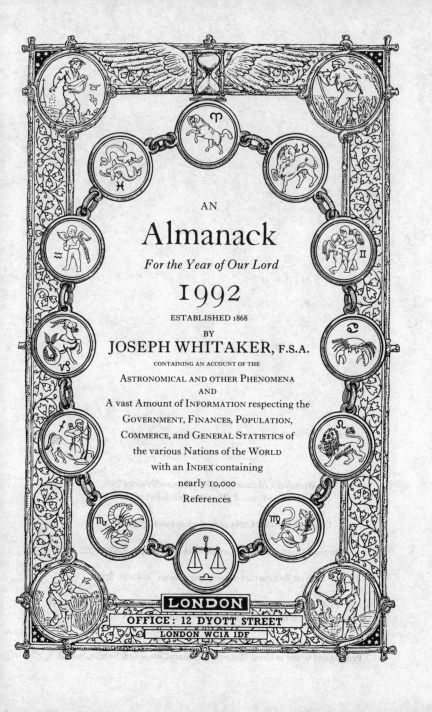

AN

Almanack

For the Year of Our Lord

1992

ESTABLISHED 1868

BY

JOSEPH WHITAKER, F.S.A.

CONTAINING AN ACCOUNT OF THE

ASTRONOMICAL AND OTHER PHENOMENA

AND

A vast Amount of INFORMATION respecting the
GOVERNMENT, FINANCES, POPULATION,
COMMERCE, and GENERAL STATISTICS of
the various Nations of the WORLD
with an INDEX containing
nearly 10,000
References

LONDON

OFFICE: 12 DYOTT STREET

LONDON WC1A 1DF

J. WHITAKER AND SONS LTD
12 Dyott Street, London WC1A 1DF

Complete Edition (1,184 pages, cloth covers)   0 85021 220 0

Library Edition (1,184 pages, maps, leather binding)   0 85021 222 7

Shorter Edition (624 pages, paper covers)   0 85021 221 9

Complete Edition distributed exclusively in the USA by Gale Research Company,
Book Tower, Detroit, Michigan 48226, USA

Typeset by Clowes Computer Composition
Printed and bound in Great Britain by William Clowes Ltd, Beccles, Suffolk

CONTENTS

CONTENTS
(of the Complete Edition and Library Edition)
continued

1992

	January	February	March	April
Sunday	.. — 5 12 19 26	.. — 2 9 16 23	.. 1 8 15 22 29	.. — 5 12 19 26
Monday	.. — 6 13 20 27	.. — 3 10 17 24	.. 2 9 16 23 30	.. — 6 13 20 27
Tuesday	.. — 7 14 21 28	.. — 4 11 18 25	.. 3 10 17 24 31	.. — 7 14 21 28
Wednesday	.. 1 8 15 22 29	.. — 5 12 19 26	.. 4 11 18 25 —	.. 1 8 15 22 29
Thursday	.. 2 9 16 23 30	.. — 6 13 20 27	.. 5 12 19 26 —	.. 2 9 16 23 30
Friday	.. 3 10 17 24 31	.. — 7 14 21 28	.. 6 13 20 27 —	.. 3 10 17 24 —
Saturday	.. 4 11 18 25 —	.. 1 8 15 22 29	.. 7 14 21 28 —	.. 4 11 18 25 —

	May	June	July	August
Sunday	— 3 10 17 24 31	.. — 7 14 21 28	.. — 5 12 19 26	— 2 9 16 23 30
Monday	— 4 11 18 25 —	.. 1 8 15 22 29	.. — 6 13 20 27	— 3 10 17 24 31
Tuesday	— 5 12 19 26 —	.. 2 9 16 23 30	.. — 7 14 21 28	— 4 11 18 25 —
Wednesday	— 6 13 20 27 —	.. 3 10 17 24 —	.. 1 8 15 22 29	— 5 12 19 26 —
Thursday	— 7 14 21 28 —	.. 4 11 18 25 —	.. 2 9 16 23 30	— 6 13 20 27 —
Friday	1 8 15 22 29 —	.. 5 12 19 26 —	.. 3 10 17 24 31	— 7 14 21 28 —
Saturday	2 9 16 23 30 —	.. 6 13 20 27 —	.. 4 11 18 25 —	1 8 15 22 29 —

	September	October	November	December
Sunday	— 6 13 20 27	.. — 4 11 18 25	.. 1 8 15 22 29	.. — 6 13 20 27
Monday	— 7 14 21 28	.. — 5 12 19 26	.. 2 9 16 23 30	.. — 7 14 21 28
Tuesday	1 8 15 22 29	.. — 6 13 20 27	.. 3 10 17 24 —	.. 1 8 15 22 29
Wednesday	2 9 16 23 30	.. — 7 14 21 28	.. 4 11 18 25 —	.. 2 9 16 23 30
Thursday	3 10 17 24 —	.. 1 8 15 22 29	.. 5 12 19 26 —	.. 3 10 17 24 31
Friday	4 11 18 25 —	.. 2 9 16 23 30	.. 6 13 20 27 —	.. 4 11 18 25 —
Saturday	5 12 19 26 —	.. 3 10 17 24 31	.. 7 14 21 28 —	.. 5 12 19 26 —

Public Holidays

	England and Wales	Scotland	Northern Ireland
New Year	January 1	January 1, 2	January 1
St Patrick's Day	—	—	March 17
Good Friday	April 17*	April 17	April 17*
Easter Monday	April 20	—	April 20
May Day	May 4	May 25	May 4
Spring	May 25	May 4	May 25
Battle of Boyne	—	—	July 13
Summer	August 31	August 3	August 31
Christmas	December 25*, 26	December 25, 26	December 25*, 26

*In England, Wales, and Northern Ireland, Christmas Day and Good Friday are common law holidays.
In the Channel Islands, Liberation Day (May 9) is a bank and public holiday.

CENTENARIES OF 1992

1892

Jan. 3	J. R. R. Tolkien, writer, born.
March 10	Dame Eva Turner, opera singer, born.
March 26	Walt Whitman, American poet, died.
April 13	Marshal of the RAF Sir Arthur ('Bomber') Harris born.
May 7	Marshal Josip Tito, Yugoslav leader, born.
June 21	Prof. Reinhold Niebuhr, American theologian, born.
June 26	Pearl S. Buck, American novelist, born.
Aug. 29	Lady Diana Cooper, society hostess and writer, born.
Sept. 4	Darius Milhaud, French composer, born.
Oct. 6	Alfred, Lord Tennyson, poet, died.
Nov. 6	Sir John Alcock, airman, born.
Dec. 15	John Paul Getty, American oil tycoon, born.
Dec. 25	Dame Rebecca West, novelist and critic, born.

1792

Feb. 23	Sir Joshua Reynolds, portrait painter, died.
Feb. 29	Gioacchino Rossini, Italian composer, born.
March 3	Robert Adam, Scottish architect, died.
March 7	Sir John Frederick Herschel, astronomer, born.

April 25	John Keble, churchman and writer, born.
July 10	Capt. Frederick Marryat, naval officer and novelist, born.
Aug. 3	Richard Arkwright, inventor of cotton-spinning machine, died.
Aug. 4	Percy Bysshe Shelley, poet, born.
Aug. 5	Frederick, 8th Lord North, statesman, died.
Aug. 18	John, 1st Earl Russell, statesman, born.
Sept. 20	Battle of Valmy.
Sept. 27	George Cruickshank, caricaturist and illustrator, born.
Oct. 28	John Smeaton, engineer, died.

1692

Feb. 13	Massacre at Glencoe.
Nov. 19	Thomas Shadwell, dramatist, died.

1592

Aug. 20	George, 1st Duke of Buckingham, statesman, born.
Sept. 13	Michel de Montaigne, French essayist, died.

1492

Aug. 3	Columbus set out on his first voyage across the Atlantic.

CENTENARIES OF 1993

1893

Jan. 12	Hermann Goering, German Nazi leader, born.
Jan. 14	Independent Labour party founded.
Jan. 15	Fanny Kemble, actress, died.
Jan. 15	Ivor Novello, actor, playwright and composer, born.
Feb. 12	Gen. Omar Bradley, American commander in Second World War, born.
March 18	Wilfred Owen, poet, born.
April 8	Mary Pickford, American actress, born.
April 20	Harold Lloyd, American actor, born.
May 26	Sir Eugene Goossens, composer and conductor, born.
June 13	Dorothy L. Sayers, writer, born.
July 6	Guy de Maupassant, French author, died.
Oct. 6	Ford Madox Brown, artist, died.
Oct. 18	Charles Gounod, French composer, died.
Nov. 6*	Piotr Tchaikovsky, Russian composer, died.

* New Style.

Dec. 12	Edward G. Robinson, American actor, born.

1793

Jan. 21	Louis XVI, King of France, executed.
March 3	William Macready, actor, born.
July 17	Charlotte Corday, French assassin of Marat, executed.
Oct. 16	Marie Antoinette, wife of Louis XVI, executed.

1693

Feb. 4	George Lillo, dramatist and jeweller, born.

1593

May 30	Christopher Marlowe, poet and playwright, died.
Aug. 9	Izaak Walton, writer, born.

PREFACE
to the 124th Annual Volume (1992)

Whitaker's Almanack 1992 looks back at a year which brought many changes, from Mrs Thatcher's resignation in November 1990 to the release of western hostages in Beirut over the past six weeks, from the victory of democracy in the USSR to England's victories against the West Indies at cricket. These and the other major events of the past year, such as the Gulf conflict and the deteriorating situation in Yugoslavia, are recorded and illustrated in this latest edition of Whitaker.

Editorial changes in this edition include revision of the coverage of the Churches and of International Organizations. In particular, the coverage of the European Community is fuller, a change suggested by many respondents to a questionnaire in the spring. We shall be addressing other matters raised by readers in future editions, including the visual appearance of Whitaker's Almanack and the layout of the information. If any readers wish to comment on the latter aspects of the Almanack, we would welcome hearing from them.

Another change is to the Whitaker's Almanack quiz. After six years we felt that we had exhausted the possibilities for quiz questions. If we were to avoid repeating ourselves, we had to change the format and so this year the quiz has been replaced by a crossword puzzle. We hope that this proves as popular with readers as the quiz.

The number of organizations and individuals we approach for information each year runs to thousands. As always, we wish to express our thanks for their help in keeping Whitaker's Almanack so up-to-date.

12 Dyott Street, London WC1A 1DF
Telephone 071–836 8911
October 1991

HILARY MARSDEN
Editor

THE YEAR 1992

Being Bissextile or leap year

RELIGIOUS, COURT, LEGAL AND OTHER DATES

Dominical Letter	ED	St George's Day	April 23
Solar Cycle	13	Coronation of HM The Queen (1953)	June 2
Roman Indiction	15	Duke of Edinburgh's Birthday (1921)	June 10
Golden Number (Lunar Cycle)	XVII	Queen's Official Birthday	June 13
Epact	25	Prince William of Wales' Birthday	
(Second epact 25 to be used as if it were 26)		(1982)	June 21
Julian Period (Year of)	6,705	Princess of Wales' Birthday (1961)	July 1
Julian Day, Jan. 1 (begins at noon)	2,448,623	Queen Elizabeth the Queen Mother's	
		Birthday (1900)	Aug. 4
New Year's Day	Jan. 1	Princess Royal's Birthday (1950)	Aug. 15
Ancient Chinese New Year (Monkey)	Feb. 4	Princess Margaret's Birthday (1930)	Aug. 21
Accession of HM The Queen (1952)	Feb. 6	Prince Henry of Wales' Birthday (1984)	Sept. 15
Duke of York's Birthday (1960)	Feb. 19	Remembrance Sunday	Nov. 8
St David's Day	March 1	Prince of Wales' Birthday (1948)	Nov. 14
Commonwealth Day	March 9	Lord Mayor's Day	Nov. 14
Prince Edward's Birthday (1964)	March 10	Wedding Day of HM The Queen (1947)	Nov. 20
St Patrick's Day	March 17	St Andrew's Day	Nov. 30
Birthday of HM The Queen (1926)	April 21		

SEASONS 1992

Northern Hemisphere

						d	*h*	
Spring Equinox	Sun enters Sign Aries					March 20	09	⎫
Summer Solstice	,,	,,	,,	Cancer	June	21	03	⎬ GMT
Autumn Equinox	,,	,,	,,	Libra	Sept.	22	19	⎬
Winter Solstice	,,	,,	,,	Capricornus	Dec.	21	15	⎭

Southern Hemisphere

						d	*h*	
Autumn Equinox	Sun enters Sign Aries					March 20	09	⎫
Winter Solstice	,,	,,	,,	Cancer	June	21	03	⎬ GMT
Spring Equinox	,,	,,	,,	Libra	Sept.	22	19	⎬
Summer Solstice	,,	,,	,,	Capricornus	Dec.	21	15	⎭

British Summer Time in 1992 begins March 29*d* 01*h* GMT and ends on October 25*d* 01*h* GMT.

RELIGIOUS CALENDARS 1992

Epiphany	Jan. 6	Pentecost (Whit Sunday)	June 7
Ash Wednesday	March 4	Trinity Sunday	June 14
Ramadan, first day	March 5	Corpus Christi	June 18
Good Friday	April 17	Islamic New Year (1413)	July 2
Passover, first day	April 18	Jewish New Year (5753)	Sept. 28
Easter Day	April 19	Day of Atonement (Yom Kippur)	Oct. 7
Greek Orthodox Easter	April 26	Feast of Tabernacles, first day	Oct. 12
Rogation Sunday	May 24	First Sunday in Advent	Nov. 29
Ascension Day	May 28	Christmas Day	Dec. 25
Feast of Weeks, first day	June 7		

LAW TERMS 1992

Hilary Term begins Jan. 11 and ends April 15
Easter Term begins April 28 and ends May 22
Trinity Term begins June 2 and ends July 31
Michaelmas Term begins Oct. 1 and ends Dec. 21

QUARTER DAYS
(England, Wales, Northern Ireland)

Lady Day	March 25
Midsummer	June 24
Michaelmas	Sept. 29
Christmas	Dec. 25

TERM DAYS
(Scotland)

Candlemas	Feb. 28
Whitsunday	May 28
Lammas	Aug. 28
Martinmas	Nov. 28

(*Removal Terms* are May 28 and Nov. 28).

(*See* **Time Measurement and Calendars** section for explanatory notes)

EVENTS IN 1992

SHOWS, PAGEANTS AND EXHIBITIONS

January 2–12	London International Boat Show	Earls Court, London
January 9–12	Cruft's Dog Show	National Exhibition Centre, Birmingham
March 12–April 5	*Daily Mail* Ideal Home Exhibition	Earls Court, London
March 22–24	London International Book Fair	Olympia, London
May 1–October 1	National Garden Festival, Wales	Ebbw Vale, Gwent
May 13–17	Royal Windsor Horse Show	Home Park, Windsor
May 21–22	Chelsea Flower Show	Royal Hospital, Chelsea, London
June 13	Trooping the Colour	Horse Guards Parade, London
July 6–9	Royal International Agricultural Show	Stoneleigh, Kenilworth, Warks.
July 8–25	Royal Tournament	Earls Court, London
August 7–29	Edinburgh Military Tattoo	Edinburgh Castle
August 13	Battle of Flowers	Jersey
September 5	Braemar Royal Highland Gathering	Braemar, Grampian
September 11–19	Southampton International Boat Show	Western Esplanade, Southampton
November 7	London to Brighton Veteran Car Run	Hyde Park to Brighton
November 14	Lord Mayor's Procession and Show	City of London
December 6–10	Royal Smithfield Show and Agricultural Machinery Exhibition	Earls Court, London

MUSIC AND DRAMA FESTIVALS

May 2–July 23	Glyndebourne Festival Opera season	Glyndebourne, Lewes, E. Sussex
May 22–June 7	Bath International Festival	Bath, Avon
May–September	Chichester Festival Theatre season	Chichester, W. Sussex
June 6–22	Aldeburgh Festival of Music and Arts	Aldeburgh, Suffolk
July 17–September 12	Promenade Concerts season	Royal Albert Hall, London
July–August	Buxton Festival	Buxton, Derbyshire
August 1–8	Royal National Eisteddfod of Wales	Aberystwyth, Dyfed
August 16–September 5	Edinburgh International Festival	Edinburgh
August 22–29	Three Choirs Festival	Gloucester
November	London International Film Festival	London

HORSE-RACING

March 12	Cheltenham Gold Cup	Cheltenham
March 21	Lincoln Handicap	Doncaster
April 4	Grand National	Aintree
April 30	One Thousand Guineas	Newmarket
May 2	Two Thousand Guineas	Newmarket
June 3	The Derby	Epsom
June 6	The Oaks	Epsom
June 16–19	Royal Ascot	Ascot
June 17	Coronation Cup	Epsom
July 25	King George VI and Queen Elizabeth Diamond Stakes	Ascot
September 12	St Leger	Doncaster
October 3	Cambridgeshire Handicap	Newmarket
October 17	Cesarewitch	Newmarket

OTHER SPORTS

January 18	Rugby Union: Ireland v. Wales	Landsdowne Road, Dublin
	Rugby Union: Scotland v. England	Murrayfield, Edinburgh
February 1	Rugby Union: Wales v. France	Cardiff Arms Park
	Rugby Union: England v. Ireland	Twickenham, London
February 8–23	Winter Olympics	Albertville, France
February 15	Rugby Union: Ireland v. Scotland	Landsdowne Road, Dublin
	Rugby Union: England v. Wales	Twickenham, London
March 7	Rugby Union: Scotland v. France	Murrayfield, Edinburgh
March 21	Rugby Union: Wales v. Scotland	Cardiff Arms Park
April 12	Athletics: London Marathon	London
May 7–10	Badminton Horse Trials	Badminton, Avon
May 9	Football: FA Cup Final	Wembley Stadium, London
June 1–12	International TT Motorcycle Races	Isle of Man
June 22–July 5	Lawn Tennis Championships	Wimbledon, London
July 1–5	Henley Royal Regatta	Henley-on-Thames
July 16–18	Golf: Open Championship	Muirfield, E. Lothian
July 27–August 9	Olympic Games	Barcelona, Spain
August 1–8	Cowes Week	Cowes, Isle of Wight
August 21–September 5	Golf: British Amateur Championship	Carnoustie and Panmure, Angus
October 6–10	Horse of the Year Show	Wembley Arena, London

The horse-racing fixtures are the copyright of The Jockey Club.

1993

	January	**February**	**March**	**April**
Sunday	.. 3 10 17 24 31	.. — 7 14 21 28	.. — 7 14 21 28	.. — 4 11 18 25
Monday	.. 4 11 18 25 —	.. 1 8 15 22 —	.. 1 8 15 22 29	.. — 5 12 19 26
Tuesday	.. 5 12 19 26 —	.. 2 9 16 23 —	.. 2 9 16 23 30	.. — 6 13 20 27
Wednesday	.. 6 13 20 27 —	.. 3 10 17 24 —	.. 3 10 17 24 31	.. — 7 14 21 28
Thursday	.. 7 14 21 28 —	.. 4 11 18 25 —	.. 4 11 18 25 —	.. 1 8 15 22 29
Friday	1 8 15 22 29 —	.. 5 12 19 26 —	.. 5 12 19 26 —	.. 2 9 16 23 30
Saturday	2 9 16 23 30 —	.. 6 13 20 27 —	.. 6 13 20 27 —	.. 3 10 17 24 —

	May	**June**	**July**	**August**
Sunday	— 2 9 16 23 30	.. — 6 13 20 27	.. — 4 11 18 25	.. 1 8 15 22 29
Monday	— 3 10 17 24 31	.. — 7 14 21 28	.. — 5 12 19 26	.. 2 9 16 23 30
Tuesday	— 4 11 18 25 —	.. 1 8 15 22 29	.. — 6 13 20 27	.. 3 10 17 24 31
Wednesday	— 5 12 19 26 —	.. 2 9 16 23 30	.. — 7 14 21 28	.. 4 11 18 25 —
Thursday	— 6 13 20 27 —	.. 3 10 17 24 —	.. 1 8 15 22 29	.. 5 12 19 26 —
Friday	— 7 14 21 28 —	.. 4 11 18 25 —	.. 2 9 16 23 30	.. 6 13 20 27 —
Saturday	1 8 15 22 29 —	.. 5 12 19 26 —	.. 3 10 17 24 31	.. 7 14 21 28 —

	September	**October**	**November**	**December**
Sunday	.. — 5 12 19 26	.. 3 10 17 24 31	.. — 7 14 21 28	.. — 5 12 19 26
Monday	.. — 6 13 20 27	.. 4 11 18 25 —	.. 1 8 15 22 29	.. — 6 13 20 27
Tuesday	.. — 7 14 21 28	.. 5 12 19 26 —	.. 2 9 16 23 30	.. — 7 14 21 28
Wednesday	.. 1 8 15 22 29	.. 6 13 20 27 —	.. 3 10 17 24 —	.. 1 8 15 22 29
Thursday	.. 2 9 16 23 30	.. 7 14 21 28 —	.. 4 11 18 25 —	.. 2 9 16 23 30
Friday	.. 3 10 17 24 —	1 8 15 22 29 —	.. 5 12 19 26 —	.. 3 10 17 24 31
Saturday	.. 4 11 18 25 —	2 9 16 23 30 —	.. 6 13 20 27 —	.. 4 11 18 25 —

Public Holidays

	England and Wales	**Scotland**	**Northern Ireland**
New Year	January 1	January 1, 2	January 1
St Patrick's Day.....	—	—	March 17
Good Friday	April 9*	April 9	April 9*
Easter Monday......	April 12	—	April 12
May Day	May 3	May 31	May 3
Spring	May 31	May 3	May 31
Battle of Boyne	—	–	July 12
Summer	August 30	August 2	August 30
Christmas	December 25*, 27	December 25, 27	December 25*, 27

* In England, Wales, and Northern Ireland, Christmas Day and Good Friday are common law holidays.
In the Channel Islands, Liberation Day (May 9) is a bank and public holiday.

Year	Month	Week		

Janus, god of the portal, facing two ways, past and future.

Sun's Longitude 300° ♒ 20ᵈ 20ʰ

Year	Month	Week	
1	1	W.	**Naming of Jesus.** J. Edgar Hoover *b.* 1895.
2	2	Th.	Fabian Bellingshausen *d.* 1852.
3	3	F.	Jeremiah Horrocks *d.* 1641. J.R.R. Tolkien *b.* 1892.*
4	4	S.	Louis Braille *b.* 1809. T.S. Eliot *d.* 1965.
5	5	S.	**2nd S. after Christmas.** Shackleton *d.* 1922.
6	6	M.	**The Epiphany.** Theodore Roosevelt *d.* 1919.
7	7	Tu.	Millard Fillimore *b.* 1800. Hirohito *d.* 1989.
8	8	W.	Galileo *d.* 1642. Elvis Presley *b.* 1935.
9	9	Th.	Napoleon III *d.* 1873. Gracie Fields *b.* 1898.
10	10	F.	Penny Post introduced 1840.
11	11	S.	HILARY LAW SITTINGS BEGIN.
12	12	S.	**1st S. after Epiphany.** Pestalozzi *b.* 1746.
13	13		Edmund Spenser *d.* 1599.
14	14	Tu.	Edmond Halley *b.* 1742. Anthony Eden *d.* 1977.
15	15	W.	Molière *bapt.* 1622. Rosa Luxemburg *d.* 1919.
16	16	Th.	Gibbon *b.* 1794. Start of Prohibition 1920.
17	17	F.	Benjamin Franklin *b.* 1706. Nevil Shute *b.* 1899.
18	18	S.	Cary Grant *b.* 1904. Kipling *d.* 1936.
19	19	S.	**2nd S. after Epiphany.** James Watt *b.* 1736.
20	20	M.	John Ruskin *d.* 1900.
21	21	Tu	Concorde entered service 1976.
22	22	W.	André Ampère *b.* 1775. Byron *b.* 1788.
23	23	Th.	William Pitt (the Younger) *d.* 1806.
24	24	F.	Charles James Fox *b.* 1749.
25	25	S.	**Conversion of St Paul.** Al Capone *d.* 1947.
26	26	S.	**3rd S. after Epiphany.**
27	27	M.	First television demonstration 1926.
28	28	Tu.	Sir Francis Drake *d.* 1596.
29	29	W.	Thomas Paine *b.* 1737. George III *d.* 1820.
30	30	Th.	Franklin D. Roosevelt *b.* 1882.
31	31	F.	First US earth satellite launched 1958.

PHENOMENA

d	h	
1	09	Venus in conjunction with Moon. Venus 5°N.
3	00	Mercury in conjunction with Moon. Mercury 3°N.
3	10	Mars in conjunction with Moon. Mars 0°.8N.
3	15	Earth at perihelion (147 million km)
5	01	Uranus in conjunction with Sun.
6	21	Saturn in conjunction with Moon. Saturn 3°S.
7	13	Neptune in conjunction with Sun.
10	20	Mars in conjunction with Mercury. Mars 0°6S.
22	21	Jupiter in conjunction with Moon. Jupiter 6°N.
29	22	Saturn in conjunction with Sun.
31	17	Venus in conjunction with Moon. Venus 1°N.

CONSTELLATIONS

The following constellations are near the meridian at

	d	h		d	h
Dec.	1	24	Dec.	16	23
Jan.	1	22	Jan.	16	21
Feb.	1	20	Feb.	15	19

Draco (below the Pole), Ursa Minor (below the Pole), Camelopardus, Perseus, Auriga, Taurus, Orion, Eridanus and Lepus.

MINIMA OF ALGOL

d	h	d	h
2	00·6	19	05·5
4	21·4	22	02·3
7	18·2	24	23·2
10	15·1	27	20·0
13	11·9	30	16·8
16	08·7		

*Centenary

MOON
Phases, Apsides & Node

	d	h	m
● New Moon	4	23	10
☽ First Quarter	13	02	32
○ Full Moon	19	21	28
☾ Last Quarter	26	15	27
Apogee (406,471 km)	6	11	40
Perigee (356,550 km)	19	22	13

Mean longitude of ascending node on Jan. 1, 280°.

MONTHLY NOTES

1. Bank Holiday in England, Wales, Scotland and Northern Ireland.

2. Bank Holiday, Scotland.

26. Australia Day. Republic Day, India.

(*See* page 62 for explanatory notes)

										Sidereal Time	Transit of First Point of Aries
Day	Right Ascension	Dec. −	Equation of Time	Rise		Transit	Set				
				52°	56°		52°	56°			
	h m s	° ′	m s	h m	h m	h m	h m	h m	h m s	h m s
1	18 42 42	23 05	− 3 03	8 08	8 31	12 03	15 58	15 35	6 39 39	17 17 31
2	18 47 07	23 00	− 3 32	8 08	8 31	12 04	16 00	15 37	6 43 35	17 13 35
3	18 51 31	22 55	− 4 00	8 08	8 31	12 04	16 01	15 38	6 47 32	17 09 39
4	18 55 56	22 49	− 4 28	8 08	8 31	12 05	16 02	15 39	6 51 28	17 05 43
5	19 00 20	22 43	− 4 55	8 08	8 30	12 05	16 03	15 40	6 55 25	17 01 47
6	19 04 44	22 36	− 5 22	8 07	8 30	12 06	16 04	15 42	6 59 21	16 57 51
7	19 09 07	22 29	− 5 49	8 07	8 29	12 06	16 06	15 43	7 03 18	16 53 56
8	19 13 30	22 22	− 6 15	8 06	8 28	12 06	16 07	15 45	7 07 14	16 50 00
9	19 17 52	22 14	− 6 41	8 06	8 28	12 07	16 08	15 46	7 11 11	16 46 04
10	19 22 14	22 06	− 7 06	8 05	8 27	12 07	16 10	15 48	7 15 08	16 42 08
11	19 26 35	21 57	− 7 31	8 05	8 26	12 08	16 11	15 50	7 19 04	16 38 12
12	19 30 55	21 48	− 7 55	8 04	8 25	12 08	16 12	15 51	7 23 01	16 34 16
13	19 35 15	21 38	− 8 18	8 03	8 24	12 08	16 14	15 53	7 26 57	16 30 20
14	19 39 35	21 28	− 8 41	8 03	8 23	12 09	16 15	15 55	7 30 54	16 26 24
15	19 43 53	21 18	− 9 03	8 02	8 22	12 09	16 17	15 57	7 34 50	16 22 28
16	19 48 11	21 07	− 9 24	8 01	8 21	12 10	16 19	15 59	7 38 47	16 18 32
17	19 52 28	20 56	− 9 45	8 00	8 20	12 10	16 20	16 01	7 42 43	16 14 36
18	19 56 45	20 44	−10 05	7 59	8 19	12 10	16 22	16 02	7 46 40	16 10 41
19	20 01 01	20 32	−10 24	7 58	8 17	12 11	16 23	16 04	7 50 37	16 06 45
20	20 05 16	20 20	−10 43	7 57	8 16	12 11	16 25	16 06	7 54 33	16 02 49
21	20 09 31	20 07	−11 01	7 56	8 15	12 11	16 27	16 08	7 58 30	15 58 53
22	20 13 44	19 54	−11 18	7 55	8 13	12 11	16 29	16 10	8 02 26	15 54 57
23	20 17 57	19 40	−11 34	7 54	8 12	12 12	16 30	16 12	8 06 23	15 51 01
24	20 22 09	19 26	−11 50	7 52	8 10	12 12	16 32	16 14	8 10 19	15 47 05
25	20 26 21	19 12	−12 05	7 51	8 09	12 12	16 34	16 16	8 14 16	15 43 09
26	20 30 31	18 57	−12 19	7 50	8 07	12 12	16 36	16 19	8 18 12	15 39 13
27	20 34 41	18 42	−12 32	7 48	8 05	12 13	16 37	16 21	8 22 09	15 35 17
28	20 38 50	18 27	−12 45	7 47	8 04	12 13	16 39	16 23	8 26 06	15 31 21
29	20 42 59	18 11	−12 57	7 46	8 02	12 13	16 41	16 25	8 30 02	15 27 26
30	20 47 06	17 55	−13 08	7 44	8 00	12 13	16 43	16 27	8 33 59	15 23 30
31	20 51 13	17 39	−13 18	7 43	7 58	12 13	16 45	16 29	8 37 55	15 19 34

THE SUN   s.d. 16′·3

Duration of Civil (C), Nautical (N) and Astronomical (A) Twilight (in minutes)

Lat.	Jan. 1			Jan. 11			Jan. 21			Jan. 31		
°	C	N	A	C	N	A	C	N	A	C	N	A
52	41	84	125	40	82	123	38	80	120	37	78	117
56	47	96	141	45	93	138	43	90	134	41	87	130

ASTRONOMICAL NOTES

MERCURY is visible as a morning object for the first few days of the month, magnitude −0·3. It may then be detected with some difficulty, very low on the ESE horizon around the time of beginning of morning civil twilight. After the 5th it will be too close to the Sun for observation.

VENUS is a brilliant object in the mornings, magnitude −4·0, though the duration of its visibility in the south-eastern sky before dawn shortens noticeably during the month. On the morning of the 1st the old crescent Moon passes 5°S. of the planet. On the 7th Venus passes 7°N. of Antares.

MARS is unsuitably placed for observation.

JUPITER, magnitude −2·3, is a brilliant morning object, visible from the late evening onwards. It is moving very slowly westwards in Leo. The gibbous Moon will be seen passing 6°S. of the planet as the two bodies rise in the east on the evening of the 21st.

SATURN is too close to the Sun for observation, conjunction occurring on the 29th.

ECLIPSE. An annular eclipse of the Sun occurs on the 4th–5th. See page 72 for details.

(See pages 62–63 for explanatory notes)

THE MOON

Day	RA	Dec.	Hor. Par.	Semi-diam.	Sun's Co-long.	PA of Bright Limb	Phase	Age	Rise 52°	Rise 56°	Transit	Set 52°	Set 56°
	h m	°	'	'	°	°	%	d	h m	h m	h m	h m	h m
1	15 32	− 22·9	55·2	15·0	220	100	14	25·8	5 17	5 44	9 11	13 00	12 33
2	16 25	− 24·4	54·8	14·9	233	95	8	26·8	6 19	6 48	10 02	13 43	13 14
3	17 18	− 24·9	54·5	14·8	245	90	3	27·8	7 11	7 39	10 53	14 36	14 08
4	18 11	− 24·1	54·2	14·8	257	85	1	28·8	7 52	8 18	11 42	15 38	15 12
5	19 02	− 22·3	54·0	14·7	269	216	0	0·0	8 24	8 46	12 30	16 44	16 22
6	19 51	− 19·5	54·0	14·7	281	252	1	1·0	8 48	9 06	13 16	17 52	17 36
7	20 38	− 15·9	54·0	14·7	293	249	4	2·0	9 08	9 21	14 00	19 01	18 50
8	21 24	− 11·7	54·1	14·7	306	247	8	3·0	9 25	9 33	14 42	20 10	20 03
9	22 08	− 7·0	54·3	14·8	318	245	14	4·0	9 40	9 44	15 23	21 18	21 16
10	22 52	− 2·1	54·6	14·9	330	244	21	5·0	9 54	9 54	16 04	22 27	22 30
11	23 36	+ 3·0	55·1	15·0	342	244	30	6·0	10 08	10 04	16 46	23 38	23 45
12	0 21	+ 8·1	55·7	15·2	354	244	39	7·0	10 24	10 16	17 30	—	—
13	1 09	+ 12·9	56·4	15·4	7	247	49	8·0	10 43	10 30	18 17	0 52	1 04
14	2 00	+ 17·3	57·3	15·6	19	251	59	9·0	11 07	10 49	19 09	2 09	2 26
15	2 54	+ 21·0	58·3	15·9	31	255	70	10·0	11 39	11 16	20 05	3 27	3 50
16	3 53	+ 23·6	59·2	16·1	43	260	80	11·0	12 24	11 56	21 06	4 44	5 11
17	4 56	+ 24·8	60·1	16·4	55	266	88	12·0	13 25	12 56	22 10	5 53	6 22
18	6 02	+ 24·3	60·9	16·6	67	272	95	13·0	14 42	14 16	23 14	6 49	7 15
19	7 07	+ 22·0	61·3	16·7	79	274	99	14·0	16 09	15 49	—	7 31	7 52
20	8 10	+ 18·2	61·5	16·8	91	154	100	15·0	17 41	17 27	0 16	8 03	8 18
21	9 10	+ 13·1	61·3	16·7	104	118	98	16·0	19 11	19 03	1 14	8 27	8 37
22	10 06	+ 7·3	60·8	16·6	116	118	93	17·0	20 38	20 36	2 09	8 47	8 51
23	11 00	+ 1·2	60·0	16·4	128	118	86	18·0	22 05	22 05	3 00	9 05	9 04
24	11 52	− 4·8	59·1	16·1	140	117	77	19·0	23 22	23 32	3 50	9 23	9 17
25	12 44	− 10·4	58·1	15·8	152	115	67	20·0	—	—	4 38	9 42	9 31
26	13 35	− 15·2	57·2	15·6	164	112	57	21·0	0 41	0 56	5 27	10 03	9 47
27	14 26	− 19·3	56·4	15·4	176	108	46	22·0	1 57	2 17	6 17	10 29	10 08
28	15 19	− 22·2	55·6	15·2	189	104	37	23·0	3 08	3 33	7 07	11 01	10 35
29	16 12	− 24·1	55·0	15·0	201	99	27	24·0	4 13	4 41	7 58	11 41	11 13
30	17 05	− 24·8	54·6	14·9	213	94	19	25·0	5 08	5 37	8 49	12 31	12 02
31	17 58	− 24·4	54·2	14·8	225	89	12	26·0	5 52	6 19	9 39	13 30	13 03

MERCURY

Day	RA	Dec. −	Diam.	Phase	Transit	5° high 52°	5° high 56°	Day	RA	Dec. −	Diam.	Phase	Transit	
	h m	°	"	%	h m	h m	h m		h m	°			h m	
1	17 09	21·5	6	73	10 29	7 14	7 45	16	18 37	23·7	—	—	11 00	
4	17 25	22·2	6	77	10 34	7 24	7 57	19	18 57	23·7	—	—	11 08	Mercury is too
7	17 42	22·8	6	81	10 39	7 34	8 09	22	19 17	23·5	—	—	11 16	close to the
10	18 00	23·3	5	85	10 45	7 44	8 21	25	19 37	23·0	—	—	11 24	Sun for
13	18 18	23·6	5	88	10 52	7 54	8 31	28	19 57	22·4	—	—	11 33	observation
16	18 37	23·7	5	90	11 00	8 03	8 41	31	20 18	21·6	—	—	11 42	

VENUS | MARS

Day	RA	Dec. −	Diam.	Phase	Transit	5° high 52°	5° high 56°	Day	RA	Dec. +	Diam.	Phase	Transit	
	h m	°	"	%	h m	h m	h m		h m	°			h m	
1	15 55	18·2	15	75	9 16	5 35	5 59	1	17 33	23·8	—	—	10 53	
6	16 20	19·4	15	76	9 21	5 49	6 16	6	17 49	23·9	—	—	10 49	Mars is too
11	16 45	20·5	14	78	9 27	6 03	6 32	11	18 05	24·0	—	—	10 46	close to the
16	17 11	21·4	14	79	9 33	6 16	6 47	16	18 21	24·0	—	—	10 42	Sun for
21	17 37	22·0	13	81	9 39	6 27	6 59	21	18 38	23·8	—	—	10 39	observation
26	18 04	22·3	13	82	9 46	6 37	7 10	26	18 54	23·6	—	—	10 36	
31	18 30	22·4	13	83	9 53	6 44	7 17	31	19 11	23·2	—	—	10 32	

(See pages 63–64 for explanatory notes)

SUNRISE AND SUNSET

Day	London 0°05′ 51°30′		Bristol 2°35′ 51°28′		Birmingham 1°55′ 52°28′		Manchester 2°15′ 53°28′		Newcastle 1°37′ 54°59′		Glasgow 4°14′ 55°52′		Belfast 5°56′ 54°35′	
	h m	h m	h m	h m	h m	h m	h m	h m	h m	h m	h m	h m	h m	h m
1	8 06	16 01	8 16	16 12	8 18	16 04	8 25	16 00	8 31	15 48	8 47	15 53	8 46	16 08
2	8 06	16 02	8 16	16 13	8 18	16 05	8 25	16 01	8 31	15 49	8 47	15 54	8 46	16 09
3	8 06	16 03	8 16	16 14	8 18	16 06	8 25	16 02	8 31	15 51	8 47	15 56	8 46	16 10
4	8 06	16 05	8 16	16 15	8 18	16 07	8 24	16 03	8 31	15 52	8 47	15 57	8 46	16 12
5	8 05	16 06	8 15	16 16	8 18	16 08	8 24	16 04	8 30	15 53	8 46	15 58	8 45	16 13
6	8 05	16 07	8 15	16 17	8 17	16 10	8 24	16 06	8 30	15 55	8 46	16 00	8 45	16 14
7	8 05	16 08	8 15	16 18	8 17	16 11	8 23	16 07	8 29	15 56	8 45	16 01	8 44	16 16
8	8 04	16 10	8 14	16 20	8 16	16 12	8 23	16 08	8 29	15 58	8 44	16 03	8 44	16 17
9	8 04	16 11	8 14	16 21	8 16	16 14	8 22	16 10	8 28	15 59	8 44	16 04	8 43	16 19
10	8 03	16 12	8 13	16 22	8 15	16 15	8 22	16 11	8 27	16 01	8 43	16 06	8 42	16 20
11	8 03	16 14	8 13	16 24	8 15	16 16	8 21	16 13	8 27	16 02	8 42	16 08	8 42	16 22
12	8 02	16 15	8 12	16 25	8 14	16 18	8 20	16 14	8 26	16 04	8 41	16 09	8 41	16 23
13	8 01	16 17	8 11	16 27	8 13	16 19	8 19	16 16	8 25	16 05	8 40	16 11	8 40	16 25
14	8 01	16 18	8 11	16 28	8 12	16 21	8 19	16 18	8 24	16 07	8 39	16 13	8 39	16 27
15	8 00	16 20	8 10	16 30	8 12	16 23	8 18	16 19	8 23	16 09	8 38	16 15	8 38	16 28
16	7 59	16 21	8 09	16 31	8 11	16 24	8 17	16 21	8 22	16 11	8 37	16 16	8 37	16 30
17	7 58	16 23	8 08	16 33	8 10	16 26	8 16	16 23	8 21	16 12	8 36	16 18	8 36	16 32
18	7 57	16 24	8 07	16 34	8 09	16 27	8 15	16 24	8 20	16 14	8 35	16 20	8 35	16 34
19	7 56	16 26	8 06	16 36	8 08	16 29	8 14	16 26	8 18	16 16	8 33	16 22	8 34	16 35
20	7 55	16 28	8 05	16 38	8 07	16 31	8 12	16 28	8 17	16 18	8 32	16 24	8 32	16 37
21	7 54	16 29	8 04	16 39	8 06	16 33	8 11	16 30	8 16	16 20	8 31	16 26	8 31	16 39
22	7 53	16 31	8 03	16 41	8 04	16 34	8 10	16 31	8 15	16 22	8 29	16 28	8 30	16 41
23	7 52	16 33	8 02	16 43	8 03	16 36	8 09	16 33	8 13	16 24	8 28	16 30	8 28	16 43
24	7 51	16 34	8 01	16 44	8 02	16 38	8 07	16 35	8 12	16 26	8 26	16 32	8 27	16 45
25	7 50	16 36	7 59	16 46	8 01	16 40	8 06	16 37	8 10	16 28	8 25	16 34	8 26	16 47
26	7 48	16 38	7 58	16 48	7 59	16 41	8 05	16 39	8 09	16 30	8 23	16 36	8 24	16 49
27	7 47	16 40	7 57	16 50	7 58	16 43	8 03	16 41	8 07	16 32	8 22	16 38	8 23	16 51
28	7 46	16 41	7 55	16 51	7 57	16 45	8 02	16 43	8 05	16 34	8 20	16 40	8 21	16 53
29	7 44	16 43	7 54	16 53	7 55	16 47	8 00	16 45	8 04	16 36	8 18	16 43	8 19	16 55
30	7 43	16 45	7 53	16 55	7 54	16 49	7 59	16 46	8 02	16 38	8 16	16 45	8 18	16 57
31	7 41	16 47	7 51	16 57	7 52	16 51	7 57	16 48	8 00	16 40	8 15	16 47	8 16	16 59

JUPITER

Day	RA	Dec. +	Transit	5° high 52°	5° high 56°
	h m	° ′	h m	h m	h m
1	11 05·2	7 08	4 25	22 18	22 15
11	11 04·5	7 15	3 45	21 37	21 34
21	11 02·7	7 30	3 04	20 55	20 52
31	10 59·8	7 50	2 21	20 10	20 07

Diameters—equatorial 42″ polar 39″

SATURN

Day	RA	Dec. −	Transit	
	h m	° ′	h m	
1	20 33·5	19 22	13 52	Saturn is too
11	20 38·2	19 06	13 17	close to the
21	20 43·0	18 48	12 43	Sun for
31	20 47·9	18 30	12 08	observation

Diameters—equatorial 15″ polar 14″
Rings—major axis 35″ minor axis 11″

URANUS

Day	RA	Dec. −	Transit	
	h m	° ′	h m	
1	18 59·6	23 06	12 18	Uranus is too
11	19 02·6	23 02	11 41	close to the Sun
21	19 04·7	22 59	11 05	for observation
31	19 07·2	22 55	10 28	

Diameter 4″

NEPTUNE

Day	RA	Dec. −	Transit	
	h m	° ′	h m	
1	19 10·0	21 44	12 28	Neptune is too
11	19 11·6	21 41	11 51	close to the Sun
21	19 13·2	21 38	11 13	for observation
31	19 14·8	21 36	10 35	

Diameter 2″

(*See* page 64 for explanatory notes)

Year	Month	Week	*Februa*, Roman festival of Purification *Sun's Longitude* 330°)(19ᵈ 10ʰ
32	1	S.	Clara Butt *b.* 1873. John Ford *b.* 1895.
33	2	S.	**Presentation of Christ. 4th S. after Epiphany.**
34	3	M.	Pres. Woodrow Wilson *d.* 1924.
35	4	Tu.	Charles Lindbergh *b.* 1902.
36	5	W.	John Dunlop *b.* 1840.
37	6	Th.	QUEEN'S ACCESSION 1952. Mrs Beeton *d.* 1865.
38	7	F.	Sinclair Lewis *b.* 1885.
39	8	S.	Jules Verne *b.* 1828.
40	9	S.	**5th S. after Epiphany.**
41	10	M.	Military conscription introduced 1916.
42	11	Tu.	Mary Quant *b.* 1934. John Buchan *d.* 1940.
43	12	W.	Kant *d.* 1804. Abraham Lincoln *d.* 1809.
44	13	Th.	Catherine Howard *exec.* 1542. Wagner *d.* 1883.
45	14	F.	VALENTINE'S DAY. P.G. Wodehouse *d.* 1975.
46	15	S.	Surrender of Singapore 1942.
47	16	S.	**9th S. before Easter.**
48	17	M.	Ruth Rendell *b.* 1930. Graham Sutherland *d.* 1980.
49	18	Tu.	Michelangelo *d.* 1564. Paganini *b.* 1784.
50	19	W.	DUKE OF YORK *b.* 1960. Copernicus *b.* 1473.
51	20	Th.	Sidney Poitier *b.* 1927.
52	21	F.	W.H. Auden *b.* 1907. Gogol *d.* 1852 os.
53	22	S.	George Washington *b.* 1732.
54	23	S.	**8th S. before Easter.** Pepys *b.* 1633.
55	24	M.	Henry Cavendish *d.* 1810.
56	25	Tu.	Caruso *b.* 1873. Anthony Burgess *b.* 1917.
57	26	W.	Frank Bridge *b.* 1879. Harry Lauder *d.* 1950.
58	27	Th.	Labour Party founded 1900.
59	28	F.	Henry James *d.* 1916.
60	29	S.	Gioacchino Rossini *b.* 1792.*

* Centenary   os Old Style

PHENOMENA

d	h	
1	12	Mars in conjunction with Moon. Mars 2°S.
3	05	Mercury in conjunction with Moon. Mercury 4°S.
3	10	Saturn in conjunction with Moon. Saturn 3°S.
4	22	Saturn in conjunction with Mercury. Saturn 1°N.
12	09	Mercury in superior conjunction
19	03	Jupiter in conjunction with Moon. Jupiter 6°N.
19	12	Mars in conjunction with Venus. Mars 0°.8S.
29	01	Jupiter at opposition
29	01	Saturn in conjunction with Venus. Saturn 0°.1S.

CONSTELLATIONS

The following constellations are near the meridian at

d	h		d	h
Jan.	1 24		Jan.	16 23
Feb.	1 22		Feb.	15 21
Mar.	1 20		Mar.	16 19

Draco (below the Pole), Camelopardus, Auriga, Taurus, Gemini, Orion, Canis Minor, Monoceros, Lepus, Canis Major and Puppis.

MINIMA OF ALGOL

d	h		d	h
2	13·6		16	21·7
5	10·4		19	18·5
8	07·3		22	15·4
11	04·1		25	12·2
14	00·9		28	09·0

MOON
Phases, Apsides & Node

	d	h	m
● New Moon	3	19	00
☽ First Quarter	11	16	15
○ Full Moon	18	08	04
☾ Last Quarter	25	07	56

	d	h	m
Apogee (406,509 km)	2	11	49
Perigee (358,096 km)	17	10	50
Apogee (405,916 km)	29	20	52

Mean longitude of ascending node on Feb. 1, 278°

MONTHLY NOTES

1. Pheasant and partridge shooting ends.
4. Ancient Chinese New Year (Year of the Monkey).
6. National Day, New Zealand.
28. Candlemas (Scottish Term Day).

(*See* page 62 for explanatory notes)

				THE SUN				s.d. 16′·2	Sidereal Time	Transit of First Point of Aries
Day	Right Ascension	Dec. −	Equation of Time	Rise		Transit	Set			
				52°	56°		52°	56°		
	h m s	° ′	m s	h m	h m	h m	h m	h m	h m s	h m s
1	20 55 19	17 22	−13 27	7 41	7 56	12 14	16 46	16 31	8 41 52	15 15 38
2	20 59 24	17 05	−13 36	7 40	7 54	12 14	16 48	16 34	8 45 48	15 11 42
3	21 03 28	16 48	−13 43	7 38	7 53	12 14	16 50	16 36	8 49 45	15 07 46
4	21 07 32	16 30	−13 50	7 36	7 51	12 14	16 52	16 38	8 53 41	15 03 50
5	21 11 34	16 13	−13 56	7 35	7 49	12 14	16 54	16 40	8 57 38	14 59 54
6	21 15 36	15 55	−14 02	7 33	7 47	12 14	16 56	16 42	9 01 35	14 55 58
7	21 19 37	15 36	−14 06	7 31	7 45	12 14	16 58	16 45	9 05 31	14 52 02
8	21 23 37	15 18	−14 10	7 30	7 42	12 14	17 00	16 47	9 09 28	14 48 06
9	21 27 37	14 59	−14 12	7 28	7 40	12 14	17 01	16 49	9 13 24	14 44 10
10	21 31 35	14 39	−14 14	7 26	7 38	12 14	17 03	16 51	9 17 21	14 40 15
11	21 35 33	14 20	−14 16	7 24	7 36	12 14	17 05	16 53	9 21 17	14 36 19
12	21 39 30	14 00	−14 16	7 22	7 34	12 14	17 07	16 56	9 25 14	14 32 23
13	21 43 26	13 41	−14 16	7 20	7 32	12 14	17 09	16 58	9 29 10	14 28 27
14	21 47 22	13 21	−14 15	7 19	7 29	12 14	17 11	17 00	9 33 07	14 24 31
15	21 51 16	13 00	−14 13	7 17	7 27	12 14	17 13	17 02	9 37 04	14 20 35
16	21 55 10	12 40	−14 10	7 15	7 25	12 14	17 14	17 04	9 41 00	14 16 39
17	21 59 03	12 19	−14 07	7 13	7 23	12 14	17 16	17 07	9 44 57	14 12 43
18	22 02 56	11 58	−14 03	7 11	7 20	12 14	17 18	17 09	9 48 53	14 08 47
19	22 06 48	11 37	−13 58	7 09	7 18	12 14	17 20	17 11	9 52 50	14 04 51
20	22 10 39	11 16	−13 52	7 07	7 16	12 14	17 22	17 13	9 56 46	14 00 56
21	22 14 29	10 54	−13 46	7 05	7 13	12 14	17 24	17 15	10 00 43	13 57 00
22	22 18 19	10 33	−13 39	7 03	7 11	12 14	17 26	17 17	10 04 39	13 53 04
23	22 22 08	10 11	−13 32	7 00	7 08	12 13	17 27	17 20	10 08 36	13 49 08
24	22 25 57	9 49	−13 24	6 58	7 06	12 13	17 29	17 22	10 12 33	13 45 12
25	22 29 45	9 27	−13 15	6 56	7 03	12 13	17 31	17 24	10 16 29	13 41 16
26	22 33 32	9 05	−13 06	6 54	7 01	12 13	17 33	17 26	10 20 26	13 37 20
27	22 37 19	8 42	−12 56	6 52	6 59	12 13	17 35	17 28	10 24 22	13 33 24
28	22 41 05	8 20	−12 46	6 50	6 56	12 13	17 36	17 30	10 28 19	13 29 28
29	22 44 51	7 57	−12 35	6 48	6 54	12 12	17 38	17 32	10 32 15	13 25 32

Duration of Civil (C), Nautical (N) and Astronomical (A) Twilight (in minutes)

Lat. °	Feb. 1			Feb. 11			Feb. 21			Feb. 28		
	C	N	A	C	N	A	C	N	A	C	N	A
52	37	77	117	35	75	114	34	74	113	34	73	112
56	41	86	130	39	83	126	38	81	125	38	81	124

ASTRONOMICAL NOTES

MERCURY is unsuitably placed for observation for most of the month as superior conjunction occurs on the 12th. However, for the last three evenings of the month it may be seen low above the western horizon for a short while around the end of evening civil twilight. Its magnitude will then be about −1.

VENUS continues to be visible as a brilliant object in the morning skies before dawn, magnitude −4·0, but will only be seen low above the south-eastern horizon for a very short period before sunrise.

MARS is unsuitably placed for observation.

JUPITER, magnitude −2·5, continues to be visible as a brilliant object in the night sky, and is now visible throughout the hours of darkness as it is at opposition on the 29th. Jupiter is in Leo.

SATURN is too close to the Sun for observation.

ZODIACAL LIGHT. The evening cone may be observed in the western sky after the end of twilight, from the 19th onwards. This faint phenomenon is only visible under good conditions in the absence of both moonlight and artificial lighting.

(*See* pages 62–63 for explanatory notes)

THE MOON

Day	RA	Dec.	Hor. Par.	Semi-diam.	Sun's Co-long.	PA of Bright Limb	Phase	Age	Rise 52°	Rise 56°	Transit	Set 52°	Set 56°
	h m	°	′	′	°	°	%	d	h m	h m	h m	h m	h m
1	18 49	−22·8	54·0	14·7	237	85	7	27·0	6 26	6 50	10 27	14 34	14 11
2	19 39	−20·3	53·9	14·7	250	84	3	28·0	6 53	7 12	11 14	15 42	15 24
3	20 27	−16·9	54·0	14·7	262	91	1	29·0	7 15	7 29	11 58	16 51	16 38
4	21 13	−12·8	54·0	14·7	274	198	0	0·2	7 33	7 43	12 41	18 00	17 51
5	21 57	− 8·3	54·2	14·8	286	234	1	1·2	7 48	7 54	13 22	19 09	19 05
6	22 41	− 3·4	54·5	14·8	298	238	5	2·2	8 03	8 04	14 03	20 18	20 18
7	23 25	+ 1·7	54·8	14·9	310	240	9	3·2	8 17	8 14	14 45	21 28	21 33
8	0 10	+ 6·7	55·2	15·0	323	242	16	4·2	8 32	8 25	15 28	22 39	22 49
9	0 57	+11·6	55·8	15·2	335	244	24	5·2	8 50	8 38	16 13	23 53	—
10	1 45	+16·1	56·4	15·4	347	247	33	6·2	9 11	8 55	17 02	—	0 09
11	2 38	+19·9	57·1	15·6	359	251	43	7·2	9 39	9 17	17 55	1 09	1 30
12	3 33	+22·8	57·9	15·8	11	256	54	8·2	10 16	9 50	18 52	2 24	2 50
13	4 33	+24·4	58·8	16·0	23	262	64	9·2	11 07	10 39	19 52	3 34	4 03
14	5 35	+24·6	59·6	16·2	36	268	75	10·2	12 14	11 46	20 53	4 34	5 02
15	6 38	+23·2	60·3	16·4	48	274	84	11·2	13 34	13 11	21 55	5 22	5 46
16	7 41	+20·1	60·9	16·6	60	278	92	12·2	15 02	14 45	22 54	5 58	6 17
17	8 41	+15·6	61·2	16·7	72	278	97	13·2	16 33	16 22	23 50	6 26	6 39
18	9 40	+10·2	61·2	16·7	84	252	100	14·2	18 02	17 57	—	6 48	6 56
19	10 35	+ 4·1	60·8	16·6	96	137	99	15·2	19 29	19 30	0 44	7 08	7 10
20	11 30	− 2·1	60·2	16·4	108	125	96	16·2	20 54	21 01	1 36	7 27	7 23
21	12 23	− 8·0	59·4	16·2	121	120	90	17·2	22 17	22 29	2 27	7 46	7 37
22	13 16	−13·3	58·5	15·9	133	116	82	18·2	23 37	23 55	3 18	8 07	7 53
23	14 09	−17·8	57·5	15·7	145	112	73	19·2	—	—	4 09	8 31	8 12
24	15 02	−21·2	56·6	15·4	157	107	63	20·2	0 53	1 16	5 00	9 02	8 38
25	15 56	−23·5	55·8	15·2	169	102	53	21·2	2 01	2 28	5 52	9 40	9 12
26	16 50	−24·6	55·1	15·0	181	97	44	22·2	3 01	3 29	6 44	10 27	9 58
27	17 43	−24·4	54·6	14·9	194	91	34	23·2	3 49	4 17	7 34	11 22	10 55
28	18 35	−23·2	54·3	14·8	206	86	26	24·2	4 27	4 52	8 23	12 25	12 01
29	19 26	−20·9	54·1	14·7	218	83	18	25·2	4 57	5 17	9 10	13 32	13 12

MERCURY

Day	RA	Dec. −	Diam.	Phase	Transit		Day	RA	Dec. −	Diam.	Phase	Transit	
	h m	°			h m			h m	°			h m	
1	20 25	21·2	—	—	11 44		16	22 09	13·4	—	—	12 30	
4	20 46	20·1	—	—	11 53	Mercury is too	19	22 30	11·2	—	—	12 39	Mercury is too
7	21 06	18·8	—	—	12 02	close to the	22	22 50	8·8	—	—	12 47	close to the
10	21 27	17·2	—	—	12 11	Sun for	25	23 11	6·3	—	—	12 56	Sun for
13	21 48	15·4	—	—	12 21	observation	28	23 30	3·7	—	—	13 03	observation
16	22 09	13·4	—	—	12 30		31	23 48	1·1	—	—	13 09	

VENUS

Day	RA	Dec. −	Diam.	Phase	Transit	5° high. 52°	5° high. 56°
	h m	°	″	%	h m	h m	h m
1	18 36	22·3	13	83	9 54	6 45	7 18
6	19 02	22·1	12	85	10 01	6 50	7 22
11	19 29	21·5	12	86	10 08	6 52	7 23
16	19 55	20·7	12	87	10 14	6 52	7 20
21	20 21	19·7	12	88	10 20	6 50	7 16
26	20 46	18·4	12	89	10 26	6 46	7 10
31	21 11	16·9	11	90	10 32	6 41	7 02

MARS

Day	RA	Dec. −	Diam.	Phase	Transit	
	h m	°			h m	
1	19 14	23·1	—	—	10 32	
6	19 30	22·7	—	—	10 28	Mars is too
11	19 46	22·1	—	—	10 25	close to the
16	20 03	21·4	—	—	10 21	Sun for
21	20 19	20·6	—	—	10 18	observation
26	20 34	19·7	—	—	10 14	
31	20 50	18·8	—	—	10 10	

(*See* pages 63–64 for explanatory notes)

SUNRISE AND SUNSET

Day	London 0°05′ 51°30′		Bristol 2°35′ 51°28′		Birmingham 1°55′ 52°28′		Manchester 2°15′ 53°28′		Newcastle 1°37′ 54°59′		Glasgow 4°14′ 55°52′		Belfast 5°56′ 54°35′	
	h m	h m	h m	h m	h m	h m	h m	h m	h m	h m	h m	h m	h m	h m
1	7 40	16 48	7 50	16 59	7 50	16 53	7 55	16 50	7 59	16 42	8 13	16 49	8 14	17 01
2	7 38	16 50	7 48	17 00	7 49	16 54	7 54	16 52	7 57	16 44	8 11	16 51	8 13	17 03
3	7 37	16 52	7 47	17 02	7 47	16 56	7 52	16 54	7 55	16 46	8 09	16 53	8 11	17 05
4	7 35	16 54	7 45	17 04	7 46	16 58	7 50	16 56	7 53	16 48	8 07	16 55	8 09	17 07
5	7 34	16 56	7 43	17 06	7 44	17 00	7 48	16 58	7 51	16 50	8 05	16 58	8 07	17 09
6	7 32	16 58	7 42	17 08	7 42	17 02	7 47	17 00	7 49	16 53	8 03	17 00	8 05	17 11
7	7 30	16 59	7 40	17 10	7 40	17 04	7 45	17 02	7 47	16 55	8 01	17 02	8 03	17 13
8	7 28	17 01	7 38	17 11	7 39	17 06	7 43	17 04	7 45	16 57	7 59	17 04	8 01	17 15
9	7 27	17 03	7 37	17 13	7 37	17 08	7 41	17 06	7 43	16 59	7 57	17 06	7 59	17 17
10	7 25	17 05	7 35	17 15	7 35	17 10	7 39	17 08	7 41	17 01	7 55	17 09	7 57	17 20
11	7 23	17 07	7 33	17 17	7 33	17 12	7 37	17 10	7 39	17 03	7 52	17 11	7 55	17 22
12	7 21	17 09	7 31	17 19	7 31	17 13	7 35	17 12	7 37	17 05	7 50	17 13	7 53	17 24
13	7 20	17 10	7 29	17 21	7 29	17 15	7 33	17 14	7 35	17 07	7 48	17 15	7 51	17 26
14	7 18	17 12	7 28	17 22	7 27	17 17	7 31	17 16	7 33	17 09	7 46	17 17	7 49	17 28
15	7 16	17 14	7 26	17 24	7 25	17 19	7 29	17 18	7 31	17 11	7 44	17 20	7 47	17 30
16	7 14	17 16	7 24	17 26	7 23	17 21	7 27	17 20	7 28	17 14	7 41	17 22	7 45	17 32
17	7 12	17 18	7 22	17 28	7 21	17 23	7 25	17 22	7 26	17 16	7 39	17 24	7 43	17 34
18	7 10	17 20	7 20	17 30	7 19	17 25	7 23	17 24	7 24	17 18	7 37	17 26	7 40	17 36
19	7 08	17 21	7 18	17 31	7 17	17 27	7 21	17 26	7 22	17 20	7 34	17 28	7 38	17 38
20	7 06	17 23	7 16	17 33	7 15	17 29	7 19	17 28	7 20	17 22	7 32	17 30	7 36	17 40
21	7 04	17 25	7 14	17 35	7 13	17 30	7 17	17 30	7 17	17 24	7 30	17 33	7 34	17 42
22	7 02	17 27	7 12	17 37	7 11	17 32	7 14	17 32	7 15	17 26	7 27	17 35	7 31	17 44
23	7 00	17 29	7 10	17 39	7 09	17 34	7 12	17 34	7 13	17 28	7 25	17 37	7 29	17 46
24	6 58	17 30	7 08	17 40	7 07	17 36	7 10	17 36	7 10	17 30	7 23	17 39	7 27	17 48
25	6 56	17 32	7 06	17 42	7 05	17 38	7 08	17 38	7 08	17 32	7 20	17 41	7 24	17 50
26	6 54	17 34	7 04	17 44	7 02	17 40	7 05	17 40	7 06	17 34	7 18	17 43	7 22	17 52
27	6 52	17 36	7 01	17 46	7 00	17 42	7 03	17 41	7 03	17 36	7 15	17 45	7 20	17 54
28	6 49	17 37	6 59	17 48	6 58	17 43	7 01	17 43	7 01	17 38	7 13	17 48	7 17	17 56
29	6 47	17 39	6 57	17 49	6 56	17 45	6 59	17 45	6 58	17 41	7 10	17 50	7 15	17 58

JUPITER

Day	RA	Dec. +	Transit	5° high 52°	5° high 56°
	h m	° ′	h m	h m	h m
1	10 59·4	7 53	2 17	20 06	20 03
11	10 55·5	8 19	1 34	19 20	19 17
21	10 50·9	8 48	0 50	18 34	18 30
31	10 46·1	9 19	0 06	17 47	17 43

Diameters—equatorial 44″ polar 42″

SATURN

Day	RA	Dec. −	Transit	
	h m	° ′	h m	
1	20 48·4	18 28	12 05	Saturn is too
11	20 53·2	18 10	11 30	close to the
21	20 58·0	17 51	10 56	Sun for
31	21 02·5	17 33	10 21	observation

Diameters—equatorial 15″ polar 14″
Rings—major axis 35″ minor axis 10″

URANUS

Day	RA	Dec. −	Transit	
	h m	° ′	h m	
1	19 07·4	22 55	10 24	Uranus is too
11	19 09·7	22 51	9 47	close to the Sun
21	19 11·8	22 48	9 10	for observation
31	19 13·7	22 45	8 32	

Diameter 4″

NEPTUNE

Day	RA	Dec. −	Transit	
	h m	° ′	h m	
1	19 14·9	21 35	10 31	Neptune is too
11	19 16·4	21 33	9 54	close to the Sun
21	19 17·7	21 30	9 16	for observation
31	19 18·9	21 28	8 37	

Diameter 2″

(*See* page 64 for explanatory notes)

Mars, Roman god of battle

Sun's Longitude 0° ♈ 20ᵈ 09ʰ

Year	Month	Week	
61	1	S.	**7th S. before Easter.** St David's Day.
62	2	M.	Cardinal Archbishop of Westminster *b.* 1923.
63	3	Tu.	Shrove Tuesday. Robert Adam *d.* 1792.*
64	4	W.	**Ash Wednesday.** RNLI founded 1824.
65	5	Th.	Sergei Prokofiev *d.* 1953. Tito Gobbi *d.* 1984.
66	6	F.	Elizabeth Barrett Browning *b.* 1806.
67	7	S.	Landseer *b.* 1802. Stevie Smith *d.* 1971.
68	8	S.	**1st S. in Lent.** William III *d.* 1702.
69	9	M.	William Cobbett *b.* 1768. Yuri Gagarin *b.* 1934.
70	10	Tu.	Prince Edward *b.* 1964. Mazzini *d.* 1872.
71	11	W.	Russian Revolution began 1917 ns.
72	12	Th.	Gabriele d'Annunzio *b.* 1864.
73	13	F.	Uranus discovered 1781.
74	14	S.	Einstein *b* 1879. Karl Marx *d.* 1883.
75	15	S.	**2nd S. in Lent.** Bessemer *d.* 1898.
76	16	M.	George Ohm *b.* 1787.
77	17	Tu.	St Patrick's Day. Edmund Kean *b.* 1787.
78	18	W.	Neville Chamberlain *b.* 1869.
79	19	Th.	**St Joseph of Nazareth.** A. J. Balfour *d.* 1930.
80	20	F.	Ibsen *b.* 1828. Vera Lynn *b.* 1917.
81	21	S.	Thomas Cranmer *exec.* 1556.
82	22	S.	**3rd S. in Lent.** Goethe *d.* 1832.
83	23	M.	Princess Eugenie of York *b.* 1990.
84	24	Tu.	William Morris *b.* 1834. Malcolm Muggeridge *b.*
85	25	W.	**The Annunciation.** Paul Scott *b.* 1920. [1903.
86	26	Th.	Robert Frost *b.* 1874. Walt Whitman *d.* 1892.*
87	27	F.	James Callaghan *b.* 1912. Arnold Bennett *d.* 1931.
88	28	S.	Neil Kinnock *b.* 1942. Gen. Eisenhower *d.* 1969.
89	29	S.	**4th S. in Lent.** John Major *b.* 1943.
90	30	M.	Goya *b.* 1746. James Cagney *d.* 1986.
91	31	Tu.	Haydn *b.* 1732. Charlotte Brontë *d.* 1855.

*Centenary   ns New Style

PHENOMENA

d	h	
1	16	Mars in conjunction with Moon. Mars 4°S.
1	23	Saturn in conjunction with Moon. Saturn 3°S.
2	04	Venus in conjunction with Moon. Venus 4°S.
6	02	Mercury in conjunction with Moon. Mercury 4°S.
6	18	Saturn in conjunction with Mars. Saturn 0°.4N.
9	21	Mercury at greatest elongation E.18°.
17	08	Jupiter in conjunction with Moon. Jupiter 5°N.
20	09	Equinox.
26	15	Mercury in inferior conjunction.
29	12	Saturn in conjunction with Moon. Saturn 4°S.
30	21	Mars in conjunction with Moon. Mars 5°S.

CONSTELLATIONS

The following are near the meridian at

	d	h		d	h
Feb.	1	24	Feb.	15	23
Mar.	1	22	Mar.	16	21
Apr.	1	20	Apr.	15	19

Cepheus (below the Pole), Camelopardus, Lynx, Gemini, Cancer, Leo, Canis Minor, Hydra, Monoceros, Canis Major and Puppis.

MINIMA OF ALGOL

d	h	d	h
2	05·8	19	10·8
5	02·7	22	07·6
7	23·5	25	04·4
10	20·3	28	01·3
13	17·1	30	22·1
16	13·9		

MOON
Phases, Apsides & Node

	d	h	m
● New Moon	4	13	22
☽ First Quarter	12	02	36
○ Full Moon	18	18	18
☾ Last Quarter	26	02	30
Perigee (362,411 km)	16	17	40
Apogee (404,904 km)	28	14	15

Mean longitude of ascending node on Mar. 1, 277°.

Summer Time in 1992 (*see* p. 70).—Begins: March 29ᵈ 01ʰ GMT Ends: October 25ᵈ 01ʰ GMT.

MONTHLY NOTES
5. First day of Ramadan.
9. Commonwealth Day.
17. Bank Holiday in Northern Ireland.
25. Lady Day (Quarter Day).
29. Mothering Sunday.
31. Financial year 1991–92 ends.

(*See* page 62 for explanatory notes)

Day	Right Ascension	Dec.	Equation of Time	Rise 52°	Rise 56°	Transit	Set 52°	Set 56°	Sidereal Time	Transit of First Point of Aries
	h m s	° ′	m s	h m	h m	h m	h m	h m	h m s	h m s
1	22 48 36	−7 34	−12 24	6 45	6 51	12 12	17 40	17 35	10 36 12	13 21 36
2	22 52 21	−7 11	−12 12	6 43	6 48	12 12	17 42	17 37	10 40 08	13 17 41
3	22 56 05	−6 48	−12 00	6 41	6 46	12 12	17 44	17 39	10 44 05	13 13 45
4	22 59 49	−6 25	−11 47	6 39	6 43	12 12	17 45	17 41	10 48 02	13 09 49
5	23 03 32	−6 02	−11 34	6 37	6 41	12 11	17 47	17 43	10 51 58	13 05 53
6	23 07 15	−5 39	−11 20	6 34	6 38	12 11	17 49	17 45	10 55 55	13 01 57
7	23 10 57	−5 16	−11 06	6 32	6 36	12 11	17 51	17 47	10 59 51	12 58 01
8	23 14 39	−4 52	−10 52	6 30	6 33	12 11	17 53	17 49	11 03 48	12 54 05
9	23 18 21	−4 29	−10 37	6 28	6 31	12 10	17 54	17 51	11 07 44	12 50 09
10	23 22 02	−4 05	−10 22	6 25	6 28	12 10	17 56	17 54	11 11 41	12 46 13
11	23 25 43	−3 42	−10 06	6 23	6 25	12 10	17 58	17 56	11 15 37	12 42 17
12	23 29 24	−3 18	− 9 50	6 21	6 23	12 10	18 00	17 58	11 19 34	12 38 21
13	23 33 04	−2 55	− 9 34	6 18	6 20	12 09	18 01	18 00	11 23 31	12 34 26
14	23 36 44	−2 31	− 9 17	6 16	6 18	12 09	18 03	18 02	11 27 27	12 30 30
15	23 40 24	−2 07	− 9 01	6 14	6 15	12 09	18 05	18 04	11 31 24	12 26 34
16	23 44 04	−1 44	− 8 43	6 12	6 12	12 09	18 07	18 06	11 35 20	12 22 38
17	23 47 43	−1 20	− 8 26	6 09	6 10	12 08	18 08	18 08	11 39 17	12 18 42
18	23 51 22	−0 56	− 8 09	6 07	6 07	12 08	18 10	18 10	11 43 13	12 14 46
19	23 55 01	−0 32	− 7 51	6 05	6 04	12 08	18 12	18 12	11 47 10	12 10 50
20	23 58 40	−0 09	− 7 33	6 02	6 02	12 07	18 14	18 14	11 51 06	12 06 54
21	0 02 18	+0 15	− 7 15	6 00	5 59	12 07	18 15	18 16	11 55 03	12 02 58
22	0 05 57	+0 39	− 6 57	5 58	5 57	12 07	18 17	18 18	11 59 00	11 59 02
23	0 09 35	+1 02	− 6 39	5 55	5 54	12 07	18 19	18 20	12 02 56	11 55 06
24	0 13 14	+1 26	− 6 21	5 53	5 51	12 06	18 20	18 22	12 06 53	11 51 11
25	0 16 52	+1 50	− 6 03	5 51	5 49	12 06	18 22	18 24	12 10 49	11 47 15
26	0 20 30	+2 13	− 5 45	5 48	5 46	12 06	18 24	18 26	12 14 46	11 43 19
27	0 24 09	+2 37	− 5 27	5 46	5 43	12 05	18 26	18 28	12 18 42	11 39 23
28	0 27 47	+3 00	− 5 08	5 44	5 41	12 05	18 27	18 31	12 22 39	11 35 27
29	0 31 26	+3 24	− 4 50	5 41	5 38	12 05	18 29	18 33	12 26 35	11 31 31
30	0 35 04	+3 47	− 4 32	5 39	5 35	12 04	18 31	18 35	12 30 32	11 27 35
31	0 38 43	+4 10	− 4 14	5 37	5 33	12 04	18 32	18 37	12 34 28	11 23 39

THE SUN   s.d. 16′·1

Duration of Civil (C), Nautical (N) and Astronomical (A) Twilight (in minutes)

Lat. °	Mar. 1 C	N	A	Mar. 11 C	N	A	Mar. 21 C	N	A	Mar. 31 C	N	A
52	34	73	112	34	73	113	34	74	116	34	76	120
56	38	81	124	37	80	125	37	82	129	38	84	136

ASTRONOMICAL NOTES

MERCURY is at its greatest eastern elongation (18°) on the 9th and thus is visible in the evenings low in the western sky around the end of civil twilight. It is best seen (because it is brighter) near the beginning of the month; at the end of its period of visibility, about the 19th–20th, its magnitude has faded to +2. This evening apparition is the most suitable one of the year for observers in the northern hemisphere.

VENUS, magnitude −3·9, is a brilliant morning object at first, but only visible low in the ESE sky for a very short while before dawn. Gradually it becomes more and more difficult to observe and by the end of the month rises at about the same time as the Sun. On the morning of the 2nd the old crescent Moon passes 4°N. of the planet.

MARS is unsuitably placed for observation.

JUPITER, magnitude −2·5, continues to be visible as a brilliant object for the greater part of the night. Jupiter is in Leo.

SATURN is too close to the Sun for observation.

ZODIACAL LIGHT. The evening cone may be observed in the western sky after the end of twilight, from the 1st to the 5th and again after the 19th.

(*See* pages 62–63 for explanatory notes)

THE MOON

Day	RA	Dec.	Hor. Par.	Semi-diam.	Sun's Co-long.	PA of Bright Limb	Phase	Age	Rise 52°	Rise 56°	Transit	Set 52°	Set 56°
	h m	°	′	′	°	°	%	d	h m	h m	h m	h m	h m
1	20 14	−17·8	54·0	14·7	230	80	11	26·2	5 20	5 36	9 55	14 40	14 25
2	21 00	−13·9	54·1	14·7	242	79	6	27·2	5 39	5 51	10 39	15 49	15 39
3	21 46	− 9·5	54·3	14·8	255	82	2	28·2	5 56	6 03	11 21	16 58	16 52
4	22 30	− 4·7	54·5	14·9	267	103	0	29·2	6 11	6 14	12 02	18 07	18 06
5	23 14	+ 0·3	54·9	14·9	279	203	0	0·4	6 25	6 24	12 44	19 17	19 21
6	23 59	+ 5·4	55·3	15·1	291	230	2	1·4	6 41	6 35	13 27	20 29	20 37
7	0 46	+10·3	55·7	15·2	303	238	6	2·4	6 58	6 48	14 12	21 43	21 56
8	1 34	+14·9	56·2	15·3	316	243	12	3·4	7 18	7 03	15 00	22 58	23 16
9	2 26	+18·9	56·7	15·5	328	248	19	4·4	7 44	7 24	15 51	—	—
10	3 20	+22·0	57·3	15·6	340	253	28	5·4	8 18	7 53	16 45	0 12	0 36
11	4 17	+23·9	57·9	15·8	352	259	38	6·4	9 03	8 35	17 43	1 23	1 50
12	5 17	+24·5	58·5	15·9	4	266	49	7·4	10 02	9 34	18 42	2 25	2 53
13	6 18	+23·6	59·1	16·1	16	272	60	8·4	11 14	10 49	19 41	3 15	3 41
14	7 19	+21·2	59·7	16·3	29	277	71	9·4	12 35	12 16	20 39	3 55	4 15
15	8 18	+17·4	60·2	16·4	41	281	81	10·4	14 02	13 48	21 35	4 25	4 40
16	9 16	+12·4	60·4	16·5	53	283	89	11·4	15 29	15 21	22 29	4 49	4 59
17	10 11	+ 6·8	60·5	16·5	65	282	95	12·4	16 56	16 54	23 21	5 10	5 14
18	11 05	+ 0·7	60·3	16·4	77	269	99	13·4	18 21	18 25	—	5 29	5 28
19	11 59	− 5·3	59·9	16·3	89	171	100	14·4	19 46	19 55	0 12	5 48	5 42
20	12 52	−11·0	59·2	16·1	102	129	98	15·4	21 09	21 23	1 04	6 08	5 57
21	13 46	−15·9	58·4	15·9	114	119	93	16·4	22 28	22 49	1 55	6 32	6 16
22	14 41	−19·8	57·6	15·7	126	112	87	17·4	23 42	—	2 48	7 00	6 39
23	15 37	−22·6	56·7	15·4	138	106	79	18·4	—	0 07	3 42	7 36	7 11
24	16 32	−24·1	55·9	15·2	150	100	70	19·4	0 47	1 15	4 35	8 20	7 52
25	17 26	−24·3	55·2	15·0	162	94	61	20·4	1 41	2 09	5 27	9 14	8 46
26	18 19	−23·4	54·7	14·9	175	88	51	21·4	2 24	2 50	6 17	10 15	9 49
27	19 10	−21·5	54·4	14·8	187	83	42	22·4	2 57	3 19	7 05	11 20	10 59
28	19 59	−18·6	54·2	14·8	199	79	33	23·4	3 23	3 40	7 51	12 28	12 11
29	20 46	−15·0	54·2	14·8	211	76	24	24·4	3 43	3 56	8 35	13 36	13 25
30	21 32	−10·8	54·3	14·8	223	75	17	25·4	4 01	4 10	9 17	14 45	14 38
31	22 17	− 6·1	54·6	14·9	236	75	10	26·4	4 17	4 21	9 59	15 54	15 51

MERCURY

Day	RA	Dec.	Diam.	Phase	Transit	5° high 52°	5° high 56°	Day	RA	Dec. +	Diam.	Phase	Transit	5° high 52°	5° high 56°
	h m	°	″	%	h m	h m	h m		h m	°	″	%	h m	h m	h m
1	23 42	− 1·9	6	81	13 07	18 29	18 24	16	0 36	7·3	9	20	12 59	19 04	19 06
4	0 00	+ 0·6	6	70	13 12	18 46	18 44	19	0 35	7·5	10	11	12 45	18 50	18 52
7	0 14	+ 3·0	7	58	13 15	19 00	19 00	22	0 30	7·1	10	5	12 28	18 29	18 31
10	0 26	+ 4·9	7	45	13 14	19 08	19 09	25	0 23	6·0	11	1	12 08	18 03	18 05
13	0 33	+ 6·4	8	32	13 09	19 10	19 12	28	0 14	4·6	11	1	11 48	17 35	17 36
16	0 36	+ 7·3	9	20	12 59	19 04	19 06	31	0 06	3·0	11	3	11 28	17 08	17 07

VENUS   MARS

Day	RA	Dec. −	Diam.	Phase	Transit	5° high 52°	5° high 56°	Day	RA	Dec. −	Diam.	Phase	Transit	
	h m	°	″	%	h m	h m	h m		h m	°			h m	
1	21 06	17·2	11	90	10 31	6 42	7 03	1	20 47	19·0	—	—	10 11	
6	21 31	15·5	11	90	10 36	6 35	6 55	6	21 03	18·0	—	—	10 07	Mars is too
11	21 55	13·6	11	91	10 40	6 28	6 45	11	21 18	16·9	—	—	10 02	close to the
16	22 19	11·6	11	92	10 44	6 20	6 34	16	21 34	15·7	—	—	9 58	Sun for
21	22 43	9·5	11	93	10 48	6 11	6 23	21	21 49	14·5	—	—	9 53	observation
26	23 06	7·2	11	94	10 52	6 02	6 12	26	22 04	13·2	—	—	9 49	
31	23 29	4·9	11	94	10 55	5 53	6 00	31	22 19	11·8	—	—	9 44	

(See pages 63–64 for explanatory notes)

SUNRISE AND SUNSET

Day	London 0°05′ 51°30′		Bristol 2°35′ 51°28′		Birmingham 1°55′ 52°28′		Manchester 2°15′ 53°28′		Newcastle 1°37′ 54°59′		Glasgow 4°14′ 55°52′		Belfast 5°56′ 54°35′	
	h m	h m	h m	h m	h m	h m	h m	h m	h m	h m	h m	h m	h m	h m
1	6 45	17 41	6 55	17 51	6 54	17 47	6 56	17 47	6 56	17 43	7 08	17 52	7 13	18 00
2	6 43	17 43	6 53	17 53	6 51	17 49	6 54	17 49	6 54	17 45	7 05	17 54	7 10	18 02
3	6 41	17 45	6 51	17 55	6 49	17 51	6 52	17 51	6 51	17 47	7 03	17 56	7 08	18 04
4	6 39	17 46	6 49	17 56	6 47	17 53	6 49	17 53	6 49	17 49	7 00	17 58	7 05	18 06
5	6 36	17 48	6 46	17 58	6 45	17 54	6 47	17 55	6 46	17 51	6 58	18 00	7 03	18 08
6	6 34	17 50	6 44	18 00	6 42	17 56	6 45	17 57	6 44	17 53	6 55	18 02	7 01	18 10
7	6 32	17 52	6 42	18 02	6 40	17 58	6 42	17 59	6 41	17 55	6 53	18 04	6 58	18 12
8	6 30	17 53	6 40	18 03	6 38	18 00	6 40	18 00	6 39	17 57	6 50	18 06	6 56	18 14
9	6 28	17 55	6 38	18 05	6 36	18 02	6 38	18 02	6 36	17 59	6 47	18 09	6 53	18 16
10	6 25	17 57	6 35	18 07	6 33	18 04	6 35	18 04	6 34	18 01	6 45	18 11	6 51	18 18
11	6 23	17 58	6 33	18 08	6 31	18 05	6 33	18 06	6 31	18 03	6 42	18 13	6 48	18 20
12	6 21	18 00	6 31	18 10	6 29	18 07	6 30	18 08	6 29	18 05	6 40	18 15	6 46	18 22
13	6 19	18 02	6 29	18 12	6 26	18 09	6 28	18 10	6 26	18 07	6 37	18 17	6 43	18 24
14	6 16	18 04	6 26	18 14	6 24	18 11	6 26	18 12	6 24	18 09	6 34	18 19	6 41	18 26
15	6 14	18 05	6 24	18 15	6 22	18 12	6 23	18 14	6 21	18 11	6 32	18 21	6 38	18 28
16	6 12	18 07	6 22	18 17	6 19	18 14	6 21	18 15	6 19	18 13	6 29	18 23	6 36	18 30
17	6 10	18 09	6 20	18 19	6 17	18 16	6 18	18 17	6 16	18 15	6 27	18 25	6 33	18 32
18	6 07	18 10	6 17	18 20	6 15	18 18	6 16	18 19	6 13	18 17	6 24	18 27	6 31	18 34
19	6 05	18 12	6 15	18 22	6 12	18 20	6 14	18 21	6 11	18 19	6 21	18 29	6 28	18 36
20	6 03	18 14	6 13	18 24	6 10	18 21	6 11	18 23	6 08	18 20	6 19	18 31	6 26	18 38
21	6 00	18 15	6 10	18 25	6 08	18 23	6 09	18 25	6 06	18 22	6 16	18 33	6 23	18 40
22	5 58	18 17	6 08	18 27	6 05	18 25	6 06	18 26	6 03	18 24	6 13	18 35	6 21	18 42
23	5 56	18 19	6 06	18 29	6 03	18 27	6 04	18 28	6 01	18 26	6 11	18 37	6 18	18 43
24	5 54	18 21	6 04	18 31	6 00	18 28	6 01	18 30	5 58	18 28	6 08	18 39	6 16	18 45
25	5 51	18 22	6 01	18 32	5 58	18 30	5 59	18 32	5 56	18 30	6 06	18 41	6 13	18 47
26	5 49	18 24	5 59	18 34	5 56	18 32	5 57	18 34	5 53	18 32	6 03	18 43	6 11	18 49
27	5 47	18 26	5 57	18 36	5 53	18 34	5 54	18 36	5 51	18 34	6 00	18 45	6 08	18 51
28	5 44	18 27	5 54	18 37	5 51	18 35	5 52	18 37	5 48	18 36	5 58	18 47	6 06	18 53
29	5 42	18 29	5 52	18 39	5 49	18 37	5 49	18 39	5 45	18 38	5 55	18 49	6 03	18 55
30	5 40	18 31	5 50	18 41	5 46	18 39	5 47	18 41	5 43	18 40	5 52	18 51	6 01	18 57
31	5 38	18 32	5 48	18 42	5 44	18 41	5 44	18 43	5 40	18 42	5 50	18 53	5 58	18 59

JUPITER

Day	RA	Dec. +	Transit	5° high 52°	5° high 56°
	h m	° ′	h m	h m	h m
1	10 46·6	9 16	0 10	6 24	6 29
11	10 41·7	9 45	23 22	5 43	5 47
21	10 37·2	10 12	22 38	5 01	5 06
31	10 33·4	10 33	21 55	4 20	4 25

Diameters—equatorial 44″ polar 42″

SATURN

Day	RA	Dec. −	Transit	
	h m	° ′	h m	
1	21 02·1	17 35	10 24	Saturn is too close to the Sun for observation
11	21 06·4	17 17	9 49	
21	21 10·4	17 01	9 14	
31	21 14·1	16 46	8 38	

Diameters—equatorial 16″ polar 14″
Rings—major axis 35″ minor axis 10″

URANUS

Day	RA	Dec. −	Transit	
	h m	° ′	h m	
1	19 13·5	22 45	8 36	Uranus is too close to the Sun for observation
11	19 15·1	22 42	7 58	
21	19 16·5	22 40	7 20	
31	19 17·4	22 39	6 42	

Diameter 4″

NEPTUNE

Day	RA	Dec. −	Transit	
	h m	° ′	h m	
1	19 18·8	21 28	8 41	Neptune is too close to the Sun for observation
11	19 19·8	21 26	8 03	
21	19 20·6	21 24	7 24	
31	19 21·2	21 23	6 46	

Diameter 2″

(See page 64 for explanatory notes)

Aperire, to open. Earth opens to receive seed.
Sun's Longitude 30° ☋ 19ᵈ20ʰ

Year	Month	Week	
92	1	W.	RAF formed 1918. VAT introduced 1973.
93	2	Th.	Zola *b.* 1840. Georges Pompidou *d.* 1974.
94	3	F.	Henry IV *b.* 1367. Sarah Vaughan *d.* 1990.
95	4	S.	North Atlantic Treaty signed 1949.
96	5	S.	**5th S. after Lent.** Fragonard *b.* 1732.
97	6	M.	USA entered First World War 1917.
98	7	Tu.	Wordsworth *b.* 1770. Henry Ford *d.* 1947.
99	8	W.	Adrian Boult *b.* 1889. Nijinsky *d.* 1950.
100	9	Th.	Lorenzo de Medici *d.* 1492*
101	10	F.	Hazlitt *b.* 1778. Gen. William Booth *b.* 1829.
102	11	S.	Treaty of Utrecht 1713. Canning *b.* 1770.
103	12	S.	**Palm Sunday.**
104	13	M.	Arthur 'Bomber' Harris *b.* 1892.*
105	14	Tu.	John Gielgud *b.* 1904. Ernest Bevin *d.* 1951.
106	15	W.	HILARY LAW SITTTINGS END. Greta Garbo *d.* 1990.
107	16	Th.	**Maundy Thursday.** Kingsley Amis *b.* 1922.
108	17	F.	**Good Friday.** Benjamin Franklin *d.* 1790.
109	18	S.	**Easter Eve.** San Francisco earthquake 1906.
110	19	S.	**Easter Day.** Disraeli *d.* 1881.
111	20	M.	Napoleon III *b.* 1808. Adolf Hitler *b.* 1889.
112	21	Tu.	QUEEN ELIZABETH II *b.* 1926. Racine *d.* 1699.
113	22	W.	Kant *b.* 1724. Campbell-Bannerman *d.* 1908.
114	23	Th.	ST GEORGE'S DAY. Turner *b.* 1775.
115	24	F.	Trollope *b.* 1815. Marshal Pétain *b.* 1856.
116	25	S.	**St Mark.** John Keble *b.* 1792.*
117	26	S.	**1st S. after Easter.** Daniel Defoe *d.* 1731.
118	27	M.	Magellan killed 1591. Gibbon *b.* 1737.
119	28	Tu.	EASTER LAW SITTINGS BEGIN. Edward IV *b.* 1442.
120	29	W.	Poincaré *b.* 1854. Alfred Hitchcock *d.* 1980.
121	30	Th.	Adolf Hitler *d.* 1945.

PHENOMENA

d	h	
1	13	Venus in conjunction with Moon. Venus 6°S.
2	05	Mercury in conjunction with Moon. Mercury 3°S.
6	13	Venus in conjunction with Mercury. Venus 2°S.
13	13	Jupiter in conjunction with Moon. Jupiter 5°N.
23	15	Mercury at greatest elongation W.27°.
25	23	Saturn in conjunction with Moon. Saturn 4°S.
29	01	Mars in conjunction with Moon. Mars 6°S.
30	15	Mercury in conjunction with Moon. Mercury 7°S.

CONSTELLATIONS

The following constellations are near the meridian at

d	h		d	h
Mar. 1	24		Mar. 16	23
Apr. 1	22		Apr. 15	21
May 1	20		May 16	19

Cepheus (below the Pole), Cassiopeia (below the Pole), Ursa Major, Leo Minor, Leo, Sextans, Hydra and Crater.

MINIMA OF ALGOL

d	h		d	h
2	18·9		17	03·0
5	15·7		19	23·8
8	12·5		22	20·6
11	09·4		25	17·5
14	06·2		28	14·3

*Centenary

MOON
Phases, Apsides & Node

	d	h	m
● New Moon	3	05	01
☽ First Quarter	10	10	06
○ Full Moon	17	04	42
☾ Last Quarter	24	21	40
Perigee (367,731 km)	13	06	54
Apogee (404,202 km)	25	09	48

Mean longitude of ascending node on Apr. 1, 275°.

See note on Summer Time, p. 22.

MONTHLY NOTES

5. Income tax year (1991–92) ends.
17. Bank Holiday in Scotland.
18. First day of Passover. Lent ends at midnight.
20. Bank Holiday in England, Wales and Northern Ireland.
26. Greek Orthodox Easter.

(*See* page 62 for explanatory notes)

Day	Right Ascension	Dec. +	Equation of Time	Rise 52°	Rise 56°	Transit	Set 52°	Set 56°	Sidereal Time	Transit of First Point of Aries
	h m s	° '	m s	h m	h m	h m	h m	h m	h m s	h m s
1	0 42 21	4 33	− 3 56	5 35	5 30	12 04	18 34	18 39	12 38 25	11 19 43
2	0 46 00	4 56	− 3 39	5 32	5 28	12 03	18 36	18 41	12 42 22	11 15 47
3	0 49 39	5 19	− 3 21	5 30	5 25	12 03	18 38	18 43	12 46 18	11 11 51
4	0 53 18	5 42	− 3 03	5 28	5 22	12 03	18 39	18 45	12 50 15	11 07 56
5	0 56 57	6 05	− 2 46	5 25	5 20	12 03	18 41	18 47	12 54 11	11 04 00
6	1 00 37	6 28	− 2 29	5 23	5 17	12 02	18 43	18 49	12 58 08	11 00 04
7	1 04 16	6 51	− 2 12	5 21	5 15	12 02	18 44	18 51	13 02 04	10 56 08
8	1 07 56	7 13	− 1 55	5 19	5 12	12 02	18 46	18 53	13 06 01	10 52 12
9	1 11 36	7 35	− 1 39	5 16	5 09	12 02	18 48	18 55	13 09 57	10 48 16
10	1 15 17	7 58	− 1 23	5 14	5 07	12 01	18 50	18 57	13 13 54	10 44 20
11	1 18 57	8 20	− 1 07	5 12	5 04	12 01	18 51	18 59	13 17 51	10 40 24
12	1 22 38	8 42	− 0 51	5 10	5 02	12 01	18 53	19 01	13 21 47	10 36 28
13	1 26 19	9 04	− 0 35	5 07	4 59	12 00	18 55	19 03	13 25 44	10 32 32
14	1 30 00	9 25	− 0 20	5 05	4 57	12 00	18 56	19 05	13 29 40	10 28 37
15	1 33 42	9 47	− 0 05	5 03	4 54	12 00	18 58	19 07	13 33 37	10 24 41
16	1 37 24	10 08	+ 0 09	5 01	4 52	12 00	19 00	19 09	13 37 33	10 20 45
17	1 41 07	10 29	+ 0 23	4 59	4 49	11 59	19 01	19 11	13 41 30	10 16 49
18	1 44 49	10 50	+ 0 37	4 56	4 47	11 59	19 03	19 13	13 45 26	10 12 53
19	1 48 33	11 11	+ 0 50	4 54	4 44	11 59	19 05	19 15	13 49 23	10 08 57
20	1 52 16	11 32	+ 0 03	4 52	4 42	11 59	19 07	19 17	13 53 20	10 05 01
21	1 56 00	11 52	+ 1 16	4 50	4 39	11 59	19 08	19 19	13 57 16	10 01 05
22	1 59 45	12 13	+ 1 28	4 48	4 37	11 58	19 10	19 21	14 01 13	9 57 09
23	2 03 30	12 33	+ 1 40	4 46	4 34	11 58	19 12	19 24	14 05 09	9 53 13
24	2 07 15	12 52	+ 1 51	4 44	4 32	11 58	19 13	19 26	14 09 06	9 49 17
25	2 11 01	13 12	+ 2 01	4 42	4 30	11 58	19 15	19 28	14 13 02	9 45 22
26	2 14 47	13 32	+ 2 11	4 40	4 27	11 58	19 17	19 30	14 16 59	9 41 26
27	2 18 34	13 51	+ 2 21	4 38	4 25	11 58	19 18	19 32	14 20 55	9 37 30
28	2 22 22	14 10	+ 2 30	4 36	4 23	11 57	19 20	19 34	14 24 52	9 33 34
29	2 26 10	14 29	+ 2 39	4 34	4 20	11 57	19 22	19 36	14 28 49	9 29 38
30	2 29 58	14 47	+ 2 47	4 32	4 18	11 57	19 24	19 38	14 32 45	9 25 42

Duration of Civil (C), Nautical (N) and Astronomical (A) Twilight (in minutes)

Lat. °	Apr. 1 C	N	A	Apr. 11 C	N	A	Apr. 21 C	N	A	Apr. 30 C	N	A
52	34	76	121	35	79	128	37	84	138	39	89	152
56	38	85	137	40	90	148	42	96	167	44	105	200

ASTRONOMICAL NOTES

MERCURY is unsuitably placed for observation from these latitudes, despite the fact that it is at greatest western elongation on the 23rd, even though it is at aphelion only five days earlier.

VENUS is unsuitably placed for observation.

MARS is unsuitably placed for observation.

JUPITER, magnitude −2·3, is a brilliant object in Leo and even by the end of the month is still visible until after 02h. The four Galilean satellites are readily observable with any small telescope or even a good pair of binoculars, provided that they are held rigidly. Times of eclipses and shadow transits of these satellites are given on page 71.

SATURN is too close to the Sun for observation at first but towards the end of the month it may be glimpsed very low in the south-eastern sky during morning nautical twilight, but only under good conditions. The magnitude of Saturn is +0·8.

(*See* pages 62–63 for explanatory notes)

THE MOON

Day	RA	Dec.	Hor. Par.	Semi- diam.	Sun's Co- long.	PA of Bright Limb	Phase	Age	Rise 52°	Rise 56°	Tran- sit	Set 52°	Set 56°
	h m	°	′	′	°	°	%	d	h m	h m	h m	h m	h m
1	23 01	− 1·1	54·9	15·0	248	77	5	27·4	4 32	4 32	10 41	17 04	17 06
2	23 46	+ 3·9	55·4	15·1	260	86	2	28·4	4 47	4 43	11 24	18 15	18 22
3	0 33	+ 8·9	55·9	15·2	272	130	0	29·4	5 04	4 56	12 09	19 29	19 41
4	1 21	+13·6	56·4	15·4	284	222	1	0·8	5 24	5 11	12 56	20 45	21 02
5	2 13	+17·8	56·9	15·5	297	240	4	1·8	5 49	5 31	13 47	22 01	22 23
6	3 07	+21·1	57·4	15·6	309	249	9	2·8	6 20	5 58	14 41	23 13	23 39
7	4 04	+23·4	57·8	15·8	321	256	15	3·8	7 02	6 36	15 38	—	—
8	5 04	+24·2	58·3	15·9	333	264	24	4·8	7 57	7 30	16 37	0 18	0 46
9	6 04	+23·7	58·7	16·0	346	270	34	5·8	9 05	8 39	17 35	1 12	1 38
10	7 04	+21·6	59·0	16·1	358	276	45	6·8	10 22	10 01	18 32	1 54	2 16
11	8 02	+18·2	59·3	16·2	10	281	57	7·8	11 44	11 29	19 27	2 26	2 43
12	8 59	+13·8	59·5	16·2	22	285	68	8·8	13 08	12 59	20 20	2 52	3 03
13	9 53	+ 8·5	59·6	16·2	34	287	78	9·8	14 32	14 28	21 11	3 13	3 19
14	10 46	+ 2·8	59·6	16·2	46	287	87	10·8	15 56	15 57	22 01	3 32	3 34
15	11 38	− 3·1	59·4	16·2	59	284	94	11·8	17 18	17 25	22 51	3 51	3 47
16	12 31	− 8·8	59·0	16·1	71	276	98	12·8	18 41	18 53	23 42	4 10	4 02
17	13 24	−13·9	58·5	16·0	83	230	100	13·8	20 02	20 19	—	4 32	4 19
18	14 19	−18·2	57·9	15·8	95	131	99	14·8	21 19	21 42	0 35	4 59	4 40
19	15 14	−21·4	57·2	15·6	107	113	96	15·8	22 29	22 56	1 28	5 31	5 08
20	16 11	−23·4	56·5	15·4	119	104	91	16·8	23 29	23 57	2 22	6 13	5 46
21	17 06	−24·2	55·8	15·2	132	97	84	17·8	—	—	3 16	7 03	6 35
22	18 01	−23·6	55·2	15·0	144	90	77	18·8	0 17	0 44	4 08	8 02	7 36
23	18 53	−22·0	54·7	14·9	156	84	68	19·8	0 55	1 18	4 58	9 07	8 44
24	19 43	−19·4	54·4	14·8	168	80	59	20·8	1 23	1 42	5 45	10 14	9 56
25	20 31	−16·0	54·3	14·8	180	76	49	21·8	1 46	2 01	6 29	11 22	11 09
26	21 17	−12·0	54·3	14·8	193	73	40	22·8	2 05	2 15	7 12	12 30	12 21
27	22 02	− 7·5	54·5	14·8	205	72	31	23·8	2 22	2 28	7 54	13 38	13 34
28	22 46	− 2·7	54·8	14·9	217	71	22	24·8	2 37	2 39	8 36	14 47	14 48
29	23 31	+ 2·3	55·3	15·1	229	72	15	25·8	2 52	2 50	9 18	15 58	16 03
30	0 17	+ 7·3	55·8	15·2	241	74	8	26·8	3 09	3 02	10 02	17 11	17 21

MERCURY

Day	RA	Dec.	Diam.	Phase	Tran- sit		Day	RA	Dec.	Diam.	Phase	Tran- sit	
	h m	°			h m			h m	°			h m	
1	0 03	+2·5	—	—	11 22		16	0 05	−1·2	—	—	10 27	
4	23 58	+1·1	—	—	11 06	Mercury is too	19	0 13	−0·9	—	—	10 23	Mercury is too
7	23 56	−0·1	—	—	10 52	close to the	22	0 22	−0·3	—	—	10 21	close to the
10	23 56	−0·8	—	—	10 41	Sun for	25	0 33	+0·7	—	—	10 20	Sun for
13	23 59	−1·2	—	—	10 32	observation	28	0 46	+1·8	—	—	10 21	observation
16	0 05	−1·2	—	—	10 27		31	1 00	+3·2	—	—	10 23	

VENUS　　　　　　　　　　　　　　MARS

Day	RA	Dec.	Diam.	Phase	Tran- sit		Day	RA	Dec.	Diam.	Phase	Tran- sit	
	h m	°			h m			h m	°			h m	
1	23 34	− 4·4	—	—	10 56		1	22 22	11·5	—	—	9 43	
6	23 56	− 2·0	—	—	10 59		6	22 36	10·1	—	—	9 38	
11	0 19	+ 0·4	—	—	11 02	Venus is too	11	22 51	8·7	—	—	9 33	Mars is too
16	0 42	+ 2·9	—	—	11 05	close to the	16	23 05	7·2	—	—	9 28	close to the
21	1 04	+ 5·3	—	—	11 08	Sun for	21	23 20	5·8	—	—	9 22	Sun for
26	1 27	+ 7·7	—	—	11 11	observation	26	23 34	4·2	—	—	9 17	observation
31	1 50	+10·0	—	—	11 14		31	23 48	2·7	—	—	9 11	

(*See* pages 63–64 for explanatory notes)

SUNRISE AND SUNSET

Day	London 0°05′ 51°30′		Bristol 2°35′ 51°28′		Birmingham 1°55′ 52°28′		Manchester 2°15′ 53°28′		Newcastle 1°37′ 54°59′		Glasgow 4°14′ 55°52′		Belfast 5°56′ 54°35′	
	h m	h m	h m	h m	h m	h m	h m	h m	h m	h m	h m	h m	h m	h m
1	5 35	18 34	5 45	18 44	5 42	18 42	5 42	18 45	5 38	18 44	5 47	18 55	5 56	19 01
2	5 33	18 36	5 43	18 46	5 39	18 44	5 40	18 47	5 35	18 46	5 45	18 57	5 53	19 03
3	5 31	18 37	5 41	18 47	5 37	18 46	5 37	18 48	5 33	18 48	5 42	19 00	5 51	19 05
4	5 29	18 39	5 39	18 49	5 35	18 48	5 35	18 50	5 30	18 50	5 39	19 02	5 48	19 06
5	5 26	18 41	5 36	18 51	5 32	18 49	5 32	18 52	5 28	18 52	5 37	19 04	5 46	19 08
6	5 24	18 42	5 34	18 52	5 30	18 51	5 30	18 54	5 25	18 54	5 34	19 06	5 43	19 10
7	5 22	18 44	5 32	18 54	5 28	18 53	5 28	18 56	5 23	18 56	5 32	19 08	5 41	19 12
8	5 20	18 46	5 30	18 56	5 26	18 55	5 25	18 57	5 20	18 58	5 29	19 10	5 38	19 14
9	5 17	18 47	5 27	18 57	5 23	18 56	5 23	18 59	5 18	18 59	5 27	19 12	5 36	19 16
10	5 15	18 49	5 25	18 59	5 21	18 58	5 21	19 01	5 15	19 01	5 24	19 14	5 33	19 18
11	5 13	18 51	5 23	19 01	5 19	19 00	5 18	19 03	5 13	19 03	5 21	19 16	5 31	19 20
12	5 11	18 52	5 21	19 02	5 16	19 01	5 16	19 05	5 10	19 05	5 19	19 18	5 28	19 22
13	5 09	18 54	5 19	19 04	5 14	19 03	5 14	19 07	5 08	19 07	5 16	19 20	5 26	19 24
14	5 06	18 56	5 17	19 06	5 12	19 05	5 11	19 08	5 05	19 09	5 14	19 22	5 24	19 26
15	5 04	18 57	5 14	19 07	5 10	19 07	5 09	19 10	5 03	19 11	5 11	19 24	5 21	19 28
16	5 02	18 59	5 12	19 09	5 07	19 08	5 07	19 12	5 01	19 13	5 09	19 26	5 19	19 29
17	5 00	19 01	5 10	19 11	5 05	19 10	5 04	19 14	4 58	19 15	5 06	19 28	5 16	19 31
18	4 58	19 02	5 08	19 12	5 03	19 12	5 02	19 16	4 56	19 17	5 04	19 30	5 14	19 33
19	4 56	19 04	5 06	19 14	5 01	19 14	5 00	19 17	4 53	19 19	5 01	19 32	5 12	19 35
20	4 54	19 06	5 04	19 16	4 59	19 15	4 58	19 19	4 51	19 21	4 59	19 34	5 09	19 37
21	4 52	19 07	5 02	19 17	4 57	19 17	4 55	19 21	4 49	19 23	4 56	19 36	5 07	19 39
22	4 50	19 09	5 00	19 19	4 54	19 19	4 53	19 23	4 46	19 25	4 54	19 38	5 05	19 41
23	4 48	19 11	4 58	19 21	4 52	19 21	4 51	19 25	4 44	19 27	4 52	19 40	5 02	19 43
24	4 46	19 12	4 56	19 22	4 50	19 22	4 49	19 27	4 42	19 29	4 49	19 42	5 00	19 45
25	4 44	19 14	4 54	19 24	4 48	19 24	4 47	19 28	4 39	19 31	4 47	19 44	4 58	19 47
26	4 42	19 16	4 52	19 26	4 46	19 26	4 44	19 30	4 37	19 33	4 45	19 46	4 56	19 49
27	4 40	19 17	4 50	19 27	4 44	19 28	4 42	19 32	4 35	19 35	4 42	19 48	4 53	19 50
28	4 38	19 19	4 48	19 29	4 42	19 29	4 40	19 34	4 33	19 36	4 40	19 50	4 51	19 52
29	4 36	19 21	4 46	19 31	4 40	19 31	4 38	19 36	4 30	19 38	4 38	19 52	4 49	19 54
30	4 34	19 22	4 44	19 32	4 38	19 33	4 36	19 37	4 28	19 40	4 35	19 54	4 47	19 56

JUPITER

Day	RA	Dec. +	Transit	5° high			
				52°	56°		
	h m	° ′	h m	h m	h m		
1	10 33·1	10 35	21 51	4 16	4 21		
11	10 30·2	10 50	21 09	3 35	3 41		
21	10 28·5	10 59	20 28	2 55	3 00		
31	10 27·9	11 01	19 48	2 15	2 21		

Diameters—equatorial 42″ polar 39″

SATURN

Day	RA	Dec. −	Transit	
	h m	° ′	h m	
1	21 14·4	16 45	8 35	Saturn is too
11	21 17·5	16 32	7 59	close to the
21	21 20·2	16 21	7 22	Sun for
31	21 22·3	16 13	6 45	observation

Diameters—equatorial 16″ polar 15″
Rings—major axis 37″ minor axis 10″

URANUS

Day	RA	Dec. −	Transit	10° high	
				52°	56°
	h m	° ′	h m	h m	h m
1	19 17·5	22 39	6 38	4 27	5 29
11	19 18·1	22 38	5 59	3 48	4 50
21	19 18·3	22 38	5 20	3 09	4 11
31	19 18·2	22 38	4 41	2 29	3 32

Diameter 4″

NEPTUNE

Day	RA	Dec. −	Transit	10° high	
				52°	56°
	h m	° ′	h m	h m	h m
1	19 21·2	21 23	6 42	4 16	5 06
11	19 21·6	21 22	6 03	3 37	4 27
21	19 21·7	21 22	5 24	2 58	3 48
31	19 21·5	21 22	4 44	2 18	3 08

Diameter 2″

(*See* page 64 for explanatory notes)

Year	Month	Week	*Maia,* goddess of growth and increase. Sun's Longitude 60° II 20ᵈ 19ʰ

Ⅱ

122	1	F.	**SS. Philip and James.** Goebbels *d.* 1945.
123	2	S.	Leonardo da Vinci *d.* 1591. Bing Crosby *b.* 1904.
124	3	S.	**2nd S. after Easter.** Machiavelli *b.* 1469.
125	4	M.	General Strike started 1926.
126	5	Tu.	Marx *b.* 1818. Napoleon Bonaparte *d.* 1821.
127	6	W.	*Hindenburg* airship disaster 1937.
128	7	Th.	Tito *b.* 1892.* Gary Cooper *b.* 1901.
129	8	F.	VE Day 1945. Pres. Truman *b.* 1884.
130	9	S.	Channel Is. liberated 1945.
131	10	S.	**3rd S. after Easter.**
132	11	M.	Irving Berlin *b.* 1888. Salvador Dali *b.* 1904.
133	12	Tu.	Massenet *b.* 1842. Masefield *d.* 1967.
134	13	W.	Arthur Sullivan *b.* 1842. Gary Cooper *d.* 1961.
135	14	Th.	**St Matthias.** Rita Hayworth *d.* 1985.
136	15	F.	Daniel O'Connell *d.* 1847. James Mason *b.* 1909.
137	16	S.	H. E. Bates *b.* 1905. Henry Fonda *b.* 1909.
138	17	S.	**4th S. after Easter.** Edward Jenner *b.* 1749.
139	18	M.	Pope John Paul II *b.* 1920. Margot Fonteyn *b.* 1919.
140	19	Tu.	Nellie Melba *b.* 1861. Nancy Astor *b.* 1879.
141	20	W.	John Stuart Mill *b.* 1806. Beerbohm *d.* 1956.
142	21	Th.	Pope *b.* 1688. Elizabeth Fry *b.* 1780.
143	22	F.	Easter Law Sittings End. Wagner *b.* 1813.
144	23	S.	Ibsen *d.* 1906. Himmler *d.* 1945.
145	24	S.	Queen Victoria *b.* 1819. Suzanne Lenglen *b.* 1899.
146	25	M.	Bulwer Lytton *b.* 1803. Holst *d.* 1934.
147	26	Tu.	Queen Mary *b.* 1867. George Formby *b.* 1904.
148	26	W.	Arnold Bennett *b.* 1867. Nehru *d.* 1964.
149	28	Th.	**Ascension Day.** Pitt (Younger) *b.* 1759.
150	29	F.	Oak Apple Day 1660. Chesterton *b.* 1874.
151	30	S.	Joan of Arc *exec.* 1431. John Barrymore *d.* 1942.
152	31	S.	**S. after Ascension (6th after Easter).**

PHENOMENA

d	h	
1	20	Venus in conjunction with Moon. Venus 5°S.
10	18	Jupiter in conjunction with Moon. Jupiter 6°N.
12	01	Pluto at opposition.
23	09	Saturn in conjunction with Moon. Saturn 5°S.
28	00	Venus in conjunction with Mercury. Venus 0°.5S.
28	04	Mars in conjunction with Moon. Mars 6°S.
31	16	Mercury in superior conjunction.
31	22	Venus in conjunction with Moon. Venus 2°S.

CONSTELLATIONS

The following constellations are near the meridian at

	d	h		d	h
Apr.	1	24	Apr.	15	23
May	1	22	May	16	21
June	1	20	June	15	19

Cepheus (below the Pole), Cassiopeia (below the Pole), Ursa Minor, Ursa Major, Canes Venatici, Coma Berenices, Bootes, Leo, Virgo, Crater, Corvus, and Hydra.

ALGOL

ALGOL is inconveniently situated for observation during May.

*Centenary

MOON
Phases, Apsides & Node

	d	h	m
● New Moon	2	17	44
☽ First Quarter	9	15	44
○ Full Moon	16	16	03
☾ Last Quarter	24	15	53

Perigee (369,586 km)   8 11 41
Apogee (404,320 km)   23 04 52

Mean longitude of ascending node on May 1, 273°.

See note on Summer Time, p. 22.

MONTHLY NOTES

4. Bank Holiday, England, Wales, Scotland and N. Ireland.
9. Liberation Day, Channel Islands.
25. Bank Holiday, England, Wales, Scotland and N. Ireland.
28. Whitsunday (Scottish Term Day and Removal Day).

(*See* page 62 for explanatory notes)

Day	THE SUN s.d. 15′·8									Sidereal Time	Transit of First Point of Aries
	Right Ascension	Dec. +	Equation of Time	Rise 52°	Rise 56°	Transit	Set 52°	Set 56°			
	h m s	° ′	m s	h m	h m	h m	h m	h m		h m s	h m s
1	2 33 47	15 05	+ 2 54	4 30	4 16	11 57	19 25	19 40		14 36 42	9 24 46
2	2 37 37	15 23	+ 3 01	4 28	4 13	11 57	19 27	19 42		14 40 38	9 17 50
3	2 41 27	15 41	+ 3 08	4 26	4 11	11 57	19 29	19 44		14 44 35	9 13 54
4	2 45 18	15 59	+ 3 13	4 24	4 09	11 57	19 30	19 46		14 48 31	9 09 58
5	2 49 09	16 16	+ 3 19	4 23	4 07	11 57	19 32	19 48		14 52 28	9 06 02
6	2 53 01	16 33	+ 3 24	4 21	4 05	11 57	19 33	19 50		14 56 24	9 02 07
7	2 56 53	16 49	+ 3 28	4 19	4 03	11 57	19 35	19 52		15 00 21	8 58 11
8	3 00 46	17 06	+ 3 31	4 17	4 01	11 56	19 37	19 54		15 04 18	8 54 15
9	3 04 40	17 22	+ 3 34	4 16	3 58	11 56	19 38	19 56		15 08 14	8 50 19
10	3 08 34	17 38	+ 3 37	4 14	3 56	11 56	19 40	19 58		15 12 11	8 46 23
11	3 12 28	17 53	+ 3 39	4 12	3 54	11 56	19 42	20 00		15 16 07	8 42 27
12	3 16 23	18 09	+ 3 40	4 11	3 53	11 56	19 43	20 01		15 20 04	8 38 31
13	3 20 19	18 24	+ 3 41	4 09	3 51	11 56	19 45	20 03		15 24 00	8 34 35
14	3 24 15	18 38	+ 3 42	4 07	3 49	11 56	19 46	20 05		15 27 57	8 30 39
15	3 28 12	18 53	+ 3 42	4 06	3 47	11 56	19 48	20 07		15 31 53	8 26 43
16	3 32 09	19 06	+ 3 41	4 04	3 45	11 56	19 49	20 09		15 35 50	8 22 47
17	3 36 07	19 20	+ 3 39	4 03	3 43	11 56	19 51	20 11		15 39 47	8 18 52
18	3 40 06	19 33	+ 3 37	4 01	3 41	11 56	19 52	20 13		15 43 43	8 14 56
19	3 44 05	19 47	+ 3 35	4 00	3 40	11 56	19 54	20 14		15 47 40	8 11 00
20	3 48 04	19 59	+ 3 32	3 59	3 38	11 56	19 55	20 16		15 51 36	8 07 04
21	3 52 04	20 12	+ 3 28	3 57	3 36	11 57	19 57	20 18		15 55 33	8 03 08
22	3 56 05	20 23	+ 3 24	3 56	3 35	11 57	19 58	20 20		15 59 29	7 59 12
23	4 00 06	20 35	+ 3 20	3 55	3 33	11 57	19 59	20 21		16 03 26	7 55 16
24	4 04 08	20 46	+ 3 14	3 54	3 32	11 57	20 01	20 23		16 07 22	7 51 20
25	4 08 10	20 57	+ 3 09	3 53	3 30	11 57	20 02	20 24		16 11 19	7 47 24
26	4 12 13	21 08	+ 3 03	3 51	3 29	11 57	20 03	20 26		16 15 16	7 43 28
27	4 16 16	21 18	+ 2 56	3 50	3 28	11 57	20 05	20 28		16 19 12	7 39 32
28	4 20 20	21 28	+ 2 49	3 49	3 26	11 57	20 06	20 29		16 23 09	7 35 36
29	4 24 24	21 37	+ 2 41	3 48	3 25	11 57	20 07	20 31		16 27 05	7 31 41
30	4 28 29	21 46	+ 2 33	3 47	3 24	11 58	20 08	20 32		16 31 02	7 27 45
31	4 32 34	21 55	+ 2 24	3 47	3 23	11 58	20 09	20 33		16 34 58	7 23 49

Duration of Civil (C), Nautical (N) and Astronomical (A) Twilight (in minutes)

Lat.	May 1			May 11			May 21			May 31		
°	C	N	A	C	N	A	C	N	A	C	N	A
52	39	90	154	41	97	179	44	106	TAN	46	116	TAN
56	45	106	209	49	121	TAN	53	143	TAN	57	TAN	TAN

ASTRONOMICAL NOTES

MERCURY is unsuitably placed for observation.

VENUS, is unsuitably placed for observation.

MARS, although 50° west of the Sun by the end of the month, continues to be unsuitably placed for observation, due to the lengthening twilight.

JUPITER is still visible as a brilliant evening object, magnitude −2·1, though by the end of the month it is low in the western sky by midnight.

SATURN, magnitude +0·7, is slowly emerging from the long morning twilight and may be detected low above the south-eastern horizon before the sky gets too bright for observation. Saturn is in Capricornus.

(*See* pages 62–63 for explanatory notes)

THE MOON

Day	RA	Dec.	Hor. Par.	Semi-diam.	Sun's Co-long.	PA of Bright Limb	Phase	Age	Rise 52°	Rise 56°	Tran-sit	Set 52°	Set 56°
	h m	°	′	′	°	°	%	d	h m	h m	h m	h m	h m
1	1 05	+12·1	56·5	15·4	254	80	4	27·8	3 28	3 16	10 49	18 26	18 41
2	1 56	+16·5	57·1	15·6	266	95	1	28·8	3 51	3 35	11 39	19 43	20 03
3	2 50	+20·1	57·7	15·7	278	205	0	0·3	4 20	3 59	12 33	20 59	21 24
4	3 48	+22·7	58·3	15·9	290	248	2	1·3	4 59	4 34	13 31	22 09	22 36
5	4 48	+24·0	58·7	16·0	303	260	6	2·3	5 51	5 24	14 30	23 07	23 34
6	5 49	+23·8	59·0	16·1	315	269	13	3·3	6 56	6 30	15 30	23 53	—
7	6 50	+22·0	59·2	16·1	327	276	21	4·3	8 12	7 50	16 28	—	0 16
8	7 49	+18·9	59·3	16·2	339	281	31	5·3	9 34	9 17	17 24	0 28	0 47
9	8 46	+14·6	59·3	16·2	352	286	43	6·3	10 57	10 45	18 16	0 56	1 09
10	9 40	+ 9·6	59·2	16·1	4	289	54	7·3	12 19	12 13	19 07	1 18	1 26
11	10 33	+ 4·1	59·1	16·1	16	290	65	8·3	13 40	13 40	19 56	1 37	1 40
12	11 24	− 1·7	58·8	16·0	28	290	76	9·3	15 01	15 06	20 45	1 56	1 54
13	12 15	− 7·2	58·5	15·9	40	289	85	10·3	16 21	16 31	21 34	2 14	2 08
14	13 07	−12·4	58·1	15·8	53	285	92	11·3	17 41	17 56	22 25	2 35	2 23
15	14 00	−16·9	57·7	15·7	65	279	97	12·3	18 59	19 19	23 17	2 59	2 43
16	14 55	−20·4	57·2	15·6	77	263	99	13·3	20 11	20 36	—	3 29	3 07
17	15 50	−22·8	56·6	15·4	89	136	100	14·3	21 16	21 43	0 11	4 06	3 41
18	16 46	−24·0	56·0	15·3	101	103	98	15·3	22 09	22 36	1 05	4 53	4 25
19	17 41	−23·8	55·5	15·1	113	93	94	16·3	22 51	23 15	1 58	5 49	5 22
20	18 35	−22·5	55·0	15·0	126	86	89	17·3	23 23	23 44	2 49	6 52	6 28
21	19 26	−20·2	54·6	14·9	138	80	82	18·3	23 48	—	3 38	7 59	7 39
22	20 15	−17·0	54·3	14·8	150	76	74	19·3	—	0 04	4 23	9 07	8 52
23	21 02	−13·2	54·2	14·8	162	72	66	20·3	0 09	0 20	5 07	10 15	10 05
24	21 46	− 8·9	54·3	14·8	174	70	56	21·3	0 26	0 34	5 49	11 23	11 17
25	22 31	− 4·2	54·5	14·9	187	69	47	22·3	0 42	0 45	6 30	12 31	12 29
26	23 15	+ 0·7	54·9	15·0	199	68	37	23·3	0 57	0 56	7 11	13 40	13 43
27	23 59	+ 5·6	55·4	15·1	211	69	28	24·3	1 13	1 08	7 54	14 51	14 58
28	0 46	+10·5	56·1	15·3	223	71	20	25·3	1 30	1 21	8 39	16 04	16 17
29	1 36	+15·0	56·9	15·5	236	74	12	26·3	1 51	1 37	9 28	17 21	17 38
30	2 29	+18·9	57·6	15·7	248	79	6	27·3	2 18	1 59	10 20	18 38	19 00
31	3 26	+21·9	58·4	15·9	260	87	2	28·3	2 53	2 29	11 17	19 51	20 18

MERCURY

Day	RA	Dec. +	Diam.	Phase	Tran-sit		Day	RA	Dec. +	Diam.	Phase	Tran-sit	
	h m	°			h m			h m	°			h m	
1	1 00	3·2	—	—	10 23		16	2 26	12·4	—	—	10 52	
4	1 15	4·8	—	—	10 27	Mercury is too	19	2 48	14·6	—	—	11 02	Mercury is too
7	1 31	6·5	—	—	10 31	close to the	22	3 11	16·7	—	—	11 13	close to the
10	1 48	8·4	—	—	10 37	Sun for	25	3 35	18·7	—	—	11 26	Sun for
13	2 07	10·4	—	—	10 44	observation	28	4 01	20·6	—	—	11 41	observation
16	2 26	12·4	—	—	10 52		31	4 29	22·3	—	—	11 56	

VENUS

Day	RA	Dec. +	Diam.	Phase	Tran-sit	
	h m	°			h m	
1	1 50	10·0	—	—	11 14	
6	2 14	12·2	—	—	11 18	
11	2 38	14·3	—	—	11 22	Venus is too
16	3 02	16·2	—	—	11 26	close to the
21	3 26	18·0	—	—	11 31	Sun for
26	3 52	19·6	—	—	11 37	observation
31	4 17	20·9	—	—	11 43	

MARS

Day	RA	Dec.	Diam.	Phase	Tran-sit	
	h m	°			h m	
1	23 48	− 2·7	—	—	9 11	
6	0 02	− 1·2	—	—	9 06	
11	0 16	+ 0·3	—	—	9 00	Mars is too
16	0 30	+ 1·8	—	—	8 54	close to the
21	0 44	+ 3·3	—	—	8 49	Sun for
26	0 58	+ 4·8	—	—	8 43	observation
31	1 12	+ 6·3	—	—	8 37	

(*See* pages 63–64 for explanatory notes)

SUNRISE AND SUNSET

Day	London 0°05′ 51°30′		Bristol 2°35′ 51°28′		Birmingham 1°55′ 52°28′		Manchester 2°15′ 53°28′		Newcastle 1°37′ 54°59′		Glasgow 4°14′ 55°52′		Belfast 5°56′ 54°35′	
	h m	h m	h m	h m	h m	h m	h m	h m	h m	h m	h m	h m	h m	h m
1	4 32	19 24	4 42	19 34	4 36	19 34	4 34	19 39	4 26	19 42	4 33	19 56	4 45	19 58
2	4 30	19 26	4 40	19 35	4 34	19 36	4 32	19 41	4 24	19 44	4 31	19 58	4 43	20 00
3	4 28	19 27	4 38	19 37	4 32	19 38	4 30	19 43	4 22	19 46	4 29	20 00	4 41	20 02
4	4 26	19 29	4 36	19 39	4 30	19 40	4 28	19 45	4 20	19 48	4 27	20 02	4 39	20 04
5	4 25	19 30	4 35	19 40	4 29	19 41	4 26	19 46	4 18	19 50	4 24	20 04	4 37	20 05
6	4 23	19 32	4 33	19 42	4 27	19 43	4 24	19 48	4 16	19 52	4 22	20 06	4 35	20 07
7	4 21	19 34	4 31	19 44	4 25	19 45	4 22	19 50	4 14	19 54	4 20	20 08	4 33	20 09
8	4 19	19 35	4 29	19 45	4 23	19 46	4 21	19 52	4 12	19 55	4 18	20 10	4 31	20 11
9	4 18	19 37	4 28	19 47	4 21	19 48	4 19	19 53	4 10	19 57	4 16	20 12	4 29	20 13
10	4 16	19 38	4 26	19 48	4 20	19 49	4 17	19 55	4 08	19 59	4 14	20 14	4 27	20 15
11	4 14	19 40	4 25	19 50	4 18	19 51	4 15	19 57	4 06	20 01	4 12	20 16	4 25	20 16
12	4 13	19 41	4 23	19 51	4 16	19 53	4 13	19 58	4 04	20 03	4 10	20 18	4 23	20 18
13	4 11	19 43	4 21	19 53	4 15	19 54	4 12	20 00	4 02	20 05	4 08	20 20	4 21	20 20
14	4 10	19 45	4 20	19 54	4 13	13 56	4 10	20 02	4 00	20 06	4 06	20 21	4 20	20 22
15	4 08	19 46	4 18	19 56	4 11	19 57	4 08	20 03	3 59	20 08	4 04	20 23	4 18	20 23
16	4 07	19 47	4 17	19 57	4 10	19 59	4 07	20 05	3 57	20 10	4 03	20 25	4 16	20 25
17	4 05	19 49	4 15	19 59	4 08	20 01	4 05	20 07	3 55	20 12	4 01	20 27	4 14	20 27
18	4 04	19 50	4 14	20 00	4 07	20 02	4 04	20 08	3 53	20 13	3 59	20 29	4 13	20 29
19	4 03	19 52	4 13	20 02	4 06	20 04	4 02	20 10	3 52	20 15	3 57	20 30	4 11	20 30
20	4 01	19 53	4 11	20 03	4 04	20 05	4 01	20 11	3 50	20 17	3 56	20 32	4 10	20 32
21	4 00	19 55	4 10	20 04	4 03	20 06	3 59	20 13	3 49	20 18	3 54	20 34	4 08	20 33
22	3 59	19 56	4 09	20 06	4 02	20 08	3 58	20 14	3 47	20 20	3 53	20 36	4 07	20 35
23	3 58	19 57	4 08	20 07	4 00	20 09	3 57	20 16	3 46	20 22	3 51	20 37	4 05	20 37
24	3 56	19 59	4 07	20 09	3 59	20 11	3 55	20 17	3 44	20 23	3 50	20 39	4 04	20 38
25	3 55	20 00	4 05	20 10	3 58	20 12	3 54	20 19	3 43	20 25	3 48	20 41	4 03	20 40
26	3 54	20 01	4 04	20 11	3 57	20 13	3 53	20 20	3 42	20 26	3 47	20 42	4 01	20 41
27	3 53	20 02	4 03	20 12	3 56	20 15	3 52	20 21	3 40	20 28	3 45	20 44	4 00	20 43
28	3 52	20 04	4 02	20 14	3 55	20 16	3 51	20 23	3 39	20 29	3 44	20 45	3 59	20 44
29	3 51	20 05	4 01	20 15	3 54	20 17	3 50	20 24	3 38	20 30	3 43	20 47	3 58	20 45
30	3 50	20 06	4 00	20 16	3 53	20 18	3 49	20 25	3 37	20 32	3 42	20 48	3 57	20 47
31	3 49	20 07	4 00	20 17	3 52	20 20	3 48	20 26	3 36	20 33	3 41	20 49	3 56	20 48

JUPITER

Day	RA	Dec. +	Transit	5° high 52°	5° high 56°
	h m	° ′	h m	h m	h m
1	10 27·9	11 01	19 48	2 15	2 21
11	10 28·4	10 56	19 09	1 36	1 41
21	10 30·1	10 44	18 32	0 57	1 03
31	10 32·8	10 26	17 55	0 19	0 24

Diameters—equatorial 38″ polar 36″

SATURN

Day	RA	Dec. −	Transit	5° high 52°	5° high 56°
	h m	° ′	h m	h m	h m
1	21 22·3	16 13	6 45	2 50	3 11
11	21 23·7	16 08	6 07	2 12	2 32
21	21 24·6	16 06	5 28	1 33	1 53
31	21 24·8	16 07	4 49	0 54	1 14

Diameters—equatorial 17″ polar 15″
Rings—major axis 39″ minor axis 10″

URANUS

Day	RA	Dec. −	Transit	10° high 52°	10° high 56°
	h m	° ′	h m	h m	h m
1	19 18·2	22 38	4 41	2 29	3 32
11	19 17·7	22 39	4 01	1 50	2 52
21	19 16·8	22 41	3 21	1 10	2 13
31	19 15·7	22 43	2 40	0 30	1 34

Diameter 4″

NEPTUNE

Day	RA	Dec. −	Transit	10° high 52°	10° high 56°
	h m	° ′	h m	h m	h m
1	19 21·5	21 22	4 44	2 18	3 08
11	19 21·2	21 22	4 04	1 39	2 29
21	19 20·6	21 23	3 25	0 59	1 49
31	19 19·9	21 25	2 44	0 19	1 10

Diameter 2″

(*See* page 64 for explanatory notes)

Year	Month	Week	

Junius, Roman *gens*
(family).
Sun's Longitude 90° ♋ 21ᵈ 03ʰ

153	1	M.	Marilyn Monroe *b.* 1926. Helen Keller *d.* 1968.
154	2	Tu.	TRINITY LAW SITTINGS BEGIN. CORONATION DAY
155	3	W.	George V *b.* 1865. [1953.
156	4	Th.	George III *b.* 1738. Kaiser Wilhelm II *d.* 1941.
157	5	F.	Six-Day War began 1967.
158	6	S.	Cavour *d.* 1861. Capt. Robert Scott *b.* 1868.
159	7	S.	**Pentecost (Whit Sunday).**
160	8	M.	Millais *b.* 1829. George Sand *d.* 1876.
161	9	Tu.	Charles Dickens *d.* 1870.
162	10	W.	DUKE OF EDINBURGH *b.* 1921.
163	11	Th.	**St Barnabas.** Jacques Cousteau *b.* 1910.
164	12	F.	Thomas Arnold *d.* 1842. George Bush *b.* 1924.
165	13	S.	Boxer Rebellion broke out 1900.
166	14	S.	**Trinity Sunday.** Logie Baird *d.* 1946.
167	15	M.	First transatlantic flight 1919.
168	16	Tu.	First woman in space 1963.
169	17	W.	John Wesley *b.* 1703. Stravinsky *b.* 1882 NS.
170	18	Th.	CORPUS CHRISTI. Amundsen *d.* 1928.
171	19	F.	Metropolitan Police founded 1829.
172	20	S.	Black Hole of Calcutta 1756.
173	21	S.	**2nd S. after Pentecost.** PRINCE WILLIAM
174	22	M.	Meryl Streep *b.* 1949. [OF WALES *b.* 1982.
175	23	Tu.	Duke of Windsor *b.* 1894. Jean Anouilh *b.* 1910.
176	24	W.	**St John the Baptist.** Solferino 1859.
177	25	Th.	Col. Custer *d.* 1876. George Orwell *b.* 1903.
178	26	F.	George IV *d.* 1830. Pearl S. Buck *b.* 1892.*
179	27	S.	Dettingen 1743. Parnell *b.* 1846.
180	28	S.	**3rd S. after Pentecost.** Rousseau *b.* 1712.
181	29	M.	**St Peter.** SS. PETER AND PAUL.
182	30	Tu.	Tower Bridge opened 1894.

PHENOMENA

	d	h	
	1	05	Mercury in conjunction with Moon. Mercury 1°S.
	7	03	Jupiter in conjunction with Moon. Jupiter 6°N.
	13	17	Venus in superior conjunction.
	19	16	Saturn in conjunction with Moon. Saturn 5°S.
	21	03	Solstice.
	26	05	Mars in conjunction with Moon. Mars 5°S.
	30	20	Venus in conjunction with Moon. Venus 2°N.

CONSTELLATIONS

The following constellations are near the meridian at

d	h		d	h
May 1	24		May 16	23
June 1	22		June 15	21
July 1	20		July 16	19

Cassiopeia (below the Pole), Ursa Minor, Draco, Ursa Major, Canes Venatici, Bootes, Corona, Serpens, Virgo and Libra.

ALGOL

ALGOL is inconveniently situated for observation during June.

*Centenary

MOON
Phases, Apsides & Node

		d	h	m
●	New Moon	1	03	57
☽	First Quarter	7	20	47
○	Full Moon	15	04	50
☾	Last Quarter	23	08	11
●	New Moon	30	12	18
	Perigee (365,329 km)	4	02	00
	Apogee (405,130 km)	19	21	55

Mean longitude of ascending node on June 1, 272°.

See note on Summer Time, p. 22.

MONTHLY NOTES

7. First day of Feast of Weeks.
13. Queen's Official Birthday.
21. Longest day.
24. Midsummer Day (Quarter Day).

(*See* page 62 for explanatory notes)

Day	Right Ascension	Dec. +	Equation of Time	Rise 52°	Rise 56°	Transit	Set 52°	Set 56°	Sidereal Time	Transit of First Point of Aries
	h m s	° ′	m s	h m	h m	h m	h m	h m	h m s	h m s
1	4 36 40	22 04	+ 2 15	3 46	3 22	11 58	20 11	20 35	16 38 55	7 19 53
2	4 40 46	22 11	+ 2 06	3 45	3 21	11 58	20 12	20 36	16 42 51	7 15 57
3	4 44 52	22 19	+ 1 56	3 44	3 20	11 58	20 13	20 37	16 46 48	7 12 01
4	4 48 59	22 26	+ 1 46	3 44	3 19	11 58	20 14	20 39	16 50 45	7 08 05
5	4 53 06	22 33	+ 1 35	3 43	3 18	11 58	20 15	20 40	16 54 41	7 04 09
6	4 57 13	22 39	+ 1 25	3 42	3 17	11 59	20 16	20 41	16 58 38	7 00 13
7	5 01 21	22 45	+ 1 14	3 42	3 16	11 59	20 16	20 42	17 02 34	6 56 17
8	5 05 28	22 51	+ 1 02	3 41	3 16	11 59	20 17	20 43	17 06 31	6 52 21
9	5 09 37	22 56	+ 0 51	3 41	3 15	11 59	20 18	20 44	17 10 27	6 48 26
10	5 13 45	23 01	+ 0 39	3 40	3 15	11 59	20 19	20 45	17 14 24	6 44 30
11	5 17 53	23 05	+ 0 27	3 40	3 14	12 00	20 19	20 46	17 18 20	6 40 34
12	5 22 02	23 09	+ 0 15	3 40	3 14	12 00	20 20	20 46	17 22 17	6 36 38
13	5 26 11	23 13	+ 0 02	3 40	3 13	12 00	20 21	20 47	17 26 14	6 32 42
14	5 30 20	23 16	− 0 10	3 39	3 13	12 00	20 21	20 48	17 30 10	6 28 46
15	5 34 29	23 19	− 0 23	3 39	3 13	12 00	20 22	20 48	17 34 07	6 24 50
16	5 38 39	23 21	− 0 35	3 39	3 13	12 01	20 22	20 49	17 38 03	6 20 54
17	5 42 48	23 23	− 0 48	3 39	3 13	12 01	20 23	20 49	17 42 00	6 16 58
18	5 46 58	23 24	− 1 01	3 39	3 13	12 01	20 23	20 50	17 45 56	6 13 02
19	5 51 07	23 25	− 1 14	3 39	3 13	12 01	20 23	20 50	17 49 53	6 09 06
20	5 55 17	23 26	− 1 27	3 40	3 13	12 02	20 24	20 50	17 53 49	6 05 11
21	5 59 26	23 26	− 1 40	3 40	3 13	12 02	20 24	20 50	17 57 46	6 01 15
22	6 03 36	23 26	− 1 53	3 40	3 13	12 02	20 24	20 51	18 01 43	5 57 19
23	6 07 45	23 26	− 2 06	3 40	3 14	12 02	20 24	20 51	18 05 39	5 53 23
24	6 11 55	23 25	− 2 19	3 41	3 14	12 02	20 24	20 51	18 09 36	5 49 27
25	6 16 04	23 23	− 2 32	3 41	3 14	12 03	20 24	20 51	18 13 32	5 45 31
26	6 20 13	23 22	− 2 45	3 41	3 15	12 03	20 24	20 50	18 17 29	5 41 35
27	6 24 23	23 19	− 2 57	3 42	3 16	12 03	20 24	20 50	18 21 25	5 37 39
28	6 28 32	23 17	− 3 10	3 42	3 16	12 03	20 24	20 50	18 25 22	5 33 43
29	6 32 40	23 14	− 3 22	3 43	3 17	12 03	20 24	20 50	18 29 19	5 29 47
30	6 36 49	23 10	− 3 34	3 44	3 18	12 04	20 23	20 49	18 33 15	5 25 51

THE SUN   s.d. 15′·8

Duration of Civil (C), Nautical (N) and Astronomical (A) Twilight (in minutes)

Lat. °	June 1 C	N	A	June 11 C	N	A	June 21 C	N	A	June 30 C	N	A
52	47	117	TAN	48	125	TAN	49	128	TAN	49	125	TAN
56	58	TAN	TAN	61	TAN	TAN	63	TAN	TAN	62	TAN	TAN

ASTRONOMICAL NOTES

MERCURY is unsuitably placed for observation, even though it is as much as 25° from the Sun by the end of June, because of the long duration of twilight.

VENUS is at superior conjunction on the 13th, actually passing behind the disk of the Sun, and thus remaining too close to the Sun for observation throughout the month.

MARS, magnitude +0·9, gradually becomes visible as a difficult morning object during the second half of the month, about 1½ hours before sunrise, until the long morning twilight inhibits observation. It may then be glimpsed low above the eastern horizon. On the morning of the 26th Mars may be detected about 5° below and to the right of the Moon, then four days before New.

JUPITER, magnitude −1·9, continues to be visible as a brilliant object in the evening sky. Jupiter is in Leo.

SATURN is a morning object low above the south-eastern horizon in the early hours; by the end of the month it is visible by 23h. Its magnitude is +0·6.

ECLIPSE. A partial eclipse of the Moon occurs on the 15th. See page 72 for details.

ECLIPSE. A total eclipse of the Sun occurs on the 30th. See page 72 for details.

(See pages 62–63 *for explanatory notes)*

THE MOON

Day	RA	Dec.	Hor. Par.	Semi-diam.	Sun's Co-long.	PA of Bright Limb	Phase	Age	Rise 52°	Rise 56°	Transit	Set 52°	Set 56°
	h m	°	'	'	°	°	%	d	h m	h m	h m	h m	h m
1	4 26	+23·7	59·1	16·1	272	123	0	29·3	3 40	3 13	12 17	20 56	21 23
2	5 29	+24·0	59·6	16·2	285	263	1	0·8	4 41	4 14	13 18	21 48	22 13
3	6 31	+22·6	59·9	16·3	297	274	5	1·8	5 55	5 32	14 19	22 29	22 48
4	7 33	+19·8	60·0	16·4	309	281	11	2·8	7 18	6 59	15 17	22 59	23 14
5	8 32	+15·7	59·9	16·3	321	287	19	3·8	8 43	8 30	16 12	23 23	23 32
6	9 27	+10·7	59·7	16·3	334	290	29	4·8	10 07	10 00	17 04	23 44	23 48
7	10 21	+ 5·2	59·3	16·2	346	292	40	5·8	11 29	11 27	17 54	—	—
8	11 12	− 0·5	58·9	16·0	358	293	52	6·8	12 50	12 53	18 42	0 02	0 02
9	12 03	− 6·1	58·4	15·9	10	292	63	7·8	14 09	14 18	19 31	0 21	0 15
10	12 54	−11·3	57·9	15·8	22	290	73	8·8	15 28	15 41	20 20	0 40	0 30
11	13 46	−15·9	57·4	15·6	35	287	82	9·8	16 45	17 04	21 11	1 03	0 48
12	14 39	−19·6	56·9	15·5	47	283	89	10·8	17 58	18 22	22 04	1 30	1 10
13	15 34	−22·3	56·4	15·4	59	278	95	11·8	19 05	19 32	22 57	2 04	1 39
14	16 29	−23·8	55·9	15·2	71	271	99	12·8	20 02	20 29	23 50	2 46	2 19
15	17 24	−24·0	55·4	15·1	83	254	100	13·8	20 48	21 13	—	3 39	3 11
16	18 18	−23·0	55·0	15·0	96	86	99	14·8	21 23	21 45	0 42	4 39	4 14
17	19 10	−21·0	54·6	14·9	108	79	97	15·8	21 51	22 09	1 31	5 45	5 24
18	20 00	−18·1	54·4	14·8	120	75	93	16·8	22 13	22 27	2 18	6 53	6 36
19	20 47	−14·4	54·2	14·8	132	71	87	17·8	22 32	22 41	3 03	8 01	7 49
20	21 32	−10·2	54·1	14·7	144	68	80	18·8	22 48	22 53	3 45	9 09	9 02
21	22 16	− 5·7	54·2	14·8	157	67	72	19·8	23 03	23 04	4 26	10 17	10 13
22	23 00	− 0·9	54·5	14·8	169	66	63	20·8	23 18	23 15	5 07	11 24	11 25
23	23 44	+ 4·0	54·9	14·9	181	66	53	21·8	23 34	23 27	5 48	12 33	12 39
24	0 29	+ 8·8	55·4	15·1	193	67	44	22·8	23 53	23 41	6 31	13 44	13 54
25	1 17	+13·4	56·1	15·3	206	70	34	23·8	—	—	7 17	14 58	15 13
26	2 08	+17·5	57·0	15·5	218	73	24	24·8	0 16	0 00	8 07	16 13	16 33
27	3 02	+20·9	57·9	15·8	230	77	16	25·8	0 46	0 25	9 01	17 28	17 53
28	4 01	+23·1	58·8	16·0	242	82	9	26·8	1 27	1 01	9 59	18 38	19 05
29	5 03	+24·1	59·6	16·2	255	88	3	27·8	2 21	1 54	11 00	19 37	20 03
30	6 06	+23·4	60·2	16·4	267	90	0	28·8	3 31	3 05	12 03	20 23	20 45

MERCURY

Day	RA	Dec. +	Diam.	Phase	Transit		Day	RA	Dec. +	Diam.	Phase	Transit	
	h m	°			h m			h m	°			h m	
1	4 38	22·8	—	—	12 02		16	6 53	24·9	—	—	13 18	
4	5 06	24·0	—	—	12 18	Mercury is too	19	7 16	24·3	—	—	13 28	Mercury is too
7	5 34	24·8	—	—	12 35	close to the	22	7 38	23·4	—	—	13 38	close to the
10	6 02	25·2	—	—	12 50	Sun for	25	7 57	22·3	—	—	13 45	Sun for
13	6 28	25·2	—	—	13 05	observation	28	8 14	21·1	—	—	13 50	observation
16	6 53	24·9	—	—	13 18		31	8 30	19·8	—	—	13 53	

VENUS

Day	RA	Dec. +	Diam.	Phase	Transit	
	h m	°			h m	
1	4 22	21·2	—	—	11 44	
6	4 48	22·3	—	—	11 50	
11	5 15	23·1	—	—	11 57	Venus is too
16	5 41	23·6	—	—	12 04	close to the
21	6 08	23·9	—	—	12 11	Sun for
26	6 35	23·8	—	—	12 18	observation
31	7 02	23·5	—	—	12 25	

MARS

Day	RA	Dec. +	Diam.	Phase	Transit	5° high 52°	5° high 56°
	h m	°	"	%	h m	h m	h m
1	1 15	6·6	5	91	8 36	2 35	2 33
6	1 29	8·0	5	91	8 30	2 22	2 19
11	1 43	9·3	5	90	8 24	2 09	2 05
16	1 57	10·7	5	90	8 19	1 57	1 51
21	2 11	11·9	6	90	8 13	1 44	1 38
26	2 25	13·2	6	90	8 07	1 32	1 25
31	2 39	14·3	6	89	8 02	1 20	1 12

(*See* pages 63–64 for explanatory notes)

SUNRISE AND SUNSET

Day	London 0°05′ 51°30′		Bristol 2°35′ 51°28′		Birmingham 1°55′ 52°28′		Manchester 2°15′ 53°28′		Newcastle 1°37′ 54°59′		Glasgow 4°14′ 55°52′		Belfast 5°56′ 54°35′	
	h m	h m	h m	h m	h m	h m	h m	h m	h m	h m	h m	h m	h m	h m
1	3 49	20 08	3 59	20 18	3 51	20 21	3 47	20 28	3 35	20 34	3 40	20 51	3 55	20 49
2	3 48	20 09	3 58	20 19	3 50	20 22	3 46	20 29	3 34	20 36	3 39	20 52	3 54	20 50
3	3 47	20 10	3 57	20 20	3 49	20 23	3 45	20 30	3 33	20 37	3 38	20 53	3 53	20 52
4	3 47	20 11	3 57	20 21	3 49	20 24	3 44	20 31	3 32	20 38	3 37	20 55	3 52	20 53
5	3 46	20 12	3 56	20 22	3 48	20 25	3 44	20 32	3 31	20 39	3 36	20 56	3 51	20 54
6	3 45	20 13	3 56	20 23	3 47	20 26	3 43	20 33	3 31	20 40	3 35	20 57	3 51	20 55
7	3 45	20 14	3 55	20 24	3 47	20 27	3 42	20 34	3 30	20 41	3 34	20 58	3 50	20 56
8	3 44	20 15	3 55	20 25	3 46	20 28	3 42	20 35	3 29	20 42	3 34	20 59	3 49	20 57
9	3 44	20 16	3 54	20 25	3 46	20 28	3 41	20 36	3 29	20 43	3 33	21 00	3 49	20 58
10	3 44	20 16	3 54	20 26	3 45	20 29	3 41	20 36	3 28	20 44	3 33	21 01	3 48	20 58
11	3 43	20 17	3 53	20 27	3 45	20 30	3 40	20 37	3 28	20 45	3 32	21 01	3 48	20 59
12	3 43	20 18	3 53	20 27	3 45	20 31	3 40	20 38	3 28	20 45	3 32	21 02	3 48	21 00
13	3 43	20 18	3 53	20 28	3 45	20 31	3 40	20 39	3 27	20 46	3 31	21 03	3 47	21 01
14	3 43	20 19	3 53	20 29	3 44	20 32	3 40	20 39	3 27	20 47	3 31	21 04	3 47	21 01
15	3 42	20 19	3 53	20 29	3 44	20 32	3 40	20 40	3 27	20 47	3 31	21 04	3 47	21 02
16	3 42	20 20	3 53	20 30	3 44	20 33	3 39	20 40	3 27	20 48	3 31	21 05	3 47	21 02
17	3 42	20 20	3 53	20 30	3 44	20 33	3 39	20 41	3 27	20 48	3 31	21 05	3 47	21 03
18	3 42	20 21	3 53	20 30	3 44	20 33	3 39	20 41	3 27	20 49	3 31	21 06	3 47	21 03
19	3 43	20 21	3 53	20 31	3 44	20 34	3 39	20 41	3 27	20 49	3 31	21 06	3 47	21 03
20	3 43	20 21	3 53	20 31	3 44	20 34	3 40	20 42	3 27	20 49	3 31	21 06	3 47	21 04
21	3 43	20 21	3 53	20 31	3 45	20 34	3 40	20 42	3 27	20 49	3 31	21 06	3 47	21 04
22	3 43	20 21	3 53	20 31	3 45	20 34	3 40	20 42	3 27	20 50	3 31	21 07	3 47	21 04
23	3 43	20 22	3 54	20 31	3 45	20 34	3 40	20 42	3 28	20 50	3 32	21 07	3 48	21 04
24	3 44	20 22	3 54	20 31	3 46	20 35	3 41	20 42	3 28	20 50	3 32	21 07	3 48	21 04
25	3 44	20 22	3 54	20 31	3 46	20 35	3 41	20 42	3 28	20 50	3 32	21 07	3 48	21 04
26	3 45	20 22	3 55	20 31	3 46	20 34	3 42	20 42	3 29	20 49	3 33	21 06	3 49	21 04
27	3 45	20 21	3 55	20 31	3 47	20 34	3 42	20 42	3 29	20 49	3 33	21 06	3 50	21 04
28	3 46	20 21	3 56	20 31	3 47	20 34	3 43	20 42	3 30	20 49	3 34	21 06	3 50	21 04
29	3 46	20 21	3 56	20 31	3 48	20 34	3 44	20 41	3 31	20 49	3 35	21 06	3 51	21 03
30	3 47	20 21	3 57	20 31	3 49	20 34	3 44	20 41	3 31	20 48	3 36	21 05	3 51	21 03

JUPITER

Day	RA	Dec. +	Transit	5° high 52°	5° high 56°
	h m	° ′	h m	h m	h m
1	10 33·2	10 24	17 52	0 15	0 20
11	10 36·9	10 00	17 16	23 34	23 39
21	10 41·5	9 31	16 41	22 57	23 01
31	10 46·9	8 58	16 07	22 20	22 24

Diameters—equatorial 35″ polar 33″

SATURN

Day	RA	Dec. −	Transit	5° high 52°	5° high 56°
	h m	° ′	h m	h m	h m
1	21 24·8	16 07	4 45	0 50	1 10
11	21 24·3	16 11	4 05	0 11	0 31
21	21 23·1	16 18	3 25	23 27	23 48
31	21 21·4	16 27	2 44	22 47	23 08

Diameters—equatorial 18″ polar 16″
Rings—major axis 41″ minor axis 10″

URANUS

Day	RA	Dec. −	Transit	10° high 52°	10° high 56°
	h m	° ′	h m	h m	h m
1	19 15·6	22 44	2 36	0 26	1 30
11	19 14·2	22 46	1 56	23 42	0 50
21	19 12·7	22 49	1 15	23 02	0 11
31	19 11·0	22 52	0 34	22 21	23 27

Diameter 4″

NEPTUNE

Day	RA	Dec. −	Transit	10° high 52°	10° high 56°
	h m	° ′	h m	h m	h m
1	19 19·8	21 25	2 40	0 15	1 06
11	19 18·9	21 27	2 00	23 31	0 26
21	19 17·8	21 29	1 20	22 51	23 42
31	19 16·7	21 31	0 39	22 11	23 02

Diameter 2″

(*See* page 64 for explanatory notes)

DAY OF			*Julius* Caesar, formerly *Quintilis*, 5th month (from March). Sun's Longitude 120° ♌ 22ᵈ 14ʰ
Year	Month	Week	

183	1	W.	PRINCESS OF WALES *b.* 1961. Blériot *b.* 1872.
184	2	Th.	Robert Peel *d.* 1850. Hemingway *d.* 1961.
185	3	F.	**St Thomas.** Robert Adam *b.* 1728.
186	4	S.	INDEPENDENCE DAY, USA. Byrd *b.* 1623.
187	5	S.	**4th S. after Pentecost.** Cocteau *b.* 1889.
188	6	M.	John Flaxman *b.* 1755. Louis Armstrong *d.* 1971.
189	7	Tu.	Mahler *b.* 1860. Marc Chagall *b.* 1887.
190	8	W.	Joseph Chamberlain *b.* 1836. von Zeppelin *b.* 1838.
191	9	Th.	David Hockney *b.* 1937.
192	10	F.	Capt. Marryat *b.* 1792.* Joe Davis *d.* 1978.
193	11	S.	Robert the Bruce *b.* 1274.
194	12	S.	**5th S. after Pentecost.** Kenneth More *d.* 1982.
195	13	M.	Titus Oates *d.* 1705. John Clare *d.* 1793.
196	14	Tu.	FÊTE NATIONALE, FRANCE.
197	15	W.	ST SWITHIN'S DAY. Gen. Pershing *d.* 1948.
198	16	Th.	Corot *b.* 1796. Tsar Nicholas II *d.* 1918.
199	17	F.	Charlotte Corday *exec.* 1793. Hardy Amies *b.* 1909.
200	18	S.	Watteau *d.* 1721. William Thackeray *b.* 1811.
201	19	S.	**6th S. after Pentecost.** Degas *b.* 1834.
202	20	M.	Petrarch *b.* 1304. Calouste Gulbenkían *d.* 1955.
203	21	Tu.	Tate Gallery opened 1897.
204	22	W.	**St Mary Magdalen.** Salamanca 1812.
205	23	Th.	Raymond Chandler *b.* 1888. Olivia Manning *d.* [1980.
206	24	F.	Simón Bolívar *b.* 1783. John Sell Cotman *d.* 1842.
207	25	S.	**St James.** First cross-Channel flight 1909.
208	26	S.	**7th S. after Pentecost.** G. B. Shaw *b.* 1856.
209	27	M.	Korean War ended 1953 James Mason *d.* 1984.
210	28	Tu.	Cyrano de Bergerac *d.* 1655 J. S. Bach *d.* 1750.
211	29	W.	William Wilberforce *d.* 1833. Van Gogh *d.* 1890.
212	30	Th.	William Penn *d.* 1718. Henry Moore *b.* 1898.
213	31	F.	TRINITY LAW SITTINGS END.

PHENOMENA

d	h	
2	09	Mercury in conjunction with Moon. Mercury 4°N.
3	12	Earth at aphelion (152 million km).
4	15	Jupiter in conjunction with Moon. Jupiter 6°N.
6	01	Mercury at greatest elongation E.26°.
7	23	Uranus at opposition.
9	13	Neptune at opposition.
16	20	Saturn in conjunction with Moon. Saturn 5°S.
25	03	Mars in conjunction with Moon. Mars 4°S.
26	16	Venus in conjunction with Mercury. Venus 6°N.
30	06	Mercury in conjunction with Moon. Mercury 1°S.
30	17	Venus in conjunction with Moon. Venus 5°N.

CONSTELLATIONS

The following constellations are near the meridian at

	d	h		d	h
June	1	24	June 15	23
July	1	22	July 16	21
Aug.	1	20	Aug. 16	19

Ursa Minor, Draco, Corona, Hercules, Lyra, Serpens, Ophiuchus, Libra, Scorpius and Sagittarius.

MINIMA OF ALGOL

d	h	d	h
3	13·0	17	21·1
6	09·8	20	17·9
9	06·7	23	14·7
12	03·5	26	11·5
15	00·3	29	08·3

* Centenary

See note on Summer Time, p. 22.

MOON
Phases, Apsides & Node

	d	h	m
☽ First Quarter	7	02	43
○ Full Moon	14	19	06
☾ Last Quarter	22	22	12
● New Moon	29	19	35
Perigee (360,619 km)	2	00	33
Apogee (406,012 km)	17	10	37
Perigee (357,674 km)	30	07	44

Mean longitude of ascending node on July 1, 270°

MONTHLY NOTES

1. National Day, Canada.
2. Islamic New Year (AH 1413).
3. Dog Days begin (end Aug. 15).
5. Tynwald Day, Isle of Man.
12. Bank Holiday, Northern Ireland.

(*See* page 62 for explanatory notes)

Day	Right Ascension	Dec. +	Equation of Time	Rise 52°	Rise 56°	Transit	Set 52°	Set 56°	Sidereal Time	Transit of First Point of Aries
	h m s	° ′	m s	h m	h m	h m	h m	h m	h m s	h m s
1	6 40 57	23 06	− 3 46	3 44	3 18	12 04	20 23	20 49	18 37 12	5 21 55
2	6 45 05	23 02	− 3 57	3 45	3 19	12 04	20 23	20 48	18 41 08	5 18 00
3	6 49 13	22 57	− 4 09	3 46	3 20	12 04	20 22	20 48	18 45 05	5 14 04
4	6 53 21	22 52	− 4 20	3 47	3 21	12 04	20 22	20 47	18 49 01	5 10 08
5	6 57 28	22 47	− 4 30	3 48	3 22	12 05	20 21	20 46	18 52 58	5 06 12
6	7 01 35	22 41	− 4 40	3 48	3 23	12 05	20 21	20 46	18 56 54	5 02 16
7	7 05 41	22 35	− 4 50	3 49	3 24	12 05	20 20	20 45	19 00 51	4 58 20
8	7 09 47	22 28	− 5 00	3 50	3 26	12 05	20 19	20 44	19 04 48	4 54 24
9	7 13 53	22 21	− 5 09	3 51	3 27	12 05	20 19	20 43	19 08 44	4 50 28
10	7 17 58	22 14	− 5 18	3 52	3 28	12 05	20 18	20 42	19 12 41	4 46 32
11	7 22 03	22 06	− 5 26	3 53	3 29	12 05	20 17	20 41	19 16 37	4 42 36
12	7 26 07	21 58	− 5 33	3 55	3 31	12 06	20 16	20 40	19 20 34	4 38 40
13	7 30 11	21 49	− 5 41	3 56	3 32	12 06	20 15	20 38	19 24 30	4 34 45
14	7 34 14	21 40	− 5 48	3 57	3 34	12 06	20 14	20 37	19 28 27	4 30 49
15	7 38 17	21 31	− 5 54	3 58	3 35	12 06	20 13	20 36	19 32 23	4 26 53
16	7 42 20	21 22	− 6 00	3 59	3 37	12 06	20 12	20 35	19 36 20	4 22 57
17	7 46 21	21 12	− 6 05	4 01	3 38	12 06	20 11	20 33	19 40 17	4 19 01
18	7 50 23	21 01	− 6 10	4 02	3 40	12 06	20 10	20 32	19 44 13	4 15 05
19	7 54 24	20 50	− 6 14	4 03	3 41	12 06	20 09	20 30	19 48 10	4 11 09
20	7 58 24	20 39	− 6 18	4 04	3 43	12 06	20 07	20 29	19 52 06	4 07 13
21	8 02 24	20 28	− 6 21	4 06	3 45	12 06	20 06	20 27	19 56 03	4 03 17
22	8 06 23	20 16	− 6 23	4 07	3 46	12 06	20 05	20 25	19 59 59	3 59 21
23	8 10 21	20 04	− 6 25	4 09	3 48	12 06	20 03	20 24	20 03 56	3 55 25
24	8 14 19	19 52	− 6 27	4 10	3 50	12 06	20 02	20 22	20 07 52	3 51 30
25	8 18 17	19 39	− 6 28	4 11	3 51	12 06	20 01	20 20	20 11 49	3 47 34
26	8 22 14	19 26	− 6 28	4 13	3 53	12 06	19 59	20 19	20 15 46	3 43 38
27	8 26 10	19 12	− 6 28	4 14	3 55	12 06	19 58	20 17	20 19 42	3 39 42
28	8 30 06	18 59	− 6 27	4 16	3 57	12 06	19 56	20 15	20 23 39	3 35 46
29	8 34 01	18 45	− 6 26	4 17	3 59	12 06	19 54	20 13	20 27 35	3 31 50
30	8 37 55	18 30	− 6 24	4 19	4 00	12 06	19 53	20 11	20 31 32	3 27 54
31	8 41 49	18 15	− 6 21	4 20	4 02	12 06	19 51	20 09	20 35 28	3 23 58

Duration of Civil (C), Nautical (N) and Astronomical (A) Twilight (in minutes)

Lat. °	July 1 C	N	A	July 11 C	N	A	July 21 C	N	A	July 31 C	N	A
52	48	124	TAN	46	116	TAN	44	107	TAN	41	98	180
56	61	TAN	TAN	58	TAN	TAN	53	144	TAN	49	122	TAN

ASTRONOMICAL NOTES

MERCURY despite being at greatest eastern elongation on the 6th, is unsuitably placed for observation.

VENUS is too close to the Sun for observation.

MARS, magnitude + 0·8, continues to be visible as a morning object, rising in the ENE after midnight. On the morning of the 25th Mars passes about 4°S. of the old crescent Moon. During the month Mars passes from Aries into Taurus, passing between the Pleiades and the Hyades at the very end of July.

JUPITER, magnitude −1·8, is a brilliant evening object in Leo, but now only visible for a short while after sunset. By the end of the month it will be difficult to detect in the long twilight.

SATURN continues to be visible as a morning object, magnitude + 0·4, in Capricornus.

URANUS is at opposition on the 7th, in the constellation of Sagittarius. Uranus is barely visible to the naked eye since its magnitude is + 5·6, but it is readily located with only small optical aid.

NEPTUNE is at opposition on the 9th, in the constellation of Sagittarius. It is not visible to the naked eye since its magnitude is + 7·9. These two outer planets, Uranus and Neptune, are now only about 3° apart, and closing.

TWILIGHT. Reference to the section just above these notes shows that astronomical twilight lasts all night for some time around the summer solstice (i.e. in June and July), even in southern England. Under these conditions the sky never gets completely dark since the Sun is always less than 18° below the horizon.

(See pages 62–63 for explanatory notes)

THE MOON

Day	RA	Dec.	Hor. Par.	Semi-diam.	Sun's Co-long.	PA of Bright Limb	Phase	Age	Rise 52°	Rise 56°	Transit	Set 52°	Set 56°
	h m	°	′	′	°	°	%	d	h m	h m	h m	h m	h m
1	7 09	+21·1	60·7	16·5	279	289	0	0·5	4 52	4 31	13 04	20 59	21 15
2	8 11	+17·3	60·8	16·6	291	289	3	1·5	6 19	6 03	14 02	21 26	21 37
3	9 09	+12·4	60·7	16·5	304	292	9	2·5	7 46	7 37	14 57	21 49	21 55
4	10 05	+ 6·9	60·3	16·4	316	295	17	3·5	9 12	9 08	15 49	22 08	22 09
5	10 58	+ 1·0	59·7	16·3	328	295	27	4·5	10 36	10 37	16 39	22 27	22 23
6	11 51	− 4·7	59·1	16·1	340	295	38	5·5	11 57	12 04	17 28	22 47	22 38
7	12 42	−10·1	58·4	15·9	352	293	49	6·5	13 17	13 29	18 18	23 08	22 55
8	13 34	−14·9	57·6	15·7	5	291	60	7·5	14 35	14 52	19 08	23 33	23 15
9	14 27	−18·8	57·0	15·5	17	287	70	8·5	15 49	16 11	20 00	—	23 42
10	15 21	−21·7	56·3	15·4	29	282	79	9·5	16 57	17 23	20 52	0 05	—
11	16 15	−23·5	55·8	15·2	41	278	87	10·5	17 57	18 24	21 45	0 44	0 18
12	17 10	−24·1	55·3	15·1	54	273	93	11·5	18 46	19 12	22 36	1 33	1 05
13	18 04	−23·4	54·9	15·0	66	270	97	12·5	19 25	19 48	23 26	2 30	2 04
14	18 56	−21·7	54·6	14·9	78	272	99	13·5	19 55	20 14	—	3 34	3 11
15	19 46	−19·0	54·3	14·8	90	36	100	14·5	20 18	20 33	0 14	4 41	4 23
16	20 34	−15·5	54·1	14·7	102	63	99	15·5	20 38	20 49	0 59	5 49	5 36
17	21 20	−11·5	54·0	14·7	115	64	96	16·5	20 55	21 01	1 43	6 57	6 48
18	22 04	− 7·0	54·0	14·7	127	63	91	17·5	21 10	21 13	2 24	8 05	8 00
19	22 48	− 2·3	54·1	14·8	139	63	85	18·5	21 25	21 23	3 05	9 12	9 12
20	23 31	+ 2·6	54·4	14·8	151	63	77	19·5	21 41	21 35	3 45	10 20	10 23
21	0 16	+ 7·3	54·8	14·9	163	64	69	20·5	21 58	21 48	4 27	11 28	11 37
22	1 01	+11·9	55·4	15·1	176	66	59	21·5	22 18	22 04	5 11	12 39	12 52
23	1 50	+16·1	56·1	15·3	188	69	49	22·5	22 44	22 25	5 58	13 52	14 10
24	2 42	+19·7	56·9	15·5	200	73	39	23·5	23 19	22 55	6 48	15 06	15 29
25	3 37	+22·3	57·8	15·8	212	78	29	24·5	—	23 38	7 43	16 17	16 43
26	4 37	+23·8	58·8	16·0	224	83	19	25·5	0 05	—	8 42	17 20	17 47
27	5 39	+23·8	59·7	16·3	237	88	11	26·5	1 06	0 39	9 43	18 13	18 37
28	6 42	+22·2	60·5	16·5	249	92	5	27·5	2 21	1 57	10 45	18 53	19 13
29	7 44	+19·1	61·0	16·6	261	90	1	28·5	3 46	3 27	11 45	19 25	19 39
30	8 45	+14·6	61·3	16·7	273	337	0	0·2	5 15	5 03	12 42	19 51	19 59
31	9 43	+ 9·2	61·2	16·7	286	303	2	1·2	6 44	6 38	13 37	20 12	20 16

MERCURY

Day	RA	Dec. +	Diam.	Phase	Transit		Day	RA	Dec. +	Diam.	Phase	Transit	
	h m	°			h m			h m	°			h m	
1	8 30	19·8	—	—	13 53		16	9 14	13·6	—	—	13 36	
4	8 43	18·5	—	—	13 54	Mercury is too	19	9 16	12·7	—	—	13 25	Mercury is too
7	8 54	17·1	—	—	13 53	close to the	22	9 14	12·1	—	—	13 12	close to the
10	9 03	15·8	—	—	13 50	Sun for	25	9 10	11·8	—	—	12 56	Sun for
13	9 10	14·6	—	—	13 44	observation	28	9 04	11·8	—	—	12 37	observation
16	9 14	13·6	—	—	13 36		31	8 56	12·2	—	—	12 17	

VENUS

Day	RA	Dec. +	Diam.	Phase	Transit	
	h m	°			h m	
1	7 02	23·5	—	—	12 25	
6	7 28	22·8	—	—	12 32	Venus is too
11	7 55	21·9	—	—	12 39	close to the
16	8 21	20·8	—	—	12 45	Sun for
21	8 46	19·3	—	—	12 51	observation
26	9 11	17·7	—	—	12 56	
31	9 36	15·9	—	—	13 01	

MARS

Day	RA	Dec. +	Diam.	Phase	Transit	5° high 52°	5° high 56°
	h m	°	″	%	h m	h m	h m
1	2 39	14·3	6	89	8 02	1 20	1 12
6	2 53	15·5	6	89	7 56	1 09	0 59
11	3 08	16·5	6	89	7 51	0 57	0 47
16	3 22	17·5	6	89	7 45	0 46	0 35
21	3 36	18·4	6	89	7 39	0 36	0 23
26	3 50	19·2	6	88	7 34	0 25	0 12
31	4 04	19·9	6	88	7 28	0 15	0 01

(*See* pages 63–64 for explanatory notes)

SUNRISE AND SUNSET

Day	London 0°05′ 51°30′		Bristol 2°35′ 51°28′		Birmingham 1°55′ 52°28′		Manchester 2°15′ 53°28′		Newcastle 1°37′ 54°59′		Glasgow 4°14′ 55°52′		Belfast 5°56′ 54°35′	
	h m	h m	h m	h m	h m	h m	h m	h m	h m	h m	h m	h m	h m	h m
1	3 48	20 21	3 58	20 30	3 49	20 33	3 45	20 41	3 32	20 48	3 36	21 05	3 52	21 03
2	3 48	20 20	3 58	20 30	3 50	20 33	3 45	20 40	3 33	20 47	3 37	21 04	3 53	21 02
3	3 49	20 20	3 59	20 30	3 51	20 32	3 46	20 40	3 34	20 47	3 38	21 04	3 54	21 02
4	3 50	20 19	4 00	20 29	3 52	20 32	3 47	20 39	3 35	20 46	3 39	21 03	3 55	21 01
5	3 51	20 19	4 01	20 29	3 53	20 31	3 48	20 39	3 36	20 46	3 40	21 02	3 56	21 00
6	3 51	20 18	4 02	20 28	3 54	20 31	3 49	20 38	3 37	20 45	3 41	21 02	3 57	21 00
7	3 52	20 18	4 03	20 27	3 54	20 30	3 50	20 37	3 38	20 44	3 42	21 01	3 58	20 59
8	3 53	20 17	4 03	20 27	3 55	20 29	3 51	20 36	3 39	20 43	3 43	21 00	3 59	20 58
9	3 54	20 16	4 04	20 26	3 56	20 29	3 52	20 36	3 40	20 42	3 45	20 59	4 00	20 57
10	3 55	20 15	4 05	20 25	3 58	20 28	3 53	20 35	3 41	20 41	3 46	20 58	4 01	20 56
11	3 56	20 15	4 07	20 24	3 59	20 27	3 54	20 34	3 43	20 40	3 47	20 57	4 02	20 55
12	3 57	20 14	4 08	20 24	4 00	20 26	3 56	20 33	3 44	20 39	3 49	20 56	4 04	20 54
13	3 59	20 13	4 09	20 23	4 01	20 25	3 57	20 32	3 45	20 38	3 50	20 54	4 05	20 53
14	4 00	20 12	4 10	20 22	4 02	20 24	3 58	20 31	3 47	20 37	3 51	20 53	4 06	20 52
15	4 01	20 11	4 11	20 21	4 03	20 23	3 59	20 30	3 48	20 36	3 53	20 52	4 08	20 51
16	4 02	20 10	4 12	20 20	4 05	20 22	4 01	20 29	3 49	20 35	3 54	20 51	4 09	20 50
17	4 03	20 09	4 13	20 19	4 06	20 21	4 02	20 27	3 51	20 33	3 56	20 49	4 10	20 48
18	4 05	20 08	4 15	20 18	4 07	20 20	4 03	20 26	3 52	20 32	3 57	20 48	4 12	20 47
19	4 06	20 07	4 16	20 16	4 09	20 18	4 05	20 25	3 54	20 31	3 59	20 46	4 13	20 46
20	4 07	20 05	4 17	20 15	4 10	20 17	4 06	20 24	3 55	20 29	4 01	20 45	4 15	20 44
21	4 08	20 04	4 19	20 14	4 11	20 16	4 08	20 22	3 57	20 28	4 02	20 43	4 16	20 43
22	4 10	20 03	4 20	20 13	4 13	20 15	4 09	20 21	3 59	20 26	4 04	20 42	4 18	20 41
23	4 11	20 01	4 21	20 11	4 14	20 13	4 11	20 19	4 00	20 25	4 06	20 40	4 20	20 40
24	4 13	20 00	4 23	20 10	4 16	20 12	4 12	20 18	4 02	20 23	4 07	20 38	4 21	20 38
25	4 14	19 59	4 24	20 09	4 17	20 10	4 14	20 16	4 03	20 21	4 09	20 37	4 23	20 36
26	4 15	19 57	4 26	20 07	4 18	20 09	4 15	20 15	4 05	20 20	4 11	20 35	4 24	20 35
27	4 17	19 56	4 27	20 06	4 20	20 07	4 17	20 13	4 07	20 18	4 13	20 33	4 26	20 33
28	4 18	19 54	4 28	20 04	4 22	20 06	4 18	20 11	4 09	20 16	4 14	20 31	4 28	20 31
29	4 20	19 53	4 30	20 03	4 23	20 04	4 20	20 10	4 10	20 14	4 16	20 29	4 30	20 30
30	4 21	19 51	4 31	20 01	4 25	20 02	4 22	20 08	4 12	20 12	4 18	20 27	4 31	20 28
31	4 23	19 50	4 33	19 59	4 26	20 01	4 23	20 06	4 14	20 11	4 20	20 25	4 33	20 26

JUPITER

Day	RA	Dec. +	Transit	5° high 52°	5° high 56°
	h m	° ′	h m	h m	h m
1	10 46·9	8 58	16 07	22 20	22 24
11	10 52·8	8 20	15 34	21 43	21 47
21	10 59·3	7 39	15 01	21 07	21 10
31	11 06·2	6 56	14 29	20 31	20 33

Diameters—equatorial 33″ polar 31″

SATURN

Day	RA	Dec. −	Transit	5° high 52°	5° high 56°
	h m	° ′	h m	h m	h m
1	21 21·4	16 27	2 44	22 47	23 08
11	21 19·3	16 39	2 02	22 07	22 28
21	21 16·7	16 52	1 20	21 27	21 48
31	21 13·8	17 06	0 38	20 46	21 08

Diameters—equatorial 18″ polar 17″
Rings—major axis 42″ minor axis 11″

URANUS

Day	RA	Dec. −	Transit	10° high 52°	10° high 56°
	h m	° ′	h m	h m	h m
1	19 11·0	22 52	0 34	2 42	1 37
11	19 09·3	22 55	23 49	2 01	0 54
21	19 07·5	22 58	23 08	1 19	0 12
31	19 05·9	23 01	22 27	0 37	23 25

Diameter 4″

NEPTUNE

Day	RA	Dec. −	Transit	10° high 52°	10° high 56°
	h m	° ′	h m	h m	h m
1	19 16·7	21 31	0 39	3 04	2 13
11	19 15·6	21 33	23 55	2 23	1 31
21	19 14·4	21 35	23 15	1 42	0 50
31	19 13·4	21 37	22 34	1 01	0 09

Diameter 2″

(See page 64 for explanatory notes)

DAY OF			Julius Caesar *Augustus*, formerly *Sextilis*, 6th month (from March). *Sun's Longitude* 150° ♍ 22ᵈ 21ʰ	

Year	Month	Week	

PHENOMENA

d h
1 08 Jupiter in conjunction with Moon. Jupiter 6°N.
2 21 Mercury in inferior conjunction.
7 10 Saturn at opposition.
12 22 Saturn in conjunction with Moon. Saturn 4°S.
21 02 Mercury at greatest elongation W.19°.
22 20 Mars in conjunction with Moon. Mars 1°S.
23 06 Jupiter in conjunction with Venus. Jupiter 0°.2S.
26 23 Mercury in conjunction with Moon. Mercury 4°N.
29 04 Jupiter in conjunction with Moon. Jupiter 6°N.
29 14 Venus in conjunction with Moon. Venus 6°N.

214	1	S.	Anne I. *d.* 1714. Yves St. Laurent *b.* 1936.
215	2	S.	**8th S. after Pentecost.** William II *d.* 1100.
216	3	M.	Richard Arkwright *d.* 1892.*
217	4	Tu.	QUEEN ELIZABETH THE QUEEN MOTHER *b.* 1900.
218	5	W.	Lord North *d.* 1792.* Neil Armstrong *b.* 1930.
219	6	Th.	**Transfiguration.** Diego Velazquez *d.* 1660.
220	7	F.	Joseph Jacquard *d.* 1834. Sidney Buller *d.* 1970.
221	8	S.	PRINCESS BEATRICE OF YORK *b.* 1988.
222	9	S.	**9th S. after Pentecost.** Philip Larkin *b.* 1922.
223	10	M.	Charles Keene *b.* 1823.
224	11	Tu.	First Royal Ascot meeting 1711.
225	12	W.	Southey *b.* 1774. George Stephenson *d.* 1848.
226	13	Th.	Hitchcock *b.* 1899. Florence Nightingale *d.* 1910.
227	14	F.	John Galsworthy *b.* 1867. Enzo Ferrari *d.* 1988.
228	15	S.	ASSUMPTION. PRINCESS ROYAL *b.* 1950.
229	16	S.	**10th S. after Pentecost.** Ted Hughes *b.* 1930.
230	17	M.	Rudolf Hess *d.* 1987.
231	18	Tu.	Earl Russell *b.* 1792.* Frederick Ashton *d.* 1988.
232	19	W.	Allied raid on Dieppe 1942.
233	20	Th.	Duke of Buckingham *b.* 1592.*
234	21	F.	PRINCESS MARGARET *b.* 1930. William IV *b.* 1765.
235	22	S.	Debussy *b.* 1862. Viscount Nuffield *d.* 1963.
236	23	S.	**11th S. after Pentecost.** Valentino *d.* 1926.
237	24	M.	**St Bartholomew.** George Stubbs *b.* 1724.
238	25	Tu.	Ivan the Terrible *b.* 1530. Michael Faraday *d.* 1867.
239	26	W.	Isherwood *b.* 1904. Vaughan Williams *d.* 1958.
240	27	Th.	Titian *d.* 1576. Krakatoa erupted 1883.
241	28	F.	Tolstoy *b.* 1828. Leigh Hunt *d.* 1859.
242	29	S.	Lady Diana Cooper *b.* 1892.*
243	30	S.	**12th S. after Pentecost.** Denis Healey *b.* 1917.
244	31	M.	John Bunyan *d.* 1688. Baudelaire *d.* 1867.

CONSTELLATIONS

The following constellations are near the meridian at

d h	d h
July 1 24	July 16 23
Aug. 1 22	Aug. 16 21
Sept. 1 20	Sept. 15 19

Draco, Hercules, Lyra, Cygnus, Sagitta, Ophiuchus, Serpens, Aquila and Sagittarius.

MINIMA OF ALGOL

d	h	d	h
1	05·1	18	10·0
4	02·0	21	06·8
6	22·8	24	03·6
9	19·6	27	00·4
12	16·4	29	21·2
15	13·2		

*Centenary.

MOON
Phases, Apsides & Node

	d	h	m
☽ First Quarter	5	10	59
○ Full Moon	13	10	27
☾ Last Quarter	21	10	01
● New Moon	28	02	42
Apogee (406,373 km)	13	15	38
Perigee (357,371 km)	27	17	37

Mean longitude of ascending node on Aug. 1, 269°.

See note on Summer Time, p. 22.

MONTHLY NOTES

3. Bank Holiday, Scotland.

12. Grouse shooting begins.

28. Lammas (Scottish Term Day).

31. Bank and General Holiday, England, Wales and N. Ireland.

(*See* page 62 for explanatory notes)

Day	Right Ascension	Dec. +	Equation of Time	Rise 52°	Rise 56°	Transit	Set 52°	Set 56°	Sidereal Time	Transit of First Point of Aries
	h m s	° ′	m s	h m	h m	h m	h m	h m	h m s	h m s
1	8 45 43	18 01	− 6 18	4 22	4 04	12 06	19 50	20 07	20 39 25	3 20 02
2	8 49 35	17 45	− 6 14	4 23	4 06	12 06	19 48	20 05	20 43 21	3 16 06
3	8 53 28	17 30	− 6 10	4 25	4 08	12 06	19 46	20 03	20 47 18	3 12 10
4	8 57 19	17 14	− 6 04	4 27	4 10	12 06	19 44	20 01	20 51 15	3 08 15
5	9 01 10	16 58	− 5 59	4 28	4 12	12 06	19 43	19 59	20 55 11	3 04 19
6	9 05 00	16 41	− 5 52	4 30	4 14	12 06	19 41	19 57	20 59 08	3 00 23
7	9 08 50	16 25	− 5 45	4 31	4 16	12 06	19 39	19 54	21 03 04	2 56 27
8	9 12 39	16 08	− 5 38	4 33	4 18	12 06	19 37	19 52	21 07 01	2 52 31
9	9 16 27	15 51	− 5 30	4 35	4 19	12 05	19 35	19 50	21 10 57	2 48 35
10	9 20 15	15 33	− 5 21	4 36	4 21	12 05	19 33	19 48	21 14 54	2 44 39
11	9 24 02	15 16	− 5 12	4 38	4 23	12 05	19 31	19 46	21 18 50	2 40 43
12	9 27 49	14 58	− 5 02	4 39	4 25	12 05	19 29	19 43	21 22 47	2 36 47
13	9 31 35	14 40	− 4 51	4 41	4 27	12 05	19 27	19 41	21 26 44	2 32 51
14	9 35 20	14 21	− 4 40	4 43	4 29	12 05	19 25	19 39	21 30 40	2 28 55
15	9 39 05	14 03	− 4 29	4 44	4 31	12 04	19 23	19 36	21 34 37	2 25 00
16	9 42 50	13 44	− 4 17	4 46	4 33	12 04	19 21	19 34	21 38 33	2 21 04
17	9 46 34	13 25	− 4 04	4 47	4 35	12 04	19 19	19 31	21 42 30	2 17 08
18	9 50 17	13 05	− 3 51	4 49	4 37	12 04	19 17	19 29	21 46 26	2 13 12
19	9 54 00	12 46	− 3 37	4 51	4 39	12 04	19 15	19 27	21 50 23	2 09 16
20	9 57 43	12 26	− 3 23	4 52	4 41	12 03	19 13	19 24	21 54 19	2 05 20
21	10 01 25	12 06	− 3 09	4 54	4 43	12 03	19 11	19 22	21 58 16	2 01 24
22	10 05 06	11 46	− 2 54	4 56	4 45	12 03	19 09	19 19	22 02 13	1 57 28
23	10 08 47	11 26	− 2 38	4 57	4 47	12 03	19 07	19 17	22 06 09	1 53 32
24	10 12 28	11 06	− 2 23	4 59	4 49	12 02	19 04	19 14	22 10 06	1 49 36
25	10 16 09	10 45	− 2 06	5 01	4 51	12 02	19 02	19 12	22 14 02	1 45 40
26	10 19 48	10 24	− 1 50	5 02	4 53	12 02	19 00	19 09	22 17 59	1 41 45
27	10 23 28	10 03	− 1 33	5 04	4 55	12 01	18 58	19 07	22 21 55	1 37 49
28	10 27 07	9 42	− 1 15	5 05	4 57	12 01	18 56	19 04	22 25 52	1 33 53
29	10 30 46	9 21	− 0 58	5 07	4 59	12 01	18 53	19 02	22 29 48	1 29 57
30	10 34 25	8 59	− 0 40	5 09	5 01	12 01	18 51	18 59	22 33 45	1 26 01
31	10 38 03	8 38	− 0 21	5 10	5 03	12 00	18 49	18 57	22 37 42	1 22 05

THE SUN s.d. 15′·8

Duration of Civil (C), Nautical (N) and Astronomical (A) Twilight (in minutes)

Lat. °	Aug. 1 C	N	A	Aug. 11 C	N	A	Aug. 21 C	N	A	Aug. 31 C	N	A
52	41	97	177	39	89	153	37	83	138	35	79	127
56	48	120	TAN	45	106	205	42	96	166	40	89	147

ASTRONOMICAL NOTES

MERCURY is unsuitably placed for observation at first, since it passes through inferior conjunction on the 2nd. During the second half of the month it may be seen as a morning object, magnitude +1 to −1, low above the ENE horizon at the beginning of morning civil twilight. On the morning of the 27th the Moon, only one day before New, rises to the right of Mercury, though this event will only be witnessed under extremely clear atmospheric conditions.

VENUS magnitude −3·9, very gradually becomes visible in the evenings at sunset, though only for a very short while, extremely low above the western horizon. The further north the observer is in Britain, the greater the difficulty of locating the planet.

MARS, magnitude +0·7, is now well placed for observation in the east and south-eastern sky after midnight. At the beginning of the month it is passing

between the Pleiades and the Hyades, almost exactly the same brightness as Aldebaran, moving steadily eastwards in Taurus throughout the month. Mars will be seen very close to the Moon as the two objects rise on the morning of the 22nd.

JUPITER is disappearing into the evening twilight and will not be seen again until October.

SATURN, magnitude +0·2, is at opposition on the 7th, and thus visible throughout the hours of darkness. On the evening of the 12th the Full Moon passes 4°N. of the planet.

METEORS. The maximum of the famous Perseid meteor shower occurs on the night of the 11th–12th. The Full Moon will be a considerable hindrance to observation.

(*See* pages 62–63 for explanatory notes)

THE MOON

Day	RA	Dec.	Hor. Par.	Semi-diam.	Sun's Co-long.	PA of Bright Limb	Phase	Age	Rise 52°	Rise 56°	Transit	Set 52°	Set 56°
	h m	°	′	′	°	°	%	d	h m	h m	h m	h m	h m
1	10 39	+ 3·3	60·9	16·6	298	300	7	2·2	8 12	8 11	14 30	20 32	20 30
2	11 33	− 2·7	60·2	16·4	310	299	15	3·2	9 37	9 41	15 22	20 52	20 45
3	12 27	− 8·4	59·4	16·2	322	296	24	4·2	11 00	11 10	16 13	21 13	21 02
4	13 20	−13·5	58·6	16·0	335	294	34	5·2	12 20	12 36	17 04	21 38	21 21
5	14 14	−17·8	57·7	15·7	347	290	45	6·2	13 37	13 58	17 56	22 08	21 46
6	15 08	−21·0	56·9	15·5	359	285	56	7·2	14·49	15·13	18 49	22 44	22 19
7	16 03	−23·1	56·1	15·3	11	280	66	8·2	15 51	16 19	19 41	23 30	23 03
8	16 57	−23·9	55·5	15·1	24	275	75	9·2	16 44	17 11	20 33	—	23 58
9	17 51	−23·6	55·0	15·0	36	271	83	10·2	17 25	17 50	21 23	0 24	—
10	18 43	−22·2	54·6	14·9	48	267	90	11·2	17 58	18 19	22 12	1 26	1 02
11	19 34	−19·7	54·3	14·8	60	265	95	12·2	18 24	18 40	22 57	2 32	2 12
12	20 22	−16·5	54·1	14·7	72	267	98	13·2	18 45	18 57	23 41	3 40	3 24
13	21 08	−12·6	54·0	14·7	85	291	100	14·2	19 02	19 10	—	4 47	4 37
14	21 53	− 8·2	54·0	14·7	97	35	100	15·2	19 18	19 22	0 23	5 55	5 49
15	22 37	− 3·6	54·0	14·7	109	53	98	16·2	19 33	19 33	1 04	7 02	7 00
16	23 20	+ 1·2	54·2	14·8	121	57	94	17·2	19 49	19 45	1 45	8 09	8 12
17	0 04	+ 6·0	54·5	14·8	133	60	89	18·2	20 05	19 57	2 26	9 18	9 24
18	0 50	+10·6	54·9	15·0	145	63	82	19·2	20 25	20 12	3 09	10 27	10 38
19	1 37	+14·9	55·4	15·1	158	66	74	20·2	20 48	20 31	3 54	11 38	11 54
20	2 27	+18·5	56·0	15·3	170	70	65	21·2	21 18	20 57	4 42	12 50	13 11
21	3 20	+21·4	56·8	15·5	182	75	55	22·2	21 58	21 33	5 33	14 00	14 25
22	4 16	+23·3	57·6	15·7	194	80	44	23·2	22 50	22 23	6 29	15 05	15 31
23	5 15	+23·8	58·5	15·9	207	86	33	24·2	23 56	23 31	7 27	16 01	16 26
24	6 16	+22·9	59·4	16·2	219	91	23	25·2	—	—	8 26	16 46	17 08
25	7 18	+20·5	60·2	16·4	231	96	14	26·2	1 14	0 53	9 26	17 21	17 38
26	8 18	+16·7	60·9	16·6	243	98	7	27·2	2 40	2 25	10 24	17 49	18 01
27	9 17	+11·8	61·3	16·7	255	94	2	28·2	4 09	4 00	11 21	18 13	18 19
28	10 14	+ 6·0	61·3	16·7	268	40	0	29·2	5 38	5 34	12 15	18 34	18 35
29	11 10	− 0·1	61·1	16·6	280	314	1	0·9	7 06	7 08	13 08	18 55	18 51
30	12 05	− 6·0	60·5	16·5	292	303	6	1·9	8 33	8 40	14 01	19 16	19 07
31	13 00	−11·5	59·8	16·3	304	298	12	2·9	9 57	10 10	14 54	19 40	19 26

MERCURY

Day	RA	Dec. +	Diam.	Phase	Transit		Day	RA	Dec. +	Diam.	Phase	Transit	5° high 52°	5° high 56°
	h m	°			h m			h m	°	″	%	h m	h m	h m
1	8 53	12·4	—	—	12 10		16	8 33	16·5	9	23	10 54	4 00	3 50
4	8 44	13·1	—	—	11 50	Mercury is too	19	8 40	17·0	8	34	10 50	3 54	3 43
7	8 37	14·0	—	—	11 31	close to the	22	8 52	17·1	7	46	10 50	3 53	3 42
10	8 32	15·0	—	—	11 14	Sun for	25	9 07	16·7	7	58	10 54	3 59	3 48
13	8 30	15·8	—	—	11 02	observation	28	9 26	16·0	6	70	11 01	4 10	4 00
16	8 33	16·5	—	—	10 54		31	9 46	14·8	6	81	11 10	4 26	4 17

VENUS

Day	RA	Dec. +	Diam.	Phase	Transit	5° high 52°	5° high 56°
	h m	°	″	%	h m	h m	h m
1	9 41	15·5	10	97	13 02	19 48	19 57
6	10 04	13·4	10	97	13 06	19 41	19 48
11	10 28	11·2	10	96	13 09	19 33	19 38
16	10 51	8·9	10	95	13 13	19 24	19 28
21	11 14	6·4	10	95	13 16	19 14	19 17
26	11 36	3·9	11	94	13 19	19 04	19 04
31	11 59	1·4	11	93	13 21	18 54	18 52

MARS

Day	RA	Dec. +	Diam.	Phase	Transit	5° high 52°	5° high 56°
	h m	°	″	%	h m	h m	h m
1	4 07	20·1	6	88	7 27	0 13	23 57
6	4 21	20·8	6	88	7 21	0 04	23 46
11	4 35	21·3	6	88	7 15	23 52	23 37
16	4 48	21·8	7	87	7 09	23 43	23 27
21	5 02	22·3	7	87	7 03	23 35	23 18
26	5 15	22·6	7	87	6 57	23 26	23 09
31	5 29	22·9	7	87	6 51	23 18	23 00

(*See* pages 63–64 for explanatory notes)

SUNRISE AND SUNSET

Day	London 0°05′ 51°30′		Bristol 2°35′ 51°28′		Birmingham 1°55′ 52°28′		Manchester 2°15′ 53°28′		Newcastle 1°37′ 54°59′		Glasgow 4°14′ 55°52′		Belfast 5°56′ 54°35′	
	h m	h m	h m	h m	h m	h m	h m	h m	h m	h m	h m	h m	h m	h m
1	4 24	19 48	4 34	19 58	4 28	19 59	4 25	20 05	4 16	20 09	4 22	20 23	4 35	20 24
2	4 26	19 46	4 36	19 56	4 29	19 57	4 27	20 03	4 17	20 07	4 24	20 21	4 36	20 22
3	4 27	19 45	4 37	19 54	4 31	19 56	4 28	20 01	4 19	20 05	4 26	20 19	4 38	20 20
4	4 29	19 43	4 39	19 53	4 32	19 54	4 30	19 59	4 21	20 03	4 27	20 17	4 40	20 18
5	4 30	19 41	4 40	19 51	4 34	19 52	4 32	19 57	4 23	20 01	4 29	20 15	4 42	20 16
6	4 32	19 39	4 42	19 49	4 36	19 50	4 33	19 55	4 25	19 59	4 31	20 13	4 44	20 14
7	4 33	19 38	4 44	19 47	4 37	19 48	4 35	19 53	4 26	19 57	4 33	20 11	4 45	20 12
8	4 35	19 36	4 45	19 46	4 39	19 46	4 37	19 51	4 28	19 55	4 35	20 09	4 47	20 10
9	4 37	19 34	4 47	19 44	4 41	19 44	4 38	19 49	4 30	19 52	4 37	20 06	4 49	20 08
10	4 38	19 32	4 48	19 42	4 42	19 43	4 40	19 47	4 32	19 50	4 39	20 04	4 51	20 06
11	4 40	19 30	4 50	19 40	4 44	19 41	4 42	19 45	4 34	19 48	4 41	20 02	4 53	20 04
12	4 41	19 28	4 51	19 38	4 46	19 39	4 44	19 43	4 36	19 46	4 43	20 00	4 54	20 02
13	4 43	19 26	4 53	19 36	4 47	19 37	4 45	19 41	4 37	19 44	4 45	19 57	4 56	20 00
14	4 44	19 24	4 55	19 34	4 49	19 34	4 47	19 39	4 39	19 41	4 47	19 55	4 58	19 57
15	4 46	19 22	4 56	19 32	4 50	19 32	4 49	19 37	4 41	19 39	4 49	19 53	5 00	19 55
16	4 48	19 20	4 58	19 30	4 52	19 30	4 50	19 35	4 43	19 37	4 51	19 50	5 02	19 53
17	4 49	19 18	4 59	19 28	4 54	19 28	4 52	19 32	4 45	19 35	4 52	19 48	5 04	19 51
18	4 51	19 16	5 01	19 26	4 55	19 26	4 54	19 30	4 47	19 32	4 54	19 46	5 05	19 48
19	4 52	19 14	5 02	19 24	4 57	19 24	4 56	19 28	4 49	19 30	4 56	19 43	5 07	19 46
20	4 54	19 12	5 04	19 22	4 59	19 22	4 57	19 26	4 51	19 28	4 58	19 41	5 09	19 44
21	4 56	19 10	5 06	19 20	5 00	19 20	4 59	19 24	4 52	19 25	5 00	19 38	5 11	19 41
22	4 57	19 08	5 07	19 18	5 02	19 18	5 01	19 21	4 54	19 23	5 02	19 36	5 13	19 39
23	4 59	19 06	5 09	19 16	5 04	19 15	5 03	19 19	4 56	19 20	5 04	19 33	5 15	19 37
24	5 00	19 04	5 10	19 14	5 05	19 13	5 04	19 17	4 58	19 18	5 06	19 31	5 16	19 34
25	5 02	19 02	5 12	19 12	5 07	19 11	5 06	19 15	5 00	19 16	5 08	19 28	5 18	19 32
26	5 04	18 59	5 14	19 09	5 09	19 09	5 08	19 12	5 02	19 13	5 10	19 26	5 20	19 30
27	5 05	18 57	5 15	19 07	5 10	19 07	5 10	19 10	5 04	19 11	5 12	19 23	5 22	19 27
28	5 07	18 55	5 17	19 05	5 12	19 04	5 11	19 08	5 06	19 08	5 14	19 21	5 24	19 25
29	5 08	18 53	5 18	19 03	5 14	19 02	5 13	19 05	5 07	19 06	5 16	19 18	5 26	19 22
30	5 10	18 51	5 20	19 01	5 15	19 00	5 15	19 03	5 09	19 03	5 18	19 16	5 27	19 20
31	5 12	18 48	5 22	18 58	5 17	18 57	5 17	19 01	5 11	19 01	5 20	19 13	5 29	19 17

JUPITER

Day	RA	Dec. +	Transit	5° high 52°	5° high 56°
	h m	° ′	h m	h m	h m
1	11 06·9	6 51	14 26	20 27	20 29
11	11 14·3	6 04	13 54	19 51	19 53
21	11 21·8	5 16	13 22	19 15	19 16
31	11 29·6	4 26	12 50	18 39	18 40

Diameters – equatorial 31″ polar 29″

SATURN

Day	RA	Dec. –	Transit	5° high 52°	5° high 56°
	h m	° ′	h m	h m	h m
1	21 13·6	17 07	0 34	4 22	4 00
11	21 10·6	17 21	23 48	3 38	3 16
21	21 07·7	17 35	23 05	2 54	2 32
31	21 04·9	17 47	22 23	2 11	1 48

Diameters – equatorial 19″ polar 17″
Rings – major axis 42″ minor axis 12″

URANUS

Day	RA	Dec. –	Transit	10° high 52°	10° high 56°
	h m	° ′	h m	h m	h m
1	19 05·8	23 01	22 23	0 33	23 21
11	19 04·3	23 03	21 42	23 48	22 39
21	19 03·1	23 05	21 01	23 07	21 58
31	19 02·1	23 06	20 21	22 27	21 17

Diameter 4″

NEPTUNE

Day	RA	Dec. –	Transit	10° high 52°	10° high 56°
	h m	° ′	h m	h m	h m
1	19 13·2	21 37	22 30	0 57	0 05
11	19 12·3	21 39	21 50	0 16	23 20
21	19 11·4	21 41	21 10	23 32	22 39
31	19 10·7	21 43	20 30	22 52	21 59

Diameter 2″

(See page 64 for explanatory notes)

DAY OF			*Septem* (seven), 7th month of Roman (pre-Julian) Calendar. *Sun's Longitude* 180° ♎ 22ᵈ 19ʰ
Year	Month	Week	

245	1	Tu.	Sedan 1870. Siegfried Sassoon *d.* 1967.
246	2	W.	Fire of London 1666. J. R. R. Tolkien *d.* 1973.
247	3	Th.	Start of Second World War 1939.
248	4	F.	Bruckner *b.* 1824. Grieg *d.* 1907.
249	5	S.	Douglas Bader *d.* 1982.
250	6	**S.**	**13th S. after Pentecost.** James II *d.* 1701.
251	7	M.	Holman Hunt *d.* 1910. Leonard Cheshire *b.* 1917.
252	8	Tu.	**Blessed Virgin Mary.** Peter Sellers *b.* 1925.
253	9	W.	End of soap rationing 1950.
254	10	Th.	Treaty of St Germain signed 1919.
255	11	F.	D. H. Lawrence *b.* 1885. Jan Smuts *d.* 1950.
256	12	S.	H. H. Asquith *b.* 1852.
257	13	**S.**	**14th S. after Pentecost.** de Montaigne *d.* 1592.*
258	14	M.	Isadora Duncan *d.* 1927.
259	15	Tu.	PRINCE HENRY OF WALES *b.* 1984.
260	16	W.	John Gay *d.* 1685. Maria Callas *d.* 1977.
261	17	Th.	Francis Chichester *b.* 1901. Laura Ashley *d.* 1985.
262	18	F.	Samuel Johnson *b.* 1809. Hazlitt *d.* 1830.
263	19	S.	George Cadbury *b.* 1839. Thomas Barnado *d.* 1905.
264	20	**S.**	**15th S. after Pentecost.** Valmy 1792.*
265	21	M.	**St Matthew.** H. G. Wells *b.* 1866.
266	22	Tu.	Michael Faraday *b.* 1791.
267	23	W.	Bellini *d.* 1835. Baroness Orczy *b.* 1865.
268	24	Th.	George Cross instituted 1940.
269	25	F.	Shostakovitch *b.* 1906. Strauss (elder) *d.* 1849.
270	26	S.	T. S. Eliot *b.* 1888. George Gershwin *b.* 1898.
271	27	**S.**	**16th S. after Pentecost.** George Cruikshank *b.* [1792.*
272	28	M.	Louis Pasteur *d.* 1895. W. H. Auden *d.* 1973.
273	29	Tu.	**St Michael and all Angels.**
274	30	W.	Lord Raglan *b.* 1788. Deborah Kerr *b.* 1921.

* Centenary

PHENOMENA

d	h	
9	00	Saturn in conjunction with Moon. Saturn 4°S.
15	04	Mercury in superior conjunction.
16	09	Jupiter in conjunction with Mercury. Jupiter 0°.4S.
17	19	Jupiter in conjunction with Sun.
20	09	Mars in conjunction with Moon. Mars 0°.9N.
22	19	Equinox.
26	00	Jupiter in conjunction with Moon. Jupiter 6°N.
27	03	Mercury in conjunction with Moon. Mercury 5°N.
28	13	Venus in conjunction with Moon. Venus 4°N.

CONSTELLATIONS

The following constellations are near the meridian at

	d	h		d	h
Aug.	1	24	Aug.	16	23
Sept.	1	22	Sept.	15	21
Oct.	1	20	Oct.	16	19

Draco, Cepheus, Lyra, Cygnus, Vulpecula, Sagitta, Delphinus, Equuleus, Aquila, Aquarius and Capricornus.

MINIMA OF ALGOL

d	h	d	h
1	18·0	18	22·9
4	14·9	21	19·7
7	11·7	24	16·5
10	08·5	27	13·3
13	05·3	30	10·1
16	02·1		

MOON
Phases, Apsides & Node

	d	h	m
☽ First Quarter	3	22	39
○ Full Moon	12	02	17
☾ Last Quarter	19	19	53
● New Moon	26	10	40
Apogee (406,080 km)	9	18	36
Perigee (359,928 km)	25	02	35

Mean longitude of ascending node on Sept. 1, 267°

See note on Summer Time, p. 22.

MONTHLY NOTES

1. Partridge shooting begins.
15. Battle of Britain Day.
28. Jewish New Year (AM 5753).
29. Michaelmas (Quarter day).

(*See* page 62 for explanatory notes)

Day	Right Ascension	Dec.	Equation of Time	Rise 52°	Rise 56°	Transit	Set 52°	Set 56°	Sidereal Time	Transit of First Point of Aries
	THE SUN						s.d. 15′·9			
	h m s	° ′	m s	h m	h m	h m	h m	h m	h m s	h m s
1	10 41 40	+8 16	− 0 02	5 12	5 05	12 00	18 47	18 54	22 41 38	1 18 09
2	10 45 18	+7 54	+ 0 17	5 14	5 06	12 00	18 44	18 51	22 45 35	1 14 13
3	10 48 55	+7 32	+ 0 36	5 15	5 08	11 59	18 42	18 49	22 49 31	1 10 17
4	10 52 32	+7 10	+ 0 56	5 17	5 10	11 59	18 40	18 46	22 53 28	1 06 21
5	10 56 09	+6 48	+ 1 16	5 18	5 12	11 59	18 38	18 44	22 57 24	1 02 25
6	10 59 45	+6 26	+ 1 36	5 20	5 14	11 58	18 35	18 41	23 01 21	0 58 30
7	11 03 21	+6 03	+ 1 56	5 22	5 16	11 58	18 33	18 38	23 05 17	0 54 34
8	11 06 57	+5 41	+ 2 17	5 23	5 18	11 58	18 31	18 36	23 09 14	0 50 38
9	11 10 33	+5 18	+ 2 37	5 25	5 20	11 57	18 28	18 33	23 13 11	0 46 42
10	11 14 09	+4 56	+ 2 58	5 27	5 22	11 57	18 26	18 30	23 17 07	0 42 46
11	11 17 44	+4 33	+ 3 19	5 28	5 24	11 57	18 24	18 28	23 21 04	0 38 50
12	11 21 20	+4 10	+ 3 41	5 30	5 26	11 56	18 21	18 25	23 25 00	0 34 54
13	11 24 55	+3 47	+ 4 02	5 31	5 28	11 56	18 19	18 22	23 28 57	0 30 58
14	11 28 30	+3 24	+ 4 23	5 33	5 30	11 55	18 17	18 20	23 32 53	0 27 02
15	11 32 05	+3 01	+ 4 45	5 35	5 32	11 55	18 14	18 17	23 36 50	0 23 06
16	11 35 40	+2 38	+ 5 06	5 36	5 34	11 55	18 12	18 14	23 40 46	0 19 10
17	11 39 15	+2 15	+ 5 27	5 38	5 36	11 54	18 10	18 12	23 44 43	0 15 15
18	11 42 51	+1 51	+ 5 49	5 40	5 38	11 54	18 07	18 09	23 48 39	0 11 19
19	11 46 26	+1 28	+ 6 10	5 41	5 40	11 54	18 05	18 07	23 52 36	0 07 23
20	11 50 01	+1 05	+ 6 32	5 43	5 42	11 53	18 03	18 04	23 56 33	{ 0 03 27 / 23 59 31
21	11 53 36	+0 42	+ 6 53	5 45	5 44	11 53	18 00	18 01	0 00 29	23 55 35
22	11 57 12	+0 18	+ 7 14	5 46	5 45	11 53	17 58	17 59	0 04 26	23 51 39
23	12 00 47	−0 05	+ 7 35	5 48	5 47	11 52	17 56	17 56	0 08 22	23 47 43
24	12 04 23	−0 29	+ 7 56	5 49	5 49	11 52	17 53	17 53	0 12 19	23 43 47
25	12 07 59	−0 52	+ 8 16	5 51	5 51	11 52	17 51	17 51	0 16 15	23 39 51
26	12 11 35	−1 15	+ 8 37	5 53	5 53	11 51	17 49	17 48	0 20 12	23 35 55
27	12 15 11	−1 39	+ 8 57	5 54	5 55	11 51	17 46	17 45	0 24 08	23 32 00
28	12 18 47	−2 02	+ 9 18	5 56	5 57	11 51	17 44	17 43	0 28 05	23 28 04
29	12 22 24	−2 25	+ 9 37	5 58	5 59	11 50	17 42	17 40	0 32 02	23 24 08
30	12 26 01	−2 49	+ 9 57	5 59	6 01	11 50	17 39	17 37	0 35 58	23 20 12

Duration of Civil (C), Nautical (N) and Astronomical (A) Twilight (in minutes)

Lat.	Sept. 1			Sept. 11			Sept. 21			Sept. 30		
°	C	N	A	C	N	A	C	N	A	C	N	A
52	35	79	127	34	76	120	34	74	115	34	73	113
56	39	89	146	38	84	135	37	82	129	37	80	126

ASTRONOMICAL NOTES

MERCURY is too close to the Sun for observation, superior conjunction occurring on the 15th.

VENUS, magnitude −3·9, continues to be visible as a difficult evening object for a very short while after sunset, very low above the WSW horizon. Although it is 8° farther from the Sun at the end of the month compared with the beginning, its rapid southward motion in declination compensates for this increase in elongation, so that the time available for observation remains almost exactly the same throughout September. On the 28th the thin crescent Moon, two days old, passes 4° S. of Venus.

MARS continues to be visible as a morning object, magnitude +0·4. It moves from Taurus into Gemini during the month. On the morning of the 20th the Moon, at Last Quarter, passes close to the planet.

JUPITER passes through conjunction on the 17th and is thus unsuitably placed for observation.

SATURN continues to be visible in the night sky, in Capricornus, but by the end of the month is no longer visible after midnight. Its magnitude is +0·4. On the night of the 8th–9th the gibbous Moon passes 4°N. of Saturn.

ZODIACAL LIGHT. The morning cone may be seen stretching up from the eastern horizon before the beginning of morning twilight from the 1st to the 9th and again after the 24th.

(See pages 62–63 for explanatory notes)

THE MOON

Day	RA	Dec.	Hor. Par.	Semi-diam.	Sun's Co-long.	PA of Bright Limb	Phase	Age	Rise 52°	Rise 56°	Transit	Set 52°	Set 56°
	h m	°	′	′	°	°	%	d	h m	h m	h m	h m	h m
1	13 55	−16·3	58·8	16·0	317	293	21	3·9	11 18	11 36	15 48	20 09	19 50
2	14 51	−19·9	57·9	15·8	329	288	30	4·9	12 34	12 57	16 42	20 44	20 21
3	15 47	−22·4	57·0	15·5	341	283	40	5·9	13 42	14 08	17 36	21 27	21 01
4	16 43	−23·6	56·1	15·3	353	278	51	6·9	14 38	15 05	18 29	22 19	21 53
5	17 37	−23·6	55·4	15·1	6	272	61	7·9	15 24	15 49	19 20	23 19	22 54
6	18 30	−22·4	54·9	14·9	18	267	70	8·9	16 00	16 21	20 09	—	—
7	19 21	−20·3	54·4	14·8	30	263	78	9·9	16 28	16 45	20 55	0 24	0 03
8	20 10	−17·2	54·2	14·8	42	260	86	10·9	16 50	17 03	21 39	1 30	1 14
9	20 57	−13·6	54·0	14·7	54	259	92	11·9	17 09	17 18	22 22	2 38	2 26
10	21 42	− 9·3	54·0	14·7	66	261	96	12·9	17 26	17 31	23 03	3 46	3 38
11	22 26	− 4·8	54·1	14·7	79	269	99	13·9	17 41	17 42	23 44	4 53	4 49
12	23 10	0·0	54·2	14·8	91	325	100	14·9	17 57	17 54	—	6 00	6 01
13	23 54	+ 4·8	54·5	14·8	103	40	99	15·9	18 13	18 07	0 26	7 08	7 13
14	0 39	+ 9·4	54·8	14·9	115	55	96	16·9	18 32	18 21	1 08	8 17	8 27
15	1 26	+13·7	55·2	15·0	127	61	92	17·9	18 54	18 39	1 52	9 28	9 42
16	2 15	+17·5	55·6	15·2	140	67	86	18·9	19 22	19 02	2 39	10 39	10 58
17	3 07	+20·6	56·2	15·3	152	72	78	19·9	19 58	19 34	3 29	11 49	12 12
18	4 02	+22·7	56·8	15·5	164	78	69	20·9	20 45	20 19	4 23	12 54	13 20
19	4 59	+23·6	57·5	15·7	176	84	59	21·9	21 44	21 18	5 18	13 52	14 18
20	5 58	+23·1	58·3	15·9	188	90	48	22·9	22 55	22 32	6 15	14 39	15 03
21	6 57	+21·3	59·0	16·1	200	95	37	23·9	—	23 57	7 13	15 17	15 36
22	7 56	+18·1	59·7	16·3	213	100	27	24·9	0 14	—	8 10	15 48	16 02
23	8 53	+13·7	60·3	16·4	225	103	17	25·9	1 39	1 27	9 05	16 13	16 22
24	9 50	+ 8·5	60·7	16·6	237	103	9	26·9	3 05	2 59	9 59	16 35	16 39
25	10 46	+ 2·6	60·9	16·6	249	99	3	27·9	4 32	4 31	10 53	16 56	16 55
26	11 41	− 3·4	60·8	16·6	262	75	0	28·9	5 59	6 04	11 46	17 17	17 11
27	12 36	− 9·1	60·4	16·5	274	325	1	0·6	7 25	7 35	12 39	17 41	17 29
28	13 32	−14·2	59·8	16·3	286	302	4	1·6	8 50	9 05	13 34	18 08	17 51
29	14 29	−18·4	59·1	16·1	298	294	9	2·6	10 11	10 31	14 29	18 41	18 20
30	15 26	−21·4	58·0	15·8	310	287	16	3·6	11 24	11 49	15 25	19 22	18 57

MERCURY

Day	RA	Dec. +	Diam.	Phase	Transit		Day	RA	Dec.	Diam.	Phase	Transit	
	h m	°			h m			h m	°			h m	
1	9 54	14·3	—	—	11 14		16	11 41	+ 3·7	—	—	12 01	
4	10 16	12·6	—	—	11 24	Mercury is too	19	12 01	+ 1·4	—	—	12 09	Mercury is too
7	10 38	10·6	—	—	11 34	close to the	22	12 20	− 1·0	—	—	12 16	close to the
10	10 59	8·4	—	—	11 44	Sun for	25	12 38	− 3·3	—	—	12 23	Sun for
13	11 20	6·1	—	—	11 53	observation	28	12 56	− 5·6	—	—	12 29	observation
16	11 41	3·7	—	—	12 01		31	13 14	− 7·8	—	—	12 35	

VENUS

Day	RA	Dec.	Diam.	Phase	Transit	5° high 52°	5° high 56°
	h m	°	″	%	h m	h m	h m
1	12 03	+ 0·9	11	93	13 22	18 52	18 49
6	12 26	− 1·7	11	92	13 25	18 41	18 36
11	12 48	− 4·3	11	91	13 27	18 30	18 23
16	13 10	− 6·8	11	90	13 30	18 19	18 09
21	13 33	− 9·3	11	89	13 33	18 08	17 56
26	13 56	−11·7	12	88	13 36	17 57	17 43
31	14 19	−14·0	12	87	13 40	17 47	17 33

MARS

Day	RA	Dec. +	Diam.	Phase	Transit	5° high 52°	5° high 56°
	h m	°	″	%	h m	h m	h m
1	5 31	23·0	7	87	6 49	23 16	22 59
6	5 44	23·2	7	87	6 43	23 08	22 50
11	5 57	23·3	7	87	6 35	23 00	22 42
16	6 09	23·4	8	87	6 28	22 53	22 34
21	6 21	23·5	8	87	6 20	22 45	22 26
26	6 33	23·5	8	87	6 12	22 37	22 18
31	6 44	23·4	8	87	6 04	22 28	22 10

(*See* pages 63–64 for explanatory notes)

SUNRISE AND SUNSET

Day	London 0°05′ 51°30′		Bristol 2°35′ 51°28′		Birmingham 1°55′ 52°28′		Manchester 2°15′ 53°28′		Newcastle 1°37′ 54°59′		Glasgow 4°14′ 55°52′		Belfast 5°56′ 54°35′	
	h m	h m	h m	h m	h m	h m	h m	h m	h m	h m	h m	h m	h m	h m
1	5 13	18 46	5 23	18 56	5 19	18 55	5 18	18 58	5 13	18 58	5 22	19 11	5 31	19 15
2	5 15	18 44	5 25	18 54	5 20	18 53	5 20	18 56	5 15	18 56	5 24	19 08	5 33	19 12
3	5 16	18 42	5 26	18 52	5 22	18 51	5 22	18 53	5 17	18 53	5 26	19 05	5 35	19 10
4	5 18	18 40	5 28	18 49	5 24	18 48	5 24	18 51	5 19	18 51	5 28	19 03	5 37	19 07
5	5 19	18 37	5 30	18 47	5 25	18 46	5 25	18 49	5 20	18 48	5 29	19 00	5 38	19 05
6	5 21	18 35	5 31	18 45	5 27	18 44	5 27	18 46	5 22	18 46	5 31	18 58	5 40	19 02
7	5 23	18 33	5 33	18 43	5 29	18 41	5 29	18 44	5 24	18 43	5 33	18 55	5 42	19 00
8	5 24	18 30	5 34	18 40	5 30	18 39	5 31	18 41	5 26	18 41	5 35	18 52	5 44	18 57
9	5 26	18 28	5 36	18 38	5 32	18 37	5 32	18 39	5 28	18 38	5 37	18 50	5 46	18 55
10	5 27	18 26	5 37	18 36	5 34	18 34	5 34	18 37	5 30	18 36	5 39	18 47	5 48	18 52
11	5 29	18 24	5 39	18 34	5 35	18 32	5 36	18 34	5 32	18 33	5 41	18 44	5 49	18 50
12	5 31	18 21	5 41	18 31	5 37	18 29	5 38	18 32	5 33	18 31	5 43	18 42	5 51	18 47
13	5 32	18 19	5 42	18 29	5 39	18 27	5 39	18 29	5 35	18 28	5 45	18 39	5 53	18 45
14	5 34	18 17	5 44	18 27	5 40	18 25	5 41	18 27	5 37	18 25	5 47	18 37	5 55	18 42
15	5 35	18 14	5 45	18 24	5 42	18 22	5 43	18 24	5 39	18 23	5 49	18 34	5 57	18 40
16	5 37	18 12	5 47	18 22	5 44	18 20	5 44	18 22	5 41	18 20	5 51	18 31	5 59	18 37
17	5 39	18 10	5 49	18 20	5 45	18 18	5 46	18 19	5 43	18 18	5 53	18 29	6 00	18 35
18	5 40	18 07	5 50	18 17	5 47	18 15	5 48	18 17	5 45	18 15	5 55	18 26	6 02	18 32
19	5 42	18 05	5 52	18 15	5 49	18 13	5 50	18 15	5 47	18 13	5 57	18 23	6 04	18 30
20	5 43	18 03	5 53	18 13	5 50	18 10	5 51	18 12	5 48	18 10	5 59	18 21	6 06	18 27
21	5 45	18 01	5 55	18 11	5 52	18 08	5 53	18 10	5 50	18 07	6 00	18 18	6 08	18 25
22	5 47	17 58	5 57	18 08	5 54	18 06	5 55	18 07	5 52	18 05	6 02	18 15	6 09	18 22
23	5 48	17 56	5 58	18 06	5 55	18 03	5 57	18 05	5 54	18 02	6 04	18 13	6 11	18 20
24	5 50	17 54	6 00	18 04	5 57	18 01	5 58	18 02	5 56	18 00	6 06	18 10	6 13	18 17
25	5 51	17 51	6 01	18 01	5 59	17 59	6 00	18 00	5 58	17 57	6 08	18 08	6 15	18 14
26	5 53	17 49	6 03	17 59	6 01	17 56	6 02	17 57	6 00	17 55	6 10	18 05	6 17	18 12
27	5 55	17 47	6 05	17 57	6 02	17 54	6 04	17 55	6 02	17 52	6 12	18 02	6 19	18 09
28	5 56	17 44	6 06	17 54	6 04	17 51	6 06	17 53	6 03	17 49	6 14	18 00	6 21	18 07
29	5 58	17 42	6 08	17 52	6 06	17 49	6 07	17 50	6 05	17 47	6 16	17 57	6 22	18 04
30	6 00	17 40	6 10	17 50	6 07	17 47	6 09	17 48	6 07	17 44	6 18	17 54	6 24	18 02

JUPITER

Day	RA	Dec. +	Transit	
	h m	° ′	h m	
1	11 30·4	4 21	12 47	Jupiter is too
11	11 38·3	3 30	12 16	close to the
21	11 46·3	2 39	11 44	Sun for
31	11 54·2	1 48	11 13	observation

Diameters—equatorial 31″ polar 29″

SATURN

Day	RA	Dec. −	Transit	5° high	
				52°	56°
	h m	° ′	h m	h m	h m
1	21 04·7	17 48	22 19	2 07	1 44
11	21 02·3	17 58	21 38	1 24	1 01
21	20 00·4	18 06	20 56	0 42	0 18
31	20 59·1	18 12	20 16	0 00	23 33

Diameters—equatorial 18″ polar 16″
Rings—major axis 41″ minor axis 12″

URANUS

Day	RA	Dec. −	Transit	10° high	
				52°	56°
	h m	° ′	h m	h m	h m
1	19 02·1	23 06	20 17	22 23	21 13
11	19 01·5	23 07	19 37	21 43	20 33
21	19 01·2	23 07	18 58	21 03	19 53
31	19 01·3	23 07	18 18	20 24	19 14

Diameter 4″

NEPTUNE

Day	RA	Dec. −	Transit	10° high	
				52°	56°
	h m	° ′	h m	h m	h m
1	19 10·6	21 43	20 26	22 48	21 55
11	19 10·2	21 44	19 46	22 08	21 15
21	19 09·9	21 45	19 06	21 28	20 35
31	19 09·8	21 45	18 27	20 48	19 56

Diameter 2″

(*See* page 64 for explanatory notes)

Year	Month	Week	

Octo (eight), 8th month
of Roman (pre-Julian)
Calendar.
Sun's Longitude 210° ♍ 23ᵈ 04ʰ

275	1	Th.	MICHAELMAS LAW SITTINGS BEGIN.
276	2	F.	Marshal Foch *b.* 1851. Graham Greene *b.* 1904.
277	3	S.	Francis of Assissi *d.* 1226. Malcolm Sargent *d.* 1967.
278	4	S.	**17th S. after Pentecost.** Rembrandt *d.* 1669.
279	5	M.	Offenbach *d.* 1880. Tea rationing ended 1952.
280	6	Tu.	Tyndale *exec.* 1536. Tennyson *d.* 1892.*
281	7	W.	Hubert Parry *d.* 1918. Mario Lanza *d.* 1959.
282	8	Th.	Clement Attlee *d.* 1967.
283	9	F.	Alfred Dreyfus *b.* 1859. André Maurois *d.* 1967.
284	10	S.	Verdi *b.* 1813. Orson Welles *d.* 1985.
285	11	S.	**18th S. after Pentecost.** Zwingli *d.* 1531.
286	12	M.	Robert E. Lee *d.* 1870. Edith Cavell *d.* 1915.
287	13	Tu.	Anatole France *d.* 1924. Sidney Webb *d.* 1947.
288	14	W.	Hastings 1066. Dwight Eisenhower *b.* 1890.
289	15	Th.	DUCHESS OF YORK *b.* 1959. C. P. Snow *b.* 1905.
290	16	F.	Parliament burned down 1834.
291	17	S.	Arnhem landings 1944.
292	18	S.	**St Luke. 19th S. after Pentecost.**
293	19	M.	Jacqueline du Pré *d.* 1987.
294	20	Tu.	Grace Darling *d.* 1842. Anna Neagle *b.* 1904.
295	21	W.	Coleridge *b.* 1772. Trafalgar 1805.
296	22	Th.	Franz Liszt *b.* 1811. Sarah Bernhardt *b.* 1845.
297	23	F.	Edgehill 1642. El Alamein began 1942.
298	24	S.	Tito Gobbi *b.* 1915. Christian Dior *d.* 1957.
299	25	S.	**9th S. before Christmas.** Chaucer *d.* 1400.
300	26	M.	Royal Marines founded 1664.
301	27	Tu.	Charles Hawtrey *d.* 1988.
302	28	W.	**SS Simon and Jude.** John Smeaton *d.* 1792.*
303	29	Th.	Wall Street Crash 1929.
304	30	F.	R. B. Sheridan *b.* 1751. Sir Barnes Wallis *d.* 1979.
305	31	S.	HALLOWMASS EVE. Keats *b.* 1795.

PHENOMENA

d	h	
6	05	Saturn in conjunction with Moon. Saturn 5°S.
18	14	Mars in conjunction with Moon. Mars 3°N.
23	19	Jupiter in conjunction with Moon. Jupiter 6°N.
27	15	Mercury in conjunction with Moon. Mercury 0°·5S.
28	15	Venus in conjunction with Moon. Venus 0°·4S.
31	16	Mercury at greatest elongation E·24°.

CONSTELLATIONS

The following constellations are near the meridian at

d	h		d	h
Sept. 1	24		Sept. 15	23
Oct. 1	22		Oct. 16	21
Nov. 1	20		Nov. 15	19

Ursa Major (below the Pole), Cepheus, Cassiopeia, Cygnus, Lacerta, Andromeda, Pegasus, Capricornus, Aquarius and Piscis Austrinus.

MINIMA OF ALGOL

d	h		d	h
3	07·0		20	11·8
6	03·8		23	08·6
9	00·6		26	05·4
11	21·4		29	02·2
14	18·2		31	23·1
17	15·0			

*Centenary.

MOON
Phases, Apsides & Node

		d	h	m
☽	First Quarter	3	14	12
○	Full Moon	11	18	03
☾	Last Quarter	19	04	12
●	New Moon	25	20	34

Apogee (405,299 km)   7 05 45
Perigee (364,778 km)   23 04 43

Mean longitude of ascending node on Oct. 1, 265°

Summer Time in 1992 (*see* p. 70).—Ends: October 25ᵈ 01ʰ GMT.

MONTHLY NOTES

1. Pheasant shooting begins.

7. Jewish Day of Atonement (Yom Kippur).

12. First day of Feast of Tabernacles.

(*See* page 62 for explanatory notes)

	THE SUN					s.d. 16'·1			Sidereal Time	Transit of First Point of Aries
Day	Right Ascension	Dec. −	Equation of Time	Rise		Transit	Set			
				52°	56°		52°	56°		

Day	h m s	° '	m s	h m	h m	h m	h m	h m	h m s	h m s
1	12 29 38	3 12	+10 17	6 01	6 03	11 50	17 37	17 35	0 39 55	23 16 16
2	12 33 16	3 35	+10 36	6 03	6 05	11 49	17 35	17 32	0 43 51	23 12 20
3	12 36 53	3 58	+10 55	6 04	6 07	11 49	17 32	17 30	0 47 48	23 08 24
4	12 40 31	4 22	+11 13	6 06	6 09	11 49	17 30	17 27	0 51 44	23 04 28
5	12 44 10	4 45	+11 31	6 08	6 11	11 48	17 28	17 24	0 55 41	23 00 32
6	12 47 48	5 08	+11 49	6 10	6 13	11 48	17 26	17 22	0 59 37	22 56 36
7	12 51 27	5 31	+12 07	6 11	6 15	11 48	17 23	17 19	1 03 34	22 52 41
8	12 55 07	5 54	+12 24	6 13	6 17	11 47	17 21	17 17	1 07 31	22 48 45
9	12 58 47	6 17	+12 40	6 15	6 19	11 47	17 19	17 14	1 11 27	22 44 49
10	13 02 27	6 39	+12 57	6 16	6 21	11 47	17 17	17 11	1 15 24	22 40 53
11	13 06 08	7 02	+13 12	6 18	6 23	11 47	17 14	17 09	1 19 20	22 36 57
12	13 09 49	7 25	+13 28	6 20	6 25	11 46	17 12	17 06	1 23 17	22 33 01
13	13 13 31	7 47	+13 43	6 22	6 27	11 46	17 10	17 04	1 27 13	22 29 05
14	13 17 13	8 09	+13 57	6 23	6 30	11 46	17 08	17 01	1 31 10	22 25 09
15	13 20 56	8 32	+14 11	6 25	6 32	11 46	17 06	16 59	1 35 06	22 21 13
16	13 24 39	8 54	+14 24	6 27	6 34	11 46	17 03	16 56	1 39 03	22 17 17
17	13 28 23	9 16	+14 36	6 28	6 36	11 45	17 01	16 54	1 43 00	22 13 21
18	13 32 08	9 38	+14 48	6 30	6 38	11 45	16 59	16 51	1 46 56	22 09 26
19	13 35 53	9 59	+14 59	6 32	6 40	11 45	16 57	16 49	1 50 53	22 05 30
20	13 39 39	10 21	+15 10	6 34	6 42	11 45	16 55	16 47	1 54 49	22 01 34
21	13 43 26	10 42	+15 20	6 36	6 44	11 45	16 53	16 44	1 58 46	21 57 38
22	13 47 13	11 04	+15 29	6 37	6 46	11 44	16 51	16 42	2 02 42	21 53 42
23	13 51 01	11 25	+15 38	6 39	6 48	11 44	16 49	16 39	2 06 39	21 49 46
24	13 54 49	11 46	+15 46	6 41	6 50	11 44	16 47	16 37	2 10 35	21 45 50
25	13 58 39	12 07	+15 53	6 43	6 53	11 44	16 45	16 35	2 14 32	21 41 54
26	14 02 29	12 27	+16 00	6 44	6 55	11 44	16 43	16 32	2 18 28	21 37 58
27	14 06 20	12 48	+16 06	6 46	6 57	11 44	16 41	16 30	2 22 25	21 34 02
28	14 10 11	13 08	+16 11	6 48	6 59	11 44	16 39	16 28	2 26 22	21 30 06
29	14 14 03	13 28	+16 15	6 50	7 01	11 44	16 37	16 26	2 30 18	21 26 11
30	14 17 56	13 48	+16 18	6 52	7 03	11 44	16 35	16 23	2 34 15	21 22 15
31	14 21 50	14 07	+16 21	6 53	7 05	11 44	16 33	16 21	2 38 11	21 18 19

Duration of Civil (C), Nautical (N) and Astronomical (A) Twilight (in minutes)

Lat. °	Oct. 1			Oct. 11			Oct. 21			Oct. 31		
	C	N	A	C	N	A	C	N	A	C	N	A
52	34	73	113	34	73	112	34	74	113	36	75	114
56	37	80	125	37	80	124	38	81	124	40	83	126

ASTRONOMICAL NOTES

MERCURY, although at greatest eastern elongation on the last day of the month, is unsuitably placed for observation.

VENUS is a brilliant object in the early evenings, magnitude −4·0, though still very low in the SW sky. By the end of the month it is visible for about half an hour after sunset, for observers in southern England. On the evening of the 28th the thin crescent Moon, only three days old, will be seen close to the planet.

MARS, magnitude 0·0, is a bright object, rising in the ENE in the late evening and crossing the meridian before sunrise. Mars is in Gemini. The slightly reddish tinge of the planet is an aid to its identification.

JUPITER is emerging from the morning twilight and after the first week of the month becomes visible as a brilliant morning object, magnitude −1·7, low above the eastern horizon for a while before twilight inhibits observation.

SATURN, magnitude +0·5, is an evening object in Capricornus, visible low in the south and south-western skies. The rings of Saturn present a beautiful spectacle to the observer with only a small telescope.

(See pages 62–63 for explanatory notes)

THE MOON

Day	RA	Dec.	Hor. Par.	Semi-diam.	Sun's Co-long.	PA of Bright Limb	Phase	Age	Rise 52°	Rise 56°	Transit	Set 52°	Set 56°
	h m	°	′	′	°	°	%	d	h m	h m	h m	h m	h m
1	16 24	−23·1	57·1	15·6	323	280	25	4·6	12 27	12 53	16 20	20 12	19 45
2	17 20	−23·5	56·2	15·3	335	274	34	5·6	13 18	13 44	17 13	21 10	20 45
3	18 15	−22·6	55·5	15·1	347	268	44	6·6	13 58	14 21	18 03	22 14	21 52
4	19 07	−20·7	54·9	15·0	359	264	54	7·6	14 29	14 48	18 51	23 20	23 02
5	19 56	−17·9	54·5	14·8	11	260	64	8·6	14 54	15 08	19 36	—	—
6	20 44	−14·4	54·2	14·8	24	257	72	9·6	15 14	15 24	20 19	0 28	0 14
7	21 29	−10·4	54·1	14·7	36	255	80	10·6	15 32	15 38	21 01	1 35	1 26
8	22 14	− 6·0	54·1	14·8	48	254	87	11·6	15 48	15 50	21 42	2 42	2 37
9	22 57	− 1·3	54·3	14·8	60	256	93	12·6	16 04	16 02	22 23	3 49	3 48
10	23 42	+ 3·5	54·6	14·9	72	260	97	13·6	16 20	16 15	23 06	4 57	5 01
11	0 27	+ 8·2	54·9	15·0	84	276	99	14·6	16 38	16 29	23 50	6 06	6 14
12	1 14	+12·6	55·3	15·1	97	10	100	15·6	17 00	16 46	—	7 17	7 29
13	2 03	+16·5	55·7	15·2	109	55	98	16·6	17 26	17 08	0 37	8 28	8 46
14	2 55	+19·8	56·2	15·3	121	67	95	17·6	18 00	17 38	1 26	9 39	10 01
15	3 49	+22·1	56·7	15·4	133	75	89	18·6	18 44	18 19	2 19	10 47	11 11
16	4 46	+23·3	57·2	15·6	145	82	82	19·6	19 39	19 13	3 14	11 46	12 12
17	5 44	+23·1	57·7	15·7	157	89	73	20·6	20 45	20 22	4 10	12 36	13 00
18	6 42	+21·6	58·3	15·9	170	95	63	21·6	22 01	21 41	5 07	13 17	13 37
19	7 40	+18·8	58·8	16·0	182	100	52	22·6	23 21	23 07	6 02	13 49	14 04
20	8 36	+14·9	59·3	16·1	194	104	41	23·6	—	—	6 56	14 15	14 25
21	9 31	+10·1	59·7	16·3	206	107	30	24·6	0 43	0 35	7 49	14 37	14 43
22	10 25	+ 4·6	60·0	16·3	218	108	20	25·6	2 07	2 03	8 41	14 58	14 59
23	11 19	− 1·1	60·1	16·4	231	107	11	26·6	3 31	3 33	9 32	15 18	15 14
24	12 13	− 6·8	60·0	16·4	243	103	5	27·6	4 55	5 02	10 24	15 40	15 31
25	13 08	−12·1	59·8	16·3	255	91	1	28·6	6 19	6 32	11 18	16 06	15 52
26	14 04	−16·7	59·3	16·2	267	353	0	0·1	7 42	8 00	12 13	16 36	16 17
27	15 02	−20·2	58·6	16·0	279	297	2	1·1	9 00	9 23	13 10	17 14	16 51
28	16 00	−22·4	57·8	15·8	292	285	6	2·1	10 09	10 35	14 06	18 01	17 35
29	16 58	−23·3	57·0	15·5	304	277	12	3·1	11 07	11 33	15 01	18 57	18 31
30	17 55	−22·9	56·3	15·3	316	270	19	4·1	11 52	12 16	15 54	20 00	19 36
31	18 49	−21·3	55·5	15·1	328	264	28	5·1	12 28	12 48	16 44	21 06	20 47

MERCURY

Day	RA	Dec. −	Diam.	Phase	Transit		Day	RA	Dec. −	Diam.	Phase	Transit	
	h m	°			h m				h m	°			h m
1	13 14	7·8	—	—	12 35		16	14 38	17·2	—	—	13 00	
4	13 31	9·9	—	—	12 40	Mercury is too	19	14 55	18·7	—	—	13 04	Mercury is too
7	13 48	11·9	—	—	12 46	close to the	22	15 10	20·1	—	—	13 08	close to the
10	14 05	13·8	—	—	12 51	Sun for	25	15 26	21·3	—	—	13 12	Sun for
13	14 22	15·6	—	—	12 55	observation	28	15 41	22·4	—	—	13 15	observation
16	14 38	17·2	—	—	13 00		31	15 54	23·2	—	—	13 17	

VENUS

Day	RA	Dec. −	Diam.	Phase	Transit	5° high 52°	5° high 56°
	h m	°	″	%	h m	h m	h m
1	14 19	14·0	12	87	13 40	17 47	17 29
6	14 43	16·1	12	86	13 44	17 37	17 16
11	15 07	18·1	12	85	13 48	17 28	17 04
16	15 32	19·9	13	84	13 53	17 20	16 52
21	15 57	21·5	13	83	13 59	17 13	16 42
26	16 22	22·9	13	81	14 05	17 08	16 32
31	16 48	24·0	13	80	14 11	17 04	16 25

MARS

Day	RA	Dec. +	Diam.	Phase	Transit	5° high 52°	5° high 56°
	h m	°	″	%	h m	h m	h m
1	6 44	23·4	8	87	6 04	22 28	22 10
6	6 55	23·3	8	87	5 55	22 20	22 01
11	7 05	23·2	9	87	5 45	22 11	21 52
16	7 14	23·1	9	88	5 35	22 01	21 43
21	7 23	23·0	9	88	5 24	21 51	21 33
26	7 31	22·9	10	88	5 12	21 40	21 22
31	7 39	22·8	10	89	5 00	21 28	21 10

(See pages 63–64 for explanatory notes)

SUNRISE AND SUNSET

Day	London 0°05′ 51°30′		Bristol 2°35′ 51°28′		Birmingham 1°55′ 52°28′		Manchester 2°15′ 53°28′		Newcastle 1°37′ 54°59′		Glasgow 4°14′ 55°52′		Belfast 5°56′ 54°35′	
	h m	h m	h m	h m	h m	h m	h m	h m	h m	h m	h m	h m	h m	h m
1	6 01	17 38	6 11	17 48	6 09	17 44	6 11	17 45	6 09	17 42	6 20	17 52	6 26	17 59
2	6 03	17 35	6 13	17 45	6 11	17 42	6 13	17 43	6 11	17 39	6 22	17 49	6 28	17 57
3	6 04	17 33	6 14	17 43	6 12	17 40	6 14	17 40	6 13	17 37	6 24	17 47	6 30	17 54
4	6 06	17 31	6 16	17 41	6 14	17 37	6 16	17 38	6 15	17 34	6 26	17 44	6 32	17 52
5	6 08	17 29	6 18	17 39	6 16	17 35	6 18	17 36	6 17	17 32	6 28	17 41	6 34	17 49
6	6 09	17 26	6 19	17 36	6 18	17 33	6 20	17 33	6 19	17 29	6 30	17 39	6 36	17 47
7	6 11	17 24	6 21	17 34	6 19	17 31	6 22	17 31	6 21	17 27	6 32	17 36	6 38	17 44
8	6 13	17 22	6 23	17 32	6 21	17 28	6 23	17 29	6 23	17 24	6 34	17 34	6 39	17 42
9	6 14	17 20	6 24	17 30	6 23	17 26	6 25	17 26	6 25	17 22	6 36	17 31	6 41	17 40
10	6 16	17 17	6 26	17 28	6 25	17 24	6 27	17 24	6 26	17 19	6 38	17 29	6 43	17 37
11	6 18	17 15	6 28	17 25	6 26	17 21	6 29	17 21	6 28	17 17	6 40	17 26	6 45	17 35
12	6 19	17 13	6 29	17 23	6 28	17 19	6 31	17 19	6 30	17 14	6 42	17 23	6 47	17 32
13	6 21	17 11	6 31	17 21	6 30	17 17	6 33	17 17	6 32	17 12	6 44	17 21	6 49	17 30
14	6 23	17 09	6 33	17 19	6 32	17 15	6 34	17 15	6 34	17 10	6 46	17 18	6 51	17 27
15	6 25	17 07	6 35	17 17	6 33	17 13	6 36	17 12	6 36	17 07	6 48	17 16	6 53	17 25
16	6 26	17 05	6 36	17 15	6 35	17 10	6 38	17 10	6 38	17 05	6 50	17 14	6 55	17 23
17	6 28	17 02	6 38	17 12	6 37	17 08	6 40	17 08	6 40	17 02	6 52	17 11	6 57	17 20
18	6 30	17 00	6 40	17 10	6 39	17 06	6 42	17 05	6 42	17 00	6 54	17 09	6 59	17 18
19	6 31	16 58	6 41	17 08	6 41	17 04	6 44	17 03	6 44	16 58	6 57	17 06	7 01	17 16
20	6 33	16 56	6 43	17 06	6 42	17 02	6 46	17 01	6 46	16 55	6 59	17 04	7 03	17 13
21	6 35	16 54	6 45	17 04	6 44	17 00	6 47	16 59	6 48	16 53	7 01	17 01	7 05	17 11
22	6 37	16 52	6 47	17 02	6 46	16 57	6 49	16 57	6 50	16 51	7 03	16 59	7 07	17 09
23	6 38	16 50	6 48	17 00	6 48	16 55	6 51	16 55	6 52	16 48	7 05	16 57	7 09	17 07
24	6 40	16 48	6 50	16 58	6 50	16 53	6 53	16 52	6 54	16 46	7 07	16 54	7 11	17 04
25	6 42	16 46	6 52	16 56	6 51	16 51	6 55	16 50	6 56	16 44	7 09	16 52	7 13	17 02
26	6 44	16 44	6 54	16 54	6 53	16 49	6 57	16 48	6 58	16 42	7 11	16 50	7 15	17 00
27	6 45	16 42	6 55	16 52	6 55	16 47	6 59	16 46	7 00	16 39	7 13	16 47	7 17	16 58
28	6 47	16 40	6 57	16 50	6 57	16 45	7 01	16 44	7 02	16 37	7 15	16 45	7 19	16 56
29	6 49	16 38	6 59	16 49	6 59	16 43	7 03	16 42	7 04	16 35	7 18	16 43	7 21	16 54
30	6 51	16 37	7 01	16 47	7 00	16 41	7 05	16 40	7 06	16 33	7 20	16 41	7 23	16 51
31	6 52	16 35	7 02	16 45	7 02	16 40	7 07	16 38	7 09	16 31	7 22	16 39	7 25	16 49

JUPITER

Day	RA	Dec.	Transit	5° high	
				52°	56°
	h m	° ′	h m	h m	h m
1	11 54·2	+1 48	11 13	5 37	5 39
11	12 02·1	+0 57	10 41	5 10	5 12
21	12 09·7	+0 08	10 10	4 42	4 46
31	12 17·1	−0 39	9 38	4 14	4 18

Diameters—equatorial 31″ polar 29″

SATURN

Day	RA	Dec. −	Transit	5° high	
				52°	56°
	h m	° ′	h m	h m	h m
1	20 59·1	18 12	20 16	0 00	23 33
11	20 58·4	18 14	19 36	23 16	22 52
21	20 58·4	18 14	18 57	22 37	22 13
31	20 59·1	18 11	18 18	21 59	21 35

Diameters—equatorial 17″ polar 16″
Rings—major axis 40″ minor axis 12″

URANUS

Day	RA	Dec. −	Transit	10° high	
				52°	56°
	h m	° ′	h m	h m	h m
1	19 01·3	23 07	18 18	20 24	19 14
11	19 01·8	23 06	17 40	19 45	18 36
21	19 02·6	23 05	17 01	19 07	17 58
31	19 03·8	23 03	16 23	18 29	17 21

Diameter 4″

NEPTUNE

Day	RA	Dec. −	Transit	10° high	
				52°	56°
	h m	° ′	h m	h m	h m
1	19 09·8	21 45	18 27	20 48	19 56
11	19 10·0	21 45	17 48	20 09	19 16
21	19 10·5	21 45	17 09	19 31	18 38
31	19 11·1	21 44	16 30	18 52	17 59

Diameter 2″

(*See* page 64 for explanatory notes)

DAY OF			Novem (nine), 9th month of Roman (pre-Julian) Calendar. Sun's Longitude 240° ‡ 22ᵈ 01ʰ
Year	Month	Week	
306	1	S.	**All Saints. 8th S. before Christmas.**
307	2	M.	ALL SOULS. Balfour Decloration 1917.
308	3	Tu.	First dog in space 1957.
309	4	W.	William III *b.* 1650. Mendelssohn *d.* 1847.
310	5	Th.	Gunpowder plot 1605. Inkerman 1854.
311	6	F.	Sousa *b.* 1854. John Alcock *b.* 1892.*
312	7	S.	Marie Curie *b.* 1867. Joan Sutherland *b.* 1926.
313	8	S.	**7th S. before Christmas.** Milton *d.* 1674.
314	9	M.	Katharine Hepburn *b.* 1909. DylanThomas *d.* 1953.
315	10	Tu.	Luther *b.* 1483. Brezhnev *d.* 1982.
316	11	W.	ARMISTICE DAY. Jerome Kern *d.* 1945.
317	12	Th.	Canute *d.* 1035. Alexander Borodin *b.* 1833.
318	13	F.	R. L. Stevenson *b.* 1850. Archbishop Carey *b.* 1935.
319	14	S.	PRINCE OF WALES *b.* 1948. Monet *b.* 1840.
320	15	S.	**6th S. before Christmas.** Gluck *d.* 1787.
321	16	M.	John Bright *b.* 1811. Suez Canal opened 1869.
322	17	Tu.	Montgomery *b.* 1887. Villa-Lobos *d.* 1959.
323	18	W.	Marcel Proust *d.* 1922. Man Ray *d.* 1976.
324	19	Th.	Thomas Shadwell *d.* 1692.* Indira Gandhi *b.* 1917.
325	20	F.	QUEEN'S WEDDING DAY 1947. Chatterton *b.* 1752.
326	21	S.	Voltaire *d.* 1694. André Gide *b.* 1869.
327	22	S.	**5th S. before Christmas.** de Gaulle *b.* 1890.
328	23	M.	Manuel de Falla *b.* 1876. Boris Karloff *b.* 1887.
329	24	Tu.	John Knox *d.* 1572. Toulouse Lautrec *b.* 1864.
330	25	W.	Isaac Watts *d.* 1748. Andrew Carnegie *b.* 1835.
331	26	Th.	William Cowper *b.* 1731. John McAdam *d.* 1836.
332	27	F.	Celsius *b.* 1701. Dumas (fils) *d.* 1895.
333	28	S.	William Blake *b.* 1757. Engels *b.* 1820.
334	29	S.	**Advent Sunday.** Puccini *d.* 1924.
335	30	M.	**St Andrew.** Crystal Palace fire 1936.

*Centenary

PHENOMENA

	d	h	
	2	13	Saturn in conjunction with Moon. Saturn 5°S.
	15	00	Pluto in conjunction with Sun.
	15	10	Mars in conjunction with Moon. Mars 5°N.
	20	12	Jupiter in conjunction with Moon. Jupiter 6°N.
	21	22	Mercury in inferior conjunction.
	24	00	Mercury in conjunction with Moon. Mercury 3°N.
	27	20	Venus in conjunction with Moon. Venus 5°S.
	30	00	Saturn in conjunction with Moon. Saturn 5°S.

CONSTELLATIONS

The following constellations are near the meridian at

	d	h		d	h
Oct.	1	24	Oct.	16	23
Nov.	1	22	Nov.	15	21
Dec.	1	20	Dec.	16	19

Ursa Major (below the Pole), Cepheus, Cassiopeia, Andromeda, Pegasus, Pisces, Aquarius and Cetus.

MINIMA OF ALGOL

d	h		d	h
3	19·9		18	03·9
6	16·7		21	00·7
9	13·5		23	21·6
12	10·3		26	18·4
15	07·1		29	15·2

MOON
Phases, Apsides & Node

	d	h	m
☽ First Quarter	2	09	11
○ Full Moon	10	09	20
☾ Last Quarter	17	11	39
● New Moon	24	09	11
Apogee (404,538 km)	3	23	25
Perigee (369,741 km)	19	00	01

Mean longitude of ascending node on Nov. 1, 264°

MONTHLY NOTES

1. Fox-hunting begins.

8. Remembrance Sunday.

14. Lord Mayor's Show.

28. Martinmas (Scottish Term Day and Removal Day).

(*See* page 62 for explanatory notes)

Day	THE SUN s.d. 16′·2								Sidereal Time	Transit of First Point of Aries
	Right Ascension	Dec. −	Equation of Time	Rise		Transit	Set			
				52°	56°		52°	56°		
	h m s	° ′	m s	h m	h m	h m	h m	h m	h m s	h m s
1	14 25 45	14 26	+16 23	6 55	7 07	11 44	16 31	16 19	2 42 08	21 14 23
2	14 29 40	14 46	+16 24	6 57	7 10	11 44	16 29	16 17	2 46 04	21 10 27
3	14 33 36	15 04	+16 25	6 59	7 12	11 44	16 28	16 15	2 50 01	21 06 31
4	14 37 33	15 23	+16 24	7 01	7 14	11 44	16 26	16 13	2 53 57	21 02 35
5	14 41 31	15 41	+16 23	7 02	7 16	11 44	16 24	16 11	2 57 54	20 58 39
6	14 45 30	15 59	+16 21	7 04	7 18	11 44	16 22	16 09	3 01 51	20 54 43
7	14 49 29	16 17	+16 18	7 06	7 20	11 44	16 21	16 07	3 05 47	20 50 47
8	14 53 29	16 35	+16 15	7 08	7 22	11 44	16 19	16 05	3 09 44	20 46 51
9	14 57 30	16 52	+16 10	7 10	7 24	11 44	16 17	16 03	3 13 40	20 42 56
10	15 01 32	17 09	+16 05	7 11	7 27	11 44	16 16	16 01	3 17 37	20 39 00
11	15 05 35	17 26	+15 59	7 13	7 29	11 44	16 14	15 59	3 21 33	20 35 04
12	15 09 38	17 42	+15 52	7 15	7 31	11 44	16 13	15 57	3 25 30	20 31 08
13	15 13 43	17 58	+15 44	7 17	7 33	11 44	16 11	15 55	3 29 26	20 27 12
14	15 17 48	18 14	+15 35	7 18	7 35	11 44	16 10	15 53	3 33 23	20 23 16
15	15 21 54	18 30	+15 25	7 20	7 37	11 45	16 09	15 52	3 37 20	20 19 20
16	15 26 01	18 45	+15 15	7 22	7 39	11 45	16 07	15 50	3 41 16	20 15 24
17	15 30 09	18 59	+15 04	7 24	7 41	11 45	16 06	15 48	3 45 13	20 11 28
18	15 34 18	19 14	+14 51	7 25	7 43	11 45	16 05	15 47	3 49 09	20 07 32
19	15 38 27	19 28	+14 38	7 27	7 45	11 45	16 03	15 45	3 53 06	20 03 36
20	15 42 38	19 42	+14 24	7 29	7 47	11 46	16 02	15 44	3 57 02	19 59 41
21	15 46 49	19 55	+14 10	7 30	7 49	11 46	16 01	15 42	4 00 59	19 55 45
22	15 51 01	20 08	+13 54	7 32	7 51	11 46	16 00	15 41	4 04 55	19 51 49
23	15 55 14	20 21	+13 38	7 34	7 53	11 47	15 59	15 40	4 08 52	19 47 53
24	15 59 28	20 33	+13 21	7 35	7 55	11 47	15 58	15 38	4 12 49	19 43 57
25	16 03 42	20 45	+13 03	7 37	7 57	11 47	15 57	15 37	4 16 45	19 40 01
26	16 07 57	20 57	+12 44	7 39	7 59	11 47	15 56	15 36	4 20 42	19 36 05
27	16 12 13	21 08	+12 25	7 40	8 00	11 48	15 55	15 35	4 24 38	19 32 09
28	16 16 30	21 19	+12 05	7 42	8 02	11 48	15 54	15 34	4 28 35	19 28 13
29	16 20 47	21 29	+11 44	7 43	8 04	11 48	15 53	15 33	4 32 31	19 24 17
30	16 25 05	21 39	+11 23	7 45	8 06	11 49	15 53	15 32	4 36 28	19 20 21

Duration of Civil (C), Nautical (N) and Astronomical (A) Twilight (in minutes)

Lat. °	Nov. 1			Nov. 11			Nov. 21			Nov. 30		
	C	N	A	C	N	A	C	N	A	C	N	A
52	36	75	115	37	78	117	38	80	120	39	82	123
56	40	84	127	41	87	130	43	90	134	45	93	137

ASTRONOMICAL NOTES

MERCURY is at inferior conjunction on the 21st, but thereafter moves rapidly away from the Sun and is visible as a morning object, magnitude about +0·5, for the last four days of the month. It may be seen low above the south-eastern horizon at the beginning of morning civil twilight.

VENUS continues to be visible as a brilliant object for a short while after sunset, low above the south-western horizon. By the end of the month it sets about two hours after the Sun. Its magnitude is −4·1. On the evening of the 27th the thin crescent Moon will be about 5° above the planet.

MARS is a bright morning object, its magnitude steadily increasing during the month from −0·2 to −0·8. Its eastward motion is decreasing and it reaches its first stationary point just before the end of November, on the borders of Gemini and Cancer, in almost a direct line south-eastwards from Castor and Pollux.

JUPITER, magnitude −1·7, is a brilliant morning object in Virgo and by the end of the month may be seen above the ESE horizon before 03 h.

SATURN continues to be visible in the south to south-western sky in the evenings, magnitude +0·7.

(See pages 62–63 for explanatory notes)

THE MOON

Day	RA	Dec.	Hor. Par.	Semi-diam.	Sun's Co-long.	PA of Bright Limb	Phase	Age	Rise 52°	Rise 56°	Transit	Set 52°	Set 56°
	h m	°	′	′	°	°	%	d	h m	h m	h m	h m	h m
1	19 40	−18·7	55·0	15·0	340	260	37	6·1	12 55	13 11	17 31	22 14	21 59
2	20 28	−15·4	54·5	14·9	353	256	46	7·1	13 17	13 29	18 15	23 22	23 11
3	21 15	−11·5	54·3	14·8	5	253	56	8·1	13 36	13 44	18 57	—	—
4	21 59	− 7·2	54·2	14·8	17	251	65	9·1	13 53	13 56	19 38	0 29	0 22
5	22 43	− 2·6	54·3	14·8	29	251	74	10·1	14 09	14 09	20 19	1 35	1 33
6	23 27	+ 2·1	54·5	14·9	41	251	82	11·1	14 25	14 21	21 01	2 43	2 45
7	0 12	+ 6·8	54·9	15·0	53	253	89	12·1	14 43	14 35	21 44	3 51	3 57
8	0 58	+11·3	55·4	15·1	66	256	94	13·1	15 03	14 51	22 31	5 01	5 12
9	1 47	+15·4	55·9	15·2	78	263	98	14·1	15 28	15 11	23 20	6 13	6 29
10	2 39	+18·9	56·4	15·4	90	287	100	15·1	16 00	15 39	—	7 25	7 46
11	3 33	+21·5	57·0	15·5	102	59	100	16·1	16 41	16 16	0 12	8 35	8 59
12	4 31	+23·0	57·5	15·7	114	78	97	17·1	17 33	17 08	1 08	9 39	10 05
13	5 30	+23·1	58·0	15·8	126	87	92	18·1	18 37	18 13	2 05	10 33	10 58
14	6 29	+21·9	58·4	15·9	138	94	86	19·1	19 51	19 31	3 02	11 17	11 38
15	7 27	+19·4	58·7	16·0	151	100	77	20·1	21 10	20 55	3 59	11 51	12 08
16	8 24	+15·7	58·9	16·1	163	105	67	21·1	22 31	22 21	4 53	12 19	12 30
17	9 18	+11·1	59·1	16·1	175	108	56	22·1	23 52	23 47	5 45	12 42	12 49
18	10 11	+ 5·9	59·3	16·1	187	110	44	23·1	—	—	6 36	13 02	13 05
19	11 04	+ 0·4	59·3	16·2	199	111	33	24·1	1 14	1 14	7 26	13 22	13 20
20	11 56	− 5·2	59·3	16·1	211	110	23	25·1	2 35	2 40	8 16	13 43	13 36
21	12 49	−10·5	59·1	16·1	224	108	14	26·1	3 57	4 07	9 07	14 06	13 54
22	13 44	−15·2	58·8	16·0	236	104	7	27·1	5 18	5 33	10 00	14 33	14 17
23	14 40	−19·0	58·4	15·9	248	98	2	28·1	6 37	6 57	10 55	15 07	14 46
24	15 37	−21·6	57·9	15·8	260	79	0	29·1	7 50	8 14	11 51	15 50	15 25
25	16 35	−23·0	57·3	15·6	272	286	0	0·6	8 53	9 19	12 47	16 42	16 16
26	17 33	−23·1	56·7	15·4	285	272	3	1·6	9 44	10 09	13 42	17 43	17 18
27	18 28	−21·9	56·0	15·3	297	265	7	2·6	10 24	10 46	14 34	18 49	18 28
28	19 21	−19·7	55·4	15·1	309	259	14	3·6	10 55	11 13	15 22	19 57	19 41
29	20 11	−16·6	54·9	15·0	321	255	21	4·6	11 20	11 33	16 08	21 06	20 54
30	20 59	−12·8	54·5	14·9	333	252	29	5·6	11 40	11 49	16 51	22 14	22 06

MERCURY

Day	RA	Dec. −	Diam.	Phase	Transit		Day	RA	Dec. −	Diam.	Phase	Transit	
	h m	°			h m			h m	°			h m	
1	15 59	23·4	—	—	13 17		16	16 18	22·7	—	—	12 33	
4	16 10	24·0	—	—	13 16	Mercury is too	19	16 06	21·2	—	—	12 09	Mercury is too
7	16 19	24·2	—	—	13 12	close to the	22	15 51	19·4	—	—	11 41	close to the
10	16 24	24·1	—	—	13 05	Sun for	25	15 36	17·7	—	—	11 15	Sun for
13	16 24	23·6	—	—	12 52	observation	28	15 26	16·4	—	—	10 54	observation
16	16 18	22·7	—	—	12 33		31	15 22	15·8	—	—	10 40	

VENUS

Day	RA	Dec. −	Diam.	Phase	Transit	5° high 52°	5° high 56°
	h m	°	″	%	h m	h m	h m
1	16 54	24·1	14	80	14 12	17 04	16 24
6	17 20	24·9	14	79	14 19	17 04	16 21
11	17 47	25·3	14	77	14 26	17 07	16 21
16	18 13	25·5	15	76	14 33	17 12	16 26
21	18 40	25·3	15	74	14 40	17 21	16 36
26	19 06	24·9	16	73	14 46	17 33	16 50
31	19 32	24·1	16	71	14 52	17 47	17 08

MARS

Day	RA	Dec. +	Diam.	Phase	Transit	5° high 52°	5° high 56°
	h m	°	″	%	h m	h m	h m
1	7 40	22·8	10	89	4 57	21 25	21 08
6	7 46	22·7	11	90	4 44	21 12	20 55
11	7 52	22·7	11	90	4 29	20 58	20 40
16	7 56	22·7	11	91	4 14	20 42	20 25
21	7 59	22·8	12	92	3 57	20 25	20 07
26	8 01	22·9	12	93	3 39	20 05	19 48
31	8 01	23·1	13	94	3 20	19 44	19 26

(*See* pages 63–64 for explanatory notes)

SUNRISE AND SUNSET

Day	London 0°05′ 51°30′		Bristol 2°35′ 51°28′		Birmingham 1°55′ 52°28′		Manchester 2°15′ 53°28′		Newcastle 1°37′ 54°59′		Glasgow 4°14′ 55°52′		Belfast 5°56′ 54°35′	
	h m	h m	h m	h m	h m	h m	h m	h m	h m	h m	h m	h m	h m	h m
1	6 54	16 33	7 04	16 43	7 04	16 38	7 08	16 36	7 11	16 29	7 24	16 36	7 27	16 47
2	6 56	16 31	7 06	16 41	7 06	16 36	7 10	16 34	7 13	16 27	7 26	16 34	7 29	16 45
3	6 58	16 29	7 08	16 40	7 08	16 34	7 12	16 32	7 15	16 25	7 28	16 32	7 31	16 43
4	6 59	16 28	7 09	16 38	7 10	16 32	7 14	16 30	7 17	16 23	7 30	16 30	7 33	16 41
5	7 01	16 26	7 11	16 36	7 12	16 30	7 16	16 28	7 19	16 21	7 32	16 28	7 35	16 39
6	7 03	16 24	7 13	16 34	7 13	16 29	7 18	16 27	7 21	16 19	7 34	16 26	7 37	16 37
7	7 05	16 23	7 15	16 33	7 15	16 27	7 20	16 25	7 23	16 17	7 37	16 24	7 39	16 36
8	7 07	16 21	7 16	16 31	7 17	16 25	7 22	16 23	7 25	16 15	7 39	16 22	7 41	16 34
9	7 08	16 19	7 18	16 30	7 19	16 24	7 24	16 21	7 27	16 13	7 41	16 20	7 43	16 32
10	7 10	16 18	7 20	16 28	7 21	16 22	7 26	16 20	7 29	16 11	7 43	16 18	7 45	16 30
11	7 12	16 16	7 22	16 27	7 22	16 20	7 27	16 18	7 31	16 10	7 45	16 16	7 47	16 28
12	7 14	16 15	7 23	16 25	7 24	16 19	7 29	16 16	7 33	16 08	7 47	16 15	7 49	16 27
13	7 15	16 14	7 25	16 24	7 26	16 17	7 31	16 15	7 35	16 06	7 49	16 13	7 50	16 25
14	7 17	16 12	7 27	16 22	7 28	16 16	7 33	16 13	7 37	16 04	7 51	16 11	7 52	16 23
15	7 19	16 11	7 29	16 21	7 30	16 14	7 35	16 12	7 39	16 03	7 53	16 09	7 54	16 22
16	7 20	16 09	7 30	16 20	7 31	16 13	7 37	16 10	7 41	16 01	7 55	16 08	7 56	16 20
17	7 22	16 08	7 32	16 18	7 33	16 12	7 39	16 09	7 43	16 00	7 57	16 06	7 58	16 19
18	7 24	16 07	7 34	16 17	7 35	16 10	7 40	16 08	7 45	15 58	7 59	16 04	8 00	16 17
19	7 25	16 06	7 35	16 16	7 37	16 09	7 42	16 06	7 47	15 57	8 01	16 03	8 02	16 16
20	7 27	16 04	7 37	16 15	7 38	16 08	7 44	16 05	7 48	15 55	8 03	16 01	8 04	16 15
21	7 29	16 03	7 39	16 14	7 40	16 07	7 46	16 04	7 50	15 54	8 05	16 00	8 06	16 13
22	7 30	16 02	7 40	16 12	7 42	16 06	7 48	16 02	7 52	15 53	8 07	15 59	8 08	16 12
23	7 32	16 01	7 42	16 11	7 43	16 04	7 49	16 01	7 54	15 51	8 09	15 57	8 09	16 11
24	7 34	16 00	7 43	16 10	7 45	16 03	7 51	16 00	7 56	15 50	8 11	15 56	8 11	16 09
25	7 35	15 59	7 45	16 09	7 47	16 02	7 53	15 59	7 58	15 49	8 13	15 55	8 13	16 08
26	7 37	15 58	7 47	16 09	7 48	16 01	7 54	15 58	7 59	15 48	8 15	15 54	8 15	16 07
27	7 38	15 58	7 48	16 08	7 50	16 01	7 56	15 57	8 01	15 47	8 16	15 52	8 16	16 06
28	7 40	15 57	7 50	16 07	7 51	16 00	7 58	15 56	8 03	15 46	8 18	15 51	8 18	16 05
29	7 41	15 56	7 51	16 06	7 53	15 59	7 59	15 55	8 05	15 45	8 20	15 50	8 20	16 04
30	7 43	15 55	7 52	16 06	7 54	15 58	8 01	15 55	8 06	15 44	8 22	15 49	8 21	16 03

JUPITER

Day	RA	Dec. −	Transit	5° high 52°	5° high 56°
	h m	° ′	h m	h m	h m
1	12 17·9	0 43	9 35	4 12	4 15
11	12 24·9	1 27	9 02	3 43	3 48
21	12 31·5	2 08	8 29	3 14	3 19
31	12 37·6	2 45	7 56	2 44	2 49

Diameters—equatorial 32″ polar 30″

SATURN

Day	RA	Dec. −	Transit	5° high 52°	5° high 56°
	h m	° ′	h m	h m	h m
1	20 59·2	18 10	18 14	21 55	21 31
11	21 00·6	18 04	17 36	21 18	20 54
21	21 02·7	17 55	16 59	20 42	20 19
31	21 05·3	17 44	16 22	20 06	19 44

Diameters—equatorial 17″ polar 15″
Rings—major axis 38″ minor axis 11″

URANUS

Day	RA	Dec. −	Transit	
	h m	° ′	h m	
1	19 04·0	23 03	16 19	Uranus is too
11	19 05·5	23 00	15 42	close to the
21	19 07·3	22 57	15 04	Sun for
31	19 09·4	22 54	14 27	observation

Diameter 4″

NEPTUNE

Day	RA	Dec. −	Transit	
	h m	° ′	h m	
1	19 11·2	21 44	16 26	Neptune is too
11	19 12·1	21 42	15 48	close to the
21	19 13·2	21 41	15 10	Sun for
31	19 14·5	21 39	14 32	observation

Diameter 2″

(*See* page 64 for explanatory notes)

DAY OF			*Decem* (ten), 10th month of Roman (pre-Julian) Calendar. *Sun's Longitude* 270° ♑ 21ᵈ 15ʰ
Year	Month	Week	

d h
9 14 Mercury at greatest elongation W·21°.
12 17 Mars in conjunction with Moon. Mars 6°N.
18 00 Jupiter in conjunction with Moon. Jupiter 6°N.
21 15 Solstice.
21 23 Saturn in conjunction with Venus. Saturn 1°N.
22 14 Mercury in conjunction with Moon. Mercury 2°N.
27 13 Saturn in conjunction with Moon. Saturn 5°S.
28 02 Venus in conjunction with Moon. Venus 6°S.

336	1	Tu.	Henry I *d.* 1135. Queen Alexandra *b.* 1844.
337	2	W.	Austerlitz 1805. Philip Larkin *d.* 1985.
338	3	Th.	John Flaxman *d.* 1826. Oswald Mosley *d.* 1980.
339	4	F.	The *Observer* first published 1791.
340	5	S.	Christina Rossetti *b.* 1830. Prohibition ended 1933.
341	6	S.	**2nd S. in Advent.** Joseph Conrad *b.* 1857.
342	7	M.	Kirsten Flagstad *d.* 1962. Robert Graves *d.* 1985.
343	8	Tu.	de Quincey *d.* 1859. John Lennon *d.* 1980.
344	9	W.	Milton *b.* 1608. Elizabeth Schwarzkopf *b.* 1915.
345	10	Th.	Royal Academy founded 1768.
346	11	F.	Hector Berlioz *b.* 1803.
347	12	S.	Browning *d.* 1889. Edward G. Robinson *b.* 1893.
348	13	S.	**3rd S. in Advent.** River Plate 1939.
349	14	M.	George Washington *d.* 1799. George VI *b.* 1895.
350	15	Tu.	John Paul Getty *b.* 1892.*
351	16	W.	Boston Tea Party 1773. Saint-Saëns *d.* 1921.
352	17	Th.	Elizabeth Garrett Anderson *d.* 1917.
353	18	F.	Slavery abolished, USA, 1865.
354	19	S.	Emily Brontë *d.* 1848. Genet *b.* 1910.
355	20	S.	**4th S. in Advent.**
356	21	M.	MICHAELMAS LAW SITTINGS END. Stalin *b.* 1879.
357	22	Tu.	George Eliot *d.* 1880. Beatrix Potter *d.* 1943.
358	23	W.	Richard Arkwright *b.* 1732. Malthus *d.* 1834.
359	24	Th.	CHRISTMAS EVE. John I *b.* 1167.
360	25	F.	**Christmas Day.** Rebecca West *b.* 1892.*
361	26	S.	**St Stephen.** BOXING DAY.
362	27	S.	**1st S. after Christmas.** Pasteur *b.* 1822.
363	28	M.	**The Holy Innocents.** Mary II *d.* 1694.
364	29	Tu.	**St John.** Becket killed 1170.
365	30	W.	Kipling *b.* 1865. Pablo Casals *b.* 1876.
366	31	Th.	John Wycliffe *d.* 1384. Matisse *b.* 1869.

The following constellations are near the meridian at

	d h		d h
Nov.	1 24	Nov.	15 23
Dec.	1 22	Dec.	16 21
Jan.	1 20	Jan.	16 19

Ursa Major (below the Pole), Ursa Minor (below the Pole), Cassiopeia, Andromeda, Perseus, Triangulum, Aries, Taurus, Cetus and Eridanus.

d	h	d	h
2	12·0	19	16·9
5	08·8	22	13·7
8	05·6	25	10·5
11	02·5	28	07·4
13	23·3	31	04·2
16	20·1		

* Centenary.

MOON
Phases, Apsides & Node

	d h m
☽ First Quarter	2 06 17
○ Full Moon	9 23 41
☾ Last Quarter	16 19 13
● New Moon	24 00 43
☽ First Quarter	32 03 38
Apogee (404,411 km)	1 20 09
Perigee (367,972 km)	13 21 06
Apogee (405,070 km)	29 17 04

Mean longitude of ascending node on Dec. 1, 262°

MONTHLY NOTES

10. Grouse shooting ends.

21. Shortest day.

25. Christmas Day (Quarter Day). Bank Holiday in Scotland.

26. Bank Holiday, England, Wales, Scotland and N. Ireland.

31. Various licences expire.

(See page 62 for explanatory notes)

Day	Right Ascension	Dec. −	THE SUN s.d. 16'·3 Equation of Time	Rise 52°	Rise 56°	Transit	Set 52°	Set 56°	Sidereal Time	Transit of First Point of Aries
	h m s	° '	m s	h m	h m	h m	h m	h m	h m s	h m s
1	16 29 24	21 48	+11 01	7 46	8 07	11 49	15 52	15 31	4 40 25	19 16 26
2	16 33 43	21 58	+10 38	7 47	8 09	11 50	15 51	15 30	4 44 21	19 12 30
3	16 38 03	22 06	+10 15	7 49	8 10	11 50	15 51	15 29	4 48 18	19 08 34
4	16 42 24	22 14	+ 9 51	7 50	8 12	11 50	15 50	15 28	4 52 14	19 04 38
5	16 46 45	22 22	+ 9 26	7 51	8 13	11 51	15 50	15 28	4 56 11	19 00 42
6	16 51 06	22 30	+ 9 01	7 53	8 15	11 51	15 50	15 27	5 00 07	18 56 46
7	16 55 28	22 37	+ 8 36	7 54	8 16	11 52	15 49	15 27	5 04 04	18 52 50
8	16 59 51	22 43	+ 8 10	7 55	8 18	11 52	15 49	15 26	5 08 00	18 48 54
9	17 04 14	22 49	+ 7 43	7 56	8 19	11 53	15 49	15 26	5 11 57	18 44 58
10	17 08 37	22 55	+ 7 16	7 57	8 20	11 53	15 49	15 25	5 15 54	18 41 02
11	17 13 01	23 00	+ 6 49	7 58	8 21	11 53	15 48	15 25	5 19 50	18 37 06
12	17 17 25	23 05	+ 6 21	7 59	8 22	11 54	15 48	15 25	5 23 47	18 33 10
13	17 21 50	23 09	+ 5 53	8 00	8 24	11 54	15 48	15 25	5 27 43	18 29 15
14	17 26 15	23 13	+ 5 25	8 01	8 25	11 55	15 48	15 25	5 31 40	18 25 19
15	17 30 40	23 16	+ 4 56	8 02	8 26	11 55	15 49	15 25	5 35 36	18 21 23
16	17 35 06	23 19	+ 4 27	8 03	8 26	11 56	15 49	15 25	5 39 33	18 17 27
17	17 39 31	23 21	+ 3 58	8 03	8 27	11 56	15 49	15 25	5 43 29	18 13 31
18	17 43 57	23 23	+ 3 29	8 04	8 28	11 57	15 49	15 26	5 47 26	18 09 35
19	17 48 24	23 25	+ 2 59	8 05	8 29	11 57	15 50	15 26	5 51 23	18 05 39
20	17 52 50	23 26	+ 2 29	8 05	8 29	11 58	15 50	15 26	5 55 19	18 01 43
21	17 57 16	23 26	+ 1 59	8 06	8 30	11 58	15 51	15 27	5 59 16	17 57 47
22	18 01 43	23 26	+ 1 29	8 06	8 30	11 59	15 51	15 27	6 03 12	17 53 51
23	18 06 09	23 26	+ 0 59	8 07	8 31	11 59	15 52	15 28	6 07 09	17 49 55
24	18 10 36	23 25	+ 0 29	8 07	8 31	12 00	15 52	15 29	6 11 05	17 46 00
25	18 15 02	23 24	0 00	8 08	8 31	12 00	15 53	15 29	6 15 02	17 42 04
26	18 19 29	23 22	− 0 30	8 08	8 32	12 01	15 54	15 30	6 18 58	17 38 08
27	18 23 55	23 20	− 1 00	8 08	8 32	12 01	15 55	15 31	6 22 55	17 34 12
28	18 28 21	23 17	− 1 30	8 08	8 32	12 02	15 55	15 32	6 26 52	17 30 16
29	18 32 47	23 14	− 1 59	8 08	8 32	12 02	15 56	15 33	6 30 48	17 26 20
30	18 37 13	23 10	− 2 28	8 08	8 32	12 03	15 57	15 34	6 34 45	17 22 24
31	18 41 38	23 06	− 2 57	8 08	8 31	12 03	15 58	15 35	6 38 41	17 18 28

Duration of Civil (C), Nautical (N) and Astronomical (A) Twilight (in minutes)

Lat. °	Dec. 1 C	N	A	Dec. 11 C	N	A	Dec. 21 C	N	A	Dec. 31 C	N	A
52	40	82	123	41	84	125	41	85	126	41	84	125
56	45	93	138	47	96	141	47	97	142	47	96	141

ASTRONOMICAL NOTES

MERCURY is at its greatest western elongation (21°) on the 9th and thus is visible in the mornings, magnitude +0·5 to −0·5. It is visible low above the ESE horizon around the time of beginning of morning civil twilight. This morning apparition is the most suitable one of the year for observers in the northern hemisphere (though it is only marginally better than the one in August). For the last ten days of the month it is too close to the Sun to be observed.

VENUS is a magnificent object in the early evening sky, magnitude −4·2, low above the south-western horizon. By the end of the month it is visible for over three hours after sunset. The thin crescent Moon will be seen near the planet on the evenings of the 27th and 28th.

MARS, magnitude −0·8 to −1·3, continues to be visible as a prominent object in the night sky for the greater part of the long winter night, and by the end of the month becomes visible low in the ENE as soon as it is dark. Mars is moving slowly westwards, south of the Heavenly Twins, Castor and Pollux.

JUPITER, magnitude −1·9, continues to be visible as a morning object in Virgo.

SATURN, magnitude +0·7, is still an evening object, low in the south-western sky, in Capricornus.

ECLIPSE. A total eclipse of the Moon, visible from the British Isles, occurs on the 9th–10th. See page 72 for details.

ECLIPSE. A partial eclipse of the Sun occurs on the 23rd–24th. See page 72 for details.

METEORS. The maximum of the well-known Geminid meteor shower occurs on the 13th. A gibbous Moon will make conditions for observing rather unfavourable.

(See pages 62–63 for explanatory notes)

THE MOON

Day	RA	Dec.	Hor. Par.	Semi-diam.	Sun's Co-long.	PA of Bright Limb	Phase	Age	Rise 52°	Rise 56°	Transit	Set 52°	Set 56°
	h m	°	'	'	°	°	%	d	h m	h m	h m	h m	h m
1	21 44	− 8·6	54·3	14·8	346	250	38	6·6	11 57	12 03	17 33	23 20	23 17
2	22 28	− 4·1	54·2	14·8	358	248	48	7·6	12 13	12 15	18 14	—	—
3	23 12	+ 0·5	54·3	14·8	10	248	57	8·6	12 29	12 27	18 55	0 27	0 27
4	23 56	+ 5·2	54·6	14·9	22	248	66	9·6	12 46	12 40	19 37	1 34	1 39
5	0 41	+ 9·7	55·1	15·0	34	250	75	10·6	13 05	12 55	20 22	2 42	2 51
6	1 29	+14·0	55·7	15·2	46	252	83	11·6	13 28	13 13	21 09	3 53	4 07
7	2 19	+17·7	56·3	15·3	58	256	90	12·6	13 56	13 37	22 00	5 05	5 23
8	3 13	+20·7	57·1	15·5	71	260	95	13·6	14 33	14 10	22 55	6 17	6 39
9	4 10	+22·6	57·8	15·7	83	266	99	14·6	15 22	14 56	23 53	7 25	7 50
10	5 09	+23·2	58·4	15·9	95	24	100	15·6	16 23	15 58	—	8 24	8 50
11	6 10	+22·4	58·9	16·1	107	95	99	16·6	17 35	17 13	0 52	9 13	9 36
12	7 10	+20·2	59·3	16·2	119	101	95	17·6	18 55	18 38	1 51	9 52	10 10
13	8 09	+16·7	59·5	16·2	131	106	89	18·6	20 18	20 06	2 47	10 22	10 36
14	9 05	+12·2	59·6	16·2	143	110	80	19·6	21 41	21 34	3 41	10 47	10 56
15	9 59	+ 7·1	59·5	16·2	155	112	70	20·6	23 02	23 01	4 33	11 09	11 12
16	10 52	+ 1·6	59·3	16·2	168	113	59	21·6	—	—	5 23	11 29	11 28
17	11 44	− 4·0	59·0	16·1	180	113	48	22·6	0 23	0 27	6 13	11 49	11 43
18	12 36	− 9·3	58·7	16·0	192	112	37	23·6	1 43	1 52	7 03	12 11	12 00
19	13 29	−14·0	58·3	15·9	204	109	26	24·6	3 03	3 17	7 54	12 36	12 20
20	14 24	−18·0	57·9	15·8	216	106	17	25·6	4 21	4 40	8 47	13 06	12 46
21	15 19	−21·0	57·5	15·7	228	101	10	26·6	5 34	5 58	9 41	13 44	13 20
22	16 16	−22·7	57·0	15·5	241	97	4	27·6	6 40	7 06	10 37	14 31	14 06
23	17 13	−23·2	56·5	15·4	253	94	1	28·6	7 36	8 02	11 31	15 28	15 03
24	18 09	−22·5	56·0	15·3	265	159	0	29·6	8 20	8 44	12 24	16 32	16 10
25	19 03	−20·6	55·5	15·1	277	253	1	1·0	8 55	9 14	13 14	17 40	17 22
26	19 54	−17·7	55·1	15·0	289	252	4	2·0	9 22	9 37	14 01	18 49	18 35
27	20 43	−14·2	54·7	14·9	302	249	9	3·0	9 44	9 55	14 46	19 58	19 48
28	21 29	−10·1	54·4	14·8	314	247	15	4·0	10 03	10 10	15 28	21 05	21 00
29	22 13	− 5·7	54·2	14·8	326	246	22	5·0	10 19	10 22	16 09	22 11	22 10
30	22 57	− 1·1	54·1	14·8	338	245	30	6·0	10 35	10 34	16 50	23 18	23 21
31	23 41	+ 3·6	54·3	14·8	350	245	39	7·0	10 51	10 47	17 31	—	—

MERCURY

Day	RA	Dec. −	Diam.	Phase	Transit	5° high 52°	5° high 56°	Day	RA	Dec. −	Diam.	Phase	Transit	5° high 52°	5° high 56°
	h m	°	"	%	h m	h m	h m		h m	°	"	%	h m	h m	h m
1	15 22	15·8	8	28	10 40	6 43	7 03	16	16 12	19·5	6	78	10 33	7 02	7 28
4	15 24	15·9	8	42	10 31	6 35	6 55	19	16 28	20·6	6	82	10 38	7 15	7 44
7	15 32	16·5	7	54	10 27	6 35	6 56	22	16 46	21·5	5	86	10 44	7 28	8 00
10	15 43	17·4	7	64	10 27	6 41	7 03	25	17 04	22·4	5	89	10 50	7 42	8 16
13	15 56	18·4	6	71	10 29	6 50	7 14	28	17 23	23·1	5	91	10 58	7 56	8 32
16	16 12	19·5	6	78	10 33	7 02	7 28	31	17 43	23·7	5	93	11 05	8 08	8 46

VENUS

Day	RA	Dec. −	Diam.	Phase	Transit	5° high 52°	5° high 56°
	h m	°	"	%	h m	h m	h m
1	19 32	24·1	16	71	14 52	17 47	17 08
6	19 57	23·1	17	70	14 58	18 02	17 27
11	20 22	21·8	17	68	15 03	18 18	17 47
16	20 46	20·3	18	66	15 07	18 35	18 07
21	21 09	18·5	18	64	15 10	18 51	18 28
26	21 32	16·6	19	62	15 13	19 08	18 47
31	21 54	14·5	20	60	15 15	19 23	19 06

MARS

Day	RA	Dec. +	Diam.	Phase	Transit	5° high 52°	5° high 56°
	h m	°	"	%	h m	h m	h m
1	8 01	23·1	13	94	3 20	19 44	19 26
6	8 00	23·4	13	95	2 59	19 21	19 03
11	7 57	23·8	14	96	2 37	18 56	18 38
16	7 53	24·2	14	97	2 13	18 30	18 10
21	7 47	24·7	15	98	1 48	18 01	17 41
26	7 40	25·2	15	99	1 21	17 31	17 11
31	7 33	25·6	15	100	0 54	17 01	16 39

(See pages 63–64 for explanatory notes)

SUNRISE AND SUNSET

Day	London 0°05′ 51°30′		Bristol 2°35′ 51°28′		Birmingham 1°55′ 52°28′		Manchester 2°15′ 53°28′		Newcastle 1°37′ 54°59′		Glasgow 4°14′ 55°52′		Belfast 5°56′ 54°35′	
	h m	h m	h m	h m	h m	h m	h m	h m	h m	h m	h m	h m	h m	h m
1	7 44	15 55	7 54	16 05	7 56	15 58	8 02	15 54	8 08	15 43	8 23	15 48	8 23	16 03
2	7 45	15 54	7 55	16 04	7 57	15 57	8 04	15 53	8 09	15 42	8 25	15 48	8 24	16 02
3	7 47	15 54	7 56	16 04	7 59	15 56	8 05	15 53	8 11	15 42	8 27	15 47	8 26	16 01
4	7 48	15 53	7 58	16 03	8 00	15 56	8 06	15 52	8 12	15 41	8 28	15 46	8 27	16 01
5	7 49	15 53	7 59	16 03	8 01	15 55	8 08	15 51	8 14	15 40	8 30	15 46	8 29	16 00
6	7 50	15 52	8 00	16 02	8 03	15 55	8 09	15 51	8 15	15 40	8 31	15 45	8 30	16 00
7	7 52	15 52	8 01	16 02	8 04	15 55	8 10	15 51	8 16	15 39	8 32	15 44	8 31	15 59
8	7 53	15 52	8 03	16 02	8 05	15 54	8 12	15 50	8 18	15 39	8 34	15 44	8 33	15 59
9	7 54	15 52	8 04	16 02	8 06	15 54	8 13	15 50	8 19	15 39	8 35	15 44	8 34	15 58
10	7 55	15 51	8 05	16 02	8 07	15 54	8 14	15 50	8 20	15 38	8 36	15 43	8 35	15 58
11	7 56	15 51	8 06	16 01	8 08	15 54	8 15	15 50	8 21	15 38	8 37	15 43	8 36	15 58
12	7 57	15 51	8 07	16 01	8 09	15 54	8 16	15 50	8 22	15 38	8 39	15 43	8 37	15 58
13	7 58	15 51	8 08	16 01	8 10	15 54	8 17	15 49	8 23	15 38	8 40	15 43	8 38	15 58
14	7 59	15 51	8 09	16 01	8 11	15 54	8 18	15 50	8 24	15 38	8 41	15 43	8 39	15 58
15	8 00	15 51	8 10	16 02	8 12	15 54	8 19	15 50	8 25	15 38	8 42	15 43	8 40	15 58
16	8 00	15 52	8 10	16 02	8 13	15 54	8 20	15 50	8 26	15 38	8 42	15 43	8 41	15 58
17	8 01	15 52	8 11	16 02	8 14	15 54	8 20	15 50	8 27	15 38	8 43	15 43	8 42	15 58
18	8 02	15 52	8 12	16 02	8 14	15 54	8 21	15 50	8 28	15 39	8 44	15 43	8 43	15 58
19	8 03	15 53	8 12	16 03	8 15	15 55	8 22	15 51	8 29	15 39	8 45	15 44	8 43	15 59
20	8 03	15 53	8 13	16 03	8 16	15 55	8 22	15 51	8 29	15 39	8 45	15 44	8 44	15 59
21	8 04	15 53	8 14	16 04	8 16	15 56	8 23	15 51	8 30	15 40	8 46	15 45	8 44	16 00
22	8 04	15 54	8 14	16 04	8 17	15 56	8 24	15 52	8 30	15 40	8 46	15 45	8 45	16 00
23	8 05	15 55	8 14	16 05	8 17	15 57	8 24	15 53	8 30	15 41	8 47	15 46	8 45	16 01
24	8 05	15 55	8 15	16 05	8 17	15 58	8 24	15 53	8 31	15 42	8 47	15 46	8 46	16 01
25	8 05	15 56	8 15	16 06	8 18	15 58	8 25	15 54	8 31	15 42	8 47	15 47	8 46	16 02
26	8 06	15 57	8 15	16 07	8 18	15 59	8 25	15 55	8 31	15 43	8 48	15 48	8 46	16 03
27	8 06	15 57	8 16	16 08	8 18	16 00	8 25	15 56	8 31	15 44	8 48	15 49	8 46	16 04
28	8 06	15 58	8 16	16 08	8 18	16 01	8 25	15 57	8 32	15 45	8 48	15 50	8 46	16 05
29	8 06	15 59	8 16	16 09	8 18	16 02	8 25	15 57	8 32	15 46	8 48	15 51	8 46	16 06
30	8 06	16 00	8 16	16 10	8 18	16 03	8 25	15 58	8 32	15 47	8 48	15 52	8 46	16 07
31	8 06	16 01	8 16	16 11	8 18	16 04	8 25	15 59	8 31	15 48	8 48	15 53	8 46	16 08

JUPITER

Day	RA	Dec. −	Transit	5° high	
				52°	56°
	h m	° ′	h m	h m	h m
1	12 37·6	2 45	7 56	2 44	2 49
11	12 43·0	3 17	7 22	2 13	2 19
21	12 47·6	3 44	6 47	1 40	1 47
31	12 51·3	4 05	6 12	1 07	1 13

Diameters—equatorial 35″ polar 33″

SATURN

Day	RA	Dec. −	Transit	5° high	
				52°	56°
	h m	° ′	h m	h m	h m
1	21 05·3	17 44	16 22	20 06	19 44
11	21 08·5	17 30	15 46	19 32	19 10
21	21 12·1	17 14	15 11	18 58	18 36
31	21 16·1	16 56	14 35	18 25	18 03

Diameters—equatorial 16″ polar 14″
Rings—major axis 36″ minor axis 10″

URANUS

Day	RA	Dec. −	Transit	
	h m	° ′	h m	
1	19 09·4	22 54	14 27	Uranus is too close to the Sun for observation
11	19 11·6	22 50	13 50	
21	19 41·1	22 46	13 13	
31	19 16·6	22 41	12 36	

Diameter 4″

NEPTUNE

Day	RA	Dec. −	Transit	
	h m	° ′	h m	
1	19 14·5	21 39	14 32	Neptune is too close to the Sun for observation
11	19 15·9	21 37	13 54	
21	19 17·4	21 34	13 16	
31	19 19·0	21 31	12 38	

Diameter 2″

(*See* page 64 for explanatory notes)

EXPLANATION OF ASTRONOMICAL SECTION

The astronomical data are given in a form suitable for those who practise naked-eye astronomy or use small telescopes. No attempt has been made to replace the *Astronomical Almanac* for professional astronomers. Positions of the heavenly bodies are given only to the degree of accuracy required by amateur astronomers for setting telescopes, or for plotting on celestial globes or star atlases. Where intermediate positions are required, linear interpolation may be employed.

All data are, unless otherwise stated, for 0ʰ Greenwich Mean Time (GMT), i.e. at the midnight at the beginning of the day named.

(*See also* notes on British Summer Time, p. 70).

Definitions of the terms used cannot be given in an ephemeris of this nature. They must be sought in astronomical literature and textbooks. Probably the best source for the amateur is Norton's *Star Atlas and Reference Handbook* (Longman, 18th edition, 1989; £16·50), which contains an excellent introduction to observational astronomy, and a series of star maps for showing stars visible to the naked eye. Certain more extended ephemerides are available in the British Astronomical Association Handbook, an annual popular among amateur astronomers. (Secretary: Burlington House, Piccadilly, London, W1V 9AG)

A special feature has been made of the times when the various heavenly bodies are visible in the British Isles. Since two columns, calculated for latitudes 52° and 56°, are devoted to risings and settings, the range 50° to 58° can be covered by interpolation and extrapolation. The times given in these columns are GMTs for the meridian of Greenwich. An observer west of this meridian must add his/her longitude (in time) and vice versa.

In accordance with the usual convention in astronomy, + and − indicate respectively north and south latitudes or declinations.

PAGE ONE OF EACH MONTH

The Zodiacal signs through which the Sun is passing during each month are illustrated. The date of transition from one sign to the next, to the nearest hour, is also given.

The **festivals and holy days** in bold type in the calendar are those observed by the Church of England.

Under the heading PHENOMENA will be found particulars of the more important conjunctions of the Sun, Moon and planets with each other, and also the dates of some other astronomical phenomena of special interest.

The CONSTELLATIONS listed each month are those that are near the meridian at the beginning of the month at 22ʰ local mean time. Allowance must be made for Summer Time if necessary. The fact that any star crosses the meridian 4ᵐ earlier each night or 2ʰ earlier each month may be used, in conjunction with the lists given each month, to find what constellations are favourably placed at any moment. The table preceding the list of constellations may be extended indefinitely at the rate just quoted.

Times of MINIMA OF ALGOL are approximate times of the middle of the period of diminished light.

The principal phases of the Moon are the GMTs when the difference between the longitude of the Moon and that of the Sun is 0°, 90°, 180° or 270°. The times of perigee and apogee are those when the Moon is nearest to, and farthest from, the Earth, respectively. The nodes or points of intersection of the Moon's orbit and the ecliptic make a complete retrograde circuit of the ecliptic in about 19 years. From a knowledge of the longitude of the ascending node and the inclination, whose value does not vary much from 5°, the path of the Moon among the stars may be plotted on a celestial globe or star atlas.

PAGE TWO OF EACH MONTH

The Sun's semi-diameter, in arc, is given once a month.

The right ascension given is that of the true Sun. The right ascension of the mean Sun is obtained by applying the equation of time, with the sign given, to the right ascension of the true Sun, or, more easily, by applying 12ʰ to the column Sidereal Time. The direction in which the equation of time has to be applied in different problems is a frequent source of confusion and error. Apparent Solar Time is equal to the Mean Solar Time plus the Equation of Time. For example at noon on August 8 the Equation of Time is −5ᵐ 34ˢ and thus at 12ʰ Mean Time on that day the Apparent Time is 12ʰ −5ᵐ 34ˢ = 11ʰ 54ᵐ 26ˢ.

The Greenwich Sidereal Time at 0ʰ and the Transit of the First Point of Aries (which is really the mean time when the sidereal time is 0ʰ) are used for converting mean time to sidereal time and vice versa.

The GMT of transit of the Sun at Greenwich may also be taken as the local mean time (LMT) of transit in any longitude. It is independent of latitude. The GMT of transit in any longitude is obtained by adding the longitude to the time given if west, and vice versa.

The legal importance of SUNRISE and SUNSET is that the Road Vehicles Lighting Regulations 1989 (SI 1989 No. 1796) make the use of front and rear position lamps on vehicles compulsory during the period between sunset and sunrise. Headlamps on vehicles are required to be used during the hours of darkness on unlit roads or where visibility is seriously reduced. The hours of darkness are defined in these Regulations as the period between half an hour after sunset and half an hour before sunrise.

In all laws and regulations 'sunset' refers to the local sunset, i.e. the time at which the Sun sets at the place in question. This common-sense interpretation has been upheld by legal tribunals. Thus the necessity for providing for different latitudes and longitudes, as already described, is evident.

The times of SUNRISE and SUNSET are those when the Sun's upper limb, as affected by refraction, is on the true horizon of an observer at sea-level. Assuming the mean refraction to be 34′, and the Sun's semi-diameter to be 16′, the time given is that when the true zenith distance of the Sun's centre is 90° + 34′ + 16′ or 90° 50′, or, in other words, when the depression of the Sun's centre below the true horizon is 50′. The upper limb is then 34' below the true horizon, but is brought there by refraction. It is true, of course, that an observer on a ship might see the Sun for a minute or so longer, because of the dip of the horizon, while another viewing the sunset over hills or mountains would record an earlier time. Nevertheless, the moment when the true zenith distance of the Sun's centre is 90° 50' is a precise time dependent only on the latitude and longitude of the place, and independent of its altitude above sea-level, the contour of its horizon, the vagaries of refraction or the small seasonal change in the Sun's semi-diameter; this moment is suitable in every way as a definition of sunset (or sunrise) for all statutory purposes. (For further information *see* footnote.)

It is well known that light reaches us before sunrise and also continues to reach us for some time after sunset. The interval between darkness and sunrise or sunset and darkness is called twilight. Astronomically speaking, twilight is considered to begin or end when the Sun's centre is 18° below the horizon, as no light from the Sun can then reach the observer. As thus defined twilight may last several hours; in high latitudes at the summer solstice the depression of 18° is not reached, and twilight lasts from sunset to sunrise.

The need for some sub-division of twilight is met by dividing the gathering darkness into four steps.

(1) *Sunrise or Sunset*, defined as above.

(2) *Civil twilight*, which begins or ends when the Sun's centre is 6° below the horizon. This marks the time when operations requiring daylight may commence or must cease. In England it varies from about 30 to 60 minutes after sunset and the same interval before sunrise.

(3) *Nautical twilight*, which begins or ends when the Sun's centre is 12° below the horizon. This marks the time when it is, to all intents and purposes, completely dark.

(4) *Astronomical twilight*, which begins or ends when the Sun's centre is 18° below the horizon. This marks theoretical perfect darkness. It is of little practical importance, especially if nautical twilight is tabulated.

To assist observers the durations of civil, nautical and astronomical twilights are given at intervals of ten days. The beginning of a particular twilight is found by subtracting the duration from the time of sunrise, while the end is found by adding the duration to the time of sunset. Thus the beginning of astronomical twilight in latitude 52°, on the Greenwich meridian, on March 11 is found as $06^h\ 23^m - 113^m = 04^h\ 30^m$ and similarly the end of civil twilight as $17^h\ 58^m + 34^m = 18^h\ 32^m$.

The letters TAN (twilight all night) are printed when twilight lasts all night.

Under the heading ASTRONOMICAL NOTES will be found notes describing the position and visibility of all the planets and also of other phenomena; these are intended to guide naked-eye observers or those using small telescopes.

PAGE THREE OF EACH MONTH

The Moon moves so rapidly among the stars that its position is given only to the degree of accuracy that permits linear interpolation. The right ascension and declination are geocentric, i.e. for an imaginary observer at the centre of the Earth. To an observer on the surface of the Earth the position is always different, as the altitude is always less on account of parallax, which may reach 1°.

The lunar terminator is the line separating the bright from the dark part of the Moon's disk. Apart from irregularities of the lunar surface, the terminator is elliptical, because it is a circle seen in projection. It becomes the full circle forming the limb, or edge, of the Moon at New and Full Moon. The selenographic longitude of the terminator is measured from the mean centre of the visible disk, which may differ from the visible centre by as much as 8°, because of libration.

Instead of the longitude of the terminator the Sun's selenographic co-longitude is tabulated. It is numerically equal to the selenographic longitude of the morning terminator, measured eastward from the mean centre of the disk. Thus its value is approximately 270° at New Moon, 360° at First Quarter, 90° at Full Moon and 180° at Last Quarter.

The Position Angle of the Bright Limb is the position angle of the midpoint of the illuminated limb, measured eastward from the north point on the disk. The column PHASE shows the percentage of the area of the Moon's disk illuminated; this is also the illuminated percentage of the diameter at right angles to the line of cusps. The terminator is a semi-ellipse whose major axis is the line of cusps, and whose semi-minor axis is determined by the tabulated percentage; from New Moon to Full Moon the east limb is dark, and vice versa.

The times given as moonrise and moonset are those when the upper limb of the Moon is on the horizon of an observer at sea-level. The Sun's horizontal parallax is about 9″, and is negligible when considering sunrise and sunset, but that of the Moon averages about 57'. Hence the computed time represents the moment when the true zenith distance of the Moon is 90° 50' (as for the Sun) minus the horizontal parallax. The time required for the Sun or Moon to rise or set is about four minutes (except in high latitudes). (For further information, *see* footnote on p. 69.)

SUNRISE, SUNSET and MOONRISE, MOONSET

The tables have been constructed for the meridian of Greenwich, and for latitudes 52° and 56°. They give Greenwich Mean Time (GMT) throughout the year. To obtain the GMT of the phenomenon as seen from any other latitude and longitude in the British Isles, first interpolate or extrapolate for latitude by the usual rules of proportion. To the time thus found the longitude (expressed in time) is to be *added* if west (as it usually is in Great Britain) or *subtracted* if east. If the longitude is expressed in degrees and minutes of arc, it must be converted to time at the rate of $1° = 4^m$ and $15' = 1^m$.

A method of calculating rise and set times for other places in the world is given on pp. 68 and 69.

The GMT of transit of the Moon over the meridian of Greenwich is given; these times are independent of latitude, but must be corrected for longitude. For places in the British Isles it suffices to add the longitude if west, and vice versa. For more remote places a further correction is necessary because of the rapid movement of the Moon relative to the stars. The entire correction is conveniently determined by first finding the west longitude λ of the place. If the place is in west longitude, λ is the ordinary west longitude; if the place is in east longitude λ is the complement to 24^h (or $360°$) of the longitude and will be greater than 12^h (or $180°$). The correction then consists of two positive portions, namely λ and the fraction $\lambda/24$ (or $\lambda°/360$) multiplied by the difference between consecutive transits. Thus for Sydney, New South Wales, the longitude is $10^h\,05^m$ east, so $\lambda = 13^h\,55^m$ and the fraction $\lambda/24$ is 0·58. The transit on the local date 1992 April 15 is found as follows:

	d	h	m
GMT of transit at Greenwich . . . . April	14	22	01
λ		13	55
$0\cdot58 \times (22^h\,51^m - 22^h\,01^m)$			29
GMT of transit at Sydney		15	12	25
Corr. to NSW Standard Time			10	00
Local standard time of transit		15	22	25

As is evident, for any given place the quantities λ and the correction to local standard time may be combined permanently, being here $23^h\,55^m$.

Positions of Mercury are given for every third day, and those of Venus and Mars for every fifth day; they may be interpolated linearly. The diameter (Di.) is given in seconds of arc. The phase (Ph.) is the illuminated percentage of the disk. In the case of the inner planets this approaches 100 at superior conjunction and 0 at inferior conjunction. When the phase is less than 50 the planet is crescent-shaped or horned; for greater phases it is gibbous. In the case of the exterior planet Mars, the phase approaches 100 at conjunction and opposition, and is a minimum at the quadratures.

Since the planets cannot be seen when on the horizon, the actual times of rising and setting are not given; instead, the time when the planet has an apparent altitude of 5° has been tabulated. If the time of transit is between 00^h and 12^h the time refers to an altitude of 5° above the eastern horizon; if between 12^h and 24^h, to the western horizon. The phenomenon tabulated is the one that occurs between sunset and sunrise; unimportant exceptions to these rules may occur because changes are not made during a month, except in the case of Mercury. The times given may be interpolated for latitude and corrected for longitude as in the case of the Sun and Moon.

The GMT at which the planet transits the Greenwich meridian is also given. The times of transit are to be corrected to local meridians in the usual way, as already described.

PAGE FOUR OF EACH MONTH

The GMTs of sunrise and sunset for seven towns, whose adopted positions in longitude (W.) and latitude (N.) are given immediately below the name, may be used not only for these phenomena, but also for lighting-up times, which, under the Road Vehicles Lighting Regulations, 1989, are from sunset to sunrise throughout the year. (*See* p. 62 for a fuller explanation.)

The particulars for the four outer planets resemble those for the planets on Page Three of each month, except that, under Uranus and Neptune, times when the planet is 10° high instead of 5° high are given; this is because of the inferior brightness of these planets. The diameters given for the rings of Saturn are those of the major axis (in the plane of the planet's equator) and the minor axis respectively. The former has a small seasonal change due to the slightly varying distance of the Earth from Saturn, but the latter varies from zero when the Earth passes through the ring plane every 15 years to its maximum opening half-way between these periods. The rings were open at their widest extent in 1988.

TIME

From the earliest ages, the natural division of time into recurring periods of day and night has provided the practical time-scale for the everyday activities of the human race. Indeed, if any alternative means of time measurement is adopted, it must be capable of adjustment so as to remain in general agreement with the natural time-scale defined by the diurnal rotation of the Earth on its axis. Ideally the rotation should be measured against a fixed frame of reference; in practice it must be measured against the background provided by the celestial bodies. If the Sun is chosen as the reference point, we obtain Apparent Solar Time, which is the time indicated by a sundial. It is not a uniform time but is subject to variations which amount to as much as a quarter of an hour in each direction. Such wide variations cannot be tolerated in a practical time scale, and this has led to the concept of Mean Solar Time in which all the days are exactly the same length and equal to the average length of the Apparent Solar Day.

The positions of the stars in the sky are specified in relation to a fictitious reference point in the sky known as the First Point of Aries (or the Vernal Equinox). It is therefore convenient to adopt this same reference point when considering the rotation of the Earth against the background of the stars. The time-scale so obtained is known as Apparent Sidereal Time.

Greenwich Mean Time

The daily rotation of the Earth on its axis causes the Sun and the other heavenly bodies to appear to cross the sky from east to west. It is convenient to represent this relative motion as if the Sun really performed a daily circuit around a fixed Earth. Noon in Apparent Solar Time may then be defined as the time at which the Sun transits across the observer's meridian. In Mean Solar Time, noon is similarly defined by the meridian transit of a fictitious Mean Sun moving uniformly in the sky with the same average speed as the true Sun. Mean Solar Time observed on the meridian of the transit circle telescope of the Old Royal Observatory at Greenwich is called Greenwich Mean Time (GMT). The mean solar day is divided into 24 hours and, for astronomical and other scientific purposes, these are numbered 0 to 23, commencing at midnight. Civil time is usually reckoned in two periods of 12 hours, designated a.m. (*ante meridiem*, i.e. before noon) and p.m. (*post meridiem*, i.e. after noon).

Universal Time

Before 1925 January 1, GMT was reckoned in 24 hours commencing at noon; since that date it has been reckoned from midnight. In view of the risk of confusion in the use of the designation GMT before and after 1925, the International Astronomical Union recommended in 1928 that astronomers should employ the term Universal Time (UT) or Weltzeit (WZ) to denote GMT measured from Greenwich Mean Midnight.

In precision work it is necessary to take account of small variations in Universal Time. These arise from small irregularities in the rotation of the Earth. Observed astronomical time is designated UT0. Observed time corrected for the effects of the motion of the poles (giving rise to a 'wandering' in longitude) is designated UT1. There is also a seasonal fluctuation in the rate of rotation of the Earth arising from meteorological causes, often called the annual fluctuation. UT1 corrected for this effect is designated UT2 and provides a time-scale free from short-period fluctuations. It is still subject to small secular and irregular changes.

Apparent Solar Time

As has been mentioned on page 64, the time shown by a sundial is called Apparent Solar Time. It differs from Mean Solar Time by an amount known as the Equation of Time, which is the total effect of two causes which make the length of the apparent solar day non-uniform. One cause of variation is that the orbit of the Earth is not a circle, but an ellipse, having the Sun at one focus. As a consequence, the angular speed of the Earth in its orbit is not constant; it is greatest at the beginning of January when the Earth is nearest the Sun. The other cause is due to the obliquity of the ecliptic; the plane of the equator (which is at right angles to the axis of rotation of the Earth) does not coincide with the ecliptic (the plane defined by the apparent annual motion of the Sun around the celestial sphere) but is inclined to it at an angle of 23° 26'. As a result, the apparent solar day is shorter than average at the equinoxes and longer at the solstices. From the combined effects of the components due to obliquity and eccentricity, the equation of time reaches its maximum values in February (−14 mins.) and early November (+16 mins.). It has a zero value on four dates during the year, and it is only on these dates (approx. April 15, June 14, September 1, and December 25) that a sundial shows Mean Solar Time.

Sidereal Time

A sidereal day is the duration of a complete rotation of the Earth with reference to the First Point of Aries. The term sidereal (or 'star') time is perhaps a little misleading since the time-scale so defined is not exactly the same as that which would be defined by successive transits of a selected star, as there is a small progressive motion between the stars and the First Point of Aries due to the precession of the

Earth's axis. This makes the length of the sidereal day shorter than the true period of rotation by 0·008 seconds. Superimposed on this steady precessional motion are small oscillations called nutation, giving rise to fluctuations in apparent sidereal time amounting to as much as 1·2 seconds. It is therefore customary to employ Mean Sidereal Time, from which these fluctuations have been removed. The conversion of GMT to Greenwich sidereal time (GST) may be performed by adding the value of the GST at 0h on the day in question (Page Two of each month) to the GMT converted to sidereal time using the table on p. 70.

Example. To find the GST at August 8d 02h 41m 11s GMT

					h	m	s
GST at 0h	..	..	..	..	21	07	01
GMT		..	..	..	2	41	11
Acceleration for 2h	..	..	..			20
„ „ 41m 11s		..	..			7
Sum = GST =		..	..	..	23	48	39

If the observer is not on the Greenwich meridian then his/her longitude, measured positively westwards from Greenwich, must be subtracted from the GST to obtain Local Sidereal Time (LST). Thus, in the above example, an observer 5h east of Greenwich, or 19h west, would find the LST as 4h 48m 39s.

Ephemeris Time

In the study of the motions of the Sun, Moon and planets, observations taken over an extended period are used in the preparation of tables giving the apparent position of the body each day. A table of this sort is known as an ephemeris, and may be used in the comparison of current observations with tabulated positions. A detailed examination of the observations made over the past 300 years shows that the Sun, Moon and planets appear to depart from their predicted positions by amounts proportional to their mean motions. The only satisfactory explanation is that the time-scale to which the observations were referred was not as uniform as had been supposed. Since the time-scale was based on the rotation of the Earth, it follows that this rotation is subject to irregularities. The fact that the discrepancies between the observed and ephemeris positions were proportional to the mean motions of the bodies made it possible to secure agreement by substituting a revised time-scale and recomputing the ephemeris positions. The time-scale which brings the ephemeris into agreement with the observations is known as Ephemeris Time (ET).

The new unit of time has been defined in terms of the apparent annual motion of the Sun. Thus the second is now defined in terms of the annual motion of the Earth in its orbit around the Sun (1/31556925·9747 of the Tropical Year for 1900 January 0d 12h ET) instead of in terms of the diurnal rotation of the Earth on its axis (1/86 400 of the Mean Solar Day). In many branches of scientific work other than astronomy there has been a demand for a unit of time that is invariable, and the second of Ephemeris time was adopted by the Comité International des Poids et Mesures in 1956. The length of the unit has been chosen to provide general agreement with UT throughout the 19th and 20th centuries. During 1992 the estimated difference ET−UT is 58 seconds. The precise determination of ET from astronomical observations is a lengthy process, as the accuracy with which a single observation of the Sun can be made is far less than that obtainable in, for instance, a comparison between clocks. It is therefore necessary to average the observations over an extended period. Largely on account of its faster motion, the position of the Moon may be observed with greater accuracy, and a close approximation to Ephemeris Time may be obtained by comparing observations of the Moon with its ephemeris position. Even in this case, however, the requisite standard of accuracy can only be achieved by averaging over a number of years.

Atomic Time

The fundamental standards of time and frequency must be defined in terms of a periodic motion adequately uniform, enduring and measurable. Progress has made it possible to use natural standards, such as atomic or molecular oscillations. Continuous oscillations are generated in an electrical circuit, the frequency of which is then compared or brought into coincidence with the frequency characteristic of the absorption or emission by the atoms or molecules when they change between two selected energy levels. The National Physical Laboratory makes regular comparisons between quartz clocks of high stability and a frequency defined by atoms of caesium.

International Atomic Time (TAI) is formed by combining the readings of many caesium clocks and was set close to the astronomically-based Universal Time (UT) near the beginning of 1958. It was formally recognized in 1971 and since 1988 January 1 has been maintained by the International Bureau of Weights and Measures (BIPM). The second markers are generated according to the SI definition of the second adopted in 1967 at the 13th General Conference of Weights and Measures: 'The second is the duration of 9 192 631 770 periods of the radiation corresponding to the transition between the two hyperfine levels of the ground state of the caesium-133 atom.'

Civil time in almost all countries is now based on Co-ordinated Universal Time (UTC), established through international collaboration and based on the readings of atomic clocks and the rotation of the Earth. It was designed to make both atomic time and UT accessible with accuracies appropriate for most users.

Radio Time-Signals

UTC is made generally available through time-signals and standard frequency broadcasts such as MSF in the UK, CHU in Canada and WWV and WWVH in the USA. These are based on national time-scales that are maintained in close agreement with UTC and provide traceability to the national timescale and to UTC. The markers of seconds in the UTC scale coincide with those of TAI.

As the rate of rotation of the Earth is variable, the time-signals are adjusted by the introduction of a leap second when necessary in order that UTC shall not depart from UT by more than 0·9ˢ. For convenience, leap seconds are introduced when necessary on the last second of the third, sixth, ninth or twelfth

month, but preferably on December 31 and/or June 30. In the case of a positive leap second, 23ʰ 59ᵐ 60ˢ is followed one second later by 0ʰ 0ᵐ 00ˢ of the first day of the month. In the case of a negative leap second, 23ʰ 59ᵐ 58ˢ is followed one second later by 0ʰ 0ᵐ 00ˢ of the first day of the month. Notices concerning the insertion of leap seconds in UTC are issued by the International Earth Rotation Service at the Observatoire de Paris.

To disseminate the national time-scale in the UK, special signals are broadcast on behalf of the National Physical Laboratory from the BT Radio Station in Rugby. The signals are controlled from a caesium beam atomic frequency standard and consist of a standard frequency carrier of 60 kHz (MSF) which switches off for half a second to denote the passing of one minute, and for a tenth of a second to denote the passing of one second. Also transmitted are two binary coded decimal (BCD) time codes giving time of day and calendar information. Summer and winter time changes are encoded on instruction from the British Government. Other broadcast signals in the UK include the BBC six pips signal, the BT Speaking Clock and a coded time-signal on the BBC 198 kHz Droitwich transmitter, which is used for timing in the electricity supply industry. From 1972 January 1 the six pips on the BBC have consisted of five short pips from second 55 to second 59 followed by one lengthened pip, the start of which indicates the exact minute. From 1990 February 5 these signals have been controlled by the BBC with respect to the broadcast MSF signal and are thus traceable to the National Physical Laboratory. Formerly they were generated by the Royal Greenwich Observatory. The BT Speaking Clock is connected to the National Physical Laboratory caesium beam atomic frequency standard at the Rugby Radio Station.

Accurate timing may also be obtained from the signals of international navigation systems, such as the ground-based Loran-C or Omega, or satellite-based Global Positioning System of the USA or the GLONASS system of the USSR.

STANDARD TIME

In the year 1880 it was enacted by statute that the word 'time', when it occurred in any legal document relating to Great Britain, was to be interpreted, unless otherwise specifically stated, as the mean time of the Greenwich meridian. Summer time is the 'legal' time during the period in which its use is ordained. Since the year 1883 the system of standard time by zones has been gradually accepted, and now almost throughout the world a standard time which differs from that of Greenwich by an integral number of hours, either fast or slow, is used.

The large territories of the United States and Canada are divided into zones approximately 7½° on either side of central meridians. The important ones are given below; there are in addition zones from two to 12 hours fast in the USSR.

Variations from the standard time of some countries occurs during part of the year; they are decided annually and are usually referred to as Summer Time or Daylight Saving Time. Countries in which variations may occur are indicated with an asterisk*.

Fast on Greenwich Time

In the Tonga Islands the time 13h fast and in Chatham Is. 12h 45m fast on Greenwich is used, as the date line is to the east of them.

12 hours fast
Fiji; Kiribati (Gilbert Is.); Kusaie I.; Marshall Is.; Nauru; *New Zealand; Tuvalu; *USSR (Zone 10).

11 hours 30 minutes fast
Kiribati (Banaba); Norfolk I.

11 hours fast
Kuril Is.; New Caledonia; Ponape I.; Sakhalin; Solomon Is.; *USSR (Zone 9); *Vanuatu.

10 hours fast
Admiralty Is.; *Australian Capital Territory; Guam; Mariana Is.; *New South Wales (except Broken Hill area); Papua New Guinea; *Queensland; *Tasmania; Truk Is.; *USSR (Zone 8); *Victoria; Yap Is.

9 hours 30 minutes fast
*New South Wales (Broken Hill area); Northern Territory (Aus); *South Australia.

9 hours fast
Irian Jaya; Japan; Korea (North and South); Molucca Is; Palau Is; *USSR (Zone 7).

8 hours fast
Bali; Brunei; *China; Hong Kong; †Kalimantan (south and east); Macao; Malaysia; *Mongolia; Philippines; Singapore; Sulawesi; Taiwan; Timor; *USSR (Zone 6); Western Australia.

7 hours fast
Cambodia; Christmas I. (Indian Ocean); Java; †Kalimantan (west and middle); Laos; Sumatra; Thailand; *USSR (Zone 5); Vietnam.

6 hours 30 minutes fast
Burma; Cocos (Keeling) Is.

6 hours fast
Bangladesh; Bhutan; *USSR (Zone 4).

5 hours 45 minutes fast
Nepal.

5 hours 30 minutes fast
India; Sri Lanka.

5 hours
Maldives; Pakistan; *USSR (Zone 3).

4 hours 30 minutes fast
Afghanistan.

4 hours fast
Mauritius; Oman; Réunion; Seychelles; United Arab Emirates; *USSR (Zone 2).

3 hours 30 minutes fast
*Iran.

3 hours fast
Bahrain; Comoro Is.; Djibouti; Ethiopia; *Iraq; Kenya; Kuwait; Madagascar; Qatar; Saudi Arabia; Somalia; Tanzania; Uganda; *USSR (Zone 1); Yemen.

2 hours fast
Botswana; *Bulgaria; Burundi; *Crete; *Cyprus; *Egypt; *Finland; *Greece; *Israel, *Jordan, *Lebanon; Lesotho; *Libya; Malawi; Mozambique; Namibia; *Romania; Rwanda; South Africa; Sudan; Swaziland; *Syria; *Turkey; USSR (Zone 0; Estonia, Latvia, Lithuania, Kaliningradskiy); Zaire (Haut-Zaire, Kasai, Kivu, Shaba); Zambia; Zimbabwe.

1 hour fast
*Albania; Algeria; *Andorra; Angola; *Austria; *Belgium; Benin; Cameroon; Central African Republic; Chad; Congo; *Czechoslovakia; *Denmark; Equatorial Guinea; *France; Gabon; *Germany; *Gibraltar; *Hungary; *Italy; *Liechtenstein; *Luxembourg; *Malta; *Monaco; *Netherlands; Niger; Nigeria; *Norway; *Poland; *San Marino; *Spain; Svalbard; *Sweden; *Switzerland; *Tunisia; *Vatican City State; *Yugoslavia; Zaire (Kinshasa, Mbandaka).

Greenwich Time

Ascension I.; Burkina; *Canary Is.; *Channel Is.; Côte d'Ivoire; *Faroe Is.; Gambia; Ghana; Greenland (Danmarks Havn and Mesters Vig); Guinea; Guinea Bissau; Iceland; *Ireland (Republic); Liberia; *Madeira; Mali; Mauritania; *Morocco; *Portugal; St Helena; São Tomé and Principe; Senegal; Sierra Leone; Togo; Tristan da Cunha; *UK (see p. 70).

Slow on Greenwich Time

1 hour slow
*Azores; Cape Verde Is.; *Greenland (Scoresby Sound).

2 hours slow
*Fernando de Noronha I.; South Georgia.

3 hours slow
*Argentina; *Brazil (eastern); French Guiana; *Greenland (Angmagssalik and W. coast); Guyana; *St Pierre and Miquelon; Suriname; *Uruguay.

3 hours 30 minutes slow
*Newfoundland.

4 hours slow (Atlantic time)
Anguilla; Antigua; Aruba; Barbados; *Bermuda; Bolivia; *Brazil (western); *Chile; *Dominica; Dominican Republic; *Falkland Is.; Greenland (Thule area); Grenada; Guadeloupe; *Labrador; Martinique; Montserrat; Netherlands Antilles; *New Brunswick; *Northwest Territories (E. of 68°W.); *Nova Scotia; *Quebec (E. of 63°W.); Paraguay; Puerto Rico; St Kitts; St Lucia; St Vincent; Tobago; Trinidad; Venezuela; Virgin Is.

5 hours slow
*Bahamas; *Brazil (Acre territory); Cayman Is.; Colombia; *Cuba; Ecuador; *Haiti; Jamaica; *Northwest Territories (68°W. to 85°W.); *Ontario (E. of 90° W.); Panama; *Peru; *Quebec (W. of 63°W.); *Turks and Caicos Is.; *USA (eastern time).

6 hours slow
Belize; Costa Rica, Guatemala; Honduras; *Manitoba; Mexico (eastern); Nicaragua; Northwest Territories (85° W. to 102° W.); *Ontario (W. of 90° W.); *El Salvador; *Saskatchewan (E. of 106°W.); *USA (central time).

7 hours slow
*Alberta; Mexico (central); Northwest Territories (102° W. to 120° W.); *Saskatchewan (W. of 106° W.); *USA (mountain time).

8 hours slow
*Alaska (SE coast); *British Columbia; Mexico (western); *USA (Pacific time); *Yukon.

8 hours 30 minutes slow
Pitcairn I.

9 hours slow
*Alaska (E. of 169°30'W.).

10 hours slow
Aleutian Is. (W. of 169°30' W.); Christmas I. (Pacific Ocean); French Polynesia; *Hawaii; Kiribati (Kiritimati I.); Society Is.; Tuamotu archipelago; Tubuai Is.

11 hours slow
Kiribati (Phoenix Is.); Midway Is.; Niue; Samoa.

---

†The Indonesian territory on Borneo

RISING AND SETTING TIMES

Table 1. Semi-diurnal arcs (hour angles at rising/setting)

Dec.	Latitude												Dec.
	0°	10°	20°	30°	40°	45°	50°	52°	54°	56°	58°	60°	
°	h m	h m	h m	h m	h m	h m	h m	h m	h m	h m	h m	h m	°
0	6 00	6 00	6 00	6 00	6 00	6 00	6 00	6 00	6 00	6 00	6 00	6 00	0
1	6 00	6 01	6 01	6 02	6 03	6 04	6 05	6 05	6 06	6 06	6 06	6 07	1
2	6 00	6 01	6 03	6 05	6 07	6 08	6 10	6 10	6 11	6 12	6 13	6 14	2
3	6 00	6 02	6 04	6 07	6 10	6 12	6 14	6 15	6 17	6 18	6 19	6 21	3
4	6 00	6 03	6 06	6 09	6 13	6 16	6 19	6 21	6 22	6 24	6 26	6 28	4
5	6 00	6 04	6 07	6 12	6 17	6 20	6 24	6 26	6 28	6 30	6 32	6 35	5
6	6 00	6 04	6 09	6 14	6 20	6 24	6 29	6 31	6 33	6 36	6 39	6 42	6
7	6 00	6 05	6 10	6 16	6 24	6 28	6 34	6 36	6 39	6 42	6 45	6 49	7
8	6 00	6 06	6 12	6 19	6 27	6 32	6 39	6 41	6 45	6 48	6 52	6 56	8
9	6 00	6 06	6 13	6 21	6 31	6 36	6 44	6 47	6 50	6 54	6 59	7 04	9
10	6 00	6 07	6 15	6 23	6 34	6 41	6 49	6 52	6 56	7 01	7 06	7 11	10
11	6 00	6 08	6 16	6 26	6 38	6 45	6 54	6 58	7 02	7 07	7 12	7 19	11
12	6 00	6 09	6 18	6 28	6 41	6 49	6 59	7 03	7 08	7 13	7 20	7 26	12
13	6 00	6 09	6 19	6 31	6 45	6 53	7 04	7 09	7 14	7 20	7 27	7 34	13
14	6 00	6 10	6 21	6 33	6 48	6 58	7 09	7 14	7 20	7 27	7 34	7 42	14
15	6 00	6 11	6 22	6 36	6 52	7 02	7 14	7 20	7 27	7 34	7 42	7 51	15
16	6 00	6 12	6 24	6 38	6 56	7 07	7 20	7 26	7 33	7 41	7 49	7 59	16
17	6 00	6 12	6 26	6 41	6 59	7 11	7 25	7 32	7 40	7 48	7 57	8 08	17
18	6 00	6 13	6 27	6 43	7 03	7 16	7 31	7 38	7 46	7 55	8 05	8 17	18
19	6 00	6 14	6 29	6 46	7 07	7 21	7 37	7 45	7 53	8 03	8 14	8 26	19
20	6 00	6 15	6 30	6 49	7 11	7 25	7 43	7 51	8 00	8 11	8 22	8 36	20
21	6 00	6 16	6 32	6 51	7 15	7 30	7 49	7 58	8 08	8 19	8 32	8 47	21
22	6 00	6 16	6 34	6 54	7 19	7 35	7 55	8 05	8 15	8 27	8 41	8 58	22
23	6 00	6 17	6 36	6 57	7 23	7 40	8 02	8 12	8 23	8 36	8 51	9 09	23
24	6 00	6 18	6 37	7 00	7 28	7 46	8 08	8 19	8 31	8 45	9 02	9 22	24
25	6 00	6 19	6 39	7 02	7 32	7 51	8 15	8 27	8 40	8 55	9 13	9 35	25
26	6 00	6 20	6 41	7 05	7 37	7 57	8 22	8 35	8 49	9 05	9 25	9 51	26
27	6 00	6 21	6 43	7 08	7 41	8 03	8 30	8 43	8 58	9 16	9 39	10 08	27
28	6 00	6 22	6 45	7 12	7 46	8 08	8 37	8 52	9 08	9 28	9 53	10 28	28
29	6 00	6 22	6 47	7 15	7 51	8 15	8 45	9 01	9 19	9 41	10 10	10 55	29
30	6 00	6 23	6 49	7 18	7 56	8 21	8 54	9 11	9 30	9 55	10 30	12 00	30

Table 2. Correction for Refraction and Semi-diameter

	m	m	m	m	m	m	m	m	m	m	m	m	
0	3	3	4	4	4	5	5	5	6	6	6	7	0
10	3	3	4	4	4	5	5	6	6	6	7	7	10
20	4	4	4	4	5	5	6	7	7	8	8	9	20
25	4	4	4	4	5	6	7	8	8	9	11	13	25
30	4	4	4	5	6	7	8	9	11	14	21	—	30

NB: Regarding Table 1. If latitude and declination are of the same sign, take out the respondent directly. If they are of opposite signs, subtract the respondent from 12ʰ. *Examples.*

Lat.	Dec.	Semi-diurnal arc
+52°	+20°	7h 51m
+52°	−20°	4h 09m

SUNRISE AND SUNSET

The local mean time of sunrise or sunset may be found by obtaining the hour angle from Table 1 and applying it to the time of transit. The hour angle is negative for sunrise and positive for sunset. A small correction to the hour angle, which always has the effect of increasing it numerically, is necessary to allow for the Sun's semi-diameter (16′) and for refraction (34′): it is obtained from Table 2. The resulting local mean time may be converted into the standard time of the country by taking the difference between the longitude of the standard meridian of the country and that of the place, adding it to the local mean time if the place is west of the standard meridian, and subtracting it if the place is east.

Example.—Required the New Zealand Mean Time (12ʰ fast on GMT) of sunset on May 23 at Auckland, latitude 36° 50′ S. (or minus), longitude 11ʰ 39ᵐ E. Taking the declination as +20°·7 (p. 31), we find

	h	m
Tabular entry for 30° Lat. and Dec. 20°, opposite signs	+	5 11
Proportional part for 6° 50′ of Lat.	−	15
Proportional part for 0°·7 of Dec.	−	2
Correction (Table 2)	+	4
Hour angle		4 58
Sun transits (p. 31)		11 57
Longitudinal correction	+	21
New Zealand Mean Time		17 16

MOONRISE AND MOONSET

It is possible to calculate the times of moonrise and moonset using Table 1, though the method is more complicated because the apparent motion of the Moon is much more rapid and also more variable than that of the Sun.

Table 3. Longitude Correction

A \ X	40^m	45^m	50^m	55^m	60^m	65^m	70^m
h	m	m	m	m	m	m	m
1	2	2	2	2	3	3	3
2	3	4	4	5	5	5	6
3	5	6	6	7	8	8	9
4	7	8	8	9	10	11	12
5	8	9	10	11	13	14	15
6	10	11	13	14	15	16	18
7	12	13	15	16	18	19	20
8	13	15	17	18	20	22	23
9	15	17	19	21	23	24	26
10	17	19	21	23	25	27	29
11	18	21	23	25	28	30	32
12	20	23	25	28	30	33	35
13	22	24	27	30	33	35	38
14	23	26	29	32	35	38	41
15	25	28	31	34	38	41	44
16	27	30	33	37	40	43	47
17	28	32	35	39	43	46	50
18	30	34	38	41	45	49	53
19	32	36	40	44	48	51	55
20	33	38	42	46	50	54	58
21	35	39	44	48	53	57	61
22	37	41	46	50	55	60	64
23	38	43	48	53	58	62	67
24	40	45	50	55	60	65	70

Notation

φ = latitude of observer
λ = longitude of observer (measured positively towards the west)
T_{-1} = time of transit of Moon on previous day
T_0 = time of transit of Moon on day in question
T_1 = time of transit of Moon on following day
δ_0 = approximate declination of Moon
δ_R = declination of Moon at moonrise
δ_S = declination of Moon at moonset
h_0 = approximate hour angle of Moon
h_R = hour angle of Moon at moonrise
h_S = hour angle of Moon at moonset
t_R = time of moonrise
t_S = time of moonset

The parallax of the Moon, about 57′, is near to the sum of the semi-diameter and refraction but has the opposite effect on these times. It is thus convenient to neglect all three quantities in the method outlined below.

Method

1. With arguments φ, δ_0 enter Table 1 on p. 68 to determine h_0 where h_0 is negative for moonrise and positive for moonset.

2. Form approximate times from
$$t_R = T_0 + \lambda + h_0$$
$$t_S = T_0 + \lambda + h_0$$

3. Determine δ_R, δ_S for times t_R, t_S respectively.

4. Re-enter Table 1 on p. 68 with—
   (a) arguments φ, δ_R to determine h_R
   (b) arguments φ, δ_S to determine h_S

5. Form $t_R = T_0 + \lambda + h_R + AX$
   $t_S = T_0 + \lambda + h_S + AX$

where $A = (\lambda + h)$

and $X = (T_0 - T_{-1})$ if $(\lambda + h)$ is negative
$X = (T_1 - T_0)$ if $(\lambda + h)$ is positive

AX is the respondent in Table 3.

Example.—To find the times of moonrise and moonset at Vancouver ($\varphi = +49°$, $\lambda = +8^h\ 12^m$) on 1992 January 2. The starting data (from p. 16) are

$$\begin{array}{ll} & \text{h\quad m} \\ T_{-1} = & 9\quad 11 \\ T_0 = & 10\quad 02 \\ T_1 = & 10\quad 53 \\ \delta = & -24° \end{array}$$

1. $h_0 = \quad 3^h\ 56^m$
2. Approximate values
$$\begin{array}{ll} t_R = & 2^d\ 10^h\ 02^m + 8^h\ 12^m + (-3^h\ 56^m) \\ = & 2^d\ 14^h\ 18^m \\ t_S = & 2^d\ 10^h\ 02^m + 8^h\ 12^m + (+3^h\ 56^m) \\ = & 2^d\ 22^h\ 10^m \end{array}$$
3. $\delta_R = -24°\cdot 7$
   $\delta_S = -24°\cdot 9$
4. $h_R = -3^h\ 52^m$
   $h_S = +3^h\ 51^m$
5. $t_R = 2^d\ 10^h\ 02^m + 8^h\ 12^m + (-3^h\ 52^m) + 9^m$
   $= 2^d\ 14^h\ 31^m$
   $t_S = 2^d\ 10^h\ 02^m + 8^h\ 12^m + (+3^h\ 51^m) + 26^m$
   $= 2^d\ 22^h\ 31^m$

To get the LMT of the phenomenon the longitude is subtracted from the GMT thus

Moonrise = $2^d\ 14^h\ 31^m - 8^h\ 12^m = 2^d\ 06^h\ 19^m$
Moonset = $2^d\ 22^h\ 31^m - 8^h\ 12^m = 2^d\ 14^h\ 19^m$

ASTRONOMICAL CONSTANTS

Solar Parallax	8″·794
Astronomical unit	149597870 km
Precession for the year 1992	50″·288
„ in Right Ascension	3^s·074
„ in Declination	20″·044
Constant of Nutation	9″·202
Constant of Aberration	20″·496
Mean Obliquity of Ecliptic (1992)	23° 26′ 26″
Moon's Equatorial Hor. Parallax	57′ 02″·70
Velocity of light in vacuo *per sec*	299792·5 km
Solar motion *per sec*	20·0 km
Equatorial radius of the Earth	6378·140 km
Polar radius of the Earth	6356·755 km

North Galactic Pole } RA 12^h 49^m (1950·0).
(IAU *Standard*). } Dec. 27°·4 N.
Solar Apex .... RA 18^h 06^m Dec. +30°

Length of Year (*In Mean Solar Days*)	Tropical	365·24220
	Sidereal	365·25636
	Anomalistic	365·25964
	(*Perihelion to Perihelion*)	
	Eclipse	346·6200

		d h m s
Length of Month (*Mean Values*)	New Moon to New	29 12 44 02·9
	Sidereal	27 07 43 11·5
	Anomalistic	27 13 18 33·2
	(*Perigee to Perigee*)	

MEAN AND SIDEREAL TIME

Acceleration						Retardation						MEAN REFRACTION	
h	m s	h	m s	m s	s	h	m s	h	m s	m s	s	Alt. Ref.	Alt. Ref.
1	0 10	13	2 08	0 00	0	1	0 10	13	2 08	0 00	0		
2	0 20	14	2 18	3 02	1	2	0 20	14	2 18	3 03	1	1 20 21	4 30 10
3	0 30	15	2 28	9 07	2	3	0 29	15	2 27	9 09	2	1 30 20	5 06 9
				15 13	3					15 15	3	1 41 19	5 50 8
4	0 39	16	2 38	21 18	4	4	0 39	16	2 37	21 21	4	1 52 18	6 44 7
5	0 49	17	2 48	27 23	5	5	0 49	17	2 47	27 28	5	2 05 17	7 54 6
6	0 59	18	2 57	33 28	6	6	0 59	18	2 57	33 34	6	2 19 16	9 27 5
7	1 09	19	3 07	39 34	7	7	1 09	19	3 07	39 40	7	2 35 15	11 39 4
8	1 19	20	3 17	45 39	8	8	1 19	20	3 17	45 46	8	2 52 14	15 00 3
9	1 29	21	3 27	51 44	9	9	1 29	21	3 26	51 53	9	3 12 13	20 42 2
				57 49	10					57 59	10	3 34 12	32 20 1
10	1 39	22	3 37	60 00		10	1 38	22	3 36	60 00		4 00 11	62 17 0
11	1 48	23	3 47			11	1 48	23	3 46			4 30	90 00
12	1 58	24	3 57			12	1 58	24	3 56				

The length of a sidereal day in mean time is $23^h 56^m 04^s.09$. Hence 1^h MT $= 1^h + 9^s.86$ ST and 1^h ST $= 1^h - 9^s.83$ MT.

To convert an interval of mean time to the corresponding interval of sidereal time, enter the acceleration table with the given mean time (taking the hours and the minutes and seconds separately) and add the acceleration obtained to the given mean time. To convert an interval of sidereal time to the corresponding interval of mean time, take out the retardation for the given sidereal time and subtract.

The columns for the minutes and seconds of the argument are in the form known as critical tables. To use these tables, find in the appropriate left-hand column the two entries between which the given number of minutes and seconds lies; the quantity in the right-hand column between these two entries is the required acceleration or retardation. Thus the acceleration for 11^m26^s (which lies between the entries 9^m07^s and 15^m13^s) is 2^s. If the given number of minutes and seconds is a tabular entry, the required acceleration or retardation is the entry in the right-hand column *above* the given tabular entry, e.g. the retardation for 45^m46^s is 7^s.

Example.—Convert $14^h27^m35^s$ from ST to MT

	h	m	s
Given ST	14	27	35
Retardation for 14^h		2	18
Retardation for 27^m35^s			5
Corresponding MT	14	25	12

For further explanation, *see* p. 65.
The refraction table is also in the form of a critical table.

THE SUMMER TIME ACTS

In 1916 an Act ordained that during a defined period of that year the legal time for general purposes in Great Britain should be one hour in advance of Greenwich Mean Time. The Summer Time Acts 1922 to 1925, defined the period during which Summer Time was to be in force, stabilizing practice until the war.

During the Second World War the duration of Summer Time was extended and in the years 1941–45 and in 1947, Double Summer Time (two hours in advance of Greenwich Mean Time) was in force. After the war, Summer Time was extended in each year from 1948–1952 and 1961–1964 by Order in Council.

Clocks were kept one hour ahead of Greenwich Mean Time throughout the year between 1968 October 27 and 1971 October 31.

The most recent legislation is the Summer Time Act, 1972, which enacted that 'the period of summer time for the purposes of this Act is the period beginning at two o'clock, Greenwich mean time, in the morning of the day after the third Saturday in March or, if that day is Easter Day, the day after the second Saturday in March, and ending at two o'clock, Greenwich mean time, in the morning of the day after the fourth Saturday in October.'

The duration of Summer Time can be varied by Order in Council and in recent years alterations have been made to bring the operation of Summer Time in Britain closer to similar provisions in other countries of the European Community. The latest Order in Council is the Summer Time Order 1989, stipulating that the duration of Summer Time in 1992 will be from March 29 to October 25. As in recent years, the hour of changeover will be 01^h Greenwich Mean Time.

The duration of Summer Time during the last few years is given in the following table.

1980 March 16–Oct. 26	1987 March 29–Oct. 25
1981 March 29–Oct. 25	1988 March 27–Oct. 23
1982 March 28–Oct. 24	1989 March 26–Oct. 29
1983 March 27–Oct. 23	1990 March 25–Oct. 28
1984 March 25–Oct. 28	1991 March 31–Oct. 27
1985 March 31–Oct. 27	1992 March 29–Oct. 25
1986 March 30–Oct. 26	

PHENOMENA OF JUPITER'S SATELLITES, 1992

January

GMT (d h m)	Sat.	Phen.
2 01 08	II	Sh.I.
2 03 56	II	Sh.E.
3 02 42	III	Ec.D.
3 06 16	III	Sh.I.
3 07 21	I	Ec.D.
5 23 10	I	Sh.I.
6 01 26	I	Sh.E.
9 03 43	II	Sh.I.
9 06 31	II	Sh.E.
10 06 39	III	Ec.D.
10 22 49	II	Ec.D.
12 03 42	I	Ec.D.
13 01 04	I	Sh.I.
13 03 20	I	Sh.E.
13 22 11	I	Ec.D.
14 00 07	III	Sh.E.
14 23 05	IV	Sh.E.
18 01 23	II	Sh.E.
19 22 24	II	Sh.I.
21 00 04	I	Ec.D.
21 00 32	III	Sh.I.
21 04 04	III	Sh.E.
21 23 41	I	Sh.E
23 03 30	IV	Ec.D.
25 03 57	II	Ec.D.
26 22 11	II	Sh.I.
27 00 59	II	Sh.E.
27 04 50	I	Sh.I.
27 07 06	I	Sh.E.
28 01 58	I	Ec.D.
28 04 30	III	Sh.I.
28 23 18	I	Sh.I.
29 01 34	I	Sh.E.

February

GMT (d h m)	Sat.	Phen.
1 06 31	II	Ec.D.
3 00 46	II	Sh.I.
3 03 35	II	Sh.E.
4 03 52	I	Ec.D.
5 01 11	I	Sh.I.
5 03 28	I	Sh.E.
5 22 20	I	Ec.D.
6 21 56	I	Sh.I.
7 22 31	III	Ec.D.
8 21 32	IV	Ec.R.
9 01 39	IV	Ec.R.
10 03 22	II	Sh.I.
10 06 11	II	Sh.I.
11 05 46	I	Ec.D.
11 22 21	II	Ec.D.
12 03 05	I	Sh.I.
12 05 21	I	Sh.E.
13 00 14	I	Ec.D.
13 21 33	I	Sh.I.
13 23 49	I	Sh.E.
15 02 30	III	Ec.D.
17 05 58	II	Sh.I.
17 06 51	IV	Sh.I.
18 19 55	III	Sh.E.
19 00 55	II	Ec.D.
19 04 58	I	Sh.I.
20 02 08	I	Ec.D.
20 19 16	II	Sh.I.
20 22 04	II	Sh.E.
20 23 27	I	Sh.I.
21 01 43	I	Sh.E.
21 20 37	I	Ec.D.
22 20 11	I	Sh.E.
25 20 22	III	Sh.I.
25 23 53	III	Sh.E.
26 03 29	II	Ec.D.
27 04 03	I	Ec.D.
27 21 53	II	Sh.I.
28 00 41	II	Sh.I.
28 01 21	I	Sh.I.
28 03 37	I	Sh.E.
28 22 31	I	Ec.D.
29 00 49	I	Ec.R.
29 19 32	II	Ec.R.
29 19 49	I	Sh.I.
29 22 05	I	Sh.E.

March

GMT (d h m)	Sat.	Phen.
1 19 17	I	Ec.R.
4 00 20	III	Sh.I.
4 03 50	III	Sh.E.
5 00 51	IV	Sh.I.
5 04 45	IV	Sh.E.
6 00 29	II	Sh.I.
6 03 14	I	Sh.I.
6 03 17	II	Sh.E.
7 02 43	I	Ec.R.
7 21 43	I	Sh.I.
7 22 06	II	Ec.R.
7 23 59	I	Sh.E.
8 21 12	I	Ec.R.
11 04 18	III	Sh.I.
13 03 06	II	Sh.I
13 05 08	I	Sh.I.
14 04 37	I	Ec.R.
14 21 56	III	Ec.R.
14 23 23	I	Sh.I.
15 00 39	II	Ec.R.
15 01 53	I	Sh.E.
15 23 06	I	Ec.R.
16 19 13	II	Sh.E.
16 20 21	I	Sh.I.
21 22 39	IV	Sh.E.
22 01 31	I	Sh.I.
22 01 54	III	Sh.I.
22 03 13	II	Ec.R.
22 03 47	I	Sh.E.
23 01 01	I	Ec.R.
23 20 00	I	Sh.I.
23 21 49	II	Sh.E.
23 22 15	I	Sh.E.
24 19 30	I	Ec.R.
29 03 25	I	Sh.I.
30 02 56	I	Ec.R.
30 03 40	IV	Ec.D.
30 21 40	II	Sh.I.
30 21 54	I	Sh.I.
31 00 09	I	Sh.E
31 00 26	II	Sh.E.
31 21 25	I	Ec.R.

April

GMT (d h m)	Sat.	Phen.
6 23 48	I	Sh.I.
7 00 17	II	Sh.I.
7 02 03	I	Sh.E.
7 03 03	II	Sh.E.
7 23 20	I	Ec.R.
8 20 14	III	Sh.I.
8 20 32	I	Sh.E.
8 21 38	II	Ec.R.
8 23 41	III	Sh.E.
14 01 43	I	Sh.I.
14 02 55	II	Sh.I.
15 01 15	I	Ec.R.
15 20 11	I	Sh.I.
15 21 44	IV	Ec.D.
15 22 26	I	Sh.E.
16 00 13	II	Ec.R.
16 00 13	III	Sh.I.
16 01 24	IV	Ec.R.
22 22 06	I	Sh.I.
23 00 21	I	Sh.E.
23 21 39	I	Ec.R.
24 21 35	II	Sh.E.
26 21 49	III	Ec.R.
30 23 34	I	Ec.R.

May

GMT (d h m)	Sat.	Phen.
1 21 28	II	Sh.I.
2 00 12	II	Sh.E.
3 22 21	III	Ec.D.
10 21 13	II	Sh.I.
11 00 57	IV	Sh.I.
15 22 18	I	Sh.I.
16 00 33	I	Sh.E.
16 21 53	I	Ec.R.
17 23 48	II	Ec.R.
21 23 32	III	Sh.E.
23 23 48	I	Ec.R.
26 21 22	II	Sh.E.
27 22 16	IV	Sh.E.

June

GMT (d h m)	Sat.	Phen.
2 23 59	II	Sh.E.
7 22 31	I	Sh.I.
8 21 43	III	Ec.R.
8 22 07	I	Ec.R.
15 22 19	III	Ec.D.
21 22 05	IV	Ec.D.

December

GMT (d h m)	Sat.	Phen.
8 02 47	I	Ec.D.
12 04 43	III	Sh.I.
15 04 40	I	Ec.D.
17 03 02	II	Ec.D.
19 05 37	III	Ec.D.
22 06 33	I	Ec.D.
23 03 51	I	Sh.I.
23 06 04	I	Sh.E.
24 05 37	II	Ec.D.
30 02 29	III	Sh.E.
30 05 45	I	Sh.I.
31 02 54	I	Ec.D.

Jupiter's satellites transit across the disk from east to west, and pass behind the disk from west to east. The shadows that they cast also transit across the disk. With the exception at times of Satellite IV, the satellites also pass through the shadow of the planet, i.e. they are eclipsed. Just before opposition the satellite disappears in the shadow to the west of the planet and reappears from occultation on the east limb. Immediately after opposition the satellite is occulted at the west limb and reappears from eclipse to the east of the planet. At times approximately two to four months before and after opposition, both phases of eclipses of Satellite III may be seen. When Satellite IV is eclipsed, both phases may be seen. The times given refer to the centre of the satellite. As the satellite is of considerable size the immersion and emersion phases are not instantaneous. Even when the satellite enters or leaves the shadow along a radius of the shadow, the phase can last for several minutes. With satellite IV, grazing phenomena can occur so that the light from the satellite may fade and brighten again without a complete eclipse taking place.

The list of phenomena gives most of the eclipses and shadow transits visible in the British Isles under favourable conditions.

Ec. = Eclipse	R.	= Reappearance
Sh. = Shadow transit	I.	= Ingress
D. = Disappearance	E.	= Egress

CELESTIAL PHENOMENA FOR OBSERVATION, 1992

ECLIPSES

There will be five eclipses during 1992, three of the Sun and two of the Moon. (Penumbral eclipses are not mentioned in this section as they are difficult to observe).

1. An annular eclipse of the Sun on January 4–5 is visible as a partial eclipse from Oceania, the Philippines, Japan, extreme coast of north-east Asia, northern part of Australia, Pacific Ocean and west coast of North America. The eclipse begins at January 4^d 20^h 04^m and ends at January 5^d 02^h 06^m. The annular phase begins at January 4^d 21^h 16^m in the Pacific Ocean and ends at January 5^d 00^h 53^m on the coast of North America. The maximum duration of the annular phase is 11^m 36^s.

2. A partial eclipse of the Moon on June 15 is visible from Antarctica, Africa (except the eastern part), southern tip of Greenland, South America, North America (except the north-west), Central America, part of the Pacific Ocean, and New Zealand. The eclipse begins at 03^h 27^m and ends at 06^h 27^m. The time of maximum eclipse is 04^h 57^m when 0.68 of the Moon's diameter is obscured.

3. A total eclipse of the Sun on June 30. The path of totality begins on the coast of Uruguay, crosses the South Atlantic and ends in the Southern Ocean south of Africa. The partial phase is visible from central South America, the South Atlantic, south-west Africa, Southern Ocean south of Madagascar and the extreme south-west Indian Ocean. The eclipse begins at 09^h 51^m and ends at 14^h 30^m; the total phase begins at 11^h 02^m and ends at 13^h 19^m. The maximum duration of totality is 5^m 26^s.

4. A total eclipse of the Moon on December 9–10 is visible from Asia (except the extreme east), Europe (including the British Isles), Africa, Atlantic Ocean, Iceland, Greenland, South America (except the south), Central America, and North America (except western coast). The eclipse begins at December 9^d 22^h 00^m and ends at December 10^d 01^h 28^m. Totality lasts from December 9^d 23^h 07^m to December 10^d 00^h 21^m.

5. A partial eclipse of the Sun on December 23–24 is visible from eastern China, Korea, Japan, the extreme east of USSR, and south-west Alaska. The eclipse begins at December 23^d 22^h 21^m and ends at December 24^d 02^h 41^m. At the time of maximum eclipse, 0.84 of the Sun's diameter is obscured.

LUNAR OCCULTATIONS

No occultations of planets or first-magnitude stars occur in 1992.

Observations of the times of occultations are made by both amateur and professional astronomers. Such observations are later analysed to yield accurate positions of the Moon; this is one method of determining the difference between ephemeris time and universal time.

Many of the observations made by amateurs are obtained with the use of a stop-watch which is compared with a time-signal immediately after the observation. Thus an accuracy of about one-fifth of a second is obtainable, though the observer's personal equation may amount to one-third or one-half of a second.

The list on the opposite page includes most of the occultations visible under favourable conditions in the British Isles. No occultation is included unless the star is at least 10° above the horizon and the Sun sufficiently far below the horizon to permit the star to be seen with the naked eye or with a small telescope. The altitude limit is reduced from 10° to 2° for stars and planets brighter than magnitude 2·0 and such occultations are also predicted in daylight.

The column Phase shows (*a*) whether a disappearance (D) or reappearance (R) is to be observed; and (*b*) whether it is at the dark limb (D) or bright limb (B). The column headed 'El. of Moon' gives the elongation of the Moon from the Sun, in degrees. The elongation increases from 0° at New Moon to 180° at Full Moon and on to 360° (or 0°) at New Moon again. Times and position angles (*P*), reckoned from the north point in the direction north, east, south, west, are given for Greenwich (lat. 51° 30′, long. 0°) and Edinburgh (lat. 56° 00′, long. 3° 12′ west).

The coefficients a and b are the variations in the GMT for each degree of longitude (positive to the west) and latitude (positive to the north) respectively; they enable approximate times (to within about 1^m generally) to be found for any point in the British Isles. If the point of observation is $\Delta\lambda$ degrees west and $\Delta\phi$ degrees north, the approximate time is found by adding $a.\Delta\lambda + b.\Delta\phi$ to the given GMT.

As an illustration, the disappearance of ZC976 on March 13 at Liverpool will be found from both Greenwich and Edinburgh.

	Greenwich	Edinburgh
	°	°
Longitude	0·0	+3·2
Long. of Liverpool	+3·0	+3·0
$\Delta\lambda$	+3·0	−0·2
Latitude	+51·5	+56·0
Lat. of Liverpool	+53·4	+53·4
$\Delta\phi$	+1·9	−2·6
	h m	h m
GMT....................	2 15·1	2 09·8
$a.\Delta\lambda$.....................	+1·5	−0·1
$b.\Delta\phi$.....................	−2·7	+3·9
	2 13·9	2 13·6

If the occultation is given for one station but not the other, the reason for the suppression is given by the following code.

N = star not occulted.
A = star's altitude less than 10° (2° for bright stars and planets).
S = Sun not sufficiently below the horizon.
G = occultation is of very short duration.

It will be noticed that in some cases the coefficients a and b are not given; this is because the occultation is so short that prediction for other places by means of these coefficients would not be reliable.

LUNAR OCCULTATIONS, 1992

Date		ZC No.	Mag.	Phase	El. of Moon	GREENWICH				EDINBURGH			
						UT	a	b	P	UT	a	b	P
					°	h m	m	m	°	h m	m	m	°
Jan.	8	3216	6·6	D.D.	41	18 45·6	−0·2	0·4	28	A			
	10	3453	4·9	D.D.	64	19 11·5	−1·4	−2·3	104	19 0·0	−1·1	−1·2	85
	14	399	5·7	D.D.	110	18 20·5	−0·6	3·1	20	N			
	15	435	5·9	D.D.	114	2 1·6	0·0	−1·0	70	1 57·3	−0·1	−0·9	62
	16	584	6·0	D.D.	127	1 49·9	−0·2	−1·2	79	1 43·8	−0·3	−1·1	71
	16	714	6·2	D.D.	136	17 40·2	−0·9	1·0	99	17 43·3	−0·7	1·4	86
	17	767	5·5	D.D.	142	4 50·6	−0·1	−0·4	42	4 48·3	−0·2	−0·4	36
Feb.	9	233	6·2	D.D.	68	19 32·1	−1·0	−1·8	98	19 22·6	−1·0	−1·1	82
	10	375	6·8	D.D.	81	22 48·3	0·3	−3·2	133	22 35·9	−0·1	−2·5	118
	11	493	6·9	D.D.	92	20 19·8	−1·3	0·0	62	20 17·1	−1·2	0·6	46
	14	839	5·3	D.D.	120	0 31·5	−0·5	−1·3	82	0 24·2	−0·6	−1·2	76
	14	983	6·0	D.D.	130	17 59·2	−0·7	2·9	49	18 17·3	G	G	16
	20	1670	5·1	R.D.	204	0 17·8	−1·5	0·5	275	0 15·8	−1·1	0·5	282
Mar.	9	459	6·7	D.D.	62	19 48·4	−0·4	−3·5	133	19 33·7	−0·7	−2·4	116
	9	472	5·0	D.D.	63	22 15·4	0·1	−1·6	100	22 8·3	0·0	−1·6	92
	12	789	6·9	D.D.	89	0 50·7	G	G	13	N			
	12	923	6·9	D.D.	99	19 8·5	−1·9	2·9	40	N			
	12	929	5·8	D.D.	100	20 39·4	−0·8	−2·4	137	20 27·1	−0·9	−1·8	125
	12	931	6·7	D.D.	100	21 15·2	−0·1	−3·8	160	20 59·3	−0·6	−2·8	146
	12	942	6·3	D.D.	100	22 7·2	0·1	−3·4	158	21 52·9	−0·3	−2·8	147
	13	976	3·2	D.D.	103	2 15·1	0·5	−1·4	115	2 9·8	0·3	−1·5	112
	13	1086	6·5	D.D.	112	19 55·0	−1·7	0·7	71	19 54·7	−1·6	1·7	56
	16	1381	6·3	D.D.	142	1 8·0	−1·0	−1·2	80	0 59·5	−1·0	−1·1	77
	22	2109	6·1	R.D.	224	2 33·3	G	G	205	2 35·5	G	G	215
Apr.	6	582	5·8	D.D.	45	21 19·7	0·1	−1·4	90	21 13·7	0·0	−1·4	83
	8	907	6·9	D.D.	71	22 57·0	0·2	−1·7	116	22 49·7	0·1	−1·7	112
	9	1054	6·8	D.D.	83	20 20·4	−1·4	−0·5	69	20 14·5	−1·5	−0·1	59
	9	1051	6·7	D.D.	83	20 37·1	G	G	183	20 18·3	0·0	−3·6	166
	10	1077	3·7	D.D.	85	0 33·9	0·5	−1·8	143	0 27·1	0·4	−1·9	140
	10	1207	5·8	D.D.	98	23 55·1	0·2	−2·1	148	23 46·0	0·1	−2·1	145
	12	1440	6·7	D.D.	122	20 52·8	−1·9	0·2	76	20 48·9	−1·9	0·8	67
May	9	1410	5·3	D.D.	92	20 5·7	−1·3	−1·1	99	S			
	10	1528	6·6	D.D.	106	20 51·8	−1·2	−1·3	111	S			
	12	1752	6·5	D.D.	132	21 35·3	−1·0	−1·2	140	21 27·3	−0·9	−0·9	138
June	11	2084	6·5	D.D.	141	21 43·1	−1·1	−1·1	152	S			
July	9	2183	5·7	D.D.	124	21 49·3	−1·4	−0·8	87	21 41·5	−1·3	−0·7	84
	12	2602	5·5	D.D.	160	22 59·7	−1·6	0·0	74	22 55·3	−1·4	0·1	69
	26	709	4·3	R.D.	308	1 24·2	0·5	1·6	238	1 32·5	0·4	1·5	247
Aug.	6	2270	5·4	D.D.	107	20 10·7	G	G	160	S			
	15	3320	5·3	R.D.	198	0 37·6	−1·6	0·6	254	0 35·1	−1·5	0·5	264
	21	487	5·3	R.D.	265	0 27·6	−0·1	1·9	240	0 35·8	−0·1	1·8	249
	22	660	4·4	R.D.	279	3 42·3	−0·8	2·1	238	3 48·3	−0·8	1·7	252
Sept.	18	599	4·5	R.D.	248	0 41·2	−0·6	1·9	247	0 47·3	−0·6	1·7	260
	21	1077	3·7	R.D.	286	2 4·3	−0·6	0·3	312	2 2·0	−0·7	−0·5	332
Oct.	4	2902	6·0	D.D.	105	22 9·4	−1·4	−2·1	109	21 57·6	−1·1	−1·5	94
	10	3501	5·3	D.D.	161	3 0·9	−0·5	−1·1	75	2 55·1	−0·5	−0·7	60
Nov.	3	3199	6·8	D.D.	105	18 18·2	−1·7	0·6	81	18 16·5	−1·4	0·8	73
	4	3326	6·4	D.D.	118	22 49·8	−1·1	−1·5	90	22 41·2	−0·9	−0·9	74
	6	3453	4·9	D.D.	129	N				0 8·5	G	G	125
	11	634	5·3	R.D.	197	18 19·9	G	G	197	18 33·0	0·6	2·2	212
	11	657	5·4	R.D.	198	21 11·0	−0·5	1·9	246	21 17·5	−0·5	1·7	258
	11	656	4·4	R.D.	198	21 12·4	−0·7	1·5	267	21 16·4	−0·7	1·3	279
Dec.	1	3287	5·9	D.D.	87	22 34·2	−0·1	0·6	25	22 40·2	G	G	360
	3	3501	5·3	D.D.	106	17 57·1	−1·5	1·1	71	17 58·2	−1·1	1·3	60
	5	89	6·5	D.D.	120	0 35·9	−0·4	−0·6	57	0 32·7	−0·5	−0·2	42

MEAN PLACES OF STARS, 1992·5

Name	Mag.	RA	Dec.	Spectrum
		h m	° ′	
α Andromedæ *Alpheratz*	2·1	0 08·0	+29 03	A0p
β Cassiopeiæ *Caph*	2·3	0 08·8	+59 06	F5
γ Pegasi *Algenib*	2·8	0 12·8	+15 09	B2
α Phœnicis	2·4	0 25·9	−42 21	K0
α Cassiopeiæ *Schedar*	2·2	0 40·1	+56 30	K0
β Ceti *Diphda*	2·0	0 43·2	−18 02	K0
γ Cassiopeiæ*	Var.	0 56·3	+60 41	B0p
β Andromedæ *Mirach*	2·1	1 09·3	+35 35	M0
δ Cassiopeiæ	2·7	1 25·3	+60 12	A5
α Eridani *Achernar*	0·5	1 37·4	−57 16	B5
β Arietis *Sheratan*	2·6	1 54·2	+20 46	A5
γ Andromedæ *Almak*	2·3	2 03·4	+42 18	K0
α Arietis *Hamal*	2·0	2 06·7	+23 26	K2
α Ursæ Minoris *Polaris*	2·0	2 23·8	+89 14	F8
β Persei *Algol**	Var.	3 07·7	+40 56	B8
α Persei *Mirfak*	1·8	3 23·8	+49 50	F5
η Tauri *Alcyone*	2·9	3 47·0	+24 05	B5p
α Tauri *Aldebaran*	0·9	4 35·5	+16 30	K5
β Orionis *Rigel*	0·1	5 14·2	− 8 13	B8p
α Aurigæ *Capella*	0·1	5 16·1	+45 59	G0
γ Orionis *Bellatrix*	1·6	5 24·7	+ 6 21	B2
β Tauri *Elnath*	1·7	5 25·8	+28 36	B8
δ Orionis	2·2	5 31·6	− 0 18	B0
α Leporis	2·6	5 32·4	−17 50	F0
ε Orionis	1·7	5 35·8	− 1 12	B0
ζ Orionis	1·8	5 40·4	− 1 57	B0
κ Orionis	2·1	5 47·4	− 9 40	B0
α Orionis *Betelgeuse**	Var.	5 54·8	+ 7 24	M0
β Aurigæ *Menkalinan*	1·9	5 59·0	+44 57	A0p
β Canis Majoris *Mirzam*	2·0	6 22·4	−17 57	B1
α Carinæ *Canopus*	−0·7	6 23·8	−52 41	F0
γ Geminorum *Alhena*	1·9	6 37·3	+16 24	A0
α Canis Majoris *Sirius*	−1·5	6 44·8	−16 42	A0
ε Canis Majoris	1·5	6 58·3	−28 58	B1
δ Canis Majoris	1·9	7 08·1	−26 23	F8p
α Geminorum *Castor*	1·6	7 34·1	+31 54	A0
α Canis Minoris *Procyon*	0·4	7 38·9	+ 5 15	F5
β Geminorum *Pollux*	1·1	7 44·9	+28 03	K0
ζ Puppis	2·3	8 03·3	−39 59	Od
γ Velorum	1·8	8 09·3	−47 19	Oap
ε Carinæ	1·9	8 22·4	−59 29	K0
δ Velorum	2·0	8 44·5	−54 41	A0
λ Velorum *Suhail*	2·2	9 07·7	−43 24	K5
β Carinæ	1·7	9 13·1	−69 41	A0
ι Carinæ	2·2	9 16·9	−59 15	F0
α Hydræ *Alphard*	2·0	9 27·2	− 8 38	K2
α Leonis *Regulus*	1·3	10 08·0	+12 00	B8
γ Leonis *Algeiba*	1·9	10 19·6	+19 53	K0
β Ursæ Majoris *Merak*	2·4	11 01·4	+56 25	A0
α Ursæ Majoris *Dubhe*	1·8	11 03·3	+61 47	K0

* γ Cassiopeiæ, 1991 mag. 2·5. β Persei, mag. 2·1 to 3·4.
  α Orionis, mag. 0·1 to 1·2.

The positions of heavenly bodies on the celestial sphere are defined by two co-ordinates, right ascension and declination, which are analogous to longitude and latitude on the surface of the Earth. If we imagine the plane of the terrestrial equator extended indefinitely, it will cut the celestial sphere in a great circle known as the celestial equator. Similarly the plane of the Earth's orbit, when extended, cuts in the great circle called the ecliptic. The two intersections of these circles are known as the First Point of Aries and the First Point of Libra. If from any star a perpendicular be drawn to the celestial equator, the length of this perpendicular is the star's declination. The arc, measured eastwards along the equator from the First Point of Aries to the foot of this perpendicular, is the right ascension. An alternative definition of right ascension is that it is the angle at the celestial pole (where the Earth's axis, if prolonged, would meet the sphere) between the great circles to the First Point of Aries and to the star.

The plane of the Earth's equator has a slow movement, so that our reference system for right ascension and declination is not fixed. The consequent alteration in these quantities from year to year is called precession. In right ascension it is an increase of about 3ˢ a year for equatorial stars, and larger or smaller changes in either direction for stars near the poles, depending on the right ascension of the star. In declination it varies between +20″ and −20″ according to the right ascension of the star.

A star or other body crosses the meridian when the sidereal time is equal to its right ascension. The altitude is then a maximum, and may be deduced by remembering that the altitude of the elevated pole is numerically equal to the latitude, while that of the equator at its intersection with the meridian is equal to the co-latitude, or complement of the latitude.

MEAN PLACES OF STARS, 1992·5

Name	Mag.	RA	Dec.	Spectrum
		h m	° ′	
δ Leonis	2·6	11 13·7	+20 34	A3
β Leonis *Denebola*	2·1	11 48·7	+14 37	A2
γ Ursæ Majoris *Phecda*	2·4	11 53·4	+53 44	A0
γ Corvi	2·6	12 15·4	−17 30	B8
α Crucis	1·0	12 26·2	−63 03	B1
γ Crucis	1·6	12 30·7	−57 04	M3
γ Centauri	2·2	12 41·1	−48 55	A0
γ Virginis	2·7	12 41·3	− 1 24	F0
β Crucis	1·3	12 47·3	−59 39	B1
ε Ursæ Majoris *Alioth*	1·8	12 53·7	+56 00	A0*p*
α Canum Venaticorum	2·9	12 55·7	+38 22	A0*p*
ζ Ursæ Majoris *Mizar*	2·1	13 23·6	+54 58	A2*p*
α Virginis *Spica*	1·0	13 24·8	−11 07	B2
η Ursæ Majoris *Alkaid*	1·9	13 47·2	+49 21	B3
β Centauri *Hadar*	0·6	14 03·3	−60 20	B1
θ Centauri	2·1	14 06·2	−36 20	K0
α Bootis *Arcturus*	0·0	14 15·3	+19 13	K0
α Centauri *Rigil Kent*	0·1	14 39·0	−60 48	G0
ε Bootis.....................	2·4	14 44·7	+27 06	K0
β Ursæ Minoris *Kochab*	2·1	14 50·7	+74 11	K5
α Coronæ Borealis *Alphecca* ..	2·2	15 34·4	+26 44	A0
δ Scorpii	2·3	15 59·9	−22 36	B0
β Scorpii	2·6	16 05·0	−19 47	B1
α Scorpii *Antares*	1·0	16 28·9	−26 25	M0
α Trianguli Australis.........	1·9	16 47·9	−69 01	K2
ε Scorpii	2·3	16 49·7	−34 17	K0
α Herculis*..................	Var.	17 14·3	+14 24	M3
λ Scorpii	1·6	17 33·1	−37 06	B2
α Ophiuchi *Rasalhague*	2·1	17 34·6	+12 34	A5
θ Scorpii	1·9	17 36·8	−43 00	F0
κ Scorpii	2·4	17 42·0	−39 02	B2
γ Draconis	2·2	17 56·4	+51 29	K5
ε Sagittarii *Kaus Australis* ...	1·9	18 23·7	−34 23	A0
α Lyræ *Vega*	0·0	18 36·7	+38 47	A0
σ Sagittarii..................	2·0	18 54·8	−26 18	B3
β Cygni *Albireo*..............	3·1	19 30·4	+27 57	K0
α Aquilæ *Altair*..............	0·8	19 50·4	+ 8 51	A5
α Capricorni	3·8	20 17·6	−12 34	G5
γ Cygni	2·2	20 22·0	+40 14	F8*p*
α Pavonis	1·9	20 25·1	−56 46	B3
α Cygni *Deneb*..............	1·3	20 41·2	+45 15	A2*p*
α Cephei *Alderamin*	2·4	21 18·4	+62 33	A5
ε Pegasi.....................	2·4	21 43·8	+ 9 50	K0
δ Capricorni	2·9	21 46·6	−16 10	A5
α Gruis	1·7	22 07·8	−47 00	B5
δ Cephei*...................	3·7	22 28·9	+58 23	*
β Gruis	2·1	22 42·2	−46 55	M3
α Piscis Austrini *Fomalhaut* ..	1·2	22 57·2	−29 40	A3
β Pegasi *Scheat*	2·4	23 03·4	+28 03	M0
α Pegasi *Markab*.............	2·5	23 04·4	+15 10	A0

* α Herculis, mag. 3·1 to 3·9.
  δ Cephei, mag. 3·7 to 4·4, Spectrum F5 to G0.

Thus in London (lat. 51° 30′) the meridian altitude of *Sirius* is found as follows:

	°	′
Altitude of equator	38	30
Declination south	16	42
Difference	21	48

The altitude of *Capella* (Dec. +45° 59′) at lower transit is:

	°	′
Altitude of pole	51	30
Polar distance of star	44	01
Difference	7	29

The brightness of a heavenly body is denoted by its magnitude. Omitting the exceptionally bright stars Sirius and Canopus, the twenty brightest stars are of the first magnitude, while the faintest stars visible to the naked eye are of the sixth magnitude. The magnitude scale is a precise one, as a difference of five magnitudes represents a ratio of 100 to 1 in brightness. Typical second magnitude stars are Polaris and the stars in the belt of Orion. The scale is most easily fixed in memory by comparing the stars with Norton's *Star Atlas* (see page 62). The stars Sirius and Canopus and the planets Venus and Jupiter are so bright that their magnitudes are expressed by negative numbers. A small telescope will show stars down to the ninth or tenth magnitude, while stars fainter than the twentieth magnitude may be photographed by long exposures with the largest telescopes.

Some of the astronomical information in this Almanack has been taken from *Astronomical Phenomena*, and is published here by arrangement with, and with the permission of, the Controller of HM Stationery Office.

ELEMENTS OF THE SOLAR SYSTEM

Orb	Mean distance from Sun		Sidereal period	Synodic period	Incl. of orbit to ecliptic	Diameter	Mass (Earth=1)	Period of rotation on axis
	(Earth=1)	km 10⁶						
			y d	days	° ′	km		d h m
Sun	...	...	...	...	...	1,392,000	332,948	25 09
Mercury	0·39	58	88	116	7 00	4,880	0·055	59
Venus	0·72	108	225	584	3 24	12,100	0·815	243
Earth	1·00	150	1 0	...	...	12,756eq	1·00	23 56
Mars	1·52	228	1 322	780	1 51	6,790	0·107	24 37
Jupiter	5·20	778	11 315	399	1 18	{ 142,800eq 134,200p	318	{ 9 50 9 56
Saturn	9·54	1427	29 167	378	2 29	{ 120,000eq 108,000p	95	{ 10 14 10 38
Uranus	19·19	2870	84 6	370	0 46	52,000	14·6	16–28
Neptune	30·07	4497	164 288	367	1 46	48,400	17·2	18–20
Pluto	39·46	5950	247 255	367	17 09	2,445	0·01	6 09

eq equatorial *p* polar

THE SATELLITES

Name	Star mag.	Mean distance from primary	Sidereal period of revolution	Name	Star mag.	Mean distance from primary	Sidereal period of revolution
		km	d	**Saturn**		km	d
Earth				Helene	18	377,000	2·737
Moon	—	384,400	27·322	Rhea	10	527,000	4·518
				Titan	8	1,222,000	15·945
Mars				Hyperion	14	1,481,000	21·277
Phobos	12	9,400	0·319	Iapetus	11	3,561,000	79·331
Deimos	13	23,500	1·262	Phoebe	16	12,954,000	550·4
Jupiter				**Uranus**			
XVI Metis	17	128,000	0·295	Cordelia	—	49,000	0·330
XV Adrastea	19	129,000	0·298	Ophelia	—	54,000	0·372
V Amalthea	14	181,000	0·498	Bianca	—	59,000	0·433
XIV Thebe	15	222,000	0·675	Cressida	—	62,000	0·463
I Io	5	422,000	1·769	Desdemona	—	63,000	0·475
II Europa	5	671,000	3·551	Juliet	—	64,000	0·493
III Ganymede	5	1,070,000	7·155	Portia	—	66,000	0·513
IV Callisto	6	1,880,000	16·689	Rosalind	—	70,000	0·558
XIII Leda	20	11,090,000	239	Belinda	—	75,000	0·622
VI Himalia	15	11,480,000	251	Puck	—	86,000	0·762
X Lysithea	18	11,720,000	259	Miranda	17	129,000	1·414
VII Elara	17	11,740,000	260	Ariel	14	191,000	2·520
XII Ananke	19	21,200,000	631	Umbriel	15	266,000	4·144
XI Carme	18	22,600,000	692	Titania	14	436,000	8·706
VIII Pasiphae	18	23,500,000	735	Oberon	14	583,000	13·463
IX Sinope	18	23,700,000	758				
				Neptune			
Saturn				(1989N6)	—	48,000	0·30
Atlas	18	138,000	0·602	(1989N5)	—	50,000	0·31
Prometheus	16	139,000	0·613	(1989N3)	—	52,000	0·33
Pandora	16	142,000	0·629	(1989N4)	—	62,000	0·40
Janus	14	151,000	0·695	(1989N2)	—	74,000	0·55
Epimetheus	15	151,000	0·694	(1989N1)	—	118,000	1·12
Mimas	13	186,000	0·942	Triton	14	355,000	5·877
Enceladus	12	238,000	1·370	Nereid	19	5,510,000	360·21
Tethys	10	295,000	1·888				
Telesto	19	295,000	1·888	**Pluto**			
Calypso	18	295,000	1·888	Charon	17	19,700	6·387
Dione	10	377,000	2·737				

THE EARTH

The shape of the Earth is that of an oblate spheroid or solid of revolution whose meridian sections are ellipses not differing much from circles, whilst the sections at right angles are circles. The length of the equatorial axis is about 12,756 kilometres, and that of the polar axis is 12,714 kilometres. The mean density of the Earth is 5·5 times that of water, although that of the surface layer is less. The Earth and Moon revolve about their common centre of gravity in a lunar month; this centre in turn revolves round the Sun in a plane known as the ecliptic, that passes through the Sun's centre. The Earth's equator is inclined to this plane at an angle of 23½°. This tilt is the cause of the seasons. In mid-latitudes, and when the Sun is high above the Equator, not only does the high noon altitude make the days longer, but the Sun's rays fall more directly on the Earth's surface; these effects combine to produce summer. In equatorial regions the noon altitude is large throughout the year, and there is little variation in the length of the day. In higher latitudes the noon altitude is lower, and the days in summer are appreciably longer than those in winter.

The average velocity of the Earth in its orbit is 30 kilometres a second. It makes a complete rotation on its axis in about 23^h 56^m of mean time, which is the sidereal day. Because of its annual revolution round the Sun, the rotation with respect to the Sun, or the solar day, is more than this by about four minutes (*see* p. 64). The extremity of the axis of rotation, or the North Pole of the Earth, is not rigidly fixed, but wanders over an area roughly 20 metres in diameter.

TERRESTRIAL MAGNETISM

A magnetic compass points along the horizontal component of a magnetic line of force. These directions converge on the 'magnetic dip-poles', the places where a freely suspended magnetized needle would become vertical. Not only do the positions of these poles change with time, but their exact locations are ill-defined, particularly as in the case of the north dip-pole where the lines of force on the north side of it, instead of converging radially, tend to bunch into a channel. Although it is therefore unrealistic to attempt to specify the locations of the dip-poles exactly, the present adopted positions are 78°·2 N., 103°·7W. and 64°·8 S., 138°·8 E. The two magnetic dip-poles are thus not antipodal, the line joining them passing the centre of the Earth at a distance of about 1,200 kilometres. The distances of the magnetic dip-poles from the north and south geographical poles are about 1,400 and 2,700 kilometres respectively.

There is also a 'magnetic equator', at all points of which the vertical component of the Earth's magnetic field is zero and a magnetized needle remains horizontal. This line runs between 2° and 10° north of the geographical equator in the eastern hemisphere, turns sharply south off the West African coast, and crosses South America through Brazil, Bolivia and Peru; it recrosses the geographical equator in mid-Pacific.

Reference has already been made to secular changes in the Earth's field. The following table indicates the changes in magnetic declination (or variation of the compass). Similar, though much smaller, changes have occurred in 'dip' or magnetic inclination. Secular changes differ throughout the world. Although the London observations strongly suggest a cycle with a period of several hundred years, an exact repetition is unlikely.

London			Greenwich		
1580	11°	15′ E.	1850	22°	24′ W.
1622	5	56 E.	1900	16	29 W.
1665	1	22 W.	1925	13	10 W.
1730	13	00 W.	1950	9	07 W.
1773	21	09 W.	1975	6	39 W.

In order that up-to-date information on the variation of the compass may be available, many governments publish magnetic charts on which there are lines (isogonic lines) passing through all places at which specified values of declination will be found at the date of the chart.

In the British Isles, isogonic lines now run approximately north-east to south-west. Though there are considerable local deviations due to geological causes, a rough value of magnetic declination may be obtained by assuming that at 50° N. on the meridian of Greenwich, the value in 1992 is 3° 58′ west and allowing an increase of 10′ for each degree of latitude northwards and one of 24′ for each degree of longitude westwards. For example, at 53° N., 5° W., declination will be about 3° 58′ + 30′ + 120′, i.e. 6° 28′ west. The average annual change at the present time is about 8′ decrease.

The number of magnetic observatories is about 200, widely scattered over the globe. There are three in Great Britain run by the British Geological Survey: at Hartland, North Devon; at Eskdalemuir, Dumfriesshire; and at Lerwick, Shetland Islands. The following are some recent annual mean values of the magnetic elements for Hartland.

Year	Declination West	Dip or inclination	Horizontal force	Vertical force
	° ′	° ′	oersted	oersted
1950	11 06	66 54	0·1848	0·4334
1955	10 30	66 49	0·1859	0·4340
1960	9 59	66 44	0·1871	0·4350
1965	9 30	66 34	0·1887	0·4354
1970	9 06	66 26	0·1903	0·4364
1975	8 32	66 17	0·1921	0·4373
1980	7 44	66 10	0·1933	0·4377
1985	6 56	66 08	0·1938	0·4380
1990	6 15	66 10	0·1939	0·4388

The normal world-wide terrestrial magnetic field corresponds approximately to that of a very strong small bar magnet near the centre of the Earth but with appreciable smooth spatial departures. The origin and slow secular change of the normal field are not yet fully understood but are generally ascribed to electric currents associated with fluid motions in the Earth's core. Superimposed on the normal field are local and regional anomalies whose magnitudes may in places exceed that of the normal field; these are due to the influence of mineral deposits in the Earth's crust. A small proportion of the field is of external origin, mostly associated with electric currents in the ionosphere. The configuration of the external field and the ionization of the atmosphere depend on the incident particle and radiation flux. There are, therefore, short-term and non-periodic as well as diurnal, 27-day, seasonal and 11-year periodic changes in the magnetic field, dependent upon the position of the Sun and the degree of solar activity.

Magnetic Storms

Occasionally, sometimes with great suddenness, the Earth's magnetic field is subject for several hours to marked disturbance. In extreme cases, departures in field intensity of as much as one tenth the normal value are experienced. In many instances, such disturbances are accompanied by widespread displays of aurorae, marked changes in the incidence of cosmic rays, an increase in the reception of 'noise' from the Sun at radio frequencies together with rapid changes in the ionosphere and induced electric currents within the Earth which adversely affect radio and telegraphic communications. The disturbances are generally ascribed to changes in the stream of neutral and ionized particles which emanates from the Sun and through which the Earth is continuously passing. Some of these changes are associated with visible eruptions on the Sun, usually in the region of sunspots. There is a marked tendency for disturbances to recur after intervals of about 27 days, the apparent period of rotation of the Sun on its axis, which is consistent with the sources being located on particular areas of the Sun.

ARTIFICIAL SATELLITES

Orbits

To consider the orbit of an artificial satellite it is best to imagine that one is looking at the Earth from a distant point in space. The Earth would then be seen to be rotating about its axis inside the orbit described by the rapidly revolving satellite. The inclination of a satellite orbit to the Earth's equator (which generally remains almost constant throughout the satellite's lifetime) gives at once the maximum range of latitudes over which the satellite passes. Thus a satellite whose orbit has an inclination of 53° will pass overhead all latitudes between S. 53° and N. 53°, but would never be seen in the zenith of any place nearer the poles than these latitudes. If we consider a particular place on the earth, whose latitude is less than the inclination of the satellite's orbit then the Earth's rotation carries this place first under the northbound part of the orbit and then under the southbound portion of the orbit, these two occurrences being always less than 12 hours apart for satellites moving in direct orbits (i.e. to the east). (For satellites in retrograde orbits the words 'northbound' and 'southbound' should be interchanged in the preceding statement.) As the value of the latitude of the observer increases and approaches the value of the inclination of the orbit, so this interval gets shorter until (when the latitude is equal to the inclination) only one overhead passage occurs each day.

Observation of satellites

The regression of the orbit around the Earth causes alternate periods of visibility and invisibility, though this is of little concern to the radio or radar observer. To the visual observer the following cycle of events normally occurs (though the cycle may start in any position): invisibility, morning observations before dawn, invisibility, evening observations after dusk, invisibility, morning observations before dawn, and so on. With reasonably high satellites and for observers in high latitudes around the summer solstice the evening observations follow the morning observations without interruption as sunlight passing over the polar regions can still illuminate satellites which are passing over temperate latitudes at local midnight. At the moment all satellites rely on sunlight to make them visible though a satellite with a flashing light has been suggested for a future launching. The observer must be in darkness or twilight in order to make any useful observations and the durations of twilight and the sunrise, sunset times given on Page Two of each month will be a useful guide.

Some of the satellites are visible to the naked eye and much interest has been aroused by the spectacle of a bright satellite disappearing into the Earth's shadow. The event is even more fascinating telescopically as the disappearance occurs gradually as the satellite traverses the Earth's penumbral shadow, and during the last few seconds before the eclipse is complete the satellite may change colour (under suitable atmospheric conditions) from yellow to red. This is because the last rays of sunlight are refracted through the denser layers of our atmosphere before striking the satellite.

Some satellites rotate about one or more axes so that a periodic variation in brightness is observed. This was particularly noticeable in several of the USSR satellites.

Satellite research has provided some interesting results. Among them may be mentioned a revised value of the Earth's oblateness, 1/298·2, and the discovery of the Van Allen radiation belts.

Launchings

Apart from their names, e.g. Cosmos 6 Rocket, the satellites are also classified according to their date of launch. Thus 1961 α refers to the first satellite launching of 1961. A number following the Greek letter indicated the relative brightness of the satellites put in orbit. From the beginning of 1963 the Greek letters were replaced by numbers and the numbers by roman letters e.g. 1963–01A. For all satellites successfully injected into orbit the table gives the designation and names of the main objects (in the order A, B, C . . . etc.), the launch date and some initial orbital data. These are the inclination to the equator (i), the nodal period of revolution (P), the eccentricity (e), and the perigee height.

Artificial Satellites Launched in 1989–1990

Desig-nation	Satellite	Launch date	i	P	e	Perigee height (km)
1989–		1989	°	m		
76	Cosmos 2045, rocket, engine	September 22	70·0	89·6	0·007	207
77	Fleetsatcom 8, rocket	September 25	5·1	1413·5	0·014	34765
78	Molniya 1-76, launcher rocket, launcher, rocket	September 27	62·8	702·1	0·733	618
79	Cosmos 2046, rocket	September 27	65·0	88·8	0·015	115
80	Intercosmos 24, Magion 2, rocket	September 28	82·6	116·0	0·126	507
81	Gorizont 19, launcher	September 28	1·4	1434·7	0·003	35647
82	Cosmos 2047, rocket	October 3	67·1	89·5	0·012	167
83	Cosmos 2048, rocket, engine	October 17	62·8	89·5	0·001	244
84	STS 34	October 18	343	90·7	0·003	299
85	Navstar 2-04, rocket	October 21	54·8	723·2	0·006	20162
86	Meteor 3-03, rocket	October 24	82·6	109·5	0·002	1188
87	Intelsat 6F-2	October 27	0·1	1435·6	0·002	35714
88	Cosmos 2049, rocket	November 17	64·8	89·8	0·004	236
89	COBE	November 18	99·0	102·9	0·001	888
90	STS 33	November 23	28·5	92·3	0·024	237
91	Cosmos 2050, launcher rocket, launcher, rocket	November 23	63·0	717·8	0·737	596
92	Cosmos 2051	November 24	64·9	92·8	0·006	369
93	Kvant 2	November 26	51·6	89·8	0·008	215
94	Molniya 3-36, rocket, launcher rocket, launcher	November 28	62·8	735·6	0·740	633
95	Cosmos 2052, rocket	November 30	67·1	89·6	0·013	163
96	Granat	December 1	52·1	5903·0	0·923	1957
97	Navstar 2-05, rocket	December 11	55·0	726·1	0·006	20211
98	Raduga 25, launcher	December 15	1·5	1475·2	0·001	36511
99	Progress-M2, rocket	December 20	51·6	91·1	0·009	271
100	Cosmos 2053, rocket	December 27	73·5	95·2	0·001	518
101	Cosmos 2054, launcher	December 27	1·5	1469·5	0·002	36374
1990–		1990				
01	Skynet 4A, JC Sat 2, rocket, rocket	January 1	3·4	1380·3	0·025	33676
02	STS 32, Leasat 5, rocket	January 9	28·5	90·8	0·005	293
03	Cosmos 2055, rocket, engine	January 17	62·8	89·6	0·001	249
04	Cosmos 2056, rocket	January 18	74·0	100·8	0·002	776
05	Spot 2, UOSAT 3, UOSAT 4, Pacsat, Dove, Webersat, LUsat	January 22	98·7	100·9	0·001	789
06	Molniya 3-37, launcher rocket, rocket, launcher	January 23	62·8	717·6	0·737	598
07	Hiten	January 24	29·7	17861	0·952	4893
08	Navstar 2-06, rocket	January 24	54·6	713·6	0·004	19975
09	Cosmos 2057, rocket	January 25	62·8	89·7	0·012	179
10	Cosmos 2058, rocket	January 30	82·5	97·8	0·002	634
11	China 26, rocket	February 4	0·1	1435·9	0·000	35782
12	Cosmos 2059, rocket	February 6	65·9	109·9	0·137	179
13	Momo 1b, Orizuru, Fuji 2	February 7	99·1	103·4	0·001	911
14	Soyuz TM9, rocket	February 11	51·6	90·7	0·003	290
15	LACE, RME	February 14	43·1	95·3	0·001	531
16	Raduga 26, launcher	February 15	1·5	1436·0	0·000	35766
17	Nadezhda 2, rocket	February 27	83·0	104·9	0·004	956
18	Okean 2, rocket	February 28	82·5	97·8	0·002	639
19	STS 36, USA 53	February 28	62·0	89·5	0·001	243
20	Progress-M3, rocket	February 28	51·6	90·5	0·004	277
21	Intelsat 6 F-3	March 14	28·3	92·1	0·002	376
22	Cosmos 2060, rocket	March 14	65·0	92·8	0·001	404
23	Cosmos 2061, rocket	March 20	82·9	105·1	0·003	973
24	Cosmos 2062, rocket	March 22	82·3	90·7	0·010	241
25	Navstar 2-07, rocket	March 26	37·5	354·0	0·605	168

Artificial Satellites Launched in 1989–1990—(*cont.*)

Desig-nation	Satellite	Launch date	i	P	e	Perigee height (km)
1990–		1990	°	m		
26	Cosmos 2063, launcher rocket, launcher, rocket	March 27	62·8	717·6	0·737	608
27	Offeq 2, rocket	April 3	143·2	102·7	0·095	207
28	Pegsat, USA 55	April 5	94·1	96·5	0·013	495
29	Cosmos 2064-2071, rocket	April 6	74·0	115·5	0·002	1463
30	Asia Sat 1, rocket	April 7	0·1	1436·6	0·000	35786
31	POGS+SSR, TEX, SCE	April 11				
32	Foton 3, rocket, engine	April 11	62·8	90·4	0·012	216
33	Cosmos 2072, rocket	April 13	64·8	89·8	0·004	241
34	Palapa 6, rocket	April 13	0·0	1436·0	0·003	35680
35	Cosmos 2073, rocket, engine	April 17	82·4	89·9	0·005	232
36	Cosmos 2074, rocket	April 20	82·9	104·9	0·003	967
37	STS 31, Hubble	April 24	28·5	96·8	0·001	613
38	Cosmos 2075, rocket	April 25	74·0	94·6	0·002	484
39	Molniya 1-77, launcher rocket, launcher, rocket	April 26	62·8	736·4	0·741	612
40	Cosmos 2076, launcher rocket, launcher, rocket	April 28	63·0	708·4	0·736	571
41	Progress 42, rocket	May 5	51·6	91·7	0·006	324
42	Cosmos 2077, rocket	May 7	62·8	90·0	0·015	174
43	Macsat 1, Macsat 2	May 9	89·9	98·6	0·011	613
44	Cosmos 2078, rocket	May 15	70·0	89·4	0·005	212
45	Cosmos 2079-2081	May 19	64·9	664·6	0·011	18565
46	Cosmos 2082, rocket	May 22	71·0	102·0	0·000	849
47	Resurs-F6, rocket	May 29	82·3	89·9	0·001	259
48	Kristall	May 31	51·6	90·1	0·011	213
49	Rosat	June 1	53·0	96·1	0·001	565
50	USA 59	June 8	60·9	93·5	0·000	448
51	Insat ID	June 12	27·3	91·0	0·011	256
52	Molniya 3-38, launcher rocket, launcher, rocket	June 13	62·8	717·7	0·742	464
53	Cosmos 2083, rocket, engine	June 19	82·6	91·7	0·009	297
54	Gorizont 20, launcher	June 20	1·5	1436·2	0·002	35718
55	Cosmos 2084, launcher rocket, launcher, rocket	June 21	62·8	98·2	0·012	585
56	Intelsat 6 F-4	June 23	0·4	1436·0	0·002	35689
57	Meteor 2-19, rocket	June 27	82·5	104·1	0·002	940
58	Gamma, rocket	July 11	51·6	93·0	0·001	417
59	Badr-1, rocket	July 16	28·5	96·4	0·056	204
60	Resurs-F7, rocket	July 17	82·3	89·9	0·001	261
61	Cosmos 2085, launcher	July 18	1·5	1436·5	0·001	35775
62	Cosmos 2086, rocket	July 20	82·3	89·6	0·002	236
63	TDF 2, DFS 2	July 24	0·1	1436·4	0·000	35781
64	Cosmos 2087, launcher rocket, launcher, rocket	July 25	62·9	718·0	0·737	615
65	CRRES	July 25	18·1	591·2	0·713	334
66	Cosmos 2088, rocket	July 30	73·6	116·1	0·003	1483
67	Soyuz TM10, rocket	August 1	51·6	91·3	0·004	312
68	Navstar 2-08, rocket	August 2	54·7	718·0	0·009	19932
69	Cosmos 2089, rocket	August 3	62·8	89·0	0·007	182
70	Cosmos 2090-2095, rocket	August 8	82·6	113·9	0·002	1391
71	Molniya 1-78, launcher rocket, launcher, rocket	August 10	62·9	717·8	0·735	647
72	Progress-M4, rocket	August 15	51·6	89·6	0·001	251
73	Resurs-F8, rocket, engine	August 16	82·3	89·9	0·001	258
74	Marcopolo 2	August 18	0·4	1436·0	0·002	35716
75	Cosmos 2096, rocket	August 23	65·0	92·8	0·001	403

TIDAL DATA

CONSTANTS

The time of high water at the undermentioned ports and places may be approximately found by taking the appropriate time of high water at the standard port (as shown on pp. 83, 84, etc.) and adding thereto the differences shown below. The columns headed 'Springs' and 'Neaps' show the height, in metres, of the tide above datum for mean high water springs and mean high water neaps respectively.

EXAMPLE.—Required times of high water at Stranraer on *January* 1, 1992:—

(a) *Morning Tide.*

Appropriate time of high
water at *Greenock* .... 0946 hrs. (*Jan.* 1)
Tidal difference .... − 0020 hrs.

High water at *Stranraer* 0926 hrs.

(b) *Afternoon Tide.*

Appropriate time of high
water at *Greenock* .... 2157 hrs. (*Jan* 1).
Tidal difference .... − 0020 hrs.

High water at *Stranraer* 2137 hrs.

Port	Diff.	Springs	Neaps
	h m	m	m
Aberdeen .... *Leith*	−1 19	4·3	3·4
Aberdovey ..... *Liverpool*	−3 00	5·0	3·5
Aberystwyth .. *Liverpool*	−3 30	5·0	3·5
Aldeburgh ...... *London*	−3 05	2·8	2·7
Alloa .... *Leith*	+0 47	5·6	4·2
Amlwch .... *Liverpool*	−0 33	7·3	5·8
Anstruther Easter . *Leith*	−0 22	5·5	4·4
Antwerp (Prosper-			
polder) .... *London*	+0 50	5·8	4·8
Appledore ... *Avonmouth*	−1 15	7·5	5·2
Arbroath .... *Leith*	−0 33	5·0	4·1
Ardrossan ..... *Greenock*	−0 15	3·2	2·7
†Arundel .... *London*	−2 03	3·1	2·2
Avonmouth .... *A'mouth*	0 00	13·2	10·0
Ayr .... *Greenock*	−0 25	3·0	2·6
Baie de Lampaul . *London*	+2 30	7·5	5·8
Ballycotton .. *Avonmouth*	−1 43	4·2	3·3
Banff............. *Leith*	−2 44	3·5	2·8
Bantry .... *Liverpool*	+5 59	3·5	2·6
Bardsey Island . *Liverpool*	−3 18	4·5	3·3
Barmouth .... *Liverpool*	−2 57	5·0	3·5
Barnstaple .. *Avonmouth*	−1 00	4·1	1·4
Barrow (Docks) *Liverpool*	+0 15	9·1	7·1
Barry ...... *Avonmouth*	−0 22	11·4	8·7
Belfast .... *London*	−2 45	3·5	3·0
Berwick........... *Leith*	−0 02	4·7	3·8
Bideford..... *Avonmouth*	−1 15	5·9	3·6
Blackpool .... *Liverpool*	−0 10	8·9	7·0
Blacktoft .... *Hull*	+0 31	5·8	4·0
Blakeney .... *Hull*	+0 44	3·4	2·0
Blyth .... *Leith*	+0 50	5·0	3·9
Boscastle .... *Avonmouth*	−1 20	7·3	5·6
Boulogne .... *London*	−2 44	8·9	7·2
Bovisand Pier... *London*	+3 55	5·3	4·3
Bowling .... *Greenock*	+0 15	4·0	3·4
Braye .... *London*	+5 33	6·3	4·7
Brest.......... *London*	+2 28	7·5	5·9
Bridgwater .. *Avonmouth*	−0 22	4·6	1·9
Bridlington....... *Leith*	+2 03	6·1	4·7
Bridport (W. Bay) *London*	+4 37	4·1	3·0
Brighton .... *London*	−2 50	6·5	5·1
Buckie .... *Leith*	−2 56	4·1	3·2
Bude Haven . *Avonmouth*	−1 33	7·7	5·8
Bull Sand Fort ..... *Hull*	−0 46	6·9	5·5
Burntisland .... *Leith*	0 00	5·6	4·5

Port	Diff.	Springs	Neaps
	h m	m	m
Calais .... *London*	−2 14	7·1	5·9
Campbeltown .. *Greenock*	+0 07	2·9	2·6
Cape Cornwall .. *A'mouth*	−2 30	6·0	4·3
Cardiff (Penarth)			
Avonmouth	−0 15	12·2	9·4
Cardigan Port . *Liverpool*	−3 37	4·7	3·4
Carmarthen . *Avonmouth*	−0 48	2·6	0·4
Cayeux.......... *London*	−2 55	10·2	7·9
Chatham .... *London*	−1 05	6·0	4·9
Chepstow.... *Avonmouth*	+0 20	No data	
Cherbourg...... *London*	−6 00	6·3	5·0
Chester ...... *Liverpool*	+1 05	4·0	2·0
Chichester Hbr. . *London*	−2 25	4·9	4·0
*Christchurch Hbr. *L'don*	−4 53	1·8	1·4
Cobh .... *Liverpool*	−5 55	4·2	3·2
Coulport ...... *Greenock*	−0 05	3·4	2·9
Coverack .... *Avonmouth*	−2 02	5·3	4·2
Cowes........... *London*	−2 23	4·0	3·5
Cromarty.......... *Leith*	−2 56	4·3	3·4
Cromer.......... *Hull*	+0 19	5·2	4·1
Dartmouth ..... *London*	+4 25	4·9	3·8
Deal .... *London*	−2 37	6·1	5·0
Dieppe .... *London*	−3 03	9·3	7·2
Dingle Hbr..... *Liverpool*	+5 38	3·9	2·9
Donegal Hbr. .. *Liverpool*	−5 24	3·9	3·0
Douglas (IOM) . *Liverpool*	−0 04	6·9	5·4
Dover .... *London*	−2 52	6·7	5·3
Duclair.......... *London*	−1 48	7·5	6·3
Duddon Bar ... *Liverpool*	+0 03	8·5	6·6
Dunbar .... *Leith*	−0 07	5·2	4·2
Dundalk (Sldr's Pt) *L'pool*	+0 22	5·1	4·2
Dundee .... *Leith*	+0 11	5·4	4·3
Dungeness...... *London*	−3 04	7·7	5·9
Dunkirk .... *London*	−1 54	5·8	4·8
Eastbourne ..... *London*	−2 50	7·3	5·6
East Loch Tarbert *G'nock*	+0 05	3·4	2·9
Exmouth Dock .. *London*	+4 55	4·0	2·8
Eyemouth .... *Leith*	−0 20	4·7	3·7
Falmouth ...... *Avonmouth*	+3 35	5·3	4·2
Ferryside.... *Avonmouth*	−0 58	6·7	4·5
Filey Bay........ *Leith*	+1 50	5·8	4·9
Fishguard ..... *Liverpool*	−4 01	4·8	3·4
Folkestone ..... *London*	−3 04	7·1	5·7
Formby .... *Liverpool*	−0 12	9·0	7·3
Fowey .... *London*	+3 53	5·4	4·3
Fraserburgh .... *Leith*	−2 29	3·7	2·9
*Freshwater Bay *London*	−4 33	2·6	2·3
Galway .... *Liverpool*	−6 08	5·1	3·9
Glasgow ...... *Greenock*	+0 28	4·7	4·1
Goole .... *Hull*	+0 59	5·7	3·7
Gorleston .... *London*	−5 00	2·4	2·0
Granton .... *Leith*	0 00	5·6	4·5
Granville .... *London*	+4 32	13·0	9·8
Grimsby.......... *Hull*	−0 28	7·0	5·6
Hartlepool......... *Leith*	+0 58	5·4	4·2
Harwich ...... *London*	−2 02	4·0	3·4
Hastings .... *London*	−2 57	7·5	5·8
Haverfordwest . *Liverpool*	−4 50	2·2	0·3
Hestan Islet ... *Liverpool*	+0 25	8·3	6·3
Holyhead ..... *Liverpool*	−0 48	5·7	4·5
Hook of Holland . *London*	−0 01	2·1	1·7
*Hurst Point ... *London*	−3 38	2·7	2·3
Ijmuiden .... *London*	+1 04	2·0	1·7
Ilfracombe.. *Avonmouth*	−1 10	9·2	6·9
Inveraray .... *Greenock*	+0 11	3·3	3·0
Invergordon ...... *Leith*	−2 49	4·4	3·5
Ipswich .... *London*	−1 42	4·2	3·4
Itchenor .... *London*	−2 23	4·8	3·8
Kinsale .... *Liverpool*	−6 03	4·1	3·2
Kirkcudbright . *Liverpool*	+0 15	7·5	5·9

† very approximate.   * 1st high water springs only.

Port	Diff. h m	Springs m	Neaps m
Kirkwall .... Leith	−4 15	2·9	2·2
Knights Town . Liverpool	+5 36	3·9	3·0
Lamlash...... Greenock	−0 26	3·2	2·7
Le Havre .... London	−3 55	7·9	6·6
Lerwick .... Leith	−3 49	2·2	1·6
Limerick Dock . Liverpool	−4 27	6·1	4·6
Littlehampton .. London	−2 38	5·8	4·6
Lizard Point . Avonmouth	−2 17	5·3	4·2
Llanddwyn Island L'pool	−1 53	5·0	4·0
Llanelli ..... Avonmouth	−0 56	7·8	5·8
Loch Moidart .. Greenock	+6 00	4·8	3·5
Londonderry .. London	−5 37	2·7	2·1
Looe .... London	+3 55	5·4	4·2
Lossiemouth ...... Leith	−3 01	4·1	3·2
Lowestoft .... London	−4 25	2·4	2·1
Lulworth Cove.. London	+5 00	2·3	1·5
Lundy Island Avonmouth	−1 23	8·0	5·9
Lyme Regis ..... London	+4 55	4·3	3·1
*Lymington .... London	−3 33	3·0	2·6
Margate .... London	−1 52	4·8	3·9
Maryport....... Liverpool	+0 24	8·6	6·6
Menai Bridge . Liverpool	−0 28	7·4	5·9
Mevagissey ..... London	+3 53	5·4	4·3
Middlesbrough ..... Leith	+1 09	5·6	4·5
Milford Haven . Liverpool	−5 07	7·0	5·2
Minehead ...Avonmouth	−0 40	10·6	8·1
Montrose........... Leith	−0 19	4·8	3·9
Morecambe .... Liverpool	+0 07	9·5	7·4
Mostyn Quay .. Liverpool	−0 17	8·5	6·7
Newburgh......... Leith	+0 48	4·1	3·0
Newcastle on Tyne . Leith	+0 54	5·3	4·1
Newhaven...... London	−2 48	6·6	5·2
Newlyn ..... Avonmouth	−2 24	5·6	4·4
Newport(Gwent) A'mouth	−0 15	12·1	9·0
Newquay .. Avonmouth	−1 58	7·0	5·3
New Quay, Cardigan Bay .... Liverpool	−3 30	4·9	3·4
North Shields ...... Leith	+0 51	5·0	3·9
North Sunderland .. Leith	+0 05	4·8	3·7
N. Woolwich.... London	−0 20	7·0	5·7
Oban.......... Greenock	+5 45	4·0	2·9
Old Lynn Road..... Hull	+0 05	7·3	5·8
Orfordness ..... London	−2 50	2·8	2·7
Ostend .... London	−1 32	5·0	4·2
Padstow...... Avonmouth	−1 45	7·3	5·6
Peel (IOM)..... Liverpool	−0 02	5·3	4·2
Peterhead .... Leith	−1 59	3·8	3·1
Plymouth .... London	+4 05	5·5	4·4
*Poole (Entrance) London	−5 03	2·0	1·6
Porlock Bay . Avonmouth	−0 50	10·2	7·8
Porthcawl ...Avonmouth	−0 53	9·9	7·5
Portmadoc..... Liverpool	−2 45	5·1	3·4
Portland ... London	+5 10	2·1	1·4
Portpatrick.... Liverpool	+0 22	3·8	3·0
Portsmouth..... London	−2 23	4·7	3·8
Port Talbot ..Avonmouth	−0 53	9·6	7·3
Preston ...... Liverpool	+0 10	5·3	3·3
Pwllheli .... Liverpool	−3 07	5·0	3·4
Ramsey (IOM) Liverpool	+0 04	7·2	5·7
Ramsgate....... London	−2 32	4·9	3·8
†Rosslare Hbr. . Liverpool	−5 23	1·9	1·4
Rosyth .... Leith	+0 07	5·8	4·7
Ryde .... London	−2 23	4·5	3·7
St Helier .... London	+4 48	11·1	8·1
St Ives ..... Avonmouth	−1 55	6·6	4·9
St Malo .... London	+4 28	12·2	9·2
St Peter Port.... London	+4 54	9·0	6·7

Port	Diff. h m	Springs m	Neaps m
Salcombe .... London	+4 10	5·3	4·1
Saltash......... London	+4 10	5·6	4·5
Scarborough....... Leith	+1 33	5·7	4·6
Scheveningen... London	+0 24	2·1	1·7
Scrabster.......... Leith	+6 04	5·0	3·7
Seaham .... Leith	+0 53	5·2	4·1
Selsey Bill ...... London	−2 28	5·3	4·4
Sennen Cove . Avonmouth	−2 30	6·1	4·8
Sharpness Dock .A'mouth	+0 42	9·3	5·8
Sheerness ...... London	−1 16	5·7	4·8
Shoreham ...... London	−2 43	6·2	5·0
Silloth .... Liverpool	+0 35	9·2	7·1
Southampton (1st high water) .... London	−2 52	4·5	3·7
Southend .... London	−1 22	5·7	4·8
Southwold...... London	−3 50	2·5	2·2
Stirling .... Leith	+1 13	2·9	1·6
Stonehaven........ Leith	−1 09	4·5	3·6
Stornoway .... Liverpool	−4 15	4·8	3·7
Stranraer ..... Greenock	−0 20	3·0	2·5
Stromness .... Leith	−5 31	3·6	2·7
Sunderland........ Leith	+0 51	5·2	4·2
*Swanage ...... London	−5 13	2·0	1·6
Swansea.... Avonmouth	−0 49	9·6	7·3
Tarn Point .... Liverpool	+0 05	8·3	6·4
Tay River (Bar) .... Leith	−0 19	5·2	4·2
Tees R. (Ent.) ...... Leith	+1 08	5·5	4·3
Teignmouth ... London	+4 37	4·8	3·6
Tenby .... Avonmouth	−1 05	8·4	6·3
Tilbury.......... London	−0 49	6·4	5·3
Tobermory .... Liverpool	−5 12	4·4	3·3
Torquay....... London	+4 40	4·9	3·7
*Totland Bay ... London	−3 53	2·7	2·3
Troon .... Greenock	−0 25	3·2	2·7
Truro .... London	+3 43	5·3	4·2
Walton-on-Naze.. London	−2 10	4·2	3·4
Waterford .... Liverpool	−4 54	4·6	3·6
Weston S. Mare .A'mouth	+0 25	12·0	9·0
†Wexford Hbr .. Liverpool	−5 03	1·7	1·4
Whitby............ Leith	+1 30	5·6	4·3
Whitehaven ...Liverpool	+0 10	8·0	6·3
Wick.............. Leith	−3 26	3·5	2·8
Wisbech Cut .... Hull	+0 01	7·0	5·1
Workington ... Liverpool	+0 20	8·2	6·4
Worthing ...... London	−2 38	6·1	4·8
*Yarmouth (IOW) London	−3 28	3·1	2·5
Youghal....... Liverpool	−5 49	4·0	3·1

† very approximate.   * 1st high water springs only.

Tidal data is no longer available for a number of places which formerly appeared in the list above. These places (with the name of the substitute now recorded) are: *Devonport* (Plymouth); *Loch Long* (Coulport); *Pembroke Dock* (Milford Haven); *Penzance* (Newlyn); *Plymouth Breakwater* (Bovisand Pier); *St Annes* (Blackpool); *Spurn Head* (Bull Sand Fort); *Ushant* (Baie de Lampaul); *Valentia Harbour* (Knights Town); *Woolwich* (N. Woolwich); *Yarmouth Roads* (Gorleston).

Tidal predictions (pp. 83–94) for London Bridge, Liverpool, Avonmouth, Hull, Dún Laoghaire and Leith are computed by the Proudman Oceanographic Laboratory, copyright reserved. Those for Greenock have been supplied by the Hydrographer of the Navy and are Crown copyright.

JANUARY, 1992

High water at the undermentioned places (GMT*)—

Day of Month	Day of Week	London Bridge †3·20 m below Mn.	Ht.	Aft.	Ht.	Liverpool †4·93 m below Mn.	Ht.	Aft.	Ht.	Avonmouth †6·50 m below Mn.	Ht.	Aft.	Ht.	Hull (Albert Dock) †3·90 m below Mn.	Ht.	Aft.	Ht.	Greenock †1·62 m below Mn.	Ht.	Aft.	Ht.	Leith †2·90 m below Mn.	Ht.	Aft.	Ht.	Dun Laoghaire ‡0·20 m above Mn.	Ht.	Aft.	Ht.
1	W	1105	6·2	2339	6·4	0830	7·9	2058	8·0	0407	10·7	1638	10·8	0317	6·3	1555	6·4	0946	3·1	2157	3·0			1200	4·7	0901	3·7	2126	3·7
2	Th		6·5	1208	6·3	0924	8·3	2150	8·2	0511	11·2	1737	11·3	0421	6·5	1647	6·6	1042	3·2	2258	3·0	0035	4·9	1254	4·9	0948	3·8	2214	3·8
3	F	0034	6·6	1259	6·5	1010	8·6	2235	8·5	0603	11·7	1827	11·7	0515	6·5	1732	6·7	1129	3·3	2348	3·0	0128	5·0	1341	5·0	1029	4·0	2253	3·8
4	Sa	0117	6·7	1341	6·6	1051	8·8	2313	8·6	0648	12·1	1910	12·1	0601	6·6	1810	6·9	1211	3·4			0213	5·0	1420	5·1	1106	4·1	2331	3·8
5	Su	0155	6·7	1420	6·7	1127	9·0	2349	8·7	0728	12·4	1947	12·1	0639	6·6	1843	7·0	0030	3·0	1249	3·4	0250	5·2	1452	5·2	1141	4·1		
6	M	0230	6·8	1456	6·8			1201	9·1	0804	12·5	2020	12·2	0713	6·8	1913	7·1	0107	3·0	1323	3·4	0324	5·1	1522	5·3	0006	3·8	1216	4·1
7	Tu	0303	6·8	1529	6·9	0021	8·7	1235	9·1	0834	12·5	2050	12·3	0744	6·8	1942	7·2	0140	3·1	1355	3·4	0358	5·1	1552	5·3	0040	3·7	1250	4·1
8	W	0335	6·9	1603	6·9	0052	8·7	1307	9·0	0904	12·3	2119	12·0	0813	6·8	2015	7·3	0212	3·1	1427	3·4	0430	5·1	1622	5·2	0114	3·7	1325	4·0
9	Th	0407	6·9	1637	6·8	0124	8·6	1340	8·9	0935	12·3	2150	12·0	0844	6·8	2049	7·3	0245	3·2	1459	3·4	0505	5·1	1658	5·1	0149	3·6	1400	3·9
10	F	0440	6·7	1711	6·7	0157	8·4	1412	8·7	1007	12·0	2223	11·7	0919	6·7	2125	7·1	0320	3·2	1534	3·3	0545	4·9	1735	5·1	0225	3·5	1440	3·8
11	Sa	0512	6·6	1744	6·5	0229	8·2	1447	8·5	1041	11·6	2255	11·3	0956	6·5	2203	6·8	0359	3·2	1611	3·3	0626	4·8	1820	4·9	0307	3·5	1514	3·6
12	Su	0544	6·4	1821	6·2	0307	8·0	1529	8·2	1115	11·2	2330	10·8	1035	6·3	2247	6·5	0441	3·1	1653	3·1	0713	4·6	1913	4·8	0354	3·3	1614	3·5
13	M	0622	6·2	1906	6·0	0353	7·8	1620	7·9	1154	10·7			1122	6·1	2339	6·3	0528	3·0	1739	3·0	0805	4·4	2011	4·6	0449	3·3	1710	3·5
14	Tu	0710	6·0	2005	5·8	0452	7·6	1726	7·7	0017	10·4	1252	10·3	0048	6·1	1340	5·9	0621	2·9	1833	2·9	0901	4·4	2116	4·6	0552	3·4	1816	3·5
15	W	0820	5·8	2122	5·8	0608	7·5	1845	7·7	0126	10·5	1419	10·4	0146	5·9	1458	5·9	0722	2·9	1945	2·8	1001	4·4	2222	4·6	0701	3·5	1925	3·6
16	Th	0946	5·9	2238	6·0	0727	7·7	2001	8·0	0256	10·5	1541	10·9	0328	6·1	1607	6·4	0837	2·9	2121	2·8	1103	4·6	2331	4·8	0902	3·5	2030	3·7
17	F	1105	6·2	2349	6·4	0837	8·2	2107	8·5	0413	11·2	1652	11·7	0437	6·4	1704	6·9	0950	3·1	2238	3·2			1205	4·8	0955	4·0	2127	3·9
18	Sa		6·7	1215	6·7	0936	8·9	2206	9·0	0522	12·1	1758	12·4	0534	6·7	1753	7·5	1051	3·3	2337	3·4	0037	5·1	1303	5·1	1043	4·2	2221	4·1
19	Su	0050	6·7	1316	7·0	1030	9·3	2258	9·3	0624	12·9	1857	13·1	0625	7·1	1836	7·7	1143	3·5			0137	5·4	1358	5·5	1130	4·3	2310	4·2
20	M	0142	7·0	1408	7·3	1120	9·7	2347	9·7	0719	13·6	1948	13·9	0714	7·5	1917	8·0	0028	3·4	1231	3·8	0233	5·7	1450	5·7	0046	4·2	1303	4·5
21	Tu	0230	7·2	1457	7·6			1207	9·8	0806	14·0	2034	13·9	0754	7·7	1959	8·1	0114	3·5	1316	3·9	0326	5·9	1541	6·0	0133	4·2	1350	4·6
22	W	0315	7·4	1543	7·7	0034	9·8	1253	9·8	0851	14·2	2117	13·8	0836	7·8	2042	8·2	0158	3·6	1400	4·1	0415	6·0	1631	6·0	0220	4·0	1440	4·6
23	Th	0359	7·5	1628	7·5	0119	9·8	1337	9·6	0934	14·1	2159	13·6	0918	7·7	2125	7·5	0241	3·6	1443	4·1	0503	5·8	1718	5·9	0310	3·8	1533	4·5
24	F	0442	7·2	1712	7·4	0202	9·4	1420	9·1	1016	13·6	2240	12·9	1003	7·1	2210	7·5	0323	3·5	1526	4·0	0550	5·6	1807	5·7	0403	3·6	1635	4·3
25	Sa	0525	7·2	1757	7·0	0246	9·0	1504	8·6	1057	13·0	2320	12·0	1049	6·6	2301	7·0	0406	3·3	1610	3·8	0637	5·3	1856	5·6	0506	3·5	1745	4·1
26	Su	0608	6·9	1842	6·7	0331	8·5	1548	8·1	1137	11·9			1143	6·2			0451	3·3	1655	3·6	0726	5·0	1946	5·0	0616	3·5	1858	3·9
27	M	0655	6·5	1931	6·3	0421	8·0	1648	7·6	0001	11·2	1221	11·0	0003	6·2	1248	6·0	0539	3·1	1744	3·3	0816	4·7	2043	4·8	0726	3·6	2007	3·7
28	Tu	0752	6·2	2030	5·9	0525	7·5	1800	7·3	0048	10·3	1317	9·7	0121	6·0	1404	5·8	0634	2·9	1840	3·0	0913	4·5	2146	4·5	0831	3·8	2109	3·5
29	W	0901	6·0	2142	5·9	0643	7·3	1928	7·0	0158	9·7	1437	9·7	0250	5·8	1524	5·8	0749	2·8	2000	2·8	1016	4·4	2301	4·4	0926	3·8	2200	3·6
30	Th	1031	5·8	2306	5·9	0805	7·5	2043	7·4	0327	9·8	1607	10·0	0407	5·9	1626	6·3	0916	2·9	2143	2·7	1126	4·4			0831	3·6	2109	3·6
31	F	1147	6·1			0907	7·9	2139	7·8	0445	10·5	1716	10·7			1716		1023	3·0	2253	2·8	0016	4·5	1233	4·6	0926	3·8	2200	3·6

* All times shown are Greenwich Mean Time.   † Difference of height in metres from Ordnance Datum (Newlyn).   ‡ Difference of height in metres from Ordnance Datum (Dublin).

FEBRUARY, 1992

High water at the undermentioned places (GMT*)—

Day of Month	Day of Week	LONDON BRIDGE †Datum 3·20 m. below Mn. h.m.	Ht. m.	Aft. h.m.	Ht. m.	LIVERPOOL †Datum 4·93 m. below Mn. h.m.	Ht. m.	Aft. h.m.	Ht. m.	AVONMOUTH †Datum 6·50 m. below Mn. h.m.	Ht. m.	Aft. h.m.	Ht. m.	HULL (Albert Dock) †Datum 3·90 m. below Mn. h.m.	Ht. m.	Aft. h.m.	Ht. m.	GREENOCK †Datum 1·62 m. below Mn. h.m.	Ht. m.	Aft. h.m.	Ht. m.	LEITH †Datum 2·90 m. below Mn. h.m.	Ht. m.	Aft. h.m.	Ht. m.	DUN LAOGHAIRE ‡Datum 0·20 m. above Mn. h.m.	Ht. m.	Aft. h.m.	Ht. m.
1	Sa	0010	6·2	1242	6·3	0956	8·3	2221	8·2	0543	11·4	1808	11·4	0504	6·2	1713	6·6	1115	3·1	2342	2·9	0115	4·7	1322	4·8	1012	3·9	2243	3·7
2	Su	0057	6·4	1324	6·4	1035	8·7	2258	8·5	0629	12·0	1852	11·9	0547	6·4	1751	6·9	1158	3·2			0158	4·9	1401	5·0	1053	4·0	2317	3·7
3	M	0137	6·6	1402	6·6	1111	9·0	2330	8·7	0709	12·4	1928	12·3	0622	6·6	1824	7·1	0021	3·0	1235	3·3	0233	5·1	1433	5·2	1127	4·0	2350	3·7
4	Tu	0212	6·8	1436	6·8	1143	9·1			0744	12·6	2001	12·5	0653	6·8	1853	7·3	0054	3·0	1308	3·4	0305	5·2	1501	5·3	1159	4·0		
5	W	0244	6·9	1508	6·9	0001	9·2	1215	9·2	0813	12·8	2029	12·7	0721	7·0	1923	7·5	0124	3·1	1339	3·4	0335	5·2	1531	5·4	0019	3·7	1229	4·0
6	Th	0315	7·0	1539	7·0	0031	9·3	1245	9·2	0843	12·9	2057	12·7	0748	7·1	1954	7·6	0154	3·2	1408	3·4	0407	5·2	1603	5·4	0046	3·7	1256	4·0
7	F	0346	7·0	1610	7·0	0100	9·4	1316	9·2	0912	12·9	2127	12·6	0819	7·1	2026	7·5	0224	3·2	1439	3·3	0441	5·0	1635	5·3	0113	3·7	1328	3·9
8	Sa	0416	6·9	1642	6·9	0130	9·4	1345	9·0	0943	12·6	2157	12·3	0851	7·0	2100	7·3	0257	3·1	1511	3·3	0516	5·0	1711	5·3	0146	3·7	1403	3·9
9	Su	0447	6·8	1713	6·8	0159	9·3	1418	8·8	1014	12·2	2227	11·9	0925	6·8	2135	7·1	0333	3·1	1546	3·0	0554	4·8	1750	5·1	0224	3·6	1446	3·8
10	M	0518	6·5	1749	6·5	0230	9·1	1454	8·5	1044	11·7	2257	11·4	1000	6·6	2214	6·8	0412	3·2	1624	3·0	0635	4·7	1837	4·8	0310	3·5	1536	3·7
11	Tu	0553	6·4	1828	6·4	0315	8·8	1542	8·1	1118	11·1	2334	10·8	1041	6·3	2304	6·5	0454	3·1	1706	3·0	0722	4·3	1937	4·6	0403	3·4	1635	3·6
12	W	0638	5·9	1920	5·9	0409	8·5	1645	7·7			1207	10·5	1134	6·0			0541	2·9	1754	2·7	0820	4·3	2045	4·5	0507	3·3	1745	3·5
13	Th	0744	5·8	2039	5·8	0526	8·0	1814	7·5	0038	10·3	1334	10·4	0008	6·2	1253	6·2	0635	2·9	1857	2·7	0926	4·3	2158	4·5	0626	3·4	1903	3·5
14	F	0915	5·9	2206	5·9	0659	8·0	1944	7·8	0218	10·5	1512	10·9	0141	6·3	1432	6·5	0747	3·0	2059	2·9	1035	4·5	2315	4·7	0743	3·5	2016	3·7
15	Sa	1045	6·1	2329	6·1	0925	8·7	2057	8·3	0349	10·9	1635	11·3	0317	6·2	1549	6·8	0920	3·2	2228	3·1	1145	4·7			0848	3·7	2118	3·9
16	Su	0035	6·7	1204	6·7	0015	8·9	1234	10·2	0506	11·9	1747	12·3	0428	6·7	1648	7·3	1031	3·5	2327	3·3	0028	5·2	1248	5·2	0942	4·0	2212	4·1
17	M	0128	7·1	1304	7·1	0106	9·3	1314	10·0	0611	12·9	1845	13·2	0525	7·5	1734	7·9	1126	3·3			0126	5·4	1345	5·4	1032	4·5	2300	4·2
18	Tu	0215	7·3	1357	7·3	0151	9·8	1355	10·1	0704	13·8	1934	13·8	0611	7·9	1817	8·2	0014	3·7	1214	3·7	0220	5·9	1437	5·9	1117	4·5		
19	W	0257	7·5	1442	7·6	0235	10·1	1437	10·0	0751	14·2	2016	14·2	0652	7·8	1857	8·4	0058	3·3	1258	3·9	0309	5·9	1524	6·1	0025	4·2	1201	4·5
20	Th	0339	7·5	1525	7·7	0314	10·0	1517	9·8	0832	14·4	2056	14·2	0733	7·9	1938	8·4	0138	3·5	1340	4·0	0354	6·1	1611	6·1	0104	4·2	1243	4·6
21	F	0419	7·5	1607	7·6	0359	9·6	1606	9·1	0911	14·4	2134	13·8	0812	7·6	2019	8·1	0218	3·5	1421	3·9	0439	5·8	1656	5·7	0144	4·2	1326	4·5
22	Sa	0459	7·5	1647	7·5	0435	9·1	1656	8·6	0950	13·7	2212	13·1	0851	7·2	2103	7·4	0256	3·5	1502	3·8	0522	5·7	1741	5·4	0227	3·9	1410	4·3
23	Su	0539	7·2	1726	7·2	0519	8·6	1741	8·0	1028	12·8	2247	12·2	0932	6·7	2146	6·8	0335	3·5	1543	3·6	0605	5·3	1826	5·3	0315	3·7	1500	4·1
24	M	0621	7·0	1804	7·0	0557	8·1	1826	7·6	1104	11·8	2320	11·2	1013	6·3	2233	6·2	0415	3·2	1624	3·3	0648	4·9	1913	4·9	0413	3·5	1557	3·9
25	Tu	0714	6·6	1848	6·6	0635	7·4	1913	7·0	1137	10·8	2357	10·1	1059	5·6	2329	5·6	0457	3·2	1708	3·0	0735	4·6	2007	4·6	0525	3·4	1709	3·8
26	W	0820	6·3	1940	6·3	0715	7·0	2022	6·8			1224	9·7	1156	5·4			0544	2·8	1756	2·7	0828	4·3	2109	4·3	0645	3·4	1827	3·7
27	Th	0948	5·8	2047	5·8	0557	7·1	2220	7·1	0100	9·3	1348	9·1	0042	5·6	1310	5·6	0645	2·7	1903	2·5	0931	4·2	2226	4·2	0800	3·4	1943	3·5
28	F	1122	5·9	2220	5·9	0733	7·1	2022	7·1	0246	9·2	1534	9·4	0222	5·4	1440	5·7	0836	2·6	2126	2·6	1045	4·2	2348	4·4	0902	3·4	2048	3·4
29	Sa			2342	5·9	0843	7·6	2118	7·6	0417	10·1	1648	10·3	0349	5·6	1556	6·0	0958	2·8	2237	2·8	1200	4·4					2142	3·5

*All times shown are Greenwich Mean Time.   †Difference of height in metres from Ordnance Datum (Newlyn).   ‡Difference of height in metres from Ordnance Datum (Dublin).

MARCH, 1992

High water at the undermentioned places (GMT*)—

Day of Month	Day of Week	LONDON BRIDGE †Datum 3·20 m. below Mn. h.m.	Ht. m.	Aft. h.m.	Ht. m.	LIVERPOOL †Datum 4·93 m. below Mn. h.m.	Ht. m.	Aft. h.m.	Ht. m.	AVONMOUTH †Datum 6·50 m. below Mn. h.m.	Ht. m.	Aft. h.m.	Ht. m.	HULL (Albert Dock) †Datum 3·90 m. below Mn. h.m.	Ht. m.	Aft. h.m.	Ht. m.	GREENOCK †Datum 1·62 m. below Mn. h.m.	Ht. m.	Aft. h.m.	Ht. m.	LEITH †Datum 2·90 m. below Mn. h.m.	Ht. m.	Aft. h.m.	Ht. m.	DUN LAOGHAIRE ‡Datum 0·20 m. above Mn. h.m.	Ht. m.	Aft. h.m.	Ht. m.
1	Su	0032	—	1218	6·3	0932	8·1	2159	8·1	0515	11·1	1742	11·2	0442	6·0	1647	6·4	1053	3·0	2323	2·8	0050	4·6	1254	4·7	0952	3·8	2223	3·6
2	M	0112	6·3	1300	6·6	1012	8·6	2234	8·5	0603	11·9	1825	12·0	0523	6·5	1725	6·8	1136	3·1	2359	2·9	0131	4·8	1333	4·9	1032	3·9	2256	3·7
3	Tu	0112	6·6	1337	6·7	1045	8·9	2305	8·8	0642	12·4	1902	12·3	0557	6·7	1758	7·2	1212	3·1	—	—	0205	5·0	1405	5·1	1105	3·9	2326	3·7
4	W	0147	6·8	1409	6·9	1118	9·2	2334	9·0	0717	12·7	1934	12·7	0627	6·9	1828	7·4	0030	3·0	1245	3·3	0237	5·2	1435	5·3	1134	3·9	2351	3·8
5	Th	0218	7·0	1440	7·0	1149	9·3	—	—	0748	13·0	2002	13·0	0653	7·1	1857	7·6	0059	3·1	1315	3·3	0309	5·3	1507	5·4	—	—	1201	3·9
6	F	0249	7·1	1511	7·1	0004	9·4	1218	9·4	0816	13·1	2030	13·1	0721	7·3	1930	7·6	0128	3·2	1345	3·3	0341	5·3	1539	5·4	0015	3·8	1226	3·9
7	Sa	0318	7·1	1542	7·1	0042	9·3	1249	9·3	0847	13·1	2101	13·0	0752	7·3	2002	7·5	0159	3·2	1415	3·3	0415	5·3	1613	5·4	0042	3·8	1257	3·9
8	Su	0349	7·1	1613	7·1	0103	9·1	1320	9·0	0918	12·9	2132	12·7	0823	7·2	2036	7·4	0232	3·2	1448	3·2	0448	5·1	1648	5·3	0113	3·8	1335	3·9
9	M	0421	7·0	1647	6·9	0134	8·9	1354	9·0	0950	12·5	2203	12·2	0856	7·0	2111	7·1	0307	3·2	1523	3·2	0524	4·9	1730	5·1	0152	3·8	1417	3·8
10	Tu	0455	6·8	1720	6·6	0209	8·7	1432	8·7	1023	11·9	2234	11·7	0931	6·7	2152	6·8	0345	3·2	1601	3·1	0603	4·7	1818	4·8	0238	3·7	1510	3·7
11	W	0534	6·6	1801	6·3	0250	8·3	1521	8·2	1058	11·3	2315	11·0	1012	6·4	2242	6·5	0426	3·1	1643	2·9	0650	4·6	1920	4·6	0332	3·5	1613	3·6
12	Th	0622	6·2	1853	5·9	0345	7·9	1627	7·7	1150	10·5	—	—	1106	6·1	2350	6·1	0511	3·0	1730	2·8	0752	4·4	2028	4·4	0440	3·4	1728	3·5
13	F	0731	5·9	2012	5·7	0505	7·5	1758	7·7	0019	10·3	1317	10·0	—	—	1224	6·0	0602	2·9	1833	2·6	0900	4·5	2143	4·4	0606	3·4	1852	3·5
14	Sa	0901	5·7	2143	5·8	0641	7·5	1931	8·0	0158	10·1	1456	10·3	0130	6·0	1408	6·0	0710	2·9	2052	2·6	1015	4·5	2300	4·6	0726	3·5	2006	3·6
15	Su	1033	6·2	2309	6·3	0804	8·0	2043	8·3	0334	11·3	1623	11·3	0308	6·6	1529	6·7	0853	2·9	2214	2·8	1126	5·0	—	—	0832	3·8	2108	4·0
16	M	1150	6·7	—	—	0908	8·7	2141	8·7	0452	11·9	1732	12·3	0416	6·9	1627	7·1	1008	3·2	2309	3·1	0011	5·0	1231	5·2	0928	4·0	2202	4·1
17	Tu	0015	6·8	1249	7·4	1000	9·3	2228	9·3	0556	12·9	1827	13·1	0508	7·4	1713	7·4	1104	3·4	2354	3·3	0111	5·4	1328	5·6	1018	4·3	2246	4·1
18	W	0109	7·2	1338	7·5	1047	9·7	2312	9·7	0646	13·6	1914	13·7	0551	7·5	1754	7·8	1152	3·6	—	—	0201	5·6	1416	5·9	1102	4·4	2326	4·2
19	Th	0155	7·3	1422	7·6	1130	10·0	2353	10·0	0730	14·0	1954	14·0	0629	7·8	1835	8·1	0035	3·4	1236	3·6	0246	5·8	1503	6·0	1143	4·5	—	—
20	F	0236	7·5	1503	7·6	—	—	1211	10·0	0809	14·1	2032	14·0	0707	7·7	1916	8·2	0114	3·4	1318	3·6	0330	5·8	1546	6·0	0002	4·2	1222	4·5
21	Sa	0317	7·5	1542	7·5	0031	9·5	1250	9·7	0847	14·0	2107	13·7	0745	7·7	1958	8·1	0151	3·4	1357	3·5	0413	5·7	1631	5·8	0036	4·1	1301	4·4
22	Su	0355	7·5	1619	7·4	0109	9·5	1328	9·4	0924	13·4	2143	13·0	0825	7·5	2042	7·6	0228	3·2	1436	3·5	0452	5·5	1713	5·5	0111	4·0	1344	4·2
23	M	0433	7·2	1654	7·2	0145	8·9	1405	8·9	1000	12·8	2217	12·1	0903	7·1	2125	7·1	0304	3·2	1515	3·3	0531	5·2	1756	5·2	0152	3·9	1432	3·9
24	Tu	0512	6·9	1729	7·0	0222	8·6	1446	8·5	1033	11·6	2248	11·1	0941	6·7	2210	6·5	0341	3·1	1554	3·1	0611	4·8	1841	4·8	0238	3·8	1528	3·7
25	W	0553	6·5	1807	6·9	0304	8·1	1532	7·9	1105	10·6	2320	10·2	1021	6·3	2301	6·2	0420	2·9	1635	2·9	0654	4·5	1931	4·4	0332	3·6	1636	3·4
26	Th	0642	6·1	1855	6·5	0357	7·5	1637	7·5	1144	9·6	—	—	1111	5·9	—	—	0502	2·8	1720	2·8	0745	4·3	2031	4·1	0443	3·4	1756	3·3
27	F	0744	5·8	1959	6·1	0512	6·9	1811	6·9	0015	9·1	1302	8·9	0007	5·9	1219	5·6	0552	2·7	1817	2·6	0845	4·1	2141	4·1	0609	3·4	1911	3·4
28	Sa	0903	5·6	2121	5·8	0645	7·0	1942	7·4	0159	9·1	1447	9·1	0134	5·2	1342	5·5	0714	2·6	2037	2·4	0954	4·1	2258	4·2	0725	3·5	2018	3·4
29	Su	1037	5·7	2257	5·7	0801	7·4	2042	7·9	0332	9·7	1606	10·0	0314	5·4	1510	5·8	0914	2·7	2158	2·5	1107	4·3	—	—	0830	3·5	2114	3·5
30	M	1142	6·1	2356	6·1	0854	7·9	2124	8·4	0435	10·7	1702	10·9	0410	6·1	1609	6·3	1015	2·8	2245	2·7	0005	4·5	1205	4·5	0922	3·6	2155	3·6
31	Tu	1227	6·5	—	—	0935	8·4	2200	8·4	0525	11·7	1747	11·7	0451	6·3	1649	6·7	1101	3·0	2323	2·9	0050	4·7	1250	4·8	1002	3·7	2228	3·6

*All times shown are Greenwich Mean Time.   †Difference of height in metres from Ordnance Datum (Newlyn).   ‡Difference of height in metres from Ordnance Datum (Dublin).

APRIL, 1992

High water at the undermentioned places (GMT*)—

Heights are given against each place under the following data: London Bridge †Datum of Predictions 3·20 m. below; Liverpool †Datum of Predictions 4·93 m. below; Avonmouth †Datum of Predictions 6·50 m. below; Hull (Albert Dock) †Datum of Predictions 3·90 m. below; Greenock †Datum of Predictions 1·62 m. below; Leith †Datum of Predictions 2·90 m. below; Dun Laoghaire ‡Datum of Predictions 0·20 m. above.

Day of Month	Day of Week	London Bridge Mn h.m.	Ht.	Aft. h.m.	Ht.	Liverpool Mn h.m.	Ht.	Aft. h.m.	Ht.	Avonmouth Mn h.m.	Ht.	Aft. h.m.	Ht.	Hull Mn h.m.	Ht.	Aft. h.m.	Ht.	Greenock Mn h.m.	Ht.	Aft. h.m.	Ht.	Leith Mn h.m.	Ht.	Aft. h.m.	Ht.	Dun Laoghaire Mn h.m.	Ht.	Aft. h.m.	Ht.
1	W	0038	6.4	1303	6.7	1012	8.8	2231	8.7	0607	12.2	1827	12.2	0525	6.7	1725	7.1	1139	3.1	2356	3.0	0128	5.0	1328	5.0	1036	3.8	2253	3.7
2	Th	0113	6.7	1337	6.8	1045	9.0	2302	9.0	0643	12.6	1900	12.6	0554	7.0	1757	7.3	1214	3.1			0203	5.1	1403	5.2	1103	3.8	2319	3.7
3	F	0145	6.9	1409	7.0	1118	9.2	2333	9.1	0717	12.9	1933	12.9	0622	7.2	1831	7.5	0027	3.1	1247	3.2	0237	5.2	1437	5.3	1130	3.9	2344	3.8
4	Sa	0218	7.0	1440	7.1	1150	9.4			0749	13.1	2004	13.2	0653	7.3	1904	7.5	0059	3.2	1319	3.2	0311	5.3	1515	5.4	1159	3.9		
5	Su	0250	7.1	1514	7.2	0005	9.4	1224	9.4	0822	13.2	2037	13.1	0726	7.3	1940	7.4	0132	3.2	1352	3.2	0345	5.2	1552	5.2	0013	4.0	1233	4.0
6	M	0324	7.1	1548	7.2	0039	9.2	1259	9.3	0857	13.1	2111	13.0	0758	7.3	2016	7.3	0207	3.2	1427	3.1	0420	5.1	1633	5.2	0049	3.9	1313	3.9
7	Tu	0400	7.2	1624	7.2	0114	9.1	1337	9.0	0934	12.9	2146	12.6	0833	7.0	2056	7.0	0244	3.2	1505	3.1	0458	5.0	1720	5.1	0130	3.9	1401	3.9
8	W	0441	7.0	1702	7.0	0152	8.8	1420	8.7	1012	12.6	2226	12.4	0911	6.8	2141	6.8	0323	3.1	1546	3.0	0541	4.9	1815	4.9	0218	3.8	1457	3.7
9	Th	0526	6.7	1747	6.7	0239	8.3	1514	8.2	1055	12.0	2313	11.8	0956	6.5	2235	6.4	0404	3.0	1630	2.9	0633	4.6	1913	4.5	0317	3.7	1603	3.6
10	F	0621	6.3	1843	6.3	0338	8.0	1623	7.7	1153	11.3			1052	6.2			0450	2.9	1723	2.8	0735	4.6	2020	4.5	0429	3.6	1721	3.5
11	Sa	0730	6.1	1958	6.1	0457	7.8	1750	7.6	0021	10.6	1313	10.4	0124	6.1	1342	6.1	0542	2.7	1838	2.7	0845	4.6	2131	4.5	0552	3.5	1841	3.5
12	Su	0851	6.1	2122	6.0	0624	7.7	1914	7.8	0148	10.4	1442	10.5	0251	6.1	1501	6.3	0649	2.7	2037	2.9	0956	4.7	2245	4.7	0708	3.6	1953	3.6
13	M	1016	6.4	2245	6.4	0741	8.2	2022	8.3	0317	11.1	1603	11.3	0355	6.3	1600	6.6	0824	3.0	2150	2.9	1107	4.9	2350	5.0	0814	3.8	2053	3.8
14	Tu	1129	6.8	2351	6.8	0844	8.7	2118	9.0	0433	11.6	1709	11.9	0445	6.6	1649	6.9	0941	3.1	2243	3.1			1209	5.2	0911	3.9	2145	3.9
15	W			1228	7.2	0938	9.2	2204	9.5	0533	12.6	1804	12.6	0527	6.9	1732	7.2	1039	3.3	2328	3.2	0048	5.3	1305	5.5	1000	4.2	2229	4.1
16	Th	0046	7.0	1317	7.3	1024	9.5	2248	9.6	0624	13.1	1849	13.1	0607	7.1	1815	7.4	1128	3.5			0137	5.5	1354	5.6	1046	4.3	2306	4.1
17	F	0133	7.1	1401	7.3	1106	9.6	2327	9.4	0707	13.4	1930	13.5	0643	7.3	1857	7.6	0009	3.3	1213	3.5	0222	5.6	1441	5.7	1126	4.3	2340	4.3
18	Sa	0215	7.2	1440	7.3	1147	9.5			0747	13.5	2006	13.5	0721	7.5	1941	7.7	0048	3.3	1255	3.5	0305	5.4	1526	5.7			1204	4.3
19	Su	0254	7.3	1517	7.3	0005	9.4	1227	9.4	0823	13.3	2043	13.3	0759	7.3	2025	7.6	0125	3.4	1335	3.4	0345	5.1	1609	5.5	0012	4.1	1242	4.2
20	M	0332	7.3	1552	7.1	0043	9.3	1304	9.2	0900	12.9	2118	12.7	0837	7.0	2107	7.3	0201	3.3	1413	3.2	0424	4.9	1650	5.3	0046	4.1	1323	4.1
21	Tu	0412	7.1	1626	6.8	0120	9.0	1341	8.8	0936	12.3	2153	12.1	0914	6.7	2149	7.0	0236	3.1	1450	3.1	0500	4.6	1731	5.0	0126	4.0	1410	3.8
22	W	0449	6.8	1659	6.6	0157	8.6	1420	8.1	1009	11.7	2224	11.3	0952	6.4	2235	6.6	0312	3.0	1529	2.8	0535	4.4	1813	4.7	0211	3.9	1503	3.6
23	Th	0530	6.5	1736	6.3	0237	8.1	1505	7.7	1042	11.0	2258	10.5	1035	6.0	2332	6.2	0350	2.8	1608	2.6	0615	4.2	1900	4.5	0304	3.7	1607	3.4
24	F	0615	6.2	1818	6.0	0327	7.6	1602	7.1	1120	9.8	2346	9.6	1136	5.7			0431	2.6	1653	2.5	0701	4.2	1954	4.2	0410	3.5	1718	3.3
25	Sa	0710	5.9	1916	5.7	0430	7.3	1716	6.9			1221	9.2	0041	5.7	1250	5.4	0518	2.5	1747	2.5	0800	4.2	2056	4.2	0527	3.4	1830	3.2
26	Su	0818	5.7	2030	5.5	0546	7.1	1839	7.3	0107	9.2	1348	9.7	0202	5.3	1405	5.6	0621	2.6	1911	2.5	0903	4.3	2201	4.4	0641	3.4	1934	3.3
27	M	0932	5.7	2150	5.6	0700	7.3	1947	7.9	0233	9.6	1507	10.5	0317	5.7	1511	6.0	0800	2.7	2051	2.7	1009	4.5	2305	4.6	0746	3.4	2028	3.4
28	Tu	1042	5.9	2259	5.9	0801	7.9	2036	8.3	0341	10.4	1607	11.1	0404	6.1	1603	6.3	0919	2.7	2151	2.7	1111	4.6			0840	3.4	2114	3.4
29	W	1137	6.2	2350	6.2	0850	8.3	2117	8.6	0434	11.1	1658	11.8	0441	6.5	1645	6.6	1014	2.8	2237	2.9	0000	4.7	1201	4.7	0922	3.5	2148	3.5
30	Th	1221	6.5			0931	8.5	2153	8.6	0520	11.8	1743	11.9	0518	6.7	1724	6.8	1059	2.9	2316	3.0	0045	4.8	1246	4.9	0958	3.6	2218	3.6

*All times shown are Greenwich Mean Time.   †Difference of height in metres from Ordnance Datum (Newlyn).
‡Difference of height in metres from Ordnance Datum (Dublin).

MAY, 1992

High water at the undermentioned places (GMT*)—

Datum of Predictions: London Bridge 3·20 m. below · Liverpool 4·93 m. below · Avonmouth 6·50 m. below · Hull (Albert Dock) 3·90 m. below · Greenock 1·62 m. below · Leith 2·90 m. below · Dun Laoghaire 0·20 m. above.

(Mn = morning h.m.; Aft = afternoon h.m.; Ht = height in metres)

Day	Wk	LB Mn	Ht	LB Aft	Ht	Liv Mn	Ht	Liv Aft	Ht	Avon Mn	Ht	Avon Aft	Ht	Hull Mn	Ht	Hull Aft	Ht	Grk Mn	Ht	Grk Aft	Ht	Leith Mn	Ht	Leith Aft	Ht	DL Mn	Ht	DL Aft	Ht
1	F	0032	6·5	1259	6·7	1009	8·8	2228	8·9	0604	12·3	1824	12·4	0516	6·8	1725	7·1	1139	3·0	2353	3·1	0124	5·0	1330	5·1	1029	3·7	2247	3·7
2	Sa	0110	6·7	1335	6·9	1045	9·1	2304	9·1	0643	12·7	1902	12·8	0551	7·1	1804	7·3	1217	3·1	—	—	0201	5·1	1411	5·2	1100	3·8	2317	3·9
3	Su	0148	6·9	1413	7·0	1123	9·3	2342	9·3	0723	12·9	1940	13·1	0627	7·2	1842	7·3	0030	3·2	1255	3·1	0239	5·2	1452	5·3	1137	3·9	2354	4·0
4	M	0226	7·1	1450	7·1	—	9·3	1203	9·3	0802	13·0	2018	13·0	0703	7·2	1923	7·2	0107	3·2	1333	3·1	0318	5·2	1537	5·3	—	4·0	1218	4·0
5	Tu	0305	7·2	1529	7·1	0019	9·3	1243	9·3	0843	12·9	2058	12·6	0740	7·1	2005	7·0	0145	3·3	1412	3·1	0358	5·2	1626	5·2	0033	4·0	1303	4·0
6	W	0348	7·3	1610	7·0	0102	9·2	1328	9·1	0925	12·4	2141	12·2	0819	6·9	2049	6·8	0225	3·3	1454	3·1	0441	5·2	1716	5·1	0118	4·0	1354	3·9
7	Th	0434	7·1	1654	6·8	0147	9·0	1418	8·7	1010	12·2	2227	11·8	0901	6·8	2138	6·5	0306	3·4	1539	3·0	0530	5·1	1811	4·9	0211	3·9	1452	3·8
8	F	0525	6·9	1743	6·5	0237	8·7	1512	8·3	1059	11·6	2319	11·1	0949	6·7	2233	6·5	0350	3·4	1628	3·0	0626	4·9	1907	4·8	0310	3·8	1557	3·7
9	Sa	0621	6·6	1839	6·2	0336	8·3	1620	8·0	1157	11·0	—	—	1044	6·3	2340	6·3	0438	3·3	1726	2·9	0726	4·7	2009	4·7	0417	3·7	1709	3·6
10	Su	0726	6·4	1947	6·1	0447	8·1	1733	7·9	0022	10·7	1304	10·4	1151	6·3	—	—	0531	3·2	1841	2·9	0830	4·6	2115	4·8	0531	3·6	1821	3·5
11	M	0836	6·4	2100	6·2	0601	8·1	1848	8·0	0134	11·0	1420	10·9	0106	6·4	1313	6·6	0635	3·1	2006	2·8	0935	4·8	2220	4·9	0644	3·7	1930	3·7
12	Tu	0950	6·6	2216	6·4	0713	8·3	1954	8·3	0251	11·7	1535	11·8	0223	6·4	1430	6·6	0754	3·1	2116	2·9	1043	4·9	2324	5·0	0750	3·8	2031	3·8
13	W	1102	6·6	2325	6·7	0816	8·6	2050	8·6	0405	12·1	1640	12·1	0327	6·9	1532	6·9	0909	3·1	2212	3·0	1145	5·1	—	—	0848	3·8	2124	3·9
14	Th	—	6·8	1203	7·0	0911	8·8	2139	8·9	0505	12·5	1736	12·5	0419	7·1	1626	7·1	1011	3·2	2300	3·1	0022	5·1	1243	5·3	0941	4·0	2207	4·0
15	F	0022	6·8	1255	7·0	1000	9·0	2224	9·1	0558	12·6	1824	12·7	0504	7·1	1715	7·3	1054	3·3	2344	3·2	0113	5·2	1335	5·4	1028	4·1	2247	4·0
16	Sa	0112	6·8	1338	7·0	1045	9·2	2305	9·2	0643	12·6	1906	12·7	0544	7·2	1801	7·3	1152	3·3	—	—	0200	5·3	1424	5·4	1109	4·0	2321	4·0
17	Su	0155	6·9	1418	6·9	1127	9·1	2344	9·1	0726	12·6	1945	12·6	0624	7·2	1845	7·2	0024	3·2	1236	3·2	0241	5·3	1509	5·3	1148	4·0	2355	4·0
18	M	0236	7·0	1454	6·6	—	8·9	1207	8·9	0804	12·1	2023	11·9	0703	7·1	1930	6·9	0102	3·2	1316	3·1	0320	5·3	1550	5·3	—	4·0	1228	3·9
19	Tu	0315	7·0	1529	6·6	0022	8·9	1245	8·7	0842	11·9	2100	11·8	0740	7·1	2011	6·8	0139	3·2	1355	3·1	0358	5·2	1630	5·1	0030	4·0	1308	3·9
20	W	0353	7·0	1603	6·6	0059	8·7	1323	8·5	0922	11·5	2134	11·3	0816	6·8	2050	6·7	0215	3·1	1432	3·1	0431	5·1	1709	4·9	0108	3·9	1353	3·8
21	Th	0431	6·8	1637	6·4	0137	8·4	1401	8·2	0952	10·9	2207	10·9	0851	6·8	2129	6·5	0251	3·1	1510	3·1	0503	4·9	1746	4·7	0153	3·8	1442	3·6
22	F	0511	6·7	1712	6·3	0216	8·1	1442	7·8	1024	10·4	2242	10·4	0927	6·4	2209	6·2	0328	3·1	1549	3·0	0541	4·7	1830	4·6	0243	3·6	1536	3·5
23	Sa	0551	6·3	1751	6·1	0300	7·7	1528	7·5	1102	9·9	2323	9·9	1007	6·1	2254	5·8	0407	3·0	1632	2·9	0624	4·5	1918	4·5	0338	3·4	1635	3·3
24	Su	0638	6·1	1838	5·9	0350	7·4	1624	7·2	1147	9·9	—	—	1058	5·7	2349	5·5	0451	2·9	1722	2·8	0716	4·4	2013	4·4	0439	3·3	1738	3·3
25	M	0731	5·9	1934	5·7	0449	7·1	1729	7·1	0018	10·1	1246	10·1	—	5·5	1200	5·7	0543	2·9	1821	2·8	0816	4·3	2111	4·3	0546	3·3	1837	3·2
26	Tu	0833	5·8	2044	5·6	0554	7·0	1836	7·2	0127	10·1	1358	10·5	0053	5·7	1310	6·0	0645	2·8	1933	2·7	0918	4·4	2211	4·3	0648	3·3	1933	3·3
27	W	0936	5·8	2152	5·7	0706	7·2	1937	7·5	0237	10·7	1505	10·9	0201	6·0	1415	6·3	0803	2·7	2045	2·7	1018	4·5	2308	4·5	0744	3·3	2021	3·3
28	Th	1035	6·0	2252	5·9	0755	7·6	2027	8·0	0338	11·3	1603	11·5	0300	6·3	1514	6·6	0914	2·7	2144	2·7	1115	4·7	—	—	0832	3·3	2102	3·4
29	F	1130	6·3	—	—	0846	8·1	2114	8·4	0433	11·9	1657	12·1	0352	6·6	1606	6·8	1013	2·8	2235	2·8	—	—	1207	4·7	0915	3·5	2139	3·6
30	Sa	—	—	1219	6·2	0932	8·6	2156	8·8	0523	12·2	1747	12·2	0438	6·8	1654	7·0	1104	2·9	2320	3·1	0045	4·8	1258	4·9	0956	3·6	2216	3·7
31	Su	0035	6·5	1306	—	1017	8·9	2240	9·1	0612	12·7	1834	12·7	0522	6·8	1740	7·0	1150	3·1	—	—	0128	5·0	1346	5·1	1037	3·8	2255	3·9

*All times shown are Greenwich Mean Time. †Difference of height in metres from Ordnance Datum (Newlyn). ‡Difference of height in metres from Ordnance Datum (Dublin).

JUNE, 1992

High water at the undermentioned places (GMT*)—

Datum of Predictions (metres): London Bridge †3·20 m. below · Liverpool †4·93 m. below · Avonmouth †6·50 m. below · Hull (Albert Dock) †3·90 m. below · Greenock †1·62 m. below · Leith †2·90 m. below · Dun Laoghaire ‡0·20 m. above

Day of Week	Day of Month	London Bridge Mn.	Ht.	Aft.	Ht.	Liverpool Mn.	Ht.	Aft.	Ht.	Avonmouth Mn.	Ht.	Aft.	Ht.	Hull Mn.	Ht.	Aft.	Ht.	Greenock Mn.	Ht.	Aft.	Ht.	Leith Mn.	Ht.	Aft.	Ht.	Dun Laoghaire Mn.	Ht.	Aft.	Ht.
M	1	0121	6·7	1351	6·9	1102	9·2	2323	9·3	0700	12·7	1920	13·0	0604	7·0	1827	7·2	0003	3·2	1235	3·1	0211	5·1	1435	5·2	1120	3·9	2337	4·0
Tu	2	0208	7·0	1434	7·0	1147	9·3	—		0747	13·0	2005	13·2	0646	7·1	1912	7·3	0045	3·3	1319	3·1	0254	5·3	1526	5·3	—		1205	4·0
W	3	0254	7·2	1518	7·1	0007	9·4	1234	9·3	0833	13·0	2051	13·2	0727	7·2	1958	7·3	0127	3·4	1403	3·2	0341	5·3	1616	5·4	0022	4·2	1254	4·0
Th	4	0341	7·3	1602	7·1	0053	9·4	1323	9·2	0921	12·9	2138	12·9	0809	7·2	2044	7·2	0210	3·5	1448	3·2	0430	5·3	1709	5·4	0110	4·2	1347	4·0
F	5	0430	7·3	1648	7·1	0142	9·3	1413	9·0	1007	12·6	2226	12·7	0854	7·1	2132	7·0	0254	3·6	1535	3·3	0522	5·3	1801	5·3	0201	4·1	1443	3·9
Sa	6	0520	7·1	1737	6·8	0233	9·1	1507	8·7	1057	12·2	2316	12·3	0941	7·1	2224	6·8	0339	3·6	1625	3·3	0616	5·2	1856	5·2	0257	4·1	1542	3·8
Su	7	0614	6·9	1829	6·6	0328	8·8	1604	8·4	1147	11·7	—		1031	6·9	2323	6·6	0427	3·5	1719	3·3	0713	5·1	1952	5·0	0359	4·0	1646	3·6
M	8	0710	6·7	1927	6·5	0427	8·6	1706	8·1	0010	11·8	1245	11·3	1130	6·7	—		0519	3·4	1819	3·0	0811	5·0	2052	5·0	0504	3·9	1753	3·6
Tu	9	0813	6·6	2032	6·4	0532	8·3	1814	8·0	0110	11·4	1348	11·0	0036	6·4	1242	6·6	0616	3·4	1928	3·0	0913	4·9	2152	4·8	0614	3·8	1859	3·6
W	10	0921	6·6	2142	6·4	0641	8·2	1921	8·1	0219	11·2	1458	11·0	0148	6·4	1357	6·6	0722	3·1	2037	3·0	1016	4·9	2254	4·8	0722	3·8	2000	3·6
Th	11	1030	6·6	2257	6·4	0748	8·3	2023	8·3	0328	11·2	1606	11·2	0253	6·5	1505	6·7	0835	3·1	2139	3·0	1120	4·9	2354	5·0	0824	3·8	2057	3·7
F	12	1136	6·5	—		0849	8·5	2117	8·5	0434	11·4	1706	11·5	0350	6·5	1609	6·8	0944	3·0	2234	3·1	—		1224	5·0	0922	3·9	2145	3·8
Sa	13	0000	6·5	1231	6·5	0942	8·5	2206	8·7	0533	11·6	1800	11·9	0442	6·8	1704	6·8	1045	3·0	2322	3·1	0048	5·0	1320	5·1	1011	3·9	2229	3·9
Su	14	0053	6·6	1319	6·6	1030	8·7	2249	8·7	0624	12·0	1846	12·2	0527	6·8	1754	6·8	1137	3·0	—		0139	5·1	1411	5·1	1056	3·9	2307	4·0
M	15	0140	6·6	1359	6·7	1113	8·7	2329	9·0	0709	12·1	1928	12·4	0610	6·9	1839	6·7	0006	3·2	1224	3·0	0222	5·2	1454	5·1	1137	3·8	2344	4·0
Tu	16	0222	6·7	1437	6·7	1153	8·7	—		0749	12·1	2008	12·4	0648	6·9	1920	6·7	0047	3·2	1305	3·0	0301	5·2	1535	5·1	—		1215	3·8
W	17	0300	6·8	1511	6·8	0007	9·0	1229	8·6	0827	12·1	2044	12·3	0724	7·0	1957	6·6	0124	3·2	1343	2·9	0335	5·1	1611	5·1	0021	4·1	1254	3·8
Th	18	0338	6·9	1545	6·9	0043	9·0	1304	8·5	0903	11·7	2117	12·1	0757	7·0	2032	6·5	0200	3·2	1419	2·9	0407	5·1	1646	5·0	0057	4·0	1335	3·7
F	19	0413	6·8	1619	6·7	0119	8·8	1340	8·4	0934	11·7	2149	11·8	0830	6·9	2105	6·5	0235	3·2	1454	2·9	0435	5·0	1720	5·0	0137	4·0	1415	3·6
Sa	20	0449	6·7	1652	6·6	0155	8·3	1416	8·2	1006	11·1	2223	11·5	0904	6·9	2141	6·4	0310	3·2	1531	2·9	0511	4·9	1800	4·9	0217	3·9	1459	3·5
Su	21	0526	6·5	1729	6·4	0232	8·4	1454	7·9	1040	11·1	2258	11·1	0942	6·5	2219	6·2	0347	3·1	1610	2·9	0552	4·8	1843	4·8	0301	3·7	1545	3·4
M	22	0605	6·1	1805	6·0	0312	8·3	1536	7·7	1115	10·7	2337	10·7	1026	6·5	2304	6·0	0426	3·1	1654	2·9	0639	4·7	1931	4·5	0347	3·5	1635	3·3
Tu	23	0646	6·1	1846	5·8	0357	7·7	1626	7·5	1156	10·3	—		1113	6·2	2356	5·8	0509	3·0	1742	2·8	0733	4·5	2026	4·5	0438	3·4	1727	3·2
W	24	0734	5·9	1937	5·8	0451	7·7	1726	7·3	0024	10·3	1246	10·1	—		1212	6·0	0558	2·9	1837	2·8	0831	4·4	2122	4·3	0535	3·3	1824	3·2
Th	25	0833	5·8	2044	5·8	0554	7·6	1834	7·4	0124	10·3	1355	10·1	0059	5·8	1321	6·1	0655	2·8	1939	2·8	0933	4·4	2220	4·5	0635	3·3	1922	3·3
F	26	0938	5·8	2156	5·8	0702	7·7	1940	7·7	0239	10·3	1510	10·5	0205	5·9	1429	6·1	0806	2·7	2048	2·7	1033	4·5	2315	4·5	0737	3·4	2014	3·4
Sa	27	1042	6·0	2302	6·0	0805	8·0	2039	8·0	0346	10·8	1614	10·8	0308	6·1	1531	6·3	0925	2·7	2153	2·7	1133	4·6	—		0835	3·5	2104	3·5
Su	28	1144	6·3	—		0903	8·4	2131	8·6	0448	11·5	1715	11·9	0406	6·4	1630	6·6	1033	2·8	2249	3·1	0007	4·7	1231	4·8	0927	3·6	2151	3·7
M	29	0005	6·3	1242	6·6	0956	8·8	2221	9·0	0549	12·1	1812	12·5	0459	6·7	1725	6·9	1130	3·0	2340	3·2	0058	5·0	1328	5·1	1018	3·8	2236	4·0
Tu	30	0103	6·7	1334	6·8	1047	9·1	2309	9·4	0645	12·6	1906	13·0	0547	7·0	1815	7·1	1220	3·1	—		0146	5·2	1422	5·3	1106	3·9	2321	4·2

*All times shown are Greenwich Mean Time.   †Difference of height in metres from Ordnance Datum (Newlyn).
‡Difference of height in metres from Ordnance Datum (Dublin).

JULY, 1992

High water at the undermentioned places (GMT*)—

Day of Month	Day of Week	London Bridge †Datum 3.20 m. below Mn. h.m.	Ht. m.	Aft. h.m.	Ht. m.	Liverpool †Datum 4.93 m. below Mn. h.m.	Ht. m.	Aft. h.m.	Ht. m.	Avonmouth †Datum 6.50 m. below Mn. h.m.	Ht. m.	Aft. h.m.	Ht. m.	Hull (Albert Dock) †Datum 3.90 m. below Mn. h.m.	Ht. m.	Aft. h.m.	Ht. m.	Greenock †Datum 1.62 m. below Mn. h.m.	Ht. m.	Aft. h.m.	Ht. m.	Leith †Datum 2.90 m. below Mn. h.m.	Ht. m.	Aft. h.m.	Ht. m.	Dun Laoghaire ‡Datum 0.20 m. above Mn. h.m.	Ht. m.	Aft. h.m.	Ht. m.
1	W	0157	7.0	1422	7.0	1136	9.4	2357	9.6	0737	13.0	1955	13.4	0632	7.2	1903	7.4	0027	3.4	1308	3.3	0237	5.4	1515	5.5	1154	4.1	1243	4.1
2	Th	0246	7.3	1507	7.2	0045	9.8	1225	9.5	0825	13.3	2043	13.6	0714	7.5	1948	7.5	0112	3.6	1353	3.4	0328	5.6	1605	5.6	0009	4.3	1333	4.1
3	F	0334	7.5	1552	7.3	0133	9.7	1313	9.5	0911	13.4	2128	13.6	0757	7.7	2033	7.5	0156	3.7	1438	3.4	0418	5.7	1656	5.6	0056	4.4	1422	4.0
4	Sa	0420	7.5	1637	7.3	0219	9.6	1401	9.4	0956	13.2	2214	13.4	0840	7.7	2119	7.4	0241	3.8	1523	3.4	0511	5.7	1746	5.6	0146	4.4	1517	3.9
5	Su	0508	7.4	1723	7.1	0308	9.2	1449	9.1	1042	12.8	2259	12.9	0925	7.6	2206	7.1	0326	3.8	1609	3.3	0601	5.6	1837	5.4	0238	4.3	1613	3.7
6	M	0557	7.1	1810	6.9	0400	8.8	1539	8.7	1127	12.2	2347	12.2	1012	7.3	2258	6.8	0412	3.6	1656	3.3	0654	5.6	1930	5.1	0332	4.2	1714	3.6
7	Tu	0646	6.8	1900	6.7	0458	8.3	1634	8.3	1215	12.2	—	—	1106	7.0	2358	6.5	0500	3.4	1846	3.0	0748	5.2	2024	4.9	0432	4.0	1820	3.5
8	W	0741	6.6	1958	6.5	0605	7.9	1737	7.9	0038	11.5	1309	11.6	—	6.3	1211	6.8	0551	3.2	1846	3.0	0846	5.0	2120	4.7	0539	3.8	1926	3.5
9	Th	0843	6.4	2107	6.3	0721	7.8	1848	7.8	0138	10.8	1415	10.8	0107	6.3	1326	6.5	0649	2.9	1954	3.0	0948	4.8	2222	4.6	0651	3.7	2028	3.6
10	F	0952	6.3	2224	6.3	0832	7.9	1958	7.9	0249	10.5	1529	10.5	0216	6.3	1444	6.4	0800	2.9	2107	3.0	1058	4.7	2326	4.7	0800	3.6	2125	3.6
11	Sa	1105	6.3	2339	6.2	0931	8.1	2100	8.1	0404	10.6	1641	10.9	0324	6.3	1557	6.4	0922	2.9	2211	3.0	1207	4.7	—	0904	3.6	2212	3.7
12	Su	—	—	1208	6.4	1020	8.5	2152	8.5	0512	11.0	1740	11.5	0423	6.5	1658	6.5	1034	2.9	2306	3.1	0030	4.8	1309	4.9	1000	3.7	2253	3.9
13	M	0038	6.4	1300	6.5	1101	8.6	2237	8.8	0607	11.8	1831	12.2	0513	6.7	1747	6.7	1131	2.9	2353	3.2	0122	4.8	1400	5.0	1047	3.7	2331	4.0
14	Tu	0128	6.5	1342	6.6	1139	8.6	2315	9.0	0655	12.0	1914	12.5	0556	6.8	1829	6.8	1217	2.9	—	—	0205	5.1	1441	5.0	1126	3.7	—	—
15	W	0208	6.6	1420	6.7	0025	9.1	1212	8.7	0735	12.2	1952	12.5	0632	7.1	1906	7.1	0034	3.3	1257	3.0	0243	5.2	1516	5.1	0006	4.1	1202	3.7
16	Th	0244	6.6	1454	6.8	0057	9.1	1316	8.7	0812	12.2	2026	12.5	0706	7.3	1938	7.3	0115	3.3	1331	3.0	0315	5.2	1550	5.1	0042	4.0	1236	3.7
17	F	0319	6.8	1527	6.9	0130	8.9	1347	8.5	0843	12.2	2057	12.5	0737	7.2	2008	7.2	0146	3.3	1403	3.0	0343	5.2	1620	5.1	0114	3.9	1310	3.7
18	Sa	0352	6.9	1600	6.7	0202	8.5	1419	8.3	0912	12.1	2127	12.7	0808	7.0	2037	7.0	0218	3.3	1435	3.0	0411	5.2	1654	5.0	0147	3.8	1343	3.6
19	Su	0426	6.9	1630	6.6	0236	8.2	1454	8.1	0942	12.1	2157	12.1	0840	6.8	2110	6.8	0250	3.3	1508	3.0	0443	5.0	1730	4.9	0222	3.7	1418	3.6
20	M	0458	6.7	1702	6.5	0314	7.9	1535	8.0	1012	12.0	2230	11.7	0915	6.5	2145	6.6	0323	3.2	1544	3.0	0520	5.0	1809	4.7	0303	3.8	1456	3.4
21	Tu	0532	6.5	1734	6.3	0359	7.6	1627	7.7	1042	11.8	2301	11.2	0953	6.4	2223	6.1	0437	3.0	1623	2.9	0603	4.9	1854	4.6	0347	3.7	1539	3.4
22	W	0607	6.3	1810	6.2	0458	7.5	1737	7.5	1115	10.9	2334	10.4	1034	6.2	2305	5.9	0520	3.0	1705	2.9	0652	4.7	1943	4.3	0439	3.6	1626	3.3
23	Th	0645	6.1	1852	6.1	0614	7.7	1857	7.6	1151	10.3	—	—	1122	6.2	2357	5.9	0607	2.9	1753	2.9	0748	4.5	2037	4.3	0541	3.3	1721	3.3
24	F	0734	6.0	1948	6.0	0734	8.2	2011	8.4	0021	10.0	1249	10.1	—	6.2	1225	5.8	0607	2.9	1847	2.9	0748	4.3	2135	4.3	0651	3.3	1826	3.3
25	Sa	0842	5.9	2108	5.8	0843	8.7	2112	9.1	0135	11.2	1416	11.7	0112	5.8	1347	5.9	0706	2.9	1953	2.9	0852	4.4	2237	4.4	0804	3.6	1933	3.4
26	Su	1000	6.1	2228	5.9	0942	9.2	2206	9.6	0305	12.7	1539	13.2	0232	6.4	1507	6.9	0837	2.7	2112	2.8	0958	4.4	2337	4.8	0908	3.6	2035	3.6
27	M	1115	6.3	2344	5.9	1034	9.6	2257	9.9	0421	13.2	1651	13.8	0342	6.6	1616	7.1	1010	3.1	2223	3.0	1105	4.8	1211	5.1	1003	3.8	2130	4.0
28	Tu	—	—	1222	6.3	1123	9.6	2343	9.8	0530	12.7	1756	13.6	0441	6.9	1713	7.3	1115	3.3	2319	3.3	0035	5.0	1311	5.1	1053	4.0	2219	4.3
29	W	0049	6.8	1319	7.0	—	—	1210	9.8	0631	13.2	1853	13.8	0530	7.5	1804	7.6	1207	3.4	1254	3.4	0130	5.3	1407	5.5	1141	4.1	2306	4.5
30	Th	0144	7.2	1406	7.3	—	—	—	—	0724	13.3	1942	13.8	0614	7.6	1849	7.5	0009	3.6	1254	3.4	0222	5.6	1500	5.7	1053	4.0	2352	4.5
31	F	0233	7.5	1451	—	—	—	—	—	0812	13.7	2029	14.1	0656	7.8	1933	7.8	0055	3.8	1337	3.5	0313	5.8	1548	5.8	—	—	1226	4.2

*All times shown are Greenwich Mean Time.   †Difference of height in metres from Ordnance Datum (Newlyn).
‡Difference of height in metres from Ordnance Datum (Dublin).

AUGUST, 1992

High water at the undermentioned places (GMT*)—

Datum of Predictions: London Bridge †3·20 m. below · Liverpool †4·93 m. below · Avonmouth †6·50 m. below · Hull (Albert Dock) †3·90 m. below · Greenock †1·62 m. below · Leith †2·90 m. below · Dun Laoghaire ‡0·20 m. above

Day of Month	Day of Week	London Bridge Mn.	Ht.	Aft.	Ht.	Liverpool Mn.	Ht.	Aft.	Ht.	Avonmouth Mn.	Ht.	Aft.	Ht.	Hull (Albert Dock) Mn.	Ht.	Aft.	Ht.	Greenock Mn.	Ht.	Aft.	Ht.	Leith Mn.	Ht.	Aft.	Ht.	Dun Laoghaire Mn.	Ht.	Aft.	Ht.
1	Sa	0319	7·6	1535	7·5	0029	10·1	1256	9·8	0856	13·9	2111	14·1	0737	8·1	2015	7·8	0139	3·9	1420	3·6	0401	6·0	1637	5·8	0037	4·6	1311	4·2
2	Su	0404	7·6	1619	7·5	0114	10·1	1340	9·6	0938	13·7	2155	13·8	0819	8·1	2057	7·6	0223	4·0	1501	3·5	0450	6·0	1724	5·7	0123	4·6	1357	4·1
3	M	0448	7·4	1701	7·3	0158	9·8	1423	9·3	1019	13·2	2237	13·1	0904	8·0	2141	7·3	0306	4·0	1544	3·5	0541	5·8	1813	5·5	0211	4·5	1445	4·0
4	Tu	0532	7·1	1744	7·1	0242	9·4	1508	8·8	1101	12·5	2318	12·3	0949	7·6	2227	6·9	0350	3·9	1627	3·2	0630	5·6	1901	5·2	0301	4·3	1535	4·0
5	W	0617	6·8	1831	6·8	0328	8·8	1557	8·3	1142	11·6	—		1041	7·0	2320	6·5	0435	3·6	1712	3·2	0722	4·9	1952	4·9	0357	3·7	1632	3·8
6	Th	0704	6·4	1924	6·4	0423	8·2	1657	7·8	0001	11·3	1227	10·7	1142	6·7	—		0522	3·4	1803	2·9	0818	4·5	2046	4·5	0504	3·5	1738	3·7
7	F	0801	6·2	2030	6·1	0532	7·6	1812	7·5	0053	10·4	1330	10·0	0024	6·2	1259	6·0	0614	3·1	1906	3·0	0920	4·5	2150	4·5	0621	3·5	1848	3·7
8	Sa	0907	5·9	2152	5·9	0657	7·3	1935	7·3	0208	9·8	1456	9·9	0138	6·2	1427	6·0	0723	3·1	2034	3·2	1033	4·5	2300	4·7	0737	3·5	1958	3·7
9	Su	1031	5·9	2319	5·9	0819	7·5	2044	7·9	0338	9·9	1620	10·5	0257	6·3	1549	6·3	0908	2·8	2152	3·1	1152	4·9	—		0850	3·6	2102	3·8
10	M	1146	6·1	—		0919	7·9	2138	8·4	0454	10·7	1722	11·4	0404	6·6	1648	6·8	1028	2·9	2251	2·5	0103	5·1	1256	5·2	0951	3·6	2156	3·9
11	Tu	0021	6·4	1241	6·4	1006	8·5	2220	8·8	0550	11·4	1812	12·0	0455	6·9	1734	7·1	1123	2·9	2339	2·5	0146	5·2	1343	5·2	1036	3·7	2239	4·0
12	W	0109	6·6	1323	6·6	1044	8·5	2257	9·0	0636	12·0	1855	12·5	0537	7·1	1811	7·4	1205	3·0	—		0220	5·2	1420	5·2	1113	3·8	2314	4·1
13	Th	0148	6·8	1359	6·8	1118	8·7	2330	9·2	0716	12·5	1931	12·7	0611	7·4	1845	7·5	0019	3·1	1241	3·3	0248	5·3	1452	5·3	1144	3·9	—	
14	F	0223	6·9	1433	6·9	1149	8·9	—		0749	12·6	2004	12·8	0643	7·5	1913	7·5	0055	3·2	1312	3·4	0316	5·4	1522	5·4	0009	4·0	1213	4·0
15	Sa	0256	6·9	1503	6·9	0001	9·3	1219	8·9	0819	12·6	2032	12·8	0712	7·5	1940	7·4	0126	3·3	1341	3·4	0345	5·4	1554	5·4	0046	4·0	1242	4·0
16	Su	0325	6·9	1532	6·9	0032	9·3	1248	8·9	0846	12·6	2100	12·8	0742	7·4	2008	7·2	0156	3·4	1410	3·4	0416	5·3	1626	5·3	0113	3·9	1308	3·9
17	M	0356	6·9	1602	6·9	0103	9·2	1317	8·8	0914	12·5	2129	12·5	0813	7·2	2039	7·1	0226	3·4	1441	3·3	0450	5·2	1700	5·3	0146	3·9	1339	3·9
18	Tu	0427	6·8	1633	6·8	0133	9·0	1347	8·6	0942	12·1	2159	12·1	0847	7·1	2111	6·9	0257	3·3	1515	3·3	0530	5·0	1735	5·0	0225	3·8	1414	3·8
19	W	0458	6·7	1705	6·6	0202	8·8	1418	8·4	1012	11·7	2228	11·5	0921	6·9	2145	6·5	0330	3·3	1552	3·3	0615	4·8	1816	4·8	0310	3·7	1456	3·7
20	Th	0532	6·5	1739	6·4	0237	8·5	1456	8·1	1040	11·2	2258	11·0	0959	6·5	2223	6·2	0406	3·3	1632	3·2	0713	4·6	1901	4·6	0403	3·5	1545	3·5
21	F	0608	6·2	1819	6·2	0319	8·1	1545	7·7	1112	10·7	2339	10·2	1044	6·2	2311	5·9	0447	3·2	1716	3·1	0820	4·5	1956	4·5	0506	3·4	1640	3·5
22	Sa	0653	5·9	1916	5·9	0417	7·7	1654	7·5	—		1204	9·9	1144	5·8	—		0531	3·1	1806	2·9	0931	4·4	2100	4·4	0624	3·4	1748	3·5
23	Su	0751	5·7	2034	5·7	0540	7·4	1825	7·4	0050	9·9	1335	10·0	0021	6·0	1314	6·3	0625	2·9	1906	2·8	1043	4·4	2205	4·3	0746	3·5	1903	3·7
24	M	0925	5·7	2204	5·9	0712	7·6	1949	7·9	0234	10·0	1514	11·4	0201	6·3	1450	6·5	0801	2·8	2034	2·7	1154	4·8	2313	4·7	0854	3·7	2013	4·1
25	Tu	1051	6·0	2329	6·4	0826	8·1	2056	8·6	0402	10·6	1634	12·6	0321	6·5	1603	6·6	0957	2·7	2158	2·9	0015	5·1	1256	5·2	0951	4·1	2112	4·4
26	W	—		1203	7·0	0928	8·8	2150	9·2	0515	12·0	1742	13·5	0421	6·6	1701	7·2	1150	2·9	2348	3·3	0111	5·5	1350	5·6	1040	4·1	2203	4·5
27	Th	0035	6·9	1300	7·3	1019	9·3	2240	9·8	0617	12·9	1838	14·1	0511	7·2	1747	7·7	1234	3·3	—		0203	5·8	1439	5·8	1124	4·2	2250	4·3
28	F	0128	7·3	1348	7·5	1106	9·8	2325	10·1	0707	13·6	1926	14·4	0553	7·7	1829	8·1	0034	3·5	1316	3·6	0252	6·1	1526	5·9	—		1206	4·4
29	Sa	0215	7·6	1432	7·6	1150	10·0	—		0752	14·0	2009	14·4	0634	8·1	1910	7·9	0118	3·9	1355	3·7	0341	6·1	1613	6·1	0016	4·6	1247	4·3
30	Su	0300	7·6	1514	7·6	0008	10·3	1232	9·9	0833	14·0	2050	14·3	0714	7·9	1949	8·3	0200	4·0	1435	3·6	0428	6·1	1658	5·7	0058	4·6	1328	4·2
31	M	0342	7·6	1556	7·6	0050	10·2	1314	9·7	0912	13·9	2129	13·9	0757	8·3	2030	7·7	0240	4·0	1515	3·6	0516	6·0	1742	5·5	0140	4·5	1409	4·1

* All times shown are Greenwich Mean Time.   † Difference of height in metres from Ordnance Datum (Newlyn).   ‡ Difference of height in metres from Ordnance Datum (Dublin).

SEPTEMBER, 1992

High water at the undermentioned places (GMT*)—

Datum of Predictions (below Ordnance Datum unless noted): London Bridge †3·20 m. below; Liverpool †4·93 m. below; Avonmouth †6·50 m. below; Hull (Albert Dock) †3·90 m. below; Greenock †1·62 m. below; Leith †2·90 m. below; Dun Laoghaire ‡0·20 m. above.

Day of Month	Day of Week	London Bridge Mn h.m.	Ht m.	Aft h.m.	Ht m.	Liverpool Mn h.m.	Ht m.	Aft h.m.	Ht m.	Avonmouth Mn h.m.	Ht m.	Aft h.m.	Ht m.	Hull (Albert Dock) Mn h.m.	Ht m.	Aft h.m.	Ht m.	Greenock Mn h.m.	Ht m.	Aft h.m.	Ht m.	Leith Mn h.m.	Ht m.	Aft h.m.	Ht m.	Dun Laoghaire Mn h.m.	Ht m.	Aft h.m.	Ht m.
1	Tu	0424	7·4	1637	7·4	0133	9·9	1354	9·4	0952	13·3	2210	13·1	0842	8·0	2112	7·4	0242	3·9	1514	3·5	0515	5·9	1743	5·5	0144	4·5	1410	4·1
2	W	0505	7·0	1719	7·1	0213	9·3	1436	8·9	1031	12·5	2248	12·5	0928	7·5	2156	6·9	0324	3·8	1555	3·4	0603	5·8	1830	5·1	0232	4·2	1457	3·9
3	Th	0546	6·7	1803	6·7	0258	8·7	1521	8·3	1109	11·5	2327	11·0	1017	6·8	2244	6·5	0407	3·5	1637	3·3	0654	5·1	1918	4·8	0325	3·9	1550	3·8
4	F	0628	6·3	1853	6·3	0349	8·1	1619	7·7	1149	10·5	—	—	1116	6·2	—	—	0451	3·3	1723	3·2	0748	4·7	2011	4·5	0433	3·6	1656	3·6
5	Sa	0719	6·0	1957	5·9	0458	7·2	1736	7·3	0014	9·9	1249	9·6	0055	5·8	1232	5·4	0541	3·0	1819	3·1	0852	4·4	2115	4·5	0555	3·4	1813	3·5
6	Su	0822	5·7	2115	5·7	0634	7·0	1909	7·3	0131	9·2	1423	9·4	0223	5·8	1411	5·6	0645	2·7	1952	2·9	1005	4·3	2226	4·5	0716	3·3	1927	3·6
7	M	0948	5·7	2252	5·9	0801	7·2	2022	7·8	0311	9·4	1556	10·2	0339	6·1	1534	5·9	0854	2·7	2126	2·9	1128	4·3	2339	4·7	0834	3·5	2037	3·7
8	Tu	1118	6·0	2357	6·4	0900	7·8	2114	8·3	0430	10·4	1658	11·3	0431	6·5	1628	6·3	1013	2·8	2228	3·0	—	—	1231	4·9	0932	3·6	2132	3·8
9	W	—	—	1214	6·7	0943	8·2	2155	8·7	0525	11·4	1746	12·1	0511	6·9	1711	6·7	1103	2·8	2315	3·1	0035	4·8	1316	5·1	1018	3·6	2215	3·9
10	Th	0043	6·7	1257	6·9	1019	8·6	2230	9·0	0610	12·0	1828	12·5	0544	7·1	1746	7·0	1142	2·9	2354	3·3	0116	5·0	1350	5·2	1053	3·7	2250	4·0
11	F	0123	6·8	1334	6·9	1051	8·8	2302	9·2	0649	12·4	1904	12·8	0615	7·4	1817	7·2	1214	3·0	—	—	0148	5·2	1422	5·3	1119	3·7	2320	4·0
12	Sa	0157	6·9	1405	7·0	1120	9·0	2333	9·4	0721	12·6	1935	12·9	0645	7·5	1843	7·3	0028	3·1	1244	3·3	0218	5·4	1452	5·3	1144	3·8	2348	4·0
13	Su	0226	6·9	1434	7·0	1150	9·1	—	—	0749	12·8	2002	13·0	0716	7·5	1910	7·4	0100	3·4	1313	3·4	0246	5·4	1522	5·3	—	—	1209	3·8
14	M	0256	7·0	1503	7·1	0003	9·3	1218	9·1	0816	12·9	2032	13·0	0748	7·2	1938	7·3	0129	3·4	1342	3·4	0318	5·4	1556	5·3	0013	4·0	1235	3·8
15	Tu	0325	7·0	1534	7·1	0034	9·4	1246	9·0	0844	12·5	2101	12·3	0820	6·9	2009	7·1	0159	3·4	1413	3·4	0350	5·3	1628	5·0	0042	3·9	1304	3·8
16	W	0356	7·0	1604	7·0	0103	9·1	1317	8·9	0914	12·5	2132	12·3	0854	6·3	2040	6·9	0230	3·3	1447	3·4	0426	5·1	1701	4·8	0115	3·8	1342	3·7
17	Th	0427	6·8	1638	6·8	0134	8·8	1349	8·7	0945	12·1	2203	11·7	0932	5·8	2112	6·3	0304	3·2	1524	3·3	0505	4·8	1739	4·5	0156	3·8	1422	3·6
18	F	0501	6·6	1716	6·6	0208	8·6	1427	8·3	1014	11·5	2235	11·1	1019	6·0	2149	5·8	0341	3·1	1604	3·2	0554	4·5	1826	4·5	0243	3·6	1513	3·5
19	Sa	0539	6·3	1801	6·3	0256	8·1	1518	7·9	1049	10·5	2319	10·5	1120	6·8	2238	6·3	0422	3·1	1647	3·1	0652	4·5	1924	4·6	0340	3·4	1613	3·5
20	Su	0625	6·0	1859	6·0	0356	7·7	1630	7·6	1144	10·3	—	—	—	—	2349	6·3	0508	3·0	1735	3·0	0801	4·6	2031	4·6	0449	3·4	1724	3·4
21	M	0731	5·7	2019	5·8	0520	7·5	1804	7·5	0035	9·9	1317	10·0	0130	7·3	1253	7·0	0612	2·9	1834	3·1	0913	4·6	2141	5·2	0611	3·5	1842	3·7
22	Tu	0900	5·7	2150	6·0	0655	7·6	1928	8·0	0216	10·0	1456	10·6	0256	7·6	1436	7·3	0757	3·0	2002	3·3	1026	5·0	2250	5·7	0733	3·5	1954	3·9
23	W	1030	6·1	2313	6·6	0811	8·2	2036	8·7	0346	11·0	1617	11·7	0357	7·7	1548	7·5	0941	3·2	2131	3·5	1135	5·6	2354	5·9	0840	3·7	2053	4·4
24	Th	1142	6·6	—	—	0910	8·9	2129	9·3	0458	12·1	1723	12·7	0447	7·5	1642	7·7	1040	3·4	2233	3·6	—	—	1237	5·9	0935	3·9	2145	4·5
25	F	0017	7·1	1238	7·1	0959	9·4	2217	9·8	0557	13·0	1818	13·5	0530	8·0	1727	7·8	1128	3·5	2324	3·8	0052	6·1	1330	5·9	1022	4·1	2230	4·6
26	Sa	0109	7·4	1327	7·5	1044	9·8	2302	10·1	0646	13·6	1904	14·0	0611	8·1	1807	8·0	1210	3·6	—	—	0143	6·1	1416	5·9	1105	4·2	2313	4·5
27	Su	0155	7·5	1411	7·6	1126	10·0	2344	10·2	0730	14·0	1947	14·2	0653	8·1	1845	8·1	0054	3·9	1250	3·7	0231	6·1	1501	5·9	1144	4·3	2355	4·4
28	M	0237	7·5	1451	7·6	—	—	1207	10·0	0809	14·1	2026	14·1	0737	8·1	1924	8·1	0136	4·0	1329	3·7	0318	6·1	1546	5·9	—	—	1221	4·3
29	Tu	0318	7·4	1532	7·6	0027	10·0	1248	9·9	0847	13·9	2105	13·7	0822	7·8	2004	8·1	0217	3·9	1407	3·7	0405	6·1	1630	5·9	0036	4·5	1258	4·2
30	W	0357	7·3	1614	7·4	0107	9·7	1327	9·4	0927	13·3	2145	12·9	—	—	2046	7·8	—	—	1445	3·6	0452	5·7	1713	5·4	0118	4·3	1339	4·1

*All times shown are Greenwich Mean Time.   †Difference of height in metres from Ordnance Datum (Newlyn).
‡Difference of height in metres from Ordnance Datum (Dublin).

OCTOBER, 1992

High water at the undermentioned places (GMT*)—

Day of Week	Day of Month	London Bridge †Datum of Predictions 3·20 m. below				Liverpool †Datum of Predictions 4·93 m. below				Avonmouth †Datum of Predictions 6·50 m. below				Hull (Albert Dock) †Datum of Predictions 3·90 m. below				Greenock †Datum of Predictions 1·62 m. below				Leith †Datum of Predictions 2·90 m. below				Dun Laoghaire ‡Datum of Predictions 0·20 m. above			
		Mn. h.m.	Ht. m.	Aft. h.m.	Ht. m.	Mn. h.m.	Ht. m.	Aft. h.m.	Ht. m.	Mn. h.m.	Ht. m.	Aft. h.m.	Ht. m.	Mn. h.m.	Ht. m.	Aft. h.m.	Ht. m.	Mn. h.m.	Ht. m.	Aft. h.m.	Ht. m.	Mn. h.m.	Ht. m.	Aft. h.m.	Ht. m.	Mn. h.m.	Ht. m.	Aft. h.m.	Ht. m.
Th	1	0437	7·0	1655	7·1	0148	9·1	1406	8·9	1004	12·4	2223	11·8	0908	7·2	2127	6·9	0258	3·6	1524	3·6	0539	5·4	1756	5·1	0207	4·1	1424	4·0
F	2	0515	6·6	1739	6·7	0230	8·5	1450	8·3	1041	11·4	2259	10·8	0956	6·5	2212	6·5	0339	3·4	1604	3·3	0628	5·0	1841	4·8	0300	3·8	1515	3·8
Sa	3	0554	6·2	1827	6·2	0319	7·8	1545	7·8	1119	10·4	2343	9·8	1051	5·9	2302	6·1	0422	3·1	1648	3·1	0720	4·6	1933	4·5	0407	3·5	1620	3·7
Su	4	0641	5·9	1926	5·9	0423	7·2	1657	7·3	----		1215	9·5	----		1200	5·4	0510	2·7	1739	3·0	0820	4·4	2033	4·3	0527	3·3	1738	3·6
M	5	0741	5·6	2037	5·7	0553	6·9	1825	7·0	0053	9·1	1345	9·2	0008	5·7	1331	5·4	0610	2·7	1856	2·9	0928	4·3	2141	4·3	0648	3·3	1852	3·6
Tu	6	0900	5·5	2207	5·8	0723	7·1	1942	7·3	0229	9·2	1515	9·9	0128	5·6	1503	5·6	0813	2·8	2042	3·0	1043	4·6	2250	4·5	0803	3·4	2000	3·6
W	7	1034	5·8	2320	6·2	0825	7·6	2037	8·1	0350	10·1	1621	10·9	0257	5·9	1559	5·8	0937	3·1	2150	3·1	1148	4·6	2350	4·7	0902	3·5	2057	3·7
Th	8	1139	6·2	----		0910	8·5	2119	8·6	0448	11·0	1711	11·7	0355	6·1	1640	6·2	1027	3·2	2239	3·2	----		1235	5·1	0946	3·7	2142	3·8
F	9	0010	6·6	1224	6·6	0946	9·1	2156	8·9	0533	11·8	1753	12·3	0438	6·7	1713	6·6	1106	3·2	2320	3·3	0035	5·0	1313	5·3	1021	3·7	2218	3·8
Sa	10	0049	6·8	1300	6·9	1019	9·3	2230	9·1	0614	12·4	1831	12·8	0513	7·0	1743	6·8	1140	3·3	2356	3·4	0111	5·2	1346	5·3	1049	3·8	2249	3·9
Su	11	0123	6·9	1333	6·9	1048	9·0	2302	9·2	0648	12·6	1903	12·8	0544	7·3	1811	7·1	1211	3·4	----		0145	5·3	1420	5·3	1112	3·8	2316	3·9
M	12	0154	6·9	1402	7·0	1118	9·2	2333	9·3	0717	13·0	1933	13·0	0617	7·3	1839	7·3	0029	3·4	1243	3·4	0214	5·4	1452	5·4	1137	3·9	2344	3·9
Tu	13	0223	7·1	1434	7·1	1149	9·2	----		0747	13·0	2005	13·0	0650	7·4	1910	7·4	0101	3·4	1314	3·5	0251	5·4	1526	5·4	----		1205	3·9
W	14	0256	7·1	1507	7·1	0005	9·3	1221	9·2	0818	12·9	2037	12·8	0724	7·3	1941	7·4	0134	3·5	1348	3·5	0330	5·4	1558	5·3	0015	3·9	1237	4·0
Th	15	0329	7·1	1542	7·1	0039	9·3	1253	9·1	0851	12·7	2112	12·4	0759	7·1	2015	7·3	0208	3·5	1423	3·5	0410	5·3	1633	5·1	0053	3·9	1315	3·9
F	16	0403	6·9	1620	7·0	0114	9·0	1330	8·9	0927	12·3	2149	11·9	0836	6·9	2049	7·1	0244	3·5	1501	3·5	0456	4·9	1715	5·0	0137	3·9	1401	3·9
Sa	17	0441	6·8	1704	6·8	0155	8·6	1413	8·5	1003	11·8	2230	11·3	0918	6·5	2129	6·5	0324	3·5	1542	3·5	0546	4·6	1803	4·9	0228	3·7	1454	3·9
Su	18	0522	6·4	1753	6·4	0244	8·2	1507	8·1	1045	11·2	2320	10·6	1007	6·2	2227	6·1	0408	3·4	1626	3·4	0645	4·6	1903	4·7	0329	3·5	1556	3·7
M	19	0611	6·1	1853	6·1	0346	7·6	1617	7·8	1146	10·6	----		1109	6·1	----		0458	3·4	1715	3·4	0750	4·6	2011	4·6	0440	3·5	1707	3·7
Tu	20	0719	5·8	2011	5·9	0508	7·6	1743	7·8	0034	10·2	1309	10·3	----		1238	6·0	0603	3·4	1815	3·3	0858	4·8	2120	4·7	0600	3·5	1824	3·7
W	21	0842	5·9	2135	6·3	0634	7·9	1903	8·3	0201	10·2	1437	10·8	0057	6·0	1413	6·3	0751	3·1	1936	3·3	1009	4·8	2230	4·7	0716	3·5	1933	3·8
Th	22	1006	6·2	2252	6·7	0747	8·3	2009	8·7	0325	11·1	1556	11·8	0225	6·3	1522	6·6	0915	3·1	2101	3·4	1115	5·0	2333	4·9	0821	3·7	2034	4·0
F	23	1116	6·7	2354	7·1	0846	8·8	2105	9·2	0435	12·0	1659	12·8	0328	6·8	1617	7·1	1013	3·5	2205	3·6	----		1213	5·3	0915	3·7	2126	4·2
Sa	24	----		1215	7·1	0935	9·3	2155	9·6	0533	12·8	1754	13·2	0421	7·1	1704	7·4	1101	3·5	2259	3·7	0030	5·6	1305	5·6	1003	4·1	2212	4·4
Su	25	0048	7·3	1304	7·2	1020	9·6	2240	9·9	0624	13·3	1842	13·5	0508	7·6	1743	7·6	1145	3·6	2346	3·8	0122	5·8	1354	5·7	1044	4·2	2256	4·4
M	26	0134	7·3	1349	7·3	1104	9·7	2323	9·9	0707	13·6	1924	13·7	0551	7·9	1822	7·9	0031	3·8	1304	3·7	0211	5·8	1439	5·7	1123	4·3	2337	4·4
Tu	27	0216	7·3	1432	7·4	1144	9·7	----		0747	13·7	2005	13·6	0636	7·9	1902	7·9	0114	3·7	1342	3·7	0300	5·9	1522	5·8	1158	4·3	----	
W	28	0256	7·2	1512	7·4	0005	9·7	1224	9·6	0825	13·6	2044	13·3	0721	7·5	1941	7·6	0154	3·6	1420	3·6	0346	5·8	1603	5·6	0018	4·3	1235	4·3
Th	29	0334	7·1	1555	7·3	0046	9·3	1303	9·3	0904	13·1	2124	12·7	0806	7·3	2022	7·3	0235	3·5	1458	3·5	0431	5·5	1645	5·4	0100	4·2	1314	4·2
F	30	0412	6·9	1635	7·0	0126	8·9	1342	8·9	0942	12·3	2202	11·7	0851	6·9	2101	6·9	0315	3·2	1537	3·4	0516	5·5	1724	5·2	0147	4·0	1359	4·1
Sa	31	0448	6·6	1718	6·7	0206	8·4	1425	8·4	1020	11·4	2238	10·8	0938	6·4	2141	6·4					0601	5·0	1805	4·9	0239	3·7	1450	3·9

*All times shown are Greenwich Mean Time.   †Difference of height in metres from Ordnance Datum (Newlyn).   ‡Difference of height in metres from Ordnance Datum (Dublin).

NOVEMBER, 1992

High water at the undermentioned places (GMT*)—

Day of Month	Day of Week	LONDON BRIDGE †Datum of Predictions 3·20 m. below				LIVERPOOL †Datum of Predictions 4·93 m. below				AVONMOUTH †Datum of Predictions 6·50 m. below				HULL (Albert Dock) †Datum of Predictions 3·90 m. below				GREENOCK †Datum of Predictions 1·62 m. below				LEITH †Datum of Predictions 2·90 m. below				DUN LAOGHAIRE ‡Datum of Predictions 0·20 m. above			
		Mn. h.m.	Ht. m.	Aft. h.m.	Ht. m.	Mn. h.m.	Ht. m.	Aft. h.m.	Ht. m.	Mn. h.m.	Ht. m.	Aft. h.m.	Ht. m.	Mn. h.m.	Ht. m.	Aft. h.m.	Ht. m.	Mn. h.m.	Ht. m.	Aft. h.m.	Ht. m.	Mn. h.m.	Ht. m.	Aft. h.m.	Ht. m.	Mn. h.m.	Ht. m.	Aft. h.m.	Ht. m.
1	Su	0526	6·3	1803	6·3	0253	7·8	1514	8·0	1057	10·6	2319	10·0	1024	5·9	2226	6·3	0357	3·1	1619	3·3	0650	4·7	1852	4·6	0342	3·5	1550	3·8
2	M	0608	6·0	1855	6·0	0348	7·3	1614	7·6	1144	9·8			1118	5·5	2319	5·9	0444	2·9	1706	3·2	0743	4·4	1948	4·5	0452	3·3	1700	3·6
3	Tu	0702	5·7	1958	5·7	0458	7·0	1726	7·3	0014	9·4	1255	9·4	0028	5·7	1224	5·7	0539	2·8	1806	3·1	0843	4·3	2050	4·4	0606	3·3	1811	3·5
4	W	0812	5·5	2110	5·7	0621	7·0	1842	7·5	0130	9·2	1416	9·6	0145	5·8	1349	5·8	0659	2·8	1932	3·0	0946	4·4	2154	4·4	0716	3·3	1918	3·6
5	Th	0931	5·6	2223	5·9	0731	7·3	1945	7·8	0249	9·7	1525	10·3	0258	6·1	1508	6·0	0832	2·9	2053	3·1	1045	4·5	2254	4·6	0816	3·4	2014	3·6
6	F	1044	5·9	2322	6·2	0823	7·8	2034	8·2	0353	10·4	1621	11·1	0352	6·5	1556	6·4	0934	3·0	2152	3·1	1145	4·8	2346	4·8	0902	3·5	2101	3·6
7	Sa	1137	5·9			0904	8·2	2117	8·6	0445	11·2	1708	11·7	0434	6·8	1633	6·8	1021	3·3	2240	3·2			1230	5·0	0941	3·6	2139	3·7
8	Su	0007	6·5	1219	6·5	0941	8·6	2155	8·9	0529	11·8	1750	12·2	0512	7·1	1705	7·0	1101	3·3	2321	3·2	0031	5·0	1309	5·1	1011	3·7	2214	3·8
9	M	0045	6·7	1256	6·7	1014	8·9	2230	9·1	0608	12·3	1828	12·5	0550	7·2	1737	7·2	1138	3·3			0113	5·2	1346	5·1	1039	3·8	2246	3·8
10	Tu	0120	6·9	1331	6·9	1048	9·1	2306	9·2	0645	12·7	1906	12·8	0627	7·3	1811	7·1	0000	3·5	1214	3·5	0154	5·3	1422	5·3	1107	3·9	2319	3·9
11	W	0155	6·9	1409	7·0	1123	9·3	2343	9·3	0721	12·9	1942	12·9	0706	7·3	1846	7·2	0037	3·5	1249	3·6	0233	5·3	1458	5·3	1140	4·0	2357	4·0
12	Th	0232	7·1	1447	7·1			1200	9·3	0758	13·0	2022	12·9	0745	7·2	1921	7·1	0114	3·3	1326	3·7	0316	5·3	1535	5·3			1218	4·1
13	F	0310	7·1	1528	7·2	0022	9·3	1239	9·1	0837	12·7	2103	13·0	0826	7·1	1958	7·0	0152	3·3	1404	3·7	0401	5·3	1616	5·2	0039	4·0	1300	4·1
14	Sa	0349	7·0	1612	7·2	0103	9·1	1321	9·1	0918	12·3	2145	13·2	0911	7·0	2037	6·9	0233	3·3	1444	3·7	0450	5·2	1701	5·1	0126	3·9	1347	4·1
15	Su	0430	6·8	1658	7·0	0148	8·8	1408	8·8	1002	11·8	2231	12·3	1002	6·6	2121	6·6	0316	3·3	1527	3·6	0541	5·1	1754	5·0	0218	3·8	1440	4·0
16	M	0515	6·6	1749	6·7	0240	8·5	1501	8·5	1049	10·8	2323	11·8	1059	6·4	2210	6·4	0401	3·2	1613	3·5	0637	5·0	1852	4·9	0320	3·6	1542	3·9
17	Tu	0605	6·3	1848	6·4	0341	8·1	1606	8·3	1147	10·1					2311	6·4	0457	3·2	1703	3·5	0737	4·9	1956	4·8	0428	3·6	1649	3·9
18	W	0706	6·1	1957	6·3	0451	7·9	1718	8·1	0025	11·1	1255	11·0	0024	6·4	1214	6·4	0602	3·1	1801	3·5	0841	4·8	2100	5·0	0541	3·7	1800	3·9
19	Th	0819	6·1	2111	6·4	0605	7·9	1832	8·3	0138	11·2	1412	11·1	0147	6·8	1340	6·6	0724	3·1	1911	3·5	0945	5·0	2205	5·0	0652	3·7	1909	3·9
20	F	0936	6·3	2224	6·6	0716	8·2	1940	8·6	0256	12·2	1527	12·1	0257	6·9	1450	6·8	0841	3·3	2028	3·5	1048	5·4	2309	5·2	0757	3·7	2010	4·0
21	Sa	1049	6·6	2330	6·9	0818	8·6	2040	8·9	0406	12·7	1633	12·5	0357	6·8	1549	6·9	0943	3·5	2137	3·5	1148	5·5			0851	3·9	2107	4·1
22	Su	1151	7·0			0911	8·9	2134	9·2	0506	13·0	1730	12·8	0451	7·3	1640	7·1	1034	3·5	2235	3·5	0009	5·4	1243	5·4	0941	4·0	2156	4·2
23	M	0027	7·0	1245	7·2	1000	9·4	2221	9·3	0558	13·2	1821	13·0	0540	7·4	1723	7·3	1121	3·6	2327	3·5	0105	5·5	1333	5·5	1025	4·1	2243	4·2
24	Tu	0114	7·0	1333	7·3	1044	9·5	2306	9·3	0645	13·2	1906	13·0	0627	7·4	1805	7·4	1203	3·6			0158	5·6	1418	5·6	1105	4·2	2324	4·2
25	W	0158	7·1	1416	7·2	1126	9·5	2349	9·2	0727	12·9	1948	13·2	0712	7·0	1845	7·2	0013	3·6	1244	3·6	0246	5·5	1501	5·6	1141	4·2		
26	Th	0237	7·0	1458	7·1			1207	9·4	0808	12·4	2029	12·8	0755	6·7	1924	7·0	0057	3·5	1323	3·6	0331	5·3	1543	5·5	0005	4·3	1218	4·3
27	F	0315	7·0	1538	7·0	0029	9·0	1245	9·2	0847	12·0	2107	12·4	0836	6·6	2002	6·7	0138	3·4	1400	3·6	0415	5·2	1620	5·3	0046	4·1	1257	4·2
28	Sa	0352	6·7	1619	6·8	0109	8·8	1324	9·0	0925	11·8	2145	12·0	0915	6·2	2039	6·6	0218	3·3	1438	3·6	0456	5·0	1656	5·2	0130	3·9	1339	4·1
29	Su	0427	6·7	1658	6·8	0148	8·4	1402	8·7	1000	11·4	2219	11·8	0953	5·9	2114	6·2	0257	3·2	1515	3·5	0537	4·9	1731	5·0	0217	3·9	1425	4·0
30	M	0504	6·5	1739	6·5	0227	8·1	1446	8·3	1035	11·1	2254	10·7			2153	6·7	0337	3·1	1555	3·4	0618	4·8	1813	4·8	0308	3·5	1518	3·8

*All times shown are Greenwich Mean Time.   †Difference of height in metres from Ordnance Datum (Newlyn).   ‡Difference of height in metres from Ordnance Datum (Dublin).

DECEMBER, 1992

High water at the undermentioned places (GMT*)—

Day of Month	Day of Week	London Bridge †Datum of Predictions 3·20 m. below				Liverpool †Datum of Predictions 4·93 m. below				Avonmouth †Datum of Predictions 6·50 m. below				Hull (Albert Dock) †Datum of Predictions 3·90 m. below				Greenock †Datum of Predictions 1·62 m. below				Leith †Datum of Predictions 2·90 m. below				Dun Laoghaire ‡Datum of Predictions 0·20 m. above			
		Mn.	Ht.	Aft.	Ht.	Mn.	Ht.	Aft.	Ht.	Mn.	Ht.	Aft.	Ht.	Mn.	Ht.	Aft.	Ht.	Mn.	Ht.	Aft.	Ht.	Mn.	Ht.	Aft.	Ht.	Mn.	Ht.	Aft.	Ht.
1	Tu	0542	6·2	1822	6·4	0311	7·7	1532	7·6	1115	10·6	2334	10·2	1035	5·9	2237	6·4	0420	3·0	1637	3·3	0703	4·6	1901	4·7	0407	3·4	1616	3·7
2	W	0625	6·0	1914	6·1	0403	7·4	1628	7·5			1201	10·1	1123	5·7	2333	6·1	0508	3·0	1726	3·3	0754	4·5	2000	4·5	0511	3·3	1720	3·5
3	Th	0720	5·7	2013	5·9	0505	7·1	1730	7·5	0027	9·8	1303	9·9			1225	5·6	0604	2·9	1824	3·1	0852	4·4	2100	4·5	0616	3·3	1824	3·4
4	F	0827	5·6	2117	5·8	0614	7·1	1838	7·5	0133	9·6	1415	9·9	0041	5·9	1337	5·8	0711	2·9	1936	3·0	0952	4·5	2200	4·5	0718	3·3	1923	3·4
5	Sa	0935	5·7	2219	5·9	0720	7·4	1940	7·8	0243	10·5	1519	10·3	0152	6·0	1444	5·8	0824	2·9	2051	3·0	1050	4·6	2258	4·6	0810	3·5	2014	3·5
6	Su	1035	5·9	2313	6·2	0815	7·8	2032	8·1	0346	11·2	1616	10·9	0257	6·2	1539	6·2	0927	3·0	2155	3·0	1143	4·7	2352	4·8	0854	3·5	2100	3·6
7	M	1129	6·2			0901	8·2	2118	8·5	0440	11·9	1708	11·6	0352	6·5	1626	6·5	1019	3·2	2247	3·1			1230	5·1	0932	3·6	2139	3·7
8	Tu	0003	6·4	1218	6·4	0943	8·6	2202	8·8	0530	12·5	1756	12·2	0440	6·8	1708	6·8	1105	3·3	2334	3·1	0043	5·0	1313	5·2	1007	3·8	2219	3·8
9	W	0048	6·7	1306	6·7	1024	9·0	2244	9·1	0617	12·9	1842	12·6	0525	7·0	1747	7·0	1147	3·4			0130	5·2	1354	5·4	1043	3·9	2259	3·9
10	Th	0133	6·9	1351	6·9	1105	9·3	2327	9·3	0702	13·2	1927	12·9	0610	7·1	1828	7·2	0018	3·4	1228	3·6	0216	5·3	1435	5·5	1120	3·9	2341	3·9
11	F	0215	7·0	1436	7·0	1146	9·4			0745	13·3	2012	13·1	0652	7·3	1907	7·3	0100	3·3	1309	3·7	0303	5·4	1518	5·5	1201	4·2		
12	Sa	0258	7·1	1519	7·1	0011	9·4	1229	9·5	0829	13·2	2057	13·1	0735	7·4	1947	7·4	0143	3·3	1350	3·8	0352	5·4	1605	5·5	0026	4·0	1246	4·3
13	Su	0341	7·2	1606	7·1	0056	9·3	1314	9·5	0912	13·0	2142	12·9	0819	7·3	2027	7·4	0226	3·4	1432	3·9	0443	5·3	1654	5·4	0114	4·0	1333	4·3
14	M	0423	7·1	1652	7·0	0142	9·2	1402	9·3	0959	12·6	2227	12·6	0904	7·2	2111	7·2	0310	3·4	1515	3·9	0533	5·3	1745	5·3	0206	4·0	1425	4·2
15	Tu	0508	6·9	1742	7·0	0232	8·9	1453	9·1	1045	12·1	2316	12·1	0950	7·0	2157	7·0	0357	3·4	1601	3·9	0626	5·1	1839	5·2	0303	3·8	1521	4·1
16	W	0556	6·8	1835	6·8	0325	8·6	1548	8·6	1136	11·5			1042	6·7	2251	6·7	0448	3·3	1650	3·8	0720	5·0	1937	5·1	0403	3·7	1625	3·9
17	Th	0649	6·5	1934	6·5	0424	8·3	1649	8·5	0008	11·1	1232	11·1	1144	6·5	2354	6·5	0544	3·2	1743	3·6	0816	4·9	2037	5·0	0510	3·6	1731	3·9
18	F	0751	6·4	2042	6·4	0532	8·0	1758	8·3	0107	11·1	1338	11·2			1259	6·4	0648	3·2	1844	3·5	0916	4·9	2139	5·0	0620	3·6	1842	3·9
19	Sa	0903	6·5	2153	6·5	0642	8·0	1910	8·2	0218	11·5	1450	11·3	0110	6·6	1413	6·6	0800	3·2	1955	3·4	1016	4·9	2245	5·1	0726	3·7	1948	4·0
20	Su	1019	6·6	2302	6·6	0751	8·2	2018	8·4	0331	11·7	1602	11·5	0227	6·7	1519	6·7	0909	3·3	2110	3·3	1122	5·0	2352	5·2	0827	3·8	2048	4·0
21	M	1129				0851	8·5	2118	8·6	0438	12·0	1706	12·0	0338	6·8	1617	6·8	1009	3·3	2218	3·3			1222	5·2	0921	3·9	2144	4·0
22	Tu	0004	6·7	1229	6·7	0945	8·8	2210	8·8	0537	12·4	1803	12·5	0441	6·9	1708	6·9	1101	3·5	2315	3·3	0054	5·3	1316	5·2	1008	4·0	2232	4·0
23	W	0057	6·7	1320	6·7	1031	9·1	2257	8·9	0628	12·7	1852	12·5	0534	6·9	1753	7·2	1147	3·3			0148	5·4	1405	5·3	1050	4·1	2316	4·0
24	Th	0142	6·8	1405	6·7	1115	9·2	2339	8·9	0713	12·7	1935	12·5	0621	6·9	1832	7·3	0005	3·5	1230	3·6	0237	5·4	1448	5·4	1128	4·2	2355	4·2
25	F	0223	6·9	1446	6·8	1154	9·3			0755	12·8	2016	12·2	0703	6·9	1909	7·3	0049	3·3	1309	3·6	0320	5·4	1526	5·4			1205	4·1
26	Sa	0300	6·9	1524	6·9	0017	8·9	1231	9·2	0833	12·6	2051	11·9	0742	6·8	1944	7·3	0129	3·2	1346	3·6	0400	5·3	1600	5·4	0033	3·9	1320	4·0
27	Su	0335	6·9	1602	7·0	0052	8·8	1306	9·1	0908	12·3	2125	11·5	0816	6·8	2016	7·2	0205	3·2	1422	3·5	0435	5·3	1631	5·3	0110	3·8	1400	4·0
28	M	0407	6·8	1637	6·9	0126	8·6	1341	8·9	0941	11·9	2156	11·4	0850	6·7	2050	7·1	0241	3·2	1456	3·5	0509	5·2	1701	5·2	0150	3·7	1443	4·1
29	Tu	0441	6·7	1712	7·0	0201	8·4	1416	8·7	1012	11·4	2227	10·9	0922	6·7	2124	7·1	0316	3·2	1532	3·5	0545	5·1	1737	5·1	0232	3·6	1531	4·0
30	W	0515	6·5	1750	6·8	0236	8·1	1454	8·5	1044	10·9	2259	10·5	0957	6·6	2156	6·8	0354	3·1	1609	3·4	0624	4·9	1820	4·9	0317	3·5	1609	3·9
31	Th	0553	6·3	1829	6·3	0315	7·8	1536	8·0	1119	10·5	2334	10·5	1037	6·2	2234	6·5	0435	3·1	1649	3·2	0711	4·9	1911	4·7	0407	3·4	1621	3·5

*All times shown are Greenwich Mean Time.   †Difference of height in metres from Ordnance Datum (Newlyn).   ‡Difference of height in metres from Ordnance Datum (Dublin).

WEATHER IN THE UNITED KINGDOM, 1990–91

(1990) **July.**—Rainfall totals were mostly below normal except in parts of north-west Scotland, the Isle of Man and parts of Cornwall. In England and Wales many places had almost no rain from the 8th to 26th. Odiham and Farnborough (both in Hants.), Easthampstead (Berks.) and Charing (Kent) were among a few places which had no rain from the 7th to the end of the month. Scattered thunderstorms occurred on the 1st and 2nd and heavy rain fell in western areas on the 3rd and 4th. At Grizedale (Cumbria) 49 mm (1·9 in) fell on the 4th. On the 5th winds reached gale force at Shoreham-by-Sea (E. Sussex). Coastal fog formed over southern Wales and south-west England on the 6th and 7th. Further heavy rain fell in western areas on the 7th and 8th; on the 8th 46 mm (1·8 in) fell at Dunstaffnage (Strathclyde). On the 9th winds reached gale force at the Forth Road Bridge and Leith Harbour (Lothian). Rain fell from the Midlands northwards on the 15th while coastal fog persisted in western Wales on the 16th. Rain fell in western and northern areas of Scotland on the 18th and coloured dust was deposited at Cavendish (Suffolk) on the 27th. Heavy rain fell in western areas on the 29th when a fall of 61 mm (2·4 in) was recorded at Princetown (Devon). Monthly mean temperatures were above normal everywhere except for a few places in south-east England. In northern and western England temperatures barely reached 14°C (57·2°F) during the first week but on the 8th the temperature rose to 26·8°C (80·2°F) at Heathrow (Gtr. London). It became hot in southern England on the 11th and hot generally by the 14th. A temperature of 26°C (77·0°F) was recorded somewhere in the United Kingdom on every day from the 11th to the 31st. On the 15th several places in southern England recorded 31°C (87·8°F) while 33°C (91·4°F) was reached over a large area of central and southern England on the 21st. The highest temperature recorded during the month was 33·3°C (91·9°F) at St Helier (Jersey) on the 21st and the lowest was −0·5°C (31·1°F) at Grendon Underwood (Bucks.) on the 3rd. Sunshine totals were above normal everywhere and Aldergrove (Co. Antrim) had 168 per cent of the normal amount. The highest monthly total was 334·4 hours at Bastreet (Cornwall) and the highest daily total was 16·3 hours at Stornoway (Western Isles) on the 23rd.

August.—Rainfall totals were below normal everywhere except for parts of Northern Ireland and western and northern Scotland. Most places had some rain on the 14th with thunder reported in the Highland Region. In some places in southern England this ended a drought which had lasted 38 days. On the 15th thunderstorms occurred over the Midlands and East Anglia and 50 mm (2·0 in) of rain fell at Falkirk (Central). Also on the 15th a gust of 61 knots (70·2 mph) was recorded at Great Dun Fell (Cumbria). The 16th brought thunderstorms to much of central and south-east England and East Anglia. Fog was widespread over England and Wales on the 23rd and on the 24th there were thunderstorms over northern Wales and northern England. During a storm at Leeming (N. Yorks.) 30 mm (1·2 in) of rain fell in one hour and 79 mm (3·1 in) fell at Newton Seahouses (Northumberland) during the day. Thunderstorms occurred in parts of south-east England and East Anglia on the 25th and 26th. On the 25th 72 mm (2·8 in) of rain fell at Pilgrims Heath (Essex). Fog formed over much of the United Kingdom on the 25th and 26th and areas of thick fog formed over East Anglia and south-east England on the 27th. There were thunderstorms in eastern England on the 29th and fog formed over central and southern England. Monthly mean temperatures were above normal

almost everywhere in the United Kingdom. At Valley (Gwynedd) the mean minimum temperature was the highest in the area since 1933. Temperatures reached 32°C (89·6°F) in parts of south-east England on the 1st and on the 3rd the temperature reached 37·1°C (98·8°F) at Cheltenham (Glos.), the highest temperature ever recorded in the United Kingdom from an officially accredited station. On the night of the 3rd–4th the temperature did not fall below 24°C (75·2°F) at Brighton (E. Sussex). The lowest temperature was 1·7°C (35·1°F) at Tomatin (Highland) on the 23rd. Sunshine totals were generally above normal over most of England and Wales but below normal over most of Scotland and Northern Ireland. At Broom's Barn (Suffolk) it was the sunniest August for 40 years. The highest monthly total was 300.8 hours at Eastbourne (E. Sussex) and the highest daily total was 15.0 hours at Bastreet (Cornwall) on the 6th.

September.—Monthly rainfall totals were well above normal in northern Scotland, the Western Isles and parts of northern Wales but below normal elsewhere. A large part of the Midlands and south-east England had less than half the normal amount. Rain fell in Scotland on the 5th and 6th and fog formed over southern Scotland and Northern Ireland on the 10th. Fog occurred, especially in the east Midlands, on the 12th and thick fog formed in East Anglia and southern England on the 14th. On the 17th rain fell in northern areas and on the 18th and 19th there was heavy rain over western Scotland when 66·5 mm (2·6 in) of rain fell at Ardgour (Highland) in 7 hours. At Eilanreach (Highland) 94 mm (3·7 in) fell on the 18th, and a combination of heavy rain and strong winds caused a landslip on the West Highland railway line at Glenfinnan. A gust of 86 knots (99 mph) was recorded at Cairngorm (Highland) on the 18th and the 19th was a very windy day generally over Scotland with gusts of over 60 knots (69 mph) being widespread. A gust of 80 knots (92 mph) was recorded at Butt of Lewis (Western Isles) and Kirkwall (Orkney) recorded two gusts of 75 knots (86 mph). There were heavy showers on the 22nd and 23rd over England and Wales, with hail and thunder in places. On the 27th 80 mm (3.15 in) of rain fell at Isle of Rhum (Highland), and 76 mm (2·99 in) fell at Princetown (Devon) on the 29th. Thunderstorms occurred over Dorset on the evening of the 29th and around London on the 30th. Thick fog formed over northern England and Northern Ireland on the 30th. Monthly mean temperatures were generally near or below normal everywhere. During the first three days temperatures reached 26°C (78·8°F) in south-east England and on the 2nd 24·5°C (76·1°F) was recorded at Dyce (Grampian). The remainder of the month was much cooler and on the 28th the temperature fell to −1·4°C (29·5°F) at Hurn (Dorset) to give the coldest night there for 50 years. The highest temperature was 26·6°C (79·9°F) at Marholm (Cambs.) on the 2nd and the lowest was −3·4°C (25·9°F) at St Harmon (Powys) on the 26th. Sunshine totals were below normal in East Anglia and much of Scotland but near or above normal elsewhere. The highest monthly total was 229 hours at Jersey (CI) and the highest daily total was 13·0 hours at North Wyke (Devon) on the 2nd and at Slapton (Devon) on the 9th.

October.—Rainfall totals were generally above normal except in parts of southern and central England. All areas had some rain during the first six days, heavy in places particularly in the west. On the 2nd 81 mm (3·2 in) fell at Dinorwic (Gwynedd) and 73 mm (2·9 in) fell at Penicuik (Lothian) on the 6th. Winds reached gale force over western Scotland on the 2nd and a gust of 65 knots (74·9 mph) was recorded at Greenock (Strathclyde). There were thunderstorms over southern Wales on the 3rd. On the 6th there were gales along southern and western coasts and in north-east England. A gust of 62 knots (71·4 mph) was recorded at Solent (Hants.) and 64 knots (73·7 mph) was recorded at Boulmer (Northumberland). On the 7th showers turned to snow on Fair Isle (Shetland). Early on the 13th fog was extensive over south-west and north-east England. On the 15th a thunderstorm produced dramatic lightning at Colchester (Essex) and there were thunderstorms in Scotland on the 16th and in eastern areas of England and Wales between the 17th and 19th. Heavy rain fell in many places on the 17th and 18th and 78·5 mm (4·48 in) of rain fell at Inkersall (Derbys.) on the 17th. At Sheffield (S. Yorks.) the 17th was its wettest day since 1933 with 45 mm (1·77 in) of rain. Dense fog affected much of eastern and southern England on the 20th. Fog formed over East Anglia and north-east England on the 24th and 25th. Thunderstorms, sometimes accompanied by hail, were widespread between the 25th and 27th. Fog formed over Cumbria and southern Scotland on the 27th and over Northern Ireland on the 27th–28th. There were scattered thunderstorms in southern England and southern Wales on the 28th and strong winds were widespread; gusts of 63 knots (72·5 mph) were recorded at Fair Isle, Lerwick and Sella Ness (Shetland) and a gust of 86 knots (99·0 mph) was recorded at Herstmonceux (E. Sussex). There were thunderstorms along the south coast on the 31st. Monthly mean temperatures were above normal everywhere and were nearly 2°C (3·60°F) above normal at Gatwick (W. Sussex). Temperatures of 24·3°C (75·7°F) at Valley (Gwynedd) and 22·3°C (72·1°F) at Kinloss (Grampian) were the highest there since 1959. October was generally the warmest for 20 years. The highest temperature recorded was 24·8°C (76·6°F) at Enfield (Gtr London) on the 12th and at Waltham Cross (Gtr London) and Pen-y-Ffridd (Gwynedd) on the 13th. The lowest temperature was −4·9°C (23·2°F) at Grantown-on-Spey (Highland) on the 30th. Sunshine totals were near normal everywhere. The highest monthly total was 143·1 hours at Folkestone (Kent) and at Levington (Suffolk). The highest daily total was 10·8 hours at Plumpton (E. Sussex) on the 8th.

November.—Rainfall totals were generally below normal except for a few places along the east coast. Thunderstorms occurred on the south coast on the 3rd. There was thick fog in places on the 10th. There were thunderstorms in the Leeds (W. Yorks.) and Glasgow (Strathclyde) areas on the 14th and winds reached gale force in places between the 16th and 18th with gusts reaching 60 knots (69 mph) at Kirkwall (Orkney) on the 16th and 62 knots (71 mph) at Greenock (Strathclyde) on the 18th. Fog was widespread over England and Wales on the 16th. Hail fell over northern Wales on the 18th and sleet fell on the Cairngorms and southern uplands of Scotland and over Shropshire, while snow lay on the Pennines. On the 20th 58 mm (2·28 in) of rain fell at Gogerddan (Dyfed) and 3 cm (1·18 in) of snow lay on the northern Pennines. There were showers of hail over Salisbury Plain (Wilts.) and the Isle of Man on the 20th. Thunderstorms with hail occurred over south-west England, southern Wales and the Isle of Wight on the 21st. Sleet or snow fell as far south as southern Wales, the Cotswolds and East Anglia, and 4 cm (1·57 in) lay on the northern Pennines. On the 22nd thunderstorms occurred in East Sussex and fog persisted all day in parts of the Midlands and eastern Wales. On the 23rd there was heavy rain in the west, with 154 mm (6·07 in) falling at Trassey Slievenaman (Co. Down), 125 mm (4·92 in) at Bryansford (Co. Down) and 50 mm (1·97 in) at Whitechurch (Dyfed). Mid Wales and the Brecon Beacons had 2–10 cm (0·8–

3·9 in) of snow lying on the 23rd and thunderstorms with hail occurred over Cumbria and Lancashire. Hail was also reported in Devon and Cornwall on the 23rd and thunderstorms occurred in East Anglia; many parts of England and Wales were foggy. Thunderstorms occurred over eastern Scotland, Cornwall and Kent on the 24th and over Fife, the Thames Valley, Kent and the Isle of Wight on the 25th. On the 24th and 25th snow fell as far south as Bristol (Avon). The 26th brought further rain to parts of south-east England. Dense fog persisted all day in parts of Northern Ireland on the 28th. Monthly mean temperatures were generally around normal. The temperature fell to −5·0°C (23·0°F) at Aviemore (Highland) on the 8th but rose to 18°C (64·4°F) at several places in England, Wales and Northern Ireland on the 11th and 12th. After the 17th temperatures fell below −6·0°C (21·2°F) at several places in the United Kingdom. The highest temperature was 18·2°C (64·8°F) at Tivington (Somerset) on the 12th and the lowest was −7·2°C (19·0°F) at Braemar (Grampian) on the 22nd. Sunshine totals were generally above normal in western and southern areas but below in central and eastern areas. At Paisley (Strathclyde) the total was the equal highest (with 1947) since 1885. The highest monthly total was 121 hours at Penzance (Cornwall) and the highest daily total was 9·5 hours at Swansea (W. Glam.) on the 3rd.

December.—Rainfall totals were generally above normal in the north and west but below in the south and east. Patchy fog over England and Wales on the 4th and 5th became widespread on the 6th. Except for East Anglia and areas along the south coast snow and sleet fell everywhere on the 7th and 8th with 30 cm (11·81 in) deposited at Emley Moor and 19 cm (7·09 in) at Wilsden (both W. Yorks.). There was heavy drifting in gale force winds and this caused considerable disruption to traffic and brought down power lines. There were also thunderstorms over west Cornwall. On the 9th there were thunderstorms in Dyfed, west Cornwall, Fife, Northumberland, Kent and East Sussex and further snow left 15 cm (5·91 in) lying at Cellarhead (Staffs.) and 10 cm (3·49 in) at Cynwyd (Powys). On the 11th and 12th there were storm force winds off the North Sea when Fair Isle (Shetland) recorded a gust of 73 knots (84 mph). On the 14th fog persisted all day in the Thames Valley and on the 15th dense fog formed in many areas of England, Wales and Northern Ireland. On the 16th fog was persistent in the Forth and Clyde Valleys. There was light snow or sleet in many parts of England and Wales on the 17th, 18th and 19th and in the north and west of Scotland on the 20th. From the 20th to 23rd there was persistent heavy rain in western Scotland, with 50·6 mm (2·21 in) falling at Isle of Rhum (Highland) on the 23rd. On the 20th 93 mm (3·66 in) fell at Cwmystwyth (Dyfed) and 75 mm (2·95 in) at Moel Cynnedd (Powys). From the 23rd to the end of the month very strong winds and heavy rain affected many areas. On the 24th 54·2 mm (2·14 in) of rain fell at Clatteringshaws (Dumfries & Galloway). On the 25th and 26th gales, thunderstorms and storm force winds affected many areas. On the 26th there were gusts of 77 knots (88·7 mph) at Greenock (Strathclyde), 75 knots (86·4 mph) at Plymouth (Devon) and 73 knots (84·1 mph) at High Bradfield (S. Yorks.). On the 25th tornadoes were reported over Devon, Somerset and Avon. Sleet and snow fell as far south as southern Wales on the 27th and hailstones (15 mm (0·59 in) in diameter fell at Towy Castle (Dyfed). On the 29th a cottage in northern Wales was hit by lightning and a whirlwind caused extensive damage to property in Gorseinon (W. Glam.). There was a whirlwind at Towy Castle (Dyfed) on the 20th. Monthly mean temperatures were mostly around normal. The highest temperature was 14·6°C (58·3°F) at Greenwich (Gtr London) on the 26th and the lowest was −8·0°C (17·6°F) at Dalwhinnie (Highland) on the 8th. Sunshine totals were above normal except in parts of western Wales, eastern England and central Scotland. The highest monthly total was 77 hours at Ventnor (Isle of Wight) and the highest daily total was 7·6 hours at Jersey (CI) on the 1st.

Year (1990).—The year 1990 will be remembered for the January and February storms and the very hot summer which produced some record-breaking temperatures. It will also be remembered in the south of England for the lack of rainfall which really began in late 1988 and continued right through 1989 and 1990. The year as a whole was very warm; in central England it was the warmest since 1659, beating the previous record set in 1989. Over England and Wales the spring (March, April, May) was the driest this century and the sunniest since 1948. The summer (June, July, August) was both warmer and drier than normal. January was a very windy month with some severe gales. A gust of 109 knots (125 mph) at Fair Isle (Shetland) on the 16th was a record for January. On the 25th very extensive damage occurred in southern England and Wales when severe gales uprooted or damaged trees over a much greater area than the storm of October 1987. Many people were injured and several killed, transport was severely disrupted and large areas were left without electricity. Thunderstorms were frequent, often with hail, and the western Highlands had more than twice the normal amount of rain. February was another very windy month, with a gust of 113 knots (130 mph) recorded at Cairngorm (Highland) on the 22nd. It was wet in parts of Scotland and the Grampain Region had 438 per cent of the normal amount of rain. It was the wettest February since 1886 at Fort Augustus (Highland) and the wettest at Paisley (Strathclyde) since 1894. On the 6th and 7th there was heavy rain over much of England and Wales which caused widespread flooding in the Wye, Severn and Thames Valleys. On the 26th and 27th gales and high spring tides combined to cause very severe flooding and wave damage along many coasts. The sea-wall at Towyn (Clwyd) was breached leading to a major disaster with many people rendered homeless. March was the wettest in Scotland since 1869 and at Fort William (Highland) more than four times the normal amount of rain fell. Parts of Kent on the other hand had only 2 mm (0·1 in) of rain in the whole month. Over England and Wales it was the driest March since 1861. A pressure reading of 1047·9 millibars in the Scilly Isles was the highest for March this century, and at Coventry it was the warmest March this century. In central England it was the warmest since 1957. Sunshine totals were above normal. In April an earthquake registering 5·2 on the Richter scale shook much of England and Wales on the 2nd. On the 3rd 11 cm (4·3 in) of snow fell in the Aviemore (Highland) region. On the 19th Hampstead Heath (London) was covered in a layer of hail during heavy thunderstorms. A total of 7 mm (0·3 in) of rain at Tynemouth (Tyne and Wear) was the lowest April total since 1912. Severe frosts damaged plants and fruit trees advanced by the previously warm weather. May was dry in England and Wales with less than half the normal amount of rain in most places and less than ten per cent of normal in central and southern England; even so there were thunderstorms in most areas. Temperatures reached the high 20's°C (80's°F) on each of the first five days, giving the hottest start to May since 1875. At London (Heathrow) a temperature of 28·1°C (82·6°F) on the 3rd was the highest for the day since 1893. A 20 m (65·6 ft) high whirlwind occurred near Towy Castle

(Dyfed) on the 27th. June was generally wet and dull with above normal rainfall in many areas and below normal sunshine. On the night of the 6th–7th the railway embankment at Carrbridge (Highland) was washed away by a stream swollen by heavy rain and the Inverness to London express was in danger of being derailed when it crossed the gap beneath the lines. The rainfall total at Edinburgh was the highest for June since 1928. On the 27th thunderstorms and hail caused flooding in Nottinghamshire and on the 30th lightning cut power supplies in north-west England. July was a mainly dry and sunny month and parts of England and Wales had almost no rain from the 8th to the 26th. A few places had no rain from the 7th to the end of the month. August was another month of below average rainfall but rain fell in many parts on the 14th and there were frequent thunderstorms, mainly in eastern areas. The month was very warm everywhere and a temperature of 37·1°C (98·8°F) at Cheltenham (Glos.) was the highest temperature ever recorded in the United Kingdom from an officially accredited station. September was a month of contrasts, with Cape Wrath (Highland) receiving 181 per cent of its normal amount of rain and Folkestone (Kent) and London receiving only 36 per cent of the normal amount. The first snow of the autumn fell on the Scottish mountains on the 19th. On the 18th and 19th very heavy rain fell in western Scotland. October was generally a wet month, although some central and southern areas had less rain than normal. Strong winds were widespread on the 28th and a gust of 86 knots (99 mph) was recorded at Herstmonceux (E. Sussex). Temperatures were above normal everywhere. Thunderstorms were frequent during the month. November was a generally dry month but the 23rd was a very wet day in the west. Temperatures were around normal for the month but sunshine totals were above average. December brought some very heavy snowfalls. On the 7th and 8th heavy drifting in gale force winds caused considerable disruption. On the 25th tornadoes were reported over Devon, Somerset and Avon, and on the 25th and 26th gales and storm force winds affected many areas. On the 29th a whirlwind caused extensive damage to property in Gorseinon (W. Glam.).

(1991) January.—Rainfall totals were above normal everywhere except eastern Scotland, the Western Isles, East Anglia and northern and eastern England and Northern Ireland. On the 1st heavy rain and melting snow caused flooding in many areas of southern Scotland; 83 mm (3·27 in) of rain fell at Dalwhinnie (Highland), 76 mm (2·99 in) at Ardentinny (Strathclyde), and 64 mm (2·52 in) at Pencelli (Powys). On the 2nd a gust of 71 knots (81·8 mph) was recorded at Butt of Lewis (Western Isles). Thunderstorms were frequent and widespread between the 3rd and 7th. Between the 3rd and 5th snow showers were frequent over Scotland and on the 5th gales and high tides caused extensive damage to western and southern coasts. There was considerable flooding and disruption of power supplies and transport. A gust of 78 knots (89·8 mph) was recorded at Greenock (Strathclyde). On the 6th and 7th snow fell as far south as the Cotswolds and there was heavy snow over southern Scotland on the 8th. A gust of 71 knots (81·8 mph) was recorded at Langdon Bay (Kent) on the 8th. Further snow extended south to Shropshire on the 9th. There were widespread thunderstorms in south-east England on the 11th. Snow fell in southern Wales on the 12th and 12 cm (4·72 in) lay on the southern uplands of Scotland. There was further snow in Scotland on the 13th, 14th and 15th. Overnight fog, dense in places, occurred on the 14th in Wales, the Midlands, East Anglia and southern England and there was dense fog in East Anglia and southern England on the 17th. There was further fog in parts of England on the 18th. There was rain in many places between the 17th and 20th. A gust of 72 knots (82·9 mph) was recorded at Benbecula (Western Isles) on the 18th and 74 mm (2·91 in) of rain fell at Kinlochewe (Highland) on the 19th. Fog formed over much of Northern Ireland and parts of England and Wales on the 21st and persisted on the 22nd in England and Wales. Further fog formed in parts of Wales and northern England on the 23rd, 24th and 25th and extended to eastern Scotland on the 25th. Snow fell on high ground in Wales on the 25th and in Wales, north-west England and the Midlands on the 27th. Further snow fell over northern Wales and eastern England on the 29th and in western and southern England on the 30th. On the 31st 15 cm (5·91 in) of snow lay in southern Wales and 10 cm (3·94 in) in north Devon. Monthly mean temperatures were above normal in northern Scotland, central and south-east England and East Anglia but were below normal elsewhere. The highest temperature was 14·6°C (58·28°F) at Madley (Herefordshire) on the 1st and the lowest was −14·4°C (6·08°F) at Kindrogan (Highland) on the 14th. Sunshine totals were above normal everywhere except in parts of western and south-western Scotland. It was the sunniest January in Northern Ireland since 1959 and the sunniest at Wick (Highland) since 1946. The highest monthly total was 97 hours at Tynemouth (Tyne and Wear) and the highest daily total was 8.3 hours at Twist (Devon) on the 19th.

February.—Rainfall totals were above normal in most eastern areas of England and Scotland but generally below normal elsewhere. There were frequent falls of snow, often heavy, during the first half of the month. On the 2nd fog formed over north-east England. On the 3rd winds reached gale force in Shetland and there was some dense freezing fog over England and Wales. Rain fell in western areas on the 4th and many areas had snow showers on the 6th. Snow fell heavily in places between the 6th and 14th. At Anvil Green (Kent) 6 cm (2·36 in) of snow lay on the 6th. There was further snow in the south-east overnight and Gatwick (W. Sussex) had 7 cm (2·76 in) by the morning of the 7th. On the 7th–8th there was snow over England and Wales, giving 47 cm (18·5 in) at Wilsden (W. Yorks.), 35 cm (13·78 in) at Pencelli (Powys) and 20 cm (7·87 in) in central London, probably the greatest depth there since 1962. There were thunderstorms in eastern areas of England on the 8th. There was further heavy snow in eastern and northern areas on the 9th and 10th. There was general rain on the 12th and Fylingdales (N. Yorks.) had 45 cm (17·72 in) of snow. On the 13th 46 cm (18·11 in) of snow fell at Long Framlingham (Northumberland). There was widespread rain on the 14th and 15 cm (5·91 in) of snow fell at East Hoathly (E. Sussex) and 46 cm (18·11 in) lay at Fylingdales (N. Yorks.). On the 19th and 20th there was persistent fog in southern and eastern England. There were gales in western areas on the 21st and 22nd and at Gwennap Head (Cornwall) a gust of 57 knots (65·6 mph) was recorded on the 21st. There was heavy rain on the 22nd, giving 133 mm (5·24 in) at Llanymawddwy (Powys), 110 mm (4·33 in) at Betws-y-Crwyn (Shrops.), and 101 mm (3·98 in) at Lake Vyrnwy (Powys). There was widespread fog in central and southern areas early on the 25th. Many parts of England and Wales had rain on the 27th and 28th. Monthly mean temperatures were below normal everywhere. Temperatures did not rise above freezing between the 5th and 10th. At Broom's Barn (Suffolk) it was the fourth coldest February this century. The highest temperature was 14·7°C (58·46°F) at Lowestoft (Suffolk) on the 24th and the lowest was −15·6°C (3·92°F) at Barbourne (Worcs.)

on the 14th. Sunshine totals were generally above normal in western areas but below normal on eastern coasts. The highest monthly total was 117 hours at Bude (Cornwall) and the highest daily total was 9·4 hours at Brawdy (Dyfed) on the 17th.

March.—Rainfall totals were above normal everywhere except in parts of eastern and central England and the northern area of the Western Isles. At Portland (Dorset) 170 per cent of the normal amount was received. On the 2nd there was heavy rain in western and northern areas and on the 3rd a tornado hit south-west Wales, uprooting trees and causing serious damage to property. There were gales in western areas on the 4th and extensive rain on the 4th and 5th, heavy at times, with 62·2 mm (2·45 in) falling at Great Dun Fell (Cumbria) on the 4th. There were periods of rain in most areas from the 6th to the 22nd. On the 7th coloured dust was deposited at several places in the West Midlands and on the 11th at Northwood (Gtr London) and Cavendish (Suffolk). There was persistent fog on the 12th especially over north-east England and eastern Scotland, and there was thick fog over southern England on the 13th. There was extensive sea and coastal fog especially over the Irish Sea, eastern Scotland and north-east England on the 12th. There were thunderstorms from East Sussex to Lincolnshire on the 16th and there was very heavy rain in places on the 18th, giving 61·5 mm (2·60 in) at Eskdalemuir (Dumfries and Galloway), 55·8 mm (2·48 in) at Sloy Power Station (Strathclyde) and 51·8 mm (2·32 in) at Fort William (Highland). There were gales between the 19th and 21st and a gust of 65 knots (74·9 mph) was recorded at the Forth Road Bridge (Lothian) on the 19th. Two gusts of 61 knots (70·2 mph) were recorded at Leeds Weather Centre on the night of the 20th–21st. Rain was heavy, mainly in the west, on the 20th. There were thunderstorms in Surrey and Berkshire on the 21st and in the Thames Valley, the Cotswolds and Cornwall on the 22nd. There were showers of sleet or snow over north-eastern coastal areas on the 23rd. There were gales in Kent on the 25th. On the 26th coloured dust was deposited at Towy Castle (Dyfed) and at Slimbridge (Glos.). Monthly mean temperatures were above normal everywhere. The temperature rose to nearly 15°C (59·0°F) in south-east England on the 6th and to 17°C (62·6°F) at Saunton Sands (Devon) on the 7th. Temperatures reached nearly 20°C (68°F) in many places on the 13th. The highest temperature was 20·8°C (69·44°F) at Barbourne (Worcs.) on the 13th and the lowest was −5·7°C (21·74°F) at Aviemore (Highland) on the 2nd. Sunshine totals were below normal everywhere except for a few places in East Anglia. The highest monthly total was 126 hours at St Mawgan (Cornwall) and the highest daily total was 11·5 hours at Belfast (Co. Antrim) on the 25th.

April.—Rainfall totals were above normal everywhere except eastern Scotland and northern England where they were a little below normal. On the 1st 71·7 mm (3·16 in) of rain fell at Inverinan (Strathclyde) and 53·3 mm (2·21 in) at Brodick (Isle of Arran). A gust of 107 knots (123·2 mph) was recorded at Cairngorm (Highland) on the 1st. On the 4th there were strong winds in exposed places in the west and gusts of 63 knots (72·5 mph) at Kilkeel (Co. Down) and two of 60 knots (69·1 mph) at Culdrose (Cornwall) were recorded. On the 4th 61·4 mm (2·56 in) of rain fell at Great Dun Fell (Cumbria). On the 6th all areas had some rain, heavy in places, and strong winds; a gust of 60 knots (69·1 mph) was recorded at Camborne (Cornwall). On the 9th 51·4 mm (2·17 in) of rain fell at Sloy Power Station (Strathclyde) and on the 10th 80·5 mm (3·35 in) fell at Korloch Castle (Isle of Rhum), its wettest April day since 1958. At Glasgow (Strathclyde) 102 mm (4·02 in) gave it its wettest April day since 1949. Several gusts of 50–59 knots (58–68 mph) were recorded in Scotland on the 11th. On the 12th there was moderate or heavy rain over western Wales and thunderstorms occurred over central and southern England. On the 18th there were frequent showers of hail, snow and sleet over eastern Scotland and there were showers, heavy and with thunder at times, over England and Wales. Many areas had heavy, blustery showers, often of hail or sleet, on the 19th and there were further wintry showers over eastern England and Scotland on the 20th when 17 cm (6·69 in) of snow lay in the Cairngorm car park (Highland). There was a thunderstorm in Essex during the evening. Rain fell in many areas on the 21st and there was rain in eastern areas on the 22nd, with hail in south-east England and East Anglia. There were further outbreaks of rain on the 25th. Thunderstorms occurred over Wales, the Midlands and Cornwall on the 26th and there was rain in all areas on the 28th which persisted until the 30th. The 29th was the wettest day since 1986 over England and Wales. Monthly mean temperatures were generally around normal. On the 14th Tummel Bridge (Tayside) recorded a maximum temperature of 16·5°C (61·7°F) and a minimum of −4·2°C (24·4°F), and 19·8°C (67·6°F) was recorded at Ardtalnaig (Tayside). The highest temperature was 23·5°C (74·3°F) at Elmstone (Kent) on the 12th and the lowest was −7·1°C (19·2°F) at Leadhills (Strathclyde) on the 20th. Sunshine totals were mainly above normal in eastern areas but below normal in the west. Stornoway (Western Isles) had its dullest April since 1975 whereas Lerwick (Shetland) had its sunniest since 1970. The highest monthly total was 194 hours at Hemsby (Norfolk) and at Leuchars (Fife). The highest daily total was 14·3 hours at Folkestone (Kent) on the 28th.

May.—Rainfall totals were well below normal everywhere except for the far north of Scotland. Cape Wrath (Highland) received 124 per cent of its normal amount of rainfall whereas western Scotland, southern Wales and most of south-west England had less than 10 per cent of the normal amount. It was the driest May over England and Wales since 1896 and Glasgow (Strathclyde) had its driest May since 1868. On the 1st a gust of 52 knots (59·9 mph) was recorded at Culdrose (Cornwall). The 3rd was generally the wettest day of the month and 21 mm (0·83 in) of rain fell at Nantmor (Gwynedd). On the 4th 15·1 mm (0·63 in) of rain fell at Wattisham (Suffolk) and a thunderstorm occurred at Cromer (Norfolk). There was hail to the west of London on the 4th and 13·3 mm (0·63 in) of rain fell at Charing (Kent) on the 5th. Hail fell in western Cornwall on the 6th and 7th and a thunderstorm occurred at Camborne on the 7th. Also on the 7th heavy showers fell over some parts of southern England and southern Wales. There were outbreaks of rain, heavy at times, over Scotland on the 11th and 12th and rain or showers occurred in all areas of England and Wales on the 13th. There were isolated showers in southern England on the 14th and a spell of general rain on the 15th, when 12 mm (0·47 in) fell at Chipping Camden (Glos.), and on the 16th. There were gales over northern Scotland on the 21st when a gust of 61 knots (70·2 mph) was recorded at Lerwick (Shetland). Monthly mean temperatures were generally around

normal, although during the first week temperatures fell to 3·0°C (26·6°F) in places with some ground temperatures as low as −9·0°C (15·8°F). On the 21st temperatures rose to the low 20's°C (70°F) over a large part of southern England and Wales. The highest temperature recorded was 26·0°C (78·8°F) at Barbourne (Worcs.) on the 21st and the lowest was −5·0°C (23·0°F) at Leadhills (Strathclyde) on the 8th and 9th. Sunshine totals were below normal everywhere except in parts of western Scotland, Devon and Cornwall, where they were just above normal. The highest total during the month was 221 hours at St Mawgan (Cornwall) and the highest daily total was 16·1 hours at Benbecula (Western Isles) on the 30th.

June.—Rainfall totals were above normal everywhere except for some scattered areas mainly in the west. Western Scotland had only half the normal amount whereas East Sussex received nearly three times the normal amount. It was the wettest June this century over a large part of the United Kingdom and the number of days with rain falling reached 25 in some places, including London. Daily falls exceeded 10 mm (0·39 in) somewhere in the United Kingdom on every day except the 20th. Sleet fell over the Grampian Mountains on the 2nd, and over the Grampians and the southern uplands of Scotland on the 3rd. Snow fell over the northern Pennines on the 3rd and there was hail at Inverness (Highland), North Yorkshire and northern Norfolk, and a thunderstorm over Salisbury Plain (Wilts.). On the 4th thunderstorms occurred in eastern and south-eastern England and there was hail in the east Midlands. On the 8th and 9th there were thunderstorms over the Moray Firth area and also over North Yorkshire. On the 11th 56 mm (2·20 in) of rain fell at Balquhidder (Central) and there were gales in exposed western areas on the 12th when a gust of 65 knots (74·9 mph) was recorded at Orlock Head (Co. Down). Thunderstorms occurred over south-east England on the 15th and 16th and over East Anglia, with hail in places, on the 19th. There were further thunderstorms over northern England and eastern Scotland on the 21st and over northern England and the Midlands, Edinburgh and the east coast of Scotland as far as Aberdeen (Grampian) on the 22nd. On the 22nd 47 mm (1·85 in) of rain fell at Falmouth (Cornwall) and 46 mm (1·81 in) fell at Princetown (Devon) on the 23rd. On the 27th 46 mm (1·81 in) fell at Llanfair Caereinion (Powys) and 66 mm (2·6 in) at Bradford (W. Yorks.). Monthly mean temperatures were below normal in all areas of the United Kingdom making it the coolest June this century in many places. Frost was widespread during the first week and at Bastreet (Cornwall) the temperature fell to −1·0°C (30·2°F) on the 2nd. The grass temperature fell to −6·0°C (21·2°F) at Birmingham (Elmdon) on the 5th and a number of places had their coldest June night since records began. The highest temperature was 23·3°C (73·94°F) at Cambridge on the 30th and the lowest was −3·8°C (25·16°F) at Carnwath (Strathclyde) on the 5th. Sunshine totals were below normal everywhere except for a few places in northern Scotland, and it was the dullest June this century in many places. The highest monthly total was 217 hours at Tiree (Strathclyde) and the highest daily total was 16·1 hours at Benbecula (Western Isles) on the 6th and at Tiree on the 20th.

AVERAGE AND GENERAL VALUES, 1989–1991 (June)

Month	Rainfall (mm)				Temperature (°C)				Bright Sunshine (hrs per day)			
	Aver. 1941–1970	1989	1990	1991	Aver. 1951–1980	1989	1990	1991	Aver. 1951–1980	1989	1990	1991
England and Wales												
January........	86	47	133	92	4·0	6·7	7·1	3·9	1·6	2·1	1·8	2·2
February.......	65	88	141	63	4·1	6·4	7·8	2·0	2·3	3·4	2·8	2·3
March	59	92	24	75	5·9	7·8	8·7	8·1	3·6	3·4	4·4	2·9
April...........	58	83	38	68	8·2	6·9	8·5	8·3	5·1	4·7	7·1	5·1
May	67	21	25	14	11·3	13·2	12·9	10·9	6·3	8·9	8·2	4·7
June	61	55	70	101	14·3	14·7	14·0	10·3	6·7	8·0	4·4	4·7
July	73	38	35	—	16·0	18·3	17·0	—	5·9	8·5	8·7	—
August.........	90	58	46	—	15·9	17·0	18·4	—	5·5	7·6	7·1	—
September......	83	41	53	—	14·0	15·1	13·6	—	4·6	4·3	5·1	—
October	83	98	103	—	11·0	12·3	12·5	—	3·3	2·9	3·3	—
November	97	61	67	—	7·1	7·2	7·5	—	2·1	2·9	2·2	—
December	90	134	97	—	5·1	5·5	4·9	—	1·5	0·9	1·5	—
YEAR	912	814	834	—	9·8	10·9	11·0	—	4·1	4·8	4·7	—
Scotland												
January........	137	206	247	146	3·5	7·3	5·7	3·2	1·3	1·3	1·3	1·7
February.......	104	240	292	83	3·4	5·2	5·6	2·6	2·4	2·7	2·1	1·7
March	92	188	241	128	5·1	5·7	7·5	6·7	3·3	3·7	3·0	2·7
April...........	90	63	95	121	7·1	6·0	7·3	7·5	5·0	4·5	5·6	5·2
May	91	53	55	43	9·9	10·7	11·0	10·4	5·7	7·0	6·6	5·1
June	92	76	124	126	12·7	12·5	12·5	8·9	5·9	6·5	4·3	5·2
July	112	49	75	—	13·9	15·6	14·6	—	4·9	7·3	6·8	—
August.........	129	184	119	—	13·9	14·1	15·1	—	4·6	4·3	4·0	—
September......	137	96	149	—	12·2	12·0	11·5	—	3·7	3·7	3·5	—
October	149	187	213	—	9·8	10·4	10·4	—	2·6	2·4	2·4	—
November	142	60	102	—	6·0	6·3	6·0	—	1·7	2·3	1·8	—
December	156	96	184	—	4·5	3·2	4·5	—	1·1	1·2	0·9	—
YEAR	1431	1496	1911	—	8·5	9·1	9·3	—	3·5	3·9	4·1	—

TEMPERATURE, RAINFALL AND WIND SPEED RECORDS

WORLD: The maximum air temperature recorded is 57·8°C (136°F) at San Louis, Mexico on August 11, 1933; the minimum air temperature recorded is −89·2°C (−128·56°F) at Vostok, Antarctica on July 21, 1983. The greatest rainfall recorded in one day is 1870 mm (73·62 in) at Cilaos, Isle de Réunion on March 16, 1952; the greatest rainfall in one calendar month is 9300 mm (366·14 in) at Cherrapunji, Assam in July 1861, the greatest annual total being 22,990 mm (905·12 in) also at Cherrapunji in 1861. The highest gust recorded is 201 knots (231 mph) at Mount Washington Observatory, New Hampshire, USA on April 12, 1934.

UNITED KINGDOM: The maximum air temperature recorded is 37·1°C (98·8°F) at Cheltenham (Glos.) on August 3, 1990; the minimum air temperature recorded is −27·2°C (−17°F) at Braemar (Grampian) on February 11, 1895 and January 10, 1982. The greatest rainfall recorded in one day is 280 mm (11 in) at Martinstown, Dorset on July 18, 1955. The greatest annual total is 6,528 mm (257 in) at Sprinkling Tarn, Cumbria in 1954. The highest gust recorded is 150 knots (173 mph) at Cairngorm (Highland) on March 20, 1986. The highest low-level (below 200 m (656 ft)) gust is 123 knots (141·7 mph) at Fraserburgh (Grampian) on February 13, 1989. The highest mean hourly speed is 92 knots (106 mph) at Great Dun Fell (Cumbria) in December 1974. The highest low-level mean hourly speed is 72 knots (83 mph) at Shoreham-by-Sea (Sussex) on October 16, 1987.

WIND FORCE MEASURES

The **Beaufort Scale** of wind force has been accepted internationally and is used in communicating weather conditions. Devised originally by Admiral Sir Francis Beaufort in 1805, it now consists of the numbers 0–17, each representing a certain strength or velocity of wind at 10 m (33 ft) above ground in the open.

Scale No.	Wind Force	Mph	Knots	Scale No.	Wind Force	Mph	Knots
0	Calm	1	1	9	Strong gale	47–54	41–47
1	Light air	1–3	1–3	10	Whole gale	55–63	48–55
2	Slight breeze	4–7	4–6	11	Storm	64–72	56–63
3	Gentle breeze	8–12	7–10	12	Hurricane	73–82	64–71
4	Moderate breeze	13–18	11–16	13	—	83–92	72–80
5	Fresh breeze	19–24	17–21	14	—	93–103	81–89
6	Strong breeze	25–31	22–27	15	—	104–114	90–99
7	High wind	32–38	28–33	16	—	115–125	100–108
8	Gale	39–46	34–40	17	—	126–136	109–118

TEMPERATURE, RAINFALL AND SUNSHINE
IN THE UNITED KINGDOM

The following table gives mean air temperature (°C), total monthly rainfall (mm) and mean daily bright sunshine (hours) at a representative selection of climatological reporting stations in the United Kingdom during the year July 1990 to June 1991 and the calendar year 1990. The heights (in metres) of the reporting stations above mean sea level are also given. (Data provided by the Met Office.)

		1990											
		July			August			September			October		
Station	Ht. m	Temp. °C	Rain mm	Sun hrs	Temp. °C	Rain mm	Sun hrs	Temp. °C	Rain mm	Sun hrs	Temp. °C	Rain mm	Sun hrs
Aberdeen (Dyce) .	65	14·1	37	7·4	15·5	47	5·2	11·4	62	3·8	9·5	121	2·3
Aberporth	134	16·4	33	9·3	16·7	43	6·3	13·1	58	5·5	12·1	109	3·0
Aldergrove	68	15·5	50	7·6	15·9	91	3·4	12·0	37	4·0	10·8	165	2·3
Aspatria	61	15·5	41	8·6	16·2	65	5·6	11·7	60	3·7	10·9	167	2·3
Bala	163	15·1	31	7·8	16·1	61	5·4	11·1	84	3·9	10·7	139	2·5
Birmingham (Elmdon)	98	17·1	22	8·9	18·5	32	7·4	13·4	39	4·8	11·9	67	3·4
Boulmer.........	23	14·3	23	8·0	16·5	51	7·2	11·9	32	4·5	10·5	103	2·7
Bournemouth (Hurn)	10	16·7	12	10·0	18·1	21	8·6	13·3	37	6·1	12·3	95	3·5
Bradford	134	15·7	46	7·5	16·9	46	5·2	11·9	35	3·5	10·8	109	1·9
Braemar	339	13·3	32	7·0	13·7	43	4·4	9·9	43	4·2	8·1	124	2·1
Buxton..........	307	14·9	51	7·9	16·1	85	5·6	11·1	107	4·4	9·8	170	2·5
Cambridge	24	17·6	17	7·3	19·7	21	7·5	13·7	37	4·6	12·9	44	4·1
Cheltenham	65	18·6	26	9·3	19·3	37	7·1	13·9	90	5·4	12·9	125	3·6
Clacton-on-Sea...	16	16·9	11	8·6	18·6	37	8·8	14·2	25	4·9	12·8	84	4·1
Douglas	85	15·0	73	8·3	15·7	48	4·6	12·5	79	4·8	11·4	181	2·5
Dumfries........	49	15·0	67	6·9	15·7	52	4·7	11·5	38	3·6	10·7	156	2·5
Dundee	45	15·1	18	8·2	16·4	48	5·4	12·1	36	4·4	10·5	126	3·0
Durham	102	15·1	31	7·2	17·0	53	6·9	12·1	43	4·2	10·8	79	2·5
East Malling	33	17·3	8	9·3	19·3	26	8·9	13·9	35	5·1	12·7	68	4·2
Edinburgh......	134	15·0	43	7·2	15·6	37	4·8	11·9	49	3·4	10·3	129	2·5
Glasgow (Abbotsinch)...	5	15·3	49	7·5	15·3	64	4·1	11·5	54	4·3	10·5	191	2·0
Gogerddan	31	16·9	53	8·7	17·3	77	5·5	12·5	106	5·2	12·6	123	2·8
Hastings	45	17·2	7	9·3	19·1	27	9·3	14·7	32	6·0	13·5	135	4·1
Hull	2	16·7	19	—	19·1	29	—	13·7	38	—	12·5	45	—
Inverness	4	15·1	33	7·2	15·7	71	3·7	11·5	87	3·0	10·0	82	2·9
Leeming.........	32	16·3	25	7·5	17·9	75	6·2	12·9	32	4·1	11·3	40	2·7
Lerwick.........	82	11·8	54	4·3	12·5	108	3·6	9·9	126	3·9	8·8	136	1·5
London (Heathrow)....	25	18·9	7	8·8	20·3	27	8·0	14·9	25	5·8	13·3	50	3·9
Long Ashton	51	17·1	51	—	17·9	40	—	13·6	54	—	12·1	105	—
Lowestoft	25	17·1	18	7·4	18·7	30	8·1	13·9	33	4·2	12·7	59	4·2
Manchester (Ringway)	75	16·5	25	8·4	17·6	71	5·1	12·5	68	4·3	11·6	111	2·5
Manston	44	17·2	7	9·7	19·3	26	9·3	14·4	40	5·3	12·7	68	4·2
Melbury.........	143	15·9	69	9·8	16·7	84	6·0	12·7	89	5·9	11·9	193	2·4
Morecambe	7	16·3	53	8·3	16·7	56	4·9	12·9	64	4·3	11·8	137	2·7
Nottingham (Watnall)......	117	16·6	30	8·4	18·4	45	7·3	13·2	24	4·1	11·7	96	3·0
Oxford	63	18·0	18	8·7	19·3	27	7·6	14·0	41	5·5	12·5	46	4·0
Penzance........	19	17·0	73	9·8	17·8	42	7·0	15·0	56	6·6	13·5	127	3·0
Plymouth	27	17·2	53	10·3	17·9	41	7·1	14·3	66	6·7	13·3	112	3·2
Prestwick	16	15·3	47	7·5	15·5	101	3·7	11·8	88	4·1	10·9	167	2·2
Rhoose..........	65	17·3	47	10·1	18·1	62	7·3	13·5	78	6·7	12·4	109	3·2
St Mawgan	103	17·1	62	10·0	17·3	55	6·3	14·5	54	6·7	12·9	116	2·9
Shawbury	72	16·6	27	9·0	18·0	35	5·9	12·7	54	4·7	11·6	59	3·0
Sheffield........	131	17·0	21	8·8	18·5	41	7·5	13·1	30	4·3	11·5	130	2·5
Skegness	5	16·2	12	8·5	18·7	40	8·3	13·1	30	4·5	12·3	50	3·6
Southampton	3	18·1	9	9·3	19·4	19	8·3	15·1	39	5·6	13·3	92	3·7
Stornoway	15	13·5	113	6·0	13·5	85	3·1	10·7	121	3·3	9·9	93	3·1
Tenby	5	16·5	41	10·1	16·9	67	6·3	13·2	64	6·7	12·9	115	2·9
Tiree...........	9	13·9	71	6·6	13·9	110	4·3	11·5	135	3·6	10·5	171	2·5
Torbay (Torquay)	8	17·5	31	10·0	18·5	31	7·8	14·9	40	7·0	13·1	55	3·1
Trawscoed	63	16·6	54	8·8	16·8	69	5·6	12·1	108	5·1	12·1	149	2·5
Ventnor.........	135	17·1	10	10·0	18·9	19	—	15·4	71	7·3	13·8	83	4·1
Waddington	68	16·7	24	8·4	18·7	50	8·1	13·5	36	4·7	11·9	55	3·5
Weymouth	21	16·9	19	9·8	18·3	29	8·7	14·9	38	7·0	13·6	84	3·5
Whitby..........	41	15·2	15	8·2	17·6	29	6·7	12·5	37	4·6	11·5	73	3·4
Worthing	2	16·9	9	9·5	18·4	29	8·9	14·2	50	6·7	13·1	146	4·3
Writtle..........	35	16·9	9	8·4	18·9	47	8·7	13·6	29	—	12·6	44	4·3

TEMPERATURE, RAINFALL AND SUNSHINE IN THE UNITED KINGDOM—*contd.*

Mean temperature of the air (°C), rainfall (mm) and bright sunshine (mean hours per day) at a representative selection of reporting stations during the year July 1990 to June 1991. Fuller details of the weather are given in the *Monthly Weather Report* published by the Met Office.

| | 1990 | | | | | | | | | 1991 | | | | | |
| | November | | | December | | | Year | | | January | | | February | | |
Station	Temp. °C	Rain mm	Sun hrs	Temp. °C	Rain mm	Sun hrs	Temp. °C	Rain mm	Sun hrs	Temp. °C	Rain mm	Sun hrs	Temp. °C	Rain mm	Sun hrs
Aberdeen (Dyce)	5·9	73	1·5	4·1	57	1·5	8·6	699	4·1	2·3	26	2·6	1·9	95	2·1
Aberporth	7·5	79	2·6	5·1	97	1·5	10·5	751	4·6	3·7	97	2·6	2·6	55	3·0
Aldergrove	6·2	73	2·3	3·9	74	2·1	9·7	979	3·9	3·1	66	2·1	2·5	46	1·9
Aspatria	5·5	34	2·1	4·0	166	1·3	9·7	1102	4·1	2·9	108	1·8	1·9	70	3·0
Bala	6·1	105	1·2	3·8	197	0·7	9·4	1366	3·6	2·5	131	1·3	1·0	112	1·8
Birmingham (Elmdon)	6·7	37	1·7	4·1	63	1·9	10·7	582	4·7	2·8	74	2·3	1·3	26	2·1
Boulmer	7·0	72	2·1	4·7	72	1·7	9·5	595	4·6	2·9	43	3·1	2·8	77	1·7
Bournemouth (Hurn)	7·5	57	3·2	4·5	67	2·3	10·9	703	5·4	4·2	97	2·4	1·5	36	3·1
Bradford	6·3	57	1·7	3·9	121	0·8	9·8	866	3·5	2·4	106	1·5	1·5	80	1·7
Braemar	3·5	53	0·8	1·7	108	0·7	—	974	3·6	0·6	70	1·6	0·1	61	1·5
Buxton	5·1	76	1·1	2·9	169	1·1	8·9	1235	3·9	1·5	94	2·1	0·5	72	2·0
Cambridge	7·1	41	1·3	4·6	46	1·4	11·3	408	4·6	3·7	30	2·4	1·4	23	1·6
Cheltenham	7·1	73	1·8	4·5	162	1·6	11·0	955	4·7	3·7	101	2·5	1·7	61	2·9
Clacton-on-Sea	7·5	51	2·3	4·7	39	1·8	11·1	465	4·5	4·7	41	2·6	1·2	37	1·6
Douglas	7·4	75	2·5	5·3	128	1·5	10·1	1082	4·3	4·3	66	1·7	2·9	72	2·1
Dumfries	5·7	39	2·1	3·9	167	1·1	9·5	1219	3·6	2·7	123	1·5	2·1	87	2·0
Dundee	5·9	51	2·1	4·2	41	1·3	9·7	646		2·5	63	2·0	3·1	64	2·5
Durham	6·3	53	1·8	4·4	93	1·5	9·7	597	4·2	2·3	47	2·7	2·1	80	1·9
East Malling	7·7	53	2·4	4·9	55	1·6	11·3	533	5·4	4·7	76	2·3	1·7	40	2·0
Edinburgh	5·9	44	2·0	4·1	68	1·1	9·3	774	3·9	2·7	73	1·9	2·5	76	2·6
Glasgow (Abbotsinch)	5·1	50	2·8	3·9	139	1·2	9·5	1349	3·7	2·7	135	1·4	1·7	59	2·4
Gogerddan	7·0	152	2·1	4·7	133	1·5	10·7	1091	4·3	3·9	100	2·2	2·5	60	2·8
Hastings	8·1	80	2·9	5·5	65	1·7	11·7	675	5·7	5·3	85	2·3	1·9	38	2·6
Hull	7·5	57	—	5·3	93	—	11·1	515	—	3·5	46	—	2·9	68	—
Inverness	5·5	65	1·2	4·7	91	0·6	9·4	925	3·3	3·5	57	1·9	2·4	21	2·2
Leeming	6·6	21	1·8	4·7	101	1·7	10·4	575	4·1	2·3	58	2·4	1·9	61	1·7
Lerwick	5·9	94	1·0	4·1	117	0·6	7·7	1529	2·8	3·9	136	1·1	2·9	56	1·5
London (Heathrow)	7·9	22	2·3	5·1	51	1·5	12·1	435	5·2	4·5	70	2·2	2·1	35	1·7
Long Ashton	7·1	32	—	4·7	88	—	11·0	799	—	3·9	135	—	2·0	42	—
Lowestoft	7·5	121	1·8	4·9	52	1·2	11·1	566	4·9	4·3	27	2·3	1·8	25	1·7
Manchester (Ringway)	6·7	65	1·4	3·9	89	1·1	10·4	800	3·9	2·7	53	2·4	2·1	29	2·6
Manston	7·7	88	2·3	4·8	41	1·5	11·3	503	5·7	4·7	38	2·3	1·7	18	2·2
Melbury	7·1	112	2·6	4·7	175	1·2	10·4	1427	4·7	3·9	175	2·0	2·0	103	3·3
Morecambe	6·9	44	2·2	4·7	91	1·5	10·5	956	4·2	3·3	63	2·0	2·5	69	2·5
Nottingham (Watnall)	6·7	47	1·3	4·1	87	1·3	10·5	640	4·4	2·7	65	2·6	1·3	45	1·6
Oxford	7·0	20	2·8	4·3	56	1·9	11·3	473	5·1	3·8	61	2·2	1·5	21	2·1
Penzance	9·6	114	4·0	7·1	149	1·8	—	—	—	6·3	152	2·4	4·9	120	3·2
Plymouth	8·9	80	3·4	6·5	82	1·9	11·8	911	5·3	5·6	108	2·3	3·5	51	3·5
Prestwick	5·6	27	3·1	4·5	107	2·5	9·7	1188	3·8	3·3	90	1·7	2·3	60	3·2
Rhoose	7·1	72	3·3	4·5	93	1·8	11·0	843	5·4	3·9	87	2·2	1·9	37	3·0
St Mawgan	8·5	116	3·7	5·9	106	2·1	11·1	1035	5·3	5·2	129	2·5	3·5	66	4·1
Shawbury	6·1	54	1·7	3·9	84	1·3	10·3	604	4·4	2·5	59	2·0	1·5	32	2·1
Sheffield	6·9	48	1·1	—	136	0·8	—	763	4·2	2·8	87	1·7	2·3	69	1·6
Skegness	7·5	65	2·2	5·1	37	1·5	10·7	447	5·1	3·9	50	2·7	2·3	33	1·8
Southampton	8·4	43	2·9	5·5	58	1·9	12·0	662	5·2	5·1	104	2·1	2·5	29	2·6
Stornoway	6·3	82	1·4	5·1	136	0·4	8·6	1542	3·2	4·3	107	1·3	3·7	53	2·4
Tenby	7·9	115	3·0	5·8	107	1·3	11·1	990	5·0	5·1	155	2·0	2·9	57	2·5
Tiree	7·4	78	2·1	5·9	134	0·9	9·3	1521	3·8	5·2	116	1·7	4·1	87	3·4
Torbay (Torquay)	9·1	68	3·3	6·1	75	1·9	12·0	799	5·4	5·7	137	1·9	3·9	49	2·6
Trawscoed*	6·6	159	2·1	4·4	183	1·3	10·3	1295	4·0	3·1	272	1·5	0·8	133	2·0
Ventnor	8·7	57	3·7	5·9	62	2·5	11·9	622	—	5·5	93	2·4	2·7	27	3·2
Waddington	6·5	35	1·5	4·3	36	1·5	10·6	459	4·8	2·8	38	2·7	1·7	63	1·7
Weymouth	8·5	74	3·5	5·7	71	2·1	11·7	666	5·6	5·3	86	2·1	2·8	33	3·3
Whitby	7·2	40	1·8	4·9	101	1·4	10·2	552	4·4	2·9	47	2·9	2·9	72	1·7
Worthing	8·3	52	3·3	5·5	57	2·0	11·5	647	5·8	5·3	82	2·1	2·0	41	3·0
Writtle	7·0	41	1·8	4·5	54	1·3	10·9	485	—	3·9	60	2·1	0·8	51	1·3

* Jan. and Feb. 1991 are for Pencelli (16 m).

TEMPERATURE, RAINFALL AND SUNSHINE IN THE UNITED KINGDOM—*contd.*

Mean temperature of the air (°C), rainfall (mm) and bright sunshine (mean hours per day) at a representative selection of reporting stations during the year July 1990 to June 1991. Fuller details of the weather are given in the *Monthly Weather Report* published by the Met Office.

						1991						
	March			April			May			June		
Station	Temp. °C	Rain mm	Sun hrs	Temp. °C	Rain mm	Sun hrs	Temp. °C	Rain mm	Sun hrs	Temp. °C	Rain mm	Sun hrs
Aberdeen (Dyce)	5·8	71	2·9	6·9	47	5·9	10·0	31	5·3	10·7	115	4·6
Aberporth	7·5	67	3·7	7·7	77	5·0	10·1	9	6·2	11·7	43	5·6
Aldergrove	7·1	74	2·8	7·7	82	4·9	11·0	7	5·1	11·7	76	4·3
Aspatria	6·9	96	2·3	7·7	75	5·3	10·7	18	5·3	11·7	82	6·1
Bala	6·9	107	2·5	7·3	138	4·2	9·9	9	4·3	11·7	99	4·1
Birmingham (Elmdon)	7·8	50	2·3	7·7	70	4·5	11·1	13	4·3	12·1	69	4·6
Boulmer	6·9	67	3·0	7·1	17	5·7	9·9	14	4·9	11·1	50	6·4
Bournemouth (Hurn)	7·9	97	3·4	7·9	44	5·7	11·3	11	5·7	12·7	111	5·4
Bradford	7·3	71	1·2	7·5	56	3·9	10·2	9	3·1	11·3	136	3·6
Braemar	4·3	62	2·5	5·3	71	4·7	9·4	38	—	9·5	129	—
Buxton.............	6·3	77	1·9	6·3	80	4·4	9·3	15	3·8	10·4	105	4·7
Cambridge	8·3	38	3·2	8·2	43	4·9	10·7	14	3·7	12·7	98	3·8
Cheltenham	8·3	84	3·0	8·3	86	4·1	11·5	17	4·3	12·1	116	4·1
Clacton-on-Sea.....	7·6	26	3·3	8·3	31	5·4	10·3	10	4·6	13·2	81	4·1
Douglas	7·0	137	2·7	7·7	82	5·1	10·7	21	6·2	11·1	69	4·1
Dumfries	6·8	103	2·3	7·3	105	5·2	10·4	18	5·1	—	—	—
Dundee	6·3	59	2·5	7·6	26	6·3	11·3	18	5·3	11·5	135	5·0
Durham	7·2	61	2·2	7·1	28	5·2	10·3	19	4·0	11·3	54	5·1
East Malling	8·5	33	3·1	8·7	61	5·6	10·3	20	4·4	12·9	127	4·9
Edinburgh..........	6·5	63	2·6	7·3	31	5·7	10·7	34	4·9	11·5	62	5·1
Glasgow (Abbotsinch)......	6·5	90	2·8	7·8	102	4·9	11·3	7	6·7	11·6	90	6·2
Gogerddan	7·9	68	3·0	8·3	123	5·1	10·3	18	5·4	12·0	84	5·0
Hastings	8·1	43	3·5	8·6	54	6·1	10·3	22	4·8	12·4	132	4·6
Hull	8·2	38	—	8·3	35	—	11·1	10	—	12·6	49	—
Inverness	6·8	60	2·6	8·0	21	5·6	11·0	29	4·7	11·9	141	4·1
Leeming............	7·5	64	1·7	7·7	32	4·5	10·7	11	4·1	11·9	40	4·5
Lerwick............	5·6	121	2·2	5·9	46	5·5	7·8	33	4·7	8·7	56	5·0
London (Heathrow)	8·9	26	3·3	8·9	53	5·3	11·7	9	4·5	13·7	89	4·5
Long Ashton........	8·2	70	—	8·2	87	—	11·5	9	—	12·3	148	—
Lowestoft	4·8	21	3·8	8·1	33	6·3	10·3	17	5·1	13·3	55	4·5
Manchester (Ringway)	7·9	54	2·0	8·1	32	5·1	10·9	8	3·6	11·8	69	4·6
Manston	8·4	15	3·8	8·3	44	6·1	10·3	25	5·3	12·9	87	5·2
Melbury............	7·5	119	3·7	7·6	121	5·2	10·5	9	6·3	11·9	130	4·6
Morecambe	7·9	93	2·2	8·7	41	5·1	11·2	26	4·5	12·6	81	5·7
Nottingham (Watnall).........	7·7	43	2·4	7·7	52	4·7	10·7	11	3·8	11·7	63	4·6
Oxford	8·3	46	2·8	8·4	56	5·2	11·3	9	4·6	12·9	75	5·0
Pencelli	7·3	139	2·8	7·3	158	4·7	10·5	3	4·6	—	—	—
Penzance	9·1	148	4·1	9·5	92	5·5	12·3	3	7·4	13·3	132	5·4
Plymouth	8·6	121	4·2	8·9	69	5·4	—	4	7·3	—	—	—
Prestwick	6·9	70	3·1	7·7	90	5·6	10·5	14	6·6	11·5	84	6·2
Rhoose	7·8	77	3·2	8·1	89	5·6	11·3	5	5·7	12·4	134	5·5
St Mawgan	8·3	112	3·9	8·5	105	5·6	10·9	7	7·1	12·5	113	5·6
Shawbury	7·3	57	2·4	7·7	54	4·7	10·8	12	4·4	11·7	64	4·9
Sheffield...........	7·9	59	2·0	7·9	67	4·3	11·1	14	4·2	12·1	69	5·1
Skegness	7·7	31	2·9	7·7	33	5·3	10·5	9	5·0	12·5	45	5·7
Southampton	8·7	79	3·2	8·9	40	5·1	12·3	11	5·2	13·3	111	4·4
Stornoway	6·6	71	2·9	6·9	82	3·8	9·3	34	4·2	9·7	69	5·5
Tenby..............	7·5	115	3·5	8·3	115	5·7	11·5	3	7·1	12·3	115	5·4
Tiree	7·1	120	3·0	7·7	115	5·7	10·0	37	5·7	10·7	83	7·2
Torbay (Torquay) ...	8·9	104	4·1	8·9	54	5·3	—	—	—	13·1	109	5·1
Ventnor............	8·1	59	4·2	8·7	41	6·4	11·2	11	6·3	12·3	101	5·6
Waddington	7·7	27	2·8	7·7	37	5·2	10·7	11	4·3	12·1	43	4·8
Weymouth	8·2	94	3·9	8·5	56	6·1	11·7	6	5·7	12·8	94	5·7
Whitby.............	7·7	37	2·1	7·3	18	5·1	10·1	14	4·3	11·9	47	5·5
Worthing	7·9	58	3·9	8·1	47	6·3	10·7	15	5·4	12·7	114	4·8
Writtle.............	8·0	31	3·3	8·1	56	5·7	10·2	18	3·7	13·1	81	3·9

METEOROLOGICAL OBSERVATIONS, LONDON (HEATHROW)

Weather Record, July 1990

Day	Max. °C	Min. °C	Wind speed knots	Rainfall mm	Sunshine hrs
1	18.9	13.1	11.3	0.0	3.4
2	19.6	8.2	5.5	0.0	9.5
3	20.2	7.8	4.7	2.0	11.0
4	18.0	11.4	10.6	2.7	2.2
5	18.8	11.5	11.7	0.5	2.9
6	20.2	8.5	7.8	1.6	4.9
7	23.3	12.5	8.3	0.0	1.6
8	26.8	16.4	11.2	0.0	9.4
9	18.3	12.0	8.7	0.0	2.4
10	20.1	10.7	6.7	0.0	8.6
11	27.3	9.3	4.9	0.0	15.1
12	27.7	15.7	5.3	0.0	9.6
13	26.8	14.4	9.0	0.0	14.9
14	24.0	13.5	11.0	0.0	15.0
15	31.3	12.6	5.5	0.0	10.8
16	24.9	16.6	6.3	0.0	3.6
17	26.4	14.6	4.0	0.0	6.3
18	27.6	14.1	3.9	0.0	14.4
19	30.1	14.0	4.1	0.0	14.6
20	31.8	15.5	3.7	0.0	14.2
21	32.5	17.7	8.1	0.0	12.6
22	24.0	15.1	11.2	0.0	11.5
23	24.1	13.5	8.7	0.0	12.3
24	23.9	11.3	5.0	0.0	13.7
25	25.9	11.3	6.0	0.0	13.9
26	24.4	12.0	9.2	0.0	10.4
27	26.1	15.9	7.4	0.1	1.0
28	26.0	15.0	6.0	0.0	7.3
29	25.3	13.0	7.8	0.0	6.0
30	23.9	17.0	6.9	0.0	2.1
31	27.3	15.0	2.9	0.0	8.0
Total	—	—	—	6.9	223.4
Mean	24.7	13.2	7.2	—	—
Temp. °F	76.5	55.8	—	—	—
Average	22.0	12.9	8.2	51.0	189.7

Weather Record, August 1990

Max. °C	Min. °C	Wind speed knots	Rainfall mm	Sunshine hrs	Day
32.5	15.8	4.7	0.0	13.7	1
34.0	18.4	6.9	0.0	11.9	2
36.5	18.3	4.2	0.0	12.7	3
34.4	19.4	5.3	0.0	13.2	4
24.2	15.1	6.1	0.0	8.9	5
21.5	12.4	6.5	0.0	8.1	6
21.3	11.7	3.3	0.0	6.8	7
25.8	11.2	4.2	0.0	9.8	8
27.6	13.7	6.8	0.0	13.0	9
28.3	14.6	4.7	0.0	6.7	10
27.5	14.5	5.0	0.0	10.1	11
29.4	16.5	4.8	0.0	12.2	12
26.0	13.7	5.9	0.0	9.7	13
23.9	14.7	5.4	0.0	1.1	14
23.6	15.4	10.6	3.6	1.2	15
22.0	13.2	11.5	0.0	12.1	16
20.5	10.4	8.8	5.1	9.0	17
18.5	12.8	4.3	8.8	0.0	18
22.2	15.3	8.5	5.5	0.2	19
21.6	13.6	8.2	0.0	10.3	20
22.0	14.4	5.3	0.0	7.1	21
26.7	12.9	3.4	0.0	9.1	22
27.6	18.0	4.3	0.0	3.8	23
27.8	17.9	3.7	0.0	7.3	24
27.7	16.9	4.5	0.0	7.2	25
26.9	16.8	4.6	0.2	4.9	26
25.2	15.5	4.3	0.0	3.1	27
27.7	15.6	6.0	0.0	11.3	28
30.3	15.6	6.1	3.6	9.1	29
21.8	10.9	6.4	0.0	11.7	30
20.9	10.4	4.7	0.0	4.0	31
—	—	—	26.8	249.3	Total
26.0	14.7	5.8	—	—	Mean
78.8	58.5	—	—	—	Temp. °F
21.6	12.7	8.0	58.0	176.4	Average

Weather Record, September 1990

Day	Max. °C	Min. °C	Wind speed knots	Rainfall mm	Sunshine hrs
1	23.8	14.1	4.1	0.0	5.6
2	25.6	14.2	4.9	0.0	8.3
3	24.5	12.7	5.1	0.0	3.1
4	20.9	11.0	4.7	0.0	7.7
5	20.8	8.9	5.8	0.0	1.8
6	18.8	12.3	8.9	0.0	9.3
7	20.2	11.5	9.9	0.0	7.7
8	19.1	9.2	5.4	0.0	5.6
9	21.8	7.7	4.3	0.0	11.1
10	20.5	9.6	3.1	0.0	6.0
11	21.9	10.9	4.1	0.0	8.0
12	21.2	12.4	4.1	0.0	10.7
13	22.2	10.5	5.4	0.0	8.3
14	22.1	10.4	4.8	0.0	4.8
15	19.5	12.5	7.1	0.0	7.1
16	18.8	11.9	3.2	0.0	0.6
17	15.3	11.0	4.0	1.9	1.6
18	22.6	7.8	7.9	1.4	2.9
19	17.7	14.4	10.5	0.1	6.6
20	15.5	6.0	8.4	0.0	6.7
21	16.7	9.6	9.6	2.0	8.3
22	15.1	9.0	4.2	0.0	0.7
23	16.6	7.6	4.7	2.2	1.8
24	17.1	5.2	6.3	0.5	8.6
25	16.7	8.5	5.3	0.0	9.9
26	17.2	6.4	2.5	0.0	8.1
27	17.3	5.3	3.7	0.0	7.7
28	21.4	5.3	5.1	0.0	9.9
29	18.1	9.6	4.5	8.1	0.3
30	20.8	13.8	6.7	8.7	0.6
31					
Total	—	—	—	24.9	179.4
Mean	19.7	10.0	5.6	—	—
Temp. °F	67.5	50.0	—	—	—
Average	19.2	10.6	7.9	56.0	144.7

Weather Record, October 1990

Max. °C	Min. °C	Wind speed knots	Rainfall mm	Sunshine hrs	Day
17.7	6.5	3.5	0.0	8.6	1
19.5	10.8	7.4	0.5	5.6	2
16.2	14.8	8.1	4.9	0.7	3
17.0	5.2	6.8	3.1	8.2	4
17.7	10.6	10.9	0.5	0.0	5
18.2	13.5	11.7	0.1	1.1	6
13.7	6.5	4.7	0.0	8.6	7
14.5	0.8	3.2	0.0	9.3	8
15.5	5.2	6.9	0.0	0.5	9
18.9	10.6	6.7	0.0	3.0	10
18.6	12.8	6.8	0.0	4.9	11
24.2	7.9	5.9	0.0	8.6	12
24.0	13.0	7.1	0.0	6.6	13
21.6	15.2	5.7	0.0	6.9	14
21.2	14.3	9.3	1.1	1.3	15
19.2	12.7	8.5	0.0	9.0	16
17.7	12.1	6.3	14.0	0.3	17
15.9	14.2	3.1	0.1	0.0	18
17.8	12.5	2.4	0.0	2.7	19
19.1	10.3	4.5	0.0	4.7	20
14.7	12.8	12.0	0.0	0.1	21
13.0	10.0	9.7	0.0	0.1	22
17.5	7.4	7.5	0.0	4.4	23
16.0	9.3	6.2	1.6	1.2	24
16.4	7.6	9.0	8.1	5.3	25
12.5	10.3	6.9	7.2	2.4	26
13.5	7.1	8.0	6.4	3.2	27
12.2	9.3	9.7	0.0	1.1	28
11.1	3.5	5.3	1.8	2.5	29
13.9	4.5	10.8	0.0	6.2	30
14.1	7.3	11.1	0.3	5.4	31
—	—	—	49.7	122.5	Total
16.9	9.6	7.3	—	—	Mean
62.4	49.3	—	—	—	Temp. °F
15.2	7.6	7.8	56.0	104.4	Average

Entries of maximum temperature cover the 24 hour period 9–9 h; minimum temperature the 24 hour period 9–9 h; rainfall is for the 24 hours commencing at 9 h on the day of entry; sunshine is for the 24 hours 0–24 h; mean wind speed is 10 metres above the ground. 100 knots = 115·1 mph; 100 mm = 3·94 in.; °F = 9/5°C + 32. Averages are for the period 1951–80 except for mean wind speed which is for 1961–80.

Weather Record, November 1990

Day	Temperature Max. °C	Temperature Min. °C	Wind speed knots	Rain-fall mm	Sun-shine hrs
1	12·8	5·1	5·4	0·0	8·8
2	10·0	4·0	4·7	0·4	2·5
3	9·6	3·2	6·0	0·0	5·8
4	10·0	3·2	5·1	0·0	5·1
5	10·9	2·6	3·3	0·0	4·9
6	11·0	2·5	3·4	0·0	5·5
7	10·3	4·7	3·6	0·1	3·2
8	8·6	2·5	9·2	0·0	5·7
9	13·5	2·7	5·0	0·2	0·0
10	15·2	5·6	4·0	1·7	0·5
11	13·0	6·6	2·7	1·0	0·1
12	14·6	9·6	3·4	0·5	0·0
13	15·6	12·1	6·4	2·3	0·3
14	14·6	10·3	6·8	0·0	2·3
15	14·3	9·2	6·3	0·1	1·8
16	16·2	8·8	9·8	0·1	0·0
17	15·7	13·0	10·2	1·7	2·1
18	11·4	9·1	10·2	0·1	6·1
19	9·5	4·8	7·0	1·9	0·3
20	8·2	3·2	5·5	0·0	3·1
21	6·3	1·1	2·8	0·4	1·3
22	4·9	2·2	2·5	0·0	0·0
23	7·5	1·6	6·7	3·8	1·6
24	6·8	3·0	7·7	0·3	0·4
25	9·0	1·6	4·4	5·8	5·4
26	8·1	4·4	13·4	1·7	0·0
27	8·3	5·9	7·9	0·0	0·8
28	7·9	2·4	4·3	0·0	1·1
29	8·0	4·4	3·8	0·0	0·0
30	8·1	4·4	5·8	0·0	1·3
31					
Total	—	—	—	22·1	70·0
Mean	10·7	5·1	5·9	—	—
Temp. °F	51·3	41·2	—	—	—
Average	10·2	3·9	8·9	62·0	64·0

Weather Record, December 1990

Temperature Max. °C	Temperature Min. °C	Wind speed knots	Rain-fall mm	Sun-shine hrs	Day
8·4	5·2	4·6	0·0	0·0	1
5·6	4·0	3·2	0·0	0·0	2
7·8	4·5	3·1	0·0	0·0	3
9·0	0·0	2·5	0·0	6·2	4
8·4	2·0	3·2	0·0	6·1	5
6·6	−1·9	2·1	0·0	0·0	6
8·0	−1·2	7·5	1·5	3·8	7
2·5	1·0	7·0	3·4	0·0	8
6·5	−1·4	8·0	6·4	2·5	9
6·8	0·9	13·4	0·2	0·0	10
9·2	5·5	7·8	1·0	0·6	11
5·8	4·3	10·6	0·0	4·0	12
6·9	2·4	7·5	0·0	3·2	13
2·5	0·1	2·4	0·0	2·2	14
5·4	−4·6	3·5	0·4	0·2	15
4·5	−2·6	5·6	0·0	1·7	16
3·7	−1·0	4·3	0·0	0·0	17
2·2	1·1	3·4	0·0	0·0	18
4·6	1·1	4·1	0·0	1·7	19
9·6	−0·8	8·4	4·4	0·0	20
11·4	4·4	4·8	0·1	0·0	21
11·3	9·4	9·3	0·0	0·0	22
10·0	8·4	10·9	1·5	0·7	23
9·5	8·2	5·8	1·1	1·9	24
9·6	3·7	12·2	14·0	0·0	25
12·9	3·6	15·7	4·4	0·0	26
7·2	4·5	10·8	0·0	6·3	27
11·6	3·4	10·5	5·2	0·2	28
9·1	5·9	8·3	6·5	0·0	29
9·7	2·9	8·2	0·1	5·0	30
9·4	4·2	7·3	1·2	1·5	31
—	—	—	51·4	47·8	Total
7·6	2·5	6·7	—	—	Mean
45·7	36·5	—	—	—	Temp. °F
7·9	2·2	7·0	55·0	43·9	Average

Weather Record, January 1991

Day	Temperature Max. °C	Temperature Min. °C	Wind speed knots	Rain-fall mm	Sun-shine hrs
1	13·1	0·3	11·6	6·1	1·3
2	13·1	1·6	12·7	7·7	0·5
3	9·5	6·1	7·4	3·6	0·8
4	9·1	2·4	8·2	5·7	1·8
5	10·0	2·4	16·5	2·2	3·6
6	8·5	3·7	10·7	6·5	4·1
7	8·6	3·7	10·4	0·1	5·2
8	11·4	3·6	12·6	7·8	0·0
9	11·5	3·2	13·9	15·6	2·6
10	9·3	5·0	12·7	4·1	1·3
11	7·4	3·6	7·2	2·1	2·5
12	6·4	0·6	3·6	0·0	4·5
13	5·6	−2·5	3·4	0·0	7·3
14	5·8	−3·2	7·0	0·0	7·3
15	4·6	0·0	6·0	0·0	7·2
16	7·2	−1·9	4·8	0·0	6·1
17	8·2	0·0	6·9	0·4	0·0
18	9·1	6·0	9·2	6·1	0·1
19	8·0	1·1	3·9	0·2	6·1
20	10·0	1·7	5·8	0·0	0·0
21	9·3	4·9	5·3	0·0	5·8
22	6·0	1·8	5·6	0·0	0·3
23	5·9	2·8	2·5	0·0	0·0
24	4·5	1·7	5·0	0·0	0·0
25	3·1	1·2	3·6	0·0	0·0
26	3·5	1·3	4·0	0·2	0·0
27	4·0	1·1	3·7	0·0	0·0
28	5·1	2·4	5·0	0·0	0·0
29	1·9	0·6	4·0	0·0	0·0
30	2·1	0·5	2·7	0·0	0·0
31	3·7	0·1	5·5	1·3	0·0
Total	—	—	—	69·7	68·4
Mean	7·3	1·8	7·1	—	—
Temp. °F	45·1	35·2	—	—	—
Average	6·7	1·1	8·6	51·0	48·8

Weather Record, February 1991

Temperature Max. °C	Temperature Min. °C	Wind speed knots	Rain-fall mm	Sun-shine hrs	Day
6·4	0·3	3·2	0·7	1·2	1
4·2	−0·9	2·6	0·0	0·3	2
2·7	−2·0	3·1	0·0	0·4	3
3·6	−3·2	3·1	0·0	1·3	4
2·5	−2·3	5·1	0·1	0·4	5
−0·6	−1·8	9·3	0·4	2·1	6
−3·4	−7·3	8·6	4·9	0·0	7
−2·1	−6·4	6·5	0·5	0·0	8
−2·5	−6·8	5·2	0·0	0·5	9
2·1	−8·9	5·0	0·4	0·4	10
2·3	−5·7	6·9	0·0	6·7	11
2·0	−5·8	3·3	5·0	1·1	12
3·0	−2·7	3·6	0·0	0·7	13
6·1	−5·6	3·4	1·8	6·4	14
9·1	−1·8	6·0	0·2	0·0	15
6·6	0·4	4·0	0·0	6·9	16
6·2	0·5	3·5	0·0	4·7	17
6·4	0·7	3·9	0·0	2·1	18
4·2	−5·0	2·2	0·0	3·6	19
6·7	−3·0	6·8	0·9	0·0	20
8·1	3·9	9·4	1·2	0·0	21
11·5	2·4	13·7	3·2	0·4	22
12·2	5·4	14·9	0·0	0·0	23
12·5	9·2	9·4	1·0	0·2	24
11·9	1·5	3·3	0·0	5·4	25
10·3	2·7	5·7	0·2	0·1	26
9·0	4·7	3·0	14·2	0·0	27
9·9	1·8	2·7	0·0	3·6	28
					29
					30
					31
—	—	—	34·7	48·5	Total
5·3	−1·2	5·6	—	—	Mean
41·5	29·8	—	—	—	Temp. °F
7·3	1·3	9·3	38·0	62·2	Average

Weather Record, March 1991

Day	Temperature Max. °C	Min. °C	Wind speed knots	Rainfall mm	Sunshine hrs
1	8.8	0.5	2.4	0.0	1.7
2	7.4	1.4	6.0	0.3	0.3
3	12.0	3.5	7.6	0.0	7.2
4	11.4	2.5	8.7	1.0	0.0
5	11.0	6.8	5.0	6.5	0.3
6	14.3	8.1	5.9	1.1	0.3
7	14.4	8.4	4.6	3.1	2.0
8	14.7	8.4	10.9	0.0	7.9
9	11.6	8.6	8.3	0.1	0.1
10	11.4	7.5	7.0	0.9	0.0
11	12.1	8.2	4.4	0.0	0.1
12	12.6	9.1	5.1	0.0	0.0
13	18.7	5.5	3.0	0.0	9.7
14	14.1	6.2	3.5	0.4	1.5
15	11.7	7.5	6.8	0.0	0.2
16	14.8	7.9	6.6	5.4	0.2
17	12.0	8.0	6.0	0.0	1.0
18	12.9	2.6	9.5	2.7	5.4
19	16.0	7.6	11.8	0.1	1.1
20	12.8	10.6	11.0	0.3	0.0
21	13.8	7.6	6.8	0.0	7.2
22	10.4	2.2	3.5	4.0	4.4
23	9.4	2.2	3.9	0.0	3.5
24	10.9	-0.4	5.8	0.0	2.9
25	11.1	3.8	11.7	0.0	9.9
26	8.4	4.6	9.6	0.0	0.0
27	13.7	2.9	7.5	0.0	10.5
28	13.8	3.0	8.0	0.0	6.8
29	12.0	5.8	5.5	0.0	5.6
30	14.1	-0.1	3.4	0.0	9.7
31	15.9	5.1	3.7	0.0	3.2
Total	—	—	—	25.9	102.7
Mean	12.5	5.3	6.6	—	—
Temp. °F	54.5	41.5	—	—	—
Average	10.2	2.6	9.5	43.0	110.8

Weather Record, April 1991

Temperature Max. °C	Min. °C	Wind speed knots	Rainfall mm	Sunshine hrs	Day
12.3	6.5	9.2	0.7	0.0	1
11.3	8.5	13.4	1.2	0.0	2
13.0	4.5	8.2	1.5	10.2	3
11.8	5.9	13.5	5.1	2.5	4
11.3	5.1	10.7	0.0	1.7	5
10.6	1.8	10.0	3.5	3.2	6
12.3	6.2	10.9	0.1	4.1	7
15.0	6.1	7.2	0.0	5.6	8
15.1	6.3	5.8	0.0	5.6	9
18.6	6.4	6.9	0.0	6.2	10
21.0	8.7	5.9	0.0	7.6	11
21.0	8.3	4.8	0.0	7.8	12
17.6	10.3	9.2	0.0	10.3	13
12.9	5.4	11.0	0.0	5.6	14
16.0	6.3	8.0	0.0	7.7	15
11.9	4.6	10.7	0.0	5.1	16
8.9	1.5	10.4	0.0	7.2	17
9.9	1.3	5.7	3.6	1.3	18
9.2	1.2	9.7	2.9	4.5	19
8.3	0.9	5.8	1.4	7.3	20
11.3	-0.7	5.5	1.7	4.2	21
11.5	4.2	6.1	0.0	9.2	22
12.3	-0.3	3.1	0.0	5.8	23
12.6	6.9	4.3	0.0	0.6	24
12.4	5.9	7.2	0.0	3.7	25
15.9	4.5	6.8	0.0	10.7	26
14.7	4.4	6.4	0.0	8.0	27
14.2	2.8	3.4	0.0	12.7	28
10.8	5.0	6.7	28.9	0.1	29
9.1	6.4	9.5	2.2	0.0	30
					31
—	—	—	52.8	158.5	Total
13.1	4.8	7.9	—	—	Mean
55.6	40.6	—	—	—	Temp. °F
13.2	4.6	8.3	41.0	146.9	Average

Weather Record, May 1991

Day	Temperature Max. °C	Min. °C	Wind speed knots	Rainfall mm	Sunshine hrs
1	11.1	5.2	10.9	0.5	0.6
2	11.4	2.2	8.1	0.1	5.0
3	11.4	2.7	6.4	4.6	4.9
4	12.3	5.0	8.2	0.2	7.1
5	10.5	5.8	9.8	0.7	0.9
6	9.7	5.2	6.2	0.0	0.9
7	11.4	6.2	4.8	0.0	2.2
8	14.1	6.8	6.8	0.0	0.9
9	14.6	2.2	4.3	0.0	13.1
10	16.8	2.2	2.7	0.0	8.1
11	15.6	7.7	3.9	0.0	1.7
12	19.1	6.2	3.9	0.0	10.7
13	20.5	10.0	6.2	0.3	3.8
14	16.1	8.8	6.6	0.0	9.5
15	15.7	5.4	6.5	0.2	6.4
16	12.4	8.6	5.9	2.2	0.0
17	12.6	8.0	3.6	0.1	0.0
18	14.1	8.8	3.5	0.2	0.3
19	17.5	9.8	4.0	0.0	0.9
20	21.7	10.6	5.1	0.0	6.9
21	24.6	11.6	4.4	0.0	9.4
22	21.2	12.0	4.9	0.0	10.5
23	18.2	10.1	4.7	0.0	3.7
24	18.4	8.0	3.3	0.0	2.3
25	21.8	10.1	4.6	0.0	10.4
26	16.9	12.5	4.4	0.0	1.0
27	20.5	9.0	6.7	0.0	8.8
28	12.5	9.7	8.4	0.0	0.0
29	15.1	8.9	8.3	0.0	3.0
30	16.2	9.4	6.3	0.0	5.6
31	13.6	8.7	6.3	0.0	0.1
Total	—	—	—	9.1	138.7
Mean	15.7	7.7	5.8	—	—
Temp. °F	60.3	45.9	—	—	—
Average	17.1	7.8	8.5	48.0	196.1

Weather Record, June 1991

Temperature Max. °C	Min. °C	Wind speed knots	Rainfall mm	Sunshine hrs	Day
14.1	8.5	8.0	0.0	2.6	1
15.5	5.9	4.5	1.6	3.7	2
14.6	6.9	6.3	0.4	5.6	3
15.8	2.9	4.0	0.0	11.7	4
16.2	4.9	7.2	7.4	5.1	5
17.2	9.7	5.0	0.6	1.4	6
16.1	10.9	4.8	5.1	0.2	7
16.3	10.4	6.0	0.8	0.0	8
19.0	11.4	12.2	0.0	10.9	9
18.9	11.8	9.5	3.0	4.2	10
16.2	7.6	9.8	1.8	3.5	11
20.0	12.5	12.3	0.0	6.7	12
18.4	11.0	12.2	0.5	8.1	13
19.2	8.5	9.0	10.5	9.3	14
16.6	8.8	8.4	1.3	1.3	15
16.5	9.2	3.8	0.8	6.3	16
15.3	9.9	4.6	0.5	1.9	17
15.6	7.0	6.2	1.5	2.2	18
17.5	9.4	7.0	0.5	3.9	19
19.1	10.6	4.9	0.1	4.6	20
22.6	10.5	8.6	0.2	8.5	21
19.9	11.9	10.2	0.0	6.6	22
15.9	11.2	7.6	14.9	0.0	23
17.0	12.0	3.9	7.4	0.0	24
18.6	13.1	7.8	6.2	0.0	25
18.1	10.6	8.4	12.0	6.5	26
19.9	9.5	5.8	5.7	3.9	27
20.5	10.9	4.1	0.0	6.7	28
20.5	9.1	5.6	2.1	8.5	29
21.3	13.1	7.4	3.7	1.1	30
					31
—	—	—	88.6	135.0	Total
17.7	9.7	7.2	—	—	Mean
63.9	49.5	—	—	—	Temp. °F
20.5	10.9	8.4	51.0	206.0	Average

Data provided by the Met Office

TIME MEASUREMENT AND CALENDARS

MEASUREMENTS OF TIME

Measurements of time are based on the time taken by the earth to rotate on its axis (day); by the moon to revolve round the earth (month); and by the earth to revolve round the sun (year). From these, which are not commensurable, certain average or mean intervals have been adopted for ordinary use.

The Day begins at midnight and is divided into 24 hours of 60 minutes, each of 60 seconds. The hours are counted from midnight up to 12 noon (when the sun crosses the meridian), and these hours are designated a.m. (*ante meridiem*); and again from noon up to 12 midnight, which hours are designated p.m. (*post meridiem*), except when the twenty-four hour reckoning is employed. The 24-hour reckoning ignores a.m. and p.m., and the hours are numbered 0 to 23 from midnight to midnight.

Colloquially the 24 hours are divided into day and night, day being the time while the sun is above the horizon (including the four stages of twilight defined on p. 63). Day is subdivided further into morning, the early part of daytime, ending at noon; afternoon, from noon to 6 p.m. ; and evening, which may be said to extend from 6 p.m. until midnight. Night, the dark period between day and night, begins at the close of astronomical twilight (*see* p. 63) and extends beyond midnight to sunrise the next day.

The names of the days are derived from Old English translations or adaptations of the Roman titles.

Sunday	Sun	Sol
Monday	Moon	Luna
Tuesday	Tiw/Tyr (god of war)	Mars
Wednesday	Woden/Odin	Mercury
Thursday	Thor	Jupiter
Friday	Frigga/Freyja (goddess of love)	Venus
Saturday	Saeternes	Saturn

The Week is a period of seven days.

The Month in the ordinary calendar is approximately the twelfth part of a year, but the lengths of the different months vary from 28 (or 29) days to 31.

The Year.—The equinoctial or tropical year is the time that the earth takes to revolve round the sun from equinox to equinox, or 365·2422 mean solar days.

The calendar year consists of 365 days, but a year the date of which is divisible by four without remainder, is called bissextile (*see* Roman Calendar) or leap year and consists of 366 days, one day being added to the month February, so that a date 'leaps over' a day of the week. The last year of a century is not a leap year unless its number is divisible by 400 (e.g. the years 1800 and 1900 had only 365 days but the year 2000 will have 366 days).

The Solstice.—A solstice is the point in the tropical year at which the sun attains its greatest distance, north or south, from the Equator. In the northern hemisphere the greatest distance north of the Equator is the summer solstice and the greatest distance south is the winter solstice.

The summer solstice is also the longest day of the year, measured from sunrise to sunset. At the solstice the sun, reaching its greatest northern declination, appears to stand still, the times of sunrise and sunset and the consequent length of the day showing no variation for several days together, before and after the longest day (June 21 or 22). For the remainder of this century the longest day in the United Kingdom will fall each year on June 21.

The date of the solstice varies according to locality. If the solstice falls on June 21 late in the day by

Greenwich time, that day will be the longest of the year at Greenwich even though it may be by only a second of time or a fraction thereof, but it will be on June 22, local date, in Japan, and so June 22 will be the longest day there and at places in eastern longitudes.

Leaving aside the question of locality, the date of the solstice is also affected by the length of the tropical year, which is 365·24 days, less about 11 minutes. If a solstice happens late on June 21 in one year, it will be nearly six hours later in the next, i.e. early on June 22, and that will be the longest day. This delay of the solstice is not permitted to continue because the extra day in leap year brings it back a day in the calendar.

However, because of the 11 minutes mentioned above, the additional day in leap year brings the solstice back too far by 44 minutes, and the time of the solstice in the calendar is earlier as the century progresses. (In the year 2000 the summer solstice reaches its earliest date for 100 years, i.e. June 21^d 02^h.) To remedy this the last year of a century is in most cases not a leap year, and the omission of the extra day puts the date of the solstice later by about six hours too much, compensation for which is made by making the fourth centennial year a leap year.

Similar considerations apply to the day of the winter solstice, the shortest day of the year. For the remainder of this century the shortest day in the United Kingdom will fall on December 21 in two years of four and on December 22 in the remaining two years. In the year 2000 the winter solstice reaches its earliest date, i.e. December 21^d 13^h. The difference due to locality also prevails in the same sense as for the longest day.

At Greenwich the sun sets at its earliest by the clock about ten days before the shortest day. The reason for this is twofold. The daily change in the time of sunset is due in the first place to the sun's movement southwards at this time of the year, which diminishes the interval between the sun's transit and its setting, and, secondly, because of the daily decrease of the Equation of Time which causes the time of apparent noon to be continuously later day by day, and so in a measure counteracts the first effect. The rates of the change of these two quantities are not equal, nor are they uniform, but are such that their combination causes the date of earliest sunset to be December 12 or 13 at Greenwich. In more southerly latitudes the effect of the movement of the sun is less, and the change in the time of sunset depends on that of the Equation of Time to a greater degree, and the date of earliest sunset is earlier than it is at Greenwich.

The Equinox is the point at which the sun crosses the Equator and day and night are of equal length all over the world. This occurs in March (vernal equinox—about March 21) and September (autumnal equinox—about September 21).

The Historical Year.—Before the year 1752, two calendar systems were in use in England. The civil or legal year began on March 25, while the historical year began on January 1. Thus the civil or legal date March 24, 1658, was the same day as the historical date March 24, 1659; and a date in that portion of the year is written as March 24, 165$\frac{8}{9}$, the lower figure showing the historical year.

The New Year.—In England in the seventh century, and as late as the thirteenth, the year was reckoned from Christmas Day, but in the twelfth century the Anglican Church began the year with the feast of the Annunciation of the Blessed Virgin (Lady Day) on March 25 and this practice was adopted generally in the fourteenth century. The civil or legal year in the British Dominions (exclusive of Scotland) began with 'Lady Day' until 1751. But in and since 1752 the civil year has begun with January 1. Certain dividends are still paid by the Bank of England on dates based on Old Style. New Year's Day in Scotland was changed from March 25 to January 1 in 1600.

On the continent of Europe, January 1 was adopted as the first day of the year by Venice in 1522, Germany in 1544, Spain, Portugal, and the Roman Catholic Netherlands in 1556, Prussia, Denmark and Sweden in 1559, France in 1564, Lorraine in 1579, the Protestant Netherlands in 1583, Russia in 1725, and Tuscany in 1751.

The Masonic Year.—Two dates are quoted in warrants, dispensations, etc., issued by the United Grand Lodge of England, those for the current year being expressed as *Anno Domini* 1992—*Anno Lucis* 5992. This *Anno Lucis* (year of light) is based on the Book of Genesis 1 : 3, the 4000 year difference being derived, in modified form, from *Ussher's Notation*, published in 1654, which places the Creation of the World in 4004 BC.

Regnal Years.—These are the years of a sovereign's reign, and each begins on the anniversary of his or her accession, e.g. regnal year 41 of the present Queen begins on Februrary 6, 1992.

The system was used for dating Acts of Parliament until 1962. The Summer Time Act, 1925, for example, is quoted as 15 and 16 Geo. V. c. 64, because it became law in the parliamentary session which extended over part of both of these regnal years. Acts of a parliamentary session during which a sovereign died were usually given two year numbers, the regnal year of the deceased sovereign and the regnal year of his or her successor. Acts passed in 1952 were dated 16 Geo. VI. and 1 Elizabeth II. Since 1962, Acts of Parliament have been dated by the calendar year.

Dog Days.—The days about the heliacal rising of the Dog Star, noted from ancient times as the hottest and most unwholesome period of the year in the northern hemisphere. Their incidence has been variously calculated as depending on the Greater or Lesser Dog Star (Sirius or Procyon) and their duration has been reckoned as from 30 to 54 days. A generally accepted period is from July 3 to August 15.

Metonic (Lunar, or Minor) **Cycle.**—In the year 432 BC, Meton, an Athenian astronomer, found that 235 lunations are very nearly, though not exactly, equal in duration to 19 solar years, and, hence, after 19 years the phases of the Moon recur on the same

days of the month (nearly). The dates of full moon in a cycle of 19 years were inscribed in figures of gold on public monuments in Athens, and the number showing the position of a year in the cycle is called the **Golden Number** of that year.

Roman Indiction.—A period of fifteen years, instituted for fiscal purposes about AD 300.

Solar (or Major) **Cycle.**—A period of twenty-eight years, in any corresponding year of which the days of the week recur on the same day of the month.

Julian Period.—Proposed by Joseph Scaliger in 1582. The period is 7980 Julian years, and its first year coincides with the year 4713 BC. The figure of 7980 is the product of the number of years in the Solar cycle, the Metonic cycle and the cycle of the Roman Indiction (28 × 19 × 15).

Epact.—The age of the calendar Moon, diminished by one day, on January 1, in the ecclesiastical lunar calendar.

THE FOUR SEASONS

Spring, the first season of the year, is defined astronomically to begin in the northern hemisphere at the vernal equinox and to end at the summer solstice. In Britain, spring in popular parlance comprises the months of March, April and May. In the southern hemisphere spring corresponds with autumn in the northern.

Summer, the second and warmest season, begins astronomically in the northern hemisphere at the summer solstice and ends at the autumnal equinox. In popular parlance summer in Britain includes the months of June, July and August. In the southern hemisphere summer corresponds with winter in the northern.

Autumn, the third season, begins astronomically in the northern hemisphere at the autumnal equinox and ends at the winter solstice. In Britain it is popularly held to include the months of September, October and November. A warm period sometimes occurs round about St Luke's Day (October 18) and is known as St Luke's Summer. A warm period occurring round about Martinmas (November 11) is known as St Martin's Summer. In the southern hemisphere autumn corresponds with spring in the northern.

Winter, the fourth and coldest season, begins astronomically in the northern hemisphere at the winter solstice and ends at the vernal equinox. In Britain the season is popularly held to comprise the months of December, January and February. In the southern hemisphere it corresponds with summer in the northern.

THE CHRISTIAN CALENDAR

In the Christian chronological system the years are distinguished by cardinal numbers before or after the Incarnation, the period being denoted by the letters BC (Before Christ) or, more rarely, AC (*Ante Christum*), and AD (*Anno Domini*—In the Year of Our Lord). The correlative dates of the epoch are the fourth year of the 194th Olympiad, the 753rd year from the foundation of Rome, AM 3761 (Jewish chronology), and the 4714th year of the Julian period.

The system was introduced into Italy in the sixth century. Though first used in France in the seventh century, it was not universally established there until about the eighth century. It has been said that the system was introduced into England by St

Augustine (AD 596), but it was probably not generally used until some centuries later. It was ordered to be used by the Bishops at the Council of Chelsea (AD 816). The actual date of the birth of Christ is somewhat uncertain.

The Julian Calendar.—In the Julian calendar all the centennial years were leap years, and for this reason towards the close of the sixteenth century there was a difference of ten days between the tropical and calendar years; the equinox fell on March 11 of the calendar, whereas at the time of the Council of Nicaea (AD 325), it had fallen on March 21. In 1582 Pope Gregory ordained that October 5 should be called October 15 and that of the end-century years only the fourth should be a leap year (*see* p. 107).

The **Gregorian Calendar** was adopted by Italy, France, Spain, and Portugal in 1582, by Prussia, the Roman Catholic German states, Switzerland, Holland and Flanders on January 1, 1583, by Poland in 1586, Hungary in 1587, the Protestant German and Netherland states and Denmark in 1700, and by Great Britain and her Dominions (including the North American colonies) in 1752, by the omission of eleven days (September 3 being reckoned as September 14). Sweden omitted the leap day in 1700 but observed leap days in 1704 and 1708, and reverted to the Julian calendar by having two leap days in 1712; the Gregorian calendar was adopted in 1753 by the omission of eleven days (February 18 being reckoned as March 1). Japan adopted the calendar in 1872, China in 1912, Bulgaria in 1915, Turkey and Soviet Russia in 1918, Yugoslavia and Romania in 1919, and Greece in February 1923.

In the same year that the change was made in England from the Julian to the Gregorian calendar, the beginning of the new year was also changed from March 25 to January 1 (*see* p. 107–8).

The **Orthodox Churches.**—Some Orthodox Churches still use the Julian reckoning, but the majority of Greek Orthodox Churches and the Romanian Orthodox Church have adopted a modified 'New Calendar', observing the Gregorian calendar for fixed feasts and the Julian for movable feasts.

The Orthodox Church year begins on September 1. There are four fast periods, and in addition to Pascha (Easter), twelve great feasts, as well as numerous commemorations of the saints of the Old and New Testaments throughout the year.

The **Dominical Letter** is one of the letters A–G which are used to denote the Sundays in successive years. If the first day of the year is a Sunday the letter is A; if the second, B; the third, C; and so on. Leap year requires two letters, the first for January 1 to February 29, the second for March 1 to December 31 (*see* page 111).

Epiphany.—The feast of the Epiphany, commemorating the manifestation of Christ, later became associated with the offering of gifts by the Magi. The day was of exceptional importance from the time of the Council of Nicaea (AD 325), as the primate of Alexandria was charged at every Epiphany feast with the announcement in a letter to the churches of the date of the forthcoming Easter. The day was of considerable importance in Britain as it influenced dates, ecclesiastical and lay, e.g. **Plough Monday**, when work was resumed in the fields, falls upon the Monday in the first full week after Epiphany.

Lent.—The Teutonic word *Lent*, which denotes the fast preceding Easter, originally meant no more than the spring season; but from Anglo-Saxon times at least, it has been used as the equivalent of the more significant Latin term **Quadragesima**, meaning the 'Forty Days' or, more literally, the fortieth day. As early as the fifth century some of the Fathers of the Church put forward the view that the forty days fast is of Apostolic origin, but this is not supported or believed by modern scholars; and it appears to some that it dates from the early years of the fourth century. There is some suggestion that the fast was kept originally for only forty hours. **Ash Wednesday** is the first day of Lent, which ends at midnight before Easter Day.

Sexagesima and Septuagesima.—It has been suggested that the unmeaning application of the names *Sexagesima* and *Septuagesima* to the second and third Sundays before Lent was made by analogy with the names *Quadragesima* and *Quinquagesima*.

A less likely conjecture is that *Septuagesima* means the seventh day before the Octave of Easter. It is not certain whether the name *Quinquagesima* is due to the fact that the Sunday in question is the fiftieth day before Easter (reckoned inclusive) or was simply formed on the analogy of *Quadragesima* (*New English Dictionary*).

Mothering Sunday is the fourth Sunday in Lent.

Palm Sunday, the Sunday before Easter and the beginning of Holy Week, commemorates the triumphal entry of Christ into Jerusalem and is celebrated in Britain (when palm is not available) by branches of willow gathered for use in the decoration of churches on that day.

Maundy Thursday is the day before Good Friday, the name itself being a corruption of *dies mandati* (day of the mandate) when Christ washed the feet of the disciples and gave them the mandate to love one another.

Easter Day is the first Sunday after the full moon which happens upon, or next after, the 21st day of March; if the full moon happens upon a Sunday, Easter Day is the Sunday after.

This definition is contained in an Act of Parliament (24 Geo. II. c. 23) and explanation is given in the preamble to the Act that the day of full moon depends on certain tables that have been prepared. These are the tables whose essential points are given in the early pages of the Book of Common Prayer. The moon referred to is not the real moon of the heavens, but a hypothetical moon on whose 'full' the date of Easter depends, and the lunations of this 'calendar' moon consist of twenty-nine and thirty days alternately, with certain necessary modifications to make the date of its full agree as nearly as possible with that of the real moon, which is known as the **Paschal Full Moon**. As at present ordained, Easter falls on one of 35 days (March 22–April 25).

A **Fixed Easter.**—On June 15, 1928, the House of Commons agreed to a motion for the third reading of a Bill proposing that Easter Day shall, in the calendar year next but one after the commencement of the Act and in all subsequent years, be the first Sunday after the second Saturday in April. Easter would thus fall between April 9 and 15 (inclusive), that is, on the second or third Sunday in April. A clause in the Bill provided that before it shall come into operation, regard shall be had to any opinion expressed officially by the various Christian Churches. Efforts by the World Council of Churches to secure a unanimous choice of date for Easter by its member Churches have so far been unsuccessful.

Holy Days and **Saints Days** were the normal factors in early times for setting the dates of future and recurrent appointments, e.g. the **Quarter Days** in England and Wales are the feast of the Nativity, the feast of the Annunciation, the feast of St John the Baptist and the feast of St Michael and All Angels, while **Term Days** in Scotland are Candlemas (feast of the Purification), Whitsunday, Lammas (Loaf Mass) and Martinmas (St Martin's Day). **Law Sittings** in England and Wales commence on the feast of St Hilary and the term which begins on Old Michaelmas Day ends on the former feast of St Thomas the Apostle.

Red-Letter Days were holy days and saints days indicated in early ecclesiastical calendars by letters printed in red ink. The days to be distinguished in this way were finally approved at the Council of Nicaea (AD 325). The judges of the Queen's Bench Division wear scarlet robes on red-letter days falling during the law sittings.

Rogation Days.—These are the Monday, Tuesday and Wednesday preceding Ascension Day and in the fifth century were ordered by the Church to be observed as public fasts with solemn processions and supplications. The processions were discontinued as religious observances at the Reformation, but survive in the ceremony known as 'Beating the Parish Bounds'. **Rogation Sunday** is the Sunday before Ascension Day.

Ascension Day is forty days after Easter Day.

Ember Days.—The Ember Days at the four seasons are the Wednesday, Friday and Saturday (*a*) before the third Sunday in Advent, (*b*) before the second Sunday in Lent, and (*c*) before the Sundays nearest to the festivals of St Peter and of St Michael and All Angels.

Pentecost or **Whit Sunday** is seven weeks after Easter Day. It is generally said that the name Whit

Sunday is a variant of White Sunday, and was so called from the albs or white robes of the newly baptized, but other derivations have been suggested.

Trinity Sunday is eight weeks after Easter Day, on the Sunday following Whit Sunday. Subsequent Sundays are sometimes reckoned in the Church of England as 'after Trinity'.

Thomas Becket (1118–70) was consecrated Archbishop of Canterbury on the Sunday after Whit Sunday and his first act was to ordain that the day of his consecration should be held as a new festival in honour of the Holy Trinity. The observance thus originated spread from Canterbury throughout the whole of Christendom.

Advent Sunday is the Sunday nearest to St Andrew's Day (November 30), which allows three Sundays between Advent and Christmas Day in all cases.

MOVABLE FEASTS TO THE YEAR 2025

Year	Ash Wednesday	Easter	Ascension	Pentecost (Whit Sunday)	Sundays after Pentecost	Advent Sunday
1992	March 4	April 19	May 28	June 7	19	Nov. 29
1993	Feb. 24	April 11	May 20	May 30	20	Nov. 28
1994	Feb. 16	April 3	May 12	May 22	21	Nov. 27
1995	March 1	April 16	May 25	June 4	20	Dec. 3
1996	Feb. 21	April 7	May 16	May 26	21	Dec. 1
1997	Feb. 12	March 30	May 8	May 18	22	Nov. 30
1998	Feb. 25	April 12	May 21	May 31	20	Nov. 29
1999	Feb. 17	April 4	May 13	May 23	21	Nov. 28
2000	March 8	April 23	June 1	June 11	19	Dec. 3
2001	Feb. 28	April 15	May 24	June 3	20	Dec. 2
2002	Feb. 13	March 31	May 9	May 19	22	Dec. 1
2003	March 5	April 20	May 29	June 8	19	Nov. 30
2004	Feb. 25	April 11	May 20	May 30	20	Nov. 28
2005	Feb. 9	March 27	May 5	May 15	22	Nov. 27
2006	March 1	April 16	May 25	June 4	20	Dec. 3
2007	Feb. 21	April 8	May 17	May 27	21	Dec. 2
2008	Feb. 6	March 23	May 1	May 11	23	Nov. 30
2009	Feb. 25	April 12	May 21	May 31	20	Nov. 29
2010	Feb. 17	April 4	May 13	May 23	21	Nov. 28
2011	March 9	April 24	June 2	June 12	18	Nov. 27
2012	Feb. 22	April 8	May 17	May 27	21	Dec. 2
2013	Feb. 13	March 31	May 9	May 19	22	Dec. 1
2014	March 5	April 20	May 29	June 8	19	Nov. 30
2015	Feb. 18	April 5	May 14	May 24	21	Nov. 29
2016	Feb. 10	March 27	May 5	May 15	22	Nov. 27
2017	March 1	April 16	May 25	June 4	20	Dec. 3
2018	Feb. 14	April 1	May 10	May 20	22	Dec. 2
2019	March 6	April 21	May 30	June 9	19	Dec. 1
2020	Feb. 26	April 12	May 21	May 31	20	Nov. 29
2021	Feb. 17	April 4	May 13	May 23	21	Nov. 28
2022	March 2	April 17	May 26	June 5	19	Nov. 27
2023	Feb. 22	April 9	May 18	May 28	21	Dec. 3
2024	Feb. 14	March 31	May 9	May 19	22	Dec. 1
2025	March 5	April 20	May 29	June 8	19	Nov. 30

NOTES:
Ash Wednesday (first day in Lent) can fall at earliest on February 4 and at latest on March 10.
Easter Day can fall at earliest on March 22 and at latest on April 25.
Ascension Day can fall at earliest on April 30 and at latest on June 3.
Pentecost (Whit Sunday) can fall at earliest on May 10 and at latest on June 13.
Trinity Sunday is the Sunday after Whit Sunday.
Corpus Christi falls on the Thursday after Trinity Sunday.
There are not less than 18 and not more than 23 Sundays after Pentecost.
Advent Sunday is the Sunday nearest to November 30.

EASTER DAYS AND SUNDAY LETTERS, 1500 TO 2025

		1500—1599	1600—1699	1700—1799	1800—1899	1900—1999	2000-2025
d	Mar. 22	1573	1668	1761	1818		
e	,, 23	1505-16	1600	1788	1845-56	1913	2008
f	,, 24		1611-95	1706-99		1940	
g	,, 25	1543-54	1627-38-49	1722-33-44	1883-94	1951	
A	,, 26	1559-70-81-92	1654-65-76	1749-58-69-80	1815-26-37	1967-78-89	
b	Mar. 27	1502-13-24-97	1608-87-92	1785-96	1842-53-64	1910-21-32	2005-16
c	,, 28	1529-35-40	1619-24-30	1703-14-25	1869-75-80	1937-48	
d	,, 29	1551-62	1635-46-57	1719-30-41-52	1807-12-91	1959-64-70	
e	,, 30	1567-78-89	1651-62-73-84	1746-55-66-77	1823-34	1902-75-86-97	
f	,, 31	1510-21-32-83-94	1605-16-78-89	1700-71-82-93	1839-50-61-72	1907-18-29-91	2002-13-24
g	April 1	1526-37-48	1621-32	1711-16	1804-66-77-88	1923-34-45-56	2018
A	,, 2	1553-64	1643-48	1727-38-52(NS)	1809-20-93-99	1961-72	
b	,, 3	1575-80-86	1659-70-81	1743-63-68-74	1825-31-36	1904-83-88-94	
c	,, 4	1507-18-91	1602-13-75-86-97	1708-79-90	1847-58	1915-20-26-99	2010-21
d	,, 5	1523-34-45-56	1607-18-29-40	1702-13-24-95	1801-63-74-85-96	1931-42-53	2015
e	April 6	1539-50-61-72	1634-45-56	1729-35-40-60	1806-17-28-90	1947-58-69-80	
f	,, 7	1504-77-88	1667-72	1751-65-76	1822-33-44	1901-12-85-96	
g	,, 8	1509-15-20-99	1604-10-83-94	1705-87-92-98	1849-55-60	1917-28	2007-12
A	,, 9	1531-42	1615-26-37-99	1710-21-32	1871-82	1939-44-50	2023
b	,, 10	1547-58-69	1631-42-53-64	1726-37-48-57	1803-14-87-98	1955-66-77	
c	April 11	1501-12-63-74-85-96	1658-69-80	1762-73-84	1819-30-41-52	1909-71-82-93	2004
d	,, 12	1506-17-28	1601-12-91-96	1789	1846-57-68	1903-14-25-36-98	2009-20
e	,, 13	1533-44	1623-28	1707-18	1800-73-79-84	1941-52	
f	,, 14	1555-60-66	1639-50-61	1723-34-45-54	1805-11-16-95	1963-68-74	
g	,, 15	1571-82-93	1655-66-77-88	1750-59-70-81	1827-38	1900-06-79-90	2001
A	April 16	1503-14-25-36-87-98	1609-20-82-93	1704-75-86-97	1843-54-65-76	1911-22-33-95	2006-17
b	,, 17	1530-41-52	1625-36	1715-20	1808-70-81-92	1927-38-49-60	2022
c	,, 18	1557-68	1647-52	1731-42-56	1802-13-24-97	1954-65-76	
d	,, 19	1500-79-84-90	1663-74-85	1747-67-72-78	1829-35-40	1908-81-87-92	
e	,, 20	1511-22-95	1606-17-79-90	1701-12-83-94	1851-62	1919-24-30	2003-14-25
f	April 21	1527-38-49	1622-33-44	1717-28	1867-78-89	1935-46-57	2019
g	,, 22	1565-76	1660	1739-53-64	1810-21-32	1962-73-84	
A	,, 23	1508	1671		1848	1905-16	2000
b	,, 24	1519	1603-14-98	1709-91	1859		2011
c	,, 25	1546	1641	1736	1886	1943	

THE JEWISH CALENDAR

The story of the Flood in the Book of Genesis relates that the Flood began on the seventeenth day of the second month, that after the end of 150 days the waters were abated, and that on the seventeenth day of the seventh month the Ark rested on Mount Ararat. This indicates the use of a calendar of some kind and that the writers recognized 30 days as the length of a lunation. There is other mention of months by their original numbers in the Book of Genesis and in establishing the rite of the Passover, Moses spoke of Abib as the month when the Israelites came out from Egypt and Abib was to be the first month of the year. In the first Book of Kings three months are mentioned by name, Ziv the second month, Ethanim the seventh and Bul the eighth, but these are not names now in use. After the dispersion, Jewish communities were left in considerable doubt as to the times of fasts and festivals. This led to the formation of the Jewish calendar as used today. It is said that this was done in AD 358 by Rabbi Hillel II, a descendant of Gamaliel, though some assert that it did not happen until much later.

The calendar is luni-solar, and is based on the lengths of the lunation and of the tropical year as found by Hipparchus (c. 120 BC), which differ little from those adopted at the present day. The year AM 5752 (1991–92) is the 14th year of the 303rd Metonic (Minor or Lunar) cycle of 19 years and the 12th year of the 206th Solar (or Major) Cycle of 28 years since the Era of the Creation. Jews hold that the Creation occurred at the time of the autumnal equinox in the year known in the Christian calendar as 3760 BC (954 of the Julian period). The epoch or starting point of Jewish chronology corresponds to October 7, 3761 BC. At the beginning of each solar cycle, the Tekufah of Nisan (the vernal equinox) returns to the same day and to the same hour.

The hour is divided into 1080 minims, and the month between one new moon and the next is reckoned as 29 days, 12 hours, 793 minims. The normal calendar year, called a Common Regular year, consists of 12 months of 30 days and 29 days alternately. Since twelve months such as these comprise only 354 days, in order that each of them shall not diverge greatly from an average place in the solar year, a thirteenth month is occasionally added after the fifth month of the civil year (which commences on the first day of the month Tishri), or as the penultimate month of the ecclesiastical year (which commences on the first day of month Nisan). The years when this happens are called Embolismic or leap years.

Of the 19 years that form a Metonic cycle, seven are leap years; they occur at places in the cycle indicated by the numbers 3, 6, 8, 11, 14, 17 and 19, these places being chosen so that the accumulated excesses of the solar years should be as small as possible.

The first of each month is called the day of New Moon, though it is not necessarily the day of astronomical new moon, that being the day on which conjunction of sun and moon occurs, but there is generally a difference of a day or two. In practice, in a month which follows one of 30 days, the day preceding its first day is also observed as a day of New Moon. The dates on which the first days of the months fall depend on that of the first of Tishri, which therefore controls the dates of fasts and festivals in the Jewish year. For certain ceremonial reasons connected with these, the first of Tishri must not fall on a Sunday, Wednesday or Friday, and if this should happen as the result of the computation it is postponed to the following day. Also, if the New Moon of Tishri falls on any day of the week at noon or later than noon, then the following day is to be taken for the celebration of that New Moon and is Tishri 1, provided that it is not one of the forbidden days, in which case there is a further postponement of a day.

These rules and others have been considered in detail, and a calendar scheme has been drawn up in

which a Jewish year is of one of the following six types:

Minimal Common	353 days
Regular Common	354 days
Full Common	355 days
Minimal Leap	383 days
Regular Leap	384 days
Full Leap	385 days

The Regular year has alternate months of 30 and 29 days. In a Full year, whether Common or Leap, Marcheshvan, the second month of the civil year, has 30 days instead of 29; in Minimal years Kislev, the third month, has 29 instead of 30. The additional month in leap years is called Adar I and precedes the month called Adar in Common years. Adar II is called Ve-Adar, in leap years. Adar I and Adar II always have 30 days, but neither this, nor the other variations mentioned, is allowed to change the number of days in the other months which still follow the alternation of the normal twelve. In leap years the month intercalated precedes Adar and usurps its name, but the usual Adar festivals are kept in Ve-Adar.

These are the main features of the Jewish calendar, which must be considered permanent because as a Jewish law it cannot be altered except by a great Sanhedrin.

The Jewish day begins between sunset and nightfall. The time used is that of the meridian of Jerusalem, which is $2h.\,21m.$ in advance of Greenwich Mean Time. Rules for the beginning of sabbaths and festivals were laid down for the latitude of London in the eighteenth century and hours for nightfall are now fixed annually by the Chief Rabbi.

Jewish Calendar 5752–53

AM 5752 (752) is a Full Leap year of 13 months, 55 sabbaths and 385 days. AM 5753 (753) is a Minimal Common year of 12 months, 50 sabbaths and 353 days.

Jewish Month					AM 5752					AM 5753	
Tishri	1	..	..	..	1991	September	9	..	..	..	1992	September	28
Marcheshvan	1	..	..	..		October	9	..	..	..		October	28
Kislev	1	..	..	..		November	8	..	..	..		November	26
Tebet	1	..	..	..		December	8	..	..	..		December	25
Shebat	1	..	..	..	1992	January	6	..	..	..	1993	January	23
*Adar	1	..	..	..		February	5	..	..			February	22
Ve-Adar	1	..	..	..		March	6					
Nisan	1	..	..	..		April	4	..	..	..		March	23
Iyar	1	..	..	..		May	4	..	..	..		April	22
Sivan	1	..	..	..		June	2	..	..	..		May	21
Tammuz	1	..	..	..		July	2	..	..	..		June	20
Ab	1	..	..	..		July	31	..	..	..		July	19
Elul	1	..	..	..		August	30	..	..	..		August	18

*Known as Adar Rishon in leap years.

Jewish Fasts and Festivals

Tishri	1–2	Rosh Hashanah (New Year).	*Tebet*	10	Fast of Tebet.
,,	3	*Fast of Gedaliah.	†*Adar*	13	§Fast of Esther.
,,	10	Yom Kippur (Day of Atonement).	,, ,,	14	Purim.
,,	15–21	Succoth (Feast of Tabernacles).	,, ,,	15	Shushan Purim.
,,	21	Hoshana Rabba.	*Nisan*	15–22	Pesach (Passover).
,,	22	Shemini Atseret (Solemn Assembly).	*Sivan*	6–7	Shavuot (Feast of Weeks).
,,	23	Simchat Torah (Rejoicing of the Law).	*Tammuz*	17	*Fast of Tammuz.
Kislev	25	Chanukah (Dedication of the Temple) begins.	*Ab*	9	*Fast of Ab.

* If these dates fall on the sabbath the fast is kept on the following day.

† Ve-Adar in leap years.

§ This fast is observed on Adar 11 (or Ve-Adar 11 in leap years) if Adar 13 falls on a sabbath.

THE MUSLIM CALENDAR

The basic date of the Muslim calendar is the *Hejira*, or flight of Muhammad from Mecca to Medina, the corresponding date of which is AD 622, July 16, in the Julian calendar. Hejira years are used principally in Iran, Turkey, Egypt, in various Arab states, in certain parts of India and in Malaysia. The system was adopted about AD 632, commencing from the first day of the month preceding the Hejira.

The years are purely lunar and consist of twelve months containing in alternate sequence 30 or 29 days, with the intercalation of one day at the end of the twelfth month at stated intervals in each cycle of 30 years. The object of the intercalation is to reconcile the date of the first of the month with the date of the actual new moon. Some adherents still take the date of the evening of the first visibility of the crescent as that of the first of the month. In each cycle of 30 years, 19 are common and contain 354 days, and 11 are intercalary (355 days), the latter being called *kabishah*.

The mean length of the Hejira year is 354 days, 8 hours, 48 minutes, and the period of mean lunation is 29 days, 12 hours, 44 minutes.

To ascertain if a Hejira year is common or *kabishah*, divide it by 30; the quotient gives the number of completed cycles and the remainder shows the place of the year in the current cycle. If the remainder is 2, 5, 7, 10, 13, 16, 18, 21, 24, 26 or 29, the year is *kabishah* and consists of 355 days.

Hejira year AH 1412 (remainder 2) is a *kabishah* year and AH 1413 (remainder 1) is a common year.

Hejira Years 1412 and 1413

Name and length of month	AH 1412		AH 1413	
Muharram (30) 1991	July	13	1992 July	2
Safar (29)	Aug.	12	Aug.	1
Rabía I (30)	Sept.	10	Aug.	30
Rabía II (29)	Oct.	10	Sep.	29
Jumâda I (30)	Nov.	8	Oct.	28
Jumâda II (29)	Dec.	8	Nov.	27
Rajab (30) 1992	Jan.	6	Dec.	26
Shaabán (29)	Feb.	5	1993 Jan.	25
Ramadán (30)	March	5	Feb.	23
Shawwâl (29)	April	4	March	25
Dhû'l-Qa'da (30)	May	3	April	23
Dhû'l-Hijja (29 or 30)	June	2	May	23

OTHER EPOCHS AND CALENDARS

China.—Until the year AD 1911 a lunar calendar was in force in China, but with the establishment of the Republic the government adopted the Gregorian calendar. The new and old systems were used simultaneously until 1930, when the publication and use of the old calendar were banned by the government, and an official Chinese calendar, corresponding with the European or Western system, compiled. The old Chinese calendar, with a cycle of 60 years, is still in use in Tibet, Hong Kong, Singapore, Malaysia and elsewhere in south-east Asia.

Ethiopia.—In the coptic Calendar, which is used by part of the population of Egypt and Ethiopia, the year is made up of 12 months of 30 days each, followed, in general, by five complementary days. Every fourth year is an intercalary or leap year and in these years there are six complementary days. The intercalary year of the Coptic calendar immediately precedes the leap year of the Julian calendar. The era is that of Diocletian or the Martyrs, the origin of which is fixed at AD 284, August 29 (Julian date).

Greece.—Ancient Greek chronology was reckoned in Olympiads, cycles of four years corresponding with the periodic Olympic Games held on the plain of Olympia in Elis once every four years, the intervening years being the first, second, etc., of the Olympiad which received the name of the victor at the Games. The first recorded Olympiad is that of Choroebus, 776 BC.

India.—In addition to the Muslim reckoning there are six eras used in India. The principal astronomical system was the Kaliyuga era, which appears to have been adopted in the fourth century AD. It began on February 18, 3102 BC. The chronological system of northern India, known as the Vikrama Samvat era, prevalent in western India, began on February 23, 57 BC. The year AD 1992 is, therefore, the year 2049 of the Vikrama era.

The Saka era of southern India dating from AD 78, March 3, was declared the uniform national calendar of the Republic of India with effect from March 22, 1957, to be used concurrently with the Gregorian calendar. As revised, the year of the new Saka era begins at the spring equinox, with five successive months of 31 days and seven of 30 days in ordinary years, and six months of each length in leap years. The year AD 1992 is 1914 of the revised Saka era.

The Saptarshi era dates from the moment when the Saptarshi, or saints, were translated and became the stars of the Great Bear in 3076 BC.

The Buddhists reckoned from the death of Buddha in 543 BC (the actual date being 487 BC); and the epoch of the Jains was the death of Vardhamana, the founder of their faith, in 527 BC.

Iran.—The chronology of Iran is the era of Hejira, which began on AD 622, July 16. The Zoroastrian Calendar was used in pre-Muslim days and is still employed by Zoroastrians in Iran and India (Parsees), with an era beginning AD 632, June 16.

Japan.—The Japanese calendar is essentially the same as the Gregorian calendar, the years, months and weeks being of the same length and beginning on the same days as those of the Gregorian calendar. The numeration of the years is different, for Japanese chronology is based on a system of epochs or periods, each of which begins at the accession of an Emperor or other important occurrence. The method is not unlike the former British system of regnal years, but differs from it in that each year of a period closes on December 31. The Japanese chronology begins about AD 650 and the three latest epochs are defined by the reigns of Emperors, whose actual names are not necessarily used:

Epoch Taishō from 1912 Aug. 1 to 1926 Dec. 25

„ Shōwa „ 1926 Dec. 26 to 1989 Jan. 7

„ Heisei „ 1989 Jan. 8

Hence the year Heisei 4 begins on January 1, 1992.

The months are not named. They are known as First Month, Second Month, etc., First Month being the equivalent to January. The days of the week are Nichiyōbi (Sun-day), Getsuyōbi (Moon-day), Kayōbi (Fire-day), Suiyōbi (Water-day), Mokuyōbi (Wood-day), Kinyōbi (Metal-day), Doyōbi (Earth-day).

THE ROMAN CALENDAR

Roman historians adopted as an epoch the foundation of Rome, which is believed to have happened in the year 753 BC. The ordinal number of the years in Roman reckoning is followed by the letters AUC (*ab urbe condita*), so that the year 1992 is 2745 AUC (MMDCCXLV). The calendar that we know has developed from one established by Romulus, who is said to have used a year of 304 days divided into ten months, beginning with March. To this Numa added January and February, making the year consist of 12 months of 30 and 29 days alternately, with an additional day so that the total was 355. It is also said that Numa ordered an intercalary month of 22 or 23 days in alternate years, making 90 days in eight years, to be inserted after February 23. However, there is some doubt as to the origination and the details of the intercalation in the Roman calendar. It is certain that some scheme of this kind was inaugurated and not fully carried out, for in the year 46 BC Julius Caesar, who was then Pontifex Maximus,

found that the calendar had been allowed to fall into some confusion. He therefore sought the help of the Egyptian astronomer Sosigenes, which led to the construction and adoption (45 BC) of the Julian calendar, and, by a slight alteration, to the Gregorian calendar now in use. The year 46 BC was made to consist of 445 days and is called the Year of Confusion.

In the Roman (Julian) calendar the days of the month were counted backwards from three fixed points, or days, and an intervening day was said to be so many days before the next coming point, the first and last being counted. These three points were the Kalends, the Nones, and the Ides. Their positions in the months and the method of counting from them will be seen in the table below. The year containing 366 days was called *bissextillis annus*, as it had a doubled sixth day (*bissextus dies*) before the March Kalends on February 24—*ante diem sextum Kalendas Martias*, or a.d. VI Kal. Mart.

Present days of the month	March, May, July, October have thirty-one days	January, August, December have thirty-one days	April, June, September, November have thirty days	February has twenty-eight days, and in leap year twenty-nine
1	Kalendis.	Kalendis.	Kalendis.	Kalendis.
2	VI ⎱ ante	IV ⎱ ante	IV ⎱ ante	IV ⎱ ante
3	V ⎰	III ⎰ Nonas.	III ⎰ Nonas.	III ⎰ Nonas.
4	IV ⎱ Nonas.	pridie Nonas.	pridie Nonas.	pridie Nonas.
5	III ⎰	Nonis.	Nonis.	Nonis.
6	pridie Nonas.	VIII ⎱	VIII ⎱	VIII ⎱
7	Nonis.	VII ⎮	VII ⎮	VII ⎮
8	VIII ⎱	VI ⎱ ante	VI ⎱ ante.	VI ⎱ ante
9	VII ⎮	V ⎰ Idus.	V ⎰ Idus.	V ⎰ Idus.
10	VI ⎱ ante	IV ⎮	IV ⎮	IV ⎮
11	V ⎰ Idus.	III ⎰	III ⎰	III ⎰
12	IV ⎮	pridie Idus.	pridie Idus.	pridie Idus.
13	III ⎰	Idibus.	Idibus.	Idibus.
14	pridie Idus.	XIX ⎱	XVIII ⎱	XVI ⎱
15	Idibus.	XVIII ⎮	XVII ⎮	XV ⎮
16	XVII ⎱	XVII ⎮	XVI ⎮	XIV ⎮
17	XVI ⎮	XVI ⎮	XV ⎮	XIII ⎮
18	XV ⎮	XV ⎮	XIV ⎮	XII ⎮
19	XIV ⎮ ante Kalendas (of the month following).	XIV ⎮ ante Kalendas (of the month following).	XIII ⎮ ante Kalendas (of the month following).	XI ⎮ ante Kalendas Martias.
20	XIII ⎮	XIII ⎮	XII ⎮	X ⎮
21	XII ⎮	XII ⎮	XI ⎮	IX ⎮
22	XI ⎮	XI ⎮	X ⎮	VIII ⎮
23	X ⎮	X ⎮	IX ⎮	VII ⎮
24	IX ⎮	IX ⎮	VIII ⎮	*VI ⎮
25	VIII ⎮	VIII ⎮	VII ⎮	V ⎮
26	VII ⎮	VII ⎮	VI ⎮	IV ⎮
27	VI ⎮	VI ⎮	V ⎮	III ⎰
28	V ⎮	V ⎮	IV ⎮	pridie Kalendas Martias.
29	IV ⎮	IV ⎮	III ⎰	
30	III ⎰	III ⎰	pridie Kalendas (Maias, Quinctilis, Octobris, Decembris).	
31	pridie Kalendas (Aprilis, Iunias, Sextilis, Novembris).	pridie Kalendas (Februarias, Septembris, Ianuarias).		* (repeated in leap year).

ROMAN NUMERALS

1..........I	9..........IX	17.......XVII	70.......LXX	600........DC
2..........II	10..........X	18.......XVIII	80....LXXX	700....DCC
3..........III	11..........XI	19.........XIX	90..........XC	800....DCCC
4..........IV	12..........XII	20..........XX	100..........C	900....CM
5..........V	13........XIII	30.........XXX	200........CC	1000........M
6.........VI	14........XIV	40..........XL	300......CCC	1500....MD
7........VII	15..........XV	50............L	400........CD	1900....MCM
8....... VIII	16........XVI	60..........LX	500..........D	2000......MM

Examples: 43=XLIII; 66=LXVI; 98=XCVIII
339=CCCXXXIX; 619=DCXIX; 988=CMLXXXVIII; 996=CMXCVI
1674=MDCLXXIV; 1962=MCMLXII; 1992=MCMXCII
A bar placed over a numeral has the effect of multiplying the number by 1,000, e.g.

6,000=V̄I; 16,000=X̄VI; 160,000=C̄LX; 666,000=D̄CLXVI.

CALENDAR FOR ANY YEAR, 1770–2025

To select the correct calendar for any year between 1770 and 2025, consult the index below

* leap year

Year		Year		Year		Year		Year		Year	
1770	C	1813	K	1856	F*	1899	A	1942	I	1985	E
1771	E	1814	M	1857	I	1900	C	1943	K	1986	G
1772	H*	1815	A	1858	K	1901	E	1944	N*	1987	I
1773	K	1816	D*	1859	M	1902	G	1945	C	1988	L*
1774	A	1817	G	1860	B*	1903	I	1946	E	1989	A
1775	A	1818	I	1861	E	1904	L*	1947	G	1990	C
1776	D*	1819	K	1862	G	1905	A	1948	J*	1991	E
1777	G	1820	N*	1863	I	1906	C	1949	M	1992	H*
1778	I	1821	C	1864	L*	1907	E	1950	A	1993	K
1779	K	1822	E	1865	A	1908	H*	1951	C	1994	M
1780	N*	1823	G	1866	C	1909	K	1952	F*	1995	A
1781	C	1824	J*	1867	E	1910	M	1953	I	1996	D*
1782	E	1825	M	1868	H*	1911	A	1954	K	1997	G
1783	G	1826	A	1869	K	1912	D*	1955	M	1998	I
1784	J*	1827	C	1870	M	1913	G	1956	B*	1999	K
1785	M	1828	F*	1871	A	1914	I	1957	E	2000	N*
1786	A	1829	I	1872	D*	1915	K	1958	G	2001	C
1787	C	1830	K	1873	G	1916	N*	1959	I	2002	E
1788	F*	1831	M	1874	I	1917	C	1960	L*	2003	G
1789	I	1832	B*	1875	K	1918	E	1961	A	2004	J*
1790	K	1833	E	1876	N*	1919	G	1962	C	2005	M
1791	M	1834	G	1877	C	1920	J*	1963	E	2006	A
1792	B*	1835	I	1878	E	1921	M	1964	H*	2007	C
1793	E	1836	L*	1879	G	1922	A	1965	K	2008	F*
1794	G	1837	A	1880	J*	1923	C	1966	M	2009	I
1795	I	1838	C	1881	M	1924	F*	1967	A	2010	K
1796	L*	1839	E	1882	A	1925	I	1968	D*	2011	M
1797	A	1840	H*	1883	C	1926	K	1969	G	2012	B*
1798	C	1841	K	1884	F*	1927	M	1970	I	2013	E
1799	E	1842	M	1885	I	1928	B*	1971	K	2014	G
1800	G	1843	A	1886	K	1929	E	1972	N*	2015	I
1801	I	1844	D*	1887	M	1930	G	1973	C	2016	L*
1802	K	1845	G	1888	B*	1931	I	1974	E	2017	A
1803	M	1846	I	1889	E	1932	L*	1975	G	2018	C
1804	B*	1847	K	1890	G	1933	A	1976	J*	2019	E
1805	E	1848	N*	1891	I	1934	C	1977	M	2020	H*
1806	G	1849	C	1892	L*	1935	E	1978	A	2021	K
1807	I	1850	E	1893	A	1936	H*	1979	C	2022	M
1808	L*	1851	G	1894	C	1937	K	1980	F*	2023	A
1809	A	1852	J*	1895	E	1938	M	1981	I	2024	D*
1810	C	1853	M	1896	H*	1939	A	1982	K	2025	G
1811	E	1854	A	1897	K	1940	D*	1983	M		
1812	H*	1855	C	1898	M	1941	G	1984	B*		

A

	January	February	March
Su.	1 8 15 22 29	5 12 19 26	5 12 19 26
M.	2 9 16 23 30	6 13 20 27	6 13 20 27
Tu.	3 10 17 24 31	7 14 21 28	7 14 21 28
W.	4 11 18 25	1 8 15 22	1 8 15 22 29
Th.	5 12 19 26	2 9 16 23	2 9 16 23 30
F.	6 13 20 27	3 10 17 24	3 10 17 24 31
S.	7 14 21 28	4 11 18 25	4 11 18 25

	April	May	June
Su.	2 9 16 23 30	7 14 21 28	4 11 18 25
M.	3 10 17 24	1 8 15 22 29	5 12 19 26
Tu.	4 11 18 25	2 9 16 23 30	6 13 20 27
W.	5 12 19 26	3 10 17 24 31	7 14 21 28
Th.	6 13 20 27	4 11 18 25	1 8 15 22 29
F.	7 14 21 28	5 12 19 26	2 9 16 23 30
S.	1 8 15 22 29	6 13 20 27	3 10 17 24

	July	August	September
Su.	2 9 16 23 30	6 13 20 27	3 10 17 24
M.	3 10 17 24 31	7 14 21 28	4 11 18 25
Tu.	4 11 18 25	1 8 15 22 29	5 12 19 26
W.	5 12 19 26	2 9 16 23 30	6 13 20 27
Th.	6 13 20 27	3 10 17 24 31	7 14 21 28
F.	7 14 21 28	4 11 18 25	1 8 15 22 29
S.	1 8 15 22 29	5 12 19 26	2 9 16 23 30

	October	November	December
Su.	1 8 15 22 29	5 12 19 26	3 10 17 24 31
M.	2 9 16 23 30	6 13 20 27	4 11 18 25
Tu.	3 10 17 24 31	7 14 21 28	5 12 19 26
W.	4 11 18 25	1 8 15 22 29	6 13 20 27
Th.	5 12 19 26	2 9 16 23 30	7 14 21 28
F.	6 13 20 27	3 10 17 24	1 8 15 22 29
S.	7 14 21 28	4 11 18 25	2 9 16 23 30

Easter Days

March 26	1815 1826 1837 1967 1978 1989
April 2	1809 1893 1899 1961
April 9	1871 1882 1939 1950 2023
April 16	1775 1786 1797 1843 1854 1865 1911
	1922 1933 1995 2006 2017
April 23	1905

B (leap year)

	January	February	March
Su.	1 8 15 22 29	5 12 19 26	4 11 18 25
M.	2 9 16 23 30	6 13 20 27	5 12 19 26
Tu.	3 10 17 24 31	7 14 21 28	6 13 20 27
W.	4 11 18 25	1 8 15 22 29	7 14 21 28
Th.	5 12 19 26	2 9 16 23	1 8 15 22 29
F.	6 13 20 27	3 10 17 24	2 9 16 23 30
S.	7 14 21 28	4 11 18 25	3 10 17 24 31

	April	May	June
Su.	1 8 15 22 29	6 13 20 27	3 10 17 24
M.	2 9 16 23 30	7 14 21 28	4 11 18 25
Tu.	3 10 17 24	1 8 15 22 29	5 12 19 26
W.	4 11 18 25	2 9 16 23 30	6 13 20 27
Th.	5 12 19 26	3 10 17 24 31	7 14 21 28
F.	6 13 20 27	4 11 18 25	1 8 15 22 29
S.	7 14 21 28	5 12 19 26	2 9 16 23 30

	July	August	September
Su.	1 8 15 22 29	5 12 19 26	2 9 16 23 30
M.	2 9 16 23 30	6 13 20 27	3 10 17 24
Tu.	3 10 17 24 31	7 14 21 28	4 11 18 25
W.	4 11 18 25	1 8 15 22 29	5 12 19 26
Th.	5 12 19 26	2 9 16 23 30	6 13 20 27
F.	6 13 20 27	3 10 17 24 31	7 14 21 28
S.	7 14 21 28	4 11 18 25	1 8 15 22 29

	October	November	December
Su.	7 14 21 28	4 11 18 25	2 9 16 23 30
M.	1 8 15 22 29	5 12 19 26	3 10 17 24 31
Tu.	2 9 16 23 30	6 13 20 27	4 11 18 25
W.	3 10 17 24 31	7 14 21 28	5 12 19 26
Th.	4 11 18 25	1 8 15 22 29	6 13 20 27
F.	5 12 19 26	2 9 16 23 30	7 14 21 28
S.	6 13 20 27	3 10 17 24 31	1 8 15 22 29

Easter Days

April 1	1804 1888 1956
April 8	1792 1860 1928 2012
April 22	1832 1984

C

	January	February	March
Su.	7 14 21 28	4 11 18 25	4 11 18 25
M.	1 8 15 22 29	5 12 19 26	5 12 19 26
Tu.	2 9 16 23 30	6 13 20 27	6 13 20 27
W.	3 10 17 24 31	7 14 21 28	7 14 21 28
Th.	4 11 18 25	1 8 15 22	1 8 15 22 29
F.	5 12 19 26	2 9 16 23	2 9 16 23 30
S.	6 13 20 27	3 10 17 24	3 10 17 24 31

	April	May	June
Su.	1 8 15 22 29	6 13 20 27	3 10 17 24
M.	2 9 16 23 30	7 14 21 28	4 11 18 25
Tu.	3 10 17 24	1 8 15 22 29	5 12 19 26
W.	4 11 18 25	2 9 16 23 30	6 13 20 27
Th.	5 12 19 26	3 10 17 24 31	7 14 21 28
F.	6 13 20 27	4 11 18 25	1 8 15 22 29
S.	7 14 21 28	5 12 19 26	2 9 16 23 30

	July	August	September
Su.	1 8 15 22 29	5 12 19 26	2 9 16 23 30
M.	2 9 16 23 30	6 13 20 27	3 10 17 24
Tu.	3 10 17 24 31	7 14 21 28	4 11 18 25
W.	4 11 18 25	1 8 15 22 29	5 12 19 26
Th.	5 12 19 26	2 9 16 23 30	6 13 20 27
F.	6 13 20 27	3 10 17 24 31	7 14 21 28
S.	7 14 21 28	4 11 18 25	1 8 15 22 29

	October	November	December
Su.	7 14 21 28	4 11 18 25	2 9 16 23 30
M.	1 8 15 22 29	5 12 19 26	3 10 17 24 31
Tu.	2 9 16 23 30	6 13 20 27	4 11 18 25
W.	3 10 17 24 31	7 14 21 28	5 12 19 26
Th.	4 11 18 25	1 8 15 22 29	6 13 20 27
F.	5 12 19 26	2 9 16 23 30	7 14 21 28
S.	6 13 20 27	3 10 17 24	1 8 15 22 29

Easter Days

March 25	1883 1894 1951
April 1	1866 1877 1923 1934 1945 2018
April 8	1787 1798 1849 1855 1917 2007
April 15	1770 1781 1827 1838 1900 1906 1979 1990 2001
April 22	1810 1821 1962 1973

E

	January	February	March
Su.	6 13 20 27	3 10 17 24	3 10 17 24 31
M.	7 14 21 28	4 11 18 25	4 11 18 25
Tu.	1 8 15 22 29	5 12 19 26	5 12 19 26
W.	2 9 16 23 30	6 13 20 27	6 13 20 27
Th.	3 10 17 24 31	7 14 21 28	7 14 21 28
F.	4 11 18 25	1 8 15 22	1 8 15 22 29
S.	5 12 19 26	2 9 16 23	2 9 16 23 30

	April	May	June
Su.	7 14 21 28	5 12 19 26	2 9 16 23 30
M.	1 8 15 22 29	6 13 20 27	3 10 17 24
Tu.	2 9 16 23 30	7 14 21 28	4 11 18 25
W.	3 10 17 24	1 8 15 22 29	5 12 19 26
Th.	4 11 18 25	2 9 16 23 30	6 13 20 27
F.	5 12 19 26	3 10 17 24 31	7 14 21 28
S.	6 13 20 27	4 11 18 25	1 8 15 22 29

	July	August	September
Su.	7 14 21 28	4 11 18 25	1 8 15 22 29
M.	1 8 15 22 29	5 12 19 26	2 9 16 23 30
Tu.	2 9 16 23 30	6 13 20 27	3 10 17 24
W.	3 10 17 24 31	7 14 21 28	4 11 18 25
Th.	4 11 18 25	1 8 15 22 29	5 12 19 26
F.	5 12 19 26	2 9 16 23 30	6 13 20 27
S.	6 13 20 27	3 10 17 24 31	7 14 21 28

	October	November	December
Su.	6 13 20 27	3 10 17 24	1 8 15 22 29
M.	7 14 21 28	4 11 18 25	2 9 16 23 30
Tu.	1 8 15 22 29	5 12 19 26	3 10 17 24 31
W.	2 9 16 23 30	6 13 20 27	4 11 18 25
Th.	3 10 17 24 31	7 14 21 28	5 12 19 26
F.	4 11 18 25	1 8 15 22 29	6 13 20 27
S.	5 12 19 26	2 9 16 23 30	7 14 21 28

Easter Days

March 24	1799
March 31	1771 1782 1793 1839 1850 1861 1907
	1918 1929 1991 2002 2013
April 7	1822 1833 1901 1985
April 14	1805 1811 1895 1963 1974
April 21	1867 1878 1889 1935 1946 1957 2019

D (leap year)

	January	February	March
Su.	7 14 21 28	4 11 18 25	3 10 17 24 31
M.	1 8 15 22 29	5 12 19 26	4 11 18 25
Tu.	2 9 16 23 30	6 13 20 27	5 12 19 26
W.	3 10 17 24 31	7 14 21 28	6 13 20 27
Th.	4 11 18 25	1 8 15 22 29	7 14 21 28
F.	5 12 19 26	2 9 16 23	1 8 15 22 29
S.	6 13 20 27	3 10 17 24	2 9 16 23 30

	April	May	June
Su.	7 14 21 28	5 12 19 26	2 9 16 23 30
M.	1 8 15 22 29	6 13 20 27	3 10 17 24
Tu.	2 9 16 23 30	7 14 21 28	4 11 18 25
W.	3 10 17 24	1 8 15 22 29	5 12 19 26
Th.	4 11 18 25	2 9 16 23 30	6 13 20 27
F.	5 12 19 26	3 10 17 24 31	7 14 21 28
S.	6 13 20 27	4 11 18 25	1 8 15 22 29

	July	August	September
Su.	7 14 21 28	4 11 18 25	1 8 15 22 29
M.	1 8 15 22 29	5 12 19 26	2 9 16 23 30
Tu.	2 9 16 23 30	6 13 20 27	3 10 17 24
W.	3 10 17 24 31	7 14 21 28	4 11 18 25
Th.	4 11 18 25	1 8 15 22 29	5 12 19 26
F.	5 12 19 26	2 9 16 23 30	6 13 20 27
S.	6 13 20 27	3 10 17 24 31	7 14 21 28

	October	November	December
Su.	6 13 20 27	3 10 17 24	1 8 15 22 29
M.	7 14 21 28	4 11 18 25	2 9 16 23 30
Tu.	1 8 15 22 29	5 12 19 26	3 10 17 24 31
W.	2 9 16 23 30	6 13 20 27	4 11 18 25
Th.	3 10 17 24 31	7 14 21 28	5 12 19 26
F.	4 11 18 25	1 8 15 22 29	6 13 20 27
S.	5 12 19 26	2 9 16 23 30	7 14 21 28

Easter Days

March 24	1940
March 31	1872 2024
April 7	1776 1844 1912 1996
April 14	1816 1968

F (leap year)

	January	February	March
Su.	6 13 20 27	3 10 17 24	2 9 16 23 30
M.	7 14 21 28	4 11 18 25	3 10 17 24 31
Tu.	1 8 15 22 29	5 12 19 26	4 11 18 25
W.	2 9 16 23 30	6 13 20 27	5 12 19 26
Th.	3 10 17 24 31	7 14 21 28	6 13 20 27
F.	4 11 18 25	1 8 15 22 29	7 14 21 28
S.	5 12 19 26	2 9 16 23	1 8 15 22 29

	April	May	June
Su.	6 13 20 27	4 11 18 25	1 8 15 22 29
M.	7 14 21 28	5 12 19 26	2 9 16 23 30
Tu.	1 8 15 22 29	6 13 20 27	3 10 17 24
W.	2 9 16 23 30	7 14 21 28	4 11 18 25
Th.	3 10 17 24	1 8 15 22 29	5 12 19 26
F.	4 11 18 25	2 9 16 23 30	6 13 20 27
S.	5 12 19 26	3 10 17 24 31	7 14 21 28

	July	August	September
Su.	6 13 20 27	3 10 17 24 31	7 14 21 28
M.	7 14 21 28	4 11 18 25	1 8 15 22 29
Tu.	1 8 15 22 29	5 12 19 26	2 9 16 23 30
W.	2 9 16 23 30	6 13 20 27	3 10 17 24
Th.	3 10 17 24 31	7 14 21 28	4 11 18 25
F.	4 11 18 25	1 8 15 22 29	5 12 19 26
S.	5 12 19 26	2 9 16 23 30	6 13 20 27

	October	November	December
Su.	5 12 19 26	2 9 16 23 30	7 14 21 28
M.	6 13 20 27	3 10 17 24	1 8 15 22 29
Tu.	7 14 21 28	4 11 18 25	2 9 16 23 30
W.	1 8 15 22 29	5 12 19 26	3 10 17 24 31
Th.	2 9 16 23 30	6 13 20 27	4 11 18 25
F.	3 10 17 24 31	7 14 21 28	5 12 19 26
S.	4 11 18 25	1 8 15 22 29	6 13 20 27

Easter Days

March 23	1788 1856 2008
April 6	1828 1980
April 13	1884 1952
April 20	1924

G

January — February — March

	January	February	March
Su.	5 12 19 26	2 9 16 23	2 9 16 23 30
M.	6 13 20 27	3 10 17 24	3 10 17 24 31
Tu.	7 14 21 28	4 11 18 25	4 11 18 25
W.	1 8 15 22 29	5 12 19 26	5 12 19 26
Th.	2 9 16 23 30	6 13 20 27	6 13 20 27
F.	3 10 17 24 31	7 14 21 28	7 14 21 28
S.	4 11 18 25	1 8 15 22	1 8 15 22 29

April — May — June

	April	May	June
Su.	6 13 20 27	4 11 18 25	1 8 15 22 29
M.	7 14 21 28	5 12 19 26	2 9 16 23 30
Tu.	1 8 15 22 29	6 13 20 27	3 10 17 24
W.	2 9 16 23 30	7 14 21 28	4 11 18 25
Th.	3 10 17 24	1 8 15 22 29	5 12 19 26
F.	4 11 18 25	2 9 16 23 30	6 13 20 27
S.	5 12 19 26	3 10 17 24 31	7 14 21 28

July — August — September

	July	August	September
Su.	6 13 20 27	3 10 17 24 31	7 14 21 28
M.	7 14 21 28	4 11 18 25	1 8 15 22 29
Tu.	1 8 15 22 29	5 12 19 26	2 9 16 23 30
W.	2 9 16 23 30	6 13 20 27	3 10 17 24
Th.	3 10 17 24 31	7 14 21 28	4 11 18 25
F.	4 11 18 25	1 8 15 22 29	5 12 19 26
S.	5 12 19 26	2 9 16 23 30	6 13 20 27

October — November — December

	October	November	December
Su.	5 12 19 26	2 9 16 23 30	7 14 21 28
M.	6 13 20 27	3 10 17 24	1 8 15 22 29
Tu.	7 14 21 28	4 11 18 25	2 9 16 23 30
W.	1 8 15 22 29	5 12 19 26	3 10 17 24 31
Th.	2 9 16 23 30	6 13 20 27	4 11 18 25
F.	3 10 17 24 31	7 14 21 28	5 12 19 26
S.	4 11 18 25	1 8 15 22 29	6 13 20 27

Easter Days

March 23	1845	1913				
March 30	1777	1823	1834	1902	1975	1986 1997
April 6	1806	1817	1890	1947	1958	1969
April 13	1800	1873	1879	1941		
April 20	1783	1794	1851	1862	1919	1930 2003
	2014	2025				

I

January — February — March

	January	February	March
Su.	4 11 18 25	1 8 15 22	1 8 15 22 29
M.	5 12 19 26	2 9 16 23	2 9 16 23 30
Tu.	6 13 20 27	3 10 17 24	3 10 17 24 31
W.	7 14 21 28	4 11 18 25	4 11 18 25
Th.	1 8 15 22 29	5 12 19 26	5 12 19 26
F.	2 9 16 23 30	6 13 20 27	6 13 20 27
S.	3 10 17 24 31	7 14 21 28	7 14 21 28

April — May — June

	April	May	June
Su.	5 12 19 26	3 10 17 24 31	7 14 21 28
M.	6 13 20 27	4 11 18 25	1 8 15 22 29
Tu.	7 14 21 28	5 12 19 26	2 9 16 23 30
W.	1 8 15 22 29	6 13 20 27	3 10 17 24
Th.	2 9 16 23 30	7 14 21 28	4 11 18 25
F.	3 10 17 24	1 8 15 22 29	5 12 19 26
S.	4 11 18 25	2 9 16 23 30	6 13 20 27

July — August — September

	July	August	September
Su.	5 12 19 26	2 9 16 23 30	6 13 20 27
M.	6 13 20 27	3 10 17 24 31	7 14 21 28
Tu.	7 14 21 28	4 11 18 25	1 8 15 22 29
W.	1 8 15 22 29	5 12 19 26	2 9 16 23 30
Th.	2 9 16 23 30	6 13 20 27	3 10 17 24
F.	3 10 17 24 31	7 14 21 28	4 11 18 25
S.	4 11 18 25	1 8 15 22 29	5 12 19 26

October — November — December

	October	November	December
Su.	4 11 18 25	1 8 15 22 29	6 13 20 27
M.	5 12 19 26	2 9 16 23 30	7 14 21 28
Tu.	6 13 20 27	3 10 17 24	1 8 15 22 29
W.	7 14 21 28	4 11 18 25	2 9 16 23 30
Th.	1 8 15 22 29	5 12 19 26	3 10 17 24 31
F.	2 9 16 23 30	6 13 20 27	4 11 18 25
S.	3 10 17 24 31	7 14 21 28	5 12 19 26

Easter Days

March 22	1818					
March 29	1807	1891	1959	1970		
April 5	1795	1801	1863	1874	1885	1931 1942
	1953	2015				
April 12	1789	1846	1857	1903	1914	1925 1998
	2009					
April 19	1778	1829	1835	1981	1987	

H (leap year)

January — February — March

	January	February	March
Su.	5 12 19 26	2 9 16 23	1 8 15 22 29
M.	6 13 20 27	3 10 17 24	2 9 16 23 30
Tu.	7 14 21 28	4 11 18 25	3 10 17 24 31
W.	1 8 15 22 29	5 12 19 26	4 11 18 25
Th.	2 9 16 23 30	6 13 20 27	5 12 19 26
F.	3 10 17 24 31	7 14 21 28	6 13 20 27
S.	4 11 18 25	1 8 15 22 29	7 14 21 28

April — May — June

	April	May	June
Su.	5 12 19 26	3 10 17 24 31	7 14 21 28
M.	6 13 20 27	4 11 18 25	1 8 15 22 29
Tu.	7 14 21 28	5 12 19 26	2 9 16 23 30
W.	1 8 15 22 29	6 13 20 27	3 10 17 24
Th.	2 9 16 23 30	7 14 21 28	4 11 18 25
F.	3 10 17 24	1 8 15 22 29	5 12 19 26
S.	4 11 18 25	2 9 16 23 30	6 13 20 27

July — August — September

	July	August	September
Su.	5 12 19 26	2 9 16 23 30	6 13 20 27
M.	6 13 20 27	3 10 17 24 31	7 14 21 28
Tu.	7 14 21 28	4 11 18 25	1 8 15 22 29
W.	1 8 15 22 29	5 12 19 26	2 9 16 23 30
Th.	2 9 16 23 30	6 13 20 27	3 10 17 24
F.	3 10 17 24 31	7 14 21 28	4 11 18 25
S.	4 11 18 25	1 8 15 22 29	5 12 19 26

October — November — December

	October	November	December
Su.	4 11 18 25	1 8 15 22 29	6 13 20 27
M.	5 12 19 26	2 9 16 23 30	7 14 21 28
Tu.	6 13 20 27	3 10 17 24	1 8 15 22 29
W.	7 14 21 28	4 11 18 25	2 9 16 23 30
Th.	1 8 15 22 29	5 12 19 26	3 10 17 24 31
F.	2 9 16 23 30	6 13 20 27	4 11 18 25
S.	3 10 17 24 31	7 14 21 28	5 12 19 26

Easter Days

March 29	1812	1964	
April 5	1896		
April 12	1868	1936	2020
April 19	1772	1840	1908 1992

J (leap year)

January — February — March

	January	February	March
Su.	4 11 18 25	1 8 15 22 29	7 14 21 28
M.	5 12 19 26	2 9 16 23	1 8 15 22 29
Tu.	6 13 20 27	3 10 17 24	2 9 16 23 30
W.	7 14 21 28	4 11 18 25	3 10 17 24 31
Th.	1 8 15 22 29	5 12 19 26	4 11 18 25
F.	2 9 16 23 30	6 13 20 27	5 12 19 26
S.	3 10 17 24 31	7 14 21 28	6 13 20 27

April — May — June

	April	May	June
Su.	4 11 18 25	2 9 16 23 30	6 13 20 27
M.	5 12 19 26	3 10 17 24 31	7 14 21 28
Tu.	6 13 20 27	4 11 18 25	1 8 15 22 29
W.	7 14 21 28	5 12 19 26	2 9 16 23 30
Th.	1 8 15 22 29	6 13 20 27	3 10 17 24
F.	2 9 16 23 30	7 14 21 28	4 11 18 25
S.	3 10 17 24	1 8 15 22 29	5 12 19 26

July — August — September

	July	August	September
Su.	4 11 18 25	1 8 15 22 29	5 12 19 26
M.	5 12 19 26	2 9 16 23 30	6 13 20 27
Tu.	6 13 20 27	3 10 17 24 31	7 14 21 28
W.	7 14 21 28	4 11 18 25	1 8 15 22 29
Th.	1 8 15 22 29	5 12 19 26	2 9 16 23 30
F.	2 9 16 23 30	6 13 20 27	3 10 17 24
S.	3 10 17 24 31	7 14 21 28	4 11 18 25

October — November — December

	October	November	December
Su.	3 10 17 24 31	7 14 21 28	5 12 19 26
M.	4 11 18 25	1 8 15 22 29	6 13 20 27
Tu.	5 12 19 26	2 9 16 23 30	7 14 21 28
W.	6 13 20 27	3 10 17 24	1 8 15 22 29
Th.	7 14 21 28	4 11 18 25	2 9 16 23 30
F.	1 8 15 22 29	5 12 19 26	3 10 17 24 31
S.	2 9 16 23 30	6 13 20 27	4 11 18 25

Easter Days

March 28	1880	1948	
April 4	1920		
April 11	1784	1852	2004
April 18	1824	1976	

K

	January	February	March
Su.	.. 3 10 17 24 31	7 14 21 28	7 14 21 28
M.	.. 4 11 18 25	1 8 15 22	1 8 15 22 29
Tu.	.. 5 12 19 26	2 9 16 23	2 9 16 23 30
W.	.. 6 13 20 27	3 10 17 24	3 10 17 24 31
Th.	.. 7 14 21 28	4 11 18 25	4 11 18 25
F.	1 8 15 22 29	5 12 19 26	5 12 19 26
S.	2 9 16 23 30	6 13 20 27	6 13 20 27

	April	May	June
Su.	.. 4 11 18 25	2 9 16 23 30	6 13 20 27
M.	.. 5 12 19 26	3 10 17 24 31	7 14 21 28
Tu.	.. 6 13 20 27	4 11 18 25	1 8 15 22 29
W.	.. 7 14 21 28	5 12 19 26	2 9 16 23 30
Th.	.. 1 8 15 22 29	6 13 20 27	3 10 17 24
F.	.. 2 9 16 23 30	7 14 21 28	4 11 18 25
S.	.. 3 10 17 24	1 8 15 22 29	5 12 19 26

	July	August	September
Su.	.. 4 11 18 25	1 8 15 22 29	5 12 19 26
M.	.. 5 12 19 26	2 9 16 23 30	6 13 20 27
Tu.	.. 6 13 20 27	3 10 17 24 31	7 14 21 28
W.	.. 7 14 21 28	4 11 18 25	1 8 15 22 29
Th.	.. 1 8 15 22 29	5 12 19 26	2 9 16 23 30
F.	.. 2 9 16 23 30	6 13 20 27	3 10 17 24
S.	.. 3 10 17 24 31	7 14 21 28	4 11 18 25

	October	November	December
Su.	.. 3 10 17 24 31	7 14 21 28	5 12 19 26
M.	.. 4 11 18 25	1 8 15 22 29	6 13 20 27
Tu.	.. 5 12 19 26	2 9 16 23 30	7 14 21 28
W.	.. 6 13 20 27	3 10 17 24	1 8 15 22 29
Th.	.. 7 14 21 28	4 11 18 25	2 9 16 23 30
F.	1 8 15 22 29	5 12 19 26	3 10 17 24 31
S.	2 9 16 23 30	6 13 20 27	4 11 18 25

Easter Days

March 28	1869	1875	1937			
April 4	1779	1790	1847	1858	1915	1926	1999
	2010	2021				
April 11	1773	1819	1830	1841	1909	1971	1982
	1993					
April 18	1802	1813	1897	1954	1965	
April 25	1886	1943				

M

	January	February	March
Su.	.. 2 9 16 23 30	6 13 20 27	6 13 20 27
M.	.. 3 10 17 24 31	7 14 21 28	7 14 21 28
Tu.	.. 4 11 18 25	1 8 15 22	1 8 15 22 29
W.	.. 5 12 19 26	2 9 16 23	2 9 16 23 30
Th.	.. 6 13 20 27	3 10 17 24	3 10 17 24 31
F.	.. 7 14 21 28	4 11 18 25	4 11 18 25
S.	1 8 15 22 29	5 12 19 26	5 12 19 26

	April	May	June
Su.	.. 3 10 17 24	1 8 15 22 29	5 12 19 26
M.	.. 4 11 18 25	2 9 16 23 30	6 13 20 27
Tu.	.. 5 12 19 26	3 10 17 24 31	7 14 21 28
W.	.. 6 13 20 27	4 11 18 25	1 8 15 22 29
Th.	.. 7 14 21 28	5 12 19 26	2 9 16 23 30
F.	.. 1 8 15 22 29	6 13 20 27	3 10 17 24
S.	.. 2 9 16 23 30	7 14 21 28	4 11 18 25

	July	August	September
Su.	.. 3 10 17 24 31	7 14 21 28	4 11 18 25
M.	.. 4 11 18 25	1 8 15 22 29	5 12 19 26
Tu.	.. 5 12 19 26	2 9 16 23 30	6 13 20 27
W.	.. 6 13 20 27	3 10 17 24 31	7 14 21 28
Th.	.. 7 14 21 28	4 11 18 25	1 8 15 22 29
F.	1 8 15 22 29	5 12 19 26	2 9 16 23 30
S.	2 9 16 23 30	6 13 20 27	3 10 17 24

	October	November	December
Su.	.. 2 9 16 23 30	6 13 20 27	4 11 18 25
M.	.. 3 10 17 24 31	7 14 21 28	5 12 19 26
Tu.	.. 4 11 18 25	1 8 15 22 29	6 13 20 27
W.	.. 5 12 19 26	2 9 16 23 30	7 14 21 28
Th.	.. 6 13 20 27	3 10 17 24	1 8 15 22 29
F.	.. 7 14 21 28	4 11 18 25	2 9 16 23 30
S.	1 8 15 22 29	5 12 19 26	3 10 17 24 31

Easter Days

March 27	1785	1842	1853	1910	1921	2005
April 3	1774	1825	1831	1983	1994	
April 10	1803	1814	1887	1898	1955	1966	1977
April 17	1870	1881	1927	1938	1949	2022
April 24	1791	1859	2011			

L (leap year)

	January	February	March
Su.	.. 3 10 17 24 31	7 14 21 28	6 13 20 27
M.	.. 4 11 18 25	1 8 15 22 29	7 14 21 28
Tu.	.. 5 12 19 26	2 9 16 23	1 8 15 22 29
W.	.. 6 13 20 27	3 10 17 24	2 9 16 23 30
Th.	.. 7 14 21 28	4 11 18 25	3 10 17 24 31
F.	1 8 15 22 29	5 12 19 26	4 11 18 25
S.	2 9 16 23 30	6 13 20 27	5 12 19 26

	April	May	June
Su.	.. 3 10 17 24	1 8 15 22 29	5 12 19 26
M.	.. 4 11 18 25	2 9 16 23 30	6 13 20 27
Tu.	.. 5 12 19 26	3 10 17 24 31	7 14 21 28
W.	.. 6 13 20 27	4 11 18 25	1 8 15 22 29
Th.	.. 7 14 21 28	5 12 19 26	2 9 16 23 30
F.	1 8 15 22 29	6 13 20 27	3 10 17 24
S.	2 9 16 23 30	7 14 21 28	4 11 18 25

	July	August	September
Su.	.. 3 10 17 24 31	7 14 21 28	4 11 18 25
M.	.. 4 11 18 25	1 8 15 22 29	5 12 19 26
Tu.	.. 5 12 19 26	2 9 16 23 30	6 13 20 27
W.	.. 6 13 20 27	3 10 17 24 31	7 14 21 28
Th.	.. 7 14 21 28	4 11 18 25	1 8 15 22 29
F.	1 8 15 22 29	5 12 19 26	2 9 16 23 30
S.	2 9 16 23 30	6 13 20 27	3 10 17 24

	October	November	December
Su.	.. 2 9 16 23 30	6 13 20 27	4 11 18 25
M.	.. 3 10 17 24 31	7 14 21 28	5 12 19 26
Tu.	.. 4 11 18 25	1 8 15 22 29	6 13 20 27
W.	.. 5 12 19 26	2 9 16 23 30	7 14 21 28
Th.	.. 6 13 20 27	3 10 17 24	1 8 15 22 29
F.	.. 7 14 21 28	4 11 18 25	2 9 16 23 30
S.	1 8 15 22 29	5 12 19 26	3 10 17 24 31

Easter Days

March 27	1796	1864	1932	2016
April 3	1836	1904	1988	
April 17	1808	1892	1960	

N (leap year)

	January	February	March
Su.	.. 2 9 16 23 30	6 13 20 27	5 12 19 26
M.	.. 3 10 17 24 31	7 14 21 28	6 13 20 27
Tu.	.. 4 11 18 25	1 8 15 22 29	7 14 21 28
W.	.. 5 12 19 26	2 9 16 23	1 8 15 22 29
Th.	.. 6 13 20 27	3 10 17 24	2 9 16 23 30
F.	.. 7 14 21 28	4 11 18 25	3 10 17 24 31
S.	1 8 15 22 29	5 12 19 26	4 11 18 25

	April	May	June
Su.	.. 2 9 16 23 30	7 14 21 28	4 11 18 25
M.	.. 3 10 17 24	1 8 15 22 29	5 12 19 26
Tu.	.. 4 11 18 25	2 9 16 23 30	6 13 20 27
W.	.. 5 12 19 26	3 10 17 24 31	7 14 21 28
Th.	.. 6 13 20 27	4 11 18 25	1 8 15 22 29
F.	.. 7 14 21 28	5 12 19 26	2 9 16 23 30
S.	1 8 15 22 29	6 13 20 27	3 10 17 24

	July	August	September
Su.	.. 2 9 16 23 30	6 13 20 27	3 10 17 24
M.	.. 3 10 17 24 31	7 14 21 28	4 11 18 25
Tu.	.. 4 11 18 25	1 8 15 22 29	5 12 19 26
W.	.. 5 12 19 26	2 9 16 23 30	6 13 20 27
Th.	.. 6 13 20 27	3 10 17 24 31	7 14 21 28
F.	.. 7 14 21 28	4 11 18 25	1 8 15 22 29
S.	1 8 15 22 29	5 12 19 26	2 9 16 23 30

	October	November	December
Su.	1 8 15 22 29	5 12 19 26	3 10 17 24 31
M.	2 9 16 23 30	6 13 20 27	4 11 18 25
Tu.	3 10 17 24 31	7 14 21 28	5 12 19 26
W.	4 11 18 25	1 8 15 22 29	6 13 20 27
Th.	5 12 19 26	2 9 16 23 30	7 14 21 28
F.	6 13 20 27	3 10 17 24	1 8 15 22 29
S.	7 14 21 28	4 11 18 25	2 9 16 23 30

Easter Days

March 26	1780		
April 2	1820	1972	
April 9	1944		
April 16	1876		
April 23	1848	1916	2000

Geological and Human Development

GEOLOGICAL TIME

The earth is thought to have come into existence approximately 4,600 million years ago, but for nearly half this time, the **Archean** era, it was uninhabited. Life is generally believed to have emerged in the succeeding **Proterozoic** era. The Archean and the Proterozoic eras are often together referred to as the **Precambrian**.

Although primitive forms of life, e.g. algae and bacteria, existed during the Proterozoic era, it is not until the strata of Palaeozoic rocks is reached that abundant fossilized remains appear, initially of small shellfish, followed by plants, primitive fishes and, in the Devonian period (c.400 million BC), land-living plants and amphibia.

Since the Precambrian, there have been three great geological eras:

Palaeozoic ('ancient life')
*c.*570–*c.*250 million BC

Cambrian.—Mainly sandstones, slate and shales; limestones in Scotland. Shelled fossils and invertebrates, e.g. trilobites and brachiopods appear.
Ordovician.—Mainly shales and mudstones, e.g. in north Wales; limestones in Scotland.
Silurian.—Shales, mudstones and some limestones, found mostly in Wales and southern Scotland.
Devonian.—Old red sandstone, shale, limestone and slate, e.g. in south Wales and the West Country. 'The age of fishes'—proliferation of fish fossils. First traces of land-living life.
Carboniferous.—Coal-bearing rocks, millstone grit, limestone and shale.
Permian.—Marls, sandstones and clays, named after the area of Russia where these strata are widespread. First large-scale appearance of reptile fossils.

There were two great phases of mountain building in the Palaeozoic era: the *Caledonian*, characterized in Britain by NE–SW lines of hills and valleys; and the later *Hercyian*, widespread in west Germany and adjacent areas, and in Britain exemplified in E.–W. lines of hills and valleys.

The end of the Palaeozoic era was marked by the extensive glaciations of the Permian period in the southern continents and the decline of amphibians. It was succeeded by an era of warm conditions.

Mesozoic ('middle forms of life')
*c.*250–*c.*65 million BC

Triassic.—Mostly sandstone, e.g. in the West Midlands.
Jurassic.—Mainly limestones and clays, typically displayed in the Jura mountains, and in England in a NE–SW belt from Lincolnshire and the Wash to the Severn and the Dorset coast.
Cretaceous.—Mainly chalk, clay and sands, e.g. in Kent and Sussex.

Giant reptiles were dominant during the Mesozoic era, but it was at this time that marsupial mammals first appeared, as well as *Archaeopteryx lithographica*, the earliest known species of bird. Coniferous trees and flowering plants also developed during the era and, with the birds and the mammals, were the main species to survive into the Caenozoic (or Cenozoic) era. The giant reptiles became extinct.

Caenozoic ('recent life')
from *c.*65 million BC

Eocene.—The emergence of new forms of life, i.e. existing species.
Oligocene.—Fossils of a few still existing species.
Miocene.—Fossil remains show a balance of existing and extinct species.

Pliocene.—Fossil remains show a majority of still existing species.
Pleistocene.—The majority of remains are those of still existing species.
Holocene.—The present, post-glacial period. Existing species only, except for a few exterminated by man.

In the last 25 million years, from the Miocene through the Pliocene periods, the Alpine-Himalayan and the circum-Pacific phases of mountain building reached their climax. During the Pleistocene period ice sheets repeatedly locked up masses of water as land ice; its weight depressed the land, but the locking-up of the water lowered the sea-level by 100–200 metres. The glaciations and interglacials of the Ice Age are extremely difficult to date and classify, but recent scientific opinion considers the Pleistocene period to have begun approximately 1·7 million years ago. The last glacial retreat, merging into the Holocene period, was 10,000 years ago.

HUMAN DEVELOPMENT

Any consideration of the history of man must start with the fact that all members of the human race belong to one species of animal, i.e. *Homo sapiens*, the definition of a species being in biological terms that all its members can interbreed. As a species of mammal it is possible to group man with other similar types, known as the primates. Amongst these is found a sub-group, the apes, which includes, in addition to man, the chimpanzees, gorillas, orang-utans and gibbons. All lack a tail, have shoulder blades at the back, and a Y-shaped chewing pattern on the surface of their molars, as well as showing the more general primate characteristics of four incisors, a thumb which is able to touch the fingers of the same hand, and finger and toe nails instead of claws. All the factors available to scientific study suggest that human beings have chimpanzees and gorillas as their nearest relatives in the animal world. However, there remains the possibility that there once lived creatures, now extinct, which were closer to modern man than the chimpanzees and gorillas, and which shared with modern man the characteristics of having flat faces (i.e. the absence of a pronounced muzzle), being bipedal, and possessing large brains.

There are two broad groups of extinct apes recognized by specialists. First the ramapithecines, the remains of which, mainly jaw fragments, have been found in east Africa, Asia, and Turkey. They lived about 14 to 8 million years ago, and from the evidence of their teeth it seems they chewed more in the manner of modern man than the other presently living apes. The second group, the australopithecines, have left much more numerous remains amongst which sub-groups may be detected, although the geographic spread is limited to south and east Africa. Living between 5 and 1·5 million years ago, they were closer relatives of modern man to the extent that they walked upright, did not have an extensive muzzle, and had similar types of pre-molars. The first australopithecine remains were recognized at Taung in South Africa in 1924, and subsequent discoveries include those at the famous site of Olduvai Gorge in Tanzania. Perhaps the most impressive discovery was made at Hadar in Ethiopia in 1974 when about half a skeleton, known as 'Lucy', was found.

Also in east Africa, between 2 million and 1·5 million years ago, lived a hominid group which not only walked upright, had a flat face, and a large brain case, but also made simple pebble and flake stone tools. On present evidence these habilines seem to have been the first people to make tools, however crude. This facility is related to the larger brain size and human beings are the only animals to make implements to be used in other processes. These early pebble tool users, because of their distinctive characteristics, have been grouped as a separate sub-species, now extinct, of the genus *Homo*, and are known as *Homo habilis*.

The use of fire, again a human characteristic, is associated with another group of extinct hominids whose remains, about a million years old, are found in south and east Africa, China, Indonesia, north Africa and Europe. No doubt the mastery of the techniques of making fire helped the colonization of the colder northern areas and in this respect the site of Vertesszollos in Hungary is of particular importance. *Homo erectus* is the name given to this group of fossils and it now includes a number of famous individual discoveries from earlier decades, for example, Solo Man, Heidelberg Man, and especially Peking Man who lived at the cave site at Choukoutien, which has yielded evidence of fire and burnt bone.

The well-known group, Neanderthal Man, or *Homo sapiens neandertalensis*, is an extinct form of modern man who lived between about 100,000 and 40,000 years ago, thus spanning the last Ice Age. Indeed, its ability to adapt to the cold climate on the edge of the ice sheets is one of its characteristic features, the remains being found only in Europe, Asia and the Middle East. Complete neanderthal skeletons were found during excavations at Tabun in Israel, together with evidence of tool-making and the use of fire. Distinguished by very large brains, it seems that neanderthal man was the first to develop recognizable social customs, especially deliberate burial rites. Why the neanderthalers became extinct is not clear, but it may be connected with the climatic changes at the end of the Ice Ages, which would have seriously affected their food supplies; possibly they became too specialized for their own good.

The Swanscombe skull is the only known human fossil remains found in England. Some specialists see Swanscombe Man (or, more probably, woman) as a neanderthaler. Others group these remains together with the Steinheim skull from Germany, seeing both as a separate sub-species, *Homo sapiens steinheimenses*. Unfortunately there is too little evidence as yet on which to form a final judgement.

Modern Man, *Homo sapiens sapiens*, the surviving sub-species of *Homo sapiens*, had evolved to our present physical condition and had colonized much of the world by about 30,000 years ago. There are many previously distinguished individual specimens, for example Cromagnon Man, which may now be grouped together as *Homo sapiens sapiens*. It was modern man who spread to the American continent by crossing the landbridge between Siberia and Alaska and thence moved south through North America and into South America. Equally it is modern man who over the last 30,000 years has been responsible for the major developments in technology, art and civilization generally.

One of the problems for those studying fossil man is the lack in many cases of sufficient quantities of fossil bone for analysis. It is important that theories should be tested against evidence, and not the evidence made to fit the theory. The celebrated Piltdown hoax is perhaps the best-known example of 'fossils' being forged to fit what was seen in some quarters as the correct theory of man's evolution.

CULTURAL DEVELOPMENT

The Eurocentric bias of early archaeologists meant that the search for a starting point for the development and transmission of cultural ideas, especially by migration, trade and warfare, concentrated unduly on Europe and the Near East. The Three Age System, whereby pre-history was divided into a Stone Age, a Bronze Age, and an Iron Age, was devised by Christian Thomsen, curator of the National Museum of Denmark in the early nineteenth century, to facilitate the classification of the museum's collections. The descriptive adjectives referred to the materials from which the implements and weapons were made, and came to be regarded as the dominant features of the societies to which they related. The refinement of the Three Age System once dominated archaeological thought and still remains a generally accepted concept in the popular mind. However, it is now seen by archaeologists as an inadequate model for human development.

Common sense alone suggests that there were no complete breaks between one so-called 'Age' and another, any more than contemporaries would have regarded 1485 as a complete break between medieval and modern English history. Nor can the Three Age System be applied universally. In some areas it is necessary to insert a Copper Age, while in Africa south of the Sahara there would seem to be no Bronze Age at all; in Australia, Old Stone Age societies survived, while in South America, New Stone Age communities existed into modern times. The civilizations in other parts of the world clearly invalidate a Eurocentric theory of human development.

The concept of the 'Neolithic Revolution', associated with the domestication of plants and animals, was a development of particular importance in the human cultural pattern. It reflected change from the primitive hunter/gatherer economies to a more settled agricultural way of life and therefore, so the argument goes, made possible the development of urban civilization. However, it can no longer be argued that this 'revolution' took place only in one area from which all development stemmed. Though it appears that the cultivation of wheat and barley was first undertaken, together with the domestication of cattle and goats/sheep in the Fertile Crescent, there is evidence that rice was first deliberately planted and pigs domesticated in south-east Asia, maize first cultivated in Central America, and llamas first domesticated in South America. It has been recognized increasingly in recent years that cultural changes can take place independently of each other in different parts of the world at different rates and different times. There is no need for a general diffusionist theory.

Although scholars will continue to study the particular societies which interest them, it may be possible to obtain a reliable chronological framework, in absolute terms of years, against which the cultural development of any particular area may be set. The development and refinement of radio-carbon dating and other scientific methods of producing absolute chronologies is enabling the cross-referencing of societies to be undertaken. As the techniques of dating become more rigorous in application and the number of scientifically obtained dates increases, the attainment of an absolute chronology for prehistoric societies throughout the world comes closer to being achieved.

WORLD GEOGRAPHICAL STATISTICS

The Earth

The shape of the Earth is that of an oblate spheroid or solid of revolution whose meridian sections are ellipses, whilst the sections at right angles are circles.

Dimensions

Equatorial diameter = 12,756·28 km (7,926·38 miles).
Polar diameter = 12,713·50 km (7,899·80 miles).
Equatorial circumference = 40,075·01 km (24,901·45 miles).
Polar circumference = 40,008·00 km (24,859·82 miles).

The equatorial circumference is divided into 360 degrees of longitude, which is measured in degrees, minutes and seconds east or west of the Greenwich meridian (0°) to 180° (the meridian 180° E. coinciding with 180° W.).

Distance north and south of the Equator is measured in degrees, minutes and seconds of latitude. The Equator is 0°, the North Pole is 90° N. and the South Pole is 90° S. The Tropics lie at 23° 26′ N. (Tropic of Cancer) and 23° 26′ S. (Tropic of Capricorn). The Arctic Circle lies at 66° 34′ N. and the Antarctic Circle at 66° 34′ S. (NB The Tropics and the Arctic and Antarctic circles are of variable latitude due to the mean obliquity of the Ecliptic; the values given are for 1991·5.)

Area, etc.

The surface area of the Earth is 510,069,120 km² (196,938,800 miles²), of which the water area is 70·92 per cent and the land area is 29·08 per cent.

The velocity of a given point of the Earth's surface at the Equator exceeds 1,000 miles an hour (24,901·8 miles in 24 hours, viz 1,037·56 m.p.h.); the Earth's velocity in its orbit round the Sun averages 66,620 m.p.h. (584,018,400 miles in 365·256366 days). The Earth is distant from the Sun 92,955,900 miles, on the average.

OCEAN AREAS

| | *Area* | |
	km²	miles²
Pacific	166,240,000	64,186,300
Atlantic	86,550,000	33,420,000
Indian	73,427,000	28,350,500
Arctic	13,223,700	5,105,700

Greatest Ocean Depths

| *Greatest depth location* | *Depth* | |
	metres	feet
Mariana Trench (Pacific)	10,916	35,839
Puerto Rico Trench (Atlantic)	8,605	28,232
Java Trench (Indian)	7,125	23,376
Eurasian Basin (Arctic)	5,450	17,880

SEA AREAS

| | *Area* | |
	km²	miles²
South China	2,974,600	1,148,500
Caribbean	2,515,900	971,400
Mediterranean	2,509,900	969,100
Bering	2,226,100	873,000
Gulf of Mexico	1,507,600	582,100
Okhotsk	1,392,000	537,500
Japan	1,015,000	391,100
Hudson Bay	730,100	281,900
East China	664,600	256,600
Andaman	564,880	218,100

| | *Area* | |
	km²	miles²
Black Sea	507,900	196,100
Red Sea	453,000	174,900
North Sea	427,100	164,900
Baltic Sea	382,000	147,500
Yellow Sea	294,000	113,500
Persian Gulf	230,000	88,800

THE CONTINENTS

There are six geographic continents, though America is often divided politically into North and Central America, and South America.

Africa is surrounded by sea except for the narrow isthmus of Suez in the north-east, through which is cut the Suez Canal. The Equator passes through the middle of the continent. Its extreme longitudes are 17° 20′ W. at Cape Verde, Senegal, and 51° 24′ E. at Ras Hafun, Somalia. The extreme latitudes are 37° 20′ N. at Cape Blanco, Tunisia, and 34° 50′ S. at Cape Agulhas, South Africa, about 4,400 miles apart.

America.—North America, including Mexico, is surrounded by ocean except in the south, where the isthmian states of **Central America** link North America with South America. Its extreme longitudes are 168° 5′ W. at Cape Prince of Wales, Alaska, and 55° 40′ W. at Cape Charles, Newfoundland. The extreme latitudes are about 82° N. in the Arctic Ocean and 15° N. in the south of Mexico. The West Indies, about 65,000 square miles in area, extend from about 27° N. to 10° N. latitude.

South America lies mostly in the southern hemisphere; the Equator passes through the north of the continent. It is surrounded by ocean except where it is joined to Central America in the north by the narrow isthmus through which is cut the Panama Canal. Its extreme longitudes are 34° 47′ W. at Cape Branco in Brazil and 81° 20′ W. at Punta Pariña, Peru. The extreme latitudes are 12° 25′ N. at Punta Gallinas, Colombia, and 55° 59′ S. at Cape Horn, Chile.

Antarctica lies almost entirely within the Antarctic Circle (66° 34′ S.) and is the largest of the world's glaciated areas. The continent has an area of about 5·5 million square miles, 99 per cent of which is permanently ice-covered. The ice amounts to some 7·2 million cubic miles and represents more than 90 per cent of the world's fresh water. The environment is too hostile for unsupported human habitation. The staff of scientific research stations are the only people present on the continent and off-lying islands.

Asia is the largest continent and occupies almost a third of the world's land surface. The extreme longitudes are about 26° E. on the west coast of Asia Minor and 169° 45′ W. at Mys Dežneva (East Cape), USSR, a distance of about 6,000 miles. Its extreme northern latitude is 77° 45′ N. at Cape Čeljuskin, USSR, and it extends over 5,000 miles south to about 1° 15′ N. of the Equator. The islands of Japan, the Philippines and Indonesia ring the continent to the east and south-east.

Australia is the smallest of the continents and lies in the southern hemisphere. It is entirely surrounded by ocean. Its extreme longitudes are 113° 9′ E. at Steep Point and 153° 38′ E. at Cape Byron. The extreme latitudes are 10° 40′ S. at Cape York and 39° S. at South East Point.

Europe, including European Russia, is the smallest continent in the northern hemisphere. Its extreme latitudes are 71° 11′ N. at North Cape in Norway, and

36° 23′ N. at Cape Matapan in southern Greece, a distance of about 2,400 miles. Its breadth from Cape da Roca in Portugal (9° 30′ W.) in the west to the Urals in the east is about 3,300 miles. The division between Europe and Asia is generally regarded as being the Ural Mountains and, in the south, the valley of the Manych, which stretches from the Caspian Sea to the mouth of the Don.

	Area	
	km²	miles²
Asia	43,998,000	16,988,000
America[1]	41,918,000	16,185,000
Africa	29,800,000	11,506,000
Antarctica	c.13,600,000	c.5,500,000
Europe[2]	9,699,000	3,745,000
Australia	7,618,493	2,941,526

[1] North and Central America has an area of 24,255,000 km² (9,365,000 miles²).
[2] Includes 5,571,000 km² (2,151,000 miles²) of USSR territory west of the Ural Mountains.

PENINSULAS

	Area	
	km²	miles²
Arabian	3,250,000	1,250,000
Southern Indian	2,072,000	800,000
Alaskan	1,500,000	580,000
Labradorian	1,300,000	500,000
Scandinavian	800,300	309,000
Iberian	584,000	225,500

LARGEST ISLANDS

Island	Ocean	Area	
		km²	miles²
Greenland	Arctic	2,175,500	840,000
New Guinea	Pacific	792,500	306,000
Borneo	Pacific	725,450	280,100
Madagascar	Indian	587,040	226,658
Baffin Island	Arctic	507,528	195,928
Sumatra	Indian	427,350	165,000
Honshu	Pacific	228,000	88,031
Great Britain[1]	Atlantic	218,040	84,186
Victoria Island	Arctic	217,290	83,895
Ellesmere Island	Arctic	196,235	75,767
Sulawesi (Celebes)	Indian	178,700	69,000
South Island, NZ	Pacific	151,010	58,305
Java	Indian	126,650	48,900
Cuba	Atlantic	114,525	44,218
North Island, NZ	Pacific	114,050	44,035
Newfoundland	Atlantic	108,855	42,030
Luzon	Pacific	105,880	40,880
Iceland	Atlantic	103,000	39,770
Mindanao	Pacific	95,247	36,775
Ireland	Atlantic	82,462	31,839

[1] Mainland only

GLACIATED AREAS

It is estimated that 15,600,000 km² (6,020,000 miles²) or 10·51 per cent of the world's land surface is permanently covered with ice.

	Area	
	km²	miles²
South Polar regions	13,597,000	5,250,000
North Polar regions (incl. Greenland)	1,965,000	758,500
Alaska-Canada	58,800	22,700
Asia	37,800	14,600
South America	11,900	4,600
Europe	10,700	4,128
New Zealand	984	380
Africa	238	92

LARGEST DESERTS

	Area (approx.)	
	km²	miles²
The Sahara (N. Africa)	8,400,000	3,250,000
Australian Desert	1,550,000	600,000
Arabian Desert	1,300,000	500,000
*The Gobi (Mongolia/China)	1,170,000	450,000
Kalahari Desert (Botswana/ Namibia/S. Africa)	520,000	200,000
Sonoran Desert (USA/ Mexico)	310,000	120,000
Namib Desert (Namibia)	310,000	120,000
†Kara Kum (USSR)	270,000	105,000
Thar Desert (India/Pakistan)	260,000	100,000
Somali Desert (Somalia)	260,000	100,000
Atacama Desert (Chile)	180,000	70,000
†Kyzyl Kum (USSR)	180,000	70,000
Dasht-e Lut (Iran)	52,000	20,000
Mojave Desert (USA)	35,000	13,500
Desierto de Sechura (Peru)	26,000	10,000

* Including the Takla Makan—320,000 km² (125,000 miles²)

† Together known as the Turkestan Desert

DEEPEST DEPRESSIONS

	Maximum depth below sea level	
	metres	feet
Dead Sea (Jordan/Israel)	395	1,296
Turfan Depression (Sinkiang, China)	153	505
Qattara Depression (Egypt)	132	436
Mangyshlak peninsula (Kazakh SSR)	131	433
Danakil Depression (Ethiopia)	116	383
Death Valley (California, USA)	86	282
Salton Sink (California, USA)	71	235
W. of Ustyurt plateau (Kazakh SSR)	70	230
Prikaspiyskaya Nizmennost' (Russian SFSR/Kazakh SSR)	67	220
Lake Sarykamysh (Uzbek/Turkmen SSR)	45	148
El Faiyûm (Egypt)	44	147
Valdies peninsula, Lago Enriquillo (Dominican Republic)	40	131

The world's largest exposed depression is the Prikaspiyskaya Nizmennost' covering the hinterland of the northern third of the Caspian Sea, which is itself 28 m (92 ft) below sea level.

Western Antarctica and Central Greenland largely comprise crypto-depressions under ice burdens. The Antarctic Wilkes subglacial basin has a bedrock 2,341 m (7,680 ft) below sea-level. In Greenland (lat. 73° N., long. 39° W.) the bedrock is 365 m (1,197 ft) below sea-level.

LONGEST MOUNTAIN RANGES

Range (Location)	Length	
	km	miles
Cordillera de Los Andes (W. South America)	7,200	4,500
Rocky Mountains (W. North America)	4,800	3,000
Himalaya-Karakoram-Hindu Kush (S. Central Asia)	3,800	2,400
Great Dividing Range (E. Australia)	3,600	2,250
Trans-Antarctic Mts. (Antarctica)	3,500	2,200
Atlantic Coast Range (E. Brazil)	3,000	1,900
West Sumatran-Javan Range (Indonesia)	2,900	1,800
Aleutian Range (Alaska and NW Pacific)	2,650	1,650
Tien Shan (S. Central Asia)	2,250	1,400
Central New Guinea Range (Irian Jaya— Papua New Guinea)	2,000	1,250

HIGHEST MOUNTAINS

The world's 8,000-metre mountains (with six subsidiary peaks) are all in the 3,800 km (2,400 mile) long Himalaya-Karakoram-Hindu Kush range of south central Asia.

Mountain	Height	
	m	ft
Mount Everest	8,863	29,078
K 2	8,607	28,238
Kangchenjunga	8,597	28,208
Lhotse	8,511	27,923
Makalu I	8,481	27,824
Lhotse Shar	8,383	27,504
Dhaulagiri I	8,167	26,795
Manaslu I (Kutang I)	8,156	26,760
Cho Oyu	8,153	26,750
Nanga Parbat (Diamir)	8,125	26,660
Annapurna I	8,091	26,546
Gasherbrum I (Hidden Peak)	8,068	26,470
Broad Peak I	8,046	26,400
Shisha Pangma (Gosainthan)	8,046	26,398
Gasherbrum II	8,034	26,360
Annapurna East	8,010	26,280
Makalu South-East	8,010	26,280
Broad Peak Central	8,000	26,246

The culminating summits in the other major mountain ranges are:—

Mountain (Range or Country)	Height	
	m	ft
Pik Pobeda (Tien Shan)	7,439	24,406
Cerro Aconcagua (Cordillera de Los Andes)	6,960	22,834
Mt. McKinley—*S. Peak* (Alaska Range)	6,194	20,320
Kilimanjaro (Tanzania)	5,894	19,340
Hkakabo Razi (Burma)	5,881	19,296
Citlaltépetl (Orizaba) (Sierra Madre Oriental, Mexico)	5,699	18,700
El'brus—*W. Peak* (Caucasus, USSR)	5,663	18,481
Vinson Massif (E. Antarctica)	4,897	16,067
Puncak Jaya (Central New Guinea Range)	4,884	16,023
Mt. Blanc (Alps)	4,807	15,771
Klyuchevskaya Sopka (Kamchatka peninsula, USSR)	4,750	15,584
Ras Dashan (Ethiopian Highlands)	4,620	15,158
Zard Kūh (Zagros Mts, Iran)	4,547	14,921
Mt. Kirkpatrick (Trans Antarctic)	4,529	14,860
Mt. Belukha (Altai Mts., USSR/ Mongolia)	4,505	14,783
Mt. Elbert (Rocky Mountains)	4,400	14,433
Mt. Rainier (Cascade Range, N. America)	4,392	14,410
Nevado de Colima (Sierra Madre Occidental, Mexico)	4,268	14,003
Jebel Toubkal (Atlas Mts, N. Africa)	4,165	13,665
Kinabalu (Crocker Range, Borneo)	4,101	13,455
Kerinci (West Sumatran-Javan Range, Indonesia)	3,800	12,467
Jabal an Nabī Shu'ayb (N. Tihāmat, Yemen)	3,760	12,336
Teotepec (Sierra Madre del Sur, Mexico)	3,703	12,149
Thaban Ntlenyana (Drakensberg, South Africa)	3,482	11,425

	m	ft
Pico de Bandeira (Atlantic Coast Range)	2,890	9,482
Shishaldin (Aleutian Range)	2,861	9,387
Kosciusko (Great Dividing Range)	2,228	7,310

HIGHEST VOLCANOES

Volcano (last major eruption) and location	Height	
	m	ft
Guallatiri (1959), Andes, Chile	6,060	19,882
Lascar (1986), Andes, Chile	5,990	19,652
Cotopaxi (1975), Andes, Ecuador	5,897	19,347
Tupungatito (1980), Andes, Chile	5,640	18,504
Sangay (1976), Andes, Ecuador	5,230	17,159
Guagua Pichincha (1982), Andes, Ecuador	4,784	15,696
Purace (1977), Colombia	4,756	15,604
Klyuchevskaya Sopka (1985), Kamchatka peninsula, USSR	4,750	15,584
Nevado de Colima (1987), Mexico	4,268	14,003
Mauna Loa (1984), Hawaii Is.	4,170	13,680
Cameroon (1982), Cameroon	4,070	13,354
Acatenango (1972), Guatemala	3,960	12,992
Fuego (1988), Guatemala	3,835	12,582
Kerinci (1987), Sumatra, Indonesia	3,800	12,467
Erebus (1988), Ross Island, Antarctica	3,794	12,450
Tacana (1988), Guatemala	3,780	12,400
Santiaguito (1902, 1988), Guatemala	3,768	12,362
Rindjani (1966), Lombok, Indonesia	3,726	12,224
Semeru (1988), Java, Indonesia	3,675	12,060
Nyirgongo (1977), Zaïre	3,475	11,400
Koryakskaya (1957), Kamchatka, USSR	3,456	11,339
Irazú (1987), Costa Rica	3,432	11,260
Slamet (1967), Java, Indonesia	3,428	11,247
Spurr (1953), Alaska, USA	3,374	11,069
Mt. Etna (1169, 1669, 1988), Sicily, Italy	3,369	11,053
Shiveluch (1964), Kamchatka, USSR	3,283	10,771
Agung (1964), Bali, Indonesia	3,142	10,308
Llaima (1988), Chile	3,128	10,239
Redoubt (1966), Alaska, USA	3,108	10,197
Tjareme (1938), Java, Indonesia	3,078	10,098
Iliamna (1978), Alaska, USA	3,076	10,092
On-Taka (1980), Japan	3,063	10,049
Nyamlagira (1988), Zaire	3,056	10,028

Other notable volcanoes

	Height	
	m	ft
Tambora (1815), Subawa, Indonesia	2,850	9,353
Mount St Helens (1986), Washington State, USA	2,530	8,300
Tristan da Cunha (1961), South Atlantic	2,060	6,760
Hekla (1981), Iceland	1,491	4,892
Mount Pelée (1902), Martinique	1,397	4,583
Vesuvius (AD 79, 1944), Italy	1,280	4,198
Kilauea (1988), Hawaii, USA	1,242	4,077
Stromboli (1986), Lipari Is., Italy	926	3,038
Krakatau (1883), Sunda Strait, Indonesia	804	2,640
Santoríni (Thíra) (1628 BC), Aegean Sea, Greece	566	1,857
Vulcano (Monte Aria), Lipari Is., Italy	499	1,637
Surtsey (1963–67), off Iceland	173	568

LARGEST LAKES

The areas of some of these lakes are subject to seasonal variation.

Lake	Location	Area		Length	
		km²	miles²	km	miles
Caspian Sea	Iran/USSR	371,000	143,000	1,171	728
Superior	Canada/USA	82,100	31,700	563	350
Victoria	Uganda, Tanzania, Kenya	69,500	26,828	362	225
Huron	Canada/USA	59,570	23,000	331	206
Michigan	USA	57,750	22,300	494	307
Aral Sea	USSR	40,400	15,600	331	235
Tanganyika	Zaïre, Tanzania, Zambia, Burundi	32,900	12,700	675	420
*Baykal (Baikal)	USSR	31,500	12,162	635	395
Great Bear	Canada	31,328	12,096	309	192
Malawi	Tanzania, Malawi and Mozambique	28,880	11,150	580	360
Great Slave	Canada	28,570	11,031	480	298
Erie	Canada/USA	25,670	9,910	388	241
Winnipeg	Canada	24,390	9,417	428	266
Ontario	Canada/USA	19,550	7,550	310	193
Balkhash	USSR	18,427	7,115	605	376
Ladozhskoye (Ladoga)	USSR	17,700	6,835	200	124

United Kingdom (by country)

Lake	Location	Area		Length	
Lough Neagh	Northern Ireland	381·73	147·39	28·90	18·00
Loch Lomond	Scotland	71·12	27·46	36·44	22·64
Windermere	England	14·74	5·69	16·90	10·50
Lake Vyrnwy	Wales (artificial)	4·53	1·75	7·56	4·70
Llyn Tegid (Bala)	Wales (natural)	4·38	1·69	5·80	3·65

* World's deepest lake (1,940 m/6,365 ft)

LONGEST RIVERS

River	Length		Source	Outflow
	km	miles		
Nile (Bahr-el-Nil)	6,670	4,145	R. Luvironza, Burundi	E. Mediterranean Sea
Amazon (Amazonas)	6,648	4,007	Lago Villafro, Peru	S. Atlantic Ocean
Mississippi-Missouri	5,970	3,710	R. Red Rock, SW Montana	Gulf of Mexico
Yenisey-Angara	5,540	3,442	W. Mongolia	Kara Sea
Yangtze-Kiang (Chang Jiang)	5,530	3,436	Kunlun Mts, W. China	Yellow Sea
Ob'-Irtysh	5,410	3,362	W. Mongolia	Kara Sea
Huang He (Yellow River)	4,830	3,000	Bayan Har Shan range, central China	Yellow Sea
Zaire (Congo)	4,700	2,920	R. Lualaba, Zaire-Zambia	S. Atlantic Ocean
Amur-Argun	4,670	2,903	R. Argun, Khingan Mts, N. China	Sea of Okhotsk
Lena-Kirenga	4,345	2,700	R. Kirenga, W. of Lake Baykal, USSR	Arctic Ocean
Mackenzie-Peace	4,240	2,635	Tatlatui Lake, British Columbia	Beaufort Sea
Mekong	4,184	2,600	Lants'an, Tibet	South China Sea
Niger	4,184	2,600	Loma Mts, Guinea	Gulf of Guinea, E. Atlantic Ocean
Rió de la Plata-Paraná	4,000	2,485	R. Paranáiba, central Brazil	S. Atlantic Ocean
Murray-Darling	3,750	2,330	SE Queensland	Lake Alexandrina, S. Australia
Volga	3,690	2,293	Valdai plateau, USSR	Caspian Sea
Zambezi	3,540	2,200	NW Zambia	S. Indian Ocean

Other notable rivers

River	Length		Source	Outflow
St Lawrence	3,130	1,945	Minnesota, USA	Gulf of St Lawrence
Ganges-Brahmaputra	2,900	1,800	R. Matsang, SW Tibet	Bay of Bengal
Indus	2,880	1,790	R. Sengge, SW Tibet	N. Arabian Sea
Danube (Donau)	2,850	1,770	Black Forest, SW Germany	Black Sea
Tigris-Euphrates	2,740	1,700	R. Murat, E. Turkey	Persian Gulf
Irrawaddy	2,090	1,300	R. Mali Hka, N. Burma	Andaman Sea
Don	1,969	1,224	SE of Novomoskovsk	Sea of Azov

British Isles

River	Length		Source	Outflow
Shannon	386	240	Co. Cavan, Rep. of Ireland	Atlantic Ocean
Severn	354	220	Powys, Wales	Bristol Channel
Thames	346	215	Gloucestershire, England	North Sea
Tay	188	117	Perthshire, Scotland	North Sea
Clyde	158	98½	Lanarkshire, Scotland	Firth of Clyde
Tweed	155	96½	Peeblesshire, Scotland	North Sea
Bann (Upper and Lower)	122	76	Co. Down, N. Ireland	Atlantic

GREATEST WATERFALLS—BY HEIGHT

Waterfall	River and Location	Total drop		Greatest single leap	
		m	ft	m	ft
Angel	Carrao, Venezuela	979	3,212	807	2,648
Tugela	Tugela, S. Africa	947	3,110	410	1,350
Utigård	Jostedal Glacier, Norway	800	2,625	600	1,970
Mongefossen	Monge, Norway	774	2,540	—	—
Yosemite	Yosemite Creek, USA	739	2,425	435	1,430
Østre Mardøla Foss	Mardals, Norway	656	2,154	296	974
Tyssestrengane	Tysso, Norway	646	2,120	289	948
Cuquenán	Arabopó, Venezuela	610	2,000	—	—
Sutherland	Arthur, NZ	580	1,904	248	815
Kjellfossen[1]	Naeröfjord, Norway	561	1,841	149	490

British Isles (by country)

Eas a' Chuàl Aluinn	Glas Bheinn, Sutherland, Scotland	200	658		
Powerscourt Falls	Dargle, Co. Wicklow, Rep. of Ireland	106	350		
Pistyll-y-Llyn	Powys-Dyfed border, Wales	c.73	230–240	(cascades)	
Pistyll Rhyadr	Clwyd-Powys border, Wales	71·5	235	(single leap)	
Caldron Snout	R. Tees, Cumbria/Durham, England	60	200	(cascades)	

[1] Volume often so low the fall atomizes into a 'bridal veil'.

GREATEST WATERFALLS—BY VOLUME

Waterfall (River and Location)	Mean Annual Flow	
	m³/sec	galls/sec
Boyoma (R. Lualaba, Zaïre)	c.17,000	c.3,750,000
*Guairá (Alto Parañá, Brazil/ Paraguay)	13,300	2,930,000
Khône (Mekong, Laos)	11,500	2,530,000
Niagara (Horseshoe) (R. Niagara/Lake Erie–Lake Ontario)	3,000	670,000
Paulo Afonso (R. São Francisco, Brazil)	2,750	605,000
Urubupunga (Alto Parañá, Brazil)	2,800	625,000
Cataratas del Iguazú (R. Iguaçu, Brazil/ Argentina)	1,725	380,000
Patos-Maribando (Rio Grande, Brazil)	1,500	330,000
Victoria (Mosi-oa-tunya) (R. Zambezi, Zambia/Zimbabwe)	1,000	220,000
Churchill (R. Churchill, Canada)	975	215,000
Kaieteur (R. Potaro, Guyana)	660	145,000

*Peak flow 50,000 m³/sec, 11,000,000 galls/sec.

TALLEST INHABITED BUILDINGS

Building and City	Height	
	metres	feet
Sears Tower, Chicago	443	[1]1,454
World Trade Center, New York	417	[2]1,368
Empire State Building, New York	381	[3]1,250
AMOCO Building, Chicago	346	1,136
John Hancock Center, Chicago	343	1,127
Chrysler Building, New York	319	1,046
C. & S. Plaza, Atlanta	312	1,024
First Interstate World Center, Los Angeles	310	1,017
Texas Commerce Tower, Houston	305	1,002
Allied Bank Plaza, Houston	302	992

[1] With TV antennae 475·18 m/1,559 ft
[2] With TV antennae, 521·2 m/1,710 ft
[3] With TV tower (added 1950–51), 430·9 m/1,414 ft

TALLEST STRUCTURES

Structure and Location	Height	
	metres	feet
*Warszawa Radio Mast, Konstantynow, Poland	646	2,120
KTHI-TV Mast, Fargo, North Dakota	629	2,063
CN Tower, Metro Centre, Toronto, Canada	555	1,822

*Collapsed during renovation, August 1991.

LONGEST BRIDGES—BY SPAN

Bridge and Location	Length	
	m	ft
Suspension Spans		
Humber Estuary, Humberside, England	1,410	4,626
Verrazano Narrows, Brooklyn-Staten I, USA	1,298	4,260
Golden Gate, San Francisco Bay, USA	1,280	4,200
Mackinac Straits, Michigan, USA	1,158	3,800
Bosporus, Istanbul, Turkey	1,074	3,524
George Washington, Hudson River, New York City, USA	1,067	3,500
Ponte 25 Abril (Tagus), Lisbon, Portugal	1,013	3,323
Firth of Forth (road), nr. Edinburgh, Scotland	1,006	3,300
Severn River, Severn Estuary, England	988	3,240
Cantilever Spans		
Pont de Québec (rail-road), St Lawrence, Canada	548·6	1,800
Ravenswood, W. Virginia, USA	525·1	1,723
Firth of Forth (rail), nr. Edinburgh, Scotland	521·2	1,710
Minato, Osaka, Japan	510·0	1,673
Commodore Barry, Chester, Pennsylvania, USA	494·3	1,622
Greater New Orleans, Algiers, Louisiana, USA	480·0	1,575
Howrah (rail-road), Calcutta, India	457·2	1,500
Steel Arch Spans		
New River Gorge, Fayetteville, W. Virginia, USA	518·2	1,700
Bayonne (Kill van Kull), Bayonne, NJ-Staten I, USA	503·5	1,652
Sydney Harbour, Sydney, Australia	502·9	1,650

The 'floating' bridging at Evergreen, Seattle, Washington State, USA is 3,839 m/12,596 ft long.

The longest stretch of bridgings of any kind are those between Mandeville and Jefferson, Louisiana, USA—the Lake Pontchartrain Causeway II 38·422 km/23·87 miles and Causeway I 38·352 km/23·83 miles.

LONGEST VEHICULAR TUNNELS

Tunnel and Location	Length	
	km	miles
*Seikan (rail), Tsugaru Channel, Japan	53·90	33·49
Moscow metro, Belyaevo-Medved Kovo, Moscow, USSR	30·70	19·07
Northern line tube, East Finchley-Morden, London	27·84	17·30
Oshimizu, Honshū, Japan	22·17	13·78
Simplon II (rail), Brigue, Switzerland-Iselle, Italy	19·82	12·31
Simplon I (rail), Brigue, Switzerland-Iselle, Italy	19·80	12·30
Shin-Kanmon (rail), Kanmon Strait, Japan	18·68	11·61
Great Appennine (rail), Vernio, Italy	18·49	11·49
St Gotthard (road), Göschenen-Airolo, Switzerland	16·32	10·14
Rokko (rail), Ōsaka-Kōbe, Japan	16·09	10·00

*Sub-aqueous

The twin rail Eurotunnel under the English Channel between Cheriton, Kent and Sargette, near Calais, is due to be opened in summer 1993. The tunnels are 49·94 km/31·03 miles in length.

The longest non-vehicular tunnelling in the world is the Delaware Aqueduct in New York State, USA, constructed in 1937–44 to a length of 168·9 km/105 miles.

British Rail

		miles	yards
Severn	Western Region	4	484
Totley	Eastern Region	3	950
Standedge	Eastern Region	3	66
Sodbury	Western Region	2	924
Disley	London Midland Region	2	346
Ffestiniog	London Midland Region	2	338
Bramhope	Eastern Region	2	241
Cowburn	London Midland Region	2	182

LONGEST SHIP CANALS

Opened	Canal		Length		Min. Depth	
			km	miles	m	ft
1933	White Sea-Baltic (formerly Stalin)	Canalized river; canal 51·5 km/32 miles	227	141·00	5·0	16·5
1869	*Suez	Links Red and Mediterranean Seas	162	100·60	12·9	42·3
1952	V. I. Lenin Volga-Don	Links Black and Caspian Seas	100	62·20	n/a	n/a
1895	Kiel (or North Sea)	Links North and Baltic Seas	98	60·90	13·7	45·0
1940	*Houston	Links inland city with sea	91	56·70	10·4	34·0
1926	Alphonse XIII	Gives Seville access to sea	85	53·00	7·6	25·0
1914	Panama	Links Pacific Ocean and Caribbean Sea; lake chain, 78·9 km/49 miles dug	82	50·71	12·5	41·0
1894	Manchester Ship	Links city with Irish Channel	64	39·70	8·5	28·0
1931	Welland	Circumvents Niagara Falls and Rapids	45	28·00	8·8	29·0
1922	Brussels (Rupel Sea)	Renders Brussels an inland port	32	19·80	6·4	21·0

*Has no locks

The first section of China's Grand Canal, running 1,780 km/1,107 miles from Beijing to Hangchou was opened AD 610 but in undredged parts is today only 1·8 m/6 ft deep.

The longest boat canal in the world is the Volga-Baltic canal from Astrakhan to St Petersburg/Leningrad with 2,300 route km/1,850 miles.

THE SEVEN WONDERS OF THE WORLD

I.   THE PYRAMIDS OF EGYPT.—From Gizeh (near Cairo) to a southern limit 60 miles distant. The oldest is that of Zoser, at Saqqara, built c. 2650 BC. The Great Pyramid of Cheops covers 13·12 acres and was originally 481 ft. in height and 756 × 756 ft. at the base.

II. THE HANGING GARDENS OF BABYLON.—Adjoining Nebuchadnezzar's palace, 60 miles south of Baghdad. Terraced gardens, ranging from 75 to 300 ft. above ground level, watered from storage tanks on the highest terrace.

III. THE TOMB OF MAUSOLUS.—At Halicarnassus, in Asia Minor. Built by the widowed Queen Artemisia about 350 BC. The memorial originated the term mausoleum.

IV. THE TEMPLE OF ARTEMIS AT EPHESUS.—Ionic temple erected about 350 BC in honour of the goddess and burned by the Goths in AD 262.

V.   THE COLOSSUS OF RHODES.—A bronze statue of Apollo, set up about 280 BC. According to legend it stood at the harbour entrance of the seaport of Rhodes.

VI. THE STATUE OF ZEUS.—At Olympia in the plain of Elis, constructed of marble inlaid with ivory and gold by the sculptor Phidias, about 430 BC.

VII. THE PHAROS OF ALEXANDRIA.—A marble watch tower and lighthouse on the island of Pharos in the harbour of Alexandria, built c. 270 BC.

THE UNITED KINGDOM

The United Kingdom comprises Great Britain (England, Wales and Scotland) and Northern Ireland.

AREA
(as at March 31, 1981)

	Land		Inland Water†		Total	
	miles²	km²	miles²	km²	miles²	km²
UK*	93,005	240,882	1,242	3,218	94,247	244,100
England	50,070	129,681	293	758	50,363	130,439
Wales	7,968	20,638	50	130	8,018	20,768
Scotland	29,761	77,080	653	1,692	30,414	78,772
Northern Ireland‡ ..	5,206	13,483	246	638	5,452	14,121

* Excludes the Isle of Man (221 sq. miles) and the Channel Islands (75 sq. miles).
† Excluding tidal water.
‡ Excluding certain tidal waters that are parts of statutory areas in Northern Ireland.

POPULATION

CENSUS RESULTS, 1801–1991

Before 1801 there existed no official return of the population of either England or Scotland. Estimates of the population of England at various periods, calculated from the number of baptisms, burials and marriages, are: in 1570, 4,160,221; 1600, 4,811,718; 1630, 5,600,517; 1670, 5,773,646; 1700, 6,045,008; 1750, 6,517,035.

Thousands

	United Kingdom‡			England and Wales			Scotland			Northern Ireland†		
	Total	Male	Female	Total	Male	Female	Total	Male	Female	Total	Male	Female
1801	—	—	—	8,893	4,255	4,638	1,608	739	869	—	—	—
1811	13,368	6,368	7,000	10,165	4,874	5,291	1,806	826	980	1,397	668	729
1821	15,472	7,498	7,974	12,000	5,850	6,150	2,092	983	1,109	1,380	665	715
1831	17,835	8,647	9,188	13,897	6,771	7,126	2,364	1,114	1,250	1,574	762	812
1841	20,183	9,819	10,364	15,914	7,778	8,137	2,620	1,242	1,378	1,649	800	849
1851	22,259	10,855	11,404	17,928	8,781	9,146	2,889	1,376	1,513	1,443	698	745
1861	24,525	11,894	12,631	20,066	9,776	10,290	3,062	1,450	1,612	1,396	668	728
1871	27,431	13,309	14,122	22,712	11,059	11,653	3,360	1,603	1,757	1,359	647	712
1881	31,015	15,060	15,955	25,974	12,640	13,335	3,736	1,799	1,936	1,305	621	684
1891	34,264	16,593	17,671	29,003	14,060	14,942	4,026	1,943	2,083	1,236	590	646
1901	38,237	18,492	19,745	32,528	15,729	16,799	4,472	2,174	2,298	1,237	590	647
1911	42,082	20,357	21,725	36,070	17,446	18,625	4,761	2,309	2,452	1,251	603	648
1921	44,027	21,033	22,994	37,887	18,075	19,811	4,882	2,348	2,535	1,258	610	648
1931	46,038	22,060	23,978	39,952	19,133	20,819	4,843	2,326	2,517	1,243	601	642
1951	50,225	24,118	26,107	43,758	21,016	22,742	5,096	2,434	2,662	1,371	668	703
1961	52,709	25,481	27,228	46,105	22,304	23,801	5,179	2,483	2,697	1,425	694	731
1971	55,515	26,952	28,562	48,750	23,683	25,067	5,229	2,515	2,714	1,536	755	781
1981	55,848	27,104	28,742	49,155	23,873	25,281	5,131	2,466	2,664	1,533*	750	783
1991p	55,500	—	—	48,960	—	—	4,957	—	—	1,583	—	—

NOTES.
1. Because of the War there was no Census in 1941.
2. The last official Census of population was taken on the night of April 21, 1991 (p preliminary).
3. ‡ Excludes the Isle of Man and the Channel Islands.
4. † All figures refer to the area which is now Northern Ireland. Figures for Northern Ireland in 1921 and 1931 are estimates based on the Censuses held in 1926 and 1937.
5. *Figures include non-enumerated persons.

ISLANDS

Populations of the Isle of Man and the Channel Islands at Census years since 1900 were:—

	Isle of Man			Jersey			Guernsey		
	Total	Male	Female	Total	Male	Female	Total	Male	Female
1901.............	54,752	25,496	29,256	52,576	23,940	28,636	43,042	21,140	21,902
1911.............	52,016	23,937	28,079	51,898	24,014	27,884	45,001	22,215	22,786
1921.............	60,284	27,329	32,955	49,701	22,438	27,263	40,529	19,303	21,226
1931.............	49,308	22,443	26,865	50,462	23,424	27,038	42,743	20,675	22,068
1951.............	55,123	25,749	29,464	57,296	27,282	30,014	45,747	22,094	23,380
1961.............	48,151	22,060	26,091	57,200	27,200	30,000	47,178	22,890	24,288
1971.............	56,289	26,461	29,828	72,532	35,423	37,109	52,708	25,382	27,326
1981.............	64,679	30,901	33,778	77,000	37,000	40,000	56,000	27,000	29,000

Source: HMSO—Annual Abstract of Statistics 1991; OPCS–1991 Census (preliminary reports)

Resident Population by Age and Sex 1989

Thousands

	0–4	5–15	16–44	45–59/64*	60/65†–79	80 and over	All ages
Males							
United Kingdom	1,950·7	3,973·5	12,357·7	6,052·5	2,958·0	614·0	27,906·5
England	1,616·7	3,269·7	10,311·4	5,064·3	2,489·6	523·9	23,275·6
Wales	97·2	201·5	596·5	308·5	158·7	31·1	1,393·5
Scotland	166·7	356·9	1,109·2	535·2	245·5	46·9	2,460·4
Northern Ireland .	70·2	145·4	340·7	144·5	64·2	12·0	777·1
Females							
United Kingdom	1,857·0	3,768·3	12,107·0	4,704·8	5,445·1	1,447·5	29,329·7
England	1,539·9	3,099·6	10,105·2	3,908·3	4,536·6	1,224·3	24,413·8
Wales	92·5	190·4	590·7	237·7	293·2	75·0	1,479·6
Scotland	158·6	339·0	1,084·3	439·1	488·9	120·4	2,630·3
Northern Ireland .	66·1	139·4	326·7	119·7	126·2	27·9	806·0

*59 for women, 64 for men.
†60 for women, 65 for men.

Birth Rates 1989

Live births per 1,000 women in age groups:

	Under 20	20–24	25–29	30–34	35–39	40 and over
United Kingdom	32	92	120	83	29	5
England	32	91	120	84	30	5
Wales	37	103	115	77	25	4
Scotland	31	82	113	72	23	4
Northern Ireland	29	102	152	107	46	10

Death Rates 1989

Deaths per 1,000 population in age groups:

	0–4	5–14	15–24	25–34	35–44	45–54	55–64	65–74	75 and over
Males									
United Kingdom	2·3	0·2	0·8	0·9	1·7	4·8	15·2	40·3	112·7
England	2·3	0·2	0·8	0·9	1·7	4·7	14·7	39·1	111·0
Wales	2·1	0·3	0·8	0·6	1·8	4·9	16·0	43·1	114·9
Scotland	2·4	0·2	1·0	1·1	2·1	6·1	19·2	48·4	126·1
Northern Ireland .	1·9	0·3	1·1	1·2	1·8	5·4	17·2	46·6	124·3
Females									
United Kingdom	1·8	0·2	0·3	0·5	1·1	3·1	9·0	23·1	86·3
England	1·8	0·1	0·3	0·4	1·1	2·9	8·7	22·4	84·9
Wales	1·8	0·2	0·3	0·4	1·1	3·1	9·1	24·4	87·3
Scotland	1·8	0·2	0·4	0·6	1·4	3·9	11·5	28·4	97·0
Northern Ireland .	1·6	0·2	0·2	0·5	1·2	3·3	9·6	24·7	95·2

Source: HMSO—Regional Trends 1991

Immigration—Acceptances for settlement in the UK by nationality

Geographical region and nationality	Number of persons			Geographical region and nationality	Number of persons		
	1987	1988	1989		1987	1988	1989
Belgium	60	90	60	Nigeria	780	970	1,370
Denmark	110	110	90	Sierra Leone	100	110	170
France	420	430	350	Somalia	70	60	160
Germany (Federal Republic)	450	480	310	South Africa	1,020	870	720
Greece	240	220	100	Sudan	70	80	80
Italy	260	300	240	Tanzania	210	230	250
Luxembourg	—	—	—	Tunisia	30	60	60
Netherlands	280	220	220	Uganda	90	120	100
Portugal	230	250	210	Zambia	150	180	180
Spain	370	370	330	Zimbabwe	350	440	460
European Community	**2,430**	**2,470**	**1,910**	**Africa: total**	**5,150**	**5,840**	**6,390**
Austria	100	90	110	Bangladesh	3,080	2,890	3,780
Cyprus	380	350	340	India	4,610	5,020	4,510
Finland	140	130	110	Pakistan	3,930	4,280	4,080
Malta	120	100	100	**Indian sub-continent**	**11,620**	**12,180**	**12,360**
Norway	180	160	130	Iran	1,450	1,500	1,980
Sweden	490	520	370	Iraq	450	450	580
Switzerland	130	170	150	Israel	300	240	310
Turkey	460	600	690	Jordan	130	120	180
Yugoslavia	170	190	240	Kuwait	10	20	10
Other Western Europe	**2,160**	**2,310**	**2,240**	Lebanon	220	330	360
				Saudi Arabia	30	20	50
Bulgaria	10	30	20	Syria	100	120	120
Czechoslovakia	40	20	20	**Middle East**	**2,690**	**2,810**	**3,590**
German Democratic Republic	—	10	10				
Hungary	50	40	20	China	120	160	170
Poland	270	650	580	Indonesia	60	70	70
Romania	20	30	10	Japan	1,300	1,340	1,410
USSR	70	60	20	Malaysia	630	740	910
Eastern Europe	**470**	**830**	**670**	Philippines	1,240	1,140	750
Europe: total	**5,060**	**5,620**	**4,820**	Singapore	140	180	150
				Sri Lanka	720	860	800
Argentina	40	50	30	Thailand	470	390	240
Barbados	60	50	40	BDTC Hong Kong*	920	1,150	1,360
Brazil	160	190	130	**Remainder of Asia**	**5,600**	**6,020**	**5,860**
Canada	1,180	1,190	1,040				
Chile	40	60	40	**Asia: total**	**19,920**	**21,010**	**21,960**
Colombia	160	220	180				
Cuba	—	—	—	Australia	3,020	3,520	3,860
Guyana	180	200	120	New Zealand	2,690	2,680	2,970
Jamaica	510	620	520	**Australasia: total**	**5,710**	**6,190**	**6,830**
Mexico	80	60	40				
Peru	50	60	60	British Overseas Citizens	1,860	1,910	1,450
Trinidad and Tobago	140	160	170	Other countries not elsewhere specified	890	960	790
USA	3,710	3,750	3,030	Stateless†	1,040	1,270	1,500
Uruguay	—	10	10	**All nationalities**	**45,980**	**49,280**	**49,060**
Venezuela	40	40	40				
Americas: total	**6,350**	**6,480**	**5,440**	Foreign	18,230	19,100	18,330
				Commonwealth	27,750	30,180	30,730
Algeria	80	100	160	**Old Commonwealth**	**6,900**	**7,380**	**7,870**
Egypt	250	300	340	New Commonwealth and Pakistan	20,850	22,800	22,860
Ethiopia	60	50	70				
Ghana	920	1,180	1,140				
Kenya	400	440	370				
Libya	100	110	150				
Mauritius	300	280	220				
Morocco	170	270	390				

Source: HMSO—Annual Abstract of Statistics 1991

*British Dependent Territories Citizens.   † Includes refugees from south-east Asia.

Births and Marriages

Thousands

		Live births				Marriages			
	United Kingdom	England and Wales		Scotland	Northern Ireland	United Kingdom	England and Wales		Scotland	Northern Ireland
		Total	Wales				Total	Wales		
1984	729·6	636·8	35·9	65·1	27·7	395·8	349·2	19·2	36·3	10·4
1985	750·7	656·4	36·8	66·7	27·6	393·1	346·4	19·1	36·4	10·3
1986	755·0	661·0	37·0	65·8	28·2	393·9	347·9	19·5	35·8	10·2
1987	755·6	681·5	37·8	66·2	27·9	397·9	351·8	19·5	35·8	10·4
1988	787·6	693·6	38·8	66·2	27·8	—	348·5	19·3	—	10·0
1989	777·3	687·7	38·0	63·5	26·1	—	—	—	—	10·0
1990†	798·6	706·1	38·9	66·0	26·5	—	—	—	—	—
1990 1st quarter†	191·3	168·3	9·2	16·1	6·8	52·9	47·1	2·7	4·7	1·1
2nd quarter†	202·4	179·3	9·8	16·3	6·8	—	—	—	10·1	2·9
3rd quarter†	207·5	184·0	10·1	16·9	6·6	—	—	—	12·7	—
4th quarter†	197·4	174·5	9·7	16·5	6·3	—	—	—	7·0	—

† provisional.   *Source: HMSO—Monthly Digest of Statistics (July 1991)*

Divorce

	1983	1984	1985	1986	1987	1988	1989
England and Wales Decrees absolute, granted:							
Number	147,479	144,501	160,300	153,903	151,007	152,633	150,872
Rate per 1,000 married couples	*12·2*	*12·0*	*13·4*	*12·9*	*12·7*	*12·8*	*12·7†*
Scotland Decrees absolute, granted:							
Number	13,238	11,906	13,371	12,800	12,133	11,472	11,659
Rate per 1,000 married couples	*11·0*	*9·9*	*11·2*	*10·7*	*10·2*	*9·8*	*10·0*
Northern Ireland Petitions filed:							
Nullity of marriage	—	6	6	6	4	1	6
Divorce.	1,577	1,749	1,986	1,630	1,834	2,217	2,385
Judicial separation	9	5	15	17	7	6	16

† provisional.   *Source: HMSO—Annual Abstract of Statistics 1991*

Deaths Registered*

Thousands

		Total				Infants under one year			
	United Kingdom	England and Wales		Scotland	Northern Ireland	United Kingdom	England and Wales		Scotland	Northern Ireland
		Total	Wales				Total	Wales		
1984	644·9	566·9	33·7	62·3	15·7	7·00	6·04	0·31	0·67	0·29
1985	670·6	590·7	35·5	64·0	16·0	7·03	6·14	0·36	0·62	0·27
1986	660·7	581·2	34·7	63·5	16·1	7·18	6·31	0·35	0·58	0·29
1987	644·3	567·0	33·9	62·0	15·3	7·08	6·27	0·36	0·56	0·24
1988	649·2	571·4	34·0	62·0	15·8	7·06	6·27	0·29	0·54	0·25
1989	657·7†	576·9	35·1	65·0	15·8	6·55†	5·81	0·30	0·56	0·18
1990	641·8†	564·8	34·0	61·5	15·4	6·27†	5·56	0·27	0·51	0·20
1990 1st quarter†	177·8	156·3	9·4	16·9	4·5	1·77	1·57	0·08	0·15	0·06
2nd quarter†	154·3	135·7	8·1	15·1	3·5	1·54	1·35	0·07	0·14	0·05
3rd quarter†	143·4	126·3	7·6	13·7	3·4	1·43	1·27	0·06	0·10	0·05
4th quarter†	166·3	146·6	8·9	15·8	3·9	1·54	1·38	0·05	0·12	0·04

* Excluding stillbirths.   † provisional.   *Source: HMSO—Monthly Digest of Statistics (July 1991)*

Deaths Analysed By Cause, 1989

	England & Wales	Scotland	N. Ireland†
Total deaths	576,872	65,017	15,844
Deaths from natural causes	556,100	62,206	15,151
Infections and parasitic diseases	2,543	307	49
Intestinal infectious diseases	185	6	—
Tuberculosis of respiratory system	333	42	10
Other tuberculosis, including late effects	316	39	3
Whooping cough	1	—	—
Meningococcal infection	203	15	6
Measles	3	—	—
Malaria	4	—	3
Syphilis	17	2	—
Neoplasms	145,120	15,054	3,571
Malignant neoplasm of stomach	9,062	877	246
Malignant neoplasm of trachea, bronchus and lung	34,581	4,234	831
Malignant neoplasm of breast	14,084	1,363	305
Malignant neoplasm of uterus	3,271	331	75
Leukaemia	3,729	325	79
Benign and unspecified neoplasms	1,275	107	49
Endocrine, nutritional and metabolic diseases and immunity disorders	10,153	765	83
Diabetes mellitus	7,872	576	38
Nutritional deficiencies	120	10	9
Other metabolic and immunity disorders	1,497	137	29
Diseases of blood and blood-forming organs	2,424	174	32
Anaemias	1,214	75	18
Mental disorders	13,718	1,105	45
Diseases of nervous system and sense organs	11,456	887	178
Meningitis	246	33	10
Diseases of the circulatory system	264,600	31,223	7,422
Rheumatic heart disease	2,314	246	55
Hypertensive disease	3,526	273	63
Ischaemic heart disease	150,794	18,107	4,508
Diseases of pulmonary circulation and other forms of heart disease	21,298	2,468	665
Cerebrovascular disease	67,692	8,437	1,804
Diseases of the respiratory system	66,712	8,668	2,886
Influenza	2,114	457	43
Pneumonia	28,777	4,565	1,908
Bronchitis, emphysema	8,680	621	150
Asthma	1,957	174	60
Diseases of the digestive system	18,679	1,961	380
Ulcer of stomach and duodenum	4,399	388	89
Appendicitis	106	13	2
Hernia of abdominal cavity and other intestinal obstruction	1,989	166	39
Chronic liver disease and cirrhosis	3,023	427	70
Diseases of the genito-urinary system	7,772	834	243
Nephritis, nephrotic syndrome and nephrosis	4,465	544	159
Hyperplasia of prostate	501	19	6
Complications of pregnancy, childbirth, etc.	56	4	—
Abortion	6	—	—
Diseases of the skin and subcutaneous tissue	823	98	31
Diseases of the musculo-skeletal system	5,374	302	45
Congenital anomalies	1,766	226	92
Certain conditions originating in the perinatal period	240	229	55
Birth trauma, hypoxia, birth asphyxia and other respiratory conditions	85	123	18
Signs, symptoms and ill-defined conditions	4,664	369	39
Sudden infant death syndrome	1,190	143	5
Deaths from accidents and violence	17,500	2,811	693
All accidents	11,491	1,829	445
Motor vehicle accidents	4,880	561	183
Suicide and self-inflicted injury	3,717	527	117
All other external causes	2,292	455	131

† provisional.

Source: HMSO—Annual Abstract of Statistics 1991

ENGLISH KINGS AND QUEENS AD 827 TO 1603

Name	Dynasty	Married	Access.	Died	Age	Rgnd. Yrs.
	Saxons and Danes					
EGBERT	King of Wessex and all England		827	839	—	12
ETHELWULF	Son of Egbert		839	858	—	19
ETHELBALD	Son of Ethelwulf		858	860	—	2
ETHELBERT	Son of Ethelwulf		858	866	—	8
ETHELRED	Son of Ethelwulf		866	871	—	5
ALFRED THE GREAT	Son of Ethelwulf	Ealhswith of Gaini	871	899	52	28
EDWARD THE ELDER	Son of Alfred the Great	1st, Egwyn; 2nd, Elfled; 3rd, Eadgifu	899	925	55	26
ATHELSTAN	Eldest son of Edward the Elder by Egwyn		925	940	45	15
EDMUND	Third son of Edward the Elder by Eadgifu	1st, Elgifu; 2nd, Ethelfled	940	946	25	6
EDRED	Fourth son of Edward the Elder by Eadgifu		946	955	32	9
EDWY	Son of Edmund by Elgifu	1st, Ethelfled; 2nd, Elfthryth	955	959	18	3
EDGAR	Second son of Edmund by Elgifu		959	975	32	17
EDWARD THE MARTYR	Son of Edgar by Ethelfled		975	978	17	4
ETHELRED II	Younger son of Edgar by Elfthryth	1st, Elgifu; 2nd, Emma, dau. of Richard, Duke of Normandy.	978	1016	48	37
EDMUND IRONSIDE	Eldest son of Ethelred II by Elfgifu	1st, Elfgifu of Deira; 2nd, Emma, widow of Ethelred II.	1016	1016	27	0
CANUTE THE DANE	By conquest and election		1017	1035	40	18
HAROLD I	Son of Canute by Elfgifu		1035	1040	—	5
HARDICANUTE	Son of Canute by Emma	Edith, dau. of Earl of Godwin.	1040	1042	24	2
EDWARD THE CONFESSOR	Son of Ethelred II by Emma		1042	1066	62	24
HAROLD II	Son of Earl Godwin		1066	1066	44	0
	The House of Normandy					
WILLIAM I	Obtained the Crown by conquest	Matilda, dau. of Baldwin, Count of Flanders	1066	1087	60	21
WILLIAM II	Third son of William I	(Died unmarried)	1087	1100	43	13
HENRY I	Youngest son of William I	1st, Matilda, dau. of Malcolm Canmore, K. of Scotland; 2nd Adelicia, dau. of Godfrey, D. of Louvaine.	1100	1135	67	35
STEPHEN	Third son of Stephen, Count of Blois, by Adela, fourth dau. of William I.	Matilda, dau. of Eustace, Count of Boulogne.	1135	1154	50	19
	The House of Plantagenet					
HENRY II	Son of Geoffrey Plantagenet by Matilda, only dau. of Henry I; his grandmother, Matilda of Scotland, was a lineal descendant of Alfred and Egbert.	Eleanor, dau. of William, D. of Aquitaine, divorced Queen of Louis VII of France.	1154	1189	56	35
RICHARD I	Eldest surviving son of Henry II	Berengaria, dau. of Sancho VI, K. of Navarre.	1189	1199	42	10
JOHN	Sixth and youngest son of Henry II	1st Avisa, dau. of E. of Gloucester, divorced upon grounds of consanguinity; 2nd Isabella dau. of Aymer, Count of Angoulême.	1199	1216	50	17
HENRY III	Elder son of John	Eleanor, dau. of Raymond, Count of Provence.	1216	1272	65	56
EDWARD I	Eldest surviving son of Henry III	1st Eleanor, dau. of Ferdinand III, K. of Castile; 2nd Margaret, dau. of Philip III, the Hardy, K. of France.	1272	1307	68	35
EDWARD II	Eldest surviving son of Edward I	Isabella, dau. of Philip IV, the Fair, K. of France.	1307	1327	43	20

Name	Dynasty	Married	Access.	Died	Age	Rgnd.
EDWARD III	Eldest son of Edward II	Philippa, dau. of William, Count of Holland and Hainault.	1327	1377	65	Yrs. 50
RICHARD II	Son of the Black Prince, eldest son of Edward III (died 1400).	1st Anne, dau. of Emp. Charles IV; 2nd Isabel, dau. of Charles VI, K. of France.	1377	dep. 1399	34	22
The House of Lancaster						
HENRY IV	Son of John of Gaunt, 4th son of Edward III.	1st Mary de Bohun, dau. of the E. of Hereford; 2nd Joanna of Navarre, widow of John de Montfort, D. of Brittany.	1399	1413	47	13
HENRY V	Eldest surviving son of Henry IV	Katherine, dau. of Charles VI, K. of France	1413	1422	34	9
HENRY VI	Only son of Henry V (died 1471)	Margaret of Anjou, dau. of René, D. of Anjou.	1422	dep. 1461	49	39
The House of York						
EDWARD IV	Son of Richard, grandson of Edmund, fifth son of Edward III; and of Anne, great-grand-daughter of Lionel, third son of Edward III.	Elizabeth Widvile (or Woodville), dau. of Sir Richard Widvile and widow of Sir John Grey of Groby.	1461	1483	41	22
EDWARD V	Eldest son of Edward IV	(Died unmarried)	1483	1483	13	75 days
RICHARD III	Younger brother of Edward IV	Anne, dau. of the E. of Warwick, and widow of Edward, Prince of Wales, son of Henry VI.	1483	1485	32	2
The House of Tudor						
HENRY VII	Son of Edmund, eldest son of Owen Tudor, by Katherine, widow of Henry V; his mother, Margaret Beaufort, was great-grand-daughter of John of Gaunt.	Elizabeth, dau. of Edward IV	1485	1509	53	24
HENRY VIII	Only surviving son of Henry VII	1st Katherine of Aragon, widow of his elder brother Arthur, (divorced); 2nd Anne, dau. of Sir Thomas Boleyn, (beheaded); 3rd Jane, dau. of Sir John Seymour, (died in childbirth of a son, after Edward VI); 4th Anne, sister of William, D. of Cleves, (divorced); 5th Catherine Howard, niece of the Duke of Norfolk, (beheaded); 6th Catherine, dau. of Sir Thomas Parr and widow of Edward Nevill, Lord Latimer.	1509	1547	56	38
EDWARD VI	Son of Henry VIII by Jane Seymour	(Died unmarried)	1547	1553	16	6
JANE	Grand-daughter of Mary, younger sister of Henry VIII, (beheaded Feb. 12, 1554).	Lord Guildford Dudley	1553	1554	17	14 days
MARY I	Daughter of Henry VIII by Katherine of Aragon.	Philip II of Spain	1553	1558	43	5
ELIZABETH I	Daughter of Henry VIII by Anne Boleyn	(Died unmarried)	1558	1603	69	44

BRITISH KINGS AND QUEENS FROM 1603

Name	Dynasty	Married	Access.	Died	Age	Rgnd.
	The House of Stuart					Yrs.
JAMES I (VI of Scotland)	Son of Mary, Queen of Scots grand-daughter of James IV and Margaret, daughter of Henry VII.	Anne, dau. of Frederick II of Denmark	1603	1625	59	22
CHARLES I	Only surviving son of James I	Henrietta-Maria, dau. of Henry IV of France	1625	beh. 1649	48	24
	Commonwealth declared May 19, 1649					
	Oliver Cromwell, Lord Protector, 1653–8: Richard Cromwell, Lord Protector, 1658–9					
CHARLES II	Eldest son of Charles I (restored 1660)	Catharine, dau. of John IV, K. of Portugal, and sister of Alphonso VI.	1649	1685	55	36
JAMES II (VII of Scotland)	Second son of Charles I (died 1701) (Interregnum, Dec. 11, 1688–Feb. 13, 1689)	1st Lady Anne Hyde, dau. of Edward, E. of Clarendon, who died before James ascended the throne; 2nd Mary Beatrice Eleanor d'Este, dau. of Alphonso, D. of Modena.	1685	dep. 1688	68	3
WILLIAM III and	Son of William, Prince of Orange and grand- son of Charles I	{	1689	{ 1702 { 1694	51 33	13 6
MARY II	Eldest daughter of James II					
ANNE	Second daughter of James II	Prince George of Denmark	1702	1714	49	12
	The House of Hanover					
GEORGE I	Son of Elector of Hanover, by Sophia, daugh- ter of Elizabeth, daughter of James I.	Sophia, dau. of George William, D. of Celle.	1714	1727	67	13
GEORGE II	Only son of George I	Wilhelmina Caroline, dau. of John Frederick, Margrave of Brandenburg-Anspach.	1727	1760	77	33
GEORGE III	Grandson of George II	Charlotte Sophia, dau. of Charles Lewis Freder- ick, D. of Mecklenburg-Strelitz.	1760	1820	81	59
GEORGE IV	Eldest son of George III (Regent from Febru- ary 5, 1811).	Caroline, dau. of Charles William Ferdinand, D. of Brunswick-Wolfenbuttel.	1820	1830	67	10
WILLIAM IV	Third son of George III	Adelaide, dau. of George Frederick Charles, D. of Saxe-Meiningen.	1830	1837	71	7
VICTORIA	Daughter of Edward, 4th son of George III	Francis Albert Augustus Charles Emmanuel, D. of Saxony, Pr. of Saxe-Coburg and Gotha.	1837	1901	81	63
	The House of Saxe-Coburg					
EDWARD VII	Eldest son of Victoria	Alexandra, dau. of Christian IX, K. of Denmark.	1901	1910	68	9
	The House of Windsor					
GEORGE V	Surviving son of Edward VII	Victoria Mary, dau. of Francis, D. of Teck.	1910	1936	70	25
EDWARD VIII	Eldest son of George V (died 1972)	Mrs Wallis Warfield (after abdication)	1936	abd. 1936	77	325 days
GEORGE VI	Second son of George V	Lady Elizabeth Bowes-Lyon, dau. of 14th Earl of Strathmore and Kinghorne (HM QUEEN ELIZ- ABETH THE QUEEN MOTHER).	1936	1952	56	15
ELIZABETH II	Elder daughter of George VI	Philip, son of Prince Andrew of Greece (HRH THE DUKE OF EDINBURGH).	1952	WHOM GOD PRESERVE.		

KINGS AND QUEENS OF SCOTS 1057 to 1603

Name	Sovereign	Married	Access.	Died
MALCOLM III (CANMORE)	Son of Duncan I	1st Ingibiorg, widow of Thorfinn, Earl of Orkney; 2nd Margaret, sister of Edgar the Atheling.	1057	1093
DONALD BÁN	Brother of Malcolm Canmore		1093	—
DUNCAN II	Son of Malcolm Canmore, by Ingibiorg		1094	1094
DONALD BÁN	(Restored)		1094	1097
EDGAR	Son of Malcolm Canmore, by Margaret	(Died unmarried)	1097	1107
ALEXANDER I (THE FIERCE)	Son of Malcolm Canmore, by Margaret	Sybilla, natural dau. of Henry I of England	1107	1124
DAVID I (THE SAINT)	Son of Malcolm Canmore, by Margaret	Matilda, dau. of Waltheof, Earl of Northumbria, widow of Simon, Earl of Northampton.	1124	1153
MALCOLM IV (THE MAIDEN)	Son of Henry, eldest son of David I	(Died unmarried)	1153	1165
WILLIAM I (THE LION)	Brother of Malcolm the Maiden	Ermengarde, dau. of Richard, Viscount of Beaumont.	1165	1214
ALEXANDER II	Son of William the Lion	1st Joanna, dau. of King John; 2nd Mary, dau. of Ingelram de Coucy (Picardy).	1214	1249
ALEXANDER III	Son of Alexander II, by Mary	1st Margaret, dau. of Henry III of England; 2nd Joleta, dau. of the Count de Dreux.	1249	1286
MARGARET (THE MAID OF NORWAY)	Daughter of Eric II of Norway, granddaughter of Alexander III.	(Died unmarried).	1286	1290
JOHN BALIOL	Grandson of eldest daughter of David, Earl of Huntingdon, brother of William the Lion.		1292	1296
ROBERT I (BRUCE)	Great-grandson of 2nd daughter of David, Earl of Huntingdon, brother of William the Lion.	1st Isabella, dau. of Donald, Earl of Mar; 2nd Elizabeth de Burgh, sister of Earl of Ulster.	1306	1329
DAVID II	Son of Robert I, by Elizabeth.	1st Joanna, dau. of Edward II of England; 2nd Margaret, widow of Sir John Logie (divorced, 1369).	1329	1371
ROBERT II (STEWART)	Son of Marjorie, daughter of Robert I by first marriage, and Walter the Steward.	1st Elizabeth, dau. of Sir Robert Mure (or More) of Rowallan; 2nd Euphemia, dau. of Hugh, Earl of Ross, widow of John, Earl of Moray.	1371	1390
ROBERT III	Son of Robert II, by Elizabeth	Annabella, dau. of Sir John Drummond of Stobhall, niece of Margaret Logie.	1390	1406
JAMES I	Son of Robert III	Jane Beaufort, dau. of John, Earl of Somerset, 4th son of John of Gaunt and grandson of Edward III of England.	1406	1437
JAMES II	Son of James I	Mary, dau. of Arnold, Duke of Gueldres.	1437	1460
JAMES III	Eldest son of James II	Margaret, dau. of Christian I of Denmark, Norway and Sweden.	1460	1488
JAMES IV	Eldest son of James III	Margaret Tudor, dau. of Henry VII	1488	1513
JAMES V	Son of James IV	1st Madeleine, dau. of Francis I of France; 2nd Mary of Lorraine, dau. of Duc de Guise, widow of Duc de Longueville.	1513	1542
MARY	Daughter of James V, by Mary (died 1587)	1st Francis, Dauphin of France; 2nd Henry, Lord Darnley; 3rd James, Earl of Bothwell.	1542	abd. 1567
JAMES VI (Ascended the Throne of England 1603)	Son of Mary, by second marriage	Anne, dau. of Frederick II of Denmark	1567	1625

WELSH SOVEREIGNS AND PRINCES

Wales was ruled by Sovereign Princes from the earliest times until the death of Llywelyn in 1282. The first English Prince of Wales was the son of Edward I, and was born in Caernarvon town on April 25, 1284. According to a discredited legend, he was presented to the Welsh chieftains as their Prince, in fulfilment of a promise that they should have a Prince who 'could not speak a word of English' and should be native born. This son, who afterwards became Edward II, was created 'Prince of Wales and Earl of Chester' at the famous Lincoln Parliament on February 7, 1301. The title Prince of Wales is borne after individual conferment and is not inherited at birth, though some Princes have been declared and styled Prince of Wales but never formally so created (s.). The title was conferred on Prince Charles by HM The Queen on July 26, 1958. He was invested at Caernarvon on July 1, 1969.

Independent Princes, AD 844 to 1282	
Rhodri the Great	844–878
Anarawd, son of Rhodri	878–916
Hywel Dda, the Good	916–950
Iago ab Idwal (or Ieuaf)	950–979
Hywel ab Ieuaf, the Bad	979–985
Cadwallon, his brother	985–986
Maredudd ab Owain ap Hywel Dda	986–999
Cynan ap Hywel ab Ieuaf	999–1008
Llywelyn ap Seisyll	1018–1023
Iago ab Idwal ap Meurig	1023–1039
Gruffydd ap Llywelyn ap Seisyll	1039–1063
Bleddyn ap Cynfyn	1063–1075
Trahaern ap Caradog	1075–1081
Gruffydd ap Cynan ab Iago	1081–1137
Owain Gwynedd	1137–1170
Dafydd ab Owain Gwynedd	1170–1194
Llywelyn Fawr, the Great	1194–1240
Dafydd ap Llywelyn	1240–1246
Llywelyn ap Gruffydd ap Llywelyn	1246–1282

English Princes, since 1301	
Edward (Edward II), cr. Pr. of Wales	1301
Edward the Black Prince, s. of Edward III	1343
Richard (Richard II), s. of the Black Prince	1376
Henry of Monmouth (Henry V)	1399
Edward of Westminster, son of Henry VI	1454
Edward of Westminster (Edward V)	1471
Edward, son of Richard III (d. 1484)	1483
Arthur Tudor, son of Henry VII	1489
Henry Tudor (Henry VIII), s. of Henry VII	1504
Henry Stuart, son of James I (d. 1612)	1610
Charles Stuart (Charles I), s. of James I	1616
Charles (Charles II), son of Charles I   ... (s.) c. 1638
James Francis Edward (The Old Pretender) (d. 1766)   (s.) 1688
George Augustus (George II), s. of George I	1714
Frederick Lewis, s. of George II (d. 1751)	1729
George William Frederick (George III)	1751
George Augustus Frederick (George IV)	1762
Albert Edward (Edward VII)	1841
George (George V)	1901
Edward (Edward VIII)	1910
Charles Philip Arthur George	1958

THE FAMILY OF QUEEN VICTORIA

QUEEN VICTORIA (Alexandrina Victoria), *born* May 24, 1819; *succeeded* to the Throne June 20, 1837; *married* Feb. 10, 1840 (Francis) Albert Augustus Charles Emmanuel, Duke of Saxony, Prince of Saxe-Coburg and Gotha (*HRH Albert, Prince Consort, born* Aug. 26, 1819, *died* Dec. 14, 1861); *died* Jan. 22, 1901. Her Majesty had *issue*:—

1. HRH Princess Victoria Adelaide Mary Louisa (*Princess Royal*) (1840–1901), *m.* 1858, Frederic (1831–88), *Emperor of Germany* March–June 1888. *Issue*:—

(1) HIM Wilhelm II (1859–1941), *Emperor of Germany* 1888–1918, *m.*, 1st, 1881 Princess Augusta Victoria of Schleswig-Holstein-Sonderburg-Augustenburg (1858–1921); 2nd, 1922 Princess Hermine of Reuss (1887–1947). *Issue*:—

(a) Prince Wilhelm (1882–1951), (*Crown Prince* 1888–1918), *m.* 1905 Duchess Cecilie of Mecklenburg-Schwerin; *issue*:—Prince Wilhelm (1906–40); Prince Ludwig Ferdinand (*b.* 1907), *m.* 1938 Grand Duchess Kira (*see* p. 138); Prince Hubertus (1909–50); Prince Friedrich Georg (1911–66); Princess Alexandrine Irene (1915–); Princess Cecilie (1917–75).

(b) Prince Eitel-Friedrich (1883–1942), *m.* 1906 Duchess Sophie of Oldenburg (marriage dissolved 1926).

(c) Prince Adalbert (1884–1948), *m.* 1914 Duchess Adelheid of Saxe-Meiningen; *issue*:—Princess Victoria Marina (1917–81); Prince Wilhelm Victor (1919–89).

(d) Prince August Wilhelm (1887–1949), *m.* 1908 Princess Alexandra of Schleswig-Holstein-Sonderburg-Glücksburg (marriage dissolved 1920); *issue*:—Prince Alexander (1912–85).

(e) Prince Oskar (1888–1958), *m.* 1914 Countess von Ruppin; *issue*:—Prince Oskar (1915–39); Prince Burchard (1917–); Princess Herzeleide (1918–89); Prince Wilhelm (*b.* 1922.

(f) Prince Joachim (1890–1920), *m.* 1916 Princess Marie of Anhalt; *issue*:—Prince Karl (1916–75).

(g) Princess Viktoria Luise (1892–1980), *m.* 1913 Ernst, Duke of Brunswick 1913–18 (1887–1953); *issue*:—Prince Ernst (1914–87); Prince Georg (*b.* 1915), *m.* 1946 Princess Sophie of Greece (*see* p. 137) and has issue (two sons, one daughter); Princess Frederika (1917–81), *m.* 1938 Paul I, King of the Hellenes (*see* p. 137); Prince Christian (1919–81); Prince Welf Heinrich (*b.* 1923).

(2) Princess Charlotte (1860–1919), *m.* 1878 Bernhard, Duke of Saxe-Meiningen 1914 (1851–1914). *Issue*:—Princess Feodora (1879–1945), *m.* 1898 Prince Heinrich XXX of Reuss.

(3) Prince Heinrich (1862–1929), *m.* 1888 Princess Irene of Hesse (*see* p. 137). *Issue*:—

(a) Prince Waldemar (1889–1945), *m.* Princess Calixsta of Lippe.

(b) Prince Sigismund (1896–1978), *m.* Princess Charlotte of Saxe-Altenburg; *issue*:—Princess Barbe (*b.* 1920); Prince Alfred (*b.* 1924).

(4) Princess Victoria (1866–1929), *m.* 1st 1890, Prince Adolf of Schaumburg-Lippe (1859–1916); 2nd, 1927 Alexander Zubkov.

(5) Prince Joachim Waldemar (1868–79).

(6) Princess Sophie (1870–1932), *m.* 1889 Constantine I (1868–1923). *King of the Hellenes* 1913–17, 1920–23. *Issue*:—

(a) George II (1890–1947), *King of the Hellenes* 1923–24 and 1935–47, *m.* 1921 Princess Elisabeth of Roumania (marriage dissolved 1935), (*see* p. 137).

(b) Alexander I (1893–1920), *King of the Hellenes* 1917–20, *m.* 1919 Aspasia Manos; *issue*:—Princess Alexandra (*b.* 1921), *m.* 1944 King Petar II of Yugoslavia (*see* p. 137).

(c) Princess Helena (1896–1982), *m.* 1921 King Carol of Roumania (*see* below), (marriage dissolved 1928).

(d) Paul I (1901–64), *King of the Hellenes* 1947–64, *m.* 1938 Princess Frederika of Brunswick (*see* p. 136); *issue*:—King Constantine II (*b.* 1940), *m.* 1964 Princess Anne-Marie of Denmark (*see* p. 138), and has issue (three sons, two daughters); Princess Sophie (*b.* 1938), *m.* 1962 Juan Carlos I of Spain (*see* p. 138); Princess Irene (*b.* 1942).

(e) Princess Irene (1904–74), *m.* 1939 4th Duke of Aosta; *issue*:—Prince Amedeo (*b.* 1943).

(f) Princess Katherine (*Lady Katherine Brandram*) (*b.* 1913), *m.* 1947 Major R. C. A. Brandram, MC, TD; *issue*:—R. Paul G. A. Brandram (*b.* 1948).

(7) Princess Margarethe (1872–1954), *m.* 1893 Prince Friedrich Karl of Hesse (1868–1940). *Issue*:—

(a) Prince Friedrich Wilhelm (1893–1916).

(b) Prince Maximilian (1894–1914).

(c) Prince Philipp (1896–1980), *m.* 1925 Princess Mafalda of Italy; *issue*:—Prince Moritz (*b.* 1926); Prince Heinrich (*b.* 1927); Prince Otto (*b.* 1937); Princess Elisabeth (*b.* 1940).

(d) Prince Wolfgang (*b.* 1896), *m.*, 1st, 1924 Princess Marie Alexandra of Baden; 2nd, 1948 Ottilie Möller.

(e) Prince Richard (1901–).

(f) Prince Christoph (1901–43), *m.* 1930 Princess Sophie of Greece (*see* below) and has issue (two sons, three daughters).

2. HRH Prince Albert Edward (HM KING EDWARD VII), *b.* Nov. 9, 1841, *m.* 1863 HRH Princess Alexandra of Denmark (1844–1925), *succeeded* to the Throne Jan. 22, 1901, *d.* May 6, 1910. *Issue*:—

(1) Albert Victor, *Duke of Clarence and Avondale* (1864–92).

(2) George (HM KING GEORGE V) (*see* p. 138).

(3) Louise (1867–1931) *Princess Royal* 1905–31, *m.* 1889 1st Duke of Fife (1849–1912). *Issue*:—

(a) Princess Alexandra, Duchess of Fife (1891–1959), *m.* 1913 Prince Arthur of Connaught (*see* p. 138).

(b) Princess Maud (1893–1945), *m.* 1923 11th Earl of Southesk (*b.* 1893); *issue*:—The Duke of Fife (*b.* 1929).

(4) Victoria (1868–1935).

(5) Maud (1869–1938), *m.* 1896 Prince Charles of Denmark (1872–1957), later King Haakon VII of Norway 1905–57. *Issue*:—

(a) Olav V, *King of Norway* 1957–91 (1903–91), *m.* 1929 Princess Märtha of Sweden (1901–54); *issue*:—Princess Ragnhild (*b.* 1930); Princess Astrid (*b.* 1932); Harald V, **King of Norway** (*b.* 1937).

(6) Alexander (April 6–7, 1871).

3. HRH Princess Alice Maud Mary (1843–78), *m.* 1862 Prince Louis (1837–92), Grand Duke of Hesse 1877–92. *Issue*:—

(1) Victoria (1863–1950), *m.* 1884 *Admiral of the Fleet* Prince Louis of Battenberg (1854–1921), *cr.* 1st Marquess of Milford Haven 1917. *Issue*:—

(a) Alice (1885–1969), *m.* 1903 Prince Andrew of Greece (1882–1914); *issue*:—Princess Margarita (1905–81) *m.* 1931 Prince Gottfried of Hohenlohe-Langenburg (*see* p. 138); Princess Theodora (1906–69), *m.* Prince Berthold of Baden (1906–63) and has issue (2 sons, one daughter); Princess Cecilie (1911–37), *m.* George, Grand Duke of Hesse (*see* below); Princess Sophie (*b.* 1914), *m.*, 1st, 1930 Prince Christoph of Hesse (*see* above); 2nd, 1946 Prince Georg of Hanover (*see* p. 136); **Prince Philip, Duke of Edinburgh** (*b.* 1921), (*see* p. 140).

(b) Louise (1889–1965), *m.* 1923 Gustaf VI Adolf (1882–1973), *King of Sweden* 1950–73.

(c) George, 2nd Marquess of Milford Haven (1892–1938), *m.* 1916 Countess Nadejda, daughter of Grand Duke Michael of Russia; *issue*:—Lady Tatiana (1917–88); David Michael, 3rd Marquess (1919–70).

(d) Louis, 1st Earl Mountbatten of Burma (1900–79), *m.* 1922 Edwina Ashley, daughter of Lord Mount Temple; *issue*:—Patricia, Countess Mountbatten of Burma (*b.* 1924), Pamela (*b.* 1929).

(2) Elizabeth (1864–1918), *m.* 1884 Grand Duke Sergius of Russia (1857–1905).

(3) Irene (1866–1953), *m.* 1888 Prince Heinrich of Prussia (*see* p. 136).

(4) Ernst Ludwig (1868–1937), Grand Duke of Hesse 1892–1918, *m.*, 1st, 1894 Princess Victoria Melita of Saxe-Coburg (*see* below), (marriage dissolved 1901); 2nd, 1905 Princess Eleonore of Solms-Hohensolmslich. *Issue*:—

(a) George, Grand Duke of Hesse (1906–37), *m.* Princess Cecilie of Greece (*see* above), and had issue, 2 sons, accidentally killed with parents 1937.

(b) Ludwig, Grand Duke of Hesse (1908–68), *m.* 1937 Margaret, daughter of 1st Lord Geddes.

(5) Frederick William (1870–73).

(6) Alix (*Tsaritsa of Russia*) (1872–1918), *m.* 1894 Nicholas II (1868–1918) *Tsar of All the Russias* 1894–1917, assassinated July 16, 1918. *Issue*:—

(a) Grand Duchess Olga (1895–1918).

(b) Grand Duchess Tatiana (1897–1918).

(c) Grand Duchess Marie (1899–1918).

(d) Grand Duchess Anastasia (1901–18).

(e) Alexis, Tsarevitch of Russia (1904–18).

(7) Marie (1874–78).

4. HRH Prince Alfred Ernest Albert, *Duke of Edinburgh, Admiral of the Fleet* (1844–1900), *m.* 1874 Grand Duchess Marie Alexandrovna of Russia (1853–1920); succeeded as *Duke of Saxe-Coburg and Gotha* Aug. 22, 1893. *Issue*:—

(1) Alfred (*Prince of Saxe-Coburg*) (1874–99).

(2) Marie (1875–1938), *m.* 1893 Ferdinand (1865–1927), *King of Roumania* 1914–27. *Issue*:—

(a) Carol II (1893–1953), *King of Roumania* 1930–40, *m.*, 2nd, Princess Helena of Greece (*see* above), (marriage dissolved 1928); *issue*:— Michael (*b.* 1921), *King of Roumania* 1927–30, 1940–47, *m.* 1948 Princess Anne of Bourbon Palma, and has issue (five daughters).

(b) Elisabeth (1894–1956), *m.* 1921 George II (1890–1947) *King of the Hellenes* (*see* p. 136).

(c) Marie (1900–61), *m.* 1922 Alexander (1888–1934), *King of Yugoslavia* 1921–34; *issue*:—Petar II (1923–70), *King of Yugoslavia* 1934–45, *m.* 1944 Princess Alexandra of Greece (*see* p. 136) and has issue (one son); Prince Tomislav (*b.* 1928), *m.*, 1st, 1957 Princess Margarita of Baden (daughter of Princess Theodora of Greece and Prince Berthold of Baden, *see* above); 2nd, 1982 Linda Bonney; and has issue (three sons, one daughter); Prince Andrej (1929–90), *m.*, 1st, Princess Christina of Hesse (daughter of Prince Christoph of Hesse and Princess Sophie of Greece, *see* above); 2nd, 1963 Princess Kira-Melita of Leiningen (*see* below); and has issue (three sons, one daughter).

(d) Prince Nicolas (1903–).

(e) Princess Ileana (1909–91), *m.*, 1st, 1931 Archduke Anton of Austria; 2nd, 1954 Dr Stefan Issarescu; *issue*:—Archduke Stefan (*b.* 1932); Archduchess Maria Ileana (1933–59); Archduchess Alexandra (*b.* 1935); Archduke Dominic (*b.* 1937); Archduchess Maria Magdalena (*b.* 1939); Archduchess Elisabeth (*b.* 1942).

(f) Prince Mircea (1913–16).

(3) Victoria Melita (1876–1936), *m.*, 1st, 1894 Grand Duke Ernst of Hesse (*see* above), (marriage dissolved 1901); 2nd, 1905 the Grand Duke Kirill of Russia (1876–1938). *Issue*:—

(a) Marie Kirillovna (1907–51), *m.* 1925 Prince Friedrich Karl of Leiningen; *issue*:—Prince Emich

(b. 1926); Prince Karl (b. 1928); Princess Kira-Melita (b. 1930), m. Prince Andrej of Yugoslavia (see p. 137); Princess Margarita (b. 1932); Princess Mechtilde (b. 1936); Prince Friedrich (b. 1938).

(b) Kira Kirillovna (1909–67), m. 1938 Prince Ludwig of Prussia (see p. 136); issue:—Prince Friedrich Wilhelm (b. 1939); Prince Michael (b. 1940); Princess Marie (b. 1942); Princess Kira (b. 1943); Prince Louis Ferdinand (1944–77); Prince Christian (b. 1946); Princess Xenia (b. 1949).

(c) Vladimir Kirillovitch (b. 1917), m., 1948, Princess Leonida Bagration-Mukhransky; issue:—Grand Duchess Maria (b. 1953).

(4) Alexandra (1878–1942), m. 1896 Ernst, Prince of Hohenlohe Langenburg. Issue:—

(a) Gottfried (1897–1960), m. 1931 Princess Margarita of Greece (see p. 137); issue:—Prince Kraft (b. 1935), Princess Beatrix (b. 1936), Prince George (b. 1938), Prince Ruprecht and Prince Albrecht (b. 1944).

(b) Maria (1899–1967), m. 1916 Prince Frederick of Schleswig-Holstein-Sonderburg-Glücksburg; issue:—Prince Peter (1922–80); Princess Marie (b. 1927).

(c) Princess Alexandra (1901–63).

(d) Princess Irma (1902–).

(5) Princess Beatrice (1884–1966), m. 1909 Alfonso of Orleans, Infante of Spain. Issue:—

(a) Prince Alvaro (b. 1910), m. 1937 Carla Parodi-Delfino; issue:—Princess Gerarda (b. 1939); Prince Alonso (1941–75); Princess Beatriz (b. 1943); Prince Alvaro (b. 1947).

(b) Prince Alonso (1912–36).

(c) Prince Ataulfo (1913–).

5. HRH Princess Helena Augusta Victoria (1846–1923), m. 1866 Prince Christian of Schleswig-Holstein-Sonderburg-Augustenburg (1831–1917). Issue:—

(1) Prince Christian Victor (1867–1900).

(2) Prince Albert (1869–1931), Duke of Schleswig-Holstein 1921–31.

(3) Princess Helena (1870–1948).

(4) Princess Marie Louise (1872–1956), m. 1891 Prince Aribert of Anhalt (marriage dissolved 1900).

(5) Prince Harold (May 12–20, 1876).

6. HRH Princess Louise Caroline Alberta (1848–1939), m. 1871 the Marquess of Lorne, afterwards 9th Duke of Argyll (1845–1914); without issue.

7. HRH Prince Arthur William Patrick Albert, Duke of Connaught, Field Marshal (1850–1942), m. 1879 Princess Louisa of Prussia (1860–1917). Issue:—

(1) Margaret (1882–1920), m. 1905 Crown Prince Gustaf Adolf (1882–1973), afterwards King of Sweden 1950–73. Issue:—

(a) Gustaf Adolf, Duke of Västerbotten (1906–47), m. 1932 Princess Sibylla of Saxe-Coburg-Gotha (see below); issue:—Princess Margaretha (b. 1934); Princess Birgitta (b. 1937); Princess Désirée (b. 1938); Princess Christina (b. 1943); Carl XVI Gustaf, **King of Sweden** (b. 1946).

(b) Count Sigvard Bernadotte (b. 1907); m., issue:—Count Michael (b. 1944).

(c) Princess Ingrid (Queen Mother of Denmark) (b. 1910), m. 1935 Frederick IX (1899–72), King of Denmark 1947–72; issue:—Margrethe II, **Queen of Denmark** (b. 1940); Princess Benedikte (b. 1944); Princess Anne-Marie (b. 1946), m. 1964 Constantine II of Greece (see p. 137).

(d) Prince Bertil, Duke of Halland (b. 1912), m. 1976 Mrs Lilian Craig.

(e) Count Carl Bernadotte (b. 1916), m., 1st, 1946 Mrs Kerstin Johnson; 2nd, 1988 Countess Gunnila Busler.

(2) Arthur (1883–1938), m. 1913 HH the Duchess of Fife (see p. 137). Issue:—

Alastair Arthur, Duke of Connaught (1914–43).

(3) (Victoria) Patricia (1886–1974), m. 1919 Adm. Hon. Sir Alexander Ramsay. Issue:—Hon. Alexander Ramsay of Mar (b. 1919), m. 1956 Hon. Flora Fraser, (Lady Saltoun).

8. HRH Prince Leopold George Duncan Albert, Duke of Albany (1853–84), m. 1882 Princess Helena of Waldeck (1861–1922). Issue:—

(1) Alice (1883–1981), m. 1904 Prince Alexander of Teck (1874–1957), cr. 1st Earl of Athlone 1917. Issue:—

(a) Lady May (b. 1906), m. 1931 Sir Henry Abel-Smith, KCMG, KCVO, DSO; issue:—Anne (b. 1932); Richard (b. 1933); Elizabeth (b. 1936).

(b) Rupert, Viscount Trematon (1907–28).

(2) Charles Edward (1884–1954), Duke of Albany 1884 until title suspended 1917, Duke of Saxe-Coburg-Gotha 1900–18, m. 1905 Princess Victoria Adelheid of Schleswig-Holstein-Sonderburg-Glücksburg. Issue:—

(a) Prince Johann (1906–72), and has issue.

(b) Princess Sibylla (1908–72) m. 1932 Prince Gustav Adolf of Sweden (see above).

(c) Prince Dietmar (1909–).

(d) Princess Caroline (1912–83).

(e) Prince Friedrich (b. 1918).

9. HRH Princess Beatrice Mary Victoria Feodore (1857–1944), m. 1885 Prince Henry of Battenberg (1858–96). Issue:—

(1) Alexander, 1st Marquess of Carisbrooke (1886–1960), m. 1917 Lady Irene Denison. Issue:—Lady Iris Mountbatten (1920–82).

(2) Victoria Eugénie (1887–1969), m. 1906 Alfonso XIII (1886–1941) King of Spain 1886–1931. Issue:—

(a) Prince Alfonso (1907–38).

(b) Prince Jaime (1908–75).

(c) Princess Beatrice (b. 1909.

(d) Princess Maria (b. 1911).

(e) Prince Juan (b. 1913) Count of Barcelona, and has issue:— Princess Maria (b. 1936); Juan Carlos I, **King of Spain** (b. 1938) m. 1962 Princess Sophie of Greece (see p. 137) and has issue (1 son, 2 daughters); Princess Margarita (b. 1939).

(f) Prince Gonzale (1914–34).

(3) Major Lord Leopold Mountbatten (1889–1922).

(4) Maurice (1891–1914), died of wounds received in action.

THE HOUSE OF WINDSOR

King George V assumed by royal proclamation (June 17, 1917) for his House and family, as well as for all descendants in the male line of Queen Victoria who are subjects of these realms, the name of **Windsor**.

KING GEORGE V (George Frederick Ernest Albert), second son of King Edward VII, born June 3, 1865; married July 6, 1893, HSH Princess Victoria Mary Augusta Louise Olga Pauline Claudine Agnes of Teck (**Queen Mary**, born May 26, 1867; died March 24, 1953); succeeded to the Throne May 6, 1910; died Jan. 20, 1936. Issue:—

1. HRH Prince Edward Albert Christian George Andrew Patrick David, born June 23, 1894, succeeded to the Throne as **King Edward VIII**, Jan. 20, 1936; abdicated Dec. 11, 1936; created Duke of Windsor, 1936; married June 3, 1937, Mrs. Wallis Warfield (Her Grace The Duchess of Windsor, born June 19, 1896; died April 24, 1986), died May 28, 1972.

2. HRH Prince Albert Frederick Arthur George, *born* Dec. 14, 1895; *married* April 26, 1923, Lady Elizabeth Bowes-Lyon, daughter of the 14th Earl of Strathmore and Kinghorne, **(HM Queen Elizabeth the Queen Mother)**, *succeeded* to the Throne as **King George VI**, Dec. 11, 1936; *died* Feb. 6, 1952, having had issue *(see* pp. 140 and 141).

3. HRH Princess (Victoria Alexandra Alice) **Mary** *(Princess Royal)*, *born* April 25, 1897, *married* Feb. 28, 1922, Viscount Lascelles, later the 6th Earl of Harewood *(born* Sept. 9, 1882; *died* May 24, 1947), *died* March 28, 1965. *Issue:*—

   (1) George Henry Hubert Lascelles, **7th Earl of Harewood**, KBE, *born* Feb. 7, 1923; *married* 1st, Sept. 29, 1949, Maria (Marion) Stein (marriage dissolved 1967); *issue,* (*a*) David Henry George, Viscount Lascelles, *born* Oct. 21, 1950; (*b*) James Edward, *born* Oct. 5, 1953; (*c*) (Robert) Jeremy Hugh, *born* Feb. 14, 1955; 2nd, July 31, 1967, Mrs Patricia Tuckwell; *issue,* (*d*) Mark Hubert, *born* July 5, 1964.

   (2) Gerald David Lascelles, *born* Aug. 21, 1924, *married* 1st, July 15, 1952, Miss Angela Dowding (marriage dissolved 1978); *issue,* (*a*) Henry Ulick, *born* May 19, 1953; 2nd, Nov. 17, 1978, Mrs Elizabeth Colvin; *issue,* (*b*) Martin David, born Feb. 9, 1962.

4. HRH Prince Henry William Frederick Albert, Duke of Gloucester, Earl of Ulster and Baron Culloden, *born* March 31, 1900, *married* Nov. 6, 1935, Lady Alice Christabel Montagu-Douglas-Scott, daughter of the 7th Duke of Buccleuch **(HRH Princess Alice, Duchess of Gloucester)**, GCB, CI, GCVO, GBE, Grand Cordon of Al Kamal, Air Chief Marshal, Colonel-in-Chief of The Royal Hussars (Prince of Wales's Own), The King's Own Scottish Borderers, Royal Corps of Transport, Royal Australian Corps of Transport, Royal New Zealand Corps of Transport, Deputy Colonel-in-Chief, The Royal Anglian Regiment, Air Chief Commandant Women's Royal Air Force, *born* Dec. 25, 1901); *died* June 10, 1974. *Issue:*

   (1) HRH Prince **William** Henry Andrew Frederick, *born* Dec. 18, 1941; *accidentally killed* Aug. 28, 1972.

   (2) HRH Prince Richard Alexander Walter George **(HRH The Duke of Gloucester)**, GCVO, Colonel-in-Chief, The Gloucestershire Regiment, Royal Pioneer Corps, Honorary Colonel Royal Monmouthshire Royal Engineers (Militia), Grand Prior of the Order of St John of Jerusalem. *Born* Aug. 26, 1944, *married* July 8, 1972, Birgitte Eva van Deurs **(HRH The Duchess of Gloucester,** GCVO), *born* June 20, 1946, Colonel-in-Chief, Royal Irish Rangers (27th (Inniskilling) 83rd and 87th), Royal Army Educational Corps, Royal Australian Army Educational Corps, Royal New Zealand Educational Corps; and has *issue:*—

   (*a*) Alexander Patrick Gregers Richard, Earl of Ulster, *born* Oct. 24, 1974;

   (*b*) Davina Elizabeth Alice Benedikte (Lady Davina Windsor), *born* Nov. 19, 1977;

   (*c*) Rose Victoria Birgitte Louise (Lady Rose Windsor), *born* March 1, 1980.

   Residences.—Kensington Palace, W8 4PU (Tel: 071–937 6374); Barnwell Manor, Peterborough, Northants PE8 5PJ.

5. HRH Prince George Edward Alexander Edmund, Duke of Kent, Earl of St Andrews and Baron Downpatrick, *born* Dec. 20, 1902, *married* Nov. 29, 1934, HRH Princess Marina of Greece and Denmark *(born* Nov. 30, 1906, OS, 1906; *died* Aug. 27, 1968); *killed on active service,* Aug. 25, 1942. *Issue:*—

   (1) HRH Prince Edward George Nicholas Paul Patrick **(HRH The Duke of Kent)**, KG, GCMG, GCVO, Personal ADC to the Queen, Major General, Hon. Air Vice-Marshal, Colonel-in-Chief The Royal Regiment of Fusiliers, The Devonshire and Dorset Regiment, The Lorne Scots Regiment (Peel, Dufferin and Hamilton Regiment), Colonel Scots Guards. *Born* Oct. 9, 1935, *married* June 8, 1961, Katharine Lucy Mary Worsley, daughter of Sir William Worsley, Bt. **(HRH The Duchess of Kent)**, GCVO, *born* Feb. 22, 1933, Hon. Major General, Colonel-in-Chief 4th/7th Royal Dragoon Guards, The Prince of Wales's Own Regiment of Yorkshire, Army Catering Corps, Controller Commandant Women's Royal Army Corps, Hon. Colonel The Yorkshire Volunteers; and has *issue:*—

   (*a*) George Philip Nicholas, Earl of St Andrews, *born* June 26, 1962, *married* Jan. 9, 1988, Sylvana Tomaselli, and has *issue,* Edward Edmund Maximilian George, Lord Downpatrick, *born* Dec. 2, 1988;

   (*b*) Helen Marina Lucy (Lady Helen Windsor), *born* April 28, 1964;

   (*c*) Nicholas Charles Edward Jonathan (Lord Nicholas Windsor), *born* July 25, 1970.

   Residences—York House, St James's Palace, SW1A 1BQ (Tel: 071–930 4872); Crocker End House, Nettlebed, Oxon.

   (2) HRH Princess Alexandra Helen Elizabeth Olga Christabel **(HRH Princess Alexandra, the Hon. Lady Ogilvy)**, GCVO, Patron Queen Alexandra's Royal Naval Nursing Service, Colonel-in-Chief, 17th/21st Lancers, The King's Own Royal Border Regiment, The Queen's Own Rifles of Canada, The Canadian Scottish Regiment (Princess Mary's), Deputy Colonel-in-Chief The Light Infantry, Deputy Hon. Colonel The Royal Yeomanry, Patron and Air Chief Commandant Princess Mary's Royal Air Force Nursing Service. *Born* Dec. 25, 1936, *married* April 24, 1963, The Hon. Sir Angus Ogilvy, KCVO, 2nd son of the 12th Earl of Airlie *(born* Sept. 14, 1928); and has *issue:*—

   (*a*) James Robert Bruce, *born* Feb. 29, 1964, *married* July 30, 1988, Miss Julia Rawlinson;

   (*b*) Marina Victoria Alexandra, *born* July 31, 1966, *married* Feb. 2, 1990, Mr Paul Mowatt and has *issue,* Zenouska, *born* May 25, 1990.

   Residence—Thatched House Lodge, Richmond Park, Surrey. *Office*—22 Friary Court, St James's Palace, SW1A 1BJ (Tel: 071–930 1860).

   (3) HRH Prince Michael George Charles Franklin **(HRH Prince Michael of Kent)**, Major (retd) The Royal Hussars (Prince of Wales's Own), Hon. Auxiliary Commodore Royal Naval Auxiliary Service. *Born* July 4, 1942, *married* June 30, 1978, Baroness Marie-Christine Agnes Hedwig Ida von Reibnitz **(HRH Princess Michael of Kent)**, *born* Jan. 15, 1945; and has *issue:*—

   (*a*) Frederick Michael George David Louis (Lord Frederick Windsor), *born* April 6, 1979;

   (*b*) Gabriella Marina Alexandra Ophelia (Lady Gabriella Windsor), *born* April 23, 1981.

   Residences.—Kensington Palace, W8 4PU (Tel: 071–938 3519); Nether Lypiatt Manor, Stroud, Glos.

6. HRH Prince John Charles Francis, *born* July 12, 1905; *died* Jan. 18, 1919.

THE SOVEREIGN

Her Most Excellent Majesty **ELIZABETH THE SECOND** (Elizabeth Alexandra Mary of Windsor) by the Grace of God, of the United Kingdom of Great Britain and Northern Ireland and of Her other Realms and Territories Queen, Head of the Commonwealth, Defender of the Faith, Sovereign of the British Orders of Knighthood and Sovereign Head of the Order of St John, Lord High Admiral of the United Kingdom, Colonel-in-Chief of The Life Guards, The Blues and Royals (Royal Horse Guards and 1st Dragoons), The Royal Scots Dragoon Guards (Carabiniers and Greys), 16th/5th The Queen's Royal Lancers, Royal Tank Regiment, Corps of Royal Engineers, Grenadier Guards, Coldstream Guards, Scots Guards, Irish Guards, Welsh Guards, The Royal Welch Fusiliers, The Queen's Lancashire Regiment, The Argyll and Sutherland Highlanders (Princess Louise's), The Royal Green Jackets, Royal Army Ordnance Corps, Corps of Royal Military Police, The Queen's Own Mercian Yeomanry, The Duke of Lancaster's Own Yeomanry, The Governor General's Horse Guards, The King's Own Calgary Regiment, Canadian Forces Military Engineers Branch, Royal 22e Regiment, Governor-General's Foot Guards, The Canadian Grenadier Guards, Le Régiment de la Chaudière, 2nd Bn. Royal New Brunswick Regiment (North Shore), The 48th Highlanders of Canada, The Argyll and Sutherland Highlanders of Canada (Princess Louise's), The Calgary Highlanders, Royal Australian Engineers, Royal Australian Infantry Corps, Royal Australian Army Ordnance Corps, Royal Australian Army Nursing Corps, The Corps of Royal New Zealand Engineers, Royal New Zealand Infantry Regiment, Royal New Zealand Army Ordnance Corps, Royal Malta Artillery, The Malawi Rifles, Captain-General of Royal Regiment of Artillery, The Honourable Artillery Company, Combined Cadet Force, Royal Regiment of Canadian Artillery, Royal Regiment of Australian Artillery, Royal Regiment of New Zealand Artillery, Royal New Zealand Armoured Corps, Air Commodore-in-Chief, Royal Auxiliary Air Force, Royal Air Force Regiment, Royal Observer Corps, Air Reserve (of Canada), Royal Australian Air Force Reserve, Territorial Air Force (New Zealand), Commandant-in-Chief Royal Air Force College, Cranwell, Hon. Air Commodore, RAF Marham, Hon. Commissioner, Royal Canadian Mounted Police, Master of the Merchant Navy and Fishing Fleets, Head of the Civil Defence Corps.

Elder daughter of HM King George VI and of HM Queen Elizabeth the Queen Mother; *born* at 17 Bruton Street, London, W1, April 21, 1926, *succeeded* to the Throne February 6, 1952, *crowned* June 2, 1953; having *married*, November 20, 1947, in Westminster Abbey, Philip, Duke of Edinburgh, Earl of Merioneth and Baron Greenwich (**HRH The Prince Philip, Duke of Edinburgh**), KG, KT, OM, GBE, AC, QSO, PC, *born* June 10, 1921, Admiral of the Fleet, Field Marshal, Marshal of the Royal Air Force, Admiral of the Fleet Royal Australian Navy, Field Marshal Australian Military Forces, Marshal of the Royal Australian Air Force, Admiral of the Fleet Royal New Zealand Navy, Field Marshal New Zealand Army, Marshal of the Royal New Zealand Air Force, Captain General Royal Marines, Admiral Sea Cadet Corps, Royal Canadian Sea Cadets, Colonel-in-Chief The Queen's Royal Irish Hussars, The Duke of Edinburgh's Royal Regiment (Berkshire and Wiltshire), The Queen's Own Highlanders (Seaforth and Camerons), Corps of Royal Electrical and Mechanical Engineers, Intelligence Corps, Army Cadet Force, The Royal Canadian Regiment, The Royal Hamilton Light Infantry (Wentworth Regiment), The Cameron Highlanders of Ottawa, The Queen's Own Cameron Highlanders of Canada, The Seaforth Highlanders of Canada, The Royal Canadian Army Cadets, The Royal Australian Electrical and Mechanical Engineers, The Australian Cadet Corps, Corps of Royal New Zealand Electrical and Mechanical Engineers, Colonel Grenadier Guards, Hon. Colonel Edinburgh and Heriot-Watt Universities Officers' Training Corps, The Trinidad and Tobago Regiment, Air Commodore-in-Chief Air Training Corps, Royal Canadian Air Cadets, Hon. Air Commodore RAF Kinloss, Master of the Corporation of Trinity House, Ranger of Windsor Park, Hon. Colonel Leicester and Derbyshire Yeomanry PAQ Sqn. *See* p. 137.

Official Residences.—Buckingham Palace, SW1A 1AA (Tel: 071–930 4832); Windsor Castle, Berks.; Palace of Holyroodhouse, Edinburgh. *Private Residences.*—Sandringham, Norfolk; Balmoral Castle, Aberdeenshire.

CHILDREN OF THE QUEEN

HRH THE PRINCE OF WALES (CHARLES Philip Arthur George), KG, KT, GCB, AK, QSO, PC, ADC, Prince of Wales and Earl of Chester, Duke of Cornwall and Duke of Rothesay, Earl of Carrick and Baron Renfrew, Lord of the Isles and Great Steward of Scotland, Personal ADC to the Queen, Great Master of the Order of the Bath, Captain Royal Navy, Group Captain Royal Air Force, Colonel-in-Chief 5th Royal Inniskilling Dragoon Guards, The Cheshire Regiment, The Royal Regiment of Wales (24th/41st Foot), The Gordon Highlanders, The Parachute Regiment, 2nd King Edward VII's Own Gurkha Rifles (The Sirmoor Rifles), The Royal Canadian Dragoons, Lord Strathcona's Horse (Royal Canadians), Royal Regiment of Canada, Royal Winnipeg Rifles, Royal Australian Armoured Corps, The Royal Pacific Islands Regiment, Colonel Welsh Guards, Air Commodore-in-Chief Royal New Zealand Air Force, Hon. Air Commodore RAF Brawdy.

Born November 14, 1948, *married* July 29, 1981, Lady Diana Frances Spencer, youngest daughter of the 8th Earl Spencer and the Hon. Mrs Shand Kydd (**HRH The Princess of Wales**), *born* July 1, 1961, Colonel-in-Chief 13th/18th Royal Hussars (Queen Mary's Own), The Royal Hampshire Regiment, The Princess of Wales's Own Regiment (of Canada), Hon. Air Commodore RAF Wittering; and has *issue*, (*a*) William Arthur Philip Louis (**HRH Prince William of Wales**), *born* June 21, 1982; and (*b*) Henry Charles Albert David (**HRH Prince Henry of Wales**), *born* Sept. 15, 1984.

Residences.—Highgrove, Doughton, Tetbury, Glos.; Kensington Palace, W8. *Office.*—St James's Palace, SW1A 1BS (Tel: 071–930 4832).

HRH THE PRINCESS ROYAL (ANNE Elizabeth Alice Louise), GCVO, FRS, Chief Commandant Women's Royal Naval Service, Colonel-in-Chief 14th/20th King's Hussars, Royal Corps of Signals, The Royal Scots (The Royal Regiment), The Worcestershire and Sherwood Foresters Regiment (29th/45th Foot), 8th Canadian Hussars (Princess Louise's), Canadian Forces Communications and Electronics Branch, Grey and Simcoe Foresters Militia, The Royal Regina Rifle Regiment, Royal Newfoundland Regiment, Royal Australian Corps of Signals, Royal New Zealand Corps of Signals, Royal New Zealand Nursing Corps, Hon. Colonel London University Officers' Training Corps, Hon. Air Commodore RAF Lyneham, Commandant-in-Chief (Ambulance and Nursing Cadets) St John Ambulance, Commandant-in-Chief, Women's Transport Service (FANY).

Born August 15, 1950, *married* Nov. 14, 1973, Capt. Mark Anthony Peter Phillips, cvo (*born* Sept. 22, 1948), Personal ADC to the Queen, *separated* August 1989; and has *issue*, (*a*) Peter Mark Andrew, *born* Nov. 15, 1977; and (*b*) Zara Anne Elizabeth, *born* May 15, 1981.

Residence.—Gatcombe Park, Minchinhampton, Stroud, Glos. *Office.*—Buckingham Palace, SW1A 1AA. (Tel: 071–930 4832).

HRH THE DUKE OF YORK (ANDREW Albert Christian Edward), Duke of York, Earl of Inverness and Baron Killyleagh, cvo, Personal ADC to the Queen, Lieutenant Royal Navy, Hon. Commander Sea Cadet Corps, Colonel-in-Chief The Staffordshire Regiment (The Prince of Wales's). *Born* Feb. 19, 1960, *married* July 23, 1986, Miss Sarah Margaret Ferguson, younger daughter of Major Ronald Ferguson and Mrs Hector Barrantes (**HRH The Duchess of York**, *born* October 15, 1959); and has *issue*, (*a*) Beatrice Elizabeth Mary (**HRH Princess Beatrice of York**), *born* Aug. 8, 1988; and (*b*) Eugenie Victoria Helena (**HRH Princess Eugenie of York**), *born* March 23, 1990.

Residences.—Sunninghill Park, Ascot, Berks.; Buckingham Palace, SW1. *Office.*—Buckingham Palace, SW1A 1AA. (Tel: 071–930 4832).

HRH THE PRINCE EDWARD Antony Richard Louis, cvo, *born* March 10, 1964.
Residence and Office.—Buckingham Palace, SW1A 1AA. (Tel: 071–930 4832).

MOTHER OF THE QUEEN

HM QUEEN ELIZABETH THE QUEEN MOTHER (Elizabeth Angela Marguerite) (daughter of the 14th Earl of Strathmore and Kinghorne), Lady of the Garter, Lady of the Thistle, CI, GMVO, GBE, Dame Grand Cross of the Order of St John, Royal Victorian Chain, Colonel-in-Chief 1st The Queen's Dragoon Guards, The Queen's Own Hussars, 9th/12th Royal Lancers (Prince of Wales's), The King's Regiment, The Royal Anglian Regiment, The Light Infantry, The Black Watch (Royal Highland Regiment), Royal Army Medical Corps, The Black Watch (Royal Highland Regiment) of Canada, The Toronto Scottish Regiment, Canadian Forces Medical Services, Royal Australian Army Medical Corps, Royal New Zealand Army Medical Corps, Hon. Colonel The Royal Yeomanry, The London Scottish, Inns of Court and City Yeomanry, Commandant-in-Chief Women's Royal Naval Service, Women's Royal Army Corps, Women's Royal Air Force, RAF Central Flying School, Patron St Andrew's Ambulance Association, Commandant-in-Chief Nursing Corps and Divisions, Commandant-in-Chief (Nursing) St John Ambulance, Lord Warden and Admiral of the Cinque Ports and Constable of Dover Castle. *Born* August 4, 1900, *married* April 26, 1923, Prince Albert Frederick Arthur George of Windsor, Duke of York, afterwards King George VI (*see* page 139).

Residences.—Clarence House, St James's Palace, SW1A 1BA (Tel: 071–930 3141); Royal Lodge, Windsor Great Park, Berks.; Castle of Mey, Caithness, Scotland.

SISTER OF THE QUEEN

HRH THE PRINCESS MARGARET, COUNTESS OF SNOWDON (Margaret Rose), CI, GCVO, Royal Victorian Chain, Colonel-in-Chief 15th/19th The King's Royal Hussars, The Royal Highland Fusiliers (Princess Margaret's Own Glasgow and Ayrshire Regiment), Queen Alexandra's Royal Army Nursing Corps, The Highland Fusiliers of Canada, The Princess Louise Fusiliers, The Bermuda Regiment, Deputy Colonel-in-Chief The Royal Anglian Regiment, Hon. Air Commodore RAF Coningsby, Grand President, St John Ambulance Association and Brigade, Dame Grand Cross of the Order of St John of Jerusalem, President of the Girl Guides Association.

Born Aug. 21, 1930, *married* May 6, 1960, Anthony Charles Robert Armstrong-Jones, GCVO (*born* March 7, 1930), son of the late Ronald Armstrong-Jones, QC, and the Countess of Rosse, *created* Earl of Snowdon, 1961, Constable of Caernarvon Castle, *marriage dissolved*, 1978; and has *issue*, (*a*) David Albert Charles, Viscount Linley, *born* Nov. 3, 1961; and (*b*) Sarah Frances Elizabeth (Lady Sarah Armstrong-Jones), *born* May 1, 1964.
Residence.—Kensington Palace, W8 4PU (Tel: 071–930 3141).

Order of Succession to the Throne

1. HRH The Prince of Wales
2. HRH Prince William of Wales
3. HRH Prince Henry of Wales
4. HRH The Duke of York
5. HRH Princess Beatrice of York
6. HRH Princess Eugenie of York
7. HRH The Prince Edward
8. HRH The Princess Royal
9. Master Peter Phillips
10. Miss Zara Phillips
11. HRH The Princess Margaret, Countess of Snowdon
12. Viscount Linley
13. Lady Sarah Armstrong-Jones
14. HRH The Duke of Gloucester
15. Earl of Ulster
16. Lady Davina Windsor
17. Lady Rose Windsor
18. HRH The Duke of Kent
19. Lord Downpatrick
20. Lord Nicholas Windsor
21. Lady Helen Windsor
22. Lord Frederick Windsor
23. Lady Gabriella Windsor
24. HRH Princess Alexandra, the Hon. Lady Ogilvy
25. Mr James Ogilvy
26. Mrs Paul Mowatt

The Earl of St Andrews and HRH Prince Michael of Kent are excluded from succession to the Throne, each having married a Roman Catholic. However, each transmits his right to his children.

THE QUEEN'S HOUSEHOLD

Lord Chamberlain, The Earl of Airlie, KT, GCVO, PC.
Lord Steward, The Viscount Ridley, TD.
Master of the Horse, The Earl of Westmorland, KCVO.
Treasurer of the Household, A. Goodlad, MP.
Comptroller of the Household, D. Lightbown, MP.
Vice Chamberlain, J. M. Taylor, MP.

Gold Stick, Maj.-Gen. Lord Michael Fitzalan Howard, GCVO, CB, CBE, MC; Gen. Sir Desmond Fitzpatrick, GCB, DSO, MBE, MC.
Vice-Adm. of the United Kingdom, Adm. Sir Anthony Morton, GBE, KCB.
Rear-Adm. of the United Kingdom, Adm. Sir James Eberle, GCB.
First and Principal Naval Aide-de-Camp, Adm. Sir Julian Oswald, GCB.
Flag Aide de Camp, Adm. Sir Jeremy Black, KCB, DSO, MBE.
Aides-de-Camp General, Gen. Sir John Chapple, GCB, CBE; Gen. Sir David Ramsbotham, KCB, CBE; Gen. Sir Peter Inge, KCB.
Air Aides-de-Camp, Air Chief Marshal Sir Peter Harding, GCB; Air Chief Marshal Sir Roger Palin, KCB, OBE.

Mistress of the Robes, The Duchess of Grafton, GCVO.
Ladies of the Bedchamber, The Countess of Airlie, CVO; The Lady Farnham..
Extra Ladies of the Bedchamber, The Marchioness of Abergavenny, DCVO; The Countess of Cromer, CVO.
Women of the Bedchamber, Hon. Mary Morrison, DCVO; Lady Susan Hussey, DCVO; Mrs John Dugdale, DCVO; The Lady Elton.
Extra Women of the Bedchamber, Mrs John Woodroffe, CVO; Lady Rose Baring, DCVO; Mrs Michael Wall, DCVO; Lady Abel Smith, DCVO; Mrs Robert de Pass.
Equerries, Lt.-Col. B. A. Stewart-Wilson, CVO; Wg Cdr. D. A. Walker; Capt. J. Giles (*temp.*).
Extra Equerries, Vice-Adm. Sir Peter Ashmore, KCB, KCVO, DSC; Lt.-Col. The Lord Charteris of Amisfield, GCB, GCVO, OBE, QSO, PC; Air Cdre the Hon. T. Elworthy, CBE; Rt Hon. Sir Robert Fellowes, KCVO; Sir Edward Ford, KCB, KCVO, ERD; Rear-Adm. Sir John Garnier, KCVO, CBE; Rear-Adm. Sir Paul Greening, KCVO, CBE; Brig. Sir Geoffrey Hardy-Roberts, KCVO, CB, CBE; The Rt. Hon. Sir William Heseltine, GCB, GCVO, AC, QSO; Rear-Adm. Sir Hugh Janion, KCVO; Lt.-Col. Sir John Johnston, GCVO, MC; Sir Peter Miles, KCVO; Lt.-Col. Sir John Miller, GCVO, DSO, MC; Air Cdre Sir Dennis Mitchell, KBE, CVO, DFC, AFC; The Lord Moore of Wolvercote, GCB, GCVO, CMG, QSO; Lt.-Col. Sir Eric Penn, GCVO, OBE, MC; Lt.-Col. W. H. M. Ross, OBE; Air Vice-Marshal Sir John Severne, KCVO, OBE, AFC; Gp Capt P. Townsend, CVO, DSO, DFC; Rear-Adm. Sir Richard Trowbridge, KCVO; Lt.-Col. G. West, CVO; Air Cdre Sir Archie Winskill, KCVO, CBE, DFC, AE.

THE PRIVATE SECRETARY'S OFFICE
Buckingham Palace, SW1A 1AA

Private Secretary to The Queen, Rt Hon. Sir Robert Fellowes, KCB, KCVO.
Deputy Private Secretary, Sir Kenneth Scott, KCVO, CMG.
Assistant Private Secretary, R. B. Janvrin, LVO.
Press Secretary, C. V. Anson, LVO.
Deputy Press Secretary, J. Haslam, LVO.
Assistant Press Secretaries, G. Crawford; R. W. Arbiter.
Chief Clerk, Mrs G. S. Coulson, MVO.
Secretary to the Private Secretary, Miss E. Pearce, MVO.

Head of Information and Correspondence Section, Mrs J. Bean, LVO.
Clerks, Mrs P. Bachelier; Miss A. Foreman; Mrs C. H. Good; Miss A. Kennedy; Miss S. Moore; Miss H. Spiller.
Press Office, Miss K. McGrigor; Mrs R. Murdo-Smith, LVO; Miss C. Sillars; Miss L. Stewart.
Lady in Waiting's Office, Mrs D. Phillips; Mrs J. Vince.

The Queen's Archives
Round Tower, Windsor Castle

Keeper of The Queen's Archives, Rt Hon. Sir Robert Fellowes, KCB, KCVO.
Assistant Keeper, O. Everett, CVO.
Registrar, Lady de Bellaigue, MVO.
Assistant Registrar, Miss P. Clark.
Curator of the Photographic Collection, Miss F. Dimond, MVO.

THE PRIVY PURSE AND TREASURER'S OFFICE
Buckingham Palace, SW1A 1AA

Keeper of the Privy Purse and Treasurer to The Queen, Maj. Sir Shane Blewitt, KCVO.
Deputy Keeper of the Privy Purse and Deputy Treasurer, J. Parsons.
Chief Accountant and Paymaster, D. Walker, LVO.
Personnel Officer, G. Franklin, CVO.
Pensions Manager, Miss P. Lloyd.
Assistant Chief Accountant and Paymaster, Miss R. Ward.
Assistant Personnel Officer, Miss C. Hall.
Superintendent of Public Enterprises, E. Hewlett.
Accountants, Mrs J. Maitland, LVO; Mrs D. Mowbray, MVO; Mrs W. Johnson.
Clerks, Mrs C. Auton, MVO; Mrs F. Burrows; Miss C. Murphy; Miss G. Wickham, MVO; Miss C. Robinson; Miss L. Buggé; Miss M. O'Connell; I. Biss.
Clerk of Stationery, W. Cotton.
Land Agent, Sandringham, J. Major.
Resident Factor, Balmoral, M. Leslie, LVO.

Finance and Property Services

Director of Finance and Property Services, M. Peat.
Deputy Director, Property Services, J. H. Tiltman.
Superintending Architect, S. Dhargalkar.
Property Administrator, Miss M. Green.
Maintenance Manager, G. Griffiths, MVO.
Deputy Maintenance Manager, R. Mole.
Assistant Maintenance Manager, M. Harmer.
Deputy Property Administrator, Miss E. Burrin.
Assistant Property Administrator, Mrs H. Dunlop.
Senior Maintenance Officers, A. Ryan; C. Anderson; J. Barrand; D. I'Anson; P. McLoughlin; R. Purdy.
Maintenance Officers, K. Appleby; A. Holdstock.
Clerks, Mrs. J. Hillyer; K. Langley; Mrs C. Sharma; Mrs J. Thomas; Miss R. Wickenden.

Windsor Castle

Maintenance Manager, E. Norton.
Deputy Maintenance Manager, M. Thresher.
Senior Maintenance Officers, J. Cox; P. Godwin.
Clerk of Works, D. Plunkett.
Maintenance Officer, P. Davies.
Clerk, G. Kirby.

Royal Almonry

High Almoner, The Rt. Rev. the Lord Bishop of St Albans.
Hereditary Grand Almoner, The Marquess of Exeter.
Sub-Almoner, Rev. W. Booth.
Secretary, P. Wright, CVO.
Assistant Secretary, D. Waters, CVO.

THE LORD CHAMBERLAIN'S OFFICE
Buckingham Palace, SW1A 1AA

Comptroller, Lt.-Col. M. Ross, OBE.
Assistant Comptroller, Lt.-Col. A. Mather, OBE.
Secretary, P. D. Hartley, MVO.
Assistant Secretary, J. Spencer.
State Invitations Assistant, J. Mordaunt, MVO.
Registrar, J. Spencer.
Clerks, Miss H. Asprey; Miss L. Pears; Miss L. Connor; Mrs V. Cunningham.
Permanent Lords-in-Waiting, Lt.-Col. The Lord Charteris of Amisfield, GCB, GCVO, OBE, QSO, PC; The Lord Moore of Wolvercote, GCB, GCVO, CMG, QSO.
Lords-in-Waiting, The Lord Somerleyton; The Viscount Boyne; The Viscount Long; The Earl of Strathmore and Kinghorne; The Lord Cavendish of Furness; The Viscount Astor; The Earl Howe.
Gentlemen Ushers, C. Greig, CVO, CBE; Gp Capt J. Slessor; Maj. N. Chamberlayne-Macdonald, LVO, OBE; Air Marshal Sir Roy Austen-Smith, KBE, CB, DFC; Vice-Adm. Sir David Loram, KCB, LVO; Capt. M. Barrow, DSO, RN; Capt. M. Fulford-Dobson, RN; Lt.-Gen. Sir Richard Vickers, KCB, LVO, OBE; Air Vice-Marshal B. Newton, CB, OBE; Col. M. Havergal, OBE.
Extra Gentlemen Ushers, Maj. T. Harvey, CVO, DSO; Maj.-Gen. Sir Cyril Colquhoun, KCVO, CB, OBE; Lt.-Col. Sir John Hugo, KCVO, OBE; Vice-Adm. Sir Ronald Brockman, KCB, CSI, CIE, CVO, CBE; Air Marshal Sir Maurice Heath, KBE, CB, CVO; Sir James Scholtens, KCVO; Sir Patrick O'Dea, KCVO; Brig.-Gen S. Cooper, CVO, OBE, CD; Adm. Sir David Williams, GCB; Capt. M. Tufnell, CVO, DSC, RN; H. Davis, CVO, CM; Maj.-Gen. R. Reid, CVO, MC, CD; Lt.-Cdr. J. Holdsworth, CVO, OBE, RN; Col. G. Leigh, CVO, CBE; Lt.-Cdr. Sir Russell Wood, KCVO, VRD; Col. D. Lawrence; Air Chief Marshal Sir Neville Stack, KCB, CVO, CBE, AFC; Maj.-Gen. Sir Desmond Rice, KCVO, CBE; Lt.-Col. Sir Julian Paget, Bt., CVO.
Gentleman Usher to the Sword of State, Gen. Sir Edward Burgess, KCB, OBE.
Gentleman Usher of the Black Rod, Air Chief Marshal Sir John Gingell, GBE, KCB.
Serjeants at Arms, M. Tims, CVO; G. Franklin, CVO; D. Walker, LVO.

Marshal of the Diplomatic Corps, Lt.-Gen. Sir John Richards, KCB, KCVO.
Vice-Marshal, R. Hervey, CMG.

Constable and Governor of Windsor Castle, Adm. Sir David Hallifax, KCB, KBE.
Keeper of the Jewel House, Tower of London, Maj.-Gen. C. Tyler, CB.
Master of The Queen's Music, Malcolm Williamson, CBE, AO.
Poet Laureate, Ted Hughes, OBE.
Bargemaster, R. Crouch.
Keeper of the Swans, F. J. Turk, MVO.
Superintendent of the State Apartments, St James's Palace, T. Taylor, MVO, MBE.

ROYAL COLLECTION DEPARTMENT
St James's Palace, SW1

Director of Royal Collection and Surveyor of The Queen's Works of Art, Sir Geoffrey de Bellaigue, KCVO, FSA.
Surveyor of The Queen's Pictures, C. Lloyd.
Librarian, The Royal Library, Windsor Castle, O. Everett, CVO.
Deputy Surveyor of The Queen's Works of Art, H. Roberts.
Surveyor Emeritus of The Queen's Pictures, Sir Oliver Millar, GCVO, FBA, FSA.
Adviser for The Queen's Works of Art, Sir Francis Watson, KCVO, FBA, FSA.

Librarian Emeritus, Sir Robin Mackworth-Young, GCVO, FSA.
Curator of the Print Room, The Hon. Mrs Roberts, MVO.
Registrar, M. Bishop, MVO.
Assistant to Registrar, Miss S. Goodbody.
Assistant to Surveyors (Military), D. Rankin-Hunt, TD.
Assistant to Surveyor of The Queen's Pictures, C. Noble, MVO.
Secretary to the Director, Miss C. Crichton-Stuart, MVO.
Inventory Assistant, Mrs S. Newton.
Clerks, Hon. C. Neville; Mrs C. Gordon Lennox; Miss H. Edwards; Miss A. Fairbank; Miss A. Leslie.

ASCOT OFFICE
St James's Palace, SW1
[071-930 9882]

Her Majesty's Representative at Ascot, Col. Sir Piers Bengough, KCVO, OBE.
Secretary, Miss L. Thompson-Royd.

ECCLESIASTICAL HOUSEHOLD
The College of Chaplains

Clerk of the Closet, Rt. Rev. Bishop of Chelmsford.
Deputy Clerk of the Closet, Rev. W. Booth.
Chaplains to The Queen, Rev. A. H. H. Harbottle, LVO; Ven. D. N. Griffiths, RD; Canon A. Glendining, LVO; Canon J. V. Bean; Rev. K. Huxley; Ven. P. Ashford; Canon G. A. Elcoat; Canon D. C. Gray, TD; Ven. D. Scott; Canon E. James; Canon J. Hester; Rev. S. Pedley; Rev. D. Tonge; Rev. Canon C. Craston; Rev. Canon N. M. Ramm; Rev. Canon D. N. Hole; Rev. Canon M. A. Moxon; Canon R. J. W. Bevan; Canon R. T. W. McDermid; Canon G. Murphy, LVO; Canon R. H. C. Lewis; Rev. D. J. Burgess; Rev. E. R. Ayerst; Rev. R. S. Clarke; Rev. Canon C. J. Hill; Ven. K. Pound; Rev. Canon J. Haslam; Rev. Canon G. Hall; Rev. Canon A. C. Hill; Rev. J. C. Priestley; Rev. Canon J. O. Colling; Rev. Canon G. Jones; Rev. D. G. Palmer; Rev. Canon D. H. Wheaton; Rev. Canon P. Boulton.
Extra Chaplains, Rev. Canon J. S. D. Mansel, KCVO, FSA; Preb. S. A. Williams, CVO; Ven. E. J. G. Ward, LVO; Rev. J. R. W. Stott; Rev. Canon A. D. Caesar, CVO.

Chapels Royal

Dean of the Chapels Royal, The Bishop of London.
Sub-Dean of Chapels Royal, Rev. W. Booth.
Priests in Ordinary, Rev. W. Booth; Rev. G. Watkins; Rev. H. Mead.
Organist, Choirmaster and Composer, R. J. Popplewell, FRCO, FRCM.
Domestic Chaplain, Buckingham Palace, Rev. W. Booth.
Domestic Chaplain, Windsor Castle, The Dean of Windsor.
Domestic Chaplain, Sandringham, Rev. C. on G. R. Hall.
Chaplain, Royal Chapel, Windsor Great Pa , Rev. Canon M. Moxon.
Chaplain, Hampton Court Palace, Rev. Ca on M. Moore.
Chaplain, Tower of London, vacant.
Organist and Choirmaster, Hampton Court Palace, Gordon Reynolds, LVO.

MEDICAL HOUSEHOLD

Head of the Medical Household and Physician, A. Dawson, MD, FRCP.
Physician, R. W. Davey, MB, BS.
Serjeant Surgeon, B. T. Jackson, MS, FRCS.

Surgeon Oculist, P. Holmes Sellors, LVO, BM, B.ch., FRCS.
Surgeon Gynaecologist, M. E. Setchell, FRCS, FRCOG.
Surgeon Dentist, N. A. Sturridge, CVO, LDS, BDS, DDS.
Orthopaedic Surgeon, D. R. Sweetnam, CBE, FRCS.
Physician to the Household, R. Thompson, DM, FRCP.
Surgeon to the Household, A. A. M. Lewis, MB, FRCS.
Surgeon Oculist to the Household, T. J. ffytche, FRCS.
Apothecary to The Queen and to the Household, N. R. Southward, LVO, MB, B.chir.
Apothecary to the Household at Windsor, J. H. D. Briscoe, MB, B.chir., D.obst.
Apothecary to the Household at Sandringham, H. K. Ford, LVO, MB, FRCGP.
Coroner of The Queen's Household, J. Burton, CBE, MB, BS.

CENTRAL CHANCERY
OF THE ORDERS OF KNIGHTHOOD
St James's Palace, SW1

Secretary, Lt.-Col. A. Mather, OBE.
Assistant Secretary, Sqn. Ldr. B. Sowerby, MVO.
Clerks, J. McGurk, MVO; Miss S. Koller, MVO; Miss R. Wells, MVO; Miss L. Dove; Miss F. Bean; Mrs T. Issac.

The Honorable Corps of Gentlemen at Arms
St James's Palace, SW1

Captain, The Lord Hesketh.
Lieutenant, Maj. T. St Aubyn.
Standard Bearer, Lt.-Col. Sir James Scott, Bt.
Clerk of the Cheque & Adjutant, Maj. Sir Torquil Matheson of Matheson, Bt.
Harbinger, Maj. the Lord Suffield, MC.

Gentlemen of the Corps

Brigadier, A. N. Breitmeyer.
Colonels, T. Hall, OBE; Sir Piers Bengough, KCVO, OBE; Hon. N. Crossley, TD; T. Wilson; D. Fanshawe, OBE; J. Baker; R. ffrench Blake.
Lieutenant-Colonels, R. Mayfield, DSO; B. Lockhart; Hon. P. H. Lewis; R. Macfarlane; Hon. G. B. Norrie; J. H. Fisher, OBE.
Majors, F. J. H. Matheson; J. A. J. Nunn; Sir Philip Duncombe, Bt.; I. B. Ramsden, MBE; M. J. Drummond-Brady; A. Arkwright; G. M. B. Colenso-Jones; T. Gooch, MBE; J. B. B. Cockcroft; C. J. H. Gurney; J. R. E. Nelson; P. D. Johnson.
Captain, The Lord Monteagle of Brandon.

The Queen's Bodyguard of the Yeoman of the Guard
St James's Palace, SW1

Captain, The Viscount Davidson.
Lieutenant, Col. A. B. Pemberton, CVO, MBE.
Clerk of the Cheque and Adjutant, Col. G. W. Tufnell.
Ensign, Lt.-Col. S. Longsdon.
Exons., Maj. C. Marriott; Maj. C. Enderby.

MASTER OF THE HOUSEHOLD'S
DEPARTMENT
Board of Green Cloth
Buckingham Palace, SW1A 1AA

Master of the Household, Rear-Adm. Sir Paul Greening, KCVO.
Deputy Master of the Household, Lt.-Col. B. A. Stewart-Wilson, CVO.
Assistants to the Master of the Household, M. D. Tims, CVO; M. T. Parker, MVO.
Chief Clerk, M. C. W. N. Jephson, MVO.
Chief Housekeeper, Miss H. Colebrook.
Deputy to Assistant F, M. Bovaird.
Senior Clerk G, S. Stacey.
Administrator F, Miss J. Cartwright.

Clerks, Miss S. Derry, MVO; Miss S. Fergus, MVO; Mrs C. Creak; K. Sharp; Miss J. Perry; Miss S. Bell; Miss L. Moran.
Palace Steward, A. Jarred, RVM.
Royal Chef, L. Mann, RVM.
Superintendent, Windsor Castle, Maj. B. Eastwood, MBE.
Assistant to Superintendent, Capt. R. McClosky, MVO.
Superintendent, The Palace of Holyroodhouse, Lt.-Col. D. Wickes, MVO.

ROYAL MEWS DEPARTMENT
Buckingham Palace, SW1A 1AA

Crown Equerry, Lt.-Col. S. Gilbart-Denham.
Veterinary Surgeon, P. Scott Dunn, LVO, MRCVS.
Supt. Royal Mews, Buckingham Palace, Maj. A. Smith, MBE.
Comptroller of Stores, Maj. L. Marsham, MVO.
Chief Clerk, P. Almond, MVO.
Deputy Chief Clerk, A. Marshall.
Assistant Chief Clerk, Mrs J. Clark.

HER MAJESTY'S HOUSEHOLD
IN SCOTLAND

Hereditary Lord High Constable, The Earl of Erroll.
Hereditary Master of the Household, The Duke of Argyll.
Lord Lyon King of Arms, Sir Malcolm Innes of Edinight, KCVO, WS.
Hereditary Bearer of the Royal Banner of Scotland, The Earl of Dundee.
Hereditary Bearer of the Scottish National Flag, The Earl of Lauderdale.
Hereditary Keepers:—
 Palace of Holyroodhouse, The Duke of Hamilton and Brandon.
 Falkland Castle, N. J. Crichton-Stuart.
 Stirling Castle, The Earl of Mar and Kellie.
 Dunstaffnage Castle, The Duke of Argyll.
 Dunconnel Castle, Sir Fitzroy Maclean, Bt, CBE.
Hereditary Carver, Sir Ralph Anstruther, KCVO, MC.
Keeper of Dumbarton Castle, Brig. A. S. Pearson, CB, DSO, OBE, MC, TD.
Governor of Edinburgh Castle, Lt.-Gen. Sir Peter Graham, KCB, CBE.
Historiographer, Prof. G. Donaldson, CBE, FBA, FRSE.
Botanist, Prof. D. Henderson, CBE, FRSE.
Painter and Limner, D. A. Donaldson, RSA, RP.
Sculptor in Ordinary, Prof. Sir Eduardo Paolozzi.
Astronomer, Prof. M. S. Longair, Ph.D.
Heralds and Pursuivants, see p. 297–8.

Ecclesiastical Household

Dean of the Order of the Thistle, The Very Rev. G. I. Macmillan.
Dean of the Chapel Royal, Very Rev. W. I. Morris, DD, LL.D.
Chaplains in Ordinary, Rev. W. J. Morris, DD, LL.D.; Rev. K. MacVicar, MBE, DFC, TD; Rev. A. J. C. Macfarlane; Rev. J. McLeod; Very Rev. G. I. Macmillan; Very Rev. W. B. Johnston, DD; Rt Rev. M. D. Craig; Rev. W. B. R. Macmillan, LL.D.; Rev. J. L. Weatherhead; Rev. M. I. Levison.
Extra Chaplains, Very Rev. R. L. Small, CBE, DD; Very Rev. W. R. Sanderson, DD; Very Rev. R. W. V. Selby Wright, CVO, TD, DD, FRSE, FSASCOT.; Rev. T. J. T. Nicol, MVO, MBE, MC, TD; Very Rev. Prof. J. McIntyre, CVO, DD, FRSE; Rev. C. Forrester-Paton; Rev. H. W. M. Cant; Very Rev. R. A. S. Barbour, KCVO, MC, DD.
Domestic Chaplain, Balmoral, Rev. J. A. K. Angus, LVO, TD.

Medical Household

Physicians in Scotland, P. Brunt, MD, FRCP; A. L. Muir, MD, FRCP.

Surgeons in Scotland, I. B. Macleod, MB, ch.B., FRCS; J. Engeset, ch.M., FRCS.

Extra Surgeons in Scotland, Prof. Sir Charles Illingworth, CBE, MD, FRCSE; Prof. Sir Donald Douglas, MBE, ch.M., MS, D.SC., FRCS.

Apothecary to the Household at Balmoral, D. J. A. Glass, MB, ch.B.

Apothecary to the Household at the Palace of Holyroodhouse, Dr J. Cormack, MD, FRCGP.

THE QUEEN'S BODY GUARD FOR SCOTLAND

Royal Company of Archers.
Archers' Hall, Edinburgh.

Captain-General and Gold Stick for Scotland, Col. the Lord Clydesmuir, KT, CB, MBE, TD.

Captains, Maj. the Lord Home of the Hirsel, KT; The Duke of Buccleuch and Queensberry, KT, VRD; Lt.-Col. Sir John Gilmour, Bt., DSO, TD; Maj. Sir Hew Hamilton-Dalrymple, Bt., KCVO.

Lieutenants, Maj. the Earl of Wemyss and March, KT; The Earl of Airlie, KT, GCVO; The Earl of Dalhousie, KT, GCVO, GBE, MC; Capt. Sir Iain Tennant, KT.

Ensigns, Capt. N. E. F. Dalrymple-Hamilton, CVO, MBE, DSC, RN; The Marquess of Lothian, KCVO; Cdre Sir John Clerk of Penicuik, Bt., CBE, VRD; The Earl of Elgin and Kincardine, KT.

Brigadiers, Col. G. R. Simpson, DSO, LVO, TD; Maj. Sir David Butter, KCVO, MC; The Earl of Minto, OBE; Maj.-Gen. Sir John Swinton, KCVO, OBE; Gen. Sir Michael Gow, GCB; The Hon. Lord Elliott, MC; Maj. the Hon. Sir Lachlan Maclean, Bt.; The Rt. Hon. George Younger, TD, MP; Capt. G. Burnet, LVO; The Marquess of Graham; Lt.-Gen. Sir Norman Arthur, KCB; The Hon. Sir William Macpherson of Cluny, TD; Sir David Nickson, KBE.

Adjutant, Maj. the Hon. Sir Lachlan Maclean, Bt.

Surgeon, Dr P. A. P. Mackenzie, TD.

Chaplain, Very Rev. R. Selby Wright, CVO, TD, DD, FRSE.

President of the Council and Silver Stick for Scotland, Maj. Sir Hew Hamilton-Dalrymple, Bt., KCVO.

Vice-President, The Earl of Dalhousie, KT, GCVO, GBE, MC.

Secretary, Col. H. F. O. Bewsher, OBE.

Treasurer, R. A. G. Douglas-Miller.

HOUSEHOLD OF THE PRINCE PHILIP, DUKE OF EDINBURGH

Private Secretary and Treasurer, B. H. McGrath, CVO.

Assistant Private Secretary, Brig. C. Robertson.

Equerry, Lt.-Cdr, M. C. Sillars.

Extra Equerries, J. B. V. Orr, CVO; Sir Richard Davies, KCVO, CBE; Lord Buxton of Alsa.

Temporary Equerries, Capt. G. Rocke; Capt. I. Grant, RM.

Chief Clerk and Accountant, V. G. Jewell, MVO.

HOUSEHOLD OF QUEEN ELIZABETH THE QUEEN MOTHER

Lord Chamberlain, Maj. the Earl of Dalhousie, KT, GCVO, GBE, MC.

Comptroller and Extra Equerry, Capt. Sir Alastair Aird, KCVO.

Private Secretary and Equerry, Lt.-Col. Sir Martin Gilliat, GCVO, MBE.

Treasurer and Equerry, Maj. Sir Ralph Anstruther, Bt., KCVO, MC.

Equerries, Maj. R. Seymour, CVO; Capt. C. Morris-Adams (*temp.*).

Extra Equerries, Maj. Sir John Griffin, KCVO; The Lord Sinclair, CVO.

Apothecary to the Household, Dr N. Southward, LVO, MB, B.chir.

Surgeon-Apothecary to the Household (Royal Lodge, Windsor), Dr J. Briscoe, D.obst.

Mistress of the Robes, vacant.

Ladies of the Bedchamber, The Dowager Viscountess Hambleden, CVO; The Lady Grimthorpe, CVO.

Women of the Bedchamber, Ruth, Lady Fermoy, DCVO, OBE; Dame Frances Campbell-Preston, DCVO; Lady Elizabeth Basset, DCVO; Lady Angela Oswald.

Extra Women of the Bedchamber, Lady Victoria Wemyss, CVO; Lady Jean Rankin, DCVO; Miss Jane Walker-Okeover; Lady Margaret Colville; The Hon. Mrs Rhodes.

Clerk Comptroller, M. Blanch, LVO.

Clerk Accountant, J. P. Kyle, LVO.

Information Officer, Mrs R. Murphy, LVO.

Clerks, Miss F. Fletcher, MVO; Mrs W. Stevens.

HOUSEHOLD OF THE PRINCE AND PRINCESS OF WALES

Private Secretary and Treasurer to The Prince of Wales, Cdr. R. J. Aylard, RN.

Deputy Private Secretary to The Prince of Wales, P. Westmacott.

Assistant Private Secretary to The Prince of Wales, H. Merrill.

Assistant Private Secretary to the Princess of Wales, P. Jephson.

Secretary to the Duchy of Cornwall and Keeper of the Records, D. W. N. Landale.

Equerry to The Prince of Wales, Lt.-Cdr. R. Fraser.

Extra Equerries to The Prince of Wales, The Hon. Edward Adeane, CVO; Maj.-Gen. Sir Christopher Airy, KCVO, CBE; Sqn. Ldr. Sir David Checketts, KCVO; Sir John Riddle, Bt., CVO; G. J. Ward, CBE; Col. J. Q. Winter, LVO.

Equerry to The Princess of Wales, Wg Cdr. D. Barton.

Ladies-in-Waiting, Miss Anne Beckwith-Smith, LVO; Viscountess Campden; Mrs Max Pike; Miss Alexandra Loyd; The Hon. Mrs Vivian Baring; Mrs James Lonsdale.

HOUSEHOLD OF THE DUKE AND DUCHESS OF YORK

Private Secretary and Treasurer to the Duke and Duchess of York, Capt. N. Blair, RN.

Comptroller and Assistant Private Secretary to the Duke and Duchess of York, Mrs Jonathan Mathias.

Equerry to The Duke of York, Capt. A. Buchanan-Baillie-Hamilton.

Extra Equerry, Maj. G. W. McLean.

Ladies-in-Waiting, Mrs John Spooner; Mrs John Floyd.

Extra Ladies-in-Waiting (temp.), Miss Lucy Manners; Mrs Harry Cotterell.

HOUSEHOLD OF THE PRINCE EDWARD

Private Secretary and Equerry to The Prince Edward, Lt.-Col. S. G. O'Dwyer.

Assistant Private Secretary, Mrs R. Warburton, MVO.

HOUSEHOLD OF THE PRINCESS ROYAL

Private Secretary, Lt.-Col. P. Gibbs, LVO.

Assistant Private Secretary, The Hon. Mrs Louloudis.

Ladies-in-Waiting, Mrs Richard Carew Pole, LVO; Mrs Andrew Feilden, LVO; The Hon. Mrs Legge-Bourke, LVO; Mrs William Nunneley; Mrs Timothy Holderness-Roddam; Mrs Charles Ritchie; Mrs David Bowes Lyon.

Extra Ladies-in-Waiting, Miss Victoria Legge-Bourke, LVO; Mrs Malcolm Innes, LVO; The Countess of Lichfield.

HOUSEHOLD OF THE PRINCESS MARGARET, COUNTESS OF SNOWDON

Private Secretary and Comptroller, The Lord Napier and Ettrick, CVO.
Personal Secretary, Miss M. Murray Brown, CVO.
Extra Ladies-in-Waiting, Lady Elizabeth Cavendish, LVO; Lady Aird, LVO; Mrs Robin Benson, LVO, OBE; Lady Juliet Townsend, LVO; Mrs Jane Stevens; The Hon. Mrs Wills, LVO; The Lady Glenconner, LVO; The Hon. Mrs Whitehead, LVO; The Countess Alexander of Tunis, LVO; Mrs Charles Vyvyan.

HOUSEHOLD OF THE DUKE AND DUCHESS OF GLOUCESTER

Private Secretary, Comptroller and Equerry, Maj. N. M. L. Barne.
Assistant Private Secretary to The Duchess of Gloucester, Miss Suzanne Marland.
Extra Equerry, Lt.-Col. Sir Simon Bland, KCVO.
Ladies-in-Waiting, Mrs Michael Wigley, CVO; Mrs Euan McCorquodale; Mrs Howard Page.
Extra Lady-in-Waiting, Miss Jennifer Thomson.

HOUSEHOLD OF PRINCESS ALICE, DUCHESS OF GLOUCESTER

Private Secretary, Comptroller and Equerry, Maj. N. M. L. Barne.
Extra Equerry, Lt.-Col. Sir Simon Bland, KCVO.
Ladies-in-Waiting, Dame Jean Maxwell-Scott, DCVO; Mrs Michael Harvey.
Extra Ladies-in-Waiting, Miss Dorothy Meynell, CVO; Miss Diana Harrison; The Hon. Jane Walsh, LVO; Miss Jane Egerton-Warburton, LVO.

HOUSEHOLD OF THE DUKE AND DUCHESS OF KENT

Private Secretary, Cdr. R. M. Walker.
Extra Equerry, Lt.-Cdr. Sir Richard Buckley, KCVO.
Equerry (temp.), Capt. the Hon. C. E. Knollys.
Ladies-in-Waiting, Mrs Fiona Henderson, CVO; Mrs David Napier, LVO; Mrs Colin Marsh, LVO.
Extra Ladies-in-Waiting, Mrs Peter Wilmot-Sitwell, LVO; Mrs Julian Tomkins; Mrs Peter Troughton.

HOUSEHOLD OF PRINCE AND PRINCESS MICHAEL OF KENT

Private Secretary and Equerry, Lt.-Col. Sir Christopher Thompson, Bt.
Ladies-in-Waiting, The Hon. Mrs Sanders; Miss Anne Frost; Lady Thompson.

HOUSEHOLD OF PRINCESS ALEXANDRA

Comptroller and Private Secretary, Rear-Adm. Sir John Garnier, KCVO, CBE.
Extra Equerry, Maj. P. C. Clarke, CVO.
Lady-in-Waiting, Lady Mary Mumford, CVO.
Extra Ladies-in-Waiting, Mrs Peter Afia; Lady Mary Colman; Lady Nicholas Gordon Lennox; The Hon. Lady Rowley; Miss Mona Mitchell, CVO.

THE CIVIL LIST

The land revenues of the Crown in England and Wales have been collected on the public account since 1760, when George III surrendered them and received a fixed annual payment or Civil List. (For details of income from the Crown Estate, *see* page 308).

The Civil List, the annuity payable to The Queen, is payable out of the Consolidated Fund under the authority of a Civil List Act following the recommendation of a Parliamentary select committee.

Until 1972, the amount of money allocated annually under the Civil List was set for the period of a reign. The system was then altered to a fixed annual payment for ten years but from 1975 high inflation made an annual review necessary. However, the system of payments reverted to the practice of a fixed annual payment for ten years from January 1, 1991. The annual payments for the years 1991–2000 are:

The Queen	£7,900,000
Queen Elizabeth The Queen Mother	640,000
The Duke of Edinburgh	360,000
The Duke of York	250,000
The Prince Edward	100,000
The Princess Royal	230,000
The Princess Margaret	220,000
Princess Alice, Duchess of Gloucester	90,000
*Duke of Gloucester	
*Duke of Kent	630,000
*Princess Alexandra	
	10,420,000
*Refunded to the Treasury by The Queen	630,000
Total	9,790,000

The Prince of Wales does not receive an allocation from the Civil List but derives his income from the revenues of the Duchy of Cornwall.

THE ROYAL ARMS

Quarters

1st and 4th quarters (representing England).—gules, three lions passant guardant in pale or.
2nd quarter (representing Scotland).—or, a lion rampant within a double tressure flory counterflory gules.
3rd quarter (representing Ireland).—azure, a harp or, stringed argent.
The whole shield is encircled with the Garter.
Scottish usage shows the Royal Arms with the Lion of Scotland in the 1st and 4th quarters, and the Lions of England in the 2nd quarter.

Supporters

Dexter (right).—a lion rampant guardant or, imperially crowned.
Sinister (left).—a unicorn argent, armed, crined, and unguled or, gorged with a coronet composed of crosses patées and fleurs-de-lis, a chain affixed, passing between the forelegs, and reflexed over the back.
Scottish usage shows the Royal Arms with the supporters transposed, the unicorn appearing on the right.

Badges

England.—the red and white rose united, slipped and leaved proper.
Scotland.—a thistle, slipped and leaved proper.
Ireland.—a shamrock leaf slipped vert; also a harp or, stringed argent.
United Kingdom.—the Rose of England, the Thistle of Scotland, and the Shamrock of Ireland engrafted on the same stem proper, and an escutcheon

charged as the Union Flag (all ensigned with the Royal Crown).

Wales.—upon a mount vert a dragon passant, wings elevated gules.

ROYAL SALUTES

A salute of 62 guns is fired on the wharf at the Tower of London on the following occasions:
- (a) the anniversaries of the birth, accession and coronation of the Sovereign;
- (b) the anniversary of the birth of HM Queen Elizabeth the Queen Mother;
- (c) the anniversary of the birth of HRH Prince Philip, Duke of Edinburgh.

A salute of 41 guns only is fired on extraordinary and triumphal occasions, e.g. on the occasion of the Sovereign opening, proroguing or dissolving Parliament in person, or when passing through London in procession, except when otherwise ordered.

A salute of 41 guns is fired from the two saluting stations in London (the Tower of London and Hyde Park) on the occasion of the birth of a Royal infant.

Constable of the Royal Palace and Fortress of London, Field Marshal Sir John Stanier, GCB, MBE.

Lieutenant of the Tower of London, Lt.-Gen. Sir Derek Boorman, KCB.

Resident Governor and Keeper of the Jewel House, Maj.-Gen. C. Tyler, CB.

Master Gunner of St James's Park, Gen. Sir Martin Farndale, KCB.

Master Gunner within the Tower, Col. D. P. Spooner, TD.

THE NATIONAL FLAG

The national flag of the United Kingdom is the Union Flag, generally known as the Union Jack. (The name 'Union Jack' derives from the use of the Union Flag on the jack-staff of naval vessels.)

The Union Flag is a combination of the cross of St George, patron saint of England; the cross of St Andrew, patron saint of Scotland; and a cross similar to that of St Patrick, patron saint of Ireland.

Cross of St George.—cross gules in a field argent (red cross on a white ground).

Cross of St Andrew.—saltire argent in a field azure (white diagonal cross on a blue ground).

Cross of St Patrick.—saltire gules in a field argent (red diagonal cross on a white ground).

The Union Flag was first introduced in 1606 after the union of England and Scotland. The cross of St Patrick was added in 1801 after the union of Great Britain and Ireland.

DAYS FOR FLYING FLAGS

The correct orientation of the Union Flag when flying is with the broader diagonal band of white uppermost in the hoist (i.e. near the pole) and the narrower diagonal band of white uppermost in the fly (i.e. farthest from the pole).

It is the practice to fly the Union Flag daily on some Customs Houses. In all other cases, flags are flown on government buildings by command of HM The Queen.

Days for hoisting the Union Flag are notified to the Department of the Environment by Her Majesty's command and communicated by the Department to the other government departments. On the days appointed, the Union Flag should be flown on all government buildings in London and elsewhere in the United Kingdom from 8 a.m. to sunset.

February 6.—The Queen's Accession.
February 19.—Birthday of The Duke of York.
March 1.—St David's Day (in Wales only).
March 9 (1992).—Commonwealth Day.
March 10.—Birthday of The Prince Edward.
April 21.—Birthday of The Queen.
April 23.—St George's Day (in England only). Where a building has two or more flagstaffs the Cross of St George may be flown in addition to the Union Jack but not in a superior position.
June 2.—Coronation Day.
June 10.—Birthday of The Duke of Edinburgh.
June 13 (1992).—Queen's Official Birthday.

July 1.—Birthday of The Princess of Wales.
Aug. 4.—Birthday of HM Queen Elizabeth the Queen Mother.
Aug. 15.—Birthday of The Princess Royal.
Aug. 21.—Birthday of The Princess Margaret.
Nov. 8 (1992).—Remembrance Sunday.
Nov. 14.—Birthday of The Prince of Wales.
Nov. 20.—The Queen's Wedding Day.
Nov. 30.—St Andrew's Day (in Scotland only).
—The occasion of the opening and closing of Parliament by The Queen, whether or not Her Majesty performs the ceremony in person (on government buildings in the Greater London area only).

Flags at half-mast

Flags will be flown at half-mast on the following occasions:
- (a) From the announcement of the death up to the funeral of the Sovereign, except on Proclamation Day, when they are hoisted right up from 11 a.m. to sunset.
- (b) The funerals of members of the Royal Family, subject to special commands from Her Majesty in each case.
- (c) The funerals of foreign rulers, subject to special commands from Her Majesty in each case.
- (d) The funerals of Prime Ministers and ex-Prime Ministers of the United Kingdom.
- (e) Other occasions by special command of Her Majesty.

On occasions when days for flying flags coincide with days for flying flags at half-mast, the following rules will be observed. Flags will be flown:
- (a) although a member of the Royal Family, or a near relative of the Royal Family, may be lying dead, unless special commands be received from Her Majesty to the contrary;
- (b) although it may be the day of the funeral of a foreign ruler.

If the body of a very distinguished subject is lying at a government office, the flag may fly at half-mast on that office until the body has left (provided it is a day on which the flag would fly) and then the flag is to be hoisted right up. On all other government buildings the flag will fly as usual.

The **Royal Standard** is to be hoisted only when The Queen is actually present in the building, and never when Her Majesty is passing in procession.

PRECEDENCE IN ENGLAND

THE SOVEREIGN.
The Prince Philip, Duke of Edinburgh.
The Prince of Wales.
The Sovereign's younger Sons.
The Sovereign's Grandsons.
The Sovereign's Cousins.
Archbishop of Canterbury.
Lord High Chancellor.
Archbishop of York.
The Prime Minister.
Lord President of the Council.
Speaker of the House of Commons.
Lord Privy Seal.
Ambassadors and High Commissioners.
Lord Great Chamberlain.
Earl Marshal.
Lord Steward of the Household.
Lord Chamberlain of the Household.
Master of the Horse.
Dukes, according to their Patent of Creation: (1) of England; (2) of Scotland; (3) of Great Britain; (4) of Ireland; (5) those created since the Union.
Ministers and Envoys.
Eldest sons of Dukes of Blood Royal.
Marquesses, according to their Patent of Creation: (1) of England; (2) of Scotland; (3) of Great Britain; (4) of Ireland; (5) those created since the Union.
Dukes' eldest Sons.
Earls, according to their Patent of Creation: (1) of England; (2) of Scotland; (3) of Great Britain; (4) of Ireland; (5) those created since the Union.
Younger sons of Dukes of Blood Royal.
Marquesses' eldest Sons.
Dukes' younger Sons.
Viscounts, according to their Patent of Creation: (1) of England; (2) of Scotland; (3) of Great Britain; (4) of Ireland; (5) those created since the Union.
Earls' eldest Sons.
Marquesses' younger Sons.
Bishops of London, Durham and Winchester.
Other English Diocesan Bishops, according to seniority of consecration.
Suffragan Bishops, according to seniority of consecration.
Secretaries of State, if of the degree of a Baron.
Barons, according to their Patent of Creation: (1) of England; (2) of Scotland; (3) of Great Britain; (4) of Ireland; (5) those created since the Union.
Treasurer of the Household.

Comptroller of the Household.
Vice-Chamberlain of the Household.
Secretaries of State under the degree of Baron.
Viscounts' eldest Sons.
Earls' younger Sons.
Barons' eldest Sons.
Knights of the Garter.
Privy Counsellors.
Chancellor of the Exchequer.
Chancellor of the Duchy of Lancaster.
Lord Chief Justice of England.
Master of the Rolls.
President of the Family Division.
Vice-Chancellor.
The Lords Justices of Appeal.
Judges of the High Court.
Viscounts' younger Sons.
Barons' younger Sons.
Sons of Life Peers.
Baronets, according to date of Patent.
Knights of the Thistle.
Knights Grand Cross of the Bath.
Members of the Order of Merit.
Knights Grand Commanders of the Star of India.
Knights Grand Cross of St Michael and St George.
Knights Grand Commanders of the Indian Empire.
Knights Grand Cross of the Royal Victorian Order.
Knights Grand Cross of the British Empire.
Companions of Honour.
Knights Commanders of the Bath.
Knights Commanders of the Star of India.
Knights Commanders of St Michael and St George.
Knights Commanders of the Indian Empire.
Knights Commanders of the Royal Victorian Order.
Knights Commanders of the British Empire.
Knights Bachelor.
Vice-Chancellor of the Co. Palatine of Lancaster.
Official Referees of the Supreme Court.
Circuit judges and judges of the Mayor's and City of London Court.
Companions of the Bath.
Companions of the Star of India.
Companions of St Michael and St George.
Companions of the Indian Empire.
Commanders of the Royal Victorian Order.
Commanders of the British Empire.

Companions of the Distinguished Service Order.
Lieutenants of the Royal Victorian Order.
Officers of the British Empire.
Companions of the Imperial Service Order.
Eldest Sons of younger Sons of Peers.
Baronets' eldest Sons.
Eldest Sons of Knights, in the same order as their Fathers.
Members of the Royal Victorian Order.
Members of the British Empire.
Younger Sons of the younger Sons of Peers.
Baronets' younger Sons.
Younger Sons of Knights, in the same order as their Fathers.
Naval, Military, Air, and other Esquires by Office.

Women

Women take the same rank as their husbands or as their brothers; but the daughter of a peer marrying a commoner retains her title as Lady or Honourable. Daughters of peers rank next immediately after the wives of their elder brothers, and before their younger brothers' wives. Daughters of peers marrying peers of lower degree take the same order of precedence as that of their husbands; thus the daughter of a Duke marrying a Baron becomes of the rank of Baroness only while her sisters married to commoners retain their rank and take precedence of the Baroness. Merely official rank on the husband's part does not give any similar precedence to the wife.

Peeresses in their own right take the same precedence as peers of the same rank, i.e. from their date of creation.

Local precedence

ENGLAND AND WALES.—No written code of county or city order of precedence has been promulgated, but in counties the Lord Lieutenant stands first, and secondly (normally) the Sheriff, and therefore in cities and boroughs the Lord Lieutenant has social precedence over the Mayor; but at city or borough functions the Lord Mayor or Mayor will preside. At Oxford and Cambridge the High Sheriff takes precedence of the Vice-Chancellor. SCOTLAND.—*See* p. 613.

THE PEERAGE

The rules which govern the creation and succession of Peerages are extremely complicated. There are, technically, five separate Peerages, the Peerage of England, of Scotland, of Ireland, of Great Britain, and of the United Kingdom. The Peerage of Great Britain dates from 1707 when an Act of Union combined the two Kingdoms of England and Scotland and separate Peerages were discontinued; and the Peerage of the United Kingdom from 1801 when Great Britain and Ireland were combined under an Act of Union. Some Scottish Peers have received additional Peerages of Great Britain or of the United Kingdom since 1707, and some Irish Peers additional Peerages of the United Kingdom since 1801. The Peerage of Ireland was not entirely discontinued from 1801 but holders of Irish Peerages, whether pre-dating or created subsequent to the Union of 1801, are not entitled to sit in the House of Lords if they have no additional English, Scottish, Great Britain or United Kingdom Peerage. (However, they are eligible for election to the House of Commons and to vote in Parliamentary elections, which other Peers are not.) An Irish Peer holding a Peerage of a lower grade which enables him to sit in the House of Lords is introduced there by the title which enables him to sit, though for all other purposes he is known by his higher title. In the Peerage of Scotland there is no rank of Baron; the equivalent rank is Lord of Parliament, abbreviated to 'Lord' (the female equivalent is 'Lady'). All Peers of England, Scotland, Great Britain or the United Kingdom who are of full age (21 years) and of British, Irish or Commonwealth nationality are entitled to sit in the House of Lords.

Most hereditary peerages pass on death to the nearest male heir; but certain ancient Peerages pass on death to the nearest heir, male or female, and several are held by women (*see also* pp. 169–70). Since the Peerage Act, 1963, women Peers in their own Right have been entitled to sit in the House of Lords, subject to the same qualifications as men.

Non-hereditary or Life Peerages, in the degree of Baron or Baroness, have been conferred by the Crown since 1876 on eminent judges, the Lords of Appeal or Law Lords, to enable them to carry out the judicial functions of the House of Lords, and since 1958 on men and women of distinction in public life, giving them seats in the House of Lords. Life Peers are addressed identically as an hereditary Peer, and their children have the same courtesy style as the children of an hereditary Peer.

No fees for dignities have been payable since 1937. The House of Lords surrendered the ancient right of Peers to be tried for treason or felony by their peers in 1948.

Peerages Extinct Since the Last Issue

BARONIES.—Portal of Hungerford (*cr.* 1945); Ebbisham (*cr.* 1928); Loch (*cr.* 1895); Allerton (*cr.* 1902).

LIFE PEERAGES.—Caradon (*cr.* 1964); Swann (*cr.* 1981); Reilly (*cr.* 1978); Caccia (*cr.* 1965); Marshall of Leeds (*cr.* 1980); Pearce (*cr.* 1962); Seebohm (*cr.* 1972); Wells-Pestell (*cr.* 1965); Lloyd of Kilgerran (*cr.* 1973); Penney (*cr.* 1967); Kaberry of Adel (*cr.* 1983); Taylor of Mansfield (*cr.* 1966); Walston (*cr.* 1961); Miles (*cr.* 1979); MacLeod of Fuinary (*cr.* 1967).

Disclaimer of Peerages

The Peerage Act 1963 enables Peers to disclaim their Peerages for life. Peers alive in 1963 could disclaim within 12 months after the passing of the Act (July 31, 1963); a person subsequently succeeding to a Peerage may disclaim within 12 months (one month if an MP) after the date of succession, or of attaining his or her majority, if later. The disclaimer is irrevocable but does not affect the descent of the Peerage after the disclaimant's death, and children of a disclaimed Peer may, if they wish, retain their precedence and any courtesy titles and styles borne as children of a Peer.

EARLS.—Durham (1970); Home (1963); Sandwich (1964).

VISCOUNTS.—Hailsham (1963); Stansgate (1963).

BARONS.—Altrincham (1963); Archibald (1975); Merthyr (1977); Reith (1972); Sanderson of Ayot (1971); Silkin (1972).

Peers Who Are Minors
(i.e. under 21 years of age)

EARLS.—Craven (*b.* 1989).

VISCOUNTS.—Dillon (*b.* 1973).

BARONS.—Gretton (*b.* 1975).

Contractions and Symbols

S. or I. appended to the date of creation denotes a Scottish or Irish title, the further addition of a * implies that the Peer in question holds also an Imperial title, which is specified (after the name) by its more definite description as *Engl., Brit.,* or *UK.* When both titles are alike, as in the case of Argyll, this star is appended to the conjoined date below, and it then denotes that such date is that of the imperial creation.

°.—there is no 'of' in the Marquessate or Earldom so designated.

b.—born.

s.—succeeded.

m.—married.

w.—widower or widow.

M.—minor.

†—Information on *Eldest Son or Heir* not ascertained at time of going to press.

ROYAL DUKES

Style, His Royal Highness The Duke of ——.
Addressed as, Sir, *or more formally,* May it please your Royal Highness.

Created

1947   *Edinburgh,* The Prince Philip, Duke of Edinburgh, KG, KT, OM, GBE, PC, *b.* 1921, *m.* (*see* p. 140).

1337   *Cornwall,* Charles, Prince of Wales, Duke of Cornwall (*Scottish Duke, Rothesay,* 1398), KG, KT, GCB, PC, *b.* 1948, *m.* (*see* p. 140).

1986   *York,* The Prince Andrew, Duke of York, CVO, *b.* 1960, *m.* (*see* p. 141).

1928   *Gloucester* (2nd), Richard, Duke of Gloucester, GCVO, *b.* 1944, *s.* 1974, *m.* (*see* p. 139).

1934   *Kent* (2nd), Edward, Duke of Kent, KG, GCMG, GCVO, *b.* 1935, *s.* 1942, *m.* (*see* p. 139).

ARCHBISHOPS

Style.—The Most Rev. and Right Hon. the Lord Archbishop of——.
Addressed as, Archbishop; *or,* Your Grace.

Introd. to House of Lords		
1991	*Canterbury* (103rd), George Leonard Carey, PH.D., *b.* 1935, *m.* Consecrated Bishop of Bath and Wells 1988, *trans.* 1991.	
1973	*York* (95th), John Stapylton Habgood, PC, PH.D., *b.* 1927, *m.* Consecrated Bishop of Durham, 1973, *trans.* 1983.	

DUKES

Coronet.—Eight strawberry leaves.
Style.—His Grace the Duke of——.
Wife's style.—Her Grace the Duchess of——.
Eldest son's style.—Takes his father's second title as a courtesy title.
Younger sons' style.—'Lord' before forename and family name.
Daughters' style.—'Lady' before forename and family name.
For forms of address, *see* page 219.

Created	Title, Order of Succession, Name, etc.	Eldest Son or Heir
1868 I.*	*Abercorn* (5th), James Hamilton (6th *Brit. Marq.,* 1790, and 14th *Scott. Earl,* 1606 both *Abercorn*), *b.* 1934, *s.* 1979, *m.*	Marquess of Hamilton, *b.* 1969.
1701 s. 1892*	} *Argyll,* Ian Campbell (12th *Scottish* and 5th *UK* Duke, *Argyll*), *b.* 1937, *s.* 1973, *m.*	Marquess of Lorne, *b.* 1968.
1703 s.	*Atholl* (10th), George Iain Murray, *b.* 1931, *s.* 1957.	John *M.*, *b.* 1929.
1682	*Beaufort* (11th), David Robert Somerset, *b.* 1928, *s.* 1984, *m.*	Marquess of Worcester, *b.* 1952.
1694	*Bedford* (13th), John Robert Russell, *b.* 1917, *s.* 1953, *m.*	Marquess of Tavistock, *b.* 1940.
1663 s.*	*Buccleuch* (9th) & *Queensberry* (11th) (1684), Walter Francis John Montagu Douglas Scott, KT, VRD (8th *Engl. Earl, Doncaster,* 1662), *b.* 1923, *s.* 1973, *m.*	Earl of Dalkeith, *b.* 1954.
1694	*Devonshire* (11th), Andrew Robert Buxton Cavendish, MC, PC, *b.* 1920, *s.* 1950, *m.*	Marquess of Hartington, *b.* 1944.
1900	*Fife* (3rd), James George Alexander Bannerman Carnegie, *b.* 1929, *s.* 1959. (*see* p. 137).	Earl of Macduff, *b.* 1961.
1675	*Grafton* (11th), Hugh Denis Charles FitzRoy, KG, *b.* 1919, *s.* 1970, *m.*	Earl of Euston, *b.* 1947.
1643 s.*	*Hamilton* (15th) & *Brandon* (12th) (*Brit.* 1711), Angus Alan Douglas Douglas-Hamilton (*Premier Peer of Scotland*), *b.* 1938, *s.* 1973, *m.*	Marquess of Douglas and Clydesdale, *b.* 1978.
1766 I.*	*Leinster* (8th), Gerald FitzGerald (*Premier Duke, Marquess and Earl of Ireland;* 8th *Brit. Visct., Leinster,* 1747), *b.* 1914, *s.* 1976, *m.*	Marquess of Kildare, *b.* 1948.
1719	*Manchester* (12th), Angus Charles Drogo Montagu, *b.* 1938, *s.* 1985, *m.*	Viscount Mandeville, *b.* 1962.
1702	*Marlborough* (11th), John George Vanderbilt Henry Spencer-Churchill, *b.* 1926, *s.* 1972, *m.*	Marquess of Blandford, *b.* 1955.
1707 s.*	*Montrose* (7th), James Angus Graham (5th *Brit. Earl, Graham,* 1722), *b.* 1907, *s.* 1954, *m.*	Marquess of Graham, *b.* 1935.
1483	*Norfolk* (17th), Miles Francis Stapleton Fitzalan-Howard, KG, GCVO, CB, CBE, MC (*Premier Duke and Earl;* 12th *Eng. Baron Beaumont,* 1309, *s.* 1971; 4th *UK Baron Howard of Glossop,* 1869, *s.* 1972), *b.* 1915, *s.* 1975, *m.* (*Earl Marshal*).	Earl of Arundel and Surrey, *b.* 1956.
1766	*Northumberland* (11th), Henry Alan Walter Richard Percy, *b.* 1953, *s.* 1988.	Lord Ralph G.A.P., *b.* 1956.
1675	*Richmond* (10th) & *Gordon* (5th) (*UK* 1876), Charles Henry Gordon Lennox (10th *Scott. Duke, Lennox,* 1675), *b.* 1929, *s.* 1989, *m.*	Earl of March and Kinrara, *b.* 1955.
1707 s.*	*Roxburghe* (10th), Guy David Innes-Ker (5th *UK Earl, Innes,* 1837), *b.* 1954, *s.* 1974. (*Premier Baronet of Scotland*)	Marquess of Bowmont and Cessford, *b.* 1981.
1703	*Rutland* (10th), Charles John Robert Manners, CBE, *b.* 1919, *s.* 1940, *m.*	Marquess of Granby, *b.* 1959.
1684	*St Albans* (14th), Murray de Vere Beauclerk, *b.* 1939, *s.* 1988, *m.*	Earl of Burford, *b.* 1965.
1547	*Somerset* (19th), John Michael Edward Seymour, *b.* 1952, *s.* 1984, *m.*	Lord Seymour, *b.* 1982.
1833	*Sutherland* (6th), John Sutherland Egerton, TD (5th *UK Earl, Ellesmere,* 1846), *b.* 1915, *s.* 1963, *m.*	Cyril R. *E.*, *b.* 1905.
1814	*Wellington* (8th), Arthur Valerian Wellesley, KG, LVO, OBE, MC (9th *Irish Earl, Mornington,* 1760), *b.* 1915, *s.* 1972, *m.*	Marquess of Douro, *b.* 1945.
1874	*Westminster* (6th), Gerald Cavendish Grosvenor, *b.* 1951, *s.* 1979, *m.*	Earl Grosvenor, *b.* 1991.

MARQUESSES

Coronet.—Four strawberry leaves alternating with four silver balls.
Style.—The Most Hon. the Marquess of——. (In Scotland
the spelling 'Marquis' is preferred for pre-Union creations.)
Wife's style.—The Most Hon. the Marchioness of——.
Eldest son's style.—Takes his father's second title as a courtesy title.
Younger sons' style.—'Lord' before forename and family name.
Daughters' style.—'Lady' before forename and family name.
For forms of address, *see* page 219.

Created	Title, Order of Succession, Name, etc.	Eldest Son or Heir
1916	*Aberdeen and Temair* (6th), Alastair Ninian John Gordon (12th *Scott. Earl, Aberdeen*, 1682), b. 1920, s. 1984, m.	Earl of Haddo, b. 1955.
1876	*Abergavenny* (5th), John Henry Guy Nevill, KG, OBE, b. 1914, s. 1954, m.	Guy R. G. N., b. 1945.
1821	*Ailesbury* (8th), Michael Sidney Cedric Brudenell-Bruce, b. 1926, s. 1974, m.	Earl of Cardigan, b. 1952.
1831	*Ailsa* (7th), Archibald David Kennedy, OBE, (19th *Scott. Earl, Cassillis*, 1509), b. 1925, s. 1957, m.	Earl of Cassillis, b. 1956.
1815	*Anglesey* (7th), George Charles Henry Victor Paget, b. 1922, s. 1947, m.	Earl of Uxbridge, b. 1950.
1789	*Bath* (6th), Henry Frederick Thynne, b. 1905, s. 1946, m.	Viscount Weymouth, b. 1932.
1826	*Bristol* (7th), (Frederick William) John Augustus Hervey, b. 1954, s. 1985.	Lord F. W. C. Nicholas W. H., b. 1961.
1796	*Bute* (6th), John Crichton-Stuart (11th *Scott. Earl, Dumfries*, 1633), b. 1933, s. 1956, m.	Earl of Dumfries, b. 1958.
1812	°*Camden* (6th), David George Edward Henry Pratt, b. 1930, s. 1983.	Earl of Brecknock, b. 1965.
1815	*Cholmondeley* (7th), David George Philip Cholmondeley (11th *Irish Viscount, Cholmondeley*, 1661), b. 1960, s. 1990. (*Lord Great Chamberlain*).	Charles G. C., b. 1959.
1816 I.*	°*Conyngham* (7th), Frederick William Henry Francis Conyngham (7th *UK Baron, Minster, UK* 1821), b. 1924, s. 1974, m.	Earl of Mount Charles, b. 1951.
1791 I.*	*Donegall* (7th), Dermot Richard Claud Chichester, LVO (7th *Brit. Baron, Fisherwick*, 1790, 6th *Brit. Baron, Templemore*, 1831), b. 1916, s. to Marquessate, 1975: to Templemore Barony, 1953, m.	Earl of Belfast, b. 1952.
1789 I.*	*Downshire* (8th), (Arthur) Robin Ian Hill (8th *Brit. Earl, Hillsborough*, 1772), b. 1929, s. 1989, m.	Earl of Hillsborough, b. 1959.
1801 I.*	*Ely* (8th) Charles John Tottenham (8th *UK Baron, Loftus*, 1801), b. 1913, s. 1969, m.	Viscount Loftus, b. 1943.
1801	*Exeter* (8th), (William) Michael Anthony Cecil, b. 1935, s. 1988, m.	Lord Burghley, b. 1970.
1800 I.*	*Headfort* (6th), Thomas Geoffrey Charles Michael Taylour (4th *UK Baron, Kenlis*, 1831), b. 1932, s. 1960, m.	Earl of Bective, b. 1959.
1793	*Hertford* (8th), Hugh Edward Conway Seymour (9th *Irish Baron, Conway*, 1712), b. 1930, s. 1940, m.	Earl of Yarmouth, b. 1958.
1599 s.*	*Huntly* (13th), Granville Charles Gomer Gordon (*Premier Marquess of Scotland*) (5th *UK Baron, Meldrum*, 1815), b. 1944, s. 1987, m.	Earl of Aboyne, b. 1973.
1784	*Lansdowne* (8th), George John Charles Mercer Nairne Petty-Fitzmaurice, PC (8th *Irish Earl, Kerry*, 1723), b. 1912, s. 1944, w.	Earl of Shelburne, b. 1941.
1902	*Linlithgow* (4th), Adrian John Charles Hope (10th *Scott. Earl, Hopetoun* 1703), b. 1946, s. 1987, m.	Earl of Hopetoun, b. 1969.
1816 I.*	*Londonderry* (9th), Alexander Charles Robert Vane-Tempest-Stewart (6th *UK Earl, Vane*, 1823), b. 1937, s. 1955, m.	Viscount Castlereagh, b. 1972.
1701 s.*	*Lothian* (12th), Peter Francis Walter Kerr, KCVO (6th *UK Baron, Kerr*, 1821), b. 1922, s. 1940, m.	Earl of Ancram, b. 1945.
1917	*Milford Haven* (4th), George Ivar Louis Mountbatten, b. 1961, s. 1970, m.	Lord Ivar A. M. M., b. 1963.
1838	*Normanby* (4th), Oswald Constantine John Phipps, KG, CBE (8th *Irish Baron, Mulgrave*, 1767), b. 1912, s. 1932, m.	Earl of Mulgrave, b. 1954.
1812	*Northampton* (7th), Spencer Douglas David Compton, b. 1946, s. 1978, m.	Earl Compton, b. 1973.
1825 I.*	*Ormonde* (7th), James Hubert Theobald Charles Butler, MBE (7th *UK Baron, Ormonde*, 1821), b. 1899, s. 1971, w.	None to Marquessate. To Earldoms of Ormonde and Ossory, Viscount Mountgarret, b. 1936 (*see* p. 158).
1682 s.	*Queensberry* (12th), David Harrington Angus Douglas, b. 1929, s. 1954.	Viscount Drumlanrig, b. 1967.
1926	*Reading* (4th), Simon Charles Henry Rufus Isaacs, b. 1942, s. 1980, m.	Viscount Erleigh, b. 1986.
1789	*Salisbury* (6th), Robert Edward Peter Cecil, b. 1916, s. 1972, m.	Viscount Cranborne, b. 1946.
1800 I.*	*Sligo* (10th), Denis Edward Browne (10th *UK Baron, Monteagle*, 1806), b. 1908, s. 1952, m.	Earl of Altamont, b. 1939.
1787	°*Townshend* (7th), George John Patrick Dominic Townshend, b. 1916, s. 1921, w.	Viscount Raynham, b. 1945.
1694 s.*	*Tweeddale* (13th), Edward Douglas John Hay (4th *UK Baron, Tweeddale*, 1881), b. 1947, s. 1979.	Lord Charles D. M. H., b. 1947.
1789 I.*	*Waterford* (8th), John Hubert de la Poer Beresford (8th *Brit. Baron, Tyrone*, 1786), b. 1933, s. 1934, m.	Earl of Tyrone, b. 1958.
1551	*Winchester* (18th), Nigel George Paulet (*Premier Marquess of England*), b. 1941, s. 1968, m.	Earl of Wiltshire, b. 1969.
1892	*Zetland* (4th), Lawrence Mark Dundas (6th *UK Earl of Zetland*, 1838, 7th *Brit. Baron Dundas*, 1794), b. 1937, s. 1989, m.	Earl of Ronaldshay, b. 1965.

EARLS

Coronet.—Eight silver balls on stalks alternating with
eight gold strawberry leaves.
Style.—The Right Hon. the Earl of——.
Wife's style.—The Right Hon. the Countess of——.
Eldest son's style.—Takes his father's second title as a courtesy title.
Younger sons' style.—'The Hon.' before forename and family name.
Daughters' style.—'Lady' before forename and family name.
For forms of address, *see* page 219.

Created	Title, Order of Succession, Name, etc.	Eldest Son or Heir
1639 s.	*Airlie* (13th), David George Coke Patrick Ogilvy, KT, GCVO, PC, *b.* 1926, *s.* 1968, *m.* (*Lord Chamberlain*).	Lord Ogilvy, *b.* 1958.
1696	*Albemarle* (10th), Rufus Arnold Alexis Keppel, *b.* 1965, *s.* 1979.	Crispian W. J. K., *b.* 1948.
1952	°*Alexander of Tunis* (2nd), Shane William Desmond Alexander, *b.* 1935, *s.* 1969, *m.*	Hon. Brian J. A., *b.* 1939.
1826	°*Amherst* (5th), Jeffery John Archer Amherst, MC, *b.* 1896, *s.* 1927.	(None.)
1662 s.	*Annandale and Hartfell* (11th), Patrick Andrew Wentworth Hope Johnstone, *b.* 1941, *claim established* 1985, *m.*	Lord Johnstone, *b.* 1971.
1789 I.	°*Annesley* (10th), Patrick Annesley, *b.* 1924, *s.* 1979, *m.*	Hon. Philip H.A., *b.* 1927.
1785 I.	*Antrim* (9th), Alexander Randal Mark McDonnell, *b.* 1935, *s.* 1977, *m.* (*Viscount Dunluce.*)	Hon. Randal A. St J. M., *b.* 1967.
1762 I.*	*Arran* (9th), Arthur Desmond Colquhoun Gore (5th *UK Baron Sudley*, 1884), *b.* 1938, *s.* 1983, *m.*	Paul A. G., CMG, CVO, *b.* 1921.
1955	°*Attlee* (3rd), John Richard Attlee, *b.* 1956, *s.* 1991.	(None.)
1714	*Aylesford* (11th), Charles Ian Finch-Knightley, *b.* 1918, *s.* 1958, *m.*	Lord Guernsey, *b.* 1947.
1937	°*Baldwin of Bewdley* (4th), Edward Alfred Alexander Baldwin, *b.* 1938, *s.* 1976, *m.*	Viscount Corvedale, *b.* 1973.
1922	*Balfour* (4th), Gerald Arthur James Balfour, *b.* 1925, *s.* 1968, *m.*	Eustace A. G. B., *b.* 1921.
1772	°*Bathurst* (8th), Henry Allen John Bathurst, *b.* 1927, *s.* 1943, *m.*	Lord Apsley, *b.* 1961.
1919	°*Beatty* (3rd), David Beatty, *b.* 1946, *s.* 1972, *m.*	Viscount Borodale, *b.* 1973.
1797 I.	*Belmore* (8th), John Armar Lowry-Corry, *b.* 1951, *s.* 1960, *m.*	Viscount Corry, *b.* 1985.
1739 I.* } 1937 }	*Bessborough*, Frederick Edward Neuflize Ponsonby (10th *Irish* and 2nd *UK Earl Bessborough*), *b.* 1913, *s.* 1956, *m.*	Arthur M. L. P., *b.* 1912 (to Irish Earldom and UK Barony only).
1815	*Bradford* (7th), Richard Thomas Orlando Bridgeman, *b.* 1947, *s.* 1981, *m.*	Viscount Newport, *b.*1980.
1677 s.	*Breadalbane and Holland* (10th), John Romer Boreland Campbell, *b.* 1919, *s.* 1959.	(None.)
1469 s.*	*Buchan* (17th), Malcolm Harry Erskine, (8th *UK Baron Erskine* 1806), *b.* 1930, *s.* 1984, *m.*	Lord Cardross, *b.* 1960.
1746	*Buckinghamshire* (10th), (George) Miles Hobart-Hampden, *b.* 1944, *s.* 1983, *m.*	Sir John Hobart, Bt., *b.* 1945.
1800	°*Cadogan* (7th), William Gerald Charles Cadogan, MC, *b.* 1914, *s.* 1933, *m.*	Viscount Chelsea, *b.* 1937.
1878	°*Cairns* (6th), Simon Dallas Cairns, *b.* 1939, *s.* 1989, *m.*	Viscount Garmoyle, *b.* 1965.
1455 s.	*Caithness* (20th), Malcolm Ian Sinclair, PC, *b.* 1948, *s.* 1965, *m.*	Lord Berriedale, *b.* 1981.
1800 I.	*Caledon* (7th), Nicholas James Alexander, *b.* 1955, *s.* 1980, *m.*	Viscount Alexander, *b.* 1990.
1661	*Carlisle* (12th), Charles James Ruthven Howard, MC (12th *Scott. Baron, Ruthven of Freeland*, 1651), *b.* 1923, *s.* 1963, *m.*	Viscount Morpeth, *b.* 1949.
1793	*Carnarvon* (7th), Henry George Reginald Molyneux Herbert, KCVO, KBE, *b.* 1924, *s.* 1987, *m.*	Lord Porchester, *b.* 1956.
1748 I.*	*Carrick* (9th), Brian Stuart Theobald Somerset Caher Butler (3rd *UK Baron, Butler*, 1912), *b.* 1931, *s.* 1957, *m.*	Viscount Ikerrin, *b.* 1953.
1800 I.	°*Castle Stewart* (8th), Arthur Patrick Avondale Stuart, *b.* 1928, *s.* 1961, *m.*	Viscount Stuart, *b.* 1953.
1814	°*Cathcart* (6th), Alan Cathcart, CB, DSO, MC (15th *Scott. Baron, Cathcart*, 1447), *b.* 1919, *s.* 1927, *m.*	Lord Greenock, *b.* 1952.
1647 I.	*Cavan* (13th), Roger Cavan Lambart, *b.* 1944, *s.* 1988.	Arthur O. R. L., *b.* 1909.
1827	°*Cawdor* (6th), Hugh John Vaughan Campbell, *b.* 1932, *s.* 1970, *m.*	Viscount Emlyn, *b.* 1962.
1801	*Chichester* (9th), John Nicholas Pelham, *b.* 1944, *s.* 1944, *m.*	Richard A. H. P., *b.* 1952.
1803 I.*	*Clancarty* (8th), William Francis Brinsley Le Poer Trench (7th *UK Visct. Clancarty*, 1823), *b.* 1911, *s.* 1975, *m.*	Nicholas P. R. *Le P. T.*, *b.* 1952.
1776 I.*	*Clanwilliam* (7th), John Herbert Meade (5th *UK Baron Clanwilliam*, 1828), *b.* 1919, *s.* 1989, *m.*	Lord Gillford, *b.* 1960.
1776	*Clarendon* (7th), George Frederick Laurence Hyde Villiers, *b.* 1933, *s.* 1955, *m.*	Lord Hyde, *b.* 1976.
1620 I.*	*Cork* (13th) *& Orrery* (13th)(I. 1660), Patrick Reginald Boyle (9th *Brit. Baron, Boyle of Marston*, 1711), *b.* 1910, *s.* 1967, *m.*	Hon. John W. *B.*, DSC, *b.* 1916.
1850	*Cottenham* (8th), Kenelm Charles Everard Digby Pepys, *b.* 1948, *s.* 1968, *m.*	Viscount Crowhurst, *b.* 1983.
1762 I.*	*Courtown* (9th), James Patrick Montagu Burgoyne Winthrop Stopford (8th *Brit. Baron, Saltersford*, 1796), *b.* 1954, *s.* 1975, *m.*	Viscount Stopford, *b.* 1988.
1697	*Coventry* (11th), George William Coventry, *b.* 1934, *s.* 1940, *m.*	Viscount Deerhurst, *b.* 1957.

Created	Title, Order of Succession, Name, etc.	Eldest Son or Heir
1857	°*Cowley* (7th), Garret Graham Wellesley, b. 1934, s. 1975, m.	Viscount Dangan, b. 1965.
1892	*Cranbrook* (5th), Gathorne Gathorne-Hardy, b. 1933, s. 1978, m.	Lord Medway, b. 1968.
1801	*Craven* (9th), Benjamin Robert Joseph Craven, b. 1989, s. 1990, M.	Rupert J. E. C., b. 1926.
1398 s.*	*Crawford* (29th) & *Balcarres* (12th) (s. 1651), Robert Alexander Lindsay, PC, (*Premier Earl on Union Roll, 5th UK Baron, Wigan, 1826,* and *Baron Balniel* (Life Peer)), b. 1927, s. 1975, m.	Lord Balniel, b. 1958.
1861	*Cromartie* (5th), John Ruaridh Blunt Grant Mackenzie, b. 1948, s. 1989, m.	Viscount Tarbat, b. 1987.
1901	*Cromer* (4th), Evelyn Rowland Esmond Baring, b. 1946, s. 1991, m.	Hon. Vivian J. R. B., b. 1950.
1633 s.*	*Dalhousie* (16th), Simon Ramsay, KT, GCVO, GBE, MC (4th *UK Baron, Ramsay*, 1875), b. 1914, s. 1950, m.	Lord Ramsay, b. 1948.
1725 i.*	*Darnley* (11th), Adam Ivo Stuart Bligh (20th *English Baron, Clifton of Leighton Bromswold*, 1608), b. 1941, s. 1980, m.	Lord Clifton of Rathmore, b. 1968.
1711	*Dartmouth* (9th), Gerald Humphry Legge, b. 1924, s. 1962, m.	Viscount Lewisham, b. 1949.
1761	°*De La Warr* (11th), William Herbrand Sackville, b. 1948, s. 1988, m.	Lord Buckhurst, b. 1979.
1622	*Denbigh* (11th) & *Desmond* (10th) (i. 1622), William Rudolph Michael Feilding, b. 1943, s. 1966, m.	Viscount Feilding, b. 1970.
1485	*Derby* (18th), Edward John Stanley, MC, b. 1918, s. 1948, w.	Edward R. W. S., b. 1962.
1553	*Devon* (17th), Charles Christopher Courtenay, b. 1916, s. 1935, m.	Lord Courtenay, b. 1942.
1800 i.*	*Donoughmore* (8th), Richard Michael John Hely-Hutchinson (8th *UK Visct., Hutchinson,* 1821), b. 1927, s. 1981, m.	Viscount Suirdale, b. 1952.
1661 i.*	*Drogheda* (12th), Henry Dermot Ponsonby Moore, (3rd *UK Baron, Moore,* 1954), b. 1937, s. 1989, m.	Viscount Moore, b. 1983.
1837	*Ducie* (6th), Basil Howard Moreton, b. 1917, s. 1952, m.	Lord Moreton, b. 1951.
1860	*Dudley* (4th), William Humble David Ward, b. 1920, s. 1969, m.	Viscount Ednam, b. 1947.
1660 s.*	*Dundee* (12th), Alexander Henry Scrymgeour, (2nd *UK Baron, Glassary,* 1954), b. 1949, s. 1983, m.	Lord Scrymgeour, b. 1982.
1669 s.	*Dundonald* (15th), Iain Alexander Douglas Blair Cochrane, b. 1961, s. 1986, m.	Lord Cochrane, b. 1991.
1686 s.	*Dunmore* (11th), Kenneth Randolph Murray, b. 1913, s. 1981, w.	Viscount Fincastle, b. 1946.
1822 i.	*Dunraven and Mount-Earl* (7th), Thady Windham Thomas Wyndham-Quin, b. 1939, s. 1965, m.	(None).
1833	*Durham.* Disclaimed for life 1970. (*Antony Claud Frederick Lambton,* b. 1922, s. 1970, m.)	Hon. Edward R. L., b. 1961.
1837	*Effingham* (6th), Mowbray Henry Gordon Howard (16th *E. Baron, Howard of Effingham,* 1554), b. 1905, s. 1946, m.	Cdr. David P. M. A. H., b. 1939.
1507 s. ⎱ 1859* ⎰	*Eglinton* (18th) & *Winton* (9th) (1600), Archibald George Montgomerie (6th *UK Earl, Winton,* 1859), b. 1939, s. 1966, m.	Lord Montgomerie, b. 1966.
1733 i.*	*Egmont* (11th), Frederick George Moore Perceval (9th *Brit. Baron, Lovel & Holland,* 1762), b. 1914, s. 1932, m.	Viscount Perceval, b. 1934.
1821	*Eldon* (5th), John Joseph Nicholas Scott, b. 1937, s. 1976, m.	Viscount Encombe, b. 1962.
1633 s.*	*Elgin* (11th), & *Kincardine* (15th) (s. 1647), Andrew Douglas Alexander Thomas Bruce (4th *UK Baron, Elgin,* 1849), KT, b. 1924, s. 1968, m.	Lord Bruce, b. 1961.
1789 i.*	*Enniskillen* (7th), Andrew John Galbraith Cole (5th *UK Baron, Grinstead,* 1815) b. 1942, s. 1989, m.	Arthur G. C., b. 1920.
1789 i.*	*Erne* (6th), Henry George Victor John Crichton (3rd *UK Baron, Fermanagh,* 1876), b. 1937, s. 1940, m.	Viscount Crichton, b. 1971.
1452 s.	*Erroll* (24th), Merlin Sereld Victor Gilbert Hay (*Hereditary Lord High Constable and Knight Marischal of Scotland*), b. 1948, s. 1978, m.	Lord Hay, b. 1984.
1661	*Essex* (10th), Robert Edward de Vere Capell, b. 1920, s. 1981, m.	Viscount Malden, b. 1944.
1711	°*Ferrers* (13th), Robert Washington Shirley, PC, b. 1929, s. 1954, m.	Viscount Tamworth, b. 1952.
1789	°*Fortescue* (7th), Richard Archibald Fortescue, b. 1922, s. 1977, m.	Viscount Ebrington, b. 1951.
1841	*Gainsborough* (5th), Anthony Gerard Edward Noel, b. 1923, s. 1927, m.	Viscount Campden, b. 1950.
1623 s.*	*Galloway* (13th), Randolph Keith Reginald Stewart (6th *Brit. Baron, Stewart of Garlies,* 1796), b. 1928, s. 1978, m.	Andrew C. S., b. 1949.
1703 s.*	*Glasgow* (10th), Patrick Robin Archibald Boyle (4th *UK Baron, Fairlie,* 1897), b. 1939, s. 1984, m.	Viscount of Kelburn, b. 1978.
1806 i.*	*Gosford* (7th), Charles David Nicholas Alexander John Sparrow Acheson (5th *UK Baron, Worlingham,* 1835), b. 1942, s. 1966, m.	Hon. Patrick B. V. M. A., b. 1915.
1945	*Gowrie* (2nd), Alexander Patric Greysteil Hore-Ruthven, PC (3rd *UK Baron, Ruthven of Gowrie,* 1919), b. 1939, s. 1955, m.	Viscount Ruthven of Canberra, b. 1964.
1684 i.*	*Granard* (9th), Arthur Patrick Hastings Forbes, AFC (4th *UK Baron, Granard,* 1806), b. 1915, s. 1948, m.	Peter A. E. H. F., b. 1957.
1833	°*Granville* (5th), Granville James Leveson-Gower, MC, b. 1918, s. 1953, m.	Lord Leveson, b. 1959.
1806	°*Grey* (6th), Richard Fleming George Charles Grey, b. 1939, s. 1963, m.	Philip K. G., b. 1940.
1752	*Guilford* (9th), Edward Francis North, b. 1933, s. 1949, m.	Lord North, b. 1971.
1619 s.	*Haddington* (13th), John George Baillie-Hamilton, b. 1941, s. 1986, m.	Lord Binning, b. 1985.
1919	°*Haig* (2nd), George Alexander Eugene Douglas Haig, OBE, b. 1918, s. 1928, m.	Viscount Dawick, b. 1961.
1944	*Halifax* (3rd), Charles Edward Peter Neil Wood (5th *UK Viscount, Halifax,* 1866), b. 1944, s. 1980, m.	Lord Irwin, b. 1977.

Created	Title, Order of Succession, Name, etc.	Eldest Son or Heir

1898   *Halsbury* (3rd), John Anthony Hardinge Giffard, FRS, *b.* 1908, *s.* 1943, *w.* — Adam E. *G.*, *b.* 1934.

1754   *Hardwicke* (10th), Joseph Philip Sebastian Yorke, *b.* 1971, *s.* 1974. — Richard C. J. *Y.*, *b.* 1916.

1812   *Harewood* (7th), George Henry Hubert Lascelles, KBE, *b.* 1923, *s.* 1947, *m.* (*See also* p. 139.) — Viscount Lascelles, *b.* 1950.

1742   *Harrington* (11th), William Henry Leicester Stanhope (8th *Brit. Viscount, Stanhope of Mahon,* 1717), *b.* 1922, *s.* 1929, *m.* — Viscount Petersham, *b.* 1945.

1809   *Harrowby* (7th), Dudley Danvers Granville Coutts Ryder, TD, *b.* 1922, *s.* 1987, *m.* — Viscount Sandon, *b.* 1951.

1605 s.   *Home.* Disclaimed for life 1963. (*See* Lord Home of the Hirsel, p. 172.) — Hon. David A. C. *D.-H.*, *b.* 1943.

1821   °*Howe* (7th), Frederick Richard Penn Curzon, *b.* 1951, *s.* 1984, *m.* — Charles M. P. *C.*, *b.* 1967.

1529   *Huntingdon* (16th), William Edward Robin Hood Hastings Bass, *b.* 1948, *s.* 1990, *m.* — Simon A. R. H. *H. B.*, *b.* 1950.

1885   *Iddesleigh* (4th), Stafford Henry Northcote, *b.* 1932, *s.* 1970, *m.* — Viscount St Cyres, *b.* 1957.

1756   *Ilchester* (9th), Maurice Vivian de Touffreville Fox-Strangways, *b.* 1920, *s.* 1970, *m.* — Hon. Raymond G. *F.-S.*, *b.* 1921.

1929   *Inchcape* (3rd), Kenneth James William Mackay, *b.* 1917, *s.* 1939, *m.* — Viscount Glenapp, *b.* 1943.

1919   *Iveagh* (3rd), Arthur Francis Benjamin Guinness, *b.* 1937, *s.* 1967. — Viscount Elveden, *b.* 1969.

1925   °*Jellicoe* (2nd), George Patrick John Rushworth Jellicoe, KBE, DSO, MC, PC, *b.* 1918, *s.* 1935, *m.* — Viscount Brocas, *b.* 1950.

1697   *Jersey* (9th), George Francis Child-Villiers (12th *Irish Visct., Grandison,* 1620), *b.* 1910, *s.* 1923, *m.* — Viscount Villiers, *b.* 1948.

1822 I.   *Kilmorey* (6th), Richard Francis Needham, MP, *b.* 1942, *s.* 1977, *m.* — Viscount Newry and Morne, *b.* 1966.

1866   *Kimberley* (4th), John Wodehouse, *b.* 1924, *s.* 1941, *m.* — Lord Wodehouse, *b.* 1951.

1768 I.   *Kingston* (11th), Barclay Robert Edwin King-Tenison, *b.* 1943, *s.* 1948, *m.* — Viscount Kingsborough, *b.* 1969.

1633 s.*   *Kinnoull* (15th), Arthur William George Patrick Hay (9th *Brit. Baron, Hay of Pedwardine,* 1711), *b.* 1935, *s.* 1938, *m.* — Viscount Dupplin, *b.* 1962.

1677 s.*   *Kintore* (13th), Michael Canning William John Keith (3rd *UK Viscount Stonehaven,* 1938), *b.* 1939, *s.* 1989, *m.* — Lord Inverurie, *b.* 1976.

1914   °*Kitchener of Khartoum* (3rd), Henry Herbert Kitchener, TD, *b.* 1919, *s.* 1937. — (None.)

1756 I.   *Lanesborough* (9th), Denis Anthony Brian Butler, TD, *b.* 1918, *s.* 1950. — Henry A. B. C. *B.*, *b.* 1909.

1624 s.   *Lauderdale* (17th), Patrick Francis Maitland, *b.* 1911, *s.* 1968, *m.* — Viscount Maitland, *b.* 1937.

1837   *Leicester* (6th), Anthony Louis Lovel Coke, *b.* 1909, *s.* 1976, *m.* — Viscount Coke, *b.* 1936.

1641 s.   *Leven* (14th) & *Melville* (13th) (s. 1690), Alexander Robert Leslie Melville, *b.* 1924, *s.* 1947, *m.* — Lord Balgonie, *b.* 1954.

1831   *Lichfield* (5th), Thomas Patrick John Anson, *b.* 1939, *s.* 1960. — Viscount Anson, *b.* 1978.

1803 I.*   *Limerick* (6th), Patrick Edmund Pery, KBE (6th *UK Baron, Foxford,* 1815), *b.* 1930, *s.* 1967, *m.* — Viscount Glentworth, *b.* 1963.

1572   *Lincoln* (18th), Edward Horace Fiennes-Clinton, *b.* 1913, *s.* 1988, *m.* — Hon. Edward G. *F.-C.*, *b.* 1943.

1633 s.   *Lindsay* (16th), James Randolph Lindesay-Bethune, *b.* 1955, *s.* 1989, *m.* — Viscount Garnock, *b.* 1990.

1626   *Lindsey* (14th) *and Abingdon* (9th) (1682), Richard Henry Rupert Bertie, *b.* 1931, *s.* 1963, *m.* — Lord Norreys, *b.* 1958.

1776 I.   *Lisburne* (8th), John David Malet Vaughan, *b.* 1918, *s.* 1965, *m.* — Viscount Vaughan, *b.* 1945.

1822 I.*   *Listowel* (5th), William Francis Hare, GCMG, PC, (3rd *UK Baron, Hare,* 1869), *b.* 1906, *s.* 1931, *m.* — Viscount Ennismore, *b.* 1964.

1905   *Liverpool* (5th), Edward Peter Bertram Savile Foljambe, *b.* 1944, *s.* 1969, *m.* — Viscount Hawkesbury, *b.* 1972.

1945   °*Lloyd George of Dwyfor* (3rd), Owen Lloyd George, *b.* 1924, *s.* 1968, *m.* — Viscount Gwynedd, *b.* 1951.

1785 I.*   *Longford* (7th), Francis Aungier Pakenham, KG, PC (6th *UK Baron, Silchester,* 1821; 1st *UK Baron, Pakenham,* 1945), *b.* 1905, *s.* 1961, *m.* — Thomas F. D. *P.*, *b.* 1933.

1807   *Lonsdale* (7th), James Hugh William Lowther, *b.* 1922, *s.* 1953, *m.* — Viscount Lowther, *b.* 1949.

1838   *Lovelace* (5th), Peter Axel William Locke King (12th *British Baron, King,* 1725), *b.* 1951, *s.* 1964, *m.* — (None.)

1795 I.*   *Lucan* (7th), Richard John Bingham (3rd *UK Baron, Bingham,* 1934), *b.* 1934, *s.* 1964, *m.* — Lord Bingham, *b.* 1967.

1880   *Lytton* (5th), John Peter Michael Scawen Lytton (18th *English Baron, Wentworth,* 1529), *b.* 1950, *s.* 1985, *m.* — Viscount Knebworth, *b.* 1989.

1721   *Macclesfield* (8th), George Roger Alexander Thomas Parker, *b.* 1914, *s.* 1975, *m.* — Viscount Parker, *b.* 1943.

1800   *Malmesbury* (6th), William James Harris, TD, *b.* 1907, *s.* 1950, *m.* — Viscount FitzHarris, *b.* 1946.

1776 &   *Mansfield and Mansfield* (8th), William David Mungo James Murray (14th *Scott. Visct., Stormont,* 1621), *b.* 1930, *s.* 1971, *m.* — Viscount Stormont, *b.* 1956.

1792

1565 s.   *Mar* (13th) & *Kellie* (15th) (s. 1616), John Francis Hervey Erskine, *b.* 1921, *s.* 1955, *m.* — Lord Erskine, *b.* 1949.

1785 I.   *Mayo* (10th), Terence Patrick Bourke, *b.* 1929, *s.* 1962, *m.* — Lord Naas, *b.* 1953.

1627 I.*   *Meath* (14th), Anthony Windham Normand Brabazon (5th *UK Baron, Chaworth,* 1831), *b.* 1910, *s.* 1949, *m.* — Lord Ardee, *b.* 1941.

1766 I.   *Mexborough* (8th), John Christopher George Savile, *b.* 1931, *s.* 1980, *m.* — Viscount Pollington, *b.* 1959.

Created	Title, Order of Succession, Name, etc.	Eldest Son or Heir
1813	*Minto* (6th), Gilbert Edward George Lariston Elliot-Murray-Kynynmound, OBE, *b.* 1928, *s.* 1975, *m.*	Viscount Melgund, *b.* 1953.
1562 s.*	*Moray* (20th) Douglas John Moray Stuart (12th *Brit. Baron, Stuart of Castle Stuart*, 1796), *b.* 1928, *s.* 1974, *m.*	Lord Doune, *b.* 1966.
1815	*Morley* (6th), John St Aubyn Parker, *b.* 1923, *s.* 1962, *m.*	Viscount Boringdon, *b.* 1956.
1458 s.	*Morton* (22nd), John Charles Sholto Douglas, *b.* 1927, *s.* 1976, *m.*	Lord Aberdour, *b.* 1952.
1789	*Mount Edgcumbe* (8th), Robert Charles Edgcumbe, *b.* 1939, *s.* 1982, *m.*	Piers V. *E.*, *b.* 1946.
1831	*Munster* (7th), Anthony Charles FitzClarence, *b.* 1926, *s.* 1983, *m.*	(None.)
1805	°*Nelson* (9th), Peter John Horatio Nelson, *b.* 1941, *s.* 1981, *m.*	Viscount Merton, *b.* 1971.
1660 s.	*Newburgh* (12th), Prince Filippo Giambattista Camillo Francesco Aldo Maria Rospigliosi, *b.* 1942, *s.* 1986, *m.*	Princess Benedetta F. M. *R.*, *b.* 1974.
1827 I.	*Norbury* (6th), Noel Terence Graham-Toler, *b.* 1939, *s.* 1955, *m.*	Viscount Glandine, *b.* 1967.
1806 I.*	*Normanton* (6th), Shaun James Christian Welbore Ellis Agar (9th *Brit. Baron, Mendip*, 1791) (4th *UK Baron, Somerton*, 1873), *b.* 1945, *s.* 1967, *m.*	Viscount Somerton, *b.* 1982.
1647 s.	*Northesk* (13th), Robert Andrew Carnegie, *b.* 1926, *s.* 1975, *m.*	Lord Rosehill, *b.* 1954.
1801	*Onslow* (7th), Michael William Coplestone Dillon Onslow, *b.* 1938, *s.* 1971, *m.*	Viscount Cranley, *b.* 1967.
1696 s.	*Orkney* (8th), Cecil O'Bryen Fitz-Maurice, *b.* 1919, *s.* 1951, *m.*	O. Peter *St John*, *b.* 1938.
1925	*Oxford and Asquith* (2nd), Julian Edward George Asquith, KCMG, *b.* 1916, *s.* 1928, *m.*	Viscount Asquith, *b.* 1952.
1929	°*Peel* (3rd), William James Robert Peel (4th *UK Viscount Peel*, 1895), *b.* 1947, *s.* 1969, *m.*	Viscount Clanfield, *b.* 1976.
1551	*Pembroke* (17th) & *Montgomery* (14th) (1605), Henry George Charles Alexander Herbert, *b.* 1939, *s.* 1969.	Lord Herbert, *b.* 1978.
1605 s.	*Perth* (17th), John David Drummond, PC, *b.* 1907, *s.* 1951, *m.*	Viscount Strathallan, *b.* 1935.
1905	*Plymouth* (3rd), Other Robert Ivor Windsor-Clive (15th *English Baron, Windsor*, 1529), *b.* 1923, *s.* 1943, *m.*	Viscount Windsor, *b.* 1951.
1785 I.	*Portarlington* (7th), George Lionel Yuill Seymour Dawson-Damer, *b.* 1938, *s.* 1959, *m.*	Viscount Carlow, *b.* 1965.
1689	*Portland* (11th), Count Henry Noel Bentinck, *b.* 1919, *s.* 1990, *m.*	Viscount Woodstock, *b.* 1953.
1743	*Portsmouth* (10th), Quentin Gerard Carew Wallop, *b.* 1954, *s.* 1984, *m.*	Viscount Lymington, *b.* 1981.
1804	*Powis* (7th), George William Herbert (8th *Irish Baron, Clive*, 1762), *b.* 1925, *s.* 1988, *m.*	Viscount Clive, *b.* 1952.
1765	*Radnor* (8th), Jacob Pleydell-Bouverie, *b.* 1927, *s.* 1968, *m.*	Viscount Folkestone, *b.* 1955.
1831 I.*	*Ranfurly* (7th), Gerald François Needham Knox (8th *UK Baron, Ranfurly*, 1826), *b.* 1929, *s.* 1988, *m.*	Viscount Northland, *b.* 1957.
1771 I.	*Roden* (9th), Robert William Jocelyn, *b.* 1909, *s.* 1956, *w.*	Viscount Jocelyn, *b.* 1938.
1801	*Romney* (7th), Michael Henry Marsham, *b.* 1910, *s.* 1975, *m.*	Julian C. *M.*, *b.* 1948.
1703 s.*	*Rosebery* (7th), Neil Archibald Primrose (3rd *UK Earl, Midlothian*, 1911), *b.* 1929, *s.* 1974, *m.*	Lord Dalmeny, *b.* 1967.
1806 I.	*Rosse* (7th), William Brendan Parsons, *b.* 1936, *s.* 1979, *m.*	Lord Oxmantown, *b.* 1969.
1801	*Rosslyn* (7th), Peter St Clair-Erskine, *b.* 1958, *s.* 1977, *m.*	Lord Loughborough, *b.* 1986.
1457 s.	*Rothes* (21st), Ian Lionel Malcolm Leslie, *b.* 1932, *s.* 1975, *m.*	Lord Leslie, *b.* 1958.
1861	°*Russell* (5th), Conrad Sebastian Robert Russell, *b.* 1937, *s.* 1987, *m.*	Viscount Amberley, *b.* 1968.
1915	°*St Aldwyn* (2nd), Michael John Hicks Beach, GBE, TD, PC, *b.* 1912, *s.* 1916, *m.*	Viscount Quenington, *b.* 1950.
1815	*St Germans* (10th), Peregrine Nicholas Eliot, *b.* 1941, *s.* 1988.	Lord Eliot, *b.* 1966.
1660	*Sandwich.* Disclaimed for life 1964. ((*Alexander*) *Victor* (*Edward Paulet*) *Montagu, b.* 1906, *s.* 1962.)	John E. H. *M.*, *b.* 1943.
1690	*Scarbrough* (12th), Richard Aldred Lumley (13th *Irish Visct., Lumley*, 1628), *b.* 1932, *s.* 1969, *m.*	Viscount Lumley, *b.* 1973.
1701 s.	*Seafield* (13th), Ian Derek Francis Ogilvie-Grant, *b.* 1939, *s.* 1969, *m.*	Viscount Reidhaven, *b.* 1963.
1882	*Selborne* (4th), John Roundell Palmer, KBE, FRS, *b.* 1940, *s.* 1971, *m.*	Viscount Wolmer, *b.* 1971.
1646 s.	*Selkirk* (10th), (George) Nigel Douglas-Hamilton, KT, GCMG, GBE, AFC, AE, PC, QC, *b.* 1906, *s.* 1940, *m.*	The Master of Selkirk, *b.* 1939.
1672	*Shaftesbury* (10th), Anthony Ashley-Cooper, *b.* 1938, *s.* 1961, *m.*	Lord Ashley, *b.* 1977.
1756 I.*	*Shannon* (9th), Richard Bentinck Boyle (8th *Brit. Baron Carleton*, 1786), *b.* 1924, *s.* 1963.	Viscount Boyle, *b.* 1960.
1442	*Shrewsbury & Waterford* (22nd) (I. 1446), Charles Henry John Benedict Crofton Chetwynd Chetwynd-Talbot (*Premier Earl of England and Ireland; Earl Talbot*, 1784), *b.* 1952, *s.* 1980, *m.*	Viscount Ingestre, *b.* 1978.
1961	*Snowdon* (1st), Antony Charles Robert Armstrong-Jones, GCVO, *b.* 1930, *m.* (See also p. 141.)	Viscount Linley, *b.* 1961 (*see also* p. 141).
1880	°*Sondes* (5th), Henry George Herbert Milles-Lade, *b.* 1940, *s.* 1970.	(None.)
1633 s.*	*Southesk* (11th), Charles Alexander Carnegie, KCVO (3rd *UK Baron, Balinhard*, 1869), *b.* 1893, *s.* 1941, *m.*	The Duke of Fife, *b.* 1929 (*see* pp. 137 and 150).
1765	°*Spencer* (8th), (Edward) John Spencer, LVO, *b.* 1924, *s.* 1975, *m.*	Viscount Althorp, *b.* 1964.
1703 s.*	*Stair* (13th), John Aymer Dalrymple, KCVO, MBE (6th *UK Baron, Oxenfoord*, 1841), *b.* 1906, *s.* 1961, *m.*	Viscount Dalrymple, *b.* 1961.
1984	*Stockton* (2nd), Alexander Daniel Alan Macmillan, *b.* 1943, *s.* 1986.	Viscount Macmillan of Ovenden, *b.* 1974.
1821	*Stradbroke* (6th), Robert Keith Rous, *b.* 1937, *s.* 1983, *m.*	Viscount Dunwich, *b.* 1961.
1847	*Strafford* (8th), Thomas Edmund Byng, *b.* 1936, *s.* 1984, *m.*	Viscount Enfield, *b.* 1964.

Created	Title, Order of Succession, Name, etc.	Eldest Son or Heir
1606 s.*	*Strathmore and Kinghorne* (18th), Michael Fergus Bowes Lyon (16th *Scottish Earl, Strathmore*, 1677, *& 18th Kinghorne*, 1606; 5th *UK Earl, Strathmore & Kinghorne*, 1937), *b.* 1957, *s.* 1987, *m.*	Lord Glamis, *b.* 1986.
1603	*Suffolk* (21st) *& Berkshire* (14th) (1626), Michael John James George Robert Howard, *b.* 1935, *s.* 1941, *m.*	Viscount Andover, *b.* 1974.
1955	*Swinton* (2nd), David Yarburgh Cunliffe-Lister, *b.* 1937, *s.* 1972, *m.*	Hon. Nicholas J. C.-L., *b.* 1939.
1714	*Tankerville* (10th), Peter Grey Bennet, *b.* 1956, *s.* 1980.	Rev. the Hon. George A. G. B., *b.* 1925.
1822	°*Temple of Stowe* (8th), (Walter) Grenville Algernon Temple-Gore-Langton, *b.* 1924, *s.* 1988, *m.*	Lord Langton, *b.* 1955.
1815	*Verulam* (7th), John Duncan Grimston (11th *Irish Visct., Grimston*, 1719; 16th *Scott. Baron, Forrester of Corstorphine*, 1633), *b.* 1951, *s.* 1973, *m.*	Viscount Grimston, *b.* 1978.
1729	°*Waldegrave* (12th), Geoffrey Noel Waldegrave, KG, GCVO, TD, *b.* 1905, *s.* 1936, *m.*	Viscount Chewton, *b.* 1940.
1759	*Warwick & *°*Brooke* (8th) (*Brit.* 1746), David Robin Francis Guy Greville (8th *Earl Brooke* and 8th *Earl of Warwick*), *b.* 1934, *s.* 1984.	Lord Brooke, *b.* 1957.
1633 s.*	*Wemyss* (12th) *& March* (8th) (s. 1697), Francis David Charteris, KT (5th *UK Baron, Wemyss*, 1821), *b.* 1912, *s.* 1937, *w.*	Lord Neidpath, *b.* 1948.
1621 I.	*Westmeath* (13th), William Anthony Nugent, *b.* 1928, *s.* 1971, *m.*	Hon. Sean C. W. N., *b.* 1965.
1624	*Westmorland* (15th), David Anthony Thomas Fane, KCVO, *b.* 1924, *s.* 1948, *m.* (*Master of the Horse*).	Lord Burghersh, *b.* 1951.
1876	*Wharncliffe* (5th), Richard Alan Montagu Stuart Wortley, *b.* 1953, *s.* 1987, *m.*	Viscount Carlton, *b.* 1980.
1801	*Wilton* (7th), Seymour William Arthur John Egerton, *b.* 1921, *s.* 1927, *m.*	Baron Ebury, *b.* 1934 (*see* p. 162).
1628	*Winchilsea* (16th) *& Nottingham* (11th) (1675), Christopher Denys Stormont Finch Hatton, *b.* 1936, *s.* 1950, *m.*	Viscount Maidstone, *b.* 1967.
1766 I.	°*Winterton* (7th), Robert Chad Turnour, *b.* 1915, *s.* 1962, *m.*	D. David T., *b.* 1943.
1956	*Woolton* (3rd), Simon Frederick Marquis, *b.* 1958, *s.* 1969, *m.*	(None.)
1837	*Yarborough* (8th), Charles John Pelham, *b.* 1963, *s.* 1991, *m.*	Lord Worsley, *b.* 1990.

VISCOUNTS

Coronet.—Sixteen silver balls.
Style.—The Right Hon. the Viscount——.
Wife's style.—The Right Hon. the Viscountess——.
Children's style.—'The Hon.' before forename and family name.
(In Scotland, the heir apparent to a Viscount may be styled
'The Master of—— (title of peer)'.)
For forms of address, *see* page 219.

Created	Title, Order of Succession, Name, etc.	Eldest Son or Heir
1945	*Addison* (3rd), Michael Addison, *b.* 1914, *s.* 1976, *m.*	Hon. William M. W. A., *b.* 1945.
1946	*Alanbrooke* (3rd), Alan Victor Harold Brooke, *b.* 1932, *s.* 1972.	(None.)
1919	*Allenby* (3rd), Lt.-Col. Michael Jaffray Hynman Allenby, *b.* 1931, *s.* 1984, *m.*	Hon. Henry J. H. A., *b.* 1968.
1911	*Allendale* (3rd), Wentworth Hubert Charles Beaumont, *b.* 1922, *s.* 1956, *m.*	Hon. Wentworth P. I. B., *b.* 1948.
1642 s.	*of Arbuthnott* (16th), John Campbell Arbuthnott, CBE, DSC, *b.* 1924, *s.* 1966, *m.*	Master of Arbuthnott, *b.* 1950.
1751 I.	*Ashbrook* (10th), Desmond Llowarch Edward Flower, KCVO, MBE, *b.* 1905. *s.* 1936, *m.*	Hon. Michael L. W. F., *b.* 1935.
1917	*Astor* (4th), William Waldorf Astor, *b.* 1951, *s.* 1966, *m.*	Hon. William W. A., *b.* 1979.
1781 I.	*Bangor* (7th), Edward Henry Harold Ward, *b.* 1905, *s.* 1950, *w.*	Hon. William M. D. W., *b.* 1948.
1925	*Bearsted* (4th), Peter Montefiore Samuel, MC, TD, *b.* 1911, *s.* 1986, *m.*	Hon. Nicholas A. S., *b.* 1950.
1963	*Blakenham* (2nd), Michael John Hare, *b.* 1938, *s.* 1982, *m.*	Hon. Caspar J. H., *b.* 1972.
1935	*Bledisloe* (3rd), Christopher Hiley Ludlow Bathurst, QC, *b.* 1934, *s.* 1979.	Hon. Rupert E. L. B., *b.* 1964.
1712	*Bolingbroke* (7th) *& St John* (8th) (1716), Kenneth Oliver Musgrave St John, *b.* 1927, *s.* 1974.	Hon. Henry F. *St J.*, *b.* 1957.
1960	*Boyd of Merton* (2nd), Simon Donald Rupert Neville Lennox-Boyd, *b.* 1939, *s.* 1983, *m.*	Hon. Benjamin A. L.-B., *b.* 1964.
1717 I.*	*Boyne* (10th), Gustavus Michael George Hamilton-Russell (4th *UK Baron, Brancepeth*, 1866), *b.* 1931, *s.* 1942, *m.*	Hon. Gustavus M. S. H.-R., *b.* 1965.
1929	*Brentford* (4th), Crispin William Joynson-Hicks, *b.* 1933, *s.* 1983, *m.*	Hon. Paul W. J.-H., *b.* 1971.
1929	*Bridgeman* (3rd), Robin John Orlando Bridgeman, *b.* 1930, *s.* 1982, *m.*	Hon. William O. C. B., *b.* 1968.
1868	*Bridport* (4th), Alexander Nelson Hood (7th *Duke of Brontë in Sicily*, 1799, *and* 6th *Irish Baron Bridport*, 1794), *b.* 1948, *s.* 1969, *m.*	Hon. Peregrine A. N. H., *b.* 1974.

Created	Title, Order of Succession, Name, etc.	Eldest Son or Heir
1952	*Brookeborough* (3rd), Alan Henry Brooke, *b.* 1952, *s.* 1987, *m.*	Hon. Christopher A. *B.*, *b.* 1954.
1933	*Buckmaster* (3rd), Martin Stanley Buckmaster, OBE, *b.* 1921, *s.* 1974.	Hon. Colin J. *B.*, *b.* 1923.
1939	*Caldecote* (2nd), Robert Andrew Inskip, KBE, DSC, *b.* 1917, *s.* 1947, *m.*	Hon. Piers J. H. *I.*, *b.* 1947.
1941	*Camrose* (2nd), (John) Seymour Berry, TD, *b.* 1909, *s.* 1954, *m.*	Baron Hartwell, MBE, TD, *b.* 1911 (see p. 172).
1954	*Chandos* (3rd), Thomas Orlando Lyttelton, *b.* 1953, *s.* 1980, *m.*	Hon. Oliver A. *L.*, *b.* 1986.
1665 I.	*Charlemont* (14th), John Day Caulfeild (18th *Irish Baron, Caulfeild of Charlemont*, 1620), *b.* 1934, *s.* 1985, *m.*	Hon. John D. *C.*, *b.* 1966.
1921	*Chelmsford* (3rd), Frederic Jan Thesiger, *b.* 1931, *s.* 1970, *m.*	Hon. Frederic C. P. *T.*, *b.* 1962.
1717 I.	*Chetwynd* (10th), Adam Richard John Casson Chetwynd, *b.* 1935, *s.* 1965, *m.*	Hon. Adam D. *C.*, *b.* 1969.
1911	*Chilston* (4th), Alastair George Akers-Douglas, *b.* 1946, *s.* 1982, *m.*	Hon. Oliver I. *A.-D.*, *b.* 1973.
1902	*Churchill* (3rd), Victor George Spencer (5th *UK Baron Churchill*, 1815), *b.* 1934, *s.* 1973.	None to Viscountcy. To Barony, Richard H. R. *S.*, *b.* 1926.
1718	*Cobham* (11th), John William Leonard Lyttelton (8th *Irish Baron, Westcote*, 1776), *b.* 1943, *s.* 1977, *m.*	Hon. Christopher C. *L.*, *b.* 1947.
1902	*Colville of Culross* (4th), John Mark Alexander Colville, QC (13th *Scott. Baron, Colville of Culross*, 1604), *b.* 1933, *s.* 1945, *m.*	Master of Colville, *b.* 1959.
1826	*Combermere* (5th), Michael Wellington Stapleton-Cotton, *b.* 1929, *s.* 1969, *m.*	Hon. Thomas R. W. *S.-C.*, *b.* 1969.
1917	*Cowdray* (3rd), Weetman John Churchill Pearson, TD (3rd *UK Baron, Cowdray*, 1910), *b.* 1910, *s.* 1933, *m.*	Hon. Michael O. W. *P.*, *b.* 1944.
1927	*Craigavon* (3rd), Janric Fraser Craig, *b.* 1944, *s.* 1974.	(None.)
1886	*Cross* (3rd), Assheton Henry Cross, *b.* 1920, *s.* 1932.	(None.)
1943	*Daventry* (3rd), Francis Humphrey Maurice FitzRoy Newdegate, *b.* 1921, *s.* 1986, *m.*	Hon. James E. *F.N.*, *b.* 1960.
1937	*Davidson* (2nd), John Andrew Davidson, *b.* 1928, *s.* 1970, *m.*	Hon. Malcolm W. M. *D.*, *b.* 1934.
1956	*De L'Isle* (2nd), Philip John Algernon Sidney, MBE, (7th *Baron De L'Isle and Dudley*, 1835), *b.* 1945, *s.* 1991, *m.*	Hon. Philip *S.*, *b.* 1985.
1776 I.	*De Vesci* (7th), Thomas Eustace Vesey (8th *Irish Baron, Knapton*, 1750), *b.* 1955, *s.* 1983, *m.*	Hon. Damian B. J. *V.*, *b.* 1985.
1917	*Devonport* (3rd), Terence Kearley, *b.* 1944, *s.* 1973.	Chester D. H. *K.*, *b.* 1932.
1964	*Dilhorne* (2nd), John Mervyn Manningham-Buller, *b.* 1932, *s.* 1980, *m.*	Hon. James E. *M.-B.*, *b.* 1956.
1622 I.	*Dillon* (22nd), Henry Benedict Charles Dillon, *b.* 1973, *s.* 1982, *M.*	Hon. Richard A. L. *D.*, *b.* 1948.
1785 I.	*Doneraile* (10th), Richard Allen St Leger, *b.* 1946, *s.* 1983, *m.*	Hon. Nathaniel W. R. St J. *St L.*, *b.* 1971.
1680 I.*	*Downe* (11th), John Christian George Dawnay (4th *UK Baron, Dawnay*, 1897), *b.* 1935, *s.* 1965, *m.*	Hon. Richard H. *D.*, *b.* 1967.
1959	*Dunrossil* (2nd), John William Morrison, CMG, *b.* 1926, *s.* 1961, *m.*	Hon. Andrew W. R. *M.*, *b.* 1953.
1964	*Eccles* (1st), David McAdam Eccles, CH, KCVO, PC, *b.* 1904, *m.*	Hon. John D. *E.*, CBE, *b.* 1931.
1897	*Esher* (4th), Lionel Gordon Baliol Brett, CBE, *b.* 1913. *s.* 1963, *m.*	Hon. Christopher L. B. *B.*, *b.* 1936.
1816	*Exmouth* (10th), Paul Edward Pellew, *b.* 1940, *s.* 1970, *m.*	Hon. Edward F. *P.*, *b.* 1978.
1620 S.	*Falkland* (15th), Lucius Edward William Plantagenet Cary (*Premier Scottish Viscount on the Roll*), *b.* 1935, *s.* 1984, *m.*	Master of Falkland, *b.* 1963.
1720	*Falmouth* (9th), George Hugh Boscawen (26th *Eng. Baron, Le Despencer*, 1264), *b.* 1919, *s.* 1962, *m.*	Hon. Evelyn A. H. *B.*, *b.* 1955.
1918	*Furness* (2nd), William Anthony Furness, *b.* 1929, *s.* 1940.	(None.)
1720 I.*	*Gage* (7th), George John St Clere Gage, (6th *Brit. Baron, Gage*, 1790), *b.* 1932, *s.* 1982.	Hon. H. Nicholas *G.*, *b.* 1934.
1727 I.	*Galway* (12th), George Rupert Monckton-Arundell, *b.* 1922, *s.* 1980, *m.*	Hon. J. Philip *M.*, *b.* 1952.
1478 I.*	*Gormanston* (17th), Jenico Nicholas Dudley Preston (*Premier Viscount of Ireland*; 5th *UK Baron, Gormanston*, 1868), *b.* 1939, *s.* 1940, *w.*	Hon. Jenico F. T. *P.*, *b.* 1974.
1816 I.	*Gort* (8th), Colin Leopold Prendergast Vereker, *b.* 1916, *s.* 1975, *m.*	Hon. Foley R.S.P. *V.*, *b.* 1951.
1900	*Goschen* (4th), Giles John Harry Goschen, *b.* 1965, *s.* 1977.	(None.)
1849	*Gough* (5th), Shane Hugh Maryon Gough, *b.* 1941, *s.* 1951.	(None.)
1937	*Greenwood* (2nd), David Henry Hamar Greenwood, *b.* 1914, *s.* 1948.	Hon. Michael G. H. *G.*, *b.* 1923.
1929	*Hailsham.* Disclaimed for life 1963. (*See* Lord Hailsham of St Marylebone, p. 172.)	Hon. Douglas M. *H.*, QC, MP, *b.* 1945.
1891	*Hambleden* (4th), William Herbert Smith, *b.* 1930, *s.* 1948, *m.*	Hon. William H. B. *S.*, *b.* 1955.
1884	*Hampden* (6th), Anthony David Brand, *b.* 1937, *s.* 1975.	Hon. Francis A. *B.*, *b.* 1970.
1936	*Hanworth* (2nd), David Bertram Pollock, *b.* 1916, *s.* 1936, *m.*	Hon. David S. G. *P.*, *b.* 1946.
1791 I.	*Harberton* (10th), Thomas de Vautort Pomeroy, *b.* 1910, *s.* 1980, *m.*	Hon. Robert W. *P.*, *b.* 1916.
1846	*Hardinge* (6th), Charles Henry Nicholas Hardinge, *b.* 1956, *s.* 1984, *m.*	Hon. Andrew H. *H.*, *b.* 1960.
1791 I.	*Hawarden* (8th), Robert Leslie Eustace Maude, *b.* 1926, *s.* 1958, *m.*	Hon. R. Connan W. L. *M.*, *b.* 1961.
1960	*Head* (2nd), Richard Antony Head, *b.* 1937, *s.* 1983, *m.*	Hon. Henry J. *H.*, *b.* 1980.

Created	Title, Order of Succession, Name, etc.	Eldest Son or Heir
1550	*Hereford* (18th), Robert Milo Leicester Devereux (*Premier Viscount of England*), b. 1932, s. 1952.	Hon. Charles R. de B. *D.*, b. 1975.
1842	*Hill* (8th), Antony Rowland Clegg-Hill, b. 1931, s. 1974.	Peter D. R. C. *C.-H.*, b. 1945.
1796	*Hood* (7th), Alexander Lambert Hood (7th *Irish Baron, Hood*, 1782), b. 1914, s. 1981, m.	Hon. Henry L. A. *H.*, b. 1958.
1956	*Ingleby* (2nd), Martin Raymond Peake, b. 1926, s. 1966, m.	(None.)
1945	*Kemsley* (2nd), (Geoffrey) Lionel Berry, b. 1909, s. 1968, m.	Richard G. *B.*, b. 1951.
1911	*Knollys* (3rd), David Francis Dudley Knollys, b. 1931, s. 1966, m.	Hon. Patrick N. M. *K.*, b. 1962.
1895	*Knutsford* (6th), Michael Holland-Hibbert, b. 1926, s. 1986, m.	Hon. Henry T. *H.-H.*, b. 1959.
1945	*Lambert* (3rd), Michael John Lambert, b. 1912, s. 1989, m.	(None.)
1954	*Leathers* (2nd), Frederick Alan Leathers, b. 1908, s. 1965, m.	Hon. Christopher G. *L.*, b. 1941.
1922	*Leverhulme* (3rd), Philip William Bryce Lever, KG, TD, b. 1915, s. 1949, w.	(None.)
1781 I.	*Lifford* (9th), (Edward) James Wingfield Hewitt, b. 1949, s. 1987, m.	Hon. James T. W. *H.*, b. 1979.
1921	*Long* (4th), Richard Gerard Long, b. 1929, s. 1967, m.	Hon. James R. *L.*, b. 1960.
1957	*Mackintosh of Halifax* (3rd), (John) Clive Mackintosh, b. 1958, s. 1980, m.	Hon. Thomas H. G. *M.*, b. 1985.
1955	*Malvern* (3rd), Ashley Kevin Godfrey Huggins, b. 1949, s. 1978.	Hon. M. James *H.*, b. 1928.
1945	*Marchwood* (3rd), David George Staveley Penny, b. 1936, s. 1979, m.	Hon. Peter G. W. *P.*, b. 1965.
1942	*Margesson* (2nd), Francis Vere Hampden Margesson, b. 1922, s. 1965, m.	Capt. Hon. Richard F. D. *M.*, b. 1960.
1660 I.*	*Massereene* (13th) & *Ferrard* (6th) (1797), John Clotworthy Talbot Foster Whyte-Melville Skeffington (6th *UK Baron, Oriel*, 1821), b. 1914, s. 1956, m.	Hon. John D. C. W.-M. F. *S.*, b. 1940.
1802	*Melville* (9th), Robert David Ross Dundas, b. 1937, s. 1971, m.	Hon. Robert H. K. *D.*, b. 1984.
1916	*Mersey* (4th), Richard Maurice Clive Bigham, b. 1934, s. 1979, m.	Hon. Edward J. H. *B.*, b. 1966.
1717 I.*	*Midleton* (12th), Alan Henry Brodrick (9th *Brit. Baron, Brodrick of Peper Harow*, 1796), b. 1949, s. 1988, m.	Hon. Ashley R. *B.*, b. 1980.
1962	*Mills* (3rd), Christopher Philip Roger Mills, b. 1956, s. 1988, m.	(None.)
1716 I.	*Molesworth* (11th), Richard Gosset Molesworth, b. 1907, s. 1961, w.	Hon. Robert B. K. *M.*, b. 1959.
1801 I.*	*Monck* (7th), Charles Stanley Monck (4th *UK Baron, Monck*, 1866), b. 1953, s. 1982.	Hon. George S. *M.*, b. 1957.
1957	*Monckton of Brenchley* (2nd), Gilbert Walter Riversdale Monckton, CB, MC, b. 1915, s. 1965, m.	Hon Christopher W. *M.*, b. 1952.
1935	*Monsell* (2nd), Henry Bolton Graham Eyres Monsell, b. 1905, s. 1969.	(None.)
1946	*Montgomery of Alamein* (2nd), David Bernard Montgomery, CBE, b. 1928, s. 1976, m.	Hon. Henry D. *M.*, b. 1954.
1550 I.*	*Mountgarret* (17th), Richard Henry Piers Butler (4th *UK Baron, Mountgarret*, 1911), b. 1936, s. 1966, m.	Hon. Piers J. R. *B.*, b. 1961.
1964	*Muirshiel* (1st), John Scott Maclay, KT, CH, CMG, PC, b. 1905, w.	(None.)
1952	*Norwich* (2nd), John Julius Cooper, b. 1929, s. 1954, m.	Hon. Jason C. D. B. *C.*, b. 1959.
1651 S.	*of Oxfuird* (13th), George Hubbard Makgill, b. 1934, s. 1986, m.	Master of Oxfuird, b. 1969.
1873	*Portman*, (9th), Edward Henry Berkeley Portman, b. 1934, s. 1967, m.	Hon. Christopher E. B. *P.*, b. 1958.
1743 I.*	*Powerscourt* (10th), Mervyn Niall Wingfield (4th *UK Baron, Powerscourt*, 1885), b. 1935, s. 1973, m.	Hon. Mervyn A. *W.*, b. 1963.
1900	*Ridley* (4th), Matthew White Ridley, TD, b. 1925, s. 1964, m. (*Lord Steward*).	Hon. Matthew W. *R.*, b. 1958.
1960	*Rochdale* (1st), John Durival Kemp, OBE, TD (2nd *UK Baron, Rochdale*, 1913), b. 1906, s. to Barony 1945, m.	Hon. St John D. *K.*, b. 1938.
1919	*Rothermere* (3rd), Vere Harold Esmond Harmsworth, b. 1925, s. 1978, m.	Hon. H. Jonathan E. V. *H.*, b. 1967.
1937	*Runciman of Doxford* (3rd), Walter Garrison Runciman, CBE, FBA (4th *UK Baron, Runciman*, 1933), b. 1934, s. 1989, m.	Hon. David W. *R.*, b. 1967.
1918	*St Davids* (3rd), Colwyn Jestyn John Philipps (20th *English Baron Strange of Knokin*, 1299, 8th *English Baron Hungerford*, 1426, and *De Moleyns*, 1445), b. 1939, s. 1991, m.	Hon. Rhodri C. *P.*, b. 1966.
1801	*St Vincent* (7th), Ronald George James Jervis, b. 1905, s. 1940, m.	Hon. Edward R. J. *J.*, b. 1951.
1937	*Samuel* (3rd), David Herbert Samuel, PH.D., b. 1922, s. 1978, m.	Hon. Dan J. *S.*, b. 1925.
1911	*Scarsdale* (3rd), Francis John Nathaniel Curzon (7th *Brit. Baron, Scarsdale*, 1761), b. 1924, s. 1977, m.	Hon. Peter G. N. *C.*, b. 1949.
1905	*Selby* (4th), Michael Guy John Gully, b. 1942, s. 1959, m.	Hon. Edward T. W. *G.*, b. 1967.
1805	*Sidmouth* (7th), John Tonge Anthony Pellew Addington, b. 1914, s. 1976, w.	Hon. Jeremy F. *A.*, b. 1947.
1940	*Simon* (2nd), John Gilbert Simon, CMG, b. 1902, s. 1954, m.	Hon. Jan D. *S.*, b. 1940.
1960	*Slim* (2nd), John Douglas Slim, OBE, b. 1927, s. 1970, m.	Hon. Mark W. R. *S.*, b. 1960.
1954	*Soulbury* (2nd), James Herwald Ramsbotham, b. 1915, s. 1971, w.	Hon. Sir Peter E. *R.*, GCMG, GCVO, b. 1919.
1776 I.	*Southwell* (7th), Pyers Anthony Joseph Southwell, b. 1930, s. 1960, m.	Hon. Richard A. P. *S.*, b. 1956.
1942	*Stansgate*. Disclaimed for life 1963. (*Rt. Hon. Anthony Neil Wedgwood Benn*, MP, b. 1925, s. 1960, m.*)	Stephen M. W. *B.*, b. 1951.

Created	*Title, Order of Succession, Name, etc.*	*Eldest Son or Heir*
1959	*Stuart of Findhorn* (2nd), David Randolph Moray Stuart, *b.* 1924, *s.* 1971, *m.*	Hon. J. Dominic *S., b.* 1948.
1957	*Tenby* (3rd), William Lloyd George, *b.* 1927, *s.* 1983, *m.*	Hon. Timothy H. G. *L. G., b.* 1962.
1952	*Thurso* (2nd), Robin Macdonald Sinclair, *b.* 1922, *s.* 1970, *m.*	Hon. John A. *S., b.* 1953.
1983	*Tonypandy* (1st), (Thomas) George Thomas, PC, *b.* 1909.	(None.)
1721	*Torrington* (11th), Timothy Howard St George Byng, *b.* 1943, *s.* 1961, *m.*	John L. *B.,* MC, *b.* 1919.
1936	*Trenchard* (3rd), Hugh Trenchard, *b.* 1951, *s.* 1987, *m.*	Hon. Alexander T. *T., b.* 1978.
1921	*Ullswater* (2nd), Nicholas James Christopher Lowther, *b.* 1942, *s.* 1949, *m.*	Hon. Benjamin J. *L., b.* 1975.
1621 I.	*Valentia* (15th), Richard John Dighton Annesley, *b.* 1929, *s.* 1983, *m.*	Hon. Francis W. D. *A., b.* 1959.
1964	*Watkinson* (1st), Harold Arthur Watkinson, CH, PC, *b.* 1910, *m.*	(None.)
1952	*Waverley* (3rd), John Desmond Forbes Anderson, *b.* 1949, *s.* 1990.	(None.)
1938	*Weir* (3rd), William Kenneth James Weir, *b.* 1933, *s.* 1975, *m.*	Hon. James W. H. *W., b.* 1965.
1983	*Whitelaw* (1st), William Stephen Ian Whitelaw, KT, CH, MC, PC, *b.* 1918, *m.*	(None.)
1918	*Wimborne* (3rd), Ivor Fox-Strangways Guest (4th *UK Baron, Wimborne,* 1880), *b.* 1939, *s.* 1967, *m.*	Hon. Ivor M.V.*G., b.* 1968.
1923	*Younger of Leckie* (3rd), Edward George Younger, OBE, TD, *b.* 1906, *s.* 1946, *w.*	Rt. Hon. George K. H. *Y.,* TD, MP, *b.* 1931.

BISHOPS

Style.—the Right Rev. the Lord Bishop of ——. *Addressed as,* My Lord.
The Bishops of London, Durham and Winchester always have seats in the House of Lords; the other 21 seats are filled by the remaining diocesan Bishops in order of seniority. The Bishop of Sodor and Man and the Bishop of Gibraltar are not eligible to sit in the House of Lords.

Introd. to House of Lords		*Election as Diocesan Bp. confirmed*	*Trans. to present See*
1990	*London* (131st), David Michael Hope, PC, *b.* 1940, *cons.* 1985.	1985	1991
1984	*Durham* (92nd), David Edward Jenkins, *b.* 1925, *cons.* 1984, *m.*	1984	—
1982	*Winchester* (95th), Colin Clement Walter James, *b.* 1926, *cons.* 1973, *m.*	1977	1985
1979	*Chichester* (102nd), Eric Waldram Kemp, DD, *b.* 1915, *cons.* 1974, *m.*	1974	
1980	*Liverpool* (6th), David Stuart Sheppard, *b.* 1929, *cons.* 1969, *m.*	1975	
1981	*Gloucester* (37th), John Yates, *b.* 1925, *cons.* 1972, *m.*	1975	
1984	*Ripon* (11th), David Nigel de Lorentz Young, *b.* 1931, *cons.* 1977, *m.*	1977	
1985	*Chelmsford* (7th), John Waine, *b.* 1930, *cons.* 1975, *m.*	1978	1986
1985	*Manchester* (9th), Stanley Eric Francis Booth-Clibborn, *b.* 1924, *cons.* 1979, *m.*	1979	
1985	*Sheffield* (5th), David Ramsay Lunn, *b.* 1930, *cons.* 1980.	1980	
1985	*St Albans* (8th), John Bernard Taylor, *b.* 1929, *cons.* 1980, *m.*	1980	
1985	*Newcastle* (10th), Andrew Alexander Kenny Graham, *b.* 1929, *cons.* 1977.	1981	
1986	*Salisbury* (76th), John Austin Baker, *b.* 1928, *cons.* 1982, *m.*	1982	
1987	*Worcester* (111th), Philip Harold Ernest Goodrich, *b.* 1929, *cons.* 1973, *m.*	1982	
1987	*Chester* (39th), Michael Alfred Baughen, *b.* 1930, *cons.* 1982, *m.*	1982	
1988	*Guildford* (7th), Michael Edgar Adie, *b.* 1929, *cons.* 1983, *m.*	1983	
1988	*Bradford* (7th), Robert Kerr Williamson, *b.* 1932, *cons.* 1984, *m.*	1984	
1989	*Lichfield* (97th), Keith Norman Sutton, *b.* 1934, *cons.* 1978, *m.*	1984	
1989	*Peterborough* (36th), William John Westwood, *b.* 1925, *cons.* 1975, *m.*	1984	
1990	*Portsmouth* (7th), Timothy John Bavin, *b.* 1935, *cons.* 1974.	1985	
1990	*Exeter* (69th), (Geoffrey) Hewlett Thompson, *b.* 1929, *cons.* 1974, *m.*	1985	
1990	*Bristol* (54th), Barry Rogerson, *b.* 1936, *cons.* 1979, *m.*	1985	

Bishops awaiting seats, in order of seniority

	Coventry (7th), Simon Barrington-Ward, *b.* 1930, *cons.* 1985, *m.*	1985	
	Norwich (70th), Peter John Nott, *b.* 1933, *cons.* 1977, *m.*	1985	
	St Edmundsbury and Ipswich (8th), John Dennis, *b.* 1931, *cons.* 1979, *m.*	1986	
	Lincoln (70th), Robert Maynard Hardy, *b.* 1936, *cons.* 1980, *m.*	1986	
	Oxford (41st), Richard Douglas Harries, *b.* 1936, *cons.* 1987, *m.*	1987	
	Birmingham (7th), Mark Santer, *b.* 1936, *cons.* 1981, *m.*	1987	
	Derby (5th), Peter Spencer Dawes, *b.* 1928, *cons.* 1988, *m.*	1988	
	Southwell (9th), Patrick Burnet Harris, *b.* 1934, *cons.* 1973, *m.*	1988	
	Rochester (105th), (Anthony) Michael (Arnold) Turnbull, *b.* 1935, *cons.* 1988, *m.*	1988	

	Election as Diocesan Bp. confirmed	Trans. to present See
Introd. to House of Lords		
Blackburn (7th), Alan David Chesters, *b.* 1937, *cons.* 1989, *m.*	1989	
Carlisle (65th), Ian Harland, *b.* 1932, *cons.* 1985, *m.*	1989	
Truro (13th), Michael Thomas Ball, *b.* 1932, *cons.* 1980.	1990	
Ely (67th), Stephen Whitefield Sykes, *b.* 1939, *cons.* 1990, *m.*	1990	
Hereford (103rd), John Keith Oliver, *b.* 1935, *cons.* 1990, *m.*	1990	
Leicester (5th), Thomas Frederick Butler, *b.* 1940, *cons.* 1985, *m.*	1991	

Bath and Wells, new Bishop to be enthroned in late 1991.
Southwark, the Bishop of Bradford is to be translated to the see of Southwark in late 1991.
Wakefield, vacant.

BARONS

Coronet.—Six silver balls.
Style.—The Right Hon. the Lord ——.
Wife's style.—The Right Hon. the Lady ——.
Children's style.—'The Hon.' before forename and family name.
(In Scotland, the heir apparent to a Lord may be styled
'The Master of —— (title of peer)'.)
For forms of address, *see* page 219.

Created	*Title, Order of Succession, Name, etc.*	*Eldest Son or Heir*
1911	*Aberconway* (3rd), Charles Melville McLaren, *b.* 1913, *s.* 1953, *m.*	Hon. H. Charles *M.*, *b.* 1948.
1873	*Aberdare* (4th), Morys George Lyndhurst Bruce, KBE, PC, *b.* 1919, *s.* 1957, *m.*	Hon. Alastair J. L. *B.*, *b.* 1947.
1835	*Abinger* (8th), James Richard Scarlett, *b.* 1914, *s.* 1943, *m.*	Hon. James H. S., *b.* 1959.
1869	*Acton* (4th), Richard Gerald Lyon-Dalberg-Acton, *b.* 1941, *s.* 1989, *m.*	Hon. John C. F. H. *L.-D.-A.*, *b.* 1966.
1887	*Addington* (6th), Dominic Bryce Hubbard, *b.* 1963, *s.* 1982.	Hon. Michael W. L. *H.*, *b.* 1965.)
1955	*Adrian* (2nd), Richard Hume Adrian, FRS, *b.* 1927, *s.* 1977, *m.*	(None.)
1907	*Airedale* (4th), Oliver James Vandeleur Kitson, *b.* 1915, *s.* 1958.	(None.)
1896	*Aldenham* (6th), and *Hunsdon of Hunsdon* (4th) (1923), Vicary Tyser Gibbs, *b.* 1948, *s.* 1986, *m.*	Hon. Humphrey W. F. *G.*, *b.* 1989.
1962	*Aldington* (1st), Toby Austin Richard William Low, KCMG, CBE, DSO, TD, PC, *b.* 1914, *m.*	Hon Charles H. S. *L.*, *b.* 1948.
1945	*Altrincham.* Disclaimed for life 1963. (*John Edward Poynder Grigg, b.* 1924, *s.* 1955, *m.*)	Hon. Anthony U. D. D. *G.*, *b.* 1934.
1929	*Alvingham* (2nd), Maj.-Gen. Robert Guy Eardley Yerburgh, CBE, *b.* 1926, *s.* 1955, *m.*	Capt. Hon. Robert R. G. *Y.*, *b.* 1956.
1892	*Amherst of Hackney* (4th), William Hugh Amherst Cecil, *b.* 1940, *s.* 1980, *m.*	Hon. H. William A. *C.*, *b.* 1968.
1881	*Ampthill* (4th), Geoffrey Denis Erskine Russell, CBE, *b.* 1921, *s.* 1973.	Hon. David W. E. *R.*, *b.* 1947.
1947	*Amwell* (3rd), Keith Norman Montague, *b.* 1943, *s.* 1990, *m.*	Hon. Ian *M.*, *b.* 1973.
1863	*Annaly* (6th), Luke Richard White, *b.* 1954, *s.* 1990, *m.*	Luke H. *W.*, *b.* 1990.
1949	*Archibald.* Disclaimed for life 1975. (*George Christopher Archibald, b.* 1926, *s.* 1975, *m.*)	(None.)
1885	*Ashbourne* (4th), Edward Barry Greynville Gibson, *b.* 1933, *s.* 1983, *m.*	Hon. Edward C. d'O. *G.*, *b.* 1967.
1835	*Ashburton* (7th), John Francis Harcourt Baring, KCVO, *b.* 1928, *s.* 1991, *m.*	Hon. Mark F. R. *B.*, *b.* 1958.
1892	*Ashcombe* (4th), Henry Edward Cubitt, *b.* 1924, *s.* 1962, *m.*	M. Robin *C.*, *b.* 1936.
1911	*Ashton of Hyde* (3rd), Thomas John Ashton, TD, *b.* 1926, *s.* 1983, *m.*	Hon. Thomas H. *A.*, *b.* 1958.
1800 I.	*Ashtown* (6th), Christopher Oliver Trench, *b.* 1931, *s.* 1979.	Sir Nigel C. C. *T.*, KCMG, *b.* 1916.
1956	*Astor of Hever* (3rd), John Jacob Astor, *b.* 1946, *s.* 1984, *m.*	Hon. Charles G. J. *A.*, *b.* 1990.
1789 I. } 1793* }	*Auckland* (9th), Ian George Eden (9th *Brit. Baron, Auckland*), *b.* 1926, *s.* 1957, *m.*	Hon. Robert I. B. *E.*, *b.* 1962.
1313	*Audley* (25th), Richard Michael Thomas Souter, *b.* 1914, *s.* 1973, *m.*	Three co-heiresses.
1900	*Avebury* (4th), Eric Reginald Lubbock, *b.* 1928, *s.* 1971, *m.*	Hon. Lyulph A. J. *L.*, *b.* 1954.
1718 I.	*Aylmer* (13th), Michael Anthony Aylmer, *b.* 1923, *s.* 1982, *m.*	Hon. A. Julian *A.*, *b.* 1951.
1929	*Baden-Powell* (3rd), Robert Crause Baden-Powell, *b.* 1936, *s.* 1962, *m.*	Hon. David M. *B.-P.*, *b.* 1940.
1780	*Bagot* (9th), Heneage Charles Bagot, *b.* 1914, *s.* 1979, *m.*	Hon. C. H. Shaun *B.*, *b.* 1944.
1953	*Baillieu* (3rd), James William Latham Baillieu, *b.* 1950, *s.* 1973, *m.*	Hon. Robert L. *B.*, *b.* 1979.
1607 S.	*Balfour of Burleigh* (8th), Robert Bruce, *b.* 1927, *s.* 1967, *m.*	Hon. Victoria B., *b.* 1973.
1945	*Balfour of Inchrye* (2nd), Ian Balfour, *b.* 1924, *s.* 1988, *m.*	(None.)
1924	*Banbury of Southam* (3rd), Charles William Banbury, *b.* 1953, *s.* 1981.	(None.)
1698	*Barnard* (11th), Harry John Neville Vane, TD, *b.* 1923, *s.* 1964, *m.*	Hon. Henry F. C. *V.*, *b.* 1959.
1887	*Basing* (5th), Neil Lutley Sclater-Booth, *b.* 1939, *s.* 1983, *m.*	Hon. Stuart W. *S.-B.*, *b.* 1969.
1917	*Beaverbrook* (3rd), Maxwell William Humphrey Aitken, *b.* 1951, *s.* 1985, *m.*	Hon. Maxwell F. *A*, *b.* 1977.

Created	Title, Order of Succession, Name, etc.	Eldest Son or Heir
1647 s.	Belhaven and Stenton (13th), Robert Anthony Carmichael Hamilton, b. 1927, s. 1961, m.	Master of Belhaven, b. 1953.
1848 I.	Bellew (7th), James Bryan Bellew, b. 1920, s. 1981, m.	Hon. Bryan E. B., b. 1943.
1856	Belper (4th), (Alexander) Ronald George Strutt, b. 1912, s. 1956.	Hon. Richard H. S., b. 1941.
1938	Belstead (2nd), John Julian Ganzoni, PC, b. 1932, s. 1958.	(None.)
1922	Bethell (4th), Nicholas William Bethell, MEP, b. 1938, s. 1967.	Hon. James N. B., b. 1967.
1938	Bicester (3rd), Angus Edward Vivian Smith, b. 1932, s. 1968.	Hugh C. V. S., b. 1934.
1903	Biddulph (5th), (Anthony) Nicholas Colin Maitland Biddulph, b. 1959, s. 1988.	Hon. William I. R. M.B., b. 1963.
1938	Birdwood (3rd), Mark William Ogilvie Birdwood, b. 1938, s. 1962, m.	(None.)
1958	Birkett (2nd), Michael Birkett, b. 1929, s. 1962, m.	Hon. Thomas B., b. 1982.
1907	Blyth (4th), Anthony Audley Rupert Blyth, b. 1931, s. 1977, m.	Hon. Riley A. J. B., b. 1955.
1797	Bolton (7th), Richard William Algar Orde-Powlett, b. 1929, s. 1963, m.	Hon. Harry A. N. O.-P., b. 1954.
1452 s.	Borthwick (23rd), John Henry Stuart Borthwick, TD, b. 1905, claim succeeded 1986, w.	Master of Borthwick, b. 1940.
1922	Borwick (4th), James Hugh Myles Borwick, MC, b. 1917, s. 1961, m.	Hon. George S. B., b. 1922.
1761	Boston (10th), Timothy George Frank Boteler Irby, b. 1939, s. 1978, m.	Hon. George W. E. B. I., b. 1971.
1942	Brabazon of Tara (3rd), Ivon Anthony Moore-Brabazon, b. 1946, s. 1974, m.	Hon. Benjamin R. M.-B., b. 1983.
1880	Brabourne (7th), John Ulick Knatchbull, b. 1924, s. 1943, m.	Lord Romsey, b. 1947 (see p. 169).
1925	Bradbury (2nd), John Bradbury, b. 1914, s. 1950, m.	Hon. John B., b. 1940.
1962	Brain (2nd), Christopher Langdon Brain, b. 1926, s. 1966, m.	Hon. Michael C. B., DM, b. 1928.
1938	Brassey of Apethorpe (3rd), David Henry Brassey, b. 1932, s. 1967, m.	Hon. Edward B., b. 1964.
1788	Braybrooke (10th), Robin Henry Charles Neville, b. 1932, s. 1990, m.	George N., b. 1943.
1957	Bridges (2nd), Thomas Edward Bridges, GCMG, b. 1927, s. 1969, m.	Hon. Mark T. B., b. 1954.
1945	Broadbridge (3rd), Peter Hewett Broadbridge, b. 1938, s. 1972, m.	Martin H. B., b. 1929.
1933	Brocket (3rd), Charles Ronald George Nall-Cain, b. 1952, s. 1967, m.	Hon. Alexander C. C. N.-C., b. 1984.
1860	Brougham and Vaux (5th), Michael John Brougham, b. 1938, s. 1967.	Hon. Charles W. B., b. 1971.
1945	Broughshane (2nd), Patrick Owen Alexander Davison, b. 1903, s. 1953, m.	Hon. W. Kensington D., DSO, DFC, b. 1914.
1776	Brownlow (7th), Edward John Peregrine Cust, b. 1936, s. 1978, m.	Hon. Peregrine E. Q. C., b. 1974.
1942	Bruntisfield (1st), Victor Alexander George Anthony Warrender, MC, b. 1899, m.	Hon. John R. W., OBE, MC, TD, b. 1921.
1950	Burden (2nd), Philip William Burden, b. 1916, s. 1970, m.	Hon. Andrew P. B., b. 1959.
1529	Burgh (7th), Alexander Peter Willoughby Leith, b. 1935, s. 1959, m.	Hon. A. Gregory D. L., b. 1958.
1903	Burnham (5th), William Edward Harry Lawson, b. 1920, s. 1963, m.	Hon. Hugh J. F. L., b. 1931.
1897	Burton (3rd), Michael Evan Victor Baillie, b. 1924, s. 1962, m.	Hon. Evan M. R. B., b. 1949.
1643	Byron (13th), Robert James Byron, b. 1950, s. 1989, m.	Hon. Charles R. G. B., b. 1990.
1937	Cadman (3rd), John Anthony Cadman, b. 1938, s. 1966, m.	Hon. Nicholas A. J. C., b. 1977.
1796	Calthorpe (10th), Peter Waldo Somerset Gough-Calthorpe, b. 1927, s. 1945, m.	(None.)
1945	Calverley (3rd), Charles Rodney Muff, b. 1946, s. 1971, m.	Hon. Jonathan E. M., b. 1975.
1383	Camoys (7th), (Ralph) Thomas Campion George Sherman Stonor, b. 1940, s. 1976, m.	Hon. R. William R. T. S., b. 1974.
1715 I.	Carbery (11th), Peter Ralfe Harrington Evans-Freke, b. 1920, s. 1970, m.	Hon. Michael P. E.-F., b. 1942.
1834 I. ⎱ 1838* ⎰	Carew (6th), William Francis Conolly-Carew, CBE (6th UK. Baron, Carew, 1838), b. 1905, s. 1927, w.	Hon. Patrick T. C.-C., b. 1938.
1916	Carnock (4th), David Henry Arthur Nicolson, b. 1920, s. 1982.	Nigel N., b. 1917.
1796 I. ⎱ 1797* ⎰	Carrington (6th), Peter Alexander Rupert Carington, KG, GCMG, CH, MC, PC, (6th Brit. Baron, Carrington, 1797), b. 1919, s. 1938, m.	Hon. Rupert F. J. C., b. 1948.
1812 I.	Castlemaine (8th), Roland Thomas John Handcock, MBE, b. 1943, s. 1973, m.	Hon. Ronan M. E. H., b. 1989.
1936	Catto (2nd), Stephen Gordon Catto, b. 1923, s. 1959, m.	Hon. Innes G. C., b. 1950.
1918	Cawley (3rd), Frederick Lee Cawley, b. 1913, s. 1954, m.	Hon. John F. C., b. 1946.
1937	Chatfield (2nd), Ernle David Lewis Chatfield, b. 1917, s. 1967, m.	(None.)
1858	Chesham (6th), Nicholas Charles Cavendish, b. 1941, s. 1989, m.	Hon. Charles G. C. C., b. 1974.
1945	Chetwode (2nd), Philip Chetwode, b. 1937, s. 1950, m.	Hon. Roger C., b. 1968.
1945	Chorley (2nd), Roger Richard Edward Chorley, b. 1930, s. 1978, m.	Hon. Nicholas R. D. C., b. 1966.
1858	Churston (5th), John Francis Yarde-Buller, b. 1934, s. 1991, m.	Hon. Benjamin F. A. Y.-B., b. 1974.
1946	Citrine (2nd), Norman Arthur Citrine, b. 1914, s. 1983, m.	Hon. Ronald E. C., b. 1919.
1800 I.	Clanmorris (8th), Simon John Ward Bingham, b. 1937, s. 1988, m.	John T. B., b. 1923.
1672	Clifford of Chudleigh (14th), Thomas Hugh Clifford, b. 1948, s. 1988, m.	Hon. Alexander T. H. C., b. 1985.

Created	*Title, Order of Succession, Name, etc.*	*Eldest Son or Heir*
1299	*Clinton* (22nd), Gerard Nevile Mark Fane Trefusis, *b.* 1934, *title called out of abeyance* 1965, *m.*	Hon. Charles P. R. F. *T.*, *b.* 1962.
1955	*Clitheroe* (2nd), Ralph John Assheton, *b.* 1929, *s.* 1984, *m.*	Hon. Ralph C. *A.*, *b.* 1962.
1919	*Clwyd* (3rd), (John) Anthony Roberts, *b.* 1935, *s.* 1987, *m.*	Hon. J. Murray *R.*, *b.* 1971.
1948	*Clydesmuir* (2nd), Ronald John Bilsland Colville, KT, CB, MBE, TD, *b.* 1917, *s.* 1954, *m.*	Hon. David R. *C.*, *b.* 1949.
1960	*Cobbold* (2nd), David Antony Fromanteel Lytton Cobbold, *b.* 1937, *s.* 1987, *m.*	Hon. Henry F. *L. C.*, *b.* 1962.
1919	*Cochrane of Cults* (4th), (Ralph Henry) Vere Cochrane, *b.* 1926, *s.* 1990, *m.*	Hon. Thomas H. V. *C.*, *b.* 1957.
1954	*Coleraine* (2nd), (James) Martin (Bonar) Law, *b.* 1931, *s.* 1980, *m.*	Hon. James P. B. *L.*, *b.* 1975.
1873	*Coleridge* (5th), William Duke Coleridge, *b.* 1937, *s.* 1984, *m.*	Hon. James D. *C.*, *b.* 1967.
1946	*Colgrain* (3rd), David Colin Campbell, *b.* 1920, *s.* 1973, *m.*	Hon. Alastair C. L. *C.*, *b.* 1951.
1917	*Colwyn* (3rd), (Ian) Anthony Hamilton-Smith, CBE, *b.* 1942, *s.* 1966, *m.*	Hon. Craig P. *H.-S.*, *b.* 1968.
1956	*Colyton* (1st), Henry Lennox d'Aubigné Hopkinson, CMG, PC, *b.* 1902, *m.*	Hon. Nicholas H. E. *H.*, *b.* 1932.
1841	*Congleton* (8th), Christopher Patrick Parnell, *b.* 1930, *s.* 1967, *m.*	Hon. John P. C. *P.*, *b.* 1959.
1927	*Cornwallis* (3rd), Fiennes Neil Wykeham Cornwallis, OBE, *b.* 1921, *s.* 1982, *m.*	Hon. F. W. Jeremy *C.*, *b.* 1946.
1874	*Cottesloe* (4th), John Walgrave Halford Fremantle, GBE, TD, *b.* 1900, *s.* 1956, *m.*	Cdr. Hon. John T. *F.*, *b.* 1927.
1929	*Craigmyle* (3rd), Thomas Donald Mackay Shaw, *b.* 1923, *s.* 1944, *m.*	Hon. Thomas C. *S.*, *b.* 1960.
1899	*Cranworth* (3rd), Philip Bertram Gurdon, *b.* 1940, *s.* 1964, *m.*	Hon. Sacha W. R. *G.*, *b.* 1970.
1959	*Crathorne* (2nd), Charles James Dugdale, *b.* 1939, *s.* 1977, *m.*	Hon. Thomas A. J. *D.*, *b.* 1977.
1892	*Crawshaw* (4th), William Michael Clifton Brooks, *b.* 1933, *s.* 1946.	Hon. David G. *B.*, *b.* 1934.
1940	*Croft* (2nd), Michael Henry Glendower Page Croft, *b.* 1916, *s.* 1947, *w.*	Hon. Bernard W. H. P. *C.*, *b.* 1949.
1797 I.	*Crofton* (7th), Guy Patrick Gilbert Crofton, *b.* 1951, *s.* 1989, *m.*	Hon. E. Harry P. *C.*, *b.* 1988.
1375	*Cromwell* (7th), Godfrey John Bewicke-Copley, *b.* 1960, *s.* 1982, *m.*	Hon. Thomas D. *B.-C.*, *b.* 1964.
1947	*Crook* (2nd), Douglas Edwin Crook, *b.* 1926, *s* 1989, *m.*	Hon. Robert D. E. *C.*, *b.* 1955.
1920	*Cullen of Ashbourne* (2nd), Charles Borlase Marsham Cokayne, MBE, *b.* 1912, *s.* 1932, *m.*	Hon. Edmund W. M. *C.*, *b.* 1916.
1914	*Cunliffe* (3rd), Roger Cunliffe, *b.* 1932, *s.* 1963, *m.*	Hon. Henry *C.*, *b.* 1962.
1927	*Daresbury* (3rd), Edward Gilbert Greenall, *b.* 1928, *s.* 1990, *m.*	Hon. Peter G. *G.*, *b.* 1953.
1924	*Darling* (2nd), Robert Charles Henry Darling, *b.* 1919, *s.* 1936, *m.*	Hon. R. Julian H. *D.*, *b.* 1944.
1946	*Darwen* (3rd), Roger Michael Davies, *b.* 1938, *s.* 1988, *m.*	Hon. Paul *D.*, *b.* 1962.
1923	*Daryngton* (2nd), Jocelyn Arthur Pike Pease, *b.* 1908, *s.* 1949.	(None.)
1932	*Davies* (3rd), David Davies, *b.* 1940, *s.* 1944, *m.*	Hon. David D. *D.*, *b.* 1975.
1812 I.	*Decies* (6th), Arthur George Marcus Douglas de la Poer Beresford, *b.* 1915, *s.* 1944, *m.*	Hon. Marcus H. T. *de la P.B.*, *b.* 1948.
1299	*de Clifford* (27th), John Edward Southwell Russell, *b.* 1928, *s.* 1982, *m.*	Hon. William S. *R.*, *b.* 1930.
1851	*De Freyne* (7th), Francis Arthur John French, *b.* 1927, *s.* 1935, *m.*	Hon. Fulke C. A. J. *F.*, *b.* 1957.
1821	*Delamere* (5th), Hugh George Cholmondeley, *b.* 1934, *s.* 1979, *m.*	Hon. Thomas P. G. *C.*, *b.* 1968.
1838	*de Mauley* (6th), Gerald John Ponsonby, *b.* 1921, *s.* 1962, *m.*	Col. Hon. Thomas M. *P.*, TD, *b.* 1930.
1937	*Denham* (2nd), Bertram Stanley Mitford Bowyer, KBE, PC, *b.* 1927, *s.* 1948, *m.*	Hon. Richard G. G. *B.*, *b.* 1959.
1834	*Denman* (5th), Charles Spencer Denman, CBE, MC, TD, *b.* 1916, *s.* 1971, *w.*	Hon. Richard T. S. *D.*, *b.* 1946.
1885	*Deramore* (6th), Richard Arthur de Yarburgh-Bateson, *b.* 1911, *s.* 1964, *m.*	(None.)
1887	*De Ramsey* (3rd), Ailwyn Edward Fellowes, KBE, TD, *b.* 1910, *s.* 1925, *w.*	Hon. John A. *F.*, *b.* 1942.
1264	*de Ros* (28th), Peter Trevor Maxwell, *b.* 1958, *s.* 1983, *m.* (*Premier Baron of England*).	Hon. Finbar J. *M.*, *b.* 1988.
1881	*Derwent* (5th), Robin Evelyn Leo Vanden-Bempde-Johnstone, LVO, *b.* 1930, *s.* 1986, *m.*	Hon. Francis P. H. *V.-B.-J.*, *b.* 1965.
1831	*De Saumarez* (7th), Eric Douglas Saumarez, *b.* 1956, *s.* 1991.	Hon. Victor T. *S.*, *b.* 1956.
1910	*de Villiers* (3rd), Arthur Percy de Villiers, *b.* 1911, *s.* 1934.	Hon. Alexander C. *de V.*, *b.* 1940.
1930	*Dickinson* (2nd), Richard Clavering Hyett Dickinson, *b.* 1926, *s.* 1943, *m.*	Hon. Martin H. *D.*, *b.* 1961.
1620 I. 1765* }	*Digby* (12th), Edward Henry Kenelm Digby, (6th *Brit. Baron, Digby*), *b.* 1924, *s.* 1964, *m.*	Hon. Henry N. K. *D.*, *b.* 1954.
1615	*Dormer* (16th), Joseph Spencer Philip Dormer, *b.* 1914, *s.* 1975.	Geoffrey H. *D.*, *b.* 1920.
1943	*Dowding* (2nd), Derek Hugh Tremenheere Dowding, *b.* 1919, *s.* 1970, *m.*	Hon. Piers H. T. *D.*, *b.* 1948.
1800 I.	*Dufferin and Clandeboye* (10th), Francis George Blackwood, *b.* 1916, *s.* 1988, *m.*	Hon. John F. *B.*, *b.* 1944.
1929	*Dulverton* (2nd), (Frederick) Anthony Hamilton Wills, CBE, TD, *b.* 1915, *s.* 1956, *m.*	Hon. G. Michael H. *W.*, *b.* 1944.
1800 I.	*Dunalley* (6th), Henry Desmond Graham Prittie, *b.* 1912, *s.* 1948, *m.*	Hon. Henry F. C. *P.*, *b.* 1948.

Created	Title, Order of Succession, Name, etc.	Eldest Son or Heir

1324 I.   *Dunboyne* (28th), Patrick Theobald Tower Butler, VRD, b. 1917, s. 1945, m.   Hon. John F. B., b. 1951.

1802   *Dunleath* (4th), Charles Edward Henry John Mulholland, TD, b. 1933, s. 1956, m.   Sir Michael H. M., Bt., b. 1915.

1439 I.   *Dunsany* (19th), Randal Arthur Henry Plunkett (20th *Irish Baron Killeen*, 1449), b. 1906, s. 1957, m.   Hon. Edward J. C. P., b. 1939.

1780   *Dynevor* (9th), Richard Charles Uryan Rhys, b. 1935, s. 1962.   Hon. Hugo G. U. R., b. 1966.

1857   *Ebury* (6th), Francis Egerton Grosvenor, b. 1934, s. 1957, m.   Hon. Julian F. M. G., b. 1959.

1963   *Egremont* (2nd), & *Leconfield* (7th) (1859), John Max Henry Scawen Wyndham, b. 1948, s. 1972, m.   Hon. George R. V. W., b. 1983.

1643   *Elibank* (14th), Alan D'Ardis Erskine-Murray, b. 1923, s. 1973, m.   Master of Elibank, b. 1964.

1802   *Ellenborough* (8th), Richard Edward Cecil Law, b. 1926, s. 1945, w.   Maj. Hon. Rupert E. H. L., b. 1955.

1509 s.*   *Elphinstone* (18th), James Alexander Elphinstone (4th *UK Baron Elphinstone*, 1885), b. 1953, s. 1975, m.   Master of Elphinstone, b. 1980.

1934   *Elton* (2nd), Rodney Elton, TD, b. 1930, s. 1973, m.   Hon. Edward P. E., b. 1966.

1964   *Erroll of Hale* (1st), Frederick James Erroll, TD, PC, b. 1914, m.   (None.)

1964   *Erskine of Rerrick* (2nd), Iain Maxwell Erskine, b. 1926, s. 1980.   (None.)

1627 s.   *Fairfax of Cameron* (14th), Nicholas John Albert Fairfax, b. 1956, s. 1964, m.   Hon. Edward N. T. F., b. 1984.

1961   *Fairhaven* (3rd), Ailwyn Henry George Broughton, b. 1936, s. 1973, m.   Hon. James H. A. B., b. 1963.

1916   *Faringdon* (3rd), Charles Michael Henderson, b. 1937, s. 1977, m.   Hon. James H. H., b. 1961.

1756 I.   *Farnham* (12th), Barry Owen Somerset Maxwell, b. 1931, s. 1957, m.   Hon. Simon K. M., b. 1933.

1856 I.   *Fermoy* (6th), Patrick Maurice Burke Roche, b. 1967, s. 1984.   Hon. E. Hugh B. R., b. 1972.

1826   *Feversham* (6th), Charles Antony Peter Duncombe, b. 1945, s. 1963, m.   Hon. Jasper O. S. D., b. 1968.

1798 I.   *ffrench* (8th), Robuck John Peter Charles Mario ffrench, b. 1956, s. 1986, m.   Hon. John C. M. J. F. ff., b. 1928.

1909   *Fisher* (3rd), John Vavasseur Fisher, DSC, b. 1921, s. 1955, m.   Hon. Patrick V. F., b. 1953.

1295   *Fitzwalter* (21st), (Fitzwalter) Brook Plumptre, b. 1914, *called out of abeyance*, 1953, m.   Hon. Julian B. P., b. 1952.

1776   *Foley* (8th), Adrian Gerald Foley, b. 1923, s. 1927, m.   Hon. Thomas H. F., b. 1961.

1445 s.   *Forbes* (22nd), Nigel Ivan Forbes, KBE (*Premier Baron of Scotland*), b. 1918, s. 1953, m.   Master of Forbes, b. 1946.

1821   *Forester* (8th), (George Cecil) Brooke Weld-Forester, b. 1938, s. 1977, m.   Hon. C. R. George W.-F., b. 1975.

1922   *Forres* (4th), Alastair Stephen Grant Williamson, b. 1946, s. 1978, m.   Hon. George A. M. W., b. 1972.

1917   *Forteviot* (3rd), Henry Evelyn Alexander Dewar, MBE, b. 1906, s. 1947, w.   Hon. John J. E. D., b. 1938.

1951   *Freyberg* (2nd), Paul Richard Freyberg, OBE, MC, b. 1923, s. 1963, m.   Hon. Valerian B. F., b. 1970.

1917   *Gainford* (3rd), Joseph Edward Pease, b. 1921, s. 1971, m.   Hon. George P., b. 1926.

1818 I.   *Garvagh* (5th), (Alexander Leopold Ivor) George Canning, b. 1920, s. 1956, m.   Hon. Spencer G. S. de R. C., b. 1953.

1942   *Geddes* (3rd), Euan Michael Ross Geddes, b. 1937, s. 1975, m.   Hon. James G. N. G., b. 1969.

1876   *Gerard* (4th), Robert William Frederick Alwyn Gerard, b. 1918, s. 1953.   Anthony R. H. G., b. 1949.

1824   *Gifford* (6th), Anthony Maurice Gifford, QC, b. 1940, s. 1961, m.   Hon. Thomas A. G., b. 1967.

1917   *Gisborough* (3rd), Thomas Richard John Long Chaloner, b. 1927, s. 1951, m.   Hon. Thomas P. L. C., b. 1961.

1960   *Gladwyn* (1st), (Hubert Miles) Gladwyn Jebb, GCMG, GCVO, CB, b. 1900, w.   Hon. Miles A. G. J., b. 1930.

1899   *Glanusk* (4th), David Russell Bailey, b. 1917, s. 1948, m.   Hon. Christopher R. B., b. 1942.

1918   *Glenarthur* (4th), Simon Mark Arthur, b. 1944, s. 1976, m.   Hon. Edward A. A., b. 1973.

1911   *Glenconner* (3rd), Colin Christopher Paget Tennant, b. 1926, s. 1983, m.   Hon. Charles E. P. T., b. 1957.

1964   *Glendevon* (1st), John Adrian Hope, PC, b. 1912, m.   Hon. Julian J. S. H., b. 1950.

1922   *Glendyne* (3rd), Robert Nivison, b. 1926, s. 1967, m.   Hon. John N., b. 1960.

1939   *Glentoran* (2nd), Daniel Stewart Thomas Bingham Dixon, KBE, PC (NI), b. 1912, s. 1950, w.   Hon. Thomas R. V. D., MBE, b. 1935.

1909   *Gorell* (4th), Timothy John Radcliffe Barnes, b. 1927, s. 1963, m.   Hon. Ronald A. H. B., b. 1931.

1953   *Grantchester* (2nd), Kenneth Bent Suenson-Taylor, CBE, QC, b. 1921, s. 1976, m.   Hon. Christopher J. S.-T., b. 1951.

1782   *Grantley* (7th), John Richard Brinsley Norton, MC, b. 1923, s. 1954, m.   Hon. Richard W. B. N., b. 1956.

1794 I.   *Graves* (8th), Peter George Wellesley Graves, b. 1911, s. 1963, m.   Evelyn P. G., b. 1926.

1445 s.   *Gray* (22nd), Angus Diarmid Ian Campbell-Gray, b. 1931, s. 1946, w.   Master of Gray, b. 1964.

1950   *Greenhill* (3rd), Malcolm Greenhill, b. 1924, s. 1989.   (None.)

1927   *Greenway* (4th), Ambrose Charles Drexel Greenway, b. 1941, s. 1975, m.   Hon. Mervyn S. K. G., b. 1942.

1902   *Grenfell* (3rd), Julian Pascoe Francis St Leger Grenfell, b. 1935, s. 1976, m.   Francis P. J. G., b. 1938.

1944   *Gretton* (4th), John Lysander Gretton, b. 1975, s. 1989, M.   (None.)

1397   *Grey of Codnor* (5th), Charles Legh Shuldham Cornwall-Legh, CBE, AE, b. 1903, *title called out of abeyance* 1989, m.   Hon. Richard H. C.-L., b. 1936.

Created	Title, Order of Succession, Name, etc.	Eldest Son or Heir
1955	*Gridley* (2nd), Arnold Hudson Gridley, *b.* 1906, *s.* 1965, *m.*	Hon. Richard D. A. *G.*, *b.* 1956.
1964	*Grimston of Westbury* (2nd), Robert Walter Sigismund Grimston, *b.* 1925, *s.* 1979, *m.*	Hon. Robert J. S. *G.*, *b.* 1951.
1886	*Grimthorpe* (4th), Christopher John Beckett, OBE, *b.* 1915, *s.* 1963, *m.*	Hon. Edward J. *B.*, *b.* 1954.
1945	*Hacking* (3rd), Douglas David Hacking, *b.* 1938, *s.* 1971, *m.*	Hon. Douglas F. *H.*, *b.* 1968.
1950	*Haden-Guest* (4th), Peter Haden Haden-Guest, *b.* 1913, *s.* 1987, *m.*	Hon. Christopher *H.-G.*, *b.* 1948.
1886	*Hamilton of Dalzell* (4th), James Leslie Hamilton, *b.* 1938, *s.* 1990, *m.*	Hon. Gavin G. *H.*, *b.* 1968.
1874	*Hampton* (6th), Richard Humphrey Russell Pakington, *b.* 1925, *s.* 1974, *m.*	Hon. John H. A. *P.*, *b.* 1964.
1939	*Hankey* (2nd), Robert Maurice Alers Hankey, KCMG, KCVO, *b.* 1905, *s.* 1963, *m.*	Hon. Donald R. A. *H.*, *b.* 1938.
1958	*Harding of Petherton* (2nd), John Charles Harding, *b.* 1928, *s.* 1989, *m.*	Hon. William A. J. *H.*, *b.* 1969.
1910	*Hardinge of Penshurst* (3rd), George Edward Charles Hardinge, *b.* 1921, *s.* 1960, *m.*	Hon. Julian A. *H.*, *b.* 1945.
1876	*Harlech* (6th), Francis David Ormsby-Gore, *b.* 1954, *s.* 1985, *m.*	Hon. Jasset D. C. *O.-G.*, *b.* 1986.
1939	*Harmsworth* (3rd), Thomas Harold Raymond Harmsworth, *b.* 1939, *s.* 1990, *m.*	Hon. Dominic M. E. *H.*, *b.* 1973.
1815	*Harris* (6th), George Robert John Harris, *b.* 1920, *s.* 1984.	Derek M. *H.*, *b.* 1916.
1954	*Harvey of Tasburgh* (2nd), Peter Charles Oliver Harvey, *b.* 1921, *s.* 1968, *m.*	Hon. John W. *H.*, *b.* 1923.
1295	*Hastings* (22nd), Edward Delaval Henry Astley, *b.* 1912, *s.* 1956, *m.*	Hon. Delaval T. H. *A.*, *b.* 1960.
1835	*Hatherton* (8th), Edward Charles Littleton, *b.* 1950, *s.* 1985, *m.*	Hon. Thomas E. *L.*, *b.* 1977.
1776	*Hawke* (10th), (Julian Stanhope) Theodore Hawke, *b.* 1904, *s.* 1985, *m.*	Hon. Edward G. *H.*, *b.* 1950.
1927	*Hayter* (3rd), George Charles Hayter Chubb, KCVO, CBE, *b.* 1911, *s.* 1967, *m.*	Hon. G. William M. *C.*, *b.* 1943.
1945	*Hazlerigg* (2nd), Arthur Grey Hazlerigg, MC, TD, *b.* 1910, *s.* 1949, *w.*	Hon. Arthur G. *H.*, *b.* 1951.
1797 I.	*Headley* (7th), Charles Rowland Allanson-Winn, *b.* 1902, *s.* 1969, *w.*	Hon. Owain G. *A.-W.*, *b.* 1906.
1943	*Hemingford* (3rd), (Dennis) Nicholas Herbert, *b.* 1934, *s.* 1982, *m.*	Hon. Christopher D. C. *H.*, *b.* 1973.
1906	*Hemphill* (5th), Peter Patrick Fitzroy Martyn Martyn-Hemphill, *b.* 1928, *s.* 1957, *m.*	Hon. Charles A. M. *M.-H.*, *b.* 1954.
1799 I.*	*Henley* (8th), Oliver Michael Robert Eden (6th *UK Baron, Northington,* 1885), *b.* 1953, *s.* 1977, *m.*	Hon. John W. O. *E.*, *b.* 1988.
1800 I.*	*Henniker* (8th), John Patrick Edward Chandos Henniker-Major, KCMG, CVO, MC (4th *UK Baron, Hartismere,* 1866), *b.* 1916, *s.* 1980, *m.*	Hon. Mark I. P. C. *H.-M.*, *b.* 1947.
1886	*Herschell* (3rd), Rognvald Richard Farrer Herschell, *b.* 1923, *s.* 1929, *m.*	(None.)
1935	*Hesketh* (3rd), Thomas Alexander Fermor-Hesketh, PC, *b.* 1950, *s.* 1955, *m.*	Hon. Frederick H. *F.-H.*, *b.* 1988.
1828	*Heytesbury* (6th), Francis William Holmes à Court, *b.* 1931, *s.* 1971, *m.*	Hon. James W. *H. à C.*, *b.* 1967.
1886	*Hindlip* (5th), Henry Richard Allsopp, *b.* 1912, *s.* 1966, *m.*	Hon. Charles H. *A.*, *b.* 1940.
1950	*Hives* (2nd), John Warwick Hives, CBE, *b.* 1913, *s.* 1965, *m.*	Matthew P. *H.*, *b.* 1971.
1912	*Hollenden* (3rd), Gordon Hope Hope-Morley, *b.* 1914, *s.* 1977, *m.*	Hon. Ian H. *H.-M.*, *b.* 1946.
1897	*Holm Patrick* (4th), Hans James David Hamilton, *b.* 1955, *s.* 1991, *m.*	Hon. Ion H. J. *H.*, *b.* 1956.
1933	*Horder* (2nd), Thomas Mervyn Horder, *b.* 1910, *s.* 1955.	(None.)
1797 I.	*Hotham* (8th), Henry Durand Hotham, *b.* 1940, *s.* 1967, *m.*	Hon. William B. *H.*, *b.* 1972.
1881	*Hothfield* (6th), Anthony Charles Sackville Tufton, *b.* 1939, *s.* 1991, *m.*	Hon. William S. *T.*, *b.* 1977.
1597	*Howard de Walden* (9th), John Osmael Scott-Ellis, TD (5th *UK Baron, Seaford,* 1826), *b.* 1912, *s.* 1946, *m.*	To Barony of Howard de Walden, four co-heiresses. To Barony of Seaford, Colin H. F. *Ellis,* *b.* 1946.
1930	*Howard of Penrith* (2nd), Francis Philip Howard, *b.* 1905, *s.* 1939, *m.*	Hon. Philip E. *H.*, *b.* 1945.
1960	*Howick of Glendale* (2nd), Charles Evelyn Baring, *b.* 1937, *s.* 1973, *m.*	Hon. David E. C. *B.*, *b.* 1975.
1796 I.	*Huntingfield* (6th), Gerard Charles Arcedeckne Vanneck, *b.* 1915, *s.* 1969, *m.*	Hon. Joshua C. *V.*, *b.* 1954.
1866	*Hylton* (5th), Raymond Hervey Jolliffe, *b.* 1932, *s.* 1967, *m.*	Hon. William H. M. *J.*, *b.* 1967.
1933	*Iliffe* (2nd), Edward Langton Iliffe, *b.* 1908, *s.* 1960, *m.*	Robert P. R. *I.*, *b.* 1944.
1543 I.	*Inchiquin* (18th), Conor Myles John O'Brien, *b.* 1943, *s.* 1982.	Murrough R. *O'B.*, *b.* 1910.
1962	*Inchyra* (2nd), Robert Charles Reneke Hoyer Millar, *b.* 1935, *s.* 1989, *m.*	Hon. C. James C. H. *M.*, *b.* 1962.
1964	*Inglewood* (2nd), (William) Richard Fletcher-Vane, MEP, *b.* 1951, *s.* 1989, *m.*	Hon. Henry W. F. *F.-V.*, *b.* 1990.
1919	*Inverforth* (4th), Andrew Peter Weir, *b.* 1966, *s.* 1982.	Hon. John V. *W.*, *b.* 1935.
1941	*Ironside* (2nd), Edmund Oslac Ironside, *b.* 1924, *s.* 1959, *m.*	Hon. Charles E. G. *I.*, *b.* 1956.
1952	*Jeffreys* (3rd), Christopher Henry Mark Jeffreys, *b.* 1957, *s.* 1986, *m.*	Hon. Arthur M. H. *J.*, *b.* 1989.
1906	*Joicey* (4th), Michael Edward Joicey, *b.* 1925, *s.* 1966, *m.*	Hon. James M. *J.*, *b.* 1953.
1937	*Kenilworth* (4th), (John) Randle Siddeley, *b.* 1954, *s.* 1981, *m.*	(None.)
1935	*Kennet* (2nd), Wayland Hilton Young, *b.* 1923, *s.* 1960, *m.*	Hon. W. A. Thoby *Y.*, *b.* 1957.

Created	Title, Order of Succession, Name, etc.	Eldest Son or Heir
1776 I. } 1886* }	*Kensington* (8th), Hugh Ivor Edwardes (5th *UK Baron, Kensington*), b. 1933, s. 1981, m.	Hon. W. Owen A. *E.*, b. 1964.
1951	*Kenswood* (2nd), John Michael Howard Whitfield, b. 1930, s. 1963, m.	Hon. Michael C. *W.*, b. 1955.
1788	*Kenyon* (5th), Lloyd Tyrell-Kenyon, CBE, b. 1917, s. 1927, m.	Hon. Lloyd *T.-K.*, b. 1947.
1947	*Kershaw* (4th), Edward John Kershaw, b. 1936, s. 1962, m.	Hon. John C. E. *K.*, b. 1971.
1943	*Keyes* (2nd), Roger George Bowlby Keyes, b. 1919, s. 1945, m.	Hon. Charles W. P. *K.*, b. 1951.
1909	*Kilbracken* (3rd), John Raymond Godley, DSC, b. 1920, s. 1950.	Hon. Christopher J. *G.*, b. 1945.
1900	*Killanin* (3rd), Michael Morris, MBE, TD, b. 1914, s. 1927, m.	Hon. G. Redmond F. *M.*, b. 1947.
1943	*Killearn* (2nd), Graham Curtis Lampson, b. 1919, s. 1964, m.	Hon. Victor M. G. A. *L.*, b. 1941.
1789 I.	*Kilmaine* (7th), John David Henry Browne, b. 1948, s. 1978, m.	Hon. John F. S. *B.*, b. 1983.
1831	*Kilmarnock* (7th), Alastair Ivor Gilbert Boyd, b. 1927, s. 1975, m.	Hon. Robin J. *B.*, b. 1941.
1941	*Kindersley* (3rd), Robert Hugh Molesworth Kindersley, b. 1929, s. 1976, m.	Hon. Rupert J. M. *K.*, b. 1955.
1223 I.	*Kingsale* (35th), John de Courcy (*Premier Baron of Ireland*), b. 1941, s. 1969.	Nevinson R. *de C.*, b. 1920.
1682 s. } 1860* }	*Kinnaird* (13th), Graham Charles Kinnaird (5th *UK. Baron, Kinnaird*), b. 1912, s. 1972, m.	(None.)
1902	*Kinross* (5th), Christopher Patrick Balfour, b. 1949, s. 1985, m.	Hon. Alan I. *B.*, b. 1978.
1951	*Kirkwood* (3rd), David Harvie Kirkwood, PH.D., b. 1931, s. 1970, m.	Hon. James S. *K.*, b. 1937.
1800 I.	*Langford* (9th), Geoffrey Alexander Rowley-Conwy, OBE, b. 1912, s. 1953, m.	Hon. Owain G. *R.-C.*, b. 1958.
1942	*Latham* (2nd), Dominic Charles Latham, b. 1954, s. 1970.	Anthony M. *L.*, b. 1954.
1431	*Latymer* (8th), Hugo Nevill Money-Coutts, b. 1926, s. 1987, m.	Hon. Crispin J. A. N. *M.-C.*, b. 1955.
1869	*Lawrence* (5th), David John Downer Lawrence, b. 1937, s. 1968.	(None.)
1947	*Layton* (3rd), Geoffrey Michael Layton, b. 1947, s. 1989, m.	Hon. David *L.*, MBE, b. 1914.
1839	*Leigh* (5th), John Piers Leigh, b. 1935, s. 1979, m.	Hon. Christopher D. P. *L.*, b. 1960.
1962	*Leighton of St Mellons* (2nd), (John) Leighton Seager, b. 1922, s. 1963, m.	Hon. Robert W. H. L. *S.*, b. 1955.
1797	*Lilford* (7th), George Vernon Powys, b. 1931, s. 1949, m.	Hon. Mark V. *P.*, b., 1975.
1945	*Lindsay of Birker* (2nd), Michael Francis Morris Lindsay, b. 1909, s. 1952, m.	Hon. James F. *L.*, b. 1945.
1758 I.	*Lisle* (7th), John Nicholas Horace Lysaght, b. 1903, s. 1919, m.	Patrick J. *L.*, b. 1931.
1850	*Londesborough* (9th), Richard John Denison, b. 1959, s. 1968, m.	Hon. James F. *D.*, b. 1990.
1541 I.	*Louth* (16th), Otway Michael James Oliver Plunkett, b. 1929, s. 1950, m.	Hon. Jonathan O. *P.*, b. 1952.
1458 s. } 1837* }	*Lovat* (15th), Simon Christopher Joseph Fraser, DSO, MC, TD (4th *UK Baron, Lovat*), b. 1911, s. 1933, m.	Master of Lovat, b. 1939.
1946	*Lucas of Chilworth* (2nd), Michael William George Lucas, b. 1926, s. 1967, m.	Hon. Simon W. *L.*, b. 1957.
1929	*Luke* (2nd), Ian St John Lawson-Johnston, KCVO, TD, b. 1905, s. 1943, m.	Hon. Arthur C. St J. *L.-J.*, b. 1933.
1839	*Lurgan* (5th), John Desmond Cavendish Brownlow, OBE, b. 1911, s. 1984.	(None.)
1914	*Lyell* (3rd), Charles Lyell, b. 1939, s. 1943.	(None.)
1859	*Lyveden* (6th), Ronald Cecil Vernon, b. 1915, s. 1973, m.	Hon. Jack L. *V.*, b. 1938.
1959	*MacAndrew* (3rd), Christopher Anthony Colin MacAndrew, b. 1945, s. 1989, m.	Hon. Oliver C. J. *M.*, b. 1983.
1776 I.	*Macdonald* (8th), Godfrey James Macdonald of Macdonald, b. 1947, s. 1970, m.	Hon. Godfrey E. H. T. *M.*, b. 1982.
1949	*Macdonald of Gwaenysgor* (2nd), Gordon Ramsay Macdonald, b. 1915, s. 1966, m.	(None.)
1937	*McGowan* (3rd), Harry Duncan Cory McGowan, b. 1938, s. 1966, m.	Hon. Harry J. C. *M.*, b. 1971.
1922	*Maclay* (3rd), Joseph Paton Maclay, b. 1942, s. 1969, m.	Hon. Joseph P. *M.*, b. 1977.
1955	*McNair* (3rd), Duncan James McNair, b. 1947, s. 1989, m.	Hon. Thomas J. *M.*, b. 1990.
1951	*Macpherson of Drumochter* (2nd), (James) Gordon Macpherson, b. 1924, s. 1965, m.	Hon. James A. *M.*, b. 1979.
1937	*Mancroft* (3rd), Benjamin Lloyd Stormont Mancroft, b. 1957, s. 1987, m.	(None.)
1807	*Manners* (5th), John Robert Cecil Manners, b. 1923, s. 1972, m.	Hon. John H. R. *M.*, b. 1956.
1922	*Manton* (3rd), Joseph Rupert Eric Robert Watson, b. 1924, s. 1968, m.	Capt. Hon. Miles R. M. *W.*, b. 1958.
1908	*Marchamley* (3rd), John William Tattersall Whiteley, b. 1922, s. 1949, m.	Hon. William F. *W.*, b. 1968.
1964	*Margadale* (1st), John Granville Morrison, TD, b. 1906, w.	Hon. James I. *M.*, TD, b. 1930.
1961	*Marks of Broughton* (2nd), Michael Marks, b. 1920, s. 1964.	Hon. Simon R. *M.*, b. 1950.
1964	*Martonmere* (2nd), John Stephen Robinson, b. 1963, s. 1989.	David A. *R.*, b. 1965.
1776 I.	*Massy* (9th), Hugh Hamon John Somerset Massy, b. 1921, s. 1958, m.	Hon. David H. S. *M.*, b. 1947.
1935	*May* (3rd), Michael St John May, b. 1931, s. 1950, m.	Hon. Jasper B. St J. *M.*, b. 1965.
1928	*Melchett* (4th), Peter Robert Henry Mond, b. 1948, s. 1973.	(None.)

Created	Title, Order of Succession, Name, etc.	Eldest Son or Heir
1925	*Merrivale* (3rd), Jack Henry Edmond Duke, *b.* 1917, *s.* 1951, *m.*	Hon. Derek J. P. *D.*, *b.* 1948.
1911	*Merthyr.* Disclaimed for life 1977. (*Trevor Oswin Lewis, Bt.*, CBE, *b.* 1935, *s.* 1977, *m.*)	David T. *L.*, *b.* 1977.
1919	*Meston* (3rd), James Meston, *b.* 1950, *s.* 1984, *m.*	Hon. Thomas J. D. *M.*, *b.* 1977.
1838	*Methuen* (6th), Anthony John Methuen, *b.* 1925, *s.* 1975.	Hon. Robert A. H. *M.*, *b.* 1931.
1711	*Middleton* (12th), (Digby) Michael Godfrey John Willoughby, MC, *b.* 1921, *s.* 1970, *m.*	Hon. Michael C. J. *W.*, *b.* 1948.
1939	*Milford* (2nd), Wogan Philipps, *b.* 1902, *s.* 1962, *m.*	Hon. Hugo J. L. *P.*, *b.* 1929.
1933	*Milne* (2nd), George Douglass Milne, TD, *b.* 1909, *s.* 1948, *m.*	Hon. George A. *M.*, *b.* 1941.
1951	*Milner of Leeds* (2nd), Arthur James Michael Milner, AE, *b.* 1923, *s.* 1967, *m.*	Hon. Richard J. *M.*, *b.* 1959.
1947	*Milverton* (2nd), Rev. Fraser Arthur Richard Richards, *b.* 1930, *s.* 1978, *m.*	Hon. Michael H. *R.*, *b.* 1936.
1873	*Moncreiff* (5th), Harry Robert Wellwood Moncreiff, *b.* 1915, *s.* 1942, *w.*	Hon. Rhoderick H. W. *M.*, *b.* 1954.
1884	*Monk Bretton* (3rd), John Charles Dodson, *b.* 1924, *s.* 1933, *m.*	Hon. Christopher M. *D.*, *b.* 1958.
1885	*Monkswell* (5th), Gerard Collier, *b.* 1947, *s.* 1984, *m.*	Hon. James A. *C.*, *b.* 1977.
1728	*Monson* (11th), John Monson, *b.* 1932, *s.* 1958, *m.*	Hon. Nicholas J. *M.*, *b.* 1955.
1885	*Montagu of Beaulieu* (3rd), Edward John Barrington Douglas-Scott-Montagu, *b.* 1926, *s.* 1929, *m.*	Hon. Ralph *D.-S.-M.*, *b.* 1961.
1839	*Monteagle of Brandon* (6th), Gerald Spring Rice, *b.* 1926, *s.* 1946, *m.*	Hon. Charles J. S. *R.*, *b.* 1953.
1943	*Moran* (2nd), (Richard) John (McMoran) Wilson, KCMG, *b.* 1924, *s.* 1977, *m.*	Hon. James M. *W.*, *b.* 1952.
1918	*Morris* (3rd), Michael David Morris, *b.* 1937, *s.* 1975, *m.*	Hon. Thomas A. S. *M.*, *b.* 1982.
1950	*Morris of Kenwood* (2nd), Philip Geoffrey Morris, *b.* 1928, *s.* 1954, *m.*	Hon. Jonathan D. *M.*, *b.* 1968.
1945	*Morrison* (2nd), Dennis Morrison, *b.* 1914, *s.* 1953.	(None.)
1831	*Mostyn* (5th), Roger Edward Lloyd Lloyd-Mostyn, MC, *b.* 1920, *s.* 1965, *m.*	Hon. Llewellyn R. L. *L.-M.*, *b.* 1948.
1933	*Mottistone* (4th), David Peter Seely, CBE, *b.* 1920, *s.* 1966, *m.*	Hon. Peter J. P. *S.*, *b.* 1949.
1945	*Mountevans* (3rd), Edward Patrick Broke Evans, *b.* 1943, *s.* 1974, *m.*	Hon. Jeffrey de C. R. *E.*, *b.* 1948.
1283	*Mowbray* (26th), *Segrave* (27th) (1283), *& Stourton* (23rd) (1448), Charles Edward Stourton, CBE, *b.* 1923, *s.* 1965, *m.*	Hon. Edward W. S. *S.*, *b.* 1953.
1932	*Moyne* (2nd), Bryan Walter Guinness, *b.* 1905, *s.* 1944, *m.*	Hon. Jonathan B. *G.*, *b.* 1930.
1929	*Moynihan* (3rd), Antony Patrick Andrew Cairnes Berkeley Moynihan, *b.* 1936, *s.* 1965, *m.*	Hon. Daniel A. P. B. *M.*, *b.* 1991.
1781 I.	*Muskerry* (9th), Robert Fitzmaurice Deane, *b.* 1948, *s.* 1988, *m.*	Hon. Jonathan F. *D.*, *b.* 1986.
1627 S.	*Napier* (14th) *& Ettrick* (5th) (*UK* 1872), Francis Nigel Napier, CVO, *b.* 1930, *s.* 1954, *m.*	Master of Napier, *b.* 1962.
1868	*Napier of Magdala* (6th), Robert Alan Napier, *b.* 1940, *s.* 1987, *m.*	Hon. James R. *N.*, *b.* 1966.
1940	*Nathan* (2nd), Roger Carol Michael Nathan, *b.* 1922, *s.* 1963, *m.*	Hon. Rupert H. B. *N.*, *b.* 1957.
1960	*Nelson of Stafford* (2nd), Henry George Nelson, *b.* 1917, *s.* 1962, *m.*	Hon. Henry R. G. *N.*, *b.* 1943.
1959	*Netherthorpe* (3rd), James Frederick Turner, *b.* 1964, *s.* 1982, *m.*	Hon. Patrick A. *T.*, *b.* 1971.
1946	*Newall* (2nd), Francis Storer Eaton Newall, *b.* 1930, *s.* 1963, *m.*	Hon. Richard H. E. *N.*, *b.* 1961.
1776 I.	*Newborough* (7th), Robert Charles Michael Vaughan Wynn, DSC, *b.* 1917, *s.* 1965, *m.*	Hon. Robert V. *W.*, *b.* 1949.
1892	*Newton* (4th), Peter Richard Legh, *b.* 1915, *s.* 1960, *m.*	Hon. Richard T. *L.*, *b.* 1950.
1930	*Noel-Buxton* (3rd), Martin Connal Noel-Buxton, *b.* 1940, *s.* 1980, *m.*	Hon. Charles C. *N.-B.*, *b.* 1975.
1957	*Norrie* (2nd), (George) Willoughby Moke Norrie, *b.* 1936, *s.* 1977, *m.*	Hon. Mark W. J. *N.*, *b.* 1972.
1884	*Northbourne* (5th), Christopher George Walter James, *b.* 1926, *s.* 1982, *m.*	Hon. Charles W. H. *J.*, *b.* 1960.
1866	*Northbrook* (6th), Francis Thomas Baring, *b.* 1954, *s.* 1990, *m.*	(None.)
1878	*Norton* (7th), John Arden Adderley, OBE, *b.* 1915, *s.* 1961, *m.*	Hon. James N. A. *A.*, *b.* 1947.
1906	*Nunburnholme* (4th), Ben Charles Wilson, *b.* 1928, *s.* 1974.	Hon. Charles T. *W.*, *b.* 1935.
1950	*Ogmore* (2nd), Gwilym Rees Rees-Williams, *b.* 1931, *s.* 1976, *m.*	Hon. Morgan R.-*W.*, *b.* 1937.
1870	*O'Hagan* (4th), Charles Towneley Strachey, MEP, *b.* 1945, *s.* 1961, *m.*	Hon. Richard T. *S.*, *b.* 1950.
1868	*O'Neill* (4th), Raymond Arthur Clanaboy O'Neill, TD, *b.* 1933, *s.* 1944, *m.*	Hon. Shane S. C. *O'N.*, *b.* 1965.
1836 I.*	*Oranmore and Browne* (4th), Dominick Geoffrey Edward Browne (2nd *UK Baron Mereworth*, 1926), *b.* 1901, *s.* 1927, *m.*	Hon. Dominick G. T. *B.*, *b.* 1929.
1933	*Palmer* (4th), Adrian Bailie Nottage Palmer, *b.* 1951, *s.* 1990, *m.*	Hon. Hugo B. R. *P.*, *b.* 1980.
1914	*Parmoor* (4th), (Frederick Alfred) Milo Cripps, *b.* 1929, *s.* 1977.	M. Anthony L. *C.*, CBE, DSO, TD, QC, *b.* 1913.
1937	*Pender* (3rd), John Willoughby Denison-Pender, *b.* 1933, *s.* 1965, *m.*	Hon. Henry J. R. *D.-P.*, *b.* 1968.
1866	*Penrhyn* (6th), Malcolm Frank Douglas-Pennant, DSO, MBE, *b.* 1908, *s.* 1967, *m.*	Hon. Nigel *D.-P.*, *b.* 1909.
1603	*Petre* (18th), John Patrick Lionel Petre, *b.* 1942, *s.* 1989, *m.*	Hon. Dominic W. *P.*, *b.* 1966.
1918	*Phillimore* (4th), Claud Stephen Phillimore, *b.* 1911, *s.* 1990, *m.*	Hon. Francis S. *P.*, *b.* 1944.
1945	*Piercy* (3rd), James William Piercy, *b.* 1946, *s.* 1981.	Hon. Mark E. P. *P.*, *b.* 1953.

Created	Title, Order of Succession, Name, etc.	Eldest Son or Heir
1827	*Plunket* (8th), Robin Rathmore Plunket, b. 1925, s. 1975, m.	Hon. Shaun A. F. S. P., b. 1931.
1831	*Poltimore* (7th), Mark Coplestone Bampfylde, b. 1957, s. 1978, m.	Hon. Henry A. W. B., b. 1985.
1690 s.	*Polwarth* (10th), Henry Alexander Hepburne-Scott, TD, b. 1916, s. 1944, m.	Master of Polwarth, b. 1947.
1930	*Ponsonby of Shulbrede* (4th), Frederick Matthew Thomas Ponsonby, b. 1958, s. 1990.	(None.)
1958	*Poole* (1st), Oliver Brian Sanderson Poole, CBE, TD, PC, b. 1911, m.	Hon. David C. P., b. 1945.
1852	*Raglan* (5th), FitzRoy John Somerset, b. 1927, s. 1964.	Hon. Geoffrey S., b. 1932.
1932	*Rankeillour* (4th), Peter St Thomas More Henry Hope, b. 1935, s. 1967.	Michael R. H., b. 1940.
1953	*Rathcavan* (2nd), Phelim Robert Hugh O'Neill, PC (NI), b. 1909, s. 1982, m.	Hon. Hugh D. T. O'N., b. 1939.
1916	*Rathcreedan* (3rd), Christopher John Norton, b. 1949, s. 1990, m.	Hon. Adam G. N., b. 1952.
1868 I.	*Rathdonnell* (5th), Thomas Benjamin McClintock–Bunbury, b. 1938, s. 1959, m.	Hon. William L. M.-B., b. 1966.
1911	*Ravensdale* (3rd), Nicholas Mosley, MC, b. 1923, s. 1966, m.	Hon. Shaun N. M., b. 1949.
1821	*Ravensworth* (8th), Arthur Waller Liddell, b. 1924, s. 1950, m.	Hon. Thomas A. H. L., b. 1954.
1821	*Rayleigh* (6th), John Gerald Strutt, b. 1960, s. 1988, m.	Hon. Hedley V. S., b. 1915.
1937	*Rea* (3rd), John Nicolas Rea, MD, b. 1928, s. 1981, m.	Hon. Matthew J. R., b. 1956.
1628 s.	*Reay* (14th), Hugh William Mackay, b. 1937, s. 1963, m.	Master of Reay, b. 1965.
1902	*Redesdale* (6th), Rupert Bertram Mitford, b. 1967, s. 1991.	(None.)
1940	*Reith*. Disclaimed for life 1972. (*Christopher John Reith*, b. 1928, s. 1971, m.	Hon. James H. J. R., b. 1971.
1928	*Remnant* (3rd), James Wogan Remnant, CVO, b. 1930, s. 1967, m.	Hon. Philip J. R., b. 1954.
1806 I.	*Rendlesham* (8th), Charles Anthony Hugh Thellusson, b. 1915, s. 1943, w.	Hon. Charles W. B. T., b. 1954.
1933	*Rennell* (3rd), (John Adrian) Tremayne Rodd, b. 1935, s. 1978, m.	Hon. James R. D. T. R., b. 1978.
1964	*Renwick* (2nd), Harry Andrew Renwick, b. 1935, s. 1973, m.	Hon. Robert J. R., b. 1966.
1885	*Revelstoke* (4th), Rupert Baring, b. 1911, s. 1934.	Hon. John B., b. 1934.
1905	*Ritchie of Dundee* (5th), (Harold) Malcolm Ritchie, b. 1919, s. 1978, m.	Hon. C. Rupert R. R., b. 1958.
1935	*Riverdale* (2nd), Robert Arthur Balfour, b. 1901, s. 1957, m.	Hon. Mark R. B., b. 1927.
1961	*Robertson of Oakridge* (2nd), William Ronald Robertson, b. 1930, s. 1974, m.	Hon. William B. E. R., b. 1975.
1938	*Roborough* (2nd), Massey Henry Edgcumbe Lopes, b. 1903, s. 1938, m.	Hon. Henry M. L., b. 1940.
1931	*Rochester* (2nd), Foster Charles Lowry Lamb, b. 1916, s. 1955, m.	Hon. David C. L., b. 1944.
1934	*Rockley* (3rd), James Hugh Cecil, b. 1934, s. 1976, m.	Hon. Anthony R. C., b. 1961.
1782	*Rodney* (9th), John Francis Rodney, b. 1920, s. 1973, m.	Hon. George B. R., b. 1953.
1651 s.*	*Rollo* (13th), Eric John Stapylton Rollo (4th *UK Baron, Dunning,* 1869), b. 1915, s. 1947, m.	Master of Rollo, b. 1943.
1959	*Rootes* (2nd), William Geoffrey Rootes, b. 1917, s. 1964, m.	Hon. Nicholas G. R., b. 1951.
1796 I. } 1838* }	*Rossmore* (7th), William Warner Westenra (6th *UK Baron, Rossmore*), b. 1931, s. 1958, m.	Hon. Benedict W. W., b. 1983.
1939	*Rotherwick* (2nd), (Herbert) Robin Cayzer, b. 1912, s. 1958, w.	Hon. H. Robin C., b. 1954.
1885	*Rothschild* (4th), (Nathaniel Charles) Jacob Rothschild, b. 1936, s. 1990, m.	Hon. Nathaniel P. V. J. R., b. 1971.
1911	*Rowallan* (3rd), Arthur Cameron Corbett, b. 1919, s. 1977.	Hon. John P. C. C., b. 1947.
1947	*Rugby* (3rd), Robert Charles Maffey, b. 1951, s. 1990, m.	Hon. Timothy J. H. M., b. 1975.
1919	*Russell of Liverpool* (3rd), Simon Gordon Jared Russell, b. 1952, s. 1981, m.	Hon. Edward C. S. R., b. 1985.
1876	*Sackville* (6th), Lionel Bertrand Sackville-West, b. 1913, s. 1965, m.	Hugh R. I. S.-W., b. 1919.
1964	*St Helens* (2nd), Richard Francis Hughes-Young, b. 1945, s. 1980, m.	Hon. Henry T. H.-Y., b. 1986.
1559	*St John of Bletso* (21st), Anthony Tudor St John, b. 1957, s. 1978.	Edmund O. St J., b. 1927.
1887	*St Levan* (4th), John Francis Arthur St Aubyn, DSC, b. 1919, s. 1978, m.	Hon. O. Piers St A., MC, b. 1920.
1885	*St Oswald* (5th), Derek Edward Anthony Winn, b. 1919, s. 1984, m.	Hon. Charles R. A. W., b. 1959.
1960	*Sanderson of Ayot*. Disclaimed for life 1971. (*Alan Lindsay Sanderson*, b. 1931, s. 1971, m.)	Hon. Michael S., b. 1959.
1945	*Sandford* (2nd), Rev. John Cyril Edmondson, DSC, b. 1920, s. 1959, m.	Hon. James J. M. E., b. 1949.
1871	*Sandhurst* (5th), (John Edward) Terence Mansfield, DFC, b. 1920, s. 1964, m.	Hon. Guy R. J. M., b. 1949.
1802	*Sandys* (7th), Richard Michael Oliver Hill, b. 1931, s. 1961, m.	Marcus T. H., b. 1931.
1888	*Savile* (3rd), George Halifax Lumley-Savile, b. 1919, s. 1931.	Hon. Henry L. T. L.-S., b. 1923.
1447	*Saye and Sele* (21st), Nathaniel Thomas Allen Fiennes, b. 1920, s. 1968, m.	Hon. Richard I. F., b. 1959.
1932	*Selsdon* (3rd), Malcolm McEacharn Mitchell-Thomson, b. 1937, s. 1963, m.	Hon. Callum M. M. M.-T., b. 1969.
1916	*Shaughnessy* (3rd), William Graham Shaughnessy, b. 1922, s. 1938, m.	Hon. Michael J. S., b. 1946.
1946	*Shepherd* (2nd), Malcolm Newton Shepherd, PC, b. 1918, s. 1954, m.	Hon. Graeme G. S., b. 1949.
1964	*Sherfield* (1st), Roger Mellor Makins, GCB, GCMG, FRS, b. 1904, w.	Hon. Christopher J. M., b. 1942.

Created	Title, Order of Succession, Name, etc.	Eldest Son or Heir
1902	*Shuttleworth* (5th), Charles Geoffrey Nicholas Kay-Shuttleworth, *b.* 1948, *s.* 1975, *m.*	Hon. Thomas E. *K.-S.*, *b.* 1976.
1950	*Silkin.* Disclaimed for life 1972. (*Arthur Silkin, b.* 1916, *s.* 1972, *m.*)	Hon. Christopher L. *S.*, *b.* 1947.
1963	*Silsoe* (2nd), David Malcolm Trustram Eve, QC, *b.* 1930, *s.* 1976, *m.*	Hon. Simon R. T. *E.*, *b.* 1966.
1947	*Simon of Wythenshawe* (2nd), Roger Simon, *b.* 1913, *s.* 1960, *m.*	Hon. Matthew *S.*, *b.* 1955.
1449 s.	*Sinclair* (17th), Charles Murray Kennedy St Clair, CVO, *b.* 1914, *s.* 1957, *m.*	Master of Sinclair, *b.* 1968.
1957	*Sinclair of Cleeve* (3rd), John Lawrence Robert Sinclair, *b.* 1953, *s.* 1985.	(None.)
1919	*Sinha* (3rd), Sudhindro Prosanno Sinha, *b.* 1920, *s.* 1967, *m.*	Hon. Susanta P. *S.*, *b.* 1953.
1828	*Skelmersdale* (7th), Roger Bootle-Wilbraham, *b.* 1945, *s.* 1973, *m.*	Hon. Andrew *B.-W.*, *b.* 1977.
1916	*Somerleyton* (3rd), Savile William Francis Crossley, *b.* 1928, *s.* 1959, *m.*	Hon. Hugh F. S. *C.*, *b.* 1971.
1784	*Somers* (8th), John Patrick Somers Cocks, *b.* 1907, *s.* 1953, *m.*	Philip S. S. *C.*, *b.* 1948.
1780	*Southampton* (6th), Charles James FitzRoy, *b.* 1928, *s.* 1989, *m.*	Hon. Edward C. *F.*, *b.* 1955.
1917	*Southborough* (4th), Francis Michael Hopwood, *b.* 1922, *s.* 1982, *w.*	(None.)
1959	*Spens* (3rd), Patrick Michael Rex Spens, *b.* 1942, *s.* 1984, *m.*	Hon. Patrick N. G. *S.*, *b.* 1968.
1640	*Stafford* (15th), Francis Melfort William Fitzherbert, *b.* 1954, *s.* 1986, *m.*	Hon. Benjamin J. B. *F.*, *b.* 1983.
1938	*Stamp* (4th), Trevor Charles Bosworth Stamp, MD, FRCP, *b.* 1935, *s.* 1987, *m.*	Hon. Nicholas C. T. *S.*, *b.* 1978.
1839	*Stanley of Alderley* (8th) & *Sheffield* (8th) (1738 I.), Thomas Henry Oliver Stanley (7th *UK Baron Eddisbury*, 1848), *b.* 1927, *s.* 1971, *m.*	Hon. Richard O. *S.*, *b.* 1956.
1318	*Strabolgi* (11th), David Montague de Burgh Kenworthy, *b.* 1914, *s.* 1953, *m.*	Andrew D. W. *K.*, *b.* 1967.
1954	*Strang* (2nd), Colin Strang, *b.* 1922, *s.* 1978, *m.*	(None.)
1955	*Strathalmond* (3rd), William Roberton Fraser, *b.* 1947, *s.* 1976, *m.*	Hon. William G. *F.*, *b.* 1976.
1936	*Strathcarron* (2nd), David William Anthony Blyth Macpherson, *b.* 1924, *s.* 1937, *m.*	Hon. Ian D. P. *M.*, *b.* 1949.
1955	*Strathclyde* (2nd), Thomas Galloway Dunlop du Roy de Blicquy Galbraith, *b.* 1960, *s.* 1985.	Hon. Charles W. du R. de B. *G.*, *b.* 1962.
1900	*Strathcona and Mount Royal* (4th), Donald Euan Palmer Howard, *b.* 1923, *s.* 1959, *m.*	Hon. Donald A. S. *H.*, *b.* 1961.
1836	*Stratheden & Campbell* (1841) (6th), Donald Campbell, *b.* 1934, *s.* 1987, *m.*	Hon. David A. *C.*, *b.* 1963.
1884	*Strathspey* (5th), Donald Patrick Trevor Grant of Grant, *b.* 1912, *s.* 1948, *m.*	Hon. James P. *G.*, *b.* 1943.
1838	*Sudeley* (7th), Merlin Charles Sainthill Hanbury-Tracy, *b.* 1939, *s.* 1941.	D. Andrew J. *H-T.*, *b.* 1928.
1786	*Suffield* (11th), Anthony Philip Harbord-Hamond, MC, *b.* 1922, *s.* 1951, *m.*	Hon. Charles A. A. *H.-H.*, *b.* 1953.
1893	*Swansea* (4th), John Hussey Hamilton Vivian, *b.* 1925, *s.* 1934, *m.*	Hon. Richard A. H. *V.*, *b.* 1957.
1907	*Swaythling* (4th), David Charles Samuel Montagu, *b.* 1928, *s.* 1990, *m.*	Hon. Charles E. S. *M.*, *b.* 1954.
1919	*Swinfen* (3rd), Roger Mynors Swinfen Eady, *b.* 1938, *s.* 1977, *m.*	Hon. Charles R. P. S. *E.*, *b.* 1971.
1935	*Sysonby* (3rd), John Frederick Ponsonby, *b.* 1945, *s.* 1956.	(None.)
1831 I.	*Talbot of Malahide* (10th), Reginald John Richard Arundell, *b.* 1931, *s.* 1987, *w.*	Hon. Richard J. T. *A.*, *b.* 1957.
1946	*Tedder* (2nd), John Michael Tedder, SC.D., PH.D., D.SC., *b.* 1926, *s.* 1967, *m.*	Hon. Robin J. *T.*, *b.* 1955.
1884	*Tennyson* (4th), Harold Christopher Tennyson, *b.* 1919, *s.* 1951.	Hon. Mark A. *T.*, DSC, *b.* 1920.
1918	*Terrington* (4th), (James Allen) David Woodhouse, *b.* 1915, *s.* 1961, *m.*	Hon. C. Montague *W.*, DSO, OBE, *b.* 1917.
1940	*Teviot* (2nd), Charles John Kerr, *b.* 1934, *s.* 1968, *m.*	Hon. Charles R. *K.*, *b.* 1971.
1616	*Teynham* (20th), John Christopher Ingham Roper-Curzon, *b.* 1928, *s.* 1972, *m.*	Hon. David J. H. I. *R.-C.*, *b.* 1965.
1964	*Thomson of Fleet* (2nd), Kenneth Roy Thomson, *b.* 1923, *s.* 1976, *m.*	Hon. David K. R. *T.*, *b.* 1957.
1792	*Thurlow* (8th), Francis Edward Hovell-Thurlow-Cumming-Bruce, KCMG, *b.* 1912, *s.* 1971, *w.*	Hon. Roualeyn R. *H.-T.-C.-B.*, *b.* 1952.
1876	*Tollemache* (5th), Timothy John Edward Tollemache, *b.* 1939, *s.* 1975, *m.*	Hon. Edward J. H. *T.*, *b.* 1976.
1564 s.	*Torphichen* (15th), James Andrew Douglas Sandilands, *b.* 1946, *s.* 1975, *m.*	Douglas R. A. *S.*, *b.* 1926.
1947	*Trefgarne* (2nd), David Garro Trefgarne, PC, *b.* 1941, *s.* 1960, *m.*	Hon. George G. *T.*, *b.* 1970.
1921	*Trevethin* (4th), *and Oaksey* (2nd), John Geoffrey Tristram Lawrence, OBE (2nd *UK Baron, Oaksey*, 1947), *b.* 1929, *s.* 1971, *m.*	Hon. Patrick J. T. *L.*, *b.* 1960.
1880	*Trevor* (4th), Charles Edwin Hill-Trevor, *b.* 1928, *s.* 1950, *m.*	Hon. Marke C. *H.-T.*, *b.* 1970.
1461 I.	*Trimlestown* (20th), Anthony Edward Barnewall, *b.* 1928, *s.* 1990, *m.*	Hon. Raymond C. *B.*, *b.* 1930.
1940	*Tryon* (3rd), Anthony George Merrik Tryon, *b.* 1940, *s.* 1976, *m.*	Hon. Charles G. B. *T.*, *b.* 1976.
1935	*Tweedsmuir* (2nd), John Norman Stuart Buchan, CBE, CD, *b.* 1911, *s.* 1940, *m.*	Hon. William *B.*, *b.* 1916.
1523	*Vaux of Harrowden* (10th), John Hugh Philip Gilbey, *b.* 1915, *s.* 1977, *m.*	Hon. Anthony W. *G.*, *b.* 1940.

Created	Title, Order of Succession, Name, etc.	Eldest Son or Heir
1800 I.	*Ventry* (8th), Andrew Wesley Daubeny de Moleyns, *b.* 1943, *s.* 1987, *m.*	Hon. Francis W. *D. de M.*, *b.* 1965.
1762	*Vernon* (10th), John Lawrance Vernon, *b.* 1923, *s.* 1963, *m.*	Col. William R. D. *Vernon-Harcourt*, OBE, *b.* 1909.
1922	*Vestey* (3rd), Samuel George Armstrong Vestey, *b.* 1941, *s.* 1954, *m.*	Hon. William G. *V.*, *b.* 1983.
1841	*Vivian* (6th), Nicholas Crespigny Laurence Vivian, *b.* 1935, *s.* 1991, *m.*	Hon. Charles H. C. *V.*, *b.* 1966.
1934	*Wakehurst* (3rd), (John) Christopher Loder, *b.* 1925, *s.* 1970, *m.*	Hon. Timothy W. *L.*, *b.* 1958.
1723	*Walpole* (10th), Robert Horatio Walpole, *b.* 1938, *s.* 1989, *m.* (*8th Brit. Baron Walpole of Wolterton*, 1756).	Hon. Jonathan R. H. *W.*, *b.* 1967.
1780	*Walsingham* (9th), John de Grey, MC, *b.* 1925, *s.* 1965, *m.*	Hon. Robert *de G.*, *b.* 1969.
1936	*Wardington* (2nd), Christopher Henry Beaumont Pease, *b.* 1924, *s.* 1950, *m.*	Hon. William S. *P.*, *b.* 1925.
1792 I.	*Waterpark* (7th), Frederick Caryll Philip Cavendish, *b.* 1926, *s.* 1948, *m.*	Hon. Roderick A. *C.*, *b.* 1959.
1942	*Wedgwood* (4th), Piers Anthony Weymouth Wedgwood, *b.* 1954, *s.* 1970, *m.*	John *W.*, CBE, MD, *b.* 1919.
1861	*Westbury* (5th), David Alan Bethell, MC, *b.* 1922, *s.* 1961, *m.*	Hon. Richard N. *B.*, MBE, *b.* 1950.
1944	*Westwood* (2nd), William Westwood, *b.* 1907, *s.* 1953, *m.*	Hon. William G. *W.*, *b.* 1944.
1935	*Wigram* (2nd), (George) Neville (Clive) Wigram, MC, *b.* 1915, *s.* 1960, *w.*	Maj. Hon. Andrew F. C. *W.*, MVO, *b.* 1949.
1491	*Willoughby de Broke* (21st), Leopold David Verney, *b.* 1938, *s.* 1986, *m.*	Hon. Rupert G. *V.*, *b.* 1966.
1946	*Wilson* (2nd), Patrick Maitland Wilson, *b.* 1915, *s.* 1964, *w.*	(None.)
1937	*Windlesham* (3rd), David James George Hennessy, CVO, PC, *b.* 1932, *s.* 1962, *w.*	Hon. James R. *H.*, *b.* 1968.
1951	*Wise* (2nd), John Clayton Wise, *b.* 1923, *s.* 1968, *m.*	Hon. Christopher J. C. *W.*, Ph.D., *b.* 1949.
1869	*Wolverton* (7th), Christopher Richard Glyn, *b.* 1938, *s.* 1988, *m.*	Hon. Andrew J. *G.*, *b.* 1943.
1928	*Wraxall* (2nd), George Richard Lawley Gibbs, *b.* 1928, *s.* 1931.	Hon. Sir Eustace H. B. *G.*, KCVO, CMG, *b.* 1929.
1915	*Wrenbury* (3rd), John Burton Buckley, *b.* 1927, *s.* 1940, *m.*	Hon. William E. *B.*, *b.* 1966.
1838	*Wrottesley* (6th), Clifton Hugh Lancelot de Verdon Wrottesley, *b.* 1968, *s.* 1977.	Hon. Stephen J. *W.*, *b.* 1955.
1919	*Wyfold* (3rd), Hermon Robert Fleming Hermon-Hodge, *b.* 1915, *s.* 1942.	(None.)
1829	*Wynford* (8th), Robert Samuel Best, MBE, *b.* 1917, *s.* 1943, *m.*	Hon. John P. *B.*, *b.* 1950.
1308	*Zouche* (18th), James Assheton Frankland, *b.* 1943, *s.* 1965, *m.*	Hon. William T. A. *F.*, *b.* 1984.

WOMEN PEERS IN THEIR OWN RIGHT

Peerages falling under this heading are the result of regular inheritance in lines which are open to females in default of males. A woman peer in her own right retains her title after marriage, and if her husband's rank is the superior she is designated by the two titles jointly, the inferior one last; her hereditary claim still holds good in spite of any marriage whether higher or lower. No rank held by a woman can confer any title or even precedence upon her husband but the rank of a woman peer in her own right is inherited by her eldest son (or perhaps daughter), to whomsoever she may have been married.

Where marked ° the 'of' is not used.

COUNTESSES IN THEIR OWN RIGHT

Style.—The Right Hon. the Countess (of) ——.
Husband.—Untitled.
Children's style.—As for children of an Earl.
For forms of address, *see* page 219.

Created	Title, Name, etc.	Eldest Son or Heir
1643 S.	*Dysart* (11th in line), Rosamund Agnes Greaves, *b.* 1914, *s.* 1975.	Lady Katherine *Grant of Rothiemurchus*, *b.* 1918.
1633 S.	*Loudoun* (13th in line), Barbara Huddleston Abney-Hastings, *b.* 1919, *s.* 1960, *m.*	Lord Mauchline, *b.* 1942.
c.1115 S.	*Mar* (31st in line), Margaret of Mar (*Premier Earldom of Scotland*), *b.* 1940, *s.* 1975, *m.*	Mistress of Mar, *b.* 1963.
1947	°*Mountbatten of Burma* (2nd in line), Patricia Edwina Victoria Knatchbull, CBE, *b.* 1924, *s.* 1979, *m.*	Lord Romsey, *b.* 1947 (*see also* p. 161).
c.1235 S.	*Sutherland* (24th in line), Elizabeth Millicent Sutherland, *b.* 1921, *s.* 1963, *m.*	Lord Strathnaver, *b.* 1947.

BARONESSES IN THEIR OWN RIGHT

Style.—The Right Hon. the Lady ——, *or* The Right Hon. the Baroness ——,
according to her preference.
Husband.—Untitled.
Children's style.—As for children of a Baron.
For forms of address, *see* page 219.

Created	Title, Name, etc.	Eldest Son or Heir
1421	*Berkeley* (17th in line), Mary Lalle Foley Berkeley, *b.* 1905, *title called out of abeyance,* 1967.	Hon. Cynthia E. *Gueterbock, b.* 1909.
1455	*Berners* (15th in line), Vera Ruby Williams, *b.* 1901, *s.* 1950, *m.*	Two co-heiresses.
1529	*Braye* (8th in line), Mary Penelope Aubrey–Fletcher, *b.* 1941, *s.* 1985, *m.*	Two co-heiresses.
1321	*Dacre* (27th in line), Rachel Leila Douglas-Home, *b.* 1929, *title called out of abeyance,* 1970, *m.*	Hon. James T. A. *D.-H., b.* 1952.
1332	*Darcy de Knayth* (18th in line), Davina Marcia Ingrams, *b.* 1938, *s.* 1943, *w.*	Hon. Caspar D. *I., b.* 1962.
1439	*Dudley* (14th in line), Barbara Amy Felicity Hamilton, *b.* 1907, *s.* 1972, *m.*	Hon. Jim A. H. *Wallace, b.* 1930.
1490 s.	*Herries of Terregles* (14th in line), Anne Elizabeth Fitzalan-Howard, *b.* 1938, *s.* 1975, *m.*	Lady Mary *Mumford,* CVO, *b.* 1940.
1602 s.	*Kinloss* (12th in line), Beatrice Mary Grenville Freeman-Grenville, *b.* 1922, *s.* 1944, *m.*	Master of Kinloss, *b.* 1953.
1663	*Lucas of Crudwell* (10th in line) **&** *Dingwall* (7th in line) (Scottish Lordship 1609), Anne Rosemary Palmer, *b.* 1919, *s.* 1958, *m.*	Hon. Ralph M. *P., b.* 1951.
1681 s.	*Nairne* (12th in line), Katherine Evelyn Constance Bigham (*Katherine, Viscountess Mersey*), *b.* 1912, *s.* 1944, *w.*	Viscount Mersey, *b.* 1934 (*see* p. 158).
1445 s.	*Saltoun* (20th in line), Flora Marjory Fraser, *b.* 1930, *s.* 1979, *m.*	Hon. Katharine I. M. I. *F., b.* 1957.
1489 s.	*Sempill* (20th in line), Ann Moira Sempill, *b.* 1920, *s.* 1965, *w.*	Master of Sempill, *b.* 1949.
1628	*Strange* (16th in line), (Jean) Cherry Drummond of Megginch, *b.* 1928, *title called out of abeyance,* 1986, *m.*	Hon. Adam H. *D. of M., b.* 1953.
1544–5	*Wharton* (11th in line), Myrtle Olive Felix Robertson, *b.* 1934, *title called out of abeyance,* 1990, *m.*	Hon. Myles C. D. *R., b.* 1964.
1313	*Willoughby de Eresby* (27th in line), (Nancy) Jane Marie Heathcote-Drummond-Willoughby, *b.* 1934, *s.* 1983.	Two co-heiresses.

LIFE PEERS

Created under the Appellate Jurisdiction Act, 1876 (as amended)

BARONS

Created		
1986	*Ackner,* Desmond James Conrad Ackner, PC, *b.* 1920, *m.*	Lord of Appeal in Ordinary.
1981	*Brandon of Oakbrook,* Henry Vivian Brandon, MC, PC, *b.* 1920, *m.*	Lord of Appeal in Ordinary.
1980	*Bridge of Harwich,* Nigel Cyprian Bridge, PC, *b.* 1917, *m.*	Lord of Appeal in Ordinary.
1982	*Brightman,* John Anson Brightman, PC, *b.* 1911, *m.*	Lord of Appeal (retired).
1957	*Denning,* Alfred Thompson Denning, PC, *b.* 1899, *m.*	Lord of Appeal (retired).
1961	*Devlin,* Patrick Arthur Devlin, PC, FBA, *b.* 1905, *m.*	Lord of Appeal (retired).
1974	*Edmund-Davies,* (Herbert) Edmund Edmund-Davies, PC, *b.* 1906, *m.*	Lord of Appeal (retired).
1986	*Goff of Chieveley,* Robert Lionel Archibald Goff, PC, *b.* 1926, *m.*	Lord of Appeal in Ordinary.
1985	*Griffiths,* (William) Hugh Griffiths, MC, PC, *b.* 1923, *m.*	Lord of Appeal in Ordinary.
1987	*Jauncey of Tullichettle,* Charles Eliot Jauncey, PC, *b.* 1925, *m.*	Lord of Appeal in Ordinary.
1977	*Keith of Kinkel,* Henry Shanks Keith, PC, *b.* 1922, *m.*	Lord of Appeal in Ordinary.
1979	*Lane,* Geoffrey Dawson Lane, AFC, PC, *b.* 1918, *m.*	Lord of Appeal (Lord Chief Justice).
1986	*Oliver of Aylmerton,* Peter Raymond Oliver, PC, *b.* 1921, *m.*	Lord of Appeal in Ordinary.
1980	*Roskill,* Eustace Wentworth Roskill, PC, *b.* 1911, *m.*	Lord of Appeal (retired).
1972	*Salmon,* Cyril Barnet Salmon, PC, *b.* 1903, *w.*	Lord of Appeal (retired).
1977	*Scarman,* Leslie George Scarman, OBE, PC, *b.* 1911, *m.*	Lord of Appeal (retired).
1982	*Templeman,* Sydney William Templeman, MBE, PC, *b.* 1920, *w.*	Lord of Appeal in Ordinary.
1964	*Wilberforce,* Richard Orme Wilberforce, CMG, OBE, PC, *b.* 1907, *m.*	Lord of Appeal (retired).

Created under Life Peerages Act, 1958

Between September 1, 1990 and August 31, 1991, the conferment of 25 life peerages was announced:

RESIGNATION HONOURS (Dec. 20, 1990): Prof. Brian Griffiths; Sir Hector Laing; Peter Palumo; Dame Joan Seccombe, DBE; Sir Jeffrey Sterling, CBE; Sir Gordon White, KBE; Sir David Wolfson.

NEW YEARS HONOURS (Dec. 31, 1990): Phyllis James, OBE.

'WORKING PEERS' (April 29): Jean Denton, CBE; Prof. Meghnad Desai; Sally Hamwee; Jennifer Hilton, QPM; Clive Hollick; Frank Judd; John Mackay; Ann Mallalieu, QC; Detta O'Cathain, OBE; Prof. Colin Renfrew; Mark Schreiber.

THE QUEEN'S BIRTHDAY HONOURS (June 15): Gp Capt Leonard Cheshire, VC, OM; Sir Norman Macfarlane; Pauline Perry; Prof. Robert Skidelsky.

GULF HONOURS (June 29): Marshal of the RAF Sir David Craig, GCB, OBE.

and upon the Rt. Hon. David Waddington (Nov. 1990).

BARONS

Created

1974   *Alexander of Potterhill*, William Picken Alexander, PH.D., *b.* 1905, *m.*
1988   *Alexander of Weedon*, Robert Scott Alexander, QC, *b.* 1936, *m.*
1976   *Allen of Abbeydale*, Philip Allen, GCB, *b.* 1912, *m.*
1961   *Alport*, Cuthbert James McCall Alport, TD, PC, *b.* 1912, *w.*
1965   *Annan*, Noel Gilroy Annan, OBE, *b.* 1916, *m.*
1970   *Ardwick*, John Cowburn Beavan, *b.* 1910, *m.*
1988   *Armstrong of Ilminster*, Robert Temple Armstrong, GCB, CVO, *b.* 1927, *m.*
1973   *Ashby*, Eric Ashby, D.SC., FRS, *b.* 1904, *m.*
1967   *Aylestone*, Herbert William Bowden, CH, CBE, PC, *b.* 1905, *m.*
1982   *Bancroft*, Ian Powell Bancroft, GCB, *b.* 1922, *m.*
1974   *Banks*, Desmond Anderson Harvie Banks, CBE, *b.* 1918, *m.*
1974   *Barber*, Anthony Perrinott Lysberg Barber, TD, PC, *b.* 1920, *m.*
1983   *Barnett*, Joel Barnett, PC, *b.* 1923, *m.*
1982   *Bauer*, Prof. Peter Thomas Bauer, D.SC., *b.* 1915.
1967   *Beaumont of Whitley*, Rev. Timothy Wentworth Beaumont, *b.* 1928, *m.*
1979   *Bellwin*, Irwin Norman Bellow, *b.* 1923, *m.*
1981   *Beloff*, Max Beloff, *b.* 1913, *m.*
1981   *Benson*, Henry Alexander Benson, GBE, *b.* 1909, *m.*
1969   *Bernstein*, Sidney Lewis Bernstein, *b.* 1899, *m.*
1971   *Blake*, Robert Norman William Blake, FBA, *b.* 1916, *m.*
1983   *Blanch*, Rt. Rev. Stuart Yarworth Blanch, PC, *b.* 1918, *m.*
1978   *Blease*, William John Blease, *b.* 1914, *m.*
1980   *Boardman*, Thomas Gray Boardman, MC, TD, *b.* 1919, *m.*
1986   *Bonham-Carter*, Mark Raymond Bonham Carter, *b.* 1922, *m.*
1976   *Boston of Faversham*, Terence George Boston, QC, *b.* 1930, *m.*
1984   *Bottomley*, Arthur George Bottomley, OBE, PC, *b.* 1907, *m.*
1972   *Boyd-Carpenter*, John Archibald Boyd-Carpenter, PC, *b.* 1908, *m.*
1987   *Bramall*, Edwin Noel Westby Bramall, KG, GCB, OBE, MC, *Field Marshal*, *b.* 1923, *m.*
1976   *Briggs*, Asa Briggs, *b.* 1921, *m.*
1974   *Briginshaw*, Richard William Briginshaw, *b.* 1910, *m.*
1976   *Brimelow*, Thomas Brimelow, GCMG, OBE, *b.* 1915, *m.*
1975   *Brookes*, Raymond Percival Brookes, *b.* 1909, *m.*
1979   *Brooks of Tremorfa*, John Edward Brooks, *b.* 1927, *m.*
1983   *Broxbourne*, Derek Colclough Walker-Smith, TD, QC, PC, *b.* 1910, *m.*
1974   *Bruce of Donington*, Donald William Trevor Bruce, *b.* 1912, *m.*
1976   *Bullock*, Alan Louis Charles Bullock, FBA, *b.* 1914, *m.*
1988   *Butterfield*, (William) John (Hughes) Butterfield, OBE, DM, *b.* 1920, *m.*
1985   *Butterworth*, John Blackstock Butterworth, CBE, *b.* 1918, *m.*
1978   *Buxton of Alsa*, Aubrey Leland Oakes Buxton, MC, *b.* 1918, *m.*
1987   *Callaghan of Cardiff*, (Leonard) James Callaghan, KG, PC, *b.* 1912, *m.*
1984   *Cameron of Lochbroom*, Kenneth John Cameron, PC, *b.* 1931, *m.*
1981   *Campbell of Alloway*, Alan Robertson Campbell, QC, *b.* 1917, *m.*
1974   *Campbell of Croy*, Gordon Thomas Calthrop Campbell, MC, PC, *b.* 1921, *m.*
1966   *Campbell of Eskan*, John (Jock) Middleton Campbell, *b.* 1912, *w.*
1987   *Carlisle of Bucklow*, Mark Carlisle, QC, PC, *b.* 1929, *m.*
1983   *Carmichael of Kelvingrove*, Neil George Carmichael, *b.* 1921.
1975   *Carr of Hadley*, (Leonard) Robert Carr, PC, *b.* 1916, *m.*
1987   *Carter*, Denis Victor Carter, *b.* 1932, *m.*
1977   *Carver*, (Richard) Michael (Power) Carver, GCB, CBE, DSO, MC, *Field Marshal*, *b.* 1915, *m.*
1990   *Cavendish of Furness*, (Richard) Hugh Cavendish, *b.* 1941, *m.*
1982   *Cayzer*, (William) Nicholas Cayzer, *b.* 1910, *m.*
1964   *Chalfont*, (Alun) Arthur Gwynne Jones, OBE, MC, PC, *b.* 1919, *m.*
1985   *Chapple*, Frank Joseph Chapple, *b.* 1921, *m.*
1978   *Charteris of Amisfield*, Martin Michael Charles Charteris, GCB, GCVO, OBE, PC, *b.* 1913, *m.*
1963   *Chelmer*, Eric Cyril Boyd Edwards, MC, TD, *b.* 1914, *m.*
1991   *Cheshire*, (Geoffrey) Leonard Cheshire, VC, OM, DSO, DFC, *b.* 1917, *m.*
1987   *Chilver*, (Amos) Henry Chilver, FRS, *b.* 1926, *m.*
1977   *Chitnis*, Pratap Chidamber Chitnis, *b.* 1936, *m.*
1979   *Cledwyn of Penrhos*, Cledwyn Hughes, CH, PC, *b.* 1916, *m.*
1990   *Clinton-Davis*, Stanley Clinton Davis, *b.* 1928, *m.*
1978   *Cockfield*, (Francis) Arthur Cockfield, PC, *b.* 1916, *m.*
1987   *Cocks of Hartcliffe*, Michael Francis Lovell Cocks, PC, *b.* 1929, *m.*
1980   *Coggan*, Rt. Rev. (Frederick) Donald Coggan, PC, Royal Victorian Chain, *b.* 1909, *m.*
1964   *Collison*, Harold Francis Collison, CBE, *b.* 1909, *m.*
1987   *Colnbrook*, Humphrey Edward Gregory Atkins, KCMG, PC, *b.* 1922, *m.*
1981   *Constantine of Stanmore*, Theodore Constantine, CBE, AE, *b.* 1910, *w.*
1991   *Craig of Radley*, David Brownrigg Craig, GCB, OBE, *Marshal of the Royal Air Force*, *b.* 1929, *m.*
1959   *Craigton*, Jack Nixon Browne, CBE, PC, *b.* 1904, *m.*

Created

1987 *Crickhowell*, (Roger) Nicholas Edwards, PC, b. 1934, m.
1978 *Croham*, Douglas Albert Vivian Allen, GCB, b. 1917, m.
1974 *Cudlipp*, Hugh Cudlipp, OBE, b. 1913, m.
1979 *Dacre of Glanton*, Hugh Redwald Trevor-Roper, b. 1914, m.
1986 *Dainton*, Frederick Sydney Dainton, PH.D., SC.D., FRS, b. 1914, m.
1974 *Davies of Penrhys*, Gwilym Elfed Davies, b. 1913, m.
1983 *Dean of Beswick*, Joseph Jabez Dean, b. 1922.
1986 *Deedes*, William Francis Deedes, MC, PC, b. 1913, m.
1976 *Delfont*, Bernard Delfont, b. 1909, m.
1991 *Desai*, Prof. Meghnad Jagdishchandra Desai, PH.D., b. 1940, m.
1970 *Diamond*, John Diamond, PC, b. 1907, m.
1967 *Donaldson of Kingsbridge*, John George Stuart Donaldson, OBE, b. 1907, m.
1988 *Donaldson of Lymington*, John Francis Donaldson, PC, b. 1920, m. (*Master of the Rolls*).
1985 *Donoughue*, Bernard Donoughue, D.Phil., b. 1934.
1987 *Dormand of Easington*, John Donkin Dormand, b. 1919, m.
1983 *Eden of Winton*, John Benedict Eden, PC, b. 1925, m.
1985 *Elliott of Morpeth*, Robert William Elliott, b. 1920, m.
1972 *Elworthy*, (Samuel) Charles Elworthy, KG, GCB, CBE, DSO, LVO, DFC, AFC, *Marshal of the Royal Air Force*, b. 1911, w.
1981 *Elystan-Morgan*, Dafydd Elystan Elystan-Morgan, b. 1932, m.
1980 *Emslie*, George Carlyle Emslie, MBE, PC, b. 1919, m.
1983 *Ennals*, David Hedley Ennals, PC, b. 1922, m.
1978 *Evans of Claughton*, (David Thomas) Gruffydd Evans, b. 1928, m.
1983 *Ezra*, Derek Ezra, MBE, b. 1919, m.
1983 *Fanshawe of Richmond*, Anthony Henry Fanshawe Royle, KCMG, b. 1927, m.
1958 *Ferrier*, Victor Ferrier Noel-Paton, ED, b. 1900, w.
1990 *Fieldhouse*, John David Elliott Fieldhouse, GCB, GBE, *Admiral of the Fleet*, b. 1928, m.
1983 *Fitt*, Gerard Fitt, b. 1926, m.
1979 *Flowers*, Brian Hilton Flowers, FRS, b. 1924, m.
1967 *Foot*, John Mackintosh Foot, b. 1909, m.
1982 *Forte*, Charles Forte, b. 1908, m.
1962 *Franks*, Oliver Shewell Franks, OM, GCMG, KCB, KCVO, CBE, PC, FBA, b. 1905, w.
1989 *Fraser of Carmyllie*, Peter Lovat Fraser, QC, PC, b. 1945, m.
1974 *Fraser of Kilmorack*, (Richard) Michael Fraser, CBE, b. 1915, m.
1982 *Galpern*, Myer Galpern, b. 1903.
1979 *Gallacher*, John Gallacher, b. 1920, m.
1975 *Gibson*, (Richard) Patrick (Tallentyre) Gibson, b. 1916, m.
1979 *Gibson-Watt*, (James) David Gibson-Watt, MC, PC, b. 1918, m.
1977 *Glenamara*, Edward Watson Short, CH, PC, b. 1912, m.
1965 *Goodman*, Arnold Abraham Goodman, CH, b. 1913.
1987 *Goold*, James Duncan Goold, b. 1934, m.
1982 *Gormley*, Joseph Gormley, OBE, b. 1917, m.
1976 *Grade*, Lew Grade, b. 1906, m.
1983 *Graham of Edmonton*, (Thomas) Edward Graham, b. 1925, m.
1967 *Granville of Eye*, Edgar Louis Granville, b. 1899, m.
1983 *Gray of Contin*, James (Hamish) Hector Northey Gray, PC, b. 1927, m.
1974 *Greene of Harrow Weald*, Sidney Francis Greene, CBE, b. 1910, m.
1974 *Greenhill of Harrow*, Denis Arthur Greenhill, GCMG, OBE, b. 1913, m.
1975 *Gregson*, John Gregson, b. 1924.
1968 *Grey of Naunton*, Ralph Francis Alnwick Grey, GCMG, GCVO, OBE, b. 1910, m.
1991 *Griffiths of Fforestfach*, Brian Griffiths, b. 1941, m.
1983 *Grimond*, Joseph Grimond, TD, PC, b. 1913, m.
1970 *Hailsham of St Marylebone*, Quintin McGarel Hogg, KG, CH, PC, b. 1907, m.
1983 *Hanson*, James Edward Hanson, b. 1922, m.
1974 *Harmar-Nicholls*, Harmar Harmar-Nicholls, b. 1912, m.
1974 *Harris of Greenwich*, John Henry Harris, b. 1930, m.
1979 *Harris of High Cross*, Ralph Harris, b. 1924, m.
1968 *Hartwell*, (William) Michael Berry, MBE, TD, b. 1911, w.
1971 *Harvey of Prestbury*, Arthur Vere Harvey, CBE, b. 1906, m.
1974 *Harvington*, Robert Grant Grant-Ferris, AE, PC, b. 1907, m.
1990 *Haslam*, Robert Haslam, b. 1923, m.
1978 *Hatch of Lusby*, John Charles Hatch, b. 1917.
1987 *Havers*, (Robert) Michael (Oldfield) Havers, PC, b. 1923, m.
1984 *Henderson of Brompton*, Peter Gordon Henderson, KCB, b. 1922, m.
1979 *Hill-Norton*, Peter John Hill-Norton, GCB, *Admiral of the Fleet*, b. 1915, m.
1967 *Hirshfield*, Desmond Barel Hirshfield, b. 1913, m.
1979 *Holderness*, Richard Frederick Wood, PC, b. 1920, m.
1991 *Hollick*, Clive Richard Hollick, b. 1945, m.
1990 *Holme of Cheltenham*, Richard Gordon Holme, CBE, b. 1936, m.
1974 *Home of the Hirsel*, Alexander Frederick Douglas-Home, KT, PC, b. 1903, w.
1979 *Hooson*, (Hugh) Emlyn Hooson, QC, b. 1925, m.
1974 *Houghton of Sowerby*, (Arthur Leslie Noel) Douglas Houghton, CH, PC, b. 1898, m.
1978 *Howie of Troon*, William Howie, b. 1924, m.
1961 *Hughes*, William Hughes, CBE, PC, b. 1911, m.
1966 *Hunt*, (Henry Cecil) John Hunt, KG, CBE, DSO, b. 1910, m.
1980 *Hunt of Tanworth*, John Joseph Benedict Hunt, GCB, b. 1919, m.

Created

1978 *Hunter of Newington*, Robert Brockie Hunter, MBE, FRCP, b. 1915, m.
1978 *Hutchinson of Lullington*, Jeremy Nicolas Hutchinson, QC, b. 1915, m.
1982 *Ingrow*, John Aked Taylor, OBE, TD, b. 1917, m.
1987 *Irvine of Lairg*, Alexander Andrew Mackay Irvine, QC, b. 1940, m.
1968 *Jacques*, John Henry Jacques, b. 1905, m.
1988 *Jakobovits*, Immanuel Jakobovits, b. 1921, m.
1959 *James of Rusholme*, Eric John Francis James, b. 1909, m.
1987 *Jay*, Douglas Patrick Thomas Jay, PC, b. 1907, m.
1987 *Jenkin of Roding*, (Charles) Patrick (Fleeming) Jenkin, PC, b. 1926, m.
1987 *Jenkins of Hillhead*, Roy Harris Jenkins, PC, b. 1920, m.
1981 *Jenkins of Putney*, Hugh Gater Jenkins, b. 1908, w.
1981 *John-Mackie*, John John-Mackie, b. 1909, m.
1987 *Johnston of Rockport*, Charles Collier Johnston, TD, b. 1915, m.
1987 *Joseph*, Keith Sinjohn Joseph, CH, PC, b. 1918, m.
1991 *Judd*, Frank Ashcroft Judd, b. 1935, m.
1981 *Kadoorie*, Lawrence Kadoorie, CBE, b. 1899, m.
1976 *Kagan*, Joseph Kagan, b. 1915, m.
1970 *Kearton*, (Christopher) Frank Kearton, OBE, FRS, b. 1911, m.
1980 *Keith of Castleacre*, Kenneth Alexander Keith, b. 1916, m.
1985 *Kimball*, Marcus Richard Kimball, b. 1928, m.
1983 *King of Wartnaby*, John Leonard King, b. 1918, m.
1965 *Kings Norton*, Harold Roxbee Cox, PH.D., b. 1902, m.
1975 *Kirkhill*, John Farquharson Smith, b. 1930, m.
1974 *Kissin*, Harry Kissin, b. 1912, m.
1987 *Knights*, Philip Douglas Knights, CBE, QPM, b. 1920, m.
1991 *Laing of Dunphail*, Hector Laing, b. 1923, m.
1990 *Lane of Horsell*, Peter Stewart Lane, b. 1925, w.
1964 *Leatherland*, Charles Edward Leatherland, OBE, b. 1898, w.
1979 *Lever of Manchester*, Harold Lever, PC, b. 1914, m.
1982 *Lewin*, Terence Thornton Lewin, KG, GCB, LVO, DSC, *Admiral of the Fleet*, b. 1920, m.
1989 *Lewis of Newnham*, Jack Lewis, FRS, b. 1928, m.
1965 *Lloyd of Hampstead*, Dennis Lloyd, QC, LL.D., b. 1915, m.
1974 *Lovell-Davis*, Peter Lovell Lovell-Davis, b. 1924, m.
1979 *Lowry*, Robert Lynd Erskine Lowry, PC, PC(NI), b. 1919, w. (*Lord of Appeal in Ordinary*).
1984 *McAlpine of West Green*, (Robert) Alistair McAlpine, b. 1942, m.
1988 *Macaulay of Bragar*, Donald Macaulay, QC, b. 1933.
1975 *McCarthy*, William Edward John McCarthy, b. 1925, m.
1976 *McCluskey*, John Herbert McCluskey, b. 1929, m.
1989 *McColl of Dulwich*, Ian McColl, FRCS, FRCSE, b. 1933, m.
1966 *McFadzean*, William Hunter McFadzean, KT, b. 1903, m.
1980 *McFadzean of Kelvinside*, Francis Scott McFadzean, b. 1915, m.
1991 *Macfarlane of Bearsden*, Norman Somerville Macfarlane, b. 1926, m.
1978 *McGregor of Durris*, Oliver Ross McGregor, b. 1921, m.
1982 *McIntosh of Haringey*, Andrew Robert McIntosh, b. 1933, m.
1991 *Mackay of Ardbrecknish*, John Jackson Mackay, b. 1938, m.
1979 *Mackay of Clashfern*, James Peter Hymers Mackay, PC, b. 1927, m. (*Lord High Chancellor*).
1988 *Mackenzie-Stuart*, Alexander John Mackenzie Stuart, , b. 1924, m.
1974 *Mackie of Benshie*, George Yull Mackie, CBE, DSO, DFC, b. 1919, m.
1982 *MacLehose of Beoch*, (Crawford) Murray MacLehose, KT, GBE, KCMG, KCVO, b. 1917, m.
1967 *Mais*, Alan Raymond Mais, GBE, TD, ERD, b. 1911, m.
1991 *Marlesford*, Mark Shuldham Schreiber, b. 1931, m.
1981 *Marsh*, Richard William Marsh, PC, b. 1928, m.
1985 *Marshall of Goring*, Walter Charles Marshall, CBE, FRS, b. 1932, m.
1987 *Mason of Barnsley*, Roy Mason, PC, b. 1924, m.
1980 *Matthews*, Victor Collin Matthews, b. 1919, m.
1983 *Maude of Stratford-upon-Avon*, Angus Edmund Upton Maude, TD, PC, b. 1912, m.
1981 *Mayhew*, Christopher Paget Mayhew, b. 1915, m.
1985 *Mellish*, Robert Joseph Mellish, PC, b. 1913, m.
1978 *Mishcon*, Victor Mishcon, b. 1915, m.
1981 *Molloy*, William John Molloy, b. 1918.
1961 *Molson*, (Arthur) Hugh (Elsdale) Molson, PC, b. 1903, m.
1986 *Moore of Wolvercote*, Philip Brian Cecil Moore, GCB, GCVO, CMG, PC, b. 1921, m.
1990 *Morris of Castle Morris*, Brian Robert Morris, D.Phil., b. 1930, m.
1985 *Morton of Shuna*, Hugh Drennan Baird Morton, b. 1930, m.
1971 *Moyola*, James Dawson Chichester-Clark, PC (NI), b. 1923, m.
1984 *Mulley*, Frederick William Mulley, PC, b. 1918, m.
1985 *Murray of Epping Forest*, Lionel Murray, OBE, PC, b. 1922, m.
1964 *Murray of Newhaven*, Keith Anderson Hope Murray, KCB, PH.D., b. 1903.
1979 *Murton of Lindisfarne*, (Henry) Oscar Murton, OBE, TD, PC, b. 1914, m.
1975 *Northfield*, (William) Donald Chapman, b. 1923.
1966 *Nugent of Guildford*, (George) Richard (Hodges) Nugent, PC, b. 1907, m.
1973 *O'Brien of Lothbury*, Leslie Kenneth O'Brien, GBE, PC, b. 1908, m.
1976 *Oram*, Albert Edward Oram, b. 1913, m.
1971 *Orr-Ewing*, (Charles) Ian Orr-Ewing, OBE, b. 1912, m.
1991 *Palumbo*, Peter Garth Palumbo, b. 1935, m.
1975 *Parry*, Gordon Samuel David Parry, b. 1925, m.

Created

1990 *Pearson of Rannoch*, Malcolm Everard MacLaren Pearson, *b.* 1942, *m.*
1982 *Pennock*, Raymond William Pennock, *b.* 1920, *m.*
1979 *Perry of Walton*, Walter Laing Macdonald Perry, OBE, FRS, FRSE, *b.* 1921, *m.*
1987 *Peston*, Maurice Harry Peston, *b.* 1931, *m.*
1983 *Peyton of Yeovil*, John Wynne William Peyton, PC, *b.* 1919, *m.*
1975 *Pitt of Hampstead*, David Thomas Pitt, *b.* 1913, *m.*
1959 *Plowden*, Edwin Noel Plowden, GBE, KCB, *b.* 1907, *m.*
1987 *Plumb*, (Charles) Henry Plumb, MEP, *b.* 1925, *m.*
1981 *Plummer of St Marylebone*, (Arthur) Desmond (Herne) Plummer, TD, *b.* 1914, *m.*
1973 *Porritt*, Arthur Espie Porritt, GCMG, GCVO, CBE, *b.* 1900, *m.*
1990 *Porter of Luddenham*, George Porter, OM, FRS, *b.* 1920, *m.*
1987 *Prior*, James Michael Leathes Prior, PC, *b.* 1927, *m.*
1975 *Pritchard*, Derek Wilbraham Pritchard, *b.* 1910, *m.*
1982 *Prys-Davies*, Gwilym Prys Prys-Davies, *b.* 1923, *m.*
1987 *Pym*, Francis Leslie Pym, MC, PC, *b.* 1922, *m.*
1982 *Quinton*, Anthony Meredith Quinton, *b.* 1925, *m.*
1978 *Rawlinson of Ewell*, Peter Anthony Grayson Rawlinson, PC, QC, *b.* 1919, *m.*
1976 *Rayne*, Max Rayne, *b.* 1918, *m.*
1983 *Rayner*, Derek George Rayner, *b.* 1926.
1987 *Rees*, Peter Wynford Innes Rees, PC, QC, *b.* 1926, *m.*
1988 *Rees-Mogg*, William Rees-Mogg, *b.* 1928, *m.*
1970 *Reigate*, John Kenyon Vaughan-Morgan, PC, *b.* 1905, *m.*
1991 *Renfrew of Kaimsthorn*, (Andrew) Colin Renfrew, FBA, *b.* 1937, *m.*
1979 *Renton*, David Lockhart-Mure Renton, KBE, TD, PC, QC, *b.* 1908, *w.*
1990 *Richard*, Ivor Seward Richard, QC, *b.* 1932, *m.*
1979 *Richardson*, John Samuel Richardson, LVO, MD, FRCP, *b.* 1910, *w.*
1983 *Richardson of Duntisbourne*, Gordon William Humphreys Richardson, KG, MBE, TD, PC, *b.* 1915, *m.*
1987 *Rippon of Hexham*, (Aubrey) Geoffrey (Frederick) Rippon, PC, QC, *b.* 1924, *m.*
1961 *Robens of Woldingham*, Alfred Robens, PC, *b.* 1910, *m.*
1977 *Roll of Ipsden*, Eric Roll, KCMG, CB, *b.* 1907, *m.*
1987 *Ross of Newport*, Stephen Sherlock Ross, *b.* 1926, *m.*
1991 *Runcie*, Rt Rev. Robert Alexander Kennedy Runcie, MC, PC, Royal Victoria Chain, *b.* 1921, *m.*
1975 *Ryder of Eaton Hastings*, Sydney Thomas Franklin (Don) Ryder, *b.* 1916, *m.*
1962 *Sainsbury*, Alan John Sainsbury, *b.* 1902, *w.*
1989 *Sainsbury of Preston Candover*, John Davan Sainsbury, *b.* 1927, *m.*
1987 *St John of Fawsley*, Norman Antony Francis St John-Stevas, PC, *b.* 1929.
1985 *Sanderson of Bowden*, Charles Russell Sanderson, *b.* 1933, *m.*
1979 *Scanlon*, Hugh Parr Scanlon, *b.* 1913, *m.*
1976 *Schon*, Frank Schon, *b.* 1912, *m.*
1978 *Sefton of Garston*, William Henry Sefton, *b.* 1915, *m.*
1958 *Shackleton*, Edward Arthur Alexander Shackleton, KG, OBE, PC, *b.* 1911, *m.*
1989 *Sharp of Grimsdyke*, Eric Sharp, CBE, *b.* 1916, *m.*
1959 *Shawcross*, Hartley William Shawcross, GBE, PC, QC, *b.* 1902, *w.*
1980 *Sieff of Brimpton*, Marcus Joseph Sieff, OBE, *b.* 1913, *m.*
1971 *Simon of Glaisdale*, Jocelyn Edward Salis Simon, PC, *b.* 1911, *m.* (*Lord of Appeal, retired*).
1991 *Skidelsky*, Robert Jacob Alexander Skidelsky, D.Phil., *b.* 1939, *m.*
1978 *Smith*, Rodney Smith, KBE, FRCS, *b.* 1914, *m.*
1965 *Soper*, Rev. Donald Oliver Soper, Ph.D., *b.* 1903, *m.*
1990 *Soulsby*, Ernest Jackson Lawson Soulsby, Ph.D., *b.* 1926, *m.*
1983 *Stallard*, Albert William Stallard, *b.* 1921, *m.*
1991 *Sterling of Plaistow*, Jeffrey Maurice Sterling, CBE, *b.* 1934, *m.*
1987 *Stevens of Ludgate*, David Robert Stevens, *b.* 1936, *m.*
1981 *Stodart of Leaston*, James Anthony Stodart, PC, *b.* 1916, *m.*
1983 *Stoddart of Swindon*, David Leonard Stoddart, *b.* 1926, *m.*
1969 *Stokes*, Donald Gresham Stokes, TD, *b.* 1914, *m.*
1979 *Strauss*, George Russell Strauss, PC, *b.* 1901, *m.*
1971 *Tanlaw*, Simon Brooke Mackay, *b.* 1934, *m.*
1978 *Taylor of Blackburn*, Thomas Taylor, CBE, *b.* 1929, *m.*
1968 *Taylor of Gryfe*, Thomas Johnston Taylor, *b.* 1912, *m.*
1982 *Taylor of Hadfield*, Francis Taylor, *b.* 1905, *m.*
1987 *Thomas of Gwydir*, Peter John Mitchell Thomas, PC, QC, *b.* 1920, *w.*
1981 *Thomas of Swynnerton*, Hugh Swynnerton Thomas, *b.* 1931, *m.*
1977 *Thomson of Monifieth*, George Morgan Thomson, KT, PC, *b.* 1921, *m.*
1967 *Thorneycroft*, (George Edward) Peter Thorneycroft, CH, PC, *b.* 1909, *m.*
1962 *Todd*, Alexander Robertus Todd, OM, D.SC., D.Phil., FRS, *b.* 1907, *w.*
1990 *Tombs*, Francis Leonard Tombs, *b.* 1924, *m.*
1981 *Tordoff*, Geoffrey Johnson Tordoff, *b.* 1928, *m.*
1974 *Tranmire*, Robert Hugh Turton, KBE, MC, PC, *b.* 1903, *m.*
1979 *Underhill*, (Henry) Reginald Underhill, CBE, *b.* 1914, *m.*
1990 *Varley*, Eric Graham Varley, PC, *b.* 1932, *m.*
1985 *Vinson*, Nigel Vinson, LVO, *b.* 1931, *m.*
1990 *Waddington*, David Charles Waddington, PC, QC, *b.* 1929, *m.*
1990 *Wade of Chorlton*, (William) Oulton Wade, *b.* 1932, *m.*
1974 *Wallace of Campsie*, George Wallace, *b.* 1915, *m.*
1974 *Wallace of Coslany*, George Douglas Wallace, *b.* 1906, *m.*
1989 *Walton of Detchant*, John Nicholas Walton, TD, FRCP, *b.* 1922, *m.*

Created
1977 *Wedderburn of Charlton*, Kenneth William Wedderburn, QC, *b.* 1927, *m.*
1976 *Weidenfeld*, (Arthur) George Weidenfeld, *b.* 1919.
1980 *Weinstock*, Arnold Weinstock, *b.* 1924, *m.*
1978 *Whaddon*, (John) Derek Page, *b.* 1927, *m.*
1991 *White of Hull*, (Vincent) Gordon (Lindsay) White, KBE, *b.* 1923, *m.*
1974 *Wigoder*, Basil Thomas Wigoder, QC, *b.* 1921, *m.*
1985 *Williams of Elvel*, Charles Cuthbert Powell Williams, CBE, *b.* 1933, *m.*
1963 *Willis*, Edward Henry Willis, *b.* 1918, *m.*
1969 *Wilson of Langside*, Henry Stephen Wilson, PC, QC, *b.* 1916, *m.*
1983 *Wilson of Rievaulx*, (James) Harold Wilson, KG, OBE, PC, FRS, *b.* 1916, *m.*
1975 *Winstanley*, Michael Platt Winstanley, *b.* 1918, *m.*
1965 *Winterbottom*, Ian Winterbottom, *b.* 1913, *m.*
1985 *Wolfson*, Leonard Gordon Wolfson, *b.* 1927, *m.*
1991 *Wolfson of Sunningdale*, David Wolfson, *b.* 1935, *m.*
1987 *Wyatt of Weeford*, Woodrow Lyle Wyatt, *b.* 1918, *m.*
1978 *Young of Dartington*, Michael Young, PH.D., *b.* 1915, *m.*
1984 *Young of Graffham*, David Ivor Young, PC, *b.* 1932, *m.*
1971 *Zuckerman*, Solly Zuckerman, OM, KCB, FRS, MD, D.SC., *b.* 1904, *m.*

BARONESSES

Created
1979 *Airey of Abingdon*, Diana Josceline Barbara Neave Airey, *b.* 1919, *w.*
1970 *Bacon*, Alice Martha Bacon, CBE, PC, *b.* 1911.
1967 *Birk*, Alma Birk, *b.* 1921, *m.*
1987 *Blackstone*, Tessa Ann Vosper Blackstone, PH.D., *b.* 1942.
1987 *Blatch*, Emily May Blatch, CBE, *b.* 1937, *m.*
1990 *Brigstocke*, Heather Renwick Brigstocke, *b.* 1929, *w.*
1964 *Brooke of Ystradfellte*, Barbara Muriel Brooke, DBE, *b.* 1908, *w.*
1962 *Burton of Coventry*, Elaine Frances Burton, *b.* 1904.
1982 *Carnegy of Lour*, Elizabeth Patricia Carnegy of Lour, *b.* 1925.
1990 *Castle of Blackburn*, Barbara Anne Castle, PC, *b.* 1910, *w.*
1982 *Cox*, Caroline Anne Cox, *b.* 1937, *m.*
1990 *Cumberlege*, Julia Frances Cumberlege, CBE, *b,* 1943, *m.*
1978 *David*, Nora Ratcliff David, *b.* 1913, *m.*
1974 *Delacourt-Smith of Alteryn*, Margaret Rosalind Delacourt-Smith, *b.* 1916, *m.*
1978 *Denington*, Evelyn Joyce Denington, DBE, *b.* 1907, *m.*
1991 *Denton of Wakefield*, Jean Denton, CBE, *b.* 19–.
1990 *Dunn*, Lydia Selina Dunn, DBE, MEC, *b.* 1940, *m.*
1990 *Eccles of Moulton*, Diana Catherine Eccles, *b.* 1933, *m.*
1972 *Elles*, Diana Louie Elles, *b.* 1921, *m.*
1958 *Elliot of Harwood*, Katharine Elliot, DBE, *b.* 1903, *w.*
1981 *Ewart-Biggs*, (Felicity) Jane Ewart-Biggs, *b.* 1929, *w.*
1975 *Faithfull*, Lucy Faithfull, OBE, *b.* 1910.
1974 *Falkender*, Marcia Matilda Falkender, CBE, *b.* 1932.
1974 *Fisher of Rednal*, Doris Mary Gertrude Fisher, *b.* 1919, *w.*
1990 *Flather*, Shreela Flather, *b.* 19–, *m.*
1981 *Gardner of Parkes*, (Rachel) Trixie (Anne) Gardner, *b.* 1927, *m.*
1991 *Hamwee*, Sally Rachel Hamwee, *b.* 19–.
1988 *Hart of South Lanark*, Judith Constance Mary Hart, DBE, PC, *b.* 1924, *m.*
1991 *Hilton of Eggardon*, Jennifer Hilton, QPM, *b.* 19–.
1990 *Hollis of Heigham*, Patricia Lesley Hollis, D.PHIL., *b.* 1941, *m.*
1985 *Hooper*, Gloria Dorothy Hooper, *b.* 1939.
1965 *Hylton-Foster*, Audrey Pellew Hylton-Foster, DBE, *b.* 1908, *w.*
1991 *James of Holland Park*, Phyllis Dorothy James (Mrs White), OBE, *b.* 1920, *w.*
1979 *Jeger*, Lena May Jeger, *b.* 1915, *w.*
1967 *Llewelyn-Davies of Hastoe*, (Annie) Patricia Llewelyn-Davies, PC, *b.* 1915, *w.*
1978 *Lockwood*, Betty Lockwood, *b.* 1924, *w.*
1979 *McFarlane of Llandaff*, Jean Kennedy McFarlane, *b.* 1926.
1971 *Macleod of Borve*, Evelyn Hester Macleod, *b.* 1915, *w.*
1991 *Mallalieu*, Ann Mallalieu, QC, *b.* 1945, *m.*
1970 *Masham of Ilton*, Susan Lilian Primrose Cunliffe-Lister, *b.* 1935, *m.* (*Countess of Swinton*).
1982 *Nicol*, Olive Mary Wendy Nicol, *b.* 1923, *m.*
1991 *O'Cathain*, Detta O'Cathain, OBE, *b.* 1938, *m.*
1989 *Oppenheim-Barnes*, Sally Oppenheim-Barnes, PC, *b.* 1930, *m.*
1990 *Park of Monmouth*, Daphne Margaret Sybil Désirée Park, CMG, OBE, *b.* 1921.
1991 *Perry of Southwark*, Pauline Perry, *b.* 1931, *m.*
1964 *Phillips*, Norah Phillips, *b.* 1910, *w.*
1974 *Pike*, (Irene) Mervyn (Parnicott) Pike, DBE, *b.* 1918.
1981 *Platt of Writtle*, Beryl Catherine Platt, CBE, *b.* 1923, *m.*
1974 *Robson of Kiddington*, Inga-Stina Robson, *b.* 1919, *w.*
1979 *Ryder of Warsaw*, (Margaret) Susan Cheshire, CMG, OBE, *b.* 1923, *m.*
1991 *Seccombe*, Joan Anna Dalziel Seccombe, DBE, *b.* 1930, *m.*
1971 *Seear*, (Beatrice) Nancy Seear, PC, *b.* 1913.
1967 *Serota*, Beatrice Serota, *b.* 1919, *m.*

Created
1973 *Sharples*, Pamela Sharples, *b.* 1923, *m.*
1974 *Stedman*, Phyllis Stedman, OBE, *b.* 1916, *w.*
1980 *Trumpington*, Jean Alys Barker, *b.* 1922, *w.*
1985 *Turner of Camden*, Muriel Winifred Turner, *b.* 1927, *m.*
1974 *Vickers*, Joan Helen Vickers, DBE, *b.* 1907.
1985 *Warnock*, Helen Mary Warnock, DBE, *b.* 1924, *m.*
1970 *White*, Eirene Lloyd White, *b.* 1909, *w.*
1971 *Young*, Janet Mary Young, PC, *b.* 1926, *m.*

COURTESY TITLES

From this list it will be seen that, for example, the Marquess of Blandford is heir to the Dukedom of Marlborough, and Viscount Althorp to the Earldom of Spencer. Titles of second heirs are also given, and the courtesy title of the father of a second heir is indicated by *; e.g., Earl of Burlington, eldest son of *Marquess of Hartington.

For forms of address, *see* page 219.

Marquesses

Blandford—*Marlborough*, D.
Bowmont and Cessford—*Roxburghe*, D.
Douglas and Clydesdale—*Hamilton*, D.
*Douro—*Wellington*, D.
*Graham—*Montrose*, D.
Granby—*Rutland*, D.
Hamilton—*Abercorn*, D.
*Hartington—*Devonshire*, D.
*Kildare—*Leinster*, D.
Lorne—*Argyll*, D.
*Tavistock—*Bedford*, D.
*Worcester—*Beaufort*, D.

Earls

*Aboyne—*Huntly*, M.
Altamont—*Sligo*, M.
Ancram—*Lothian*, M.
Arundel and Surrey—*Norfolk*, D.
*Bective—*Headfort*, M.
*Belfast—*Donegall*, M.
*Brecknock—*Camden*, M.
Burford—*St Albans*, D.
Burlington—*Hartington*, M.
*Cardigan—*Ailesbury*, M.
Cassillis—*Ailsa*, M.
Compton—*Northampton*, M.
*Dalkeith—*Buccleuch*, D.
*Dumfries—*Bute*, M.
*Euston—*Grafton*, D.
Glamorgan—*Worcester*, D.
Grosvenor—*Westminster*, D.
*Haddo—*Aberdeen and Temair*, M.
Hillsborough—*Downshire*, M.
Hopetoun—*Linlithgow*, M.
Macduff—*Fife*, D.
March and Kinrara—*Richmond*, D.
*Mount Charles—*Conyngham*, M.
Mornington—*Douro*, M.
Mulgrave—*Normanby*, M.

Offaly—*Kildare*, M.
Ronaldshay—*Zetland*, M.
*St Andrews—*Kent*, D.
*Shelburne—*Lansdowne*, M.
*Tyrone—*Waterford*, M.
Ulster—*Gloucester*, D.
*Uxbridge—*Anglesey*, M.
Wiltshire—*Winchester*, M.
Yarmouth—*Hertford*, M.

Viscounts

Althorp—*Spencer*, E.
Amberley—*Russell*, E.
Andover—*Suffolk and Berkshire*, E.
Anson—*Lichfield*, E.
Asquith—*Oxford & Asquith*, E.
Boringdon—*Morley*, E.
Borodale—*Beatty*, E.
Boyle—*Shannon*, E.
Brocas—*Jellicoe*, E.
Calne and Calstone—*Shelburne*, E.
Campden—*Gainsborough*, E.
Carlow—*Portarlington*, E.
Carlton—*Wharncliffe*, E.
Castlereagh—*Londonderry*, M.
Chelsea—*Cadogan*, E.
Chewton—*Waldegrave*, E.
Chichester—*Belfast*, E.
Clanfield—*Peel*, E.
Clive—*Powis*, E.
Coke—*Leicester*, E.
Corry—*Belmore*, E.
Corvedale—*Baldwin of Bewdley*, E.
Cranborne—*Salisbury*, M.
Cranley—*Onslow*, E.
Crichton—*Erne*, E.
Crowhurst—*Cottenham*, E.
Dalrymple—*Stair*, E.
Dangan—*Cowley*, E.
Dawick—*Haig*, E.
Deerhurst—*Coventry*, E.
Drumlanrig—*Queensberry*, M.
Dunwich—*Stradbroke*, E.
Dupplin—*Kinnoull*, E.
Ebrington—*Fortescue*, E.

Ednam—*Dudley*, E.
Elveden—*Iveagh*, E.
Emlyn—*Cawdor*, E.
Encombe—*Eldon*, E.
Ennismore—*Listowel*, E.
Enfield—*Strafford*, E.
Erleigh—*Reading*, M.
Feilding—*Denbigh*, E.
Fincastle—*Dunmore*, E.
FitzHarris—*Malmesbury*, E.
Folkestone—*Radnor*, E.
Garmoyle—*Cairns*, E.
Garnock—*Lindsay*, E.
Glandine—*Norbury*, E.
Glenapp—*Inchcape*, E.
Glentworth—*Limerick*, E.
Grimstone—*Verulam*, E.
Gwynedd—*Lloyd George of Dwyfor*, E.
Hawkesbury—*Liverpool*, E.
Ikerrin—*Carrick*, E.
Ingestre—*Shrewsbury*, E.
Ipswich—*Euston*, E.
Jocelyn—*Roden*, E.
Kelburn—*Glasgow*, E.
Kingsborough—*Kingston*, E.
Knebworth—*Lytton*, E.
Lascelles—*Harewood*, E.
Lewisham—*Dartmouth*, E.
Linley—*Snowdon*, E.
Loftus—*Ely*, M.
Lowther—*Lonsdale*, E.
Lumley—*Scarbrough*, E.
Lymington—*Portsmouth*, E.
Macmillan of Ovenden—*Stockton*, E.
Maidstone—*Winchilsea and Nottingham*, E.
Maitland—*Lauderdale*, E.
Malden—*Essex*, E.
Mandeville—*Manchester*, D.
Melgund—*Minto*, E.
Merton—*Nelson*, E.
Moore—*Drogheda*, E.
Morpeth—*Carlisle*, E.
Mount Stuart—*Dumfries*, E.
Newport—*Bradford*, E.
Newry and Mourne—*Kilmorey*, E.
Northland—*Ranfurly*, E.
Parker—*Macclesfield*, E.
Perceval—*Egmont*, E.

Petersham—*Harrington*, E.
Pollington—*Mexborough*, E.
Quenington—*St Aldwyn*, E.
Raynham—*Townshend*, M.
Reidhaven—*Seafield*, E.
Ruthven of Canberra—*Gowrie*, E.
St Cyres—*Iddesleigh*, E.
Sandon—*Harrowby*, E.
Savernake—*Cardigan*, E.
Slane—*Mount Charles*, E.
Somerton—*Normanton*, E.
Stopford—*Courtown*, E.
Stormont—*Mansfield*, E.
Strathallan—*Perth*, E.
Stuart—*Castle Stewart*, E.
Suirdale—*Donoughmore*, E.
Tamworth—*Ferrers*, E.
Tarbat—*Cromartie*, E.
Vaughan—*Lisburne*, E.
Villiers—*Jersey*, E.
Weymouth—*Bath*, M.
Windsor—*Plymouth*, E.
Wolmer—*Selborne*, E.
Woodstock—*Portland*, E.

Barons (Lord—)

Aberdour—*Morton*, E.
Apsley—*Bathurst*, E.
Ardee—*Meath*, E.
Ashley—*Shaftesbury*, E.
Balgonie—*Leven & Melville*, E.
Balniel—*Crawford and Balcarres*, E.
Berriedale—*Caithness*, E.
Bingham—*Lucan*, E.
Binning—*Haddington*, E.
Brooke—*Warwick*, E.
Bruce—*Elgin*, E.
Buckhurst—*De La Warr*, E.
Burghersh—*Westmorland*, E.
Burghley—*Exeter*, M.
Cardross—*Buchan*, E.
Clifton of Rathmore—*Darnley*, E.
Cochrane—*Dundonald*, E.

Courtenay—*Devon*, E.
Dalmeny—*Rosebery*, E.
Doune—*Moray*, E.
Downpatrick—*St Andrews*, E.
Eliot—*St Germans*, E.
Erskine—*Mar & Kellie*, E.
Eskdail—*Dalkeith*, E.
Fintrie—*Graham*, M.
Formartine—*Haddo*, E.
Gillford—*Clanwilliam*, E.
Glamis—*Strathmore*, E.
Greenock—*Cathcart*, E.
Guernsey—*Aylesford*, E.
Hay—*Erroll*, E.

Herbert—*Pembroke*, E.
Howland—*Tavistock*, M.
Hyde—*Clarendon*, E.
Inverurie—*Kintore*, E.
Irwin—*Halifax*, E.
Johnstone—*Annandale and Hartfell*, E.
Kenlis—*Bective*, E.
Langton—*Temple of Stowe*, E.
La Poer—*Tyrone*, E.
Leslie—*Rothes*, E.
Leveson—*Granville*, E.
Loughborough—*Rosslyn*, E.

Maltravers—*Arundel and Surrey*, E.
Mauchline—*Loudoun*, C.
Medway—*Cranbrook*, E.
Montgomerie—*Eglinton and Winton*, E.
Moreton—*Ducie*, E.
Naas—*Mayo*, E.
Neidpath—*Wemyss & March*, E.
Norreys—*Lindsey & Abingdon*, E.
North—*Guilford*, E.
Ogilvy—*Airlie*, E.
Oxmantown—*Rosse*, E.

Paget de Beaudesert—*Uxbridge*, E.
Porchester—*Carnarvon*, E.
Ramsay—*Dalhousie*, E.
Romsey—*Mountbatten of Burma*, C.
Rosehill—*Northesk*, E.
Scrymgeour—*Dundee*, E.
Seymour—*Somerset*, D.
Strathnaver—*Sutherland*, C.
Wodehouse—*Kimberley*, E.
Worsley—*Yarborough*, E.

PEERS' SURNAMES WHICH DIFFER FROM THEIR TITLES

The following symbols indicate the rank of the peer holding each title: *C.* Countess; *D.* Duke; *E.* Earl; *M.* Marquess; *V.* Viscount; **Life Peer. Where no designation is given, the title is that of an hereditary Baron or Baroness.

Abney-Hastings—*Loudoun*, C.
Acheson—*Gosford*, E.
Adderley—*Norton*
Addington—*Sidmouth*, V.
Agar—*Normanton*, E.
Airey—*A. of Abingdon*
Aitken—*Beaverbrook*
Akers-Douglas—*Chilston*, V.
Alexander—*A. of Potterhill*
Alexander—*A. of Tunis*, E.
Alexander—*A. of Weedon*
Alexander—*Caledon*, E.
Allen—*A. of Abbeydale*
Allen—*Croham*
Allanson-Winn—*Headley*
Allsopp—*Hindlip*
Anderson—*Waverley*, V.
Annesley—*Valentia*, V.
Anson—*Lichfield*, E.
Armstrong—*A. of Ilminster*
Armstrong-Jones—*Snowdon*, E.
Arthur—*Glenarthur*
Arundell—*Talbot of Malahide*
Ashley-Cooper—*Shaftesbury*, E.
Ashton—*A. of Hyde*
Asquith—*Oxford & Asquith*, E.
Assheton—*Clitheroe*
Astley—*Hastings*
Astor—*A. of Hever*
Atkins—*Colnbrook*
Aubrey-Fletcher—*Braye*
Bailey—*Glanusk*
Baillie—*Burton*
Baillie Hamilton—*Haddington*, E.
Baldwin—*B. of Bewdley*, E.
Balfour—*B. of Inchrye*
Balfour—*Kinross*
Balfour—*Riverdale*
Bampfylde—*Poltimore*
Banbury—*B. of Southam*
Baring—*Ashburton*

Baring—*Cromer*, E.
Baring—*Howick of Glendale*
Baring—*Northbrook*
Baring—*Revelstoke*
Barker—*Trumpington*
Barnes—*Gorell*
Barnewall—*Trimlestown*
Bathurst—*Bledisloe*, V.
Beauclerk—*St Albans*, D.
Beaumont—*Allendale*, V.
Beaumont—*B. of Whitley*
Beavan—*Ardwick*
Beckett—*Grimthorpe*
Bellow—*Bellwin*
Benn—*Stansgate*, V.
Bennet—*Tankerville*, E.
Bentinck—*Portland*, E.
Beresford—*Decies*
Beresford-Waterford*, M.
Berry—*Camrose*, V.
Berry—*Hartwell*
Berry—*Kemsley*, V.
Bertie—*Lindsey*, E.
Best—*Wynford*
Bethell—*Westbury*
Bewicke-Copley—*Cromwell*
Bigham—*Mersey*, V.
Bigham—*Nairne*
Bingham—*Clanmorris*
Bingham—*Lucan*, E.
Blackwood—*Dufferin & Clandeboye*
Bligh—*Darnley*, E.
Bootle-Wilbraham—*Skelmersdale*
Boscawen—*Falmouth*, V.
Boston—*Boston of Faversham*
Bourke—*Mayo*, E.
Bowden—*Aylestone*
Bowes Lyon—*Strathmore*, E.
Bowyer—*Denham*
Boyd—*Kilmarnock*
Boyle—*Cork & Orrery*, E.
Boyle—*Glasgow*, E.
Boyle—*Shannon*, E.
Brabazon—*Meath*, E.
Brand—*Hampden*, V.
Brandon—*B. of Oakbrook*

Brassey—*B. of Apethorpe*
Brett—*Esher*, V.
Bridge—*B. of Harwich*
Bridgeman—*Bradford*, E.
Brodrick—*Midleton*, V.
Brooke—*Alanbrooke*, V.
Brooke—*Brookeborough*, V.
Brooke—*B. of Ystradfellte*
Brooks—*B. of Tremorfa*
Brooks—*Crawshaw*
Brougham—*Brougham and Vaux*
Broughton—*Fairhaven*
Browne—*Craigton*
Browne—*Kilmaine*
Browne—*Oranmore and Browne*
Browne—*Sligo*, M.
Brownlow—*Lurgan*
Bruce—*Aberdare*
Bruce—*Balfour of Burleigh*
Bruce—*B. of Donington*
Bruce—*Elgin and Kincardine*, E.
Brudenell-Bruce—*Ailesbury*, M.
Buchan—*Tweedsmuir*
Buckley—*Wrenbury*
Burton—*B. of Coventry*
Butler—*Carrick*, E.
Butler—*Dunboyne*
Butler—*Lanesborough*, E.
Butler—*Mountgarret*, V.
Butler—*Ormonde*, M.
Buxton—*B. of Alsa*
Byng—*Strafford*, E.
Byng—*Torrington*, V.
Callaghan—*C. of Cardiff*
Cameron—*C. of Lochbroom*
Campbell—*Argyll*, D.
Campbell—*Breadalbane and Holland*, E.
Campbell—*C. of Alloway*
Campbell—*C. of Croy*
Campbell—*C. of Eskan*
Campbell—*Cawdor*, E.
Campbell—*Colgrain*
Campbell—*Stratheden and Campbell*
Campbell-Gray—*Gray*

Canning—*Garvagh*
Capell—*Essex*, E.
Carington—*Carrington*
Carlisle—*C. of Bucklow*
Carmichael—*C. of Kelvingrove*
Carnegie—*Fife*, D.
Carnegie—*Northesk*, E.
Carnegie—*Southesk*, E.
Carr—*C. of Hadley*
Cary—*Falkland*, V.
Castle—*C. of Blackburn*
Caulfeild—*Charlemont*, V.
Cavendish—*C. of Furness*
Cavendish—*Chesham*
Cavendish—*Devonshire*, D.
Cavendish—*Waterpark*
Cayzer—*Rotherwick*
Cecil—*Amherst of Hackney*
Cecil—*Exeter*, M.
Cecil—*Rockley*
Cecil—*Salisbury*, M.
Chaloner—*Gisborough*
Chapman—*Northfield*
Charteris—*C. of Amisfield*
Charteris—*Wemyss and March*, E.
Cheshire—*Ryder of Warsaw*
Chetwynd-Talbot—*Shrewsbury*, E.
Chichester—*Donegall*, M.
Chichester-Clark—*Moyola*
Child-Villiers—*Jersey*, E.
Cholmondeley—*Delamere*
Chubb—*Hayter*
Clegg-Hill—*Hill*, V.
Clifford—*Clifford of Chudleigh*
Cochrane—*C. of Cults*
Cochrane—*Dundonald*, E.
Cocks—*C. of Hartcliffe*
Cocks—*Somers*
Cokayne—*Cullen of Ashbourne*
Coke—*Leicester*, E.
Cole—*Enniskillen*, E.

Collier—*Monkswell*
Colville—*Clydesmuir*
Colville—*C. of Culross, V.*
Compton—*Northampton, M.*
Conolly-Carew—*Carew*
Constantine—*C. of Stanmore**
Cooper—*Norwich, V.*
Corbett—*Rowallan*
Courtenay—*Devon, E.*
Cox—*Kings Norton**
Craig—*C. of Radley**
Craig—*Craigavon, V.*
Crichton—*Erne, E.*
Crichton-Stuart—*Bute, M.*
Cripps—*Parmoor*
Crossley—*Somerleyton*
Cubitt—*Ashcombe*
Cunliffe-Lister—*Masham of Ilton**
Cunliffe-Lister—*Swinton, E.*
Curzon—*Howe, E.*
Curzon—*Scarsdale, V.*
Cust—*Brownlow*
Dalrymple—*Stair, E.*
Daubeny de Moleyns—*Ventry*
Davies—*Darwen*
Davies—*D. of Penrhys**
Davis—*Clinton-Davis**
Davison—*Broughshane*
Dawnay—*Downe, V.*
Dawson-Damer—*Portarlington, E.*
Dean—*D. of Beswick**
Deane—*Muskerry*
de Courcy—*Kingsale*
de Grey—*Walsingham*
Delacourt-Smith—*Delacourt Smith of Alteryn**
Denison—*Londesborough*
Denison-Pender—*Pender*
Denton—*D. of Wakefield**
Devereux—*Hereford, V.*
Dewar—*Forteviot*
De Yarburgh-Bateson—*Deramore*
Dixon—*Glentoran*
Dodson—*Monk Bretton*
Donaldson—*D. of Kingsbridge**
Donaldson—*D. of Lymington**
Dormand—*D. of Easington**
Douglas—*Morton, E.*
Douglas—*Queensberry, M.*
Douglas-Hamilton—*Hamilton, D.*
Douglas-Hamilton—*Selkirk, E.*
Douglas-Home—*Dacre*
Douglas-Home—*Home of the Hirsel**
Douglas-Pennant—*Penrhyn*
Douglas-Scott-Montagu—*Montagu of Beaulieu*
Drummond—*Perth, E.*
Drummond of Megginch—*Strange*

Dugdale—*Crathorne*
Duke—*Merrivale*
Duncombe—*Feversham*
Dundas—*Melville, V.*
Dundas—*Zetland, M.*
Eady—*Swinfen*
Eccles—*E. of Moulton**
Eden—*Auckland*
Eden—*E. of Winton**
Eden—*Henley*
Edgcumbe—*Mount Edgcumbe, E.*
Edmondson—*Sandford*
Edwardes—*Kensington*
Edwards—*Chelmer**
Edwards—*Crickhowell**
Egerton—*Sutherland, D.*
Egerton—*Wilton, E.*
Eliot—*St Germans, E.*
Elliot—*E. of Harwood**
Elliot-Murray-Kynynmound—*Minto, E.*
Elliott—*E. of Morpeth**
Erroll—*E. of Hale*
Erskine—*Buchan, E.*
Erskine—*E. of Rerrick*
Erskine—*Mar & Kellie, E.*
Erskine-Murray—*Elibank*
Evans—*E. of Claughton**
Evans—*Mountevans*
Evans-Freke—*Carbery*
Eve—*Silsoe*
Eyres Monsell—*Monsell, V.*
Fairfax—*F. of Cameron*
Fane—*Westmorland, E.*
Feilding—*Denbigh, E.*
Fellowes—*De Ramsey*
Fermor-Hesketh—*Hesketh*
Fiennes—*Saye & Sele*
Fiennes-Clinton—*Lincoln, E.*
Finch Hatton—*Winchilsea, E.*
Finch-Knightley—*Aylesford, E.*
Fisher—*F. of Rednal**
Fitzalan-Howard—*Herries of Terregles*
Fitzalan-Howard—*Norfolk, D.*
FitzClarence—*Munster, E.*
FitzGerald—*Leinster, D.*
Fitzherbert—*Stafford*
Fitz-Maurice—*Orkney, E.*
FitzRoy—*Grafton, D.*
FitzRoy—*Southampton*
FitzRoy Newdegate—*Daventry, V.*
Fletcher-Vane—*Inglewood*
Flower—*Ashbrook, V.*
Foley Berkeley—*Berkeley*
Foljambe—*Liverpool, E.*
Forbes—*Granard, E.*
Fox-Strangways—*Ilchester, E.*
Frankland—*Zouche*
Fraser—*F. of Carmyllie**
Fraser—*F. of Kilmorack**

Fraser—*Lovat*
Fraser—*Saltoun*
Fraser—*Strathalmond*
Freeman-Grenville—*Kinloss*
Fremantle—*Cottesloe*
French—*De Freyne*
Galbraith—*Strathclyde*
Ganzoni—*Belstead*
Gardner—*G. of Parkes**
Gathorne-Hardy—*Cranbrook, E.*
Gibbs—*Aldenham*
Gibbs—*Wraxall*
Gibson—*Ashbourne*
Giffard—*Halsbury, E.*
Gilbey—*Vaux of Harrowden*
Glyn—*Wolverton*
Godley—*Kilbracken*
Goff—*G. of Chieveley**
Gordon—*Aberdeen, M.*
Gordon—*Huntly, M.*
Gordon Lennox—*Richmond, D.*
Gore—*Arran, E.*
Gough-Calthorpe—*Calthorpe*
Graham—*G. of Edmonton**
Graham—*Montrose, D.*
Graham-Toler—*Norbury, E.*
Grant of Grant—*Strathspey*
Grant-Ferris—*Harvington**
Granville—*G. of Eye**
Gray—*G. of Contin**
Greaves—*Dysart, C.*
Greenall—*Daresbury*
Greene—*G. of Harrow Weald**
Greenhill—*G. of Harrow**
Greville—*Warwick, E.*
Grey—*G. of Naunton**
Griffiths—*G. of Fforestfach**
Grigg—*Altrincham*
Grimston—*G. of Westbury*
Grimston—*Verulam, E.*
Grosvenor—*Ebury*
Grosvenor—*Westminster, D.*
Guest—*Wimborne, V.*
Guinness—*Iveagh, E.*
Guinness—*Moyne*
Gully—*Selby, V.*
Gurdon—*Cranworth*
Gwynne Jones—*Chalfont**
Hamilton—*Abercorn, D.*
Hamilton—*Belhaven and Stenton*
Hamilton—*Dudley*
Hamilton—*H. of Dalzell*
Hamilton—*Holm Patrick*
Hamilton-Russell—*Boyne, V.*
Hamilton-Smith—*Colwyn*
Hanbury-Tracy—*Sudeley*
Handcock—*Castlemaine*
Harbord-Hamond—*Suffield*

Harding—*H. of Petherton*
Hardinge—*H. of Penshurst*
Hare—*Blakenham, V.*
Hare—*Listowel, E.*
Harmsworth—*Rothermere, V.*
Harris—*H. of Greenwich**
Harris—*H. of High Cross**
Harris—*Malmesbury, E.*
Hart—*H. of South Lanark**
Harvey—*H. of Prestbury**
Harvey—*H. of Tasburgh*
Hastings Bass—*Huntingdon, E.*
Hatch—*H. of Lusby**
Hay—*Erroll, E.*
Hay—*Kinnoull, E.*
Hay—*Tweeddale, M.*
Heathcote-Drummond-Willoughby—*Willoughby de Eresby*
Hely-Hutchinson—*Donoughmore, E.*
Henderson—*Faringdon*
Henderson—*H. of Brompton**
Hennessy—*Windlesham*
Henniker-Major—*Henniker*
Hepburne-Scott—*Polwarth*
Herbert—*Carnarvon, E.*
Herbert—*Hemingford*
Herbert—*Pembroke, E.*
Herbert—*Powis, E.*
Hermon-Hodge—*Wyfold*
Hervey—*Bristol, M.*
Hewitt—*Lifford, V.*
Hicks Beach—*St Aldwyn, E.*
Hill—*Downshire, M.*
Hill—*Sandys*
Hill-Trevor—*Trevor*
Hilton—*H. of Eggardon**
Hobart-Hampden—*Buckinghamshire, E.*
Hogg—*Hailsham of St Marylebone**
Holland-Hibbert—*Knutsford, V.*
Hollis—*H. of Heigham**
Holme—*H. of Cheltenham**
Holmes à Court—*Heytesbury*
Hood—*Bridport, V.*
Hope—*Glendevon*
Hope—*Linlithgow, M.*
Hope—*Rankeillour*
Hope Johnstone—*Annandale and Hartfell, E.*
Hope-Morley—*Hollenden*
Hopkinson—*Colyton*
Hopwood—*Southborough*
Hore Ruthven—*Gowrie, E.*
Houghton—*H. of Sowerby**
Hovell-Thurlow-Cumming-Bruce—*Thurlow*
Howard—*Carlisle, E.*

C. Countess; *D.* Duke; *E.* Earl; *M.* Marquess; *V.* Viscount; * Life Peer.

Howard—*Effingham, E.*
Howard—*H. of Penrith*
Howard—*Strathcona*
Howard—*Suffolk and Berkshire, E.*
Howie—*H. of Troon**
Hubbard—*Addington*
Huggins—*Malvern, V.*
Hughes—*Cledwyn of Penrhos**
Hughes-Young—*St Helens*
Hunt—*H. of Tanworth**
Hunter—*H. of Newington**
Hutchinson—*H. of Lullington**
Ingrams—*Darcy de Knayth*
Innes-Ker—*Roxburghe, D.*
Inskip—*Caldecote, V.*
Irby—*Boston*
Irvine—*I. of Lairg**
Isaacs—*Reading, M.*
James—*J. of Holland Park**
James—*J. of Rusholme**
James—*Northbourne*
Jauncey—*J. of Tullichettle**
Jebb—*Gladwyn*
Jenkin—*J. of Roding**
Jenkins—*J. of Hillhead**
Jenkins—*J. of Putney**
Jervis—*St Vincent, V.*
Jocelyn—*Roden, E.*
Johnston—*J. of Rockport**
Jolliffe—*Hylton*
Joynson-Hicks—*Brentford, V.*
Kay-Shuttleworth—*Shuttleworth*
Kearley—*Devonport, V.*
Keith—*K. of Castleacre**
Keith—*K. of Kinkel**
Keith—*Kintore, E.*
Kemp—*Rochdale, V.*
Kennedy—*Ailsa, M.*
Kenworthy—*Strabolgi*
Keppel—*Albemarle, E.*
Kerr—*Lothian, M.*
Kerr—*Teviot*
King—*Lovelace, E.*
King—*K. of Wartnaby**
King-Tenison—*Kingston, E.*
Kitchener—*K. of Khartoum, E.*
Kitson—*Airedale*
Knatchbull—*Brabourne*
Knatchbull—*Mountbatten of Burma, C.*
Knox—*Ranfurly, E.*
Laing—*L. of Dunphail**
Lamb—*Rochester*
Lambart—*Cavan, E.*
Lambton—*Durham, E.*
Lampson—*Killearn*
Lane—*L. of Horsell**
Lascelles—*Harewood, E.*
Law—*Coleraine*
Law—*Ellenborough*

Lawrence—*Trevethin and Oaksey*
Lawson—*Burnham*
Lawson-Johnston—*Luke*
Legge—*Dartmouth, E.*
Legh—*Grey of Codnor*
Legh—*Newton*
Leith—*Burgh*
Lennox-Boyd—*Boyd of Merton, V.*
Le Poer Trench—*Clancarty, E.*
Leslie—*Rothes, E.*
Leslie Melville—*Leven and Melville, E.*
Lever—*Leverhulme, V.*
Lever—*L. of Manchester**
Leveson-Gower—*Granville, E.*
Lewis—*L. of Newnham**
Lewis—*Merthyr*
Liddell—*Ravensworth*
Lindesay-Bethune—*Lindsay, E.*
Lindsay—*Crawford, E.*
Lindsay—*L. of Birker*
Littleton—*Hatherton*
Llewelyn-Davies—*Llewelyn-Davies of Hastoe**
Lloyd—*L. of Hampstead**
Lloyd George—*Lloyd George of Dwyfor, E.*
Lloyd George—*Tenby, V.*
Lloyd-Mostyn—*Mostyn*
Loder—*Wakehurst*
Lopes—*Roborough*
Low—*Aldington*
Lowry-Corry—*Belmore, E.*
Lowther—*Lonsdale, E.*
Lowther—*Ullswater, V.*
Lubbock—*Avebury*
Lucas—*L. of Chilworth*
Lumley—*Scarbrough, E.*
Lumley-Savile—*Savile*
Lyon-Dalberg-Acton—*Acton*
Lysaght—*Lisle*
Lyttelton—*Chandos, V.*
Lyttelton—*Cobham, V.*
Lytton Cobbold—*Cobbold*
McAlpine—*M. of West Green**
Macaulay—*M. of Bragar**
McClintock-Bunbury—*Rathdonnell*
McColl—*M. of Dulwich**
Macdonald—*M. of Gwaenysgor*
Macdonald of Macdonald—*Macdonald*
McDonnell—*Antrim, E.*
McFadzean—*M. of Kelvinside**
Macfarlane—*M. of Bearsden**
McFarlane—*M. of Llandaff**
McGregor—*M. of Durris**
McIntosh—*M. of Haringey**
Mackay—*Inchcape, E.*

Mackay—*M. of Ardbrecknish**
Mackay—*M. of Clashfern**
Mackay—*Reay*
Mackay—*Tanlaw**
Mackenzie—*Cromartie, E.*
Mackie—*John-Mackie**
Mackie—*M. of Benshie**
Mackintosh—*M. of Halifax, V.*
McLaren—*Aberconway*
Maclay—*Muirshiel, V.*
MacLehose—*M. of Beoch**
Macleod—*M. of Borve**
Macmillan—*Stockton, E.*
Macpherson—*M. of Drumochter*
Macpherson—*Strathcarron*
Maffey—*Rugby*
Maitland—*Lauderdale, E.*
Makgill—*Oxfuird, V.*
Makins—*Sherfield*
Manners—*Rutland, D.*
Manningham-Buller—*Dilhorne, V.*
Mansfield—*Sandhurst*
Marks—*M. of Broughton*
Marquis—*Woolton, E.*
Marshall—*M. of Goring**
Marsham—*Romney, E.*
Martyn-Hemphill—*Hemphill*
Mason—*M. of Barnsley**
Maude—*Hawarden, V.*
Maude—*M. of Stratford-upon-Avon**
Maxwell—*de Ros*
Maxwell—*Farnham*
Meade—*Clanwilliam, E.*
Mercer Nairne Petty-Fitzmaurice—*Lansdowne, M.*
Millar—*Inchyra*
Milles-Lade—*Sondes, E.*
Milner—*M. of Leeds*
Mitchell-Thomson—*Selsdon*
Mitford—*Redesdale*
Monckton—*M. of Brenchley, V.*
Monckton-Arundell—*Galway, V.*
Mond—*Melchett*
Money-Coutts—*Latymer*
Montagu—*Manchester, D.*
Montagu—*Sandwich, E.*
Montagu—*Swaythling*
Montagu Douglas Scott—*Buccleuch, D.*
Montagu Stuart Wortley—*Wharncliffe, E.*
Montague—*Amwell*
Montgomerie—*Eglinton, E.*
Montgomery—*M. of Alamein, V.*
Moore—*Drogheda, E.*
Moore—*M. of Wolvercote**

Moore-Brabazon—*Brabazon of Tara*
Moreton—*Ducie, E.*
Morris—*Killanin*
Morris—*M. of Castle Morris**
Morris—*M. of Kenwood*
Morrison—*Dunrossil, V.*
Morrison—*Margadale*
Morton—*M. of Shuna**
Mosley—*Ravensdale*
Mountbatten—*Milford Haven, M.*
Muff—*Calverley*
Mulholland—*Dunleath*
Murray—*Atholl, D.*
Murray—*Dunmore, E.*
Murray—*Mansfield and Mansfield, E.*
Murray—*M. of Epping Forest**
Murray—*M. of Newhaven**
Murton—*M. of Lindisfarne**
Nall-Cain—*Brocket*
Napier—*Napier and Ettrick*
Napier—*N. of Magdala*
Needham—*Kilmorey, E.*
Nelson—*N. of Stafford*
Nevill—*Abergavenny, M.*
Neville—*Braybrooke*
Nicolson—*Carnock*
Nivison—*Glendyne*
Noel—*Gainsborough, E.*
Noel-Paton—*Ferrier**
North—*Guilford, E.*
Northcote—*Iddesleigh, E.*
Norton—*Grantley*
Norton—*Rathcreedan*
Nugent—*N. of Guildford**
Nugent—*Westmeath, E.*
O'Brien—*Inchiquin*
O'Brien—*O'Brien of Lothbury**
Ogilvie-Grant—*Seafield, E.*
Ogilvy—*Airlie, E.*
Oliver—*O. of Aylmerton**
O'Neill—*Rathcavan*
Orde-Powlett—*Bolton*
Ormsby-Gore—*Harlech*
Page—*Whaddon**
Paget—*Anglesey, M.*
Pakenham—*Longford, E.*
Pakington—*Hampton*
Palmer—*Lucas of Crudwell*
Palmer—*Selborne, E.*
Park—*P. of Monmouth**
Parker—*Macclesfield, E.*
Parker—*Morley, E.*
Parnell—*Congleton*
Parsons—*Rosse, E.*
Paulet—*Winchester, M.*
Peake—*Ingleby, V.*
Pearson—*Cowdray, V.*
Pearson—*P. of Rannoch**
Pease—*Daryngton*
Pease—*Gainford*
Pease—*Wardington*
Pelham—*Chichester, E.*
Pelham—*Yarborough, E.*
Pellew—*Exmouth, V.*

Penny—*Marchwood, V.*
Pepys—*Cottenham, E.*
Perceval—*Egmont, E.*
Percy—*Northumberland, D.*
Perry—*P. of Southwark**
Perry—*P. of Walton**
Pery—*Limerick, E.*
Peyton—*P. of Yeovil**
Philipps—*Milford*
Philipps—*St Davids, V.*
Phipps—*Normanby, M.*
Pitt—*P. of Hampstead**
Platt—*P. of Writtle**
Pleydell-Bouverie—*Radnor, E.*
Plummer—*P. of St Marylebone**
Plumptre—*Fitzwalter*
Plunkett—*Dunsany*
Plunkett—*Louth*
Pollock—*Hanworth, V.*
Pomeroy—*Harberton, V.*
Ponsonby—*Bessborough, E.*
Ponsonby—*de Mauley*
Ponsonby—*P. of Shulbrede*
Ponsonby—*Sysonby*
Porter—*P. of Luddenham**
Powys—*Lilford*
Pratt—*Camden, M.*
Preston—*Gormanston, V.*
Primrose—*Rosebery, E.*
Prittie—*Dunalley*
Ramsay—*Dalhousie, E.*
Ramsbotham—*Soulbury, V.*
Rawlinson—*R. of Ewell**
Rees-Williams—*Ogmore*
Renfrew—*R. of Kaimsthorn**
Rhys—*Dynevor*
Richards—*Milverton*
Richardson—*R. of Duntisbourne**
Rippon—*R. of Hexham**
Ritchie—*R. of Dundee*
Robens—*R. of Woldingham**
Roberts—*Clwyd*
Robertson—*R. of Oakridge*
Robertson—*Wharton*
Robinson—*Martonmere*
Robson—*R. of Kiddington**
Roche—*Fermoy*
Rodd—*Rennell*
Roll—*R. of Ipsden**
Roper-Curzon—*Teynham*
Rospigliosi—*Newburgh, E.*
Ross—*R. of Newport**
Rous—*Stradbroke, E.*
Rowley-Conwy—*Langford*

Royle—*Fanshawe of Richmond**
Runciman—*R. of Doxford, V.*
Russell—*Ampthill*
Russell—*Bedford, D.*
Russell—*de Clifford*
Russell—*R. of Liverpool*
Ryder—*Harrowby, E.*
Ryder—*R. of Eaton Hastings**
Ryder—*R. of Warsaw**
Sackville—*De La Warr, E.*
Sackville-West—*Sackville*
Sainsbury—*S. of Preston Candover**
St Aubyn—*St Levan*
St Clair—*Sinclair*
St Clair-Erskine—*Rosslyn, E.*
St John—*Bolingbroke and St John, V.*
St John—*St John of Blesto*
St John-Stevas—*St John of Fawsley**
St Leger—*Doneraile, V.*
Samuel—*Bearsted, V.*
Sanderson—*S. of Ayot*
Sanderson—*S. of Bowden**
Sandilands—*Torphichen*
Saumarez—*De Saumarez*
Savile—*Mexborough, E.*
Scarlett—*Abinger*
Schreiber—*Marlesford**
Sclater-Booth—*Basing*
Scott—*Eldon, E.*
Scott-Ellis—*Howard de Walden*
Scrymgeour—*Dundee, E.*
Seager—*Leighton of St Mellons*
Seely—*Mottistone*
Sefton—*S. of Garston**
Seymour—*Hertford, M.*
Seymour—*Somerset, D.*
Sharp—*S. of Grimsdyke**
Shaw—*Craigmyle*
Shirley—*Ferrers, E.*
Short—*Glenamara**
Siddeley—*Kenilworth*
Sidney—*De L'Isle, V.*
Sieff—*S. of Brimpton**
Simon—*S. of Glaisdale**
Simon—*S. of Wythenshawe*
Sinclair—*Caithness, E.*
Sinclair—*S. of Cleeve*
Sinclair—*Thurso, V.*
Skeffington—*Massereene, V.*
Smith—*Bicester*
Smith—*Hambleden, V.*
Smith—*Kirkhill**
Somerset—*Beaufort, D.*
Somerset—*Raglan*

Souter—*Audley*
Spencer—*Churchill, V.*
Spencer-Churchill—*Marlborough, D.*
Spring Rice—*Monteagle of Brandon*
Stanhope—*Harrington, E.*
Stanley—*Derby, E.*
Stanley—*Stanley of Alderley & Sheffield*
Stapleton-Cotton—*Combermere, V.*
Sterling—*S. of Plaistow**
Stevens—*S. of Ludgate**
Stewart—*Galloway, E.*
Stodart—*S. of Leaston**
Stoddart—*S. of Swindon**
Stonor—*Camoys*
Stopford—*Courtown, E.*
Stourton—*Mowbray*
Strachey—*O'Hagan*
Strutt—*Belper*
Strutt—*Rayleigh*
Stuart—*Castle Stewart, E.*
Stuart—*Moray, E.*
Stuart—*S. of Findhorn, V.*
Suenson-Taylor—*Grantchester*
Taylor—*Ingrow**
Taylor—*T. of Blackburn**
Taylor—*T. of Gryfe**
Taylor—*T. of Hadfield**
Taylour—*Headfort, M.*
Temple-Gore-Langton—*Temple of Stowe, E.*
Tennant—*Glenconner*
Thellusson—*Rendlesham*
Thesiger—*Chelmsford, V.*
Thomas—*T. of Gwydir**
Thomas—*T. of Swynnerton**
Thomas—*Tonypandy, V.*
Thomson—*T. of Fleet*
Thomson—*T. of Monifieth**
Thynne—*Bath, M.*
Tottenham—*Ely, M.*
Trefusis—*Clinton*
Trench—*Ashtown*
Trevor-Roper—*Dacre of Glanton**
Tufton—*Hothfield*
Turner—*Netherthorpe*
Turner—*T. of Camden**
Turnour—*Winterton, E.*
Turton—*Tranmire**
Tyrell-Kenyon—*Kenyon*
Vanden-Bempde-Johnstone—*Derwent*
Vane—*Barnard*
Vane—*Inglewood*
Vane-Tempest-Stewart—*Londonderry, M.*
Vanneck—*Huntingfield*
Vaughan—*Lisburne, E.*

Vaughan-Morgan—*Reigate**
Vereker—*Gort, V.*
Verney—*Willoughby de Broke*
Vernon—*Lyveden*
Vesey—*De Vesci, V.*
Villiers—*Clarendon, E.*
Vivian—*Swansea*
Wade—*W. of Chorlton**
Walker-Smith—*Broxbourne**
Wallace—*W. of Campsie**
Wallace—*W. of Coslany**
Wallop—*Portsmouth, E.*
Walton—*W. of Detchant**
Ward—*Bangor, V.*
Ward—*Dudley, E.*
Warrender—*Bruntisfield*
Watson—*Manton*
Wedderburn—*W. of Charlton**
Weir—*Inverforth*
Weld-Forester—*Forester*
Wellesley—*Cowley, E.*
Wellesley—*Wellington, D.*
Westenra—*Rossmore*
White—*Annaly*
White—*W. of Hull**
Whiteley—*Marchamley*
Whitfield—*Kenswood*
Williams—*Berners*
Williams—*W. of Elvel**
Williamson—*Forres*
Willoughby—*Middleton*
Wills—*Dulverton*
Wilson—*Moran*
Wilson—*Nunburnholme*
Wilson—*W. of Langside**
Wilson—*W. of Rievaulx**
Windsor—*Gloucester, D.*
Windsor—*Kent, D.*
Windsor-Clive—*Plymouth, E.*
Wingfield—*Powerscourt, V.*
Winn—*St Oswald*
Wodehouse—*Kimberley, E.*
Wolfson—*W. of Sunningdale**
Wood—*Halifax, E.*
Wood—*Holderness**
Woodhouse—*Terrington*
Wyatt—*W. of Weeford**
Wyndham—*Egremont & Leconfield*
Wyndham-Quin—*Dunraven, E.*
Wynn—*Newborough*
Yarde-Buller—*Churston*
Yerburgh—*Alvingham*
Yorke—*Hardwicke, E.*
Young—*Kennet*
Young—*Y. of Dartington**
Young—*Y. of Graffham**
Younger—*Y. of Leckie, V.*

C. Countess; *D.* Duke; *E.* Earl; *M.* Marquess; *V.* Viscount; * Life Peer.

ORDERS OF CHIVALRY

The Most Noble Order of the Garter (1348)—KG

Ribbon, Garter Blue. *Motto*, Honi soit qui mal y pense (*Shame on him who thinks evil of it*).
The number of Knights Companions is limited to 24.

SOVEREIGN OF THE ORDER—THE QUEEN

Lady of the Garter—HM QUEEN ELIZABETH THE QUEEN MOTHER, 1936.

Royal Knights

HRH The Duke of Edinburgh, 1947.
HRH The Prince of Wales, 1958.
HRH The Duke of Kent, 1985.

Extra Knights Companions and Ladies

Princess Juliana of the Netherlands, 1958.
HM The King of The Belgians, 1963.
HRH The Grand Duke of Luxembourg, 1972.
HM The Queen of Denmark, 1979.
HM The King of Sweden, 1983
HM The King of Spain, 1988.
HM The Queen of the Netherlands, 1989.

Knights and Lady Companions

Sir Cennydd Traherne, 1970.
The Earl Waldegrave, 1971.
The Earl of Longford, 1971.
The Lord Shackleton, 1974.
The Marquess of Abergavenny, 1974.
The Lord Wilson of Rievaulx, 1976.
The Duke of Grafton, 1976.
The Lord Elworthy, 1977.
The Lord Hunt, 1979.
Sir Paul Hasluck, 1979.
The Duke of Norfolk, 1983.
The Lord Lewin, 1983.
The Lord Richardson of Duntisbourne, 1983.
The Marquess of Normanby, 1985.
The Lord Carrington, 1985.

The Lord Callaghan of Cardiff, 1987.
The Viscount Leverhulme, 1988.
The Lord Hailsham of St Marylebone, 1988.
Lavinia, Duchess of Norfolk, 1990.
The Duke of Wellington, 1990.
Field Marshal Lord Bramall, 1990.

Prelate, The Bishop of Winchester.
Chancellor, The Marquess of Abergavenny, KG, OBE.
Register, The Dean of Windsor.
Garter King of Arms, Sir Colin Cole, KCVO, TD.
Gentleman Usher of the Black Rod, Air Chief Marshal Sir John Gingell, GBE, KCB.
Secretary, D. H. B. Chesshyre, LVO.

The Most Ancient and Most Noble Order of the Thistle (revived 1687)—KT

Ribbon, Green. *Motto*, Nemo me impune lacessit (*No one provokes me with impunity*).
The number of Knights is limited to 16.

SOVEREIGN OF THE ORDER—THE QUEEN

Lady of the Thistle—HM QUEEN ELIZABETH THE QUEEN MOTHER, 1937

Royal Knights

HRH The Duke of Edinburgh, 1952.
HRH The Prince of Wales (*Duke of Rothesay*), 1977.

Knights

The Lord Home of the Hirsel, 1962.
The Earl of Wemyss and March, 1966.
The Earl of Dalhousie, 1971.
The Lord Clydesmuir, 1972.
The Viscount Muirshiel, 1973.

Sir Donald Cameron of Lochiel, 1973.
The Earl of Selkirk, 1976.
The Lord McFadzean, 1976.
The Hon. Lord Cameron, 1978.
The Duke of Buccleuch and Queensberry, 1978.
The Earl of Elgin and Kincardine, 1981.
The Lord Thomson of Monifieth, 1981.
The Lord MacLehose of Beoch, 1983.

The Earl of Airlie, 1985.
Capt. Sir Iain Tennant, 1986.
The Viscount Whitelaw, 1990.

Chancellor, The Lord Home of the Hirsel.
Dean, The Very Rev. G. I. Macmillan.
Secretary and Lord Lyon King of Arms, Sir Malcolm Innes of Edingight, KCVO, WS.
Usher of the Green Rod, Rear-Admiral D.A. Dunbar-Nasmith, CB, DSC.

The Most Honourable Order of the Bath (1725)

GCB, Knight (or Dame) Grand Cross; KCB, Knight Commander; DCB, Dame Commander; CB, Companion

GCB Mil.   *Ribbon*, Crimson. *Motto*, Tria juncta in uno (*Three joined in one*).   GCB Civ.

Remodelled 1815, and enlarged many times since. The Order is divided into civil and military divisions. Women became eligible for the Order from January 1, 1971.

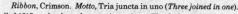

THE SOVEREIGN; *Great Master and First or Principal Knight Grand Cross*, HRH The Prince of Wales, KG, KT, GCB; *Dean of the Order*, The Dean of Westminster; *Bath King of Arms*, Air Chief Marshal Sir David Evans, GCB, CBE; *Registrar and Secretary*, Rear-Adm. D. E. Macey, CB; *Genealogist*, Dr C. Swan, CVO, PH.D.; *Gentleman Usher of the Scarlet Rod*, Air Vice-Marshal Sir Richard Peirse, KCVO, CB; *Deputy Secretary*, The Secretary of the Central Chancery of the Orders of Knighthood; *Chancery*, Central Chancery of the Orders of Knighthood, St James's Palace, SW1A 1BH.

The Order of Merit (1902)—OM

Ribbon, Blue and Crimson.

OM Mil.

This Order is designed as a special distinction for eminent men and women without conferring a knighthood upon them. The Order is limited in numbers to 24, with the addition of foreign honorary members. Membership is of two kinds, Military and Civil, the badge of the former having crossed swords, and the latter oak leaves. Membership is denoted by the suffix OM, which follows the first class of the Order of the Bath and precedes the letters designating membership of the inferior classes of the Bath and all classes of the lesser Orders of Knighthood.

OM Civ.

THE SOVEREIGN
HRH THE DUKE OF EDINBURGH (1968)

Dorothy Hodgkin, 1965.
The Lord Zuckerman, 1968.
Dame Veronica Wedgwood, 1969.
Sir Isaiah Berlin, 1971.
Sir George Edwards, 1971.
Sir Alan Hodgkin, 1973.
The Lord Todd, 1977.
The Lord Franks, 1977.
Gp. Capt. The Lord Cheshire, VC, 1981.

Sir Andrew Huxley, 1983.
Sir Sidney Nolan, 1983.
Sir Michael Tippett, 1983.
Rev. Prof. Owen Chadwick, KBE, 1983.
Frederick Sanger, 1986.
Air Commodore Sir Frank Whittle, 1986.
Sir Yehudi Menuhin, 1987.

Prof. Sir Ernst Gombrich, 1988.
Dr Max Perutz, 1988.
Dame Cicely Saunders, 1989.
The Lord Porter of Luddenham, 1990.
Rt. Hon. Margaret Thatcher, 1990.
Honorary Member, Mother Teresa, 1983.

Secretary and Registrar, Sir Edward Ford, KCB, KCVO, ERD.
Chancery, Central Chancery of the Orders of Knighthood, St James's Palace, SW1A 1BH.

The Most Exalted Order of the Star of India (1861)

GCSI, Knight Grand Commander; KCSI, Knight Commander; CSI, Companion

Ribbon, Light Blue, with White Edges. *Motto,* Heaven's Light our Guide.

THE SOVEREIGN; *Registrar,* The Secretary of the Central Chancery of the Orders of Knighthood. No conferments have been made since 1947.

The Most Distinguished Order of St Michael and St George (1818)

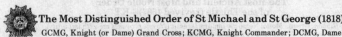

GCMG, Knight (or Dame) Grand Cross; KCMG, Knight Commander; DCMG, Dame Commander; CMG, Companion

GCMG

Ribbon, Saxon Blue, with Scarlet centre. *Motto,* Auspicium melioris aevi (Token of a better age)

KCMG

THE SOVEREIGN; *Grand Master,* HRH The Duke of Kent, KG, GCMG, GCVO, ADC; *Prelate,* The Rt. Rev. the Bishop of Coventry; *Chancellor,* The Lord Carrington, KG, GCMG, CH, MC, PC; *Secretary,* Sir David Gillmore, KCMG; *Registrar,* Sir John Graham, Bt., GCMG; *King of Arms,* Sir Oliver Wright, GCMG, GCVO, DSC; *Gentleman Usher of the Blue Rod,* Sir John Moreton, KCMG, KCVO, MC; *Dean,* The Dean of St Paul's; *Deputy Secretary,* The Secretary of the Central Chancery of the Orders of Knighthood; *Chancery,* Central Chancery of the Orders of Knighthood, St James's Palace, SW1A 1BH.

The Most Eminent Order of the Indian Empire (1868)

GCIE, Knight Grand Commander; KCIE, Knight Commander; CIE, Companion

Ribbon, Imperial Purple. *Motto,* Imperatricis auspiciis (*Under the auspices of the Empress*).

THE SOVEREIGN; *Registrar,* The Secretary of the Central Chancery of the Orders of Knighthood. No conferments have been made since 1947.

The Imperial Order of the Crown of India (for Ladies)—CI

Instituted 1877. *Badge,* the royal cipher in jewels within an oval, surmounted by an Heraldic Crown and attached to a bow of light blue watered ribbon, edged white. The honour does not confer any rank or title upon the recipient. No conferments have been made since 1947.

HM THE QUEEN, 1947.
HM Queen Elizabeth the Queen Mother, 1931.

HRH The Princess Margaret, Countess of Snowdon, 1947.

HRH The Princess Alice, Duchess of Gloucester, 1937.
HH Maharani of Travancore, 1929.

The Royal Victorian Order (1896)

GCVO, Knight or Dame Grand Cross; KCVO, Knight Commander; DCVO, Dame Commander; CVO, Commander; LVO, Lieutenant; MVO, Member

Ribbon, Blue, with Red and White Edges. *Motto,* Victoria.

GCVO

THE SOVEREIGN; *Grand Master,* HM Queen Elizabeth The Queen Mother; *Chancellor,* The Lord Chamberlain; *Secretary,* The Keeper of the Privy Purse; *Registrar,* The Secretary of the Central Chancery of the Orders of Knighthood; *Chaplain,* The Rev. J. Robson. *Hon. Genealogist,* D. H. B. Chesshyre, LVO.

KCVO

The Most Excellent Order of the British Empire (1917)

(The Order was divided into *Military* and *Civil* divisions in December 1918)

GBE, Knight or Dame Grand Cross; KBE. Knight Commander; DBE, Dame Commander;
CBE, Commander; OBE, Officer; MBE, Member

GBE   *Ribbon*, Rose pink edged with pearl grey with vertical pearl stripe in centre (Military   KBE
Division); without vertical pearl stripe (Civil Division). *Motto*, For God and the Empire.

THE SOVEREIGN: *Grand Master*, HRH The Prince Philip, Duke of Edinburgh, KG, KT, OM, GBE, PC, FRS; *Prelate*, The Bishop of London; *King of Arms*, Admiral Sir Anthony Morton, GBE, KCB; *Registrar*, The Secretary of the Central Chancery of the Orders of Knighthood; *Secretary*, Sir Robin Butler, KCB, CVO; *Dean*, The Dean of St Paul's; *Gentleman Usher of the Purple Rod*, Sir Robin Gillett, Bt., GBE, RD; *Chancery*, Central Chancery of the Orders of Knighthood, St James's Palace, SW1A 1BH.

Order of the Companions of Honour (1917)—CH

Ribbon, Carmine, with Gold Edges.

This Order consists of one Class only and carries with it no title. It ranks after the 1st Class of the Order of the British Empire, i.e. Knights and Dames Grand Cross (Military and Civil Divisions). The number of awards is limited to 65 (excluding honorary members) and the Order is open to both sexes.

Anthony, Rt. Hon. John, 1981.
Ashley, Rt. Hon. Jack, 1975.
Aylestone, The Lord, 1975.
Brenner, Sydney, 1986.
Carrington, The Lord, 1983.
Casson, Sir Hugh, 1984.
Cledwyn of Penrhos, The Lord, 1976.
de Valois, Dame Ninette, 1981.
Eccles, The Viscount, 1984.
Fraser, Rt. Hon. Malcolm, 1977.
Freud, Lucian, 1983.
Gielgud, Sir John, 1977.
Glenamara, The Lord, 1976.
Goodman, The Lord, 1972.
Gorton, Rt. Hon. Sir John, 1971.

Hailsham of St Marylebone, The Lord, 1974.
Hawking, Prof. Stephen, 1989.
von Hayek, Prof. Friedrich, 1984.
Healey, Rt. Hon. Denis, 1979.
Houghton of Sowerby, The Lord, 1967.
Jones, James, 1977.
Joseph, The Lord, 1986.
Lange, Rt. Hon. David, 1989.
Muirshiel, The Viscount, 1962.
Muldoon, Rt. Hon. Sir Robert, 1977.
Pasmore, Victor, 1980.
Perutz, Prof. Max, 1975.
Piper, John, 1972.
Popper, Prof. Sir Karl, 1982.
Powell, Anthony, 1987.

Powell, Sir Philip, 1984.
Runciman, Hon. Sir Steven, 1984.
Rylands, George, 1987.
Sanger, Frederick, 1981.
Smith, Arnold Cantwell, 1975.
Somare, Rt. Hon. Sir Michael, 1978.
Summerson, Sir John, 1986.
Talboys, Rt. Hon. Sir Brian, 1981.
Tebbit, Rt. Hon. Norman, 1987.
Thorneycroft, The Lord, 1979.
Tippett, Sir Michael, 1979.
Trudeau, Rt. Hon. Pierre, 1984.
Watkinson, The Viscount, 1962.
Whitelaw, The Viscount, 1974.
Honorary Members, Lee Kuan Yew, 1970; Dr Joseph Luns, 1971.

Secretary and Registrar, The Secretary of the Central Chancery of the Orders of Knighthood.

The Distinguished Service Order (1886)—DSO

Ribbon, Red, with Blue Edges.

Bestowed in recognition of especial services in action of commissioned officers in the Navy, Army and Royal Air Force and (since 1942) Mercantile Marine. The members are Companions only and rank immediately before the 4th Class of the Royal Victorian Order. A Bar may be awarded for any additional act of service.

The Imperial Service Order (1902)—ISO

Ribbon, Crimson, with Blue Centre.

Appointment of Companion of this Order shall be open to those members of the Civil Services whose eligibility shall be determined by the grade held by such persons. The Order consists of THE SOVEREIGN and Companions (not exclusively male) to a number not exceeding 1,900, of whom 1,300 may belong to the Home Civil Services and 600 to Overseas Civil Services. *Secretary*, Sir Robin Butler, KCB, CVO. *Registrar*, The Secretary of the Central Chancery of the Orders of Knighthood, St James's Palace, SW1A 1BH.

The Royal Victorian Chain (1902)

Founded by King Edward VII, in 1902. It confers no precedence on its holders.
HM THE QUEEN
HM QUEEN ELIZABETH THE QUEEN MOTHER, 1937.

Princess Juliana of the Netherlands, 1950.
HM The King of Thailand, 1960.
HIH The Crown Prince of Ethiopia, 1965.
HM The King of Jordan, 1966.
HM King Zahir Shah of Afghanistan, 1971.

HM The Queen of Denmark, 1974.
HM The King of Nepal, 1975.
HM The King of Sweden, 1975.
The Lord Coggan, 1980.
HM The Queen of the Netherlands, 1982.
General Antonio Eanes, 1985.
HM The King of Spain, 1986.

HM The King of Saudi Arabia, 1987.
HRH The Princess Margaret, Countess of Snowdon, 1990.
The Lord Runcie, 1991.

BARONETAGE AND KNIGHTAGE

Badge of Baronets
of the United Kingdom

Badge of Ulster

Badge of Baronets
of Nova Scotia

BARONETS

Style.—'Sir' before forename and surname, followed by 'Bt.'
Wife's style.—'Lady' followed by surname.
For forms of address, *see* page 219.

There are five different creations of Baronetcies: Baronets of England (creations dating from 1611); Baronets of Ireland (creations dating from 1611); Baronets of Scotland or Nova Scotia (creations dating from 1625); Baronets of Great Britain (creations after the Act of Union 1707 which combined the Kingdoms of England and Scotland); and Baronets of the United Kingdom (creations after the union of Great Britain and Ireland in 1801). The patent of creation limits the destination of a baronetcy, usually to male descendants of the first baronet, although special remainders allow the baronetcy to pass, if the male issue of sons fail, to the male issue of daughters of the first baronet. In the case of baronetcies of Scotland or Nova Scotia, a special remainder of 'heirs male and of tailzie' allows the baronetcy to descend to heirs general, including women. There are four existing Scottish baronets with such a remainder, one of whom, the holder of the Dunbar of Hempriggs creation, is a Baronetess.

The Official Roll of Baronets is kept at the Home Office by the Registrar of the Baronetage. Anyone who considers that he is entitled to be entered on the Roll may petition the Crown through the Home Secretary. Every person succeeding to a Baronetcy must exhibit proofs of succession to the Home Secretary. A person whose name is not entered on the Official Roll will not be addressed or mentioned by the title of Baronet in any official document, nor will he be accorded precedence as a Baronet.

KNIGHTS

Style.—'Sir' before forename and surname, followed by appropriate post-nominal initials if a Knight Grand Cross, Knight Grand Commander or Knight Commander.
Wife's style.—'Lady' followed by surname.
For forms of address, *see* page 219.

The prefix 'Sir' is not used by knights who are clerics of the Church of England, who do not receive the accolade. (Their wives are entitled to precedence as the wife of a knight but not to the style of 'Lady'.)

Orders of Knighthood

Knight Grand Cross, Knight Grand Commander, and Knight Commander are the higher classes of the Orders of Chivalry (*see* pp. 181–183). Honorary knighthoods of these Orders may be conferred on men who are citizens of countries of which the Queen is not head of state. As a rule, the prefix 'Sir' is not used by honorary knights.

Knights Bachelor

The Knights Bachelor do not constitute a Royal Order, but comprise the surviving representation of the ancient State Orders of Knighthood. The Register of Knights Bachelor, instituted by James I in the 17th century, lapsed, and in 1908 a voluntary association under the title of The Society of Knights (now The Imperial Society of Knights Bachelor by Royal command) was formed with the primary objects of continuing the various registers dating from 1257 and obtaining the uniform registration of every created Knight Bachelor. In 1926 a design for a badge to be worn by Knights Bachelor was approved and adopted, a miniature reproduction being shown above; in 1974 a neck badge and miniature were added.

The Officers of the Society are: *Knight Principal,* Sir Colin Cole, KCVO, TD; *Chairman of Council,* Sir David Napley; *Prelate,* Rt. Rev. and Rt. Hon. The Bishop of London; *Hon. Registrar,* Sir Kenneth Newman, GBE, QPM; *Hon. Treasurer,* The Lord Lane of Horsell; *Clerk to the Council,* R. M. Esden; *Deputy Clerk,* Lt.-Col. G. H. H. Coles; *Office,* 21 Old Buildings, Lincoln's Inn, WC2A 3UJ.

LIST OF BARONETS AND KNIGHTS
(Revised to August 31, 1991)
Peers are not included in this list

When an obelisk (†) precedes a name it indicates that, at the time of going to press, the Baronet concerned has not been registered on the Official Roll of the Baronetage. The date of creation of the Baronetcy is given in parenthesis ( ).
I.—Baronet of Ireland; NS—Baronet of Nova Scotia; S.—Baronet of Scotland.
If a Baronet or Knight has a double barrelled or hyphenated surname, he is listed under the final element of the name.
A full entry in italic type indicates that the recipient of a Knighthood died during the year in which the honour was conferred. The name is included for purposes of record.

Abal, Sir Tei, Kt., CBE.
Abbott, Sir Albert Francis, Kt., CBE.

Abdy, Sir Valentine Robert Duff, Bt. (1850).

Abel, Sir Seselo (Cecil) Charles Geoffrey, Kt., OBE.

Abeles, Sir (Emil Herbert) Peter, Kt.

Abell, Sir Anthony Foster, KCMG.

Abercromby, Sir Ian George, Bt. (s. 1636).

Abraham, Sir Edward Penley, Kt., CBE, FRS.

Acheson, *Prof.* Sir (Ernest) Donald, KBE.

Ackers, Sir James George, Kt.

Ackroyd, Sir John Robert Whyte, Bt. (1956).

Acland, Sir Antony Arthur, GCMG, GCVO.

Acland, *Maj.* Sir (Christopher) Guy (Dyke), Bt., MVO. (1890).

†Acland, Sir John Dyke, Bt. (1644).

Acland, *Maj.-Gen.* Sir John Hugh Bevil, KCB, CBE.

Acton, Sir Harold Mario Mitchell, Kt., CBE.

Adam, Sir Christopher Eric Forbes, Bt. (1917).

Adams, Sir Philip George Doyne, KCMG.

Adams, Sir William James, KCMG.

Adams-Schneider, *Rt. Hon.* Sir Lancelot Raymond, KCMG.

Adamson, Sir (William Owen) Campbell, Kt.

Addison, Sir William Wilkinson, Kt.

Ademola, *Rt. Hon.* Sir Adetokunbo Adegboyega, KBE.

Adrien, *Hon.* Sir Maurice Latour-, Kt.

Agnew, Sir Crispin Hamlyn, Bt. (s. 1629).

Agnew, Sir (John) Anthony Stuart, Bt. (1895).

Agnew, Sir (William) Godfrey, KCVO, CB.

Ah-Chuen, Sir Moi Lin Jean Etienne, Kt.

Aiken, *Air Chief Marshal* Sir John Alexander Carlisle, KCB.

Ainley, Sir (Alfred) John, Kt., MC.

Ainsworth, Sir (Thomas) David, Bt. (1916).

Aird, *Capt.* Sir Alastair Sturgis, KCVO.

Aird, Sir (George) John, Bt. (1901).

Airey, Sir Lawrence, KCB.

Airy, *Maj.-Gen.* Sir Christopher John, KCVO, CBE.

Aisher, Sir Owen Arthur, Kt.

Aitchison, Sir Charles Walter de Lancey, Bt. (1938).

Aitken, Sir Robert Stevenson, Kt., MD, D.Phil.

Akehurst, *Gen.* Sir John Bryan, KCB, CBE.

Akers-Jones, Sir David, KBE, CMG.

Albert, Sir Alexis François, CMG, VRD.

Albu, Sir George, Bt. (1912).

Aldington, Sir Geoffrey William, KBE, CMG.

Aldous, *Hon.* Sir William, Kt.

Alexander, Sir Alexander Sandor, Kt.

Alexander, Sir Charles Gundry, Bt. (1945).

Alexander, Sir Claud Hagart-, Bt. (1886).

Alexander, Sir Douglas, Bt. (1921).

Alexander, Sir (John) Lindsay, Kt.

Alexander, *Prof.* Sir Kenneth John Wilson, Kt.

Alexander, Sir Michael O'Donal Bjarne, KCMG.

Alexander, Sir Norman Stanley, Kt., CBE.

†Alexander, Sir Patrick Desmond William Cable-, Bt. (1809).

Allan, Sir Anthony James Allan Havelock-, Bt. (1858).

Allan, Sir Colin Hamilton, KCMG, OBE.

Allard, Sir Gordon Laidlaw, Kt.

Allen, *Rear-Adm.* Sir David, KCVO, CBE.

Allen, *Prof.* Sir Geoffrey, Kt., PH.D., FRS.

Allen, *Hon.* Sir Peter Austin Philip Jermyn, Kt.

Allen, Sir Peter Christopher, Kt.

Allen, Sir Richard Hugh Sedley, KCMG.

Allen, Sir William Guilford, Kt.

Allen, Sir (William) Kenneth (Gwynne), Kt.

Alleyne, Sir George Allanmoore Ogarren, Kt.

Alleyne, *Rev.* Sir John Olpherts Campbell, Bt. (1769).

Alliance, Sir David, Kt., CBE.

Allinson, Sir (Walter) Leonard, KCVO, CMG.

Alliott, *Hon.* Sir John Downes, Kt.

Alment, Sir (Edward) Anthony John, Kt.

Althaus, Sir Nigel Frederick, Kt.

Alun-Jones, Sir (John) Derek, Kt.

Ambo, *Rt. Rev.* George, KBE.

Amies, Sir (Edwin) Hardy, KCVO.

Amis, Sir Kingsley William, Kt., CBE.

Amory, Sir Ian Heathcoat, Bt. (1874).

Anderson, *Prof.* Sir (James) Norman (Dalrymple), Kt., OBE, QC, FBA.

Anderson, *Maj.-Gen.* Sir John Evelyn, KBE.

Anderson, Sir John Muir, Kt., CMG.

Anderson, Sir Kenneth, KBE, CB.

Anderson, *Hon.* Sir Kevin Victor, Kt.

Anderson, *Vice-Adm.* Sir Neil Dudley, KBE, CB.

Anderson, *Prof.* Sir (William) Ferguson, Kt., OBE.

Anderton, Sir (Cyril) James, Kt., CBE, QPM.

Andrew, Sir Robert John, KCB.

Andrews, Sir Derek Henry, KCB, CBE.

Andrews, *Hon.* Sir Dormer George, Kt.

Angus, Sir Michael Richardson, Kt.

Ansell, *Col.* Sir Michael Picton, Kt., CBE, DSO.

Anson, *Vice-Adm.* Sir Edward Rosebery, KCB.

Anson, Sir John, KCB.

Anson, *Rear-Adm.* Sir Peter, Bt., CB (1831).

Anstey, *Brig.* Sir John, Kt., CBE, TD.

Anstruther, Sir Ralph Hugo, Bt. KCVO, MC (s. 1694).

Antico, Sir Tristan Venus, Kt.

Antrobus, Sir Philip Coutts, Bt. (1815).

Appleyard, Sir Raymond Kenelm, KBE.

Arbuthnot, Sir John Sinclair-Wemyss, Bt., MBE, TD (1964).

Arbuthnot, Sir Keith Robert Charles, Bt. (1823).

Archdale, *Capt.* Sir Edward Folmer, Bt., DSC, RN (1928).

Archer, *Gen.* Sir (Arthur) John, KCB, OBE.

Archer, Sir Clyde Vernon Harcourt, Kt.

Arculus, Sir Ronald, KCMG, KCVO.

Armitage, *Air Chief Marshal* Sir Michael John, KCB, CBE.

Armstrong, Sir Andrew Clarence Francis, Bt., CMG (1841).

Armstrong, Sir Thomas Henry Wait, Kt., D.MUS..

Armytage, Sir John Martin, Bt. (1738).

Arnold, *Rt. Hon.* Sir John Lewis, Kt.

Arnold, Sir Thomas Richard, Kt., MP.

Arnott, Sir Alexander John Maxwell, Bt. (1896).

Arnott, *Prof.* Sir (William) Melville, Kt., TD, MD.

Arrindell, Sir Clement Athelston, GCMG, GCVO, QC.

Arrowsmith, Sir Edwin Porter, KCMG.

Arthur, *Lt.-Gen.* Sir (John) Norman Stewart, KCB.

Arthur, Sir Stephen John, Bt. (1841).

Ash, *Prof.* Sir Eric Albert, Kt., CBE, FRS.

Ashburnham, Sir Denny Reginald, Bt. (1661).

Ashe, Sir Derick Rosslyn, KCMG.

Ashley, Sir Bernard Albert, Kt.

Ashmore, *Admiral of the Fleet* Sir Edward Beckwith, GCB, DSC.

Ashmore, *Vice-Adm.* Sir Peter William Beckwith, KCB, KCVO, DSC.

Ashworth, Sir Herbert, Kt.

Aske, *Rev.* Sir Conan, Bt. (1922).

Askew, Sir Bryan, Kt.

Astley, Sir Francis Jacob Dugdale, Bt. (1821).

Aston, Sir Harold George, Kt., CBE.

Aston, *Hon.* Sir William John, KCMG.

Astor, *Hon.* Sir John Jacob, Kt., MBE.

Astwood, *Hon.* Sir James Rufus, Kt.

Astwood, *Lt.-Col.* Sir Jeffrey Carlton, Kt., CBE, ED.

Atcherley, Sir Harold Winter, Kt.

Atiyah, Sir Michael Francis, Kt., PH.D., FRS.

Atkinson, *Air Marshal* Sir David William, KBE.

Atkinson, Sir Frederick John, KCB.

Atkinson, Sir John Alexander, KCB, DFC.

Atkinson, Sir Robert, Kt., DSC.

Attenborough, Sir David Frederick, Kt., CVO, CBE, FRS.

Attenborough, Sir Richard Samuel, Kt., CBE.

Atwell, Sir John William, Kt., CBE, FRSE.

Atwill, Sir (Milton) John (Napier), Kt.

Audland, Sir Christopher John, KCMG.

Audley, Sir George Bernard, Kt.

Auld, *Hon.* Sir Robin Ernest, Kt.

Austin, Sir Michael Trescawen, Bt. (1894).

Austin, *Vice-Adm.* Sir Peter Murray, KCB.

Aykroyd, Sir Cecil William, Bt. (1929).

Aykroyd, Sir William Miles, Bt., MC (1920).

Aylmer, Sir Richard John, Bt. (I. 1622).

Backhouse, Sir Jonathan Roger, Bt. (1901).

Bacon, Sir Nicholas Hickman Ponsonby, Bt. *Premier Baronet of England* (1611 and 1627).

Bacon, Sir Sidney Charles, Kt., CB.

Baddeley, Sir John Wolsey Beresford, Bt. (1922).

Baddiley, *Prof.* Sir James, Kt., PH.D., D.SC., FRS, FRSE.

Badenoch, Sir John, Kt., DM, FRCP.

Badger, Sir Geoffrey Malcolm, Kt.

Bagge, Sir (John) Jeremy Picton, Bt. (1867).

Bagnall, *Field Marshal* Sir Nigel Thomas, GCB, CVO, MC.

Bailey, Sir Alan Marshall, KCB.

Bailey, Sir Brian Harry, Kt., OBE.

Bailey, Sir Derrick Thomas Louis, Bt., DFC (1919).

Bailey, *Prof.* Sir Harold Walter, Kt., D.Phil., FBA.

Bailey, Sir John Bilsland, KCB.

Bailey, Sir Richard John, Kt., CBE.

Bailey, Sir Stanley Ernest, Kt., CBE, QPM.

Baillie, Sir Gawaine George Hope, Bt. (1823).

Baines, *Prof.* Sir George Grenfell-, Kt., OBE.

Baird, Sir David Charles, Bt. (1809).

Baird, *Lt.-Gen.* Sir James Parlane, KBE, MD.

Baird, Sir James Richard Gardiner, Bt., MC (s. 1695).

Baird, *Vice-Adm.* Sir Thomas Henry Eustace, KCB.

Bairsto, *Air Marshal* Sir Peter Edward, KBE, CB.

Baker, Sir (Allan) Ivor, Kt., CBE.

Baker, Sir Robert George Humphrey Sherston-, Bt. (1796).

Baker, *Hon.* Sir (Thomas) Scott (Gillespie), Kt.

Balcombe, *Rt. Hon.* Sir (Alfred) John, Kt.

Balderstone, Sir James Schofield, Kt.

Baldwin, Sir Peter Robert, KCB.

Balfour, *Gen.* Sir (Robert George) Victor FitzGeorge-, KCB, CBE, DSO, MC.

Ball, *Air Marshal* Sir Alfred Henry Wynne, KCB, DSO, DFC.

Ball, Sir Charles Irwin, Bt. (1911).

Ball, Sir Christopher John Elinger, Kt.

Ball, *Prof.* Sir Robert James, Kt., ph.D.

Balmer, Sir Joseph Reginald, Kt.

Bamford, Sir Anthony Paul, Kt.

Bannerman, Sir David Gordon, OBE, Bt. (s. 1682).

Bannister, Sir Roger Gilbert, Kt., CBE, DM, FRCP.

Barber, Sir Derek Coates, Kt.

Barber, *Hon.* Sir (Edward Hamilton) Esler, Kt.

Barber, Sir William Francis, Bt., TD (1960).

Barbour, *Very Rev.* Sir Robert Alexander Stewart, KCVO, MC.

Barclay, Sir Colville Herbert Sanford, Bt. (s. 1668).

Barclay, Sir Roderick Edward, GCVO, KCMG.

Barford, Sir Leonard, Kt.

Baring, *Hon.* Sir John Francis Harcourt, Kt., KCVO.

Barker, Sir Alwyn Bowman, Kt., CMG.

Barker, Sir Colin, Kt.

Barker, Sir Harry Heaton, Kt., KBE.

Barker, Sir William, KCMG, OBE.

Barlow, Sir Christopher Hilaro, Bt. (1803).

Barlow, Sir (George) William, Kt.

Barlow, Sir John Kemp, Bt. (1907).

Barlow, Sir Thomas Erasmus, Bt., DSC (1902).

Barnard, Sir (Arthur) Thomas, Kt., CB, OBE.

Barnard, *Capt.* Sir George Edward, Kt.

Barnard, Sir Joseph Brian, Kt.

Barnes, Sir Denis Charles, KCB.

Barnes, Sir (Ernest) John (Ward), KCMG, MBE.

Barnes, Sir James George, Kt., MBE.

Barnes, Sir Kenneth, KCB.

Barnett, *Air Chief Marshal* Sir Denis Hensley Fulton, GCB, CBE, DFC.

Barnett, Sir Oliver Charles, Kt., CBE, QC.

Barnewall, Sir Reginald Robert, Bt. (I. 1623).

Barraclough, *Air Chief Marshal* Sir John, KCB, CBE, DFC, AFC.

Barraclough, Sir Kenneth James Priestley, Kt., CBE, TD.

Barran, Sir David Haven, Kt.

Barran, Sir John Napoleon Ruthven, Bt. (1895).

Barratt, Sir Lawrence Arthur, Kt.

Barratt, Sir Richard Stanley, Kt., CBE, QPM.

Barrett, *Lt.-Gen.* Sir David William Scott-, KBE, MC.

Barrett, *Lt.-Col.* Sir Dennis Charles Titchener, Kt., TD.

Barrett, Sir Stephen Jeremy, KCMG.

Barrington, Sir Alexander (Fitzwilliam Croker), Bt. (1831).

Barrington, Sir Nicholas John, KCMG, CVO.

Barron, Sir Donald James, Kt.

Barrow, *Capt.* Sir Richard John Uniacke, Bt. (1835).

Barrowclough, Sir Anthony Richard, Kt., QC.

Barry, Sir (Lawrence) Edward (Anthony Tress), Bt. (1899).

Barry, Sir (Philip) Stuart Milner-, KCVO, CB, OBE.

Bartlett, Sir John Hardington, Bt. (1913).

Barton, *Prof.* Sir Derek Harold Richard, Kt., FRS, FRSE.

Barttelot, *Lt.-Col.* Sir Brian Walter de Stopham, Bt., OBE (1875).

Barwick, *Rt. Hon.* Sir Garfield Edward John, GCMG.

Basten, Sir Henry Bolton, Kt., CMG.

Batchelor, Sir Ivor Ralph Campbell, Kt., CBE.

Bate, Sir David Lindsay, KBE.

Bate, Sir (Walter) Edwin, Kt., OBE.

Bateman, Sir Cecil Joseph, KBE.

Bateman, Sir Geoffrey Hirst, Kt., FRCS.

Bateman, Sir Ralph Melton, KBE.

Bates, *Prof.* Sir David Robert, Kt., D.SC., FRS.

Bates, *Maj.-Gen.* Sir (Edward) John (Hunter), KBE, CB, MC.

Bates, Sir Geoffrey Voltelin, Bt., MC (1880).

Bates, Sir John David, Kt., CBE, VRD.

Bates, Sir (John) Dawson, Bt., MC (1937).

Batho, Sir Peter Ghislain, Bt. (1928).

Bathurst, *Adm.* Sir (David) Benjamin, GCB.

Bathurst, Sir Frederick Peter Methuen Hervey-, Bt. (1818).

Bathurst, Sir Maurice Edward, Kt., CMG, CBE, QC.

Batten, Sir John Charles, KCVO.

Battishill, Sir Anthony Michael William, KCB.

Batty, Sir William Bradshaw, Kt., TD.

Baxendell, Sir Peter Brian, Kt., CBE.

Bayliss, *Prof.* Sir Noel Stanley, Kt., CBE.

Bayliss, Sir Richard Ian Samuel, KCVO, MD, FRCP.

Bayly, *Vice-Adm.* Sir Patrick Uniacke, KBE, CB, DSC.

Baynes, Sir John Christopher Malcolm, Bt. (1801).

Bazley, Sir Thomas Stafford, Bt. (1869).

Beach, *Gen.* Sir (William Gerald) Hugh, GBE, KCB, MC.

Beale, Sir William Francis, Kt., OBE.

Beament, Sir James William Longman, Kt., SC.D., FRS.

Beattie, *Hon.* Sir Alexander Craig, Kt.

Beattie, *Hon.* Sir David Stuart, GCMG, GCVO.

Beauchamp, Sir Christopher Radstock Proctor-, Bt. (1745).

Beaumont, Sir George (Howland Francis), Bt. (1661).

Beaumont, Sir Richard Ashton, KCMG, OBE.

Beavis, *Air Chief Marshal* Sir Michael Gordon, KCB, CBE, AFC.

Becher, Sir William Fane Wrixon, Bt., MC (1831).

Beck, Sir Edgar Charles, Kt., CBE.

Beck, Sir Edgar Philip, Kt.

Beckett, *Capt.* Sir (Martyn) Gervase, Bt., MC (1921).

Beckett, Sir Terence Norman, Kt., KBE.

Bedbrook, Sir George Montario, Kt., OBE.

Bedingfeld, *Capt.* Sir Edmund George Felix Paston-, Bt. (1661).

Beecham, Sir John Stratford Roland, Bt. (1914).

Beeley, Sir Harold, KCMG, CBE.

Beetham, *Marshal of the Royal Air Force* Sir Michael James, GCB, CBE, DFC, AFC.

Beevor, Sir Thomas Agnew, Bt. (1784).

Begg, Sir Neil Colquhoun, KBE.

Begg, *Admiral of the Fleet* Sir Varyl Cargill, GCB, DSO, DSC.

Beit, Sir Alfred Lane, Bt. (1924).

Beith, Sir John Greville Stanley, KCMG.

Beldam, *Rt. Hon.* Sir (Alexander) Roy (Asplan), Kt.

Belich, Sir James, Kt.

Bell, Sir Gawain Westray, KCMG, CBE.

Bell, Sir (George) Raymond, KCMG, CB.

Bell, Sir John Lowthian, Bt. (1885).

Bell, Sir Timothy John Leigh, Kt.

Bell, Sir (William) Ewart, KCB.

Bell, Sir William Hollin Dayrell Morrison-, Bt. (1905).

Bellew, Hon. Sir George Rothe, KCB, KCVO, FSA.

Bellew, Sir Henry Charles Gratton-, Bt. (1838).

Bellinger, Sir Robert Ian, GBE.

Bellingham, Sir Noel Peter Roger, Bt. (1796).

Bengough, *Col.* Sir Piers, KCVO, OBE.

Benn, Sir James Jonathan, Bt. (1914).

Benn, *Capt.* Sir (Patrick Ion) Hamilton, Bt. (1920).

Bennett, Sir Charles Moihi Te Arawaka, Kt., DSO.

Bennett, *Air Vice-Marshal* Sir Erik Peter, KBE, CB.

Bennett, *Rt. Hon.* Sir Frederic Mackarness, Kt.

Bennett, Sir Hubert, Kt.

Bennett, Sir John Mokonuiarangi, Kt.

Bennett, *Gen.* Sir Phillip Harvey, KBE, DSO.

Bennett, Sir Reginald Frederick Brittain, Kt., VRD.

Bennett, Sir Ronald Wilfrid Murdoch, Bt. (1929).

Benson, Sir Christopher John, Kt.

Benson, Sir (William) Jeffrey, Kt.

Benthall, Sir (Arthur) Paul, KBE.

Bentley, Sir William, KCMG.

Beresford, Sir Alexander Paul, Kt.

Berger, *Vice-Adm.* Sir Peter Egerton Capel, KCB, MVO, DSC.

Berghuser, *Hon.* Sir Eric, Kt., MBE.

Berlin, Sir Isaiah, Kt., OM, CBE.

Bernard, Sir Dallas Edmund, Bt. (1954).

Berney, Sir Julian Reedham Stuart, Bt. (1620).

Berrill, Sir Kenneth Ernest, GBE, KCB.

Berriman, Sir David, Kt.

Berthon, *Vice-Adm.* Sir Stephen Ferrier, KCB.

Berthoud, Sir Martin Seymour, KCVO, CMG.

Best, Sir Richard Radford, KCVO, CBE.

Bethune, Sir Alexander Maitland Sharp, Bt. (s. 1683).

Bethune, *Hon.* Sir (Walter) Angus, Kt.

Bevan, Sir Martyn Evan Evans, Bt. (1958).

Bevan, Sir Timothy Hugh, Kt.

Beverley, *Lt.-Gen.* Sir Henry York La Roche, KCB, OBE, RM.

Beynon, *Prof.* Sir (William John) Granville, Kt., CBE, PH.D., D.SC., FRS.

Bibby, Sir Derek James, Bt., MC (1959).

Bickersteth, *Rt. Rev.* John Monier, KCVO.

Biddulph, Sir Ian D'Olier, Bt. (1664).

Bide, Sir Austin Ernest, Kt.

Bidwell, Sir Hugh Charles Philip, GBE.

Biggs, Sir Norman Paris, Kt.

Billière, *Gen.* Sir Peter Edgar de la Cour de la, KCB, KBE, DSO, MC.

Bing, Sir Rudolf Franz Josef, KBE.

Bingham, *Hon.* Sir Eardley Max, Kt., QC.

Bingham, *Rt. Hon.* Sir Thomas Henry, Kt.

Bird, *Col.* Sir Richard Dawnay Martin-, Kt., CBE, TD.

Bird, Sir Richard Geoffrey Chapman, Bt. (1922).

Birkin, Sir John Christian William, Bt. (1905).

Birkin, Sir (John) Derek, Kt., TD.

Birkmyre, Sir Henry, Bt. (1921).

Birley, Sir Derek Sydney, Kt.

Birtwistle, Sir Harrison, Kt.

Bishop, Sir Frederick Arthur, Kt., CB, CVO.

Bishop, Sir George Sidney, Kt., CB, OBE.

Bishop, Sir Michael David, Kt., CBE.

Bisson, *Rt Hon.* Sir Gordon Ellis, Kt.

Black, Sir Cyril Wilson, Kt.

Black, *Prof.* Sir Douglas Andrew Kilgour, Kt., MD, FRCP.

Black, Sir James Whyte, Kt., FRCP, FRS.

Black, *Adm.* Sir (John) Jeremy, GCB, DSO, MBE.

Black, Sir Robert Brown, GCMG, OBE.

Black, Sir Robert David, Bt. (1922).

Blacker, *Gen.* Sir Cecil Hugh, GCB, OBE, MC.

Blackett, Sir George William, Bt. (1673).

Blackman, Sir Frank Milton, KCVO, OBE.

Blackwell, Sir Basil Davenport, Kt.

Blair, Sir Alastair Campbell, KCVO, TD, WS..

Blair, *Lt.-Gen.* Sir Chandos, KCVO, OBE, MC.

Blair, Sir Edward Thomas Hunter, Bt. (1786).

Blake, Sir Alfred Lapthorn, KCVO, MC.

Blake, Sir Francis Michael, Bt. (1907).

Blake, Sir (Thomas) Richard (Valentine), Bt. (I. 1622).

Blaker, Sir John, Bt. (1919).

Blaker, *Rt. Hon.* Sir Peter Allan Renshaw, KCMG, MP.

Blakiston, Sir Ferguson Arthur James, Bt. (1763).

Bland, Sir Henry Armand, Kt., CBE.

Bland, *Lt.-Col.* Sir Simon Claud Michael, KCVO.

Blelloch, Sir John Nial Henderson, KCB.

Blennerhassett, Sir (Marmaduke) Adrian Francis William, Bt. (1809).

Blewitt, *Maj.* Sir Shane Gabriel Basil, KCVO.

Blofield, *Hon.* Sir John Christopher Calthorpe, Kt.

Blois, Sir Charles Nicholas Gervase, Bt. (1686).

Blomefield, Sir Thomas Charles Peregrine, Bt. (1807).

Bloomfield, *Hon.* Sir John Stoughton, Kt., QC.

Bloomfield, Sir Kenneth Percy, KCB.

Blosse, *Capt.* Sir Richard Hely Lynch-, Bt. (1622).

Blount, Sir Walter Edward Alpin, Bt., DSC (1642).

Blundell, Sir Michael, KBE.

Blunden, Sir George, Kt.

Blunden, Sir Philip Overington, Bt. (I. 1766).

Blunt, Sir David Richard Reginald Harvey, Bt. (1720).

Blyth, Sir James, Kt.

Boardman, *Prof.* Sir John, Kt., FSA, FBA.

Boardman, Sir Kenneth Ormrod, Kt.

Bodilly, *Hon.* Sir Jocelyn, Kt., VRD.

Bodmer, Sir Walter Fred, Kt., PH.D., FRS.

Body, Sir Richard Bernard Frank Stewart, Kt., MP.

Boevey, Sir Thomas Michael Blake Crawley-, Bt. (1784).

Boileau, Sir Guy (Francis), Bt. (1838).

Boles, Sir Jeremy John Fortescue, Bt. (1922).

Boles, Sir John Dennis, Kt., MBE.

Bolland, Sir Edwin, KCMG.

Bollers, *Hon.* Sir Harold Brodie Smith, Kt.

Bolton, Sir Frederic Bernard, Kt., MC.

Bonallack, Sir Richard Frank, Kt., CBE.

Bonar, Sir Herbert Vernon, Kt., CBE.

Bond, Sir Kenneth Raymond Boyden, Kt.

Bondi, *Prof.* Sir Hermann, KCB, FRS.

Bonham, *Maj.* Sir Antony Lionel Thomas, Bt. (1852).

Bonsall, Sir Arthur Wilfred, KCMG, CBE.

Bonsor, Sir Nicholas Cosmo, Bt., MP (1925).

Boolell, Sir Satcam, Kt.

Boon, Sir Peter Coleman, Kt.

Boord, Sir Nicolas John Charles, Bt. (1896).

Boorman, *Lt.-Gen.* Sir Derek, KCB.

Booth, Sir Angus Josslyn Gore-, Bt. (t. 1760).

Booth, Sir Christopher Charles, Kt., MD, FRCP.

Booth, Sir Douglas Allen, Bt. (1916).

Booth, Sir Gordon, KCMG, CVO.

Booth, Sir Robert Camm, Kt., CBE, TD.

Boothby, Sir Brooke Charles, Bt. (1660).

Boreel, Sir Francis David, Bt. (1645).

Boreham, Sir (Arthur) John, KCB.

Boreham, *Hon.* Sir Leslie Kenneth Edward, Kt.

Bornu, The Waziri of, KCMG, CBE.

Borrie, Sir Gordon Johnson, Kt., QC.

Borthwick, Sir John Thomas, Bt. MBE (1908).

Bossom, *Hon.* Sir Clive, Bt. (1953).

Boswall, Sir (Thomas) Alford Houstoun-, Bt. (1836).

Boswell, *Lt.-Gen.* Sir Alexander Crawford Simpson, KCB, CBE.

Bosworth, Sir Neville Bruce Alfred, Kt., CBE.

Bottomley, Sir James Reginald Alfred, KCMG.

Boughey, Sir John George Fletcher, Bt. (1798).

Boulton, Sir Clifford John, KCB.

Boulton, Sir (Harold Hugh) Christian, Bt. (1905).

Boulton, Sir William Whytehead, Bt., CBE, TD (1944).

Bourn, Sir John Bryant, KCB.

Bourne, Sir (John) Wilfrid, KCB.

Bovell, *Hon.* Sir (William) Stewart, Kt.

Bowater, Sir Euan David Vansittart, Bt. (1939).

Bowater, Sir (John) Vansittart, Bt. (1914).

Bowden, Sir Frank, Bt. (1915).

Bowen, Sir Geoffrey Fraser, Kt.

Bowen, Sir Mark Edward Mortimer, Bt. (1921).

Bowen, *Hon.* Sir Nigel Hubert, KBE.

Bowlby, Sir Anthony Hugh Mostyn, Bt. (1923).

Bowman, Sir George, Bt. (1961).

Bowman, Sir Jeffery Haverstock, Kt.

Bowman, Sir John Paget, Bt. (1884).

Bowmar, Sir Charles Erskine, Kt.

Bowness, Sir Alan, Kt., CBE.

Bowness, Sir Peter Spencer, Kt., CBE.

Boxer, *Air Vice-Marshal* Sir Alan Hunter Cachemaille, KCVO, CB, DSO, DFC.

Boyce, Sir Robert Charles Leslie, Bt. (1952).

Boyd, Sir Alexander Walter, Bt. (1916).

Boyd, *Prof.* Sir Robert Lewis Fullarton, Kt., CBE, D.SC., FRS.

Boyes, Sir Brian Gerald Barratt-, KBE.

Boyle, *Marshal of the Royal Air Force* Sir Dermot Alexander, GCB, KCVO, KBE, AFC.

Boyle, Sir Stephen Gurney, Bt. (1904).

Boyne, Sir Henry Brian, Kt., CBE.

Boynton, Sir John Keyworth, Kt., MC.

Boyson, *Rt. Hon.* Sir Rhodes, Kt., MP.

Brabham, Sir John Arthur, Kt., OBE.

Bradbeer, Sir John Derek Richardson, Kt., OBE, TD.

Bradbury, *Surgeon Vice-Adm.* Sir Eric Blackburn, KBE, CB.

Bradford, Sir Edward Alexander Slade, Bt. (1902).

Bradlaw, *Prof.* Sir Robert Vivian, Kt., CBE.

Bradley, Sir Burton Gyrth Burton-, Kt., OBE.

Bradman, Sir Donald George, Kt.

Bradshaw, Sir Kenneth Anthony, KCB.

Bradshaw, *Lt.-Gen.* Sir Richard Phillip, KBE.

Brain, Sir (Henry) Norman, KBE, CMG.

Braine, *Rt. Hon.* Sir Bernard Richard, Kt., MP.

Braithwaite, Sir (Joseph) Franklin Madders, Kt.

Braithwaite, Sir Rodric Quentin, KCMG.

Bramall, Sir (Ernest) Ashley, Kt.

Bramley, *Prof.* Sir Paul Anthony, Kt.

Branch, Sir William Allan Patrick, Kt.

Brancker, Sir (John Eustace) Theodore, Kt., QC.

Branigan, Sir Patrick Francis, Kt., QC.

Bray, Sir Theodor Charles, Kt., CBE.

Braynen, Sir Alvin Rudolph, Kt.

Bremridge, Sir John Henry, KBE.

Brennan, *Hon.* Sir (Francis) Gerard, KBE.

Brett, Sir Charles Edward Bainbridge, Kt., CBE.

Brickwood, Sir Basil Greame, Bt. (1927).

Bridges, *Hon.* Sir Phillip Rodney, Kt., CMG.

Brierley, Sir Ronald Alfred, Kt.

Brierley, Sir Zachry, Kt., CBE.

Briggs, *Hon.* Sir Geoffrey Gould, Kt.

Bright, Sir Keith, Kt.

Brinckman, Sir Theodore George Roderick, Bt. (1831).

Brisco, Sir Donald Gilfrid, Bt. (1782).

Briscoe, Sir John Leigh Charlton, Bt., DFC (1910).

Brise, Sir John Archibald Ruggles-, Bt., CB, OBE, TD (1935).

Bristow, *Hon.* Sir Peter Henry Rowley, Kt.

Brittan, *Rt. Hon.* Sir Leon, Kt., QC.

Britton, Sir Edward Louis, Kt., CBE.

Broackes, Sir Nigel, Kt.

Broadbent, Sir Ewen, KCB, CMG.

Broadbent, Sir George Walter, Bt. (1893).

Broadhurst, *Air Chief Marshal* Sir Harry, GCB, KBE, DSO, DFC, AFC.

Brockhoff, Sir Jack Stuart, Kt.

Brocklebank, Sir Aubrey Thomas, Bt. (1885).

Brockman, *Vice-Adm.* Sir Ronald Vernon, KCB, CVO, CSI, CIE, CBE.

Brockman, *Hon.* Sir Thomas Charles Drake-, Kt., DFC.

Brodie, Sir Benjamin David Ross, Bt. (1834).

Brogan, *Lt.-Gen.* Sir Mervyn Francis, KBE, CB.

Bromhead, Sir John Desmond Gonville, Bt. (1806).

Bromley, Sir Rupert Charles, Bt. (1757).

Bromley, Sir Thomas Eardley, KCMG.

Brook, Sir Robin, Kt., CMG, OBE.

†Brooke, Sir Alistair Weston, Bt. (1919).

Brooke, Sir Francis George Windham, Bt. (1903).

Brooke, *Hon.* Sir Henry, Kt.

Brooke, Sir Richard Neville, Bt. (1662).

Brookes, Sir Wilfred Deakin, Kt., CBE, DSO.

Brooksbank, Sir (Edward) Nicholas, Bt. (1919).

Broom, *Air Marshal* Sir Ivor Gordon, KCB, CBE, DSO, DFC, AFC.

Broughton, *Air Marshal* Sir Charles, KBE, CB.

Broughton, Sir Evelyn Delves, Bt. (1661).

Broun, Sir Lionel John Law, Bt. (s. 1686).

Brown, Sir Allen Stanley, Kt., CBE.

Brown, Sir (Arthur James) Stephen, KBE.

Brown, *Adm.* Sir Brian Thomas, KCB, CBE.

Brown, *Lt.-Col.* Sir Charles Frederick Richmond, Bt. (1863).

Brown, Sir (Cyril) Maxwell Palmer, KCB, CMG.

Brown, Sir David, Kt.

Brown, *Vice-Adm.* Sir David Worthington, KCB.

Brown, Sir Derrick Holden-, Kt.

Brown, Sir Douglas Denison, Kt.

Brown, *Hon.* Sir Douglas Dunlop, Kt.

Brown, *Prof.* Sir (Ernest) Henry Phelps, Kt., MBE, FBA.

Brown, Sir (Frederick Herbert) Stanley, Kt., CBE.

Brown, *Prof.* Sir (George) Malcolm, Kt., FRS.

Brown, Sir George Noel, Kt.

Brown, Sir John Douglas Keith, Kt.

Brown, Sir John Gilbert Newton, Kt., CBE.

Brown, Sir Mervyn, KCMG, OBE.

Brown, *Hon.* Sir Ralph Kilner, Kt., OBE, TD.

Brown, Sir Raymond Frederick, Kt., OBE.

Brown, Sir Robert Crichton-, KCMG, CBE, TD.

Brown, *Hon.* Sir Simon Denis, Kt.

Brown, *Rt. Hon.* Sir Stephen, Kt.

Brown, Sir Thomas, Kt.

Brown, Sir William Brian Piggott-, Bt. (1903).

Browne, *Rt. Hon.* Sir Patrick Reginald Evelyn, Kt., OBE, TD.

Brownrigg, Sir Nicholas (Gawen), Bt. (1816).

Bruce, Sir Arthur Atkinson, KBE, MC.

Bruce, Sir (Francis) Michael Ian, Bt. (s. 1628).

Bruce, Sir Hervey James Hugh, Bt. (1804).

Bruce, *Rt. Hon.* Sir (James) Roualeyn Hovell-Thurlow-Cumming-, Kt.

Brunner, Sir John Henry Kilian, Bt. (1895).

Brunton, Sir (Edward Francis) Lauder, Bt. (1908).

Brunton, Sir Gordon Charles, Kt.

Bryan, Sir Arthur, Kt.

Bryan, Sir Paul Elmore Oliver, Kt., DSO, MC.

Bryce, *Hon.* Sir (William) Gordon, Kt., CBE.

Bryson, *Vice-Adm.* Sir Lindsay Sutherland, KCB.

Buchan, Sir John, Kt., CMG.

Buchanan, Sir Andrew George, Bt. (1878).

Buchanan, Sir Charles Alexander James Leith-, Bt. (1775).

Buchanan, *Prof.* Sir Colin Douglas, Kt., CBE.

Buchanan, *Vice-Adm.* Sir Peter William, KBE.

Buchanan, Sir Robert Wilson (Robin), Kt.

Buchanan, Sir Ronald Dennis, Kt., MBE.

Buck, Sir (Philip) Antony (Fyson), Kt., QC, MP.

Buckley, *Rt. Hon.* Sir Denys Burton, Kt., MBE.

Buckley, Sir John William, Kt.

Buckley, *Rear-Adm.* Sir Kenneth Robertson, KBE.

Buckley, *Lt.-Cdr.* Sir (Peter) Richard, KCVO.

Buckley, *Hon.* Sir Roger John, Kt.

Bulkeley, Sir Richard Harry David Williams-, Bt., TD (1661).

Bull, Sir Simeon George, Bt. (1922).

Bull, Sir Walter Edward Avenon, KCVO.

Bullard, Sir Giles Lionel, KCVO, CMG.

Bullard, Sir Julian Leonard, GCMG.

Bullus, Sir Eric Edward, Kt.

Bulmer, Sir William Peter, Kt.

Bultin, Sir Bato, Kt., MBE.

Bunbury, Sir Michael William, Bt. (1681).

Bunbury, Sir (Richard David) Michael Richardson-, Bt. (I. 1787).

Bunch, Sir Austin Wyeth, Kt., CBE.

Bunting, Sir (Edward) John, KBE.

Bunyard, Sir Robert Sidney, Kt., CBE, QPM.

Burbidge, Sir Herbert Dudley, Bt. (1916).

Burbury, *Hon.* Sir Stanley Charles, KCMG, KCVO, KBE.

Burdett, Sir Savile Aylmer, Bt. (1665).

Burgen, Sir Arnold Stanley Vincent, Kt., FRS.

Burgess, *Gen.* Sir Edward Arthur, KCB, OBE.

Burgh, Sir John Charles, KCMG, CB.

Burke, Sir James Stanley Gilbert, Bt. (I. 1797).

Burke, *Prof.* Sir Joseph Terence, KBE.

Burke, Sir (Thomas) Kerry, Kt.

Burley, Sir Victor George, Kt., CBE.

Burman, Sir (John) Charles, Kt.

Burman, Sir Stephen France, Kt., CBE.

Burnet, Sir James William Alexander (Sir Alastair Burnet), Kt.

Burnett, *Air Chief Marshal* Sir Brian Kenyon, GCB, DFC, AFC.

Burnett, Sir David Humphery, Bt., MBE, TD (1913).

Burnett, Sir John Harrison, Kt.

Burnett, Sir Walter John, Kt.

Burney, Sir Cecil Denniston, Bt. (1921).

Burns, Sir Terence, Kt.

Burns, *Maj.-Gen.* Sir (Walter Arthur) George, GCVO, CB, DSO, OBE, MC.

Burrell, Sir John Raymond, Bt. (1774).

Burrenchobay, Sir Dayendranath, KBE, CMG, CVO.

Burrows, Sir Bernard Alexander Brocas, GCMG.

Burston, Sir Samuel Gerald Wood, Kt., OBE.

Burt, *Hon.* Sir Francis Theodore Page, KCMG.

Burton, Sir Carlisle Archibald, Kt., OBE.

Burton, Sir George Vernon Kennedy, Kt., CBE.

Burton, *Air Marshal* Sir Harry, KCB, CBE, DSO.

Busby, Sir Matthew, Kt., CBE.

Bush, *Adm.* Sir John Fitzroy Duyland, GCB, DSC.

Butler, *Rt. Hon.* Sir Adam Courtauld, Kt.

Butler, Sir Clifford Charles, Kt., Ph.D., FRS.

Butler, Sir (Frederick) (Edward) Robin, KCB, CVO.

Butler, Sir Michael Dacres, GCMG.

Butler, Sir (Reginald) Michael (Thomas), Bt. (1922).

Butler, *Hon.* Sir Richard Clive, Kt.

Butler, *Col.* Sir Thomas Pierce, Bt., CVO, DSO, OBE (1628).

Butt, Sir (Alfred) Kenneth Dudley, Bt. (1929).

Butter, *Maj.* Sir David Henry, KCVO, MC.

Butterworth, Sir (George) Neville, Kt.

Buxton, Sir Thomas Fowell Victor, Bt. (1840).

Buzzard, Sir Anthony Farquhar, Bt. (1929).

Byatt, Sir Hugh Campbell, KCVO, CMG.

Byers, Sir Maurice Hearne, Kt., CBE, QC.

Byford, Sir Lawrence, Kt., CBE, QPM.

Byrne, Sir Clarence Askew, Kt., OBE, DSC.

Cable, Sir James Eric, KCVO, CMG.

Cadbury, Sir (George) Adrian (Hayhurst), Kt.

Cadell, *Vice-Adm.* Sir John Frederick, KBE.

Cadogan, *Prof.* Sir John Ivan George, Kt., CBE, FRS, FRSE.

Cadwallader, Sir John, Kt.

Cahn, Sir Albert Jonas, Bt. (1934).

Cain, Sir Edward Thomas, Kt., CBE.

Cain, Sir Henry Edney Conrad, Kt.

Caine, Sir Michael Harris, Kt.

Caines, Sir John, KCB.

Cairncross, Sir Alexander Kirkland, KCMG.

Calcutt, Sir David Charles, Kt., QC.

Calderwood, Sir Robert, Kt.

Caldwell, *Surgeon Vice-Adm.* Sir (Eric) Dick, KBE, CB.

Callaghan, Sir Allan Robert, Kt., CMG.

Callaghan, Sir Bede Bertrand, Kt., CBE.

Callard, Sir Eric John, Kt.

Callaway, *Prof.* Sir Frank Adams, Kt., CMG, OBE.

Calley, Sir Henry Algernon, Kt., DSO, DFC.

Callinan, Sir Bernard James, Kt., CBE, DSO, MC.

Calne, *Prof.* Sir Roy Yorke, Kt., FRS.

Calthorpe, Sir Euan Hamilton Anstruther-Gough-, Bt. (1929).

Cameron of Lochiel, Sir Donald Hamish, KT, CVO, TD.

Cameron, Sir (Eustace) John, Kt., CBE.

Cameron, Sir James Clark, Kt., CBE, TD.

Cameron, *Hon.* Sir John, KT, DSC, QC (Lord Cameron).

Cameron, Sir John Watson, Kt., OBE.

Campbell, Sir Alan Hugh, GCMG.

Campbell, Sir Clifford Clarence, GCMG, GCVO.

Campbell, Sir Colin Moffat, Bt., MC (s. 1668).

Campbell, *Col.* Sir Guy Theophilus Halswell, Bt., OBE, MC (1815).

Campbell, *Maj.-Gen.* Sir Hamish Manus, KBE, CB.

Campbell, Sir Ian Tofts, Kt., CBE, VRD.

Campbell, Sir Ilay Mark, Bt. (1808).

Campbell, Sir Matthew, KBE, CB, FRSE.

Campbell, Sir Niall Alexander Hamilton, Bt. (1831).

Campbell, Sir Robin Auchinbreck, Bt. (s. 1628).

Campbell, Sir Thomas Cockburn-, Bt. (1821).

Campbell, *Hon.* Sir Walter Benjamin, Kt.

Campbell, *Hon.* Sir William Anthony, Kt.

Campion, Sir Harry, Kt., CB, CBE.

Cantley, *Hon.* Sir Joseph Donaldson, Kt., OBE.

Carden, *Lt.-Col.* Sir Henry Christopher, Bt., OBE (1887).

Carden, Sir John Craven, Bt. (I. 1787).

Carew, Sir Rivers Verain, Bt. (1661).

Carey, Sir Peter Willoughby, GCB.

Carlill, *Vice-Adm.* Sir Stephen Hope, KBE, CB, DSO.

Carlisle, Sir John Michael, Kt.

Carmichael, Sir David Peter William Gibson-Craig-, Bt. (s. 1702 and 1831).

Carmichael, Sir John, KBE.

Carnac, *Rev. Canon* Sir (Thomas) Nicholas Rivett-, Bt. (1836).

Carnegie, *Lt.-Gen.* Sir Robin Macdonald, KCB, OBE.

Carnegie, Sir Roderick Howard, Kt.

Carnwath, Sir Andrew Hunter, KCVO.

Caro, Sir Anthony Alfred, Kt., CBE.

Carpenter, *Very Rev.* Edward Frederick, KCVO.

Carr, Sir (Albert) Raymond (Maillard), Kt.

Carr, *Air Marshal* Sir John Darcy Baker-, KBE, CB, AFC.

Carrick, *Hon.* Sir John Leslie, KCMG.

Carsberg, *Prof.* Sir Bryan Victor, Kt.

Carswell, *Hon.* Sir Robert Douglas, Kt.

Carter, Sir Charles Frederick, Kt., FBA.

Carter, Sir Derrick Hunton, Kt., TD.

Carter, Sir John, Kt., QC.

Carter, Sir John Alexander, Kt.

Carter, Sir Philip David, Kt., CBE.

Carter, Sir William Oscar, Kt.

Cartland, Sir George Barrington, Kt., CMG.

Cartledge, Sir Bryan George, KCMG.

Cary, Sir Roger Hugh, Bt. (1955).

Casey, *Rt. Hon.* Sir Maurice Eugene, Kt.

Cash, Sir Gerald Christopher, GCMG, GCVO, OBE.

Cass, Sir John Patrick, Kt., OBE.

Cassel, Sir Harold Felix, Bt., TD, QC (1920).

Cassels, *Field Marshal* Sir (Archibald) James Halkett, GCB, KBE, DSO.

Cassels, Sir John Seton, Kt., CB.

Cassels, *Adm.* Sir Simon Alastair Cassillis, KCB, CBE.

Cassidi, *Adm.* Sir (Arthur) Desmond, GCB.

Casson, Sir Hugh Maxwell, CH, KCVO, PPRA, FRIBA.

Cater, Sir Jack, KBE.

Cater, Sir John Robert, Kt.

Catherwood, Sir (Henry) Frederick (Ross), Kt., MEP.

Catling, Sir Richard Charles, Kt., CMG, OBE.

Cato, *Hon.* Sir Arnott Samuel, KCMG.

Caughey, Sir Thomas Harcourt Clarke, KBE.

Caulfield, *Hon.* Sir Bernard, Kt.

Cave, Sir Charles Edward Coleridge, Bt. (1896).

Cave, Sir (Charles) Philip Haddon-, KBE, CMG.

Cave, Sir Robert Cave-Browne-, Bt. (1641).

Cawley, Sir Charles Mills, Kt., CBE, ph.D.

Cayley, Sir Digby William David, Bt. (1661).

Cayzer, Sir James Arthur, Bt. (1904).

Cazalet, *Hon.* Sir Edward Stephen, Kt.

Cazalet, Sir Peter Grenville, Kt.

Cecil, *Rear-Adm.* Sir (Oswald) Nigel Amherst, KBE, CB.

Chacksfield, *Air Vice-Marshal* Sir Bernard Albert, KBE, CB.

Chadwick, *Rev. Prof.* Henry, KBE.

Chadwick, Sir Joshua Kenneth Burton, Bt. (1935).

Chadwick, *Rev. Prof.* (William) Owen, OM, KBE, FBA.

Chalk, *Hon.* Sir Gordon William Wesley, KBE.

Chamberlain, *Hon.* Sir Reginald Roderic St Clair, Kt.

Chan, *Rt. Hon.* Sir Julius, KBE.

Chance, Sir (George) Jeremy ffolliott, Bt. (1900).

Chandler, Sir Colin Michael, Kt.

Chandler, Sir Geoffrey, Kt., CBE.

Chaney, *Hon.* Sir Frederick Charles, KBE, AFC.

Chaplin, Sir Malcolm Hilbery, Kt., CBE.

Chapman, Sir David Robert Macgowan, Bt. (1958).

Chapman, Sir George Alan, Kt.

Chapple, *Gen.* (*Field Marshal* w.e.f. Feb. 1992) Sir John Lyon, GCB, CBE.

Charles, Sir Joseph Quentin, Kt.

Charnley, Sir (William) John, Kt., CB.

Chaytor, Sir George Reginald, Bt. (1831).

Cheadle, Sir Eric Wallers, Kt., CBE.

Checketts, *Sqn. Ldr.* Sir David John, KCVO.

Cheetham, Sir Nicolas John Alexander, KCMG.

Chesterman, Sir (Dudley) Ross, Kt., ph.D.

Chesterton, Sir Oliver Sidney, Kt., MC.

Chetwood, Sir Clifford Jack, Kt.

Chetwynd, Sir Arthur Ralph Talbot, Bt. (1795).

Cheung, Sir Oswald Victor, Kt., CBE.

Cheyne, Sir Joseph Lister Watson, Bt., OBE (1908).

Chichester, Sir (Edward) John, Bt. (1641).

Child, Sir (Coles John) Jeremy, Bt. (1919).

Chilton, *Air Marshal* Sir (Charles) Edward, KBE, CB.

Chilton, *Brig.* Sir Frederick Oliver, Kt., CBE, DSO.

Chilwell, *Hon.* Sir Muir Fitzherbert, Kt.

Chinn, Sir Trevor Edwin, Kt., CVO.

Chitty, Sir Thomas Willes, Bt. (1924).

Cholmeley, Sir Montague John, Bt. (1806).

Christie, Sir George William Langham, Kt.

Christie, *Hon.* Sir Vernon Howard Colville, Kt.

Christie, Sir William, Kt., MBE.

Christison, *Gen.* Sir (Alexander Frank) Philip, Bt., GBE, CB, DSO, MC (1871).

Christofas, Sir Kenneth Cavendish, KCMG, MBE.

Christopherson, Sir Derman Guy, Kt., OBE, D.Phil., FRS.

Chung, Sir Sze-yuen, Kt., GBE.

Clapham, Sir Michael John Sinclair, KBE.

†Clark, Sir Colin Douglas, Bt. (1917).

Clark, Sir Francis Drake, Bt. (1886).

Clark, Sir John Allen, Kt.

Clark, Sir John Stewart-, Bt., MEP (1918).

Clark, Sir Robert Anthony, Kt., DSC.

Clark, Sir Robin Chichester-, Kt.

Clark, Sir Terence Joseph, KBE, CMG, CVO.

Clark, Sir Thomas Edwin, Kt.

Clark, *Rt. Hon.* Sir William Gibson, Kt., MP.

Clarke, Sir (Charles Mansfield) Tobias, Bt. (1831).

Clarke, *Prof.* Sir Cyril Astley, KBE, MD, SC.D., FRS, FRCP.

Clarke, Sir Ellis Emmanuel Innocent, GCMG.

Clarke, Sir (Henry) Ashley, GCMG, GCVO.

Clarke, Sir Jonathan Dennis, Kt.

Clarke, Sir Rupert William John, Bt., MBE (1882).

Clay, Sir Richard Henry, Bt. (1841).

Clayton, Sir David Robert, Bt., (1732).

Clayton, *Air Marshal* Sir Gareth Thomas Butler, KCB, DFC.

Clayton, Sir Robert James, Kt., CBE.

Cleary, Sir Joseph Jackson, Kt.

Clegg, Sir Walter, Kt.

Cleminson, Sir James Arnold Stacey, KBE, MC.

Clerk, Sir John Dutton, Bt., CBE, VRD (s. 1679).

Clerke, Sir John Edward Longueville, Bt. (1660).

Clifford, Sir Roger Joseph, Bt. (1887).

Clothier, Sir Cecil Montacute, KCB, QC.

Clowes, *Col.* Sir Henry Nelson, KCVO, DSO, OBE.

Clucas, Sir Kenneth Henry, KCB.

Clutterbuck, *Vice-Adm.* Sir David Granville, KBE, CB.

Coates, Sir Ernest William, Kt., CMG.

Coates, Sir Frederick Gregory Lindsay, Bt. (1921).

Coats, Sir Alastair Francis Stuart, Bt. (1905).

Coats, Sir William David, Kt.

Cobban, Sir James Macdonald, Kt., CBE, TD.

Cochrane, Sir (Henry) Marc (Sursock), Bt. (1903).

Cockburn, Sir John Elliot, Bt. (s. 1671).

Cockburn, Sir Robert, KBE, CB, Ph.D.

Cockcroft, Sir Wilfred Halliday, Kt., D.Phil.

Cockerell, Sir Christopher Sydney, Kt., CBE, FRS.

Cockram, Sir John, Kt.

Codrington, Sir Simon Francis Bethell, Bt. (1876).

Codrington, Sir William Alexander, Bt. (1721).

Coghill, Sir Egerton James Nevill Tobias, Bt. (1778).

Cohen, Sir Edward, Kt.

†Cohen, Sir Stephen Harry Waley-, Bt. (1961).

Coldstream, Sir George Phillips, KCB, KCVO, QC.

Cole, Sir (Alexander) Colin, KCVO, TD.

Cole, Sir David Lee, KCMG, MC.

Cole, Sir (Robert) William, Kt.

Coles, Sir (Arthur) John, KCMG.

Colfox, Sir (William) John, Bt. (1939).

Collett, Sir Christopher, GBE.

Collett, Sir Ian Seymour, Bt. (1934).

Collins, Sir Arthur James Robert, KCVO.

Collyear, Sir John Gowen, Kt.

Colman, Sir Michael Jeremiah, Bt. (1907).

Colquhoun, *Maj.-Gen.* Sir Cyril Harry, KCVO, CB, OBE.

Colquhoun of Luss, Sir Ivar Iain, Bt. (1786).

Colt, Sir Edward William Dutton Bt. (1694).

Colthurst, Sir Richard La Touche, Bt. (1744).

Combs, Sir Willis Ide, KCVO, CMG.

Compston, *Vice-Adm.* Sir Peter Maxwell, Kt.

Compton, Sir Edmund Gerald, GCB, KBE.

Compton Miller, Sir John (Francis), Kt., MBE, TD.

Comyn, *Hon.* Sir James, Kt.

Conant, Sir John Ernest Michael, Bt. (1954).

Conran, Sir Terence Orby, Kt.

Cons, *Hon.* Sir Derek, Kt.

Constable, Sir Robert Frederick Strickland-, Bt. (1641).

Constantine, *Air Chief Marshal* Sir Hugh Alex, KBE, CB, DSO.

Cook, *Prof.* Sir Alan Hugh, Kt.

Cook, Sir Christopher Wymondham Rayner Herbert, Bt. (1886).

Cooke, Sir Charles Fletcher-, Kt., QC.

Cooke, *Lt.-Col.* Sir David William Perceval, Bt. (1661).

Cooke, *Rt. Hon.* Sir Robin Brunskill, KBE.

Cooley, Sir Alan Sydenham, Kt., CBE.

Coop, Sir Maurice Fletcher, Kt.

Cooper, *Rt. Hon.* Sir Frank, GCB, CMG.

Cooper, Sir (Frederick Howard) Michael Craig-, Kt., CBE, TD.

Cooper, *Gen.* Sir George Leslie Conroy, GCB, MC.

Cooper, Sir Patrick Graham Astley, Bt. (1821).

Cooper, Sir Richard Powell, Bt. (1905).

Cooper, *Maj.-Gen.* Sir Simon Christie, KCVO.

Cooper, Sir William Daniel Charles, Bt. (1863).

Cooper, *Prof.* Sir (William) Mansfield, Kt.

Coote, Sir Christopher John, Bt., *Premier Baronet of Ireland* (I. 1621).

Copas, *Most Rev.* Virgil, KBE, DD.

Cope, *Rt. Hon.* Sir John Ambrose, Kt., MP.

Copisarow, Sir Alcon Charles, Kt.

Corbet, Sir John Vincent, Bt., MBE (1808).

Corby, Sir (Frederick) Brian, Kt.

Corfield, *Rt. Hon.* Sir Frederick Vernon, Kt., QC.

Corfield, Sir Kenneth George, Kt.

Cork, Sir Kenneth Russell, GBE.

Corley, Sir Kenneth Sholl Ferrand, Kt.

Cormack, Sir Magnus Cameron, KBE.

Corness, Sir Colin Ross, Kt.

Cornford, Sir (Edward) Clifford, KCB.

Cornforth, Sir John Warcup, Kt., CBE, D.Phil., FRS.

Corry, Sir William James, Bt. (1885).

Cortazzi, Sir (Henry Arthur) Hugh, GCMG.

Cory, Sir (Clinton Charles) Donald, Bt. (1919).

Costar, Sir Norman Edgar, KCMG.

Cotter, *Lt.-Col.* Sir Delaval James Alfred, Bt., DSO (I. 1763).

Cotterell, Sir John Henry Geers, Bt. (1805).

Cotton, Sir John Richard, KCMG, OBE.

Cotton, *Hon.* Sir Robert Carrington, KCMG.

Cottrell, Sir Alan Howard, Kt., Ph.D., FRS.

Cotts, Sir (Robert) Crichton Mitchell, Bt. (1921).

Coulson, Sir John Eltringham, KCMG.

Couper, Sir (Robert) Nicholas (Oliver), Bt. (1841).

Court, *Hon.* Sir Charles Walter Michael, KCMG, OBE.

Coutts, Sir David Burdett Money-, KCVO.

Couzens, Sir Kenneth Edward, KCB.

Covacevich, Sir (Anthony) Thomas, Kt., DFC.

Cowan, Sir Robert, Kt.

Coward, *Vice-Adm.* Sir John Francis, KCB, DSO.

Cowen, *Rt. Hon. Prof.* Sir Zelman, GCMG, GCVO, QC.

Cowley, *Lt.-Gen.* Sir John Guise, GC, KBE, CB.

Cowperthwaite, Sir John James, KBE, CMG.

Cox, Sir Anthony Wakefield, Kt., CBE, FRIBA.

Cox, *Prof.* Sir David Roxbee, Kt., FRS.

Cox, Sir (Ernest) Gordon, KBE, TD, D.SC., FRS.

Cox, Sir Geoffrey Sandford, Kt., CBE.

Cox, Sir (George) Trenchard, Kt., CBE, FSA.

Cox, *Vice-Adm.* Sir John Michael Holland, KCB.

Cox, Sir Mencea Ethereal, Kt., Cradock, Sir Percy, GCMG.

Craig, Sir (Albert) James (Macqueen), GCMG.

Cramer, *Hon.* Sir John Oscar, Kt.

Crane, Sir James William Donald, Kt., CBE.

Craufurd, Sir Robert James, Bt. (1781).

Craven, *Air Marshal* Sir Robert Edward, KBE, CB, DFC.

Crawford, *Prof.* Sir Frederick William, Kt.

Crawford, *Hon.* Sir George Hunter, Kt.

Crawford, Sir (Robert) Stewart, GCMG, CVO.

Crawford, *Prof.* Sir Theodore, Kt.

Crawford, *Vice-Adm.* Sir William Godfrey, KBE, CB, DSC.

Crawshay, *Col.* Sir William Robert, Kt., DSO, ERD, TD.

Creagh, *Maj.-Gen.* Sir (Kilner) Rupert Brazier-, KBE, CB, DSO.

Cresswell, *Hon.* Sir Peter John, Kt.

Crichton, Sir Andrew James Maitland-Makgill-, Kt.

Crill, Sir Peter Leslie, Kt., CBE.

Cripps, Sir Cyril Humphrey, Kt.

Cripps, Sir John Stafford, Kt., CBE.

Crisp, Sir (John) Peter, Bt. (1913).

Critchett, Sir Ian (George Lorraine), Bt. (1908).

Croft, Sir Owen Glendower, Bt. (1671).

Croft, Sir Thomas Stephen Hutton, Bt. (1818).

†Crofton, Sir Hugh Denis, Bt. (1801).

Crofton, *Prof.* Sir John Wenman, Kt.

Crofton, Sir Malby Sturges, Bt. (1838).

Croker, Sir Walter Russell, KBE.

Crookenden, *Lt.-Gen.* Sir Napier, KCB, DSO, OBE.

Cross, Sir Barry Albert, Kt., CBE, FRS.

Cross, *Air Chief Marshal* Sir Kenneth Brian Boyd, KCB, CBE, DSO, DFC.

Crossland, *Prof.* Sir Bernard, Kt., CBE.

Crossland, Sir Leonard, Kt.

Crossley, Sir Nicholas John, Bt. (1909).

Crouch, Sir David Lance, Kt.

Cruthers, Sir James Winter, Kt.

Cubbon, Sir Brian Crossland, GCB.

Cubitt, Sir Hugh Guy, Kt., CBE.

Cuckney, Sir John Graham, Kt.

Cullen, Sir (Edward) John, Kt., F.Eng.

Cumming, Sir William Gordon Gordon-, Bt. (1804).

Cuninghame, Sir John Christopher Foggo Montgomery-, Bt. (NS 1672).

†Cuninghame, Sir William Henry Fairlie-, Bt. (s. 1630).

Cunliffe, Sir David Ellis, Bt. (1759)

Cunningham, Sir Charles Craik, GCB, KBE, CVO.

Cunningham, *Lt.-Gen.* Sir Hugh Patrick, KBE.

Cunynghame, Sir Andrew David Francis, Bt. (s. 1702).

Curle, Sir John Noel Ormiston, KCVO, CMG.

Curran, Sir Samuel Crowe, Kt., D.SC., Ph.D., FRS, FRSE.

Currie, *Prof.* Sir Alastair Robert, Kt., FRCP, FRCPE, FRSE.

†Currie, Sir Donald Scott, Bt. (1847).

Currie, Sir Neil Smith, Kt., CBE.

Curtis, Sir (Edward) Leo, Kt.

Curtis, Sir William Peter, Bt. (1802).

Curtiss, *Air Marshal* Sir John Bagot, KCB, KBE.

Curwen, Sir Christopher Keith, KCMG.

Cuthbertson, Sir Harold Alexander, Kt.

Cutler, Sir (Arthur) Roden, VC, KCMG, KCVO, CBE.

Cutler, Sir Charles Benjamin, KBE, ED.

Cutler, Sir Horace Walter, Kt., OBE.

Dacie, *Prof.* Sir John Vivian, Kt., MD, FRS.

Dalais, Sir Adrien Pierre, Kt.

Dale, Sir William Leonard, KCMG.

Dalrymple, *Maj.* Sir Hew Fleetwood Hamilton-, Bt., KCVO (s. 1697).

Dalton, Sir Alan Nugent Goring, Kt., CBE.

Dalton, *Vice-Adm.* Sir Geoffrey Thomas James Oliver, KCB.

Dalton, *Vice-Adm.* Sir Norman Eric, KCB, OBE.

Daly, *Lt.-Gen.* Sir Thomas Joseph, KBE, CB, DSO.

Dalyell, Sir Tam, Bt., MP (NS 1685).

Daniel, Sir Goronwy Hopkin, KCVO, CB, D.Phil.

Daniell, Sir Peter Averell, Kt., TD.

Danks, Sir Alan John, KBE.

Darby, *Prof.* Sir Henry Clifford, Kt., CBE.

Darby, Sir Peter Howard, Kt., CBE, QFSM.

Darell, Sir Jeffrey Lionel, Bt., MC (1795).

Dargie, Sir William Alexander, Kt., CBE.

Darling, Sir Clifford, Kt.

Darling, Sir James Ralph, Kt., CMG, OBE.

Darling, *Gen.* Sir Kenneth Thomas, GBE, KCB, DSO.

Darlington, *Rear-Adm.* Sir Charles Roy, KBE.

Darvall, Sir (Charles) Roger, Kt., CBE.

Dashwood, Sir Francis John Vernon Hereward, Bt., *Premier Baronet of Great Britain* (1707).

Dashwood, Sir Richard James, Bt. (1684).

Daunt, Sir Timothy Lewis Achilles, KCMG.

David, Sir Jean Marc, Kt., CBE, QC.

Davidson, Sir Robert James, Kt.

Davie, Sir Antony Francis Ferguson-, Bt. (1847).

Davies, *Air Marshal* Sir Alan Cyril, KCB, CBE.

Davies, *Hon.* Sir (Alfred William) Michael, Kt.

Davies, Sir Alun Talfan, Kt., QC.

Davies, Sir David Henry, Kt.

Davies, *Hon.* Sir (David Herbert) Mervyn, Kt., MC, TD.

Davies, *Vice-Adm.* Sir Lancelot Richard Bell, KBE.

Davies, Sir Oswald, Kt., CBE.

Davies, Sir Peter Maxwell, Kt., CBE.

Davies, Sir Richard Harries, KCVO, CBE.

Davies, Sir Victor Caddy, Kt., OBE.

Davis, Sir Charles Sigmund, Kt., CB.

Davis, Sir Colin Rex, Kt., CBE.

Davis, *Hon.* Sir (Dermot) Renn, Kt., OBE.

Davis, Sir (Ernest) Howard, Kt., CMG, OBE.

Davis, Sir John Gilbert, Bt. (1946).

Davis, Sir John Henry Harris, Kt.

Davis, Sir Maurice Herbert, Kt., OBE.

Davis, Sir Rupert Charles Hart-, Kt.

Davis, *Hon.* Sir Thomas Robert Alexander Harries, KBE.

Davis, Sir (William) Allan, GBE.

Davison, *Rt. Hon.* Sir Ronald Keith, GBE, CMG.

Dawbarn, Sir Simon Yelverton, KCVO, CMG.

Dawson, *Hon.* Sir Daryl Michael, KBE, CB.

Dawson, Sir Hugh Michael Trevor, Bt. (1920).

Dawson, *Air Chief Marshal* Sir Walter Lloyd, KCB, CBE, DSO.

Dawtry, Sir Alan (Graham), Kt., CBE, TD.

Day, Sir Derek Malcolm, KCMG.

Day, Sir (Judson) Graham, Kt.

Day, Sir Robin, Kt.

Deakin, Sir (Frederick) William (Dampier), Kt., DSO.

Dean, *Rt. Hon.* Sir (Arthur) Paul, Kt., MP.

Dean, Sir Patrick Henry, GCMG.

Deane, *Hon.* Sir William Patrick, KBE.

Dearing, Sir Ronald Ernest, Kt., CB.

de Bellaigue, Sir Geoffrey, KCVO.

Debenham, Sir Gilbert Ridley, Bt. (1931).

Deer, Sir (Arthur) Frederick, Kt., CMG.

de Hoghton, Sir (Richard) Bernard (Cuthbert), Bt. (1611).

De la Bère, Sir Cameron, Bt. (1953).

Delacombe, *Maj.-Gen.* Sir Rohan, KCMG, KCVO, KBE, CB, DSO.

de la Mare, Sir Arthur James, KCMG, KCVO.

Delamere, Sir Monita Eru, KBE.

de la Rue, Sir Andrew George Ilay, Bt. (1898).

Dellow, Sir John Albert, Kt., CBE.

de Lotbinière, *Lt.-Col.* Sir Edmond Joly, KC.

Delve, Sir Frederick William, Kt., CBE.

de Montmorency, Sir Arnold Geoffroy, Bt. (I. 1631).

Denholm, Sir John Ferguson (Ian), Kt., CBE.

Denman, Sir (George) Roy, KCB, CMG.

Denny, Sir Alistair Maurice Archibald, Bt. (1913).

Denny, Sir Anthony Coningham de Waltham, Bt. (I. 1782).

Dent, Sir John, Kt., CBE.

Denton, *Prof.* Sir Eric James, Kt., CBE, FRS.

Derbyshire, Sir Andrew George, Kt.

Derham, Sir Peter John, Kt..

de Trafford, Sir Dermot Humphrey, Bt. (1841).

Deverell, Sir Colville Montgomery, GBE, KCMG, CVO.

Devesi, Sir Baddeley, GCMG, GCVO.

De Ville, Sir Harold Godfrey Oscar, Kt., CBE.

Devitt, Sir Thomas Gordon, Bt. (1916).

de Waal, Sir (Constant Henrik) Henry, KCB, QC.

Dewey, Sir Anthony Hugh, Bt. (1917).

Dewhurst, *Prof.* Sir (Christopher) John, Kt.

d'Eyncourt, Sir Mark Gervais Tennyson-, Bt. (1930).

Dhenin, *Air Marshal* Sir Geoffrey Howard, KBE, AFC, GM, MD.

Dhrangadhra, HH the Maharaja Raj Saheb of, KCIE.

Dibela, *Hon.* Sir Kingsford, GCMG.

Dick, Sir John Alexander, Kt., MC, QC.

Dickenson, Sir Aubrey Fiennes Trotman-, Kt.

Dickinson, Sir Harold Herbert, Kt.

Dickinson, Sir Samuel Benson, Kt.

Dilbertson, Sir Geoffrey, Kt., CBE.

Dilke, Sir John Fisher Wentworth, Bt. (1862).

Dill, Sir Nicholas Bayard, Kt., CBE.

Dillon, *Rt. Hon.* Sir (George) Brian (Hugh), Kt.

Dillon, Sir John Vincent, Kt., CMG.

Dillon, Sir Max, Kt.

Diver, *Hon.* Sir Leslie Charles, Kt.

Dixon, Sir John George, Bt. (1919).

Dobbs, *Capt.* Sir Richard Arthur Frederick, KCVO.

Dobson, Sir Denis William, KCB, OBE, QC.

Dobson, *Gen.* Sir Patrick John Howard-, GCB.

Dobson, Sir Richard Portway, Kt.

Dodds, Sir Ralph Jordan, Bt. (1964).

Dodson, Sir Derek Sherborne Lindsell, KCMG, MC.

Dodsworth, Sir John Christopher Smith-, Bt. (1784).

Doll, *Prof.* Sir (William) Richard (Shaboe), Kt., OBE, FRS, DM, MD, D.SC.

Dollery, Sir Colin Terence, Kt.

Donald, Sir Alan Ewen, KCMG.

Donald, *Air Marshal* Sir John George, KBE.

Donne, *Hon.* Sir Gaven John, KBE.

Donne, Sir John Christopher, Kt.

Dookun, Sir Dewoonarain, Kt.

Dorman, *Lt.-Col.* Sir Charles Geoffrey, Bt., MC (1923).

Dorman, Sir Maurice Henry, GCMG, GCVO.

Dos Santos, Sir Errol Lionel, Kt., CBE.

Dougherty, *Maj.-Gen.* Sir Ivan Noel, Kt., CBE, DSO, ED.

Doughty, Sir William Roland, Kt.

Douglas, *Prof.* Sir Donald Macleod, Kt., MBE.

Douglas, Sir (Edward) Sholto, Kt.

Douglas, Sir Robert McCallum, Kt., OBE.

Douglas, *Hon.* Sir Roger Owen, Kt.

Douglas, *Rt. Hon.* Sir William Randolph, KCMG.

Dover, *Prof.* Sir Kenneth James, Kt., D.Litt., FBA, FRSE.

Down, Sir Alastair Frederick, Kt., OBE, MC, TD.

Downes, Sir Edward Thomas, Kt., CBE.

Downey, Sir Gordon Stanley, KCB.

Downs, Sir Diarmuid, Kt., CBE.

Downward, Sir William Atkinson, Kt.

Dowson, Sir Philip Manning, Kt., CBE, ARA.

Doyle, Sir Reginald Derek Henry, Kt., CBE.

D'Oyly, Sir Nigel Hadley Miller, Bt. (1663).

Drake, Sir (Arthur) Eric (Courtney), Kt., CBE.

Drake, *Hon.* Sir (Frederick) Maurice, Kt., DFC.

Drew, Sir Arthur Charles Walter, KCB.

Dreyer, *Adm.* Sir Desmond Parry, GCB, CBE, DSC.

Drinkwater, Sir John Muir, Kt., QC.

Driver, Sir Antony Victor, Kt.

Driver, Sir Eric William, Kt.

Drury, Sir (Victor William) Michael, Kt., OBE.

Dryden, Sir John Stephen Gyles, Bt. (1733 and 1795).

du Cann, *Rt. Hon.* Sir Edward Dillon Lott, KBE.

Duckmanton, Sir Talbot Sydney, Kt., CBE.

Duckworth, *Maj.* Sir Richard Dyce, Bt. (1909).

du Cros, Sir Claude Philip Arthur Mallet, Bt. (1916).

Duff, *Rt. Hon.* Sir (Arthur) Antony, GCMG, CVO, DSO, DSC.

Duffus, *Hon.* Sir William Algernon Holwell, Kt.

Duffy, Sir (Albert) (Edward) Patrick, Kt., MP, Ph.D.

Dugdale, Sir William Stratford, Bt., MC (1936).

Duke, *Maj.-Gen.* Sir Gerald William, KBE, CB, DSO.

Dunbar, Sir Archibald Ranulph, Bt. (s. 1700).

Dunbar, Sir David Hope-, Bt. (s. 1664).

Dunbar, Sir Drummond Cospatrick Ninian, Bt., MC (s. 1698).

Dunbar, Sir Jean Ivor, Bt. (s. 1694).

Dunbar of Hempriggs, Dame Maureen Daisy Helen (Lady Dunbar of Hempriggs), Btss. (s. 1706).

Duncan, Sir James Blair, Kt.

Duncombe, Sir Philip Digby Pauncefort-, Bt. (1859).

Dundas, Sir Hugh Spencer Lisle, Kt., CBE, DSO, DFC.

Dunham, Sir Kingsley Charles, Kt., Ph.D., FRS, FRSE.

Dunlop, Sir (Ernest) Edward, Kt., CMG, OBE.

Dunlop, Sir Thomas, Bt. (1916).

Dunlop, Sir William Norman Gough, Kt.

Dunn, *Air Marshal* Sir Eric Clive, KBE, CB, BEM.

Dunn, *Lt.-Col.* Sir (Francis) Vivian, KCVO, OBE.

Dunn, *Air Marshal* Sir Patrick Hunter, KBE, CB, DFC.

Dunn, *Rt. Hon.* Sir Robin Horace Walford, Kt., MC.

Dunnett, Sir (Ludovic) James, GCB, CMG.

Dunning, Sir Simon William Patrick, Bt. (1930).

Dunphie, *Maj.-Gen.* Sir Charles Anderson Lane, Kt., CB, CBE, DSO.

Dunstan, *Lt.-Gen.* Sir Donald Beaumont, KBE, CB.

†Duntze, Sir Daniel Evans, Bt. (1774).

Dupree, Sir Peter, Bt. (1921).

Durand, *Rev.* Sir (Henry Mortimer) Dickon, Bt. (1892).

Durant, Sir (Robert) Anthony (Bevis), Kt., MP.

Durham, Sir Kenneth, Kt.

Durie, Sir Alexander Charles, Kt., CBE.

Durkin, *Air Marshal* Sir Herbert, KBE, CB.

Durrant, Sir William Henry Estridge, Bt. (1784).

Duthie, *Prof.* Sir Herbert Livingston, Kt.

Duthie, Sir Robert Grieve (Robin), Kt., CBE.

Duval, Sir (Charles) Gaetan, Kt.

Duxbury, *Air Marshal* Sir (John) Barry, KCB, CBE.

Dyer, *Prof.* Sir (Henry) Peter (Francis) Swinnerton-, Bt., KBE, FRS (1678).

Dyke, Sir David William Hart, Bt. (1677).

Earle, Sir (Hardman) George (Algernon), Bt. (1869).

East, Sir (Lewis) Ronald, Kt., CBE.

Eastham, *Hon.* Sir (Thomas) Michael, Kt.

Easton, Sir Robert William Simpson, Kt., CBE.

Eastwood, Sir John Bealby, Kt..

Eaton, *Vice-Adm.* Sir Kenneth John, KCB.

Eberle, *Adm.* Sir James Henry Fuller, GCB.

Ebrahim, Sir (Mahomed) Currimbhoy, Bt. (1910).

Eburne, Sir Sidney Alfred William, Kt., MC.

Eccles, Sir John Carew, Kt., D.Phil., FRS.

Echlin, Sir Norman David Fenton, Bt. (I. 1721).

Eckersley, Sir Donald Payze, Kt., OBE.

†Edge, Sir William, Bt. (1937).

Edmenson, Sir Walter Alexander, Kt., CBE.

Edmonston, Sir Archibald Bruce Charles, Bt. (1774).

Edwardes, Sir Michael Owen, Kt.

Edwards, Sir Christopher John Churchill, Bt. (1866).

Edwards, Sir George Robert, Kt., OM, CBE, FRS.

Edwards, Sir (John) Clive (Leighton), Bt. (1921).

Edwards, Sir Llewellyn Roy, Kt.

Edwards, *Prof.* Sir Samuel Frederick, Kt., FRS.

Egan, Sir John Leopold, Kt.

Egerton, Sir John Alfred Roy, Kt.

Egerton, Sir (Philip) John (Caledon) Grey-, Bt. (1617).

Egerton, Sir Seymour John Louis, GCVO.

Egerton, Sir Stephen Loftus, KCMG.

Eggleston, *Hon.* Sir Richard Moulton, Kt.

Eichelbaum, *Rt. Hon.* Sir Thomas, GBE.

Eliott of Stobs, Sir Charles Joseph Alexander, Bt. (s. 1666)

Elliot, Sir Gerald Henry, Kt.

Elliott, Sir Clive Christopher Hugh, Bt. (1917).

Elliott, Sir Norman Randall, Kt., CBE.

Elliott, Sir Randal Forbes, KBE.

Elliott, *Prof.* Sir Roger James, Kt., FRS.

Elliott, Sir Ronald Stuart, Kt.

Ellis, Sir John Rogers, Kt., MBE, MD, FRCP.

Ellis, Sir Ronald, Kt.

Ellison, *Rt. Rev.* and *Rt. Hon.* Gerald Alexander, KCVO.

Ellison, *Col.* Sir Ralph Harry Carr-, Kt., TD.

Ellwood, *Air Marshal* Sir Aubrey Beauclerk, KCB, DSC.

Elphinstone, Sir John, Bt. (s. 1701).

Elphinstone, Sir (Maurice) Douglas (Warburton), Bt., TD (1816).

Elton, Sir Arnold, Kt., CBE.

Elton, Sir Charles Abraham Grierson, Bt. (1717).

Elton, *Prof.* Sir Geoffrey Rudolph, Kt., FBA.

Elwood, Sir Brian George Conway, Kt., CBE.

Elworthy, Sir Peter Herbert, Kt.

Elyan, Sir (Isadore) Victor, Kt.

Emery, Sir Peter Frank Hannibal, Kt., MP.

Empson, *Adm.* Sir (Leslie) Derek, GBE, KCB.

Emson, *Air Marshal* Sir Reginald Herbert, KBE, CB, AFC.

Engineer, Sir Noshirwan Phirozshah, Kt.

Engle, Sir George Lawrence Jose, KCB, QC.

English, Sir Cyril Rupert, Kt.

English, Sir David, Kt.

English, Sir Terence Alexander Hawthorne, KBE, FRCS.

Entwistle, Sir (John Nuttall) Maxwell, Kt.

Epstein, *Prof.* Sir (Michael) Anthony, Kt., CBE, FRS.

Ereaut, Sir (Herbert) Frank Cobbold, Kt.

Eri, Sir Vincent Serei, GCMG.

Errington, *Col.* Sir Geoffrey Frederick, Bt. (1963).

Errington, Sir Lancelot, KCB.

Erskine, Sir (Thomas) David, Bt. (1821).

Esmonde, Sir Thomas Francis Grattan, Bt. (I. 1629).

Espie, Sir Frank Fletcher, Kt., OBE.

Esplen, Sir John Graham, Bt. (1921).

Eustace, Sir Joseph Lambert, GCMG, GCVO.

Evans, *Hon.* Sir Anthony Howell Meurig, Kt., RD.

Evans, *Air Chief Marshal* Sir David George, GCB, CBE.

Evans, *Air Chief Marshal* Sir David Parry-, GCB, CBE.

Evans, Sir Francis Loring Gwynne-, Bt. (1913).

Evans, Sir Geraint Llewellyn, Kt., CBE.

Evans, *Hon.* Sir Haydn Tudor, Kt.

Evans, Sir Richard Mark, KCMG, KCVO.

Evans, Sir (Robert) Charles, Kt.

Evans, Sir (William) Vincent (John), GCMG, MBE, QC.

Eveleigh, *Rt. Hon.* Sir Edward Walter, Kt., ERD.

Everard, *Maj.-Gen.* Sir Christopher Earle Welby-, KBE, CB.

Everard, Sir Robin Charles, Bt. (1911).

Everson, Sir Frederick Charles, KCMG.

Every, Sir Henry John Michael, Bt. (1641).

Ewans, Sir Martin Kenneth, KCMG.

Ewart, Sir (William) Ivan (Cecil), Bt., DSO (1887).

Ewbank, *Hon.* Sir Anthony Bruce, Kt.

Ewin, Sir (David) Ernest Thomas Floyd, Kt., OBE, MVO.

Ewing, *Vice-Adm.* Sir (Robert) Alastair, KBE, CB, DSC.

Ewing, Sir Ronald Archibald Orr-, Bt. (1886).

Eyre, Sir Graham Newman, Kt., QC.

Eyre, *Maj.-Gen.* Sir James Ainsworth Campden Gabriel, KCVO, CBE.

Eyre, Sir Reginald Edwin, Kt.

Faber, Sir Richard Stanley, KCVO, CMG.

Fadahunsi, Sir Joseph Odeleye, KCMG.

Fagge, Sir John William Frederick, Bt. (1660).

Fairbairn, *Hon.* Sir David Eric, KBE, DFC.

Fairbairn, Sir (James) Brooke, Bt. (1869).

Fairbairn, Sir Nicholas Hardwick, Kt., QC, MP.

Fairclough, Sir John Whitaker, Kt.

Fairfax, Sir Vincent Charles, Kt., CMG.

Fairgrieve, Sir (Thomas) Russell, Kt., CBE, TD.

Fairhall, *Hon.* Sir Allen, KBE.

Falconer, *Hon.* Sir Douglas William, Kt., MBE.

Falk, Sir Roger Salis, Kt., OBE.

Falkiner, Sir Edmond Charles, Bt. (I. 1778).

Falkner, Sir (Donald) Keith, Kt.

Falle, Sir Samuel, KCMG, KCVO, DSC.

Fareed, Sir Djamil Sheik, Kt.

Farmer, Sir (Lovedin) George Thomas, Kt.

Farndale, *Gen.* Sir Martin Baker, KCB.

Farquhar, Sir Michael Fitzroy Henry, Bt. (1796).

Farquharson, *Rt. Hon.* Sir Donald Henry, Kt.

Farquharson, Sir James Robbie, KBE.

Farr, Sir John Arnold, Kt., MP.

Farrer, Sir Charles Matthew, KCVO.

Farrington, Sir Henry Francis Colden, Bt. (1818).

Fat, Sir Maxime Edouard Lim Man Lim-, Kt.

Faulkner, Sir Eric Odin, Kt., MBE.

Faulkner, Sir (James) Dennis (Compton), Kt., CBE, VRD.

Fawcus, Sir (Robert) Peter, KBE, CMG.

Fawkes, Sir Randol Francis, Kt.

Fay, Sir (Humphrey) Michael Gerard, Kt.

Fayrer, Sir John Lang Macpherson, Bt. (1896).

Fearn, Sir (Patrick) Robin, KCMG.

Feilden, Sir Bernard Melchior, Kt., CBE.

Feilden, Sir Henry Wemyss, Bt., (1846).

Feldman, Sir Basil Samuel, Kt.

Fell, Sir Anthony, Kt.

Fellowes, *Rt. Hon.* Sir Robert, KCB, KCVO.

Fenn, Sir Nicholas Maxted, KCMG.

Fennell, *Hon.* Sir (John) Desmond Augustine, Kt., OBE.

Fennessy, Sir Edward, Kt., CBE.

Ferens, Sir Thomas Robinson, Kt., CBE.

Ferguson, *Lt.-Col.* Sir Neil Edward Johnson-, Bt., TD (1906).

Fergusson of Kilkerran, Sir Charles, Bt. (s. 1703).

Fergusson, Sir Ewan Alastair John, KCMG.

Fergusson, Sir James Herbert Hamilton Colyer-, Bt. (1866).

Feroze, Sir Rustam Moolan, Kt., FRCS.

Ferris, *Hon.* Sir Francis Mursell, Kt., TD.

ffolkes, Sir Robert Francis Alexander, Bt, OBE (1774).

Field, Sir Malcolm David, Kt.

Fielding, Sir Colin Cunningham, Kt., CB.

Fielding, Sir Leslie, KCMG.

Fiennes, Sir John Saye Wingfield Twisleton-Wykeham-, KCB, QC.

Fiennes, Sir Maurice Alberic Twisleton-Wykeham-, Kt.

Fiennes, Sir Ranulph Twisleton-Wykeham-, Bt. (1916).

Figg, Sir Leonard Clifford William, KCMG.

Figgess, Sir John George, KBE, CMG.

Figures, Sir Colin Frederick, KCMG, OBE.

Fingland, Sir Stanley James Gunn, KCMG.

Finlay, Sir David Ronald James Bell, Bt. (1964).

Finley, Sir Peter Hamilton, Kt., OBE, DFC.

Finsberg, Sir Geoffrey, Kt., MBE, MP.

Firth, *Prof.* Sir Raymond William, Kt., Ph.D., FBA.

Fish, Sir Hugh, Kt., CBE.

Fisher, Sir George Read, Kt., CMG.

Fisher, *Hon.* Sir Henry Arthur Pears, Kt.

Fisher, Sir Nigel Thomas Loveridge, Kt., MC.

Fison, Sir (Richard) Guy, Bt., DSC (1905).

Fitch, *Adm.* Sir Richard George Alison, KCB.

Fitzgerald, *Rev.* (Sir) Edward Thomas, Bt. (1903).

FitzGerald, Sir George Peter Maurice, Bt., MC (*The Knight of Kerry*) (1880).

FitzHerbert, Sir Richard Ranulph, Bt. (1784).

Fitzmaurice, *Lt.-Col.* Sir Desmond FitzJohn, Kt., CIE.

Fitzpatrick, *Gen.* Sir (Geoffrey Richard) Desmond, GCB, DSO, MBE, MC.

Fitzpatrick, *Air Marshal* Sir John Bernard, KBE, CB.

Flanagan, Sir James Bernard, Kt., CBE.

Flavelle, Sir (Joseph) David Ellsworth, Bt. (1917).

Fleming, *Instructor Rear-Adm.* Sir John, KBE, DSC.

Fletcher, *Hon.* Sir Alan Roy, Kt.

Fletcher, Sir James Muir Cameron, Kt.

Fletcher, Sir John Henry Lancelot Aubrey-, Bt. (1782).

Fletcher, Sir Leslie, Kt., DSC.

Fletcher, *Air Chief Marshal* Sir Peter Carteret, KCB, OBE, DFC, AFC.

Floyd, Sir Giles Henry Charles, Bt. (1816).

Foley, Sir (Thomas John) Noel, Kt., CBE.

Foot, Sir Geoffrey James, Kt.

Foots, Sir James William, Kt.

Forbes, *Hon.* Sir Alastair Granville, Kt.

Forbes of Pitsligo, Sir Charles Edward Stuart-, Bt. (s. 1626).

Forbes of Brux, *Hon.* Sir Ewan, Bt. (s. 1630).

Forbes, *Maj.* Sir Hamish Stewart, Bt., MBE, MC (1823).

Forbes, *Vice-Adm.* Sir John Morrison, KCB.

Ford, Sir Andrew Russell, Bt. (1929).

Ford, Sir David Robert, KBE, LVO, OBE.

Ford, *Maj.* Sir Edward William Spencer, KCB, KCVO.

Ford, *Air Marshal* Sir Geoffrey Harold, KBE, CB.

Ford, *Prof.* Sir Hugh, Kt., FRS.

†Ford, Sir James Anson St Clair-, Bt. (1793).

Ford, Sir John Archibald, KCMG, MC.

Ford, Sir Richard Brinsley, Kt., CBE.

Ford, *Gen.* Sir Robert Cyril, GCB, CBE.

Foreman, Sir Philip Frank, Kt., CBE.

Forman, Sir John Denis, Kt., OBE.

Forrest, *Prof.* Sir (Andrew) Patrick (McEwen), Kt.

Forrest, Sir James Alexander, Kt.

Forrest, *Rear-Adm.* Sir Ronald Stephen, KCVO.

Forster, Sir Archibald William, Kt.

Forster, Sir Oliver Grantham, KCMG, MVO.

Forwood, Sir Dudley Richard, Bt. (1895).

Foster, *Prof.* Sir Christopher David, Kt.

Foster, Sir John Gregory, Bt. (1930).

Foster, Sir Norman Robert, Kt.

Foster, Sir Robert Sidney, GCMG, KCVO.

Foulis, Sir Ian Primrose Liston-, Bt. (s. 1634).

Foulkes, Sir Nigel Gordon, Kt.

Fowden, Sir Leslie, Kt., FRS.

†Fowke, Sir David Frederick Gustavus, Bt. (1814).

Fowler, Sir (Edward) Michael Coulson, Kt.

Fowler, *Rt. Hon.* Sir (Peter) Norman, Kt., MP.

Fox, Sir (Henry) Murray, GBE.

Fox, Sir (John) Marcus, Kt., MBE, MP.

Fox, *Rt. Hon.* Sir Michael John, Kt.

Fox, Sir Paul Leonard, Kt., CBE.

Frame, Sir Alistair Gilchrist, Kt.

France, Sir Arnold William, GCB.

France, Sir Christopher Walter, KCB.

Francis, Sir Horace William Alexander, Kt., CBE.

Francis, Sir Richard Trevor Langford, KCMG.

Frank, Sir Douglas George Horace, Kt., QC.

Frank, Sir (Frederick) Charles, Kt., OBE, FRS.

Frank, Sir Robert Andrew, Bt. (1920).

Frankel, Sir Otto Herzberg, Kt., D.SC., FRS.

Franklin, Sir Eric Alexander, Kt., CBE.

Franklin, Sir Michael David Milroy, KCB, CMG.

Franks, Sir Arthur Temple, KCMG.

Fraser, Sir Angus McKay, KCB, TD.

Fraser, Sir Basil Malcolm, Bt. (1921).

Fraser, Sir Bruce Donald, KCB.

Fraser, Sir Charles Annand, KCVO.

Fraser, *Gen.* Sir David William, GCB, OBE.

Fraser, Sir Douglas Were, Kt., ISO.

Fraser, *Air Marshal Rev.* Sir (Henry) Paterson, KBE, CB, AFC.

Fraser, Sir Ian, Kt., DSO, OBE.

Fraser, Sir Ian James, Kt., CBE, MC.

Fraser, Sir (James) Campbell, Kt.

Fraser, *Prof.* Sir James David, Bt. (1943).

Fraser, Sir William Kerr, GCB.

Frederick, Sir Charles Boscawen, Bt. (1723).

Freeland, Sir John Redvers, KCMG.

Freeman, Sir James Robin, Bt. (1945).

Freeman, Sir Ralph, Kt., CVO, CBE.

Freer, *Air Chief Marshal* Sir Robert William George, GBE, KCB.

Freeth, *Hon.* Sir Gordon, KBE.

French, *Hon.* Sir Christopher James Saunders, Kt.

Fretwell, Sir (Major) John (Emsley), GCMG.

Freud, Sir Clement Raphael, Kt.

Froggatt, Sir Leslie Trevor, Kt.

Froggatt, Sir Peter, Kt.

Frossard, Sir Charles Keith, Kt.

Frost, *Hon.* Sir (Thomas) Sydney, Kt.

Fry, *Hon.* Sir William Gordon, Kt.

Fryberg, Sir Abraham, Kt., MBE.

Fuchs, Sir Vivian Ernest, Kt., PH.D.

Fuller, *Hon.* Sir John Bryan Munro, Kt.

Fuller, Sir John William Fleetwood, Bt. (1910).

Fung, *Hon.* Sir Kenneth Ping-Fan, Kt., CBE.

Furness, Sir Stephen Roberts, Bt. (1913).

Gadsden, Sir Peter Drury Haggerston, GBE.

Gage, Sir Berkeley Everard Foley, KCMG.

Gairy, *Rt. Hon.* Sir Eric Matthew, Kt.

Gaius, *Rt. Rev.* Saimon, KBE.

Gallwey, Sir Philip Frankland Payne-, Bt. (1812).

Galsworthy, Sir John Edgar, KCVO, CMG.

Gamble, Sir David Hugh Norman, Bt. (1897).

Ganilau, *Ratu* Sir Penaia Kanatabatu, GCMG, KCVO, KBE, DSO.

Gardiner, Sir George Arthur, Kt., MP.

Gardner, Sir Douglas Bruce Bruce-, Bt. (1945).

Gardner, Sir Edward Lucas, Kt., QC.

Garland, *Hon.* Sir Patrick Neville, Kt.

Garland, *Hon.* Sir Ransley Victor, KBE.

Garlick, Sir John, KCB.

Garner, Sir Anthony Stuart, Kt.

Garnier, *Rear-Adm.* Sir John, KCVO, CBE, LVO.

Garrett, *Hon.* Sir Raymond William, Kt., AFC.

Garrioch, Sir (William) Henry, Kt.

Garrod, *Lt.-Gen.* Sir (John) Martin Carruthers, KCB, OBE.

Garthwaite, Sir William Francis Cuthbert, Bt., DSC (1919).

Gaskell, Sir Richard Kennedy Harvey, Kt.

Gatehouse, *Hon.* Sir Robert Alexander, Kt.

Geddes, Sir (Anthony) Reay (Mackay), KBE.

Gentry, *Maj.-Gen.* Sir William George, KBE, CB, DSO.

George, Sir Arthur Thomas, Kt.

Gerken, *Vice-Adm.* Sir Robert William Frank, KCB, CBE.

Gery, Sir Robert Lucian Wade-, KCMG, KCVO.

Gethin, Sir Richard Joseph St Lawrence, Bt. (I. 1665).

Ghurburrun, Sir Rabindrah, Kt.

Gibb, Sir Francis Ross (Frank), Kt., CBE.

Gibbings, Sir Peter Walter, Kt.

Gibbon, *Gen.* Sir John Houghton, GCB, OBE.

Gibbons, Sir (John) David, KBE.

Gibbons, Sir William Edward Doran, Bt. (1752).

Gibbs, *Hon.* Sir Eustace Hubert Beilby, KCVO, CMG.

Gibbs, *Air Marshal* Sir Gerald Ernest, KBE, CIE, MC.

Gibbs, *Rt. Hon.* Sir Harry Talbot, GCMG, KBE.

Gibbs, *Col.* Sir Martin St John Valentine, KCVO, CB, DSO, TD.

Gibbs, *Field Marshal* Sir Roland Christopher, GCB, CBE, DSO, MC.

Gibson, Sir Alexander Drummond, Kt., CBE.

Gibson, Sir Christopher Herbert, Bt. (1931).

Gibson, *Rev.* Sir David, Bt. (1926).

Gibson, *Vice-Adm.* Sir Donald Cameron Ernest Forbes, KCB, DSC.

Gibson, Sir Donald Evelyn Edward, Kt., CBE.

Gibson, *Hon.* Sir Peter Leslie, Kt.

Gibson, *Rt. Hon.* Sir Ralph Brian, Kt.

Giddings, *Air Marshal* Sir (Kenneth Charles) Michael, KCB, OBE, DFC, AFC.

Gielgud, Sir (Arthur) John, Kt., CH.

Giffard, Sir (Charles) Sydney (Rycroft), KCMG.

Gilbert, *Air Chief Marshal* Sir Joseph Alfred, KCB, CBE.

Gilbey, Sir (Walter) Derek, Bt. (1893).

Gilchrist, Sir Andrew Graham, KCMG.

Giles, *Rear-Adm.* Sir Morgan Charles Morgan-, Kt., DSO, OBE, GM.

Gilkison, Sir Alan Fleming, Kt., CBE.

Gill, Sir Anthony Keith, Kt., F. Eng.

Gillett, Sir Robin Danvers Penrose, Bt., GBE, RD (1959).

Gilliat, *Lt.-Col.* Sir Martin John, GCVO, MBE.

Gillmore, Sir David Howe, KCMG.

Gilmour, *Col.* Sir Allan Macdonald, KCVO, OBE, MC.

Gilmour, *Rt. Hon.* Sir Ian Hedworth John Little, Bt., MP (1926)..

Gilmour, Sir John Edward, Bt., DSO, TD (1897).

Gina, Sir Lloyd Maepeza, KBE.

Gingell, *Air Chief Marshal* Sir John, GBE, KCB.

Girolami, Sir Paul, Kt.

Gladstone, Sir (Erskine) William, Bt. (1846).

Glasspole, Sir Florizel Augustus, GCMG, GCVO.

Glen, Sir Alexander Richard, KBE, DSC.

Glenn, Sir (Joseph Robert) Archibald, Kt., OBE.

Glidewell, *Rt. Hon.* Sir Iain Derek Laing, Kt.

Glock, Sir William Frederick, Kt., CBE.

Glover, *Gen.* Sir James Malcolm, KCB, MBE.

Glover, Sir Victor Joseph Patrick, Kt.

Glyn, Sir Alan, Kt., ERD, MP.

Glyn, Sir Anthony Geoffrey Leo Simon, Bt. (1927).

Glyn, Sir Richard Lindsay, Bt. (1759 and 1800).

Goad, Sir (Edward) Colin (Viner), KCMG.

Godber, Sir George Edward, GCB, DM.

Goff, Sir Robert (William) Davis-, Bt. (1905).

Gohel, Sir Jayvantsinhji Kayaji, Kt., CBE.

Gold, Sir Arthur Abraham, Kt., CBE.

Gold, Sir Joseph, Kt.

Goldberg, *Prof.* Sir Abraham, Kt., MD, DSC, FRCP.

Golding, Sir John Simon Rawson, Kt., OBE.

Golding, Sir William Gerald, Kt., CBE.

Goldman, Sir Samuel, KCB.

Goldsmith, Sir James Michael, Kt.

Gombrich, *Prof.* Sir Ernst Hans Josef, Kt., OM, CBE, PH.D., FBA, FSA.

Gooch, Sir (Richard) John Sherlock, Bt. (1746).

Gooch, Sir Robert Douglas, Bt. (1866).

Goodall, Sir (Arthur) David Saunders, GCMG.

Goodenough, Sir Richard Edmund, Bt. (1943).

Goodhart, Sir Philip Carter, Kt., MP.

Goodhart, Sir Robert Anthony Gordon, Bt. (1911).

Goodhart, Sir William Howard, Kt., QC.

Goodhew, Sir Victor Henry, Kt.

Goodison, Sir Alan Clowes, KCMG.

Goodison, Sir Nicholas Proctor, Kt.

Goodson, Sir Mark Weston Lassam, Bt. (1922).

Goodwin, Sir Matthew Dean, Kt., CBE.

Goody, *Most Rev.* Launcelot John, KBE.

Goold, Sir George Leonard, Bt. (1801).

Gordon, Sir Alexander John, Kt., CBE.

Gordon, Sir Andrew Cosmo Lewis Duff-, Bt. (1813).

Gordon, Sir Charles Addison Somerville Snowden, KCB.

Gordon, Sir Keith Lyndell, Kt., CMG.

Gordon, Sir (Lionel) Eldred (Peter) Smith-, Bt. (1838).

Gordon, Sir Robert James, Bt. (s. 1706).

Gordon, Sir Sidney Samuel, Kt., CBE.

Gordon Lennox, Lord Nicholas Charles, KCMG, KCVO.

Gore, Sir Richard Ralph St George, Bt. (I. 1622).

Goring, Sir William Burton Nigel, Bt. (1627).

Gorton, *Rt. Hon.* Sir John Grey, GCMG, CH.

Goschen, Sir Edward Christian, Bt., DSO (1916).

Gosling, Sir (Frederick) Donald, Kt.

Goswell, Sir Brian Lawrence, Kt.

Goulding, Sir (Ernest) Irvine, Kt.

Goulding, Sir (William) Lingard Walter, Bt. (1904).

Gourlay, *Gen.* Sir (Basil) Ian (Spencer), KCB, OBE, MC, RM.

Gourlay, Sir Simon Alexander, Kt.

Govan, Sir Lawrence Herbert, Kt.

Gow, Sir (James) Michael, GCB.

Gow, Sir Leonard Maxwell Harper, Kt., MBE.

Gowans, Sir James Learmonth, Kt., CBE, FRCP, FRS.

Gowans, *Hon.* Sir (Urban) Gregory, Kt.

Graaff, Sir de Villiers, Bt., MBE (1911).

Grabham, Sir Anthony Henry, Kt.

Graesser, *Col.* Sir Alastair Stewart Durward, Kt., DSO, OBE, MC, TD.

Graham, Sir Alexander Michael, GBE.

Graham, Sir Charles Spencer Richard, Bt. (1783).

Graham, Sir James Bellingham, Bt. (1662).

Graham, Sir James Thompson, Kt., CMG.

Graham, Sir John Alexander Noble, Bt., GCMG (1906).

Graham, Sir John Moodie, Bt. (1964).

Graham, Sir (John) Patrick, Kt.

Graham, Sir Norman William, Kt., CB.

Graham, Sir Peter Alfred, Kt., OBE.

Graham, *Lt.-Gen.* Sir Peter Walter, KCB, CBE.

Graham, Sir Ralph Wolfe, Bt. (1629).

Graham, *Hon.* Sir Samuel Horatio, Kt., CMG, OBE.

Grandy, *Marshal of the Royal Air Force* Sir John, GCB, GCVO, KBE, DSO.

Grant, Sir Archibald, Bt. (s. 1705).

Grant, Sir Clifford, Kt.

Grant, Sir (John) Anthony, Kt., MP.

Grant, Sir Patrick Alexander Benedict, Bt. (s. 1688).

Grantham, *Adm.* Sir Guy, GCB, CBE, DSO.

Gray, Sir (Francis) Anthony, KCVO.

Gray, Sir John Archibald Browne, Kt., SC.D., FRS.

Gray, *Vice-Adm.* Sir John Michael Dudgeon, KBE, CB.

Gray, *Lt.-Gen.* Sir Michael Stuart, KCB, OBE.

Gray, Sir William Hume, Bt. (1917).

Gray, Sir William Stevenson, Kt.

Graydon, *Air Chief Marshal* Sir Michael James, KCB, CBE.

†Grayson, Sir Jeremy Brian Vincent Harrington, Bt. (1922).

Green, Sir Allan David, KCB, QC.

Green, Sir (Edward) Stephen (Lycett), Bt., CBE (1886).

Green, Sir George Ernest, Kt.

Green, *Hon.* Sir Guy Stephen Montague, KBE.

Green, Sir Kenneth, Kt.

Green, Sir Owen Whitley, Kt.

Green, Sir Peter James Frederick, Kt.

Greenaway, Sir Derek Burdick, Bt., CBE (1933).

Greenborough, Sir John, KBE.

Greene, Sir (John) Brian Massy-, Kt.

Greengross, Sir Alan David, Kt.

Greening, *Rear-Adm.* Sir Paul Woollven, KCVO.

Greenwell, Sir Edward Bernard, Bt. (1906).

Greeves, *Maj.-Gen.* Sir Stuart, KBE, CB, DSO, MC.

Gregson, Sir Peter Lewis, KCB.

Grenside, Sir John Peter, Kt., CBE.

Gretton, *Vice-Adm.* Sir Peter William, KCB, DSO, OBE, DSC.

Grey, Sir Anthony Dysart, Bt. (1814).

Grey, Sir Roger de, KCVO, PRA.

Grierson, Sir Michael John Bewes, Bt. (s. 1685).

Grierson, Sir Ronald Hugh, Kt.

Grieve, *Prof.* Sir Robert, Kt.

Griffin, *Adm.* Sir Anthony Templer Frederick Griffith, GCB.

Griffin, *Maj.* (Arthur) John (Stewart), KCVO.

Griffin, Sir (Charles) David, Kt., CBE.

Griffin, Sir John Bowes, Kt., QC.

Griffiths, Sir Eldon Wylie, Kt., MP.

Griffiths, Sir (Ernest) Roy, Kt.

Griffiths, Sir John Norton-, Bt. (1922).

Griffiths, Sir Percival Joseph, KBE, CIE.

Grimwade, Sir Andrew Sheppard, Kt., CBE.

Grindrod, *Most Rev.* John Basil Rowland, Kt.

Grinstead, Sir Stanley Gordon, Kt.

Grose, *Vice-Adm.* Sir Alan, KBE.

Grotrian, Sir Philip Christian Brent, Bt. (1934).

Grove, Sir Charles Gerald, Bt. (1874).

Grove, Sir Edmund Frank, KCVO.

Groves, Sir Charles Barnard, Kt., CBE.

Grugeon, Sir John Drury, Kt..

Guinness, Sir Alec, Kt., CBE.

Guinness, Sir Howard Christian Sheldon, Kt., VRD.

Guinness, Sir Kenelm Ernest Lee, Bt. (1867).

Guise, Sir John, GCMG, KBE.

Guise, Sir John Grant, Bt. (1783).

Gujadhur, Sir Radhamohun, Kt., CMG.

Gull, Sir Rupert William Cameron, Bt. (1872).

Gunn, *Prof.* Sir John Currie, Kt., CBE.

Gunn, Sir William Archer, KBE, CMG.

†Gunning, Sir Charles Theodore, Bt. (1778).

†Gunston, Sir John Wellesley, Bt. (1938).

Guthrie, *Gen.* Sir Charles Ronald Llewelyn, KCB, LVO, OBE.

Guthrie, Sir Malcolm Connop, Bt., (1936)

Guy, *Gen.* Sir Roland Kelvin, GCB, CBE, DSO.

Habakkuk, Sir John Hrothgar, Kt., FBA.

Hackett, *Gen.* Sir John Winthrop, GCB, CBE, DSO, MC.

Hadlee, Sir Richard John, Kt., MBE.

Hadley, Sir Leonard Albert, Kt.

Hadow, Sir Gordon, Kt., CMG, OBE.

Hadow, Sir (Reginald) Michael, KCMG.

Hague, *Prof.* Sir Douglas Chalmers, Kt., CBE.

Halberg, Sir Murray Gordon, Kt., MBE.

Hale, *Prof.* Sir John Rigby, Kt.

Hall, Sir Arnold Alexander, Kt., FRS.

Hall, Sir Basil Brodribb, KCB, MC, TD.

Hall, *Air Marshal* Sir Donald Percy, KCB, CBE, AFC.

Hall, Sir Douglas Basil, Bt., KCMG (s. 1687).

Hall, Sir (Frederick) John (Frank), Bt. (1923).

Hall, Sir John, Kt.

Hall, Sir John Bernard, Bt. (1919).

Hall, Sir Peter Reginald Frederick, Kt., CBE.

Hall, Sir Robert de Zouche, KCMG.

Hall, *Brig.* Sir William Henry, KBE, DSO, ED.

Halliday, *Vice-Adm.* Sir Roy William, KBE, DSC.

Hallifax, *Adm.* Sir David John, KCB, KBE.

Hallinan, Sir (Adrian) Lincoln, Kt.

Halpern, Sir Ralph Mark, Kt.

Halsey, *Rev.* Sir John Walter Brooke, Bt. (1920).

Halstead, Sir Ronald, Kt., CBE.

Ham, Sir David Kenneth Rowe-, GBE.

Hambling, Sir (Herbert) Hugh, Bt. (1924).

Hamburger, Sir Sidney Cyril, Kt., CBE.

Hamer, *Hon.* Sir Rupert James, KCMG, ED.

Hamill, Sir Patrick, Kt., QPM.

Hamilton, Sir Edward Sydney, Bt. (1776 and 1819).

Hamilton, Sir James Arnot, KCB, MBE.

Hamilton, *Adm.* Sir John Graham, GBE, CB.

†Hamilton, Sir Malcolm William Bruce Stirling-, Bt. (s. 1673).

Hamilton, Sir Michael Aubrey, Kt.

Hamilton, Sir Patrick George, Bt. (1937).

Hamilton, Sir (Robert Charles) Richard Caradoc, Bt. (s. 1646).

Hammett, *Hon.* Sir Clifford James, Kt.

Hammick, Sir Stephen George, Bt. (1834).

Hampshire, Sir Stuart Newton, Kt., FBA.

Hanbury, Sir John Capel, Kt., CBE.

Hancock, Sir David John Stowell, KCB.

Hancock, *Air Marshal* Sir Valston Eldridge, KBE, CB, DFC.

Hand, *Most Rev.* Geoffrey David, KBE.

Handley, Sir David John Davenport-, Kt., OBE.

Hanham, Sir Michael William, Bt., DFC (1667).

Hanley, Sir Michael Bowen, KCB.

Hanmer, Sir John Wyndham Edward, Bt. (1774).

Hannay, Sir David Hugh Alexander, KCMG.

Hanson, Sir Anthony Leslie Oswald, Bt. (1887).

Hanson, Sir (Charles) John, Bt. (1918).

Harders, Sir Clarence Waldemar, Kt., OBE.

Hardie, Sir Charles Edgar Mathewes, Kt., CBE.

Hardie, Sir Douglas Fleming, Kt., CBE.

Harding, Sir Christopher George Francis, Kt.

Harding, Sir George William, KCMG, CVO.

Harding, *Air Chief Marshal* Sir Peter Robin, GCB.

Harding, Sir Roy Pollard, Kt., CBE.

Hardinge, Sir Robert Arnold, Bt. (1801).

Hardingham, Sir Robert Ernest, Kt., CMG, OBE.

Hardman, Sir Henry, KCB.

Hardy, Sir James Gilbert, Kt., OBE.

Hardy, Sir Rupert John, Bt. (1876).

Hare, Sir Thomas, Bt. (1818).

Harford, Sir James Dundas, KBE, CMG.

Harford, Sir (John) Timothy, Bt. (1934).

Hargroves, *Brig.* Sir Robert Louis, Kt., CBE.

Harington, *Gen.* Sir Charles Henry Pepys, GCB, CBE, DSO, MC.

Harington, Sir Nicholas John, Bt. (1611).

Harland, *Air Marshal* Sir Reginald Edward Wynyard, KBE, CB.

Harman, *Gen.* Sir Jack Wentworth, GCB, OBE, MC.

Harman, *Hon.* Sir Jeremiah LeRoy, Kt.

Harmer, Sir Frederic Evelyn, Kt., CMG.

Harmsworth, Sir Hildebrand Harold, Bt. (1922).

Harpham, Sir William, KBE, CMG.

Harris, *Prof.* Sir Alan James, Kt., CBE.

Harris, Sir Anthony Kyrle Travers, Bt. (1953).

Harris, *Prof.* Sir Charles Herbert Stuart-, Kt., CBE, MD.

Harris, *Lt.-Gen.* Sir Ian Cecil, KBE, CB, DSO.

Harris, Sir Jack Wolfred Ashford, Bt. (1932).

Harris, Sir Philip Charles, Kt.

Harris, Sir Ronald Montague Joseph, KCVO, CB.

Harris, Sir William Gordon, KBE, CB.

Harrison, Sir Donald Frederick Norris, Kt., FRCS.

Harrison, Sir Ernest Thomas, Kt., OBE..

Harrison, Sir Francis Alexander Lyle, Kt., MBE, QC.

Harrison, *Surgeon Vice-Adm.* Sir John Albert Bews, KBE.

Harrison, *Hon.* Sir (John) Richard, Kt., ED.

Harrison, Sir Michael James Harwood, Bt. (1961).

Harrison, *Prof.* Sir Richard John, Kt., FRS.

Harrison, Sir (Robert) Colin, Bt. (1922).

Harrop, Sir Peter John, KCB.

Hart, Sir Francis Edmund Turton-, KBE.

Hartley, *Air Marshal* Sir Christopher Harold, KCB, CBE, DFC, AFC.

Hartley, Sir Frank, Kt., CBE, Ph.D.

Hartopp, Sir John Edmund Cradock-, Bt. (1796).

Hartwell, Sir Brodrick William Charles Elwin, Bt. (1805).

Harvey, Sir Charles Richard Musgrave, Bt. (1933).

Haskard, Sir Cosmo Dugal Patrick Thomas, KCMG, MBE.

Haslam, *Hon.* Sir Alec Leslie, Kt.

Haslam, *Rear-Adm.* Sir David William, KBE, CB.

Hasluck, *Rt. Hon.* Sir Paul Meernaa Caedwalla, KG, GCMG, GCVO.

Hassan, Sir Joshua Abraham, GBE, KCMG, LVO, QC.

Hassett, *Gen.* Sir Francis George, KBE, CB, DSO, MVO.

Hastings, Sir Stephen Lewis Edmonstone, Kt., MC.

Hatty, *Hon.* Sir Cyril James, Kt.

Haughton, Sir James, Kt., CBE, QPM.

Havelock, Sir Wilfrid Bowen, Kt.

Hawkins, Sir Arthur Ernest, Kt.

Hawkins, Sir Humphry Villiers Caesar, Bt. (1778).

Hawkins, Sir Paul Lancelot, Kt., TD.

Hawley, Sir Donald Frederick, KCMG, MBE.

†Hawley, Sir Henry Nicholas, Bt. (1795).

Haworth, Sir Philip, Bt. (1911).

Hawthorne, *Prof.* Sir William Rede, Kt., CBE, SC.D., FRS.

Hay, Sir Arthur Thomas Erroll, Bt., ISO (s. 1663).

Hay, Sir David Osborne, Kt., CBE, DSO.

Hay, Sir David Russell, Kt., CBE, FRCP, MD.

Hay, Sir Hamish Grenfell, Kt.

Hay, Sir James Brian Dalrymple-, Kt.

†Hay, Sir Ronald Frederick Hamilton, Bt. (s. 1703).

Hayday, Sir Frederick, Kt., CBE.

Haydon, Sir Walter Robert, KCMG.

Hayes, Sir Brian David, GCB.

Hayes, Sir Claude James, KCMG.

Hayes, *Vice-Adm.* Sir John Osier Chattock, KCB, OBE.

Hayhoe, *Rt. Hon.* Sir Bernard John (Barney), Kt., MP.

Hayman, Sir Peter Telford, KCMG, CVO, MBE.

Hayr, *Air Marshal* Sir Kenneth William, KCB, KBE, AFC.

Hayter, Sir William Goodenough, KCMG.

Hayward, Sir Anthony William Byrd, Kt.

Hayward, Sir Jack Arnold, Kt., OBE.

Hayward, Sir Richard Arthur, Kt., CBE.

Haywood, Sir Harold, KCVO, OBE.

Head, Sir Francis David Somerville, Bt. (1838).

Healey, Sir Charles Edward Chadwyck-, Bt. (1919).

Heap, Sir Desmond, Kt.

Heath, Sir Mark Evelyn, KCVO, CMG.

Heath, *Air Marshal* Sir Maurice Lionel, KBE, CB, CVO.

Heathcote, *Brig.* Sir Gilbert Simon, Bt., CBE (1733).

Heathcote, Sir Michael Perryman, Bt. (1733).

Heatley, Sir Peter, Kt., CBE.

Heaton, Sir Yvo Robert Henniker-, Bt. (1912).

Heiser, Sir Terence Michael, KCB.

Hele, Sir Ivor Thomas Henry, Kt., CBE.

Hellaby, Sir (Frederick Reed) Alan, Kt.

Henderson, Sir Denys Hartley, Kt.

Henderson, Sir James Thyne, KBE, CMG.

Henderson, Sir (John) Nicholas, GCMG, KCVO.

Henderson, *Adm.* Sir Nigel Stuart, GBE, KCB.

Henderson, Sir William MacGregor, Kt., D.Sc., FRS.

Henley, Sir Douglas Owen, KCB.

Henley, *Rear-Adm.* Sir Joseph Charles Cameron, KCVO, CB.

Hennessy, Sir James Patrick Ivan, KBE, CMG.

Hennessy, Sir John Wyndham Pope-, Kt., CBE, FBA, FSA.

Henniker, *Brig.* Sir Mark Chandos Auberon, Bt., CBE, DSO, MC (1813).

Henry, Sir Denis Aynsley, Kt., OBE, QC.

Henry, *Hon.* Denis Robert Maurice, Kt.

Henry, Sir James Holmes, Bt., CMG, MC, TD, QC (1923).

Henry, *Hon.* Sir Trevor Ernest, Kt.

Hepburn, Sir Ninian Buchan Archibald John Buchan-, Bt. (1815).

Herbecq, Sir John Edward, KCB.

Herbert, *Adm.* Sir Peter Geoffrey Marshall, KCB, OBE.

Hermon, Sir John Charles, Kt., OBE, QPM.

Heron, Sir Conrad Frederick, KCB, OBE.

Herries, Sir Michael Alexander Robert Young-, Kt., OBE, MC.

Heseltine, *Rt. Hon.* Sir William Frederick Payne, GCB, GCVO.

Hetherington, Sir Arthur Ford, Kt., DSC.

Hetherington, Sir Thomas Chalmers, KCB, CBE, TD, QC.

Heward, *Air Chief Marshal* Sir Anthony Wilkinson, KCB, OBE, DFC, AFC.

Hewetson, Sir Christopher Raynor, Kt., TD.

Hewetson, *Gen.* Sir Reginald Hackett, GCB, CBE, DSO.

†Hewett, Sir Peter John Smithson, Bt., MM (1813).

Hewitt, Sir (Cyrus) Lenox (Simson), Kt., OBE.

Hewitt, Sir Nicholas Charles Joseph, Bt. (1921).

Heygate, Sir George Lloyd, Bt. (1831).

Heyman, Sir Horace William, Kt.

Heywood, Sir Oliver Kerr, Bt. (1838).

Hezlet, *Vice-Adm.* Sir Arthur Richard, KBE, CB, DSO, DSC.

Hibbert, Sir Jack, KCB.

Hibbert, Sir Reginald Alfred, GCMG.

Hickey, Sir Justin, Kt.

Hickman, Sir (Richard) Glenn, Bt. (1903).

Hidden, *Hon.* Sir Anthony Brian, Kt.

Hielscher, Sir Leo Arthur, Kt.

Higgins, Sir Christopher Thomas, Kt.

Higgins, *Hon.* John Patrick Basil, Kt.

Higgs, Sir (John) Michael (Clifford), Kt.

Hildreth, *Maj.-Gen.* Sir (Harold) John (Crossley), Kt.

Hildyard, Sir David Henry Thoroton, KCMG, DFC.

Hiley, *Hon.* Sir Thomas Alfred, KBE.

Hill, Sir Alexander Rodger Erskine-, Bt. (1945).

Hill, Sir Arthur Alfred, Kt., CBE.

Hill, Sir Brian John, Kt.

Hill, Sir James Frederick, Bt. (1917).

Hill, Sir John McGregor, Kt., Ph.D.

Hill, Sir John Maxwell, Kt., CBE, DFC.

Hill, Sir Richard George Rowley, Bt., MBE (I. 1779).

Hill, *Vice-Adm.* Sir Robert Charles Finch, KBE.

Hillary, Sir Edmund, KBE.

Hillhouse, Sir (Robert) Russell, KCB.

Hills, Sir Graham John, Kt.

Himsworth, Sir Harold Percival, KCB, MD, FRS.

Hine, *Air Chief Marshal* Sir Patrick Bardon, GCB, GBE.

Hines, Sir Colin Joseph, Kt., OBE.

Hinsley, *Prof.* Sir Francis Harry, Kt., OBE, FBA.

Hirsch, *Prof.* Sir Peter Bernhard, Kt., Ph.D., FRS.

Hirst, *Hon.* Sir David Cozens-Hardy, Kt.

Hoare, Sir Peter Richard David, Bt. (1786).

Hoare, Sir Timothy Edward Charles, Bt. (I. 1784).

Hobart, Sir John Vere, Bt. (1914).

Hobday, Sir Gordon Ivan, Kt.

†Hobhouse, Sir Charles John Spinney, Bt. (1812).

Hobhouse, *Hon.* Sir John Stewart, Kt.

Hobson, Sir Harold, Kt., CBE.

Hockaday, Sir Arthur Patrick, KCB, CMG.

Hockley, *Gen.* Sir Anthony Heritage Farrar-, GBE, KCB, DSO, MC.

Hodge, Sir John Rowland, Bt., MBE (1921).

Hodge, Sir Julian Stephen Alfred, Kt.

Hodges, *Air Chief Marshal* Sir Lewis MacDonald, KCB, CBE, DSO, DFC.

Hodgkin, *Prof.* Sir Alan Lloyd, OM, KBE, FRS, SC.D.

Hodgkinson, *Air Chief Marshal* Sir (William) Derek, KCB, CBE, DFC, AFC.

Hodgson, Sir Maurice Arthur Eric, Kt.

Hodgson, *Hon.* Sir (Walter) Derek (Thornley), Kt.

Hodson, Sir Michael Robin Adderley, Bt. (I. 1789).

Hoffenberg, *Prof.* Sir Raymond, KBE.

Hoffman, *Hon.* Sir Leonard Hubert, Kt.

Hogg, *Maj.* Sir Arthur Ramsay, Bt., MBE (1846).

Hogg, Sir Christopher Anthony, Kt.

Hogg, Sir Edward William Lindsay-, Bt. (1905).

Hogg, *Vice-Adm.* Sir Ian Leslie Trower, KCB, DSC.

Hogg, Sir John Nicholson, Kt., TD.

Holcroft, Sir Peter George Culcheth, Bt. (1921).

Holden, Sir David Charles Beresford, KBE, CB, ERD.

Holden, Sir Edward, Bt. (1893).

Holden, Sir John David, Bt. (1919).

Holder, Sir John Henry, Bt. (1898).

Holder, *Air Marshal* Sir Paul Davie, KBE, CB, DSO, DFC, Ph.D.

Holderness, Sir Richard William, Bt. (1920).

Holdsworth, Sir (George) Trevor, Kt.

Holland, Sir Clifton Vaughan, Kt.

Holland, Sir Geoffrey, KCB.

Holland, Sir Guy (Hope), Bt. (1917).

Holland, Sir Kenneth Lawrence, Kt., CBE, QFSM.

Holland, Sir Philip Welsby, Kt.

Holliday, *Prof.* Sir Frederick George Thomas, Kt., CBE, FRSE.

Hollings, *Hon.* Sir (Alfred) Kenneth, Kt., MC.

Hollis, *Hon.* Sir Anthony Barnard, Kt.

Hollom, Sir Jasper Quintus, KBE.

Holloway, *Hon.* Sir Barry Blyth, KBE.

Holm, Sir Carl Henry, Kt., OBE.

Holmes, *Prof.* Sir Frank Wakefield, Kt.

Holmes, Sir Maurice Andrew, Kt.

Holmes, Sir Peter Fenwick, Kt., MC.

Holroyd, *Air Marshal* Sir Frank Martyn, KBE, CB.

Holt, *Prof.* Sir James Clarke, Kt.

Holt, Sir John Anthony Langford-, Kt.

Home, Sir David George, Bt. (s. 1671).

Hone, *Maj.-Gen.* Sir (Herbert) Ralph, KCMG, KBE, MC, TD, QC.

Honeycombe, *Prof.* Sir Robert William Kerr, Kt., FRS.

Honywood, Sir Filmer Courtenay William, Bt. (1660).

Hood, Sir Alexander William Fuller-Acland-, Bt. (1806).

Hood, Sir Harold Joseph, Bt., TD (1922).

Hookway, Sir Harry Thurston, Kt.

Hoole, Sir Arthur Hugh, Kt.

Hooper, Sir Leonard James, KCMG, CBE.

Hope, Sir (Charles) Peter, KCMG, TD.

Hope, Sir John Carl Alexander, Bt. (s. 1628).

Hope, Sir Robert Holms-Kerr, Bt. (1932).

Hopkin, Sir David Armand, Kt.

Hopkin, Sir (William Aylsham) Bryan, Kt., CBE.

Hopkins, Sir James Sidney Rawdon Scott-, Kt., MEP.

Hordern, Sir Michael Murray, Kt., CBE.

Hordern, Sir Peter Maudslay, Kt., MP.

Horlick, *Vice-Adm.* Sir Edwin John, KBE.

Horlick, Sir John James Macdonald, Bt. (1914).

Hornby, Sir Derek Peter, Kt.

Hornby, Sir Simon Michael, Kt.

Horne, Sir Alan Gray Antony, Bt. (1929).

Horsfall, Sir John Musgrave, Bt., MC, TD (1909).

Horsley, *Air Marshal* Sir (Beresford) Peter (Torrington), KCB, CBE, MVO, AFC.

Hort, Sir James Fenton, Bt. (1767).

Hoskyns, Sir Benedict Leigh, Bt. (1676).

Hoskyns, Sir John Austin Hungerford Leigh, Kt.

Houghton, Sir John Theodore, Kt., CBE, FRS.

†Houldsworth, Sir Richard Thomas Reginald, Bt. (1887).

Hounsfield, Sir Godfrey Newbold, Kt., CBE.

House, *Lt.-Gen.* Sir David George, GCB, KCVO, CBE, MC.

Houssemayne du Boulay, Sir Roger William, KCVO, CMG.

Howard, Sir (Hamilton) Edward de Coucey, Bt., GBE (1955).

Howard, Sir John Philip, Bt. (1841).

Howard, *Prof.* Sir Michael Eliot, Kt., CBE, MC.

Howard, *Maj.-Gen.* Lord Michael Fitzalan-, GCVO, CB, CBE, MC.

Howard, Sir Walter Stewart, Kt., MBE.

Howe, *Rt. Hon.* Sir (Richard Edward) Geoffrey, Kt., QC, MP.

Howie, Sir James William, Kt.

Howlett, *Gen.* Sir Geoffrey Hugh Whitby, KBE, MC.

Hoyle, *Prof.* Sir Fred, Kt., FRS.

Hoyos, *Hon.* Sir Fabriciano Alexander, Kt.

Huckle, Sir (Henry) George, Kt., OBE.

Huddie, Sir David Patrick, Kt.

Hudleston, *Air Chief Marshal* Sir Edmund Cuthbert, GCB, CBE.

Hudson, Sir Havelock Henry Trevor, Kt.

Hudson, *Lt.-Gen.* Sir Peter, KCB, CBE.

Huggins, *Hon.* Sir Alan Armstrong, Kt.

Hugh-Jones, Sir Wynn Normington, Kt., MVO.

Hughes, Sir David Collingwood, Bt. (1773).

Hughes, *Prof.* Sir Edward Stuart Reginald, Kt., CBE.

Hughes, Sir Jack William, Kt.

Hughes, *Air Marshal* Sir (Sidney Weetman) Rochford, KCB, CBE, AFC.

Hughes, Sir Trevor Denby Lloyd-, Kt.

Hughes, Sir Trevor Poulton, KCB.

Hugo, *Lt.-Col.* Sir John Mandeville, KCVO, OBE.

Hulse, Sir (Hamilton) Westrow, Bt. (1739).

Hulton, Sir Geoffrey Alan, Bt. (1905).

Hume, Sir Alan Blyth, Kt., CB.

Humphreys, Sir Olliver William, Kt., CBE.

Humphreys, Sir (Raymond Evelyn) Myles, Kt.

Hunn, Sir Jack Kent, Kt., CMG.

Hunt, Sir David Wathen Stather, KCMG, OBE.

Hunt, Sir John Leonard, Kt., MP.

Hunt, *Adm.* Sir Nicholas John Streynsham, GCB, LVO.

Hunt, Sir Rex Masterman, Kt., CMG.

Hunt, Sir Robert Frederick, Kt., CBE.

Hunter, *Hon.* Sir Alexander Albert, KBE.

Hunter, Sir Ian Bruce Hope, Kt., MBE.

Hurley, Sir John Garling, Kt., CBE.

Hurrell, Sir Anthony Gerald, KCVO, CMG.

Hutchinson, *Hon.* Sir Ross, Kt., DFC.

Hutchison, *Lt.-Cdr.* Sir (George) Ian Clark, Kt., RN.

Hutchison, *Hon.* Sir Michael, Kt.

Hutchison, Sir Peter, Bt. (1939).

Hutchison, Sir Peter Craft, Bt. (1956).

Hutson, Sir Francis Challenor, Kt., CBE.

Hutton, *Rt. Hon.* Sir (James) Brian Edward, Kt.

Huxley, *Prof.* Sir Andrew Fielding, Kt., OM, FRS.

Huxtable, *Gen.* Sir Charles Richard, KCB, CBE.

Hyatali, *Hon.* Sir Isaac Emanuel, Kt.

Ibbs, Sir (John) Robin, KBE.

Ihaka, *Ven.* Sir Kingi Matutaera, Kt., MBE.

Imbert, Sir Peter Michael, Kt., QPM.

Inch, Sir John Ritchie, Kt., CVO, CBE.

Inge, *Gen.* Sir Peter Anthony, KCB.

Ingham, Sir Bernard, Kt.

Ingilby, Sir Thomas Colvin William, Bt. (1866).

Inglefield, Sir Gilbert Samuel, GBE, TD.

Inglis, Sir Brian Scott, Kt.

Inglis of Glencorse, Sir Roderick John, Bt. (s. 1703).

Ingram, Sir James Herbert Charles, Bt. (1893).

†Innes, Sir David Charles Kenneth Gordon, Bt. (NS 1686).

Innes of Edingight, Sir Malcolm Rognvald, KCVO.

Innes, Sir Peter Alexander Berowald, Bt. (s. 1628).

Inniss, *Hon.* Sir Clifford de Lisle, Kt.

Irish, Sir Ronald Arthur, Kt., OBE.

Irvine, *Rt. Hon.* Sir Bryant Godman, Kt.

Irvine, *Dr.* Sir Robin Orlando Hamilton, Kt.

Irving, Sir Charles Graham, Kt., MP.

Irwin, Sir James Campbell, Kt., OBE, ED.

Isham, Sir Ian Vere Gyles, Bt. (1627).

Jack, *Hon.* Sir Alieu Sulayman, Kt.

Jack, Sir David, GCMG, MBE.

Jackman, *Air Marshal* Sir (Harold) Douglas, KBE, CB.

Jackson, *Air Chief Marshal* Sir Brendan James, KCB.

Jackson, Sir (John) Edward, KCMG.

Jackson, *Hon.* Sir Lawrence Walter, KCMG.

Jackson, Sir Michael Roland, Bt. (1902).

Jackson, Sir Nicholas Fane St George, Bt. (1913).

Jackson, *Air Vice-Marshal* Sir Ralph Coburn, KBE, CB.

Jackson, Sir Robert, Bt. (1815).

Jackson, *Gen.* Sir William Godfrey Fothergill, GBE, KCB, MC.

Jackson, Sir William Thomas, Bt. (1869).

Jacob, *Lt.-Gen.* Sir (Edward) Ian (Claud), GBE, CB.

Jacob, Sir Isaac Hai, Kt., QC.

Jacobi, *Dr.* Sir James Edward, Kt., OBE.

Jacobs, Sir David Anthony, Kt.

Jacobs, *Hon.* Sir Kenneth Sydney, KBE.

Jacobs, Sir Piers, KBE.

Jacobs, Sir Wilfred Ebenezer, GCMG, GCVO, OBE, QC.

Jacomb, Sir Martin Wakefield, Kt.

Jaffray, Sir William Otho, Bt. (1892).

Jakeway, Sir (Francis) Derek, KCMG, OBE.

James, Sir Cynlais Morgan, KCMG.

James, Sir Gerard Bowes Kingston, Bt. (1823).

James, Sir Robert Vidal Rhodes, Kt., MP.

Jamieson, *Air Marshal* Sir David Ewan, KBE, CB.

Janion, *Rear-Adm.* Sir Hugh Penderel, KCVO.

Jansen, Sir Ross Malcolm, KBE.

Janvrin, *Vice-Adm.* Sir (Hugh) Richard Benest, KCB, DSC.

Jardine, Sir Andrew Colin Douglas, Bt. (1916).

Jardine, *Maj.* Sir (Andrew) Rupert (John) Buchanan-, Bt., MC (1885).

Jardine of Applegirth, Sir Alexander Maule, Bt. (s. 1672).

Jarratt, Sir Alexander Anthony, Kt., CB.

Jarrett, Sir Clifford George, KBE, CB.

Jawara, *Hon.* Sir Dawda Kairaba, Kt.

Jay, Sir Antony Rupert, Kt.

Jeewoolall, Sir Ramesh, Kt.

Jeffcoate, Sir (Thomas) Norman (Arthur), Kt., MD, FRCS.

Jefferson, Sir George Rowland, Kt., CBE.

Jefferson, Sir Mervyn Stewart Dunnington-, Bt. (1958).

Jehangir, Sir Hirji, Bt. (1908).

Jejeebhoy, Sir Rustom, Bt. (1857).

Jellicoe, Sir Geoffrey Alan, Kt., CBE, FRIBA.

Jenkins, Sir Michael Romilly Heald, KCMG.

Jenkins, Sir Owain Trevor, Kt.

Jenkinson, Sir John Banks, Bt. (1661).

Jenks, Sir Richard Atherley, Bt. (1932).

Jennings, Sir Albert Victor, Kt.

Jennings, Sir Raymond Winter, Kt., QC.

Jennings, *Prof.* Sir Robert Yewdall, Kt., QC.

Jenour, Sir (Arthur) Maynard (Chesterfield), Kt., TD.

Jephcott, Sir (John) Anthony, Bt. (1962).

Jessel, Sir Charles John, Bt. (1883).

Jewkes, Sir Gordon Wesley, KCMG.

Joel, *Hon.* Sir Asher Alexander, KBE.

John, Sir Rupert Godfrey, Kt.

Johnson, *Rt. Hon.* Sir David Powell Croom-, Kt., DSC, VRD.

Johnson, *Lt.-Gen.* Sir Garry Dene, KCB, OBE, MC.

Johnson, Sir John Rodney, KCMG.

Johnson, Sir Peter Colpoys Paley, Bt. (1755).

Johnson, *Hon.* Sir Robert Lionel, Kt.

†Johnson, Sir Robin Eliot, Bt. (1818).

Johnson, Sir Ronald Ernest Charles, Kt., CB.

Johnston, Sir Alexander, GCB, KBE.

Johnston, Sir (David) Russell, Kt., MP.

Johnston, Sir Edward Alexander, KBE, CB.

Johnston, Sir John Baines, GCMG, KCVO.

Johnston, *Lt.-Col.* Sir John Frederick Dame, GCVO, MC.

Johnston, *Lt.-Gen.* Sir Maurice Robert, KCB, OBE.

Johnston, Sir Thomas Alexander, Bt. (s. 1626).

Johnstone, Sir Frederic Allan George, Bt. (s. 1700).

Jolliffe, Sir Anthony Stuart, GBE.

Jones, *Gen.* Sir (Charles) Edward Webb, KCB, CBE.

Jones, Sir Christopher Lawrence-, Bt. (1831).

Jones, *Air Marshal* Sir Edward Gordon, KCB, CBE, DSO, DFC.

Jones, Sir (Edward) Martin Furnival, Kt., CBE.

Jones, *Rt. Hon.* Sir Edward Warburton, Kt.

Jones, Sir Ewart Ray Herbert, Kt., D.SC., Ph.D., FRS.

Jones, Sir Francis Avery, Kt., CBE, FRCP.

Jones, *Air Marshal* Sir George, KBE, CB, DFC.

Jones, Sir Glyn Smallwood, GCMG, MBE.

Jones, Sir Gordon Pearce, Kt.

Jones, Sir Harry Ernest, Kt., CBE.

Jones, Sir James Duncan, KCB.

Jones, Sir John Henry Harvey-, Kt., MBE.

Jones, Sir (John) Kenneth (Trevor), Kt., CBE, QC.

Jones, Sir John Lewis, KCB, CMG.

Jones, Sir John Prichard-, Bt. (1910).

Jones, Sir Keith Stephen, Kt.

Jones, *Hon.* Sir Kenneth George Illtyd, Kt.

Jones, *Air Marshal* Sir Laurence Alfred, KCB, CB, AFC.

Jones, Sir (Owen) Trevor, Kt.

Jones, Sir (Peter) Hugh (Jefferd) Lloyd-, Kt.

Jones, Sir Richard Anthony Lloyd, KCB.

Jones, Sir Robert Edward, Kt.

Jones, Sir Simon Warley Frederick Benton, Bt. (1919).

Jones, Sir (Thomas) Philip, Kt., CB.

Jones, Sir (William) Emrys, Kt.

Jones, *Hon.* Sir William Lloyd Mars-, Kt., MBE.

Jordan, *Air Marshal* Sir Richard Bowen, KCB, DFC.

Joseph, *Maj.* Sir (Herbert) Leslie, Kt.

Joughin, Sir Michael, Kt., CBE.

Jowitt, *Hon.* Sir Edwin Frank, Kt.

Judge, *Hon.* Sir Igor, Kt.

Jugnauth, *Rt. Hon.* Sir Anerood, KCMG, QC.

Jungius, *Vice-Adm.*, Sir James George, KBE.

Junor, Sir John Donald Brown, Kt.

Jupp, *Hon.* Sir Kenneth Graham, Kt., MC.

Kaberry, *Hon.* Sir Christopher Donald, Bt. (1960).

Kadoorie, Sir Horace, CBE.

Kalo, Sir Kwamala, Kt., MBE.

Kan Yuet-Keung, Sir, GBE.

Kapi, *Hon.* Sir Mari, Kt., CBE.

Karimjee, Sir Tayabali Hassanali Alibhoy, Kt.

Katsina, The Emir of, KBE, CMG.

Katz, Sir Bernard, Kt., FRS.

Kavali, Sir Thomas, Kt., OBE.

Kawharu, *Prof.* Sir Ian Hugh, Kt.

Kay, *Prof.* Sir Andrew Watt, Kt.

Kaye, Sir David Alexander Gordon, Bt. (1923).

Kaye, Sir Emmanuel, Kt., CBE.

Kaye, Sir John Phillip Lister Lister-, Bt. (1812).

Keane, Sir Richard Michael, Bt. (1801).

Keatinge, Sir Edgar Mayne, Kt., CBE.

Keeble, Sir (Herbert Ben) Curtis, GCMG.

Keith, *Prof.* Sir James, KBE.

Kellett, Sir Brian Smith, Kt.

Kellett, Sir Stanley Charles, Bt. (1801).

Kelliher, Sir Henry Joseph, Kt.

Kelly, *Rt. Hon.* Sir (John William) Basil, Kt.

Kelly, Sir William Theodore, Kt., OBE.

Kemball, *Air Marshal* Sir (Richard) John, KCB, CBE.

Kemp, Sir (Edward) Peter, KCB.

Kemsley, *Col.* Sir Alfred Newcombe, KBE, CMG, ED.

Kendrew, Sir John Cowdery, Kt., CBE, SC.D., FRS.

Kenilorea, *Rt. Hon.* Sir Peter, KBE.

Kennard, *Lt.-Col.* Sir George Arnold Ford, Bt. (1891).

Kennaway, Sir John Lawrence, Bt. (1791).

Kennedy, Sir Albert Henry, Kt.

Kennedy, Sir Clyde David Allen, Kt.

Kennedy, Sir Francis, KCMG, CBE.

Kennedy, *Hon.* Sir Ian Alexander, Kt.

Kennedy, Sir Michael Edward, Bt., (1836).

Kennedy, *Hon.* Sir Paul Joseph Morrow, Kt.

Kennedy, *Air Chief Marshal* Sir Thomas Lawrie, GCB, AFC.

Kennedy-Good, Sir John, KBE.

Kenny, *Gen.* Sir Brian Leslie Graham, GCB, CBE.

Kent, Sir Harold Simcox, GCB, QC.

Kenyon, Sir George Henry, Kt.

Kermode, Sir (John) Frank, Kt., FBA.

Kermode, Sir Ronald Graham Quale, KBE.

Kerr, *Hon.* Sir Alastair Blair-, Kt.

Kerr, *Adm.* Sir Edwin Beverley, KCB.

Kerr, Sir John Olav, KCMG.

Kerr, *Rt. Hon.* Sir Michael Robert Emanuel, Kt.

Kerruish, Sir (Henry) Charles, Kt., OBE.

Kerry, Sir Michael James, KCB, QC.

Kershaw, Sir (John) Anthony, Kt., MC.

Keville, Sir (William) Errington, Kt., CBE.

Kidd, Sir Robert Hill, KBE, CB.

Kidu, *Hon.* Sir Buri (William), Kt.

Kikau, *Ratu* Sir Jone Latianara, KBE.

Kiki, *Hon.* Sir (Albert) Maori, KBE.

Killen, *Hon.* Denis James, KCMG.

Killick, Sir John Edward, GCMG.

Kilpatrick, *Prof.* Sir Robert, Kt., CBE.

Kimber, Sir Charles Dixon, Bt. (1904).

Kinahan, Sir Robert George Caldwell, Kt., ERD.

King, Sir Albert, Kt., OBE.

King, *Gen.* Sir Frank Douglas, GCB, MBE.

King, Sir John Christopher, Bt. (1888).

King, *Vice-Adm.* Sir Norman Ross Dutton, KBE.

King, Sir Richard Brian Meredith, KCB, MC.

King, Sir Sydney Percy, Kt., OBE.

King, Sir Wayne Alexander, Bt. (1815).

Kingman, *Prof.* Sir John Frank Charles, Kt., FRS.

Kingsland, Sir Richard, Kt., CBE, DFC.

Kingsley, Sir Patrick Graham Toler, KCVO.

Kinloch, Sir David, Bt. (s. 1686).

Kinloch, Sir John, Bt. (1873).

Kirby, *Hon.* Sir Richard Clarence, Kt.

Kirkpatrick, Sir Ivone Elliott, Bt. (s. 1685).

Kirwan, Sir (Archibald) Laurence Patrick, KCMG, TD.

Kitson, *Gen.* Sir Frank Edward, GBE, KCB, MC.

Kitson, Sir Timothy Peter Geoffrey, Kt.

Kitto, *Rt. Hon.* Sir Frank Walters, KBE.

Kleinwort, Sir Kenneth Drake, Bt. (1909).

Klug, Sir Aaron, Kt.

Knight, Sir Allan Walton, Kt., CMG.

Knight, Sir Arthur William, Kt.

Knight, Sir Harold Murray, KBE, DSC.

Knight, *Air Chief Marshal* Sir Michael William Patrick, KCB, AFC.

Knill, Sir John Kenelm Stuart, Bt. (1893).

Knipe, Sir Leslie Francis, Kt., MBE.

Knott, Sir John Laurence, Kt., CBE.

Knowles, Sir Charles Francis, Bt. (1765).

Knowles, Sir Leonard Joseph, Kt., CBE.

Knowles, Sir Richard Marchant, Kt.

Knox, Sir Bryce Muir, KCVO, MC, TD.

Knox, *Hon.* Sir John Leonard, Kt.

Knox, *Hon.* Sir William Edward, Kt.

Kornberg, *Prof.* Sir Hans Leo, Kt., D.SC., SC.D., Ph.D., FRS.

Krusin, Sir Stanley Marks, Kt., CB.

Kurongku, *Most. Rev.* Peter, KBE.

Labouchere, Sir George Peter, GBE, KCMG.

Lacon, Sir Edmund Vere, Bt. (1818).

Lacy, Sir Hugh Maurice Pierce, Bt. (1921).

Lagesen, *Air Marshal* Sir Philip Jacobus, KCB, DFC, AFC.

Laidlaw, Sir Christophor Charles Fraser, Kt.

Laing, Sir (John) Maurice, Kt.

Laing, Sir (William) Kirby, Kt.

Lake, Sir (Atwell) Graham, Bt. (1711).

Laker, Sir Frederick Alfred, Kt.

Lakin, Sir Michael, Bt. (1909).

Laking, Sir George Robert, KCMG.

Lamb, Sir Albert (Larry), Kt.

Lamb, Sir Albert Thomas, KBE, CMG, DFC.

Lamb, Sir Lionel Henry, KCMG, OBE.

Lambert, Sir Anthony Edward, KCMG.

Lambert, Sir Edward Thomas, KBE, CVO.

Lambert, Sir John Henry, KCVO, CMG.

†Lambert, Sir Peter John Biddulph, Bt. (1711).

Lampl, Sir Frank William, Kt.

Lancaster, *Vice-Adm.* Sir John Strike, KBE, CB.

Landau, Sir Dennis Marcus, Kt.

Lane, Sir David William Stennis Stuart, Kt.

Lang, *Lt.-Gen.* Sir Derek Boileau, KCB, DSO, MC.

Langham, Sir James Michael, Bt. (1660).

Langley, *Maj.-Gen.* Sir Henry Desmond Allen, KCVO, MBE.

Langrishe, Sir Hercules Ralph Hume, Bt. (I. 1777).

Lapsley, *Air Marshal* Sir John Hugh, KBE, CB, DFC, AFC.

Lapun, *Hon.* Sir Paul, Kt.

Larcom, Sir (Charles) Christopher Royde, Bt. (1868).

Larmour, Sir Edward Noel, KCMG.

Lartigue, Sir Louis Cools-, Kt., OBE.

Lasdun, Sir Denys Louis, Kt., CBE, FRIBA.

Latey, *Rt. Hon.* Sir John Brinsmead, Kt., MBE.

Latham, Sir Richard Thomas Paul, Bt. (1919).

Latimer, Sir (Courtenay) Robert, Kt., CBE.

Latimer, Sir Graham Stanley, KBE.

Laucke, *Hon.* Sir Condor Louis, KCMG.

Lauder, Sir Piers Robert Dick-, Bt. (s. 1690).

Laughton, Sir Anthony Seymour, Kt.

Laurantus, Sir Nicholas, Kt., MBE.

Laurence, Sir Peter Harold, KCMG, MC.

Laurie, Sir Robert Bayley Emilius, Bt. (1834).

Lauti, *Rt. Hon.* Sir Toaripi, GCMG.

Lavan, *Hon.* Sir John Martin, Kt.

Law, *Adm.* Sir Horace Rochfort, GCB, OBE, DSC.

Lawes, Sir (John) Michael Bennet, Bt. (1882).

Lawler, Sir Peter James, Kt., OBE.

Lawrence, Sir David Roland Walter, Bt. (1906).

Lawrence, Sir Guy Kempton, Kt., DSO, OBE, DFC.

Lawrence, Sir John Patrick Grosvenor, Kt., CBE.

Lawrence, Sir John Waldemar, Bt., OBE (1858).

Lawrence, Sir William Fettiplace, Bt. (1867).

Lawson, Sir Christopher Donald, Kt.

Lawson, *Col.* Sir John Charles Arthur Digby, Bt., DSO, MC (1900).

Lawson, *Hon.* Sir Neil, Kt.

Lawson, *Gen.* Sir Richard George, KCB, DSO, OBE.

Lawton, *Prof.* Sir Frank Ewart, Kt.

Lawton, *Rt. Hon.* Sir Frederick Horace, Kt.

Layden, Sir John (Jack), Kt.

Layfield, Sir Frank Henry Burland Willoughby, Kt., QC.

Lazarus, Sir Peter Esmond, KCB.

Lea, *Vice-Adm.*, Sir John Stuart Crosbie, KBE.

†Lea, Sir Thomas William, Bt. (1892).

Leach, *Admiral of the Fleet* Sir Henry Conyers, GCB.

Leach, Sir Ronald George, GBE.

Leahy, Sir John Henry Gladstone, KCMG.

Learmont, *Lt.-Gen.* Sir John Hartley, KCB, CBE.

Leask, *Lt.-Gen.* Sir Henry Lowther Ewart Clark, KCB, DSO, OBE.

Leather, Sir Edwin Hartley Cameron, KCMG, KCVO.

Leaver, Sir Christopher, GBE.

Le Bailly, *Vice-Adm.* Sir Louis Edward Stewart Holland, KBE, CB.

Le Cheminant, *Air Chief Marshal* Sir Peter de Lacey, GBE, KCB, DFC.

Lechmere, Sir Berwick Hungerford, Bt. (1818).

Ledger, Sir Frank, (Joseph Francis), Kt.

Ledwidge, Sir (William) Bernard (John), KCMG.

Lee, Sir Arthur James, KBE, MC.

Lee, *Air Chief Marshal* Sir David John Pryer, GBE, CB.

Lee, Sir (Henry) Desmond (Pritchard), Kt.

Lee, *Brig.* Sir Leonard Henry, Kt., CBE.

Lee, Sir Quo-wei, Kt., CBE.

Lee, *Col.* Sir William Allison, Kt., OBE, TD.

Leech, Sir William Charles, Kt., CBE

Leeds, Sir Christopher Anthony, Bt. (1812).

Lees, Sir David Bryan, Kt.

Lees, Sir Thomas Edward, Bt. (1897).

Lees, Sir Thomas Harcourt Ivor, Bt. (1804).

Lees, Sir (William) Antony Clare, Bt. (1937).

Leese, Sir John Henry Vernon, Bt. (1908).

Le Fanu, *Maj.* Sir (George) Victor (Sheridan), KCVO.

le Fleming, Sir Quintin John, Bt. (1705).

Legard, Sir Charles Thomas, Bt. (1660).

Leggatt, *Rt. Hon.* Sir Andrew Peter, Kt.

Leggatt, Sir Hugh Frank John, Kt.

Leggett, Sir Clarence Arthur Campbell, Kt., MBE.

Leigh, Sir Geoffrey Norman, Kt.

Leigh, Sir John, Bt. (1918).

Leigh, Sir Neville Egerton, KCVO.

Leighton, Sir Michael John Bryan, Bt. (1693).

Leitch, Sir George, KCB, OBE.

Leith, Sir Andrew George Forbes-, Bt. (1923).

Le Marchant, Sir Francis Arthur, Bt. (1841).

Le Masurier, Sir Robert Hugh, Kt., DSC.

Lemon, Sir (Richard) Dawnay, Kt., CBE.

Leng, *Gen.* Sir Peter John Hall, KCB, MBE, MC.

Lennard, *Rev.* Sir Hugh Dacre Barrett-, Bt. (1801).

Leon, Sir John Ronald, Bt. (1911).

Leonard, *Rt. Rev.* Graham Douglas, KCVO.

Leonard, *Hon.* Sir (Hamilton) John, Kt.

Lepping, Sir George Geria Dennis, GCMG, MBE.

Le Quesne, Sir (Charles) Martin, KCMG.

Le Quesne, Sir (John) Godfray, Kt., QC.

Leslie, Sir Colin Alan Bettridge, Kt.

Leslie, Sir John Norman Ide, Bt. (1876).

†Leslie, Sir (Percy) Theodore, Bt. (s. 1625).

Leslie, Sir Peter Evelyn, Kt.

Lethbridge, Sir Thomas Periam Hector Noel, Bt. (1804).

Leuchars, Sir William Douglas, KBE.

Leupena, Sir Tupua, GCMG, MBE.

Levene, Sir Peter Keith, KBE.

Lever, Sir (Tresham) Christopher Arthur Lindsay, Bt. (1911).

Levey, Sir Michael Vincent, Kt., MVO.

Levine, Sir Montague Bernard, Kt.

Levinge, Sir Richard George Robin, Bt. (I. 1704).

Levy, Sir Ewart Maurice, Kt. (1913).

Lewando, Sir Jan Alfred, Kt., CBE.

Lewis, Sir Allen Montgomery, GCMG, GCVO, QC.

Lewis, *Adm.* Sir Andrew Mackenzie, KCB.

Lewis, Sir Kenneth, Kt.

Lewis, Sir Terence Murray, Kt., OBE, QPM.

Lewthwaite, Sir William Anthony, Bt. (1927).

Ley, Sir Francis Douglas, Bt., MBE, TD (1905).

Leyland, Sir Philip Vyvyan Naylor-, Bt. (1895).

Lickley, Sir Robert Lang, Kt., CBE.

Lidbury, Sir John Towersey, Kt.

Lidderdale, Sir David William Shuckburgh, KCB.

Liggins, Sir Edmund Naylor, Kt., TD.

Liggins, *Prof.* Sir Graham Collingwood, Kt., CBE, FRS.

Lighthill, Sir (Michael) James, Kt., FRS.

Lighton, Sir Christopher Robert, Bt., MBE (I. 1791).

Lim, Sir Han-Hoe, Kt., CBE.

Linacre, Sir (John) Gordon (Seymour), Kt., CBE, AFC, DFM.

Lincoln, Sir Anthony Handley, KCMG, CVO.

Lindley, Sir Arnold Lewis George, Kt.

Lindop, Sir Norman, Kt.

Lindsay, Sir James Harvey Kincaid Stewart, Kt.

Lindsay, Sir Ronald Alexander, Bt., (1962).

Lintott, Sir Henry John Bevis, KCMG.

Lipworth, Sir (Maurice) Sydney, Kt.

Lithgow, Sir William James, Bt. (1925).

Little, *Hon.* Sir Douglas Macfarlan, Kt.

Little, *Most Rev.* Thomas Francis, KBE.

Littler, Sir (James) Geoffrey, KCB.

Livesay, *Adm.* Sir Michael Howard, KCB.

Llewellyn, Sir David Treharne, Kt.

Llewellyn, Sir Henry Morton, Bt., CBE (1922).

Llewellyn, *Lt.-Col.* Sir Michael Rowland Godfrey, Bt. (1959).

Llewelyn, Sir John Michael Dillwyn-Venables-, Bt. (1890).

Lloyd, *Rt. Hon.* Sir Anthony John Leslie, Kt.

Lloyd, Sir Ian Stewart, Kt., MP.

Lloyd, Sir (John) Peter (Daniel), Kt.

Lloyd, Sir Nicholas Markley, Kt.

Lloyd, Sir Richard Ernest Butler, Bt. (1960).

Loader, Sir Leslie Thomas, Kt., CBE.

Loane, *Most Rev.* Marcus Lawrence, KBE.

Lobo, Sir Rogerio Hyndman, Kt., CBE.

Lock, *Cdr.* Sir (John) Duncan, Kt.

Lockhart, Sir Simon John Edward Francis Sinclair-, Bt. (s. 1636).

Loder, Sir Giles Rolls, Bt. (1887).

Lodge, Sir Thomas, Kt.

Loehnis, Sir Clive, KCMG.

Logan, Sir Donald Arthur, KCMG.

Logan, Sir Raymond Douglas, Kt.

Lokoloko, Sir Tore, GCMG, GCVO, OBE.

Longden, Sir Gilbert James Morley, Kt., MBE.

Longland, Sir John Laurence, Kt.

Longley, Sir Norman, Kt., CBE.

Looker, Sir Cecil Thomas, Kt.

Loram, *Vice-Adm.* Sir David Anning, KCB, MVO.

Lorimer, Sir (Thomas) Desmond, Kt.

Lousada, Sir Anthony Baruh, Kt.

Love, Sir Makere Rangiatea Ralph, Kt.

Lovell, Sir (Alfred Charles) Bernard, Kt., OBE, FRS.

Lovelock, Sir Douglas Arthur, KCB.

Loveridge, Sir John Henry, Kt., CBE.

Loveridge, Sir John Warren, Kt.

Lovill, Sir John Roger, Kt., CBE.

Low, Sir Alan Roberts, Kt.

Low, Sir James Richard Morrison-, Bt. (1908).

Lowe, *Air Chief Marshal* Sir Douglas Charles, GCB, DFC, AFC.

Lowe, *Air Vice-Marshal* Sir Edgar Noel, KBE, CB.

Lowe, Sir Thomas William Gordon, Bt. (1918).

Lowry, Sir John Patrick, Kt., CBE.

Lowson, Sir Ian Patrick, Bt. (1951).

Lowther, *Maj.* Sir Charles Douglas, Bt. (1824).

Loyd, Sir Francis Alfred, KCMG, OBE.

Loyd, Sir Julian St John, KCVO.

Lu, Sir Tseng Chi, Kt.

Lucas, Sir Cyril Edward, Kt., CMG, FRS.

Lucas, Sir Thomas Edward, Bt. (1887).

Luce, *Rt Hon.* Sir Richard Napier, Kt., MP.

Luckhoo, *Hon.* Sir Joseph Alexander, Kt.

Luckhoo, Sir Lionel Alfred, KCMG, CBE, QC.

Lucy, Sir Edmund John William Hugh Cameron-Ramsay-Fairfax-, Bt. (1836).

Luddington, Sir Donald Collin Cumyn, KBE, CMG, CVO.

Lumsden, Sir David James, Kt.

Lus, *Hon.* Sir Pita, Kt., OBE.

Lush, *Hon.* Sir George Hermann, Kt.

Lushington, Sir John Richard Castleman, Bt. (1791).

Luyt, Sir Richard Edmonds, GCMG, KCVO, DCM.

Lyell, *Rt. Hon.* Sir Nicholas Walter, Kt., QC, MP.

Lygo, *Adm.* Sir Raymond Derek, KCB.

Lyle, Sir Gavin Archibald, Bt. (1929).

Lyons, Sir Edward Houghton, Kt.

Lyons, Sir James Reginald, Kt.

Lyons, Sir John, Kt.

McAdam, Sir Ian William James, Kt., OBE.

Macadam, Sir Peter, Kt.

McAlpine, Sir Robin, Kt., CBE.

McAlpine, Sir William Hepburn, Bt. (1918).

Macara, Sir (Charles) Douglas, Bt. (1911).

Macartney, Sir John Barrington, Bt. (I. 1799).

McAvoy, Sir (Francis) Joseph, Kt., CBE.

McCaffrey, Sir Thomas Daniel, Kt.

McCall, Sir (Charles) Patrick Home, Kt., MBE, TD.

McCallum, Sir Donald Murdo, Kt., CBE.

McCamley, Sir Graham Edward, Kt., MBE.

McCarthy, *Rt. Hon.* Sir Thaddeus Pearcey, KBE.

McCaw, *Hon.* Sir Kenneth Malcolm, Kt., QC.

McClellan, *Col.* Sir Herbert Gerard Thomas, Kt., CBE, TD.

McClintock, Sir Eric Paul, Kt.

McColl, Sir Colin Hugh Verel, KCMG.

McCollum, *Hon.* Sir William, Kt.

McConnell, Sir Robert Shean, Bt.

McCowan, *Rt. Hon.* Sir Anthony James Denys, Kt..

McCowan, Sir Hew Cargill, Bt. (1934).

McCrea, *Prof.* Sir William Hunter, Kt., FRS.

McCrindle, Sir Robert Arthur, Kt., MP.

McCullough, *Hon.* Sir (Iain) Charles (Robert), Kt.

McCusker, Sir James Alexander, Kt.

MacDermott, *Rt. Hon.* Sir John Clarke, Kt.

McDermott, Sir (Lawrence) Emmet, KBE.

MacDonald, *Gen.* Sir Arthur Leslie, KBE, CB.

McDonald, *Air Chief Marshal* Sir Arthur William Baynes, KCB, AFC.

McDonald, Sir Duncan, Kt., CBE.

Macdonald, Sir Herbert George deLorme, KBE.

Macdonald of Sleat, Sir Ian Godfrey Bosville, Bt. (s. 1625).

Macdonald, Sir Kenneth Carmichael, KCB.

McDonald, *Vice-Adm.* Sir Roderick Douglas, KBE.

McDonald, Sir Tom, Kt., OBE.

McDonald, *Hon.* Sir William John Farquhar, Kt.

MacDougall, Sir (George) Donald (Alastair), Kt., CBE, FBA.

McDowell, Sir Eric Wallalce, Kt., CBE.

McDowell, Sir Henry McLorinan, KBE.

Mace, *Lt.-Gen.* Sir John Airth, KBE, CB.

McEvoy, *Air Chief Marshal* Sir Theodore Newman, KCB, CBE.

McEwen, Sir John Roderick Hugh, Bt. (1953).

McFarland, Sir John Talbot, Bt. (1914).

Macfarlane, Sir (David) Neil, Kt., MP.

Macfarlane, Sir George Gray, Kt., CB.

McFarlane, Sir Ian, Kt.

Macfarlane, Sir James Wright, Kt.

McGeoch, *Vice-Adm.* Sir Ian Lachlan Mackay, KCB, DSO, DSC.

Macgregor, Sir Edwin Robert, Bt. (1828).

MacGregor of MacGregor, Sir Gregor, Bt. (1795).

McGregor, Sir Ian Alexander, Kt., CBE, FRS.

MacGregor, Sir Ian Kinloch, Kt.

McGrigor, *Capt.* Sir Charles Edward, Bt. (1831).

McInerney, *Hon.* Sir Murray Vincent, Kt.

McIntosh, *Vice-Adm.* Sir Ian Stewart, KBE, CB, DSO, DSC.

McIntosh, Sir Ronald Robert Duncan, KCB.

McKaig, *Adm.* Sir (John) Rae, KCB, CBE.

Mackay, Sir (George Patrick) Gordon, Kt., CBE.

McKay, Sir James Wilson, Kt.

McKay, Sir John Andrew, Kt., CBE.

Mackay, Sir William Calder, Kt., OBE, MC.

McKee, *Maj.* Sir (William) Cecil, Kt., ERD.

McKellen, Sir Ian Murray, Kt., CBE.

McKenzie, Sir Alexander, KBE.

Mackenzie, Sir Alexander Alwyne Henry Charles Brinton Muir-, Bt. (1805).

Mackenzie, Sir (Alexander George Anthony) Allan, Bt. (1890).

Mackenzie, *Vice-Adm.* Sir Hugh Stirling, KCB, DSO, DSC.

†Mackenzie, Sir Peter Douglas, Bt. (s. 1673).

†Mackenzie, Sir Roderick McQuhae, Bt. (s. 1703).

McKenzie, Sir Roy Allan, KBE.

Mackeson, Sir Rupert Henry, Bt. (1954).

Mackie, Sir Maitland, Kt., CBE.

MacKinlay, Sir Bruce, Kt., CBE.

McKinnon, *Hon.* Sir Stuart Neil, Kt.

McKissock, Sir Wylie, Kt., OBE, FRCS.

Macklin, Sir Bruce Roy, Kt., OBE.

Mackworth, *Cdr.* Sir David Arthur Geoffrey, Bt. (1776).

McLaren, Sir Robin John Taylor, KCMG.

MacLaurin, Sir Ian Charter, Kt.

Maclean, Sir Donald Og Grant, Kt.

Maclean, Sir Fitzroy Hew, Bt., CBE (1957).

McLean, Sir Francis Charles, Kt., CBE.

MacLean, *Vice-Adm.* Sir Hector Charles Donald, KBE, CB, DSC.

Maclean, Sir Lachlan Hector Charles, Bt. (NS 1631).

Maclean, Sir Robert Alexander, KBE.

McLennan, Sir Ian Munro, KCMG, KBE.

McLeod, Sir Charles Henry, Bt. (1925).

MacLeod, Sir (Hugh) Roderick, Kt.

McLeod, Sir Ian George, Kt.

†MacLeod, *Hon.* Sir John Maxwell Norman, Bt. (1924).

McLintock, Sir Michael William, Bt. (1934).

Maclure, Sir John Robert Spencer, Bt. (1898).

McMahon, Sir Brian Patrick, Bt. (1817).

McMahon, Sir Christopher William, Kt.

McMichael, Sir John, Kt., MD, FRS, FRCP.

Macmillan, Sir (Alexander McGregor) Graham, Kt.

McMillan, *Lt.-Gen.* Sir John Richard Alexander, KCB, CBE.

MacMillan, Sir Kenneth, Kt.

McMullin, *Rt. Hon.* Sir Duncan Wallace, Kt.

Macnab, *Brig.* Sir Geoffrey Alex Colin, KCMG, CB.

Macnaghten, Sir Patrick Alexander, Bt. (1836).

McNair-Wilson, Sir Patrick Michael Ernest David, Kt., MP.

McNair-Wilson, Sir (Robert) Michael Conal, Kt., MP.

McNamara, *Air Chief Marshal* Sir Neville Patrick, KBE.

Macnaughton, *Prof.* Sir Malcolm Campbell, Kt.

McNee, Sir David Blackstock, Kt., QPM.

McNeice, Sir (Thomas) Percy (Fergus), Kt., CMG, OBE.

MacPherson, Sir Keith Duncan, Kt.

Macpherson of Cluny, *Hon.* Sir William Alan, Kt., TD.

McQuarrie, Sir Albert, Kt.

Macrae, *Col.* Sir Robert Andrew Scarth, KCVO, MBE.

Macready, Sir Nevil John Wilfrid, Bt. (1923).

Macrory, Sir Patrick Arthur, Kt.

McShine, *Hon.* Sir Arthur Hugh, Kt.

Mactaggart, Sir John Auld, Bt. (1938).

Madden, *Adm.* Sir Charles Edward, Bt., GCB (1919).

Maddocks, Sir Kenneth Phipson, KCMG, KCVO.

Maddox, Sir (John) Kempson, Kt., VRD, MD.

Madigan, Sir Russel Tullie, Kt., OBE.

Magarey, Sir James Rupert, Kt.

Magnus, Sir Laurence Henry Philip, Bt. (1917).

Maguire, *Air Marshal* Sir Harold John, KCB, DSO, OBE.

Mahon, Sir (John) Denis, Kt., CBE.

Mahon, Sir William Walter, Bt. (1819).

Main, Sir Peter Tester, Kt., ERD.

Maini, Sir Amar Nath, Kt., CBE.

Mais, *Hon.* Sir (Robert) Hugh, Kt.

Maitland, Sir Donald James Dundas, GCMG, OBE.

Maitland, Sir Richard John, Bt. (1818).

Makins, Sir Paul Vivian, Bt. (1903).

Malcolm, Sir David Peter Michael, Bt. (s. 1665).

†Malet, Sir Harry Douglas St Lo, Bt.

Mallaby, Sir Christopher Leslie George, KCMG.

Mallinson, Sir William John, Bt. (1935).

Malone, *Hon.* Sir Denis Eustace Gilbert, Kt.

Mamo, Sir Anthony Joseph, Kt., OBE.

Manchester, Sir William Maxwell, KBE.

Mander, Sir Charles Marcus, Bt. (1911).

Manduell, Sir John, Kt., CBE.

Mann, *Rt. Hon.* Sir Michael, Kt.

Mann, *Rt. Rev.* Michael Ashley, KCVO.

Mann, Sir Rupert Edward, Bt. (1905).

Mansel, *Rev. Canon* James Seymour Denis, KCVO.

Mansel, Sir Philip, Bt. (1622).

Mansfield, *Vice-Adm.* Sir (Edward) Gerard (Napier), KBE, CVO.

Mansfield, Sir Philip (Robert Aked), KCMG.

Mantell, *Hon.* Sir Charles Barrie Knight, Kt.

Manzie, Sir (Andrew) Gordon, KCB.

Mara, *Rt. Hon. Ratu* Sir Kamisese Kapaiwai Tuimacilai, GCMG, KBE.

March, Sir Derek Maxwell, KBE.

Margetson, Sir John William Denys, KCMG.

Marjoribanks, Sir James Alexander Milne, KCMG.

Mark, Sir Robert, GBE.

Markham, Sir Charles John, Bt. (1911).

Marking, Sir Henry Ernest, KCVO, CBE, MC.

Marling, Sir Charles William Somerset, Bt. (1882).

Marr, Sir Leslie Lynn, Bt. (1919).

Marriner, Sir Neville, Kt., CBE.

Marriott, Sir Hugh Cavendish Smith-, Bt. (1774).

Marsden, Sir Nigel John Denton, Bt. (1924).

Marshall, Sir Arthur Gregory George, Kt., OBE.

Marshall, Sir Colin Marsh, Kt.

Marshall, Sir Denis Alfred, Kt.

Marshall, *Prof.* Sir (Oshley) Roy, Kt., CBE.

Marshall, Sir Peter Harold Reginald, KCMG.

Marshall, Sir Robert Braithwaite, KCB, MBE.

Marshall, Sir (Robert) Michael, Kt., MP.

Martell, *Vice-Adm.* Sir Hugh Colenso, KBE, CB.

Martin, *Vice-Adm.* Sir John Edward Ludgate, KCB, DSC.

Martin, *Prof.* Sir (John) Leslie, Kt., ph.D.

Martin, *Col.* Sir Robert Andrew St George, KCVO, OBE.

Martin, Sir Sidney Launcelot, Kt.

Marwick, Sir Brian Allan, KBE, CMG.

Marychurch, Sir Peter Harvey, KCMG.

Masefield, Sir Peter Gordon, Kt.

Mason, *Hon.* Sir Anthony Frank, KBE.

Mason, Sir (Basil) John, Kt., CB, D.SC., FRS.

Mason, Sir Frederick Cecil, KCVO, CMG.

Mason, Sir John Charles Moir, KCMG.

Mason, *Prof.* Sir Ronald, KCB, FRS.

Matane, Sir Paulias Nguna, Kt., CMG, OBE.

Mather, Sir (David) Carol (Macdonell), Kt., MC.

Mather, Sir William Loris, Kt., CVO, OBE, MC, TD.

Mathers, Sir Robert William, Kt.

Matheson, Sir (James Adam) Louis, KBE, CMG.

Matheson of Matheson, Sir Torquhil Alexander, Bt. (1882).

Matthews, Sir Peter Alec, Kt.

Matthews, Sir Peter Jack, Kt., CVO, OBE, QPM.

Matthews, Sir Stanley, Kt., CBE.

Mavor, *Air Marshal* Sir Leslie Deane, KCB, AFC.

†Maxwell, Sir Michael Eustace George, Bt. (s. 1681).

Maxwell, Sir Nigel Mellor Heron-, Bt. (s. 1683).

Maxwell, Sir Robert Hugh, KBE.

May, *Hon.* Sir Anthony Tristram Kenneth, Kt.

May, *Rt. Hon.* Sir John Douglas, Kt.

May, Sir Kenneth Spencer, Kt., CBE.

Mayall, Sir (Alexander) Lees, KCVO, CMG.

Mayhew, *Rt. Hon.* Sir Patrick Barnabas Burke, Kt., QC, MP.

Maynard, *Hon.* Sir Clement Travelyan, Kt.

Maynard, *Air Chief Marshal* Sir Nigel Martin, KCB, CBE, DFC, AFC.

Meade, Sir (Richard) Geoffrey (Austin), KBE, CMG, CVO.

Meaney, Sir Patrick Michael, Kt.

Medlycott, Sir Mervyn Tregonwell, Bt. (1808).

Megarry, *Rt. Hon.* Sir Robert Edgar, Kt., FBA.

Megaw, *Rt. Hon.* Sir John, Kt., CBE, TD.

Meinertzhagen, Sir Peter, Kt., CMG.

Mellon, Sir James, KCMG.

Melville, Sir Harry Work, KCB, ph.D., D.SC., FRS.

Melville, Sir Leslie Galfreid, KBE.

Melville, Sir Ronald Henry, KCB.

Mensforth, Sir Eric, Kt., CBE, F.Eng.

Menter, Sir James Woodham, Kt., ph.D., SC.D., FRS.

Menteth, Sir James Wallace Stuart-, Bt. (1838).

Menuhin, Sir Yehudi, OM, KBE.

Menzies, Sir Peter Thomson, Kt.

Messervy, Sir (Roney) Godfrey (Collumbell), Kt.

Meyer, Sir Anthony John Charles, Bt., MP (1910).

Meyjes, Sir Richard Anthony, Kt.

Meyrick, Sir David John Charlton, Bt. (1880).

Meyrick, Sir George Christopher Cadafael Tapps-Gervis-, Bt. (1791).

Miakwe, *Hon.* Sir Akepa, KBE.

Michael, Sir Peter Colin, Kt., CBE.

Micklethwait, Sir Robert Gore, Kt., QC.

Middleton, Sir George Humphrey, KCMG.

Middleton, Sir Peter Edward, GCB.

Middleton, Sir Stephen Hugh, Bt. (1662).

Miers, Sir (Henry) David Alastair Capel, KBE, CMG.

Milbank, Sir Anthony Frederick, Bt. (1882).

Milburn, Sir Anthony Rupert, Bt. (1905).

Miles, Sir Peter Tremayne, KCVO.

Miles, Sir William Napier Maurice, Bt. (1859).

Millais, Sir Ralph Regnault, Bt. (1885).

Millar, Sir Oliver Nicholas, GCVO, FBA.

Millar, Sir Ronald Graeme, Kt.

Millard, Sir Guy Elwin, KCMG, CVO.

Miller, Sir Donald John, Kt., FRSE.

Miller, Sir Douglas Sinclair, KCVO, CBE.

Miller, Sir Hilary Duppa (Hal), Kt., MP.

Miller, Sir (Ian) Douglas, Kt.

Miller, Sir John Holmes, Bt. (1705).

Miller, *Lt.-Col.* Sir John Mansel, GCVO, DSO, MC.

Miller, Sir (Joseph) Holmes, Kt., OBE.

Miller, Sir (Oswald) Bernard, Kt.

Miller, Sir Peter North, Kt.

Miller, Sir Stephen James Hamilton, KCVO, MD, FRCS.

†Miller of Glenlee, Sir Stephen William Macdonald, Bt. (1788).

Millett, *Hon.* Sir Peter Julian, Kt.

Millichip, Sir Frederick Albert (Bert), Kt.

Milling, *Air Marshal* Sir Denis Crowley-, KCB, CBE, DSO, DFC.

Mills, *Vice-Adm.* Sir Charles Piercy, KCB, CBE, DSC.

Mills, Sir Frank, KCVO, CMG.

Mills, Sir John Lewis Ernest Watts, Kt., CBE.

Mills, *Air Marshal* Sir Nigel Holroyd, KBE.

Mills, Sir Peter Frederick Leighton, Bt. (1921).

Mills, Sir Peter McLay, Kt.

Milne, Sir John Drummond, Kt.

Milner, Sir (George Edward) Mordaunt, Bt. (1717).

Milnes Coates, Sir Anthony Robert, Bt. (1911).

Minhinnick, Sir Gordon Edward George, KBE.

Minogue, *Hon.* Sir John Patrick, Kt., QC.

Miskin, *Hon.* Sir James William, Kt., QC.

Mitchell, *Air Cdre* Sir (Arthur) Dennis, KBE, CVO, DFC, AFC.

Mitchell, Sir David Bower, Kt., MP.

Mitchell, Sir Derek Jack, KCB, CVO.

Mitchell, *Prof.* Sir (Edgar) William John, Kt., CBE, FRS.

Mobbs, Sir (Gerald) Nigel, Kt.

Moberly, Sir John Campbell, KBE, CMG.

Moberly, Sir Patrick Hamilton, KCMG.

Moffat, *Lt.-Gen.* Sir (William) Cameron, KBE.

Mogg, *Gen.* Sir (Herbert) John, GCB, CBE, DSO.

Moir, Sir Ernest Ian Royds, Bt. (1916).

Moller, *Hon.* Sir Lester Francis, Kt.

†Molony, Sir Thomas Desmond, Bt. (1925).

Monro, Sir Hector Seymour Peter, Kt., MP.

Monson, Sir (William Bonnar) Leslie, KCMG, CB.

Montgomery, Sir (Basil Henry) David, Bt. (1801).

Montgomery, Sir (William) Fergus, Kt., MP.

Mookerjee, Sir Birendra Nath, Kt.

Moollan, Sir Abdool Hamid Adam, Kt.

Moollan, *Hon.* Sir Cassam (Ismael), Kt.

Moon, Sir Peter Wilfred Giles Graham-, Bt. (1855).

†Moon, Sir Roger, Bt. (1887).

Moore, Sir Edward Stanton, Bt., OBE (1923).

Moore, Sir Francis Thomas, Kt.

Moore, Sir Henry Roderick, Kt., CBE.

Moore, *Hon.* Sir John Cochrane, Kt.

Moore, *Maj.-Gen.* Sir (John) Jeremy, KCB, OBE, MC.

Moore, Sir John Michael, KCVO, CB, DSC.

Moore, *Prof.* Sir Norman Winfrid, Bt. (1919).

Moore, Sir William Roger Clotworthy, Bt., TD (1932).

Moores, Sir John, Kt., CBE.

Mootham, Sir Orby Howell, Kt.

Morauta, Sir Mekere, Kt.

Mordaunt, Sir Richard Nigel Charles, Bt. (1611).

Moreton, Sir John Oscar, KCMG, KCVO, MC.

Morgan, *Maj.-Gen.* Sir David John Hughes-, Bt., CB, CBE (1925).

Morgan, Sir Ernest Dunstan, KBE.

Morgan, Sir John Albert Leigh, KCMG.

Morland, *Hon.* Sir Michael, Kt.

Morland, Sir Robert Kenelm, Kt.

Morpeth, Sir Douglas Spottiswoode, Kt., TD.

Morris, *Air Marshal* Sir Arnold Alec, KBE, CB.

Morris, Sir Robert Byng, Bt. (1806).

Morrison, *Hon.* Sir Charles Andrew, Kt., MP.

Morrison, Sir Howard Leslie, Kt., OBE.

Morrison, *Rt. Hon.* Sir Peter Hugh, Kt., MP.

Morritt, *Hon.* Sir (Robert) Andrew, Kt., CVO.

Morrow, Sir Ian Thomas, Kt.

Morse, Sir Christopher Jeremy, KCMG.

Morton, *Adm.* Sir Anthony Storrs, GBE, KCB.

Morton, Sir (Robert) Alastair (Newton), Kt.

Morton, Sir William David, Kt., CBE.

Moseley, Sir George Walker, KCB.

Moser, *Prof.* Sir Claus Adolf, KCB, CBE, FBA.

†Moss, Sir David John Edwards-, Bt. (1868).

Mostyn, *Gen.* Sir (Joseph) David Frederick, KCB, CBE.

†Mostyn, Sir William Basil John, Bt. (1670).

Mott, Sir John Harmer, Bt. (1930).

Mott, Sir Nevill Francis, Kt., FRS.

Mount, Sir James William Spencer, Kt., CBE, BEM.

Mount, Sir William Malcolm, Bt. (1921).

Mountain, Sir Denis Mortimer, Bt. (1922).

Mowbray, Sir John, Kt.

Mowbray, Sir John Robert, Bt. (1880).

Moynihan, Sir Noel Henry, Kt.

Muir, Sir John Harling, Bt. (1892).

Muir, Sir Laurence Macdonald, Kt.

Muir Wood, Sir Alan Marshall, Kt., FRS.

Muirhead, Sir David Francis, KCMG, CVO.

Muldoon, *Rt. Hon.* Sir Robert David, GCMG, CH.

Mulholland, Sir Michael Henry, Bt. (1945).

Mullens, *Lt.-Gen.* Sir Anthony Richard Guy, KCB, OBE.

Mummery, *Hon.* Sir John Frank, Kt.

Munn, Sir James, Kt., OBE.

Munro, Sir Alan Gordon, KCMG.

Munro, Sir Alasdair Thomas Ian, Bt. (1825).

Munro, Sir Ian Talbot, Bt. (s. 1634).

Munro, *Hon.* Sir Robert Lindsay, Kt., CBE.

Munro, Sir Sydney Douglas Gun-, GCMG, MBE.

Murley, Sir Reginald Sydney, KBE, TD, FRCS.

Murphy, Sir Leslie Frederick, Kt.

Murray, *Rt. Hon.* Sir Donald Bruce, Kt.

Murray, Sir Donald Frederick, KCVO, CMG.

Murray, Sir James, KCMG.

Murray, Sir John Antony Jerningham, Kt., CBE.

Murray, Sir Nigel Andrew Digby, Bt. (s. 1628).

Murray, Sir Patrick Ian Keith, Bt. (s. 1673).

Murray, Sir Rowland William Patrick, Bt. (s. 1630).

Murrie, Sir William Stuart, GCB, KBE.

Mursell, Sir Peter, Kt., MBE.

Musgrave, Sir Christopher Patrick Charles, Bt. (1611).

Musgrave, Sir Richard James, Bt. (i. 1782).

Musker, Sir John, Kt.

Musson, *Gen.* Sir Geoffrey Randolph Dixon, GCB, CBE, DSO.

Mustill, *Rt. Hon.* Sir Michael John, Kt.

Myers, Sir Kenneth Ben, Kt., MBE.

Myers, Sir Philip Alan, Kt., OBE, QPM.

Myers, *Prof.* Sir Rupert Horace, KBE.

Mynors, Sir Richard Baskerville, Bt. (1964).

Nabarro, Sir John David Nunes, Kt., MD, FRCP.

Naipaul, Sir Vidiadhar Surajprasad, Kt.

Nairn, Sir Michael, Bt. (1904).

Nairn, Sir Robert Arnold Spencer-, Bt. (1933).

Nairne, *Rt. Hon.* Sir Patrick Dalmahoy, GCB, MC.

Nalder, *Hon.* Sir Crawford David, Kt.

Nall, Sir Michael Joseph, Bt., RN (1954).

Napier, Sir John Archibald Lennox, Bt. (s. 1627).

Napier, Sir Oliver John, Kt.

Napier, Sir Robin Surtees, Bt. (1867).

Napley, Sir David, Kt.

Narain, Sir Sathi, KBE.

Neal, Sir Eric James, Kt.

Neal, Sir Leonard Francis, Kt., CBE.

Neale, Sir Alan Derrett, KCB, MBE.

Neale, Sir Gerrard Anthony, Kt., MP.

Neave, Sir Arundell Thomas Clifton, Bt. (1795).

Nedd, *Hon.* Sir Robert Archibald, Kt.

Neill, *Rt. Hon.* Sir Brian Thomas, Kt.

Neill, Sir Francis Patrick, Kt., QC.

Neill, *Rt. Hon.* Sir Ivan, Kt.

Nelson, *Maj.-Gen.* Sir (Eustace) John (Blois), KCVO, CB, DSO, OBE, MC.

†Nelson, Sir Jamie Charles Vernon Hope, Bt. (1912).

Nelson, *Air Marshal* Sir (Sidney) Richard (Carlyle), KCB, OBE, MD.

Nepean, *Lt.-Col.* Sir Evan Yorke, Bt. (1802).

Ness, *Air Marshal* Sir Charles Ernest, KCB, CBE.

Neubert, Sir Michael John, Kt., MP.

Neville, Sir Richard Lionel John Baines, Bt. (1927).

New, *Maj.-Gen.* Sir Laurence Anthony Wallis, Kt., CB, CBE.

Newbold, Sir Charles Demorée, KBE, CMG, QC.

Newman, Sir Francis Hugh Cecil, Bt. (1912).

Newman, Sir Geoffrey Robert, Bt. (1836).

Newman, Sir Jack, Kt., CBE.

Newman, Sir Kenneth Leslie, GBE, QPM.

Newns, Sir (Alfred) Foley (Francis Polden), KCMG, CVO.

Newsam, Sir Peter Anthony, Kt.

Newton, Sir (Harry) Michael (Rex), Bt. (1900).

Newton, Sir Kenneth Garnar, Bt., OBE, TD (1924).

Newton, Sir (Leslie) Gordon, Kt.

Ngata, Sir Henare Kohere, KBE.

Niall, Sir Horace Lionel Richard, Kt., CBE.

Nicholas, Sir David, Kt., CBE.

Nicholas, Sir Herbert Richard, Kt., OBE.

Nicholas, Sir John William, KCVO, CMG.

Nicholls, *Rt. Hon.* Sir Donald James, Kt.

Nicholls, *Air Marshal* Sir John Moreton, KCB, CBE, DFC, AFC.

Nichols, Sir Edward Henry, Kt., TD.

Nicholson, Sir Bryan Hubert, Kt.

Nicholson, *Hon.* Sir David Eric, Kt.

Nicholson, Sir John Norris, Bt., KBE, CIE (1912).

Nicholson, *Hon.* Sir Michael, Kt.

Nicholson, Sir Robin Buchanan, Kt., ph.D., FRS.

Nickson, Sir David Wigley, KBE.

Nicolson, Sir David Lancaster, Kt.

Nield, Sir Basil Edward, Kt., CBE, QC.

Nield, Sir William Alan, GCMG, KCB.

Nightingale, Sir Charles Manners Gamaliel, Bt. (1628).

Nightingale, Sir John Cyprian, Kt., CBE, BEM, QPM.

Nimmo, *Hon.* Sir John Angus, Kt., CBE.

Niven, Sir (Cecil) Rex, Kt., CMG, MC.

Nixon, Sir Edwin Ronald, Kt., CBE.

Nixon, *Rev.* Sir Kenneth Michael John Basil, Bt. (1906).

Pasley, Sir John Malcolm Sabine, Bt. (1794).

Paterson, Sir Dennis Craig, Kt.

Paterson, Sir George Mutlow, Kt., OBE, QC.

Paterson, Sir John Valentine Jardine, Kt.

Paton, Sir (Thomas) Angus (Lyall), Kt., CMG, FRS.

Paton, *Prof.* Sir William Drummond Macdonald, Kt., CBE, DM, FRS, FRCP.

Pattie, *Rt. Hon.* Sir Geoffrey Edwin, Kt., MP.

Pattinson, *Hon.* Sir Baden, KBE.

Pattinson, Sir (William) Derek, Kt.

Paul, Sir John Warburton, GCMG, OBE, MC.

Paul, *Air Marshal* Sir Ronald Ian Stuart, KBE.

Payne, Sir Norman John, Kt., CBE.

Peach, Sir Leonard Harry, Kt.

Peacock, *Prof.* Sir Alan Turner, Kt., DSC.

Pearce, Sir Austin William, Kt., CBE, Ph.D.

Pearce, Sir (Daniel Norton) Idris, Kt., CBE, TD.

Pearce, Sir Eric Herbert, Kt., OBE.

Peard, *Rear-Adm.* Sir Kenyon Harry Terrell, KBE.

Pearman, *Hon.* Sir James Eugene, Kt., CBE.

Pearson, Sir Francis Nicholas Fraser, Bt. (1964).

Pearson, Sir (James) Denning, Kt.

Pearson, *Gen.* Sir Thomas Cecil Hook, KCB, CBE, DSO.

Peart, *Prof.* Sir William Stanley, Kt., MD, FRS.

Pease, Sir (Alfred) Vincent, Bt. (1882).

Pease, Sir Richard Thorn, Bt. (1920).

Peat, Sir Gerrard Charles, KCVO.

Peat, Sir Henry, KCVO, DFC.

Peck, Sir Edward Heywood, GCMG.

Peck, Sir John Howard, KCMG.

Pedder, *Vice-Adm.* Sir Arthur Reid, KBE, CB.

Pedder, *Air Marshal* Sir Ian Maurice, KCB, OBE, DFC.

Peek, Sir Francis Henry Grenville, Bt. (1874).

Peek, *Vice-Adm.* Sir Richard Innes, KBE, CB, DSC.

Peel, Sir John Harold, KCVO.

Peel, Sir (William) John, Kt.

Peierls, Sir Rudolf Ernst, Kt., CBE, D.SC., D.Phil., FRS.

Peirse, Sir Henry Grant de la Poer Beresford-, Bt. (1814).

Peirse, *Air Vice-Marshal* Sir Richard Charles Fairfax, KCVO, CB.

Pelly, Sir John Alwyne, Bt. (1840).

Pemberton, Sir Francis Wingate William, Kt., CBE.

Penn, *Lt.-Col.* Sir Eric Charles William Mackenzie, GCVO, OBE, MC.

Percival, Sir Anthony Edward, Kt., CB.

Percival, *Rt. Hon.* Sir (Walter) Ian, Kt., QC.

Pereira, Sir (Herbert) Charles, Kt., D.SC., FRS.

Perkins, *Surgeon Vice-Adm.* Sir Derek Duncombe Steele-, KCB, KCVO.

Perring, Sir Ralph Edgar, Bt. (1963).

Perris, Sir David (Arthur), Kt., MBE.

Perry, Sir David Howard, KCB.

Perry, Sir (David) Norman, Kt., MBE.

Pestell, Sir John Richard, KCVO.

Peterkin, Sir Neville, Kt.

Petersen, Sir Jeffrey Charles, KCMG.

Petersen, Sir Johannes Bjelke-, KCMG.

Petit, Sir Dinshaw Manockjee, Bt. (1890).

Peto, Sir Henry George Morton, Bt. (1855).

Peto, Sir Michael Henry Basil, Bt. (1927).

Petrie, Sir Peter Charles, Bt., CMG (1918).

Pettigrew, Sir Russell Hilton, Kt.

Pettit, Sir Daniel Eric Arthur, Kt.

Philips, *Prof.* Sir Cyril Henry, Kt.

Philipson, Sir Robert James, (Sir Robin Philipson), Kt., RA.

Phillips, *Prof.* Sir David Chilton, KBE, Ph.D., FRS.

Phillips, Sir Fred Albert, Kt., CVO.

Phillips, Sir Henry Ellis Isidore, Kt., CMG, MBE.

Phillips, Sir Horace, KCMG.

Phillips, *Hon.* Sir Nicholas Addison, Kt.

Phillips, Sir Peter John, Kt., OBE.

Phillips, Sir Robin Francis, Bt. (1912).

Pickard, Sir Cyril Stanley, KCMG.

Pickering, Sir Edward Davies, Kt.

Pickthorn, Sir Charles William Richards, Bt. (1959).

Pidgeon, Sir John Allan Stewart, Kt.

Piers, Sir Charles Robert Fitzmaurice, Bt. (I. 1661).

Pigot, Sir George Hugh, Bt. (1764).

Pigott, Sir Berkeley Henry Sebastian, Bt. (1808).

Pike, Sir Michael Edmund, KCVO, CMG.

Pike, Sir Philip Ernest Housden, Kt., QC.

Pike, *Lt.-Gen.* Sir William Gregory Huddleston, KCB, CBE, DSO.

Pilcher, Sir (Charlie) Dennis, Kt., CBE.

Pilditch, Sir Richard Edward, Bt. (1929).

Pile, Sir Frederick Devereux, Bt. MC (1900).

Pile, Sir William Dennis, GCB, MBE.

Pilkington, Sir Antony Richard, Kt.

Pilkington, Sir Lionel Alexander Bethune, (Sir Alastair), Kt., FRS.

Pilkington, Sir Thomas Henry Milborne-Swinnerton-, Bt. (s. 1635).

Pill, *Hon.* Sir Malcolm Thomas, Kt.

Pillar, *Adm.* Sir William Thomas, GBE, KCB.

Pindling, *Rt. Hon.* Sir Lynden Oscar, KCMG.

Pinker, Sir George Douglas, KCVO.

Pinsent, Sir Christopher Roy, Bt. (1938).

Pippard, *Prof.* Sir (Alfred) Brian, Kt., FRS.

Pirie, *Gp. Capt.* Sir Gordon Hamish, Kt., CVO, CBE.

Pitblado, Sir David Bruce, KCB, CVO.

Pitoi, Sir Sere, Kt., CBE.

Pitt, Sir Harry Raymond, Kt., PH.D., FRS.

Pitts, Sir Cyril Alfred, Kt.

Pixley, Sir Neville Drake, Kt., MBE, VRD.

Pizey, *Adm.* Sir (Charles Thomas) Mark, GBE, CB, DSO.

Plastow, Sir David Arnold Stuart, Kt.

†Platt, Sir (Frank) Lindsey, Bt. (1958).

Platt, *Prof.* Hon. Sir Peter, Bt. (1959).

Playfair, Sir Edward Wilder, KCB.

Pliatzky, Sir Leo, KCB.

Plowman, Sir (John) Anthony, Kt.

Plowman, *Hon.* Sir John Robin, Kt., CBE.

Plumb, *Prof.* Sir John Harold, Kt.

Poett, *Gen.* Sir (Joseph Howard) Nigel, KCB, DSO.

Pole, *Col.* Sir John Gawen Carew, Bt., DSO, TD (1628).

Pole, Sir Peter Van Notten, Bt. (1791).

Pollen, Sir John Michael Hungerford, Bt. (1795).

Pollock, Sir George Frederick, Bt. (1866).

Pollock, Sir Giles Hampden Montagu-, Bt. (1872).

Pollock, *Admiral of the Fleet* Sir Michael Patrick, GCB, MVO, DSC.

Pollock, Sir William Horace Montagu-, KCMG.

Ponsonby, Sir Ashley Charles Gibbs, Bt., MC (1956).

Pontin, Sir Frederick William, Kt.

Poore, Sir Herbert Edward, Bt. (1795).

Pope, *Vice-Adm.* Sir (John) Ernle, KCB.

Pope, Sir Joseph Albert, Kt., D.SC., Ph.D.

Popper, *Prof.* Sir Karl Raimund, Kt., CH, Ph.D., FRS.

Popplewell, *Hon.* Sir Oliver Bury, Kt.

Portal, Sir Jonathan Francis, Bt. (1901).

Porter, Sir John Simon Horsbrugh-, Bt. (1902).

Porter, Sir Leslie, Kt.

Porter, *Air Marshal* Sir (Melvin) Kenneth (Drowley), KCB, CBE.

Porter, *Hon.* Sir Murray Victor, Kt.

Porter, *Rt. Hon.* Sir Robert Wilson, Kt., QC.

Posnett, Sir Richard Neil, KBE, CMG.

Potter, Sir (Joseph) Raymond (Lynden), Kt.

Potter, *Hon.* Sir Mark Howard, Kt.

Potter, *Maj.-Gen.* Sir (Wilfrid) John, KBE, CB.

Potter, Sir (William) Ian, Kt.

Potts, *Hon.* Sir Francis Humphrey, Kt.

Pound, Sir John David, Bt. (1905).

Pountain, Sir Eric John, Kt.

Powell, Sir (Arnold Joseph) Philip, Kt., CH, OBE, RA, FRIBA.

Powell, Sir Charles David, KCMG.

Powell, Sir Nicholas Folliott Douglas, Bt. (1897).

Powell, Sir Richard Royle, GCB, KBE, CMG.

Power, Sir Alastair John Cecil, Bt. (1924).

Powles, Sir Guy Richardson, KBE, CMG, ED.

Poynton, Sir (Arthur) Hilton, GCMG.

Prendergast, Sir John Vincent, KBE, CMG, GM.

Prentice, *Rt. Hon.* Sir Reginald Ernest, Kt.

Prentice, *Hon.* Sir William Thomas, Kt., MBE.

Prescott, Sir Mark, Bt. (1938).

Preston, Sir Kenneth Huson, Kt.

Preston, Sir Peter Sansome, KCB.

Preston, Sir Ronald Douglas Hildebrand, Bt. (1815).

Prevost, Sir Christopher Gerald, Bt. (1805).

Price, Sir Charles Keith Napier Rugge-, Bt. (1804).

Price, Sir David Ernest Campbell, Kt., MP.

Price, Sir Francis Caradoc Rose, Bt. (1815).

Price, Sir Frank Leslie, Kt.

Price, Sir (James) Robert, KBE.

Price, Sir Leslie Victor, Kt., OBE.

Price, Sir Norman Charles, KCB.

Price, Sir Robert John Green-, Bt. (1874).

Prickett, *Air Chief Marshal* Sir Thomas Other, KCB, DSO, DFC.

Prideaux, Sir Humphrey Povah Treverbian, Kt., OBE.

Prideaux, Sir John Francis, Kt., OBE.

†Primrose, Sir John Ure, Bt. (1903).

Pringle, *Air Marshal* Sir Charles Norman Seton, KBE.

Pringle, *Lt.-Gen.* Sir Steuart (Robert), Bt., KCB, RM (s. 1683).

Pritchard, Sir Neil, KCMG.

Pritchett, Sir Victor Sawdon, Kt., CBE.

Proby, Sir Peter, Bt. (1952).

Proctor, Sir Roderick Consett, Kt., MBE.

Proud, Sir John Seymour, Kt.

Prout, Sir Christopher James, Kt., TD, QC, MEP.

Pryke, Sir David Dudley, Bt. (1926).

Pugh, Sir Idwal Vaughan, KCB.

Pugsley, *Prof.* Sir Alfred Grenville, Kt., OBE, D.SC., FRS.

Pullen, Sir William Reginald James, KCVO.

Pullinger, Sir (Francis) Alan, Kt., CBE.

Pumphrey, Sir (John) Laurence, KCMG.

Purchas, *Rt. Hon.* Sir Francis Brooks, Kt.

Quicke, Sir John Godolphin, Kt., CBE.

Quilliam, *Hon.* Sir (James) Peter, Kt.

Quilter, Sir Anthony Raymond Leopold Cuthbert, Bt. (1897).

Quinlan, Sir Michael Edward, GCB.

Quinton, Sir James Grand, Kt.

Quirk, *Prof.* Sir (Charles)Randolph, Kt., CBE, FBA.

Rabukawaqa, Sir Josua Rasilau, KBE, MVO.

Radcliffe, Sir Sebastian Everard, Bt. (1813).

Radclyffe, Sir Charles Edward Mott-, Kt.

Radford, Sir Ronald Walter, KCB, MBE.

Radzinowicz, *Prof.* Sir Leon, Kt., LL.D.

Rae, *Hon.* Sir Wallace Alexander Ramsay, Kt.

Raeburn, Sir Michael Edward Norman, Bt. (1923).

Raeburn, *Maj.-Gen.* Sir (William) Digby (Manifold), KCVO, CB, DSO, MBE.

Raffray, Sir Piat Joseph Raymond Andre, Kt.

Raikes, *Vice-Adm.* Sir Iwan Geoffrey, KCB, CBE, DSC.

Raison, *Rt. Hon.* Sir Timothy Hugh Francis, Kt., MP.

Ralli, Sir Godfrey Victor, Bt., TD (1912).

Ramdanee, Sir Mookteswar Baboolall Kailash, Kt.

Ramphal, Sir Shridath Surendranath, Kt., GCMG.

Ramphul, Sir Baalkhristna, Kt.

Ramphul, Sir Indurduth, Kt.

Rampton, Sir Jack Leslie, KCB.

Ramsay, Sir Alexander William Burnett, Bt. (1806).

Ramsay, Sir Thomas Meek, Kt., CMG.

Ramsbotham, *Gen.* Sir David John, KCB, CBE.

Ramsbotham, *Hon.* Sir Peter Edward, GCMG, GCVO.

Ramsden, Sir John Charles Josslyn, Bt. (1689).

Ramsey, Sir Alfred Ernest, Kt.

Randle, *Prof.* Sir Philip John, Kt.

Ranger, Sir Douglas, Kt., FRCS.

Rank, Sir Benjamin Keith, Kt., CMG.

Rankin, Sir Ian Niall, Bt. (1898).

Rasch, *Maj.* Sir Richard Guy Carne, Bt. (1903).

Rashleigh, Sir Richard Harry, Bt. (1831).

Rattee, *Hon.* Sir Donald Keith, Kt.

Rault, Sir Louis Joseph Maurice, Kt.

Rawlins, *Surgeon Vice-Adm.* Sir John Stuart Pepys, KBE.

Rawlinson, Sir Anthony Henry John, Bt. (1891).

Rayne, Sir Edward, Kt., CVO.

Read, *Air Marshal* Sir Charles Frederick, KBE, CB, DFC, AFC.

Read, *Gen.* Sir (John) Antony (Jervis), GCB, CBE, DSO, MC.

Read, Sir John Emms, Kt.

Reade, Sir Clyde Nixon, Bt. (1661).

Reay, *Lt.-Gen.* Sir (Hubert) Alan John, KBE.

Redgrave, *Maj.-Gen.* Sir Roy Michael Frederick, KBE, MC.

Redmayne, Sir Nicholas, Bt. (1964).

Redmond, Sir James, Kt.

Redwood, Sir Peter Boverton, Bt. (1911).

Reece, Sir Charles Hugh, Kt.

Reece, Sir James Gordon, Kt.

Reed, *Hon.* Sir Nigel Vernon, Kt., CBE.

Rees, Sir (Charles William)Stanley, Kt., TD.

Reeve, Sir (Charles) Trevor, Kt.

Reeves, *Most Rev.* Paul Alfred, GCMG, GCVO.

Reffell, *Adm.* Sir Derek Roy, KCB.

Refshauge, *Maj-Gen.* Sir William Dudley, Kt., CBE.

Reid, Sir Alexander James, Bt. (1897).

Reid, *Hon.* Sir George Oswald, Kt., QC.

Reid, Sir (Harold) Martin (Smith), KBE, CMG.

Reid, Sir Hugh, Bt. (1922).

Reid, Sir John James Andrew, KCMG, CB, TD.

Reid, Sir Norman Robert, Kt.

Reid, Sir Robert Basil, Kt., CBE.

Reid, Sir Robert Paul, Kt.

Reilly, Sir (D'Arcy) Patrick, GCMG, OBE.

Reilly, *Lt.-Gen.* Sir Jeremy Calcott, KCB, DSO.

Renals, Sir Stanley, Bt. (1895).

Rendell, Sir William, Kt.

Rennie, Sir John Shaw, GCMG, OBE.

Renouf, Sir Clement William Bailey, Kt.

Renouf, Sir Francis Henry, Kt.

Renshaw, Sir (Charles) Maurice Bine, Bt. (1903).

Renwick, Sir Richard Eustace, Bt. (1921).

Renwick, Sir Robin William, KCMG.

Reporter, Sir Shapoor Ardeshirji, KBE.

Rex, *Hon.* Sir Robert Richmond, KBE, CMG.

Reynolds, Sir David James, Bt. (1923).

Reynolds, Sir Peter William John, Kt., CBE.

Rhodes, Sir Basil Edward, Kt., CBE, TD.

Rhodes, Sir John Christopher Douglas, Bt. (1919).

Rhodes, Sir Peregrine Alexander, KCMG.

Rice, *Maj.-Gen.* Sir Desmond Hind Garrett, KCVO, CBE.

Richards, *Hon.* Sir Edward Trenton, Kt., CBE.

Richards, Sir (Francis) Brooks, KCMG, DSC.

Richards, Sir James Maude, Kt., CBE.

Richards, *Lt.-Gen.* Sir John Charles Chisholm, KCB, KCVO, RM.

Richards, Sir Rex Edward, Kt., D.SC., FRS.

Richardson, Sir Anthony Lewis, Bt. (1924).

Richardson, *Gen.* Sir Charles Leslie, GCB, CBE, DSO.

Richardson, *Air Marshal* Sir (David) William, KBE.

Richardson, Sir Egerton Rudolf, Kt., CMG.

Richardson, *Rt. Hon.* Sir Ivor Lloyd Morgan, Kt.

Richardson, Sir (John) Eric, Kt., CBE.

Richardson, Sir (Lionel) Earl George, Kt.

Richardson, Sir Michael John de Rougemont, Kt.

Richardson, *Lt.-Gen.* Sir Robert Francis, KCB, CVO, CBE.

Richardson, Sir Simon Alaisdair Stewart-, Bt. (s. 1630).

Riches, Sir Derek Martin Hurry, KCMG.

Riches, *Gen.* Sir Ian Hurry, KCB, DSO.

Richmond, Sir Alan James, Kt.

Richmond, *Rt. Hon.* Sir Clifford Parris, KBE.

Richmond, Sir John Frederick, Bt. (1929).

Richmond, *Prof.* Sir Mark Henry, Kt., FRS.

Rickett, Sir Denis Hubert Fletcher, KCMG, CB.

Rickett, Sir Raymond Mildmay Wilson, Kt., CBE, PH.D.

Ricketts, Sir Robert Cornwallis Gerald St Leger, Bt. (1828).

Ricks, Sir John Plowman, Kt.

Riddell, Sir John Charles Buchanan, Bt., CVO (s. 1628).

Ridley, Sir Adam (Nicholas), Kt.

Ridley, Sir Sidney, Kt.

Ridsdale, Sir Julian Errington, Kt., CBE, MP.

Rigby, *Lt.-Col.* Sir (Hugh) John (Macbeth), Bt. (1929).

Riley, Sir Ralph, Kt., FRS.

Ring, Sir Lindsay Roberts, GBE.

Ringadoo, *Hon.* Sir Veerasamy, GCMG.

Ripley, Sir Hugh, Bt. (1880).

Risk, Sir Thomas Neilson, Kt.

Risson, *Maj.-Gen.* Sir Robert Joseph Henry, Kt., CB, CBE, DSO, ED.

Ritchie, Sir James Edward Thomson, Bt., TD (1918).

Rix, Sir Brian Norman Roger, Kt., CBE.

Rix, Sir John, Kt., MBE.

Roberts, Sir Bryan Clieve, KCMG, QC.

Roberts, *Hon.* Sir Denys Tudor Emil, KBE, QC.

Roberts, Sir (Edward Fergus) Sidney, Kt., CBE.

Roberts, Sir Frank Kenyon, GCMG, GCVO.

Roberts, Sir Geoffrey Newland, Kt., CBE, AFC.

Roberts, *Brig.* Sir Geoffrey Paul Hardy-, KCVO, CB, CBE.

Roberts, Sir Gilbert Howland Rookehurst, Bt. (1809).

Roberts, Sir Gordon James, Kt., CBE.

Roberts, *Rt. Hon.* Sir (Ieuan) Wyn Pritchard, Kt., MP.

Roberts, Sir Samuel, Bt. (1919).

Roberts, Sir Stephen James Leake, Kt.

Roberts, Sir William James Denby, Bt. (1909).

Robertson, Sir Lewis, Kt., CBE, FRSE.

Robertson, *Prof.* Sir Rutherford Ness, Kt., CMG.

Robins, Sir Ralph Harry, Kt.

Robinson, Sir Albert Edward Phineas, Kt.

†Robinson, Sir Christopher Philipse, Bt. (1854).

Robinson, *Prof.* Sir (Edward) Austin (Gossage), Kt., CMG, OBE, FBA.

Robinson, Sir John James Michael Laud, Bt. (1660).

Robinson, *Rt. Hon.* Sir Kenneth, Kt.

Robinson, Sir Niall Bryan Lynch-, Bt., DSC (1920).

Robinson, Sir Wilfred Henry Frederick, Bt. (1908).

Robotham, *Hon.* Sir Lascelles Lister, Kt.

Robson, *Prof.* Sir James Gordon, Kt., CBE.

Robson, Sir John Adam, KCMG.

Roch, *Hon.* Sir John Ormond, Kt.

Roche, Sir David O'Grady, Bt. (1838).

Rodger, Sir William Glendinning, Kt., OBE.

Rodgers, Sir John Charles, Bt. (1964).

Rodrigues, Sir Alberto Maria, Kt., CBE, ED.

Roe, *Air Chief Marshal* Sir Rex David, GCB, AFC.

Rogers, Sir Frank Jarvis, Kt.

Rogers, *Air Chief Marshal* Sir John Robson, KCB, CBE.

Rogers, Sir Philip James, Kt., CBE.

Rogers, Sir Richard George, Kt., RA.

Roll, *Rev.* Sir James William Cecil, Bt. (1921).

Rooke, Sir Denis Eric, Kt., CBE.

Roper, *Hon.* Sir Clinton Marcus, Kt.

Ropner, Sir John Bruce Woollacott, Bt. (1952).

Ropner, Sir Robert Douglas, Bt. (1904).

Roscoe, Sir Robert Bell, KBE.

Rose, *Hon.* Sir Christopher Dudley Roger, Kt.

Rose, Sir Clive Martin, GCMG.

Rose, Sir David Lancaster, Bt. (1874).

Rose, Sir Julian Day, Bt. (1872 and 1909).

Rosier, *Air Chief Marshal* Sir Frederick Ernest, GCB, CBE, DSO.

Ross, Sir Alexander, Kt.

Ross, Sir Archibald David Manisty, KCMG.

Ross, Sir (James) Keith, Bt., RD, FRCS (1960).

Ross, Sir Lewis Nathan, Kt., CMG.

Rosser, Sir Melvyn Wynne, Kt.

Rossi, Sir Hugh Alexis Louis, Kt., MP.

Roth, *Prof.* Sir Martin, Kt., MD, FRCP.

Rothenstein, Sir John Knewstub Maurice, Kt., CBE, PH.D.

Rothnie, Sir Alan Keir, KCVO, CMG.

Rothschild, Sir Evelyn Robert Adrian de, Kt.

Rougier, *Hon.* Sir Richard George, Kt.

Rous, Sir Anthony Gerald Roderick, KCMG, OBE.

Row, *Hon.* Sir John Alfred, Kt.

Rowe, Sir Henry Peter, KCB, QC.

Rowe, Sir Jeremy, Kt., CBE.

Rowell, Sir John Joseph, Kt., CBE.

Rowland, *Air Marshal* Sir James Anthony, KBE, DFC, AFC.

Rowlands, *Air Marshal* Sir John Samuel, GC, KBE.

Rowley, Sir Charles Robert, Bt. (1836).

Rowley, Sir Joshua Francis, Bt. (1786).

Rowling, *Rt. Hon.* Sir Wallace Edward, KCMG.

Roxburgh, *Vice-Adm.* Sir John Charles Young, KCB, CBE, DSO, DSC.

Royden, Sir Christopher John, Bt. (1905).

Rumbold, Sir Henry John Sebastian, Bt. (1779).

Rumbold, Sir (Horace) Algernon (Fraser), KCMG, CIE.

Rumbold, Sir Jack Seddon, Kt.

Runciman, *Hon.* Sir James Cochran Stevenson (Sir Steven Runciman), Kt., CH.

Rusby, *Vice-Adm.* Sir Cameron, KCB, MVO.

Russell, Sir Archibald Edward, Kt., CBE, FRS.

Russell, Sir Charles Ian, Bt. (1916).

Russell, Sir Evelyn Charles Sackville, Kt.

Russell, Sir George Michael, Bt. (1812).

Russell, Sir (Robert) Mark, KCMG.

Russell, Sir Spencer Thomas, Kt.

Russell, *Rt. Hon.* Sir (Thomas) Patrick, Kt.

Rutter, Sir Frank William Eden, KBE.

†Ryan, Sir Derek Gerald, Bt. (1919).

Rycroft, Sir Richard Newton, Bt. (1784).

Ryrie, Sir William Sinclair, KCB.

Sainsbury, Sir Robert James, Kt.

St Aubyn, Sir (John) Arscott Molesworth-, Bt. (1689).

St George, Sir George Bligh, Bt. (I. 1766).

St Johnston, Sir Kerry, Kt.

Sainty, Sir John Christopher, KCB.

Sakzewski, Sir Albert, Kt.

†Salt, Sir Patrick MacDonnell, Bt. (1869).

Salt, Sir (Thomas) Michael John, Bt. (1899).

Samuel, Sir Jon Michael Glen, Bt. (1898).

Samuelson, Sir (Bernard) Michael (Francis), Bt. (1884).

Sandberg, Sir Michael Graham Ruddock, Kt., CBE.

Sanders, Sir John Reynolds Mayhew-, Kt.

Sanders, Sir Robert Tait, KBE, CMG.

Sanderson, Sir (Frank Philip) Bryan, Bt. (1920).

Sandilands, Sir Francis Edwin Prescott, Kt., CBE.

Sarei, Sir Alexis Holyweek, Kt., CBE.

Slynn, *Hon.* Sir Gordon, Kt.

Smallpeice, Sir Basil, KCVO.

Smallwood, *Air Chief Marshal* Sir Denis Graham, GBE, KCB, KBO, DFC.

Smart, *Prof.* Sir George Algernon, Kt., MD, FRCP.

Smart, Sir Jack, Kt., CBE.

Smedley, Sir Harold, KCMG, MBE.

Smeeton, *Vice-Adm.* Sir Richard Michael, KCB, MBE.

†Smiley, *Lt.-Col.* Sir John Philip, Bt. (1903).

Smith, Sir Alan, Kt., CBE, DFC.

Smith, Sir Alexander Mair, Kt., Ph.D.

Smith, Sir Charles Bracewell-, Bt. (1947).

Smith, Sir Christopher Sydney Winwood, Bt. (1809).

Smith, Sir Cyril, Kt., MBE, MP.

Smith, *Prof.* Sir David Cecil, Kt., FRS.

Smith, *Air Chief Marshal* Sir David Harcourt-, GBE, KCB, DFC.

Smith, Sir David Iser, KCVO.

Smith, Sir Dudley (Gordon), Kt., MP.

Smith, *Maj.-Gen.* Sir (Francis) Brian Wyldbore-, Kt., CB, DSO, OBE.

Smith, *Prof.* Sir (Francis) Graham, Kt., FRS.

Smith, Sir (Frank) Ewart, Kt.

Smith, Sir Geoffrey Johnson, Kt., MP.

Smith, *Col.* Sir Henry Abel, KCMG, KCVO, DSO.

Smith, Sir Howard Frank Trayton, GCMG.

Smith, *Hon.* Sir James Alfred, Kt., CBE, TD.

Smith, Sir John Hamilton-Spencer-, Bt. (1804).

Smith, Sir John Kenneth Newson-, Bt. (1944).

Smith, Sir John Lindsay Eric., Kt., CBE.

Smith, Sir John Wilson, Kt., CBE.

Smith, Sir Joseph William Grenville, Kt., MD, FRCP.

Smith, Sir Leslie Edward George, Kt.

Smith, *Rt. Hon.* Sir Murray Stuart-, Kt.

Smith, Sir Raymond Horace, KBE.

Smith, Sir Reginald Beaumont, Kt.

Smith, Sir Richard Rathbone Vassar-, Bt., TD (1917).

Smith, Sir (Richard) Robert Law-, Kt., CBE, AFC.

Smith, Sir Robert Courtney, Kt., CBE.

Smith, Sir Robert Hill, Bt. (1945).

Smith, *Prof.* Sir Roland, Kt.

Smith, *Air Marshal* Sir Roy David Austen-, KBE, CB, DFC.

Smith, Sir (Thomas) Gilbert, Bt. (1897).

Smith, *Adm.* Sir Victor Alfred Trumper, KBE, CB, DSC.

Smith, Sir William Reardon Reardon-, Bt. (1920).

Smith, Sir (William) Reginald Verdon, Kt.

Smith, Sir (William) Richard Prince-, Bt. (1911).

Smithers, *Prof.* Sir David Waldron, Kt., MD.

Smithers, Sir Peter Henry Berry Otway, Kt., VRD, D.Phil.

Smithers, *Hon.* Sir Reginald Allfree, Kt.

Smyth, Sir Thomas Weyland Bowyer-, Bt. (1661).

Smyth, Sir Timothy John, Bt. (1955).

Snelling, Sir Arthur Wendell, KCMG, KCVO.

Snelson, Sir Edward Alec Abbott, KBE.

Soame, Sir Charles John Buckworth-Herne-, Bt. (1697).

Sobell, Sir Michael, Kt.

Sobers, Sir Garfield St Auburn, Kt.

Solomon, Sir David Arnold, Kt., MBE.

Solomon, Sir Harry, Kt.

Solomons, *Hon.* Sir (Louis) Adrian, Kt.

Solti, Sir Georg, KBE.

Somare, *Rt. Hon.* Sir Michael Thomas, GCMG, CH.

Somers, *Rt. Hon.* Sir Edward Jonathan, Kt.

Somerset, Sir Henry Beaufort, Kt., CBE.

Somerville, *Brig.* Sir John Nicholas, Kt., CBE.

Somerville, Sir Quentin Charles Somerville Agnew-, Bt. (1957).

Somerville, Sir Robert, KCVO.

Sopwith, Sir Charles Ronald, Kt.

Soutar, *Air Marshal* Sir Charles John Williamson, KBE.

South, Sir Arthur, Kt.

Southby, Sir John Richard Bilbe, Bt. (1937).

Southern, Sir Richard William, Kt., FBA.

Southern, Sir Robert, Kt., CBE.

Southey, Sir Robert John, Kt., CMG.

Southward, Sir Leonard Bingley, Kt., OBE.

Southward, Sir Ralph, KCVO, FRCP.

Southwood, *Prof.* Sir (Thomas) Richard (Edmund), Kt., FRS.

Southworth, Sir Frederick, Kt., QC.

Souyave, *Hon.* Sir (Louis) Georges, Kt.

Sowrey, *Air Marshal* Sir Frederick Beresford, KCB, CBE, AFC.

Soysa, Sir Warusahennedige Abraham Bastian, Kt., CBE.

Sparkes, Sir Robert Lyndley, Kt.

Sparrow, Sir John, Kt.

Spearman, Sir Alexander Young Richard Mainwaring, Bt. (1840).

Speed, Sir Robert William Arney, Kt., CB, QC.

Speelman, Sir Cornelis Jacob, Bt. (1686).

Speight, *Hon.* Sir Graham Davies, Kt.

Speir, Sir Rupert Malise, Kt.

Spencer, Sir Kelvin Tallent, Kt., CBE, MC.

Spender, *Prof.* Sir Stephen Harold, Kt., CBE.

Spicer, Sir James Wilton, Kt., MP.

Spicer, Sir Peter James, Bt. (1906).

Spooner, Sir James Douglas, Kt.

Spotswood, *Marshal of the Royal Air Force* Sir Denis Frank, GCB, CBE, DSO, DFC.

Spratt, *Col.* Sir Greville Douglas, GBE, TD.

Spreckley, Sir (John) Nicholas (Teague), KCVO, CMG.

Springer, Sir Hugh Worrell, GCMG, GCVO, CBE.

Spry, *Brig.* Sir Charles Chambers Fowell, Kt., CBE, DSO.

Spry, *Hon.* Sir John Farley, Kt.

Stabb, *Hon.* Sir William Walter, Kt., QC.

Stack, *Air Chief Marshal* Sir (Thomas) Neville, KCB, CVO, CBE, AFC.

Stainton, Sir (John) Ross, Kt., CBE.

Stakis, Sir Reo Argiros, Kt.

Stallard, Sir Peter Hyla Gawne, KCMG, CVO, MBE.

Stallworthy, Sir John Arthur, Kt., FRCS.

Stamer, Sir (Lovelace) Anthony, Bt. (1809).

Stanbridge, *Air Vice-Marshal* Sir Brian Gerald Tivy, KCVO, CBE, AFC.

Stanier, *Brig.* Sir Alexander Beville Gibbons, Bt., DSO, MC (1917).

Stanier, *Field Marshal* Sir John Wilfred, GCB, MBE.

Stanley, *Rt. Hon.* Sir John Paul, Kt., MP.

†Staples, Sir Thomas, Bt. (I. 1628).

Stapleton, Sir (Henry) Alfred, Bt. (1679).

Stark, Sir Andrew Alexander Steel, KCMG, CVO.

Starke, *Hon.* Sir John Erskine, Kt.

Starkey, Sir John Philip, Bt. (1935).

Starrit, Sir James, KCVO.

Statham, Sir Norman, KCMG, CVO.

Staughton, *Rt. Hon.* Sir Christopher Stephen Thomas Jonathan Thayer, Kt.

Staveley, Sir John Malfroy, KBE, MC.

Staveley, *Admiral of the Fleet* Sir William Doveton Minet, GCB.

Stear, *Air Marshal* Sir Michael James Douglas, KCB, CBE.

Steedman, *Air Chief Marshal* Sir Alasdair (Alexander McKay Sinclair), GCB, CBE, DFC.

Steel, Sir David Edward Charles, Kt., DSO, MC, TD.

Steel, *Rt. Hon.* Sir David Martin Scott, KBE, MP.

Steel, *Maj.* Sir (Fiennes) William Strang, Bt. (1938).

Steel, Sir James, Kt., CBE.

Steele, Sir (Philip John) Rupert, Kt.

Steere, Sir Ernest Henry Lee-, KBE.

Stenhouse, Sir Nicol, Kt.

Stening, *Col.* Sir George Grafton Lees, Kt., ED.

Stephen, *Rt. Hon.* Sir Ninian Martin, GCMG, GCVO, KBE.

Stephenson, Sir Henry Upton, Bt. (1936).

Stephenson, *Rt. Hon.* Sir John Frederick Eustace, Kt.

Sternberg, Sir Sigmund, Kt.

Stevens, Sir Laurence Houghton, Kt., CBE.

Stevenson, *Vice-Adm.* Sir (Hugh) David, KBE.

Stevenson, Sir Simpson, Kt.

Stewart, Sir Alan, KBE.

Stewart, Sir Alan d'Arcy, Bt. (I. 1623).

Stewart, *Rt. Hon.* Sir (Bernard) (Harold) Ian (Halley), Kt., RD, FBA, FRSE, MP.

Stewart, Sir David Brodribb, Bt., TD (1960).

Stewart, Sir David James Henderson-, Bt. (1957).

Stewart, Sir Edward Jackson, Kt.

Stewart, *Prof.* Sir Frederick Henry, Kt., PH.D., FRS, FRSE.

Stewart, Sir Houston Mark Shaw-, Bt., MC, TD (S. 1667).

Stewart, Sir Hugh Charlie Godfray, Bt. (1803).

Stewart, Sir James Douglas, Kt.

Stewart, Sir (John) Simon (Watson), Bt. (1920).

Stewart, Sir Michael Norman Francis, KCMG, OBE.

Stewart, Sir Robertson Huntly, Kt., CBE.

Stewart, Sir Ronald Compton, Bt. (1937).

Steyn, *Hon.* Sir Johan Van Zyl, Kt.

Stibbon, *Gen.* Sir John James, KCB, OBE.

Stirling, Sir Alexander John Dickson, KBE, CMG.

Stockdale, Sir Arthur Noel, Kt.

Stockdale, Sir Thomas Minshull, Bt. (1960).

Stocker, *Rt. Hon.* Sir John Dexter, Kt., MC, TD.

Stoddart, *Wg Cdr.* Sir Kenneth Maxwell, KCVO, AE.

Stoker, *Prof.* Sir Michael George Parke, Kt., CBE, FRCP, FRS, FRSE.

Stokes, Sir John Heydon Romaine, Kt., MP.

Stone, *Prof.* Sir (John) Richard (Nicholas), Kt., CBE.

Stones, Sir William Frederick, Kt., OBE.

Stonhouse, Sir Philip Allan, Bt. (1628).

Stonor, *Air Marshal* Sir Thomas Henry, KCB.

Storey, *Hon.* Sir Richard, Bt. (1960).

Stormonth Darling, Sir James Carlisle, Kt., CBE, MC, TD.

Stott, Sir Adrian George Ellingham, Bt. (1920).

Stow, Sir Christopher Philipson-, Bt., DFC (1907).

Stow, Sir John Montague, GCMG, KCVO.

Stowe, Sir Kenneth Ronald, GCB, CVO.

Stracey, Sir John Simon, Bt. (1818).

Strachey, Sir Charles, Bt. (1801).

Straker, Sir Michael Ian Bowstead, Kt., CBE.

Strawson, *Prof.* Sir Peter Frederick, Kt., FBA.

Street, *Hon.* Sir Laurence Whistler, KCMG.

Streeton, Sir Terence George, KBE, CMG.

Strong, Sir Roy Colin, Kt., PH.D., FSA.

Stronge, Sir James Anselan Maxwell, Bt. (1803).

Stroud, *Prof.* Sir (Charles) Eric, Kt., FRCP.

Strutt, Sir Nigel Edward, Kt., TD.

Stuart, Sir James Keith, Kt.

Stuart, Sir Kenneth Lamonte, Kt.

†Stuart, Sir Phillip Luttrell, Bt. (1660).

Stubblefield, Sir (Cyril) James, Kt., D.SC., FRS.

Stubbs, Sir James Wilfrid, KCVO, TD.

Stucley, *Lt.* Sir Hugh George Coplestone Bampfylde, Bt. (1859).

Studd, Sir Edward Fairfax, Bt. (1929).

Studd, Sir Peter Malden, GBE, KCVO.

Studholme, Sir Henry William, Bt. (1956).

Style, *Lt. Cdr.* Sir Godfrey William, Kt., CBE, DSC, RN.

†Style, Sir William Frederick, Bt. (1627).

Suffield, Sir (Henry John) Lester, Kt.

Sugden, Sir Arthur, Kt.

Sullivan, Sir Desmond John, Kt.

Sullivan, Sir Richard Arthur, Bt. (1804).

Summerfield, *Hon.* Sir John Crampton, Kt., CBE.

Summers, Sir Felix Roland Brattan, Bt. (1952).

Summerson, Sir John Newenham, Kt., CH, CBE, FBA, FSA.

Sunderland, *Prof.* Sir Sydney, Kt., CMG.

Sutherland, Sir John Brewer, Bt. (1921).

Sutherland, Sir Maurice, Kt.

Sutherland, Sir William George MacKenzie, Kt.

Suttie, Sir (George) Philip Grant-, Bt. (S. 1702).

Sutton, Sir Frederick Walter, Kt., OBE.

Sutton, *Air Marshal* Sir John Matthias Dobson, KCB.

Sutton, Sir Richard Lexington, Bt. (1772).

Sutton, Sir Stafford William Powell Foster-, KBE, CMG, QC.

Swaffield, Sir James Chesebrough, Kt., CBE, RD.

Swallow, Sir William, Kt.

Swan, Sir John William David, KBE.

Swann, Sir Michael Christopher, Bt., TD (1906).

Swanwick, Sir Graham Russell, Kt., MBE.

Swartz, *Hon.* Sir Reginald William Colin, KBE, ED.

Swayne, Sir Ronald Oliver Carless, Kt., MC.

Swinburn, *Lt.-Gen.* Sir Richard Hull, KCB.

Swinson, Sir John Henry Alan, Kt., OBE.

Swinton, *Maj.-Gen.* Sir John, KCVO, OBE.

Swire, Sir Adrian Christopher, Kt.

Swire, Sir John Anthony, Kt., CBE.

Swiss, Sir Rodney Geoffrey, Kt., OBE.

Swynnerton, Sir Roger John Massy, Kt., CMG, OBE, MC.

Sykes, Sir Francis John Badcock, Bt. (1781).

Sykes, Sir John Charles Anthony le Gallais, Bt. (1921).

Sykes, *Prof.* Sir Malcolm Keith, Kt.

Sykes, Sir Tatton Christopher Mark, Bt. (1783).

Symington, *Prof.* Sir Thomas, Kt., MD, FRSE.

Symons, *Vice-Adm.* Sir Patrick Jeremy, KBE.

Synge, Sir Robert Carson, Bt. (1801).

Tait, *Adm.* Sir (Allan) Gordon, KCB, DSC.

Tait, Sir James Sharp, Kt., D.SC., LID., PH.D.

Tait, Sir Peter, KBE.

Talbot, *Vice-Adm.* Sir (Arthur Allison) FitzRoy, KBE, CB, DSO.

Talbot, *Hon.* Sir Hilary Gwynne, Kt.

Talboys, *Rt. Hon.* Sir Brian Edward, Kt., CH.

Tancred, Sir Henry Lawson-, Bt. (1662).

Tangaroa, *Hon.* Sir Tangoroa, Kt., MBE.

Tange, Sir Arthur Harold, Kt., CBE.

Tansley, Sir Eric Crawford, Kt., CMG.

Tapsell, Sir Peter Hannay Bailey, Kt., MP.

Tate, *Lt.-Col.* Sir Henry, Bt. (1898).

Taukala, Sir David Dawea, Kt., MBE.

Tavaiqia, *Ratu* Sir Josaia, KBE.

Tavare, Sir John, Kt., CBE.

Taylor, *Lt.-Gen.* Sir Allan Macnab, KBE, MC.

Taylor, Sir Alvin Burton, Kt.

Taylor, Sir (Arthur) Godfrey, Kt.

Taylor, Sir Cyril Julian Hebden, Kt.

Taylor, Sir Edward Macmillan (Teddy), Kt., MP.

Taylor, Sir George, Kt., D.SC., FRS, FRSE.

Taylor, Sir Henry Milton, Kt.

Taylor, Sir James, Kt., MBE, D.SC.

Taylor, Sir John Lang, KCMG.

Taylor, Sir Nicholas Richard Stuart, Bt. (1917).

Taylor, *Rt. Hon.* Sir Peter Murray, Kt.

Taylor, *Prof.* Sir William, Kt., CBE.

Tebbit, Sir Donald Claude, GCMG.

Te Heuheu, Sir Hepi Hoani, KBE.

Telford, Sir Robert, Kt., CBE.

Temple, Sir Ernest Sanderson, Kt., MBE, QC.

Temple, Sir John Meredith, Kt.

Temple, Sir Rawden John Afamado, Kt., CBE, QC.

Temple, *Maj.* Sir Richard Anthony Purbeck, Bt., MC (1876).

Templeton, Sir John Marks, Kt.

Tennant, *Capt.* Sir Iain Mark, KT.

Tennant, Sir Peter Frank Dalrymple, Kt., CMG, OBE.

Teo, Sir Fiatau Penitala, GCMG, GCVO, ISO, MBE.

Terry, Sir George Walter Roberts, Kt., CBE, QPM.

Terry, Sir John Elliott, Kt.

Terry, Sir Michael Edward Stanley Imbert-, Bt. (1917).

Terry, *Air Chief Marshal* Sir Peter David George, GCB, AFC.

Tetley, Sir Herbert, KBE, CB.

Tett, Sir Hugh Charles, Kt.

Thatcher, Sir Denis, Bt., MBE, TD (1990).

Thiess, Sir Leslie Charles, Kt., CBE.

Thomas, Sir Derek Morison David, KCMG.

Thomas, Sir Frederick William, Kt.

Thomas, Sir (Godfrey) Michael (David), Bt. (1694).

Thomas, Sir Jeremy Cashel, KCMG.

Thomas, Sir John Maldwyn, Kt.

Thomas, *Prof.* Sir John Meurig, Kt., FRS.

Thomas, Sir Keith Vivian, Kt.

Thomas, Sir Robert Evan, Kt.

Thomas, *Hon.* Sir Swinton Barclay, Kt.

Thomas, Sir William James Cooper, Bt., TD (1919).

Thomas, Sir (William) Michael (Marsh), Bt. (1918).

Thomas, *Adm.* Sir (William) Richard Scott, KCB, OBE.

Thompson, Sir Christopher Peile, Bt. (1890).

Thompson, Sir Edward Hugh Dudley, Kt., MBE, TD.

Thompson, *Surgeon Vice-Adm.* Sir Godfrey James Milton-, KBE.

Thompson, *Vice-Adm.* Sir Hugh Leslie Owen, KBE.

Thompson, Sir (Humphrey) Simon Meysey-, Bt. (1874).

Thompson, *Hon.* Sir John, Kt.

Thompson, *Prof.* Sir Michael Warwick, Kt., D.SC.

Thompson, Sir Paul Anthony, Bt. (1963).

Thompson, Sir Peter Anthony, Kt.

Thompson, Sir Ralph Patrick, Kt.

Thompson, Sir Richard Hilton Marler, Bt. (1963).

Thompson, Sir Robert Grainger Ker, KBE, CMG, DSO, MC.

Thompson, Sir (Thomas) Lionel Tennyson, Bt. (1806).

Thomson, Sir Adam, Kt., CBE.

Thomson, *Air Marshal* Sir (Charles) John, KCB, CBE, AFC.

Thomson, Sir Evan Rees Whitaker, Kt.

Thomson, Sir (Frederick Douglas) David, Bt. (1929).

Thomson, Sir Ivo Wilfrid Home, Bt. (1925).

Thomson, Sir John, KBE, TD.

Thomson, Sir John Adam, GCMG.

Thomson, Sir John (Ian) Sutherland, KBE, CMG.

Thomson, Sir Thomas James, Kt., CBE, FRCP.

Thorn, Sir John Samuel, Kt., OBE.

Thorne, *Maj.-Gen.* Sir David Calthrop, KBE.

Thorne, Sir Peter Francis, KCVO, CBE.

Thornton, *Lt.-Gen.* Sir Leonard Whitmore, KCB, CBE.

Thornton, Sir Peter Eustace, KCB.

Thorold, Sir Anthony Henry, Bt., OBE, DSC (1642).

Thorpe, *Hon.* Sir Mathew Alexander, Kt.

Thorpe, *Col.* Sir Ronald Gardner-, GBE, TD.

Thouron, Sir John Rupert Hunt, KBE.

†Throckmorton, Sir Anthony John Benedict, Bt. (1642).

Thwaites, Sir Bryan, Kt., PH.D.

Thwin, Sir U, Kt.

Tibbits, *Capt.* Sir David Stanley, Kt., DSC.

Tickell, Sir Crispin Charles Cervantes, GCMG, KCVO.

Tidbury, Sir Charles Henderson, Kt.

Tikaram, Sir Moti, KBE.

Tilney, Sir John Dudley Robert Tarleton, Kt., TD.

Tippet, *Vice-Adm.* Sir Anthony Sanders, KCB.

Tippett, Sir Michael Kemp, Kt., OM, CH, CBE.

Tirvengadum, Sir Harry Krishnan, KBE.

Titman, Sir John Edward Powis, KCVO.

Tizard, Sir John Peter Mills, Kt.

Tod, *Air Marshal* Sir John Hunter Hunter-, KBE, CB.

Todd, Sir Ian Pelham, KBE, FRCS.

Todd, *Hon.* Sir (Reginald Stephen) Garfield, Kt.

Tollemache, Sir Lyonel Humphry John, Bt. (1793).

Tololo, Sir Alkan, KBE.

Tomkins, Sir Alfred George, Kt., CBE.

Tomkins, Sir Edward Emile, GCMG, CVO.

Tomkys, Sir (William) Roger, KCMG.

Tomlinson, *Prof.* Sir Bernard Evans, Kt., CBE.

Tomlinson, Sir (Frank) Stanley, KCMG.

Tooley, Sir John, Kt.

Tooth, Sir (Hugh) John Lucas-, Bt. (1920).

Tooth, *Hon.* Sir (Seymour) Douglas, Kt.

ToRobert, Sir Henry Thomas, KBE.

Tory, Sir Geofroy William, KCMG.

Touche, Sir Anthony George, Bt. (1920).

Touche, Sir Rodney Gordon, Bt. (1962).

Tovey, Sir Brian John Maynard, KCMG.

ToVue, Sir Ronald, Kt., OBE.

Townsend, *Rear-Adm.* Sir Leslie William, KCVO, CBE.

Townsing, Sir Kenneth Joseph, Kt., CMG.

Traherne, Sir Cennydd George, KG, TD.

Traill, Sir Alan Towers, GBE.

Trant, *Gen.* Sir Richard Brooking, KCB.

Travers, Sir Thomas à'Beckett, Kt.

Treacher, *Adm.* Sir John Devereux, KCB.

Trehane, Sir (Walter) Richard, Kt.

Trelawny, Sir John Barry Salusbury-, Bt. (1628).

Trench, Sir Nigel Clive Cosby, KCMG.

Trench, Sir Peter Edward, Kt., CBE, TD.

Trescowthick, Sir Donald Henry, KBE.

Trethowan, *Prof.* Sir William Henry, Kt., CBE, FRCP.

Trevelyan, Sir George Lowthian, Bt. (1874).

Trevelyan, Sir Norman Irving, Bt. (1662).

Trewby, *Vice-Adm.* Sir (George Francis) Allan, KCB.

Tritton, Sir Anthony John Ernest, Bt. (1905).

†Trollope, Sir Anthony Simon, Bt. (1642).

Trotter, Sir Ronald Ramsay, Kt.

Troubridge, Sir Thomas Richard, Bt. (1799).

Troup, *Vice-Adm.* Sir (John) Anthony (Rose), KCB, DSC.

Trowbridge, *Rear-Adm.* Sir Richard John, KCVO.

Truscott, Sir George James Irving, Bt. (1909).

Tuck, Sir Bruce Adolph Reginald, Bt. (1910).

Tucker, *Hon.* Sir Richard Howard, Kt.

Tudor, *Hon.* Sir James Cameron, KCMG.

Tugendhat, Sir Christopher Samuel, Kt.

Tuite, Sir Christopher Hugh, Bt., PH.D. (1622).

Tuivaga, Sir Timoci Uluiburotu, Kt.

Tuke, Sir Anthony Favill, Kt.

Tupper, Sir Charles Hibbert, Bt. (1888).

Turbott, Sir Ian Graham, Kt., CMG, CVO.

Turing, Sir John Dermot, Bt. (s. 1638).

Turnbull, Sir George Henry, Kt.

Turnbull, Sir Richard Gordon, GCMG.

Turner, *Rt. Hon.* Sir Alexander Kingcome, KBE.

Turner, *Adm.* Sir (Arthur) Francis, KCB, DSC.

Turner, *Hon.* Sir Michael John, Kt.

Tuti, *Rev.* Dudley, KBE.

Tuzo, *Gen.* Sir Harry Craufurd, GCB, OBE, MC.

Twiss, *Adm.* Sir Frank Roddam, KCB, KCVO, DSC.

Tyler, *Maj.-Gen.* Sir Leslie Norman, KBE, CB.

Tyree, Sir (Alfred) William, Kt., OBE.

Tyrrell, Sir Murray Louis, KCVO, CBE.

Tyrwhitt, Sir Reginald Thomas Newman, Bt. (1919).

Udoma, *Hon.* Sir (Egbert) Udo, Kt.

Unsworth, Hon. Sir Edgar Ignatius Godfrey, Kt., CMG.

Unwin, Sir (James) Brian, KCB.

Ure, Sir John Burns, KCMG, LVO.

Urquhart, Sir Brian Edward, KCMG, MBE.

Urwick, Sir Alan Bedford, KCVO, CMG.

Usher, Sir Leonard Gray, KBE.

†Usher, Sir Robert Edward, Bt. (1899).

Ustinov, Sir Peter Alexander, Kt., CBE.

Utting, Sir William Benjamin, Kt., CB.

Vallat, Sir Francis Aimé, GBE, KCMG, QC.

Vallings, *Vice-Adm.* Sir George Montague Francis, KCB.

Vanderfelt, Sir Robin Victor, KBE.

van der Post, Sir Laurens Jan, Kt., CBE.

Vane, Sir John Robert, Kt., D.Phil., D.SC., FRS.

Vanneck, *Air Cdre* Hon. Sir Peter Beckford Rutgers, GBE, CB, AFC.

van Straubenzee, Sir William Radcliffe, Kt., MBE.

Vasquez, Sir Alfred Joseph, Kt., CBE, QC.

Vaughan, Sir (George) Edgar, KBE.

Vaughan, Sir Gerard Folliott, Kt., MP, FRCP.

Vavasour, *Cdr.* Sir Geoffrey William, Bt., DSC, RN (1828).

Veale, Sir Alan John Ralph, Kt.

Veira, Sir Philip Henry, KBE.

Verco, Sir Walter John George, KCVO.

Verney, Sir John, Bt., MC, TD (1946).

Verney, Sir Ralph Bruce, Bt., KBE (1818).

Vernon, Sir James, Kt., CBE.

Vernon, Sir Nigel John Douglas, Bt. (1914).

Vesey, Sir (Nathaniel) Henry (Peniston), Kt., CBE.

Vestey, Sir (John) Derek, Bt. (1921).

Vial, Sir Kenneth Harold, Kt., CBE.

Vick, Sir (Francis) Arthur, Kt., OBE, Ph.D.

Vickers, *Lt.-Gen.* Sir Richard Maurice Hilton, KCB, MVO, OBE.

Victoria, Sir (Joseph Aloysius) Donatus, Kt., CBE.

Villiers, Sir Charles Hyde, Kt., MC.

Vincent, *Field Marshal* Sir Richard Frederick, GBE, KCB, DSO.

Vincent, Sir William Percy Maxwell, Bt. (1936).

Vinelott, *Hon.* Sir John Evelyn, Kt.

Vines, Sir William Joshua, Kt., CMG.

Vyse, *Lt.-Gen.* Sir Edward Dacre Howard-, KCB, CB, MC.

Vyvyan, Sir John Stanley, Bt. (1645).

Waddell, Sir Alexander Nicol Anton, KCMG, DSC.

Waddell, Sir James Henderson, Kt., CB.

Wade, *Prof.* Sir Henry William Rawson, Kt., QC, FBA.

Wade, *Air Chief Marshal* Sir Ruthven Lowry, KCB, DFC.

Wagner, Sir Anthony Richard, KCB, KCVO.

Waite, *Hon.* Sir John Douglas, Kt.

Wake, Sir Hereward, Bt. MC (1621).

Wakefield, Sir (Edward) Humphry (Tyrell), Bt. (1962).

Wakefield, Sir Norman Edward, Kt.

Wakefield, Sir Peter George Arthur, KBE, CMG.

Wakeford, *Air Marshal* Sir Richard Gordon, KCB, OBE, MVO, AFC.

Wakeley, Sir John Cecil Nicholson, Bt., FRCS (1952).

†Wakeman, Sir Edward Offley Bertram, Bt. (1828).

Walker, *Rev.* Alan Edgar, Kt., OBE.

Walker, Sir Allan Grierson, Kt., QC.

Walker, *Gen.* Sir Antony Kenneth Frederick, KCB.

Walker, Sir Baldwin Patrick, Bt. (1856).

Walker, Sir (Charles) Michael, GCMG.

Walker, Sir Colin John Shedlock, Kt., OBE.

Walker, Sir David Alan, Kt.

Walker, Sir Gervas George, Kt.

Walker, Sir Harold Berners, KCMG.

Walker, *Maj.* Sir Hugh Ronald, Bt. (1906).

Walker, Sir James Graham, Kt., MBE.

Walker, Sir James Heron, Bt. (1868).

Walker, Sir Michael Leolin Forestier-, Bt. (1835).

Walker, Sir Patrick Jeremy, KCB.

Walker, *Gen.* Sir Walter Colyear, KCB, CBE, DSO.

Wall, *Dr Hon.* Sir Gerard Aloysius, Kt.

Wall, Sir Patrick Henry Bligh, Kt., MC, VRD.

Wall, Sir Robert William, Kt., OBE.

Wallace, Sir Ian James, Kt., CBE.

Waller, *Hon.* Sir (George) Mark, Kt.

Waller, *Rt. Hon.* Sir George Stanley, Kt., OBE.

Waller, Sir (John) Keith, Kt., CBE.

Waller, Sir John Stainer, Bt. (1815).

Waller, Sir Robert William, Bt. (I. 1780).

Walley, Sir John, KBE, CB.

Walsh, Sir Alan, Kt., D.SC., FRS.

Walsh, *Prof.* Sir John Patrick, KBE.

Walsham, *Rear-Adm.* Sir John Scarlett Warren, Bt., CB, OBE (1831).

Walter, Sir Harold Edward, Kt.

Walters, *Prof.* Sir Alan Arthur, Kt.

Walters, Sir Dennis Murray, Kt., MBE, MP.

Walters, Sir Frederick Donald, Kt.

Walters, Sir Peter Ingram, Kt.

Walters, Sir Roger Talbot, KBE, FRIBA.

Walton, Sir John Robert, Kt.

Wan, Sir Wamp, Kt., MBE.

Wanstall, *Hon.* Sir Charles Gray, Kt.

Ward, *Hon.* Sir Alan Hylton, Kt.

Ward, Sir Arthur Hugh, KBE.

Ward, *Gen.* Sir Dudley, GCB, KBE, DSO.

Ward, Sir Joseph James Laffey, Bt. (1911).

Ward, *Maj.-Gen.* Sir Philip John Newling, KCVO, CBE.

Ward, Sir Terence George, Kt., CBE.

Wardale, Sir Geoffrey Charles, KCB.

Wardlaw, Sir Henry (John), Bt. (s. 1631).

Wardle, Sir Thomas Edward Jewell, Kt.

Waring, Sir (Alfred) Holburt, Bt. (1935).

Warmington, *Lt.-Cdr.* Sir Marshall George Clitheroe, Bt., RN (1908).

Warner, Sir (Edward Courtenay) Henry, Bt. (1910).

Warner, Sir Edward Redston, KCMG, OBE.

Warner, Sir Frederick Archibald, GCVO, KCMG.

Warner, Sir Frederick Edward, Kt., FRS.

Warner, *Hon.* Sir Jean-Pierre Frank Eugene, Kt.

Warnock, Sir Geoffrey James, Kt.

Warren, Sir Brian Charles Pennefather, Bt. (1784).

Warren, Sir Frederick Miles, KBE.

Warren, Sir (Harold) Brian (Seymour), Kt.

Wass, Sir Douglas William Gretton, GCB.

Waterhouse, *Hon.* Sir Ronald Gough, Kt.

Waterlow, Sir Christopher Rupert, Bt. (1873).

Waterlow, Sir (James) Gerard, Bt. (1930).

Waters, *Gen.* Sir (Charles) John, KCB, CBE.

Wates, Sir Christopher Stephen, Kt.

Watkins, *Rt. Hon.* Sir Tasker, VC, GBE.

Watson, Sir Bruce Dunstan, Kt.

Watson, Sir Francis John Bagott, KCVO, FBA, FSA.

Watson, Sir (James) Andrew, Bt. (1866).

Watson, Sir John Forbes Inglefield-, Bt. (1895).

Watson, Sir Michael Milne-, Bt., CBE (1937).

Watson, Sir (Noel) Duncan, KCMG.

Watson, *Vice-Adm.* Sir Philip Alexander, KBE, MVO.

Watt, *Surgeon Vice-Adm.* Sir James, KBE, FRCS.

Watt, Sir James Harvie-, Bt. (1945).

Watts, Sir Arthur Desmond, KCMG.

Watts, *Lt.-Gen.* Sir John Peter Barry Condliffe, KBE, CB, MC.

Wauchope, Sir Roger (Hamilton) Don-, Bt. (s. 1667).

Way, Sir Richard George Kitchener, KCB, CBE.

Weatherall, *Prof.* Sir David John, Kt., FRS.

Weatherall, *Vice-Adm.* Sir James Lamb, KBE.

Weatherstone, Sir Dennis, KBE.

Weaver, Sir Tobias Rushton, Kt., CB.

Webb, *Lt.-Gen.* Sir Richard James Holden, KBE, CB.

Webb, Sir Thomas Langley, Kt.

Webster, *Very Rev.* Alan Brunskill, KCVO.

Webster, *Vice-Adm.* Sir John Morrison, KCB.

Webster, *Hon.* Sir Peter Edlin, Kt.

Wedderburn, Sir Andrew John Alexander Ogilvy-, Bt. (1803).

Wedgwood, Sir (Hugo) Martin, Bt. (1942).

Weeks, Sir Hugh Thomas, Kt., CMG.

Weinberg, Sir Mark Aubrey, Kt.

Weir, Sir Michael Scott, KCMG.

Weir, Sir Roderick Bignell, Kt.

Welby, Sir (Richard) Bruno Gregory, Bt. (1801).

Welch, Sir John Reader, Bt. (1957).

Weld, *Col.* Sir Joseph William, Kt., OBE, TD.

Weldon, Sir Anthony William, Bt. (l. 1723).

Welensky, *Rt. Hon.* Sir Roy, (Roland), KCMG.

Wellings, Sir Jack Alfred, Kt., CBE.

Wells, Sir Charles Maltby, Bt., TD (1944).

Wells, Sir John Julius, Kt.

West-Russell, *Hon.* Sir David Sturrock, Kt.

Westbrook, Sir Neil Gowanloch, Kt., CBE.

Westerman, Sir (Wilfred) Alan, Kt., CBE.

Weston, Sir Michael Charles Swift, KCMG, CVO.

Wheeler, Sir Frederick Henry, Kt., CBE.

Wheeler, Sir Harry Anthony, Kt., OBE.

Wheeler, *Air Chief Marshal* Sir (Henry) Neil (George), GCB, CBE, DSO, DFC, AFC.

Wheeler, Sir John Daniel, Kt., MP.

Wheeler, Sir John Hieron, Bt. (1920).

Wheeler, *Hon.* Sir Kenneth Henry, Kt.

Wheler, Sir Edward Woodford, Bt. (1660).

Whishaw, Sir Charles Percival Law, Kt.

Whitaker, *Maj.* Sir James Herbert Ingham, Bt. (1936).

White, Sir Christopher Robert Meadows, Bt. (1937).

White, Sir Dick Goldsmith, KCMG, KBE.

White, Sir Frederick William George, KBE, Ph.D., FRS.

White, Sir George Stanley James, Bt. (1904).

White, Sir Harold Leslie, Kt., CBE.

White, *Wg-Cdr.* Sir Henry Arthur Dalrymple-, Bt., DFC (1926).

White, *Vice-Adm.* Sir Hugo Moresby, KCB, CBE.

White, *Hon.* Sir John Charles, Kt., MBE.

White, Sir John Woolmer, Bt. (1922).

White, Sir Lynton Stuart, Kt., MBE. TD.

White, *Adm.* Sir Peter, GBE.

White, Sir Thomas Astley Woollaston, Bt. (1802).

Whitehead, Sir John Stainton, KCMG, CVO.

Whitehead, Sir Rowland John Rathbone, Bt. (1889).

Whiteley, Sir Hugo Baldwin Huntington-, Bt. (1918).

Whiteley, *Gen.* Sir Peter John Frederick, GCB, OBE, RM.

Whitford, *Hon.* Sir John Norman Keates, Kt.

Whitley, *Air Marshal* Sir John René, KBE, CB, DSO, AFC.

Whitmore, Sir Clive Anthony, GCB, CVO.

Whitmore, Sir John Henry Douglas, Bt. (1954).

Whitteridge, Sir Gordon Coligny, KCMG, OBE.

Whittle, *Air Cdre* Sir Frank, OM, KBE, CB, FRS.

Whittome, Sir Leslie Alan, Kt.

Wickerson, Sir John Michael, Kt.

Wicks, Sir James Albert, Kt.

Wigan, Sir Alan Lewis, Bt. (1898).

Wiggin, Sir John Henry, Bt., MC (1892).

Wigglesworth, Sir Vincent Brian, Kt., CBE, MD, FRS.

Wigram, *Rev. Canon* Sir Clifford Woolmore, Bt. (1805).

Wilbraham, Sir Richard Baker, Bt. (1776).

Wilford, Sir (Kenneth) Michael, GCMG.

Wilkes, *Lt.-Gen.* Sir Michael John, KCB, CBE.

Wilkins, Sir Graham John, Kt.

Wilkins, *Lt.-Gen.* Sir Michael Compton Lockwood, KCB, OBE.

Wilkinson, Sir (David) Graham (Brook) Bt. (1941).

Wilkinson, *Prof.* Sir Denys Haigh, Kt., FRS.

Wilkinson, *Prof.* Sir Geoffrey, Kt., FRS.

Wilkinson, *Rt. Hon.* Sir Nicolas Christopher Henry Browne-, Kt.

Wilkinson, Sir Peter Allix, KCMG, DSO, OBE.

Wilkinson, Sir Philip William, Kt.

Wilkinson, Sir William Henry Nairn, Kt.

Willatt, Sir (Robert) Hugh, Kt.

Willcocks, Sir David Valentine, Kt., CBE, MC.

Williams, Sir Alastair Edgcumbe James Dudley-, Bt. (1964).

Williams, Sir Alwyn, Kt., Ph.D., FRS.

Williams, Sir Arthur Dennis Pitt, Kt.

Williams, Sir (Arthur) Gareth Ludovic Emrys Rhys, Bt. (1918).

Williams, *Prof.* Sir Bruce Rodda, KBE.

Williams, *Adm.* Sir David, GCB.

Williams, *Prof.* Sir David Glyndwr Tudor, Kt.

Williams, Sir David Innes, Kt.

Williams, *Hon.* Sir Denys Ambrose, Kt.

Williams, Sir Donald Mark, Bt. (1866).

Williams, Sir Edgar Trevor, Kt., CB, CBE, DSO.

Williams, *Prof.* Sir (Edward) Dillwyn, Kt., FRCP.

Williams, *Hon.* Sir Edward Stratten, KCMG, KBE.

Williams, Sir Francis John Watkin, Bt., QC (1798).

Williams, Sir Henry Sydney, Kt., OBE.

Williams, Sir (John) Leslie, Kt., CBE.

Williams, Sir John Robert, KCMG.

Williams, Sir Leonard, KBE, CB.

Williams, Sir Osmond, Bt., MC (1909).

Williams, Sir Peter Watkin, Kt.

Williams, *Prof.* Sir Robert Evan Owen, Kt., MD, FRCP.

Williams, Sir (Robert) Philip Nathaniel, Bt. (1915).

Williams, Sir Robin Philip, Bt. (1953).

Williams, Sir (William) Maxwell (Harries), Kt.

Williamson, *Marshal of the Royal Air Force* Sir Keith Alec, GCB, AFC.

Williamson, Sir (Nicholas Frederick) Hedworth, Bt. (1642).

Willink, Sir Charles William, Bt. (1957).

Willis, *Hon.* Sir Eric Archibald, KBE, CMG.

Willis, *Vice-Adm.* Sir (Guido) James, KBE.

Willison, *Lt.-Gen.* Sir David John, KCB, OBE, MC.

Willison, Sir John Alexander, Kt., OBE.

Wills, Sir David Seton, Bt. (1904).

Wills, Sir (Hugh) David Hamilton, Kt., CBE, TD.

Wills, Sir John Spencer, Kt.

Wills, Sir John Vernon, Bt., TD (1923).

Wilmot, Sir Henry Robert, Bt. (1759).

Wilmot, *Cdr.* Sir John Assheton Eardley-, Bt., MVO, DSC, RN (1821).

Wilsey, *Lt.-Gen.* Sir John Finlay Willasey-, Kt.

Wilson, Sir Alan Herries, Kt., FRS.

Wilson, *Lt.-Gen.* Sir (Alexander) James, KBE, MC.

Wilson, Sir Anthony, Kt.

Wilson, Sir Austin George, Kt., OBE.

Wilson, *Vice-Adm.* Sir Barry Nigel, KCB.

Wilson, Sir Charles Haynes, Kt.

Wilson, Sir David, Bt. (1920).

Wilson, Sir David Clive, GCMG.

Wilson, Sir David Mackenzie, Kt.

Wilson, Sir Geoffrey Masterman, KCB, CMG.

Wilson, Sir James William Douglas, Bt. (1906).

Wilson, Sir John Foster, Kt., CBE.

Wilson, Sir John Gardiner, Kt., CBE.

Wilson, Sir John Martindale, KCB.

†Wilson, *Brig.* Sir Mathew John Anthony, Bt., OBE, MC (1874).

Wilson, Sir Reginald Holmes, Kt.

Wilson, Sir Robert, Kt., CBE.

Wilson, Sir Robert Donald, Kt.

Wilson, *Rt. Rev.* Roger Plumpton, KCVO, DD.

Wilson, Sir Roland, KBE.

Wilson, *Air Marshal* Sir (Ronald) Andrew (Fellowes), KCB, AFC.

Wilson, *Hon.* Sir Ronald Darling, KBE, CMG.

Wilton, Sir (Arthur) John, KCMG, KCVO, MC.

Wiltshire, Sir Frederick Munro, Kt., CBE.

Windeyer, Sir Brian Wellingham, Kt.

Wingate, *Capt.* Sir Miles Buckley, KCVO.

Winnifrith, Sir (Alfred) John (Digby), KCB.

Winnington, Sir Francis Salwey William, Bt. (1755).

Winskill, *Air Cdre* Sir Archibald Little, KCVO, CBE, DFC.

Winterbottom, Sir Walter, Kt., CBE.

Wiseman, Sir John William, Bt. (1628).

Wolfson, Sir Brian Gordon, Kt.

Wolseley, Sir Charles Garnet Richard Mark, Bt. (1628).

Wolseley, Sir Garnet, Bt. (I. 1745).

Wolstenholme, Sir Gordon Ethelbert Ward, Kt., OBE.

Wombwell, Sir George Philip Frederick, Bt. (1778).

Womersley, Sir Peter John Walter, Bt. (1945).

Wontner, Sir Hugh Walter Kingwell, GBE, CVO.

Wood, Sir Anthony John Page, Bt. (1837).

Wood, Sir David Basil Hill-, Bt. (1921).

Wood, Sir Frederick Ambrose Stuart, Kt.

Wood, Sir Henry Peart, Kt., CBE.

Wood, *Prof.* Sir John Crossley, Kt., CBE.

Wood, *Hon.* Sir John Kember, Kt., MC.

Wood, Sir Martin Francis, Kt., OBE.

Wood, Sir Russell Dillon, KCVO, VRD.

Wood, Sir William Alan, KCVO, CB.

Woodcock, Sir John, Kt., CBE, QPM.

Woodfield, Sir Philip John, KCB, CBE.

Woodhouse, *Rt. Hon.* Sir (Arthur) Owen, KBE, DSC.

Woodroffe, *Most Rev.* George Cuthbert Manning, KBE.

Woodroofe, Sir Ernest George, Kt., ph.D.

Woodruff, *Prof.* Sir Michael Francis Addison, Kt., D.SC., FRS, FRCS.

Woods, Sir Colin Philip Joseph, KCVO, CBE.

Woods, *Most Rev.* Frank, KBE, DD.

Woods, *Rt. Rev.* Robert Wilmer, KCMG, KCVO.

Woodward, *Hon.* Sir (Albert) Edward, Kt., OBE.

Woodward, *Adm.* Sir John Forster, GBE, KCB.

Woolf, *Rt. Hon.* Sir Harry Kenneth, Kt.

Woolf, Sir John, Kt.

Woollaston, Sir (Mountford) Tosswill, Kt.

Wordie, Sir John Stewart, Kt., CBE, VRD.

Worsley, *Gen.* Sir Richard Edward, GCB, OBE.

Worsley, Sir (William) Marcus (John), Bt. (1838).

Worsthorne, Sir Peregrine Gerard, Kt.

Worthington, *Air Vice-Marshal* Sir Geoffrey Luis, KBE, CB.

Wraight, Sir John Richard, KBE, CMG.

Wratten, *Air Vice Marshal* Sir William John, KBE, CB, AFC.

Wraxall, Sir Charles Frederick Lascelles, Bt. (1813).

Wrey, Sir (Castel Richard) Bourchier, Bt. (1628).

Wrigglesworth, Sir Ian William, Kt.

Wright, Sir Allan Frederick, KBE.

Wright, Sir Denis Arthur Hepworth, GCMG.

Wright, Sir Edward Maitland, Kt., D.Phil.,Ll.D., D.SC., FRSE.

Wright, *Hon.* Sir (John) Michael, Kt.

Wright, Sir (John) Oliver, GCMG, GCVO, DSC.

Wright, Sir Patrick Richard Henry, GCMG.

Wright, Sir Paul Hervé Giraud, KCMG, OBE.

Wright, Sir Richard Michael Cory-, Bt. (1903).

Wrightson, Sir Charles Mark Garmondsway, Bt. (1900).

Wykeham, *Air Marshal* Sir Peter Guy, KCB, DSO, OBE, DFC, AFC.

Wylie, Sir Campbell, Kt., ED, QC.

Wynn, Sir David Watkin Williams-, Bt. (1688).

Yang, *Hon.* Ti Liang, Kt.

Yapp, Sir Stanley Graham, Kt.

Yarrow, Sir Eric Grant, Bt., MBE (1916).

Yeend, Sir Geoffrey John, Kt., CBE.

Yellowlees, Sir Henry, KCB.

Yocklunn, Sir John (Soong Chung), KCVO.

Youens, Sir Peter William, Kt., CMG, OBE.

Young, Sir Brian Walter Mark, Kt.

Young, *Lt.-Gen.* Sir David Tod, KBE, CB, DFC.

Young, Sir George Samuel Knatchbull, Bt., MP (1813).

Young, *Hon.* Sir Harold William, KCMG.

Young, Sir John Kenyon Roe, Bt. (1821).

Young, *Hon.* Sir John McIntosh, KCMG.

Young, Sir Leslie Clarence, Kt., CBE.

Young, Sir Norman Smith, Kt.

Young, Sir Richard Dilworth, Kt.

Young, Sir Robert Christopher Mackworth-, GCVO.

Young, Sir Roger William, Kt.

Young, Sir Stephen Stewart Templeton, Bt. (1945).

Young, Sir William Neil, Bt. (1769).

Younger, *Maj.-Gen.* Sir John William, Bt., CBE (1911).

Younger, Sir William McEwan, Bt., DSO (1964).

Zeeman, *Prof.* Sir Erik Christopher, Kt., FRS.

Zeidler, Sir David Ronald, Kt., CBE.

Zoleveke, Sir Gideon Pitabose, KBE.

Zunz, Sir Gerhard Jacob (Jack), Kt.

Zurenuo, *Rt. Rev.* Zurewe Kamong, Kt., OBE.

Baronetcies Extinct (since last issue).—Harmood-Banner (UK, 1924); Mellor (UK, 1924); Mathias (UK, 1917); Blades (UK, 1922) by the death of 2nd Baron Ebbisham; Nicholson (UK, 1958).

DAMES GRAND CROSS AND DAMES COMMANDERS

Style.—'Dame' before forename and surname, followed by appropriate post-nominal initials. Where such an award is made to a lady already in enjoyment of a higher title, the appropriate initials follow her name.

Husband.—Untitled.

For forms of address, *see* page 219.

Dame Grand Cross and Dames Commander are the higher classes for women of the Order of the Bath, the Order of St Michael and St George, the Royal Victorian Order, and the Order of the British Empire. Dames Grand Cross rank after the wives of Baronets and before the wives of Knights Grand Cross. Dames Commanders rank after the wives of Knights Grand Cross and before the wives of Knights Commanders.

Honorary Dame Commanders may be conferred on women who are citizens of countries of which the Queen is not head of state.

LIST OF DAMES
(Revised to August 31, 1991)

Women Peers in their own right and Life Peers are not included in this list.

HM Queen Elizabeth The Queen Mother, KG, KT, CI, GMVO.
HRH The Princess Royal, GCVO.
HRH The Princess Margaret, Countess of Snowdon, CI, GCVO.
HRH The Duchess of Gloucester, GCVO.
HRH The Princess Alice, Duchess of Gloucester, GCB, CI, GCVO, GBE.
HRH The Duchess of Kent, GCVO.
HRH The Princess Alexandra of Kent, GCVO.
Abaijah, Dame Josephine, DBE.
Abel Smith, Lady, DCVO.
Abergavenny, The Marchioness of, DCVO.
Albemarle, The Countess of, DBE.
Anderson, Dame Judith, DBE.
Anderson, *Brig.* Hon. Dame Mary Mackenzie (Mrs Pihl), DBE.
Anglesey, The Marchioness of, DBE.
Baker, Dame Janet Abbott (Mrs Shelley), DBE.
Baring, Lady Rose Gwendolen Louisa, DCVO.
Barnes, Dame (Alice) Josephine (Mary Taylor), DBE, FRCP, FRCS.
Barrow, Dame (Ruth) Nita, GCMG.
Basset, Lady Elizabeth, DCVO.
Beaurepaire, Dame Beryl Edith, DBE.
Berry, Dame Alice Miriam, DBE.
Bishop, Dame (Margaret) Joyce, DBE.
Blaize, Dame Venetia Ursula, DBE.
Blaxland, Dame Helen Frances, DBE.
Booth, *Hon.* Dame Margaret Myfanwy Wood, DBE.
Bottomley, Dame Bessie Ellen, DBE.
Bowman, Dame (Mary) Elaine Kellett-, DBE, MP.
Boyd, Dame Vivienne Myra, DBE.
Bracewell, *Hon.* Dame Joyanne Winifred (Mrs Copeland), DBE.
Brazill, Dame Josephine (Sister Mary Philippa), DBE.
Breen, Dame Marie Freda, DBE.
Bridges, Dame Mary Patricia, DBE.
Brown, Dame Beryl Paston, DBE.
Brown, Dame Gillian Gerda, DCVO, CMG.
Browne, Lady Moyra Blanche Madeleine, DBE.
Bryans, Dame Anne Margaret, DBE.
Bryce, Dame Isabel Graham, DBE.
Burnside, Dame Edith, DBE.
Buttfield, Dame Nancy Eileen, DBE.
Bynoe, Dame Hilda Louisa, DBE.

Cartland, Dame Barbara Hamilton, DBE.
Cartwright, Dame Mary Lucy, DBE, SC.D., D.Phil., FRS.
Cartwright, Dame Silvia Rose, DBE.
Casey, Dame Stella Katherine, DBE.
Cayford, Dame Florence Evelyn, DBE.
Chesterton, Dame Elizabeth Ursula, DBE.
Clay, Dame Marie Mildred, DBE.
Clayton, Dame Barbara Evelyn (Mrs Klyne), DBE.
Cleland, Dame Rachel, DBE.
Clode, Dame (Emma) Frances (Heather), DBE.
Coles, Dame Mabel Irene, DBE.
Cooper, Dame Whina, DBE.
Coulshed, Dame (Mary) Frances, DBE, TD.
Cozens, *Brig.* Dame (Florence) Barbara, DBE, RRC.
Crowe, Dame Sylvia, DBE.
Davies, Dame Gwen Ffrangcon-, DBE.
Daws, Dame Joyce Margaretta, DBE.
De La Warr, Sylvia, Countess, DBE.
Dell, Dame Miriam Patricia, DBE.
Dench, Dame Judith Olivia (Mrs Williams), DBE.
de Valois, Dame Ninette, CH, DBE.
Digby, Lady, DBE.
Donaldson, Dame (Dorothy) Mary (Lady Donaldson of Lymington), GBE.
Doyle, *Air Cmdt.* Dame Jean Lena Annette Conan (Lady Bromet), DBE.
Drake, *Brig.* Dame Jean Elizabeth Rivett-, DBE.
Dugdale, Kathryn Edith Helen (Mrs John Dugdale), DCVO.
Durack, Dame Mary (Mrs H. C. Miller), DBE.
Emerton, Dame Audrey Caroline, DBE.
Fenner, Dame Peggy Edith, DBE, MP.
Fermoy, Ruth Sylvia, Lady, DCVO, OBE.
Fitton, Dame Doris Alice (Mrs Mason), DBE.
Fookes, Dame Janet Evelyn, DBE, MP.
Fraser, Dame Dorothy Rita, DBE.
Friend, Dame Phyllis Muriel, DBE.
Frink, Dame Elisabeth, DBE, RA.
Frost, Dame Phyllis Irene, DBE.
Fry, Dame Margaret Louise, DBE.

Gallagher, Dame Monica Josephine, DBE.
Gardiner, Dame Helen Louisa, DBE, MVO.
Gibbs, Dame Molly Peel, DBE.
Giles, *Air Cmdt.* Dame Pauline (Mrs Parsons), DBE, RRC.
Godwin, Dame (Beatrice) Anne, DBE.
Golding, Dame (Cecilie) Monica, DBE.
Goodman, Dame Barbara, DBE.
Gordon, Dame Minita Elmira, GCMG, GCVO.
Gow, Dame Jane Elizabeth, DBE.
Grafton, The Duchess of, GCVO.
Green, Dame Mary Georgina, DBE.
Grey, Dame Beryl Elizabeth (Mrs Svenson), DBE.
Guilfoyle, Dame Margaret Georgina Constance, DBE.
Hall, Dame Catherine Mary, DBE.
Hambleden, Patricia, Viscountess, GCVO.
Hammond, Dame Joan Hood, DBE.
Harris, Dame (Muriel) Diana Reader-, DBE.
Heilbron, *Hon.* Dame Rose, DBE.
Henrison, Dame Anne Elizabeth Rosina, DBE.
Herbison, Dame Jean Marjory, DBE, CMG.
Hercus, *Hon.* Dame (Margaret) Ann, DCMG.
Hill, Dame Elizabeth Mary, DBE.
Hill, *Air Cdre* Dame Felicity Barbara, DBE.
Hiller, Dame Wendy (Mrs Gow), DBE.
Horsman, Dame Dorothea Jean, DBE.
Howard, Dame Rosemary Christian, DBE.
Hunter, Dame Pamela, DBE.
Hurley, *Prof.* Dame Rosalinde (Mrs Gortvai), DBE.
Hussey, Lady Susan Katharine, DCVO.
Isaacs, Dame Albertha Madeline, DBE.
James, Dame Naomi Christine (Mrs Haythorne), DBE.
Jenkins, Dame (Mary) Jennifer (Lady Jenkins of Hillhead), DBE.
Jessel, Dame Penelope, DBE.
Jones, Dame Gwyneth (Mrs Haberfeld-Jones), DBE.
Kekedo, Dame Mary, DBE, BEM.

Kelleher, Dame Joan, DBE.

Kettlewell, *Cmdt.* Dame Marion Mildred, DBE.

Kilroy, Dame Alix Hester Marie (Lady Meynell), DBE.

Kirk, Dame (Lucy) Ruth, DBE.

Knight, Dame (Joan Christabel) Jill, DBE, MP.

Kramer, *Prof.* Dame Leonie Judith, DBE.

Lancaster, Dame Jean, DBE.

Lister, Dame Unity Viola, DBE.

Litchfield, Dame Ruby Beatrice, DBE.

Lloyd, *Prof.* Dame June Kathleen, DBE, FRCP.

Lowrey, *Air Cmdt.* Dame Alice, DBE, RRC.

Lynn, Dame Vera (Mrs Lewis), DBE.

Mackinnon, Dame (Una) Patricia, DBE.

Macknight, Dame Ella Annie Noble, DBE, MD.

Macmillan of Ovenden, Katharine, Viscountess, DBE.

Maconchy, Dame Elizabeth Violet (Mrs Le Fanu), DBE.

Major, Dame Malvina Lorraine (Mrs Fleming), DBE.

Mann, Dame Ida Caroline, DBE, D.SC., FRCS.

Markova, Dame Alicia, DBE.

Martin, Rosamund Mary Holland-, Lady, DBE.

Menzies, Dame Pattie Maie, GBE.

Metge, Dr Dame (Alice) Joan, DBE.

Miles, Dame Margaret, DBE.

Miller, Dame Mabel Flora Hobart, DBE.

Miller, Dame Mary Elizabeth Hedley-, DCVO, CB.

Mitchell, *Hon.* Dame Roma Flinders, DBE.

Morrison, *Hon.* Dame Mary Anne, DCVO.

Mueller, Dame Anne Elisabeth, DCB.

Munro, Dame Alison, DBE.

Murdoch, Dame Elisabeth Joy, DBE.

Murdoch, Dame (Jean) Iris (Mrs Bayley), DBE.

Murray, Dame (Alice) Rosemary, DBE, D.Phil.

Niccol, Dame Kathleen Agnes, DBE.

Ollerenshaw, Dame Kathleen Mary, DBE, D.Phil.

Park, Dame Merle Florence (Mrs Bloch), DBE.

Parker, Dame Marjorie Alice Collett, DBE.

Paterson, Dame Betty Fraser Ross, DBE.

Pepys, Lady (Mary) Rachel, DCVO.

Plowden, The Lady, DBE.

Porter, Dame Shirley (Lady Porter), DBE.

Prendergast, Dame Simone Ruth, DBE.

Prentice, Dame Winifred Eva, DBE.

Preston, Dame Frances Olivia Campbell-, DCVO.

Purves, Dame Daphne Helen, DBE.

Pyke, Lady, DBE.

Quinn, Dame Sheila Margaret Imelda, DBE.

Railton, *Brig.* Dame Mary, DBE.

Railton, Dame Ruth (Mrs King), DBE.

Rankin, Lady Jean Margaret Florence, DCVO.

Raven, Dame Kathleen Annie (Mrs Ingram), DBE.

Riddelsdell, Dame Mildred, DCB, CBE.

Ridley, Dame (Mildred) Betty, DBE.

Ridsdale, Dame Victoire Evelyn Patricia (Lady Ridsdale), DBE.

Rie, Dame Lucie, DBE.

Roberts, Dame Joan Howard, DBE.

Roberts, Dame Shelagh Marjorie, DBE.

Robertson, *Cmdt.* Dame Nancy Margaret, DBE.

Roe, Dame Raigh Edith, DBE.

Rue, Dame (Elsie) Rosemary, DBE.

Salas, Dame Margaret Laurence, DBE.

Saunders, Dame Cicely Mary Strode, OM, DBE, FRCP.

Scott, Dame Catherine Campbell, DBE.

Scott, Dame Jean Mary Monica Maxwell-, DCVO.

Scott, Dame Margaret, (Dame Catherine Margaret Mary Denton), DBE.

Shenfield, Dame Barbara Estelle, DBE.

Sherlock, *Prof.* Dame Sheila Patricia Violet, DBE, MD, FRCP.

Sloss, *Rt. Hon.* Dame (Ann) Elizabeth (Oldfield) Butler-, DBE.

Smieton, Dame Mary Guillan, DBE.

Smith, Dame Margaret Natalie (Maggie) (Mrs Cross), DBE.

Smith, Dame Margot, DBE.

Snagge, Dame Nancy Marion, DBE.

Soames, Mary, Lady, DBE.

Stark, Dame Freya (Mrs Perowne), DBE.

Stephens, *Air Cmdt.* Dame Anne, DBE.

Stewart, Dame Muriel Acadia, DBE.

Sutherland, Dame Joan (Mrs Bonynge), DBE.

Szaszy, Dame Miraka Petricevich, DBE.

Taylor, Dame Jean Elizabeth, DCVO.

Te Atairangikaahu, Te Arikinui, Dame, DBE.

Te Kanawa, Dame Kiri Janette (Mrs Park), DBE.

Tilney, Dame Guinevere (Lady Tilney), DBE.

Tinson, Dame Sue, DBE.

Tizard, Dame Catherine Anne, GCMG, DBE.

Tokiel, Dame Rosa, DBE.

Turner, *Brig.* Dame Margot, DBE, RRC.

Tyrwhitt, *Brig.* Dame Mary Joan Caroline, DBE, TD.

Uatioa, Dame Mere, DBE.

Uvarov, Dame Olga, DBE.

Varley, Dame Joan Fleetwood, DBE.

Vaughan, Dame Janet Maria (Mrs Gourlay), DBE, FRS.

Wakehurst, Margaret, Lady, DBE.

Walker, Dame Susan Armour, DBE.

Wall, (Alice) Anne, (Mrs Michael Wall), DCVO.

Warburton, Dame Anne Marion, DCVO, CMG.

Warwick, Dame Margaret Elizabeth Harvey Turner-, DBE, FRCP, FRCPE.

Waterhouse, Dame Rachel Elizabeth, DBE, Ph.D.

Wedega, Dame Alice, DBE.

Wedgwood, Dame (Cicely) Veronica, OM, DBE.

Weston, Dame Margaret Kate, DBE.

Williamson, Dame (Elsie) Marjorie, DBE, Ph.D.

Winstone, Dame Dorothy Gertrude, DBE, CMG.

Wormald, Dame Ethel May, DBE.

Yonge, Dame (Ida) Felicity (Ann), DBE.

THE ORDER OF ST. JOHN

The Most Venerable Order of the Hospital of St. John of Jerusalem

St. John's Gate, Clerkenwell, EC1M 4DA

Grand Prior, HRH The Duke of Gloucester, GCVO.

Lord Prior, The Lord Vestey.
Chancellor, Prof. A. R. Mellows, TD.

FORMS OF ADDRESS

It is only possible to cover here the forms of address for peers, their wife and children. Greater detail should be sought in one of the publications devoted to the subject.

Both formal and social forms of address are given where usage differs; increasingly, the social form is preferred to the formal, though this is used for official documents and on very formal occasions.

In the forms of address given below, F—— represents forename, S—— represents surname.

Baron.—*Envelope (formal)*, The Right Hon. Lord ——; *(social)*, The Lord ——. *Letter (formal)*, My Lord; *(social)*, Dear Lord ——. *Spoken*, Lord ——.

Baron's wife.—*Envelope (formal)*, The Right Hon. Lady ——; *(social)*, The Lady ——. *Letter (formal)*, My Lady; *(social)*, Dear Lady ——. *Spoken*, Lady ——.

Baron's children.—*Envelope*, The Hon. F—— S——. *Letter*, Dear Mr/Miss/Mrs S——. *Spoken*, Mr/ Miss/Mrs [F——] S——.

Baroness in own right.—*Envelope*, may be addressed in same way as a Baron's wife or, if she prefers *(formal)*, The Right Hon. the Baroness ——; *(social)*, The Baroness ——. Otherwise as for a **Baron's wife**.

Baronet.—*Envelope*, Sir F—— S——, Bt. *Letter (formal)*, Dear Sir; *(social)*, Dear Sir F——. *Spoken*, Sir F——.

Baronet's wife.—*Envelope*, Lady S——. *Letter (formal)*, Dear Madam; *(social)*, Dear Lady S——. *Spoken*, Lady S——.

Countess in own right.—As for an **Earl's wife**.

Courtesy titles.—The heir apparent to a Duke, Marquess or Earl uses the highest of his father's other titles as a courtesy title. (For list, *see* pp. 176-7.) The holder of a courtesy title is not styled The Most Hon. or The Right Hon., and in correspondence 'The' is omitted before the title. The heir apparent to a Scottish title may use the title 'Master' (*see* below).

Dame.—*Envelope*, Dame F—— S——, followed by appropriate post-nominal letters. *Letter (formal)*, Dear Madam; *(social)*, Dear Dame F——. *Spoken*, Dame F——.

Duke.—*Envelope (formal)*, His Grace the Duke of ——; *(social)*, The Duke of ——. *Letter (formal)*, My Lord Duke; *(social)*, Dear Duke. *Spoken (formal)*, Your Grace; *(social)*, Duke.

Duke's wife.—*Envelope (formal)*, Her Grace the Duchess of ——; *(social)*, The Duchess of ——. *Letter (formal)*, Dear Madam; *(social)*, Dear Duchess. *Spoken*, Duchess.

Duke's eldest son.—See **Courtesy titles**.

Duke's younger sons.—*Envelope*, Lord F—— S——. *Letter (formal)*, My Lord; *(social)*, Dear Lord F——. *Spoken (formal)*, My Lord; *(social)*, Lord F——.

Duke's daughter.—*Envelope*, Lady F—— S——. *Letter (formal)*, Dear Madam; *(social)*, Dear Lady F——. *Spoken*, Lady F——.

Earl.—*Envelope (formal)*, The Right Hon. the Earl of ——; *(social)*, The Earl of ——. *Letter (formal)*, My Lord; *(social)*, Dear Lord ——. *Spoken (formal)*, My Lord; *(social)*, Lord.

Earl's wife.—*Envelope (formal)*, The Right Hon. the Countess ——; *(social)*, The Countess of ——. *Letter (formal)*, Madam; *(social)*, Lady ——. *Spoken (formal)*, Madam; *(social)*, Lady ——.

Earl's children.—*Eldest son*, see **Courtesy titles**. *Younger sons*, The Hon. F—— S—— (for forms of address, see **Baron's children**). *Daughters*, Lady F—— S—— (for forms of address, see **Duke's daughter**).

Knight (Bachelor).—*Envelope*, Sir F—— S——. *Letter (formal)*, Dear Sir; *(social)*, Dear Sir F——. *Spoken*, Sir F——.

Knight (Orders of Chivalry).—*Envelope*, Sir F—— S——, followed by appropriate post-nominal letters. Otherwise as for **Knight Bachelor**.

Knight's wife.—As for **Baronet's wife**.

Marquess.—*Envelope (formal)*, The Most Hon. the Marquess of ——; *(social)*, The Marquess of ——. *Letter (formal)*, My Lord; *(social)*, Dear Lord ——. *Spoken (formal)*, My Lord; *(social)*, Lord ——.

Marquess's wife.—*Envelope (formal)*, The Most Hon. the Marchioness of ——; *(social)*, The Marchioness of ——. *Letter (formal)*, Madam; *(social)*, Dear Lady ——. *Spoken*, Lady ——.

Marquess's children.—*Eldest son*, see **Courtesy titles**. *Younger sons*, Lord F—— S—— (for forms of address, see **Duke's younger sons**). *Daughters*, Lady F—— S—— (for forms of address, see **Duke's daughter**).

Master.—The title is used by the heir apparent to a Scottish peerage, though usually the heir apparent to a Duke, Marquess or Earl uses his courtesy title rather than 'Master'. *Envelope*, The Master of ——. *Letter (formal)*, Dear Sir; *(social)*, Dear Master of ——. *Spoken (formal)*, Master, or Sir; *(social)*, Master, or Mr S——.

Master's wife.—Addressed as for the wife of the appropriate peerage style, otherwise as Mrs S——.

Privy Counsellor.—*Envelope*, The Right (or Rt.) Hon. F—— S——. *Letter*, Dear Mr/Miss/Mrs S——. *Spoken*, Mr/Miss/Mrs S——. It is incorrect to use the letters PC after the name, unless the Privy Counsellor is a peer below the rank of Marquess and so is styled The Right Hon. In this case the post-nominal letters may be used in conjunction with the prefix The Right Hon.

Viscount.—*Envelope (formal)*, The Right Hon. the Viscount ——; *(social)*, The Viscount ——. *Letter (formal)*, My Lord; *(social)*, Dear Lord ——. *Spoken*, Lord ——.

Viscount's wife.—*Envelope (formal)*, The Right Hon. the Viscountess of ——; *(social)*, The Viscountess ——. *Letter (formal)*, Madam; *(social)*, Dear Lady ——. *Spoken*, Lady ——.

Viscount's children.—As for **Baron's children**.

CHIEFS OF CLANS AND NAMES IN SCOTLAND

Only chiefs of whole Names or Clans are included, except certain special instances (marked *), who though not chiefs of a whole name, were, or are, for some reason, (e.g. the Macdonald forfeiture), independent. Under decision (*Campbell-Gray*, 1950) that a bearer of a 'double or triple-barrelled' surname cannot be held chief of a part of such, several others cannot be included in the list at present.

THE ROYAL HOUSE: HM The Queen

AGNEW: Sir Crispin Agnew of Lochnaw, Bt., 6 Palmerston Road, Edinburgh.

ANSTRUTHER: Sir Ralph Anstruther of that Ilk, Bt., KCVO, MC, Balcaskie, Pittenweem, Fife.

ARBUTHNOTT: The Viscount of Arbuthnott, CBE, DSC, Arbuthnott House, Laurencekirk, Kincardineshire.

BARCLAY: Peter C. Barclay of that Ilk, Gatemans, Stratford St Mary, Colchester, Essex.

BORTHWICK: The Lord Borthwick, TD, Crookston, Heriot, Midlothian.

BOYD: The Lord Kilmarnock, Casa de Mondragon, Ronda (Malaga), Spain.

BOYLE: The Earl of Glasgow, Kelburn, Fairlie, Ayrshire.

BRODIE: Ninian Brodie of Brodie, Brodie Castle, Forres, Morayshire.

BRUCE: The Earl of Elgin and Kincardine, KT, Broomhall, Dunfermline, Fife.

BUCHAN: David S. Buchan of Auchmacoy, Auchmacoy, Ellon, Aberdeenshire.

BURNETT: J. C. A. Burnett of Leys, Crathes Castle, Kincardineshire.

CAMERON: Sir Donald Cameron of Lochiel, KT, CVO, TD, Achnacarry, Spean Bridge, Inverness-shire.

CAMPBELL: The Duke of Argyll, Inveraray, Argyll.

CARMICHAEL: Richard J. Carmichael of Carmichael, Carmichael, Thankerton, Biggar, Lanarkshire.

CARNEGIE: The Earl of Southesk, KCVO, Kinnaird Castle, Brechin.

CATHCART: Maj.-Gen. The Earl Cathcart, CB, DSO, MC, 2 Pembroke Gardens, W8.

CHARTERIS: The Earl of Wemyss and March, KT, Gosford House, Longniddry, East Lothian.

CLAN CHATTAN: M. K. Mackintosh of Clan Chattan, Maxwell Park, Gwelo, Zimbabwe.

CHISHOLM: Alastair Chisholm of Chisholm (*The Chisholm*), Silver Willows, Bury St Edmunds.

COCHRANE: The Earl of Dundonald, Lochnell Castle, Ledaig, Argyllshire.

COLQUHOUN: Sir Ivar Colquhoun of Luss, Bt., Camstraddan, Luss, Dunbartonshire.

CRANSTOUN: David A. S. Cranstoun of that Ilk, Corehouse, Lanark.

CRICHTON: Charles Crichton of that Ilk, Monzie, Perth.

DARROCH: Capt. Duncan Darroch of Gourock, The Red House, Branksome Park Road, Camberley, Surrey.

DEWAR: Kenneth M. J. Dewar of that Ilk and Vogrie, The Dower House, Grayshott, Nr. Hindhead, Surrey.

DRUMMOND: The Earl of Perth, PC, Stobhall, Perth.

DUNBAR: Sir Jean Dunbar of Mochrum, Bt., 45–55 39th Street, Long Island City, New York.

DUNDAS: David D. Dundas of Dundas, 8 Derna Road, Kenwyn 7700, South Africa.

DURIE: Raymond V. D. Durie of Durie, Court House, Pewsey, Wilts.

ELIOTT: Mrs Margaret Eliott of Redheugh, Redheugh, Newcastleton, Roxburghshire.

ERSKINE: The Earl of Mar and Kellie, Claremont House, Alloa.

FARQUHARSON: Capt. A. A. C. Farquharson of Invercauld, MC, Invercauld, Braemar.

FERGUSSON: Sir Charles Fergusson of Kilkerran, Bt., Kilkerran, Maybole, Ayrshire.

FORBES: The Lord Forbes, KBE, Balforbes, Alford, Aberdeenshire.

FORSYTH: Alistair Forsyth of that Ilk, Ethie Castle, by Arbroath, Angus.

FRASER: The Lady Saltoun, Cairnbulg Castle, Fraserburgh, Aberdeenshire.

*FRASER (OF LOVAT): The Lord Lovat, DSO, MC, TD, Balblair House, Beauly, Inverness-shire.

GAYRE: Lt.-Col. Robert Gayre of Gayre and Nigg, 1–3 Gloucester Lane, Edinburgh.

GORDON: The Marquess of Huntly, Aboyne Castle, Aberdeenshire.

GRAHAM: The Duke of Montrose, Auchmar, Drymen, Stirlingshire.

GRANT: The Lord Strathspey, 111 Elms Ride, West Wittering, W. Sussex.

GRIERSON: Sir Michael Grierson of Lag, Bt., 40C Palace Road, London.

HAIG: The Earl Haig, OBE, Bemersyde, Melrose, Roxburghshire.

HALDANE: Alexander N. C. Haldane of Gleneagles, Auchterarder, Perthshire.

HANNAY: Ramsey W. R. Hannay of Kirkdale and of that Ilk, Cardoness House, Gatehouse-of-Fleet, Kirkcudbrightshire.

HAY: The Earl of Erroll, Wolverton Farm, Wolverton, Basingstoke, Hants.

HENDERSON: John W. P. Henderson of Fordell, 7 Owen Street, Toowoomba, Queensland, Australia.

HUNTER: Neil A. Hunter of Hunterston, Tour d'Escas, Carretera d'Escas, La Massana, Andorra.

IRVINE OF DRUM: C. F. Irvine of Drum, 29 Forest Road, Hcylake, Wirral, Merseyside.

JARDINE: Sir Alexander Jardine of Applegirth, Bt., Ash House, Thwaites, Millom, Cumbria.

JOHNSTONE: The Earl of Annandale and Hartfell, Raehills, Lockerbie, Dumfriesshire.

KEITH: The Earl of Kintore, Glenton House, Rickarton, Stonehaven, Kincardineshire.

KENNEDY: The Marquess of Ailsa, OBE, Blanefield, Kirkoswald, Ayrshire.

KERR: The Marquess of Lothian, KCVO, Monteviot, Ancrum, Roxburghshire.

KINCAID: Mrs Heather V. Kincaid of Kincaid, 4A Bristol Gardens, Brighton, E. Sussex.

LAMONT: Peter N. Lamont of that Ilk, St Patrick's College, Manley, NSW 2095, Australia.

LEASK: Madam Leask of Leask, 1 Vincent Road, Sheringham, Norfolk.

LENNOX: Edward J. H. Lennox of that Ilk, Pools Farm, Downton on the Rock, Ludlow, Shropshire.

LESLIE: The Earl of Rothes, Tanglewood, West Tytherley, Salisbury, Wilts.

LINDSAY: The Earl of Crawford and Balcarres, PC, Balcarres, Colinsburgh, Fife.

LOCKHART: Angus H. Lockhart of the Lee, Newholme, Dunsyre, Lanark.

LUMSDEN: Gillem Lumsden of that Ilk and Blanerne, Kinderslegh, Bois Avenue, Chesham Bois, Amersham, Bucks.

MCBAIN: J. H. McBain of McBain, 7025, North Finger Rock Place, Tucson, Arizona, USA.

MALCOLM (MACCALLUM): Robin N. L. Malcolm of Poltalloch, Duntrune Castle, Lochgilphead, Argyll.

MACDONALD: The Lord Macdonald (*The Macdonald of Macdonald*), Ostaig House, Skye.

*MACDONALD OF CLANRANALD: Ranald A. Macdonald of Clanranald, 55 Compton Road, N1.

*MACDONALD OF SLEAT (CLAN HUSTEAIN): Sir Ian Bosville Macdonald of Sleat, Bt., Thorpe Hall, Rudston, Driffield, N. Humberside.

*MACDONELL OF GLENGARRY: Air Cdre Aeneas R. MacDonell of Glengarry, CB, DFC, Elonbank, Castle Street, Fortrose, Ross-shire.

MACDOUGALL: vacant.

MACDOWELL: Fergus D. H. Macdowell of Garthland, 16 Tower Road, Nepean, Ontario, Canada.

MACGREGOR: Sir Gregor MacGregor of MacGregor, Bt., Bannatyne, Newtyle, Angus.

MACINTYRE: James W. McIntyre of Glencoe, 15301 Pine Orchard Drive, Apartment 3H, Silver Spring, Maryland, USA.

MACKAY: The Lord Reay, 11 Wilton Crescent, SW1.

MACKENZIE: The Earl of Cromartie, MC, TD, Castle Leod, Strathpeffer, Ross-shire.

MACKINNON: Madam Anne Mackinnon of Mackinnon, 16 Purleigh Road, Bridgewater, Somerset.

MACKINTOSH: The Mackintosh of Mackintosh, OBE, Moy Hall, Inverness.

MACLACHLAN: Madam Marjorie MacLachlan of MacLachlan, Castle Lachlan, Argyll.

MACLAREN: Donald MacLaren of MacLaren and Achleskine, c/o Foreign and Commonwealth Office, London SW1.

MACLEAN: The Hon. Sir Lachlan Maclean of Duart, Bt., Duart Castle, Mull.

MACLENNAN: vacant.

MACLEOD: J. MacLeod of MacLeod, Dunvegan Castle, Skye.

MACMILLAN: George MacMillan of MacMillan, Finlaystone, Langbank, Renfrewshire.

MACNAB: J. C. Macnab of Macnab (*The Macnab*), Finlarig, Killin, Perthshire.

MACNAGHTEN: Sir Patrick Macnaghten of Macnaghten and Dundarave, Bt., Dundarave, Bushmills, Co. Antrim.

MACNEACAIL: Iain Macneacail of Macneacail and Scorrybreac, 12 Fox Street, Ballina, NSW, Australia.

MACNEIL OF BARRA: Ian R. Macneil of Barra (*The Macneil of Barra*), Kisimul Castle, Barra.

MACPHERSON: The Hon. Sir William Macpherson of Cluny, TD, Newtown Castle, Blairgowrie, Perthshire.

MACTHOMAS: Andrew P. C. MacThomas of Finegand, c/o The Clan MacThomas Society, 19 Warriston Avenue, Edinburgh 3.

MAITLAND: The Earl of Lauderdale, 12 St Vincent Street, Edinburgh.

MAKGILL: The Viscount of Oxfuird, Hill House, St Mary Bourne, Andover, Hants.

MAR: The Countess of Mar, St Michael's Farm, Great Witley, Worcs.

MARJORIBANKS: William Marjoribanks of that Ilk, Kirklands of Forglen, Turriff, Aberdeenshire.

MATHESON: Sir Torquhil Matheson of Matheson, Bt., Sanderwick Court, Frome, Somerset.

MENZIES: David R. Menzies of Menzies, 20 Nardina Crescent, Dalkeith, Western Australia.

MOFFAT: Francis Moffat of that Ilk, Redacres, Moffat, Dumfriesshire.

MONCREIFFE: vacant.

MONTGOMERIE: The Earl of Eglinton and Winton, The Dutch House, West Green, Hartley Wintney, Hants.

MORRISON: Dr Iain M. Morrison of Ruchdi, Todhurst Farm, Lake Lane, Barnham, W. Sussex.

MUNRO: Patrick G. Munro of Foulis, TD, Foulis Castle, Ross.

MURRAY: The Duke of Atholl, Blair Castle, Blair Atholl, Perthshire.

NICOLSON: The Lord Carnock, 90 Whitehall Court, SW1.

OGILVY: The Earl of Airlie, KT, GCVO, PC, Cortachy Castle, Kirriemuir, Angus.

RAMSAY: The Earl of Dalhousie, KT, GCVO, GBE, MC, Brechin Castle, Angus.

RATTRAY: James S. Rattray of Rattray, Craighall, Rattray, Perthshire.

ROBERTSON: Alexander G. H. Robertson of Struan (*Struan-Robertson*), The Breach Farm, Goudhurst Road, Cranbrook, Kent.

ROLLO: The Lord Rollo, Pitcairns, Dunning, Perthshire.

ROSE: Miss Elizabeth Rose of Kilravock, Kilravock Castle, Croy, Inverness.

ROSS: David C. Ross of that Ilk, The Old Schoolhouse, Fettercairn, Kincardineshire.

RUTHVEN: The Earl of Gowrie, PC, Castlemartin, Kilcullen, Co. Kildare, Republic of Ireland.

SCOTT: The Duke of Buccleuch and Queensberry, KT, VRD, Bowhill, Selkirk.

SCRYMGEOUR: The Earl of Dundee, Birkhill, Cupar, Fife.

SEMPILL: The Lady Sempill, Druminnor Castle, Rhynie, Aberdeenshire.

SHAW: John Shaw of Tordarroch, Newhall, Balblair, By Conon Bridge, Ross-shire.

SINCLAIR: The Earl of Caithness, Finstock Manor, Finstock, Oxon.

STIRLING: Fraser J. Stirling of Cader, 17 Park Row, Farnham, Surrey.

SUTHERLAND: The Countess of Sutherland, House of Tongue, Brora, Sutherland.

SWINTON: vacant.

URQUHART: Kenneth T. Urquhart of that Ilk, 4713 Orleans Boulevard, Jefferson, Louisiana, USA.

WALLACE: Ian F. Wallace of that Ilk, 5 Lennox Street, Edinburgh EH4 1QB.

WEDDERBURN OF THAT ILK: The Master of Dundee, Birkhill, Cupar, Fife.

WEMYSS: David Wemyss of that Ilk, Invermay, Forteviot, Perthshire.

PRINCIPAL DECORATIONS AND MEDALS (in order of Precedence)

Victoria Cross (VC), 1856.

George Cross (GC), 1940.

British Orders of Knighthood, Etc. (for order in which worn, *see* pp. 181–83).

Baronet's Badge

Knight Bachelor's Badge

Decorations

Royal Red Cross (Class I—RRC), 1883.—For ladies.

Distinguished Service Cross (DSC), 1914.—For officers of RN below the rank of Captain, and Warrant Officers.

Military Cross (MC), Dec. 1914.—Awarded to Captains, Lieutenants, and Warrant Officers (I and II) in the Army and Indian and Colonial Forces.

Distinguished Flying Cross (DFC), 1918.—For officers and Warrant Officers in the RAF and Fleet Air Arm from April 9, 1941) for acts of gallantry when flying in active operations against the enemy.

Air Force Cross (AFC), 1918.—Instituted as preceding but for acts of courage or devotion to duty when flying, although not in active operations against the enemy (extended to Fleet Air Arm since April 9, 1941).

Royal Red Cross (Class II—ARRC).

Order of British India.

Kaisar-i-Hind Medal.

Order of St John.

Medals for Gallantry and Distinguished Conduct

Union of South Africa Queen's Medal for Bravery, in Gold.

Distinguished Conduct Medal (DCM), 1854.—Awarded to warrant officers, non-commissioned officers and men of the Army and RAF.

Conspicuous Gallantry Medal (CGM), 1874.—Is bestowed upon warrant officers and men of the RN and since 1942 of Mercantile Marine and RAF.

The George Medal (GM), 1940.

Queen's Police Medal for Gallantry.

Queen's Fire Service Medal for Gallantry.

Royal West African Frontier Force Distinguished Conduct Medal.

King's African Rifles Distinguished Conduct Medal.

Indian Distinguished Service Medal.

Union of South Africa Queen's Medal for Bravery, in Silver.

Distinguished Service Medal (DSM), 1914.—For chief petty officers, petty officers and men, of all branches of the Royal Navy, and since 1942 of Mercantile Marine; non-commissioned officers and men of the Royal Marines; all other persons holding corresponding positions in Her Majesty's service afloat.

Military Medal (MM), 1916.—For warrant and non-commissioned officers and men and serving women.

Distinguished Flying Medal (DFM), 1918, and the Air Force Medal (AFM)—For warrant and non-commissioned officers and men for equivalent services as for DFC and AFC (extended to Fleet Air Arm, 1941).

Constabulary Medal (Ireland).

Medal for Saving Life at Sea.

Indian Order of Merit (Civil).

Indian Police Medal for Gallantry.

Ceylon Police Medal for Gallantry.

Sierra Leone Police Medal for Gallantry.

Sierra Leone Fire Brigades Medal for Gallantry.

Colonial Police Medal for Gallantry (CPM)

Queen's Gallantry Medal, 1974.

Royal Victorian Medal (RVM)—(Gold, Silver and Bronze).

British Empire Medal (BEM), (formerly the Medal of the Order of the British Empire, for Meritorious Service; also includes the Medal of the Order awarded before Dec. 29, 1922).

Queen's Police (QPM) and Fire Services Medals (QFSM) for Distinguished Service.

Queen's Medal for Chiefs.

War Medals and Stars (in order of date).

Polar Medals (in order of date).

Imperial Service Medal.

Police Medals for Valuable Service.

Badge of Honour.

Jubilee, Coronation and Durbar Medals.

King George V, King George VI and Queen Elizabeth II Long and Faithful Service Medals.

Efficiency and Long Service Decorations and Medals.

Medal for Meritorious Service.

Long Service and Good Conduct Medal (Military).

Naval Long Service and Good Conduct Medal.

Royal Marine Meritorious Service Medal.

Royal Air Force Meritorious Service Medal.

Royal Air Force Long Service and Good Conduct Medal.

Medal for Long Service and Good Conduct (Ulster Defence Regiment).

Police Long Service and Good Conduct Medal.

Fire Brigade Long Service and Good Conduct Medal.

Colonial Police and Fire Brigades Long Service Medal.

Colonial Prison Service Medal.

Army Emergency Reserve Decoration (ERD), 1952.

Volunteer Officer's Decoration (VD)

Volunteer Long Service Medal.

Volunteer Officer's Decoration (for India and the Colonies).

Volunteer Long Service Medal (for India and the Colonies).

Colonial Auxiliary Forces Officer's Decoration.

Colonial Auxiliary Forces Long Service Medal.

Medal for Good Shooting (Naval).

Militia Long Service Medal.

Imperial Yeomanry Long Service Medal.

Territorial Decoration (TD), 1908.

Efficiency Decoration (ED).

Territorial Efficiency Medal.

Efficiency Medal.

Special Reserve Long Service and Good Conduct Medal.

Decoration for Officers, Royal Navy Reserve (RD), 1910.

Decoration for Officers, RNVR (VRD)

Royal Naval Reserve Long Service and Good Conduct Medal.

RNVR Long Service and Good Conduct Medal.

Royal Naval Auxiliary Sick Berth Reserve Long Service and Good Conduct Medal.

Royal Fleet Reserve Long Service and Good Conduct Medal.

Royal Naval Wireless Auxiliary Reserve Long Service and Good Conduct Medal.

Air Efficiency Award (AE), 1942.

Ulster Defence Regiment Medal.

The Queen's Medal.—(For champion shots in the RN, RM, RNZN, Army, RAF).

Cadet Forces Medal, 1950.

Coast Life Saving Corps Long Service Medal, 1911.

Special Constabulary Long Service Medal.

Royal Observer Corps Medal.

Civil Defence Long Service Medal.

Royal Ulster Constabulary Service Medal.

Service Medal of the Order of St John.

Badge of the Order of the League of Mercy.

Voluntary Medical Service Medal, 1932.

Women's Royal Voluntary Service Medal.

Colonial Special Constabulary Medal.

Foreign Orders, Decorations and Medals (in order of date).

THE VICTORIA CROSS, VC (1856)

For Conspicuous Bravery

Ribbon, Crimson, for all Services (until 1918 it was *Blue* for Royal Navy).

Instituted on January 29, 1856, the Victoria Cross was awarded retrospectively to 1854, the first being held by Lt. C. D. Lucas, RN, for bravery in the Baltic Sea on June 21, 1854 (gazetted February 24, 1857). The first 62 Crosses were presented by Queen Victoria in Hyde Park, London, on June 26, 1857.

The VC is worn before all other decorations, on the left breast, and consists of a cross-pattée of bronze, 1½ inches in diameter, with the Royal Crown surmounted by a lion in the centre, and beneath there is the inscription 'For Valour'. Holders of the VC receive a tax-free annuity of £100, irrespective of need or other conditions. In 1911, the right to receive the Cross was extended to Indian soldiers, and in 1920 a Royal Warrant extended the right to Matrons, Sisters and Nurses, and the staff of the Nursing Services and other services pertaining to hospitals and nursing, and to civilians of either sex regularly or temporarily under the orders, direction or supervision of the Naval, Military, or Air Forces of the Crown.

Surviving Recipients of the Victoria Cross
(as at August 31, 1991)

Agansing Rai, *Havildar*, MM (Gurkha Rifles), *World War* 1944

Ali Haidar, *Jemadar* (Frontier Force Rifles), *World War* 1945

Annand, *Capt.* R. W. (Durham Light Infantry), *World War* 1940

Bhan Bhagta Gurung, *Capt.* (2nd Gurkha Rifles), *World War* 1945

Bhandari Ram, *Capt.* (Baluch R.), *World War* ..1944

Burton, *Cpl.* R. H. (Duke of Wellington's R.), *World War* 1944

Chapman, *Sgt.* E. T., BEM (Monmouthshire R.), *World War* 1945

Cheshire, *Group Capt.* The Lord, OM, DSO, DFC (RAF), *World War* 1944

Cruickshank, *Flt. Lt.* J. A. (RAFVR), *World War* 1944

Cutler, Sir Roden, AK, KCMG, KCVO, CBE (Australia), *World War* 1941

Eardley, *Sgt.* G. H., MM (KSLI), *World War* 1944

Ervine-Andrews, *Lt.-Col.* H. M. (E. Lancs. R.), *World War* 1940

Foote, *Maj.-Gen.* H. R. B., CB, DSO (R. Tank R.), *World War* 1942

Fraser, *Lt. Cdr.* I. E., DSC (RNR), *World War* 1945

Gaje Ghale, *Subedar* (Gurkha Rifles), *World War* 1943

Ganju Lama, *Jemadar*, MM (Gurkha Rifles), *World War* 1944

Gardner, *Capt.* P. J., MC (RTR), *World War* 1941

Gian Singh, *Jemadar* (Punjab R.), *World War* ..1945

Gould, *Lt.* T. W. (RN), *World War* 1942

Hinton, *Sgt.* J. D. (NZMF), *World War* 1941

Jackson, *WO* N. C. (RAFVR), *World War* 1944

Jamieson, *Maj.* D. A., CVO (R. Norfolk R.), *World War* 1944

Kenna, *Pte.* E. (Australian M. F.), *World War* ..1945

Kenneally, *C-Q-M-S* J. P. (Irish Guards), *World War* 1943

Lachiman Gurung, *Rifleman* (Gurkha Rifles), *World War* 1945

Learoyd, *Wg Cdr.* R. A. B. (RAF), *World War* ..1940

Merritt, *Lt.-Col.* C. C. I., CD (S. Saskatchewan R.), *World War* 1942

Norton, *Capt.* G. R., MM (SAMF), *World War* 1944

Payne, *WO* K. (Australian Army), *Vietnam* 1969

Place, *Rear-Adm.* B. C. G., CB, CVO, DSC (RN), *World War* 1943

Porteous, *Col.* P. A. (RA), *World War* 1942

Rambahadur Limbu, *Lt.*, MVO (Gurkha Rifles), *Sarawak* 1965

Reid, *Flt. Lt.* W. (RAFVR), *World War* 1943

Smith, *Sgt.* E. A., CD (Seaforth Highlanders of Canada), *World War* 1944

Smythe, *Capt.* Q. G. M. (SAMF), *World War* 1942

Speakman-Pitt, *Sgt.* W. (Black Watch), *Korea* ..1951

Tilston, *Maj.* F. A., CD (Essex Scottish, Canada), *World War* 1945

Tulbahadur Pun, *WOI* (Gurkha Rifles), *World War* 1944

Umrao Singh, *Sub-Major* (IA), *World War* 1944

Upham, *Capt.* C. H. (and Bar, 1942), (NZMF), *World War* 1941

Watkins, *Maj. Rt. Hon.* Sir Tasker, GBE (Welch R.), *World War* 1944

Wilson, *Lt.-Col.* E. C. T. (E. Surrey R.), *World War* 1940

THE GEORGE CROSS, GC (1940)

For Gallantry

Ribbon, Dark Blue, threaded through a bar adorned with laurel leaves.

Instituted September 24, 1940 (with amendments, November 3rd, 1942).

The George Cross is worn before all other decorations (except the VC) on the left breast (when worn by a woman it may be worn on the left shoulder from a ribbon of the same width and colour fashioned into a bow). It consists of a plain silver cross with four equal limbs, the cross having in the centre a circular medallion bearing a design showing St George and the Dragon. The inscription 'For Gallantry' appears round the medallion and in the angle of each limb of the cross is the Royal cypher 'G VI' forming a circle concentric with the medallion. The reverse is plain and bears the name of the recipient and the date of the award. The cross is suspended by a ring from a bar adorned with laurel leaves on dark blue ribbon 1½ inches wide.

The cross is intended primarily for civilians; awards to the fighting services are confined to actions for which purely military honours are not normally granted. It is awarded only for acts of the greatest heroism or of the most conspicuous courage in circumstances of extreme danger. From April 1, 1965, holders of the Cross have received a tax-free annuity of £100.

Empire Gallantry Medal.—The Royal Warrant which ordained that the grant of the Empire Gallantry Medal should cease authorized holders of that medal to return it to the Central Chancery of the Orders of Knighthood and to receive in exchange the George Cross. A similar provision applied to posthumous awards of the Empire Gallantry Medal made after the outbreak of war in 1939.

In October 1971 all surviving holders of the Albert Medal and the Edward Medal exchanged those decorations for the George Cross.

Surviving Recipients of the George Cross
(as at August 31, 1991)

(If the recipient originally received the Empire Gallantry Medal, the Albert Medal or the Edward Medal, this is indicated by the initials in parenthesis after the name.)

Archer, *Col.* B. S. T., GC, OBE, ERD...............1941
Ashburnham Ruffner, Mrs D., GC (AM).........1917
Atkinson, T., GC (EGM)..........................1939
Babington, J. H., GC, OBE.......................1940
Baker, J. T., GC (EM)............................1929
Baldwin, W. C. G., GC, PH.D. (EM)..............1943
Bamford, J., GC..................................1952
Barkat Singh, *Ex. Sub.*, GC (EGM).............1938
Baxter, W. F., GC (EM)..........................1942
Beaton, J., GC, LVO..............................1974
Biggs, *Maj.* K. A., GC..........................1946
Blackburn, R., GC (EGM).........................1936
Blackburn, S., GC (EM)..........................1947
Bridge, *Cdr.* J., GC, GM........................1944
Butson, *Col.* A. R. C., GC, CD, MD (AM).........1948
Bywater, R. A. S., GC, GM........................1944
Cobham, *Cdr.* A. J., GC, MBE (EGM)............1930
Copperwheat, *Lt. Cdr.* D. A., GC................1942
Cowley, *Lt.-Gen.* Sir John, GC, KCB, CBE (AM)...1935
Durrani, *Lt.-Col.* M. K., GC.....................1946
Easton, J. M. C., GC.............................1941
Errington, J., GC................................1941
Fairfax, F. W., GC...............................1953
Farrow, K., GC (AM)..............................1948
Fisher, B., GC (EM)..............................1939
Flintoff, H. H., GC (EM).........................1944
Gibbs, S., GC (AM)...............................1927
Gledhill, A. J., GC..............................1967
Goad, W., GC (AM)................................1943
Goldsworthy, *Lt. Cdr.* L. V., GC, DSC, GM.......1944
Gregson, J. S., GC (AM)..........................1943
Hallowes, Mrs O. M. C., GC, MBE, Légion d'Honneur..1946
Hawkins, E., GC (AM).............................1943
Hodge, *Capt.* A. M., GC, VRD (EGM)..............1940

Idris, Shawish Taha, GC (EGM)..................1934
Johnson, *WO1 (SSM)* B., GC.....................1990
Kinne, D. G., GC.................................1954
Lowe, A. R., GC (AM).............................1949
Lynch, J., GC, BEM (AM)..........................1948
McAloney, *Gp. Capt.* W. S., GC, OBE (AM).......1938
McClymont, J. M., GC (EGM)......................1940
Manwaring, T. G., GC (EM).......................1949
May, P. R. S., GC (AM)...........................1947
Miller, *Lt. Cdr.* J. B. P., GC..................1941
Moore, R. V., GC.................................1940
Moss, B., GC....................................1940
Naughton, F., GC (EGM)..........................1937
Nix, F. E., GC (EM).............................1944
Patton, The Hon. John, GC, CBE.................1940
Pearson, Miss J. D. M., GC (EGM)...............1940
Pratt, M. K., GC.................................1978
Purves, Mrs M., GC (AM).........................1949
Purvis, J. S., GC (EM)..........................1929
Raweng, Awang anak, GC..........................1951
Riley, G., GC (AM)..............................1944
Rimmer, R., GC (EGM)............................1931
Rogerson, S., GC.................................1946
Rowlands, *Air Marshal* Sir John, GC, KBE.......1943
Sinclair, *Air Vice-Marshal* Sir Laurence, GC, KCB, CBE, DSO.................................1941
Stevens, H. W., GC...............................1958
Stronach, *Capt.* G. P., GC......................1943
Styles, *Lt.-Col.* S. G., GC.....................1972
Sylvester, W. G., GC (EGM).......................1940
Taylor, *Lt. Cdr.* W. H., GC, MBE...............1941
Walker, C., GC...................................1972
Walker, C. H., GC (AM)...........................1942
Walton, E. W. K., GC (AM).......................1948
Wastie, G. C., GC (EM)..........................1930
Western, D., GC (AM)............................1948
Wilcox, C., GC (EM).............................1949
Wiltshire, S. N., GC (EGM)......................1930
Yates, P. W., GC (EM)...........................1932
Younger, W., GC (EM)...........................1948

THE MILITARY KNIGHTS OF WINDSOR

The Military Knights of Windsor take part in all ceremonies of the Noble Order of the Garter and attend Sunday morning service in St George's Chapel, Windsor Castle, as representatives of the Knights of the Garter. The Knights receive a small stipend in addition to their army pensions and quarters in Windsor Castle.

The Knights of Windsor were originally founded in 1348 after the wars in France to assist English knights, who, having been prisoners in the hands of the French, had become impoverished by the payments of heavy ransoms. When Edward III founded the Order of the Garter later the same year, he incorporated the Knights of Windsor and the College of St George into its foundation and raised the number of Knights to 26 to correspond with the number of the Knights of the Garter. Known later as the Alms Knights or Poor Knights of Windsor, their establishment was reduced under the will of King Henry VIII to 13 and Statutes were drawn up by Queen Elizabeth I.

In 1833 King William IV changed their designation to The Military Knights and granted them their present uniform which consists of a scarlet tail-coat with white cross sword-belt, crimson sash and cocked hat with plume. The badges are the Shield of St George and the Star of the Order of the Garter.

Governor, Maj.-Gen. Peter Downward, CB, DSO, DFC.
Military Knights, Maj. A. E. Wollaston, MVO; Brig. A. L. Atkinson, OBE; Brig. J. F. Lindner, OBE, MC; Brig. A. C. Tyler, CBE, MC; Maj. W. L. Thompson, MVO, MBE, DCM; Maj. L. W. Dickerson; Maj. J. C. Cowley, DCM; Lt.-Col. N. L. West; Maj. G. R. Mitchell; MBE, BEM; Lt.-Col. R. L. C. Tamplin; Maj. P. H. Bolton, MBE.
Supernumerary, Lt.-Col. A. R. Clark, MC.

THE PRIVY COUNCIL

Apart from Cabinet Ministers, who must be Privy Counsellors and are sworn in on first assuming office, membership of the Council (retained for life) is accorded by the Sovereign on the recommendation of the Prime Minister to eminent people in independent monarchical countries of the Commonwealth.

HRH The Duke of Edinburgh	1951
HRH The Prince of Wales	1977
Aberdare, Lord	1974
Ackner, Lord	1980
Adams-Schneider, Sir Lancelot	1980
Ademola, Sir Adetokunbo	1963
Airlie, Earl of	1984
Aldington, Lord	1954
Alebua, Ezekiel	1988
Alison, Michael	1981
Alport, Lord	1960
Amery, Julian	1960
Anthony, Douglas	1971
Archer, Peter	1977
Armstrong, Ernest	1979
Arnold, Sir John	1979
Ashdown, Paddy	1989
Ashley, Jack	1979
Avonside, Lord	1962
Aylestone, Lord	1962
Azikiwe, Nnamdi	1960
Bacon, Baroness	1966
Baker, Kenneth	1984
Balcombe, Sir John	1985
Barber, Lord	1963
Barnett, Lord	1975
Barwick, Sir Garfield	1964
Beldam, Sir Roy	1989
Belstead, Lord	1983
Benn, Anthony	1964
Bennett, Sir Frederic	1985
Bevins, John	1959
Biffen, John	1979
Bingham, Sir Thomas	1986
Bird, Vere	1982
Bisson, Sir Gordon	1987
Blaker, Sir Peter	1983
Blanch, Lord	1975
Bolger, James	1991
Booth, Albert	1976
Bottomley, Lord	1952
Boyd-Carpenter, Lord	1954
Boys, Michael	1989
Boyson, Sir Rhodes	1987
Braine, Sir Bernard	1985
Braithwaite, Nicholas	1991
Brandon of Oakbrook, Lord	1978
Bridge of Harwich, Lord	1975
Brightman, Lord	1979
Brittan, Sir Leon	1981
Brooke, Peter	1988
Brown, Sir Stephen	1983
Browne, Sir Patrick	1974
Browne-Wilkinson, Sir Nicolas	1983
Broxbourne, Lord	1957
Buckley, Sir Denys	1970
Butler, Sir Adam	1984
Butler-Sloss, Dame Elizabeth	1988
Caithness, Earl of	1990
Callaghan of Cardiff, Lord	1964

Cameron of Lochbroom, Lord	1984
Campbell of Croy, Lord	1970
Canterbury, The Archbishop of	1991
Carlisle of Bucklow, Lord	1979
Carr of Hadley, Lord	1963
Carrington, Lord	1959
Casey, Sir Maurice	1986
Castle of Blackburn, Baroness	1964
Cato, Robert	1981
Chalfont, Lord	1964
Chalker, Lynda	1987
Chan, Sir Julius	1981
Channon, Paul	1980
Charteris of Amisfield, Lord	1972
Chataway, Christopher	1970
Clark, Alan	1991
Clark, Helen	1990
Clark, Sir William	1990
Clarke, Kenneth	1984
Cledwyn of Penrhos, Lord	1966
Cockfield, Lord	1982
Cocks of Hartcliffe, Lord	1976
Coggan, Lord	1961
Colman, Fraser	1986
Colnbrook, Lord	1973
Colyton, Lord	1952
Compton, John	1983
Concannon, John	1978
Cooke, Sir Robin	1977
Cooper, Sir Frank	1983
Cope, Sir John	1988
Corfield, Sir Frederick	1970
Cowen, Sir Zelman	1981
Craigton, Lord	1961
Crawford and Balcarres, Earl of	1972
Crickhowell, Lord	1979
Croom-Johnson, Sir David	1984
Cumming-Bruce, Sir Roualeyn	1977
Davies, Denzil	1978
Davison, Sir Ronald	1978
Dean, Sir Paul	1991
Deedes, Lord	1962
Dell, Edmund	1970
Denham, Lord	1981
Denning, Lord	1948
Devlin, Lord	1960
Devonshire, Duke of	1964
Diamond, Lord	1965
Dillon, Sir Brian	1982
Donaldson of Lymington, Lord	1979
Douglas, Sir William	1977
du Cann, Sir Edward	1964
Duff, Sir Antony	1980
Dunn, Sir Robin	1980
Ercles, Viscount	1951
Eden of Winton, Lord	1972
Edmund-Davies, Lord	1966
Eichelbaum, Sir Thomas	1989
Ellison, Rt. Rev. Gerald	1973

Emslie, Lord	1972
Ennals, Lord	1970
Erroll of Hale, Lord	1960
Esquivel, Manuel	1986
Eveleigh, Sir Edward	1977
Farquharson, Sir Donald	1989
Fellowes, Sir Robert	1990
Fernyhough, Ernest	1970
Ferrers, Earl	1982
Foot, Michael	1974
Fowler, Sir Norman	1979
Fox, Sir Michael	1981
Franks, Lord	1949
Fraser, Malcolm	1976
Fraser of Carmyllie, Lord	1989
Freeman, John	1966
Freeson, Reginald	1976
Gairy, Sir Eric	1977
Georges, Telford	1986
Gibbs, Sir Harry	1972
Gibson, Sir Ralph	1985
Gibson-Watt, Lord	1974
Gilbert, John	1978
Gilmour, Sir Ian, Bt	1973
Glenamara, Lord	1964
Glendevon, Lord	1959
Glidewell, Sir Iain	1985
Goff of Chieveley, Lord	1982
Gorton, Sir John	1968
Gowrie, Earl of	1984
Gray of Contin, Lord	1982
Griffiths, Lord	1980
Grimond, Lord	1961
Gummer, John	1985
Hailsham of St Marylebone, Lord	1956
Hamilton, Archie	1991
Harrison, Walter	1977
Hart of South Lanark, Baroness	1967
Harvington, Lord	1971
Hasluck, Sir Paul	1966
Hattersley, Roy	1975
Havers, Lord	1977
Hayhoe, Sir Barney	1985
Healey, Denis	1964
Heath, Edward	1955
Herbison, Margaret	1964
Heseltine, Michael	1979
Heseltine, Sir William	1986
Hesketh, Lord	1991
Higgins, Terence	1979
Holderness, Lord	1959
Home of the Hirsel, Lord	1951
Hope, *Hon.* Lord	1989
Houghton of Sowerby, Lord	1964
Howard, Michael	1990
Howe, Sir Geoffrey	1972
Howell, David	1979
Howell, Denis	1976
Hughes, Lord	1970
Hunt, David	1990
Hunt, Jonathan	1989
Hurd, Douglas	1982
Hutton, Sir Brian	1988

Waldegrave, William	1990	Whitelaw, Viscount	1967	Withers, Reginald	1977
Walker, Harold	1979	Wilberforce, Lord	1964	Woodhouse, Sir Owen	1974
Walker, Peter	1970	Williams, Alan	1977	Woolf, Sir Harry	1986
Waller, Sir George	1976	Williams, Shirley	1974	Wylie, *Hon.* Lord	1970
Watkins, Sir Tasker	1980	Wilson of Langside, Lord	1967	York, The Archbishop of	1983
Watkinson, Viscount	1955	Wilson of Rievaulx, Lord	1947	Young, Baroness	1981
Weatherill, Bernard	1980	Windlesham, Lord	1973	Young of Graffham, Lord	1984
Welensky, Sir Roy	1960	Wingti, Paias	1987	Younger, George	1979

Clerk of the Council, G. I. de Deney, cvo   *Deputy Clerk of the Council,* R. P. Bulling.

PRIME MINISTERS SINCE 1782

Marquess of Rockingham, *Whig,* March 27, 1782.
Earl of Shelburne, *Whig,* July 13, 1782.
Duke of Portland, *Coalition,* April 4, 1783.
William Pitt, *Tory,* December 7, 1783.
Henry Addington, *Tory,* March 21, 1801.
William Pitt, *Tory,* May 16, 1804.
Lord Grenville, *Whig,* February 10, 1806.
Duke of Portland, *Tory,* March 31, 1807.
Spencer Perceval, *Tory,* December 6, 1809.
Earl of Liverpool, *Tory,* June 16, 1812.
George Canning, *Tory,* April 30, 1827.
Viscount Goderich, *Tory,* September 8, 1827.
Duke of Wellington, *Tory,* January 26, 1828.
Earl Grey, *Whig,* November 24, 1830.
Viscount Melbourne, *Whig,* July 13, 1834.
Sir Robert Peel, *Tory,* December 26, 1834.
Viscount Melbourne, *Whig,* March 18, 1835.
Sir Robert Peel, *Tory,* September 6, 1841.
Lord John Russell, *Whig,* July 6, 1846.
Earl of Derby, *Tory,* February 28, 1852.
Earl of Aberdeen, *Peelite,* December 28, 1852.
Viscount Palmerston, *Liberal,* February 10, 1855.
Earl of Derby, *Conservative,* February 25, 1858.
Viscount Palmerston, *Liberal,* June 18, 1859.
Earl Russell, *Liberal,* November 6, 1865.
Earl of Derby, *Conservative,* July 6, 1866.
Benjamin Disraeli, *Conservative,* February 27, 1868.
W. E. Gladstone, *Liberal,* December 9, 1868.
Benjamin Disraeli, *Conservative,* February 21, 1874.
W. E. Gladstone, *Liberal,* April 28, 1880.
Marquess of Salisbury, *Conservative,* June 24, 1885.
W. E. Gladstone, *Liberal,* February 6, 1886.

Marquess of Salisbury, *Conservative,* August 3, 1886.
W. E. Gladstone, *Liberal,* August 18, 1892.
Earl of Rosebery, *Liberal,* March 3, 1894.
Marquess of Salisbury, *Conservative,* July 2, 1895.
A. J. Balfour, *Conservative,* July 12, 1902.
Sir H. Campbell-Bannerman, *Liberal,* December 5, 1905.
H. H. Asquith, *Liberal,* April 8, 1908.
H. H. Asquith, *Coalition,* May 26, 1915.
D. Lloyd-George, *Coalition,* December 7, 1916.
A. Bonar Law, *Conservative,* October 23, 1922.
S. Baldwin, *Conservative,* May 22, 1923.
J. R. MacDonald, *Labour,* January 22, 1924.
S. Baldwin, *Conservative,* November 4, 1924.
J. R. MacDonald, *Labour,* June 8, 1929.
J. R. MacDonald, *Coalition,* August 25, 1931.
S. Baldwin, *Coalition,* June 7, 1935.
N. Chamberlain, *Coalition,* May 28, 1937.
W. S. Churchill, *Coalition,* May 11, 1940.
W. S. Churchill, *Conservative,* May 23, 1945.
C. R. Attlee, *Labour,* July 26, 1945.
Sir W. S. Churchill, *Conservative,* October 26, 1951.
Sir Anthony Eden, *Conservative,* April 6, 1955.
H. Macmillan, *Conservative,* January 13, 1957.
Sir Alec Douglas-Home, *Conservative,* October 19, 1963.
J. H. Wilson, *Labour,* October 16, 1964.
E. R. G. Heath, *Conservative,* June 19, 1970.
J. H. Wilson, *Labour,* March 4, 1974.
L. J. Callaghan, *Labour,* April 5, 1976.
Mrs M. H. Thatcher, *Conservative,* May 4, 1979.
J. Major, *Conservative,* November 28, 1990.

SPEAKERS OF THE COMMONS SINCE 1660

PARLIAMENT OF ENGLAND

1660 Sir Harbottle Grimston.
1661 Sir Edward Turner.
1673 Sir Job Charlton.
1673 Sir Edward Seymour.
1678 Sir Robert Sawyer.
1679 Sir William Gregory.
1680 Sir William Williams.
1685 Sir John Trevor.
1688 Henry Powle.
1694 Paul Foley.
1698 Sir Thomas Lyttelton.
1700 Robert Harley (*Earl of Oxford and Mortimer*).
1702 John Smith.

PARLIAMENT OF GREAT BRITAIN

1708 Sir Richard Onslow (*Lord Onslow*).
1710 William Bromley.
1713 Sir Thomas Hanmer.
1715 Spencer Compton (*Earl of Wilmington*).
1727 Arthur Onslow.
1761 Sir John Cust.
1770 Sir Fletcher Norton.
1780 Charles Cornwall.

1788 Hon. William Grenville (*Lord Grenville*).
1789 Henry Addington (*Viscount Sidmouth*).

PARLIAMENT OF UNITED KINGDOM

1801 Sir John Mitford (*Lord Redesdale*).
1802 Charles Abbot (*Lord Colchester*).
1817 Charles M. Sutton (*Viscount Canterbury*).
1835 James Abercromby (*Lord Dunfermline*).
1839 Charles Shaw-Lefevre (*Viscount Eversley*).
1857 J. Evelyn Denison (*Viscount Ossington*).
1872 Sir Henry Brand (*Viscount Hampden*).
1884 Arthur Wellesley Peel (*Viscount Peel*).
1895 William C. Gully (*Viscount Selby*).
1905 James W. Lowther (*Viscount Ullswater*).
1921 John H. Whitley.
1928 Hon. Edward A. FitzRoy.
1943 Col. D. Clifton Brown (*Viscount Ruffside*).
1951 William S. Morrison (*Viscount Dunrossil*).
1959 Sir Harry Hylton-Foster.
1965 Horace M. King (*Lord Maybray-King*).
1971 Selwyn Lloyd (*Lord Selwyn-Lloyd*).
1976 George Thomas (*Viscount Tonypandy*).
1983 (Bruce) Bernard Weatherill.

THE CONSTITUTION OF THE UNITED KINGDOM

The United Kingdom constitution is not contained in any single document but has evolved in the course of time, formed partly by statute, partly by common law and partly by convention. A constitutional monarchy, the United Kingdom is governed by Ministers of the Crown in the name of the Sovereign, who is head both of the state and of the government.

The organs of government are the legislature (Parliament), the executive and the judiciary. The executive consists of Her Majesty's Government (Cabinet and other Ministers), government departments (*see* pp. 293–376), local authorities (*see* Index), and public corporations operating nationalized industries or social or cultural services (*see* pp. 293–376). The judiciary (*see* **Law Courts and Offices**) pronounces on the law, both written and unwritten, interprets statutes and is responsible for the enforcement of the law; the judiciary is independent of both the legislature and the executive.

THE MONARCHY

The Sovereign personifies the state and is, in law, an integral part of the legislature, head of the executive, head of the judiciary, the Commander-in-Chief of all armed forces of the Crown and the 'Supreme Governor' of the Church of England. The seat of the monarchy is in the United Kingdom. In the Channel Islands and the Isle of Man, which are Crown dependencies, the Sovereign is represented by a Lieutenant-Governor; in the member states of the Commonwealth of which the Sovereign is head of state, her representative is a Governor-General (*see also* p. 625); in United Kingdom dependencies the Sovereign is usually represented by a Governor, who is responsible to the British Government.

Although the powers of the monarchy are now very limited, restricted mainly to the advisory and ceremonial, there are important acts of government which require the participation of the Sovereign. These include summoning, proroguing and dissolving Parliament, giving Royal Assent to Bills passed by Parliament, appointing important office-holders, e.g. government ministers, judges, bishops, and governors, conferring peerages, knighthoods and other honours, and granting pardon to a person wrongly convicted of a crime. An important function is appointing a Prime Minister, by convention the leader of the political party which enjoys, or can secure, a majority of votes in the House of Commons. In international affairs the Sovereign as head of State has the power to declare war and make peace, to recognize foreign states and governments, to conclude treaties and to annex or cede territory. However, as the Sovereign entrusts executive power to Ministers of the Crown and acts on the advice of her Ministers, which she cannot ignore, in practice royal prerogative powers are exercised by Ministers, who are responsible to Parliament.

Ministerial responsibility does not diminish the Sovereign's importance to the smooth working of government. She holds meetings of the Privy Council, gives audiences to her Ministers and other officials at home and overseas, receives accounts of Cabinet decisions, reads dispatches and signs state papers; she must be informed and consulted on every aspect of national life; and she must show complete impartiality.

Counsellors of State

In the event of the Sovereign's absence abroad, it is necessary to appoint Counsellors of State under Letters Patent to carry out the chief functions of the Monarch, including the holding of Privy Councils

and giving Royal Assent to Acts passed by Parliament. The normal procedure is to appoint as Counsellors three or four members of the Royal family among those remaining in the United Kingdom. In the event of the Sovereign on accession being under the age of eighteen years, or at any time unavailable or incapacitated by infirmity of mind or body for the performance of the royal functions, provision is made for a Regency.

THE PRIVY COUNCIL

The Sovereign in Council, or Privy Council, was the chief source of executive power until the system of Cabinet government developed. Now its main function is to advise the Sovereign to approve Orders in Council and to advise on the issue of royal proclamations. The Council's own statutory responsibilities (independent of the powers of the Sovereign in Council) include powers of supervision over the registering bodies for the medical and allied professions. A full Council is summoned only on the death of the Sovereign or when the Sovereign announces his or her intention to marry. (For full list of Counsellors, *see* pp. 225–7.)

There are a number of advisory Privy Council committees, whose meetings the Sovereign does not attend. Some are prerogative committees, such as those dealing with legislative matters submitted by the legislatures of the Channel Islands and the Isle of Man or with applications for charters of incorporation; and some are provided for by statute, e.g. those for the universities of Oxford and Cambridge and the Scottish universities.

The Judicial Committee of the Privy Council is the final court of appeal from courts of the United Kingdom dependencies, courts of independent Commonwealth countries which have retained the right of appeal, courts of the Channel Islands and the Isle of Man, some professional and disciplinary committees, and church sources. The Committee is composed of all Privy Counsellors who hold, or have held, high judicial office, although usually only three or five hear each case.

Administrative work is carried out by the Privy Council Office under the direction of the Lord President of the Council, a Cabinet Minister.

PARLIAMENT

Parliament is the supreme law-making authority and can legislate for the United Kingdom as a whole or for any parts of it separately (the Channel Islands and the Isle of Man are Crown dependencies and not part of the United Kingdom). The main functions of Parliament are to pass laws, to provide (by voting taxation) the means of carrying on the work of government and to scrutinize government policy and administration, particularly proposals for expenditure. International treaties and agreements are by custom presented to Parliament before ratification.

Parliament emerged during the late thirteenth and early fourteenth centuries. The officers of the King's household and the King's judges were the nucleus of early Parliaments, joined by such ecclesiastical and lay magnates as the King might summon to form a prototype 'House of Lords', and occasionally by the knights of the shires, burgesses and proctors of the lower clergy. By the end of Edward III's reign a 'House of Commons' was beginning to appear; the first known Speaker was elected in 1377.

Parliamentary procedure is based on custom and precedent, partly formulated in the Standing Orders of both Houses (*see* **Standing Orders**, p. 236), and each House has the right to control its own internal proceedings and to commit for contempt. The system of debate in the two Houses is similar; when a motion has been moved, the Speaker proposes the question as the subject of a debate. Members speak from wherever they have been sitting. Questions are decided by a vote on a simple majority. Draft legislation is introduced, in either House, as a Bill. Bills can be introduced by a Government Minister or a private Member, but in practice the majority of Bills which become law are introduced by the Government. To become law, a Bill must be passed by each House (for parliamentary stages, *see* **Bill**, p. 232) and then sent to the Sovereign for the Royal Assent, after which it becomes an Act of Parliament.

Proceedings of both Houses are public, except on extremely rare occasions. The minutes (called Votes and Proceedings in the Commons, and Minutes of Proceedings in the Lords) and the speeches (The Official Report of Parliamentary Debates, *Hansard*) are published daily. Proceedings are also recorded for transmission on radio and television and preserved by the Parliamentary Sound Archive. Television cameras have been allowed into the House of Lords since January 1985, and into the House of Commons since November 1989; committee meetings may also be televised.

By the Parliament Act of 1911, the maximum duration of a Parliament is five years (if not previously dissolved), the term being reckoned from the date given on the writs for the new Parliament. The maximum life has been prolonged by legislation in such rare circumstances as the two world wars (Jan. 31, 1911–Nov. 25, 1918; Nov. 26, 1935–June 15, 1945). Dissolution and writs for a general election are ordered by The Queen on the advice of the Prime Minister. The life of a Parliament is divided into sessions, usually of one year in length, beginning and ending most often in October or November.

THE HOUSE OF LORDS
SW1A 0PW
[071-219 3000]

The House of Lords consists of the Lords Spiritual and Temporal. The Lords Spiritual are the Archbishops of Canterbury and York, the Bishops of London, Durham and Winchester, and the 21 senior diocesan bishops of the Church of England. The Lords Temporal consist of all hereditary Peers and Peeresses of England, Scotland, Great Britain and the United Kingdom who have not disclaimed their Peerages, Life Peers and Peeresses created under the Life Peerages Act 1958, and those Lords of Appeal in Ordinary created Life Peers under the Appellate Jurisdiction Act 1876, as amended (Law Lords). Disclaimants of an hereditary Peerage lose their right to sit in the House of Lords but gain the right to vote at Parliamentary elections and to offer themselves for election to the House of Commons. (*See also* p. 149.) Peers who do not wish to attend sittings of the House of Lords may apply for leave of absence for the duration of a Parliament.

Until the beginning of this century the House of Lords had considerable power, being able to veto any Bill submitted to it by the House of Commons, but those powers were greatly reduced by the Parliament Act of 1911 and subsequently by the Parliament Act of 1949 (*see* **Parliament Acts 1911 and 1949**, p. 233).

Combined with its legislative role, the House of Lords has judicial powers as the ultimate Court of Appeal for courts in Great Britain and Northern Ireland, except for criminal cases in Scotland. These powers are exercised by the Lord Chancellor and the Law Lords.

Members of the House of Lords are unpaid. However, they are entitled to reimbursement of travelling expenses on parliamentary business within the UK and certain other expenses incurred for the purpose of attendance at sittings of the House, within a maximum for each day of £68·00 for overnight subsistence, £26·00 for day subsistence and incidental travel, and £27·00 for secretarial costs, postage and certain additional expenses.

Composition
(as at July 31, 1991)

Archbishops and Bishops	26
Peers by succession	760
	(20 women)
Hereditary Peers of first creation (including the Prince of Wales)	20
Life Peers under the Appellate Jurisdiction Act 1876	18
Life Peers under the Life Peerages Act 1958	374
	(61 women)
TOTAL	1,198

Of whom:

Peers without Writs of Summons	84
Peers on leave of absence from the House	137

State of Parties
(as at July 31, 1991)

About half of the members of the House of Lords take the whip of one of the political parties. The other members sit on the cross-benches or as independents.

Conservative	454
Labour	116
Liberal Democrats	55
Social Democrat	15
Cross-bench	255
Other (including Bishops)	161

Officers

The House is presided over by the Lord Chancellor, who is *ex officio* Speaker of the House. A panel of deputy Speakers is appointed by Royal Commission. The first deputy Speaker is the Chairman of Committees, appointed at the beginning of each session, a salaried officer of the House who takes the chair in committee of the whole House and in some select committees. He is assisted by a panel of Deputy Chairmen, headed by the salaried Principal Deputy Chairman of Committees, who is also Chairman of the European Communities Committee of the House. The permanent officers include the Clerk of the Parliaments, who is in charge of the administrative staff collectively known as the Parliament Office; the Gentleman Usher of the Black Rod, who is also Serjeant-at-Arms in attendance upon the Lord Chancellor and is responsible for security and for accommodation and services in the House of Lords; and the Yeoman Usher who is Deputy Serjeant-at-Arms and assists Black Rod in his duties.

OFFICERS

Speaker, The Rt. Hon. the Lord Mackay of Clashfern £14,693
   Private Secretary, Ms J. Rowe.
Chairman of Committees, The Rt. Hon. the Lord Aberdare, KBE £44,232
Principal Deputy Chairman of Committees, The Baroness Serota £40,424
Clerk of the Parliaments, M. A. J. Wheeler-Booth £82,780
Clerk Assistant and Clerk of the Journals, J. M. Davies .... £59,020–£69,120
Reading Clerk, P. D. G. Hayter ..... £50,380–£58,010
Counsel to Chairman of Committees, D. Rippengal, CB, QC .... £59,020–£69,120

Second Counsel, Mrs E. Denza, CMG
£50,380–£58,010
Assistant Counsel, N. J. Adamson, CB, QC
£38,747–£52,210
Principal Clerks, J. A. Vallance White
(*Judicial Office and Fourth Clerk at the
Table*); M. G. Pownall (*Committees*); B.
P. Keith (*Private Bills*) .... £43,431–£48,501
Chief Clerks, C. A. J. Mitchell; R. H.
Walters, D.Phil.; D. R. Beamish; Mrs F.
M. Martin; D. F. Slater (*Seconded as
Secretary to the Leader of the House and
Chief Whip*) .... £35,720–£46,747
Senior Clerks, Dr F. P. Tudor;
E. C. Ollard; Miss M. E. De Groose;
A. Makower; E. J. J. Wells;
T. V. Mohan; W. G. Sleath ...... £24,641–£34,301
Clerk, S. P. Burton .... £12,867–£22,480
Clerk of the Records, D. J. Johnson, FSA
£35,720–£46,746
Assistant Clerks of the Records, J. C.
Morgan (*Sound Archives*); S. K. Ellison
£24,641–£34,301
Accountant, C. Preece............ £24,641–£34,301
Assistant Accountant, Miss J. M.
Lansdown .... £19,117–£26,296
Judicial Taxing Clerk, C. G. Osborne
£19,117–£26,296
Librarian, D. L. Jones. .... £35,720–£46,746
Library Clerks, P. G. Davis, Ph.D.; Miss I. L.
Victory, Ph.D.; Ms S. Taylor ..... £24,641–£34,301
Examiners of Petitions for Private Bills,
B. P. Keith; R. J. Willoughby.
*Gentleman Usher of the Black Rod and
Serjeant-at-Arms*, Air Chief Marshal Sir
John Gingell, GBE, KCB .... £50,380–£58,010
*Yeoman Usher of the Black Rod and Deputy
Serjeant-at-Arms*, Air Cdre A. C. Curry,
OBE .... £24,641–£34,301
Staff Superintendent, Maj. F. P. Horsfall, MBE.
Shorthand Writer, Mrs E. M. C. Holland ...... *fees*
Editor, Official Report (*Hansard*), Mrs M. E.
Villiers........................ £33,682–£44,046
Deputy Editor, Official Report, G. R. Good-
barne .... £25,259–£37,854

THE HOUSE OF COMMONS
SW1A 0AA
[071-219 3000]

The Members of the House of Commons are elected
by universal adult suffrage. For electoral purposes,
the United Kingdom is divided into constituencies,
each of which returns one Member to the House of
Commons, the Member being the candidate who
obtains the largest number of votes cast in the
constituency. To ensure equitable representation
the four Boundary Commissions keep constituency
boundaries under review and recommend any redistribution of seats which may seem necessary because
of population movements, etc. The number of seats
was raised to 640 in 1945, then reduced to 625 in 1948,
and subsequently rose to 630 in 1955, 635 in 1970 and
650 in 1983. (The number of seats will increase to 651
at the next General Election.) Of the present 650
seats, there are 523 for England, 38 for Wales, 72 for
Scotland and 17 for Northern Ireland.

Elections

Elections are by secret ballot, each elector casting
one vote; voting is not compulsory. When a seat
becomes vacant between General Elections, a by-
election is held.

British subjects and citizens of the Irish Republic
can stand for election as Members of Parliament

(MPs) provided they are 21 or over and not subject to
disqualification. Those disqualified from sitting in
the House include undischarged bankrupts, people
sentenced to more than one year's imprisonment,
clergy of the Church of England, Church of Scotland,
Church of Ireland and Roman Catholic Church,
members of the House of Lords, and holders of certain
offices listed in the House of Commons Disqualification Act 1975 (e.g. members of the judiciary, Civil
Service, regular armed forces, police forces, some
local government officers and some members of public
corporations and government commissions).

A candidate does not require any party backing
but his or her nomination for election must be
supported by the signatures of ten people registered
in the constituency. A candidate must also deposit
with the returning officer £500, which is forfeit
if the candidate does not receive more than 5 per cent
of the votes cast. All election expenses, except the
candidate's personal expenses, are subject to a
statutory limit of £4,144, plus 3·5 pence for each
elector in a borough constituency or 4·7 pence for
each elector in a county constituency. (*See* pp. 241–
248 for an alphabetical list of MPs, pp. 249–275 for the
results of the last General Election, and pp. 239–40
for the results of subsequent by-elections.)

Business

The week's business of the House is outlined each
Thursday by the Leader of the House, after consultation between the Chief Government Whip and the
Chief Opposition Whip. A quarter to a third of the
time will be taken up by the Government's legislative
programme, and the rest by other business, e.g.
question time. As a rule Bills likely to raise political
controversy are introduced in the Commons before
going on to the Lords, and the Commons claims
exclusive control in respect of national taxation and
expenditure. Bills such as the Finance Bill, which
imposes taxation, and the Consolidated Fund Bills,
which authorize expenditure, must begin in the
Commons. A Bill of which the financial provisions
are subsidiary may begin in the Lords; and the
Commons may waive its rights in regard to Lords'
amendments affecting finance.

The Commons has a public register of MPs'
financial, and certain other, interests. Members must
also disclose any relevant financial interest or benefit
in a matter before the House when taking part in a
debate, in certain other proceedings of the House or
in consultations with other Members, with Ministers
or civil servants.

Members' pay, etc.

Since 1911 Members of the House of Commons have
received salary payments; facilities for free travel
were introduced in 1924. Members are entitled to
claim income tax relief on expenses incurred in the
course of their Parliamentary duties. Salary rates
since 1911 are as follows:

	p.a.		p.a.
1911..........	£400	1979 June	£9,450
1931..........	360	1980 June	11,750
1934..........	380	1981 June	13,950
1935..........	400	1982 June	14,510
1937..........	600	1983 June	15,308
1946..........	1,000	1984 Jan......	16,106
1954..........	1,250	1985 Jan......	16,904
1957..........	1,750	1986 Jan......	17,702
1964..........	3,250	1987 Jan......	18,500
1972 Jan......	4,500	1988 Jan......	22,548
1975 June	5,750	1989 Jan......	24,107
1976 June	6,062	1990 Jan......	26,701
1977 July	6,270	1991 Jan......	28,970
1978 June	6,897		

In October 1969 Members were granted an allowance for secretarial and research expenses. In 1987 this became known as the Office Costs Allowance, and in April 1990 rose to £27,166 a year.

Since January 1972 Members can claim reimbursement for the additional cost of staying overnight away from their main residence while on Parliamentary business. This was set at £10,570 for the 1990–91 financial year. Since 1984 this has been non-taxable.

From March 1980 provision was made enabling each Member in receipt of Office Costs Allowance to contribute sums to an approved pension scheme for the provision of a pension, or other benefits, for or in respect of persons whose salary is met by him/her from the Office Costs Allowance.

The cost of travel allowances for 1990–91 was stated in July 1991 to be £7,107,460.

Members' pensions

A contributory pension fund exists to provide pensions for former Members of Parliament and for dependants of deceased former Members. The arrangements currently provide a pension of one-fiftieth of salary for each year of pensionable service with a maximum of two-thirds of salary at age 65. Pension is payable normally at age 65, for men and women, or on later retirement. Pensions may be paid earlier, e.g. on ill-health retirement. The widow/widower of a former Member receives a pension of one-half of the late Member's pension. Pensions are index-linked. Members contribute 9 per cent of salary to the pension fund; there is an Exchequer contribution, currently slightly less than half the amount contributed by Members.

The House of Commons Members' Fund provides for annual or lump sum grants to ex-Members, their widows or widowers, and children whose incomes are below certain limits. Alternatively, payments of £1,884 per annum to ex-Members with at least ten years' service and who left the House of Commons before October 1964, and £942 per annum to their widows or widowers are made as of right. Members contribute £24 per annum and the Exchequer £115,000 per annum to the Fund. The net assets of the Fund as at September 30, 1988 amounted to £1,478,531.

Officers

The House of Commons is presided over by the Speaker, who has considerable powers to maintain order in the House. His deputy, the Chairman of Ways and Means, and two Deputy Chairmen may preside over sittings of the House of Commons; they are elected by the House, and, like the Speaker, neither speak nor vote other than in their official capacity. The staff of the House are employed by a Commission chaired by the Speaker. The Heads of House of Commons Departments (see below) are permanent officers of the House, not MPs. The Clerk of the House is the principal adviser to the Speaker on the privileges and procedures of the House, the conduct of the business of the House, and Committees. The Serjeant-at-Arms is responsible for security, ceremonial, and for accommodation in the Commons part of the Palace of Westminster.

OFFICERS AND OFFICIALS

Speaker, The Rt. Hon. Bernard Weatherill, MP for Croydon North East £59,914
Chairman of Ways and Means, The Rt. Hon. Harold Walker, MP for Doncaster Central . £48,771
First Deputy Chairman of Ways and Means, Rt. Hon. Sir Paul Dean, MP for Woodspring £45,505

Second Deputy Chairman of Ways and Means, Miss Betty Boothroyd, MP for West Bromwich West £45,505

Offices of the Speaker and Chairman of Ways and Means

Speaker's Secretary, P. J. Kitcatt, CB
£35,720–£40,360
Speaker's Counsel, H. Knorpel, CB, QC; G. E. Gammie, CB, QC .... £50,380–£58,010
Assistant to Speaker's Counsel, P. Harvey, CB .... £26,747–£31,559
Chaplain to the Speaker, The Rev. Canon D. Gray, TD.
Secretary to the Chairman of Ways and Means, R. I. S. Phillips.

Department of the Clerk of the House

Clerk of the House of Commons, Sir Clifford Boulton, KCB £82,780
Clerk Assistant, D. W. Limon £59,020
Clerk of Committees, J. F. Sweetman, CB, TD . £59,020
Principal Clerks (£50,380–£58,010):—
  Public Bills, W. R. McKay.
  Table Office, C. B. Winnifrith.
  Select Committees, R. B. Sands.
  Overseas Office, G. Cubie.
  Journals, A. J. Hastings.
  Private Bills, R. J. Willoughby.
  Second Clerk of Select Committees, D. G. Millar.
  Standing Committees, M. R. Jack, PH.D.
  Financial Committees, R. W. G. Wilson.
Deputy Principal Clerks, S. A. L. Panton; Mrs J. Sharpe; Ms A. Milner-Barry; W. A. Proctor; F. A. Cranmer; R. J. Rogers; C. R. M. Ward, PH.D.; Ms H. E. Irwin; D. W. N. Doig; A. Sandall; D. L. Natzler; E. P. Silk; A. R. Kennon; D. W. Robson; L. C. Laurence Smyth; S. J. Patrick; D. F. Harrison; S. J. Priestley; A. H. Doherty; P. A. Evans; R. I. S. Phillips ..... £35,720–£40,360
Senior Clerks, D. J. Gerhold; C. J. Poyser; R. G. James; Ms P. A. Helme; D. R Lloyd; R. A. Lambert; B. M. Hutton; J. S. Benger; Ms E. C. Samson; N. P. Walker; M. D. Hamlyn; J. M. Hope *(acting)*; H. R. Neilson *(acting)*; M. J. Reeves *(acting)*; D. Steel *(acting)* .... £24,641–£29,049
Clerk of Services Sub-Committees, K. J. Brown £27,871
Examiners of Petitions for Private Bills, R. J. Willoughby; B. P. Keith.
Registrar of Members' Interests, R. B. Sands.
Taxing Officer, R. J. Willoughby.

Department of the Serjeant-at-Arms

Serjeant-at-Arms, Sir Alan Urwick, KCVO, CMG. .... £50,380–£58,010
Deputy Serjeant-at-Arms, P. N. W. Jennings
£35,720–£40,360
Assistant Serjeant-at-Arms, M. J. A. Cummins .... £26,747–£34,301
Deputy Assistant Serjeants-at-Arms, P. A. J. Wright; J. F. Collins .... £24,641–£29,049

Department of the Library

Librarian, D. J. T. Englefield ...... £50,380–£58,010
Deputy Librarian, Miss J. B. Tanfield
£43,431–£45,057

Library and Information Service

Assistant Librarians, S. Z. Young; Miss P. J. Baines .... £35,720–£40,360

Deputy Assistant Librarians,; Mrs H. R.
Coates; K. G. Cuninghame; Mrs J. M.
Wainwright; C. C. Pond, ph.d.; Mrs C. B.
Andrews; R. C. Clements; Mrs J. M.
Lourie; R. J. Ware, d.phil.; C. R. Barclay
.... £27,871–£35,720
Senior Library Clerks, Ms F. Poole; Mrs J. M.
Fiddick; Mrs C. M. Gillie; Miss C. E. Nield;
R. J. Twigger; T. N. Edmonds; R. J.
Cracknell; Miss O. M. Gay; Miss E. M.
McInnes; Mrs G. L. Allen; Miss M. Baber;
Ms A. Muir; Mrs H. V. Holden; Miss J.
Seaton; Mrs P. L. Carling .... £24,641–£29,049

Vote Office

Deliverer of the Vote, G. R. Russell . £27,871–£35,720
Deputy Deliverer of the Vote, H. C. Foster
.... £24,641–£29,049

Department of Finance and Administration

Director of Finance and Administration,
J. Rodda .... £50,380–£58,010
Accountant, A. J. Lewis........... £43,431–£45,057
Deputy Accountant, A. R. Marskell (*acting*)
.... £35,720–£40,360
Senior Assistant Accountant, M. J. Barram (*acting*)
.... £27,871–£35,720

Assistant Accountants, Miss M. M. McColl;
M. Fletcher; R. H. A. Russell; Mrs G.
Crowther (*acting*) .... £24,641–£29,049
Head of Establishments Office, B. A. Wilson
.... £35,720–£40,360
Deputy Head of Establishments Office, J. A.
Robb .... £27,871–£35,720
Computer Officer, R. S. Morgan .... £35,720–£40,360
Internal Auditor, A. A. Cameron... £24,641–£29,049
Staff Inspector, R. C. Collins .... £24,641–£29,049

Department of the Official Report

Editor, I. D. Church .... £43,431–£45,057
Deputy Editor, P. Walker .... £27,871–£35,720
Principal Assistant Editors, R. V. Hadlow;
J. Gourley; J. Withers; W. G. Garland
.... £26,209–£33,601
Assistant Editors, Miss V. Grainger; Miss
V. A. A. Clarke; Miss H. Hales; Miss G. L.
Sutherland; S. Hutchinson ..... £23,655–£30,276

Refreshment Department

General Manager, W. J. J. Smillie .. £27,871–£35,720
Deputy General Manager, E. J. Nash
.... £24,641–£29,049
Catering Accountant, D. R. W. Wood
.... £24,641–£29,049

PARLIAMENTARY INFORMATION
The following is a short glossary of aspects of the work of Parliament
(Unless otherwise stated, references are to House of Commons procedures.)

Adjournment Debate.—Usually a half-hour debate introduced by a backbencher at the end of
business for the day. The subjects raised are often
local or personal issues.

Bill.—Proposed legislation is termed a Bill. The
stages of a Public Bill (for **Private Bills**, *see* p. 233) in
the House of Commons are as follows:

First Reading: There is no debate at this stage,
which nowadays merely constitutes an order to have
the Bill printed.

Second Reading: The debate on the principles of
the Bill.

Committee Stage: The detailed examination of a
Bill, clause by clause. In most cases this takes place
in a Standing Committee, or the whole House may
act as a Committee. A Special Standing Committee
may take evidence before embarking on detailed
scrutiny of the Bill. Very rarely, a Bill may be
examined by a Select Committee (*see* below).

Report Stage: Detailed review of a Bill as amended
in Committee.

Third Reading: Final debate on a Bill.

Public Bills go through the same stages in the
House of Lords, except that in almost all cases the
Committee stage is taken in Committee of the Whole
House.

A Bill may start in either House, and has to pass
through both Houses to become law.

Both Houses have to agree the same text of a Bill,
so that the amendments made by the second House
are then considered in the originating House, and if
not agreed, sent back or themselves amended, until
agreement is reached.

Chiltern Hundreds.—A legal fiction, a nominal
office of profit under the Crown, the acceptance of
which requires a Member to vacate his seat. The
Manor of Northstead is similar. These are the only
means by which an MP may resign.

Closure and Guillotine.—To prevent deliberate
waste of time of either House, a motion may be made
that the question be now put. In the House of
Commons, if the Speaker decides that the rights of a
minority are not being prejudiced and 100 members
support the closure motion in a division, if carried,
the original motion is put to the House without
further debate.

The guillotine represents a more rigorous and
systematic application of the closure. Under this
system, a Bill proceeds in accordance with a rigid
timetable and discussion is limited to the time allotted
to each group of clauses. The closure is hardly ever
used in the Lords, and there is no procedure for a
guillotine. The completion of business in the Lords
is ensured by agreement from all sides of the House.

Consolidated Fund Bill.—A Bill to authorize
issue of money to maintain Government services.
The Bill is dealt with without debate, but afterwards
members may raise topics of public or local importance.

Delegated Legislation.—Many Statutes empower Ministers to make delegated legislation, with
little or no reference back to Parliament, usually by
means of Statutory Instruments. These fall into four
broad categories:—

(i) Affirmative Instruments, which are subject to
approval by resolutions of both Houses before they
can come into or remain in force;

(ii) Negative Instruments, which are subject to
annulment by resolution of either House;

(iii) General Instruments, which include those not required to be laid before Parliament and those which are required to be so laid but are not subject to approval or annulment;

(iv) Special Procedure Orders, against which parties outside Parliament may lodge petitions.

Dissolution.—Parliament comes to an end either by dissolution by the Sovereign, on the advice of the Prime Minister, or on the expiration of the term of five years for which the House of Commons was elected. Dissolution is normally effected by a Royal Proclamation.

Early Day Motion.—A motion put on the Notice Paper by an MP without in general the real prospect of its being debated. Such motions are expressions of back-bench opinion.

Emergency Debate.—In the Commons a method of obtaining prompt discussion of a matter of urgency is by moving the adjournment under Standing Order No. 20 for the purpose of discussing a specific and important matter that should have urgent consideration. A member may ask leave to make this motion by giving written notice to the Speaker, usually before 12 noon, and if the Speaker considers the matter of sufficient importance and the House agrees, it is discussed usually at 7 p.m. on the following day.

Father of the House.—The Member whose continuous service in the House of Commons, is the longest. The present Father of the House is the Rt. Hon. Sir Bernard Braine, elected first in 1950.

General Synod Measure.—A measure passed by the national assembly of the Church of England under the Church of England Assembly (Powers) Act 1919. These measures are considered by the Joint Ecclesiastical Committee, who make a report. They are then considered by both Houses, and if approved, sent for the Royal Assent.

Hansard.—The official report of debates in both Houses (and in Standing Committees) published by HMSO, normally on the day after the sitting concerned.

Hours of Meeting.—The House of Commons meets on Monday, Tuesday, Wednesday and Thursday at 2.30 p.m., and on Friday at 9.30 a.m. The House of Lords normally meets at 2.30 p.m. on Monday, Tuesday and Wednesday and at 3 p.m. on Thursday. In the latter part of the session, the House of Lords sometimes sits on Fridays at 11 a.m.

Hybridity.—A Public Bill which is considered to affect specific private or local interests, as distinct from all such interests of a single category, is called a Hybrid Bill and is subject to a special form of scrutiny to enable people affected to object. In the House of Lords, affirmative instruments (*see* **Delegated Legislation** above) may also be treated as hybrid.

Leader of the Opposition.—In 1937 the office of Leader of the Opposition was recognized and a salary of £2,000 per annum was assigned to the post. From January 1991 the salary was £56,746 (including Parliamentary salary of £21,809). The present Leader of the Opposition is the Rt. Hon. Neil Kinnock.

The Lord Chancellor.—The Lord High Chancellor of Great Britain is (*ex officio*) the Speaker of the House of Lords. Unlike the Speaker of the House of Commons, he is a member of the Government, takes part in debates and votes in divisions. He has none of the powers to maintain order that the Speaker in the Commons has, these powers being exercised in the Lords by the House as a whole. The Lord Chancellor sits in the Lords on one of the Woolsacks, couches covered with red cloth and stuffed with wool. If he wishes to address the House in any way except formally as Speaker, he leaves the Woolsack.

Naming.—When a member has been named by the Speaker for a breach of order, i.e. contrary to the practice of the House, called by surname and not addressed as the 'Hon. Member for ... (her/his constituency)', the Leader of the House moves that the offender 'be suspended from the service of the House' for (in the case of a first offence) a period of five sitting days. Should the member offend again, the period of suspension is increased.

Opposition Day.—A day on which the topic for debate is chosen by the Opposition. There are 20 such days in a normal session. On 17 days, subjects are chosen by the Leader of the Opposition; on the remaining three days by the leader of the next largest opposition party.

Parliament Acts 1911 and 1949.—Under these Acts Bills may become law without the consent of the Lords.

Since at least the 18th century the Commons have had the privilege of having bills concerned with supply (i.e. taxation and money matters) passed without amendment by the Lords, though until 1911 the Lords retained the right to reject such bills outright.

By the Parliament Act 1911 a Bill which has been endorsed by the Speaker of the House of Commons as a Money Bill, and has been passed by the Commons and sent up to the Lords at least one month before the end of a session, can become law without the consent of the Lords if it is not passed by them without amendment within a month.

Under the Parliament Acts 1911 and 1949, if the Lords reject any other Public Bill (except one to prolong the life of a Parliament) which has been passed by the Commons in two successive sessions, then that Bill shall (unless the Commons direct to the contrary) become law without the consent of the Lords. The Lords have power, therefore, to delay a Public Bill for thirteen months from its first Second Reading in the House of Commons.

Prime Minister's Questions.—The Prime Minister answers questions from 3.15 to 3.30 p.m. on Tuesdays and Thursdays. Nowadays the 'open question' predominates. Members tend to ask the Prime Minister what are her or his official engagements for the day; a supplementary question on virtually any topic can then be put.

Private Bill.—A Bill promoted by a body or an individual to give powers additional to, or in conflict with, the general law, and to which a special procedure applies to enable people affected to object.

Private Members' Bill.—A Public Bill promoted by a Member who is not a member of HM Government.

Private Notice Question.—A question adjudged of urgent importance on submission to the Speaker (in the Lords, the Leader of the House), answered at the end of oral questions—usually at 3.30 p.m.

Privilege.—The following are covered by the privilege of Parliament:—

(i) freedom from interference in going to, attending at, and going from, Parliament;

(ii) freedom of speech in Parliamentary proceedings;

(iii) the printing and publishing of anything relating to the proceedings of the two Houses is subject to privilege;

(iv) each House is the guardian of its dignity and may punish any insult to the House as a whole.

Prorogation.—The bringing to an end, by the Sovereign on the advice of the Government, of a session of Parliament. Public Bills which have not completed all their stages lapse on Prorogation.

Queen's Speech.—The Speech delivered by The Queen at the State Opening of Parliament, in which the Government's programme for the session is set forth. The Speech is, in fact, drafted by Civil Servants and approved by the Cabinet.

Question Time.—Oral questions are answered by Ministers in the Commons from 2.30 to 3.30 p.m. every day except Friday. They are also taken at the start of the Lords sittings, with a daily limit of four oral questions.

Royal Assent.—The Royal Assent is signified by Letters Patent to such Bills and Measures as have passed both Houses of Parliament (or Bills which have been passed under the Parliament Acts 1911 and 1949). The Sovereign has not given Royal Assent in person since 1854. On occasion, for instance in the Prorogation of Parliament, Royal Assent may be pronounced to the two Houses by Lords Commissioners; but more usually Royal Assent is notified to each House sitting separately in accordance with the Royal Assent Act 1967. The old French formulae for Royal Assent are then endorsed on the Acts by the Clerk of the Parliaments.

The power to withhold assent resides with the Sovereign, but has not been exercised in the United Kingdom since 1707, in the reign of Queen Anne.

Select Committees consisting usually of 10–15 members of all parties are a means used by both Houses in order to investigate certain matters.

Most select committees in the House of Commons are now tied to departments; each committee investigates subjects within a government department's remit.

There are other House of Commons select committees dealing with Public Accounts (i.e. the spending by HM Government of money voted by Parliament) and European Legislation, and also domestic committees dealing, for example, with Privilege and Services. Major select committees usually take evidence in public; their evidence and reports are published by HMSO.

The principal select committee in the House of Lords is that on the European Communities, which has, at present, six sub-committees dealing with all areas of Community policy. The House of Lords also has a select committee on Science and Technology, which appoints sub-committees to deal with specific subjects. In addition, *ad hoc* select committees have been set up from time to time to investigate specific subjects, e.g. overseas trade, murder and life imprisonment. There are also some joint committees of the two Houses, e.g. the Joint Committee on Statutory Instruments.

Departmental Committees

Agriculture.—Chair, J. Wiggin, MP; *Clerk*, D. W. Robson.

Defence.—Chair, M. Mates, MP; *Clerk*, D. L. Natzler.

Education, Science and Arts.—Chair, M. Thornton, MP; *Clerk*, A. Sandall.

Employment.—Chair, R. Leighton, MP; *Clerk*, S. J. Patrick.

Energy.—Chair, Dr M. Clark, MP; *Clerk*, D. J. Gerhold.

Environment.—Chair, Sir Hugh Rossi, MP; *Clerk*, S. J. Priestley.

Foreign Affairs.—Chair, D. Howell, MP; *Clerk*, R. W. G. Wilson.

Health.—Chair, N. Winterton, MP; *Clerk*, Ms H. E. Irwin.

Home Affairs.—Chair, Sir John Wheeler, MP; *Clerk*, E. P. Silk.

Scottish Affairs.—Committee not appointed.

Social Security.—Chair, F. Field, MP; *Clerk*, D. Lloyd.

Trade and Industry. —Chair, K. Warren, MP; *Clerk*, A. R. Kennon.

Transport.—Chair, D. Marshall, MP; *Clerk*, A. H. Doherty.

Treasury and Civil Service.—Chair, T. Higgins, MP; *Clerk*, D. G. Millar.

Welsh Affairs.—Chair, G. Wardell, MP; *Clerk*, D. F. Harrison.

Non-departmental Committees

European Legislation.—Chair, N. Spearing, MP; *Clerk*, C. R. M. Ward.

Members' Interests.—Chair, Sir Geoffrey Smith, MP; *Clerk*, A. J. Hastings.

Parliamentary Commissioner for Administration.—Chair, Sir Anthony Buck, MP; *Clerk*, C. G. Lee.

Privileges.—Chair, J. MacGregor, MP; *Clerk*, W. R. McKay.

Procedure.—Chair, Sir Peter Emery, MP; *Clerk*, D. W. N. Doig.

Public Accounts.—Chair, R. Sheldon, MP; *Clerk*, Mrs E. J. Flood.

The Speaker.—The Speaker of the House of Commons is the spokesman and president of the Chamber. He is elected by the House at the beginning of each Parliament or when the previous Speaker retires or dies. He neither speaks in debates nor votes in divisions except when the voting is equal.

Standing Orders.—Rules which have from time to time been agreed by each House of Parliament to regulate the conduct of its business. These orders may be amended or repealed, and are from time to time suspended or dispensed with.

State Opening.—This marks the start of each new session of Parliament. Parliament is normally opened, in the presence of both Houses, by the Queen in person, who makes the Speech from the Throne which outlines the Government's policies for the coming session (*see* **Queen's Speech**). In the absence of the Queen, Parliament is opened by Royal Commission, and the Queen's Speech is read by one of the Lords Commissioners specially appointed by Letters Patent for the occasion.

Strangers.—Anyone who is not a Member or Officer of the House is a stranger. Visitors are generally admitted to debates of both Houses but may be excluded if the House so decides. In practice this happens only in time of war.

Ten Minute Rule.—A colloquial term for Standing Order No. 19, under which back-benchers have an opportunity on Tuesdays and Wednesdays to state for about ten minutes why a Bill on a certain subject should be introduced. Time is also available for a short opposing speech.

Vacant Seats.—When a vacancy occurs in the House of Commons during a session of Parliament, the Writ for the by-election is moved by a Whip of the party to which the member whose seat has been vacated belonged. If the House is in recess, the Speaker can issue a warrant for a writ, should two members certify to him that a seat is vacant.

Whips.—In order to secure the attendance of Members of a particular party in Parliament on all occasions, and particularly on the occasion of an important vote, Whips (originally known as 'Whippers-in') are appointed. The written appeal or circular letter issued by them is also known as a 'whip', its urgency being denoted by the number of times it is underlined. Failure to respond to a three-line whip, headed 'Most important', is tantamount in the Commons to secession (at any rate temporarily) from the party. Whips are officially recognized by Parliament and are provided with office accommodation in both Houses. In both Houses, Government and some Opposition Whips receive salaries from public funds.

Public Information Services

HOUSE OF COMMONS.—Public Information Office, House of Commons, SW1A 0AA (Tel: 071-219 4272).

HOUSE OF LORDS.—The Journal and Information Office, House of Lords, SW1A 0PW (Tel: 071-219 3107).

THE GOVERNMENT

The Government is the body of Ministers responsible for the administration of national affairs, determining policy and introducing into Parliament any legislation necessary to give effect to government policy. The majority of Ministers are members of the House of Commons but members of the House of Lords or of neither House may also hold Ministerial responsibility. The Lord Chancellor is always a member of the House of Lords. The Prime Minister is, by current convention, always a member of the House of Commons.

The Prime Minister

The office of Prime Minister, which had been in existence for nearly 200 years, was officially recognized in 1905 and its holder was granted a place in the table of precedence. The Prime Minister, by tradition also First Lord of the Treasury and Minister for the Civil Service, is appointed by the Sovereign and is usually the leader of the party which enjoys, or can secure, a majority in the House of Commons. Other Ministers are appointed by the Sovereign on the recommendation of the Prime Minister, who also allocates functions amongst Ministers and has the power to obtain their resignation or dismissal individually.

The Prime Minister informs the Sovereign of state and political matters, advises on the dissolution of Parliament, and makes recommendations for important Crown appointments, the award of honours, etc.

As the chairman of Cabinet meetings and leader of a political party, the Prime Minister is responsible for translating party policy into government activity. As leader of the Government, the Prime Minister is responsible to Parliament and to the electorate for the policies and their implementation.

The Prime Minister also represents the nation in international affairs, e.g. summit conferences.

The Cabinet

The Cabinet developed during the 18th century as an inner committee of the Privy Council, which was the chief source of executive power until that time. The Cabinet is composed of about 20 Ministers chosen by the Prime Minister, usually the heads of government departments (generally known as Secretaries of State unless they have a special title, e.g. Chancellor of the Exchequer), the leaders of the two Houses of Parliament, and the holders of various traditional offices.

The Cabinet's functions are the final determination of policy, control of government and co-ordination of government departments. The exercise of its functions is dependent upon enjoying majority support in the House of Commons. Cabinet meetings are held in private, taking place once or twice a week during parliamentary sittings and less often during a recess. Proceedings are confidential, the members being bound by their oath as Privy Counsellors not to disclose information about the proceedings.

The convention of collective responsibility means that the Cabinet acts unanimously even when Cabinet Ministers do not all agree on a subject. The policies of departmental Ministers must be consistent with the policies of the Government as a whole, and once the Government's policy has been decided, each Minister is expected to support it or resign.

The convention of Ministerial responsibility holds a Minister, as the political head of his or her department, accountable to Parliament for the department's work. Departmental Ministers usually decide all matters within their responsibility, although on matters of political importance they normally consult their colleagues collectively. A decision by a departmental Minister is binding on the Government as a whole.

Her Majesty's Government as at July 31, 1991

THE CABINET

Prime Minister, First Lord of the Treasury and Minister for the Civil Service, THE RT. HON. JOHN MAJOR, MP, *born* March 29, 1943.

Lord High Chancellor, The Rt. Hon. the Lord Mackay of Clashfern, *born* July 2, 1927.

Secretary of State for Foreign and Commonwealth Affairs, The Rt. Hon. Douglas Richard Hurd, CBE, MP, *born* March 8, 1930.

Lord Privy Seal and Leader of the House of Lords, The Lord Waddington, PC, QC, *born* August 2, 1929.

Secretary of State for the Home Department, The Rt. Hon. Kenneth Wilfred Baker, MP, *born* November 3, 1934.

Chancellor of the Exchequer, The Rt. Hon. Norman Stewart Hughson Lamont, MP, *born* May 8, 1942.

Secretary of State for the Environment, The Rt. Hon. Michael Ray Dibdin Heseltine, MP, *born* March 21, 1933.

Secretary of State for Defence, The Rt. Hon. Thomas Jeremy King, MP, *born* June 13, 1933.

Secretary of State for Education, and Science, The Rt. Hon. Kenneth Henry Clarke, QC, MP, *born* July 2, 1940.

Lord President of the Council and Leader of the House of Commons, The Rt. Hon. John Roddick Russell MacGregor, OBE, MP, *born* February 14, 1937.

Secretary of State for Transport, The Rt. Hon. Malcolm Leslie Rifkind, QC, MP, *born* June 21, 1946.

Secretary of State for Energy, The Rt. Hon. John Wakeham, MP, *born* June 22, 1932.

Secretary of State for Social Security, The Rt. Hon. Antony Harold Newton, OBE, MP, *born* August 29, 1937.

Chancellor of the Duchy of Lancaster, The Rt. Hon. Christopher Francis Patten, MP, *born* May 12, 1944.

Secretary of State for Northern Ireland, The Rt. Hon. Peter Leonard Brooke, MP, *born* March 3, 1934.

Minister of Agriculture, Fisheries and Food, The Rt. Hon. John Selwyn Gummer, MP, *born* November 26, 1939.
Secretary of State for Employment, The Rt. Hon. Michael Howard, QC, MP, *born* July 7, 1941.
Secretary of State for Wales, The Rt. Hon. David James Fletcher Hunt, MBE, MP, *born* May 21, 1942.
Secretary of State for Trade and Industry, The Rt. Hon. Peter Bruce Lilley, MP, *born* August 23, 1943.
Secretary of State for Health, The Rt. Hon. William Arthur Waldegrave, MP, *born* August 15, 1946.
Secretary of State for Scotland, The Rt. Hon. Ian Bruce Lang, MP, *born* June 27, 1940.
Chief Secretary to the Treasury, The Rt. Hon. David John Mellor, QC, MP, *born* March 12, 1949.

LAW OFFICERS

Attorney-General, The Rt. Hon. Sir Patrick Barnabas Burke Mayhew, QC, MP.
Lord Advocate, The Lord Fraser of Carmyllie, PC, QC.
Solicitor-General, The Rt. Hon. Sir Nicholas Walter Lyell, QC, MP.
Solicitor-General for Scotland, Alan Ferguson Rodger, QC*
   (* not a member of the House of Commons)

OTHER MINISTERS

Parliamentary Secretary to the Treasury, The Rt. Hon. Richard Ryder, OBE, MP.
Financial Secretary to the Treasury, The Hon. Francis Maude, MP.

MINISTERS OF STATE

Agriculture, Fisheries and Food, The Baroness Trumpington.
Defence, The Rt. Hon. Archibald Hamilton, MP (*Armed Forces*); The Rt. Hon. Alan Clark, MP (*Defence Procurement*).
Education and Science, Timothy Eggar, MP.
Employment, (no appointment made).
Energy, (no appointment made).
Environment, Sir George Young, MP (*Housing, Planning*); Michael Portillo, MP (*Local Government, Inner Cities*); David Trippier, RD, MP (*Environment and Countryside*); The Baroness Blatch, CBE (*Heritage*).
Foreign and Commonwealth Affairs, The Rt. Hon. Lynda Chalker, MP (*Minister for Overseas Development*); Tristan Garel-Jones, MP; The Earl of Caithness, PC; The Hon. Douglas Hogg, QC, MP.
Health, Mrs Virginia Bottomley, MP.
Home Office, The Earl Ferrers, PC; The Rt. Hon. John Patten, MP; The Rt. Hon. Angela Rumbold, CBE, MP.
Northern Ireland, The Lord Belstead, PC (Paymaster General); Dr. Brian Mawhinney, MP.
Privy Council Office, The Rt. Hon. Timothy Renton, MP (*Minister for the Arts*).
Scottish Office, Michael Forsyth, MP.
Social Security, The Rt. Hon. Nicholas Scott, MBE, MP (*Social Security and Disabled People*).
Trade and Industry, The Hon. Timothy Sainsbury, MP (*Trade*); John Redwood, MP (*Corporate Affairs*).
Transport, Roger Freeman, MP (*Public Transport*); The Lord Brabazon of Tara (*Aviation and Shipping*).

Treasury, Gillian Shephard, MP; John Maples, MP (*Economic Secretary*).
Welsh Office, The Rt. Hon. Sir Wyn Roberts, MP.

UNDER-SECRETARIES OF STATE

Agriculture, Fisheries and Food, David Maclean, MP; David Curry, MP.
Defence, The Earl of Arran (*Armed Forces*); Kenneth Carlisle, MP (*Defence Procurement*).
Education and Science, Alan Howarth, CBE, MP; Michael Fallon, MP; Robert Atkins, MP (*Minister of Sport*).
Employment, Robert Jackson, MP; Eric Forth, MP; The Viscount Ullswater.
Energy, The Hon. Colin Moynihan, MP; David Heathcoat-Amory, MP.
Environment, Robert Key, MP; Anthony Baldry, MP; Timothy Yeo, MP.
Foreign and Commonwealth Affairs, The Hon. Mark Lennox-Boyd, MP.
Health, The Baroness Hooper; Stephen Dorrell, MP.
Home Office, Peter Lloyd, MP.
Northern Ireland Office, Richard Needham, MP; Jeremy Hanley, MP.
Scottish Office, Lord James Douglas-Hamilton, MP; The Lord Strathclyde; Allan Stewart, MP.
Social Security, The Lord Henley; Ann Widdicombe, MP; Michael Jack, MP.
Trade and Industry, Edward Leigh, MP (*Industry and Consumer Affairs*); The Lord Reay (*Industry and Technology*).
Transport, Patrick McLoughlin, MP (*Shipping*); Christopher Chope, MP (*Roads and Traffic*).
Treasury, The Lords Commissioners (see Government Whips).
Welsh Office, Nicholas Bennett, MP.

GOVERNMENT WHIPS

HOUSE OF LORDS

Captain of the Honourable Corps of Gentlemen-at-Arms (Chief Whip), The Rt. Hon. The Lord Hesketh.
Captain of the Queen's Bodyguard of the Yeoman of the Guard (Deputy Chief Whip), The Viscount Davidson.
Lords-in-Waiting, The Viscount Long; The Earl of Strathmore and Kinghorne; The Lord Cavendish of Furness; The Viscount Astor; The Earl Howe.

HOUSE OF COMMONS

Parliamentary Secretary to the Treasury (Chief Whip), The Rt. Hon. Richard Ryder, OBE, MP.

Treasurer of HM Household (Deputy Chief Whip), Alastair Goodlad, MP.
Comptroller of HM Household, David Lightbown, MP.
Vice-Chamberlain of HM Household, John Taylor, MP.
Lords Commissioners, The Hon. Thomas Sackville, MP; Sydney Chapman, MP; Gregory Knight, MP; Irvine Patnick, OBE, MP; Nicholas Baker, MP.
Assistant Whips, Timothy Wood, MP; Neil Hamilton, MP; Timothy Boswell, MP; Timothy Kirkhope, MP; David Davis, MP.

GOVERNMENT BY PARTY

Before the reign of William and Mary the principal Officers of State were chosen by and were responsible to the Sovereign alone and not to Parliament or the nation at large. Such officers acted sometimes in concert with one another, but more often independently, and the fall of one did not, of necessity, involve that of others, although all were liable to be dismissed at any moment.

In 1693 the Earl of Sunderland recommended to William III the advisability of selecting a Ministry from the political party which enjoyed a majority in the House of Commons and the first united Ministry was drawn in 1696 from the Whigs, to which party the King owed his throne. This group became known as the Junto and was regarded with suspicion as a novelty in the political life of the nation, being a small section meeting in secret apart from the main body of Ministers. It may be regarded as the forerunner of the Cabinet and in course of time it led to the establishment of the principle of joint responsibility of Ministers, so that internal disagreement caused a change of personnel or resignation of the whole body of Ministers.

The accession of George I, who was unfamiliar with the English language, led to a disinclination on the part of the Sovereign to preside at meetings of his Ministers and caused the appearance of a Prime Minister, a position first acquired by Robert Walpole in 1721 and retained without interruption for 20 years and 326 days.

Development of Parties

In 1828 the old party of the Whigs became known as **Liberals**, a name originally given to it by its opponents to imply laxity of principles, but gradually accepted by the party to indicate its claim to be pioneers and champions of political reform and progressive legislation. In 1861 a Liberal Registration Association was founded and Liberal Associations became widespread. In 1877 a National Liberal Federation was formed, with headquarters in London. The Liberal Party was in power for long periods during the second half of the nineteenth century and for several years during the first quarter of the twentieth century, but after a split in the party the numbers elected were small from 1931. In March 1988, the Liberals and the Social Democratic Party merged under the title **Social and Liberal Democrats**. Since October 1989 they have been known as the **Liberal Democrats**.

Soon after the change from Whig to Liberal the Tory Party became known as **Conservative**, a name traditionally believed to have been invented by John Wilson Croker in 1830 and to have been generally adopted about the time of the passing of the Reform Act of 1832 to indicate that the preservation of national institutions was the leading principle of the party. After the Home Rule crisis of 1886 the dissentient Liberals entered into a compact with the Conservatives, under which the latter undertook not to contest their seats, but a separate **Liberal Unionist** organization was maintained until 1912, when it was united with the Conservatives.

Labour candidates for Parliament made their first appearance at the General Election of 1892, when there were 27 standing as Labour or Liberal-Labour. In 1900 the Labour Representation Committee was set up in order to establish a distinct Labour group in Parliament, with its own whips, its own policy, and a readiness to co-operate with any party which might be engaged in promoting legislation in the direct interest of labour. In 1906 the LRC became known as **The Labour Party**.

The Council for Social Democracy was announced by four former Labour Cabinet Ministers on January 25, 1981. Subsequently a number of sitting Labour Members of Parliament, together with one Conservative, joined the new group, and on March 26, 1981 the **Social Democratic Party** was launched. Later in the year the SDP and the Liberal Party formed an electoral alliance. In 1988 a majority of the SDP agreed on a merger with the Liberal Party (*see* above) but a minority continued as a separate party under the SDP title. In June 1990 it was decided to wind up the party organization.

Government and Opposition

The government of the day is formed by the party which wins the largest number of seats in the House of Commons at a General Election, or which has the support of a majority of members in the House of Commons. By tradition, the leader of the majority party is asked by the Sovereign to form a government, while the largest minority party becomes the official Opposition with its own leader and 'Shadow Cabinet'. Leaders of the Government and Opposition sit on the front benches of the Commons with their supporters (the back-benchers) sitting behind them.

When a party is in Opposition and its leadership becomes vacant, it makes its free choice among the various personalities available; but if the party is in office, the Sovereign's choice may anticipate, and in a certain sense forestall, the decision of the party.

POLITICAL PARTIES

The parties included here are those with MPs sitting in the House of Commons.

CONSERVATIVE AND UNIONIST PARTY, Central Office, 32 Smith Square, SW1P 3HH. (Tel: 071–222 9000).—*Party Chairman*, The Rt. Hon. C. Patten, MP; *Deputy Chairman*, The Rt. Hon. Sir John Cope, MP; *Vice Chairmen*, Sir Thomas Arnold, MP; The Baroness Seccombe, DBE; Sir James Spicer, MP; The Rt. Hon. Sir Geoffrey Pattie, MP; M. Stern, MP; *Hon. Treasurers*, Lord Laing of Dunphail; Lord Beaverbrook; The Rt. Hon. Sir John Cope, MP.

SCOTTISH CONSERVATIVE PARTY, Central Office, Suite 1/1, 14 Links Place, Leith, Edinburgh EH6 7EZ. (Tel: 031–555 2900).—*Chairman*, Lord Sanderson of Bowden; *Deputy Chairman*, W. Hughes, CBE; Sir Matthew Goodman, CBE; Mrs N. Milne; *Hon. Treasurer*, D. Mitchell; *Dir.*, J. Goodsman.

LABOUR PARTY, 150 Walworth Road, SE17 1JT. (Tel: 071–703 0833).—*Chair*, T. Sawyer; *Vice Chair*, J. Evans, MP; *Treasurer*, S. McCluskie; *Gen. Sec.*, L. Whitty; *Parliamentary Party Leader*, The Rt. Hon. Neil Kinnock, MP; *Deputy Leader*, The Rt. Hon. Roy Hattersley, MP; *Leader of the Labour Peers*, Lord Cledwyn of Penrhos, CH.

Shadow Cabinet 1990–91

Leader, The Rt. Hon. Neil Kinnock, MP.
Home Affairs, The Rt. Hon. Roy Hattersley, MP.
Treasury and Economic Affairs, The Rt. Hon. John Smith, MP.
Trade and Industry, Gordon Brown, MP.

Chief Secretary to the Treasury, Margaret Beckett, MP.

Health and Community Care, Robin Cook, MP.

Foreign and Commonwealth Affairs, The Rt. Hon. Gerald Kaufman, MP.

Education, Jack Straw, MP.

Food, Agriculture and Rural Affairs, Dr David Clark, MP.

Employment, Tony Blair, MP.

Scotland, Donald Dewar, MP.

Social Security, Michael Meacher, MP.

Development and Co-operation, Ann Clwyd, MP.

Environmental Protection, Ann Taylor, MP.

Leader of the House, Dr John Cunningham, MP.

Wales, Barry Jones, MP.

Women, Jo Richardson, MP.

Energy, Frank Dobson, MP.

Environment, Bryan Gould, MP.

Transport, John Prescott, MP.

Chief Whip, Derek Foster, MP.

Chief of Parliamentary Labour Party, The Rt. Hon. Stan Orme, MP.

Leader of the Labour Peers, The Rt. Hon. Lord Cledwyn of Penrhos, CH.

Opposition Chief Whip, Lords, Lord Graham of Edmonton.

Peers Representative, Lord Dean of Beswick.

Additional Party Spokesmen

Defence, Martin O'Neill, MP.

Northern Ireland, Kevin McNamara, MP.

Arts, Mark Fisher, MP.

Children, Joan Lestor, MP.

Disabled, The Rt. Hon. Alf Morris, MP.

Attorney-General, The Rt. Hon. John Morris, QC, MP.

Science and Technology, Dr Jeremy Bray, MP.

Labour Chief Whip in the House of Lords is Lord Graham of Edmonton. Labour Chief Whip in the House of Commons is Derek Foster, MP.

LIBERAL DEMOCRATS, 4 Cowley Street, SW1P 3NB. (Tel: 071–222 7999).—*President*, C. Kennedy, MP; *Deputy Chair*, T. C. Jones; *Hon. Treasurer*, T. Razzall; *Gen. Sec.*, G. Elson; *Leader of the Party*, The Rt. Hon. Paddy Ashdown, MP; *Leader in the Lords*, The Rt. Hon. the Lord Jenkins of Hillhead.

SCOTTISH LIBERAL DEMOCRATS, 4 Clifton Terrace, Edinburgh EH12 5DR. (Tel: 031–337 2314).—*Chairman*, R. Thomson; *Hon. Treasurer*, K. Smith; *Party President*, Sir Russell Johnston, MP; *Party Leader*, M. G. Bruce, MP.

WELSH LIBERAL DEMOCRATS, 91 St Mary Street, Cardiff CF1 1DW. (Tel: 0222–382210).—*Chairman*, G. Williams; *Treasurer*, B. Lopez; *Secretary*, Ms K. Lloyd; *Party President*, Rev. R. Roberts; *Party Leader*, R. Livsey, MP.

Party Spokesmen

Foreign Affairs, Rt. Hon. Sir David Steel, MP.

Defence and Disarmament, Menzies Campbell, MP.

Europe, Sir Russell Johnston, MP.

Treasury, Alan Beith, MP.

Environment, Natural Resources and Food, Simon Hughes, MP.

Trade and Industry, Alex Carlile, MP.

Employment/Fisheries, Jim Wallace, MP.

Agriculture, Geraint Howells, MP.

Tourism/Housing and Transport, Ronnie Fearn, MP.

Home Affairs, Robert Maclennan, MP.

Northern Ireland, Lord Holme (Sir Russell Johnston in Commons).

Wales, Richard Livsey, MP.

Local Government and Community Care, David Bellotti, MP.

Scotland, Malcolm Bruce, MP/Ray Michie, MP.

North of England, Sir Cyril Smith, MP.

Social Security, Archy Kirkwood, MP.

Health, Charles Kennedy, MP.

Education, Science and Training, Matthew Taylor, MP/Michael Carr, MP.

Liberal Democrat Whips in the House of Lords are: *Chief Whip*, Lord Tordoff; *Deputy Whip*, Viscount of Falkland. Whips in the House of Commons are: *Chief Whip*, Jim Wallace, MP; *Deputy Whips*, Simon Hughes, MP; Archy Kirkwood, MP.

PLAID CYMRU, 51 Cathedral Road, Cardiff CF1 9HD. (Tel: 0222–231944).—*Chairman*, I. W. Jones, MP; *Deputy Chairman*, J. Dixon; *Hon. Treasurer*, S. R. Morgan; *Sec.*, D. Williams; *Party President*, D. E. Thomas, MP; *Vice-President*, D. Iwan.

SCOTTISH NATIONAL PARTY, 6 North Charlotte Street, Edinburgh EH2 4JH. (Tel: 031–226 3661).— *National Convener*, A. Salmond, MP; *Deputy Vice Convener*, A. Morgan; *National Treasurer*, T. Chalmers; *National Sec.*, J. Swinney; *Parliamentary Party Leader*, Mrs M. Ewing, MP; *Chief Whip*, A. Welsh, MP.

NORTHERN IRELAND

SOCIAL DEMOCRATIC AND LABOUR PARTY, 24 Mount Charles, Belfast BT7 1NZ. (Tel: 0232–323428).— *Chairman*, M. Durkan; *Deputy Chairmen*, Ms A. Hegarty; G. Murphy; *Hon. Treasurer*, D. Field; *Gen. Sec.*, P. McGlone; *Parliamentary Party Leader*, J. Hume, MP; *Deputy Leader*, S. Mallon, MP; *Chief Whip*, E. McGrady, MP.

ULSTER DEMOCRATIC UNIONIST PARTY, 296 Albertbridge Road, Belfast BT5 4GX. (Tel: 0232–458597).— *Chairman*, J. McClure; *Deputy Chairman*, S. Gibson; *Hon. Treasurer*, D. Herron; *Sec.*, A. Kane; *Parliamentary Party Leader*, Dr I. Paisley, MP; *Deputy Leader*, P. Robinson, MP.

ULSTER UNIONIST COUNCIL, 3 Glengall Street, Belfast BT12 5AE. (Tel: 0232–324601).—*Chairman*, J. Nicholson, MEP; *Vice Chairman*, A. J. Wilson; *Hon. Treasurer*, J. Allen; *Party Sec.*, J. Wilson; *Party Leader*, The Rt. Hon. J. H. Molyneaux, MP.

BY–ELECTIONS 1987–91

Kensington (Gtr. London)
(July 14, 1988)

J. D. Fishburn, *C.*		9,829
Mrs A. Holmes, *Lab.*		9,014
W. Goodhart *SLD*		2,546
J. Martin *SDP*		1,190
P. Hobson, *Grn.*		572
Mrs C. Payne, *Rainbow Alliance Payne and Pleasure Party*		193
'Lord' Sutch, *Monster Raving Loony Rock Music Party*		61
J. Duignan, *London Class War*		60
B. Goodier, *Anti Left Wing Fascist*		31
B. McDermott, *Free Trade Liberal Party–Europe Out*		31
R. Edey, *Fair Wealth Distribution Fair Housing Provision*		30
W. Scola, *The Leveller Party*		27
J. Crowley, *Anti-Yuppie Revolutionary Crowleyist Vegetarian Visionary*		24
J. Connell, *Peace—Stop ITN Manipulation*		20
Dr K. Trivedi, *Independent Janata Party*		5
C. maj.		815

Glasgow Govan (S'clyde)
(Nov. 10, 1988)

J. Sillars, *SNP*		14,677
R. Gillespie, *Lab.*		11,123
G. Hamilton, *C.*		2,207
B. Ponsonby, *SLD*		1,246
G. Campbell, *Grn.*		345
D. Chalmers, *Comm.*		281
'Lord' Sutch, *Monster Raving Loony Party*		174
F. Clark, *Rainbow Zippy Alliance*		51
SNP maj.		3,554

Epping Forest (Essex)
(Dec. 15, 1988)

S. J. Norris, *C.*		13,183
A. J. Thompson, *SLD*		8,679
S. W. Murray, *Lab.*		6,261
M. G. Pettman, *SDP*		4,077
A. M. Simms, *Grn.*		672
Ms T. Wingfield, *Independent National Front*		286
'Lord' Sutch, *Monster Raving Loony Liberal Christmas*		208
J. Moore, *Rainbow Alliance Change the World*		33
B. G. Goodier, *Vote No Belsen for South Africans*		16
C. maj.		4,504

Pontypridd (Mid Glam)
(Feb. 23, 1989)

Dr K. Howells, *Lab.*		20,549
S. Morgan, *PC*		9,755
N. Evans, *C.*		5,212
T. Ellis, *SLD*		1,500
T. Thomas, *SDP*		1,199
D. Richards, *Comm.*		239
D. Black, *Ind.*		57
Lab. maj.		10,794

Richmond (N. Yorks.)
(Feb. 23, 1989)

W. Hague, *C.*		19,543
M. Potter, *SDP*		16,909
Mrs B. Pearce, *SLD*		11,589
F. Robson, *Lab.*		2,591
Dr R. Upsall, *Grn.*		1,473
'Lord' Sutch, *Monster Raving Loony Party*		167
A. Mills, *University Information Officer*		113
Miss L. St Claire, *Corrective Party*		106
N. Watkins, *Official Liberal*		70
C. maj.		2,634

Vale of Glamorgan (S. Glam)
(May 4, 1989)

J. Smith, *Lab.*		23,342
R. Richards, *C.*		17,314
F. Leavers, *SLD*		2,017
J. Dixon, *PC*		1,672
K. Davies, *SDP*		1,098
Miss M. Wakefield, *Grn.*		971
C. Tiarks, *Protect the NHS*		847
'Lord' Sutch, *Monster Raving Loony Party*		266
E. Roberts, *Welsh Independence*		148
Miss L. St Claire, *Corrective Party*		39
D. Black, *Ind.*		32
Lab. maj.		6,028

Glasgow Central (S'clyde)
(June 15, 1989)

M. Watson , *Lab.*		14,480
A. Neil, *SNP*		8,018
A. Hogarth, *C.*		2,028
Ms I. Brandt, *Grn.*		1,019
R. McCreadie, *SLD*		411
P. Kerr, *SDP*		253
Ms L. Murdoch, *Revolutionary Communist*		141
W. Kidd, *Scottish Socialist*		137
D. Lettice, *Workers Revolutionary*		48
Lab. maj.		6,462

Vauxhall (Gtr. London)
(June 15, 1989)

Miss C. L. Hoey, *Lab.*		15,191
M. Keegan, *C.*		5,425
M. Tuffrey, *SLD*		5,043
H. Bewley, *Grn.*		1,767
H. Andrew, *People's Candidate*		302
J. Allen, *The Greens*		264
R. Narayan, *Barrister, Civil Liberties Activist in Brixton*		179
D. Milligan, *Revolutionary Communist*		177
P. Harrington, *Official National Front*		127
'Lord' Sutch, *Monster Raving Loony Mad Hatters*		106
D. Black, *Christian Alliance*		86
E. Budden, *National Front*		83
G. Rolth, *Fellowship*		21
W. Scola, *Leveller*		21
Lab. maj.		9,766

Staffordshire, Mid
(March 22, 1990)

Mrs S. Heal, *Lab.*		27,649
C. C. L. Prior, *C.*		18,200
T. A. Jones, *Lib. Dem.*		6,315
I. W. Wood, *SDP*		1,422
R. Saunders, *Grn.*		1,215
J. G. Bazeley, *Anti-Thatcher C.*		547
'Lord' Sutch, *Monster Raving Loony Green Teeth*		336
C. J. G. Hill, *National Front*		311
C. A. Abell, *NHS Supporters*		102
N. Parker-Jervis, *Against Immigration C. Green*		71
S. B. F. Hughes, *Raving Loony Green Giant Supercalafragalistic*		59
L. St C. Love, *National Independent Correct Edification*		51
B. R. A. Mildwater, *Save the 2CV*		42
D. M. Black, *Christian Patriotic Alliance/Save Britain Campaign*		39
Lab. maj.		9,449

Upper Bann
(May 17, 1990)

D. Trimble, *OUP*		20,547
Mrs B. Rodgers, *SDLP*		6,698
Ms S. Campbell, *SF*		2,033
Rev. H. Ross, *Ulster Independence*		1,534
T. French, *Workers' Party*		1,083
Mrs C. Jones, *C.*		1,038
Dr W. Ramsay, *All.*		948
G. McMichael, *DUP*		600
P. Doran, *Grn.*		576
E. Holmes, *Right to Vote Labour*		235
A. Dunn, *SDP*		154
OUP maj.		13,849

Bootle
(May 24, 1990)

M. Carr, *Lab.*		26,737
J. Clappison, *C.*		3,220
J. Cunningham, *Lib. Dem.*		3,179
S. Brady, *Grn.*		1,267
K. White, *Lib.*		474
D. Sutch, *Monster Raving Loony Cavern Rock*		418
J. Holmes, *SDP*		155
T. Schofield, *Ind.*		27
Lab. maj.		23,517

Knowsley South
(Sept. 27, 1990)

E. O'Hara, *Lab.*		14,581
L. Byrom, *C.*		3,214
Mrs C. Hancox, *Lib. Dem.*		1,809
R. Georgeson, *Grn.*		656
I. Smith, *Lib.*		628
'Lord' D. Sutch, *Monster Loony*		197
'Lady' C. Whiplash, *Corrective*		99
Lab. maj.		11,367

Eastbourne
(Oct. 18, 1990)

D. F. Bellotti, *Lib. Dem.* . . .	23,415
R. Hickmet, *C.*	18,865
Ms C. Atkins, *Lab.*	2,308
D. Aherne, *Grn.*	553
Ms T. Williamson, *Lib.*	526
Ms L. St. Clair, *Corrective* .	216
J. McAuley, *NF*	154
E. Page, *Ironside*	35
Lib. Dem. maj.	4,550

Bootle
(Nov. 8, 1990)

J. E. Benton, *Lab.*	22,052
J. Clappison, *C.*	2,587
J. Cunningham, *Lib. Dem.*	2,216
S. Brady, *Grn.*	557
'Lord' D. Sutch, *Monster*	
Raving Loony	310
K. White, *Lib.*	291
D. Black, *Christian Alliance*	
. . . .	132
Lab. maj.	19,465

Bradford North
(Nov. 8, 1990)

T. H. Rooney, *Lab.*	18,619
D. Ward, *Lib. Dem.*	9,105
Ms J. Atkin, *C.*	6,048
D. Pidcock, *Islamic GB* . . .	800
M. Knott, *Grn.*	447
R. Tenney, *NF*	305
J. Floyd, *Christian Alliance*	219
W. Beckett, *Raving Loony* .	210
N. Nowosielski, *Lib.*	187
M. Wrigglesworth, *Ind. C.*	
Anti-Poll Tax	89
Lab. maj.	9,514

Paisley North
(Nov. 29, 1990)

Ms I. Adams, *Lab.*	11,353
R. Mullin, *SNP.*	7,583
E. Marwick, *C.*	3,835
J. Bannerman, *Lib. Dem.* . .	2,139
D. Mellor, *Grn.*	918
Lab. maj.	3,770

Paisley South
(Nov. 29, 1990)

G. McMaster, *Lab.*	12,485
I. Lawson, *SNP.*	7,455
J. Workman, *C.*	3,627
A. Reid, *Lib. Dem.*	2,660
L. Collie, *Grn.*	835
Lab. maj.	5,030

Ribble Valley
(March 7, 1991)

M. Carr, *Lib. Dem.*	22,377
N. Evans, *C.*	17,776
Mrs J. Farrington, *Lab.* . . .	4,356
D. Brass, *Ind. C.*	611
H. Ingham, *Grn.*	466
'Lord' D. Sutch, *Monster*	
Raving Loony	278
S. Taylor, *Lib.*	133
Ms L. St Clair-Whiplash,	
Corrective	72
S. B. F. Hughes, *Raving*	
Loony Green Giant Clith-	
eroe Kid	60
Lib. Dem. maj.	4,601

Neath
(April 5, 1991)

P. G. Hain, *Lab.*	17,962
D. Evans, *PC*	8,132
R. Evans, *C.*	2,995
D. Lloyd, *Lib. Dem.*	2,000
J. Warman, *SDP*	1,826
R. Jeffries, *Local Ind. Lab.* .	1,253
'Lord' D. Sutch, *Monster*	
Raving Loony	263
B. Kirk, *Bean Party*	262
Lab. maj.	9,830

Monmouth
(May 16, 1991)

W. E. H. Edwards, *Lab.* . . .	17,733
R. Evans, *C.*	15,327
Mrs F. David, *Lib. Dem.* . . .	11,164
'Lord' D. Sutch, *Monster*	
Raving Loony.	314
M. Witherden, *PC/Grn.* . . .	277
P. Carpenter, *Unitax Ind.* .	164
Ms L. St Clair-Whiplash,	
Corrective	121
Lab. maj.	2,406

Liverpool Walton
(July 4, 1991)

P. Kilfoyle, *Lab.*	21,317
P. Clark, *Lib. Dem.*	14,457
Ms L. Mahmood, *Walton*	
Real Lab.	2,613
B. Greenwood, *C.*	1,155
'Lord' D. Sutch, *Monster*	
Raving Loony	546
E. G. L. Delisle, *G. L. Delisle*	
Party	63
Lab. maj.	6,860

Vacant
(as at Aug. 31, 1991)

Kincardine and Deeside.

WOMEN MEMBERS

The number of women MPs returned in June 1987 (41) was the highest ever.

Ms Diane Abbott (*Lab.*, *Hackney N. and Stoke Newington*); Ms Hilary Armstrong (*Lab.*, *Durham, NW*); *Mrs Rosemary Barnes (*SDP/All.*, *Greenwich*); *Mrs Margaret Beckett (*Lab.*, *Derby S.*); *Miss Betty Boothroyd (*Lab.*, *West Bromwich W.*); *Miss Virginia Bottomley (*C.*, *Surrey, SW*); *Mrs Lynda Chalker (*C.*, *Wallasey*); *Mrs Ann Clwyd (*Lab.*, *Cynon Valley*); *Mrs Edwina Currie (*C.*, *Derbyshire S.*); *Hon. Mrs Gwyneth Dunwoody (*Lab.*, *Crewe and Nantwich*); Mrs Margaret Ewing (*SNP*, *Moray*); *Dame Peggy Fenner (*C.*, *Medway*); *Miss Janet Fookes (*C.*, *Plymouth Drake*); Mrs Maria Fyfe (*Lab.*, *Glasgow Maryhill*); *Mrs Llinos Golding (*Lab.*, *Newcastle under Lyme*); Mrs Mildred Gordon (*Lab.*, *Bow and Poplar*); Mrs Theresa Gorman (*C.*, *Billericay*); *Ms Harriet Harman (*Lab.*, *Peckham*); Mrs Maureen Hicks (*C.*, *Wolverhampton NE*); *Mrs Elaine Kellett-Bowman (*C.*, *Lancaster*); *Dame Jill Knight (*C.*, *Birmingham Edgbaston*); Miss Joan Lestor (*Lab.*, *Eccles*); Mrs Alice Mahon (*Lab.*, *Halifax*); Mrs Ray Michie (*L./All.*, *Argyll and Bute*); Dr Marjorie Mowlam (*Lab.*, *Redcar*); Miss Emma Nicholson (*C.*, *Devon W. and Torridge*); *Mrs Elizabeth Peacock (*C.*, *Batley and Spen*); Ms Dawn Primarolo (*Lab.*, *Bristol S.*); Miss Joyce Quin (*Lab.*, *Gateshead E.*); *Ms Jo Richardson (*Lab.*, *Barking*); *Mrs Marion Roe (*C.*, *Broxbourne*); Ms Joan Ruddock (*Lab.*, *Lewisham Deptford*); *Mrs Angela Rumbold (*C.*, *Mitcham and Morden*); Mrs Gillian Shephard (*C.*, *Norfolk SW*); *Ms Clare Short (*Lab.*, *Birmingham Ladywood*); Mrs Ann Taylor (*Lab.*, *Dewsbury*); *Rt. Hon. Mrs Margaret Thatcher (*C.*, *Finchley*); Ms Joan Walley (*Lab.*, *Stoke-on-Trent*); Miss Ann Widdecombe (*C.*, *Maidstone*); *Mrs Ann Winterton (*C.*, *Congleton*); Mrs Audrey Wise (*Lab.*, *Preston*).

The number of women MPs was 44 in July 1991 following the election of Kate Hoey (*Lab.*, *Vauxhall*), Sylvia Heal (*Lab.*, *Staffordshire Mid*) and Irene Adams (*Lab.*, *Paisley N.*).

MEMBERS OF THE HOUSE OF COMMONS
(as at end Aug. 1991)

Lib. Dem. = Liberal Democrat. *SD* = Independent Social Democrat. For other abbreviations, *see* page 249
* Denotes membership of the last Parliament.

Maj.

Abbott, Ms Diane J. (*b.* 1953), *Lab.*, *Hackney N. and Stoke Newington* 7,678
*Adams, Gerard (*b.* 1948), *SF, Belfast W.* .. 2,221
Adams, Mrs Irene (*b.* 1948), *Lab.*, *Paisley N.* 3,770
*Adley, Robert J. (*b.* 1935), *C., Christchurch* 22,374
*Aitken, Jonathan W. P. (*b.* 1942), *C., Thanet S.* 13,683
*Alexander, Richard T. (*b.* 1934), *C., Newark* 13,543
*Alison, Rt. Hon. Michael J. H. (*b.* 1926), *C., Selby* 13,779
Allason, Rupert W. S. (*b.* 1951), *C., Torbay* 8,820
Allen, Graham W. (*b.* 1953), *Lab.*, *Nottingham N.* 1,665
*Alton, David P. P. (*b.* 1951), *Lib. Dem.*, *Liverpool, Mossley Hill* 2,226
*Amery, Rt. Hon. H. Julian (*b.* 1919), *C., Brighton, Pavilion* 9,142
*Amess, David A. A. (*b.* 1952), *C., Basildon* 2,649
Amos, Alan T. (*b.* 1952), *C., Hexham* 8,066
*Anderson, Donald (*b.* 1939), *Lab.*, *Swansea E.* 19,338
Arbuthnot, James N. (*b.* 1952), *C., Wanstead and Woodford* 16,412
*Archer, Rt. Hon. Peter K., QC (*b.* 1926), *Lab.*, *Warley W.* 5,393
Armstrong, Ms Hilary J. (*b.* 1945), *Lab.*, *Durham NW* 10,162
Arnold, Jacques A. (*b.* 1947), *C., Gravesham* 8,792
*Arnold, Sir Thomas (*b.* 1947), *C., Hazel Grove* 1,840
*Ashby, David G. (*b.* 1940), *C., Leicestershire NW* 7,828
*Ashdown, Rt. Hon. J. J. D. (Paddy) (*b.* 1941), *Lib. Dem.*, *Yeovil* 5,700
*Ashley, Rt. Hon. Jack, CH (*b.* 1922), *Lab.*, *Stoke-on-Trent S.* 5,053
*Ashton, Joseph W. (*b.* 1933), *Lab.*, *Bassetlaw* 5,613
*Aspinwall, Jack H. (*b.* 1933), *C., Wansdyke* 16,144
*Atkins, Robert J. (*b.* 1946), *C., S. Ribble* .. 8,430
*Atkinson, David A. (*b.* 1940), *C., Bournemouth E.* 14,683
*Baker, Rt. Hon. Kenneth W. (*b.* 1934), *C., Mole Valley* 16,076
*Baker, Nicholas B. (*b.* 1938), *C., Dorset N.* . 11,907
*Baldry, Antony B. (*b.* 1950), *C., Banbury* . 17,330
*Banks, Robert G. (*b.* 1937), *C., Harrogate* . 11,902
*Banks, Tony L. (*b.* 1943), *Lab.*, *Newham NW* 8,496
Barnes, Harold (*b.* 1936), *Lab.*, *Derbyshire NE* 3,720
*Barnes, Mrs Rosemary S. (*b.* 1946), *SD, Greenwich* 2,141
*Barron, Kevin J. (*b.* 1946), *Lab.*, *Rother Valley* 15,790
*Batiste, Spencer L. (*b.* 1945), *C., Elmet* 5,356
Battle, John D. (*b.* 1951), *Lab.*, *Leeds W.* .. 4,692
*Beaumont-Dark, Anthony M. (*b.* 1932), *C., Birmingham, Selly Oak* 2,584
*Beckett, Mrs Margaret M. (*b.* 1943), *Lab.*, *Derby S.* 1,516
*Beggs, J. Roy (*b.* 1936), *OUP, Antrim E.* .. 15,360
*Beith, Alan J. (*b.* 1943), *Lib. Dem.*, *Berwickupon-Tweed* 9,503
*Bell, Stuart (*b.* 1938), *Lab.*, *Middlesbrough* 14,958
*Bellingham, Henry C. (*b.* 1955), *C., Norfolk NW* 10,825
Bellotti, David F. (*b.* 1943), *Lib. Dem.*, *Eastbourne* 4,550

Maj.

*Bendall, Vivian W. H. (*b.* 1938), *C., Ilford N.* 12,090
*Benn, Rt. Hon. Anthony N. W. (*b.* 1925), *Lab.*, *Chesterfield* 8,577
*Bennett, Andrew F. (*b.* 1939), *Lab.*, *Denton and Reddish* 8,250
Bennett, Nicholas J. (*b.* 1949), *C., Pembroke* 5,700
Benton, Joseph E. (*b.* 1933), *Lab.*, *Bootle* .. 19,465
*Benyon, William R. (*b.* 1930), *C., Milton Keynes* 13,701
*Bermingham, Gerald E. (*b.* 1940), *Lab.*, *St Helens S.* 13,801
*Bevan, A. David G. (*b.* 1928), *C., Birmingham, Yardley* 2,522
*Bidwell, Sydney J. (*b.* 1917), *Lab.*, *Ealing, Southall* 7,977
*Biffen, Rt. Hon. W. John (*b.* 1930), *C., Shropshire N.* 14,415
*Blackburn, John G. (*b.* 1933), *C., Dudley W.* 10,244
*Blair, Anthony C. L. (*b.* 1953), *Lab.*, *Sedgefield* 13,058
*Blaker, Rt. Hon. Sir Peter KCMG (*b.* 1922), *C., Blackpool S.* 6,744
Blunkett, David (*b.* 1947), *Lab.*, *Sheffield, Brightside* 24,191
Boateng, Paul Y. (*b.* 1951), *Lab.*, *Brent S.* 7,931
*Body, Sir Richard (*b.* 1927), *C., Holland with Boston* 17,595
*Bonsor, Sir Nicholas, Bt. (*b.* 1942), *C., Upminster* 16,857
*Boothroyd, Miss Betty (*b.* 1929), *Lab.*, *West Bromwich W.* 5,253
*Boscawen, Hon. Robert T., MC (*b.* 1923), *C., Somerton and Frome* 9,538
Boswell, Timothy E. (*b.* 1942), *C., Daventry* 19,690
*Bottomley, Peter J. (*b.* 1944), *C., Eltham* .. 6,460
*Bottomley, Mrs Virginia H. B. M. (*b.* 1948), *C., Surrey SW* 14,343
*Bowden, Andrew, MBE (*b.* 1930), *C., Brighton, Kemptown* 9,260
*Bowden, Gerald F., TD (*b.* 1935), *C., Dulwich* 180
Bowis, John C. (*b.* 1945), *C., Battersea* 857
*Boyes, Roland (*b.* 1937), *Lab.*, *Houghton and Washington* 20,193
*Boyson, Rt. Hon. Sir Rhodes (*b.* 1925), *C., Brent N.* 15,720
Bradley, Keith J. C. (*b.* 1950), *Lab.*, *Manchester, Withington* 3,391
*Braine, Rt. Hon. Sir Bernard (*b.* 1914), *C., Castle Point* 19,248
*Brandon-Bravo, Martin M. (*b.* 1932), *C., Nottingham S.* 2,234
*Bray, Dr Jeremy W. (*b.* 1930), *Lab.*, *Motherwell S.* 16,930
Brazier, Julian W. H. (*b.* 1953), *C., Canterbury* 14,891
*Bright, Graham F. J. (*b.* 1942), *C., Luton S.* 5,115
*Brooke, Rt. Hon. Peter L. (*b.* 1934), *C., City of London and Westminster S.* 12,042
*Brown, Dr J. Gordon (*b.* 1951), *Lab.*, *Dunfermline E.* 19,589
*Brown, Michael R. (*b.* 1951), *C., Brigg and Cleethorpes* 12,248
*Brown, Nicholas H. (*b.* 1950), *Lab.*, *Newcastle upon Tyne E.* 12,500
*Brown, Ronald D. M. (*b.* 1940), *Lab.*, *Edinburgh, Leith* 11,327

Maj.

*Browne, John E. D. D. (b. 1938), C., Winchester 7,479
Bruce, Ian C. (b. 1947), C., Dorset S. 15,067
*Bruce, Malcolm G. (b. 1944), Lib. Dem., Gordon 9,519
*Buck, Sir Antony, QC (b. 1928), C., Colchester N. 13,623
Buckley, George J. (b. 1935), Lab., Hemsworth 20,700
*Budgen, Nicholas W. (b. 1937), C., Wolverhampton SW 10,318
Burns, Simon H. M. (b. 1952), C., Chelmsford 7,761
*Burt, Alistair J. H. (b. 1955), C., Bury N. .. 6,911
*Butcher, John P. (b. 1946), C., Coventry SW 3,210
Butler, Christopher J. (b. 1950), C., Warrington S. 3,609
*Butterfill, John V. (b. 1941), C., Bournemouth W. 12,651
*Caborn, Richard G. (b. 1943), Lab., Sheffield, Central 19,342
*Callaghan, James (b. 1927), Lab., Heywood and Middleton 6,848
Campbell, Ronald (b. 1943), Lab., Blyth Valley 853
Campbell W. Menzies, CBE, QC (b. 1941), Lib. Dem., Fife NE 1,447
*Campbell-Savours, Dale N. (b. 1943), Lab., Workington 7,019
*Canavan, Dennis A. (b. 1942), Lab., Falkirk W. 13,552
*Carlile, Alexander C., QC (b. 1948), Lib. Dem., Montgomery 2,558
*Carlisle, John R. (b. 1942), C., Luton N. ... 15,573
*Carlisle, Kenneth M. (b. 1941), C., Lincoln 7,483
Carr, Michael (b. 1946), Lib. Dem., Ribble Valley 4,601
Carrington, Matthew H. M. (b. 1947), C., Fulham 6,322
*Carttiss, Michael R. H. (b. 1938), C., Great Yarmouth 10,083
*Cartwright, John C. (b. 1933), SD, Woolwich 1,937
*Cash, William N. P. (b. 1940), C., Stafford . 13,707
*Chalker, Rt. Hon. Mrs Lynda (b. 1942), C., Wallasey 279
*Channon, Rt. Hon. H. Paul G. (b. 1935), C., Southend W. 8,400
*Chapman, Sydney B. (b. 1935), C., Chipping Barnet 14,871
*Chope, Christopher R., OBE (b. 1947), C., Southampton, Itchen 6,716
*Churchill, Winston S. (b. 1940), C., Davyhulme 8,199
*Clark, Rt. Hon. Alan K. M. (b. 1928), C., Plymouth, Sutton 4,013
*Clark, Dr David G. (b. 1939), Lab., South Shields 13,851
*Clark, Dr Michael (b. 1935), C., Rochford . 19,694
*Clark, Rt. Hon. Sir William (b. 1917), C., Croydon S. 19,063
*Clarke, Rt. Hon. Kenneth H., QC (b. 1940), C., Rushcliffe 20,839
*Clarke, Thomas, CBE (b. 1941), Lab., Monklands W. 18,333
*Clay, Robert A. (b. 1946), Lab., Sunderland N. 14,672
*Clelland, David G. (b. 1943), Lab., Tyne Bridge 15,573
*Clwyd, Mrs Ann (b. 1937), Lab., Cynon Valley 21,571
*Cohen, Harry M. (b. 1949), Lab., Leyton .. 4,641
*Colvin, Michael K. B. (b. 1932), C., Romsey and Waterside 15,272

Maj.

*Conway, Derek L. (b. 1953), C., Shrewsbury and Atcham 9,064
*Cook, Francis (b. 1935), Lab., Stockton N. . 8,801
*Cook, R. F. (Robin) (b. 1946), Lab., Livingston 11,105
Coombs, Anthony M. V. (b. 1952), C., Wyre Forest 7,224
*Coombs, Simon C. (b. 1947), C., Swindon .. 4,857
*Cope, Rt. Hon. Sir John (b. 1937), C., Northavon 14,270
*Corbett, Robin (b. 1933), Lab., Birmingham, Erdington 2,467
*Corbyn, Jeremy B. (b. 1949), Lab., Islington N. 9,657
*Cormack, Patrick T. (b. 1939), C., Staffordshire S. 25,268
*Couchman, James R. (b. 1942), C., Gillingham 12,549
Cousins, James M. (b. 1944), Lab., Newcastle upon Tyne, Central 2,483
*Cox, Thomas M. (b. 1930), Lab., Tooting .. 1,441
Cran, James D. (b. 1944), C., Beverley 12,595
*Critchley, Julian M. G. (b. 1930), C., Aldershot 17,784
*Crowther, J. Stanley (b. 1925), Lab., Rotherham 16,012
Cryer, G. Robert (b. 1934), Lab., Bradford S. 309
Cummings, John S. (b. 1943), Lab., Easington 24,639
*Cunliffe, Lawrence F. (b. 1929), Lab., Leigh 16,606
*Cunningham, Dr John A. (b. 1939), Lab., Copeland 1,894
*Currie, Mrs Edwina (b. 1946), C., Derbyshire S. 10,311
Curry, David M. (b. 1944), C., Skipton and Ripon 17,174
*Dalyell, Tam (Sir Thomas Dalyell of the Binns, Bt.) (b. 1932), Lab., Linlithgow .. 10,373
Darling, Alistair M. (b. 1953), Lab., Edinburgh, Central 2,262
*Davies, Rt. Hon. D. J. Denzil (b. 1938), Lab., Llanelli 20,935
Davies, J. Quentin (b. 1944), C., Stamford and Spalding 13,991
*Davies, Ronald (b. 1946), Lab., Caerphilly . 19,167
Davis, David M. (b. 1948), C., Boothferry .. 18,970
*Davis, Terence A. G. (b. 1938), Lab., Birmingham, Hodge Hill 4,789
Day, Stephen R. (b. 1948), C., Cheadle 10,631
*Dean, Rt. Hon. Sir Paul (b. 1924), C., Woodspring 17,852
Devlin, Timothy R. (b. 1959), C., Stockton S. 774
*Dewar, Donald C. (b. 1937), Lab., Glasgow, Garscadden 18,977
*Dickens, Geoffrey K. (b. 1931), C., Littleborough and Saddleworth 6,202
*Dicks, Terence P. (b. 1937), C., Hayes and Harlington 5,965
*Dixon, Donald (b. 1929), Lab., Jarrow 18,795
*Dobson, Frank G. (b. 1940), Lab., Holborn and St Pancras 8,853
Doran, Frank (b. 1949), Lab., Aberdeen S. . 1,198
*Dorrell, Stephen J. (b. 1952), C., Loughborough 17,648
*Douglas, Richard G. (b. 1932), Independent, Dunfermline W. 9,402
*Douglas-Hamilton, Lord James (b. 1942), C., Edinburgh W. 1,234
*Dover, Densmore R. (b. 1938), C., Chorley . 8,057
*Duffy, Sir Patrick (b. 1920), Lab., Sheffield, Attercliffe 17,191
*Dunn, Robert J. (b. 1946), C., Dartford 14,929
Dunnachie, James F. (b. 1930), Lab., Glasgow, Pollok 17,983

Maj.

*Dunwoody, Hon. Mrs Gwyneth P. (b. 1930), Lab., Crewe and Nantwich 1,092
*Durant, Sir Anthony (b. 1928), C., Reading W. 16,753
*Dykes, Hugh J. M. (b. 1939), C., Harrow E. 18,273
*Eadie, Alexander, BEM (b. 1920), Lab., Midlothian 12,253
*Eastham, Kenneth (b. 1927), Lab., Manchester, Blackley 10,122
Edwards, W. E. Huw (b. 1953), Lab., Monmouth 2,406
*Eggar, Timothy J. C. (b. 1951), C., Enfield N. 14,015
*Emery, Sir Peter (b. 1926), C., Honiton 16,562
Evans, David J. (b. 1935), C., Welwyn Hatfield 10,903
*Evans, John (b. 1930), Lab., St Helens N. .. 14,260
*Evennett, David A. (b. 1949), C., Erith and Crayford 6,994
*Ewing, Harry (b. 1931), Lab., Falkirk E. .. 14,023
Ewing, Mrs Margaret A. (b. 1945), SNP, Moray 3,685
*Fairbairn, Sir Nicholas, QC (b. 1933), C., Perth and Kinross 5,676
*Fallon, Michael (b. 1952), C., Darlington .. 2,661
*Farr, Sir John (b. 1922), C., Harborough .. 18,810
*Fatchett, Derek J. (b. 1945), Lab., Leeds, Central 11,505
*Faulds, Andrew M. W. (b. 1923), Lab., Warley E. 5,585
*Favell, Anthony R. (b. 1939), C., Stockport 2,853
Fearn, Ronald C. (b. 1931), Lib. Dem., Southport 1,849
*Fenner, Dame Peggy, DBE (b. 1922), C., Medway 9,929
Field, Barry J. A. (b. 1946), C., Isle of Wight 6,442
*Field, Frank (b. 1942), Lab., Birkenhead .. 15,372
*Fields, Terence (b. 1937), Lab., Liverpool, Broadgreen 6,047
*Finsberg, Sir Geoffrey, MBE (b. 1926), C., Hampstead and Highgate 2,221
Fishburn, J. Dudley (b. 1946), C., Kensington 815
*Fisher, Mark (b. 1944), Lab., Stoke-on-Trent, Central 9,770
*Flannery, Martin H. (b. 1918), Lab., Sheffield, Hillsborough 3,286
Flynn, Paul P. (b. 1935), Lab., Newport W. 2,708
*Fookes, Dame Janet, DBE (b. 1936), C., Plymouth, Drake 3,125
*Foot, Rt. Hon. Michael M. (b. 1913), Lab., Blaenau Gwent 27,861
*Forman, F. Nigel (b. 1943), C., Carshalton and Wallington 14,409
*Forsyth, Michael B. (b. 1954), C., Stirling . 948
*Forsythe, Clifford (b. 1929), OUP, Antrim S. 19,587
*Forth, M. Eric (b. 1944), C., Worcestershire, Mid 14,911
*Foster, Derek (b. 1937), Lab., Bishop Auckland 7,035
*Foulkes, George (b. 1942), Lab., Carrick, Cumnock and Doon Valley 16,802
*Fowler, Rt. Hon. Sir Norman (b. 1938), C., Sutton Coldfield 21,183
*Fox, Sir Marcus, MBE (b. 1927), C., Shipley 12,630
*Franks, Cecil S. (b. 1935), C., Barrow and Furness 3,927
*Fraser, John D. (b. 1934), Lab., Norwood .. 4,723
*Freeman, Roger N. (b. 1942), C., Kettering 11,327
French, Douglas C. (b. 1944), C., Gloucester 12,035
*Fry, Peter D. (b. 1931), C., Wellingborough 14,070
Fyfe, Mrs Maria (b. 1938), Lab., Glasgow, Maryhill 19,364
Galbraith, Samuel L. (b. 1945), Lab., Strathkelvin and Bearsden 2,452

Maj.

*Gale, Roger J. (b. 1943), C., Thanet N. 17,480
Galloway, George (b. 1954), Lab., Glasgow, Hillhead 3,251
*Gardiner, Sir George (b. 1935), C., Reigate 18,173
*Garel-Jones W. A. T. Tristan (b. 1941), C., Watford 11,736
Garrett, John L. (b. 1931), Lab., Norwich S. 336
*Garrett, William E. (b. 1920), Lab., Wallsend 19,384
*George, Bruce T. (b. 1942), Lab., Walsall S. 1,116
*Gilbert, Dr the Rt. Hon. John W. (b. 1927), Lab., Dudley E. 3,473
Gill, Christopher J. F., RD (b. 1936), C., Ludlow 11,699
*Gilmour, Rt. Hon. Sir Ian, Bt. (b. 1926), C., Chesham and Amersham 19,440
*Glyn, Sir Alan, ERD (b. 1918), C., Windsor and Maidenhead 17,836
*Godman, Dr Norman A. (b. 1938), Lab., Greenock and Port Glasgow 20,055
*Golding, Mrs Llinos (b. 1933), Lab., Newcastle under Lyme 5,132
*Goodhart, Sir Philip (b. 1925), C., Beckenham 13,464
*Goodlad, Alastair R. (b. 1943), C., Eddisbury 15,835
Goodson-Wickes, Dr Charles (b. 1945), C., Wimbledon 11,301
Gordon, Mrs Mildred (b. 1923), Lab., Bow and Poplar 4,631
Gorman, Mrs Theresa E. (b. 1931), C., Billericay 17,986
*Gorst, John M. (b. 1928), C., Hendon N. ... 10,932
*Gould, Bryan C. (b. 1939), Lab., Dagenham 2,469
Graham, Thomas (b. 1944), Lab., Renfrew W. and Inverclyde 4,053
*Grant, Sir Anthony (b. 1925), C., Cambridgeshire SW 18,251
Grant, Bernard A. M. (b. 1944), Lab., Tottenham 4,141
*Greenway, Harry (b. 1934), C., Ealing N. . 15,153
Greenway, John R. (b. 1946), C., Ryedale . 9,740
*Gregory, Conal R. (b. 1947), C., York 147
*Griffiths, Sir Eldon (b. 1925), C., Bury St Edmunds 21,458
Griffiths, Nigel (b. 1955), Lab., Edinburgh S. 1,859
*Griffiths, Peter H. S. (b. 1928), C., Portsmouth N. 18,401
Griffiths, Winston J. (b. 1943), Lab., Bridgend 4,380
*Grist, Ian (b. 1938), C., Cardiff, Central ... 1,986
Grocott, Bruce J. (b. 1940), Lab., The Wrekin 1,456
*Ground, R. Patrick, QC (b. 1932), C., Feltham and Heston 5,430
*Grylls W. Michael J. (b. 1934), C., Surrey NW 23,575
*Gummer, Rt. Hon. John S. (b. 1939), C., Suffolk, Coastal 15,280
Hague, William J. (b. 1961), C., Richmond 2,634
Hain, Peter G. (b. 1950), Lab., Neath 9,830
*Hamilton, Rt Hon. Archibald G. (b. 1941), C., Epsom and Ewell 20,761
*Hamilton, M. Neil (b. 1949), C., Tatton 17,094
*Hampson, Dr Keith (b. 1943), C., Leeds NW 5,201
*Hanley, Jeremy J. (b. 1945), C., Richmond and Barnes 1,766
*Hannam, John G. (b. 1929), C., Exeter 7,656
*Hardy, Peter (b. 1931), Lab., Wentworth .. 20,092
Hargreaves, Andrew R. (b. 1955), C., Birmingham, Hall Green 7,621
*Hargreaves, J. Kenneth (b. 1939), C., Hyndburn 2,220
*Harman Ms Harriet (b. 1950), Lab., Peckham 9,489
*Harris, David A. (b. 1937), C., St Ives 7,555

Maj.

*Haselhurst, Alan G. B. (b. 1937), C., Saffron Walden 16,602
*Hattersley, Rt. Hon. Roy S. G. (b. 1932), Lab., Birmingham, Sparkbrook 11,859
*Hawkins, Christopher J. (b. 1937), C., High Peak 9,516
*Hayes, Jeremy J. J. (b. 1953), C., Harlow .. 5,877
*Hayhoe, Rt. Hon. Sir Barney (b. 1925), C., Brentford and Isleworth 7,953
*Haynes, D. F. (Frank) (b. 1926), Lab., Ashfield 4,400
*Hayward, Robert A., OBE (b. 1949), C., Kingswood 4,393
Heal, Mrs Sylvia Lloyd (b. 1942), Lab., Staffordshire Mid 9,449
*Healey, Rt. Hon. Denis W., CH, MBE (b. 1917), Lab., Leeds E. 9,526
*Heath, Rt. Hon. Edward R. G., MBE (b. 1916), C., Old Bexley and Sidcup 16,274
*Heathcoat-Amory, David P. (b. 1949), C., Wells 8,541
Henderson, Douglas J. (b. 1949), Lab., Newcastle upon Tyne N. 5,243
*Heseltine, Rt. Hon. Michael R. D. (b. 1933), C., Henley 17,082
Hicks, Mrs Maureen P. (b. 1948), C., Wolverhampton NE 204
*Hicks, Robert A. (b. 1938), C., Cornwall SE 6,607
*Higgins, Rt. Hon. Terence L. (b. 1928), C., Worthing 18,501
*Hill S. James A. (b. 1926), C., Southampton, Test 6,954
Hinchliffe, David M. (b. 1948), Lab., Wakefield 2,789
*Hind, Kenneth H. (b. 1949), C., Lancashire W. 1,353
Hoey, Catharine (Kate) L. (b. 1946), Lab., Vauxhall 9,766
*Hogg, Hon. Douglas M. (b. 1945), C., Grantham 21,303
*Hogg, Norman (b. 1938), Lab., Cumbernauld and Kilsyth 14,403
*Holt, J. Richard (b. 1931), C., Langbaurgh 2,088
*Home Robertson, John D. (b. 1948), Lab., E. Lothian 10,105
Hood, James (b. 1949), Lab., Clydesdale ... 10,502
*Hordern, Sir Peter (b. 1929), C., Horsham 23,907
*Howard, Rt. Hon. Michael, QC (b. 1941), C., Folkestone and Hythe 9,126
*Howarth, Alan T., CBE (b. 1944), C., Stratford-upon-Avon 21,165
*Howarth, George E. (b. 1949), Lab., Knowsley N. 21,098
*Howarth, J. Gerald D. (b. 1947), C., Cannock and Burntwood 2,689
*Howe, Rt. Hon. Sir Geoffrey, QC (b. 1926), C., Surrey E. 18,126
*Howell, Rt. Hon. David A. R. (b. 1936), C., Guildford 12,607
*Howell, Rt. Hon. Denis H. (b. 1923), Lab., Birmingham, Small Heath 15,521
*Howell, Ralph F. (b. 1923), C., Norfolk N. .. 15,310
*Howells, Geraint W. (b. 1925), Lib. Dem., Ceredigion and Pembroke N. 4,700
Howells, Dr Kim S. (b. 1946), Lab., Pontypridd 10,794
*Hoyle E. Douglas H. (b. 1930), Lab., Warrington N. 8,013
Hughes, John (b., 1925), Lab., Coventry NE 11,867
*Hughes, Robert (b. 1932), Lab., Aberdeen N. 16,278
Hughes, Robert G. (b. 1951), C., Harrow W. 15,444
*Hughes, Royston J. (b. 1925), Lab., Newport E. 7,064
*Hughes, Simon H. W. (b. 1951), Lib. Dem., Southwark and Bermondsey 2,779

Maj.

*Hume, John (b. 1937), SDLP, Foyle 9,860
*Hunt, Rt. Hon. David J. F., MBE (b. 1942), C., Wirral W. 12,723
*Hunt, Sir John (b. 1929), C., Ravensbourne 16,919
*Hunter, Andrew R. F. (b. 1943), C., Basingstoke 17,893
*Hurd, Rt. Hon. Douglas R., CBE (b. 1930), C., Witney 18,464
Illsley, Eric E. (b. 1955), Lab., Barnsley, Central 19,051
Ingram, Adam P. (b. 1947), Lab., East Kilbride 12,624
Irvine, Michael F. (b. 1939), C., Ipswich ... 874
*Irving, Sir Charles (b. 1926), C., Cheltenham 4,896
Jack, J. Michael (b. 1946), C., Fylde 17,772
*Jackson, Robert V. (b. 1946), C., Wantage . 12,156
Janman, Timothy S. (b. 1957), C., Thurrock 690
*Janner, Hon. Greville E., QC (b. 1928), Lab., Leicester W. 1,201
*Jessel, Toby F. H. (b. 1934), C., Twickenham 7,127
*Johnson Smith, Sir Geoffrey (b. 1924), C., Wealden 20,110
*Johnston, Sir Russell (b. 1932), Lib. Dem., Inverness, Nairn and Lochaber 5,431
*Jones, Gwilym H. (b. 1947), C., Cardiff N. . 8,234
Jones, Ieuan W. (b. 1949), PC, Ynys Môn . 4,298
Jones, Martyn D. (b. 1947), Lab., Clwyd SW 1,028
*Jones, Robert B. (b. 1950), C., Hertfordshire W. 14,924
*Jones S. Barry (b. 1938), Lab., Alyn and Deeside 6,416
*Jopling, Rt. Hon. T. Michael (b. 1930), C., Westmorland and Lonsdale 14,920
*Kaufman, Rt. Hon. Gerald B. (b. 1930), Lab., Manchester, Gorton 14,065
*Kellett-Bowman, Dame Elaine, DBE (b. 1924), C., Lancaster 6,453
*Kennedy, Charles P. (b. 1959), Lib. Dem., Ross, Cromarty and Skye 11,319
*Key, S. Robert (b. 1945), C., Salisbury 11,443
*Kilfedder, James A. (b. 1928), UPUP, Down N. 3,953
Kilfoyle, Peter (b. 1946), Lab., Liverpool Walton 6,860
*King, Roger D. (b. 1943), C., Birmingham, Northfield 3,135
*King, Rt. Hon. Thomas J. (b. 1933), C., Bridgwater 11,195
*Kinnock, Rt. Hon. Neil G. (b. 1942), Lab., Islwyn 22,947
Kirkhope, Timothy J. R. (b. 1945), C., Leeds NE 8,419
*Kirkwood, Archibald J. (b. 1946), Lib. Dem., Roxburgh and Berwickshire 4,008
Knapman, Roger M. (b. 1944), C., Stroud .. 12,375
*Knight, Gregory (b. 1949), C., Derby N. ... 6,325
*Knight, Dame Jill, DBE (b. 1923), C., Birmingham, Edgbaston 8,581
*Knowles, Michael (b. 1942), C., Nottingham E. 456
*Knox, David L. (b. 1933), C., Staffordshire, Moorlands 14,427
*Lambie, David (b. 1925), Lab., Cunninghame S. 16,633
*Lamond, James A. (b. 1928), Lab., Oldham Central and Royton 6,279
*Lamont, Rt. Hon. Norman S. H. (b. 1942), C., Kingston upon Thames 11,186
*Lang, Ian B. (b. 1940), C., Galloway and Upper Nithsdale 3,673
*Latham, Michael A. (b. 1942), C., Rutland and Melton 23,022
*Lawrence, Ivan J., QC (b. 1936), C., Burton 9,830
*Lawson, Rt. Hon. Nigel (b. 1932), C., Blaby 22,176

Maj.

*Leadbitter, Edward (b. 1919), Lab., Hartlepool 7,289
*Lee, John R. L. (b. 1942), C., Pendle 2,639
*Leigh, Edward J. E. (b. 1950), C., Gainsborough and Horncastle 9,723
*Leighton, Ronald (b. 1930), Lab., Newham NE 8,236
*Lennox-Boyd, Hon. Mark A. (b. 1943), C., Morecambe and Lunesdale 11,785
*Lester, James T. (b. 1932), C., Broxtowe ... 16,651
Lestor, Miss Joan (b. 1931), Lab., Eccles .. 9,699
*Lewis, Terence (b. 1935), Lab., Worsley ... 7,337
*Lightbown, David L. (b. 1932), C., Staffordshire SE 10,885
*Lilley, Rt. Hon. Peter B. (b. 1943), C., St Albans 10,881
*Litherland, Robert K. (b. 1930), Lab., Manchester, Central 19,867
Livingstone, Ken R. (b. 1945), Lab., Brent E. 1,653
*Livsey, Richard A. L. (b. 1935), Lib. Dem., Brecon and Radnor 56
*Lloyd, Anthony J. (b. 1950), Lab., Stretford 9,402
*Lloyd, Sir Ian (b. 1921), C., Havant 16,510
*Lloyd, Peter R. C. (b. 1937), C., Fareham .. 18,795
*Lofthouse, Geoffrey (b. 1925), Lab., Pontefract and Castleford 21,626
*Lord, Michael N. (b. 1938), C., Suffolk, Central 16,290
*Loyden, Edward (b. 1923), Lab., Liverpool, Garston 13,777
*Luce, Rt. Hon. Sir Richard (b. 1936), C., Shoreham 17,070
*Lyell, Rt. Hon. Sir Nicholas, QC (b. 1938), C., Bedfordshire, Mid. 22,851
McAllion, John (b. 1948), Lab., Dundee E. 1,015
McAvoy, Thomas (b. 1943), Lab., Glasgow, Rutherglen 13,995
McCartney, Ian (b. 1951), Lab., Makerfield 15,558
*McCrea, Rev. Robert T. W. (b. 1948), DUP, Ulster, Mid. 9,360
*McCrindle, Sir Robert (b. 1929), C., Brentwood and Ongar 18,921
MacDonald, Calum A. (b. 1956), Lab., Western Isles 2,340
McFall, John (b. 1944), Lab., Dumbarton .. 5,222
*Macfarlane, Sir Neil (b. 1936), C., Sutton and Cheam 15,718
McGrady, Edward K. (b. 1943), SDLP, Down S. 731
*MacGregor, Rt. Hon. John R. R., OBE (b. 1937), C., Norfolk S. 12,418
*McKay, Allen (b. 1927), Lab., Barnsley W. and Penistone 14,191
*MacKay, Andrew J. (b. 1949), C., Berkshire E. 22,626
*McKelvey, William (b.1934), Lab., Kilmarnock and Loudoun 14,127
*Maclean, David J. (b. 1953), C., Penrith and the Border 17,366
McLeish, Henry B. (b. 1948), Lab., Fife, Central 15,709
*Maclennan, Robert A. R. (b. 1936), Lib. Dem., Caithness and Sutherland 8,494
*McLoughlin, Patrick A. (b. 1957), C., Derbyshire W. 10,527
McMaster, Gordon J. (b.1960), Lab., Paisley S. 5,030
*McNair-Wilson, Sir Patrick (b. 1929), C., New Forest 21,732
*McNair-Wilson, Sir Michael (b. 1930), C., Newbury 16,658
*McNamara, J. Kevin (b. 1934), Lab., Kingston upon Hull N. 12,169
*McWilliam, John D. (b.1941), Lab., Blaydon 12,488

Maj.

*Madden, Maxwell F. (b. 1941), Lab., Bradford W. 7,551
*Madel, William D. (b. 1938), C., Bedfordshire SW 22,305
*Maginnis, Kenneth (b. 1938), OUP, Fermanagh and S. Tyrone 12,823
Mahon, Mrs Alice (b. 1937), Lab., Halifax . 1,212
*Major, Rt. Hon. John (b. 1943), C., Huntingdon 27,044
*Malins, Humfrey J. (b. 1945), C., Croydon NW 3,988
*Mallon, Seamus (b. 1936), SDLP, Newry and Armagh 5,325
Mans, Keith D. R. (b. 1946), C., Wyre 14,661
*Maples, John C. (b. 1943), C., Lewisham W. 3,772
*Marek, Dr John (b. 1940), Lab., Wrexham . 4,152
*Marland, Paul (b. 1940), C., Gloucestershire W. 11,679
*Marlow, Antony R. (b. 1940), C., Northampton N. 9,256
*Marshall, David (b. 1941), Lab., Glasgow, Shettleston 18,981
Marshall, James (b. 1941), Lab., Leicester S. 1,877
Marshall, John L. (b, 1940), C., Hendon S. . 11,124
*Marshall, Sir Michael (b. 1930), C., Arundel 18,880
Martin, David J. P. (b. 1945), C., Portsmouth S. 205
*Martin, Michael J. (b. 1945), Lab., Glasgow, Springburn 22,063
Martlew, Eric A. (b. 1949), Lab., Carlisle .. 916
*Mates, Michael J. (b. 1934), C., Hampshire E. 23,786
*Maude, Hon. Francis A. A. (b. 1953), C., Warwickshire N. 2,829
*Mawhinney, Dr Brian S. (b. 1940), C., Peterborough 9,784
*Maxton, John A. (b. 1936), Lab., Glasgow, Cathcart 11,203
*Maxwell-Hyslop, R. J. (Robin) (b. 1931), C., Tiverton 9,212
*Mayhew, Rt. Hon. Sir Patrick B. B., QC (b. 1929), C., Tunbridge Wells 16,122
*Meacher, Michael H. (b. 1939), Lab., Oldham W. 5,967
Meale, J. Alan (b. 1949), Lab., Mansfield .. 56
*Mellor, Rt. Hon. David J., QC (b. 1949), C., Putney 6,907
*Meyer, Sir Anthony, Bt. (b. 1920), C., Clwyd NW 11,781
Michael, Alun E. (b. 1943), Lab., Cardiff S. and Penarth 4,574
Michie, Mrs J. Ray (b. 1934), Lib. Dem., Argyll and Bute 1,394
*Michie, William (b. 1935), Lab., Sheffield, Heeley 14,440
*Miller, Sir Hilary (Hal) (b. 1929), C., Bromsgrove 16,685
*Mills, Iain C. (b. 1940), C., Meriden 16,820
*Miscampbell, Norman A., QC (b. 1925), C., Blackpool N. 7,321
Mitchell, Andrew J. B. (b. 1956), C., Gedling 16,539
*Mitchell, Austin V. (b. 1934), Lab., Great Grimsby 8,784
*Mitchell, Sir David (b. 1928), C., Hampshire NW 13,437
*Moate, Roger D. (b. 1938), C., Faversham . 13,978
*Molyneaux, Rt. Hon. James H. (b. 1920), OUP, Lagan Valley 23,373
*Monro, Sir Hector (b. 1922), C., Dumfries . 7,493
*Montgomery, Sir Fergus (b. 1927), C., Altrincham and Sale 14,228
Moonie, Dr Lewis G. (b. 1947), Lab., Kirkcaldy 11,570
*Moore, Rt. Hon. John E. M. (b. 1937), C., Croydon, Central 12,617

Maj.

Morgan, H. Rhodri (b. 1939), Lab., Cardiff W. 4,045
Morley, Elliot A. (b. 1952), Lab., Glanford and Scunthorpe 512
*Morris, Rt. Hon. Alfred (b. 1928), Lab., Manchester, Wythenshawe 11,855
*Morris, Rt. Hon. John, QC (b. 1931), Lab., Aberavon 20,609
*Morris, Michael W. L. (b. 1936), C., Northampton S. 17,803
*Morrison, Hon. Sir Charles A. (b. 1932), C., Devizes 17,830
*Morrison, Rt. Hon. Sir Peter (b. 1944), C., City of Chester 4,855
Moss, Malcolm D. (b. 1943), C., Cambridgeshire NE 1,428
Mowlam, Dr Marjorie (b. 1949), Lab., Redcar 7,735
*Moynihan, Hon. Colin B. (b. 1955), C., Lewisham E. 4,814
*Mudd W. David (b. 1933), C., Falmouth and Camborne 5,039
Mullin, Christopher J. (b. 1947), Lab., Sunderland S. 12,613
Murphy, Paul P. (b. 1948), Lab., Torfaen .. 17,550
*Neale, Sir Gerrard (b. 1941), C., Cornwall N. 5,682
*Needham, Richard F. (b. 1942), C., Wiltshire N. 10,939
*Nellist, David J. (b. 1952), Lab., Coventry SE. 6,653
*Nelson, R. Anthony (b. 1948), C., Chichester 20,177
*Neubert, Sir Michael (b. 1933), C., Romford 13,471
*Newton, Rt. Hon. Antony H., OBE (b. 1937), C., Braintree 16,857
*Nicholls, Patrick C. M. (b. 1948), C., Teignbridge 10,425
Nicholson, David J. (b. 1944), C., Taunton 10,380
Nicholson, Miss Emma H. (b. 1941), C., Devon W. and Torridge 6,468
Norris, Steven J. (b. 1945), C., Epping Forest 4,504
*Oakes, Rt. Hon. Gordon J. (b. 1931), Lab., Halton 14,578
*O'Brien, William (b. 1929), Lab., Normanton 7,287
O'Hara, Edward (b. 1937), Lab., Knowsley S. 11,367
*O'Neill, Martin J. (b. 1945), Lab., Clackmannan 12,401
*Onslow, Rt. Hon. Cranley G. D. (b. 1926), C., Woking 16,544
*Oppenheim, Phillip A. C. L. (b. 1956), C., Amber Valley 9,500
*Orme, Rt. Hon. Stanley (b. 1923), Lab., Salford E. 12,056
*Owen, Dr the Rt. Hon. David A. L. (b. 1938), SD, Plymouth, Devonport 6,470
*Page, Richard L. (b. 1941), C., Hertfordshire SW 15,784
Paice, James E. T. (b. 1949), C., Cambridgeshire SE 17,502
*Paisley, Rev. Ian R. K. (b. 1926), DUP, Antrim N. 23,234
*Parkinson, Rt. Hon. Cecil E. (b. 1931), C., Hertsmere 18,106
*Parry, Robert (b. 1933), Lab., Liverpool, Riverside 20,689
*Patchett, Terry (b. 1940), Lab., Barnsley E. 23,511
Patnick, C. Irvine, OBE, (b. 1929), C., Sheffield, Hallam 7,637
*Patten, Rt. Hon. Christopher F. (b. 1944), C., Bath 1,412
*Patten, Rt. Hon. John H. C. (b. 1945), C., Oxford W. and Abingdon 4,878
*Pattie, Rt. Hon. Sir Geoffrey (b. 1936), C., Chertsey and Walton 17,469

Maj.

*Pawsey, James F. (b. 1933), C., Rugby and Kenilworth 16,264
*Peacock, Mrs Elizabeth J. (b. 1937), C., Batley and Spen 1,362
*Pendry, Thomas (b. 1934), Lab., Stalybridge and Hyde 5,663
*Pike, Peter L. (b. 1937), Lab., Burnley 7,557
Porter, David J. (b. 1948), C., Waveney 11,783
*Porter, George B. (b. 1939), C., Wirral S. .. 10,963
*Portillo, Michael D. X. (b. 1953), C., Enfield, Southgate 18,345
*Powell, Raymond (b. 1928), Lab., Ogmore . 22,292
*Powell, William R. (b. 1948), C., Corby 1,805
*Prescott, John L. (b. 1938), Lab., Kingston upon Hull E. 14,689
*Price, Sir David (b. 1924), C., Eastleigh ... 13,355
Primarolo, Ms Dawn (b. 1954), Lab., Bristol S. 1,404
Quin, Miss Joyce G. (b. 1944), Lab., Gateshead E. 17,228
*Radice, Giles H. (b. 1936), Lab., Durham N. 18,433
*Raffan, Keith W. T. (b. 1949), C., Delyn ... 1,224
*Raison, Rt. Hon. Sir Timothy (b. 1929), C., Aylesbury 16,558
*Randall, Stuart J. (b. 1938), Lab., Kingston upon Hull W. 8,130
*Rathbone, J. R. (Tim) (b. 1933), C., Lewes . 13,620
*Redmond, Martin (b. 1937), Lab., Don Valley 11,467
Redwood, John A. (b. 1951), C., Wokingham 20,387
*Rees, Rt. Hon. Merlyn (b. 1920), Lab., Leeds S. and Morley 6,711
Reid, Dr John (b. 1947), Lab., Motherwell N. 23,595
*Renton, Rt. Hon. R. Timothy (b. 1932), C., Sussex, Mid 18,292
*Rhodes James, Sir Robert (b. 1933), C., Cambridge 5,060
*Richardson, Ms Josephine (b. 1923), Lab., Barking 3,409
Riddick, Graham E. G. (b. 1955), C., Colne Valley 1,677
*Ridley, Rt. Hon. Nicholas (b. 1929), C., Cirencester and Tewkesbury 12,662
*Ridsdale, Sir Julian, CBE (b. 1915), C., Harwich 12,082
*Rifkind, Rt. Hon. Malcolm L., QC (b. 1946), C., Edinburgh, Pentlands 3,745
*Roberts, Rt. Hon. Sir Wyn (b. 1930), C., Conwy 3,024
*Robertson, George I. M. (b. 1946), Lab., Hamilton 21,662
*Robinson, Geoffrey (b. 1939), Lab., Coventry NW 5,663
*Robinson, Peter D. (b. 1948), DUP, Belfast E. 9,798
*Roe, Mrs Marion A. (b. 1936), C., Broxbourne 22,995
*Rogers, Allan R. (b. 1932), Lab., Rhondda . 30,754
*Rooker, Jeffrey W. (b. 1941), Lab., Birmingham, Perry Barr 6,933
Rooney, Terrence H. (b. 1950), Lab., Bradford N. 9,514
*Ross, Ernest (b. 1942), Lab., Dundee W. ... 16,526
*Ross, William (b. 1936), OUP, Londonderry E. 20,157
*Rossi, Sir Hugh (b. 1927), C., Hornsey and Wood Green 1,779
*Rost, Peter L. (b. 1930), C., Erewash 9,754
*Rowe, Andrew J. B. (b. 1935), C., Kent, Mid. 14,768
*Rowlands, Edward (b. 1940), Lab., Merthyr Tydfil and Rhymney 28,130
Ruddock, Ms Joan M. (b. 1943), Lab., Lewisham, Deptford 6,771

Maj.

Rumbold, Rt. Hon. Angela C. R., CBE (b. 1932), C., Mitcham and Morden 6,183
Ryder, Richard A., OBE (b. 1949), C., Norfolk, Mid 18,008
Sackville, Hon. Thomas G. (b. 1950), C., Bolton W. 4,593
Sainsbury, Hon. Timothy A. D. (b. 1932), C., Hove 18,218
Salmond, Alexander E. A. (b. 1954), SNP, Banff and Buchan 2,441
Sayeed, Jonathan (b. 1948), C., Bristol E. . 4,123
Scott, Rt. Hon. Nicholas P., MBE (b. 1933), C., Chelsea 13,319
Sedgemore, Brian C. J. (b. 1937), Lab., Hackney S. and Shoreditch 7,522
Shaw, David L. (b. 1950), C., Dover 6,541
Shaw, Sir Giles (b. 1931), C., Pudsey 6,436
Shaw, Sir Michael (b. 1920), C., Scarborough 13,626
Sheerman, Barry J. (b. 1940), Lab., Huddersfield 7,278
Sheldon, Rt. Hon. Robert E. (b. 1923), Lab., Ashton-under-Lyne 9,286
Shelton, Sir William (b. 1929), C., Streatham 2,407
Shephard, Mrs Gillian P. (b. 1940), C., Norfolk SW 20,436
Shepherd, Colin R. (b. 1938), C., Hereford . 1,413
Shepherd, Richard C. S. (b. 1942), C., Aldridge-Brownhills 12,396
Shersby, J. Michael (b. 1933), C., Uxbridge 15,970
Shore, Rt. Hon. Peter D. (b. 1924), Lab., Bethnal Green and Stepney 5,284
Short, Ms Clare (b. 1946), Lab., Birmingham, Ladywood 10,028
Sillars, James (b. 1937), SNP, Glasgow Govan 3,554
Sims, Roger E. (b. 1930), C., Chislehurst ... 14,507
Skeet, Sir Trevor (b. 1918), C., Bedfordshire N. 16,505
Skinner, Dennis E. (b. 1932), Lab., Bolsover 14,120
Smith, Andrew D. (b. 1951), Lab., Oxford E. 1,288
Smith, Christopher R. (b. 1951), Lab., Islington S. and Finsbury 805
Smith, Sir Cyril, MBE (b. 1928), Lib. Dem., Rochdale 2,779
Smith, Sir Dudley (b. 1926), C., Warwick and Leamington 13,982
Smith, Rt. Hon. John, QC (b. 1938), Lab., Monklands E. 16,389
Smith, John W. P. (b. 1951), Lab., Vale of Glamorgan 6,028
Smith, Timothy J. (b. 1947), C., Beaconsfield 21,339
Smyth, Rev. W. Martin (b. 1931), OUP, Belfast S. 11,954
Snape, Peter C. (b. 1942), Lab., West Bromwich E. 983
Soames, Hon. A. Nicholas W. (b. 1948), C., Crawley 12,138
Soley, Clive S. (b. 1939), Lab., Hammersmith 2,415
Spearing, Nigel J. (b. 1930), Lab., Newham S. 2,766
Speed, H. Keith, RD (b. 1934), C., Ashford . 15,488
Speller, Antony (b. 1929), C., Devon N. 4,469
Spicer, Sir James (b. 1925), C., Dorset W. ... 12,364
Spicer W. Michael H. (b. 1943), C., Worcestershire S. 13,645
Squire, Robin C. (b. 1944), C., Hornchurch 10,694
Stanbrook, Ivor R. (b. 1924), C., Orpington 12,732
Stanley, Rt. Hon. Sir John (b. 1942), C., Tonbridge and Malling 16,429
Steel, Rt. Hon. Sir David (b. 1938), Lib. Dem., Tweeddale, Ettrick and Lauderdale 5,942
Steen, Anthony D. (b. 1939), C., South Hams 13,146
Steinberg, Gerald N. (b. 1945), Lab., Durham, City of 6,125
Stern, Michael C. (b. 1942), C., Bristol NW 6,952

Maj.

Stevens, Lewis D., MBE (b. 1936), C., Nuneaton 5,655
Stewart, Andrew S. (b. 1937), C., Sherwood 4,495
Stewart, Rt. Hon. Sir Ian, RD (b. 1935), C., Hertfordshire N. 11,442
Stewart, J. Allan (b. 1942), C., Eastwood . 6,014
Stokes, Sir John (b. 1917), C., Halesowen and Stourbridge 13,808
Stott, Roger, CBE (b. 1943), Lab., Wigan ... 20,462
Strang, Gavin S. (b. 1943), Lab., Edinburgh E. 9,295
Straw, J. W. (Jack) (b. 1946), Lab., Blackburn 5,497
Sumberg, David A. G. (b. 1941), C., Bury S. 2,679
Summerson, Hugo H. F. (b. 1950), C., Walthamstow 1,512
Tapsell, Sir Peter (b. 1930), C., Lindsey E. . 8,616
Taylor, Sir Edward (Teddy) (b. 1937), C., Southend E. 13,847
Taylor, Ian C., MBE, (b. 1945), C., Esher ... 19,068
Taylor, Rt. Hon. John D. (b. 1937), OUP, Strangford 20,646
Taylor, John M. (b. 1941), C., Solihull 21,786
Taylor, Matthew O. J. (b. 1963), Lib. Dem., Truro 4,753
Taylor, Mrs W. Ann (b. 1947), Lab., Dewsbury 445
Tebbit, Rt. Hon. Norman B., CH (b. 1931), C., Chingford 17,955
Temple-Morris, Peter (b. 1938), C., Leominster 14,075
Thatcher, Rt. Hon. Margaret H., OM (b. 1925), C., Finchley 8,913
Thomas, Dafydd E. (b. 1946), PC, Meirionnydd Nant Conwy 3,026
Thompson, Donald (b. 1931), C., Calder Valley 6,045
Thompson, H. Patrick (b. 1935), C., Norwich N. 7,776
Thompson, John (b. 1928), Lab., Wansbeck 16,789
Thorne, Neil G., OBE, TD (b. 1932), C., Ilford S. 4,572
Thornton, G. Malcolm (b. 1939), C., Crosby 6,847
Thurnham, Peter G. (b. 1938), C., Bolton NE 813
Townend, John E. (b. 1934), C., Bridlington 17,321
Townsend, Cyril D. (b. 1937), C., Bexleyheath 11,687
Tracey, Richard P. (b. 1943), C., Surbiton . 9,741
Tredinnick, David A. S. (b. 1950), C., Bosworth 17,016
Trimble W. David (b. 1944), OUP, Upper Bann 13,849
Trippier, David A., RD (b. 1946), C., Rossendale and Darwen 4,982
Trotter, Neville G. (b. 1932), C., Tynemouth 2,583
Twinn, Dr Ian D. (b. 1950), C., Edmonton . 7,286
Turner, Dennis (b. 1942), Lab., Wolverhampton SE 6,398
Vaughan, Sir Gerard (b. 1923), C., Reading E. 16,217
Vaz, N. Keith A. S. (b. 1956), Lab., Leicester E. 1,924
Viggers, Peter J. (b. 1938), C., Gosport 13,723
Wakeham, Rt. Hon. John (b. 1932), C., Colchester S. and Maldon 15,483
Waldegrave, Rt. Hon. William A. (b. 1946), C., Bristol W. 7,703
Walden, George G. H., CMG (b. 1939), C., Buckingham 18,526
Walker, A. Cecil (b. 1924), OUP, Belfast N. 8,560
Walker, Rt. Hon. Harold (b. 1927), Lab., Doncaster, Central 8,196
Walker, Rt. Hon. Peter E., MBE (b. 1932), C., Worcester 10,453
Walker, William C. (b. 1929), Tayside N. .. 5,016

Maj.

Wallace, James R. (b. 1954), Lib. Dem., Orkney and Shetland 3,922
Waller, Gary P. A. (b. 1945), C., Keighley .. 5,606
Walley, Ms Joan L. (b. 1949), Lab., Stoke-on-Trent N. 8,513
Walters, Sir Dennis, MBE (b. 1928), C., Westbury 10,097
Ward, John D., CBE (b. 1925), C., Poole 14,808
Wardell, Gareth L. (b. 1944), Lab., Gower . 5,764
Wardle, Charles F. (b. 1939), C., Bexhill and Battle 20,519
Wareing, Robert N. (b. 1930), Lab., Liverpool, West Derby 20,496
Warren, Kenneth R. (b. 1926), C., Hastings and Rye 7,347
Watson, Michael (b. 1949), Lab., Glasgow Central* 6,462
Watts, John A. (b. 1947), C., Slough 4,090
Weatherill, Rt. Hon. B. Bernard (b. 1920), The Speaker, Croydon NE 12,519
Wells, Bowen (b. 1935), C., Hertford and Stortford 17,140
Welsh, Andrew (b. 1944), SNP, Angus E. . 1,544
Welsh, Michael C. (b. 1926), Lab., Doncaster N. 19,935
Wheeler, Sir John (b. 1940), C., Westminster N. 3,310
Whitney, Raymond W., OBE (b. 1930), C., Wycombe 13,819
Widdecombe, Miss Ann N. (b. 1947), C., Maidstone* 10,364
Wiggin, A. W. (Jerry), TD (b. 1937), C., Weston-super-Mare 7,998
Wigley, Dafydd W. (b. 1943), PC, Caernarfon 12,802

Maj.

Wilkinson, John A. D. (b. 1940), C., Ruislip-Northwood 16,971
Williams, Rt. Hon. Alan J. (b. 1930), Lab., Swansea W. 7,062
Williams, Alan W. (b. 1945), Lab., Carmarthen* 4,317
Wilshire, David (b. 1943), C., Spelthorne .. 20,050
Wilson, Brian D. H. (b. 1948), Lab., Cunninghame N.* 4,467
Winnick, David J. (b. 1933), Lab., Walsall N. 1,790
Winterton, Mrs J. Ann (b. 1941), C., Congleton 7,969
Winterton, Nicholas R. (b. 1938), C., Macclesfield 19,092
Wise, Mrs Audrey (b. 1935), Lab., Preston 10,645
Wolfson, G. Mark (b. 1934), C., Sevenoaks . 17,345
Wood, Timothy J. R. (b. 1940), C., Stevenage 5,340
Woodcock, Michael (b. 1943), C., Ellesmere Port and Neston 1,853
Worthington, Anthony (b. 1941), Lab., Clydebank and Milngavie* 16,304
Wray, James (b. 1938), Lab., Glasgow, Provan* 18,372
Yeo, Timothy S. K. (b. 1945), C., Suffolk S. 16,243
Young, David W. (b. 1930), Lab., Bolton SE 11,381
Young, Sir George, Bt. (b. 1941), C., Ealing, Acton 12,243
Younger, Rt. Hon. George K. H., TD (b. 1931), C., Ayr 182

RETIRING MEMBERS

The following MPs have announced that they will not stand for election at the next General Election (as at July 31, 1991):

Rt. Hon. Julian Amery (C.); Rt. Hon. Peter Archer (Lab.); Rt. Hon. Jack Ashley (Lab.); William Benyon (C.); Rt. Hon. Sir Peter Blaker (C.); Hon. Robert Boscawen (C.); Rt. Hon. Sir Bernard Braine (C.); John Browne (C.); Sir Antony Buck (C.); Rt. Hon. Sir William Clark (C.); Stanley Crowther (Lab.); Rt. Hon. Sir Paul Dean (C.); Richard Douglas (Ind.); Sir Patrick Duffy (Lab.); Alexander Eadie (Lab.); Harry Ewing (Lab.); John Farr (C.); Sir Geoffrey Finsberg (C.); Martin Flannery (Lab.); Rt. Hon. Michael Foot (Lab.); William Garrett (Lab.); Sir Alan Glyn (C.); Sir Philip Goodhart (C.); Sir Eldon Griffiths (C.); Christopher Hawkins (C.); Rt. Hon. Sir Barney Hayhoe (C.); Frank Haynes (Lab.); Rt. Hon. Denis Healey (Lab.); Rt. Hon. Sir Geoffrey Howe (C.); Sir Charles Irving (C.); David Lambie (Lab.); James Lamond (Lab.); Michael Latham (C.); Rt. Hon. Nigel Lawson (C.); Edward Leadbitter (Lab.); Sir Ian Lloyd (C.); Sir Robert McCrindle (C.); Sir Neil Macfarlane (C.); Allen McKay (Lab.); Sir Michael McNair-Wilson (C.); Robin Maxwell-Hyslop (C.); Sir Hal Miller (C.); Norman Miscampbell (C.); Rt. Hon. John Moore (C.); Hon. Sir Charles Morrison (C.); Rt. Hon. Sir Peter Morrison (C.); David Mudd (C.); Rt. Hon. Cecil Parkinson (C.); Sir David Price (C.); Keith Raffan (C.); Rt. Hon. Sir Timothy Raison (C.); Rt. Hon. Merlyn Rees (Lab.); Sir Robert Rhodes James (C.); Rt. Hon. Nicholas Ridley (C.); Sir Julian Ridsdale (C.); Peter Rost (C.); Sir Michael Shaw (C.); Sir Cyril Smith (Lib. Dem.); Ivor Stanbrook (C.); Sir John Stokes (C.); Rt. Hon. Norman Tebbit (C.); Rt. Hon. Margaret Thatcher (C.); Dafydd Thomas (PC.); Rt. Hon. John Wakeham (C.); Rt. Hon. Peter Walker (C.); Sir Dennis Walters (C.); Kenneth Warren (C.); Rt. Hon. Bernard Weatherill (The Speaker); Michael Welsh (Lab.); Rt. Hon. George Younger (C.).

The following MPs have not been selected to stand for their present constituency at the next General Election (as at July 31, 1991):

Sydney Bidwell (Lab.); Ronald Brown (Lab.); John Hughes (Lab.); Sir Anthony Meyer (C.).

THE HOUSE OF COMMONS BY CONSTITUENCIES, JUNE 1987

The figures following the name of each constituency denote the total number of electors in the Parliamentary division at the General Election of June 11, 1987.

An asterisk * denotes membership of the last Parliament. The majority in the 1983 General Election (and in any subsequent by-election) is shown below the 1987 result. For **by-elections** since the 1987 General Election, *see* pp. 239–40.

Abbreviations — *C.* = Conservative; *DUP* = Democratic Unionist Party; *Ind.* = Independent; *L./All., SDP/ All.* = Liberal and Social Democratic Alliance; *Lab.* = Labour; *OUP* = Official Unionist Party; *PC* = Plaid Cymru; *SDLP* = Social Democratic and Labour Party; *SDP* = Social Democratic Party; *SF* = Sinn Fein; *SLD* = Social and Liberal Democrat; *SNP* = Scottish National Party; *UPUP* = Ulster Popular Unionist Party.

All. = Alliance Party (NI); *BN* = British Nationalist; *Bread* = Creek Road Fresh Bread Party; *BT* = Blancmange Thrower; *CD* = Christian Democrat; *CMNHY* = Common Market No, Hanging Yes; *Comm.* = Communist Party; *CPRP* = Capital Punishment Referendum Party; *CPWSML* = Capital Punishment Will Save More Lives; *CS* = Christian Socialist Opposing Secret Masonic Government; *DC* = Democratic Commonwealth Party; *Dem.* = Independent Democrat; *Ecol.* = Ecology (NI); *Ex. Lab. Mod.* = Ex Labour Moderate; *Falk.* = Right of Falkland Islands to elect Westminster MP; *FDP* = Fancy Dress Party; *Fell.* = Fellowship Party; *FP* = Feudal Party; *Gait. Lab.* = Gaitskell Labour; *Gold* = Gold Party; *Grem.* = Gremloid; *Grn.* = Green Party; *HP* = Human Party; *ICC* = Independent Community Campaigner, East Oxford People; *ICN* = Independent Christian Nationalist; *LAO* = Law and Order; *LAPP* = Let's Have Another Party Party; *LM* = Loony Official Monster Raving Party; *ML* = Moderate Labour Party; *NFFG* = National Front Flag Group; *NPR* = National People's Rally; *OFP* = Official Fidgeyitous Party; *OOBPC* = Only Official Best Party Candidate; *OSM* = Orkney and Shetland Movement; *PIP* = Public Independent Plaintiff; *Prot. U.* = Protestant Unionist; *PRP* = Protestant Reformation Party; *RABIES* = Rainbow Alliance Brixton Insane Extremist Section; *RCP* = Return Capital Punishment; *Real U.* = Real Unionist; *RF* = Red Front; *Ret.* = Retired; *RRPRC* = Revolutionary Reform Party Representative of Christ; *SE* = Spare the Earth; *SPGB* = Socialist Party of Great Britain; *WP* = Workers' Party (NI); *WRP* = Workers' Revolutionary Party.

ENGLAND

Aldershot (Hants)
E. 80,797

*J. M. G. Critchley, C.	....	35,272
R. A. Hargreaves, *L./All.*	.	17,488
I. H. Pearson, *Lab.*	....	7,061
C. maj.	......	17,784
(June '83, C. maj. 12,218)		

Aldridge-Brownhills
(W. Midlands)
E. 62,129

*R. C. S. Shepherd, C.	.....	26,434
C. Duncan, *Lab.*	....	14,038
G. Betteridge, *SDP/All.*		9,084
C. maj.	....	12,396
(June '83, C. maj. 12,284)		

Altrincham and Sale
(Gtr. Manchester)
E. 67,611

*Sir F. Montgomery, C.	....	27,746
J. Mulholland, *L./All.*	....	13,518
D. Hinder, *Lab.*	....	10,617
C. maj.	....	14,228
(June '83, C. maj. 10,911)		

Amber Valley (Derbys)
E. 68,478

*P. A. C. L. Oppenheim, C.		28,603
D. M. Bookbinder, *Lab.*	..	19,103
S. Reynolds, *L./All.*	......	7,904
C. maj.	....	9,500
(June '83, C. maj. 3,318)		

Arundel (W. Sussex)
E. 78,683

*R. M. Marshall, C.	....	34,356
Dr. J. M. M. Walsh, *L./All.*		15,476
P. Slowe, *Lab.*	....	6,177
C. maj.	....	18,880
(June '83, C. maj. 15,705)		

Ashfield (Notts)
E. 70,937

*D. F. Haynes, Lab.	....	22,812
B. G. Coleman, *C.*	....	18,412
Mrs. F. B. Stein, *L./All.*	..	13,542
Lab. maj.	....	4,400
(June '83, Lab. maj. 6,087)		

Ashford (Kent)
E. 70,052

*H. K. Speed, C.	....	29,978
N. N. Macmillan, *SDP/All.*		14,490
M. J. Wiggins, *Lab.*	......	7,775
Dr. C. A. Porter, *Grn.*	....	778
C. maj.	....	15,488
(June '83, C. maj. 13,911)		

Ashton-under-Lyne
(Gtr. Manchester)
E. 58,440

*Rt. Hon. R. E. Sheldon, Lab.		22,389
H. L. Cadman, *C.*	....	13,103
M. J. Hunter, *L./All.*	......	7,760
Lab. maj.	....	9,286
(June '83, Lab. maj. 7,697)		

Aylesbury (Bucks)
E. 76,919

*Rt. Hon. T. H. F. Raison,		
C.	....	32,970
M. A. Soole, *SDP/All.*	...	16,412
Ms. J. Larner, *Lab.*	......	7,936
C. maj.	....	16,558
(June '83, C. maj. 14,920)		

Banbury (Oxon)
E. 69,455

*A. B. Baldry, C.	....	29,716
D. C. Rowland, *SDP/All.*		12,386
J. A. Honeybone, *Lab.*	...	10,789
C. maj.	....	17,330
(June '83, C. maj. 13,025)		

Barking (Gtr. London)
E. 51,639

*Ms. J. Richardson, Lab.	..	15,307
W. K. Sharp, *C.*	....	11,898
J. K. Gibb, *L./All.*	....	7,336
Lab. maj.	....	3,409
(June '83, Lab. maj. 4,026)		

Barnsley (S. Yorks)
E. 55,902

CENTRAL *E.* 55,902

E. E. Illsley, Lab.	....	26,139
Mrs. V. Prais, *C.*	....	7,088
Mrs. S. A. M. Holland, *L./ All.*	....	5,928
Lab. maj.	....	19,051
(June '83, Lab. maj. 14,173)		

EAST *E.* 53,505

*T. Patchett, Lab.	....	28,948
W. J. Clappison, *C.*	......	5,437
G. J. Griffiths, *L./All.*	....	4,482
Lab. maj.	....	23,511
(June '83, Lab. maj. 17,492)		

WEST AND PENISTONE *E.* 61,091

*A. McKay, Lab.	....	26,498
A. J. C. Duncan, *C.*	......	12,307
R. Hall, *SDP/All.*	....	7,409
Lab. maj.	....	14,191
(June '83, Lab. maj. 10,342)		

Barrow and Furness (Cumbria)
E. 69,288

*C. S. Franks, C.	....	25,431
P. Phizacklea, *Lab.*	......	21,504
R. W. Phelps, *SDP/All.*	...	7,799
C. maj.	....	3,927
(June '83, C. maj. 4,577)		

Basildon (Essex)
E. 68,500

*D. A. A. Amess, C.	....	21,858
J. G. H. Fulbrook, *Lab.*	...	19,209
R. M. Auvray, *L./All.*	....	9,139
C. maj.	....	2,649
(June '83, C. maj. 1,379)		

Basingstoke (Hants)
E. 78,003

*A. R. F. Hunter, C.	....	33,657
D. Bennett, *SDP/All.*	....	15,764
P. Daden, *Lab.*	....	10,632
C. maj.	....	17,893
(June '83, C. maj. 12,450)		

Bassetlaw (Notts)
E. 68,043

*J. W. Ashton, *Lab.*		25,385
D. R. J. Selves, *C.*		19,772
W. G. Smith, *SDP/All.*	...	7,616
Lab. maj.		5,613
(June '83, Lab. maj. 3,831)		

Bath (Avon)
E. 65,246

C. F. Patten, C.		23,515
J. M. Dean, *SDP/All.*	...	22,103
Mrs. J. Smith, *Lab.*		5,507
D. N. Wall, *Grn.*		687
C. maj.		1,412
(June '83, C. maj. 5,304)		

Batley and Spen (W. Yorks)
E. 74,347

Mrs. E. J. Peacock, C.	....	25,512
K. J. Woolmer, *Lab.*		24,150
K. Burke, *SDP/All.*		8,372
A. Harrison, *ML*		689
C. maj.		1,362
(June '83, C. maj. 870)		

Battersea (Gtr. London)
E. 66,979

J. C. Bowis, *C.*		20,945
*A. Dubs, *Lab.*		20,088
D. I. Harries, *SDP/All.*	...	5,634
Ms. S. G. Willington, *Grn.*		559
A. B. Bell, *WRP.*		116
C. maj.		857
(June '83, Lab. maj. 3,276)		

Beaconsfield (Bucks)
E. 67,713

T. J. Smith, C.		33,324
D. H. Ive, *L./All.*		11,985
K. J. Harper, *Lab.*		5,203
C. maj.		21,339
(June '83, C. maj. 18,300)		

Beckenham (Gtr. London)
E. 60,110

Sir P. C. Goodhart, C.	....	24,903
C. G. Darracott, *L./All.*	...	11,439
K. G. Ritchie, *Lab.*		7,888
C. maj.		13,464
(June '83, C. maj. 12,670)		

Bedfordshire

MID E. 80,673

N. W. Lyell, QC, C.		37,411
N. C. Hills, *SDP/All.*		14,560
J. Heywood, *Lab.*		11,463
C. maj.		22,851
(June '83, C. maj. 17,381)		

NORTH E. 73,536

Sir T. H. H. Skeet, C.	.....	29,845
Mrs. J. V. Lennon, *L./All.*		13,340
C. B. Henderson, *Lab.*	....	13,140
C. D. Slee, *OOBPC*		435
C. maj.		16,505
(June '83, C. maj. 13,849)		

SOUTH WEST E. 78,956

W. D. Madel, C.	...	36,140
J. R. Burrow, *SDP/All.*	...	13,835
P. H. Dimoldenberg, *Lab.*	..	11,352
P. J. Rollings, *Grn.*		822
C. maj.		22,305
(June '83, C. maj. 15,731)		

Berkshire East
E. 87,820

A. J. MacKay, C.		39,094
Mrs. L. A. Murray, *SDP/All.*		16,468
R. J. E. Evans, *Lab.*		9,287
C. maj.		22,626
(June '83, C. maj. 16,099)		

Berwick-upon-Tweed (Nthmb)
E. 54,378

A. J. Beith, L./All.	...	21,903
T. Middleton, *C.*		12,400
S. Lambert, *Lab.*		7,360
N. Pamphilion, *Grn.*		379
L./All. maj.		9,503
(June '83, L./All. maj. 8,215)		

Bethnal Green and Stepney
(Gtr. London)
E. 55,769

*Rt. Hon. P. D. Shore, *Lab.*	15,490
J. A. Shaw, *L./All.*		10,206
Lady O. H. Maitland, *C.*	..	6,176
Ms. S. Gasquoine, *Comm.*	.	232
Lab. maj.		5,284
(June '83, Lab. maj. 6,358)		

Beverley (Humberside)
E. 78,923

J. D. Cran, *C.*		31,459
J. Bryant, *L./All.*		18,864
M. Shaw, *Lab.*		9,901
C. maj.		12,595
(June '83, C. maj. 13,869)		

Bexhill and Battle
(E. Sussex)
E. 65,288

C. F. Wardle, C.		33,570
R. Kiernan, *SDP/All.*	....	13,051
D. K. Watts, *Lab.*		3,903
C. maj.		20,519
(June '83, C. maj. 19,746)		

Bexleyheath
(Gtr. London)
E. 59,448

C. D. Townsend, C.	......	24,866
B. C. Standen, *L./All.*	....	13,179
J. F. Little, *Lab.*		8,218
C. maj.		11,687
(June '83, C. maj. 10,258)		

Billericay (Essex)
E. 79,535

Mrs. T. E. Gorman, C.	....	33,741
M. Birch, *SDP/All.*		15,755
R. Howitt, *Lab.*		11,942
C. maj.		17,986
(June '83, C. maj. 14,615)		

Birkenhead (Merseyside)
E. 65,662

*F. Field, *Lab.*		27,883
K. J. Costa, *C.*		12,511
R. Kemp, *L./All.*		7,095
Lab. maj.		15,372
(June '83, Lab. maj. 9,714)		

Birmingham (W. Midlands)

EDGBASTON E. 54,416

Dame J. C. J. Knight, DBE, C.		18,595
J. Wilton, *Lab.*		10,014
J. C. Binns, *SDP/All.*		7,843
P. Simpson, *Grn.*		559
S. T. Hardwick, *Ind. C.*	...	307
C. maj.		8,581
(June '83, C. maj. 11,418)		

ERDINGTON E. 54,179

*R. Corbett, *Lab.*		17,037
P. J. Johnston, *C.*	......	14,570
N. Biddlestone, *SDP/All.*	5,530
Lab. maj.		2,467
(June '83, Lab. maj. 231)		

HALL GREEN E. 61,148

A. R. Hargreaves, *C.*	...	20,478
Mrs. E. Brook, *Lab.*		12,857
M. Wilkes, *SDP/All.*		12,323
C. maj.		7,621
(June '83, C. maj. 9,373)		

HODGE HILL E. 59,296

*T. A. G. Davis, *Lab.*		19,872
S. Eyre, *C.*		15,083
K. G. Hardeman, *L./All.*	...	5,868
Lab. maj.		4,789
(June '83, Lab. maj. 5,092)		

LADYWOOD E. 58,761

*Ms. C. Short, *Lab.*	......	21,971
S. T. Lee, *C.*		11,943
G. S. Sangha, *SDP/All.*	..	3,532
Ms. J. Millington, *Grn.*	...	650
Lab. maj.		10,028
(June '83, Lab. maj. 9,030)		

NORTHFIELD E. 73,319

*R. D. King, *C.*		24,024
J. F. Spellar, *Lab.*		20,889
J. Gordon, *SDP/All.*		8,319
C. maj.		3,135
(June '83, C. maj. 2,760)		

PERRY BARR E. 73,767

*J. W. Rooker, *Lab.*	....	25,894
J. D. B. Taylor, *C.*		18,961
D. D. Webb, *L./All.*		6,514
Lab. maj.		6,933
(June '83, Lab. maj. 7,402)		

SELLY OAK E. 72,213

A. M. Beaumont-Dark, C.	23,305
A. Bore, *Lab.*		20,721
Mrs. C. Cane, *L./All.*		8,128
Ms. M. Hackett, *Grn*	.....	611
C. maj.		2,584
(June '83, C. maj. 5,396)		

SMALL HEATH *E.* 56,722
Rt. Hon. D. H. Howell, Lab. 22,787
P. Nischal, *C.* 7,266
J. A. M. Hemming, *L./All.* 3,600
A. Clawley, *Grn.* 559
P. R. Sheppard, *Comm.* ... 154
Lab. maj. 15,521
(June '83, Lab. maj. 15,252)

SPARKBROOK *E.* 53,093
*Rt. Hon. R. S. G. Hattersley,
Lab.* 20,513
N. A. Khan, *C.* 8,654
R. Dimmick, *SDP/All.* 3,803
R. Ambler, *Grn.* 526
P. Khan, *RF.* 229
Lab. maj. 11,859
(June '83, Lab. maj. 10,548)

YARDLEY *E.* 56,957
A. D. G. Bevan, C. 17,931
G. Edge, *Lab.* 15,409
L. Smith, *L./All.* 8,734
C. maj. 2,522
(June '83, C. maj. 2,865)

Bishop Auckland (Durham)
E. 72,147
D. Foster, Lab. 25,648
R. Wight, *C.* 18,613
G. Irwin, *L./All.* 9,195
Lab. maj. 7,035
(June '83, Lab. maj. 4,306)

Blaby (Leics)
E. 77,094
Rt. Hon. N. Lawson, C. ... 37,732
R. E. Lustig, *L./All.* 15,556
J. M. Roberts, *Lab.* 9,046
C. maj. 22,176
(June '83, C. maj. 17,116)

Blackburn (Lancs)
E. 74,801
J. W. Straw, Lab. 27,965
Mrs. A. C. Cheetham, *C.* .. 22,468
M. A. Ali, *SDP/All.* 5,602
Lab. maj. 5,497
(June '83, Lab. maj. 3,055)

Blackpool (Lancs)
NORTH *E.* 58,893
N. A. Miscampbell, QC, C. 20,680
E. Kirton, *Lab.* 13,359
C. J. Heyworth, *L./All.* ... 9,032
C. maj. 7,321
(June '83, C. maj. 10,152)

SOUTH *E.* 57,567
*Rt. Hon. Sir P. A. R. Blaker,
KCMG, C.* 20,312
Mrs. S. Baugh, *Lab.* 13,568
J. Allitt, *SDP/All.* 8,405
C. maj. 6,744
(June '83, C. maj. 10,138)

Blaydon (Tyne & Wear)
E. 66,301
J. D. McWilliam, Lab. ... 25,277
V. P. Nunn, *SDP/All.* ... 12,789
P. R. Pescod, *C.* 12,147
Lab. maj. 12,488
(June '83, Lab. maj. 7,222)

Blyth Valley (Nthmb)
E. 59,104

R. Campbell, *Lab.* 19,604
Miss R. M. Brownlow,
SDP/All. 18,751
Dr R. Kinghorn, *C.* 7,823
Lab. maj. 853
(June '83, Lab. maj. 3,243)

Bolsover (Derbys)
E. 65,452
D. E. Skinner, Lab. 28,453
M. R. Lingens, *C.* 14,333
M. H. Fowler, *SDP/All.* .. 7,836
Lab. maj. 14,120
(June '83, Lab. maj. 13,848)

Bolton (Gtr. Manchester)
NORTH EAST *E.* 59,382
P. G. Thurnham, C. 20,742
F. R. White, *Lab.* 19,929
J. H. Alcock, *SDP/All.* ... 6,060
C. maj. 813
(June '83, C. maj. 2,443)

SOUTH EAST *E.* 65,932
D. W. Young, Lab. 26,791
S. Windle, *C.* 15,410
F. Harasiwka, *L./All.* 7,161
Lab. maj. 11,381
(June ' 83, Lab. maj. 8,753)

WEST *E.* 69,843
T. G. Sackville, C. 24,779
G. J. Harkin, *Lab.* 20,186
D. T. Eccles, *SDP/All.* 10,936
C. maj. 4,593
(June '83, C. maj. 7,152)

Boothferry (Humberside)
E. 75,176

D. M. Davis, *C.* 31,716
Mrs. J. D. Davies, *L./All.* .. 12,746
R. Donson, *Lab.* 12,498
C. maj. 18,970
(June '83, C. maj. 17,420)

Bootle (Merseyside)
E. 71,765
A. Roberts, Lab. 34,975
P. R. Papworth, *C.* 10,498
P. Denham, *SDP/All.* 6,820
Lab. maj. 24,477
(June '83, Lab. maj. 15,139)
(*See also* pp. 239, 240)

Bosworth (Leics)
E. 77,186

D. A. S. Tredinnick, *C.* ... 34,145
D. C. Bill, *L./All.* 17,129
R. S. Hall, *Lab.* 10,787
Mrs. D. Freer, *Grn* 660
C. maj. 17,016
(June '83, C. maj. 17,294)

Bournemouth (Dorset)
EAST *E.* 75,232
D. A. Atkinson, C. 30,925
Dr. J. Millward, *L./All.* ... 16,242
I. A. Taylor, *Lab.* 5,885
C. maj. 14,683
(June '83, C. maj. 11,416)

WEST *E.* 74,444
J. V. Butterfill, C. 30,117
P. G. M. Craven, *SDP/All.* 17,466
R. W. Jones, *Lab.* 7,018
C. maj. 12,651
(June '83, C. maj. 13,331)

Bow and Poplar (Gtr. London)
E. 59,178

Ms. M. Gordon, *Lab.* 15,746
E. Flounders, *L./All.* 11,115
D. C. Hughes, *C.* 6,810
P. S. Chappell, *WRP* 274
Lab. maj. 4,631
(June '83, Lab. maj. 5,861)

Bradford (W. Yorks)
NORTH *E.* 67,430
C. P. Wall, *Lab.* 21,009
G. J. Lawler, C. 19,376
A. M. Berkeley, *SDP/All.* 8,656
Lab. maj. 1,633
(June '83, C. maj. 1,602)
(*See also* p. 240)

SOUTH *E.* 69,588
G. R. Cryer, *Lab.* 21,230
G. T. Hall, *C.* 20,921
T. Lindley, *SDP/All.* 9,109
Lab. maj. 309
(June '83, Lab. maj. 110)

WEST *E.* 70,763
M. F. Madden, Lab. 25,775
I. Duncan-Smith, *C.* 18,224
M. Moghal, *SDP/All.* 5,657
Lab. maj. 7,551
(June '83, Lab. maj. 3,337)

Braintree (Essex)
E. 76,994
A. H. Newton, OBE, C. 32,978
I. G. Bing, *SDP/All.* 16,121
B. Stapleton, *Lab.* 11,764
C. maj. 16,857
(June '83, C. maj. 13,441)

Brent (Gtr. London)
EAST *E.* 61,020
K. R. Livingstone, *Lab.* ... 16,772
Miss H. S. Crawley, *C.* ... 15,119
D. W. Finkelstein, *SDP/
All.* 5,710
R. Q. Dooley, *Ind. Lab.* ... 1,035
M. Litvinoff, *Grn.* 716
Lab. maj. 1,653
(June '83, Lab. maj. 4,834)

NORTH *E.* 63,081
Dr. R. Boyson, C. 26,823
P. Patel, *Lab.* 11,103
C. Mularczyk, *SDP/All.* 6,868
C. maj. 15,720
(June '83, C. maj. 14,651)

SOUTH *E.* 62,772
P. Y. Boateng, *Lab.* 21,140
A. J. Paterson, *C.* 13,209
M. T. Harskin, *L./All.* 6,375
Lab. maj. 7,931
(June '83, Lab. maj. 10,519)

Brentford and Isleworth
(Gtr. London)
E. 71,715

*Rt. Hon. Sir B. J. Hayhoe, C.		26,230
Ms. A. Keen, *Lab.*		18,277
Dr. D. M. W. Wilks, *SDP/ All.*		9,626
T. Cooper, *Grn.*		849
C. maj.		7,953
(June '83, C. maj. 9,387)		

Brentwood and Ongar (Essex)
E. 67,521

*R. A. McCrindle, C.		32,258
N. R. Amor, *L./All.*		13,337
J. W. Orpe, *Lab.*		7,042
Mrs. M. E. Willis, *Grn.*		686
C. maj.		18,921
(June '83, C. maj. 14,202)		

Bridgwater (Somerset)
E. 67,480

*Rt. Hon. T. J. King, C.		27,177
C. Clarke, *SDP/All.*		15,982
J. Turner, *Lab.*		9,594
C. maj.		11,195
(June '83, C. maj. 10,697)		

Bridlington (Humberside)
E. 80,126

*J. E. Townend, C.		32,351
E. I. Marshall, *SDP/All.*		15,030
L. M. Bird, *Lab.*		10,653
R. D. Myerscough, *Grn.*		983
C. maj.		17,321
(June '83, C. maj. 16,609)		

Brigg and Cleethorpes
(Humberside)
E. 80,096

*M. R. Brown, C.		29,723
I. Powney, *L./All.*		17,475
T. Geraghty, *Lab.*		13,876
C. maj.		12,248
(June '83, C. maj. 12,189)		

Brighton (E. Sussex)

KEMPTOWN *E.* 60,271

*A. Bowden, MBE, C.		24,031
J. S. Bassam, *Lab.*		14,771
C. Berry, *L./All.*		6,080
C. maj.		9,260
(June '83, C. maj. 9,378)		

PAVILION *E.* 58,910

*Rt. Hon. H. J. Amery, C.		22,056
D. S. Hill, *Lab.*		12,914
K. F. Carey, *SDP/All.*		8,459
C. maj.		9,142
(June '83, C. maj. 11,132)		

Bristol (Avon)

EAST *E.* 63,840

*J. Sayeed, C.		21,906
R. R. Thomas, *Lab.*		17,783
D. M. E. Foster, *L./All.*		10,247
P. M. Kingston, *NFFG*		286
C. maj.		4,123
(June '83, C. maj. 1,789)		

NORTH WEST *E.* 72,876

*M. C. Stern, C.		26,953
T. W. Walker, *Lab.*		20,001
J. M. G. Kirkaldy, *SDP/ All.*		10,885
C. maj.		6,952
(June '83, C. maj. 6,327)		

SOUTH *E.* 68,733

Ms. D. Primarolo, *Lab.*		20,798
P. S. Cutcher, *C.*		19,394
Mrs. H. S. Long, *SDP/All.*		9,952
G. R. Vowles, *Grn.*		600
Ms. C. M. Meghji, *RF*		149
Lab. maj.		1,404
(June '83, Lab. maj. 4,419)		

WEST *E.* 72,357

*Hon. W. A. Waldegrave, C.		24,695
G. R. P. Ferguson, *L./All.*		16,992
Mrs. M. C. Georghiou, *Lab.*		11,337
Mrs. G. A. Dorey, *Grn.*		1,096
Ms. V. Ralph, *Comm.*		134
C. maj.		7,703
(June '83, C. maj. 10,178)		

Bromsgrove (H & W)
E. 69,494

*H. D. Miller, C.		29,051
J. D. Ward, *Lab..*		12,366
D. L. Cropp, *SDP/All.*		11,663
C. maj.		16,685
(June '83, C. maj. 17,175)		

Broxbourne (Herts)
E. 70,631

*Mrs. M. A. Roe, C.		33,567
Mrs. E. Yates, *L./All.*		10,572
P. Parry, *Lab.*		8,984
C. maj.		22,995
(June '83, C. maj. 17,466)		

Broxtowe (Notts)
E. 71,780

*J. T. Lester, C.		30,462
K. Fleet, *Lab.*		13,811
K. M. Melton, *L./All.*		12,562
C. maj.		16,651
(June '83, C. maj. 15,078)		

Buckingham
E. 70,036

*G. G. H. Walden, CMG, C.		32,162
C. M. Burke, *L./All.*		13,636
M. Groucutt, *Lab.*		9,053
C. maj.		18,526
(June '83, C. maj. 13,968)		

Burnley (Lancs)
E. 65,956

*P. L. Pike, Lab.		25,140
H. Elletson, *C.*		17,583
R. H. Baker, *SDP/All.*		9,241
Lab. maj.		7,557
(June '83, Lab. maj. 770)		

Burton (Staffs)
E. 73,252

*I. J. Lawrence, QC, C.		29,160
D. Heptonstall, *Lab.*		19,330
K. A. Hemsley, *L./All.*		9,046
C. maj.		9,830
(June '83, C. maj. 11,647)		

Bury (Gtr. Manchester)

NORTH *E.* 67,961

*A. J. H. Burt, C.		28,097
D. Crausby, *Lab.*		21,186
D. Vasmer, *L./All.*		6,804
C. maj.		6,911
(June '83, C. maj. 2,792)		

SOUTH *E.* 65,039

*D. A. G. Sumberg, C.		23,878
D. Boden, *Lab.*		21,199
D. A. Eyre, *SDP/All.*		6,772
C. maj.		2,679
(June '83, C. maj. 3,720)		

Bury St. Edmunds (Suffolk)
E. 76,619

*Sir E. W. Griffiths, C.		33,672
Sir R. Harland, *SDP/All.*		12,214
C. L. Greene, *Lab.*		9,841
Ms. I. M. J. Wakelam, *Grn.*		1,057
C. maj.		21,458
(June '83, C. maj. 16,122)		

Calder Valley (W. Yorks)
E. 73,398

*D. Thompson, C.		25,892
D. M. Chaytor, *Lab.*		19,847
D. T. Shutt, *L./All.*		13,761
C. maj.		6,045
(June '83, C. maj. 7,999)		

Cambridge
E. 69,336

*R. V. Rhodes James, C.		21,624
Mrs. S. V. T. B. Williams, *SDP/All.*		16,564
C. J. Howard, *Lab.*		15,319
Ms. M. E. Wright, *Grn.*		597
C. maj.		5,060
(June '83, C. maj. 5,968)		

Cambridgeshire

NORTH EAST *E.* 74,231

M. D. Moss, *C.*		26,983
*C. R. Freud, *L./All.*		25,555
R. J. Harris, *Lab.*		4,891
C. maj.		1,428
(June '83, L./All. maj. 5,195)		

SOUTH EAST *E.* 73,216

J. E. T. Paice, *C.*		32,901
P. C. Lee, *SDP/All.*		15,399
T. G. Ling, *Lab.*		7,694
C. maj.		17,502
(June '83, C. maj. 13,764)		

SOUTH WEST *E.* 81,658

*Sir J. A. Grant, C.		36,622
D. C. Nicholls, *L./All.*		18,371
Ms. J. Billing, *Lab.*		8,434
C. maj.		18,251
(June '83, C. maj. 13,867)		

Cannock and Burntwood (Staffs)
E. 68,137

*J. G. D. Howarth, C.		24,186
G. E. Roberts, *Lab.*		21,497
N. Stanley, *L./All.*		8,698
C. maj.		2,689
(June '83, C. maj. 2,045)		

Canterbury (Kent)
E. 76,062

J. W. H. Brazier, *C.* 30,273
J. Purchese, *L./All.* 15,382
Ms. L. A. Keen, *Lab.* 9,494
S. Dawe, *Grn.* 947
Miss J. M. White, *ICN* ... 157
  C. maj. 14,891
(June '83, C. maj. 15,742)

Carlisle (Cumbria)
E. 55,053

E. A. Martlew, *Lab.* 18,311
W. G. Hodgson, *C.* 17,395
R. S. Hunt, *SDP/All* 7,655
  Lab. maj. 916
(June '83, Lab. maj. 71)

Carshalton and Wallington
(Gtr. London)
E. 69,120

*F. N. Forman, *C.* 27,984
J. D. Grant, *SDP/All.* 13,575
Mrs. J. G. Baker, *Lab.* 9,440
R. W. Steel, *Grn.* 843
  C. maj. 14,409
(June '83, C. maj. 10,755)

Castle Point (Essex)
E. 65,992

*Rt. Hon. Sir B. R. Braine,
  C. 29,681
Miss A. P. Bastow, *SDP/
  All.* 10,433
W. A. Deal, *Lab.* 9,422
  C. maj. 19,248
(June '83, C. maj. 15,417)

Cheadle
(Gtr. Manchester)
E. 68,332

S. R. Day, *C.* 30,484
A. B. Leah, *L./All.* 19,853
Ms. A. Coffey, *Lab.* 5,037
  C. maj. 10,631
(June '83, C. maj. 9,380)

Chelmsford (Essex)
E. 82,564

S. H. M. Burns, *C.* 35,231
S. G. Mole, *L./All.* 27,470
C. E. Playford, *Lab.* 4,642
A. C. Slade, *Grn.* 486
  C. maj. 7,761
(June '83, C. maj. 378)

Chelsea
(Gtr. London)
E. 49,534

*N. P. Scott, MBE, *C.* 18,443
Mrs. J. M. Ware, *L./All.* .. 5,124
D. J. Ward, *Lab.* 4,406
Ms. N. Kortvelyessy, *Grn.* 587
  C. maj. 13,319
(June '83, C. maj. 12,021)

Cheltenham (Glos)
E. 79,234

*C. G. Irving, *C.* 31,371
R. G. Holme, *L./All.* 26,475
M. Luker, *Lab.* 4,701
  C. maj. 4,896
(June '83, C. maj. 5,518)

Chertsey and Walton (Surrey)
E. 71,448

*G. E. Pattie, *C.* 32,119
Mrs. S. K. Stapely, *SDP/
  All.* 14,650
H. G. Trace, *Lab.* 7,185
  C. maj. 17,469
(June '83, C. maj. 15,699)

Chesham and Amersham
(Bucks)
E. 71,751

*Rt. Hon. Sir I. H. J. L.
  Gilmour, Bt., *C.* 34,504
A. T. Ketteringham, *L./All.* 15,064
P. A. Goulding, *Lab.* 5,170
Mrs. A. G. Darnbrough,
  Grn. 760
  C. maj. 19,440
(June '83, C. maj. 15,879)

Chester, City of
E. 65,845

*Hon. P. H. Morrison, *C.* .. 23,582
D. Robinson, *Lab.* 18,727
R. A. Stunell, *L./All.* 10,262
  C. maj. 4,855
(June '83, C. maj. 9,099)

Chesterfield (Derbys)
E. 70,357

*Rt. Hon. A. N. W. Benn,
  Lab. 24,532
A. H. Rogers, *L./All.* 15,955
R. P Grant, *C.* 13,472
  Lab. maj. 8,577
(June '83, Lab. maj. 7,763)
(March '84, Lab. maj. 6,264)

Chichester (W. Sussex)
E. 81,019

*R. A. Nelson, *C.* 37,274
P. F. Weston, *L./All.* 17,097
D. Morrison, *Lab.* 4,751
I. F. N. Bagnall, *Grn.* 1,196
  C. maj. 20,177
(June '83, C. maj. 20,117)

Chingford (Gtr. London)
E. 56,797

*Rt. Hon. N. B. Tebbit, *C.* .. 27,110
J. G. Williams, *L./All.* 9,155
Ms. M. I. Cosin, *Lab.* 6,650
Ms. E. Newton, *Grn.* 634
  C. maj. 17,955
(June '83, C. maj. 12,414)

Chipping Barnet (Gtr. London)
E. 60,876

*S. B. Chapman, *C.* 24,686
J. Skinner, *L./All.* 9,815
D. Perkin, *Lab.* 8,115
  C. maj. 14,871
(June '83, C. maj. 12,393)

Chislehurst (Gtr. London)
E. 55,535

*R. E. Sims, *C.* 24,165
R. A. Younger-Ross, *L./All.* 9,658
S. H. Ward, *Lab.* 8,115
  C. maj. 14,507
(June '83, C. maj. 12,061)

Chorley (Lancs)
E. 78,541

*D. R. Dover, *C.* 29,015
A. J. Watmough, *Lab.* 20,958
I. A. Simpson, *L./All.* 9,706
A. S. Holgate, *Grn.* 714
  C. maj. 8,057
(June '83, C. maj. 10,275)

Christchurch (Dorset)
E. 70,964

*R. J. Adley, *C.* 35,656
Miss H. J. McKenzie, *SDP/
  All.* 13,282
Ms. C. E. Longhurst, *Lab.* 5,174
  C. maj. 22,374
(June '83, C. maj. 19,738)

Cirencester and Tewkesbury
(Glos)
E. 84,071

*Rt. Hon. N. Ridley, *C.* ... 36,272
P. T. Beckerlegge, *L./All.* .. 23,610
J. D. Naysmith, *Lab.* 5,342
M. A. Curtis, *Male OAP* ... 283
  C. maj. 12,662
(June '83, C. maj. 13,827)

**The City of London and
Westminster South**
E. 57,428

*Hon. P. L. Brooke, *C.* 19,333
Ms. J. C. G. Smithard, *SDP/
  All* 7,291
Ms. R. E. Bush, *Lab.* 6,821
  C. maj. 12,042
(June '83, C. maj. 13,387)

Colchester (Essex)
E. 82,420

NORTH   E. 84,392
*Sir P. A. F. Buck, QC, *C.* .. 32,747
A. Hayman, *SDP/All.* 19,124
R. A. Green, *Lab.* 10,768
  C. maj. 13,623
(June '83, C. maj. 15,048)

SOUTH, AND MALDON   E. 84,392
*Rt. Hon. J. Wakeham, *C.* .. 34,894
J. W. Stevens, *SDP/All.* .. 19,411
Ms. S. Bigwood, *Lab.* 9,229
  C. maj. 15,483
(June '83, C. maj. 12,165)

Colne Valley (W. Yorks)
E. 70,199

G. E. G. Riddick, *C.* 20,457
N. J. Priestley, *L./All.* 18,780
J. A. Harman, *Lab.* 16,353
M. R. Mullany, *Grn.* 614
  C. maj. 1,677
(June '83, L./All. maj. 3,146)

Congleton (Cheshire)
E. 68,172

*Mrs. J. A. Winterton, *C.* .. 26,513
I. M. Brodie-Browne, *L./
  All.* 18,544
M. Knowles, *Lab.* 9,810
  C. maj. 7,969
(June '83, C. maj. 8,459)

Copeland (Cumbria)
E. 54,695

Dr. J. A. Cunningham, Lab.		20,999
A. R. M. Toft, *C.*		19,105
E. T. Colgan, *SDP/All.*		4,052
R. A. Gibson, *Grn.*		319
Lab. maj.		1,894
(June '83, Lab. maj. 1,837)		

Corby (Northants)
E. 66,119

W. R. Powell, C.		23,323
H. A. Feather, *Lab.*		21,518
T. G. Whittington, *L./All.*		7,805
C. maj.		1,805
(June '83, C. maj. 3,168)		

Cornwall

NORTH *E.* 72,375

G. A. Neale, C.		29,862
M. N. Mitchell, *L./All.*		24,180
Ms. C. Herries, *Lab.*		3,719
C. maj.		5,682
(June '83, C. maj. 5,059)		

SOUTH EAST *E.* 70,248

R. A. Hicks, C.		28,818
I. P. Tunbridge, *L./All.*		22,211
P. A. Clark, *Lab.*		4,847
C. maj.		6,607
(June '83, C. maj. 8,354)		

Coventry (W. Midlands)

NORTH EAST *E.* 67,479

J. Hughes, *Lab.*		25,832
C. Prior, *C.*		13,965
S. Wood, *L./All.*		7,502
A. McNally, *Comm.*		310
Lab. maj.		11,867
(June '83, Lab. maj. 8,775)		

NORTH WEST *E.* 53,090

G. Robinson, Lab.		19,450
J. Powell, *C.*		13,787
T. Jones, *SDP/All.*		6,455
Lab. maj.		5,663
(June '83, Lab. maj. 3,038)		

SOUTH EAST *E.* 51,880

D. J. Nellist, Lab.		17,969
A. Grant, *C.*		11,316
F. Devine, *SDP/All.*		8,095
N. Hutchinson, *Grn.*		479
Lab. maj.		6,653
(June '83, Lab. maj. 2,682)		

SOUTH WEST *E.* 65,567

J. P. Butcher, C.		22,318
R. E. G. Slater, *Lab.*		19,108
R. Wheway, *L./All.*		10,166
C. maj.		3,210
(June '83, C. maj. 6,447)		

Crawley (W. Sussex)
E. 72,076

Hon. A. N. W. Soames, C.		29,259
P. J. Leo, *Lab.*		17,121
D. N. Simmons, *SDP/All.*		12,674
C. maj.		12,138
(June '83, C. maj. 11,814)		

Crewe and Nantwich (Cheshire)
E. 72,961

Hon. Mrs. G. P. Dunwoody, Lab.		25,457
Mrs. A. F. Browning, *C.*		24,365
Dr. K. N. Roberts, *SDP/All.*		8,022
Lab. maj.		1,092
(June '83, Lab. maj. 290)		

Crosby (Merseyside)
E. 83,914

G. M. Thornton, C.		30,836
A. F. S. Donovan, *SDP/All.*		23,989
C. W. Cheetham, *Lab.*		11,992
C. maj.		6,847
(June '83, C. maj. 3,401)		

Croydon (Gtr. London)

CENTRAL *E.* 55,410

Rt. Hon. J. E. M. Moore, C.		22,133
Mrs. B. T. Prentice, *Lab.*		9,516
T. Burgess, *SDP/All.*		7,435
C. maj.		12,617
(June '83, C. maj. 11,821)		

NORTH EAST *E.* 63,129

Rt. Hon. B. B. Weatherill, (The Speaker)		24,188
Miss C. Patrick, *Lab.*		11,669
J. D. Goldie, *SDP/All.*		8,128
The Speaker maj.		12,519
(June '83, C. maj. 11,627)		

NORTH WEST *E.* 57,369

H. J. Malins, C.		18,665
M. H. Wicks, *Lab.*		14,677
L. A. Rowe, *L./All.*		6,363
C. maj.		3,988
(June '83, C. maj. 4,092)		

SOUTH *E.* 65,085

Sir W. G. Clark, C.		30,732
I. Morrison, *L./All.*		11,669
G. R. Davies, *Lab.*		4,679
P. C. Baldwin, *Grn.*		900
C. maj.		19,063
(June '83, C. maj. 17,440)		

Dagenham (Gtr. London)
E. 61,714

B. C. Gould, Lab.		18,454
R. J. M. Neill, *C.*		15,985
J. Carter, *SDP/All*		7,088
Lab. maj.		2,469
(June '83, Lab. maj. 2,997)		

Darlington (Durham)
E. 65,940

M. Fallon, C.		24,831
O. O'Brien, *Lab.*		22,170
A. Collinge, *L./All.*		6,289
C. maj.		2,661
(June '83, C. maj. 3,438)		

Dartford (Kent)
E. 72,632

R. J. Dunn, C.		30,685
B. J. Clarke, *Lab.*		15,756
M. G. Bruce, *SDP/All.*		10,439
K. J. Davenport, *FDP*		491
C. maj.		14,929
(June '83, C. maj. 13,563)		

Daventry (Northants)
E. 69,241

T. E. Boswell, *C.*		31,353
I. R. Miller, *L./All.*		11,663
Mrs. L. M. A. W. Koumi, *Lab.*		11,097
C. maj.		19,690
(June '83, C. maj. 13,136)		

Davyhulme (Gtr. Manchester)
E. 65,558

W. S. Churchill, C.		23,633
J. Nicholson, *Lab.*		15,434
D. I. Wrigley, *L./All.*		11,637
C. maj.		8,199
(June '83, C. maj. 9,014)		

Denton and Reddish
(Gtr. Manchester)
E. 69,533

A. F. Bennett, Lab.		26,023
P. Slater, *C.*		17,773
T. I. Huffer, *SDP/All.*		8,697
Lab. maj.		8,250
(June '83, Lab. maj. 5,125)		

Derby

NORTH *E.* 71,738

G. Knight, C.		26,561
P. Whitehead, *Lab.*		20,236
S. F. Connolly, *L./All.*		7,268
E. Wall, *Grn.*		291
C. maj.		6,325
(June '83, C. maj. 3,506)		

SOUTH *E.* 68,825

Mrs. M. M. Beckett, Lab.		21,003
P. F. Leighton, *C.*		19,487
Ms. P. N. Mellor, *SDP/All.*		7,608
Lab. maj.		1,516
(June '83, Lab. maj. 421)		

Derbyshire

NORTH EAST *E.* 70,314

H. Barnes, *Lab.*		24,747
J. H. Hayes, *C.*		21,027
S. P. Hardy, *SDP/All.*		9,985
Lab. maj.		3,720
(June '83, Lab. maj. 2,006)		

SOUTH *E.* 80,045

Mrs. E. Currie, C.		31,927
J. D. Whitby, *Lab.*		21,616
J. Edgar, *SDP/All.*		11,509
C. maj.		10,311
(June '83, C. maj. 8,613)		

WEST *E.* 70,782

P. A. McLoughlin, C.		31,224
C. R. Walmsley, *L./All.*		20,697
W. Moore, *Lab.*		6,875
C. maj.		10,527
(June '83, C. maj. 15,325)		
(May '86, C. maj. 100)		

Devizes (Wilts)
E. 86,047

Hon. C. A. Morrison, C.		36,372
Mrs. L. E. Siegle, *L./All.*		18,542
R. W. Buxton, *Lab.*		11,487
C. maj.		17,830
(June '83, C. maj. 15,624)		

Devon

NORTH *E.* 67,474

*A. Speller, C		28,071
M. A. Pinney, *L./All.*		23,602
Ms. A. Marjoram, *Lab.*		3,467
C. maj.		4,469
(June '83, C. maj. 8,727)		

WEST AND TORRIDGE *E.* 74,550

Miss E. H. Nicholson, C.	..	29,484
J. P. A. Burnett, *L./All.*	..	23,016
D. G. Brenton, *Lab.*		4,990
F. Williamson, *Grn.*		1,168
C. maj.		6,468
(June '83, C. maj. 12,351)		

Dewsbury (W. Yorks)
E. 70,836

Mrs. W. A. Taylor, *Lab.*	..	23,668
*J. Whitfield, C.		23,223
A. Mills, *SDP/All.*		8,907
Lab. maj.		445
(June '83, C. maj. 2,086)		

Doncaster (S. Yorks)

CENTRAL *E.* 69,699

*Rt. Hon. H. Walker, Lab.		26,266
Miss P. E. Rawlings, *C.*	...	18,070
J. A. Gore-Browne, *SDP/All.*		7,004
Lab. maj.		8,196
(June '83, Lab. maj. 2,508)		

NORTH *E.* 72,986

*M. C. Welsh, Lab.		32,950
R. J. Shepherd, *C.*		13,015
P. Norwood, *SDP/All.*		7,394
Lab. maj.		19,935
(June '83, Lab. maj. 12,711)		

Don Valley (S. Yorks)
E. 74,500

*M. Redmond, Lab.		29,200
C. H. Gallagher, *C.*		17,733
W. K. Whitaker, *L./All.*	..	8,027
Lab. maj.		11,467
(June '83, Lab. maj. 6,466)		

Dorset

NORTH *E.* 72,844

*N. B. Baker, C.		32,854
Dr. G. W. Tapper, *L./All.*	.	20,947
J. Hanley, *Lab.*		3,819
C. maj.		11,907
(June '83, C. maj. 11,380)		

SOUTH *E.* 72,855

I. C. Bruce, *C.*		30,184
B. Ellis, *L./All.*		15,117
Ms. B. Dench, *Lab.*		9,494
A. Hayler, *Ind.*		244
C. maj.		15,067
(June '83, C. maj. 15,098)		

WEST *E.* 64,360

*J. W. Spicer, C.		28,305
T. Jones, *L./All.*		15,941
D. Watson, *Lab.*		6,123
C. maj.		12,364
(June '83, C. maj. 13,952)		

Dover (Kent)
E. 68,997

D. L. Shaw, *C.*		25,343
S. S. E. W. Love, *Lab.*		18,802
G. Nice, *SDP/All.*		10,942
C. maj.		6,541
(June '83, C. maj. 9,220)		

Dudley (W. Midlands)

EAST *E.* 75,206

*Rt. Hon. Dr. J. W. Gilbert, Lab.		24,942
Mrs. E. Jones, *C.*		21,469
K. Monks, *SDP/All.*		7,965
Lab. maj.		3,473
(June '83, Lab. maj. 5,816)		

WEST *E.* 81,789

*J. G. Blackburn, C.		32,224
G. Titley, *Lab.*		21,980
G. P. T. Lewis, *L./All.*		10,477
C. maj.		10,244
(June '83, C. maj. 8,723)		

Dulwich (Gtr. London)
E. 56,355

*G. F. Bowden, C.		16,563
Miss C. L. Hoey, *Lab.*		16,383
Dr. A. N. G. Harris, *SDP/All.*		5,664
A. Goldie, *Grn.*		432
C. maj.		180
(June '83, C. maj. 1,859)		

Durham

CITY OF *E.* 66,567

G. N. Steinberg, *Lab.*		23,382
D. Stoker, *SDP/All.*		17,257
C. M. Colquhoun, *C.*		11,408
Lab. maj.		6,125
(June '83, Lab. maj. 1,973)		

NORTH *E.* 72,115

*G. H. Radice, Lab.		30,798
Dr. D. Jeary, *SDP/All.*	...	12,365
N. C. Gibbon, *C.*		11,602
Lab. maj.		18,433
(June '83, Lab. maj. 13,437)		

NORTH WEST *E.* 61,302

Ms. H. J. Armstrong, *Lab.*		22,947
D. Iceton, *C.*		12,785
C. Foote Wood, *L./All.*	...	9,349
Lab. maj.		10,162
(June '83, Lab. maj. 6,356)		

Ealing (Gtr. London)

ACTON *E.* 67,176

*Sir G. S. K. Young, Bt., C.	..	25,499
P. J. Portwood, *Lab.*		13,256
S. R. D. Brooks, *SDP/All.*		8,973
C. maj.		12,243
(June '83, C. maj. 10,092)		

NORTH *E.* 71,634

*H. Greenway, C.		30,100
H. J. Benn, *Lab.*		14,947
A. H. J. Miller, *L./All.*		8,149
Mrs. K. Fitzherbert, *Grn.*		577
C. maj.		15,153
(June '83, C. maj. 6,291)		

Southall *E.* 74,843

*S. J. Bidwell, Lab.		26,480
M. A. Truman, *C.*		18,503
Mrs. M. Howes, *L./All.*		6,947
R. F. Lugg, *WRP*		256
Lab. maj.		7,977
(June '83, Lab. maj. 11,116)		

Easington (Durham)
E. 64,863

J. S. Cummings, *Lab.*		32,396
W. J. Perry, *C.*		7,757
G. Morpeth, *L./All.*		7,447
Lab. maj.		24,639
(June '83, Lab. maj. 14,792)		

Eastbourne (E. Sussex)
E. 74,144

*I. Gow, TD, C.		33,587
P. G. Driver, *L./All.*		16,664
A. Patel, *Lab.*		4,928
Ms. R. Addison, *Grn.*		867
C. maj.		16,923
(June '83, C. maj. 13,486)		

(See also p. 240)

Eastleigh (Hants)
E. 87,552

*Sir D. E. C. Price, C.		35,584
M. J. Kyrle, *L./All.*		22,229
D. J. C. Bull, *Lab.*		11,599
C. maj.		13,355
(June '83, C. maj. 13,008)		

Eccles (Gtr. Manchester)
E. 66,961

Miss J. Lestor, *Lab.*		25,346
Mrs. M. E. J. Packalow, *C.*		15,647
P. C. W. Beatty, *SDP/All.*		8,924
Lab. maj.		9,699
(June '83, Lab. maj. 6,005)		

Eddisbury (Cheshire)
E. 73,894

*A. R. Goodlad, C.		29,474
R. I. Fletcher, *L./All.*		13,639
Mrs. C. Grigg, *Lab.*		13,574
A. Basden, *Grn.*		976
C. maj.		15,835
(June '83, C. maj. 14,846)		

Edmonton (Gtr. London)
E. 66,080

*Dr. I. D. Twinn, C.		24,556
B. G. Grayston, *Lab.*		17,270
M. Lawson, *SDP/All.*		6,115
C. maj.		7,286
(June '83, C. maj. 1,193)		

Ellesmere Port and Neston
(Cheshire)
E. 71,344

*M. Woodcock, C.		25,664
Miss H. M. Jones, *Lab.*	...	23,811
S. A. Holbrook, *SDP/All.*		8,143
D. J. E. Carson, *PRP*		185
C. maj.		1,853
(June '83, C. maj. 7,087)		

Elmet (W. Yorks)
E. 69,024

*S. L. Batiste, C.		25,658
C. Burgon, *Lab.*		20,302
J. D. Macarthur, *SDP/All.*		8,755
C. maj.		5,356
(June '83, C. maj. 7,856)		

Eltham (Gtr. London)
E. 54,063

*P. J. Bottomley, C.		19,752
D. Vaughan, *Lab.*		13,292
E. J. Randall, *L./All.*		8,542
C. maj.		6,460
(June '83, C. maj. 7,592)		

Enfield (Gtr. London)

NORTH   E. 69,488

*T. J. C. Eggar, C.		28,758
M. Upham, *Lab.*		14,743
Ms. H. Leighter, *SDP/All.*		7,633
M. Chantler, *Grn.*		644
C. maj.		14,015
(June '83, C. maj. 11,716)		

SOUTHGATE   E. 66,600

*M. D. X. Portillo, C.		28,445
N. Harvey, *L./All.*		10,100
R. Course, *Lab.*		9,114
S. Rooney, *Grn.*		696
C. maj.		18,345
(June '83, C. maj. 15,819)		
(Dec. '84, C. maj. 4,711)		

Epping Forest (Essex)
E. 67,804

*Sir J. A. Biggs-Davison, C.		31,536
A. Humphris, *SDP/All.*		10,023
S. Murray, *Lab.*		9,499
R. Denhard, *Grn.*		695
C. maj.		21,513
(June '83, C. maj. 15,378)		
(See also p. 239)		

Epsom and Ewell (Surrey)
E. 70,683

*Hon. A. G. Hamilton, C.		33,145
Mrs. M. J. Joachim, *L./All.*		12,384
Mrs. D. B. Follett, *Lab.*		7,751
C. maj.		20,761
(June '83, C. maj. 17,195)		

Erewash (Derbys)
E. 76,545

*P. L. Rost, C.		28,775
R. W. Jones, *Lab.*		19,021
Ms. C. P. Moss, *SDP/All.*		11,442
C. maj.		9,754
(June '83, C. maj. 11,319)		

Erith and Crayford
(Gtr. London)
E. 59,292

*D. A. Evennett, C.		20,203
C. F. Hargrave, *Lab.*		13,209
*A. J. Wellbeloved, *SDP/ All.*		11,300
C. maj.		6,994
(June '83, C. maj. 920)		

Esher (Surrey)
E. 62,117

I. C. Taylor, MBE, C.		31,334
A. J. Barnett, *L./All.*		12,266
N. J. V. Lucas, *Lab.*		4,197
C. maj.		19,068
(June '83, C. maj. 15,912)		

Exeter (Devon)
E. 75,208

*J. G. Hannam, C.		26,922
M. S. Thomas, *SDP/All.*		19,266
J. A. Vincent, *Lab.*		13,643
R. J. Vail, *Grn.*		597
N. D. Byles, *LAPP*		209
C. maj.		7,656
(June '83, C. maj. 9,880)		

Falmouth and Camborne
(Cornwall)
E. 68,612

*W. D. Mudd, C.		23,725
J. C. Marks, *SDP/All.*		18,686
J. Cosgrove, *Lab.*		11,271
F. Zapp, *LM*		373
C. maj.		5,039
(June '83, C. maj. 11,025)		

Fareham (Hants)
E. 76,974

*P. R. C. Lloyd, C.		36,781
T. Slack, *L./All.*		17,986
M. Merritt, *Lab.*		5,451
C. maj.		18,795
(June '83, C. maj. 16,316)		

Faversham (Kent)
E. 79,039

*R. D. Moate, C.		31,074
E. M. Goyder, *SDP/All.*		17,096
P. Dangerfield, *Lab.*		12,616
C. maj.		13,978
(June '83, C. maj. 14,597)		

Feltham and Heston
(Gtr. London)
E. 81,062

*R. P. Ground, QC, C.		27,755
C. Hinds, *Lab.*		22,325
J. Daly, *SDP/All.*		9,623
C. maj.		5,430
(June '83, C. maj. 2,148)		

Finchley (Gtr. London)
E. 57,727

*Rt. Hon. Mrs. M. H. Thatcher, C.		21,603
J. Davies, *Lab.*		12,690
D. Howarth, *L./All.*		5,580
'Lord' Buckethead, *Grem.*		131
Miss M. St. Vincent, *Gold*		59
C. maj.		8,913
(June '83, C. maj. 9,314)		

Folkestone and Hythe (Kent)
E. 64,406

*M. Howard, QC, C.		27,915
J. R. MacDonald, *L./All.*		18,789
V. S. Anand, *Lab.*		3,720
C. maj.		9,126
(June '83, C. maj. 11,670)		

Fulham (Gtr. London)
E. 54,498

M. H. M. Carrington, C.		21,752
*W. R. N. Raynsford, *Lab.*		15,430
P. A. C. Marshall, *SDP/All.*		4,365
Ms. J. Grimes, *Grn.*		465
C. maj.		6,322
(June '83, C. maj. 4,789)		
(April '86, Lab. maj. 3,503)		

Fylde (Lancs)
E. 63,246

J. M. Jack, C.		29,559
Mrs. E. A. Smith, *L./All.*		11,787
G. Smith, *Lab.*		6,955
H. Fowler, *RCP*		405
C. maj.		17,772
(June '83, C. maj. 17,102)		

Gainsborough and Horncastle
(Lincs)
E. 69,760

*E. J. E. Leigh, C.		28,621
D. A. Grace, *L./All.*		18,898
R. Naylor, *Lab.*		6,156
C. maj.		9,723
(June '83, C. maj. 5,067)		

Gateshead East (Tyne & Wear)
E. 67,953

Miss J. G. Quin, *Lab.*		28,895
F. W. Rogers, *C.*		11,667
N. G. Rippeth, *SDP/All.*		8,231
Lab. maj.		17,228
(June '83, Lab. maj. 10,322)		

Gedling (Notts)
E. 68,398

A. J. B. Mitchell, C.		29,492
V. R. Coaker, *Lab.*		12,953
D. Morton, *SDP/All.*		11,684
C. maj.		16,539
(June '83, C. maj. 14,664)		

Gillingham (Kent)
E. 71,847

*J. R. Couchman, C.		28,711
L. R. Andrews, *L./All.*		16,162
D. J. Bishop, *Lab.*		9,230
C. maj.		12,549
(June '83, C. maj. 10,843)		

Glanford and Scunthorpe
(Humberside)
E. 72,816

E. A. Morley, *Lab.*		24,733
*R. S. Hickmet, C.		24,221
C. Nottingham, *SDP/All.*		7,762
K. S. Trivedi, *Ind.*		104
Lab. maj.		512
(June '83, C. maj. 637)		

Gloucester
E. 76,910

D. C. French, C.		29,826
D. Hulme, *Lab.*		17,791
J. Hilton, *L./All.*		12,417
C. maj.		12,035
(June '83, C. maj. 12,537)		

Gloucestershire West
E. 77,994

**P. Marland, *C.*	....	29,257
P. E. S. Nielson, *Lab.*	.....	17,578
J. T. Watkinson, *SDP/All.*		16,440
C. maj.	....	11,679
(June '83, C. maj. 9,652)		

Gosport (Hants)
E. 68,113

**P. J. Viggers, *C.*	....	29,804
P. J. Chegwyn, *L./All.*	....	16,081
A. Lloyd, *Lab.*	....	5,053
C. maj.	....	13,723
(June '83, C. maj. 14,451)		

Grantham (Lincs)
E. 79,434

**Hon. D. M. Hogg, *C.*	...	33,988
J. P. Heppell, *L./All.*	....	12,685
M. B. Gent, *Lab.*	....	12,197
Mrs. P. A. Hewis, *Grn.*	...	700
C. maj.	....	21,303
(June '83, C. maj. 18,911)		

Gravesham (Kent)
E. 72,759

J. A. Arnold, *C.*	......	28,891
M. A. Coleman, *Lab.*	.....	20,099
R. I. Crawford, *L./All.*	...	8,724
C. maj.	....	8,792
(June '83, C. maj. 8,463)		

Great Grimsby (Humberside)
E. 68,501

**A. V. Mitchell, *Lab.*	......	23,463
C. F. Robinson, *C.*	....	14,679
P. W. Genney, *SDP/All.*		13,457
Lab. maj.	....	8,784
(June '83, Lab. maj. 731)		

Great Yarmouth
(Norfolk)
E. 65,770

**M. R. H. Carttiss, *C.*	.....	25,336
J. Cannell, *Lab.*	....	15,253
S. D. Maxwell, *SDP/All.*		8,387
C. maj.	....	10,083
(June '83, C. maj. 11,200)		

Greenwich (Gtr. London)
E. 50,830

**Mrs. R. S. Barnes, *SDP/*		
All.	....	15,149
Mrs. D. F. M. Wood, *Lab.*	.	13,008
J. G. C. Antcliffe, *C.*	......	8,695
Ms. J. Thomas, *Grn.*	.....	346
R. Mallone, *Fell.*	....	59
Ms. P. Clinton, *Comm.*	...	58
SDP/All. maj.	....	2,141
(June '83, Lab. maj. 1,211)		
(Feb. '87, SDP/All. maj. 6,611)		

Guildford (Surrey)
E. 77,872

**Rt. Hon. D. A. R. Howell, *C.*		32,504
Mrs. M. L. Sharp, *SDP/All.*		19,897
R. J. Wolverson, *Lab.*	....	6,216
C. maj.	....	12,607
(June '83, C. maj. 11,824)		

Hackney (Gtr. London)
NORTH AND STOKE NEWINGTON
E. 66,771

*Ms. D. J. Abbott, *Lab.*	....	18,912
O. Letwin, *C.*	....	11,234
S. H. Taylor, *SDP/All.*	...	7,446
D. J. Fitzpatrick, *Grn.*	...	997
Ms. Y. T. Anwar, *RF.*	....	228
Lab. maj.	....	7,678
(June '83, Lab. maj. 8,545)		

SOUTH AND SHOREDITCH *E.* 70,873

**B. C. J. Sedgemore, *Lab.*	..	18,799
M. C. Northcroft-Brown, *C.*	11,277
J. D. Roberts, *L./All.*	.....	8,812
D. Green, *Comm.*	....	403
Lab. maj.	....	7,522
(June '83, Lab. maj. 7,691)		

Halesowen and Stourbridge
(W. Midlands)
E. 78,017

**J. H. R. Stokes, *C.*	....	31,037
T. J. Sunter, *Lab.*	....	17,229
D. C. A. Simon, *SDP/All.*		13,658
C. maj.	....	13,808
(June '83, C. maj. 13,316)		

Halifax (W. Yorks)
E. 73,392

*Mrs. A. Mahon, *Lab.*	......	24,741
**R. Galley, *C.*	....	23,529
F. L. Cockcroft, *SDP/All.*		8,758
Lab. maj.	....	1,212
(June '83, C. maj. 1,869)		

Halton (Cheshire)
E. 73,848

**Rt. Hon. G. J. Oakes, *Lab.*	.	32,065
J. Hardman, *C.*	....	17,487
Ms. H. Clucas, *SDP/All.*		8,272
Lab. maj.	....	14,578
(June '83, Lab. maj. 6,829)		

Hammersmith (Gtr. London)
E. 48,285

**C. S. Soley, *Lab.*	....	15,811
N. J. A. Deva, *C.*	....	13,396
S. H. J. A. Knott, *L./All.*	..	5,241
D. P. Kirk, *Grn.*	....	453
P. J. F. Fitzpatrick, *RF*	...	125
Miss M. M. A. Carrick,		
Humanist	....	98
Lab. maj.	....	2,415
(June '83, Lab. maj. 1,954)		

Hampshire

EAST *E.* 86,363

**M. J. Mates, *C.*	....	43,093
R. Booker, *L./All.*	....	19,307
C. Lloyd, *Lab.*	....	4,443
C. maj.	....	23,786
(June '83, C. maj. 18,327)		

NORTH WEST *E.* 69,965

**D. B. Mitchell, *C.*	....	31,470
I. H. Wills, *L./All.*	....	18,033
Ms. A. Burnage, *Lab.*	.....	4,980
C. maj.	....	13,437
(June '83, C. maj. 12,122)		

Hampstead and Highgate
(Gtr. London)
E. 63,301

**Sir G. Finsberg, MBE, *C.*	..	19,236
P. J. Turner, *Lab.*	....	17,015
Mrs. A. Sofer, *SDP/All.*	...	8,744
G. Weiss, *Rainbow*	....	137
Ms. S. Ellis, *Humanist*	....	134
C. maj.	....	2,221
(June '83, C. maj. 3,370)		

Harborough (Leics)
E. 74,700

**Sir J. A. Farr, *C.*	....	35,216
T. J. Swift, *L./All.*	....	16,406
P. Harley, *Lab.*	....	7,646
C. maj.	....	18,810
(June '83, C. maj. 18,485)		

Harlow (Essex)
E. 70,286

**J. J. J. Hayes, *C.*	....	26,017
A. S. Newens, *Lab.*	......	20,140
Mrs. M. C. Eden-Green,		
SDP/All.	....	8,915
C. maj.	....	5,877
(June '83, C. maj. 3,674)		

Harrogate (N. Yorks)
E. 75,761

**R. G. Banks, *C.*	....	31,167
J. R. Leach, *SDP/All.*	....	19,265
A. J. Wright, *Lab.*	....	5,671
C. maj.	....	11,902
(June '83, C. maj. 15,888)		

Harrow (Gtr. London)

EAST *E.* 81,124

**H. J. M. Dykes, *C.*	....	32,302
D. J. Brough, *Lab.*	......	14,029
Mrs. Z. Gifford, *L./All.*	...	13,251
C. maj.	....	18,273
(June '83, C. maj. 12,668)		

WEST *E.* 74,041

*R. G. Hughes, *C.*	....	30,456
S. P. Bayliss, *SDP/All.*	...	15,012
C. Bastin, *Lab.*	....	9,665
C. maj.	....	15,444
(June '83, C. maj. 11,021)		

Hartlepool (Cleveland)
E. 68,686

**E. Leadbitter, *Lab.*	....	24,296
P. C. Catchpole, *C.*	......	17,007
A. Preece, *L./All.*	....	7,047
I. J. Cameron, *Ind.*	....	1,786
Lab. maj.	....	7,289
(June '83, Lab. maj. 3,090)		

Harwich (Essex)
E. 77,149

**Sir J. E. Ridsdale, CBE, *C.*		29,344
Miss E. Lynne, *L./All.*	.....	17,262
R. Knight, *Lab.*	....	9,920
C. A. Humphrey, *OFP*	...	161
C. maj.	....	12,082
(June '83, C. maj. 12,502)		

Hastings and Rye (E. Sussex)
E. 72,758

*K. R. Warren, C.		26,163
D. J. Amies, L./All.		18,816
Ms. J. Hurcombe, Lab.	...	6,825
D. Howell, LM.		242
S. P. Davies, NPR		194
C. maj.		7,347
(June '83, C. maj. 10,980)		

Havant (Hants)
E. 76,344

*Sir I. S. Lloyd, C.		32,527
Mrs. E. E. Cleaver, SDP/ All.		16,017
J. A. Phillips, Lab.		8,030
G. W. Fuller, Bread		373
C. maj.		16,510
(June '83, C. maj. 11,956)		

Hayes and Harlington
(Gtr. London)
E. 58,240

*T. P. Dicks, C.		21,355
P. F. Fagan, Lab.		15,390
Ms. S. Slipman, SDP/All.		6,641
C. maj.		5,965
(June '83, C. maj. 4,234)		

Hazel Grove (Gtr. Manchester)
E. 65,717

*T. R. Arnold, C.		24,396
A. M. Vos, L./All.		22,556
J. G. Ford, Lab.		6,354
Ms. F. K. Chapman, Grn.		346
C. maj.		1,840
(June '83, C. maj. 2,022)		

Hemsworth (W. Yorks)
E. 54,951

G. J. Buckley, Lab.		27,859
E. H. Garnier, C.		7,159
J. D. Wooffindin, L./All.		6,568
Lab. maj.		20,700
(June '83, Lab. maj. 14,190)		

Hendon (Gtr. London)

NORTH   E. 55,095

*J. M. Gorst, C.		20,155
Ms. J. Manson, Lab.		9,223
Ms. E. Davies, SDP/All.		6,859
C. maj.		10,932
(June '83, C. maj. 9,025)		

SOUTH   E. 54,560

J. L. Marshall, C.		19,341
M. O. Palmer, L./All.		8,217
Miss L. Christian, Lab.	...	7,261
C. maj.		11,124
(June '83, C. maj. 6,433)		

Henley (Oxon)
E. 65,443

*Rt. Hon. M. R. D. Heseltine, C.		29,978
J. Madeley, L./All.		12,896
M. B. Barber, Lab.		6,173
C. maj.		17,082
(June '83, C. maj. 13,781)		

Hereford
E. 67,075

*C. R. Shepherd, C.		24,865
C. F. Green, L./All.		23,452
V. S. Woodell, Lab.		4,031
C. maj.		1,413
(June '83, C. maj. 2,277)		

Hertford and Stortford
E. 75,508

*B. Wells, C.		33,763
R. E. Wotherspoon, SDP/ All.		16,623
Mrs. P. R. E. Sumner, Lab.		7,494
G. C. Cole, Grn.		814
C. maj.		17,140
(June '83, C. maj. 12,929)		

Hertfordshire

NORTH   E. 78,694

*B. H. I. H. Stewart, RD, C.		31,750
G. W. Binney, L./All.		20,308
A. Gorst, Lab.		11,782
C. maj.		11,442
(June '83, C. maj. 9,943)		

SOUTH WEST   E. 75,643

*R. L. Page, C.		32,791
I. M. Blair, L./All.		17,007
I. Willmore, Lab.		8,966
C. maj.		15,784
(June '83, C. maj. 12,194)		

WEST   E. 78,966

*R. B. Jones, C.		31,760
N. A. Hollinghurst, SDP/ All.		16,836
A. McBrearty, Lab.		15,317
C. maj.		14,924
(June '83, C. maj. 9,576)		

Hertsmere (Herts)
E. 73,367

*Rt. Hon. C. E. Parkinson, C.		31,278
L. S. Brass, L./All.		13,172
F. Ward, Lab.		10,835
C. maj.		18,106
(June '83, C. maj. 14,870)		

Hexham (Nthmb)
E. 56,360

A. T. Amos, C.		22,370
E. M. Robson, L./All.		14,304
M. R. Wood, Lab.		8,103
Mrs. S. M. Wood, Grn.		336
C. maj.		8,066
(June '83, C. maj. 8,308)		

Heywood and Middleton
(Gtr. Manchester)
E. 59,487

*J. Callaghan, Lab.		21,900
R. E. Walker, C.		15,052
I. Greenhalgh, SDP/All.		6,953
Lab. maj.		6,848
(June '83, Lab. maj. 3,974)		

High Peak (Derbys)
E. 69,926

*C. J. Hawkins, C.		25,715
Mrs. J. McCrindle, Lab.	..	16,199
Dr. J. Oldham, SDP/All.		14,389
C. maj.		9,516
(June '83, C. maj. 9,940)		

Holborn and St. Pancras
(Gtr. London)
E. 70,589

*F. G. Dobson, Lab.		22,966
P. J. Luff, C.		14,113
S. McGrath, L./All.		7,994
M. J. Gavan, RF		300
Lab. maj.		8,853
(June '83, Lab. maj. 7,259)		

Holland with Boston (Lincs)
E. 65,539

*Sir R. B. F. S. Body, C.	...	27,412
Mrs. C. Le Brun, L./All.	..	9,817
J. D. Hough, Lab.		9,734
D. James, Local Voice		405
C. maj.		17,595
(June '83, C. maj. 11,736)		

Honiton (Devon)
E. 77,259

*Sir P. F. H. Emery, C.	....	34,931
G. Tatton-Brown, SDP/ All.		18,369
S. Pollentine, Lab.		4,988
S. Hughes, LM		747
C. maj.		16,562
(June '83, C. maj. 14,769)		

Hornchurch (Gtr. London)
E. 62,397

*R. C. Squire, C.		24,039
A. R. Williams, Lab.		13,345
M. L. C. Long, L./All.		9,609
C. maj.		10,694
(June '83, C. maj. 9,184)		

Hornsey and Wood Green
(Gtr. London)
E. 80,594

*Sir H. A. L. Rossi, C.		25,397
Mrs. B. M. R. Roche, Lab.		23,618
D. Eden, SDP/All.		8,928
Ms. E. Crosbie, Grn.		1,154
C. maj.		1,779
(June '83, C. maj. 3,899)		

Horsham (W. Sussex)
E. 86,135

*Sir P. M. Hordern, C.	....	39,775
Mrs. J. Pearce, SDP/All.		15,868
M. Shrimpton, Lab.		5,435
T. Metheringham, Grn.	..	1,383
C. maj.		23,907
(June '83, C. maj. 21,785)		

Houghton and Washington
(Tyne & Wear)
E. 77,906

*R. Boyes, Lab.		32,805
M. Callanan, C.		12,612
R. F. Kenyon, SDP/All.	..	10,090
Lab. maj.		20,193
(June '83, Lab. maj. 13,821)		

Hove (E. Sussex)
E. 72,626

*Hon. T. A. D. Sainsbury, C.		28,952
Mrs. M. E. Collins, *SDP/		
All.*		10,734
D. K. Turner, *Lab.*		9,010
T. A. Layton, *SE*		522
C. maj.		18,218
(June '83, C. maj. 17,219)		

Huddersfield (W. Yorks)
E. 66,413

*B. J. Sheerman, Lab.		23,019
N. J. Hawkins, *C.*		15,741
J. Smithson, *L./All.*		10,773
N. A. L. Harvey, *Grn.*		638
Lab. maj.		7,278
(June '83, Lab. maj. 3,955)		

Huntingdon (Cambs)
E. 86,186

*Rt. Hon. J. Major, C.		40,530
A. J. Nicholson, *SDP/All.*		13,486
D. M. Brown, *Lab.*		8,883
B. Lavin, *Grn.*		874
C. maj.		27,044
(June '83, C. maj. 20,348)		

Hyndburn (Lancs)
E. 60,529

*J. K. Hargreaves, C.		21,606
K. Coombes, *Lab.*		19,386
J. Strak, *SDP/All.*		7,423
F. Smith, *Grn.*		297
C. maj.		2,220
(June '83, C. maj. 21)		

Ilford (Gtr. London)

NORTH E. 60,433

*V. W. H. Bendall, C.		24,110
P. Jeater, *Lab.*		12,020
G. Tobbell, *SDP/All.*		7,757
C. maj.		12,090
(June '83, C. maj. 11,201)		

SOUTH E. 58,572

*N. G. Thorne, OBE, TD, C.		20,351
K. Jones, *Lab.*		15,779
R. J. Scott, *L./All.*		5,928
C. maj.		4,572
(June '83, C. maj. 4,566)		

Ipswich (Suffolk)
E. 68,165

*M. F. Irvine, C.		23,328
*K. T. Weetch, *Lab.*		22,454
H. P. Nicholson, *SDP/All.*		6,596
D. T. Lettice, *WRP*		174
C. maj.		874
(June '83, Lab. maj. 1,077)		

Isle of Wight
E. 98,694

*B. J. A. Field, C.		40,175
M. Young, *L./All.*		33,733
K. Pearson, *Lab.*		4,626
C. maj.		6,442
(June '83, L./All. maj. 3,503)		

Islington (Gtr. London)

NORTH E. 58,917

*J. B. Corbyn, Lab.		19,577
E. G. Noad, *C.*		9,920
A. Whelan, *SDP/All.*		8,560
C. Ashby, *Grn.*		1,131
Lab. maj.		9,657
(June '83, Lab. maj. 5,607)		

SOUTH AND FINSBURY E. 57,910

*C. R. Smith, Lab.		16,511
G. Cunningham, *SDP/All.*		15,706
A. Mitchell, *C.*		8,482
P. Powell, *Grn.*		382
S. Dowsett, *SPGB*		81
Ms. J. Early, *HP*		56
Lab. maj.		805
(June '83, Lab. maj. 363)		

Jarrow (Tyne & Wear)
E. 62,845

*D. Dixon, Lab.		29,651
P. Yeoman, *C.*		10,856
P. Freitag, *L./All.*		6,230
Lab. maj.		18,795
(June '83, Lab. maj. 13,877)		

Keighley (W. Yorks)
E. 65,831

*G. P. A. Waller, C.		23,903
A. Rye, *Lab.*		18,297
J. H. Wells, *L./All.*		10,041
C. maj.		5,606
(June '83, C. maj. 2,774)		

Kensington (Gtr. London)
E. 48,212

*Sir B. M. Rhys Williams,		
Bt., *C.*		14,818
B. T. Bousquet, *Lab.*		10,371
W. H. Goodhart, *SDP/All.*		5,379
R. E. Shorter, *Grn.*		528
Miss L. Carrick, *Humanist*		65
Mrs. M. Hughes, *PIP*		30
C. maj.		4,447
(June '83, C. maj. 5,101)		
(See also p. 239)		

Kent Mid
E. 72,456

*A. J. B. Rowe, C.		28,719
G. D. Colley, *L./All.*		13,951
J. A. Hazelgrove, *Lab.*		9,420
C. maj.		14,768
(June '83, C. maj. 12,543)		

Kettering (Northants)
E. 65,965

*R. N. Freeman, C.		26,532
Mrs. C. M. Goodhart, *SDP/		
All.*		15,205
A. M. Minto, *Lab.*		10,229
C. maj.		11,327
(June '83, C. maj. 8,586)		

Kingston upon Hull

EAST E. 68,657

*J. L. Prescott, Lab.		27,287
P. Jackson, *C.*		12,598
T. Wright, *L./All.*		8,572
Lab. maj.		14,689
(June '83, Lab. maj. 10,074)		

North E. 73,288

*J. K. McNamara, Lab.		26,123
Miss A. O'Brien, *C.*		13,954
S. W. Unwin, *SDP/All.*		10,962
Lab. maj.		12,169
(June '83, Lab. maj. 6,028)		

WEST E. 55,636

*S. J. Randall, Lab.		19,527
M. R. C. Humphrys, *C.*		11,397
M. Bond, *SDP/All.*		6,669
Lab. maj.		8,130
(June '83, Lab. maj. 3,654)		

Kingston upon Thames
(Gtr. London)
E. 54,839

*Rt. Hon. N. S. H. Lamont,		
C.		24,198
R. M. Hayes, *L./All.*		13,012
R. Markless, *Lab.*		5,676
J. Baker, *CPWSML*		175
C. maj.		11,186
(June '83, C. maj. 8,872)		

Kingswood (Avon)
E. 73,089

*R. A. Hayward, C.		26,300
R. L. Berry, *Lab.*		21,907
Mrs. P. Whittle, *SDP/All.*		10,382
C. maj.		4,393
(June '83, C. maj. 1,797)		

Knowsley (Merseyside)

NORTH E. 52,960

*G. E. Howarth, Lab.		27,454
Ms. R. Cooper, *L./All.*		6,356
R. C. A. Brown, *C.*		4,922
D. Hallsworth, *RF*		538
Lab. maj.		21,098
(June '83, Lab. maj. 17,191)		
(Nov. '86, Lab. maj. 6,724)		

SOUTH E. 65,643

*S. F. Hughes, Lab.		31,378
A. J. Hall, *C.*		10,532
Mrs. R. Watmough, *SDP/		
All.*		6,760
Lab. maj.		20,846
(June '83, Lab. maj. 11,769)		
(See also p. 239)		

Lancashire West
E. 76,094

*K. H. Hind, C.		26,500
C. Pickthall, *Lab.*		25,147
R. Jermyn, *SDP/All.*		8,972
C. maj.		1,353
(June '83, C. maj. 6,858)		

Lancaster (Lancs)
E. 57,229

*Mrs. M. E. Kellett-Bow-		
man, *C.*		21,142
J. Gallacher, *Lab.*		14,689
Mrs. K. C. Brooks, *L./All.*		9,003
P. F. F. Jones, *Grn.*		473
C. maj.		6,453
(June '83, C. maj. 10,636)		

Langbaurgh (Cleveland)
E. 79,193

*J. R. Holt, C.	26,047
P. Harford, Lab.	23,959
R. A. J. Ashby, L./All.	12,405
C. maj.	2,088
(June '83, C. maj. 6,024)	

Leeds (W. Yorks)

CENTRAL E. 59,019

*D. J. Fatchett, Lab.	21,270
D. Schofield, C.	9,765
Dr. Karen Lee, SDP/All.	6,853
W. Innis, Comm.	355
Lab. maj.	11,505
(June '83, Lab. maj. 8,222)	

EAST E. 61,178

*Rt. Hon. D. W. Healey, CH, MBE, Lab.	20,932
J. S. W. Sheard, C.	11,406
Miss M. G. Clay, L./All.	10,630
Lab. maj.	9,526
(June '83, Lab. maj. 6,095)	

NORTH EAST E. 64,631

T. J. R. Kirkhope, C.	22,196
P. M. Crystal, SDP/All.	13,777
O. B. Glover, Lab.	12,292
Ms. C. D. Nash, Grn.	416
C. maj.	8,419
(June '83, C. maj. 8,995)	

NORTH WEST E. 68,227

*Dr. K. Hampson, C.	22,480
B. Peters, L./All.	17,279
Ms. J. Thomas, Lab.	11,210
A. Stevens, Grn.	663
C. maj.	5,201
(June '83, C. maj. 8,537)	

SOUTH AND MORLEY E. 60,726

*Rt. Hon. M. Rees, Lab.	21,551
Mrs. T. C. Holdroyd, C.	14,840
E. J. V. Dawson, SDP/All.	7,099
Lab. maj.	6,711
(June '83, Lab. maj. 5,854)	

WEST E. 66,344

J. D. Battle, Lab.	21,032
*M. J. Meadowcroft, L./All.	16,340
P. D. Allott, C.	11,276
Lab. maj.	4,692
(June '83, L./All. maj. 2,048)	

Leicester

EAST E. 66,372

N. K. A. S. Vaz, Lab.	24,074
*P. N. E. Bruinvels, C.	22,150
Mrs. A. M. Ayres, SDP/All.	5,935
Lab. maj.	1,924
(June '83, C. maj. 933)	

SOUTH E. 73,236

J. Marshall, Lab.	24,901
*D. H. Spencer, QC, C.	23,024
R. Pritchard, L./All.	7,773
B. Fewster, Grn.	390
M. M. Mayat, Ind. Lab.	192
Ms. R. F. Manners, WRP	96
Lab. maj.	1,877
(June '83, C. maj. 7)	

WEST E. 67,829

*G. E. Janner, QC, Lab.	22,156
J. S. W. Cooper, C.	20,955
W. Edgar, SDP/All.	6,708
Lab. maj.	1,201
(June '83, Lab. maj. 1,712)	

Leicestershire North West
E. 70,633

*D. G. Ashby, C.	27,872
Mrs. S. A. Waddington, Lab.	20,044
D. S. Emmerson, L./All.	10,034
Miss H. T. Michetschlager, Grn.	570
C. maj.	7,828
(June '83, C. maj. 6,662)	

Leigh (Gtr. Manchester)
E. 69,155

*L. F. Cunliffe, Lab.	30,064
L. B. A. Browne, C.	13,458
S. D. Jones, SDP/All.	7,743
Lab. maj.	16,606
(June '83, Lab. maj. 12,314)	

Leominster (H & W)
E. 69,977

*P. Temple-Morris, C.	31,396
S. C. Morris, L./All.	17,321
A. C. R. Chappell, Lab.	4,444
Mrs. F. M. Norman, Grn.	1,102
C. maj.	14,075
(June '83, C. maj. 9,786)	

Lewes (E. Sussex)
E. 73,181

*J. R. Rathbone, C.	32,016
D. F. Bellotti, L./All.	18,396
R. P. Taylor, Lab.	4,973
A. G. P. Sherwood, Grn.	970
C. maj.	13,620
(June '83, C. maj. 13,904)	

Lewisham (Gtr. London)

DEPTFORD E. 58,151

Ms. J. M. Ruddock, Lab.	18,724
M. C. Punyer, C.	11,953
Ms. A. M. E. Braun, SDP/All.	6,513
P. K. Makepeace, Grn.	568
Lab. maj.	6,771
(June '83, Lab. maj. 6,032)	

EAST E. 59,627

*Hon. C. B. Moynihan, C.	19,873
M. R. Profitt, Lab.	15,059
Mrs. V. W. Stone, SDP/All.	9,118
C. maj.	4,814
(June '83, C. maj. 1,909)	

WEST E. 62,923

*J. C. Maples, C.	20,995
J. P. Dowd, Lab.	17,223
Ms. S. C. Titley, L./All.	7,247
C. maj.	3,772
(June '83, C. maj. 2,506)	

Leyton (Gtr. London)
E. 57,662

*H. M. Cohen, Lab.	16,536
S. Banks, L./All.	11,895
D. N. Gilmartin, C.	11,692
Lab. maj.	4,641
(June '83, Lab. maj. 4,516)	

Lincoln
E. 77,049

*K. M. Carlisle, C.	27,097
N. J. Butler, Lab.	19,614
P. Zentner, SDP/All.	11,319
T. B. Kyle, RRPRC	232
C. maj.	7,483
(June '83, C. maj. 10,286)	

Lindsey East (Lincs)
E. 74,027

*Sir P. H. B. Tapsell, C.	29,048
J. C. L. Sellick, L./All.	20,432
K. Stevenson, Lab.	6,206
C. maj.	8,616
(June '83, C. maj. 7,517)	

Littleborough and Saddleworth
(Gtr. Manchester)
E. 66,074

*G. K. Dickens, C.	22,027
C. Davies, L./All.	15,825
P. Stonier, Lab.	13,299
C. maj.	6,202
(June '83, C. maj. 5,650)	

Liverpool

BROADGREEN E. 63,091

*T. Fields, Lab.	23,262
R. Pine, L./All.	17,215
M. R. G. Seddon, C.	7,413
Lab. maj.	6,047
(June '83, Lab. maj. 3,800)	

GARSTON E. 61,280

*E. Loyden, Lab.	24,848
P. B. Feather, C.	11,071
R. Isaacson, SDP/All.	10,370
K. Timlin, WRP	98
Lab. maj.	13,777
(June '83, Lab. maj. 4,002)	

MOSSLEY HILL E. 60,954

*D. P. P. Alton, L./All.	20,012
J. A. Devaney, Lab.	17,786
W. M. Lightfoot, C.	8,005
L./All. maj.	2,226
(June '83, L./All. maj. 4,195)	

RIVERSIDE E. 53,328

*R. Parry, Lab.	25,505
S. Fitzsimmons, C.	4,816
B. S. Chahal, SDP/All.	3,912
Ms. C. A. Gardner, Comm.	601
Lab. maj.	20,689
(June '83, Lab. maj. 17,378)	

WALTON E. 73,118

*E. S. Heffer, Lab.	34,661
P. R. Clark, L./All.	11,408
I. A. Mays, C.	7,738
Lab. maj.	23,253
(June '83, Lab. maj. 14,115)	
(See also p. 240)	

WEST DERBY *E.* 60,522
*R. N. Wareing, *Lab.*		29,021
J. E. Backhouse, *C.*		8,525
M. Ferguson, *SDP/All.*		6,897
	Lab. maj.	20,496
(June '83, Lab. maj. 11,843)		

Loughborough (Leics)
E. 73,660
*S. J. Dorrell, *C.*	31,931
C. J. Wrigley, *Lab.*	14,283
R. G. Fox, *SDP/All.*	11,499
R. Gupta, *Grn.*	656
C. maj.	17,648
(June '83, C. maj. 16,180)	

Ludlow (Salop)
E. 66,187
C. J. F. Gill, RD, *C.*		27,499
D. Phillips, *L./All.*		15,800
K. Harrison, *Lab.*		7,724
	C. maj.	11,699
(June '83, C. maj. 11,303)		

Luton (Beds)
NORTH *E.* 74,235
*J. R. Carlisle, *C.*	30,997
M. Wright, *Lab.*	15,424
J. D. Stephen, *SDP/All.*	11,166
C. maj.	15,573
(June '83, C. maj. 11,981)	

SOUTH *E.* 71,231
*G. F. J. Bright, *C.*	24,762
W. D. McKenzie, *Lab.*	19,647
P. Chapman, *L./All.*	9,146
C. maj.	5,115
(June '83, C. maj. 4,621)	

Macclesfield (Cheshire)
E. 76,093
*N. R. Winterton, *C.*	33,208
A. B. Haldane, *L./All.*	14,116
Ms. C. Pinder, *Lab.*	11,563
C. maj.	19,092
(June '83, C. maj. 20,679)	

Maidstone (Kent)
E. 72,987
Miss A. N. Widdecombe, *C.*		29,100
C. J. Sutton-Mattocks, *L./All.*		18,736
K. P. Brooks, *Lab.*		6,935
Mrs. P. A. Kemp, *Grn.*		717
	C. maj.	10,364
(June '83, C. maj. 7,226)		

Makerfield (Gtr. Manchester)
E. 70,819
I. McCartney, *Lab.*	30,190
L. A. Robertson, *C.*	14,632
B. Hewer, *L./All.*	8,838
Lab. maj.	15,558
(June '83, Lab. maj. 10,876)	

Manchester
BLACKLEY *E.* 58,814
*K. Eastham, *Lab.*	22,476
K. Nath, *C.*	12,354
H. Showman, *SDP/All.*	8,041
Lab. maj.	10,122
(June '83, Lab. maj. 6,456)	

CENTRAL *E.* 62,928
*R. K. Litherland, *Lab.*	27,428
M. R. W. Banks, *C.*	7,561
B. W. McColgan, *SDP/All.*	5,250
Lab. maj.	19,867
(June '83, Lab. maj. 18,485)	

GORTON *E.* 64,243
*Rt. Hon. G. B. Kaufman, *Lab.*		24,615
J. Kershaw, *C.*		10,550
K. A. Whitmore, *L./All.*		9,830
Ms. P. Lawrence, *RF*		253
	Lab. maj.	14,065
(June '83, Lab. maj. 9,965)		

WITHINGTON *E.* 65,343
K. J. C. Bradley, *Lab.*	21,650
*F. J. Silvester, *C.*	18,259
Mrs. A. Jones, *L./All.*	9,978
M. T. Abberton, *Grn.*	524
Lab. maj.	3,391
(June '83, C. maj. 2,373)	

WYTHENSHAWE *E.* 58,287
*Rt. Hon. A. Morris, *Lab.*		23,881
D. G. Sparrow, *C.*		12,026
Ms. J. Butterworth, *SDP/All.*		5,921
Ms. S. Connelly, *RF*		216
	Lab. maj.	11,855
(June '83, Lab. maj. 10,684)		

Mansfield (Notts)
E. 66,764
J. A. Meale, *Lab.*		19,610
C. Hendry, *C.*		19,554
B. Answer, *SDP/All.*		11,604
B. Marshall, *ML*		1,580
	Lab. maj.	56
(June '83, Lab. maj. 2,216)		

Medway (Kent)
E. 64,103
*Dame P. Fenner, DBE, *C.*		23,889
V. Hull, *Lab.*		13,960
Mrs. J. Horne-Roberts, *SDP/All.*		8,450
Ms. J. V. Rosser, *Grn.*		504
	C. maj.	9,929
(June '83, C. maj. 8,656)		

Meriden (W. Midlands)
E. 78,444
*I. C. Mills, *C.*		31,935
R. H. Burden, *Lab.*		15,115
Ms. C. E. Parkinson, *SDP/All.*		10,896
	C. maj.	16,820
(June '83, C. maj. 15,018)		

Middlesbrough (Cleveland)
E. 60,789
*S. Bell, *Lab.*	25,747
R. J. Orr-Ewing, *C.*	10,789
P. A. Hawley, *L./All.*	6,554
Lab. maj.	14,958
(June '83, Lab. maj. 9,669)	

Milton Keynes (Bucks)
E. 97,041
*W. R. Benyon, *C.*	35,396
W. T. Rodgers, *SDP/All.*	21,695
Ms. Y. V. A. Brownfield-Pope, *Lab.*	16,111
A. H. Francis, *Grn.*	810
C. maj.	13,701
(June '83, C. maj. 11,522)	

Mitcham and Morden
(Gtr. London)
E. 63,089
*Mrs. A. C. R. Rumbold, CBE, *C.*		23,002
Ms. S. McDonagh, *Lab.*		16,819
B. L. H. Douglas-Mann, *SDP/All.*		7,930
	C. maj.	6,183
(June '83, C. maj. 6,451)		

Mole Valley (Surrey)
E. 67,715
*Rt. Hon. K. W. Baker, *C.*	31,689
Mrs. S. P. Thomas, *L./All.*	15,613
C. M. B. King, *Lab.*	4,846
C. maj.	16,076
(June '83, C. maj. 14,718)	

Morecambe and Lunesdale
(Lancs)
E. 55,718
*Hon. M. A. Lennox-Boyd, *C.*		22,327
Mrs. J. Greenwell, *SDP/All.*		10,542
D. Smith, *Lab.*		9,535
	C. maj.	11,785
(June '83, C. maj. 12,194)		

Newark (Notts)
E. 67,555
*R. T. Alexander, *C.*	28,070
D. Barton, *Lab.*	14,527
G. A. Emerson, *SDP/All.*	9,833
C. maj.	13,543
(June '83, C. maj. 14,283)	

Newbury (Berks)
E. 75,187
*R. M. C. McNair-Wilson, *C.*	35,266
D. D. Rendel, *L./All.*	18,608
R. C. Stapley, *Lab.*	4,765
C. maj.	16,658
(June '83, C. maj. 13,038)	

Newcastle under Lyme (Staffs)
E. 66,053
*Mrs. L. Golding, *Lab.*		21,618
A. L. Thomas, *L./All.*		16,486
P. C. J. Ridgway, *C.*		14,863
M. J. Nicklin, *Ex Lab. Mod.*		397
	Lab. maj.	5,132
(June '83, Lab. maj. 2,804)		
(July '86, Lab. maj. 799)		

Newcastle upon Tyne
CENTRAL *E.* 63,682
J. M. Cousins, *Lab.*	20,416
*P. R. G. Merchant, *C.*	17,933
Dr. N. Martin, *SDP/All.*	7,304
R. J. Bird, *Grn.*	418
K. Williams, *RF*	111
Lab. maj.	2,483
(June '83, C. maj. 2,228)	

EAST *E.* 59,369
*N. H. Brown, Lab. 23,677
Miss J. G. A. Riley, *C.* 11,177
P. J. Arnold, *L./All.* 6,728
J. Keith, *Comm.* 362
Lab. maj. 12,500
(June '83, Lab. maj. 7,492)

NORTH *E.* 69,178
D. J. Henderson, Lab. 22,424
J. W. Shipley, *L./All.* 17,181
J. W. Tweddle, *C.* 12,915
Lab. maj. 5,243
(June '83, Lab. maj. 2,556)

New Forest (Hants)
E. 75,083

**P. M. E. D. McNair-Wilson,
C.* 37,188
R. Karn, *L./All.* 15,456
J. I. Hampton, *Lab.* 4,856
C. maj. 21,732
(June '83, C. maj. 20,925)

Newham (Gtr. London)

NORTH EAST *E.* 60,787
*R. Leighton, Lab. 20,220
P. Davis, *C.* 11,984
Ms. H. Steele, *L./All.* 6,772
Lab. maj. 8,236
(June '83, Lab. maj. 8,509)

NORTH WEST *E.* 47,568
*T. L. Banks, Lab. 15,677
J. C. Wylie, *C.* 7,181
R. H. Redden, *SDP/All.* .. 4,920
Ms. A. V. Degrandis-
Harrison, *Grn.* 497
Lab. maj. 8,496
(June '83, Lab. maj. 6,918)

SOUTH *E.* 50,244
*N. J. Spearing, Lab. 12,935
J. Fairrie, *C.* 10,169
A. J. Kellaway, *SDP/All.* .. 6,607
Lab. maj. 2,766
(June '83, Lab. maj. 7,311)

Norfolk

MID *E.* 73,893
*R. A. Ryder, OBE, C. 32,758
G. J. E. Graham, *SDP/All.* 14,750
K. Luckey, *Lab.* 10,272
C. maj. 18,008
(June '83, C. maj. 15,515)

NORTH *E.* 69,790
*R. F. Howell, C. 28,822
N. R. Anthony, *SDP/All.* 13,512
A. Earle, *Lab.* 10,765
M. G. Filgate, *Grn.* 960
C. maj. 15,310
(June '83, C. maj. 13,223)

NORTH WEST *E.* 73,739
*H. C. Bellingham, C. 29,393
C. Brocklebank-Fowler,
SDP/All. 18,568
F. Dignan, *Lab.* 10,184
C. maj. 10,825
(June '83, C. maj. 3,147)

SOUTH *E.* 78,372
**Rt. Hon. J. R. R. Mac-
Gregor, OBE, C.* 33,912
R. A. P. Carden, *L./All.* ... 21,494
L. Addison, *Lab.* 8,047
C. maj. 12,418
(June '83, C. maj. 12,135)

SOUTH WEST *E.* 74,240
Mrs. G. P. Shephard, C. .. 32,519
M. Scott, *L./All.* 12,083
Ms. M. Page, *Lab.* 11,844
C. maj. 20,436
(June '83, C. maj. 14,910)

Normanton (W. Yorks)
E. 62,899

*W. O'Brien, Lab. 23,303
M. D. M. Smith, *C.* 16,016
R. J. Macey, *SDP/All.* 7,717
Lab. maj. 7,287
(June '83, Lab. maj. 4,183)

Northampton

NORTH *E.* 69,294
*A. R. Marlow, C. 24,816
O. J. Granfield, *Lab.* 15,560
A. S. Rounthwaite, *L./All.* 10,690
M. Green, *Grn.* 471
S. Colling, *WRP* 156
C. maj. 9,256
(June '83, C. maj. 9,860)

SOUTH *E.* 76,071
*M. W. L. Morris, C. 31,864
J. Dickie, *Lab.* 14,061
G. Hopkins, *SDP/All.* 10,639
Mrs. M. Hamilton, *Grn.* ... 647
C. maj. 17,803
(June '83, C. maj. 15,126)

Northavon (Avon)
E. 78,483

*J. A. Cope, C. 34,224
Mrs. C. Willmore, *L./All.* . 19,954
D. Norris, *Lab.* 8,762
C. maj. 14,270
(June '83, C. maj. 12,983)

Norwich (Norfolk)

NORTH *E.* 62,725
*H. P. Thompson, C. 22,772
Miss M. H. R. Honeyball,
Lab. 14,996
T. P. Nicholls, *L./All.* 11,922
C. maj. 7,776
(June '83, C. maj. 5,879)

SOUTH *E.* 64,421
J. L. Garrett, Lab. 19,666
*J. A. Powley, C. 19,330
C. J. M. Hardie, *SDP/All.* 12,896
Lab. maj. 336
(June '83, C. maj. 1,712)

Norwood (Gtr. London)
E. 56,602

*J. D. Fraser, Lab. 18,359
D. C. R. Grieve, *C.* 13,636
M. M. Noble, *SDP/All.* ... 12,579
F. M. Jackson, *RABIES* ... 171
R. J. Hammond, *CD.* 151
Lab. maj. 4,723
(June '83, Lab. maj. 2,883)

Nottingham

EAST *E.* 68,266
*M. Knowles, C. 20,162
M. Aslam, *Lab.* 19,706
S. Parkhouse, *L./All.* 6,887
K. Malik, *RF* 212
C. maj. 456
(June '83, C. maj. 1,464)

NORTH *E.* 69,620
G. W. Allen, Lab. 22,713
*R. G. J. Ottaway, C. 21,048
S. C. Fernando, *SDP/All.* 5,912
J. H. Peck, *Comm.* 879
Lab. maj. 1,665
(June '83, C. maj. 362)

SOUTH *E.* 72,807
*M. M. Brandon-Bravo, C. . 23,921
A. Simpson, *Lab.* 21,687
L. V. Williams, *SDP/All.* ... 7,517
C. maj. 2,234
(June '83, C. maj. 5,715)

Nuneaton (Warwicks)
E. 68,287

*L. D. Stevens, MBE, C. 24,630
Mrs. V. A. Veness, *Lab.* .. 18,975
A. Trembath, *SDP/All.* ... 10,550
Dr. J. Morrissey, *Grn.* 719
C. maj. 5,655
(June '83, C. maj. 5,061)

Old Bexley and Sidcup
(Gtr. London)
E. 50,831

**Rt. Hon. E. R. G. Heath,
MBE, C.* 24,350
T. H. Pearce, *L./All.* 8,076
H. J. A. Stoate, *Lab.* 6,762
C. maj. 16,274
(June '83, C. maj. 12,718)

Oldham (Gtr. Manchester)

CENTRAL AND ROYTON
E. 65,277
*J. A. Lamond, Lab. 21,759
J. A. Farquhar, *C.* 15,480
Mrs. A. Dunn, *SDP/All.* ... 7,956
Lab. maj. 6,279
(June '83, Lab. maj. 3,312)

WEST *E.* 57,178
*M. H. Meacher, Lab. 20,291
Mrs. J. M. Jacobs, *C.* 14,324
Miss M. R. Mason, *L./All.* . 6,478
Lab. maj. 5,967
(June '83, Lab. maj. 3,180)

Orpington (Gtr. London)
E. 59,608

*I. R. Stanbrook, C. 27,261
J. H. Fryer, *L./All.* 14,529
S. J. Cowan, *Lab.* 5,020
C. maj. 12,732
(June '83, C. maj. 10,151)

Oxford

EAST *E.* 62,145
A. D. Smith, *Lab.* 21,103
*S. J. Norris, C. 19,815
Mrs. M. Godden, *L./All.* .. 7,648
D. Dalton, *Grn.* 441
P. S. Mylvaganam, *ICC* ... 60
Lab. maj. 1,288
(June '83, C. maj. 1,267)

WEST AND ABINGDON *E.* 69,193
*J. H. C. Patten, C. 25,171
C. M. P. Huhne, *SDP/All.* 20,293
J. G. Power, *Lab.* 8,108
D. Smith, *Grn.* 695
  C. maj. 4,878
(June '83, C. maj. 7,151)

Peckham (Gtr. London)
E. 59,261

*Ms. H. Harman, Lab. 17,965
Mrs. L. K. F. Ingram, *C.* .. 8,476
R. H. Shearman, *L./All.* .. 5,878
Miss D. Robinson, *Grn.* ... 628
  Lab. maj. 9,489
(June '83, Lab. maj. 8,824)

Pendle (Lancs)
E. 63,588

*J. R. L. Lee, C. 21,009
Mrs. S. Renilson, *Lab.* 18,370
A. G. Lishman, *L./All.* ... 12,662
  C. maj. 2,639
(June '83, C. maj. 6,135)

Penrith and the Border
(Cumbria)
E. 70,994

*D. J. Maclean, C. 33,148
D. J. Ivison, *L./All.* 15,782
J. M. P. Hutton, *Lab.* 6,075
  C. maj. 17,366
(June '83, C. maj. 15,421)
(July '83, C. maj. 552)

Peterborough (Cambs)
E. 84,284

*Dr. B. S. Mawhinney, C. . 30,624
A. MacKinlay, *Lab.* 20,840
D. W. Green, *L./All.* 9,984
N. A. Callaghan, *Grn.* 506
  C. maj. 9,784
(June '83, C. maj. 10,439)

Plymouth (Devon)

DEVONPORT *E.* 64,741
*Rt. Hon. Dr. D. A. L. Owen,
  SDP/All. 21,039
T. Jones, *C.* 14,569
I. Flintoff, *Lab.* 14,166
  SDP/All. maj. 6,470
(June '83, SDP/All. maj. 4,936)

DRAKE *E.* 51,186
*Miss J. E. Fookes, C. 16,195
D. Astor, *SDP/All.* 13,070
D. Jamieson, *Lab.* 9,451
Ms. P. Barber, *Grn.* 493
  C. maj. 3,125
(June '83, C. maj. 8,585)

SUTTON *E.* 64,120
*Hon. A. K. M. Clark, C. .. 23,187
B. Tidy, *L./All.* 19,174
R. D. Maddern, *Lab.* 8,310
  C. maj. 4,013
(June '83, C. maj. 11,687)

Pontefract and Castleford
(W. Yorks)
E. 64,414

*G. Lofthouse, Lab. 31,656
J. H. Mallins, *C.* 10,030
M. F. Taylor, *L./All.* 5,334
D. M. Lees, *RF* 295
  Lab. maj. 21,626
(June '83, Lab. maj. 13,691)

Poole (Dorset)
E. 76,673

*J. D. Ward, CBE, C. 34,159
R. J. Whitley, *SDP/All.* ... 19,351
M. Shutler, *Lab.* 5,901
  C. maj. 14,808
(June '83, C. maj. 14,429)

Portsmouth (Hants)

NORTH *E.* 80,501
*P. H. S. Griffiths, C. 33,297
Mrs. E. Mitchell, *SDP/All.* 14,896
D. Miles, *Lab.* 12,016
  C. maj. 18,401
(June '83, C. maj. 17,999)

SOUTH *E.* 76,292
D. Martin, *C.* 23,534
*M. T. Hancock, SDP/All. 23,329
K. Gardiner, *Lab.* 7,047
R. Hughes, *657 Party* 455
  C. maj. 205
(June '83, C. maj. 12,335)
(June '84, SDP/All. maj. 1,341)

Preston (Lancs)
E. 64,459

Mrs. A. Wise, *Lab.* 23,341
Dr. R. T. Chandran, *C.* ... 12,696
J. P. Wright, *L./All.* 8,452
  Lab. maj. 10,645
(June '83, Lab. maj. 6,978)

Pudsey (W. Yorks)
E. 71,681

*J. G. D. Shaw, C. 25,457
J. P. F. Cummins, *L./All.* . 19,021
N. Taggart, *Lab.* 11,461
  C. maj. 6,436
(June '83, C. maj. 5,314)

Putney (Gtr. London)
E. 63,108

*D. J. Mellor, C. 24,197
P. G. Hain, *Lab.* 17,290
Ms. S. Harlow, *L./All.* ... 5,934
S. Desorgher, *Grn.* 508
  C. maj. 6,907
(June '83, C. maj. 5,019)

Ravensbourne (Gtr. London)
E. 59,365

*J. L. Hunt, C. 28,295
G. Campbell, *SDP/All.* ... 11,376
M. D'Arcy, *Lab.* 5,087
A. Waide, *BN* 184
  C. maj. 16,919
(June '83, C. maj. 15,512)

Reading (Berks)

EAST *E.* 72,311
*Sir G. Vaughan, C. 28,515
Mrs. S. M. Baring, *SDP/*
  All. 12,298
M. J. Salter, *Lab.* 11,371
P. J. Unsworth, *Grn.* 667
A. B. Shone, *CS* 125
  C. maj. 16,217
(June '83, C. maj. 11,508)

WEST *E.* 70,391
*R. A. B. Durant, C. 28,122
K. H. Lock, *L./All.* 11,369
M. E. Orton, *Lab.* 10,819
E. P. Wilson, *Grn.* 542
  C. maj. 16,753
(June '83, C. maj. 11,399)

Redcar (Cleveland)
E. 63,393

Dr. Marjorie Mowlam, *Lab.* 22,824
P. J. Bassett, *C.* 15,089
G. Nightingale, *SDP/All.* 10,298
  Lab. maj. 7,735
(June '83, Lab. maj. 3,104)

Reigate (Surrey)
E. 71,940

*G. A. Gardiner, C. 30,925
Mrs. E. A. Pamplin, *SDP/*
  All. 12,752
R. P. Spencer, *Lab.* 7,460
G. Brand, *Grn.* 1,026
  C. maj. 18,173
(June '83, C. maj. 16,307)

Ribble Valley (Lancs)
E. 62,644

*Rt. Hon. D. C. Waddington,
  QC, *C.* 30,136
M. Carr, *SDP/All.* 10,608
G. Pope, *Lab.* 8,781
  C. maj. 19,528
(June '83, C. maj. 18,591)
(*See also* p. 240)

Richmond and Barnes
(Gtr. London)
E. 54,700

*J. J. Hanley, C. 21,729
A. J. Watson, *L./All.* 19,963
M. D. Gold, *Lab.* 3,227
Miss C. M. Matthews, *Grn.* 610
  C. maj. 1,766
(June '83, C. maj. 74)

Richmond (N. Yorks)
E. 79,277

*Rt. Hon. L. Brittan, QC,
  C. 34,995
D. Lloyd-Williams, *L./All.* 15,419
F. Robson, *Lab.* 6,737
  C. maj. 19,576
(June '83, C. maj. 18,066)
(*See also* p. 239)

Rochdale (Gtr. Manchester)
E. 68,703

*C. Smith, MBE, L./All. 22,245
D. Williams, *Lab.* 19,466
C. Condie, *C.* 9,561
  L./All. maj. 2,779
(June '83, L./All. maj. 7,587)

Rochford (Essex)
E. 76,048

*Dr. M. Clark, C.	....	35,872
P. Young, L./All.	......	16,178
D. Weir, Lab.	....	7,308
C. maj.	....	19,694
(June '83, C. maj. 13,102)		

Romford (Gtr. London)
E. 55,668

*M. J. Neubert, C.	....	22,745
N. J. M. Smith, Lab.	......	9,274
J. H. Bates, L./All.	......	8,195
F. J. Gibson, Grn.	......	385
C. maj.	....	13,471
(June '83, C. maj. 10,574)		

Romsey and Waterside (Hants)
E. 79,136

*M. K. B. Colvin, C.	....	35,303
A. T. Bloss, SDP/All.	......	20,031
S. J. Roberts, Lab.	......	7,213
C. maj.	....	15,272
(June '83, C. maj. 13,690)		

Rossendale and Darwen (Lancs)
E. 75,038

*D. A. Trippier, C.	....	28,056
Mrs. J. Anderson, Lab.	...	23,074
P. J. Hulse, L./All.	......	9,097
C. maj.	....	4,982
(June '83, C. maj. 8,821)		

Rotherham (S. Yorks)
E. 61,521

*J. S. Crowther, Lab.	......	25,422
J. C. C. Stevens, C.	....	9,410
P. J. Bowler, L./All.	......	7,766
Lab. maj.	....	16,012
(June '83, Lab. maj. 11,709)		

Rother Valley (S. Yorks)
E. 66,416

*K. J. Barron, Lab.	....	28,292
P. R. Rayner, C.	....	12,502
J. R. Boddy, SDP/All.	....	9,240
M. R. Driver, WRP.	......	145
Lab. maj.	....	15,790
(June '83, Lab. maj. 8,625)		

Rugby and Kenilworth (Warwicks)
E. 76,654

*J. F. Pawsey, C.	....	31,485
J. Airey, Lab.	....	15,221
D. R. Owen-Jones, L./All.	..	14,343
C. maj.	....	16,264
(June '83, C. maj. 14,241)		

Ruislip-Northwood (Gtr. London)
E. 56,365

*J. A. D. Wilkinson, C.	....	27,418
Mrs. D. Darby, L./All.	....	10,447
Ms. H. A. Smith, Lab.	....	5,913
C. maj.	....	16,971
(June '83, C. maj. 12,982)		

Rushcliffe (Notts)
E. 72,797

*Rt. Hon. K. H. Clarke, QC, C.	....	34,214
L. George, SDP/All.	.....	13,375
P. Tipping, Lab.	....	9,631
Ms. H. Wright, Grn.	.....	991
C. maj.	....	20,839
(June '83, C. maj. 20,220)		

Rutland and Melton (Leics)
E. 77,846

*M. A. Latham, C.	....	37,073
R. C. Renold, L./All.	.....	14,051
L. C. Burke, Lab.	....	8,680
C. maj.	....	23,022
(June '83, C. maj. 18,353)		

Ryedale (N. Yorks)
E. 83,205

J. R. Greenway, C.	....	35,149
*Mrs. E. L. Shields, L./All.	..	25,409
J. Beighton, Lab.	....	5,340
C. maj.	....	9,740
(June '83, C. maj. 16,142)		
(May '86, L./All. maj. 4,940)		

Saffron Walden (Essex)
E. 73,185

*A. G. B. Haselhurst, C.	...	33,354
M. P. Hayes, L./All.	......	16,752
R. Gifford, Lab.	....	6,674
G. B. Hannah, Grn.	......	816
W. O. Smedley, CMNHY	......	217
C. maj.	....	16,602
(June '83, C. maj. 15,363)		

St. Albans (Herts)
E. 75,281

*P. B. Lilley, C.	....	31,726
A. S. B. Walkington, L./All.	20,845
A. McWalter, Lab.	......	6,922
Ms. E. V. Field, Grn.	.....	788
W. H. Pass, CPRP	....	110
C. maj.	....	10,881
(June '83, C. maj. 8,561)		

St. Helens (Merseyside)

NORTH E. 70,836

*J. Evans, Lab.	....	28,989
Miss M. J. Libby, C.	......	14,729
N. P. Derbyshire, L./All.	..	10,300
Lab. maj.	....	14,260
(June '83, Lab. maj. 9,259)		

SOUTH E. 69,449

*G. E. Bermingham, Lab.	..	27,027
A. J. Brown, C.	....	13,226
P. J. Briers, SDP/All.	....	9,252
Lab. maj.	....	13,801
(June '83, Lab. maj. 9,662)		

St. Ives (Cornwall)
E. 67,448

*D. A. Harris, C.	....	25,174
H. H. J. Carter, SDP/All.	..	17,619
I. Hope, Lab.	....	9,275
C. maj.	....	7,555
(June '83, C. maj. 7,859)		

Salford East (Gtr. Manchester)
E. 58,087

*Rt. Hon. S. Orme, Lab.	...	22,555
C. W. H. McFall, C.	......	10,499
P. Keaveney, SDP/All.	...	5,105
S. G. Murray, WRP	......	201
Lab. maj.	....	12,056
(June '83, Lab. maj. 9,541)		

Salisbury (Wilts)
E. 76,221

*S. R. Key, C.	....	31,612
P. A. Mitchell, SDP/All.	..	20,169
Ms. T. E. Seabourne, Lab.	..	5,455
S. W. Fletcher, Ind.	......	372
C. maj.	....	11,443
(June '83, C. maj. 7,174)		

Scarborough (N. Yorks)
E. 74,612

*Sir M. N. Shaw, C.	....	27,672
Mrs. H. Callan, SDP/All.	..	14,046
M. Wolstenholme, Lab.	..	12,913
C. maj.	....	13,626
(June '83, C. maj. 13,929)		

Sedgefield (Durham)
E. 60,866

*A. C. L. Blair, Lab.	......	25,965
N. B. S. Hawkins, C.	.....	12,907
R. I. Andrew, SDP/All.	...	7,477
Lab. maj.	....	13,058
(June '83, Lab. maj. 8,281)		

Selby (N. Yorks)
E. 71,378

*Rt. Hon. M. J. H. Alison, C.	....	28,611
J. T. Grogan, Lab.	....	14,832
J. E. F. Longman, L./All.	.	12,010
C. maj.	....	13,779
(June '83, C. maj. 15,965)		

Sevenoaks (Kent)
E. 73,179

*G. M. Wolfson, C.	....	32,945
S. R. Jakobi, L./All.	.....	15,600
G. A. Green, Lab.	....	7,379
C. maj.	....	17,345
(June '83, C. maj. 15,706)		

Sheffield (S. Yorks)

ATTERCLIFFE E. 67,051

*A. E. P. Duffy, Lab.	......	28,266
G. J. Perry, C.	....	11,075
Ms. H. E. Woolley, SDP/ All.	....	9,549
Lab. maj.	....	17,191
(June '83, Lab. maj. 11,612)		

BRIGHTSIDE E. 64,982

D. Blunkett, Lab.	....	31,208
Miss M. C. Glyn, C.	......	7,017
J. A. Leeman, L./All.	.....	6,434
Lab. maj.	....	24,191
(June '83, Lab. maj. 15,209)		

CENTRAL *E.* 61,156
*R. G. Caborn, *Lab.* 25,872
B. Oxley, *C.* 6,530
Ms. F. C. Hornby, *SDP/All.* 5,314
C. T. Dingle, *RF.* 278
K. E. Petts, *Comm.* 203
   Lab. maj. 19,342
   (June '83, Lab. maj. 16,790)

HALLAM *E.* 74,158
C. I. Patnick, *C.* 25,649
P. J. Gold, *L./All.* 18,012
M. C. Savani, *Lab.* 11,290
Ms. L. M. Spencer, *Grn.* .. 459
   C. maj. 7,637
   (June '83, C. maj. 11,774)

HEELEY *E.* 73,931
*W. Michie, *Lab.* 28,425
N. P. Mearing-Smith, *C.* .. 13,985
P. Moore, *SDP/All.* 10,811
   Lab. maj. 14,440
   (June '83, Lab. maj. 8,368)

HILLSBOROUGH *E.* 76,312
*M. H. Flannery, *Lab.* 26,208
D. Chadwick, *L./All.* 22,922
J. D. Sykes, *C.* 10,396
   Lab. maj. 3,286
   (June '83, Lab. maj. 1,546)

Sherwood (Notts)
E. 71,378
*A. S. Stewart, *C.* 26,816
W. S. G. Bach, *Lab.* 22,321
S. R. Thompstone, *SDP/All.* 9,343
   C. maj. 4,495
   (June '83, C. maj. 658)

Shipley (W. Yorks)
E. 68,705
*Sir J. M. Fox, MBE, *C.* 26,941
W. J. L. Wallace, *L./All.* .. 14,311
C. R. B. Butler, *Lab.* 12,669
C. M. Harris, *Grn.* 507
   C. maj. 12,630
   (June '83, C. maj. 11,445)

Shoreham (W. Sussex)
E. 71,318
*Rt. Hon. R. N. Luce, *C.* ... 33,660
J. A. Ingram, *L./All.* 16,590
P. Godwin, *Lab.* 5,053
   C. maj. 17,070
   (June '83, C. maj. 15,766)

Shrewsbury and Atcham (Salop)
E. 70,689
*D. L. Conway, *C.* 26,027
R. Hutchison, *L./All.* 16,963
Mrs. E. Owen, *Lab.* 10,797
G. Hardy, *Grn.* 660
   C. maj. 9,064
   (June '83, C. maj. 8,624)

Shropshire North
E. 77,122
*Rt. Hon. W. J. Biffen, *C.* .. 30,385
G. Smith, *L./All.* 15,970
R. Hawkins, *Lab.* 11,866
   C. maj. 14,415
   (June '83, C. maj. 11,667)

Skipton and Ripon
(N. Yorks)
E. 72,199

D. M. Curry, *C.* 33,128
S. J. Cooksey, *L./All.* 15,954
T. L. Whitfield, *Lab.* 6,264
Ms. L. S. Williams, *Grn.* .. 825
   C. maj. 17,174
   (June '83, C. maj. 15,046)

Slough (Berks)
E. 73,424

*J. A. Watts, *C.* 26,166
E. Lopez, *Lab.* 22,076
M. Goldstone, *SDP/All.* ... 7,490
   C. maj. 4,090
   (June '83, C. maj. 3,106)

Solihull (W. Midlands)
E. 78,123

*J. M. Taylor, *C.* 35,844
G. E. Gadie, *L./All.* 14,058
Mrs. S. E. Knowles, *Lab.* . 8,791
   C. maj. 21,786
   (June '83, C. maj. 17,394)

Somerton and Frome
(Somerset)
E. 68,773

*Hon. R. T. Boscawen, MC, *C.* 29,351
R. G. Morgan, *L./All.* 19,813
I. S. Kelly, *Lab.* 5,461
   C. maj. 9,538
   (June '83, C. maj. 9,227)

Southampton (Hants)

ITCHEN *E.* 72,687
*C. R. Chope, OBE, *C.* 24,419
J. Y. Denham, *Lab.* 17,703
R. C. Mitchell, *SDP/All.* .. 13,006
   C. maj. 6,716
   (June '83, C. maj. 5,290)

TEST *E.* 73,918
*S. J. A. Hill, *C.* 25,722
A. P. V. Whitehead, *Lab.* . 18,768
Mrs. V. Rayner, *L./All.* ... 11,950
   C. maj. 6,954
   (June '83, C. maj. 9,346)

Southend (Essex)

EAST *E.* 59,073
*E. M. Taylor, *C.* 23,753
H. J. Berkeley, *SDP/All.* .. 9,906
D. R. Scully, *Lab.* 7,296
   C. maj. 13,847
   (June '83, C. maj. 10,691)

WEST *E.* 68,415
*Rt. Hon. H. P. G. Channon, *C.* 28,003
G. Grant, *L./All.* 19,603
Mrs. A. Smith, *Lab.* 3,899
   C. maj. 8,400
   (June '83, C. maj. 8,033)

South Hams (Devon)
E. 78,583

*A. D. Steen, *C.* 34,218
R. F. Chave, *L./All.* 21,072
*W. W. Hamilton, *Lab.* 5,060
C. G. Titmuss, *Grn.* 1,178
T. C. Langsford, *LM* 277
   C. maj. 13,146
   (June '83, C. maj. 12,401)

Southport (Merseyside)
E. 71,443

R. C. Fearn, *L./All.* 26,110
N. M. Thomas, *C.* 24,261
Mrs. A. Moore, *Lab.* 3,483
J. R. G. Walker, *Grn.* 653
   L./All. maj. 1,849
   (June '83, C. maj. 5,039)

South Ribble (Lancs
E. 72,177

*R. J. Atkins, *C.* 28,133
D. F. Roebuck, *Lab.* 19,703
J. A. Holleran, *L./All.* 11,746
   C. maj. 8,430
   (June '83, C. maj. 12,659)

South Shields (Tyne & Wear)
E. 60,754

*Dr. D. G. Clark, *Lab.* 24,882
M. L. D. Fabricant, *C.* 11,031
Ms. M. Meling, *SDP/All.* .. 6,654
E. G. Dunn, *Dem.* 408
   Lab. maj. 13,851
   (June '83, Lab. maj. 6,402)

Southwark and Bermondsey
(Gtr. London)
E. 55,438

*S. H. W. Hughes, *L./All.* .. 17,072
J. Bryan, *Lab.* 14,293
O. Heald, *C.* 4,522
P. N. Power, *Comm.* 108
   L./All. maj. 2,779
   (June '83, L./All. maj. 5,164)

Spelthorne (Surrey)
E. 72,967

D. Wilshire, *C.* 32,440
Mrs. M. Cunningham, *SDP/All.* 12,390
D. F. J. Welfare, *Lab.* 9,227
   C. maj. 20,050
   (June '83, C. maj. 13,506)

Stafford
E. 72,431

*W. N. P. Cash, *C.* 29,541
C. B. Phipps, *SDP/All.* ... 15,834
Ms. N. Hafeez, *Lab.* 12,177
   C. maj. 13,707
   (June '83, C. maj. 14,277)
   (May '84, C. maj. 3,980)

Staffordshire

MID *E.* 71,252
*B. J. Heddle, *C.* 28,644
C. R. St. Hill, *Lab.* 13,990
T. A. Jones, *L./All.* 13,114
J. G. Bazeley, *Ind. C.* 836
   C. maj. 14,654
   (June '83, C. maj. 13,880)
   (*See also* p. 239)

MOORLANDS *E.* 74,302
*D. L. Knox, C. 31,613
Mrs. V. Ivers, *Lab.* 17,186
J. P. Corbett, *SDP/All.* 10,950
   C. maj. 14,427
   (June '83, C. maj. 16,566)

SOUTH *E.* 79,261
*P. T. Cormack, C. 37,708
Mrs. F. Oborski, *L./All.* .. 12,440
P. Bateman, *Lab.* 11,805
   C. maj. 25,268
   (June '83, C. maj. 19,760)

SOUTH EAST *E.* 66,176
*D. L. Lightbown, C. 25,115
Miss E. Gluck, *SDP/All.* .. 14,230
D. Spilsbury, *Lab.* 13,874
   C. maj. 10,885
   (June '83, C. maj. 10,898)

Stalybridge and Hyde
(Gtr. Manchester)
E. 67,983
*T. Pendry, Lab. 24,401
R. N. Greenwood, *C.* 18,738
P. J. Ashenden, *SDP/All.* .. 7,311
   Lab. maj. 5,663
   (June '83, Lab. maj. 4,362)

Stamford and Spalding (Lincs)
E. 70,560
J. Q. Davies, *C.* 31,000
Miss R. Bryan, *L./All.* 17,009
P. E. Lowe, *Lab.* 6,882
   C. maj. 13,991
   (June '83, C. maj. 11,756)

Stevenage (Herts)
E. 69,525
*T. J. R. Wood, C. 23,541
B. R. M. Stoneham, *SDP/*
  All. 18,201
M. R. C. Withers, *Lab.* ... 14,229
   C. maj. 5,340
   (June '83, C. maj. 1,755)

Stockport (Gtr. Manchester)
E. 60,059
*A. R. Favell, C. 19,410
Mrs. S. Haines, *Lab.* 16,557
J. L. Begg, *SDP/All.* 10,365
M. Shipley, *Grn.* 573
   C. maj. 2,853
   (June '83, C. maj. 5,786)

Stockton (Cleveland)
NORTH *E.* 70,329
*F. Cook, Lab. 26,043
D. J. C. Faber, *C.* 17,242
N. F. G. Bosanquet, *SDP/*
  All. 9,712
   Lab. maj. 8,801
   (June '83, Lab. maj. 1,870)

SOUTH *E.* 75,279
T. R. Devlin, *C.* 20,833
*I. W. Wrigglesworth, SDP/
  All. 20,059
J. M. Scott, *Lab.* 18,600
   C. maj. 774
   (June '83, SDP/All. maj. 102)

Stoke-on-Trent (Staffs)
CENTRAL *E.* 65,987
*M. Fisher, Lab. 23,842
D. Stone, *C.* 14,072
I. Cundy, *SDP/All.* 7,462
   Lab. maj. 9,770
   (June '83, Lab. maj. 8,250)

NORTH *E.* 74,184
Ms. J. L. Walley, *Lab.* 25,459
R. Davies, *C.* 16,946
S. J. Simmonds, *SDP/All.* .. 11,665
   Lab. maj. 8,513
   (June '83, Lab. maj. 8,203)

SOUTH *E.* 70,806
*Rt. Hon. J. Ashley, CH, Lab. 24,794
D. Hartshorne, *C.* 19,741
P. Wild, *L./All.* 7,669
   Lab. maj. 5,053
   (June '83, Lab. maj. 7,105)

Stratford-upon-Avon (Warwicks)
E. 81,263
*A. T. Howarth, CBE, C. .. 38,483
D. G. Cowcher, *L./All.* ... 17,318
R. H. Rhodes, *Lab.* 6,335
   C. maj. 21,165
   (June '83, C. maj. 17,917)

Streatham (Gtr. London)
E. 60,519
*W. J. M. Shelton, C. 18,916
Ms. A. Tapsall, *Lab.* 16,509
M. Tuffrey, *L./All.* 6,663
   C. maj. 2,407
   (June '83, C. maj. 5,902)

Stretford (Gtr. Manchester)
E. 57,568
*A. J. Lloyd, Lab. 22,831
D. Dougherty, *C.* 13,429
D. Lee, *SDP/All.* 5,125
   Lab. maj. 9,402
   (June '83, Lab. maj. 4,342)

Stroud (Glos)
E. 81,275
R. M. Knapman, *C.* 32,883
A. A. Walker-Smith, *L./All.* 20,508
T. Levitt, *Lab.* 12,145
   C. maj. 12,375
   (June '83, C. maj. 11,714)

Suffolk
CENTRAL *E.* 79,199
*M. N. Lord, C. 32,422
T. Dale, *L./All.* 16,132
M. Walker, *Lab.* 11,817
   C. maj. 16,290
   (June '83, C. maj. 14,731)

COASTAL *E.* 75,684
*Rt. Hon. J. S. Gummer, C. 32,834
Mrs. J. M. Miller, *SDP/All.* 17,554
Mrs. S. A. Reeves, *Lab.* ... 7,534
J. W. Holloway, *Grn.* 1,049
   C. maj. 15,280
   (June '83, C. maj. 15,622)

SOUTH *E.* 81,954
*T. S. K. Yeo, C. 33,972
C. M. N. Bradford, *L./All.* 17,729
A. C. Bavington, *Lab.* 11,876
   C. maj. 16,243
   (June '83, C. maj. 11,269)

Sunderland
(Tyne & Wear)
NORTH *E.* 75,674
*R. A. Clay, Lab. 29,767
I. S. Picton, *C.* 15,095
T. Jenkinson, *L./All.* 8,518
   Lab. maj. 14,672
   (June '83, Lab. maj. 7,196)

SOUTH *E.* 74,947
C. J. Mullin, *Lab.* 28,823
G. E. Howe, *C.* 16,210
K. Hudson, *SDP/All.* 7,768
D. N. Jacques, *Grn.* 516
   Lab. maj. 12,613
   (June '83, Lab. maj. 5,548)

Surbiton (Gtr. London)
E. 45,428
*R. P. Tracey, C. 19,861
D. T. Burke, *SDP/All.* 10,120
A. McGowan, *Lab.* 5,111
Ms. J. Vidler, *Grn.* 465
   C. maj. 9,741
   (June '83, C. maj. 8,749)

Surrey
EAST *E.* 59,528
*Rt. Hon. Sir R. E. G. Howe,
  QC, C. 29,126
M. A. J. Anderson, *L./All.* 11,000
M. Davis, *Lab.* 4,779
D. Newell, *Grn.* 1,044
   C. maj. 18,126
   (June '83, C. maj. 15,436)

NORTH WEST *E.* 83,083
*W. M. J. Grylls, C. 38,535
C. Brodie, *L./All.* 14,960
J. Cooper, *Lab.* 6,751
   C. maj. 23,575
   (June '83, C. maj. 21,018)

SOUTH WEST *E.* 73,018
*Mrs. V. H. B. M. Bottomley,
  C. 34,024
G. D. Scott, *L./All.* 19,681
J. K. P. Evers, *Lab.* 3,224
M. J. Green, *Ind. C.* 299
   C. maj. 14,343
   (June '83, C. maj. 14,351)
   (May '84, C. maj. 2,599)

Sussex Mid
E. 80,147
*R. T. Renton, C. 37,781
N. S. E. Westbrook, *L./All.* 19,489
R. Hughes, *Lab.* 4,573
   C. maj. 18,292
   (June '83, C. maj. 16,744)

Sutton and Cheam
(Gtr. London)
E. 63,850
*D. N. Macfarlane, C. 29,710
R. D. Grieg, *L./All.* 13,992
Ms. L. Monk, *Lab.* 5,202
   C. maj. 15,718
   (June '83, C. maj. 10,264)

Sutton Coldfield (W. Midlands)
E. 72,329

*Rt. Hon. P. N. Fowler, C. .	34,475
T. Bick, *L./All.*	13,292
P. McLoughlin, *Lab.*	6,104
C. maj.	21,183
(June '83, C. maj. 18,984)	

Swindon (Wilts)
E. 86,150

*S. C. Coombs, C.	29,385
Ms. G. Johnston, *Lab.*	24,528
D. J. Scott, *SDP/All.*	13,114
C. maj.	4,857
(June '83, C. maj. 1,395)	

Tatton (Cheshire)
E. 71,904

*M. N. Hamilton, C.	30,128
Ms. B. Gaskin, *SDP/All.*	13,034
Ms. H. A. Blears, *Lab.*	11,760
M. G. Gibson, *FP.*	263
C. maj.	17,094
(June '83, C. maj. 13,960)	

Taunton (Somerset)
E. 74,145

D. J. Nicholson, C.	30,248
M. A. K. Cocks, *SDP/All.* ..	19,868
Dr. G. Reynolds, *Lab.*	8,754
C. maj.	10,380
(June '83, C. maj. 12,567)	

Teignbridge (Devon)
E. 71,872

*P. C. M. Nicholls, C.	30,693
R. D. Ryder, *L./All.*	20,268
J. Greenwood, *Lab.*	6,413
A. Hope, *LM*	312
C. maj.	10,425
(June '83, C. maj. 8,218)	

Thanet (Kent)

NORTH *E.* 69,723

*R. J. Gale, C.	29,225
N. R. M. Cranston, *SDP/*	
All.	11,745
A. M. Bretman, *Lab.*	8,395
D. R. Condor, *Grn.*	996
C. maj.	17,480
(June '83, C. maj. 14,545)	

SOUTH *E.* 62,761

*J. W. P. Aitken, C.	25,135
W. H. Pitt, *L./All.*	11,452
C. Wright, *Lab.*	9,673
C. maj.	13,683
(June '83, C. maj. 14,051)	

Thurrock (Essex)
E. 67,594

T. S. Janman, *C.*	20,527
*Dr. O. A. McDonald, Lab.	19,837
D. S. Benson, *SDP/All.* ...	7,970
C. maj.	690
(June '83, Lab. maj. 1,722)	

Tiverton (Devon)
E. 68,210

*R. J. Maxwell-Hyslop, C. .	29,875
D. J. Morrish, *L./All.*	20,663
Mrs. J. A. Northam, *Lab.* ..	3,400
W. J. Jones, *LAO*	434
C. maj.	9,212
(June '83, C. maj. 7,886)	

Tonbridge and Malling (Kent)
E. 76,797

*Rt. Hon. J. P. Stanley, C. .	33,990
M. J. Ward, *SDP/All.*	17,561
D. G. Still, *Lab.*	7,803
M. D. S. Easter, *BN.*	369
C. maj.	16,429
(June '83, C. maj. 13,520)	

Tooting (Gtr. London)
E. 68,116

*T. M. Cox, Lab.	21,457
M. A. Winter, *C.*	20,016
J. N. Ambache, *SDP/All.* ..	6,423
Ms. M. Vickery, *Grn.*	621
Lab. maj.	1,441
(June '83, Lab. maj. 2,659)	

Torbay (Devon)
E. 70,435

R. W. S. Allason, *C.*	29,029
N. D. Bye, *L./All.*	20,209
G. R. Taylor, *Lab.*	4,538
C. maj.	8,820
(June '83, C. maj. 6,555)	

Tottenham (Gtr. London)
E. 76,092

B. A. L. Grant, *Lab.*	21,921
P. L. Murphy, *C.*	17,780
S. Etherington, *L./All.* ...	8,983
D. Nicholls, *Grn.*	744
P. Nealon, *Gait. Lab.*	638
Ms. C. L. Dixon, *WRP*	205
Lab. maj.	4,141
(June '83, Lab. maj. 9,396)	

Truro (Cornwall)
E. 72,432

*M. O. J. Taylor, L./All. ...	28,368
N. F. St. Aubyn, *C.*	23,615
J. R. King, *Lab.*	5,882
L./All. maj.	4,753
(June '83, L./All. maj. 10,480)	
(March '87, L./All. maj. 14,617)	

Tunbridge Wells (Kent)
E. 76,291

*Sir P. B. B. Mayhew, QC, C.	33,111
Mrs. D. A. Buckrell, *L./All.*	16,989
P. L. Sloman, *Lab.*	6,555
C. maj.	16,122
(June '83, C. maj. 15,126)	

Twickenham (Gtr. London)
E. 64,661

*T. F. H. Jessel, C.	27,331
J. Waller, *L./All.*	20,204
Ms. V. C. M. Vaz, *Lab.* ...	4,415
D. S. Batchelor, *Grn.*	746
C. maj.	7,127
(June '83, C. maj. 4,792)	

Tyne Bridge
(Tyne & Wear)
E. 58,152

*D. G. Clelland, Lab.	23,131
M. W. Bates, *C.*	7,558
J. C. Mansfield, *SDP/All.*	6,005
Lab. maj.	15,573
(June '83, Lab. maj. 11,693)	
(Dec '85, Lab. maj. 6,575)	

Tynemouth
(Tyne & Wear)
E. 74,407

*N. G. Trotter, C.	25,113
P. Cosgrove, *Lab.*	22,530
D. F. Mayhew, *L./All.*	10,446
C. maj.	2,583
(June '83, C. maj. 9,609)	

Upminster (Gtr. London)
E. 66,613

*Sir N. C. Bonsor, Bt., C. ..	27,946
J. Martin, *SDP/All.*	11,089
D. R. O'Flynn, *Lab.*	11,069
C. maj.	16,857
(June '83, C. maj. 12,814)	

Uxbridge (Gtr. London)
E. 63,157

*J. M. Shersby, C.	27,292
D. Keys, *Lab.*	11,322
A. Goodman, *SDP/All.* ...	9,164
I. Flindall, *Grn.*	549
C. maj.	15,970
(June '83, C. maj. 12,837)	

Vauxhall (Gtr. London)
E. 66,538

*S. K. Holland, Lab.	21,364
D. R. Lidington, *C.*	12,345
S. H. V. Acland, *SDP/All.*	7,764
Ms. J. Owens, *Grn.*	770
D. J. S. Cook, *Comm.*	223
K. Oluremi, *RF.*	117
Lab. maj.	9,019
(June '83, Lab. maj. 7,780)	
(*See also* p. 239)	

Wakefield (W. Yorks)
E. 69,580

D. M. Hinchliffe, *Lab.*	24,509
N. J. Hazell, *C.*	21,720
Dr. L. Kamal, *SDP/All* ...	6,350
Lab. maj.	2,789
(June '83, Lab. maj. 360)	

Wallasey (Merseyside)
E. 67,216

*Mrs. L. Chalker, C.	22,791
L. Duffy, *Lab.*	22,512
J. K. Richardson, *SDP/*	
All.	8,363
C. maj.	279
(June '83, C. maj. 6,708)	

Wallsend (Tyne & Wear)
E. 76,688

*W. E. Garrett, Lab.	32,709
D. Milburn, *C.*	13,325
Mrs. J. Phylactou, *SDP/*	
All.	11,508
Lab. maj.	19,384
(June '83, Lab. maj. 12,514)	

Walsall (W. Midlands)

NORTH *E.* 68,331

*D. J. Winnick, Lab.	......	21,458
Mrs. L. Hertz, *C.*	......	19,668
I. Shires, *L./All.*	....	9,285
Lab. maj.	....	1,790

(June '83, Lab. maj. 2,824)

SOUTH *E.* 66,746

*B. T. George, Lab.	......	22,629
G. E. Postles, *C.*	....	21,513
L. A. King, *L./All.*	......	6,241
Lab. maj.	....	1,116

(June '83, Lab. maj. 702)

Walthamstow (Gtr. London)
E. 48,691

H. H. F. Summerson, *C.*	..	13,748
*E. P. Deakins, Lab.	....	12,236
P. L. Leighton, *SDP/All.*		8,852
Dr. Z. I. Malik, *DC*	....	396
C. maj.	....	1,512

(June '83, Lab. maj. 1,305)

Wansbeck (Nthmb)
E. 62,639

*J. Thompson, Lab.	......	28,080
Mrs. S. Mitchell, *L./All.*	..	11,291
D. Walton, *C.*	....	9,490
Lab. maj.	....	16,789

(June '83, Lab. maj. 7,831)

Wansdyke (Avon)
E. 75,239

*J. H. Aspinwall, C.	......	31,537
R. B. Blackmore, *L./All.*	..	15,393
I. White, *Lab.*	....	14,231
C. maj.	....	16,144

(June '83, C. maj. 13,066)

Wanstead and Woodford
(Gtr. London)
E. 57,921

J. N. Arbuthnot, *C.*	......	25,701
J. R. Bastick, *L./All.*	.....	9,289
Mrs. L. Hilton, *Lab.*	......	6,958
C. maj.	....	16,412

(June '83, C. maj. 14,354)

Wantage (Oxon)
E. 66,499

*R. V. Jackson, C.	....	27,951
Mrs. W. Tumin, *SDP/All.*		15,795
S. Ladyman, *Lab.*	....	8,055
C. maj.	....	12,156

(June '83, C. maj. 10,125)

Warley (W. Midlands)

EAST *E.* 55,706

*A. M. W. Faulds, Lab.	...	19,428
A. Antoniou, *C.*	....	13,843
J. J. Jordan, *SDP/All.*	...	5,396
Lab. maj.	....	5,585

(June '83, Lab. maj. 3,391)

WEST *E.* 57,526

*Rt. Hon. P. K. Archer, QC,		
Lab.	....	19,825
W. Williams, *C.*	....	14,432
Miss E. Todd, *L./All.*	.....	6,027
Lab. maj.	....	5,393

(June '83, Lab. maj. 5,268)

Warrington (Cheshire)

NORTH *E.* 75,627

*E. D. H. Hoyle, Lab.	....	27,422
L. Jones, *C.*	....	19,409
C. Bithel, *SDP/All.*	......	10,046
Lab. maj.	....	8,013

(June '83, Lab. maj. 5,277)

SOUTH *E.* 76,219

C. J. Butler, C,	....	24,809
A. Booth, *Lab.*	....	21,200
I. Marks, *L./All.*	....	13,112
C. maj.	....	3,609

(June '83, C. maj. 6,465)

Warwick and Leamington
E. 72,763

*Sir D. G. Smith, C.	......	27,530
K. P. O'Sullivan, *SDP/All.*		13,548
Ms. A. Christina, *Lab.*	...	13,019
Ms. J. A. Alty, *Grn.*	......	1,214
C. maj.	....	13,982

(June '83, C. maj. 13,032)

Warwickshire

NORTH *E.* 70,687

*Hon. F. A. A. Maude, C.	..	25,453
M. O'Brien, *Lab.*	....	22,624
Mrs. S. J. Neale, *SDP/All.*		8,382
C. maj.	....	2,829

(June '83, C. maj. 2,585)

Watford (Herts)
E. 73,540

*W. A. T. T. Garel-Jones, C.		27,912
M. J. Jackson, *Lab.*	......	16,176
Mrs. F. M. Beckett, *SDP/*		
All.	....	13,202
C. maj.	....	11,736

(June '83, C. maj. 12,006)

Waveney (Suffolk)
E. 81,889

D. J. Porter, *C.*	....	31,067
J. A. Lark, *Lab.*	....	19,284
D. Beaven, *SDP/All.*	.....	13,845
C. maj.	....	11,783

(June '83, C. maj. 14,298)

Wealden (E. Sussex)
E. 73,057

*Sir G. J. Johnson Smith,		
C.	....	35,154
D. Sinclair, *SDP/All.*	.....	15,044
C. Ward, *Lab.*	....	4,563
C. maj.	....	20,110

(June '83, C. maj. 17,185)

Wellingborough (Northants)
E. 70,450

*P. D. Fry, C.	....	29,038
J. Currie, *Lab.*	....	14,968
L. E. Stringer, *L./All.*	...	11,047
C. maj.	....	14,070

(June '83, C. maj. 12,056)

Wells (Somerset)
E. 67,195

*D. P. Heathcoat-Amory, C.		28,624
A. A. S. Butt Philip, *L./All.*		20,083
P. James, *Lab.*	....	4,637
J. S. Fish, *Falk.*	....	134
C. maj.	....	8,541

(June '83, C. maj. 6,575)

Welwyn Hatfield (Herts)
E. 73,607

D. J. Evans, C.	....	27,164
Miss L. P. Granshaw, *SDP/*		
All.	....	16,261
C. R. Pond, *Lab.*	....	15,699
B. I. Dyson, *Ind. C.*	......	401
C. maj.	....	10,903

(June '83, C. maj. 12,246)

Wentworth (S. Yorks)
E. 63,886

*P. Hardy, Lab.	....	30,205
W. J. Hague, *C.*	....	10,113
D. M. Eglin, *SDP/All.*	....	6,031
Lab. maj.	....	20,092

(June '83, Lab. maj. 15,935)

West Bromwich (W. Midlands)

EAST *E.* 58,239

*P. C. Snape, Lab.	....	18,162
R. F. Woodhouse, *C.*	.....	17,179
M. G. Smith, *L./All.*	......	7,268
Lab. maj.	....	983

(June '83, Lab. maj. 298)

WEST *E.* 58,944

*Miss B. Boothroyd, Lab.	..	19,925
F. A. Betteridge, *C.*	......	14,672
A. Collingbourne, *SDP/*		
All.	....	4,877
Lab. maj.	....	5,253

(June '83, Lab. maj. 6,639)

Westbury (Wilts)
E. 84,860

*D. M. Walters, MBE, *C.*	....	34,256
D. J. Hughes, *L./All.*	.....	24,159
H. W. Thomas, *Lab.*	......	7,982
C. maj.	....	10,097

(June '83, C. maj. 8,506)

Westminster North
(Gtr. London)
E. 59,263

*J. D. Wheeler, C.	....	19,941
Ms. J. F. Edwards, *Lab.*	..	16,631
R. J. De Ste Croix, *SDP/*		
All.	....	5,116
D. Stutchfield, *Grn.*	......	450
C. maj.	....	3,310

(June '83, C. maj. 1,710)

Westmorland and Lonsdale
(Cumbria)
E. 70,237

*Rt. Hon. T. M. Jopling, C.	..	30,259
S. Collins, *L./All.*	....	15,339
C. Halfpenny, *Lab.*	......	6,968
C. maj.	....	14,920

(June '83, C. maj. 16,587)

Weston-super-Mare (Avon)
E. 76,341

*A. W. Wiggin, TD, *C.*	.....	28,547
J. R. Crockford-Hawley,		
SDP/All.	....	20,549
P. J. Loach, *Lab.*	....	6,584
Dr. R. H. Lawson, *Grn.*	...	2,067
C. maj.	....	7,998

(June '83, C. maj. 9,491)

Wigan (Gtr. Manchester)
E. 72,064

R. Stott, CBE, Lab.	....	33,955
K. R. Wade, C.	....	13,493
K. J. White, L./All.	....	7,732
Lab. maj.	....	20,462
(June '83, Lab. maj. 17,305)		

Wiltshire North
E. 80,712

R. F. Needham, C.	....	35,309
C. S. M. Graham, L./All.	..	24,370
Mrs. C. Reid, Lab.	....	4,343
C. maj.	....	10,939
(June '83, C. maj. 7,232)		

Wimbledon (Gtr. London)
E. 63,353

Dr. C. Goodson-Wickes, C.		24,538
A. C. Slade, L./All.	....	16,144
Ms. C. M. Bickerstaff, Lab.		10,428
C. maj.	....	11,301
(June '83, C. maj. 11,546)		

Winchester (Hants)
E. 76,507

J. E. D. D. Browne, C.	....	32,195
J. L. MacDonald, SDP/		
All.	....	24,716
F. C. Inglis, Lab.	....	4,028
Ms. J. P. Walker, Grn.	....	565
C. maj.	....	7,479
(June '83, C. maj. 13,047)		

Windsor and Maidenhead
(Berks)
E. 79,319

Dr. A. Glyn, ERD, C.	......	33,980
S. J. Jackson, L./All.	.....	16,144
Ms. H. B. De Lyon, Lab.	..	6,678
W. O. Board, Ind. C.	.....	1,938
P. Gordon, Grn.	....	711
Ms. P. H. Stephenson, BT		328
C. maj.	....	17,836
(June '83, C. maj. 18,203)		

Wirral (Merseyside)

SOUTH *E.* 62,251

G. B. Porter, C.	....	24,821
J. S. Swarbrooke, Lab.	...	13,858
P. N. Gilchrist, L./All.	...	10,779
C. maj.	....	10,963
(June '83, C. maj. 13,838)		

WEST *E.* 63,597

D. J. F. Hunt, MBE, C.	....	25,736
A. H. Dunn, Lab.	....	13,013
A. J. Brame, L./All.	....	10,015
D. Burton, Grn.	....	806
C. maj.	....	12,723
(June '83, C. maj. 15,151)		

Witney (Oxon)
E. 75,284

Rt. Hon. D. R. Hurd, CBE,		
C.	....	33,458
Miss M. E. Burton, L./All.		14,994
Ms. C. Collette, Lab.	.....	9,733
C. maj.	....	18,464
(June '83, C. maj. 12,712)		

Woking (Surrey)
E. 82,476

C. G. D. Onslow, C.	......	35,990
P. Goldenberg, L./All.	....	19,446
Miss A. J. Pollack, Lab.	..	6,537
C. maj.	....	16,544
(June '83, C. maj. 16,237)		

Wokingham (Berks)
E. 85,474

J. A. Redwood, C.	......	39,808
J. C. Leston, L./All.	......	19,421
P. J. Morgan, Lab.	......	5,622
C. maj.	....	20,387
(June '83, C. maj. 15,698)		

Wolverhampton (W. Midlands)

NORTH EAST *E.* 63,464

Mrs. M. P. Hicks, C.	.....	19,857
K. Purchase, Lab.	......	19,653
M. Pearson, L./All.	......	7,623
C. maj.	....	204
(June '83, Lab. maj. 214)		

SOUTH EAST *E.* 55,710

D. Turner, Lab.	....	19,760
J. P. Mellor, C.	....	13,362
R. F. Whitehouse, L./All.	.	7,258
Lab. maj.	....	6,398
(June '83, Lab. maj. 5,012)		

SOUTH WEST *E.* 68,586

N. W. Budgen, C.	....	26,235
R. Lawrence, Lab.	......	15,917
B. Lamb, SDP/All.	......	9,616
C. maj.	....	10,318
(June '83, C. maj. 11,520)		

Woodspring (Avon)
E. 76,289

Sir P. Dean, C.	....	34,134
Mrs. C. R. Coleman, L./All.		16,282
D. L. T. Chapple, Lab.	...	8,717
Dr. B. R. Keeble, Grn.	...	1,208
C. maj.	....	17,852
(June '83, C. maj. 15,132)		

Woolwich (Gtr. London)
E. 58,071

J. C. Cartwright, SDP/All.		17,137
J. Austin Walker, Lab.	...	15,200
A. Salter, C.	....	8,723
SDP/All. maj.	....	1,937
(June '83, SDP/All. maj. 2,725)		

Worcester
E. 68,980

Rt. Hon. P. E. Walker, MBE,		
C.	....	25,504
M. J. Webb, Lab.	......	15,051
J. J. Caiger, SDP/All.	...	12,386
C. maj.	....	10,453
(June '83, C. maj. 10,871)		

Worcestershire

MID *E.* 80,591

M. E. Forth, C.	....	31,854
P. Pinfield, Lab.	......	16,943
E. Harwood, SDP/All.	...	12,954
C. maj.	....	14,911
(June '83, C. maj. 14,205)		

SOUTH *E.* 77,237

W. M. H. Spicer, C.	......	32,277
P. J. Chandler, L./All.	....	18,632
R. J. Garnett, Lab.	....	6,374
G. M. H. Woodford, Grn.	.	1,089
C. maj.	....	13,645
(June '83, C. maj. 11,389)		

Workington (Cumbria)
E. 56,911

D. N. Campbell-Savours,		
Lab.	....	24,019
Miss A. C. B. McIntosh, C.		17,000
G. W. Badger, L./All.	.....	4,853
Lab. maj.	....	7,019
(June '83, Lab. maj. 7,128)		

Worsley (Gtr. Manchester)
E. 73,208

T. Lewis, Lab.	....	27,157
Mrs. V. Horman, C.	......	19,820
D. Cowpe, L./All.	......	9,507
Lab. maj.	....	7,337
(June '83, Lab. maj. 4,139)		

Worthing (W. Sussex)
E. 77,000

Rt. Hon. T. L. Higgins, C.	.	34,573
B. A. Clare, L./All.	....	16,072
J. Deen, Lab.	....	5,387
C. maj.	....	18,501
(June '83, C. maj. 15,253)		

The Wrekin (Salop)
E. 82,520

B. J. Grocott, Lab.	......	27,681
P. W. Hawksley, C.	......	26,225
G. Cook, SDP/All.	......	10,737
Lab. maj.	....	1,456
(June '83, C. maj. 1,331)		

Wycombe (Bucks)
E. 71,918

R. W. Whitney, OBE, C.	...	28,209
T. E. G. Hayhoe, SDP/All.		14,390
J. R. W. Huddart, Lab.	...	9,773
C. maj.	....	13,819
(June '83, C. maj. 13,197)		

Wyre (Lancs)
E. 67,066

K. D. R. Mans, C.	....	26,800
I. C. Murdoch, SDP/All.		12,139
P. Ainscough, Lab.	......	10,725
R. Brown, Grn.	....	874
C. maj.	....	14,661
(June '83, C. maj. 14,811)		

Wyre Forest (H & W)
E. 70,784

A. M. V. Coombs, C.	.....	25,877
A. J. Batchelor, L./All.	...	18,653
N. Knowles, Lab.	....	10,365
C. maj.	....	7,224
(June '83, C. maj. 8,177)		

Yeovil (Somerset)
E. 70,390

J. J. D. Ashdown, L./All.	.	28,841
G. D. S. Sandeman, C.	...	23,141
J. Fitzmaurice, Lab.	.....	4,099
L./All. maj.	....	5,700
(June '83, L./All. maj. 3,406)		

York (N. Yorks)
E. 79,297

*C. R. Gregory, C.	....	25,880
H. Bayley, *Lab.*		25,733
J. V. Cable, *SDP/All.*	......	9,898
A. D. Dunnett, *Grn.*	......	637
C. maj.	....	147
(June '83, C. maj. 3,647)		

WALES

Aberavon (W. Glam)
E. 52,280

*Rt. Hon. J. Morris, QC, *Lab.*	27,126
Mrs. M. Harris, *L./All.*	...	6,517
P. Warrick, *C.*		5,861
Miss A. Howells, *PC.*	......	1,124
Lab. maj.	....	20,609
(June '83, Lab. maj. 15,539)		

Alyn and Deeside (Clwyd)
E. 58,674

*S. B. Jones, *Lab.*	....	22,916
N. J. Twilley, *C.*	....	16,500
E. C. H. Owen, *SDP/All.*	....	7,273
J. D. Rogers, *PC.*	....	478
Lab. maj.	....	6,416
(June '83, Lab. maj. 1,368)		

Blaenau Gwent
E. 56,011

*Rt. Hon. M. M. Foot, *Lab.*	..	32,820
A. R. Taylor, *C.*	....	4,959
D. I. McBride, *L./All.*	.....	3,847
S. Morgan, *PC.*	....	1,621
Lab. maj.	....	27,861
(June '83, Lab. maj. 23,705)		

Brecon and Radnor (Powys)
E. 49,394

*R. A. L. Livsey, *L./All.*	....	14,509
J. P. Evans, *C.*	....	14,453
F. R. Willey, *Lab.*	....	12,180
J. H. Davies, *PC*	....	535
L./All. maj.	....	56
(June '83, C. maj. 8,784)		
(July '84, L./All. maj. 559)		

Bridgend (Mid Glam)
E. 57,389

W. J. Griffiths, *Lab.*	......	21,893
*P. C. Hubbard-Miles, *C.*	..	17,513
R. Smart, *SDP/All.*	......	5,590
Miss L. McAllister, *PC*	....	1,065
Lab. maj.	....	4,380
(June '83, C. maj. 1,327)		

Caernarfon (Gwynedd)
E. 45,661

*D. W. Wigley, *PC.*	....	20,338
F. F. E. Aubel, *C.*	....	7,536
D. Rhys Williams, *Lab.*	.....	5,632
J. H. Parsons, *L./All.*	....	2,103
PC maj.	....	12,802
(June '83, PC maj. 10,989)		

Caerphilly (Mid Glam)
E. 64,154

*R. Davies, *Lab.*	....	28,698
M. E. Powell, *C.*	....	9,531
M. G. Butlin, *L./All.*	....	6,923
L. G. Whittle, *PC*	....	3,955
Lab. maj.	....	19,167
(June '83, Lab. maj. 11,553)		

Cardiff (S. Glam)

CENTRAL *E.* 52,980

*I. Grist, *C.*	....	15,241
J. O. Jones, *Lab.*	....	13,255
M. J. German, *L./All.*	.....	12,062
Ms. S. M. Caiach, *PC*	.....	535
C. maj.	....	1,986
(June '83, C. maj. 3,452)		

NORTH *E.* 54,704

*G. H. Jones, *C.*	....	20,061
S. H. Tarbet, *Lab.*	....	11,827
A. W. Jeremy, *SDP/All.*	.....	11,725
Ms. E. M. Bush, *PC*	......	692
C. maj.	....	8,234
(June '83, C. maj. 6,848)		

SOUTH AND PENARTH *E.* 58,714

A. E. Michael, *Lab.*	.....	20,956
G. J. J. Neale, *C.*	....	16,382
Mrs. J. E. Randerson, *L./All.*		6,900
Ms. S. A. Edwards, *PC*	...	599
Lab. maj.	....	4,574
(June '83, Lab. maj. 2,276)		

WEST *E.* 57,363

H. R. Morgan, *Lab.*	......	20,329
*S. Terlezki, *C.*	....	16,284
R. G. Drake, *SDP/All.*	....	7,300
P. J. Keelan, *PC*	....	736
Lab. maj.	....	4,045
(June '83, C. maj. 1,774)		

Carmarthen (Dyfed)
E. 65,252

A. W. Williams, *Lab.*	.....	19,128
R. Richards, *C.*	....	14,811
H. T. Edwards, *PC*	.....	12,457
G. G. Jones, *SDP/All.*	.....	7,203
G. E. Oubridge, *Grn.*	.....	481
Lab. maj.	....	4,317
(June '83, Lab. maj. 1,154)		

Ceredigion and Pembroke North
(Dyfed)
E. 63,141

*G. W. Howells, *L./All.*	....	17,683
O. J. Williams, *C.*	....	12,983
J. R. Davies, *Lab.*	....	8,965
C. G. Davis, *PC*	....	7,848
Mrs. M. A. Wakefield, *Grn.*		821
L./All. maj.	....	4,700
(June '83, L./All. maj. 5,639)		

Clwyd

NORTH WEST *E.* 66,118

*Sir A. J. C. Meyer, Bt., *C.*	.	24,116
K. L. Thomas, *Lab.*	......	12,335
O. G. Griffiths, *L./All.*	.....	11,279
R. K. Davies, *PC*	....	1,966
C. maj.	....	11,781
(June '83, C. maj. 9,989)		

SOUTH WEST *E.* 58,158

M. D. Jones, *Lab.*	....	16,701
*R. L. Harvey, *C.*	....	15,673
R. T. Ellis, *SDP/All.*	.....	10,778
E. L. Jones, *PC*	....	3,987
Lab. maj.	....	1,028
(June '83, C. maj. 1,551)		

Conwy (Gwynedd)
E. 52,862

*I. W. P. Roberts, *C.*	....	15,730
J. R. Roberts, *L./All.*	.....	12,706
Ms. E. Williams, *Lab.*	....	9,049
R. Davies, *PC*	....	3,177
C. maj.	....	3,024
(June '83, C. maj. 4,268)		

Cynon Valley (Mid Glam)
E. 49,621

*Mrs. A. Clwyd, *Lab.*	.....	26,222
K. D. Butler, *SDP/All.*	....	4,651
M. A. Bishop, *C.*	....	4,638
Mrs. D. L. Richards, *PC*	..	2,549
Lab. maj.	....	21,571
(June '83, Lab. maj. 13,074)		
(May '84, Lab. maj. 12,835)		

Delyn (Clwyd)
E. 63,541

*K. W. T. Raffan, *C.*	......	21,728
D. G. Hanson, *Lab.*	......	20,504
D. J. Evans, *L./All.*	......	8,913
D. J. Owen, *PC*	....	1,329
C. maj.	....	1,224
(June '83, C. maj. 5,944)		

Gower (W. Glam)
E. 58,871

*G. L. Wardell, *Lab.*	......	22,138
G. A. L. Price, *C.*	....	16,374
D. H. O. Elliott, *SDP/All.*	..	7,645
J. G. M. Edwards, *PC*	....	1,341
Lab. maj.	....	5,764
(June '83, Lab. maj. 1,205)		

Islwyn (Gwent)
E. 50,414

*Rt. Hon. N. G. Kinnock, *Lab.*	28,901
J. Twitchen, *C.*	....	5,954
Ms. J. Gasson, *SDP/All.*	..	3,746
A. Richards, *PC*	....	1,932
Lab. maj.	....	22,947
(June '83, Lab. maj. 14,380)		

Llanelli (Dyfed)
E. 63,845

*Rt. Hon. D. J. D. Davies, *Lab.*	29,506
P. J. Circus, *C.*	....	8,571
M. J. Shrewsbury, *L./All.*	.	6,714
A. Price, *PC*	....	5,088
Lab. maj.	....	20,935
(June '83, Lab. maj. 13,606)		

Meirionnydd Nant Conwy
(Gwynedd)
E. 31,632

*D. E. Thomas, *PC*	....	10,392
D. T. Jones, *C.*	....	7,366
H. G. Roberts, *Lab.*	......	4,397
D. L. Roberts, *SDP/All.*	..	3,847
PC maj.	....	3,026
(June '83, PC maj. 2,643)		

Merthyr Tydfil and Rhymney
(Mid Glam)
E. 58,285

*E. Rowlands, Lab.	....	33,400
N. M. Walters, *C.*	....	5,270
P. Verma, *L./All.*	....	3,573
Mrs. J. Davies, *PC*	......	2,085
Lab. maj.	....	28,130

(June '83, Lab. maj. 22,730)

Monmouth (Gwent)
E. 58,468

*Sir J. Stradling Thomas, C.		22,387
Ms. K. Gass, *Lab.*	....	13,037
C. Lindley, *SDP/All.*	......	11,313
Mrs. S. Meredudd, *PC* ...		363
C. maj.	....	9,350

(June '83, C. maj. 9,343)
(*See also* p. 240)

Montgomery (Powys)
E. 39,808

*A. C. Carlile, qc L./All.	...	14,729
D.M. Evans, *C.*	....	12,171
E. D. W. Llewellyn Jones, *Lab.*	....	3,304
C. Clowes, *PC*	....	1,412
L./All. maj.	....	2,558

(June '83, L./All. maj. 668)

Neath (W. Glam)
E. 55,261

*D. R. Coleman, Lab.	.....	27,612
M. R. T. Howe, *C.*	....	7,034
J. Warman, *SDP/All.*	.....	6,132
H. John, *PC*	....	2,792
Lab. maj.	....	20,578

(June '83, Lab. maj. 13,604)
(*See also* p. 240)

Newport (Gwent)
EAST *E.* 52,199

*R. J. Hughes, Lab.	....	20,518
G. R. Webster-Gardiner, *C.*		13,454
Mrs. F. A. David, *SDP/All.*		7,383
G. Butler, *PC*	....	458
Lab. maj.	....	7,064

(June '83, Lab. maj. 2,630)

WEST *E.* 55,455

P. P. Flynn, *Lab.*	....	20,887
*M. N. F. Robinson, C.	....	18,179
G. W. Roddick, *L./All.*	.....	5,903
D. J. Bevan, *PC*	....	377
Lab. maj.	....	2,708

(June '83, C. maj. 581)

Ogmore (Mid Glam)
E. 51,255

*R. Powell, Lab.	....	28,462
M. F. Barratt, *C.*	....	6,170
Ms. M. James, *SDP/All.*		3,954
J. G. Jones, *PC*	....	1,791
T. H. Spence, *Ind. Lab.*	....	652
Lab. maj.	....	22,292

(June '83, Lab. maj. 17,364)

Pembroke (Dyfed)
E. 70,360

N. J. Bennett, *C.*	....	23,314
B. J. Rayner, *Lab.*	....	17,614
P. E. C. Jones, *L./All.*	....	14,832
O. Osmond, *PC*	....	1,119
C. maj.	....	5,700

(June '83, C. maj. 9,356)

Pontypridd (Mid Glam)
E. 61,255

*B. T. John, Lab.	....	26,422
D. Swayne, *C.*	....	9,145
P.G.Sain-Ley-Berry, *SDP/All.*	....	8,865
D. L. Bowen, *PC*	....	2,498
Lab. maj.	....	17,277

(June '83, Lab. maj. 8,744)
(*See also* p. 239)

Rhondda (Mid Glam)
E. 60,931

*A. R. Rogers, Lab.	....	35,015
G. R. Davies, *PC*	....	4,261
J. R. YorkWilliams, *SDP/All.*	....	3,930
S. H. Reid, *C.*	....	3,611
A. True, *Comm.*	....	869
Lab. maj.	....	30,754

(June '83, Lab. maj. 21,370)

Swansea (W. Glam)
EAST *E.* 57,200

*D. Anderson, Lab.	....	27,478
R. D. Lewis, *C.*	....	8,140
Rev. D. W. Thomas, *L./All.*		6,330
C. Reid, *PC*	....	1,145
Lab. maj.	....	19,338

(June '83, Lab. maj. 13,535)

WEST *E.* 59,836

*Rt. Hon. A. J. Williams, Lab.	....	22,089
N. M. Evans, *C.*	....	15,027
M. Ford, *L./All.*	....	7,019
N. Williams, *PC*	....	902
Mrs. J. V. Harman, *Grn.* ..		469
Lab. maj.	....	7,062

(June '83, Lab. maj. 2,350)

Torfaen (Gwent)
E. 59,896

P. P. Murphy, *Lab.*	......	26,577
G. R. Blackburn, *L./All.* ...		9,027
R. Gordon, *C.*	....	8,632
J. Evans, *PC*	....	577
M. Witherden, *Grn.*		450
Lab. maj.	....	17,550

(June '83, Lab. maj. 8,285)

Vale of Glamorgan (S. Glam)
E. 65,310

*Sir H. R. Gower, C.	......	24,229
J. W. P. Smith, *Lab.*	......	17,978
D. K. Davies, *SDP/All.* ...		8,633
P. G. Williams, *PC*	....	946
C. maj.	....	6,251

(June '83, C. maj. 10,393)
(*See also* p. 239)

Wrexham (Clwyd)
E. 62,401

*Dr. J. C. Marek, Lab.	....	22,144
R. H. W. Graham-Palmer, *C.*	....	17,992
M. Thomas, *L./All.*	......	9,808
D. Watkins, *PC*	....	539
Lab. maj.	....	4,152

(June '83, Lab. maj. 424)

Ynys Môn/Anglesey
(Gwynedd)
E. 52,633

I. W. Jones, *PC*	....	18,580
R. Evans, *C.*	....	14,282
C. Parry, *Lab.*	....	7,252
I. L. Evans, *SDP/All.*		2,863
PC maj.	....	4,298

(June '83, C. maj. 1,684)

SCOTLAND

Aberdeen (Grampian)
NORTH *E.* 63,214

*R. Hughes, Lab.	....	24,145
R. Smith, *SDP/All.*	......	7,867
Mrs. G. E. C. Scanlan, *C.* .		6,330
P. Greenhorn, *SNP*		5,827
Lab. maj.	....	16,278

(June '83, Lab. maj. 9,144)

SOUTH *E.* 62,943

F. Doran, *Lab.*	....	15,917
*G. P. Malone, C.	....	14,719
I. G. Philip, *SDP/All.*		8,844
M. F. Weir, *SNP*	....	2,776
Lab. maj.	....	1,198

(June '83, C. maj. 3,581)

Angus East (Tayside)
E. 61,060

A. Welsh, *SNP*	....	19,536
*P. L. Fraser, qc, C.	....	17,992
R. Mennie, *Lab.*	....	4,971
I. Mortimer, *SDP/All.* ...		3,592
SNP maj.	....	1,544

(June '83, C. maj. 3,527)

Argyll and Bute (S'clyde)
E. 48,700

Mrs. J. R. Michie, *L./All.* .		13,726
*J. J. MacKay, C.	....	12,332
R. Shaw, *SNP*	....	6,297
D. Tierney, *Lab.*	....	4,437
L./All. maj.	....	1,394

(June '83, C. maj. 3,844)

Ayr (S'clyde)
E. 66,450

*Rt. Hon. G. K. H. Younger, TD, C.	....	20,942
K. MacDonald, *Lab.*	.....	20,760
K. M. Moody, *L./All.*	.....	7,859
C. Weir, *SNP*	....	3,548
C. maj.	....	182

(June '83, C. maj. 7,987)

Banff and Buchan (Grampian)
E. 62,149

A. E. A. Salmond, *SNP* ..		19,462
*A. McQuarrie, C.	....	17,021
G. M. Burness, *SDP/All.*		4,211
J. Livie, *Lab.*	....	3,281
SNP maj.	....	2,441

(June '83, C. maj. 937)

Caithness and Sutherland
(H'land)
E. 31,279

*R. A. R. Maclennan, SDP/		
All.		12,338
R. L. Hamilton, *C.*		3,844
A. Byron, *Lab.*		3,437
K. MacGregor, *SNP*		2,371
W. A. Mowat, *Ind. L.*		686
B. Planterose, *Grn.*		333
SDP/All. maj.		8,494
(June '83, SDP/All. maj. 6,843)		

Carrick, Cumnock and Doon
Valley (S'clyde)
E. 56,360

*G. Foulkes, *Lab.*		25,669
S. Stevenson, *C.*		8,867
Mrs. M. Ali, *SDP/All.*		4,106
C. D. Calman, *SNP*		4,094
Lab. maj.		16,802
(June '83, Lab. maj. 11,370)		

Clackmannan (Central)
E. 49,083

*M. J. O'Neill, *Lab.*		20,317
Dr. A. Macartney, *SNP*		7,916
J. Parker, *C.*		5,620
Mrs. A. Watters, *SDP/All.*		3,961
Lab. maj.		12,401
(June '83, Lab. maj. 9,639)		

Clydebank and Milngavie
(S'clyde)
E. 50,152

A. Worthington, *Lab.*		22,528
K. Hirstwood, *C.*		6,224
R. Ackland, *SDP/All.*		5,891
S. Fisher, *SNP*		4,935
Lab. maj.		16,304
(June '83, Lab. maj. 7,715)		

Clydesdale (S'clyde)
E. 61,620

J. Hood, *Lab.*		21,826
R. Robertson, *C.*		11,324
J. Boyle, *SDP/All.*		7,909
M. Russell, *SNP*		7,125
Lab. maj.		10,502
(June '83, Lab. maj. 4,866)		

Cumbernauld and Kilsyth
(S'clyde)
E. 45,427

*N. Hogg, *Lab.*		21,385
T. Johnston, *SNP*		6,982
C. S. Deans, *SDP/All.*		4,059
Mrs. A. E. Thomson, *C.*		3,227
Lab. maj.		14,403
(June '83, Lab. maj. 9,928)		

Cunninghame (S'clyde)

NORTH *E.* 54,817

B. D. H. Wilson, *Lab.*		19,061
*J. A. Corrie, *C.*		14,594
D. J. Herbison, *SDP/All.*		5,185
M. Brown, *SNP*		4,076
Lab. maj.		4,467
(June '83, C. maj. 1,637)		

SOUTH *E.* 49,842

*D. Lambie, *Lab.*		22,728
E. R. Gibson, *C.*		6,095
J. A. Boss, *L./All.*		4,426
Mrs. K. Ullrich, *SNP*		4,115
Lab. maj.		16,633
(June '83, Lab. maj. 11,768)		

Dumbarton (S'clyde)
E. 58,968

J. McFall, *Lab.*		19,778
R. F. Graham, *C.*		14,556
R. Mowbray, *SDP/All.*		6,060
Ms. J. Herriot, *SNP*		5,564
Lab. maj.		5,222
(June '83, Lab. maj. 2,115)		

Dumfries (D & G)
E. 59,347

*Sir H. S. P. Monro, *C.*		18,785
Ms. C. W. Phillips, *Lab.*		11,292
J. R. McCall, *SDP/All.*		8,064
T. McAlpine, *SNP*		6,391
P. M. Thomas, *Grn.*		349
C. maj.		7,493
(June '83, C. maj. 8,694)		

Dundee (Tayside)

EAST *E.* 60,805

J. McAllion, *Lab.*		19,539
*R. G. Wilson, *SNP*		18,524
P. Cook, *C.*		5,938
Mrs. M. von Romberg, *L./		
All.*		2,143
Lab. maj.		1,015
(June '83, SNP maj. 5,016)		

WEST *E.* 61,926

*E. Ross, *Lab.*		24,916
J. A. Donnelly, *C.*		8,390
A. N. Morgan, *SNP*		7,164
Ms. R. Lonie, *SDP/All.*		5,922
S. R. Mathewson, *Comm.*		308
Lab. maj.		16,526
(June '83, Lab. maj. 10,150)		

Dunfermline (Fife)

EAST *E.* 51,175

*Dr. J. G. Brown, *Lab.*		25,381
C. Shenton, *C.*		5,792
Ms. E. Harris, *L./All.*		4,122
Mrs. A. McGarny, *SNP*		3,901
Lab. maj.		19,589
(June '83, Lab. maj. 11,301)		

WEST *E.* 51,063

*R. G. Douglas, *Lab.*		18,493
P. R. Gallie, *C.*		9,091
F. A. Moyes, *SDP/All.*		8,288
G. Hughes, *SNP*		3,435
Lab. maj.		9,402
(June '83, Lab. maj. 2,474)		

East Kilbride (S'clyde)
E. 63,097

A. P. Ingram, *Lab.*		24,491
D. R. E. Sullivan, *SDP/All.*		11,867
P. M. Walker, *C.*		7,344
J. H. Taggart, *SNP*		6,275
Lab. maj.		12,624
(June '83, Lab. maj. 4,336)		

East Lothian
E. 65,046

*J. D. Home Robertson,		
Lab.*		24,583
S. M. Langdon, *C.*		14,478
A. Robinson, *L./All.*		7,929
A. Burgon-Lyon, *SNP*		3,727
A. Marland, *Grn.*		451
Lab. maj.		10,105
(June '83, Lab. maj. 6,241)		

Eastwood (S'clyde)
E. 61,872

*J. A. Stewart, *C.*		19,388
R. Leishman, *SDP/All.*		13,374
P. A. Grant-Hutchison,		
Lab.*		12,305
J. Findlay, *SNP*		4,033
C. maj.		6,014
(June '83, C. maj. 8,595)		

Edinburgh (Lothian)

CENTRAL *E.* 59,529

A. M. Darling, *Lab.*		16,502
*Sir A. Fletcher, *C.*		14,240
A. Myles, *L./All.*		7,333
B. Shaw, *SNP*		2,559
Mrs. L. M. Hendry, *Grn.*		438
Lab. maj.		2,262
(June '83, C. maj. 2,566)		

EAST *E.* 48,895

*G. S. Strang, *Lab.*		18,257
J. F. Renz, *C.*		8,962
Mrs. J. Aitken, *L./All.*		5,592
M. Bovey, *SNP*		3,434
Lab. maj.		9,295
(June '83, Lab. maj. 5,866)		

LEITH *E.* 60,359

*R. D. M. Brown, *Lab.*		21,104
D. A. Y. Menzies, *C.*		9,777
Mrs. S. Wells, *SDP/All.*		7,843
W. Morrison, *SNP*		4,045
Lab. maj.		11,327
(June '83, Lab. maj. 4,973)		

PENTLANDS *E.* 58,125

*Rt. Hon. M. L. Rifkind, QC,		
C.*		17,278
M. Lazarowicz, *Lab.*		13,533
K. A. Smith, *SDP/All.*		11,072
D. N. MacCormick, *SNP*		3,264
C. maj.		3,745
(June '83, C. maj. 4,309)		

SOUTH *E.* 63,842

N. Griffiths, *Lab.*		18,211
*M. A. F. J. K. Ancram (Earl		
of Ancram), *C.*		16,352
D. A. Graham, *SDP/All.*		10,900
Mrs. R. Moore, *SNP*		2,455
Mrs. R. Clark, *Grn.*		440
Lab. maj.		1,859
(June '83, C. maj. 3,655)		

WEST *E.* 62,214

*Lord James Douglas-Ham-		
ilton, *C.*		18,450
D. G. King, *L./All.*		17,216
M. McGregor, *Lab.*		10,957
N. Irons, *SNP*		2,774
C. maj.		1,234
(June '83, C. maj. 498)		

Falkirk (Central)

EAST *E.* 52,564
*H. Ewing, Lab.		21,379
K. H. Brookes, C.		7,356
R. N. F. Halliday, SNP		6,056
Mrs. E. G. Dick, SDP/All.		4,624
Lab. maj.		14,023
(June '83, Lab. maj. 10,061)		

WEST *E.* 50,222
*D. A. Canavan, Lab.		20,256
D. R. D. Thomas, C.		6,704
I. R. Goldie, SNP		6,696
M. J. Harris, L./All.		4,841
Lab. maj.		13,552
(June '83, Lab. maj. 8,978)		

Fife

CENTRAL *E.* 56,090
H. B. McLeish, Lab.		22,827
R. E. Aird, C.		7,118
Mrs. T. M. Little, L./All.		6,487
D. Hood, SNP		6,296
Lab. maj.		15,709
(June '83, Lab. maj. 7,794)		

NORTH EAST *E.* 52,266
W. M. Campbell, CBE, QC, L./All.		17,868
*J. S. B. Henderson, C.		16,421
A. M. E. Gannon, Lab.		2,947
F. D. Roche, SNP		2,616
L./All. maj.		1,447
(June '83, C. maj. 2,185)		

Galloway and Upper Nithsdale
(D & G)
E. 53,429
*I. B. Lang, C.		16,592
S. F. Norris, SNP		12,919
J. McKercher, L./All.		6,001
J. Gray, Lab.		5,298
D. Kenny, Ret.		230
C. maj.		3,673
(June '83, C. maj. 5,461)		

Glasgow (S'clyde)

CATHCART *E.* 49,307
*J. A. Maxton, Lab.		19,623
W. A. Harvey, C.		8,420
Miss M. Craig, SDP/All.		5,722
W. A. Steven, SNP		3,883
Lab. maj.		11,203
(June '83, Lab. maj. 4,230)		

CENTRAL *E.* 51,137
*R. McTaggart, Lab.		21,619
B. Jenkin, C.		4,366
Dr. J. Bryden, L./All.		3,528
A. Wilson, SNP		3,339
A. Brooks, Grn.		290
J. P. McGoldrick, Comm.		265
D. Owen, RF		126
Lab. maj.		17,253
(June '83, Lab. maj. 10,962)		
(See also p. 239)		

GARSCADDEN *E.* 47,958
*D. C. Dewar, Lab.		23,178
A. Brophy, SNP		4,201
T. N. A. Begg, C.		3,660
S. Callison, SDP/All.		3,211
Lab. maj.		18,977
(June '83, Lab. maj. 13,474)		

GOVAN *E.* 50,616
*Rt. Hon. B. Millan, Lab.		24,071
A. Ferguson, SDP/All.		4,562
Mrs. J. R. Girsman, C.		4,411
F. McCabe, SNP		3,851
D. Chalmers, Comm.		237
Lab. maj.		19,509
(June '83, Lab. maj. 13,057)		
(See also p. 239)		

HILLHEAD *E.* 57,836
G. Galloway, Lab.		17,958
*Rt Hon. R. H. Jenkins, SDP/All.		14,707
B. D. Cooklin, C.		6,048
W. Kidd, SNP		2,713
A. Whitelaw, Grn.		443
Lab. maj.		3,251
(June '83, SDP/All. maj. 1,164)		

MARYHILL *E.* 52,371
Mrs. M. Fyfe, Lab.		23,482
Miss E. M. A. Attwooll, L./All.		4,118
G. Roberts, SNP		3,895
S. R. R. Kirk, C.		3,307
D. Spaven, Grn.		539
Lab. maj.		19,364
(June '83, Lab. maj. 11,203)		

POLLOK *E.* 51,396
J. Dunnachie, Lab.		23,239
Mrs. G. French, C.		5,256
J. Shearer, L./All.		4,445
A. Doig, SNP		3,528
D. Fogg, Grn.		362
Lab. maj.		17,983
(June '83, Lab. maj. 11,532)		

PROVAN *E.* 43,744
J. Wray, Lab.		22,032
W. Ramsay, SNP		3,660
Miss A. Strutt, C.		2,336
J. Morrison, SDP/All.		2,189
Lab. maj.		18,372
(June '83, Lab. maj. 15,385)		

RUTHERGLEN *E.* 57,313
T. McAvoy, Lab.		24,790
R. E. Brown, L./All.		10,795
G. Hamilton, C.		5,088
J. Higgins, SNP		3,584
Lab. maj.		13,995
(June '83, Lab. maj. 9,126)		

SHETTLESTON *E.* 53,604
*D. Marshall, Lab.		23,991
J. M. S. Fisher, C.		5,010
J. MacVicar, SNP		4,807
Miss P. Clarke, L./All.		3,942
Lab. maj.		18,981
(June '83, Lab. maj. 12,416)		

SPRINGBURN *E.* 51,563
*M. J. Martin, Lab.		25,617
B. O'Hara, SNP		3,554
M. Call, C.		2,870
D. Rennie, L./All.		2,746
Lab. maj.		22,063
(June '83, Lab. maj. 17,599)		

Gordon (Grampian)
E. 73,479
*M. G. Bruce, L./All.		26,770
P. R. Leckie, C.		17,251
Mrs. M. C. Morrell, Lab.		6,228
G. E. Wright, SNP		3,876
L./All. maj.		9,519
(June '83, L./All. maj. 850)		

Greenock and Port Glasgow
(S'clyde)
E. 57,756
*Dr. N. A. Godman, Lab.		27,848
J. H. Moody, L./All.		7,793
T. J. D. Pearson, C.		4,199
T. Lenehan, SNP		3,721
(June '83, Lab. maj. 4,625)		20,055

Hamilton (S'clyde)
E. 62,205
*G. I. M. Robertson, Lab.		28,563
G. S. Mond, C.		6,901
T. Mackay, L./All.		6,302
C. Crossley, SNP		6,093
Lab. maj.		21,662
(June '83, Lab. maj. 15,019)		

Inverness, Nairn and Lochaber
(H'land)
E. 66,743
*Sir D. R. Johnston, L./All.		17,422
D. Stewart, Lab.		11,991
Mrs. A. T. Keswick, C.		10,901
N. P. Johnson, SNP		7,001
L./All. maj.		5,431
(June '83, L./All. maj. 7,298)		

Kilmarnock and Loudoun
(Grampian)
E. 62,648
*W. McKelvey, Lab.		23,713
Mrs. A. K. Bates, C.		9,586
G. Leslie, SNP		8,881
P. Kerr, SDP/All.		6,698
Lab. maj.		14,127
(June '83, Lab. maj. 8,800)		

Kincardine and Deeside
(Grampian)
E. 63,587
*Rt. Hon. A. L. Buchanan-Smith, C.		19,438
N. R. Stephen, L./All.		17,375
J. K. Thomaneck, Lab.		7,624
Mrs. F. E. Duncan, SNP		3,082
Mrs. L. M. Perica, Grn.		299
C. maj.		2,063
(June '83, C. maj. 7,796)		

Kirkcaldy (Fife)
E. 53,439
Dr. L. G. Moonie, Lab.		20,281
I. G. Mitchell, C.		8,711
D. Stewart, SDP/All.		7,118
W. A. R. Mullin, SNP		4,794
Lab. maj.		11,570
(June '83, Lab. maj. 5,331)		

Linlithgow (Lothian)
E. 59,542

*T. Dalyell, Lab.	....	21,869
J. Sillars, *SNP*	....	11,496
T. R. Armstrong Wilson, *C.*		6,828
Mrs. H. McDade, *SDP/All.*		5,840
J. Glassford, *Comm.*	......	154
Lab. maj.	....	10,373
(June '83, Lab. maj. 11,361)		

Livingston (Lothian)
E. 56,583

*R. F. Cook, Lab.	....	19,110
R. McCreadie, *L./All.*	....	8,005
Dr. M. N. A. Mayall, *C.*	...	7,860
K. MacAskill, *SNP*	......	6,969
Lab. maj.	....	11,105
(June '83, Lab. maj. 4,951)		

Midlothian
E. 60,549

*A. Eadie, BEM, *Lab.*	......	22,553
A. R. Dewar, *SDP/All.*	.....	10,300
Dr. F. Riddell, *C.*	....	8,527
I. Chisholm, *SNP*	....	4,947
I. Smith, *Grn.*	....	412
Lab. maj.	....	12,253
(June '83, Lab. maj. 6,156)		

Monklands (S'clyde)

EAST *E.* 49,644

*Rt. Hon. J. Smith, QC, *Lab.*		22,649
J. Love, *C.*	....	6,260
K. Gibson, *SNP*	....	4,790
Mrs. S. Grieve, *L./All.*	....	3,442
Lab. maj.	....	16,389
(June '83, Lab. maj. 9,799)		

WEST *E.* 50,874

*T. Clarke, CBE, *Lab.*	......	24,499
G. Lind, *C.*	....	6,166
Ms. A. McQueen, *SDP/All.*		4,408
K. Bovey, *SNP*	....	4,260
Lab. maj.	....	18,333
(June '83, Lab. maj. 12,264)		

Moray (Grampian)
E. 62,201

Mrs. M. Ewing, *SNP*	.....	19,510
*A. Pollock, C.	....	15,825
C. R. C. Smith, *Lab.*	......	5,118
D. G. M. Skene, *L./All.*	...	4,724
SNP maj.	....	3,685
(June '83, C. maj. 1,713)		

Motherwell (S'clyde)

NORTH *E.* 57,632

Dr. J. Reid, Lab.	....	29,825
A. Currie, *SNP*	....	6,230
R. Hargrave, *C.*	....	4,939
G. Swift, *L./All.*	....	3,558
Lab. maj.	....	23,595
(June '83, Lab. maj. 17,894)		

SOUTH *E.* 52,127

*Dr. J. W. Bray, Lab.	.....	22,957
J. Wright, *SNP*	....	6,027
J. S. Bercow, *C.*	....	5,702
W. R. MacGregor, *SDP/ All.*	....	4,463
R. Somerville, *Comm.*	....	223
Lab. maj.	....	16,930
(June '83, Lab. maj. 12,349)		

Orkney and Shetland
E. 31,047

*J. R. Wallace, L./All.	.....	8,881
R. W. A. Jenkins, *C.*	.....	4,959
J. H. Aberdein, *Lab.*	.....	3,995
J. Goodlad, *OSM*	....	3,095
G. K. Collister, *Grn.*	......	389
L./All. maj.	....	3,922
(June '83, L./All. maj. 4,150)		

Paisley (S'clyde)

NORTH *E.* 49,487

*A. S. Adams, Lab.	......	20,193
Mrs. E. F. Laing, *C.*	.....	5,751
Miss E. P. McCartin,*SDP/ All.*	....	5,741
I. Taylor *SNP*	....	4,696
Lab. maj.	....	14,442
(June '83, Lab. maj. 7,587)		
(*See also* p. 240)		

SOUTH *E.* 51,127

*N. F. Buchan, Lab.	......	21,611
A. M. Carmichael, *L./All*		5,826
Miss D. A. Williamson, *C.*		5,644
J. R. Mitchell, *SNP*	......	5,398
Lab. maj.	....	15,785
(June '83, Lab. maj. 6,529)		
(*See also* p. 240)		

Perth and Kinross (Tayside)
E. 63,443

*N. H. Fairbairn, QC, *C.*	...	18,716
J. M. Fairlie, *SNP*	......	13,040
S. Donaldson, *L./All.*	....	7,969
J. W. McConnell, *Lab.*	...	7,490
C. maj.	....	5,676
(June '83, C. maj. 6,733)		

Renfrew West and Inverclyde (S'clyde)
E. 56,189

T. Graham, *Lab.*	....	17,525
*Mrs. A. A. McCurley, C.	...	13,472
Dr. J. D. Mabon, *SDP/All.*		9,669
C. Campbell, *SNP*	....	4,578
Lab. maj.	....	4,053
(June '83, C. maj. 1,322)		

Ross, Cromarty and Skye (H'land)
E. 52,369

*C. P. Kennedy, SDP/All.		18,809
F. Spencer Nairn, *C.*	.....	7,490
M. M. MacMillan, *Lab.*	...	7,287
R. M. Gibson, *SNP*	......	4,492
S.D.P./All. maj.	....	11,319
(June '83 SDP/All. maj. 1,704)		

Roxburgh and Berwickshire (Borders)
E. 43,140

*A. J. Kirkwood, L./All.	....	16,388
Dr. L. Fox, *C.*	....	12,380
T. Luckhurst, *Lab.*	......	2,944
M. Douglas, *SNP*	....	1,586
L./All. maj.	....	4,008
(June '83, L./All. maj. 3,396)		

Stirling (Central)
E. 57,836

*M. B. Forsyth, C.	....	17,591
M. Connarty, *Lab.*	......	16,643
I. McFarlane, *L./All.*	.....	6,804
I. M. Lawson, *SNP*	......	4,897
C. maj.	....	948
(June '83, C. maj. 5,133)		

Strathkelvin and Bearsden (S'clyde)
E. 62,676

S. L. Galbraith, *Lab.*	.....	19,639
*M. W. Hirst, C.	....	17,187
J. Bannerman, *L./All.*	....	11,034
G. Paterson, *SNP*	....	3,654
Lab. maj.	....	2,452
(June '83, C. maj. 3,700)		

Tayside North
E. 53,985

*W. C. Walker, C.	....	18,307
K. J. N. Guild, *SNP*	.....	13,291
P. F. Regent, *L./All.*	......	5,201
J. Whytock, *Lab.*	....	3,550
C. maj.	....	5,016
(June '83, C. maj. 10,099)		

Tweeddale, Ettrick and Lauderdale (Borders)
E. 37,875

*Rt. Hon. D. M. S. Steel, L./ All.	....	14,599
Mrs. S. Finlay-Maxwell, *C.*		8,657
N. Glen, *Lab.*	....	3,320
A. Lumsden, *SNP*	....	2,660
L./All. maj.	....	5,942
(June '83, L./All. maj. 8,539)		

Western Isles
E. 23,507

C. A. MacDonald, *Lab.*	...	7,041
I. Smith, *SNP*	....	4,701
K. MacIver, *SDP/All.*	....	3,419
M. Morrison, *C.*	....	1,336
Lab. maj.	....	2,340
(June '83 SNP maj. 3,712)		

NORTHERN IRELAND

Antrim

EAST *E.* 60,587

*J. R. Beggs, OUP	....	23,942
S. Neeson, *All.*	....	8,582
A. Kelly, *WP*	....	936
OUP maj.	....	15,360
(June '83, OUP maj. 367)		
(Jan. '86, OUP maj. 24,981)		

NORTH *E.* 65,733

*Rev. I. R. K. Paisley, DUP		28,383
S. Farren, *SDLP*	....	5,149
G. Williams, *All.*	....	5,140
S. Reagan, *SF*	....	2,633
DUP maj.	....	23,234
(June '83, DUP maj. 13,173)		
(Jan. '86, DUP maj. 33,024)		

SOUTH *E.* 61,649

*C. Forsythe, OUP	....	25,395
G. Mawhinney, *All.*	......	5,808
D. McClelland, *SDLP*	....	3,611
H. Cushinan, *SF*	....	1,592
OUP maj.	....	19,587
(June '83, OUP maj. 6,792)		
(Jan. '86, OUP maj. 28,217)		

Belfast

EAST E.54,628
*P. D. Robinson, DUP	...	20,372
Dr. J. Alderdice, All.	....	10,574
F. Cullen, WP	....	1,314
J. O'Donnell, SF	....	649
DUP maj.	....	9,798

(June '83, DUP maj. 7,989)
(Jan. '86, DUP maj. 21,690)

NORTH E.59,124
*A. C. Walker, OUP	......	14,355
A. Maginness, SDLP	....	5,795
G. Seawright, Prot. U.	...	5,671
P. McManus, SF	....	5,062
S. Lynch, WP	....	3,062
T. Campbell, All.	....	2,871
OUP maj.	....	8,560

(June '83, OUP maj. 7,079)
(Jan. '86, OUP maj. 16,577)

SOUTH E.54,208
*Rev. W. M. Smyth, OUP		18,917
D. Cook, All.	....	6,963
Dr. A. McDonnell, SDLP		4,268
G. Carr, WP	....	1,528
S. McKnight, SF	....	1,030
OUP maj.	....	11,954

(June '83, OUP maj. 9,724)
(Jan. '86, OUP maj. 14,136)

WEST E.59,324
*G. Adams, SF	....	16,862
Dr. J. G. Hendron, SDLP	.	14,641
F. Miller, OUP	....	7,646
Mrs. M. McMahon, WP	...	1,819
SF maj.	....	2,221

(June '83, SF maj. 5,445)

Down

NORTH E.65,018
*J. A. Kilfedder, UPUP	...	18,420
R. McCartney, Real U.	...	14,467
J. Cushnahan, All.	....	7,932
UPUP maj.	....	3,953

(June '83, UPUP maj. 13,846)
(Jan. '86, UPUP maj. 22,727)

SOUTH E.71,235
E. K. McGrady, SDLP	...	26,579
*Rt. Hon. J. E. Powell, MBE, OUP		25,848
Ms. G. Ritchie, SF	....	2,363
Miss S. E. Laird, All.	.....	1,069
D. O'Hagan, WP	....	675
SDLP maj.	....	731

(June '83, OUP maj. 548)
(Jan. '86, OUP maj. 1,842)

Fermanagh and South Tyrone E.68,979
*K. Maginnis, OUP	....	27,446
P. Corrigan, SF	....	14,623
Mrs. R. Flanagan, SDLP	.	10,581
D. Kettyles, WP	....	1,784
J. Haslett, All.	....	941
OUP maj.	....	12,823

(June '83, OUP maj. 7,676)
(Jan. '86, OUP maj. 12,579)

Foyle E.70,519
*J. Hume, SDLP	....	23,743
G. Campbell, DUP	....	13,883
M. McGuiness, SF	....	8,707
Mrs. E. Zammitt, All.	....	1,276
E. Melaugh, WP	....	1,022
SDLP maj.	....	9,860

(June '83, SDLP maj. 8,148)

Lagan Valley E.64,873
*Rt. Hon. J. H. Molyneaux, OUP		29,101
S. A. Close, All.	....	5,728
B. McDonnell, SDLP	.....	2,888
P. J. Rice, SF	....	2,656
J. T. Lowry, WP	....	1,215
OUP maj.	....	23,373

(June '83, OUP maj. 17,216)
(Jan. '86, OUP maj. 29,186)

Londonderry East E.71,031
*W. Ross, OUP	....	29,532
A. Doherty, SDLP	....	9,375
J. Davey, SF	....	5,464
P. McGowan, All.	....	3,237
F. Donnelly, WP	....	935
M. H. Samuel, Ecol.	......	281
OUP maj.	....	20,157

(June '83, OUP maj. 7,262)
(Jan. '86, OUP maj. 28,921)

Newry and Armagh E.66,027
*S. Mallon, SDLP	....	25,137
J. F. Nicholson, OUP	...	19,812
J. McAllister, SF	....	6,173
W. H. Jeffrey, All.	....	664
J. O'Hanion, WP	....	482
SDLP maj.	....	5,325

(June '83, SDLP maj. 1,554)
(Jan. '86, SDLP maj. 2,583)

Strangford E.64,429
*Rt. Hon. J. D. Taylor, OUP		28,199
A. J. Morrow, All.	....	7,553
Miss I. E. Hynds, WP	....	1,385
OUP maj.	....	20,646

(June '83, OUP maj. 7,370)
(Jan. '86, OUP maj. 30,634)

Ulster, Mid- E.67,256
*Rev. R. T. W. McCrea, DUP		23,004
P. D. Haughey, SDLP	....	13,644
S. Begley, SF	....	12,449
P. Bogan, All.	....	1,846
P. J. McClean, WP	....	1,133
DUP maj.	....	9,360

(June '83, DUP maj. 78)
(Jan. '86, DUP maj. 9,697)

Upper Bann E.64,540
*J. H. McCusker, OUP	....	26,037
Mrs. B. Rodgers, SDLP	..	8,676
B. P. Curran, SF	....	3,126
Mrs. M. F. A. Cook, All.	..	2,487
T. French, WP	....	2,004
OUP maj.	....	17,361

(June '83, OUP maj. 17,081)
(Jan. '86, OUP maj. 22,333)
(See also p. 239)

(For by-elections since 1987 General Election, see pp. 239–240)

EUROPEAN PARLIAMENT—UK MEMBERS
(as at end July 1991)

An asterisk* denotes membership of the last Parliament.

	Maj.
*Adam, Gordon J. (b. 1934), Lab., Northumbria	60,040
*Balfe, Richard A. (b. 1944), Lab. Co-op, London S. Inner	45,018
Barton, Roger (b. 1945), Lab., Sheffield	69,276
*Beazley, Christopher J. P. (b. 1952), C., Cornwall and Plymouth	19,817
*Beazley, Peter G. (b. 1922), C., Bedfordshire S.	2,977
*Bethell, The Lord (b. 1938), C., London NW	7,400
*Bird, John A. W. (b. 1926), Lab. Co-op, Midlands W.	42,364
Bowe, David (b. 1955), Lab., Cleveland and Yorkshire N.	24,092
*Buchan, Mrs Janey O. (b. 1926), Lab., Glasgow	59,232
*Cassidy, Bryan M. D. (b.1934), C., Dorset E. and Hampshire W.	61,774
*Catherwood, Sir Frederick (b. 1925), C., Cambridge and Bedfordshire N.	32,321
Coates, Kenneth (b. 1939), Lab., Nottingham	14,513
*Collins, Kenneth D. (b. 1939), Lab., Strathclyde E.	60,317
Crampton, Peter D. (b. 1932), Lab., Humberside	16,328
*Crawley, Mrs Christine M. (b. 1950), Lab., Birmingham E.	46,948
*Daly, Mrs Margaret E. (b. 1938), C., Somerset and Dorset W.	52,220
David, Wayne (b. 1957), Lab., Wales S.	62,557
Donnelly, Alan J. (b. 1957), Lab., Tyne and Wear	95,780
*Elles, James E. M. (b. 1949), C., Oxford and Buckinghamshire	47,518
*Elliott, Michael N. (b. 1932), Lab., London W.	14,808
*Ewing, Mrs Winifred M. (b. 1929), SNP, Highlands and Islands	44,695
*Falconer, Alec (b. 1940), Lab., Scotland Mid and Fife	52,157
*Ford, J. Glyn (b. 1950), Lab., Greater Manchester E.	34,501
Green, Ms Pauline (b. 1948), Lab. Co-op, London N.	5,837
Harrison, Lyndon (b. 1947), Lab., Cheshire W.	23,201
*Hindley, Michael J. (b. 1947), Lab., Lancashire E.	39,148
*Hoon, Geoffrey W. (b. 1953), Lab., Derbyshire	33,388
*Howell, Paul F. (b. 1951), C., Norfolk	20,907
*Hughes, Stephen S. (b.1952), Lab., Durham	86,848
*Hume, John, MP (b. 1937), SDLP, N. Ireland	—
Inglewood, The Lord (Richard Fletcher-Vane) (b. 1951), C., Cumbria and Lancashire N.	2,391
*Jackson, Mrs Caroline F. (b. 1946), C., Wiltshire	46,313
*Jackson, Christopher M. (b. 1935), C., Kent E.	28,961
*Kellett-Bowman, Edward T. (b. 1931), C., Hampshire Central	27,674
*Lomas, Alfred (b. 1928), Lab., London NE	47,767
*McGowan, Michael (b. 1940), Lab., Leeds	42,518
McCubbin, Henry (b. 1942), Lab., Scotland NE	2,613
McIntosh, Miss Anne C. B. (b. 1954), C., Essex NE	39,398
*McMahon, Hugh R. (b. 1938), Lab., Strathclyde W.	39,591

	Maj.
*McMillan-Scott, Edward H. C. (b. 1949), C., York	15,102
*Martin, David W. (b. 1954), Lab., Lothians	38,826
*Megahy, Thomas (b. 1929), Lab., Yorkshire SW	65,901
*Moorhouse, C. James O. (b. 1924), C., London S. and Surrey E.	30,816
*Morris, Rev. David R. (b. 1930), Lab., Wales Mid and W.	51,912
*Newens, A. Stanley (b. 1930), Lab. Co-op, London Central	11,542
*Newman, Edward (b. 1953), Lab., Greater Manchester Central	38,867
*Newton Dunn, William F. (b. 1941), C., Lincolnshire	20,650
Nicholson, James F. (b. 1945), OUP, N. Ireland	—
Oddy, Ms Christine M. (b. 1955), Lab., Midlands Central	5,093
*O'Hagan, The Lord (b. 1945), C., Devon	57,298
*Paisley, Rev. Ian R. K., MP (b. 1926), DUP, N. Ireland	—
*Patterson, G. Benjamin (Ben) (b. 1939), C., Kent W.	24,050
*Plumb, The Lord (b.1925), C., The Cotswolds	45,678
Pollack, Ms Anita J. (b.1946), Lab., London SW	518
*Prag, Derek (b. 1923), C., Hertfordshire	43,342
*Price, Peter N. (b. 1942), C., London SE	7,590
*Prout, Sir Christopher, TD, QC (b. 1942), C., Shropshire and Stafford	2,544
Rawlings, Miss Patricia (b. 1939), C., Essex SW	9,403
Read, Ms Mel (b. 1939), Lab., Leicester	15,322
*Scott-Hopkins, Sir James (b. 1921), C., Hereford and Worcester	25,665
*Seal, Barry H. (b. 1937), Lab., Yorkshire W.	37,927
*Seligman, R. Madron (b. 1918), C., Sussex W.	46,233
*Simmonds, Richard J. (b. 1944), C., Wight and Hampshire E.	39,430
*Simpson, Anthony M. H., TD (b. 1935), C., Northamptonshire	20,447
Simpson, Brian (b. 1953), Lab., Cheshire E.	1,864
Smith, Alexander (b. 1943), Lab., Scotland S.	15,693
*Smith, Llewellyn T. (b. 1944), Lab., Wales SE	108,488
Spencer Thomas N. B. (b. 1948), C., Surrey W.	49,342
Stevens, John C. C. (b. 1955), C., Thames Valley	26,491
*Stevenson, George W. (b. 1938), Lab., Staffordshire E.	31,769
*Stewart, Kenneth A. (b. 1925), Lab., Merseyside W.	49,817
*Stewart-Clark, Sir John, Bt. (b. 1929), C., Sussex E.	53,294
Titley, Gary (b. 1950), Lab., Greater Manchester W.	50,135
*Tomlinson, John E. (b. 1939), Lab., Birmingham W.	30,860
*Tongue, Miss Carole (b. 1955), Lab., London E.	27,385
*Turner, Amédée E., QC (b. 1929), C., Suffolk	25,693
*Welsh, Michael J. (b. 1942), C., Lancashire Central	5,688
*West, Norman (b. 1935), Lab., Yorkshire S.	91,784
White, Ian (b. 1947), Lab., Bristol	9,982
Wilson, Joseph (b. 1937), Lab., Wales N.	4,460
Wynn, Terence (b. 1946), Lab., Merseyside E.	76,867

EUROPEAN PARLIAMENT—UK CONSTITUENCIES
(June 15, 1989)

(*Corr.* = Corrective Party: *Hum.* = Humanist Party; *ICP* = International Communist Party; *Lab. RG* = Labour for Regional Government; *MK* = Mebyon Kernow; *W. Reg.* = Wessex Regionalists. For other abbreviations, *see* p. 249)

Bedfordshire South
E. 569,506

*P. G. Beazley, C.	73,406
T. McWalter, *Lab.*	70,429
D. Everett, *Grn.*	34,508
W. M. Johnston, *SLD*	8,748
R. Muller, *SDP*	3,067
C. maj.	*2,977*

(June '84, C. maj. 14,982)

Birmingham East
E. 531,081

*Mrs. C. M. Crawley, Lab.	96,588
M. J. C. Harbour, *C.*	49,640
P. M. Simpson, *Grn.*	22,589
J. C. Binns. *SDP*	5,424
J. M. E. C. Roodhouse, *SLD*	4,010
M. Wingfield, *NF*	1,471
Lab. maj.	*46,948*

(June '84, Lab maj. 21,383)

Birmingham West
E. 515,817

*J. E. Tomlinson, Lab.	86,545
C. F. Robinson, *C.*	55,685
J. D. Bentley, *Grn.*	21,384
S. Reynolds, *SLD*	7,673
Lab. maj.	*30,860*

(June '84, Lab. maj. 6,244)

Bristol
E. 562,277

I. White, *Lab.*	87,753
*R. J. Cottrell, C.	77,771
D. N. Wall, *Grn.*	39,436
C. Boney, *SLD.*	16,309
G. McEwen *W. Reg.*	1,017
Lab. maj.	*9,982*

(June '84, C. maj. 17,644)

Cambridge and Bedfordshire North
E. 562,539

*Sir F. Catherwood, C.	84,044
M. Strube, *Lab.*	51,723
Ms. M. E. Wright, *Grn.*	37,956
A. N. Duff, *SLD*	15,052
C. maj.	*32,321*

(June '84, C. maj. 47,216)

Cheshire East
E. 518,311

B. Simpson, *Lab.*	74,721
*Sir T. Normanton, C.	72,857
C. C. White, *Grn.*	21,456
Mrs. B. Fraenkel, *SLD*	12,344
Lab. maj.	*1,864*

(June '84, C. maj. 18,376)

Cheshire West
E. 543,256

L. Harrison, *Lab.*	102,962
*A. Pearce, C.	79,761
G. L. Nicholls, *Grn.*	25,933
J. Rankin, *SLD*	9,333
Lab. maj.	*23,201*

(June '84, C. maj. 9,692)

Cleveland and Yorkshire North
E. 571,254

D. Bowe, *Lab.*	94,953
*Sir P. Vanneck, C.	70,861
O. Dumpleton, *Grn.*	17,225
T. M. Mawston, *SLD*	8,470
R. I. Andrew *SDP*	7,970
Lab. maj.	*24,092*

(June '84, C. maj. 2,625)

Cornwall and Plymouth
E. 542,527

*C. J. P. Beazley, C.	88,376
P. A. Tyler, *SLD*	68,559
Ms. D. Kirk, *Lab.*	41,466
H. Hoptrough, *Grn.*	24,581
C. Lawry, *MK*	4,224
C. maj.	*19,817*

(June '84, C. maj. 17,751)

The Cotswolds
E. 558,115

*Lord Plumb, C.	94,852
Mrs. S. Limb, *Grn.*	49,174
T. Levitt, *Lab.*	48,180
L. A. Rowe, *SLD*	18,196
C. maj.	*45,678*

(June '84, C. maj. 48,942)

Cumbria and Lancashire North
E. 561,263

W. R. Fletcher-Vane, C..	84,035
J. M. P. Hutton, *Lab.*	81,644
Mrs C. E. Smith, *Grn.*	21,262
E. E. Hill, *SLD*	12,590
J. Bates, *SDP*	4,206
C. maj.	*2,391*

(June '84, C. maj. 23,795)

Derbyshire
E. 564,429

*G. W. Hoon, Lab.	105,018
P. Jenkinson, *C.*	72,630
E. Wall, *Grn.*	20,781
S. Molloy, *SLD*	4,613
Mrs. A. M. Ayres, *SDP*	3,858
Lab. maj.	*33,388*

(June '84, Lab maj. 6,853)

Devon
E. 596,671

*Lord O'Hagan, C.	110,518
P. S. Christie, *Grn.*	53,220
W. J. Cairns, *Lab.*	40,675
M. Edmunds, *SLD*	23,306
R. Edwards, *SDP*	7,806
S. B. F. Hughes, *LM*	2,241
Lady Rous *W. Reg.*	385
C. maj.	*57,298*

(June '84, C. maj. 56,610)

Dorset East and Hampshire West
E. 608,895

*B. M. D. Cassidy, C.	111,469
Ms. K. I. Bradbury, *Grn.*	49,695
H. R. White, *Lab.*	38,011
H. R. Legg, *SLD*	21,809
C. maj.	*61,774*

(June '84, C. maj. 59,891)

Durham
E. 530,137

*S. S. Hughes, Lab.	124,448
R. Hull, *C.*	37,600
Ms. H. I. Lennox, *Grn.*	18,770
P. Freitag, *SLD*	8,369
Lab. maj.	*86,848*

(June '84, Lab. maj. 61,227)

Essex North East
E. 598,542

Miss A. C. B. McIntosh, C.	92,758
Ms. H. J. Bryan, *Lab.*	53,360
C. R. Keene, *Grn.*	45,163
Miss D. P. Wallis, *SLD*	16,939
C. maj.	*39,398*

(June '84, C. maj. 54,302)

Essex South West
E. 569,011

Miss P. E. Rawlings, C.	77,408
J. W. Orpe, *Lab.*	68,005
Mrs. M. E. Willis, *Grn.*	32,242
T. P. Allen, *SLD*	10,618
C. maj.	*9,403*

(June '84, C. maj. 16,021)

Glasgow
E. 487,199

*Mrs. J. O. Buchan, Lab.	107,818
A. Brophy, *SNP*	48,586
Mrs. A. K. Bates, *C.*	20,761
D. L. Spaven, *Grn.*	12,229
J. Morrison, *SLD.*	3,887
D. Chalmers, *Comm.*	1,164
J. Simons, *ICP*	193
Lab. maj.	*59,232*

(June '84, Lab. maj. 65,733)

Greater Manchester Central
E. 481,023

*E. Newman, Lab.	86,914
Miss C. E. Gillan, *C.*	48,047
B. Candeland, *Grn.*	19,742
J. H. Mulholland, *SLD*	9,437
S. M. Millson, *SDP*	2,769
S. Knight, *Hum.*	1,045
Lab. maj.	*38,867*

(June '84, Lab. maj. 28,077)

Greater Manchester East
E. 506,930

*J. G. Ford, Lab.	93,294
R. N. Greenwood, *C.*	58,793
M. J. Shipley, *Grn.*	19,090
A. B. Leah, *SLD*	16,645
Lab. maj.	*34,501*

(June '84, Lab. maj. 8,651)

Greater Manchester West
E. 522,476

G. Titley, *Lab.*	109,228
P. H. Twyman, *C.*	59,093
D. W. Milne, *Grn.*	22,778
A. H. Cruden, *SLD*	6,940
Mrs. B. Archer, *SDP*	4,526
Lab. maj.	*50,135*

(June '84, Lab. maj. 37,698)

Hampshire Central
E. 546,630

E. T. Kellett-Bowman, C.		78,651
Ms A. Mawle, *Lab.*		50,977
Mrs S.J. Penton, *Grn.*		33,186
D. W. G. Chidgey, *SLD*		18,418
C. maj.		*27,674*
(June '84, C. maj. 44,821)		
(Dec. '88, C. maj. 21,442)		

Hereford and Worcester
E. 595,504

Sir J. Scott-Hopkins, C.		87,898
C. A. Short, *Lab.*		62,233
Ms F. M. Norman, *Grn.*		49,296
Mrs J. D. Davies, *SLD*		13,569
C. maj.		*25,665*
(June '84, C. maj. 39,934)		

Hertfordshire
E. 517,137

D. N. Prag, C.		86,898
V. S. Anand, *Lab.*		43,556
M. F. Ames, *Grn.*		37,277
M. D. Phelan, *SLD*		13,456
Mrs. C. Treves Brown, *SDP*		5,048
C. maj.		*43,342*
(June '84, C. maj. 45,932)		

Highlands and Islands
E. 313,877

Mrs. W. M. Ewing SNP		66,297
Sir A. McQuarrie, *C.*		21,602
N. MacAskill, *Lab.*		17,848
M. Gregson, *Grn.*		12,199
N. Michison, *SLD*		10,644
SNP maj.		*44,695*
(June '84, SNP maj. 16,277)		

Humberside
E. 504,219

P. D. Crampton *Lab.*		74,163
R. C. Battersby, C.		57,835
Mrs. J. C. Clark, *Grn.*		23,835
F. L. Parker, *SLD*		3,989
S. W. Unwin, *SDP*		3,419
Lab. maj.		*16,328*
(June '84, C. maj. 8,015)		

Kent East
E. 575,789

C. M. Jackson, C.		85,667
G. N. J. Perry, *Lab.*		56,706
Ms. P. A. Kemp, *Grn.*		36,931
A. F. C. Morris, *SLD*		15,470
C. maj.		*28,961*
(June '84, C. maj. 48,867)		

Kent West
E. 569,725

G. B. Patterson, C.		82,519
P. L. Sloman, *Lab.*		58,469
J. Tidy, *Grn.*		33,202
J. B. Doherty, *SLD.*		16,087
C. maj.		*24,050*
(June '84, C. maj. 34,630)		

Lancashire Central
E. 537,610

M. J. Welsh, C.		81,125
G. W. T. Smith, *Lab.*		75,437
Mrs. H. Ingham, *Grn.*		28,777
Ms. J. Ross-Mills, *SLD*		7,378
C. maj.		*5,688*
(June '84, C. maj. 26,195)		

Lancashire East
E. 529,740

M. J. Hindley, Lab.		96,926
R. W. Sturdy, *C.*		57,778
S. Barker, *Grn.*		20,728
M. Hambley, *SLD*		12,661
Lab. maj.		*39,148*
(June '84, Lab. maj. 7,905)		

Leeds
E. 519,631

M. McGowan, Lab.		97,385
J. W. Tweddle, *C.*		54,867
C. R. Lord, *Grn.*		22,558
Mrs. J. Ewens, *SLD*		11,720
Lab. maj.		*42,518*
(June '84, Lab. maj. 10,357)		

Leicester
E. 579,050

Ms. I. M. Read, *Lab.*		90,798
F. A. Tuckman, C.		75,476
C. J. Davis, *Grn.*		33,081
A. G. Barrett, *Ind. C.*		6,996
G. W. Childs, *SLD*		6,791
Lab. maj.		*15,322*
(June '84, C. maj. 2,892)		

Lincolnshire
E. 586,156

W. F. Newton Dunn, C.		92,043
S. Taggart, *Lab.*		71,393
Ms J. Steranka, *Grn.*		24,908
J. P. Heppell, *SLD*		14,341
C. maj.		*20,650*
(June '84, C. maj. 45,445)		

London Central
E. 486,558

A. S. Newens, Lab. Co-op.		78,561
Ms. H. S. Crawley, *C.*		67,019
Ms. N. Kortvelyessy, *Grn.*		28,087
Miss S. A. Ludford, *SLD*		7,864
W. D. E. Mallinson, *SDP*		2,957
'Lord' D. E. Sutch, *LM*		841
Ms. L. St-Claire, *Corr.*		707
J. S. Swinden, *Hum.*		304
Lab. Co-op maj.		*11,542*
(June '84, Lab. maj. 13,297)		

London East
E. 530,548

Miss C. Tongue, Lab.		92,803
A. R. Tyrrell, *C.*		65,418
Ms. E. L. Crosbie, *Grn.*		21,388
J. K. Gibb, *SLD*		7,341
D. A. O'Sullivan, *ICP*		717
Lab. maj.		*27,385*
(June '84, Lab. maj. 12,159)		

London North
E. 573,043

Ms. P. Green, *Lab. Co-op.*		85,536
R. M. Lacey, *C.*		79,699
S. Clark, *Grn.*		30,807
Ms. H. F. Leighter, *SLD*		8,917
P. Burns, *Ind.*		2,016
Ms. L. Reith, *Comm.*		850
Lab. Co-op. maj.		*5,837*
(June '84, Lab. maj. 4,853)		

London North East
E. 510,138

A. Lomas, Lab.		76,085
M. Trend, *C.*		28,318
Mrs. J. D. Lambert, *Grn.*		25,949
S. Banks, *SLD*		9,575
Ms. N. C. Temple, *Comm.*		1,129
Lab. maj.		*47,767*
(June '84, Lab. maj. 52,665)		

London North West
E. 506,707

Lord Bethell, C.		74,900
A. K. Toms, *Lab.*		67,500
I. E. Flindall, *Grn.*		28,275
C. D. Noyce, *SLD*		10,553
C. maj.		*7,400*
(June '84, C. maj. 7,422)		

London South and Surrey East
E. 495,942

C. J. O. Moorhouse, C.		78,256
R. J. E. Evans, *Lab.*		47,440
G. F. Brand, *Grn.*		31,854
P. H. Billenness, *SLD*		14,967
C. maj.		*30,816*
(June '84, C. maj. 44,657)		

London, South East
E. 558,815

P. N. Price, C.		80,619
D. J. Earnshaw, *Lab.*		73,029
Dr. E. C. McPhee, *Grn.*		37,576
A. A. Kinch, *SDP*		10,196
Mrs. M. C. Williams, *SLD*		9,052
W. E. Turner, *Ind.*		456
C. maj.		*7,590*
(June '84, C. maj. 20,015)		

London, South Inner
E. 528,188

R. A. Balfe, Lab Co-op		90,378
R. J. Wheatley, *C.*		45,360
Ms. P. A. Shepherd, *Grn.*		26,230
M. J. Pindar, *SLD.*		10,277
P. N. Power, *Comm.*		1,277
Ms. D. Weppler, *Comm. League*		323
Lab. Co-op maj.		*45,018*
(June '84, Lab. maj. 31,481)		

London South West
E. 486,412

Ms A. J. Pollack, *Lab.*		74,298
Dame S. M. Roberts, C.		73,780
Ms. M. A. Elson, *Grn.*		35,476
J. C. Field, *SLD*		10,400
Lab. maj.		*518*
(June '84, C. maj. 6,867)		

London West
E. 515,581

M. N. Elliott, Lab.		92,959
B. Donnelly, *C.*		78,151
J. R. Hywell-Davies, *Grn.*		32,686
J. G. Parry, *SLD.*		9,309
J. Rogers-Davies, *SDP*		2,877
Lab. maj.		*14,808*
(June '84, Lab. maj. 5,229)		

Lothians
E. 523,506

*D. W. Martin, *Lab.*	90,840
Mrs. C. M. Blight, *C.*	52,014
J. Smith, *SNP*	44,935
R. C. M. Harper, *Grn*	22,983
K. Leadbetter, *SLD*	9,222
Lab. maj.	*38,826*

(June '84, Lab. maj. 25,924)

Merseyside East
E. 519,514

*T. Wynn, *Lab.*	107,288
E. N. Farthing, *C.*	30,421
R. L. Georgeson, *Grn.*	20,018
R. M. Clayton, *SLD*	5,658
Lab. maj.	*76,867*

(June '84, Lab. maj. 49,039)

Merseyside West
E. 508,722

*K. A. Stewart, *Lab.*	93,717
M. D. Byrne, *C.*	43,900
L. Brown, *Grn.*	23,052
Mrs. H. F. Clucas, *SLD* . . .	16,327
D. J. E. Carson, *PRP*	1,747
Lab. maj.	*49,817*

(June '84, Lab. maj. 13,197)

Midlands Central
E. 539,211

Ms. C. M. Oddy, *Lab.*	76,736
*J. de Courcy Ling, *C.*	71,643
Ms. J. A. Alty, *Grn.*	42,622
I. Cundy, *SLD.*	8,450
Lab. maj.	*5,093*

(June '84, C. maj. 12,729)

Midlands West
E. 529,505

*J. A. W. Bird, *Lab. Co-op.*	105,529
M. J. Whitby, *C.*	63,165
J. Raven, *Grn.*	21,787
Mrs. F. M. Oborski, *SLD*	6,974
Lab. Co-op maj.	*42,364*

(June '84, Lab. maj. 19,685)

Norfolk
E. 577,576

*P. F. Howell, *C.*	92,385
Ms. M. Page, *Lab.*	71,478
M. Macartney-Filgate, *Grn.*	40,575
R. A. Lawes, *SLD*	8,902
S. D. Maxwell, *SDP*	4,934
C. maj.	*20,907*

(June '84, C. maj. 36,857)

Northamptonshire
E. 587,733

*A. M. H. Simpson, *C.*	86,695
M. Coyne, *Lab.*	66,248
Ms. A. T. Bryant, *Grn.*	43,071
R. Church, *SLD.*	11,619
C. maj.	*20,447*

(June '84, C. maj. 39,859)

Northumbria
E. 514,083

*G. J. Adam, *Lab.*	110,688
P. Yeoman, *C.*	50,648
Ms. A. Lipman, *Grn.*	24,882
Viscount Morpeth, *SLD*	10,983
Lab. maj.	*60,040*

(June '84, Lab. maj. 15,700)

Nottingham
E. 565,354

K. Coates, *Lab.*	92,261
*M. L. Kilby, *C.*	77,748
Mrs. S. E. Blount, *Grn.* . . .	34,097
A. Swift, *SLD*	6,693
Lab. maj.	*14,513*

(June '84, C. maj. 16,126)

Oxford and Buckinghamshire
E. 560,730

*J. E. M. Elles, *C.*	92,483
R. Gifford, *Lab.*	44,965
T. H. Andrewes, *Grn.*	42,058
R. Johnston, *SLD*	14,405
R. C. Turner, *Ind.*	3,696
C. maj.	*47,518*

(June '84, C. maj. 49,081)

Scotland Mid and Fife
E. 534,638

*A. Falconer, *Lab.*	102,246
K. W. MacAskill, *SNP* . . .	50,089
A. Christie, *C.*	46,505
G. Moreton, *Grn.*	14,165
M. Black, *SLD*	8,857
Lab. maj.	*52,157*

(June '84, Lab. maj. 27,166)

Scotland North East
E. 554,408

H. McGubbin, *Lab.*	65,348
Dr. A. Macartney, *SNP*	62,735
*J. L. C. Provan, *C.*	56,835
M. Hill, *Grn.*	15,584
S. Horner, *SLD*	12,704
Lab. maj.	*2,613*

(June '84, C. maj. 9,171)

Scotland South
E. 491,865

A. Smith, *Lab.*	81,366
*A. H. Hutton, *C.*	65,673
M. Brown, *SNP*	35,155
J. Button, *Grn.*	11,658
J. E. McKercher, *SLD* . . .	10,368
Lab. maj.	*15,693*

(June '84, C. maj. 3,137)

Sheffield
E. 564,409

R. Barton, *Lab.*	109,677
T. S. R. Mort, *C.*	40,401
P. L. Scott, *Grn.*	26,844
A. H. Rogers, *SLD*	10,910
D. E. Hyland, *ICP*	657
Lab. maj.	*69,276*

(June '84, Lab. maj. 46,283)

Shropshire and Stafford
E. 597,554

*C. J. Prout, *C.*	85,896
D. J. A. Hallam, *Lab.*	83,352
R. T. C. Saunders, *Grn.* . .	29,637
C. Hards, *SLD*	10,568
C. maj.	*2,544*

(June '84, C. maj. 24,932)

Somerset and Dorset West
E. 582,098

*Mrs. M. E. Daly, *C.*	106,716
Dr. R. H. Lawson, *Grn.* . .	54,496
Ms. D. M. Organ, *Lab.* . . .	46,210
M. Mactaggart, *SLD*	28,662
A. P. B. Mockler *W. Reg.*	930
C. maj.	*52,220*

(June '84, C. maj. 40,251)

Staffordshire East
E. 581,127

*G. W. Stevenson, *Lab.* . . .	94,873
M. F. Spungin, *C.*	63,104
S. Parker, *Grn.*	23,415
R. C. Dodson, *SLD*	7,046
Lab. maj.	*31,769*

(June '84, Lab. maj. 7,867)

Strathclyde East
E. 494,274

*K. D. Collins, *Lab.*	109,170
G. A. Leslie, *SNP*	48,853
M. Dutt, *C.*	22,233
A. Whitelaw, *Grn.*	9,749
G. Lait, *SLD*	4,276
Lab. maj.	*60,317*

(June '84, Lab. maj. 63,462)

Strathclyde West
E. 493,067

*H. R. McMahon, *Lab.*	89,627
C. M. Campbell, *SNP* . . .	50,036
S. J. Robin, *C.*	45,872
G. Campbell, *Grn.*	16,461
D. J. Herbison, *SLD.*	8,098
Lab. maj.	*39,591*

(June '84, Lab. maj. 23,038)

Suffolk
E. 550,131

*A. E. Turner, *C.*	82,481
M. D. Cornish, *Lab.*	56,788
A. C. Slade, *Grn.*	37,305
P. R. Odell, *SLD*	12,660
C. maj.	*25,693*

(June '84, C. maj. 47,098)

Surrey West
E. 515,881

T. N. B. Spencer, *C.*	89,674
E. Haywood, *Grn.*	40,332
H. G. Trace, *Lab.*	28,313
A. Davies, *SLD*	18,042
B. M. Collignon, *SDP* . .	3,676
C. maj.	*49,342*

(June '84, Lab. maj. 52,588)

Sussex East
E. 553,536

Sir J. Stewart-Clark, Bt.,	
C.	96,388
Ms G. Roles, *Lab.*	43,094
Ms R. Addison, *Grn*	42,316
Mrs D. Venables, *SLD* . . .	16,810
D. Howells, *LM*	1,181
C. maj.	*53,294*

(June '84, C. maj. 65,621)

Sussex West
E. 554,664

*R. M. Seligman, *C.*	95,821
I. F. N. Bagnall, *Grn.*	49,588
M. Shrimpton, *Lab.*	32,006
Dr. J. M. M. Walsh, *SLD.*	24,855
C. maj.	*46,233*

(June '84, C. maj. 57,502)

Thames Valley
E. 542,855

J. C. C. Stevens, *C.*	73,070
Ms. H. B. de Lyon, *Lab.* . .:	46,579
P. Gordon, *Grn.*	36,865
D. B. Griffiths, *SLD*	14,603
C. maj.	*26,491*

(June '84, C. maj. 38,805)

Tyne and Wear
E. 530,953

A. J. Donnelly, *Lab.*	126,682
N. C. Gibbon, *C.*	30,902
R. Stather, *Grn.*	18,107
P. J. Arnold, *SLD*	6,101
T. P. Kilgallon, *SPGB*	919
Lab. maj.	*95,780*
(June '84, Lab. maj. 49,414)	

Wales Mid and West
E. 547,740

*Rev. D. R. Morris, *Lab.*	105,670
O. J. Williams, *C.*	53,758
Ms. B. I. McPake, *Grn.*	29,852
Dr. P. J. S. Williams, *PC*	26,063
G. A. Sinclair, *SLD*	10,031
Lab. maj.	*51,912*
(June '84, Lab. maj. 36,452)	

Wales North
E. 540,230

J. Wilson, *Lab.*	83,638
*Miss B. A. Brookes, *C.*	79,178
Dr. D. E. Thomas, *PC*	64,120
P. H. W. Adams, *Grn.*	15,832
R. K. Marshall, *SLD*	10,056
Lab. maj.	*4,460*
(June '84, C. maj. 12,278)	

Wales South
E. 520,911

W. David, *Lab.*	108,550
A. R. Taylor, *C.*	45,993
G. P. Jones, *Grn.*	25,993
P. J. Keelan, *PC*	10,727
P. K. Verma, *SLD*	4,037
D. A. T. Thomas, *SDP*	3,513
Lab. maj.	*62,557*
(June '84, Lab. maj. 44,258)	

Wales South East
E. 561,068

*L. T. Smith, *Lab.*	138,872
R. J. Young, *C.*	30,384
M. J. Witherden, *Grn.*	27,869
Ms. J. Evans, *PC*	14,152
P. Nicholls-Jones, *SLD*	4,661
Lab. maj.	*108,488*
(June '84, Lab. maj. 95,557)	

Wight and Hampshire East
E. 574,332

*R. J. Simmonds, *C.*	90,658
Dr. A. D. Burnett, *Lab.*	51,228
S. L. Rackett, *Grn.*	40,664
Ms. V. A. Rayner, *SLD*	19,569
C. maj.	*39,430*
(June '84, C. maj. 42,928)	

Wiltshire
E. 568,875

*Mrs. C. F. Jackson, *C.*	93,200
G. A. Harris, *Lab.*	46,887
J. V. Hughes, *Grn.*	46,735
P. N. Crossley, *SLD*	18,302
J. A. Cade, *Ind.*	4,809
C. maj.	*46,313*
(June '84, C. maj. 26,469)	

York
E. 542,998

E. H. C. McMillan-Scott, C.	81,453
J. T. Grogan, *Lab.*	66,351
R. Bell, *Grn.*	27,525
A. Collinge, *SLD*	12,542
C. maj.	*15,102*
(June '84, C. maj. 36,402)	

Yorkshire South
E. 518,995

*N. West, *Lab.*	121,060
W. J. Clappison, *C.*	29,276
A. Grace, *Grn.*	19,063
B. Boulton, *SLD*	5,039
Lab. maj.	*91,784*
(June '84, Lab. maj. 67,749)	

Yorkshire South West
E. 523,322

*T. Megahy, *Lab.*	108,444
G. T. Horton, *C.*	42,543
Mrs. S. Leyland, *Grn.*	25,677
J. A. D. Ridgway, *SLD*	10,352
Lab. maj.	*65,901*
(June '84, Lab. maj. 44,173)	

Yorkshire West
E. 564,001

*B. H. Seal, *Lab.*	108,644
G. T. Hall, *C.*	70,717
N. Parrott, *Grn.*	28,308
P. Wrigley, *SLD*	9,765
Lab. maj.	*37,927*
(June '84, Lab. maj. 20,854)	

Northern Ireland
E. 1,105,551

*Rev. I. R. K. Paisley, *MP*, DUP*	160,110
*J. Hume, *MP*, *SDLP*	136,335
J. F. Nicholson, *OUP*	118,785
D. Morrison *SF*	48,914
J. T. Alderdice, *All.*	27,905
A. Kennedy, *C.*	25,789
M. H. Samuel, *Ecol.*	6,569
S. Lynch, *WP*	5,590
M. Langhammer, *Lab. RG*	3,540
B. Caul, *Lab.* 87	1,274

Rev. I. R. K. Paisley, J. Hume and *J. F. Nicholson* were elected by the single transferable voting system.

PARLIAMENT, 1990–91

For the first time in 19 years Parliament was recalled during the 1990 summer recess, meeting on September 6 and 7 to debate the Iraqi invasion of Kuwait on August 2. The Prime Minister (Margaret Thatcher) called it 'a flagrant and blatant case of aggression'. The Leader of the Opposition (Neil Kinnock) said that 'our unrelenting purpose must be to ensure that Saddam Hussein gets out of Kuwait and legitimate government is restored in that country'. Although the debate in the Commons was on a procedural motion for the adjournment of the House, which would not normally lead to a vote, a division was forced by some Labour MPs against the wishes of their front bench; the vote was 437 in favour and 35 against. Whilst this was technically a vote on 'whether the House should adjourn', in practice the vote was on support for government policy.

The House of Lords returned from the summer recess on October 8 and the House of Commons on October 15.

On October 8, the Government was defeated in the Lords on an amendment to the Environmental Protection Bill, setting out a series of principles to be applied to companies to ensure that their tasks are audited in such a way as to promote sustainable development. On October 11 the Government agreed to withdraw its controversial amendment to the Broadcasting Bill covering impartiality. On October 17, the sitting of the House on the Environmental Protection Bill was suspended following complaints that the Goverment spokesman (Baroness Blatch) had announced the detail of the members and powers of the various replacement bodies for the Nature Conservancy Council too quickly and in too much detail for the Lords to appreciate without seeing the text. On October 18, a final attempt to amend the Human Fertilization and Embryology Bill to decrease the number of weeks at which an abortion could legally be carried out was defeated by 133 votes to 89 and the figure agreed by the Commons (24 weeks) was therefore approved.

On October 24 the Foreign Secretary (Douglas Hurd) made a statement on developments in the Gulf since the Commons debated the issue in September. The Secretary of State for Social Security (Tony Newton) announced the annual uprating of social security benefits to come into effect in the week beginning April 8, 1991; he announced a £1 increase in child benefit for the first child after several years of this benefit being frozen. His Labour Shadow (Michael Meacher) welcomed the 'small but useful increases' but criticized the Government for failing to honour its manifesto promises on child benefit. On October 29 Tony Newton announced the publication of a White Paper, *Children Come First*, outlining the Government's proposals for securing the maintenance of children. Michael Meacher said that Labour strongly supported the principle of the state assisting with the collection of child maintenance and agreed that fathers should be expected to accept responsibility for their children.

The Commons overturned two defeats suffered by the Goverment in the Lords on the Environmental Protection Bill, rejecting Lords' amendments concerning the so-called Valdez principles (without division) and on setting up a dog registration scheme (by 274 votes to 271). For the second vote the Government business managers had recalled Ministers from visits all around the globe to vote, to ensure that their view prevailed; as it was, some dozen Opposition MPs missed the vote. On October 31 the Environment Secretary (Chris Patten) announced details of the local government financial settlement

for England for 1991–92, suggesting that the average community charge for that year should be £380.

The Queen's Speech

The 1989–90 Parliamentary session ended on November 1 and The Queen opened the new session of Parliament on November 7. The Queen's Speech outlined the Government's legislative programme, of which the following were the main features:

Atomic Weapons Establishment Bill—to enable the privatization of the Atomic Weapons Establishment

Child Support Bill—to make provisions for the assessment, collection and enforcement of maintenance for children

Criminal Justice Bill—to reform the sentencing system and make easier provision for child witnesses

Disability Living and Disability Working Allowance Bill—to introduce two new benefits for the disabled

Export and Investment Guarantees Bill—to enable the privatization of the insurance services business of the Export Credit Guarantee Department

Natural Heritage (Scotland) Bill—to create a national heritage agency to achieve an integrated approach to conservation and countryside matters

New Roads and Street Works Bill—to allow for the private funding of roads and the introduction of toll roads and to reform the law on utilities' street works

Northern Ireland (Emergency Provisions) Bill—to replace existing anti-terrorist legislation in Northern Ireland which is due to expire in 1992

Planning and Compensation Bill—to improve arrangements for compensation for compulsory purchase of land and buildings and to make the town and country planning system more efficient

Ports Bill—to enable the privatization of various trust ports and the sale by the Port of London Authority of the port of Tilbury

Road Traffic Bill—a measure in two parts, first to implement the recommendations of the North report on drinking and driving, and second to reform the management of traffic in London, with particular emphasis on red routes

School Teachers' Pay and Conditions Bill—to establish new machinery for negotiating the pay and conditions of school teachers in England and Wales

Severn Bridge Bill—to allow for a second tolled road bridge and to provide the necessary framework for it to be privately financed

War Crimes Bill—to enable the prosecution of alleged war criminals resident in the UK (reintroduced)

Other minor bills would also be introduced.

Debate on the Queen's Speech

Neil Kinnock said that the speech contained 'measures that the Opposition are likely to support' and in particular he pledged to continue to support the United Nations policy for securing a complete and unconditional Iraqi withdrawal from Kuwait. He was particularly critical of the Prime Minister, most pointedly on her attitude to Europe, claiming 'She is incapable of making the alliances Britain needs. She is incapable of making the arguments that are essential to the exercise of our influence at this time of great change . . . her economic, industrial and social policies and her style of government are putting our country on the sidelines within the European Community'. The Liberal Democrat leader (Paddy Ashdown) described the speech as 'a sad little programme for the last year of a government who have claimed to be a reforming and radical government; a programme that is definite, precise and active about a number of rather small measures ... but where it should have been precise and definite on the great issues ... it is instead confused, opaque and indecisive'. There were the usual six days of debate on the speech and the vote at the end was 333 in favour, 225 against.

Financial Statement

On November 8 the Chancellor of the Exchequer (John Major) presented his autumn financial statement. Mr Major told the Commons that planned public expenditure in the current year was expected to be £180,600 million, rather less than 1 per cent above the planning total set in 1989. Most of this increase was due to an increase in the financing requirements of the nationalized industries, to a surge in common agricultural policy spending on agricultural market support, and to expenditure on the Gulf crisis. Despite this, public expenditure remained under tight control. Inflation had been higher than forecast but it had not been allowed to feed through fully into expenditure. The ratio of spending to national income in the year was likely to be slightly lower than that projected at the time of the Budget.

The main points of the Financial Statement were:

Public expenditure
Public spending planning total for 1991–92 to increase to over £200,000. Planning totals for 1992–93 to be £215,000 and for 1993–94 to be £226,000

Spending programmes
Central government support for local authorities to increase by £2,500 million
Defence spending to fall by 6 per cent in real terms over the next three years
Education spending to increase by over £500 million
Health spending to increase by £3,000 million
Public transport finance to be double the level of the past three years, with an extra £500 million for improvements to British Rail and London Underground
Social security spending to increase by nearly £3,000 million
Arts spending to keep pace with inflation
Extra resources for environmental research and in support of environmental bodies

National Insurance
Lower earning limit of national insurance contributions raised to £52 a week
Upper earning limit of national insurance contributions raised to £390 a week
Main contribution rate to fall to 10.4 per cent in April 1991 and each of lower rates to be cut by 0.4 per cent

Economic forecast
Economic growth in 1991 expected to be 0.5 per cent
Manufacturing output expected to fall by 0.5 per cent
Current account deficit expected to fall to £11,000 million in 1991–92
Inflation expected to fall to around 5.5 per cent by the end of 1991

Mr Major commended his plans to the House, saying that they 'are consistent with the tight fiscal and monetary policies that will lead to a falling trade deficit and to a sharp reduction in inflation'. (The Autumn Statement was approved on February 13 by 321 votes to 216.)

On November 12 the Energy Secretary (John Wakeham) announced the publication of the report into the Piper Alpha disaster. He said that the Government accepted all the recommendations and

conclusions of the report, most importantly the transfer of responsibility for offshore safety from the Department of Energy to the Health and Safety Executive. His Labour Shadow (Frank Dobson) hoped that everyone who worked in the environment would now 'work together to create a new safe regime in the North Sea'. On November 13, Sir Geoffrey Howe, the former Leader of the House, made a personal statement to the Commons giving the reasons for his resignation from the Government on November 2: 'The Prime Minister's perceived attitude to Europe is running increasingly serious risks for the future of our nation ... The conflict of loyalty has become all too great; I no longer believe that it is possible to resolve that conflict from within the Government. That is why I resigned.'

On November 19 the Northern Ireland (Emergency Provisions) Bill was given a second reading in the Commons by 234 votes to 113. In the Lords, the Natural Heritage (Scotland) Bill had its second reading. On November 20 the Criminal Justice Bill received a second reading in the Commons by 350 votes to 190. In the Lords, the New Roads and Street Works Bill has its second reading. On November 21 the Disability Living and Disability Working Allowance Bill was given an unopposed second reading in the Commons, as was the Armed Forces Bill, to enable the various discipline acts for the armed forces to remain in force for a further five years.

On November 22 the Prime Minister, Margaret Thatcher, announced her decision not to stand in the second round of elections for the leadership of the Conservative party and said that she would continue as Prime Minister only until the outcome of that ballot was known. The Defence Secretary (Tom King) announced in the Commons further troop deployments in the Gulf, detailing the provision of an extra brigade, divisional HQ and supporting arms and two more mine counter-measure vessels, which would raise the operating costs by £10 million a week. The Government survived an Opposition debate on a motion of no confidence by 367 votes to 247, during which Mrs Thatcher, making what amounted to her resignation speech, said 'I'm enjoying this'.

On November 27, John Major failed by two votes to win an outright majority in the second ballot for the leadership of the Conservative party, but the third ballot was cancelled when his two opponents, Douglas Hurd and Michael Heseltine, effectively stood down, and so he became Prime Minister. In the Commons the School Teachers' Pay and Conditions Bill received its second reading by 328 votes to 177. In the Lords, the Planning and Compensation Bill was given its second reading. On November 28 Douglas Hurd brought the Commons up to date on developments in the Middle East since his last statement, in particular announcing the restoration of diplomatic relations with Syria.

On December 3 the Minister of State at the Foreign and Commonwealth Office (Douglas Hogg) replied to a private notice question from Gerald Kauffman (Labour foreign affairs spokesman), welcoming the United States' invitation to Iraq for talks on the crisis in the Gulf. This was followed by a statement by the Minister for Trade (Tim Sainsbury) on exports to Iraq, with particular reference to an article in the *Sunday Times* concerning the Minister for Defence Procurement (Alan Clark) and the Machine Tool Technologies Association. The Community Charges (Substitute Setting) Bill, a measure introduced by the Government at short notice following a legal case, to ensure that when a local authority has been capped, the reduction in spending is passed on in full to the community charge payers, had its second reading by 307 votes to 224. On December 4 in answer to a private notice question from his Labour Shadow (Robin Cook), the Secretary of State for Health (William Waldegrave) gave the details of his decision to establish 56 National Health Service trusts in April 1991. The Scottish Secretary (Ian Lang) gave the details of planned public expenditure in Scotland; for 1991–92 the total sum would be just over £11,000 million. On December 5 during an Opposition debate on the abolition of the community charge, the Environment Secretary (Michael Heseltine) moved an amendment offering an overall and fundamental review of the tax, including discussion with Opposition parties. This was approved by 310 votes to 232.

On December 10, Peter Lilley reported to the Commons on the breakdown of the GATT negotiations in Brussels, expressing the hope that they would be continued, with a view to completion, in Geneva early in the New Year. One of Labour's trade team (Joyce Quin) called this failure to reach agreement 'serious and the only sign of hope is that there is, at least, a commitment to resume talks.' The Road Traffic Bill was given an unopposed second reading in the Commons. On December 11 there was a debate on a government motion on developments in the Gulf. This was intended to show the strength and unity of Parliament on the issue, but a back-bench Labour MP (Tony Benn) forced a division of the Commons, when normally there would not have been one and against the wishes of his front bench; his motion was defeated by 455 votes to 42.

On December 17 there was a special committee stage debate on the Criminal Justice Bill on the floor of the Commons to deal with new clauses relating to capital punishment. The following votes were taken on back-bench clauses introducing the death penalty:

(i) For murder of a police officer—defeated by 350 votes to 215
(ii) for murder, except for those under 18— defeated by 367 votes to 182
(iii) for murder, covering terrorism and police-men—defeated by 349 votes to 186
(iv) on the abolition of the death penalty, still in effect for treason and piracy—defeated by 289 votes to 257.

On December 18 the Atomic Weapons Establishment Bill was given a second reading in the Commons by 292 votes to 221. In the Lords, the Government was defeated by 106 votes to 88 in the report stage of the Natural Heritage (Scotland) Bill on an amendment moved by an independent peer (Lady Saltoun) to ensure that Scottish Natural Heritage should take account of the interests of local communities in all its decisions. On December 19 the Overseas Development Minister (Lynda Chalker) announced an emergency package of £5 million of aid for the starving in Ethiopia and Sudan. The Arts Minister (Tim Renton) made a statement on the structure of arts funding in England.

After the return from the Christmas recess on January 14 the Secretary of State for Transport (Malcolm Rifkind) made a statement on the railway accident at Cannon Street station on January 8 in which one person was killed and over 500 were injured. The Severn Bridges Bill was given an unopposed second reading in the Commons. In the Lords, the Government suffered two defeats on the committee stage of the Statutory Sick Pay Bill: by 132 votes to 80 on an amendment introduced by a Conservative peer (Lord Mottistone) with cross-party support, to cut the State's contribution from 100 per cent rebates to 91 per cent rebates, rather than the 80 per cent proposed by the Government; and by 106 votes to 71 on an amendment moved by a Liberal Democrat peer (Earl Russell) to force the

Government to introduce further new legislation if it wanted to alter the percentage that employers deducted. On January 15 both Houses debated the situation in the Gulf; in the Commons there was criticism from some Opposition MPs that there was no opportunity to vote on a substantive motion and so they forced a vote on the adjournment of the House in an attempt to test opinion. In the event the vote was 534 to 57 in favour of the Government's policy. On January 17 John Major came to the Commons to make a statement on the outbreak of hostilities in the Gulf. In support Neil Kinnock said that just by having a debate 'we are demonstrating the superiority of democracy over any form of dictatorship'. There were also announcements by the Environment Secretary, the Welsh Secretary and the Scottish Secretary on local government finance in 1991–92 in England, Wales and Scotland respectively.

On January 21 both Houses again debated the Gulf crisis, this time in the Commons with a substantive motion expressing full support for the British forces and their contribution to the implementation of the United Nations resolutions, and with an agreed Opposition amendment commending the instruction to minimize civilian casualties. These were approved by 563 votes to 34. In his summing-up the Defence Secretary (Tom King) announced the setting up of the Gulf Trust to co-ordinate the efforts to help the dependents of those involved in the fighting. On January 22 the Export and Investment Guarantees Bill was given an unopposed second reading in the Commons. In the Lords the Government was defeated in the third reading debate on the Natural Heritage (Scotland) Bill by 65 votes to 45 on an amendment moved by Lady Saltoun to create an appeal mechanism over planning.

On January 28 the Ports Bill was given its second reading in the Commons by 260 votes to 204. In the Lords the Government was defeated in the third reading of the Statutory Sick Pay Bill by 128 votes to 84 on an amendment moved by a Conservative peer (Lord Stanley of Alderley) to limit the costs to be imposed on small firms. On January 29 in a debate to approve the local government revenue support grants, Michael Heseltine said that his review of the community charge would have made significant progress by the spring. He also said that the average community charge in England should be under £300 for the next year. In the following debate on Welsh revenue support grants, the failure of the Deputy Speaker (Betty Boothroyd, MP) to call any member of Plaid Cymru to speak in the debate led to the tabling of a motion of no confidence in the Deputy Speaker by the leader of Plaid Cymru (Dafydd Wigley). On January 31 while updating the Commons on the military situation in the Gulf, Tom King announced that the Government had agreed to allow the US Air Force to station B52 bombers at RAF Fairford, to undertake missions with conventional munitions. Several government ministers went against convention and voted against the carryover motion on the Private Bill to allow for the construction of the Southampton Rapid Transport system, and it was rejected by 138 votes to 49. On February 1 on the second reading of the National Health Service (Compensation) Bill, a Private Member's Bill introduced by an independent social democrat MP (Rosie Barnes) to provide no-fault compensation for those people injured during care by the NHS, the Government opposed the measure and it was defeated by 193 votes to 81.

On February 4 the Coal Mining Subsidence Bill, a measure introduced by the Government, following back-bench pressure, to provide compensation for certain cases of subsidence, was given an unopposed second reading in the Commons. On February 5 Tom King made a statement about the closure of the US Navy submarine support facility at Holy Loch and the changes to the US Air Force deployments at RAF Upper Heyford and RAF Lakenheath. His Labour Shadow (Martin O'Neill) said, 'the withdrawal of Poseidon missile submarines is expected and welcome'. In the Commons the Government overturned the three defeats it had suffered in the Lords on the Statutory Sick Pay Bill. On February 7 the Home Secretary (Kenneth Baker) reported to the Commons on the mortar attack on 10 Downing Street that morning. His Labour Shadow (Roy Hattersley) joined in the condemnation of 'this act of terrorism'. On February 8 the Parliamentary Under Secretary of State at the Department of Education (Tim Yeo) announced the allocation of 500 extra bed places in emergency shelters for the duration of the very cold weather. On February 11 the Minister for Social Security and Disabled People (Nicholas Scott) gave details of the cold weather payments outlined by the Prime Minister in the previous week, but stressed that these would apply for one week only. On February 12 the British Technology Group Bill, a privatization measure, was given its second reading in the Commons by 275 votes to 198. In the Lords, the Government accepted in principle an amendment introduced by a Conservative peer (Lord Swinfen) in the third reading of the New Roads and Street Works Bill, concerning re-instatement of special features for the disabled. On February 13 the Minister for the Armed Forces (Archie Hamilton) made a statement in response to a private notice question from a Conservative MP (Tony Speller) concerning the provision of an area of the Bristol Channel for the possible dumping of unused bombs by US B52 bombers flying on Gulf missions from their UK bases.

On February 18 Douglas Hurd made a statement to the Commons on the developments in the Gulf, including the alleged offer by Iraq of compliance with the UN Resolutions contained in an Iraqi radio broadcast on February 14. On February 20 Malcolm Rifkind responded to a question from his Labour Shadow (John Prescott) on the transport problems faced by commuters in London on February 18–19 because of bombs placed at railway stations. A government clause on sexual offenders was added to the Criminal Justice Bill in its remaining stages in the Commons. On February 25 Tom King made a statement in the Commons on the final phase of action in the Gulf. In the remaining stages of debate on the Criminal Justice Bill, the Government accepted an amendment from a Conservative MP (John Greenway) to allow experiments with privatization in all types of prisons. In the Lords the Child Support Bill had its second reading. On February 28 John Major came to the Commons to announce the ceasefire in the Gulf; he said 'The whole nation is proud of our forces, proud of their families and proud that through their valour, freedom and justice have prevailed. It has been a victory for what is right.'

On March 5 Peter Lilley announced the publication of a White Paper, *Competition and Choice: Telecommunications Policy for the 1990s*, including proposals for the ending of the duopoly of British Telecom and Mercury. Malcolm Rifkind announced the lifting of restrictions on air traffic distribution rules at Heathrow airport. In the Lords on March 7 the Government was defeated in the committee stage of the Disability Living and Disability Working Allowance Bill by 125 votes to 103 on an amendment introduced by an independent peer (Lord Henderson of Brompton) which would enable local authorities to have responsibility for those helped by the Independent Living Fund beyond the five years initially envisaged when

it was set up in 1988. On March 11 Malcolm Rifkind replied to a question from one of Labour's transport spokesmen (Peter Snape) on the collapse of Air Europe, absolving the Civil Aviation Authority of any criticism of their handling of the affair. He then went on to make an announcement on the outcome of the UK–US air negotiations, offering major new opportunities to British airlines on transatlantic routes. On March 13 William Waldegrave made a statement on the implementation of the General Practitioners' Fund Holding Scheme from April 1; some 306 practices, involving 1,720 GPs, had applied.

During questions to Ministers from the Northern Ireland Office on March 14, the Secretary of State for Northern Ireland (Peter Brooke) announced that he had been able to draw up a text which would provide a sound basis for formal political talks on all the key issues in the Anglo-Irish Agreement. He hoped this would 'give a real chance to move forward together with substantive talks, that would offer the prospect of a significant transfer of power to local politicians in Northern Ireland and a new beginning for relationships between both parts of Ireland and amongst the peoples of the whole of the UK.' Kenneth Baker made a statement on the decision by the Court of Appeal to quash the convictions of the Birmingham Six and announced the setting up of a Royal Commission to inquire into the criminal investigations of prosecution and appeal cases. Roy Hattersley said 'we must all feel relief that so grotesque a miscarriage of justice has at last been righted'.

On March 18 the War Crimes Bill was re-introduced after being defeated in the Lords in the 1989–90 session of Parliament and received its second reading in the Commons by 254 votes to 88. The Commons approved a measure empowering the Home Secretary to evoke the Parliament Act to force the measure through if the Lords again declined to give the bill a second reading.

The Budget

On March 19 the Chancellor of the Exchequer (Norman Lamont) gave his first Budget Statement. Mr Lamont departed from recent tradition and started with a joke at his own expense—referring to the fact that a recent poll had shown that he was almost as well-known as the racehorse Desert Orchid—but he then reverted to the usual format of paying tribute to his immediate predecessors, John Major and Nigel Lawson, saying of the latter, 'my admiration and respect for him remain undimmed'. He said that his central aim was to bring inflation down and keep it down. Beyond that his objective was to encourage enterprise by creating a broadly based tax system that allowed markets to do their job with the minimum of distortion and government interference. 'Although there is no scope this year for an overall reduction in taxes, the Budget will include measures to help business through the recession in the short term and to encourage it to invest for the longer term. It will provide assistance for families. It will also further the process of tax reform and make some radical changes in the tax system.'

As usual he began his speech with a review of the economic situation and prospects. Mr Lamont said 'The past year has brought recession to a number of major industrial countries ... In five of the seven leading industrial nations, industrial output is now lower than it was a year ago. The basic cause is the same everywhere: very rapid growth in the industrialized world during the 1980s led to the re-emergence of inflationary pressures. A period of slower growth was needed to stop inflation taking hold again.' The Gulf crisis had not helped.

The main points of the Budget were:

Economic forecast
Output expected to increase by about 2 per cent between the first half of 1991 and the first half of 1992
Current account deficit expected to be £6,000 million in 1991
Inflation expected to fall to an average of 4 per cent by the end of 1991, and to below 4 per cent by mid 1992
Unemployment expected to continue to rise

Monetary policy
Target for the annual rate of growth of M0 (the narrow measure of money) to be within a range of 0 to 4 per cent
No plans to move sterling to a narrow band in the exchange rate mechanism (ERM) at present

Public sector finance
Deficit in the public sector borrowing rate (PSBR) expected to be £8,000 million in 1991–92, with a slightly larger deficit in 1992–93

Taxation*
VAT increased by 2.5 per cent to 17.5 per cent, with effect from April 1, 1991
Abolition of higher rate of mortgage interest relief
Capital gains tax—reduction in qualifying age for retirement relief, increase in amount exempted from tax
Corporation tax—cut in rate of tax, increase in higher rate tax thresholds
Profit related pay to be free of tax up to present limits
Improvements in share schemes for employees
Tax relief on fees for training paid by individuals
More tax relief for seafarers working mainly overseas
*For details, *see* **Taxation** section

Charities
Concessions intended to increase company donations:
New relief from income and corporation tax
Abolition of the limit on the gift aid scheme
A cut in the pools betting duty to 37.5 per cent to support a new foundation for sport and the arts, on the understanding that all the main pools companies agree to participate and that the full amount of the cut in duty is passed on to the foundation

Excise duties
Duties on drinks increased by 9.3 per cent
Duties on tobacco increased by 15 per cent
Duties on petrol and DERV increased by 15 per cent

Income tax*
Personal allowances increased in line with inflation
Threshold for higher rate of tax increased to £23,700
Employees who had intended to work in Kuwait or Iraq for a year or more but were forced to return home early are not to be taxed on their foreign earnings
*For details, *see* **Taxation** section

Benefits in kind
Tax on company cars increased by 20 per cent
Mobile telephones to become taxable

Savings
Concessions on personal equity plans (PEPs), increasing the amount that can be invested, allowing investment in EC shares, and allowing transfers between PEPs
New National Savings bond for children under 16 to be introduced
Abolition of restrictions on friendly societies writing tax-exempt life insurance for children

Child benefit
Child benefit to be increased by £1 a week for the first eligible child in each family, and by 25p a week for other children
Government pledge to increase the benefit in line with inflation in future

Community charge
Extra government grant to be given to local authorities to enable community charge to be reduced—all community charges in England, Wales and Scotland to be cut by £140

In the course of his speech Mr Lamont also announced that the Government intended to sell part of its holding of British Telecom shares in the coming year.

Debate on the Budget

Neil Kinnock, as usual, congratulated the Chancellor on the way in which he delivered his speech, but went on to say 'My congratulations are even warmer than they would otherwise have been because he has provided us with what must be the biggest climb-down in modern political history. After two years of wasting £10,000 million on the misery, injustice and inefficiency of the poll tax we find the Government backing off that which was, but less than a year ago, their flagship.' But while welcoming some elements, he concluded, 'In the depth of recession we needed a Budget to build out of recession. We needed a Budget that helped to lay foundations for future economic strength. Instead, we got a Budget from a Government who will not learn from their own failures and—even worse—will not learn from the success of others'. The debate continued for the usual four days and the vote at the end was 336 in favour, 226 against. In his speech on March 25, former Chancellor Nigel Lawson said he thought it was basically a very good Budget, but he was scathing about the proposals for the reform of local government taxation because he considered it was a 'muddle' and he issued this warning to the Government, 'It was Pierre Mendes France who said that to govern was to choose. I agree with that. To appear to be unable to choose is to appear to be unable to govern.'

In the Lords on March 19 the Government was defeated in the committee stage of the Child Support Bill by 110 votes to 106 on an amendment introduced by Earl Russell to remove Clause 22 of the bill, which would give the Government the power to pay reduced benefit to mothers who refused to name the father of their child. On March 20 Peter Brooke outlined proposals for the privatization of the electricity supply industry in Northern Ireland, published in a White Paper. On March 21 Michael Heseltine announced the outcome of the review of local government finance, with the publication of three consultation papers: one on the structure of local government, one on the management of local government, and the third on the financing of local government. He announced the ending of the community charge, which is to be replaced by a tax based on both property values and the number of adults living in a property. The details would be worked out during the consultation period. Similar announcements were made by David Hunt for Wales and Ian Lang for Scotland. The Labour Shadow environment spokesman (Bryan Gould) said, 'We have just heard the most complete capitulation, the most startling U-turn and the most shameless abandonment of consistency and principle in modern political history'. The Education Secretary (Kenneth Clarke) announced plans for the reorganization of further education in England, whereby sixth form colleges and colleges of further education would be removed from local authority control and would be funded directly by the Government through a council appointed by and responsible to the Secretary of State.

On March 25 the Minister for Local Government and the Inner Cities (Michael Portillo) announced significant changes to the community charge reduction scheme for 1991–92, giving extra assistance to some 16 million people. On March 26 Peter Brooke was able to announce the agreement of all parties involved to begin formal political talks on the long-term solution to the problems of Northern Ireland. The Community Charges (General Reduction) Bill, foreshadowed in the Budget speech announcement of additional local authority funding to reduce community charges, completed all its Commons' stages in one day, without division on the principle. On March 27 Neil Kinnock introduced a debate on a motion of no confidence in the Government in the light of its inability to rectify the damage done to the nation by the community charge. This was defeated by 358 votes to 238. In the series of pre-recess adjournment debates on March 28, the Parliamentary Under Secretary of State at the Department of Health (Stephen Dorrell) announced that the Government would be commissioning an inquiry into the state and nature of ritual and satanic child abuse.

On return from the Easter recess on April 15 Douglas Hurd made a statement on the relief efforts for the Kurds fleeing from Iraq. In the Lords, replying to a debate on medicinal products, Lord Hesketh outlined government policy on patent term restoration in the light of EC proposals; they were in favour of the introduction of a safeguard such that, provided the overall patent term was not duly extended, industry would be able to count on having thirteen years of protected life rather than the sixteen years proposed by the Commission. They also considered that the maximum extension should be for five years rather than ten. On April 16 local MPs opposed to plans in the Private Bill to allow for the construction of the Cardiff Bay Barrage mounted an all-night fillibuster which led to the Leader of the House (John MacGregor) announcing that the Private Bill was being withdrawn by the sponsors and that the Government would be introducing its own bill later in this session. On April 17 Douglas Hurd made a statement on plans for the relief of the suffering of the Kurds in Iraq. Kenneth Clarke announced that the School Teachers' Pay and Conditions Bill was being withdrawn and that teachers' pay and conditions should be determined by an independent review body in future; a new bill to enact this would be introduced without delay. His Labour Shadow (Jack Straw) thought that the statement highlighted 'the chaos, confusion and indecision into which the Government has descended and displays contempt for the House and the grossest breach of faith with the teaching profession'. On April 18 Tom King gave details of the assistance which UK armed forces were providing to the relief efforts for the Kurds in Iraq. In the Lords the Government was defeated twice in the committee stage of the Criminal Justice Bill. On an amendment abolishing the mandatory life sentence, introduced by an independent peer (Lord Nathan) and supported by the Lord Chief Justice (Lord Lane) the vote was 177 to 79, and on another amendment moved by Lord Nathan on courts' duty on passing the sentence of life imprisonment, the vote was 120 to 68.

On April 22 Lynda Chalker reported to the Commons on her visit to the Kurds in Iraq and outlined the Government's intention to relieve the suffering in Turkey and Iran, announcing a doubling of its contributions. On April 23 Michael Heseltine announced the publication of two more consultation documents on the structure of local government in England and on the Government's proposal for a new

council tax to replace the community charge; this would have a property and a personal element. Similar announcements were made by David Hunt for Wales and Ian Lang for Scotland. Bryan Gould felt that it was 'remarkable that we have still not had a single word of apology from the Government for the billions of pounds that they have wasted, the chaos and confusion they have inflicted and the misery they have caused to millions of people'. In the Lords on April 25 the Lord Chancellor (Lord Mackay of Clashfern) said during the report stage of the Child Support Bill that the Government would not be legislating against so-called 'virgin births'. The School Teachers' Pay and Conditions (No 2) Bill, replacing the Government's original bill, was given a second reading by 310 votes to 200 on April 29.

On April 30 the Finance Bill, detailing the Budget proposals, was given a second reading by 310 votes to 209. In the Lords the second reading of the War Crimes Bill was rejected by 131 votes to 109. On May 1 in the Commons, the Speaker (Bernard Weatherill, MP) announced that due to the rejection of the War Crimes Bill by the Lords for the second time, the provisions of the Parliament Act would come into force and the Lords would be asked to return the bill to the Commons, where it would be prepared for Royal Assent with no further proceedings. On May 7 the Speaker made a statement to the Commons on the *Hansard* report of Prime Minister's question time from the preceeding Thursday, clarifying the confusion surrounding the actual words used by Mr Major (in a reference to the support of a medical journal for NHS reforms) and the reported text, which seemed to have different implications. On May 8 Lynda Chalker gave further details of the Government's response to the cyclone disaster in Bangladesh, announcing that a further £2 million was being made available, bringing the total to £6.5 million.

On May 20 Kenneth Clark detailed the Government's proposals for further and higher education for all young people over the age of 16, and announced the publication of three White Papers, *Education and Training for the 21st Century, The Challenge to Colleges*, and *Higher Education: A New Framework*. His Labour Shadow (Jack Straw) said, 'the country's failure in education and training has been built on a lack of commitment, a lack of funding and a lack of clarity of thinking by this Government'. There was also a statement by the Employment Secretary (Michael Howard) on the dovetailing arrangements for training set out in the White Papers. A motion to ensure that all future Private Bills have been subject to an environmental assessment before presentation was approved. On May 21 the Government overturned in the Commons its three defeats suffered in the Lords on the Disability Living and Disability Working Allowance Bill. On May 22 Kenneth Baker announced the Government's decision to bring forward legislation to ban the breeeding and ownership of dangerous dogs; Roy Hattersley gave the Opposition's support for any measures to reduce the number of attacks by such dogs. In the remaining stages of debate on the New Roads and Street Works Bill the Government introduced a new clause covering charges for occupation of the highway where works were unreasonably prolonged and accepted an amendment from a Conservative MP (Graham Riddick) on the power of a street authority or district council to undertake street works.

Returning from the Spring recess on June 3, the Agriculture Secretary (John Gummer) reported on the 1991 settlement of farm prices reached by the EC on May 24. The Minister for Health (Virginia Bottomley) made a statement on the report on residential care for children published by Staffordshire County Council, following an enquiry by Allan

Levy, QC, and Mrs Barbara Kahan into the so-called pindown approach. The Local Government Finance and Valuation Bill, designed to strengthen the capping powers of the Government before 1992–93 and to provide the powers needed for the banding of domestic properties before the introduction of the new council tax in April 1993, was given its second reading by 275 votes to 200. In the Lords the Government was defeated on the third reading of the Criminal Justice Bill by 79 votes to 75 on an amendment moved by a Conservative peer (Baroness Faithfull) proposing that youth courts should meet outside normal hours for the convenience of the parents and guardians of young people.

On June 10 the Dangerous Dogs Bill, to prohibit persons from having in their possession or custody dogs belonging to types bred for fighting and to impose restrictions in respect of such dogs, received an unopposed second reading in the Commons. All the remaining stages were then taken and a Conservative back-bench amendment to introduce compulsory dog registration for all breeds was defeated by 303 votes to 260. On June 21 the Minister for Defence Procurement (Alan Clark) announced the decision to replace the Chieftain tank with the Vickers Challenger II tank. On June 24 there was a row in the Commons debate on the consideration of Lords' amendments to the Natural Heritage (Scotland) Bill. Scottish Labour MPs accused the Government of inserting a revised clause during the Lords' consideration of the bill which the Commons had originally rejected. On June 25 the Government overturned in the Commons the defeats it had suffered in the Lords on mandatory life sentencing in the Criminal Justice Bill. On June 26 Tony Newton made a statement about recent developments in pension provisions following the European Court of Justice ruling on the case of Barber v. GRE. He announced that the Government was planning to treat men and women equally in the state pension scheme and to force companies to practise sex equality in occupational pensions. Margaret Thatcher made her first speech in the Commons since her resignation as Prime Minister, in a debate on the European Community. On June 27 the Leader of the Commons (John MacGregor) announced the setting up of a special select committee to undertake a review of the operation of the work of the Commons, including MPs' working hours. In the annual debate on the Royal Navy Kenneth Carlisle announced an invitation to tender for up to three more Type 23 frigates and studies into the design of a new hunter-killer submarine.

On July 2 Kenneth Baker made a statement on the Government's plans to change the regulations covering those seeking political asylum in the UK, announcing that it would introduce a bill to allow substantial acceleration and simplification of the procedures at the earliest parliamentary opportunity. On July 3 Peter Brooke announced the ending of the all-party talks on Northern Ireland, insisting that there was a good prospect for future discussions but the likelihood of talks restarting before the next general election was remote. Douglas Hurd made a statement on developments in Yugoslavia. The consideration of the Commons' reasons for disagreeing with the Lords on their amendments to the Criminal Justice Bill over life sentencing, saw the Lords, with a series of amendments moved by Lord Nathan, insist that four of their amendments be reinstated and therefore sent back to the Commons for further consideration.

On July 8 the Economic Secretary to the Treasury (John Maples) made a statement about the decision of the Bank of England to secure control of the assets

of the Bank of Credit and Commerce International (BCCI) group on July 5. The Shadow Chancellor (John Smith) thought that the most disturbing feature was that the system of regulation appeared to have failed completely, with serious consequences and losses for all customers. On July 10 the Minister for Housing and Planning (Sir George Young) made a statement about the housing action trust and estate action programmes by which the Government is attempting to tackle the problems of rundown local authority estates; he announced the issue of new guidelines to local authorities under which the Government would consider proposals for the establishment of schemes for next year. On July 12 Sir George announced the Government's decision to introduce freehold ownership and communal management of flats and other interdependent buildings with shared facilities, called commonhold.

On July 16 by 153 votes to 52 the Commons again rejected the Lords' amendments concerning life sentencing in the Criminal Justice Bill and, in effect, restored to the Home Secretary the right to determine when murderers sentenced to mandatory life imprisonment could be released. On July 17 Tom King announced the Government's intentions for the rationalization of the Royal Navy support arrangements; this followed a row the previous day when the details appeared to have been released in a press conference rather than being announced to MPs first. On July 18 in the Lords a government amendment was introduced to the Dangerous Dogs Bill exempting police dogs and military guard dogs from the penalties provided in the bill against owners or handlers of dogs that cause injury. Following pressure earlier in the week for a further statement on BCCI, the Chancellor (Norman Lamont) announced on July 19 that in the light of widespread public concern, the Governor of the Bank of England and he had agreed that there should be an independent inquiry into the supervision of BCCI.

On July 22 John Major had to answer a private notice question from Neil Kinnock on his own knowledge of and understanding of the operations of BCCI in the years before June 1991. Mr Major said that the inquiry announced by the Chancellor would be headed by Lord Justice Bingham and gave its terms of reference. He went on to make a statement on the publication of a White Paper on the Government's Citizens' Charter, outlining the action that would be expected from all public services to improve standards and give wider choice. He also announced that there would be a special unit set up in the Cabinet Office to identify new areas for action to help carry the programme forward. Neil Kinnock summed up the Charter as 'a mixture of the belated, the ineffectual, the banal, the vague and the damaging'. The Minister for the Environment and Countryside (David Trippier) made a statement about the failure of disinfection over the weekend in water supplied by Three Valleys' Water Services PLC. On July 23 Tom King gave the details of the Government's plans for restructuring the British Army; the total strength by the mid-1990s would be reduced to 116,000. No regiments would be abolished but there would be a certain number of mergers and amalgamations. Michael Heseltine announced the Government's proposals for the local government finance settlement in England for 1992–93, and proposals for future years; there would be a 7.2 per cent increase in external support, which should give an average community charge bill of approximately £256 for the year, and there would be an extra band added to the seven already proposed for the new council tax, covering properties worth more than £320,000. For Wales, David Hunt announced figures of £118 for the community charge and £240,000 for the extra band.

For Scotland, Ian Lang gave no target figure for the community charge, expressing the hope that they should not increase significantly, and set the eighth band at £212,000. The Lords finally accepted the directive from the Commons on mandatory life

sentencing in the Criminal Justice Bill and removed their objection. The Commons agreed to accept a consequential amendment stemming from this. On July 25 both Houses rose for the summer recess.

PUBLIC ACTS OF PARLIAMENT 1990–91

This list commences with two Acts of Parliament which received the Royal Assent before September 1990 and which were mentioned briefly in the last summary. Those Public Acts which follow received the Royal Assent after August 1990. The date stated after each Act is that came into operation.

Appropriation Act 1990, c. 28 (July 26, 1990) applies a sum out of the Consolidated Fund to the service of the year ended March 31, 1991; appropriates supplies granted in this session of Parliament and repeals certain Consolidated Fund and Appropriation Acts.

Aviation and Maritime Security Act 1990, c. 31 (various dates) gives effect to the Protocol for the Suppression of Unlawful Acts of Violence at Airports Serving International Civil Aviation which supplements the Convention for the Suppression of Unlawful Acts against the Safety of Civil Aviation; makes further provision with respect to aviation security and civil aviation; gives effect to the Convention for the Suppression of Unlawful Acts against the Safety of Maritime Navigation and to the Protocol for the Suppression of Unlawful Acts against the Safety of Fixed Platforms Located on the Continental Shelf which supplements that Convention; and for connected purposes.

Human Fertilization and Embryology Act 1990, c. 37 (April 1, 1991) makes provisions relating to the development of human embryos, specifically prohibiting certain practices connected to embryos and gametes; amends the Surrogacy Arrangements Act 1985; clarifies who in law should be treated as the parents of a child; provides for the establishment of a Human Fertilization and Embryology Authority.

Employment Act 1990, c. 38 (various dates ending with Feb. 1, 1991) makes it unlawful for a person to be refused employment or any service of an employment agency on grounds related to trade union membership and amends the law relating to industrial action and ballots; and connected purposes.

Landlord and Tenant (Licensed Premises) Act 1990, c. 39 (Jan. 1, 1991) repeals section 43(1)(d) of the Landlord and Tenant Act 1954, Part II, which exempts tenancies of premises licensed for the sale of intoxicating liquor for consumption on the premises.

Law Reform (Miscellaneous Provisions) (Scotland) Act 1990, c. 40 (various dates, some to be appointed) provides for the regulation of charities in Scotland; provides for the establishment of a Board having functions with respect to the provision of conveyancing and executry services by persons other than solicitors, advocates and incorporated practices; makes provision for a Scottish legal services ombudsman to replace the Legal Observer for Scotland; extends eligibility for senior judicial appointments and provides for the appointment of temporary judges; amends the standard permitted opening hours for licensed premises; and makes various other reforms relating to, e.g. prisons, housing and mental health.

Courts and Legal Services Act 1990, c. 41 (various dates, some to be appointed) makes provision relating

to legal services and procedures in and the allocation of business between the High Court and other courts; amends the law relating to judicial and related pensions, the limitation of actions, arbitration, solicitors and also the Children Act 1989. Amongst other provisions it provides for the establishment of a Conveyancing Appeal Tribunal, a Lord Chancellor's Advisory Committee on Legal Education and for a Legal Services Ombudsman.

Broadcasting Act 1990, c. 42 (various dates, some to be appointed) provides for the provision and regulation of independent television and sound programme services, encompassing a number of other services provided on television and radio frequencies; substantially amends the law relating to broadcasting and provision of television and sound programme services; establishes a Broadcasting Standards Council; makes provision as to the transfer of the property, rights and liabilities of the IBA and the Cable Authority; and for connected purposes.

Environmental Protection Act 1990, c. 43 (various dates, some to be appointed) makes provisions relating to pollution encompassing waste on land and its collection and disposal; restates the law defining statutory nuisances, emissions into the air; provides for the extension of the Clean Air Acts to prescribed gases, and the disposal of waste at sea. It also provides for the regulation of the clearing of litter from public places and the importation, exportation, use, supply and storage of prescribed substances and articles, and the importation and exportation of prescribed wastes. Consequential amendments are made to the Radioactive Substances Act 1960, the Water Act 1989, the Control of Pollution Act 1974, and the Food and Environment Protection Act 1985.

Caldey Island Act 1990, c. 44 (Nov. 1, 1990) makes provision for the islands of Caldey and St Margaret's in the county of Dyfed to be included in the district of South Pembrokeshire for the purposes of elections and local taxation and for other purposes such as the Pembrokeshire Health Authority.

Import and Export Control Act 1990, c. 45 (Dec. 6, 1990) provides for the continuance in force of the Import and Export Customs Powers (Defence) Act 1959 by repealing section 9(3) of that Act.

Consolidated Fund (No. 2) Act 1990, c. 46 (Dec. 20, 1990) applies certain sums out of the Consolidated Fund to the service of the years ending March 31, 1991 and 1992.

Development Board for Rural Wales 1991, c. 1 (Feb. 12, 1991) increases the statutory financial limit of the Board from £100 million to £175 million.

Caravans (Standard Community Charge and Rating) Act 1991, c. 2 (Feb. 12, 1991) makes provision to amend existing legislation concerning the liability of certain caravans and their pitches to standard community charges and non-domestic rates.

Statutory Sick Pay Act 1991, c. 3 (various dates ending with April 1, 1991) reduces the amount of statutory sick pay which employers are entitled to recover and repeals section 9(1A) of the Social Security and Housing Benefits Act 1982.

Namibia Act 1991, c. 4 (Feb. 28, 1991, backdated to March 21, 1990) makes provision in connection with the admission of Namibia as a member of the Commonwealth on March 21, 1990 and subsequently provides for the modification of certain UK enactments relating to the Commonwealth Institute, the services and visiting forces, and to shipping.

Ministerial and other Pensions and Salaries Act 1991, c. 5 (Feb. 28, 1991) provides for improvements in the pensions of the holders of the offices of Prime Minister, Lord Chancellor and Speaker; relates the salary of the Lord Chancellor to that of the Lord Chief Justice and makes provision concerning the granting of pensions to persons ceasing to hold ministerial and certain other offices.

Census (Confidentiality) Act 1991, c. 6 (March 7, 1991) amends section 8(2) of the Census Act 1920 and substitutes a new offence in respect of the unlawful disclosure of personal Census information.

Consolidated Fund Act 1991, c. 7 (March 21, 1991) applies certain sums out of the Consolidated Fund to the service of the years ended March 31, 1990, 1991 and 1992.

Community Charges (Substitute Setting) Act 1991, c. 8 (March 21, 1991) amends the law imposed by section 35 of the Local Government Act 1988 on charging authorities for the setting of substitute amounts for personal community charges in certain circumstances in relation to future financial years and establishes the appropriate formula to be used in specific situations.

Community Charges (General Reduction) Act 1991, c. 9 (March 28, 1991) provides for the general reduction of community charge by a fixed amount and specifies the conditions for application.

Consolidated Fund (No. 2) Act 1991, c. 10 (May 9, 1991) applies certain sums out of the Consolidated Fund to the service of the year ended March 31, 1992.

Representation of the People Act 1991, c. 11 (day to be appointed) makes provisions with respect to charges for returning officer's services rendered and expenses incurred for or in connection with a parliamentary election.

Civil Jurisdiction and Judgments Act 1991, c. 12 (day to be appointed) provides for effect to be given to the Lugano Convention on jurisdiction and the enforcement of judgments in civil and commercial matters.

War Crimes Act 1991, c. 13 (day to be appointed) confers jurisdiction on UK courts in respect of certain grave violations of the laws and customs of war committed in German-held territory during the Second World War, and for connected purposes.

Motor Vehicles (Safety Equipment for Children) Act 1991, c. 14 (June 27, 1991) makes provision in relation to safety equipment for children in motor vehicles.

Local Government Finance (Publicity for Auditors' Reports) Act 1991, c. 15 (Aug. 27, 1991) makes further provision with respect to the furnishing or making of copies and inspection of auditors' immediate reports made under section 15(3) of the Local Government Finance Act 1982.

Oversea Superannuation Act 1991, c. 16 (Aug. 27, 1991) authorizes the making of schemes under Overseas Pensions Act 1973 for provision of pensions, allowances and gratuities to or in respect of persons who have contributed to the Oversea Superannuation Fund.

Maintenance Enforcement Act 1991, c. 17 (day or days to be appointed) gives the courts powers to make orders specifying the method of payment to be employed when making or dealing with a maintenance order requiring periodical payment.

Crofter Forestry (Scotland) Act 1991, c. 18 (day or days to be appointed) extends the powers of grazing committees in relation to the use of crofting land for forestry purposes and makes them eligible for certain grants in respect of such use.

Football (Offences) Act 1991, c. 19 (day or days to be appointed) makes further provision with respect to disorderly conduct by persons attending football matches (including two hours before and one hour after the advertised starting time) and for connected purposes.

Registered Homes (Amendment) Act 1991, c. 20 (day to be appointed) amends Part I of the 1984 Act so as to require registration in respect of small (i.e. less than four 'patients') residential care homes and for connected purposes.

Disability Living Allowance and Disability Working Allowance Act 1991, c. 21 (day or days to be appointed) introduces the two allowances as social security benefits. The first is non-contributory and the second income-related.

New Roads and Street Works Act 1991, c. 22 (day or days to be appointed) amends the law relating to roads so as to enable new roads to be provided by new means, makes new provision with respect to street and road-works and for connected purposes.

Children and Young Persons (Protection from Tobacco) Act 1991, c. 23 (day or days to be appointed) increases the penalties for the sale of tobacco to persons under the age of 16 and enacts certain other provisions relating to the sale or advertising of tobacco.

Northern Ireland (Emergency Powers) Act 1991, c. 24 (various dates) re-enacts with amendments the 1978 and 1987 Acts and Part VI of the Prevention of Terrorism (Temporary Provisions) Act 1989 and makes further provision for the preservation of peace and maintenance of order in Northern Ireland.

Criminal Procedure (Insanity and Unfitness to Plead) Act 1991, c. 25 (day to be appointed) amends the law relating to the special verdict and unfitness to plead; increases the courts' powers where the defendant is found to be insane or unfit to plead and provides for a trial of the facts in such cases.

Road Traffic (Temporary Restrictions) Act 1991, c. 26 (day to be appointed) makes new provision in place of the Road Traffic Regulation Act 1984, ss. 14 and 15 (temporary prohibitions and restrictions on traffic); and for connected purposes.

Radioactive Material (Road Transport) Act 1991, c. 27 (except for s. 8, Aug. 27, 1991) makes new provision with respect to the transport of radioactive material (i.e. specific activity of 70 becquerels per kg or such lesser activity as may be ordered) by road; repeals Radioactive Substances Act 1948, s. 5(2); and for connected purposes.

Natural Heritage (Scotland) Act 1991, c. 28 (day or days to be appointed) establishes Scottish Natural Heritage and makes provision for management of water resources in Scotland; and for connected purposes.

Property Misdescriptions Act 1991, c. 29 (June 27, 1991) prohibits making of false or misleading statements about property made in the course of estate agency business and property development business.

Welfare of Animals at Slaughter Act 1991, c. 30 (Aug. 27, 1991) makes further provision for the welfare of animals at slaughter, e.g. provides for codes of practice and amends the provisions relating to slaughtermen's licences.

Finance Act 1991, c. 31 (July 25, 1991) grants certain duties, alters others and amends the law relating to the National Debt and the Public Revenue.

Appropriation Act 1991, c. 32 (July 25, 1991) applies a sum out of the Consolidated Fund to the service of the year ended March 31, 1992, appropriates supplies granted in this session of Parliament and repeals certain Consolidated Fund and Appropriation Acts.

Agriculture and Forestry (Financial Provisions) Act 1991, c. 33 (various dates) repeals the statutory provisions relating to the Agricultural Mortgage Corporation and the Scottish Agricultural Securities Corporation; provides for the recovery of the cost of government supervision of Community livestock carcass grading at slaughterhouses and for other purposes connected with, e.g. suckler cow premiums and the expenses of New Forest verderers.

Planning and Compensation Act 1991, c. 34 (day or days to be appointed) amends the law relating to town and country planning (e.g. planning contravention notices); extends the powers to acquire by agreement land which may be affected by carrying out public works; amends the law relating to compulsory acquisition of land and to compensation where people are displaced from land, or the value of land or its enjoyment may be affected by public works by, e.g. amending the rules relating to home loss payments; and for connected purposes.

Badgers (Further Provision) Act 1991, c. 35 (Sept. 25, 1991) confers additional powers on a court where a dog has been used in or was present at the commission of certain offences under the 1977 Act, e.g. owners may be disqualified from having custody of a dog and/or the destruction of the dog may be ordered.

Badgers Act 1991, c. 36 (Oct. 25, 1991) makes provision for the protection of badger sets and connected purposes.

Smoke Detection Act 1991, c. 37 (day to be appointed) makes provision for the fitting of smoke detectors in new buildings.

Medical Qualifications (Amendment) Act 1991, c. 38 (day to be appointed) amends the definition of a primary UK qualification for registration as a medical practitioner to include the Royal College of Surgeons.

Wildlife and Countryside (Amendment) Act 1991, c. 39 (Sept. 25, 1991) makes it an offence knowingly to cause or permit certain acts within ss. 5 and 11 of the 1981 Act relating to the taking and killing of wild birds and animals.

Road Traffic Act 1991, c. 40 (day or days to be appointed) amends the law relating to road traffic.

Arms Control and Disarmament (Inspections) Act 1991, c. 41 (day to be appointed) facilitates the carrying out in the UK of inspections under the Protocol on Inspection incorporated in the Treaty on Conventional Armed Forces in Europe signed in Paris on November 19, 1990; and for connected purposes.

Social Security (Contributions) Act 1991, c. 42 (July 25, 1991) introduces contributions under the Social Security Act 1975 in respect of cars made available for private use and car fuel as from the tax year beginning April 6, 1991.

Forestry Act 1991, c. 43 (Sept. 25, 1991) increases from nine to 12 the maximum number of members of a regional advisory committee maintained under section 37 of the 1967 Act.

Foreign Corporations Act 1991, c. 44 (Sept. 25, 1991) makes provision about the status in the UK of bodies incorporated or formerly incorporated under the laws of certain territories outside the UK.

Coal Mining Subsidence Act 1991, c. 45 (day or days to be appointed) repeals and re-enacts with amendments the 1957 Act and part of the Coal Industry Act 1975, and for connected purposes; e.g. the Act redefines subsidence damage.

Child Support Act 1991, c. 48 (day or days to be appointed) makes provision for the assessment, collection and enforcement of periodical maintenance payable by certain parents with respect to children of theirs who are not in their care; for the collection and enforcement of certain other kinds of maintenance; and for connected purposes.

School Teachers' Pay and Conditions Act 1991, c. 49 (day or days to be appointed) makes provision with respect to the remuneration and other conditions of employment of school teachers, and for connected purposes; e.g. it establishes a review body.

Local Government Finance and Valuation Act 1991, c. 51 (various dates) abolishes restrictions on the Secretary of State's powers to designate authorities under the Local Government Finance Act 1988, s. 100; amends the grounds on which he may make a report under Schedule 3 to the Abolition of Domestic Rates, etc. (Scotland) Act 1987; makes provision for the valuation of domestic property; and for connected purposes.

Ports Act 1991, c. 52 (various dates) provides for the transfer to companies of certain statutory port undertakings (including the Port of London Authority) and for the disposal of securities of those companies; amends the law with respect to lighthouses, buoys and beacons and the authorities responsible for them; and for connected purposes.

Criminal Justice Act 1991, c. 53 (day or days to be appointed) makes further provision with respect to the treatment of offenders, and the position of children and young persons and the persons having responsibility for them; makes provision with respect to certain services provided or proposed to be provided for purposes connected with the administration of justice or the treatment of offenders; makes financial provision with respect to that administration; and for connected purposes.

Deer Act 1991, c. 54 (Oct. 25, 1991) consolidates certain enactments relating to deer with amendments to give effect to recommendations of the Law Commission.

Water Resources Act 1991, c. 57 (Dec. 1, 1991) consolidates enactments relating to the National Rivers Authority and the matters in relation to which it exercises functions, with amendments to give effect to recommendations of the Law Commission.

Statutory Water Companies Act 1991, c. 58 (Dec. 1, 1991) consolidates certain enactments relating to statutory water companies.

Land Drainage Act 1991, c. 59 (Dec. 1, 1991) consolidates the enactments relating to internal drainage boards and to the functions of such boards, and of local authorities in relation to land drainage, with amendments to give effect to recommendations of the Law Commission.

Water Consolidation (Consequential Provisions) Act 1991, c. 60 (Dec. 1, 1991) makes provision for consequential amendments and repeals and for transitional and transitory matters and savings in connection with the consolidation of certain enactments in the Water Resources, Water Industry, Land Drainage and Statutory Water Companies Acts 1991.

Statute Law Revision (Isle of Man) Act 1991, c. 61 (July 25, 1991) revises the statute law by repealing obsolete, spent, unnecessary or superseded enactments so far as they continue to form part of the law of the Isle of Man.

Armed Forces Act 1991, c. 62 (day or days to be appointed) continues the Army Act 1955, the Air Force Act 1955 and the Naval Discipline Act 1957; amends those Acts and others relating to the armed forces; makes provision for compensation for miscarriages of justice before courts-martial; makes provision for orders for the assessment and emergency protection of children forming part of or staying with service families abroad; and for connected purposes.

British Railways Board (Finance) Act 1991, c. 63 (July 25, 1991) increases the limits under section 42(6) of the Transport Act 1968 relating to the indebtedness of the Board and the limits on the amount of compensation payable in respect of certain public service obligations of the Board.

Breeding of Dogs Act 1991, c. 64 (Sept. 25, 1991) extends the powers of inspection for the purposes of the 1973 Act to premises not covered by a licence under that Act.

Dangerous Dogs Act 1991, c. 65 (day or days to be appointed) prohibits persons from having in their possession or custody dogs belonging to types bred for fighting; imposes restrictions in respect of such dogs pending the coming into force of the prohibition; enables restrictions to be imposed in relation to other types of dogs which present a serious danger to the public; makes further provision for securing that dogs are kept under control, and for connected purposes.

Atomic Weapons Establishment Act 1991, c. 46.

Mental Health (Detention) (Scotland) Act 1991, c. 47.

Age of Legal Capacity (Scotland) Act 1991, c. 50.

Agricultural Holdings (Scotland) Act 1991, c. 55.

Water Industry Act 1991, c. 56 (Dec. 1, 1991).

SMALL MAJORITIES

The following Members were returned in June 1987 with majorities of fewer than 1,000 votes.

*Richard Livsey (*L/All., Brecon and Radnor*)	56	Elliott Morley (*Lab., Glanford and Scunthorpe*)	512
Alan Meale (*Lab., Mansfield*)	56	Timothy Janman (*C., Thurrock*)	690
*Conal Gregory (*C., York*)	147	Edward McGrady (*SDLP, Down S.*)	731
*Gerald Bowden (*C., Dulwich*)	180	Timothy Devlin (*C., Stockton S.*)	774
*Rt. Hon. George Younger (*C., Ayr*)	182	*Christopher Smith (*Lab., Islington S. and Finsbury*)	805
Mrs Maureen Hicks (*C., Wolverhampton NE*)	204	*Peter Thurnham (*C., Bolton NE*)	813
David Martin (*C., Portsmouth S.*)	205	Ronald Campbell (*Lab., Blyth Valley*)	853
*Mrs Lynda Chalker (*C., Wallasey*)	279	John Bowis (*C., Battersea*)	857
Robert Cryer (*Lab., Bradford S.*)	309	Michael Irvine (*C., Ipswich*)	874
John Garrett (*Lab., Norwich S.*)	336	Eric Martlew (*Lab., Carlisle*)	916
Mrs Ann Taylor (*Lab., Dewsbury*)	445	*Michael Forsyth (*C., Stirling*)	948
*Michael Knowles (*C., Nottingham E.*)	456	*Peter Snape (*Lab., West Bromwich E.*)	983

PARLIAMENTARY ASSOCIATIONS

COMMONWEALTH PARLIAMENTARY ASSOCIATION (1911)

The Commonwealth Parliamentary Association consists of 119 branches in the national, state, provincial or territorial parliaments in the countries of the Commonwealth. Commonwealth parliamentary conferences and general assemblies are held every year in different countries of the Commonwealth.

President (1990–91), Hon. Rabi Ray, MP, Speaker of the Lok Sabha (*India*).
Vice-President (1990–91), Hon. Darrell Rolle, MP, Minister of National Security and Leader of the House (*The Bahamas*).
Chairman of the Executive Committee (1990–93), Hon. Clive Griffiths, MLC, President of the Legislative Council (*Western Australia*).
Secretary-General, D. Tonkin, 7 Old Palace Yard, SW1P 3JY.

United Kingdom Branch

Hon. Presidents, The Lord Chancellor; Mr Speaker.

Chairman of Branch, The Rt. Hon. John Major, MP.
Chairman of Executive Committee, C. Shepherd, MP.
Secretary, P. Cobb, OBE, Westminster Hall, Palace of Westminster, SW1.

THE INTER-PARLIAMENTARY UNION (1889)

To facilitate personal contact between members of all Parliaments in the promotion of representative institutions, peace and international co-operation.
Secretary-General, P. Cornillon, Place du Petit-Saconnex, BP 99, 1211 Geneva 19, Switzerland.

British Group
Palace of Westminster, SW1A 0AA

Hon. Presidents, The Lord Chancellor; Mr Speaker.
President, The Rt. Hon. John Major, MP.
Chairman, Dr M. Clark, MP.
Secretary, D. Ramsay.

THE PRINCIPAL PARTIES IN PARLIAMENT (1931–1987)

General Election	Conservative	Liberal	Labour
1931............	471	72 (a)	65 (b)
1935............	387	54 (c)	166 (d)
1945............	189	25 (e)	396 (f)
1950............	298 (g)	9	315 (h)
1951............	320 (i)	6	296 (h)
1955............	344 (i)	6	277 (j)
1959............	365 (i)	6	258 (k)
1964............	303 (i)	9	317
1966............	253 (i)	12	363 (l)
1970............	330 (m)	6	287 (n)
1974 (February) .	296	14	301 (o)
1974 (October) ..	276	13	319 (p)
1979............	339	11	268 (q)
1983............	397	23 (r)	209 (s)
1987............	376	22 (t)	229 (u)

NOTES.—(a) Liberal National 35 (Simon); Liberal 33 (Samuel); 4 (Lloyd George). (b) National Labour 13 (MacDonald); Labour 52 (Henderson). (c) Liberal National 33; Liberal 21. (d) National Labour 8; Labour 154; ILP 4. (e) Liberal National 13; Liberal 12. (f) Labour 393; ILP 3. (g) Incl. Nat. Liberal. (h) Irish Nationalists (2) and Speaker make total of 625.

(i) Including associates. (j) Sinn Fein (2) and Speaker make total of 630. (k) Independent (1) makes total of 630. (l) Republican Labour (1) makes total of 630. (m) Including Ulster Unionists. (n) Scottish Nationalist (1); Independent (5) and Speaker make total of 630. (o) United Ulster Unionist Council (11), Scottish Nationalist (7), Plaid Cymru (2); Social Democratic and Labour Party (1); Social Democrat (1); Independent Labour (1); and Speaker make total of 635. (p) Scottish Nationalist (11); United Ulster Unionist (10); Plaid Cymru (3); Social Democratic and Labour Party (1); Independent (1) and Speaker make a total of 635. (q) Ulster Unionist (5); Democratic Unionist (3); Plaid Cymru (2); Scottish Nationalist (2); Social Democratic and Labour (1); United Ulster Unionist (1); Independent (2) and Speaker make a total of 635. (r) Liberal 17; SDP 6. (s) Official Unionist (11); Democratic Unionist (3); Scottish Nationalist (2); Plaid Cymru (2); Ulster Popular Unionist (1); Social Democratic and Labour Party (1) and Provisional Sinn Fein (1) make a total of 650. (t) Liberal 17; SDP 5. (u) Ulster Unionist (9); Scottish Nationalist (3); Plaid Cymru (3); Democratic Unionist (3); Social Democratic and Labour Party (3); Ulster Popular Unionist (1); Sinn Fein (1) make a total of 650.

PARLIAMENTS SINCE 1945

Assembled	Dissolved	Duration yrs. m. d.	Assembled	Dissolved	Duration yrs. m. d.
1945 Aug. 1	1950 Feb. 3	4 6 2	1970 June 29	1974 Feb. 8	3 7 10
1950 March 1	1951 Oct. 5	1 7 4	1974 March 6	1974 Sept. 20	0 6 14
1951 Oct. 31	1955 May 6	3 6 6	1974 Oct. 22	1979 April 7	4 5 16
1955 June 7	1959 Sept. 18	4 3 11	1979 May 9	1983 May 13	4 0 4
1959 Oct. 20	1964 Sept. 25	4 11 5	1983 June 15	1987 May 18	3 11 3
1964 Oct. 27	1966 March 10	1 4 11	1987 June 17		
1966 April 18	1970 May 29	4 1 11			

MAJORITIES IN THE HOUSE OF COMMONS SINCE 1945

Year	Party	Majority	Year	Party	Majority
1945	Labour	146	1970	Conservative	31
1950	Labour	8	1974 (Feb.)	No majority	
1951	Conservative	16	1974 (Oct.)	Labour	5
1955	Conservative	59	1979.............	Conservative	43
1959	Conservative	100	1983.............	Conservative	144
1964	Labour	5	1987.............	Conservative	102
1966	Labour	99			

VOTES CAST AT UK GENERAL ELECTIONS, 1974–87

General Election, October, 1974*

Labour	11,456,597
Conservative	10,464,675
Liberal	5,346,800
Scottish Nationalist	839,628
Plaid Cymru	166,321
Others	195,065

General Election, 1983*

Conservative	13,012,602
Labour	8,457,124
Liberal/SDP Alliance	7,780,587
Scottish Nationalist	331,975
Plaid Cymru	125,309
Others	198,383

General Election, 1979*

Conservative	13,697,753
Labour	11,506,741
Liberal	4,305,324
Scottish Nationalist	504,259
National Front	191,706
Plaid Cymru	132,544
Others	188,063

General Election, 1987*

Conservative	13,760,525
Labour	10,029,944
Liberal/SDP Alliance	7,341,152
Scottish Nationalist	416,873
Plaid Cymru	123,589
†Green	89,753
Others	37,576

*Excluding Northern Ireland seats   †Excluding Ecology candidate in Northern Ireland

GOVERNMENT AND PUBLIC OFFICES

SALARIES 1991–92

Ministerial Salaries
(as at January 1, 1991)

Prime Minister	£50,724
Secretary of State	£38,105
Minister of State (Lords)	£43,010
Minister of State (Commons)	£26,962
Parliamentary Under Secretary (Lords)	£36,066
Parliamentary Under Secretary (Commons)	£20,463

(Ministers who are Members of the House of Commons receive a reduced Parliamentary salary (£21,809 in 1991) in addition to this ministerial salary.)

Civil Service (Basic) Salaries
(as at April 1, 1991)

+Secretary to the Cabinet and Head of the Home Civil Service	£102,930
+Permanent Secretary to the Treasury	£96,210
+Head of the Diplomatic Service	£96,210
+Grade 1	£82,780
+Grade 1A	£76,060
+Grade 2	£59,020
Grade 3	£47,090*
Grade 4	£40,116–£46,751
Grade 5	£32,551–£44,996
Grade 6	£24,977–£33,970
Grade 7	£21,905–£32,551
Senior Executive Officer	£17,367–£21,724
Higher Executive Officer (D)	£15,244–£19,177
Higher Executive Officer	£13,885–£17,723
Executive Officer	£8,180–£14,170
Administration Trainee	£12,119–£14,122

*£48,380 if in London.
+These grades do not attract London weighting.
London weighting, since July 1, 1989, is:

Inner zone	£1,750 a year
Intermediate zone	£1,000 a year
Outer zone	£725 a year

The Home Civil Service's unified pay and grading structure for senior personnel represents the following:

Grade	Title
1	Permanent Secretary.
1A	Second Permanent Secretary.
2	Deputy Secretary.
3	Under Secretary.
4	Chief Scientific Officer B, Professional and Technology Directing A.
5	Assistant Secretary, Deputy Chief Scientific Officer, Professional and Technology Directing B.
6	Senior Principal, Senior Principal Scientific Officer, Professional and Technology Superintending Grade.
7	Principal.

ADVISORY, CONCILIATION AND ARBITRATION SERVICE
27 Wilton Street, SW1X 7AX
[071–210 3000]

The Advisory, Conciliation and Arbitration Service (ACAS) is an independent organization set up under the Employment Protection Act, 1975. ACAS is directed by a Council consisting of a chairman and employer, trade union and independent members, all appointed by the Secretary of State for Employment. The functions of the Service are to provide facilities for conciliation, mediation and arbitration as means of avoiding and resolving industrial disputes, and to provide advisory services to industry on industrial relations and matters affecting the quality of working life.

ACAS also has offices in Birmingham, Bristol, Cardiff, Fleet, Glasgow, Leeds, Liverpool, Manchester, Newcastle upon Tyne and Nottingham.
Chairman, D. B. Smith, CB.
Chief Conciliation Officer (G4), D. G. Boyd, CBE.
Director of Resources and General Policy Branch (G5), E. Norcross.

MINISTRY OF AGRICULTURE, FISHERIES AND FOOD
Whitehall Place, SW1A 2HH†
[071–270 3000]

The Ministry of Agriculture, Fisheries and Food is responsible for administering government policy for agriculture, horticulture and fisheries in England and for policies relating to the safety and quality of food in the United Kingdom as a whole. In association with the other Agricultural Departments in the UK and the Intervention Board for Agricultural Produce, the Ministry is responsible for the negotiation and administration of the EC common agricultural and fisheries policies and for matters relating to the single European market.

The Ministry administers policies for the control and eradication of animal, plant and fish diseases and for assistance to capital investment in farm and horticultural businesses; it exercises responsibilities relating to the protection and enhancement of the countryside and the marine environment as well as to flood defence and other rural issues and appropriate research and development.

The Ministry has responsibility for ensuring public health standards in the manufacture, preparation and distribution of basic foods, and planning to safeguard essential food supplies in times of emergency. The Ministry is responsible for government relations with the UK food and drink manufacturing industries, and the food and drink importing, distributive and catering trades.

The Food Safety Directorate is responsible for many aspects of food safety and quality. These include analytical and research work, pesticide safety approval, biotechnology, meat hygiene, animal health and welfare, and related public health issues.

Minister, THE RT. HON. JOHN GUMMER, MP.
Principal Private Secretary (G7), T. D. Rossington.
Asst. Private Secretary, M. D. K. Harrison.
Parliamentary Private Secretary, J. Paice, MP.
Special Adviser, K. Adams.
Minister of State (Lords), THE BARONESS TRUMPINGTON *(Countryside).*
Private Secretary, C. L. Young.
Parliamentary Private Secretary, J. Greenway, MP.
Parliamentary Secretary, DAVID CURRY, MP *(Farming and Fisheries).*
Private Secretary, Ms A. M. Gartland.
Parliamentary Secretary, DAVID MACLEAN, MP *(Food).*
Private Secretary, S. C. Tanner.
Parliamentary Clerk, I. Pearson.
Permanent Secretary (G1), Sir Derek Andrews, KCB, CBE.
Private Secretary, Miss S. E. Hendry.

ESTABLISHMENT DEPARTMENT
Director of Establishments (G3), D. H. Griffiths.

---

†Unless otherwise stated, this is the main address of Divisions of the Ministry.

Staff Resources and Organization
Victory House, 30–34 Kingsway, WC2B 6TU
[071–405 4310]
Head of Division (G5), A. G. Kuyk.

Establishments (General) Division
Victory House, 30–34 Kingsway, WC2B 6TU
[071–405 4310]
Head of Division (G5), Mrs A. M. Pickering.

Staff Training Branch*
Principal (G7), Miss E. M. Berthoud.

Welfare Branch
Victory House, 30–34 Kingsway, WC2B 6TU
[071–405 4310]
Chief Welfare Officer (SEO), D. J. Jones.

Personnel Division
Victory House, 30–34 Kingsway, WC2B 6TU
[071–405 4310]
Head of Division (G5), Miss L. J. Neville-Rolfe.

FINANCE DEPARTMENT

Principal Finance Officer (G3), A. R. Cruickshank.

Financial Planning Division*
Head of Division (G5), Miss V. A. Smith.

Financial Management Division*
Head of Division (G5), vacant.

Audit Division*
Director of Audit (G5), D. V. Fisher.
Deputy Director of Audit (G6), D. J. Littler.

Purchasing and Supply Unit*
Director (G5), G. Lander.

LEGAL DEPARTMENT
55 Whitehall, SW1A 2EY
[071–270 3000]

Legal Adviser and Solicitor (G2), G. J. Jenkins, QC.
Principal Assistant Solicitors (G3), A. E. Munir; B. T. Atwood.

Legal Division A1
Assistant Solicitor (G5), P. D. Davis.

Legal Division A2
Assistant Solicitor (G5), Mrs C. Davis.

Legal Division A3
Assistant Solicitor (G5), M. C. P. Thomas.

Legal Division A4
Assistant Solicitor (G5), Miss E. A. Stephens.

Legal Division A5
Assistant Solicitor (G5), L. Gunatilleke.

Legal Division B1
Assistant Solicitor (G5), Ms C. A. Crisham.

Legal Division B2
Assistant Solicitor (G5), D. J. Pearson.

Legal Division B3
Assistant Solicitor (G5), A. I. Corbett.

Legal Division B4
Assistant Solicitor (G5), M. Parke.

---

*At Nobel/Ergon House, 17 Smith Square, SW1P 3JR [071-238 3000].

Investigation Unit
Chief Investigation Officer (SEO), A. F. N. Maloney.

MANAGEMENT SERVICES

Under Secretary (G3), M. T. Haddon.

Information Technology Directorate
Government Buildings, Epsom Road,
Guildford, Surrey GU1 2LD
[0483-68121]
Director (G4), D. Selwood.
Assistant Directors (G5), A. G. Matthews; D. J. Dunthorne; (G6), D. D. Brown; R. F. Syrett.

Building and Estate Management
Eastbury House, 30–34 Albert
Embankment, SE1 7TL
[071-238 3000]
Head of Division (G5), J. S. Buchanan.

Office Services Division*
Head of Division (G6), vacant.

Departmental Health and Safety Unit
Head of Unit (G7), P. A. Greatorex.

Management Services Division
Hampton House, 20 Albert
Embankment, SE1 7TL
[071-238 3000]
Head of Division (G5), P. A. Cocking.

Information Division
Chief Information Officer (G5), S. Dugdale.
Chief Press Officer, M. Smith.
Principal Librarian (G7), T. Cullen.

AGRICULTURAL COMMODITIES

Deputy Secretary (G2), R. J. Packer.

EUROPEAN COMMUNITY

Under Secretary (G3), R. J. D. Carden.

European Community Division I
Head of Division (G5), C. I. Llewelyn.

European Community Division II
Head of Division (G6), D. Maskell.

ARABLE CROPS

Under Secretary (G3), C. J. Barnes.

Cereals, Set-Aside and Extensification Division
Head of Division (G5), Ms J. Allfrey.

Sugar, Tobacco, Oilseeds and Proteins Division
Head of Division (G5), R. S. Thomas.

Horticulture and Potatoes Division
Head of Division (G5), R. A. Saunderson.

LIVESTOCK PRODUCTS

Under Secretary (G3), S. Wentworth.

Beef Division
Head of Division (G5), J. R. Cowan.

Sheep and Livestock Subsidies Division
Head of Division (G5), A. J. Lebrecht.

Pigs, Eggs and Poultry Division
Head of Division (G5), G. W. Noble.

Milk and Milk Products
Head of Division (G5), P. Elliott.

FOOD, DRINK AND MARKETING POLICY

Under Secretary (G3), J. W. Hepburn.

Food Industry, Marketing and Competition Policy Division
Head of Division (G5), R. E. Melville.

Alcoholic Drinks Division
Head of Division (G5), D. V. Orchard.

External Relations and Trade Promotion Division
Head of Division (G5), G. Belchamber.

Trade Policy and Tropical Foods
Head of Division (G5), D. P. Hunter.
Special Duties (Food Trade Gap) (G5), H. B. Brown.

COUNTRYSIDE, MARINE ENVIRONMENT AND FISHERIES

Deputy Secretary (G2), B. J. G. Hilton.

LANDS

Under Secretary (G3), G. R. Waters.*

Rural Structures and Grants Division*
Head of Division (G5), T. E. D. Eddy.

Land Use and Tenure Division*
Head of Division (G5), G. P. McLachlan.

Environmental Protection Division*
Head of Division (G5), P. P. Nash.

Conservation Policy Division*
Head of Division (G5), C. R. Bodrell.

Environment Task Force
Head of Division (G5), J. Robbs.

FISHERIES DEPARTMENT*

Fisheries Secretary (G3), C. R. Cann.

Marine Environmental Protection Division
Head of Division (G5), P. M. Boyling.

Fisheries Division I
Head of Division (G5), I. C. Redfern.

Fisheries Division II
Head of Division (G5), A. R. Burne.

Fisheries Division III
Head of Division (G5), Mrs A. M. Blackburn.

Sea Fisheries Inspectorate
Chief Inspector (G6), M. G. Jennings.

Fisheries Research
Director of Fisheries Research and Development for Great Britain (G4), D. J. Garrod, Ph.D.
Deputy Directors of Fisheries Research (G5), Dr J. G. Shepherd; Dr C. E. Purdom.

Fisheries Laboratory
Pakefield Road, Lowestoft, Suffolk NR33 0HT
[0502–62244]

Fisheries Laboratory
Remembrance Avenue, Burnham-on-Crouch, Essex CM0 8HA
[0621–782658]

Fisheries Experiment Station
Benarth Road, Conwy, Gwynedd LL32 8UB
[049–263 3883]

———————

*At Nobel/Ergon House, 17 Smith Square, SW1P 3JR [071-238 3000].

Fish Diseases Laboratory
The Nothe, Weymouth, Dorset DT4 8UB
[03057–72137]
Officer-in-Charge (Principal Scientific Officer) (G7), B. J. Hill, Ph.D.

FLOOD DEFENCE, PLANT PROTECTION AND AGRICULTURAL RESOURCES

Under Secretary (G3), M. Madden.

Agricultural Resources Policy Division
Head of Division (G5), R. C. McIvor.

Plant Variety, Rights Office and Seeds
White House Lane, Huntingdon Road, Cambridge CB3 0LF
[0223–277151]
Head of Division (G5), J. Harvey.

Plant Health Division*
Head of Division (G5), J. C. Edwards.

Flood Defence Division*
Eastbury House, 30–34 Albert Embankment, SE1 7TL
[071-238 3000]
Head of Division (G5), J. R. Park, Ph.D.

ECONOMICS AND STATISTICS

Under Secretary (G3), R. E. Mordue.

Economics (Farm Business) Division
Senior Economic Adviser (G5), J. P. Muriel.

Economics (International) Division
Senior Economic Adviser (G5), R. W. Irving.

Economics (Resource Use) Division
Senior Economic Adviser (G5), A. P. Power, Ph.D.

Statistics (Agricultural Commodities) Division*
Chief Statistician (G5), P. J. Lund, Ph.D.

Statistics (Census and Prices) Division
Government Buildings, Epsom Road, Guildford GU1 2LD
[0483–68121]
Chief Statistician (G5), D. E. Bradbury.

Economics and Statistics (Food)
Senior Economic Adviser (G5), J. M. Slater, Ph.D.

FOOD SAFETY

Deputy Secretary (G2), C. W. Capstick, CMG.

ANIMAL HEALTH AND VETERINARY GROUP

Under Secretary (G3), Mrs E. A. J. Attridge.
Chief Veterinary Officer (G3), K. C. Meldrum.

Animal Health (Disease Control) Division
Government Buildings, Hook Rise South, Tolworth, Surbiton, Surrey KT6 7NF
[081–330 4411]
Head of Division (G5), R. C. Lowson.

Animal Health (International Trade) Division
Government Buildings, Hook Rise South, Tolworth, Surbiton, Surrey KT6 7NF
[081-330 4411]
Head of Division (G5), R. A. Bell.

Animal Welfare Division
Government Buildings, Hook Rise South, Tolworth, Surbiton, Surrey KT6 7NF
[081–330 4411]
Head of Division (G5), A. J. Perrins.

Meat Hygiene Division
Tolworth Tower, Surbiton, Surrey KT6 7DX
[081–330 4411]
Head of Division (G5), Mrs K. J. A. Brown.

Resource Management Division
Government Buildings, Hook Rise South,
Tolworth, Surbiton, Surrey KT6 7NF
[081-330 4411]
Head of Division (G5), W. A. Edwards.

STATE VETERINARY SERVICE
Government Buildings, Hook Rise South,
Tolworth, Surbiton, Surrey KT15 3NB
[081–330 4411]
Director of Veterinary Field Services (G3), I. Crawford.

Lasswade Veterinary Laboratory,
East of Scotland College of Agriculture,
The Bush Estate, Penicuik,
Midlothian EH26 09N
[031–445 4811]

FOOD SAFETY

Under Secretary (G3), B. H. B. Dickinson.
Chief Scientist (Fisheries and Food) (G3), M. E. Knowles, ph.D.*

Chemical Safety of Food Division*
Head of Division (G5), R. C. McKinley.

Consumer Protection Division*
Head of Division (G5), C. A. Cockbill.

Microbiological Safety of Food Division
Head of Division (G5), J. C. Suich.

Food Science Division I*
Head of Division (G5), J. Bell, ph.D.

Food Science Division II*
Head of Division (G5), W. H. B. Denner, ph.D.

Food Science Laboratory
Colney Lane,
Norwich NR4 7UQ
[0603–501102]
Head of Laboratory (G6), D. J. McWeeny.

Torry Research Station
PO Box 31, 135 Abbey Road,
Aberdeen AB9 8DG
[0224–877071]
Director (G5), G. Hobbs, ph.D.

PESTICIDES, VETERINARY MEDICINES AND
EMERGENCIES

Under Secretary (G3), P. W. Murphy.

Emergencies and Food Protection Division
Head of Division (G5), G. F. Meekings.

Pesticides Safety Division
Head of Division (G5), G. A. Hollis.

Biotechnology Unit
Head of Unit (G7), J. A. Bainton.

CHIEF SCIENTIFIC ADVISER

Chief Scientific Adviser (G2), P. J. Bunyan, DSC, Ph.D.
Chief Scientist (Agriculture and Horticulture) (G3), D. W. F. Shannon, ph.D.*

---

*At Nobel/Ergon House, 17 Smith Square, SW1P 3JR [071-238 3000].

Research and Development Requirements Division*
Head of Division (G5), A. T. Cahn.

REGIONAL ORGANIZATION

Director of Regional Administration (G3), D. J. Coates.*

Eastern, Block C, Government Buildings, Brooklands Avenue, Cambridge CB2 2DR (0223–358911).—*Regional Director (G4)*, G. K. Bruce.

Northern, Block 2, Government Buildings, Lawnswood, Leeds LS16 5PY (0532–611223).—*Regional Director (G4)*, A. F. Baines.

South Eastern, Block A, Government Offices, Coley Park, Reading RG1 6DT (0734–581222).—*Regional Director (G4)*, G. M. Trevelyan.

South Western, Block 3, Government Buildings, Burghill Road, Westbury-on-Trym, Bristol BS10 6NJ (0272–500000).—*Regional Director (G4)*, B. F. Shorney.

Midlands and Western, Woodthorne, Wolverhampton WV6 8TQ (0902–754190).—*Regional Director (G4)*, A. D. Bailey.

Wales, Trawsgoed, Aberystwyth SY23 1PQ.—*Chief Officer (G5)*, T. M. K. Evans.

Regional Management Division
Head of Division (G5), B. J. Harding.*

EXECUTIVE AGENCIES

Central Veterinary Laboratory
New Haw, Weybridge, Surrey KT15 3NB
[0932–341111]
The Central Veterinary Laboratory provides scientific and technical expertise in animal and public health.
Director of Laboratory (G3), T. W. A. Little, ph.D.

Veterinary Medicines Directorate
Woodham Lane, New Haw, Weybridge, Surrey
KT15 3NB
[0932–336911]
The Veterinary Medicines Directorate is responsible for all aspects of licensing and control of animal medicines, including the protection of the consumer from hazardous or unacceptable residues.
Director (G4), J. M. Rutter, ph.D.

(from April 1, 1992)
Central Science Laboratory
Chief Executive (G3), P. I. Stanley, ph.D.
Deputy Director (G5), A. R. Hardy.

Comprising:
Central Science Laboratory Slough
London Road, Slough, Berks. SL3 7HJ
[0753–534626]

Central Science Laboratory Harpenden
Hatching Green, Harpenden, Herts. AL5 2BD
[0582–75241]

Agricultural Development and Advisory Service (ADAS)

The Agricultural Development and Advisory Service (ADAS) Agency provides scientific, technical and professional services in support of the Ministry's statutory functions, and advice to farmers, growers and ancillary industries. It also commissions research to assist in the formulation and assessment of policy.

Chief Executive (G2), Dr J. Walsh.
Director of Farm and Countryside Service (G3), P. Needham.*
Head of Product Services (G4), J. B. Finney, CBE.
Director of Field Research and Development (G4), A. D. Hughes.*
Staff Officers (G6), I. M. Tring; W. J. Stubbs.

ADAS Marketing Unit
Head of Unit (G5), D. E. Bawcutt.*

ADAS Information Services Unit
Rivershill House, St Georges Road
Cheltenham
Head of Unit (G5), R. W. Swain.

AGRICULTURAL AND FOOD RESEARCH COUNCIL
Polaris House, North Star Avenue,
Swindon SN2 1UH
[0793-413200]

The Agricultural and Food Research Council (AFRC) is an independent body established by Royal Charter. It is funded from the Science Budget of the Department of Education and Science, receives commissions from the Ministry of Agriculture, Fisheries and Food, and does research for industry and other bodies.

The Council is responsible for research done in its institutes and in UK university departments funded through its research grants scheme. It advises the Department of Agriculture and Fisheries for Scotland (DAFS) on research in the Scottish Agricultural Research Institutes.

The institutes funded through AFRC and DAFS, and the university groups supported, form the Agricultural and Food Research Service.

Chairman, M. A. Grant.
Deputy Chairman and Secretary, Prof. T. L. Blundell, FRS.
Members, Dr P. J. Bunyan; Prof. E. C. D. Cocking, FRS; Prof. J. M. M. Cunningham, CBE; Sir Sam Edwards, FRS; Dr D. A. Evans; D. F. R. George; D. F. Goodwin; L. P. Hamilton, CB; B. J. G. Hilton; Prof. W. F. H. Jarrett, FRS; R. M. Knapman, MP; Dr M. Knowles; Prof. J. R. Krebs, FRS; Prof. C. J. Leaver, FRS; Prof. T. Mansfield; Prof. J. R. Norris; J. L. C. Provan; G. T. Pryce; Dr D. W. F. Shannon; Prof. N. V. Shaw; Prof. R. Whittenbury.
Assessors, Dr R. F. Coleman, FRSE; J. I. Davies, MBE; K. Meldrum; Dr C. McMurray; Prof. H. Smith, FRS.
Deputy Secretary (G2), vacant.
Director of Central Office (G3), B. G. Jamieson, Ph.D.
Heads of Divisions (G5), S. H. Visscher *(Finance)*; R. J. Price *(Personnel)*; Dr J. N. Wingfield *(Research)*; Dr A. V. Harrison *(Policy)*.
Commercial Policy Section (G7), S. M. Lawrie.
Principal Information Officer (G7), M. A. Winstanley.
For institutes and units of the Agricultural and Food Research Service, *see* p. 964.

*At Nobel/Ergon House, 17 Smith Square, SW1P 3JR [071-238 3000].

COLLEGE OF ARMS OR HERALDS COLLEGE
Queen Victoria Street, EC4V 4BT
[071-248 2762]

The College is the official repository of the Arms and pedigrees of English, Northern Irish, and Commonwealth families and their descendants, and its records include official copies of the records of Ulster King of Arms, the originals of which remain in Dublin. The 13 officers of the College specialize in genealogical and heraldic work for their respective clients.

Arms have been and still are granted by Letters Patent from the Kings of Arms under authority delegated to them by the Sovereign, such authority having been expressly conferred on them since at least the fifteenth century. A right to Arms can only be established by the registration in the official records of the College of Arms of a pedigree showing direct male line descent from an ancestor already appearing therein as being entitled to Arms, or by making application through the College of Arms for a Grant of Arms.

The College of Arms is open Mon.–Fri. 10–4, when an Officer of Arms is in attendance to deal with enquiries by the public, though such enquiries may also be directed to any of the Officers of Arms, either personally or by letter.

Earl Marshal, His Grace the Duke of Norfolk, KG, GCVO, CB, CBE, MC.

Kings of Arms

Garter, Sir Colin Cole, KCVO, TD, FSA.
Clarenceux, Sir Anthony Wagner, KCB, KCVO, FSA.
Norroy and Ulster, J. P. B. Brooke-Little, CVO, FSA.

Heralds

York (and Registrar), C. M. J. F. Swan, CVO, Ph.D., FSA.
Chester, D. H. B. Chesshyre, LVO, FSA.
Windsor, T. D. Mathew.
Lancaster, P. L. Gwynn-Jones.
Somerset, T. Woodcock, FSA.
Richmond, P. L. Dickinson.

Earl Marshal's Secretary, Sir Walter Verco, KCVO, Surrey Herald Extraordinary.

Pursuivants

Portcullis, P. B. Spurrier.
Bluemantle, T. D. McCarthy.
Rouge Croix, H. E. Paston-Bedingfeld.
Rouge Dragon, T. H. S. Duke.

COURT OF THE LORD LYON
HM New Register House, Edinburgh EH1 3YT
[031-556 7255]

The Court of the Lord Lyon is the Scottish Court of Chivalry, (including the genealogical jurisdiction of the *Ri-Sennachie* of Scotland's Celtic Kings) and adjudicates rights to arms and administration of the Scottish Public Register of All Arms and Bearings and Public Register of All Genealogies. The Lord Lyon presides and judicially establishes rights to existing arms or succession to Chiefship, or for cadets with scientific 'differences' showing position in clan or family. Pedigrees are also established by decrees of Lyon Court and by Letters Patent. As Royal Commissioner in Armory, he grants Patents of Arms (which constitute the grantee and heirs noble in the Noblesse of Scotland) to 'virtuous and well-deserving' Scotsmen, and petitioners (personal or corporate) in

Her Majesty's overseas realms of Scottish connection, and issues birthbrieves.
Lord Lyon King of Arms, Sir Malcolm Innes of Edingight, KCVO, WS, FSA scot.

Heralds

Albany, J. A. Spens, RD, WS.
Rothesay, Sir Crispin Agnew of Lochnaw, Bt.
Ross, C. J. Burnett, FSA scot.

Pursuivants

Kintyre, J. C. G. George, FSA scot.
Unicorn, Alastair Campbell of Airds, FSA scot.

Lyon Clerk and Keeper of Records, Mrs C. G. W. Roads, MVO, FSA scot.
Procurator-Fiscal, I. R. Guild, CBE, FRSE WS.
Herald Painter, Mrs J. Phillips.
Macer, T. C. Gray.

OFFICE OF ARTS AND LIBRARIES
Horse Guards Road, SW1P 3AL
[071–270 3000]

The Office of Arts and Libraries, formerly part of the Department of Education and Science, was established in its present form in 1983. It has general responsibilities for government arts policy and its objectives are to assist the development of artistic and cultural activity throughout the country and to promote public interest in, and appreciation of, the arts and cultural heritage.

It directly funds over 20 bodies including the Arts Council, the eleven national museums and galleries, the British Library and its St Pancras project. The Office of Arts and Libraries also has policy responsibilities towards the public library and local museum services. The Government Art Collection, which is responsible for the acquisition, maintenance and display of works of art in major government buildings in this country and abroad, also forms part of the Office.

Minister for the Arts, THE RT. HON. TIMOTHY RENTON, MP.
  Private Secretary, M. Le Jeune.
  Special Adviser, P. Moman.
  Parliamentary Private Secretary, G. Bowden, MP.
Head of the Office of Arts and Libraries (G2), C. E. Henderson.

Arts

Assistant Secretary (G5), Miss S. E. Brown.
Principals (G7), P. J. Fallon; Miss J. C. Mole; F. V. Rees.

Heritage

Principal (G7), Miss C. R. Morrison.

Museums, Galleries and Finance

Assistant Secretary (G5), N. Pittman.
Principals (G7), I. D. Baxter; K. Gray; E. A. Yeo.

Libraries and Information Services

Assistant Secretary (G5), C. C. Leamy.
Principal (G7), A. Poulter.
Library Adviser, P. J. Beauchamp.

British Library Project St Pancras

Project Director (G5), J. R. W. Pardey.

Government Art Collection
St Christopher House Annexe,
Sumner Street, SE1 9LA
[071-928 8516]

Advisory Committee

Chairman, Prof. Sir John Hale, FBA, FSA.
Members, Dr W. Baron; L. Greene; Dr J. Hayes, CBE; N. MacGregor; N. Serota; R. Shone.

Officers

Director, Dr W. Baron.
Head of Conservation and Research, Dr M. Beal.
Registrar, Miss J. Toffolo.

ARTS COUNCIL OF GREAT BRITAIN
14 Great Peter Street, SW1P 3NQ
[071-333 0100]

The Arts Council, an independent body established in 1946, is the principal channel for the Government's support of the arts. It funds the major arts organizations in England, the Regional Arts Boards (which replaced the Regional Arts Associations in October 1991) and the Scottish and Welsh Arts Councils. It also provides a service of advice, information and help to artists, arts organizations and the general public.

Its objectives are to develop and improve the understanding and practice of the arts and to increase their accessibility to the public.

The Council distributes an annual grant from the Office of Arts and Libraries, and for the year 1991–92 the amount is £194 million.
Chairman, Lord Palumbo.
Secretary-General, A. Everitt.

Regional Arts Boards

Arts Board North West, 12 Harter Street, Manchester M1 6HY (061-228 3062). *Chair*, M. Unger.

East Midlands Arts Board, Mountfields House, Forest Road, Loughborough, Leics. LE11 3HU (0509-218292). *Chair*, M. Hutchinson.

Eastern Arts Board, Cherry Hinton Hall, Cherry Hinton Road, Cambridge CB1 4DW (0223-215355). *Chair*, Prof. D. Hargreaves.

London Arts Board, Coriander House, Gainsford Street, Butlers Wharf, SE1 2NE (071-403 9013). *Chair*, C. Priestley.

Northern Arts Board, 9–10 Osborne Terrace, Newcastle-upon-Tyne NE2 1NZ (091-281 6334). *Chair*, vacant.

South East Arts Board, 10 Mount Ephraim, Tunbridge Wells, Kent TN4 8AS (0892-515210). *Chair*, B. Nicholson.

South West Arts Board, Bradninch Place, Gandy Street, Exeter EX4 3LS (0392-218188). *Chair*, Ms M. Guillebaud.

Southern Arts Board, 13 St Clement Street, Winchester SO23 9DQ (0962-855099). *Chair*, D. Reid.

West Midlands Arts Board, 82 Granville Street, Birmingham B1 2LH (021-631 3121). *Chair*, vacant.

Yorkshire and Humberside Arts Board, Dean Clough Office Park, Dean Clough, Halifax, W. Yorks. HX3 5AX (0422-345631). *Chair*, E. Hall.

Scottish Arts Council
12 Manor Place, Edinburgh EH3 7DD

Chairman, Prof. A. Peacock.

Welsh Arts Council
Holst House, 9 Museum Place, Cardiff CF1 3NX

Chairman, M. Prichard.

ART GALLERIES, ETC.

ROYAL FINE ART COMMISSION
7 St James's Square, SW1Y 4JU
[071–839 6537]

Established in 1924, the Commission is an autonomous authority on the aesthetic implications of any project or development, primarily but not exclusively architectural, which affects the visual environment.

Chairman, The Lord St John of Fawsley, PC.
Commissioners, R. D. Carter, CBE,; Dame Elizabeth Chesterton, DBE; Sir Philip Dowson, CBE, RA; M. Girouard, PH.D.; Sir Alexander Gordon, CBE; The Duke of Grafton, KG, FSA; M. J. Hopkins, CBE; S. A. Lipton; R. MacCormac; H. T. Moggridge, OBE; Mrs J. Nutting; D. Hamilton Fraser, RA; Sir Philip Powell, CH, OBE, RA; J. Sutherland; Miss W. Taylor, CBE; W. Whitfield, CBE; J. Winter, MBE.
Secretary (G6), S. Cantacuzino, CBE.

ROYAL FINE ART COMMISSION FOR SCOTLAND
9 Atholl Crescent,
Edinburgh EH3 8HA
[031–229 1109]

Chairman, The Hon. Lord Prosser.
Commissioners, Miss K. Borland; J. Boys, FRIBA; W. D. Campbell; Dr Deborah Howard, PH.D., FSA; W. K. Mackay; A. S. Matheson, FRIBA; G. Ogilvie-Laing; R. R. Steedman, RSA; Mrs F. M. E. Walker; Prof. R. Walker; R. Wedgwood.
Secretary, C. Prosser.

NATIONAL GALLERY
Trafalgar Square, WC2N 5DN
[071–839 3321]

Hours of opening.—Weekdays 10–6, Sun. 2–6. Closed on Good Friday, Christmas Eve, Christmas Day, Boxing Day, New Year's Day and May Day Bank Holiday.

The National Gallery was founded in 1824, following a Parliamentary grant of £60,000 for the purchase and exhibition of the Angerstein collection of pictures. The present site was first occupied in 1838 and enlarged and improved at various times throughout the years. A substantial extension to the north of the building with a public entrance in Orange Street was opened in 1975, and a new wing, the Sainsbury wing, was opened by HM The Queen on July 9, 1991. Expenses for 1991–92 are estimated at £23,231,000.

Board of Trustees

Chairman, The Lord Rothschild.
Trustees, HRH The Prince of Wales, KG, KT, GCB, PC; Lord Alexander of Weedon, QC; F. St J. Gore, CBE; B. Gascoigne; P. Troughton; Sir Rex Richards, FRS D.Phil.; The Countess of Airlie, CVO; Sir Derek Oulton, KCB, QC; N. Baring; E. Uglow; Hon. Simon Sainsbury; Sir Keith Thomas.

Officers

Director, R. N. MacGregor £54,100
Chief Curator (G5), Dr C. P. H. Brown.

Senior Curators (G5), Dr A. J. W. Braham; (G6), Dr N. Penny; (G7), Dr S. Foister; Dr D. Gordon; M. Helston.
Chief Restorer (G5), M. H. Wyld.
Head of Exhibitions (G6), M. J. Wilson.
Scientific Adviser (G6), Dr A. Roy.
Director of Administration (G5), M. A. Cowdy.
Head of Finance and Personnel (G6), T. Tarkowski.
Head of Building, Mrs J. Evans.
Head of Press and Public Relations, Miss J. Liddiard.

NATIONAL PORTRAIT GALLERY
St Martin's Place, WC2H 0HE
[071–306 0055]

Open Mon.–Fri. 10–5, Sat. 10–6, Sun. 2–6.

A grant was made in 1856 to form a gallery of the portraits of the most eminent persons in British history. The present building was opened in 1896, £80,000 being contributed to its cost by Mr W. H. Alexander; an extension erected at the expense of Lord Duveen was opened in 1933. There are four outstations displaying portraits in appropriate settings: Montacute House, Gawthorpe Hall, Beningbrough Hall and Bodelwyddan Castle.

Chairman, The Rev. Prof. W. O Chadwick, OM, KBE, FBA.
Trustees, The Lord President of the Council (*ex officio*); The President of the Royal Academy of Arts (*ex officio*); The Duke of Grafton, KG, FSA; Sir Oliver Millar, GCVO, FBA, FSA; J. Roberts, D.Phil.; The Lord Morris of Castle Morris, D.Phil.; Mrs S. Crosland; Prof. M. Gowing, CBE, FBA; H. Keswick; Prof. N. Lynton; The Lord Sieff of Brimpton, OBE; The Lord Weidenfeld; Sir Eduardo Paolozzi; J. Tusa; Sir Antony Acland.

Director, J. T. Hayes, CBE, PH.D., FSA £45,057
Keeper and Deputy Director, M. Rogers, D.Phil.
£41,866

TATE GALLERY
Millbank, SW1P 4RG
[071–821 1313]

Hours of opening.—Weekdays 10–5.50, Sun. 2–5.50. Closed on New Year's Day, Good Friday, May Day Holiday, Christmas Eve, Christmas Day and Boxing Day.

The Tate Gallery comprises the National Collections of British painting and 20th century painting and sculpture. The Gallery was opened in 1897, the cost of erection (£80,000) being defrayed by Sir Henry Tate, who also contributed the nucleus of the present collection. The Turner Wing, built at the expense of Sir Joseph Duveen, was opened in 1920. Lord Duveen defrayed the cost of galleries to contain the collection of modern foreign painting, completed in 1926, and a new sculpture hall, completed in 1937. In 1979 a further extension was built with a contribution from the Calouste Gulbenkian Foundation. The latest extension to the Tate Gallery, the Clore Gallery for the Turner Collection, was opened by HM The Queen on April 1, 1987. The Tate Gallery Liverpool, sited in the Albert Dock, opened in May 1988. The Tate Gallery St Ives is due to open in 1993. Total government funding for 1991–92 is £15,126,000.

Board of Trustees

Chairman, D. Stevenson.
Trustees, The Countess of Airlie, CVO; G. de Botton; R. Deacon; C. LeBrun; D. Puttnam, CBE; Sir Mark Weinberg; Mrs C. Hubbard; W. Govett; Mrs P. Ridley; M. Craig-Martin.

Officers
Salaries 1991

Director £54,100
Grade 5 .... £35,721–£46,746
Grade 6 .... £24,997–£41,866

Director, N. Serota.
Deputy Director, F. Carnwath.
Keeper of the British Collection (G5), A. Wilton.
Keeper of the Modern Collection (G5), R. Morphet.
Deputy Keepers (G6), L. A. Parris; J. Lewison.

Tate Gallery Liverpool
Albert Dock, Liverpool L3 4BB
[051–709 3223]
Open Wed.–Sun., 10–6, Tues. 11–6. Closed Mondays.
Curator (G6), L. Biggs.

WALLACE COLLECTION
Hertford House, Manchester Square, W1M 6BN
[071–935 0687]

Admission free. Open on weekdays 10–5, Sun. 2–5.
Closed on Good Friday, December 24–26, January 1
and May Day.
    The Wallace Collection was bequeathed to the
nation by the widow of Sir Richard Wallace, Bt., on
her death in 1897, and Hertford House was subsequently acquired by the Government. The collection
includes pictures, drawings and miniatures, French
furniture, sculpture, bronzes, porcelain, armour and
miscellaneous *objets d'art*. The total net expenses for
1991–92 were estimated at £2,146,000.
Director, J. A. S. Ingamells.
Assistants to Director, P. Hughes; Miss R. J. Savill.
Head of Administration, A. W. Houldershaw.

NATIONAL GALLERIES OF SCOTLAND
The Mound, Edinburgh EH2 2EL
[031–556 8921]

Trustees

Chairman of the Trustees, A. M. Grossart, CBE.
Trustees, The Countess of Rosebery; J. Packer, OBE;
A. R. Cole-Hamilton; Mrs L. W. Gibbs; Sir Norman
Macfarlane; Dr T. Johnston; Prof. A. A. Tait; E.
Hagman; Prof. E. Fernie.

Officers
Salaries 1991

Director .... £40,116–£41,681
Keeper .... £24,997–£32,551
Assistant Keeper/Curator .... £21,905–£26,121

Director, T. Clifford.
Keeper of Conservation, J. P. Dick.
Keeper of Information (Asst. Keeper), Miss L. S.
Callander.
Keeper of Education (Asst. Keeper), Ms L. B. Shaw.
Registrar (Asst. Keeper), J. Patterson.
Secretary (Keeper), Ms S. Edwards.
Buildings (Asst. Keeper), C. P. Fotheringham.

Comprising:

National Gallery of Scotland
The Mound, Edinburgh
[031–556 8921]

Open: Mon.–Sat. 10–5, Sun. 2–5. Closed December
25, 26, 31, January 1, 2, 3.
Keeper, M. Clarke.
Assistant Keepers, Miss L. M. Errington, PH.D.; Ms J.
Lloyd Williams.
Keeper of Prints and Drawings, H. Macandrew.
Assistant Keeper, R. M. M. Campbell.

Scottish National Portrait Gallery
1 Queen Street, Edinburgh
[031–556 8921]

Hours: as for National Gallery of Scotland.
Keeper, D. Thomson, PH.D.
Assistant Keepers, Miss R. K. Marshall, PH.D.; J. E.
Holloway.
Curator of Photography, Miss S. F. Stevenson.

Scottish National Gallery of Modern Art
Belford Road, Edinburgh EH4 3DR
[031–556 8921]

Hours: as for National Gallery of Scotland.
Keeper, R. Calvocoressi.
Assistant Keepers, K. S. Hartley; P. Elliott.

(For other British Art Galleries, *see* Index.)

UNITED KINGDOM ATOMIC ENERGY AUTHORITY
11 Charles II Street, SW1Y 4QP
[071–389 6565]

The UKAEA was established by the Atomic Energy
Authority Act 1954, and is responsible for research
and development support for the UK nuclear power
programme and for public information. Since April
1986 the UKAEA has been required by the Government to operate on a quasi-commercial footing and in
1990 it adopted the trading name AEA Technology.
It provides scientific and technical services, products
and consultancy on a commercial basis to govern-
ments, utilities and industries worldwide. The
UKAEA has seven research and engineering centres.
Chairman, J. N. Maltby, CBE (*part-time*).
Deputy Chairman and Chief Executive, Dr B. L. Eyre.
Members (part-time) Prof. Sir Peter Hirsch, FRS; J.
Bullock; R. Sanderson, OBE; Prof. Sir Roger Elliott,
FRS; J. A. Gardiner.
Secretary, J. R. Bretherton.
Executive Director, Finance, P. G. Daffern.
Managing Director, Sites and Personnel, A. W. Hills.
Managing Director, Industrial Business Group, Dr R.
S. Nelson.
Managing Director, Nuclear Business Group, Dr D.
Pooley.

THE AUDIT COMMISSION FOR LOCAL AUTHORITIES AND THE NATIONAL HEALTH SERVICE IN ENGLAND AND WALES
1 Vincent Square, SW1P 2PN
[071–828 1212]

The Audit Commission was set up in 1983 with
responsibility for the external audit of local authorities. This remit was extended from October 1990 to
include the audit of the National Health Service
bodies in England and Wales. The Commission
appoints the auditors, who may be from the District
Audit Service or from a private firm of accountants.
The Commission also has responsibility for promoting
value for money in the services provided by local
authorities and health bodies.
    The Commission has 15–17 members appointed by
the Secretary of State for the Environment in
consultation with the Secretaries of State for Wales
and for Health. Though appointed by the Secretary
of State the Commissioners are responsible to Parliament.
Chairman, D. J. S. Cooksey.
Deputy Chairman, C. M. Stuart.
Controller of Audit, H. J. Davies.
Deputy Controller, J. C. Nicholson, CBE.

THE COMMISSION FOR LOCAL AUTHORITY ACCOUNTS IN SCOTLAND
18 George Street, Edinburgh EH2 2QU
[031-226 7346]

The Commission was set up in 1975. It is responsible for securing the audit of the accounts of Scottish local authorities and certain joint boards and joint committees. Amongst its duties the Commission is required to deal with reports made by the Controller of Audit on items of account contrary to law; incorrect accounting; and losses due to misconduct, negligence and failure to carry out statutory duties. Since 1988 the Commission has had responsibility for value-for-money audits of authorities.

Members are appointed by the Secretary of State for Scotland.

Chairman, Prof. J. R. Small, CBE.
Controller of Audit, J. Broadfoot.
Secretary, J. Ritchie.

THE BANK OF ENGLAND
Threadneedle Street, EC2R 8AH
[071-601 4444]

The Bank of England was incorporated in 1694 under Royal Charter. It is the banker of the Government on whose behalf it manages the Note Issue and the National Debt. As the central reserve bank of the country, the Bank keeps the accounts of British banks, who maintain with it a proportion of their cash resources, and of most overseas central banks.

Governor, Rt. Hon. Robin Leigh-Pemberton.
Deputy Governor, E. A. J. George.
Directors, Dr D. V. Atterton, CBE; Sir Adrian Cadbury; A. L. Coleby; Sir Frederick Corby; Sir Colin Corness; A. D. Crockett; The Lord Haslam; Sir Martin Jacomb; Prof. M. A. King; G. H. Laird; D. B. Lees; B. Quinn; Sir David Scholey, CBE; Prof. R. Smith; C. G. Southgate; D. A. Walker.
Associate Directors, P. H. Kent; H. C. E. Harris; I. Plenderleith.
Advisers to the Governor, J. P. Charkham; Sir Peter Petrie.
Assistant Director, R. A. Barnes.
Chief of Banking Department (*Chief Cashier*), G. Kentfield.
Chief Registrar, D. A. Bridger.
General Manager, Printing Works, A. W. Jarvis.
Secretary, G. A. Croughton.
Head of Information Division, J. R. E. Footman.
The Auditor, M. J. W. Phillips.

BOUNDARY COMMISSIONS

The Commissions are constituted under the Parliamentary Constituencies Act, 1986. The Speaker of the House of Commons is ex-officio chairman of all four Commissions in the United Kingdom. Each of the four Commissions is required by law to keep the parliamentary constituencies in their part of the United Kingdom under review. Each of the three Commissions in Great Britain is required by law to keep the European Parliamentary constituencies in their part of Great Britain under review.

England
St Catherines House, 10 Kingsway, WC2B 6JP
[071-242 0262]

Deputy Chairman, The Hon. Mr Justice Knox.
Joint Secretaries, R. McLeod; Mrs J. S. Morris.

Wales
St Catherines House, 10 Kingsway, WC2B 6JP
[071-242 0262]

Deputy Chairman, The Hon. Mr Justice Anthony Evans.
Joint Secretaries, R. McLeod; Mrs J. S. Morris.

Scotland
St Andrew's House, Edinburgh EH1 3DE
[031-244 2196-8]

Deputy Chairman, The Hon. Lord Davidson.
Secretary, D. K. C. Jeffrey.

Northern Ireland
c/o Northern Ireland Office,
Whitehall, SW1A 2AZ
[071-210 6569]

Deputy Chairman, His Hon. Mr Justice Higgins.
Secretary, J. R. Fisher.

BRITISH BROADCASTING CORPORATION
Broadcasting House, W1A 1AA
[071-580 4468]

The BBC was incorporated under Royal Charter as successor to the British Broadcasting Company Ltd, whose licence expired on December 31, 1926. Its present Charter came into force on August 1, 1981, for 15 years. The Chairman, Vice-Chairman and other Governors are appointed by the Queen in Council. The BBC is financed by revenue from receiving licences for the Home services and by grant-in-aid from Parliament for the External services. The total number of receiving licences in the UK at March 31, 1991 was 19,545,830, of which 1,435,213 were for monochrome receivers and 18,110,617 for colour receivers. Annual television licence fees are: monochrome £25.50; colour £77. Television licence fees became index-linked from April 1, 1988.

Board of Governors
(as at August 1, 1991)

Chairman, M. Hussey. £50,365
Vice-Chairman, The Lord Barnett, PC £12,920
Governors, Sir Kenneth Bloomfield, KCB (*N. Ireland*); J. Parry, CBE (*Wales*); Sir Graham Hills, FRSE (*Scotland*) . . . . (*each*) £12,920
Dr J. Roberts; W. B. Jordan; J. K. Oates; OBE; The Baroness James of Holland Park; Miss J. Glover, D.phil; Mrs S. Sadeque; Lord Nicholas Gordon Lennox, KCMG, KCVO . . . . (*each*) £6,460

Board of Management

Director-General, M. Checkland.
Deputy Director-General, J. Birt.
Managing Directors, W. Wyatt (*Network Television*); D. Hatch (*Network Radio*); J. Tusa (*World Service*); R. Neil (*Regional Broadcasting*).
Directors, W. Dennay (*Engineering*); H. James (*Corporate Affairs*); I. Phillips (*Finance*); Ms M. Salmon (*Personnel*).

Other Senior Staff

Director, News and Current Affairs, I. Hargreaves.
Director, Resources, Radio, D. Thomas.
Director, Resources, Television, C. Taylor.
Deputy Managing Director, World Service, D. Witherow.
Deputy Director of Engineering, C. Sandbank.
Head of Policy and Planning Unit, Ms P. Hodgson.
Controller, BBC-1, J. Powell.
Controller, BBC-2, A. Yentob.

Assistant Managing Director, Network Television, Ms J. Drabble.
Controller, Radio 1, J. Beerling.
Controller, Radio 2, Ms F. Line.
Controller, Radio 3, J. Drummond.
Controller, Radio 4, M. Green.
Controller, Radio 5, Ms P. Ewing.
Controller, Scotland, P. Chalmers.
Controller, Wales, G. Talfan Davies.
Controller, N. Ireland, R. Walsh.
Chief Political Adviser, Ms M. Douglas.
Controller, Editorial Policy, J. Wilson.
Controller, Information Services and International Relations, D. Barlow.
The Secretary, J. McCormick.
Legal Adviser, G. Roscoe.
Chief Executive, BBC Enterprises, J.Arnold-Baker.

BRITISH COAL CORPORATION
Hobart House, Grosvenor Place, SW1X 7AE
[071–235 2020]

The British Coal Corporation (formerly the National Coal Board) was constituted in 1946 and took over the mines on January 1, 1947.
Chairman, J. N. Clarke.
Deputy Chairman, J. H. Northard, CBE.
Executive Members, M. J. Edwards, CBE (*Commercial Director*); M. H. Butler (*Finance Director*); K. Moses, CBE (*Technical Director*); A. Wheeler, CBE (*Operations*); K. Hunt (*Employee Relations*).
Non-Executive Members, Dr D. V. Atterton, CBE; Dr T. J. Parker; D. B. Walker; J. P. Erbé.
Secretary, M. S. Shelton.

THE BRITISH COUNCIL
10 Spring Gardens, SW1A 2BN
[071–930 8466]

The British Council was established in 1934 and incorporated by Royal Charter in 1940.
It is an independent, non-political organization which promotes Britain abroad. It provides access to British ideas, talents and experience in education and training, books and periodicals, the English language, the arts, the sciences and technology.
The Council is represented in 90 countries and runs 155 offices, 116 libraries and 55 English language schools around the world.
The Council's annual turnover in 1991–92 is estimated at £395 million, including grants from the Foreign and Commonwealth Office and the Overseas Development Administration. The Council's own revenue now exceeds £90 million.
Chairman, Sir David Orr, MC.
Chairman-designate, Sir Martin Jacomb (*from Jan. 1992*).
Director-General, Sir Richard Francis, KCMG.
    £77,500

BRITISH RAILWAYS BOARD
Euston House, 24 Eversholt Street,
PO Box 100, NW1 1DZ
[071–928 5151]

The British Railways Board came into being in 1963 under the terms of the Transport Act, 1962. The Board became responsible for the provision of railway services in Great Britain and for catering and other services formerly carried on by the British Transport Commission.
Chairman, Sir Robert Reid £200,000
Chief Executive, Railways, J. K. Welsby.
Members, Ms A. Biss*; Miss K. T. Kantor*; J. B. Cameron, CBE*; D. E. Rayner; J. C. P. Edmonds; K.

H. M. Dixon*; Sir Fred Holliday, CBE*; J. J. Jerram; E. Sanderson*; Dr P. Watson.
    * part-time members.

BSI (BRITISH STANDARDS INSTITUTION)
2 Park Street, W1A 2BS
[Enquiry Section: BSI, Linford Wood, Milton Keynes, MK14 6LE. Tel. 0908–221166]

BSI (the British Standards Institution) is the recognized authority in the UK for the preparation and publication of national standards for industrial and consumer products. In consultation with the interests concerned, BSI prepares standards relating to nearly every sector of the nation's industry and trade. It also represents the UK at European and international standards meetings.
British Standards are issued for voluntary adoption, though in a number of cases compliance with a British Standard is required by legislation. BSI operates certification schemes under which industrial and consumer products are certified as complying with the relevant British Standard and may carry the Institution's certification trade marks, known as the 'Kitemark' and the 'Safety Mark'. It assesses and registers companies which meet the requirements of the quality management standard, BS5750. BSI runs one of the largest testing laboratories in Europe and has an advisory service for exporters, Technical Help to Exporters.
BSI is financed by voluntary subscriptions, an annual Government grant, the sale of its publications, and fees for testing and certification. There are more than 27,000 subscribing members of BSI.
Director General, Dr I. Dunstan.

BRITISH TECHNOLOGY GROUP
101 Newington Causeway, SE1 6BU
[071–403 6666]

British Technology Group (BTG) is a self-financing technology transfer organization. It searches for new technology in research laboratories and companies worldwide, licenses new scientific and engineering products to industry, and provides finance for the development of new technology. It is due to be privatized by the end of 1991.
Chairman, Sir Colin Barker.
Chief Executive, I. A. Harvey.

BRITISH TOURIST AUTHORITY
Thames Tower, Black's Road, W6 9EL
[081–846 9000]

Established under the Development of Tourism Act 1969, the British Tourist Authority has specific responsibility for promoting tourism to Great Britain from overseas. It also has a general responsibility for the promotion and development of tourism and tourist facilities within Great Britain as a whole, and for advising the Government on tourism matters.
Chairman, W. Davis (*part-time*).
Chief Executive, M. G. Medlicott.

BRITISH WATERWAYS BOARD
Greycaine Road, Watford, Herts. WD2 4JR
[0923–226422]

The British Waterways Board is the navigational authority for over 2,000 miles of canals and river navigations in England, Scotland and Wales. Some 380 miles are maintained and are being developed as commercial waterways for use by freight-carrying vessels, and another 1,100 miles, the cruising waterways, are being developed for boating, fishing and other leisure activities. The remaining 600 miles, the remainder waterways, are maintained with due regard to safety, public health and the preservation of amenities. Of this remaining mileage, nearly two-thirds is navigable or has been restored to navigation over the last twenty years.

Chairman, D. C. Ingman *(part-time)*.
Vice-Chairman, Sir Peter Hutchison, Bt. *(part-time)*.
Members (all part-time), J. Gordon; Dr B. Goodman; M. Golder; D. H. R. Yorke; M. Cairns.
Chief Executive, B. C. Dice.
Secretary and Solicitor, R. J. Duffy.

BROADCASTING STANDARDS COUNCIL
5–8 The Sanctuary, SW1P 3JS
[071–233 0544]

The Council was set up in 1988 but received its statutory powers under the Broadcasting Act 1990. It monitors the portrayal of sex, violence and matters of taste and decency in any television or radio programme or broadcast advertisement. The Council publishes a code of practice, considers complaints and undertakes relevant research. Members of the Council are appointed by the Home Secretary. (The appointments are part-time.)

Chairman, The Lord Rees-Mogg £33,725
Deputy Chairman, Miss J. Barrow, OBE £25,465
Members, R. Baker, OBE, RD; The Bishop of Peterborough; A. Dubs; Dr R. Brinley Jones; Dr Jean Curtis-Raleigh; Rev. C. Robertson £10,130
Director, C. Shaw.
Deputy Director, T. Cobley.

THE BROADS AUTHORITY
Thomas Harvey House, 18 Colegate,
Norwich NR3 1BQ
[0603–610734]

The Broads Authority is a special statutory authority set up under the Norfolk and Suffolk Broads Act 1988, with powers and responsibilities similar to those of National Park Authorities. The functions of the Authority are: to conserve and enhance the natural beauty of the Broads; to promote the enjoyment of the Broads by the public; and to protect the interests of navigation.

The Authority comprises 35 members, appointed by Norfolk County Council (4); Suffolk County Council (2); Broadland District Council (2); Great Yarmouth Borough Council (2); North Norfolk District Council (2); Norwich City Council (2); South Norfolk District Council (2); Waveney District Council (2); the Countryside Commission (2); English Nature (1); the Great Yarmouth Port Authority (2); National Rivers Authority (Anglian Region) (1); the Secretary of State for the Environment (9); and two from amongst members of the Authority's statutory Navigation Committee who are not already members of the Authority.

Chairman, J. S. Peel, MC.
Chief Executive, M. A. Clark.

CABINET OFFICE

The Cabinet Office comprises the Secretariat, who support Ministers collectively in the conduct of Cabinet business; and the Office of the Minister for the Civil Service (OMCS) which is responsible for the management and organization of the Civil Service and recruitment into it, efficiency, and senior appointments. Other functions are from time to time laid on the Office, some ephemerally and some permanently. Non-departmental Ministers may be attached to the Office.

The functions of the OMCS are in support of the Prime Minister in his capacity as Minister for the Civil Service, with responsibility for day-to-day supervision delegated to the Minister of State, Privy Council Office.

(For **Salaries**, *see* page 293)

PRIME MINISTER'S OFFICE

Prime Minister and Minister for the Civil Service, THE RT. HON. JOHN MAJOR, MP.
Principal Private Secretary to the Prime Minister, *(G2)*, A. Turnbull, CB.
Private Secretaries to the Prime Minister, J. S. Wall *(Overseas Affairs)*; B. Potter *(Economic Affairs)*; D. Morris *(Parliamentary Affairs)*; W. Chapman *(Home Affairs)*.
Personal Assistant to the Prime Minister, Miss S. Phillips.
Secretary for Appointments (G5), J. R. Catford, CBE.
Foreign Affairs Adviser, Sir Percy Cradock, GCMG.
Political Secretary, Mrs J. Chaplin.
Policy Unit, Mrs S. Hogg; Miss C. Sinclair; J. Mills; H. Harris-Hughes; N. True; J. Hill; A. Rosling.
Chief Press Secretary, A. T. O'Donnell.
Deputy Chief Press Secretary, J. Haslam.
Assistant Private Secretaries to Prime Minister, Miss A. Hordern; Miss J. L. Wilkinson.
Parliamentary Private Secretary, G. Bright, MP.
Adviser on Efficiency, Sir Angus Fraser, KCB, TD.

Efficiency Unit
70 Whitehall, SW1A 2AS

Head of Unit (G3), D. Brereton.
Assistant Secretaries (G5), Dr G. D. Coley; Dr I. V. Howell.

Cabinet Office

Secretary to the Cabinet and Head of Home Civil Service, Sir Robin Butler, KCB, CVO.

Ceremonial Branch

Ceremonial Officer (G5), J. H. Thompson, CB.

SECRETARIAT
70 Whitehall, SW1A 2AS
[071–270 3000]

Deputy Secretaries (G2), Sir Christopher Curwen, KCMG; D. Hadley, CB; P. F. Owen, CB.
Chief Scientific Adviser, Prof. W. P. D. Stewart D.SC., FRS, FRSE.
Under Secretaries (G3), G. Barrass; W. D. Reeves; T. J. Burr; C R. Walker; M. Russell; B. G. Bender.
Assistant Secretaries (G5), Brig. J. A. J. Budd; A. Charlton; R. P. Short; L. Parker; Mrs G. Craig; P. I. Bailey; D. Gowan; Dr D. J. W. Lumley; Air Cdre N. J. G. Hodnett, CBE; P. L. Thomas; M. B. Nicholson; S. H. D. Hawker.
Senior Principals (G6), C. K. Davies; P. C. F. Gilbert; P. F. Tero; Dr J. A. Leather; J. C. Dilling.

ESTABLISHMENT OFFICER'S GROUP

Principal Establishment and Finance Officer (G3), S. R. Davie.

Information Services
Chief Press Officer (G6), J. P. Lawson.

Establishment Division
Deputy Establishment Officer (G5), G. S. Royston.

Finance Division
Senior Finance Officer (G6), Miss J. M. E. Buchan.

Internal Audit
Principal (G7), I. C. R. Boulton.

Historical Section
Hepburn House, Marsham Street, SW1P 4HW
[071–217 6032]

Departmental Records Adviser (G6), Miss. P. M. Andrews.

OFFICE OF THE MINISTER FOR THE CIVIL SERVICE (OMCS)
Horse Guards Road, SW1P 3AL
[071–270 3000]

Project Manager–Next Steps Initiative, (G1A), Sir Peter Kemp, KCB.
Director, Management Development and Training (G2), B. T. Gilmore.
First Civil Service Commissioner (G2), J. H. Holroyd.
Director, Top Management Programme Group (G3), Miss M. T. Neville-Rolfe.
Course Directors, Top Management Programmme Group (G5), Mrs S. R. Street; T. J. Rose.

Management Development Group
Grade 3, Dr E. G. Finer.
Assistant Secretaries (G5), R. D. J. Wright; Miss S. Haird; M. Gibson; H. H. Taylor.

Senior and Public Appointments Group and European Staffing
Grade 3, A. J. Merifield.
Grade 5, D. Laughrin (SPA); Mrs K. B. Elliott (ES).

Machinery of Government
Assistant Secretary (G5), A. D. Whetnall.

Security Division
Assistant Secretary (G5), H. H. Taylor.

Information Officer Management Unit
Chief Information Officer A (G5), T. J. Perks.

Office of the Civil Service Commissioners (OCSC)
Alencon Link, Basingstoke, Hants. RG21 1JB
[0256–29222]

First Commissioner (G2), J. H. Holroyd (London).
Commissioners (G3), M. Geddes (*Chief Exec., RAS*); *(G4)*, J. K. Moore (*Head of OCSC*).
Commissioners (part-time), G. L. Dennis; Miss D. Whittingham; Miss U. Prashar.

EXECUTIVE AGENCIES

Occupational Health Service
18–20 Hill Street, Edinburgh EH2 3NB
[031-220 4177]

Medical Adviser and Director, Dr G. S. Sorrie.
Deputy Medical Advisers, Dr P. Brown.

Civil Service College
Sunningdale Park, Ascot, Berks. SL5 0QE
[0344–23444]
11 Belgrave Road, SW1V 1RB
[071–834 6644]

Chief Executive (G3), Miss M. T. Neville-Rolfe.
Director of Services and Resources (G5), I. Cameron.
Business Group Directors (G5/G6), Ms C. M. Bentley; Ms E. Chennells; P. A. Daffern; J. G. Fuller; P. J. C. O'Connell; P. G. Tebby; Miss J. A. Topham.
College Secretary (G6), Miss M. A. Wood.

Recruitment and Assessment Services (RAS)
Alencon Link, Basingstoke, Hants. RG21 1JB
[0256-29222]
24 Whitehall, SW1A 2ED
[071-210 3000]

Chief Executive, M. D. Geddes.
Grade 5, A. S. Halford (*London*); C. J. Parry.
Grade 6, F. D. Bedford (*London*); P. Cook; K. N. Bastin.

CENTRAL STATISTICAL OFFICE
Great George Street, SW1P 3AQ
[071–270 6363/6364]

The work of the Central Statistical Office encompasses data collection from businesses; the preparation and publication of macro-economic statistics and social statistics abstracts; statistics relating to institutional sectors and financial statistics; the retail prices index and the family expenditure survey; liaison with international statistical bodies; and central management of the Government Statistical Service (GSS).

Director and Head of the Government Statistical Service (G1A), Sir Jack Hibbert, KCB.
Private Secretary, Mrs A. French.
Deputy Director and Director of National Accounts (G3), D. C. L. Wroe.
Head of Division 1 (G3), R. G. Ward.
Head of Division 2 (G3), N. Harvey.
Head of Division 3 (G3), J. E. Kidgell.
Head of Division 4 and Principal Establishment and Finance Officer (G4), F. Martin.
Head of Information (G5), J. B. Wright.

Division 1
Heads of Branches (G5):
Branch 1, D. C. K. Stirling (*GSS policy and management*).
Branch 2, T. J. Griffin (*Social, regional and international*).
Branch 3, D. J. Sellwood (*Consumer prices; family expenditure survey; distribution and redistribution of income*).
Branch 4, R. J. Scott (*Registers; energy and materials inquiries; classifications; survey control*).

Deputy Director's Office
Heads of Branches (G5):
Branch 5, Miss S. P. Carter (*Central national accounts coordination; national accounts training; economic assessment*).
Branch 6, P. B. Kenny (*Research, development and evaluation*).

Division 2
Heads of Branches (G5):
Branch 7, K. Francombe (*Index of production and manufacturing output*).
Branch 8, C. J. Spiller (*Annual censuses of production and construction; stocks and capital expenditure inquiries*).
Branch 9, R. M. Norton (*Distribution and services*).
Branch 10, R. G. Lynch (*Producer prices; annual and quarterly sales inquiries*).
Branch 11, K. Mansell (*Consumers' expenditure; capital formation; output other than production industries*).

Division 3
Heads of Branches (G5):
Branch 12, G. Jenkinson (*External trade*).

Branch 13, B. J. Buckingham (*Balance of payments*).
Branch 14, Mrs P. Walker (*Company and personal sector accounts*).
Branch 15, P. Turnbull (*Financial statistics; public sector accounts; R&D statistics*).

Division 4

Heads of Branches (G5):
Branch 16, Dr J. Ludley (*Information systems*).
Branch 17, J. B. Wright (*Press, publications and publicity*).
Branch 18, D. R. Lewis (*Establishment and finance*).

CERTIFICATION OFFICE FOR TRADE UNIONS AND EMPLOYERS' ASSOCIATIONS
27 Wilton Street, SW1X 7AZ
[071–210 3733/4]

The Certification Office is an independent statutory authority. The Certification Officer is appointed by the Secretary of State for Employment and is responsible for receiving and scrutinizing annual returns from trade unions and employers' associations; for reimbursing certain costs of trade unions' postal ballots; for dealing with complaints concerning trade union elections; for ensuring observance of statutory requirements governing political funds and trade union mergers; and for certifying the independence of trade unions.
Certification Officer, M. Wake.
Assistant Certification Officer, G. S. Osborne.

Scotland
58 Frederick Street, Edinburgh EH2 1LN
[031–226 3224]

Assistant Certification Officer for Scotland, J. L. J. Craig.

CHARITY COMMISSION
St Alban's House, 57–60 Haymarket, SW1Y 4QX
[071–210 3000]
Graeme House, Derby Square, Liverpool L2 7SB
[051–227 3191]
Woodfield House, Tangier, Taunton, Somerset TA1 4BL
[0823–345000]

The Charity Commissioners are appointed under the Charities Act, 1960, principally to further the work of charities in England and Wales by giving advice and information, and by investigating and checking abuses. The Commissioners maintain a register of charities; give consent to land transactions; help to modernize the purposes and administrative machinery of charities; and, in the name of some of their staff, the Official Custodian for Charities, hold investments for charities.

At the end of 1990 the total number of registered charities was 171,434.
Chief Commissioner, R. I. L Guthrie.
Commissioners, J. Farquharson; R. M. C. Venables.
Commissioners (part-time), M. Webber; Mrs D. H. Yeo.
(*Commissioners* .... £47,090–£56,010)
Deputy Commissioners (G5), J. A. Dutton; J. F. Claricoat; G. S. Goodchild; K. M. Dibble; S. Slack.
Secretary and Asst. Commissioner (G5), D. Forrest.
Director of Operations and Asst. Commissioner (G5), J. H. Vining.
Grade 6, Mrs H. M. Phillips; Miss D. F. Taylor; S. K. Sen; P. P. White; N. M. Mackenzie; M. J. Harbottle; C. Noon; V. Mitchell.
Senior Legal Assistants, A. H. Bilbrough; I. M. Davies.

Grade 7, R. E. Hatton; A. O. Polak; M. C. T. Seymour; K. M. Dickin; M. J. McManus; R. E. Edwards; G. B. Ward; R. Kilby; Miss V. A. Nuttall; Mrs M. E. Whittaker; J. S. Holdsworth; M. Pearson; B. Deal; P. W. Somerfield; R. G. Dawes; Miss G. Fletcher; A. J. George.
Official Custodian for Charities (G6), Mrs S. E. Gillingham.
Deputy Official Custodian (G7), M. Fry.
Establishment Officer (G5), D. Truman.

The departments responsible for charities in Scotland and Northern Ireland are:

Scotland.—Scottish Home and Health Department, Charities Division, New St Andrews House, Edinburgh EH1 3DE. (Tel: 031-244 2206).

Northern Ireland.—Department of Finance and Personnel, Charities Branch, Rosepark House, Upper Newtownards Road, Belfast BT4 3NR. (Tel: 0232-484567).

OFFICE OF THE CHIEF ADJUDICATION OFFICER
Priestley House, 3 Park Row,
Leeds LS1 5LA
[0532-467676]

The Chief Adjudication Officer is an independent authority under the Social Security Act, 1975 (as amended), appointed by the Secretary of State for Social Security to give advice to adjudication officers (who make decisions of first instance on all claims for social security cash benefits), to keep under review the operation of the system of adjudication and to report annually to the Secretary of State on adjudication standards. The Office also enters written observations on all appeals made to the Social Security Commissioners.
Chief Adjudication Officer, K. Bellamy.

CHURCH COMMISSIONERS
1 Millbank, SW1P 3JZ
[071–222 7010]

The Church Commissioners were established in 1948 by the amalgamation of Queen Anne's Bounty (established 1704) and the Ecclesiastical Commissioners (established 1836).

The Commissioners are responsible for the management of the Church of England's assets, the income from which is predominantly used to pay, house and pension the clergy. The Commissioners own over 150,000 acres of agricultural land, a number of residential estates in central London, and commercial property in Great Britain and the USA. They also carry out administrative duties in connection with pastoral reorganization and redundant churches, and have been designated by the General Synod as the central stipends authority of the Church of England.

The Commissioners' income for the year ended December 31, 1990, was derived from the following sources:—

	£ million
Stock exchange investments	64·9
Land and property	67·4
Mortgages, loans, etc.	32·2
Trust income, and diocesan/parish contributions for stipends	65·8
	£230·3

This income was applied as follows:—

Clergy stipends	127·3
Clergy and widows' pensions	53·0
Clergy houses	15·9
Episcopal administration and payments to Chapters	9·1
Church buildings	5·0
Administrative expenses of the Commissioners and related bodies	11·8
Carried forward	8.2
	£230·3

Constitution

The Archbishops of Canterbury and of York; the 41 diocesan Bishops; five deans or provosts, ten other clergy and ten laymen appointed by the General Synod; four laymen nominated by the Queen; four persons nominated by the Archbishop of Canterbury; The Lord Chancellor; The Lord President of the Council; the First Lord of the Treasury; The Chancellor of the Exchequer; The Secretary of State for the Home Department; The Speaker of the House of Commons; The Lord Chief Justice; The Master of the Rolls; The Attorney-General; The Solicitor-General; The Lord Mayor and two Aldermen of the City of London; The Lord Mayor of York and one representative from each of the Universities of Oxford and Cambridge.

Church Estates Commissioners

First, Sir Douglas Lovelock, KCB.
Second, Rt. Hon. Michael Alison, MP.
Third, Mrs M. H. Laird.

Officers

Secretary, J. E. Shelley, CBE.
Deputy Secretary, P. Locke.
Assistant Secretaries:
Chief Accountant, D. I. Archer.
Deputy Accountant and Trust Officer, G. C. Baines.
Bishoprics, C. P. Canton.
Commercial Property, M. G. S. Farrell.
Computer Manager, J. W. Ferguson.
Establishment Officer, W. R. Herbert.
Estates, P. H. P. Shaw, LVO.
General Purposes, Press and Information, M. D. Elengorn.
Houses, D. J. B. Long.
Investments Manager, P. G. Brealey.
Pastoral, D. N. Goodwin.
Redundant Churches, J. M. Davies.
Stipends and Allocations, R. S. Hopgood.
Senior Architect, J. A. Taylor.
Senior Surveyor, R. N. May.
Senior Principals, A. S. Hardy; B. J. Hardy; E. G. Peacock.
Principals, A. W. Atkins; P. D. Chadwick; Miss A. M. Mackie; G. Wills; J. A. W. Elloy; C. R. Bullen; N. M. Waring; D. W. H. Lewis; N. J. Neil-Smith; J. W. Wallace; R. A. Scott.

Legal Department

Official Solicitor, E. W. Wills.
Deputy Solicitor, J. P. Guy.
Solicitors, Miss J. M. Bland; J. D. Carter; Miss J. A. Egar; Miss S. M. S. Jones; R. D. C. Murray; T. Tayleur.

CIVIL AVIATION AUTHORITY
CAA House, 45–59 Kingsway, WC2B 6TE
[071–379 7311]

The CAA is responsible for the economic regulation of UK airlines by licensing air routes, air travel organizers and approving fares; for the safety regulation of UK civil aviation by the certification of airlines and aircraft, and by licensing aerodromes, flight crew and aircraft engineers; and, through the National Air Traffic Services, for the provision of air traffic control and telecommunications services.

Chairman, The Rt. Hon. C. Chataway (*part-time*) £57,750
Managing Director, T. Murphy, CBE.
Secretary, Miss G. M. E. White.

CLYDE PORT AUTHORITY
16 Robertson Street, Glasgow G2 8DS
[041-221 8733]

The Authority is a self-governing statutory body established by individual Act of Parliament. It provides sea port facilities within a 450 sq. mile area of jurisdiction which encompasses the River Clyde, its estuary and sea lochs.

Chairman, Sir Robert Easton, CBE.
Managing Director, J. Mather.
Director and Secretary, G. P. Johnston.
Director, Ports and Marketing, H. A. C. Ross.

COMMONWEALTH DEVELOPMENT CORPORATION
1 Bessborough Gardens, SW1V 2JQ
[071–828 4488]

The Corporation's area of operations covers British dependent territories and, with Ministerial approval, any Commonwealth or other developing country. At present, the Corporation is authorized to operate in 38 Commonwealth and 16 non-Commonwealth countries in addition to the British dependent territories. The Corporation is authorized to borrow up to £750,000,000.

Chairman (part-time), Sir Peter Leslie.
Deputy Chairman (part-time), Sir Michael Caine.
Members (part-time), Mrs A. Wright; V. Robertson, OBE; M. D. Nightingale, OBE; Prof. M. Faber; M. Robinson; E. B. Waide, OBE; M. D. McWilliam.
Chief Executive, J. D. Eccles, CBE.

COMMONWEALTH SECRETARIAT
(*see* p. 626)

COMMONWEALTH WAR GRAVES COMMISSION
2 Marlow Road, Maidenhead, Berkshire SL6 7DX
[0628–34221]

The Commonwealth War Graves Commission (formerly Imperial War Graves Commission) was founded by Royal Charter in 1917. It is responsible for the commemoration of 1,695,000 members of the forces of the Commonwealth who fell in the two world wars. More than one million graves are maintained in 23,102 burial grounds throughout the world. Over three-quarters of a million men and women who have no known grave or who were cremated are commemorated by name on memorials built by the Commission.

The funds of the Commission are derived from the six Governments participating in its work—the UK, Australia, Canada, India, New Zealand and South Africa.

President, HRH The Duke of Kent, KG, GCMG, GCVO, ADC.
Chairman, The Secretary of State for Defence in the UK.
Vice-Chairman, Gen. Sir Robert Ford, GCB, CBE.
Members, The Secretary of State for the Environment in the UK; The High Commissioners in London for Australia, Canada, India, and New Zealand; the Ambassador in London for the Republic of South Africa; The Rt. Hon. J. D. Concannon; Dame Janet Fookes, DBE, MP; Sir Derek Day, KCMG; Sir Nigel Mobbs; Adm. Sir Nicholas Hunt, GCB, LVO; Air Chief Marshal Sir Joseph Gilbert, KCB, CBE; The Viscount Ridley, TD; Prof. R. J. O'Neill, AO.
Director-General, J. Saynor.
Deputy Director-Generals, D. Kennedy (*Administration*); N. B. Osborn, OBE (*Operations*).
Directors, R. D. Wilson (*Finance*); A. Coombe (*Works*); P. J. Noakes (*Horticulture*); H. Mackay (*Management Services*); T. F. Penfold (*Personnel*); J. P. D. Gee (*Information and Secretariat*).
Legal Adviser and Solicitor, G. C. Reddie.
Hon. Artistic Adviser, Prof. Sir Peter Shepheard, CBE.
Hon. Botanical Adviser, Prof. G. T. Prance, D.Phil., FLS.

Imperial War Graves Endowment Fund

Trustees, Gen. Sir Robert Ford, GCB, CBE; H. U. A. Lambert; The Lord Remnant, CVO.
Hon. Secretary to the Trustees, R. D. Wilson.

COUNTRYSIDE COMMISSION
John Dower House, Crescent Place,
Cheltenham, Glos. GL50 3RA
[0242–521381]

The Countryside Commission is an independent agency set up in 1968 to promote the conservation and enhancement of landscape beauty in England and Wales, to encourage the provision and improvement of facilities in the countryside for enjoyment, including the need to secure access for open air recreation. Since April 1982 the Commission has been funded by annual grant from the Department of the Environment. Members of the Commission are appointed by the Secretary of State for the Environment.

Since April 1, 1991, the Countryside Commission's responsibilities in Wales have been discharged by the new Countryside Council for Wales.
Chairman, John Johnson.
Director General (G3), A. A. C. Phillips.
Directors (G5), R. Clarke (*Policy*); M. J. Kirby (*Operations*); M. Taylor (*Resources*).
Deputy Director (*Operations*) (G6), D. E. Coleman.
National Heritage Adviser, P. Walshe.
Head of Corporate Planning (G7), T. Robinson.
Head of Land Use Branch (G7), R. Roberts.
Head of Recreation and Access Branch (G7), J. W. B. Worth.
Head of Communications Branch (G7), C. Pugsley.
Head of Finance and Establishments (G7), V. Ellis.
Head of National Parks and Planning Branch (G7), R. Lloyd.
Head of Environmental Protection Branch (G7), I. Mitchell.
Regional Officers (G7), K. Buchanan, (*Newcastle*); Dr M. Carroll (*Cambridge*); Dr S. A. Bucknall (*Leeds*); E. Holdaway (*Bristol*); R. T. Thomas (*Manchester*); H. McIlwaine, L. Leeson (*London*); F. S. Walmsley (*Birmingham*).
Special Initiatives, Dr M. Rawson (*Community Forests*); S. Bell (*New National Forest*); T. Allen (*Countryside Stewardship*).

COUNTRYSIDE COMMISSION FOR SCOTLAND
Battleby, Redgorton, Perth, PH1 3EW
[0738–27921]

The Commission was established under the Countryside (Scotland) Act, 1967, with functions for the provision, development and improvement of facilities for the enjoyment of the Scottish countryside, and for the conservation and enhancement of its natural beauty and amenity.

From April 1, 1992, the Countryside Commission for Scotland will merge with the Nature Conservancy Council for Scotland to create a new agency, Scottish Natural Heritage (*see* p. 358).
Chairman, J. R. Carr, CBE (*part-time*).
Commissioners, J. M. S. Arnott (*Vice-Chairman*); Prof. C. H. Gimingham; Q. Brown; R. B. Cowe, MBE; R. D. Cramond, CBE; Mrs S. Harvey; A. W. Henry; E. Langmuir, MBE; I. Miller; Dr W. E. S. Mutch; Prof. J. C. Smyth, OBE; W. M. Turnbull; Dr A. Watson.
Director, D. Campbell.
Asst. Directors, J. M. Fladmark (*Planning*); J. R. Turner (*Research and Development*); M. A. Payne (*Communications and Training*); W. T. Band (*Finance and Administration*); R. I. Fairley (*Policy Officer*).

COUNTRYSIDE COUNCIL FOR WALES (CYNGOR CEFN GWLAD CYMRU)
Plas Penrhos, Fford Penrhos, Bangor, Gwynedd
LL57 2LQ
[0248-37044]

The Countryside Council for Wales took over the functions of the Nature Conservancy Council in Wales and the Countryside Commission in Wales on April 1, 1991. It is accountable to the Secretary of State for Wales and exists to promote the conservation and enhancement of the quality of the Welsh landscape and to encourage opportunities for public access and enjoyment of the counryside.
Chairman, E. M. W. Griffith, CBE.
Chief Executive, I. Mercer.

COVENT GARDEN MARKET AUTHORITY
Covent House, New Covent Garden Market,
SW8 5NX
[071–720 2211]

The Covent Garden Market Authority is constituted under the Covent Garden Market Acts, 1961 to 1966, the members being appointed by the Minister of Agriculture, Fisheries and Food. The Authority owns and operates the 56-acre New Covent Garden Markets (fruit, vegetable, flowers) which have been trading since 1974.
Chairman, W. P. Bowman, OBE (*part-time*).
Members (*part-time*), P. J. Hunt; E. I. Kingston; J. A. Harvey; R. Smith, OBE; Sir Peter Reynolds, CBE.
General Manager, Dr P. M. Liggins.
Secretary, P. R. Taylor.

CRIMINAL INJURIES COMPENSATION BOARD
Blythswood House, 200 West Regent Street,
Glasgow G2 4SW
[041–221 0945]
LONDON OFFICE: Whittington House,
19 Alfred Place, WC1E 7LG
[071–636 9501 and 071–636 2812]

The Board was constituted in 1964 to administer the Government scheme for *ex gratia* payments of compensation to victims of crimes of violence.

Chairman, The Lord Carlisle of Bucklow, PC, QC (*part-time*) £24,050
Members, J. F. A. Archer, QC; Sir Derek Bradbeer, OBE; D. Brennan, QC; D. Calcutt, QC; H. Carlisle, QC; B. W. Chedlow, QC; J. Cherry, QC; Miss B. Cooper, QC; Miss D. Cotton, QC; J. D. Crowley, QC; T. Dawson, QC; T. A. K. Drummond, QC; C. Fawcett, QC; W. Gage, QC; B. Green, QC; G. M. Hamilton, QC; Sir Arthur Hoole; J. Kingham; J. Law, QC; M. E. Lewer, QC; J. Leighton Williams, QC; C. Lindsay, QC; Lord Macaulay of Bragar, QC; L. McCreery; D. MacKay, QC; Sir Denis Marshall; Mrs B. Mills, QC; Sir John Palmer; I. M. S. Park, CBE; T. Preston, QC; Miss S. Ritchie, QC; D. B. Robertson, QC; C. Seagroatt, QC; L. S. Shields, QC; Mrs J. Smith, QC; R. Smith, QC; E. Stone, QC; D. M. Thomas, OBE; D. O. Thomas, QC; P. Weitzman, QC; Sir David West Russell; C. H. Whitby, QC.
Secretary and Solicitor, D. J. White.

CROFTERS COMMISSION
4–6 Castle Wynd, Inverness IV2 3EQ
[0463–237231]

The Crofters Commission was established by Act of Parliament in 1955 and is responsible for re-organizing, developing and regulating crofting in the seven crofting (and former county) areas of Argyll, Caithness, Inverness, Orkney, Ross and Cromarty, Shetland and Sutherland. The Commission keeps under review all matters relating to crofting, advises the Secretary of State for Scotland on crofting matters and liaises with other relevant bodies. The Commission also administers the Crofting Counties Agricultural Grants (Scotland) Scheme 1972.
Chairman, H. A. M. Maclean.
Members (*part-time*), B. T. Hunter; D. A. Morrison; P. Morrison; D. Macdonald; A. Cameron; W. Ritchie.
Secretary (G6), A. Johnston.

CROWN AGENTS FOR OVERSEA GOVERNMENTS AND ADMINISTRATIONS
St Nicholas House, St Nicholas Road, Sutton, Surrey, SM1 1EL
[081–643 3311]

The Crown Agents act on behalf of governments and public authorities in the developing world. Incorporated by Act of Parliament, they provide commercial, financial and professional services to public sector authorities and the major international development agencies. They do not act for individuals or for commercial concerns in the private sector.
Chairman, D. H. Probert.
Managing Director, P. F. Berry.

CROWN ESTATE
16 Carlton House Terrace, SW1Y 5AH
[071–210 3000]

The land revenues of the Crown in England and Wales have been collected on the public account since 1760, when George III surrendered them and received a fixed annual payment or Civil List. At the time of the surrender the gross revenues amounted to about £89,000 and the net return to about £11,000.
In the year ended March 31, 1991, the gross income from the Crown Estate totalled £106,000,000. The sum of £61,000,000 was paid to the Exchequer in 1990–91 as surplus revenue.
The land revenues in Ireland have been carried to the Consolidated Fund since 1820; from April 1, 1923, as regards Southern Ireland, they have been collected and administered by the Irish Government.
The land revenues in Scotland were transferred to the Crown Estate Commissioners in 1833.

First Commissioner and Chairman (*part-time*), The Earl of Mansfield and Mansfield.
Second Commissioner and Chief Executive (G2), C. K. Howes.
Commissioners (*part-time*), R. B. Caws, CBE; P. Sober; G. D. I. Lillingston, CBE; J. N. C. James, CBE; A. S. Macdonald, CBE; J. H. M. Norris, CBE.
Deputy Chief Executive, H. B. Clarke.
Corporate Services Manager, M. E. Beckwith.
Crown Estate Surveyor, C. F. Hynes.
Asset Managers (*Urban Estates*), M. W. Dillon; J. S. Ellingford; B. T. O'Connoll; M. Tree.
Housing Manager, R. Wyatt.
Property Services and Technical Manager, P. Shearmur.
Head of Valuation and Investment Analysis, R. Spence.
Head of Building Services, R. Turner.
Business Manager, Agricultural Estates, R. J. Mulholland.
Asset Manager, Agricultural Estates, J. Stumbke.
Business Manager, Marine Estates, F. G. Parrish.
Accountant and Receiver-General, D. E. G. Griffiths.
Information Systems Manager, D. Kingston-Smith.
Head of Internal Audit, J. E. Ford.
Head of Finance Branch, J. G. Lelliott.
Legal Adviser, M. L. Davies.
Deputy Legal Adviser, H. Turnsek.
Solicitors, A. S. Dawson; J. B. Postgate; R. T. Hayward; M. Drayton; P. Horner; D. R. Apthorpe.
Senior Legal Assistant, M. A. J. Cordingley.
Head of Personnel Group, R. J. Blake.

Scotland
10 Charlotte Square, Edinburgh EH2 4BR
[031–226 2741]

Crown Estate Receiver for Scotland, M. J. Gravestock.
Solicitor, D. Clark.
Planning Adviser, Dr P. McGovern.

Windsor Estate
The Great Park, Windsor, Berks. SL4 2HT
[0753-860222]

Surveyor and Deputy Ranger, A. R. Wiseman, MVO.
Keeper of Gardens, J. Bond.

BOARD OF CUSTOMS AND EXCISE
New King's Beam House, 22 Upper Ground, SE1 9PJ
[071–620 1313]

Commissioners of Customs were first appointed in 1671 and housed by the King in London. The present 'Long Room' in the Custom House, Lower Thames Street, EC3, replaced that built by Charles II and was rebuilt after destruction by fire in 1718 and 1814. The Excise Department was formerly under the Inland Revenue Department and was amalgamated with the Customs Department on April 1, 1909.
HM Customs and Excise is responsible for collecting and administering customs and excise duties and value added tax, and advises the Chancellor of the Exchequer on any matters connected with them. The Department is also responsible for preventing and detecting the evasion of revenue laws and for enforcing a range of prohibitions and restrictions on the importation of certain classes of goods. In addition, the Department undertakes certain agency work on behalf of other departments, including the compilation of UK overseas trade statistics from customs import and export documents.
(For *Salaries*, *see* page 293).

The Board
Chairman (G1), Sir Brian Unwin, KCB.

Private Secretaries, S. Harlen; Miss J. C. Huneburg.
Deputy Chairmen (*G2*), Mrs V. P. M. Strachan, CB; P. Jefferson Smith.
Commissioners (*G3*), D. J. Howard; A. W. Russell; Ms D. J. Seammen; P. R. H. Allen; D. F. O. Battle; A. C. Sawyer.

Headquarters Office

Head of Information Technology (*G4*), A. G. H. Paynter.
Assistant Secretaries (*G5*), P. Kent; D. A. Walton; J. W. Tracey; M. R. Brown; I. Walton; A. Killikelly; M. J. Eland; M. Peach; K. M. Romanski; Ms D. Barrett; B. E. G. Banks; J. P. Bone; D. C. Hewett; A. Ferguson; A. F. Cross-Rudkin; C. J. Holloway; P. Trevett; B. G. Dawbarn; Mrs M. Smith; J. Campbell; V. C. Whittington; P. A. Blomfield; C. Arnott; D. P. Child; J. Strachan; R. Kellaway; M. F. Knox; M. W. Summers; F. A. D. Rush; W. L. Parker; L. I. Stark; A. P. Allen; J. Meyler.
Head of Information (*G7*), Ms L. J. Sinclair.

VAT Central Unit

Controller (*G5*), M. J. Wardle.
Deputy Controller (*G6*), B. Smith.

Solicitor's Office

Solicitor (*G2*), M. L. Saunders, CB.
Principal Assistant Solicitors (*G3*), G. F. Butt; R. D. S. Wylie.
Assistant Solicitors (*G5*), M. Michael; M. A. Cooper; D. E. T. S. Keefe; M. C. K. Gasper; Miss A. E. Bolt; D. Pratt; Miss S. G. Linton; J. A. Quin; I. D. Napper; G. Fotherby; G. W. H. McFarlane; D. J. C. McIntyre; D. M. North.

Accountant and Comptroller-General's Office

Accountant and Comptroller-General (*G5*), P. A. Blomfield.
Deputy Accountants-General (*G6*), M. Deedman; G. B. Fox.

Statistical Office

Controller (*G5*), A. H. Cowley.

Investigation Division

Chief Investigation Officer (*G5*), F. D. Tweddle.

Collectors of Customs and Excise (G5)

England and Wales

Birmingham, R. A. Flavill.
Dover, R. Crossley.
East Anglia, R. C. Shephard.
East Midlands, M. D. Patten.
Leeds, W. J. G. Prollins.
Liverpool, C. Roberts.
London Airports, J. Bugge.
London Central, Mrs F. Boardman.
London North and West, C. A. Bray.
London Port, R. L. H. Lawrence.
London South, T. S. Archer.
Manchester, J. C. Barnard.
Northampton, P. E. St Quinton.
Northern England, J. McKenzie.
Reading, A. Bowen.
Southampton, C. J. Packman.
South Wales and the Borders, W. I. Stuttle.
South West England, P. B. Grange.

Scotland

Edinburgh, W. F. Coghill.
Glasgow and Clyde, T. F. Jessop.

Northern Ireland

Belfast, R. N. McAfee.

OFFICE OF THE DATA PROTECTION REGISTRAR
Springfield House, Water Lane, Wilmslow, Cheshire SK9 5AX
[Admin: 0625–535711; Enquiries: 0625–535777]

The Office of the Data Protection Registrar was created by the Data Protection Act, 1984. It is the Registrar's duty to compile and maintain the Register of Data Users and Computer Bureaux and provide facilities for members of the public to examine the Register; to promote observance of the data protection principles; to consider complaints made by data subjects; to disseminate information about the Act; to encourage the production of codes of practice by trade associations and other bodies; to guide data users in complying with the data protection principles; to co-operate with other parties to the Council of Europe Convention and act as UK authority for the purposes of Article 13 of the Convention; to report annually to Parliament on the performance of his functions under the Act.
Registrar, E. J. Howe, CBE.

MINISTRY OF DEFENCE
See pp. 394–6

DESIGN COUNCIL
28 Haymarket, SW1Y 4SU
[071–839 8000]

The Design Council's aim is to improve the design of British products and hence their competitiveness by: advising companies on up-to-date practice in engineering and industrial design; presenting the annual British Design Awards; publishing information to help manufacturers, designers, and others professionally involved in design; and promoting improvements in design education and training at all levels. There is a Design Centre in London and offices in Glasgow, Leeds, Newcastle upon Tyne, Belfast, Wolverhampton, Manchester and Treforest in Wales. The Design Council is funded partly by a Government grant-in-aid and partly by earned revenues.
Chairman, Sir Simon Hornby.
Director, I. Owen.

THE DUCHY OF CORNWALL
10 Buckingham Gate, SW1E 6LA
[071–834 7346]

The Duchy of Cornwall was instituted by Edward III in 1337 for the support of his eldest son, Edward, the Black Prince, and since 1503 the eldest surviving son of the Sovereign has, as heir apparent, succeeded to the dukedom by inheritance. As the oldest of the English duchies, it has enjoyed a long association with the Crown. Before elevation to a dukedom, it was an earldom from 1227, when Richard, King of the Romans and younger brother of Henry III, was created Earl of Cornwall.

The Prince's Council

HRH The Prince of Wales, KG, KT, GCB; Hon. Sir John Baring, KCVO; (*Lord Warden of the Stannaries*); The Earl Cairns (*Receiver General*); R. J. A. Carnwath, QC (*Attorney-General to the Prince of Wales*); D. W. N. Landale (*Secretary and Keeper of the Records*); The Earl of Shelburne; Cdr. R. J. Aylard, RN; J. E. Pugsley; J. N. C. James, CBE; A. M. J. Galsworthy; C. Howes.

Other Officers of the Duchy of Cornwall

Auditors, Sir Jeffery Bowman; P. L. Ainger; H. Hughes.
Sheriff (1991–92), D. C. Treffry, OBE.

THE DUCHY OF LANCASTER
Lancaster Place, Strand, WC2E 7ED
[071–836 8277]

The estates and jurisdiction known as the Duchy and County Palatine of Lancaster have been attached to the Crown since 1399, when John of Gaunt's son came to the throne as Henry IV. As the Lancaster inheritance it goes back to 1265. Edward III erected Lancashire into a County Palatine in 1351.

Chancellor of the Duchy of Lancaster, THE RT. HON. CHRISTOPHER PATTEN, MP.

Private Secretary, R. Canniff.

Attorney-General and Attorney and Serjeant within the County Palatine of Lancaster, J. F. Parker, QC.

Receiver-General, Maj. Sir Shane Blewitt, KCVO.

Vice-Chancellor, The Hon. Mr Justice Morritt, CVO.

Clerk of the Council and Keeper of Records, M. K. Ridley.

Solicitor, I. J. Dicker.

Chief Clerk, P. C. Clarke, CVO.

ECONOMIC AND SOCIAL RESEARCH COUNCIL
Polaris House, North Star Avenue,
Swindon SN2 1UJ
[0793–413000]

The ESRC is an independent, government-funded body established by Royal Charter in 1965. It supports research into economic life and social behaviour carried out in universities, polytechnics and research centres in Britain. The Council carries out its role by awarding research grants, by initiating research and research contracts, by funding designated research centres, and by awarding postgraduate studentships and bursaries. In addition, the Council provides advice and disseminates knowledge on the social sciences.

Chairman, Prof. H. Newby.

Secretary, W. Solesbury.

For research centres of the Economic and Social Science Research Council, *see* pp. 964–5.

DEPARTMENT OF EDUCATION AND SCIENCE
Elizabeth House, York Road, SE1 7PH
[071–934 9000]

The Government Department of Education was, until the establishment of a separate office, a Committee of the Privy Council appointed in 1839 to supervise the distribution of certain grants which had been made by Parliament since 1834. The Act of 1899 established the Board of Education, with a President and Parliamentary Secretary, and created a Consultative Committee. The Education Act of 1944 established the Ministry of Education. In April 1964 the office of the Minister of Science was combined with the Ministry to form the Department of Education and Science.

(For *Salaries*, *see* page 293.)

Secretary of State for Education and Science, THE RT. HON. KENNETH CLARKE, QC, MP.

Private Secretary, C. Bienkowska.

Parliamentary Private Secretary, P. Oppenheim, MP.

Minister of State, TIMOTHY EGGAR, MP.

Private Secretary, Ms C. Durkin.

Parliamentary Under Secretaries of State, ALAN HOWARTH, CBE, MP; MICHAEL FALLON, MP; ROBERT ATKINS, MP (*Minister for Sport*).

Permanent Secretary (*G1*), Sir John Caines, KCB.

Private Secretary, R. Read.

Deputy Secretaries (*G2*), N. W. Stuart, CB; J. M. M. Vereker; A. J. Wiggins.

Under Secretaries (*G3*), M. M. Capey (*Director of*

Establishments); A. E. D. Chamier; C. A. Clark; J. E. Coleman; R. N. Ricks (*Legal Adviser*); D. M. Forester; J. C. Hedger; R. D. Horne; D. G. Libby; B. M. Norbury; N. J. Sanders (*Accountant General*); C. H. Saville; N. Summers; D. A. Wilkinson; (G4) D. Allnut.

Chief Architect (*G4*), P. Benwell.

Schools Branch 1

Assistant Secretaries (*G5*), M. J. Richardson; Miss S. L. Scales; A. D. Adamson.

Principals (*G7*), B. C. Willett; M. E. Malt; C. P. Barnham; A. G. Short; T. C. Tarrant; Miss L. M. Clarke; N. R. Flint; P. V. D. Swift; M. J. Rabarts; Mrs A. C. Jeffery; C. Dee; R. S. Daruwalla.

Schools Branch 2

Assistant Secretaries (*G5*), Miss D. C. Fordham; Ms J. F. Cramphorn; A. J. Shaw.

Senior Principal (*G6*), P. S. Lewis.

Principals (*G7*), C. Dowe; I. C. Loveless; Mrs P. A. Masters; Mrs J. D. Nisbet; N. Cornwell; D. Noble; G. A. Holley; I. M. Hughes; A. W. Wilshaw; Mrs S. C. West; M. Spearing.

Schools Branch 3

Assistant Secretaries (*G5*), Miss A. J. Benham; M. B. Baker; H. W. B. Davies; Mrs C. M. Chattaway.

Principals (*G7*), Mrs S. G. Evans; Mrs S. Jetha; A. B. Thompson; Mrs M. E. P. Farthing; R. A. V. Jacobs; J. Webb; Mrs J. Baker; D. A. Jones; M. Wardle; Mrs S. G. Murton; Mrs A. Curtis.

Schools Branch 4

Assistant Secretaries (*G5*), Miss A. Stewart; A. G. B. Woollard; Miss P. Laidlaw; R. L. Smith.

Senior Principal (*G6*), L. Webb.

Principals (*G7*), Miss N. Bartman; S. Hillier; R. Troedson; S. E. Burt; J. P. Moore; Mrs P. Bailey; P. Daglish; S. James; P. Otley; G. D. Sandeman.

Architects and Building Branch

Chief Architect (*G4*), P. Benwell.

Deputy Chief Architect (*G5*), A. J. Branton.

Chief Quantity Surveyor (*G5*), B. G. Whitehouse.

Superintending Architects, M. S. Hacker; G. J. Parker; J. J. Wilson; D. H. Griffin.

Principals (*G7*), K. L. R. English; A. G. Myatt.

Principal Research Officer, Dr G. B. Kenny.

Principal Architects, E. C. Bissell; Mrs D. Holt; Miss E. J. Lloyd-Jones, OBE; P. Lenessen; D. S. Nightingale; Miss B. M. T. Sanders; D. F. Wicks; A. J. Benson-Wilson; J. R. C. Brook; A. C. Thompson.

Principal Quantity Surveyors, A. A. Jones; W. Horsnell; M. E. H. Sturt.

Principal Engineer, M. J. Patel.

Principal Furniture Designer, N. J. Carter.

SPTO Architects, G. E. Hughes; Miss L. Watson; T. J. Williamson; W. Beadling; R. H. Bishop; W. A. Fletcher; A. V. Brock; F. G. Cassidy; K. Goften; S. A. Legg.

SPTO Quantity Surveyors, T. W. A. Carden; G. Wonnacott.

SPTO Engineer, R. L. Daniels.

Further and Higher Education Branch 1

Assistant Secretaries (*G5*), A. Clarke; E. R. Morgan.

Senior Principal (*G6*), Dr E. J. Herbert.

Principals (*G7*), K. Baxter; A. Sevier; W. Smyth; M. P. Markus; P. Cohen.

Further and Higher Education Branch 2

Assistant Secretaries (*G5*), R. D. Hull; Miss M. D'Armenia; S. T. Crowne.

Principals (*G7*), A. J. Coles; K. Davey; G. H. N. Evans; P. W. Fulford-Jones; Miss C. E. Treen; D.

Barwick; M. P. Howarth; E. G. Hartman; Ms S. P. Gane; Ms C. E. Dale; B. D. Glickman.

Further and Higher Education Branch 3

Assistant Secretaries (*G5*), T. B. Jeffery; M. D. Phipps; A. J. Wye; J. S. Street; S. R. Williams.
Senior Principal (*G6*), D. I. B. Hardy.
Principals (*G7*), Miss A. Barlow; M. L. Lyons; D. D. Cook; P. S. Sharples; J. K. Bushnell; D. M. Carter; Dr G. Ingle; C. T. Moorcroft; Ms S. A. Gray; R. H. Campbell; J. Abbott; P. V. Chorley; Ms V. Berkeley; E. D. Foster; O. A. Pereira; Mrs M. Pegg; R. M. Johnston.

Science Branch

Assistant Secretaries (*G5*), R. P. Ritzema; P. J. Thorpe; Miss J. P. Partington.
Senior Principal (*G6*), K. D. J. Root.
Principals (*G7*), L. J. R. Dando; D. M. Mainwood; P. J. Hodgman; M. H. Sharpe; J. Adams; C. De Grouchy; Ms A. S. J. Frost; M. McBride; D. K. Timms.

Information Branch

Assistant Secretary (*G5*), J. W. Coe.
Senior Principal Information Officer (*G6*), K. B. Kerslake.
Chief Information Officer (*G7*), M. Paterson.

Teachers Pay and General Branch

Assistant Secretaries (*G5*), R. W. Chattaway; A. J. Sargent.
Principals (*G7*), M. Barker; T. P. Franklin; M. Thompson; J. A. Tarsh.

Pensions Branch

Mowden Hall, Staindrop Road,
Darlington, Co. Durham DL3 9BG
[0325–460155]

Assistant Secretary (*G5*), J. Wilde.
Principals (*G7*), D. G. Halladay; P. M. Bleasdale; A. Allison.

Teachers Supply, Training and International Relations Branch

Assistant Secretaries (*G5*), B. Bekhradnia; S. R. C. Jones; J. W. Whitaker.
Principals (*G7*), J. C. Sheridan; Ms E. Slater; Mrs G. W. Dishart; S. A. Mellor; R. J. Wood; Miss L. Hanmer.

Information Systems Branch

Assistant Secretary (*G5*), A. F. Cowan.
Senior Principals (*G6*), P. D. Gott; A. K. C. Gibson; N. Rudd.
Principals (*G7*), B. Lillburn; Mrs N. A. T. Malt; Mrs J. M. Craggs; M. Midwood; A. P. Thompson; D. Craggs; E. S. Simpson; J. Winkle.

Analytical Services Branch

Chief Statisticians (*G5*), J. W. Gardner; H. M. Dale; R. B. Ladley; B. D. Cullen.
Statisticians (*G7*), A. J. Barnett; R. K. Jain; S. N. Kew; J. Pascoe; T. C. Knight; M. J. Davidson; N. Rudoe; Mrs H. E. Evans; G. W. Goodwin; S. K. Cook; Miss A. C. Kennedy.

Legal Branch

Legal Adviser (*G3*), R. Ricks.
Assistant Legal Advisers (*G5*), D. J. Aries; A. D. Preston; M. Harris.
Assistant Solicitor (*G6*), Ms J. L. C. Brooks.
Senior Legal Assistants (*G6*), N. P. Beach; S. T. Harker.

Library

Chief Librarian, J. L. Birch.

Finance Branch

Assistant Secretaries (*G5*), M. C. Stark; Mrs H. M. Williams; P. F. Slade.
Senior Principal (*G6*), P. J. Edwards (*Assistant Accountant General*).
Principals (*G7*), P. L. Jones; D. R. Pollard; B. G. Townsend; Miss S. A. Clarke; R. J. Gardner; S. A. Marston; S. N. Jardine; S. M. Philpotts; K. Fleay; J. Browning.

HM Inspectorate (England)

Senior Chief Inspector (*G2*), vacant.
Chief Inspectors (*G4*), J. A. Everson; T. P. Melia; Miss A. C. Millett; A. J. Rose; B. D. Short; Mrs M. M. Smart; M. J. Tomlinson; Mrs S. P. Twite.
Divisional Inspectors (*G5*), R. G. Booth; R. J. Brake; B. A. Chaplin; E. Scott; D. E. Walker.
Staff Inspectors (*G5*), Mrs C. A. Agambar; D. W. Airey; T. H. Bennetts; P. L. Bradbury; E. F. H. Brittain; P. Brown; R. A. Callender; M. J. Caton; B. J. Chopping; Miss D. Chorley; P. R. Clarke; M. J. Convey; D. A. Cormican; A. T. Cox; L. S. Crickmore; Miss K. Cross; D. A. Denegri; P. D. Edwards; Mrs V. E. Emmett; Mrs G. Everson; J. H. Fairhurst; Ms C. Farrell; D. Fraser; G. R. Frater; A. Gibson; G. Goldstein; V. Green; R. H. Griffiths; R. A. S. Hennessey; G. A. Hicks; P. Highfield; M. W. Himsworth; D. G. Labon; Miss B. J. Lewis; E. R. B. Little; M. R. E. Mealing; B. E. Merton; R. W. Mycock; Ms S. M. Nicholls; G. T. Peaker; P. J. Pearson; Miss J. M. Phillips; C. Potts; W. J. Rea; C. M. Richards; G. Robson; P. L. Seaborne; P. Singh; D. E. Soulsby; Mrs B. Staniland; J. Stanyer; D. W. Taylor; A. F. Thomas; J. V. Townshend; D. R. Trainor; A. D. J. Turner; Mrs J. W. Turner; J. R. Ungoed-Thomas; D. L. West; D. G. Whittaker; C. C. B. Wightwick; J. B. Willcock; T. Wylie; F. P. Young.
HM Inspectors (*G6*), W. Agnew; Mrs G. M. V. Alexander; Mrs C. Anderson-Frost; Ms J. C. Andrae; P. L. Armitage; D. G. Arrell; A. Ashworth; D. Baillie; W. G. Bakehouse; Mrs C. A. Baker; Mrs E. M. Baker; Mrs O. M. Baldock; Mrs M. T. Banbury; C. Banks; Miss D. M. L. Barlow; J. H. Barnes; Mrs J. M. Barnes; G. Barratt; R. E. Barrett; Ms E. P. Baxell; Mrs I. M. B. Beckett; J. F. Bennett; J. Bennetts; N. Blackett; Ms S. B. Blatton; A. J. Boddington; Mrs C. M. Bond; Mrs E. J. Boucher; Miss E. Bourne; Mrs M. T. Boyd-Clarke; D. J. Bradbury; M. H. Bradley; Miss P. A. Brain; T. E. Brand; Mrs H. S. Bridge; F. Brook; Mrs J. M. Brookes; Miss C. M. Brooks; Mrs M. E. Brooks; A. W. Brown; Mrs M. A. Buckingham; M. J. Buckley; P. N. Bufton; Miss K. Bull; J. M. Burgess; Mrs G. M. Burke; D. R. Butler; Ms M. E. Caistor; M. J. Campbell; P. Candlish; N. Carr; B. Chandler; M. Charnley; Ms J. A. Cheong; Mrs M. S. Christie; D. Clare; C. R. Clark; P. Clarke; G. Clay; R. S. W. Clements; D. G. Close; D. A. Coe; J. E. M. Cohn; B. Colbeck; Mrs M. E. Coleman; M. J. Collier; Mrs P. M. Collins; Mrs M. A. Cooke; P. Cradock; G. Cranmer; Mrs G. K. Crawford; J. Creedy; M. Cribb; Ms O. Cupid; Ms B. J. Cusdin; D. K. Dana; C. M. Davies; P. A. Davies; M. C. Davis; R. V. Davis; J. Dawson; T. Dickinson, OBE; T. Dillon; A. Dobson; Ms C. R. Donoughue; J. A. S. Dossett; P. W. Dougill; M. A. Dowling; R. G. Dyke; K. H. Dyson; Mrs M. E. Eade; Mrs C. Elliott; D. L. Elliott; J. A. Elliott; L. J. Ellis; M. A. Emery; Mrs J. E. Ensing; C. B. L. Evans; Mrs B. E. Fawcett; Ms F. D. Findlay; B. P. Fitzgerald; J. Fitzpatrick; I. G. Forrest; D. H. M. Foster; Ms M. C. Fraser; P. S. Friend; B. Frost; C. C. Frost; D. J. Frost; B. S. Furniss; P. Gannon; D. A. Gardiner; V. Gardiner; Ms J. M. Gaukroger; I. Gera; Mrs P. Gibbon; Mrs J. E. A. Gifford; K. Gilbert; Mrs J. M. Giles; G. A.

Gill; C. R. Gillings; C. Goodhead; Mrs E. M.
Goodwin; C. D. Gould; C. Goulding; D. I. Grant; J.
D. Green; N. M. J. Green; B. Gregson-Allcott; N.
Grenyer; M. Griffiths; P. Griffiths; S. Grounds;
Mrs F. Hadley; Mrs C. E. Hague; E. E. J. Haidon;
D. S. Hale; M. Halle; D. J. Halligan; N. J. Hallmark;
J. A. Hamer; P. G. Hancock; Ms S. C. Hands; J. N.
Hardwick; J. S. Hardwick; R. A. Hargreaves; B. R.
Harris; S. M. Harrison; D. J. Hart; R. Hartley; A.
Harvey; R. C. Harvey; Mrs G. M. Hayes; G. M.
Hearnshaw; Miss L. M. Hencher; M. L. Hening;
Mrs J. S. Herbert; J. A. Hetrich; D. Hibbert; J. M.
Hibbs; J. F. H. Hilbourne; Mrs E. M. Hill; I. A. E.
Hill; W. J. Hill; D. Hinchcliffe; D. G. Holford; T.
Holland; Ms M. H. Hollingsworth; J. R. Holmes; C.
Hooper; F. X. Horan; M. J. Horn; J. E. Hosegood;
D. J. House; B. A. F. Hubbard; B. R. Hudson; V. C.
Hughes; Ms D. M. Hunt; J. E. Hunt; P. J. Hunt; J.
E. Hurley; J. B. Huskins; Mrs M. A. V. Huxley; J.
S. Ingleson; P. F. J. Irvine; A. R. Ivatts; M. J. Ive;
N. J. Jackson; H. A. James; R. K. James; T. M.
Jardine; B. D. Jelly; R. L. Johns; Miss S. H. Johns;
P. W. R. Johnson; H. B. Joicey; B. Jones; Mrs M.
E. Jones; M. G. Jones; P. R. Jones; M. Jutsum; Mrs
G. N. Kanji; R. Kapadia; W. D. Kaye; Mrs A. C.
Keelan-Towner; M. Kerrigan; T. J. Key; M. A.
Khan; B. L. King; D. P. King; K. King; A. V.
Kirwan; D. Knighton; J. B. Knox; A. J. Lacey; G.
N. E. Lageard; Miss E. J. M. Layson; D. Lewis; D.
F. Lewis, OBE; D. J. Lewis; Mrs J. M. Lingard; G.
R. Little; A. W. Littlewood; W. K. G. Lloyd; A. B.
Lomax; R. Long; J. A. Low; T. L. Lusty; Mrs S.
Lyons; J. A. Mabey; Mrs E. M. McAndrew; B.
McCafferty; C. McCall; Mrs H. M. Macdonald; D.
G. McEnhill; D. C. McIntosh; Ms J. D. McKenley;
M. McLaughlin; Miss T. McLaughlin; Mrs P. R.
Maclay; Mrs J. McLean; G. W. McLeman; I. A.
McNally; Mrs H. P. McVeigh; M. E.Madden; Mrs
J. P. Maddick; J. R. Marriott; G. D. Marrow; E. S.
Martin; Mrs M. M. Martin; W. P. Massam; Miss E.
M. Matthews; J. E. Mattick; B. R. Meech; G.
Merlane; K. Miller; H. Millington; Ms J. I. Mills;
P. Milton; Miss H. A. Moffat; Ms J. L. Mokades; A.
R. H. Monk; D. Moon; D. L. Moore; P. R. Moore;
K. J. Morgan; S. H. Morris; Mrs A. M. Mukhopa-
dhyay; Miss F. A. Munday; Mrs A. A. H. Murrell;
P. Muschamp; C. Needham; A. J. Nisbett; P. M.
Nixon; M. Norman; K. Oldfield; Mrs G. I. Oldham;
P. I. Orr; B. C. O'Sullivan; Mrs S. O'Sullivan; W.
E. Owen; H. M. Page; R. L. Page-Jones; Mrs E. I.
Pagliacci; A. C. Parfitt; D. J. Parks; J. M. Parsons;
Miss E. L. Passmore; I. M. Paterson; P. Piddock;
M. W. A. Pitts; E. A. Pollard; R. D. Ponchaud; M.
R. Potter; C. P. Power; Mrs B. F. Pratley; Mrs M.
P. Pryce; M. E. Pullee; P. C. Purdy; C. J. Redman;
Mrs J. F. C. Reeves; J. D. Reid; J. C. Richardson;
B. Roberts; A. S. Robertson; C. Robinson; I. A.
Rodger; S. J. A. Rogers; Mrs M. C. Rosen; A. C.
Rowe; C. Rowe; M. J. Ryder; W. H. Salaman; Mrs
J. Sartain; Mrs K. J. Saunders; B. Sayer; Ms M.
Sayer; J. C. W. Schenk; D. J. Scott; Ms S. M. Scott;
G. W. Searle; Mrs P. J. Sellwood; R. V. L. Shannon;
D. T. V. Sharman; D. I. Shelton; R. Shippam; A. R.
Shirley; K. A. Shooter; D. Shortland; Mrs V. M.
Sida; P. J. Silvester; Mrs D. E. Simmonds; D.
Singleton; G. Sleightholme; B. J. Smeaton; B. J.
Smith; G. K. Smith; P. J. C. Smith; P. R. Smith;
Ms S. P. Soul-Gray; Mrs M. F. Spence; J. D.
Stannard; Ms O. M. Stannard; D. Starling; J. M.
Steels; J. B. Stevenson; Mrs M. T. Stiles; M. M.
Stone; R. Storrs; Ms M. E. Stride; R. Summersby;
D. P. Swain; A. Sykes; D. W. Sylvester; Mrs A. M.
Tapsfield; F. Taylor; J. A. Taylor; R. S. Taylor; M.
D. Thirkell; Mrs M. E. Thomas; D. L. Thorburn; J.
Tierney; D. S. Tobin; M. J. Todd; P. N. Toft; Ms E.
Tombs; B. D. Tomkins; J. E. Trickey; Ms L. J.
Tumman; G. C. Turner; T. Turner; E. A. Vallis; M.

Wardlow; Mrs A. P. Warren; R. K. Warren; N. G.
Warwick; J. M. Watson; M. R. Webb; Mrs J. M.
Webberley; R. R. Weir; D. J. Wells; K. J. Wheeldon;
R. Whitburn; Miss F. White; J. White; F. White-
man; Mrs A. J. Whitlam; Ms S. M. Wiles; J. R.
Williams; K. G. Williams; Mrs S. A. Williams; Mrs
M. H. Williamson; G. R. Wilson; J. D. Woodhouse;
Mrs S. A. Woodroffe; R. D. Woods; J. I. Wragg;
Miss B. M. Wright; D. Wynne; Miss A. P. Yeomans;
R. E. Yorke; A. J. Youngs.

HM Inspectorate Support Services

Principals (G7), C. Boxall; R. C. Knight; R. Dew.

HM Inspectorate (Wales)

(*See* Welsh Office)

Establishments and Organization Branch

Assistant Secretaries (G5), E. B. Granshaw, CBE; Miss
J. Gilbey; Miss C. E. Hodkinson.
Senior Principals (G6), H. H. Barrick; N. J. Beggs; T.
A. H. Tyler.
Principals (G7), C. Bramley; Miss A. F. Brown; K. R.
Fitzgerald; K. M. Miles; D. A. Robins; Mrs M. J.
Lawrence; M. Hipkins; Mrs S. Trundle; H. Tomlin-
son; S. J. Bishop.

OFFICE OF ELECTRICITY REGULATION
Hagley House, Hagley Road,
Birmingham B16 8QG
[021–456 2100]

The Office of Electricity Regulation (OFFER) is a
regulatory body set up under the Electricity Act
1989. It is headed by the Director General of
Electricity Supply, who is independent of Ministerial
control.
Director General of Electricity Supply, Prof. S. C.
Littlechild.
Deputy Director General, Ms P. A. Boys.
Deputy Director General for Scotland, R. N. Irvine.

DEPARTMENT OF EMPLOYMENT
Caxton House, Tothill Street, SW1H 9NF
[071–273 3000]

The Department of Employment is responsible for the
government policy of promoting a competitive and
efficient labour market conducive to the growth of
employment and the reduction of unemployment. Its
main tasks are to help people acquire and improve
their skills and competence for work, to help unemployed people, to promote the creation and growth of
small firms and self-employment, to encourage industries to train their workforce, and to develop tourism.
The Secretary of State for Employment is responsible
for setting the strategic policy framework in consultation with the Secretaries of State for Scotland and
Wales.
  Many of the executive functions carried out in the
Department's area of policy interest are exercised by
separate public agencies reporting to the Secretary
of State for Employment. These include the Health
and Safety Commission and ACAS and, within the
Department, the Employment Service. The training,
enterprise and education functions of the Department are carried out by the Training, Enterprise and
Education Directorate; the responsibility for planning and delivering many government-funded training and enterprise programmes rests with the
network of 82 independent Training and Enterprise
Councils in England and Wales and 22 local enterprise
companies in Scotland (for addresses, see local
telephone directories).
(For **Salaries**, *see* page 293).

Secretary of State for Employment, THE RT. HON. MICHAEL HOWARD, QC, MP.
 Principal Private Secretary (G5), M. Waring.
 Parliamentary Private Secretary, R. King, MP.
Under Secretaries of State, ROBERT JACKSON, MP; ERIC FORTH, MP; THE VISCOUNT ULLSWATER.
 Private Secretaries, A. Loy; M. Daly; Ms C. Pride.
 Special Adviser, B. Baldwin.
 Parliamentary Private Secretary, P. Thurnham, MP.
Parliamentary Clerk, S. J. Loach.
Permanent Secretary (G1), Sir Geoffrey Holland, KCB.
 Private Secretary, Ms S. Morgan.
Deputy Secretaries (G2+), R. Dawe; (G2), G. Reid, CB; Ms J. Bacon.
Legal Adviser (G3), H. R. L. Purse.
Special Advisers, T. Collins; Ms C. Stratton.

The Employment Service

(An executive agency within the Department of Employment.)
Chief Executive (G3+), M. E. G. Fogden.
Deputy Chief Executive (G3), J. Turner.
Director of Field Operations (G4), J. W. Cooper, CBE.
Director of Personnel and Business Services (G4), D. B. Price.
Director of Programmes (G4), M. Emmott.

Training, Enterprise and Education Directorate
Moorfoot, Sheffield S1 4PQ
[0742-753275]

Director General (G2), R. J. Dawe, CB, OBE.
Deputy Director General (G3+), I. A. Johnston.

Education

Director (G3), Mrs V. Bayliss.
Heads of Branches (G5):
 TVEI and Partnerships, J. West.
 Higher Education, G. Macnair.
 Strategy and Further Education, K. Franklin.
 Careers Service, A. G. Davies.

Training, Strategy and Standards

Director (G3), D. Grover.
Heads of Branches (G5/G6):
 Industry Training Organizations, J. Wiltshire.
 Qualifications and Standards, J. Fuller.
 Standards and Methodology, G. Debling.
 Skills Enterprise Unit, E. Galvin.
 Training, Strategy and Secretariat, B. Shaw.

Training and Systems

Director (G4), K. White.
Heads of Branches (G5):
 Budgets, N. Atkinson.
 Learning Systems and Access, R. Wye.
 Training Quality, J. Blizard.
 Europe, M. Brimmer.

Operations (South and East)

Director (G3), J. Surr.
Head of TEC Operations (G5), P. Lauener.

Operations (North and West)

Director (G3), J. Lambert.
Head of Field System (G5), M. Christie.

Youth and Adult Training

Director (G3), S. Loveman.
Heads of Branches (G5):
 Training Credits, G. Dyche.
 Special Needs, and Health and Safety, M. Nicholas.
 TEC Training Strategy, B. Heatley.
 Clients and Delivery, J. Smith.
 Operational Plans, I. Randall.

Business and Enterprise

Director (G4), N. Schofield.
Heads of Branches (G5):
 Business Communications, P. Keen.
 Business and Enterprise, J. Reid.
 Small Firms Policy, Ms S. Newton.

Training Standards Advisory Service

Chief Inspector (G4), D. Tinsley.

Industrial Relations and International Directorate

Director (G2), G. Reid.
International and Tourism Division (G3), L. Lewis.
Industrial Relations Division I (G3), C. Tucker.
Industrial Relations Division II (G3), R. Hillier.
Statistical Services Division (G3), P. Stibbard.
Chief Wages Inspector (G6), C. Beach.
Secretary of Wages Councils, G. Knorpel.

Resources and Strategy Directorate

Director (G2), Ms J. Bacon.
Finance and Resource Management Division (G3), M. Addison.
Economics, Research and Evaluation Division (G3), D. Stanton.
Strategy and Employment Policy Division (G3), D. Normington.
Personnel and Development Division (G3), E. Whybrew.
Information Systems and Management Services Division (G4), P. Makeham.
Information Branch (G5), B. Sutlieff.

DEPARTMENT OF ENERGY
1 Palace Street, SW1E 5HE
[071–238 3000]

The Department of Energy is responsible for the development of government policy in relation to all forms of energy. It also discharges governmental functions connected with the coal and electricity industries. It is responsible for the UK Atomic Energy Authority; is the sponsoring department for the nuclear power industry and is responsible for the development of oil and gas resources on the British sector of the continental shelf. It is the sponsoring department for the oil industry and is responsible for international aspects of energy problems, including relations and co-operation with oil producing countries. The Department is the co-ordinating body for energy efficiency policy and for encouraging the development of new sources of energy.
(For **Salaries,** *see* page 293).

Secretary of State for Energy, THE RT. HON. JOHN WAKEHAM, MP.
 Principal Private Secretary, J. S. Neilson.
 Parliamentary Private Secretary, A. Mitchell, MP.
Parliamentary Under-Secretaries of State, DAVID HEATHCOAT-AMERY, MP; THE HON. COLIN MOYNIHAN, MP.
Permanent Under Secretary of State (G1A), J. R. S. Guinness.
 Private Secretary, Ms M. Jackson.
Deputy Secretary (G2), R. J. Priddle.
Chief Scientific Adviser, Prof. Sir Richard Norman, KBE, FRS.
Parliamentary Clerk, T. Collingridge.

Establishment and Finance Division

Principal Establishment and Finance Officer (G3), M. S. Buckley.
Director of Resource Management (G4), A. J. Dorken.
Assistant Secretaries (G5), J. Morris; P. D. Atkinson; B. Hampton.

Electricity Division A

Under Secretary (G3), C. C. Wilcock.
Assistant Secretaries (G5), M. Higson; S. F. Powell.

Electricity Division B

Under Secretary (G3), C. C. Wilcock.
Assistant Secretary (G5), M. Higson.
Chief Electrical Engineering Inspector (G7), J. G. Lindsay.

Coal Division

Under Secretary (G3), R. Heathcote.
Assistant Secretaries (G5), Dr D. H. Metz; J. A. V. Collett.

Atomic Energy Division

Under Secretary (G3), Dr T. Walker.
Assistant Secretaries (G5), P. H. Agrell; Mrs J. Britton; J. Bird; Dr D. P. Hauser; Mrs H. Haddon.

Energy Technology Division

Chief Scientist (G3), Dr W. D. Evans.
Deputy Chief Scientific Officers (G5), Dr A. Eggington; G. Bevan.
Senior Principal Scientific Officers (G6), R. A. Meir; W. Macpherson; Dr A. Heyes; A. J. Hyde; W. T. Morris; D. Irving.

International Unit

Assistant Secretary (G5), S. W. Freemantle.

Energy Efficiency Office

Director General (G3), W. Rickett.
Directors (G5), J. E. P. Miles; Dr N. Williams; C. Myerscough.
Director (G6), Mrs A. Wadsworth.

Economics and Statistics Division

Under Secretary (G3), E. H. M. Price.
Chief Statistician (G5), G. White.
Senior Economic Advisers (G5), S. A. Price; D. Hodgson.

Oil and Gas Division

Under Secretary (G3), D. R. Davis.
Assistant Secretaries (G5), W. C. F. Butler; Ms A. Beaton; N. A. C. Hirst; J. R. Wakely.

Gas and Oil Measurement Branch

Government Buildings, Saffron Road, Wigston, Leicester
[0533–785354]

Director (G5), J. Plant.
Senior Chief Examiner (G6), G. A. Paul-Clark.

Petroleum Engineering Division

Director (G3), P. T. Harding.
Reservoir Evaluation Specialist I, I. W. G. Hughes.
Reservoir Evaluation Specialists II, J. H. Aitken; D. W. Mann.
Assistant Director Engineer (G6), G. N. Marriott.

Offshore Supplies Office

Alhambra House, 45 Waterloo Street, Glasgow G2 6AS
[041–221 8777]

Director General (G3), J. E. d'Ancona.
Director Industry (G5), H. M. Whiteside.
Director Policy and Administration (G5), A. E. Maule.
Director Research and Development (G5), C. P. Carter.
Senior Principal Business Development (G6), H. Holden.
Senior Principal Scientific Officer (G6), Dr K. Tregonning.
Assistant Director Engineer (G6), P. R. Taylor.

Information Division

Head of Information (G5), N. W. Hayes.
Deputy Head of Information and Chief Press Officer (G7), D. Price.

DEPARTMENT OF THE ENVIRONMENT
2 Marsham Street, SW1P 3EB
[071–276 3000]

The Department of the Environment is responsible for planning and land use; local government; housing and construction; inner city areas; new towns; environmental protection; conservation areas and countryside affairs; royal parks and palaces; historic buildings and ancient monuments; and property holdings.
See p. 353 for PSA Services.
(For **Salaries**, *see* page 293)

Secretary of State for the Environment, THE RT. HON. MICHAEL HESELTINE, MP.
Private Secretary, P. Ward.
Special Advisers, Lady Eileen Strathnaver; T. Burke.
Private Secretary, J. Cressy.
Special Advisers (part-time), Sir Peter Levene, Prof. P. Hall, Prof. D. Pearce, Dr A. Kemp.
Private Secretary, A. Swyer.
Parliamentary Private Secretary, W. Powell MP.
Minister for Local Government and Inner Cities, MICHAEL PORTILLO, MP.
Private Secretary, T. F. Beattie.
Parliamentary Private Secretary, D. Amess, MP.
Minister for Environment and Countryside, DAVID TRIPPIER, RD, MP.
Private Secretary, C. R. Bates.
Parliamentary Private Secretary, Dr I. Twinn, MP.
Minister for Housing and Planning, SIR GEORGE YOUNG, Bt. MP.
Private Secretary, A. Allberry.
Parliamentary Private Secretary, G. Howarth, MP.
Minister for the Heritage, BARONESS BLATCH, CBE.
Private Secretary, S. E. S. Stringer.
Special Adviser to Ministers of State, Ms A. Broom.
Personal Secretary, Miss C. Martyres.
Parliamentary Under Secretaries of State, ROBERT KEY, MP; TIM YEO, MP; TONY BALDRY, MP.
Private Secretaries, N. Ratcliffe; Ms K. Jennings; G. Cory.
Lord in Waiting, Viscount Astor.
Private Secretary, Miss A. Moore.
Parliamentary Clerk, D. S. Demorais.
Permanent Secretary (G1), Sir Terence Heiser, KCB.
Private Secretary, Mrs B. Houlden.
Chief Executive, PSA (G1A), G. H. Chipperfield, CB.
Private Secretary, Mrs N. Baxter.

ORGANIZATION AND ESTABLISHMENTS
Lambeth Bridge House, SE1 7SB
[071 238 3000]

Principal Establishments and Finance Officer (G2), D. J. Burr.

Personnel

Director (G3), J. A. Owen.
Grade 5, C. P. Evans; K. G. Arnold; L. B. Hicks.
Grade 6, M. A. L. Ross; R. E. Vidler; Miss J. A. Clark; J. Kingdom.
Chief Librarian (G6), P. Kirwan.
Chief Welfare Officer (G7), R. J. Lintern.

Central Finance

Under Secretary (G3), R. S. Dudding.

Heads of Divisions (G5), J. Adams; B. Redfern; D. A. C. Heigham; C. Whaley; (*G6*), G. Knowles.
Head of Internal Audit (G6), M. R. Haselip.

Administrative Resources

Director (G3), D. A. R. Peel.
Grade 4, B. G. Rosser.
Grade 5, Miss P. E. Alexander; I. C. McBrayne; M. J. Bailey.
Grade 6, R. H. Cheeseman; D. Tridgell; R. Bendall.
Grade 7, Miss C. Rees-Jenkins.

Heritage and Royal Estate

Director (G3), J. A. L. Gunn.
Grade 5, J. J. Rendell; A. H. Corner; C. P. Douglas.
Grade 6, Mrs J. Adams.

Historic Royal Palaces Agency
The Birdwood Annexe, Hampton Court Palace, East Molesey, Surrey KT8 9AU

An executive agency within the Department of the Environment, the Historic Royal Palaces Agency manages the Tower of London, Hampton Court Palace, Kensington Palace, Kew Palace with Queen Charlotte's Cottage, and the Banqueting House, Whitehall.

Chief Executive (G3), D. C. Beeton.
Director of Finance and Resources (G5), Ms S. A. Booth.
Director of Marketing (G6), D. Hammond.
Administrator, Hampton Court Palace (G6), D. J. C. MacDonald.
Resident Governor, HM Tower of London (G5), Maj.-Gen. C. Tyler (retd.).
Curator, Kensington Palace, N. J. Arch.

PLANNING INSPECTORATE

Chief Planning Inspector (G3), H. S. Crow.
Deputy Chief Planning Inspector (G4), J. R. Mossop.
Director of Planning Appeals (G4), A. J. M. Morgan.
Assistant Chief Planning Inspectors (G5), Miss G. M. Pain; J. T. Graham; M. I. Montague-Smith; J. Acton; J. T. Dunlop; D. F. Harris; R. E. Wilson.
Head of Administration (G5), D. A. C. Marshall.
Head of Finance and Management Services (G5), M. Brasher.

REGIONAL OFFICES

West Midlands, Birmingham.—*Regional Director (G3)*, D. R. Ritchie. *Regional Controllers (G5)*, J. E. Northover; D. L. Saunders; Mrs P. M. Holland.
Yorkshire and Humberside, Leeds.—*Regional Director (G3)*, J. P. Henry. *Regional Controllers (G5)*, I. H. Crowther; Mrs E. A. Kerry.
North West, Manchester.—*Regional Director (G3)*, D. C. Renshaw. *Regional Controllers (G5)*, B. C. Isherwood; P. Styche.
Northern, Newcastle upon Tyne.—*Regional Director (G3)*, P. A. Shaw. *Regional Controllers (G5)*, Ms D. Caudle; R. G. Bell.
South West, Bristol.—*Regional Director (G3)*, Ms E. A. Hopkins. *Regional Controller (G5)*, S. McQuillin.
East Midlands, Nottingham.—*Regional Director (G4)*, D. J. Morrison. *Regional Controller (G6)*, G. Meynell, MBE; R. J. Smith.
South East, London W14.—*Regional Director (G3)*, J. W. Fellows. *Regional Controllers (G5)*, Mrs J. A. Bridges; R. Williams; R. Ash; (*G6*), E. G. Everett.
Eastern, Bedford.—*Regional Director (G3)*, P. F. Emms. *Regional Controllers (G5)*, A. Z. Levy; R. A. Bird.

LONDON REGIONAL OFFICE

Under Secretary (G3), A. A. Pelling.
Grade 5, A. Buchanan; B. Strong; B. H. Leonard; R. K. Madders.

Information

Director (G3), D. A. McDonald.
Grade 5, J. Gee.

PLANNING, RURAL AFFAIRS AND HERITAGE

Deputy Secretary (G2), P. C. McQuail.

Planning and Development Control

Director (G3), P. J. Fletcher.
Grade 5, D. N. Donaldson; R. S. Horsman; R. G. Wakeford; C. L. L. Braun; J. M. Leigh-Pollitt.

Planning Services

Director (G4), J. B. Wilson.
Grade 5, R. C. Mabey; J. A. Zetter; A. F. Richardson.
Grade 6, D. C. Stroud.

Directorate of Rural Affairs

Under Secretary (G3), R. J. A. Sharp.
Grade 4, P. L. Leonard.
Grade 5, R. Bunce; R. M. Pritchard.
Grade 6, J. C. Peters.

MERSEYSIDE TASK FORCE

Director (G3), Dr R. C. Dobbie.
Controllers (G5), S. P. Sage; I. Urquhart.

CHIEF ARCHITECTURAL ADVISER ON THE BUILT ENVIRONMENT

Grade 2, J. B. Jefferson, CB.
Grade 5, J. E. Turner.

HOUSING AND INNER CITIES

Deputy Secretary (G2), Miss E. C. Turton.

Inner Cities

Director (G3), M. B. Gahagan.
Head of Divisions (G5), A. C. B. Ramsay; G. L. Laufer; P. F. Unwin; Mrs R. Le Guin.

Housing Associations and Private Sector

Under Secretary (G3), J. F. Ballard.
Heads of Divisions (G5), R. J. Dorrington; P. F. Everall; Mrs L. A. Heath; R. Jones.
Grade 6, J. S. Gill.

Housing Monitoring and Analysis

Under Secretary (G3), vacant.
Grade 5, J. E. Turner; A. E. Holmans, CBE; Mrs J. Littlewood; M. Hughes; J. E. Roberts.

Public Housing Management and Resources

Under Secretary (G3), Mrs M. McDonald.
Heads of Divisions (G5), J. Stevens; I. H. Nicol; N. Kinghan; R. A. Mills.
Grade 6, P. J. Radley.

PROPERTY HOLDINGS CONSTRUCTION AND CENTRAL SUPPORT SERVICES

Deputy Secretary (G2), Miss D. A. Nichols.
Principal Finance Officer (G3), Mrs D. S. Phillips.
Director, Property Holdings (G3), N. E. Borrett.

Directorate of Estate Planning

Grade 4, D. O. McCreadie.
Grade 5, R. J. Dinwiddy.
Grade 6, N. Lee; J. H. Bilsby.

Directorate of Estate Operations

Grade 4, vacant.
Head of Operations Division (G5), R. W. P. Brice.
Grade 6, M. S. Jennett; G. R. Southey; J. Glen.

Heads of Outstations (G6), Scotland, P. R. Stewart; *North East*, G. M. Searjeant; *North West*, A. R. Jones; *Midlands*, M. J. Hathaway; *Thames North*, A. J. Partridge; *Thames South*, C. G. H. Young; *South West/Wales*, R. M. Barry.
Head of Central London Division (G5), A. R. Edwards.

Finance

Grade 5, M. Nelson.

TCS Privatization Unit

Grade 5, Ms D. S. Khan.

PSA Privatization Unit

Grade 5, J. W. M. Rogers.

Central Policy Division

Grade 5, M. H. Bowles.

Directorate of Central Support Services

Grade 4, M. J. Wanstall.
Grade 5, J. C. King.
Grade 6, W. J. Marsh; B. C. Sewell; R. Window; A. Makepeace.

Construction Policy Directorate

Under Secretary (G3), T. R. Hornsby.
Heads of Divisions (G5), A. D. Fagin; G. I. Fuller; I. C. Macpherson; F. D. Sando.

Queen Elizabeth II Conference Centre

(An executive agency within the Department of the Environment.)
Chief Executive (G5), R. E. Kendrick.

Building Research Establishment

(An executive agency within the Department of the Environment).
Chief Executive (G3), R. G. Courtney.
Deputy Chief Executive (G4), J. M. Baker.
Directors of Groups and Stations (G5), N. O. Milbank; B. O. Hall; Dr W. D. Woolley.
Heads of Services/Research (G6), A. J. M. Harrison; Dr J. F. A. Moore; Dr A. B. Birties; R. E. Baldwin; Dr V. A. C. Crisp; B. B. Pigott; C. R. Durham; P. A. MacDermott; H. W. Harrison; J. R. Britten; R. M. C. Driscoll; Dr P. J. Nixon; Dr J. R. F. Burdett; Dr J. P. Cornish; A. J. Butler; Dr P. R. Warren; H. Gulvanessian; Dr A. J. Bravery; Dr J. W. Llewellyn.
Heads of Laboratories and Services (G7), P. W. Staff; Dr D. J. T. Webb; C. J. Judge; R. H. Welsh.

LOCAL GOVERNMENT

Deputy Secretary (G2), C. J. S. Brearley.

Local Government Finance Policy

Director, Local Government Finance Policy (G4), P. J. Britton.
Heads of Divisions (G5), P. Rowsell; Mrs C. Wells; M. H. Coulshed; Mrs H. J. Chipping; R. J. Gibson; A. C. B. Ramsay.

Local Government Review Team

Under Secretary (G3), R. U. Young.
Grade 5, Ms L. F. Bell; I. J. Scotter; A. M. Wells.

Local Government

Under Secretary (G3), R. J. Green.
Heads of Divisions (G5), A. J. C. Simcock; H. C. T. Fawcett; (*G6*), P. G. Iredale.

LEGAL

Solicitor and Legal Adviser (G2), M. J. Ware, CB, QC.
Deputy Solicitors (G3), J. A. Catlin; Mrs M. A. Morgan.
Assistant Solicitors (G5), J. L. Comber; Mrs J. L. Weinberg; P. J. Szell; I. D. Day; C. M. Vine; Mrs S. Headley; Miss R. A. Lester; Mrs P. J. Conlon; Mrs G. Hedley-Dent; Ms S. D. Unerman.

CHIEF SCIENTIST

Chief Scientist (G3), Dr D. J. Fisk.
Head of Division (G5), C. L. Robson.

ENVIRONMENT PROTECTION

Deputy Secretary (G2), F. A. Osborn, CB.

HM Inspectorate of Pollution

Director and Chief Inspector (G3), Dr D. H. Slater.
Deputy Chief Inspector (G4), Dr A. Duncan.
Heads of Division (G5), M. F. Tunnicliffe; A. Windsor; L. N. Stuffins; L. Packer; Dr D. J. Bryce.

Directorate of Air, Climate and Toxic Substances

Under Secretary (G3), Dr D. J. Fisk.
Heads of Division (G5), A. Davis; Dr N. J. King; M. J. C. Faulkner.
Grade 6, Dr A. J. Apling; D. L. Pounder; Dr P. J. Corcoran; R. Derwent.

Directorate of Pollution Control and Wastes

Under Secretary (G3), J. Hobson.
Heads of Division (G5), J. Grevatt; Mrs L. A. C. Simcock; Dr M. W. Jones; N. Sanders.

Environmental Policy and Analysis

Director (G3), A. G. Watson.
Heads of Division (G5), J. Stoker; P. S. MacCormack; N. J. Hartley; J. P. Plowman; Miss F. McConnell, CBE.

Water Directorate

Director (G3), N. W. Summerton.
Heads of Divisions (G5), D. L. H. Roberts; D. R. Lewis; J. Jacobs; N. Dorling.

Drinking Water Inspectorate

Grade 5, M. G. Healey.

ROYAL COMMISSION ON ENVIRONMENTAL POLLUTION
Church House, Great Smith Street, SW1P 3BZ
[071–276 2080]

The Commission was set up in 1970, to advise on matters, both national and international, concerning the pollution of the environment; on the adequacy of research in this field; and the future possibilities of danger to the environment.

Chairman, The Lord Lewis of Newnham, FRS.
Members, Prof. H. Charnock, FRS; Prof. Dame Barbara Clayton, DBE; The Earl of Cranbrook; H. R. Fell; P. R. A. Jacques, CBE; Prof. J. H. Lawton, FRS; Prof. J. G. Morris; J. J. R. Pope, OBE; D. A. D. Reeve, CBE; W. N. Scott, OBE; Dr C. W. Suckling, CBE; Prof. E. M. Rothschild; Prof. Z. A. Silberston, OBE.
Secretary, B. Glicksman.

EQUAL OPPORTUNITIES COMMISSION

Overseas House, Quay Street, Manchester M3 3HN
[061–833 9244]

Press Office: Swan House, 53 Poland Street, W1V 3DF (071–287 3953)

Regional Offices: St Andrew House, 141 West Nile Street, Glasgow G1 2RN (041–332 8018); Caerwys House, Windsor Place, Cardiff (0222–43552)

The Commission was set up by Parliament in 1975 as a result of the passing of the Sex Discrimination Act. It works towards the elimination of discrimination by virtue of sex or marital status and to promote equality of opportunity between men and women generally.

Chair, Mrs J. Foster £48,990
Deputy Chair, Mrs J. Bridgeman £24,000
Members, A. Simpkin; Miss M. Monk; Mrs M. Prosser; Lady Brittan; Mrs A. Hasan; Ms B. Hillon; Ms A. Watts; Ms N. Bray; Ms A. Gibson; Mrs B. Kelly; Miss J. Trotter; Ms C. Wells.
Chief Executive, Miss V. Amos.

Equal Opportunities Commission for Northern Ireland

Chamber of Commerce House, 22 Great Victoria Street, Belfast BT2 2BA
[0232-242752]

Chief Executive, Mrs M. B. Clark-Glass, CBE.

EXCHEQUER AND AUDIT DEPARTMENT
See National Audit Office

ECGD (EXPORT CREDITS GUARANTEE DEPARTMENT)

PO Box 2200, 2 Exchange Tower, Harbour Exchange Square, E14 9GS
[071-934 9000]

ECGD (Export Credits Guarantee Department), the official export credit insurer, is a separate government department responsible to the Secretary of State for Trade and Industry and functions under the Export Guarantees and Overseas Investment Act 1978. This enables ECGD to encourage UK exports by making available export credit insurance to British firms engaged in selling overseas and to guarantee repayment to banks in Britain providing finance for export credit for goods sold on credit terms of two years or more. Guarantees under Section 1 of the Act are given after consultation with an Advisory Council of bankers and businessmen.

The Act also empowers ECGD to insure British private investment overseas against political risks, such as war, expropriation and restrictions on remittances.

The Insurance Services Group of the ECGD is due to be privatized by the end of 1991, subject to parliamentary legislation.

Chief Executive, M. G. Stephens, CB.
Directors (G3), C. Foxall; M. T. Hawtin; R. Wild (T); J. R. Weiss.
Heads of Divisions (G5), G. Bromley; R. P. Burnett; P. J. Callagham; D. C. Cooper; R. I. Fear; A. P. Fowell; T. M. Jaffray; K. G. Lockwood; V. P. Lunn Rockliffe; R. W. MacGregor; M. D. Pentecost; Mrs

V. A. Randall; R. A. Ranson; G. C. Bird (T); B. M. Sidwell, TD (T); J. S. Snowden (T); Miss J. West.
Senior Principals (G6), J. M. Foster (T); R. P. D. Crick (T); S. J. Johnson; Mrs M. E. Maddox; Ms S. Rice; E. Walsby.
Principals (G7), J. S. Astruc; D. I. Calvert; Mrs A. C. Cowie; G. P. Cox; A. B. Coyne; M. J. Crane; J. C. W. Croall; S. R. Dodgson; R. X. Fear; G. C. Fisher; Mrs J. A. Fulwood; P. C. Gaudoin; N. F. George; R. Gotts; R. Hardy; P. Jackson; C. D. Jones; K. Jones; R. Jones; N. A. Lambert; D. J. M. Lucas; I. Mackay; S. Merchack; A. J. E. Muckersie; P. L. Neal; G. A. Newhouse; S. C. Pond; P. J. Radford; A. B. Redmayne; S. Rosenthal; R. Scott; K. R. Smith; Miss V. M. Taylor; D. A. H. Tickner; R. N. Tolliday; J. A. Tyler; A. R. Watt; R. A. Watt; T. West; F. Whitehead; J. M. Willis; D. L. Wyatt; J. A. Youd; G. A. Young; M. R. Hodson; C. J. Leeds; P. J. Rossington; A. C. Faulkner (T); I. Wilson.
Principal Information Officer, J. Peacock.

(T = temporary)

Export Guarantees Advisory Council

Chairman, Sir Peter Leslie.
Deputy Chairman, A. G. Gormly.
Other Members, The Hon. D. Douglas-Home; D. Eustace; M. Riding; R. T. Fox.

OFFICE OF FAIR TRADING
Field House, Bream's Buildings, EC4A 1PR
[071–242 2858]

The Office of Fair Trading is a non-ministerial government department, headed by the Director General of Fair Trading. It keeps commercial activities in the UK under review and seeks to protect consumers against unfair trading practices. The Director General's consumer protection duties under the Fair Trading Act 1973, together with his responsibilities under the Consumer Credit Act 1974, the Estate Agents Act 1979, and Control of Misleading Advertisements Regulations 1988, are administered by the Office's Consumer Affairs Division. The Competition Policy Division is concerned with monopolies and mergers (under the Fair Trading Act 1973), and the Director General's other responsibilities for competition matters, including those under the Restrictive Trade Practices Act 1976, the Resale Prices Act 1976, the Competition Act 1980 and the Financial Services Act 1986. The Office is the UK competent authority on the application of the European Commission's competition rules, and also liaises with the Commission on consumer protection initiatives.

Director General, Sir Gordon Borrie, QC.
Deputy Director General (G2), J. W. Preston, CB.

Consumer Affairs Division

Director (G3), R. J. Thomas.
Assistant Directors (G5), M. Lanyon; D. W. Lightfoot; J. Chapman.

Competition Policy Division

Director (G3), Dr M. Howe.
Assistant Directors (G5), A. G. Atkinson; A. J. White; D. Roots-Parsons.
Head of International Section (G6), H. L. Emden.

Legal Division

Director (G3), R. Woolman.
Assistant Directors (G5), M. A. Khan; P. T. Rostron.

Senior Economic Adviser (G5), D. Elliot.
Establishment and Finance Officer (G5), Miss C. Banks.
Chief Information Officer (G6), J. Stubbs.

FOREIGN AND COMMONWEALTH OFFICE
Downing Street, SW1A 2AL
[071-270 3000]

The Foreign and Commonwealth Office provides, mainly through diplomatic missions, the means of communication between the British Government and other governments and international governmental organizations for the discussion and negotiation of all matters falling within the field of international relations. It is responsible for alerting the British Government to the implications of developments overseas; for protecting British interests overseas; for protecting British citizens abroad; for explaining British policies to, and cultivating friendly relations with, governments overseas; and for the discharge of British responsibilities to the dependent territories.

Salaries

For Ministerial salaries, *see* page 293.

Diplomatic Service
(since April 1, 1991)

Permanent Under Secretary and Head of the Diplomatic Service	£96,210
Senior Grade Salary Point 1 (SP1)	£82,780
Senior Grade Salary Point 2 (SP2)	£69,120
Senior Grade Salary Point 3 (SP3)	£59,020
Senior Grade Salary Point 4 (SP4)	£55,540
Senior Grade Salary Point 5 (SP5)	£50,380
Diplomatic Service Grade 4 (DS4)	£35,720–£40,360
Diplomatic Service Grade 5 (DS5)	£24,641–£29,049

Secretary of State, THE RT. HON. DOUGLAS HURD, CBE, MP.
 Private Secretary, R. H. T. Gozney.
 Assistant Private Secretaries, S. L. Gass; C. N. R. Prentice; S. L. Hall.
 Social Secretary, Miss D. J. Pearey, MBE.
 Special Adviser, E. Bickham.
 Parliamentary Private Secretary, D. Martin, MP.
Minister of State for Foreign and Commonwealth Affairs (Minister for Overseas Development), THE RT. HON. LYNDA CHALKER, MP.
 Private Secretary, S. Chakrabarti.
 Special Adviser, M. Fraser.
 Parliamentary Private Secretary, D. Nicholson, MP.
Ministers of State for Foreign and Commonwealth Affairs, THE HON. DOUGLAS HOGG, QC, MP; THE EARL OF CAITHNESS, PC; TRISTAN GAREL-JONES, MP.
 Private Secretaries, Hon. D. Asquith; P. H. Tibber; T. M. Hitchens.
Parliamentary Under Secretary of State, THE HON. MARK LENNOX-BOYD, MP.
 Private Secretary, P. A. Speller.
Parliamentary Relations Unit, M. C. Bates. (*Head*); J. P. Rodgers (*Deputy Head and Parliamentary Clerk*).
Permanent Under Secretary of State and Head of the Diplomatic Service, Sir David Gillmore, KCMG.
 Private Secretary, T. M. J. Simmons.
Deputy Under Secretaries (SP2), J. D. I. Boyd, CMG, (*Chief Clerk*); P. S. Fairweather, CMG; N. P. Bayne, CMG; L. V. Appleyard, CMG (*Political Director*); N. H. R. A. Broomfield, CMG; Sir John Coles, KCMG.
HM Vice-Marshal of the Diplomatic Corps, R. B. R. Hervey, CMG.
Assistant Under Secretaries (SP5), A. J. Beamish, CMG; P. J. Goulden, CMG; Mrs V. E. Sutherland, CMG; (*Deputy Chief Clerk*); R. J. S. Muir (*Principal Finance Officer and Chief Inspector*); The Hon. D. Gore-Booth, CMG; S. N. P. Hemans, CVO; D. Slater,

CMG; R. A. Burns; J. Ling, CMG (*Director of Communications & Technical Services*); Miss R. J. Spencer, CMG; M. L. Tait, CMG, LVO; J. Q. Greenstock, CMG; R. O. Miles, CMG; M. H. Jay.
Legal Adviser, Sir Arthur Watts, KCMG, QC.
Second Legal Adviser, D. H. Anderson, CMG.
Deputy Legal Advisers, F. D. Berman, CMG; K. J. Chamberlain.
Legal Counsellors, M. C. Wood; Mrs A. Glover; Miss S. Brooks.
International Labour Adviser, A. E. Smith.
Overseas Police Adviser (DS4), J. W. Kelland, LVO, QPM.

Heads of Departments (*DS4*) and Assistant Heads of Department (*DS5*)

Aid Policy Dept., P. D. M. Freeman. *Asst.*, D. Lyscom.
Arms Control and Disarmament Dept., P. W. M. Vereker; *Asst.*, A. Auckle.
Aviation and Maritime Dept., E. J. Hughes.
Central and Southern African Dept., R. N. Dales; *Asst.*, C. Jennings.
Commonwealth Co-ordination Dept., T. C. S. Stitt; *Asst.*, M. W. Powles.
Conference on Security and Co-operation in Europe Unit, D. J. Johnson.
Consular Dept., C. J. A. Denne; *Asst.*, J. W. MacDonald.
Cultural Relations Dept., J. N. Elam; *Assts.*, I. Rawlinson, OBE; S. F. Howarth.
East African Dept., R. Edis; *Asst.*, M. R. Crompton.
Eastern European Dept., C. Hulse, OBE; *Assts.*, J. M. G. Freeman; J. C. R. Gray.
Economic Advisers, S. H. Broadbent; *Asst.*, N. R. Chrimes.
Economic Relations Dept., R. Bone; *Asst.*, P. J. Millett.
Environment Science and Energy Dept., A. R. Brenton; *Asst.*, M. Bourke.
European Community Dept. (External), E. Jones Parry; *Asst.*, Q. M. Quayle.
European Community Dept. (Internal), M. Arthur; *Asst.*, N. Sheinwald.
Far Eastern Dept., H. L. Davies; *Asst.*, D. Warren.
Finance Dept., G. F. Griffiths; *Asst.*, A. R. Ingle.
Home Estate and Services Dept., D. Brown; *Asst.*, F. J. Savage, LVO, OBE.
Hong Kong Dept., A. R. Paul; *Asst.*, Miss R. Marsden.
Information Dept. A. D. Harris, LVO; *Assts.*, C. J. Ingham; D. Wyatt.
Information Systems Division (Operations), R. Cowling; *Assts.*, D. Carrol; C. Ford.
Information Systems Division (Projects), K. Willis.
Information Systems Division (Resources), D. Wright, OBE; *Assts.*, T. N. Guina, MVO; J. Bambrough.
Information Systems Division (Services), D. Briggs; *Asst.*, N. Paget.
Latin America Dept., A. R. Murray; *Asst.*, W. B. Sinton.
Library and Records Dept., R. Bone; *Assts.*, R. L. E. Foreman; I. S. Lockhart, MBE; B. Barrett.
Management Review Staff, A. C. Hunt, CMG; *Deputy Head*, J. Anning.
Medical and Staff Welfare Unit, E. A. Burner; *Deputy Head*, Mrs J. Newby.
Middle East Dept., P. M. Nixon, CMG, OBE.
Migration and Visa Dept., A. E. Montgomery; *Assts.*, M. J. Peart, LVO; D. Cockaham.
Narcotics Control and Aids Dept., T. J. David; *Asst.* B. E. Stewart.
Nationality, Treaty and Claims Dept., M. F. Sullivan, MBE; *Asst.*, A. Harrington.

---

*Joint Foreign and Commonwealth Office/Overseas Development Administration Dept.

Near East and North Africa Dept., S. W. J. Fuller; *Asst.*, E. Glover.

News Dept., B. Mower.

Non-Proliferation and Defence Dept., R. H. Smith; *Asst.*, J. A. Noakes.

North America Dept., D. A. Burns; *Asst.*, R. French.

Overseas Estate Dept., M. H. R. Bertram; *Deputy Head*, J. Owen, MBE.

Overseas Inspectorate, R. J. S. Muir (*Chief Inspector and Principal Finance Officer*); *Inspectors*, D. I. Lewty; S. D. M. Jack; D. Carter; I. J. Rawlinson, OBE.

*Overseas Trade Services Directorate, Dir. Gen., R. O. Miles, CMG; *Dir.*, M. G. Dougal.

Permanent Under Secretary's Dept., I. R. Callan, CMG; *Deputy Head*, A. Charlton.

Personnel Management Dept., E. Clay; *Deputy Head*, S. M. J. Lamport.

Personnel Policy Dept., D. Walker.

Personnel Services Dept., R. G. Short, MVO; *Assts.*, J. Long; M. Greenstreet.

Policy Planning Staff, R. Cooper, MVO; *Asst.*, J. Powell.

Protocol Dept., D. C. B. Beaumont; *Assts.*, T. C. Almond, OBE; S. W. F. Martin, LVO (*First Assistant Marshal of the Diplomatic Corps*).

Republic of Ireland Dept., G. R. Archer; *Asst.*, D. F. G. Farr.

Research and Analysis Dept., Director, A. St J. Figgis; *Regional Directors*, C. J. S. Rundle, OBE (*Africa and Middle East*); K. C. Walker (*Asia*); Miss S. Morphet (*Atlantic*); J. R. Banks, OBE (*Soviet Union and Eastern Europe*).

Resource Management Dept., R. J. Chase; *Asst.*, J. A. Dew.

Security Dept., J. W. Hodge; *Asst.*, W. P. Hartshorne.

Security Policy Dept., S. J. Gomersall; *Asst.*, P. Ricketts.

South Asian Dept., M. J. Williams, CVO, OBE; *Asst.*, R. Codrington.

South Atlantic and Antarctic Dept., M. Baker-Bates; *Asst.*, P. L. Hunt.

South-east Asian Dept., D. H. Colvin; *Asst.*, J. W. Guy, OBE.

Southern European Dept., D. C. A. Madden; *Asst.*, D. D. Pearey.

South Pacific Dept., R. Thomas; *Asst.*, A. C. Walder.

Soviet Dept., R. M. J. Lyne; *Asst.*, C. R. V. Stagg.

Technical Security Dept., M. J. B. Smith; *Assts.*, R. Read; J. Gould.

Training Dept., T. D. Curran; *Director of Language Centre*, J. Moore.

United Nations Dept., Miss M. G. D. Evans; *Asst.*, J. Watt.

West African Dept., M. E. Cook.

West Indian and Atlantic Dept., G. M. Baker; *Asst.*, P. A. Penfold, OBE.

Western European Dept., Miss M. MacGlashen; *Assts.*, N. Cox; E. Callway.

CORPS OF QUEEN'S MESSENGERS
Foreign and Commonwealth Office, SW1A 2AH
[071-270 2779]

Superintendent of the Corps of Queen's Messengers, Maj. I. G. M. Bamber.

Queen's Messengers, Maj. J. E. A. Andre; Cdr. R. D. D. Bamford; Cdr. D. H. Barraclough; Lt.-Cdr. B. R. Bezance; Maj. A. N. D. Bols; Lt. Cdr. K. E. Brown; Lt.-Col. W. P. A. Bush; Lt.-Col. M. B. de S. Clayton; Capt. G. Courtauld; Maj. F. C. W. Courtenay-Thompson; Maj. P. C. H. Dening-Smitherman; Maj.

---

*Joint Foreign and Commonwealth Office/Overseas Development Administration Dept.

P. T. Dunn; Sqn. Ldr. J. S. Frizzell; Capt. N. C. E. Gardner; Cdr. P. G. Gregson; Maj. D. A. Griffiths; Wg Cdr. J. O. Jewiss; Lt.-Col. P. S. Kerr-Smiley; Lt.-Col. J. M. C. Kimmins; Lt.-Col. R. C. Letchworth; G. F. Miller; Lt.-Col. A. R. Murray; Maj. D. R. Nevile; Maj. K. J. Rowbottom; Maj. M. R. Senior; Cdr. K. M. C. Simmons, AFC; Maj. P. M. O. Springfield; Maj. J. S. Steele; Col. D. W. F. Taylor.

FOREIGN COMPENSATION COMMISSION
Old Admiralty Building, SW1A 2AF
[071-210 6158]

The Commission was set up by the Foreign Compensation Act 1950 primarily to distribute under Orders in Council funds received from other governments in accordance with agreements to pay compensation for expropriated British property and other losses sustained by British nationals.

The Commission has the further duty of registering claims for British-owned property in contemplation of agreements with other countries, and it has done so in seven instances since 1950.

Chairman, A. W. E. Wheeler, CBE.
Commissioner, J. A. S. Hall, DFC, QC.
Secretary and Chief Examiner, D. H. Wright.

FORESTRY COMMISSION
231 Corstorphine Road, Edinburgh EH12 7AT
[031-334 0303]

The Forestry Commission has the legal status of and functions as a government department. It reports directly to Forestry Ministers (i.e. the Minister of Agriculture, Fisheries and Food, the Secretary of State for Scotland, and the Secretary of State for Wales), to whom it is responsible for advice on forestry policy and for the implementation of that policy in Great Britain. There is a statutorily-appointed Chairman and Board of Commissioners (four full-time and six part-time) with prescribed duties and powers. The full-time Commissioners form the Executive Board.

As the forestry authority for Great Britain, the Commission is also responsible for carrying out certain regulatory functions in connection with plant health and felling licensing, for conducting forestry research, and for administering grant-aid schemes for private woodlands. As the forestry enterprise, the Commission has a primary responsibility to provide timber for industry. In discharging their functions, the Forestry Commissioners are charged with endeavouring to achieve a reasonable balance between the needs of forestry and conservation.

Chairman, J. R. Johnstone, CBE (*part-time*) £31,206
Director-General and Deputy Chairman, T. R. Cutler.................................£59,020
Commissioner for Private Forestry and Development, R. T. Bradley £49,560
Commissioner for Administration and Finance, D. S. Grundy.........................£47,090
Commissioner for Operations, D. L. Foot £47,090
Secretary to the Commissioners, P. J. Clarke . £43,307

REGISTRY OF FRIENDLY SOCIETIES
15 Great Marlborough Street, W1V 2AX
[071-437 9992]

The Registry of Friendly Societies is a government department serving two statutory bodies, the Building Societies Commission, and the Central Office of the Registry of Friendly Societies, together with the Assistant Registrar of Friendly Societies for Scotland.

The Building Societies Commission was established

by the Building Societies Act 1986. The Commission is responsible for the supervision of building societies, and administers the system of regulation. It also advises the Treasury and other government departments on matters relating to building societies.

The Central Office of the Registry of Friendly Societies provides a public registry for mutual organizations registered under the Building Societies Act 1986, Friendly Societies Act 1974, and the Industrial and Provident Societies Act 1965. It is responsible for the supervision of friendly societies and credit unions, and advises the Government on issues affecting those societies. The Chief Registrar has certain powers to arbitrate in disputes between members and registered societies. He also acts as the Industrial Assurance Commissioner.

(For **Salaries**, *see* page 293)

Building Societies Commission

Chairman, Mrs R. E. J. Gilmore.
Deputy Chairman, H. G. Walsh.
Commissioners, D. Hobson, CBE; T. F. Mathews; S. Proctor, CBE; G. Sammons; H. R. C. Walden, CBE; F. E. Worsley.

Central Office

Chief Registrar, Mrs R. E. J. Gilmore.
Assistant Registrars, A. Wilson; D. W. Lee; A. J. Perrett; R. N. Williams.

The Registry

First Commissioner and Chief Registrar (G2), Mrs R. E. J. Gilmore.

Staff serving the Building Societies Commission:
Grade 3, H. G. Walsh.
Grade 4, T. F. Matthews.
Grade 5, D. A. W. Stevens; J. M. Palmer; A. T. Gosling.
Grade 6, N. F. Digance.
Grade 7, A. G. Tebbutt; Mrs S. A. Russell; E. Engstrom; M. E. Duff; N. J. Lock; B. Champion; B. Morbin; M. Turner.

Staff serving the Central Office:
Assistant Registrar (G4), A. Wilson.
Assistant Registrar (G5), D. W. Lee.
Grade 7, F. da Rocha; N. J. F. Fawcett; C. T. Martyn.

Central Services
Assistant Registrar (G5), A. J. Perrett.
Legal Staff (G6), Mrs V. Edwards; P. G. Ashcroft; P. V. H. Smith.
Establishment and Finance Officer (G6), M. L. Battenti.

Registry of Friendly Societies, Scotland
58 Frederick Street, Edinburgh, EH2 1NB
[031–226 3224]

Assistant Registrar (G5), J. L. J. Craig, WS.

GAMING BOARD FOR GREAT BRITAIN
Berkshire House, 168–173 High Holborn,
WC1V 7AA
[071–240 0821]

The Board was established on October 25, 1968, to keep under review the extent and character of gaming in Great Britain, to approve prospective gaming licensees' management and staff, to inspect gaming establishments, and to advise the Home Secretary on changes in the law which may be needed for the further control of gaming.

Chairman (part-time), N. A. Ward Jones, CBE, VRD
£28,860
Members (part-time), Sir Richard Barratt, CBE, QPM; Lady Ibbs; W. B. Kirkpatrick; M. H. Hogan.
£11,575
Secretary, B. O. Bubbear.

OFFICE OF GAS SUPPLY
Southside, 105 Victoria Street, SW1E 6QT
[071–828 0898]

The Office of Gas Supply (Ofgas) is a regulatory body set up under the Gas Act 1986. It is headed by the Director General of Gas Supply, who is independent of ministerial control.

The principal function of Ofgas is to monitor British Gas' activities as a public gas supplier and, where necessary, enforce the conditions of that company's authorization to act as a public gas supplier. Other functions are: to grant authorizations to other suppliers of gas through pipes; to investigate complaints on matters where enforcement powers may be exercisable; to fix and publish maximum charges for reselling gas; to publish information and advice for the benefit of tariff customers; to keep under review developments concerning the gas supply industry, including competition; and to settle the terms on which other suppliers have access to British Gas' pipelines in the event of disagreement.

Director General, J. McKinnon.
Deputy Director General, M. R. Keay.
Legal Adviser, D. R. M. Long.
Business Adviser, G. McGregor.
Public Affairs Adviser, I. Cooke.
Consumer Affairs Adviser, W. Macleod.

THE GOVERNMENT ACTUARY
22 Kingsway, WC2B 6LE
[071–242 6828]

The Government Actuary provides a consulting service to government departments, the public sector, and overseas governments. His actuaries advise on social security schemes and superannuation arrangements within the public sector at home and abroad, on population and other statistical studies, and on government supervision of insurance companies and friendly societies.

Government Actuary, C. D. Daykin.
Directing Actuaries, D. G. Ballantine; D. H. Loades; M. A. Pickford.
Chief Actuaries, P. L. Burt; J. L. Field; R. T. Foster; T. W. Hewitson; P. H. Hinton; A. I. Johnston; A. G. Young.
Actuaries, E. I. Battersby; A. B. Chughtai; W. H. P. Davies; A. P. Gallop; T. A. Grant; C. A. Harris; F. A. Honeysett; V. P. Knowles; Mrs I. W. Lane; J. M. MacLeod; A. J. Macnair; P. Merricks; S. M. O'Ceallaigh; A. P. Pavelin; J. W. Peers; H. J. Prescott; J. C. Rathbone; D. F. Renn; A. H. Silverman; J. G. Spain; D. M. Webber.

GOVERNMENT HOSPITALITY FUND
8 Cleveland Row, SW1A 1DH
[071–210 3000]

The Government Hospitality Fund was instituted in 1908 for the purpose of organizing official hospitality on a regular basis, with a view to the promotion of international goodwill.

Minister in Charge, The Earl of Caithness, PC.
Secretary, Brig. A. Cowan, MBE.

DEPARTMENT OF HEALTH
Richmond House, 79 Whitehall, SW1A 2NS
[071–210 3000]

The Department of Health is responsible for the administration of the National Health Service in England and for the personal social services run by local authorities in England for children, the elderly, the infirm, the handicapped and other persons in need. It has functions relating to food hygiene and welfare foods. The Department is also concerned with the medical treatment of war pensioners, and is responsible for the ambulance and emergency first aid services, under the Civil Defence Act 1948. The Department represents the UK at the World Health Organization.
(For **Salaries**, *see* page 293)

Secretary of State for Health, THE RT. HON. WILLIAM WALDEGRAVE, MP.
  Private Secretary, S. Alcock.
  Special Advisers to the Secretary of State, Mrs L. Campey; R. Marsh.
Minister of State, MRS VIRGINIA BOTTOMLEY, MP.
  Private Secretary, T. Sands.
  Parliamentary Private Secretary, K. Mans, MP.
Parliamentary Under Secretaries of State, THE BARONESS HOOPER; STEPHEN DORRELL, MP.
  Private Secretary, Mrs Y. Baxter.
Permanent Secretary (G1), Sir Christopher France, KCB.
  Private Secretary (G7), Ms K. Wright.
Chief Medical Officer (G1A), Dr K. Calman.
Director of Research and Development, Prof. M. Peckham.

NATIONAL HEALTH SERVICE POLICY BOARD

Chairman, The Secretary of State.
Deputy Chairman, Sir Roy Griffiths.
Members, Sir Donald Acheson, KBE (*Chief Medical Officer*); Sir James Ackers; Mrs V. Bottomley, MP (*Minister of State*); Prof. C. Chantler; The Baroness Cumberledge, CBE; Sir Graham Day; S. Dorrell, MP (*Parliamentary Under Secretary*); Sir Kenneth Durham; Sir Christopher France, KCB (*Permanent Secretary*); D. Nichol, CBE; Sir Robert Scholey, CBE.

NATIONAL HEALTH SERVICE MANAGEMENT EXECUTIVE

Chief Executive, D. Nichol, CBE.
Deputy Chief Executive and Director of Operations, M. Malone-Lee.
Director of Planning & Information, M. J. Fairey.
Director of Personnel, E. Caines.
Director of Financial Management, Ms S. Masters.
Medical Director, Dr D. Walford.
Director, Family Practitioner Services, B. Rayner, CB.
Deputy Chief Nursing Officer, Ms C. McLoughlin.
Property Adviser, I. Oddy.

HEALTH AND PERSONAL SOCIAL SERVICES GROUP

Deputy Secretary (G2), T. S. Heppell, CB

Environmental Health and Food Safety

Under Secretary (G3), Miss R. O. B. Pease.
Assistant Secretaries (G5), J. C. Dobson; J. A. Parker.
Senior Principals (G6), P. W. Otley; Mrs M. Fry.

Hotel and Dietetic Services Branch

Chief Officer, Mrs M. Fry.
Deputy Chief Officer, Hotel and Dietetic Services (G7), R. E. Brown.

Priority and Health Services Division

Under Secretary (G3), C. H. Wilson.
Assistant Secretaries (G5), Miss P. M. C. Winterton; K. Jacobsen; P. R. Grant; J. C. Stopes-Roe; I. Jewesbury.

Community Services Division

Under Secretary (G3), T. Luce.
Assistant Secretaries (G5), Mrs A. De Peyer; N. Boyd; R. P. S. Hughes, CBE; A. McKeon.

Child Health, Maternity and Prevention Division and Aids Unit

Under Secretary (G3), N. M. Hale.
Assistant Secretaries (G5), J. E. Knight; W. Burroughs; J. F. Sharpe; J. C. Middleton.

FAMILY PRACTITIONERS SERVICES AND MEDICINES

Deputy Secretary (G2), B. R. Rayner.

Division FHS1

Under Secretary (G3), J. H. Barnes.
Assistant Secretaries (G5), D. Walden; Miss H. Gwyn; D. Wild; B. A. R. Smith, CBE; G. J. F. Podger.

Division FHS2

Under Secretary (G3), B. Bridges.
Assistant Secretaries (G5), Miss I. Nisbet; S. J. Furniss; J. Tross.

Medicines Control Agency

(An executive agency within the Department of Health.)
Chief Executive (G3), Dr K. H. Jones.
Grade 4, D. O. Hagger; R. K. Alder; D. H. Hartley; Dr J. B. Jefferys; Dr S. M. Wood.
Grade 5, Dr A. R. Rogers.

NHS MANAGEMENT BOARD OPERATIONS GROUP

Director of Operations (G2), M. Malone-Lee.

Regional Liaison Division

Under Secretary (G3), J. F. Shaw.
Assistant Secretaries (G5), Ms C. James; B. Slater; Miss S. O'Toole.

NHS ESTATES

Chief Executive (G3), J. C. Locke.
Estate Policy Director (G5), G. G. Mayers.
Estate Management Director and Chief Accountant (G5), P. L. Ward.
Head of Policy and Administration (G5), T. Whiteley.
Head of Consultancy Services (G5), C. Davies.
Chief Engineer (G5), L. W. M. Arrowsmith.
Chief Surveyor (G5), D. A. Eastwood.
Principal Nursing Adviser (G6), Miss S. B. R. Scott.

NHS PROCUREMENT DIRECTORATE

Acting Director of Procurement and Distribution (G3), E. M. Sutherland.
Assistant Directors (G5), E. H. W. Luxton; E. Evans; J. Oldham.
Commercial Executives (G6), F. G. Doyle; A. Doveston; T. Bird; K. Gill; J. Smith; R. Coxford; C. J. Uden; B. A. Bell.

MEDICAL DEVICES DIRECTORATE

Director (G4), A. B. Barton.
Assistant Director (G5), Miss M. N. Duncan (*Safety and Quality*); Dr D. Potter (*Technical Support*).
Senior Medical Officer (G5), Dr H. Sutton; Dr S. P. Vahl.
Product Group Heads (G6), R. W. B. Allen (*Implants*

and Materials); C. Bray (*Sterilization, Pharmacy, Pathology, Anaesthesia*); A. D. C. Shipley (*Rehabilitation and Community Care*); Dr N. A. Slark (*Electro-Medical and Imaging*).
Head of Planning and Budgeting (*G6*), T. F. Crawley.

NHS MANAGEMENT BOARD PERSONNEL GROUP

Director of Operations (Personnel) (*G2*), E. Caines.

Division HAP

Under Secretary (*G3*), R. W. D. Venning.
Assistant Secretaries (*G4*), R. M. Drury; (*G5*), R. M. Orton; I. Jewesbury; Mrs P. Hurley.

Information Systems Directorate

Director of Information Systems (*G2*), M. J. Fairey, CB.
Deputy Director (*G4*), R. T. Rogers.
Assistant Secretaries (*G5*), M. A. O'Flynn; vacant.
Senior Principals (*G6*), M. C. McCurry; P. Mason.

Research and Management Division

Director of Research and Development, Prof. M. Peckham.
Director of Research Management (*G4*), Dr W. J. Burroughs.
Principal Medical Officer (*G4*), Dr H. Pickles.
Assistant Secretaries (*G5*), D. M. Woolley; Mrs J. Griffin; Miss M. Edwards; Dr B. Soper.
Senior Medical Oficers (*G5*), Dr E. Wilson; (*G6*) Dr C. Hemshall.
Senior Principal Research Officer (*G6*), Ms A. Kauder.

Social Services Inspectorate

Chief Inspector (*G2*), H. Laming, CBE.
Deputy Chief Inspectors (*G4*), D. C. Brand; Miss C. Hey.
Assistant Chief Inspectors (*HQ*), Miss J. Baraclough; J. Kennedy; S. Mitchell; J. G. Smith; Mrs W. Rose.
Assistant Chief Inspectors (*Regions*), S. Allard; J. K. Corcoran; J. Cypher; D. Gilroy; B. D. Harrison; A. Jones; D. G. Lambert; Miss A. Taylor; Mrs P. K. Hall.

MEDICAL DIVISIONS (HEALTH AND PERSONAL SOCIAL SERVICES)

Chief Medical Officer (*G1A*), Sir Donald Acheson, KBE.
Deputy Chief Medical Officers (*G2*), Dr M. E. Abrams; Dr J. S. Metters; Dr D. Walford.

MEDICAL DIVISIONS UNDER DR ABRAMS

Division HPS

Senior Principal Medical Officer (*G3*), Dr N. P. Halliday.
Senior Medical Officers (*G5*), Dr P. J. Bourdillon; Dr N. P. Melia; Dr M. J. Prophet; Dr J. Hangartner; Dr D. Rothman.

Division MCD

Senior Principal Medical Officer (*G3*), Dr E. Rubery.
Principal Medical Officers (*G4*), Dr G. Lewis; Dr R. Skinner.
Senior Medical Officers (*G5*), Dr P. E. Exon; Dr D. Salisbury; Dr A. Dawson; Dr G. Greenberg; Dr L. Robinson; Dr M. Dunne; Dr S. Lader; Dr C. Swinson; Dr J. Hilton; Dr J. Leese; Dr E. Tebbs; Dr M. McGovern; Dr A. Wright.

Division TEH

MasterSenior Principal Medical Officer (*G3*), Dr J. H. S. Steadman.

Principal Medical Officers (*G4*), Dr E. Smales; Dr G. E. Diggle.
Senior Medical Officers (*G5*), Dr M. Waring; Dr R. B. Singh; Dr N. Lazarus; Dr T. Meredith; Dr R. L. Maynard; Dr T. Marrs; Dr H. Williams.

Division E

Principal Medical Officer (*G4*), Dr J. D. F. Bellamy.

MEDICAL DIVISIONS UNDER DR METTERS

Division CPNM

Senior Principal Medical Officer (*G3*), Dr P. R. Greenfield.
Principal Medical Officer (*G4*), Dr J. M. Graham.
Senior Medical Officers (*G5*), Dr E. Cloake; Dr D. Ernaelsteen; Dr W. J. Modle; Dr I. A. Lister-Cheese; Dr P. Clarke; Dr M. J. Wiseman; Dr H. Markowe; Dr F. Harvey; Dr S. Shepherd.
Medical Officer (*G6*), Dr J. G. Ablett.

Division MHIE

Senior Principal Medical Officer (*G3*), Dr J. L. Reed.
Principal Medical Officers (*G4*), Dr J. E. Shanks; Dr R. Jenkins.
Senior Medical Officers (*G5*), Dr P. Mason; Dr J. Brooksbank; Dr D. Jones.

Division ISD

Senior Principal Medical Officer (*G3*), Dr G. Jones.
Principal Medical Officers (*G4*), Dr H. Pickles; Dr P. A. Hyzler.
Senior Medical Officers (*G5*), Dr S. A. Munday; Dr A. Rawson; Dr P. R. Dendy; Dr P. Furnell; Dr S. P. Vahl; Dr H. Sutton; Dr A. Rejman; Dr C. Collier.

MEDICAL DIVISIONS UNDER DR WALFORD

Division MPO

Principal Medical Officer (*G4*), Dr D. Cunningham.
Senior Medical Officers (*G5*), Dr A. L. J. Martin; Dr W. Thorne; Dr G. N. Brown; Dr D. Holt; Dr D. MacPherson; Dr I. H. Nicholas.

Division PCR

Senior Principal Medical Officer (*G3*), Dr G. C. Rivett.
Senior Medical Officers (*G5*), Dr. W. Miller; Dr V. Press; Dr P. Leech; Dr T. Mann; Dr T. Van Zwanenberg; Dr A. Clark; Dr D. Milner.

Division MME

Senior Principal Medical Officer (*G3*), Dr A. J. Isaacs.
Senior Medical Officers (*G5*), Dr H. S. Bloom; Dr M. Smith; Dr B. Ely; Dr P. J. Doyle; Dr J. Ashwell.
Assistant Secretary (*G5*), N. F. Duncan.
Principals (*G7*), J. Gooderham; A. McNeil; T. G. Bennett.

Dental Division

Chief Dental Officer, R. B. Mouatt.
Senior Dental Officers, C. Howard; J. M. G. Hunt; G. A. Wells.

Nursing Division

Chief Nursing Officer, Mrs A. A. B. Poole.
Director of Nursing/Acting Deputy Chief Nursing Officer, M. A. Clark.
Principal Nursing Officers, J. Tait, OBE; Miss C. Clifford; Miss S. Norman; P. Gibbons.
Acting Principal Nursing Officer, Miss D. Horridge.

Pharmaceutical Division

Chief Pharmaceutical Officer (*G3*), B. H. Hartley.
Deputy Chief Pharmaceutical Officer (*G5*), Dr J. R. V. Merrills.

Senior Principal Pharmaceutical Officer (G6), P. E. Green.

Information Division
Director of Information (G4), Miss R. Christopherson.
Deputy Directors (G6), C. P. Wilson (*news*); G. Meredith (*publicity*).

NATIONAL HEALTH SERVICE
Regional Health Authorities

The chairmen and members of Regional Health Authorities are appointed by the Secretary of State for Health.

Northern, Benfield Road, Walker Gate, Newcastle upon Tyne. *Chairman,* P. Carr, CBE. *Regional General Manager,* D. Hague.

Yorkshire, Park Parade, Harrogate. *Chairman,* Sir Bryan Askew. *Regional General Manager,* A. Foster.

Trent, Fulwood House, Old Fulwood Road, Sheffield. *Chairman,* Sir Michael Carlisle. *Regional General Manager,* B. Edwards, CBE.

East Anglia, Union Lane, Chesterton, Cambridge. *Chairman,* Sir Colin Walker, OBE. *Regional General Manager,* A. Liddell.

North East Thames, 40 Eastbourne Terrace, W2 3QR. *Chairman,* T. Chessells. *Regional General Manager,* T. Hunt.

North West Thames, 40 Eastbourne Terrace, W2 3QR. *Chairman,* Sir William Doughty. *Regional General Manager,* D. J. Kenny, CBE.

South East Thames, Thrift House, Collington Avenue, Bexhill-on-Sea, E. Sussex. *Chairman,* P. Barker. *Regional General Manager,* G. N. V. Green.

South West Thames, 40 Eastbourne Terrace, W2 3QR. *Chairman,* The Baroness Cumberlege, CBE. *Regional General Manager,* C. Spry.

Wessex, Highcroft, Romsey Road, Winchester, Hants. *Chairman,* Sir Robin Buchanan. *Regional General Manager,* K. Jarrold.

Oxford, Old Road, Headington, Oxford. *Chairman,* Sir Gordon Roberts, CBE. *Regional General Manager,* R. M. Nicholls.

South Western, King Square House, 26–27 King Square, Bristol. *Chairman,* C. Stuart. *Regional General Manager,* Miss C. E. Hawkins.

West Midlands, Arthur Thompson House, 146–150 Hagley Road, Birmingham. *Chairman,* Sir James Ackers. *Regional General Manager,* K. F. Bales, CBE.

Mersey, Hamilton House, 24 Pall Mall, Liverpool L3 6AL. *Chairman,* Sir Donald Wilson. *Regional General Manager,* G. Scaife.

North Western, Gateway House, Piccadilly South, Manchester M60 7LP. *Chairman,* R. B. Martin, QC. *Regional General Manager,* D. Allison, CB.

Special Health Authorities

Health Education Authority, Hamilton House, Mabledon Place, WC1H 9TX. *Chairman,* Sir Donald Maitland, GCMG, OBE; *Chief Executive,* Dr Spencer Hagard.

Disablement Services Authority, 14 Russell Square, WC1. *Chairman,* Lord Holderness, PC; *Chief Executive,* M. G. Jeremiah.

Special Hospitals Service Authority
Charles House, Kensington High Street, W14

The Special Hospitals Service is provided by four hospitals: Rampton; Broadmoor; Moss Side; and Park Lane.
Chairman, Dr D. E. Edmond.
Chief Executive, C. Kaye.

NATIONAL HEALTH SERVICE, SCOTLAND
See p. 362

DEPARTMENTS OF HEALTH AND SOCIAL SECURITY—COMMON SERVICES ADMINISTRATION AND FINANCE GROUP
Principal Establishments and Finance Officer (G2), Mrs A. E. Bowtell, CB.

FINANCE DIRECTORATE

Financial Management Directorate
Director of Finance NHSHE (G2), Mr. S. V. Master.
Heads of Finance Directorate Units (G3), R. Jefferies; T. Scott; R. M. Jordan.

Finance Division A
Director of Finance and Corporate Information (G3), G. Greenshields.
Under Secretary (G4), Mrs J. Firth.
Assistant Secretaries (G5), M. A. Harris; P. Garland; C. P. Kendall; Mrs E. Hunter-Johnson; Miss A. Simkins.

Finance Division B
Under Secretary (Health) (G3), Ms M. E. Stuart.
Assistant Secretaries (G5), P. F. Slade; Miss A. Mithani; J. M. Brownlee; K. J. Guinness.
Senior Principals (G6), R. J. Tredgett; A. C. Symes.

Finance Division D
Under Secretary (Social Security) (G3), Mrs E. A. Woods.
Assistant Secretaries (G5), J. T. Hughes; J. R. Simpson; C. N. Leivers; Mrs J. Clayton.

NHS Superannuation Branch
Executive Director (Personnel) (G4), R. M. Drury.
Senior Principal (G6), D. Napier.

Statistics and Management Information Division (SMI)
Director of Statistics and Management Information (G3), Mrs R. J. Butler.
Chief Statisticians (G5), Miss P. W. Annesley; J. N. Lithgow; R. K. Willmer; J. Ashe; G. J. O. Phillpotts.

Economics and Operational Research Division (Health)
Chief Economic Adviser (G3), C. H. Smee.
Senior Economic Advisers (G5), M. A. Parsonage; J. W. Hurst.

Central Resource Management
Assistant Secretary (G5), M. Brown.
Senior Principal (G6), T. Thorne.

Departmental Personnel Management
Principal Establishment Officer (G3), Miss A. Perkins.
Assistant Secretaries (G5), R. J. Tilney; P. E. Turner; I. Magee; B. K. Gilbert.

Solicitor's Office
Solicitor (G2), P. K. J. Thompson.
Principal Assistant Solicitors (G3), Mrs G. S. Kerrigan; A. D. Roberts.
Proceedings Operational Director (G4), P. C. Nilsson.

HEALTH AND SAFETY COMMISSION
Baynards House, 1 Chepstow Place,
Westbourne Grove, W2 4TF
[071–243 6000]

The Health and Safety Commission was created under the Health and Safety at Work etc. Act 1974, with duties to reform health and safety law, to propose new regulations, and generally to promote the protection of people at work and of the public from hazards arising from industrial (including commercial) activity, including major industrial accidents and the transportation of hazardous materials.

The Commission members are appointed by the Secretary of State for Employment, although the Commission assists a number of Secretaries of State concerned with aspects of its functions. It is made up of representatives of employers, trades unions and local authorities. The Chairman is full time.

The Commission can appoint agents, and it works in conjunction with local authorities who enforce the Act in such premises as offices and warehouses.
Chairman, Sir John Cullen.
Members, Dr M. C. Shannon, CBE; P. Jacques, CBE; A. Tuffin; R. Symons; P. Gallagher; J. Marvin; E. Carrick, Dame Rachel Waterhouse, DBE, PH.D; N. J. Pitcher.
Secretary, J. Grubb.

HEALTH AND SAFETY EXECUTIVE
Baynards House, 1 Chepstow Place,
Westbourne Grove, W2 4TF
[071–221 0870]

The Health and Safety Executive is the Health and Safety Commission's major instrument. Through its inspectorates it enforces health and safety law in the majority of industrial premises, to protect both people at work and the public. The Executive advises the Commission in its major task of laying down safety standards through regulations and practical guidance for many industrial processes, liaising as necessary with government departments and other institutions. The Executive is also the licensing authority for nuclear installations. In carrying out its functions the Executive acts independently of the Government, guided only by the Commission as to general health and safety policy.
Director General (G2), J. D. Rimington, CB.
Deputy Director General (G2), D. C. T. Eves.
Member of the Executive, D. J. Hodgkins.

HM Factory Inspectorate
HM Chief Inspector of Factories (G3), A. J. Linehan.

HM Agricultural Inspectorate
HM Chief Agricultural Inspector (G3), C. Boswell.

HM Mines Inspectorate
HM Chief Inspector of Mines (G3), Dr M. D. Jones.

HM Nuclear Installations Inspectorate
HM Chief Inspector of Nuclear Installations (G3), E. A. Ryder.

HM Railway Inspectorate
HM Chief Inspector of Railways (G3), R. Seymour.

Safety and General Policy Division
Director (G3), D. J. Hodgkins.

Technology Division
(includes HM Explosives Inspectorate).
Director (G3), Dr A. Ellis.

Hazardous Installations Division
Director (G3), R. J. Allison.

Research and Laboratory Services Division
Director (G3), Dr J. McQuaid.

Health Policy Division
(includes the Employment Medical Advisory Service).
Director of Medical Services (G3), Dr J. T. Carter.

Solicitor's Office
Solicitor (G4), B. J. Ecclestone.

Resources and Planning Division
(including the Accident Prevention Advisory Unit).
Director (G3), A. W. Brown.

Offshore Safety Division
Chief Executive (G3), A. C. Barrell.

HIGHLANDS AND ISLANDS ENTERPRISE
Bridge House, 20 Bridge Street,
Inverness IV1 1QR
[0463–234171]

Highlands and Islands Enterprise is the core body of a network of ten local enterprise companies, which encourage and deliver economic and social development plans and training and environmental renewal schemes at local level. It brings together the powers of the former Highlands and Islands Development Board (HIDB), the Training Agency in the former HIDB area, and the land renewal functions of the Scottish Development Agency in the former HIDB area.
Chairman, Sir Robert Cowan.
Chief Executive, I. A. Robertson.

HISTORIC BUILDINGS AND MONUMENTS COMMISSION FOR ENGLAND (ENGLISH HERITAGE)
Fortress House,
23 Savile Row, W1X 1AB
[071–973 3000]

Under the National Heritage Act, 1983, the duties of the Commission are: to secure the preservation of ancient monuments and historic buildings; to promote the preservation and enhancement of conservation areas; to promote the public's enjoyment of, and advance their knowledge of, ancient monuments and historic buildings and their preservation. The Commission has advisory committees on historic buildings, ancient monuments, historic areas, and London.
Chairman, The Lord Montagu of Beaulieu (*until March 1992*); J. Stevens (*from April 1992*).
Commissioners, HRH The Duke of Gloucester; Miss J. A. Page (*Chief Executive*); Dr R. W. Brunskill; A. Chancellor; M. B. Caroe; Viscountess Cobham; Dr N. Cossons; Sir Hugh Cubitt; Prof. B. Cunliffe; T. Farrell; The Baroness Hollis of Heigham; Sir George Moseley; D. Somerset; J. Stevens.

HISTORIC BUILDINGS COUNCIL FOR WALES
Brunel House, 2 Fitzalan Road,
Cardiff CF2 1UY
[0222–465511]

The Council's function is to advise the Secretary of State for Wales through Cadw: Welsh Historic Monuments (*see* p. 374), which is an executive agency within the Welsh Office.
Chairman, The Marquess of Anglesey, FSA, FRS.
Members, W. Lindsay Evans; Prof. J. Eynon, OBE, FRIBA, FSA; The Earl Lloyd George of Dwyfor; T. Lloyd; R. Haslam; Dr P. Morgan.
Secretary, R. W. Hughes.

HISTORIC BUILDINGS COUNCIL FOR SCOTLAND
20 Brandon Street, Edinburgh EH3 5RA
[031–556 8400]

Chairman, Sir Nicholas Fairbairn, QC, MP.
Members, Sir Ilay Campbell, Bt.; Mrs P. Chalmers; Prof. J. D. Dunbar-Nasmith, CBE, FRSA, FRSE; M. Ellington; J. Hunter Blair; I. Hutchison, OBE; The Lord Jauncey, PC; K. Martin; J. A. M. Mitchell, CB, CVO, MC; Miss G. Nayler; Rev. C. Robertson; Prof. A. J. Rowan.
Secretary, I. G. Dewar.

ROYAL COMMISSION ON THE HISTORICAL MONUMENTS OF ENGLAND
Fortress House, 23 Savile Row, W1X 2JQ
[071–973 3500]

The Royal Commission on the Historical Monuments of England was established in 1908. It is the national body charged with the recording and analysing of ancient and historical monuments and buildings. It compiles, preserves and makes publicly available the national archive of such material, which is housed in the National Monuments Record.
Chairman, The Baroness Park of Monmouth, CMG, OBE.
Commissioners, Prof. R. Bradley, FSA; R. A. Buchanan, Ph.D.; Prof. J. D. Evans, Ph.D., Litt.D., FBA, FSA; D. J. Keene, Ph.D.; Prof. G. H. Martin, CBE, D.Phil., FSA; Prof. G. I. Meirion-Jones, Ph.D., FSA; Prof. J. K. Downes, Ph.D., FSA; Prof. A. C. Thomas, CBE, D.Litt., FSA; Prof. M. Biddle, FBA, FSA; Prof. M. Todd, FSA; Mrs B. K. Cherry, FSA; R. D. H. Gem, Ph.D., FSA; T. R. M. Longman.
Secretary, T. G. Hassall, FSA.

ROYAL COMMISSION ON ANCIENT AND HISTORICAL MONUMENTS IN WALES
The Crown Building, Plas Crug,
Aberystwyth SY23 2HP
[0970–624381]

The Commission was appointed in 1908 to make an inventory of the ancient and historical monuments in Wales and Monmouthshire. The Commission also includes the National Monuments Record for Wales.
Chairman, Prof. J. B. Smith.
Commissioners, M. R. Apted, Ph.D., FSA; R. W. Brunskill, OBE, Ph.D.; Prof. D. Ellis Evans, D.Phil., FBA; Prof. R. A. Griffiths, Ph.D.; R. M. Haslam, FSA; Prof. G. B. D. Jones, D.Phil., FSA; S. B. Smith; G. J. Wainwright, MBE, Ph.D., FSA; Prof. J. G. Williams.
Secretary, P. Smith, FSA.

ROYAL COMMISSION ON ANCIENT AND HISTORICAL MONUMENTS OF SCOTLAND
54 Melville Street, Edinburgh EH3 7HF
[031–225 5994]

The Commission was appointed in 1908 to make an inventory of the ancient and historical monuments of Scotland and to specify those that seem most worthy of preservation. The Commission also includes the National Monuments Record of Scotland.
Chairman, The Earl of Crawford and Balcarres, PC.
Commissioners, Prof. A. A. M. Duncan, FBA, FRSE; Prof. J. D. Dunbar-Nasmith, CBE, FRIBA; Prof. Rosemary Cramp, CBE, FSA; Prof. L. Alcock, FSA, FRSE; Mrs P. E. Durham; Prof. T. C. Smout, Ph.D.; The Hon. Lord Cullen; Dr D. J. Howard, FSA; The Hon. P. D. E. M. Moncreiffe.
Secretary, R. J. Mercer, FSA.

ANCIENT MONUMENTS BOARD FOR WALES
Brunel House, 2 Fitzalan Road, Cardiff CF2 1UY
[0222–465511]

Chairman, Prof. G. Williams, CBE, FBA, FSA.
Members, R. B. Heaton, FRIBA; Prof. R. R. Davies, D.Phil.; Dr H. S. Green, FSA; R. G. Keen; Miss F. Lynch, FSA; Prof. W. H. Manning, FSA; D. Moore, RD, FSA; P. Smith, FSA.
Secretary, S. Morris.

ANCIENT MONUMENTS BOARD FOR SCOTLAND
20 Brandon Street, Edinburgh EH3 5RA
[031–244 3076]

Chairman, Prof. E. C. Fernie, FSA, FSA SCOT.
Members, Prof. A. Fenton, CBE, FRSE, FSA SCOT.; J. Simpson, FSA SCOT.; Sir Jamie Stormonth Darling, CBE, MC, TD, WS; Mrs E. V. W. Proudfoot, FSA, FSA SCOT.; Mrs K. Dalyell; J. H. A. Gerrard, FRSA; T. R. H. Godden, CB; L. J. Masters, FSA; Dr A. Ritchie, FSA; R. D. Kernohan, OBE; Dr J. Morgan; Prof. C. D. Morris, FSA, FSA Scot.
Secretary, Ms J. Hutchison.
Assessor, D. J. Breeze, Ph.D., FSA.

HOME-GROWN CEREALS AUTHORITY
Hamlyn House, Highgate Hill, N19 5PR
[071–263 3391]

Constituted under the Cereals Marketing Act 1965, the Authority consists of nine members representing UK cereal growers, nine representing dealers in, or processors of, grain and three independent members. The purpose of the Authority is to improve the production and marketing of UK grain. The Authority also provides certain agency services to the Intervention Board for Agricultural Produce in connection with the application of the Common Agricultural Policy in the UK.
Chairman, G. B. Nelson.
General Manager, C. J. Ames.

British Cereal Exports

Chairman, R. J. Cherrington.
Manager, J. B. Rose.

HOME OFFICE
50 Queen Anne's Gate, SW1H 9AT
[071–273 3000]

The Home Office deals with those internal affairs in England and Wales which have not been assigned to other Government Departments. The Home Secretary is particularly concerned with the administration of justice; criminal law; the treatment of offenders, including probation and the prison service; the police; immigration and nationality; passport policy matters; community relations; certain public safety matters; fire and civil emergencies services; and also with questions of national broadcasting policy. The Home Secretary personally is the link between The Queen and the public, and exercises certain powers on her behalf, including that of the Royal Pardon.

Other subjects dealt with include electoral arrangements; addresses and petitions to The Queen; ceremonial and formal business connected with honours; requests for extradition of criminals; scrutiny of local authority byelaws; granting of licences for scientific procedures involving animals; cremations, burials and exhumations; firearms; dangerous drugs and poisons; general policy on laws relating to shops, liquor licensing, gaming and lotteries, charitable collections and marriage; theatre and cinema licensing; co-ordination of government action in relation to the voluntary social services; and sex discrimination and race relations policy.

The Home Secretary is also the link between the UK government and the governments of the Channel Islands and the Isle of Man.

(For **Salaries**, *see* page 293)

Secretary of State for the Home Department, THE RT. HON. KENNETH BAKER, MP.
  Principal Private Secretary (G5), C. J. Walters.
  Private Secretaries, P. W. Pugh; Miss H. J. Wilkinson.
  Special Adviser, A. Kerpel, MBE.
  Parliamentary Private Secretary, S. J. Norris, MP.
Ministers of State, THE EARL FERRERS, PC; THE RT. HON. JOHN PATTEN, MP; THE RT. HON. MRS ANGELA RUMBOLD, CBE, MP.
  Special Adviser, C. M. Grantham.
Parliamentary Under Secretary of State, PETER LLOYD, MP.
  Parliamentary Private Secretaries:
  To Mrs Rumbold, J. Q. Davies, MP.
  To Mr Patten, M. Carrington, MP.
Parliamentary Clerk, B. E. R. Kinney.
Permanent Under Secretary of State (G1), Sir Clive Whitmore, GCB, CVO.
  Private Secretary, K. D. Sutton.
Chief Medical Officer (at Department of Health), Dr K. Calman.

Legal Adviser's Branch

Legal Adviser (G2), A. H. Hammond.
Principal Assistant Legal Advisers (G3), D. J. Bentley; Miss P. A. Edwards.
Assistant Legal Advisers, R. J. Clayton; Mrs S. A. Evans; A. M. C. Inglese; D. Seymour; A. W. D. Wilson.
Senior Principal Legal Assistants, Mrs J. M. Jones; J. O'Meara; C. M. L. Osborne; Mrs C. Price.

CRIMINAL RESEARCH AND STATISTICS DEPARTMENTS

Deputy Under Secretary (G2), J. F. Halliday.

Criminal Policy Department

Assistant Under Secretary of State (G3), G. L. Angel.
Heads of Divisions (G5), R. J. Baxter; A. Cogbill; A. Harding; Miss J. MacNaughton; Miss S. Marshall; L. P. Wright.
Senior Principal (G6), A. Norbury.
Principals (G7), Miss D. Collings; D. Cole; Ms R. Collins Rice; F. E. Cook; R. G. W. Dyce; L. D. Hay; L. T. Hughes; Ms H. Jackson; N. Jordon; Ms K. Lidbetter; K. MacKenzie; Mrs M. Manolias; Mrs R. M. Mitev; T. C. Morris; A. Pickersgill; Ms S. A. Rex; D. Rigby; Ms L. Rogerson; Mrs E. A. Sandars; G. Sutton; Ms F. Taylor; G. Underwood; P. F. Vallance; R. J. Weatherill.
Chief Inspector, Drugs Branch (G6), A. McFarlane.

Research and Statistics Department

Assistant Under Secretary of State (G3), C. P. Nuttall.

Research and Planning Unit

Head of Unit (G5), R. Tarling.
Grade 6, J. M. Hough; P. J. Jordan; Mrs P. Mayhew; G. R. Walmsley.
Principals (G7), A. C. Barton; D. C. Brown; J. A. Ditchfield; Dr P. J. Ekblom; Dr S. Field; J. H. Graham; Dr P. Grove; Dr T. Hope; Mrs K. E. Howard; Mrs C. L. Lehmann; T. Marshall; Ms P. M. Morgan; Miss J. W. Mott; Dr G. I. U. Mair; J. F. Mcleod; A. D. Moxon; W. E. Saulsbury; Dr L. J.

F. Smith; F. P. E. Southgate; Ms J. Vennard; Dr I. P. Williamson.

Statistics Department

Chief Statisticians (G5), C. G. Lewis; J. L. Walker; P. W. Ward.
Statisticians (G7), Ms A. Barber; G. G. Barclay; W. D. Burns; K. Childs; L. Davidoff; Mrs P. Dowdeswell; P. F. Collier; Miss G. Goddard; Mrs S. Keith; M. Lock; Mrs R. Passmore; Z. J. Frosztega; K. M. Jackson; Miss A. Maxwell; Ms C. D. Morgan; R. Pape; Mrs R. Passmore; Mrs P. A. Penneck; P. E. Ramell; R. M. Taylor; M. Uglow.

Criminal Justice and Constitutional Department

Assistant Under Secretary of State (G3), R. M. Morris.
Heads of Divisions (G5), E. A. Grant; Miss P. C. Drew; P. J. Honour.
Grade 6, A. F. C. Crook; P. H. Duffin.
Principals (G7), Mrs P. A. Almond; Ms J. Cooke; S. L. Cox; Miss R. M. Fletton; J. Gilhespy; Mrs G. Hetherington; H. D. Hillier; Mrs C. J. Jenkins; Mrs S. M. McCarthy; D. Massey; D. Ross; K. W. Smalldon; F. Smith; J. Wake; Mrs J. S. Waters; S. M. K. Willmington; T. J. Wilson; R. W. Wootton.
Chief Inspector of Probation (G4), C. H. Thomas, OBE.
Deputy Chief Inspector of Probation (G5), J. C. Haines.
Grade 7, Dr C. Kershaw.

Animals (Scientific Procedure) Inspectorate

Chief Inspector, Dr R. M. Watt.

POLICE DEPARTMENT

Deputy Under Secretary (G2), I. M. Burns, CB.

Police Department

Assistant Under Secretaries of State (G3), Miss M. A. Clayton; S. W. Boys Smith; G. J. Wasserman.
Heads of Divisions (G5), Mrs P. G. W. Catto; J. W. Cane; Miss A. M. Edwards; P. C. Ewards; J. L. Goddard; R. A. Harrington; K. H. Heal; J. Le Vay; C. B. J. Sutton.
Senior Principals (G6), D. R. Birleson; R. Creedon; R. Crick; R. A. Ginman; M. P. Gore; D. D. O'Brien *(acting)*.
Principals (G7), J. W. Bradley; M. P. Cook; P. R. Curwen; N. Hancock; Mrs C. Heald; M. J. I. Hill; K. Hopley; R. Korniki; Dr G. K. Laycock; Mrs S. G. Mann; M. R. Matthews; N. F. Montgomery-Pott; Mrs G. I. Moody; D. Pooley; M. Phillips; P. W. Pugh; C. Roden; S. J. Rimmer; Miss J. B. Rumble; P. T. Smith; D. Theobald; A. G. Thomson; P. Tomlinson; Mrs A. Underhill; Ms A. E. Wickington; A. Wolfenden; Miss M. S. Wooldridge.

Police Scientific Development Branch
Sandridge Laboratories, Woodcock Hill,
Sandridge, St Albans, Herts. AL4 9HQ
[0727–865051]

Head of Laboratory (G6), Dr P. A. Young.
Principal Scientific Officers (G7), C. J. Aldridge; E. C. Brown; A. J. Ford; R. Harry; T. Kent; Dr R. J. Lacey; Dr S. R. Lewis; C. D. Payne; Dr J. Tan.

Langhurst House, Langhurstwood Road,
Nr. Horsham, Sussex RH12 4WX
[0403–55451]

Principal Scientific Officers (G7), Dr N. D. Custance; A. G. Lindfield; M. J. Thompson.

Headquarters Forensic Science Service
Horseferry House
Dean Ryle Street, SW1
[071–217 3000]

(An executive agency within the Home Office.)

Director General (G4), Dr J. Thompson.
Head of Personnel and Administration (G6), J. P. Emery.
Grade 6, Dr T. Rothwell.
Grade 7, J. Glaze (*policy*); C. Passey (*personnel and administration*).

Police National Computer Organization
Horseferry House,
Dean Ryle Street, SW1
[071–217 3000]

Head of Organization (G6), J. Ladley.
Senior Principal (G6), Dr G. Turnbull.
Principals (G7), B. J. Blain; E. L. Brannan; Mrs P. Cocks; G. T. Coulthard; B. G. Cox; D. H. Faulks; J. A. Henderson; P. D. Hill-Jones; A. F. G. Hitchman; D. C. Moulton; Dr F. Preston; P. T. Price; R. J. Reason; D. G. Skene; R. H. Watt.

DTELS (Directorate of Telecommunications)
Horseferry House,
Dean Ryle Street, SW1
[071–217 3000]

Head of Directorate (G5), N. F. K. Finlayson.
Assistant Director (G6), J. F. Nicholson.
Head of Operations (G6), I. Aitken.
Head of Marketing (G6), vacant.
Head of Engineering Consultancy (G6), J. L. Mumford.
Principals (G7), B. Albon; F. W. Catterall; S. R. Cole; W. Hogg; A. Hulme; A. N. Keret; T. J. Logan; J. L. Mumford; K. O'Sullivan; M. A. Parker; R. J. Sanders; A. A. Sipson; K. Staves; L. T. Whiteside.

HM Inspectorate of Constabulary
HM Chief Inspector of Constabulary, Sir John Woodcock, CBE, QPM £67,499
HM Inspectors, C. J. Dear, QPM; D. Elliott, CBE, QPM; B. Hayes, QPM; T. A. Morris, QPM; Sir Philip Myers, OBE, QPM; C. Smith, CVO, QPM; J. A. Smith, QPM
£61,029.

Police Staff College
Bramshill House, Basingstoke, Hampshire
RG27 0JW
[025 126–2931]

Commandant, Sir Robert Bunyard, KBE, QPM.
Deputy Commandant and Director of Courses, P. J. Lewis.
Secretary (G7), K. J. Sheehan.

BROADCASTING, EQUAL OPPORTUNITIES, IMMIGRATION AND NATIONALITY DEPARTMENTS

Deputy Under Secretary (G2), A. J. Langdon.

Broadcasting and Miscellaneous Department
Assistant Under Secretary of State (G3), M. E. Head, CVO.
Heads of Divisions (G5), Miss J. M. Goose, CBE; S. B. Hickson; P. R. C. Storr.
Principals (G7), D. A. L. Cooke; Ms C. Craig; R. Eagle; Miss G. F. Harrison; N. M. McLean; G. H. Marriage; J. Sibson; C. P. Stevens; R. Thew.

Equal Opportunities and General Department
Assistant Under Secretary of State (G3), A. R. Rawsthorne.
Heads of Divisions (G5), N. M. Johnson; J. Sibson.
Senior Principal (G6), J. Daly.
Principals (G7), Dr S. R. E. Atkins; Mrs M. K. Bramwell; Mrs D. Grice; C. C. R. Hudson; Mrs J. S. Morris; S. Pike.

Voluntary Services Unit
Assistant Secretary (G5), Mrs B. H. Fair.

Principals (G7), Miss C. Byrne; Miss V. R. Hatcher; A. V. H. Stainer; Ms J. Thorpe.

Immigration and Nationality Department
Lunar House, 40 Wellesley Road, Croydon, Surrey,
CR9 2BY
[081–760 plus ext.]

Assistant Under Secretaries of State (G3), R. J. Fries; T. C. Platt.
Heads of Divisions (G5), J. I. Chisholm; M. J. Gillespie; T. J. Kavanagh; E. B. Nicholls; N. C. Sanderson; N. R. Varney; R. G. Yates.
Senior Principal (G6), G. Boiling, MBE; D. M. McQueen; C. J. Saunders.
Principals (G7), C. A. Allison; Mrs H. Bayne; Mrs M. Bishop; W. F. Bryant; J. G. Burgess; J. Casey; A. Cunningham; J. Gilbert; Dr S. Hadjipavlou; Mrs C. Kellas; J. Kelly; R. W. Knight; C. R. Miller; J. S. Page; D. A. Peters; Miss G. M. Romney; S. Spence; G. Stadlen; P. A. Stanton; A. Walmsley; P. N. Wrench.

Immigration Service
Director (Ports) (G5), Miss K. J. Collins.
Director (Immigration Service Enforcement) (G5), C. B. Manchip.
Deputy Directors (G6), T. Farrage; D. J. McDonough.
Assistant Directors (G7), B. R. Barrett; W. Downiett; J. M. Durose; Miss G. M. Griffith; V. Hogg; D. I. Ingham; G. Maguire; K. Richardson.

Passport Agency
Clive House, Petty France, SW1H 9HD
[071–271 3000]

(An executive agency within the Home Office.)
Head of Division (G5), J. E. Hayzelden.
Deputy Heads of Division (Directors of Operations) (G6), N. S. Benger; J. Lonsdale; Miss A. Smith.
Principals (G7), J. Burgess; M. Copley; E. Downham; R. G. Le Marechal; R. I. Henderson; J. McColl.

PRISON SERVICE
Cleland House, Page Street, SW1P 4LN
[071–217 3000]

Non-Civil Service grade salaries
HM Chief Inspector of Prisons £57,550
Prison Service Governor 1 . . . . £42,887
Prison Service Governor 2 . . . . £38,726
Prison Service Governor 3 . . . . £33,445
Prison Service Governor 4 . . . . £26,500–£28,763

Director-General of the Prison Service (G2), J. G. Pilling.

Prisons Department
Assistant Under Secretaries of State (Directors) (G3); Mrs J. E. Reisz (*Building and Services*); B. A. Emes (*Inmate Programmes*); W. J. A. Innes (*Custody*); I. Dunbar (*Inmate Administration*); A. J. Butler (*Personnel and Finance*); Dr J. Wool (*Prison Medical Services*).
Non-Executive Members, Mrs U. Banerjee; F. W. Bentley.
Heads of Divisions (G5), P. E. Bolton; B. M. Caffarey; W. R. Fittall; Miss L. F. Gill; Mrs E. J. Grimsey; G. E. Guy; Mrs V. V. R. Harris; J. A. Ingman; W. A. Jeffrey; J. M. Lyon; Miss C. J. Stewart; R. R. Tilt.
Assistant Director of Prison Medical Services (G4), Dr P. J. Hynes.
Principal Medical Officers (G4), Dr P. Arrowsmith; Dr R. Gooch; Dr M. Longfield; Dr P. B. Pattison; Dr G. Penton; Dr R. Ralli; Dr D. Speed; Dr A. Todd.
Senior Principals (G6), T. K. Cobley; P. Cook; R. E. Corrigan; C. F. Drewitt; M. Ireson; B. Johnson; R.

W. Lockett; B. S. Luetchford; Dr C. McDougall; P. Sleightholme.

Governors (1), J. W. Dring; R. Jacques; G. Gregory-Smith; I. Ward.

Principals (*G7*), D. M. Ackland; A. J. Adams; D. Aldridge; J. H. Attridge; R. M. Bradley; M. J. Brown; A. D. Burgess; H. M. C. Crudge; P. Dawson; M. Dent; B. J. Derry; P. Done; Miss J. Erwteman; D. H. Gannon; Ms V. Gray; Mrs M. Hollocks; N. F. M. Home; S. S. Horlock; Ms L. M. Jackson; M. W. Jarvis; F. N. Jasper; R. S. H. Kettle; C. J. Lawton; Ms P. Lowe; Mrs S. McDougall; K. Marshall; D. Neal; K. R. North; J. S. Nottingham; T. E. Russell; R. Rhodes; R. E. Smith; R. M. Sutcliffe; G. H. Thomas; G. Utteridge; T. A. Ward; Miss S. Weinel; S. C. Wells; W. F. Whiteing; A. T. Williams; Mrs H. Wood; R. J. Wood; D. I. H. Wright; P. Wright; R. A. Wright.

Governors (2), C. T. Erickson; A. J. Fitzpatrick; C. Lambert; P. J. Leonard; Miss S. F. McCormick; M. Morrison; R. J. Perry; S. C. A. Pryor; D. Roberts; S. R. Robinson; D. Shaw.

Chaplain General and Archdeacon of the Prison Service, Ven. K. Pound.

Chief Education Officer (*G6*), I. G. Benson.

Chief Physical Education Officer (*G6*), M. W. Denton.

Governors (3), N. D. Clifford; R. Daly; J. R. Dovell; W. S. Duff; P. L. Hanaway; S. O'Neill; R. Reveley; C. D. Sherwood; I. Truffet; J. Uzzell; D. Waplington; J. H. Whetton; I. G. Windebank; W. A. Wood.

Directorate of Works
Abell House, John Islip Street, SW1P 4LH
[071–217 3000]

Director of Works (*G4*), W. L. Sparks.
Group Managers:
Superintending Architect (*G6*), S. Mahraj.
Chief Civil Structural Engineer (*G6*), R. W. T. Haines.
Chief Mechanical and Electrical Engineer (*G6*), R. Putland.
Chief Quantity Surveyor (*G6*), A. W. Gillman.
Grade 6, B. Stickley.
Principals (*G7*), O. Astaniotis; P. J. Attwater; B. J. Bleet; J. K. Chamberlain; M. J. Davies; J. B. Dawson; A. Dick; J. A. Doohan; J. V. Gleed; M. C. Hayes; G. E. Hickey; C. J. Lawton; R. T. Lewis; C. W. Nicholls; J. W. Plumb; S. Richards; M. Ryland; M. Sweeny; R. J. Tricker; N. L. Wilson.

Prison Service Industries and Farms
Lunar House, Wellesley Road, Croydon,
Surrey CR9 2BY
[081–760 plus ext.]

Director (*G5*), P. R. A. Fulton.
Group Managers (*G6*), J. D. Cleary; M. Codd; G. C. Robertson; A. Sweeney; J. Weller.
Principals (*G7*), C. Allars; J. A. Byrd; J. Cairns; B. D. Feist; R. Fisher; Mrs J. M. Flaschner; J. A. Gillcrist; C. Handley; W. Heppolette; D. E. Neville; T. Senior; A. S. Wilson.

Supply and Transport Branch
Crown House, 52 Elizabeth Street,
Corby, Northants.
[0536–202101]

Director (*G5*), D. J. Hardwick.
Principals (*G7*), R. C. Brett; P. Broadhurst; D. J. Brown; B. David; M. Fitzgerald; A. Frith; S. Sirikanda.

Area Managers (Governors 1)

Directorate of Custody (*DOC*)

East Anglia, J. Simmons.
Kent, J. Hunter.
London North, A. J. Pearson.
London South, I. Boon.
South Coast, P. Kitteridge.

Directorate of Inmate Administration (*DIA*)

Central, M. D. Jenkins.
Mercia, T. Bone.
Chilterns, A. de Frisching.
Wales and the West, J. Wilkinson.
Wessex, R. J. May.

Directorate of Inmate Programmes (*DIP*)

East Midland, P. Wheatley.
North East, A. H. Papps.
North West, D. I. Lockwood.
Yorkshire, A. Stapleton.

PRISONS
Governors

Acklington (*DIP*), *Northumberland*, C. Harder.
Albany (*DOC*), *IOW*, R. Mitchell.
Aldington (*DOC*), *Kent*, J. Hone.
Ashwell (*DIA*), *Leics.*, H. Reid.
Askham Grange (*DIP*), *Yorks.*, P. M. Quin.
Bedford (*DOC*), R. B. Clark.
Belmarsh (*DOC*), H. D. Jones.
Birmingham (*DIA*), C. B. Scott.
Blantyre House (*DOC*), J. Semple.
Blundeston (*DOC*), *Suffolk*, Miss J. M. Fowler.
Bristol (*DIA*), R. Smith.
Brixton (*DOC*), *SW2*, Dr A. Coyle.
Bullingdon (*DIA*), J. Thomas-Ferrand.
Bullwood Hall (*DOC*), Miss S. Ryan.
Camp Hill (*DOC*), *IOW*, T. W. Abbott.
Canterbury (*DOC*), D. Twiner.
Cardiff (*DIA*), A. K. Rawson.
Channings Wood (*DIA*), *Devon*, J. C. Mullens.
Chelmsford (*DOC*), D. B. Sinclair.
Coldingley (*DIA*), *Surrey*, J. Capel.
Cookham Wood (*DOC*), R. Chapman.
Dartmoor (*DIA*), R. J. Kendrick.
Dorchester (*DIA*), B. Coatsworth.
Downview (*DOC*), *Surrey*, D. Aram.
Drake Hall (*DIA*), *Stafford*, R. J. Crouch.
Durham (*DIP*), M. Mogg.
Erlestone Park (*DIA*), R. S. Brandon.
Exeter (*DIA*), D. Alderson.
Featherstone (*DIA*), *Wolverhampton*, L. M. Wiltshire.
Ford (*DOC*), *Sussex*, Maj. B. Smith.
Frankland (*DIP*), *Durham*, P. Buxton.
Full Sutton (*DIP*), J. W. Staples.
Garth (*DIP*), D. Curtis,
Gartree (*DIA*), *Leics.*, R. S. Duncan.
Gloucester (*DIA*), J. Alldridge.
Grendon and Spring Hill (*DOC*), *Bucks*, M. F. S. Selby.
Haslar (*DOC*), T. Hinchcliffe.
Haverigg (*DIP*), *Cumbria*, B. Wilson.
Highpoint (*DOC*), *Newmarket*, R. Curtis.
Hindley (*DIP*), *Lancs.*, A. F. Jennings.
Holloway (*DOC*), *N7*, T. M. O'Sullivan.
Hull (*DIP*), R. Daly.
Kingston (*DOC*), *Portsmouth*, R. Merricks.
Kirkham (*DIP*), *Lancs.*, Maj. R. B. Coombs.
Lancaster (*DIP*), D. G. McNaughton.
Leeds (*DIP*), R. P. Halward.
Leicester (*DIA*), C. J. Williams.
Lewes (*DOC*), T. M. Turner.
Leyhill (*DIA*), *Glos.*, N. W. A. Wall.
Lincoln (*DIP*), W. J. MacGowan.
Lindholme (*DIP*), *Doncaster*, P. Leonard.
Littlehey (*DOC*), S. J. Twinn.
Liverpool (*DIP*), A. N. Joseph, OBE.
Long Lartin (*DIA*), *Worcs.*, A. H. Rayfield.
Maidstone (*DOC*), K. Brewer.
Manchester (*DIP*), W. J. Ginn.
Moorland (*DIP*), M. Sheldrick.
Morton Hall (*DIP*), *Lincoln*, M. F. Clarke.
New Hall (*DIP*), D. England.
Northeye (*DOC*), *Sussex*, D. A. Godfrey.

North Sea Camp (*DIP*), M. L. Knight.
Norwich (*DOC*), M. R. J. Gander.
Nottingham (*DIP*), L. Lavender.
Oxford (*DIA*), R. J. Talbot.
Parkhurst (*DOC*), M. R. J. Marriott.
Pentonville (*DOC*), N7, W. J. Abbott.
Preston (*DIP*), R. Doughty.
Ranby (*DIP*), F. Abbott.
Reading (*DIA*), D. Myers.
Rochester (*DOC*), D. Wilson.
Rudgate (*DIP*), W. Yorks., H. Jones.
Send (*DOC*), Surrey, A. C. Smith.
Shepton Mallet (*DIA*), C. T. Nellins.
Shrewsbury (*DIA*), G. Ross.
Stafford (*DIA*), D. Shaw.
Standford Hill (*DOC*), W. J. Cooper.
Stocken (*DIP*), R. P. Feeney.
Styal (*DIP*), Cheshire, G. Walker.
Sudbury Fosten (*DIA*), Derbys., Miss M. A. Carden.
Swaleside (*DOC*), Kent, B. W. Sutton.
Swansea (*DIA*), J. Heyes.
Thorp Arch (*DIP*), W. Yorks., G. Barnard.
Usk and Prescoed (*DIA*), B. T. Williams.
The Verne (*DIA*), Dorset, D. G. Longley.
Wakefield (*DIP*), T. J. Gadd.
Wakefield Service College (*DOC*), S. R. Robinson.
Wandsworth (*DOC*), SW18, C. G. Clarke.
Wayland (*DOC*), T. C. H. Newth.
Wellingborough (*DOC*), P. Atherton.
Whatton (*DIP*), M. A. Lewis.
Whitemoor (*DOC*), A. J. Barclay.
Winchester (*DOC*), J. C. Newell.
Wormwood Scrubs (*DOC*), W12, J. F. Perriss.
Wymott (*DIP*), Preston, W. J. Mansfield.

Young Offender Institutions
Governors

Aylesbury (*DIA*), C. Welsh.
Brinsford (*DIA*), P. J. Earnshaw.
Bullwood Hall, Essex (*DOC*), Miss S. Ryan.
Castington (*DIP*), J. W. Mullen.
Deerbolt (*DIP*), P. A. Whitehouse.
Dover (*DOC*), T. G. Murtagh, OBE.
Drake Hall (*DIA*), R. J. Crouch.
East Sutton Park (*DOC*), Kent, G. Gibson.
Eastwood Park (*DIA*), Glos., R. J. Summers.
Everthorpe (*DIP*), Humberside, T. Davies.
Feltham (*DOC*), J. Whitty.
Glen Parva (*DIA*), Leics., J. H. Rumball.
Grendon/Spring Hill (*DOC*), M. F. G. Selby.
Guys Marsh (*DIA*), Dorset, P. B. Tucker.
Hatfield (*DIP*), Yorks., W. J. Clark.
Hewell Grange (*DIA*), Worcs., D. W. Bamber.
Hollesley Bay Colony (*DOC*), Suffolk, Miss J. M. King.
Huntercombe and Finnamore Wood (*DIA*), Oxon.,
  Miss A. W. Hair.
Kirklevington (*DIP*), Cleveland, M. K. Lees.
The Mount (*DIA*), Mrs M. Donnelly.
New Hall (*DIP*), D. England.
Northallerton (*DIP*), J. N. Brooke.
Onley (*DIA*), Warwicks., J. O'Neill.
Portland (*DIA*), Dorset, B. McLuckie.
Stoke Heath (*DIA*), Salop, J. L. Harrison.
Styal (*DIP*), Cheshire, G. Walker.
Swinfen Hall (*DIA*), Staffs., C. Scott.
Thorn Cross (*DIP*), C. R. Griffiths.
Usk and Prescoed (*DIA*), Gwent, D. T. Williams.
Werrington (*DIA*), Staffs., P. E. Salter.
Wetherby (*DIP*), Yorks., P. J. Atkinson.
Whatton (*DIP*), Notts., M. A. Lewis.

Remand Centres
Governors

Brinsford (*DIA*), P. J. Earnshaw.
Brockhill (*DIA*), Worcs., P. T. Hanglin.
Cardiff (*DIA*), A. K. Rawson.
Exeter (*DIA*), D. Alderson.

Feltham (*DOC*), J. Whitty.
Glen Parva (*DIA*), J. H. Rumball.
Latchmere House, (*DOC*) Surrey, P. J. Meakings.
Low Newton (*DIP*), Co. Durham, A. H. Olman.
Norwich (*DOC*), M. R. J. Gander.
Pucklechurch (*DIA*), Bristol, vacant.
Risley (*DIP*), Cheshire, F. B. O'Friel.

Inspectorate of Prisons

HM Chief Inspector of Prisons, His Hon. Judge
  Tumim.
HM Deputy Chief Inspector of Prisons (*G5*), B. V.
  Smith.
HM Inspectors (*Gov. 1*), C. Allen; D. M. Brooke;
  (*Gov. 4*), J. Gallagher; D. A. Strong; (*G7*), J. J.
  Courtney; B. J. Wells.
Principal (*G7*), S. E. Bass.

ESTABLISHMENT, FINANCE AND MANPOWER, FIRE AND EMERGENCY PLANNING DEPARTMENTS

Deputy Under Secretary (*G2*), D. E. R. Faulkner.

Establishment Department

Assistant Under Secretary of State (*G3*), C. L. Scoble
  (*Personnel, Organization and Management Ser-
  vices*).
Heads of Divisions (*G5*), B. W. Buck; P. Canovan;
  Mrs C. Crawford; T. J. Flesher; Mrs E. I. France;
  R. M. Whalley.
Senior Principals (*G6*), R. C. Case; D. J. Grant; F. R.
  Hayhurst; M. H. Rumble.
Principals (*G7*), K. Aylen; F. Bannister; J. A. Black;
  W. Black; D. J. Blackwood; Mrs M. E. Bowden; G.
  Brown; P. Buley; M. Carr; R. C. Case; Mrs E. Cook;
  G. J. Edwards; A. Fishwick; J. Fleming; D. H.
  Gannon; I. C. Gaskell; J. A. Greenland; R. A.
  Hemmings; D. G. Jones; B. J. Jordan; J. A. Leake;
  Mrs J. Morgan; D. Mould; Mrs M. E. Moxon; R.
  Ritchie; K. E. R. Rogers; G. R. Sampher; J. S.
  Sarjantson; A. Silver; S. E. Wharton; Mrs V. M.
  Wilsdon.

Home Office Unit at Civil Service Selection Board
  Kirkland House, 24 Whitehall, SW1A 2ED
  [071–210 plus extension]

Director (*G5*), Miss S. E. Paul.
Deputy Director (*G6*), R. G. Evans.
Principal Psychologist (*G7*), D. J. Murray.

Public Relations Branch

Director of Information Services (*G4*), A. M. Moorey.
Deputy Director of Information Services (*G6*), J.
  Haslam.
Head Publicity Officer (*G6*), C. Skinner.
Chief Press Officer (*Prisons*), (*G7*), Miss A. Nelson.

Finance and Manpower Department

Assistant Under Secretary of State (*Principal Finance
  Officer*) (*G3*), S. G. Norris.
Heads of Divisions (*G5*), M. P. Bolt; G. C. Robertson;
  G. K. Sandiford.
Senior Principals (*G6*), T. A. S. Devon; D. W.
  Diamond; A. K. Holman.
Principals (*G7*), Ms J. Bonelle; R. Braganza; G.
  Brindle; G. Cassell; K. I. Cole; Mrs M. Cooper; T.
  A. S. Daniels; R. Davies; C. I. Dickinson; F. H.
  Eggleston; B. Elliott; B. R. Gange; C. Harnett; P.
  W. Jones; D. J. Kent; M. Lee; M. R. Matthews; P.
  Mullarky; P. T. Quibell; R. P. Ritchie; I. F. Smith;
  G. L. Thomas.

Fire and Emergency Planning Department

Assistant Under Secretary of State (*G3*), A. H. Turney,
  CB.
Civil Emergencies Adviser, D. C. G. Brook, CB, CBE.

Heads of Divisions (G5), R. J. Miles; Dr D. M. S. Peace; J. R. K. de Quidt; E. Soden; P. G. Spurgeon.
Grade 6, D. R. Dewick; Dr J. R. Stealey.
Principals (G7), Mrs P. R. Atkins; B. Bishop; Dr G. A. Carr-Hill; N. M. Clowes; E. Cook; R. C. Eaton; Ms J. Harrison; Dr J. A. Harwood; R. Haugh; A. J. Lewis; J. Maloney; A. E. Mantle; Mrs I. Posen; Dr G. E. Scott; R. C. Stephen; Dr M. D. Thomas; P. Topping; K. Wallace.

HM Fire Service Inspectorate

HM Chief Inspector, Sir Reginald Doyle, CBE.
HM Inspectors , B. H. A. Buswell; S. D. Christian; B. T. A. Collins, OBE; T. Greenwood, OBE; A. F. Kilford; P. A. Kilshaw; W. Lumb; D. N. McCallum, OBE; N. Musselwhite, QFSM; W. C. Perry, MBE; K. T. Phillips; R. W. Rawlinson; H. V. Reed; D. F. Robins, CBE; G. J. Tinley.
Senior Engineering Inspector, R. M. Simpson, OBE.
Principal (G7), R. G. W. Cooke.

Fire Service College
Moreton-in-Marsh, Gloucestershire GL56 0RH
[0608–50831]

Commandant, B. Fuller, CBE.
Deputy Commandant, A. Salisbury.
Director of Studies, Dr R. Willis-Lee.
Secretary (G7), J. A. Gundersen.

Emergency Planning College
The Hawkhills, Easingwold, Yorks. YO6 3EG
[0347–21406]

Head of College (G5), J. B. Bettridge, CBE.
Vice-Principal, Col. D. W. Smith, DFC.

Home Office HQ UK Warning and Monitoring Organization
James Wolfe Road, Cowley, Oxford OX4 2PT
[0865–776005]

Director (G6), R. F. Cooke.
Deputy Director I (G7), W. P. Lawrie.
Deputy Director II (G7), D. L. Warden.

HORSERACE TOTALISATOR BOARD
74 Upper Richmond Road, SW15 2SU
[081–874 6411]

The Horserace Totalisator Board was established by the Betting, Gaming and Lotteries Act 1963, as successor to the Racecourse Betting Control Board. Its function is to operate totalisators on approved racecourses in Great Britain, and it also provides on- and off-course cash and credit offices. Under the Horserace Totalisator and Betting Levy Board Act 1972, it is further empowered to offer bets at starting price (or other bets at fixed odds) on any sporting event.
Chairman, Lord Wyatt of Weeford £82,000
Chief Executive, B. McDonnell.
Members, P. S. Winfield; J. F. Sanderson; T. J. Phillips; Hon. D. Sieff; Lord Swaythling.

HOUSING CORPORATION
149 Tottenham Court Road, W1P 0BN
[071–387 9466]

Established by Parliament in 1964, the Housing Corporation registers, promotes, funds and supervises housing associations. There are over 2,300 registered associations in England providing more than half a million homes. Housing associations are non-profit making bodies run by voluntary committees.

The Corporation's duties have been extended under the provisions of the Housing Act 1988 to cover responsibilities for the payments of capital and revenue grants to housing associations, for helping

tenants interested in Tenants' Choice, and the approval and revocation of potential new landlords under this policy.
Chairman, Sir Christopher Benson.
Chief Executive, A. Meyer.

HUMAN FERTILIZATION AND EMBRYOLOGY AUTHORITY
Clements House, 14–18 Gresham Street, EC2V 7JE
[071-600 3272]

The Authority was established under the Human Fertilization and Embryology Act 1990. Its function is to license persons carrying out any of the following activities: the creation or use of embryos outside the body in the provision of infertility treatment services; the use of donated gametes in infertility treatment; the storage of gametes or embryos; and research on human embryos. The Authority also keeps under review information about embryos and, when requested to do so, gives advice to the Secretary of State for Health.
Chairman, Prof. C. Campbell.
Deputy Chairman, Lady Brittan.
Members, Ms M. Auld; Prof. R. J. Berry; Prof. I. Cooke; Prof. A. Cox; Ms E. Forgan; Ms J. Harbison; S. Hillier; PH.D; Prof. B. Hoggett, QC; The Rt. Rev. R. Holloway; Dr H. Houston; Ms P. Keith; Ms A. Mays; Dr A. McLaren; Rabbi Julia Neuberger; Prof. R. W. Shaw; D. Shilson; Prof. R. Snowden; Ms C. Walby; Prof. D. Whittingham.
Chief Executive, Mrs F. Goldhill.

INDEPENDENT TELEVISION COMMISSION
70 Brompton Road, SW3 1EY
[071–584 7011]

The Independent Television Commission replaced the Independent Broadcasting Authority at the beginning of 1991 under the terms of the Broadcasting Act 1990. The Commission is responsible for licensing and regulating all commercially funded UK television services.
Chairman, G. Russell, CBE.
Deputy Chairman, J. Stevens.
Members, The Earl of Dalkeith; Prof. J. F. Fulton; Ms P. Mathias; Lady Popplewell; Prof. J. Ring; P. Sheth; R. Goddard; Mrs E. Wynne Jones.
Chief Executive, D. Glencross.

INDUSTRIAL INJURIES ADVISORY COUNCIL
The Adelphi, 1–11 John Adam Street, WC2N 6HT
[071–962 8066]

The Industrial Injuries Advisory Council is a statutory body under the Social Security Act 1975 which considers and advises the Secretary of State for Social Services on regulations and other questions relating to industrial injuries benefits or their administration.
Chairman, Prof. J. M. Harrington.
Members, G. Appleby; P. Arscott; Dr J. Asherson; Miss J. C. Brown; Prof. M. J. Cinnamond; Dr D. Coggon; Prof. A. Dayan; J. Henry; P. R. A. Jacques; Dr C. P. Juniper; Dr A. J. Newman Taylor; R. Pickering; Dr E. Roman; Dr A. Sinclair; O. Tudor.
Secretary, R. Heigh.

CENTRAL OFFICE OF INFORMATION
Hercules Road, SE1 7DU
[071–928 2345]

The Central Office of Information is an executive agency which produces information and publicity material, and supplies publicity services, for other government departments on a repayment basis. In the UK it conducts government press, television, radio and poster advertising; produces and distributes booklets, leaflets, films, television and radio material, exhibitions, photographs and other visual material; and distributes departmental press notices. For the overseas departments it supplies British information posts overseas with press, radio and television material, booklets, magazines, films, exhibitions, photographs, display and reading room material.

Administrative responsibility for the Central Office of Information rests with HM Treasury Ministers, while the ministers whose departments it serves are responsible for the policy expressed in its work.
(For **Salaries,** *see* page 293)

Director-General and Head of the Government Information Service (G3), G. M. Devereau.
Private Secretary, Ms R. Leech.
Deputy Director-General (G5), J. Bolitho.

Marketing and Client Services Group

Group Director (G5), R. N. Hooper.
Director, Client Services and Project Management (G6), Miss J. Luke.
Head, Business Development and Communications Services (G7), W. Roberts.

Campaigns Group

Group Director (G5), R. Windsor.
Director, Advertising (G6), M. Brodie.
Director, Research (G6), M. Warren.
Director, Direct Marketing (G7), C. Noble.

Publications, Press and Exhibitions

Group Director (G5), D. A. Low.
Director, Press and PR (G6), G. Stickland.
Director, Publications (G6), J. Murray.
Director, Reference and Translations (G6), D. Beynon.
Director, Exhibitions and Pictures (G6), D. Beynon.
Director, Films Television and Radio Division (G6), M. Nisbet.
Principal Finance Officer (G5), K. Williamson.
Principal Establishment Officer (G6), M. Langhorne.

Regional Services and Emergency Planning Group

Group Director (G5), P. Brazier.

Regional Offices

North Eastern, Wellbar House, Gallowgate, Newcastle upon Tyne NE1 4TB.—*Regional Director (G7),* H. Cozens.
Yorkshire and Humberside, City House, New Station Street, Leeds LS1 4JG.—*Regional Director (G6),* R. P. Haslam.
Eastern, Three Crowns House, 72–80 Hills Road, Cambridge CB2 1LL.—*Regional Director (G7),* Mrs V. Burdon.
London and South Eastern, Lincoln House, Westminster Bridge Road, SE1 7DU.—*Regional Director (G6),* D. Smith.
South Western, The Pithay, Bristol BS1 2NF.—*Regional Director (G7),* P. D. Yorke.
Midlands, Five Ways Tower, Frederick Road, Edgbaston, Birmingham B15 1SH.—*Regional Director (G6),* O. J. B. Prince-White.
North Western, Sunley Tower, Piccadilly Plaza, Manchester M1 4BD.—*Regional Director (G7),* Mrs E. Jones.

BOARD OF INLAND REVENUE
Somerset House, WC2R 1LB
[071–438 6622]

The Board of Inland Revenue was constituted under the Inland Revenue Board Act, 1849, by the consolidation of the Board of Excise and the Board of Stamps and Taxes. In 1909 the administration of excise duties was transferred to the Board of Customs. The Board of Inland Revenue administers and collects direct taxes—mainly income tax, corporation tax, capital gains tax, inheritance tax, stamp duty, development land tax and petroleum revenue tax—and advises the Chancellor of the Exchequer on policy questions involving them. The Head Office is in London and there are Inspectors of Taxes offices and Collection offices throughout the United Kingdom. In 1989–90 the Inland Revenue collected over £76,500 million in tax.
(For **Salaries,** *see* page 293)

The Board

Chairman (G1), Sir Anthony Battishill, KCB.
Private Secretary, Miss J. McClatchey.
Deputy Chairmen (G2), A. J. G. Isaac, CB; T. J. Painter, CB.
Private Secretary, Miss F. Huskisson.
Directors General (G2), L. J. H. Beighton; S. C. T. Matheson.
Commissioner: Chief Valuer (G2), R. R. B. Shutler.

Subject Divisions

Directors (G3), P. Lewis; B. T. Houghton, CB; E. McGivern; D. Y. Pitts; M. A. Johns; J. H. Roberts; B. A. Mace; M. F. Cayley; E. F. Gribbon.
Senior Principal Inspector of Taxes (G4), R. E. Creed; M. D. E. Newstead; J. M. L. Davenport; D. W. Hugo; I. N. Hunter; B. Sadler; J. M. Phalp; R. M. Elliss; R. C. Mountain; R. E. Haigh; R. H. Allen; R. N. Page, CBE; M. A. Keith; P. R. P. Stokes; A. J. O'Brien; P. C. Fielder.
Grade 5, D. J. Farmer; D. L. Shaw; R. Warden; J. H. Reed; M. J. G. Elliott; J. P. B. Bryce; P. W. Fawcett; J. B. Shepherd; B. O'Connor; L. E. Jaundoo; C. Stewart; A. W. Kuczys; C. D. Sullivan; M. D. R. Haigh; Miss R. A. Dyall; M. T. Evans; S. P. Norris; Miss M. Hay; R. D. Golding.
Principal Inspectors of Taxes (G5), M. L. Gordon; J. W. Calder; J. Potter; T. R. Evans; A. Cummins; A. Beauchamp; A. Harrison; D. F. Parratt; J. T. Cawdron; A. C. Williams; D. A. Hartnett; C. R. Massingale; B. Jones; Mrs M. E. Williams; D. C. Howard; D. Newlyn; A. H. Williams; S. M. Hartlib; B. E. Quigley; J. Mawson; E. M. Griffin.
Controller of Oil Taxation Office (G4), M. Templeman.

Central Division

Grade 3, C. W. Corlett.
Grade 5, R. B. Willis; I. Fraser; M. Waters; R. W. Skelley.
Senior Economic Adviser (G5), W. M. McNie.

Management Divisions

Director of Personnel (G3), P. B. G. Jones, CB.
Assistant Directors (G4), G. Findley, CBE; N. C. Munro; (G5) R. Neilson; Mrs C. Hubbard; M. K. Robins; J. Eastman; A. J. Walker; M. D. Phelps.
Director of Manpower and Support Services (G3), M. Crawley.
Assistant Directors (G5), D. Ward; Miss M. A. Hill; A. W. Bryant; J. Gray.
Head of Operational Research (G5), R. P. R. Tilley.
Director of Information Technology (G3), G. H. Bush.
Deputy Director of Information Technology (G4), C. J. Thompson.
Assistant Directors (G5), A. M. Paterson; R. A. Hamilton; I. P. Crump; E. Wilson; D. Topple; B. T. Glassberg; R. Assirati.
Director of Operations (G3), K. V. Deacon.
Deputy Directors of Operations (G4), D. W. Muir; J. E. Yard; J. Gant.
Assistant Directors (G5), J. H. Keelty; E. C. Jones; Miss M. James; J. M. Thomas; R. S. Hurcombe; D. J. Timmons; S. J. McManus; C. H. Coleman; J. P. Gilbody; S. H. Banyard; Miss M. Boulton; M. Oakley.

Controller, Enforcement Office (G5), K. Burns.
Head of Communications Group (G5), Mrs S. Cullum.
Press Secretary (G7), D. I. Richardson.

Finance Division

Principal Finance Officer (G3), J. M. Crawley.
Assistant Secretaries (G5), I. R. Spence; R. R. Martin.
Controller, Central Accounting Office (G6), D. Easey.
Chief Internal Auditor (G6), N. Buckley.

Statistics Division

Director (G3), J. R. Calder.
Chief Statisticians (G5), J. B. Dearman; G. A. Keenay;
I. Stewart; R. J. Eason.
Computing (G6), R. James.

The Stamp Office
South-West Wing, Bush House, Strand, WC2B 4QN
and Barrington Road, Worthing, W. Sussex
BN12 4XH

Controller (G6), K. S. Hodgson.

Capital Taxes Office
Minford House, Rockley Road, W14 0DF

Controller (G4), B. D. Kent.
Deputy Controllers/Assistant Secretaries (G5), R. J.
Draper; A. G. Nield; H. Capon.
Assistant Controllers/Senior Principals (G6), D. J.
Ferley; C. A. Oldridge; T. J. Plumb; R. Shanks; N.
Tant; F. A. Cook; M. J. Francis; B. K. Lakhanpaw;
P. R. Twiddy; A. D. Tytherleigh.
Boards Actuarial Adviser (G6), D. R. Erasmus.

Solicitor of Inland Revenue
Somerset House, WC2R 1LB

Solicitor (G2), B. E. Cleave.
Principal Assistant Solicitors (G3), J. D. H. Johnston;
P. L. Ridd; J. G. H. Bates.
Assistant Solicitors (G5), C. J. C. Baron; Miss M. P.
Boland; S. Bousher; K. Brown; A. P. Douglas; A.
J. Gunz; Miss A. Hawkins; N. R. Phillips; A. K. S.
Shaw; R. W. Thornhill; R. F. Walters; R. Waterson;
Miss A. E. Wyman.

Superannuation Funds Office
Lynwood Road, Thames Ditton, Surrey KT7 0DP

Controller (G5), R. G. Lusk.
Assistant Controllers (G6), P. E. P. Berry; D. J.
Sankey.

Crown Property Unit
Jameson House, 69 Notting Hill Gate, W11 3JU
[071-273 7000]

Director, T. J. Cundall.

Inspector of Foreign Dividends Office
Lynwood Road, Thames Ditton, Surrey KT7 0DP

Inspector of Foreign Dividends (G6), J. Steele.

The Valuation Office
Executive Agency
New Court, 48 Carey Street, WC2A 2JE
[071-324 1183/1057]

Meldrum House, 15 Drumsheugh Gardens,
Edinburgh EH3 7UN
[031-225 8511]

The Valuation Office Agency is responsible for the
valuation of land and buildings for taxes administered
by the Board of Inland Revenue. It also advises and
assists other departments by furnishing valuations
and conducting negotiations in connection with the
acquisition, lease and sale of land. Similar functions
are performed on behalf of local authorities and other
public and local bodies. The Agency is also responsible
for preparing and maintaining rating lists in England
and Wales. A full advisory service is available to any

department concerned with land, covering advice on
policy proposals and legislation, and the associated
administrative, executive and professional work.
Chief Executive (G2), R. R. B. Shutler.
Deputy Chief Executives (G3), A. J. Langford (*Management*); R. J. Pawley (*Technical*).
Chief Valuer, Scotland (G4), J. A. Sutherland.

INLAND REVENUE (SCOTLAND)
80 Lauriston Place, Edinburgh EH3 9SL

Controller (G4), O. J. D. Clarke.
Group Controllers (G5), J. Brown; J. McCloskey; G.
Watson; B. Ritchie.

The Stamp Office (Scotland)
16 Picardy Place, Edinburgh EH1 3NB

Controller, D. G. Hunter.

Capital Taxes Office (Scotland)
Mulberry House, 16 Picardy Place, Edinburgh
EH1 3NB

Registrar (G5), P. G. Bruce, MBE.
Deputy Registrar (G7), W. Young.
Chief Examiners (G7), Mrs J. A. Templeton; J.
Telford; T. E. Naysmith; C. G. Hogg; Miss A.
Forbes; Miss K. M. Patrick; D. M. Paterson.

Solicitor's Office (Scotland)
80 Lauriston Place, Edinburgh EH3 9SL

Solicitor, T. H. Scott.
Senior Principals (Legal) (G6), I. K. Laing; D. S.
Wishart.
Principal (Legal), H. M. Milne.

THE INTERCEPTION COMMISSIONER
c/o The Home Office, 50 Queen Anne's Gate,
SW1H 9AT

The Commissioner is appointed by the Prime Minister. He keeps under review the issue by the Secretary
of State of warrants under the Interception of
Communications Act 1985 and safeguards made in
respect of intercepted material obtained through the
use of such warrants. He is also required to give all
such assistance as the Interception of Communications Tribunal may require to enable it to carry out
its functions and to submit an annual report to the
Prime Minister with respect to the carrying out of
his functions.
Commissioner, The Right Hon. Lord Justice Lloyd.

INTERCEPTION OF COMMUNICATIONS
TRIBUNAL
PO Box 44, London SE1 0TX

The Tribunal comprises senior members of the legal
profession who are appointed by HM the Queen.
Under the Interception of Communications Act 1985,
the Tribunal is required to investigate applications
from any person who believes that communications
sent to or by them have been intercepted in the
course of their transmission by post or by means of a
public telecommunications system.
President, The Hon. Mr Justice Macpherson of Cluny.
Vice President, Sir Cecil Clothier, KCB, QC.
Members, Sir David Calcutt, QC; I. Guild, CBE; P.
Scott, QC.

INTERVENTION BOARD
Fountain House, Queen's Walk,
Reading RG1 7QW
[0734-583626]

The Intervention Board was formed as a government
department in 1972, becoming operational on Febru-

ary 1, 1973. It became an executive agency in April 1990. The Board is responsible for the implementation of European Community regulations covering the market support arrangements of the Common Agricultural Policy. Members of the Board are appointed by and are responsible to the Minister of Agriculture and the Secretaries of State for Scotland, Wales and Northern Ireland.

(For **Salaries**, *see* page 293)

Chairman, A. J. Ellis, CBE.
Chief Executive (G3), G. Stapleton.

Heads of Divisions

Finance Division (G5), J. N. Diserens.
External Trade Division (G5), G. N. Dixon.
Crops Division (G5), H. MacKinnon.
Livestock Products Division (G5), M. J. Griffiths.
Corporate Services Division (G5), J. W. M. Peffers.
Accountancy Services (G6), R. Bryant.
Procurement and Supply Services (G6), P. J. Offer.
Establishments Services (G6), R. J. Lovell.
Computer Services (G6), T. T. Simpson.

UK Seeds Executive

Chairman, Prof. J. C. Murdoch, OBE, PH.D.
Members, T. M. Clucas; J. M. Harley; J. Harvey; Prof. J. D. Hayes, PH.D.; P. R. Hayward, OBE; I. C. Henderson; D. R. Thomas; I. M. Whitelaw.

LAND AUTHORITY FOR WALES
The Custom House, Customhouse Street,
Cardiff CF1 5AP
[0222–223444]

The Authority is responsible for acquiring and disposing of land needed for private development in Wales.

Chairman, G. D. Inkin, OBE *(part-time)* £29,015
Chief Executive, B. Ryan.

LAND REGISTRIES

HM LAND REGISTRY
Lincoln's Inn Fields, WC2A 3PH
[071–405 3488]

The registration of title to land was first introduced in England and Wales by the Land Registry Act 1862; HM Land Registry operates today under the Land Registration Acts 1925 to 1988. The object of registering title to land is to create and maintain a register of land owners whose title is guaranteed by the state and so to simplify the transfer, mortgage and other dealings with real property. Compulsory registration on sale was introduced in stages affecting only certain areas but it is now compulsory throughout England and Wales. The register, which used to be private and could only be inspected with the consent of the registered proprietor, became open to inspection by the public on December 3, 1990.

HM Land Registry is an executive agency administered under the Lord Chancellor by the Chief Land Registrar. The work is decentralized to a number of regional offices. The Chief Land Registrar is also responsible for the Land Charges Department and the Agricultural Credits Department.

(For **Salaries**, *see* page 293)

Headquarters Office

Chief Land Registrar and Chief Executive (G2), J. J. Manthorpe.
Solicitor to Land Registry (G3), C. J. West.
Senior Land Registrar (G5), Mrs J. G. Totty.
Principal Establishment Officer (G5), E. G. Beardsall.

Controller (Registration) (G5), G. N. French.
Controller (Information Technology) (G5), R. J. Fenn.
Controller (Management Services) (G6), P. J. Smith.
Land Registrar (G5), M. L. Wood.

Birkenhead District Land Registry
Old Market House, Hamilton Street,
Birkenhead L41 5JW
[051–647 2377]

District Land Registrar (G5), M. G. Garwood.
Area Manager (G6), J. Eccles.

Coventry District Land Registry
Greyfriars Business Centre,
2 Eaton Road, Coventry CV1 2SD
[0203–632442]

District Land Registrar (G5), S. P. Kelway.
Area Manager (G6), J. C. Lillistone.

Croydon District Land Registry
Sunley House, Bedford Park, Croydon CR9 3LE
[081–686 8833]

District Land Registrar (G5), D. M. J. Moss.
Area Manager (G6), V. J. C. Shorney.

Durham District Land Registry
Southfield House, Southfield Way,
Durham DH1 5TR
[091–3866151]

District Land Registrar (G5), C. W. Martin.
Area Manager (G6), D. J. Long.

Gloucester District Land Registry
Twyver House, Bruton Way,
Gloucester GL1 1DQ
[0452–511111]

District Land Registrar (G5), W. W. Budden.
Area Manager (G6), D. J. Thomas.

Harrow District Land Registry
Lyon House, Lyon Road, Harrow,
Middx. HA1 2EU
[081–427 8811]

District Land Registrar (G5), J. V. Timothy.
Area Manager (G6), M. J. Wyatt.

Kingston upon Hull District Land Registry
Earle House, Portland Street, Hull HU2 8JN
[0482–223244]

District Land Registrar (G5), S. R. G. Coveney.
Area Manager (G6), E. Howard.

Land Charges and Agricultural Credits Department
Burrington Way, Plymouth PL5 3LP
[0752–779831]

Superintendent of Land Charges (G7), H. Myers.

Leicester District Land Registry
Thames Tower, 99 Burleys Way,
Leicester LE1 3UB
[0533–510010]

District Land Registrar (G6), L. M. Pope.
Area Manager (G7), B. Warriner.

Lytham District Land Registry
Birkenhead House, Lytham St Annes,
Lancs. FY8 5AB
[0253–736999]

District Land Registrar (G5), J. G. Cooper.
Area Manager (G6), E. J. Stringer.

Nottingham District Land Registry
Chalfont Drive, Nottingham NG8 3RN
[0602–291166]

District Land Registrar (G5), P. J. Timothy.
Area Manager, (G6), W. Whitaker.

Peterborough District Land Registry
Touthill Close, City Road,
Peterborough PE1 1XN
[0733–555666]

District Land Registrar (G5), M. Avens.
Area Manager (G6), B. J. Andrews.

Plymouth District Land Registry
Plumer House, Tailyour Road,
Crownhill, Plymouth PL6 5HY
[0752–701234]

District Land Registrar (G5), A. J. Pain.
Area Manager(G6), K. Robinson.

Portsmouth District Land Registry
St Andrews Court, St Michael's Road,
Portsmouth PO1 2JH
[0705–865022]

District Land Registrar (G6), S. R. Sehrawat.
Area Manager (G7), A. W. Howarth.

Stevenage District Land Registry
Brickdale House, Swingate, Stevenage,
Herts. SG1 1XG
[0438–313003]

District Land Registrar (G5), D. M. T. Mullett.
Area Manager (G6), A. D. Gould.

Swansea District Land Registry
Tybryn Glas, High Street,
Swansea SA1 1PW
[0792–458877]

District Land Registrar (G5), G. A. Hughes.
Area Manager (G6), B. E. G. Martin.

Telford District Land Registry
Stafford Park 15, Telford,
Shropshire TF3 3AL
[0952–290355]

District Land Registrar (G5), M. A. Roche.
Area Manager (G6), R. D. Moseley.

Tunbridge Wells District Land Registry
Curtis House, Hawkenbury, Tunbridge Wells,
Kent TN2 5AQ
[0892–510015]

District Land Registrar (G5), G. R. Tooke.
Area Manager (G6), B. S. Crozier.

Weymouth District Land Registry
1 Cumberland Drive, Weymouth,
Dorset DT4 9TT
[0305–776161]

District Land Registrar (G5), Mrs P. M. Reeson.
Area Manager (G6), J Dodd.

Computer Services Division
Burrington Way,
Plymouth PL5 3LP
[0752–779831]

Head of Division (G6), A. A. Restorick.

**DEPARTMENT OF THE REGISTERS OF
SCOTLAND (EXECUTIVE AGENCY)**
Meadowbank House, 153 London Road,
Edinburgh EH8 7AU
[031–659 6111]

The Registers of Scotland consist of: General Register
of Sasines and Land Register of Scotland; Register
of Deeds in the Books of Council and Session; Register
of Protests; Register of English and Irish Judgments;
Register of Service of Heirs; Register of the Great
Seal; Register of the Quarter Seal; Register of the
Prince's Seal; Register of Crown Grants; Register of
Sheriffs' Commissions; Register of the Cachet Seal;

Register of Inhibitions and Adjudications; Register
of Entails; Register of Hornings.

The General Register of Sasines and the Land
Register of Scotland form the chief security in
Scotland of the rights of land and other heritable (or
real) property.

Keeper of the Registers of Scotland (G4), J. W. Barron.
Senior Director (G5), R. C. Brown.
Senior Assistant Directors (G6), A. M. Falconer; A.
   W. Ramage; A. G. Rennie.
Assistant Directors (G7), B. J. Corr (*computers*); R.
   Glen (*personnel*); J. Knox (*Land Register*); D.
   McCallum (*Land Register*); L. J. Mitchell (*manage-
   ment services*); A. G. T. New (*Land Register*); I. M.
   Nicol (*finance*); Mrs P. M. Stewart (*training*).
Assistant Keeper (G7), Mrs A. McDonald.
Grade 7, J. Anderson; R. C. Clark; J. Cogle; I. A.
   Davis; A. B. Farmer; H. Hosken; D. Lorimer; J. S.
   McKinlay; D. Manson; J. B. Marshall; J. Rynn; M.
   J. Wilczynski.

**LAW COMMISSION
(England and Wales)**
Conquest House, 37–38 John Street,
Theobalds Road, WC1N 2BQ
[071–411 1220]

The Law Commission was set up in 1965, under the
Law Commissions Act 1965, to make proposals to the
Government for the examination of the law and for
its revision where it is unsuited for modern requirements, obscure, or otherwise unsatisfactory. It
recommends to the Lord Chancellor programmes for
the examination of different branches of the law and
suggests whether the examination should be carried
out by the Commission itself or by some other body.
The Commission is also responsible for the preparation of Consolidation and Statute Law (Repeals)
Bills.

Chairman, The Hon. Mr Justice (Peter) Gibson.
Members, T. M. Aldridge; J. Beatson; R. Buxton, QC;
   Prof. B. M. Hoggett, QC.
Secretary, M. H. Collon.

SCOTTISH LAW COMMISSION
140 Causewayside, Edinburgh EH9 1PR
[031–668 2131]

Chairman, The Hon. Lord Davidson.
Commissioners, Dr E. M. Clive; I. D. MacPhail, QC
   (*full-time*); Prof. P. N. Love, CBE; W. Nimmo Smith,
   QC (*part-time*).
Secretary, K. F. Barclay.

LAW OFFICERS' DEPARTMENTS
Attorney-General's Chambers,
9 Buckingham Gate, SW1E 6JP
[071–828 7155]
Attorney General's Chambers,
Royal Courts of Justice, Belfast BT1 3JY
[0232–235111]

The Law Officers of the Crown for England and Wales
are the Attorney General and the Solicitor General.
The Attorney General is the Minister responsible for
the work of the Law Officers' Departments: the
Treasury Solicitor's Department, the Crown Prose-
cution Service, the Serious Fraud Office, and the
Legal Secretariat to the Law Officers. The Director
of Public Prosecutions (who is head of the Crown
Prosecution Service), the Director of Public Prose-
cutions for Northern Ireland, and the Director of the
Serious Fraud Office are responsible to the Attorney
General for the performance of their duties.

The Attorney General is the Government's principal legal adviser, dealing with questions of law arising on Bills, issues of legal policy, and major international and domestic litigation involving the Government. The Solicitor General is responsible for such matters as the Attorney General delegates to him.

Attorney General, THE RT. HON. SIR PATRICK MAY-
HEW, QC, MP .... £40,492†
  Parliamentary Private Secretary, M. Irvine, MP.
Solicitor General, THE RT. HON SIR NICHOLAS LYELL,
QC, MP .... £33,201†
  Parliamentary Private Secretary, P. Ground, QC,
  MP.
Legal Secretary (G3), Miss J. L. Wheldon.
Asst. Legal Secretary (G4), M. L. Carpenter.

† Excluding reduced Parliamentary salary of £21,809.

LEGAL AID BOARD
5th Floor, Newspaper House,
8–16 Great New Street, EC4A 3BN
[071–353 7411]

The Legal Aid Board has the general function of ensuring that advice, assistance and representation are available, in accordance with the Legal Aid Act 1988. It took over from the Law Society on April 1, 1989 responsibility for administering legal aid. The Board is a non-departmental government body whose members are appointed by the Lord Chancellor.
Chairman, J. Pitts.
Members, M. Acland; Ms D. Beale; A. Blake; L. Devonald; K. Farrow; G. Hibbert; D. Sinker; J. Smith; P. Soar.
Chief Executive, S. Orchard.

SCOTTISH LEGAL AID BOARD
44 Drumsheugh Gardens,
Edinburgh EH3 7SW
[031–226 7061]

The Scottish Legal Aid Board was set up under the Legal Aid (Scotland) Act 1986. It is responsible for ensuring that advice, assistance and representation are available in accordance with the Act. The Board is a non-departmental government body whose members are appointed by the Secretary of State for Scotland.
Chairman, Mrs C. A. M. Davis.
Members, G. Barrie; Prof. T. F. Carbery, OBE; Miss L. Clark, QC; B. G. Donald; A. Gilchrist; G. D. Holmes, CB; D. A. Leitch; R. J. Livingstone; Mrs I. McColl; C. N. McEachran, QC; R. G. McEwan, QC; G. H. Speirs; Mrs M. Tait.
Chief Executive, A. E. M. Douglas.

OFFICE OF THE LEGAL SERVICES OMBUDSMAN
22 Oxford Court, Oxford Street,
Manchester M2 3WQ
[061–236 9532]

The Legal Services Ombudsman is appointed by the Lord Chancellor under the Courts and Legal Services Act 1990 to oversee the handling of complaints against solicitors, barristers and licensed conveyancers by their professional bodies. The Ombudsman replaced the Lay Observer on January 1, 1991. He is independent of the legal profession and his services are free of charge.
Legal Services Ombudsman, M. Barnes.
Secretary, K. Fox.

LIBRARIES

OFFICE OF ARTS AND LIBRARIES
(*see* entry on page 298)

THE BRITISH LIBRARY
2 Sheraton Street, W1V 4BH
[071–636 1544]

The British Library is the UK's national library and occupies the central position in the library and information network. The Library aims to serve scholarship, research, industry, commerce and all other major users of information. Its services are based on collections which include over 18 million volumes, 1 million discs, and 55,000 hours of tape recordings, at 18 buildings in London and one complex in West Yorkshire.

The British Library was established on July 1, 1973 and brought together the library departments of the British Museum, the National Central Library, the National Lending Library for Science and Technology, the British National Bibliography Ltd and, in 1974, the Office for Scientific and Technical Information. Subsequently the Library took responsibility for the India Office Library and Records, the HMSO Binderies, and the National Sound Archive.

Access to the Humanities and Social Sciences reading rooms in Great Russell Street is limited to holders of a British Library Reader's Pass, and information about eligibility is available from the Reader Admissions Office. The Aldwych and Holborn reading rooms of the Science Reference and Information Service are open to the general public without charge or formality.

The Library's exhibition galleries are housed in the British Museum building in Great Russell Street.

The British Library is in the process of moving to purpose-built accommodation at St Pancras, London NW1 (open to the public in 1993).

British Library Board
96 Euston Road, St Pancras, NW1 2DB
[071-323 7262]

Chairman, Cdr. L. M. M. Saunders Watson.
Chief Executive and Deputy Chairman, B. Lang.
Directors General, J. M. Smethurst; D. Russon.
Part-time Members, The Lord Adrian, MD, FRS; The Lord Windlesham, CVO, PC; Prof. A. S. Forty, PH.D., D.SC.; Sir Robin Mackworth-Young, KCVO, FSA; R. E. Utiger, CBE; T. J. Rix; Dame Anne Warburton, DCVO, CMG; H. Heaney; D. Peake; The Rt. Rev. M. A. Mann, KCVO.

BRITISH LIBRARY, BOSTON SPA
Boston Spa, Wetherby, W. Yorks. LS23 7BQ
[0937–546000]

Director General, D. Russon.

Document Supply Centre
[0937–546000]

Director, D. Bradbury.

National Bibliographic Service
[0937–546585]

Director, S. J. Ede.

London Unit
2 Sheraton Street, W1V 4BH
[071–323 7077]

Acquisitions Processing and Cataloguing*
2 Sheraton Street, W1V 4BH
[071–323 7186]

Director, Mrs J. E. Butcher.

Computing and Telecommunications*
2 Sheraton Street, W1V 4BH
[071–323 7210]

Director, J. R. Mahoney.

*Scheduled to relocate to Yorkshire by the mid-1990s.

BRITISH LIBRARY, LONDON
Great Russell Street, WC1B 3DG
[071–636 1544]

Director General, J. M. Smethurst.

Humanities and Social Sciences
[071–323 7676]

Director, A. Phillips.

West European Collections, Slavonic and East European Collections, English Language Collections
[071–323 7676]

Information Branch, Official Publications and Social Science Service
[071–323 7676]

Exhibitions and Education Service
[071–323 7595]

Reader Admissions
[071–323 7677]

Collections and Preservation
[071–323 7676]

Director, Dr M. Foot.

Preservation Service (National Preservation Office)
[071–323 7612]

Special Collections
[071–323 7513]

Director, Mrs S. Tyacke.

Western Manuscripts, Map Library, Music Library, Philatelic Collections
[071–323 7513]

Information Sciences Service (BLISS)
Ridgmount Street, WC1E 7AE
[071–323 7688]

Newspaper Library
Colindale Avenue, NW9 5HE
[071–323 7353]

National Sound Archive
29 Exhibition Road, SW7 2AS
[071–589 6603]

Director, Dr C. H. Roads.

Oriental and India Office Collections
197 Blackfriars Road, SE1 8NG
[071–412 7873]

Science Reference and Information Service
25 Southampton Buildings, WC2A 1AW
[071–323 7494]
9 Kean Street, WC2B 4AT
[071–323 7288]

Director, A. Gomersall.

Research and Development Department
2 Sheraton Street, W1V 4BH
[071–323 7060]

Director, B. J. Perry.

Administration
2 Sheraton Street, W1V 4BH
[071–323 7132]

Director, R. Ball.

Press and Public Relations
96 Euston Road, NW1 2DB
[071–323 7111]

Head, I. C. Haydon.

NATIONAL LIBRARY OF SCOTLAND
George IV Bridge, Edinburgh EH1 1EW
[031–226 4531]

Reading Room, weekdays, 9.30–8.30 (Wed., 10–8.30); Sat. 9.30–1. Map Library, weekdays, 9.30–5; Sat. 9.30–1. Exhibition, weekdays, 9.30–5; Sat. 9.30–1; Sun. 2–5. Scottish Science Library, weekdays, 9.30–5 (Wed., 10–8.30).

The Library, which was founded as the Advocates' Library in 1682, became the National Library of Scotland by Act of Parliament in 1925. Its collections of printed books and MSS, augmented by purchase and gift, are very large and it has an unrivalled Scottish collection.

The Reading Room is for reference and research which cannot conveniently be pursued elsewhere. Admission is by ticket issued to an approved applicant.

Salaries

Librarian	£40,116–£44,996
Keeper	£24,997–£38,610
Curator Grade C	£21,905–£31,150

Chairman of the Trustees, The Earl of Crawford and Balcarres, PC.
Librarian and Secretary to the Trustees, I. D. McGowan.
Secretary of the Library, M. C. Graham.
Curators Grade C, A. Cameron; W. Jackson; J. E. McIntyre.
Keepers of Printed Books, A. M. Marchbank, PH.D.; Ms A. Matheson, PH.D.
Curators Grade C, T. A. Cherry; Ms A. E. Harvey Wood; B. P. Hillyard, D.PHIL.; S. Holland; Ms R. I. Hope; W. A. Kelly; J. M. Morris.
Keeper of Manuscripts, I. C. Cunningham.
Curators Grade C, I. G. Brown, PH.D., FSA; R. Duce; I. F. Maciver; S. M. Simpson; Ms J. M. Wilkes; Ms E. D. Yeo.
Director of Computer Services and Research (Keeper), B. Gallivan.
Curator Grade C, R. F. Guy.
Director of Scottish Science Library (Keeper), Ms A. J. Bunch.

THE NATIONAL LIBRARY OF WALES
Llyfrgell Genedlaethol Cymru
Aberystwyth, Dyfed SY23 3BU
[0970–623816]

Readers' room open on weekdays, 9.30–6 (Saturdays, 9.30–5); closed on Sundays, Bank Holidays and first week of October. Admission by Reader's Ticket.

The National Library of Wales was founded by Royal Charter in 1907, and is maintained by annual grant from the Treasury. It contains about 4,000,000 printed books, 40,000 manuscripts, 4,000,000 deeds and documents, and numerous maps, prints and drawings, and an audio-visual collection. It specializes in manuscripts and books relating to Wales and the Celtic peoples. It is the repository for pre-1858 Welsh probate records. It is approved by the Master of the Rolls as a repository for manorial records and tithe documents, and by the Lord Chancellor for certain legal records. It is the Bureau of the Regional Libraries Scheme for Wales.

Librarian, B. F. Roberts, PH.D., FSA.
Secretary, D. B. Lloyd.
Heads of Departments, D. Huws (*Manuscripts and Records*); J. L. Madden (*Printed Books*); D. H. Owen (*Pictures and Maps*).

LIGHTHOUSE AUTHORITIES

CORPORATION OF TRINITY HOUSE
Trinity House, Tower Hill, EC3N 4DH
[071–480 6601]

Trinity House, the first general lighthouse and pilotage authority in the Kingdom, was a body of importance when Henry VIII granted the institution its first charter in 1514. The Corporation is the general lighthouse authority for England, Wales and the Channel Islands, with certain statutory jurisdiction over aids to navigation maintained by local harbour authorities. It is also responsible for dealing with wrecks dangerous to navigation, except those occurring within port limits or wrecks of HM ships. The Trinity House Lighthouse Service is maintained out of the General Lighthouse Fund which is provided from light dues levied on ships at ports of the UK and Republic of Ireland. The Corporation is also a deep-sea pilotage authority and a charitable organization.

The affairs of the Corporation are controlled by a board of Elder Brethren, who are master mariners with long experience of command in the Royal or Merchant Navy, together with figures from the world of commerce, and the Secretary. A separate board, which comprises Elder Brethren, senior staff and outside representatives currently controls the Lighthouse Service. The Board is assisted by administrative and technical staff. The Elder Brethren also act as nautical assessors in marine cases in the Admiralty Division of the High Court of Justice.

Elder Brethren

Master, HRH The Duke of Edinburgh, KG, KT.
Deputy Master, Capt. P. M. Edge.
Elder Brethren, Capt. I. R. C. Saunders; Capt. P. F. Mason, CBE; HRH The Prince of Wales, KG, KT; Capt. Sir George Barnard, FRSA; Capt. R. N. Mayo, CBE; Capt. Sir David Tibbits, DSC, RN; Capt. D. A. G. Dickens; Capt. J. E. Bury; Capt. J. A. N. Bezant, DSC, RD, RNR (*ret.*); Capt. D. J. Cloke; The Lord Wilson of Rievaulx, KG, OBE, PC, FRS; Capt. Sir Miles Wingate, KCVO; Rt. Hon. Edward Heath, MBE, MP; Capt. T. Woodfield, OBE; Sir Eric Drake, CBE; The Lord Simon of Glaisdale, PC; Admiral of the Fleet the Lord Lewin, KG, GCB, LVO, DSC; Capt. D. T. Smith, RN; Commander Sir Robin Gillett, GBE, RD, RNR; The Lord Shackleton, KG, OBE, PC, FRS; Sir John Cuckney; Capt. D. J. Orr; The Lord Carrington, KG, GCMG, CH, MC, PC; Sir Brian Shaw; The Lord Mackay of Clashfern, PC; Sir Adrian Swire; Capt. N. M. Turner, RD; HRH The Duke of York, CVO; Capt. P. H. King; Capt. The Lord Sterling of Plaistow, CBE, RNR.

Officers

Secretary, J. B. Fuller.
Deputy Secretary, M. J. Faulkner.
Director of Finance, K. W. Clark.
Director of Engineering, D. A. S. Vennings.
Personnel and General Services Manager, Mrs B. C. Heesom.
Navigation Manager, N. J. Cutmore.
Legal and Information Manager, D. I. Brewer.
General Manager Operations, Capt. J. M. Barnes.
Operations Administration Manager, S. J. W. Dunning.
Deputy Director of Engineering, F. E. J. Holden.
Senior Inspector of Shipping, J. Sedgwick.
Manager, Corporate Department, R. Dobb.
Information Officer, H. L. Cooper.

COMMISSIONERS OF NORTHERN LIGHTHOUSES
84 George Street, Edinburgh EH2 3DA
[031-226 7051]

The Commissioners of Northern Lighthouses are the general lighthouse authority for Scotland and the Isle of Man. The present board owes its origin to an Act of Parliament passed in 1786. At present the Commissioners operate under the Merchant Shipping Act 1894 and are 19 in number.

The Commissioners control 25 major manned lighthouses, 59 major automatic lighthouses, 112 minor lights and many lighted and unlighted buoys. They have a fleet of two motor vessels.

Commissioners

The Lord Advocate; the Solicitor General for Scotland; the Lord Provosts of Edinburgh, Glasgow and Aberdeen; the Provost of Inverness; the Chairman of Argyll and Bute District Council; the Sheriffs-Principal of North Strathclyde, Tayside, Central, Fife, Grampian, Highlands and Islands, South Strathclyde, Dumfries and Galloway, Lothians and Borders, and Glasgow and Strathkelvin; T. Macgill; Capt. A. F. Dickson, OBE; Capt. D. M. Cowell; A. J. Struthers; W. F. Hay, CBE; J. Hann, CBE.

Officers

General Manager, Cdr. J. M. Mackay, MBE.
Secretary, I. A. Dickson.
Engineer-in-Chief, W. Paterson.

LOCAL COMMISSIONERS

COMMISSION FOR LOCAL ADMINISTRATION IN ENGLAND
21 Queen Anne's Gate, SW1H 9BU
[071–222 5622]

Local Commissioners (Local Government Ombudsmen) are responsible for investigating complaints from members of the public against local authorities (but not town and parish councils); police authorities; the Commission for New Towns and new town development corporations (housing functions); and urban development corporations (town and country planning functions). The Commissioners are appointed by the Crown on the recommendation of the Secretary of State for the Environment.

Certain types of action are excluded from investigation, particularly personnel matters and commercial transactions unless they relate to the purchase or sale of land. Complaints can be sent direct to the Local Government Ombudsman or through a councillor, although the Local Government Ombudsman will not consider a complaint unless the Council has had an opportunity to investigate and reply to a complainant.

A free booklet *Complaint about the Council? How to Complain to the Local Government Ombudsman* is available from the Commission's office.

Chairman of the Commission and Local Commissioner, D. C. M. Yardley, D.Phil. £82,780
Vice Chairman and Local Commissioner, F. G. Laws
£60,020
Local Commissioner, Mrs P. A. Thomas £59,020
Member (*ex officio*), The Parliamentary Commissioner for Administration.
Secretary, G. D. Adams £41,070

COMMISSION FOR LOCAL ADMINISTRATION IN WALES
Derwen House, Court Road, Bridgend CF31 1BN
[0656–661325]

The Local Commissioner for Wales has similar powers to the Local Commissioners in England. The Commissioner is appointed by the Crown on the recommendation of the Secretary of State for Wales. A free booklet *Your Local Ombudsman in Wales* is available from the Commission's office.
Local Commissioner, H. F. Jones.
Secretary, D. Bowen.
Member (*ex officio*), The Parliamentary Commissioner for Administration.

COMMISSIONER FOR LOCAL ADMINISTRATION IN SCOTLAND
5 Shandwick Place, Edinburgh EH2 4RG
[031–229 4472]

The Local Commissioner for Scotland has similar powers to the Local Commissioners in England, and is appointed by the Crown on the recommendation of the Secretary of State for Scotland.
Local Commissioner, R. G. E. Peggie, CBE.
Secretary, Ms J. H. Renton.

LONDON REGIONAL TRANSPORT
55 Broadway, SW1H 0BD
[071–222 5600]

Subject to the financial objectives and principles approved by the Secretary of State for Transport, London Regional Transport has a general duty to provide or secure the provision of public transport services for Greater London.
Chairman, C. W. Newton £100,000
Members, J. Telford Beasley; A. J. Sheppeck
£75,000

LORD ADVOCATE'S DEPARTMENT
Fielden House, 10 Great College Street,
SW1P 3SL
[071–276 3000]

The Law Officers for Scotland are the Lord Advocate and the Solicitor-General for Scotland. The Lord Advocate's Department is responsible for drafting Scottish legislation, for providing legal advice to other departments on Scottish questions and for assistance to the Law Officers for Scotland in certain of their legal duties.
Lord Advocate, THE LORD FRASER OF CARMYLLIE, PC,
QC £48,457
Solicitor-General for Scotland, ALAN F. RODGER, QC.
£42,433
Legal Secretary and First Scottish Parliamentary Counsel, J. C. McCluskie, QC £59,020
Assistant Legal Secretaries and Scottish Parliamentary Counsel, G. M. Clark; D. J. S. Duncan; G. Kowalski; P. J. Layden, TD . . . . . . £48,380–£56,010

Assistant Legal Secretaries and Depute Scottish Parliamentary Counsel, J. D. Harkness; D. C. Macrae; C. A. M. Wilson . . . . £45,057–£46,746
Assistant Legal Secretaries and Assistant Scottish Parliamentary Counsel, Miss M. Mackenzie
£27,871

LORD CHANCELLOR'S DEPARTMENT
House of Lords, SW1A 0PW
[071–219 3000]

The Lord Chancellor is responsible for promoting general reforms in the civil law, for the procedure of the civil courts and for the administration of the Supreme Court (Court of Appeal, High Court and Crown Court) and county courts in England and Wales, and for legal aid schemes. He is responsible for advising the Crown on the appointment of judges and certain other officers and is himself responsible for the appointment of Masters and Registrars of the High Court, Judges of the Principal Registry of the Family Division, District Judges and magistrates. He is responsible for ensuring that letters patent and other formal documents are passed in the proper form under the Great Seal of the Realm, of which he is the custodian. The work in connection with this is carried out under his direction in the Office of the Clerk of the Crown in Chancery.
(For **Salaries**, *see* page 293)

Lord Chancellor, THE LORD MACKAY OF CLASHFERN, PC £106,750
Private Secretary, Miss J. Rowe.
Permanent Secretary (*G1*), T. S. Legg, CB, QC.
Private Secretary, N. P. Chibnall.

Crown Office

Clerk of the Crown in Chancery (*G1*), T. S. Legg, CB, QC.
Deputy Clerk of the Crown in Chancery (*G2*), R. Potter, CB.
Clerk of the Chamber, Miss J. L. Waine.

JUDICIAL APPOINTMENTS GROUP
House of Lords, SW1A 0PW
[071–219 4311]

Head of Group (*G3*), J. L. Heritage, CB.
Grade 5, D. E. Staff; M. Sayers; R. V. Grobler; G. Norman; P. G. Taylor.

LAW AND POLICY GROUPS
Trevelyan House, Great Peter Street, SW1P 2BY
[071–210 8734]

Head of Group (*G2*), M. Huebner.

Legal and Law Reform Group
26 Old Queen Street, SW1H 9HF
[071–210 3508]

Grade 3, L. Oates.
Grade 5, R. Venne; J. Watherston; R. White.

Policy and Legal Services Group
Trevelyan House, Great Peter Street, SW1P 2BY
[071–210 8769]

Grade 3, C. Everett.
Grade 5, Mrs N. A. Oppenheimer; M. Kron; P. G. Harris.

COURT SERVICE GROUP
Trevelyan House, Great Peter Street, SW1P 2BY
[071–210 8719]

Head of Group (*G2*), R. Potter, CB.

Court Service Management Group

Grade 4, J. F. Brindley.
Grade 5, R. Stoate; R. J. Clark.

ESTABLISHMENT AND FINANCE GROUP
Trevelyan House, Great Peter Street, SW1P 2BY
[071-210 8803]

Head of Group (G3), B. Cousins, CBE.
Grade 5, D. S. Mortimer; R. A. Vincent; D. Nooney.
Grade 6, R. Sams; J. Isaacs.

**LORD CHANCELLOR'S ADVISORY
COMMITTEE ON STATUTE LAW**
House of Lords, SW1A 0PW

The Advisory Committee advises the Lord Chancellor on all matters relating to the revision, modernization and publication of the statute book.
Chairman, T. S. Legg, CB.
Members, M. A. J. Wheeler-Booth; Sir Clifford Boulton, KCB; The Hon. Mr Justice (Peter) Gibson; The Hon. Lord Davidson; P. Graham, CB, QC; J. C. McCluskie, QC; T. R. Erskine, CB; J. Nursaw, CB, QC; R. Brodie, CB; L. Oates; J. Gibson.
Secretary, J. D. Saunders.
   See also **Law Courts and Offices.**

LORD GREAT CHAMBERLAIN'S OFFICE
House of Lords, SW1A 0PW
[071-219 3100]

The Lord Great Chamberlain is a Great Officer of State, the office being hereditary since the grant of Henry I to the family of De Vere, Earls of Oxford.
Lord Great Chamberlain, The Marquess of Cholmondeley.
Secretary to the Lord Great Chamberlain, Air Chief Marshal Sir John Gingell, GBE, KCB.
Clerk to the Lord Great Chamberlain, Mrs S. E. Douglas.

LORD PRIVY SEAL'S OFFICE
Privy Council Office,
68 Whitehall, SW1A 2AT
[071-270 3000]

As leader of the House of Lords, the Lord Privy Seal is responsible to the Prime Minister for the arrangement of government business in the House. He also has a responsibility to the House itself to advise it on procedural matters and other difficulties which arise.
Lord Privy Seal, and Leader of the House of Lords, THE LORD WADDINGTON, PC, QC.
Private Secretary, Miss G. M. Kirton.
Assistant Private Secretary, W. J. S. Hawkins.

OFFICE OF MANPOWER ECONOMICS
22 Kingsway, WC2B 6JY
[071-405 5944]

The Office of Manpower Economics was set up in 1971. It is an independent non-statutory organization which is responsible for servicing independent review bodies which advise on the pay of various public service groups (*see* **Review Bodies**, p. 356), the Pharmacists Review Panel, the Police Negotiating Board and the Civil Service Arbitration Tribunal. The Office is also responsible for servicing *ad hoc* bodies of inquiry and for undertaking research into pay and associated matters as requested by the Government.
Director, D. G. Talintyre.
Assistant Secretaries (G5), H. E. Miller; P. J. H. Edwards; Dr M. E. McDowall.

MEDICAL RESEARCH COUNCIL
20 Park Crescent, W1N 4AL
[071-636 5422]

The Medical Research Council is the main government agency for the promotion of medical and related biological research. The council employs its own research staff and also provides grants for other institutions and for individuals who are not members of its own staff, thus complementing the research resources of the universities and hospitals.
Chairman, Sir David Plastow.
Deputy Chairman and Secretary, D. A. Rees, PH.D., D.SC., FRS.
Members, Sir Donald Acheson, KBE, DM, FRCP; Prof. I. V. Allen, D.SC., MD; Dr D. T. Baird, D.SC., MD, FRCPath.; Prof. C. L. Berry, PH.D.; Prof. M. Bobrow, D.SC.; K. C. Calman, MD, PH.D., FRCS Glas., FRCP; J. T. Carter, FRCP; P. Doyle, PH.D.; Prof. Sir Aaron Klug, SC.D., FRS; Prof. C. D. Marsden, D.SC., FRCP, FRS; Prof. M. J. Peckham, FRCP, FRCPGlas, FRCR; Prof. G. K. Radda, D.phil., FRS; Prof. R. Shields, MD, FRCS, FRCSE; Mrs R. Short; J. W. G. Smith, MD, FRCP.
Administrative Secretary, Ms N. Morris.

Neurobiology and Mental Health Board
Chairman, Prof. I. V. Allen, D.SC., MD, FRCPath.

Cell Biology and Disorders Board
Chairman, Prof. G. Radda.

Physiological Systems and Disorders Board
Chairman, Prof. C. L. Berry, PH.D., MD, FRCPath.

Tropical Medicine Research Board
Chairman, D. C. Evered, D.SC., MD, FRCP.

Health Services Research Committee
Chairman, Prof. J. Grimley Evans, MD, FRCP, FRCM.

HEADQUARTERS OFFICE
Second Secretary, D. Evered, D.SC., MD, FRCP.

Administrative Division
Administrative Secretary, Ms N. Morris.
Assistant Secretaries, B. C. Dodd; J. E. A. Hay; D. Smith, PH.D.

Secretariat
Assistant Secretary, N. H. Winterton.

Medical Division
Scientific Programme Managers, K. Levy, PH.D.; J. Alwen, PH.D.
Director of Operations, Dr D. Dunstan.
Deputy Director, Dr M. Davies.
Executive Board Secretaries, Dr M. B. Kemp; Dr J. E. Dowman; Dr J. E. Cope; Dr A. B. Stone.

For units of Medical Research Council, *see* pp. 965–6.

MENTAL HEALTH ACT COMMISSION
Maid Marian House, 56 Hounds Gate, Nottingham
NG1 6BG
[0602-504040]

The Mental Health Act Commission was established in 1983. Its functions are to keep under review the operation of the Mental Health Act 1983; to visit and interview patients detained under the Act; to investigate complaints falling within the Commission's remit; to monitor the implementation of the Code of Practice; and to advise ministers. Commissioners are appointed by the Secretary of State for Health in the following categories: lay; legal; medical; nursing; psychology; social worker; and specialist.
Chairman, L. Blom-Cooper, QC.
Vice-Chairman, Prof. E. Murphy.
Chief Executive (G6), W. Bingley.

MONOPOLIES AND MERGERS COMMISSION
New Court, 48 Carey Street, WC2A 2JT
[071–324 1467]

The Commission was established in 1948 as the Monopolies and Restrictive Practices Commission and became the Monopolies and Mergers Commission in 1973. The Commission has the duty of investigating and reporting on questions referred to it with respect to: the existence or possible existence of monopolies not registrable under the Restrictive Trade Practices Act 1976 and relating to the supply of goods or services in the UK or part of the UK or to the supply of goods for export; the transfer of a newspaper or newspaper's assets; the creation or possible creation of a merger qualifying for investigation within the meaning of the Fair Trading Act 1973.

References may be made to the Commission on the general effect on the public interest of specified monopoly or other uncompetitive practices and of restrictive labour practices.

The Competition Act 1980 provides for the reference to the Commission of particular anti-competitive practices and of questions of efficiency, costs, service provided and possible abuse of monopolies in the public sector. In respect of recently-privatized industries, references to the Commission may be made in certain circumstances, with regard to their respective industries, by the Director General of Telecommunications, the Civil Aviation Authority, the Director General of Gas Supply, the Director General of Water Services and the Director General of Electricity Supply.

Under the Broadcasting Act 1990 the Commission can investigate and report on the competition aspects of networking arrangements between holders of regional Channel 3 licences.

Chairman, Sir Sydney Lipworth £82,780
Deputy Chairmen, H. H. Liesner, CB; P. H. Dean; D. G. Goyder £29,015
Members, A. G. Armstrong; C. C. Baillieu; I. Barter; Prof. M. E. Beesley, CBE; Mrs C. Blight; F. E. Bonner, CBE; *P. Brenan; J. S. Bridgeman; L. Britz; K. S. Carmichael, CBE; R. Davies; Prof. S. Eilon; J. Evans; A. Ferry, MBE; M. R. Hoffman; J. D. Keir, QC; *A. L. Kingshott; Miss P. K. R. Mann; G. C. S. Mather; *N. F. Matthews; L. A. Mills; Prof. P. Minford; J. D. Montgomery; B. C. Owens; *Prof. J. Pickering; *L. Priestley; D. P. Thomson; C. A. Unwin, MBE; Prof. G. Whittington; R. Young.
each £11,680 (*£7,786)
Secretary, S. N. Burbridge.

MUSEUMS

MUSEUMS AND GALLERIES COMMISSION
16 Queen Anne's Gate, SW1H 9AA
[071–233 4200]

Established in 1931 as the Standing Commission on Museums and Galleries, the Commission was renamed and took up new functions in September 1981. Its sponsor department is the Office of Arts and Libraries. The Commission advises the Government, including the Department of Education for Northern Ireland, the Scottish Education Department and the Welsh Office, on museum affairs. There are 15 Commissioners, appointed by the Prime Minister.

The Commission's executive functions include the services of the National Museums Security Adviser; allocation of grants to the seven Area Museum Councils in England; funding and monitoring of the work of the Museum Documentation Association;

directly administering a capital grant scheme for non-national museums, and various other grant schemes. The Commission administers the arrangements for government indemnities and the acceptance of works of art in lieu of Inheritance Tax, and it has responsibility for the two purchase grant funds for local museums managed on its behalf by the Victoria and Albert Museum and the Science Museum. The Commission's Conservation Unit advises on conservation and operates grants schemes for conservators. The Travelling Exhibitions Unit promotes and encourages travelling exhibitions. A Disability Adviser promotes better provision for disabled people in museums, and an Environmental Adviser is drawing up guidelines on environmental standards in museums. A registration scheme for museums in the UK is being implemented with the assistance of the Commission.

Chairman, G. Greene, CBE.
Members, The Marchioness of Anglesey, DBE; F. Atkinson, OBE; L. Brandes, CB; The Lord Dainton, FRS; F. Dunning, OBE; Prof. Sir John Hale, FBA; J. Last, CBE; Sir Hugh Leggatt; The Lord O'Neill, TD; The Lord Rees, PC, QC; R. H. Smith; Dame Margaret Weston, DBE; Adm. Sir David Williams, GCB.
Director and Secretary, P. Longman.

THE BRITISH MUSEUM
Great Russell Street, WC1B 3DG
[071–636 1555]

Antiquities collections, coins and medals, prints and drawings. Open weekdays (including Bank Holidays) 10–5 and Sun. 2.30–6. Closed on Good Friday, Christmas Eve, Christmas Day, Boxing Day, New Year's Day and the first Monday in May. The ethnographical collections are displayed in the Museum of Mankind, 6 Burlington Gardens, W1. Opening times as above.

The British Museum may be said to date from 1753, when Parliament granted funds to purchase the collections of Sir Hans Sloane and the Harleian manuscripts, and for their proper housing and maintenance. The building (Montagu House) was opened in 1759. The present buildings were erected between 1823 and the present day, and the original collection has increased to its present dimensions by gifts and purchases. Government grants for running costs and works and building projects were estimated at £29,944,000 in 1991–92.

Board of Trustees
Appointed by the Sovereign: HRH The Duke of Gloucester, GCVO. *Appointed by the Prime Minister:* The Lord Windlesham, CVO, PC (*Chairman*); Sir Matthew Farrer, KCVO; G. C. Greene, CBE; Prof. E. T. Hall, D.Phil., FSA, FBA; C. E. A. Hambro; Sir Peter Harrop, KCB; S. Keswick; Hon. Mrs Marten, OBE; Mrs M. Moore; Sir John Morgan, KCMG; Sir Timothy Raison, MP; S. Towneley, D.Phil.; Prof. G. H. Treitel, DCL., FBA, QC; The Lord Weinstock; Prof. W. Whitfield, CBE; Sir Oliver Wright, GCMG, GCVO, DSC.
Nominated by the learned Societies: The Lord Adrian, MD, FRS (*Royal Society*); A. Jones, RA (*Royal Academy*); Sir Claus Moser, KCB, CBE, FBA (*British Academy*); Prof. A. C. Renfrew, FBA, FSA (*Society of Antiquaries*).
Appointed by the Trustees of the British Museum: Sir David Attenborough, CBE, FRS; Prof. Rosemary Cramp, CBE, FSA; Prof. Sir John Hale, FSA, FBA; Prof. P. Lasko, CBE, FSA, FBA; The Lord Egremont.

Salaries

Grade 2	£60,100
Grade 4	£41,681–£43,307
Grade 5	£33,970–£38,610
Grade 6	£26,121–£33,970
Grade 7	£22,891–£27,299
Head of Press and PR	£16,176–£20,467
Press and PR Officer	£13,262–£16,822

Officers

Director (G2), Dr R. G. W. Anderson.
Deputy Director (G4), Miss J. M. Rankine.
Secretary (G6), G. B. Morris.
Assistant to the Director (G7), Ms M. L. Caygill.
Head of Public Services (G6), G. A. L. House.
Head of Design (G6), Margaret Hall, OBE.
Head of Education (G7), J. F. Reeve.
Head of Press and Public Relations, A. E. Hamilton.
Press and Public Relations Officer, Miss A. F. Dunkels.
Head of Administration (G5), C. E. I. Jones.
Head of Building and Security Services (G6), K. T. Stannard.
Head of Architectural and Building Services (G7), C. J. Walker.
Head of Finance (G7), D. E. Williams.
Head of Personnel and Office Services (G7), Miss B. A. Hughes.
Keeper of Prints and Drawings (G5), vacant.
Deputy Keeper (G6), A. V. Griffiths.
Keeper of Coins and Medals (G5), M. Jones.
Deputy Keeper (G6), M. J. Price.
Keeper of Egyptian Antiquities (G5), W. V. Davies.
Keeper of Western Asiatic Antiquities (G5), J. E. Curtis.
Keeper of Greek and Roman Antiquities (G5), B. F. Cook.
Deputy Keeper (G6), vacant.
Keeper of Medieval and Later Antiquities (G5), N. M. Stratford.
Deputy Keepers (G6), G. H. Tait; J. Cherry; Ms L. E. Webster.
Keeper of Prehistoric and Romano-British Antiquities (G5), I. H. Longworth.
Deputy Keepers (G6), I. M. Stead; T. W. Potter.
Keeper of Japanese Antiquities (G5), L. R. H. Smith.
Keeper of Oriental Antiquities (G5), Ms J. M. Rawson.
Deputy Keeper (G6), J. R. Knox.
Keeper of Ethnography (G5), J. B. Mack.
Deputy Keeper (G6), B. Durrans.
Keeper of Scientific Research (G5), Ms S. G. E. Bowman.
Principal Scientific Officers (G7), P. T. Craddock; M. J. Hughes; I. C. Freestone; A. P. Middleton; E. J. Neville; M. Cowell.
Keeper of Conservation (G5), W. A. Oddy.
Principal Scientific Officers (G7), V. D. Daniels; Ms S. M. Bradley.
Principal Conservator (G7), Ms H. P. Lane.

THE NATURAL HISTORY MUSEUM
Cromwell Road and Exhibition Road, SW7 5BD
[071–938 9123]

Open Mon.–Sat. (except New Year's Day, Good Friday, Christmas Eve, Christmas Day and Boxing Day) 10–6, Sun. 11–6. Admission, £3·50.

The Natural History Museum originates from the natural history departments of the British Museum. During the 19th century the natural history collections grew extensively and in 1881 they were moved to South Kensington. In 1963 the Natural History Museum became completely independent with its own body of Trustees. The Zoological Museum, Tring, bequeathed by the second Lord Rothschild, has formed part of the Museum since 1938. The Geological Museum merged with the Natural History Museum in 1985 (opening times are as given above). Research workers are admitted to the libraries and study collections by Student's Ticket, applications for which should be made in writing to the Director.

The administrative expenses were estimated at £21,680,000 in 1990–91.

(For **Salaries,** *see* page 293).

Board of Trustees

Chairman, Sir Walter Bodmer, FRS.
Appointed by the Prime Minister: Sir Owen Green; Prof. J. M. Thomas, FRS; G. M. Ronson; E. N. K. Clarkson, FRS; Mrs J. M. d'Abo; Sir Denys Henderson; Prof. R. May, FRS.
Nominated by the Royal Society: Prof. J. L. Harper, FRS.
Appointed by the Trustees of the British Museum (Natural History): R. J. Carter; Prof. B. K. Follett, FRS; Sir Anthony Laughton, FRS.
Director (G3), N. R. Chalmers, Ph.D.
Associate Director (Scientific Development) (G5), J. F. Peake.
Secretary (G5), C. J. E. Legg.
Assistant to the Director (G7), Miss R. P. Baillon.

Marketing and Development Department

Head (G6), vacant.

Department of Zoology

Keeper (G5), C. R. Curds, D.SC.
Deputy Keepers (G6), R. J. Lincoln, Ph.D.; I. R. Bishop, OBE (acting).
Grade 6 , J. D. Taylor, Ph.D.

Bird Section
Park Street, Tring, Herts.
[044 282-4181]

Grade 6, I. R. Bishop, OBE.

Department of Entomology

Keeper (G5), L. A. Mound, D.SC.
Deputy Keeper (G6), I. D. Gauld, Ph.D.
Grade 6, R. L. Blackman Ph.D.; R. I. Vane-Wright.
Principal Research Fellow, P. D. Ready, Ph.D.

Department of Botany

Keeper (G5), S. Blackmore, Ph.D.
Deputy Keeper (G6), D. A. Sutton, Ph.D.
Grade 6, C. J. Humphries, Ph.D.

Department of Palaeontology

Keeper (G5), L. R. M. Cocks, D.SC.
Deputy Keepers (G6), M. K. Howarth, Ph.D.; H. G. Owen, Ph.D.
Grade 6, C. Patterson, Ph.D.; R. A. Fortey, SC.D.; P. J. Andrews, Ph.D.

Department of Mineralogy

Keeper (G5), P. Henderson, D.phil.
Deputy Keeper (G6), A. L. Graham, Ph.D.
Grade 6, R. Hutchison, Ph.D.; A. R. Woolley, Ph.D.

Department of Administrative Services

Head of Finance and Establishment Officer (G5), C. J. E. Legg.
Building Manager (G6), R. H. Essex.
Personnel Officer (G7), Mrs P. H. I. Orchard.
Head of Finance and Accounts (G6), P. M. Hackwell.
Grade 7, B. S. Martin; N. H. Thomson.

Department of Library Services

Head (G6), R. E. R. Banks.
Deputy Head (G7), Miss P. Gilbert.

Department of Public Services

Head (*G5*), R. S. Miles, D.SC.
Deputy Head (*G6*), G. C. S. Clarke, Ph.D.
Operations Manager (*G6*), M. B. McBratney.
Contracts and Production Manager (*G7*), R. G. Nash.
Technical Services Manager (*G7*), J. Furlong.
Head of Exhibition and Design (*G7*), R. M. Bloomfield, Ph.D.

MUSEUM OF LONDON
London Wall, EC2Y 5HN
[071-600 3699]

Open Tues.–Sat. 10–6, Sun. 2–6. Closed Mons., Christmas Day and Boxing Day. Admission, £3 (three months), £6 (one year); concessions, £1.50/£3.00.

The Museum of London opened in 1976. It is based on the amalgamation of the former Guildhall Museum and London Museum. The Museum is controlled by a Board of Governors, appointed (nine each) by the Government and the Corporation of London. The exhibition illustrates the history of London from prehistoric times to the present day.
Chairman of Board of Governors, P. Revell-Smith, CBE.
Director, M. G. Hebditch, FSA.

THE SCIENCE MUSEUM
South Kensington, SW7 2DD
[071–938 8000]

Open on Mon.–Sat. 10–6, Sun. 11–6. Closed on New Year's Day, Christmas Eve, Christmas Day and Boxing Day. Admission charge.

The Science Museum, part of the National Museum of Science & Industry, houses the national collections of science, technology, industry and medicine. The Museum began as the science collection of the South Kensington Museum and first opened in 1857. In 1883 it acquired the collections of the Patent Museum and in 1909 the science collections were transferred to the new Science Museum, leaving the art collections with the Victoria and Albert Museum.

Some of the Museum's commercial aircraft, agricultural machinery, and road and rail transport collections are at Wroughton, near Swindon, Wilts., and are open for public viewing on selected weekends during the summer.

The Museum is responsible for the Concorde Exhibition at the Fleet Air Arm Museum, Yeovilton.

The total running expenses, including building costs, of the Museum, the Science Museum Library, the National Railway Museum and the National Museum of Photography, Film and Television are estimated at £23,927,000 for 1991–92.
(For **Salaries**, see page 293.)

Board of Trustees

Chairman, Sir Austin Pearce, CBE.
Members, HRH The Duke of Kent, KG, GCMG, GCVO, ADC; Dr M. Archer; Prof. Sir Eric Ash, CBE, FRS; The Lord Brabourne; Adm. Sir Desmond Cassidi, GCB; Sir Kenneth Corfield, The Viscount Downe; Miss M. S. Goldring, OBE; Prof. E. T. Hall, CBE, FBA, FSA; Mrs A. Higham; Sir Robert Reid; Sir Dennis Rooke, CBE, FRS; L. de Rothschild, CBE; Prof. J. M. Thomas, FRS; Sir Christopher Wates.
Director, Dr N. Cossons, OBE.

RESOURCE MANAGEMENT DIVISION

Assistant Director (*G5*), J. J. Defries.
Head of Personnel and Training (*G7*), C. Gosling.
Head of Finance (*G7*), J. Reid.

Estate Development Manager (*SPTO*), R. Maisey.
Building Manager (*SEO*), J. Bevin.

COLLECTIONS MANAGEMENT DIVISION

Assistant Director (*G5*), Dr T. Wright.

Science Group

Head of Group (*G5*), Dr D. A. Robinson.
Curators (*G7*), Dr D. Vaughan; Dr A. Q. Morton; C. N. Brown; Dr P. Morris.

Life Sciences and the Environment Group

Head of Group (*G5*), Dr R. F. Bud.
Curators (*G7*), Dr G. M. Lawrence; P. R. Mann; A. Nahum; J. Robinson.

Technology Group

Head of Group (*G5*), Dr E. J. S. Becklake.
Curators (*G7*), Dr B. P. Bowers; D. D. Swade; R. McWilliam.

Services Group

Head of Group (*G6*), vacant.
Curators (*G7*), Dr R. Price; Dr A. K. Newmark.

MARKETING DIVISION

Assistant Director (*G5*), C. M. Pemberton.
Marketing Manager (*G7*), M. Sullivan.

PUBLIC SERVICES DIVISION

Assistant Director (*G5*), T. Suthers.
Head of Operations and House Management (*G6*), I. M. Ball.
Head of Interpretation (*G7*), Dr G. Farmelo.

RESEARCH AND INFORMATION SERVICES DIVISION
[071–938 8234]

A national library of science, specializing in the history of science and technology. Bibliographies supplied. Photocopying and microfilm service. Open Mon.–Sat. 10–5.30. Closed on Sundays and Bank Holiday weekends.
Assistant Director (*G5*), Prof. J. R. Durant.
Head of Library and Information Services (*G6*), Dr L. D. Will.

NATIONAL RAILWAY MUSEUM
Leeman Road, York YO2 4XJ
[0904–621261]

The Museum, opened in 1975, houses the national rail transport collection. Locomotives, rolling stock and carriages are displayed to illustrate the technical, social and economic story of the development of railways in Britain. Open Mon.–Sat. 10–6, Sun. 11–6.
Head of Museum (*G5*), Dr J. A. Coiley.

NATIONAL MUSEUM OF PHOTOGRAPHY, FILM AND TELEVISION
Prince's View, Bradford BD5 0TR
[0274–727488]

The Museum, opened in 1983, collects, conserves and displays photography, film and television materials and equipment. It has the only IMAX cinema in the UK. Open Tues.–Sun. 11–6, with special exhibition galleries open to 7.30.
Head of Museum (*G5*), C. J. Ford.

THE VICTORIA AND ALBERT MUSEUM
South Kensington, SW7 2RL
[071–938 8500]

Open Mon.–Sat. 10–5.50, Sun. 2.30–5.50. Closed
Christmas Eve, Christmas Day, Boxing Day, New
Year's Day and May Day. The National Art Library
is open Tues.–Sat. 10–5 (closed 1–2 Sat.) and the Print
Room Tues.–Fri. 10–5, Sat. 10–1, 2–4.30. Donations
are invited.

A museum of all branches of fine and applied art,
the Victoria and Albert Museum descends directly
from the Museum of Manufactures, which opened in
Marlborough House in 1852 after the Great Exhibition of 1851. The Museum was moved in 1857 to
become part of the collective South Kensington
Museum. It was renamed the Victoria and Albert
Museum in 1899. The branch museum at Bethnal
Green was opened in 1872 and the building is the
most important surviving example of the type of glass
and iron construction used by Paxton for the Great
Exhibition. The Victoria and Albert Museum also
administers the Wellington Museum (Apsley House),
Ham House, Osterley Park, and the Theatre Museum.

Board of Trustees
Chairman, The Lord Armstrong of Ilminster, GCB,
CVO.
Deputy Chairman, Sir Michael Butler, GCMG.
Members, Lord Barnett, PC; Miss N. Campbell; Sir
Clifford Chetwood; Mr I. H. Davison; Mr T. Dawe;
Mr R. Fitch, CBE; Prof. C. Frayling, PH.D.; Pamela,
Lady Harlech; Mr. R. Gorlin; Sir Nevil Macready,
CBE; Miss J. Muir, CBE; Miss A. Plowden; Prof. M.
Podro, PH.D.; Mr M. Saatchi; Prof. J. Steer, FSA.

Director and Secretary (G3), Mrs E. A. L. Esteve-Coll.
Assistant Directors (G5), J. D. W. Murdoch *(Collections);* J. W. Close *(Administration).*

Ceramics Collection
Curator (G6), Dr O. Watson.
Deputy Curators (D), Mrs J. Opie; P. Greenhalgh.

Department of Conservation
Head of Conservation (G5), Dr J. Ashley-Smith.

Far Eastern Collection
Curator (G6), Miss R. Kerr.
Deputy Curators (G7), Dr A. C. Clunas; *(D)* R.
Faulkner.

Furniture and Woodwork Collection
Curator (G6), C. Wilk.
Deputy Curators (G7), Dr T. Murdoch; C. Wain-
wright.

Indian and South East Asian Collection
Curator (G6), Dr D. Swallow.
Deputy Curators (G7), J. S. Guy; *(D)* Miss R. Crill.

National Art Library
Curator and Chief Librarian (G5), J. F. van den
Wateren.
Head of Special Collections (G7), Dr R. Watson.
Head of Public Services (G7), Mrs G. Varley.
Head of Collections Management (G7), D. Dodds.

Metalwork Collection
Curator (G6), Mrs P. Glanville.
Deputy Curators (G7), Miss M. Campbell; E. R.
Edgecumbe.

Prints, Drawings, Photographs and Paintings Collection
Curator (G6), Miss S. B. Lambert.
Head of Paintings (G7), L. Lambourne.
Head of Designs (G7), M. Snodin.

Head of Photographs (G7), M. Haworth-Booth.
Head of Documentation (D), Miss G. Saunders.
Deputy Curator (D), Miss M. Timmers.

Sculpture Collection
Curator (G6), P. E. D. Williamson.
Deputy Curators (D), Ms P. Evelyn; Ms M. Trusted.

Textiles and Dress Collection
Curator (G6), Mrs V. D. Mendes.
Deputy Curator (G7), Miss W. Hefford; Mrs L. L.
Parry.

Marketing and Communications Department
Head of Marketing and Communications (G5), R.
Cole-Hamilton.

BETHNAL GREEN MUSEUM OF CHILDHOOD
Cambridge Heath Road, Bethnal Green, E2 9PA
[081–980 3204]

Open Mon.–Thurs. and on Sat. 10–6, Sun. 2.30–6.
Closed every Friday, May Day, Christmas Eve,
Christmas Day, Boxing Day and New Year's Day.
Head of the Museum (G6), A. P. Burton.

THEATRE MUSEUM
1E Tavistock Street, WC2E 7PA
[071–836 7891]

Open Tues.–Sun. 11–7. Closed Mon. except Bank
Holidays. Admission £2.25, concessions £1.25.
Head of the Museum (G6), Ms M. Benton.

THE COMMONWEALTH INSTITUTE
Kensington High Street, W8 6NQ
[071–603 4535]

Open Mon.–Sat. 10–5, Sun. 2–5. Admission free.
Closed Good Friday, May Day, Christmas Eve,
Christmas Day, Boxing Day and New Year's Day.

The Commonwealth Institute is a centre for
information about the Commonwealth. It is funded
by the British government with contributions from
other Commonwealth governments. The Institute is
controlled by a Board of Governors which includes
the High Commissioners of all Commonwealth countries represented in London. The Institute has
permanent exhibitions on all Commonwealth nations, plus educational resource, information and
conference centres.
Director General, S. Cox.
Director of Education, G. Brandt.
Chief Administrative Officer, P. Kennedy.
Head of Exhibitions and Information, J. Stevenson.

IMPERIAL WAR MUSEUM
Lambeth Road, SE1 6HZ
[071–416 5000]

Open daily 10–6. Closed Christmas Eve, Christmas
Day, Boxing Day and New Year's Day. Admission,
£3·30; concessions, £1·65; free day on Fridays. The
Reference departments are open Mon.–Sat. 10–5, Sat.
by appointment only.

The Museum, founded in 1917, illustrates and
records all aspects of the two world wars and other
military operations involving Britain and the Commonwealth since 1914. It was opened in its present
home, formerly Bethlem Hospital or Bedlam, in 1936.
The Museum also administers HMS *Belfast* in the
Pool of London, Duxford Airfield near Cambridge
and the Cabinet War Rooms in Westminster.

Expenses for 1991–92 are estimated at £18,897,000.
(For **Salaries,** *see* page 293.)

Director General (G4), A. C. N. Borg, CBE, PH.D., FSA.
Deputy Director General (G5), R. W. K. Crawford.
Secretary (G6), J. J. Chadwick.

Personnel Officer (G7), P. L. Cracknell.
Finance Officer (G7), Mrs P. A. Whitfield.
Museum Superintendent (G7), D. A. Needham.
Office of Information Systems (G7), J. C. Barrett.
Senior Keeper and Keeper of Audio-Visual Records (G5), G. T. C. Coultass.
Director of Duxford Airfield (G5), E. O. Inman.
Director of HMS Belfast (G6), Capt. F. A. Collins, RN.

Keepers

Department of Museum Services (G6), C. Dowling, D.Phil.
Department of Documents (G6), R. W. A. Suddaby.
Department of Exhibits and Firearms (G6), D. J. Penn.
Department of Printed Books (G6), G. M. Bayliss, Ph.D.
Department of Art (G6), Miss A. H. Weight.
Department of Film (G6), R. B. N. Smither.
Department of Photographs (G6), Miss K. J. Carmichael.
Department of Sound Records (G6), Mrs M. A. Brooks.
Department of Marketing and Training (G6), Miss A. Godwin.
Curator of the Cabinet War Rooms (G7), E. J. Wenzel.

NATIONAL MARITIME MUSEUM
Greenwich, SE10 9NF
[081–858 4422]

Open Mon.–Sat., 10–6 (10–5 in winter); Sun. 2–6 (2–5 in winter). Closed Jan. 1, Good Friday and Dec. 24–26. Admission charge. Reading Room open Mon.–Fri., 10–5; readers' tickets available on written application to Reader Services Section.

Established by Act of Parliament in 1934, the National Maritime Museum illustrates the maritime history of Great Britain in the widest sense, underlining the importance of the sea and its influence on the nation's power, wealth, culture, technology and institutions. The Museum is in two groups of buildings in Greenwich Park—the main buildings centred around the Queen's House (built by Inigo Jones, 1616–35) and the Old Royal Observatory (including Wren's Flamsteed House) to the south—and also includes the *Cutty Sark* and a Special Exhibitions Centre. The collections include paintings, actual craft and ship models, ships' lines, prints and drawings, atlases and charts, navigational and astronomical instruments, uniforms and relics, books and MSS.
Director, R. L. Ormond.

NATIONAL ARMY MUSEUM
Royal Hospital Road, SW3 4HT
[071–730 0717]

Open daily, 10–5.30. Closed Dec. 24–26, Jan. 1, Good Friday and May Bank Hols.

The National Army Museum was established by Royal Charter (1960). It covers the history of five centuries of the British Army, including the story of the Indian Army up to independence in 1947. The Indian Army room at the Royal Military Academy Sandhurst, Camberley, Surrey may be viewed by appointment.
Director, I. G. Robertson.
Personal Assistant to the Director, Mrs E. Carpenter.
Assistant Directors, D. K. Smurthwaite; A. J. Guy; Maj. P. R. Bateman.

ROYAL AIR FORCE MUSEUM
Grahame Park Way,
Hendon, NW9 5LL
[081–205 2266]

Open daily, 10–6. Closed Dec. 24, 25, 26, Jan. 1. Admission charge.

Situated on the former airfield at Hendon, the Museum illustrates the development of aviation from before the Wright brothers to the present-day RAF. Over 60 historic aircraft are on display from the Museum's collection. The complex includes Battle of Britain and Bomber Command halls and the 'Battle of Britain Experience'.
Director, Dr M. A. Fopp.
Deputy Director, J. D. Freeborn.
Keepers, D. C. R. Elliott; P. G. Murton; P. Elliott; D. F. Lawrence.

THE NATIONAL MUSEUMS AND GALLERIES ON MERSEYSIDE
William Brown Street, Liverpool L3 8EN
[051–207 0001]

All museums and galleries are open all year except Jan. 1, Dec. 24–26 and Good Friday. Opening times (except for the Maritime Museum) are Mon.–Sat. 10–5, Sun. 12–5. Opening times for the Merseyside Maritime Museum are daily 10.30–5.30. Admission charge.

The Board of Trustees of the National Museums and Galleries on Merseyside was established in 1986 to take over responsibility for the museums and galleries previously administered by Merseyside County Council. Various stores ancillary to the collections are also the responsibility of the body. It is grant-aided by the Minister for Arts.
Chairman of the Board of Trustees, Sir Leslie Young, CBE.
Director, R. Foster.
Head of Central Services, P. Sudbury, Ph.D.
Keeper of Art Galleries, J. Treuherz.
Keeper of Conservation, J. France.

Liverpool Museum
William Brown Street, Liverpool
Keeper, E. Greenwood.

Merseyside Maritime Museum
Albert Dock, Liverpool
[051–207 0001]
Keeper, M. Stammers.

Walker Art Gallery
William Brown Street, Liverpool

Lady Lever Art Gallery
Port Sunlight Village, Bebington, Wirral

Sudley Art Gallery
Mossley Hill Road, Liverpool

THE NATIONAL MUSEUM OF WALES
(Amgueddfa Genedlaethol Cymru)
Main Building, Cathays Park, Cardiff CF1 3NP
[0222–397951]

Open Tues.–Sat., 10–5. Sun. 2.30–5. Closed on Mondays (except Bank Holidays), Christmas Eve, Christmas Day, Boxing Day, New Year's Day and Good Friday. Admission charge.
President, Hon. J. Davies.
Vice-President, C. R. T. Edwards.
Director, A. Wilson.
Head of Administration, T. Arnold.
Keepers, M. G. Bassett, Ph.D. (*Geology*); B. A. Thomas, Ph.D. (*Botany*); P. M. Morgan (*Zoology*); H. S. Green, Ph.D. (*Archaeology*); T. J. Stevens, Ph.D. (*Art*).

Welsh Folk Museum
(Amgueddfa Werin Cymru)
St Fagans, Nr. Cardiff

Open April–Oct., daily 10–5; Nov.–March, Mon.–Sat. 10–5. Admission charge. Closed on Christmas Eve, Christmas Day, Boxing Day, New Year's Day and Good Friday.

Curator, vacant.
Keepers, E. Scourfield, PH.D; E. Williams, PH.D.

Roman Legionary Museum, Caerleon
Caerleon, Gwent.

Contains material found on the site of the Roman fortress of Isca and its suburbs. Open Mon.–Sat. 10–6, Sun. 2–6 (closes 4.30 p.m. mid–Oct. to mid-March). Closed Dec. 24–26, Jan. 1, May Day and Good Friday. Admission charge.

Officer in Charge, D. Zienkiewicz.

Turner House Art Gallery
Plymouth Road, Penarth, Nr. Cardiff

Open Tues.–Fri. 11–12.45 and 2–5, Sun. 2–5. Closed Mondays, except Bank Holidays, Saturdays and on Christmas Eve, Christmas Day, Boxing Day, New Year's Day, Good Friday, and May Day.

Keeper in Charge, T. Stevens, PH.D.

Museum of the North
Llanberis, Gwynedd

A multi-media presentation of the history of Wales, and about the electricity supply industry. Open June to mid-Sept. 9.30–6; mid-Sept.–Jan. and March–May, 10–5; Feb. 10.30–4. . Closed Nov. and Dec., Jan. 1 and Good Friday. Admission charge.

Keeper, D. Roberts, PH.D.

Welsh Slate Museum
Llanberis, Gwynedd

Open Easter–Sept. 30 daily 9.30–5.30. Admission charge.

Keeper in Charge, D. Roberts, PH.D.

Segontium Roman Fort Museum
Beddgelert Road, Caernarfon, Gwynedd

Open weekdays at 9.30, Sundays at 2. Closes at 6 from May to September, at 5.30 in March, April and October (5 on Suns.), and at 4 from November to February. Closed Christmas Eve, Christmas Day, Boxing Day, New Year's Day and Good Friday. On the site of the fort, the museum is in the guardianship of the Welsh Office. Contains mostly material excavated there.

Officer in Charge, R. J. Brewer.

Museum of the Welsh Woollen Industry
Dre-fach Felindre, nr. Llandysul, Dyfed

It occupies part of a working mill. Open April–Sept., Mon.–Sat. 10–5; Oct.–March, Mon.–Fri. 10–5. Admission charge.

Keeper in Charge, E. Scourfield, PH.D.

Welsh Industrial and Maritime Museum
Bute Street, Cardiff

Open Tues.–Sat. 10–5; Sun. 2.30–5. Closed Mondays, Christmas Eve, Christmas Day, Boxing Day, New Year's Day and Good Friday. Admission charge.

Keeper, S. Owen-Jones, PH.D.

The Graham Sutherland Gallery and Picton Castle Grounds
The Rhos, Haverfordwest
[0437–751296]

Open Easter–end Oct., Tues.–Sun. 10.30–12.30, 1.30–5.00. Closed Mondays (except Bank Holidays). Admission charge.

Officer in Charge, S. Moss.

NATIONAL MUSEUMS OF SCOTLAND
Chambers Street, Edinburgh EH1 1JF
[031–225 7534]

Royal Museum of Scotland open Mon.–Sat., 10–5 and Sun., 2–5. Closed Dec. 25 and 26 and Jan. 1 and 2. Other museums, opening times vary.

The National Museums of Scotland include the Royal Museum of Scotland, Chambers Street, and the Royal Museum of Scotland, Queen Street in Edinburgh, as well as the Scottish United Services Museum at Edinburgh Castle, the Scottish Agricultural Museum at Ingliston, the Museum of Flight at East Fortune, Shambellie House Museum of Costume near Dumfries (which will be closed for refurbishment during 1992) and Biggar Gasworks Museum. The Museums are governed by a board of Trustees.

Board of Trustees

NATIONAL AUDIT OFFICE
157–197 Buckingham Palace Road, SW1W 9SP
[071–798 7000]

The National Audit Office came into existence under the National Audit Act 1983, to replace and continue the work of the former Exchequer and Audit Department. The Act reinforced the Office's total financial and operational independence from the Government and brought its head, the Comptroller and Auditor General, into a closer relationship with Parliament as an officer of the House of Commons.

The National Audit Office provides independent information, advice and assurance to Parliament and the public about all aspects of the financial operations of government departments and many other bodies receiving public funds. This it does by examining and certifying the accounts of these organizations and by regularly publishing reports to Parliament on the results of its value for money investigations of the economy, efficiency and effectiveness with which public resources have been used. The National Audit Office is also the auditor by agreement of the accounts of certain international and other organizations. In addition, the office authorizes the issue of public funds to government departments.

Comptroller and Auditor General, Sir John Bourn, KCB.
Private Secretary, M. Sinclair.
Deputy Comptroller and Auditor General, R. N. Le Marechal.

Assistant Auditor Generals, D. A. Dewar; M. J. Goodson; J. A. Higgins; P. J. C. Keemer; L. H. Hughes.
Directors, P. J. Beck; J. A. Davies; I. R. W. Hargest; R. W. Locke; P. O'Keefe; A. G. Brown; T. J. Lovett; G. J. S. Frith; C. L. Press; B. D. Baker; C. K. Beauchamp; M. C. Pfleger; R. M. Bennett; B. Hogg; G. G. Jones; R. J. McCourt; J. Marshall; A. R. Murray; J. Parsons; J. M. Pearce; A. G. Roberts; R. A. Skeen; R. E. Spurgeon; M. Easteal; A. Fiander.
Deputy Directors, C. J. Day; G. J. McKeown; M. V. Pettet; A. Cunningham; K. Maclean; M. L. Daynes; D. R. Corsby; R. W. Tycer; J. J. Jones; D. J. Woodward; A. Burchell; J. B. Cavanagh; J. Darling; P. R. Duncombe; R. J. Eales; D. A. Ferguson; N. Gale; T. Griffiths; K. Hawkswell; J. Hirst; Miss J. Lawler; J. S. McEwen; Miss C. Mawhood; R. Parker; R. A. Pocock; M. J. Reeves; N. Sloan; P. G. Woodward; R. Goacher; M. Whitehouse; P. Cannon.

NATIONAL CONSUMER COUNCIL
20 Grosvenor Gardens, SW1W 0DH
[071–730 3469]

The National Consumer Council was set up by the Government in 1975 to give an independent voice to consumers in the UK. Its job is to advocate the consumer interest to decision-makers in business, industry, the public utilities, the professions, and central and local government. It does this through a combination of research and campaigning. It is funded by a grant-in-aid from the Department of Trade and Industry.
Chairman, Lady Wilcox.
Vice-Chairman, Mrs A. Scully.
Members, Miss B. Brookes; Prof. K. Bhattacharyya; A. Burton, OBE; P. Circus; Prof. P. Fairest; Miss J. Francis; J. Hughes; Mrs D. Hutton; Prof. G. Jones; J. Mitchell; Ms M. McAnally; Lady McCollum; Mrs J. Moore, OBE; J. Nelson-Jones; Mrs J. Varnam; A. White; M. Wolfe.
Director, M. Healy.

NATIONAL DEBT OFFICE
see National Investment and Loans Office.

NATIONAL ECONOMIC DEVELOPMENT COUNCIL
Millbank Tower, Millbank, SW1P 4QX
[071–217 4000]

The National Economic Development Council brings together the Government, management and trades unions to tackle issues vital to jobs and economic growth, by identifying obstacles to economic development and promoting change.

Council
Government Members, The Chancellor of the Exchequer (*Chairman*); the Secretaries of State for Education and Science, Employment, Energy, Environment, and Trade and Industry.
Management Members, J. M. M. Banham; Sir Brian Corby; T. J. O'Connor; Sir Thomas Risk; Sir Allen Sheppard; R. Smith.
Trade Union Members, R. Bickerstaffe; Miss B. Dean; J. Edmonds; W. Jordan; R. Todd; N. Willis.
Independent Members, Sir James Ackers; E. A. Hammond, OBE; The Rt. Hon. Robin Leigh-Pemberton; Sir Bryan Nicholson; Dame Rachel Waterhouse, DBE; Sir Brian Wolfson.

Office
Director-General, W. A. Eltis.
Secretary to the Council, M. Couchman.
Industrial Director, D. Fraser.
Economic Director, Prof. M. Ricketts.

NATIONAL GALLERIES
See Art Galleries

NATIONAL HERITAGE MEMORIAL FUND
10 St James's Street, SW1A 1EF
[071–930 0963]

The National Heritage Memorial Fund was established in 1980 as an independent body, and is intended as a memorial to those who have died for the UK. The Fund is empowered, by the National Heritage Act 1980, to give financial assistance towards the cost of acquiring, maintaining or preserving land, buildings, works of art and other objects of outstanding interest which are also of importance to the national heritage. The Fund is administered by up to eleven Trustees, appointed by the Prime Minister.
The Fund's major sources of money are the Department of the Environment and the Office of Arts and Libraries, each of which gives annual grants. In its first 11 years, the Fund spent £127 million in carrying out its responsibilities.

Trustees
Chairman, The Lord Charteris of Amisfield.
Members, The Marquess of Anglesey; R. Carew Pole; Sir Nicholas Goodison; Sir Martin Jacomb; Sir Oliver Millar; Sir Norman Macfarlane; Prof. P. J. Newbould; Mrs C. Porteous; Cdr. L. M. M. Saunders Watson.
Director, Miss G. Nayler.

NATIONAL INSURANCE JOINT AUTHORITY
The Adelphi, 1–11 John Adam Street, WC2N 6HT
[071–962 8000]

The Authority's function is to co-ordinate the operation of social security legislation in Great Britain and Northern Ireland, including the necessary financial adjustments between the two National Insurance Funds.
Members, The Secretary of State for Social Security; the Head of the Department of Health and Social Services for Northern Ireland.
Secretary, Mrs D. M. Joannou.

NATIONAL INVESTMENT AND LOANS OFFICE
Royex House, Aldermanbury Square, EC2V 7LR
[071–606 7321]

The National Investment and Loans Office was set up on April 1, 1980 by merging the staffs of the National Debt Office and the Public Works Loan Board. The Department provides staff and services for the National Debt Commissioners and the Public Works Loan Commissioners.
Director, I. H. Peattie.
Establishment Officer, A. G. Ladd.

National Debt Office
Comptroller General, I. H. Peattie.

Public Works Loan Board

Chairman, R. J. Dent.
Deputy Chairman, Miss F. M. Cook.
Other Commissioners, Miss V. J. Di Palma, OBE; G. Ross Russell; P. Brackfield; D. H. Adams; R. A. Chapman; B. Fieldhouse; A. Morton; I. C. Wilson, OBE; G. G. Williams; R. G. Tettenborn.
Secretary, I. H. Peattie.
Assistant Secretary, D. L. Hammond.

NATIONAL RADIOLOGICAL PROTECTION BOARD
Chilton, Didcot, Oxon. OX11 0RQ
[0235–831600]

The National Radiological Protection Board is an independent statutory body created by the Radiological Protection Act 1970. It is intended to act as a national point of authoritative reference concerning radiological protection.
Chairman, Sir Richard Southwood, FRS.
Director, Dr R. H. Clarke.

NATIONAL RIVERS AUTHORITY
Rivers House, Waterside Drive, Aztec West,
Almondsbury, Bristol BS12 4UD
[0454–624400]

The National Rivers Authority (NRA) is an independent body set up under the Water Act 1989. Its responsibilities include monitoring the quality of water, controlling pollution, and the management of water resources, flood defence and fisheries. The NRA has a board of 15 members, two of whom are appointed by the Minister of Agriculture, Fisheries and Food, one by the Secretary of State for Wales, and the rest by the Secretary of State for the Environment.
Chairman, The Lord Crickhowell, PC.
Chief Executive, J. Wheatley.
Chief Scientist, Dr J. Pentreath.
Technical Director, Dr C. Swinnerton.
Finance Director, C. Savory.
Personnel Director, P. Humphreys.
Corporate Affairs Director, Ms M. Evans.

DEPARTMENT FOR NATIONAL SAVINGS
Charles House, 375 Kensington High Street,
W14 8SD
[071–605 9300]

The Department for National Savings was established as a government department in 1969. The Department is responsible for the administration of a wide range of schemes for personal savers. (For details of schemes, *see* **National Savings** section).
(For **Salaries**, *see* page 293)

Director of Savings (G2), J. A. Patterson, CB.
Deputy Director (G3), C. D. Butler.
Establishment Officer (G5), D. S. Speedie.
Finance Officer (G5), C. Ward.
Controllers (G5), Miss A. Nash (*Marketing & Information*); A. S. McGill; D. H. Monaghan; E. B. Senior; P. N. S. Hickman Robertson.
Senior Principals (G6), D. W. Kellaway; R. H. Lee; I. Forsyth; M. A. Nicholls; D. Newton; T. Threlfall.
Principals (G7), W. J. Herd; D. K. Paterson; A. J. V. Cummings; Dr A. Fort; W. J. Ferrier; H. Johnson; J. W. Davison; A. B. Wood; P. Finnie; C. E. Funk; I. Jordinson; A. Brown; B. Paley; A. T. Stevenson; H. Webster; J. Wheatley; T. J. F. McMahon; C. McVey; R. A. Nichol; N. Thistlethwaite; J. B. Dunphy; J. C. Foreman; D. Wilson; P. B. Robinson; G. V. Wise; A. S. Lamond; D. Jeffrey; J. Bolam; R. W. Day; I. S. Campbell; C. Dodsworth; J. C.

Foreman; R. R. Hesketh; J. C. Lunn; R. J. McLelland; M. J. Tan; M. McDade; I. Rich; Miss J. S. Clark.

NATIONAL TRAINING TASK FORCE
214 Gray's Inn Road, WC1X 8HL
[071–278 0363]

The National Training Task Force was established by the Government to advise the Secretary of State for Employment and to assist him in carrying out his training responsibilities throughout Great Britain.
Chairman, Sir Brian Wolfson.
Members, Sir Peter Bowness; L. Spencer; Sir Melvyn Rosser; Sir Peter Thompson; T. Cleaver; Mrs P. Leith; M. Rowarth; Ms S. Elliott; Sir James Ackers; W. Jordan; Sir Allen Sheppard; A. Collier; I. Dixon; Sir Bob Reid; I. Wood; T. Farmer; C. Darby.
Secretary, R. Dawe.

NATURAL ENVIRONMENT RESEARCH COUNCIL
Polaris House, North Star Avenue,
Swindon SN2 1EU
[0793–411500]

The Natural Environment Research Council was established in 1965 to encourage, plan and conduct research in the physical and biological sciences which relate to the natural environment and its resources. The Council carries out research and training through its own institutes and by grants, fellowships and post-graduate awards to universities and other institutions of higher education.
Chairman, Prof. J. Knill, PH.D., D.SC.
Secretary, Dr Eileen Buttle.
Director of Earth Sciences, Prof. J. C. Briden, PH.D.
Director of Terrestrial and Fresh Water Sciences, P. B. Tinker, D.SC., PH.D.
Director of Marine and Atmospheric Sciences, J. D. Woods, CBE, PH.D.

CENTRAL SERVICES

NERC Scientific Services
Polaris House, North Star Avenue, Swindon,
Wilts. SN2 1EU
[0793–411000]

Director, B. J. Hinde.

Research Vessel Services
No. 1 Dock, Barry, S. Glamorgan
[0446–737451]

Head, Dr C. Fay.

NERC Computer Service
Holbrook House, Station Road,
Swindon, Wilts. SN1 1DE
[0793–411000]

Director, H. J. Down.

For research institutes and units of the Natural Environment Research Council, *see* p. 966.

NATURE CONSERVANCY COUNCIL FOR ENGLAND (ENGLISH NATURE)
Northminster House, Peterborough PE1 1UA
[0733–340345]

English Nature was established by Act of Parliament in 1991 as a result of the dissolution of the Nature Conservancy Council and the creation of three new independent bodies responsible for promoting nature conservation in the three component countries of Great Britain. English Nature is responsible for advising the Government on nature conservation in

England. It promotes, directly and through others, the conservation of England's wildlife and natural features. It selects, establishes and manages National Nature Reserves and identifies and notifies Sites of Special Scientific Interest. It provides advice and information about nature conservation, and supports and conducts research relevant to these functions. Through the Joint Nature Conservation Committee, it works with sister organizations in Scotland and Wales on UK and international nature conservation issues.

Chairman, The Earl of Cranbrook.
Chief Executive, Dr D. R. Langslow.
Chief Scientist, Dr K. L. Duff.
Director, Operations, E. T. Idle.
Director, Resources, Miss C. E. M. Wood.
Director, Policy, Mrs S. Collins.
Director, Communications, I. Dair.
Environmental Audit Manager, M. R. Felton.
Head of Lands, W.J. Hopkin.
Director, East Region, J. M. Schofield.

NATURE CONSERVANCY COUNCIL FOR SCOTLAND
12 Hope Terrace, Edinburgh EH9 2AS
[031–447 4784]

The Nature Conservancy Council for Scotland was established by Act of Parliament in 1991. It is a government-funded agency which furthers the aims of nature conservation in Scotland. Responsible to the Secretary of State for Scotland, it provides advice on nature conservation to all those whose activities affect wildlife, landforms and features of geological interest throughout Scotland. On April 1, 1992, the NCCS will merge with the Countryside Commission for Scotland to form Scottish Natural Heritage, whose remit will be to protect Scotland's wildlife, culture, communities and natural resources (*see* p. 358).

Chairman, M. Magnusson, KBE.
Chief Executive, Dr J. M. Francis.
Council Secretary, A. Laing.
Chairman, South East Region, Dr W. E. S. Mutch, OBE.
Director, Miss J. E. Dalgleish.
Chairman, South West Region, The Earl of Dalkeith.
Director, C. H. C. Fox
Chairman, North East Region, D. L. Laird.
Director, Dr I. Jardine.
Chairman, North West Region, Sir John Lister-Kaye, Bt.
Director, Dr P. Tilbrook.

JOINT NATURE CONSERVATION COMMITTEE
Monkstone House, City Road,
Peterborough PE1 1JY
[0733–62626]

The Committee was established under the Environmental Protection Act 1990 and began work on April 1, 1991. It advises the Government on UK and international nature conservation issues and provides guidance to the Nature Conservancy Council for England (English Nature), the Nature Conservancy Council for Scotland, the Countryside Council for Wales and the Department of the Environment for Northern Ireland on the maintenance of standards for species and habitat conservation.
Chairman, Prof. Sir Frederick Holliday, CBE.

NORTHERN IRELAND OFFICE
The Northern Ireland Office is the UK government department in which the Secretary of State for Northern Ireland exercises overall responsibility for the government of Northern Ireland. The Secretary of State is directly responsible for constitutional developments, law and order, security and electoral matters. Under the Northern Ireland Act 1974, the Northern Ireland departments are also subject to the direction and control of the Secretary of State during direct rule.

Whitehall, SW1A 2AZ
[071–210 3000]
Secretary of State for Northern Ireland, THE RT. HON. PETER BROOKE, MP.
  Parliamentary Private Secretary, K. Hind, MP.
HM Paymaster General and Deputy to the Secretary of State, THE LORD BELSTEAD, PC.
  Private Secretary, D. Kyle.
  Parliamentary Private Secretary, J. Sayeed, MP.
Minister of State, DR BRIAN MAWHINNEY, MP.
  Parliamentary Private Secretary, J. Butterfill, MP.
Parliamentary Under Secretaries of State, RICHARD NEEDHAM, MP; JEREMY HANLEY, MP.
Permanent Under Secretary of State, J. A. Chilcot, CB.
Second Permanent Under Secretary of State, Head of the NICS, D. Fell, CB.

Northern Ireland Civil Service (NICS)
Stormont Castle, Belfast BT4 3TT
[0232–763011]

Department of Agriculture for Northern Ireland
Dundonald House, Upper Newtownards Road,
Belfast BT4 3SB
[0232–650111]

Department of Economic Development Northern Ireland
Netherleigh, Massey Avenue, Belfast BT4 2JP
[0232–63244]

Department of Education for Northern Ireland
Rathgael House, Balloo Road, Bangor,
Co. Down BT19 2PR
[0247–270077]

Department of the Environment for Northern Ireland
Parliament Buildings, Stormont, Belfast BT4 3SS
[0232–763210]

Department of Finance and Personnel
Parliament Buildings, Stormont, Belfast BT4 3SW
[0232–763210]

Department of Health and Social Services Northern Ireland
Dundonald House, Upper Newtownards Road,
Belfast BT4 3SF
[0232–650111]

OCCUPATIONAL PENSIONS BOARD
PO Box 2EE, Newcastle upon Tyne NE99 2EE
[091–2256414]

The Occupational Pensions Board (OPB) is an independent statutory body set up under the Social Security Act 1973 to administer the contracting-out of occupational pensions from the State Earnings Related Pension Scheme (SERPS), and to advise the Secretary of State. Its functions have been extended by subsequent legislation and it is now responsible also for administering equal access, preservation and appropriate personal pension schemes. Following the Social Security Act 1990, the OPB was appointed as Registrar of Occupational and Personal Pension Schemes. Under new powers in the Act to make grants to approved bodies in the field, from April 1991 the OPB has funded the operation of the Occupational Pensions Advisory Service (OPAS).

Chairman, Sir Jeremy Rowe CBE.

Members, R. J. Amy; Mrs R. Brown; Miss C. H. Dawes; R. Ellison; R. J. Hebblethwaite, TD; U. Lyburn; R. Neal; A. Pickering; W. M. R. Ramsey, D.Phil.; K. R. Thomas; The Baroness Turner of Camden; Miss H. Wiesner.

Secretary and Controller of Executive Office (G6), A. Scaife.

OMBUDSMAN, *see* Local Commissioners, *and* Parliamentary Commissioner. For non-statutory Ombudsmen, *see* Index

ORDNANCE SURVEY

Romsey Road, Maybush, Southampton SO9 4DH
[0703–792000]

The Ordnance Survey is the national mapping agency for Britain. It became an executive agency in May 1990 and reports to the Secretary of State for the Environment.

The Ordnance Survey has military origins. It produces over 220,000 large scale maps of the country at three basic scales. These are 1:1,250 (50 inches to 1 mile) for urban areas; 1:2,500 (25 inches to 1 mile) for rural areas; and 1:10,000 (6 inches to 1 mile) for mountain and moorland. Additionally, Ordnance Survey produces a range of small scale maps and other products for general use.

Director-General, Prof. D. Rhind.

Directors:

Surveys and Production, A. S. Macdonald.
Marketing, Planning and Development, J. Leonard.
Establishments and Finance, I. Lock.
Heads of Functions:
Production, D. Davies.
Topographic Surveys, P. Wesley.
Marketing, D. Toft.
Research and Development, M. Sowton.
Finance, D. James.
Establishments, I. Logan.
Information and Computer Service, B. W. Nanson.
OS International, E. Gilbert.

OVERSEAS DEVELOPMENT ADMINISTRATION

94 Victoria Street, SW1E 5JL
[071–917 7000]
Abercrombie House, Eaglesham Road, East Kilbride,
Glasgow G75 8EA
[03552–41199]

The Overseas Development Administration deals with British development assistance to overseas countries. This includes both capital aid on concessional terms and technical assistance (mainly in the form of specialist staff abroad and training facilities in the United Kingdom), whether provided directly to developing countries or through the various multilateral aid organizations, including the United Nations and its specialized agencies.

(For **Salaries**, *see* page 293)

Minister for Overseas Development, THE RT. HON. LYNDA CHALKER, MP.

Private Secretary (G7), S. Chakrabarti.

Parliamentary Private Secretary, D. Nicholson, MP.
Permanent Secretary (G1A), T. P. Lankester.
Private Secretary, Ms G. J. Lyons.
Deputy Secretary (G2), R. M. Ainscow, CB.
Under Secretaries (G3), N. B. Hudson; B. R. Ireton; J. V. Kerby; R. G. Manning; A. J. Bennett; J. B. Wilmshurst.

Economic and Social Division

Head of the Economic Service (G3), J. B. Wilmshurst.
Senior Economic Advisers (G5), J. C. H. Morris; A. G. Coverdale; B. P. Thomson; J. Roberts; M. Foster.
Economic Advisers (G6), P. J. Ackroyd; P. L. Owen; (G7), P. D. Balacs; B. Carstairs; Dr F. C. Clift; J. G. Clarke; D. B. Crapper; P. J. Dearden; D. Donaldson; P. D. Grant; N. F. Gregory; K. E. Gubbins; Dr G. Haley; A. B. D. Hall; E. Hawthorn; N. Highton; J. L. Hoy; W. Kingsmill; P. J. A. Landymore; M. Lewis; A. Moon; R. Teuten; Ms R. Turner; Mrs J. White; A. Whitworth.
Chief Statistician (G5), R. M. Allen.
Statisticians (G6), A. B. Williams; (G7), J. R. B. King; P. J. Crook.
Principal Finance Management and Administration Adviser (G5), K. L. Sparkhall.
Senior Finance Management and Administration Adviser (G6), E. A. Gill.
Senior Finance and Management Advisers (G6), D. W. Heffer; D. J. Wood.
Senior Social Development Advisers (G6), Dr E. Hanley; Dr R. J. Eyben.
Social Development Advisers (G7), Ms P. Holden; M. Schultz.

Information Department

Head of Information Dept. (G5), A. Bearpark.
Principal Information Officer (G7), R. W. Fosker.

Development Divisions

Heads of Divisions (G5):
Caribbean (Bridgetown), M. G. Bawden.
East Africa (Nairobi), D. Sands Smith.
Pacific (Suva), Mrs P. M. Wilkinson.
South-east Asia (Bangkok), M. J. Dinham.
Southern Africa (Lilongwe), Ms S. E. Unsworth.
Assistant Secretaries (G5), Miss A. M. Archbold; J. H. S. Chard; R. Elias; D. S. Fish; P. D. M. Freeman; B. W. Hammond; W. Hobman; J. Hodges; Mrs B. M. Kelly; M. C. McCulloch; J. C. Machin; V. J. McLean; C. Myhill; Dr D. Nabarro; M. A. Power; C. P. Raleigh; D. L. Stanton; G. M. Stegmann; D. F. Turner; M. Wickstead; R. J. Wilson.
Senior Principals (G6), J. A. Anning; F. Crampsey; D. R. Curran; K. D. Grimshaw; S. Ray; D. Richards; D. Trotter; G. A. Williams.
Principals (G7), G. F. H. Aicken; J. D. Aitken; R. Allen; G. A. Armstrong; C. B. Austin; N. Bailey; D. W. Baker; D. G. Bell; F. Black; H. Britton; W. A. Brownlie; P. J. Burton; R. T. Calvert; P. H. Charters; D. J. Church; T. F. G. Connor; R. G. Cousins; G. Crabtree; Ms M. E. Cund; A. O. Davies; A. D. Davis; P. Dean; J. R. Drummond; M. J. Ellis; J. R. Gilbert; M. A. Hammond; Ms V. M. Harris; S. Hefferon; Ms P. J. Hilton; M. I. Holland; Ms B. Holt; N. Hoult; W. Jardine; Mrs J. Laurence; D. Lawless; G. G. Leader; J. Lingham; M. A. B. Lowcock; M. Mallalieu; G. H. Malley; P. S. Mason; J. Maund; C. A. Metcalf; J. C. H. Millett; D. J. Moran; J. D. Moye; G. A. Mustard; P. T. Perris; G. M. Porter; Mrs J. Radice; S. R. J. Robbins; P. T. Rose; C. R. Roth; Dr P. W. K. Rundell; Ms P. Schofield; J. M. Scoular; Mrs P. A. Scutt; S. J. Sharpe; R. J. Smith; Miss R. B. Stevenson; M. J. Sexton; A. J. Sutherland; D. J. C. Taylor; E. C. N. Taylor; N. Thomas; B. A. Thorpe; R. G. Toulmin; N. A. Tranter; Miss M. H. Vowles; Ms S. T.

Wardell; C. W. Warren; R. S. White; J. M. Winter; A. K. C. Wood; M. S. S. Wyatt.

Advisory and Specialist Staff

Chief Education Adviser (G5), Dr R. O. Iredale.
Senior Education Advisers (G6), M. D. Francis; Ms M. Harrison; M. E. Seath; Dr D. G. Swift.
Chief Engineering Adviser (G5), T. D. Pike.
Senior Engineering Advisers (G6), J. N. Bulman; A. G. Colley; C. I. Ellis; D. Gillett; B. Dolton; H. B. Jackson; P. W. D. H. Roberts; M. F. Sergeant.
Engineering Advisers (G7), R. J. Cadwallader; A. Barker; A. Smallwood; M. McCarthy; D. Robson; C. Hunt.
Senior Renewable Energy and Research Adviser (G6), Dr J. L. D. Harrison.
Senior Electrical and Mechanical Engineering Adviser (G6), R. P. Jones.
Senior Architectural and Physical Planning Advisers (G6), M. W. Parkes; W. M. Housego-Woolgar.
Senior Health and Population Advisers (G6), Dr P. Key, OBE; Miss J. Isard; Dr M. Kapila; Ms S. Simmonds; J. Lambert.
Chief Natural Resources Adviser (G3), A. J. Bennett.
Deputy Chief Natural Resources and Principal Agricultural Adviser (G5), J. M. Scott.
Deputy Chief Natural Resources Adviser (G5), Dr J. C. Davies, OBE (*Research*).
Senior Natural Resources Advisers (G6), B. E. Grimwood; Dr I. Haines; J. R. F. Hansell; D. J. Salmon; A. J. Tainsh; D. Trotman; J. B. Warren; M. F. Watson; M. J. Wilson; (G7), G. A. Gilman; J. A. Harvey; Dr H. Potter.
Animal Health Advisers (G6), G. G. Freeland; Dr A. D. Irvin.
Senior Fisheries Advisers (G6), Dr J. Tarbit; R. W. Beales.
Senior Forestry Advisers (G6), W. J. Howard; R. Jenkin; P. Wood.
Senior Procurement Adviser (G6), R. C. Morgan.
Contract Adviser (G7), R. Davidson.
Senior Technical Education Advisers (G6), Dr R. C. Skelton; Dr G. R. H. Jones.
Senior Industrial Training Adviser (G6), H. E. M. Crofton.
Industrial Training Adviser (G7), A. Wray.
Senior Small-Scale Enterprise Adviser (G6), D. L. Wright.
Senior Adviser on Administration and Management (G6), Dr G. Glentworth.
Public Administration and Management Development Adviser(G7), Dr M. J. Greaves.

Natural Resources Institute
Central Avenue, Chatham Maritime,
Chatham, Kent ME4 4TB
[0634–880088]

(An executive agency within the ODA)
Director (G3), G. A. Beattie.

OFFICE OF THE PARLIAMENTARY COMMISSIONER AND HEALTH SERVICE COMMISSIONER
Church House, Great Smith Street, SW1P 3BW
[071–276 3000]

The Parliamentary Commissioner for Administration (the Ombudsman) is responsible for investigating complaints referred to him by Members of the House of Commons from members of the public who claim to have sustained injustice in consequence of maladministration by or on behalf of government departments and certain non-departmental public bodies. Certain types of action by government departments or bodies are excluded from investigation. Actions taken by other public bodies (such as local authorities, the police, the Post Office and nationalized industries) are outside the Commissioner's scope.

The Health Service Commissioners for England, for Scotland and for Wales are responsible for investigating complaints against National Health Service authorities that are not dealt with by those authorities to the satisfaction of the complainant. Complaints can be referred direct by the member of the public who claims to have sustained injustice or hardship in consequence of the failure in a service provided by a relevant body, failure of that body to provide a service or in consequence of any other action by that body. Certain types of action are excluded, in particular, action taken solely in consequence of the exercise of clinical judgment. The three offices are presently held by the Parliamentary Commissioner.

(For **Salaries**, *see* page 293)
Parliamentary Commissioner and Health Service Commissioner (G1), W. K. Reid, CB.
Deputy Parliamentary Commissioner (G3), J. E. Avery.
Deputy Health Service Commissioner (G3), R. A. Oswald.
Directors (G5), Mrs J. M. Fowler; M. D. Randall; J. C. Bateman; M. A. Johnson; M. P. Cornwell-Kelly; P. J. Belsham.
Principals (G7), G. M. Keil; Mrs C. Bentley; Miss D. M. Pace; T. J. Corkett; R. A. Bourley; D. S. Burn; A. C. Beer (*Establishment Officer*); Mrs E. A. Cooper; S. J. Drummond; J. D. Jarvis; D. Hall; B. P. Jones; D. G. Tempest; K. O'Brien.

PARLIAMENTARY COUNSEL
36 Whitehall, SW1A 2AY
[071–210 6633]

Parliamentary Counsel draft all government Bills (i.e. primary legislation) except those relating exclusively to Scotland, the latter being drafted by the Lord Advocate's Department. They also advise on all aspects of parliamentary procedure in connection with such Bills and draft government amendments to them as well as any motions (including financial resolutions) necessary to secure their introduction into, and passage through, Parliament.

First Counsel, P. Graham, CB, QC £76,320
Second Counsel, J. C. Jenkins, CB £64,300
Counsel, J. D. M. Rennie, CB; J. S. Mason, CB; D. W. Saunders, CB; E. G. Caldwell, CB; E. G. Bowman, CB; G. B. Sellers, CB; E. R. Sutherland; P. F. A. Knowles; S. C. Laws. . . . . *up to* £54,900

PAROLE BOARD FOR ENGLAND AND WALES
Abell House, John Islip Street, SW1P 4LH
[071–217 5705]

The Board was constituted under section 59 of the Criminal Justice Act 1967. Its function is to advise the Secretary of State for the Home Department with respect to: release on licence under section 60 (i) or 61 and recall under section 62 of the Criminal Justice Act 1967 of persons whose cases have been referred to the Board by the Secretary of State; the conditions of such licences, and the variation and cancellation of such conditions; and any other matter so referred which is connected with release on licence or recall of persons to whom section 60 or 61 of the Act applies.
Chairman, The Viscount Colville of Culross, QC.
Vice-Chairman, The Hon. Mr Justice Schiemann.
Secretary, T. E. Russell.

PAROLE BOARD FOR SCOTLAND
Calton House, 5 Redheughs Rigg
Edinburgh EH12 9HW
[031–244 8530]

The Board advises the Secretary of State for Scotland on the release of prisoners on licence, and related matters.
Chairman, Mrs J. D. O. Morris, CBE.
Vice-Chairman, J. M. Scott.
Secretary, Miss W. M. Doonan.

PATENT OFFICE
Cardiff Road, Newport, Gwent
NP9 1RH
[0633–814000]

The Patent Office is an executive agency of the Department of Trade and Industry. The duties of the Patent Office consist in the administration of the Patent Acts, the Registered Designs Act and the Trade Marks Act and in dealing with questions relating to the Copyright Designs and Patents Act 1988. The Search and Advisory Service will carry out commercial searches through patent information. In 1990 the Office granted 9,396 patents and registered 9,171 designs and 28,389 trade and service marks.
Comptroller-General (G3), P. R. S. Hartnack.
Assistant Comptroller Industrial Property & Copyright Dept. (G4), V. Tarnofsky, CBE.
Assistant Comptroller Patents and Designs (G4), T. W. Sage.
Assistant Registrar, Trade Marks (G4), J. M. Myall.
Head of Marketing and Information Services (Supt. Examiner), E. F. Blake.
Head of Administration and Resources (G5), P. Bunn.
Head of ADP Unit (G6), G. Bennett.

PAYMASTER GENERAL'S OFFICE
Northern Ireland Office, Old Admiralty Building,
Whitehall, SW1A 2AZ
[071–210 6498]
Sutherland House, Russell Way, Crawley, West
Sussex RH10 1UH
[0293–560999]

The Paymaster General's Office was formed by the consolidation in 1835 of various separate pay departments then existing, some of which dated back at least to 1660. Its function is that of paying agent for government departments, other than the revenue departments. Most of its payments are made through banks, to whose accounts the necessary transfers are made at the Bank of England. The payment of over one million public service pensions is an important feature of its work.
Paymaster General, THE LORD BELSTEAD, PC.
Assistant Paymaster General (G5), K. Sullens.
Grade 6, G. Thomas; M. D. West.
Grade 7, D. R. Alexander; Mrs D. F. Ambrose; M. L. Card; T. R. George; R. G. Hollands; J. A. Payne; C. A. Ulph.

OFFICE OF THE PENSIONS OMBUDSMAN
11 Belgrave Road, SW1V 1RB
[071–834 9144]

The Pensions Ombudsman is appointed by the Secretary of State for Social Security under the Social Security Act 1990 to deal with complaints against, and disputes with, occupational and personal pension schemes. He is completely independent.
Pensions Ombudsman, M. Platt.

POLICE COMPLAINTS AUTHORITY
10 Great George Street, SW1P 3AB
[071–273 6450]

The Police Complaints Authority was established under the Police and Criminal Evidence Act 1984 to introduce a further independent element into the procedure for dealing with complaints by members of the public against police officers in England and Wales. (In Scotland, complaints are investigated by independent public prosecutors.) The Authority has powers to supervise the investigation of certain categories of serious complaints and certain statutory functions in relation to the disciplinary aspects of complaints. It does not as a rule deal with complaints about police operations; these are usually dealt with by the Chief Constable of the relevant force.
Chairman, His Hon. Judge Petre.
Deputy Chairman (Investigations), Brig. J. Pownall.
Deputy Chairman (Discipline), P. W. Moorhouse.
Members, Mrs L. Cawsey; M. Chapman; J. Crawford; G. V. Marsh; W. McCall; K. Singh; Capt. N. Taylor; Brig. A. Vivian; Miss B. Wallis; E. Wignall; Mrs R. Wolff.

POLITICAL HONOURS SCRUTINY COMMITTEE
Cabinet Office, 53 Parliament Street, SW1A 2NG
[071–210 5058]

The function of the Political Honours Scrutiny Committee is set out in an Order in Council dated May 31, 1979. The Prime Minister submits certain particulars to the Committee about persons proposed to be recommended for honour for their political services. The Committee, after such enquiry as they think fit, report to the Prime Minister whether, so far as they believe, the persons whose names are submitted to them are fit and proper persons to be recommended.
Chairman, The Lord Shackleton, KG, OBE, PC, FRS.
Members, The Lord Grimond, TD, PC; The Lord Pym, MC, PC.
Secretary, J. H. Thompson, CB.

THE POLYTECHNICS AND COLLEGES FUNDING COUNCIL
Northavon House, Coldharbour Lane, Bristol
BS16 1QD
[0272–317317]

The Polytechnics and Colleges Funding Council (PCFC) was established as a result of the Education Act 1988 to oversee the sector of higher education formerly controlled by local authorities. The Council consists of 15 members appointed by the Secretary of State for Education and Science.

The PCFC distributes over £1,000 million of public funds in England each year to all the polytechnics, the largest colleges of higher education, and a number of specialist colleges. It also funds certain higher education courses in further education colleges. The PCFC sector comprises 84 institutions serving over 400,000 students (*see* p. 450). The PCFC also advises the Secretary of State on the funding of higher education. For this it has established Programme Advisory Groups to review provision in nine subject areas. It also establishes *ad hoc* committees of enquiry on particular issues.
Chairman, Sir Ronald Dearing.
Chief Executive, W. H. Stubbs.
Director of Finance, R. McClure.
Secretary, N. Brown.

OFFICE OF POPULATION CENSUSES AND SURVEYS
St Catherine's House, 10 Kingsway,
WC2B 6JP
[071–242 0262]

The Office of Population Censuses and Surveys was created by the merger in May 1970 of the General Register Office and the Government Social Survey Department. The Registrar General controls the local registration service in England and Wales in the exercise of its registration and marriage duties. Copies of the original registrations of births, still births, marriages and deaths are kept in London. A register of adopted children is held at Titchfield, Hants. Central indexes are compiled annually and certified copies of entries may be obtained on payment of certain fees. Since 1841 the Registrar General has been responsible for taking the census of population. He also prepares and publishes a wide range of statistics and appropriate commentary relating to population, fertility, births, still births, marriages, deaths and cause of death and infectious diseases. The Registrar General is also responsible for conducting surveys on a range of subjects for other government departments. He maintains, at Southport, the National Health Service Central Register.

Hours of access to Public Search Room, St Catherine's House, Mon.–Fri., 8.30 a.m.–4.30 p.m.

Director and Registrar General (G2), P. J. Wormald, CB.

Deputy Director (G3), E. J. Thompson.

Chief Medical Statistician (G3), A. J. Fox, Ph.D.

Grade 5, R. Barnes; J. Craig; J. V. Ribbins (*Deputy Registrar General*); I. K. G. Arnold; J. A. Rowntree; B. H. Mahon; B. S. Smith.

Senior Statisticians (Medical), J. S. A. Ashley; A. G. McCormick; A. J. Swerdlow.

Grade 6, B. S. T. Alcock; E. Barton; Mrs M. Bone; R. J. Butcher; A. M. Clark; J. Denton; Mrs K. H. Dunnell; W. Jenkins; I. B. Knight; D. L. Pearce; R. K. Thomas; R. McLeod; T. D. Proudfoot; Mrs J. Martin.

Grade 7, R. I. Armitage; F. L. Ashwood; Mrs P. E. Astbury; Ms J. Atkinson; N. E. Auckland; R. A. P. Bailey; R. J. Beacham; D. E. Birch; Mrs B. J. Botting; A. F. Bradley; M. J. Bradley; T. B. Bryson; L. Bulusu; D. Capron; R. J. Carpenter; J. Cloyne; Mrs J. Cooper; C. J. Denham; T. L. F. Devis; J. M. Dixie; Mrs J. C. Dobbs; Ms P. A. Dodd; D. Elliot; Miss C. M. Ellis; Ms E. M. Goddard; I. Golds; Mrs J. R. Gregory; P. C. Gregory; J. Haskey; A. J. H. Hay; P. J. Heady; Mrs J. Humby; B. G. Little; Miss C. S. J. Lloyd; D. Lockyer; W. F. Loomes; Mrs S. M. McCartney; Miss E. M. McCrossan; Mrs I. MacDonald-Davies; Miss M. Machin; A. J. Manners; R. Massingham; Ms J. Matheson; B. W. Meakings; I. D. Mills; D. J. Mountjoy; A. Parr (*Chief Inspector of Registration*); M. Quinn; Mrs I. Rauta; A. P. Read; R. U. Redpath; Miss J. M. R. Rosenbaum; T. A. Russell; J. A. Salvetti; C. Savage; Ms J. M. Sharp; D. Stewart; Mrs L. M. Street; A. W. Tester; Miss J. Todd; Mrs M. J. Wagget; Miss S. Wallace (*Press Officer*); I. S. G. White; P. H. White.

PORT OF LONDON AUTHORITY
International House, World Trade Centre,
E1 9UN
[071–481 1954]

The Port of London Authority is a public trust constituted under the Port of London Act 1968 (as amended) and a Harbour Revision Order of 1975. The Board comprises a chairman and up to ten non-executive members appointed by the Secretary of State for Transport, and up to six executive members appointed by the Board.

The Port of London Authority is the governing body for the Port of London, covering the tidal portion of the River Thames from Teddington to the seaward limit. The enclosed dock at Tilbury is wholly-owned by the PLA. Some cargo-handling facilities along the river are owned by the PLA.

Chairman, Sir Brian Kellett.

Vice-Chairman, R. Crawford, CBE.

Chief Executive, River, D. Jeffery.

Chief Executive, Property, J. C. Jenkinson, MVO.

Chief Executive, Tilbury, J. S. McNab.

Secretary, G. E. Ennals.

THE POST OFFICE
30 St James's Square, SW1Y 4PY
[071–490 2888]

Crown services for the carriage of government despatches were set up in about 1516. The conveyance of public correspondence began in 1635 and the mail service was made a parliamentary responsibility with the setting up of a Post Office in 1657. Telegraphs came under the Post Office control in 1870 and the Post Office Telephone Service began in 1880. The National Girobank service of the Post Office began in 1968. The Post Office ceased to be a government department on October 1, 1969 and responsibility for the running of the postal, telecommunications, giro and remittance services was transferred to a public authority called the Post Office. The 1981 British Telecommunications Act separated the functions of the Post Office, making it solely responsible for postal services and Girobank (privatized in 1990).

The chairman and members of the Post Office Board are appointed by the Secretary of State for Trade and Industry but responsibility for the running of the Post Office as a whole rests with the Board in its corporate capacity.

Financial Results

	1989–90 £m.	1990–91 £m.
Post Office Group		
Turnover	4,459·0	4,719·0
Trading profit before tax	116·4	153·0*
Royal Mail and Parcel force		
Turnover	3,615·1	3,979·0
Trading profit before tax and interest on long-term loans	32·1	96·0*
Post Office Counters		
Turnover	875·1	959·0
Trading profit before tax and interest on long-term loans	21·7	28·0

* Before exceptional items.

Post Office Board

Chairman, Sir Bryan Nicholson.

Deputy Chairman, K. M. Young, CBE.

Members, W. Cockburn, CBE, TD (*Managing Director, Royal Mail*); P. Howarth (*Managing Director, Parcelforce*); A. J. Roberts, CBE (*Managing Director, Counters*); R. Close (*Corporate Finance and Planning*).

Secretary, Miss M. MacDonald.

PRIVY COUNCIL OFFICE
Whitehall, SW1A 2AT
[071-270 3000]

The Office is responsible for the arrangements leading to the making of all Royal Proclamations and Orders in Council; for certain formalities connected with ministerial changes; for considering applications for the grant (or amendment) of Royal Charters; for the scrutiny and approval of by-laws and statutes of chartered bodies; and for the appointment of High Sheriffs and many Crown and Privy Council appointments to governing bodies.

Lord President of the Council (and Leader of the House of Commons), THE RT. HON. JOHN MAC-GREGOR, OBE, MP.
  Private Secretary, T. Sutton.
Minister of State, THE RT. HON. TIMOTHY RENTON, MP.
Clerk of the Council, G. I. de Deney, CVO £50,300
Deputy Clerk of the Council, R. P. Bulling . . . £37,201
Senior Clerk, Miss J. Fairbairn £20,380

PSA SERVICES
2 Marsham Street, SW1P 3EB
[071-276 3000]

PSA Services (formerly the Property Services Agency) is an executive agency within the Department of the Environment. It is responsible for all construction activities, supplies and transport at home and abroad for all government departments and some repayment clients including British Telecom. PSA Services is due to be privatized in 1992.
(For Salaries, *see* page 293)
Chief Executive (G1A), G. Chipperfield, CB.
  Private Secretary, Mrs N. Baxter.

Privatization and Strategy Directorate

Grade 3, Mrs J. Williams.
Grade 5, J. Clayton; J. Rogers.

Group Personnel Directorate

Director (G3), P. D. Draper.
Grade 5, J. Bird; A. Hazeldine.

Group Finance Directorate

Director (G3), A. Marson.
Grade 5, M. Taylor; Mrs H. Parker-Brown.
Head of Internal Audit (G5), M. Reece.
Group Management Accountant (G5), J. Tomlinson.

PSA PROJECTS

Chairman (G2), J. B. Jefferson, CB, CBE.
Managing Director (G2), J. P. G. Rowcliffe.

Operations 1

Director and Chairman (G3), S. G. D. Duguid.

Managing Directors, Projects Offices
Project Management (G4), M. R. Sutton.
London A (G4), K. Jeavons.
Edinburgh (G4), J. T. Wilson.
Leeds (G5), G. Sowden.
Birmingham (G5), A. Towers.
Cardiff (G4), J. Clemits.

Operations 2

Director and Chairman (G3), A. S. Kennedy.
Managing Director, London B (G4), F. Rymill.
Managing Director, PSA Specialist Services (G4), H. P. Webber.
Director, Building and Quantity Surveying (G4), M. Barnes.
Director, Civil Engineering Services (G4), H. P. Webber.
Director, Mechanical and Electrical Engineering Services (G5), J. Fisher.

Marketing & Planning

Director (G3), R. Gray.
Sales Director (G3), A. G. Gosling.
Personnel Director (G5), R. G. Jones.
Finance Director (G5), B. Neale.

PSA INTERNATIONAL

Chairman (G2), J. P. G. Rowcliffe.
Managing Director (G3), R. G. S. Johnston.

Operations

Director (G5), J. Reynolds.
Director, Central Services and Personnel (G5), A. D. Ring.
Director, Finance (G5), T. Sannia.

Germany

Director (G4), R. B. Perry.

PSA BUILDING MANAGEMENT

Director of Operations (G3), P. Butter.
Finance Director (G5), D. Cheal.
Personnel Director (G5), Dr M. Barrett.

Managing Directors/Directors of Regional Offices

London (G4), P. Livesey.
Scotland (G4), B. Taylor.
Wales (G5), R. Kent.
Southern (G4), M. Newey.
South West (G4), S. Todd.
South East (G4), P. Pryke.
North East (G4), G. Flanagan.
North West and Midland (G4), M. Harrison.
Eastern (G4), A. Staveley.

PUBLIC HEALTH LABORATORY SERVICE
61 Colindale Avenue, NW9 5DF
[081-200 1295]

The Public Health Laboratory Service comprises 52 regional or area laboratories distributed throughout England and Wales, the Central Public Health Laboratory and the Communicable Disease Surveillance Centre at Colindale, and the Centre for Applied Microbiology and Research, Porton Down. The PHLS provides diagnostic microbiological services to hospitals, and has reference facilities that are available nationally. It collates information on the incidence of infection, and when necessary it institutes special inquiries into outbreaks and the epidemiology of infectious disease. It also undertakes bacteriological surveillance of the quality of food and water for local authorities and others. The PHLS is often called upon to advise central and local government and the hospital service on many aspects of infectious disease. It maintains close contact with veterinary organizations in areas of mutual interest, and collaborates with the World Health Organization and with national laboratory and epidemiological services overseas.

The Board

Chairman, Dr M. P. W. Godfrey, CBE, FRCP.
Members, D. F. R. Crofton; E. Doorbar; A. E. Eames; Prof. C. S. F. Easmon; Dr J. M. Forsythe; Dr A. M. George; J. Godfrey; A. Graham-Dixon, QC; Prof. P. R. Grob, MD; Dr E. L. Harris, CB, FRCP; Dr H. H. John; Prof. M. D. Lilly; D. Noble, CBE; Dr M. J. Painter; Prof. J. R. Pattison; Prof. C. S. Peckham; Prof. I. Phillips; J. J. Skehel, PH.D., FRS.
Staff Assessors, J. P. Alexander; P. J. Greenaway; Dr A. T. Willis.

Head Office
Colindale Avenue, NW9 5DF

Director, Sir Joseph Smith.
Deputy Directors, Dr E. M. Cooke; Dr C. Roberts.

Deputy Director (Administration) and Board Secretary, K. M. Saunders.
Deputy Secretary, J. M. Harker.

Central Public Health Laboratory
Colindale Avenue, NW9 5HT

Director, Dr M. C. Timbury.
Division of Enteric Pathogens, B. Rowe, TD.
Food Hygiene Laboratory, R. J. Gilbert, Ph.D.
Division of Hospital Infection, B. D. Cookson.
Division of Microbiological Reagents, A. G. Taylor, Ph.D.
Mycological Reference Laboratory, Prof. D. W. R. Mackenzie, Ph.D.
National Collection of Type Cultures, L. R. Hill, D.SC.
Quality Assurance Laboratory, J. J. Snell.
Virus Reference Laboratory, P. P. Mortimer, MD.

Communicable Diseases Surveillance Centre
Colindale Avenue, NW9 5EQ

Director, Dr C. L. R. Bartlett.

Statistics Unit
Colindale Avenue, NW9 5EQ

Head, A. Swann, Ph.D.

Centre for Applied Microbiology and Research
Porton Down, Salisbury,
Wilts. SP4 0JG

Director, Dr P. M. Sutton.
Director of Pathology Division, Dr A. Baskerville.
Director of Biologics Division, Prof. J. Melling, Ph.D.
Director of Biotechnology Division, Prof. A. Atkinson, Ph.D.

Other Special Laboratories and Units
Anaerobe Reference Unit, Public Health Laboratory, Cardiff.—Prof. B. I. Duerden.
Cryptosproidium Reference Unit, Public Health Laboratory, Rhyl.—D. P. Casemore, Ph.D.
Gonococcus Reference Unit, Public Health Laboratory, Bristol.—A. E. Jephcott, MD.
Leptospira Reference Laboratory, Public Health Laboratory, Hereford.—I. R. Fergusson, TD.
Malaria Reference Laboratory, London School of Hygiene and Tropical Medicine, WC1.—Prof. D. J. Bradley, DM; Prof. W. Peters, MD, D.SC.
Meningococcal Reference Laboratory, Public Health Laboratory, Manchester.—D. M. Jones, MD.
Mycobacterium Reference Unit, Public Health Laboratory, Cardiff.—P. A. Jenkins, Ph.D.
Toxoplasma Reference Laboratories, Public Health Laboratory, Leeds.—R. N. Peel; Public Health Laboratory, Swansea.—D. H. M. Joynson; Public Health Laboratory, Tooting.—R. E. Holliman.
Water and Environmental Laboratory, Public Health Laboratory, Nottingham.—J. V. Lee, Ph.D.

Regional Laboratories
Birmingham, I. D. Farrell, Ph.D.; *Bristol*, A. E. Jephcott; *Cambridge*, vacant; *Cardiff*, Prof. B. I. Duerden; *Leeds*, R. N. Peel; *Liverpool*, J. H. Pennington, MD; *Manchester*, D. M. Jones, MD; *Newcastle*, N. F. Lightfoot; *Oxford*, J. B. Selkon, TD; *Portsmouth*, O. A. Okubadejo, MD; *Sheffield*, P. Norman.

Area Laboratories
Ashford, C. Dulake, TD; *Bath*, D. G. White; *Brighton*, B. T. Thom; *Carlisle*, M. A. Knowles; *Carmarthen*, M. D. Simmons (*acting*); *Chelmsford*, R. E. Tettmar, D.path.; *Chester*, P. Hunter, MD; *Coventry*, P. R. Mortimer, MD; *Dorchester*, A. Rampling, Ph.D.; *Epsom*, S. A. Chambers; *Exeter*, J. G. Cruickshank,

MD; *Gloucester*, K. A. V. Cartwright; *Guildford*, Prof. R. Y. Cartwright; *Hereford*, I. R. Ferguson, TD; *Hull*, S. L. Mawer; *Ipswich*, P. H. Jones; *Leicester*, C. J. Mitchell; *Lincoln*, E. R. Youngs; LONDON: *Central Middlesex Hospital*, M. S. Shafi (*acting*); *Dulwich*, A. H. C. Uttley, Ph.D.; *Tooting*, Prof. A. R. M. Coates; *Whipps Cross*, B. Chattopadhyay, MD; *Luton*, A. T. Willis, MD; *Middlesbrough*, E. McKay-Ferguson, MD; *Norwich*, P. M. B. White; *Nottingham*, M. J. Lewis, MD; *Peterborough*, R. S. Jobanputra, MD; *Plymouth*, P. J. Wilkinson; *Poole*, W. L. Hooper; *Preston*, D. N. Hutchinson, MD; *Reading*, J. V. Dadswell; *Rhyl*, D. N. Looker; *Salisbury*, S. Patrick; *Shrewsbury*, C. A. Morris, MD; *Southampton*, J. A. Lowes; *Stoke-on-Trent*, J. Gray; *Swansea*, D. H. M. Joynson; *Taunton*, J. V. S. Pether; *Truro*, W. A. Telfer Brunton; *Watford*, M. T. Moulsdale; *Wolverhampton*, R. G. Thompson.

REGISTRAR OF PUBLIC LENDING RIGHT
Bayheath House, Prince Regent Street,
Stockton-on-Tees, TS18 1DF
[0642–604699]

Under the Public Lending Right system, in operation since January 1983, payment is made from public funds to authors whose books are lent out from public libraries. Payment is made once a year (in February) and the amount each author receives is proportionate to the number of times (established from a sample) that each registered book was lent out during the previous year.

The Registrar of PLR, who is appointed by the Minister for the Arts, compiles the register of authors and books. Only living authors resident in the UK or West Germany are eligible to apply. (The term 'author' covers writers, illustrators, translators, and some editors/compilers.)

A payment of 1·37 pence was made in 1990–91 for each estimated loan of a registered book, up to a top limit of £6,000 for the books of any one registered author; the money for loans above this level is used to augment the remaining PLR payments.

In February 1991, the sum of £2,969,000 was made available for distribution to 15,481 registered authors and assignees as the annual payment of PLR.

The PLR Advisory Committee advises the Minister for the Arts and the Registrar of Public Lending Right. Its members are appointed by the Minister.
Chairman of Advisory Committee, D. H. Whitaker, OBE.
Registrar, Dr J. Parker.

PUBLIC RECORD OFFICE
See p. 355.

PUBLIC TRUST OFFICE
Stewart House, 24 Kingsway, WC2B 6JX
[071–269 7000]

The Public Trustee is a trust Corporation created to undertake the business of executorship and trusteeship; he can act as executor or administrator of the estate of a deceased person, or as trustee of a will or settlement. The Public Trustee is also responsible for the performance of all the administrative, but not the judicial, tasks required of the Court of Protection under Part VII of the Mental Health Act 1983, relating to the management and administration of the property and affairs of persons suffering from mental disorder. The Public Trustee also acts as Receiver when so directed by the Court, usually where there is no other person willing or able so to act.

The Accountant General of the Supreme Court, through the Court Funds Office, is responsible for the investment and accounting of funds in court for persons under a disability, monies in Court subject to litigation and statutory deposits.

The Court Funds Office is at 22 Kingsway, WC2B 6LE (071-936 6000).

Public Trustee and Accountant General, P. J. Farmer.
Assistant Public Trustee (Legal), H. N. Mather.
Investment Manager, H. Stevenson.
Chief Property Adviser, A. Nightingale.

Client Services Sector

Head, E. J. Dober.
Receivership Division, Mrs H. Bratton.
Protection Division, I. S. Price.

Internal Services Sector

Head, I. J. MacBean.
Court Funds Office, F. J. Eddy.

PUBLIC WORKS LOAN BOARD
see National Investment and Loans Office

COMMISSION FOR RACIAL EQUALITY
Elliot House, 10–12 Allington Street, SW1E 5EH
[071–828 7022]

The Commission was established in 1977, under the Race Relations Act 1976, to work towards the elimination of discrimination and promote equality of opportunity and good relations between different racial groups generally.

Chairman, M. Day, OBE.
Deputy Chairmen, J. Abrams, OBE; R. Singh.
Members, Mrs S. Sadeque; M. Skillicorn; D. A. C. Lambert; Dr D. Ray; R. Kent; Rev. E. A. Brown; Dr M. C. K. Chan, MBE; T. A. Khan; A. Rose, OBE; R. Sondhi; A. Ward; Miss P. Scotland, QC.
Chief Executive, Dr P. Sanders.

THE RADIO AUTHORITY
70 Brompton Road, SW3 1EY
[071-581 2888]

The Radio Authority was established in January 1991 under the Broadcasting Act 1990 as one of the two successor bodies to the Independent Broadcasting Authority. Its function is to assign frequencies, to grant licences to provide independent radio services, and to regulate the output of the services in accordance with published codes dealing with standards for programming, advertising and sponsorship.

Members of the Authority are appointed by the Secretary of State for the Home Department. Senior executive staff are appointed by the Authority.

Chairman, The Lord Chalfont OBE, MC, PC.
Deputy Chairman, Mrs J. McIvor.
Members, Mrs M. Corrigan; J. Grant; R. Hooper; R. Sondhi; M. Moriarty, CB.
Chief Executive, P. Baldwin.
Deputy Chief Executive and Head of Regulation, P. Brown.
Head of Development, D. Vick.
Head of Finance, N. Romain.
Head of Engineering, M. Thomas.
Secretary to the Authority, J. Norrington.

RECORD OFFICES, ETC.

ADVISORY COUNCIL ON PUBLIC RECORDS
Public Record Office, Chancery Lane, WC2A 1LR
[081–876 3444]

Council members are appointed by the Lord Chancellor, under the Public Records Act 1958, to advise him

on matters concerning public records in general and, in particular, on those aspects of the work of the Public Record Office which affect members of the public who make use of it. The Council meets quarterly and produces an annual report which is published alongside the Report of the Keeper of Public Records as a House of Commons sessional paper.

Chairman, The Master of the Rolls.
Members, Prof. B. W. E. Alford; Miss S. Beesley; A. C. Carlile, QC, MP; Rt. Hon. Sir Frank Cooper, GCB, CMG; Miss V. Cromwell; T. A. G. Davis, MP; Prof. R. B. Dobson; J. S. W. Gibson; M. A. Latham, MP; Prof. Shula Marks; Sir George Moseley, KCB; Prof. H. Roseveare; Prof. W. Saunders; Prof. R. Skidelsky; D. G. Vaisey.
Assessors, B. Cousins, CBE; M. Roper.
Secretary, C. R. H. Cooper.

THE PUBLIC RECORD OFFICE
Chancery Lane, WC2A 1LR
[081-876 3444]
Ruskin Avenue, Kew,
Richmond, Surrey TW9 4DU
[081–876 3444]

The Office, originally established in 1838 under the Master of the Rolls, was placed by the Public Records Act 1958 under the direction of the Lord Chancellor. He appoints a Keeper of Public Records, whose duties are to co-ordinate and supervise the selection of records of government departments and the English law courts for permanent preservation, to safeguard the records under his charge, and to make them available to the public.

The Office holds records of central government dating from *Domesday Book* (1086) to the present. Under the Public Records Act 1967 they are normally open to inspection when 30 years old, and are then available, without charge, in the reading rooms, Mon.–Fri., 9.30–5. The museum at Chancery Lane is open Mon.–Fri., 10–5.

The Public Records Office is to become an executive agency on April 1, 1992.
Chief Executive-designate (G3), Mrs S. Tyacke.
Keeper of Public Records (G3), M. Roper.

Public Services Division

Director (G5), C. D. Chalmers.
Reader Services Department (G6), Miss G. L. Beech.
Editorial Services Department (G6), Dr D. L. Thomas.
Publishing and Public Relations Department (G6), Dr J. B. Post.
Preservation Department (G7), Dr H. Forde.

Government Services Division

Director (G5), Dr N. G. Cox.
Appraisal and Accessions Department (G6), Mrs A. N. Nicol.
Team leaders (G7), A. H. W. Medlicott; E. J. Higgs; K. J. Smith.

Corporate Services Division

Director (G5), W. Arnold.
Management Support Department (G6), J. L. Walford.
IT Department (G7), Miss J. K. Lawlor.
Finance Department (G7), vacant.
Personnel Department (SEO), Mrs M. Bull.
Purchasing and Contracts Department (SEO), Mrs S. Flatman.

HOUSE OF LORDS RECORD OFFICE
House of Lords, SW1A 0PW
[071–219 3074]

Since 1497, the records of Parliament have been kept within the Palace of Westminster. They are in the custody of the Clerk of the Parliaments. In 1946 a record department was established to supervise their preservation and their availability to the public. The search room of the office is open to the public Mon.–Fri., 9.30–5.

Some 3,000,000 documents are preserved, including Acts of Parliament from 1497, journals of the House of Lords from 1510, minutes and committee proceedings from 1610, and papers laid before Parliament from 1531. Amongst the records are the Petition of Right, the Death Warrant of Charles I, the Declaration of Breda, and the Bill of Rights. The House of Lords Record Office also has charge of the journals of the House of Commons (from 1547), and other surviving records of the Commons (from 1572), which include plans and annexed documents relating to Private Bill legislation from 1818. Among other documents are the records of the Lord Great Chamberlain, the political papers of certain members of the two Houses, and documents relating to Parliament acquired on behalf of the nation. All the manuscripts and other records are preserved in the Victoria Tower of the Houses of Parliament. A permanent exhibition was established in the Royal Gallery in 1979.

Clerk of the Records, D. J. Johnson, FSA
£35,720–£46,746
Assistant Clerks of the Records, J. C. Morgan (*Sound Archives*); S. K. Ellison .... £24,641–£34,301

ROYAL COMMISSION ON HISTORICAL MANUSCRIPTS
Quality House, Quality Court, Chancery Lane,
WC2A 1HP
[071–242 1198]

The Commission was set up by Royal Warrant in 1869 to enquire and report on collections of papers of value for the study of history which were in private hands. In 1959 a new warrant enlarged these terms of reference to include all historical records, wherever situated, outside the Public Records and gave it added responsibilities as a central co-ordinating body to promote, assist and advise on their proper preservation and storage. The Commission has published over 200 volumes of reports. It holds a further 34,000 unpublished reports and computerized indices in the National Register of Archives, which is available for consultation in its search room. It also administers the Manorial and Tithe Documents Rules on behalf of the Master of the Rolls.

Chairman, G. E. Aylmer, FBA.
Commissioners, The Lord Kenyon, CBE, FSA; The Lord Blake, FBA; J. P. W. Ehrman, FBA, FSA; Prof. S. F. C. Milsom, FBA; P. T. Cormack, FSA, MP; The Marquess of Anglesey; Prof. Owen Chadwick, OM, KBE, FBA; D. G. Vaisey, FSA; The Viscount of Arbuthnott, CBE, DSC; The Lord Camoys; The Lord Egremont and Leconfield; Mrs J. Thirsk, FBA; Sir Matthew Farrer, KCVO; Miss B. Harvey, FBA, FSA; Sir John Sainty, KCB, FSA.
Secretary, B. S. Smith, FSA.

SCOTTISH RECORD OFFICE
HM General Register House, Edinburgh EH1 3YY
[031–556 6585]

The history of the national archives of Scotland can be traced back to the 13th century. The present headquarters of the Scottish Record Office, the General Register House, was founded in 1774. Here are preserved the administrative records of pre-Union Scotland, the registers of central and local courts of law, the public registers of property rights and legal documents, and many collections of local and church records and private archives. Certain groups of records, mainly the modern records of

government departments in Scotland, the Scottish railway records, the plans collection, and private archives of an industrial or commercial nature are preserved in the branch repository at the West Register House in Charlotte Square. The search rooms in both buildings open Mon.–Fri., 9–4.45. A permanent exhibition at the West Register House and changing exhibitions at the General Register House are open to the public on weekdays, 10–4. The National Register of Archives (Scotland), which is a branch of the Scottish Record Office, is based in the West Register House.

Keeper of the Records of Scotland, P. M. Cadell.

CORPORATION OF LONDON RECORDS OFFICE
Guildhall, EC2P 2EJ
[071–260 1251]

The Corporation of London Records Office contains the municipal archives of the City of London which are regarded as the most complete collection of ancient municipal records in existence. The collection includes charters of William the Conqueror, Henry II, and later Kings and Queens to 1957; ancient custumals: Liber Horn, Dunthorne, Custumarum, Ordinacionum, Memorandorum and Albus, Liber de Antiquis Legibus, and collections of Statutes; continuous series of judicial rolls and books from 1252 and Council minutes from 1275; records of the Old Bailey and Guildhall Sessions from 1603; financial records from the 16th century; the records of London Bridge from the 12th century; and numerous subsidiary series and miscellanea of historical interest. Readers' Room open Mon.–Fri., 9.30–4.45.

Keeper of the City Records, The Town Clerk.
City Archivist, J. R. Sewell.
Deputy City Archivist, Mrs J. M. Bankes.

RED DEER COMMISSION
Knowsley, 82 Fairfield Road, Inverness IV3 5LH
[0463–231751]

The Red Deer Commission has the general functions of furthering the conservation and control of red and sika deer in Scotland and of keeping under review all matters relating to roe deer. It has the statutory duty, with powers, to prevent damage to agriculture and forestry by red and sika deer. The Commission also has the power to advise in the interest of conservation any owner of land on questions relating to the carrying of stocks of red deer, sika deer and roe deer on that land, and to carry out research into matters of scientific importance relating to deer.

Chairman, I. K. Mackenzie, OBE (*part time*) .. £17,500
Secretary, A. Rinning £21,000
Senior Field Officer, L. A. H. K. Stewart, MBE.

REVIEW BODIES

The secretariat for these bodies is provided by the Office of Manpower Economics (*see* page 339).

ARMED FORCES PAY
The Review Body on Armed Forces Pay was appointed in September 1971 to advise the Prime Minister on the pay and allowances of members of Naval, Military and Air Forces of the Crown and of any women's service administered by the Defence Council.

Chairman, Sir Peter Cazalet.
Members, P. Ball; G. M. Hourston; D. P. M. Hudson; Mrs J. Hughes; R. Sanderson, OBE; Gen. Sir Richard Trant, KCB; Prof. J. White, CBE.

DOCTORS' AND DENTISTS' REMUNERATION

The Review Body on Doctors' and Dentists' Remuneration was set up in July 1971 to advise the Prime Minister on the remuneration of doctors and dentists taking any part in the National Health Service.
Chairman, Sir Trevor Holdsworth.
Members, Mrs J. d'Abo; D. G. Boyd; D. Fredjohn, MBE; Sir Geoffrey Leigh; Prof. G. F. Thomason, CBE; J. K. Warburton, CBE.

NURSING STAFF, MIDWIVES, HEALTH VISITORS AND PROFESSIONS ALLIED TO MEDICINE

The Review Body for nursing staff, midwives, health visitors and professions allied to medicine was set up in July 1983 to advise the Prime Minister on the remuneration of nursing staff, midwives and health visitors employed in the National Health Service; and also of physiotherapists, radiographers, remedial gymnasts, occupational therapists, orthoptists, chiropodists, dietitians and related grades employed in the National Health Service.
Chairman, M. Bett, CBE.
Members, Mrs M. Cameron; J. Hildreth; Miss A. Mackie, OBE; Dame Anne Mueller, DCB; Mrs R. Pickavance; Prof. G. F. Thomason, CBE; Miss D. Whittingham.

TOP SALARIES

The Review Body on Top Salaries was set up in May 1971 to advise the Prime Minister on the remuneration of the higher judiciary and other judicial appointments, senior civil servants, and senior officers of the armed forces. The Review Body has also been asked on a number of occasions to advise on the remuneration of Members of Parliament and of Ministers and on the level of parliamentary allowances.
Chairman, Sir David Nickson, KBE.
Members, Sir Terence Beckett, KBE; Ms L. Botting; Ms A. Burdus; Sir Peter Cazalet; Sir Cecil Clothier, KCB, QC; A. G. Gormley; H. S. Pigott; J. J. R. Pope, OBE; Sir Anthony Wilson.

ROYAL BOTANIC GARDEN EDINBURGH
Inverleith Row, Edinburgh EH3 5LR
[031–552 7171]

The Royal Botanic Garden (RBG) Edinburgh, which originated as the Physic Garden established in 1670 beside the Palace of Holyroodhouse, became the direct responsibility of the Commissioners of HM Works and Public Buildings (later the Department of Public Works) in 1889, transferring to the Department of Agriculture and Fisheries for Scotland in 1969. Since 1986, RBG Edinburgh has been administered by a Board of Trustees established under the National Heritage (Scotland) Act 1985.

RBG Edinburgh is an international centre for scientific research on plant diversity, maintaining collections of living plants and reference resources, including a herbarium of some two million specimens of preserved plants. Other statutory functions of RBG Edinburgh include provision of education and information on botany and horticulture, and the provision of public access to the living plant collections.

The Garden moved to its present site at Inverleith, Edinburgh in 1821. There are also three specialist gardens: Younger Botanic Garden, Benmore, near Dunoon, Argyllshire; Logan Botanic Garden, near Stranraer, Wigtownshire; and Dawyck Botanic Garden, near Stobo, Peeblesshire. Public opening hours:

RBG Edinburgh – daily (except Dec. 25, Jan 1) 9 to sunset (1 hour earlier in summer) (Sun. 11 to sunset); specialist gardens – April–Oct. 10–6.
Chairman of the Board of Trustees, Sir Peter Hutchison, Bt.
Regius Keeper, Dr D. S. Ingram.
Assistant Keeper, Dr D. J. Mann.

ROYAL BOTANIC GARDENS KEW
Richmond, Surrey TW9 3AB
[081-940 1171]
Wakehurst Place, Ardingly, nr. Haywards Heath,
West Sussex RH17 6TN
[0444–892701]

The Royal Botanic Gardens (RBG) Kew were founded in 1759 by HRH Princess Augusta. In 1841 they became a public institution; in 1847 the Museums of Economic Botany were opened; and in 1852 the Herbarium and Library were established. The Jodrell Laboratory opened in 1876. In 1965 the garden at Wakehurst Place was acquired; it is owned by the National Trust and managed by RBG Kew. From 1903 to 1984 RBG Kew was part of the Ministry of Agriculture, Fisheries and Food. Under the National Heritage Act 1983 a Board of Trustees was set up to administer the Gardens which in 1984 became an independent body supported by a grant-in-aid.

The functions of RBG Kew are to carry out research into plant sciences, to disseminate knowledge about plants and to provide the public with the opportunity to gain knowledge and enjoyment from the Gardens' collections. There are extensive national reference collections of living and preserved plants and a comprehensive library and archive. The main emphasis is on tropical and subtropical plants.

Open daily, except Christmas Day and New Year's Day, from 9.30 a.m. The closing hour varies from 4 p.m. in mid-winter to 6.30 p.m. on week-days, and 8 p.m. on Sundays and Bank Holidays, in mid-summer. Admission (1991), £3. Concessionary schemes available. Museums open 9.30 a.m.; Glasshouses, 9.30–4.30 (weekdays); to 5.30 p.m. (Sundays). No dogs except guide-dogs for the blind.

BOARD OF TRUSTEES

Chairman, Hon. J. D. Eccles, CBE.
Members, Sir David Attenborough, CBE, FRS; R. P. Bauman; Prof. W. G. Chaloner, FRS; Prof. E. C. D. Cocking, FRS; Sir Philip M. Dowson, CBE; Sir Leslie Fowden, FRS; R. A. E. Herbert; Mrs A. Lennox-Boyd; Prof. Elizabeth B. Robson, PH.D.; Mrs V. R. Wakefield; Cdr. L. M. Saunders Watson.
Director, Dr G. T. Prance.

ROYAL COMMISSION FOR THE EXHIBITION OF 1851
Sherfield Building,
Imperial College of Science and Technology,
SW7 2AZ
[071–225 6110]

The Royal Commission was incorporated by supplemental charter as a permanent Commission after winding up the affairs of the Great Exhibition of 1851. It has for its object the promotion of scientific and artistic education by means of funds derived from its Kensington estate, purchased with the surplus left over from the Great Exhibition.
President, HRH The Duke of Edinburgh, KG, KT, PC.
Chairman, Board of Management, Sir Denis Rooke, CBE, FRS.
Secretary to Commissioners, M. C. Neale, CB.

THE ROYAL MINT
Llantrisant, nr. Pontyclun,
Mid-Glamorgan CF7 8YT
[0443–222111]

The Royal Mint became an executive agency in April 1990, the Minister to whom the Mint is responsible being the Chancellor of the Exchequer.

The prime responsibility of the Royal Mint is the provision of United Kingdom coinage, but it actively competes in world markets for a share of the available circulating coin business and, on average, two-thirds of the 15,000 tonnes of coins produced annually are exported to over 100 countries. The Mint also manufactures special proof and uncirculated quality coins in gold, silver and other metals; military and civil decorations and medals; commemorative and prize medals; and royal and official seals.

Master of the Mint, The Chancellor of the Exchequer (*ex officio*).
Deputy Master and Comptroller, A. D. Garrett.

ROYAL NATIONAL THEATRE BOARD
South Bank, SE1 9PX
[071–928 2033]

Chairman, The Lady Soames, DBE.
Members, P. Benson; The Hon. Lady Cazalet; The Lord Chorley; R. Clutton; M. Codron, CBE; Dame Judi Dench, DBE; J. Hannam, MP; S. Lipton; Sonia Melchett; R. M. Mills; Sir Derek Mitchell, KCB, CVO; The Rt. Hon. Sir Michael Palliser, GCMG; L. Sieff, OBE; B. Simons; T. Stoppard, OBE; J. Whitney.
Company Secretary and Head of Finance, A. Blackstock.
Board and Committee Secretary, Ms Y. Bird, MBE.

RURAL DEVELOPMENT COMMISSION
11 Cowley Street, SW1P 3NA
[071-276 6969]
141 Castle Street, Salisbury,
Wilts. SP1 3TP.
[0722-336255]

The Rural Development Commission was formed in 1988 by the merger of the Development Commission for Rural England and the Council for Small Industries in Rural Areas. It is a statutory body funded by government grant-in-aid which undertakes to alleviate economic and social problems in rural areas and advises the Government on related rural matters in England. It concentrates its resources in Rural Development Areas but some assistance is also available outside the RDAs.

Chairman, The Lord Shuttleworth.
Deputy Chairman, G. Gray.
Chief Executive, R. Butt.
Deputy Chief Executive, J. Taylor.

SCIENCE AND ENGINEERING RESEARCH COUNCIL
Polaris House, North Star Avenue,
Swindon, Wilts. SN2 1ET
[0793–411000]

The Science and Engineering Research Council (SERC) is one of five research councils funded through the Department of Education and Science. Its purpose is to develop the natural and social sciences, including engineering, to maintain a fundamental capacity of research and scholarship and to support relevant postgraduate education. SERC's role is to encourage and support research and advanced training in UK universities and polytechnics in all the basic areas of science and engineering.

Chairman, Sir Mark Richmond, FRS.
Members, Prof. T. L. Blundell; Prof. P. G. Burke; D.

A. Davis; Prof. A. Donnachie; G. H. Fairtlough; Prof. R. E. Hester; Dr G. R. Higginson; Dr N. W. Horne; Prof. C. J. Humphreys; Dr A. Ledwith; D. P. Nash; Prof. E. R. Oxburgh; Prof. J. T. Stuart; Prof. J. O. Thomas; Prof. A. W. Wolfendale.

For research establishments, *see* p. 966.

SCOTTISH ENTERPRISE
120 Bothwell Street, Glasgow G2 7JP
[041-248 2700]

On April 1, 1991 Scottish Enterprise took over the economic development and environmental improvement functions of the Scottish Development Agency and the training functions of the Training Agency in lowland Scotland. Its remit is to further the development of Scotland's economy, to enhance the skills of the Scottish workforce, to promote Scotland's international competitiveness and to improve the environment. Many of its functions are contracted-out to a network of local enterprise companies. Through Locate in Scotland, Scottish Enterprise is also concerned with attracting firms to Scotland.

Chairman, Sir David Nickson.
Chief Executive, C. Beveridge.
Managing Director, Strategy and Local Enterprise Company Operations, J. Condliffe.
Managing Director, Corporate Services, L. Gold.

SCOTTISH NATURAL HERITAGE
Battleby, Redgorton, Perth PH1 3EW
[0738–27921]
12 Hope Terrace, Edinburgh EH9 2AS
[031–447 4784]

Scottish Natural Heritage will come into existence on April 1, 1992 under the Natural Heritage (Scotland) Bill 1991. It will be created by the merger of the Countryside Commission for Scotland and the Nature Conservancy Council in Scotland and will combine the functions of those bodies.

Chairman, M. Magnusson, KBE.
Chief Executive, R. Crofts.
Chief Scientific Adviser, M. B. Usher.

SCOTTISH OFFICE

The Secretary of State for Scotland is responsible in Scotland for a wide range of statutory functions which in England and Wales are the responsibility of a number of departmental ministers. He also works closely with ministers in charge of Great Britain departments on topics of special significance to Scotland within their fields of responsibility. His statutory functions are administered by five main departments: the Scottish Office Agriculture and Fisheries Department, the Scottish Office Education Department, the Scottish Office Environment Department, the Scottish Office Home and Health Department, and the Scottish Office Industry Department. These departments (plus Central Services embracing the Solicitor's Office, the Scottish Office Information Directorate, Establishment, Liaison and Finance Divisions) are collectively known as The Scottish Office. In addition there are a number of other Scottish departments for which the Secretary of State has some degree of responsibility; these include the Scottish Courts Administration, the Department of the Registrar General for Scotland (the General Register Office), the Scottish Record Office and the Department of the Registers of Scotland. The Secretary of State also bears ministerial responsibility for the activities in Scotland of several statutory bodies whose functions extend throughout Great Britain, such as the Training Commission and the Forestry Commission.

(For **Salaries**, *see* page 293)

Dover House, Whitehall, SW1A 2AU
[071–270 3000]

Secretary of State for Scotland, THE RT. HON. IAN
LANG, MP.
Private Secretary (G5), J. D. Gallagher
Assistant Private Secretaries, J. S. Hynd; Mrs L. J.
Stirling.
Special Adviser, A. Young.
Parliamentary Private Secretary, C. Wardle, MP.
Minister of State, MICHAEL FORSYTH, MP *(Education
and Health)*.
Private Secretary, I. D. Kernohan.
Parliamentary Under Secretaries of State, LORD
JAMES DOUGLAS–HAMILTON, MP; J. ALLAN STEW-
ART, MP*; THE LORD STRATHCLYDE.
Private Secretaries, O. D. Kelly *(Lord James
Douglas–Hamilton)*; K. A. L. Thomson* *(J. Allan
Stewart)*; Dr P. J. Rycroft *(Lord Strathclyde)*.
Parliamentary Clerk, I. Campbell.
Permanent Under Secretary of State (G1), Sir Russell
Hillhouse, KCB.
Private Secretary, A. I. Wilson.
Liaison Staff:
Assistant Secretary (G5), E. W. Ferguson.

St Andrew's House,
Edinburgh EH1 3DG
[031–556 8400]

MANAGEMENT GROUP SUPPORT STAFF

Principal (G7), D. A. Stewart.

CENTRAL SERVICES

Grade 2, G. R. Wilson, CB.

Personnel Group
16 Waterloo Place Edinburgh, EH1 3DN
[031–556 8400]

Principal Establishment Officer (G3), J. Hamill.
Assistant Secretaries (G5), D. J. Chalmers; C. C.
MacDonald.
Senior Principals (G6), C. D. Henderson; I. C.
Henderson; R. Tait.

Administrative Services
James Craig Walk, Edinburgh EH1 3BA
[031–556 8400]

Director of Administrative Services (G4), R. S. B.
Gordon.
Assistant Secretary (G5), D. Stevenson.
Director of Information Technology (G5), J. Duffy.
Deputy Director (G6), I. W. Goodwin.
Director of Telecommunications (G6), A. F. Harrison.
Director of Office Management (G6), B. V. Surridge,
ISO.

Finance Division
New St Andrew's House, Edinburgh EH1 3TB
[031–556 8400]
Finance Group

Principal Finance Officer (G3), H. H. Mills.
Assistant Secretaries (G5), T. A. Cameron; S. F.
Hampson; L. Mosco; B. Naylor; A. J. Rushworth;
W. T. Tait.

Solicitor's Office
*(For the Scottish departments and certain UK
services, including HM Treasury, in Scotland.)*
Solicitor (G2), R. Brodie, CB.
Deputy Solicitor (G3), N. W. Boe.

---

*Based at New St Andrew's House.

Divisional Solicitors (G5), J. B. Allan; †K. F. Barclay;
R. Bland; G. C. Duke; I. H. Harvie; R. M.
Henderson; G. Jackson; J. L. Jamieson; †Mrs L. A.
Lilliker; H. F. Macdiarmid; Mrs L. A. Wallace.
†Seconded to Scottish Law Commission

Scottish Office Information Directorate
*(For the Scottish departments and certain
UK services)*

Director (G5), C. F. Corbett.
Deputy Director (G6), D. C. M. Beveridge, OBE.

Statistics
Chief Statistician (G5), Dr J. R. Cuthbert.

SCOTTISH OFFICE AGRICULTURE AND
FISHERIES DEPARTMENT
Pentland House, 47 Robb's Loan, Edinburgh
EH14 1TW
[031–556 8400]

Dover House, Whitehall, SW1A 2AU
[071–270 3000]

Secretary (G2), L. P. Hamilton, CB.
Under Secretary (G3), K. J. MacKenzie.
Fisheries Secretary (G3), G. Robson.
Assistant Secretaries (G5), P. S. Collings; E. C.
Davison; I. W. Gordon; R. A. Grant; T. J. Kelly; A.
K. MacLeod; K. W. Moore; A. J. A. Rennie; I. M.
Whitelaw.
Chief Agricultural Officer (G4), J. F. Hutcheson.
Deputy Chief Agricultural Officer (G5), W. A. Macgre-
gor.
Assistant Chief Agricultural Officers (G6), D. R. J.
Craven; J. A. Hardie; J. G. Muir; A. Robb; J. I.
Woodrow.
Chief Agricultural Economist (G6), J. R. Wildgoose,
D.Phil.
Chief Meat and Livestock Inspector (G7), J. Miller.
Chief Food and Dairy Officer (G7), D. J. MacDonald.
Chief Surveyor (G6), N. Taylor.
Scientific Adviser (G5), T. W. Hegarty, PH.D.
Senior Principal Scientific Officers (G6), R. J. Dowdell,
PH.D.; D. Thornton.

Agricultural Scientific Services
East Craigs, Edinburgh EH12 8NJ
[031–556 8400]

Director (G5), Dr R. K. M. Hay.
Deputy Director (G6), J. R. Cutler, OBE.
Senior Principal Scientific Officers (G6), S. R. Cooper;
M. J. Richardson.

Fisheries Research Services
Marine Laboratory, PO Box 101,
Victoria Road, Torry, Aberdeen AB9 8DB
[0224–876544]

Director of Fisheries Research for Scotland (G4), Prof.
A. D. Hawkins, PH.D., FRSE.
Deputy Director (G5), D. N. MacLennan.
Senior Principal Scientific Officers (G6), R. M. Cook,
PH.D.; J. M. Davies, PH.D.; A. L. S. Munro, PH.D.; P.
A. M. Stewart, PH.D.; C. S. Wardle, PH.D.

Freshwater Fisheries Laboratory
Faskally, Pitlochry, Perthshire PH16 5LB
[0796–2060]

Senior Principal Scientific Officers (G6), R. G. J.
Shelton, PH.D.; J. E. Thorpe, PH.D.
*Inspector of Salmon and Freshwater Fisheries for
Scotland (G7)*, R. B. Williamson.

Scottish Fisheries Protection Agency
Pentland House, 47 Robb's Loan,
Edinburgh EH14 1TW
[031–556 8400]

Chief Executive (G5), A. K. MacLeod.

Director of Policy and Resources (G6), J. B. Roddin.
Chief Inspector of Sea Fisheries (G6), J. F. Fenton.
Marine Superintendent, Capt. R. M. Mill-Irving.

SCOTTISH OFFICE ENVIRONMENT DEPARTMENT
St Andrew's House, Edinburgh EH1 3DG
[031–556 8400]
Dover House, Whitehall, SW1A 2AU
[071–270 3000]

Secretary and Chief Economic Adviser (G2), Dr R. C. L. McCrone, CB, FRSE.
Under Secretaries (G3), J. S. Graham; J. F. Laing; Miss E. A. MacKay.
Assistant Secretaries (G5), C. M. Baxter; T. J. Birley; Ms L. Clare; R. S. Crofts; W. J. Fearnley; I. C. Freeman; Mrs M. B. Gunn; K. W. McKay; D. F. Middleton; J. N. Randall; E. C. Reavley; R. E. S. Robinson; Mrs G. M. Stewart; J. A. Thomson.

Professional Staff

Chief Engineer (G3), A. C. Paton.
Deputy Chief Engineer (G5), T. D. Macdonald.
Assistant Chief Engineers (G6), T. Bolton; N. G. Semple.
Director of Building and Chief Architect (G3), J. E. Gibbons, Ph.D.
Deputy Director of Building and Deputy Chief Architect (G5), M. R. Miller.
Deputy Director of Building and Chief Quantity Surveyor (G5), D. C. Russell.
Deputy Director (G5), A. F. Affolter.
Assistant Directors (G6), G. Gray; H. R. McCallum.
Chief Planner (G4), A. Mackenzie.
Deputy Chief Planner (G5), D. R. Dare.
Assistant Chief Planners (G6), T. Williamson; A. W. Denham; I. R. Duncan; S. G. Fulton.
Chief Research Officer (G5), Dr C. P. A. Levein.
Senior Principal Research Officers (G6), Mrs B. Doig; Dr Jacqueline Tombs.
HM Chief Industrial Pollution Inspector (G5), I. W. W. Wright.
Chief Estates Officer (G6), R. I. K. White.

Historic Scotland
20 Brandon Street, Edinburgh EH3 5RA
[031–244 3141]

(An executive agency within the Scottish Office.)
Director (G3), G. N. Munro.
Deputy Directors (G5), F. J. Lawrie; D. Macniven, TD.
Assistant Directors (G6), I. J. MacKenzie; I. Maxwell.
Chief Inspector of Historic Buildings (G6), D. M. Walker, FSA, FSAScot.
Chief Inspector of Ancient Monuments (G6), D. J. Breeze, Ph.D., FSA, FSAScot.
Head of Corporate Planning and Resources (G6), A. Rosie.
Head of Finance (G7), vacant.

Local Government Finance Group
New St Andrew's House, Edinburgh EH1 3TB
[031–556 8400]

Assistant Secretaries (G5), C. M. Baxter; K. W. McKay.

Inquiry Reporters
16 Waterloo Place, Edinburgh EH1 3DN
[031–556 8400]

Chief Reporter (G3), A. G. Bell, CB.
Deputy Chief Reporter (G5), R. M. Hickman.

SCOTTISH OFFICE INDUSTRY DEPARTMENT
New St Andrew's House, Edinburgh EH1 3TA
[031–556 8400]
Dover House, Whitehall, SW1A 2AU
[071–270 3000]

Secretary (G2), P. MacKay.

Under Secretaries (G3), A. D. F. Findlay; E. J. Weeple.
Assistant Secretaries (G5), D. A. Brew; G. D. Calder; D. A. Campbell; J. W. Elvidge; I. F. Gray; J. S. B. Martin; Mrs N. S. Munro; D. N. G. Reid; Mrs A. Robson.
Senior Economic Advisers (G5), A. Goudie; J. A. Peat.

Professional Staff

Director of Roads and Chief Engineer (G4), J. A. L. Dawson.
Deputy Chief Engineer (Roads) (G5), G. S. Marshall.
Deputy Chief Engineer (Bridges) (G5), J. Innes.
Assistant Chief Engineers (G6), N. B. MacKenzie; R. D. Udall; J. A. Howison.

Industrial Expansion
Alhambra House, 45 Waterloo Street, Glasgow G2 6AT
[041–248 2855]

Under Secretary (G3), H. Morison.
Industrial Adviser, Dr C. K. Benington.
Scientific Adviser, Prof. J. Lamb.
Assistant Secretaries (G5), A. W. Fraser; J. Meldrum.
Senior Principal (G6), J. McGhee.

Locate in Scotland
120 Bothwell Street, Glasgow G2 7JP
[041–248 2700]

Director (G4), E. Frizzell.
Senior Principal (G6), W. Malone.
Principal (G7), R. Whyte.
Director (North America), R. Crawford.

SCOTTISH OFFICE EDUCATION DEPARTMENT
New St Andrew's House, Edinburgh EH1 3SY
[031–556 8400]
Dover House, Whitehall, SW1A 2AU
[071–270 3000]

Secretary (G2), G. R. Wilson, CB.
Under Secretaries (G3), W. A. P. Weatherston; H. Robertson, MBE.
Assistant Secretaries (G5), P. Brady; D. S. Henderson; R. D. Jackson; J. W. L. Lonie; G. McHugh; Miss M. MacLean; K. Macrae; D. Salmond (*Chief Statistician*).
Senior Principal (G6), D. Wann.

HM Inspectors of Schools

Senior Chief Inspector (G3), T. N. Gallacher.
Deputy Senior Chief Inspectors (G4), W. T. Beveridge; D. W. Mack.
Chief Inspectors (G5), W. F. L. Bigwood; G. P. D. Donaldson; J. T. Donaldson; J. Howgego; J. J. McDonald; A. S. McGlynn; D. A. Osler; A. M. Rankin; H. M. Stacker.
Inspectors (G6), J. N. Alison; D. T. G. Allan; M. T. J. Axford; P. Banks; Mrs W. Binnie; A. D. Blair; Mrs J. M. Bowen; J. Boyes; Miss C. L. Boyle; M. J. Brown; Mrs M. M. Browning; J. W. Burdin; D. C. Burgess; T. N. Carr; W. Clark; M. Q. Cramb; Mrs A. D. Craw; F. Crawford; R. F. Dick; J. C. Dignan; Mrs M. Docherty; D. W. Duncan; Miss K. M. Fairweather; B. Fryer; A. R. Gallon; I. K. Gamble; W. Geddes; M. Gibson, Ph.D.; A. B. Giovanazzi; G. D. Gray, Ph.D.; T. O. Greig; R. A. Hawke; R. Hogg; K. A. Hope; L. A. Hunter; Mrs C. Hutchinson; M. Jack; J. Jackson, Ph.D.; E. S. Kelly; D. E. Kelso; Ms A. Kennedy; D. G. Kirkpatrick; I. Lawson; M. McAllan; I. M. MacAskill; L. McCallum; Mrs M. A. Macfarlane; Ms I. S. McGregor; C. McIlroy; S. McKilligan, Ph.D.; R. E. McKinstry; C. R. MacLean; A. J. Macpherson; D. MacQuarrie; A. Maltby; R. H. Manser; A. F. Marquis; D. Martin; H. L. Martin; G. Mathison; W. M. Mein; Mrs J. M. Millar; J.

Mitchell; Miss E. R. Mowat; B. Nickerson, PH.D.; F. S. O'Hagan, PH.D.; I. P. Pascoe; W. M. Patterson; N. A. Pepin; J. Picken; T. A. Rankin; M. C. Rhodes; S. A. Ritchie; I. D. S. Robertson; Mrs M. A. Robertson; Mrs P. A. Robertson; S. M. Robertson; A. L. Robson; M. Roebuck; I. S. Rowley; D. M. Russell; A. L. Small; E. P. Spencer; K. Srinivassan; A. M. Steel; W. Stevenson; A. Stewart; Mrs J. A. Stewart; W. P. Stewart; T. Straiton, PH.D.; J. W. Thomson; R. M. S. Tuck; R. S. Weir; J. G. L. Wright; R. W. J. Young, PH.D.

SCOTTISH OFFICE HOME AND HEALTH DEPARTMENT
St Andrew's House, Edinburgh EH1 3DE
[031–556 8400]
Dover House, Whitehall, SW1A 2AU
[071–270 3000]

Secretary (G2), G. A. Hart, CB.
Under Secretaries (G3), D. Belfall; N. G. Campbell; D. J. Essery; J. E. Fraser, CB.
Assistant Secretaries (G5), Mrs M. H. Brannan; J. T. Brown; A. M. Burnside; C. M. A. Lugton; C. K. McIntosh; P. M. Russell; R. H. Scott.
Senior Principal (G6), N. MacLeod.

National Health Service in Scotland Management Executive
Chief Executive, D. Cruickshank.
 Private Secretary, Ms J. A. Stirton.
Director of Strategic Management, G. A. Anderson.
Director of Finance, M. Collier.
Director of Administration, D. Steel.
Director of Information Services, C. B. Knox.
Director of Manpower, A. J. Matheson.
Assistant Secretaries (G5), W. J. Farquhar; Ms I. M. Low; W. Moyes; G. M. D. Thomson; G. W. Tucker.
Assistant Director (G6), H. R. McCallum.
Senior Principal (G6), Miss J. McGregor.

Medical Services
Chief Medical Officer (G2), Prof. R. E. Kendell.
Deputy Chief Medical Officer (G3), Dr A. B. Young.
Principal Medical Officers, J. V. Basson; C. F. Fleming; G. Gilray; Margaret Hennigan; A. D. McIntyre; A. Rourke.
Senior Medical Officers, R. E. G. Aitken, TD; I. R. Bashford; P. W. Brooks; S. Capewell; W. Dodd; Dr A. Findlay; Dr Margaret Hally; D. U. Sinclair; Dr R. D. Skinner, Dr Elisabeth Sowler; Dr M. A. R. Thomson; O. A. Thores.
Senior Regional Medical Officers, I. G. Conn; K. Inglis; H. McBain.
Regional Medical Officers, I. Arthurson; P. I. Brown; J. E. Durkacz; G. W. G. Hunter; G. McKay; A. S. Mackenzie; J. P. Reid.
Chief Scientist, Prof. R. D. Weir, OBE.
Chief Dental Officer, N. K. Colquhoun.
Deputy Chief Dental Officer, J. R. Wild.
Regional Dental Officers, K. J. McKenzie; M. G. Platt; Miss A. J. Power; G. A. Reid.
Chief Nursing Officer, Mrs Y. Moores.
Chief Pharmacist (G6), G. Calder.

Social Work Services Group
43 Jeffrey Street, Edinburgh EH1 1DN
[031–556 8400]

The Social Work Services Group, which is attached to the Scottish Office Home and Health Department, administers the provisions of the Social Work (Scotland) Act 1968. A Social Work Services Inspectorate is being set up and should be operational by January 1992.
Assistant Secretaries (G5), M. J. P. Cunliffe; J. W. Sinclair; D. Wishart.
Chief Social Work Adviser, A. Skinner.

Senior Advisers, Ms M. L. Hunt; F. A. O'Leary; I. C. Robertson; A. R. Sabine; J. I. Smith.

Miscellaneous Appointments
HM Chief Inspector of Constabulary, C. Sampson, CBE, QPM.
HM Chief Inspector of Prisons , A. H. Bishop, CB.
Commandant, Scottish Police College, T. J. Whitson, OBE.
HM Chief Inspector of Fire Services, A. Winton, QFSM.
Commandant, Scottish Fire Service Training School, C. F. McManus, QFSM.
Secretary, Scottish Health Service Advisory Council, W. J. Farquhar.

Scottish Prison Service
Calton House, 5 Redheughs Rigg,
Edinburgh EH12 9HW
[031–556 8400]

Director of Scottish Prison Service (G3), P. McKinlay.
Deputy Director (Operations) and Assistant Director (G5), A. R. Walker.
Deputy Director, Personnel (G5), vacant.
Deputy Director, Regime Services and Supplies (G6), N. Harvey.
Deputy Director, Planning and Development (G5), J. W. H. Irvine.
Deputy Director, Estates (G6), D. D. Sutherland.
Deputy Director, Training (G5), W. J. Fearnley.

Prison Governors
Aberdeen, W. A. R. Rattray.
Barlinnie, P. Withers.
Barlinnie Special Unit, I. A. Bannatyne.
Castle Huntly Young Offenders Institution, E. J. Brownsmith.
Cornton Vale, P. L. Abernethy.
Dumfries Young Offenders Institution, G. Taylor.
Dungavel, A. P. Spencer.
Edinburgh, J. Pearce.
Friarton, J. A. Harker.
Glenochil Prison and Young Offenders Institution, J. Milne.
Greenock, D. E. Gunn.
Inverness, L. W. G. Hewitson.
Longriggend Remand Institution, A. F. King.
Low Moss, W. Davidson.
Noranside, J. C. Stuart.
Penninghame, R. B. Carrek.
Perth, R. Kite.
Peterhead, M. J. Milne.
Polmont Young Offenders Institution, G. R. Bond.
Shotts, E. J. Campbell.
Shotts Alternative Unit, A. MacDonald.
Scottish Prison Service College, R. L. Houchin.

Mental Welfare Commission for Scotland
25 Drumsheugh Gardens, Edinburgh EH3 7NS
[031–225 7034]

Chairman, Sheriff H. J. Aronson.
Commissioners, Mrs A. Baxter; Dr D. Blaney; P. H. Brodie; R. G. Davis; Mrs A. M. Glen; Ms A. M. Green; Mrs H. L. Grieve; Mrs J. I. D. Isbister; D. A. Macdonald, OBE; Mrs H. S. Mein; Sir David Montgomery; M. O'Reilly; J. G. Sutherland.
Medical Commissioners, J. A. T. Dyer; A. A. McKechnie.
Social Work Commissioner, J. H. L. Richards.
Secretary, D. Wishart.

Counsel to the Secretary of State for Scotland under the Private Legislation Procedure (Scotland) Act 1936 (50 Frederick Street, Edinburgh (031–226 6499)).

Senior Counsel, G. S. Douglas, QC.
Junior Counsel, N. M. P. Morrison.

NATIONAL HEALTH SERVICE, SCOTLAND
Health Boards

Argyll and Clyde, Gilmour House, Paisley. *Chairman*, P. R. Reid; *General Manager*, I. C. Smith.

Ayrshire and Arran, PO Box 13, Hunters Avenue, Ayr. *Chairman*, W. S. Fyfe, OBE; *General Manager*, J. M. Eckford, OBE.

Borders, Huntlyburn, Melrose, Roxburghshire. *Chairman*, Dr D. H. Pringle, CBE; *General Manager*, D. A. Peters.

Dumfries and Galloway, Nithbank, Dumfries. *Chairman*, J. A. M. McIntyre, OBE; *General Manager*, M. D. Cook.

Fife, Glenrothes House, North Street, Glenrothes. *Chairman*, Mrs P. A. H. Ferguson; *General Manager*, F. F. Gibb, CBE.

Forth Valley, 33 Spittal Street, Stirling. *Chairman*, Mrs J. D. Isbister; *General Manager*, C. C. Nunn (acting).

Grampian, 1–7 Albyn Place, Aberdeen. *Chairman*, J. Kyle, CBE; *General Manager*, F. Harbrett.

Greater Glasgow, 112 Ingram Street, Glasgow. *Chairman*, Sir Thomas Thomson, CBE; *General Manager*, L. Peterken, CBE.

Highland, Reay House, 17 Old Edinburgh Road, Inverness. *Chairman*, J. D. M. Robertson, OBE; *General Manager*, R. R. W. Stewart.

Lanarkshire, 14 Beckford Street, Hamilton, Lanarkshire. *Chairman*, Mrs B. M. Gunn, OBE; *General Manager*, F. Clark, CBE.

Lothian, 148 The Pleasance, Edinburgh. *Chairman*, Dr J. W. Baynham; *General Manager*, J. Lusby.

Orkney, Balfour Hospital, New Scapa Road, Kirkwall, Orkney. *Chairman*, J. Leslie; *General Manager*, Dr J. I. Cromarty.

Shetland, 28 Burgh Road, Lerwick. *Chairman*, Mrs F. Grains; *General Manager*, B. J. Atherton.

Tayside, PO Box 75, Vernonholme, Riverside Drive, Dundee. *Chairman*, J. C. MacFarlane; *General Manager*, Dr R. C. Graham.

Western Isles, 37 South Beach Street, Stornoway, Isle of Lewis. *Chairman*, Mrs M. A. MacMillan; *General Manager*, J. J. Glover.

Health Education Board for Scotland
Woodburn House, Canaan Lane,
Edinburgh EH10 4SG

Chairman, E. Walker.
General Manager, Dr A. Tannahill.

State Hospital
Carstairs Junction, Lanark ML11 8RP

Chairman, P. Hamilton-Grierson.
General Manager, R. Manson.

Common Services Agency
Trinity Park House, South Trinity Road,
Edinburgh EH5 3SE

Chairman, D. G. Cruickshank.
General Manager, J. T. Donald.

GENERAL REGISTER OFFICE (Scotland)
New Register House, Edinburgh EH1 3YT
[031–334 0380]

The General Register Office for Scotland is the Scottish equivalent of the Office of Population Censuses and Surveys. The main records in the custody of the Registrar General for Scotland are: the statutory registers of births, deaths, marriages, still births, adoptions and divorces; the old parish registers (recording births, marriages, deaths, etc. before civil registration began in 1855); and records of censuses of the population in Scotland.

Hours of public access: Mon.–Thurs. 9–4.30; Fri. 9–4.

Registrar General (G4), Dr C. M. Glennie.
Deputy Registrar General (G5), B. V. Philp.
Senior Principal (G6), D. A. Orr.
Principals (G7), D. B. L. Brownlee; R. C. Lawson; D. M. Robertson.
Statisticians (G7), J. Arrundale; G. W. L. Jackson; F. G. Thomas.

SEA FISH INDUSTRY AUTHORITY
Sea Fisheries House, 10 Young Street,
Edinburgh EH2 4JQ
[031–225 2515]

Chairman, Lord Mackay of Ardbrecknish.
Chief Executive, C. H. Davies.
Deputy Chief Executive, P. D. Chaplin.
Secretary and Administration Director, R. A. Davie.
Technical Director, A. G. Hopper.
Marketing Director, R. M. Kennedy.
Training Director, K. Waind.

SECURITIES AND INVESTMENTS BOARD LTD
Gavrelle House, 2–14 Bunhill Row, EC1Y 8RA
[071–638 1240]
[*Central register of authorized firms*: 071–929 3652]

The Securities and Investments Board (SIB) became in 1987 the designated agency, under the Financial Services Act 1986, for regulating the activities of investment businesses in the UK. Although not a statutory body, the Board has powers under the 1986 Act to recognize self-regulating organizations, professional bodies, investment exchanges and clearing houses, and directly to authorize firms to do investment business in the UK. The Board also has the power to act as a prosecuting authority in respect of persons carrying on investment business without being authorized.

Members of the Board are appointed by agreement between the Secretary of State for Trade and Industry and the Governor of the Bank of England. The chairman and executive directors are full-time Board members; the others are part-time and non-executive.

The Board

Chairman, Sir David Walker.
Deputy Chairmen, The Viscount Runciman of Doxford, CBE; R. N. Quartano, CBE.
Chief Operating Officer, R. H. F. Croft, CB.
Members (part-time), D. M. Child, CBE; J. A. Craven; J. A. Gardiner; N. Lessels; P. J. Manser; J. Palmer, CBE; G. R. Russell; Lady Scott, CBE; L. Warwick; Dame Rachel Waterhouse, DBE; R. B. Williamson, CBE.

Management

The Chairman.
The Chief Operating Officer.
Group Directors:
  Legal, M. C. Blair.
  Retail Markets, C. Bowe.
  Compliance and Enforcement, J. D. Orme.
  Capital Markets, M. J. Vile.

Directors of Divisions:
  Finance, R. B. A. Purcell.
  Financial Regulation, A. J. Thrall.
  Information Services, B. W. Smith.
  Intermediaries, A. C. Pirie.
  Markets, R. J. Britton.
  Policy, M. B. Gittins.
Deputy Directors:
  Central Monitoring, A. M. A. Smith.
  Collective Investment Schemes, M. J. Borland.
  Compliance and Enforcement, R. L. Devlin; J. M. Thomas.
  Legal Services, A. Whittaker; J. Welch.
  Marketing Policy, R. B. Ferguson.
  Markets, B. A. Muston.
  Personnel and Administration, R. J. Woodley.
  Policy, P. E. Thompson.
  Public Affairs, B. I. Powell.
  Secretary to the Board, T. E. Allen.

Advisers, J. P. Coakley; R. M. Hudson; A. Jameson; J. A. Ridley; L. A. A. Stratford.

RECOGNIZED BODIES
(as at July 1, 1991)

Self-regulating Organizations

The Financial Intermediaries, Managers and Brokers Regulatory Association Ltd (FIMBRA).
*The Investment Management Regulatory Organization Ltd (IMRO).
*The Life Assurance and Unit Trust Regulatory Organization Ltd (LAUTRO).
The Securities Association Ltd.
*These two bodies are also recognized self-regulating organizations for friendly societies.

International Securities Self-regulating Organization
(recognized by DTI)

The International Securities Market Association (ISMA).

Recognized Investment Exchanges

UK Exchanges
The Baltic Futures Exchange (BFE).
The International Petroleum Exchange of London Ltd (IPE).
The International Stock Exchange of Great Britain and the Republic of Ireland Ltd (ISE).
The London Commodity Exchange (1986) Ltd (London FOX).
The London International Financial Futures Exchange Ltd (LIFFE).
The London Metal Exchange Ltd (LME).
OM London Ltd

Overseas Exchanges (recognized by the Secretary of State for Trade and Industry)
The National Association of Securities Dealers Automated Quotations System.
Sydney Futures Exchange Ltd

Recognized Professional Bodies

The Institute of Chartered Accountants in England and Wales.
The Institute of Chartered Accountants of Scotland.
The Institute of Chartered Accountants in Ireland.
The Chartered Association of Certified Accountants.
The Institute of Actuaries.
The Insurance Brokers Registration Council.
The Law Society of England and Wales.
The Law Society of Scotland.
The Law Society of Northern Ireland.

Recognized Clearing Houses

London Commodities Clearing House Ltd (ICCH).
GAFTA Clearing House Company Ltd.

THE SECURITY SERVICE COMMISSIONER
c/o The Home Office, 50 Queen Anne's Gate,
SW1H 9AT

The Commissioner is appointed by the Prime Minister. He keeps under review the issue of warrants by the Secretary of State under the Security Service Act 1989 and is required to give the Security Service Tribunal all such assistance in discharging its functions as it may require. He is also required to submit an annual report on the discharge of his functions to the Prime Minister.
Commissioner, The Rt. Hon. Lord Justice Stuart-Smith.

SECURITY SERVICE TRIBUNAL
PO Box 18, London SE1 0TZ

The Security Service Act 1989 established a tribunal of three to five senior members of the legal profession, independent of the Government and appointed by The Queen, to investigate complaints from any person about anything which they believe the Security Service has done to them or to their property.
President, The Hon. Mr Justice Simon Brown.
Vice President, Sheriff J. McInnes, QC.
Member, Sir Richard Gaskell.

SERIOUS FRAUD OFFICE
Elm House, 10–16 Elm Street, WC1X 0BJ
[071–239 7272]

The Serious Fraud Office is an autonomous department under the superintendence of the Attorney General. Its remit is to investigate and prosecute serious and complex fraud. The scope of its powers covers England, Wales and Northern Ireland. The staff includes lawyers, accountants and other support staff; investigating teams work closely with the police.
Director, Mrs B. Mills, QC.
Deputy Director, J. Knox.

OFFICE OF THE SOCIAL FUND COMMISSIONER
New Court, Carey Street, WC2A 2LS
[071–412 1503]
4th Floor, Centre City Podium, 5 Hill Street,
Birmingham B5 4UB
[021–631 4000]

The Social Fund Commissioner is appointed by the Secretary of State for Social Security. The Commissioner appoints Social Fund Inspectors, who provide an independent review of decisions made by Social Fund Officers in the Benefits Agency of the Department of Social Security.
Social Fund Commissioner, Mrs R. Mackworth.

DEPARTMENT OF SOCIAL SECURITY
Richmond House, 79 Whitehall, SW1A 2NS
[071-210 3000]

The Department of Social Security is responsible for the provision of social security services in England, Wales and Scotland.
(For **Salaries**, *see* page 293)

Secretary of State for Social Security, THE RT. HON. ANTONY NEWTON, OBE, MP.
  Private Secretary, A. Woods.
  Special Adviser, I. Stewart.

Parliamentary Private Secretary, J. Marshall, MP.
Minister of State, RT. HON. NICHOLAS SCOTT, MBE, MP. (*Social Security and Disabled People*).
Private Secretary, K. Sadler.
Parliamentary Private Secretary, R. Hughes, MP.
Parliamentary Under Secretary of State (*Lords*), THE LORD HENLEY.
Private Secretary, T. Lowe.
Parliamentary Under Secretaries of State (*Commons*), ANN WIDDECOMBE, MP; MICHAEL JACK, MP.
Private Secretary, Ms U. Dudley.
Spokesman, House of Lords, THE VISCOUNT ASTOR.
Permanent Secretary (G1), Sir Michael Partridge, KCB.
Private Secretary, Mrs V. Andrews.

SOCIAL SECURITY OPERATIONS GROUP

Deputy Secretary (G2), N. L. J. Montagu.

BENEFITS AGENCY
Euston Tower, 286 Euston Road, NW1 3DN
[071-388 1188]

(An executive agency within the Department of Social Security.)
Chief Executive (G2), M Bichard.
Private Secretary, S. G. Appleton.
Directors (G3), Mrs M. A. Robinson (*policy and planning*); D. Riggs (*finance*); G. Bardwell (*personnel*).

Benefits Agency Territories

Scotland/Northern England, Sandyford House, Archbold Terrace, Newcastle upon Tyne NE2 1AA.—*Director (G3)*, A. J. Laurance.
Southern England, Olympic House, Olympic Way, Wembley, Middx. HA9 0DL.—*Director (G3)*, I. Magee.
Wales/Central England, Five Ways Tower, Frederick Road, Edgbaston, Birmingham B15 1ST.—*Director (G3)*, J. T. Green.

Benefits Agency Medical Services

Director (G3), Dr W. R. O. Eggington.
Principal Medical Officers, Dr K. A. Cameron; Dr P. Castaldi; Dr T. J. G. Phillips; Dr D. R. Findlay.

Information Technology Services Agency

(An executive agency within the Department of Social Security.)
Chief Executive, F. J. Kenworthy.
Deputy Chief Executive, P. T. F. Dunn.
Directors, A. Smith; Ms A. Cleveland; K. Caldwell; G. McCorkell; S. Williams; J. Y. Marshall.
Non-Executive Directors, J. M. Bankier, CBE; G. Beavan.

Contributions Agency

(An executive agency within the Department of Social Security.)
Chief Executive (G5), Miss A. Chant.

SOCIAL SECURITY POLICY GROUP

Deputy Secretary (G2), R. A. Birch.

Social Security Division A

Under Secretary (G3), Mrs S. Maunsell.
Assistant Secretaries (G5), Mrs U. Brennan; A. H. Baker; J. W. White.

Social Security Division B

Under Secretary (G3), Miss M. Pierson.
Assistant Secretaries (G5), D. Allsop; A. Stott; Miss S. Fraenkel.

Social Security Division C

Under Secretary (G3), D. J. Clarke.
Assistant Secretaries (G5), S. Hewitt; Mrs C. Souter; Miss P. Barnett.
Senior Principal (G6), A. Thompson.

Social Security Division D

Under Secretary (G3), B. J. Ellis.
Assistant Secretaries (G5), M. Street; P. Tansley; A. Herscovitch.
Senior Principal (G6), I. Williams.

Information Division

Head of Information (G5), S. Reardon.
Press Officer (G7), J. Bretherton.

SOCIAL SECURITY ADVISORY COMMITTEE
New Court, Carey Street, WC2A 2LS
[071-972 1507]

The Social Security Advisory Committee (SSAC) was established by the Social Security Act 1980 to advise the Secretary of State for Social Security and the Department of Health and Social Services for Northern Ireland on all Social Security matters except those relating to benefits for industrial injuries and diseases and occupational pensions. The Social Security Housing Benefit Act 1982 added housing benefit to the Committee's responsibilities.
Chairman, P. M. Barclay, CBE.
Members, Mrs J. Anelay, OBE; Rev. G. H. Good, OBE; H. Hodge; P. F. Naish; Hon. Mrs R. H. P. Price; Lady Scott, CBE; A. M. Sealey; Dr A. V. Stokes, OBE; Prof. Olive Stevenson; O. Tudor; R. G. Wendt; D. I. Willetts.
Secretary, L. C. Smith.

SPORTS COUNCIL
16 Upper Woburn Place, WC1H 0QP
[071-388 1277]

The Sports Council, created under Royal Charter, promotes the development of sport and fosters the provision of facilities for sport and recreation in Great Britain.
Chairman, P. G. Yarranton.

HMSO (HER MAJESTY'S STATIONERY OFFICE)
St Crispins, Duke Street, Norwich NR3 1PD
[0603-622211]

HMSO (Her Majesty's Stationery Office) was established in 1786 and is the government executive agency that provides printing, binding and business supplies to government departments and publicly funded organizations. HMSO is also the Government's publisher and has bookshops for the sale of government publications in six major cities, as well as appointed agents in other cities. HMSO obtains most of its supplies and printing from commercial sources by competitive tender, apart from about 20 per cent of its printing requirement, such as Hansard and Bills and Acts of Parliament, which are produced in its own printing works. HMSO is a self-financing government trading fund and competes for its business with other commercial suppliers.
(For *Salaries*, *see* page 293)

Controller and Chief Executive, P. I. Freeman.
Executive Assistant, Mrs J. B. Ward.
Deputy Chief Executive, M. D. Lynn.
Director General of Corporate Services, P. J. Macdonald.

Heads of Divisions

Publications, C. J. Penn.
Business Supplies, C. N. Southgate.
Production, D. G. Forbes.
Print Procurement, B. Ekers.
Corporate Development, V. G. Bell.
Finance, A. M. Cole.
Personnel Services, A. J. Davies.
Industrial Personnel, A. Mackie.
Marketing, C. E. Harrold.
Information Technology, D. C. Kerry.
Quality and Innovation, J. R. Eveson.

Birmingham

Bookshop: 258 Broad Street, Birmingham B1 2HE.

Bristol

Ashton Vale Road, Bristol BS3 2HN

Bookshop: Southey House, Wine Street, Bristol BS1 2BH.

London

Publications Centre: 51 Nine Elms Lane, SW8 5DR.
Bookshop: 49 High Holborn, WC1V 6HB.

Manchester

Broadway, Chadderton, Oldham, Lancs. OL9 9QH
Bookshop: 9–21 Princess Street, Manchester M60 8AS.

Scotland

Bankhead Avenue, Edinburgh EH11 4AB
Director Edinburgh, G. W. Bedford.
Bookshop: 71 Lothian Road, Edinburgh EH3 9AZ.

Northern Ireland

IDB House, Chichester Street, Belfast BT1 4PS

Director Belfast, Miss V. J. Wilson, OBE.
Retail and Trade Bookshop: 80 Chichester Street, Belfast BT1 4JY.

STUDENT LOANS COMPANY LTD
100 Bothwell Street, Glasgow G2 7JD
[041-306 2000]

The Company was established on July 5, 1989. It administers the student loans scheme on behalf of the Government.
Managing Director, R. J. Harrison.

OFFICE OF TELECOMMUNICATIONS
Export House, 50 Ludgate Hill, EC4M 7JJ
[071–822 1600]

The Office of Telecommunications (Oftel) is a non-ministerial government department which is responsible for supervising telecommunications activities in the UK. Its principal functions are to ensure that holders of telecommunications licences comply with their licence conditions; to maintain and promote effective competition in telecommunications; and to promote, in respect of prices, quality and variety the interests of consumers, purchasers and other users of telecommunication services and apparatus.

The Director General has powers to deal with anti-competitive practices and monopoly situations. He also has a duty to consider all reasonable complaints and representations about telecommunication apparatus and services.

Director General, Prof. Sir Brian Carsberg.
Deputy Director General, W. R. B. Wigglesworth.
Director of PTO Licensing, G. P. Knight.
Director of Consumer and International Affairs, D. G. Hyde.
Head of Information, D. C. Redding.

TOURIST BOARDS

The English Tourist Board, the Scottish Tourist Board, the Wales Tourist Board and the Northern Ireland Tourist Board are responsible for developing and marketing the tourist industry in their respective countries. The Boards' main objectives are to promote holidays and to encourage the provision and improvement of tourist amenities.

English Tourist Board, Thames Tower, Black's Road, W6 9EL (081–846 9000).–*Chief Executive*, J. East.

Scottish Tourist Board, 23 Ravelston Terrace, Edinburgh EH4 3EU (031–332 2433).–*Chief Executive*, T. M. Band.

Wales Tourist Board, Brunel House, 2 Fitzalan Road, Cardiff CF2 1UY (0222–499909).–*Chief Executive*, P. Loveluck.

Northern Ireland Tourist Board, River House, 48 High Street, Belfast BT1 2DS (0232-235906).–*Chief Executive*, B. O'Harra.

DEPARTMENT OF TRADE AND INDUSTRY
Ashdown House, 123 Victoria Street, SW1E 6RB
[071–215 5000]
[*Enterprise Initiative:* 0800–500200]
[*Single European Market:* 081–200 1992]
[*Environmental Enquiries:* 0800-585794]

The Department is responsible for:
(a) international trade policy, including the promotion of UK trade interests in the European Community, GATT, OECD, UNCTAD and other international organizations.

(b) the promotion of UK exports and assistance to exporters.

(c) policy in relation to industry and commerce, including the promotion of enterprise, open markets and measures to help industry strengthen its competitiveness; regional policy and regional industrial assistance (some of this applying only to England); and policy in relation to British Shipbuilders and the Post Office.

(d) competition policy and consumer protection, including relations with the Office of Fair Trading, the Office of Telecommunications and the Monopolies and Mergers Commission; co-ordination of policy on deregulation.

(e) policy on science and technology and research and development matters, space, standards, quality and design and the following executive agencies: the Laboratory of the Government Chemist; the National Engineering Laboratory; the National Physical Laboratory; the National Weights and Measures Laboratory; Warren Springs Laboratory.

(f) company legislation and Companies House executive agency; the Insolvency Service executive agency; the regulation of financial services and the insurance industries; the Radiocommunications Agency (executive agency); and the Patent Office executive agency.

(For **Salaries**, *see* page 293).

Secretary of State for Trade and Industry and President of the Board of Trade, THE RT. HON. PETER LILLEY, MP.
Principal Private Secretary, M. Stanley.
Private Secretaries, S. Speed; Ms S. Bishop.
Special Advisers, J. Mayhew; L. Anisfeld.
Parliamentary Private Secretary, J. Arbuthnot, MP.
Minister for Trade, THE HON. TIMOTHY SAINSBURY, MP.
Private Secretary, Ms J. Knight.
Parliamentary Private Secretary, D. Fishburn, MP.
Minister for Corporate Affairs, JOHN REDWOOD, MP.

Private Secretary, Mrs H. Dunstan.
Parliamentary Private Secretary, D. Evans, MP.
Parliamentary Under Secretary of State for Industry and Consumer Affairs, EDWARD LEIGH, MP.
Principal Private Secretary, C. Thresh.
Parliamentary Under Secretary of State for Industry and Technology and Spokesman in the House of Lords, THE LORD REAY.
Private Secretary, W. Jones.
British Overseas Trade Board Chairman, Sir Derek Hornby.
Permanent Secretary (G1), Sir Peter Gregson, KCB.
Private Secretary, J. Foggo.
Deputy Secretaries (G2), Dr R. F. Coleman (*Chief Engineer and Scientist*); R. Mountfield, CB; C. W. Roberts, CB; R. Williams, CB (*Regional Organization*); A. Lane, CB; G. A. Hosker, CB, QC (*The Solicitor*); W. M. Knighton, CB.
Parliamentary Clerk, T. Williams.

LINE DIVISION ORGANIZATION

Business Task Forces Division 1
151 Buckingham Palace Road, SW1W 9SS
[071–215 5000]

Under Secretary (G3), R. W. Simpson.
Heads of Branch (G5), C. L Jackson; M. R. Cohen; Miss S. E. Harding; B. D. Winkett.

Business Task Forces Division 2
151 Buckingham Palace Road, SW1W 9SS
[071–215 5000]

Under Secretary (G3), A. J. Nieduszynski.
Heads of Branch (G5), C. E. Blundell; C. L. Bridge; Dr G. T. Coleman; (*G6*), M. O. Ralph.

Companies Division
10–18 Victoria Street, SW1H 0NN
[071–215 5000]

Under Secretary (G3), Mrs S. E. Brown.
Heads of Branch (G5), M. J. C. Butcher; C. W. Johnston; J. Healey; D. Marsh.
Grade 6, F. C. Jenkins.

Companies House
Companies House, Crown Way, Cardiff
CF4 3UZ
[0222-388588]

(An executive agency of the Department of Trade and Industry.)
Registrar of Companies for England and Wales (G4), D. Durham.
London Search Room, 55–71 City Road, EC1Y 1BB
[071–253 9393]

102 George Street, Edinburgh EH2 3DJ
[031–225 5774]
Registrar for Scotland, J. D. Leithead.

Competition Policy Division
Ashdown House, 123 Victoria Street, SW1E 6RB
[071–215 5000]

Under Secretary (G3), Dr C. E. D. Bell.
Heads of Branch (G5), G. C. Riggs; Mrs A. Walker.

Consumer Affairs Division
10–18 Victoria Street, SW1H 0NN
[071–215 5000]

Under Secretary (G3), C. T. Newton, CB.
Heads of Branch (G5), D. Jones; M. A. R. Lunn; M. Oldham; D. W. Hellings.

Deregulation Unit
Ashdown House, 123 Victoria Street, SW1E 6RB
[071–215 5000]

Director (G3), J. A. Cooke.
Heads of Branch (G5), I. Freeman; R. Allpress.

Enterprise Initiative Division
Kingsgate House, 66–74 Victoria Street,
SW1E 6SW
[071–215 5000]

Under Secretary (G3), A. R. Titchener.
Heads of Branches (G5), H. P. Brown; M. Garrod; T. Roberts; Mrs E. Ryle.

External European Policy Division
Ashdown House, 123 Victoria Street, SW1E 6RB
[071–215 5000]

Under Secretary (G3), T. Muir.
Heads of Branch (G5), M. D. C. Johnson; E. Allen; S. J. Bowen.

Financial Services Division
10–18 Victoria Street, SW1H 0NN
[071–215 5000]

Under Secretary (G3), W. B. Willott.
Heads of Branch (G5), Dr J. P. Compton; P. Loughead; Miss R. M. Thompson.

The Insolvency Service
Bridge Place, 88–89 Eccleston Square, SW1V 1PT
[071–215 5000]

(An executive agency of the Department of Trade and Industry.)
Inspector General of the Insolvency Service and Chief Executive, P. R. Joyce.
Deputy Inspectors General, D. J. Flynn; J. R. Donnison.

Information Technology Division
151 Buckingham Palace Road, SW1W 9SS
[071–215 5000]

Director (G3), Dr K. C. Shotton.
Directors (G5), R. C. Louth; B. L. Nuttall; J. T. Cast; Prof. J. N. Buxton; J. P. Hobday; H. J. Ivey.

British National Space Centre
Dean Bradley House, Horseferry Road, SW1P 2AG
[071–276 2688]

Director General (G2), A. J. Pryor.
Deputy Director General, J. S. Shrimplin.
Heads of Branch (G5), Dr J. E. Harries; Dr R. Jude; K. Inglis; (*G6*), Dr G. W. D. Findlay; Dr D. Williams; J. Thomas.

Inner Cities Unit
Ashdown House, 123 Victoria Street, SW1E 6RB
[071–215 5000]

Head of Unit (G4), M. K. O'Shea.
Deputy Head of Unit (G5), R. Palmer.

Insurance Division
10–18 Victoria Street, SW1H 0NN
[071–215 5000]

Under Secretary (G3), A. C. Russell.
Heads of Branch (G5), M. G. Roberts; Ms S. Seymour; Miss A. Lambert; Miss V. Evans.

Internal European Policy Division
Ashdown House, 123 Victoria Street, SW1E 6RB
[071–215 5000]

Under Secretary (G3), N. R. Thornton.
Heads of Branch (G5), Dr A. W. C. Keddie; D. I. Richardson; W. L. Stow.

Investment, Development and Accountancy Services Division
Kingsgate House, 66–74 Victoria Street,
SW1E 6SW
[071–215 5000]

Director (G3), P. M. S. Corley.
Directors, IDU (G3), C. R. Jenkins; Mrs D. A. King; C. Crombie.

Heads of Branch (G5), R. H. S. Wells; J. C. S. Priston; K. Holt; Mrs A. Taylor; Dr H. N. M. Stewart; C. Blundell; *(G6),* K. R. Timmins.

Joint Directorate (FCO/DTI)
Kingsgate House, 66–74 Victoria Street, SW1E 6SW
[071-215 5000]

Under Secretary (G3), R. O. Miles, CMG.

Manufacturing Technology Division
151 Buckingham Palace Road, SW1W 9SS
[071–215 5000]

Under Secretary (G3), J. E. Cammell.
Heads of Branch (G5), J. Octon; B. N. Steele; A. Berry; Dr K. Poulter; R. King.

Overseas Trade Divisions
Ashdown House, 123 Victoria Street, SW1E 6RB
[071–215 5000]

Division 1 (*Projects and Export Policy*)

Under Secretary (G3), C. C. W. Adams.
Heads of Branch (G5), R. I. Rogers; P. Casey; N. Worman; A. P. Vinall.

Division 2
(*North America, NE and SE Asia, China, Hong Kong and Export Licensing Operation*)

Under Secretary (G3), R. J. Meadway.
Heads of Branch (G5), J. V. Hagestadt; D. E. Love; M. V. Coolican.

Division 3

Under Secretary (G3), P. Bryant.
Head of Export Promotion Policy Unit (G5), D. Saunders.
Head of Exports to Europe Branch (G5), K. D. Levinson.
Head of Export Data Branch (G6), A. Reynolds.
Head of Fairs and Promotions Branch (G5), G. J. Bradshaw.
Director of Eastern Europe Branch (G4), K. W. N. George, CBE.
Head of Expo 92 Branch (G5), B. D. Avery.

Division 4

Under Secretary (G3), M. M. Baker.
Head of Middle East and North Africa Branch (G5), M. G. Petter.
Head of Mexico, Central America, Caribbean, South America and Australasia Branch (G5), J. M. Bowder.
Head of Sub-Saharan Africa and South Asia Branch (G5), G. Berg.

Research and Technology Policy Division
151 Buckingham Palace Road, SW1W 9SS
[071–215 5000]

Under Secretary (G3), Dr C. Hicks.
Heads of Branch (G5), Mrs M. Bloom; J. H. Chapman; R. Foster; J. D. Howarth.

Research Establishment Council
Chairman, Dr F. Coleman, CB.

National Physical Laboratory
Teddington, Middx. TW11 0LW
[081–977 3222]

(An executive agency of the Department of Trade and Industry.)
Director (G3), Dr P. B. Clapham.

Laboratory of the Government Chemist
Queens Road, Teddington, Middx. TW11 0LY
[081–943 7000]

(An executive agency of the Department of Trade and Industry.)
Government Chemist (G3), Dr R. Worswick.

National Engineering Laboratory
East Kilbride, Glasgow G75 0QU
[03552–20222]

(An executive agency of the Department of Trade and Industry.)
Chief Executive (G3), W. Edgar.

Warren Spring Laboratory
Gunnels Wood Road, Stevenage, Herts SG1 2BX
[0438–741122]

(An executive agency of the Department of Trade and Industry.)
Director (G3), Dr J. S. S. Reay.

National Weights and Measures Laboratory
Stanton Avenue, Teddington, Middx. TW11 0JZ
[081–943 7272]

(An executive agency of the Department of Trade and Industry.)
Chief Executive (G5), S. Bennett.

Radiocommunications Agency
Waterloo Bridge House, Waterloo Road, SE1 8UA
[071–215 5000]

(An executive agency of the Department of Trade and Industry.)
Chief Executive (G3), M. J. Michell.
Heads of Branch (G5), M. Goddard; S. Spivey; R. A. Bedford; D. Reed; R. M. Skiffins; *(G6)* B. A. Maxwell.

Telecommunications and Posts Division
151 Buckingham Palace Road, SW1W 9SS
[071–215 5000]

Under Secretary (G3), P. Salvidge.
Grade 4, S. R. Temple.
Heads of Branch (G5), J. Phillips; D. D. Sibbick; P. Smith; S. Pride.

Patent Office and Industrial Property and Copyright Department
see entry on p. 351

SERVICE DIVISION ORGANIZATION

Central Unit
Ashdown House, 123 Victoria Street, SW1E 6RB
[071–215 5000]

Head of Unit (G3), J. A. Cooke.
Grade 5, J. Green.

Economics, Market Intelligence and Statistics Division
Ashdown House, 123 Victoria Street, SW1E 6RB
[071–215 5000]

Chief Economic Adviser (G3), D. R. Coates.
Head of Industrial and Regional Economics (G4), Dr J. A. S. Robertson.
Heads of Branch (G5), Dr D. S. Higham; P. J. Goate; B. M. Nonhebel; J. M. Barber; M. S. Bradbury; Dr R. Van Slooten; P. G. Waller; Mrs M. Howarth.

Finance and Resource Management Division
Ashdown House, 123 Victoria Street, SW1E 6RB
[071–215 5000]

Under Secretary (G3), A. Whiting.
Heads of Branch (G5), D. M. Hoddinott; D. T. Smith.

Accounts Branch
PO Box 100, Government Buildings, Cardiff Road, Newport, Gwent NP9 1ZA
[0633–810636]

Director of Accounts, D. M. Hoddinott.

Internal Audit
151 Buckingham Palace Road, SW1W 9SS
[071–215 5000]

Head of Internal Audit (G5), A. C. Elkington.

Information Division
Ashdown House, 123 Victoria Street, SW1E 6RB
[071–215 5000]

Head of Information (G4), Ms J. M. Caines.
Head of News (G6), Miss A. MacLean.

Publicity
Bridge Place, 88–89 Eccleston Square, SW1V 1PT
[071-215 5000]

Grade 5, S. Lyle-Smythe.

Investigation Division
Ashdown House, 123 Victoria Street, SW1E 6RB
[071–215 5000]

Head of Branch (G3), H. V. B. Brown.
Head of Legal Services (G4), Mrs T. J. Dunstan.
Inspector of Companies, G. Harp.
Heads of Branch (G5), B. J. Welch; R. Burns; D. Fitzgerald; M. Osborne; A. Mier; R. Burton.

Management Services and Manpower Division
Kingsgate House, 66–74 Victoria Street, SW1E 6SW
[071–215 5000]

Under Secretary (G3), R. M. Rumbelow.
Director of Administrative Information Technology Services (G4), R. J. Wheeler.
Heads of Branch (G5), Miss D. Gane; K. M. Long.

Personnel Management Division
Allington Towers,
19 Allington Street, SW1E 5EB
[071–215 5000]

Under Secretary (G3), A. C. Hutton.
Heads of Branch (G5), J. P. Spencer; D. W. F. Johnson; A. Mantle.

Solicitor's Office
10–18 Victoria Street, SW1H 0NN
[071–215 5000]

The Solicitor (G2), G. A Hosker, CB, QC.
Grade 3, P. H. Bovey; C. S. Kerse; J. M. Stanley.
Assistant Solicitors (G5), H. D. M. Bailey; Mrs N. M. P. Chappell; R. D. Fayers; Miss P. A. E. Granados; R. D. B. Green; R. Higgins, CBE; D. S. Mangat; I. K. Mathers; S. Morgan; Miss K. Morton; Miss E. N. O'Flynn; S. A. Parker; Miss J. Richardson; J. W. Roberts; Miss J. V. Stokes; A. M. Susman; Miss V. C. Woodbridge.

BRITISH OVERSEAS TRADE BOARD
Kingsgate House, 66–74 Victoria Street, SW1E 6SW
[071–215 5000]

President, The Secretary of State for Trade and Industry.
Chairman, Sir Derek Hornby.
Vice-Chairman, HRH The Duke of Kent, KG, GCMG, GCVO.
Members, J. M. Banham; N. P. Bayne, CMG; C. J. Bull; R. Burman; A. B. Cleaver; T. P. Frost; A. G. Gormly; Dr A. Hayes; The Earl of Limerick, KBE; R. O. Miles, CMG; H. B. G. Montgomery; J. W. Parsons, CBE; M. S. Perry, CBE; C. W. Roberts, CB; M. G. Stephens; B. D. Taylor.
Chief Executive, D. M. Dell, CB.
Secretary (G5), D. Saunders.

REGIONAL OFFICES
DTI North East, Stanegate House, 2 Groat Market, Newcastle upon Tyne NE1 1YN. (091–232 4722).—*Regional Director (G3)*, P. A. Denham; *Regional Industrial Adviser (G3)*, J. W. Armstrong.

DTI North West, Sunley Tower, Piccadilly Plaza, Manchester M1 4BA. (061–236 2171).—*Regional Director (G3)*, J. H. Pownall.

DTI Yorkshire and Humberside, 25 Queen Street, Leeds LS1 2TW. (0532 443171).—*Regional Director (G3)*, E. Wright.

DTI East Midlands, Severns House, 20 Middle Pavement, Nottingham NG1 7DW. (0602 506181).—*Regional Director (G5)*, R. M. Anderson.

DTI West Midlands, 77 Paradise Circus, Queensway, Birmingham B1 2DT. (021–212 5000).—*Regional Director (G3)*, S. G. Linstead.

DTI East, Westbrook Centre, Milton Road, Cambridge CB4 1YG. (0223–461939).—*Regional Director (G5)*, W. J. Hall; *Deputy Regional Director (G6)*, R. D. Dennis.

DTI South East, Bridge Place, 88–89 Eccleston Square, SW1V 1PT. (071–215 5000).—*Regional Director (G5)*, I. Jones; *Deputy Regional Director (G6)*, Dr A. Thorpe.

DTI South West, The Pithay, Bristol BS1 2PB. (0272–272666).—*Regional Director (G5)*, D. B. Lodge; *Deputy Regional Directors (G6)*, D. H. Johnson; P. J. Adkin.

DEPARTMENT OF TRANSPORT
2 Marsham Street, SW1P 3EB
[071–276 3000]

The Department of Transport is responsible for land, sea and air transport, including sponsorship of the rail and bus industries; airports; domestic and international civil aviation; shipping and the ports industry; navigational lights, pilotage, HM Coastguard and marine pollution; motorways and other trunk roads; oversight of road transport including vehicle standards, registration and licensing, driver testing and licensing, bus and road freight licensing, regulation of taxis and private hire cars, road safety; and oversight of local authorities transport planning including payment of Transport Supplementary Grant.

(For **Salaries**, *see* page 293).

Secretary of State for Transport, THE RT. HON. MALCOLM RIFKIND, QC, MP.
  Private Secretary, S. C. Whiteley.
  Special Adviser, P. Miller; Prof. B. Hoskins.
  Parliamentary Private Secretary, H. Bellingham, MP.
Minister of State for Public Transport, ROGER FREEMAN, MP.
  Private Secretary, Ms S. M. Watkin.
  Parliamentary Private Secretary, G. Jones, MP.
Minister of State for Aviation, THE LORD BRABAZON OF TARA.
  Private Secretary, Ms P. J. Rennie.
Parliamentary Under Secretaries, CHRISTOPHER CHOPE, OBE, MP (*Road and Traffic*); PATRICK McLOUGHLIN, MP (*Aviation and Shipping*).
  Private Secretaries, M. H. Capstick; S. L. J. Buck.
  Parliamentary Private Secretary to Parliamentary Under Secretaries, G. Jones, MP.
Parliamentary Clerk, Mrs L. C. Jones.
Permanent Under Secretary of State (G1), A. P. Brown.
  Private Secretary, S. Ghagan.

Information
Director of Information (G5), Miss G. P. Samuel.

PUBLIC TRANSPORT AND RESEARCH
Deputy Secretary (G2), E. B. C. Osmotherly.

Railways
Under Secretary (G3), J. R. Coates.
Heads of Division (G5), S. K. Reeves; R. S. Peal; A. T. Baker; J. R. Fells; A. Burchell; B. Wadsworth.

Public Transport

Under Secretary (G3), R. E. Clarke.
Heads of Division (G5), Miss S. J. Lambert; M. N. Lambirth; G. J. Skinner.

Transport and Road Research Laboratory

Director (G3), D. F. Cornelius.
Deputy Director (G4), D. I. Robertson.
Grade 5, P. H. Bly; G. Maycock; J. Porter; Dr G. P. Tilly; Dr R. M. Kimber.
Grade 6, J. S. Yerrell; G. F. Salt.

Science and Research Policy and Programmes

Grade 5, vacant.

ESTABLISHMENT AND FINANCE OFFICER
2 Marsham Street, SW1 3EB

Principal Establishment and Finance Officer (G2), J. W. S. Dempster.

Personnel
Lambeth Bridge House, SE1 7SB
[071–238 3000]

Director of Personnel (G3), R. A. Allan.
Grade 5, P. Stringfellow; Mrs M. Clare; R. T. Bishop.
Chief Welfare Officer (G7), R. J. Lintern.
Grade 6, K. A. Wyatt; K. Wight; C. Payne; I. R. Heawood.
Chief Librarian (G6), P. Kirwan.

Finance

Under Secretary (G3), H. M. G. Stevens.
Heads of Division (G5), Mrs G. M. Ashmore; D. M. Smith; P. G. Davies; M. J. Fuhr; J. S. Parker; P. G. Collis; H. C. S. Derwent.
Accounting Adviser (G4), A. R. Allum.

Internal Audit

Head of Branch (G6), P. Houston.

Freight

Under Secretary (G3), D. J. Lyness.
Grade 5, L. Moyle.
Grade 6, J. Winder; D. J. Blackman.

Traffic Area Offices
Traffic Commissioners and Licensing Authorities

Eastern (Nottingham and Cambridge), Brig. C. M. Boyd.
North Eastern (Newcastle upon Tyne and Leeds), F. Whalley.
North Western (Manchester), M. S. Albu.
Scottish (Edinburgh), K. R. Waterworth.
South Eastern and Metropolitan (Eastbourne), Brig. M. H. Turner.
West Midlands (Birmingham), J. M. C. Pugh.
Western (Bristol), Air Vice-Marshal R. G. Ashford, CBE.
South Wales (Cardiff), J. M. C. Pugh.

Economics

Chief Economic Adviser (G3), M. J. Spackman.
Grade 5, T. E. Worsley; M. C. Mann.

Statistics

Under Secretary (G3), D. W. Flaxen.
Grade 5, Miss B. J. Wood; H. Collings; G. R. Emes; R. P. Donachie.

Vehicle Inspectorate Executive Agency

Chief Executive (G4), R. J. Oliver.
Deputy Chief Executive (G5), J. A. T. David.
Director of Administration (G6), K. Walton.

Driving Standards Executive Agency

Chief Executive (G5), Dr C. M. Woodman.

Transport Policy Unit

Grade 5, A. J. Nichols.
Consultant Professor, B. J. Hopkins.

Driver and Vehicle Licensing Executive Agency

Director (G3), S. R. Curtis.
Deputy Director (G4), M. A. Robinson.
Heads of Division (G5), R. J. Verge; T. J. Horton; Dr R. J. M. Irvine; J. K. Griffiths.
Grade 6, P. G. Desborough.

HIGHWAYS, SAFETY AND TRAFFIC

Deputy Secretary (G2), D. Holmes, CB.

Road Programme

Director (G3), A. Whitfield.

Highways Programme Support Services

Director (G4), D. A. Holland.
Heads of Division (G5), Ms A. Munro; J. B. W. Robins; M. R. Nevard.
Grade 7, Mrs G. M. Holt.

Motorway Widening Unit

Director (G4), Dr J. H. Denning.
Grade 5, N. E. Firkins.
Grade 6, D. E. Oddy.

Construction Programme Division

Eastern.—Director (G4), A. J. Homer; *G5,* J. P. Boud.
North West.—Director (G4), G. E. Hancock; *G5,* E. A. Sherwin.
South East.—Director (G4), B. A. Sperring; *G5,* M. G. Quinn.
South West.—Director (G4), W. E. Gallagher; *G5,* G. D. Rowe.
West Midlands.—Director (G4), vacant; *G5,* J. M. Bradley.
Yorkshire and Humberside.—Director (G5), D. York.

Network Management and Construction

East Midlands.—Director (G5), S. Rose.
Northern.—Director (G5), D. W. Ward.

Network Management and Maintenance

Under Secretary (G3), B. J. Billington.
Heads of Division (G5), P. R. Smith; N. T. Rees; A. S. D. Whybrow; R. S. Wilson.

Highways Policy and Resources

Grade 3, P. Wood.
Grade 5, B. R. A. Blaxall; P. J. Coby; D. J. Kershaw; P. E. Pickering; Miss P. M. Williams.

Engineering Policy

Director and Chief Highway Engineer (G3), T. A. Rochester.
Grade 5, P. H. Dawe; J. A. Kerman; N. S. Organ.

Road and Vehicle Safety

Under Secretary (G3), R. Bird.
Heads of Division (G5), D. R. Instone; I. R. Jordan; Dr P. H. Martin.

Chief Mechanical Engineer's Office

Director and Chief Mechanical Engineer (G4), E. Dunn.

Vehicle Certification Executive Agency

Chief Executive (G5), D. W. Harvey.
Departmental Medical Adviser (G4), Dr J. F. Taylor, CBE.
Head of Medical Advisory Board (G5), Dr R. J. M. Irvine.

London Region

Under Secretary (G3), I. Yass.
Grade 4, P. R. Smethurst; R. M. C. Edridge.
Heads of Division (G5), R. J. Mance; P. E. Butler; Dr S. Chatterjee.

REGIONAL OFFICES

West Midlands, Birmingham.—*Regional Director (G3)*, D. R. Ritchie; *Director, Network Management (G5)*, W. S. C. Wadrup.

Yorkshire and Humberside, Leeds.—*Regional Director (G3)*, J. P. Henry; *Director, Network Management (G5)*, J. R. Wilkins.

North West, Manchester.—*Regional Director (G3)*, D. C. Renshaw; *Director, Network Management (G5)*, M. M. Niven.

Northern, Newcastle upon Tyne.—*Regional Director (G3)*, P. A. Shaw; *Director, Network Management and Construction (G5)*, D. W. Ward.

South West, Bristol.—*Regional Director (G3)*, Ms E. A. Hopkins; *Director, Network Management (G5)*, A. P. Moss.

East Midlands, Nottingham.—*Regional Director (G4)*, D. J. Morrison; *Director Network Management and Construction (G5)*, S. Rose.

South East, London.—*Regional Director (G3)*, J. W. Fellows; *Director, Network Management (G5)*, A. D. Rowland.

Eastern, London.—*Regional Director (G3)*, P. F. Emms; *Director, Network Management (G5)*, P. E. Nutt.

AVIATION, SHIPPING AND INTERNATIONAL

Deputy Secretary (G2), G. R. Sunderland, CB.

Civil Aviation Policy Directorate

Under Secretary (G3), A. J. Goldman.
Grade 5, D. S. Evans; E. C. Neve.
Grade 6, C. C. Thame.

International Aviation Directorate

Under Secretary (G3), D. C. Moss.
Heads of Division (G5), D. B. Cooke; M. L. Fielder; R. S. Balme; F. A. Neal.

Air Accidents Investigation Branch

Chief Inspector of Air Accidents (G4), K. P. R. Smart.
Grade 5, R. C. Mckinlay.

International Transport Directorate

Under Secretary (G3), J. D. Henes.
Grade 5, P. D. Burgess; A. J. Hunt.

Channel Tunnel Safety Unit

Grade 3, A. B. Martin.

Shipping Policy, Emergencies and Security Directorate

Under Secretary (G3), D. J. Rowlands, CB.
Heads of Division (G5), P. Kitchen; A. Fortnam; H. Ditmas; J. Jack, MBE.
Grade 7, A. Crosswell.

Marine Directorate

Under Secretary (G3), H. B. Wenban-Smith.
Heads of Division (G5), Mrs A. M. Moss; M. W. Jackson.

Marine Emergency Operations and Marine Pollution Control Unit

Director (G4), C. J. Harris.
Chief Coastguard (G5), Cdr. D. T. Ascona, RN (ret.).
Surveyor General (G4), G. Thompson.
Grade 5, P. J. Hambling; W. A. Graham.

Marine Accidents Investigation Branch

Chief Inspector of Marine Accidents (G5), Capt. P. B. Marriott.

THE TREASURY
Parliament Street, SW1P 3AG
[071–233 3000]

The Office of the Lord High Treasurer has been continuously in commission for well over 200 years. The Lord High Commissioners of HM Treasury consist of the First Lord of the Treasury (who is also the Prime Minister), the Chancellor of the Exchequer and five junior Lords. This Board of Commissioners is assisted at present by the Chief Secretary, a Parliamentary Secretary who is also the government Chief Whip, a Financial Secretary, an Economic Secretary, a Minister of State, and the Permanent Secretary.

The Prime Minister and First Lord is not primarily concerned in the day-to-day aspects of Treasury business. The junior lords are government whips in the House of Commons. The management of the Treasury devolves upon the Chancellor of the Exchequer and, under him, the Chief Secretary, the Financial Secretary, the Economic Secretary and the Paymaster General.

The Chief Secretary is responsible for the control of public expenditure; nationalized industry pay; and efficiency in the public sector.

The Financial Secretary discharges the traditional responsibility of the Treasury for the largely formal procedure for the voting of funds by Parliament. He also has responsibility for other parliamentary financial business; Inland Revenue duties and taxes; privatization policy; competition and deregulation policy; and European Community business.

The Minister of State is responsible for Customs and Excise duties and taxes; Civil Service pay; management and industrial relations; procurement policy; environment; women's issues; charities; the legislative programme; and ministerial correspondence.

The Economic Secretary has responsibility for monetary policy; the Royal Mint; the financial system (including banks, building societies and other financial institutions); HMSO, the Central Office of Information, the Government Actuary's Department, and the Civil Service catering organization; international financial business (other than EC); the Central Computer and Telecommunications Agency; the North Sea fiscal regime; the Valuation Office; the Department for National Savings; the Registry of Friendly Societies; the National Loans Office; industrial casework; and the Treasury Bulletin and Economic Briefing.

The Paymaster General's Office acts as a clearing bank and provides financial information for all government departments; it has particular responsibility for public sector pensions. All Treasury Ministers are concerned in tax matters.

Prime Minister and First Lord of the Treasury, THE RT. HON. JOHN MAJOR, MP.
Chancellor of the Exchequer, THE RT. HON. NORMAN LAMONT, MP £38,105
    Principal Private Secretary, J. Heywood.
    Private Secretary, Miss S. M. A. James.
    Special Advisers, W. Lightfoot; Dr W. Robinson; A. R. Goobey; A. Tyrie.
    Parliamentary Private Secretary, W. Hague, MP.
Parliamentary Clerk, B. O. Dyer.
Chief Secretary to the Treasury, THE RT. HON. DAVID MELLOR, QC, MP £38,105
    Private Secretary, N. I. Holgate.
    Assistant Private Secretary, S. Bowden.
    Parliamentary Private Secretary, A. Coombs, MP.

Paymaster General, THE LORD BELSTEAD, PC
....£26,962
  Private Secretary, D. Kyle.
  Parliamentary Private Secretary, J. Sayeed, MP.
Financial Secretary to the Treasury, THE HON.
FRANCIS MAUDE, MP £26,962
  Private Secretary, P. M. Rutnam.
  Parliamentary Private Secretary, G. Riddick, MP.
Minister of State, MRS GILLIAN SHEPHARD, MP
                       £26,962
  Private Secretary, P. Child.
  Parliamentary Private Secretary, J. Brazier, MP.
Economic Secretary, JOHN MAPLES, MP £20,463
  Private Secretary, M. R. Buckler.
Parliamentary Secretary to the Treasury and Government Chief Whip, THE RT. HON. RICHARD RYDER,
OBE, MP £31,715
  Private Secretary, M. Maclean.
Treasurer of HM Household and Deputy Chief Whip,
ALASTAIR GOODLAD, MP £26,962
Lord Commissioners of the Treasury, The Hon. T.
Sackville, MP; S. Chapman, MP; G. Knight, MP; I.
Patnick, OBE, MP; N. Baker, MP.......... £17,349
  Assistant Whips, T Wood, MP; N. Hamilton, MP; T.
Boswell, MP; T. Kirkhope, MP; D. Davis, MP.
                       £17,349
(NOTE. All salaries shown above do not include
Parliamentary salary).
(For Civil Service **Salaries,** *see* page 293).

Permanent Secretary of the Treasury, Sir Terence
Burns.
  Private Secretary, R. J. Evans.
Second Permanent Secretaries (G1A), N. L. Wicks,
CVO, CBE *(Overseas Finance);* N. J. Monck *(Public
Expenditure).*
*Head of Government Economics Service and Chief
Economic Adviser to the Treasury,* Prof. A. Budd.
Head of Government Accountancy Service, A. J.
Hardcastle.
Deputy Secretaries (G2), M. C. Scholar, CB *(Public
Finance);* H. P. Evans *(Overseas Finance);* A. J. C.
Edwards *(Public Services, and General Expenditure);* R. Wilson, CB *(Industry);* G. H. Phillips, CB
(Civil Service Management and Pay).
Deputy Chief Economic Adviser to the Treasury (G2),
Mrs J. R. Lomax.

INDUSTRY

Industry, Agriculture and Employment Group

Under Secretary (G3), G. Monger.
Assistant Secretaries (G5), Miss J. Barber; Miss M.
O'Mara; D. Revolta.

Public Enterprises Group

Under Secretary (G3), S. A. Robson.
Assistant Secretaries (G5), R. Bent; M. L. Williams.

Home Transport and Education Group

Under Secretary (G3), M. Whippman.
Assistant Secretaries (G5), C. Farthing; D. J. Batt.

PUBLIC SERVICES AND GENERAL EXPENDITURE
Social Services and Territorial Group

Under Secretary (G3), C. W. Kelly.
Assistant Secretaries (G5), Mrs P. Diggle; J. W. Grice;
S. Kelly.

Local Government Group

Under Secretary (G3), R. I. G. Allen.
Assistant Secretaries (G5), N. J. Ilett; S. N. Wood.

Central Unit on Purchasing
Director, P. Forshaw.
Deputy Director, M. J. Hoare.

Treasury Officer of Accounts Group
Under Secretary (G3), J. S. Beastall.
Assistant Secretary (G5), I. S. Thomson.

Central Computer and Telecommunications Agency

Under Secretary (G3), I. P. Wilson.
Assistant Secretaries (G5), W. Houldsworth; C. R.
Muid; M. Gladwyn; R. E. Dibble; J. Winup; A. R.
Williams.

GENERAL EXPENDITURE
General Expenditure Policy Group

Under Secretary (G3), M. C. S. Allan.
Assistant Secretaries (G5), J. F. Gilhooly; F. K. Jones;
I. W. V. Taylor.

Defence Policy, Manpower and Material Group

Under Secretary (G3), D. J. L. Moore.
Assistant Secretaries (G5), H. J. Bush; T. R. Fellgett.

OVERSEAS FINANCE
International Finance Group

Under Secretary (G3), P. N. Sedgwick.
Assistant Secretaries (G5), C. L. Melliss; C. R.
Pickering.

Aid and Export Finance Group
Under Secretary (G3), J. E. Mortimer.
Assistant Secretaries (G5), J. M. Halligan; Mrs S. D.
Brown.

European Community Group
Under Secretary (G3), D. J. Bostock.
Assistant Secretaries (G5), R. C. Pratt; N. J. Kroll.

Accountancy Advice Group
Grade 4, D. Cooke.
Assistant Secretary (G5), D. Jamieson.
Senior Principals (G6), K. E. Bradley; J. L. Constantine.

DEPUTY CHIEF ECONOMIC ADVISER'S SECTOR
Deputy Secretary (G2), Mrs J. R. Lomax.
Assistant Secretary (G5), vacant.

Economics Assessment Group
Under Secretary (G3), C. J. Mowl.
Senior Economic Advisers (G5), J. S. Hibberd; D. E.
Owen.

Medium Term and Policy Analysis Group
Under Secretary (G3), C. Riley.
Assistant Secretaries (G5), D. Savage; C. Kelly.

Economics of Industry Division
Under Secretary (G3), Dr J. H. Rickard.
Assistant Secretaries (G5), A. J. Meyrick; R. Weeden;
R. B. Stannard.

PUBLIC FINANCE
Fiscal Policy Group
Under Secretary (G3), R. P. Culpin.
Assistant Secretary (G5), Miss J. K. Rutter; S.
Matthews.

Monetary Group

Under Secretary (G3), P. R. C. Gray.
Assistant Secretaries (G5), S. J. Davies; J. P. McIntyre.

Financial Institutions and Markets Group

Under Secretary (G3), E. J. W. Gieve.
Assistant Secretaries (G5), L. Watts (*Accounts*); Miss G. M. Noble; J. M. G. Taylor.

Public Sector Finance

Assistant Secretary (G5), A. W. Ritchie.
Economic Adviser (G7), Ms S. Owen.
Statistician (G7), Mrs H. F. Patterson.

CIVIL SERVICE MANAGEMENT AND PAY

Pay and Industrial Relations Group

Under Secretary (G3), Mrs A. F. Case.
Assistant Secretaries (G5), J. S. Cunliffe; J. Dixon; Ms E. I. Young.
Grade 6, F. S. G. Easton.

Personnel Policy Group

Under Secretary (G3), L. J. Harris.
Assistant Secretaries (G5), D. G. Pain; D. W. Rayson; S. Kingaby; N. M. Hansford.

Management Policy and Running Costs

Under Secretary (G3), W. L. St Clair.
Assistant Secretaries (G5), P. M. Rayner; M. Perfect.

Specialist Support Group

Grade 4, C. J. A. Chivers.
Grade 5, J. B. Jones.
Grade 6, J. A. Barker.

CENTRAL DIVISIONS

Establishment and Organization Division

Under Secretary (G3), B. M. Fox.
Assistant Secretaries (G5), E. I. Cooper; A. J. T. MacAuslan; D. Todd.
Senior Principals (G6), R. N. Edwards; J. W. Stevens; B. J. Porteus; D. Rampton.

Economic Briefing Division

Assistant Secretary (G5), M. C. Mercer.

Information Division

Assistant Secretary (G5), R. B. Saunders.
Deputy Head of Division (G6), P. L. Patterson.

TREASURY REPRESENTATIVES IN USA

Economic Minister and UK Representative IMF/ IBRD, D. L. C. Peretz.

CIVIL SERVICE CATERING ORGANIZATION

Executive Director (G4), R. V. Wheeler.

THE TREASURY SOLICITOR
Department of HM Procurator-General and Treasury Solicitor
Queen Anne's Chambers, 28 Broadway, SW1H 9JS
[071–210 3000]

The Treasury Solicitor's Department provides legal services for many government departments. Those that do not have their own lawyers are given legal advice, and both they and many other departments are provided with litigation and conveyancing services. The Department also deals with Bona Vacantia. The Treasury Solicitor is also the Queen's Proctor.
(For **Salaries**, *see* page 293).

Procurator-General and Treasury Solicitor (G1), J. Nursaw, CB, QC.
Deputy Treasury Solicitor (G2), T. J. G. Pratt.

Central Advisory Division

Principal Assistant Solicitor (G3), M. A. Blythe.
Assistant Solicitors (G5), F. L. Croft; M. J. Hemming.
Grade 6, Mrs P. Dayer; C. J. Gregory; Miss P. F. Henderson; Ms V. Selzer.

Litigation Divisions

Principal Assistant Solicitors (G3), D. A. Hogg; D. F. W. Pickup.
Assistant Solicitors (G5), D. Brummell; I. Hood; A. Leithead; R. Lines; A. J. Sandal; S. Sargant; P. F. O. Whitehurst; R. J. Phillips.
Grade 6, N. Ash; A. P. M. Aylett; Mrs D. Babar; Miss R. M. Caudwell; M. R. M. Davis; J. N. Desai; A. K. Fraser; P. D. F. Grant; J. D. Howes; A. D. Lawton; P. Messer; D. Palmer; D. A. Stalker; A. Turek; R. J. Walter.
Senior Legal Assistant, Miss P. J. Carroll.
Principals (G7), T. C. Adcock; L. Blake; Mrs J. Bonsey; Miss S. Brzezina; N. M. Fleischman; Mrs G. Fuller; A. D. Gafoor; M. P. Gold; C. J. Hales; S. Hudson; Mrs K. Lester; Miss E. Long; Miss M. A. McNally; N. Magyar; Miss C. R. Musaala-Mukasa; A. C. Nwanodi; F. G. O'Connell; R. C. J. Opie; H. O. J. R. Shepheard; C. Stephens; D. Trinchero; M. G. Truran; J. C. Youedll; J. Ziegel.

Queen's Proctor Division

Queen's Proctor, J. Nursaw, CB, QC.
Assistant Queen's Proctor, I. Hood.

Property Division

Principal Assistant Solicitor (G3), A. D. Osborne.
Assistant Solicitors (G5), R. W. M. Cooper; Miss G. Gilder; P. L. Noble; P. F. Nockles; M. F. Rawlins; A. M. Scarfe; J. Wyer.
Grade 6, R. L. Coward; M. Drayton; R. D. Harris; J. B. Howe; C. L. Oastler; R. M. Pierce; A. W. Prior; S. W. Rock; M. R. Rosenfeld; R. J. B. Stenhouse; T. Sylvester-Jones; B. D. Thurley.
Senior Legal Assistants, M. V. Cooper; T. Forrester; A. R. Lilleystone; S. A. Tobin; W. F. Williams.
Grade 7, I. Adams; D. G. Ager; H. S. Davis; Mrs A. M. Foxhuntley; C. R. Irving; R. S. Lugg; J. H. McFarland; G. J. Norris; P. Page; D. A. Reid; N. P. Rex; G. T. Tuttle; J. M. Williamson.

Establishment, Finance and General Services Division

Principal Establishment and Finance Officer (G6), A. J. E. Hollis.
Deputy Establishment Officer (G7), vacant.
Head of Costs Branch (G6), P. Moran.
Chief Accountant (G7), R. B. Smith.

Bona Vacantia Division

Assistant Solicitor (G5), Miss S. L. Sargant.
Senior Legal Assistant, M. R. M. Davies.
Grade 7, Miss H. Donnelly; Mrs P. L. Woods.

Ministry of Defence Branch
Neville House, Page Street, SW1P 4LS
[071–218 4691]

Grade 4, R. P. Ellis.
Grade 5, J. R. G. Braggins; R. A. D. Jackson.
Grade 6, A. L. Norris; M. B. Sturdy.

Department of Education and Science Branch
Elizabeth House, York Road, SE1 7PH
[071–934 9000]

Principal Assistant Solicitor (G3), R. N. Ricks.
Assistant Solicitors (G5), D. J. Aries; M. Harris; A. D. Preston.
Grade 6, Miss J. L. C. Brooks; S. T. Harker.
Senior Legal Assistant, N. P. Beach.

Department of Employment Branch
Caxton House, Tothill Street, SW1H 9NF
[071–273 3000]

Principal Assistant Solicitor (G3), H. R. L. Purse.
Assistant Solicitors (G5), R. J. Baker; Mrs A. Leale; S. G. Milligan; Miss V. Rice-Pyle.
Grade 6, R. H. Britten; G. W. M. Galliford; C. House; N. A. D. Lambert; Miss M. Trefgarne; J. K. Winayak.
Senior Legal Assistant, J. Hall.
Grade 7, P. H. Kilgarriff.

Department of Energy Branch
1 Palace Street, SW1E 5HE
[071–238 3000]

Principal Assistant Solicitor (G3), D. E. J. Nissen.
Assistant Solicitors (G5), D. Hogg; D. H. M. Ingham; S. G. Milligan; D. F. Pascho; G. B. Claydon.
Grade 6, M. R. Brocklehurst; F. D. W. Clarke; Miss V. F. Dewhurst; Mrs C. V. Fox; R. C. Perkins.

Department of Transport Branch
2 Marsham Street, SW1P 3EB
[071–276 3000]

Principal Assistant Solicitor (G3), G. H. Beetham.
Assistant Solicitors (G5), R. G. Bellis; P. D. Coopman; C. W. M. Ingram; B. W. James; A. G. Jones.
Grade 6, Miss A. Lind-Smith; B. McHenry; N. C. Thomas,.
Senior Legal Assistants, B. J. Hammersley; A. K. Johnston.
Grade 7, Mrs A. Heilpern; Miss A. Lancaster; A. W. Stewart.

COUNCIL ON TRIBUNALS
7th Floor, 22 Kingsway, WC2B 6LE
[071-936 7045]

The Council on Tribunals is an independent statutory body. It keeps under review the constitution and working of the various tribunals which have been placed under its general supervision, and considers and reports on administrative procedures relating to statutory inquiries. It is consulted by government departments on proposals for legislation affecting tribunals and inquiries, and on proposals where the need for an appeals procedure may arise. It also offers advice on draft primary legislation.

Some 60 tribunals are currently under the Council's supervision. The matters with which they deal range from agriculture to immigration, pensions, road traffic, taxation, and the allocation of school places.

The Scottish Committee of the Council generally considers Scottish tribunals and matters relating only to Scotland.

Members of the Council are appointed by the Lord Chancellor and the Lord Advocate. The Scottish Committee is composed partly of members of the Council designated by the Lord Advocate and partly of others appointed by him. The Parliamentary Commissioner for Administration is *ex officio* a member of both the Council and the Scottish Committee.

Chairman, Sir Cecil Clothier, KCB, QC.
Members, The Parliamentary Commissioner for Administration; G. A. Anderson; T. N. Biggart, CBE;
M. B. Dempsey; Prof. D. L. Foulkes; T. R. H. Godden, CB; B. Hill, CBE; Prof. M. J. Hill; Miss J. Horsham, CBE; G. V. Hyde; W. N. Hyde; Mrs J. U. Kellock; L. F. Read, QC; M. E. J. Rush, CBE.
Secretary, C. W. Dyment.

Scottish Committee
20 Walker Street, Edinburgh EH3 7HR
[031–220 1236]

Chairman, T. N. Biggart, CBE.
Members, The Parliamentary Commissioner for Administration; G. A. Anderson; W. J. Campbell; Mrs C. A. M. Davis; T. R. H. Godden, CB; J. Langan; Lady Scott, CBE.
Secretary, Ms L. Wilkie.

TRIBUNALS
(*see* **pages 389–90**)

UNIVERSITIES FUNDING COUNCIL
Northavon House, Coldharbour Lane,
Bristol BS16 1QD
[0272–317317]

The Universities Funding Council was established under the provisions of the Education Reform Act 1988, and came into existence formally on April 1, 1989.

Chairman, Sir Ronald Dearing.
Chief Executive, Prof. G. Davies.
Members, Prof. J. P. Barron; Prof. M. R. Bond; Mrs R. Chapman; Prof. D. Dilks; Prof. B. Follett, FRS; Sir Kenneth Green; Prof. Marian Hicks; R. B. Horton; Prof. H. Newby; Sir Idris Pearce; Sir Charles Reece; Prof. J. Shaw; Prof. H. Wood.
Secretary, F. M. Scott.
Assistant Secretaries (G5), E. C. Appleyard; J. H. Farrant; M. S. Hedges.

UNRELATED LIVE TRANSPLANT REGULATORY AUTHORITY
Department of Health, Room 518, Eileen House,
80–94 Newington Causeway, SE1 6EF
[071-972 2736]

The Unrelated Live Transplant Regulatory Authority (ULTRA) is a statutory body established on January 1, 1990. In every case where the transplant of an organ within the definition of the Human Organ Transplants Act 1989 is proposed between a living donor and a recipient who are not genetically related, the proposal must be referred to ULTRA. Applications must be made by registered medical practitioners.

The Authority comprises a chairman and 11 members appointed by the Secretary of State for Health. The secretariat is provided by Department of Health Officials.

Chairman, Prof. M. Bobrow.
Members, Rev. Prof. G. R. Dunstan; Dr P. A. Dyer; Mrs D. Eccles; Prof. M. G. McGeown; Sir Michael McNair-Wilson, MP; S. G. Macpherson; Dr N. P. Mallick; Prof. J. R. Salaman; Miss S. M. Taber; J. Wellbeloved; Mrs C. Wight.
Secretary, Mrs J. Ferguson.

OFFICE OF WATER SERVICES
Centre City Tower, 7 Hill Street,
Birmingham B5 4UA
[021–625 1300]

The Office of Water Services (Ofwat) was set up under the Water Act 1989 and came into being on September 1, 1989. Its role is to support the Director General of Water Services who regulates the economic frame-

work of the water industry in England and Wales. His main duties are to ensure that water companies comply with the terms of their appointments (or licences) and to protect the interests of water consumers. The Director General has established ten regional customer service committees which investigate complaints and identify customer concerns. The Director General is independent of ministerial control and directly accountable to Parliament.
Director General of Water Services, I. C. R. Byatt.

WELSH OFFICE

The Welsh Office has responsibility in Wales for ministerial functions relating to health and personal social services; education, except for terms and conditions of service, student awards and the University; the Welsh language and culture; local government; housing; water and sewerage; environmental protection; sport; agriculture and fisheries; forestry; land use, including town and country planning and countryside and nature conservation; new towns; ancient monuments and historic buildings; roads; tourism; a range of matters affecting the careers service and training activities in Wales; financial assistance to industry; the urban programme in Wales; the operation of the European Regional Development Fund in Wales and other European Community matters; civil emergencies and all financial aspects of these matters, including Welsh rate support grant. It has oversight responsibilities for economic affairs and regional planning in Wales. (For **Salaries,** *see* page 293).

Gwydyr House, Whitehall, SW1A 2ER
[071–270 3000]
Secretary of State for Wales, THE RT. HON. DAVID HUNT, MBE, MP.
Private Secretary, Miss J. C. Simpson.
Assistant Private Secretaries, Mrs F. Adams Jones; Miss D. E. Coleman.
Special Adviser, R. Richards.
Parliamentary Private Secretary, J. Bowis, MP.
Minister of State, THE RT. HON. SIR WYN ROBERTS, MP.
Private Secretary, H. O. Jones.
Parliamentary Private Secretary, D. Tredinnick, MP.
Parliamentary Under-Secretary, NICHOLAS BENNETT, MP.
Private Secretary, W. H. Rees.
Parliamentary Clerk, V. R. Watkin.
Permanent Secretary (G1), Sir Richard Lloyd Jones, KCB.
Private Secretary, I. R. Miller.

Cathays Park, Cardiff CF1 3NQ
[0222–825111]
Deputy Secretaries (G2), J. W. Lloyd; F. J. Craig.

Establishment Group

Principal Establishment Officer (G3), G. C. G. Craig.
Heads of Divisions (G5), R. M. Abel; W. L. Chapman.
Senior Economic Adviser (G5), O. T. Hooker.
Chief Statistician (G5), Dr M. P. G. Pepper.
Head of Health Intelligence Unit (G6), G. J. Cockell.
Principals (G7), R. J. Callen; P. Davenport; C. Tudor.
Economic Adviser (G7), V. W. F. McPherson.
Principal Research Officers (G7), E. Darwin; Mrs M. A. J. Gronow.
Statisticians (G7), D. D. Baird; M. R. Brand; G. P. Davies; J. T. Fletcher; K. Francombe; Ms C. Fullerton; P. J. Fullerton; E. Swires Hennessy; J. D. James; H. M. Jones; R. Jones; J. D. Kinder; Mrs S. Stansfield.

Cadw: Welsh Historic Monuments
Brunel House, Fitzalan Road, Cardiff CF2 1UY
[0222–465511]
(An executive agency of the Welsh Office.)
Chief Executive, E. A. J. Carr.
Conservation Architect (G6), J. D. Hogg.
Principal Inspector of Ancient Monuments and Historic Buildings, J. R. Avent.

Cathays Park, Cardiff CF1 3NQ
Inspectors of Ancient Monuments and Historic Buildings, J. K. Knight; A. D. McLees; Dr S. E. Rees; R. C. Turner; M. J. Yates.

Finance Group

Principal Finance Officer (G3), R. A. Wallace.
Grade 4, C. L. Jones.
Heads of Divisions (G5), D. H. Jones; L. A. Pavelin; J. Shortridge; Mrs E. Taylor; B. Wilcox.
Grade 6, M. G. Horlock.
Principals (G7), Mrs J. Blamire; B. R. Davies; J. Kilner; R. D. Macey; D. A. Powell; H. Rawlings; B. O. Valentine.
Head of Internal Audit (G7), D. Howarth.
Head of NHS Audit (G7), P. Brown.

Housing, Health and Social Services Policy Group

Head of Group (G3), R. W. Jarman.
Heads of Divisions (G5), D. Adams; R. J. Davies; S. H. Martin; A. Thornton.
Chief Social Work Service Officer (G5), D. G. Evans.
Chief Architect (G6), C. Eyres *(acting).*
Grade 6, A. C. Elmer.
Deputy Chief Social Work Service Officer, J. K. Fletcher.
Principals (G7), J. A. Atkins; C. Coombs; P. Godden-Kent; D. B. Hilbourne; Miss E. M. Jones; R. Patterson; I. Price Jones; D. M. Rolph; M. Shannahan; I. I. Thomas; A. C. Wood.
Social Work Service Officers (G7), D, Barker; D. A. Brushett; G. H. Davies; Miss R. E. Evans; J. K. Fletcher; I. Forster; J. F. Mooney; C. D. Vyvyan; Mrs P. White; R. C. Woodward.
Principal Professional and Technology Officers (G7), T. A. Campden; G. N. Harding; W. Ross.

Health Professional Group

Medical Officer	£33,017
Dental Officer	£34,464

Chief Medical Officer (G3), Dr D. J. Hine.
Deputy Chief Medical Officers (G4), Dr A. M. George; Dr D. Ferguson Lewis.
Senior Medical Officers (G5), Dr B. Davies; Dr E. J. Ludlow; D. Owen; Ms R. Jacobs; J. K. Richmond; Ms A. K. Thomas.
Chief Dental Officer, Dr M. Heap.
Medical Officers, J. D. Andrews; J. W. Crossley; T. I. Evans; Dr L. Hamilton-Kirkwood; N. E. Thomas.
Dental Officers, T. M. Davies; J. D. O. Parkholm; T. A. Williams.
Scientific Adviser (G5), Dr J. A. V. Pritchard.
Pharmaceutical Adviser (G6), Dr G. B. A. Veitch.
Environmental Health Adviser (G6), R. J. Alexander.

National Health Service Directorate

Director of the NHS in Wales, J. W. Owen.
Heads of Divisions (G5), M. Betenson; D. A. Pritchard; N. E. Thomas; B. Wilcox; Mrs B. J. M. Wilson.
Principals (G7), Mrs J. Annand; M. A. C. Brooke; M. D. Chown; P. Davenport; J Duggan; M. H. Harper; R. J. Keveren; E. J. McDonald; Miss C. Maddocks; K. Orchard; R. O'Sullivan; K. S. Sleight; M. F. Webb.
Ambulance Adviser (G7), P. J. Hunt.

Nursing Division

Chief Nursing Officer (G3), Miss M. Bull.
Deputy Chief Nursing Officer (G4), Mrs B. Melvin.
Nursing Officers (G6), Mrs R. Cohen; Mrs S. M. Drayton; Miss G. Harris; Dr D. Keyzer; M. F. Tonkin; Mrs D. J. Vass.

Legal Division

Legal Adviser (G3), D. G. Lambert.
Assistant Solicitor (G5), P. J. Murrin.
Grade 6, J. D. H. Evans; A. K. Gillard; C. P. Jones; C. G. Longville; A. J. Park; J. H. Turnbull; A. J. Watkins; A. Widdrington.
Senior Legal Assistants (G7), Miss A. L. Ferguson; Mrs A. T. Parkes; Mrs R. J. Wiles; D. H. J. Williams.

Information Division

Director of Information (G5), H. G. Roberts.
Chief Press Officer (G7), E. M. Bowen, MVO.
Principal Publicity Officer (G7), W. J. Edwards.

Economic and Regional Policy Group

Head of Group (G3), M. J. Cochlin.
Heads of Divisions (G5), M. E. Bevan; Miss E. N. M. Davies; M. L. Evans; D. T. Richards.
Principals (G7), D. Beames; M. H. Bendon; C. J. Burdett; M. C. Dunn; Ms J. M. Gordon; Mrs A. M. Jackson; A. D. Lansdown; Miss J. E. Paulett; J. N. Roberts.

Industry Department

Director (G3), C. D. Stevens.
Industrial Director (G4), T. E. Morgan, MBE.
Heads of Divisions (G5), D. Jones; G. T. Evans.
Senior Principal Scientific Officer (G6), Dr R. J. Loveland.
Principals (G7), N. Barry; C. F. Francis; J. A. Grimes; G. Jones; I. C. Lawrence; J. H. Roberts; K. Smith; R. Waller; J. W. Wallington.

Education Department

Head of Department (G3), R. H. Jones, CVO.
Heads of Divisions (G5), H. Evans; B. J. Mitchell.
Head of Division (G6), R. C. Simpson.
Principals (G7), Mrs J. Booker; P. F. Brown; D. A. Bullen; Mrs L. L. Changkee; C. E. J. Daniels; R. O. Evans; B. Hayward-Blake; Mrs J. Hopkins; J. R. Howells; Mrs J. Milligan; M. G. Richards; Mrs H. Thomas; A. Whittaker.

HM Inspectorate

Chief Inspector (G4), R. L. James.
Staff Inspectors (G5), S. J. Adams; W. R. Jenkins; T. E. Parry; G. Thomas; P. Thomas; R. Thomas; M. J. F. Wynn.
HM Inspectors (G6), C. Abbott; G. Adams; R. A. Charles; Mrs G. Briwnant Jones; D. G. Evans; J. R. N. Evans; N. B. Evans; Mrs L. Gainsbury; G. C. Griffiths; J. Griffiths; M. G. Haines; A. Hamilton Jones; I. G. Higginbotham; A. Higgins; D. Ioto; I. L. James; Mrs R. James; M. John; G. D. Jones; G. W. Jones; H. L. Jones; G. T. J. Jones; O. E. Jones; Mrs A. Keane; A. R. Large; J. M. Laugharne; M. J. Law; Miss S. Lewis; Mrs M. E. R. Lloyd; A. Lowndes; A. Morgan; I. G. Morgan; Miss P. A. Nicholas; Miss E. Ogwen; T. G. Prosser; D. G. H. Rees; Miss D. Selleck; Mrs V. Scott; R. I. Swain; R. Taylor; Mrs I. Thomas; Miss L. Thomas; J. N. Vaughan; P. B. Walker; B. Wigley; W. E. L. Williams; D. P. Williams.

Transport, Planning, Water and Environment Group

Head of Group (G3), P. R. Gregory.
Director of Highways (G4), K. J. Thomas°.
Heads of Divisions (G5), A. H. H. Jones; D. I. Westlake°; C. J. Curry (*Chief Planner*); H. R. Bollington°; (G6), D. M. Timlin.
Superintending Engineers (G6), J. G. Evans°; B. H. Hawker*.
Superintending Estates Officer (G6), G. K. Hoad.
Superintending Engineer (G6), J. R. Rees.
Senior Principal (G6), P. R. Marsden.
Principals (G7), P. M. Bishop; W. M. P. Cooper; G. Davies; M. D. Evans; T. W. Hunter; H. R. Payne; D. Powell°; G. R. Jones; D. Hadfield°; D. C. Quinlan; W. P. Roderick.
Principal Planning Officers (G7), D. B. Courtier; J. O. Pryce; J. V. Spear.
Principal Research Officers (G7), A. S. Dredge; Ms L. J. Roberts.
Principal Estates Officer (G7), R. W. Wilson.
Principal Professional and Technology Officers (G7), C. Hardman; J. E. Saunders.
Principal Professional and Technology Officers, Highways Directorate (G7), P. Dunstan°; M. J. Gilbert; I. A. Grindulais; J. A. L. Harries*; A. P. Howcroft; B. J. W. Martin°; A. L. Perry; R. H. Powell°; S. C. Shouler; C. W. W. Smart°; J. Collins°; K. J. Alexander°; R. H. Hooper*.

Planning Inspectorate

Principal Planning Inspectors (G5), F. Cosgrove; R. Pierce; D. Sheers.
Senior Housing and Planning Inspectors (G6), T. W. B. Barnes; J. H. Chadwick; R. Davies; P. V. Farrow; M. Griffin; G. Rees; G. Sloan; S. B. Wild; D. N. Wilks.

HM Inspectorate of Pollution for Wales

Inspector, Hazardous Wastes (G7), G. Taylor.
Inspector, Radiation and Chemicals (G7), Dr C. Hardman.
Inspector, Water (G7), A. A. Houlden.

Agriculture Department

Head of Department (G3), O. Rees, CB.
Heads of Divisions (G5), G. Podmore; D. R. Thomas; L. K. Walford.
Principals (G7), J. C. Alexander; A. G. Huws; R. A. Norris; R. F. Patterson; C. E. Taylor°; B. E. Price°.
Divisional Executive Officers (G7), W. K. Griffiths (*Carmarthen*); E. Hughes (*Caernarfon*); R. J. E. Wilcox (*Llandrindod Wells*); P. N. S. Wolfenden (*Ruthin*).

Based at:
°Ty Glas Road, Llanishen, Cardiff CF4 5PL (0222–753271)
*Government Buildings, Pinerth Road, Rhos on Sea, Colwyn Bay LL28 4UL (0492–44261)
†Plas Crug, Aberystwyth SY23 1NG (0970-3162)

WOMEN'S NATIONAL COMMISSION

Government Offices, Horse Guards Road, SW1P 3AL
[071–270 5903]

The Women's National Commission is an advisory committee to the Government whose terms of reference are to ensure by all possible means that the informed opinions of women are given their due weight in the deliberations of the Government. The Commission's fifty members are all women who are elected or appointed by national organizations with a large and active membership of women. The organizations include the women's sections of the major political parties, trades unions, religious groups, professional women's organizations and other bodies broadly representative of women.
Government Co-Chairman, Mrs V. Bottomley, MP (*nominated by the Prime Minister* 1991).
Elected Co-Chairman, Mrs E. Martin (*elected* 1991).
Secretary, Ms M. Jones.

WOMEN'S ROYAL VOLUNTARY SERVICE
234–244 Stockwell Road, SW9 9SP
[071–416 0146]

The Women's Royal Voluntary Service (WRVS) assists government departments, local authorities and voluntary bodies in organizing and carrying out welfare and emergency work for the community on a nationwide network operated through area, county, district and London borough organizers. Activities include work for the elderly and handicapped, for young families, and for prisoners and their families; non-medical work in hospitals; welfare work for HM Forces and for Service families; and trained teams to assist in national and local emergencies. Administrative costs are met from an annual Home Office grant. *National Chairman,* The Hon. Mrs M. Corsar.

CIVIL SERVICE STAFF

Analysis by ministerial responsibility at April 1 in each year

† Full-time equivalents (thousands)

	1984	1985	1986	1987	1988	1989	1990
Total civil and defence departments	624·0	599·0	594·4	597·8	579·6	569·2	562·4
of which Non-industrials	504·3	498·0	498·2	507·5	506·6	499·8	495·2
Industrials	119·7	101·0	96·2	90·3	73·0	69·4	67·2
Total civil departments	424·8	425·0	424·9	433·8	436·2	427·9	421·0
Agriculture, Fisheries and Food	12·1	12·1	11·7	11·3	11·1	10·9	10·7
Chancellor of the Exchequer's							
Departments:	112·4	111·9	110·0	110·1	108·6	109·1	109·2
Customs and Excise	25·1	25·4	25·1	25·8	26·3	26·4	26·9
Inland Revenue	69·8	69·8	69·3	67·8	66·6	67·0	66·0
Department for National Savings	8·0	7·8	7·8	7·7	7·4	7·3	7·0
Treasury and others	9·5	8·9	8·8	8·8	8·3	8·3	9·3
Education and Science	2·4	2·4	2·4	2·4	2·5	2·5	2·6
Employment	56·4	54·7	55·7	60·5	58·3	55·0	52·4
Energy	1·1	1·1	1·0	1·0	1·0	1·1	1·2
Environment	36·6	35·8	34·9	34·2	33·0	30·6	29·2
Foreign and Commonwealth	10·0	9·8	9·6	9·5	9·6	9·6	9·5
Home	36·4	36·6	37·5	37·6	39·2	40·8	42·7
Industry	–	–	–	–	–	–	–
Scotland	12·8	13·0	12·9	13·0	13·0	12·3	12·6
Social Services	92·6	94·9	94·9	97·7	102·3	94·3	88·4
Trade	–	–	–	–	–	–	–
Trade and Industry	14·7	14·8	14·8	14·8	14·6	14·7	13·6
Transport	14·2	14·4	14·7	12·3	14·1	14·1	15·5
Wales	2·2	2·3	2·3	2·3	2·2	2·2	2·3
Other civil departments	20·9	21·2	21·5	25·1	26·7	30·7	31·0
Total Ministry of Defence	199·2	174·0	169·5	164·0	143·4	141·3	141·4

† Part-time employees are counted as half units.   *Source: HMSO—Annual Abstract of Statistics 1991*

LAW COURTS AND OFFICES

THE JUDICIAL COMMITTEE
OF THE PRIVY COUNCIL

The Judicial Committee of the Privy Council is the final court of appeal from courts of the United Kingdom dependencies, courts of independent Commonwealth countries which have retained the right of appeal, courts of the Channel Islands and the Isle of Man, some professional and disciplinary committees, and church sources.

The Judicial Committee includes the Lord Chancellor, the Lords of Appeal in Ordinary (*see* below) and other members of the Privy Council who hold or have held high judicial office, and certain judges from the Commonwealth. Usually, only three or five hear each case.

Privy Council Office (Judicial Department), Downing Street, SW1A 2AJ.
Registrar of the Privy Council, D. H. O. Owen.
Chief Clerk, R. W. Trendall.

THE JUDICATURE OF
ENGLAND AND WALES

The legal system of England and Wales is separate from those of Scotland and Northern Ireland and differs from them in law, judicial procedure and court structure, although there is a common distinction between civil law (disputes between individuals) and criminal law (acts harmful to the community).

The supreme judicial authority for England and Wales is the House of Lords, which is the ultimate Court of Appeal from all courts in Great Britain and Northern Ireland (except criminal courts in Scotland). As a Court of Appeal it consists of the Lord Chancellor and the Lords of Appeal in Ordinary (Law Lords).

The Supreme Court of Judicature comprises the Court of Appeal, the Crown Court and the High Court of Justice. The High Court of Justice is the superior civil court and is divided into three divisions. The Chancery Division is concerned mainly with equity, bankruptcy and contentious probate business; the Queen's Bench Division deals with commercial and maritime law, with civil cases not assigned to other courts, and hears appeals from lower courts; and the Family Division deals with matters relating to family law. Sittings are held at the Royal Courts of Justice in London or at 27 Crown Court centres outside the capital. High Court judges sit alone to hear cases at first instance. Appeals from lower courts are heard by two or three judges, or by single judges of the appropriate division.

The decision to prosecute in the majority of cases rests with the Crown Prosecution Service, an independent prosecuting body established in 1986 to serve all of England and Wales (*see* p. 384–5). At the head of the service is the Director of Public Prosecutions, who discharges his duties under the superintendence of the Attorney-General. Certain categories of offence continue to require the consent for prosecution of the Attorney-General.

Minor criminal offences (summary offences) are dealt with in magistrates' courts, which usually consist of three unpaid lay magistrates (Justices of the Peace) sitting without a jury, who are advised on points of law and procedure by a legally-qualified clerk to the justices. (There were approximately 30,000 Justices of the Peace at June 1, 1991.) In busier courts a full-time, salaried and legally-qualified stipendiary magistrate presides alone. Cases involving people under 17 are heard in juvenile courts, specially constituted magistrates' courts which sit apart from other courts. Preliminary proceedings in a serious case to decide whether there is evidence to justify committal for trial in the Crown Court are also held in the magistrates' courts. Appeals from magistrates' courts against sentence or conviction are made to the Crown Court. Appeals upon a point of law are made to the High Court, and may go on to the House of Lords.

The Crown Court sits in about 90 centres, divided into six circuits, and is presided over by High Court judges, full-time circuit judges, and part-time recorders, sitting with a jury in all trials which are contested. It deals with trials of the more serious criminal offences, the sentencing of offenders committed for sentence by magistrates' courts (when the magistrates consider their own power of sentence inadequate), and appeals from lower courts. Magistrates usually sit with a circuit judge or recorder to deal with appeals and committals for sentence. Appeals from the Crown Court, either against sentence or conviction, are made to the Court of Appeal (Criminal Division), presided over by the Lord Chief Justice. A further appeal from the Court of Appeal to the House of Lords can be brought if a point of law of general public importance is considered to be involved.

Most minor civil cases are dealt with by the county courts, of which there are about 300 (details may be found in the local telephone directory). For cases involving small claims there are special arbitration facilities and simplified procedures. Where there are financial limits on county court jurisdiction, claims which exceed those limits may be tried in the county courts with the consent of the parties, or in certain circumstances on transfer from the High Court. Undefended divorce cases and, outside London, bankruptcy proceedings can be heard in designated county courts. Magistrates' courts can deal with certain classes of civil case, mostly those relating to the family, and committees of magistrates licence public houses, clubs and betting shops. Appeals in matrimonial, adoption and guardianship proceedings heard in the magistrates' courts go to the Family Division of the High Court; affiliation appeals and appeals from decisions of the licensing committees of magistrates go to the Crown Court. Appeals from the High Court and county courts are heard in the Court of Appeal (Civil Division), presided over by the Master of the Rolls, and may go on to the House of Lords, the final court of appeal in civil cases.

Coroners' courts investigate violent and unnatural deaths or sudden deaths where the cause is unknown. Cases may be brought before a local coroner (a senior lawyer or doctor) by doctors, the police, various public authorities or members of the public. Where a death is sudden and the cause is unknown, the coroner may order a post-mortem examination to determine the cause of death rather than hold an inquest in court.

THE HOUSE OF LORDS
(as final Court of Appeal)

The Lord High Chancellor
The Rt. Hon. the Lord Mackay of Clashfern
(*born* 1927, *apptd* 1987)
Lords of Appeal in Ordinary (each £97,000)

Rt. Hon. Lord Keith of Kinkel, *born* 1922, *apptd* 1977.
Rt. Hon. Lord Bridge of Harwich, *born* 1917, *apptd* 1980.
Rt. Hon. Lord Templeman, MBE, *born* 1920, *apptd* 1982.
Rt. Hon. Lord Griffiths, MC, *born* 1923, *apptd* 1985.

Rt. Hon. Lord Ackner, *born* 1920, *apptd* 1986.
Rt. Hon. Lord Oliver of Aylmerton, *born* 1921, *apptd* 1986.
Rt. Hon. Lord Goff of Chieveley, *born* 1926, *apptd* 1986.
Rt. Hon. Lord Jauncey of Tullichettle, *born* 1925, *apptd* 1988.
Rt. Hon. Lord Lowry, *born* 1919, *apptd* 1988.
Registrar, The Clerk of the Parliaments (M. Wheeler-Booth).

SUPREME COURT OF JUDICATURE
COURT OF APPEAL

Ex officio Judges.—The Lord High Chancellor, the Lord Chief Justice of England, the Master of the Rolls, the President of the Family Division, and the Vice-Chancellor.

The Master of the Rolls (£97,000)
The Rt. Hon. the Lord Donaldson of Lymington
(*born* 1920, *apptd* 1982)
Secretary, Miss V. Seymour; *Clerk*, D. G. Grimmett.

Lords Justices of Appeal (each £93,000)
Rt. Hon. Sir Tasker Watkins, vc, gbe, *born* 1918, *apptd* 1980.
Rt. Hon. Sir Michael Fox, *born* 1921, *apptd* 1981.
Rt. Hon. Sir Francis Purchas, *born* 1919, *apptd* 1982.
Rt. Hon. Sir Brian Dillon, *born* 1923, *apptd* 1982.
Rt. Hon. Sir Roger Parker, *born* 1923, *apptd* 1983.
Rt. Hon. Sir Anthony Lloyd, *born* 1929, *apptd* 1984.
Rt. Hon. Sir Brian Neill, *born* 1923, *apptd* 1985.
Rt. Hon. Sir Michael Mustill, *born* 1931, *apptd* 1985.
Rt. Hon. Sir Martin Nourse, *born* 1932, *apptd* 1985.
Rt. Hon. Sir Iain Glidewell, *born* 1924, *apptd* 1985.
Rt. Hon. Sir John Balcombe, *born* 1925, *apptd* 1985.
Rt. Hon. Sir Ralph Gibson, *born* 1922, *apptd* 1985.
Rt. Hon. Sir John Stocker, mc, td, *born* 1918, *apptd* 1986.
Rt. Hon. Sir Harry Woolf, *born* 1933, *apptd* 1986.
Rt. Hon. Sir Donald Nicholls, *born* 1933, *apptd* 1986.
Rt. Hon. Sir Thomas Bingham, *born* 1933, *apptd* 1986.
Rt. Hon. Sir Patrick Russell, *born* 1926, *apptd* 1987.
Rt. Hon. Dame Elizabeth Butler-Sloss, dbe, *born* 1933, *apptd* 1988.
Rt. Hon. Sir Peter Taylor, *born* 1930, *apptd* 1988.
Rt. Hon. Sir Murray Stuart-Smith, *born* 1927, *apptd* 1988.
Rt. Hon. Sir Christopher Staughton, *born* 1933, *apptd* 1988.
Rt. Hon. Sir Michael Mann, *born* 1930, *apptd* 1988.
Rt. Hon. Sir Donald Farquharson, *born* 1928, *apptd* 1989.
Rt. Hon. Sir Anthony McCowan, *born* 1928, *apptd* 1989.
Rt. Hon. Sir Roy Beldam, *born* 1925, *apptd* 1989.
Rt. Hon. Sir Andrew Leggatt, *born* 1930, *apptd* 1990.
Rt. Hon. Sir Michael Nolan, *born* 1928, *apptd* 1991.

Court of Appeal (Criminal Division)

Judges, The Lord Chief Justice of England, the Master of the Rolls, Lords Justices of Appeal and Judges of the High Court of Justice.

Courts-Martial Appeal Court

Judges, The Lord Chief Justice of England, the Master of the Rolls, Lords Justices of Appeal, and Judges of the High Court of Justice.

HIGH COURT OF JUSTICE
CHANCERY DIVISION

President, The Lord High Chancellor

The Vice-Chancellor (£93,000)
The Rt. Hon. Sir Nicolas Browne-Wilkinson
(*born* 1930, *apptd* 1985)
Clerk, W. Northfield, bem.

Judges (each £84,250)
Hon. Sir John Vinelott, *born* 1923, *apptd* 1978.
Hon. Sir Jean-Pierre Warner, *born* 1924, *apptd* 1981.
Hon. Sir Peter Gibson, *born* 1934, *apptd* 1981.
Hon. Sir Mervyn Davies, mc, td, *born* 1918, *apptd* 1982.
Hon. Sir Jeremiah Harman, *born* 1930, *apptd* 1982.
Hon. Sir Richard Scott, *born* 1934, *apptd* 1983.
Hon. Sir Leonard Hoffman, *born* 1934, *apptd* 1985.
Hon. Sir John Knox, *born* 1925, *apptd* 1985.
Hon. Sir Peter Millett, *born* 1932, *apptd* 1986.
Hon. Sir Andrew Morritt, cvo, *born* 1938, *apptd* 1988.
Hon. Sir William Aldous, *born* 1936, *apptd* 1988.
Hon. Sir John Mummery, *born* 1938, *apptd* 1989.
Hon. Sir Francis Ferris, td, *born* 1932, *apptd* 1990.
Hon. Sir John Chadwick, ed, *born* 1941, *apptd* 1991.

High Court of Justice in Bankruptcy

Judges, The Master of the Rolls, the Vice-Chancellor, the Lords Justices, and other members of the Court of Appeal.

Companies Court

Judges, The Vice Chancellor and judges of the Chancery Division of the High Court.

Patent Court (Appellate Section)
[071-936 6000]

Judges, The Hon. Mr Justice Aldous; The Hon. Mr Justice Mummery; The Hon. Mr Justice Morritt; The Hon. Mr Justice Hoffman.

QUEEN'S BENCH DIVISION

The Lord Chief Justice of England (£104,750)
The Rt. Hon. the Lord Lane, afc
(*born* 1918, *apptd* 1980)
Secretary, Mrs J. Simpson; *Clerk*, J. Bond.

Judges (each £84,250)
Hon. Sir Leslie Boreham, *born* 1918, *apptd* 1972.
Hon. Sir Haydn Tudor Evans, *born* 1920, *apptd* 1974.
Hon. Sir Derek Hodgson, *born* 1917, *apptd* 1977.
Hon. Sir Ronald Waterhouse, *born* 1926, *apptd* 1978.
Hon. Sir Maurice Drake, dfc, *born* 1923, *apptd* 1978.
Hon. Sir Barry Sheen, *born* 1918, *apptd* 1978.
Hon. Sir Christopher French, *born* 1925, *apptd* 1979.
Hon. Sir Peter Webster, *born* 1924, *apptd* 1980.
Hon. Sir Charles McCullough, *born* 1931, *apptd* 1981.
Hon. Sir John Leonard, *born* 1926, *apptd* 1981.
Hon. Sir David Hirst, *born* 1925, *apptd* 1982.
Hon. Sir John Stewart Hobhouse, *born* 1932, *apptd* 1982.
Hon. Sir Oliver Popplewell, *born* 1927, *apptd* 1983.
Hon. Sir William Macpherson, td, *born* 1926, *apptd* 1983.
Hon. Sir Philip Otton, *born* 1933, *apptd* 1983.
Hon. Sir Paul Kennedy, *born* 1935, *apptd* 1983.
Hon. Sir Michael Hutchison, *born* 1933, *apptd* 1983.
Hon. Sir Simon Brown, *born* 1937, *apptd* 1984.
Hon. Sir Anthony Evans, *born* 1934, *apptd* 1984.
Hon. Sir Mark Saville, *born* 1936, *apptd* 1985.
Hon. Sir Johan Steyn, *born* 1932, *apptd* 1985.
Hon. Sir Christopher Rose, *born* 1937, *apptd* 1985.
Hon. Sir Swinton Thomas, *born* 1931, *apptd* 1985.
Hon. Sir Richard Tucker, *born* 1931, *apptd* 1985.
Hon. Sir Robert Gatehouse, *born* 1924, *apptd* 1985.
Hon. Sir Patrick Garland, *born* 1929, *apptd* 1985.
Hon. Sir John Roch, *born* 1934, *apptd* 1985.
Hon. Sir Michael Turner, *born* 1931, *apptd* 1985.
Hon. Sir John Alliott, *born* 1932, *apptd* 1986.
Hon. Sir Harry Ognall, *born* 1934, *apptd* 1986.

Hon. Sir Konrad Schiemann, *born* 1937, *apptd* 1986.
Hon. Sir John Owen, *born* 1925, *apptd* 1986.
Hon. Sir Denis Henry, *born* 1931, *apptd* 1986.
Hon. Sir Humphrey Potts, *born* 1931, *apptd* 1986.
Hon. Sir Richard Rougier, *born* 1932, *apptd* 1986.
Hon. Sir Ian Kennedy, *born* 1930, *apptd* 1986.
Hon. Sir Nicholas Phillips, *born* 1938, *apptd* 1987.
Hon. Sir Robin Auld, *born* 1937, *apptd* 1988.
Hon. Sir Malcolm Pill, *born* 1938, *apptd* 1988.
Hon. Sir Stuart McKinnon, *born* 1938, *apptd* 1988.
Hon. Sir Mark Potter, *born* 1937, *apptd* 1988.
Hon. Sir Henry Brooke, *born* 1936, *apptd* 1988.
Hon. Sir Igor Judge, *born* 1941, *apptd* 1988.
Hon. Sir Edwin Jowitt, *born* 1929, *apptd* 1988.
Hon. Sir Michael Morland, *born* 1929, *apptd* 1989.
Hon. Sir Mark Waller, *born* 1940, *apptd* 1989.
Hon. Sir Roger Buckley, *born* 1939, *apptd* 1989.
Hon. Sir Anthony Hidden, *born* 1936, *apptd* 1989.
Hon. Sir Desmond Fennell, OBE, *born* 1933, *apptd* 1990.
Hon. Sir Michael Wright, *born* 1932, *apptd* 1990.
Hon. Sir Charles Mantell, *born* 1937, *apptd* 1990.
Hon. Sir John Blofeld, *born* 1932, *apptd* 1990.
Hon. Sir Peter Cresswell, *born* 1944, *apptd* 1991.
Hon. Sir Anthony May, *born* 1940, *apptd* 1991.

FAMILY DIVISION
President (£93,000)
Rt. Hon. Sir Stephen Brown
(*born* 1929, *apptd* 1977)
Secretary, Mrs S. Leung; *Clerk*, Mrs S. Bell.

Judges (each £84,250)
Hon. Sir Kenneth Hollings, MC, *born* 1918, *apptd* 1971.
Hon. Sir John Wood, MC, *born* 1922, *apptd* 1977.
Hon. Sir Michael Eastham, *born* 1920, *apptd* 1978.
Hon. Dame Margaret Booth, DBE, *born* 1933, *apptd* 1979.
Hon. Sir Anthony Ewbank, *born* 1925, *apptd* 1980.
Hon. Sir John Waite, *born* 1932, *apptd* 1982.
Hon. Sir Anthony Hollis, *born* 1927, *apptd* 1982.
Hon. Sir Mathew Thorpe, *born* 1938, *apptd* 1988.
Hon. Sir Edward Cazalet, *born* 1936, *apptd* 1988.
Hon. Sir Alan Ward, *born* 1938, *apptd* 1988.
Hon. Sir Scott Baker, *born* 1937, *apptd* 1988.
Hon. Sir Robert Johnson, *born* 1933, *apptd* 1989.
Hon. Sir Douglas Brown, *born* 1931, *apptd* 1989.
Hon. Sir Donald Rattee, *born* 1937, *apptd* 1989.
Hon. Dame Joyanne Bracewell, DBE, *born* 1934, *apptd* 1990.

RESTRICTIVE PRACTICES COURT
President, vacant.
Judicial Members, The Hon. Mr Justice Warner; The Hon. Lord Sutherland; The Hon. Mr Justice Murray.
Lay Members, N. L. Salmon; I. G. Stewart; B. M. Currie; L. Robertson; R. Garrick.

OFFICIAL REFEREES' COURTS
St Dunstan's House,
133–137 Fetter Lane,
EC4A 1HD

His Hon. Judge Newey, QC; His Hon. Judge Lewis, QC; His Hon. Judge Davies, QC; His Hon. Judge Fox-Andrews, QC; His Hon. Judge Bowsher, QC; His Hon. Judge Loyd, QC; His Hon. Judge Forbes, QC................................. £73,250

LORD CHANCELLOR'S DEPARTMENT
See **Government and Public Offices.**

SUPREME COURT DEPARTMENTS AND OFFICES
Royal Courts of Justice, WC2A 2LL
[071–936 6000]

Administrator, G. A. Calvett. ...... £36,178–£41,120

Central Office of the Supreme Court
Royal Courts of Justice, WC2A 2LL

Senior Master of the Supreme Court (QBD), and Queen's Remembrancer, W. K. Topley £66,500
Masters of the Supreme Court (QBD), P. B. Creightmore; D. L. Prebble; A. A. Grant; G. H. Hodgson; R. L. Turner; J. Trench; M. Tennant; P. Miller; N. O. G. Murray; I. H. Foster £59,900
Chief Clerk (Central Office), C. F. Jones £24,379–£29,073

Court of Appeal (Civil Division) Office
Royal Courts of Justice, WC2A 2LL
[071–936 6000]

Registrar, J. D. R. Adams £66,500
Chief Clerk, Miss H. M. Goddard ... £17,367–£21,724

Criminal Appeal Office
Royal Courts of Justice, WC2A 2LL
[071–936 6000]

Registrar, M. McKenzie, QC £66,500
Deputy Registrar, J. P. Stockton ... £36,178–£41,120
Chief Clerk, K. M. Dickerson ...... £24,379–£29,073

Courts-Martial Appeals Office
Royal Courts of Justice, WC2A 2LL
[071–936 6000]

Registrar, M. McKenzie, QC.
Chief Clerk, K. M. Dickerson.

Crown Office of the Supreme Court
Royal Courts of Justice, WC2A 2LL
[071–936 6000]

Master of the Crown Office, and Queen's Coroner and Attorney, M. McKenzie, QC £66,500
Head of Crown Office, Mrs L. Knapman £39,402–£44,390

Supreme Court Taxing Office
Chief Master, F. G. Berkeley £66,500
Masters of the Supreme Court, C. R. N. Martyn; M. N. Devonshire, TD; P. T. Hurst; C. A. Prince; M. Ellis; T. H. Seager Berry (*Taxing Master*) £59,900
Chief Clerk, vacant.
Principal Taxing Officer, T. J. Ryan £24,379–£29,073

Examiners of the Court
(Empowered to take examination of witnesses in all Divisions of the High Court)
M. F. Meredith-Hardy; B. Rathbone; N. W. Briggs; R. Jacobs.

Chancery Chambers,
Royal Courts of Justice, WC2A 2LL
[071–936 6000]

Chief Master of the Supreme Court, R. D. Munrow £66,500
Masters of the Supreme Court, M. B. Cholmondeley Clarke; J. M. Dyson; J. S. Gowers; G. A. Barratt £59,900
Chief Clerk, G. Robinson .... £17,367–£21,724
Conveyancing Counsel of the Supreme Court, J. Monckton; S. G. Maurice; M. J. Roth.

Bankruptcy Department
Thomas More Building, Royal Courts of Justice, Strand, WC2A 2LL
[071–936 6000]

Chief Registrar, T. L. Dewhurst £66,500
Chief Clerk, M. Brown .... £17,367–£21,724

Official Receivers' Department
21 Bloomsbury Street, WC1B 3SS
[071–323 3090]

Senior Official Receiver, J. R. Donnison.
Official Receivers, M. J. Pugh; L. T. Cramp; M. W. A. Sanderson; G. J. A. Harp.

Companies Court
Thomas More Building,
Royal Courts of Justice, WC2A 2LL
[071–936 6000]

Registrar, M. Buckley.
Chief Clerk, vacant.
Senior Official Receiver, Companies Department, J. R. Donnison.

Restrictive Practices Court
Thomas More Building,
Royal Courts of Justice, WC2A 2LL
[071–936 6000]

Clerk of the Court, M. Buckley.
Chief Clerk, vacant.

Principal Registry (Family Division)
Somerset House, WC2R 1LP
[071–936 6000]

Senior District Judge, G. B. N. A. Angel £66,500
District Judges, T. G. Guest; D. E. Morris; J. E. Artro-Morris; R. B. Rowe; B. P. F. Kenworthy-Browne; Mrs K. T. Moorhouse; D. T. A. Davies; Mrs N. Pearce; M. J. Segal; R. Conn; Miss I. M. Plumstead; G. J. Maple; Miss H. C. Bradley; K. J. White
£59,900
Secretary, R. P. Knight . . . . £24,379–£29,073

District Probate Registrars
Birmingham and Stoke-on-Trent, C. Marsh.
Brighton and Maidstone, M. N. Emery.
Bristol, Exeter and Bodmin, P. L. Speyer.
Ipswich, Norwich and Peterborough, E. R. Alexander.
Leeds, Lincoln and Sheffield, A. P. Dawson.
Liverpool, Lancaster and Chester, B. J. Thomas.
Llandaff, Bangor, Carmarthen and Gloucester, R. F. Yeldham.
Manchester and Nottingham, M. A. Moran.
Newcastle, Carlisle, York and Middlesbrough, P. Sanderson.
Oxford, R. R. Da Costa.
Winchester, A. K. Biggs.

Admiralty and Commercial Registry and Marshal's Office
Royal Courts of Justice, WC2A 2LL
[071–936 6000]

Registrar, W. K. Topley £66,500
Marshal and Chief Clerk, A. Ferrigno
£23,379–£29,073

Court of Protection
Stewart House, 24 Kingsway, WC2B 6HD
[071-269 7000]

Master, Mrs A. B. Macfarlane £66,500

Official Solicitor's Department
81 Chancery Lane, WC2A 1DD

Official Solicitor to the Supreme Court, H. D. S. Venables . . . . £48,000–£55,700
Deputy Official Solicitor, H. J. Baker £39,402–£44,390
Chief Clerk, Mrs V. J. Carter . . . . . . £24,379–£29,073

Election Petitions Office
Room 184, Royal Courts of Justice, Strand,
WC2A 2LL
[071-936 6131]

The office accepts petitions and deals with all matters relating to the questioning of Parliamentary, European Assembly and Local Government elections and with applications for relief under the Representation of the People legislation.

The Prescribed Officer, who is normally the Senior Master of the Supreme Court Queen's Bench Division, is appointed by the Lord Chief Justice.

Prescribed Officer, K. W. Topley.
Chief Clerk, C. I. P. Denyer.

OFFICE OF THE LORD CHANCELLOR'S VISITORS
Trevelyan House, 30 Great Peter Street, SW1
[071–210 8563]

Legal Visitor, A. R. Tyrrell.
Medical Visitors, A. G. Fullerton; F. E. Kenyon; K. Kahn; P. A. Morris; D. Parr; J. Roberts.

OFFICE OF THE JUDGE ADVOCATE OF THE FLEET
The Law Courts, Barker Road, Maidstone ME16 8EQ
[0622-754966]

Judge Advocate of the Fleet, His Hon. Judge Waley, VRD, QC.

OFFICE OF THE JUDGE ADVOCATE GENERAL OF THE FORCES
(*Joint Service for the Army and the Royal Air Force*)
22 Kingsway, WC2B 6LE
[071-430 5335]

Judge Advocate General, His Honour Judge J. W. Rant, QC £65,250
Vice Judge Advocate General, G. L. Chapman
£58,800
Assistant Judge Advocates General, E. G. Moelwyn-Hughes; A. P. Pitts; D. M. Berkson; M. A. Hunter; T. R. King; T. G. Pontius; J. P. Camp
£37,100–£42,800
Deputy Judge Advocates, Miss S. E. Woollam; R. C. C. Seymour . . . . £25,950–£36,400

HIGH COURT AND CROWN COURT CENTRES

First-tier centres deal with both civil and criminal cases and are served by High Court and circuit judges. Second-tier centres deal with criminal cases only and are served by High Court and circuit judges. Third-tier centres deal with criminal cases only and are served only by circuit judges.

Midland and Oxford Circuit

First-tier—Birmingham, Lincoln, Nottingham, Oxford, Stafford, Warwick.
Second-tier—Leicester, Northampton, Shrewsbury, Worcester.
Third-tier—Coventry, Derby, Grimsby, Hereford, Peterborough, Stoke-on-Trent, Wolverhampton.
Circuit Administrator, R. E. K. Holmes, 2 Newton Street, Birmingham B4 7LU.
Courts Administrators, Birmingham Group, V. C. Grove; *Nottingham Group*, Mrs E. A. Folman; *Stafford Group*, A. F. Parker.

North Eastern Circuit

First-tier—Leeds, Newcastle upon Tyne, Sheffield, Teesside.
Second-tier—York.
Third-tier—Beverley, Doncaster, Durham, Huddersfield, Wakefield.
Circuit Administrator, S. W. L. James, West Riding House, 17th Floor, Albion Street, Leeds LS1 5AA.
Courts Administrators, Leeds Group, P. Delany; *Newcastle upon Tyne Group*, K. Budgeon; *Sheffield Group*, G. Bingham.

Northern Circuit

First-tier—Carlisle, Liverpool, Manchester, Preston.
Third-tier—Barrow-in-Furness, Bolton, Burnley, Lancaster.
Circuit Administrator, P. M. Harris, Aldine House, West Riverside, New Bailey Street, Salford M3 5EU.
Courts Administrators, Manchester Group, A. H. Howard; *Liverpool Group*, D. A. Beaumont; *Preston Group*, Mrs A. Prior.

South Eastern Circuit

First-tier—Chelmsford, Lewes, Norwich.
Second-tier—Ipswich, London (Central Criminal Court), Maidstone, Reading, St Albans.
Third-tier—Aylesbury, Bury St Edmunds, Cambridge, Canterbury, Chichester, Guildford, King's Lynn, London (Croydon, Harrow, Inner London Session House, Isleworth, Kingston upon Thames, Knightsbridge, Middlesex Guildhall, Snaresbrook, Southwark and Wood Green), Southend.
The High Court in Greater London sits at the Royal Courts of Justice.
Circuit Administrator, B. Cooke, New Cavendish House, 18 Maltravers Street, WC2.
Deputy Circuit Administrator, Miss B. J. Kenny.
Courts Administrators, Chelmsford Group, P. Handcock; *Maidstone Group*, Mrs H. Hartwell; *Kingston Group*, P. M. Thomas; *London (Civil)*, P. Risk; *London (Crime)*, G. F. Addicott.

Wales and Chester Circuit

First-tier—Caernarfon, Cardiff, Chester, Mold, Swansea.
Second-tier—Carmarthen, Merthyr Tydfil, Newport, Welshpool.
Third-tier—Dolgellau, Haverfordwest, Knutsford, Warrington.
Circuit Administrator, D. Howe, Churchill House, Churchill Way, Cardiff.
Courts Administrators, Cardiff Group, G. Jones; *Chester Group*, T. D. Beckett.

Western Circuit

First-tier—Bristol, Exeter, Truro, Winchester.
Second-tier—Dorchester, Gloucester, Plymouth.
Third-tier—Barnstaple, Bournemouth, Devizes, Newport (IOW), Portsmouth, Salisbury, Southampton, Swindon, Taunton.
Circuit Administrator, G. Jones, Bridge House, Clifton, Bristol BS8 4BN.
Courts Administrators, Bristol Group, A. C. Butler; *Exeter Group*, J. Ardern; *Winchester Group*, P. Matthews.

CIRCUIT JUDGES

(*Senior Circuit Judges, £66,500; Circuit Judges, £59,900 from Dec. 1, 1991)

Midland and Oxford Circuit

W. A. L. Allardice; F. A. Allen; B. J. Appleby, QC; M. J. Astill; I. J. Black, QC; J. F. Blythe, TD; D. W. Brunning; F. L. Clark, QC; P. N. R. Clark; R. R. B. Cole; P. F. Crane; P. J. Crawford, QC; R. H. Curtis, QC; I. T. R. Davidson, QC; T. M. Dillon, QC; C. H. Durman; J. F. Evans, QC; B. A. Farrer, QC; Miss E. N. Fisher; J. E. Fletcher; R. J. H. Gibbs, QC; H. G. A. Gosling; J. Hall; M. K. Harrison-Hall; T. R. Heald; J. R. Hopkin; R. H. Hutchinson; J. E. M. Irvine; R. P. V. Jenkins; J. G. Jones; J. T. C. Lee; M. H. Mander; K. Matthewman, QC; R. G. May; P. W. Medd, OBE, QC; K. S. W. Mellor, QC; N. Micklem; A. J. H. Morrison; M. D. Mott; A. J. D. Nicholl; J. F. F. Orrell; C. J. Pitchers; R. F. D. Pollard; F. M. Potter; J. R. Pyke; D. E. Roberts; J. A. O. Shand; J. R. S. Smyth; P. J. Stretton; C. S. Stuart-White; H. C. Tayler; K. J. Taylor; R. J. Toyn; M. B. Ward; R. L. Ward, QC; D. J. R. Wilcox; D. H. Wild; H. Wilson; J. W. Wilson; B. Woods; G. H. Wootton; C. G. Young.

Northern Circuit

H. H. Andrew, QC; J. R. Arthur, DFC; A. W. Bell; R. C. W. Bennett; Miss I. Bernstein; M. S. Blackburn; A. S. Booth, QC; R. Brown; I. B. Campbell; F. B. Carter, QC; D. Clark; G. P. Crowe, QC; *R. E. Davies, QC (*Recorder of Manchester); M. Dean, QC; Miss A. E. Downey; B. R. Duckworth; S. B. Duncan; Miss A. M. Ebsworth; A. A. Edmondson; D. M. Evans, QC; S. J. D. Fawcus; D. G. F. Franks; R. G. Hamilton; J. A. Hammond; R. J. Hardy; F. D. Hart, QC; T. D. T. Hodson; Miss M. Holt; G. W. Humphries; A. C. Jolly; H. A. Kershaw; P. M. Kershaw, QC (*Commercial Circuit Judge*); H. L. Lachs; C. N. Lees; J. M. Lever, QC; R. Lockett; J. H. Lord; D. Lynch; B. C. Maddocks; C. J. Mahon; J. A. Morgan; I. H. Morris-Jones, QC; M. O'Donoghue; F. D. Owen, TD; F. D. Paterson; R. E. I. Pickering; D. A. Pirie; A. J. Proctor; M. A. G. Sachs; H. S. Singer; J. A. Stannard (*Commercial Circuit Judge*); Miss A. H. Steel; I. R. Taylor, QC; *Sir Sanderson Temple, MBE, QC (*Recorder of Liverpool*); J. P. Townend; I. S Webster; W. R. Wickham; B. Woodward.

North Eastern Circuit

T. G. F. Atkinson; G. Baker, QC; P. M. Baker, QC; J. M. A. Barker; G. N. Barr Young; D. R. Bentley, QC; D. M. A. Bryant; J. W. M. Bullimore; B. Bush; M. C. Carr; P. J. Charlesworth; J. G. K. Coles, QC; J. A. Cotton; J. Crabtree; M. T. Cracknell; W. H. R. Crawford, QC; P. J. Fox, QC; A. N. Fricker, QC; M. S. Garner; W. Hannah; G. F. R. Harkins; J. A. Henham; D. Herrod, QC; P. M. L. Hoffman; R. Hunt; V. R. Hurwitz; A. E. Hutchinson, QC; J. R. Johnson; T. D. Kent-Jones, TD; C. F. Kolbert; G. M. Lightfoot; A. C. Macdonald; Miss M. B. M. MacMurray, QC; A. L. Myerson, QC; D. A. Orde; Miss H. E. Paling; R. A. Percy; *D. M. Savill, QC; A. Simpson; J. Stephenson; R. A. R. Stroyan, QC; R. C. Taylor; G. M. Vos; M. Walker; P. H. C. Walker.

South Eastern Circuit

J. R. S. Adams; F. J. Aglionby; M. J. Anwyl-Davies, QC; J. A. Baker; J. B. Baker, QC; M. J. D. Baker; P. V. Baker, QC; A. F. Balston; R. M. N. Band, MC, QC; C. J. A. Barnett, QC; R. A. Barr; K. Bassingthwaighte; N. G. A. Bathurst; P. T. S. Batterbury, TD; P. J. L. Beaumont, QC; N. E. Beddard; F. E. Beezley; G. J. Binns; M. Birks; J. Bolland; P. C. Bowsher, QC; P. N. Brandt; L. J. Bromley, QC; A. E. Brooks; J. M. Bull, QC; G. N. Butler, QC; *N. M. Butter, QC; H. J. Byrt, QC; C. V. Callman; B. E. Capstick, QC; B. L. Charles, QC; A. W. Clark; D. J. Clarkson, QC; P. C. Clegg; M. Cohen, QC; S. H. Colgan; C. C. Colston, QC; C. D. Compston; R. D. Connor; M. J. Cook; R. A. Cooke; R. K. Cooke, OBE; G. H. Coombe; M. R. Coombe; A. Cooray; Margaret D. Cosgrave; R. C. Cox; D. L. Croft, QC; G. L. Davies; I. H. Davies, TD; L. J. Davies, QC; W. L. M. Davies, QC; W. N. Denison, QC; K. M. Devlin; A. E. J. Diamond; G. L. S. Dobry, CBE, QC; A. H. Durrant; C. M. Edwards; Q. T. Edwards, QC; F. P. L. Evans; J. K. Q. Evans; S. J. Evans; J. D.

Farnworth; A. L. Figgis; J. J. Finney; T. J. Forbes, QC; P. Ford; J. J. Fordham; G. C. F. Forrester; J. Fox-Andrews, QC; Ms D. A. Freedman.

A. Garfitt; R. Gee; L. Gerber; S. A. Goldstein; P. W. Goldstone; M. B. Goodman; C. G. M. Gordon; J. B. Gosschalk; J. H. Gower, QC; M. Graham, QC; P. B. Greenwood; D. J. Griffiths; G. D. Grigson; R. B. Groves, TD, VRD; N. T. Hague, QC; P. J. Halnan; J. Hamilton; R. E. Hammerton; B. Hargrove, OBE, QC; J. P. Harris, DSC, QC; R. G. Hawkins, QC; J. D. W. Hayman; A. H. Head; M. R. Hickman; J. C. Hicks, QC; A. N. Hitching; D. Holden; A. C. W. Hordern, QC; R. W. Howe; Sir David Hughes-Morgan, Bt., CB, CBE; J. Hunter; M. J. Hyam; C. P. James; M. Kennedy, QC; A. M. Kenny; L. G. Krikler; L. H. C. Lait; P. St J. H. Langan, QC; Capt. J. B. R. L. Langdon, RN; G. F. B. Laughland, QC; R. Laurie; T. Lawrence; E. Lewis, QC; A. Lipfriend; D. T. Lloyd; F. R. Lockhart; G. D. Lovegrove, QC; D. B. D. Lowe; R. H. Lownie; Mrs N. M. Lowry; R. J. Lowry, QC; J. A. T. Loyd, QC; R. D. Lymbery, QC (*Common Serjeant*); K. M. McHale; K. A. Machin, QC; I. G. McLean; M. B. McMullan; M. J. P. Macnair; K. C. Macrae; J. R. Main, QC; B. A. Marder, QC; F. J. M. Marr-Johnson; O. S. Martin, QC; N. A. Medawar, QC; D. J. Mellor; J. H. E. Mendl; A. L. Mildon, QC; D. Q. Miller; S. G. Mitchell, QC; E. F. Monier-Williams; D. Morton Jack; J. I. Murchie.

Mrs N. F. Negus; M. H. D. Neligan; J. H. R. Newey, QC; C. W. F. Newman, QC; Mrs M. F. Norrie; Suzanne F. Norwood; P. W. O'Brien; C. R. Oddie; A. Owen; D. A. Paiba; R. H. S. Palmer; M. C. Parker, QC; Miss V. A. Pearlman; J. R. Peppitt, QC; F. H. L. Petre; A. J. Phelan; D. C. Pitman; P. B. Pollock; H. C. Pownall, QC; R. J. C. V. Prendergast; B. H. Pryor, QC; J. E. Pullinger; J. W. Rant, QC; E. V. P. Reece; G. K. Rice; K. A. Richardson, QC; G. Rivlin, QC; J. H. P. Roberts; D. A. H. Rodwell, QC; G. H. Rooke, TD, QC; P. C. R. Rountree; K. W. R. Rubin; J. H. Rucker; T. R. G. Ryland; R. B. Sanders; J. D. Sheerin; *G. J. Shindler, QC; D. R. A. Sich; A. G. Simmons; K. T. Simpson; P. R. Simpson; M. Singh, QC; J. K. E. Slack, TD; P. M. J. Slot; F. B. Smedley, QC; C. M. Smith, QC; R. J. Southan; S. B. Spence; *R. O. C. Stable, QC; E. Stockdale; C. J. Sumner; W. F. C. Thomas; A. G. Y. Thorpe; A. H. Tibber; C. H. Tilling; A. M. Troup; S. Tumim; J. T. Turner; C. J. M. Tyrer; Mrs A. P. Uziell-Hamilton; J. E. van der Werff; L. J. Verney, TD (*Recorder of London*); A. O. R. Vick, QC; Miss M. S. Viner, QC; B. J. Wakley, MBE; A. F. Waley, VRD, QC; R. Walker; D. B. Watling, QC; V. B. Watts; F. J. White; S. M. Willis; C. G. P. Woodford; G. N. Worthington; E. G. Wrintmore; K. H. Zucker, QC.

Wales and Chester Circuit

T. R. Crowther, QC; G. H. M. Daniel; R. D. G. David, QC; J. B. S. Diehl, QC; D. E. H. Edwards; G. O. Edwards, QC; Lord Elystan-Morgan; T. M. Evans, QC; W. N. Francis; M. Gibbon, QC; D. M. Hughes; G. J. Jones; G. E. Kilfoil; T. E. I. Lewis-Bowen; D. G. Morgan; T. H. Moseley, QC; D. A. Phillips; D. W. Powell; E. J. Prosser, QC; H. W. J. ap Robert; H. E. P. Roberts, QC; *J. C. Rutter; S. M. Stephens, QC; D. B. Williams, TD, QC; H. V. Williams, QC; R. G. Woolley.

Western Circuit

M. F. Addison; S. T. Bates, QC; C. L. Boothman; M. J. L. Brodrick; R. D. H. Bursell, QC; J. R. Chalkley; Sir Jonathan Clarke; M. G. Cotterill; Hazel Counsell; J. A. Cox; J. W. Da Cunha; M. Dyer; *P. Fallon, QC; P. D. Fanner; B. J. F. Galpin; D. L. Griffiths; I. S. Hill, QC; G. B. Hutton; J. H. Inskip, QC; R. E. Jack, QC; A. C. Lauriston, QC; D. McCarraher, VRD; Miss S. M. D. McKinney; I. S. McKintosh; J. G. McNaught; E. G. Neville; S. K. O'Malley; S. K. Overend; J. N. P. Rudd; D. A. Smith, QC; W. E. M. Taylor; H. J. M. Tucker, QC; D. M. Webster, QC; J. H. Weeks, QC; J. R.

Whitley; J. A. J. Wigmore; K. M. Willcock, QC; J. C. Willis; J. H. Wroath.

RECORDERS

I. D. G. Alexander, QC; M. P. Allweis; J. Altman; Miss C. Alton; W. P. Andreae-Jones, QC; P. J. Andrews, QC; A. R. L. Ansell; Ms L. E. Appleby, QC; J. F. Appleton; J. F. A. Archer, QC; Rt. Hon. P. K. Archer, QC, MP; A. J. Arlidge, QC; E. K. Armitage; R. Ashton; P. Ashworth, QC; J. M. Aspinall; B. Atchley; N. J. Atkinson, QC; M. G. Austin-Smith; W. S. Aylen, QC; J. F. Badenoch, QC; P. G. N. Badge; A. B. Baillie; M. F. Baker, QC; N. R. J. Baker, QC; T. W. Barber; G. S. Barham; A. Barker, QC; B. J. Barker, QC; D. Barker, QC; R. O. Barlow; D. M. W. Barnes, QC; T. P. Barnes, QC; W. E. Barnett, QC; J. E. Barry; G. R. Bartlett, QC; J. C. T. Barton, QC; D. C. Bate; S. D. Batten, QC; J. J. Baughan, QC; J. F. Beashel; C. H. Beaumont; C. O. M. Bedingfield, TD, QC; R. W. Belben; R. Bell, QC; The Hon. M. J. Beloff, QC; D. P. Bennett; H. P. D. Bennett, QC; P. Bennett, QC; R. S. A. Benson; K. C. Bentall; H. L. Bentham; D. M. Berkson; M. Bethel, QC; J. P. V. Bevan; J. C. Beveridge, QC; P. V. Birkett, QC; P. W. Birts, QC; J. E. Bishop; B. M. Black; J. A. Blair-Gould; A. N. H. Blake; C. Bloom, QC; D. J. Blunt, QC; J. G. Boal; G. T. K. Boney, QC; D. J. Boulton; P. H. Bowers; J. J. Boyle; A. V. Bradbury; R. W. A. Bray; D. J. Brennan; M. L. Brent, QC; G. J. B. G. Brice, QC; J. N. W. Bridges-Adams; A. J. Brigden; A. N. J. Briggs; P. J. Briggs; D. K. Brown; R. G. Brown; A. J. N. Brunner; A. Bueno, QC; D. L. Bulmer; J. M. J. Burford, QC; J. P. Burgess; J. K. Burke, QC; J. P. Burke, QC; M. A. B. Burke-Gaffney, QC; H. W. Burnett, QC; M. R. Burr; M. J. Burton, QC; A. J. Butcher, QC; A. N. L. Butterfield, QC; R. J. Buxton, QC.

Mrs B. A. Calvert, QC; D. Calvert-Smith; Miss S. M. C. Cameron, QC; A. N. B. Campbell; J. Q. Campbell; G. M. C. Carey, QC; A. C. Carlile, QC, MP; The Lord Carlisle of Bucklow, PC, QC; H. B. H. Carlisle, QC; M. L. Cartlidge; R. Carus, QC; B. I. Caulfield; J. J. Cavell; J. A. Chadwin, QC; N. M. Chambers, QC; F. A. Chapman; B. W. Chedlow, QC; J. M. Cherry, QC; C. F. Chruszcz; C. H. Clark, QC; A. P. Clarke, QC; C. S. C. S. Clarke, QC; D. C. Clarke, QC; P. W. Clarke; R. N. B. Clegg, QC; G. M. Clifton; C. D. Cochrane, QC; P. J. Cockcroft; D. J. Cocks, QC; J. J. Coffey; T. A. Coghlan; W. J. Coker; J. R. Cole; N. J. Coleman; N. B. C. Coles, QC; P. N. Collier; A. D. Collins, QC; J. M. Collins; P. H. Collins; A. D. Colman, QC; S. S. Coltart; Ms M. Colton; Viscount Colville of Culross, QC; J. S. Colyer, QC; Mrs J. R. Comyns; P. R. C. Coni, QC; T. A. C. Coningsby, QC; G. D. Conlin; M. B. Connell, QC; J. G. Connor; C. S. Cook; Miss B. P. Cooper, QC; S. M. Corkhill; T. G. E. Corrie; E. Cotran; G. W. A. Cottle; Miss D. R. Cotton, QC; J. S. Coward, QC; B. R. E. Cox, QC; P. J. Cox, DSC, QC; C. J. Crespi, QC; D. I. Crigman, QC; M. L. S. Cripps; C. A. Critchlow; J. F. Crocker; I. W. Crompton; F. P. Crowder, QC; J. D. Crowley, QC; E. J. R. Crowther, OBE; W. R. H. Crowther, QC; Miss E. A. M. Curnow, QC; J. W. O. Curtis; M. J. Curwen; Ms J. M. P. Daley; A. J. G. Dalziel; S. C. Darwall-Smith; Mrs S. P. Darwall-Smith; G. W. Davey; C. P. M. Davidson; D. T. A. Davies; Mrs J. Davies; Ms L. H. Davies; A. W. Dawson; D. H. Day, QC; J. J. Deave; J. B. Deby, QC; C. F. Dehn, QC; P. A. de la Piquerie; P. N. De Mille; M. A. de Navarro, QC; W. E. Denny, CBE, QC; R. L. Denyer, QC; S. C. Desch, QC; H. A. D. de Silva; J. E. Devaux; M. N. Devonshire; A. D. Dinkin, QC; I. J. Dobkin; Ms B. Dohmann, QC; A. M. Donne, QC; R. Du Cann, QC; S. M. Duffield; P. R. Dunkels; W. H. Dunn, QC; J. A. Dyson, QC.

D. Eady, QC; Ms D. B. Eaglestone; T. K. Earnshaw; J. S. Eastwood; H. W. P. Eccles, QC; D. F. Elfer, QC; G. Elias, QC; B. J. Elliott; D. R. Ellis; R. M. Englehart, QC; G. A. Ensor; D. A. Evans, QC; D. R. Evans, QC; E.

C. Evans-Lombe, QC; Sir Graham Eyre, QC; W. D. Fairclough; D. J. Farrer, QC; K. J. Farrow; E. J. Faulks; M. H. Fauvelle; R. Fernyhough, QC; P. Fingret; D. P. Fisher; G. D. Flather, QC; P. E. J. Focke, QC; J. D. Foley; R. A. Fordham; J. R. Foster, QC; R. M. Foster; R. H. K. Frisby, QC; J. H. Fryer-Spedding, OBE.

W. M. Gage, QC; M. Gale, QC; J. R. B. Geake; A. C. Geddes; A. H. Gee, QC; D. S. Gee; D. S. Geey; L. N. H. George; C. A. H. Gibson; J. A. D. Gilliland, QC; N. B. D. Gilmour, QC; L. Giovene; A. T. Glass, QC; H. B. Globe; Miss A. F. Goddard, QC; H. K. Goddard, QC; Ms L. S. Godfrey, QC; J. B. Goldring, QC; A. R. Goldsack, QC; P. H. Goldsmith; I. F. Goldsworthy; A. J. J. Gompertz, QC; A. A. Gordon; J. P. Gorman, QC; T. J. C. Goudie, QC; C. O. G. Gould; A. A. Goymer; A. S. Grabiner, QC; C. A. St J. Gray, QC; G. Gray, QC; J. M. Gray; R. I. Gray, QC; R. M. K. Gray, QC; B. S. Green, QC; H. Green, QC; S. P. Grenfell; R. D. Grey, QC; J. C. Griffiths, CMG, QC; J. P. G. Griffiths; L. Griffiths; J. D. Griggs; M. G. Grills; M. S. E. Grime, QC; Mrs H. M. Grindrod, QC; P. Grobel; M. A. W. Grundy; S. J. Gullick.

A. S. Hacking, QC; Mrs C. M. A. Hagen; M. F. Haigh; J. W. Haines; D. R. Halbert; D. J. Hale; J. C. Hall; V. E. Hall; D. T. Hallchurch; Ms H. C. Hallett, QC; A. B. R. Hallgarten, QC; G. Hallon; A. W. Hamilton, QC; D. R. D. Hamilton; G. M. Hamilton, TD, QC; S. T. Hammond; J. Hampton; J. L. Hand, QC; C. R. H. Hardy; Miss R. S. A. Hare, QC; R. D. Harman, QC; P. J. Harrington; D. M. Harris, QC; G. C. W. Harris, QC; M. F. Harris; M. G. V. Harrison, QC; R. M. Harrison, QC; C. P. Hart-Leverton, QC; C. S. Harvey, MBE, TD; M. L. T. Harvey, QC; R. O. Havery, QC; T. S. A. Hawkesworth, QC; R. J. Haworth; R. W. P. Hay; R. Hayward-Smith, QC; M. Hedley; T. B. Hegarty; G. E. Heggs; R. A. Henderson, QC; R. H. Q. Henriques, QC; P. J. M. Heppel; R. B. Hickman; B. J. Higgs, QC; E. M. Hill, QC; J. W. Hillyer; A. J. H. Hilton, QC; Ms E. J. Hindley; J. D. Hitchen; S. A. Hockman, QC; C. R. Hodson; The Hon. Mary Hogg, QC; A. J. C. Hoggett, QC; Ms B. M. Hoggett, QC; D. A. Hollis, VRD, QC; F. R. B. Holloway; C. J. Holmes; R. M. Hone; A. T. Hoolahan, QC; A. Hooper, QC; The Lord Hooson, QC; M. Horowitz, QC; C. P. Hotten; B. F. Houlder; R. Houlker, QC; M. Howard, QC, MP; N. J. G. Howarth; M. J. Hubbard, QC; A. P. G. Hughes, QC; T. M. Hughes; J. Hugill, QC; J. G. Hull, QC; D. R. N. Hunt, QC; P. J. Hunt, QC; I. G. A. Hunter, QC; M. Hussain; B. A. Hytner, QC.

N. J. Inglis-Jones, QC; D. A. Inman; A. B. Issard-Davies; M. R. Jackson; P. J. E. Jackson; R. M. Jackson, QC; I. E. Jacob; C. E. F. James; N. F. B. Jarman, QC; D. A. Jeffreys, QC; J. Jeffs, QC; J. D. Jenkins, QC; D. B. Johnson, QC; M. H. Johnson; A. G. H. Jones; G. R. Jones; H. D. H. Jones; N. H. Jones, QC; S. E. Jones; T. G. Jones; W. H. Joss; P. S. L. Joyce, QC; M. D. L. Kalisher, QC; M. L. Kallipetis, QC; H. Kamil; J. W. Kay, QC; M. R. Kay, QC; D. St J. Keane, QC; M. L. Keane; K. R. Keen, QC; D. W. Keene, QC; C. L. Kelly; C. J. B. Kemp; D. A. M. Kemp, QC; L. D. Kershen; G. M. Khayat; R. I. Kidwell, QC; A. W. P. King; T. R. A. King, QC; W. M. Kingston; A. T. H. Kirkwood, QC; R. C. Klevan, QC; B. J. Knight, QC; S. E. Kramer.

L. P. Laity; C. A. Lamb; D. G. Lane, QC; G. J. H. Langley, QC; D. N. R. Latham, QC; R. B. Latham, QC; S. W. Lawler; I. J. Lawrence, QC, MP; J. G. M. Laws; M. H. Lawson, QC; G. S. Lawson Rogers; L. D. Lawton, QC; D. Lederman; M. K. Lee, QC; R. T. L. Lee; B. W. T. Leech; I. Leeming, QC; C. H. de V. Leigh, QC; Sir Godfrey Le Quesne, QC; A. P. Lester, QC; B. H. Leveson, QC; S. Levine; D. M. Levy, QC; M. E. Lewer, QC; A. K. Lewis, QC; M. ap G. Lewis, QC; R. S. Lewis; C. C. D. Lindsay, QC; S. J. Linehan; J. S. Lipton; B. J. E. Livesey, QC; R. J. D. Livesey, QC; C. G. Llewellyn-Jones, QC; H. J. Lloyd, QC; J. Lloyd-Eley, QC; A. J. C.

Lodge, Q.C.; A. G. Longden; D. C. Lovell-Pank; R. P. Lowden; G. W. Lowe; G. W. Lowther; F. D. L. Loy; G. Lumley; Sir Nicholas Lyell, QC, MP; E. Lyons, QC; Capt. S. Lyons, RN.

A. G. McCallum; A. W. McCreath; A. G. MacDuff; D. D. McEvoy, QC; R. D. Machell, QC; E. A. Machin, QC; D. I. Mackay; T. N. MacKean; N. R. B. Macleod, QC; N. J. C. McLusky; J. B. MacMillan; D. G. Maddison; T. Maher; Miss V. H. Mairants; A. R. Malcolm; The Baroness Mallalieu, QC; J. H. Mance, QC; M. E. Mann, QC; A. C. B. Markham-David; L. A. Marshall; R. G. Marshall-Andrews, QC; D. N. N. Martineau; H. R. A. Martineau; C. G. Masterman; D. Matheson, QC; W. D. Matthews; P. B. Mauleverer, QC; R. B. Mawrey, QC; H. R. Mayor, QC; M. Meggeson; D. B. Meier; G. D. Mercer; M. K. Mettyear; J. T. Milford, QC; R. A. Miller; T. J. Milligan; Mrs B. J. L. Mills, QC; J. B. M. Milmo, QC; N. A. Miscampbell, QC, MP; C. R. Mitchell; J. E. Mitting, QC; E. G. Moelwyn-Hughes; H. J. Montlake; M. J. Moore-Bick, QC; H. M. Morgan; W. G. O. Morgan, QC; G. E. Moriarty, QC; T. R. A. Morison, QC; P. R. Morrell; A. P. Morris, QC; D. G. Morris; The Rt. Hon. J. Morris, QC, MP; J. I. Morris; W. P. Morris; D. C. Morton; A. G. Moses, QC; R. T. Moss; P. C. Mott, QC; R. W. Moxon-Browne, QC; J. H. Muir; J. Mulcahy, QC; F. J. Muller, QC; I. P. Murphy; M. J. A. Murphy; N. J. Mylne, QC.

T. M. E. Nash; R. F. Nelson; D. E. Neuberger, QC; R. E. Newbold; A. R. H. Newman, QC; G. M. Newman, QC; J. D. Newton; G. Nice, QC; C. A. A. Nicholls, QC; C. V. Nicholls, QC; M. C. Nicholson; A. S. T. E. Nicol; B. Nolan; P. H. Norris; J. Q. Nutting; D. P. O'Brien, QC; E. M. Ogden, QC; B. R. Oliver; S. J. L. Oliver, QC; C. P. L. Openshaw, QC; M. A. Oppenheimer; R. T. N. Orme; R. C. C. O'Rorke; G. V. Owen, QC; R. M. Owen, QC; S. R. Page; D. C. J. Paget; A. W. Palmer, QC; A. D. W. Pardoe, QC; S. A. B. Parish; A. E. W. Park, QC; J. F. Parker, QC; G. C. Parkins, QC; G. E. Parkinson; M. P. Parroy, QC; D. J. Parry; E. O. Parry; M. A. Parry Evans; N. S. K. Pascoe, QC; A. Patience, QC; J. G. Paulusz; Mrs N. Pearce; D. H. Penry-Davey, QC; Sir Ian Percival, QC; D. S. Perrett, QC; M. Pert; B. J. Phelvin; W. B. Phillips; N. A. J. Philpot; C. J. Pitchford, QC; A. P. Pitts; Miss E. F. Platt, QC; J. R. Platt; J. R. Playford, QC; A. G. S. Pollock, QC; D. A. Poole, QC; L. R. Portnoy; M. J. Pratt, QC; S. Pratt; T. W. Preston, QC; J. E. Previté, QC; G. A. L. Price; J. A. Price, QC; N. P. L. Price; P. J. Price, QC; R. N. M. Price; R. C. Pryor, QC; A. C. Pugh, QC; G. V. Pugh, QC; D. P. Pugsley; C. P. B. Purchas, QC; R. M. Purchas, QC; N. R. Purnell, QC; P. O. Purnell, QC.

D. A. Radcliffe; Ms A. J. Rafferty, QC; A. Rankin, QC; A. D. Rawley, QC; L. F. Read, QC; A. R. F. Redgrave; J. Reeder, QC; P. Rees; J. R. Reid, QC; R. E. Rhodes, QC; D. G. Rice; M. S. Rich, QC; D. W. Richards; H. A. Richardson; S. V. Riordan; Miss S. A. Ritchie, QC; B. A. Rix, QC; S. D. Robbins; J. A. Roberts, QC; J. D. Roberts; J. H. Roberts; J. M. G. Roberts, QC; P. B. Roberts; P. E. Robertshaw; V. Robinson, QC; D. E. H. Robson, QC; G. W. Roddick, QC; J. M. T. Rogers, QC; J. W. Rogers, QC; K. S. Rokison, QC; J. J. Rowe, QC; R. J. Royce, QC; Ms G. D. Ruaux; R. J. Rubery; A. A. Rumbelow, QC; R. R. Russell; G. C. Ryan, QC.

J. E. A. Samuels, QC; J. H. B. Saunders, QC; M. P. Sayers, QC; R. J. Scholes, QC; R. M. Scott; A. F. B. Scrivener, QC; R. J. Seabrook, QC; A. T. Seader; C. Seagroatt, QC; H. M. Self, QC; M. R. Selfe; O. M. Sells; D. H. D. Selwood; D. Serota, QC; J. L. Sessions; A. J. Seys-Llewellyn; R. M. Shawcross; P. P. Shears; S. J. Sher, QC; M. D. Sherrard, QC; L. S. Shields, QC; J. M. Shorrock, QC; S. R. Silber, QC; J. P. Singer, QC; P. F. Singer; J. C. N. Slater, QC; S. P. Sleeman; A. T. Smith, QC; J. H. Smith, QC; R. S. Smith, QC; S. A. R. Smith; W. P. Smith; Ms Z. P. Smith; R. E. Snape; S. M. Solley, QC; R. F. Solman; E. Somerset Jones, QC; R. C.

E. Southwell; Miss J. M. Southworth, QC; M. H. Spence, QC; D. H. Spencer, QC; J. Spencer, QC; M. G. Spencer, QC; S. M. Spencer, QC; L. Spittle; J. A. C. Spokes, QC; R. W. Spon-Smith; D. P. Stanley; Ms E. M. Steel; D. Steer; M. T. Steiger; D. H. Stembridge, QC; Mrs L. J. Stern, QC; J. S. H. Stewart, QC; R. M. Stewart, QC; G. J. C. Still; D. M. A. Stokes, QC; M. G. T. Stokes; E. D. R. Stone, QC; P. L. Storr; T. M. F. Stow, QC; D. M. A. Strachan, QC; M. Stuart-Moore, QC; J. Stuart-Smith, QC; G. C. Styler; F. R. C. Such; A. B. Suckling, QC; J. M. Sullivan, QC; Ms L. E. Sullivan; D. M. Sumner; Mrs L. Sutcliffe; L. Swift, QC; M. R. Swift, QC.

J. A. Tackaberry, QC; G. F. Tattersall; A. B. Taylor; E. Taylor; N. Taylor, QC; J. J. Teare; A. D. Temple, QC; V. B. A. Temple; M. I. Tennant; K. J. Tetley; C. B. Tetlow; Lord Thomas of Gwydir, PC, QC; D. M. Thomas, OBE, QC; D. O. Thomas, QC; P. M. Thomas; R. J. L. Thomas, QC; R. L. Thomas; R. U. Thomas, QC; A. A. R. Thompson, QC; J. Tiley; M. B. Tillett; R. N. Titheridge, QC; J. K. Toulmin, QC; R. G. Toulson, QC; J. B. S. Townend, QC; C. M. Treacy, QC; H. B. Trethowan; I. J. C. Trigger; A. D. H. Trollope, QC; S. L. Tuckey, QC; H. W. Turcan; D. A. Turner, QC; P. A. Twigg, QC; A. R. Tyrrell, QC; J. G. G. Ungley; P. W. G. Urquhart; N. P. Valios, QC; A. R. Vandermeer, QC; M. J. D. Vere-Hodge; T. L. Viljoen; C. D. Voelcker.

Rt. Hon. D. C. Waddington, QC, MP; J. P. Wadsworth, QC; D. St J. Wagstaff; R. M. Wakerley, QC; W. H. Waldron, QC; J. D. G. Walford; R. J. Walker, QC; T. E. Walker, QC; J. J. Walker-Smith; N. P. R. Wall, QC; B. Walsh, QC; D. E. B. Waters; Sir James Watson, Bt.; C. D. G. Waud; P. A. Webster; M. Weisman; P. Weitzman, QC; C. P. C. Whelon; G. Whitburn, QC; C. H. Whitby, QC; W. J. M. White; D. R. B. Whitehouse, QC; P. G. Whiteman, QC; P. J. M. Whiteman, TD; A. Whitfield, QC; D. G. Widdicombe, QC; R. Wigglesworth; J. S. Wiggs; A. D. F. Wilcken; S. R. Wilkinson; D. B. Williams; G. H. G. Williams, QC; G. W. Williams, QC; J. G. Williams, QC; J. L. Williams, QC; The Hon. J. M. Williams, QC; S. W. Williamson, QC; A. M. Wilson, QC; N. A. R. Wilson, QC; C. Wilson-Smith, QC; G. W. Wingate-Saul, QC; M. E. Wolff; H. Wolton, QC; D. A. Wood, QC; D. R. Wood; W. R. Wood; L. G. Woodley, QC; S. Woodley; J. T. Woods; W. C. Woodward, QC; Ms A. F. W. Woolley; D. R. Woolley, QC; N. G. Wootton; A. M. Worrall, QC; N. J. Worsley; P. F. Worsley, QC; D. E. M. Young, QC.

STIPENDIARY MAGISTRATES
PROVINCIAL
(each £48,200)

Cheshire, P. K. Dodd, OBE, *apptd* 1991.
Greater Manchester, W. D. Fairclough, *apptd* 1982; C. T. Latham, OBE, *apptd* 1976; Miss J. E. Hayward, *apptd* 1991.
Hampshire, T. G. Cowling, *apptd* 1989.
Humberside, N. H. White, *apptd* 1985.
Merseyside, N. G. Wootton, *apptd* 1976.
Middlesex, N. A. McKittrick, *apptd* 1989; S. Somjee, *apptd* 1991; S. N. Day, *apptd* 1991.
Mid Glamorgan, B. R. Oliver, *apptd* 1983; J. T. Curran, *apptd* 1990.
Nottinghamshire, P. F. Nuttall, *apptd* 1991; M. L. R. Harris, *apptd* 1991.
South Glamorgan, Sir Lincoln Hallinan, *apptd* 1976.
South Yorkshire, I. W. Crompton, *apptd* 1983; J. E. Barry, *apptd* 1985; W. D. Thomas, *apptd* 1989.
Staffordshire, P. G. G. Richards, *apptd* 1991.
West Midlands, F. H. Hatchard, *apptd* 1981; W. M. Probert, *apptd* 1983; B. Morgan, *apptd* 1989.
West Yorkshire, F. D. L. Loy, *apptd* 1972; Mrs P. A. Hewitt, *apptd* 1990; G. H. Kamil, *apptd* 1990.

METROPOLITAN

Chief Metropolitan Stipendiary Magistrate and Chairman of Committee of Magistrates for Inner London Area, Sir David Hopkin (*Bow Street*) £57,500

Committee of Magistrates for Inner London Area
3rd Floor, North West Wing,
Bush House, Aldwych, WC2B 4PJ

Principal Chief Clerk and Clerk to the Committee, I. Fowler £45,174
Chief Clerk (Training), J. W. Greenhill £40,563

Magistrates
(each £46,700)

Bow Street, The Chief Magistrate; R. D. Bartle; J. G. Connor; Miss G. B. Babington Browne.
Camberwell Green, C. P. M. Davidson; P. Fingret; Mrs H. Mitcham; J. R. D. Phillips; T. H. Workman.
Clerkenwell, M. L. R. Romer; C. J. Bourke; M. A. Johnstone.
Greenwich and Woolwich, Mrs K. R. Keating; B. Loosley; W. A. Kennedy.
Highbury Corner, D. Barr; Miss D. Quick; G. Wicks; C. L. Pratt.
Horseferry Road, Miss P. A. Long; A. R. Davies; R. T. Moss; T. Maher.
Marlborough Street, K. J. H. Nichols; J. Q. Campbell.
Marylebone, G. L. J. Noel; Sir Bryan Roberts, KCMG, QC; B. Black.
Old Street, D. B. Meier; D. L. Thomas.
South Western, S. G. Clixby; C. D. Voelcker.
Thames, P. G. N. Badge; N. Crichton; Miss D. Wickham; G. E. Parkinson.
Tower Bridge, Mrs J. R. Comyns; T. M. English; A. T. Evans.
Wells Street, Miss A. M. Jennings; D. M. Fingleton; K. L. Maitland-Davies; I. M. Baker; A. C. Baldwin.
West London, H. J. Cook; D. Kennett Brown.
Unattached Magistrates, G. B. Breen; A. W. Ormerod; I. Bing.

CROWN PROSECUTION SERVICE
Headquarters: 4/12 Queen Anne's Gate, SW1H 9AZ
[071–273 8152]

Headquarters, Casework: 10 Furnival Street, EC4A 1PE [071–831 3038]

The Crown Prosecution Service (CPS) is responsible for the independent review and conduct of criminal proceedings instituted by police forces in England and Wales (with the exception of cases conducted by the Serious Fraud Office and certain minor cases).

The Director of Public Prosecutions is the head of the CPS and discharges his statutory functions under the superintendence of the Attorney-General.

The CPS comprises a headquarters office and 31 areas covering England and Wales. Each of the 31 CPS Areas is supervised by a Chief Crown Prosecutor.

Basic Salaries
(as at April 1, 1991)

Grade 1	£82,780
Grade 2	£59,020
Grade 3	£47,090–£48,380*
Grade 4	£40,116–£46,751
Grade 5	£32,551–£44,996
London weighting = £1,750 p.a.	* In London

Director of Public Prosecutions (G1), Sir Allan Green, KCB, QC.
Deputy Director and Chief Executive (G2), D. S. Gandy, CB, OBE.
Principal Establishment and Finance Officer (G3), D. J. Wiblin.
Director, Headquarters Casework (G3), C. Newell.

Field Director, Operations (G3), G. Duff.
Field Director, Resources (G3), G. D. Etherington.
Head, Policy and Communications Group (G3), K. Ashken.

CPS AREAS

AVON/SOMERSET, 1st Floor, Block A, Froomsgate House, Rupert Street, Bristol BS1 2QJ.—*Chief Crown Prosecutor (G5)*, C. T. Jones.

CAMBRIDGESHIRE/LINCOLNSHIRE, Justinian House, Spitfire Close, Ermine Business Park, Huntingdon, Cambs. PE18 6XY.—*Chief Crown Prosecutor (G5)*, D. G. Lewis.

CHESHIRE, 2nd Floor, Windsor House, Pepper Street, Chester CH1 1TD.—*Chief Crown Prosecutor (G5)*, Mrs N. E. Hollingsworth.

CLEVELAND/NORTH YORKSHIRE, 6th Floor, Rydale Building, 60 Piccadilly, York YO1 1NS.—*Chief Crown Prosecutor (G5)*, D. M. Sharp.

DERBYSHIRE, Celtic House, Heritage Gate, Friary Street, Derby DE1 1QX.—*Chief Crown Prosecutor (G5)*, D. R. K. Seddon.

DEVON/CORNWALL, Hawkins House, Pynes Hill, Rydon Lane, Exeter EX2 5SS.—*Chief Crown Prosecutor (G5)*, R. J. Green.

DORSET/HAMPSHIRE, Black Horse House, 8–10 Leigh Road, Eastleigh, Hants. SO5 4FH.—*Chief Crown Prosecutor (G5)*, P. Boeuf.

ESSEX, Gemini Centre, 88 New London Road, Chelmsford, Essex CM2 0BR.—*Chief Crown Prosecutor (G5)*, J. J. Goodwin.

GLOUCESTERSHIRE/WILTSHIRE, 7 Avon Reach, Monkton Hill, Chippenham, Wilts. SN15 1EE.—*Chief Crown Prosecutor (G5)*, R. A. Prickett.

GREATER MANCHESTER, PO Box 377, Sunlight House, Quay Street, Manchester M60 3LU.—*Chief Crown Prosecutor (G4)*, A. R. Taylor.

HERTFORDSHIRE/BEDFORDSHIRE, Queens House, 58 Victoria Street, St Albans AL1 3HZ.—*Chief Crown Prosecutor (G5)*, C. Ingham.

HUMBERSIDE, Queens House, Paragon Street, Hull HU1 3DA.—*Chief Crown Prosecutor (G5)*, L. M. Bell.

KENT, Kent House, Lower Stone Street, Maidstone, Kent ME15 6JT.—*Chief Crown Prosecutor (G5)*, R. A. Crabb.

LANCASHIRE/CUMBRIA, Robert House, 2 Starkie Street, Preston, Lancs. PR1 3NY.—*Chief Crown Prosecutor (G5)*, J. V. Bates.

LEICESTERSHIRE/NORTHAMPTONSHIRE, Princes Court, 34 York Road, Leicester LE1 5TU.—*Chief Crown Prosecutor (G5)*, P. J. M. Hollingworth.

LONDON (INNER), Portland House, Stag Place, SW1E 5BH.—*Chief Crown Prosecutor (G4)*, B. McArdle.

LONDON (NORTH), Solar House, 1 Romford Road, Stratford E15 4LJ.—*Chief Crown Prosecutor (G4)*, R. J. Chronnell.

LONDON (SOUTH)/SURREY, Tolworth Tower, Surbiton KT6 7DS.—*Chief Crown Prosecutor (G4)*, D. E. Dracup.

MERSEYSIDE, 7th Floor (South), Royal Liver Building, Liverpool L3 1HN.—*Chief Crown Prosecutor (G4)*, E. C. Woodcock.

NORFOLK/SUFFOLK, Saxon House, 1 Cromwell Square, Ipswich, Suffolk IP1 1TS.—*Chief Crown Prosecutor (G5)*, M. F. C. Harvey.

NORTHUMBRIA/DURHAM, Benton House, 136 Sandyford Road, Newcastle upon Tyne NE1 1QE.—*Chief Crown Prosecutor (G5)*, D. A. Farmer.

NORTH WALES/DYFED/POWYS, 491 Abergele Road, Old Colwyn, Colwyn Bay, Clwyd LL29 9AE.—*Chief Crown Prosecutor (G5)*, A. S. R. Clarke.

NOTTINGHAMSHIRE, 2 King Edward Court, King Edward Street, Nottingham NG1 1EL.—*Chief Crown Prosecutor (G5)*, D. C. Beal.

SOUTH WALES/GWENT, Pearl Assurance House, Greyfriars Road, Cardiff CF1 3PL.—*Chief Crown Prosecutor (G4)*, H. G. Wallace.

SOUTH YORKSHIRE, Belgrave House, 47 Bank Street, Sheffield S1 2EH.—*Chief Crown Prosecutor (G4)*, M. J. Rose.

STAFFORDSHIRE/WARWICKSHIRE, Government Buildings, 11A Princes Street, Stafford ST16 2EU.—*Chief Crown Prosecutor (G5)*, D. V. Dickenson.

SUSSEX, Unit 3, Clifton Mews, Clifton Hill, Brighton, E. Sussex BN1 3HR.—*Chief Crown Prosecutor (G5)*, D. Thompson.

THAMES VALLEY, The Courtyard, Lombard Street, Abingdon, Oxon. OX14 5SE.—*Chief Crown Prosecutor (G5)*, J. Wilcox.

WEST MERCIA, Orchard House, Victoria Square, Droitwich, Worcester WR9 8QT.—*Chief Crown Prosecutor (G5)*, D. R. Stott.

WEST MIDLANDS, Dale House, Dale End, Birmingham B4 7NR.—*Chief Crown Prosecutor (G3)*, T. M. McGowan.

WEST YORKSHIRE, 4–5 South Parade, Wakefield WF1 1LR.—*Chief Crown Prosecutor (G4)*, R. Otley.

THE SCOTTISH JUDICATURE

Scotland has a legal system separate from and differing greatly from the English legal system in enacted law, judicial procedure and the structure of courts.

There is in Scotland a system of public prosecution headed by the Lord Advocate which is independent of the police, who have no say in the decision to prosecute. The Lord Advocate, discharging his functions through the Crown Office in Edinburgh, is responsible for prosecutions in the High Court, sheriff courts and district courts. Prosecutions in the High Court are prepared by the Crown Office and conducted in court by one of the Law Officers or an advocate-depute. In the inferior courts the decision to prosecute is made and prosecution is preferred by procurators fiscal, who are lawyers and full-time civil servants, subject to the directions of the Crown Office. A permanent legally-qualified civil servant known as the Crown Agent is responsible for the running of the Crown Office and the organization of the Procurator Fiscal Service, of which he is the head.

Scotland is divided into six Sheriffdoms, each with a full-time Sheriff Principal. The Sheriffdoms are further divided into sheriff court districts, each of which has a legally-qualified, resident sheriff or sheriffs, who are the judges of the court.

In criminal cases sheriffs principal and sheriffs have the same powers; sitting with a jury of 15 members, they may try more serious cases on indictment, or, sitting alone, may try lesser cases under summary procedure. Minor summary offences are dealt with in district courts which are administered by the district and the islands local government authorities and presided over by lay justices of the peace, and, in Glasgow only, by stipendiary magistrates. Juvenile offenders (children under 16) may be brought before an informal children's hearing comprising three local lay people. The superior criminal court is the High Court of Justiciary which is both a trial and an appeal court. Cases on indictment are tried by a High Court judge, sitting with a jury of 15, in Edinburgh and on circuit in other towns. Appeals from the lower courts against conviction or sentence are heard also by the High Court, which sits as an appeal court only in Edinburgh. There is no further appeal to the House of Lords in criminal cases.

In civil cases the jurisdiction of the sheriff court extends to most kinds of action. Appeal against decisions of the sheriff may be made to the Sheriff Principal and thence to the Court of Session, or direct to the Court of Session, which sits only in Edinburgh. The Court of Session is divided into the Inner and the Outer House. The Outer House is a court of first instance in which cases are heard by judges sitting singly, sometimes with a jury of 12. The Inner House, itself subdivided into two divisions of equal status, is mainly an appeal court. Appeals may be made to the Inner House from the Outer House as well as from the sheriff court. An appeal may be made from the Inner House to the House of Lords.

The judges of the Court of Session are the same as those of the High Court of Justiciary, the Lord President of the Court of Session also holding the office of Lord Justice General in the High Court. Senators of the College of Justice are Lords Commissioners of Justiciary as well as judges of the Court of Session.

The office of coroner does not exist in Scotland. The local procurator fiscal inquires privately into sudden and suspicious deaths and may report findings to the Crown Agent. In some cases a fatal accident inquiry may be held before the sheriff.

COURT OF SESSION and HIGH COURT OF JUSTICIARY

The Lord President and Lord Justice General, (£95,130)
The Rt. Hon. Lord Hope
(*born* 1938, *apptd* 1989)

INNER HOUSE

Lords of Session (each £91,400)

FIRST DIVISION

The Lord President.
Hon. Lord Allanbridge (William Ian Stewart), *born* 1925, *apptd* 1977.
Hon. Lord Cowie (William Lorn Kerr Cowie), *born* 1926, *apptd* 1977.
Hon. Lord Mayfield (Ian MacDonald, MC), *born* 1921, *apptd* 1981.

SECOND DIVISION

Lord Justice Clerk (£92,400), The Rt. Hon. Lord Ross, (Donald MacArthur Ross), *born* 1927, *apptd* 1985.
Rt. Hon. Lord Murray (Ronald King Murray), *born* 1922, *apptd* 1979.
Hon. The Lord McCluskey, *born* 1929, *apptd* 1984.
Hon. Lord Morison (Alastair Malcolm Morison), *born* 1931, *apptd* 1985.

OUTER HOUSE

Lords of Session (each £82,800)

Hon. Lord Davidson (Charles Kemp Davidson), (*seconded to Scottish Law Commission*) *born* 1929, *apptd* 1983.
Hon. Lord Sutherland (Ranald Iain Sutherland), *born* 1932, *apptd* 1985.
Hon. Lord Weir (David Bruce Weir), *born* 1931, *apptd* 1985.
Hon. Lord Clyde (James John Clyde), *born* 1932, *apptd* 1985.
Hon. Lord Cullen (William Douglas Cullen), *born* 1935, *apptd* 1986.

Hon. Lord Prosser (William David Prosser), *born* 1934, *apptd* 1986.
Hon. Lord Kirkwood (Ian Candlish Kirkwood), *born* 1932, *apptd* 1987.
Hon. Lord Coulsfield (John Taylor Cameron), *born* 1934, *apptd* 1987.
Hon. Lord Milligan (James George Milligan), *born* 1934, *apptd* 1988.
Hon. The Lord Morton of Shuna, *born* 1930, *apptd* 1988.
Hon. Lord Caplan (Philip Isaac Caplan), *born* 1929, *apptd* 1989.
Rt. Hon. The Lord Cameron of Lochbroom, *born* 1931, *apptd* 1989.
Hon. Lord Marnoch (Michael Stewart Rae Bruce), *born* 1938, *apptd* 1990.
Hon. Lord MacLean (Ranald Norman Munro MacLean), *born* 1938, *apptd* 1990.
Hon. Lord Penrose (George William Penrose), *born* 1938, *apptd* 1990.
Hon. Lord Osborne (Kenneth Hilton Osborne), *born* 1937, *apptd* 1990.

COURT OF SESSION AND HIGH COURT OF JUSTICIARY

Parliament House, Parliament Square, Edinburgh

Principal Clerk of Session and Justiciary, H. S. Foley .... £34,667–£39,402
Deputy Principal Clerk of Justiciary and Administration, J. Robertson .... £23,329–£27,819
Deputy Principal Clerk of Session and Principal Extractor, M. Weir .... £23,329–£27,819
Deputy Principal Clerk (Keeper of the Rolls), M. G. Bonar .... £23,329–£27,819
Depute Clerks of Session and Justiciary, W. Gillon; T. D. McIntosh; A. Hogg; N. J. Dowie; J. M. Clark; I. Smith; J. A. R. Cowie; T. Higgins; T. B. Cruickshank; Q. Oliver; F. Shannly; R. D. Sinclair; Mrs A. Leighton; T. M. Thomson; D. D. Mackay; A. S. Moffat; J. Atkinson; D. J. Shand; G. Ellis; Mrs G. McKeand; K. MacKenzie; D. G. Lynn
£16,675–£20,857

SCOTTISH COURTS ADMINISTRATION
26–27 Royal Terrace, Edinburgh EH7 5AH

Director, G. Murray.

SHERIFF COURT OF CHANCERY
16 North Bank Street, Edinburgh EH1 2NJ

Sheriff of Chancery, C. G. B. Nicholson, QC.

HM COMMISSARY OFFICE
16 North Bank Street, Edinburgh EH1 2NJ

Commissary Clerk, D. B. White.

SCOTTISH LAND COURT
1 Grosvenor Crescent, Edinburgh

Chairman, The Hon. Lord Elliott, MC £63,300
Members, A. B. Campbell, OBE; D. D. McDiarmid; R MacDonald.

SHERIFFDOMS
Salaries

Sheriff Principal £63,30
Sheriff £57,05
Regional Sheriff Clerk .... £24,997–£43,30
Sheriff Clerk .... £17,017–£43,30

GRAMPIAN, HIGHLAND AND ISLANDS

Sheriff Principal, R. D. Ireland, QC.
Regional Sheriff Clerk, J. S. Doig.

Sheriffs and Sheriff Clerks

Aberdeen and Stonehaven, D. J. Risk; D. W. Bogie;
D. Kelbie; L. A. S. Jessop; *Sheriff Clerks,* J. Rodden;
W. A. Mouser.

Banff and Peterhead, K. A. McLernan; *Sheriff Clerks,*
W. H. Connon; H. Hempseed.

Elgin, N. McPartlin; *Sheriff Clerk,* A. Lynch.

*Inverness, Lochmaddy, Portree, Stornoway, Dingwall,
Tain, Wick and Dornoch,* W. J. Fulton; D. Booker-
Milburn; J. O. A. Fraser; E. Stewart; *Sheriff Clerk,*
J. S. Doig.

Kirkwall and Lerwick, A. A. MacDonald; *Sheriff
Clerks,* Miss H. M. Phillips; A. C. Norris.

Fort William, D. Noble (also *Oban and Campbeltown*);
Sheriff Clerks, C. Morrison; W. M. Cochrane.

TAYSIDE, CENTRAL AND FIFE

Sheriff Principal, J. J. Maguire, QC.
Regional Sheriff Clerk, B. J. Young.

Sheriffs and Sheriff Clerks

Arbroath and Forfar, S. O. Kermack; *Sheriff Clerks,*
M. Herbertson; P. Dougan.

Dundee, G. L. Cox; A. L. Stewart; *Sheriff Clerk,* B. J.
Young.

Perth, J. F. Wheatley; J. C. McInnes, QC; *Sheriff
Clerk,* Miss J. Telfer.

Falkirk, A. V. Sheehan; A. J. Murphy; *Sheriff Clerk,*
D. Nicoll.

Stirling, W. C. Henderson; R. E. G. Younger; *Sheriff
Clerk,* P. Crow.

Alloa, R. E. G. Younger; *Sheriff Clerk,* J. M. Murphy.

Cupar, C. Smith (also *Dundee*); *Sheriff Clerk,* B.
Sullivan.

Dunfermline, J. S. Forbes; W. M. Reid; *Sheriff Clerk,*
J. Ross.

Kirkcaldy, W. J. Christie; C. R. Macarthur, QC;
Sheriff Clerk, T. Fyffe.

LOTHIAN AND BORDERS

Sheriff Principal, C. G. B. Nicholson, QC.
Regional Sheriff Clerk, D. B. White, OBE.

Sheriffs and Sheriff Clerks

Edinburgh, N. E. D. Thomson; J. L. M. Mitchell; P.
G. B. McNeill, PH.D.; Miss H. J. Aronson, QC; R. G.
Craik, QC; G. I. W. Shiach; Miss I. A. Poole; R. J.
D. Scott; A. M. Bell; J. M. S. Horsburgh; G. W. S.
Presslie; J. A. Farrell*; I. A. Cameron; *Sheriff
Clerk,* D. B. White.

Peebles, N. E. D. Thomson (also *Edinburgh*); *Sheriff
Clerk,* D. B. White.

Linlithgow, M. Stone; H. R. MacLean; *Sheriff Clerk,*
R. Sinclair.

Haddington, G. W. S. Presslie (also *Edinburgh*);
Sheriff Clerk, B. W. S. Manthorpe.

Jedburgh and Duns, J. V. Paterson; *Sheriff Clerk,* J.
W. Williamson.

Selkirk, J. V. Paterson; *Sheriff Clerk,* L. McFarlane.

NORTH STRATHCLYDE

Sheriff Principal, R. C. Hay, CBE.
Regional Sheriff Clerk, A. A. Brown.

Sheriffs and Sheriff Clerks

Oban and Campbeltown, D. Noble (also *Fort William*);
Sheriff Clerks, W. M. Cochrane; K. L. Graham.

Dumbarton, J. T. Fitzsimons; T. Scott; S. W. H.
Fraser; *Sheriff Clerk,* N. R. Weir.

Paisley, R. G. Smith; C. N. Stoddart; J. Spy; C. K.
Higgins; C. W. Palmer; C. G. McKay*; *Sheriff
Clerk,* A. A. Brown.

Greenock, J. Irvine Smith (also *Rothesay*); Sir
Stephen Young; *Sheriff Clerk,* P. G. Corcoran.

Kilmarnock, T. M. Croan; D. B. Smith; T. F. Russell;
Sheriff Clerk, J. Shaw.

Dunoon, C. W. Palmer (also *Dumbarton*); *Sheriff
Clerk,* Mrs C. Carson.

GLASGOW AND STRATHKELVIN

Sheriff Principal, N. D. MacLeod, QC.
Regional Sheriff Clerk, C. McLay.

Sheriffs and Sheriff Clerks

Glasgow, A. C. Horsfall (*seconded to Scottish Lands
Tribunal*); J. J. Maguire; A. A. Bell, QC; B.
Kearney; G. H. Gordon, QC; A. C. McKay; A.
Lothian; J. C. M. Jardine; Mrs D. J. B. Robertson;
B. A. Lockhart; I. G. Pirie; Mrs A. L. A. Duncan;
W. G. Stevenson, QC; G. J. Evans; E. H. Galt; F. J.
Keane; A. C. Henry; J. K. Mitchell; A. G. Johnston;
J. P. Murphy; M. Sischy; A. B. Wilkinson; *Sheriff
Clerk,* C. McLay.

SOUTH STRATHCLYDE, DUMFRIES AND GALLOWAY

Sheriff Principal, J. S. Mowat, QC.
Regional Sheriff Clerk, H. Findlay.

Sheriffs and Sheriff Clerks

Hamilton, L. S. Lovat; A. C. MacPherson; W. F.
Lunny; I. A. MacMillan, CBE; V. J. Canavan (also
Airdrie); W. E. Gibson; *Sheriff Clerk,* J. Cumming.

Lanark, J. D. Allan; *Sheriff Clerk,* D. M. Cameron.

Ayr, N. Gow, QC; R. G. McEwan, QC; *Sheriff Clerk,* E.
A. Cumming.

Stranraer and Kirkcudbright, J. R. Smith; *Sheriff
Clerk,* N. L. Hodgson.

Dumfries, K. G. Barr; L. Cameron; *Sheriff Clerk,*
P. McGonigle.

Airdrie, J. H. Stewart; V. J. Canavan (also *Hamilton*);
R. H. Dickson; I. C. Simpson; *Sheriff Clerk,* H.
Findlay.

CROWN OFFICE
Regent Road, Edinburgh EH7 5BL
[031-557 3800]

Crown Agent, J. D. Lowe £60,100
Deputy Crown Agent, A. D. Vannet......... £43,307

PROCURATOR FISCAL SERVICE

Salaries

Regional Procurator Fiscal–grade 3 .... £47,090
Regional Procurator Fiscal–grade 4 £40,116–£41,861
Procurator Fiscal–upper level ...... £32,551–£36,997
Procurator Fiscal–lower level ...... £23,407–£31,851

Grampian, Highlands and Islands Region

Regional Procurator Fiscal, S. W. Lockhart, CBE
(*Aberdeen*).

Procurators Fiscal, J. D. McNaughton (*Stonehaven*);
A. J. M. Colley (*Banff*); I. S. McNaughtan (*Peter-
head*); A. Wither (*Elgin*); A. C. P. Reith (*Wick*); C.
B. McClory (*Portree and Lochmaddy*); C. S. Mack-

---

*Floating Sheriff

enzie (*Stornoway*); H. T. Westwater (*Dornoch and Tain*); W. W. Orr (*Inverness*); A. C. P. Reith (*Kirkwall*); Miss A. Thom (*Lerwick*); J. I. M. MacGillivray (*Fort William*); D. R. Hingston (*Dingwall*).

Tayside, Central and Fife Region

Regional Procurator Fiscal, B. K. Heywood (*Dundee*).
Procurators Fiscal, C. D. G. Hillary (*Arbroath*); A. L. Ingram (*Forfar*); M. MacPhail (*Perth*); G. E. Scott (*Falkirk*); K. Valentine (*Stirling*); I. D. Douglas (*Alloa*); R. A. S. Brown (*Cupar*); R. T. Hamilton (*Dunfermline*); F. R. Crowe (*Kirkcaldy*).

Lothian and Borders Region

Regional Procurator Fiscal, R. F. Lees (*Edinburgh*).
Procurators Fiscal, F. J. M. Brown (*Peebles*); H. R. Annan (*Linlithgow*); A. N. MacDonald (*Haddington*); J. C. Whitelaw (*Duns* and *Jedburgh*); D. McNeill (*Selkirk*).

North Strathclyde Region

Regional Procurators Fiscal, J. D. Friel (*Paisley*).
Procurators Fiscal, I. Henderson (*Campbeltown*); J. Cardle (*Dumbarton*); C. C. Donnelly (*Greenock* and *Rothesay*); D. L. Webster (*Dunoon*); J. G. MacGlennan (*Kilmarnock*); B. R. Maguire (*Oban*).

Glasgow and Strathkelvin Region

Regional Procurator Fiscal, A. C. Normand (*Glasgow*).

South Strathclyde, Dumfries and Galloway Region

Regional Procurator Fiscal, W. G. Carmichael (*Hamilton*).
Procurators Fiscal, S. R. Houston (*Lanark*); N. G. O'Brien (*Ayr*); F. Walkingshaw (*Stranraer*); J. T. MacDougall (*Dumfries* and *Kirkcudbright*); A. T. Wilson (*Airdrie*).

NORTHERN IRELAND JUDICATURE

In Northern Ireland the legal system and the structure of courts closely resemble those of England and Wales; there are, however, often differences in enacted law.

The Supreme Court of Judicature of Northern Ireland comprises the Court of Appeal, the High Court of Justice and the Crown Court. The practice and procedure of these Courts is similar to that in England. The superior civil court is the High Court of Justice, from which an appeal lies to the Court of Appeal; the House of Lords is the final civil appeal court.

The Crown Court, served by High Court and county court judges, deals with criminal trials on indictment. Cases are heard before a judge and, except those involving offences specified under emergency legislation, a jury. Appeals from the Crown Court against conviction or sentence are heard by the Northern Ireland Court of Appeal; the House of Lords is the final court of appeal.

The decision to prosecute in cases tried on indictment and in summary cases of a serious nature rests in Northern Ireland with the Director of Public Prosecutions, who is responsible to the Attorney General. Minor summary offences are prosecuted by the police.

Minor criminal offences are dealt with in magistrates' courts by a full-time, legally qualified resident magistrate and, where an offender is under 17, by juvenile courts consisting of the resident magistrate and two lay members specially qualified to deal with juveniles (at least one of whom must be a woman). Appeals from magistrates' courts are heard by the county court.

Magistrates' courts in Northern Ireland can deal with certain classes of civil cases but most minor civil cases are dealt with in county courts. Judgments of all civil courts are enforceable through a centralized procedure administered by the Enforcement of Judgments Office.

SUPREME COURT OF JUDICATURE
The Royal Courts of Justice
Belfast BT1 3JF
[0232–235111]

Lord Chief Justice of Northern Ireland (£97,000)
The Rt. Hon. Sir Brian Hutton
(*born* 1931, *apptd* 1988)

Lords Justices of Appeal (each £93,000)

Rt. Hon. Sir Basil Kelly, *born* 1920, *apptd* 1984.
Rt. Hon. Sir John MacDermott, *born* 1927, *apptd* 1987.

Rt. Hon. Sir Donald Murray, *born* 1923, *apptd* 1975.

Puisne Judges (each £84,250)
Hon. Sir John Higgins, *born* 1927, *apptd* 1984.
Hon. Sir Robert Carswell, *born* 1934, *apptd* 1984.
Hon. Sir Michael Nicholson, *born* 1933, *apptd* 1986.
Hon. Sir William McCollum, *born* 1933, *apptd* 1987.
Hon. Sir William Campbell, *born* 1936, *apptd* 1988.
Hon. Sir John Sheil, *born* 1938, *apptd* 1989.

Lord Chief Justice's Office

Principal Secretary to the Lord Chief Justice and Clerk of the Crown for Northern Ireland, J. A. L. McLean, QC.
Legal Secretary to the Lord Chief Justice, Mrs D. M. Kennedy.

Masters of Supreme Court
(£49,100)

Master, Central Office, V. A. Care, QC.
Master, High Court, J. W. Wilson, QC.
Master, Office of Care and Protection, F. B. Hall.
Master, Chancery Office, V. G. Bridges.
Master, Bankruptcy and Companies Office, J. B. C. Glass.
Master, Probate and Matrimonial Office, R. T. Millar.
Master, Taxing Office, J. C. Napier.

Accountant, Court Funds Office, J. Jackson.

Recorders
(£66,500)

Belfast, Judge Pringle, QC.
Londonderry, Judge Higgins, QC.

County Court Judges
(£66,500)

Judge Babington, DSC, QC; Judge Chambers, QC; Judge Curran, QC; Judge Gibson, QC; Judge McKee, QC; Judge Petrie, QC; Rt. Hon. Judge Sir Robert Porter, QC; Judge Russell, QC; Judge Hart, QC; Judge Smyth, QC; Judge Martin, QC.

Crown Solicitor's Office
Royal Courts of Justice, Belfast

Crown Solicitor, H. A. Nelson.

Department of the Director of Public Prosecutions
Royal Courts of Justice, Belfast

Director of Public Prosecutions, A. Fraser, QC.
Deputy Director of Public Prosecutions, D. Magill.

TRIBUNALS

COMMONS COMMISSIONERS
Golden Cross House, Duncannon Street
WC2N 4JF
[071–210 4584]

The Commons Commissioners are responsible for deciding disputes arising under the Commons Registration Act 1965 and the Common Land (Rectification of Registers) Act 1989. They also enquire into the ownership of unclaimed common land. Commissioners are appointed by the Lord Chancellor.

Chief Commons Commissioner, P. G. Langdon-Davies.
Commissioners, M. Roth; I. L. R. Romer; D. M. Burton.
Clerk, Miss F. A. A. Buchan.

COPYRIGHT TRIBUNAL
Room 4/6, Hazlitt House,
45 Southampton Buildings, WC2A 1AR
[071–438 4776]

The Copyright Tribunal is the successor to the Performing Right Tribunal which was established by the Copyright Act 1956 to resolve various classes of copyright dispute, principally in the field of collective licensing. Its jurisdiction was extended by the Copyright, Designs and Patents Act 1988 and the Broadcasting Act 1990.

The Chairman and two Deputy Chairmen are appointed by the Lord Chancellor. Up to eight ordinary members are appointed by the Secretary of State for Trade and Industry.

Chairman, J. M. Bowers.
Secretary, C. Brook.

EMPLOYMENT APPEAL TRIBUNAL
Central Office, 4 St James's Square, SW1Y 4JU (Tel: 071-210 3848).
Divisional Office, 11 Melville Crescent, Edinburgh, EH3 7LU (Tel: 031-225 3963).

The Employment Appeal Tribunal was established as a superior court of record under the provisions of the Employment Protection Act 1975, hearing appeals on a question of law arising from any decision of an industrial tribunal.

A tribunal consists of a legally-qualified chairman and two lay members, one from each side of industry. They are appointed by The Queen on the recommendation of the Lord Chancellor and the Secretary of State for Employment.

President, The Hon. Mr Justice Wood.
Scottish Chairman, The Hon. Lord Mayfield, MC.
Registrar, Miss V. J. Selio.

IMMIGRATION APPELLATE AUTHORITIES
Thanet House, 231 Strand, WC2R 1DA
[071–353 8060]

The Immigration Appeal Adjudicators hear appeals from immigration decisions concerning the need for, and refusal of, leave to enter or remain in the UK, decisions to make deportation orders and directions to remove persons subject to immigration control from this country. The Immigration Appeal Tribunal hears appeals direct from decisions to make deportation orders in matters concerning conduct contrary to the public good. Its principal jurisdiction is, however, the hearing of appeals from Adjudicators by the party (Home Office or individual) who is aggrieved by the decision. Most such appeals are subject to leave being granted by the Tribunal.

An Adjudicator sits alone. The Tribunal sits in divisions of three—normally a legally qualified member and two lay members. Members of the Tribunal and Adjudicators are appointed by the Lord Chancellor.

Immigration Appeal Tribunal
President, G. W. Farmer.
Vice-Presidents, Prof. D. C. Jackson; vacant.

Immigration Appeal Adjudicators
Chief Adjudicator, M. Patey, MBE.

THE INDUSTRIAL TRIBUNALS
Central Office (England and Wales)
93 Ebury Bridge Road, SW1W 8RE
[071-730 9161]

Industrial Tribunals for England and Wales sit in 11 regions. The tribunals deal with matters of employment law, redundancy, dismissal, sexual and racial discrimination and related areas of dispute which may arise in the workplace. The tribunals are funded by the Department of Employment.

Chairmen, who may be full-time or part-time, are legally qualified. They are appointed by the Lord Chancellor. Tribunal members are nominated by the CBI and TUC, and appointed by the Secretary of State for Employment.

President, His Hon. Judge T. Lawrence.

Central Office (Scotland)
St Andrew House, 141 West Nile Street,
Glasgow G1 2RU
[041–331 1601]

Tribunals in Scotland have the same remit as those in England and Wales. Chairmen are appointed by the Lord President of the Court of Session and lay members by the Secretary of State for Employment.

President, Mrs D. Littlejohn £65,250

LANDS TRIBUNAL
48–49 Chancery Lane, WC2A 1JR
[071–936 7200]

The Lands Tribunal is an independent judicial body constituted by the Lands Tribunal Act 1949 for the purpose of determining a wide range of questions relating to the valuation of land, rating appeals from local Valuation Courts and the discharge or modification of restrictive covenants. The Act also empowers the tribunal to accept the function of arbitration under references by consent. The tribunal consists of a President and a number of other members, who are appointed by the Lord Chancellor.

President, V. G. Wellings, QC £60,000
Members, C. R. Mallett; Dr T. Hoyes; His Hon. Judge B. Marder, QC; His Hon. Judge M. O'Donoghue
. . . . £54,000
Members (part-time), J. C. Hill, TD; M. St. J. Hopper
£267 per day
Registrar, C. A. McMullan.

LANDS TRIBUNAL FOR SCOTLAND
1 Grosvenor Crescent, Edinburgh EH12 5ER
[031–225 7996]

The Lands Tribunal for Scotland was constituted by the Lands Tribunal Act 1949. Its remit is the same as the tribunal for England and Wales but also covers questions relating to tenants rights. The President is appointed by the Lord President of the Court of Session.

President, The Hon. Lord Elliott, MC £63,300
Members, Sheriff A. C. Horsfall, QC; A. R. MacLeary;
J. Devine (*full-time*); R. A. Edwards, CBE, WS (*part-time*) £57,050
Clerk, D. Pentland.

NHS TRIBUNAL

The NHS Tribunal inquires into representations that the continued inclusion of a family practitioner (doctor, dentist, pharmacist or optician) on a Family Practitioner Committee's list would be prejudicial to the efficiency of the services concerned. The tribunal sits when required, about eight times a year, and usually in London.

Chairman, R. Bell, QC.
Clerk, I. D. Keith, 1–2 Judges Terrace, East Grinstead, W. Sussex RH19 3AA (Tel : 0342–321111).

PENSIONS APPEAL TRIBUNALS
Central Office (England and Wales)
48–49 Chancery Lane, WC2A 1JR
[071–936 7034]

The Pensions Appeal Tribunals are responsible for hearing appeals from ex-servicemen or women and widows who have had their claims for a war pension rejected by the Secretary of State for Social Services. The Entitlement Appeal Tribunals hear appeals in cases where the Secretary of State has refused to grant a war pension. The Assessment Appeal Tribunals hear appeals against the Secretary of State's assessment of the degree of disablement caused by the accepted condition.

The Tribunal members are appointed by the Lord Chancellor.

President, M. H. Fauvelle £46,700
Secretary, S. J. Pye.

Pensions Appeal Tribunals for Scotland
20 Walker Street, Edinburgh EH3 7HS
[031–220 1404]

President, J. A. Cameron.

OFFICE OF THE PRESIDENT OF SOCIAL SECURITY APPEAL TRIBUNALS, MEDICAL APPEAL TRIBUNALS AND VACCINE DAMAGE TRIBUNALS
Clements House, Gresham Street, EC2V 7DN
[071–606 2106]

An independent statutory authority which exercises judicial and administrative control over social security appeal tribunals, medical appeal tribunals and vaccine damage tribunals.

President, His Hon. Judge D. Holden £56,000
Chief Administrator, J. Read.

OFFICE OF THE SOCIAL SECURITY COMMISSIONERS
London: Harp House, 83–86 Farringdon Street, EC4A 4DH (Tel: 071–353 5145)
Edinburgh: 23 Melville Street, EH3 7PW (Tel: 031–225 2201)

The Social Security Commissioners are the final statutory authority to decide appeals relating to entitlement to social security benefits. Appeals may be made only on a point of law. The Commissioners' jurisdiction covers England, Wales and Scotland. The Commissioners are all qualified lawyers.

Chief Social Security Commissioner, His Hon. Judge K. Machin, QC.
Secretary, Mrs M. White (*London*); R. Lindsay (*Edinburgh*).

OFFICE OF THE SOCIAL SECURITY COMMISSIONERS FOR NORTHERN IRELAND
Lancashire House, 5 Linenhall Street, Belfast BT2 8AA
[0232–332344]

Chief Commissioner, His Hon. Judge Chambers, QC.
Secretary, J. E. P. Millar.

THE SOLICITORS' DISCIPLINARY TRIBUNAL
16 Bell Yard, WC2A 1PL
[071–242 0219]

The Solicitors' Disciplinary Tribunal was constituted under the provisions of the Solicitors Act 1974. It is an independent statutory body whose members are appointed by the Master of the Rolls. The tribunal considers applications made to it alleging either professional misconduct and/or a breach of the statutory rules by which solicitors are bound against an individually named solicitor, or former solicitor. The Tribunal's jurisdiction extends to solicitor's clerks, in respect of whom they may make an order restricting that clerk's employment by solicitors.

President, G. B. Marsh.
Clerk, Mrs S. C. Elson.

SPECIAL COMMISSIONERS OF INCOME TAX
15–19 Bedford Avenue, WC1B 3AS
[071–631 4242]

The Special Commissioners are an independent body appointed by the Lord Chancellor to hear appeals concerning income taxes, etc.

Presiding Special Commissioner, His Hon. Judge Medd, OBE, QC £65,250
Special Commissioners, T. H. K. Everett; D. A. Shirley £49,100
Deputy Special Commissioners, D. C. Potter, QC; R. H. Widdows, CB.
Clerk, R. P. Lester £21,724

VAT TRIBUNALS
15–19 Bedford Avenue, WC1B 3AS
[071–631 4242]

VAT Tribunals are administered by the Lord Chancellor's Department (the Secretary of State in Scotland). They are independent and decide disputes between taxpayers and the Commissioners of Customs and Excise, who manage VAT. In England and Wales, the President and chairmen are appointed by the Lord Chancellor, and members are appointed by the Treasury. Chairmen in Scotland are appointed by the Lord President of the Court of Session.

President, His Hon. Judge Medd, OBE, QC . . . £65,250
Vice-President, Scotland, R. A. Bennett, CBE, QC
£48,200
Registrar, R. P. Lester.

Tribunal Centres
London (*including Belfast*), 15–19 Bedford Avenue, WC1B 3AS (Tel: 071–631 4242).
Edinburgh, 44 Palmerston Place, Edinburgh EH12 5BJ (Tel: 031–226 3551).
Manchester, Warwickgate House, Warwick Road, Old Trafford, Manchester M16 0GP (Tel: 061–872 6471).

THE POLICE SERVICE

There are 52 police forces in the United Kingdom, each responsible for law enforcement in its area. Most forces' area is conterminous with an English or Welsh county or Scottish region, though there are several combined forces. Law enforcement in London is carried out by the Metropolitan Police and the City of London Police; in Northern Ireland by the Royal Ulster Constabulary; and by the Isle of Man, States of Jersey, and Guernsey forces in their respective islands and bailiwicks.

Each police force is maintained by a police authority. The authorities of English and Welsh forces comprise committees of local councillors and magistrates; in Scotland, the regional and islands councils are the authorities. The authority for the Metropolitan Police is the Home Secretary. In Northern Ireland the Secretary of State appoints the police authority.

Police authorities are financed by central and local government. Subject to the approval of the Home Secretary and to regulations, they appoint the chief constable, decide the maximum size of the force and provide buildings and equipment.

The Home Secretary and the Secretaries of State for Scotland and Northern Ireland are responsible for the organization, administration and operation of the police service. They make regulations covering matters such as police ranks, discipline, hours of duty, and pay and allowances.

All police forces (including the Metropolitan Police at the request of the Commissioner) are subject to inspection by HM Inspectors of Constabulary, who report to the respective Secretary of State.

The investigation of a serious complaint against a police officer is supervised by the Police Complaints Authority in England and Wales. In Scotland, complaints are investigated by independent public prosecutors.

Basic rates of police pay
(since Sept. 1, 1991)

Chief Constable	£52,095–£66,216
Deputy Chief Constable	£45,885–£52,974
Assistant Chief Constable	£43,701
Chief Superintendent	£37,071–£39,360
Superintendent	£33,342–£36,204
Chief Inspector	£24,510–£27,264
Inspector	£21,588–£24,510
Sergeant	£18,819–£21,588
Constable	£11,790–£19,674

Metropolitan Police
(Including London weighting and London allowance for ranks from Inspector to Commissioner)

Metropolitan Commissioner	£82,780*
Deputy Commissioner	£70,551
Assistant Commissioner	£62,241
Deputy Assistant Commissioner	£49,794
Commander	£43,701
Chief Superintendent	£37,071–£39,360
Superintendent	£34,191–£36,204
Chief Inspector	£25,686–£28,431
Inspector	£22,749–£25,686
Sergeant	£18,819–£21,588
Constable	£11,790–£19,674

*Since April 1, 1991.

The Special Constabulary

The Special Constabulary is the part-time volunteer branch of the police force. Special Constables have full police powers within their force area and undertake regular officers' routine policing duties when required, thus freeing regulars at times of emergency for those tasks which only they can perform. There were 15,902 Special Constables in England and Wales at the end of December 1990.

POLICE AUTHORITIES IN THE UNITED KINGDOM

Police Force	Headquarters	Actual Strength	Chief Constable (a) Chief Officer	Chairman of Police Authority/Committee
England				
Avon and Somerset	Bristol	3,081	D. Shattock, QPM	R. Mullett
Bedfordshire	Bedford	1,094	A. Dyer, QPM	(Elected at each meeting)
Cambridgeshire	Huntingdon	1,209	I. H. Kane, QPM	K. Spink, OBE
Cheshire	Chester	1,888	D. J. Graham, QPM	J. H. Collins, OBE
Cleveland	Middlesbrough	1,487	K. Hellawell, QPM	I. Jeffrey
Cumbria	Penrith	1,185	L. Sharp, QPM	R. Watson
Derbyshire	Ripley	1,733	J. F. Newing, QPM	R. W. Jones
Devon and Cornwall	Exeter	2,865	J. S. Evans, QPM	S. J. Day
Dorset	Dorchester	1,272	B. H. Weight, QPM	Maj.-Gen. H. M. G. Bond
Durham	Durham	1,369	F. W. Taylor, QPM	Mrs J. Parkin
Essex	Chelmsford	2,876	J. H. Burrow, OBE	G. C. Waterer, MBE
Gloucestershire	Cheltenham	1,168	A. H. Pacey, QPM	Lt.-Col. G. S. Furtado
Greater Manchester	Manchester 16	6,980	D. Wilmot, QPM	S. Murphy
Hampshire	Winchester	3,177	J. C. Hoddinott, QPM	B. L. P. Blacker
Hertfordshire	Welwyn Garden City	1,668	B. H. Skitt, BEM, QPM	F. Cogan, CBE
Humberside	Hull	1,998	D. Hall, CBE, QPM	S. J. Bayes
Kent	Maidstone	3,020	P. Condon, QPM	C. R. Carr
Lancashire	Preston	3,200	R. B. Johnson, CBE, QPM	Mrs R. B. Henig
Leicestershire	Leicester	1,817	M. J. Hirst, QPM	R. R. Angrave, CBE
Lincolnshire	Lincoln	1,218	N. G. Ovens, QPM	M. D. Kennedy
Merseyside	Liverpool 69	4,670	J. Sharples, QPM	G. Bundred, CBE
Norfolk	Norwich	1,399	P. J. Ryan, QPM	R. Chase
Northamptonshire	Northampton	1,138	D. J. O'Dowd, QPM	A. A. Morby
Northumbria	Newcastle upon Tyne	3,592	J. A. Stevens	G. Gill
North Yorkshire	Northallerton	1,369	D. M. Burke, QPM.	J. H. G. Parfect, MBE
Nottinghamshire	Nottingham	2,344	D. Crompton, QPM	C. Winterton

Police Force	Headquarters	Actual Strength	Chief Constable (a) Chief Officer	Chairman of Police Authority/Committee
South Yorkshire	Sheffield	2,996	R. Wells, QPM	Sir John Layden
Staffordshire	Stafford	2,203	C. H. Kelly, CBE, QPM	Miss I. H. Moseley
Suffolk	Ipswich	1,204	A. T. Coe, QPM	Capt. R. J. Sheepshanks, CBE
Surrey	Guildford	1,646	D. J. Williams	Mrs D. James
Sussex	Lewes	2,965	R. Birch, CBE, QPM	J. P. Sheridan
Thames Valley	Oxford	3,685	C. Pollard, QPM	F. Robinson, OBE
Warwickshire	Warwick	1,022	P. D. Joslin, QPM	J. L. Findon
West Mercia	Worcester	2,064	D. Blakey	R. A. H. Lloyd, TD
West Midlands	Birmingham 4	6,890	R. Hadfield, QPM	L. V. Jones
West Yorkshire	Wakefield	5,213	P. J. Nobes, QPM	T. Brennan
Wiltshire	Devizes	1,087	W. R. Girven, QPM	Lt.-Col. D. B. W. Jarvis, DFC
Wales				
Dyfed-Powys	Carmarthen	942	R. White, QPM	A. L. Pritchard
Gwent	Cwmbran	993	J. E. Over, QPM, CPM	B. Sutton
North Wales	Colwyn Bay	1,351	D. Owen, CBE, QPM	R. H. Roberts, OBE
South Wales	Bridgend	3,140	W. R. Lawrence, QPM	D. McDonald
Scotland				
Central Scotland	Stirling	643	W. Wilson, QPM	H. Brown
Dumfries and Galloway	Dumfries	358	G. Esson, QPM	R. L. Brown
Fife	Kirkcaldy	780	W. M. Moodie, CBE, QPM	C. J. Groom
Grampian	Aberdeen	1,145	I. Oliver, QPM	J. K. A. Thomaneck
Lothian and Borders	Edinburgh 4	2,486	Sir William Sutherland, QPM	J. Cook
Northern	Inverness	631	H. C. MacMillan, QPM	Mrs I. Rhind
Strathclyde	Glasgow 2	6,954	L. Sharp, QPM	J. Jennings
Tayside	Dundee	1,040	J. W. Bowman, QPM	W. Smith
Northern Ireland				
Royal Ulster Constabulary	Belfast 5	8,242	H. N. Annesley, QPM	T. Rainey
Islands				
Isle of Man	Douglas	212	R. E. N. Oake	†Hon. E. G. Lowey, MLC
States of Jersey	St Helier	230	(a) D. Parkinson	M. Wavell
Guernsey	St Peter Port	145	(a) M. Le Moignan, QPM	M. W. Torode

† Minister for Home Affairs

METROPOLITAN POLICE FORCE
New Scotland Yard, Broadway, SW1H 0BG
[071–230 1212]
Establishment, 28,524

Commissioner, Sir Peter Imbert, QPM.
Deputy Commissioner, J. A. Smith, QPM.
Receiver, D. H. J. Hilary, CB £59,020
Deputy Receiver, R. M. Gregory £43,307

Territorial Operations Department
Assistant Commissioner, R. A. Hunt, OBE.
Deputy Assistant Commissioner, D. N. Meynell, OBE.
Commanders, D. A. Ray; D. N. Stevens; D. C. Veness.
Head of Administration, Miss B. Arnold
£26,121–£40,116

Area Headquarters
Deputy Assistant Commissioners, W. E. E. Boreham, OBE; M. B. Taylor, QPM; D. J. Osland, QPM; J. E. Metcalfe, QPM; M. J. Sullivan, QPM; A. G. Fry, QPM; L. T. Roach, QPM; A. J. Speed, QPM.
Commanders, C. A. Couch; J. A. Coo; M. G. Far-brother; D. Flanders; D. M. T. Kendrick; B. G. Moss; B. J. Luckhurst; T. D. Laidlow; A. V. Comben; B. S. Plaxton; J. D. Gibson; J. P. O'Connor; B. F. Aitchison; I. Quinn; M. R. Campbell, QPM; J. Taylor.

Specialist Operations Department
Assistant Commissioner, W. Taylor, QPM.
Deputy Assistant Commissioners, S. R. A. Crawshaw, QPM; P. Phelan, OBE, QPM; C. J. Rideout, QPM.

Commanders, K. G. Churchill-Coleman, QPM; D. G. Gunn; G. M. Ness, QPM; P. R. Nove; R. A. Penrose; D. C. Stockley; D. Buchanan; R. C. Marsh, QPM; D. M. Tucker.

Metropolitan Police Laboratory
Director, Dr B. Sheard £42,494
Deputy Directors, G. J. O. Lee; M. R. Loveland; P. D. Martin; Dr W. D. C. Wilson ..... £26,121–£40,116
Senior Principal Scientific Officer, vacant
£26,121–£40,116

Personnel and Training Department
Assistant Commissioner, G. W. Jones, QPM.
Deputy Assistant Commissioner, E. Mitchell, QPM.
Commanders, D. Y. Cooke; J. G. D. Grieve.
Welfare Officer, K. F. T. Rivers, MBE £22,891–£32,551

Metropolitan Police Cadet Corps
Commander, J. G. D. Grieve.

Medical and Dental Branch
Chief Medical Officer, Dr E. C. A. Bott, CBE £41,050

Management Support Department
Assistant Commissioner, P. J. J. Winship, QPM.
Deputy Assistant Commissioner, J. A. Howley, QPM.

Complaints Investigation Bureau
Commander, E. Humphrey, QPM.

Central Staff
Commander, M. Briggs.

Directorate of Public Affairs
Director of Public Affairs, M. S. D. Granatt
£33,970–£44,996
Deputy Director of Public Affairs, D. H. Dowle
£26,121–£40,116

Directorate of Management Services
Director, Mrs S. M. Merchant (*temp.*)
£33,970–£44,996
Deputy Director, P. I. May . . . . £26,121–£40,116

Force Inspectorate

Deputy Assistant Commissioner, T. J. Siggs, OBE
Commanders, J. J. Allinson; R. C. Adams, BEM

Solicitor's Department

Solicitor, C. S. Porteous £50,850
Assistant Solicitors, P. A. Shawdon; D. S. Hamilton . . . . £36,997–£50,460

The following departments are responsible to the Receiver through the Deputy Receiver.

'E' Department

Establishment Officer, R. B. Jones . . £33,970–£44,996
Deputy Establishment Officers, D. F. F. Hannaford; J. S. Steele . . . . £26,121–£40,116

'F' Department

Director of Finance, J. A. Crutchlow £33,970–£44,996
Deputy Directors of Finance, D. H. Burr; J. P. Nicholson; M. W. Maidment . . . . . £26,121–£40,116

Supplies and Services Department

Director, D. Wilson . . . . £26,121–£40,116

Catering Department

Director of Catering, A. Thompson. . £26,121–£40,116

Property Services Department

Director of Property Services, T. G. Lawrence
£33,970–£44,996
Deputy Directors, K. R. Sewell; D. F. Hobart
£26,121–£40,116

Chief Engineer's Department

Chief Engineer, N. Boothman . . . . . . £33,970–£44,996
Deputy Chief Engineers, D. A. Woolgar; G. C. Sudbury; J. T. Clifton; R. J. Perham
£26,121–£40,116

Department of Computing Services

Director, DCS, D. K. Dunkin . . . . . . £33,970–£44,996
Deputy Directors, DCS, K. G. Daly; T. Egan
£26,121–£40,116

CITY OF LONDON POLICE
26 Old Jewry, EC2R 8DJ
[071-601 2222]

Strength of Force (June 1991), 831

Commissioner, O. Kelly, QPM £63,105
Assistant Commissioner, C. Coxall £49,191
Commander, H. J. Moore £40,278
Chief Superintendents (£34,167–£36,750):
  '*B*' *Division*, G. Marshall.
  '*C*' *Division*, T. Dickinson.
  CID, P. Gwynn.
  CID/Fraud, R. Knevett.
  Management Support, R. Friend.
  Operational Support, T. Hillier.

BRITISH TRANSPORT POLICE
15 Tavistock Place, WC1H 9SJ
[071–388 7541]

Strength of Force (April 1991), 2,017

The Force provides a policing service to the British Railways Board and London Underground Ltd Police posts are located throughout England, Wales and Scotland.

The Chief Constable reports to the British Transport Police Committee, a statutory body set up under the Transport Act 1962. The members of the Committee are appointed by the British Railways Board and London Regional Transport.
Chief Constable, D. O'Brien, OBE.
Deputy Chief Constable, G. E. Coles.
Assistant Chief Constables:
  London Underground Division, W. Palmer.
  Support Services, A. Parker.
  Operations, W. I. McGregor.
  Scotland Division, A. Mackenzie.

MINISTRY OF DEFENCE POLICE
Ministry of Defence, Empress State Building,
Lillie Road, SW6 1TR
[071–385 1244]

Strength of Force (May 1991), 5,021

The Ministry of Defence Police is a statutory police force directly responsible to the Secretary of State for Defence for the policing of all military land, stations and establishments in the United Kingdom.
Chief Constable, J. Reddington, QPM
Deputy Chief Constable, N. L. Chapple, QPM
Head of MDP Secretariat, W. A. T. Aves.
Assistant Chief Constables:
  Inspectorate and Firearms, S. G. Edwards.
  Operations, R. E. Murray.
  Personnel and Training, A. A. J. Scale.
  Scotland, A. F. Grant.
  Support, C. Bucke.

ROYAL PARKS CONSTABULARY
2 Marsham Street, SW1P 3EB
[071-276 3761/3]

Strength of Force (June 1991), 155

The Royal Parks Constabulary is maintained by the Department of the Environment and is responsible, through the Bailiff of the Royal Parks, for the policing of twenty Royal Parks and Gardens in and around London. These comprise an area in excess of 6,000 acres. Officers of the Force are appointed under the Parks Regulations Act 1872, as amended by the Parks Regulations (Amendment) Act 1974.
Chief Officer, W. Ross.
Deputy Chief Officer, M. J. Loader.

UNITED KINGDOM ATOMIC ENERGY AUTHORITY CONSTABULARY
11 Charles II Street, SW1Y 4QP
[071-389 6565]

Strength of Force (June 1991), 555

The Constabulary is responsible for policing United Kingdom Atomic Energy Authority and British Nuclear Fuels PLC establishments and for escorting nuclear material between establishments.

The Chief Constable is responsible, through the Atomic Energy Authority Police Committee, to the Secretary of State for Energy.
Chief Constable, H. J. McMorris, QPM
Deputy Chief Constable, E. H. Miller.

THE ARMED FORCES

MINISTRY OF DEFENCE
Main Building, Whitehall, SW1A 2HB
[071–218 9000]

The Ministry of Defence is concerned with the control, administration, equipment and support of the Armed Forces of the Crown. The research, development, production and purchase of weapons systems and equipment for the Armed Forces is the concern of the Procurement Executive of the Ministry of Defence.

Salaries

Secretary of State	£38,105
Minister of State (Commons)	£26,962
Minister of State (Lords)	£43,010
Parliamentary Under Secretary (Commons)	£20,463
Parliamentary Under Secretary (Lords)	£36,066
Grade 1	£84,250
Grade 1A	£77,500
Grade 2	£60,100–£70,400
Grade 3	£48,000–£55,700*
Grade 4	£40,116–£44,996*
Grade 5	£32,551–£43,307*

*Plus £1,500 London allowance.
(For Services salaries, *see* pp. 404–9)

Secretary of State for Defence, THE RT. HON. THOMAS KING, MP.
  Private Secretary (G5), S. Webb.
  Parliamentary Private Secretary, A. McKay, MP.
Minister of State for the Armed Forces, THE RT. HON. ARCHIBALD HAMILTON, MP.
  Private Secretary, J. A. Miller.
  Parliamentary Private Secretary, R. Knapman, MP.
Minister of State for Defence Procurement, THE RT. HON. ALAN CLARK, MP.
  Private Secretary, P. Watkins.
  Parliamentary Private Secretary, D. Wilshire, MP.
Parliamentary Under Secretary of State for the Armed Forces, THE EARL OF ARRAN.
  Private Secretary, P. A. Wilson.
Parliamentary Under Secretary of State for Defence Procurement, KENNETH CARLISLE, MP.
  Private Secretary, C. R. C. Holderness.
Permanent Under Secretary of State (G1), Sir Michael Quinlan, GCB.
  Private Secretary., T. C. McKane.
Chief of Defence Staff, Field Marshal Sir Richard Vincent, GBE, KCB, DSO.

Defence Staff

Vice Chief of the Defence Staff, Adm. Sir Benjamin Bathurst, KCB.
Deputy Under Sec. (Policy) (G2), R. C. Mottram.
Defence Services Secretary, Maj.-Gen. B. T. Pennicott.
Deputy CDS (Commitments), Air Marshal Sir Kenneth Hayr, KCB, CBE, AFC.
Asst. Under Sec. (Commitments) (G3), N. Bevan, CB.
Asst. CDS (NATO/UK), Rear-Adm. M. G. T. Harris.
Asst. CDS (Overseas), Maj.-Gen. A. G. H. Harley, OBE.
Asst. CDS (Logistics), Air Vice-Marshal D. J. Saunders, CBE.
Deputy CDS (Systems), Lt.-Gen. Sir Anthony Mullens, KCB, OBE.
Asst. CDS (Concepts), Air Vice-Marshal A. L. Roberts, CBE, AFC.
Asst. CDS, Operational Requirements (Sea), Rear-Adm. R. F. Cobbold.
Asst. CDS, Operational Requirements (Land), Maj.-Gen. S. Cowan, CBE.
Asst. CDS, Operational Requirements (Air), Air Vice-Marshal I. D. Macfadyen, CB, OBE.
Asst. CDS (CIS), Rear-Adm. R. Walmsley.

Asst. CDS (Policy and Nuclear), Rear-Adm. J. J. R. Tod, CBE.
Asst. Under Sec. (Policy) (G3), H. Griffiths.
Deputy CDS (Programmes and Personnel), Vice-Adm. Sir Barry Wilson, KCB.
Asst. CDS (Programmes), Maj.-Gen. the Hon. T. P. J. Boyd-Carpenter, MBE.
Surgeon Gen. and Dir. Gen. Medical Services (RAF), Air Marshal Sir Nigel Mills, KBE, QHP.
Deputy Surgeon Gen. (Ops. and Plans) and Medical Dir. Gen. (Naval), Surgeon Rear-Adm. D. A. Lammiman, LVO, QHS.
Deputy Surgeon Gen. (Health Services) and Dir. Gen. Army Medical Services, Maj.-Gen. P. J. Beale, QHP.
Dir., Defence Nursing Services, Brig. J. M. Field, OBE, QHNS.
Dir., Defence Dental Services, Maj.-Gen. F. E. Ashenhurst, QHDS.
Defence Medical Services (Fin. and Sect. Div.) (G5), G. J. Gammon.
Dir., Army Medicine and Consulting Physician, Maj.-Gen. I. C. Crawford, CBE, QHP.
Dir., Army Surg. and Consulting Surgeon, Maj.-Gen. J. T. Coull, QHS.
Dir., Army Psychiatry and Consulting Psychiatrist, Brig. P. Abraham, QHP.

Defence Intelligence Staff

Dir., Defence Intelligence (Secretariat) (G5), J. N. L. Morrison.

Naval Department

Chief of Naval Staff and First Sea Lord, Adm. Sir Julian Oswald, GCB, ADC.
Asst. Chief of Naval Staff, Rear-Adm. P. C. Abbott.
Commandant General Royal Marines, Lt.-Gen. Sir Henry Beverley, KBE, OBE, ADC.
Chief of Naval Personnel and Second Sea Lord, Vice-Adm. Sir Michael Livesay, KCB.
Naval Secretary, Rear-Adm. C. C. Morgan.
Dir. Gen., Naval Manpower and Training, Rear-Adm. M. H. G. Layard, CBE.
Dir. Gen., Naval Personal Services, Rear-Adm. D. M. Dow.
Asst. Under Sec. (Naval Personnel) (G3), J. M. Moss.
Chief of Fleet Support, Vice-Adm. N. Purvis.
Chief Executive, Hydrographic Office Defence Support Agency, Rear-Adm. J. A. L. Myres.
Asst. Under Sec. (Fleet Support) (G3), D. C. R. Heyhoe.
Dir. Gen., Ship Refitting (G3), G. A. Allin.
Dir. Gen., Supplies and Transport (G3), J. T. Baugh.
  Principal Dir., Supplies and Transport (Ops.) (G4), W. N. Cooke.
  Principal Dir., Supplies and Transport (Stores and Victualling) (G4), G. E. Miller.
  Principal Dir., Supplies and Transport (Armaments) (G4), M. A. Holder.
Dir. Gen., Fleet Support (Policy and Services), Rear-Adm. G. N. Davis.
Dir., Naval Shore Telecommunications (G5), P. Woodger.
Dir. Gen., Aircraft (Navy), Rear-Adm. R. H. Burn, AFC.
Dir., Women's Royal Naval Services, Cmdt. A. C. Spencer, ADC.
Chaplain of The Fleet, Ven. M. H. G. Henley, QHC.

Army Department

Chief of the General Staff, Gen. Sir John Chapple, GCB, CBE, ADC (Gen.); (w.e.f. Feb. 14, 1992, Gen. Sir Peter Inge, KCB, ADC (Gen.)).

Asst. Chief of the General Staff, Maj.-Gen. R. N. Wheeler, CBE.
Dir. Gen., Military Survey, Maj.-Gen. R. Wood.
Dir. Gen., TA and Organization, Maj.-Gen. D. M. Naylor, MBE.
Dir. Gen., Training (Army), Maj.-Gen. S. C. Grant.
Inspector Gen., Doctrine and Training, Lt.-Gen. Sir Garry Johnson, KCB, OBE, MC.
Dir., Royal Armoured Corps, Maj.-Gen. R. E. Barron.
Dir., Royal Artillery, Maj.-Gen. M. T. Tennant.
Dir., Infantry, Maj.-Gen. R. J. Hodges, CB, OBE.
Dir., Army Air Corps, Maj.-Gen. S. W. St J. Lytle (*w.e.f. Feb. 1992*).
Engineer in Chief (Army), Maj.-Gen. J. A. J. P. Barr, CBE.
Dir. Gen., CCIS Signals Officer in Chief (Army), Maj.-Gen. R. F. L. Cook.
Military Secretary, Lt.-Gen. The Hon. W. E. Rous, OBE.
Adjutant-General, Gen. Sir David Ramsbotham, KCB, CBE, ADC (*Gen.*).
Asst. Under Sec. (Army) (G3), M. Gainsborough.
Dir. Gen., Army Manning and Recruiting, Maj.-Gen. J. F. J. Johnston, CBE.
Paymaster in Chief, Maj.-Gen. P. S. Bray.
Dir. Gen., Personal Services (Army), Maj.-Gen. D. A. Grove, OBE.
Dir. Security (Army), Maj.-Gen. P. D. Alexander, CB, MBE (retd).
Provost Marshal (Army), Brig. A. R.Bell, MBE.
Dir., Army Legal Services, Maj.-Gen. D. H. D. Selwood.
Dir., Army Education, Maj.-Gen. C. A. Kinvig.
Quartermaster General, Lt.-Gen. Sir John Learmont, KCB, CBE.
Asst. Under Sec. (Quartermaster) (G3), N. J. Beaumont.
Dir. Gen., Logistics Policy (Army), Maj.-Gen. G. W. Field, OBE.
Dir. Gen., Transport and Movements, Maj.-Gen. J. D. Macdonald, CBE.
Dir., Army Veterinary and Remount Services, Brig. G. R. Durrant, CBE, QHVS.
Dir. Gen., Management and Support of Intelligence, Maj.-Gen. A. L. Meier, OBE.
Dir. Gen., Ordnance Services, Maj.-Gen. D. F. E. Botting, CBE.
Dir. Gen., Electrical and Mechanical Engineering, Maj.-Gen. M. S. Heath.
Chaplain General, Rev. J. Harkness, OBE, QHC.

Air Force Department

Chief of the Air Staff, Air Chief Marshal Sir Peter Harding, GCB, ADC.
Asst. Chief of Air Staff, Air Vice-Marshal T. Garden.
Cmdt. Gen. and Dir. Gen. of Security (RAF), Air Vice-Marshal D. R. Hawkins, MBE.
Chief Exec., National Air Traffic Services (G3), D. J. McLauchlan.
Dir. Gen., Policy and Planning, National Air Traffic Services, Air Vice-Marshal M. J. Gibson, OBE.
Air Member for Personnel, Air Chief Marshal Sir Roger Palin, KCB, CBE, ADC.
Air Secretary, Air Vice-Marshal R. J. Honey, CB, CBE.
Dir. Gen., RAF Personal Services, Air Vice-Marshal D. O. Crwys-Williams, CB.
Dir. Gen., Training, Air Vice-Marshal J. F. Willis, CB, CBE.
Dir., Legal Services (RAF) Air Vice-Marshal R. T. Dawson, CBE.
Chief of Logistic Support (RAF), Air Marshal R. J. M. Alcock, CB.
Asst. Under Sec. (Personnel (Air)) (G3), M. D. Tidy.
Air Member for Supply and Organization, Air Chief Marshal Sir Brendan Jackson, KCB.
Dir. Gen., Support Services (RAF), Air Vice-Marshal J. P. R. Browne, CBE.

Dir. Gen., Support Management (RAF), Air Vice-Marshal C. P. Baker, CB.
Ass. Under Sec. (Supply and Organization (Air)) (G3), T. F. W. Knapp.
Chaplain-in-Chief, Ven. B. H. Lucas, CB, QHC.

Defence Scientific Staff

Chief Scientific Adviser (G1A), Prof. E. R. Oxburgh, PH.D.
Deputy Chief Scientific Adviser (G2), Dr G. G. Pope, CB.
Dir. Gen., Chemical and Biological Defence Establishment (G3), Dr G. S. Pearson, CB.
Asst. Chief Scientific Advisers (G3), J. E. Britton (*Projects and Research*); Mrs M. J. Bourne, OBE (*Capabilities*); Dr T. Buckley (*Research*); (G4) Dr G. Pocock (*Nuclear*).
Dir., Defence Operational Analysis Establishment (G3), Dr D. Leadbeater.
Dir. Gen., Strategic Defence Initiative Participation Office (G5), A. L. C. Quigley.

Office of Management and Budget

Second Permanent Under Secretary of State (G1A), J. M. Stewart, CB.
Deputy Under Secs. (G2), M. J. V. Bell (*Finance*); R. M. Hastie-Smith, CB (*Civilian Management*); R. L. L. Facer (*Personnel and Logistics*); R. Jackling, CBE (*Resources and Programmes*).
Asst. Under Secs. of State (G3), T. J. Brack (*General Finance*); M. J. Culham (*Civilian Management (Administration)*); Dr M. J. Harte (*Resources*); M. J. Dymond (*Dir. Gen. Defence Accounts*); A. G. Rucker (*Security and Common Services*); A. J. Cragg (*Dir. Gen. of Management Audit*); J. F. Howe, OBE (*Personnel and Logistics*); D. B. Omand (*Programmes*); N. H. Nicholls, CBE (*Systems*); D. J. L. Smith, PH.D. (*Civilian Management (Specialists)*); B. F. Rule (*Dir. Gen., Information Technology Services*); B. W. Stanley (*Dir., Works Services*).
Head, Statistics (G4), M. V. Wilde.
Chief of Ministry of Defence Police, J. Reddington.

Public Relations

Chief of Public Relations (G4), H. B. Colver, CBE.
Deputy Chief of Public Relations (G5), C. Verey.
Dir. of Public Relations (Navy), Capt. P. A. Voute, RN.
Dir. of Public Relations (Army), Brig. B. H. Dutton, CBE.
Dir. of Public Relations (RAF), Air Cdre M. Barnes.

PROCUREMENT EXECUTIVE

Chief of Defence Procurement (G1), Dr M. K. McIntosh.
Private Secretary, Miss S. Scholefield.

Procurement Executive Policy and Administration

Deputy Under Secretary (Defence Procurement) (G2), A. J. P. Macdonald, CB.
Asst. Under Secretary (International and Domestic Procurement) (G3), J. A. Gulvin.
President of the Ordnance Board, Air Vice-Marshal J. M. P. Calnan.
Dir. Gen., Defence Quality Assurance (G3), B. Miller.
Dir. Gen., Defence Contracts (G3), G. E. Roe.
Principal Dir., Accountancy, Estimating and Pricing Services (G4), J. V. A. Crawford.
Principal Dir., Patents (G4), E. J. Mansfield.
Commandant, Aeroplane and Armament Experimental Establishment, Air Cdre D. L. Bywater.

DEFENCE RESEARCH AGENCY

The Defence Research Agency (DRA) was set up on April 1, 1991. It incorporates the Royal Aerospace Establishment (now Aerospace Division), the Admiralty Research Establishment (now Maritime Division), the Royal Armament Research and Development Establishment (now Military Division), and the Royal Signals and Radar Establishment (now Electronics Division).

Chief Exec. (G2), J. A. R. Chisholm.
Directors, (G3) Dr D. C. Tyte (*technical*); (G4) A. J. H. Ward (*personnel*); (G5) J. R. Corkhill (*marketing*); A. L. Reeves (*finance*).
Managing Dir., Maritime Division (G3), P. D. Ewins.
Directors, (G3) P. M. Sutcliffe; (G4) B. P. Blaydes.
Managing Dir., Aerospace Division (G3), J. M. Flood.
Managing Dir., Military Division (G3).
Managing Dir., Electronics Division (G3), S. J. Robinson, OBE.
Directors, (G3) Dr A. L. Mears; (G4) Dr J.Prior.
Company Sec. (G5), Mrs E. Peace.

Nuclear Programmes

Deputy Controller (Nuclear) (G3), G. N. Beavan.
Dir., Atomic Weapons Establishment (G2), B. H. Richards.

Sea Systems Controllerate

Controller of the Navy, Vice-Adm. Sir Kenneth Eaton, KCB.
Asst. Under Sec. (*Material Naval*) (G3), B. R. Hawtin.
Principal Dir., Navy and Nuclear Contracts (G4), A. T. Phipps.
Chief, Abovewater Systems Executive and Deputy Controller, Vice-Adm. Sir Robert Hill, KBE.
Dir. Gen., Surface Ships (G3), H. Perkins.
Dir. Gen., Surface Weapons (G4), Cdre F. P. Scourse, MBE.
Dir. Gen., Marine Engineering, Cdre R. F. James, ADC.
Naval Ships Acceptance, Cdre P. Dalrymple Smith.
Chief, Underwater Systems Executive (G3), A. J. Creighton.
Dir. Gen., Submarines (G3), W. G. Sanders, CB.
Dir. Gen., Underwater Weapons (G4), D. McArthur.
Dir., Naval Architect/Submarines (G5), P. Davies.
Chief, Strategic Systems Executive, Rear-Adm. I. H. Pirnie.
Deputy Chief, Strategic Systems Executive, Cdre P. L. Bryan.
Dir. Gen., Strategic Weapons Systems, Cdre G. Bryan.
Dir., Strategic Systems (Finance and Sect.) (G5), J. P. Colston.
Dir. Gen., Procurement and Support Organization (Navy), Rear-Adm. D. M. Pulvertaft, CB.
Dir., Abovewater Systems (Finance and Sect.) (G5), P. A. Rotheram.
Dir., Technical Services (Warships) and Naval Architect/Surface Ships (G5), P. C. Bryan.

Dir., Underwater Systems (Finance and Sect.) (G5), E. J. Hitt.
Dir., Future Projects (Naval) (G5), A. Jenkins.

Land Systems Controllerate

Master-General of the Ordnance, Lt.-Gen. A. S. J. Blacker, CBE.
Dir. Gen., Policy and Special Projects, Maj.-Gen. A. C. P. Stone.
Asst. Under Sec. (*Ordnance*) (G3), Dr A. Fox.
Principal Dir., Contracts (Ordnance) (G4), R. C. Harford.
Dir. Gen., Guided Weapons and Electronics (G3), J. D. Maines.
Dir. Gen., Land Fighting Systems, Maj.-Gen. R. J. Hayman-Joyce, CBE.

Air Systems Controllerate

Controller, Aircraft, D. M. Spiers, CB, TD.
Dep. Controller, Aircraft, Air Marshal Sir Michael Simmons, KCB, AFC.
Asst. Under Sec. (*Air (Procurement Executive)*) (G3), B. A. E. Taylor.
Principal Dir., Contracts (Air) (G4), D. A. Oakley.
Dir. Gen., Aircraft 1, (G3), J. A. Gordon.
Dir. Gen., Aircraft 2, Air Vice-Marshal D. Cousins, CB, AFC.
Dir. Gen., Aircraft 3, (G3), K. G. Hambleton.
Dir. Gen., Strategic Electronic Systems (G3), J. C. Mabberley.

Defence Export Services Organization

Head of Defence Export Services (G2), J. A. Thomas.
Military Deputy to Head of DES, Rear-Adm. P. B. Rowe, CBE, LVO.
Dir. Gen. Saudi Armed Forces Project, Air Marshal Sir Ronald Stuart-Paul, KBE.
Dir. Gen., Marketing (G3), N. Paren.
Asst. Under Sec. (DES Admin.) (G3), C. T. Sandars.
Malaysian Project Office (G5), J. B. Taylor.

METEOROLOGICAL OFFICE
London Road, Bracknell, Berks. RG12 2SZ
[0344-420242]

The Meteorological Office is the national meteorological service. It became an executive agency within the Ministry of Defence in April 1990. It provides meteorological services for the Services departments and civilian aviation, shipping, public services, the press, industry and the general public. It collects, distributes and publishes meteorological information from all parts of the world and undertakes research related to meteorology and climate.

Chief Executive (G2), Sir John Houghton, CBE, FRS.
Dir. of Operations (G3), Dr P. Ryder.
Dir. of Research (G4), Dr K. A. Browning.

THE ROYAL NAVY

THE QUEEN

Admirals of the Fleet

HRH The Prince Philip, Duke of Edinburgh, KG, KT, OM, GBE, AC, QSO, PC, *born* June 10, 1921 ..... Jan. 15, 1953
Sir Varyl Begg, GCB, DSO, DSC, *born* Oct. 1, 1908 .... Aug. 12, 1968
The Lord Hill-Norton, GCB, *born* Feb. 8, 1915 .... March 12, 1971
Sir Michael Pollock, GCB, LVO, DSC, *born* Oct. 19, 1916 .... March 1, 1974
Sir Edward Ashmore, GCB, DSC, *born* Dec. 11, 1919 .... Feb. 9, 1977
The Lord Lewin, KG, GCB, LVO, DSC, *born* Nov. 19, 1920 .... July 6, 1979
Sir Henry Leach, GCB, *born* Nov. 18, 1923 .... Dec. 1, 1982
The Lord Fieldhouse, GCB, GBE, *born* Feb. 12, 1928 .... Aug. 2, 1985
Sir William Staveley, GCB, *born* Nov. 10, 1928 .... May 25, 1989

Admirals

Oswald, Sir Julian, GCB, ADC (*Chief of Naval Staff and First Sea Lord*).

Bathurst, Sir Benjamin, GCB (*Vice Chief of the Defence Staff*).

Slater, Sir Jock, KCB, LVO, (*C.-in-C. Fleet, Allied C.-in-C. Channel and C.-in-C. Eastern Atlantic Area*).

Livesay, Sir Michael, KCB (*Chief of Personnel and Second Sea Lord*).

Kerr, Sir John, KCB (*C.-in-C. Naval Home Command*).

Vice-Admirals

Symons, Sir Patrick, KBE (*Representative to Supreme Allied Command Atlantic in Europe*).

Grose, Sir Alan, KBE (*Flag Officer Plymouth and Naval Base Comd. Devonport*).

Coward, Sir John, KCB, DSO (*Comdt. Royal College of Defence Studies*).

Wilson, Sir Barry, KCB (*Deputy CDS (Programmes and Personnel)*).

Eaton, Sir Kenneth, KCB (*Controller of the Navy*).

Hill, Sir Robert, KBE (*Chief Abovewater Systems Executive*).

Hill-Norton, The Hon. Sir Nicholas, KCB (*Flag Officer Flotilla Three*).

Purvis, N., (*Chief of Fleet Support*).

Dobson, D. S. (*Chief of Staff to Commander, Allied Naval Forces Southern Europe*).

White, Sir Hugo, KCB, CBE (*Flag Officer Scotland and N. Ireland, Commander Northern Atlantic, and Commander NORE Sub. Area Channel*).

Newman, R. T., CB (*Chief of Staff to C.-in-C. Fleet*).

Woodhead, A. P. (*Deputy Supreme Allied Commander Atlantic*).

Rear-Admirals

Pirnie, I. H., (*Chief Strategic Systems Executive*).

Frere, R. T. (*Flag Officer Submarines and Comd. Sub. Area East Atlantic*).

Layard, M. H. G., CBE (*Dir. Gen., Naval Manpower and Training*).

Dow, D. M., CB (*Dir. Gen. Naval Personal Services*).

Cooke-Priest, C. H. D. (*Flag Officer Naval Aviation*).

Tod, J. J. R., CBE (*Asst. CDS (Policy and Nuclear)*).

Harris, M. G. T. (*Asst. CDS (NATO/UK)*).

Abbott, P. C. (*Asst. Chief of the Naval Staff*).

Richardson, A. B. (*Flag Officer First Flotilla*).

Middleton, J. P. W. (*Chief Staff Officer (Support)*).

Biggs, G. W. R. (*Flag Officer Gibraltar, Gibraltar Naval Base Commander and COMGIBMED*).

Walmsley, R. (*Asst. CDS (CIS)*).

Rowe, P. B., CBE, LVO (*Military Deputy to Head of DES*).

Myres, J. A. L. (*Chief Exec., Hydrographic Office Defence Support Agency*).

Hoddinott, A. P., OBE (*Commander British Naval Staff Washington, Naval Attaché Washington and UK National Liaison Representative to SACLANT*).

Burn, R. H., AFC (*Dir. Gen. Aircraft (Naval)*).

Pulvertaft, D. M., CB (*Dir. Gen., Procurement Support Org. (Navy)*).

Musson, J. G. R. (*Senior Directing Staff (Naval) RCDS*).

Bawtree, D. K. (*Flag Officer Portsmouth and Naval Base Commander Portsmouth*).

Woodard, R. N. (*Flag Officer Royal Yachts*).

Moore, M. A. C., LVO (*Deputy Asst. Chief of Staff (Operations) on the Staff of the Supreme Allied Commander Europe*).

Morgan, C. C. (*Naval Secretary*).

Wilkinson, N. J. (*DOPT*).

Brigstocke, J. R. (*Flag Officer Flotilla Two*).

Cobbold, R. F. (*Asst. CDS Operational Requirements (Sea Systems)*).

Davis, G. N. (*Dir. Gen., Fleet Support (Policy and Services)*).

Boyce, M. C., OBE (*Flag Officer Sea Training and Naval Base Commander Portland*).

Shiffner, J. R. (*Chief of Staff to C.-in-C. Naval Home Command*).

Lang, J. S. (*w.e.f. Jan. 7, 1992*).

HER MAJESTY'S FLEET
(as at July 1, 1991)

Type/Class	No.	Operational or engaged in preparing for service, trials or training	No.	Undergoing refit or on standby, etc.
Submarines				
Polaris	3	Repulse, Resolution, Revenge	1	Renown
Fleet	14	Courageous, Sovereign, Swiftsure, Superb, Sceptre, Spartan, Talent, Trafalgar, Turbulent, Tireless, Torbay, Trenchant, Triumph*, Valiant	1	Splendid
Type 2400	2	Upholder†, Unseen*		
Oberon Class	6	Otus, Ocelot, Opportune, Osiris, Oracle, Opossum		
ASW Carriers	2	Ark Royal, Invincible	1	Illustrious
Assault Ships	1	Fearless	1	Intrepid
Destroyers				
Type 42	9	Birmingham, Cardiff, Edinburgh, Exeter, Glasgow, Gloucester, Manchester, Newcastle, York	3	Southampton, Liverpool, Nottingham
Frigates				
Type 23	4	Norfolk†, Argyll, Lancaster*, Marlborough†		
Type 22	13	Battleaxe, Boxer, Brave, Brazen†, Brilliant, Broadsword, Campbeltown, Chatham, Cornwall, Coventry, Cumberland, London, Sheffield	1	Beaver
Type 21	6	Amazon, Ambuscade, Active, Avenger, Alacrity, Arrow		
Leander Class	8	Argonaut, Charybdis, Cleopatra, Jupiter, Minerva, Hermione, Sirius†, Scylla	1	Andromeda
Navigation Training Ship	1	Juno†		

Type/Class	No.	Operational or engaged in preparing for service trials or training	No.	Undergoing refit or on standby, etc.
Offshore Patrol				
Castle Class	2	*Leeds Castle, Dumbarton Castle*		
Island Class	7	*Alderney, Guernsey, Orkney, Shetland, Anglesey, Jersey, Lindisfarne*		
MCMVs				
Minesweepers Ton Class	1	*Soberton*		
River Class**	11	*Waveney, Carron, Dovey, Helford, Blackwater, Itchen, Helmsdale, Orwell, Ribble, Spey, Arun*	1	*Humber*
Minehunters Ton Class	7	*Brinton, Iveston, Kedleston, Kellington, Nurton, Sheraton, Wilton*		
Hunt Class	13	*Brecon, Brocklesby, Ledbury, Cottesmore, Dulverton, Middleton†, Chiddingford†, Hurworth, Bicester, Atherstone, Berkeley, Quorn, Cattistock*		
Single Role Minehunter	3	*Sandown, Inverness†, Cromer**		
Patrol Craft				
Bird Class	3	*Kingfisher, Redpole, Cygnet*		
Coastal Training Craft†	13	*Attacker, Fencer, Hunter, Chaser, Striker, Archer, Biter, Smiter, Pursuer, Blazer, Dasher, Puncher, Charger*		
Peacock Class	3	*Peacock, Plover, Starling*		
Gibraltar Search and Rescue Craft	2	*Ranger, Trumpeter*		
Support Ships				
Submarine Tender	1	*Sentinel*		
Royal Yacht/Hospital Ship ..	1	*Britannia*		
Training Ships				
Fleet Tenders†	4	*Manly, Mentor, Messina, Milbrook*		
Ice Patrol Ship	1	*Endurance*		
Survey Ships	7	*Bulldog, Beagle, Fawn, Herald, Gleaner, Hecla, Roebuck*		

Notes:
(1) This table includes ships due for completion or disposal during the course of 1991–92; the numbers of each type are not therefore an accurate indication of the ships available at any one time. Ships solely engaged in harbour training duties are not included.
(2) All submarines, ASW Carriers, Assault Ships, Guided Missile Destroyers, Frigates, Offshore Patrol Ships and MCMVs are assigned to NATO, or will be so assigned on becoming operational. Other ships could be made available in support of NATO operations if national requirements permitted.
(3) Ships marked * were under construction on April 1, 1991 and are planned to enter service during 1991–92.
(4) Ships marked † are engaged in trials or training.
(5) River Class vessels, marked **, apart from HMS *Blackwater*, are operated by the Royal Naval Reserve.
(6) Coastal Training Craft are operated by the Royal Naval Reserve and the University Royal Naval Units.
(7) Ships approved for disposal or sale during 1991–92: Conqueror, Onslaught, Odin, Phoebe, Gavinton, Kirkliston, Peterel, Sandpiper, Challenger, Churchill, Warspite, Onyx, Penelope, Cuxton, Upton, Hubberston, Cormorant, Hart and Hecate.

Royal Naval Reserve (RNR).—The Royal Naval Reserve is a totally integrated part of the Royal Navy. It comprises about 6,000 men and women nationwide who volunteer to train in their spare time for a variety of sea and shore tasks which they would carry out in time of tension or war.
Chief Staff Officer, Capt. C. W. Pile.

Royal Naval Auxiliary Service (RNXS).—The RNXS is a uniformed, unarmed and, in peacetime, volunteer civilian service of some 2,700 men and women, under the direction of the Commander-in-Chief Naval Home Command. Members train in their spare time in units around the coasts of the United Kingdom for duties in times of tension and war. Their role includes manning port headquarters in support of the Naval Control of Shipping Organization, and providing crews for vessels engaged in the defence of ports and anchorages.
Patron and Hon. Auxiliary Commodore, HRH Prince Michael of Kent.
Captain, Capt. J. M. Neville-Rolfe, RN.

ROYAL MARINES

The Corps of Royal Marines was formed in 1664 and is part of the Naval Service. The Royal Marines provide Britain's sea soldiers and in particular 3 Commando Brigade Royal Marines, two-thirds of which is trained and equipped for arctic warfare. Royal Marines also serve in HM Ships, provide landing craft crews, special boat sections and other detachments for naval and amphibious operations. They also provide the Naval Band Service. The Corps is about 7,000 strong.
Commandant General, Royal Marines, Lt.-Gen. Sir Henry Beverley, KCB, OBE.
Major-Generals, A. F. Whitehead, DSO (*Chief of Staff*); R. J. Ross, OBE (*Commando Forces*); P. T. Stevenson; M. P. J. Hunt, OBE (*Royal College Defence Studies*).

Royal Marines Reserve (RMR).—The Royal Marines Reserve is a force of commando-trained volunteers who train to combat-readiness in order to support the regular Royal Marines should the need arise. About 50 per cent are trained and equipped for arctic warfare and most regular Royal Marine specializations are open to the reservist. There are RMR centres in London, Glasgow, Bristol, Liverpool and Newcastle, each with a number of outlying detachments. The present strength of the RMR is about 1,200.
Director, Brig. J. S. Chester, OBE.

QUEEN ALEXANDRA'S ROYAL NAVAL NURSING SERVICE

The first nursing sisters were appointed to naval hospitals in 1884 and the Queen Alexandra's Royal Naval Nursing Service (QARNNS) gained its current title under the patronage of Queen Alexandra in 1902. Nursing ratings were introduced in 1960 and men were integrated into the Service in 1982; both men and women serve as officers and ratings. Qualified staff and learners are mainly based at the UK Royal Naval Hospitals, and continue their responsibility for the health and fitness of naval personnel. The strength is about 530.
Patron, HRH Princess Alexandra, the Hon. Lady Ogilvy.
Matron-in-Chief, Principal Nursing Officer Miss J. Titley.

WOMEN'S ROYAL NAVAL SERVICE

Originally founded in 1917, the Women's Royal Naval Service (WRNS) was temporarily disbanded between the First and Second World Wars. The contribution of the Service is now firmly established as a professional and integral part of the Royal Navy with personnel serving in the United Kingdom and abroad in a wide range of specialist roles. From February 6, 1990, the role of the WRNS was expanded to include sea service , and from January 1, 1991 to include aircrew. WRNS officers adopted Royal Navy rank titles from December 1, 1990. The strength of the WRNS is about 3,500.
Chief Commandant, HRH The Princess Royal.
Director, Commandant A. C. Spencer, ADC.

THE ARMY

THE QUEEN

Field Marshals

HRH The Prince Philip, Duke of Edinburgh, KG, KT, OM, GBE, AC, QSO, PC, *born* June 10, 1921 . . . . . Jan. 15, 1953
Sir James Cassels, GCB, KBE, DSO, *born* Feb. 28, 1907 . . . . Feb. 29, 1968
The Lord Carver, GCB, CBE, DSO, MC, *born* April 24, 1915 . . . . July 18, 1973
Sir Roland Gibbs, GCB, CBE, DSO, MC, *born* June 22, 1921 . . . . July 13, 1979
The Lord Bramall, KG, GCB, OBE, MC, *born* Dec. 18, 1923 . . . . Aug. 1, 1982
Sir John Stanier, GCB, MBE, *born* Oct. 6, 1925 . . . . July 10, 1985
Sir Nigel Bagnall, GCB, CVO, MC, *born* Feb. 10, 1927 . . . . Sept. 9, 1988
Sir Richard Vincent, GBE, KCB, DSO (*Chief of Defence Staff*), *born* Aug. 10, 1927 . . . . April 2, 1991
Sir John Chapple, GCB, CBE, ADC (*Gen.*), *born* May 27, 1931 . . . . *w.e.f* Feb. 13, 1992

Generals

Kenny, Sir Brian, GCB, CBE, Col. Cmdt. RAVC, Col. QRIH, Col. Cmdt. RAC (*S. SACEUR*).

Palmer, Sir Patrick, KBE, Col. A. & S. H. (*C.-in-C. AFNORTH*).

Inge, Sir Peter, KCB, ADC (*Gen.*), Col. Green Howards, Col. Cmdt. RMP, Col. Cmdt. APTC (*Chief of the General Staff w. e. f. Feb. 14, 1992*).

Walker, Sir Anthony, KCB (*Comdt. Royal College of Defence Studies*).

Waters, Sir John, KCB, CBE, Col. Cmdt. POW Div. (*C.-in-C. UK Land Forces*).

Ramsbotham, Sir David, KCB, CBE, ADC (*Gen.*), Col. Comdt. 2 RGJ (*Adjutant General*).

Billière, Sir Peter de la, KCB, KBE, DSO, MC (*Military Adviser to Chief of the Defence Staff*).

Guthrie, Sir Charles, KCB, LVO, OBE, Col. Cmdt. Int. Corps (*C.-in-C. BAOR and Comdt, Northern Army Group*).

Jones, Sir Edward, KCB, CBE, Col. Cmdt. RAEC, Col. Cmdt. 3 RGJ (*UK Military Rep. to NATO*) (*w. e. f. Jan. 13, 1992*).

Lieutenant-Generals

Learmont, Sir John, KCB, CBE, Col. Cmdt. AAC, Col. Cmdt. RHA, Col. 2 Wessex (V) (*Quartermaster General*).

Mullens, Sir Anthony, KCB, OBE (*Deputy Chief of the Defence Staff (Systems)*).

Johnson, Sir Garry, KCB, OBE, MC, Col. Cmdt. The Light Division (*Comd. Doctrine and Training*).

Swinburn, Sir Richard, KCB (*GOC SE District*).

Wilsey, Sir John, KCB, CBE, Col. D and D, Col. Cmdt ACC (*GOC and D. Mil. Ops. Northern Ireland*).

Wilkes, Sir Michael, KCB, CBE, Col. Cmdt. RA (*Cmdt. UK Fd. Army and Inspector Gen. TA*).

Graham, Sir Peter, KCB, CBE, Col. Gordons, Col. Cmdt. The Scottish Division (*GOC Scotland and Governor Edinburgh Castle*).

Blacker, A. S. J., CBE, Col. Cmdt. REME, Col. Cmdt. RTR (*Master-General of the Ordnance*).

Rous, The Hon. W. E., OBE (*Military Secretary*).

MacKenzie, J. J. G., OBE, Col. Cmdt. WRAC (*Cmdt. 1 (Br) Corps*).

Major-Generals

Pollard, A. J. G., CBE, Col. Comdt. SASC, Col. Cmdt. The Queen's Division, Dep. Col. R. Anglian (*GOC SW District*).

Hodges, R. J., CB, OBE, Col. Kings Own Border (*Dir. Infantry*).

Naylor, D. M., MBE (*Dir. Gen. TA and Organization*).

Boyd-Carpenter, The Hon. T. P. J., MBE (*Asst. Chief of Defence Staff (Programmes)*).

Corbett, R. J. S., CB (*GOC London District and Maj.-Gen. Comdt. The Household Division*).

Hayman-Joyce, R. J., CBE (*Dir. Gen. Land Fighting Systems*).

Beale, P. J., QHP (*DGAMS and DSG (Hlth Svcs)*).

Bray, P. S., CB (*Paymaster in Chief (Army)*).
Cowan, S., CBE, Col. QGS, Col. Cmdt. ALC (*Asst. Chief of the Defence Staff OR (Land)*).
Pennicott, B. T. (*Defence Services Secretary*).
Coull, J. T., QHS (*DA Surg.*).
Barr, J. A. J. P., CBE (*Engineer-in-Chief (Army)*).
Cook, R. F. L. (*Signal Officer in Chief (Army)*).
Duffell, P. R., CBE, MC (*CBF Hong Kong*).
Evans, W. A. (*GOC E. District*).
Wheeler, R. N., CBE, Col. R. Irish (*Asst. Chief of General Staff*).
Crawford, I. P., GM, QHP, (*Cmdt. Royal Army Medical College*).
Rose, H. M., OBE, QGM (*Comdt. Staff College*).
Barron, R. E. (*Dir. Royal Armoured Corps*).
Grist, R. D., OBE, Col. Glocesters (*Dir. Gen. AG Corps*).
Shellard, M. F. L., CBE.
Thomson, D. P., CBE, MC (*Senior Army Member, Royal College of Defence Studies, w. e. f. Jan. 20, 1992*).
Selwood, D. H. D. (*Dir. Army Legal Services*).
Denison-Smith, A. A., MBE (*Comdt. 4 Armd Division*).
Johnston, J. F. J., CBE (*Dir. Gen. Army Manning and Recruiting*).
Makepeace-Warne, A., MBE (*Cmdt. Joint Services Defence College*).
Alexander, J. O. C., CB, OBE (*Comd. Comms. BAOR*).
Field, G. W., OBE (*Dir. Gen. Logistics Policy (Army)*).
Shellard, M. F. L., CBE.
Ashenhurst, F. E., QHDS (*Dir. of Defence Dental Services*).
Crawford, I. C., CBE, QHP (*Dir. Army Medicine*).
Botting, D. F. E., CBE (*Dir. Gen. Ordnance Services LE (A)*).
Stone, A. C. P. (*Dir. Gen. Policy and Special Projects*).
Wallace, C. B. Q., OBE (*Cmdt. 3 Armed Division*).

Harley, A. G. H., CB, OBE (*Asst. Chief of the Defence Staff (Overseas)*).
Kinvig, C. A. (*Dir. Army Education*).
Baskervyle-Glegg, J., MBE (*SBLSO RAO*).
Smith, R. A., DSO, OBE, QGM, (*Cmdt. 1 Armed Division*).
Ticehurst, A. C., MB (*Cmdt. MED. UK Land Forces*).
Wood, R. (*Dir. Gen. Military Survey*).
Courage, W. J., MBE (*Chief Joint Services Liaison Organization Bonn*).
Mayes, F. B., QHS (*Cmdt. Med. BAOR*).
Toyne Sewell, T. P. (*Cmdt. RMAS*).
Tennant, M. T. (*Dir. Royal Artillery*).
Macdonald, J. D., CBE (*Dir. Gen. Transport and Movements*).
Heath, M. S. (*Dir. Gen. Electrical and Mechanical Engineering*).
Burton, E. F. G., OBE (*Cmdt. RMCS*).
Grove, D. A., OBE (*Dir. Gen. Personal Services*).
Meier, A. L., OBE (*Dir. Gen. Management and Support of Intelligence, MOD*).
Pett, R. A., MBE (*Dep. Chief of Staff (Support) AFNORTH*).
Grant, S. C. (*Dir. Gen. Army Training*).
Gordon, J. (*Chief of Staff HQ UK Land Forces*).
Sheppard, P. J., OBE (*Chief of Staff HQ BAOR*).
Walker, M. J. D., OBE (*GOC NE District Cmdt. 2 Inf. Division*).
Regan, M. D., OBE (*GOC W District*).
Freer, I. L., CBE, Col. Staffords (*CLF and DD Ops. Northern Ireland*).
Foley, J. P., CB, OBE, MC (*DGI (ROW*)) (*w. e. f. Feb. 1992*).
Hollands, G. S. (*Cmdt. Artillery 1 (Br) Corps*) (*w. e. f. Feb. 1992*).
Lytle, S. W. St J. (*Dir. Army Air Corps*) (*w. e. f. Feb. 1992*).

CONSTITUTION OF THE BRITISH ARMY

The Defence Secretary confirmed in July 1991 that the strength of the army would be reduced to 116,000 by the mid-1990s, and that 22 regiments would be amalgamated.

The Regular Forces include the following Arms, Branches and Corps. Soldiers' record offices are shown at the end of each group; records of officers are maintained at the Ministry of Defence.

The Arms

Household Cavalry.—The Life Guards; The Blues and Royals (Royal Horse Guards and 1st Dragoons). *Records*, Horse Guards, London, SW1.

Royal Armoured Corps.—Cavalry Regiments: 1st The Queen's Dragoon Guards; The Royal Scots Dragoon Guards (Carabiniers and Greys); 4th/7th Royal Dragoon Guards; 5th Royal Inniskilling Dragoon Guards; The Queen's Own Hussars; The Queen's Royal Irish Hussars; 9th/12th Royal Lancers (Prince of Wales's); The Royal Hussars (Prince of Wales's Own), 13th/18th Royal Hussars (Queen Mary's Own); 14th/20th King's Hussars; 15th/19th The King's Royal Hussars; 16th/5th The Queen's Royal Lancers; 17th/21st Lancers; Royal Tank Regiment comprising four regular regiments. *Records*, Queen's Park, Chester.

Artillery.—Royal Regiment of Artillery. *Records*, Imphal Barracks, Fulford Road, York.

Engineers.—Corps of Royal Engineers. *Records*, Kentigern House, Brown Street, Glasgow.

Signals.—Royal Corps of Signals. *Records*, Kentigern House, Brown Street, Glasgow.

The Infantry

The Foot Guards and Regiments of Infantry of the Line are grouped in Divisions as follows:—

Guards Division.—Grenadier, Coldstream, Scots,

Irish and Welsh Guards. *Divisional HQ*, HQ Household Division, Horse Guards, SW1. *Depot*, Pirbright Camp, Brookwood, Surrey. *Records*, Imphal Barracks, Fulford Road, York.

Scottish Division.—The Royal Scots (The Royal Regiment); The Royal Highland Fusiliers (Princess Margaret's Own Glasgow and Ayrshire Regiment); The King's Own Scottish Borderers; The Black Watch (Royal Highland Regiment); Queen's Own Highlanders (Seaforth and Camerons); The Gordon Highlanders; The Argyll and Sutherland Highlanders (Princess Louise's). *Divisional HQ*, The Castle, Edinburgh. *Depots*, Scottish Divisional Depots, Glencorse, Milton Bridge, Midlothian; Albemarle Barracks, Ouston, Newcastle. *Records*, Imphal Barracks, Fulford Road, York.

Queen's Division.—The Queen's Regiment, The Royal Regiment of Fusiliers, The Royal Anglian Regiment. *Divisional HQ*, Bassingbourn Barracks, Royston, Herts. *Depot*, Bassingbourn Barracks, Royston, Herts. *Records*, Higher Barracks, Exeter, Devon.

King's Division.—The King's Own Royal Border Regiment; The King's Regiment; The Prince of Wales's Own Regiment of Yorkshire; The Green Howards (Alexandra, Princess of Wales's Own Yorkshire Regiment); The Royal Irish Rangers (27th (Inniskilling) 83rd and 87th); The Queen's Lancashire Regiment; The Duke of Wellington's Regiment (West Riding). *Divisional HQ*, Imphal Barracks, York. *Depots*, The King's Division Depot (Yorkshire), Queen Elizabeth Barracks, Strensall, Yorks.; Albemarle Barracks, Ouston, Newcastle. The King's Division Depot (Royal Irish Rangers), St Patrick's Barracks, Ballymena, Northern Ireland. *Records*, Imphal Barracks, Fulford Road, York.

Prince of Wales's Division.—The Devonshire

and Dorset Regiment; The Cheshire Regiment; The Royal Welch Fusiliers; The Royal Regiment of Wales (24th/41st Foot); The Gloucestershire Regiment; The Worcestershire and Sherwood Foresters Regiment (29th/45th Foot); The Royal Hampshire Regiment; The Staffordshire Regiment (The Prince of Wales's); The Duke of Edinburgh's Royal Regiment (Berkshire and Wiltshire). *Divisional HQ*, Whittington Barracks, Lichfield, Staffs. *Depot*, The Prince of Wales's Division Depot, Whittington Barracks, Lichfield. Staffs. *Records*, Imphal Barracks, Fulford, York.

Light Division.—The Light Infantry; The Royal Green Jackets. *Divisional HQ*, Sir John Moore Barracks, Winchester, Hants. *Depot*, Sir John Moore Barracks, Winchester, Hants. *Records*, Higher Barracks, Exeter.

Brigade of Gurkhas.—2nd King Edward VII's Own Gurkha Rifles (The Sirmoor Rifles); 6th Queen Elizabeth's Own Gurkha Rifles; 7th Duke of Edinburgh's Own Gurkha Rifles; 10th Princess Mary's Own Gurkha Rifles; The Queen's Gurkha Engineers; Queen's Gurkha Signals; Gurkha Transport Regt. *Brigade HQ*, HMS *Tamar*, Hong Kong, BFPO 1. *Depot*, Training Depot, Brigade of Gurkhas, Malaya Lines, Sek Kong, BFPO 1. *Records*, Record Office, Brigade of Gurkhas, Hong Kong, BFPO 1.

The Parachute Regiment (Three regular battalions).—*Depot*, Browning Barracks, Aldershot, Hants. *Records*, Higher Barracks, Exeter.

Special Air Service Regiment.—*Regimental HQ*, Duke of York's Headquarters, Sloane Square, SW3. *Depot*, Stirling Lines, Hereford. *Records*, Higher Barracks, Exeter, Devon.

Army Air Corps.—*Regimental HQ* and *Depot*, Middle Wallop, Hants. *Records*, Higher Barracks, Exeter.

The Services

Royal Army Chaplain's Department.—*Regimental HQ* and *Depot*, Bagshot Park, Surrey.

Royal Corps of Transport.—*Records*, Kentigern House, Brown Street, Glasgow.

Royal Army Medical Corps, Royal Army Dental Corps, Queen Alexandra's Royal Army Nursing Corps, and Women's Royal Army Corps.—*Records*, Queen's Park, Chester.

Royal Army Ordnance Corps, Corps of Royal Electrical and Mechanical Engineers.—*Records*, Glen Parva Barracks, Saffron Road, Wigston, Leicester.

Small Arms School Corps.—*Records*, Higher Barracks, Exeter.

General Service Corps.—*Records*, Imphal Barracks, Fulford Road, York.

Corps of Royal Military Police, Royal Army Pay Corps, Royal Army Veterinary Corps, Royal Pioneer Corps, Intelligence Corps, Army Catering Corps, Military Provost Staff Corps, Royal Army Educational Corps, Army Physical Training Corps, Army Legal Corps, Sandhurst, Officers Training Corps.—*Records*, Higher Barracks, Exeter, Devon.

The Ulster Defence Regiment (UDR) was raised under authority of the UDR Act 1969 and assists the Regular Army in Northern Ireland.—*HQ*, Magheralave Road, Lisburn, Co. Antrim. *Records*, Imphal Barracks, Fulford Road, York.

The Territorial Army (TA).—The Territorial Army is designed to provide a highly-trained and well-equipped force which will complete the Regular Army order of battle in a time of national emergency. Its establishment is approximately 91,000. A new element of the TA, the Home Service Force, designed to produce a low-cost guard force, is currently being expanded to some 4,500 posts.

QUEEN ALEXANDRA'S ROYAL ARMY NURSING CORPS

The Queen Alexandra's Royal Army Nursing Corps (QARANC) was founded in 1902 as Queen Alexandra's Imperial Military Nursing Service (QAIMNS) and gained its present title in 1949. The QARANC has trained nurses for the register and roll since 1950 and has eight other employment categories. A non-nursing officer element was introduced in 1959 for personnel work. The QARANC provides service in military hospitals in the United Kingdom (including Northern Ireland), BAOR, Hong Kong, Cyprus, Falkland Islands and Belize.
Colonel-in-Chief, HRH The Princess Margaret, Countess of Snowdon, GCVO, CI.
Matron-in-Chief (Army) and Director of Defence Nursing Services, Brig. J. M. Field, QHNS.

WOMEN'S ROYAL ARMY CORPS

The Women's Royal Army Corps (WRAC) was formed on February 1, 1949 as a Corps of the Regular Army. The Corps predecessors were Queen Mary's Army Auxiliary Corps (QMAAC) in World War I, and the Auxiliary Territorial Service (ATS) in World War II. The present role of the WRAC is to be organized and trained, as an integral part of the Army, to carry out those tasks for which its members are best suited and qualified, so that it will contribute to the maximum efficiency of the Army as a whole. The Corps is approximately 8,500 (Regular and TA) and is employed by 36 sponsors in 30 employments in 500 units worldwide in the British Army.
Commandant-in-Chief, HM Queen Elizabeth The Queen Mother.
Controller Commandant, HRH The Duchess of Kent, GCVO.
Deputy Controller Commandant, Brig. A. Field, CB.
Director, Brig. G. K. Ramsey, MBE, ADC.

THE ROYAL AIR FORCE

THE QUEEN

Marshals of the Royal Air Force

HRH The Prince Philip, Duke of Edinburgh, KG, KT, OM, GBE, AC, QSO, PC, *born* June 10, 1921 ..... Jan. 15, 1953
Sir Dermot A. Boyle, GCB, KCVO, KBE, AFC, *born* Oct. 2, 1904 .... Jan 1, 1958
The Lord Elworthy, KG, GCB, CBE, DSO, MVO, DFC, AFC, *born* March 23, 1911 .... April 1, 1967
Sir John Grandy, GCB, GCVO, KBE, DSO, *born* Feb. 8, 1913 .... April 1, 1971
Sir Denis Spotswood, GCB, CBE, DSO, DFC, *born* Sept. 26, 1916 .... March 31, 1974
Sir Michael Beetham, GCB, CBE, DFC, AFC, *born* May 17, 1923 .... Oct. 15, 1982
Sir Keith Williamson, GCB, AFC, *born* Feb. 25, 1928 .... Oct. 15, 1985
Lord Craig of Radley, GCB, OBE, *born* Sept. 17, 1929 .... Nov. 14, 1988

Air Chief Marshals

Harding, Sir Peter, GCB, ADC (*Chief of the Air Staff*).
Skingsley, Sir Anthony, KCB (*Deputy C.-in-C., Allied Forces Central Europe*).
Parry-Evans, Sir David, GCB, CBE.
Jackson, Sir Brendan, KCB (*Air Member for Supply and Organization*).
Graydon, Sir Michael, KCB, CBE (*AOC-in-C Strike Command*).
Palin, Sir Roger, KCB, OBE, ADC (*Air Member for Personnel*).

Air Marshals

Hayr, Sir Kenneth, KCB, CBE, AFC (*Deputy CDS (Commitments)*).
Simmons, Sir Michael, KCB, AFC (*Deputy Controller Aircraft*).
Stear, Sir Michael, KCB, CBE (*AOC No. 18 Group*).
Stuart-Paul, Sir Ronald, KBE (*Dir. Gen. Saudi Armed Forces Project*).
Kemball, Sir John, KCB, CBE (*Chief of Staff and Deputy C.-in-C. Strike Command*).
Mills, Sir Nigel, KBE, QHP (*Surgeon General and Dir. Gen. Medical Services (RAF)*).
Thomson, Sir John, KCB, CBE, AFC (*AOC-in-C. RAF Support Command*).
Wilson, Sir Andrew, KCB, AFC (*C.-in-C. RAF Germany*).
Alcock, R. J. M., CB (*Chief of Logistic Support*).
Walker, J. R., CBE, AFC.

Air Vice-Marshals

Pilkington, M. J., CB, CBE (*Air Officer Training RAF Support Command*).
Roberts, A. L., CBE, AFC (*Asst. Chief of Defence Staff (Concepts)*).
Honey, R. J., CB, CBE (*Air Secretary and Air Officer Commanding RAF Personnel Management Centre*).
Austin, R. M., AFC (*Air Officer Commanding and Cmdt. RAF College, Cranwell*).
Woodford, A. A. G., CB (*Asst. Chief of Staff (Policy)*).
Harris, J. H., CB, CBE (*Chief of Staff HQ No. 18 Group*).
Crwys-Williams, D. O., CB (*Dir. Gen. of Personal Services (RAF)*).
Blackley, A. B., CBE, AFC (*Air Officer Scotland and N. Ireland*).
Johns, R. E., CB, CBE, LVO (*AOC No. 1 Group*).
Evans, C. E., CBE (*Senior Directing Staff, Royal College of Defence Studies*).
Willis, J. F., CB, CBE (*Dir. Gen. of Training (RAF)*).
Harding, P. J., CBE, AFC (*Deputy Chief of Staff (Operations) Allied Air Forces Central Europe*).
Wratten, Sir William, KBE, CB, AFC.
Hunter, A. F. C., CBE, AFC (*Comd. British Forces Cyprus*).
Browne, J. P. R., CBE (*Dir. Gen. Support Services (RAF)*).
Dicken, M. J. C. W., CB (*Air Officer Administration, RAF Support Command*).
Cousins, D., CB, AFC (*Dir. Gen. Aircraft 2*).
Davies, D. B. A. L., QHP (*Principal Medical Officer RAF Support Command*).

Dawson, R. T., CBE (*Dir. of Legal Services (RAF)*).
Allison, J. S., CBE (*AOC No. 11 Group*).
Baker, C. P., CB (*Dir. Gen. of Support Management (RAF)*).
Calnan, J. M. P. (*President of the Ordnance Board*).
Peters, R. G. (*Cmdt. RAF Staff College, Bracknell*).
Ernsting, J., OBE, QHS, Ph.D (*Senior Consultant*).
Dodworth, P., OBE, AFC (*Defence Attaché and Head of British Defence Staff, Washington*).
Garden, T. (*Asst. Chief of the Air Staff*).
Baird, J. A., QHP (*Principal Medical Officer Strike Command*).
Beer, P. G., CBE, LVO (*Commander British Forces Falkland Islands*).
Clark, P. D. (*Air Officer Engineering Strike Command*).
Ferguson, G. M., CBE (*Air Officer Admin. Strike Command*).
French, D. R., MBE (*Air Officer Maintenance RAF Support Command*).
Gibson, M. J., OBE (*Dir. Gen. Policy and Planning, National Air Traffic Services*).
Hawkins, D. R., MBE (*Dir. Gen. of Security (RAF)*).
Macfadyen, I. D., CB, OBE (*Asst. CDS Operational Requirements (Air Systems)*).
Saunders, D. J., CBE (*Asst. CDS (Logistics)*).
Squire, P. T., DFC, AFC (*Senior Air Staff Officer Strike Command*).
Robertson, G. A. (*Deputy Commander, RAF Germany*).
Lucas, B. H., QHC (*Chaplain-in-Chief (RAF)*).
Davison, D. J., QHS (*Dean of Air Force Medicine, w. e. f. Dec. 3, 1991*).

CONSTITUTION OF THE ROYAL AIR FORCE

The Royal Air Force consists of three Commands: Strike Command and Support Command in the United Kingdom, and RAF Germany. Strike Command is responsible for providing the air defence of the United Kingdom and reinforcement forces for NATO; its roles include strike/attack, air defence, control and reporting, maritime surveillance, air reconnaissance, air-to-air refuelling, offensive support, air transport, aero-medical facilities, and search and rescue. Support Command is responsible for air and ground training, communications, engineering support, logistics, hospitals and for providing a range of administrative support. RAF Germany provides tactical air support in NATO's Central Region; its roles include strike/attack, interdiction, counter air operations, air defence, close air support of land forces, tactical reconnaissance and helicopter support.

To carry out its tasks, the Royal Air Force is equipped with Victor, Tornado, Buccaneer, Phantom, Harrier, Jaguar, Canberra, Nimrod, Shackleton, VC10, Tristar, Hercules, Hawk, Jet Provost, Tucano, Chipmunk and Bulldog aircraft; Puma, Wessex, Sea King and Chinook helicopters; miscellaneous communications aircraft, etc.; Bloodhound and Rapier missiles; and the Skyguard system.

Royal Auxiliary Air Force (RAUXAF).—Formed in 1924, the Auxiliary Air Force served with great distinction in the Second World War and in recognition of its war record King George VI conferred the prefix 'Royal' in 1947. Following a major reduction of units in the late 1950s, the benefits to be gained by using auxiliary forces in certain roles has resulted in a subsequent expansion. Today, the Royal Auxiliary Air Force supports the RAF in maritime air operations, air and ground defence of major airfields, air movements and aeromedical evacuation.
Air Commodore-in-Chief, HM The Queen.
Director of Reserve Forces (RAF), Air Cdre R. P. Skelley.

Royal Air Force Volunteer Reserve (RAFVR).—The Royal Air Force Volunteer Reserve was created in 1936 with the object of providing training for the increased number of aircrew who were seen as necessary for

the forthcoming conflict. The RAFVR was reconstituted in 1947 following war service and today is a small but important part of the Air Force Reserve. There are RAFVR aircrew with the Harrier, Nimrod and Tornado Forces, and RAFVR units specializing in intelligence-orientated duties and public relations.
Director of Reserve Forces (RAF), Air Cdre R. P. Skelley.

PRINCESS MARY'S ROYAL AIR FORCE NURSING SERVICE

The Princess Mary's Royal Air Force Nursing Service (PMRAFNS) is open to both male and female candidates. Commissions are offered to those who are Registered General Nurses (RGN) and possess a second qualification suitable to the needs of the service. RGNs with no additional experience or qualification are also recruited as non-commissioned officers in the grade of Staff Nurse.
Air Chief Commandant, HRH Princess Alexandra, the Hon. Lady Ogilvy, GCVO.
Matron-in-Chief, Group Captain E. M. Hancock.

WOMEN'S ROYAL AIR FORCE

Formed on April 1, 1918, the Women's Royal Air Force (WRAF) was disbanded on April 1, 1920 and re-formed on February 1, 1949 from the Women's Auxiliary Air Force, the Second World War service which had been formed on June 28, 1939, and from the RAF companies of the Auxiliary Territorial Service.

WRAF officers and airwomen serve in most of the RAF branches and trades including as aircrew. WRAF personnel are employed at RAF stations and higher formations at home and abroad, and they compete on equal terms with their RAF counterparts for appointments, promotion and places on training courses.
Commandant-in-Chief, HM Queen Elizabeth The Queen Mother.
Air Chief Commandant, HRH Princess Alice, Duchess of Gloucester.
Director, Air Commodore, R. M. B. Montague, ADC.

ROYAL OBSERVER CORPS
Bentley Priory, Stanmore, Middlesex

Established in 1925, the Royal Observer Corps is a uniformed voluntary civilian organization originally set up to identify and track the movement of aircraft in war. In 1955 the Corps assumed the modern role of detecting nuclear bursts and monitoring radio-active fall-out in support of the United Kingdom Warning and Monitoring Organization. The Corps is affiliated to the Royal Air Force and is administered by the Ministry of Defence. The Home Secretary announced in July 1991 that the ROC would be disbanded; the Corps will stand down on March 31, 1992.
Air Commodore-in-Chief, HM The Queen.
Commandant, Air Cdre G. M. Boddy, OBE.

RELATIVE RANK—SEA, LAND AND AIR

ROYAL NAVY	ARMY	ROYAL AIR FORCE
1. Admiral of the Fleet.	1. Field Marshal.	1. Marshal of the RAF.
2. Admiral (Adm.).	2. General (Gen.).	2. Air Chief Marshal.
3. Vice-Admiral (Vice-Adm.).	3. Lieutenant-General (Lt.-Gen.).	3. Air Marshal.
4. Rear-Admiral (Rear-Adm.).	4. Major-General (Maj.-Gen.).	4. Air Vice-Marshal.
5. Commodore (1st & 2nd Class) (Cdre).	5. Brigadier (Brig.).	5. Air Commodore (Air Cdre).
6. Captain (Capt.).	6. Colonel (Col.).	6. Group Captain (Gp Capt).
7. Commander (Cdr.).	7. Lieutenant-Colonel (Lt.-Col.).	7. Wing Commander (Wg Cdr.).
8. Lieutenant Commander (Lt. Cdr.).	8. Major (Maj.).	8. Squadron Leader (Sqn. Ldr.).
9. Lieutenant (Lt.).	9. Captain (Capt).	9. Flight Lieutenant (Flt. Lt.).
10. Sub-Lieutenant (Sub-Lt.).	10. Lieutenant (Lt.).	10. Flying Officer (FO).
11. Acting Sub-Lieutenant (Acting Sub-Lt.).	11. Second Lieutenant (2nd Lt.).	11. Pilot Officer (PO).

SERVICE SALARIES AND PENSIONS

The following rates of pay have been introduced as part of the 1991 pay award for Service personnel.

Salaries for the women's services reflect equal pay for equal work and conditions, and the X-Factor addition for men and women is now the same (11·5 per cent).

Since 1970 the determining factor of the Review Bodies' recommendations has been the relation of forces' salaries to civilian earnings by a carefully detailed process of job evaluation.

ROYAL NAVY AND ROYAL MARINES
Normal Rates

Rank	Daily	Annual
	£	£
Midshipman		
On appointment	22·56	8,234
After 1 year	28·04	10,235
Sub-Lieutenant and Acting Lieutenant RM		
On appointment	32·14	11,731
After 2 years in rank	42·49	15,509
After 3 years in rank	45·85	16,735
Lieutenant		
On appointment	54·10	19,747
After 1 year in rank	55·56	20,279
After 2 years in rank	57·02	20,812
After 3 years in rank	58·48	21,345
After 4 years in rank	59·94	21,878
After 5 years in rank	61·40	22,411
After 6 years in rank	62·86	22,944
Lieutenant Commander/Captain RM		
On appointment	68·17	24,882
After 1 year in rank	69·86	25,449
After 2 years in rank	71·55	26,116
After 3 years in rank	73·24	26,733
After 4 years in rank	74·93	27,349
After 5 years in rank	76·62	27,966
After 6 years in rank	78·31	28,583
After 7 years in rank	80·00	29,200
After 8 years in rank	81·69	29,817
Commander/Major RM		
On appointment with less than 19 years service	95·63	34,905
After 2 years in rank or with 19 years service	98·15	35,825
After 4 years in rank or with 21 years service	100·67	36,745
After 6 years in rank or with 23 years service	103·19	37,664
After 8 years in rank or with 25 years service	105·71	38,584
Captain/Lieutenant-Colonel RM		
On appointment	111·37	40,650
After 2 years in rank	114·30	41,720
After 4 years in rank	117·23	42,789
With 6 years seniority/Colonel RM	136·62	49,866
Rear-Admiral/Major-General RM	145·21	53,000
Vice-Admiral/Lieutenant-General RM	166·03	60,600
Admiral/General RM	230·82	84,250
Admiral of the Fleet	286·00	104,750

ARMY, WRAC AND QARANC
Normal Rates

Rank	Daily	Annual
	£	£
Second Lieutenant	32·14	11,731
Lieutenant		
On appointment	42·49	15,509
After 1 year in rank	43·61	15,918
After 2 years in rank	44·73	16,326
After 3 years in rank	45·85	16,735
After 4 years in rank	46·97	17,144
Captain		
On appointment	54·10	19,747
After 1 year in rank	55·56	20,279
After 2 years in rank	57·02	20,812
After 3 years in rank	58·48	21,345
After 4 years in rank	59·94	21,878
After 5 years in rank	61·40	22,411
After 6 years in rank	62·86	22,944
Major		
On appointment	68·17	24,882
After 1 year in rank	69·86	25,499
After 2 years in rank	71·55	26,116
After 3 years in rank	73·24	26,733
After 4 years in rank	74·93	27,349
After 5 years in rank	76·62	27,966
After 6 years in rank	78·31	28,583
After 7 years in rank	80·00	29,200
After 8 years in rank	81·69	29,817
Special List Lieutenant-Colonel	93·99	34,306
Lieutenant-Colonel		
On appointment with less than 19 years service	95·63	34,905
After 2 years in rank or with 19 years service	98·15	35,825
After 4 years in rank or with 21 years service	100·67	36,745
After 6 years in rank or with 23 years service	103·19	37,664
After 8 years or with 25 years service	105·71	38,584
Colonel		
On appointment	111·37	40,650
After 2 years in rank	114·30	41,720
After 4 years in rank	117·23	42,789
After 6 years in rank	120·16	43,858
After 8 years in rank	123·09	44,928
Brigadier	136·62	49,866
Major-General	145·21	53,000
Lieutenant-General	166·03	60,600
General	230·82	84,250
Field Marshal	286·00	104,750

ROYAL AIR FORCE, WRAF AND PMRAFNS (Male and Female)

Rank	Daily	Annual	Rank	Daily	Annual
	£	£		£	£
Acting Pilot Officer			**Squadron Leader** (*cont.*)		
On appointment..............	28·04	10,235	After 7 years in rank	80·00	29,200
After 6 months in rank	28·69	10,472	After 8 years in rank	81·69	29,817
Pilot Officer	32·14	11,731	**Wing Commander**		
Flying Officer			On appointment with less than		
On appointment..............	42·49	15,509	19 years service	95·63	34,905
After 1 year in rank	43·61	15,918	After 2 years in rank or with		
After 2 years in rank	44·73	16,326	19 years service	98·15	35,825
After 3 years in rank	45·85	16,735	After 4 years in rank or with		
After 4 years in rank	46·97	17,144	21 years service	100·67	36,745
Flight Lieutenant			After 6 years in rank or with		
On appointment..............	54·10	19,747	23 years service	103·19	37,664
After 1 year in rank	55·56	20,279	After 8 years in rank or with		
After 2 years in rank	57·02	20,812	25 years service	105·71	38,584
After 3 years in rank	58·48	21,345	**Group Captain**		
After 4 years in rank	59·94	21,878	On appointment..............	111·37	40,650
After 5 years in rank	61·40	22,411	After 2 years in rank	114·30	41,720
After 6 years in rank	62·86	22,944	After 4 years in rank	117·23	42,789
Squadron Leader			After 6 years in rank	120·16	43,858
On appointment..............	68·17	24,882	After 8 years in rank	123·09	44,928
After 1 year in rank	69·86	25,499	Air Commodore	136·62	49,866
After 2 years in rank	71·55	26,116	Air Vice-Marshal	145·21	53,000
After 3 years in rank	73·24	26,733	Air Marshal	166·03	60,600
After 4 years in rank	74·93	27,349	Air Chief Marshal	230·82	84,250
After 5 years in rank	76·62	27,966	Marshal of the Royal Air Force .	286·00	104,750
After 6 years in rank	78·31	28,583			

ROYAL NAVY AND ROYAL MARINES SPECIAL DUTIES LIST OFFICERS, ARMY MALE OFFICERS COMMISSIONED FROM THE RANKS, ROYAL AIR FORCE BRANCH OFFICERS

Years of commissioned service	Years of non-commissioned service from age 18					
	Less than 12 years		12 years but less than 15 years		15 years or more	
	Daily	Annual	Daily	Annual	Daily	Annual
	£	£	£	£	£	£
On appointment...................	58·40	21,316	61·36	22,396	64·32	23,586
After 1 year service..............	59·88	21,856	62·84	22,936	65·43	23,882
After 2 years service.............	61·36	22,396	64·32	23,477	66·54	24,287
After 3 years service.............	62·84	22,937	65·53	23,918	67·65	24,692
After 4 years service.............	64·42	23,477	66·54	24,287	68·76	25,097
After 5 years service.............	65·43	23,882	67·65	24,692	69·87	25,507
After 6 years service.............	66·54	24,287	68·76	25,097	70·98	25,908
After 8 years service.............	67·65	24,692	69·87	25,503	72·09	26,313
After 10 years service............	68·76	25,097	70·98	25,908	72·09	26,313
After 12 years service............	69·87	25,503	72·09	26,313	72·09	26,313
After 14 years service............	70·98	25,908	72·09	26,313	72·09	26,313
After 16 years service............	72·09	26,313	72·09	26,313	72·09	26,313

ROYAL NAVY/WRNS (SEA SERVICE) (Artificers, Medical and Communications Technicians)

Rank	Uncommitted	Intermediate	Career
	£	£	£
WO Artificer/Technician	61·05	61·35	61·80
CCPO Artificer/Technician	58·84	59·14	59·59
CPO Artificer/1st Class Technician Scale A	56·57	56·87	57·32
Scale B	54·40	54·70	55·15
PO Artificer/2nd Class Technician	47·72	48·02	48·47
Probationary or Acting PO Artificer/3rd Class Technician	45·52	45·82	46·27
4th Class Technician (Leading)	39·86	40·16	40·61
Leading Artificer/Acting 4th Class Technician	37·38	37·68	38·13
Acting Leading Artificer/Comms Tech	33·74	34·04	34·49
5th Class Technician (Able)	31·94	32·24	32·69

ROYAL NAVY (Other Branches)/WRNS (Other Branches) and QARNNS MAs (SEA SERVICE)

Rank	Uncommitted	Intermediate	Career
	£	£	£
Warrant Officer	55·85	56·15	56·60
Chief Petty Officer—Scale A	49·43	49·73	50·18
—Scale B	48·54	48·84	49·29
Petty Officer/Sergeant—Scale A	44·22	44·52	44·97
—Scale B	44·42	44·27	44·17
Leading Rating—Scale A	39·86	40·16	40·16
—Scale B	37·38	37·68	38·13
Able Rating—Scale A	31·94	32·24	32·69
—Scale B	30·00	30·30	30·75
—Scale C	26·15	26·45	26·90
Ordinary Rating—Scale A	21·87	22·17	22·62
—Scale B	20·10	20·40	20·85
QARNNS MAs and WRNS Ordinary Ratings under 17½ years	15·20		

ARMY

Daily rates of pay for those committed to serve for:

Rank	Less than 6 years Scale A			6 years but less than 9 years Scale B			9 years or more Scale C		
	Band 1	Band 2	Band 3	Band 1	Band 2	Band 3	Band 1	Band 2	Band 3
	£	£	£	£	£	£	£	£	£
Private Class IV ...	20·10	—	—	20·40	—	—	20·85	—	—
Class III ...	22·51	26·15	30·18	22·81	26·45	30·48	23·26	26·90	30·93
Class II	25·19	28·83	32·86	25·49	29·13	33·16	25·94	29·58	33·61
Class I	27·33	30·97	35·00	27·63	31·27	35·30	28·08	31·72	35·75
Lance Corporal									
Class III ...	27·33	30·97	35·00	27·63	31·27	35·30	28·08	31·72	35·75
Class II	29·20	32·84	37·20	29·50	33·14	37·50	29·95	33·59	37·95
Class I	31·42	35·06	39·42	31·72	35·36	39·72	32·17	35·81	40·17
Corporal Class II ...	33·74	37·38	41·74	34·04	37·68	42·04	34·49	38·13	42·49
Class I	36·22	39·86	44·22	36·52	40·16	44·52	36·97	40·61	44·97

	Band 4	Band 5	Band 6	Band 7	Band 4	Band 5	Band 6	Band 7	Band 4	Band 5	Band 6	Band 7
	£	£	£	£	£	£	£	£	£	£	£	£
Sergeant	39·49	43·42	47·72	—	39·79	43·72	48·02	—	40·24	44·17	48·47	—
Staff Sergeant	41·76	45·69	49·99	55·19	42·06	45·99	50·29	55·49	42·51	46·44	50·74	55·94
Warrant Officer												
Class II	44·66	48·59	52·89	58·09	44·96	48·89	53·19	58·39	45·41	49·34	53·64	58·84
Class I	47·62	51·55	55·85	61·05	47·92	51·85	56·15	61·35	48·37	52·30	56·60	61·80

ROYAL AIR FORCE AIRMEN/AIRWOMEN (Aircrew, Ground Trades, Apprentices and PMRAFNS)

Daily rates of pay for those committed to serve for:

Rank/Category	Less than 6 years Scale A			6 years but less than 9 years Scale B			9 years or more Scale C		
	Band 1	Band 2	Band 3	Band 1	Band 2	Band 3	Band 1	Band 2	Band 3
	£	£	£	£	£	£	£	£	£
Aircraftman over 17 on entry	20·10	20·10	20·10	20·40	20·40	20·40	20·85	20·85	20·85
Leading Aircraftman	22·51	26·15	30·51	22·81	26·45	30·81	23·26	26·90	31·26
Senior Aircraftman	27·33	30·97	35·00	27·63	31·27	35·30	28·08	31·72	35·75
Junior Technician	31·42	35·06	39·42	31·72	35·36	39·72	32·17	35·81	40·17
Corporal	35·78	39·42	44·22	36·08	39·72	44·52	36·53	40·17	44·97

	Band 4	Band 5	Band 6	Band 7	Band 4	Band 5	Band 6	Band 7	Band 4	Band 5	Band 6	Band 7
	£	£	£	£	£	£	£	£	£	£	£	£
Sergeant	39·49	53·42	47·72	—	39·79	43·02	48·02	—	40·24	44·17	48·47	—
Chief Technician	41·33	45·26	49·56	54·60	41·63	45·56	49·86	55·06	42·08	46·01	50·31	55·51
Flight Sergeant	43·17	47·10	51·40	56·60	43·47	47·40	51·70	56·90	43·92	47·85	52·15	57·35
Warrant Officer	47·62	51·55	55·85	61·05	47·92	51·85	56·15	61·35	48·39	52·37	56·60	61·80

ROYAL AIR FORCE—AIRMEN (AIRCREW)
Daily rates for those committed to serve for:

Rank	Less than 6 years Scale A			6 years but less than 9 years Scale B			9 years or more Scale C		
	Band 5	Band 6	Band 7	Band 5	Band 6	Band 7	Band 5	Band 6	Band 7
	£	£	£	£	£	£	£	£	£
Pilot, Navigator, Air Engineer (A) and Air Signallers (A)									
Sergeant	—	47·72	—	—	48·02	—	—	48·47	—
Flight Sergeant ..	—	—	56·60	—	—	56·90	—	—	57·35
Master Aircrew ..	—	—	61·05	—	—	61·35	—	—	61·80
Air Electronics Operators									
Sergeant	47·72	—	—	48·02	—	—	48·47	—	—
Flight Sergeant ..	—	51·40	—	—	51·70	—	—	52·15	—
Master Aircrew ..	—	55·85	—	—	56·15	—	—	56·60	—

WOMEN'S SERVICES
(where rates of pay differ from men's rates)

OFFICERS OF WRNS AND FEMALE OFFICES OF QARNNS

Rank	Daily	Annual
	£	£
Sub-Lieutenant/Nursing Officer		
On confirmation	42·49	15,509
After 1 year..................	43·49	15,509
After 2 years.................	44·73	16,326
After 3 years.................	45·85	16,735
After 4 years.................	46·97	17,144
Lieutenant/Senior Nursing Officer		
On appointment	54·10	19,747
After 1 year in rank	56·56	20,279
After 2 years in rank	57·02	20,812
After 3 years in rank	58·48	21,345
After 4 years in rank	59·94	21,878
After 5 years in rank	61·40	22,411
After 6 years in rank	62·86	22,944
Lieutenant Commander/ Superintending Nursing Officer		
On appointment...............	68·17	24,882
After 1 year in rank	69·86	25,499
After 2 years in rank	71·55	26,116
After 3 years in rank	73·24	26,733
After 4 years in rank	74·93	27,349
After 5 years in rank	76·62	27,966
After 6 years in rank	78·31	28,583
After 7 years in rank	80·00	29,200
After 8 years in rank	81·69	29,817
Commander/Chief Nursing Officer		
On appointment with less than 19 years service	95·63	34,905
After 2 years in rank or with 19 years service................	98·15	35,825
After 4 years in rank or with 21 years service................	100·67	36,745
After 6 years in rank or with 23 years service................	103·19	37,664
After 8 years in rank or with 25 years service................	105·71	38,584

Rank	Daily	Annual
	£	£
Captain/Principal Nursing Officer		
On appointment...............	111·37	40,650
After 2 years in rank	114·30	41,720
After 4 years in rank	117·23	42,789
After 6 years in rank	120·16	43,858
After 8 years in rank	123·09	44,928
Director QARNNS/Matron-in-Chief WRNS	136·62	49,666

FEMALE WRNS AND QARNNS RATINGS (NON-SEA SERVICE)

Rank	Band 1	Band 2	Band 3
	£	£	£
Ordinary Rating under 17½........	15·20	—	—
Ordinary Rating at 17½...............	20·10	20·10	—
Able Rating Scale C	22·51	26·15	30·51
Scale B	26·36	30·00	34·36
Scale A	28·30	31·94	36·30
Leading Rating			
Scale B	33·74	37·38	41·74
Scale A	36·22	39·86	44·22

	Band 4	Band 5	Band 6	Band 7
	£	£	£	£
Petty Officer Scale B	39·06	42·99	47·29	52·49
Scale A	39·92	43·85	48·15	53·35
CPO Scale B	42·06	45·99	50·29	55·49
Scale A	43·08	47·01	51·31	56·51
Warrant Officer	47·62	51·55	55·85	61·05

WRAC and QARANC
Daily rates of pay for those who have served for:

Rank	Less than 6 years			6 years but less than 9 years			9 years or more		
	Band 1	Band 2	Band 3	Band 1	Band 2	Band 3	Band 1	Band 2	Band 3
	£	£	£	£	£	£	£	£	£
Private Class IV Age 17–17½ ..	14·81	—	—	—	—	—	—	—	—
Class IV	19·59	—	—	19·89	—	—	20·34	—	—
Class III	21·94	25·49	29·42	22·24	25·79	29·72	22·69	26·24	30·17
Class II	24·55	28·10	32·03	24·85	28·40	32·33	25·30	28·85	32·78
Class I	26·64	30·19	34·12	26·94	30·49	34·42	27·39	30·94	34·87
Lance Corporal Class III	26·64	30·19	34·12	26·94	30·49	34·42	27·39	30·94	34·87
Class II	28·46	32·01	36·26	28·76	32·31	36·56	29·21	32·76	37·01
Class I	30·63	34·18	38·43	30·93	34·48	38·73	31·38	34·93	39·18
Corporal Class II	32·89	36·44	40·69	33·19	36·74	40·99	33·64	37·19	41·44
Class I	35·31	38·86	43·11	35·61	39·16	43·41	36·06	39·61	43·86

	Band 4	Band 5	Band 6	Band 7	Band 4	Band 5	Band 6	Band 7	Band 4	Band 5	Band 6	Band 7
	£	£	£	£	£	£	£	£	£	£	£	£
Sergeant	38·50	42·44	46·52	—	38·80	42·63	46·82	—	39·25	43·08	47·27	—
Staff Sergeant	40·71	44·54	48·73	53·80	41·01	44·84	49·03	54·10	41·46	45·29	49·48	54·55
Warrant Officer Class II	43·54	47·37	51·56	56·63	43·84	47·67	51·86	56·93	44·29	48·12	52·31	57·38
Class I	46·42	50·25	54·45	59·52	46·72	50·55	54·75	59·82	47·17	51·00	55·20	60·27

WRAF AIRWOMEN (Aircrew, Ground Trades, Apprentices and PMRAFNS)
Daily rates of pay for those who have served for:

Rank/Category	Less than 6 years			6 years but less than 9 years			9 years or more		
	Band 1	Band 2	Band 3	Band 1	Band 2	Band 3	Band 1	Band 2	Band 3
	£	£	£	£	£	£	£	£	£
Aircraftwoman under age 17 .	15·20	—	—	—	—	—	—	—	—
Aircraftwoman at age 17	20·10	20·10	20·10	—	—	—	—	—	—
Leading Aircraftwoman	22·51	26·15	30·51	22·89	26·45	30·81	23·26	26·90	31·26
Senior Aircraftwoman	27·33	30·97	35·00	27·63	31·27	35·30	28·08	31·72	35·75
Junior Technician	31·42	35·06	39·42	31·72	35·36	39·27	32·17	35·81	40·17
Corporal	35·78	39·42	44·22	36·08	39·72	44·52	36·53	40·17	44·97

	Band 4	Band 5	Band 6	Band 7	Band 4	Band 5	Band 6	Band 7	Band 4	Band 5	Band 6	Band 7
	£	£	£	£	£	£	£	£	£	£	£	£
Sergeant	39·49	43·42	47·72	—	39·79	43·72	48·02	—	40·24	44·17	48·47	—
Chief Technician	41·33	45·26	49·56	54·60	41·93	45·56	49·86	55·06	42·08	46·01	50·31	55·51
Flight Sergeant	43·17	47·10	51·40	56·60	43·47	47·40	51·70	56·90	43·92	47·85	52·15	57·35
Warrant Officer	47·62	51·55	55·85	61·05	47·92	51·85	56·15	61·35	48·39	52·37	56·60	61·80

SERVICE RETIREMENT BENEFITS, ETC.

Those who leave the Forces having served at least five years, but not long enough to qualify for the appropriate immediate pension, now qualify for a preserved pension and terminal grant both of which are payable at age 60. The tax-free resettlement grants shown below are payable on release to those who qualify for a preserved pension and who have completed nine years service from age 21 (officers) or 12 years from age 18 (other ranks). The annual rates for the Army are given.

Officers*—Men and Women

No. of years reckonable service over age 21	Capt. (incl. QM) and below	Major (incl. QM)	Lt.-Col.	Col. (incl. Deputy Chaplain General)	Brigadier	Major-General	Lieu-tenant-General	General
	£ p.a.	£ p.a.	£ p.a.	£ p.a.	£ p.a.	£ p.a.	£ p.a.	£ p.a.
16	6,557	7,816	10,238	11,923	14,251			
17	6,858	8,187	10,712	12,475	14,807			
18	7,159	8,559	11,185	13,026	15,362			
19	7,460	8,930	11,659	13,578	15,918			
20	7,761	9,302	12,133	14,129	16,473			
21	8,063	9,673	12,607	14,681	17,029			
22	8,364	10,044	13,080	15,232	17,584			
23	8,665	10,416	13,554	15,784	18,140			
24	8,966	10,787	14,028	16,335	18,695	19,480		
25	9,267	11,159	14,501	16,887	19,251	20,059		
26	9,568	11,530	14,975	17,438	19,807	20,638		
27	9,869	11,901	15,449	17,990	20,362	21,217	22,519	
28	10,170	12,273	15,923	18,541	20,918	21,796	24,870	
29	10,471	12,644	16,396	19,093	21,473	22,375	25,530	
30	10,773	13,015	16,870	19,644	22,029	22,953	26,191	36,478
31	11,074	13,387	17,344	20,196	22,584	23,532	26,851	37,398
32	11,375	13,758	17,818	20,747	23,140	24,111	27,512	38,318
33	11,676	14,130	18,291	21,299	23,695	24,690	28,172	39,238
34	11,977	14,501	18,765	21,850	24,251	25,269	28,833	40,158

* These figures apply to equivalent ranks in all services, including the nursing services.

Ratings, Soldiers and Airmen*—Men and Women

Number of years reckonable service	Below Corporal	Corporal	Sergeant	Staff Sergeant	Warrant Officer Class II	Warrant Officer Class I
	£ p.a.	£ p.a.	£ p.a.	£ p.a.	£ p.a.	£ p.a.
22	3,812	4,871	5,350	6,058	6,232	6,827
23	3,945	5,041	5,537	6,270	6,453	7,073
24	4,078	5,211	5,723	6,481	6,674	7,319
25	4,211	5,381	5,910	6,693	6,895	7,565
26	4,344	5,551	6,097	6,904	7,116	7,811
27	4,477	5,721	6,284	7,116	7,337	8,057
28	4,610	5,891	6,470	7,327	7,558	8,303
29	4,743	6,061	6,657	7,539	7,779	8,549
30	4,877	6,232	6,844	7,750	8,001	8,795
31	5,010	6,402	7,031	7,962	8,222	9,041
32	5,143	6,572	7,217	8,173	8,443	9,287
33	4,682	6,022	6,616	7,495	7,741	9,287
34	5,409	6,912	7,591	8,596	8,885	9,779
35	5,542	7,082	7,778	8,808	9,106	10,025
36	5,675	7,252	7,964	9,019	9,327	10,271
37	5,808	7,422	8,151	9,231	9,548	10,517

* These figures apply to equivalent ranks in all services, including the nursing services.

Terminal Grants and Gratuities

Terminal grants are in each case three times the rate of retired pay or pension. There are special rates of retired pay for Chaplains, Flight Lieutenants (Specialist Aircrew), and certain other ranks not shown above. Lower rates are payable in cases of voluntary retirement.

A gratuity is payable for officers with short service commissions of £2,230 for each year completed. Resettlement grants are: officers £7,669; non-commissioned ranks £5,076.

THE CHURCHES

THE ANGLICAN COMMUNION

The Anglican Communion consists of 26 independent provincial or national Christian Churches or extra-provincial dioceses throughout the world, many of which are in Commonwealth countries and originated from missionary activity by the Church of England. There is no single world authority linking the Communion, but all recognize the leadership of the Archbishop of Canterbury and have strong ecclesiastical and historical links with the Church of England. Every ten years all the bishops in the Communion meet at the Lambeth Conference, convened by the Archbishop of Canterbury. The Conference has no policy-making authority but is an important forum for the discussion of issues of common concern. The Anglican Consultative Council was set up in 1968 to function between conferences and the meeting of the Primates every two years.

There are about 70 million Anglicans and 605 archbishops, bishops and clergy world-wide.

THE CHURCH OF ENGLAND

The Church of England is the established (i.e. state) church in England and the mother church of the Anglican Communion. It originated in the conflicts between church and state throughout the Middle Ages, culminating in the Act of Supremacy issued by Henry VIII in 1534. This broke with Rome and declared the King to be the supreme head of the Church in England. Since 1534 the English monarch has been termed the Supreme Governor of the Church of England. The Thirty-Nine Articles, a set of doctrinal statements defining the position of the Church of England, were adopted in their final form in 1571 and include the emphasis on personal faith and the authority of the scriptures common to the Protestant Reformation throughout Europe.

The Church of England is divided into the two provinces of Canterbury and York, each under an archbishop. The two provinces are subdivided into 44 dioceses. Decisions on matters concerning the Church of England are made by the General Synod, established in 1970. It also discusses and expresses opinion on any other matter of religious or public interest. The General Synod has 574 members in total, divided between three houses: the House of Bishops, the House of Clergy and the House of Laity. It is presided over jointly by the Archbishops of Canterbury and York and normally meets three times a year. The Synod has the power, delegated by Parliament, to frame statute law (known as a Measure) on any matter concerning the Church of England. A Measure must be laid before both Houses of Parliament, who may accept or reject it but cannot amend it. Once accepted the Measure is submitted for Royal Assent and then has the full force of law. The Synod appoints a number of committees, boards and councils which deal with, or advise the synod on, a wide range of matters. In addition to the General Synod, there are synods of clergy and laity at diocesan level.

The Church of England has an estimated 1·6 million members, of whom about 1·2 million regularly attend Sunday services. There are two archbishops, 109 bishops, 10,867 full-time stipendiary clergy, and over 16,500 churches and places of worship.

GENERAL SYNOD OF THE CHURCH OF ENGLAND, Church House, Dean's Yard, SW1P 3NZ (Tel: 071-222 9011).—*Sec.-Gen.*, P. Mawer.
HOUSE OF BISHOPS—*Chairman*, The Archbishop of Canterbury; *Vice-Chairman*, The Archbishop of York.
HOUSE OF CLERGY—*Joint Chairmen*, The Archdeacon of Leicester and Canon J. Stanley.
HOUSE OF LAITY—*Chairman*, Prof. J. D. McClean; *Vice Chairman*, Dr Christina Baxter.

Stipends 1991–92

Archbishop of Canterbury £40,960
Archbishop of York £35,880
Bishop of London £33,440
Bishop of Durham £29,510
Bishop of Winchester £24,600
Other Diocesan Bishops £22,200
Suffragan Bishops £18,250
Deans and Provosts £18,250
Residentiary Canons £14,920

Province of Canterbury

CANTERBURY

103rd *Archbishop and Primate of All England*, Most Rev. and Rt. Hon. George Leonard Carey, *cons.* 1987, *trs.* 1991, *apptd* 1991; Lambeth Palace, SE1 7JU. *Signs* George Cantuar:

Bishops Suffragan

Dover, Rt. Rev. Richard Henry McPhail Third, *cons.* 1976, *apptd* 1980; Upway, St Martin's Hill, Canterbury, CT1 1PR.
Maidstone, Rt. Rev. David James Smith, *cons.* 1987, *apptd* 1987; Bishop's House, Pett Lane, Charing, Ashford TN27 0DL.

Assistant Bishops

Rt. Rev. Ross Hook, MC, *cons.* 1965, *apptd* 1986; Rt. Rev. William Franklin, OBE, *cons.* 1972, *apptd* 1987; Rt. Rev. Richard Say, KCVO, *cons.* 1961, *apptd* 1988.

Dean

Very Rev. John Arthur Simpson, *apptd* 1986.

Canons Residentiary

J. H. R. De Sausmarez, *apptd* 1981; P. Brett, *apptd* 1983; Ven. M. Till, *apptd* 1986; C. A. Lewis, *apptd* 1987.
Organist, D. Flood, *apptd* 1988.

Archdeacons

Canterbury, Ven. M. Till, *apptd* 1986.
Maidstone, Ven. P. Evans, *apptd* 1989.

Stipendiary Male Clergy, 189.
Stipendiary Women Deacons, 11.

Vicar-General of Province and Diocese, Chancellor S. Cameron, QC.
Commissary General, J. H. R. Newey, QC, *apptd* 1971.
Joint Registrars of the Province, F. E. Robson, OBE, 16 Beaumont Street, Oxford; B. J. T. Hanson, Church House, Dean's Yard, SW1P 3NZ.

Registrar of the Diocese of Canterbury, A. O. E. Davies, 9 The Precincts, Canterbury CT1 2EQ.

LONDON

131*st Bishop,* Rt. Rev. and Rt. Hon. David Michael Hope, D.phil., *cons.* 1985, *trans.* 1991, *apptd* 1991; 8 Barton Street, SW1P 3NE. *Signs* David Londin:

Area Bishops

Edmonton, Rt. Rev. Brian John Masters, *cons.* 1982, *apptd* 1984; 1 Regent's Park Terrace, NW1 7EE.
Kensington, Rt. Rev. John Hughes, ph.d., *cons.* 1987, *apptd* 1987; 19 Campden Hill Square, W8 7JY.
Stepney, vacant; 63 Coborn Road, E3 2DB.
Willesden, vacant; 173 Willesden Lane, NW6 7YN.

Bishop Suffragan

Fulham, Rt. Rev. (Charles) John Klyberg, *cons.* 1985, *apptd* 1985; 4 Cambridge Place, W8 5PB.

Assistant Bishops

Rt. Rev. Maurice Wood, DSC, *cons.* 1971, *apptd* 1985; Rt. Rev. Michael Marshall, *cons.* 1975, *apptd* 1984.

Dean of St Paul's

Very Rev. (Thomas) Eric Evans, *apptd* 1988.

Canons Residentiary

Ven. G. Cassidy, *apptd* 1987; C. J. Hill, *apptd* 1989; R. J. Halliburton, *apptd* 1990; M. J. Saward, *apptd* 1991.
Organist, J. Scott.
Receiver of St Paul's, Brig. R. Ackworth.

Archdeacons

Charing Cross, Rt. Rev. C. J. Klyberg, *apptd* 1989.
Hackney, Ven. R. E. D. Sharpley, *apptd* 1981.
Hampstead, Ven. R. A. W. Coogan, *apptd* 1985.
London, Ven. G. Cassidy, *apptd* 1987.
Middlesex, Ven. T. J. Raphael, *apptd* 1983.
Northolt, Ven. E. Shirras, *apptd* 1985.

Stipendiary Male Clergy, 568.
Stipendiary Women Deacons, 49.

Chancellor and Commissary of the Dean and Chapter, G. H. Newsom, QC, *apptd* 1971.
Registrar, D. W. Faull, 35 Great Peter Street, SW1P 3LR.

WESTMINSTER

The Collegiate Church of St Peter (A Royal Peculiar)
Dean, Michael Clement Otway Mayne, *apptd* 1986.
Sub Dean and Archdeacon, A. E. Harvey, *apptd* 1987.

Canons of Westminster

A. E. Harvey, *apptd* 1982; D. C. Gray, *apptd* 1987; C. D. Semper, *apptd* 1987; P. S. Bates, *apptd* 1990.
Chapter Clerk and Receiver General, Rear-Adm. K. A. Snow, CB, *apptd* 1987.
Organist, M. Neary, FRCO, *apptd* 1988.
Legal Secretary, C. L. Hodgetts, *apptd* 1973.
Registrar, S. J. Holmes, MVO, *apptd* 1984, 20 Dean's Yard, SW1P 3PA.

WINCHESTER

95*th Bishop,* Rt. Rev. Colin Clement Walter James, *cons.* 1973, *trs.* 1977 and 1985, *apptd* 1985; Wolvesey, Winchester SO23 9ND. *Signs* Colin Winton:

Bishops Suffragan

Basingstoke, Rt. Rev. Michael Richard John Manktelow, *cons.* 1977, *apptd* 1977; Bishop's Lodge, Skippetts Lane West, Basingstoke RG21 3HP.

Southampton, Rt. Rev. John Freeman Perry, *cons.* 1989, *apptd* 1989; Ham House, The Crescent, Romsey SO51 7NG.

Assistant Bishops

Rt. Rev. Hassan Dehqani-Tafti, *cons.* 1961, *apptd* 1982; Rt. Rev. Leslie Rees, *cons.* 1980, *apptd* 1986.

Dean

Very Rev. Trevor Randall Beeson, *apptd* 1987.

Dean of Jersey (A Peculiar), Very Rev. Basil Arthur O'Ferrall, CB, *apptd* 1985.
Dean of Guernsey (A Peculiar), Very Rev. Jeffery Fenwick, *apptd* 1989.

Canons Residentiary

E. G. Job, *apptd* 1979; P. A. Britton, *apptd* 1980; A. K. Walker, *apptd* 1987; Ven. A. F. Knight, *apptd* 1991.
Organist, D. Hill, FRCO, *apptd* 1988.

Archdeacons

Basingstoke, Ven. A. F. Knight, *apptd* 1990.
Winchester, Ven. A. G. Clarkson, *apptd* 1984.

Stipendiary Male Clergy, 274.
Stipendiary Women Deacons, 10.

Chancellor, J. Spokes, QC, *apptd* 1985.
Registrar and Legal Secretary, P. M. White, 19 St Peter Street, Winchester SO23 8BU.

BATH AND WELLS

76*th Bishop,* Rt. Rev. James Lawton Thompson, *cons.* 1978, *apptd* 1991; The Palace, Wells BA5 2PD. *Signs* James Bath & Wells.

Bishop Suffragan

Taunton, Rt. Rev. Nigel Simeon McCulloch, *cons.* 1986, *apptd* 1986; Sherford Farm House, Sherford, Taunton TA1 3RF.

Dean

Very Rev. Richard Lewis, *apptd* 1990.

Canons Residentiary

S. R. Cutt, *apptd* 1979; C. E. Thomas, *apptd* 1983; P. de N. Lucas, *apptd* 1988.
Organist, A. Crossland, FRCO, *apptd* 1970.

Archdeacons

Bath, Ven. J. E. Burgess, *apptd* 1975.
Taunton, Ven. L. E. Olyott, *apptd* 1977.
Wells, Ven. C. E. Thomas, *apptd* 1983.

Stipendiary Male Clergy, 253.
Stipendiary Women Deacons, 8.

Chancellor, G. H. Newsom, QC, *apptd* 1970.
Registrar, Secretary and Chapter Clerk, N. M. Cavender, Diocesan Registry, Market Place, Wells BA5 2RE.

BIRMINGHAM

7*th Bishop,* Rt. Rev. Mark Santer, *cons.* 1981, *apptd* 1987; Bishop's Croft, Harborne, Birmingham B17 0BG. *Signs* Mark Birmingham.

Stipendiary Assistant Bishop

Rt. Rev. Michael Whinney, *cons.* 1982, *apptd* 1989.

Provost

Very Rev. Peter Austin Berry, *apptd* 1986.

Canons Residentiary

L. M. Davies, *apptd* 1981; Ven. C. J. G. Barton, *apptd* 1990.
Organist, M. R. Huxley, FRCO, *apptd* 1986.

Archdeacons

Aston, Ven. C. J. G. Barton, *apptd* 1990.
Birmingham, Ven. J. F. Duncan, *apptd* 1985.
Coleshill, Ven. J. L. Cooper, *apptd* 1990.

Stipendiary Male Clergy, 210.
Stipendiary Women Deacons, 15.

Chancellor, His Honour Judge Aglionby, *apptd* 1970.
Registrar and Legal Secretary, M. B. Shaw, St Philip's House, St Philip's Place, Birmingham B3 2PP.

BRISTOL

54th Bishop, Rt. Rev. Barry Rogerson, *cons.* 1979, *apptd* 1985; Bishop's House, Clifton Hill, Bristol BS8 1BW. *Signs* Barry Bristol.

Bishop Suffragan

Malmesbury, Rt. Rev. Peter James Firth, *cons.* 1983, *apptd* 1983; 7 Ivywell Rd., Bristol BS9 1NX.

Dean

Very Rev. Wesley Arthur Carr, *apptd* 1987.

Canons Residentiary

J. Rogan, *apptd* 1983; A. L. J. Redfern, *apptd* 1987; J. L. Simpson, *apptd* 1989; P. F. Johnson, *apptd* 1990.
Organist, C. Brayne, FRCO, *apptd* 1990.

Archdeacons

Bristol, Ven. D. J. Banfield, *apptd* 1990.
Swindon, Ven. K. J. Clark, *apptd* 1982.

Stipendiary Male Clergy, 162.
Stipendiary Women Deacons, 19.

Chancellor, Sir David Calcutt, QC, *apptd* 1971.
Registrar and Secretary, T. R. Urquhart, 30 Queen Charlotte Street, Bristol BS13 8HE.

CHELMSFORD

7th Bishop, Rt. Rev. John Waine, *cons.* 1975, *apptd* 1986; Bishopscourt, Margaretting, Ingatestone CM4 0HD. *Signs* John Chelmsford.

Bishops Suffragan

Barking, Rt. Rev. Roger Frederick Sainsbury, *cons.* 1991, *apptd* 1991; 110 Capel Road, Forest Gate, London E7 0JS.
Bradwell, Rt. Rev. Charles Derek Bond, *cons.* 1976, *apptd* 1976; 21 Elmhurst Avenue, Benfleet SS7 5RY.
Colchester, Rt. Rev. Michael Edwin Vickers, *cons.* 1988, *apptd* 1988; 1 Fitzwalter Road, Lexden, Colchester CO3 3SS.

Provost

Very Rev. John Henry Moses, PH.D., *apptd* 1982.

Canons Residentiary

P. G. Brett, *apptd* 1985; P. G. Southwell-Sander, *apptd* 1985; T. Thompson, *apptd* 1988; B. P. Thompson, *apptd* 1988.
Organist, G. Elliott, PH.D., FRCO, *apptd* 1981.

Archdeacons

Colchester, Ven. E. C. F. Stroud, *apptd* 1983.
Southend, Ven. J. S. Bailey, *apptd* 1982.
West Ham, Ven. T. J. Stevens, *apptd* 1991.

Stipendiary Male Clergy, 480.
Stipendiary Women Deacons, 22.

Chancellor, Miss S. M. Cameron, QC, *apptd* 1970.
Diocesan Registrar, B. Hood, 53 New Street, Chelmsford CM1 1NG.

CHICHESTER

102nd Bishop, Rt. Rev. Eric Waldram Kemp, DD, *cons.* 1974, *apptd* 1974; The Palace, Chichester PO19 1PY. *Signs* Eric Cicestr:

Bishops Suffragan

Horsham, Rt. Rev. John William Hind, *cons.* 1991, *apptd* 1991; Bishop's Lodge, Worth, nr. Crawley RH10 4RT.
Lewes, Rt. Rev. Peter John Ball, *cons.* 1977, *apptd* 1977; Litlington Rectory, nr. Polegate BN26 5RB.

Assistant Bishops

Rt. Rev. William Hunt, *cons.* 1955, *apptd* 1980; Rt. Rev. Mark Green, *cons.* 1972, *apptd* 1982; Rt. Rev. Simon Phipps, *cons.* 1968, *apptd* 1987; Rt. Rev. Edward Knapp-Fisher, *cons.* 1960, *apptd* 1987; Rt. Rev. Morris Maddocks, *cons.* 1972, *apptd* 1987.

Dean

Very Rev. John David Treadgold, LVO, *apptd* 1989.

Canons Residentiary

R. T. Greenacre, *apptd* 1975; J. F. Hester, *apptd* 1985.
Organist, A. J. Thurlow, FRCO, *apptd* 1980.

Archdeacons

Chichester, Ven. K. Hobbs, *apptd* 1981.
Horsham, Ven. W. C. L. Filby, *apptd* 1983.
Lewes and Hastings, Ven. H. Glaisyer, *apptd* 1991.

Stipendiary Male Clergy, 362.
Stipendiary Women Deacons, 5.

Chancellor, His Honour Judge Q. T. Edwards, QC, *apptd* 1978.
Legal Secretary to the Bishop, and Diocesan Registrar, C. L. Hodgetts, 5 East Pallant, Chichester PO19 1TS.

COVENTRY

7th Bishop, Rt. Rev. Simon Barrington-Ward, *cons.* 1985, *apptd* 1985; The Bishop's House, 23 Davenport Road, Coventry CV5 6PW. *Signs* Simon Coventry.

Bishop Suffragan

Warwick, Rt. Rev. George Clive Handford, *cons.* 1990, *apptd* 1990; 139 Kenilworth Road, Coventry CV4 7AF.

Assistant Bishops

Rt. Rev. John Daly, *cons.* 1935, *apptd* 1968; Rt. Rev. Vernon Nicholls, *cons.* 1974, *apptd* 1984.

Provost

Very Rev. John Fitzmaurice Petty, *apptd* 1987.

Canons Residentiary

P. Oestreicher, *apptd* 1986; M. Sadgrove, *apptd* 1987; G. T. Hughes, *apptd* 1989.
Organist, A. P. Leddington Wright, FRCO, *apptd* 1984.

Archdeacons

Coventry, Ven. H. I. L. Russell, *apptd* 1989.
Warwick, Ven. M. J. J. Paget-Wilkes, *apptd* 1990.

Stipendiary Male Clergy, 177.
Stipendiary Women Deacons, 17.

Chancellor, W. M. Gage, *apptd* 1980.
Registrar, D. J. Dumbleton, 8 The Quadrant, Coventry CV1 2EL.

DERBY

5th Bishop, Rt. Rev. Peter Spencer Dawes, *cons.* 1988, *apptd* 1988; The Bishop's House, 6 King Street, Duffield, Derby DE6 4EU. *Signs* Peter Derby.

Bishop Suffragan

Repton, Rt. Rev. Francis Henry Arthur Richmond, *cons.* 1986, *apptd* 1986; Repton House, Lea, Matlock DE4 5JP.

Provost

Very Rev. Benjamin Hugh Lewers, *apptd* 1981.

Canons Residentiary

Ven. R. S. Dell, *apptd* 1981; I. Gatford, *apptd* 1984; G. R. Orchard, *apptd* 1986; G. A. Chesterman, *apptd* 1989.
Organist, P. Gould, FRCO, *apptd* 1982.

Archdeacons

Chesterfield, Ven. G. R. Phizackerley, *apptd* 1978.
Derby, Ven. R. S. Dell, *apptd* 1973.

Stipendiary Male Clergy, 210.
Stipendiary Women Deacons, 14.

Chancellor, J. W. M. Bullimore, *apptd* 1981.
Registrar, J. S. Battie, Derby Church House, Full Street, Derby DE1 3DR.

ELY

67th Bishop, Rt. Rev. Stephen Whitfield Sykes, *cons.* 1990, *apptd* 1990; The Bishop's House, Ely CB7 4DW. *Signs* Stephen Ely.

Bishop Suffragan

Huntingdon, Rt. Rev. William Gordon Roe, D.Phil., *cons.* 1980, *apptd* 1980; 14 Lynn Road, Ely, Cambs. CB6 1DA.

Dean

Very Rev. Michael Higgins, *apptd* 1991.

Canons Residentiary

D. J. Green, *apptd* 1980; J. Rone, *apptd* 1989.
Organist, P. Trepte.

Archdeacons

Ely, Ven. D. Walser, *apptd* 1981.
Huntingdon, Ven. R. K. Sledge, *apptd* 1978.
Wisbech, Ven. D. Fleming, *apptd* 1984.

Stipendiary Male Clergy, 170.
Stipendiary Women Deacons, 7.

Chancellor, W. Gage, QC.
Registrar, W. H. Godfrey, 18 The Broadway, St Ives, Huntingdon PE17 4BS.
Joint Registrar, P. F. B. Beesley, 1 The Sanctuary, SW1P 3JT.

EXETER

69th Bishop, Rt. Rev. Geoffrey Hewlett Thompson, *cons.* 1974, *apptd* 1985; The Palace, Exeter EX1 1HY. *Signs* Hewlett Exon:

Bishops Suffragan

Crediton, Rt. Rev. Peter Everard Coleman, *cons.* 1984, *apptd* 1984; 10 The Close, Exeter EX1 1EZ.
Plymouth, Rt. Rev. Richard Stephen Hawkins, *cons.* 1988, *apptd* 1988; 31 Riverside Walk, Tamerton Foliot, Plymouth PL5 4AQ.

Assistant Bishops

Rt. Rev. Ronald Goodchild, *cons.* 1964, *apptd* 1983; Rt. Rev. Philip Pasterfield, *cons.* 1974, *apptd* 1984; Rt. Rev. Richard Cartwright, *cons.* 1972, *apptd* 1988; Rt. Rev. Colin Docker, *cons.* 1975, *apptd* 1991.

Dean

Very Rev. Richard Montague Stephens Eyre, *apptd* 1981.

Canons Residentiary

A. C. Mawson, *apptd* 1979; Ven. J. Richards, *apptd* 1981; K. C. Parry, *apptd* 1991.
Organist, L. Nethsingha, FRCO, *apptd* 1972.

Archdeacons

Barnstaple, Ven. T. Lloyd, *apptd* 1989.
Exeter, Ven. J. Richards, *apptd* 1981.
Plymouth, Ven. R. G. Ellis, *apptd* 1982.
Totnes, Ven. A. F. Tremlett, *apptd* 1988.

Stipendiary Male Clergy, 300.
Stipendiary Women Deacons, 5.

Chancellor, Sir David Calcutt, QC, *apptd* 1971.
Registrar, J. F. G. Michelmore, TD, 18 Cathedral Yard, Exeter EX1 1HE.
Diocesan Secretary, Rev. R. R. Huddleson, Diocesan House, Palace Gate, Exeter EX1 1HX.

GIBRALTAR IN EUROPE

1st Bishop, Rt. Rev. John Richard Satterthwaite, CMG, *cons.* 1970, *apptd* 1970; 5A Gregory Place, W8 4NG. *Signs* John Gibraltar.

Bishop Suffragan

In Europe, Rt. Rev. Edward Holland, *apptd* 1986.

Auxiliary Bishops

Rt. Rev. E. M. H. Capper, OBE, *cons.* 1967, *apptd* 1973; Rt. Rev. D. de Pina Cabral, *cons.* 1967, *apptd* 1976; Rt. Rev. A. W. M. Weeks, CB, *cons.* 1977, *apptd* 1988.

Vicar-General, Rev. Canon P. O. Deacon.
Bishop's Commissaries, Canon L. Tyzack; Canon J. D. Beckwith; Canon D. H. Palmer; A. M. Apostol.
Dean, Cathedral Church of the Holy Trinity, Gibraltar, Very Rev. B. W. Horlock, OBE.
Chancellor, Pro-Cathedral of St Paul, Valletta, Malta, Canon P. Cousins.
Chancellor, Pro-Cathedral of the Holy Trinity, Brussels, Belgium, Ven. J. Lewis.

Archdeacons

Aegean, Ven. G. B. Evans.
North-west Europe, Ven. J. Lewis.
North France, Ven. M. B. Lea.
Gibraltar, Rt. Rev. D. de Pina Cabral.
Italy, Ven. G. L. C. Westwell.
Riviera, Ven. J. Livingstone.
Scandinavia, Ven. G. A. C. Brown.
Switzerland, Ven. P. J. Hawker.

Chancellor, Sir David Calcutt, QC.
Diocesan Registrar and Legal Secretary, J. G. Underwood, 37A Walbrook, EC4 8BS.

GLOUCESTER

Bishop, vacant. Bishopscourt, Gloucester GL1 2BQ.

Bishop Suffragan

Tewkesbury, Rt. Rev. Geoffrey David Jeremy Walsh, *cons.* 1986, *apptd* 1986; Green Acre, Hempsted, Gloucester GL2 6LS.

Dean

Very Rev. Kenneth Neal Jennings, *apptd* 1982.

Canons Residentiary

A. L. Dunstan, *apptd* 1978; R. D. M. Grey, *apptd* 1982; P. R. Greenwood, *apptd* 1986.
Organist, J. D. Sanders, FRCO, *apptd* 1967.

Archdeacons

Cheltenham, Ven. J. A. Lewis, *apptd* 1988.
Gloucester, Ven. C. J. H. Wagstaff, *apptd* 1982.

Stipendiary Male Clergy, 185.
Stipendiary Women Deacons, 12.

Chancellor and Vicar-General, Ms D. J. Rogers, *apptd* 1990.
Registrar, C. G. Peak, 34 Brunswick Road, Gloucester GL1 1JW.
Diocesan Secretary, R. Anderton, Church House, College Green, Gloucester GL1 2LY.

GUILDFORD

7th Bishop, Rt. Rev. Michael Edgar Adie, *cons.* 1983, *apptd* 1983; Willow Grange, Woking Road, Guildford GU4 7QS. *Signs* Michael Guildford.

Bishop Suffragan

Dorking, Rt. Rev. David Peter Wilcox, *cons.* 1986, *apptd* 1986; 13 Pilgrims Way, Guildford GU4 8AD.

Dean

Very Rev. Alexander Gillan Wedderspoon, *apptd* 1987.

Canons Residentiary

F. S. Telfer, *apptd* 1973; P. G. Croft, *apptd* 1983; R. D. Fenwick, *apptd* 1990.
Organist, A. T. S. Millington, FRCO, *apptd* 1983.

Archdeacons

Dorking, Ven. C.W. Herbert, *apptd* 1990.
Surrey, Ven. J. S. Went, *apptd* 1989.

Stipendiary Male Clergy, 194.
Stipendiary Women Deacons, 15.

Chancellor, M. B. Goodman.
Legal Secretary and Registrar, P. F. B. Beesley, 1 The Sanctuary, SW1P 3JT.

HEREFORD

103rd Bishop, Rt. Rev. John Oliver, *cons.* 1990, *apptd* 1990; The Palace, Hereford HR4 9BN. *Signs* John Hereford.

Bishop Suffragan

Ludlow, Rt. Rev. Ian MacDonald Griggs, *cons.* 1987, *apptd* 1987; Halford Vicarage, Craven Arms, Shropshire SY7 9BT.

Dean

Very Rev. Peter Haynes, *apptd* 1982.

Canons Residentiary

P. Iles, *apptd* 1983; J. Tiller, *apptd* 1984.
Organist, R. Massey, FRCO, *apptd* 1974.

Archdeacons

Hereford, vacant.
Ludlow, Ven. J. H. R. Lewis, *apptd* 1987.

Stipendiary Male Clergy, 135.
Stipendiary Women Deacons, 6.

Chancellor, J. M. Henty.
Joint Registrars, V. T. Jordan, 44 Bridge Street, Hereford; P. Beesley, 1 The Sanctuary, Westminster, SW1P 3JT.

LEICESTER

5th Bishop, Rt. Rev. Thomas Frederick Butler, PH.D., *cons.* 1985, *apptd* 1991; Bishop's Lodge, 10 Springfield Road, Leicester LE2 3BD. *Signs* Thomas Leicester.

Assistant Bishops

Rt. Rev. John Mort, CBE, *cons.* 1952, *apptd* 1972; Rt. Rev. Godfrey Ashby, *cons.* 1980, *apptd* 1988.

Provost

Very Rev. Alan Christopher Warren, *apptd* 1978.

Canons Residentiary

M. T. H. Banks, *apptd* 1988; M. Wilson, *apptd* 1988.
Organist, P. White, FRCO, *apptd* 1968.

Archdeacons

Leicester, Ven. R. D. Silk, *apptd* 1980.
Loughborough, Ven. T. H. Jones, *apptd* 1986.

Stipendiary Male Clergy, 170.
Stipendiary Women Deacons, 12.

Chancellor, N. Seed, *apptd* 1989.
Registrar, G. K. J. Moore, 10 Friar Lane, Leicester LE1 5QD.

LICHFIELD

97th Bishop, Rt. Rev. Keith Norman Sutton, *cons.* 1978, *apptd* 1984; Bishop's House, The Close, Lichfield WS13 7LG. *Signs* Keith Lichfield.

Bishops Suffragan

Shrewsbury, Rt. Rev. John Dudley Davies, *cons.* 1987, *apptd* 1987; Athlone House, 68 London Road, Shrewsbury SY2 6PG.
Stafford, Rt. Rev. Michael Charles Scott-Joynt, *cons.* 1987, *apptd* 1987; Ash Garth, Broughton Crescent, Barlaston ST12 9DD.
Wolverhampton, Rt. Rev. Christopher John Mayfield, *cons.* 1985, *apptd* 1985; 61 Richmond Road, Wolverhampton WV3 9JH.

Dean

Very Rev. John Harley Lang, *apptd* 1980.

Canons Residentiary

Ven. R. B. Ninis, *apptd* 1974; A. N. Barnard, *apptd* 1977; W. J. Turner, *apptd* 1983; J. Howe, *apptd* 1988.
Organist, A. Lumsden, *apptd* 1992.

Archdeacons

Lichfield, Ven. R. B. Ninis, *apptd* 1974.
Salop, Ven. G. Frost, *apptd* 1987.
Stoke-on-Trent, Ven. D. Ede, *apptd* 1989.

Stipendiary Male Clergy, 406.
Stipendiary Women Deacons, 24.

Chancellor, His Honour Judge Shand.
Diocesan Registrar, J. P. Thorneycroft, St Mary's House, The Close, Lichfield WS13 7LD.

LINCOLN

70th Bishop, Rt. Rev. Robert Maynard Hardy, *cons.* 1980, *apptd* 1987; Bishop's House, Eastgate, Lincoln LN2 1QQ. *Signs* Robert Lincoln.

Bishops Suffragan

Grantham, Rt. Rev. William Ind, *cons.* 1987, *apptd* 1987; Fairacre, Barrowby High Road, Grantham NG31 8NP.
Grimsby, Rt. Rev. David Tustin, *cons.* 1979, *apptd* 1979; Bishop's House, Church Lane, Ireby-upon-Humber, Grimsby DN37 7JR.

Assistant Bishops

Rt. Rev. Gerald Colin, *cons.* 1966, *apptd* 1979; Rt. Rev. Harold Darby, *cons.* 1975, *apptd* 1989.

Dean

Very Rev. Brandon Donald Jackson, *apptd* 1989.

Canons Residentiary

B. R. Davis, *apptd* 1977; J. S. Nurser, PH.D., *apptd* 1977; Ven. J. H. C. Laurence, *apptd* 1985.
Organist, C. Walsh, FRCO, *apptd* 1988.

Archdeacons

Lincoln, Ven. M. P. Brackenbury, *apptd* 1988.
Lindsey, Ven. J. H. C. Laurence, *apptd* 1985.
Stow, Ven. R. J. Wells, *apptd* 1989.

Stipendiary Male Clergy, 254.
Stipendiary Women Deacons, 16.

Chancellor, His Honour Judge Goodman, *apptd* 1971.
Registrar and Legal Secretary, D. M. Wellman, 28 West Parade, Lincoln LN1 1JT.

NORWICH

70th Bishop, Rt. Rev. Peter John Nott, *cons.* 1977, *apptd* 1985; Bishop's House, Norwich, NR3 1SB. *Signs* Peter Norvic:

Bishops Suffragan

Lynn, Rt. Rev. David Edward Bentley, *cons.* 1986, *apptd* 1986; The Old Vic, Castle Acre, King's Lynn PE32 2AA.
Thetford, vacant.

Dean

Very Rev. John Paul Burbridge, *apptd* 1983.

Canons Residentiary

D. H. Bishop, *apptd* 1980; C. Beswick, *apptd* 1984; M. S. McLean, *apptd* 1986.
Organist, M. B. Nicholas, FRCO, *apptd* 1971.

Archdeacons

Lynn, Ven. A. C. Foottit, *apptd* 1987.
Norfolk, Ven. P. Dawson, *apptd* 1977.
Norwich, Ven. A. M. Handley, *apptd* 1981.

Stipendiary Male Clergy, 238.
Stipendiary Women Deacons, 7.

Chancellor, His Honour J. H. Ellison, VRD, *apptd* 1955.
Registrar and Secretary, J. W. F. Herring, Francis House, 3–7 Redwell Street, Norwich NR2 4TJ.

OXFORD

41st Bishop, Rt. Rev. Richard Douglas Harries, *cons.* 1987, *apptd* 1987; Diocesan Church House, North Hinksey, Oxford OX2 0NB. *Signs* Richard Oxon:

Area Bishops

Buckingham, Rt. Rev. Simon Hedley Burrows, *cons.* 1974, *apptd* 1974; Sheridan, Grimms Hill, Great Missenden HP16 9BD.
Dorchester, Rt. Rev. Anthony John Russell, *cons.* 1988, *apptd* 1988; Holmby House, Sibford Ferris, Banbury, Oxon. OX15 5RG.
Reading, Rt. Rev. John Frank Ewan Bone, *cons.* 1989, *apptd* 1989; Greenbanks, Old Bath Road, Sonning, Reading RG4 0SY.

Assistant Bishops

Rt. Rev. Albert Cragg, DD, *cons.* 1970, *apptd* 1982; Rt. Rev. Leonard Ashton, CB, *cons.* 1974, *apptd* 1984; Rt. Rev. Richard Watson, *cons.* 1970, *apptd* 1988; Rt. Rev. Peter Walker, *cons.* 1972, *apptd* 1990; Rt. Rev. Maurice Wood, *cons.* 1971, *apptd* 1991; Rt. Rev. Stephen Verney, *cons.* 1977, *apptd* 1991.

Dean of Christ Church

Very Rev. John Henry Drury, *apptd* 1991.

Canons Residentiary

Ven. F. V. Weston, *apptd* 1982; O. M. T. O'Donovan, D.Phil., *apptd* 1982; R. D. Williams, D.Phil., *apptd* 1985; J. M. Pierce, *apptd* 1987; J. S. K. Ward, *apptd* 1991; Rt. Rev. A. R. M. Gordon, *apptd* 1991.
Organist, S. Darlington, FRCO.

Archdeacons

Berkshire, Ven. D. N. Griffiths, *apptd* 1987.
Buckingham, Ven. J. A. Morrison, *apptd* 1989.
Oxford, Ven. F. V. Weston, *apptd* 1982.

Stipendiary Male Clergy, 449.
Stipendiary Women Deacons, 29.

Chancellor, P. T. S. Boydell, QC, *apptd* 1958.
Registrar and Legal Secretary, Dr F. E. Robson, OBE, 16 Beaumont Street, Oxford OX1 2LZ.

WINDSOR

The Queen's Free Chapel of St George within Her Castle of Windsor (A Royal Peculiar)
Dean, Very Rev. Patrick Reynolds Mitchell, FSA, *apptd* 1989.

Canons Residentiary

J. A. White, *apptd* 1982; D. M. Stanesby, *apptd* 1985; A. A. Coldwells, *apptd* 1987; D. M. Moxon, *apptd* 1990.
Organist, J. Rees-Williams, FRCO, *apptd* 1991.
Chapter Clerk, Lt.-Col. N. J. Newman, *apptd* 1990.

PETERBOROUGH

36th Bishop, Rt. Rev. William John Westwood, *cons.* 1975, *apptd* 1984; The Palace, Peterborough PE1 1YA. *Signs* William Petriburg:

Bishop Suffragan

Brixworth, Rt. Rev. Paul Everard Barber, *cons.* 1989, *apptd* 1989; 4 The Avenue, Dallington, Northampton NN1 4RZ.

Dean

Very Rev. Randolph George Wise, *apptd* 1981.

Canons Residentiary

T. R. Christie, *apptd* 1980; J. Higham, *apptd* 1983; T. Willmott, *apptd* 1989.
Organist, C. S. Gower, FRCO, *apptd* 1977.

Archdeacons

Northampton, Ven. M. R. Chapman, *apptd* 1991.
Oakham, Ven. B. Fernyhough, *apptd* 1977.

Stipendiary Male Clergy, 175.
Stipendiary Women Deacons, 9.

Chancellor, T. A. C. Coningsby, QC, *apptd* 1989.
Registrar and Legal Secretary, R. Hemingray, 4 Holywell Way, Longthorpe, Peterborough PE3 6SS.

PORTSMOUTH

7th Bishop, Rt. Rev. Timothy John Bavin, *cons.* 1974, *apptd* 1985; Bishopswood, Fareham, Hants. PO14 1NT. *Signs* Timothy Portsmouth.

Provost

Very Rev. David Staffurth Stancliffe, *apptd* 1982.

Canons Residentiary

R. Eckersley, *apptd* 1984; M. D. Doe, *apptd* 1989; C. J. Bradley, *apptd* 1990; D. T. Isaac, *apptd* 1990.
Organist, A. Lucas, FRCO.

Archdeacons

Isle of Wight, Ven. A. H. M. Turner, *apptd* 1986.
Portsmouth, Ven. N. H. Crowder, *apptd* 1985.

Stipendiary Male Clergy, 143.
Stipendiary Women Deacons, 10.

Chancellor, His Honour Judge Aglionby, *apptd* 1978.
Registrar, Miss H. A. G. Tyler, 132 High Street, Portsmouth PO1 2HR.

ROCHESTER

105*th Bishop*, Rt. Rev. Anthony Michael Arnold Turnbull, *cons.* 1988, *apptd* 1988; Bishopscourt, Rochester ME1 1TS. *Signs* Michael Roffen:

Bishop Suffragan

Tonbridge, Rt. Rev. David Henry Bartleet, *cons.* 1982, *apptd* 1982; Bishop's Lodge, St Botolph's Road, Sevenoaks TN13 3AG.

Assistant Bishops

Rt. Rev. Colin Buchanan, *cons.* 1985, *apptd* 1989; Rt. Rev. John Flagg, *cons.* 1969, *apptd* 1987.

Dean

Very Rev. Edward Frank Shotter, *apptd* 1990.

Canons Residentiary

E. R. Turner, *apptd* 1981; R. J. R. Lea, *apptd* 1988; J. Armson, *apptd* 1989; N. Warren, *apptd* 1989.
Organist, B. Ferguson, FRCO, *apptd* 1977.

Archdeacons

Bromley, Ven. E. R. Francis, *apptd* 1979.
Rochester, Ven. N. L. Warren, *apptd* 1989.
Tonbridge, Ven. R. J. Mason, *apptd* 1977.

Stipendiary Male Clergy, 231.
Stipendiary Women Deacons, 16.

Chancellor, His Honour Judge M. B. Goodman, *apptd* 1971.
Registrar, O. R. Woodfield, The Precinct, Rochester ME1 1SZ.
Secretary, D. W. Faull, 35 Great Peter Street, SW1P 3LR.

ST ALBANS

8*th Bishop*, Rt. Rev. John Bernard Taylor, *cons.* 1980, *apptd* 1980; Abbey Gate House, St Albans AL3 4HD. *Signs* John St Albans.

Bishops Suffragan

Bedford, Rt. Rev. David John Farmbrough, *cons.* 1981, *apptd* 1981; 168 Kimbolton Road, Bedford MK41 8DN.
Hertford, Rt. Rev. Robin Jonathan Norman Smith, *cons.* 1990, *apptd* 1990; Hertford House, Abbey Mill Lane, St Albans AL3 4HE.

Assistant Bishop

Rt. Rev. The Lord Runcie, *cons.* 1970, *apptd* 1991.

Dean

Very Rev. Peter Clement Moore, D.PHIL., *apptd* 1973.

Canons Residentiary

B. G. E. Pettifer, *apptd* 1985; C. B. Slee, *apptd* 1982; C. Garner, *apptd* 1984; G. R. S. Ritson, *apptd* 1987; M. Sansom, *apptd* 1988.
Organist, B. Rose, FRCO (1988).

Archdeacons

Bedford, Ven. M. G. Bourke, *apptd* 1986.
St Albans, Ven. P. B. Davies, *apptd* 1987.

Stipendiary Male Clergy, 313.
Stipendiary Women Deacons, 19.

Chancellor, G. H. Newsom, QC, *apptd* 1958.
Registrar and Legal Secretary, D. N. Cheetham, Holywell Lodge, 41 Holywell Hill, St Albans AL1 1HE.

ST EDMUNDSBURY AND IPSWICH

8*th Bishop*, Rt. Rev. John Dennis, *cons.* 1979, *apptd* 1986; Bishop's House, Ipswich IP1 3ST. *Signs* John St Edmunds & Ipswich.

Bishop Suffragan

Dunwich, Rt. Rev. Eric Nash Devenport, *cons.* 1980, *apptd* 1980; The Old Vicarage, Stowupland, Stowmarket IP14 4BQ.

Provost

Very Rev. Raymond Furnell, *apptd* 1981.

Canons Residentiary

G. J. Tarris, *apptd* 1982; R. Garrard, *apptd* 1987; A. M. Shaw, *apptd* 1989.

Archdeacons

Ipswich, Ven. T. A. Gibson, *apptd* 1987.
Sudbury, Ven. R. Garrard, *apptd* 1992.
Suffolk, Ven. N. Robinson, *apptd* 1987.

Stipendiary Male Clergy, 192.
Stipendiary Women Deacons, 11.

Chancellor, His Honour Judge Blofeld, QC, *apptd* 1974.
Registrar, J. D. Mitson, 22–28 Museum Street, Ipswich IP1 1JA.

SALISBURY

76*th Bishop*, Rt. Rev. John Austin Baker, *cons.* 1982, *apptd* 1982; South Canonry, The Close, Salisbury SP1 2ER. *Signs* John Sarum.

Bishops Suffragan

Ramsbury, Rt. Rev. Peter St George Vaughan, *cons.* 1989, *apptd* 1989; Bishop's House, Urchfont, Devizes, Wilts. SN10 4QH.
Sherborne, Rt. Rev. John Dudley Galtrey Kirkham, *cons.* 1976, *apptd* 1976; Little Bailie, Sturminster Marshall, Wimborne BH21 4AD.

Assistant Bishop

Rt. Rev. John Cavell, *cons.* 1972, *apptd* 1988.

Dean

Very Rev. the Hon. Hugh Geoffrey Dickinson, *apptd* 1986.

Canons Residentiary

I. G. D. Dunlop, FSA, *apptd* 1972; D. J. C. Davies, *apptd* 1985; J. R. Stewart, *apptd* 1990.
Organist, R. G. Seal, FRCO, *apptd* 1968.

Archdeacons

Dorset, Ven. G. E. Walton, *apptd* 1982.
Sarum, Ven. B. J. Hopkinson, *apptd* 1986.
Sherborne, Ven. P. C. Wheatley, *apptd* 1991.
Wilts, Ven. B. J. Smith, *apptd* 1980.

Stipendiary Male Clergy, 264.
Stipendiary Women Deacons, 7.

Chancellor of the Diocese, His Honour. J. H. Ellison, VRD, *apptd* 1955.
Registrar and Legal Secretary, F. M. Broadbent, 42 Castle Street, Salisbury SP1 3TX.

SOUTHWARK

8th Bishop designate, Rt. Rev. Robert Kerr Williamson, *cons.* 1984, *trs.* 1991, *apptd* 1991; Bishop's House, 38 Tooting Bec Gardens, SW16 1QZ. *Signs* Robert Southwark.

Bishops Suffragan

Croydon, Rt. Rev. Wilfred Denniston Wood, DD, *cons.* 1985, *apptd* 1985; St Matthew's House, George Street, Croydon CR0 1PE.
Kingston upon Thames, Rt. Rev. Peter Stephen Maurice Selby, PH.D., *cons.* 1984, *apptd* 1984; *Office*, Whitelands College, West Hill, SW15 3SN.
Woolwich, Rt. Rev. Albert Peter Hall, *cons.* 1984, *apptd* 1984; 8B Hillyfields Crescent, SE4 1QA.

Assistant Bishops

Rt. Rev. Edmund Capper, OBE, *cons.* 1967, *apptd* 1981; Rt. Rev. John Hughes, *cons.* 1956, *apptd* 1986; Rt. Rev. Hugh Montefiore, *cons.* 1970, *apptd* 1987; Rt. Rev. Simon Phipps, *cons.* 1976, *apptd* 1987; Rt. Rev. Michael Nazir-Ali, *cons.* 1984, *apptd* 1990.

Provost

Very Rev. David Lawrence Edwards, *apptd* 1983.

Canons Residentiary

I. G. Smith-Cameron, *apptd* 1972; P. B. Price, *apptd* 1988; D. Painter, *apptd* 1991.
Organist, P. Wright, *apptd* 1989.

Archdeacons

Croydon, Ven. F. R. Hazell, *apptd* 1984.
Lambeth, Ven. C. R. B. Bird, *apptd* 1988.
Lewisham, Ven. G. Kuhrt, *apptd* 1989.
Reigate, Ven. P. B. Coombs, *apptd* 1988.
Southwark, Ven. D. L. Bartles-Smith, *apptd* 1985.
Wandsworth, Ven. D. Gerrard, *apptd* 1989.

Stipendiary Male Clergy, 396.
Stipendiary Women Deacons, 31.

Chancellor, R. Gray, QC, *apptd* 1990.
Joint Registrars, D. W. Faull and P. Morris, 35 Great Peter Street, SW1P 3LR.

TRURO

13th Bishop, Rt. Rev. Michael Thomas Ball, *cons.* 1980, *apptd* 1990; Lis Escop, Truro TR3 6QQ. *Signs* Michael Truro.

Bishop Suffragan

St Germans, Rt. Rev. Richard Llewellin, *cons.* 1985, *apptd* 1985; 32 Falmouth Road, Truro TR1 2HX.

Assistant Bishops

Rt. Rev. Richard Cartwright, *cons.* 1972, *apptd* 1982; Rt. Rev. Conrad Meyer, *cons.* 1979, *apptd* 1991.

Dean

Very Rev. David John Shearlock, *apptd* 1982.

Canons Residentiary

W. J. P. Boyd, PH.D., *apptd* 1985; Ven. R. L. Ravenscroft, *apptd* 1988; R. O. Osborne, *apptd* 1988.
Organist, D. J. Briggs, FRCO (1989).

Archdeacons

Cornwall, Ven. R. L. Ravenscroft, *apptd* 1988.
Bodmin, Ven. R. D. C. Whiteman, *apptd* 1989.

Stipendiary Male Clergy, 149.
Stipendiary Women Deacons, 2.

Chancellor, P. T. S. Boydell, QC, *apptd* 1957.
Registrar and Secretary, M. J. Follett, Messrs Follett Blair, Riverside Business Centre, Malpas Road, Truro TR1 1QH.

WORCESTER

111th Bishop, Rt. Rev. Philip Harold Ernest Goodrich, *cons.* 1973, *apptd* 1982; The Bishop's House, Hartlebury Castle, Kidderminster DY11 7XX. *Signs* Philip Worcester.

Bishop Suffragan

Dudley, Rt. Rev. Anthony Charles Dumper, *cons.* 1977, *apptd* 1977; The Bishop's House, Brooklands, Halesowen Road, Cradley Heath B64 7JF.

Assistant Bishops

Rt. Rev. David Allenby, *cons.* 1962, *apptd* 1968; Rt. Rev. John Maund, CBE, MC, *cons.* 1950, *apptd* 1984; Rt. Rev. Kenneth Woollcombe, *cons.* 1971, *apptd* 1989; Rt. Rev. George Briggs, *cons.* 1973, *apptd* 1990.

Dean

Very Rev. Robert Martin Colquhoun Jeffery, *apptd* 1987.

Canons Residentiary

Ven. F. Bentley, *apptd* 1984; D. G. Thomas, *apptd* 1987; I. M. MacKenzie, *apptd* 1989.
Organist, D. Hunt, MUS.D., FRCO, *apptd* 1975.

Archdeacons

Dudley, Ven. J. Gathercole, *apptd* 1987.
Worcester, Ven. F. Bentley, *apptd* 1984.

Stipendiary Male Clergy, 150.
Stipendiary Women Deacons, 14.

Chancellor, P. T. S. Boydell, QC, *apptd* 1959.
Registrar, Rev. Canon J. A. Dale, Diocesan Registry, The Old Palace, Deansway, Worcester WR1 2JE.

Province of York

YORK

95th Archbishop and Primate of England, Most Rev. and Rt. Hon. John Stapylton Habgood, PH.D., *cons.* 1973, *trs.* 1983, *apptd* 1983; Bishopthorpe, York YO2 1QE. *Signs* John Ebor:

Bishops Suffragan

Hull, Rt. Rev. Donald George Snelgrove, TD, *cons.* 1981, *apptd* 1981; Hullen House, Woodfield Lane, Hessle, Hull HU13 0ES.
Selby, Rt. Rev. Humphrey Vincent Taylor, *cons.* 1991, *apptd* 1991; 8 Bankside Close, Upper Poppleton, York YO2 6LH.
Whitby, Rt. Rev. Gordon Bates, *cons.* 1983, *apptd* 1983; 60 West Green, Stokesley, Middlesbrough TS9 5BD.

Assistant Bishops

Rt. Rev. George Cockin, *cons.* 1959, *apptd* 1969; Rt. Rev. Richard Wimbush, *cons.* 1963, *apptd* 1977; Rt. Rev. Richard Wood, *cons.* 1973, *apptd* 1985; Rt. Rev. Ronald Foley, *cons.* 1982, *apptd* 1989; Rt. Rev. David Galliford, *cons.* 1975, *apptd* 1991.

Dean

Very Rev. John Eliot Southgate, *apptd* 1984.

Canons Residentiary

R. A. Hockley, *apptd* 1976; R. Mayland, *apptd* 1982; J. Toy, PH.D., *apptd* 1983; R. Metcalfe, *apptd* 1988.
Organist, P. J. Moore, FRCO.

Archdeacons

Cleveland, Ven. C. J. Hawthorn, *apptd* 1991.
East Riding, Ven. H. F. Buckingham, *apptd* 1988.
York, Ven. G. B. Austin, *apptd* 1988.

Stipendiary Male Clergy, 328.
Stipendiary Women Deacons, 24.

Official Principal and Auditor of the Chancery Court, J. A. D. Owen, QC.
Chancellor of the Diocese, T. A. C. Coningsby, QC, *apptd* 1977.
Vicar-General of the Province and Official Principal of the Consistory Court, T. A. C. Coningsby, QC.
Registrar and Legal Secretary, L. P. M. Lennox, 1 Peckitt Street, York YO1 1SG.

DURHAM

92nd Bishop, Rt. Rev. David Edward Jenkins, *cons.* 1984, *apptd* 1984; Auckland Castle, Bishop Auckland DL14 7NR. *Signs* David Dunelm.

Bishop Suffragan

Jarrow, Rt. Rev. Alan Smithson, *cons.* 1990, *apptd* 1990; The Old Vicarage, Hallgarth, Pittington, Durham DH6 1AB.

Dean

Very Rev. John Robert Arnold, *apptd* 1989.

Canons Residentiary

Ven. M. C. Perry, *apptd* 1970; R. L. Coppin, *apptd* 1974; Ven. J. D. Hodgson, *apptd* 1983; T. Hart, *apptd* 1983; D. W. Brown, *apptd* 1990.
Organist, J. B. Lancelot, FRCO, *apptd* 1985.

Archdeacons

Auckland, Ven. J. D. Hodgson, *apptd* 1983.
Durham, Ven. M. C. Perry, *apptd* 1970.

Stipendiary Male Clergy, 286.
Stipendiary Women Deacons, 23.

Chancellor, His Honour Judge R. D. H. Bursell, QC, *apptd* 1989.
Registrar and Legal Secretary, D. M. Robertson, Diocesan Registry, Auckland Castle, Bishop Auckland DL14 7QJ.

BLACKBURN

7th Bishop, Rt. Rev. Alan David Chesters, *cons.* 1989, *apptd* 1989; Bishop's House, Ribchester Road, Blackburn BB1 9EF. *Signs* Alan Blackburn.

Bishops Suffragan

Burnley, Rt. Rev. Ronald James Milner, *cons.* 1988, *apptd* 1988; Dean House, 449 Padiham Road, Burnley BB12 6TE.
Lancaster, Rt. Rev. John Nicholls, *cons.* 1990, *apptd* 1990; Wheatfields, 7 Dallas Road, Lancaster LA1 1TN.

Provost

Very Rev. Lawrence Jackson, *apptd* 1973.

Canons Residentiary

J. M. Taylor, *apptd* 1976; B. M. Beaumont, *apptd* 1977; G. I. Hirst, *apptd* 1987; M. A. Kitchener, *apptd* 1990.
Organist, D. A. Cooper, FRCO, *apptd* 1983.

Archdeacons

Blackburn, Ven. W. D. Robinson, *apptd* 1986.
Lancaster, Ven. K. H. Gibbons, *apptd* 1989.

Stipendiary Male Clergy, 267.
Stipendiary Women Deacons, 3.

Chancellor, J. W. M. Bullimore, *apptd* 1990.
Registrar, T. A. Hoyle, Diocesan Registry, Cathedral Close, Blackburn BB1 5AB.

BRADFORD

7th Bishop, Rt. Rev. Robert Kerr Williamson, *cons.* 1984, *apptd* 1984; Bishopscroft, Ashwell Road, Heaton, Bradford BD9 4AU. *Signs* Robert Bradford.
(Bishop Williamson is to become Bishop of Southwark in late 1991.)

Assistant Bishop

Rt. Rev. David Evans, *cons.* 1978, *apptd* 1988.

Provost

Very Rev. John Stephen Richardson, *apptd* 1990.

Canons Residentiary

K. H. Cook, *apptd* 1977; C. J. Hayward, *apptd* 1983.
Organist, A. Horsey, *apptd* 1986.

Archdeacons

Bradford, Ven. D. H. Shreeve, *apptd* 1984.
Craven, Ven. B. A. Smith, *apptd* 1987.

Stipendiary Male Clergy, 136.
Stipendiary Women Deacons, 8.

Chancellor, D. M. Savill, QC, *apptd* 1976.
Registrar and Secretary, J. G. H. Mackrell, 6–14 Devonshire Street, Keighley BD21 2AY.

CARLISLE

65th Bishop, Rt. Rev. Ian Harland, *cons.* 1985, *apptd* 1989; Rose Castle, Dalston, Carlisle CA5 7BZ. *Signs* Ian Carliol:

Bishop Suffragan

Penrith, Rt. Rev. George Lanyon Hacker, *cons.* 1979, *apptd* 1979; The Rectory, Great Salkeld, Penrith CA11 9NA.

Dean

Very Rev. Henry Edward Champneys Stapleton, *apptd* 1988.

Canons Residentiary

R. A. Chapman, *apptd* 1978; Ven. C. P. Stannard, *apptd* 1984; R. C. Johns, *apptd* 1989.
Organist, J. Suter, *apptd* 1991.

Archdeacons

Carlisle, Ven. C. P. Stannard, *apptd* 1984.
West Cumberland, J. R. Packer, *apptd* 1991.
Westmorland and Furness, Ven. L. J. Peat, *apptd* 1989.

Stipendiary Male Clergy, 194.
Stipendiary Women Deacons, 5.

Chancellor, His Honour Judge F. Aglionby, *apptd* 1991.
Registrar and Secretary, Mrs S. Holmes, Woodside, Great Corby, Carlisle CA4 8LL.

CHESTER

39th Bishop, Rt. Rev. Michael Alfred Baughen, *cons.* 1982, *apptd* 1982; Bishop's House, Chester CH1 2JD. *Signs* Michael Cestr:

Bishops Suffragan

Birkenhead, Rt. Rev. Ronald Brown, *cons.* 1974, *apptd* 1974; Trafford House, Queen's Park, Chester CH4 7AX.
Stockport, Rt. Rev. Frank Pilkington Sargeant, *cons.* 1984, *apptd* 1984; 32 Park Gate Drive, Cheadle Hulme, Cheshire SK8 7DF.

Dean

Very Rev. Stephen Stewart Smalley, *apptd* 1986.

Canons Residentiary

C. D. Biddell, *apptd* 1986; R. M. Rees, *apptd* 1990; C. J. Bennetts, *apptd* 1990; O. A. Conway, *apptd* 1991.
Organist, R. A. Fisher, FRCO, *apptd* 1967.

Archdeacons

Chester, Ven. M. F. Gear, *apptd* 1988.
Macclesfield, Ven. J. S. Gaisford, *apptd* 1986.

Stipendiary Male Clergy, 322.
Stipendiary Women Deacons, 7.

Chancellor, H. H. Lomas, *apptd* 1977.
Registrar and Legal Secretary, A. K. McAllester, Friars, 20 White Friars, Chester CH1 1XS.

LIVERPOOL

6th Bishop, Rt. Rev. David Stuart Sheppard, *cons.* 1969, *apptd* 1975; Bishop's Lodge, Woolton Park, Liverpool L25 6DT. *Signs* David Liverpool.

Bishop Suffragan

Warrington, Rt. Rev. Michael Henshall, *cons.* 1976, *apptd* 1976; Martinsfield, Elm Avenue, Great Crosby, Liverpool L23 2SX.

Assistant Bishops

Rt. Rev. Graham Chadwick, *cons.* 1976, *apptd* 1990; Rt. Rev. James Roxburgh, *cons.* 1983, *apptd* 1991.

Dean

Very Rev. Rhys Derrick Chamberlain Walters, *apptd* 1983.

Canons Residentiary

M. M. Wolfe, *apptd* 1982; D. J. Hutton, *apptd* 1983; K. J. Riley, *apptd* 1983; H. Thomas, *apptd* 1988.
Organist, I. Tracey, *apptd* 1980.

Archdeacons

Liverpool, Ven. S. Durant, *apptd* 1991.
Warrington, Ven. C. D. S. Woodhouse, *apptd* 1981.

Stipendiary Male Clergy, 274.
Stipendiary Women Deacons, 23.

Chancellor, R. G. Hamilton.
Registrar and Cathedral Chapter Clerk, R. H. Arden, 1 Hanover Street, Liverpool L1 3DW.

MANCHESTER

9th Bishop, Rt. Rev. Stanley Eric Francis Booth-Clibborn, *cons.* 1979, *apptd* 1979; Bishopscourt, Bury New Road, Manchester M7 0LE. *Signs* Stanley Manchester.

Bishops Suffragan

Bolton, Rt. Rev. David Bonser, *cons.* 1991, *apptd* 1991; 4 Sandfield Drive, Lostock, Bolton BL6 4DU.
Hulme, Rt. Rev. Colin John Fraser Scott, *cons.* 1984, *apptd* 1984; 1 Raynham Avenue, Didsbury, Manchester M20 0BW.
Middleton, Rt. Rev. Donald Alexander Tytler, *cons.* 1982, *apptd* 1982; The Hollies, Manchester Road, Rochdale OL11 3QY.

Assistant Bishop

Rt. Rev. Edward Wickham, *cons.* 1959, *apptd* 1982.

Dean

Very Rev. Robert Murray Waddington, *apptd* 1984.

Canons Residentiary

Ven. R. B. Harris, *apptd* 1980; J. R. Atherton, PH.D., *apptd* 1984; B. Duncan, *apptd* 1986; A. E. Radcliffe, *apptd* 1991.
Organist, G. Stewart.

Archdeacons

Bolton, Ven. W. S. Brison, *apptd* 1985.
Manchester, Ven. R. B. Harris, *apptd* 1980.
Rochdale, Ven. J. M. M. Dalby, *apptd* 1991.

Stipendiary Male Clergy, 377.
Stipendiary Women Deacons, 16.

Chancellor, G. C. H. Spafford, *apptd* 1976.
Registrar and Bishop's Secretary, M. Darlington, 90 Deansgate, Manchester M3 2GH.

NEWCASTLE

10th Bishop, Rt. Rev. Andrew Alexander Kenny Graham, *cons.* 1977, *apptd* 1981; Bishop's House, 29 Moor Road South, Gosforth, Newcastle upon Tyne NE3 1PA. *Signs* A. Newcastle.

Assistant Bishop

Rt. Rev. Kenneth Gill, *cons.* 1972, *apptd* 1980.

Provost

Very Rev. Nicholas Guy Coulton, *apptd* 1990.

Canons Residentiary

W. J. Thomas, *apptd* 1983; R. Langley, *apptd* 1985; P. R. Strange, *apptd* 1986; I. F. Bennett, *apptd* 1988.
Organist, T. Hone, *apptd* 1987.

Archdeacons

Lindisfarne, Ven. M. E. Bowering, *apptd* 1987.
Northumberland, Ven. W. J. Thomas, *apptd* 1983.

Stipendiary Male Clergy, 176.
Stipendiary Women Deacons, 6.

Chancellor, His Honour A. J. Blackett-Ord, CVO, *apptd* 1971.
Registrar and Secretary, R. R. V. Nicholson, 46 Grainger Street, Newcastle upon Tyne NE1 5LB.

RIPON

11th Bishop, Rt. Rev. David Nigel de Lorentz Young, *cons.* 1977, *apptd* 1977; Bishop Mount, Ripon HG4 5DP. *Signs* David Ripon.

Bishop Suffragan

Knaresborough, Rt. Rev. Malcolm James Menin, *cons.* 1986, *apptd* 1986; 16 Shaftesbury Avenue, Roundhay, Leeds LS8 1DT.

Assistant Bishops

Rt. Rev. John Howe, (*cons.* 1955, *apptd* 1985; Rt. Rev. Ralph Emmerson, *cons.* 1972, *apptd* 1986; Rt. Rev. Derek Rawcliffe, *cons.* 1974, *apptd* 1991.

Dean

Very Rev. Christopher Russell Campling, *apptd* 1984.

Canons Residentiary

D. G. Ford, *apptd* 1980; P. J. Marshall, *apptd* 1985; M. R. Glanville Smith, *apptd* 1990.
Organist, R. Perrin, FRCO, *apptd* 1966.

Archdeacons

Leeds, Ven. A. J. Comber, *apptd* 1982.
Richmond, Ven. N. G. L. R. McDermid, *apptd* 1983.

Stipendiary Male Clergy, 174.
Stipendiary Women Deacons, 17.

Chancellor, D. M. Savill, QC, *apptd* 1987.
Registrar and Legal Secretary, J. R. Balmforth, York House, York Place, Knaresborough HG5 0AD.
Diocesan Secretary, G. M. Royal, Diocesan Office, St Mary's Street, Leeds LS9 7DP.

SHEFFIELD

5th Bishop, Rt. Rev. David Ramsay Lunn, cons. 1980, apptd 1980; Bishopscroft, Snaithing Lane, Sheffield S10 3LG. Signs David Sheffield.

Bishop Suffragan

Doncaster, Rt. Rev. William Michael Dermot Persson, cons. 1982, apptd 1982; Bishops Lodge, Rotherham S65 4PF.

Assistant Bishops

Rt. Rev. Kenneth Skelton, CBE, cons. 1962, apptd 1984; Rt. Rev. Kenneth Pillar, cons. 1982, apptd 1989.

Provost

Very Rev. John Warren Gladwin, apptd 1988.

Canons Residentiary

T. M. Page, apptd 1982; Ven. S. R. Lowe, apptd 1988; J. R. Giles, apptd 1988; C. M. Smith, apptd 1991. Organist, P. Brough, apptd 1991.

Archdeacons

Doncaster, Ven. D. Carnelley, apptd 1985.
Sheffield, Ven. S. R. Lowe, apptd 1988.

Stipendiary Male Clergy, 216.
Stipendiary Women Deacons, 16.

Chancellor, G. B. Graham, QC, apptd 1971.
Registrar and Legal Secretary, C. P. Rothwell, 30 Bank Street, Sheffield S1 2DS.

SODOR AND MAN

79th Bishop, Rt. Rev. Noel Debroy Jones, CB, cons. 1989, apptd 1989; The Bishop's House, Quarterbridge Road, Douglas, IOM. Signs Noel Sodor and Man.

Canons

B. H. Kelly, apptd 1980; J. D. Gelling, apptd 1980; B. H. Partington, apptd 1985; J. Sheen, apptd 1991.

Archdeacon

Isle of Man, Ven. D. A. Willoughby, apptd 1982.

Stipendiary Male Clergy, 21.

Vicar-General and Registrar, P. W. S. Farrant, 24 Athol Street, Douglas.

SOUTHWELL

9th Bishop, Rt. Rev. Patrick Burnet Harris, cons. 1973, apptd 1988; Bishop's Manor, Southwell NG25 0JR. Signs Patrick Southwell.

Bishop Suffragan

Sherwood, Rt. Rev. Alan Wyndham Morgan, cons. 1989, apptd 1989; Sherwood House, High Oakham Road, Mansfield NG18 5AJ.

Provost

Very Rev. David Leaning, apptd 1991.

Canons Residentiary

D. P. Keene, apptd 1981; I. G. Collins, apptd 1985. Organist, P. R. Hale, FRCO, apptd 1989.

Archdeacons

Newark, vacant.
Nottingham, Ven. T. Walker, apptd 1991.

Stipendiary Male Clergy, 212.
Stipendiary Women Deacons, 9.

Chancellor, J. Shand, apptd 1981.
Registrar, C. C. Hodson, Diocesan Office, Westgate, Southwell NG25 0JL.

WAKEFIELD

Bishop, vacant (Bishop's Lodge, Woodthorpe Lane, Wakefield WF2 6JJ).

Bishop Suffragan

Pontefract, Rt. Rev. Thomas Richard Hare, cons. 1971, apptd 1971; 306 Barnsley Road, Wakefield WF2 6AX.

Provost

Very Rev. John Edward Allen, apptd 1982.

Canons Residentiary

C. Dawson, apptd 1982; R. D. Baxter, apptd 1986; I. C. Knox, apptd 1989.
Organist, J. L. Bielby, FRCO, apptd 1971.

Archdeacons

Halifax, Ven. D. Hallett, apptd 1989.
Pontefract, Ven. K. Unwin, apptd 1981.

Stipendiary Male Clergy, 211.
Stipendiary Women Deacons, 11.

Chancellor, G. B. Graham, QC, apptd 1959.
Registrar and Secretary, E. Chapman, Burton Street, Wakefield WF1 2DA.

THE CHURCH IN WALES

The Anglican Church was the established church in Wales from the 16th century until 1920, when the estrangement of the majority of Welsh people from Anglicanism, in particular in favour of Presbyterianism, resulted in disestablishment. Since then the Church in Wales has been an autonomous province consisting of six sees, with one of the diocesan bishops being elected Archbishop of Wales by an electoral college comprising elected lay and clerical members.

The legislative body of the Church in Wales is the Governing Body, which has 345 members in total, divided between the three orders of bishops, clergy and laity. It is presided over by the Archbishop of Wales and meets twice annually. Its decisions are binding upon all members of the Church. There are 120,892 members of the Church in Wales, with six bishops, about 600 clergy and 1,178 parishes.

THE GOVERNING BODY OF THE CHURCH IN WALES, 39 Cathedral Road, Cardiff CF1 9XF. (Tel: 0222–231638).—Sec. Gen., J. W. D. McIntyre.

ARCHBISHOP OF WALES, vacant.

BANGOR

79th Bishop, Rt. Rev. John Cledan Mears, b. 1922, cons. 1982, apptd 1982; Tŷ'r Esgob, Bangor LL57 2SS. Signs Cledan Bangor.

Stipendiary clergy, 70.

LLANDAFF

101st Bishop, Rt. Rev. Roy Thomas Davies, b. 1934, cons. 1985, apptd 1985; Llys Esgob, The Cathedral Green, Llandaff, Cardiff CF5 2YE. Signs Roy Landav.

Stipendiary clergy, 158.

MONMOUTH

Bishop, vacant (Bishopstow, Stow Hill, Newport NP9 4EA).

Stipendiary clergy, 110.

ST ASAPH

74th Bishop, Rt. Rev. Alwyn Rice Jones, *b.*, 1934, *cons.* 1982, *apptd* 1982; Esgobty, St Asaph, Clwyd LL17 0TW. *Signs* Alwyn St Asaph.

Stipendiary clergy, 112.

ST DAVID'S

Bishop, vacant (Llys Esgob, Abergwili, Dyfed SA31 2JG).

Stipendiary clergy, 129.

SWANSEA AND BRECON

7th Bishop, Rt. Rev. Dewi Morris Bridges, *b.* 1933, *cons.* 1988, *apptd* 1988; Ely Tower, Brecon, Powys LD3 9DE. *Signs* Dewi Swansea & Brecon.

Stipendiary clergy, 100.

(Stipend of diocesan bishop of the Church in Wales is £22,497 a year from Jan. 1, 1992.)

THE EPISCOPAL CHURCH IN SCOTLAND

The Episcopal Church in Scotland was founded after the Act of Settlement (1690) established the presbyterian nature of the Church of Scotland. The Episcopal Church is in full communion with the Church of England but is autonomous. The governing authority is the General Synod, an elected body of 160 members which meets once a year. The diocesan bishop who convenes and presides at meetings of the General Synod is called the Primus and is elected by his fellow bishops.

There are 61,000 members of the Episcopal Church in Scotland, of whom 35,281 are communicants. There are seven bishops, 206 clergy, and 341 churches and places of worship.

THE GENERAL SYNOD OF THE EPISCOPAL CHURCH IN SCOTLAND, 21 Grosvenor Crescent, Edinburgh EH12 5EE. (Tel: 031–225 6357).—*Sec.. Gen.,* J. G. Davies.

PRIMUS OF THE EPISCOPAL CHURCH IN SCOTLAND, Most Rev. George Henderson (Bishop of Argyll and the Isles), *elected* 1990.

The Rt. Rev. Bishops

Aberdeen and Orkney, Frederick Charles Darwent, *b.* 1927, *cons.* 1978, *apptd* 1978. *Clergy* 14.
Argyll and the Isles, George Kennedy Buchanan Henderson, *b.* 1921, *cons.* 1977, *apptd* 1977. *Clergy* 10.
Brechin, Robert Taylor Halliday, *b.* 1932, *cons.* 1990, *apptd* 1990. *Clergy* 17.
Edinburgh, Richard Frederick Holloway, *b.* 1933, *cons.* 1986, *apptd* 1986. *Clergy* 65.
Glasgow and Galloway, John Mitchell Taylor, *b.* 1932, *cons.* 1991, *apptd* 1991. *Clergy* 42.

Moray, Ross and Caithness, George Minshull Sessford, *b.* 1928, *cons.* 1970, *apptd* 1970. *Clergy* 17.
St Andrews, Dunkeld and Dunblane, Michael Geoffrey Hare-Duke, *b.* 1925, *cons.* 1969, *apptd* 1969. *Clergy* 30.

(Stipend of diocesan bishop of the Episcopal Church in Scotland is £15,210 in 1991.)

THE CHURCH OF IRELAND

The Anglican Church was the established church in Ireland from the 16th century but never secured the allegiance of a majority of the Irish, and was disestablished in 1871. The Church in Ireland is divided into the provinces of Armagh and Dublin, each under an archbishop. The provinces are subdivided into ten dioceses.

The legislative body is the General Synod, which has 660 members in total, divided between the House of Bishops and the House of Representatives. The Archbishop of Armagh is elected by the House of Bishops; other episcopal elections are made by an electoral college.

There are about 395,000 members of the Church of Ireland, with two archbishops, ten bishops, about 613 clergy and about 1,100 churches and places of worship.

CENTRAL OFFICE, Church of Ireland House, Church Avenue, Rathmines, Dublin 6. (Tel: 0001–978422).—*Asst. Sec. of the General Synod*, J. F. Buttimore.

PROVINCE OF ARMAGH

Archbishop of Armagh and Primate of All Ireland, Most Rev. Robert Henry Alexander Eames, PH.D., *b.* 1937, *cons.* 1975, *trs.* 1986. *Clergy* 55.

The Rt. Rev. Bishops

Clogher, Brian Desmond Anthony Hannon, *b.* 1936, *cons.* 1986, *apptd* 1986. *Clergy* 28.
Connor, Samuel Greenfield Poyntz, PH.D., *b.* 1926, *cons.* 1978, *trs.* 1987. *Clergy* 113.
Derry and Raphoe, James Mehaffey, PH.D., *b.* 1931, *cons.* 1980, *apptd* 1980. *Clergy* 54.
Down and Dromore, Gordon McMullan, PH.D., *b.* 1934, *cons.* 1980, *trs.* 1986. *Clergy* 117.
Kilmore, Elphin and Ardagh, William Gilbert Wilson, ph.D., *b.* 1918, *cons.* 1981, *apptd* 1981. *Clergy* 24.
Tuam, Killala and Achonry, John Robert Winder Neill, *b.* 1945, *cons.* 1986, *apptd* 1986. *Clergy* 10.

PROVINCE OF DUBLIN

Archbishop of Dublin, Bishop of Glendalough, and Primate of Ireland, Most Rev. Donald Arthur Caird, DD, *b.* 1925, *cons.* 1970, *trans.* 1976, 1985. *Clergy* 87.

The Rt. Rev. Bishops

Cashel and Ossory, Noel Vincent Willoughby, *b.* 1926, *cons.* 1980, *apptd* 1980. *Clergy* 35.
Cork, Cloyne and Ross, Robert Alexander Warke, *b.* 1930, *cons.* 1988, *apptd* 1988. *Clergy* 27.
Limerick and Killaloe, Edward Flewett Darling, *b.* 1933, *cons.* 1985, *apptd* 1985. *Clergy* 24.
Meath and Kildare, Most Rev. Walton Newcombe Francis Empey, *b.* 1934, *cons.* 1981, *trs.* 1985. *Clergy* 20.

ANGLICAN COMMUNION OVERSEAS

ANGLICAN CHURCH OF AUSTRALIA

Primate of Australia, vacant.

Province of New South Wales

Metropolitan

Archbishop of Sydney, The Most Rev. Donald William Bradley Robinson, *cons.* 1973, *trans.* 1982.

The Rt. Rev. Bishops

Armidale, P. Chiswell, *cons.* 1976, *apptd* 1976.
Bathurst, B. W. Wilson, *cons.* 1984, *trans.* 1989.
Canberra and Goulburn, O. D. Dowling, *cons.* 1981, *trans.* 1983.
Grafton, B. A. Schultz, *cons.* 1985, *apptd* 1985.
Newcastle, A. C. Holland, *cons.* 1970, *trans.* 1978.
Riverina, B. R. Hunter, *cons.* 1971, *apptd* 1971.

Province of Queensland

Metropolitan

Archbishop of Brisbane, The Most Rev. Peter Hollingworth, *cons.* 1985, *trans.* 1990.

The Rt. Rev. Bishops

Carpentaria, A. F. B. Hall-Matthews, *cons.* 1984.
North Queensland, H. J. Lewis, *cons.* 1971.
Northern Territory, vacant.
Rockhampton, G. A. Hearn, *cons.* 1981.

Province of South Australia

Metropolitan

Archbishop of Adelaide, The Most Rev. Ian Gordon George, *cons.* 1989, *trans.* 1991.

The Rt. Rev. Bishops

The Murray, G. H. Walden, *cons.* 1981, *trans.* 1989.
Willochra, W. D. H. McCall, *cons.* 1987, *apptd* 1987.

Province of Victoria

Metropolitan

Archbishop of Melbourne, The Most Rev. Keith Rayner, *cons.* 1969, *trans.* 1975, 1990.

The Rt. Rev. Bishops

Ballarat, J. Hazlewood, *cons.* 1975, *apptd* 1975.
Bendigo, vacant.
Gippsland, C. D. Sheumack, *cons.* 1987, *apptd* 1987.
Wangaratta, R. G. Beal, *cons.* 1985, *apptd* 1985.

Province of Western Australia

Metropolitan

Archbishop of Perth, The Most Rev. Peter Frederick Carnley, PH.D., *cons.* 1981, *apptd* 1981.

The Rt. Rev. Bishops

Bunbury, H. J. U. Jamieson, *cons.* 1974, *trans.* 1984.
North-west Australia, G. B. Muston, *cons.* 1971, *trans.* 1982.

Extra-Provincial Diocese

Tasmania, P. K. Newell, *cons.* 1982, *apptd* 1982.

EPISCOPAL CHURCH OF BRAZIL
(Igreja Episcopal Do Brasil)

Primate, The Most Rev. Olavo Ventura Luiz (Bishop of South Western Brazil), *cons.* 1976, *elected* 1986.

The Rt. Rev. Bishops

Brasilia, A. Santos, *cons.* 1989, *apptd* 1989.
Central Brazil, S. A. Ruiz, *cons.* 1985, *apptd* 1985.
Northern Brazil, C. E. Rodrigues, *cons.* 1985, *apptd* 1986.
Pelotas, L. O. P. Prado, *cons.* 1987, *apptd* 1989.
South Central Brazil, G. Soares de Lima, *cons.* 1989, *apptd* 1989.
Southern Brazil, C. V. S. Gastal, *cons.* 1984, *apptd* 1984.
South Western Brazil, (see above), *apptd* 1976.

CHURCH OF THE PROVINCE OF BURUNDI, RWANDA AND ZAIRE

Archbishop of Province, The Most Rev. Samuel Sindamuka (Bishop of Matana), *cons.* 1975, *apptd* 1989.

The Rt. Rev. Bishops

Boga Zaire, Byanka Njojo, *apptd* 1980.
Bujumbura, Pie Ntukamazina, *cons.* 1990, *apptd* 1990.
Bukavu, Balufuga Dirokpa, *apptd* 1982.
Butare, Justin Ndandali, *cons.* 1975, *apptd* 1975.
Buye, Samuel Ndayisenga, *apptd* 1979.
Gitega, Jean Nduwayo, *apptd* 1985.
Kigali, Adonia Sebununguri, *cons.* 1965.
Kisangani, Tibefa Mugera, *apptd* 1980.
Matana (see above).
Shaba, Mbona Kolini.
Shyira, Augustin Nshamihigo, *cons.* 1984, *apptd* 1984.

ANGLICAN CHURCH OF CANADA

Archbishop and Primate, The Most Rev. Michael Geoffrey Peers, *cons.* 1977, *trans.* 1986.

Province of British Columbia

Metropolitan

Archbishop of New Westminster, The Most Rev. Douglas Walter Hambidge, *cons.* 1969, *trans.* 1981.

The Rt. Rev. Bishops

British Columbia, Ronald Shepherd, *cons.* 1984, *apptd* 1984.
Caledonia, John Hannen, *cons.* 1981, *apptd* 1981.
Cariboo, vacant.
Kootenay, David Crawley, *cons.* 1990, *apptd* 1990.
Yukon, Ronald Ferris, *cons.* 1981, *apptd* 1981.

Province of Canada

Metropolitan

Archbishop of West Newfoundland, Most Rev. Stewart S. Payne, *cons.* 1978, *trans.* 1990.

The Rt. Rev. Bishops

Central Newfoundland, Edward Marsh, *cons.* 1990, *apptd* 1990.
Eastern Newfoundland and Labrador, Martin Mate, *cons.* 1980, *apptd* 1980.
Fredericton, George Lemon, *cons.* 1989, *apptd* 1989.
Montreal, Andrew Hutchison, *cons.* 1990, *apptd* 1990.
Nova Scotia, Arthur Peters, *cons.* 1981, *apptd* 1982.
Quebec, Bruce Stavert, *cons.* 1991, *apptd* 1991.
Western Newfoundland (see above).

Province of Ontario

Metropolitan

Archbishop of Niagara, The Most Rev. John Charles Bothwell, *cons.* 1971, *trans.* 1985.

The Rt. Rev. Bishops

Algoma, Leslie Peterson, *cons.* 1983, *apptd* 1983.

Huron, Percival O'Driscoll, *cons.* 1990, *apptd* 1990.
Moosonee, Caleb Lawrence, *cons.* 1980, *apptd* 1980.
Ontario, Allan Read, *cons.* 1972, *trans.* 1981.
Ottawa, Edwin Lackey, *cons.* 1981, *apptd* 1981.
Toronto, Terence Finlay, *cons.* 1986, *apptd* 1990.

Province of Rupert's Land

Metropolitan

Archbishop of Rupert's Land, The Most Rev. Walter Heath Jones, *cons.* 1970, *trans.* 1988.

The Rt. Rev. Bishops

Arctic, J. C. R. Williams, *cons.* 1987, *apptd* 1991.
Athabasca , Garry Woolsey, *cons.* 1983, *apptd* 1983.
Brandon, John Conlin, *cons.* 1975, *apptd* 1975.
Calgary, Barry Curtis, *cons.* 1983, *apptd* 1983.
Edmonton, Kenneth Genge, *cons.* 1988, *apptd* 1988.
Keewatin, vacant.
Qu' Appelle, Eric Bays, *cons.* 1986, *apptd* 1986.
Rupert's Land (see above).
Saskatchewan, Thomas Morgan, *cons.* 1985, *apptd* 1985.
Saskatoon, Roland Wood, *cons.* 1981, *apptd* 1981.

CHURCH OF THE PROVINCE OF CENTRAL AFRICA

Archbishop of Province, The Most Rev. Walter P. K. Makhulu (Bishop of Botswana), *cons.* 1979, *apptd* 1980.

The Rt. Rev. Bishops

Botswana (see above).
Central Zambia, Clement Shaba, *cons.* 1984, *apptd* 1984.
Harare, Ralph Hatendi, *cons.* 1979, *apptd* 1981.
Lake Malawi, Peter Nyanja, *cons.* 1978, *apptd* 1978.
The Lundi, Jonathan Siyachitema, *cons.* 1981, *apptd* 1981.
Lusaka, Stephen Mumba, *cons.* 1981, *apptd* 1981.
Manicaland, Elijah Masuko, *cons.* 1981, *apptd* 1981.
Matabeleland, Theophilus Naledi, *cons.* 1987, *apptd* 1987.
Northern Zambia, Bernard Malango, *cons.* 1988, *apptd* 1988.
Southern Malawi, Nathaniel Aipa, *cons.* 1987, *apptd* 1987.

CHURCH OF THE PROVINCE OF THE INDIAN OCEAN

Archbishop of Province, The Most Rev. French Chang-Him (Bishop of Seychelles), *cons.* 1979, *apptd* 1984.

The Rt. Rev. Bishops

Antananarivo, Remi Rabenirina, *cons.* 1984, *apptd* 1984.
Antsiranana, Keith Benzies, *cons.* 1982, *apptd* 1982.
Mauritius, Rex Donat, *cons.* 1984, *apptd* 1984.
Seychelles, (see above).
Toamasina, Donald Smith, *cons.* 1990, *apptd* 1990.

THE HOLY CATHOLIC CHURCH IN JAPAN (Nippon Sei Ko Kai)

Primate

The Most Rev. Christopher Ichiro Kikawada (Bishop of Osaka), *cons.* 1975, *apptd* 1986.

The Rt. Rev. Bishops

Chubu, Samuel Wataru Hoyo, *cons.* 1987, *apptd* 1987.
Hokkaido, Augustine Hideaki Amagi, *cons.* 1987, *apptd* 1987.
Kita Kanto, James Takashi Yashiro, *cons.* 1985, *apptd* 1985.

Kobe, vacant.
Kyoto, John Toshiharu Okano, *cons.* 1991, *apptd* 1991.
Kyushu, Joseph Noriaki Iida, *cons.* 1982, *apptd* 1982.
Okinawa, Paul Saneaki Nakamura, *cons.* 1972, *apptd* 1972.
Osaka, (see above).
Tohoku, Cornelius Yasuo Tazaki, *cons.* 1979, *apptd* 1979.
Tokyo, John Makoto Takeda, *cons.* 1988, *apptd* 1988.
Yokohama, Raphael Shiro Kajiwara, *cons.* 1984, *apptd* 1984.

THE EPISCOPAL CHURCH IN JERUSALEM AND THE MIDDLE EAST

President-Bishop, Rt. Rev. Samir Kafity, *apptd* 1986.
Jerusalem, Samir Kafity, *cons.* 1984.
Iran, Iraj Mottahedeh, *cons.* 1990.
Egypt, Ghais Abdel Malik, *cons.* 1984.
Cyprus and the Gulf, John Brown, *cons.* 1986.

CHURCH OF THE PROVINCE OF KENYA

Archbishop of Province, The Most Rev. Manasses Kuria (Bishop of Nairobi), *cons.* 1970, *apptd* 1980.

The Rt. Rev. Bishops

Eldoret, vacant.
Embu, Moses Njue.
Kirinyaga, David Gitari, *cons.* 1975, *apptd* 1975.
Machakos, Benjamin Nzimbi, *cons.* 1985, *apptd* 1985.
Maseno North, James Mundia, *cons.* 1970, *apptd* 1970.
Maseno South, Henry Okullu, *cons.* 1974, *apptd* 1974.
Maseno West, Daniel Omolo, *cons.* 1982, *apptd* 1985.
Mombasa, Crispus Nzano, *cons.* 1975, *apptd* 1981.
Mount Kenya Central, John Mahiaini, *cons.* 1984, *apptd* 1984.
Mount Kenya South, George Njuguna, *cons.* 1984, *apptd* 1985.
Nairobi, (see above).
Nakuru, vacant.
Nambale, Isaac Namango, *cons.* 1984, *apptd* 1987.

CHURCH OF THE PROVINCE OF MELANESIA

Archbishop of Province, The Most Rev. Amos Stanley Waiaru (Bishop of Central Melanesia), *cons.* 1981, *apptd* 1988.

The Rt. Rev. Bishops

Central Melanesia, (see above).
Hanuato'o, James Mason, *cons.* 1991, *apptd* 1991.
Malaita, Raymond Aumae, *cons.* 1990, *apptd* 1990.
Temotu, Lazarus Munamua, *cons.* 1987, *apptd* 1987.
Vanuatu, Michael Tavoa, *cons.* 1990, *apptd* 1990.
Ysabel, Ellison Pogo, *cons.* 1981, *apptd* 1981.

CHURCH OF THE PROVINCE OF MYANMAR

Archbishop of Province, The Most Rev. Andrew Mya Han (Bishop of Yangon), *cons.* 1988, *apptd* 1988.

The Rt. Rev. Bishops

Mandalay, T. Mya Wah, *cons.* 1984, *apptd* 1984.
Myitkyina, A. Hla Aung, *cons.* 1988, *apptd* 1988.
Hpa'an, G. Kyaw Mya, *cons.* 1979, *apptd* 1979.
Yangon (Rangoon), (see above).
Sittwe, B. Theaung Hawi, *cons.* 1978, *apptd* 1980.

CHURCH OF THE PROVINCE OF NEW ZEALAND

Primate

Archbishop of New Zealand, The Most Rev. Brian Newton Davis (Bishop of Wellington), *cons.* 1980, *apptd* 1986.

The Rt. Rev. Bishops

Aotearoa, W. Vercoe, *cons.* 1981, *apptd* 1981.
Auckland, Bruce Gilberd, *cons.* 1985, *apptd* 1985.
Christchurch, David Coles, *cons.* 1990, *apptd* 1990.
Dunedin, Penelope Jamieson, *cons.* 1990, *apptd* 1990.
Nelson, Derek Eaton, *cons.* 1990, *apptd* 1990.
Polynesia, Jabez Bryce, *cons.* 1975, *apptd* 1975.
Waiapu, vacant.
Waikato, Roger Herft, *cons.* 1986, *apptd* 1986.
Wellington, (*see* above).

CHURCH OF THE PROVINCE OF NIGERIA

Archbishop of the Province, The Most Rev. Abiodun Adetiloye, *apptd* 1988.

The Rt. Rev. Bishops

Aba, A. O. Iwuagwu, *apptd* 1985.
Abuja, Peter Akinola, *apptd* 1989.
Akoko, J. O. K. Olowokure, *apptd* 1986.
Akure, Emmanuel Gbonigi, *apptd* 1983.
Asaba, Roland Nwosu, *apptd* 1977.
Awka, Maxwell Anikwenwa, *apptd* 1987.
Bauchi, E. O. Chukwuma, *apptd* 1990.
Benin, John George, *apptd* 1985.
Egbado, Timothy Bolaji.
Egba-Egbado, T. I. Akintayo, *apptd* 1977.
Ekiti, C. A. Akinbola, *apptd* 1986.
Enugu, Gideon Otubelu, *apptd* 1969.
Ibadan, Gideon Olajide, *apptd* 1988.
Ife, Gabriel Oloniyo.
Ijebu, Abraham Olowoyo, *apptd* 1990.
Ijebu Remo, E. O. I. Ogundana, *apptd* 1984.
Ilesha, E. A. Ademowo, *apptd* 1989.
Jos, Timothy Adesola, *apptd* 1985.
Kaduna, Titus Ogbonyomi, *apptd* 1975.
Kafanchan, W. Diya, *apptd* 1990.
Kano, B. O. Omoseibi, *apptd* 1990.
Katsina, J. S. Kwasu, *apptd* 1990.
Kwara, Herbert Haruna, *apptd* 1974.
Lagos, Jospeh Adetiloye, *apptd* 1985.
Maiduguri, E. K. Mani, *apptd* 1990.
Makurdi, J. T. Iyangemar, *apptd* 1990.
Minna, J. A. Yisa, *apptd* 1990.
The Niger, Jonathan Onyemelukwe, *apptd* 1975.
Niger Delta, Samuel Elenwa, *apptd* 1981.
Okigwe/Orlu, Samuel Ebo, *apptd* 1984.
Ondo, Samuel Aderin, *apptd* 1981.
Osun, Seth Fagbemi, *apptd* 1987.
Owerri, Benjamin Nwankiti, *apptd* 1968.
Owo, Abraham Awosan, *apptd* 1983.
Sokoto, J. A. Idowu-Fearon, *apptd* 1990.
Warri, John Dafiewhare, *apptd* 1980.
Yola, C. O. Efobi, *apptd* 1990.

ANGLICAN CHURCH OF PAPUA NEW GUINEA

Archbishop of Province, The Most Rev. Bevan Meredith (Bishop of New Guinea Islands), *cons.* 1967, *apptd* 1990.

The Rt. Rev. Bishops

Aipo Rongo, Paul Richardson, *cons.* 1987, *apptd* 1987.
Dogura, Blake Kerina, *cons.* 1981, *apptd* 1990.
New Guinea Islands, (*see* above).
Popondota, Walter Siba, *cons.* 1990, *apptd* 1990.
Port Moresby, Isaac Gadebo, *cons.* 1983, *apptd* 1983.

PHILIPPINE EPISCOPAL CHURCH

Prime Bishop, Rt. Rev. Richard Abellon (Bishop of Northern Luzon).

The Rt. Rev. Bishops

Central Philippines, Manuel Capuyan Lumpias, *cons.* 1977, *apptd* 1978.

North Central Philippines, Artemio Masweng Zabala.
Northern Luzon, Richard Abellon, *cons.* 1975, *apptd* 1983.
Northern Philippines, Robert Lee Longid, *cons.* 1983, *apptd* 1983.
Southern Philippines, Narisco Ticobay, *cons.* 1986, *apptd* 1986.

CHURCH OF THE PROVINCE OF SOUTHERN AFRICA

Metropolitan

Archbishop of Cape Town, The Most Rev. Desmond Mpilo Boy Tutu, *cons.* 1976, *trans.* 1986.

The Rt. Rev. Bishops

Bloemfontein, Thomas Stanage, *cons.* 1978, *apptd* 1982.
Christ the King, Peter Lee, *cons.* 1990, *apptd* 1990.
George, Derek Damant, *cons.* 1985, *apptd* 1985.
Grahamstown, David Russell, *cons.* 1986, *apptd* 1987.
Johannesburg, Duncan Buchanan, *cons.* 1986, *apptd* 1986.
Kimberley and Kuruman, W. N. Ndungane, *cons.* 1991, *apptd* 1991.
Klerksdorp, David Nkwe, *cons.* 1990, *apptd* 1990.
Lebombo, Dinis Sengulane, *cons.* 1976, *apptd* 1976.
Lesotho, Philip Mokuku, *cons.* 1978, *apptd* 1978.
Namibia, James Kauluma, *cons.* 1978, *apptd* 1981.
Natal, Michael Nuttall, *cons.* 1975, *apptd* 1982.
Niassa, Paulino Manhique, *cons.* 1986, *apptd* 1986.
Port Elizabeth, Bruce Evans, *cons.* 1975, *apptd* 1975.
Pretoria, Richard Kraft, *cons.* 1982, *apptd* 1982.
St Helena, John Ruston, *cons.* 1985, *apptd* 1991.
St John's, Jacob Dlamini, *cons.* 1980, *apptd* 1985.
St Mark the Evangelist, Rollo Le Feuvre, *cons.* 1987, *apptd* 1987.
South Eastern Transvaal, David Beetge, *cons.* 1990, *apptd* 1990.
Swaziland, Bernard Mkhabela, *cons.* 1975, *apptd* 1975.
Zululand, Lawrence Zulu, *cons.* 1975, *apptd* 1975.

Order of Ethiopia, Sigqibo Dwane, *cons.* 1983, *apptd* 1983.

ANGLICAN CHURCH OF THE SOUTHERN CONE OF AMERICA

Presiding Bishop, Rt. Rev. Colin Bazley.

The Rt. Rev. Bishops

Argentina, David Leake.
Chile, Colin Bazley, *cons.* 1969, *apptd* 1977.
Northern Argentina, Maurice Sinclair.
Paraguay, John Ellison.
Peru, Alan Winstanley.
Uruguay, Harold Godfrey.

CHURCH OF THE PROVINCE OF THE SUDAN

Archbishop of Province, The Most Rev. Benjamina Wani Yugusuk (Bishop of Juba).

The Rt. Rev. Bishops

Bor, Nathaniel Garang.
Juba, (*see* above).
Kadugli, Mubarek Khamis.
Kajo-Kaji, Manasse Dawidi.
Khartoum, Bulus Idris Tia.
Maridi, Joseph Marona.
Mundri, Eluzai Munda.
Rumbek, Gabriel Jur.
Yei, Seme Solomona.
Yambio, Daniel Zindo, *cons.* 1984, *apptd* 1984.
Wau, Gabriel Jur (*acting*).

CHURCH OF THE PROVINCE OF TANZANIA

Archbishop of Province The Most Rev. John Acland Ramadhani (Bishop of Zanzibar and Tanga), *cons.* 1980, *apptd* 1984.

The Rt. Rev. Bishops

Central Tanganyika, Godfrey Mhogolo, *cons.* 1989, *apptd* 1989.
Dar es Salaam, Christopher Mlangwa, *cons.* 1984, *apptd* 1984.
Kagera, Christopher Ruhuza, *cons.* 1985, *apptd* 1985.
Mara, Gershom Nyaronga, *cons.* 1985, *apptd* 1985.
Masasi, Richard Norgate, *cons.* 1984, *apptd* 1984.
Morogoro, Dudley Mageni, *cons.* 1987, *apptd* 1987.
Mount Kilimanjaro, S. Makundi, *cons.* 1991, *apptd* 1991.
Mpwapwa, S. Chiwanga, *cons.* 1991, *apptd* 1991.
Rift Valley, A. Mohamed, *cons.* 1982, *apptd* 1991.
Ruaha, D. Mtetemela, *cons.* 1982, *apptd* 1990.
Ruvuma, Stanford Shauri, *cons.* 1989, *apptd* 1989.
South-west Tanganyika, Charles Mwaigoga, *cons.* 1983, *apptd* 1983.
Tabora, Francis Ntiruka, *cons.* 1989, *apptd* 1989.
Victoria Nyanza, vacant.
Western Tanganyika, George Mpango, *cons.* 1983, *apptd* 1983.
Zanzibar and Tanga, (see above).

CHURCH OF THE PROVINCE OF UGANDA

Archbishop of the Province, The Most Rev. Dr Yona Okoth (Bishop of Kampala), *cons.* 1972, *apptd* 1984.

The Rt. Rev. Bishops

Bukedi, Nicodemus Okille, *apptd* 1984.
Bunyoro-Kitara, Wilson Turumanya, *apptd* 1981.
Busoga, Cyprian Bamwoze, *apptd* 1972.
East Ankole, Amos Betungura, *apptd* 1970.
Kampala, (see above).
Karamoja, Peter Lomongin, *apptd* 1987.
Kigezi, William Rukirande.
Lango, Melchizedek Otim, *apptd* 1976.
Madi and West Nile, vacant.
Mbale, Akisoferi Wesonga, *apptd* 1981.
Mityana, Nelson Mutebi, *apptd* 1977.
Mukono, Livingstone Mpalanyi-Nkoyoyo, *apptd* 1985.
Namirembe, Misaeri Kauma, *apptd* 1985.
North Kigezi, Yustasi Ruhindi, *apptd* 1981.
Northern Uganda, Benon Ogwal-Abwang, *apptd* 1974.
Ruwenzori, Eustace Kamanyire, *apptd* 1981.
Soroti, Geresom Ilukor, *apptd* 1976.
South Ruwenzori, Zebidee Masereka.
West Ankole, Yorumu Bamunoba, *apptd* 1977.
West Buganda, Christopher Senyonjo, *apptd* 1974.

EPISCOPAL CHURCH IN THE USA

Presiding Bishop and Primate, Most Rev. Edmond Lee Browning, DD, *cons.* 1968, *apptd* 1986.

Rt. Rev. Bishops
(*Missionary Diocese)

Province I

Connecticut, Arthur E. Walmsley, *cons.* 1979, *apptd* 1981.
Maine, Edward C. Chalfant, *cons.* 1984, *apptd* 1986.
Massachusetts, David E. Johnson, *cons.* 1985, *apptd* 1986.
New Hampshire, Douglas E. Theuner, *cons.* 1986, *apptd* 1986.
Rhode Island, George N. Hunt, *cons.* 1980, *apptd* 1980.
Vermont, Daniel L. Swensen, *cons.* 1986, *apptd* 1987.
Western Massachusetts, Andrew F. Wissemann, *cons.* 1984, *apptd* 1984.

Province II

Albany, David S. Ball, *cons.* 1984, *apptd* 1984.
Central New York, O'Kelley Whitaker, *cons.* 1981, *apptd* 1983.
Europe, Convocation of American Churches in, Matthew P. Bigliardi.
Haiti, Luc A. J. Garnier, *cons.* 1971, *apptd* 1971.
Long Island, Robert C. Witcher, *cons.* 1975, *apptd* 1977.
New Jersey, G. P. Mellick Belshaw, *cons.* 1975, *apptd* 1983.
New York, Richard Grein, *cons.* 1981, *apptd* 1989.
Newark, John S. Spong, *cons.* 1976, *apptd* 1979.
Rochester, William G. Burrill, *cons.* 1984, *apptd* 1984.
Virgin Islands, Don. E. Taylor, *cons.* 1987, *apptd* 1987.
Western New York, David C. Bowman, *cons.* 1986, *apptd* 1987.

Province III

Bethlehem, J. Mark Dyer, *cons.* 1982, *apptd* 1983.
Central Pennsylvania, Charles F. McNutt, *cons.* 1980, *apptd* 1982.
Delaware, C. Cabell Tennis, *cons.* 1986, *apptd* 1986.
Easton, Elliott L. Sorge, *cons.* 1971, *apptd* 1983.
Maryland, A. Theodore Eastman, *cons.* 1982, *apptd* 1986.
North-western Pennsylvania, Robert D. Rowley jun.
Pennsylvania, Allen L. Bartlett, *cons.* 1986, *apptd* 1987.
Pittsburgh, Alden M. Hathaway, *cons.* 1981, *apptd* 1983.
Southern Virginia, C. Charles Vaché, *cons.* 1976, *apptd* 1978.
South-western Virginia, Arthur H. Light, *cons.* 1979, *apptd* 1979.
Virginia, Peter J. Lee, *cons.* 1984, *apptd* 1985.
Washington, Ronald Haines.
West Virginia, John H. Smith, *cons.* 1989, *apptd* 1989.

Province IV

Alabama, Robert O. Miller, *cons.* 1988, *apptd* 1988.
Atlanta, Frank K. Allan, *cons.* 1988, *apptd* 1989.
Central Florida, John Howe.
Central Gulf Coast, Charles F. Duvall, *cons.* 1981, *apptd* 1981.
East Carolina, B. Sidney Sanders, *cons.* 1979, *apptd* 1983.
East Tennessee, William E. Sanders, *cons.* 1979, *apptd* 1985.
Florida, Frank S. Cerveny, *cons.* 1974, *apptd* 1975.
Georgia, Harry W. Shipps, *cons.* 1984, *apptd* 1985.
Kentucky, David B. Reed, *cons.* 1964, *apptd* 1974.
Lexington, Don A. Wimberley, *cons.* 1984, *apptd* 1985.
Louisiana, James B. Brown, *cons.* 1976, *apptd* 1976.
Mississippi, Duncan M. Gray jun., *cons.* 1974, *apptd* 1974.
North Carolina, Robert W. Estill, *cons.* 1980, *apptd* 1983.
South Carolina, Edward Salmon jun.
South-east Florida, Calvin O. Schofield jun., *cons.* 1979, *apptd* 1980.
South-west Florida, Roger Harris, *cons.* 1989, *apptd* 1989.
Tennessee, George L. Reynolds, *cons.* 1985, *apptd* 1985.
Upper South Carolina, William A. Beckham, *cons.* 1979, *apptd* 1979.
West Tennessee, Alex D. Dickson jun., *cons.* 1983, *apptd* 1983.
Western Louisiana, Robert Hargrove jun.
Western North Carolina, Robert Johnson.

Province V

Chicago, Frank T. Griswold III, cons. 1985, apptd 1987.
Eau Claire, William C. Wantland, cons. 1980, apptd 1980.
Fond Du Lac, William L. Stevens, cons. 1980, apptd 1980.
Indianapolis, Edward W. Jones, cons. 1977, apptd 1977.
Michigan, R. Stewart Wood, cons. 1990, apptd 1990.
Milwaukee, Roger J. White, cons. 1984, apptd 1985.
Missouri, Hayes Rockwell.
Northern Indiana, Francis C. Gray, cons. 1986, apptd 1987.
Northern Michigan, Thomas K. Ray, cons. 1982, apptd 1982.
Ohio, James R. Moodey, cons. 1983, apptd 1984.
Quincy, Edward Macburney.
Southern Ohio, William G. Black, cons. 1979, apptd 1980.
Springfield, Donald M. Hultstrand, cons. 1982, apptd 1982.
Western Michigan, Edward L. Lee jun., cons. 1989, apptd 1989.

Province VI

Colorado, William Winterrowd.
Iowa, C. Christopher Epting, cons. 1988, apptd 1988.
Minnesota, Robert M. Anderson, cons. 1978, apptd 1978.
Montana, Charles I. Jones, cons. 1986, apptd 1986
Nebraska, James E. Krotz, cons. 1989, apptd 1989.
*North Dakota, Andrew H. Fairfield, cons. 1990, apptd 1990.
South Dakota, Craig B. Anderson, cons. 1984, apptd 1984.
Wyoming, Bob G. Jones, cons. 1977, apptd 1977.

Province VII

Arkansas, Herbert A. Donovan jun., cons. 1980, apptd 1981.
Dallas, Donis D. Patterson, cons. 1983, apptd 1983.
Fort Worth, Clarence C. Pope jun., cons. 1985, apptd 1986.
Kansas, William E. Smalley, cons. 1989, apptd 1989.
North-west Texas, Sam B. Hulsey, cons. 1980, apptd 1980.
Oklahoma, Robert M. Moodey, cons. 1988, apptd 1989.
Rio Grande, Terence Kelshaw, cons. 1989, apptd 1989.
Texas, Maurice M. Benitez, cons. 1980, apptd 1980.
West Missouri, John C. Buchanan, cons. 1989, apptd 1989.
West Texas, John H. MacNaughton, cons. 1986, apptd 1987.
Western Kansas, John F. Ashby, cons. 1981, apptd 1981.

Province VIII

Alaska, Stephen Charleston.
Arizona, Joseph T. Heistand, cons. 1976, apptd 1979.
California, William E. Swing, cons. 1979, apptd 1980.
El Camino Real, Richard L. Skimpfky.
Eastern Oregon, Rustin R. Kimsey, cons. 1980, apptd 1980.
Hawaii, Donald P. Hart, cons. 1986, apptd 1986.
Idaho, John Thornton.
Los Angeles, Frederick L. Borsch, cons. 1988, apptd 1988.
*Navajoland Area Mission, Steven T. Plummer, cons. 1989, apptd 1989.
Nevada, Stewart C. Zabriskie, cons. 1986, apptd 1986.
Northern California, John L. Thompson III, cons. 1978, apptd 1978.

Olympia, Vincent W. Warner, cons. 1989, apptd 1990.
Oregon, Robert L. Ladehoff, cons. 1985, apptd 1986.
San Diego, C. Brinkley Morton, cons. 1982, apptd 1982.
San Joaquin, John-David Schofield, cons. 1988, apptd 1989.
Spokane, Frank Terry.
*Taiwan, John C. T. Chien, cons. 1988, apptd 1988.
Utah, George E. Bates, cons. 1986, apptd 1986.

Province IX

*Central Ecuador, Neptali Larrea Moreno.
*Colombia, Bernardo Merino-Botero, cons. 1979, apptd 1979.
Cuernavaca, Jose G. Saucedo, cons. 1958, apptd 1989.
*Dominican Republic, Telesfaro A. Isaac, cons. 1972, apptd 1972.
*Guatemala, Armando Guerra-Soria, cons. 1982, apptd 1982.
*Honduras, Leopold Frade, cons. 1984, apptd 1984.
*Mexico, Sergio Cananga-Gomez, cons. 1989, apptd 1989.
*Nicaragua, Sturdie W. Downs, cons. 1985, apptd 1985.
*Northern Mexico, German Martinez-Marquez, cons. 1987, apptd 1987.
*Panama, James H. Ottley, cons. 1984, apptd 1984.
*El Salvador, James H. Ottley, cons. 1984, apptd 1989.
*South-east Mexico, Claro Huerta-Rames, cons. 1980, apptd 1989.
*Western Mexico, Samuel Espinoza-Venegas, cons. 1981, apptd 1983.

Extra-Provincial

Costa Rica, Cornelius J. Wilson, cons. 1978, apptd 1978.
Puerto Rico, David Alvarez.
Venezuela, Onell A. Soto, cons. 1987, apptd 1987.

CHURCH OF THE (ON-GOING) PROVINCE OF WEST AFRICA

Archbishop of Province, The Most Rev. George Daniel Browne, DD, (Bishop of Liberia), cons. 1970, apptd 1982.

The Rt. Rev. Bishops

Accra, Francis Thompson, cons. 1983, apptd 1983.
Bo, Michael Keili, OBE, cons. 1981, apptd 1981.
Cape Coast, vacant.
Freetown, Prince Thompson, cons. 1981, apptd 1981.
Gambia, Solomon Johnson, cons. 1990, apptd 1990.
Guinea, vacant.
Koforidua, Robert Okine, cons. 1981, apptd 1981.
Kumasi, Edmund Yeboah, cons. 1985, apptd 1985.
Liberia, (see above)
Sekondi, Theophilus Annobil, cons. 1981, apptd 1981.
Sunyani/Tamale, Joseph Dadson, cons. 1981, apptd 1981.
The Anglican Church of Cameroon is a missionary area of the Province.

CHURCH IN THE PROVINCE OF THE WEST INDIES

Archbishop of Province, The Most Rev. Orland Lindsay (Bishop of North-eastern Caribbean and Aruba), cons. 1970, apptd 1986.

The Rt. Rev. Bishops

Barbados, Drexel Gomez, cons. 1972, apptd 1972.
Belize, Desmond Smith, cons. 1989, apptd 1989.
Guyana, Randolph George, cons. 1976, apptd 1980.
Jamaica, Neville de Souza, cons. 1973, apptd 1979.

Nassau and the Bahamas, Michael Eldon, CMG, *cons.* 1971, *apptd* 1972.
North-eastern Caribbean and Aruba (*see above*).
Trinidad and Tobago, Clive Abdulah, *cons.* 1970, *apptd* 1970.
Windward Islands, Philip Elder, *cons.* 1966.

OTHER CHURCHES AND EXTRA-PROVINCIAL DIOCESES

Anglican Church of Bermuda, Rt. Rev. William Down, *apptd* 1990.
Episcopal Church of Cuba, Rt. Rev. Emilio Hernandez Albalate.
Anglican Church in Korea:
  Pusan, Rt. Rev. Bundo Kim, *apptd* 1988.

Seoul, Rt. Rev. Simon Kim.
  Taejon, Rt. Rev. Paul Hwan Yoon, *apptd* 1988.
Hong Kong and Macao, Rt. Rev. Peter Kwong.
Kuching, Rt. Rev. Datuk John Leong Chee Yun.
Sabah, Rt. Rev. Yong Ping Chung.
Singapore, Rt. Rev. Moses Leng Kong Tay, *apptd* 1982.
West Malaysia, Rt. Rev. Tan Sri John Savarimuthu, *apptd* 1973.
Lusitanian Church (Portuguese Episcopal Church), Rt. Rev. Fernando Soares, *apptd* 1971.
Spanish Reformed Church, Rt. Rev. Arturo Sánchez Galan, *apptd* 1982.

THE ROMAN CATHOLIC CHURCH

The Roman Catholic Church is one world-wide Christian Church acknowledging as its head the Bishop of Rome, known as the Pope (Father). The Pope is held to be the successor of St Peter and thus invested with the power which was entrusted to St Peter by Jesus Christ. A direct line of succession is therefore claimed from the earliest Christian communities. Papal authority over the doctrine and jurisdiction of the Church in western Europe developed early and was unrivalled after the split with the Eastern Orthodox Church until the Protestant Reformation in the 16th century. With the fall of the Roman Empire the Pope also became an important political leader. His temporal power is now limited to the 107 acres of the Vatican City State.

The Pope exercises spiritual authority over the Church with the advice and assistance of the Sacred College of Cardinals, the supreme council of the Church. He is also advised about the concerns of the Church locally by his ambassadors, who liaise with the Bishops' Conference in each country.

In addition to advising the Pope, those members of the Sacred College of Cardinals who are under the age of 80 also elect a successor following the death of a Pope. The assembly of the Cardinals at the Vatican for the election of a new Pope is known as the Conclave in which, in complete seclusion, the Cardinals elect by a secret ballot; a two-thirds majority is necessary before the vote can be accepted as final. When a Cardinal receives the necessary votes, the Dean of the Sacred College formally asks him if he will accept election and the name by which he wishes to be known. On his acceptance of the office the Conclave is dissolved and the First Cardinal Deacon announces the election to the assembled crowd in St Peter's Square. On the first Sunday or Holyday following the election, the new Pope assumes the pontificate at High Mass in St Peter's Square. A new pontificate is dated from the assumption of the pontificate.

The number of cardinals was fixed at 70 by Pope Sixtus V in 1586, but has been steadily increased since the pontificate of John XXIII and now stands at 164 (as at June 28, 1991). The governing body of the Church is the Curia, which is made up of the Secretariat of State, the Sacred Council for the Public Affairs of the Church, and various congregations, secretariats and tribunals assisted by commissions and offices. All are headed by cardinals.

The Vatican State has its own diplomatic service, with representatives known as nuncios. Papal nuncios with full diplomatic recognition are given precedence over all other ambassadors to the country

to which they are appointed; where precedence is not recognized, as in Britain, the Papal representative is known as a pro-nuncio. Where the representation is only to the local churches and not to the government of a country, the Papal representative is known as an Apostolic Delegate. The Roman Catholic Church has an estimated 890,907,000 adherents world-wide.

SOVEREIGN PONTIFF

His Holiness Pope John Paul II (Karol Wojtyla), *born* Wadowice, Poland, May 18, 1920; *ordained priest* 1946; *appointed Archbishop* of Krakow 1964; *created Cardinal* 1967; *assumed Pontificate* Oct. 16, 1978.

GREAT BRITAIN AND IRELAND

The Roman Catholic Church in England and Wales is governed by the Bishops' Conference, membership of which includes the Diocesan Bishops, the Apostolic Exarch of the Ukrainians, the Bishop of the Forces and the Auxiliary Bishops; the Conference is headed by the President (Cardinal Basil Hume, Archbishop of Westminster) and Vice-President (Archbishop Worlock, Archbishop of Liverpool). There are five departments, each with an episcopal chairman: the Department for Christian Life and Worship (the Archbishop of Southwark), the Department for Mission and Unity (the Bishop of East Anglia), the Department for Christian Doctrine and Formation (the Bishop of Leeds), the Department for Christian Responsibility and Citizenship (the Bishop of Middlesbrough), and the Department for International Affairs (the Bishop of Salford).

The Bishops' Standing Committee, made up of all the Archbishops and the chairman of each of the above departments, has general responsibility for continuity and policy between the plenary sessions of the Conference. It prepares the Conference agenda and implements its decisions. It is serviced by a General Secretariat. There are also agencies and consultative bodies affiliated to the Conference.

The Bishops' Conference of Scotland has as its president Archbishop Winning of Glasgow and is the permanently constituted assembly of the Bishops of Scotland. To promote its work, the Conference establishes various agencies which have an advisory function in relation to the Conference. The more important of these agencies are called Commissions and each one has a Bishop President who, with the other members of the Commissions, are appointed by the Conference.

The Irish Episcopal Conference has as its Acting President Archbishop Connell of Dublin. Its membership comprises all the Archbishops and Bishops of Ireland and it appoints various Commissions to assist it in its work. There are three types of Commissions: (a) those made up of lay and clerical members chosen for their skills and experience, and staffed by full-time expert secretariats; (b) Commissions whose members are selected from existing institutions and whose services are supplied on a part-time basis; and (c) Commissions of Bishops only.

The Roman Catholic Church in Britain and Ireland has an estimated 8,992,092 members, 11 archbishops, 67 bishops, 12,698 priests, and 8,588 churches and chapels open to the public.

Catholic Bishops' Conferences secretariats:

ENGLAND AND WALES, 39 Eccleston Square, SW1V 1PD. Tel: 071-630 8279. *Gen. Sec.*, Mgr. Vincent Nichols.

SCOTLAND, Candida Casa, 8 Corsehill Road, Ayr, Scotland KA7 2ST. Tel: 0292-256750. *Gen. Sec.*, Rt. Rev. Maurice Taylor, Bishop of Galloway.

IRELAND, Iona, 67 Newry Road, Dundalk, Co. Louth. *Exec. Sec.*, Rev. Gerard Clifford.

GREAT BRITAIN

Apostolic Pro-Nuncio to the United Kingdom of Great Britain and Northern Ireland, The Most Revd Luigi Barbarito.

England and Wales

The Most Revd Archbishops

	Cons.	Clgy.
Westminster, HE Cardinal Basil Hume ...	1976	839
Auxil., John Crowley	1986	
Auxil., Victor Guazzelli	1970	
Auxil., Gerald Mahon	1970	
Auxil., James J. O'Brien	1977	
Birmingham, Maurice Couve de Murville (1982)	1982	426
Auxil., Terence Brain	1991	
Auxil., Philip Pargeter	1989	
Cardiff, John A. Ward (1983)	1981	163
Liverpool, Derek Worlock (1976)	1965	515
Auxil., Kevin O'Connor	1979	
Auxil., John Rawsthorne	1981	
Auxil., Vincent Malone	1989	
Southwark, Michael Bowen (1977)	1970	518
Auxil., Charles Henderson	1972	
Auxil., Howard Tripp	1980	
Auxil., John Jukes	1980	

The Rt. Rev. Bishops

	Cons.	Clgy.
Arundel and Brighton, Cormac Murphy-O'Connor	1977	255
Brentwood, Thomas McMahon (1980)	1980	188
Clifton, Mervyn Alexander (1975)	1972	242
East Anglia, Alan Clark (1976)	1969	112
Hallam, Gerald Moverley (1980)	1968	100
Hexham and Newcastle, Hugh Lindsay (1974)	1969	309
Auxil., Owen Swindelhurst	1977	
Lancaster, John Brewer (1985)	1971	228
Leeds, David Konstant (1985)	1977	225
Menevia (Wales), Daniel Mullins (1987)	1970	59
Middlesbrough, Augustine Harris (1978)	1966	201
Auxil., Thomas O'Brien	1981	
Northampton, Patrick Leo McCartie	1977	
Nottingham, James McGuinness (1975)	1972	224
Plymouth, Christopher Budd	1986	168
Portsmouth, F. Crispian Hollis (1989)	1987	282
Salford, Patrick Kelly	1984	455
Shrewsbury, Joseph Gray (1980)	1969	226

	Cons.	Clgy.
Wrexham (Wales), James Hannigan (1987)	1983	94

Scotland

The Most Revd Archbishops

	Cons.	Clgy.
St Andrews and Edinburgh, Keith Patrick O'Brian	1985	213
Auxil., Kevin Rafferty	1990	
Glasgow, Thomas Winning (1974)	1972	338
Auxil., Charles Renfrew	1977	

The Rt. Rev. Bishops

	Cons.	Clgy.
Aberdeen, Mario Conti	1977	59
Argyll and the Isles, Roderick Wright	1990	35
Dunkeld, Vincent Logan	1981	67
Galloway, Maurice Taylor	1981	75
Motherwell, Joseph Devine (1983)	1977	190
Paisley, John A. Mone (1988)	1984	98

IRELAND

There is one hierarchy for the whole of Ireland. Several of the dioceses have territory partly in the Republic of Ireland and partly in Northern Ireland. *Nuncio to Ireland*, Most Revd Emanuele Gerada (titular Archbishop of Nomenta).

The Most Rev. Archbishops

	Cons.	Clgy.
Armagh, HE Cardinal Cahal B. Daly	1990	271
Auxil., Gerard Clifford	1991	
Cashel, Dermot Clifford	1986	122
Dublin, Desmond Connell (1988)	1988	994
Auxil., Donal Murray	1982	
Auxil., Dermot O'Mahony	1975	
Auxil., Eamonn Walsh	1990	
Auxil., Desmond Williams	1985	
Tuam, Joseph Cassidy (1987)	1979	165

The Rt. Rev. Bishops

	Cons.	Clgy.
Achonry, Thomas Flynn	1975	55
Ardagh and Clonmacnois, Colm O'Reilly	1983	108
Clogher, Joseph Duffy	1979	124
Clonfert, Joseph Kirby	1988	76
Cloyne, John Magee	1987	155
Cork and Ross, Michael Murphy	1976	360
Auxil., John Buckley	1984	
Derry, Edward Daly	1974	149
Auxil., Francis Lagan	1988	
Down and Connor, Patrick J. Walsh	1991	324
Auxil., Anthony Farquhar	1983	
Auxil., William Philbin	1991	
Dromore, Francis Brooks	1976	71
Elphin, Dominic Conway	1970	104
Ferns, Brendon Comiskey	1980	148
Galway and Kilmacduagh, Eamonn Casey	1969	134
Kerry, Dermot O'Sullivan	1985	143
Kildare and Leighlin, Laurence Ryan	1984	225
Killala, Thomas Finnegan	1970	51
Killaloe, Michael Harty	1967	186
Kilmore, Francis McKiernan	1972	103
Limerick, Jeremiah Newman	1974	234
Meath, Michael Smith (1990)	1984	270
Ossory, Laurence Forristal	1980	125
Raphoe, Seamus Hegarty	1984	102
Waterford and Lismore, Michael Russell	1965	206

RESIDENTIAL ARCHBISHOPRICS THROUGHOUT THE WORLD

This list is set out with the name of the relevant country first; then the name of the diocese; and finally the Archbishop's name. It does not include

England and Wales, Scotland or Ireland which are above.

Albania

Durrës, vacant. (Apostolic Administrator, Mgr. Nicola Troshani).
Shkodër, vacant. (Apostolic Administrator, Mgr. Ernesto Coba).

Algeria

Algiers, Henri Teissier.

Angola

Huambo, Francisco Viti.
Luanda, HE Cardinal Alexandre do Nascimento.
Lubango, Manuel Franklin da Costa.

Argentina

Bahia Blanca, Romulo Garcia.
Buenos Aires, HE Cardinal Antonio Quarracino.
Córdoba, HE Cardinal Raúl Francisco Primatesta.
Corrientes, Fortunato A. Rossi.
La Plata, Carlos Galán.
Mendoza, Candido Genaro Rubiolo.
Paraná, Estanislao Esteban Karlic.
Resistencia, Juan J. Iriarte.
Rosario, Jorge Manuel López.
Salta, Moises J. Blanchoud.
San Juan de Cuyo, Italo Severino Di Stefano.
Santa Fe, Edgardo Gabriel Storni.
Tucumán, Horatio A. Bozzoli.

Australia

Adelaide, Leonard Anthony Faulkner.
Brisbane, Francis Roberts Rush.
Canberra, Francis P. Carroll.
Hobart, Joseph E. D'Arcy.
Melbourne, Thomas Francis Little.
Perth, vacant.
Sydney, HE Cardinal Edward B. Clancy.

Austria

Salzburg, Georg Eder.
Vienna, HE Cardinal Hans Hermann Groer.

Bangladesh

Dhaka, Michael Rozario.

Belgium

Malines-Bruxelles, HE Cardinal Godfried Danneels.

Benin

Cotonou, Isidore de Souzá.

Bolivia

Cochabamba, Rene Fernandez Apaza.
La Paz, Luis Sainz Hinojosa.
Santa Cruz de la Sierra, Julio T. Sandoval.
Sucre, Jesus G. Pérez Rodriguez.

Brazil

Aparacida, Geraldo Maria de Morais Penido.
Aracaju, Luciano José Cabral Duarte.
Bélem do Pará, Vicente Joaquim Zico.
Belo Horizonte, Serafim Fernandes de Araújo.
Botucatu, Antonio M. Mucciolo.
Brasilia, HE Cardinal Jose Freire Falcao.
Campinas, Gilberto Pereira Lopes.
Campo Grande, Vitorio Pavanello.
Cascavel, Armando Cirio.
Cuiaba, Bonifacio Piccinini.
Curitiba, Pedro Antonio Fedalto.
Diamantina, Geraldo Majelo Reis.
Florianópolis, Eusebio Oscar Scheid.
Fortaleza, HE Cardinal Aloisio Lorscheider.
Goiania, Antonio Ribeiro de Oliveira.
Juiz de Fora, Clovis Frainer.

Londrina, Geraldo Majela Agnelo.
Maceió, Edvaldo G. Amaral.
Manaus, vacant.
Mariana, Luciano Mendes de Almeida.
Maringá, Jaime Luis Coelho.
Natal, Alair V. Fernandes de Melo.
Niteroi, Carlos A. Navarro.
Olinda & Recife, José Cardoso Sobrinho.
Paraiba, José M. Pires.
Porto Alegre, Claudio Colling.
Porto Velho, José Martins da Silva.
Pouso Alegre, João Bergese.
Ribeirão Preto, Arnaldo Ribeiro.
São Luis do Maranhão, Paulo Eduardo Andrade Ponte.
São Paulo, HE Cardinal Paulo Evaristo Arns.
São Salvador da Bahia, HE Cardinal Lucas Moreira Neves.
São Sebastião do Rio de Janeiro, HE Cardinal Eugenio de Araújo Sales.
Teresina, Miguel F. Camara Filho.
Uberaba, Benedito de Ulhôa Vieira.
Vitória, Silvestre L. Scandian.

Burkina

Ouagadougou, HE Cardinal Paul Zoungrana.

Burundi

Gitega, Joachim Ruhuna.

Cameroon

Bamenda, Paul Verdzekov.
Douala, Simon Tonyé.
Garoua, HE Cardinal Christian W. Tumi.
Yaoundé, Jean Zoa.

Canada

Edmonton, Joseph N. MacNeil.
Gatineau-Hull, Roger Ebacher.
Grouard-McLennon, Henri Légaré.
Halifax, Austin-Emile Burke.
Keewatin-Le Pas, Peter Alfred Sutton.
Kingston, Francis John Spence.
Moncton, Donat Chiasson.
Montreal, Jean-Claude Turcotte.
Ottawa, Marcel A. Gervais.
Quebec, Maurice Couture.
Regina, Charles Halpin.
Rimouski, Gilles Ouellet.
St Boniface, Antoine Hacault.
St Johns, Newfoundland, James H. MacDonald.
Sherbrooke, Jean Marie Fortier.
Toronto, Aloysius Matthew Ambrosic.
Vancouver, Adam J. Exner.
Winnipeg, Ukrainian Rite–Maxim Hermaniuk.

Central African Republic

Bangui, Joachim N'Dayen.

Chad

Ndjamena, Charles Vandame.

Chile

Antofagasta, Patricio Infante Alfonso.
Concepción, Antonio M. Casamitjana.
La Serena, Francisco J. C. Huneeus.
Puerto Montt, Savino B. C. Bertollo.
Santiago de Chile, Carlos Oviedo Cavada.

China

Anking, Huai-Ning, vacant.
Canton, Dominic Tang Yee-Ming.
Changsha, vacant.
Chungking, vacant.
Foochow, Min-Hou, vacant.
Hangchow, vacant.
Hankow, vacant.

Kaifeng, vacant.
Kunming, vacant.
Kweiyang, vacant.
Lanchow, vacant.
Mukden, vacant.
Nanchang, vacant.
Nanking, vacant.
Nanning, vacant.
Peking, vacant.
Sian, vacant.
Suiyüan, Francis Wang Hsueh-Ming.
Taiyuan, vacant; Archbishop Emeritus Dominic Luke Capozi (expelled April 11, 1946, now living in Nazareth, Israel).
Tsinan, vacant.

Colombia

Barranquilla, Felix Maria Torres Parra.
Bogotá, HE Cardinal Mario Revollo Bravo.
Bucaramanga, Hector Rueda Hernández.
Cali, Pedro Rubiano Sáenz.
Cartagena, Carlos Jose Ruiseco Vieira.
Ibague, José Joaquin Flórez Hernández.
Manizales, José de Jesús Pimiento Rodriguez.
Medellin, vacant.
Nueva Pamplona, Rafael Sarmiento Peralta.
Popayán, Alberto G. Jaramillo.
Sante Fe de Antioquia, Eladio Acosta Arteaga.
Tunja, Augusto Trujillo Arango.

Congo

Brazzaville, Barthélémy Batantu.

Costa Rica

San José, Román Arrieta Villalobos.

Côte d'Ivoire

Abidjan, HE Cardinal Bernard Yago.

Cuba

San Cristóbal de la Habana, Jaime Lucas Ortega y Alamino.
Santiago de Cuba, Pedro Meurice Estiu.

Cyprus

Cyprus (Maronite Seat at Nicosia), Boutros Gemayel.

Czechoslovakia

Olomouc, František Vanak.
Praha, Miloslav Vlk.
Trnava, Jan Sokol.

Dominican Republic

Santo Domingo, HE Cardinal Nicolás de Jesús López Rodriguez.

Ecuador

Cuenca, Alberto Luna Tobar.
Guayaquil, Ignacio Larrea Holguin.
Quito, Antonio J. González Zumárraga.

Equatorial Guinea

Malabo, Idlefonso Obama Obono.

Ethiopia

Addis Ababa, HE Cardinal Paul Tzadua.

France

Aix, Bernard Panafieu.
Albi, Roger Meindre.
Auch, Gabriel Vanel.
Avignon, Raymond Bouchex.
Besançon, Lucien Daloz.
Bordeaux, Pierre Eyt.
Bourges, Pierre Plateau.
Cambrai, Jacques Delaporte.
Chambéry, Claude Feidt.

Lyon, HE Cardinal Albert Decourtray.
Marseilles, HE Cardinal Robert Coffy.
Paris, HE Cardinal J. M. Lustiger.
Reims, Jean Balland.
Rennes, Jacques Jullien.
Rouen, Joseph Duval.
Sens, Gérard Defois.
Strasbourg, Charles Amarin Brand.
Toulouse, André Collini.
Tours, Jean Honoré.

French Polynesia

Papeete, Michel Coppenrath.

Gabon

Libreville, André Fernand Anguilé.

Germany

Bamberg, Elmar Maria Kredel.
Cologne, HE Cardinal Joachim Meisner.
Essen, vacant.
Freiburg im Breisgau, Oskar Saier.
Munich & Freising, HE Cardinal Friedrich Wetter.
Paderborn, Johannes Joachim Degenhardt.

Ghana

Cape Coast, John Kodwo Amissah.
Tamale, Peter Poreiku Dery.

Greece

Athens, Nicholaos Foscolos.
Corfu, Antonio Varthalitis.
Naxos, Jean Perris.
Rhodes, vacant (Apostolic administrator, Michel Pierre Franzidis).

Guatemala

Guatemala, Prospero Penandos del Barrio.

Guinea

Conakry, Robert Sarah.

Haiti

Cap-Haitien, François Gayot.
Port au Prince, vacant. (Apostolic Administrator, Joseph Lafontant.)

Honduras

Tegucigalpa, Hector Enrique Santos Hernández.

Hong Kong

Hong Kong, HE Cardinal J. B. Wu Cheng Chung.

Hungary

Eger, Istvan Seregely.
Esztergom, HE Cardinal Laslo Paskai.
Kalocsa, Laszlo Danko.

India

Agra, Cecil de Sa.
Bangalore, Alphonsus Mathias.
Bhopal, Eugene D'Souza.
Bombay, HE Cardinal I. Pimenta.
Calcutta, Henry Sebastian D'Souza.
Changanacherry, Joseph Powathil.
Cuttack-Bhubaneswar, Raphael Cheenath.
Delhi, Alan de Lastic.
Ernakulam, HE Cardinal Anthony Padiyara.
Goa and Daman, Raul Nicolau Gonsalves.
Hyderabad, Saminini Arulappa.
Madras and Mylapore, Casimir Gnanadickam.
Madurai, Marianus Arokiasamy.
Nagpur, Leobard D'Souza.
Pondicherry and Cuddalore, Venmani S. Selvanather.
Ranchi, Telesphore P. Toppo.
Shillong-Gauhati, Hubert D'Rosario.

Trivandrum (Syrian Melekite Rite), Benedict Varghese Mar Gregorios Thangalathil.
Verapoly, Cornelius Elanjikal.

Indonesia

Ende, Donatus Djagom.
Jakarta, Leo Soekoto.
Kupang, Gregorius Manteiro.
Medan, Alfred Gonti Pius Datubara.
Merauke, Jacobus Duivenvoorde.
Pontianak, Hieronymus Herculanus Bumbun.
Semarang, Julius R. Darmaatmadja.
Ujung Pandang, R. P. Francis van Roessel.

Iran

Ahváz, Hanna Zora.
Tehran, Youhannan Semaan Issayi.
Urmyā, Thomas Meram.

Iraq

Arbil, Stephane Babaca.
Baghdad, (Latin Rite), Paul Dahdah; (Syrian Rite), Athanase M. S. Matoka; (Armenian Rite), Paul Coussa.
Basra, Yousif Thomas.
Kirkuk, André Sana.
Mosul, Georges Garmo.

Israel

Akka (Greek Melekite Catholic Rite), Maximos Salloum.

Italy

Acerenza, Michele Scandiffio.
Amalfi, Beniamino De Palma.
Ancona, Franco Festorazzi.
Bari, Mariano Magrassi.
Benevento, Carlo Minchiatti.
Bologna, HE Cardinal Giacomo Biffi.
Brindisi, Settimio Todisco.
Cagliari, Otterino Pietro Alberti.
Camerino, Francesco Gioia.
Campobasso-Boiano, Ettore Di Filippo.
Capua, Luigi Diligenza.
Catania, Luigi Bommarito.
Catanzaro, Antonio Cantisani.
Chieti, Antonio Valentini.
Conza, Mario Milano.
Cosenza, Dino Trabalzini.
Crotone-Santa Severina, Giuseppi Agostino.
Fermo, Cleto Bellucci.
Ferrara, Luigi Maverna.
Florence, HE Cardinal Silvano Piovanelli.
Foggia, Giuseppe Casale.
Gaeta, Vincenzo Farano.
Genoa, HE Cardinal Giovanni Canestri.
Gorizia and Gradisca, Antonio Vitale Bommarco.
Lanciano, Enzio d'Antonio.
L'Aquila, Mario Peressin.
Lecce, Cosmo F. Ruppi.
Lucca, Bruno Tommasi.
Manfredonia, Vincenzo D'Addario.
Matera, Ennio Appignanesi.
Messina, Ignazio Cannavó.
Milan, HE Cardinal Carlo Maria Martini.
Modena, Santo B. Quadri.
Monreale, Salvatore Cassisa.
Naples, HE Cardinal Michele Giordano.
Oristano, Pier Luigi Tiddia.
Otranto, Vincenzo Franco.
Palermo, HE Cardinal Salvatore Pappalardo.
Perugia, Ennio Antonelli.
Pescara-Penne, Francesco Cuccarese.
Pisa, Alessandro Plotti.
Potenza, Guiseppe Vairo.
Ravenna, Luigi Amaducci.
Reggio Calabria, Vittorio L. Mondello.

Rossano, Serafino Sprovieri.
Salerno, Guerino Grimaldi.
Sassari, Salvatore Isgrò.
Siena, Gaetano Bonicelli.
Siracusa, Giuseppe Costanzo.
Sorrento, Felice Cece.
Spoleto, Antonio Ambrosanio.
Taranto, Luigi Papa.
Turin, HE Cardinal Giovanni Saldarini.
Trani and Barletta, Carmelo Cassati.
Trento, Giovanni Sartori.
Udine, Alfredo Battisti.
Urbino, Donato U. Bianchi.
Vercelli, Tarcisio Bertone.

Jamaica

Kingston, Samuel Emmanuel Carter.

Japan

Nagasaki, Francis Xavier Shimamoto.
Osaka, Paul Hisao Yasuda.
Tōkyō, Peter Seiichi Shirayanagi.

Jordan

Petra and Filadelfia (Greek Melekite Catholic Rite), Saba Youakim.

Kenya

Kisumu, Zaccharus Okoth.
Mombasa, John Njenga.
Nairobi, HE Cardinal Maurice Otunga.
Nyeri, Nicodemus Kirima.

Korea

Kwangju, Victorinus Kong-Hi Youn.
Seoul, HE Cardinal Stephen Sou Hwan Kim.
Taegu, Paul Moun-Hi Ri.

Latvia

Riga, Jānis Pujats.

Lebanon

Antelias (Maronite Rite), Joseph Mohsen Bechara.
Baalbek, Eliopoli (Greek Melekite Catholic Rite), Salim Bustros.
Baniyas (Greek Melekite Catholic Rite), Antoine Hayek.
Beirut (Greek Melekite Catholic Rite), Habib Bacha; (Maronite Rite), Khalil Abinader.
Saïda (Greek Melekite Catholic Rite), Georges Kwaiter.
Tripoli (Maronite Rite), Antoine Joubeir; (Greek Melekite Catholic Rite), Elias Nijmé.
Tyre (Greek Melekite Catholic Rite), Jean A. Haddad; (Maronite Rite), Joseph Khoury.
Zahle and Furzol (Greek Melekite Catholic Rite), Andre Haddad.

Lesotho

Maseru, Bernard Mohlalisi.

Liberia

Monrovia, Michael Kpakala Francis.

Lithuania

Kaunas, HE Cardinal Vincentas Sladkevicius.
Vilnius, vacant.

Luxembourg

Luxembourg, Fernand Franck.

Madagascar

Antananarive, HE Cardinal Victor Razafimahatratra.
Antsiranana, Albert Joseph Tsiahoana.
Fianarantsoa, Gilbert Ramanantoanina.

Malaysia

Kuala Lumpur, Anthony S. Fernandez.
Kuching, Peter Chung Hoan Ting.

Mali

Bamako, Luc Auguste Sangaré.

Malta

Malta, Joseph Mercieca.

Martinique

Fort de France, Maurice Marie-Sainte.

Mauritius

Port Louis, HE Cardinal Jean Margeot.

Mexico

Acapulco, Rafael Bello Ruiz.
Antequera, Bartolomé Carrasco Briseno.
Chihuahua, Adalberto Almeida Merino.
Durango, Antonio L. Avina.
Guadalajara, HE Cardinal Juan J.P. Ocampo.
Hermosillo, Carlos Quintero Arce.
Jalapa, Sergio Obeso Rivero.
Mexico City, HE Cardinal Ernesto Corripio Ahumada.
Monterrey, Adolfo Suarez Rivera.
Morelia, Estanislao Alcarez Figueroa.
Puebla de los Angeles, Rosendo Huesca Pacheco.
San Luis Potosi, Arturo A. Szymanski Ramirez.
Tlalnepantla, Manuel P. Gil Gonzalez.
Yucatán, Manuel Castro Ruiz.

Monaco

Monaco, Joseph-Marie Sardou.

Morocco

Rabat, Hubert Michon.
Tangier, Antonio J. Peteiro Freire.

Mozambique

Beira, Jaime P. Goncalves.
Maputo, HE Cardinal Alexandre José Maria dos Santos.
Nampula, Manuel Vieira Pinto.

Myanmar (Burma)

Mandalay, Alphonse U. Than Aung.
Yangon (Rangoon), Gabriel Thohey Mahn Gaby.

Netherlands

Utrecht, HE Cardinal Adrianus J. Simonis.

New Zealand

Wellington, HE Cardinal Thomas Stafford Williams.

Nicaragua

Managua, HE Cardinal Miguel Obando Bravo.

Nigeria

Kaduna, Peter Yariyok Jatau.
Lagos, Anthony Okogie.
Onitsha, Stephen Nweke Ezeanya.

Oceania

Agaña, Anthony Sablan Apuron.
Honiara, Adrian Thomas Smith.
Nouméa, Michel-Marie-Bernard Calvet.
Samoa, Apia and Tokelau, HE Cardinal Pio Taofino'u.
Suva, Petero Mataca.

Pakistan

Karachi, HE Cardinal Joseph Cordeiro.

Panama

Panama, Marcos Gregorio McGrath.

Papua New Guinea

Madang, Benedict To Varpin.
Mount Hagen, Michael Meier.
Port Moresby, Peter Kurongku.
Rabaul, Karl Hesse.

Paraguay

Asuncion, Felipe Santiago B. Avalos.

Peru

Arequipa, Fernando Vargas Ruiz de Somocurcio.
Ayacucho o Huamanga, vacant.
Cuzco, Alcides Mendoza Castro.
Huancayo, Emilio Vallebuona Merea.
Lima, Augusto Vargas Alzamora.
Piura, Oscar Rolando Cantuarias Pastor.
Trujillo, Manuel Prado Pérez-Rosas.

Philippines

Caceres, Leonardo Legazpi.
Cagayan de Oro, Jesus B. Tuquib.
Capiz, Onesimo C. Gordoncillo.
Cebu, Nome di Gesù, HE Cardinal Ricardo Vidal.
Cotabato, Philip Frances Smith.
Davao, Antonio Mabutas.
Jaro, Alberto J. Piamonte.
Lingayan-Dagupen, Oscar V. Cruz.
Lipa, Mariano Gaviola.
Manila, HE Cardinal Jaime L. Sin.
Nueva Segovia, Orlando Quevedo.
Ozamiz, Jesus Dosado.
Palo, Pedro R. Dean.
San Fernando, Paciano Aniceto.
Tuguegarao, Diosdado A. Talamayan.
Zamboanga, Francisco Raval Cruces.

Poland

Gniezno, HE Cardinal Józef Glemp (*also* Warsaw).
Kraków, HE Cardinal Franciszek Macharski.
Poznan, Jerzy Stroba.
Warsaw, HE Cardinal Józef Glemp.
Wroclaw, HE Cardinal Henryk Roman Gulbinowicz.

Portugal

Braga, Eurico Dias Nogueira.
Evora, Maurilio Jorge Quintal de Gouveia.

Puerto Rico

San Juan, HE Cardinal Luis Aponte Martinez.

Romania

Alba Julia (Latin Rite), Lajos Balint.
Bucarest, Ioan Robu.
Fagaras and Alba Julia (Romanian Byzantine Rite), HE Cardinal Alexandru Todea.

Rwanda

Kigali, Vincent Nsengiyumva.

El Salvador

San Salvador, Arturo Rivera Damas.

Senegal

Dakar, HE Cardinal Hyacinthe Thiandoum.

Sierra Leone

Freetown & Bo, Joseph Ganda.

Singapore

Singapore, Gregory Yong Sooi Nghean.

South Africa

Bloemfontein, Peter John Butelezi.
Cape Town, Lawrence Patrick Henry.
Durban, Denis Eugene Hurley.
Pretoria, George Francis Daniel.

Spain

Barcelona, Ricardo Maria Carles Gordó.
Burgos, Theodoro C. Fernandez.
Granada, José Méndez Asensio.
Madrid, HE Cardinal Angel Suquia Goicoechea.
Oviedo, Gabino Diaz Merchán.
Pamplona, José Mariá Cirardo Lachiondo.
Santiago de Compostela, Antonio Rouco Varela.
Sevilla, Carlos Amigo Vallejo.
Tarragona, Ramon Torrella Cascante.
Toledo, HE Cardinal Marcelo González Martin.
Valencia, Miguel Roca Cabanellas.
Valladolid, José Delicado Baeza.
Zaragoza, Elíaz Yanez Alvarez.

Sri Lanka

Colombo, Nicholas Marcus Fernando.

Sudan

Khartoum, Gabriel Zubeir Wako.

Syria

Alep, Beroea, Halab (Greek Melekite Catholic Rite), Néophytes Edelby; (Syrian Rite), Raboula A. Beylouni; (Maronite Rite), Pierre Callaos; (Armenian Rite), Boutros Marayati.
Baniyas (Greek Melekite Catholic Rite), Antoine Hayek.
Bosra, Bostra, Boulos Nassif Borkhoche.
Damascus (Greek Melekite Catholic Rite), vacant; (Syrian Rite), Eustache J. Mounayer; (Maronite Rite), Hamid A. Mourany.
Hassaké-Nisibi, Georges Habib Hafouri.
Homs, Emesa (Syrian Catholic Rite), Jean Dahi.
Laodicea (Greek Melekite Catholic Rite), Michel Yatim.

Taiwan

Taipei, Joseph Ti-Kang.

Tanzania

Dar es Salaam, HE Cardinal Laurean Rugambwa.
Mwanza, Antony Mayala.
Tabora, Mario E. A. Mgulunde.

Thailand

Bangkok, HE Cardinal Michael Michai Kitbunchu.
Tharé and Nonseng, Lawrence Khai Saen-Phon-On.

Togo

Lomé, Robert Casimir Dosseh-Anyron.

Trinidad

Port of Spain, Gordon Anthony Pantin.

Turkey

Diarbekir, Paul Karatas.
Istanbul (Constantinople), Jean Tcholakian.
Izmir, Giuseppe G. Bernardini.

Uganda

Kampala, Emmanuel Wamala.

Uruguay

Montevideo, José Gottardi Cristelli.

USA

Anchorage, Francis Thomas Hurley.
Atlanta, James P. Lyke.
Baltimore, William Henry Keeler.
Boston, HE Cardinal Bernard F. Law.
Chicago, HE Cardinal Joseph L. Bernardin.
Cincinnati, Daniel E. Pilarczyk.
Denver, James Francis Stafford.
Detroit, Adam J. Maida.
Dubuque, Daniel W. Kucera.

Hartford, John F. Whealon.
Indianapolis, Edward T. O'Meara.
Kansas City, Ignatius J. Strecker.
Los Angeles, HE Cardinal Roger M. Mahony.
Louisville, Thomas C. Kelly.
Miami, Edward A. McCarthy.
Milwaukee, Rembert G. Weakland.
Mobile, Oscar H. Lipscomb.
Newark, Theodore E. McCarrick.
New Orleans, Francis B. Schulte.
New York, HE Cardinal John J. O'Connor.
Oklahoma City, Charles A. Salatka.
Omaha, Daniel E. Sheehan.
Philadelphia, HE Cardinal Anthony J. Beuilacqua; (Ukrainian Rite), Stephen Sulyk.
Pittsburgh (Byzantine Rite), Stephen J. Kocisko.
Portland (Oregon), William J. Levada.
St Louis (Missouri), John L. May.
St Paul & Minneapolis, John Robert Roach.
San Antonio, Patrick F. Flores.
San Francisco, John R. Quinn.
Santa Fe, Robert F. Sanchez.
Seattle, Thomas J. Murphy.
Washington, HE Cardinal James A. Hickey.

USSR

Latin Rite
   Karaganda Apostolic Administration (covering Kazakhstan), Apostolic Administrator, Fr Jan Lenga (titular Bishop of Arba).
   Lvov, Marian Jaworski (Archbishop of Lvov of the Latins).
   Minsk-Mohilev Archdiocese (covering Belorussia), Kazimierz Swiatek.
   Moscow Apostolic Administration (covering European Russia), Apostolic Administrator, Archbishop Tadeusz Kondrusiewicz.
   Novosibirsk Apostolic Administration (covering Siberia), Apostolic Administrator, Fr Joseph Werth, SJ (titular Bishop of Bulna).

Ukrainian Rite
   Lvov, HE Cardinal Myroslav I. Lubachivsky (Major Archbishop of Lvov of the Ukrainians); Archbishop Volodymir Sterniuk is 'locum tenens'.

Venezuela

Barquisimeto, Julio Manuel Chirivella Varela.
Caracas, HE Cardinal José Ali Lebrún Moratinos; (Greek Melekite Catholic Rite), Pierre Rai.
Ciudad Bolivar, Medardo Luzardo Romero.
Maracaibo, Domingo Roa Pérez.
Mérida, Miguel Antonio Salas Salas.
Valencia, Jorge Liberato Urosa Savino.

Vietnam

Hanoi, vacant.
Hue, vacant.
Thanh-Phô Hôchiminh, Paul Nguyên Van Binh.

West Indies

Castries, Kelvin Edward Felix.

Yugoslavia

Bar, Petar Perkolić.
Belgrade, Franc Perko.
Ljubljana, Alojzij Suštar.
Rijeka-Senj, Anton Tamarut.
Split-Makarska, Ante Juric.
Vrhbosna & Sarajevo, Vinko Puljic.
Zadar, Marijan Oblak.
Zagreb, HE Cardinal Franjo Kuharić.

Zaire

Bukavu, Mulindwa Mutabesha Mweru.
Kananga, Bakole wa Ilunga.

Kinshasa, HE Cardinal Frederick Etsou-Nzabi-Bamungwabi.
Kisangani, Laurent Monsengwo Pasinya.
Lubumbashi, Kabanga Songasonga.
Mbandaka-Bikoro, (Apostolic Administrator) HE Cardinal Etsou-Nzabi-Bamungwabi.

Zambia

Kasama, James Spaita.
Lusaka, Adrian Mungandu.

Zimbabwe

Harare, Patrick Chakaipa.

ARCHBISHOPS OF TITULAR SEES

Abari, Carlo Furno.
Adana (Greek Melekite Catholic Rite), Gregoire Haddad.
Amantia, Edward Idris Cassidy.
Amasya, James Patrick Carroll.
Amiterno, Agostino Cacciavillan.
Aquileia, Marcello Costalunga.
Balneoregium, Mario Rizzi.
Beroe, Victor Sartre.
Cadi, Stefan M. Marusyn.
Celene, Gabriel Montaluo.
Cesariana, Giovanni Lajolo.
Cesarea in Palaestina (Greek Melekite Catholic Rite), Hilarion Capucci.
Claudiopolis in Honoriade, Alfredo Bruniera.
Corinthus, Gennaro Verolino.
Dara, Nicholas T. Elko.
Doclea, Pier Luigi Celata.
Drivastum, Bruno Bertagna.
Edessa in Osrhoëne (Syrian Catholic Rite), Gregoire Ephrem Jarjour.
Ephesus, John Henry Boccella.
Fidene, Giacinto Berloco.
Fiorentino, Luigi Barbarito.
Forum Novum, Giovanni Battista Re.
Gabala, Gérard de Milleville.
Gradum, José López Ortiz.
Hadrianopolis in Haemimonto, Lino Zanini.
Heraclea, Jozef Kowalczyk.
Horta, Paul Marcinkus.
Idicra, Georg Weinhold.
Kaškar, Emmanuel-Karim Delly.
Macra, John Dooley.
Madaurus, Janusz Bolonek.
Marcianopolis, Volodymyr Sterniuk.
Mesembria, Loris Francesco Capovilla.
Meta, Audrys J. Backis.
Neapoli, HE Cardinal Jacques Martin.
Nicaea Parva, Paolino Limongi.
Novaliciana, Faustino Sainz Munoz.
Nubia, Paul Antaki.
Octava, Blasco Francisco Collaco.
Otriculum, Pietro Biggio.
Pia, Osvaldo Padilla.
Razia Ria, Marian Oles.
Rebellum, Giovanni Marray.
Rusellae, Lorenzo Antonetti.
Salamis, Joseph Kuo Joshih.
Satrianum, Patrick Coveney.
Scytopolis, Joseph Raya.
Severiana, Luigi Bressan.
Silli, Jan Schotte.
Sinna, Paul F. Tabet.
Soteropolis, Ettore Cunial.
Tagase, Giovanni Ceirano.
Tagora, Cipriano Calderon Polo.
Tarsus (Greek Melekite Catholic Rite), Loutfi Laham.
Tharros, Giuseppe Uhač.

Tiburnia, Donato Squicciarini.
Tiddi, Eugenio Sbarbaro.
Turris, Vincenzo Moreni.
Vannida, Felix del Blanco Prieto.
Villamagna, Giulio Einaudi.
Viminacium, Franco Brambilla.
Volsinium, Justin Francis Rigali.

PATRIARCHS IN COMMUNION WITH THE ROMAN CATHOLIC CHURCH

Alexandria, HB Stephanos II Ghattas (Patriarch for Catholic Copts).
Antioch, HB Ignace Antoine II Hayek (Patriarch for Syrian Rite Catholics); HB Maximos V. Hakim (Patriarch for Greek Melekite Rite Catholics); HB Nasrallah Piere Sfeir (Patriarch for Maronite Rite Catholics).
Jerusalem, HB Michel Sabbah (Patriarch for Latin Rite Catholics).
Babilonia of the Chaldeens, HB Raphael I Bidawid.
Cilicia of the Armenians, HB Jean Pierre XVIII Kasparian (Patriarch for Armenian Rite Catholics).
Oriental India, Archbishop Raul Nicolau Gonsalves.
Lisbon, HE Cardinal Antonio Ribeiro.
Venice, HE Cardinal Marco Ce.

THE BAPTIST CHURCH

Baptists trace their origins to John Smyth, who in 1609 in Amsterdam reinstituted the baptism of conscious believers as the basis of the fellowship of a gathered church. Members of Smyth's church established the first Baptist church in England in 1612. They came to be known as 'General' Baptists and their theology was Arminian, whereas a later group of Calvinists who adopted the baptism of believers came to be known as 'Particular' Baptists. The two sections of the Baptists were united into one body, the Baptist Union of Great Britain and Ireland, in 1891. In 1988 the title was changed to the Baptist Union of Great Britain.

Baptists emphasize the complete independence of the local church, although individual churches are linked in various kinds of associations. There are international bodies (such as the Baptist World Alliance) and national bodies, but many Baptist churches belong to neither. However, in Great Britain the majority of churches and associations belong to the Baptist Union of Great Britain. There are also Baptist Unions in Wales, Scotland and Ireland which are much smaller than the Baptist Union of Great Britain, and there is some overlap of membership.

There are over 37 million Baptist church members world-wide; in the Baptist Union of Great Britain there are 160,800 members, 1,585 pastors and 2,000 churches. In the Baptist Union of Scotland there are 16,212 members, 130 pastors and 166 churches. In the Baptist Union of Wales there are 27,700 members, 117 pastors and 560 churches. In the Baptist Union of Ireland there are 8,505 members, 72 pastors and 103 churches.

President of the Baptist Union of Great Britain (1991–92), Rev. R. Jenkins.
Gen. Sec., Rev. D. R. Coffey, Baptist House, PO Box 44, 129 Broadway, Didcot, Oxon. OX11 8RT. (Tel: 0235–512077).

THE CHURCH OF CHRIST, SCIENTIST

The Church of Christ, Scientist, was founded by Mary Baker Eddy in the United States of America in 1879 to 'reinstate primitive Christianity and its lost element of healing'. Christian Science is concerned with spiritual regeneration and salvation from sin, but is best known for its reliance on prayer alone in the healing of sickness. Adherents believe that such healing is in direct line with that practised by Jesus Christ (revered, not as God, but as the Son of God) and by the early Christian Church.

The denomination consists of the First Church of Christ, Scientist, in Boston, Massachusetts, USA (the Mother Church) and its branch churches in over 60 countries worldwide. Branch churches are democratically governed by their members. There is also a five-member Board of Directors which oversees Church matters. There are no clergy. Those engaged in full-time healing ministry are called practitioners, of whom there are 3,500 world-wide.

No membership figures are available, since Mary Baker Eddy felt that numbers are no measure of spiritual vitality and ruled that such statistics should not be published. There are over 2,500 branch churches worldwide, including 215 in the United Kingdom.

CHRISTIAN SCIENCE COMMITTEE ON PUBLICATION, 108 Palace Gardens Terrace, W8 4RT. (Tel: 071–221 5650).—*District Manager for Great Britain and Ireland*, G. Phaup.

THE CHURCH OF SCOTLAND

The Church of Scotland is the established church of Scotland. The Church is Calvinistic and evangelical in doctrine, and presbyterian in constitution. In 1560 the jurisdiction of the Roman Catholic Church was abolished and the first assembly of the Church of Scotland ratified the Confession of Faith, drawn up by John Knox. In 1592 Parliament passed an Act guaranteeing the liberties of the Church and its presbyterian government. James VI (James I of England) and later Stuart monarchs attempted to restore episcopacy, but a presbyterian church was finally restored in 1690 and secured by the Act of Settlement (1690) and the Act of Union (1707). The Free Church of Scotland was formed in 1843 in a dispute over patronage and state interference; in 1900 it merged with the United Presbyterian Church (formed in 1847) as the United Free Church of Scotland. In 1929 most of this body rejoined the Church of Scotland to form the United Church of Scotland.

The Church of Scotland is presbyterian in its organization, i.e. based on a hierarchy of councils of ministers and elders. At local level the kirk session consists of the parish minister and ruling elders, and at district level the presbyteries, of which there are 46, consist of all the ministers in the district and one ruling elder from each congregation. The 12 provincial synods comprise three or more presbyteries. The General Assembly is the supreme authority, and is presided over by a Moderator chosen annually by the Assembly. The Sovereign, if not present in person, is represented by a Lord High Commissioner who is appointed each year by the Crown.

The Church of Scotland has about 790,000 members, 1,250 ministers and 1,700 churches. There are about 100 ministers and other personnel working overseas.
Lord High Commissioner (1991), The Rt. Hon. Lord Ross.
Moderator of the General Assembly (1991), Rt. Rev. W. B. R. Macmillan.
Principal Clerk, Rev. J. L. Weatherhead.
Deputy Clerk, Rev. A. G. McGillivray.
Procurator, A. Dunlop, QC.

Law Agent and Solicitor of the Church, R. A. Paterson.
Parliamentary Agent, I. McCulloch (*London*).
General Treasurer, W. G. P. Colledge.
CHURCH OFFICE, 121 George Street, Edinburgh EH2 4YN. (Tel: 031–225 5722).

THE CONGREGATIONAL FEDERATION

The Congregational Federation was founded by members of Congregational churches in England and Wales who did not join the United Reformed Church in 1972. There are also churches in Scotland and Australia. The Federation exists to encourage congregations of believers to worship in free assembly, but has no authority over them and emphasizes their right to independence and self-government.

The Federation has 9,515 members, 116 ministers, 38 pastors, about 270 lay preachers and 282 churches.
President of the Federation (1991–92), Rev. J. E. Bourne.
Gen. Sec., G. M. Adams, The Congregational Centre, 4 Castle Gate, Nottingham NG1 7AS. (Tel: 0602-413801).

THE FREE CHURCH OF ENGLAND

The Free Church of England, also known as the Reformed Episcopal Church, traces its beginnings to a dispute over the influence of the Oxford Movement in the established church between the Bishop of Exeter and one of his clergy, James Shore, in 1843. The Church defined its beliefs in 1863, accepting the Church of England's Thirty-Nine Articles and recognizing the legitimacy of the principle of episcopacy. Although its government was at first presbyterian, the Church later became affiliated to the Reformed Episcopal Church in the USA (a connection which has not been maintained) and adopted episcopal organization.

The Free Church of England has 1,700 members, 35 ministers and 30 churches in England. It also has three churches and three ministers in New Zealand, and one church and one minister in Leningrad, USSR.
Gen. Sec., Rt. Rev. A. Ward, 28 Sedgebrook, Liden, Swindon, Wilts. SN3 6EY. (Tel: 0793–695838).

THE FREE PRESBYTERIAN CHURCH OF SCOTLAND

The Free Presbyterian Church of Scotland was formed in 1893 by two ministers of the former Free Church of Scotland who refused to accept a Declaratory Act passed by the Free Church General Assembly in 1892. The Free Presbyterian Church of Scotland is Calvinistic in doctrine and emphasizes observance of the Sabbath. It adheres strictly to the Westminster Confession of Faith drawn up in 1643.

The Church has 5,000 members, 26 ministers and 34 churches.
Moderator, Rev. D. Ross, Free Presbyterian House, Laide, Ross-shire, Scotland. (Tel: 0445–731340).
Clerk of Synod, Rev. D. B. MacLeod, 8 Colinton Road, Edinburgh EH10 5DS. (Tel: 031–447 1920).

THE INDEPENDENT METHODIST CHURCHES

The Independent Methodist Churches seceded from the Wesleyan Methodist Church in 1805 and remained independent when the Methodist Church in Great Britain was formed in 1932. They are mainly concentrated in the industrial areas of the north of England.

The churches are Methodist in doctrine but their

organization is congregational. All the churches are members of the Independent Methodist Connexion of Churches. The controlling body of the Connexion is the Annual Meeting, to which churches send delegates. The Connexional President is elected annually. Between Annual Meetings the affairs of the Connexion are handled by Departmental Committees. Ministers are appointed by the churches and trained through the Connexion, but are not titled 'Reverend'. The ministry is open to both men and women and is unpaid.

There are 3,700 members, 112 ministers and 106 churches in Great Britain.

Connexional President (1991–92), D. E. Yates.
Gen. Sec., Rev. J. M. Day, The Old Police House, Croxton, Stafford ST21 6PE. (Tel: 063 082 671).

THE LUTHERAN CHURCH

Lutheranism is based on the teachings of Martin Luther, the German leader of the Protestant Reformation. The authority of the scriptures is held to be supreme over Church tradition and creeds, and the key doctrine is that of justification by faith alone.

Lutheranism is one of the largest Protestant denominations and it is particularly strong in northern Europe and the USA. Some Lutheran churches are episcopal, while others have a synodal form of organization; unity is based on doctrine rather than structure. Most Lutheran churches are members of the Lutheran World Federation, based in Geneva.

Lutheran services in Great Britain are held in many languages to serve members of different nationalities. English-language congregations are members either of the Lutheran Church in Great Britain–United Synod, or of the Evangelical Lutheran Church of England. The United Synod and most of the various national congregations are members of the Lutheran Council of Great Britain.

There are over 70 million Lutherans world-wide; in Great Britain there are 27,000 members, 45 ministers and 100 churches.

Chairman of the Lutheran Council of Great Britain, Very Rev. R. J. Patkai, 8 Collingham Gardens, SW5 0HW. (Tel: 071–373 1141).

THE METHODIST CHURCH

The Methodist movement started in England in 1729 when the Rev. John Wesley, an Anglican priest, and his brother Charles met with others in Oxford and resolved to conduct their lives and study by 'rule and method'. In 1739 the Wesleys began evangelistic preaching and the first Methodist chapel was founded in Bristol in the same year. In 1744 the first annual conference was held, at which the Articles of Religion were drawn up. Doctrinal emphases included repentance, faith, the assurance of salvation, social concern and the priesthood of all believers. After John Wesley's death in 1791 the Methodists withdrew from the established Church to form the Methodist Church. Methodists gradually drifted into many groups, but in 1932 the Wesleyan Methodist Church, the United Methodist Church and the Primitive Methodist Church united to form the Methodist Church in Great Britain as it now exists.

The governing body and supreme authority of the Methodist Church is the Conference, but there are also 33 district synods, consisting of all the ministers and selected lay people in each district, and circuit meetings of the ministers and lay people of each circuit.

There are over 54 million Methodists world-wide; in Great Britain (1989 figures) there are 431,549 members, 3,514 ministers, 10,359 lay preachers and 7,207 churches.

The Methodist Church in Ireland has 19,408 members, 196 ministers, 295 lay preachers and 234 churches.

President of the Conference in Great Britain (1991–92), Rev. R. W. C. Hoar.
Vice-President of the Conference (1991–92), I. Weekes.
Secretary of the Conference, Rev. B. E. Beck, Methodist Church, Conference Office, 1 Central Buildings, Storeys Gate, SW1H 9NH. (Tel: 071–222 8010).
President of the Conference in Ireland (1991–92), Rev. J. W. Good.
Secretary of the Conference in Ireland, Rev. E. T. I. Mawhinney, 1 Fountainville Avenue, Belfast BT9 6AN. (Tel: 0232–324554).

THE ORTHODOX CHURCH

The Orthodox Church (or Eastern Orthodox Church) is a communion of self-governing Christian Churches recognizing the honorary primacy of the Ecumenical Patriarch of Constantinople.

In the first millennium of the Christian era the faith was slowly formulated. Between AD 325 and 787 there were seven Ecumenical Councils at which bishops from the entire Christian world assembled to resolve various doctrinal disputes which had arisen. The estrangement between East and West began after Constantine moved the centre of the Roman Empire from Rome to Constantinople, and it gained momentum after the temporal administration was divided. Linguistic and cultural differences between Greek East and Latin West served to encourage separate ecclesiastical developments which became pronounced in the tenth and early eleventh centuries.

The administration of the church was divided between five ancient patriarchates: Rome and all the West, Constantinople (the imperial city – the 'New Rome'), Jerusalem and all Palestine, Antioch and all the East, and Alexandria and all Africa. Of these, only Rome was in the Latin West and after the Great Schism in 1054, Rome developed a structure of authority centralized on one source, the Papacy, while the Orthodox East maintained the style of localized administration. To the older patriarchates were later added the Patriachates of Russia, Georgia, Serbia, Bulgaria and Romania. The Orthodox Church also includes autocephalous (self-governing) national churches in Greece, Cyprus, Poland, Albania, Czechoslovakia and Sinai, and autonomous national churches in Finland and Japan. The Estonian and Latvian Orthodox Churches are in practice part of the Moscow Patriarchate. The Belorussians and Ukrainians have recently been given greater autonomy by Moscow, but some Ukrainians have broken away to establish an independent Ukrainian Patriarchate. In Macedonia the local hierarchy has declared itself independent of the Serbian Patriarchate. The Russian dioceses in the diaspora fall into four groups: those under the direct control of the Moscow Patriarchate; the Russian Orthodox Church Outside Russia, sometimes known as the Synod in Exile; the Russian Archdiocese centred at the cathedral in Rue Daru, Paris, which is part of the Patriarchate in Constantinople; and the Orthodox Church in America, which was granted autocephalous status in 1970.

The position of Orthodox Christians is that the faith was fully defined during the period of the Ecumenical Councils. In doctrine it is strongly trinitarian, and stresses the mystery and importance of the sacraments. It is episcopal in government. The structure of the Orthodox Christian year differs from that of Western Churches (*see* p. 109).

Orthodox Christians throughout the world are estimated to number about 150 million.

The Greek Orthodox Church
(Patriarchate of Constantinople)

The presence of Greek Orthodox Christians in Britain dates back to 1677 when Archbishop Joseph Geogirenes of Samos fled from Turkish persecution and came to London, where a church was built for him in Soho. The present Greek cathedral in Moscow Road, Bayswater, was opened for public worship in 1879 and the Diocese of Thyateira and Great Britain was established in 1922. There are now 87 parishes in Great Britain, served by eight bishops and 87 churches.

In Great Britain the Patriarchate of Constantinople is represented by Archbishop Gregorios of Thyateira and Great Britain, 5 Craven Hill, London W2 3EN. (Tel: 071–723 4787).

The Russian Orthodox Church (Patriarchate of Moscow) and The Russian Orthodox Church Outside Russia

The earliest records of Russian Orthodox Church activities in Britain date from the visit to England of Tsar Peter I at the beginning of the 18th century. Clergy were sent from Russia to serve the chapel established to minister to the staff of the Imperial Russian Embassy in London.

After 1917 the Church of Russia was persecuted. The Patriarch of Moscow, St Tikhon the New Martyr, anathematized both the atheistic persecutors of the Church and all who collaborated with them. Because of the civil war normal administrative contact with Russian Orthodox Christians outside the country was impossible, and he therefore authorized the establishment of a higher church administration, i.e. a synod in exile, by Russian bishops who were then outside Russia. This is the origin of the Russian Orthodox Church Outside Russia. The attitude of the Church to the Soviet regime has always been a source of contention between the two hierarchies and remains unresolved.

In Britain the Patriarchate of Moscow is represented by Metropolitan Anthony of Sourozh, 67 Ennismore Gardens, SW7 1NH. (Tel: 071–584 0096). There are 15 parishes, with two bishops and 13 priests.

The Russian Orthodox Church Outside Russia is represented by Archbishop Mark of Richmond and Great Britain (who is also Archbishop of Berlin and Germany), 14 St Dunstan's Road, W6 8RB. (Tel: 081–748 4232). There are eight parishes and two monasteries, served by six priests.

The Serbian Orthodox Church
(Patriarchate of Serbia)

There was a small congregation of Orthodox Christian Serbs in London before the Second World War, but most Serbian parishes in Britain have been established since 1945. There is no resident bishop as the parishes are part of the Serbian Orthodox Diocese of Western Europe, which has its centre in Germany. There are five main parishes in Britain and several smaller communities served by seven priests.

In Britain the Patriarchate of Serbia is represented by the Episcopal Vicar, the Very Rev. Milun Kostic, 89 Lancaster Road, W11 1QQ. (Tel: 071–727 8367).

Other Nationalities

Latvian, Polish and some Belorussian Orthodox parishes in Britain are under the care of the Patriarchate of Constantinople. The Patriarchates of Antioch, Bulgaria and Romania are represented by one priest each. Both the Ukrainian Autocephalous Orthodox Church and the Belorussian Autoce-

phalic Orthodox Church have a few parishes in Britain.

Orthodox Church Public Relations Office, St George Orthodox Information Service, 64 Prebend Gardens, W6 0XU. (Tel: 081–741 9624).—*Sec.,* A. Bond.

THE PRESBYTERIAN CHURCH IN IRELAND

The Presbyterian Church in Ireland is Calvinistic in doctrine and presbyterian in constitution. Presbyterianism was established in Ireland as a result of the Ulster plantation in the early 17th century, when English and Scottish Protestants settled in the north of Ireland.

There are 21 presbyteries and five regional synods under the chief court known as the General Assembly. The General Assembly meets annually and is presided over by a Moderator who is elected for one year. The ongoing work of the Church is undertaken by 18 boards under which there are a number of specialist committees.

There are about 350,000 Presbyterians in Ireland, mainly in the north, in 565 congregations and with 400 ministers.

Moderator (1991–92), The Rt. Rev. Dr R. Sterritt.
Clerk of Assemby and Gen. Sec., The Rev. Samuel Hutchinson, Church House, Belfast BT1 6DW. (Tel: 0232–322284).

THE PRESBYTERIAN CHURCH OF WALES

The Presbyterian Church of Wales or Calvinistic Methodist Church of Wales is Calvinistic in doctrine and presbyterian in constitution. It was formed in 1811 when Welsh Calvinists severed the relationship with the established church by ordaining their own ministers. It secured its own confession of faith in 1823 and a Constitutional Deed in 1826, and since 1864 the General Assembly has met annually, presided over by a Moderator elected for a year. The doctrine and constitutional structure of the Presbyterian Church of Wales was confirmed by Act of Parliament in 1931–32.

The Church has 61,616 members, 136 ministers and 1,025 churches.

Moderator (1991–92), Rev. Principal Elfed ap Nefydd Roberts.
Gen. Sec., Rev. D. H. Owen, 53 Richmond Road, Cardiff CF2 3UP. (Tel: 0222–494913).

THE RELIGIOUS SOCIETY OF FRIENDS (QUAKERS)

Quakerism is a movement, not a church, which was founded in the 17th century by George Fox and others in an attempt to revive what they saw as 'primitive Christianity'. The movement was based originally in the Midlands, Yorkshire and north-west England, but there are now Quakers in 36 countries around the world. The colony of Pennsylvania, founded by William Penn, was originally Quaker.

Emphasis is placed on the experience of God in daily life rather than on sacraments or religious occasions. There is no church calendar. Worship is largely silent and there are no appointed ministers; the responsibility for conducting a meeting is shared equally among those present. Social reform and religious tolerance have always been important to Quakers, together with a commitment to non-violence in resolving disputes.

There are 213,800 Quakers world-wide, with 18,070 in Great Britain and Ireland. There are 464 meeting houses in Great Britain.

Central Offices: (Great Britain) Friends House, Euston Road, NW1 2BJ. (Tel: 071–387 3601); *(Ireland)* Swanbrook House, Morehampton Road, Dublin 4. (Tel: 0001–683684).

THE SALVATION ARMY

The Salvation Army was founded by William Booth in the east end of London in 1865, and has since become established in 93 countries world-wide. It was first known as the Christian Mission, and took its present name in 1878 when it adopted a quasi-military command structure intended to inspire and regulate its endeavours and to reflect its view that the Church was engaged in spiritual warfare. Salvationists emphasize evangelism, social work and the relief of poverty.

The world leader, known as the General, is elected by a High Council composed of the Chief of Staff and other senior commissioned officers, who are full-time ministers.

There are about 1·5 million soldiers, 16,982 active officers and 14,249 corps (churches) world-wide. In Great Britain and Ireland there are 55,000 soldiers, 1,642 active officers and 839 corps.

General, Eva Burrows.

Territorial Commander (UK Territory), Commissioner John Larsson.

INTERNATIONAL AND TERRITORIAL HEADQUARTERS, PO Box 249, 101 Queen Victoria Street, EC4P 4EP. (Tel: 071–236 5222).

THE SEVENTH-DAY ADVENTIST CHURCH

The Seventh-day Adventist Church was founded in 1863 in the USA. Its members look forward to the second coming of Christ and observe the Sabbath as a day of rest, worship and ministry. The Church bases its faith and practice wholly on the Bible and has developed 27 fundamental beliefs.

The World Church is divided into 12 divisions, each made up of unions of churches. The Seventh-day Adventist Church in the British Isles is known as the British Union of Seventh-day Adventists and is a member of the Trans-European Division. In the British Isles the administrative organization of the church is arranged in three tiers: the local churches, the regional conferences for South England, North England, Wales, Scotland and Ireland, which are held every three years, and the national 'union' conference which is held every five years.

There are over 6 million Adventists and 25,000 churches in 190 countries world-wide. In the United Kingdom and Ireland there are 17,750 members, 150 ministers and 236 churches.

President of the British Union Conference (1991–96), Pastor C. Perry.

BRITISH ISLES HEADQUARTERS, Stanborough Park, Watford WD2 6JP. (Tel: 0923–672251).

UNDEB YR ANNIBYNWYR CYMRAEG (The Union of Welsh Independents)

The Union of Welsh Independents is entirely Welsh-speaking and dates back to 1639 when the first Welsh Congregational Church was opened in Gwent. It is Calvinistic in doctrine and congregationalist in organization. Each church has complete independence in the government and administration of its affairs.

The Union has 52,027 members, 130 ministers and 649 chapels.

President of the Union (1991–92), Rev. M. Islwyn Lake.

Gen. Sec., Rev. Derwyn Morris Jones, Tŷ John Penry, 11 Heol Sant Helen, Swansea SA1 4AL. (Tel: 0792–467040).

UNITARIAN AND FREE CHRISTIAN CHURCHES

Unitarianism has its historical roots in the Judaeo-Christian tradition but allows the individual to embrace insights from all the world's faiths and philosophies, as there is no formal creed. It is accepted that beliefs may evolve in the light of personal experience.

Unitarian communities first became established in Poland and Transylvania in the 16th century. The first avowedly Unitarian place of worship in the British Isles opened in London in 1774. The General Assembly of Unitarian and Free Christian Churches came into existence in 1928 as the result of the amalgamation of two earlier organizations.

There are about 10,000 Unitarians in Great Britain and Ireland, and 150 Unitarian ministers. About 250 self-governing congregations and fellowship groups, including a small number overseas, are members of the General Assembly.

Gen. Sec. of the General Assembly of Unitarian and Free Christian Churches, Dr R. W. Smith, Essex Hall, 1–6 Essex Street, Strand, WC2R 3HY. (Tel: 071–240 2384).

THE UNITED REFORMED CHURCH

The United Reformed Church was formed by the union of most of the Congregational churches in England and Wales with the Presbyterian Church of England in 1972.

Congregationalism dates from the mid 16th century. It was Calvinistic in doctrine, and its followers formed independent self-governing congregations bound under God by covenant, a principle laid down in the writings of Robert Browne (1550–1633). From the late 16th century the movement was driven underground by persecution, but the cause was defended at the Westminster Assembly in 1643 and the Savoy Declaration of 1658 laid down its principles. Congregational churches formed county associations for mutual support and in 1832 these associations merged to form the Congregational Union of England and Wales.

The Presbyterian Church in England also dates from the mid 16th century, and was Calvinistic and evangelical in its doctrine. It was governed by a hierarchy of courts.

In the 1960s there was close co-operation locally and nationally between Congregational and Presbyterian Churches. This led to union negotiations and a Scheme of Union, supported by Act of Parliament in 1972. In 1981 a further unification took place, with the Reformed Association of Churches of Christ becoming part of the URC. In its basis the United Reformed Church reflects local church initiative and responsibility with a conciliar pattern of oversight. The General Assembly is the central body, and is made up of equal numbers of ministers and lay members.

The United Reformed Church is divided into 12 Provinces, each with a Provincial Moderator who chairs the Synod, and 70 Districts. There are 126,000 members, 730 full-time ministers and 1,800 local churches.

Gen. Sec. of the United Reformed Church, Rev. B. G. Thorogood (*from July 1992,* Rev. A. G. Burnham). 86 Tavistock Place, WC1H 9RT. (Tel: 071–837 7661).

THE WESLEYAN REFORM UNION

The Wesleyan Reform Union was founded by Methodists who left or were expelled from Wesleyan Methodism in 1849 following a period of internal conflict. Its doctrine is Methodist but its organization is congregational, each church having complete independence in the government and administration of its affairs. The main concentration of churches is in Yorkshire.

The Union has 2,933 members, 19 ministers, 140 lay preachers and 127 churches.

President (1991), J. R. Evans.

Gen. Sec., Rev. E. W. Downing, Wesleyan Reform Church House, 123 Queen Street, Sheffield S1 2DU. (Tel: 0742–721928).

JUDAISM IN THE UNITED KINGDOM

Judaism is the oldest monotheistic faith. The Hebrew Bible, which records how the descendants of Abraham were led by Moses out of their slavery in Egypt to Mount Sinai where God's law (*Torah*) was revealed to them as the chosen people, is the primary authority of Judaism. The *Talmud*, which consists of commentaries on the *Mishnah* (the first text of rabbinical Judaism), is also held to be authoritative, and may be divided into two main categories: the *halakah* (dealing with legal and ritual matters) and the *Aggadah* (dealing with theological and ethical matters not directly concerned with the regulation of conduct). The *halakah* has become a source of division; Orthodox Jews regard Jewish law as derived from God and therefore unalterable; Reform and Liberal Jews seek to interpret it in the light of contemporary considerations; and Conservative Jews aim to maintain most of the traditional rituals but to allow changes in accordance with that tradition. Reconstructionist Judaism, a 20th century movement, regards Judaism as a culture rather than a theological system and therefore accepts all forms of Jewish practice.

The family is the basic unit of Jewish ritual, with the synagogue playing an important role as the centre for public worship and religious study. A synagogue is led by a group of laymen who are elected to office; there are no priestly roles. The Rabbi is primarily a teacher and spiritual guide. The Sabbath is the central religious observance. (For details of the Jewish calendar, fasts and festivals, *see* pp. 111–2). Most British Jews are descendants of either the Ashkenazim of central and eastern Europe or the Sephardim of Spain and Portugal.

The Chief Rabbi of the United Hebrew Congregation and the Commonwealth is appointed by a Chief Rabbinate Conference, and is the rabbinical authority only to the Orthodox sector of the Jewish community, whose main organization is the United Hebrew Congregation. His authority is not recognized by the Reform Synagogues of Great Britain (the largest progressive group), the Union of Liberal and Progressive Synagogues, the Union of Orthodox Hebrew Congregations, the Federation of Synagogues, the Sephardi community, or the Assembly of Masorti Synagogues. He is, however, generally recognized both outside the Jewish community and within it as the public religious representative of the totality of British Jewry. The *Beth Din* (Court of Judgement) is the rabbinic court. The *Dayanim* (Assessors) adjudicate in disputes or on matters of Jewish law and tradition; they also oversee dietary law administration. The Chief Rabbi is President of the *Beth Din* of the United Synagogue.

The Board of Deputies of British Jews was established in 1760 and is the representative body of British Jewry. The basis of representation is mainly synagogal, but communal organizations are also represented. It watches over the interests of British Jewry and seeks to counter anti-Jewish discrimination.

There are over 12·5 million Jews world-wide; in Great Britain and Ireland there are an estimated 326,000 adherents, 150 rabbis and ministers under the jurisdiction of the Chief Rabbi, and 357 synagogues. *Chief Rabbi*, Dr Jonathan Sacks.

BETH DIN (COURT OF THE CHIEF RABBI), Adler House, Tavistock Square, WC1H 0EP. (Tel: 071–387 5772).—*Executive Director*, J. Kestenbaum; *Registrar*, J. Phillips; *Dayanim*, Rabbi C. Ehrentreu; Rabbi Dr I. Lerner; Rabbi C. D. Kaplin; Rabbi I. D. Berger.

UNITED SYNAGOGUE HEAD OFFICE, Woburn House, Upper Woburn Place, WC1H 0EZ. (Tel: 071–387 4300).—*Chief Exec.*, J. M. Lew.

REFORM SYNAGOGUES OF GREAT BRITAIN, The Sternberg Centre, Manor House, 80 East End Road, N3 2SY. (Tel: 081–349 4731).—*Executive Director*, R. M. Goldman.

UNION OF LIBERAL AND PROGRESSIVE SYNAGOGUES (JEWISH RELIGIOUS UNION), 109 Whitfield Street, W1P 5RP. (Tel: 071–580 1663).—*Director*, Mrs R. Rosenberg.

UNION OF ORTHODOX HEBREW CONGREGATIONS, 40 Queen Elizabeth's Walk, N16 0HH. (Tel: 081–802 6226).—*Sec.*, vacant.

FEDERATION OF SYNAGOGUES, 9–11 Greatorex Street, E1 5NF. (Tel: 071–247 4471).—*Administrator*, G. Kushner.

SEPHARDI COMMUNAL CENTRE, Montefiore Hall, 2 Ashworth Road, W9 1JY. (Tel: 071–289 2573).

ASSEMBLY OF MASORTI SYNAGOGUES, 33 Abbey Road, NW8 0AT. (Tel: 071–624 0539).

BOARD OF DEPUTIES OF BRITISH JEWS, Woburn House, Tavistock Square, WC1H 0EZ. (Tel: 071–387 3952).—*President*, His Hon. I. Finestein, QC; *Chief Exec.*, N. A. Nagler.

EDUCATION IN THE UNITED KINGDOM

(For addresses of national education departments, *see* **Government and Public Offices**. For other addresses, *see* **Education Directory**.)

Responsibility for education in the United Kingdom is largely decentralized. The Secretary of State for Education and Science has overall responsibility for all aspects of education in England, and for government policy and support for universities throughout Britain in consultation with the Secretaries of State for Wales and Scotland. Responsibility in Wales for nursery, primary and secondary education, and for all non-university institutions of higher and further education, the youth and community services, and adult education lies with the Secretary of State for Wales. The general supervision of the national system of education in Scotland, except for the universities, is the responsibility of the Secretary of State for Scotland acting through the Scottish Office Education Department. All aspects of education in Northern Ireland, schools, further education and universities, are the responsibility of the Secretary of State for Northern Ireland.

The main concerns of the education departments (the Department of Education and Science (DES), the Welsh Office, the Scottish Office Education Department (SOED), and the Department of Education for Northern Ireland (DENI)) are the formulation of national policies for education, and the maintenance of consistency in educational standards. They are responsible for the broad allocation of resources for education, for the rate and distribution of educational building and for the supply, training and superannuation of teachers. Hitherto, none of the education departments have run any schools or colleges directly, nor employed any teachers. However, under the provisions of the Education Reform Act 1988 and the Self-Governing Schools etc. (Scotland) Act 1989, the Department of Education and Science in England and Wales and the Scottish Office Education Department funds individual schools which have opted out of local education authority control and applied for direct funding from the Secretaries of State. In addition, the Department of Education and Science, in association with sponsors from industry, funds the new City Technology Colleges and the City College for the Technology of the Arts. Technology Academies are to be instituted on a similar basis in Scotland.

Schools in Northern Ireland providing integrated education will be able to apply for grant-maintained status from the Department of Education for Northern Ireland.

Expenditure

The Department of Education and Science, the Welsh Office, the Scottish Office and the Northern Ireland Office act within a framework of estimates approved by Parliament.

In real terms expenditure on education by central government departments was as follows (£ million):

	1990–91 estimated outturn	1991–92 planned
DES	6,654	7,293
Welsh Office	88	97
SOED	537	650
DENI	994	1,120

In the United Kingdom in 1988–89, central government provisional expenditure on education was apportioned as follows (£million):

Schools	13,069
Further and higher education	5,591
Other education and related expenditure	1,026

Most of this expenditure is incurred by local authorities which make their own expenditure decisions according to their local situations and needs and which are also responsible for funding most further education courses. The bulk of direct expenditure by central government is by the DES, which supports the universities in England, Wales and Scotland through the Universities Funding Council (UFC). It also supports higher education courses in polytechnics and colleges of higher education, and prescribed higher education courses in local education authority colleges in England through the Polytechnics and Colleges Funding Council (PCFC), and grant-maintained schools and CTCs.

The Welsh Office funds grants for adult, higher and further education and supports bilingual education and the Welsh language.

In Scotland, as in England and Wales, the bulk of expenditure on education is at a local level by the regional and islands councils. The main elements of central government expenditure are grant-aided special schools, self-governing schools, student awards, and the capital and recurrent grants to central institutions and colleges of education.

The Department of Education for Northern Ireland finances higher education, teacher education, teacher salaries and superannuation, student awards, grant-maintained integrated schools, and voluntary grammar schools. Remaining expenditure is by education and library boards at local level.

Local education administration

The education service at present is a national service in which the provision of school education and post-school further education is locally administered and its administration is still largely decentralized.

England and Wales.—In England and Wales the education service is administered by local education authorities (LEAs), which carry the day-to-day responsibility for providing most state primary and secondary education and some further education to meet the needs of their areas.

Each local education authority is required by statute to appoint an education committee, or committees, authorized to exercise on its behalf any of the authority's functions with respect to education, except the power to borrow money. Members of the council make up a majority of these committees, but a number of people with experience in education and knowledge of the local education situation are also included.

The LEAs own and maintain schools and colleges, build new ones and provide equipment. Most of the public money spent on education is disbursed by the local authorities. LEAs are financed largely from the community charge and Aggregate External Finance (AEF) from the Department of the Environment in England and the Welsh Office in Wales.

The powers of local education authorities as regards the control of their schools have been modified in recent years. The Education (No. 2) Act 1986 legislated for equal numbers of parents and local authority representatives as governors in most maintained schools. This modification was continued by the Education Reform Act 1988, which delegated control of their budgets directly to secondary and larger primary schools, although LEAs can exercise their discretion to delegate to primary schools. It also provided for schools to opt out of local authority control and to be funded directly by central government.

Scotland.—The duty of providing education locally in Scotland rests with the nine regional and three islands councils. They are responsible for the construction of buildings, the employment of teachers and other staff, and the provision of equipment and materials. Their responsibility for the curricula taught in schools is delegated at the moment to individual headteachers, but discussions are taking place on the standardization of curricula to allow for new assessment procedures.

The powers of local authorities over educational institutions under their control have been reduced also in Scotland. Under the School Boards (Scotland) Act 1988, education authorities are required to establish school boards consisting of parents and teachers as well as co-opted members, responsible among other things for the appointment of staff. The Self-Governing Schools etc. (Scotland) Act 1989 provides for schools to withdraw from local authority control and become self-governing; for the institution of Technology Academies directly funded by central government; and for the composition of further education college councils on which at least half the members are employers, and for the delegation of substantial functions to these new councils.

Northern Ireland.—Education is administered locally in Northern Ireland by five education and library boards. All grant-aided schools include elected parents and teachers on their boards of governors. Provision has been made for schools wishing to provide integrated education to have grant-main-tained integrated status from the outset. All secondary schools and colleges of further education have had full responsibility for their own budgets, including staffing costs, since April 1991. Primary and nursery schools have partly delegated budgets, although the Boards were able to delegate fully if they wish.

The Council for Catholic Maintained Schools forms an upper tier of management for Catholic schools and provides advice on matters relating to management and administration.

The Inspectorate

In England, Wales and Scotland Her Majesty's Inspectors (HMIs) inspect state and independent schools and all other educational establishments apart from universities. The same function is performed in Northern Ireland by the Education and Training Inspectorate of the Department of Education. The Inspectors assess standards and trends and advise the Secretaries of State on the performance of the system in the United Kingdom. They identify and make more widely known good practice and promising developments, and draw attention to weaknesses. They provide advice and help to those with responsibilities for, or in, the institutions through day-to-day contacts, contributions to training, and their publications. Inspection visits are the main way in which the Inspectors perform their functions. There were, in 1991–92, 475 HMIs in England, 54 in Wales, 105 in Scotland and 62 members of the Inspectorate in Northern Ireland.

SCHOOLS AND PUPILS

Schooling is compulsory in the United Kingdom for all children between five and 16 years. Some provision is made for children under five and many pupils remain at school after the minimum leaving age. No fees are charged in any publicly maintained school in England, Wales and Scotland. In Northern Ireland, fees are paid by pupils in preparatory departments of grammar schools, but pupils admitted to the secondary departments of grammar schools do not pay fees.

In the United Kingdom, parents have a right to express a preference for a particular school and have a right to appeal if dissatisfied. Parental choice has been increased by the introduction of a policy known as more open enrolment whereby schools are required to admit children up to the limit of their capacity if there is a demand for places, and to publish their criteria for selection if they are over-subscribed.

Schools are now required to make available information about themselves and their examination results. Corporal punishment is no longer legal in publicly maintained schools in the United Kingdom.

Fall and rise in numbers

In primary education, and increasingly in secondary education, pupil numbers in the United Kingdom have declined. In primary schools pupil numbers reached their lowest figure of 4·3 million in 1985–86. Numbers stood at 4·8 million in 1988–89 and are expected to increase gradually year by year until by 1999 they reach about 5·6 million. In secondary schools pupil numbers rose to 4·6 million in 1981. They stood at 3·5 million in 1988–89 and are projected to decrease to 3·4 million in 1991, before rising to 3·8 million in 1999.

England and Wales

There are two main categories of school in England and Wales: those maintained by local education authorities (27,335), which charge no fees; and independent schools (2,437), which charge fees (*see* p. 444). To these two categories may be added two more as a result of the Education Reform Act 1988, consisting of institutions funded directly by the Secretary of State. These comprise primary and secondary schools which, although still providing free education, have applied to opt out of local education authority control in favour of grant-maintained status; and City Technology Colleges (*see* below).

Maintained schools are of two types: (i) county schools (15,580 in 1990) which are owned by LEAs and wholly funded by them. They are non-denominational and provide primary and secondary education; (ii) voluntary schools (7,458 in 1990) which also provide primary and secondary education. Although the buildings are in many cases provided by the voluntary bodies (mainly religious denominations) they are financially maintained by an LEA.

All publicly maintained schools have a governing body usually made up of an equal number of parent representatives and governors appointed by the LEA, the headteacher (unless he or she chooses otherwise), and serving teachers. Parental involvement in the running of their children's schools has increased considerably in recent years, and parents have also been given the power to decide by ballot whether their child's school should opt out of local authority control. The responsibilities of governors under the Education (No. 2) Act 1986 were extended to cover the overall policies of schools and their academic aims and objectives. The governors also now control matters of school discipline and the appointment and dismissal of staff. The Education Reform Act 1988 delegated control of the administration of the major part of school budgets, including staffing costs, from LEAs directly to the larger primary and secondary schools under an initiative known as Local Management of Schools (LMS).

Voluntary schools are of three kinds: controlled (3,070), aided (4,314) and special agreement (74). In controlled schools the LEA bears all costs. In aided schools the building is usually provided by the voluntary body. The managers or governors are responsible for repairs to the outside of the school building and for improvements and alterations to it, though the Department of Education and Science may reimburse part of approved capital expenditure. The LEA pays for internal maintenance and other running costs. Special agreement schools are those where the LEA may, by special agreement, pay between one-half and three-quarters of the cost of building a new, or extending an existing, voluntary school, almost always a secondary school. There are no special agreement schools in Wales.

In voluntary schools the majority of the managers or governors are appointed by the voluntary body and at least one by the LEA. The managers or governors control the appointment of teachers. Expenditure is normally apportioned between the authority and the voluntary body.

Grant-maintained (GM) schools.—All secondary schools and larger primary schools are eligible to apply for grant-maintained status, subject to a ballot of parents. GM schools are maintained directly by the Secretary of State, not the LEA, and are wholly run by their own governing body. By September 1991 there were at least 100 GM schools, of which 56 per cent were comprehensive schools.

City Technology Colleges (CTCs) and City Colleges for the Technology of the Arts (CCTAs).—These schools are state-aided but independent of LEAs. Their aim is to widen the choice of secondary education in disadvantaged urban areas and to teach a broad curriculum with an emphasis on science, technology, business understanding and arts technologies. Capital costs are shared by government and sponsors from industry and commerce, and running costs are covered by a per capita grant from the DES in line with comparable costs in an LEA maintained school.

The first city technology college opened in September 1988 in Solihull. By September 1991 there were thirteen. The first CCTA, known as Britschool, opened in Croydon in September 1991.

Scotland

Schools in Scotland fall into three main categories: education authority schools (3,778) (known as public schools), which are financed and managed by the regional and islands councils; grant aided schools (9), conducted by voluntary managers who receive grants direct from the Scottish Office Education Department; and independent schools (121), which receive no direct grant and charge fees, but are subject to inspection and registration. An additional category is created under the provisions of the Self-Governing Schools etc. (Scotland) Act 1989, of schools opting to be managed entirely by a board of management consisting of the headmaster, parent and staff representatives and co-opted members. The change of status will require a ballot of parents and the publication of proposals by the board, and the achievement of self-government is subject to a final decision by the Secretary of State. These schools will remain in the public sector and will be funded by direct government grant set to match the resources the school would have received under education authority management.

Under the School Boards (Scotland) Act 1988, education authorities are required to establish school boards to participate in the administration and management of schools. These boards consist of elected parents and staff members as well as co-opted members.

Technology Academies (TAs).—The Self-Governing Schools etc. (Scotland) Act 1989 provides for setting up technology academies in areas of urban deprivation. These secondary schools are intended to be so placed as to draw on a wide catchment, and will offer a broad curriculum with an emphasis on science and technology. They are to be founded and managed in partnership with industrial sponsors, with central government meeting the running costs by grant-aid thereafter.

Northern Ireland

There are three main categories of grant-aided school in Northern Ireland: controlled schools (713), which are controlled by the education and library boards with all costs paid from public funds; voluntary maintained schools (586), mainly under Roman Catholic management, which receive grants towards capital costs and running costs in whole or in part; and voluntary grammar schools (52), which may be under Roman Catholic or non-denominational management and receive grants from the Department of Education for Northern Ireland. All grant-aided schools include elected parents and teachers on their boards of governors, whose responsibilities also include financial management under the Local Management of Schools (LMS) initiative. There are also 16 independent schools in Northern Ireland.

The majority of children in Northern Ireland are educated in schools which in practice are segregated on religious lines. The Education Reform (Northern Ireland) Order 1989, however, makes provision for parents to opt for integrated education more easily. These provisions include arrangements to fund new integrated schools from the outset and procedure for balloting parents in existing segregated schools to determine whether they want instead to have integrated schools.

THE STATE SYSTEM

Nursery education.—Nursery education is for children from two to five years and is not compulsory. In the United Kingdom it takes place in nursery schools or nursery classes in primary schools. In 1988–89, 722,000 pupils under five years of age were receiving education in maintained nursery and primary schools, an increase of 22,000 on the previous year. Of the total, 81,700 were in nursery schools, 590,100 in nursery classes in primary schools, and 43,900 in non-maintained nursery schools. Expressed as a percentage of the population aged three and four years, the 722,000 represented 49 per cent, compared to 48·4 per cent in the previous year.

Many children also attend pre-school playgroups organized by parents and voluntary bodies such as the Pre-School Playgroups Association.

Primary education.—Primary education begins at five years and is almost always co-educational. In England, Wales and Northern Ireland the transfer to secondary school is generally made at 11 years. In Scotland, the primary school course lasts for seven years and pupils transfer to secondary courses at about the age of 12.

Primary schools consist mainly of infants' schools for children aged five to seven, junior schools for those aged seven to 11, and combined junior and infant schools for both age groups. In addition, first schools in some parts of England cater for ages five to ten. (They are the first stage of a three-tier system: first, middle and secondary). Many primary schools provide nursery classes for children under five (see above).

The number of primary schools in the United Kingdom in 1988–89 was 24,334, which was 148 fewer than in 1987–88, with 4,792,000 full- and part-time pupils, of which 768,000 were under five. Between 1989 and 1999 primary school pupil numbers are projected to rise by about 15 per cent.

Pupil-teacher ratios in maintained primary schools in the United Kingdom are:

	1987–88	1988–89
England	22·0	22·0
Wales	22·1	22·3
Scotland	20·4	20·3
Northern Ireland	23·5	23·2
UK	21·9	21·9

The average size of classes 'as taught' has fallen from 25·5 in 1981 to 25·1 in 1989.

Middle schools.—Middle schools (which take children from first schools), mostly in England, cover varying age ranges between eight and 14 and usually lead on to comprehensive upper schools.

Secondary education.—Secondary schools are for children aged 11 to 16 and for those who choose to stay on to 18. At 16, many students prefer to move on to tertiary or sixth form colleges (*see* p. 447). Most secondary schools in England, Wales and Scotland are co-educational. The largest secondary schools have over 2,000 pupils but only 20 per cent of the schools take over 1,000 pupils.

In England and Wales the main types of secondary schools are: comprehensive schools (85·9 per cent of pupils in England, 98·9 in Wales), whose admission arrangements are without reference to ability or aptitude; middle deemed secondary schools for children aged variously between eight and 14 years who then move on to senior comprehensive schools at 12, 13 or 14 (6·3 per cent of pupils in England only); secondary modern schools (3·9 per cent of pupils in England, 0·2 per cent in Wales) providing a general education with a practical bias; secondary grammar schools (3·4 per cent of pupils in England, 0·2 per cent in Wales) with selective intake providing an academic course from 11 to 16–18 years; and technical schools (0·1 per cent) in England only, providing an integrated academic and technical education.

In January 1990 there were in England and Wales 3,048,323 pupils in maintained secondary schools, including 11 per cent (England) and 11·5 per cent (Wales) who were 16 or over. After falling by 12 per cent between 1987 and 1991, numbers are projected to rise by 8·7 per cent by 1998.

Pupil-teacher ratios have improved steadily from 16·1 in 1985–86 to 15·3 in 1990 in England and Wales. The average class size in England was 20·7 in 1990. In Wales the average class size in 1990 was 18·9.

In Scotland all pupils in education authority secondary schools attend schools with a comprehensive intake. Most of these schools provide a full range of courses appropriate to all levels of ability from first to sixth year. In 1989–90 there were 298,603 pupils in education authority schools, of whom 17·4 per cent were 16 or over. Numbers are not expected to increase much between 1990 and 1995. Pupil-teacher ratios have improved from 14·4 in 1981–82 to 12·3 in 1990. The average class size in 1990 was 18·5.

In most areas of Northern Ireland there is a selective system of secondary education with pupils transferring either to grammar schools or secondary schools at 11–12 years of age. Parents can choose the school they would like their children to attend and all those who apply must be admitted. If a school is over-subscribed beyond its statutory admissions number, selection is on the basis of published criteria. In drawing up their criteria most grammar schools place emphasis on performance in the transfer procedure tests which are centrally administered by the Department of Education. When parents consider that a school has not applied its criteria fairly they have access to independent appeals tribunals. Grammar schools provide an academic type of secondary

education with A-levels at the end of the seventh year, while secondary non-grammar schools follow a curriculum suited to a wider range of aptitudes and abilities.

In 1988–89 there were 143,099 pupils in public sector secondary schools, of whom 89,968 (62·9 per cent) attended non-grammar secondary and 53,131 (37·1 per cent) attended grammar schools. Of these 23·8 per cent were 16 or over. Pupil-teacher ratios in Northern Ireland have improved from 15·5 in 1982 to 15·1 in 1990.

Special education.—Special education is provided for children with special educational needs, usually because they have a disability which either prevents or hinders them from making use of educational facilities of a kind generally provided for children of their age in schools within the area of the local authority concerned. Maintained special schools are run by education authorities which pay all the costs of maintenance, although the government is looking to extend Local Management of Schools (LMS) to them also. Non-maintained special schools are run by voluntary bodies; they may receive some grant from central government for capital expenditure and for equipment, but their current expenditure is met primarily from the fees charged to the education authorities for pupils placed in the schools. Some independent schools provide education wholly or mainly for children with special educational needs and are required to meet similar standards to those for maintained and non-maintained special schools. The national curriculum also applies to children with a statement of special needs, but there is provision for them to be exempt from it, or for it to be modified to suit the individual child's capabilities.

In January 1989 in the United Kingdom there was a total of 114,100 full-time pupils in special schools (of whom 2,800 were in hospital schools in England, Wales and Northern Ireland). Of the total, 97,500 were in England, 3,800 in Wales, 8,900 in Scotland and 3,800 in Northern Ireland. Numbers have decreased since 1975–76 as education authorities in England, Wales and Northern Ireland must now ensure that children with special needs are educated as far as possible in ordinary schools with support teaching.

In Scotland, school placing is a matter of agreement between education authorities and parents. Parents have the right to say which school they want their child to attend, and a right of appeal where their wishes are not being met. Whenever possible, children with special needs are integrated into ordinary schools. However, for those who require a different environment or specialized facilities, there are special schools, both grant-aided and independent, and special classes within ordinary schools. The Self-Governing Schools etc. (Scotland) Act 1989 obliges education authorities to respond to reasonable requests for independent special schools, and provides for them to send children with special needs to schools outside Scotland if appropriate provision is not available within the country.

Alternative provision

There is no legal obligation on parents in the United Kingdom to educate their children at school provided that the local education authority is satisfied that the child is receiving full-time education suited to its age, abilities and aptitudes. The education authority need not be informed that a child is being educated at home unless the child is already registered at a state school. In this case the parents must arrange for the child's name to be removed from the school's register (by writing to the headteacher) before education at home can begin. Failure to de-register a child leaves the parents liable to prosecution for condoning non-attendance.

In most cases an initial visit is made by an education adviser or education welfare officer, and sometimes subsequent inspections are made, but practice varies according to the individual education authority. There is no requirement for parents educating their children at home to be in possession of a teaching qualification.

Further advice on educating children other than at school can be obtained from Education Otherwise (*see* p. 456).

INDEPENDENT SCHOOLS

Independent schools receive no grants from public funds. They charge fees, and are owned and managed under special trusts, with profits being used for the benefit of the schools concerned. There is a wide variety of provision, from kindergartens to large day and boarding schools, and from experimental schools to traditional institutions. A number of independent schools have been instituted by religious and ethnic minorities.

All independent schools in the United Kingdom are open to inspection by the Inspectorate (*see* p. 441) and must register with the appropriate government education department. The education departments lay down certain minimum standards and can make schools remedy any unacceptable features of their building or instruction and exclude any unsuitable teacher or proprietor. Most independent schools offer a similar range of courses to state schools and enter pupils for the same public examinations. Introduction of the national curriculum and the associated education targets and assessment procedures is not obligatory in the independent sector.

The term public schools is often applied to those independent schools in membership of the Headmasters' Conference, the Governing Bodies Association or the Governing Bodies of Girls' Schools Association. Most public schools are single-sex (about half of them for girls) but there are some mixed schools and an increasing number of schools have mixed sixth forms.

Preparatory schools are so called because they prepare children for the Common Entrance Examination to senior independent schools. Most cater for boys from about seven to 13 years, some are for girls, and an increasing number are co-educational. The Common Entrance Examination is set by the Common Entrance Examination Board, but marked by the independent school to which the pupil intends to go. It is taken at 13 by boys, and from 11 to 13 by girls.

In 1990 there were in England 2,280 independent schools with 558,700 full-time pupils and a pupil-teacher ratio of 10·9.

In Wales in 1989–90 there were 67 independent schools, with 12,075 pupils and a pupil-teacher ratio of 10·5.

In Scotland in 1989–90 there were 121 registered independent schools with 33,100 pupils. Most independent schools in Scotland follow the English examination system, i.e. GCSE followed by A-levels, although some take the Scottish Education Certificate at Ordinary/Standard grade followed by Highers.

There are 16 independent schools in Northern Ireland with 959 pupils and a pupil-teacher ratio of 13·3.

Assisted Places Scheme

The Assisted Places Scheme enables children to attend independent secondary schools which their parents could not otherwise afford. The scheme provides help with tuition fees and other expenses, except boarding costs, on a sliding scale depending on the family's income. The take-up rate for places

available at age 11 to 13 at the 303 participating schools in England and Wales is around 90 per cent, and the proportion of pupils receiving full fee remission is 32 per cent. Over 34,000 places were offered in England and Wales in the academic year 1990–91. The 59 participating schools in Scotland admitted 2,900 pupils on the scheme, which, unlike that in England and Wales, is cash-limited. The proportion of pupils receiving full fee remission is 43 per cent.

The scheme is administered and funded in England by the Department of Education and Science, in Wales by the Welsh Office, and in Scotland by the Scottish Office Education Department.

The scheme does not operate in Northern Ireland as the independent sector admits non-fee paying pupils. There is, however, a similar scheme known as the Talented Children's Scheme to help pupils gifted in music and dance.

Further information can be obtained from the Independent Schools Information Service (*see* p. 456).

THE CURRICULUM

England and Wales

The Education Reform Act 1988 legislated for the progressive introduction of a national curriculum in primary and secondary schools from autumn 1989. During the period of compulsory schooling for children aged five to 16 the curriculum will include mathematics, English and science as core subjects and history, geography, technology, music, art, physical education and (for pupils in secondary schools) a modern foreign language as foundation subjects. For the core and foundation subjects there will be attainment targets and assessment procedures at the ages of seven, 11 and 14; at 16 the GCSE will be the main form of assessment. It is intended that pupils with special educational needs should have access to as much of the national curriculum as possible. Religious education is required to be available in schools, with the curriculum devised locally, but parents have the right to remove their children if they wish.

In Wales in 1989–90 the Welsh language was in use as the main or secondary medium of instruction in 34·5 per cent of primary and 18·2 per cent of secondary schools. Following the introduction of the national curriculum it will constitute a core subject in Welsh speaking schools and a foundation subject in the others, although there is provision for exemptions to be made.

In England the National Curriculum Council, funded by the Department of Education and Science, is responsible for the promotion and support of curriculum development, in addition to advising the Secretary of State on the national curriculum. In Wales this function is performed by the Curriculum Council for Wales, funded by the Welsh Office.

Scotland

The content and management of the curriculum in Scotland is the responsibility of education authorities and individual headteachers. Advice and guidance is provided by the Scottish Office Education Department and the Scottish Consultative Council on the Curriculum. Scotland effectively has a national curriculum for 14–16 year-olds, who are required to study English, mathematics and a science subject plus five other subjects. These form the core area supplemented by other activities forming the elective area. There is a recommended percentage of class time to be devoted to each area over the two years. Provision is made for teaching in Gaelic in Gaelic speaking areas.

The Scottish Consultative Council on the Curriculum, which is responsible for development and advisory work on the curriculum in Scotland, has been asked to undertake a major review of the balance of the primary curriculum, and to produce new guidelines for each of the subject areas for the age group five to 14. There will be new guidelines on assessment across the whole curriculum, and standardized tests will be introduced in English and mathematics for nine and 12 year-olds. For 16–18 year-olds, there is available a modular system of vocational courses in addition to academic courses.

Northern Ireland

Major programmes of curriculum review and development are in progress in primary and secondary schools. A curriculum common to all schools is being introduced over a three-year period to 1992–93, with six broad areas of study within which ten subjects will be compulsory; religious education will also be a compulsory part of the curriculum. The Irish language will be a compulsory subject in Irish-medium primary schools and can be chosen as the compulsory foreign language in secondary schools. Arrangements for the assessment of pupils, broadly in line with those in England and Wales, are proposed at the ages of eight, 11, 14 and 16.

The Northern Ireland Curriculum Council advises the Government on all matters concerning the curriculum for grant-aided schools in Northern Ireland.

Records of achievement

National records of achievement are documents which set down the range of school-leavers' achievements and activities both inside and outside the classroom, including those not tested by examination. They are being issued to all those leaving school in England and Wales from summer 1991 and will be introduced in Scotland. It is also intended that by 1991 parents in England and Wales will receive a yearly progress report on all aspects of their children's achievements. There is a similar commitment for Northern Ireland. In Scotland the report card system is being reformed to give parents more information on their children's progress.

Technical and Vocational Initiative

The Technical and Vocational Initiative (TVEI) operates across the curriculum within a framework of general education in England, Wales and Scotland. It aims to make the secondary curriculum more relevant to adult life and work. Following pilot projects, it is now a national scheme with newly established criteria which complement and are compatible with the requirements of the new national curriculum in England and Wales. Participation is voluntary, and is open to all maintained schools and colleges providing for young people of all abilities aged 14–18. TVEI is not an examination or a qualification.

THE PUBLIC EXAMINATION SYSTEM
England, Wales and Northern Ireland

Until the end of 1987, secondary school pupils at the end of compulsory schooling around the age of 16, and others, took the General Certificate of Education (GCE) Ordinary-level or the Certificate of Secondary Education (CSE). From 1988 these were replaced by a single system of examinations, the General Certificate of Secondary Education (GCSE), which is usually taken after five years of secondary education. The first examinations took place in summer 1988.

The GCSE differs from its predecessors in that there are: syllabuses based on national criteria covering course objectives, content and assessment methods; differentiated assessment (i.e. different papers or questions for different ranges of ability); and grade-related criteria (i.e. grades awarded on absolute rather than relative performance).

The GCSE certificates are awarded on a seven-point scale, A to G. Grades A to C are the equivalent of the corresponding O-level grades A to C, or CSE grade 1. Grades D, E, F and G record achievement at least as high as that represented by CSE grades 2 to 5. There is no restriction on entry to any examination. All GCSE syllabuses, assessments and grading procedures are monitored by the School Examinations and Assessment Council (*see* below) to ensure that they conform to the national criteria.

Of school leavers in the United Kingdom who left school without A-levels or SCE H-grades in 1988–89, 36·1 per cent had achieved one or more graded GCE O-level, CSE, GCSE or SCE O-grade results.

From September 1991, maintained schools will be able to offer BTEC Firsts (*see* below) and it is hoped that more schools will offer BTEC Nationals than do so at present.

Certificate of Extended Education.—The Certificate of Extended Education (CEE) comprises a number of single-subject examinations set and awarded by certain GCSE examining boards and taken a year after GCSE. Apart from English and mathematics, subjects are non-traditional and include social, environmental, technological, business and health studies.

Advanced levels.—Advanced (A-level) examinations, taken by those who choose to continue their education after GCSE, continue as before although changes have been made to the grading system.

A-level courses last two years and have traditionally provided the foundation for entry to higher education. A-levels are marked on a seven-point scale, from A to E, N (narrow failure) and U (unclassified), which latter grade will not be certificated.

Advanced Supplementary Levels.—As an alternative to, and to complement, A-level examinations, Advanced Supplementary level (AS-level) examinations were introduced in September 1987, with the first examinations taking place in summer 1989. AS-levels are for full-time A-level students but also open to other students. An AS-level syllabus covers not less than half the amount of ground covered by the corresponding A-level syllabus and, where possible, is related to it. An AS-level course lasts two years and requires not less than half the teaching time of the corresponding A-level course, and two AS-levels are equivalent to one A-level. AS-level courses are intended to supplement and broaden A-level studies, and examinations are held at the same time as A-levels. AS-level passes are graded A to E, with grade standards related to the A-level grades.

A mixture of A-level courses in the subjects to be specialized in and AS-levels will form the standard for admission to higher education.

In the United Kingdom in 1988–89, 23 per cent of all 17 year olds (22 per cent of boys, 24 per cent of girls) achieved one or more A-level or SCE H-grade result. This figure includes those continuing their education in maintained further education establishments including tertiary colleges, as well as school leavers.

Of school leavers alone (755,000), 19·1 per cent achieved at least one A-level or SCE H-grade (18·5 per cent of boys, 19·8 per cent of girls). Of those in Great Britain obtaining two or more A-levels, or three or more SCE H-grades, 16 per cent studied sciences (22 per cent of boys, 11 per cent of girls), 41 per cent studied arts/social studies (32 per cent of boys, 50 per cent of girls), and 43 per cent (46 per cent of boys, 39 per cent of girls) studied science and arts/social studies.

S-levels.—Most examining boards allow the option of an additional paper of greater difficulty to be taken by A-level candidates to obtain what is known as a Special-level or Scholarship-level qualification. S-level papers are available in most of the traditional academic subjects and are marked on a three-point scale, grade A or 1, grade B or 2, and unclassified.

The Certificate of Pre-Vocational Education.—The Certificate of Pre-Vocational Education (CPVE) is a one-year full-time (or two years part-time) course available at schools and colleges in England, Wales and Northern Ireland. It is intended for a wide ability range at 16+, including pupils who might not go on to A-levels but would like to continue their education on completion of their secondary schooling. The qualification is offered by the City and Guilds of London Institute.

There are no formal examinations but credits for work achieved during CPVE can be built up towards further study. Within guidelines schools and colleges design their own courses, which stress activity-based learning, basic numeracy and work experience. The CPVE is mainly for those who want to find out what aptitudes they may have and to prepare themselves for work, but who are not yet committed to a particular occupation. Over a two-year period from September 1991 CPVE is to be phased out and the Diploma of Vocational Education will take its place.

Co-ordination and advisory bodies.—The School Examinations and Assessment Council (SEAC) has been set up to advise the Government on all school examinations and assessment matters in England and Wales. It is also responsible for the development of the assessment system for the national curriculum. The Council is funded wholly by the Department of Education and Science.

The Northern Ireland Schools Examinations and Assessment Council performs the same function in Northern Ireland, funded by the Department of Education for Northern Ireland.

Scotland

The system of public examinations in Scotland is different from that elsewhere in the United Kingdom. At the end of the fourth year of secondary education (equivalent to the fifth year in the rest of the United Kingdom), at about the age of 16, pupils take either the Ordinary grade of the Scottish Certificate of Education Examination (corresponding to the old GCE Ordinary level) or the Standard grade. The Ordinary grade will be replaced by 1993 by the new Standard grade courses and examinations, which have been designed to suit every level of ability, with assessment against nationally determined standards of performance.

For most courses there are three separate examination papers at the end of the two-year Standard grade course. They are set at Credit (leading to awards at grade 1 or 2), General (leading to awards at grade 3 or 4) and Foundation (leading to awards at grade 5 or 6) levels. Grade 7 is available to those who, although they have completed the course, have shown no significant level of attainment. Normally pupils will take examinations covering two pairs of grades, either grades 1–4 or grades 3–6.

Pupils may attempt as many of a wide range of subjects as they are capable of, on either the Ordinary/Standard grades, or on the Higher grade which is normally taken one year after Ordinary/Standard grades, at the age of 17 or thereabouts. The shorter length of course means that Higher grades are normally studied to a lesser depth than A-levels; on the other hand it is common for pupils to be presented for four or more Higher grades at a single diet of the examination.

The Certificate of Sixth Year Studies (CSYS) is designed to give direction and purpose to sixth-year work by encouraging pupils who have completed their main subjects at Higher grade to study a maximum of three of these subjects in depth. Pupils may also use the sixth year to gain improved or additional Higher grades or Ordinary/Standard grades.

The Scottish Certificate of Education Examination and the Certificate of Sixth Year Studies are conducted by the Scottish Examination Board.

National Certificates.—National Certificates were introduced in 1984–85 as an alternative to, and to complement, Highers and CSYS. They are awarded to pupils over the age of 16 who have successfully completed a programme of vocational courses based on modular study units, and the assessment system is based on national criteria. The modules are now being introduced in schools for pupils aged 14–16, and other short courses are being devised for use in schools. National Certificates are validated by the Scottish Vocational Education Council (*see also* p. 448).

The International Baccalaureate

The International Baccalaureate is an internationally recognized two-year pre-university course and examination designed to facilitate the mobility of students and to promote international understanding. Candidates must offer one subject from each of six subject groups, at least three at higher level and the remainder at subsidiary level. Single subjects can be offered, for which a certificate is received. There are 22 schools and colleges in the United Kingdom which offer the International Baccalaureate diploma. Further information can be obtained from International Baccalaureate London.

TEACHERS
England and Wales

Teachers are appointed by local education authorities, school governing bodies, or school managers. Those in publicly maintained schools must be approved as qualified by the Department of Education and Science. To become a qualified teacher it is necessary to have successfully completed a course of initial teacher training, usually either a Bachelor of Education (B.Ed.) degree or the Postgraduate Certificate of Education (PGCE). Teacher training has hitherto been largely integrated with the rest of higher education, with training places concentrated in universities, polytechnics and institutes or colleges of education, but under the articled teacher scheme, graduates will be paid a bursary in addition to a salary to complete a school-based PGCE course over two years involving a progressively increasing teaching load.

With certain exceptions the profession now has an all-graduate entry. Teachers in further education are not required to have qualified teacher status, though roughly half have a teaching qualification and most have industrial, commercial or professional experience.

The licensed teacher scheme is designed to attract into the teaching profession entrants over 24 years of age without formal teaching qualifications but with relevant training and experience. All licensees are required to have the equivalent of two years' higher education in the United Kingdom and the equivalent of grade C in GCSE maths and English. Local education authorities will be involved in devising a suitable two-year training programme for any licensed teachers they may appoint to their schools; for grant-maintained schools and City Technology Colleges this will be a matter for the schools themselves. LEAs have discretion to recommend qualified teacher status after one year for a licensee with at least two years' experience as an instructor prior to becoming a licensed teacher.

Scotland

All teachers in maintained schools must be registered with the General Teaching Council for Scotland. They are registered provisionally for a two-year probationary period which can be extended if necessary. Only graduates are accepted as entrants to the teaching profession in Scotland.

Northern Ireland

Teacher training in Northern Ireland is provided by the two universities and two colleges of education. The colleges are concerned with teacher education mainly for the primary school sector. They also provide B.Ed. courses for intending secondary school teachers of religious education, commercial studies, and craft, design and technology. With these exceptions, the training of teachers for secondary schools is provided in the education departments of the universities.

Accreditation of training courses

The Council for the Accreditation of Teacher Education (CATE) advises on course accreditation in England, Wales and Northern Ireland, and monitors and disseminates good practice. In Scotland all training courses in colleges of education must be approved by the Scottish Office Education Department and a validating body.

Newly-trained teachers

Of teachers who in 1988 had successfully completed initial training courses in the United Kingdom, 10,200 had completed a postgraduate course and 8,200 a course for non-graduates.

In the year to January 1990, 13,800 teachers took up first full-time appointments, either permanently or for at least one term's duration, in maintained nursery, primary and secondary schools in England

and Wales. In Scotland and Northern Ireland, figures for 1990 were 1,366 and 550 respectively.

Shortage subjects.—Because of a shortage of teachers in a number of secondary subjects, a tax-free bursary scheme for trainee teachers on one- or two-year courses has been introduced. The subjects are mathematics, chemistry, biology, modern languages (including Welsh in Wales), and technology, which attract a bursary of £1,500, and physics, which attracts a bursary of £2,000.

Serving teachers

In 1988–89 there were 616,000 teachers (full-time and full-time equivalent) in public sector schools and establishments of further education in the United Kingdom. Of these, 494,000 were in maintained schools and 112,000 in further education. There were 209,000 full-time teachers in public sector primary schools, 244,000 in public sector secondary schools and 19,000 in special schools.

Salaries

All qualified teachers in England and Wales, other than heads and deputy heads, are paid on a ten-point scale ranging from £10,404 to £17,502 (£10,212 to £17,208 in Northern Ireland) (January 1992 figures). Entry points vary depending on qualification and according to the discretion of the appointing authority. In addition, incentive allowances are payable on a range of five rates. Headteachers' salaries range from £21,310 to £46,678 (principals from £20,640 to £40,746 in Northern Ireland); deputy headteachers' salaries range from £20,633 to £33,940 (vice-principals from £19,674 to £29,670 in Northern Ireland). There is a statutory superannuation scheme in maintained schools.

Teachers in Scotland are paid (January 1992 figures) on a ten-point scale from £10,746 to £17,862. As in the rest of the United Kingdom, the entry point depends on type of qualification, and additional allowances are payable under certain circumstances. Headteachers are paid on a scale from £20,820 to £36,936 and deputy headteachers from £21,624 to £28,203, depending on whether the school is primary or secondary and the size of school roll.

FURTHER EDUCATION

The Education Reform Act 1988 defines further education as all provision outside schools to people aged over 16 of education up to and including A-level and its equivalent. All education authorities have a duty to secure provision of adequate facilities for further education in their area.

England and Wales

Responsibility for co-ordinating further education provision rests with ten Regional Advisory Councils set up by the local education authorities (LEAs) in each region. There are nine for England, and the Welsh Joint Education Committee acts as the council for Wales. The councils operate in accordance with terms of reference agreed between the participating LEAs, which meet staffing and other expenses. Members include representatives from LEAs, polytechnics and universities, further education institutions, employers and employees in industry and commerce. HM Inspectors attend as assessors.

Proposals are at present under consideration for all further education and sixth form colleges to be taken out of local authority control by mid-1993, and

funded directly by central government through national further education councils.

In England and Wales further education courses are taught at a variety of institutions. These range from polytechnics and colleges of further and higher education (most of which also offer higher education courses) to tertiary colleges and sixth form colleges, which concentrate on the provision of normal sixth form school courses as well as a range of vocational courses. A number of institutions specific to a particular form of training, e.g. the Royal College of Music, are also involved. All such courses are funded at present by local education authorities, including further education courses in polytechnics and colleges of higher education.

Every institution maintained by a local education authority and providing full-time further education under a further education scheme is required to appoint a board of governors. At least half the governors must represent employment interests or be independent of local authority or college interests. Local authorities must delegate to these bodies extensive powers over the appointment of staff and the management of college budgets under the local management of further and higher education colleges initiative.

The position of teaching staff in further education establishments is similar to that in schools with respect to qualifications and regular appraisal of teachers' performance.

Much of the post-school provision outside the higher education sector is broadly vocational in purpose. It ranges from lower-level technical and commercial courses through courses for those aiming at higher-level posts in industry, commerce and administration, to professional courses. Facilities for GCSE courses, CEE (Certificate of Extended Education), CPVE (Certificate of Pre-Vocational Education), AS-levels and A-level courses are also provided (see pp. 445–6). These courses can form the foundation for progress to higher education qualifications (see below).

The main courses and examinations in the vocational field are offered by the following bodies, but there are also many others:

Business and Technician Education Council (BTEC) provides awards across a wide range of subject areas and four main qualifications: the BTEC First Certificate (one year part-time), the BTEC First Diploma (one year full-time or two years part-time), the BTEC National Certificate (two years part-time), and the BTEC National Diploma (two years full-time or three years part-time or as a sandwich course).

City and Guilds of London Institute (C&G) offers a wide range of technical and vocational qualifications and has sole responsibility for administering CPVE (see p. 446). Most courses are part-time for students already in employment, but some full-time courses are available.

RSA (Royal Society of Arts) Examinations Board schemes cover a wide range of vocational qualifications, including business and administration, language schemes and teaching qualifications. Many schemes are offered at levels matching those established by the NCVQ (see below), and a policy operates of credit accumulation, so that candidates can take a single unit or complete qualifications.

There are 486 further education establishments in England and Wales with 2,782 adult education centres. In 1989–90 there were 400,282 full-time and sandwich students and 853,898 part-time students on further education courses.

Scotland

Education authorities in Scotland provide further education comprising non-advanced courses up to SCE Highers grade, GCE A-level and SCOTVEC vocational courses, but as in England and Wales it is proposed that funding of further education colleges should be transferred to central government by April 1993. Courses are taught mainly at colleges of further education, including technical colleges, and in some schools.

The Self-Governing Schools etc. (Scotland) Act 1989 legislated for Further Education College Councils to be set up with extensive powers to run their colleges. The Act specifies that at least half the members of college councils must be private or public sector employers and not more than one-fifth local authority representatives; that education authorities must delegate substantial functions to the new councils; and that colleges must be allowed to earn income from commercial activities.

The Scottish Vocational Education Council (SCOTVEC) provides national qualifications, known as the National Certificate, across a similar range of occupational sectors to the Business and Technician Education Council in England and Wales. The system is completely comprehensive and covers the whole range of non-advanced further education provision in Scotland. Students may study for the National Certificate on a full-time, part-time, or day- or block-

release basis. The system is based on modules an National Certificate modules and modular pro grammes can be taken in further education colleges central institutions or in secondary schools from th age of 16 onwards. Scottish Vocational Qualification (SVQS) combine programmes of SCOTVEC's Na tional Certificate modules or Higher National Unit with skills gained in the work-place.

In 1988–89 there were 33,765 full-time and sandwic students, 169,449 part-time students on non-advance vocational courses of further education in the 4' further education colleges, 12 central institution and five colleges of education.

Northern Ireland

Education and library boards are obliged to prepar and submit for approval to the Department o Education for Northern Ireland, schemes setting ou the principles to be applied by the boards in plannin the further education provision to be made by college under their management.

Although the colleges of further education ar maintained by the education and library boards proposals along the lines of those in England an Wales were implemented in 1991 for the delegation c financial powers and responsibilities to the boards c governors of the colleges and the proposed change in the structure of further education in England Wales and Scotland are being studied for thei relevance to Northern Ireland. The composition o the boards themselves is to be changed to include 5(per cent membership from the professions, loca business or industry, or other fields of employmen relevant to the activities of the college.

On reaching school-leaving age, pupils may attenc colleges of further education to pursue the same type of vocational courses as are provided in colleges ir England and Wales, administered by the sam examining bodies.

Northern Ireland has 24 institutions of furthe education with 287 out-centres. In 1989–90 ther were 16,208 full-time students and 33,112 part-tim students on non-advanced vocational courses o further education.

Course Information

Applications for further education courses ar generally made directly to the colleges concerned Information on further education courses in the United Kingdom and addresses of colleges can be found in the *Directory of Further Education* publishec annually by the Careers Research and Advisory Council.

National Council for Vocational Qualifications

The National Council for Vocational Qualification (NCVQ) was set up by the Government in Octobe 1986 to achieve a coherent national framework fo vocational qualifications. The Council does not award qualifications but works with and through the established examining and awarding bodies to reform the existing vocational qualifications system anc introduce simplified arrangements. The new system should be fully operational in England, Wales anc Northern Ireland by the end of 1992. It does not apply to Scotland, where a reformed framework already exists under the SCOTVEC National Certificate (see above).

The name and style National Vocational Qualifi cation will be accorded to qualifications accreditec by NCVQ and awarded by bodies it has approved The NVQ framework is currently based on four levels incorporating qualifications up to and including the Higher National standard.

A National Record of Vocational Achievement has been introduced which allows small elements of competence acquired at different times and in different ways to be recorded in a standard form and to be built up into a full NVQ.

HIGHER EDUCATION

The term higher education is used to describe education above A-level and Higher grade or their equivalent, which is provided in universities, polytechnics and colleges of higher education.

Students

In 1988–89, there were 863,000 full-time and sandwich students in higher education in the United Kingdom, of whom 65,100 were from overseas. The number of part-time students in the United Kingdom, including the Open University, was 377,000. The proportion of 18 to 20 year-olds entering full-time higher education in Great Britain rose from 16·7 per cent in 1985–86 to 17·3 per cent in 1988–89. The number of mature entrants to higher education in 1988 (excluding those at the Open University) was 204,000, up by 46 per cent on 1981. The number of full-time students on science courses in 1988–89 was 131,700, of which 43,400 were female.

Academic staff

Each university appoints its own academic staff on its own conditions, though there is a common salary structure and, except for Oxford and Cambridge, a common career structure. The University Commissioners were appointed under the Education Reform Act 1988 to secure changes in university statutes to abolish the granting of tenure, thus enabling staff to be dismissed for good cause and for redundancy.

The Education Reform Act 1988 took polytechnics and higher education colleges in England and Wales out of local education authority control, turning them into employers on their own account. The Polytechnics and Colleges Employers Forum was set up to look after terms and conditions of employment and has negotiated the introduction of an academic contract similar to that obtaining in the universities.

Teaching staff in higher education require no formal teaching qualification, but teacher trainers are required to spend a certain amount of time in schools to ensure that they have sufficient recent practical experience.

In 1989–90 there were 53,565 full-time and part-time academic staff in universities in the United Kingdom and 114,257 in public sector further and higher education.

The 1991–92 salary scales for non-clinical academic staff in universities are under negotiation. Those for 1990–91 were: lecturer grade A £11,399–£16,755; lecturer grade B £17,455–£22,311; senior lecturer £23,423–£28,616; professor £27,013 (minimum). Salary scales for lecturers in polytechnics and colleges of higher education (as from September 1990) were: lecturer £9,993–£18,735; senior lecturer £18,108–£23,106; principal lecturer £21,855–£27,477; head of department £26,304 (minimum). The salaries of clinical academic staff are kept broadly comparable to those of doctors and dentists in the National Health Service.

UNIVERSITIES

Universities are self-governing institutions, usually established by Royal Charter, which are responsible for their own academic appointments, curricula and student admissions. The universities have freedom in academic matters but the Government, through the University Funding Council, determines the total size of the university student population, its distribution between arts, science, medicine, etc., and the part which the university sector plays in the higher education system.

Overall responsibility for universities in Great Britain rests with the Secretary of State for Education and Science, who consults with the Secretaries of State for Scotland and Wales as necessary. Universities in Northern Ireland are the responsibility of the Secretary of State for Northern Ireland.

Advice to the Government on university matters is provided by the Universities Funding Council (UFC). The UFC acts as a buffer between the Government, from which it receives a block grant of money, and the universities, to which it allocates its grant. Its brief is to secure more effective use of public funds allocated to higher education.

There are 46 universities in the United Kingdom. Of these, 35 are in England, one (a federal institution) in Wales, eight in Scotland and two in Northern Ireland. In 1989–90 there was a total of 350,981 full-time students at universities in the United Kingdom (12,575 from EC countries; 40,923 from other overseas countries) and 53,850 part-time students. Women form 43·1 per cent of both the full-time total and part-time total.

The non-residential Open University provides courses leading to degrees nationally. Teaching is through a combination of television and radio programmes, correspondence, tutorials, short residential courses and local audio-visual centres. No qualifications are needed for entry. The Open University offers undergraduate, post-experience and postgraduate courses. The University also has a programme of higher degrees: B.Phil., M.Phil. and Ph.D. through research, and MA, MBA and M.Sc. through taught courses.

The Open University is grant-aided directly by the Department of Education and Science and does not come under the Universities Funding Council. For Open University purposes, Northern Ireland is administered as a separate section of the United Kingdom and the cost is met by the Department of Education for Northern Ireland.

In 1990, 72,622 undergraduates were registered at the Open University, of whom 34,200 were women and 38,422 were men. Estimated cost (1991) of a BA general degree was around £2,300 and of a BA Hons. degree over £2,700.

The independent University of Buckingham provides a two-year course leading to a bachelor's degree and its tuition fees were £7,460 for 1991. It receives no capital or recurrent income from the Government but its students are eligible for mandatory awards from local education authorities. Its academic year consists of four terms of ten weeks each.

Courses

All universities award their own degrees and sometimes act as awarding and validating bodies for neighbouring colleges of higher education, though this function is usually performed by the Council for National Academic Awards (*see* below). With the exception of certain Scottish universities where Master is sometimes used for a first degree in arts subjects, undergraduate courses lead to the title of Bachelor—Bachelor of Arts (BA) and Bachelor of

Science (B.Sc.) being the most common—and for a higher degree, Master of Arts (MA), Master of Science (M.Sc.) (usually taught courses) and the research degrees of Master of Philosophy (M.Phil.) and Doctor of Philosophy (Ph.D. or, at a few universities, D.Phil.).

Most undergraduate programmes at British universities run for three years, except in Scotland and at the University of Keele where they may take four years. Professional courses in subjects such as medicine, dentistry and veterinary science take longer. Details of courses on offer and of entry requirements to first degree courses can be found in the annual handbook produced co-operatively by the universities, *University Entrance: The Official Guide*, published by the Association of Commonwealth Universities (for address, *see* p. 457).

Postgraduate programmes vary in length. Taught courses which lead to certificates, diplomas or master's degrees usually take one year full-time or two years part-time. Research degrees take from two to three years full-time and much longer if completed on a part-time basis. Details of taught courses and research degree opportunities can be found in *Graduate Studies* published annually for the Careers Research and Advisory Centre by Hobsons Publishing PLC (for address, *see* p. 457).

Post-experience short courses are forming an increasing part of university provision, reflecting the need to update professional and technical training. Most of these courses finance themselves.

Admissions

Constraints are imposed by the Government on the number of home students which a university is able to admit, but the individual university decides which students to accept and which to reject. Students applying for admission to a first degree course at most universities do not apply direct but through a clearing-house, the Universities' Central Council on Admissions (UCCA). All universities in the United Kingdom participate in the UCCA scheme except the Open University, which conducts its own admissions direct. The *UCCA handbook* is issued free for use in completing UCCA application forms, and is available from schools, colleges, or direct from the Universities' Central Council on Admissions (for address, *see* p. 458).

For admission as a postgraduate student, universities normally require a good first degree in a subject related to the proposed course of study or research, but each candidate is considered on his or her merits. Application is normally to the institution direct.

Finance

Universities are being expected to look to a much wider range of funding sources than before, and to generate additional revenue in collaboration with industry.

In the academic year 1990–91 the total recurrent income of universities in the United Kingdom was £4,040,217. The exchequer grant was £1,792,575, forming 44·4 per cent of total income, compared to 1976–77 when it formed 75 per cent. The total non-recurrent exchequer grant for 1987–88 was £121 million. Income from contracts with industry, commerce and public corporations was £763,441, an increase of 16·2 per cent on the previous year.

NON-UNIVERSITY SECTOR
England and Wales

Polytechnics, colleges of higher education, and other major establishments provide both further and higher education courses in England and Wales.

Until April 1989 these public sector higher education establishments were under local education authority control, except for institutions for teacher training and a few others which were grant-maintained directly from central government. However, the Education Reform Act 1988 legislated for the polytechnics and higher education colleges in England to be removed from local education authority control and incorporated as independent institutions, each run by a Higher Education Corporation (HEC). The HECs are responsible for providing higher education and carrying out research in these institutions. HECs are controlled by boards of governors appointed by the Secretary of State. At least half the members of each board must be drawn from industry, business, commerce and the professions.

The HECs are funded by the Polytechnics and Colleges Funding Council (PCFC), which allocates funds between individual institutions for the provision of higher education, both in its own sector, and in colleges under local education authority control. The PCFC also advises the Secretary of State for Education on matters relevant to its sector. Until March 1992 the Wales Advisory Body for Local Authority Higher Education (WAB) performs the same function for the Secretary of State for Wales, but thereafter institutions of higher education in Wales will become independent and receive their funding directly from the Welsh Office. WAB will concurrently be dissolved, but will advise the Secretary of State on funding for the sector for 1992–93. The independent higher education institutions are, like the universities, expected to supplement their income by undertaking consultancy work and exploiting commercial possibilities.

In 1989–90, there was a total of 301,019 students enrolled at polytechnics: 285,519 (44 per cent of them women) were on higher education courses, and of this number, 194,874 (45 per cent of them women) were full-time or sandwich course students. In those colleges of higher education now in the PCFC sector there were (1989–90) 148,600 students, 112,442 on higher education courses, of which 71,000 were full-time or sandwich course students.

There are 377 major establishments of higher education (maintained, assisted by LEAs, in receipt of direct grant from the DES, or voluntary) in addition to the polytechnics. In England and Wales in 1989–90 they catered for 134,779 students on higher education courses including 32,957 on full-time or sandwich courses.

Courses

Higher education courses comprise courses for the further training of teachers, and other courses which last full-time for at least four weeks or, if part-time, involve more than 60 hours of instruction. They include first degree and postgraduate courses (including research) leading to the same qualifications as those awarded by universities, courses for Diplomas of Higher Education, Higher National Diploma and Higher National Certificate, courses in preparation for professional examinations, and other courses of above GCE A-level or Ordinary National Certificate standard. Facilities are available for full-time and part-time study, and day release, sandwich or bloc release courses are more commonly available than in universities. Higher education courses are offered in some 400 institutions outside the universities.

The Diploma of Higher Education (Dip.H.E.) is a two-year diploma usually intended to serve as a stepping-stone to a degree course or other further study. The Dip.H.E. is usually awarded by the Council for National Academic Awards (*see* below).

The BTEC Higher National Certificate (HNC) is awarded after two years part-time study. The BTEC

Higher National Diploma (HND) is awarded after two years full-time, or three years sandwich or part-time study.

The Council for National Academic Awards (CNAA) was established by Royal Charter in 1964 as a self-governing body to award degrees to students taking courses approved by it in non-university institutions. However, academic responsibility is now increasingly being devolved to accredited institutions which control the academic standards of their own taught courses as well as having the authority to validate new courses and to modify existing ones. Thirty six institutions, including all the polytechnics, have so far been accredited.

More than 140 colleges in Britain conduct courses leading to CNAA degrees: BA, B.Ed., B.Sc., and higher degrees including MA and M.Sc. (for postgraduate course work) and M.Phil. and Ph.D. (for research which may be undertaken jointly in industry and an academic institution). Some colleges of higher education have retained their traditional links with a university which validates and awards their degrees.

Admissions

Information on all higher education courses in polytechnics including postgraduate courses, can be found in the *Polytechnic Courses Handbook* available from the Committee of Directors of Polytechnics (for address, *see* p. 458). Postgraduate courses in all PCFC institutions are included in *Graduate Studies* (*see* p. 450).

The entry requirements in this sector are much the same as those for universities, i.e. two or three GCSEs at grades A to C, or equivalent, and two or three A-levels for first degrees, and a good first degree in a related subject for postgraduate study, although each candidate is considered on his or her merits. Polytechnics and colleges are, however, often more flexible than universities in accepting alternative entry qualifications, particularly technician-level awards.

The Polytechnics Central Admissions System (PCAS) acts as a clearing-house for all full-time and sandwich first degree, HND and Dip.H.E. courses at participating polytechnics and colleges, except for art and design courses (*see* p. 454). Applicants can obtain a copy of the *Guide for Applicants* and the PCAS application form either from their school or college or from PCAS.

For CNAA first degree and postgraduate courses in art and design and BTEC HND courses in design and associated studies, applications should be made through the Art and Design Admissions Registry.

For polytechnic courses other than the above, applications are made to the institution direct, using the Polytechnic Standard Application Form, available in schools or colleges or from the Committee of Directors of Polytechnics. Applications for courses at colleges of higher education outside the clearing-house schemes are also made direct to the institutions.

Scotland

Advanced full-time courses outside the universities in Scotland are provided by the twelve central institutions, five colleges of education, the agricultural college, and 49 local education authority colleges. These are funded by central government mainly through the Scottish Office Education Department. Each is managed by an independent governing body which includes representatives of industrial, commercial, professional and educational interests. Most of the courses at the central institutions have a vocational orientation and are of the sandwich type. They are intended to complement provision in the universities. Most of the degrees are

validated by the CNAA, though some degree courses such as agriculture, fine art and planning are run in collaboration with nearby universities which validate and award the degrees.

In 1988–89, 69,592 students were enrolled on advanced courses of higher education (40 per cent of them women): 32,575 at central institutions, 5,302 at colleges of education, and 31,715 at education authority colleges. Of the total number, 36,109 were on full-time or sandwich courses (51 per cent of them women).

Applications to the central institutions are made direct to the college concerned, with the exception of those courses offered by certain agricultural and art central institutions which are run in conjunction with universities. Application for these courses is made through UCCA. Application for teacher training courses is made to TEACH (*see* p. 458). Further information can be obtained from the institutions themselves or from the Conference of Scottish Centrally-Funded Colleges (*see* p. 457).

Northern Ireland

In Northern Ireland advanced courses are provided by 26 institutions of further education and by the University of Ulster. As well as offering first and postgraduate degrees, the University runs courses leading to the BTEC Higher National Diploma and professional qualifications. Applications to undertake courses other than degree courses are made to the institutions direct.

In 1989–90, 3,444 students were enrolled on advanced courses of higher education in the institutions of further education (44·8 per cent of them women). There were 854 students on full-time or sandwich courses, including 513 women.

FEES

The tuition fees for students with mandatory awards (*see* p. 452) are paid by the grant-awarding body. Students from member states of the European Community pay fees at home student rates. Since 1980–81 students from outside the EC have paid fees that are meant to cover the cost of their education, but financial help is available under a number of schemes. Information about these schemes is available from British Council offices worldwide.

The recommended minimum fees at universities in England, Wales and Scotland for students from non-EC countries in 1991–92 are £5,000 (£3,810 in Northern Ireland) for arts students, £6,630 (£5,075–£6,630 in Northern Ireland) for science students, and £12,210 throughout the UK for students following clinical courses in medicine, dentistry and veterinary science. These compare with undergraduate fees for home and EC students of £1,755 for arts courses, £2,650 for science courses and £4,770 for clinical courses in the academic year 1991–92.

At polytechnics and higher education colleges the same fees apply as at universities for home students and EC nationals. At institutions in the maintained sector, recommended fees for higher education courses are as follows: £5,019 (England and Wales); £4,920 (Scotland); £3,810 (Northern Ireland). No recommended minimum fees have been set for non-EC overseas students for 1991–92 at polytechnics.

For postgraduate students, the maximum tuition fee that will be reimbursed through the awards system is £2,104 in 1991–92.

GRANTS FOR STUDENTS

Students in the United Kingdom who plan to take a full-time or sandwich course of further study after leaving school may be eligible for a grant. A parental contribution is deductible on a sliding scale dependent on income. For married students this may be deducted from their spouse's income instead. However, parental contribution is not deducted from the grant to students over 25 years of age who have been self-supporting for at least three years. The main rates of mandatory grant have been frozen from 1991–92, as it is envisaged that students will increasingly support themselves by loans (*see* below). Tuition fees are paid in full for all students in receipt of a grant, regardless of parental income, and they are usually paid direct to the university or college by the education authority.

Grants are paid by local education authorities in England, Wales and Northern Ireland, and by the Scottish Office Education Department in Scotland. Applications are made to the authority in the area in which the student normally lives. Applications should not, however, be made earlier than the January preceding the start of the course.

Types of grant

Grants are of two kinds: mandatory and discretionary. Mandatory grants are those which awarding authorities must pay to students who are attending designated courses (*see* below) and who can satisfy certain other conditions. Such a grant is awarded normally to enable the student to attend only one designated course and there is no general entitlement to an award for any particular number of years. Discretionary grants are those for which each awarding authority has discretion to decide its own policy.

Designated courses are those full-time or sandwich courses leading to: a degree; the Diploma of Higher Education (Dip.H.E.); the Higher National Diploma (HND) of the Business and Technician Education Council; initial teacher-training courses, including those for the postgraduate certificate of education and the art teachers' certificate or diploma; a university certificate or diploma course lasting at least three years; other qualifications which are specifically designated as being comparable to first degree courses; and the SCOTVEC Higher National Diploma.

Eligibility.—To be eligible for a mandatory grant, students admitted to a designated course must usually have been ordinarily resident in the United Kingdom for the three years immediately preceding the academic year in which the course begins; have not previously attended a course of advanced further education of more than two years' duration; and apply for the grant before the end of the first term of the course. (The local education authority should be consulted for advice about eligibility.)

Students taking designated courses who do not satisfy the residency condition may be eligible for a mandatory grant if they come from other member states of the EC and can establish migrant worker status, or their parents are migrant workers; or if they, or their spouse and children, are asylees or refugees.

Value.—A means-tested maintenance grant, usually paid once a term, covers periods of attendance during term as well as the Christmas and Easter vacations, but not the summer vacation. It is subject to deduction on account of the student's own income and her/his parents' or spouse's income. The basic grant rates are: £2,845 if living in a hall of residence or lodgings and studying within the London area; £2,265 as above but outside the London area; £1,795 if living at the parental home. Additional allowances are available if, for example, the course requires a period of study abroad.

Cost.—Education authority and Scottish Office Education Department expenditure on student maintenance in 1988–89 was £812·7 million.

Student loans.—The Education (Student Loans) Act 1990 legislates for interest-free but indexed top-up loans of up to £660 in 1991–92 to be made available to eligible students in the United Kingdom. This will increase the resources available to students by 31 per cent. The government expects that at least £231 million will be taken up in loans in 1991–92.

Students apply direct to the Student Loans Company Ltd, which will require a certificate of eligibility from their place of study. Loans are available to students on designated courses within the scope of mandatory awards and the same residency conditions apply. Repayment is normally over five to seven years, although it can be deferred if income is low.

Postgraduate awards

Unlike funding for undergraduates, which is mandatory for most degree and equivalent level courses, grants for postgraduate study are usually discretionary. Grants are also often dependent on the class of first degree, especially for research degrees.

A number of schemes of postgraduate bursaries or studentships for residents in England and Wales are funded by the Department of Education and Science the five government research councils, the Ministry of Agriculture, Fisheries and Food, and the British Academy, which awards grants for study in the humanities.

In Scotland postgraduate funding is provided by the Scottish Office Education Department, the Scottish Office Agriculture and Fisheries Department and the research councils as in England and Wales.

Awards in Northern Ireland are made by the Department of Education for Northern Ireland, the Department of Agriculture for Northern Ireland, and the Medical Research Council.

In 1988–89 in the United Kingdom 24,200 awards were made.

Value.—The national rates for twelve-month studentships in 1991–92 were: £4,970 in college or lodgings in London; £3,950 in college or lodging outside London; £2,915 for those living with parents or spouse's parents. The rates for 30-week bursaries for 1991–92 were: £2,950 in college or lodgings in London; £2,330 in college or lodgings outside London £1,760 if living with parents or spouse's parents.

ADULT AND CONTINUING EDUCATION

The term adult education covers a broad spectrum of educational activities ranging from non-vocational courses of general interest, through the acquiring of special vocational skills needed in industry or commerce, to study for a degree at the Open University.

Providers

Courses specifically for adults are funded and/or provided by many bodies. They include, in the

statutory sector: local education authorities in England and Wales; the regional and islands education authorities in Scotland and the Scottish Office Education Department; education and library board in Northern Ireland; the Open University; the extra-mural departments of other universities and Birkbeck College of the University of London; residential colleges; the Open College; the BBC, independent television and local radio stations. There are, in addition, a number of voluntary bodies.

The local education authorities in England and

Wales operate through 'area' adult education centres (2,782 in 1989), institutes or colleges, and the adult studies departments of colleges of further education. The regional and islands education authorities in Scotland fund adult education including that provided by the universities and the Workers' Educational Association at vocational further education colleges (49 in 1990). In addition, the Scottish Office Education Department provides grants to a number of voluntary organizations. Provision in the statutory sector in Northern Ireland is the responsibility of the universities and the education and library boards, which operate 26 further education colleges and a number of community schools.

More than 30 universities have extra-mural, adult education or continuing education departments which serve their local areas or regions, and Birkbeck College in the University of London caters solely for part-time students. Institutions in the PCFC sector in England and Wales, because of their range of courses and flexible patterns of student attendance, provide substantial opportunities in the field of adult and continuing education. The Polytechnic Association for Continuing Education (PACE) exists to promote collaboration between polytechnics and colleges of higher education active in this area. The Open University, in partnership with the BBC, provides distance teaching leading to ordinary or honours first degrees, and also offers post-experience and higher degree courses (*see* p. 449–50). The Open College uses radio and television to provide open learning courses in areas of vocational and technical competence, leading to nationally recognized qualifications or credits towards them.

Of the voluntary bodies, the biggest is the Workers' Educational Association (WEA) which operates throughout the United Kingdom and comprises about 900 branches, organized into 19 districts, and nearly 1,500 affiliated educational and workers' organizations, reaching about 180,000 adult students annually. The Department of Education and Science (DES), Welsh Office, Scottish Office Education Department, Department of Education for Northern Ireland and local education authorities make grants towards provision.

The National Institute of Adult Continuing Education (England and Wales) (NIACE) provides information and advice to organizations and individuals on all aspects of adult continuing education. NIACE manages a number of agencies and special units, including the Adult Literacy and Basic Skills Unit, which receive funding from the DES and the Welsh Office. The Welsh committee, NIACE Cymru, receives financial support from the Welsh Office Education Department, support in kind from the Welsh Joint Education Committee, and advises government, voluntary bodies and education providers on adult continuing education and training matters in Wales.

The Scottish Institute of Adult and Continuing Education (SIACE) advises on policy, conducts research, provides information, arranges conferences and produces publications. Its membership comprises all the major funders and providers of adult and continuing education in Scotland.

The Northern Ireland Council for Continuing Education has an advisory role. Its membership includes representatives of most organizations involved in the field, together with appointees of the Northern Ireland Minister responsible for education.

The Universities Council for Adult and Continuing Education consists of one or two representatives from each university in the United Kingdom. It was established in 1947 for the interchange of ideas and the formulation of common policies on extra-mural education.

Courses

Although lengths vary, most courses are part-time. Long-term residential colleges, which are grant-aided by the DES, the Welsh Office or the Scottish Office, provide full-time courses lasting one or two years.

Some colleges and centres offer short-term residential courses, lasting from a few days to a few weeks, in a wide range of subjects. Local education authorities directly sponsor many of the colleges, while others are sponsored by universities or voluntary organizations. A booklet listing courses, *Residential Short Courses*, is published by NIACE.

Grants

Although full-time courses at degree level attract mandatory awards regardless of the age of the student, for courses below that level all students over the age of 19 must pay a fee. However, discretionary grants may be available. Adult education bursaries for students at the long-term residential colleges of adult education are the responsibility of the colleges themselves. The awards are administered for the colleges by the Awards Officer of the Residential Colleges Committee for students resident in England; by the Welsh Office Education Department for those resident in Wales; by the Scottish Office Education Department for those resident in Scotland; and by the Department of Education for Northern Ireland for students resident there. The bursaries are paid in accordance with the rates and conditions set from time to time by the DES. *Adult and Continuing Education Bursaries* can be obtained from the Awards Officer, Adult Education Bursaries, c/o Ruskin College (*see* p. 466).

Numbers

There are no comprehensive statistics covering all aspects of adult education. However, it is known that enrolments on evening courses in further education establishments in the United Kingdom numbered 2,564,000 in 1988–89 (64 per cent women). This number included 1,617,000 students at adult education centres. In 1989–90, 324,922 students attended courses of liberal adult education provided by university extra-mural departments, including joint courses with the WEA, in the United Kingdom.

EDUCATION DIRECTORY

LOCAL EDUCATION AUTHORITIES

ENGLAND

County Councils

AVON, PO Box 57, Avon House North, St James Barton, Bristol BS99 7EB. (Tel: 0272-290777).—*Dir.*, G. Badman.

BEDFORDSHIRE, County Hall, Cauldwell Street, Bedford MK42 9AP. (Tel: 0234-363222).—*Dir.*, D. G. Wadsworth.

BERKSHIRE, Shire Hall, Shinfield Park, Reading RG2 9XD. (Tel: 0734-233400).—*Chief Education Officer*, S. R. Goodchild.

BUCKINGHAMSHIRE, County Hall, Aylesbury HP20 1UZ. (Tel: 0296-395000).—*Chief Education Officer*, S. Sharp.

CAMBRIDGESHIRE, Castle Court, Castle Hall, Cambridge CB3 0AP. (Tel: 0223-317667).—*Dir.*, J. Ferguson.

CHESHIRE, County Hall, Chester CH1 1SF. (Tel: 0244-602424).—*Dir.*, D. Cracknell.

CLEVELAND, Woodlands Road, Middlesbrough TS1 3BN. (Tel: 0642-248155).—*County Education Officer*, B. Worthy.

CORNWALL, New County Hall, Truro TR1 3AY. (Tel: 0872-74282).—*Sec. of Education*, D. W. Fryer.

CUMBRIA, 5 Portland Square, Carlisle CA1 1PU. (Tel: 0228-23456).—*Dir.*, Ms P. Black.

DERBYSHIRE, County Offices, Matlock DE4 3AG. (Tel: 0629-580000).—*Chief Education Officer*, G. Lennox.

DEVON, County Hall, Exeter EX2 4QG. (Tel: 0392-382000).—*Chief Education Officer*, S. W. Jenkin.

DORSET, County Hall, Dorchester DT1 1XJ. (Tel: 0305-251000).—*Dir.*, P. L. Gedling.

DURHAM, County Hall, Durham DH1 5UJ. (Tel: 091-386 4411).—*Dir.*, K. Mitchell.

EAST SUSSEX, PO Box 4, County Hall, St Anne's Crescent, Lewes BN7 1SG. (Tel: 0273-481000).—*County Education Officer*, D. Mallen.

ESSEX, Threadneedle House, Market Road, Chelmsford CM1 1LD. (Tel: 0245-492211).—*County Education Officer*, R. M. Sharp.

GLOUCESTERSHIRE, Shire Hall, Gloucester GL1 2TP. (Tel: 0452-425300).—*Dir.*, K. D. Anderson.

HAMPSHIRE, The Castle, Winchester SO23 8UJ. (Tel: 0962-841841).—*County Education Officer*, P. J. Coles.

HEREFORD AND WORCESTER, Castle Street, Worcester WR1 3AG. (Tel: 0905-763763).—*County Education Officer*, J. W. Turnbull.

HERTFORDSHIRE, County Hall, Hertford SG13 8DF. (Tel: 0992-555700).—*County Education Officer*, Mrs H. du Quesnay.

HUMBERSIDE, County Hall, Beverley HU17 9BA. (Tel: 0482-867131).—*Dir.*, Dr M. W. Garnett.

ISLE OF WIGHT, County Hall, Newport PO30 1UD. (Tel: 0983-821000).—*Dir.*, J. A. Williams.

KENT, Springfield, Maidstone ME14 2LJ. (Tel: 0622-671411).—*Dir.*, R. Pryke.

LANCASHIRE, PO Box 61, County Hall, Preston PR1 8RJ. (Tel: 0772-261701).—*Chief Education Officer*, A. J. Collier.

LEICESTERSHIRE, County Hall, Glenfield, Leicester LE3 8RA. (Tel: 0533-323232).—*Dir.*, K. H. Wood-Allum.

LINCOLNSHIRE, County Offices, Newland, Lincoln LN1 1YL. (Tel: 0522-552222).—*Dir.*, A. M. Ridings.

NORFOLK, County Hall, Martineau Lane, Norwich NR1 2DL. (Tel: 0603-222146).—*Dir.*, M. H. Edwards.

NORTHAMPTONSHIRE, Northampton House, Northampton NN1 2HX. (Tel: 0604-236250).—*Dir.*, J. R. Atkinson.

NORTHUMBERLAND, County Hall, Morpeth NE61 2EF. (Tel: 0670-514343).—*Dir.*, C. C. Tipple.

NORTH YORKSHIRE, County Hall, Racecourse Lane, Northallerton DL7 8AE. (Tel: 0609-780780).—*Dir.* F. F. Evans.

NOTTINGHAMSHIRE, County Hall, West Bridgford, Nottingham NG2 7QP. (Tel: 0602-823823).—*Dir.*, P. J. Housden.

OXFORDSHIRE, Macclesfield House, New Road, Oxford OX1 1NA. (Tel: 0865-792422).—*Chief Education Officer*, Mrs J. Stephens.

SHROPSHIRE, The Shirehall, Abbey Foregate, Shrewsbury SY2 6ND. (Tel: 0743-254307).—*County Education Officer*, P. B. Cates.

SOMERSET, County Hall, Taunton TA1 4DY. (Tel: 0823-333451).—*Chief Education Officer*, Mrs J. Wisker.

STAFFORDSHIRE, Tipping Street, Stafford ST16 2DH. (Tel: 0785-223121).—*Chief Education Officer*, Dr P. J. Hunter.

SUFFOLK, St Andrew House, County Hall, Ipswich IP4 1LJ. (Tel: 0473-230000).—*County Education Officer*, T. R. Cornthwaite.

SURREY, County Hall, Penrhyn Road, Kingston upon Thames KT1 2DJ. (Tel: 081-541 9999).—*County Education Officer*, M. C. Pinchin.

WARWICKSHIRE, PO Box 24, 22 Northgate Street, Warwick CV34 4SR. (Tel: 0926-410410).—*Dir.*, M. M. Maden.

WEST SUSSEX, County Hall, Chichester PO19 1RH. (Tel: 0243-777100).—*Dir.*, R. D. C. Bunker.

WILTSHIRE, County Hall, Bythesea Road, Trowbridge BA14 8JN. (Tel: 0225-753641).—*Dir.*, I. M. Slocombe.

Metropolitan District Councils

BARNSLEY, Berneslai Close, Barnsley. (Tel: 0226 733252).—*Dir.*, T. Brooks.

BIRMINGHAM, Council House, Margaret Street, B 3BU. (Tel: 021-235 2590).—*Chief Education Officer*, D. Hammond.

BOLTON, Paderborn House, Civic Centre, BL1 1JW (Tel: 0204-22311).—*Education Officer*, B. Hughes.

BRADFORD, Provincial House, BD1 1NP. (Tel: 027-752500).—*Education Officer*, Mrs S. Conway.

BURY, Athenaeum House, Market Street, BL9 0BN (Tel: 061-705 5000).—*Education Officer*, M. Gray.

CALDERDALE.—Northgate House, Halifax HX1 1UN (Tel: 0422-357257).—*Education Officer*, A. Pickvance.

COVENTRY, Council House, Earl Street, CV1 5R (Tel: 0203-831500).—*Dir.*, C. Farmer.

DONCASTER, Princegate, DN1 3EP. (Tel: 030 734105).—*Dir.*, A. M. Taylor.

DUDLEY, Westox House, 1 Trinity Road, DY1 1J (Tel: 0384-456000).—*Chief Education Officer*, R. Westerby.

GATESHEAD, Civic Centre, Regent Street, NE8 1H (Tel: 091-477 1011).—*Dir.*, D. Arbon.

KIRKLEES, Oldgate House, 2 Oldgate, Huddersfie HD1 6QW. (Tel: 0484-422133).—*Chief Education Officer*, Ms J. Devlin.

KNOWSLEY, Huyton Hey Road, Huyton, Merseysi L36 5YM. (Tel: 051-443 3220).—*Education Officer* A. Culley.

LEEDS, Merrion House, Woodhouse Lane, LS2 8D' (Tel: 0532-475587).—*Chief Education Officer*, R. Johnson, CBE.

LIVERPOOL, 14 Sir Thomas Street, L1 6BJ. (Tel: 05 227 3911).—*Dir.*, M. F. Cogley.

MANCHESTER, Cumberland House, Crown Square, M60 3BB. (Tel: 061-234 5000).—*Education Officer,* R. Jobson.

NEWCASTLE UPON TYNE, Civic Centre, NE99 2BN. (Tel: 091-232 8520).—*Education Officer,* W. B. Downer.

NORTH TYNESIDE, The Chase, North Shields NE29 1RW. (Tel: 091-257 6621).—*Education Officer,* J. A. Taylor.

OLDHAM, Old Town Hall, Middleton Road, Chadderton, OL9 6PP. (Tel: 061-624 0505).—*Education Officer,* W. R. Kneen, PH.D.

ROCHDALE, PO Box 70, Municipal Offices, Smith Street, OL16 1YD. (Tel: 0706-47474).—*Education Officer,* Mrs D. Cavanagh.

ROTHERHAM, Norfolk House, Walker Place, Rotherham. (Tel: 0709-382121).—*Education Officer,* B. H. Yemm.

ST HELENS, Century House, Hardshaw Street, St Helens WA10 1RN. (Tel: 0744-24061).—*Dir.,* N. D. Nelson.

SALFORD, Chapel Street, M3 5LT. (Tel: 061-832 9751).—*Chief Education Officer,* A. Lockhart.

SANDWELL, PO Box 41, Shaftesbury House, 402 High Street, West Bromwich B70 9LT. (Tel: 021-525 7366).—*Dir.,* vacant.

SEFTON, Town Hall, Bootle, Merseyside L20 7AE. (Tel: 051-922 4040).—*Education Officer,* J. A. Marsden.

SHEFFIELD, PO Box 67, Leopold Street, S1 1RJ. (Tel: 0742-726341).—*Dir.,* Mrs A. Muller.

SOLIHULL, PO Box 18, Council House, B91 3QS. (Tel: 021-704 6000).—*Dir.,* M. E. Sweet.

SOUTH TYNESIDE, Town Hall and Civic Offices, South Shields, NE33 2RL. (Tel: 091-427 1717).— *Education Officer,* I. L. Reid.

STOCKPORT, Stopford House, SK1 3XE (Tel: 061-474 3808).—*Dir.,* J. E. Hendy.

SUNDERLAND, PO Box 101, Town Hall and Civic Centre, SR2 7DN. (Tel: 091-567 6161).—*Education Officer,* D. A. Bowers.

TAMESIDE, Council Offices, Wellington Road, Ashton-under-Lyne OL6 6DL. (Tel: 061-330 8355).—*Dir,* A. M. Webster.

TRAFFORD, PO Box 19, Tatton Road, Sale M33 1YR. (Tel: 061-872 2101).—*Chief Education Officer,* C. J. Radley.

WAKEFIELD, County Hall, WF1 2QW. (Tel: 0924-290900).—*Education Officer,* A. Lenney.

WALSALL, Civic Centre, Darwall Street, WS1 1DQ. (Tel: 0922-650000).—*Education Officer,* vacant.

WIGAN, Gateway House, Standishgate, WN1 1AE. (Tel: 0942-44991).—*Education Officer,* J. K. Hampson.

WIRRAL, Hamilton Building, Conway Street, Birkenhead L41 4FD. (Tel: 051-666 2121).—*Dir.,* D. Rigby.

WOLVERHAMPTON, Civic Centre, St Peter's Square, WV1 1RR. (Tel: 0902-27811).—*Dir.,* Ms C. Adams.

London

The ILEA was abolished on April 1, 1990 and from that date the inner London boroughs(*) and the Corporation of the City of London assumed responsibility for the provision of education within their own areas.

BARKING AND DAGENHAM, Town Hall, Barking, Essex IG11 7LU. (Tel: 081-592 4500).—*Education Officer,* A. Larbalastier.

BARNET, Town Hall, Friern Barnet, N11 3DL. (Tel: 081-368 1255).—*Education Officer,* N. M. Gill.

BEXLEY, Hill View, Hill View Drive, Welling, Kent DA16 3RS. (Tel: 081-303 7777).—*Dir.,* G. Hall.

BRENT, PO Box 1, 9 Park Lane, Wembley, Middx. HA9 7RW. (Tel: 081-900 5443).—*Dir.,* G. Benham.

BROMLEY, Town Hall, Tweedy Road, Bromley, Kent BR1 1SB. (Tel: 081-464 3333).—*Dir.,* G. Grainge.

*CAMDEN, Crowndale Centre, 216–220 Eversholt Street, NW1 1BE (Tel: 071-860 1525).—*Education Officer,* P. Mitchell.

*CITY OF LONDON, Clements House, 14–18 Gresham Street, EC2P 2EJ. (Tel: 071-260 1465).—*City Education Officer,* D. Smith.

*CITY OF WESTMINSTER, City Hall, PO Box 240, Victoria Street, SW1E 6QP. (Tel: 071-828 8070).— *Education Officer,* Mrs D. Tuck.

CROYDON, Taberner House, Park Lane, CR9 1TP. (Tel: 081-686 4433).—*Dir.,* P. Benians.

EALING, Perceval House, 14–16 Uxbridge Road, W5 2HL. (Tel: 081-579 2424).—*Dir.,* M. Herman (*acting*).

ENFIELD, PO Box 56, Civic Centre, Silver Street, EN1 3XQ. (Tel: 081-366 6565).—*Education Officer,* G. Hutchinson.

*GREENWICH, Riverside House, 9th Floor, Beresford Street, Woolwich, SE18 6DF. (Tel: 081-854 8888).— *Dir.,* N. McClelland.

*HACKNEY, 77–83 East Road, N1 6AH. (Tel: 071-490 8838).—*Dir.,* G. John.

*HAMMERSMITH AND FULHAM, Cambridge House, Cambridge Grove, W6 9JU. (Tel: 081-748 3020).— *Dir.,* Ms C. Whatford.

HARINGEY, 48 Station Road, N22 6UX. (Tel: 081-975 9700).—*Education Officer,* R. L. Jones.

HARROW, Civic Centre, Station Road, Harrow HA1 2UW. (Tel: 081-863 5611).—*Dir.,* H. Fielding.

HAVERING, Mercury House, Mercury Gardens, Romford RM1 3DX. (Tel: 0708-766999).—*Dir.,* B. H. Laister.

HILLINGDON, Civic Centre, Uxbridge, Middx. UB8 1UW. (Tel: 0895-250111).—*Education Officer,* Ms K. Higgins.

HOUNSLOW, Civic Centre, Lampton Road, Hounslow, Middx. TW3 4DN. (Tel: 081-570 7728).—*Dir.,* J. D. Trickett.

*ISLINGTON, Barnsbury Complex, Barnsbury Park, N1 1QF. (Tel: 071-226 1234).—*Education Officer,* C. Webb.

*KENSINGTON AND CHELSEA, Town Hall, Hornton Street, W8 7NX. (Tel: 071-937 5464).—*Education Officer,* M. Stoten.

KINGSTON UPON THAMES, Guildhall, KT1 1EU. (Tel: 081-547 5220).—*Dir.,* W. Dickinson.

*LAMBETH, 50 Acre Lane, SW2 5SS. (Tel: 071-926 3350).— *Chief Education Officer,* B. Burchell.

*LEWISHAM, Laurence House, Catford, SE6 4SW. (Tel: 081-695 6000).—*Dir.,* L. Fullick.

MERTON, Crown House, London Road, Morden, Surrey SM4 5DX. (Tel: 081-543 2222).—*Dir.,* R. Davies.

NEWHAM, Broadway House, 322 High Street, E15 1AJ. (Tel: 081-555 5552).—*Education Officer,* S. Lawless.

REDBRIDGE, Lynton House, 255–259 High Road, Ilford, IG1 1NN. (Tel: 081-478 3020).—*Dir.,* K. G. M. Ratcliffe.

RICHMOND UPON THAMES, Regal House, London Road, Twickenham, TW1 3QB. (Tel: 081-891 1411).—*Dir.,* G. Alexander.

*SOUTHWARK, 1 Bradenham Close, SE17. (Tel: 071-237 4551).—*Education Officer,* G. Mott.

SUTTON, The Grove, Carshalton, Surrey SM5 3AL. (Tel: 081-770 6500).—*Dir.,* C. Blurton.

*TOWER HAMLETS, Birkbeck Street Complex, 27 Birkbeck Street, E2 6LA. (Tel: 081-980 4831).— *Education Officer,* Mrs A. Sofer.

WALTHAM FOREST, Municipal Offices, High Road, Leyton E10 5QJ. (Tel: 081-527 5544).—*Dir.,* J. M. Shepherd.

*WANDSWORTH, Town Hall, Wandsworth High Street, SW18 2PU. (Tel: 081-871 7890).—*Dir.,* D. Naismith.

WALES
County Councils

CLWYD, Shire Hall, Mold CH7 6NB. (Tel: 0352-752121).—*Dir.*, H. K. Evans.

DYFED, Pibwrlwyd, Carmarthen SA31 2NH. (Tel: 0267-233333).—*Dir.*, J. G. Ellis.

GWENT, County Hall, Cwmbran NP44 2XG. (Tel: 0633-838838).—*Dir.*, G. V. Drought.

GWYNEDD, County Offices, Caernarfon LL55 1SH. (Tel: 0286-672255).—*Dir.*, G. E. Humphreys.

MID GLAMORGAN, County Hall, Cathays Park, Cardiff CF1 3NF. (Tel: 0222-780200).—*Dir.*, E. Roberts.

POWYS, County Hall, Llandrindod Wells LD1 5LG. (Tel: 0597-826422).—*Dir.*, R. W. Bevan.

SOUTH GLAMORGAN, County Hall, Atlantic Wharf, Cardiff CF1 5UW. (Tel: 0222-872000).—*Dir.*, D. Orrell.

WEST GLAMORGAN, County Hall, Swansea SA1 3SN. (Tel: 0792-471111).—*Dir.*, J. Beale.

SCOTLAND
Regional and Islands Councils

BORDERS, Regional Headquarters, Newtown St Boswells, Melrose TD6 0SA. (Tel: 0835-23301).—*Dir.*, I. Dutton.

CENTRAL, Regional Council Offices, Viewforth, Stirling FK8 2ET. (Tel: 0786-442000).—*Dir.*, I. Collie.

DUMFRIES AND GALLOWAY, 30 Edinburgh Road, Dumfries DG1 1JQ. (Tel: 0387-61234).—*Dir.*, W. C. Fordyce.

FIFE, Fife House, North Street, Glenrothes KY7 5LT. (Tel: 0592-754411).—*Dir.*, M. More.

GRAMPIAN, Woodhill House, Westburn Road, Aberdeen AB9 2LU. (Tel: 0224-682222).—*Dir.*, J. Graham.

HIGHLAND, Regional Buildings, Glenurquhart Road, Inverness IV3 5NX. (Tel: 0463-234121).—*Dir.*, Dr C. E. Stewart.

LOTHIAN, 40 Torphichen Street, Edinburgh EH3 8JJ. (Tel: 031-229 9166).—*Dir.*, W. D. C. Semple.

ORKNEY, Council Offices, Kirkwall KW15 1NY. (Tel: 0856-3535).—*Dir.*, J. Anderson.

SHETLAND, 1 Harbour Street, Lerwick ZE1 0LS. (Tel: 0595-2810).—*Dir.*, W. A. Smith.

STRATHCLYDE, 20 India Street, Glasgow G2 4PF. (Tel: 041-204 2900).—*Dir.*, F. Pignatelli.

TAYSIDE, Tayside House, 28 Crichton Street, Dundee DD1 3RJ. (Tel: 0382-23281).—*Dir.*, A. B. Watson.

WESTERN ISLES, Council Offices, Sandwick Road, Stornoway, Isle of Lewis PA87 2BW. (Tel: 0851-703773).—*Dir.*, N. R. Galbraith.

NORTHERN IRELAND
Education and Library Boards

BELFAST, Board Headquarters, 40 Academy Street, Belfast BT1 2NQ. (Tel: 0232-329211).—*Chief Exec.*, T. G. J. Moag.

NORTH EASTERN, County Hall, 182 Galgorm Road, Ballymena, Co. Antrim BT42 1HN. (Tel: 0266-653333).—*Chief Exec.*, R. A. Hamilton.

SOUTH EASTERN, 18 Windsor Avenue, Belfast BT9 6EF. (Tel: 0232-381188).—*Chief Exec.*, T. Nolan, OBE.

SOUTHERN, 3 Charlemont Place, The Mall, Armagh BT61 9AX. (Tel: 0861-523811).—*Chief Exec.*, J. G. Kelly.

WESTERN, 1 Hospital Road, Omagh, Co. Tyrone BT79 0AW. (Tel: 0662-240240).—*Chief Exec.*, M. H. F. Murphy, OBE.

ISLANDS, ETC.

GUERNSEY, PO Box 32, Grange Road, St Peter Port. (Tel: 0481-710821).—*Dir.*, M. D. Hutchings.

JERSEY, PO Box 142, St Saviour. (Tel: 0534-71065).—*Dir.*, B. Grady.

ISLE OF MAN, Government Offices, Buck's Road, Douglas. (Tel: 0624-626262).—*Dir.*, A. Davies.

ISLES OF SCILLY, Town Hall, St Mary's TR21 0LW. (Tel: 0720-22537).—*Sec. for Education*, P. S. Hygate (*acting*).

ADVISORY BODIES
Schools

EDUCATION OTHERWISE, 25 Common Lane, Hemmingford Abbots, Cambridge PE18 9AN. *Helpline*, tel: 0480-63130.

INTERNATIONAL BACCALAUREATE, Examinations Office, Pascal Close, Cardiff CF3 0YP. (Tel: 0222-770770).—*Dir. of Examinations*, C. Carthew.

SCHOOLS EXAMINATION AND ASSESSMENT COUNCIL Newcombe House, 45 Notting Hill Gate, W11 3JB (Tel: 071-229 1234).—*Chief Exec.*, P. Halsey, CB LVO; *Sec.*, Dr R. Dorrance, CBE.

Independent Schools

ASSISTED PLACES COMMITTEE, 26 Queen Anne's Gate, SW1H 9AN. (Tel: 071-222 9595).—*Sec.*, Mrs M. L. Shaw.

COMMON ENTRANCE BOARD, Drax House, Tilshead, Salisbury, Wilts. SP3 4SJ. (Tel: 0980-620473).—*Sec.*, Mrs E. J. Twiston-Davies.

GOVERNING BODIES ASSOCIATION, Windleshaw Lodge Withyham, Nr. Hartfield, E. Sussex TN7 4DB. (Tel 0892-770879).—*Sec.*, D. G. Banwell.

GOVERNING BODIES OF GIRLS' SCHOOLS ASSOCIATION Windleshaw Lodge, Withyham, Nr. Hartfield, E Sussex TN7 4DB. (Tel: 0892-770879).—*Sec.*, D. G. Banwell.

INDEPENDENT SCHOOLS INFORMATION SERVICE, 56 Buckingham Gate, SW1E 6AG. (Tel: 071-630 8793/4).—*National Dir.*, D. J. Woodhead.

Further Education

FURTHER EDUCATION UNIT, 2–6 Orange Street, WC2H 7WE. (Tel: 071-962 1280).—*Chief Officer*, G. Stanton

NATIONAL COUNCIL FOR VOCATIONAL QUALIFICA TIONS, 222 Euston Road, NW1 2BZ. (Tel. 071-387 9898). *Chief Exec.*, P. Reay.

Regional Advisory Councils

CENTRA (NORTH WESTERN REGIONAL ADVISORY COUNCIL FOR FURTHER EDUCATION), Walkden Road Worsley, Manchester M28 4QE. (Tel: 061-702 8700).—*Manager*, R. S. Welsh.

EAST ANGLIAN REGIONAL ADVISORY COUNCIL FOR FURTHER EDUCATION, 2 Looms Lane, Bury St Edmunds, Suffolk IP33 1HE. (Tel: 0284-764977).—*Dir.*, Mrs H. Herrington.

EAST MIDLAND FURTHER EDUCATION COUNCIL, Robins Wood House, Robins Wood Road, Aspley, Nottingham NG8 3NH. (Tel: 0602-293291).—*Sec.*, R Ainscough.

LONDON AND SOUTH EAST ADVISORY COUNCIL FOR EDUCATION AND TRAINING, 232 Vauxhall Bridge Road, SW1V 1AU. (Tel: 071-233 6199).—*Dir.*, L South.

NORTHERN COUNCIL FOR FURTHER EDUCATION, 8 Grosvenor Villas, Grosvenor Road, Newcastle upon Tyne NE2 2RU. (Tel: 091-281 3242).—*Sec.*, J. F Pearce.

SOUTHERN REGIONAL COUNCIL FOR FURTHER EDUCA TION, 26 Bath Road, Reading RG1 6NT. (Tel: 0734 572120).—*Sec.*, B. J. Knowles.

SOUTH WEST ASSOCIATION FOR FURTHER EDUCATION AND TRAINING, Bishops Hull House, Bishops Hull Taunton, Somerset TA1 5RA. (Tel: 0823-335491).—*Sec.*, F. S. Fisher.

WELSH JOINT EDUCATION COMMITTEE, 245 Western Avenue, Cardiff CF5 2YX. (Tel: 0222-561231).—*Sec.*, C. Heycock.

WEST MIDLANDS ADVISORY COUNCIL FOR FURTHER EDUCATION AND TRAINING, Norfolk House, Smallbrook Queensway, Birmingham B5 4NB. (Tel: 021-643 8924).—*Chief Officer*, C. H. Smith.

YORKSHIRE AND HUMBERSIDE ASSOCIATION FOR FURTHER AND HIGHER EDUCATION, Bowling Green Terrace, Leeds LS11 9SX. (Tel: 0532-440751).—*Sec.*, M. J. Hudson.

Higher Education

THE ASSOCIATION OF COMMONWEALTH UNIVERSITIES, John Foster House, 36 Gordon Square, WC1H 0PF. (Tel: 071-387 8572).—*Sec.-Gen.*, Dr A. Christodoulou, CBE.

COMMITTEE OF VICE-CHANCELLORS AND PRINCIPALS OF THE UNIVERSITIES OF THE UNITED KINGDOM, 29 Tavistock Square, WC1H 9EZ. (Tel: 071-387 9231).—*Sec.*, T. U. Burgner.

POLYTECHNICS AND COLLEGES FUNDING COUNCIL, Northavon House, Coldharbour Lane, Bristol BS16 1QD. (*see also* Government Offices).

UNIVERSITIES' FUNDING COUNCIL, Northavon House, Coldharbour Lane, Bristol BS16 1QD. (*see also* Government Offices).

WALES ADVISORY BODY FOR LOCAL AUTHORITY HIGHER EDUCATION, 24 Cathedral Road, Cardiff CF1 9LJ. (Tel: 0222-397844).—*Sec.*, Dr R. Wynne.

Curriculum Councils, etc.

NATIONAL CURRICULUM COUNCIL, Albion Wharf, 25 Skeldergate, York YO1 2XL. (Tel: 0904-622533).—*Chief Exec.*, vacant.

NORTHERN IRELAND CURRICULUM COUNCIL, Stranmillis College, Stranmillis Road, Belfast BT9 5DY. (Tel: 0232-381414).—*Chief Exec.*, Mrs C. Coxhead.

SCOTTISH CONSULTATIVE COUNCIL ON THE CURRICULUM, 17 St John Street, Edinburgh EH8 8DG. (Tel: 031-557 4888).—*Chief Exec.*, C. E. Harrison.

CURRICULUM COUNCIL FOR WALES, Castle Buildings, Womanby Street, Cardiff CF1 9SX. (Tel: 0222-344946).—*Chief Exec.*, B. Jones.

TVEI UNIT, Training Agency, Moorfoot, Sheffield S1 4PQ. (Tel: 0742-758316).

EXAMINING BODIES
GCSE

LONDON EAST ANGLIAN GROUP, The Lindens, 139 Lexden Road, Colchester CO3 3RL. (Tel: 0206-549595); Stewart House, 32 Russell Square, WC1B 5DN. (Tel: 071-436 5351).—*Chief Exec.*, A. Smith.

NORTHERN EXAMINING ASSOCIATION, c/o Joint Matriculation Board, Manchester M15 6EU. (Tel. 061-273 2565).—*Joint Sec.*, C. Vickerman.

NORTH REGIONAL EXAMINATIONS BOARD, Wheatfield Road, Westerhope, Newcastle upon Tyne NE5 5JZ. (Tel: 091-286 2711).—*Sec.*, D. Kelly.

NORTH WEST REGIONAL EXAMINATIONS BOARD,Orbit House, Albert Street, Eccles, Manchester M30 0WL. (Tel: 061-953 1185).—*Sec.*, Ms M. E. Hutchinson (*acting*).

SOUTHERN EXAMINING GROUP, Stag Hill House, Guildford, Surrey GU2 5XJ. (Tel. 0483-506506).—*Joint Secs.*, J. A. Day ; J. Pailing.

WEST MIDLANDS EXAMINATIONS BOARD, Norfolk House, Smallbrook Queensway, Birmingham B5 4NJ. (Tel: 021-631 2151).—*Sec.*, B. Swift.

NORTHERN IRELAND SCHOOLS EXAMINATIONS AND ASSESSMENT COUNCIL, Beechill House, 42 Beechill Road, Belfast BT8 4RS. (Tel. 0232-704666).—*Chief Officer*, W. J. Caves.

WELSH JOINT EDUCATION COMMITTEE, 245 Western Avenue, Cardiff CF5 2YX. (Tel. 0222-561231).—*Sec.*, C. Heycock.

A-level

ASSOCIATED EXAMINING BOARD, Stag Hill House, Guildford, Surrey GU2 5XJ. (Tel: 0483-506506).—*Sec-Gen.*, J. A. Day.

UNIVERSITY OF CAMBRIDGE LOCAL EXAMINATIONS SYNDICATE, Syndicate Buildings, 1 Hills Road, Cambridge CB1 2EU. (Tel: 0223-61111).—*Sec.*, J. L. Reddaway.

JOINT MATRICULATION BOARD, Manchester M15 6EU. (Tel: 061-273 2565).—*Sec.*, Ms K. Tattersall.

OXFORD AND CAMBRIDGE SCHOOLS EXAMINATION BOARD, Purbeck House, Purbeck Road, Cambridge CB2 2PU. (Tel: 0223-411211).—*Sec.*, H. F. King.

OXFORD AND CAMBRIDGE SCHOOLS EXAMINATION BOARD, Elsfield Way, Oxford OX2 8EP. (Tel: 0865-54421).—*Deputy Sec.*, J. G. Lloyd.

SOUTHERN UNIVERSITIES' JOINT BOARD, Cotham Road, Bristol BS6 6DD. (Tel: 0272-736042).—*Sec.*, Dr S. T. Smith.

UNIVERSITY OF LONDON SCHOOL EXAMINATIONS BOARD, Stewart House, 32 Russell Square, WC1B 5DN. (Tel: 071-331 4000).—*Sec.*, Dr A. J. Woodthorpe (*acting*).

UNIVERSITY OF OXFORD DELEGACY OF LOCAL EXAMINATIONS, Ewert House, Ewert Place, Summertown, Oxford OX2 7BZ. (Tel: 0865-54291).—*Sec.*, J. Pailing.

Scotland

SCOTTISH EXAMINATION BOARD, Ironmills Road, Dalkeith, Midlothian EH22 1LE. (Tel: 031-663 6601).—*Dir.*, H. A. Long, PH.D.

SCOTTISH VOCATIONAL EDUCATION COUNCIL, Hanover House, 24 Douglas Street, Glasgow G2 7NQ. (Tel: 041-248 7900).—*Chief Exec.*, T. J. McCool.

Further Education

BUSINESS AND TECHNICIAN EDUCATION COUNCIL, Central House, Upper Woburn Place, WC1H 0HH. (Tel: 071-413 8400).—*Chief Exec.*, J. E. Sellars.

CITY AND GUILDS OF LONDON INSTITUTE, 76 Portland Place, W1N 4AA. (Tel: 071-278 2468).— *Dir. Gen.*, J. Barnes.

JOINT UNIT FOR CPVE AND FOUNDATION PROGRAMMES, 46 Britannia Street, WC1X 9RG. (Tel: 071-278 3344).—*Chairman*, A. Ainsworth ; *Head of Unit*, Ms S. Fifer.

RSA EXAMINATIONS BOARD, Westwood Way, Coventry CV4 8HS. (Tel: 0203-470033).—*Chief Exec.*, M. F. Cross.

Higher Education

COUNCIL FOR NATIONAL ACADEMIC AWARDS, 344–354 Gray's Inn Road, WC1X 8BP. (Tel: 071-278 4411).—*Chairman*, Sir Raymond Rickett, CBE ; *Chief Exec.*, M. Frazer, PH.D.

ADMISSIONS INFORMATION

ART AND DESIGN ADMISSIONS REGISTRY, Penn House, 9 Broad Street, Hereford HR4 9AP. (Tel: 0432-266653).—*Registrar*, T. W. M. Gourdie.

CAREERS RESEARCH AND ADVISORY CENTRE, Sheraton House, Castle Park, Cambridge CB3 0AX. (Tel: 0223-460277).—*Dir.*, D. Blandford. *Publishers*, Hobsons Publishing PLC, Bateman Street, Cambridge CB2 1LZ.

THE CENTRAL INSTITUTIONS INFORMATION OFFICE, Conference of Scottish Centrally-Funded Colleges, Room 54, Moray House College, Holyrood Road, Edinburgh EH8 8AQ. (Tel: 031-557 6309).—*Sec.*, Dr J. Robinson.

COMMITTEE OF DIRECTORS OF POLYTECHNICS, Kirkman House, 12–14 Whitfield Street, W1P 6AX. (Tel: 071-637 9939).—*Sec.*, R. P. Blows.

GRADUATE TEACHER TRAINING REGISTRY, PO Box 239, Cheltenham, Glos. GL50 3SL.

POLYTECHNICS CENTRAL ADMISSIONS SYSTEM, Fulton House, Jessop Avenue, Cheltenham, Glos. GL50 3SH. (Tel: 0242-227788).—*Chief Exec.*, M. A. Higgins.

TEACHER EDUCATION ADMISSIONS CLEARING HOUSE (TEACH), (Scotland only), PO Box 165, Holyrood Road, Edinburgh EH8 8AT.—*Registrar*, Miss R. C. Williamson.

UNIVERSITIES' CENTRAL COUNCIL ON ADMISSIONS, PO Box 28, Cheltenham, Glos. GL50 3SA. (Tel: 0242-222444).—*Gen. Sec.*, P. A. Oakley.

UNIVERSITIES

ASTON UNIVERSITY (1966)
Aston Triangle, Birmingham B4 7ET
[021-359 3611]

Full-time Students (1990–91), 4,791.
Chancellor, Sir Adrian Cadbury (1979).
Vice-Chancellor, Prof. Sir Frederick Crawford, PH.D., D.Eng., D.SC, F.ENG.
Registrar and Secretary, R. D. A. Packham.

UNIVERSITY OF BATH (1966)
Claverton Down, Bath BA2 7AY
[0225-826826]

Full-time Students (1990–91), 4,336.
Chancellor, The Lord Kearton, OBE, D.SC., FRS (1980).
Vice-Chancellor, Prof. J. R. Quayle, PH.D., FRS.
Secretary and Registrar, R. M. Mawditt, OBE, FRSA.

THE UNIVERSITY OF BIRMINGHAM (1900)
Edgbaston, Birmingham B15 2TT
[021-414 3344]

Full-time Students (1990-91), 9,742.
Chancellor, Sir Alexander Jarratt, CB (1983).
Vice-Chancellor, Prof. Sir Michael Thompson, D.SC.
Registrar and Secretary, D. R. Holmes.

UNIVERSITY OF BRADFORD (1966)
Bradford BD7 1DP

Full-time Students (1990–91), 5,305.
Chancellor, Sir John Harvey-Jones, MBE (1986).
Vice-Chancellor, Prof. D. J. Johns, PH.D., D.SC. (1989).
Registrar and Secretary, D. W. Granger, MBE.

THE UNIVERSITY OF BRISTOL (1909)
Bristol BS8 1TH
[0272-303030]

Full-time Students (1990–91), 8,429.
Chancellor, Sir Jeremy Morse, KCMG (1989).
Vice-Chancellor, Sir John Kingman, FRS.
Registrar, Mrs C. M. Cunningham.
Secretary, J. H. M. Parry.

BRUNEL UNIVERSITY (1966)
Uxbridge, Middx. UB8 3PH
[0895-274000]

Full-time Students (1990–91), c. 3,123.
Chancellor, The Earl of Halsbury, FRS (1966).
Vice-Chancellor, Prof. M. J. H. Sterling.
Registrar and Secretary, D. Neave.

UNIVERSITY OF BUCKINGHAM (1983)
(Founded 1976 as University College at Buckingham). Independent of state finance.
Buckingham MK18 1EG
[0280-814080]

Full-time Students (1991–92), 862.
Chancellor, The Lord Hailsham of St Marylebone, KG, CH, PC, FRS (1983).
Vice-Chancellor, vacant.
Registrar and Secretary, M. Lavis, PH.D.

THE UNIVERSITY OF CAMBRIDGE

Number of Undergraduates in Residence 1991–92:
Men, 6,121; *Women*, 4,261

UNIVERSITY OFFICERS, etc.†	Elect.
Chancellor, HRH The Duke of Edinburgh, KG, KT, OM, GBE, PC.	1977
Vice-Chancellor, Prof. Sir David Williams (*Wolfson*)	1989
High Steward, The Lord Runcie, DD	1991
Deputy High Steward, The Lord Richardson of Duntisbourne, PC, MBE, TD.	1983
Commissary, The Lord Oliver, PC (*Trinity Hall*)	1989
Proctors, J. N. King (*Wolfson*); C. Y. Barlow, PH.D. (*Newnham*)	1991
Orator, J. Diggle, Litt.D. (*Queens'*)	1982
Registrary, S. G. Fleet, PH.D. (*Downing*)	1983
Deputy Registrary, R. F. Holmes (*Darwin*)	1972
Librarian, F. W. Ratcliffe, PH.D. (*Corpus Christi*)	1980
Treasurer, M. P. Halstead, PH.D. (*Gonville & Caius*)	1985
Secretary General of the Faculties, vacant.	
Director of the Fitzwilliam Museum, S. S. Jervis (*Corpus Christi*)	1990

Cambridge Colleges and Halls, etc.
(With dates of foundation)

Christ's (1505), *Master*, Prof. Sir Hans Kornberg, PH.D., D.SC., SC.D., FRS (1983).

Churchill (1960), *Master*, Prof. A. N. Broers, PH.D., FRS (1990).

Clare (1326), *Master*, Prof. R. C. O. Matthews, CBE, FBA (1975).

Clare Hall (1966), *President*, Prof. D. A. Low, PH.D. (1987).

Corpus Christi (1352), *Master*, M. W. McCrum (1980).

Darwin (1964), *Master*, Prof. G. E. R. Lloyd, PH.D., FBA (1989).

Downing (1800), *Master*, P. Mathias, CBE, Litt.D., FBA (1987).

Emmanuel (1584), *Master*, The Lord St John of Fawsley, PC, PH.D. (1991).

Fitzwilliam (1966), *Master*, Prof. A. W. Cuthbert, PH.D., FRS (1991).

Girton (1869), *Mistress*, Mrs J. J. d'A. Campbell, CMG (1992).

Gonville & Caius (1348), *Master*, Prof. P. Gray, SC.D., FRS (1988).

Homerton (1824) (for B. Ed. Students), *Principal*, Mrs K. B. Pretty, PH.D. (1991).

Hughes Hall (1885), (for post-graduate students), *President*, T. D. Hawkins (1989).

Jesus (1496), *Master*, Prof. Lord Renfrew, SC.D. (1986).

King's (1441), *Provost*, Prof. P. P. G. Bateson, SC.D., FRS (1987).

---

† Correspondence for the Vice-Chancellor and other administrative officers should be sent to the University Offices, The Old Schools, Cambridge CB2 1TN. (Tel: 0223-337733).

Lucy Cavendish College (1965) (for women research students and mature and affiliated undergraduates), *President*, Dame Anne Warburton, DCVO, CMG (1985).

Magdalene (1542), *Master*, Sir David Calcutt, QC (1985).

New Hall (1954), *President*, Mrs V. L. Pearl, PH.D. (1981).

Newnham (1871), *Principal*, Miss S. J. Browne, CB (1983).

Pembroke (1347), *Master*, Prof. the Lord Adrian, MD, FRS (1981).

Peterhouse (1284), *Master*, Prof. H. Chadwick, KBE, DD, FBA (1987).

Queens' (1448), *President*, Rev. J. C. Polkinghorne, SC.D., FRS (1989).

Robinson (1977), *Warden*, Prof. the Lord Lewis of Newnham, SC.D., FRS (1977).

St Catharine's (1473), *Master*, Prof. B. E. Supple, PH.D. (1984).

St Edmund's (1896), *Master*, R. M. Laws, CBE, PH.D. (1986).

St John's (1511), *Master*, Prof. R. A. Hinde, SC.D., FRS (1989).

Selwyn (1882), *Master*, Prof. Sir Alan Cook, SC.D., FRS (1983).

Sidney Sussex (1596), *Master*, Prof. D. H. Northcote, PH.D., SC.D., FRS (1976).

Trinity (1546), *Master*, Sir Michael Atiyah, PH.D., FRS, FRSE (1990).

Trinity Hall (1350), *Master*, Sir John Lyons, PH.D. (1984).

Wolfson (1965), *President*, Prof. Sir David Williams (1980).

* Colleges for women only.

CITY UNIVERSITY (1966)
Northampton Square, EC1V 0HB
[071-253 4399]

Full-time Students (1990–91), 4,468.
Chancellor, The Rt. Hon. Lord Mayor of London.
Vice-Chancellor and Principal, Prof. R. N. Franklin, D.Phil., D.SC.
Registrar, A. H. Seville, PH.D.
Secretary, M. M. O'Hara.

THE UNIVERSITY OF DURHAM
(Founded 1832; re-organized 1908, 1937 and 1963)
Old Shire Hall, Durham DH1 3HP
[091-374 2000]

Full-time Students (1990–91), 5,592.
Chancellor, vacant.
Vice-Chancellor and Warden, Prof. E. A. V. Ebsworth, D.SC., FRSE.
Registrar and Secretary, J. C. F. Hayward.

Colleges

Collingwood.—Principal, G. H. Blake, PH.D.
Graduate Society.—Principal, M. Richardson, PH.D.
Grey.—Master, V. E. Watts.
Hatfield.—Master, J. P. Barber, PH.D.
St Aidan's.—Principal, R. J. Williams.
St Chad's.—Principal, vacant.
St Cuthbert's Society.—Principal, S. G. C. Stoker.
St Hild and St Bede.—Principal, J. V. Armitage, PH.D.
St John's.—Principal, Rev. A. C. Thiselton, PH.D.
St Mary's.—Principal, Miss J. M. Kenworthy.
Trevelyan.—Principal, Miss D. Lavin.
University.—Master, E. C. Salthouse, PH.D.
Ushaw.—President, Rt. Rev. Mgr. P. F. J. Walton.
Van Mildert.—Principal, Ms J. Turner, PH.D.

THE UNIVERSITY OF EAST ANGLIA (1963)
Norwich NR4 7TJ
[0603-56161]

Full-time Students (1990–91), 4,786.
Chancellor, Rev. Prof. W. O. Chadwick, OM, KBE, DD, FBA (1985).
Vice-Chancellor, Prof. D. C. Burke, PH.D.
Registrar and Secretary, M. G. E. Paulson-Ellis.

THE UNIVERSITY OF ESSEX (1964)
Wivenhoe Park, Colchester CO4 3SQ
[0206-873333]

Full-time Students (1990–91), 3,293.
Chancellor, The Rt. Hon. Sir Patrick Nairne, GCB, MC (1983).
Vice-Chancellor, Prof. M. Harris, PH.D.
Registrar and Secretary, E. Newcomb.

THE UNIVERSITY OF EXETER (1955)
Exeter EX4 4QJ
[0392-263263]

Full-time Students (1990–91), 6,340.
Chancellor, Sir Rex Richards, D.SC., FRS (1981).
Vice-Chancellor, D. Harrison, CBE, PH.D., SC.D., F.Eng.
Academic Registrar and Secretary, I. H. C. Powell.

THE UNIVERSITY OF HULL (1954)
Cottingham Road, Hull HU6 7RX

Full-time Students (1990–91), 6,819.
Chancellor, The Lord Wilberforce, CMG, OBE, PC (1978).
Vice-Chancellor, Prof. D. Dilks.
Registrar and Secretary, F. T. Mattison.

THE UNIVERSITY OF KEELE (1962)
Keele, Newcastle under Lyme, Staffs. ST5 5BG
[0782-621111]

Full-time Students (1990–91), 3,715.
Chancellor, Sir Claus Moser, KCB, CBE, FBA (1986).
Vice-Chancellor, Prof. B. E. Fender, CMG, PH.D.
Registrar, D. Cohen, PH.D.

UNIVERSITY OF KENT AT CANTERBURY (1965)
Canterbury CT2 7LX
[0227-764000]

Full-time Students (1990–91), 4,886.
Chancellor, R. Horton (1990).
Vice-Chancellor, D. J. E. Ingram, CBE, D.Phil., D.SC.
Registrar, T. Mead, PH.D.

THE UNIVERSITY OF LANCASTER (1964)
Lancaster LA1 4YW
[0524-65201]

Full-time Students (1990–91), 5,318.
Chancellor, HRH Princess Alexandra, the Hon. Lady Ogilvy, GCVO (1964).
Vice-Chancellor, Prof. H. J. Hanham, PH.D.
Secretary, G. M. Cockburn.

THE UNIVERSITY OF LEEDS (1904)
Leeds LS2 9JT
[0532-431751]

Full-time Students (1990–91), 12,393.
Chancellor, HRH The Duchess of Kent, GCVO (1966).
Vice-Chancellor, Prof. A. G. Wilson.
Registrar, J. J. Walsh.

THE UNIVERSITY OF LEICESTER (1957)
Leicester LE1 7RH
[0533-522522]

Full-time Students (1990–91), 6,203.
Chancellor, Prof. Sir George Porter, FRS, PH.D., SC.D. (1985).
Vice-Chancellor, K. J. R. Edwards, PH.D.
Registrar, Prof. G. Bernbaum.

THE UNIVERSITY OF LIVERPOOL (1903)
PO Box 147, Liverpool L69 3BX
[051-794 2000]

Full-time Students (1990–91), 9,504.
Chancellor, The Viscount Leverhulme, KG, TD (1980).
Vice-Chancellor, Prof. J. N. Tarn, PH.D (*acting*).
Registrar and Secretary, M. D. Carr.

THE UNIVERSITY OF LONDON (1836)
Senate House, WC1E 7HU
[071-636 8000]

Internal Students (1988–89), 54,521, External Students, 24,856.
Visitor, HM The Queen in Council.
Chancellor, HRH The Princess Royal, GCVO, FRS (1981).
Vice-Chancellor, Prof. S. R. Sutherland.
Chairman of the Court, The Lord Goff of Chieveley, PC, DCL.
Chairman of Convocation, Prof. C. D. Cowan, CBE, PH.D.
Principal, P. Holwell.

Principal Officers
Clerk of the Court, P. J. Griffiths.
Clerk of the Senate, J. R. Davidson.
Academic Registrar, Mrs G. F. Roberts.
Secretary to School Examinations Council, vacant.

Schools of the University
Birkbeck College, Malet Street, WC1E 7HX.—*Master*, The Baroness Blackstone, PH.D.
Goldsmiths' College, Lewisham Way, New Cross, SE14 6NW.—*Warden*, Prof. A. Rutherford.
Imperial College of Science, Technology and Medicine, Prince Consort Road, SW7 2AZ.—*Rector*, Prof. Sir Eric Ash, CBE, PH.D., FRS.
Institute of Education, 20 Bedford Way, WC1H 0AL.—*Dir.*, Sir Peter Newsam.
King's College London (includes former Chelsea College and Queen Elizabeth College), Strand, WC2R 2LS.—*Principal*, Prof. J. D. E. Beynon, PH.D.
London School of Economics and Political Science, Houghton Street, WC2A 2AE.—*Dir.*, Prof. J. M. Ashworth, PH.D., D.SC.
Queen Mary and Westfield College, Mile End Road, E1 4NS.—*Principal*, Prof. G. Zellick.
Royal Holloway and Bedford New College, Egham Hill, Egham, Surrey TW20 0EX.—*Principal*, Prof. N. Gowar.
Royal Veterinary College, Royal College Street, NW1 0TU.—*Principal and Dean*, Prof. L. E. Lanyon, PH.D.
School of Oriental and African Studies, Malet Street, WC1E 7HP.—*Dir.*, M. D. McWilliam.
School of Pharmacy, 29–39 Brunswick Square, WC1N 1AX.—*Dean*, Prof. A. T. Florence, PH.D., FRSE.
University College, Gower Street, WC1E 6BT.—*Provost*, Dr D. H. Roberts, CBE, FRS.
Wye College, Wye, Ashford, Kent TN25 5AH.—*Principal*, Prof. J. H. D. Prescott, PH.D.
*Heythrop College, 11–13 Cavendish Square, W1M 0AN.—*Principal*, Rev. B. A. Callaghan, SJ.

---

*Not in receipt of UFC grants.

Medical Schools
Charing Cross and Westminster Medical School, The Reynolds Building, St Dunstan's Road, W6 8RP.—*Dean*, J. E. H. Pendower; *Sec.*, G. K. Buckley.
Royal Free Hospital School of Medicine, Rowland Hill Street, NW3 2PF.—*Dean*, Prof. A. J. Zuckerman, MD, FRCP; *Sec.*, B. A. Blatch.
The Royal London Hospital Medical College, Turner Street, E1 2AD.—*Dean*, Prof. R. Duckworth, CBE, MD, FRCS, FRCPath; *Sec.*, J. W. Walmsley.
St Bartholomew's Hospital Medical College, West Smithfield, EC1A 7BE.—*Dean*, Prof. L. H. Rees, MD, FRCP; *Sec.*, Dr J. C. Axe.
St George's Hospital Medical School, Cranmer Terrace, SW17 0RE.—*Dean*, Prof. A. W. Asscher, MD, FRCP; *Sec.*, R. B. Hill.
United Medical and Dental Schools of Guy's and St Thomas's Hospitals, Guy's: London Bridge, SE1 9RT; St Thomas's: Lambeth Palace Road, SE1 7EH.—*Dean*, Prof. I. R. Cameron, DM, FRCP; *Sec.*, C. S. Argles.

Postgraduate Medical Institutions
London School of Hygiene and Tropical Medicine, Keppel Street, WC1E 7HT.—*Dean*, Prof. R. G. Feachem, PH.D.
Royal Postgraduate Medical School, Du Cane Road, W12 0SH.—*Dean*, Prof. Sir Colin Dollery.
British Postgraduate Medical Federation (University of London), 33 Millman Street, WC1N 3EJ.—*Dir.*, Dr M. Green, DM, FRCP.
Comprises:
Institute of Cancer Research, Royal Cancer Hospital, 17A Onslow Gardens, SW7 3AL.—*Dir.*, Prof. R. A. Weiss, PH.D.
Institute of Child Health, 30 Guilford Street, WC1N 1EH.—*Dean*, Prof. R. J. Levinsky, MD, FRCP.
Institute of Dental Surgery, Eastman Dental Hospital, Gray's Inn Road, WC1X 8LD.—*Dean*, Prof. G. B. Winter, D.CH., FDS.
National Heart and Lung Institute, Fulham Road, SW3 6HP.—*Dean*, Prof. T. Clark, MD, FRCP.
Hunterian Institute, Royal College of Surgeons of England, Lincoln's Inn Fields, WC2A 3PN.—*Master*, Prof. Sir Stanley Peart, FRS, FRCP; *Academic Dean*, Prof. G. P. Lewis, PH.D.
Institute of Neurology, National Hospital, Queen Square, WC1N 3BG.—*Dean*, Prof. D. N. Landon.
Institute of Ophthalmology, Judd Street, WC1H 9QS.—*Dean*, R. K. Blatch, MD, FRCS.
Institute of Psychiatry, De Crespigny Park, Denmark Hill, SE5 8EF.—*Dean*, D. S. Checkley, MD.

Senate Institutes
British Institute in Paris, 9–11 Rue de Constantine, 75007, Paris.—*Dir.*, Prof. C. L. Campos, L-ès-L., PH.D. *London office*: Senate House, Malet Street, WC1E 7HU.
Centre for Defence Studies, King's College London, Strand, WC2R 2LS.—*Dir.*, Prof. L. Freedman.
Courtauld Institute of Art, North Block, Somerset House, Strand, WC2R 2LS.—*Dir.*, Prof. C. M. Kauffman, PH.D.
Institute of Advanced Legal Studies, Charles Clore House, 17 Russell Square, WC1B 5DR.—*Dir.*, Prof. T. C. Daintith.
Institute of Classical Studies, 31–34 Gordon Square, WC1H 0PY.—*Dir.*, Prof. R. R. K. Sorabji.
Institute of Commonwealth Studies, 27–28 Russell Square, WC1B 5DS.—*Dir.*, Prof. Shula E. Marks, PH.D.
Institute of Germanic Studies, 29 Russell Square, WC1B 5DP.—*Hon. Dir.*, Prof. M. W. Swales, PH.D.

Institute of Historical Research (including the Institute of United States Studies), Senate House, Malet Street, WC1E 7HU.—*Dir.*, Prof. P. K. O'Brien, D.Phil.

Institute of Latin American Studies, 31 Tavistock Square, WC1H 9HA.—*Dir.*, Prof. L. M. Bethell, Ph.D.

Institute of Romance Studies, Senate House, Malet Street, WC1E 7HU.—*Dir.*, Prof. M. M. Bowie, D.Phil.

School of Slavonic and East European Studies, Senate House, Malet Street, WC1E 7HU.—*Dir.*, Prof. M. A. Branch, Ph.D.

Warburg Institute, Woburn Square, WC1H 0AB.— *Dir.*, Dr N. Mann.

Institute of Zoology, Royal Zoological Society, Regent's Park, NW1 4RY.—*Dir.*, Prof. A. P. F. Flint, Ph.D., D.SC.

Institutions having Recognized Teachers

Jews' College, 44A Albert Road, NW4 2SJ.—*Principal*, Rabbi I. Jacobs.

London Business School, Sussex Place, NW1 4SA.— *Principal*, Prof. G. Bain, D.Phil.

Royal Academy of Music, Marylebone Road, NW1 5HT.—*Principal*, Sir David Lumsden, D.phil., FRCM.

Royal College of Music, Prince Consort Road, SW7 2BS.—*Dir.*, M. G. Matthews, FRSA, FRCM.

Trinity College of Music, Mandeville Place, W1M 6AQ.—*Principal*, P. Jones, CBE, FRCM.

LOUGHBOROUGH UNIVERSITY OF TECHNOLOGY (1966)
Loughborough LE11 3TU

Full-time Students (1990–91), 5,887.
Chancellor, Sir Denis Rooke, CBE, FRS (1989).
Vice-Chancellor, Prof. D. E. N. Davies, CBE, Ph.D., D.SC., FRS.
Registrar, D. E. Fletcher, Ph.D.
Academic Secretary, N. A. McHard.

THE UNIVERSITY OF MANCHESTER
(Founded 1851; re-organized 1880 and 1903).
Oxford Road, Manchester M13 9PL

Full-time Students (1990–91), 13,000.
Chancellor, Prof. J. A. G. Griffiths, FBA (1986).
Vice-Chancellor, S. A. Moore (*acting*).
Registrar and Secretary, K. E. Kitchen.

UNIVERSITY OF MANCHESTER INSTITUTE OF SCIENCE AND TECHNOLOGY (1824)
PO Box 88, Manchester M60 1QD
[061-2363311]

Full-time Students (1990–91), 5,100.
President, Sir John Mason, CB, D.SC., FRS (1986).
Principal, Prof. H. C. A. Hankins, Ph.D.
Secretary and Registrar, P. C. C. Stephenson.

THE UNIVERSITY OF NEWCASTLE UPON TYNE
(Founded 1852; re-organized 1908, 1937 and 1963)
6 Kensington Terrace, Newcastle upon Tyne
NE1 7RU
[091-222 6000]

Full-time Students (1990–91), 9,090.
Chancellor, The Viscount Ridley, TD (1989).
Vice-Chancellor, J. R. G. Wright.
Registrar, D. E. T. Nicholson.

THE UNIVERSITY OF NOTTINGHAM (1948)
University Park, Nottingham NG7 2RD
[0602-484848]

Full-time Students (1990–91), 8,500.
Chancellor, Sir Gordon Hobday, Ph.D. (1979).
Vice-Chancellor, Prof. C. M. Campbell.
Registrar, G. E. Chandler.

THE UNIVERSITY OF OXFORD

Number of Students in Residence 1991–92: *Men*, 8,620; *Women*, 5,328

UNIVERSITY OFFICERS, etc.†	Elect.
Chancellor, The Lord Jenkins of Hillhead, PC (*Balliol*)	1987
High Steward, The Lord Goff of Chieveley (*Lincoln* and *New College*)	1990
Vice-Chancellor, Sir Richard Southwood, D.SC., FRS (*Merton*)	1989
Proctors, J. Norbury (*Lincoln*); H. Morphy (*Linacre*)	1991
Assessor, M. Mingos, D.Phil. (*Keble*)	1991
Public Orator, G. W. Bond (*Pembroke*)	1980
Bodley's Librarian, D. G. Vaisey (*Exeter*)	1986
Keeper of Archives, J. Hackney (*Wadham*)	1988
Director of the Ashmolean Museum, C. J. White (*Worcester*)	1985
Registrar of the University, A. J. Dorey, D.Phil. (*Linacre*)	1979
Surveyor to the University, D. W. Bending (*Linacre*)	1985
Secretary of Faculties, A. P. Weale (*Worcester*)	1984
Secretary of the Chest and Chief Accountant, I. G. Thompson (*Merton*)	1986
Deputy Registrar (General), P. W. Jones (*Green*)	1989

Oxford Colleges and Halls
(With dates of foundation)

All Souls (1438), *Warden*, Sir Patrick Neill, QC (1977).
Balliol (1263), *Master*, B. S. Blumberg (1989).
Brasenose (1509), *Principal*, The Lord Windlesham, CVO, PC (1989).
Christ Church (1546), *Dean*, Very Rev. J. H. Drury (1991).
Corpus Christi (1517), *President*, Prof. Sir Keith Thomas, FBA (1986).
Exeter (1314), *Rector*, Sir Richard Norman, KBE, D.SC., FRS (1987).
Green (1979), *Warden*, Sir Crispin Tickell, GCMG, KCVO (1990).
Hertford (1874), *Principal*, Prof. Sir Erik Zeeman, KBE, FRS (1988).
Jesus (1571), *Principal*, Dr P. M. North, CBE, DCL (1984).
Keble (1868), *Warden*, G. B. Richardson, CBE (1989).
Lady Margaret Hall (1878), *Principal*, D. M. Stewart (1979).
Linacre (1962), *Principal*, Sir Bryan Cartledge, KCMG (1988).
Lincoln (1427), *Rector*, Sir Maurice Shock (1987).
Magdalen (1458), *President*, A. D. Smith, CBE (1988).
Merton (1264), *Warden*, J. M. Roberts, D.phil. (1985).
New College (1379), *Warden*, H. McGregor, QC, DCL (1985).

† Correspondence for the Vice-Chancellor and other administrative officers should be sent to the University Offices, Wellington Square, Oxford OX1 2JD. (Tel: 0865-270001).

Nuffield (1937), *Warden*, Sir David Cox, FRS (1988).
Oriel (1326), *Provost*, E. W. Nicholson, DD, FBA (1990).
Pembroke (1624), *Master*, Sir Roger Bannister, CBE, DM, FRCP (1985).
Queen's (1340), *Provost*, J. Moffatt, D.phil. (1987).
Rewley House (1990), *President*, G. P. Thomas, Ph.D. (1990).
St Anne's (1952) (Originally Society of Oxford Home-Students (1879)), *Principal*, Mrs R. L. Deech (1991).
St Antony's (1950), *Warden*, R. Dahrendorf, HON. KBE, ph.D., FBA (1987).
St Catherine's (1962), *Master*, E. B. Smith, D.Sc. (1988).
St Cross (1965), *Master*, R. C. Repp, D.phil. (1987).
St Edmund Hall (*c.* 1278), *Principal*, J. C. B. Gosling (1983).
*St Hilda's (1893), *Principal*, Miss E. Llewellyn-Smith, CB (1990).
St Hugh's (1886), *Principal*, D. Woods, QC (1991).
St John's (1555), *President*, W. Hayes, D.phil. (1987).
St Peter's (1929), *Master*, Prof. G. E. Aylmer, D.Phil., FBA (1978).
*Somerville (1879), *Principal*, Miss C. E. Pestell, CMG (1989).
Trinity (1554), *President*, Sir John Burgh, KCMG, CB (1987).
University (1249), *Master*, W. J. Albery, D.Phil., FRS (1989).
Wadham (1612), *Warden*, Sir Claus Moser, KCB, CBE, FBA (1984).
Wolfson (1966), *President*, Sir Raymond Hoffenberg, KBE, FRCP (1985).
Worcester (1714), *Provost*, R. G. Smethurst (1991).
Campion Hall (1896), *Master*, Rev. J. A. Munitiz (1989).
St Benet's Hall (1897), *Master*, Rev. P. F. Cowper, OSB (1989).
Mansfield (1886), *Principal*, D. J. Trevelyan, CB (1989).
Regent's Park (1810), *Principal*, Rev. P. S. Fiddes, D.phil. (1989).
Greyfriars (1910), *Warden*, Rev. M. W. Sheehan, D.phil. (1990).
Manchester (1990), *Principal*, Rev. R. Waller, ph.D. (1990).

* Colleges for women only.

THE UNIVERSITY OF READING (1926)
Whiteknights, PO Box 217, Reading RG6 2AH
[0734-875123]

Full-time Students (1990–91), 7,600.
Chancellor, The Lord Sherfield, GCB, GCMG, FRS (1970).
Vice-Chancellor, E. S. Page, ph.D.
Registrar, T. Bottomley.

UNIVERSITY OF SALFORD (1967)
Salford M5 4WT
[061-745 5000]

Full-time Students (1990–91), 4,325.
Chancellor, HRH The Duchess of York (1990).
Vice-Chancellor, Prof. T. M. Husband, ph.D, F.Eng.
Registrar, S. R. Bosworth, OBE.

THE UNIVERSITY OF SHEFFIELD (1905)
Western Bank, Sheffield S10 2TN

Full-time Students (1989–90), 8,884.
Chancellor, The Lord Dainton, ph.D., SC.D., FRS (1979).
Vice-Chancellor, Prof. G. G. Roberts.
Registrar and Secretary, Dr J. S. Padley.

THE UNIVERSITY OF SOUTHAMPTON (1952)
Highfield, Southampton SO9 5NH
[0703-595000]

Full-time Students (1990–91), 7,822.
Chancellor, The Earl Jellicoe, KBE, DSO, MC, PC (1984).
Vice-Chancellor, G. R. Higginson, ph.D.
Secretary and Registrar, D. A. Schofield.
Academic Registrar, Miss A. E. Clarke.

UNIVERSITY OF SURREY (1966)
Guildford, Surrey GU2 5XH
[0483-300800]

Full-time Students (1990–91), 4,546.
Chancellor, HRH The Duke of Kent, KG, GCMG, GCVO (1977).
Vice-Chancellor, Prof. A. Kelly, CBE, SC.D., FRS, F.Eng.
Secretary, L. J. Kail.

THE UNIVERSITY OF SUSSEX (1961)
Falmer, Brighton BN1 9RH

Full-time Students (1990–91), 6,014.
Chancellor, The Earl of March and Kinrara (1985).
Vice-Chancellor, Sir Leslie Fielding, KCMG.
Registrar and Secretary, G. Lockwood, D.Phil.

THE UNIVERSITY OF WARWICK (1965)
Coventry CV4 7AL

Full-time Students (1990–91), 7,222.
Chancellor, Sir Shridath Surendranath Ramphal, GCMG, QC (1989).
Vice-Chancellor, C. L. Brundin, ph.D.
Registrar, M. L. Shattock, OBE.

THE UNIVERSITY OF YORK (1963)
Heslington, York YO1 5DD
[0904-430000]

Full-time Students (1990–91), 4,516.
Chancellor, Dame Janet Baker, DBE.
Vice-Chancellor, Prof. S. B. Saul, Ph.D.
Registrar, D. J. Foster.

CRANFIELD INSTITUTE OF TECHNOLOGY (1969)
Cranfield, Bedford MK43 0AL
[0908-672974]

Under Royal Charter (1969) the Cranfield Institute of Technology grants degrees in applied science, engineering, technology and management.
Full-time Students (1990–91), 2,091.
Chancellor, The Lord Kings Norton, ph.D., F.Eng. (1969).
Vice-Chancellor, Prof. F. R. Hartley, D.Sc.
Secretary and Registrar, J. K. Pettifer.

THE OPEN UNIVERSITY (1969)
Walton Hall, Milton Keynes MK7 6AA
[0908-274066]

Students and clients (1991), 185,000.
Tuition by correspondence linked with special radio and television programmes, video and audio cassettes, residential schools and a locally-based tutorial and counselling service. Under Royal Charter the University awards degrees of BA, B.Phil., MA, MBA, M.SC., M.Phil., ph.D., D.SC. and D.Litt. There are seven faculties—arts, education, management, mathematics, science, social sciences and technology and a wide range of continuing education courses and study packs.
Chancellor, The Lord Briggs, FBA (1978).
Vice-Chancellor, Dr J. S. Daniel.
Secretary, D. J. Clinch.

ROYAL COLLEGE OF ART (1837)
Kensington Gore, SW7 2EU
[071-584 5020]

Under Royal Charter (1967) the Royal College of Art grants the degrees of Doctor, Doctor of Philosophy, Master of Arts, Master of Design and Master of Design (Engineering) (RCA).
Students (1990–91), 635 (all postgraduate).
Provost, The Earl of Gowrie, PC (1986).
Registrar, A. Selby.

THE UNIVERSITY OF WALES (1893)
King Edward VII Avenue, Cathays Park,
Cardiff CF1 3NS
[0222-382656]

Chancellor, HRH The Prince of Wales, KG, KT, GCB, PC (1976).
Vice-Chancellor, Sir Aubrey Trotman-Dickenson.
Registrar, D. P. L. Davies.

Colleges

University College of Wales, Aberystwyth.—*Princ.*, Prof. K. O. Morgan, D.Phil. (1979).
University College of North Wales, Bangor.—*Princ.*, Prof. E. Sunderland, Ph.D. (1984).
University of Wales College of Cardiff, Cardiff.—*Princ.*, Sir Aubrey Trotman-Dickenson, Ph.D., D.Sc. (1968).
St David's College, Lampeter.—*Princ.*, The Lord Morris of Castle Morris (1990).
University College, Swansea.—*Princ.*, Prof. B. L. Clarkson, Ph.D., (1982).
University of Wales College of Medicine, Cardiff.—*Provost*, Prof. Sir Herbert Duthie, MD, Ch.M., FRCS (1979).

SCOTLAND

UNIVERSITY OF ABERDEEN (1495)
Regent Walk, Aberdeen AB9 1FX
[0224-272000]

Full-time Students (1990–91), 7,200.
Chancellor, Sir Kenneth Alexander, FRSE (1987).
Principal, Prof. J. Maxwell Irvine, Ph.D.
Secretary, N. R. D. Begg.
Rector, C. Bell (1991–1993).

UNIVERSITY OF DUNDEE (1967)
Dundee DD1 4HN
[0382-23181]

Full-time Students (1990–91), 4,308.
Chancellor, The Earl of Dalhousie, KT, GCVO, GBE, MC (1977).
Vice-Chancellor, Prof. M. J. Hamlin, F.Eng.
Secretary, R. Seaton.
Rector, P. H. Scott, CMG (1989–92).

UNIVERSITY OF EDINBURGH (1583)
Old College, South Bridge, Edinburgh EH8 9YL
[031-667 1011]

Full-time Students (1990–91), 12,158.
Chancellor, HRH The Prince Philip, Duke of Edinburgh, KG, KT, OM, GBE, PC, FRS (1952).
Vice-Chancellor and Principal, Sir David Smith, D.Phil., FRS.
Secretary, Dr M. J. B. Lowe.
Rector, D. Munro (1991–94).

UNIVERSITY OF GLASGOW (1451)
Glasgow G12 8QQ
[041-339 8855]

Full-time Students (1990–91), 13,142.
Chancellor, Sir Alexander Cairncross, KCMG, FBA (1972).
Vice-Chancellor, Sir William Fraser, GCB, FRSE.
Registrar, J. M. Black.
Secretary, R. Ewen, OBE, TD.
Rector, P. Kane (1990–93).

HERIOT-WATT UNIVERSITY (1966)
Riccarton, Edinburgh EH14 4AS
[031-449 5111]

Full-time Students (1990–91), 6,000.
Chancellor, The Lord Mackay of Clashfern, PC, QC, FRSE (1979).
Principal and Vice-Chancellor, Prof. A. G. J. Mac-Farlane, CBE, Ph.D., FRS, F.Eng. (1989).
Secretary, P. L. Wilson.
Registrar, D. Sturgeon.

UNIVERSITY OF ST. ANDREWS (1411)
College Gate, St Andrews KY16 9AJ
[0334-76161]

Full-time Students (1990–91), 4,298.
Chancellor, Sir Kenneth Dover, D.Litt., FRSE, FBA (1981).
Vice-Chancellor, Prof. S. Arnott, Ph.D., FRS, FRSE.
Secretary of Court, D. J. Corner.
Rector, N. Parsons (1989–91).

UNIVERSITY OF STIRLING (1967)
Stirling FK9 4LA
[0786-73171]

Full-time Students (1990–91), 3,600.
Chancellor, The Lord Balfour of Burleigh, FRSE (1988).
Principal and Vice-Chancellor, Prof. A. J. Forty, CBE, Ph.D., D.Sc., FRSE.
Registrar, D. J. Farrington, D.Phil.
Secretary, R. G. Bomont.

UNIVERSITY OF STRATHCLYDE (1964)
16 Richmond Street, Glasgow G1 1XQ
[041-552 4400]

Full-time Students (1990–91), 8,500.
Chancellor, The Lord Tombs, F.Eng. (1990).
Principal and Vice-Chancellor, Prof. J. P. Arbuthnott.
Secretary, P. W. A. West.

NORTHERN IRELAND

THE QUEEN'S UNIVERSITY OF BELFAST (1908)
Belfast BT7 1NN
[0232-245133]

Full-time Students (1990–91), 7,867.
Chancellor, vacant.
President and Vice-Chancellor, G. Beveridge, Ph.D., FRSE.
Secretary, D. Wilson.

UNIVERSITY OF ULSTER (1984)
(Amalgamation of New University of Ulster and
Ulster Polytechnic)
Cromore Road, Coleraine BT52 1SA
[0232-852926]

Full-time Students (1990–91), 11,140.
Chancellor, The Lord Grey of Naunton, GCMG, GCVO, OBE (1985).
Vice-Chancellor, Prof. T. A. Smith.
Academic Registrar, K. Millar, PH.D.
Secretary, J. A. Hunter.

NON-UNIVERSITY SECTOR

POLYTECHNICS

(ENGLAND AND WALES)

The number of students (full-time equivalent) for
the academic year 1990–91 is shown in parenthesis.

ANGLIA POLYTECHNIC, Victoria Road South, Chelmsford, Essex CM1 1LL. (Tel: 0245-493131). (6,361).—*Dir.,* M. J. Salmon. *Head of Student Administration,* D. Davies.
BIRMINGHAM POLYTECHNIC, Perry Barr, Birmingham B42 2SU (7,689).—*Dir.,* P. C. Knight, D.Phil.; *Registrar,* Ms M. Penlington.
BOURNEMOUTH POLYTECHNIC, Poole House, Talbot Campus, Fern Barrow, Dorset BH12 5BB. (Tel: 0202-524111). (4,670).—*Dir.,* B. R. MacManus, PH.D.; *Registrar,* Miss B. Chamberlain.
BRIGHTON POLYTECHNIC, Lewes Road, Brighton BN2 4AT. (Tel: 0273-600900). (c. 6,800).—*Dir.,* Prof. D. Watson; *Registrar,* P. Reynolds.
BRISTOL POLYTECHNIC, Coldharbour Lane, Frenchay, Bristol BS16 1QY. (Tel: 0272-656261). (9,450).—*Dir.,* A. C. Morris; *Registrar,* Mrs H. K. Croft.
CITY OF LONDON POLYTECHNIC, 31 Jewry Street, EC3N 2EY. (Tel: 071-283 1030). (6,986).—*Dir.,* Prof. R. Floud, D.Phil.; *Registrar,* B. High.
COVENTRY POLYTECHNIC, Priory Street, Coventry CV1 5FB. (Tel: 0203-631313). (8,300).—*Dir.,* M. Goldstein, PH.D., D.SC., FRSC; *Registrar,* Ms S. Haselgrove.
HATFIELD POLYTECHNIC, College Lane, Hatfield, Herts AL10 9AB. (Tel: 0707-279000). (6,750).—*Dir.,* Prof. N. K. Buxton, PH.D.; *Registrar,* P. G. Jeffreys.
HUMBERSIDE POLYTECHNIC, Cottingham Road, Hull HU6 7RT. (Tel: 0482-440550). (8,000).—*Principal,* R. P. King; *Registrar,* Mrs P. Jackson.
KINGSTON POLYTECHNIC, Penrhyn Road, Kingston upon Thames KT1 2EE. (Tel: 081-547 2000). (6,555).—*Dir.,* R. C. Smith, CBE, PH.D.; *Registrar,* Ms A. Hynes.
LANCASHIRE POLYTECHNIC, Preston PR1 2TQ. (Tel: 0772-201201). (7,700).—*Rector,* B. G. Booth; *Sec.,* D. Sharrocks.
LEEDS POLYTECHNIC, Calverley Street, Leeds LS1 3HE. (Tel: 0532-832600). (8,187).—*Dir.,* C. Price.
LEICESTER POLYTECHNIC, PO Box 143, Leicester LE1 9BH. (Tel: 0533-551551). (9,196).—*Dir.,* K. Barker; *Registrar,* H. E. J. Woolls.
LIVERPOOL POLYTECHNIC, Rodney House, 70 Mount Pleasant, Liverpool L3 5UX. (Tel: 051-207 3581). (c. 8,500).—*Rector,* Prof. P. Toyne; *Head of Academic Affairs,* Miss A. Richardson.
MANCHESTER POLYTECHNIC, All Saints, Manchester M15 6BH. (Tel: 061-247 2000). (c. 12,500).—*Dir.,* Sir Kenneth Green; *Registrar,* J. D. M. Karczewski-Slowikowski.
MIDDLESEX POLYTECHNIC, Trent Park, Bramley Road, N14 4XS. (Tel: 081-368 1299). (8,145).—*Dir.,* Prof. D. Melville, PH.D.; *Registrar,* G. Jones.

NEWCASTLE UPON TYNE POLYTECHNIC, Newcastle upon Tyne NE1 8ST. (Tel: 091-232 6002). (10,043)—*Dir.,* Prof. L. Barden, CBE, PH.D., D.SC.; *Registrar,* R. A. Bott.
NOTTINGHAM POLYTECHNIC, Burton Street, Nottingham NG1 4BU. (Tel: 0602-418418). (10,445).—*Dir.,* Prof. R. Cowell, PH.D.; *Registrar,* A. E. Foster.
OXFORD POLYTECHNIC, Headington, Oxford OX3 0BP. (Tel: 0865-741111). (6,262).—*Dir.,* Dr C. Booth; *Registrar,* R. Tulloch.
POLYTECHNIC OF CENTRAL LONDON, 309 Regent Street, W1R 8AL. (Tel: 071-911 5000). (4,000).—*Rector.,* Prof. T. E. Burlin, D.SC., PH.D.; *Registrar,* Ms J. Hopkinson.
POLYTECHNIC OF EAST LONDON, Romford Road, E15 4LZ. (Tel: 081-590 7722). (6,900).—*Rector,* Prof. G. T. Fowler; *Registrar,* G. D. Miller.
POLYTECHNIC OF HUDDERSFIELD, Queensgate, Huddersfield HD1 3DH. (Tel: 0484-422288). (6,400).—*Rector,* Prof. K. J. Durrands; *Registrar,* M. Bond.
POLYTECHNIC OF NORTH LONDON, Holloway Road, N7 8DB. (Tel: 071-607 2789). (6,019)—*Dir.,* L. Wagner; *Registrar,* Dr M. Starey.
POLYTECHNIC OF WEST LONDON, St Mary's Road, W5 5RF. (Tel: 081-579 5000). (*Also* at Wellington Street, Slough SL1 1YG. (5,925).—*Dir.,* Dr M. Fitzgerald; *Academic Registrar,* Ms A. Denton.
POLYTECHNIC SOUTH WEST, Drake Circus, Plymouth PL4 8AA. (Tel: 0752-600600). (8,470).—*Dir.,* R. J. Bull; *Registrar,* Dr C. J. Sparrow.
PORTSMOUTH POLYTECHNIC, Ravelin House, Museum Road, Portsmouth PO1 2QQ. (Tel: 0705-827681). (7,343).—*Pres.,* Prof. N. Merritt; *Registrar,* Brig. B. R. Biggs.
SHEFFIELD CITY POLYTECHNIC, Pond Street, Sheffield S1 1WB. (Tel: 0742-720911). (12,246).—*Principal,* J. M. Stoddart; *Registrar,* Ms J. Tory.
SOUTH BANK POLYTECHNIC, 103 Borough Road, SE1 0AA. (Tel: 071-928 8989). (7,109).—*Dir.,* The Baroness Perry of Southwark; *Registrar,* N. Andrew.
STAFFORDSHIRE POLYTECHNIC, College Road, Stoke-on-Trent, ST4 2DE. (Tel: 0782-744531). (c. 8,000).—*Dir.,* K. B. Thompson; *Academic Registrar,* Mrs F. Francis.
SUNDERLAND POLYTECHNIC, Langham Tower, Ryhope Road, Sunderland SR2 7EE. (Tel: 091-515 2000). (6,530).—*Rector,* Ms A. Wright, PH.D.; *Registrar,* S. Porteous.
TEESSIDE POLYTECHNIC, Middlesbrough, Cleveland TS1 3BA. (Tel: 0642-218121). (7,239).—*Dir.,* M. D. Longfield, PH.D.; *Registrar,* M. McClintock.
THAMES POLYTECHNIC, Wellington Street, Woolwich, SE18 6PF. (Tel: 081-316 8000). (7,970).—*Dir.,* N. Singer, CBE, PH.D.; *Registrar,* A. I. Mayfield.
WOLVERHAMPTON POLYTECHNIC, Molineux Street, Wolverhampton WV1 1SB. (Tel: 0902-321000). (13,174).—*Dir.,* Prof. M. J. Harrison; *Head of Academic Affairs,* Ms A. M. Cooper.

POLYTECHNIC OF WALES, Pontypridd, Mid Glamorgan CF37 1DL. (Tel: 0443-480480). (5,500).—*Dir.,* J. D. Davies, OBE, PH.D., D.SC; *Registrar,* J. O'Shea.

SCOTTISH CENTRAL INSTITUTIONS

DUNCAN OF JORDANSTONE COLLEGE OF ART, Perth Road, Dundee DD1 4HT. (Tel: 0382-23261).—*Principal,* R. Miller-Smith.
DUNDEE INSTITUTE OF TECHNOLOGY, Bell Street, Dundee DD1 1HG. (Tel: 0382-308000).—*Principal,* H. G. Cuming, CBE, PH.D.
EDINBURGH COLLEGE OF ART, Lauriston Place, Edinburgh EH3 9DF. (Tel: 031-229 9311).—*Principal,* Prof. A. J. Rowan, PH.D.

GLASGOW POLYTECHNIC, Cowcaddens Road, Glasgow G4 0BA. (Tel: 041-331 3000).—*Principal*, Prof. J. S. Mason.

GLASGOW SCHOOL OF ART, 167 Renfrew Street, Glasgow G3 6RQ. (Tel: 041-332 9797).—*Dir.*, Dr J. Whiteman.

NAPIER POLYTECHNIC, Colinton Road, Edinburgh EH14 1DJ. (Tel: 031-444 2266).—*Principal*, W. A. Turmeau, CBE, Ph.D, FRSE.

PAISLEY COLLEGE OF TECHNOLOGY, High Street, Paisley PA1 2BE. (Tel: 041-848 3000).—*Principal*, Prof. R. W. Shaw.

QUEEN MARGARET COLLEGE, Clerwood Terrace, Edinburgh EH12 8TS. (Tel: 031-317 3000).—*Principal*, D. F. Leach.

THE QUEEN'S COLLEGE, GLASGOW, 1 Park Drive, Glasgow G3 6LP. (Tel: 041-337 4000).—*Principal*, Prof. J. C. Phillips.

ROBERT GORDON INSTITUTE OF TECHNOLOGY, Schoolhill, Aberdeen AB9 1FR. (Tel: 0224-633611).—*Principal*, D. A. Kennedy, Ph.D.

ROYAL SCOTTISH ACADEMY OF MUSIC AND DRAMA, 100 Renfrew Street, Glasgow G2 3DB. (Tel: 041-332 4101).—*Principal*, Dr P. Ledger, CBE, FRSE.

SCOTTISH AGRICULTURAL COLLEGE, Cleeve Gardens, Oakbank Road, Perth PH1 1HF. (Tel: 0738-36611). Campuses at Aberdeen, Auchincruive, and Edinburgh.—*Principal*, Prof. P. C. Thomas.

SCOTTISH COLLEGE OF TEXTILES, Netherdale, Galashiels, Selkirkshire TD1 3HF. (Tel: 0896-3351).—*Principal*, C. E. R. Maddox, Ph.D.

COLLEGES

It is not possible to name here all the colleges offering courses of higher or further education. The list of English colleges that follows is confined to those in the PCFC sector; there are many more colleges in England providing higher education courses, some with PCFC funding. The list of colleges in Wales, Scotland and Northern Ireland includes institutions providing at least one full-time course leading to a first degree granted by a university or by the Council for National Academic Awards (CNAA). It does not include colleges forming part of a polytechnic or a university, nor does it include Scottish central institutions.

ENGLAND

PCFC Sector

BATH COLLEGE OF HIGHER EDUCATION, Newton Park, Newton St Loe, Bath BA2 9BN. (Tel: 0225-873701).—*Dir.*, B. L. Gomes da Costa.

BISHOP GROSSETESTE COLLEGE, Lincoln LN1 3DY. (Tel: 0522-527347).—*Principal*, Prof. L. Marsh, D.Phil.

BOLTON INSTITUTE OF HIGHER EDUCATION, Deane Road, Bolton BL3 5AB. (Tel: 0204-28851).—*Principal*, R. Oxtoby, Ph.D.

BRETTON HALL, West Bretton, Wakefield, W. Yorks. WF4 4LG. (Tel: 0924-830261).—*Principal*, Prof. J. L. Taylor, OBE, Ph.D.

BUCKINGHAMSHIRE COLLEGE OF HIGHER EDUCATION, Queen Alexandra Road, High Wycombe, Bucks. HP11 2JZ. (Tel: 0494-522141).—*Dir.*, P. B. Mogford.

CAMBORNE SCHOOL OF MINES, Pool, Redruth, Cornwall TR15 3SE. (Tel: 0209-714866).—*Principal*, P. Hackett, OBE, Ph.D, F.Eng.

CANTERBURY CHRIST CHURCH COLLEGE, North Holmes Road, Canterbury, Kent CT1 1QU. (Tel: 0227-767700).—*Principal*, M. H. A. Berry, TD.

THE CENTRAL SCHOOL OF SPEECH AND DRAMA, Embassy Theatre, Eton Avenue, NW3 3HY. (Tel: 071-722 8183).—*Principal*, R. S. Fowler.

CHARLOTTE MASON COLLEGE OF EDUCATION, Rydal Road, Ambleside, Cumbria LA22 9BB. (Tel: 05394-33066).—*Principal*, Prof. J. Thorley, Ph.D.

CHELTENHAM AND GLOUCESTER COLLEGE OF HIGHER EDUCATION, PO Box 220, The Park, Cheltenham GL50 2QF. (Tel: 0242-532701).—*Principal*, Miss J. O. Trotter, OBE.

CHESTER COLLEGE, Cheyney Road, Chester CH1 4BJ. (Tel: 0244-375444).—*Principal*, Rev. E. V. Binks.

COLLEGE OF RIPON AND YORK ST JOHN, Lord Mayor's Walk, York YO3 7EX. (Tel: 0904-656771).—*Principal*, Dr G. P. McGregor.

COLLEGE OF ST MARK AND ST JOHN, Derriford Road, Plymouth PL6 8BH. (Tel: 0752-777188).—*Principal*, J. E. Anderson.

CREWE AND ALSAGER COLLEGE OF HIGHER EDUCATION, Crewe Green Road, Crewe CW1 1DU. (Tel: 0270-500661).—*Dir.*, Miss B. P. R. Ward, CBE.

DARTINGTON COLLEGE OF ARTS, Totnes, Devon TQ9 6EJ.—*Principal*, G. Dowrick.

DERBYSHIRE COLLEGE OF HIGHER EDUCATION, Kedleston Road, Derby DE3 1GB. (Tel: 0332-47181).—*Dir.*, R. Waterhouse.

EDGE HILL COLLEGE OF HIGHER EDUCATION, St Helens Road, Ormskirk, Lancs. L39 4QP. (Tel: 0695-575171).—*Dir.*, Prof. R. Gee.

FALMOUTH SCHOOL OF ART AND DESIGN, Woodlane, Falmouth, Cornwall TR11 4RA. (Tel: 0326-211077).—*Principal*, Prof. A. G. Livingston.

HARPER ADAMS AGRICULTURAL COLLEGE, Newport, Shropshire TF10 8NB. (Tel: 0952-820280).—*Principal*, A. G. Harris.

HOMERTON COLLEGE, Cambridge CB2 2PH. (Tel: 0223-411141).—*Principal*, Mrs K. Pretty, Ph.D.

INSTITUTE OF ADVANCED NURSING, Royal College of Nursing, 20 Cavendish Square, W1M 0AB.—*Principal*, J. C. A. Wells.

KENT INSTITUTE OF ART AND DESIGN, Oakwood Park, Oakwood Road, Maidstone ME16 8AG (*also* New Dover Road, Canterbury CT1 3AN; and Fort Pitt, Rochester ME1 1DZ). (Tel: 0622-757286).—*Dir.*, P. I. Williams.

KING ALFRED'S COLLEGE, Sparkford Road, Winchester SO22 4NR. (Tel: 0962-841515).—*Principal*, J. A. Cranmer.

LIVERPOOL INSTITUTE OF HIGHER EDUCATION, PO Box 6, Stand Park Road, Liverpool L16 9JD. (Tel: 051-722 2361).—*Rector*, J. Burke, OBE, Ph.D.

THE LONDON INSTITUTE, 388–396 Oxford Street, W1R 1FE.—*Rector*, Prof. J. C. McKenzie. Comprising:

Camberwell College of Arts, Peckham Road, SE5 8UF.

Central St Martins College of Art and Design, Southampton Row, WC1B 4AP.

Chelsea College of Art and Design, Manresa Road, SW3 6LS.

London College of Fashion, 20 John Prince's Street, W1M 9HE.

London College of Printing and Distributive Trades, Elephant and Castle, SE1 6SB.

LOUGHBOROUGH COLLEGE OF ART AND DESIGN, Radmoor, Loughborough, Leics. LE11 3BT. (Tel: 0509-261515).—*Principal*, I. Pugh.

LSU COLLEGE OF HIGHER EDUCATION, The Avenue, Southampton SO9 5HB. (Tel: 0703-228761).—*Principal*, Dr A. C. Chitnis.

LUTON COLLEGE OF HIGHER EDUCATION, Park Square, Luton LU1 3JU. (Tel: 0582-34111).—*Dir.*, A. J. Wood, Ph.D.

NENE COLLEGE, Moulton Park, Northampton NN2 7AL. (Tel: 0604-715000).—*Dir.*, Dr S. M. Gaskell.

NEWMAN COLLEGE, Genners Lane, Bartley Green, Birmingham B32 3NT. (Tel: 021-476 1181).—*Principal*, Joan S. Cuming, Ph.D.

NORTH RIDING COLLEGE, Filey Road, Scarborough, N. Yorks. YO11 3AZ. (Tel: 0723-362392).—*Principal*, R. A. Withers, Ph.D.

RAVENSBOURNE COLLEGE OF DESIGN AND COMMUNI-
CATION, Walden Road, Chislehurst, Kent BR7 5SN.
(Tel: 081-468 7071).—*Dir.*, N. J. Frewing.

ROEHAMPTON INSTITUTE, Senate House, Roehampton
Lane, SW15 5PU. Comprises Digby Stuart College,
Froebel Institute, Southlands College and White-
lands College. (Tel: 081-878 8117).—*Rector*, Prof. S.
C. Holt, PH.D.

ROSE BRUFORD COLLEGE OF SPEECH AND DRAMA,
Lamorbey Park, Burnt Oak Lane, Sidcup, Kent
DA15 9DF. (Tel: 081-300 3024).—*Principal*, P.
Robins.

ROYAL ACADEMY OF MUSIC, Marylebone Road, NW1
5HT. (071-935 1665).—*Principal*, Sir David Lumsden, D.phil.

ROYAL COLLEGE OF MUSIC, Prince Consort Road,
London SW7 2BS. (Tel: 071-589 3643).—*Dir.*, M. G.
Matthews.

ROYAL NORTHERN COLLEGE OF MUSIC, 124 Oxford
Road, Manchester M13 9RD.—*Principal*, Sir John
Manduell, CBE.

S. MARTIN'S COLLEGE LANCASTER, Lancaster LA1
3JD. (Tel: 0524-63446).—*Principal*, D. Edynbry,
PH.D.

ST MARY'S COLLEGE, Strawberry Hill, Twickenham
TW1 4SX. (Tel: 081-892 0051).—*Principal*, Rev.
Father D. A. Beirne.

SALFORD COLLEGE OF TECHNOLOGY, Frederick Road,
Salford M6 6PU. (Tel: 061-736 6541).—*Principal*, Dr
R. Allerton.

SOUTHAMPTON INSTITUTE OF HIGHER EDUCATION, East
Park Terrace, Southampton SO9 4WW. (Tel: 0703-
229381).—*Dir.*, D. G. Leyland.

TRINITY AND ALL SAINTS' COLLEGE, Brownberrie
Lane, Horsforth, Leeds LS18 5HD. (Tel: 0532-
584341).—*Principal*, Dr G. L. Turnbull.

TRINITY COLLEGE OF MUSIC, 11–13 Mandeville Place,
W1M 6AQ. (Tel: 071-935 5773).—*Principal*, P.
Jones, CBE.

WESTHILL COLLEGE, Hamilton Building, Weoley Park
Road, Selly Oak, Birmingham B29 6LL. (Tel: 021-
472 7245).—*Principal*, Dr G. Priestley.

WEST LONDON INSTITUTE OF HIGHER EDUCATION,
Lancaster House, Borough Road, Isleworth, Middx.
TW7 5DU. (Tel: 081-568 8741).—*Principal*, J. E.
Kane, OBE, PH.D.

WESTMINSTER COLLEGE, Oxford OX2 9AT. (Tel: 0865-
247644).—*Principal*, Rev. Dr K. B. Wilson.

WEST SURREY COLLEGE OF ART AND DESIGN, Falkner
Road, The Hart, Farnham, Surrey GU9 7DS. (Tel:
0252-722441).—*Dir.*, N. J. Taylor.

WEST SUSSEX INSTITUTE OF HIGHER EDUCATION, The
Dome, Upper Bognor Road, Bognor Regis, West
Sussex PO21 1HR. (Tel: 0243-865581).—*Dir.*, J. F.
Wyatt.

WINCHESTER SCHOOL OF ART, Park Avenue, Winchester, Hants. SO23 8DL. (Tel: 0962-842500).—*Principal*, M. Sadler-Forster.

WORCESTER COLLEGE OF HIGHER EDUCATION, Hen-
wick Grove, Worcester WR2 6AJ. (Tel: 0905-
748080).—*Principal*, D. R. Shadbolt, OBE, D.phil.

WALES

BANGOR NORMAL COLLEGE, Bangor, Gwynedd LL57
2PX. (Tel: 0248-370171).—*Principal*, R. Williams.

GWENT COLLEGE OF HIGHER EDUCATION, College
Crescent, Caerleon, Newport, Gwent NP6 1XJ.
(Tel: 0633-421292).—*Principal*, Dr K. J. Overshott.

THE NORTH EAST WALES INSTITUTE OF HIGHER
EDUCATION, Kelsterton Road, Connah's Quay,
Deeside, Clwyd CH5 4BR. (Tel: 0244-831531).—
Principal, Prof. G. O. Phillips, PH.D., D.SC.

SOUTH GLAMORGAN INSTITUTE OF HIGHER EDUCATION,
Western Avenue, Llandaff, Cardiff CF5 2YB.—
Principal, E. J. Brent, PH.D.

TRINITY COLLEGE, Carmarthen, Dyfed, SA31 3EP.
(Tel: 0267-237971).—*Principal*, D. C. Jones-Davies.

WELSH AGRICULTURAL COLLEGE, Llanbadarn Fawr,
Aberystwyth, Dyfed SY23 3AL. (Tel: 0970-
624471).—*Principal*, J. R. Gill.

WELSH COLLEGE OF MUSIC AND DRAMA, Castle
Grounds, Cathays Park, Cardiff CF1 3ER. (Tel:
0222-342854).—*Principal*, E. Fivet.

WEST GLAMORGAN INSTITUTE OF HIGHER EDUCATION,
Townhill Road, Swansea SA2 0UT. (Tel: 0792-
203482).—*Principal*, G. Stockdale, PH.D.

SCOTLAND

CRAIGIE COLLEGE OF EDUCATION, Ayr KA8 0SR. (Tel:
0292-260321).—*Principal*, G. M. Wilson, PH.D.

JORDANHILL COLLEGE OF EDUCATION, 73 Southbrae
Drive, Jordanhill, Glasgow G13 1PP. (Tel: 041-950
3200).—*Principal*, T. R. Bone, CBE, PH.D.

MORAY HOUSE COLLEGE OF EDUCATION, Holyrood
Road, Edinburgh EH8 8AQ. (Tel: 031-556 8455).—
Principal, G. Kirk.

NORTHERN COLLEGE OF EDUCATION, Hilton Place,
Aberdeen AB9 1FA. (Tel: 0224-283500); Gardyne
Road, Dundee DD5 1NY. (Tel: 0382-453433).—
Principal, D. A. Adams.

ST ANDREW'S COLLEGE OF EDUCATION, Duntocher
Road, Bearsden, Glasgow G61 4QA. (Tel: 041-943
1424).—*Principal*, B. J. McGettrick.

NORTHERN IRELAND

ST MARY'S COLLEGE, 191 Falls Road, Belfast BT12
6FE. (Tel: 0232-327678).—*Principal*, J. I. O'Connell.

STRANMILLIS COLLEGE, Stranmillis Road, Belfast BT9
5DY. (Tel: 0232-381271).—*Principal*, R. J. Rodgers,
PH.D.

ADULT AND CONTINUING EDUCATION

NATIONAL INSTITUTE OF ADULT CONTINUING EDUCA-
TION, 19B De Montfort Street, Leicester LE1 7GE.
(Tel: 0533-551451).—*Dir.*, A. Tuckett.

NIACE CYMRU, 245 Western Avenue, Cardiff CF5
2YX. (Tel: 0222-571201).—*National Officer for
Wales*, Ms A. Poole.

NORTHERN IRELAND COUNCIL FOR CONTINUING EDU-
CATION, Department of Education for Northern
Ireland, Rathgael House, Balloo Road, Bangor
BT19 2PR. (Tel: 0247-270077).—*Sec.*, Miss S. Pid-
duck.

OPEN COLLEGE, 101 Wigmore Street, W1H 9AA.
(Tel: 0800 300760).—*Managing Dir.*, M. Colenso.

THE POLYTECHNIC ASSOCIATION FOR CONTINUING
EDUCATION, Educational Development Officer,
Polytechnic of Wales, Pontypridd, Mid Glam. CF37
1DL. (Tel: 0443-480480).—*Sec.*, P. Race.

THE RESIDENTIAL COLLEGES COMMITTEE, c/o Ruskin
College, Oxford OX1 2HE. (Tel: 0865-56360).—
Awards Officer, Mrs F. A. Bagchi.

SCOTTISH INSTITUTE OF ADULT AND CONTINUING
EDUCATION, 30 Rutland Square, Edinburgh EH1
2BW. (Tel: 031-229 0331).—*Dir.*, Mrs H. Johnston.

THE UNIVERSITIES COUNCIL FOR ADULT AND CONTIN-
UING EDUCATION, Department of Continuing Education, The University of Warwick, Coventry CV4

7AL. (Tel: 0203-523835).—*Hon. Sec.*, Prof. C. Duke, PH.D.

THE WORKER'S EDUCATIONAL ASSOCIATION, Temple House, 9 Upper Berkeley Street, W1H 8BY. (Tel: 071-402 5608).—*Gen. Sec.*, R. Lochrie.

Long-term Residential Colleges for Adult Education

COLEG HARLECH, Harlech, Gwynedd LL46 2PU. (Tel: 0766-780363).—*Warden*, J. W. England.

CO-OPERATIVE COLLEGE, Stanford Hall, Loughborough, Leics. LE12 5QR. (Tel: 0509-852333).—*Principal*, Dr R. Houlton.

FIRCROFT COLLEGE, 1018 Bristol Road, Selly Oak, Birmingham B29 6LH. (Tel: 021-472 0116).—*Principal*, K. Jackson.

HILLCROFT COLLEGE, South Bank, Surbiton, Surrey KT6 6DF. (Tel: 081-399 2688). (For women only).—*Principal*, Ms E. Aird.

NEWBATTLE ABBEY COLLEGE, Dalkeith, Midlothian EH22 3LL. (Tel: 031-662 1921).—*Principal*, W. M. Conboy (*acting*).

NORTHERN COLLEGE, Wentworth Castle, Stainborough, Barnsley, S. Yorks. S75 3ET. (Tel: 0226-285426).—*Principal*, R. H. Fryer.

PLATER COLLEGE, Pullens Lane, Oxford OX3 0DT. (Tel: 0865-741676).—*Principal*, D. G. Chiles.

RUSKIN COLLEGE, Walton Street, Oxford OX1 2HE. (Tel: 0865-54331).—*Principal*, S. Yeo, D.PHIL.

PROFESSIONAL EDUCATION
(excluding postgraduate study)

NOTE.—References to courses at universities, polytechnics and colleges in the sections following are not claimed to be comprehensive and cover only full-time courses leading to first degrees. Full lists appear in *University Entrance: The Official Guide* and in the *CNAA Directory of First Degree and Diploma of Higher Education Courses*. Both are published annually.

Postgraduate study and research are not covered here.

ACCOUNTANCY

(*See also* **Business, Management and Administration**).

First degrees in *Accounting* or *Accountancy* are granted by most universities. At several universities one of these subjects can be combined, e.g. with Financial Administration, Finance or Economics.

Courses leading to first degrees in *Accounting, Accountancy* or *Accounting and Finance* granted by the CNAA are provided by most polytechnics.

The main bodies granting membership on examination after a period of practical work are:

INSTITUTE OF CHARTERED ACCOUNTANTS IN ENGLAND AND WALES, Chartered Accountants' Hall, PO Box 433, Moorgate Place, EC2P 2BJ. (Tel: 071-628 7060).—*Sec.*, A. J. Colquhoun.

INSTITUTE OF CHARTERED ACCOUNTANTS OF SCOTLAND, 27 Queen Street, Edinburgh EH2 1LA. (Tel: 031-225 5673).—*Sec.*, P. W. Johnston.

CHARTERED ASSOCIATION OF CERTIFIED ACCOUNTANTS, 29 Lincolns Inn Fields, WC2A 3EE.—*Sec.*, A. W. Sansom.

CHARTERED INSTITUTE OF MANAGEMENT ACCOUNTANTS, 63 Portland Place, W1N 4AB.—*Sec.*, Sir George Vallings, KCB.

CHARTERED INSTITUTE OF PUBLIC FINANCE AND ACCOUNTANCY, 3 Robert Street, WC2N 6BH. (Tel: 071-895 8823).—*Sec.*, N. P. Hepworth, OBE.

ACTUARIAL SCIENCE

First degrees in *Actuarial Science* are granted by the City University and the Universities of Kent and London (London School of Economics and Political Science); and in *Actuarial Studies* and either *Mathematics* or *Economics* by Southampton University.

Two professional organizations grant qualifications after examination:

INSTITUTE OF ACTUARIES, Staple Inn Hall, High Holborn, WC1V 7QJ. (Tel: 071-242 0106).—*Sec. Gen.*, A. G. Tait.

FACULTY OF ACTUARIES IN SCOTLAND, 23 St Andrew Square, Edinburgh EH2 1AQ.—*Sec.*, W. W. Mair.

AERONAUTICS
and Aeronautical Engineering

First degrees in *Aeronautical Engineering* are granted by the Universities of Bath, Belfast, Bristol, Cambridge, the City University (also *Air Transport Engineering*), Cranfield Institute of Technology (Shrivenham College), the Universities of Glasgow, London (Imperial College of Science and Technology, Queen Mary and Westfield College, also *Avionics—Aeronautical/Electrical*), Liverpool (*Aerospace Engineering*), Loughborough, Manchester, Salford and Southampton (*Aeronautics and Astronautics* and *Aerospace Systems Engineering*).

First degrees in *Aeronautical Engineering* granted by the CNAA are provided at Hatfield Polytechnic and Kingston Polytechnic.

AGRICULTURE

First degrees in *Agriculture* or *Agricultural Science(s)* are granted by the Universities of Aberdeen, Belfast, Edinburgh, London (Wye College), Newcastle upon Tyne, Nottingham, Reading and Wales (University Colleges of Aberystwyth and Bangor); and in *Horticulture* by London (Wye College), Nottingham, Reading and Strathclyde.

First degrees in *Agriculture* granted by the CNAA are provided at Harper Adams College, Middlesex, South West and Wolverhampton Polytechnics; and in *Horticulture* by Hatfield and Lancashire Polytechnics.

ARCHAEOLOGY

First degrees in *Archaeology* or *Archaeological Sciences/Studies* are granted by the Universities of Belfast, Birmingham, Bradford, Cambridge, Durham, Edinburgh, Exeter, Glasgow, Leicester, Liverpool, London (King's College, University College), Manchester, Newcastle upon Tyne, Nottingham, Oxford, Reading, Sheffield, Southampton, Wales (University College Cardiff, Bangor UC, St David's UC, Lampeter) and York. At several of the above universities archaeology must be combined with another subject, e.g. ancient history or anthropology.

ARCHITECTURE

(*See also* **Building**, and **Town and Country Planning**).

First degrees in *Architecture/Architectural Studies* are granted by the Universities of Bath, Belfast, Cambridge, Dundee, Edinburgh, Glasgow, Heriot-Watt, Leeds, Liverpool, London (University College), Manchester, Newcastle upon Tyne, Nottingham, Sheffield, Strathclyde, Wales (Cardiff).

First degrees in *Architecture/Architectural Studies* granted by the CNAA are provided by the Polytechnics of Birmingham, Brighton, Huddersfield, Humberside, Kingston, Leeds, Leicester, Liverpool, Manchester, Oxford, Central London, East London, North London, Polytechnic South West, Portsmouth, South Bank and Thames, and by Kent Institute and Robert Gordon's Institute.

Other schools of architecture include THE ARCHITECTURAL ASSOCIATION, 34–36 Bedford Square, WC1B 2ES.—*Sec.*, E. A. Le Maistre.

THE ROYAL INSTITUTE OF BRITISH ARCHITECTS
66 Portland Place, W1N 4AD
[Tel: 071-580 5533]

The Education and Professional Development Committee of the Royal Institute of British Architects sets standards and guides the whole system of architectural education throughout the United Kingdom. Courses at Schools recognized by the RIBA exempt students from the RIBA's own examinations.
Pres., R. MacCormac.
Dir.-Gen. The Rt. Hon. W. Rodgers.

ART AND DESIGN

First degrees in *Art, Fine Art* or *History of Art* are granted by the Universities of Aberdeen, Bristol (*provisional*), Cambridge, East Anglia, Edinburgh, Essex, Glasgow, Lancaster (*Visual Arts*), Leeds, Leicester, London (Courtauld Institute of Art, Birkbeck, University and Queen Mary and Westfield Colleges, School of Oriental and African Studies, Goldsmiths' College), Loughborough (*Design and Technology*), Manchester, Manchester Institute of Science and Technology (*Textile Design*), Newcastle upon Tyne, Nottingham, Oxford, Reading, St Andrews, Sussex, Wales (University College, Aberystwyth) and Warwick. At several other universities art or history of art can be combined with another subject. The degrees in *Art* granted by the Royal College of Art are higher degrees.

Courses leading to first degrees in *Art and Design, Fine Art, Graphic Design, Textiles/Fashion* or *Three-Dimensional Design* granted by the CNAA are provided by more than 40 colleges/schools of art and polytechnics, some of which also offer CNAA degree courses in other subjects in the field of Art and Design, including *Furniture Design, Industrial Design* and *Interior Design*.

ASTRONOMY

First degrees in *Astronomy* are granted by the Universities of Glasgow, London (University and Queen Mary and Westfield Colleges), Newcastle, St Andrew's; in *Astrophysics* by the Universities of Edinburgh, London (Queen Mary and Westfield College, University College), Newcastle, St Andrews and Wales (University College, Cardiff); and in *Physics and Astronomy/Astrophysics* at the Universities of Birmingham, Glasgow, Kent, Leeds, Leicester, London (King's College, Royal Holloway & Bedford New College, University College), Manchester, Sheffield, Southampton and Sussex. Various combinations of Astronomy and Astrophysics with other subjects are also available.
Astronomy may be taken as part of a CNAA degree course at certain polytechnics.

BANKING

First degrees with specialization in *Banking and Finance* are granted by the Universities of Birmingham (*Money, Banking and Finance*), Loughborough, Ulster, Wales (University College, Cardiff and Bangor

UC), and the City University (*Banking and International Finance*).
Finance may be taken as part of a CNAA degree course at many polytechnics/colleges.
Professional organizations granting qualifications after examination:

CHARTERED INSTITUTE OF BANKERS, 10 Lombard Street, EC3V 9AS. (Tel: 071-623 5071).—*Sec. Gen.*, E. Glover.

INSTITUTE OF BANKERS IN SCOTLAND, 19 Rutland Square, Edinburgh EH1 2DE. (Tel: 031-229 9869).—*Sec.*, Dr C. W. Munn.

BIOLOGY, CHEMISTRY, PHYSICS

First degrees in these subjects are granted by many universities. Courses leading to first degrees granted by the CNAA are provided by many polytechnics. Professional qualifications are awarded by:—

INSTITUTE OF BIOLOGY, 20 Queensberry Place, SW7 2DZ. (Tel: 071-581 8333).—*Pres.*, Prof. P. M. Biggs, CBE, FRS; *Gen. Sec.*, Dr R. H. Priestley.

ROYAL SOCIETY OF CHEMISTRY, Burlington House, Piccadilly, W1V 0BN. (Tel: 071-437 8656).—*Pres.*, Sir Rex Richards, FRS; *Sec.*, J. S. Gow, PH.D., FRSC, FRSE.

INSTITUTE OF PHYSICS, 47 Belgrave Square, SW1X 8QX. (Tel: 071-235 6111).—*Chief Exec.*, Dr A. Jones.

BREWING

First degrees in *Brewing and Distilling* are granted by Heriot-Watt University.

BUILDING
(*See also* Architecture, Estate and Land Management and Surveying)

First degrees in *Building, Building Engineering, Building Services Engineering* or *Building Technology* are granted by the following Universities: Bath, Heriot-Watt, Liverpool, London (University College), Loughborough, Manchester (Manchester Institute of Science and Technology), Reading, Salford (*Building Surveying, Quantity Surveying*), Strathclyde (*Building Design Engineering*), and Ulster. Courses covering other aspects of building and construction are also available.

First degrees in *Building, Building Management, Building Engineering, Construction, Construction Management* and *Residential Development* granted by the CNAA are provided by Brighton, Bristol, Coventry, Lancashire, Leeds, Newcastle, Nottingham, Central London, Sheffield, South Bank and Thames and Wolverhampton Polytechnics, the Polytechnic of Wales, Anglia HE College, Glasgow College, Luton College of HE and Napier Polytechnic of Edinburgh.

Examinations are also conducted by:—

CHARTERED INSTITUTE OF BUILDING, Englemere, King's Ride, Ascot, Berks. SL5 8BJ. (Tel: 0344-23355).—*Chief Exec.*, K. Banbury.

INSTITUTE OF BUILDING CONTROL, 21 High Street, Ewell, Epsom, Surrey KT17 1SB. (Tel: 081-393 6860).—*Sec.*, Ms R. Raywood.

INSTITUTE OF CLERKS OF WORKS OF GREAT BRITAIN, 41 The Mall, W5 3TJ. (Tel: 081-579 2917-8).—*Sec.*, A. P. Macnamara.

BUSINESS, MANAGEMENT AND ADMINISTRATION

First degrees in *Business, Management, Administration* or various aspects or combinations of these subjects are granted by most Universities.
Courses leading to first degrees in *Business Studies,*

Business Administration, or other aspects of business, granted by the CNAA, are provided by all polytechnics. The CNAA also grants first degrees in *Marketing*.

Professional bodies conducting training and/or examinations in *Business, Administration, Management* or *Commerce* include:

ROYAL INSTITUTE OF PUBLIC ADMINISTRATION, 3 Birdcage Walk, SW1H 9JH. (Tel: 071-222 2248).— *Dir.-Gen.*, D. Falcon.

CAM FOUNDATION, Abford House, 15 Wilton Road, SW1V 1NJ. (Tel: 071-828 7506).—*Registrar*, Ms K. Hutchinson.

CHARTERED INSTITUTE OF MARKETING, Moor Hall, Cookham, Maidenhead, Berks. SL6 9QH.—*Dir. Gen.*, T. J. Nash.

CHARTERED INSTITUTE OF TRANSPORT, 80 Portland Place, W1N 4DP.—*Dir. Gen.*, R. P. Botwood.

FACULTY OF SECRETARIES AND ADMINISTRATORS, 15 Church Street, Godalming, Surrey GU7 1EL.— *Sec.*, Mrs D. M. Rummery.

INSTITUTE OF ADMINISTRATIVE MANAGEMENT, 40 Chatsworth Parade, Petts Wood, Orpington, Kent BR5 1RW. (Tel: 0689-875555).—*Chief Exec.*, Ms C. Hayhurst.

INSTITUTE OF CHARTERED SECRETARIES AND ADMINISTRATORS, 16 Park Crescent, W1N 4AH. (Tel: 071-580 4741).—*Sec.*, M. J. Ainsworth.

INSTITUTE OF CHARTERED SHIPBROKERS, 24 St Mary Axe, EC3A 8DE. (Tel: 071-283 1361).—*Sec.*, J. H. Parker.

INSTITUTE OF EXPORT, Export House, 64 Clifton Street, EC2A 4HB. (Tel: 071-247 9812).—*Sec.*, D. J. Langham.

INSTITUTE OF HEALTH SERVICES MANAGEMENT, 75 Portland Place, W1N 4AN. (Tel: 071-580 5041).— *Dir.*, Ms M. P. Charlwood.

INSTITUTE OF HOUSING, Octavia House, Westwood Way, Coventry CV4 8JP. (Tel: 0203-694433).—*Dir.*, P. McGurk.

INSTITUTION OF INDUSTRIAL MANAGERS, Rochester House, 66 Little Ealing Lane, W5 4XX.—*Chief Exec.*, G. J. Rawlins, OBE

INSTITUTE OF PERSONNEL MANAGEMENT, IPM House, Camp Road, SW19 4UX. (Tel: 081-946 9100).—*Dir. Gen.*, K. B. Ward Lilley.

INSTITUTE OF PRACTITIONERS IN ADVERTISING, 44 Belgrave Square, SW1X 8QS. (Tel: 071-235 7020).— *Sec.*, J. Raad.

INSTITUTE OF PURCHASING AND SUPPLY, Easton House, Easton on the Hill, Stamford, Lincs. PE9 3NZ. (Tel: 0780-56777).—*Dir. Gen.*, P. Thomson.

HENLEY MANAGEMENT COLLEGE, Greenlands, Henley on Thames, Oxon., RG9 3AU. (Tel: 0491-571454).— *Princ.*, Prof. R. Wild.

LONDON BUSINESS SCHOOL, Sussex Place, Regent's Park, NW1 4SA. (Tel: 071-262 5050).—*Princ.*, Prof. G. Bain, PH.D.

MANCHESTER BUSINESS SCHOOL, Booth Street West, Manchester M15 6PB. (Tel: 061-275 6333).—*Dir.*, Prof. T. Cannon.

ASSOCIATION FOR MANAGEMENT EDUCATION AND TRAINING IN SCOTLAND, c/o University of Stirling, Stirling FK9 4LA. (Tel: 0786-50906).—*Vice-Chairman*, M. Makower.

LONDON CHAMBER OF COMMERCE AND INDUSTRY EXAMINATIONS BOARD, Marlowe House, Station Road, Sidcup, Kent DA15 7BJ. (Tel: 081-302 0261).—*Dir.*, Prof. C. Bateson.

COMPUTER SCIENCE

First degrees covering various aspects of *Computer/ Computing Science, Data Processing, Information Systems* and *Information Technology* are available at all universities.

Courses leading to first degrees in computer science

subjects granted by the CNAA are provided by all the polytechnics.

These subjects also form part of other degree courses, often as *Mathematics/Statistics and Computer Science*, at many universities, polytechnics and colleges.

DANCE

(*See also* **Recreation, Sport,** etc.)

First degrees in *Dance in Society* are granted by the University of Surrey.

First degrees in *Dance Theatre* are granted by the CNAA for which courses are provided at the Laban Centre for Movement and Dance; dance also forms part of other CNAA degree courses, often called *Performing Arts* or *Creative Arts*, at several polytechnics and colleges.

ROYAL ACADEMY OF DANCING, 36 Battersea Square, SW11 3RA. (Tel: 071-223 0091).—*Dirs*, D. Watchman; J. Byrne.

ROYAL BALLET SCHOOL, 155 Talgarth Road, W14 9DE, and White Lodge, Richmond Park, Surrey TW10 5HR.—*Dir.*, Dame Merle Park, DBE.

IMPERIAL SOCIETY OF TEACHERS OF DANCING, Euston Hall, Birkenhead Street, WC1H 8BE. (Tel: 071-837 9967).—*Gen. Sec.*, M. J. Browne.

DEFENCE

First degrees in *Peace Studies* are granted by the Universities of Bradford and Ulster, and in *War Studies* by the University of London (King's College).

Royal Naval Colleges

ROYAL NAVAL COLLEGE, Greenwich, SE10 9NN.— *Admiral President*, Vice-Adm. Sir Michael Livesay, KCB; *Dean of the College*, Prof. G. Till.

BRITANNIA ROYAL NAVAL COLLEGE, Dartmouth, Devon TQ6 0HJ. (Tel: 0803-832141).—Initial officer training.
Captain, Capt. R. G. Hastilow.

ROYAL NAVAL ENGINEERING COLLEGE, Manadon, Plymouth PL5 3AQ.—BA, B.Eng., M.Sc. and specialist training in naval engineering. Students are selected uniformed officers of the Royal Navy, Commonwealth and foreign navies, and civilians.
Captain, Capt. T. J. England.
Dean, Capt. J. N. McGrath.
Exec. Officer, Cdr. B. V. C. Reeves, LVO.

INSTITUTE OF NAVAL MEDICINE, Alverstoke, Gosport, Hants. PO12 2DL. (Tel: 0705-822351).—Higher professional and postgraduate training for officers of all three services, and some civilians.
Medical Officer in Charge, Surgeon Capt. J. W. Davies.

Military Colleges

STAFF COLLEGE, Camberley, Surrey GU15 4NP. (Tel: 0276-412614).—*Commandant*, Maj.-Gen. H. M. Rose, CBE.

ROYAL MILITARY ACADEMY, Sandhurst, Camberley, Surrey GU15 4PQ. (Tel: 0276-63344).—*Commandant*, Maj.-Gen. T. P. Toxne Sewell.

ROYAL MILITARY COLLEGE OF SCIENCE, Shrivenham, Swindon, Wilts. SN6 8LA.—Students from UK and overseas study from degree to postgraduate levels in management, science and technology. There is an increasing range of research and consultancy activity as the College is now a Faculty of the Cranfield Institute of Technology.
Commandant, Maj.-Gen. S. Cowan, CBE.
Principal, Prof. A. C. Baynham, PH.D.

INSTITUTE OF ARMY EDUCATION, Court Road, Eltham, SE9 5NR. (Tel: 081-854 2242).—*Director*, Maj.-Gen. C. A. Kinvig.

Royal Air Force Colleges

ROYAL AIR FORCE STAFF COLLEGE, Bracknell, Berks. RG12 3DD.—Prepares selected senior officers for high-grade command and staff appointments. The majority of students are RAF officers but officers from the other UK services and from foreign air forces also attend.

Air Officer Commanding and Commandant, Air Vice-Marshal R. G. Peters.

ROYAL AIR FORCE COLLEGE, Cranwell, Sleaford, Lincs NG34 8HB.—Initial officer training for officers of the RAF, WRAF and PMRAFNS, and initial specialist training for officers of the Engineer and Supply Branches. Advanced specialist training is provided for officers of the General Duties, Engineer and Supply Branches and basic flying training for pilots of the General Duties Branch.

Air Officer Commanding and Commandant, Air Vice-Marshal R. M. Austin, AFC.

ROYAL AIR FORCE SCHOOL OF EDUCATION AND TRAINING SUPPORT, RAF Newton, Nottingham NG13 8HL. (Tel: 0949-20771).—*Commanding Officer*, Gp. Capt. J. Rennie.

DENTISTRY

First degrees in Dentistry are granted by the Universities of Belfast, Birmingham, Bristol, Dundee, Glasgow, Leeds, Liverpool, London (United Medical and Dental Schools of Guy's and St Thomas's Hospitals, King's College School of Medicine and Dentistry, London Hospital Medical College), Manchester, Newcastle upon Tyne, Sheffield, Wales (College of Medicine).

To be entitled to be registered in the Dentists Register, a person must hold the degree or diploma in dental surgery of a University in the United Kingdom or Republic of Ireland or the diploma of any of the licensing authorities (The Royal College of Surgeons of England, of Edinburgh and in Ireland, and the Royal College of Physicians and Surgeons of Glasgow). Nationals of an EC member state holding an appropriate European diploma, and holders of certain overseas diplomas, may also be registered. The Dentists Register is maintained by THE GENERAL DENTAL COUNCIL, 37 Wimpole Street, W1M 8DQ. *Registrar*, N. T. Davies.

DIETETICS
(*See also* **Food and Nutrition Science**)

Courses in *Nutrition and Dietetics* leading to first degrees granted by the University of Wales are provided by South Glamorgan Institute of Higher Education. The Universities of Bradford, London (King's College), Nottingham, Southampton, Surrey and Ulster grant first degrees in *Nutrition* and related subjects.

First degrees in *Dietetics* and *Nutrition and Dietetics* granted by the CNAA are provided by Huddersfield and Leeds Polytechnics, Queen Margaret College, Edinburgh, the Queen's College, Glasgow and Robert Gordon's Institute.

The professional association is THE BRITISH DIETETIC ASSOCIATION, 7th Floor, Elizabeth House, 22 Suffolk Street, Queensway, Birmingham B1 1LS. Full membership is open to dietitians holding a recognized qualification, who may also become State Registered Dietitians through the Council for Professions Supplementary to Medicine (*q.v.*).

DRAMA

First Degrees in *Drama* are granted by the Universities of Birmingham (*Drama and Theatre Arts*), Bristol, East Anglia, Exeter, Glasgow (*Theatre Studies*), Hull, Kent (*Drama and Theatre Studies*), Lancaster (*Theatre Studies*), London (Royal Holloway and Bedford New College, *Drama and Theatre Studies*, Goldsmiths', *Drama and Theatre Arts*), Loughborough, Manchester and Wales (University College of Aberystwyth) and Warwick (*Theatre Studies and Dramatic Arts*). Drama also forms part of degree courses in other universities.

First degrees in *Drama Studies, Theatre, Theatre Arts* and *Drama, Theatre and TV Studies* granted by the CNAA are provided at a number of polytechnics and colleges.

The national validating body for courses providing training in drama is THE NATIONAL COUNCIL FOR DRAMA TRAINING, 5 Tavistock Place, WC1H 9SS. *Chief Exec.*, Miss E. M. McKay. It currently has accredited courses at the following: Academy of Live and Recorded Arts; Arts Educational Schools; Birmingham School of Speech Training & Dramatic Art; Bristol Old Vic Theatre School; Central School of Speech and Drama; Drama Centre, London; Drama Studio; Guildford School of Acting; Guildhall School of Music and Drama; London Academy of Music and Dramatic Art; Manchester Polytechnic School of Theatre; Mountview Theatre School; Rose Bruford College of Speech and Drama; Royal Academy of Dramatic Art; Royal Scottish Academy of Music and Drama; Webber Douglas Academy of Dramatic Art; Welsh College of Music and Drama. (The accreditation of a course in a school does not necessarily imply that other courses of different type or duration in the same school are also accredited.)

ECONOMICS

Almost all universities grant first degrees in *Economics*. Courses leading to first degrees in *Economics* granted by the CNAA are provided by many polytechnics and colleges.

ENGINEERING
(*See separate subjects below*)

THE ENGINEERING COUNCIL, 10 Maltravers Street, WC2R 3ER, supervises the engineering profession through the 47 nominated engineering institutions who are represented on its system of a Board for Engineers' Registration. Working with and through the institutions, the Council sets the standards for the registration of individuals, and also the accreditation for academic courses in universities, polytechnics and technical colleges and the practical training in industry.—*Sec.*, L. Chelton. The principal qualifying bodies are:

BRITISH COMPUTER SOCIETY, PO Box 1454, Station Road, Swindon SN1 1TG. (Tel: 0793 480269).—*Chief Exec.*, J. R. Brookes.

CHARTERED INSTITUTION OF BUILDING SERVICES ENGINEERS, Delta House, 222 Balham High Road, SW12 9BS. (Tel: 071-675 5211).—*Sec.*, A. V. Ramsay.

INSTITUTION OF CHEMICAL ENGINEERS, The Davis Building, 165–171 Railway Terrace, Rugby, Warks. CV21 3HQ. (Tel: 0788-758214).—*Gen. Sec.*, Dr T. J. Evans.

INSTITUTION OF CIVIL ENGINEERS, Great George Street, SW1P 3AA.—*Sec.*, R. Dobson.

INSTITUTION OF ELECTRICAL ENGINEERS, Savoy Place, WC2R 0BL. (Tel: 071-240 1871).—*Sec.*, Dr J. C. Williams, F.Eng.

INSTITUTE OF ENERGY, 18 Devonshire Street, W1N 2AU. (Tel: 071-580 7124).—*Sec.* C. Rigg, TD.

INSTITUTION OF GAS ENGINEERS, 17 Grosvenor Crescent, SW1X 7ES. (Tel: 071-245 9811).—*Sec.*, D. J. Chapman.

INSTITUTE OF MARINE ENGINEERS, The Memorial Building, 76 Mark Lane, EC3R 7JN. (Tel: 071-481 8493).—*Sec.*, J. E. Sloggett.

INSTITUTE OF MEASUREMENT AND CONTROL, 87 Gower Street, WC1E 6AA. (Tel: 071-387 4949).—*Sec.*, M. J. Yates.

INSTITUTION OF MECHANICAL ENGINEERS, 1 Birdcage Walk, SW1H 9JJ. (Tel: 071-222 7899).—*Sec.* R. Mellor, CBE.

INSTITUTE OF METALS, 1 Carlton House Terrace, SW1Y 5DB. (Tel: 071-839 4071).—*Sec.*, Dr J. A. Catterall.

INSTITUTION OF MINING ENGINEERS, Danum House, 6A South Parade, Doncaster DN1 2DY. (Tel: 0302-320486).—*Sec.*, W. J. W. Bourne, OBE.

INSTITUTION OF MINING AND METALLURGY, 44 Portland Place, W1N 4BR.—*Sec.*, M. J. Jones.

INSTITUTION OF PRODUCTION ENGINEERS, Rochester House, 66 Little Ealing Lane, W5 4XX.—*Sec.*, Brig. P. V. Crooks.

INSTITUTION OF STRUCTURAL ENGINEERS, 11 Upper Belgrave Street, SW1X 8BH. (Tel: 071-235 4535).—*Sec.*, D. J. Clark.

ROYAL AERONAUTICAL SOCIETY, 4 Hamilton Place, W1V 0BQ. (Tel: 071-499 3515).—*Dir.*, R. J. Kennett.

ROYAL INSTITUTION OF NAVAL ARCHITECTS, 10 Upper Belgrave Street, SW1X 8BQ. (Tel: 071-235 4622).—*Sec.*, J. Rosewarn.

ENGINEERING, GENERAL AND ENGINEERING SCIENCE

First degrees in *General Engineering* or *Engineering Science* are granted by the Universities of Aberdeen, Aston, Belfast (*Integrated Engineering*), Cambridge, Durham, Edinburgh, Exeter, Hull, Lancaster, Leicester, Liverpool, London (Queen Mary and Westfield College), Loughborough, Manchester (foundation year), University of Manchester Institute of Science and Technology (*Integrated Engineering*), Oxford, Reading, Stirling, Sussex, Ulster, Wales (University College, Cardiff and Swansea) and Warwick.

Courses leading to first degrees in *Engineering* granted by the CNAA are provided by some 12 polytechnics and colleges.

Aeronautical Engineering

See also **Aeronautics and Aeronautical Engineering**

Agricultural Engineering

First degrees in *Agricultural Engineering* are granted by the University of Newcastle upon Tyne. Courses in *Agricultural Engineering* leading to degrees granted by Cranfield Institute of Technology are provided at Silsoe College.

Chemical Engineering

First degrees are granted by the Universities of Aston, Bath, Belfast, Birmingham, Bradford, Cambridge, Edinburgh, Exeter (*Chemical & Process Engineering*), Heriot-Watt, Leeds, London (Imperial College of Science and Technology, University College), Loughborough, Manchester (Manchester Institute of Science and Technology), Newcastle upon Tyne (*Chemical & Process Engineering*), Nottingham, Sheffield (*Chemical Process Engineering*), Strathclyde, Surrey and Wales (University College, Swansea).

Courses leading to first degrees in *Chemical Engineering* granted by the CNAA are provided by

Paisley College of Technology, Polytechnic of the South Bank, Teesside Polytechnic and Polytechnic of Wales.

Civil and Mechanical Engineering

First degrees in *Civil* (or *Civil and Structural*), and *Mechanical Engineering* are granted by the Universities of Aberdeen, Aston, Bath (*M.*), Belfast, Birmingham, Bradford, Bristol, Brunel, Cambridge, the City University, Cranfield Institute, the Universities of Dundee, Durham, Edinburgh, Exeter, Glasgow, Heriot-Watt, Lancaster (*M.*), Leeds, Leicester (*M.*), Liverpool, London (Imperial College of Science and Technology, King's College (*M.*), Queen Mary and Westfield College, University College), Loughborough, Manchester, Manchester Institute of Science and Technology, Newcastle upon Tyne, Nottingham, Oxford, Reading (*M.*), Salford, Sheffield, Southampton, Strathclyde, Surrey, Sussex (*M.*), Ulster, Wales (University Colleges at Cardiff and Swansea) and Warwick.

Many polytechnics and colleges provide courses in *civil engineering* or *mechanical engineering,* or both, leading to first degrees granted by the CNAA.

Electrical and Electronic Engineering and Electronics

First degrees in *Electronic Engineering* or *Electronics* or *Electrical and Electronic Engineering* or *Electrical Engineering (including Electronics)* are granted by almost all universities.

Courses leading to first degrees in *Electronic Engineering* or in *Electrical and Electronic Engineering* granted by the CNAA are provided by many polytechnics and colleges.

Marine Engineering and Naval Architecture

First degrees in *Marine Engineering* and *Naval Architecture* are granted by the University of Newcastle upon Tyne; in *Naval Architecture* by the Universities of Glasgow, London (University College) and Strathclyde; in *Offshore Engineering* by Heriot-Watt University; and in *Ship Science* by the University of Southampton.

First degrees in *Mechanical Engineering (Marine)* granted by the CNAA are provided at Liverpool Polytechnic.

Nuclear Engineering

First degrees in *Nuclear Engineering* are granted by the University of Manchester.

Production Engineering

First degrees in *Production Engineering, Manufacturing Engineering* or *Industrial Engineering* are granted by the Universities of Aberdeen (*Engineering (Manufacturing Systems)*), Aston, Bath, Belfast, Birmingham, Brunel, Cambridge, Exeter (*Engineering (Operations & Manufacturing)*), Hull (*Engineering Design and Manufacture*), Loughborough, Manchester Institute of Science and Technology (*Manufacturing Systems Engineering*), Strathclyde and Warwick (*Engineering (Manufacturing Systems)*).

First degrees in *Production Engineering, Industrial Engineering, Manufacturing Engineering, Manufacturing Systems Engineering,* and *Plant Engineering* granted by the CNAA are provided by nearly all polytechnics.

Structural Engineering

First degrees in *Civil and Structural Engineering* are granted by the Universities of Aberdeen, Bradford, Heriot-Watt (*Structural Engineering*), Liverpool, London (University College, *Structural Engineering*), and Sheffield.

ESTATE AND LAND MANAGEMENT
(*See also* Building and Surveying)

First degrees are granted by the Universities of Aberdeen (*Land Economy*), Reading (*Land Management* and *Rural Land Management*) and Ulster (*Estate Management*).

First degrees in *Estate Management, Housing, Housing Studies, Land Administration, Land Economics, Land Management, Minerals Estate Management, Urban Estate Management, Urban Land Administration, Urban Land Economics* and *Valuation and Estate Management* granted by the CNAA are provided at most polytechnics.

FOOD AND NUTRITION SCIENCE
(*See also* Dietetics and Home Economics)

First degrees in *Food Science* are granted by the Universities of Belfast (also *Food Technology*), Leeds, London (King's College), Newcastle (*Agricultural & Food Marketing*), Nottingham, Reading, Strathclyde, Surrey, Ulster (*Food Technology Management*) and Wales (University College, Aberystwyth, *Agricultural & Food Marketing*); in *Nutrition* by the Universities of London (King's College), Nottingham and Surrey; and in *Human Nutrition* by the University of Ulster.

First degrees in *Food Science*; *Catering and Applied Nutrition*; *Food and Accommodation Studies*; *Food Marketing Sciences*; *Industrial Food Technology*; *Nutrition and Dietetics* granted by the CNAA are provided at many polytechnics.

Scientific and professional bodies include:

INSTITUTE OF FOOD SCIENCE & TECHNOLOGY, 5 Cambridge Court, 210 Shepherd's Bush Road, W6 7NL. (Tel: 071-603 6316).—*Exec. Sec.*, Ms H. G. Wild.

NUTRITION SOCIETY, Grosvenor Gardens House, 35–37 Grosvenor Gardens, SW1W 0BS.—*Hon. Sec.*, Dr R. F. Grimble.

FORESTRY AND TIMBER STUDIES

First degrees in *Forestry* are granted by the Universities of Aberdeen, Edinburgh (also *Agriculture, Forestry & Rural Economy*), and Wales (University College, Bangor, also *Wood Science* and *Agroforestry*).

First degrees in *Timber Technology* granted by the CNAA are provided at Buckinghamshire HE College.

Professional organizations include:

ROYAL FORESTRY SOCIETY OF ENGLAND, WALES AND NORTHERN IRELAND, 102 High Street, Tring, Herts., HP23 4AF. (Tel: 044 282-2028).—*Dir.*, J. E. Jackson, PH.D.

ROYAL SCOTTISH FORESTRY SOCIETY, 11 Atholl Crescent, Edinburgh EH3 8HE. (Tel: 031-229 8180).—*Sec.*, W. B. C. Walker.

INSTITUTE OF CHARTERED FORESTERS, 22 Walker Street, Edinburgh EH3 7HR.—*Sec.*, Mrs M. W. Dick.

COMMONWEALTH FORESTRY ASSOCIATION, c/o Oxford Forestry Institute, South Parks Road, Oxford OX1 3RB. (Tel: 0865-275072).—*Sec.*, P. J. Wood (*acting*).

FUEL AND ENERGY STUDIES
(*See also* Nuclear Engineering)

First degrees in *Fuel and Combustion Science* and in *Fuel and Energy Engineering* are granted by the University of Leeds; in *Petroleum Engineering* by London (Imperial College of Science and Technol-

ogy); and in *Chemical Process Engineering and Fuel Technology* by the University of Sheffield. These subjects may also form part of other degree courses.

First degrees in *Energy Engineering* are granted by the CNAA.

The principal professional bodies are:—

INSTITUTE OF ENERGY, 18 Devonshire Street, W1N 2AU. (Tel: 071-580 7124).—*Sec.*, C. Rigg, TD.

INSTITUTION OF GAS ENGINEERS, 17 Grosvenor Crescent, SW1X 7ES. (Tel: 071-245 9811).—*Sec.*, D. J. Chapman.

INSTITUTE OF PETROLEUM, 61 New Cavendish Street, W1M 8AR. (Tel: 071-636 1004).—*Dir. Gen.*, A. E. H. Williams.

GEOLOGY

First degrees in *Geology* or *Geological Sciences* or *Applied Geology* are granted by the Universities of Aberdeen (with *Petroleum Geology*), Belfast, Birmingham, Bristol, Cambridge, Durham, Edinburgh, Glasgow, Keele, Leeds, Leicester, Liverpool, London (Birkbeck College, Imperial College of Science and Technology (also *Mining Geology*), Royal Holloway & Bedford New College, University College), Manchester, Oxford (*Earth Sciences*), St Andrews (*Geoscience*), Southampton, Wales (University Colleges at Aberystwyth and Cardiff).

Degree courses in *Geophysics* and *Geophysical Sciences* are provided by the Universities of East Anglia, Edinburgh, Lancaster, Leeds, Leicester, Liverpool, London (University College), Newcastle and Southampton.

First degrees in *Geology, Earth Sciences*, etc. granted by the CNAA are provided by some 11 polytechnics and colleges.

HOME ECONOMICS AND CATERING, HOTELKEEPING AND INSTITUTIONAL MANAGEMENT
(*See also* Dietetics, and Food)

First degrees in *Home Economics* are granted by the University of Wales (University College, Cardiff); in *Hotel and Catering Management* by the Universities of Strathclyde, Surrey (also *Hotel Management*), Ulster (*Hotel and Tourism Management*, also *Hospitality Management*) and Wales (University College, Cardiff, *Hotel and Institutional Management*).

First degrees are granted by the CNAA in *Home Economics, Hotel and Catering Administration/Management/Studies, Applied Consumer Science, Hospitality Management, International Hotel Management* and combinations of these subjects. Courses are available at over 20 polytechnics and colleges.

Qualifying professional body in the subjects is:

HOTEL CATERING AND INSTITUTIONAL MANAGEMENT ASSOCIATION, 191 Trinity Road, SW17 7HN.—*Dir.*, Ms. E. Gadsby.

INDUSTRIAL RELATIONS

First degrees in *Industrial Relations* are granted by the University of Kent. *Industrial relations* also forms part of degree courses at other universities.

INSURANCE

First degrees in *Banking, Insurance and Finance* are granted by the University of Wales (University College, Bangor) and in *Insurance and Investment* by the City University.

First degrees in *Risk Management* granted by the CNAA are provided at Glasgow College.

Organizations conducting examinations and awarding diplomas:—

ASSOCIATION OF AVERAGE ADJUSTERS, HQS *Wellington*, Temple Stairs, Victoria Embankment, WC2R 2PN. (Tel: 071-240 5516).—*Sec.*, Mrs P. J. Albano.

CHARTERED INSURANCE INSTITUTE, 20 Aldermanbury, EC2V 7HY. (Tel: 071-606 3835).—*Dir. Gen.*, Dr D. E. Bland.

CHARTERED INSTITUTE OF LOSS ADJUSTERS, Manfield House, 376 The Strand, WC2R 0LR. (Tel: 071-240 1496).—*Dir.*, A. F. Clack.

JOURNALISM

Courses for trainee newspaper journalists are available at 11 centres. One-year full-time courses are available for selected students. Particulars of all these courses are available from the Director of the NATIONAL COUNCIL FOR TRAINING OF JOURNALISTS, Carlton House, Hemnall Street, Epping, Essex CM16 4NL. (Tel: 0378-72395).—*Dir.*, D. K. Hall. Short courses for experienced journalists are also arranged by the National Council.

For periodical journalists, there are four centres running courses approved by THE PERIODICALS TRAINING COUNCIL, Imperial House, 15–19 Kingsway, WC2B 6UN. (Tel: 071-836 8798).—*Dir.*, D. Longbottom, MBE.

LANGUAGES

First Degrees in *English* and in a wide range of other languages are granted by most universities. Degrees in *Linguistics* are awarded by the Universities of Cambridge, East Anglia, Edinburgh, Essex (also *Language Studies* and *Psycholinguistics*), Lancaster, Leeds (*Linguistics and Phonetics*), London (School of Oriental and African Studies, University College), Manchester (*provisional*), Newcastle upon Tyne, Reading, Sussex and Wales (University College, Bangor); in *Applied Languages* by the University of Ulster; and in *Modern Languages and Linguistics* by the University of York. These subjects also form part of degree courses at many other universities.

Courses leading to first degrees in *English* and other languages granted by the CNAA are provided by many polytechnics and colleges.

LAW

First Degrees in *Law* are granted by most universities.

Courses leading to first degrees in *Law* granted by the CNAA are provided by most polytechnics.

THE BAR

Admission to the Bar of England and Wales is controlled by the Inns of Court, and admission to the Bar of Northern Ireland by the Honorable Society of the Inn of Court of Northern Ireland. Admission as an Advocate of the Scottish Bar is controlled by the Faculty of Advocates.

England and Wales

THE GENERAL COUNCIL OF THE BAR
11 South Square, Gray's Inn, WC1R 5EL

The governing body of the Barristers' branch of the legal profession, established in 1987 in succession to the Senate of the Inns of Court and the Bar.
Chairman, A. Scrivener, QC.
Chief Executive, J. Mottram, CB, LVO, OBE.

THE INNS OF COURT

THE INNER TEMPLE, EC4Y 7HL.—*Treasurer*, F. Petre Crowder, QC; *Sub-Treasurer*, Capt. P. T. Sheehan, CBE, RN.

THE MIDDLE TEMPLE, EC4Y 9AT.—*Treasurer*, A. Heyman, QC; *Deputy Treasurer*, Rear-Adm. J. R. Hill.

GRAY'S INN, 8 South Square, WC1R 5EU.—*Treasurer*, R. Stone, QC; *Under-Treasurer*, D. Machin.

LINCOLN'S INN, WC2A 3TL.—*Treasurer*, The Hon. Mr Justice Michael Davies; *Under-Treasurer*, Capt. P. M. Carver, RN.

The education and examination of students for the Bar of England and Wales is superintended by the COUNCIL OF LEGAL EDUCATION, Inns of Court School of Law, 4 Gray's Inn Place, WC1R 5DX.
Chairman, The Hon. Mr Justice Hoffmann.
Dean, Inns of Court School of Law, Mrs M. A. Phillips.

Scotland

FACULTY OF ADVOCATES, Advocates Library, Parliament House, Edinburgh EH1 1RF.—*Dean*, A. C. M. Johnston, QC; *Clerk*, J. R. Doherty.

Northern Ireland

THE HONORABLE SOCIETY OF THE INN OF COURT OF NORTHERN IRELAND, Royal Courts of Justice, Belfast BT1 3JF.—*Treasurer* (1991), J. A. Creaney, OBE, TD, QC; *Under-Treasurer*, J. A. L. McLean, QC.

SOLICITORS

Qualifications for Solicitor are obtainable only from one of the Law Societies, which control the education and examination of articled clerks, and the admission of solicitors.

LAW SOCIETY OF ENGLAND AND WALES, 113 Chancery Lane, WC2A 1PL.—*President* (1991–92), P. T. Ely; *Vice-Pres.* (1991–92), M. H. Sheldon; *Sec.-Gen.*, J. W. Hayes.

Courses for The Law Society examinations are provided by THE COLLEGE OF LAW, at Braboeuf Manor, St Catherine's, Guildford, Surrey GU3 1HA; 33–35 Lancaster Gate, W2 3LU; 2 Breams Buildings, Chancery Lane, EC4A 1DP; Christleton Hall, Chester CH3 7AB; and Bishopthorpe Road, York YO2 1QA.

The SOLICITORS COMPLAINTS BUREAU, Portland House, Stag Place, SW1E 5BL, is an independent arm of the Law Society set up to handle complaints about solicitors.

LAW SOCIETY OF SCOTLAND, Law Society's Hall, 26 Drumsheugh Gardens, Edinburgh EH3 7YR.—*Pres.* (1991–92), J. H. Campbell; *Sec.*, K. W. Pritchard.

LAW SOCIETY OF NORTHERN IRELAND, Law Society House, 90–106 Victoria Street, Belfast BT1 3JZ. (Tel: 0232-231614).—*Sec.*, M. C. Davey.

LIBRARIANSHIP AND INFORMATION SCIENCE/INFORMATION MANAGEMENT

First degrees are granted by the University of Loughborough (*Library Studies*), Strathclyde (*Information Science*), and the University of Wales (Aberystwyth) (*Librarianship* with another subject).

First degrees in *Librarianship* or *Librarianship/Library Studies and Information Studies/Science* granted by the CNAA are provided at the Polytechnics of Birmingham, Brighton, Leeds, Liverpool, Manchester (*Information and Library Management*), Newcastle upon Tyne, North London (*Information and Communication Studies*) and West London (*Information Management*), Queen Margaret College, Edinburgh (*Information Management*), and Robert Gordon's Institute of Technology.

Two-thirds of entrants into librarianship/information work are graduates in other subjects, who take a one- or two-year postgraduate course.

THE LIBRARY ASSOCIATION, 7 Ridgmount Street, WC1E 7AE, maintains a professional register of Chartered Members. A full list of accredited degree and postgraduate courses is available from the Education Department.—*Chief Exec.*, G. Cunningham.

MATERIALS STUDIES
(including Metallurgy)

First degrees in *Materials Science, Materials Technology, or Materials Science and Technology* are granted by the Universities of Bath, Birmingham, Brunel, Cambridge (*Materials Science and Metallurgy*), Leeds, Liverpool, London (Imperial College of Science and Technology, Queen Mary and Westfield College), Manchester and Manchester Institute of Science and Technology, Sheffield (*Materials Science and Engineering*), Strathclyde (*Science of Engineering Materials*), Surrey and Wales (University College, Swansea, *Materials Engineering*). First degrees in *Polymer Science and Engineering* are granted by London (Queen Mary and Westfield College) and Manchester Institute of Science and Technology (*Polymer Science and Technology*). First degrees in *Ceramics Science and Engineering* are granted by the Universities of Leeds and Sheffield; and in *Glass Science and Engineering* by the University of Sheffield. First degrees in *Metallurgy* and/or *Metallurgical Engineering* are granted by the Universities of Birmingham (*Metallurgy/Materials Engineering*), Brunel, Cambridge (*Materials Science and Metallurgy*), Leeds, Liverpool (*Metallurgy and Materials Science*), Manchester and Manchester Institute of Science and Technology, Oxford (*Metallurgy and Science of Materials*), Sheffield (*Metal Science and Engineering*), Strathclyde and Surrey.

First degrees in *Materials Science/Technology* or *Metallurgy* or *Metallurgy and Materials* or *Polymer Science* granted by the CNAA are provided at Coventry, Manchester, North London, Sheffield, Sunderland, Thames and Wolverhampton Polytechnics, and at Robert Gordon's Institute.

INSTITUTE OF METALS, 1 Carlton House Terrace, SW1Y 5DB, is a qualifying body.—*Sec.*, Dr J. A. Catterall.

MEDICINE

First degrees in *Medicine* are granted by the Universities of Aberdeen, Belfast, Birmingham, Bristol, Cambridge (*Medical Sciences*), Dundee, Edinburgh, Glasgow, Leeds, Leicester, Liverpool, London medical schools/colleges (University College and Middlesex SM, King's College SMD, St Mary's HMS, and those listed on p. 460), Manchester, Newcastle upon Tyne, Nottingham, Oxford, St Andrews (*Medical Science*), Sheffield, Southampton, and University of Wales College of Medicine.

Licensing Corporations granting Diplomas

ROYAL COLLEGE OF PHYSICIANS OF LONDON AND THE ROYAL COLLEGE OF SURGEONS OF ENGLAND, Examining Board in England, 35–43 Lincoln's Inn Fields, WC2A 3PN. (Tel: 071-405 3474).

SOCIETY OF APOTHECARIES OF LONDON, Black Friars Lane, EC4V 6EJ. (Tel: 071-236 1189).—*Clerk*, Maj. J. C. O'Leary; *Registrar*, D. H. C. Barrie.

SCOTTISH TRIPLE QUALIFICATION BOARD, Nicolson Street, Edinburgh EH8 9DW and 242 St Vincent Street, Glasgow.

Colleges holding postgraduate membership and diploma examinations

ROYAL COLLEGE OF GENERAL PRACTITIONERS, 14 Princes Gate, SW7 1PU.—*Pres.*, Dr S. Carne.

ROYAL COLLEGE OF OBSTETRICIANS AND GYNAECOLOGISTS, 27 Sussex Place, NW1 4RG. (Tel: 071-262 5425).—*Pres.*, S. Simmons; *Sec.*, P. A. Barnett.

ROYAL COLLEGE OF PATHOLOGISTS, 2 Carlton House Terrace, SW1Y 5AF. (Tel: 071-930 5863).—*Pres.*, Prof. P. J. Lachmann, FRS, FRCP; *Sec.*, K. Lockyer.

ROYAL COLLEGE OF PHYSICIANS IN ENGLAND, 11 St Andrews Place, NW1 4LE. (Tel: 071-935 1174).—*Pres.*, Prof. Dame Margaret Turner-Warwick, DBE; *Sec.*, D. B. Lloyd.

ROYAL COLLEGE OF PHYSICIANS OF EDINBURGH, 9 Queen Street, Edinburgh EH2 1JQ. (Tel: 031-225 7324).—*Pres.*, Prof. J. Richmond, MD; *Sec.*, Dr J. L. Anderton.

ROYAL COLLEGE OF PHYSICIANS AND SURGEONS OF GLASGOW, 234–242 St Vincent Street, Glasgow G2 5RJ. (Tel: 041-221 6072).—*Pres.*, Dr R. Hume; *Hon. Sec.*, Dr A. D. Beattie.

ROYAL COLLEGE OF PSYCHIATRISTS, 17 Belgrave Square, SW1X 8PG. (Tel: 071-235 2351).—*Pres.*, Prof. A. Sims; *Sec.*, Mrs V. Cameron.

ROYAL COLLEGE OF RADIOLOGISTS, 38 Portland Place, W1N 3DG. (Tel: 071-636 4432).—*Pres.*, Dr O. Craig; *Sec.*, A. J. Cowles.

ROYAL COLLEGE OF SURGEONS OF ENGLAND, 35 Lincoln's Inn Fields, WC2A 3PN. (Tel: 071-405 3474).—*Pres.*, Sir Terence English, KBE; *Sec.*, R. H. E. Duffett.

ROYAL COLLEGE OF SURGEONS OF EDINBURGH, Nicolson Street, Edinburgh EH8 9DW. (Tel: 031-556 6206).—*Pres.*, Prof. P. S. Boulter; *Sec.*, Prof. A. G. D, Maran.

PROFESSIONS SUPPLEMENTARY TO MEDICINE

The standard of professional education in chiropody, dietetics, medical laboratory sciences, occupational therapy, orthoptics, physiotherapy and radiography is the responsibility of seven professional boards, which also publish an annual register of qualified practitioners. The work of the Boards is coordinated by THE COUNCIL FOR PROFESSIONS SUPPLEMENTARY TO MEDICINE, Park House, 184 Kennington Park Road, SE11 4BU. *Registrar*, R. Pickis.

Biomedical/Medical Laboratory Sciences

First degrees in *Biomedical Sciences* are granted by the Universities of Belfast, Bradford, Keele and Ulster.

First degrees in *Biomedical Sciences* and *Medical Laboratory Science* granted by the CNAA are provided at Kingston, Lancashire, Liverpool, Portsmouth, Sunderland and Wolverhampton Polytechnics, and combinations including these subjects are available at other polytechnics and colleges.

Qualifications from higher or further education establishments and training in medical laboratories are required for progress to the professional examinations and qualifications of the INSTITUTE OF MEDICAL LABORATORY SCIENCES, 12 Queen Anne Street, W1M 0AU. *Chief Exec.*, A. Potter.

Chiropody

Professional qualifications are granted by THE SOCIETY OF CHIROPODISTS, 53 Welbeck Street, W1M 7HE, to students who have passed the qualifying examination after attending a course of full-time training for three years at one of the 14 recognized schools in the UK (11 in England and Wales, two in Scotland and one in Northern Ireland). Qualifications granted by the Society are approved by the Chiropodists Board for the purpose of State Registration, which is a condition of employment within the National Health Service. *Gen. Sec.*, J. G. C. Trouncer.

Dietetics
(*See* p. 470)

Occupational Hygiene

First degrees in *Occupational Hygiene* granted by the CNAA are provided at South Bank Polytechnic.

Occupational Therapy

First degrees in *Occupational Therapy* are granted by the Universities of East Anglia and Ulster; first degrees in *Occupational Therapy* granted by the CNAA are provided by Coventry and Newcastle upon Tyne Polytechnics and Queen Margaret College, Edinburgh.

Professional qualifications are awarded by THE COLLEGE OF OCCUPATIONAL THERAPISTS, 6–8 Marshalsea Road, SE1 1HL, upon completion of one of the 27 training courses approved by the College. *Sec.*, Air Cdre G. J. B. Claridge, CBE.

Orthoptics

Orthoptists undertake the diagnosis and treatment of all types of squint and other anomalies of binocular vision, working in close collaboration with ophthalmologists. The training and maintenance of professional standards are the responsibility of the Orthoptists Board of the Council for the Professions Supplementary to Medicine. The examining and qualifying body is the BRITISH ORTHOPTIC SOCIETY, Tavistock House North, Tavistock Square, WC1H 9HX. *Sec.*, Ms J. Voller. Training consists of a three-year course at one of nine approved Orthoptic Schools in England and Wales and one in Scotland.

(*See also* **Ophthalmic Optics**, p. 476)

Physiotherapy

First degrees in *Physiotherapy* are granted by the Universities of Bradford, East Anglia, London (King's College, University College), Manchester and Ulster; first degrees in *Physiotherapy* granted by the CNAA are provided at Brighton, Coventry, Newcastle upon Tyne, East London, Central London, Sheffield, Teesside and Wolverhampton Polytechnics, and at Queen Margaret College, Edinburgh, and Queen's College, Glasgow.

Full-time three- or four-year degree or diploma courses are available at 32 recognized Schools in the UK. Information about courses leading to eligibility for Membership of The Chartered Society of Physiotherapy and to State Registration is available from THE CHARTERED SOCIETY OF PHYSIOTHERAPY, 14 Bedford Row, London WC1R 4ED.—*Sec.*, T. Simon.

Radiography and Radiotherapy

First degrees in *Radiography* are granted by the Universities of London (King's College), Ulster and Wales (University College, Swansea) (*Diagnostic Radiotherapy, provisional*).

First degrees in *Radiography* granted by the CNAA are provided at Portsmouth and South Bank Polytechnics and Suffolk College.

In order to practise both diagnostic and therapeutic radiography in the United Kingdom it is necessary to have successfully completed a course of education and training recognized by the Privy Council. Such courses are offered by universities, polytechnics and colleges throughout the United Kingdom and lead to the award of either a degree in radiography or the Diploma of the College of Radiographers. Further information is available from THE COLLEGE OF RADIOGRAPHERS, 14 Upper Wimpole Street, W1M 8BN.

METEOROLOGY

First degrees in *Meteorology* are granted by the University of Reading. The subject is also included in degree courses at some other universities.

MINING AND MINING ENGINEERING

First degrees in *Mining* or *Mining Engineering* are granted by the following universities: Leeds (also *Mineral Engineering*), London (Imperial College of Science and Technology) and Nottingham.

First degrees granted by the CNAA in *Mining Engineering* and *Mineral Engineering* are provided at Camborne School of Mines.

Miscellaneous Authorities

ENGINEERING COUNCIL, 10 Maltravers Street, WC2R 3ER. *See* p. 470.

INSTITUTION OF MINING ENGINEERS, Danum House, 6A South Parade, Doncaster DN1 2DY. (Tel: 0302-320486).—*Sec.*, W. J. W. Bourne, OBE.

MUSIC

First degrees in *Music* are granted by the Universities of Belfast, Birmingham, Bristol, Cambridge, the City University, the Universities of Durham, East Anglia, Edinburgh, Exeter, Glasgow, Hull, Lancaster, Leeds, Liverpool, London (King's College, Royal Holloway and Bedford New College; *also* Goldsmiths' College, Royal Academy of Music and Royal College of Music), Manchester, Newcastle upon Tyne, Nottingham, Oxford, Reading, Sheffield, Southampton, Surrey (*Academic & Practical Applications of Music*; *Music & Sound Recording (Tonmeister)*), Sussex, Ulster, Wales (University Colleges at Bangor and Cardiff) and York.

Courses leading to first degrees in *Music* granted by the CNAA are provided by several polytechnics and colleges.

ASSOCIATED BOARD OF THE ROYAL SCHOOLS OF MUSIC, 14 Bedford Square, WC1B 3JG.—Conducts the local examinations in centres throughout the world in music and speech for the Royal Academy of Music and the Royal College of Music in London, the Royal Northern College of Music, Manchester and the Royal Scottish Academy of Music and Drama, Glasgow.
Chief Exec., R. Smith.

ROYAL ACADEMY OF MUSIC, Marylebone Road, NW1 5HT. (Tel: 071-935 1665).—*Principal*, Sir David Lumsden, D.Phil.

ROYAL COLLEGE OF MUSIC, Prince Consort Road, SW7 2BS. (Tel: 071-589 3643).—*Director*, M. G. Matthews.

ROYAL NORTHERN COLLEGE OF MUSIC, 124 Oxford Road, Manchester M13 9RD.—*Principal*, Sir John Manduell, CBE.

ROYAL SCOTTISH ACADEMY OF MUSIC AND DRAMA, 100 Renfrew Street, Glasgow G2 3DB.—*Principal*, Dr P. Ledger, CBE.

ROYAL COLLEGE OF ORGANISTS, 7 St Andrew Street, EC4A 3LQ. (Tel: 071-936 3606).—*Clerk*, V. Waterhouse.

GUILDHALL SCHOOL OF MUSIC AND DRAMA, Silk Street, EC2Y 8DT. (Tel: 071-628 2571).—*Principal*, I. Horsbrugh.

LONDON COLLEGE OF MUSIC AT EALING, Polytechnic of West London, St Mary's Road, W5 5RF.—*Director*, W. Webb.

TRINITY COLLEGE OF MUSIC, 11–13 Mandeville Place, W1M 6AQ. (Tel: 071-935 5773).—*Principal*, P. Jones, CBE.

NAUTICAL STUDIES
(*See also* Marine Engineering)

The University of Wales grants first degrees in *Maritime Studies, Maritime Commerce* and *Maritime Geography* (courses at University College, Cardiff).

First degrees in *Maritime Studies* and *Fishery Studies* granted by the CNAA are provided at Humberside and Liverpool Polytechnics and Polytechnic South West.

Merchant Navy Training Schools
For Officers

THE COLLEGE OF MARITIME STUDIES, Southampton Institute of Higher Education, Warsash Campus, Warsash, Southampton SO3 6ZL. (Tel: 0489-576161).

For Seamen

INDEFATIGABLE AND NATIONAL SEA TRAINING SCHOOL FOR BOYS, Plas Llanfair, Llanfairpwllgwyngyll, Gwynedd LL61 6NT.—*Captain Headmaster*, Capt. T. R. Beggs.

NATIONAL SEA TRAINING COLLEGE, Denton, Gravesend, Kent DA12 2HR. (Tel: 0474-363656).—*Princ.*, Capt. C. G. W. Hunter.

NURSING

Courses in which academic study leading to a degree at a University may be combined with nursing training/practical nursing in hospitals are provided by the Universities of Birmingham, Bradford, the City University, Edinburgh, Glasgow, Hull, Liverpool, London (King's College), Manchester, Nottingham, Southampton, Surrey, Ulster and Wales (College of Medicine).

First degrees in *Nursing* granted by the CNAA are provided at many polytechnics and at Anglia HE college, Buckinghamshire College, Dundee Institute, Cheltenham and Gloucester College, Glasgow College, NE Surrey College and Queen Margaret College.

Three-year courses are undertaken for State Registration in general, sick children's, mental and mental deficiency nursing. Two-year courses lead to State enrolment. There are training schools in many parts of Great Britain.

THE ROYAL COLLEGE OF NURSING
OF THE UNITED KINGDOM
20 Cavendish Square, W1M 0AB

The Royal College of Nursing, within its Institute of Advanced Nursing Education, provides education at post-basic level in hospital, occupational health and community health fields. Advanced courses are held in preparation for senior posts in management and teaching; and other short and special courses.
Gen. Sec., Miss C. Hancock.
Director of Education, T. Bolger.
Principal of the Institute of Advanced Nursing Education, J. C. A. Wells.

ENGLISH NATIONAL BOARD FOR NURSING, MIDWIFERY AND HEALTH VISITING, Victory House, 170 Tottenham Court Road, W1P 0HA. (Tel: 071-388 3131).—*Chief Exec. Officer*, A. P. Smith.

WELSH NATIONAL BOARD FOR NURSING, MIDWIFERY AND HEALTH VISITING, Floor 13, Pearl Assurance House, Greyfriars Road, Cardiff CF1 3AG. (Tel: 0222-395535).—*Chief Exec. Officer*, D. A. Ravey.

NATIONAL BOARD FOR NURSING, MIDWIFERY AND HEALTH VISITING FOR SCOTLAND, 22 Queen Street, Edinburgh EH2 1JX. (Tel: 031-226 7371).—*Chief Exec. Officer.*, Mrs E. C. Mitchell.

NATIONAL BOARD FOR NURSING, MIDWIFERY AND HEALTH VISITING FOR NORTHERN IRELAND, RAC House, 79 Chichester Street, Belfast BT1 4JE. (Tel: 0232-238152).—*Chief Exec. Officer*, J. J. Walsh.

OPHTHALMIC OPTICS

First degrees in *Ophthalmic Optics* or *Optometry* are granted by the Universities of Aston, Bradford, the City University, Liverpool (*provisional*), Manchester (Manchester Institute of Science and Technology), Sheffield and Wales (University College, Cardiff).

First degrees in *Optometry* granted by the CNAA are provided at Glasgow College.

THE BRITISH COLLEGE OF OPTOMETRISTS, 10 Knaresborough Place, SW5 0TG, grants qualifications as an optometrist. (Tel: 071-373 7765).—*Gen. Sec.*, T. H. Collingridge.

THE ASSOCIATION OF BRITISH DISPENSING OPTICIANS, 6 Hurlingham Business Park, Sulivan Road, SW6 3DU, grants qualifications as a dispensing optician. (Tel: 071-736 0088).—*Registrar*, D. G. Baker.

PHARMACY

First degrees in *Pharmacy* are granted by the Universities of Aston, Bath, Belfast, Bradford, London (King's College and the School of Pharmacy), Manchester, Nottingham, Strathclyde, Wales (University College, Cardiff).

First degrees in *Pharmacy* and *Pharmacology* granted by the CNAA are provided at Brighton, Leicester, Liverpool, East London, Portsmouth and Sunderland Polytechnics, and Robert Gordon's Institute.

Information may be obtained from The Secretary and Registrar, ROYAL PHARMACEUTICAL SOCIETY OF GREAT BRITAIN, 1 Lambeth High Street, SE1 7JN. *Sec. and Registrar*, J. Ferguson.

PHOTOGRAPHY, FILM AND TV STUDIES

First degrees are awarded by the Universities of Glasgow (*Theatre Studies/Film & TV Studies*), Kent (*Drama/Film Studies*) and Reading (*Film & Drama*). At some other universities these subjects may be studied as part of a first degree course.

First degrees in *Photography, Photographic Arts/Sciences/Studies* and various aspects of film, video and television are granted by the CNAA and courses are available at some 11 polytechnics and colleges.

BRITISH INSTITUTE OF PROFESSIONAL PHOTOGRAPHY, Amwell End, Ware, Herts. SG12 9HN. (Tel: 0920-464011).—*Chief Exec.*, A. M. Berkeley.

PRINTING

First degrees in *Typography and Graphic Communication* are awarded by the University of Reading.

First degrees in *Graphic Design* granted by the CNAA are provided at many polytechnics and colleges. First degrees in *Printing and Packaging Technology* granted by the CNAA are provided by Watford College in association with Hatfield Polytechnic.

Courses in general and technical design and administrative aspects of printing are available at technical colleges throughout the United Kingdom. Details can be obtained from the Institute of Printing and the British Printing Industries Federation (*see* below).

In addition to the examining and organizing bodies listed below, examinations are held by various independent regional examining boards in further education.

BRITISH PRINTING INDUSTRIES FEDERATION, 11 Bedford Row, WC1R 4DX. (Tel: 071-242 6904).—*Dir.-Gen.*, C. Stanley.

INSTITUTE OF PRINTING, 8 Lonsdale Gardens, Tunbridge Wells, Kent TN1 1NU. (Tel: 0892-38118).—*Sec.*, C. F. Partridge.

RECREATION, SPORT, AND HUMAN MOVEMENT STUDIES
(*See also* **Dance**)

First degrees are granted by the University of Birmingham (*Sport and Recreation Studies*), Lancaster (*Physical Education*), Leeds, (*Physical Education*), Liverpool (*Physical Education*), Loughborough (*Physical Education and Sports Science*; also *Physical Education, Sports Science and Recreation Management*), Ulster (*Sport and Leisure Studies*), Wales (Bangor) and Warwick. *Physical Education* and various aspects of recreation may also be studied as part of other first degree courses at several universities.

First degrees in various aspects of physical education, recreation and sports science/studies are granted by the CNAA; *Physical Education and Sports Science/Studies* also form part of a degree course at many other colleges/polytechnics.

ROBOTICS

First degrees in *Electronic Control and Robot Engineering* are granted by the University of Hull.

SOCIAL WORK

First degrees in *Social Studies* or in *Social Sciences* are granted by most universities. Courses leading to first degrees in *Social Science* or *Social Sciences/Applied Social Science* or *Sociology* granted by the CNAA are provided by many polytechnics and colleges.

CENTRAL COUNCIL FOR EDUCATION AND TRAINING IN SOCIAL WORK, Derbyshire House, St Chad's Street, WC1H 8AD.—*Dir.*, A. Hall. The Council promotes education and training for social work and social care throughout the UK. It approves training programmes, including those leading to one of three social work qualifying awards: the Certificate of Qualification in Social Work, the Certificate in Social Service, and the Diploma in Social Work.

SPEECH SCIENCE
(*See also* **Languages**)

First degrees are awarded in *Speech Science* by the University of Sheffield; in *Speech Sciences* by the University of London (University College); in *Speech Pathology* by the University of Manchester; in *Speech* by the University of Newcastle upon Tyne; and in *Speech Therapy* by the University of Ulster.

First degrees in various aspects of speech therapy and speech pathology granted by the CNAA are provided at Birmingham, Leeds, Leicester and Manchester Polytechnics, and at the Central School of Speech and Drama and Queen Margaret College.

THE COLLEGE OF SPEECH AND LANGUAGE THERAPISTS, Harold Poster House, 6 Lechmere Road, NW2 5BU, provides details of courses leading to qualification as a speech therapist. The College also sponsors advanced clinical courses. Associate Membership is available for professionals in other disciplines. A Directory of Members of the College is published triennially. *Gen. Sec.*, D. J. C. Wiseman.

SURVEYING
(*See also* **Building** and **Estate and Land Management**)

First degrees in *Surveying Science* are granted by the University of Newcastle upon Tyne; in *Building*

Economics and Quantity Surveying and in *Building Surveying* by Heriot-Watt University; in *Quantity Surveying* by Ulster University; in *Property Valuation and Finance* by the City University; in *Quantity Surveying* and *Building Surveying* by the Universities of Reading and Salford.

First degrees in *Quantity Surveying, Surveying and Mapping Sciences* and *Urban Estate Surveying* granted by the CNAA are provided by most polytechnics.

Qualifying professional bodies include:

ROYAL INSTITUTION OF CHARTERED SURVEYORS (incorporating The Institute of Quantity Surveyors), 12 Great George Street, SW1P 3AD. (Tel: 071-222 7000).—*Sec. Gen.*, M. Pattison.
ARCHITECTS AND SURVEYORS INSTITUTE, 15 St Mary Street, Chippenham, Wilts. SN15 3JN. (Tel: 0249-444505).—*Chief Exec.*, B. A. Hunt.
INCORPORATED ASSOCIATION OF ARCHITECTS AND SURVEYORS, Jubilee House, Billing Brook Road, Weston Favell, Northampton NN3 4NW. (Tel: 0604-404121).—*Administrator*, B. D. Hughes.
INSTITUTE OF REVENUES, RATING AND VALUATION, 41 Doughty Street, WC1N 2LF. (Tel: 071-831 3505).—*Dir.*, C. Farrington.
INCORPORATED SOCIETY OF VALUERS AND AUCTIONEERS (1968), 3 Cadogan Gate, SW1X 0AS. (Tel: 071-235 2282).—*Sec.*, H. Whitty.

TEACHING

To become a qualified teacher it is necessary to have successfully completed a course of initial teacher training. Non-graduates usually qualify by way of a three- or four-year course leading to a Bachelor of Education (B.Ed.) honours degree, but some universities offer first degree courses (BA, B.Sc.) taken concurrently with a certificate of education. Graduates take a one-year postgraduate certificate of education (PGCE).

Details of courses in England and Wales are contained in the *Handbook of Degree and Advanced Courses* published annually by the National Association of Teachers in Further and Higher Education.

Applications for B.Ed. courses in England and Wales at institutions other than universities are made through the Central Register and Clearing House Ltd, from which application forms can be obtained. For all PGCE courses in England and Wales, applications are handled by the Graduate Teacher Training Registry at the same address. (For address, *see* p. 458.)

Details of courses in Scotland can be obtained from the colleges of education and from TEACH (*see* p. 458). Details of courses in Northern Ireland can be obtained from the Department of Education for Northern Ireland. Applications for teacher training courses in Scotland and Northern Ireland are made to the institutions direct.

TECHNICAL EDUCATION

First degrees in one or more technologies are awarded by almost all universities; and many polytechnics and colleges of technology provide courses leading to first degrees granted by the CNAA. Details are given under individual subject headings.

Industry Training Bodies

AGRICULTURAL, Stoneleigh Park Pavilion, National Agricultural Centre, Kenilworth, Warks. CV8 2UG. (Tel: 0203-696996).—*Chief Exec.*, N. M. Snook.
CLOTHING AND ALLIED PRODUCTS, 80 Richardshaw Lane, Pudsey, Leeds LS28 6BN. (Tel: 0532-393355).—*Chief Exec.*, J. W. Dearden.

CONSTRUCTION, Bircham Newton, Nr. King's Lynn, Norfolk PE31 6RH. (Tel: 0553-776677).—*Sec.*, M. Smith.

ENGINEERING, 41 Clarendon Road, Watford, Herts. WD1 1HS. (Tel: 0923-38441).—*Sec.*, E. P. Jones.

HOTEL AND CATERING, International House, High Street, W5 5DB. (Tel: 081-579 2400).—*Sec.*, D. Rutter.

LOCAL GOVERNMENT TRAINING BOARD, Arndale House, Arndale Centre, Luton, Beds. LU1 2TS. (Tel: 0582-451166).—*Chief Exec.*, M. G. Clarke.

MAN-MADE FIBRES INDUSTRY TRAINING ADVISORY BOARD, Central House, Gate Lane, Sutton Coldfield, W. Midlands B73 5TS. (Tel: 021-355 7022).— *Sec.*, P. Grice.

OFFSHORE PETROLEUM, Offshore Training Centre, Forties Road, Montrose, Angus DD10 9ET.—*Sec.*, G. A. R. Stark.

PLASTICS PROCESSING, Coppice House, Halesfield 7, Telford, Shropshire TF7 4NA.—*Chief Exec.*, J. C. Shearman.

ROAD TRANSPORT, Capitol House, Empire Way, Wembley, Middx. HA9 0NG.—*Dir. Gen.*, D. C. Barnett.

TEXTILES

First degrees are awarded by the Universities of Leeds (*Textile Chemistry* and *Textile Studies*) and Manchester (Manchester Institute of Science and Technology, *Textile Science and Technology*).

Courses leading to first degrees granted by the CNAA in various aspects of Textiles, Clothing Studies, and Textile Marketing are provided by many polytechnics and colleges.

THE TEXTILE INSTITUTE, 10 Blackfriars Street, Manchester M3 5DR. (Tel: 061-834 8457).—*Gen. Sec.*, R. G. Denyer.

THEOLOGY

First degrees in *Theology, Divinity, Religious Studies,* or combinations of these subjects, are granted by most universities.

Courses leading to first degrees in *Theology* or *Theological Studies* granted by the CNAA are provided by about half a dozen polytechnics and colleges.

Theological Colleges

Anglican

The number of students for the academic year 1990–91 is shown in parenthesis.

CHICHESTER THEOLOGICAL COLLEGE, Chichester, W. Sussex PO19 1SG.—*Princ.*, Rev. P. Atkinson.

COATES HALL, Rosebery Crescent, Edinburgh EH12 5JT. (26).—*Princ.*, Rev. Canon K. Mason.

CRANMER HALL, St John's College, Durham DH1 3RJ. (62).—*Warden*, Rev. I. P. M. Cundy.

LINCOLN THEOLOGICAL COLLEGE, Drury Lane, Lincoln LN1 3BP. (63).—*Warden*, Rev. Canon W. M. Jacob, PH.D.

OAK HILL COLLEGE, Chase Side, N14 4PS. (120).— *Princ.*, Rev. Canon G. Bridger.

COLLEGE OF THE RESURRECTION, Mirfield, W. Yorks. WF14 0BW. (28).—*Princ.*, Rev. D. J. Lane.

RIDLEY HALL, Cambridge CB3 9HG. (56).—*Princ.*, Rev. Canon H. F. de Waal.

RIPON COLLEGE, Cuddesdon, Oxford OX9 9EX. (70).— *Princ.*, Rev. Canon J. H. Garton.

ST DEINIOL'S LIBRARY, Hawarden, Deeside, Clwyd CH5 3DF.—*Princ.*, Rev. P. J. Jagger.

ST JOHN'S COLLEGE, Bramcote, Nottingham NG9 3DS. (115).—*Princ.*, Rev. Dr J. Goldingay.

ST MICHAEL'S THEOLOGICAL COLLEGE, Llandaff, Cardiff CF5 2YJ. (35).—*Warden.*, Rev. Canon J. H. L. Rowlands.

ST STEPHEN'S HOUSE, 16 Marston Street, Oxford OX4 1JX. (60).—*Princ.*, Rev. E. R. Barnes.

SALISBURY AND WELLS THEOLOGICAL COLLEGE, 19 The Close, Salisbury SP1 2EE. (67).—*Princ.*, Rev. P. A. Crowe.

TRINITY COLLEGE, Stoke Hill, Bristol BS9 1JP. (130).— *Princ.*, Canon D. Gillett.

WESTCOTT HOUSE, Jesus Lane, Cambridge CB5 8BP. (50).—*Princ.*, Rev. Dr R. W. N. Hoare.

WYCLIFFE HALL, 54 Banbury Road, Oxford OX2 6PW. (80).—*Princ.*, Rev. Dr R. T. France.

Church of Scotland

CHRIST'S COLLEGE, Aberdeen AB1 1YD. (191).— *Master*, Rev. H. R. Sefton, PH.D.

NEW COLLEGE, Mound Place, Edinburgh EH1 2LU. (380).—*Princ.*, Rev. Prof. D. B. Forrester.

TRINITY COLLEGE, 4 The Square, University of Glasgow, Glasgow G12 8QQ. (130).—*Princ.*, Very Rev. Prof. R. Davidson, DD.

Presbyterian Church of Wales

UNITED THEOLOGICAL COLLEGE, Aberystwyth SY23 2LT. (52).—*Princ.*, Rev. Prof. E. ap Nefydd Roberts.

Presbyterian

UNION THEOLOGICAL COLLEGE, Belfast BT7 1JT. (76).—*Princ.*, Rev. Prof. R. F. G. Holmes.

Methodist

EDGHILL THEOLOGICAL COLLEGE, 9 Lennoxvale, Belfast BT9 5BY. (92).—*Princ.*, Rev. W. D. D. Cooke, PH.D.

WESLEY COLLEGE, College Park Drive, Henbury Road, Bristol BS10 7QD. (68).—*Princ.*, Dr H. McKeating.

WESLEY HOUSE, Cambridge CB5 8BJ. (39).—*Princ.*, Rev. Dr I. H. Jones.

Baptist

BRISTOL BAPTIST COLLEGE, Woodland Road, Bristol BS8 1UN. (40).—*Princ.*, Rev. Dr J. E. Morgan-Wynne.

NORTHERN BAPTIST COLLEGE, Luther King House, Brighton Grove, Rusholme, Manchester M14 5JP. (45).—*Princ.*, Rev. Dr B. Haymes.

NORTH WALES BAPTIST COLLEGE, Ffordd Ffriddoedd, Bangor, Gwynedd LL57 2EH. (5).—*Princ.*, Rev. J. R. Rowlands.

REGENT'S PARK COLLEGE, Oxford OX1 2LB. (75).— *Princ.*, Rev. Dr P. S. Fiddes.

THE SCOTTISH BAPTIST COLLEGE, 12 Aytoun Road, Glasgow G41 5RT. (28).—*Princ.*, Rev. I. J. N. Oakley.

SOUTH WALES BAPTIST COLLEGE, 54 Richmond Road, Cardiff CF2 3UR. (15).—*Princ.*, Rev. D. H. Matthews.

SPURGEON'S COLLEGE, South Norwood Hill, SE25 6DJ. (67).—*Princ.*, P. Beasley-Murray, PH.D.

United Reformed

BALA-BANGOR INDEPENDENT COLLEGE, Bangor LL57 2EH. (15).—*Princ.*, R. T. Jones, D.PHIL., DD.

MANSFIELD COLLEGE, Mansfield Road, Oxford OX1 3TF. (30).—*Princ.*, D. J. Trevelyan, CB.

NORTHERN COLLEGE, Luther King House, Brighton Grove, Rusholme, Manchester M14 5JP. (45).— *Princ.*, Rev. R. J. McKelvey, PH.D.

WESTMINSTER COLLEGE, Madingley Road, Cambridge CB3 0AA. (36).—*Princ.*, Rev. M. H. Cressey.

Congregational

COLLEGE OF THE WELSH INDEPENDENTS, 38 Pier Street, Aberystwyth, Dyfed.—*Princ.*, Rev. Dr E. S. John.

SCOTTISH CONGREGATIONAL COLLEGE, Rosebery Crescent, Edinburgh EH12 5YN. (8).—*Princ.*, Rev. Dr J. W. S. Clark.

Unitarian

MANCHESTER COLLEGE, Mansfield Road, Oxford OX1 3TF. (90).—*Princ.*, Rev. Dr R. Waller.

UNITARIAN COLLEGE, Luther King House, Brighton Grove, Rusholme, Manchester M14 5JP. (5).—*Principal*, Rev. L. Smith, PH.D.

Ecumenical

QUEEN'S COLLEGE, Somerset Road, Edgbaston, Birmingham B15 2QH. (75).—*Princ.*, Rev. Dr J. B. Walker.

Non-Denominational

ST MARY'S COLLEGE, The University, St Andrews, Fife KY16 9JU. (190).—*Princ.*, Very Rev. D. W. D. Shaw.

Roman Catholic

ALLEN HALL COLLEGE, 28 Beaufort Street, SW3 5AA.—*Princ.*, Rev. K. Barltrop.

CAMPION HOUSE COLLEGE, 112 Thornbury Road, Isleworth, Middx. TW7 4NN. (35).—*Princ.*, Rev. M. Barrow, SJ.

CHESTERS COLLEGE, 2 Chesters Road, Bearsden, Glasgow G61 4AG. (45).—*Rector*, Very Rev. P. Tartaglia.

OSCOTT COLLEGE, Chester Road, Sutton Coldfield, W. Midlands B73 5AA. (73).—*Rector*, Rt. Rev. Mgr. P. McKinney.

ST JOHN'S SEMINARY, Wonersh, Guildford, Surrey GU5 0QX. (42).—*Rector*, Rt. Rev. Mgr. P. Smith.

USHAW COLLEGE, Durham DH7 9RH. (110).—*Princ.*, Rt. Rev. Mgr. R. Atherton.

Jewish

JEWS' COLLEGE, Albert Road, NW4 2SJ. (135).—*Princ.*, Rabbi I. Jacobs.

LEO BAECK COLLEGE, Sternberg Centre for Judaism, 80 East End Road, N3 2SY (30).—*Princ.* Rabbi Dr J. Magonet.

TOWN AND COUNTRY PLANNING

First degrees are granted by the Universities of Belfast (*Environmental Planning*), Dundee (*Town and Regional Planning*), Heriot-Watt (*Town Planning*), Kent (*Urban Studies*), London (University College, *Environmental Studies* and *Town and Country Planning*), Manchester (*Town and Country Planning*), Newcastle upon Tyne (*Town and Country Planning*), Sheffield (*Urban Studies*), Strathclyde (*Planning*), and Wales (University College, Cardiff, *City and Regional Planning*).

First degrees in *Town Planning, Town and Country Planning, Environmental/Urban Planning*, and other aspects of planning granted by the CNAA are provided at Birmingham, Bristol, Leeds, Oxford, Central London and South Bank Polytechnics.

The ROYAL TOWN PLANNING INSTITUTE, 26 Portland Place, W1N 4BE, recognizes a number of degree and diploma courses in town planning. *Sec. Gen.*, D. Fryer.

TRANSPORT

First degrees are granted by the Universities of Aston (*Transport Management*), Loughborough (*Transport Management and Planning*), and Wales (University College, Cardiff, *International Transport*).

The CHARTERED INSTITUTE OF TRANSPORT, 80 Portland Place, London W1N 4DP, conducts qualifying examinations in transport management leading to chartered professional status. *Dir. Gen.*, R. P. Botwood.

VETERINARY STUDIES

First degrees in *Veterinary Science/Medicine and Surgery* are granted by the Universities of Bristol, Cambridge, Edinburgh, Glasgow, Liverpool and London (Royal Veterinary College).

INDEPENDENT SCHOOLS

The following pages list those independent schools whose Head is a member of the Headmasters' Conference, the Society of Headmasters and Headmistresses of Independent Schools or the Girls' Schools Association.

THE HEADMASTERS' CONFERENCE

Chairman (1992), Revd D. L. Milroy (Ampleforth College); *Sec.*, V. S. Anthony, 130 Regent Road, Leicester LE1 7PG; *Membership Sec.*, R. N. P. Griffiths, 1 Russell House, Bepton Road, Midhurst, W. Sussex GU29 9NB. The annual meetings are, as a rule, held at the end of September.

The Headmasters of some maintained schools are by invitation Additional Members of the HMC. These include the following: Aylesbury Grammar School; The Cavendish School; Easingwold School; Haberdashers' Aske's Hatcham Boys' School; Haywards Heath Sixth Form College; The John Fisher School; The Judd School; Liskeard School; The London Oratory School; Longsands Community College; Prescot School; The Richard Huish College; Richmond School; The Royal Grammar School, High Wycombe; The Royal Grammar School, Lancaster; St Bartholomew's School; Sir Roger Manwood's School.

Name of School	Founded	No. of pupils	Annual fees B'ding	Annual fees Day	Headmaster (With date of appointment)
England and Wales					
Abbotsholme School, Staffs.	1889	244‡	£9,207	£6,138	D. J. Farrant (1984)
Abingdon School, Oxon.	1256	740	£8,082	£4,082	M. St J. Parker (1975)
Aldenham School, Herts.	1597	375†	£9,975	£6,450	M. Higginbottom (1983)
Alleyn's School, SE22	1619	929‡	....	£4,905	D. A. Fenner (1976)
Allhallows School, Dorset	1515	285‡	£9,552	£4,776	P. S. Larkman, LVO (1983)
Ampleforth College (*RC*), Yorks. ...	1802	687	£9,570	£7,917	Rev. D. L. Milroy, OSB (1980)
*Ardingly College, W. Sussex	1858	480‡	£9,360	£7,575	J. W. Flecker (1980)
Arnold School, Blackpool	1896	820‡	£6,054	£2,997	J. A. B. Kelsall (1987)
Ashville College, Harrogate	1877	490‡	£7,599	£3,999	M. H. Crosby (1987)
Bancroft's School, Essex	1727	730‡	....	£4,482	Dr P. C. D. Southern (1985)
Barnard Castle School, Co. Durham	1883	500†	£6,650	£3,950	F. S. McNamara (1980)
Batley Grammar School, W. Yorks..	1612	617†	....	£2,826	C. S. Parker (1986)
Bedales School, Hants.	1893	403‡	£10,445	£7,494	E. A. M. MacAlpine (1981)
Bedford School	1552	725	£8,670	£5,505	Dr I. P. Evans (1990)
Bedford Modern School	1566	990	£6,474	£3,489	P. J. Squire (1977)
Berkhamsted School, Herts.	1541	500	£8,478	£3,549	Rev. K. H. Wilkinson (1989)
Birkenhead School, Merseyside	1860	750	....	£2,865	S. J. Haggett (1988)
Bishop's Stortford College, Herts...	1868	365†	£8,130	£5,880°	S. G. G. Benson (1984)
*Bloxham School, Oxon.	1860	365†	£9,270	£6,954	D. K. Exham (1991)
Blundell's School, Devon	1604	469†	£9,750	£6,015	A. J. D. Rees (1980)
Bolton School	1524	850	....	£3,354	A. W. Wright (1983)
Bootham School, York.	1823	335‡	£7,800	£5,400	I. M. Small (1988)
Bradfield College, Berks.	1850	580†	£10,350	£7,765	P. B. Smith (1985)
Bradford Grammar School	1662	1,032†	....	£2,850	D. A. G. Smith (1974)
Brentwood School, Essex	1557	960†	£8,142	£4,650	J. A. E. Evans (1981)
Brighton College, E. Sussex	1845	498‡	£9,630	£6,330	J. D. Leach (1987)
Bristol Cathedral School	1542	460†	....	£3,327	R. A. Collard (1990)
Bristol Grammar School	1532	980‡	....	£3,228	C. E. Martin (1986)
Bromsgrove School, Worcs.........	1553	560‡	£8,460	£5,295	T. M. Taylor (1986)
Bryanston School, Dorset	1928	670‡	£9,750°	......	T. D. Wheare (1983)
Bury Grammar School, Lancs.	1634	670	....	£2,790	K. Richards (1990)
Canford School, Dorset	1923	520†	£10,375	£7,575	M. Marriott (1974)
Caterham School, Surrey	1811	450†	£8,310	£4,530	S. R. Smith (1976)
Charterhouse, Surrey	1611	700†	£9,795°	£8,100°	P. J. Attenborough (1982)
Cheadle Hulme School, Cheshire ...	1855	912‡	£7,260	£3,360	D. J. Wilkinson (1990)
Cheltenham College, Glos..........	1841	570†	£10,425	£7,875	P. D. V. Wilkes (1990)
Chigwell School, Essex	1629	340†	£7,839	£5,154	A. R. M. Little (1989)
Christ College, Brecon	1541	350†	£7,029	£5,328	S. W. Hockey (1982)
Christ's Hospital, W. Sussex	1553	821‡	varies	......	R. C. Poulton (1987)
Churcher's College, Hants.	1722	480‡	£7,850	£4,050	G. W. Buttle (1988)
City of London, EC4	1442	850	....	£4,734	B. G. Bass (1990)
City of London Freemen's School, Surrey	1854	365‡	£7,449	£4,779	D. C. Haywood (1987)
Clifton College, Bristol.............	1862	670‡	£10,320	£7,200	H. Monro (1990)
Colfe's School, SE12	1652	698†	....	£3,870	Dr D. Richardson (1990)
Colston's School, Bristol	1710	300†	£7,380	£4,455	S. B. Howarth (1988)
Coventry School	—	1,678‡	....	£2,883	R. Cooke (*Director*) (1977)
Cranleigh School, Surrey	1863	560†	£10,530	£7,905	A. Hart (1984)
Culford School, Suffolk	1881	400‡	£8,019	£5,211	D. Robson (1971)
Dame Allan's School, Newcastle upon Tyne.....................	1705	434†	....	£2,868	T. A. Willcocks (*Principal*) (1988)

* Woodard Corporation School. ‡ Co-educational. † Girls in VI form. ° 1991 figure. °°1990 figure.

Name of School	Founded	No. of pupils	Annual fees B'ding	Annual fees Day	Headmaster (With date of appointment)
Dauntsey's School, Wiltshire	1543	606‡	£8,658	£5,385	C. R. Evans (1985)
Dean Close School, Cheltenham	1884	450‡	£9,780	£6,780	C. J. Bacon (1979)
*Denstone College, Staffs.	1873	330‡	£8,880	£6,330	H. C. K. Carson (1990)
Douai School (RC), Berks.	1903	280	£8,700	£5,490	Dom. G. Scott, OSB (1987)
Dover College, Kent	1871	310‡	£8,580	£5,670	M. P. G. Wright (1990)
Downside School (RC), Somerset	1607	401	£9,186	£5,874	Dom. A. Bellenger (1991)
Dulwich College, SE21	1619	1,398	£10,710	£5,355	A. C. F. Verity (*Master*) (1986)
Durham School	1414	380†	£9,744	£6,495	M. A. Lang (1982)
Eastbourne College, E. Sussex	1867	540†	£9,807	£7,251	C. J. Saunders (1981)
*Ellesmere College, Shropshire	1884	370†	£8,790	£6,230	D. R. du Croz (1988)
Eltham College, SE9	1842	530†	£8,172	£3,870	D. M. Green (1990)
Emanuel School, SW11	1594	750	£9,807	£3,525	P. F. Thomson (1984)
Epsom College, Surrey	1855	650†	£9,405	£6,600	Dr J. B. Cook (1982)
Eton College, Berks.	1440	1,270	£18,900	......	Dr W. E. K. Anderson (1980)
Exeter School	1633	700†	£6,147	£3,282	G. T. Goodall (1979)
Felsted School, Essex	1564	450†	£10,170	£8,025	E. J. H. Gould (1983)
Forest School, E17	1834	787†	£6,861	£4,449	J. C. Gough (*Warden*) (1983)
Framlingham College, Suffolk	1864	420‡	£7,974	£5,118	J. F. X. Miller (1989)
Frensham Heights, Surrey	1925	282‡	£10,050	£6,330	A. L. Pattinson (1973)
Giggleswick School, N. Yorks.	1512	310‡	£9,468	£6,279	P. Hobson (1986)
Gresham's School, Norfolk	1555	480‡	£8,895	£6,225	J. H. Arkell (1991)
Haberdashers' Aske's School, Herts.	1690	1,100	......	£4,680	K. Dawson (1987)
Haileybury, Herts.	1862	640†	£10,545	£7,380	D. J. Jewell (1987)
Hampton School, Middx.	1557	875	......	£3,690	G. G. Able (1988)
Harrow School, Middx.	1571	770	£11,175	......	N. R. Bomford (1991)
Hereford Cathedral School	1384	595‡	£6,330	£3,675	Dr H. C. Tomlinson (1987)
Highgate School, N6	1565	585	£9,660	£5,694	R. P. Kennedy (1989)
Hulme Grammar School, Oldham	1611	740	......	£2,430°°	G. F. Dunkin (1987)
*Hurstpierpoint College, W. Sussex	1849	380	£9,555	£7,650	S. A. Watson (1986)
Hymers College, Hull	1889	700‡	......	£2,835	J. C. Morris (1990)
Ipswich School, Suffolk	1390	620†	£6,840	£4,020	Dr J. M. Blatchly (1972)
John Lyon School, Middx.	1876	495	......	£4,155	Rev. T. J. Wright (1986)
Kelly College, Devon	1877	320‡	£9,492	£6,330	C. H. Hirst (1985)
Kent College, Canterbury	1885	560‡	£8,034	£4,500	R. J. Wicks (1980)
Kimbolton School, Cambs.	1600	540‡	£7,290	£4,230	R. V. Peel (1987)
King Edward VI School, Southampton	1553	962†	......	£3,762	T. R. Cookson (1990)
King Edward VII School, Lytham	1908	540	......	£2,715	D. Heap (1982)
King Edward's School, Bath	1552	685†	......	£3,321	J. P. Wroughton (1982)
King Edward's School, Birmingham	1552	825	......	£3,255	H. R. Wright (*Chief Master*) (1991)
King Edward's School, Witley, Surrey	1553	515‡	£7,485	£5,520	R. J. Fox (1988)
*King's College, Taunton	1880	470‡	£9,630	£7,020	R. S. Funnell (1988)
King's College School, SW19	1829	660	......	£5,070	R. M. Reeve (1980)
King's School, Bruton, Somerset	1519	337†	£9,300	£6,585	A. H. Beadles (1985)
King's School, Canterbury	600	710‡	£9,300°	£6,510°	Rev. Canon A. C. J. Phillips (1986)
King's School, Chester	1541	480	......	£3,615	A. R. D. Wickson (1981)
King's School, Ely, Cambs.	970	420‡	£9,732	£6,204	H. Ward (1970)
King's School, Macclesfield	1502	870†	......	£3,465	A. G. Silcock (1987)
King's School, Rochester, Kent	604	367‡	£8,712	£5,223	Dr I. R. Walker (1986)
King's School, Tynemouth	1860	706†	......	£2,880	W. T. Gillen (1986)
King's School, Worcester	1541	706‡	£7,284	£4,440	Dr J. M. Moore (1984)
Kingston Grammar School, Surrey	1561	587‡	......	£4,290	C. D. Baxter (1991)
Kingswood School, Bath	1748	460‡	£9,135	£5,940	G. M. Best (1987)
*Lancing College, W. Sussex	1848	550	£10,065	£7,545	J. S. Woodhouse (1981)
Leeds Grammar School	1552	1,020	......	£3,321	B. W. Collins (1986)
Leighton Park School, Reading	1890	350†	£8,794°	£6,651°	J. A. Chapman (1986)
The Leys School, Cambridge	1875	388†	£10,035	£7,425	Rev. J. C. A. Barrett (1990)
Liverpool College	1840	359†	......	£3,075	R. V. Haygarth (1979)
Llandovery College, Dyfed	1848	220‡	£7,362	£4,803	Dr C. E. Evans (*Warden*) (1988)
Lord Wandsworth College, Hants.	1912	440†	£7,908	£6,118	G. A. G. Dodd (1982)
Loughborough Grammar School	1495	910	£6,657	£3,528	D. N. Ireland (1984)
Magdalen College School, Oxford	1480	500	£7,260	£3,825	P. M. Tinniswood (*Master*) (1991)
Malvern College, Worcs.	1865	600	£9,210°	£6,705°	R. de C. Chapman (1983)
Manchester Grammar School	1515	1,445	......	£3,400	J. G. Parker (*High Master*) (1985)

* Woodard Corporation School.　　‡ Co-educational.　　† Girls in VI form.　　° 1991 figure.　　°° 1990 figure.

Name of School	Founded	No. of pupils	Annual fees B'ding	Annual fees Day	Headmaster (With date of appointment)
Marlborough College, Wilts........	1843	856‡	£10,500	......	D. R. Cope (*Master*) (1986)
Merchant Taylors' School, Liverpool....................	1620	724	....	£3,168	S. J. R. Dawkins (1986)
Merchant Taylors' School, Middx..	1561	720	£8,040°	£5,040°	D. J. Skipper (1982)
Mill Hill School, NW7..........	1807	575†	£9,660	£6,390	A. C. Graham (1979)
Monkton Combe School, Bath	1868	328†	£9,720	£7,170	M. J. Cuthbertson (1990)
Monmouth School, Gwent........	1614	535	£6,957	£4,176	R. D. Lane (1982)
Mount St Mary's College (*RC*), Derbys....................	1842	322‡	£7,329	£4,950	P. Fisher (1991)
Newcastle under Lyme School	1874	1,204†	....	£2,931°	R. M. Reynolds (*Principal*) (1990)
Norwich School	1250	609	£6,663	£3,663	C. D. Brown (1984)
Nottingham High School	1513	830	....	£3,450	D. T. Witcombe, Ph.D. (1970)
Oakham School, Rutland	1584	1000‡	£9,510	£5,265	G. Smallbone (1985)
The Oratory School (*RC*), Berks....	1859	360	£8,621°	£6,036°	M. K. Lynn (1989)
Oundle School, Northants	1556	820‡	£10,800	£4,200	D. B. McMurray (1984)
Pangbourne College, Berks.	1917	350	£9,210	£6,300	A. B. E. Hudson (1988)
Perse School, Cambridge	1615	500	£6,561°	£3,261°	Dr G. M. Stephen (1987)
Plymouth College	1877	685	£6,915	£3,585	A. M. Joyce (1983)
Pocklington School, York........	1514	576‡	£7,167	£3,834	A. D. Pickering (1981)
Portsmouth Grammar School	1732	760‡	....	£3,480	A. C. V. Evans (1983)
Prior Park College (*RC*), Bath	1830	417‡	£8,508	£4,704	J. W. R. Goulding (1989)
Queen Elizabeth GS, Wakefield ...	1591	735‡	£4,926	£3,393	R. P. Mardling (1985)
Queen Elizabeth's GS, Blackburn ..	1567	1,100†	....	£3,333	P. F. Johnston (1978)
Queen Elizabeth's Hospital, Bristol.	1590	485	£5,835	£3,324	Dr R. Gliddon (1985)
Queen's College, Taunton	1843	450‡	£7,620	£4,980	C. T. Bradnock (1991)
Radley College, Oxon...........	1847	610	£10,350	......	R. M. Morgan (*Warden*) (1991)
Ratcliffe College (*RC*), Leicester ...	1844	450‡	£7,278	£4,854	Rev. L. G. Hurdidge (1985)
Reed's School, Surrey...........	1813	350†	£8,445	£6,375	D. E. Prince (1983)
Reigate Grammar School, Surrey ..	1675	850‡	....	£3,942	J. G. Hamlin (1982)
Rendcomb College, Glos.	1920	265†	£8,910	......	J. Tolputt (1987)
Repton School, Derby	1557	560‡	£9,765	£7,326	G. E. Jones (1987)
RNIB New College, Worcester	1987	121‡	£14,361°°	£9,576°°	Rev. B. R. Manthorp (1980)
Rossall School, Lancs.	1844	485‡	£9,765	£6,810	R. D. W. Rhodes (1987)
Royal Grammar School, Guildford .	1552	800	....	£3,540°°	J. Daniel (1972)
Royal Grammar School, Newcastle upon Tyne	1545	956	....	£2,895	A. S. Cox (1972)
Royal Grammar School, Worcester .	1291	760	£6,147	£3,654	T. E. Savage, TD (1978)
Rugby School, Warwicks.	1567	672†	£10,725	£6,300	M. B. Mavor, CVO (1990)
Rydal School, Clwyd	1885	358‡	£7,680	£5,838	N. W. Thorne (1991)
Ryde School, Isle of Wight	1921	322‡	£6,579	£3,222	M. D. Featherstone (1990)
St Albans School, Herts.	1570	670	....	£4,185	S. C. Wilkinson (1984)
St Ambrose College, Cheshire......	1946	640	....	£2,517	G. E. Hester (1991)
St Anselm's College (*RC*), Birkenhead.	1933	650	....	£2,592	Rev. Br. C. J. Sreenan, OBI (1987)
St Bede's College (*RC*), Manchester	1876	880‡	....	£2,793°	J. Byrne (1983)
St Bees School, Cumbria	1583	360‡	£7,800°	£5,460°	P. A. Chamberlain (1988)
St Benedict's School (*RC*), W5 ...	1902	600†	....	£3,750	Dr A. J. Dachs (1987)
St Dunstan's College, SE6	1888	650	....	£3,942	B. D. Dance (1973)
St Edmund's College (*RC*), Herts. ..	1568	507‡	£7,608	£4,875	D. J. J. McEwen (1984)
St Edmund's School, Canterbury ...	1749	315‡	£9,510	£6,210	J. V. Tyson (1978)
St Edward's College (*RC*), Liverpool	1853	650†	....	£2,805	Rev. Br. B. D. Sassi (1984)
St Edward's School, Oxford	1863	575†	£10,350	£7,770	D. Christie (1988)
St George's College (*RC*), Surrey ...	1869	540†	£7,380	£4,920	Rev. J. W. Munton (1987)
St John's School, Surrey	1851	450†	£8,400	£6,000	D. E. Brown (1985)
St Lawrence College, Kent	1879	400‡	£8,940	£5,985	J. H. Binfield (1983)
St Mary's College (*RC*), Merseyside	1919	565‡	....	£2,862	W. Hammond (1991)
St Paul's School, SW13	1509	757	£10,200	£6,450	Rev. Canon P. Pilkingtor (*High Master*) (1986)
St Peter's School, York	627	470‡	£8,745	£5,205	R. N. Pittman (1985)
Sedbergh School, Cumbria	1525	495	£9,900	£6,930	Dr R. G. Baxter (1982)
Sevenoaks School, Kent...........	1418	910‡	£9,540	£5,790	R. P. Barker (1981)
Sherborne School, Dorset	1550	650	£11,045	£8,025	P. H. Lapping (1988)
Shrewsbury School	1552	665	£10,125	£7,140	F. E. Maidment (1988)
Silcoates School, W. Yorks........	1820	302‡	£7,473	£4,176	A. P. Spillane (1991)
Solihull School, Warwicks	1560	830†	....	£3,138	A. Lee (1983)
Stamford School, Lincs.	1532	560	£6,600	£3,300	G. J. Timm (1978)
Stockport Grammar School.......	1487	1,010‡	....	£3,258	D. R. J. Bird (1985)
Stonyhurst College (*RC*), Lancs. ...	1593	435	£9,465	£5,136	Dr R. G. G. Mercer (1985)
Stowe School, Bucks.............	1923	580‡	£9,786	£6,846	J. G. L. Nichols (1989)

‡ Co-educational.   † Girls in VI form.   ° 1991 figure.   °° 1990 figure.

Name of School	Founded	No. of pupils	Annual fees B'ding	Annual fees Day	Headmaster (With date of appointment)
Sutton Valence School, Kent	1576	400‡	£8,800	£5,600	M. R. Haywood (1980)
Taunton School	1847	600‡	£7,680°°	£4,975°°	B. B. Sutton (1987)
Tettenhall College, Staffs.	1863	300‡	£6,870	£4,230	W. J. Dale (1968)
Tonbridge School, Kent	1553	640	£10,425	£7,350	J. M. Hammond (1990)
Trent College, Derbys.	1868	640†	£8,697	£5,301	J. S. Lee (1988)
Trinity School, Surrey	1596	840	....	£4,233	R. J. Wilson (1972)
Truro School	1879	885‡	£7,020	£3,780	B. K. Hobbs (1986)
University College School, NW3	1830	520	....	£5,460	G. D. Slaughter (1983)
Uppingham School, Leics.	1584	680†	£10,710	....	S. C. Winkley (1991)
Warwick School	914	800	£8,040	£3,720	P. J. Cheshire (1989)
Wellingborough School, Northants.	1595	440‡	£7,410	£4,500	G. Garrett (1973)
Wellington College, Berks.	1856	824†	£10,395	£7,590	C. J. Driver (1989)
Wells Cathedral School, Somerset	1180	601‡	£7,371	£4,332	J. S. Baxter (1986)
West Buckland School, Devon	1858	475‡	£7,055	£3,885	M. Downward (1979)
Westminster School, SW1	1560	600†	£10,425	£6,900	D. M. Summerscale (1986)
Whitgift School, Surrey	1596	935	....	£4,440	C. A. Barnett (1991)
William Hulme's GS, Manchester	1887	790‡	....	£3,432	P. D. Briggs (1987)
Winchester College, Hants.	1382	656	£10,800	£8,100	J. P. Sabben-Clare (1985)
Wolverhampton Grammar School	1512	650†	....	£3,828	B. St J. Trafford (1990)
Woodbridge School, Suffolk	1662	550‡	£7,530	£4,590	Dr D. Younger (1985)
*Woodhouse Grove School, Bradford	1812	580	£6,975	£4,170	D. W. Welsh (1991)
*Worksop College, Notts.	1895	400‡	£7,875	£5,400	R. D. V. Knight (1990)
Worth School (*RC*), W. Sussex	1959	309	£9,600	£7,200	Rev. R. S. Ortiger (1983)
Wrekin College, Shropshire	1880	380‡	£9,270	£6,435	P. Johnson (1991)
Wycliffe College, Glos.	1882	310‡	£9,990	£6,975	A. P. Millard (1987)
Scotland					
Daniel Stewart's and Melville College, Edinburgh	1832	790	£6,507°	£3,366°	P. F. J. Tobin (1989)
Dollar Academy, Clackmannanshire	1818	765‡	£6,285°	£2,835°	L. Harrison (*Rector*) (1984)
Dundee High School, Tayside	1239	750‡	....	£3,168	R. Nimmo (*Rector*) (1977)
The Edinburgh Academy	1824	563‡	£8,985	£4,245	L. E. Ellis (*Rector*) (1977)
Fettes College, Edinburgh	1870	379	£9,360°	£6,285°	M. T. Thyne (1988)
George Heriot's School, Edinburgh	1659	1,370‡	....	£3,160	K. P. Pearson (1983)
George Watson's College, Edinburgh	1741	1,275‡	£6,675	£3,375	F. E. Gerstenberg (*Principal*) (1985)
Glasgow Academy	1845	500‡	....	£3,510	C. W. Turner (*Rector*) (1983)
Glenalmond College, Perth.	1841	310†	£9,900	£6,930	J. F. Wainwright (*Warden*) (1991)
Gordonstoun School, Moray	1934	474‡	£9,960	£6,420	M. C. S.-R. Pyper (1990)
The High School of Glasgow	1124	580‡	....	£3,030°	R. G. Easton (1983)
Hutcheson's Grammar School, Glasgow	1641	1,231	....	£2,916	D. R. Ward (*Rector*) (1987)
Kelvinside Academy, Glasgow	1878	500	....	£3,500	J. H. Duff (*Rector*) (1980)
Loretto School, E. Lothian	1827	306†	£8,850	....	Rev. N. W. Drummond (1984)
Merchiston Castle School, Edinburgh	1833	380	£9,480	£6,120	D. M. Spawforth (1981)
Morrison's Academy, Perthshire	1860	550‡	£7,782	£2,880	H. A. Ashmall (*Rector*) (1979)
Robert Gordon's College, Aberdeen	1729	910‡	£6,650	£3,050	G. A. Allan (1978)
Strathallan School, Perth	1913	400‡	£9,450	....	C. D. Pighills (1975)
Northern Ireland					
Bangor Grammar School, Co. Down	1856	890	....	£1,700°	T. W. Patton (1979)
Belfast Royal Academy	1785	1,300‡	....	£65	W. M. Sillery (1980)
Campbell College, Belfast	1894	540	£6,900	£3,500	Dr R. J. I. Pollock (1987)
Coleraine Academical Institution	1856	850	£4,350	£1,900	R. S. Forsythe (1984)
Methodist College, Belfast	1868	1,600‡	£4,257°	£1,920°	T. W. Mulryne (1988)
Portora Royal School, Enniskillen	1618	346	£4,902	£45	R. L. Bennett (1983)
Royal Belfast Academical Institution	1810	940	....	£210	R. M. Ridley (1990)
Channel Islands and Isle of Man					
Elizabeth College, Guernsey	1563	540	£5,025	£1,935	J. H. F. Doulton (1988)
Victoria College, Jersey	1852	580	£6,912	£1,431	vacant
King William's College, Isle of Man	1668	385‡	£8,580	£6,060	S. A. Westley (1989)

Woodard Corporation School.   ‡ Co-educational.   † Girls in VI form.   ° 1991 figure.   °°1990 figure.

HMC SCHOOLS OVERSEAS
Fees are given in local currency

Name of School	Founded	No. of pupils	Annual fees B'ding	Day	Headmaster *(With date of appointment)*
Africa					
Falcon College, Esigodini, Zimbabwe	1954	450	Z$9,000	....	P. N. Todd (1985)
Hilton College, Natal, SA	1872	482†	R19,800	....	P. Marsh (1987)
Michaelhouse, Natal, SA	1896	480	R19,100	....	J. Pluke (1987)
Peterhouse, Marondera, Zimbabwe	1955	791†	Z$9,150	Z$1,820	Rev. Dr A. J. Megahey (*Rector*) (1984)
St George's College, Harare, Zimbabwe	1896	800	Z$6,693	....	vacant
St John's College, Johannesburg, SA	—	620†	R16,185	R9,075	W. W. MacFarlane (1983)
St Stithian's College, Randburg, SA	1953	618†	R14,310	R7,770	D. B. Wylde (1989)
Australia					
Anglican Church GS, Queensland	1912	1,313	$A10,260	$A4,560	C. V. Ellis (1987)
Brighton GS, Victoria	1882	700	....	$A7,140	R. L. Rofe (1967)
Camberwell GS, Victoria	1886	975	....	$A6,734	C. F. Black (1987)
Canberra GS, ACT	1929	1,241	$A12,100	$A5,620	T. C. Murray (1986)
Caulfield GS, Victoria	1881	1,500†	$A13,650	$A7,020	Rev. A. S. Holmes (*Principal*) (1977)
Christ Church GS, W. Australia	—	932	$A11,860	$A5,560	J. S. Madin (1988)
Cranbrook School, NSW	1918	772	$A13,905	$A7,110	Dr B. N. Carter (1985)
The Geelong College, Victoria	1861	850‡	$A15,400	$A7,600	A. P. Sheahan (1986)
Geelong GS, Victoria	1855	1,200‡	$A15,380	$A7,220	J. E. Lewis (1980)
Guildford GS, W. Australia	1896	763	$A11,184	$A5,184	J. M. Moody (1979)
Haileybury College, Victoria	1892	850	....	$A7,200	A. M. H. Aikman (*Principal*) (1974)
Hale School, W. Australia	1858	722	$A11,480	$A5,480	J. Inverarity, MBE (1989)
King's School, Parramatta, NSW	1831	900	$A14,080	$A7,900	J. A. Wickham (1984)
Kinross Wolardi School, NSW	1886	620‡	$A11,940	$A5,670	A. E. S. Anderson (1978)
Knox, NSW	1924	1,261	$A13,910	$A6,690	Dr I. W. Paterson (1969)
Melbourne C. of E. GS, Victoria	1856	1,133	$A13,920	$A8,000	A. J. de V. Hill (1988)
Newington College, NSW	1863	1,135	$A10,650	$A8,250	A. J. Rae (1972)
The Peninsula School, Victoria	1961	930	$A13,000	$A7,000	R. T. Hille (1992)
St Peter's College, S. Australia	1847	760	$A13,040	$A6,140	Dr A. J. Shinkfield (1978)
Scotch College, Adelaide, S. Australia	1919	650‡	$A14,870	$A6,960	W. M. Miles (1975)
Scotch College, Hawthorn, Victoria	1851	1,408	$A14,505	$A7,320	Dr F. G. Donaldson (1983)
Scotch College, Swanbourne, W. Australia	1897	729	$A11,520	$A5,440	W. R. Dickinson (1972)
Scots College, Sydney, NSW	1893	1,000	$A14,970	$A7,800	G. A. W. Renney (*Principal*) (1980)
Sydney C. of E. GS, NSW	1889	985	$A13,446	$A6,888	R. A. I. Grant (1983)
Sydney GS, NSW	1857	1,110	....	$A2,795	Dr R. D. Townsend, D. phil. (198?)
Wesley College, Melbourne, Victoria	1866	2,099‡	....	$A7,260	D. H. Prest (*Principal*) (1972)
Canada					
Brentwood College School, Vancouver	1961	380‡	C$17,000	C$8,400	W. T. Ross (1976)
Glenlyon-Norfolk School, BC	—	302‡	....	C$6,345	D. S. S. Brooks (1987)
Hillfield Strathallan College, Ontario	1901	968‡	....	C$7,995	M. B. Wansbrough (1969)
Pickering College, Ontario	1842	175	C$18,800	C$9,800	S. H. Clark (1978)
St Andrew's College, Ontario	1899	370	C$19,350	C$11,500	R. P. Bedard (1981)
Toronto French School, Ontario	1962	1,165‡	C$16,980	C$9,005	A. S. Troubetzkoy (1987)
Trinity College School, Ontario	1865	403	C$16,350°°	C$9,000°°	R. C. N. Wright (1983)
Upper Canada College, Toronto	1829	640	C$20,000	C$10,950	J. D. Blakey (*Principal*) (1991)
Europe					
Aiglon College, Switzerland	1949	280‡	Frs.44,190	....	P. Parsons (1976)
British School in the Netherlands	¿1935	530‡	....	Fl.16,500	M. J. Cooper (1990)
British School of Brussels	1970	495‡	....	Frs.492,885	Dr J. Jackson (1983)
British School of Paris, France	1954	310‡	Frs.102,840	Frs.75,100	A. W. Livingstone-Smith (1986)

† Girls in VI form.   ‡ Co-educational.   ° 1991 figure.   °° 1990 figure.

Name of School	Founded	No. of pupils	Annual fees B'ding	Day	Headmaster (With date of appointment)
The English School, Nicosia, Cyprus	1900	820‡	. . . .	C£1,250	A. M. Hudspeth (1988)
The International School of Paris	1964	250‡	. . . .	Frs.72,000	N. M. Prentki (1988)
King's College, Madrid	—	1,060‡	P. 1,506,000	P. 726,000	Dr G. R. Percy (1991)
St Columba's College, Dublin	1843	275‡	IR£5,070	IR£2,700	T. E. Macey (Warden) (1988)
St George's English School, Rome	1958	430‡	. . . .	L15,000,000	F. Ruggiero (1991)
Hong Kong					
Island School	1967	1,200‡	. . . .	HK$40,700	D. J. James (Principal) (1988)
King George V School	1900	1,050‡	. . . .	HK$36,300°	M. J. Behennah (1989)
India					
Birla Public School, Pilani	—	600	Rs.11,500	Rs.4,000	N. K. Ojha (Principal) (1991)
Lawrence School, Ootacamund . .	1858	500‡	Rs.14,000°	. . . .	D. Lahiri (1991)
Lawrence School, Sanawar	1847	533†	Rs.14,500	. . . .	S. B. Singh (1988)
The Scindia School, Gwalior	1897	750	Rs.13,500	. . . .	Dr S. D. Singh (1978)
New Zealand					
Christ's College, Christchurch . . .	1850	600	NZ$9,600	NZ$5,250	Dr M. J. Rosser (1985)
Collegiate School, Wanganui	1854	512†	NZ$12,993	NZ$7,273	T. S. McKinlay (1988)
King's College, Auckland	1896	800†	NZ$10,620°	NZ$6,285°	J. S. Taylor (1988)
Rathkeale College, Masterton . . .	1964	333†	NZ$12,810	NZ$6,030	B. R. Levick (1991)
St Andrew's College, Christchurch	1916	606	NZ$10,515	NZ$6,075	Dr A. J. Rentoul (Rector) (1982)
South America					
Academia Britanica Cuscatleca, El Salvador	1971	630‡	. . . .	US$1,500	A. J. McQuiggan (1986)
Markham College, Peru	1946	800	. . . .	US$3,000	W. J. Baker (1990)
St Andrew's Scots School, Argentina	—	600‡	. . . .	US$10,680	K. Prior (1982)
St George's College, Argentina . .	1898	220‡	US$19,200	US$12,000	N. P. O. Green (1991)
St Paul's School, Brazil	1926	700‡	. . . .	US$5,000°	C. McCann (1990)
USA					
The Rivers School, Massachusetts	1915	260‡	. . . .	$10,000°	R. A. Bradley (1981)

‡ Co-educational. † Girls in VI form. ° 1991 figure.

SOCIETY OF HEADMASTERS AND HEADMISTRESSES OF INDEPENDENT SCHOOLS

Hon. Secretary, A. E. R. Dodds, Mantons, Park Road, Winchester, Hants. SO23 7BE.

The Society was founded in 1961 and, in general, represents smaller boarding schools. A Headmaster may be a member of both HMC and SHMIS. This is the case for the Headmasters of the following schools, details of which appear in the HMC list:

Abbotsholme School, Bedales School, Churcher's College, City of London Freemen's School, Colston's School, King's School, Tynemouth, Lord Wandsworth College, Pangbourne College, Reed's School, Rendcomb College, Ryde School, St George's College, Silcoates School, Tettenhall College, Wells Cathedral School, West Buckland School and Woodbridge School.

Name of School	Founded	No. of pupils	Annual fees B'ding	Day	Headmaster (With date of appointment)
Ackworth School, W. Yorks	1779	440‡	£7,368	£4,140	D. S. Harris (1989)
Austin Friars School (RC), Carlisle	1951	307‡	£6,015	£3,435	Rev. T. Lyons, OSA (1981)
Bearwood College, Berks.	1827	320	£8,400	£4,650	The Hon. M. C. Penney (1980)
Bedstone College, Shropshire	1948	220‡	£5,685°	£3,420°	M. S. Symonds (1989)
Belmont Abbey (RC), Hereford	1926	220	£7,125	£4,260	Rev. D. C. Jenkins, OSB (1988)
Bembridge School, Isle of Wight . . .	1919	200‡	£7,485	£4,035	J. High (1986)
Bentham School, N. Yorks	1726	274‡	£6,555	£3,240	J. E. Rigg (1988)
Bethany School, Kent	1866	260‡	£7,668	£4,908	W. M. Harvey (1988)
Box Hill School, Surrey	1959	290‡	£8,685	£5,235	Dr R. A. S. Atwood (1987)

‡ Co-educational. ° 1991 figure.

Name of School	Founded	No. of pupils	Annual fees B'ding	Annual fees Day	Headmaster (With date of appointment)
Carmel College (*Jewish*), Oxon.	1948	260‡	£12,636	£6,750	P. D. Skelker (1984)
Claremont Fan Court School, Surrey	1932	402‡	£7,650	£5,085	J. H. Scott (1987)
Clayesmore School, Dorset	1896	300‡	£9,390	£6,615	D. J. Beeby (1986)
Cokethorpe School, Oxon.	1957	180‡	£9,666	£6,444	D. G. Crawford (1989)
Ewell Castle School, Surrey	1926	350	......	£3,600	R. A. Fewtrell (1983)
Friends' School, Essex	1702	300‡	£7,650	£4,794	Miss S. H. Evans (1989)
Fulneck Boys' School, W. Yorks.	1753	312‡	£5,550°°	£2,865°°	I. D. Cleland (1980)
*Grenville College, Devon	1954	374	£7,965	£3,906	D. Young (*acting*) (1991)
Halliford School, Middx.	1956	320†	......	£3,510	J. R. Crook (1984)
Hipperholme Grammar School, Halifax.........................	1648	370‡	......	£2,580	C. C. Robinson (1988)
Keil School, Dumbarton	1915	214‡	£7,419	£4,155	C. H. Tongue (1984)
Kingham Hill School, Oxon.	1886	210	£7,194	£4,320	M. Payne (*Warden*) (1990)
King's School, Gloucester	1541	360‡	£6,888	£4,077	Rev. A. C. Charters (1983)
Kirkham Grammar School, Lancs. ..	1549	510‡	£5,160	£2,865	B. Stacey (1991)
Lord Mayor Treloar College, Hants.	1908	280‡	£7,859	£5,895	H. Heard (1990)
Milton Abbey School, Dorset	1954	275	£9,450	......	R. H. Hardy (1987)
Oswestry School, Shropshire	1407	300‡	£7,500	£4,470	I. G. Templeton (1985)
Pierrepont School, Surrey.........	1947	220‡	£8,505	£5,118	J. D. Payne (1983)
The Purcell School (music), Middx. .	1962	108‡	£12,033	£7,116	K. J. Bain (1983)
Rannoch School, Perthshire.......	1959	258‡	£8,385	£4,950	M. Barratt (1982)
Reading Blue Coat School, Berks. ..	1646	560†	£7,170	£3,930	Rev. A. C. E. Sanders (1974)
Rishworth School, W. Yorks.	1724	480†	£7,650	£4,050	A. J. Morsley (1986)
Rougemont School, Gwent	1919	254†	......	£3,576	G. R. Sims (1991)
Royal Hospital School, Ipswich	1712	650‡	£5,700	......	M. A. B. Kirk (1983)
Royal Russell School, Surrey	1853	691‡	£8,385	£4,410	R. D. Balaam (1981)
Royal School, Dungannon, N. Ireland	1614	600‡	£4,372	£2,050	P. D. Hewitt (1984)
Royal Wolverhampton School	1850	320‡	£7,120	£4,120	P. Gorring (1985)
Ruthin School, Clwyd	1574	170‡	£7,005°	£4,575°	F. R. Ullmann (1986)
St Bede's School, E. Sussex	—	350‡	£9,150	£5,745	R. A. Perrin (1978)
St David's College, Gwynedd	1965	200	£7,740	£4,995	W. Seymour (1991)
Scarborough College, N. Yorks.	1898	415‡	£7,968	£4,323	D. S. Hempsall, PH.D. (1985)
Seaford College, W. Sussex	1884	360	£7,590	......	R. C. Hannaford (1990)
Shebbear College, Devon	1841	260†	£7,410	£4,050	R. J. Buley (1983)
Shiplake College, Oxon.	1959	335	£8,610°	£5,655°	N. V. Bevan (1988)
Sidcot School, Avon	1808	300‡	£7,830	£4,620	C. J. Greenfield (1986)
Stanbridge Earls School, Hants.	1952	165‡	£8,850°	£6,600°	H. Moxon (1984)
Warminster School, Wilts.	1707	320†	£7,335	£4,410	T. D. Holgate (1990)
Wisbech GS, Cambs.	1379	610‡	......	£3,750	R. S. Repper (1988)
Yarm School, Cleveland	1978	440†	......	£3,918	R. Neville Tate (1978)

*Woodard Corporation School.   ‡Co-educational.   †Girls in VI form.   °1991 figure.   °°1990 figure.

GIRLS' SCHOOLS ASSOCIATION

THE GIRLS' SCHOOLS ASSOCIATION, 130 Regent Road, Leicester LE1 7PG. (Tel: 0533-541619)
President (1991–92), Miss E. Diggory; *Sec.*, Miss A. C. Parkin.

Name of School	Founded	No. of pupils	Annual fees B'ding	Annual fees Day	Headmistress (a) Headmaster (With date of appointment)
Abbey School, Reading............	1887	768	......	£3,399	Miss B. C. L. Sheldon (1991)
Abbot's Hill, Herts.	1912	160	£8,445	£4,980	Mrs J. Kingsley (1979)
Adcote School, Shropshire	1907	100	£7,290	£4,320	Mrs S. B. Cecchet (1979)
Alice Ottley School, Worcester	1883	602	£7,197	£3,756	Miss C. Sibbit (1986)
Amberfield School, Ipswich........	1952	173	......	£3,225	Mrs P. F. Webb (1979)
Ashford School, Kent	1910	450	£7,569	£4,365	Mrs A. T. D. Macaire (1984)
Assumption School, N. Yorks.	1852	100	£6,654	£3,729	Mrs V. Fisher (1990)
Atherley School, Southampton (CSC)	1926	320	......	£3,429	Mrs M. Williams (1988)
Badminton School, Bristol	1858	300	£9,000	£5,000	(a) C. J. T. Gould (1981)
‡Bath High School	1875	381	......	£3,156	Miss M. A. Winfield (1985)

‡Girls' Public Day School Trust.   *CSC* Church Schools Company.

Name of School	Founded	No. of pupils	Annual fees B'ding	Annual fees Day	Headmistress (a) Headmaster (b) Principal (With date of appointment)
Battle Abbey School, E. Sussex	1912	126†	£6,870	£4,140	(a) D. J. A. Teall (1982)
Bedford High School..............	1882	774	£7,572	£3,969	Mrs D. M. Willis (1987)
Bedgebury School, Kent	1860	340	£8,721	£5,400	Mrs M. E. A. Kaye (1987)
‡Belvedere School, Liverpool	1880	435	......	£3,156	Miss S. Downs (1972)
Benenden School, Kent	1923	414	£10,500	......	Mrs G. D. duCharme (1985)
Beresford House School, E. Sussex .	1902	195	£8,475	£4,575	Miss S. B. Jackson (1988)
Berkhamsted School, Herts.	1888	452	£7,061	£3,926	Miss V. E. M. Shepherd (1980)
‡Birkenhead High School	1901	750	......	£3,156	Mrs K. R. Irving (1986)
‡Blackheath High School, SE3	1880	335	......	£3,684	Miss R. K. Musgrave (1989)
Bolton School, Lancs.	1877	935	......	£3,585	Mrs M. A. Spurr (1979)
Bradford Girls' Grammar School ...	1875	690	......	£2,796°	Mrs L. J. Warrington (1987)
‡Brighton and Hove High School ...	1876	510	£5,724	£3,156	Miss R. A. Woodbridge (1989)
Brigidine Convent, Windsor	1948	325	......	£2,985°	Mrs M. B. Cairns (1986)
‡Bromley High School, Kent	1883	510	......	£3,684	Mrs E. J. Hancock (1989)
Bruton School, Somerset	1900	518	£5,430	£2,940	Mrs J. M. Wade (1987)
Burgess Hill School, W. Sussex	1906	315	£7,350	£4,350	Mrs B. H. Webb (1979)
Bury Grammar School, Lancs.	1884	826	......	£2,790	Miss J. M. Lawley (1987)
Casterton School, Cumbria	1823	323	£7,332	£4,512	(a) A. F. Thomas (1990)
‡Central Newcastle High School	1895	570	......	£3,156	Mrs A. M. Chapman (1985)
Channing School, N6	1885	455	......	£4,545	Mrs I. R. Raphael (1984)
‡Charters-Ancaster School, E. Sussex	1906	179	£6,732	£3,432	Mrs K. Lewis (1990)
Cheltenham Ladies' College, Glos...	1853	850	£10,110	£6,420	(b) Miss E. Castle (1987)
City of London School for Girls, EC2.....................	1894	550	......	£4,100	Lady France (1986)
Clarendon School, Bedford	1898	183	£8,160	£4,740	Mrs M. Crane (1990)
Clifton High School, Bristol	1877	490	£6,750	£3,465	Mrs J. D. Walters (1985)
Cobham Hall, Kent	1962	250	£9,570°	£6,420°	Mrs R. J. McCarthy (1989)
Colston's Girls' School, Bristol	1891	625	......	£2,934	Mrs J. P. Franklin (1989)
Combe Bank School, Kent	1868	250	£6,450	£4,095	Mrs A. J. K. Austin (1982)
Commonweal Lodge School, Surrey	1916	150	......	£3,135	Miss J. M. Brown (1982)
Cranford House School, Oxon.	1931	102	......	£3,330	Miss T. A. Spencer (1980)
Croft House School, Dorset	1941	200	£7,725	£5,370	Mrs S. Rawlinson (1985)
Croham Hurst School, Surrey	1899	333	......	£3,480	Mrs J. M. Shelmerdine (1986)
‡Croydon High School, Surrey	1874	704	......	£3,684	Mrs P. E. Davies (1990)
Dame Alice Harpur School, Bedford	1882	800	......	£3,261	Mrs R. Randle (1990)
Dame Allan's Girls' School, Newcastle upon Tyne	1705	460†	......	£2,868	(b) T. A. Willcocks (1988)
*Derby High School	1892	286	......	£3,540	(a) Dr G. H. Goddard (1983)
Downe House, Berks.	1907	432	£9,855	£7,140	Miss S. Cameron (1989)
Dunottar School, Surrey	1926	448	......	£1,905	Miss J. Burnell (1985)
Durham High School	1884	287	......	£2,583°	Miss B. E. Stephenson (1978)
Edgbaston Church of England College......................	1886	300	......	£3,543	(a) I. J. Walkley (1979)
Edgbaston High School	1876	559	......	£3,510	Mrs S. J. Horsman (1987)
Edgehill College, Devon	1884	370	£7,545	£4,725	Mrs E. M. Burton (1987)
Ellerslie, Worcs.	1922	250	£8,925	£5,805	Mrs E. M. Baker (1988)
*Elmslie Girls' School, Lancs.	1918	350	......	£2,892	Miss E. M. Smithies (1978)
Eothen School, Surrey (CSC)	1892	160	......	£3,855	Miss D. C. Raine (1973)
Farlington School, W. Sussex	1896	243	£7,095	£4,380	Mrs P. Metham (1987)
Farnborough Hill, Hants.	1889	500	......	£3,489	Sr E. McCormack (1988)
Farringtons, Kent...............	1911	300	£7,356	£4,026	Mrs B. J. Stock (1987)
Felixstowe College, Suffolk	1929	270	£8,085°	£4,950°	Mrs A. F. Woodings (1989)
Fernhill Manor School, Hants.	1890	176	£6,795	£4,335	(a) Rev. A. J. Folks (1985)
Francis Holland School, NW1......	1878	360	......	£4,140	Mrs P. H. Parsonson (1988)
Francis Holland School, SW1	1881	175	......	£4,560	Mrs J. A. Anderson (1982)
Gateways School, Leeds	1941	210	......	£2,850	Miss L. M. Brown (1984)
Godolphin School, Wilts.	1726	345	£8,865	£5,265	Mrs H. Fender (1990)
Godolphin and Latymer School, W6	1905	700	......	£4,200	Miss M. Rudland (1986)
Greenacre School, Surrey	1933	360	£7,284	£3,831	Mrs P. M. Wood (1990)
The Grove School, Hindhead, Surrey	1877	200	£6,810	£4,185	(a) C. Brooks (1984)
Guildford High School (CSC)	1888	446	......	£3,582°	Mrs S. H. Singer (1991)
Haberdashers' Aske's School for Girls, Herts.	1873	840	......	£3,030	Mrs P. Penney (1991)
Haberdashers' Monmouth School, Gwent	1891	533	£6,213	£3,288	Miss H. L. Gichard (1986)
Harrogate Ladies' College	1893	400	£7,485	£5,025	Mrs J. C. Lawrance (1974)
Headington School, Oxford........	1915	570	£7,146	£3,648	Miss E. M. Tucker (1982)
Heathfield School, Ascot, Berks. ...	1900	220	£10,500	......	Mrs S. E. Watkins (1982)

*Woodard Corporation School.   ‡Girls' Public Day School Trust.   *CSC* Church Schools Company.
†Boys in VI form.   °1991 figure.

Name of School	Founded	No. of pupils	Annual fees B'ding	Annual fees Day	Headmistress (a) Headmaster (b) Principal (With date of appointment)
‡Heathfield School, Pinner, Middx. . .	1900	354	......	£3,684	Mrs J. Merritt (1988)
Hethersett Old Hall School, Norwich	1928	220	£6,450	£3,345	Mrs V. M. Redington (1983)
Highclare School, W. Midlands	1932	340†	......	£2,745	Mrs C. A. Hanson (1974)
Hollygirt School, Nottingham	1877	316	......	£2,940	Mrs M. R. Banks (1985)
Holy Child School, Birmingham ...	1933	222	£6,870	£3,852	Miss J. M. Johnson (1987)
Holy Trinity Convent School, Bromley......................	1886	305	......	£3,498	Sr B. Wetz (1986)
Holy Trinity School, Kidderminster	1903	232	......	£2,550	Mrs S. M. Bell (1990)
Howell's School, Denbigh, Clwyd...	1859	298	£8,400	£5,400	Mrs M. Steel (1991)
‡Howell's School, Llandaff, Cardiff . .	1860	573	£6,456	£3,156	Mrs C. J. Fitz (1991)
Hull High School (*CSC*)	1890	420	£4,872	£3,045	Miss C. M. B. Radcliffe (1976)
Hulme Grammar School, Oldham ...	1895	500	......	£2,667°	Mrs A. Groom (1985)
Huyton College, Liverpool	1894	207	£6,720°	£2,955°	Mrs C. Bradley (1991)
‡Ipswich High School	1878	406	......	£3,156	Miss P. M. Hayworth (1971)
James Allen's Girls' School, SE22 ..	1741	720	......	£3,750°	Mrs B. Davies (1984)
School of Jesus and Mary, Suffolk ..	1860	200	......	£3,210	Mrs E. A. McKay (1982)
Kent College......................	1885	276	£8,355	£4,980	Miss B. Crompton (1990)
King Edward VI High School for Girls, Birmingham	1883	550	......	£3,381	Miss E. W. Evans (1977)
King's HS for Girls, Warwick......	1879	550	......	£3,126	Mrs J. M. Anderson (1987)
Kingsley School, Warwicks.	1884	412	£6,420°	£2,970°	Mrs M. A. Webster (1988)
Lady Eleanor Holles School, Middx.	1711	620	......	£3,900	Miss E. M. Candy (1981)
La Retraite School, Wilts.	1953	200	......	£3,450	Mrs M. Paisey (1986)
La Sagesse Convent High School, Newcastle upon Tyne	1906	360	......	£2,916	Mrs D. C. Parker (1988)
La Sagesse Convent School, Hants..	1896	135	......	£2,400	Sr Thomas Cox (1977)
Lavant House School, W. Sussex ...	1952	150	£7,605	£4,545	Mrs Y. Graham (1990)
Lawnside, Worcs.	1818	100	£8,685	£4,980	Miss J. Harvey (1991)
Leeds Girls' High School	1876	600	......	£3,129°	Miss P. A. Randall (1977)
Leicester High School	1906	290	......	£3,210	Mrs D. Buchan (1982)
Loughborough High School	1850	535	£5,085	£3,160	Miss J. E. L. Harvatt (1978)
Luckley-Oakfield School, Berks. ..	1895	290	£6,585	£4,080	(a) R. C. Blake (1984)
Malvern Girls' College, Worcs. ...	1893	525	£9,468	£6,312	Dr V. B. Payne (1986)
Manchester High School	1874	732	......	£3,195	Miss M. M. Moon (1983)
Maynard School, Exeter	1877	477	......	£3,048	Miss F. Murdin (1980)
Merchant Taylors' School, Liverpool......................	1888	635	......	£3,168	Miss E. J. Panton (1988)
Micklefield School, E. Sussex	1910	170	£8,250	£4,725	(a) E. Reynolds (1987)
Moira House School, E. Sussex	1875	300	£8,958	£5,784	(a) A. R. Underwood (1975)
More House School, SW1	1953	235	......	£4,200	Miss M. Connell (1991)
Moreton Hall, Shropshire	1913	346	£9,270	£6,450	(b) M. J. Maloney (1990)
Mount School, York	1831	285	£7,620	£5,070	Miss B. J. Windle (1986)
Newcastle upon Tyne Church HS ..	1885	375	......	£2,985	Miss P. E. Davies (1974)
New Hall, Essex	1642	550	£8,175°	£5,235°	Sr. M. M. Horton (1986)
Northampton High School	1878	527	......	£3,105	Mrs L. A. Mayne (1988)
North Foreland Lodge, Hants.	1909	187	£8,850	......	Miss D. L. Matthews (1983)
North London Collegiate School ..	1850	702	......	£3,942	Mrs J. L. Clanchy (1986)
Northwood College, Middx.	1878	480	......	£3,960	Mrs J. A. Mayou (1991)
‡Norwich High School	1875	598	......	£3,156	Mrs V. C. Bidwell (1985)
‡Nottingham High School..........	1875	561	......	£3,684	Mrs C. Bowering (1984)
‡Notting Hill and Ealing High School	1873	810	......	£3,156	Mrs S. M. Whitfield
Ockbrook School, Derby	1799	225	£5,046	£2,745	Dr M. Rennie (1987)
Old Palace School, Surrey	1887	600	......	£3,222	Miss K. L. Hilton (1974)
‡Oxford High School	1875	557	......	£3,156	Mrs J. Townsend (1981)
Palmers Green High School, N21 ..	1905	320	......	£3,150	Mrs S. Grant (1989)
Park School, Somerset	1851	95	£5,280°°	£3,150°°	Mrs M. J. Hannon (1987)
Parsons Mead, Surrey	1897	470	£7,350	£3,930	Miss E. B. Plant (1990)
Penrhos College, Clwyd	1880	274	£7,140°	£4,890°	(a) N. C. Peacock (1974)
Perse School for Girls, Cambridge ..	1881	550	......	£3,570	Miss H. S. Smith (1989)
*Peterborough High School	1939	225	£6,540	£3,255	Mrs A. Storey (1977)
Pipers Corner School, Bucks.	1930	375	£7,620	£4,230	Dr M. M. Wilson (1986)
Polam Hall, Co. Durham	1848	350	£6,990	£3,420	Mrs H. C. Hamilton (1987)
‡Portsmouth High School	1882	503	......	£3,156	Mrs J. M. Dawtrey (1984)
Princess Helena College, Herts. ..	1820	150	£8,250	£5,850	Miss H. Davidson-Wall (1990)
Prior's Field, Surrey	1902	250	£8,010	£5,055	Mrs J. M. McCallum (1987)
‡Putney High School, SW15	1893	596	......	£3,684	Mrs P. A. Penney (1987)

‡ Girls' Public Day School Trust.   *CSC* Church Schools Company.   † Boys in VI form.   ° 1991 figure.
°° 1990 figure.

Name of School	Founded	No. of pupils	Annual fees B'ding	Annual fees Day	Headmistress (a) Headmaster (b) Principal (With date of appointment)
Queen Anne's School, Berks.	1698	400	£8,136°	£5,085°	Miss A. M. Scott (1977)
*Queen Ethelburga's College, York .	1912	150	£7,080	£4,245	Mrs J. M. Town (1988)
*Queen Margaret's School, York	1901	360	£8,400	£5,325	(a) C. S. McGarrigle (1983)
Queen Mary School, Lytham, Lancs.	1930	600	......	£2,715	Miss M. C. Ritchie (1981)
Queen's College, W1	1848	410	£5,625°	£3,825°	Mrs P. J. Fleming (1983)
Queen's Gate School, SW7.........	1891	180	......	£1,428	(b) Mrs A. M. Holyoak (1987)
Queen's School, Chester	1878	430	......	£3,012	Miss D. M. Skilbeck (1989)
Queenswood, Herts.	1894	410	£9,600	£6,075	Mrs A. M. B. Butler (1981)
Redland High School, Bristol	1882	455	......	£3,165	Mrs C. Lear (1989)
Red Maids' School, Bristol	1634	479	£6,396	£3,198	Miss S. Hampton (1987)
Rickmansworth Masonic School, Herts.	1788	530	£6,249	£3,582	(a) D. L. Curtis (1980)
Roedean School, Brighton.........	1885	475	£10,740	......	Mrs A. R. Longley (1984)
Rosemead, W. Sussex	1919	166	£8,085	£4,680	(b) Mrs H. Kingham (1991)
Royal Naval School, Surrey	1840	290	£7,812	£5,208	Dr J. L. Clough (1987)
Royal School, Bath	1864	326	£9,198	£5,871°	Dr J. McClure (1987)
Runton and Sutherland School, Norfolk	1911	155	£6,765	£4,059	Miss A. Ritchie (1990)
Rye St Antony School (RC), Oxford	1930	400	£6,540	£3,675	Miss A. M. Jones (1990)
Sacred Heart School (RC), Kent ...	1915	200	£9,240	£5,250	(a) Dr J. A. Fallon (1979)
St Albans High School, Herts.	1889	710	......	£3,375°	Miss E. M. Diggory (1983)
St Andrew's School, Bedford	1897	200	......	£2,625	Mrs J. E. Stephen (1991)
St Anne's School, Cumbria	1863	400	£7,220	£5,460	(a) M. P. Hawkins (1986)
St Antony's-Leweston School (RC), Dorset	1891	400	£7,440°	£4,725°	Mrs P. Cartwright (1983)
St Catherine's School, Surrey	1885	451	£7,125	£4,350	(a) J. R. Palmer (1982)
*School of St Clare, Penzance	1889	130	£6,765	£3,579	Mrs I. Halford (1986)
St David's School, Middx.	1716	250†	£7,245°	£4,185	Mrs J. G. Osborne (1985)
St Dunstan's Abbey, Devon	1850	234	£5,490	£3,390	Mrs R. A. Bye (1991)
*St Elphin's School, Derbys.	1844	250	£8,193	£4,770	(a) A. P. C. Pollard (1979)
St Felix School, Suffolk	1897	330	£7,689°	£4,755°	Mrs S. R. Campion (1991)
St Francis' College (RC), Herts. ...	1933	216	£7,740	£3,975	Mrs J. Frith (1987)
S. Gabriel's School, Berks.	1929	160	......	£3,585°	(a) D. Cobb (1990)
St George's School, Ascot, Berks. ..	1923	285	£8,850	£4,950	Mrs A. M. Griggs (1989)
School of S. Helen and S. Katharine, Oxon.	1903	519	£6,075	£3,150	Miss Y. Paterson (1973)
St Helen's School, Middx.	1899	550	£7,356	£3,900	Mrs Y.A. Burne, PH.D. (1987)
*S. Hilary's School, Cheshire	1880	200	......	£3,360	Mrs J. Tracey (1985)
St Hilary's School, Sevenoaks, Kent	1942	160	......	£4,590	Mrs P. Miles (1977)
St James's and the Abbey, Worcs. ..	1896	190	£8,640	£5,760	Miss E. M. Mullenger (1986)
St Joseph's Convent School (RC), Berks.	1909	500	......	£3,225	Mrs V. Brookes (1990)
St Joseph's School, Lincoln	1905	200	£5,940	£2,940	Mrs A. Scott (1983)
St Leonards-Mayfield School, E. Sussex	1850	540	£8,150	£5,430	Sr J. Sinclair (1980)
St Margaret's School, Bushey, Herts.	1749	406	£7,050	£4,500	Mrs S. K. Law (1985)
*St Margaret's School, Exeter	1904	455	£4,608°	£2,817°	Mrs J. M. Giddings (1984)
St Martin's School, Solihull	1941	250	......	£3,585°	Mrs S. J. Williams (1988)
*School of St Mary and St Anne, Abbots Bromley, Staffs	1874	300	£8,655	£5,490	(a) A. Grigg (1989)
St Mary's Hall, Brighton	1836	245	£7,626	£4,779	Mrs M. T. Broadbent (1988)
St Mary's School (RC), Ascot, Berks.	1885	330	£8,940	£5,364	Sr M. M. Orchard (1982)
St Mary's School, Calne, Wilts.	1872	318	£9,525	£5,484	Miss D. H. Burns (1985)
St Mary's School, Cambridge	1898	565	£5,415	£3,045	Miss M. Conway (1989)
St Mary's School, Colchester	1908	300	......	£2,955	Mrs G. M. G. Mouser (1981)
St Mary's School, Gerrards Cross ..	1872	200	......	£3,870	Mrs J. P. G. Smith (1984)
St Mary's School (RC), Shaftesbury	1945	310	£8,070	£5,160	Sr M. Campion Livesey (1985)
St Mary's School, Wantage, Oxon. .	1873	300	£8,700	......	Mrs P. H. Johns (1980)
*S. Michaels Burton Park, W. Sussex	1844	182	£8,190	£5,400	Mrs L. J. Griffin (1991)
St Michael's, Limpsfield, Surrey ...	1850	133	£7,725	£4,245	M. J. Hustler, PH.D. (1989)
St Paul's Girls' School, W6	1904	622	......	£5,010	Mrs H. Williams (High Mistress) (1989)
St Swithun's School, Winchester ..	1884	441	£9,210	£5,565	Miss J. E. Jefferson (1986)
St Teresa's Convent School, Dorking	1928	340	£6,705°	£3,426°	(a) L. Allan (1987)
Selwyn School, Glos..............	—	262	£6,030	£3,450	(a) A. Beatson (1990)

*Woodard Corporation School.   °1991 figure.   †Boys in VI form.

Name of School	Founded	No. of pupils	Annual fees B'ding	Annual fees Day	Headmistress (a) Headmaster (With date of appointment)
‡Sheffield High School	1878	503	......	£3,156	Mrs M. A. Houston (1989)
Sherborne School for Girls, Dorset	1899	464	£8,280°	£5,520°	Miss J. M. Taylor (1985)
‡Shrewsbury High School	1885	393	......	£3,156	Miss S. Gardner (1990)
Sir William Perkins's School, Surrey	1725	496	......	£3,085	Mrs A. F. Darlow (1982)
‡South Hampstead High School, NW3	1876	533	......	£3,684	Mrs D. A. Burgess (1975)
Stamford High School, Lincs.	1876	740	£6,600	£3,300	Miss G. K. Bland (1978)
Stonar School, Wilts.	1921	401	£7,908	£4,380	Mrs S. Hopkinson (1985)
Stover School, Devon	1932	265	£5,265°°	£2,742°°	Mrs W. E. Lunel (1984)
Stratford House School, Kent	1912	246	......	£3,915	Mrs A. A. Williamson (1974)
‡Streatham Hill and Clapham High School, SW2	1887	386	......	£3,684	Miss G. M. Ellis (1979)
Sunderland Church High School (CSC)	1884	233†	......	£3,285	Mrs M. Thrush (1980)
Surbiton High School (CSC), Surrey	1884	436	......	£3,390	Mrs R. A. Thynne (1979)
‡Sutton High School, Surrey	1884	566	......	£3,684	Miss A. E. Cavendish (1980)
‡Sydenham High School, SE26	1887	452	......	£3,684	Mrs G. Baker (1988)
Talbot Heath, Dorset	1886	481	£6,948	£3,975	Mrs C. Dipple (1991)
Teesside High School, Cleveland	1970	540	......	£2,850°	Mrs H. Coles (1982)
Tormead School, Surrey	1905	300	......	£4,080	Mrs H. E. M. Alleyne (1992)
Truro High School	1880	300	£6,627	£3,630	Mrs J.F. Marshall (1984)
*Tudor Hall School, Oxon.	1850	250	£8,790	£5,610	Miss N. Godfrey (1984)
Upper Chine, Isle of Wight	1799	198	£7,500	£3,990	Dr H. Harvey (1990)
Ursuline Convent School, Kent	1904	300	£7,968	£4,035	Sr M. Murphy (1977)
Ursuline High School, Ilford	1903	400	......	£3,441	Miss J. Reddington (1990)
Wadhurst College, E. Sussex	1930	210	£8,385	£5,340	(a) R. Purdom (1989)
Wakefield Girls' High School	1878	800	......	£3,339	Mrs P. A. Langham (1987)
Walthamstow Hall, Kent	1838	386	£8,610	£4,665	Mrs J. S. Lang (1984)
Wentworth Milton Mount, Dorset	1962	315	£7,305	£4,545	Miss S. Coe (1991)
Westfield School, Newcastle upon Tyne	1962	212	......	£3,339	Mrs M. Farndale (1990)
West Heath, Kent	1867	168	£9,000	£6,846	(b) Mrs L. Cohn-Sherbok (1988)
Westholme School, Lancs.	1923	620	......	£2,670	(b) Mrs L. Croston (1988)
Westonbirt, Glos.	1928	280	£8,880	£5,712	Mrs G. Hylson-Smith (1986)
‡Wimbledon High School, SW19	1880	486	......	£3,684	Mrs R. A. Smith (1982)
Wispers School, Surrey	1946	190	£7,305	£4,710	(a) L. H. Beltran (1978)
Withington Girls' School, Manchester	1890	470	......	£3,075	Mrs M. Kenyon (1986)
Woldingham School, Surrey	1842	450	£9,045	£5,472	Dr P. Dineen (1985)
Wroxhall Abbey School, Warwick	1872	100	£8,196	£4,938	Mrs I. D. M. Iles (1980)
Wychwood School, Oxford	1897	160	£5,970	£3,570	Mrs M. L. Duffill (1981)
Wycombe Abbey School, Bucks.	1896	490	£9,072°	......	Mrs J. M. Goodland (1989)
Wykeham House School, Fareham, Hants	1913	190	......	£3,141	Mrs E. M. Moore (1983)
York College for Girls (CSC)	1908	301	......	£3,372	Mrs J. L. Clare (1982)
Scotland					
Kilgraston School, Perthshire	1930	245	£7,350	£3,780	Sr B. Farquharson (1987)
Laurel Bank School, Glasgow	1903	280	......	£3,342	Miss L. G. Egginton (1984)
Mary Erskine School, Edinburgh	1694	570	£6,507	£3,366	(b) P. F. J. Tobin (1989)
Oxenfoord Castle School, Midlothian	1931	80	£8,970	£4,140	Miss M. Carmichael (1979)
Park School, Glasgow	1880	300	......	£3,195	Mrs M. E. Myatt (1986)
St Denis and Cranley School, Edinburgh	1858	220	£7,260	£3,615	Mrs J. M. Munro (1984)
St George's School, Edinburgh	1888	550	£6,915	£3,525	Mrs J. G. Scott (1986)
St Leonards School, St Andrews	1877	330	£9,930	£5,220	Mrs L. E. James (1988)
St Margaret's School, Aberdeen	1846	402	......	£2,883	Miss L. M. Ogilvie (1989)
St Margaret's School, Edinburgh	1890	500	£6,648	£3,350	Mrs M. J. Cameron (1984)
Wellington School for Girls, Ayr	1849	480	£7,350	£3,690	Mrs D. A. Gardner (1988)
Channel Islands					
The Ladies' College, Guernsey	1872	325	......	£1,575°	Miss J. Honey (1976)

‡ Girls' Public Day School Trust, 26 Queen Anne's Gate, SW1H 9AN. * Woodard Corporation School.
CSC Church Schools Company, 1A Doughty Street, WC1N 2PH. † Boys in VI form. ° 1991 figure.
°° 1990 figure.

EVENTS OF THE YEAR
September 1, 1990–August 31, 1991

BRITISH AFFAIRS

(For the Gulf conflict and the events leading up to it, including certain British domestic events, *see* **The Gulf Conflict**.)

(1990). Sept. 1. The Prince of Wales underwent a second operation on his broken right arm. **3.** The Trades Union Congress annual conference opened in Blackpool. **6.** The House of Commons was recalled for a two-day emergency debate on the Gulf crisis; the Government's policy on the Gulf crisis was supported by 437 votes to 35. **7.** Michael Forsyth, MP, resigned as chairman of the Scottish Conservative Party and was replaced by Lord Sanderson of Bowden, who relinquished his post as Minister of State at the Scottish Office. He was replaced there by Mr Forsyth. **10.** At a meeting in Paris, miners' leaders agreed to transfer a large sum of disputed money from the International Miners' Organization to the National Union of Mineworkers; on Sept. 13 the NUM executive decided to drop their High Court action against NUM president Arthur Scargill over the use of Soviet funds during the miners' strike of 1984–85. **11.** The official report on the Lockerbie disaster was published. **15.** The Social and Liberal Democrat conference opened in Blackpool. The Government announced that it would sue British Aerospace for the repayment of £44·4 million, paid as a 'sweetener' to the company when it bought the Rover group. **19.** The Scottish National Party conference opened in Perth. **20.** Shares in Polly Peck International were suspended at the company's request after falling from 245p to 108p in a few hours as a result of investigations into the company by the Serious Fraud Office. **24.** The Government imposed a statutory ban on the use of specified cattle offal in the manufacture of all animal food, following confirmation that a pig had contracted bovine spongiform encephalopathy (BSE). **27.** The Knowsley South by-election took place. The Foreign Secretary (Douglas Hurd) announced that Britain would resume diplomatic relations with Iran. **29.** The Labour Party conference opened in Blackpool. On Oct. 3 the conference voted for defence spending to be cut to the average of other western European countries, against the advice of the party leadership, but supported the leadership's stance on the Gulf crisis.

Oct. 1. Britain joined the European exchange rate mechanism. **9.** The Conservative Party conference opened in Bournemouth. **10.** Delegates to a special conference of the NUM cleared Arthur Scargill, president, and Peter Heathfield, general secretary, of allegations

that they had misapplied funds during the 1984–85 strike. **11.** Patrick Nicholls, an Under-Secretary of State at the Department of the Environment, resigned after being charged with drinking and driving while attending the Conservative Party conference in Bournemouth. **14.** The Prime Minister (Margaret Thatcher) held talks with President de Klerk of South Africa at Chequers. **18.** The Eastbourne by-election took place. The report on the Kegworth air disaster was published. **20.** A protest against the community charge in Brixton, London, ended in violent clashes between police and demonstrators; eleven people were treated in hospital and 105 arrests were made. **23.** President Cossiga of Italy arrived in Britain for a five-day State visit. **24.** The directors of Polly Peck International applied to have administrators appointed after failing to raise fresh capital to pay the company's creditors; the administrators confirmed on Oct. 25 that the company owed a total of £1·3 million million, and Barclays de Zoete Wedd sued chairman Asil Nadir for bankruptcy. **30.** The drilling of a two-inch borehole linked the two halves of the Channel Tunnel service tunnel.

Nov. 1. The Parliamentary session ended. Sir Geoffrey Howe, Leader of the House of Commons, resigned from the Cabinet in protest at Mrs Thatcher's attitude to the European Community. **2.** John MacGregor was appointed Leader of the House of Commons and was replaced as Education Secretary by Kenneth Clarke. William Waldegrave succeeded Mr Clarke as Health Secretary. It was announced that Sky Television and British Satellite Broadcasting would merge their operations. **4.** The CBI annual conference opened in Glasgow. **5.** The George Cross was awarded to an army bomb disposal officer who was badly wounded while defusing a bomb in Londonderry in Oct. 1989. **7.** The State Opening of Parliament took place. **8.** By-elections took place in Bradford North and Bootle. **11.** A man set himself on fire during the two-minute silence at the Remembrance Day ceremony in Whitehall. **12.** The Prince and Princess of Wales attended the enthronement of Emperor Akihito of Japan. The report on the Piper Alpha disaster was published. **13.** In a speech to the Commons explaining the reasons for his resignation, Sir Geoffrey Howe attacked Mrs Thatcher's style of government and her hostility to closer links with the rest of Europe. **14.** Michael Heseltine, MP, announced that he would challenge Mrs Thatcher for the leadership of the Conservative Party. **16.** Mrs Thatcher arrived in Paris for the three-day Conference on Security and Co-operation in Europe. **20.** In the ballot for the leadership of the Conservative Party, Margaret Thatcher received 204 votes and Michael Heseltine 152 votes; there were 16 abstentions. Both candidates declared their intention to stand in the second round of the contest. The Leader of the Opposition (Neil Kinnock) tabled a motion of no confidence in Mrs Thatcher's government; on Nov. 22 the motion was defeated by 367 votes to 247 votes. **22.** Margaret Thatcher announced that she would not be standing in the second round of the contest for the leadership of the Conservative Party. Douglas Hurd (the Foreign Secretary) and John Major (the Chancellor of the Exchequer) put their names forward for the second ballot. **27.** In the second ballot for the leadership of the Conservative Party, John Major received 185 votes, Michael Heseltine 131 votes, and Douglas Hurd 56 votes. Mr Heseltine and Mr Hurd pledged their support for Mr Major and it was decided not to hold a third ballot. **28.** Mrs Thatcher resigned as Prime Minister. The Queen asked John Major to form a new administration and Mr Major kissed hands upon his appointment as Prime Minister. Britain restored diplomatic relations with Syria. **29.** By-elections were held in Paisley North and Paisley South.

Dec. 1. Opposition members called for the resignation of Alan Clark, the Minister for Defence Procurement, for assisting the export of munitions-making machinery to Iraq after Britain had imposed an arms embargo in 1984. The first stage in the building of the Channel Tunnel was completed with the breakthrough of the service tunnel. **5.** The Environment Secretary (Michael Heseltine) announced in the House of Commons a full review of the structure and finance of local government, and offered the opposition parties a part in the discussions. The Levitt Group, one of Britain's largest financial advisory firms, went into receivership; chairman and chief executive Roger Levitt resigned amid allegations of financial irregularities. **8.** Severe weather hit many parts of Britain; the snow continued on Dec. 9, causing the deaths of at least ten people. **11.** The Prime Minister (John Major) announced that an extra £42 million would be made available in an out-of-court settlement to haemophiliacs who had been infected with the Aids virus by contaminated blood supplied by the NHS. The Cheltenham Conservative Association voted to expel Bill Galbraith, a party member who had used racially abusive language about John Taylor, the party's black parliamentary candidate for the constituency. **16.** Cahal Daly was installed as the new Archbishop of Armagh and Primate of All Ireland. **17.** The Minister of State for Health (Virginia Bottomley) signed an agreement with the British Medical Association and the royal medical colleges with the ultimate aim of a maximum 72-hour working

week for junior doctors. The report into the Purley train crash was published. **19.** The national executive committee of the Labour Party voted to suspend meetings of the Birkenhead constituency party, where the sitting MP, Frank Field, was deselected in 1989, pending an inquiry into its activities. **20.** The Prime Minister flew to Washington for talks with President Bush. **22.** The Prince of Wales visited British forces in Saudi Arabia. **24.** Salman Rushdie announced that he had accepted the Islamic faith, and undertook not to publish a paperback edition of *The Satanic Verses* while any risk of further offence existed. **25.** Gales and heavy rain from Dec. 25–27 caused the deaths of at least three people. **29.** Classified information outlining allied deployments in the Gulf were stolen from the car of an RAF staff officer in London; the documents were later recovered and the thief returned a computer by post to the Ministry of Defence.

(1991) Jan. 4. The Education Secretary announced that the full national curriculum of ten subjects would be taught to children only up to the age of 14, and not to 16 as originally intended. **5–6.** Thirty people died in gales affecting many parts of Britain and Ireland. **7.** The Department of Education published final details of the national curriculum for seven year-olds in English, mathematics and science. **8.** The Prime Minister visited British troops in Saudi Arabia. **10.** The Cabinet put Britain on a war footing. **12.** A large demonstration took place in central London against war in the Gulf. **13.** The Prime Minister held talks with the US Secretary of State, James Baker, in London. Kuwaiti exiles demonstrated in London. **14.** The Home Secretary announced a new five-year licence fee agreement with the BBC. **15.** MPs voted 534–57 in support of the Government after a debate in the Commons on its handling of the Gulf crisis; 53 Labour MPs voted against the Government, including two frontbenchers, Maria Fyfe and John McFall, who later resigned, and a further 31 Labour MPs abstained. A War Cabinet was formed, comprising the Prime Minister, the Foreign Secretary, the Defence Secretary, the Energy Secretary and the Attorney-General. **17.** The Prime Minister told the Commons that the first 24 hours of the Gulf conflict had been very successful; he later made a television broadcast to explain the reasons for British involvement in the conflict. An anti-war demonstration took place in London. The Environment Secretary announced that the community charge transitional relief scheme would be replaced by the community charge reduction scheme. **18.** The Home Office announced that all Iraqis would be refused entry to Britain from Jan. **19.** Seven Palestinians were arrested and served with deportation orders. **20.** The Supreme Council of British Muslims called on Britain and the USA to withdraw their troops from the Gulf. The Board of Deputies of British Jews praised the Israeli government for not retaliating to Iraqi Scud missile attacks. **21.** In a debate on the Gulf conflict in the Commons, the Prime Minister ruled out any prospect of a ceasefire until Iraq had withdrawn from Kuwait. MPs voted 563–34 in support of British action in the Gulf; the Opposition front bench spokesman on social security, Tony Banks, voted against the motion and later resigned from the Shadow Cabinet. The Iraqi ambassador in London, Dr Azmi Shafiq al-Salihi, was summoned to the Foreign Office and told that Iraq's treatment of prisoners of war captured since the Gulf conflict began contravened the Geneva Convention. The chairman of the Islamic Society for the Promotion of Religious Tolerance denounced the refusal of the Supreme Council of British Muslims to condemn Iraq's invasion of Kuwait. **22.** The Prime Minister condemned the latest Iraqi Scud missile attack on Israel and expressed the hope that Israel would continue to refrain from retaliation. John Battle resigned as a Labour Party whip in protest at his party's support of the use of force in the Gulf. **23.** Fourteen Iraqi students were deported and 31 Iraqis were arrested. The Education Minister (Tim Eggar) announced that grant-maintained schools would receive funding equivalent to £240 per child for 1991–92 and that local authority-funded schools would receive £100 per child. **24.** The Home Office announced that 33 detained Iraqis would be handed over to the Ministry of Defence as prisoners of war. **25.** Two Iraqis and two Palestinians were deported. The Education Secretary announced a new examination for 14 year-olds, consisting mainly of written tests in at least seven subjects. **28.** The Chancellor of the Exchequer (Norman Lamont) attended a meeting in Brussels of EC finance ministers; he attempted to secure financial assistance towards the cost of Britain's war effort in the Gulf. **29.** The Iraqi ambassador in London was summoned to the Foreign Office to receive a protest after reports that an allied POW had been killed in an air raid in Baghdad. **30.** The Foreign Secretary visited Bonn for talks with Chancellor Kohl and the German Foreign Minister; Germany pledged £270 million and extra equipment to Britain's war effort. The Iraqi ambassador to London left Britain at the end of his tour of duty and was not replaced. The national executive committee of the Labour party issued a policy statement reaffirming support for allied aims in the Gulf. The Prince of Wales and the Princess Royal attended the funeral in Oslo of King Olav of Norway. The Government announced that up to 20 conventionally armed US B-52 bombers would be based at RAF Fairford, Glos.; the first arrived

on Feb. 5. The department store group Lewis's went into receivership.

Feb. 6. Snow fell in many areas of Britain. Four Palestinian detainees were released. **7.** Three IRA mortar bombs were fired at Downing Street from a van parked in Whitehall; one of the bombs exploded in the garden of No. 10 Downing Street during a meeting of the War Cabinet, causing some damage but no injuries. **10.** A special meeting of the Cheltenham Conservative Party endorsed the adoption of John Taylor as their parliamentary candidate. **11.** The Prime Minister held talks with Chancellor Kohl in Bonn and then visited the families of British Gulf servicemen at Munster and RAF Bruggen. **13.** Hundreds of Iraqi civilians were killed when American planes bombed an air raid shelter in Baghdad; the Foreign Secretary later told the House of Commons that all possible care was being taken to minimize civilian casualties. **14.** Clare Short resigned as the opposition social security spokesman after the Leader of the Opposition asked her to refrain from making public statements about the Gulf war. **15.** The Prime Minister called a conditional offer of withdrawal from Kuwait by Iraq 'a bogus sham'. **16.** President Zhelev of Bulgaria began an official visit to Britain. **18.** Two bombs planted by the IRA exploded at Paddington and Victoria stations in London. No-one was injured at Paddington but one man was killed and about 40 people injured at Victoria. **19.** The Prime Minister rejected a Soviet plan for peace in the Gulf, saying that the conflict would continue until Iraq withdrew totally and unconditionally from Kuwait. **21.** The Trade and Industry select committee published a report in which Lord Young, the former Trade and Industry Secretary, was criticized for his handling of the sale of Rover to British Aerospace in 1988. **22.** Shares in National Power and PowerGen went on sale to the public at 175 pence each. **24.** The Prime Minister said that the land offensive in the Gulf (which began at 0100 GMT) had started well but that increased resistance from the Iraqis should be anticipated. The Queen made a television and radio broadcast to the nation in which she expressed hope for a just and lasting peace in the Gulf. Hundreds of Muslims marched through London to protest at the start of the allied land offensive. **25.** A bomb exploded on the London Midland Railway line at St Albans; no-one was injured and there was no admission of responsibility. The public inquiry into the rail crash at Cannon Street station on Jan. 8 opened at Church House, Westminster. The report by Lord Justice Woolf into the prison riots in 1990 was published; the Home Secretary announced a programme of prison reform. **26.** Dr George Carey, the archbishop-designate of Canterbury, was criticized for using the word 'heresy' in a magazine interview to describe opposition to the ordination of women priests; Dr Carey said that he regretted speaking of heresy rather than theological error. **27.** Nine children in Orkney were taken into care amid allegations of ritual sexual abuse; on April 4 the children were returned to their parents after Sheriff Kelbie found at Kirkwall Sheriff Court that proceedings had been 'fundamentally flawed'. The Department of Health announced that there would be an inquiry into the extent of ritual abuse in Britain. **28.** After a ceasefire had been called at 0500 GMT, the Prime Minister, said in the Commons that a durable peace must now be established in the Gulf and called on the people of Iraq to overthrow Saddam Hussein. Lord Palumbo was given permission by the House of Lords to demolish eight listed buildings in the City of London.

March 3. The Defence Secretary visited British troops in Bahrain, Kuwait and Saudi Arabia. **5.** The Prime Minister flew to the Gulf to visit British troops, to meet the Crown Prince of Kuwait, and to hold talks with King Fahd of Saudi Arabia. The last American cruise missiles based in Britain were flown out from RAF Greenham Common, Berks. **6.** Thirty-two Iraqis held as prisoners of war in Britain were released. Lord Jakobovits was awarded the Templeton Prize. **7.** The Ribble Valley by-election took place. Mr Justice Douglas Brown ruled at the High Court in Manchester that ten of the children taken into care in Rochdale in 1990 amid allegations of ritual sexual abuse should be returned to their parents immediately. **8.** The Home Secretary ordered the release of 33 Iraqi and Arab detainees. **10.** The British Pregnancy Advisory Service said that a woman who had never had sexual intercourse was receiving fertility treatment at their Birmingham clinic. **14.** Following the release of the Birmingham Six, the Home Secretary announced that a Royal Commission into the criminal justice system in England and Wales would be set up under Lord Runciman. **16.** The Prime Minister met President Bush in Bermuda for talks. **17.** The Dalai Lama arrived in Britain for a five-day visit. **18.** An all-party Commons motion was tabled calling for the removal from office of Lord Lane, who heard the 1989 appeal case brought by the Birmingham Six, and was signed by 102 MPs. **19.** The Education Secretary said that further education and sixth form colleges would be taken out of local authority control. The Labour Party tabled a motion of no-confidence in the Government due to its 'inability to rectify the damage done to the British people by the poll tax'; the motion was debated on March 27 and defeated by 358 votes to 238. **26.** The Community Charge (General Reduction) Bill passed through the House of Commons in a single day. **27.** Thirteen Labour councillors in the London Borough of Lambeth were suspended by the Labour Party's national executive committee pending further investigations into their running of the council. The House of Keys rejected a move to legalize homosexual acts between consenting adults in the Isle of Man.

April 2. Roger Cooper, a British businessman held in Iran since December 1985, returned to Britain. **3.** The Prime Minister authorized aid to be sent to the Kurdish refugees in northern Iraq. **4.** The by-election in Neath took place. **5.** Fourteen Kurdish protesters stormed the Iraqi Embassy in London; after a four-hour siege they surrendered to police. **10.** The Shadow Environment spokesman, Bryan Gould, announced Labour Party proposals for a 'fair rates' scheme to replace the community charge. **19.** Dr George Carey was enthroned as Archbishop of Canterbury. **21.** The 1991 Census was carried out. **22.** In the Shakespeare birthday lecture in Stratford-upon-Avon, the Prince of Wales criticized standards of education in British schools. The Prince and Princess of Wales left Heathrow for a five-day official visit to Brazil. The Prime Minister held talks with President de Klerk of South Africa at Downing Street. **23.** President Walesa of Poland arrived in Britain at the start of a four-day State visit. The Secretary of State for the Environment announced that the Government would replace the community charge from April 1993 with a council tax based on the value of the property and the number of adults in the household. He also published proposals for a single-tier structure of local government for England and Wales. **24.** The Prime Minister held talks with Nelson Mandela, the deputy leader of the African National Congress, at Downing Street. **25.** Sydney Bidwell, the Labour MP for Ealing, Southall, was deselected by his local constituency party.

May 2. Local government elections were held in England and Wales. **4.** A Gulf war service of thanksgiving and remembrance conducted by the Archbishop of York was held in Glasgow Cathedral. **6.** The Prince and Princess of Wales arrived in Czechoslovakia for a five-day official visit. **8.** A man was seriously injured when he was savaged by two pit bull terriers in Lincoln. **9.** The Charity Commission told the trustees of Oxfam that they had breached the laws governing charitable status and should stop using their funds for political campaigning rather than charitable work. **12.** A pop concert, The Simple Truth, was held at Wembley, to raise money for the relief of Kurdish refugees. **14.** The Queen and the Duke of Edinburgh arrived in Washington, USA, for a three-day State visit; they subsequently visited Florida and Texas. On May 16 the Queen addressed a joint meeting of the United States Congress. **16.** The Monmouth by-election took place. **18.** A six-year-old girl,

Rucsana Khan, was savaged by a pit bull terrier in Bradford and suffered multiple injuries; on May 21 the Home Secretary announced that the import of pit bull terriers and other dogs bred for fighting was banned from midnight and that emergency legislation regarding the dogs would be introduced. **20.** The leisure and property company Brent Walker announced losses of £246.8 million for 1990; on May 30 George Walker was sacked as the company's chief executive. **22.** Britain and Albania agreed to restore diplomatic relations. **23.** British Telecom announced profits of £3,080 million and 10,000 job losses. **24.** The Prince of Wales and the Foreign Secretary attended the funeral of Rajiv Gandhi in Delhi. Creditors of Polly Peck International agreed to a restructuring of the company devised by its administrators. **31.** A report by Allan Levy, QC, and Barbara Kahan was published; it severely criticized Staffordshire social services for operating a system of punishment known as 'pindown' in some of its children's homes.

June 3. Prince William underwent an operation for a depressed fracture of the skull after being accidentally hit by a golf club at school. **4.** The Dangerous Dogs Bill was given its first reading in the Commons. **6.** The Foreign and Commonwealth Office said that proposals from Col. Gaddafi intended to restore diplomatic relations between Britain and Libya were insufficient and that Libya would have to renounce its support for international terrorism. British Rail announced that it had halted all new investment projects because of a cash shortage. **10.** The High Court approved terms of settlement for compensation claims against the Government by 1,200 haemophiliacs infected by the Aids virus through contaminated blood supplied by the NHS. The Prince and Princess of Wales attended a memorial service in Münster, Germany, for British soldiers who died in the Gulf conflict. **12.** The Minister of State for Health (Virginia Bottomley) announced an agreement with doctors under which 40 per cent of junior doctors would have their working week cut to 72 hours by the end of 1994, and the rest by the end of 1996. **13.** The Government increased British Rail's public service obligations grant by £185 million, and on June 19 it loaned British Rail £215 million for its investment programme. **17.** Douglas Brand, jailed for life on spying charges in Iraq on May 17, was released after the intervention of the former Prime Minister Edward Heath. **19.** Liverpool City Council voted to privatize the city's refuse collection service in spite of a work-to-rule by refuse collectors which had left uncollected 12,000 tonnes of refuse; on June 20, 200 council staff went on strike, but on June 25 the refuse collectors reached an agreement with the council and began to clear the rubbish. **21.** The Defence Procure-

ment Minister announced that the contract for 140 new tanks for the army had been awarded to Vickers Defence Systems for the Challenger 2 tank. A Welcome Home Parade of troops from Britain's Gulf forces was held in the City of London; the Queen took the salute from a balcony at the Mansion House. **22.** Frank Field, the Labour MP for Birkenhead, was reselected as the Labour candidate for the constituency at the next election. **23.** Lloyd's announced record losses of £509.7 million.

July 2. The Armed Forces Minister announced that four RAF bases would close. **4.** The by-election at Liverpool, Walton, took place. The Defence Secretary announced that jobs at the Ministry of Defence would be cut by 35,000 over the next four years. **5.** The Bank of Credit and Commerce International (BCCI) was closed down and its assets frozen after the discovery of suspected widespread fraud. **7.** Two suspected IRA terrorists escaped from Brixton prison, London. On July 8 the Home Secretary announced an inquiry into the breakout. **11.** The Western Isles Council finance director, Donald Macleod, was suspended pending an investigation into the loss of £23 million as a result of the collapse of BCCI; on July 16 councillors set up an independent inquiry. **12.** Kurdish protesters stormed the Turkish Embassy in London after three mourners at the funeral of a political activist in Turkey were shot dead by security forces; 53 demonstrators were arrested. **15.** The meeting of the Group of Seven (G7) leaders opened in London. **16.** The Defence Secretary announced that the naval base at Rosyth would remain open but with the loss of hundreds of jobs. **17.** President Gorbachev met the G7 leaders. **18.** The Prime Minister held talks with President Gorbachev at Downing Street. **19.** The Chancellor of the Exchequer announced that an independent inquiry would be held into the closure of BCCI. **21.** James Saunders, a convicted child rapist, escaped from Broadmoor high security hospital; he was recaptured on July 22. **22.** The Prime Minister launched the 'Citizen's Charter'. An application by the Bank of England to wind up BCCI was adjourned by the High Court to allow time for a proposed rescue package and interim compensation for small investors to be considered; on July 30 the application was adjourned until Dec. **23.** The Defence Secretary confirmed in the House of Commons that the strength of the army would be reduced to 116,000 by the mid-1990s and announced plans to amalgamate 22 regiments. President Mubarak of Egypt arrived in London on a four-day State visit. The Prime Minister denied in the House of Commons that he had been aware of irregularities in the running of BCCI before June 28, 1991. The governor of the Bank of England explained to members of the Treasury select committee his decision to close the bank. 24. The official inquiry into the deaths of nine British soldiers killed in a missile attack by US planes during the Gulf war failed to establish why the pilots wrongly identified their target. 26. It was disclosed in written evidence to a Commons committee that Britain was exporting materials with military and nuclear uses to Iraq until three days after the invasion of Kuwait.

Aug. 1. Violent thunderstorms caused flooding in south-east England. 5. Extracts from a report on the escape of two IRA suspects from Brixton prison on July 7 criticized security provisions at the prison and disclosed that the police had warned in February that the prisoners were seeking to escape. 8. John McCarthy, a British hostage kidnapped in Beirut on April 17, 1986, was released from captivity; on August 11 he met the UN Secretary General at RAF Lyneham to deliver a letter from his kidnappers. 12. A man was shot dead by police after an armed siege in Telford, Shropshire. 13. Neville Norton, a building contractor detained in Saudi Arabia for nearly 16 years, was allowed to leave the country and flew back to Britain. 15. The official report into the *Marchioness* disaster was published. 19. The Government condemned the coup against President Gorbachev. 20. Prisoners rioted at Lindholme prison, Doncaster, starting fires and causing extensive damage. 26. The Prime Minister flew to the USA for a three-day visit; on Aug. 29 he agreed a programme of aid for the Soviet Union with President Bush. 27. Britain recognized the independent status of Estonia, Latvia and Lithuania. 31. Dr Jonathan Sacks was installed as Chief Rabbi of the United Hebrew Congregations of the Commonwealth.

ACCIDENTS AND DISASTERS

(1990). Sept. 14. After an explosion at a nuclear fuel processing plant at Ust-Kamenogorsk, a region of Kazakhstan, USSR, was contaminated by the toxic heavy metal beryllium and the region was declared a disaster zone.

Oct. 2. Over 130 people were killed when a plane hijacked from Xiamen crashed into two aircraft while landing at Canton airport in China.

Nov. 6. Six people died and seven were injured in a crash involving 11 vehicles on the M42 near Solihull, West Midlands. An earthquake registering 6·8 on the Richter scale struck in southern Iran, killing at least 22 people and making 12,000 homeless. 14. An aircraft crashed into a hillside on its approach to Zurich airport, killing 46. 21. A Soviet

airliner crashed near Yakutsk in Siberia, killing 176. 22. Four fishermen were drowned when their trawler *Antares* was accidentally sunk by a submarine, HMS *Trenchant*, in the Firth of Clyde.

Dec. 3. Eight people were killed when two airliners collided at Detroit Metropolitan Airport. 6. At least 12 people died when a military aircraft crashed into a secondary school near Bologna, Italy. 12. Six fishermen were drowned when their trawler *Premier* capsized in force ten gales 50 miles east of Shetland. 13. An earthquake measuring 4·7 on the Richter scale struck Sicily, killing over 12 people and leaving hundreds homeless.

(1991) Jan. 8. One person was killed and more than 500 injured when a commuter train crashed into the buffers at Cannon Street station in London; a second person died on Jan. 11.

Feb. 1. An earthquake measuring 6·7 on the Richter Scale struck an area on the Afghan–Pakistan border, killing over 1,000 people. A Boeing 737 crashed into a smaller aircraft on the runway at Los Angeles airport, killing at least 35 people. 15. In Thailand, a lorry carrying dynamite exploded, killing over 150 people.

March 13. Ten people were killed and 25 injured in a multi-vehicle crash in fog on the M4 in Berkshire.

April 10. Six fishermen were drowned when their trawler, *Wilhelmina J*, collided in fog with a cargo ship in the English Channel. 10. An Italian ferry, *Moby Prince*, caught fire after colliding with an oil tanker, the *Agip Abruzzo*, outside the port of Livorno, northern Italy; 139 people were killed. 11. A tanker, the *Haven*, exploded in the bay of Genoa during a pumping operation; five people were killed and thousands of tons of oil leaked into the sea. 14. The *Haven* sank. 22. An earthquake measuring 7·5 on the Richter scale struck Costa Rica and Panama, killing over 80 people. 29. A cyclone hit south-east Bangladesh, killing at least 140,000 people. An earthquake measuring 7·2 on the Richter scale hit Georgia, USSR; over 100 people were killed.

May 6. More than 1,000 people were evacuated from their homes when two 24-ton tanker trailers containing ethyl acrylate were washed up at Weybourne, Norfolk. 13. Parts of north-eastern Bangladesh were flooded when the river Surma burst its banks; 52 people died. 16. A freight train carrying 660 tons of petrol, kerosene and diesel oil was derailed near Taunton, Somerset, and exploded. 26. An Austrian airliner exploded in mid-air shortly after taking off from Bangkok, killing all 223 aboard.

June 1. Hundreds of people were killed when a cyclone hit southern Bangladesh. **3.** Mount Unzen in Japan erupted, killing over 30 people and causing widespread destruction; further eruptions took place. **12.** Mount Pinatubo in the Philippines erupted in a series of explosions after becoming active in April; the death toll was over 500 by late Aug. **15.** A typhoon and earthquakes hit the Philippines.

July 10. Days of torrential rain in central and eastern China caused widespread flooding; nearly 1,300 people died and millions were left homeless. **11.** All 261 people aboard an aeroplane carrying Muslim pilgrims back to Nigeria from Mecca were killed when it crashed near Jeddah, Saudi Arabia. The Januna and Brahmaputra rivers in northern Bangladesh burst their banks; the flooding left 300,000 people homeless. **18.** Torrential rain continued to fall on central and eastern China; the death toll reached 1,700. **21.** Four people were killed and more than 30 injured when two passenger trains collided at Newton station, near Glasgow. **29.** Up to 100 people died in India when the River Indravati flooded after monsoon rains. **30.** Up to 100 people died and 500 were missing after the River Wardha in India burst its banks because of monsoon rains.

Aug. 3. The Greek-registered cruise ship *Oceanis* sank off the coast of South Africa; the passengers and crew were all rescued. **11.** One man died and four others were feared drowned when the trawler *Ocean Hound* sank in fog in the Strait of Dover. **15.** An oil barge capsized and sank in the South China Sea with the loss of at least 17 lives; 174 people were rescued but four men died after being trapped in the vessel's decompression chamber.

ARTS, SCIENCE AND MEDIA

(1990). Sept. 7. Mark Elder, the conductor who was to have led the last night of the Proms, was replaced by Andrew Davis after saying that he would consider removing nationalist anthems from the programme if war broke out in the Gulf.

Oct. 6. Astronauts on the space shuttle *Discovery* launched the European Space Agency's *Ulysses* probe. **15.** Vivienne Westwood was named Designer of the Year at the British Fashion Awards ceremony.

Nov. 2. It was announced that Sky Television and British Satellite Broadcasting would merge. **3.** The Royal Shakespeare Company closed both its London theatres. **9.** It was announced that the Arts Council grant for

1991–92 would rise by 11 per cent to £175 million and that an enhancement fund of £22·5 million over three years would be created. **27.** The *Sunday Correspondent* newspaper closed.

Dec. 2. A Japanese journalist, Toychiro Akiyama, joined two Soviet cosmonauts on a flight to the space station *Mir.* **17.** The Independent Television Commission published a new code on television advertising standards and practices.

(1991) Jan. 8. The Gaelic poet Sorley Mac-Lean was awarded the Queen's Gold Medal for Poetry. **17.** Richard Branson and Per Lindstrand completed the first hot-air balloon crossing of the Pacific Ocean. **23.** The first implantation of an artificial lung into a British patient was carried out at St George's Hospital, London. **29.** The Sainsbury family launched a set of annual awards worth £250,000 intended to encourage educational activities in the arts.

Feb. 15. Researchers at St Mary's Hospital Medical School, London, said that they had discovered a genetic mutation to be the cause of inherited Alzheimer's disease. **28.** The Independent Television Commission published the final version of its broadcasting impartiality code.

March 21. The Royal Shakespeare Company re-opened at its London base in the Barbican Centre. **24.** The Liverpool Playhouse, which had been threatened with closure, secured a temporary rescue deal with five local authorities. **28.** It was announced that the Almeida theatre in north London would close after losing most of its grant; it was rescued on July 26 by a £100,000 donation from Andrew Lloyd Webber.

April 3. Derbyshire County Council was expelled from the Museums Association after deciding to sell objects from Buxton Museum to make up a shortfall in its education budget. **8.** The chairman of the Royal Opera House, Lord Sainsbury of Preston Candover, resigned, saying that because of the financial pressures on the Royal Opera House the job demanded more time than he was able to give to it. **12.** The Secretary of State for the environment launched a campaign to raise £1.5 million to prevent the closure of the Liverpool Playhouse Theatre. The British musical *Miss Saigon* opened on Broadway after weeks of protests from groups who said it was racist and sexist.

May 15. Forty bidders for the 16 ITV franchises submitted their applications to the Independent Television Commission. The *Independent* newspaper announced that it would merge its daily and Sunday newspapers. **17.** An appeal by the National Art Collections Fund to raise £8.6 million to prevent the export of the Badminton Cabinet failed to reach its target and the export ban on the Cabinet was lifted. **18.** Helen Sharman became the first British astronaut, taking part in an eight-day Anglo-Soviet mission to the Soviet space station *Mir*. With two Soviet astronauts, she travelled to *Mir* aboard a Juno Soyuz rocket launched at Baikonur, USSR.

June 17. Independent Television News (ITN) agreed a budget involving redundancies and other cost-cutting measures.

July 30. A free open-air concert was given in Hyde Park by the Italian tenor Luciano Pavarotti.

CRIMES AND LEGAL AFFAIRS

(1990). Sept. 3. The driver of a British Rail passenger train which crashed near Purley in 1989, was sentenced to six months in prison after admitting manslaughter. **7.** Criminal charges were laid against Arthur Scargill and Peter Heathfield, president and general secretary respectively of the National Union of Mineworkers, alleging failure to keep proper accounts. **10.** The trial of four crew members of the *Herald of Free Enterprise* and three members of P & O Ferries, accused of manslaughter following the Zeebrugge disaster, opened; on Oct. 19 the charges were dropped and the jury instructed to find the defendants not guilty. **13.** The Calcutt inquiry found that Colin Wallace, a former army information officer who alleged that MI5 ran a propaganda campaign code-named Clockwork Orange, was unfairly dismissed in 1975 and should be awarded £30,000 compensation. At the inquest into the Clapham rail disaster of December 1988, the jury returned a verdict of unlawful killing. **23.** A four-year-old boy, Simon Jones, was abducted in Hemel Hemstead; on Nov. 18 he was found at a men's hostel in the town and a man at the hostel was arrested. **24.** Three appeal court judges ruled that the Secretary of State for the Environment had no power to set community charge levels for capped councils. **25.** Sir Jack Lyons, one of the financiers convicted in the Guinness case, was fined £3 million for his offences.

Oct. 1. The fatal accident inquiry into the Lockerbie air disaster of December 1988 opened in Dumfries. **14.** An 11-year-old girl was raped in her hospital bed in the children's ward of St Helier's hospital, Carshalton, Surrey. **19.** The Appeal Court ruled that a severely handicapped five-month-old baby should be allowed to die if he fell critically ill, setting a legal precedent.

Nov. 7. Terry Marsh, the former world light-welterweight boxing champion, was acquitted at the Central Criminal Court of the attempted murder of Frank Warren, his former manager, in November 1989. A disabled 77-year-old woman was sexually assaulted in her hospital bed at Newton Green hospital, Leeds. **18.** Twelve female employees of Barclays Bank who were compelled to retire five years before their male counterparts, won compensation for lost earnings and were offered their jobs back after an Appeal Court hearing. **23.** The former world light-middleweight boxing champion, Maurice Hope, was awarded £50,000 damages against the Metropolitan Police in the High Court, after claiming false imprisonment and malicious prosecution on drugs charges in 1988. **26.** Two senior consultant plastic surgeons were murdered at Pinderfields hospital in Wakefield, W. Yorks; a man was convicted of the murders in July 1991 and committed indefinitely to Rampton security hospital. **27.** An armed robber was killed and a second man was wounded when police officers ambushed a gang hijacking a security van in Surrey.

Dec. 3. Mrs Josephine Wood was awarded £8,155 damages and costs at Birmingham High Court, when Mr Justice Hodgson ruled that West Midlands police had made a series of errors in their handling of a fatal shooting incident in 1980 in which Mrs Wood's daughter, Gail Kinchin, was used as a shield by her former boyfriend. **7.** Harry Greenway, MP, was charged with accepting bribes in connection with British Rail contracts. Seven police officers accused of beating a man unconscious after a pub brawl in 1987 were dismissed from the Metropolitan Police. Bryan Wright became the first person to be jailed for non-payment of the community charge; he was sentenced to 21 days imprisonment. **10.** The inquest into the death of 11 bandsmen in the IRA bomb attack at the Royal Marines School of Music at Deal, Kent, in September 1989, opened; on Dec. 13 the jury returned a verdict of unlawful killing. **13.** Russell Bishop was sentenced to life imprisonment at Lewes Crown Court for the attempted murder of a seven-year-old girl in February 1990. Roger Levitt, chairman and chief executive of the Levitt Group, was arrested and charged with two counts of theft totalling £665,000. **15.** Rodney Witchelo was found guilty at the Central Criminal Court of blackmailing Heinz Baby Foods and Pedigree Pet Foods from 1988 to 1989. **16.** Asil Nadir, chairman of the Polly Peck group of companies, was charged with 18 offences of theft and false accounting. **18.** An armed gang stole over £1 million from a Securicor van after holding hostage the wife of one of the guards. **20.** Karen Smith was sentenced in Thailand to 25 years imprisonment for heroin smuggling. **21.** Sonia Sutcliffe, the wife of the 'Yorkshire Ripper', lost a libel action against the *News of the World* and costs estimated at £300,000 were awarded against her. **31.** A man was arrested after attempting to cut down the Christmas tree in Trafalgar Square with a chainsaw.

(1991) Jan. 8. The South West Water Authority was fined £10,000 at Exeter Crown Court after being found guilty of causing a public nuisance; the charge was brought over the pollution of drinking water supplies in the Camelford area of Cornwall in July 1988. **9.** Mrs Brenda Dunn, whose husband worked at the Sellafield nuclear reprocessing plant from 1978–82 and who died of leukaemia in 1989, was given £150,000 compensation by British Nuclear Fuels in an out-of-court settlement. **24.** The House of Lords ruled that all interest rate swap deals by local government councils are illegal. **31.** In a High Court test case, Mr Justice Hidden ruled that eight out of nine representative claimants against the American manufacturer of the arthritis drug Opren could not pursue the claims as they had been launched outside the statutory time-limit for bringing civil actions.

Feb 5. Bankruptcy proceedings against Asil Nadir were dropped after he reached a £50 million agreement with eight creditors, including the Inland Revenue. Three of the policemen involved in the questioning of the Guildford Four in 1974 were charged with conspiring to pervert the course of justice and remanded on bail. **11.** The trial of three corporate and seven individual defendants accused of fraud in connection with the Blue Arrow rights issue in 1987 opened at the Central Criminal Court. **13.** Paul Burton, who kidnapped seven-year-old Gemma Lawrence from her family's holiday caravan in Dorset in August 1990, was sent to Broadmoor without time limit. **25.** Counsel for the Director of Public Prosecutions said in the Appeal Court that the DPP would no longer claim the convictions of the Birmingham Six were 'safe and satisfactory'.

March 5. A teacher in Bristol was shot and injured in class by a 15-year-old boy who later gave himself up to police. Mrs Margaret Smith, the wife of a millionaire businessman, was found tied up in an empty flat in Hemel Hempstead by a milkman; she had been abducted on March 1. **14.** The Birmingham Six (Hugh Callaghan, Richard McIlkenny, Patrick Hill, William Power, Gerard Hunter and John Walker) who were convicted of the Birmingham pub bombings in 1974, were released after their appeal was successful. In a test case in the Court of Appeal, five judges dismissed an appeal by a man who had been jailed for attempting to rape his estranged wife; the Lord Chief Justice said that the principle that a man could not be convicted of raping his wife if they were still living

together was 'a common law fiction which has become anachronistic and offensive'. **15.** Det. Con. Paul Hughes was shot and seriously wounded during a police raid in north-west London in which over £500,000 worth of drugs was seized. **22.** The report of the inquiry into the Lockerbie air disaster was published. **25.** Mark Gaynor was sentenced to life imprisonment for the murder of PC Laurence Brown in August 1990. Derek Hatton, former deputy leader of Liverpool city council, was charged with conspiracy to defraud the ratepayers and released on bail. Susan Whybrow and Dennis Saunders were found guilty at Norwich Crown Court of attempting to murder Mrs Whybrow's husband by staging an accident with his lawnmower. **26.** A 33-year-old man became the first husband in England and Wales to be convicted of raping his wife and was sentenced at the Central Criminal Court to five years imprisonment. **28.** At an inquest in Sheffield, verdicts of accidental death were returned on the 95 victims of the Hillsborough disaster in 1989.

April 5. Nine fire bombs were detonated in the main shopping precinct in Manchester. **13.** The trial of the captain of the *Bowbelle* dredger involved in the *Marchioness* disaster in August 1989, ended at the Central Criminal Court with the jury unable to reach a verdict. **19.** The first man to be convicted in England and Wales of raping his wife while they still lived together was jailed for five years at Winchester Crown Court. **30.** In the Court of Appeal three judges ruled that local councils seeking injunctions against shops trading on a Sunday must be prepared to pay for losses incurred by the retailers if the House of Lords or the European Court of Justice should eventually rule that restrictions on Sunday trading were illegal.

May 2. The body of Rachel McLean, a student at Oxford University who had been missing since April 15, was found under the floorboards at her lodgings in Oxford; her boyfriend, John Tanner, was subsequently charged with her murder. **3.** The Appeal Court reversed a ruling that 15 relatives of victims of the Hillsborough disaster could seek compensation for severe nervous shock from South Yorkshire police. A fire started by the Animal Liberation Front damaged part of the new Queen Mother stand at Aintree racecourse. **10.** Yvonne Sleightholme was convicted of murdering the wife of her ex-fiancé in December 1988 and was sentenced to life imprisonment. **13.** Mr Justice Hollis ruled in the High Court that a 12-year-old girl who was 19 weeks pregnant could have an abortion without her mother's consent. **14.** Edwina Currie, MP, was awarded £5,000 damages against the *Observer*. Five law lords decided in a test case in the House of Lords to seek further guidance from the European Court of

Justice on the validity of restrictions on Sunday trading. **15.** Kenneth Carrera, who stabbed to death a mugger who attacked him in August 1990, was acquitted of murder and manslaughter. **16.** The five-year jail sentence imposed on Ernest Saunders, former chairman and chief executive of Guinness, was cut to two and a half years by the Court of Appeal. The sentence imposed on Anthony Parnes was cut from two and a half years to 21 months. **21.** Patricia Cahill was sentenced in Thailand to 18 years and 9 months imprisonment for heroin smuggling. **23.** Thames Water Utilities pleaded guilty to discharging industrial effluent into a two-mile stretch of the River Kennet in Nov. 1990. **24.** Norman Tebbit, MP won a libel case brought against him by David Bookbinder, the Labour leader of Derbyshire County Council. **30.** Three fishermen from Ullapool, Scotland, were convicted of smuggling £100 million worth of cocaine into Britain. **31.** Hani Elrayes was sentenced to 12 years imprisonment for holding hostage 150 people in Tokyo Joe's nightclub in London, in July 1990.

June 1. The body of a student, Catherine Ayling, was found in the boot of a car at Gatwick Airport. Curtis Howard, an American former friend of Miss Ayling, was arrested in Boston, USA, and on June 6 he was charged with her murder. **6.** A business woman, Ruth Bell, was found murdered in her car outside a swimming pool in west London. **7.** Michael Kyte was sentenced at Winchester Crown Court to life imprisonment after being convicted of murdering his ex-girlfriend Ruth Stevens in December 1989. **11.** Charges of conspiracy to pervert the course of justice against three Surrey detectives involved in the interrogation of the Guildford Four were dismissed on the grounds that the lapse of time and adverse publicity had prejudiced the chances of a fair trial. **12.** In the Court of Session three appeal judges ruled that Sheriff Kelbie was wrong to dismiss the allegations of ritual sexual abuse of nine children in the Orkneys so early in the proceedings and that he had breached elementary rules of natural justice. **14.** Leslie Bailey was sentenced to life imprisonment after he admitted assaulting and murdering six-year-old Barry Lewis in 1985. British Rail was fined £250,000 after admitting to safety failures that led to the Clapham Junction train crash in Dec. 1988. **19.** Criminal charges against Arthur Scargill and Peter Heathfield, president and general secretary respectively of the NUM, over their handling of the Union's finances were dismissed. **20.** Harry Collinson, principal planning officer for Derwentside District Council, was shot dead by a man whose bungalow was about to be demolished under a demolition order; two people were injured. Rosemary Aberdour, who claimed to be the daughter of the Earl of Morton, was charged with stealing

£1·7 million from the National Hospital Development Foundation, of which she had been deputy director. Three former members of the disbanded West Midlands serious crimes squad were cleared at Oxford Crown Court of perjury and attempting to pervert the course of justice in relation to a conviction which was later quashed. **26.** The conviction of the Maguire family in 1976 for running an IRA bomb factory in London was quashed as unsafe and unsatisfactory at the Court of Appeal in London. Patrick Pottle and Michael Randle were acquitted of helping George Blake, the Soviet spy, escape from prison and from Britain in 1966. **28.** Wg Cdr. David Farquhar was severely reprimanded and stripped of seniority after being convicted at a court martial of negligence over the theft of classified information about the Gulf conflict from his car in Dec. 1990.

July 3. Michael Shorey was sentenced to life imprisonment for murdering his girlfriend Elaine Forsyth and their flatmate Patricia Morrison in July 1990. **5.** A man was shot in the hand in Newport, Gwent, after being held hostage at gunpoint in his car for 29 hours. **11.** Terry Fields, MP, was sentenced to 60 days imprisonment for refusing to pay his community charge. **12.** Hitoshi Igarashi, who translated *The Satanic Verses* into Japanese, was murdered in Tokyo. **24.** Police in Milwaukee, USA, found the dismembered bodies of at least 11 men in the flat of Jeffrey Dahmer. **26.** In a reserved judgment concerning an asylum seeker from Zaire who had wrongly been sent back to his country, Mr Justice Simon Brown ruled that the Crown and its individual officers were immune from proceedings for contempt. **22.** The Bank of Credit and Commerce International, two of its founders and four affiliated companies were charged in New York with fraud, theft, falsifying bank records and illegal money laundering. Twenty-nine Kenyan schoolboys were charged with the manslaughter of 19 schoolgirls at St Kizito's Secondary School near Nairobi on July 13. **31.** Teresa Gorman, MP, was awarded £150,000 damages for libel and costs of up to £200,000 against businessman Anthony Mudd. The captain of the dredger *Bowbelle* was cleared of negligence at his retrial after the jury failed to reach a verdict.

Aug. 1. An armed gang held a woman and her two sons hostage for 18 hours until her husband, the manager of an Ipswich store, paid £70,000 in ransom. **3.** Two men were killed and four seriously wounded in a shooting incident at the Bell public house, Walworth, London. **5.** The manager of a travel agency was kidnapped from his home in Kent by two men and forced to hand over £50,000 from his office safe. **11.** Seven-year-old Angela Flaherty, who had gone missing on August 10, was found murdered near her home in Huddersfield. **12.** Six-year-old Rebecca McBride, who had gone missing on August 10, was found drowned in a lake 20 miles from her home in Swansea; on August 14 a 15-year-old boy was charged with her murder. **13.** A woman was abducted from her home in Dartford, Kent, and held captive for 22 hours while her kidnappers forced her son-in-law to hand over about £200,000 from a Post Office security van. **15.** Seven-year-old Paul Pearson, who had gone missing on August 14, was found murdered near his home in Cleveland; on August 16 a man was charged with his murder. **20.** Police arrested 23 people following a series of drug raids in Moss Side, Manchester. **26.** A man was stabbed to death at the Notting Hill Carnival in London. The judicial inquiry into the conduct of the case of alleged ritual abuse in the Orkneys opened at Kirkwall Town Hall under Lord Clyde.

ENVIRONMENT

(1990). Sept. 19. Canada, China, Japan, the Soviet Union and the Scandinavian countries signed an agreement on joint environmental and scientific research in the Arctic. **29.** The World Bank suspended funding of new tropical timber projects because of the damage to rainforests caused by past and current projects.

Oct. 23. The Japanese government announced that it would stabilize the level of carbon dioxide emissions from fossil fuels at 1990 levels by the year 2000. **29.** European Community environment and energy ministers reached a common position on stabilizing emissions of carbon dioxide by EC states by the year 2000, although Britain maintained its separate objective of the year 2005. The Second World Climate Conference opened in Geneva. A meeting of the London Dumping Convention began in London; the 44 signatories present agreed that the dumping of industrial waste, including the submarine deposit of nuclear waste, would cease by 1995.

Nov. 5. EFTA members agreed to stabilize emissions of carbon dioxide by the year 2000. **7.** At the World Climate Conference, the 137 countries present agreed to negotiate by June 1992 a convention to limit the emissions contributing to global warming and to provide scientific and technical assistance to developing countries to help them meet the requirements of a convention without losing the benefits of industrialization. **19.** A three-week meeting of the parties to the 1961 Antarctic Treaty began in Chile; on Nov. 21 Britain refused to support a proposal to declare Antarctica a world park. Delegates agreed a draft environmental protocol to the 1961 Antarctic Treaty for later discussion.

Dec. 21. The European Community unanimously agreed to end the production, import and use of chlorofluorocarbons in member states by July 1997; new limits were also imposed on vehicle exhaust fumes, in effect making catalytic converters obligatory on new cars by 1993. **28.** The Government announced a ban on fishing for sand-eels on Shetland because of the breeding failure of sea birds in the area since 1984.

(1991) Jan. 22. Iraq began pumping millions of gallons of crude oil from Kuwaiti installations into the Gulf, causing a slick 33 miles long and ten miles wide. **28.** An international effort was mounted to combat the environmental pollution caused by the oil slick in the Gulf. **31.** The environment ministers of all OECD members agreed that all sectors of their economies should be held accountable for the environmental consequences of their activities.

Feb. 3. It was announced that RSPCA wildlife experts would go to Saudi Arabia to help treat birds and animals affected by the oil slick in the Gulf. **5.** Experts from 11 international organizations met in Geneva to discuss the environmental impact of the Gulf conflict. **8.** Soviet scientists and ecologists said that 16 per cent of the Soviet Union was now an ecological disaster area. **14.** The Department of the Environment announced plans to develop forests on the outskirts of nine large cities. **22.** Hundreds of Kuwaiti oil wells were set alight by Iraqi soldiers.

March 6. The Environment Secretary said that the Government would contribute £1 million to a fund set up by the IMO to cover the costs of cleaning up the oil slick in the Gulf. **26.** Firefighters plugged the first of hundreds of damaged Kuwaiti oil wells.

April 21. A meeting of the parties to the 1961 Antarctic Treaty opened in Madrid; on April 22 agreement was reached on a 50-year moratorium on mineral exploitation in Antarctica. **25.** The Minister of Agriculture, Fisheries and Food (John Gummer) said that Britain would not support the resumption of commercial whaling until a humane method of killing whales had been devised.

May 27. The annual meeting of the International Whaling Commission opened in Reykjavik; on May 31 the Commission agreed to continue a moratorium on commercial whaling but said that licences could be issued where stocks are sufficiently high.

June 3. Iceland resigned from the International Whaling Commission because of the Commission's failure to lift the moratorium on commercial whale hunting. **17.** Norwegian whalers announced that they would resume hunting minke whales from July 4.

July 31. British Steel was fined £200,000 at Cardiff Crown Court for an oil leak from its Llanwern plant in February 1991 which polluted the Severn Estuary.

NORTHERN IRELAND

(1990). Sept. 10. A bomb planted by the IRA exploded on the roof of an Army and Royal Navy careers office in Derby. **15.** In south Armagh an off-duty RUC officer was kidnapped and later shot dead by the IRA. **17.** An army colour sergeant was shot and wounded by the IRA outside an army recruiting centre in London. **18.** Air Vice-Marshal Sir Peter Terry was shot and wounded by the IRA at his home near Stafford. **27.** A bomb planted by the IRA was discovered and defused at the Royal Overseas League in London before the opening of an international conference on terrorism. **30.** Two teenagers driving a stolen car were killed by soldiers who opened fire when the car failed to stop at a checkpoint in west Belfast.

Oct. 5. The anti-racketeering squad of the RUC searched republican homes and offices in Northern Ireland as part of a drive against illegal fund-raising by the IRA. **9.** In Co. Armagh the army shot dead two men, Desmond Grew and Martin McCaughey, who had arrived at a farm to collect weapons and ammunition and who were suspected of being IRA terrorists. **10.** Charges against five men relating to possession of intelligence documents on IRA suspects were dropped at Belfast Magistrates Court; the charges had been brought as a result of the Stevens investigation into intelligence leaks from the security forces. **24.** In separate incidents in Londonderry, Newry and Omagh, a bomb was attached to a civilian who was then instructed to drive to an army checkpoint. The explosion at the checkpoint in Londonderry killed five soldiers and the driver of the car, and the explosion at Newry killed one soldier. The third bomb, driven to barracks in Omagh, was defused. The IRA claimed responsibility.

Nov. 2. A part-time UDR soldier was killed in Cookstown, Co. Tyrone, by a bomb brought by a women in her car to the garage where he worked; the IRA later claimed responsibility. **10.** Four men, including an RUC officer, were killed by the IRA while duck shooting on the shores of Lough Neagh, Co. Armagh. **11.** Police raided two flats in Kilburn, London, and found a store of arms and ammunition; six people were arrested. **13.** Alex Patterson, a suspected IRA terrorist, was killed at Victoria Bridge, Co. Tyrone, when the army opened fire on republicans attempting to attack the home of a UDR soldier. **14.**

Desmond Ellis lost his appeal against extradition at the Supreme Court in Dublin, becoming the first IRA suspect to be extradited to Britain from the Republic of Ireland; he was later charged in London with conspiracy to cause explosions and possessing explosives. **23.** The IRA abducted a man in Co. Fermanagh and forced him to take a 3,500 lb bomb to an army checkpoint on the border; only the detonator exploded and no-one was hurt.

Dec. 5. Three suspected members of the IRA were arrested and a cache of arms was seized by Belgian police in a raid on a house in Antwerp. **6.** Liam O'Dhuibhir and Damien McComb were each sentenced at the Central Criminal Court to 30 years imprisonment for involvement in IRA terrorist activities. **14.** Vivian McDonald was sentenced at Belfast Crown Court to 18 years imprisonment for the attempted murder of two UDR soldiers in May 1990. **18.** The Director of Public Prosecutions in Northern Ireland announced that two soldiers who shot dead three men who were robbing a bookmaker's shop in Belfast in January 1990 would not be prosecuted. **30.** A man was killed and his brother injured by troops who opened fire when their car failed to stop at an army checkpoint in south Armagh.

(1991) Jan. 2. Patrick Sheehy, believed by police to be involved in the IRA's bombing campaign in Britain, was found shot dead outside a post office at Nenagh, Co. Tipperary; on Jan. 16 a report from the Irish state pathologist found that he had committed suicide. **11.** Nine men involved in an IRA plot to kill 12 soldiers in 1988 were jailed for between seven and 25 years at Belfast Crown Court.

March 1. A member of the UDR was killed and three others seriously injured when an IRA landmine exploded on the outskirts of Armagh; one of the injured died on March 5. **6.** Five Irishmen received jail sentences ranging from five to seven years in Paris for their part in an attempt to smuggle Libyan arms to the IRA on the coaster *Eksund* in 1987. **19.** The Northern Ireland Secretary (Peter Brooke) said that two of the 18 permanent vehicle checkpoints along the border with the Republic would be closed, and that 500 soldiers from the Cheshire Regiment had been deployed for an indefinite tour of duty in Co. Fermanagh. **21.** Margaret Cooke, whose husband was murdered by the IRA in 1987, was shot and seriously wounded by the IRA in Londonderry. **25.** The Unionist leaders James Molyneaux and Ian Paisley issued a statement agreeing to join in talks with nationalists and the Dublin government according to proposals laid out by the Secretary of State for Northern Ireland; on March 26

Mr Brooke outlined to the House of Commons a three-month timetable for the talks. **28.** Two teenage girls and a man were shot dead in a mobile shop in Craigavon, Co. Armagh by the Protestant Action Force.

April 2. Gerard Harte, a suspected member of the IRA, was sentenced in the Netherlands to 18 years imprisonment for the murder of two Australian tourists in Roermond in May 1990; three other defendants were acquitted. **10.** A member of the IRA, Colm Marks, was killed by the RUC while preparing a mortar attack at Downpatrick, Co. Down. **17.** The Ulster Volunteer Force and the Ulster Defence Association said that they would suspend 'aggressive operational hostilities' during talks about the future government of Northern Ireland; on April 22 the IRA said that it would monitor the situation and act accordingly. **30.** The Secretary of State for Northern Ireland started talks on the future government of Northern Ireland with leaders of the four main political parties in Belfast. The first plenary session was due to start on May 7 but was delayed by disagreement over procedure and over the venue for future talks with the Irish government.

May 2. An RUC sergeant died from injuries he sustained in an IRA rocket attack in Belfast on May 1; on May 9 three men appeared at Belfast Magistrates Court charged with his murder. **8.** Danny Morrison, the former publicity director of Sinn Fein, was convicted in Belfast of falsely imprisoning a police informer in Jan. 1990. **21.** The director of a fruit and vegetable company was shot dead by the IRA in Belfast because his company sold produce to the security forces. **25.** A soldier was killed and another critically injured in a bomb attack on a barracks in Belfast. **31.** Three soldiers were killed and 18 people injured in an IRA bomb attack on a UDR barracks in Glennan, Co. Armagh.

June 2. A senior civil servant was seriously injured when a bomb exploded under her car in Drumbeg, Co. Antrim. **3.** Three members of the IRA, believed to be on their way to attack a group of Protestant men, were shot dead by undercover soldiers in Coagh, Co. Tyrone. **8.** Three IRA members were sentenced in Florida to four years imprisonment for conspiring to buy a Stinger anti-aircraft missile. **9.** Houses on a Protestant housing estate in Donaghcloney, Co. Down, were seriously damaged by a 600 lb car bomb planted by the IRA. **17.** The first full session of talks on the political future of Northern Ireland started at Stormont Castle, Belfast, and after weeks of disagreements over the chairman of the later stages of the talks, Sir Ninian Stephen was accepted by all parties. **29.** The Queen visited Northern Ireland. **30.** Army bomb disposal officers carried out a controlled explosion when a bomb, believed to have been planted by the IRA, was found outside an RAF careers office in Preston, Lancs.

July 3. The Secretary of State for Northern Ireland announced that the inter-party talks on the future government of the province had broken down. **5.** In the Court of Appeal in the Netherlands, the conviction of Gerard Harte (*see* April 2) was found to be unsafe because of a conflict in eye-witness evidence, and he was therefore acquitted. The acquittal of the other three defendants was upheld. On July 12 all four defendants were cleared of being members of the IRA. **29.** In Dublin Adrian Hopkins was sentenced to eight years imprisonment, five of them suspended, after pleading guilty to possessing Libyan arms and explosives intended for the IRA on board his coaster *Eksund* in 1987.

Aug. 5. An incendiary device planted by the IRA caused a fire which destroyed part of the Cambridge public house in Charing Cross Road, London; a second unexploded device was later found in the pub. **17.** Two Roman Catholic men who had been warned by the IRA to leave Ireland because of their 'criminal' activities took refuge in Newry Cathedral and claimed sanctuary; on Aug. 27 the two men left Newry Cathedral and went into hiding. A British soldier was killed when an IRA land-mine exploded in South Armagh. **28.** A 1,000 lb IRA bomb exploded in Markethill, Co. Armagh, injuring a soldier and causing extensive damage. An incendiary device planted by the IRA was found in a bookshop in Charing Cross Road, London.

SPORT

(1990). Sept. 1. Lancashire achieved the unique double of winning the NatWest and Benson and Hedges trophies in the same season. **23.** The Jockey Club confirmed that Bravefoot and Norwich, two horses who ran disappointingly at the St Leger meeting on Sept. 13 and 14, had been illegally given a tranquilliser before the races. An investigation was launched by the Jockey Club; it later emerged that the same sedative had been given to Flying Diva at Yarmouth on Sept. 20.

Oct. 12. The International Rugby Football Board announced plans to allow rugby union players to benefit financially from activities unconnected with rugby without damaging their amateur status. **22.** The Football Association charged Manchester United and Arsenal with bringing the game into disrepute after a brawl between their players during a match on Oct. 20: on Nov. 12 the Football Association deducted two league points from Arsenal and one point from Manchester United. **23.** Pat Eddery became the first jockey since 1952 to ride 200 winners in a British flat race season.

Nov. 6. Two American world record holders, the 400 metres runner Harry Reynolds and the shot putter Randy Barnes, were suspended for two years by the International Amateur Athletic Federation after returning positive drug tests. **20.** The Aga Khan's horse, Aliysa, which won the 1989 Oaks, was disqualified from the race by the Jockey Club's disciplinary committee after they decided that a post-race urine test showed the presence of a prohibited substance. On Dec. 4 the Aga Khan announced that he was withdrawing all his horses from British racing until the Jockey Club changed its drugs-testing procedures. **27.** Yorkshire Cricket Club decided to allow players not born in the county to play for the club, subject to a residential qualification.

Dec. 19. Tony Adams, the England footballer and Arsenal captain, was jailed for four months for drinking and driving, and reckless driving. **26.** Desert Orchid became the first horse to win the King George VI Chase four times. Gary Kasparov retained his world chess title when he drew the 22nd game of his match against Anatoly Karpov. **27.** Martin Pipe, the trainer, had his 1,000th National Hunt winner. **29.** The British yacht *Rothmans* was disqualified after winning the Sydney-Hobart race for using a sail showing the sponsor's logo, in contravention of race rules.

(1991). Jan. 10. The International Cricket Council decided that a paid referee would be present at all international cricket matches from September 1991, and that umpires should always be from a neutral country. **11.** The Football League fined Chelsea £105,000 for making irregular payments to three players. **17.** The England A team cricket tour of Pakistan was abandoned due to the Gulf crisis. The Princess Royal launched the Sports Council's Year of Sport. **19.** The England rugby union players and team manager refused to attend a press conference after the match against Wales. **21.** The England cricketers David Gower and John Morris were reprimanded by the tour manager Peter Lush after flying low in Tiger Moth biplanes over the Queensland ground where their team was playing; they were later fined £1,000 each. The Welsh Rugby Union banned the Wales B international player Richard Griffiths for two years after he was found to have taken steroids.

Feb. 4. Martin Crowe and Andrew Jones of New Zealand broke the world record for the highest partnership in Test cricket when they put on 467 for the third wicket against Sri Lanka in Wellington. **5.** The Home Affairs

select committee published *Policing Football Hooliganism*; it also presented the Football (Offences) Bill to the Commons as a Private Member's Bill. **12.** A working party was set up by the Rugby Football Union to deal with issues raised by the IRFB's revised regulations on amateurism. **17.** The foreign ministers of nine Commonwealth countries decided at a meeting in London that sporting links with South Africa could be resumed on a sport-by-sport basis by individual countries in the Commonwealth as soon as each country judged that racial discrimination in that sport had ended. **22.** Kenny Dalglish resigned as manager of Liverpool football club. **23.** The WBO middleweight champion Chris Eubank retained his title despite having two points deducted by the referee for head-butting his challenger Dan Sherry; Eubank was fined £10,000 and severely reprimanded by the British Boxing Board of Control.

March 15. The High Court ruled that the terms of the contract between Commonwealth middleweight champion Mike Watson and his promoter-manager Micky Duff were unfair because of the dual role of Mr Duff. **23.** The inaugural match in the World League of American football was played in Germany between Frankfurt Galaxy and the London Monarchs. **24.** A delegation from the International Olympic Committee arrived in South Africa; it gave sports officials six months to meet five conditions concerning non-racially segregated sport in South Africa before readmitting the country to the Olympic movement. **29.** The Italian soccer federation confirmed that drugs tests showed that the Napoli player and former Argentinian captain Diego Maradona had taken cocaine.

April 2. Diego Maradona was suspended from all sporting activity by the Italian football league and on April 6 he was banned from the game worldwide until June 30, 1992. **8.** The Football Association rejected proposals by the Football League for power-sharing between the two bodies, and informally proposed a premier league. **25.** Brian Moore, the England rugby player, was given a four-month suspended sentence and fined £500 for assaulting a student in a pub in October 1990.

May 3. The Rugby Football Union gave its approval in principle to a £2 million sponsorship scheme to reward England players for undertaking promotional activities. **17.** The Horserace Betting Levy Board announced funding cuts of £8·685 million and advocated a restructured fixture list for horseracing in Britain. **18.** Tottenham Hotspur won the FA Cup for a record eighth time. **20.** The Home Affairs select committee published a report on the future of horseracing in Britain. **30.** The British light-heavyweight boxing champion, Steve McCarthy, pulled out of a title defence hours before it was due to start after failing to increase his share of the television rights; on June 12 McCarthy was stripped of his title.

June 9. Graham Gooch carried his bat through England's innings in the Test match against West Indies at Headingley, scoring 154 runs. **10.** England won the first Test match, their first victory against the West Indies in England for 22 years. **13.** A spectator was killed and five others injured when they were struck by lightning during the US Open golf championship. **19.** The Football Association published *Blueprint for the Future of Football*, which included plans for a separate premier league from the 1992–93 season. **21.** Monica Seles, the top seed at Wimbledon, withdrew three days before the start of the tournament; she was fined $6,000. **22.** Terry Venables, the manager of Tottenham Hotspur football club, and businessman Alan Sugar, announced that they had signed a £7·25 million deal to take over the club, ending a year of uncertainty over the club's future. **30.** Play at the Wimbledon tennis championships continued on the middle Sunday of the fortnight for the first time, to catch up with a backlog of matches caused by rain in the first week. At the European athletics championships in Frankfurt, the Soviet Union were disqualified in the men's 4 × 400 metres relay but were reinstated after appealing.

July 7. With his victory in the French grand prix, Nigel Mansell overtook Stirling Moss's total of 16 grand prix victories. **9.** The International Olympic Committee said that South Africa would be readmitted as a member and invited to participate in the 1992 Olympic Games in Barcelona. **10.** The International Cricket Council voted to readmit South Africa to Test cricket. Yorkshire Cricket Club announced that it would allow overseas players and Englishmen not born in Yorkshire to play for the county. **14.** The World Student games were opened in Sheffield by the Princess Royal. **20.** The Aston Villa and England footballer David Platt was bought by the Italian club Bari for £5·5 million. **25.** Tottenham Hotspur football club agreed a £5·5 million fee with the Italian club Lazio for the transfer of Paul Gascoigne. **31.** The High Court ruled that the Football Association was entitled to set up an independent premier league and dismissed the Football League's claim that the FA had acted unlawfully.

Aug. 7. A spectator at the US PGA golf championships died after being struck by lightning. **10.** In the final Test match between England and West Indies at the Oval, Phil Tufnell took six wickets for 25 runs. **15.** The French grand prix driver Bertrand Gachot was sentenced to 18 months imprisonment for

spraying CS gas in the face of a taxi driver after a minor traffic accident in London. **16.** All 22 first division football clubs handed in notice of resignation to the Football League. **25.** Carl Lewis set a new world record for the 100 metres at the world athletics championships in Tokyo; six of the finalists ran under 10 seconds. **30.** At the world athletics championships in Tokyo the longest-standing world record, the long jump record set by Bob Beamon in 1968, was broken by Mike Powell.

AFRICA

(1990). Sept. 9. Samuel Doe, President of Liberia, was captured and killed by Prince Yormie Johnson's rebel group. Johnson proclaimed himself President the next day. Doe's army chose David Nimley as their new leader. **13.** Twenty-six blacks were hacked to death and over a hundred injured when a commuter train was attacked in Johannesburg, South Africa. **22.** A cease-fire was declared in Liberia between opposing factions but collapsed within six days.

Oct. 1. Thousands of refugee Tutsi tribesmen invaded Rwanda from Uganda in an attempt to topple the Hutu-led Rwandan government. **11.** Egypt voted in a referendum to give President Mubarak a mandate to call a general election, following a court ruling in May 1990 that the existing parliament had been elected illegally. **18.** President de Klerk formally ended South Africa's four-year state of emergency. **19.** The ruling South African National Party formally opened its membership to all races.

Nov. 2. The People's Assembly in Mozambique voted to introduce a multi-party constitution and a free market economy on Nov. 30. **12.** King Letsie III of Lesotho was sworn in as the country's new monarch. **28.** The three warring Liberian factions signed a cease-fire after talks in Mali.

Dec. 1. President Habré of Chad was overthrown by the Popular Salvation Movement led by Idriss Deby, which took the capital, N'djamena. **2.** Fighting broke out in the Johannesburg townships between ANC and *Inkatha* supporters, in which at least 60 died. **6.** The second round of the general election was held in Egypt and was won by the ruling party. **12.** The Zimbabwean Parliament passed legislation allowing the nationalization of white-owned farms for fixed compensation and without appeal. **21.** The three rival Liberian factions agreed to the creation of a national conference within 60 days to initiate an interim government; sporadic fighting continued.

(1991). Jan. 1. United Somali Congress (USC) rebels claimed to have occupied most of

Mogadishu, but fighting continued for much of the month. 12. *Inkatha* supporters killed at least 35 people attending a funeral in Sebokeng, South Africa. 13. At least 40 football spectators were killed in a stampede at Orkney, South Africa, after fighting between rival supporters. 14. A general strike took place in Morocco in protest at price rises; at least 100 died in clashes between security forces and demonstrators, which continued sporadically for three days. 23. Civil war continued in Rwanda as Tutsi rebels again entered the country from Uganda. 27. President Barre of Somalia fled to Kenya after his palace in Mogadishu was overrun by rebels; on Jan. 29 the USC appointed Ali Mahdi Muhammad as President.

Feb. 4. The trial of Winnie Mandela on charges of murder and kidnapping began. 11. The civil war in Somalia recommenced. 13. The leaders of three Liberian factions signed a cease-fire monitoring accord in Togo. 26. Eight died during riots in the French overseas department of Réunion.

March 3. Miguel Trovoada, an independent opposition leader, was elected President of São Tome and Príncipe. 12. A two-day general strike began in Algeria in protest at price rises. 15. The government of Zaire resigned; a transitional government was appointed. 17. A cease-fire between government and the Rwandan Popular Front forces was announced. 26. After several days of pro-democracy riots Mali, President Traoré was overthrown by the army.

April 5. The ANC threatened to break off negotiations with the South African government unless it took steps to halt township violence. 15. A national conference of all Liberian political groups convened in Monrovia; on March 19 it reconfirmed Amos Sawyer as interim president, although the rebel group led by Charles Taylor had earlier walked out. 30. It was reported that forces of the Liberian National Patriotic Liberation Front had seized areas of neighbouring Sierra Leone after several weeks of cross-border raids. The government of Lesotho was overthrown in a coup led by Col. Elias Ramaema.

May 13. Winnie Mandela was found guilty of kidnapping and accessory to assault; the following day she was sentenced to six years imprisonment but was released on bail pending an appeal. 15. A cease-fire between government and UNITA forces began in Angola. 17. The Somali National Movement declared the north of Somalia independent. 18. The ANC ended constitutional negotiations with the South African government, partly because of its failure to ban traditional Zulu weapons. 20. After talks with the South African government, Zulu leaders agreed to

restrictions on the use of arms, including ceremonial weapons. 21. President Mengistu of Ethiopia fled to Zimbabwe as rebel forces closed in on Addis Ababa. 25. A general strike began in Algeria. 27. Talks were held in London between Tesfaye Dinka, the Ethiopian Prime Minister, and leaders of the Ethiopian People's Democratic Revolutionary Front (EPDRF). The US government recommended a rebel advance into Addis Ababa, which the government was powerless to prevent; the capital was fully occupied by the EPDRF on May 28. 29. The Eritrean People's Liberation Front announced that it would form a provisional government in Eritrea until a UN-supervised referendum on independence could be held. 30. President Dos Santos of Angola and Jonas Savimbi, leader of UNITA, signed a peace agreement ending the civil war.

June 4. An ammunition dump exploded in Addis Ababa, Ethiopia, killing over 100 people, including John Mathai, a BBC journalist. Security forces shot dead at least 20 people during rioting by supporters of the Islamic Salvation Front in Algiers; Mouloud Hamrouche, the Prime Minister, resigned. 5. The President of Algeria declared a state of siege, postponed elections and appointed Sid Ahmed Ghozali Prime Minister. 7. The Islamic Salvation Front ended its protests in exchange for a government agreement to hold parliamentary and presidential elections before the end of 1991. 30. Abassi Madani, leader of the Islamic Salvation Front, and hundreds of Front members were arrested after Madani threatened a holy war against the Algerian army. The Liberian rebel leader Charles Taylor recognized Amos Sawyer as interim president, and declared an end to the civil war.

July 5. A two-year transitional government was formed in Ethiopia following a national conference of political groups. 8. The ANC resumed negotiations with the South African government, broken off in May. 19. The South African government admitted that it had made secret payments to the *Inkatha* Freedom Party to organize rallies and other anti-ANC activities. 22. Under pressure to introduce political reform, President Mobutu of Zaire appointed Etienne Tshisekedi, an opposition leader, as Prime Minister; Mr Tshisekedi declined the post and on July 24 President Mobutu reappointed the former incumbent, Mulumba Lukoji. 23. A state of emergency was declared in Madagascar after opposition demonstrators demanding popular rule occupied government ministries; President Ratsiraka subsequently sacked the government and promised a referendum on a new constitution. 29. President de Klerk reshuffled the South African Cabinet, demoting Adriaan Vlok, Minister for Law and Order, and

Magnus Malan, Defence Minister, who were implicated in the covert funding scandal; the following day the President announced the immediate ending of secret funding.

Aug. 4. Renewed fighting broke out in the Western Sahara between Moroccan forces and Polisario guerrillas. **7.** Guy Razanamasy became Prime Minister of Madagascar. **9.** At least three people were killed in clashes between the police and neo-Nazis besieging a National Party meeting at Ventersdorp, South Africa. **16.** The South African government declared a general amnesty for political exiles. **19.** Opposition forces in Madagascar declared a rival interim government; President Ratsiraka remained in office. **27.** In Togo, a national conference chose Kokou Koffigoh to be the new Prime Minister.

THE AMERICAS

(1990). Sept. 11. Three youths were sentenced to maximum terms of imprisonment for beating and raping a woman jogger in New York. **26.** A two-month siege at an Indian reservation at Oka, Quebec, Canada, ended when Mohawk protesters surrendered to Canadian troops; the siege began because a sacred tribal burial ground was threatened by development. **27.** Prime Minister Mulroney of Canada asked the Queen to appoint eight new Conservative senators so that the Liberal majority in the Senate would be outnumbered and tax legislation could be passed.

Oct. 5. The US House of Representatives rejected the federal budget by 254 votes to 179; all non-essential federal services began to close down the following day after President Bush refused to sign a bill granting emergency financing. He later signed four such bills before the budget was agreed. **8.** A British minister, Tristan Garel-Jones, arrived in Argentina for the highest-level Anglo-Argentine talks since the Falklands conflict. **16.** A coup was attempted against President Endara of Panama by disaffected police and army officers. **26.** The Mayor of Washington DC, Marion Barry, was jailed for six months for possession of cocaine. **27.** The US House of Representatives passed a federal budget, imposing cuts of $492 billion over five years. **28.** The US Senate passed the federal budget.

Nov. 6. Congressional elections were held in the USA. **12.** Presidential, national and local elections were held in Guatemala. **28.** Britain and Argentina agreed to share sovereignty over disputed territorial waters between 150 and 200 miles east of the Falkland Islands.

Dec. 3. Twenty-one soldiers and civilians were killed during an army rebellion in Argentina which was suppressed after 24 hours. **5.** A coup against President Endara of Panama was put down by US troops. The first ever presidential and National Assembly elections were held in Haiti. **24.** President Shankar of Suriname was overthrown in a military coup led by Lt.-Col. Desi Bouterse. **29.** President Menem of Argentina pardoned military officers charged with human rights abuses and others connected with the excesses of military rule.

(1991). Jan. 2. FMLN guerrillas in El Salvador killed two US military advisers after shooting down their helicopter. **7.** In Haiti, a coup attempt by the Interior Minister, Roger Lafontant, was put down by army units loyal to the President-elect, Fr. Jean-Bertrande Aristide. **8.** Guatemala and Belize joined the Organization of American States.

Feb. 14. The Peruvian cabinet resigned after division over the country's economic crisis.

March 5. A general election was held in Greenland and won by Jonathan Motzfeldt; however, Motzfeldt was the subject of allegations of financial mismanagement and was replaced by Lars Emil Johansen. **16.** The Peruvian Health Minister, Carlos Vidal Layseca, resigned in protest at the government's policy on the country's cholera epidemic; the epidemic broke out in Jan. and by end March nearly 100,000 people had been infected and over 500 had died. **27.** In Canada, the Belanger-Campeau Commission presented its report on the political and constitutional future of Quebec to the provincial legislature.

April 1. William vander Zalm, the premier of British Columbia, Canada, resigned after violating conflict-of-interest rules; he was replaced by Rita Johnston. **19.** The cholera epidemic in Peru was reported to be spreading across South America. **27.** In Mexico City, the Salvadorean government and the FMLN guerrilla movement reached agreement on political reforms. **30.** A 29-year-old woman alleged that she was raped by William Smith, a Senator for Massachusetts and a nephew of Edward Kennedy, at the Kennedy family's house in Florida; Mr Smith was charged with rape and battery on May 9.

May 4. President Bush was taken to hospital after becoming ill while jogging; he was discharged on May 6. **5.** Riots broke out in the Mount Pleasant district of Washington DC, after a Hispanic was shot and wounded by a black policewoman; after a second night of rioting a state of emergency was declared in the area. **18.** The members of the Andean Pact (Bolivia, Colombia, Ecuador, Peru and Venezuela) signed a declaration providing for the estalishment of free trade between them by Jan. 1992. **21.** An Australian nun and four other people were killed by Shining Path guerrillas in Peru.

June 8. A parade in celebration of victory in the Gulf took place in Washington DC; a larger ticker-tape parade was held in New York City on June 10.

July 6. In Colombia, a new constitution came into force at midnight; simultaneously the Medillin drug cartel disbanded its military wing.

Aug. 19. Several days of anti-Semitic rioting began in the Crown Heights district of New York after a car driven by a Hassidic Jew ran over two black children, killing one of them.

ASIA

(1990). Sept. 4. In Seoul, the South Korean Prime Minister, Kang Young Hoon, met his North Korean counterpart, Yon Hyong Muk, in the highest-level talks between the two states since 1945. **10.** The four Cambodian factions agreed to create a Supreme National Council (SNC) to embody national sovereignty while the United Nations administered free elections. In Pakistan, Benazir Bhutto, the former Prime Minister, was charged with abuse of power. **19.** A Brahmin student set fire to himself in protest at plans to reserve government jobs for low castes, a move which sparked widespread unrest throughout northern India and led to several self-immolations.

Oct. 3. A military coup against the Philippine government began on the southern island of Mindanao but was put down by troops loyal to the government two days later. **10.** In Bangladesh, the first of many student demonstrations took place, demanding the resignation of President Ershad and calling for fresh elections. **23.** The Hindu right-wing Bharatiya Janata Party (BJP) withdrew its support from the minority government of India led by V. P. Singh, following the arrest of its leader, L. K. Advani, for leading a march on the holy city of Ayodhya where Hindu militants wanted to build a temple on the site of the Babri mosque, claiming that it was the birthplace of the Lord Rama. **29.** A 100-mile police cordon was thrown around the Babri mosque at Ayodhya. **30.** A few Hindu zealots succeeded in reaching the Babri mosque; it was reported that five were killed and 300,000 arrested during the rioting.

Nov. 4. Hindu militants called off their five-day siege of the Babri mosque at Ayodhya after L. K. Advani was released. **5.** The ruling Janata Dal Party in India divided into rival factions as a consequence of the Ayodhya dispute; Chandra Shekhar founded the Jan-

ata Dal (Socialist) Party with a third or Janata's Dal's 140 MPs. **7.** V. P. Singh resigned as Prime Minister of India after losing a vote of confidence. **8.** Rajiv Gandhi, leader of Congress (I), the largest party in the Indian parliament, turned down an invitation to form a government but agreed to support, though not to join, an administration formed by Mr Shekhar. **12.** Emperor Akihito of Japan was enthroned. **20.** President Najibullah of Afghanistan held talks in Geneva with moderate Mujahidin groups and representatives of the former King about the establishment of a coalition government.

Dec. 4. President Ershad of Bangladesh resigned after weeks of popular protest. **19.** Burmese opposition leaders set up a rival government at Manerplaw; the following day the Burmese military regime banned the National League for Democracy, although the winner of the May 1990 elections had been prevented from taking office. **23.** Cambodian opposition leaders and the Vietnamese-backed Cambodian government agreed in principle to a UN peace plan to end the country's civil war.

(1991). Jan. 5. The trials of pro-democracy activists involved in the Tiananmen Square demonstrations began in Beijing. **13.** During Sino-Hong Kong negotiations, the Chinese delegation called for a halt to the construction of the new Hong Kong airport. **26.** Wang Dan a leader of the Tiananmen Square protests was sentenced to four years in prison.

Feb. 12. Wang Juntao and Chen Ziming leaders of the Tiananmen Square protests were each sentenced to 13 years imprisonment. **23.** The Thai army staged a bloodless coup and declared martial law.

March 4. In China, three Hong Kong residents were sentenced for up to five years imprisonment each for aiding pro-democracy activists. **6.** The Indian Prime Minister, Chandra Shekar, resigned, causing the collapse of the government. **26.** In Singapore, four Pakistani hijackers seized an aeroplane and demanded the release of a number of prisoners held in Pakistan; the aircraft was later stormed by Singaporean commandoes and all the hijackers were shot dead.

April 4. The Foreign Secretary, Douglas Hurd, began a four-day visit to Beijing. **20.** In Afghanistan, over 300 people were killed when two Scud missiles, fired by Afghan government forces, landed in the Mujahidin-controlled town of Asadabad. **26.** In South Korea, the death of a student killed by riot police led to weeks of student protests and the sacking of the Interior Minister, Chun Doo Hwan.

May 6. Pro-democracy parties won the majority of seats contested in local council elections in Hong Kong. **15.** Jiang Qing, the widow of Mao Tse Tung and leader of the Gang of Four, committed suicide. **20.** General elections began in India, following the most violent campaign in Indian history. **21.** Rajiv Gandhi, President of the Congress (I) Party, was assassinated by a Tamil suicide bomber at Sriperumbudur, southern India; voting in the general election was postponed. **29.** P. V. Narasimha Rao was elected President of the Congress (I) Party after Rajiv Gandhi's widow rejected the office. David Gladstone, the British High Commissioner in Sri Lanka, was declared *persona non grata* by the Sri Lanka government, which accused him of interfering in the country's internal affairs by alleging irregularities in recent local elections.

June 11. At least 40 people were killed during clashes between security forces and Muslim separatists in Srinagar, Kashmir. **12.** The second round of voting began in the Indian general election, and the third was held on June 15; the Congress (I) Party emerged with the largest number of seats but failed to gain a majority. Former President Ershad of Bangladesh was found guilty of illegal possession of firearms and sentenced to ten years hard labour. **24.** Yoshihisa Tabuchi, president of Nomura Securities, and Takuya Iwasaki, president of Nikko Securities, resigned after it was revealed that their companies had made loans to criminals and that they had illegally gained clients by promising to compensate them for potential losses on Japan's financial markets. **26.** At a meeting of the Cambodian Supreme National Council in Thailand, members agreed to a permanent cease-fire.

July 4. Britain and China announced that they had reached an agreement on the proposed new Hong Kong airport. **10.** In Sri Lanka, Tamil Tiger guerrillas began a siege of the Elephant Pass army base. **24.** In order to obtain IMF and World Bank assistance to avoid bankruptcy, the Indian government abandoned centralized planning and introduced reforms liberalizing the economy.

Aug. 3. Sri Lankan forces lifted the siege of Elephant Pass by Tamil Tigers. **6.** The Bangladeshi Parliament passed a constitutional amendment abandoning the presidential system of government and returning the country to parliamentary rule. **20.** Indian forces stormed the Bangalore hideout of Sivarasan, who masterminded the assassination of Rajiv Gandhi; they found that Sivarasan and six accomplices had committed suicide. **27.** At a meeting of the Supreme National Council, Cambodian factions agreed to cut their forces by 70 per cent and place the remainder under

UN supervision. **31.** A general election was held in Singapore.

AUSTRALASIA AND THE PACIFIC

(1990). Sept. 3. Geoffrey Palmer resigned as Prime Minister of New Zealand and was replaced by Mike Moore; a general election was called.

Oct. 27. The opposition National Party won the general election in New Zealand. **29.** Sir Joh Bjelke-Petersen, the former premier of Queensland, was charged with corruption.

Dec. 6. Alan Bond, the Australian entrepreneur, was arrested after it was disclosed that he had wrongfully concealed receipt of a $A16,000,000 payment from the failed Rothwell merchant bank. **22.** The UN Security Council voted to terminate the UN Trust Territory status of the Federated States of Micronesia, the Marshall Islands and the Northern Marianas.

(1991). Jan. 24. The Papua New Guinea government and the secessionist Bougainville Revolutionary Army signed an accord ending the two-year civil war.

April 5. Western Samoa's first election under universal suffrage was held. **29.** In Wellington, New Zealand, the French Prime Minister, Michel Rocard, apologized for the bombing in Auckland harbour in 1985 of the Greenpeace ship *Rainbow Warrior*.

May 8. A general election was held in Kiribati. **11.** Bailey Olter was elected President of the Federated States of Micronesia by the country's parliament. **30.** The Prime Minister of Australia, Bob Hawke, was challenged for the leadership of the Labor Party by Paul Keating, the Deputy Prime Minister and Treasurer.

June 3. Bob Hawke won the majority of votes at a meeting of Australian Labor federal MPs and remained Labor Party leader; Paul Keating resigned from the government.

July 30. The New Zealand government reformed the country's welfare system.

Aug. 1. Britain recognized the Federated States of Micronesia and the Marshall Islands as independent states.

EUROPE
(For Eastern Europe, *see* separate summary below)

(1990). Sept. 12. The Second World War formally ended with the signing in Moscow by the four wartime allies and the two Germanies of a treaty unifying the two

German republics. **20.** The East German parliament and the West German parliament voted to accept the treaty reuniting the two German states.

Oct. 2. Germany was reunited at midnight. **3.** The reunified state of Germany became a member of NATO. **7.** Riots broke out, and continued for several days, at Vauix-en-Velin, Lyons, France, after the death of a young motorcyclist in a confrontation with the police. **12.** The German Interior Minister, Wolfgang Schäulbe, was shot and wounded by a schizophrenic drug addict while electioneering at Oppenau, Baden-Württemburg. **25.** In the Republic of Ireland it was alleged that Brian Lenihan, the Deputy Prime Minister and a candidate for the presidency, had lied about his role in attempting to persuade the Irish President not to dissolve parliament in 1982, in breach of the constitution. **31.** Brian Lenihan was dropped from the government by the Prime Minister, to ensure that the government won a motion of no confidence in the Irish Parliament; Mr Lenihan continued his campaign for the presidency.

Nov. 5. Thousands of French high school students took part in protests throughout France at overcrowding and poor security in schools; the demonstrations began in Sept. and continued sporadically until Nov. 16, often ending in rioting. **12.** After two nights of rioting in Berlin, police stormed tenements occupied by squatters; 300 were arrested and 85 wounded during the operation.

Dec. 2. A general election took place in Germany. **17.** Lothar de Mazière, the former East German Prime Minister and a minister in the united German cabinet, resigned from his post after allegations that he had been a East German police informant; he was later cleared and reinstated. **28.** The Greek government announced that it would pardon three leaders and ten other members of the military junta which ruled the country between 1967 and 1974; it reversed its decision after popular protest.

(1991). Jan. 9. Greek students rioted in Athens after a teacher was shot dead by unknown assailants in Patras. The protests, also against planned educational reforms, continued for several days; four people were killed and many injured. **12.** The Belgian government freed a Palestinian terrorist in exchange for four Belgians held captive by the Fatah Revolutionary Council. The Spanish Prime Minister, Felipe González, sacked the Deputy Prime Minister, Alfonso Guerra, after Guerra was implicated in a financial scandal. **17.** King Olav V of Norway died and was succeeded by his son, Harald V.

Feb. 25. King Constantine of Greece accepted the result of a 1974 referendum abolishing the Greek monarchy and handed over most of his remaining Greek property to the state.

March 8. The German government approved investment aid of £3·5 billion for the former eastern German länder. **11.** The trial began in Athens of Andreas Papandreou, the former Greek Prime Minister, and ministers of his PASOK government, on charges of corruption and embezzlement. **26.** A North African was shot dead by a security guard in the Sartrouville suburb of Paris, leading to three nights of rioting. **29.** Prime Minister Giulio Andreotti of Italy resigned.

April 1. Detlev Rohwedder, the head of the German government agency set up to privatize industry in the former east Germany, was assassinated by the Red Army Faction. **9.** In Istanbul, 36 people were killed when a Turk set fire to a Greek tourist bus. **12.** The Turkish parliament passed legislation removing constitutional prohibitions on the expression of communist and Islamic fundamentalist opinion. **13.** The new Italian government, led by Giulio Andreotti, was sworn in.

May 10. A week of sporadic rioting by North African immigrants began in Brussels after an Arab had allegedly been assaulted by police. **15.** Edith Cresson was appointed Prime Minister of France after Michel Rocard resigned. **16.** Karl Otto Pohl announced his resignation as President of the Bundesbank after differences with the German government over monetary policy. **29.** Basque terrorists bombed a civil guard barracks at Vic, near Barcelona, killing nine people; the leader of the ETA group responsible was shot dead by police the following day and a number of other terrorist suspects arrested.

June 9. Italians voted in a referendum to alter electoral laws to reduce Mafia influence. **13.** The Belgian parliament changed the Belgian constitution to allow women to accede to the throne. **20.** The German *Bundestag* voted to move the federal capital from Bonn to Berlin.

July 18. Hundreds of anti-American demonstrators rioted in Athens during President Bush's visit to Greece.

Aug. 8. Albanian ships carrying over 10,000 refugees forced their way into the Italian port of Bari. Several days of rioting by the refugees followed as the Italian government refused to admit them; the majority were later repatriated.

EASTERN EUROPE

(1990). Sept. 1. The withdrawal of Soviet troops from East Germany began. **2.** The main Russian-speaking region of the Soviet republic of Moldavia declared its independence as the Dnestr Soviet Republic. **20.** The East German parliament voted to accept the treaty reuniting East and West Germany. The autonomous region of South Ossetia declared itself a full union republic independent of Georgia. **24.** The USSR Supreme Soviet gave President Gorbachev power to rule by decree until March 1992. East Germany left the Warsaw Pact. **29.** In Yugoslavia, the Serbian parliament adopted a new constitution stripping the regions of Kosovo and Vojvodina of their autonomy; in Kosovo the majority Albanian population continued to defy Serbian direct rule, imposed in June 1990.

Oct. 1. After a referendum the minority Serb community in Croatia, Yugoslavia, declared autonomy. **2.** Germany was reunited at midnight. The Soviet government agreed to hold formal independence talks with Lithuania. **14.** In the second round of voting, the Azerbaijani Communist Party emerged overwhelming victors of republican elections. **24.** The RSFSR Supreme Soviet declared that all-union laws would only take effect in the RSFSR after ratification by the RSFSR Supreme Soviet; in an emergency session the USSR Supreme Soviet passed legislation reaffirming the supremacy of all-union laws over republican laws within the areas of its responsibility, pending a new union treaty. **25.** The Soviet republic of Kazakhstan declared its sovereignty. **26.** The Moldavian Supreme Soviet declared a state of emergency in Gauguz districts after the Gauguz (ethnic Turkish) inhabitants started to hold elections; the state of emergency was lifted on Dec. 6. **28.** Soviet troops were sent into southern Moldavia to prevent clashes between Gauguz and ethnic Romanian populations. **30.** The Soviet republic of Kirghizia declared its sovereignty.

Nov. 8. The Chancellor of West Germany and the Prime Minister of Poland met at Frankfurt-an-der-Oder on the German–Polish border to conclude a 'good neighbour' treaty and agreed to negotiate a new border treaty; the treaty, recognizing the Oder-Neisse line as the definitive frontier between the two countries, was signed on Nov. 14. With domestic unrest growing, President Alia of Albania proposed that secret ballots and independent candidates should be allowed in elections scheduled for February; this was approved on Nov. 14. **11.** The second round of elections in the Soviet republic of Georgia completed the victory of the nationalist Round Table bloc. **17.** The USSR Supreme Soviet voted to support a plan to reinforce the central leadership and the republics' share in it and gave President Gorbachev executive authority over all central bodies. **25.** In the first round of the Polish presidential election Lech Walesa received 40 per cent of the vote. In Moldavia, ethnic Russians held elections to the 'Transdnestr Republic' Supreme Soviet despite Moldavian opposition. **29.** Andrei Lukanov resigned as Prime Minister of Bulgaria after several days of anti-government demonstrations.

Dec. 1. President Gorbachev issued a decree reasserting the authority of the central government in defence matters and invalidating legislation in some republics which had set up local defence forces. The Soviet Socialist Republic of Azerbaijan changed its name to the Republic of Azerbaijan. **2.** President Gorbachev sacked the liberal Interior Minister Vadim Bakatin, and replaced him with Boris Pugo. **9.** Lech Walesa won the second round of the Polish presidential election. A presidential election in Serbia, Yugoslavia, was won by Slobodan Milosovic. Anti-government demonstrations began in Tirana, Albania, and spread to other cities; these later developed into riots and pro-democracy protesters attacked Communist Party buildings in Skhöder on Dec. 13. The Albanian government announced that independent political parties would be allowed in the February elections. **11.** The Republic of Georgia abolished the autonomous region of South Ossetia, which was seeking union with North Ossetia in the RSFSR; a state of emergency was declared in the capital of South Ossetia, Tskhinvali, the following day. After anti-government demonstrations, the Romanian government postponed the abolition of price controls until June 1991. **12.** A Soviet presidential decree ordered Moldavia to obey Soviet law and to normalize the situation in the republic, where ethnic conflict continued. **13.** The Soviet Socialist Republic of Kirghizia changed its name to the Republic of Kirghizia. **14.** Tadeusz Mazowiecki resigned as Prime Minister of Poland. **20.** The Soviet Foreign Minister, Eduard Shevardnadze, resigned. **23.** In defiance of federal warnings and threats from the Yugoslav army, 94 per cent of Slovenes voted for independence in a plebiscite; Croatia had already adopted a constitution which declared its sovereignty and allowed secession. **25.** Prime Minister Ryzkhov of the Soviet Union suffered a heart attack and resigned from office. The Soviet Congress of People's Deputies formally approved a number of constitutional changes subordinating the government to the President. Gennadi Yanayev was elected Vice-President of the Soviet Union.

(1991). Jan. 7. President Gorbachev decreed that South Ossetia's secession from Georgia in September 1990 was illegal, as was the removal of South Ossetia's autonomy by the Georgian government. **13.** In Lithuania, Soviet troops stormed the Vilnius Television station, killing an estimated 15 people and wounding many more. **14.** Valentin Pavlov became the Soviet Union's new Prime Minister. The Yugoslav Constitutional Court annulled Slovenia's declaration of sovereignty. **15.** Alexsander Bessmertnykh, was appointed Soviet Foreign Minister. **16.** The Albanian government postponed elections from Feb. 10 to March 31, after opposition parties threatened to boycott the elections, claiming that there was insufficient time to prepare. **20.** Soviet troops attacked the Latvian Interior Ministry; four people were killed. The province of the Crimea voted in a referendum to become an autonomous republic independent of the Ukraine. **27.** President Gorbachev granted the KGB and the Interior Ministry new powers which came close to imposing a state of emergency.

Feb. 9. Lithuania held a referendum on independence; over 90 per cent voted in favour, including two thirds of the Russian and Polish minorities. **15.** A declaration of economic and political co-operation was signed by the leaders of Czechoslovakia, Hungary and Poland in Hungary. **20.** In Albania, demonstrators toppled a statue of the former dictator Enver Hoxha; in response to unrest President Alia announced presidential rule and the formation of a new government. The Slovene parliament voted to dissociate Slovenia from Yugoslavia, removing federal powers over the next six months; the following day Croatia declared the primacy of its constitution and laws over those of the federation. **28.** Ethnic Serb municipalities in the province of Knin, Yugoslavia, voted to secede from Croatia.

March 3. Referendums on independence were held in the Baltic republics of Latvia and Estonia; 74 per cent voted in favour in Latvia and 78 per cent in Estonia. **6.** Over 20,000 Albanians fled to southern Italy, evading Italian attempts to prevent them landing in Italy, and causing chaos in Bari and Brindisi. **10.** Albanian refugees in Italy, disillusioned with their reception, began to return home. **15.** Boris Jovic, Serbian representative on the collective Yugoslav Presidency and current chairman, resigned after the majority of his colleagues rejected proposals for martial law; the representatives of Montenegro, Kosovo and Vojvodina later resigned. **17.** In a referendum, 76 per cent of Soviet voters supported the retention of the USSR as a renewed union; six republics refused to take part. **19.** The Yugoslav army declared that it would only intervene in politics to defend the territorial integrity of the country; following the army's refusal to support the imposition of martial law, the representatives who had

resigned from the federal Presidency resumed their posts. **31.** Albania held its first multiparty elections; a second round on April 7 confirmed the victory of the ruling Communist Party. In Georgia the Georgian majority voted in a referendum to become independent of the Soviet Union; the Abkhaz minority voted to remain in the Soviet Union, and no vote took place in South Ossetia.

April 2. Opposition supporters destroyed the Albanian Communist Party headquarters in Shkodër after clashes with police in which three people were shot dead. **9.** The Georgian parliament voted unanimously to restore Georgian independence. Soviet troops began to withdraw from Poland. **10.** Soviet troops ended the blockade of Tskinvali, South Ossetia, by Georgians. **23.** President Gorbachev and leaders of nine of the 15 Soviet republics agreed on measures to renew the Soviet economy, maintain order and make the Soviet Union a looser confederation. **27.** The Georgian parliament formally dissolved the autonomous region of South Ossetia and absorbed it into neighbouring Georgian districts. **30.** Boris Yeltsin persuaded miners, who had been on strike since early March, to return to work, explaining that the central government would give control of the mines to the RSFSR. The Armenian government alleged that 35 Armenians were killed by Soviet and local Azeri troops who attacked two Armenian villages in Azerbaijan; sporadic fighting continued throughout May.

May 6. Agreements were signed between the central Soviet government and the RSFSR transferring control of Russian coalmines to the RSFSR and establishing a separate Russian KGB. Thousands of Croats attacked federal buildings in Split, Croatia, killing a soldier; the federal army began to mobilize the following day. **9.** The Yugoslav Presidency ordered the federal army to disarm all civilian and paramilitary groups in Croatia; the Croatian government and ethnic Serbs in Croatia refused to co-operate. **12.** The 'autonomous region' of Kraijina voted in a referendum to secede from Croatia and join Serbia. **15.** Serbia and its supporters on the Yugoslav collective Presidency prevented the succession of Stipe Mesic as the next President in rotation. **19.** Croats voted in a referendum to declare independence from Yugoslavia.

June 4. The Albanian government was brought down by a general strike; Yilli Bufi was appointed Prime Minister at the head of a coalition government. **12.** The presidential election in the RSFSR was won by Boris Yeltsin. **19.** The last Soviet troops left Hungary. **25.** Croatia and Slovenia both declared their independence from Yugoslavia, although their sovereignty was not recognized internationally. The last Soviet troops left

MRS THATCHER RESIGNS

Margaret Thatcher, the longest-serving Prime Minister this century, resigned in November 1990 after eleven years in office (*Syndication International*)

THE BIRMINGHAM SIX

The six men convicted of the pub bombings in Birmingham in 1974 had their convictions quashed in March 1991 (*The Times*)

One of the western hostages held in Beirut, John McCarthy, was released in August 1991 with a message for the UN Secretary-General, holding out hope of further releases (*Press Association*)

THE GULF WAR

Allied land forces attacked the Iraqi forces occupying Kuwait in February 1991 and liberated the country (*Mike Moore/Rex Features*)

THE GULF WAR

Allied and Iraqi commanders met on March 3 to negotiate the terms of a permanent ceasefire (*Associated Press*)

KURDISH REFUGEES

Civil war in Iraq after the Gulf war caused thousands of Kurds to flee over the mountains into Turkey and Iran (*Colin Boyle/Select*)

Volcanic activity by Mount Pinatubo throughout the summer killed over 500 people and covered the surrounding area, including a US military base, with volcanic ash (*Associated Press*)

COUP IN THE USSR

A hardline Communist coup in the USSR in August 1991 collapsed after three days in the face of popular protests and international pressure (*Associated Press*)

The declarations of independence of Estonia, Latvia and Lithuania were resisted, sometimes violently, by the Soviet Union until September 1991 (*Associated Press*)

YUGOSLAVIA

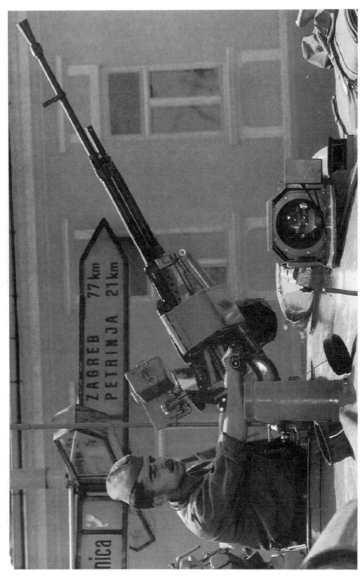

Yugoslavia hovered on the brink of civil war in September 1991 as several cease-fires were broken by clashes between Croats and Serbs (*Associated Press*)

George Carey, the Archbishop of Canterbury (*top left*), John Major, the Prime Minister (*top right*), Mikhail Gorbachev, Soviet President (*bottom left*), Boris Yeltsin, Russian President (*Camera Press*)

OBITUARIES

Dame Peggy Ashcroft (*top left*), Dame Margot Fonteyn (*top right*), Rajiv Gandhi (**bottom left*), Graham Greene (*Camera Press/*Associated Press*)

ENGLAND v WEST INDIES

Ian Botham (*left*) hits the winning stroke in the final Test match, which drew the series. The match was the last Test for West Indies captain Viv Richards
(*Allsport/Philip Brown*)

MOTOR RACING SUCCESSES

Nigel Mansell celebrating one of his five grand prix victories so far this season (*Popperfoto*)

WORLD CHAMPIONSHIPS IN TOKYO

Carl Lewis set a new world record in the 100 m final, in which six finalists ran under 10 seconds (*Allsport*)

WORLD CHAMPIONSHIPS IN TOKYO

Mike Powell set a new world record in the long jump, breaking Bob Beamon's record, which had stood since 1968 (*Allsport*)

Czechoslovakia. 27. The Yugoslav federal army moved to seize border posts in Slovenia; several people were killed. 28. The Yugoslav air force attacked Slovenian forces. A troika of EC foreign ministers (those of Luxembourg, the Netherlands and Italy) attempted to mediate; the federal government and the rebel Croatian and Slovenian republics appeared to reach a cease-fire agreement. 30. Stipe Mesic was appointed head of the Yugoslav Presidency; fighting between federal and Slovenian forces continued after Slovenia refused to suspend its declaration of independence. The EC troika returned to Yugoslavia in an attempt to revive peace negotiations.

July 1. In Yugoslavia, the second cease-fire brokered by the EC troika collapsed. 2. Yugoslav federal troops moved from their bases in Croatia and Serbia towards Slovenia; fighting broke out in Croatia as local militia attempted to prevent this. 3. An emergency CSCE meeting was held in Prague to discuss sending international observers to Yugoslavia. 4. The Yugoslav Presidency issued an ultimatum to Slovenia; the ultimatum was rejected. 5. Slovenia demobilized some of its forces and released prisoners of war; sporadic fighting continued in Croatia between Croat and Serbian militia. 7. Yugoslav leaders accepted an accord brokered by the EC troika; the accord was accepted by the Yugoslav Presidency on Aug. 8 and by the Slovenian parliament on Aug. 10. 15. The head of the EC monitoring team in Yugoslavia announced that it would not operate in Croatia where clashes were occurring daily between Croat and Serbian militia. 16. The second round of talks between the collective Yugoslav Presidency and republican leaders failed to start when Serbia and its allies refused to attend; a number of leaders met later in Belgrade. 18. The Yugoslav Presidency announced the withdrawal of all federal troops from Slovenia, apparently recognizing its independence. 22. Peace talks between the Yugoslav Presidency and republican leaders collapsed when the Croatian President walked out. 24. President Gorbachev and ten republican leaders reached agreement on a new union treaty; five other republics said that they would not sign and Armenia cooperated pending a referendum on independence. 26. A Central Committee meeting of the Soviet Communist Party approved President Gorbachev's draft party programme embracing the free market and multi-party democracy. 30. President Gorbachev and President Bush began a two-day summit in Moscow.

Aug. 2. The EC troika arrived in Yugoslavia amid continuing fighting; they left on Aug. 4, having made no progress. 18. Tengiz Sigua, the Prime Minister of Georgia, was sacked. 19. In the Soviet Union, hardliners headed by Vice President Yanayev mounted a coup and declared a six-month state of emergency; President Gorbachev had been placed under house arrest in the Crimea the previous day. In Moscow, President Yeltsin called for a general strike and incited troops to join resistance to the coup. 20. Tanks attempted to remove barricades from around the Russian parliament in Moscow, killing three Yeltsin supporters; however, the coup had already begun to collapse, having received little support in the republics. Estonia declared full, renewed independence from the Soviet Union. 21. President Gorbachev returned to Moscow and revoked all emergency restrictions; army units stood down; the coup plotters attempted to flee. Latvia declared full, renewed independence from the Soviet Union. 22. President Gorbachev expressed continued support for a reformed Communist Party; President Yeltsin ordered Communist Party cells in the armed forces on Russian soil to be disbanded. 23. The Communist Party was suspended in Russia. 24. President Gorbachev resigned as General-Secretary of the Communist Party of the Soviet Union, banned the party from all state organizations and handed its property over to the Soviet parliament. The Ukrainian Supreme Soviet declared the Ukraine's independence from the Soviet Union, subject to a referendum. 25. Belorussia declared its independence from the Soviet Union. 27. In a speech to the Soviet Congress of People's Deputies, President Gorbachev promised an acceleration of political and economic reform; he also acknowledged the right of republics to leave the Union. Russia declared that it would not allow other republics to leave the Soviet Union if they took largely Russian-inhabited areas with them. In Yugoslavia, Serbian forces launched an offensive to capture the Croatian town of Vukovar. 27. The EC recognized the independence of the Baltic states. Moldova declared independence from the Soviet Union. 28. The Soviet government was formally dismissed. 29. The Soviet Congress of People's Deputies suspended the Soviet Communist Party and seized its assets. 30. Azerbaijan declared independence from the Soviet Union. The Polish government resigned.

EUROPEAN COMMUNITY

(1990). Sept. 11. The European Parliament voted to give emergency powers to the EC Commission to integrate East Germany into the Community. 21. The European Commission assumed the power to vet all large-scale mergers within the EC and to veto any that restrict competition.

Oct. 8. Britain joined the exchange rate mechanism (ERM) at a central rate against the Deutsche Mark of DM 2·95. 27. A meeting of heads of government began in Rome. On Oct. 28, 11 of the EC leaders agreed to begin the second stage of economic and monetary union on Jan. 1, 1994, involving the creation of a EC central bank with powers over domestic monetary policy, and to achieve a single currency by the year 2000. The British Prime Minister, Margaret Thatcher, opposed the decisions, describing the plan on Oct. 30 as the 'back door to a federal Europe'.

Nov. 6. In response to US demands for radical cuts in EC agricultural subsidies, EC agriculture ministers agreed a 30 per cent reduction in direct subsidies to farmers over ten years and a limit to export refunds. **27.** Italy signed the Schengen Agreement, which will remove customs and immigration controls on common frontiers and strengthen such controls on external borders from 1993.

Dec. 15. An EC summit of heads of government began in Rome, at which it was agreed that discussions on political and on economic and monetary union would start and would proceed in parallel, concluding in Oct. 1991. **20.** The Commission suspended court action against the British government over dirty beaches in exchange for assurances that these would be cleaned up and that bathing waters would achieve EC standards by 1995.

(1991). Jan. 9. The Commission demanded that Greece sack 60,000 civil servants and improve tax collection to obtain a £1·5 billion loan.

March 11. The British Prime Minister pledged closer British co-operation in European integration; Mr Major declared that Britain 'was at the very heart of Europe', and saw no limits to the development of common foreign and security policies.

April 8. In Luxembourg, a special heads of government summit supported the British Prime Minister's proposal to establish a safe haven for Kurds in northern Iraq; EC leaders also supported Mr Major's call for a UN register to monitor and control all arms sales. **15.** The EC lifted most of its sanctions on South Africa; bans on arms sales, military co-operation and sporting links remained. **19.** The Commission announced plans to create an affiliate EC membership as a stage towards full membership for eastern European countries.

May 11. The President of the Commission, Jacques Delors, suggested a compromise to secure Britain's consent to the proposed treaty on European monetary union; the compromise allows the British Parliament to delay or veto the implementation of a single European currency in Britain.

June 17. An EC foreign ministers meeting was held in Luxembourg; Britain was isolated when it opposed a draft treaty on economic and political union. **24.** EC finance ministers meeting in Luxembourg compromised over Commission proposals for a minimum EC VAT rate. **26.** The Commission announced new proposed reforms of CAP; Britain opposed proposed compensation payments to farmers which appeared to favour smaller continental farms. **28.** An EC heads of government meeting began in Luxembourg; a draft treaty was agreed on June 29 which contained no reference to federalism and stated that a single European currency would not be created until there was greater economic convergence between EC members. The EC leaders also reaffirmed, with British reservations, their commitment to establish a European central bank from 1994.

July 1. Sweden applied to join the EC. **7.** The Commission approved new proposals to reform the CAP, cutting cereal prices by 35 per cent, beef prices by 25 per cent and milk quotas by 15 per cent. **18.** The EC signed an agreement with Japan on economic and political co-operation. **25.** The European Court of Justice ruled that British legislation designed to prevent foreign-owned trawlers from registering in British ports and fishing British quotas was illegal. **31.** The EC and Japan reached agreement on the sale of new Japanese cars in the Community.

MIDDLE EAST

(1990). Oct. 8. At least 18 Palestinians were shot dead and over a hundred were wounded after Israeli police opened fire on protesters on the Temple Mount, Jerusalem; the Palestinians had allegedly began the disturbance by throwing stones at Jewish worshippers at the Wailing Wall below. In Iran, elections to the Constituent Assembly of Experts were held, returning a majority of supporters of President Rafsanjani. **11.** Syrian forces in the Lebanon began to move against positions occupied by the forces of General Michel Aoun. **12.** The UN Security Council adopted Resolution 672 which condemned the Temple Mount shootings in Israel and supported sending a UN mission to recommend ways of protecting Palestinians in the Occupied Territories. **13.** General Michel Aoun ordered his followers to surrender and sought refuge in the French Embassy in Beirut. **14.** Iran and Iraq re-established diplomatic relations. **15.** The British Foreign Secretary, Douglas Hurd, began a three-day visit to Israel and encountered a hostile reception because of his critical remarks about the Temple Mount killings. **26.** The official Israeli report into the Temple Mount shootings criticized the police handling of the incident but said that the use of live ammunition was justified.

Nov. 7. The Lebanese government of President Hrawi began a planned reunification of Beirut with the gradual withdrawal of militia and their replacement by the Lebanese army. **14.** The Iranian Foreign Minister, Ali Akbar Velayti, met President Saddam Hussein of Iraq in Baghdad, the first high-level contact between Iran and Iraq since 1979. **23.** President Bush of the USA met President Assad of Syria in Geneva.

Dec. 20. UN Resolution 681 was passed, deploring Israel's deportation of Palestinians and calling on the UN to monitor their safety; a separate non-binding Security Council statement declared that an international conference should be held to help settle the Arab–Israeli conflict. **26.** Iran's spiritual leader, Ayatollah Khamenei, refused to lift the *fatwa* calling for the death of the author Salman Rushdie, despite Rushdie's declared acceptance of Islam.

(1991). March 4. The Crown Prince of Kuwait returned to the country. **7.** The Israeli government rejected the land-for-peace formula put forward as a solution to the Arab–Israeli conflict. **14.** The Amir of Kuwait returned to the country. **20.** The Kuwaiti government resigned after widespread public anger at the chaotic handling of the return to peace. **26.** Iran and Saudi Arabia restored diplomatic relations. Firefighters extinguished the first of Kuwait's burning oil wells.

April 1. Roger Cooper, a British businessman accused of spying and held without trial in Iran since 1985, was released. **8.** Israel agreed in principle to take part in a peace conference with Arab states under joint US–Soviet auspices. **12.** The Syrian government demanded that the UN play a significant role in the proposed Middle East peace conference. **20.** A new Kuwaiti government was formed but was rejected by opposition groups as it was dominated by the al-Sabah ruling family. **26.** The Israeli Foreign Minister, David Levy, met the US Secretary of State and agreed to EC participation in the proposed Middle East peace conference; he also agreed to Soviet involvement if full diplomatic relations were restored between Israel and the Soviet Union.

May 17. Douglas Brand, a British engineer arrested in September 1990 while trying to escape from Iraq, was jailed for life in Iraq for alleged spying. **19.** In Kuwait the trials began of 200 people accused of collaborating with the Iraqis during the occupation. **22.** Lebanon and Syria signed a Treaty of Brotherhood, Co-ordination and Co-operation, giving Syria *de facto* control over its neighbour.

June 8. A Kuwait court passed the first of a number of death sentences on alleged collaborators with the Iraqis. **16.** The Prime Minister of Turkey, Yildirim Akbulut, resigned; he was replaced by Mesnut Yilmaz the following day. **17.** The Iraqi government announced that Douglas Brand would be released; Mr Brand was handed over to British authorities in Jordan on June 20. **19.** Mudar Badran resigned as Prime Minister of Jordan and was replaced by Taher al-Masri. **26.** Martial law was lifted in Kuwait; the death sentences imposed on alleged Iraqi collaborators were commuted.

July 1. Several days of fighting began as the Lebanese army took control of Sidon and surrounding districts from PLO guerrillas, who surrendered on July 5 and agreed to move to the Bekaa valley. **14.** Syria accepted US proposals for a Middle East peace conference. **16.** Israel lifted its objections to the participation of the UN as an observer in a Middle East peace conference. **18.** An Israeli judicial inquiry blamed police incompetence and not Palestinian provocation for the deaths in the Temple Mount incident. **19.** President Mubarak of Egypt said that Arab states would suspend their economic boycott of Israel if Israel stopped building settlements in the Occupied Territories; the offer was supported by Lebanon, Saudi Arabia and Syria. **21.** The PLO dropped its insistence on attending a Middle East peace conference; Jordan announced that it would be prepared to attend such a conference.

Aug. 1. Prime Minister Shamir of Israel agreed to attend a Middle East peace conference. **8.** John McCarthy, a Briton held hostage in Beirut for five years, was released; Jerome Leyraud, a French aid worker, was kidnapped in Beirut a few hours later. Leyraud was released on Aug. 11. **11.** The UN Secretary-General, Javier Pérez de Cuellar, met John McCarthy to receive a letter from his captors. An American hostage, Edward Tracy, was released in Beirut.

THE GULF CONFLICT

(1990). Sept. 1. The first group of British hostages to leave Iraq arrived in Britain. In Jordan two days of talks between the UN Secretary-General, Javier Pérez de Cuellar, and the Iraqi Foreign Minister, Tariq Aziz, failed to find a solution to the Gulf crisis. A multi-national airlift began to repatriate refugees stranded in Jordan and Turkey. **4.** The US Navy intercepted the Iraqi vessel *Zanubia* and seized the cargo, the first seizure since the UN blockade was implemented. **6.** The House of Commons was recalled from recess for a two-day debate on the Gulf crisis; President Bush accepted Saddam Hussein's offer to broadcast direct to the Iraqi people. The Iraqi Foreign Minister met President Gorbachev for talks in Moscow. **9.** President Gorbachev and President Bush met in Helsinki and called for an unconditional Iraqi withdrawal from Kuwait. **14.** The British Defence Secretary announced that additional troops and aircraft were to be sent to the Gulf. The UN Security Council passed Resolution 666 allowing emergency food shipments to foreigners trapped in Kuwait and Iraq. The UN Security Council unanimously passed Resolution 667 condemning Iraqi raids on foreign embassies in Kuwait. In reaction to Iraqi abuses of diplomatic immunity, France expelled 29 Iraqi diplomats and nationals and Italy expelled Iraqi military attachés. **17.** The remaining EC states expelled all Iraqi military diplomats and restricted the movements of those remaining; Britain expelled two military attachés, six support staff and 23 non-diplomats. The Chief of Staff of the US Air Force, General Michael Dugan, was sacked after disclosing US plans to bomb Baghdad and to target Saddam Hussein personally in the event of war. **21.** Iraq expelled the military diplomats of 11 EC states. **24.** The UN Security Council unanimously passed Resolution 669 requiring its sanctions committee to investigate aid requests from countries affected by the trade embargo against Iraq. **25.** The UN Security Council passed Resolution 670 imposing an air blockade on Iraq.

Oct. 1. Lt.-Gen. Sir Peter de la Billière replaced Air Vice-Marshal Wilson as Commander British Forces Middle East. **20.** Anti-war demonstrations took place in the USA. **23.** The former British Prime Minister Edward Heath returned from Baghdad with 33 male hostages and five dependants, having secured the release of an additional 69 who returned later. **29.** The UN Security Council passed Resolution 674 condemning Iraq for taking hostages and oppressing the Kuwaitis.

Nov. 6. The Saudi Foreign Minister and the US Secretary of State agreed a joint military command in the event of war with Iraq. Following a visit to Iraq by the former Japanese Prime Minister Yasuhiro Nakasone, over 100 hostages, mainly Japanese, were released. **7.** The former West German Chancellor Willi Brandt met Saddam Hussein and secured the release of over 150 hostages. **8.** President Bush announced the dispatch of additional troops, tanks and ships to the Gulf. **12.** A British diplomat was expelled from Iraq after allegedly using 'inappropriate language' when addressing demonstrators outside the British embassy in Baghdad; Britain expelled an Iraqi diplomat. **22.** The British Defence Secretary announced that Britain was sending more troops and ships to the Gulf. **26.** The German magazine *Der Spiegel* published evidence of continued German involvement in Iraqi chemical warfare production despite the imposition of the UN trade embargo in August. **29.** The UN Security Council passed Resolution 678 authorizing 'all necessary

means' to ensure the complete withdrawal of Iraq from Kuwait if Iraq did not comply with existing UN resolutions by Jan. 15. Resolution 677 condemning Iraqi attempts to change the population profile of Kuwait was passed unanimously.

Dec. 6. Saddam Hussein ordered the release of all remaining hostages in Iraq. **15.** The Iraqi Foreign Minister, Tariq Aziz, cancelled his trip to Washington, where he was due to meet the US Secretary of State on Dec. 17. **16.** The British ambassador and the consul in Kuwait vacated the British embassy after a 111-day siege.

(1991). Jan. 3. Declaring his willingness to make 'one last attempt to go the extra mile for peace', President Bush proposed direct talks with Iraq in Geneva. Britain expelled eight Iraqi diplomats and 67 Iraqi nationals, mainly students. Iran declared that it would defend its borders and neutrality in event of war spilling over its frontiers. **4.** Iraq agreed to hold direct talks with the USA on Jan. 9. EC foreign ministers held an emergency meeting in Luxembourg to discuss the Gulf crisis. **6.** Saddam Hussein declared that he had no intention of withdrawing from Kuwait and said that Iraq was ready for the 'mother of battles'. **9.** At talks in Geneva James Baker and Tariq Aziz failed to find common ground. **10.** The British ambassador to Baghdad and four members of his staff left the city. **13.** In talks with Saddam Hussein the UN Secretary-General offered a UN peace plan for an Iraqi withdrawal but made no progress. Britain ordered 28 Iraqi diplomats and embassy staff to leave the country within 48 hours; four, including the ambassador, were allowed to remain. **16.** The Gulf conflict started with the launch of Operation Desert Storm, large-scale allied air raids on Iraq and occupied Kuwait; the first aircraft took off from Saudi airfields at 2150 GMT. **17.** US aircraft started to fly missions from south-eastern Turkey. **18.** Iraq fired seven Scud missiles at Tel Aviv and Haifa in Israel; nobody was killed. In response, the USA sent Patriot anti-ballistic missiles and US operators to Israel, which threatened military retaliation against Iraq. A Scud missile was fired at Dhahran, Saudi Arabia, but was shot down by a Patriot missile. **19.** The first ground action of the war took place near Khafji when Iraqi artillery shelled US Marine positions; four Marines were wounded. Allied naval forces attacked oil platforms off the Kuwait coast and captured the Iraqi garrisons. Sixteen people were injured in a Scud attack on Israel. **20.** Seven allied airmen, including two Britons, were shown on Iraqi television. **22.** A Scud missile struck Tel Aviv, Israel, killing three and injuring many. Iraq began to pump millions of gallons of crude oil from Kuwaiti installations into the Gulf. **24.** Allied naval orces recaptured the Kuwaiti island of Qaruh. 25. One person died in a Scud attack n Saudi Arabia and another in a Scud attack n Israel. 26. It was confirmed that Iraqi military aircraft had flown to Iran. 27. Allied aircraft attacked the Kuwaiti installations pumping oil into the Gulf and stopped the flow. 28. Saddam Hussein claimed that Iraq had the capacity to fit chemical, biological and nuclear warheads to its missiles and would use these if it had to. 29. Iraq launched a number of land and sea raids; in one an Iraqi armoured brigade occupied the town of Khafji as allied troops retreated. Eleven US Marines were killed in the fighting around Khafji, eight by their own side. 30. Oil began to be pumped from an Iraqi oil terminal into the Gulf, forming another slick. 31. Allied troops recaptured Khafji after heavy fighting.

Feb. 6. Iraq broke off diplomatic relations with Britain, Egypt, France, Italy, Saudi Arabia and the USA. 12. It was reported that Iraq had set over 50 oil wells alight in Kuwait in an atttempt to hide Iraqi troop positions. 3. About 300 civilians, mainly women and children, were killed when US planes bombed an air raid shelter in Baghdad in the belief that it was an Iraqi command centre; Iraq claimed that over 130 died when a stray RAF bomb hit a market in Falloujah during a raid on bridges over the Euphrates. 15. Iraq offered to withdraw from Kuwait and comply with UN resolution 660 but stipulated a number of conditions which were unacceptable to the allies. 18. The Iraqi Foreign Minister held talks in Moscow with President Gorbachev and discussed a Soviet peace plan. 19. President Bush rejected the Soviet peace plan. 21. Iraq agreed to the Soviet peace plan after further talks between Tariq Aziz and President Gorbachev in Moscow; however, in an Iraqi radio broadcast Saddam Hussein declared that he would not surrender. 22. President Bush gave Saddam Hussein until 1700 GMT on Feb. 23 to begin a complete and unconditional withdrawal from Kuwait or face a ground assault. Iraq began to destroy oil wells and other installations in Kuwait. 23. Destruction and atrocities escalated in Kuwait. 24. Allied forces began a ground offensive at 0100 GMT, encountering light opposition. 25. US troops reached the Iraqi town of Nasiriyah on the Euphrates. A Scud missile hit Khobar City, Saudi Arabia, killing 28 US soldiers. 26. Iraqi forces were routed; allied units engaged Republican Guard units in southern Iraq. Allied forces and local resistance fighters liberated Kuwait City. The Amir placed Kuwait under martial law. 7. Tariq Aziz rescinded the Iraqi annexation of Kuwait and offered reparations in return for a cease-fire and an end to sanctions; the Security Council demanded that all UN resolutions be accepted, and Iraq complied. Allied forces engaged the Iraqi Republican

Guard in a tank battle west of Basra. Nine British soldiers were killed by US fire. 28. The allied offensive was suspended at 0500 GMT.

Statistics

No precise figures of casualties have been released. The following statistics have been compiled from a variety of sources and are only approximations. The number of Iraqi casualties was distorted by propaganda claims and the civil war, and figures are necessarily imprecise.

Allied casualties

Killed in action: 224 (American 147, British 24, Egyptian 10, French 2, Italian 1, Kuwaiti 1, Saudi 33, UAE 6).

Wounded: 281+ (American 213, British 43, French 25).

POWs: 45 (British 12).

Air sorties flown: c. 100,000 (RAF 6,500), about half in combat (RAF 3,000).

Aircraft lost in action: 39 (American 30, British 6, Italian 1, Kuwaiti 1, Saudi 1).

Helicopters lost: 1 (American).

Israeli casualties

Dead: 14, of which 12 deaths were indirect.
Wounded: over 200.
Scud missile attacks: c. 40.

Iraqi casualties

Killed in action: about 35,000.
Wounded in action: about 65,000.
Civilian dead: about 1,000 (during Gulf conflict).
Aircraft lost: about 141 in action or on the ground; about 147 flown to Iran.
Tanks lost: about 3,500.
Artillery lost: over 2,000 pieces.
Armoured personnel carriers lost: over 2,000.

(For post-war events in Iraq, *see* below; for post-war events in Kuwait, *see* **Middle East.**)

POST-WAR EVENTS

March 1. A popular revolt against the Iraqi government began in Basra. The rebellion spread to other Shi'ite cities; a separate Kurdish revolt began in north Iraq. 2. The UN Security Council passed Resolution 686, calling for the release of all allied POWs, the rescinding of the annexation of Kuwait and the provision of details of minefields before a formal cease-fire could be signed. 3. The terms of Resolution 686 were accepted by Iraq. The allied commanders met Iraqi generals at Safwan, Iraq, to dictate the detail of the cease-fire terms; these included a prohibition on the use of military aircraft. Ten allied POWs were released, including three Britons. 5. Iraq released 35 POWs, including nine Britons. 15. The USA expressed concern at the failure to sign a cease-fire and moved its forces 30 miles further into southern Iraq. 17. Iraqi pleas to be allowed to move aircraft were rejected; on March 20 an Iraqi aircraft was shot down by the US Air Force. **19.** Kurdish *peshmerga* guerrillas claimed to have captured most of 'Kurdistan'. **20.** The US Air Force shot down an Iraqi aircraft flying over Kurdish areas; it shot down another Iraqi aircraft on March 22; in spite of this, Iraqi bombing of rebels continued. **28.** Iraqi government forces began a counter-offensive against the Kurds in northern Iraq, after suppressing the Shi'ite revolt in southern Iraq with great loss of life. **30.** Iraqi government forces recaptured most of the country, leading to a wave of reprisals against opponents.

April 1. Kurdish *peshmerga* guerrillas retreated to the Zagros Mountains, followed by thousands of refugees. **3.** Over a million Kurds camped on the Iraqi-Iranian and Iraqi-Turkish borders; many Kurds began to die in the freezing conditions. **4.** Saddam Hussein offered an amnesty to all Kurds who had taken part in the rebellion; this was rejected by Kurdish leaders. **5.** The UN Security Council passed Resolution 688, condemning the repression of civilians in Iraq; it decided that circumstances in Iraq threatened international peace and security, thus allowing UN intervention in the domestic affairs of Iraq. **7.** An international relief effort started. President Ozal of Turkey proposed a UN buffer zone in northern Iraq where Kurds could be protected from Iraqi forces. **8.** An EC heads of government meeting in Luxembourg supported a British proposal for the immediate establishment of a Kurdish enclave under UN protection in northern Iraq. **9.** The UN Security Council and the US government failed to endorse British-sponsored proposals for a safe haven for Kurds in Iraq. The UN Secretary-General appointed Prince Sadruddin Aga Khan head of the UN Inter-Agency Humanitarian Programme for Iraq, Kuwait, and Turkish and Iranian Border Areas. **11.** Iraq continued attacks on Kurdish guerrillas within the US exclusion zone. **15.** UN relief agencies were allowed access to Iraq to aid Kurdish refugees. **17.** British, French and US troops started to enter northern Iraq to establish and guard camps for Kurdish refugees. **19.** The Iraqi government condemned the presence of foreign troops on its soil. **23.** US and Iraqi troops confronted each other in Zakho after the Iraqis had ignored an allied order to leave the town. Iraq asked the UN to take control of the refugee camps established by allied troops in northern Iraq. The US government agreed to Iran's request for relief supplies for Kurdish refugees in Iran. **24.** Kurdish leaders announced that agreement with the Iraqi government had been reached in principle to implement a 1970 accord establishing Kurdish autonomy. **25.** Britain, France and the USA issued Iraqi forces with a 48-hour ultimatum to leave Zakho; all Iraqis, except for a permitted 50 policemen, had

withdrawn by April 26 when allied forces began patrols in the town. **27.** Allied officers met Kurdish guerrilla leaders in Iraq in an attempt to persuade them to lead Kurds down from the mountains into the safe haven; the guerrillas refused because of the continued Iraqi military presence in the area. The safe haven was extended east towards the Iranian border. **30.** Kurdish refugees were reported to be coming down from the mountains at the rate of 20,000 per day. The UN opened its first base in northern Iraq.

May 8. US troops completed their withdrawal from southern Iraq; the UN buffer zone was established the following day. **13.** The UN replaced allied forces in charge of the Kurdish refugee camp at Zakho. **20.** The UN Security Council passed Resolution 692 establishing a war reparation fund into which Iraq is to pay future oil revenues. **24.** The allied safe haven in northern Iraq was extended to include Dahuk. **25.** The mass repatriation of Kurdish refugees to Dahuk began.

June 17. EC foreign ministers agreed not to withdraw from northern Iraq in a way that would leave the Kurds in danger from Saddam Hussein; the US government made the same commitment on June 20. **28.** The UN Security Council demanded that Iraq allow an UN inspection team access to Iraqi nuclear weapons installations, after Iraqi police fired shots over the heads of UN inspectors photographing equipment at Falloujah, Iraq.

July 3. The UN nuclear inspection team left Iraq, having been prevented from examining all Iraq's possible nuclear sites. **8.** The Iraqi ambassador to the UN was required by the Security Council to produce a list of Iraqi nuclear installations and materials. **14.** Iraq delivered a new list of nuclear facilities and materials to the UN; this was rejected by the US government as incomplete. **15.** Allied forces completed their withdrawal from northern Iraq and formed a rapid reaction force to protect the Kurds from south-eastern Turkey. **19.** Iraq admitted that it had been developing a 'supergun'. **31.** UN inspectors visiting Muthanna, Iraq, discovered 46,000 warheads and 3,000 tons of chemical agents.

Aug. 5. Iraq admitted to the UN that it had conducted germ warfare experiments and that it had produced small amounts of plutonium. **8.** Following an attack by Kurdish guerrillas on a Turkish border post, Turkish forces launched raids on Kurdish positions in northern Iraq and established a three-mile buffer zone inside Iraq to prevent further border incursions. **11.** UN inspectors in Iraq were shown a supergun. **15.** The UN Security Council passed Resolution 705, which requires that a minimum of 30 per cent of Iraq's oil revenue is set aside for reparations

Resolution 706, which allows Iraq to sell up to £1,000 million of oil over a period of six months; and Resolution 707, which condemned Iraq for hindering the work of the UN inspectors.

INTERNATIONAL RELATIONS

(1990). Sept. 9. A summit was held between President Bush and President Gorbachev in Helsinki. **13.** Germany and the Soviet Union signed a 'Treaty of Good Neighbourliness, Partnership and Co-operation'. **25.** The US Senate ratified two bilateral US-Soviet treaties, the Threshold Test Ban Treaty and the Peaceful Nuclear Explosions Treaty; the treaties were ratified by the USSR Supreme Soviet on Oct. 9. **27.** Britain and Iran announced the restoration of diplomatic relations. **30.** Leaders from over 70 countries attended the World Summit for Children at the UN.

Oct. 4. The US Secretary of State and the Soviet Foreign Minister (Eduard Shevadnardze) reached agreement on a treaty reducing conventional armed forces in Europe (signed on Nov. 19). **10.** The Conference on Security and Co-operation in the Mediterranean was set up in Rome. **16.** Iran and Iraq restored diplomatic relations.

Nov. 14. The Soviet Union was persuaded to accept the inclusion of a non-circumvention clause in the Conventional Armed Forces in Europe (CFE) Treaty after Western concern at thousands of tanks being moved east of the Urals and thus outside the treaty's scope. **19.** A three-day summit of the Conference on Security and Co-operation in Europe (CSCE) began in Paris, attended by all 34 members; the 16 NATO and seven Warsaw Pact countries signed the CFE Treaty, limiting both sides to 20,000 tanks, 20,000 artillery pieces, 30,000 armoured personnel carriers, 6,800 combat aircraft and 2,000 attack helicopters. **21.** The Charter of Paris for a New Europe was signed by all the CSCE members, endorsing multi-party democracy, free market economics, human rights and a commitment to co-operation on environmental protection. **28.** Britain and Syria restored diplomatic relations.

Dec. 3. Talks began in Brussels in an attempt to prevent the collapse of the GATT Uruguay Round of negotiations; 25,000 EC farmers rioted in the city in protest at the possibility of cuts in farm subsidies. The talks ended without agreement on Dec. 7. **18.** NATO foreign ministers accused the USSR of supplying false data in the CFE Treaty. **28.** The UN Food and Agriculture Organization announced that Africa was facing a severe famine and would require substantial food aid in 1991 to prevent a disaster.

(1991). Jan. 28. After talks in Washington between the US Secretary of State and the Soviet Foreign Minister (Alexsandr Bessmertnykh) the superpower summit arranged for Feb. 11 was postponed due to a deadlock in the strategic arms reduction negotiations and to the Gulf crisis. **30.** Hungary was accepted as an associate member of the North Atlantic Council, the parliamentary arm of NATO.

Feb. 6. The US government announced that it would not submit the CFE Treaty to Senate for ratification after evidence of Soviet bad faith. **11.** The Unrepresented Nations and People's Organization (UNPO) was established at The Hague to represent ethnic groups not recognized by the UN. **20.** The Uruguay Round of GATT talks was saved from collapse when EC and US representatives agreed on a formula for negotiating food subsidy cuts; talks resumed on Feb. 26.

March 1. In Monreal, 41 countries, including Britain, signed a Convention on the Marking of Plastic Explosives for the Purposes of Detection. **14.** Germany accused the Soviet Union of violating international law after the former East German leader Erich Honecker was smuggled out of a Soviet military hospital in eastern Germany and flown to the Soviet Union. **31.** The military structure of the Warsaw Pact was dissolved.

April 12. In London, the European Bank of Reconstruction and Development was inaugurated. **16.** President Gorbachev visited Japan; talks ended three days later without reaching agreement on Japanese economic aid for the Soviet Union, on Soviet plans for an Asian-Pacific security network, or on disputed sovereignty over the Kurile Islands.

May 7. African, Caribbean and Pacific developing countries agreed to EC aid being linked to improve human rights in their respective countries. **14.** The Albanian and British governments agreed to re-establish diplomatic relations. **28.** A meeting of NATO defence ministers in Brussels approved the creation of a NATO rapid deployment force in which Britain would take the major role; they also agreed to reduce NATO forces overall. **29.** President Bush invited the world's leading arms producers (Britain, France, China, the Soviet Union and the USA) to join discussions on guidelines for the sale of weapons of mass destruction and associated technology to the Middle East.

June 3. France announced that it would sign the Non-Proliferation Treaty. **14.** Delegates from 22 countries approved a compromise arms control package which resolved Soviet circumventions of the CFE Treaty and allowed the treaty's ratification. **20.** The CSCE agreed to emergency procedures to solve crises threatening 'peace, security and stability'. **28.** The Council for Mutual Economic Assistance (Comecon) was formally dissolved.

July 1. Representatives of the six remaining Warsaw Pact countries met in Prague to sign a protocol terminating the Pact. **15.** The annual summit of the Group of Seven (Britain, Canada, France, Germany, Italy, Japan, the USA) opened in London. **17.** President Gorbachev met G7 leaders but failed to obtain direct economic aid. The G7 leaders gave their backing to the completion of the GATT Uruguay Round by the end of 1991. **22.** The

US government vetoed the fulfilment of a $267 million Iranian civil aircraft order by British Aerospace because the aircraft involved contains US components whose export to Iran is banned. **30.** President Bush and President Gorbachev began a two-day summit in Moscow; on July 31 they signed the START Treaty reducing their long-range nuclear weapons by a third.

Aug. 2. It was announced that Greece and Turkey had agreed in principle to take part in a UN conference to settle the dispute over Cyprus. **10.** China announced that it would sign the Non-Proliferation Treaty.

OBITUARIES

September 1, 1990–August 31, 1991

Acland, Sir Richard, Bt., Liberal MP for Barnstaple 1935–45, Labour MP for Gravesend 1947–55, aged 83—Nov. 24, 1990.

Adams, Allen, MP, Labour MP for Paisley North since 1979, aged 44—Sept. 5, 1990.

Allerton, 3rd Baron, aged 87—July 1.

Annaly, 5th Baron, aged 63—Sept. 30, 1990.

Arrau, Claudio, Chilean concert pianist, aged 88—June 9.

Arthur, Jean, American actress, aged *c.* 90—June 19.

Ashburton, 6th Baron, KG, KCVO, banker, aged 93—June 12.

Ashcroft, Dame Peggy, DBE, actress, aged 83—June 14.

Attlee, 2nd Earl, aged 63—July 27.

Bakhtiar, Shapour, Prime Minister of Iran Jan.–Feb. 1979, aged 77—*assassinated* August 8.

Bardeen, John, American physicist, co-inventor of the transistor and Nobel prizewinner in 1956 and 1972, aged 82—Jan. 30.

Batsford, Sir Brian, painter, publisher and Conservative MP for Ealing South 1958–74, aged 80—March 5.

Bennett, Jill, actress, aged 58—Oct. 4, 1990.

Bennett, Joan, American film actress, aged 80—Dec. 7, 1990.

Bernstein, Leonard, pianist, conductor and composer, aged 72—Oct. 14, 1990.

Bevan, Brian, rugby league player, aged 66—June 3.

Blakey, Art, American jazz drummer, aged 71—Oct. 16, 1990.

Bonar, Eric Watt, GC, aged 91—Feb. 26.

Boskovsky, Willi, Austrian violinist and conductor, aged 81—April 21.

Brown, Sir Edward, MBE, Conservative MP for Bath 1964–79, aged 78—August 27.

Brown, Freddie, CBE, cricketer, aged 80—July 24.

Browne, Coral, actress, aged 77—May 29.

Buchan, Norman, MP, Labour MP for Paisley South since 1983, aged 67—Oct. 23, 1990.

Buchanan-Smith, Rt. Hon. Alick, MP, Conservative MP for North Angus and Mearns 1964–83, and Kincardine and Deeside since 1983, aged 59—August 29.

Bunnage, Avis, actress, aged 67—Oct. 4, 1990.

Caccia, Lord, GCMG, GCVO, diplomat, aged 84—Oct. 31, 1990.

Campbell of Airds, Brig. Lorne, VC, DSO, OBE, TD, aged 88—May 25.

Caradon, Lord (formerly Sir Hugh Foot), GCMG, KCVO, PC, colonial administrator and diplomat, aged 82—Sept. 5, 1990.

Churston, 4th Baron, VRD, aged 81—April 9.

Coleman, Donald, CBE, MP, Labour MP for Neath since 1964, aged 65—Jan. 14.

Copland, Aaron, American composer and conductor, aged 90—Dec. 2, 1990.

Cromer, 5th Earl, KG, GCMG, MBE, PC, banker and diplomat, aged 72—March 16.

Cugat, Xavier, band leader, aged 90—Oct. 27, 1990.

Cummings, Robert, American film and television actor, aged 80—Dec. 2, 1990.

Dahl, Roald, author and scriptwriter, aged 74—Nov. 23, 1990.

Day, Jill, singer, aged 59—Nov. 16, 1990.

De L'Isle, 1st Viscount, VC, KG, GCMG, GCVO, PC, soldier, businessman, politician, Governor-General of Australia 1961–65, aged 81—April 5.

De Saumarez, 6th Baron, aged 66—Jan. 20.

Demy, Jacques, French film director, aged 59—Oct. 27, 1990.

Dewhurst, Colleen, Canadian-born actress, aged 65—August 22.

Doe, Samuel, president of Liberia since 1980, aged 40—Sept. 10, 1990.

Donat-Cattin, Carlo, Italian Minister for Labour 1969–73 and since July 1989, aged 71—March.

Douglas, Bill, film director, aged 57—June 18.

Dring, William, RA, artist, aged 86—Sept. 29, 1990.

Dunne, Irene, film actress, aged 88—Sept. 4, 1990.

Dunpark, Hon. Lord (Alastair Macpherson Johnston), Scottish Lord of Session 1974–90, aged 75—August 31.

Durrell, Lawrence, writer, aged 78—Nov. 7, 1990.

Dürrenmatt, Friedrich, Swiss playwright, novelist and critic, aged 69—Dec. 14, 1990.

Ebbisham, 2nd Baron, TD, international trade delegate, aged 78—April 12.

Elias, Dr Taslim, Nigerian lawyer, President of the International Court of Justice 1982–85, aged 76—August.

Elton, Charles, FRS, researcher into animal ecology, aged 91—May 1.

Figgures, Sir Frank, KCB, CMG, former chairman of the Pay Board and first secretary of EFTA, aged 80—Nov. 27, 1990.

Finniston, Sir Monty, PH.D., FRS, chairman of the British Steel Corporation 1973–76, aged 78—Feb. 2.

Fletcher, Raymond, Labour MP for Ilkeston 1964–83, aged 69—March 16.

Fodor, Eugene, Hungarian-born travel guide writer, aged 85—Feb. 18.

Fonteyn de Arias, Dame Margot, DBE, ballerina, aged 71—Feb. 21.

Frisch, Max, Swiss playwright and novelist, aged 79—April 4.

Frye, H. Northrop, Canadian literary critic, aged 78—Jan. 23.

Gaillard, Bulee 'Slim', jazz musician, aged 75—Feb. 26.

Gandhi, Rajiv, prime minister of India 1984–89, aged 46—*assassinated* May 21.

Garnett, Eve, author and illustrator, aged 91—April 5.

Getz, Stan, jazz saxophonist, aged 64—June 6.

Gibbs, Rt. Hon. Sir Humphrey, GCVO, KCMG, OBE, Governor of Southern Rhodesia 1959–69, aged 87—Nov. 4, 1990.

Gilbert, Joan, broadcaster, aged 84—Jan. 29.

Gowing, Sir Lawrence, CBE, RA, artist and art historian, aged 72—Feb. 5.

Graham, Martha, American dancer and choreographer, aged 96—April 1.

Green, Alan, CBE, Conservative MP for Preston South 1955–64 and 1970–74, aged 79—Feb. 2.

Greene, Graham, OM, CH, novelist, aged 86—April 3.

Hammer, Dr Armand, American businessman and philanthropist, aged 92—Dec. 10, 1990.

Heffer, Eric, MP, Labour MP for Liverpool Walton since 1964, aged 69—May 27.

Hellings, Gen. Sir Peter, KCB, DSC, MC, RM, aged 74—Nov. 2, 1990.

Henson, Basil, actor, aged 72—Dec. 19, 1990.

Hill, Sir Austin Bradford, CBE, FRS, medical statistician, aged 93—April 18.

Hill, Robert, FRS, biochemist, aged 91—March 15.

Ho Dam, North Korean politician and foreign minister 1970–83, aged 62—May 11.

Holmes à Court, Robert, Australian businessman, aged 52—Sept. 2, 1990.

Holmpatrick, 3rd Baron, aged 62—Feb.

Hosking, Eric, bird photographer, aged 81—Feb. 22.

Hothfield, 5th Baron, TD, aged 86—Feb. 5.

Hunter, Adam, Labour MP for Dunfermline Burghs (later Dunfermline) 1964–79, aged 82—April 9.

Hutton, Sir Leonard, cricketer, aged 74—Sept. 7, 1990.

Huxtable, Rev. Dr. John, first moderator of the United Reformed Church, aged 78—Nov. 16, 1990.

Hyde White, Wilfred, actor, aged 87—May 6.

Irwin, Col. James, lunar astronaut, aged 61—August 8.

Jaffa, Max, violinist and orchestra leader, aged 79—July 30.

Jiang Qing, widow of Mao Tse-tung and former Chinese Communist Party politburo member, aged 77—May 14.

Kaberry of Adel, Lord, TD, Conservative MP for North West Leeds 1950–83, aged 83—March 13.

Kahane, Rabbi Meir, extreme Jewish nationalist, aged 58—Nov. 5, 1990.

Kerr, Rt Hon. Sir John, AK, GCMG, GCVO, Governor-General of Australia 1974–77, aged 76—March 24.

Land, Edwin, inventor of Polaroid system of instant photography, aged 81—March 1.

Landon, Michael, American actor, aged 54—July 1.

Langdon, Michael, CBE, opera singer and director, National Opera Studio 1978–86, aged 70—March 12.

Le Duc Tho, Vietnamese Communist leader, aged 78—Oct. 13, 1990.

Lean, Sir David, CBE, film director, aged 83—April 16.

Lefebvre, Archbishop Marcel, excommunicated French Roman Catholic archbishop, aged 85—March 25.

LeMay, General Curtis, US Air Force commander in Second World War, aged 83—Oct. 1, 1990.

Lewis, Sir Arthur, economist and Nobel laureate, aged 76—June 15.

Lewis, Richard, CBE, opera singer, aged 76—Nov. 13, 1990.

Lincoln, Hon. Sir Anthony, High Court judge (Family Division) since 1979 and President of the Restrictive Practices Court, aged 71—August 12.

Lindsay, Kenneth, MP for Kilmarnock Burghs 1933–45 and for Combined English Universities 1945–50, junior minister in the Baldwin government of 1933–37, aged 93—March 4.

Lloyd of Kilgerran, Lord, CBE, QC, president of the Liberal Party 1973–74, aged 83—Jan. 30.

Loch, 4th Baron, MC, aged 70—June 24.

Lockspeiser, Sir Ben, KCB, FRS, scientist and administrator, aged 99—Oct. 18, 1990.

Love, Geoff, bandleader, aged 73—July 8.

Luard, Evan, Labour MP for Oxford 1966–70 and 1974–79, aged 64—Feb. 8.

McCrea, Joel, American film actor, aged 84—Oct. 20, 1990.

MacLeod of Fuinary, The Very Rev. Lord, Bt., MC, Church of Scotland minister and founder of the Iona Community, aged 96—June 27.

Mahony, Lt.-Col. Jack, VC, CD, aged 79—Dec. 15, 1990.

Marshall of Leeds, Lord, aged 75—Nov. 1, 1990.

Martin, Mary, American stage and film actress, aged 76—Nov. 4, 1990.

Michener, Rt. Hon. Roland, Governor-General of Canada 1967–74, aged 91—August 6.

Miles, Lord (Bernard), CBE, actor, director and founder of the Mermaid Theatre, aged 83—June 14.

Moravia, Alberto, Italian novelist and journalist, aged 82—Sept. 27, 1990.

Mortensen, Stanley, footballer, aged 69—May 22.

Motherwell, Robert, American artist, aged 76—July 16.

Moynihan, Rodrigo, CBE, RA, artist, aged 80—Nov. 6, 1990.

Mucha, Jiří, Czech writer, aged 76—April 6.

Muggeridge, Malcolm, journalist, broadcaster and author, aged 87—Nov. 14, 1990.

Murdoch, Richard, actor and comedian, aged 83—Oct. 9, 1990.

Muwanga, Paulo, vice-president of Uganda 1980–85, aged 67—April 1.

Namuth, Hans, German-born photographer, aged 75—Nov. 1990.

Nicholson, Sir Godfrey, Bt., Conservative MP for Morpeth 1931–35 and for Farnham 1937–66, aged 89—July 14.

Northbrook, 5th Baron, aged 75—Dec. 4, 1990.

Oakeshott, Michael, political philosopher, aged 89—Dec. 18, 1990.

O'Faolain, Sean, Irish writer, aged 91—April 21.

Olav V, KG, KT, GCB, GCVO, King of Norway since 1957, aged 87—Jan. 17.

Oswald, Thomas, Labour MP for Edinburgh Central 1951–74, aged 86—Oct. 23, 1990.

Parham, Adm. Sir Frederick, GBE, KCB, DSO, aged 90—March 20.

Parkash Singh, Major, VC, aged 77—March 23.

Pearce, Lord, PC, Lord of Appeal in Ordinary 1962–69, aged 89—Nov. 26, 1990.

Pearson, Sir Francis, Bt., MBE, Conservative MP for Clitheroe 1959–70, aged 79—Feb. 17.

Penney, Lord, OM, KBE, FRS, mathematician and physicist, director of British atomic weapon development in 1940s and 1950s, aged 81—March 3.

Petersen, Jack, OBE, British and Commonwealth heavyweight boxing champion 1932–36 and president of the British Boxing Board of Control since 1986, aged 79—Nov. 1990.

Pickering, Ron, OBE, sports commentator and athletics coach, aged 60—Feb. 13.

Ponsford, William (Bill), Australian Test cricketer, aged 90—April 6.

Portal of Hungerford, Baroness (2nd in line), aged 67—Sept. 29, 1990.

Pounder, Rafton, Ulster Unionist MP for Belfast South 1963–Feb. 1974, aged 57—April 16.

Priestland, Gerald, broadcaster and writer, aged 64—June 20.

Pugo, Maj.-Gen. Boris, Soviet Interior Minister and coup leader, aged 54—*committed suicide* August 22.

Rahman, Tunku Abdul, CH, first prime minister of Malaya and of Malaysia, aged 87—Dec. 6, 1990.

Rashid bin Said al-Maktoum, Sheikh, ruler of Dubai and Vice-President and Prime Minister of the United Arab Emirates, aged 76—Oct. 7, 1990.

Reading, Bertice, jazz singer and actress, aged 58—June 8.

Redesdale, 5th Baron, aged 58—March 3.

Reilly, Lord, director of the Design Council 1960–77, aged 78—Oct. 11, 1990.

Remick, Lee, American actress, aged 55—July 2.

Roberts, Emrys, Liberal MP for Merioneth 1945–51, chairman of the Development Board for Rural Wales 1968–81, aged 80—Oct. 29, 1990.

Roberts, Wilfrid, Liberal MP for North Cumberland 1935–50, aged 90—May 26.

Rose, Sir Alec, round-the-world yachtsman, aged 82—Jan. 12.

St Davids, 2nd Viscount, aged 74—June 10.

Sanders, Christopher, RA, artist, aged 85—August.

Seebohm, Lord, TD, banker and social work innovator, aged 81—Dec. 15, 1990.

Seton, Anya, American novelist, aged 86—Nov. 8, 1990.

Seyler, Athene, CBE, actress, aged 101—Sept. 12, 1990.

Siegel, Don, American film director, aged 78—April 20.

Singer, Isaac Bashevis, writer, aged 87—July 24.

Siskind, Aaron, American photographer, aged 87—Feb. 8.

Smith, Dodie, novelist and dramatist, aged 94—Nov 24, 1990.

Stanford, Adm. Sir Peter, GCB, LVO, aged 61—May 22

Stanton-Jones, Richard, engineer, aged 64—Jan. 30

Stirling, Col. Sir David, DSO, OBE, founder of the SA: Regiment, aged 74—Nov. 4, 1990.

Stradling Thomas, Sir John, MP, Conservative MI for Monmouth since 1970, aged 65—March 29.

Swann, Lord, PH.D., FRS, FRSE, chairman of the BBC 1973–80, aged 70—Sept. 22, 1990.

Taylor, A. J. P., historian and journalist, aged 84—Sept. 7, 1990.

Taylor of Mansfield, Lord, CBE, Labour MP for Mansfield 1941–66, aged 95—April 11.

Tortelier, Paul, French cellist, aged 76—Dec. 18, 1990

Trethowan, Sir Ian, director general of the BBC 1977–82, aged 68—Dec. 12, 1990.

Trimlestown, 19th Baron, aged 91—Oct. 9, 1990.

Tsedenbal, Yumjaagiyn, Communist Party leader o Mongolia 1958–84 and president of Mongolia 1974–84, aged 74—April 18.

Vivian, 5th Baron, impresario, aged 85—June 24.

Wainwright, Alfred, walker and writer, aged 84—Jan. 20.

Walston, Lord, CVO, farmer and politician, aged 78—May 29.

Walwyn, Fulke, CVO, racehorse trainer, aged 80—Feb. 18.

Watkins-Pitchford, Denys ('BB'), MBE, author and artist, aged 85—Sept. 8, 1990.

Wells-Pestell, Lord, CBE, aged 80—Jan. 17.

White, Patrick, Australian novelist and Nobel lau reate, aged 78—Sept. 30, 1990.

Wilkes, Lyall, Labour MP for Newcastle Central from 1945–51 and former circuit judge, aged 76—March 28.

Williams, Rt. Rev. Gwilym, Archbishop of Wales 1971–82, aged 77—Dec. 23, 1990.

Wilson, Sir Angus, CBE, novelist and academic, aged 77—May 31.

Winters, Bernie, comedian, aged 58—May 4.

Wolfson, Sir Isaac, Bt., FRS, businessman and philanthropist, aged 93—June 20.

Wright, Sir Rowland, CBE, Chancellor of The Queen's University of Belfast since 1984, aged 75—June 14.

Wroth, Prof. Peter, PH.D., Master of Emmanuel College, Cambridge, since 1990, aged 61—Feb. 3.

Yarborough, 7th Earl, aged 70—March 21.

ONE HUNDRED YEARS AGO

Events of 100 Years Ago (1892).—A selection follows of 'Remarkable Occurrences' (as 'Events of the Year' was then called), as printed in the 1893 and 1894 editions of *Whitaker's Almanack* covering the year 1892.

The year started with the Marquis of Salisbury as Prime Minister of a Conservative government but the elections in July resulted in a victory for the Liberal Party and Gladstone became Prime Minister for the fourth time in August. In Pennsylvania the Homestead strike by steelworkers against the Carnegie company lasted 143 days and ended in victory for the company but only after considerable violence and a number of deaths. On a lighter note, *Whitaker* hailed Baron de Hersch's horse La Flèche as 'the best three-year-old of the year' after it won the 1,000 Guineas, the Oaks, the St Leger, the Cambridgeshire, the Newmarket Oaks, the Lancashire Plate and came second (to Sir Hugo) in the Derby.

January

7. Death of HH Mohammed Tewfik Pasha, Khedive of Egypt, aged 39.

— Successful military operations of Major Yule's column in Upper Burma.

14. Death of HRH Prince Albert Victor of Wales, Duke of Clarence and Avondale, aged 28, elder son of Prince and Princess of Wales, and grandson of Queen Victoria.

— Death of his Eminence Cardinal Manning, Archbishop of Westminster, the head of the Roman Catholic Church in England, aged 83.

23 Polling in Rossendale division, Lancashire; Mr J. H. Maden elected by a majority of 1,225 over his Unionist opponent, Sir Thomas Brooks (since created Lord Crawshaw).

26. Deaths from influenza in London rose to 46 per 1,000.

February

1. Wall of Bridgwater lock on Manchester Canal destroyed by gale.

— Zanzibar declared a free port by the British Agent and Consul-General, Mr (now Sir) Gerald Herbert Portal.

6. Mr John Morley, MP, addressed a large gathering of his constituents at Newcastle-on-Tyne (Old Age Pensions).

7. Great fire at Hotel Royal, New York; 60 persons burned to death.

8. Mr Joseph Chamberlain MP, unanimously elected leader of the Liberal Unionist party in the House of Commons.

10. Strike of coal porters in the City.

13. Death of Admiral of the Fleet Sir Provo W. Parry Wallis, GCB, the 'Father of the Fleet', who in the *Shannon* was one of the captors of the American frigate *Chesapeake*, off Boston harbour, in 1813, aged 100 years, 10 months.

15. Mr James Alexander Willox, proprietor and editor of the *Liverpool Courier*, elected unopposed for Everton division of the city of Liverpool, in place of Mr. Edward Whitley, MP, deceased.

18. Mr Arthur Balfour, MP, introduced the Irish Local Government Bill into the House of Commons.

20. Heavy snow-storms in Ireland; traffic on railways greatly impeded.

23. The Commons refused by majority of 47 to consider the question of Disestablishment of the Church in Wales.

26. Mr E. S. W. Cobain, MP for East Belfast, expelled from the House of Commons.

27. Disaster among seal-fishers at Trinity Bay, Newfoundland; 40 frozen to death and many others severely injured by the cold.

March

1. Evicted Tenants (Ireland) Bill rejected by majority of 55 in the House of Commons.

3. Chertsey division, Surrey, election, Mr Charles Harvey Combe (*C.*), a brewer, returned by a majority of 1838 over Mr L. J. Baker (*G.*).

4. Polling in South Derbyshire: Mr Harrington Evans Broad (*G.*) elected by majority of 1,250 over Mr B. Melville (*C.*).

7. Extensive relief given to famine-stricken sufferers in Vienna.

9. Polling in East Belfast: Mr Gustav Wilhelm Wolff returned by a majority of 2,141 over Sir William Charley, both candidates being Conservatives.

11. Mr Thomas Joseph Healy returned unopposed for North Wexford.

— Mr James Henry Dalziel (*L.*) elected for Kirkcaldy Burghs by a majority of 1,036 over his opponent, Mr Cox (*U.*).

— Mr George Woodyatt Hastings, MP for East Worcestershire, sentenced to 5 years' penal servitude for fraud as a trustee.

— Explosion of dynamite in Boulevard St Germain, Paris.

12. General strike of miners at Durham—the price of coal rose considerably.

21. Mr G. W. Hastings expelled from the House of Commons.

23. The Commons rejected the Eight Hours Bill by majority of 112.

25. Payment of Members' Bill rejected by 65 votes in the Lower House.

27. Explosion of dynamite in Paris (Rue de Clichy); some persons injured.

28. Destruction of property by dynamite rendered a capital offence by the French Chamber.

— Victory of Lord Sheffield's cricket team over combined Australia by an innings and 230 runs.

30. Mr Austen Chamberlain, son of the Right Hon. Joseph Chamberlain, MP, leader of the Liberal Unionist party, returned unopposed for East Worcestershire, in place of Mr G. W. Hastings, convicted of fraud.

— Arrest of Ravachol, the dynamitard, in Café Véry, Paris.

31. Great fire at Mandalay, the chief city in Upper Burma; many families rendered homeless.

April

4. Termination of Walsall Anarchist trials at Stafford, with varying terms of penal servitude.

12. Fatal collision of workmen's trains at Bishopsgate station.

14. Sultan's firman of Investiture of HH Abbas Pasha as Khedive of Egypt read at Cairo.

18. Disaster at Hampstead Heath railway station, 8 persons crushed to death and 13 others wounded.

25. Café Véry destroyed by dynamite in revenge for Ravachol's arrest, six persons injured, the proprietor and one other subsequently dying.

27. Trial of dynamitards in Paris; Ravachol and his accomplice Simon condemned to penal servitude for life—*extenuating circumstances* being found.

— Women's Suffrage Bill rejected in Lower House by majority of 23, only 227 members voting.

29. Terrible hurricane at Mauritius; the western half of the island destroyed, and sugar crop entirely demolished, 600 persons in Port Louis alone killed.

30. Mr Thos Usborne (*C.*) elected unopposed for Chelmsford division of Essex, in the place of Mr W. J. Beadel, deceased.

May

12. Sir Charles Euan-Smith entered Fez on special mission to establish a commercial treaty with the Sultan of Morocco.

19. Action against two MP's for refusing to present a petition to Parliament lost with costs.

23. End of the 'Revolution in Gauges' on Great Western Railway.

— Frederick Deeming, author of a series of atrocious murders both in England and Australia, executed at Melbourne.

24. Second reading of Local Government (Ireland) Bill carried in the House of Commons by a majority of ninety-two, 612 members voting.

June

1. Close of Durham miners' strike after 90 days absence from the mines, in which about 200,000 participated, a reduction of 10 per cent in wages being agreed upon.

7. Meeting of the Emperors of Russia and Germany at Kiel.

8. Terrible fire and explosion in silver mines at Birkenberg (Bohemia), 319 lives lost.

12. A Protectorate assumed by the British Government over the Gilbert Islands in the Pacific.

17. Two immense gatherings of Unionists at Belfast to protest against Home Rule.

18. Principal streets of Oxford lighted by electric light.

21. Official reports received in Berlin confirming German reverse at Kilima-Njaro (East Africa).

22. Great Unionist meeting at St James's Hall, London, at which several delegates from Ulster Convention speak.

— The Duke of Devonshire addressed a large Unionist meeting at Bath.

23. Ravachol condemned to death for murder of the Hermit of Chambles.

— Unionist Convention, representing provinces of Leinster, Munster and Connaught, at Dublin.

27. Collapse of a bridge at Fettykil Paper Works (Fife), 5 drowned.

28. Dissolution of Her Majesty's Twelfth Parliament, the new Parliament to re-assemble 4th August.

29. Fatal balloon accident at the Crystal Palace.

July

5. Disturbances in Morocco, Sir C. Euan-Smith being met with hostile demonstration at Fez.

6. Struggle between employers and employed at Carnegie's Iron Works, Pittsburg (Pennsylvania). A gang of 250 armed men defeated by rioters; 10 killed and 40 wounded.

— Fierce riot at Tashkend, Russian Tartary, owing to attempted enforcement of sanitary precautions against cholera; over 160 killed and wounded.

7. Terrible fire at St John's, Newfoundland; more than half the city destroyed and 10,000 persons rendered homeless. Buildings of the wealthier classes covered by insurance, but those of poorer persons entirely uninsured.

— Eruption of Mount Etna devastated villages, fields and vineyards.

9. Nearly 100 labourers killed by explosion of Berkeley magazine, San Francisco.

11. Terrible disaster at St Gervais-les-Bains (Savoie) through flood caused by falling away of the de Bionnay glacier from side of Mont Blanc; 120 persons killed.

— Several persons killed in struggle between Union and non-Union men at Coeur d'Alene mines (Idaho).

— Ravachol executed at Montbrison.

12. Failure of Sir Charles Euan-Smith's mission to Morocco, through opposition of Sultan.

— First ascent of the Matterhorn by an English lady with two Zermatt guides.

19. A four-oared boat crossed from Folkestone to Boulogne in 5½ hours.

23. Mr Frick (Carnegie's manager) shot by a Russian Jew; action denounced by strikers.

31. Boiler explosion on Lake Geneva steamboat; six persons scalded to death and several injured.

August

3. Miners' Federation at Birmingham resolved unanimously to urge the new Parliament to adopt an eight hours labour law, with no exemption or local option.

— Great historical procession at Genoa in honour of Columbus.

4. Her Majesty's 13th Parliament assembled. Right Hon. A. W. Peel re-elected Speaker.

5. Supposed first case of cholera at Moscow.

8. Mr H. H. Asquith moved a vote of want of confidence in Her Majesty's Ministers.

— Carnegie's men resume work at Pittsburg.

10. Disturbances in Morocco; the Sultan's troops defeated outside Tangier by the Angherites.

11. In a closely-packed House the 'No-Confidence' vote is carried by 350 votes against 310.

12. Lord Salisbury's resignation and Mr Gladstone's succession to the Premiership accepted by Her Majesty at Osborne.

15. Outbreak of Buffalo Creek switchmen; a large amount of rolling-stock burned.

16. £20,700 collected and greater part sent to sufferers from the calamitous fire at St John's, Newfoundland.

17. Several cases of cholera at Hamburg.

18. Three thousand strikers attacked convicts' guard at Coal Creek Railway, Tennessee.

23. The strike at Coal Creek crushed out by military and civil forces.

— General increase of cholera on the Continent owing to intense heat.

25. Polling at Newcastle: Mr John Morley re-elected by majority of 1,739 over M. Pandeli Ralli (*U.*).

26. Disastrous explosion at Tondu Colliery, near Brecon: 112 persons killed.

— Winding-up of Sir Titus Salt's business at Saltaire; failure attributed to McKinley Tariff.

27. Neill committed for trial at Bow Street on charges of poisoning various girls in Lambeth.

30. Peace Congress at Berne, to recommend the establishment of International Arbitration Courts.

September

2. Strike and riots at salt works, Cheshire.

4. Terrific fire among shipping at Ichang, Hong Kong; over 150 lives lost.

8. Launch of the Cunard twin screw steamer *Campania*, the largest vessel afloat (600 × 75 ft.).

9. Resolution passed at Trade Union Congress for legal eight hours working day, except for miners, and admitting of exemption.

12. Run on the Birkbeck Bank through failure of Building Societies: all claims met.

14. Proclamations issued in Dublin removing remaining provisions of Criminal Law and Procedure Act (1887); the National League no longer styled a Dangerous Association.

— . Cases of cholera at Hamburg from 17th Aug. to this day 15,663, of which 6,764 proved fatal.

29. Polling in South Bedfordshire. Mr Whitbread (*L.*) gained majority of 242 over Colonel Duke (*U.*).

30. Opening of the Borough Road Polytechnic in Southwark by the Earl of Rosebery.

October

6. Death of Lord Tennyson, Poet Laureate.

— Resolution of East India and China section of London Chamber of Commerce to urge the Government to prevent fluctuation of exchange between silver and gold using countries.

8. Heavy storms of wind and rain, with damage to crops in North Wales.

9. Wreck of Norwegian three-masted *Irene* (667 tons) at Blackpool, with partial destruction of northern pier.

13. Cirencester election: Col. Chester Master (*U.*) gained majority of 3 over Mr H. Lawson (*L.*).

14. Riots at Carmaux mines.

19. The Home Secretary (Mr Asquith) announced the repeal of the Trafalgar Square restriction of meetings.

20. Great meeting of unemployed at Tower Hill.

24. Definition (unofficial) published of New German Army Bill. Two years' service to be adopted to obtain an army of 4,400,000 men by the year 1916.

31. News received by French Government of Colonel Dodds' victory at Kotopa over Dahomeyans.

November

1. The Southampton Docks passed into the hands of the L. & S.W. Railway.

3. Strike of Lancashire cotton workers against reduction of 5 p.c. in wages: about 45,000 out of work.

8. Presidential election in United States. Mr Grover Cleveland elected by large majority over President Harrison.

— Explosion of dynamite at office of police in Bois de Boulogne, the bomb being intended for the Carmaux Mines office.

18. Trial of Walsall election petition. Mr James unseated on account of his agent having paid for badges to be worn by his supporters.

— A steamer collided with lighthouse in Belfast Lough and knocked it completely over; two of inmates drowned.

29. Trial of Hexham election petition. Mr Clayton unseated on account of corrupt expenditure by his agent.

30. Trial of South Meath election petition. Mr Fullam's election declared void on account of intimidation by priests.

December

1. Murder of the ruling Monarch of Chitral, and the sovereignty of the State usurped by Sher Afzul Khan.

2. Shelling of seven villages in Solomon Islands by HM cruiser *Rapid*.

6. A Greek MS of 'The Gospel of Peter,' &c., discovered in a tomb in Upper Egypt.

12. Jabez Spencer Balfour, MP for Burnley, resigned his seat, and subsequently absconded on account of the 'Liberator' and other frauds.

21. Nizam-ul-Mulk, son and heir of the late Mehtar of Chitral, expels the usurper, placing himself and the State at the disposal of the Indian Government.

— The Ontario Law Society decides to admit women to practice.

23. North Meath election petition. Mr Davitt's seat declared void on account of spiritual intimidation exercised by Bishop Nulty's pastoral.

— Labour riots at Bristol.

24. Dynamite explosion at Dublin detective office.

27. New gold fields discovered in Utah, USA.

31. Serious labour riots in Holland.

WEDDING ANNIVERSARIES

First	Cotton	Fourteenth	Ivory
Second	Paper	Fifteenth	Crystal
Third	Leather	Twentieth	China
Fourth	Fruit and Flower	Twenty-fifth	Silver
Fifth	Wood	Thirtieth	Pearl
Sixth	Sugar/Iron	Thirty-fifth	Coral
Seventh	Wool	Fortieth	Ruby
Eighth	Bronze/Electrical appliances	Forty-fifth	Sapphire
Ninth	Copper/Pottery	Fiftieth	Gold
Tenth	Tin	Fifty-fifth	Emerald
Eleventh	Steel	Sixtieth	Diamond
Twelfth	Silk and Fine Linen	Seventieth	Platinum
Thirteenth	Lace		

GROSS DOMESTIC PRODUCT BY INDUSTRY

(Before depreciation but after stock appreciation)

£ million

	1983	1984	1985	1986	1987	1988	1989
Agriculture, forestry and fishing...	5,214	6,265	5,553	6,026	6,123	5,984	6,561
Energy and water supply	30,085	29,750	32,659	23,945	24,415	22,394	22,619
Manufacturing	61,401	66,446	72,615	77,831	82,579	91,196	97,380
Construction	15,711	16,928	17,748	20,127	23,051	26,953	30,274
Distribution; hotels and catering; repairs	33,230	36,188	40,497	44,827	48,937	56,561	62,133
Transport and communication.....	18,285	19,846	21,243	23,025	24,830	27,614	30,074
Banking, finance, insurance, business services and leasing	35,553	39,080	46,518	54,209	62,239	74,378	86,628
Ownership of dwellings	15,945	16,732	17,960	19,583	21,104	23,331	25,482
Public administration, national defence and compulsory social security	18,821	20,167	21,409	23,019	24,934	27,504	29,571
Education and health services	23,380	24,649	26,570	29,996	33,237	37,606	42,547
Other services	15,107	16,557	18,401	20,748	23,250	26,226	29,715
Total	272,732	292,608	321,173	343,336	374,699	419,747	462,984
Adjustment for financial services ..	11,148	13,000	14,450	16,373	16,671	18,969	25,242
Statistical discrepancy (income adjustment)	−367	619	126	−530	242	−749	1,032
Gross domestic product (average estimate)	261,217	280,227	306,849	326,433	358,270	400,029	438,774

Source: HMSO—Annual Abstract of Statistics 1991

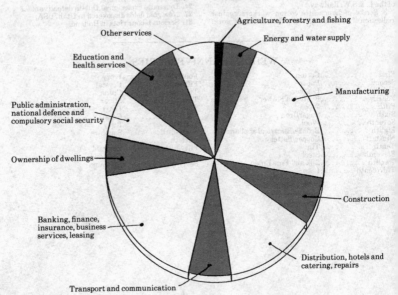

GDP by industry 1989

HOME FINANCE

Central government funds and accounts transactions   £ million

| | Consolidated Fund | | | National Loans Fund | | | | Central government borrowing requirement |
| | | | | | Other transactions | | Other funds and accounts | |
	Revenue	Expenditure	Consolidated Fund surplus/deficit	Receipts	Payments	Borrowing required		
1987	119,517	120,828	−1,311	16,452	21,441	6,299	2,240	4,059
1988	129,739	125,940	3,799	17,772	21,593	22	4,955	−4,933
1989	141,388	134,504	6,884	18,655	22,960	−2,579	2,556	−5,135
1990	151,260	157,668	−6,408	18,165	17,219	5,463	10,067	−4,605
Financial years								
1988–89	133,593	128,002	5,591	18,239	22,218	−1,612	5,507	−7,119
1989–90	144,920	141,492	3,428	18,857	20,395	−1,890	3,740	−5,630
1990–91	162,366	164,024	−1,658	17,706	18,333	2,287	4,770	−2,485
1991 1st quarter..	54,822	47,355	7,467	5,017	5,289	−7,194	−4,617†	−2,578
2nd quarter .	32,232†	45,135†	−12,903†	3,698†	3,577†	12,783†	6,121	6,662
1990 June	9,157	13,148	−3,991	842	634	3,783	1,613	2,170†
July	14,003	12,406	1,597	2,105	2,215	−1,487	1,964	−3,451
August	11,639	13,715	−2,076	1,393	845	1,528	547	981
September	10,384	12,847	−2,463	1,568	1,647	2,543	633	1,911
October	15,349	11,880	3,469	1,485	1,690	−3,263	−756	−2,508
November ..	11,914	13,168	−1,254	1,675	1,786	1,364	219†	1,145
December ..	12,511	11,663	848	475	902	−420	1,816	−2,237
1991 January ...	18,563	12,388	6,175	675	2,046	−4,804	4	−4,807
February ...	12,257	13,167	−910	2,821	1,568	−343	−47	−297
March	24,002	21,800	2,202	1,521	1,675	−2,047	−4,574	2,526
April	11,882	15,078	−3,196	1,344	1,000	2,852	2,022	831
May	11,033	17,428	−6,395	1,631	2,337	7,101	3,010	4,091
June	9,317†	12,629†	−3,312†	723†	240†	2,830†	1,089	1,740

† provisional.

Public sector borrowing requirement   £ million

	Total		Contributions by			Financed by				
						Banks and building societies/Overseas sector			Other private sector	
						External finance				
	Not seasonally adjusted	Seasonally adjusted‡	Central government*	Local authorities	Public corporations	Borrowing in sterling from banks	Foreign currency borrowing from banks	Other external finance	Notes and coin	Other
1987	−1,436	−1,671	4,059	4,664	831	−1,252	−365	−6,234	708	8,018
1988	−11,868	−11,960	−4,933	4,223	2,712	−686	−572	−734	1,040	−7,170
1989	−9,278†	−9,402†	−5,135	1,993†	2,150†	−3,581	−46	3,882†	1,040	−7,170
1990	−2,041	−2,047	−4,605	−3,153	589	169	−22†	−4,760	−93†	1,170†
Financial years										
1988–89	−14,659	−14,659	−7,119	4,604	2,936	−4,004	8	793	407	−8,021
1989–90	−7,933	−7,933	−5,630	941	1,362	−623	−85	1,330	849	−9,532
1990–91	−422	−422	−2,485	−2,045	−18	−478	121	−3,054	743	—
1990 1st quarter	−4,245	−2,710	−4,698	−1,187†	734	−1,611	−225	−2,018	−338	−1,130
2nd quarter	−5,847	−4,720	4,252	−1,647	52	1,333†	62	298	420	2,299
3rd quarter	−476	−1,551	−559	105	−188	−1,038	8	370	−116†	245
4th quarter	−3,167	−2,506	−3,600	−424	−9	−1,485	133†	−3,410	−59	−244†
1991 1st quarter	−2,626	−1,085	−2,578†	−79	127	−2,258	−82	−312	498	—
2nd quarter	6,922	5,795	6,662	−159	−101	—	—	—	—	—

† provisional.   ‡ Financial year constrained.   *An increase in debt is shown positive.

Source: HMSO—Monthly Digest of Statistics (July 1991)

BUDGET 1991 STATISTICS

The Finances of the Public Sector (£ billion)

	1990–91		1991–92 Forecast
	1990 Budget	Latest estimate	
RECEIPTS			
Inland Revenue:			
Income tax	55·0	55·5	59·6
Corporation tax[1]	20·7	21·6	19·5
Petroleum revenue tax	1·1	0·9	0·0
Capital gains tax	2·1	1·9	1·4
Inheritance tax	1·2	1·3	1·3
Stamp duties	1·9	1·7	2·1
Total Inland Revenue	81·9	82·9	83·9
Customs and Excise:			
Value added tax	32·1	30·8	35·7
Petrol, derv duties etc.	9·7	9·6	10·9
Tobacco duties	5·4	5·6	6·1
Alcohol duties	4·9	4·9	5·2
Betting and gaming duties	1·0	1·0	1·1
Car tax	1·5	1·4	1·3
Customs duties	1·9	1·7	1·7
Agricultural levies	0·1	0·1	0·2
Total Customs and Excise	56·7	55·3	62·2
Vehicle excise duties	3·0	3·0	3·0
Oil royalties	0·7	0·6	0·5
Rates[2]	12·2	12·2	14·4
Other taxes and royalties	3·2	3·5	3·8
Total taxes and royalties	157·7	157·5	167·6
Social security receipts[3]	35·4	34·9	36·7
Community charge receipts	11·2	10·4	7·6
Interest and dividends	6·4	6·4	6·1
Gross trading surpluses and rent	3·0	3·4	3·3
Other receipts	4·9	4·0	5·1
General government receipts	218·6	216·6	226·5
EXPENDITURE			
Central government's own expenditure	138·7	140·6	152·1
of which:			
Social Security	52·0	51·8	58·2
Health and OPCS	22·1	22·5	24·9
Defence	21·2	22·1	22·8
Scotland	4·9	4·9	5·8
Wales	2·3	2·2	2·5
Northern Ireland	5·9	5·9	6·4
Other departments	30·4	31·9	31·5
Overseas contributions to costs of Gulf conflict	—	− 0·7	—
Central government support for local authorities	41·8	42·6	52·5[4]
Financing requirements of nationalized industries	0·5	2·5	2·3
Privatization proceeds	−5·0	−5·3	−5·5
Reserve	3·0	—	3·5
Planning total	179·0	180·4	205·0
Local authority self financed expenditure	13·3	14·7	9·1
Central government debt interest	17·0	17·6	16·7
Accounting adjustments	3·4	3·4	3·9
General government expenditure	212·7	216·0	234·8

[1] Includes advance corporation tax (net of repayments): 7·5   7·6   7·9
  —also includes North Sea corporation tax after ACT set off and corporation tax on gains.
[2] Local authority rates and national non-domestic rates.
[3] Including National Insurance contributions.
[4] Includes additional support to finance reduction in the community charge.

Public Expenditure (£ billion)

	1989–90 Outturn	1990–91 Estimated outturn	1991–92 Plans	1992–93 Plans	1993–94 Plans
Central government's own expenditure[1]	127·5	140·6	152·1	161·6	167·9
of which:					
Dept. of Social Security	46·9	51·8	58·2	62·6	66·7
Dept. of Health and OPCS	19·9	22·5	24·9	26·3	27·5
Ministry of Defence	20·8	22·1	22·8	23·4	23·4
Scotland	4·4	4·9	5·8	6·0	6·2
Wales	1·9	2·2	2·5	2·6	2·7
Northern Ireland	5·7	5·9	6·4	6·8	7·1
Other departments	27·9	31·9	31·5	33·9	34·3
Overseas contributions to cost of Gulf conflict		− 0·7			
Central government support for local authorities	38·4	42·6	52·5	55·7	56·6
of which:					
Revenue/Rate Support Grant	13·0	13·1	13·6 ⎫		
Non-domestic rate payments	11·4	12·1	14·3 ⎬	49·9	50·7
Current specific grants	9·7	12·2	18·9 ⎭		
Capital grants	0·9	1·1	1·5	1·5	1·5
Credit approvals	3·4	4·0	4·3	4·3	4·4
Financing requirements of nationalized industries	1·1	2·5	2·3	2·1	2·0
Privatization proceeds	− 4·2	− 5·3	− 5·5	− 5·5	− 5·5
Reserve			3·5	7·0	10·5
Planning total	162·9	180·4	205·0	221·0	231·5
Local authority self-financed expenditure[2]	14·5	14·7	9·1	9¼	11¼
Central government debt interest[3]	17·8	17·6	16·7	17	17¼
Other adjustments[3]	4·2	3·4	3·9	5	5¼
General government expenditure	199·4	216·0	234·8	252	266

[1] Includes the financing requirements of public corporations other than the nationalized industries.
[2] Local authority self-financed expenditure is the difference between total local authority expenditure and central government support to local authorities.
[3] 1992–93 and 1993–94 figures rounded to nearest £¼ billion.

Public expenditure 1989–90 Outturn

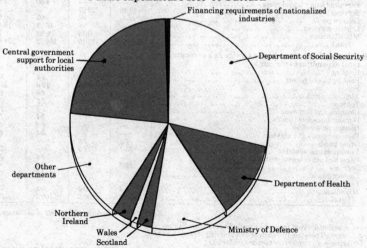

Financing requirements of nationalized industries

Central government support for local authorities

Department of Social Security

Other departments

Northern Ireland

Wales

Scotland

Department of Health

Ministry of Defence

HOUSEHOLDS AND THEIR EXPENDITURE[1]

(United Kingdom)

	1985	1986	1987	1988
Number of households supplying data	7,012	7,178	7,396	7,265
Total number of persons	18,206	18,330	18,735	18,280
Total number of adults[2]	13,401	13,554	13,902	13,640
Household percentage distribution by tenure				
Rented unfurnished	*34·9*	*33·9*	*32·5*	*30·3*
Rented furnished	*2·5*	*3·0*	*3·3*	*2·8*
Rent-free	*2·1*	*2·0*	*2·1*	*1·7*
Owner-occupied	*60·5*	*61·1*	*62·2*	*65·1*
Average number of persons per household				
All persons	2·596	2·554	2·533	2·516
Males	1·258	1·236	1·223	1·229
Females	1·339	1·317	1·310	1·288
Adults[2]	1·911	1·888	1·880	1·877
Persons under 65	1·552	1·526	1·512	1·504
Persons 65 and over	0·359	0·362	0·368	0·374
Children[2]	0·685	0·665	0·653	0·639
Children under 2	0·077	0·073	0·078	0·073
Children 2 and under 5	0·114	0·118	0·118	0·111
Children 5 and under 18	0·495	0·474	0·457	0·455
Persons working	1·164	1·160	1·161	1·168
Persons not working	1·433	1·394	1·372	1·348
Men 65 and over, women 60 and over	0·407	0·403	0·408	0·406
Others	1·026	0·991	0·965	0·942
Average weekly household expenditure on commodities and services (£)				
Housing[3]	26·63	29·92	30·42	35·81
Fuel, light and power	9·95	10·43	10·55	10·48
Food	32·70	34·97	35·79	38·28
Alcoholic drink	7·95	8·21	8·70	9·19
Tobacco	4·42	4·55	4·67	4·45
Clothing and footwear	11·92	13·46	13·32	14·52
Durable household goods	—	13·67	13·48	15·01
Household services	—	—	8·23	9·80
Personal goods and services	—	—	7·02	8·13
Other goods	12·59	13·87	—	—
Transport and vehicles	24·56	25·43	23·80	25·31
Fares and other travel costs	—	—	4·60	4·88
Services	19·48	22·67	—	—
Leisure goods	—	—	9·03	9·65
Leisure services	—	—	18·11	18·13
Miscellaneous	0·68	0·74	0·88	0·78
Total	162·50	178·10	188·62	204·41
Expenditure on commodity or service as a percentage of total expenditure (per cent)				
Housing[3]	*16·4*	*16·8*	*16·1*	*17·5*
Fuel, light and power	*6·1*	*5·9*	*5·6*	*5·1*
Food	*20·1*	*19·6*	*19·0*	*18·7*
Alcoholic drink	*4·9*	*4·6*	*4·6*	*4·5*
Tobacco	*2·7*	*2·6*	*2·5*	*2·2*
Clothing and footwear	*7·3*	*7·5*	*7·1*	*7·1*
Durable household goods	—	*7·7*	*7·1*	*7·3*
Household services	—	—	*4·4*	*4·8*
Personal goods and services	—	—	*3·7*	*4·0*
Other goods	*7·8*	*7·8*	—	—
Transport and vehicles	*15·1*	*14·3*	—	*12·4*
Fares and other travel costs	—	—	*2·4*	*2·4*
Services	*12·0*	*12·7*	*12·6*	—
Leisure goods	—	—	*4·8*	*4·7*
Leisure services	—	—	*9·6*	*8·9*
Miscellaneous	*0·4*	*0·4*	*0·5*	*0·4*
Total	*100·0*	*100·0*	*100·0*	*100·0*

Source: HMSO—Annual Abstract of Statistics 1991

[1] Information derived from the Family Expenditure Survey.
[2] Adults = all persons 18 and over and married persons under 18.
   Children = all unmarried persons under 18.
[3] Excludes mortgage payments but includes imputed expenditure (i.e. the weekly equivalent of rateable value).

Average Weekly Household Expenditure 1988

Weekly expenditure

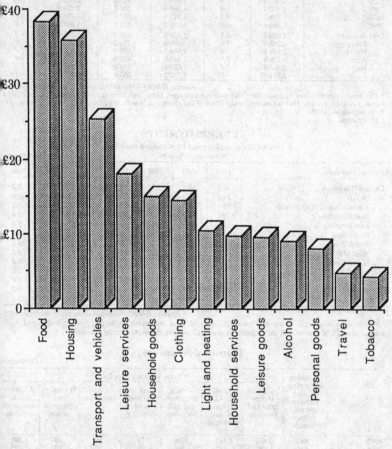

Commodities and Services

Unemployment in the United Kingdom

Thousands

	Not seasonally adjusted		Seasonally adjusted*			
	Total	% rate	Males	Females	Total	% rate
1985................	3,271·3	*11·8*	2,106·5	921·5	3,027·9	*10·9*
1986................	3,289·1	*11·8*	2,139·0	959·0	3,097·9	*11·1*
1987................	2,953·4	*10·6*	1,955·3	851·2	2,806·5	*10·0*
1988................	2,370·4	*8·4*	1,588·1	686·8	2,274·9	*8·1*
1989................	1,798·7	*6·3*	1,277·4	507·0	1,784·4	*6·3*
1990................	1,664·5	*5·8*	1,230·3	431·4	1,661·7	*5·8*
1991 January	1,959·7	*6·9*	1,425·6	466·0	1,891·6	*6·7*
February	2,045·4	*7·2*	1,495·6	484·2	1,979·8	*7·0*
March	2,142·1	*7·5*	1,581·2	509·8	2,091·0	*7·4*
April	2,198·5	*7·7*	1,644·8	528·8	2,173·6	*7·6*
May	2,213·8	*7·8*	1,697·4†	543·9†	2,241·3†	*7·9*
June	2,241·0†	*7·9†*	1,745·2	555·8	2,301·0	*8·1†*

Source: HMSO—Monthly Digest of Statistics (July 1991)

* The seasonally adjusted figures relate only to claimants aged 18 or over, in order to maintain the consistent series, available back to 1971, allowing for the effect of the change in benefit regulations for under 18 year-olds from September 1988.
† provisional.

UNEMPLOYMENT
Rates of Unemployment by standard regions.
Seasonally adjusted

Percentages

Annual averages	1983	1984	1985	1986	1987	1988	1989
United Kingdom	*10·5*	*10·7*	*11·0*	*11·2*	*10·1*	*8·1*	*6·3*
North	*14·6*	*15·3*	*15·5*	*15·4*	*14·3*	*12·1*	*10·0*
Yorkshire and Humberside	*11·4*	*11·7*	*12·1*	*12·6*	*11·5*	*9·6*	*7·7*
East Midlands	*9·5*	*9·9*	*9·9*	*10·1*	*9·2*	*7·4*	*5·6*
East Anglia	*8·0*	*7·9*	*8·1*	*8·5*	*7·3*	*5·2*	*3·6*
South East	*7·5*	*7·8*	*8·1*	*8·3*	*7·2*	*5·3*	*3·9*
South West	*8·7*	*9·0*	*9·3*	*9·5*	*8·1*	*6·2*	*4·5*
West Midlands	*12·9*	*12·7*	*12·8*	*12·9*	*11·4*	*8·9*	*6·6*
North West	*13·4*	*13·6*	*13·7*	*13·8*	*12·5*	*10·4*	*8·4*
England	*10·0*	*10·6*	*11·0*	*11·3*	*10·1*	*8·0*	*6·2*
Wales	*12·9*	*13·2*	*13·7*	*13·6*	*12·1*	*10·0*	*7·4*
Scotland	*12·3*	*12·6*	*12·9*	*13·4*	*13·1*	*11·3*	*9·3*
Northern Ireland	*15·5*	*15·9*	*16·0*	*17·4*	*17·2*	*16·0*	*15·1*

Source: HMSO—Annual Abstract of Statistics 1991

[1] Percentages calculated using mid-year estimates of total employees in employment, unemployed, self-employed and HM Forces, and participants in work-related government training schemes.

Industrial Stoppages

Thousands

	Workers beginning involvement in period in any dispute	Total working days lost						
		All industries and services	Coal, coke, mineral oil and natural gas	Metals, engineering and vehicles	Textiles, footwear and clothing	Construction	Transport and communication	All other industries and services
1985..........	643	6,402	4,143	590	31	50	197	1,391
1986..........	538	1,920	143	895	38	33	190	622
1987..........	884	3,546	217	458	50	22	1,705	1,095
1988..........	759	3,702	222	1,456	90	17	1,490	428
1989..........	727	4,128	52	655	16	128	625	2,652
1990†	285	1,903	94	953	24	14	177	641
1991 January .	6	44†	5†	2	—	4	2	31†
February	14	35	4	3	—	—	4	25
March ...	40	56	1	5	—	3	2	46
April	9†	100	—	10†	—	2†	2	87
May	14	87	2	43	—	—	31†	11

† provisional.

Source: HMSO—Monthly Digest of Statistics (July 1991)

AGRICULTURE

Estimated quantity of crops and grass harvested

Thousand tonnes

	1984	1985	1986	1987	1988	1989
Cereals						
Wheat	14,970	12,050	13,910	11,940	11,720	n/a
Barley	11,070	9,740	10,010	9,225	8,705	n/a
Oats	515	615	505	452	545	n/a
Mixed corn for threshing	35	31	29	26	22	n/a
Rye for threshing	28	35	32	32	34	n/a
Potatoes						
Early crop	396	401	360	395	420	368
Main crop	6,982	6,462	6,051	6,322	6,479	5,847
Fodder crops						
Beans for stockfeeding	125	155	230	294	—	n/a
Turnips and swedes	3,960	3,300	3,855	3,451	3,327	n/a
Fodder beet and mangolds	570	815	845	782	735	n/a
Maize for threshing or stockfeeding	580	770	915	782	876	n/a
Rape, kale, cabbage, savoys and kohlrabi						
for stockfeeding	1,805	1,555	1,380	1,320	735	n/a
Peas harvested dry for stockfeeding	170	215	330	310	—	n/a
Other crops						
Sugar beet	9,015	7,715	8,120	7,992	8,152	n/a
Rape grown for oilseed	925	895	965	1,326	—	n/a
Hops	8	6	5	5	3	5
Hay	5,700	4,650	4,675	n/a	n/a	n/a
Horticultural crops						
Vegetables grown in the open:						
Brussels sprouts	169	152	168	161	156	141
Cabbage (including savoys and spring greens)	670	683	688	692	670	678
Cauliflowers	344	356	360	373	361	365
Carrots	572	600	635	568	591	509
Parsnips	57	62	68	62	69	50
Turnips and swedes	143	140	163	166	127	120
Beetroot	115	114	95	101	102	90
Onions, dry bulb	238	268	247	287	355	251
Onions, salad	22	25	30	31	27	28
Leeks	53	60	71	72	64	66
Broad beans	21	19	14	11	9	9
Runner beans including French	77	65	67	51	54	48
Peas, green for market	27	26	20	13	15	18
Peas, green for processing	241	206	239	182	203	180
Celery	57	53	65	55	61	71
Lettuce	153	166	158	174	156	178
Rhubarb	26	26	28	27	24	24
Protected crops						
Tomatoes	129	125	131	130	117	130
Cucumbers	68	71	76	79	95	94
Lettuce	48	49	50	52	55	54
Fruit crops						
Total dessert apples	184	161	163	165	134	236
Total culinary apples	163	145	139	125	124	159
Pears	48	51	47	66	32	28
Plums	34	24	33	36	24	13
Cherries	5	5	4	4	2	4
Soft fruit	114	111	109	106	105	89

Source: HMSO—Annual Abstract of Statistics 1991

Cattle, Sheep, Pigs and Poultry on Agricultural Holdings

Thousands

At June each year	1983	1984	1985	1986	1987	1988	1989
Cattle and calves: total	13,290	13,213	12,911	12,533	12,158	11,872	11,977
Dairy herd	3,333	3,281	3,150	3,138	3,042	2,911	2,865
Beef herd	1,358	1,351	1,333	1,308	1,343	1,373	1,495
Heifers in calf (first calf)	847	811	874	879	774	834	793
Bulls for service	83	80	78	76	74	75	78
Other cattle:							
Two years old and over	904	905	852	769	732	726	733
One year old and under two	3,059	3,069	3,012	2,819	2,749	2,669	2,600
Six months old and under one year	1,924	1,949	1,905	1,876	1,844	1,702	1,775
Under six months old	1,783	1,768	1,707	1,668	1,599	1,581	1,637
Sheep and lambs: total	34,069	34,802	35,628	37,016	38,701	40,942	42,967
Breeding ewes	13,310	13,648	13,893	14,252	14,780	15,461	16,154
Rams for service	383	393	406	419	437	461	491
Other sheep	3,764	3,680	3,763	3,961	4,107	4,433	4,740
Lambs under one year old	16,612	17,080	17,566	18,384	19,377	20,587	21,582
Pigs: total	8,174	7,689	7,865	7,937	7,942	7,980	7,509
Breeding herd	856	800	828	824	820	804	757
Boars for service	45	42	44	44	44	43	42
Gilts not yet in pig	82	77	80	79	81	73	74
Barren sows for fattening	15	12	12	12	11	12	10
Other pigs:							
110 kg and over	100	91	89	80	67	62	45
80 kg and under 110 kg	605	599	589	603	615	621	613
50 kg and under 80 kg	1,868	1,787	1,813	1,863	1,890	1,898	1,779
20 kg and under 50 kg	2,362	2,198	2,260	2,270	2,253	2,263	2,131
Under 20 kg	2,241	2,082	2,151	2,163	2,160	2,204	2,058
Poultry: total	127,618	127,507	128,968	—	—	—	120,198
Fowls: total	117,854	118,846	119,456	120,740	128,628	130,809	120,198
Growing pullets	11,828	12,536	12,503	12,502	12,230	11,236	9,411
Laying flock	41,127	40,573	39,538	38,096	38,498	37,389	33,957
Breeding flock	6,012	6,396	6,104	6,334	7,146	6,879	6,788
Table birds	58,887	59,341	61,311	63,807	70,754	75,305	70,042
Ducks and Geese	1,566	1,530	1,654	1,747	1,757	1,836	2,101
Turkeys	8,198	7,134	7,864	—	—	—	—

Agricultural land: area

Thousand hectares

	1983	1984	1985	1986	1987	1988	1989
Total tillage	5,124	5,196	5,265	5,287	5,313	5,311	5,202
All grasses under five years old	1,846	1,794	1,796	1,723	1,691	1,613	1,534
Total arable	6,970	6,990	7,061	7,011	7,004	6,924	6,736
All grasses five years old and over	5,107	5,105	5,019	5,077	5,112	5,161	5,251
Total crops and grass	12,078	12,095	12,080	12,088	12,116	12,085	11,987
Rough grazings							
Sole rights	4,927	4,895	4,872	4,829	4,743	4,712	4,710
Common (estimated)	1,212	1,212	1,216	1,216	1,216	1,216	1,236
Woodland on agricultural holdings	292	299	312	316	322	333	347
All other land on agricultural holdings	227	218	223	227	225	229	273
Total area of agricultural land	18,735	18,720	18,703	18,676	18,622	18,575	18,553
Total area of the United Kingdom	24,088	24,088	24,085	24,086	24,086	24,086	24,086

Source: HMSO—Annual Abstract of Statistics 1991

TRANSPORT

Goods transport in Great Britain

	1984	1985	1986	1987	1988	1989
Total tonne kilometres (thousand millions)	182·2	187·1	187·1	195·2	217·9	222·4
Road	99·4	102·9	105·4	113·3	129·8	137·4
Rail (British Rail only)	12·7	15·4	16·5	17·3	18·0	17·9
Water: coastwise oil products*	41·0	39·4	34·4	31·6	34·3	34·3
Water: other*	18·7	18·2	20·4	22·5	25·0	23·4
Pipelines (except gases)	10·4	11·2	10·4	10·5	10·8	9·4
Total (million tonnes)	1,696	1,797	1,835	1,909	2,142	2,176
Road	1,390	1,445	1,471	1,542	1,751	1,807
Rail (British Rail only)	78	122	140	141	150	143
Water: coastwise oil products*	53	50	46	43	47	46
Water: other*	87	92	99	100	109	109
Pipelines (except gases)	88	89	79	83	85	71

*'Coastwise' includes all sea traffic within the UK, Isle of Man and Channel Islands. 'Other' means other coastwise plus inland waterway traffic and one-port traffic.

Seaport traffic of Great Britain

Million gross tonnes

	1984	1985	1986	1987	1988	1989
Foreign traffic						
Imports						
Bulk fuel traffic	60·0	57·2	61·7	57·3	62·9	64·2
Other bulk traffic	34·6	36·7	37·3	42·0	45·0	47·0
Container and roll-on traffic	28·1	29·8	31·1	34·0	38·0	40·9
Semi-bulk traffic	14·6	14·5	15·8	16·9	18·9	18·1
Conventional traffic	2·3	1·7	1·5	1·6	1·6	1·2
All imports	139·6	139·9	147·4	151·8	166·4	171·4
Exports						
Bulk fuel traffic	97·3	103·1	101·9	100·2	91·1	72·9
Other bulk traffic	18·7	17·7	21·1	20·4	18·5	19·5
Container and roll-on traffic	20·3	21·3	22·1	23·9	26·5	29·4
Semi-bulk traffic	3·6	4·1	4·0	5·1	4·6	4·6
Conventional traffic	1·8	1·6	1·2	1·2	1·0	0·7
All exports	141·7	147·8	150·4	150·7	141·7	127·1
Domestic traffic						
Bulk fuel traffic	123·2	119·9	112·2	108·1	115·3	108·3
Other bulk traffic	31·0	31·7	32·7	34·8	41·0	45·8
Container and roll-on traffic	5·4	5·9	6·2	7·3	7·6	8·1
Semi-bulk traffic	0·4	0·3	0·2	0·2	0·3	0·3
Conventional traffic	0·2	0·3	0·3	0·3	0·3	0·4
Non-oil traffic with UK offshore installations	3·2	3·6	2·9	3·1	3·5	3·6
All domestic traffic	163·5	161·6	154·5	153·9	168·1	166·4
Total foreign and domestic traffic	444·7	449·3	452·3	456·3	476·3	464·9

Passenger transport in Great Britain
(Estimated passenger kilometres)

Thousand million passenger kilometres

	1984	1985	1986	1987	1988	1989†
Total	529	536	557	588	618	654
Air	3	4	4	4	5	5
Rail*	35	36	37	39	41	40
Road:						
Public service vehicles	42	42	41	41	41	41
Cars and taxis	434	440	462	490	519	556
Motorcycles	9	8	8	7	7	7
Pedal cycles	6	6	5	6	5	5

*including London Regional Transport and Passenger Transport Executive railway systems.
†provisional.

Source: HMSO—Annual Abstract of Statistics 1991

Air Passengers by Type of Operator, 1990

Airport	Total terminal and transit	Scheduled UK and overseas		Charter UK and overseas	
		Terminal	Transit	Terminal	Transit
All UK airports: total	104,142,662	77,682,906	1,335,893	24,734,856	389,007
London area airports: total .	68,352,225	56,443,078	416,558	11,418,172	74,417
Battersea Heliport	7,236	—	—	7,236	—
Gatwick....................	21,178,762	12,249,760	100,691	8,792,810	35,501
Heathrow	42,950,832	42,512,224	313,994	62,744	1,870
London City	230,260	228,433	—	1,827	—
Luton	2,695,641	956,412	230	1,722,685	16,314
Southend..................	118,781	48,596	—	70,185	—
Stansted	1,177,949	387,653	1,643	767,872	20,732
Other UK airports: total	35,783,201	21,239,828	919,335	13,309,448	389,007
Aberdeen..................	1,974,406	1,097,377	26,699	849,805	525
Barrow-in-Furness	352	—	—	352	—
Belfast	2,304,974	1,897,846	19	395,903	11,206
Belfast City...............	547,912	541,607	338	5,965	2
Bembridge.................	360	—	—	346	14
Benbecula.................	34,089	31,372	1,794	913	10
Birmingham	3,618,704	2,050,197	109,817	1,441,415	17,275
Blackpool	137,471	86,522	676	50,273	—
Bournemouth..............	142,356	77,269	543	59,292	5,252
Bristol	815,062	212,323	26,884	561,634	14,221
Cambridge.................	29,811	24,663	—	5,148	—
Cardiff	624,304	82,250	15,240	510,557	16,257
Carlisle	1,288	—	—	1,268	20
Coventry	27,227	13,212	10,396	3,480	86
Dundee	7,647	3,964	2,489	1,186	8
East Midlands	1,284,209	553,626	383	726,655	3,545
Edinburgh.................	2,602,568	2,292,710	107,494	199,403	2,961
Exeter	237,190	125,234	15,012	92,011	4,933
Glasgow...................	4,405,819	3,074,774	105,235	1,211,499	14,311
Gloucester/Cheltenham.....	4,794	—	—	4,794	—
Hawarden	1,393	—	—	1,317	6
Humberside	154,564	87,636	18,647	47,862	419
Inverness	222,988	213,179	6,586	3,214	9
Islay	21,091	20,347	40	704	—
Isle of Man	551,173	525,050	18,681	7,203	239
Isles of Scilly–St Mary's.....	115,036	114,141	—	895	—
—Tresco	20,016	19,464	499	27	26
Kirkwall	123,177	101,340	15,803	4,357	1,677
Leeds/Bradford	865,561	625,087	23,758	209,048	7,668
Lerwick (Tingwall).........	14,485	9,536	1,710	3,212	27
Liverpool..................	485,506	431,610	10,276	42,552	1,068
Londonderry	40,962	39,310	216	1,436	—
Lydd	35,348	29,496	—	5,800	52
Manchester................	10,475,645	4,741,416	273,518	5,404,525	56,186
Manston	22,665	90	—	18,518	4,057
Newcastle	1,616,841	765,784	44,150	789,228	17,679
Norwich	218,964	152,703	13,163	52,817	284
Penzance Heliport..........	96,693	94,989	—	1,704	—
Plymouth	138,753	121,758	15,757	1,238	—
Prestwick	195,117	40,370	8,288	54,457	92,002
Scatsta...................	12,902	—	—	12,898	4
Shoreham	205	—	—	205	—
Southampton	493,184	475,918	3,662	12,990	614
Stornoway	83,658	82,598	63	770	157
Sumburgh.................	470,720	79,343	496	352,576	38,305
Swansea...................	346	—	—	340	6
Teesside...................	374,636	265,744	29,841	76,076	2,975
Tiree.....................	6,183	5,192	837	154	—
Unst	83,064	1,959	—	80,614	491
Wick	41,852	30,699	10,325	812	16
Channel Is. airports: total ...	2,951,593	2,666,584	113,608	169,232	2,169
Alderney	105,458	105,163	—	295	—
Guernsey..................	933,735	853,182	70,768	9,785	—
Jersey.....................	1,912,400	1,708,239	42,840	159,152	2,169

Source: Civil Aviation Authority.

AERODROMES AND AIRPORTS

The following aerodromes in Great Britain, Northern Ireland, the Isle of Man and the Channel Islands are either state owned or licensed for use for use by civil aircraft. A number of unlicensed aerodromes not included in this list are also available for private use by permission of the owner or controlling authority.

Aerodromes designated as Customs airports are printed in small capitals. Customs facilities are available at certain other aerodromes by special arrangement.

BAA = Owned by BAA PLC.
H = Licensed helicopter aerodrome.
HIAL = Operated by Highland and Islands Airports Ltd

J = Military aerodromes available for civil use by prior permission.
M = Owned by the municipal authority.
P = Private ownership.
S = Owned and operated by the Government.

ENGLAND AND WALES

Aberporth, Dyfed. J
Abingdon, Oxon. J
Andrewsfield, Essex.
Barrow (Walney Island), Cumbria.
Bedford/Thurleigh. J
Bembridge, IOW.
Benson, Oxon. J
BIGGIN HILL, Kent. P
BIRMINGHAM, W. Midlands. P
Blackbushe, Hants.
BLACKPOOL, Lancs. P
Bodmin, Cornwall.
Bourn, Cambridge.
BOURNEMOUTH, Dorset. P
BRISTOL, Avon. P
Brize Norton, Oxford. J
Brough, N. Humberside.
Caernarfon, Gwynedd.
CAMBRIDGE. P
CARDIFF, S. Glamorgan. P
Carlisle, Cumbria. M
Chichester (Goodwood), Sussex.
Chivenor, Devon. J
Church Fenton, N. Yorks. J
Clacton, Essex.
Compton Abbas, Dorset.
Cosford, Wolverhampton. J
COVENTRY, W. Midlands. M
Cranfield, Beds.
Cranwell, Lincs. J
Crowfield, Suffolk.
Culdrose, Cornwall. J
Denham, Bucks.
Dishforth, N. Yorks. J
Doncaster, S. Yorks.
Dunkeswell, Devon.
Dunsfold, Surrey. M
Duxford, Cambs. M
Eaglescott, Devon.
Earls Colne, Halstead.
EAST MIDLANDS, Derbys. P
Elstree, Herts.
EXETER, Devon.
Fairoaks, Surrey.
Farnborough, Hants. S
Fenland, Lincs.
Filton, Bristol.
Finningley, S. Yorks. J
Fowlmere, Cambs.
Gloucestershire (Staverton). P
Great Yarmouth (North Denes), Norfolk.
Halfpenny Green, Staffs.
Halton, Bucks. J
Hatfield, Herts.
Haverfordwest, Dyfed. M
Hawarden, Clwyd.
Hucknall, Notts.
HUMBERSIDE. P
Ipswich, Suffolk.
Isle of Wight/Sandown.

Kemble, Glos. J
Land's End (St Just), Cornwall.
Lashenden, Headcorn, Kent.
Leavesden, Herts.
LEEDS/BRADFORD, Yorks. P
Lee-on-Solent, Hants. J
Leicester, Leics.
Linton-on-Ouse, Yorks. J
LIVERPOOL, Merseyside. P
Llanbedr, Gwynedd. J
LONDON/CITY.
LONDON/GATWICK. BAA
LONDON/HEATHROW. BAA
LONDON/STANSTED. BAA
London/Westland Heliport. H
LUTON, Beds. P
LYDD, Kent.
Lyneham, Wilts. J
MANCHESTER. BAA
Manchester (Barton).
MANSTON, Kent. J
Marston Moor, York.
Netherthorpe, S. Yorks.
NEWCASTLE, Tyne and Wear. P
Newton, Notts. J
Northampton (Sywell), Northants.
Northolt, Middx. J
NORWICH, Norfolk. M
Nottingham, Notts.
Old Sarum, Wilts.
Oxford (Kidlington), Oxfordshire.
Panshanger, Herts.
Penzance, Cornwall. H
Peterborough (Conington).
Peterborough (Sibson), Cambs.
PLYMOUTH (ROBOROUGH), Devon.
Portland Naval, Dorset. JH
Redhill, Surrey.
Retford/Gamston, Notts.
Rochester, Kent.
St Mawgan, Cornwall. J
Sandtoft, Humberside.
Scilly Isles (St Mary's). M
Seething, Norfolk.
Shawbury, Shropshire. J
Sherburn-in-Elmet, N. Yorks.
Shipdham, Norfolk.
Shobdon, Herefordshire.
SHOREHAM, W. Sussex. P
Silverstone, Northants.
Skegness (Ingoldmells), Lincs.
Sleap, Shropshire.
SOUTHAMPTON/Eastleigh, Hants. P
SOUTHEND, Essex. P
Stapleford, Essex.
Sturgate, Lincs.
Swansea, W. Glam. M
TEESSIDE, Cleveland. P
Thruxton, Hants.
Tresco, Isles of Scilly. H
Turweston, Northants.
Valley, Gwynedd. J
Warton, Lancs.

Wattisham, Suffolk. J
Wellesbourne Mountford, Warwick.
Weston, Avon. H
White Waltham, Berks.
Wickenby, Lincs.
Woodford, Gtr. Manchester.
Woodvale, Merseyside. J
Wycombe Air Park (Booker), Bucks.
Yeovil, Somerset.
Yeovilton, Somerset. J

SCOTLAND

ABERDEEN (DYCE). BAA
Barra, Hebrides.
Benbecula, Hebrides. HIAL
Cumbernauld, Strathclyde.
Dounreay (Thurso). S
Dundee, Angus. M
Eday. M
EDINBURGH. BAA
Fair Isle.
Fife/Glenrothes. M
Flotta, Orkneys.
GLASGOW. BAA
Inverness (Dalcross). HIAL
Islay (Port Ellen). HIAL
Kirkwall. HIAL
Lerwick (Tingwall). M
Leuchars, Fife. J
Machrihanish, Kintyre. J
North Ronaldsay, Orkneys. M
Papa Westray, Orkneys. M
Perth (Scone).
PRESTWICK. BAA
Sanday, Orkneys. M
Scatsta.
Stornoway, Hebrides. HIAL
Stronsay, Orkneys. M
SUMBURGH, Shetlands. HIAL
Tiree. HIAL
Unst, Shetlands. M
West Freugh, Dumfries. S
Westray, Orkneys. M
Whalsay, Shetlands. M
Wick. HIAL

NORTHERN IRELAND

BELFAST (ALDERGROVE). S
Belfast (City).
Enniskillen (St Angelo). P
Londonderry (Eglinton). M
Newtownards.

ISLE OF MAN

RONALDSWAY. S

CHANNEL ISLANDS

ALDERNEY. S
GUERNSEY. S
JERSEY. S

PRINCIPAL MERCHANT FLEETS OF THE WORLD

Flag	1980 No.	1980 Gross Tonnage	1985 No.	1985 Gross Tonnage	1989 No.	1989 Gross Tonnage	1990 No.	1990 Gross Tonnage
Liberia	2,401	80,285,176	1,808	58,179,717	1,455	47,892,529	1,688	54,699,564
Panama	4,090	24,190,680	5,512	40,674,201	5,121	47,365,362	4,748	39,298,123
Japan	10,568	40,959,683	10,288	39,940,135	9,830	28,030,425	10,000	27,077,943
USSR	8,279	23,443,534	7,154	24,745,435	6,555	25,853,712	7,383	26,737,418
Norway	2,501	22,007,490	2,219	15,338,557	2,304	15,596,900	2,557	23,429,000
*USA	5,579	18,464,271	6,447	19,517,571	6,375	20,587,812	6,348	21,328,131
Greece	3,922	39,471,744	2,599	31,031,544	1,839	21,324,340	1,814	20,521,561
China, People's Republic of	955	6,873,608	1,408	10,568,236	1,907	13,513,578	1,948	13,899,448
China, Republic of (Taiwan)	497	2,039,123	583	4,327,487	641	5,169,937	660	5,766,283
Cyprus	688	2,091,089	844	8,196,056	1,278	18,134,011	1,270	18,335,929
Bahamas	91	87,320	195	3,907,267	724	11,578,891	807	13,626,335
Philippines	723	1,927,969	1,000	4,593,979	1,424	9,384,757	1,420	8,514,876
Italy	1,739	11,095,694	1,573	8,843,181	1,571	7,602,032	1,616	7,991,404
Singapore	988	7,664,229	758	6,504,682	712	7,272,506	774	7,927,866
Korea (South)	1,426	4,344,114	1,847	7,168,940	1,974	7,832,453	2,110	7,783,075
United Kingdom	3,181	27,135,155	2,378	14,343,512	2,053	7,645,750	1,998	6,716,325
Hong Kong	187	1,717,230	396	6,888,099	366	6,151,261	375	6,664,987
India	616	5,911,367	741	6,604,548	834	6,315,135	855	6,475,615
Brazil	607	4,533,663	702	6,057,364	716	6,078,150	691	6,015,684
Denmark	1,253	5,390,365	1,070	4,992,175	1,256	4,962,706	1,260	5,188,105
Iran	229	1,283,629	347	2,379,957	386	4,732,551	393	4,738,202
Malta	60	132,861	235	1,855,807	410	3,329,120	524	4,518,682
Germany, Federal Republic of	1,906	8,355,638	1,816	6,177,032	1,185	3,966,571	1,179	4,300,786
Bermuda	114	1,723,682	79	980,707	107	4,076,093	105	4,258,282
Romania	317	1,856,292	410	3,023,770	468	3,783,444	483	4,004,625
France	1,241	11,924,557	1,136	8,237,418	921	4,413,464	900	3,882,388
Yugoslavia	486	2,466,674	479	2,699,302	500	3,680,687	501	3,815,980
Spain	2,767	8,112,245	2,477	6,256,188	2,341	3,961,941	2,338	3,807,103
Netherlands	1,263	5,723,845	1,344	4,301,324	1,218	3,654,973	1,227	3,784,767
Turkey	508	1,454,838	817	3,684,357	855	3,239,825	869	3,718,641
Poland	842	3,639,078	761	3,315,285	710	3,416,014	698	3,369,183
Sweden	700	4,233,977	694	3,161,939	644	2,166,918	679	2,774,808
Canada	1,324	3,180,126	1,286	3,343,823	1,227	2,824,852	1,224	2,744,221
Australia	497	1,642,594	652	2,088,349	706	2,494,021	721	2,511,785
Indonesia	1,180	1,411,688	1,653	1,936,420	1,722	2,035,060	1,884	2,178,646
Vanuatu	14	12,541	28	138,025	177	920,333	273	2,163,618
Gibraltar	5	2,291	79	583,270	85	2,611,304	57	2,008,466
Belgium	290	1,809,829	344	2,400,292	333	2,043,594	330	1,964,478
St Vincent	35	19,679	71	235,183	414	1,486,102	521	1,936,814
Argentina	537	2,546,305	549	2,457,337	465	1,832,518	479	1,889,999
Kuwait	266	2,529,491	245	2,349,904	220	1,865,066	225	1,854,583
Malaysia	221	702,145	467	1,773,115	491	1,668,014	498	1,717,479

* Including ships of the United States Reserve Fleet.

CLASSIFICATION WITH LLOYD'S REGISTER OF SHIPPING.—Ships classed or to be classed with Lloyd's Register at June 30, 1990, totalled 8,598 with an aggregate of

Source: Lloyd's Register of Shipping

MERCHANT SHIPS COMPLETED IN THE WORLD DURING 1990

Country of Build	No.	Gross Tonnage	For Registration in	No.	Gross Tonnage
Japan	633	6,824,119	Liberia	76	3,585,085
Korea, South	110	3,459,786	Panama	158	2,910,071
*China, People's Republic of	46	366,828	Japan	419	1,325,557
China, Republic of (Taiwan)	10	667,220	China, People's Republic of	24	249,066
Germany, Federal Republic of	97	856,071	China, Republic of (Taiwan)	9	556,871
Yugoslavia	25	456,853	Singapore	40	750,038
Denmark	29	394,677	USSR	212	541,205
Italy	27	371,810	Bahamas	27	535,384
*USSR	142	367,395	Germany, Federal Republic of	54	459,315
Spain	97	363,100	Hong Kong	12	438,257
Brazil	7	256,350	Norway	41	420,715
Finland	16	247,098	Italy	24	365,505
Netherlands	65	163,293	Sweden	15	360,199
*Romania	14	159,752	Denmark	33	356,425
United Kingdom	29	130,660	Korea (South)	34	328,445
Poland	34	103,580	Cyprus	17	218,136
Bulgaria	10	80,213	Brazil	6	215,177
Norway	40	79,828	Australia	17	201,933
Portugal	16	73,519	Vanuatu	7	162,188
India	11	70,163	Netherlands	44	158,749
France	26	59,639	Romania	7	154,537
Belgium	6	58,381	Philippines	7	150,289
Singapore	29	38,614	Czechoslovakia	3	106,050
Turkey	10	31,132	Spain	56	97,736
Sweden	14	28,994	Yugoslavia	9	95,006
Australia	20	26,935	United Kingdom	25	91,202
Mexico	1	23,236	Finland	6	86,326
Greece	17	22,096	Greece	17	85,730
Malaysia	5	20,605	Belgium	8	79,809
Indonesia	10	19,312	Malaysia	11	77,030
USA	16	14,695	India	12	75,333
Other countries	60	49,433	Other countries	242	648,006
WORLD TOTAL	1,672	15,885,375	WORLD TOTAL	1,672	15,885,375

Source: Lloyd's Register of Shipping

* Information incomplete.
Of the ships completed in the world during the year 3,226,090 gross tonnage (20·3 per cent) is to be classed with Lloyd's Register.

BRITISH RAILWAYS

The British Railways Board was set up by the Transport Act, 1962, and assumed its responsibilities on January 1, 1963. (For members, see **Government and Public Offices.**)

Management of the railways is currently being reorganized into the business sectors of InterCity, Network SouthEast, Regional Railways, Trainload Freight and Railfreight Distribution. The former geographical regions of London Midland, Western, Eastern, Anglia, Scottish and Southern will no longer exist. A new organization, European Passenger Services Ltd, has been set up to manage international rail services through the Channel Tunnel.

Financial Results

The profit and loss account for 1990–91 showed a deficit of £93·1 million, £10·9 million after interest and extraordinary items, compared with a surplus of £269·8 million after interest in 1989–90. The railway operating deficit was £42·4 million compared with a surplus of £26·4 million for the previous year.

Railways	£ million 1990–91
Gross receipts:	
Passenger (including grants)	2,824·7
Freight (incl. parcels and mails).....	798·1
Other	874·0
TOTAL.........................	3,776·8
Working expenses:	
Train services	1,554·5
Terminals	379·4
Miscellaneous traffic expenses	183·9
Track and signalling...............	820·8
General expenses..................	630·8
Capital renewal provision	95·0
Other expenses....................	154·8
TOTAL EXPENDITURE...........	3,819·2
Railway net deficit	(93·2)
Surplus from subsidiaries and property sales	82·2
GROUP OPERATING DEFICIT	(10·9)

Staff

On March 31, 1991, British Rail employed 131,430 staff (129,696 at March 31, 1990). Including subsidi-

aries, the group total at March 31, 1991, was 137,277 (134,361 at March 31, 1990).

OPERATING STATISTICS

At March 31, 1991, British Rail had 23,494 miles of standard gauge lines and sidings in use, representing 10,305 miles of route of which 3,052 miles were electrified. Standard rail on main line has a weight of 110 lb. per yard. British Rail had 2,030 locomotives (2 diesel, 1,750 diesel-electric and 278 electric); 2,131 diesel multiple-unit vehicles, 7,220 electric multiple-unit vehicles and 2,372 locomotive-hauled vehicles.

Loaded train miles run in passenger service totalled 213·5m. 746·4m. passenger journeys were made during the year, including 364·9m. made by holders of season tickets. The average distance of each passenger journey on ordinary fare was 35·6 miles; and on season ticket, 17·7 miles. Passenger stations in use in 1991 numbered 2,488 and freight terminals 127.

Freight

There were 20,763 freight vehicles and 1,609 other vehicles in the non-passenger-carrying stock. Train miles run in freight service totalled 36m.

Accidents on Railways

	1988	1989
Train accidents: total	1,330	1,434
Persons killed : total	40	18
Passengers	34	6
Railway staff	2	6
Others	4	6
Persons injured : total	705	404
Passengers	615	311
Railway staff	68	71
Others	22	22
Other accidents through movement of railway vehicles		
Persons killed...................	53	41
Persons injured	3,010	2,759
Other accidents on railway premises		
Persons killed...................	4	10
Persons injured	7,351	7,628
Trespassers and suicides		
Persons killed...................	324	293
Persons injured	70	92

ROADS

Highway Authorities

The powers and responsibilities of highway authorities in England and Wales are set out in the Highways Acts 1980; for Scotland there is separate legislation.

Responsibility for trunk road motorways and other trunk roads in Great Britain rests in England with the Secretary of State for Transport, in Scotland with the Secretary of State for Scotland, and in Wales with the Secretary of State for Wales. The costs of construction, improvement and maintenance are paid for by central government. The highway authority for non-trunk roads in England and Wales is, in general, the county council, metropolitan district council or London borough council in whose area the roads lie, and in Scotland the regional or islands council. In Northern Ireland the Northern Ireland Department of the Environment is responsible for public roads and their maintenance and construction.

Expenditure

Transport Supplementary Grant (TSG) is a block grant and was introduced in England and Wales on April 1, 1975, to replace a variety of specific grants paid towards local transport expenditure.

In England grant was paid towards capital and current spending on transport by county councils and the GLC from 1975–76 to 1984–85. From April 1, 1985, TSG has only been paid towards capital spending on highways and the regulation of traffic, current expenditure having been subsumed by rate support grant. With the abolition of the GLC and the metropolitan county councils on April 1, 1986, grant has become payable to London boroughs, the Common Council of the City of London and metropolitan district councils. From April 1, 1991 TSG has also been paid towards capital spending on bridge assessment and strengthening. In Wales, grant was also paid to the Welsh county councils towards current and capital expenditure on transport. Since April 1982, TSG became payable on capital expenditure only; current expenditure having been subsumed into the rate support grant. From April 1, 1990, the grant for Wales has been renamed Transport Grant.

Grant rates are determined by the respective Secretaries of State; at present grant is paid at 50 per cent of expenditure accepted for grant in England and Wales.

For the financial year 1991–92 local authorities in England will receive £318 million in TSG. Total expenditure on building and maintaining motorways and trunk roads in 1990–91 was £1,738 million in England.

In the financial year 1991–92, local authorities in Wales will receive £36 million in TG. Total expenditure on roads in Wales in 1989–90 was £220 million.

Total expenditure on roads during the financial year 1989–90 was £300 million in Scotland.

Road lengths (miles)
(at April 1990)

	Total roads	Trunk roads (incl. motorways)	*Motorways
England	169,716	6,758	1,672
Wales	20,689	1,056	74
Scotland ...	32,063	1,969	161
N. Ireland ..	14,963	1,443†	70
UK	237,431	11,226	1,977

*There were in addition 42 miles of local authority motorway in England and 15 miles in Scotland.
†Renamed Class 1 Roads in 1984.

Motorways

The network in England and Wales is based on five main routes—London–Yorkshire (M1), London–South Wales (M4), Birmingham–Bristol–Exeter (M5), Birmingham–Carlisle (M6), and Lancashire–North Humberside (M62).

Other important motorways in use include: Medway Towns (M2); London–Winchester (M3); London–Cambridge (M11); Rotherham–Goole (M18); London–Folkestone (M20); London orbital route (M25); London–Birmingham (M40); North Cheshire (M56); and South Humberside (M180).

Motorways in use in Scotland include: Edinburgh–Glasgow–Greenock (M8); Edinburgh–Stirling (M9); Maryville–Mollisburn (M73); Millbank–Maryville (M74); Stirling–Haggs (M80); Friarton Bridge–Perth (M85); Inverkeithing–Perth (M90), and (M80)–Kincardine Bridge (M876).

Driving Tests

The number of driving tests conducted in Great Britain in 1990 was 2,059,975, of which 52·31 per cent resulted in a pass. In addition 97,811 HGV/PSV tests were undertaken, of which 51·46 per cent were successful.

Motor Vehicles

The number of vehicles in Great Britain with current licences in 1989 was:

Private and light goods	21,277,000
Motor cycles, scooters, mopeds	876,000
Public transport vehicles	122,000
Heavy goods vehicles	675,000
Agricultural tractors	384,000
Others	77,000
TOTAL	24,196,000

This total includes 785,000 Crown vehicles and vehicles exempt from licensing.

Buses and Coaches 1989–90
(Great Britain)

No. of vehicles (average)	72,900
Vehicle kilometres (millions)	3,846
Passenger journeys (millions)...........	5,686
Passenger receipts (£ million)	2,730

Road Accidents 1989

Road accidents...........................	260,759
Vehicles involved:	
Pedal cycles	29,327
Motor vehicles	429,237
Total casualties	341,592
Pedestrians..........................	60,080
Vehicle users	281,512
Killed*.................................	5,373
Pedestrians	1,706
Pedal cycles	294
All two-wheeled motor vehicles	683
Cars and taxis	2,426
Others	264

*Died within 30 days of accident.

Year	Killed	Injured	Year	Killed	Injured
1965	7,952	389,985	1985	5,165	312,359
1970	7,499	355,869	1987	5,125	306,348
1975	6,366	318,584	1988	5,052	317,253
1980	6,010	323,000	1989	5,373	336,219

VEHICLE LICENCES, ETC.

Since October 1, 1974, registration and first licensing of vehicles has been done through local offices (known as Vehicle Registration Offices) of the Department of Transport's Driver and Vehicle Licensing Centre in Swansea. The records of existing vehicles are held at Swansea. Local facilities for relicensing are available as follows:—

   (i) with a licence reminder (form V11) in person at any post office which deals with vehicle licensing or post it to the post office, shown on the form.

   (ii) with a vehicle licence renewal (form V10). You may normally apply in person at any licensing post office. You will need to take your vehicle registration document with you: if this is not available you must complete form V62 which is held at post offices. Postal applications can be made to the post offices shown on form V100, available at any post office. This form also provides guidance on registering and licensing vehicles.

Details of the present duties chargeable on motor vehicles are available at post offices and Vehicle Registration Offices. The Vehicles (Excise) Act 1971 provides *inter alia* that any vehicle kept on a public road but not used on roads is chargeable to excise duty as if it were in use.

Rates of duty for motor car and motor cycle licences are shown below.

Type of Vehicle	Exceeding	Not exceeding	12 months	6 months
			£	£
Motor Cars				
Those first constructed before January 1, 1947....	—	—	60·00	33·00
Other than above	—	—	100·00	55·00
Motor Cycles				
With or without sidecar	—	150 cc	15·00	—
With or without sidecar	150 cc	250 cc	30·00	—
With or without sidecar	250 cc	—	50·00	27·50
If first constructed before January 1, 1933 and weighs not more than 101·6 kgs...............	250 cc	—	30·00	—
Three Wheelers				
Other than pedestrian-controlled	—	—	50·00	27·50
Hackney Carriages				
Seating less than 9 persons	—	—	100·00	55·00
Seating 9–16 persons...........................	—	—	130·00	71·50
Seating 17–35 persons..........................	—	—	200·00	110·00
Seating 36–60 persons..........................	—	—	300·00	165·00
Seating over 60 persons	—	—	450·00	247·50

Driving Licences—Fees

On or after 1.2.91

FULL LICENCE	
First full licence	£17·00*
Changing a provisional to a full licence after passing a driving test	free
Renewal of full licence if last full licence was issued after Jan. 1, 1976................................	free
New licence after a period of disqualification	£5·00
PROVISIONAL LICENCE	
First provisional licence	£17·00*
First renewal of provisional licence issued before Oct. 1, 1982	£17·00
DUPLICATE LICENCE..................	£5·00
EXCHANGE LICENCE	£5·00

* Once you have paid the life fee for either a provisional or a full licence all renewals are free except where additional entitlement is required.

The minimum age for driving motor cars, light goods vehicles and motor cycles is 17 (moped, 16).

There are proposals to revise the driving licence fee structure.

Driving Test–Fees
(weekday rate (Saturday rate))

For cars ....£21·50 (£35)	
For motor cycles, part I* ....n/a	
part II ....£28·50 (£44)	
For lorries, buses £48 (£75)	

*Part I of the motor cycle test, now known as Basic Training, is no longer conducted by the Department of Transport but by appointed motor cycle training organizations, who conduct the majority of part I tests within the framework of their own training courses and are free to set their own fee. Part II is now known as the Accompanied Motor Cycle test.

Driving tests for invalid carriages are free.

MoT Testing

Cars, motor cycles, motor caravans, light goods and dual-purpose vehicles more than three years old must be covered by a current MoT test certificate. Copies of the legislation governing MoT testing can be obtained from any bookshop which stocks HMSO publications. The legislation comprises The Road Traffic Act 1988 (Sections 45 and 46), The Motor Vehicles (Test) Regulations 1981, and subsequent amendments.

FUEL AND POWER

Coal: supply and demand

Million tonnes

	1984	1985	1986	1987	1988	1989
SUPPLY						
Production of deep-mined coal	35·2	75·3	90·4	86·0	83·8	79·6
Production of opencast coal	14·3	15·6	14·3	15·8	17·9	18·7
Recovered slurry, fines, etc.	1·6	3·3	3·5	2·8	2·4	2·8
Imports	8·9	12·7	10·6	9·8	11·7	12·1
Change in colliery stocks	−7·9	−5·3	+0·3	−1·1	+0·7	+1·3
Change in stocks at opencast sites	+4·7	−6·3	−0·8	−1·5	+0·5	+1·5
Total supply	63·2	118·3	119·2	116·9	114·6	110·6
HOME CONSUMPTION						
Electricity supply industry	53·4	73·9	82·7	86·2	82·5	80·6
Coke ovens	8·2	11·1	11·1	10·9	10·9	10·8
Low temperature carbonization plants	1·1	1·4	1·0	1·0	0·8	0·8
Manufactured fuel plants	0·2	0·8	1·0	1·0	1·2	0·9
Railways	—	—	—	—	—	—
Collieries	0·2	0·3	0·3	0·2	0·2	0·1
Industry (disposals to users)	6·1	7·4	8·2	8·0	8·1	7·5
Domestic (disposals to users)	6·5	6·6	8·4	7·2	6·6	5·7
Public services	1·3	1·3	1·3	1·2	1·0	0·9
Miscellaneous	0·5	0·4	0·2	0·2	0·2	0·2
Total home consumption	77·3	105·4	114·2	115·9	111·5	107·6
Overseas shipments and bunkers	2·3	2·4	2·7	2·4	1·8	2·0
Total consumption and shipments	79·6	107·8	116·9	118·2	113·3	109·6
Change in distributed stocks*	−18·2	+10·0	+4·0	−2·8	+1·7	+0·4
Balance	+1·9	+0·5	−1·8	+1·3	−0·4	+0·6

*Stock change excludes industrial and domestic stocks.
†This is the balance between supply and consumption, shipments and changes in known distributed stocks.

Fuel input and gas output: gas sales

	1984	1985	1986	1987	1988	1989
FUEL INPUT TO GAS INDUSTRY:			million tonnes			
Petroleum	0·1	0·1	—	—	—	—
			million therms			
Petroleum gases†	30	28	36	6	1	3
Natural gas	—	—	—	—	—	—
Coke oven gas	—	—	—	—	—	—
Total to gas works	56	57	55	20	6	3
Natural gas for direct supply	17,739	18,988	19,215	20,198	19,083	18,828
Total fuel input	17,794	19,046	19,270	20,218	19,089	18,831
GAS OUTPUT AND SALES			million therms			
Gas output:						
Town gas	21	20	18	13	4	1
Natural gas supplied direct	17,764	19,017	19,243	20,205	19,083	18,828
Gross total available	17,785	19,038	19,261	20,218	19,087	18,829
Own use	−129	−140	−152	−137	−120	−101
Statistical difference*	−351	−531	−613	−708	−328	−379
Total sales	17,305	18,367	18,496	19,373	18,639	18,349
Analysis of gas sales						
Power stations	178	197	75	79	83	82
Final users:						
Iron and steel industry	449	449	419	468	449	471
Other industries	5,249	5,310	4,804	5,275	4,811	4,915
Domestic	8,933	9,684	10,242	10,500	10,255	9,914
Public administration	1,095	1,184	1,286	1,326	1,242	1,188
Miscellaneous	1,314	1,463	1,597	1,636	1,725	1,699

†Butane, propane, ethane and refinery tail gases.
*Supply greater than recorded demand (−). Includes losses in distribution.

Source: HMSO—Annual Abstract of Statistics 1991

THE ELECTRICITY SUPPLY INDUSTRY

Under the Electricity Act 1989 twelve new public electricity supply companies were formed from the twelve Area Electricity Boards in England and Wales. These companies were floated on the stock market in November 1990. Four new companies were formed from the Central Electricity Generating Board; three new generating companies (National Power PLC, Nuclear Electric PLC and PowerGen PLC) and the National Grid Company PLC. National Power PLC and PowerGen PLC were floated on the stock market in February 1991, the Government retaining a 40 per cent holding in both companies.

In Scotland, there are three new companies; Scottish Power PLC, Scottish Hydro-Electric PLC and Scottish Nuclear Ltd Flotation of Scottish Power PLC and Scottish Hydro-Electric PLC on the stock market took place in May 1991.

A new trade and representational organization, the Electricity Association, has been created by the newly formed British electricity companies; its trading arm is Electricity Association Services Ltd.

ELECTRICITY ASSOCIATION SERVICES LTD, 30 Millbank, SW1P 4RD. (Tel: 071–834 2333).—*Chief Exec.*, R. Farrance.

CEGB Successor Companies

THE NATIONAL GRID COMPANY PLC, National Grid House, Sumner Street, SE1 9JU. (Tel: 071–620 8000).—*Chief Exec.*, B. Kerss.

NATIONAL POWER PLC, Sudbury House, 15–20 Newgate Street, EC1A 7AU. (Tel: 071–634 5111).—*Chief Exec.*, J. Baker.

NUCLEAR ELECTRIC PLC, Barnett Way, Barnwood, Glos. GL4 7RS. (Tel: 0452–652222).—*Chairman*, J. Collier.

POWERGEN PLC, 53 New Broad Street, EC2M 1JJ. (Tel: 071–638 5742.—*Chief Exec.*, E. Walliss.

Regional Electricity Companies

EAST MIDLANDS ELECTRICITY PLC, PO Box 4 North PDO, 398 Coppice Road, Arnold, Nottingham NG5 7HX.

EASTERN ELECTRICITY PLC, PO Box 40, Wherstead Ipswich IP2 9AQ.

LONDON ELECTRICITY PLC, Templar House, 81–87 High Holborn, WC1V 6NU.

MANWEB PLC, Sealand Road, Chester CH1 4LR.

MIDLANDS ELECTRICITY PLC, Mucklow Hill, Halesowen, W. Midlands B62 8BP.

NORTHERN ELECTRIC PLC, Carliol House, Newcastle upon Tyne NE99 1SE.

NORWEB PLC, Talbot Road, Manchester M16 0MQ.

SEEBOARD PLC, Grand Avenue, Hove, E. Sussex BN3 2LS.

SOUTH WALES ELECTRICITY PLC, St Mellons, Cardiff CF3 9XW.

SOUTH WESTERN ELECTRICITY PLC, 800 Park Avenue, Aztec West, Almondsbury, Avon BS12 4SE.

SOUTHERN ELECTRIC PLC, Littlewick Green, Maidenhead, Berks. SL6 3QB.

YORKSHIRE ELECTRICITY GROUP PLC, Scarcroft, Leeds LS14 3HS.

Scottish Companies

SCOTTISH HYDRO-ELECTRIC PLC, 16 Rothesay Terrace, Edinburgh EH3 7SE. (Tel: 031–225 1361).—*Chief Exec.*, R. Young.

SCOTTISH NUCLEAR LTD, Minto Building, 6 Inverlair Avenue, Glasgow G44 4AD. (Tel: 041–633 1166).—*Chief Exec.*, R. M. Yeoman.

SCOTTISH POWER PLC, Cathcart House, Spean Street Glasgow G44 4BE. (Tel: 041–637 7177).—*Chief Exec.*, Dr I. Preston.

Electricity: production and fuel used

	1984	1985	1986	1987	1988	1989
Electricity generated: total (GWh*)	266,645	280,602	282,913	283,320	289,220	293,577
England and Wales	227,010	242,248	246,895	246,521	250,303	255,382
South Scotland Electricity Board	22,938	25,771	23,748	25,814	23,942	26,006
North Scotland Hydro-Electric Board	10,451	6,015	5,611	4,204	7,933	4,887
Northern Ireland	5,591	5,938	6,018	6,157	6,366	6,636
Railway and transport authorities	655	630	641	625	677	666
Method of generation (GWh*)						
Steam plant, nuclear	49,498	56,354	54,005	50,282	58,867	66,740
Steam plant, other	209,711	216,830	221,981	226,957	223,527	220,346
Gas turbines and oil engines	2,012	1,138	609	562	533	577
Hydro-electric plant other than pumped storage plant	3,368	3,447	3,925	3,313	3,973	3,845
Pumped storage plant	2,055	2,831	2,394	2,207	2,320	2,067
Fuel used (thousand tonnes)						
Coal	53,411	73,940	82,652	86,177	82,465	80,633
Coke and coke breeze	19	—	—	—	—	—
Oil	21,313	10,638	6,097	4,812	5,391	5,522
Natural gas†	712	762	285	298	332	329
Electricity sales total (GWh*)	224,660	235,570	242,969	250,927	256,317	261,811
Domestic and farm premises	85,667	90,068	93,496	94,927	93,951	93,769
Domestic and commercial	1,987	1,712	1,417	1,408	1,395	1,427
Shops, offices, other commercial premises	51,113	55,459	59,242	62,012	65,164	68,199
Factories and other industrial premises	81,105	83,419	83,870	87,531	90,687	93,354
Public lighting	2,296	2,335	2,316	2,345	2,381	2,413
Traction	2,492	2,577	2,627	2,704	2,739	2,649

Source: HMSO—Annual Abstract of Statistics 1991

*GWH = gigawatt-hour.   † Expressed in thousand tonnes of coal equivalent.

THE GAS INDUSTRY

The gas industry in the United Kingdom was nationalized in 1949 under the Gas Act 1948, and operated as the Gas Council. The Gas Act 1972 replaced the Gas Council with the British Gas Corporation and led to greater centralization of the industry. The British Gas Corporation was privatized in 1986 as British Gas PLC and remains the main supplier of gas in Great Britain.

The principal business of British Gas is the purchase, transmission and sale of natural gas to domestic, industrial and commercial customers in Great Britain. British Gas has hydrocarbon exploration and production operations offshore and onshore, both in Great Britain and overseas, and it has an interest in gas-related activities world-wide.

BRITISH GAS PLC, Rivermill House, 152 Grosvenor Road, SW1V 3JL. Tel: 071-821 1444.—*Chairman and Chief Executive*, R. Evans, CBE.

Regions

The Regions are largely concerned with the management of the gas business locally, including distribution and sale of gas, installation and servicing of appliances, meter reading, and the maintenance of emergency services.

Gas Regions

EAST MIDLANDS, PO Box 145, De Montfort Street, Leicester LE1 9DB.
EASTERN, Star House, Potters Bar, Herts. EN6 2PD.
NORTH EASTERN, New York Road, Leeds LS2 7PE.
NORTH THAMES, North Thames House, London Road, Staines, Middx. TW19 4AE.
NORTH WESTERN, Welman House, Altrincham, Cheshire WA15 8AE.
NORTHERN, PO Box 1GB, Killingworth, Newcastle upon Tyne NE99 1GB.
SCOTLAND, Granton House, 4 Marine Drive, Edinburgh EH5 1YB.
SOUTH EASTERN, Katherine Street, Croydon CR9 1JU.
SOUTH WESTERN, Riverside, Temple Street, Keynsham, Bristol BS19 1EQ.
SOUTHERN, 80 St Mary's Road, Southampton SO9 5AT.
WALES, Helmont House, Churchill Way, Cardiff CF1 4NB.
WEST MIDLANDS, Wharf Lane, Solihull, West Midlands B91 2JP.

Supply and transmission

British Gas obtains natural gas from fields on mainland Britain, in coastal waters and in the North Sea. It also imports gas from other countries. In 1990 total gas production from UK continental shelf and Norwegian fields with gas contracted to British Gas was 57,379 million cubic metres, of which 57,331 million cubic metres was offshore production and 48 million cubic metres was onshore production.

The mainland national transmission system is operated by British Gas, with other gas suppliers entering contracts with British Gas to use the system. British Gas operates six reception terminals and 3,400 miles of pipeline. The length of mains in use in 1990 was 157,400 miles: 146,200 miles of distribution mains and 11,100 miles of transmission mains.

Sales

Total gas sold and used (1990) was (million therms):
Domestic 9,890
Commercial 2,919
Industrial 5,743
Used for own purposes 96
    TOTAL 18,648

Charges for domestic use are (from April 1, 1991):
Quarterly standing charge .... £9·40
Unit charges (pence per therm)
Annual consumption
1–5,000 therms .... 45·9
5,001–10,000 therms...................... 43·9
10,001–15,000 therms..................... 42·9
15,001–25,000 therms..................... 41·9

British Gas finance

Year ended March 31	1989–90	1990–91
	£ million	
Turnover		
UK gas supply	6,909	7,930
Overseas gas supply	—	378
Exploration and production ...	622	978
UK marketing activities	719	745
Other activities	61	87
Less: intra-group sales	(328)	(627)
TOTAL	7,983	9,491
Operating costs include:		
UK gas supply (includes levy)..	3,285	3,674
Overseas gas supply	—	266
Payroll costs	1,235	1,390
Current cost depreciation less replacement expenditure....	528	726
Current cost working capital adjustments	45	79
TOTAL...................	7,836	13,701
Current cost operating profit ..	1,107	1,655
Gearing adjustment	29	41
Net interest payable	(73)	(140)
Current cost profit before tax ..	1,063	1,556
Current cost profit after tax ...	695	916
Minority shareholders' interest	(3)	2
Current cost profit attributable to British Gas shareholders .	692	918
Dividends	(447)	(533)
Current cost profit retained ...	245	385

THE WATER INDUSTRY

ENGLAND AND WALES

In England and Wales the Secretaries of State for the Environment and for Wales, and the Director General of Water Services, are responsible for the general oversight of the industry and for ensuring that the private water companies fulfil their statutory obligation to provide water supply and sewerage services.

The Minister of Agriculture, Fisheries and Food and the Secretary of State for Wales are responsible for policy relating to land drainage, flood protection, sea defences and the protection and development of fisheries.

The National Rivers Authority is responsible for water quality and the control of pollution, the management of water resources and nature conservation.

The Water Companies

Until the end of 1989, nine regional water authorities in England and the Welsh Water Authority in Wales were responsible for water supply and the development of water resources, sewerage and sewage disposal, pollution control, freshwater fisheries, flood protection, water recreation, and environmental conservation. The Water Act 1989, which received Royal Assent on July 6, 1989, provided for the creation of a privatized water industry under public regulation.

Of the 99 per cent of the population of England and Wales who are connected to a public water supply, 75 per cent are supplied by the new water companies (through their principal operating subsidiaries, the water service companies), which have replaced the regional water authorities. The remaining 25 per cent were supplied by 24 statutory water companies which were already in the private sector. Many of these have now converted to public limited company (PLC) status. The ten water service companies are also responsible for sewerage and sewage disposal throughout England and Wales.

The water service companies are:

ANGLIAN WATER SERVICES LTD, Compass House, Chivers Way, Histon, Cambs. CB4 4ZY.

DWR CYMRU (WELSH WATER), Cambrian Way, Brecon, Powys LD3 7HP.

NORTHUMBRIAN WATER LTD, Abbey Road, Pity Me, Durham DH1 5FS.

NORTH WEST WATER LTD, Dawson House, Liverpool Road, Great Sankey, Warrington WA5 3LW.

SEVERN TRENT WATER LTD, 2297 Coventry Road, Sheldon, Birmingham B26 3PU.

SOUTHERN WATER SERVICES LTD, Southern House, Yeoman Road, Worthing, W. Sussex BN13 3NX.

SOUTH WEST WATER SERVICES LTD, Peninsula House, Rydon Lane, Exeter EX2 7HR.

THAMES WATER UTILITIES LTD, Nugent House, Vastern Road, Reading RG1 8DB.

WESSEX WATER SERVICES PLC, Wessex House, Passage Street, Bristol BS2 0JQ.

YORKSHIRE WATER SERVICES LTD, West Riding House, 67 Albion Street, Leeds LS1 5AA.

Regulatory Bodies

A Director General of Water Services has been appointed by the Secretaries of State for the Environment and for Wales. Independent of Ministers and directly accountable to Parliament, his main duties are to ensure that the water companies comply with the terms of their appointments (or licences) and to protect the interests of the consumer. All 34 water companies are subject to a system of price control which sets a limit on the average increase in their prices each year. The Office of Water Services, similar to the Office of Telecommunications and the Office of Gas Supply, has been set up to support the Director General's activities.

An independent national body, the National Rivers Authority (see page 347) was established under the Water Act 1989 to take over the regulatory and river management functions of the regional water authorities. It has statutory duties and powers in relation to water resources, pollution control, flood defence, fisheries, recreation, conservation and navigation in England and Wales.

The Drinking Water Inspectorate (see page 316) was established under the Water Act 1989, and is responsible for assessing the quality of the drinking water supplied by the 34 companies in England and Wales and for inspecting the companies themselves. The Inspectors look at records, check operational manuals, visit laboratories and water treatment works, and question company officials. They also investigate any accidents affecting drinking water quality. The Chief Inspector presents an annual report in July to the Secretary of State for the Environment.

Methods of charging

In England and Wales, householders have up to now paid for domestic water supply and sewerage services through charges based on the assessed value of their property under the old domestic rating system. Industrial and most commercial users are charged according to consumption, which is recorded by meter.

The abolition of domestic rates necessitates new methods of charging the private consumer for water and sewerage services. The Water Act 1989 gave the water companies until the end of the century to decide on and introduce a suitable method of charging. Three options under consideration are a flat rate licence fee, property banding, and metering. Trials of domestic metering are currently taking place.

SCOTLAND

Overall responsibility for national water policy in Scotland rests with the Secretary of State for Scotland. Most aspects of water policy are administered through the Scottish Office Environment Department, but fisheries and certain aspects of land drainage are the responsibility of the Scottish Office Agriculture and Fisheries Department. The supply of water and sewerage services and the development of water resources are administered by separate authorities from those responsible for the control of water pollution.

Water supply and sewerage services are local authority responsibilities and are provided by the nine Regional Councils and the three Islands Councils.

Seven river purification boards and the Islands Councils of Orkney, Shetland and the Western Isles have the specific duty of restoring and maintaining the quality of water in Scotland's rivers, lochs and coastal waters. The Islands Councils of Orkney, Shetland and the Western Isles are responsible for the prevention of pollution within their own areas.

The Water (Scotland) Act 1967 brought into being a bulk water supply authority, the Central Scotland Water Development Board. The main statutory function of the board is to develop new sources of water supply for the purpose of providing water in bulk to water authorities whose limits of supply are within the board's area, i.e. Central, Fife, Lothian, Strathclyde and Tayside Regional Councils.

The community charge, which was introduced in Scotland in April 1989, includes a community water charge set by each Regional and Islands Council.

CENTRAL SCOTLAND WATER DEVELOPMENT BOARD, Balmore, Torrance, Glasgow G64 4AJ.—*Director*, W. G. Mitchell

NORTHERN IRELAND

In Northern Ireland ministerial responsibility for water services lies with the Secretary of State for Northern Ireland. The Department of the Environment for Northern Ireland, operating through the Water Service, is responsible for policy and co-ordination with regard to supply and distribution of water, and provision and maintenance of sewerage services.

The Water Service is divided into four regions, the Eastern, Northern, Western and Southern Divisions. These are based in Belfast, Ballymena, Londonderry and Craigavon respectively.

On all major policy issues the Department of the Environment for Northern Ireland seeks the views of the Northern Ireland Water Council, a body appointed to advise the Department on the exercise of its water and sewerage functions. The Council includes representatives from agriculture, angling, industry, commerce, tourism, trade unions and local government.

Usually householders do not pay directly for water and sewerage services; the costs of these services are allowed for in the Northern Ireland regional rate. Water consumed by industry, commerce and agriculture in excess of 100 cubic metres (22,000 gallons) per half year is charged through meters.

THE CINQUE PORTS

As their name implies, the Cinque Ports were originally five in number; Hastings, New Romney, Hythe, Dover and Sandwich. They existed before the Norman Conquest and were the Anglo-Saxon successors to the Roman system of coast defence organized from the Wash to Spithead to resist Saxon onslaughts. William the Conqueror reconstituted them and granted peculiar jurisdiction, most of which was abolished in 1855. Only jurisdiction in Admiralty still survives.

At some time after the Conquest the 'antient towns' of Winchelsea and Rye were added with equal privileges. The other members of the Confederation, known as Limbs, are Lydd, Faversham, Folkestone, Deal, Tenterden, Margate and Ramsgate.

The Barons of the Cinque Ports have the ancient privilege of attending the Coronation ceremony and are allotted special places in Westminster Abbey.

Lord Warden of the Cinque Ports, HM Queen Elizabeth the Queen Mother.
Judge, Court of Admiralty, Gerald Darling, RD, QC.
Registrar, I. G. Gill, LVO, PO Box 9, Margate, Kent CT9 1XZ (Tel: 0843–225511).

LORD WARDENS OF THE CINQUE PORTS SINCE 1904

Marquess Curzon	1904
The Prince of Wales	1905
Earl Brassey	1908
Earl Beauchamp	1913
Marquess of Reading	1934
Marquess of Willingdon	1936
Sir Winston Churchill	1941
Sir Robert Menzies	1965
HM Queen Elizabeth the Queen Mother	1978

CRIMINAL STATISTICS

ENGLAND AND WALES
Notifiable offences recorded by the police (thousands)

	1985	1986	1987	1988	1989
Total	3,611·9	3,847·4	3,892·2	3,715·8	3,870·1
Violence against the person	121·7	125·5	141·0	158·2	176·9
Sexual offences	21·5	22·7	25·2	26·5	29·7
Burglary	866·7	931·6	900·1	817·8	825·8
Robbery	27·5	30·0	32·6	31·4	33·2
Theft and handling stolen goods	1,884·1	2,003·9	2,052·0	1,931·3	2,012·4
Fraud and forgery	134·8	133·4	133·0	133·9	134·5
Criminal damage	539·0	583·6	589·0	594·0	630·0
Other offences	16·7	16·7	19·3	22·7	27·7

SCOTLAND
Crimes and offences recorded by the police (thousands)

	1985	1986	1987	1988	1989
Total crimes and offences	800·4	822·4	858·2	855·6	902·0
Total crimes	462·0	463·8	481·2	470·0	493·4
Non-sexual crimes of violence against the person	15·1	15·7	18·4	17·9	18·4
Crimes involving indecency	5·7	5·4	5·3	5·1	5·7
Crimes involving dishonesty	342·3	342·5	356·5	344·5	355·5
Fire-raising, vandalism, etc	79·5	78·9	76·4	73·5	79·1
Other crimes	19·2	21·4	24·6	29·0	34·7
Total offences	338·4	358·5	377·0	385·6	408·6
Miscellaneous offences	118·1	120·4	127·3	124·9	124·9
Motor vehicle offences	220·3	238·1	249·7	260·7	283·8

PRISONS

Receptions into prison: by number of previous convictions (England and Wales)

	1981	1982	1983*†	1984	1985	1986	1987	1988	1989
Number of previous convictions									
Males: total	43,388	46,779	42,716	39,930	43,626	40,004	41,442	41,385	39,773
None	1,518	1,773	1,848	1,765	1,686	2,004	1,655	2,562	2,320
1–2 sentences	3,002	3,164	2,969	2,924	3,394	3,165	3,046	2,808	2,303
3–5 sentences	7,161	7,312	6,104	5,694	6,273	5,727	5,619	4,911	4,098
6–10 sentences	11,152	11,845	10,048	9,009	9,861	8,695	8,427	7,977	6,563
11 or more sentences	13,343	14,057	13,632	13,169	13,835	11,855	11,363	10,716	9,060
Previous conviction information not recorded	7,212	8,628	8,115	7,369	8,577	8,558	11,332	12,411	15,429
Females: total	2,533	2,692	2,349	2,388	2,475	2,374	2,388	2,235	2,167
None	177	176	271	289	208	300	247	324	244
1–2 sentences	234	261	273	252	241	289	258	217	204
3–5 sentences	423	445	419	374	347	349	338	344	238
6–10 sentences	434	443	401	397	360	327	351	271	217
11 or more sentences	267	322	294	265	261	258	242	261	196
Previous conviction information not recorded	998	1,045	691	811	1,058	851	952	818	1,068

* From 1983 data are not comparable with previous years because of the Criminal Justice Act 1982.
† Youth custody for offenders aged 15–20 replaced imprisonment on May 24, 1983.

Source: HMSO—Annual Abstract of Statistics 1991

LOCAL GOVERNMENT

ENGLAND AND WALES

The London Government Act 1963 and the Local Government Acts of 1972 and 1985 have brought about the present system of local government in England and Wales. The system is based on two tiers of local authorities, county and district councils, in the non-metropolitan areas; and a single tier, of metropolitan district and London borough councils, in the six metropolitan areas of England and in London respectively.

Structures and areas in England

England outside Greater London is divided into counties. Each county is divided into districts. Six *metropolitan counties* cover the main conurbations outside Greater London; Tyne and Wear, West Midlands, Merseyside, Greater Manchester, West Yorkshire and South Yorkshire. They are divided into 36 *metropolitan districts*, most of which have a population of over 200,000. There are 39 *non-metropolitan counties*; each of these is divided into *non-metropolitan districts*, of which there are 296. These districts have populations broadly in the range of 60,000 to 100,000; some however, have larger populations, because of the need to avoid dividing large towns, and some in mainly rural areas have smaller populations. Greater London is divided into 32 *London boroughs*, with populations between 130,000 and 300,000, and the *City*, with a daytime population of 340,000 but only 4,000 by night.

There are also about 10,000 parishes, in 219 of the non-metropolitan and 18 of the metropolitan districts.

A permanent Local Government Boundary Commission keeps the areas and electoral arrangements under review, and makes proposals to the Secretary of State for changes found necessary.

Constitution and elections

For districts, non-metropolitan counties, London boroughs, the City, and for about 8,000 parishes, there are elected councils, consisting of directly elected councillors. Broadly, county councils range from 60–100 members; metropolitan district councils 50–80 members; non-metropolitan district councils 30–60 members. The councillors elect annually one of their number as chairman.

The general pattern in England is that councillors serve four years and there are no elections of district and parish councillors in county elections years. In metropolitan districts one-third of the councillors for each ward are elected each year except in the year of county elections. Non-metropolitan districts can choose whether to have elections by thirds or whole council elections. In the former case, one-third of the council is elected in each year of metropolitan district elections. If whole council elections are chosen, these are held in the year midway between county elections. The London boroughs have whole council elections, in the year immediately following the county council election years. Local elections are normally held on the first Thursday in May.

Generally speaking, all British subjects or citizens of the Republic of Ireland of 18 years or over, resident on the qualifying date in the area for which the election is being held, are entitled to vote at local government elections. A register of electors is prepared and published annually by local electoral registration officers.

A returning officer has the overall responsibility for an election. Voting takes place at polling stations,

arranged by the local authority and under the supervision of a presiding officer specially appointed for the purpose. Candidates, who are subject to various statutory qualifications and disqualifications designed to ensure that they are suitable persons to hold office, must be nominated by electors for the electoral area concerned.

Internal organization

Local authorities increasingly are organized along party political lines and over 80 per cent are now controlled by groups of councillors having allegiance to one of the main political parties. However, the council as a whole is the final decision-making body within any authority. Councils are free to a great extent to make their own internal organizational arrangements. Normally, questions of major policy are settled by the full council, while the administration of the various services is the responsibility of committees of members. Day-to-day decisions are delegated to the council's officers, who act within the policies laid down by the members.

Functions

Local authorities are empowered or required by various Acts of Parliament to carry out functions in their areas. The legislation concerned comprises public general Acts and 'local' Acts which local authorities have promoted as private bills. In non-metropolitan areas, functions are divided between the districts and counties, those requiring the larger area or population for their efficient performance going to the county. The metropolitan district councils, with the larger population in their areas, already had wider functions than non-metropolitan councils, and following abolition of the metropolitan county councils have now been given most of their functions also. A few functions continue to be exercised over the larger area by joint bodies, made up of councillors from each district.

The allocation of functions is as follows:

county councils: education; strategic planning; traffic, transport and highways; police; fire service; consumer protection; refuse disposal; smallholdings; social services; libraries.

non-metropolitan district councils: local planning; housing; highways (maintenance of certain urban roads and off-street car parks); building regulations; environmental health; refuse collection; cemeteries and crematoria.

metropolitan district and London borough councils: their functions are all those listed above, except that fire, civil defence (and in some cases, refuse disposal) in all areas and police and passenger transport in the metropolitan counties only are exercised by joint bodies.

Functions exercised concurrently by county and district councils and London boroughs: recreation (parks, playing fields, swimming pools); museums; encouragement of the arts, tourism and industry.

The sewerage and sewage disposal functions of local authorities were transferred to nine water authorities in England and the Welsh Water Authority. These functions were transferred in 1989 to the National Rivers Authority (NRA) and privatized public water companies.

The personal health functions of local authorities were transferred in 1977 to area health authorities, whose areas were the same as non-metropolitan and Welsh counties and metropolitan districts. From April 1982 this two-tier structure was replaced by about 199 District Health Authorities. They work in close collaboration with local education, social services and environmental health authorities.

Residuary Bodies

Residuary bodies were set up in 1985 to deal with the business of the Greater London and metropolitan county councils which had not already devolved on to other bodies at the time of the councils' abolition in 1986. They have all now been wound up, *see* page 579 (page 598 for Greater London).

Parish councils

Parishes with 200 or more electors must generally have parish councils, and about three-quarters of the parishes have councils. A parish council comprises at least five members, the number being fixed by the district council. Elections are held every four years, in the year in which the local district council is elected. All parishes have parish meetings, comprising the electors of the parish. Where there is no council, the meeting must be held at least twice a year.

Parish council functions include: allotments; encouragement of arts and crafts; community halls, recreational facilities (e.g. open spaces, swimming pools), cemeteries and crematoria; and many minor functions. They must also be given an opportunity to comment on planning applications. They may, like county and district councils, spend limited sums for the general benefit of the parish. They levy a precept on the district councils for their funds.

Civic dignities

District councils may petition for a Royal Charter granting borough status to the district. In boroughs the chairman of the council is the mayor. The status 'City' and the right to call the mayor 'Lord Mayor' may also be granted by letters patent. Parish councils may call themselves 'town councils', in which case their chairman is the 'town mayor'.

Charter trustees were established for those former boroughs which were too large to have parish councils when local government was reorganized in 1974 and they became part of districts without city or borough status. The charter trustees are the district councillors representing the area of the former borough and they elect a town mayor, continue civic tradition, and look after the charters, insignia and civic plate of the former borough.

Local Commissioners for England and Wales

Commissioners for Local Administration in England and in Wales (*see* pp. 337–8) have been appointed with the duty of investigating complaints of maladministration in aspects of local government; they report to the local council concerned.

WALES

Since 1974 Wales, including the former Monmouthshire, has been divided into eight counties; Gwynedd, Clwyd, Powys, Dyfed, Mid Glamorgan, South Glamorgan, West Glamorgan, and Gwent. There are 37 districts in Wales, many of those in the less populated parts reflecting the areas of former Welsh counties.

The arrangements for Welsh counties and districts are generally similar to those for English nonmetropolitan counties and districts. There are some differences in functions; Welsh district councils have refuse disposal as well as refuse collection functions

and they may provide on-street as well as off-stree car parks with the consent of the county council. *A* few districts have also been designated as librar authorities.

Community councils

In Wales parishes have been replaced by com munities. Unlike England, where many areas are no in any parish, communities have been established fo the whole of Wales, approximately 865 communitie in all. Community meetings may be convened as an when desired. Community councils exist in abou 735 communities and further councils may be estab lished at the request of a community meeting Community councils have broadly the same range o powers as English parish councils. Communit: councillors are elected en bloc on the same basis a parish councillors in England, i.e. at the same time a a district council election and for a term of four years

LOCAL GOVERNMENT FINANCE

Local government is financed from various source:

Community charges

Community charges replaced domestic rates o April 1, 1990 under the provisions of the Loca Government Finance Act 1988. They are raised b the charging authorities (district councils and, i London, borough councils and the City Corporation Liability to pay a community charge arises from a entry in the community charges register which i compiled by the community charges registratio officer of each charging authority. Sums required b county and parish councils and joint boards fo police, fire and transport are included by the chargin authority when calculating its community charg: There are three types of charge: the person: community charge, payable by people aged 18 or ove (unless exempt); the collective community charg: paid in respect of certain designated buildings whos occupants move frequently and are difficult t register, and who will therefore pay their communit charge contributions to the landlord; and the stanc ard community charge which is payable in respect « domestic property which is not occupied.

The Community Charges (General Reduction) Ac provides for the personal community charges set b charging authorities in England and Wales to t reduced by £140, or to zero where the original charg was less than £140. In addition, the Person: Community Charge (Reductions) (England) Regula tions provide for a scheme to limit househol increases over rates. In general, reductions ar awarded to individuals and households where th total community charge liability would otherwi: have exceeded the rates payable in 1989–90 by mor than £52 for the first two adults plus £52 for eac successive chargepayer. There is additional help fc the elderly or disabled who were not ratepayers.

Non-domestic rates

Non-domestic (business) rates are collected fror April 1, 1990 by charging authorities, i.e. by distric councils, the Council of the Isles of Scilly and i London by the borough councils and the Commo: Council of the City of London. The Local Goverr ment Finance Act 1988 provides for liability for rate to be assessed on the basis of a poundage (multiplie: tax on the rateable value of property (hereditaments The multiplier is to be set by central Governmer and rates collected by the charging authority for th area where a property is located. Rate income collected by charging authorities is paid into a central national non-domestic rating (NNDR) pool and redistributed to individual authorities on the basis of adult resident population. For the years 1990–91 to 1994–95 actual payment of rates in certain cases will be subjected to transitional arrangements, to phase in the larger increases and reductions in rates resulting from the combined effects of the 1990 revaluation and the introduction of a uniform national business rate (UBR).

Rateable values for the rating lists came into force on April 1, 1990. They are derived from the rental value of property as at April 1, 1988 and determined on certain statutory assumptions by valuation officers of the Board of Inland Revenue. New property is added to the list, and significant changes to existing property necessitate amendments to the rateable value, on the same basis. Rating lists remain in force until the next general revaluation, which is scheduled for April 1, 1995.

Certain types of property are exempt from rates, e.g. agricultural land and buildings, and places of public religious worship. Charities and other non-profit-making organizations may receive full or partial relief. Specified classes of empty property are liable to pay rates at 50 per cent.

Government grants

In addition to specific grants in support of revenue expenditure on particular services, central Government pays revenue support grant to local authorities. This grant is paid to each charging authority so that if all authorities in its area spend at a level sufficient to provide a standard level of service, it can set the same community charge before taking account of any transitional arrangements. In 1991–92 there are a number of transitional arrangements in operation to ease the transition from the old system of local authority finance. Also, grants are being paid to charging authorities to compensate them for the effects of the general reduction in the level of community charges for 1991–92 following the passage of the Community Charges (General Reduction) Act 1991.

The 1991–92 revenue support grant settlement provided for a total of £9,673 million in revenue support grants to be paid to local authorities.

Expenditure 1991–92

Local authority budgeted net revenue expenditure for 1991–92 in England was as follows. The amounts given are at 1991–92 cash prices.

Service	£m
Education	18,759
School catering	370
Libraries, museums and art galleries ..	660
Personal social services	4,570
Police	4,840
Fire	1,053
Other Home Office services	697
Local transport	2,393
Local environmental services	4,612
Agricultural services	32
Consumer protection and trading standards	112
Employment	165
Non-housing revenue account housing	318
Housing benefits	1,910
Total Current Expenditure	**40,490**

Capital charges	3,429
Capital charged to revenue	594
Other non-current	2,830
Interest receipts	−984
Total Revenue Expenditure	**46,359**
Specific grants	−8,202
Community charge benefit grant	−1,842
Other	−21
Net Revenue Expenditure	**36,295**

Aggregate external finance for 1991–92 was originally determined at £26,000 million. Of this, specific grants were estimated at £340 million and transitional grants at £600 million. £9,700 million was in respect of revenue support grant and £12,400 million was support from the national non-domestic rate pool. Following the Budget, community charge grant of £4,800 million was also paid to local authorities enabling community charges to be reduced by £140. Total standard spending by local authorities considered for grant purposes was £39,000 million.

Average community charges.—The average charges levied in England for 1991–92 were: London Boroughs, £241; Metropolitan Districts, £262; Shire Districts, £249. The average charge levied in England was £251.

Non-domestic rates.—National non-domestic rate (or uniform business rate). The rate in England for 1991–92 is 38·6p. The amount estimated to be raised is £12·3bn. Total rateable value held on local authority lists at December 1, 1990 was £29·3bn.

SCOTLAND

Since 1975, mainland Scotland has been divided for local government purposes into nine regions within which there are 53 districts. Regional and district councils have separate responsibility for specific functions. In the three islands areas, Orkney, Shetland and the Western Isles, there are single tier Islands Councils responsible for most local authority functions.

Local government electors.—In 1991 the Register shows 3,912,528 electors in Scotland. Elections took place in 1990 for regional and island councils, and are due in 1992 for district councils.

Functions

Regional Councils are responsible for education; social work; strategic planning; the provision of infrastructure such as roads, water and sewerage; consumer protection; flood prevention; coast protection; and valuation and rating. They also have responsibility for the police and fire services; civil defence; electoral registration; public transport; registration of births, deaths and marriages.

District Councils deal with more local matters such as housing; leisure and recreation, including tourism, parks, libraries, museums and galleries; development control and building control; environmental health, including cleansing, refuse collection and disposal, food hygiene, inspection of shops, offices and factories, clean air, markets and slaughterhouses, burial and cremation; licensing, including liquor, cinemas and theatres, taxis, street traders, betting and gaming, and charitable collections; allotments; public conveniences; the administration of district courts.

Community Councils

Unlike the parish councils of England or community councils of Wales, Scottish community councils are not local authorities. Their purpose as defined in statute is to ascertain and express the views of the communities which they represent, and to take in the interests of their communities such action as appears to be expedient or practicable. Over 1,000 community councils have been established under schemes drawn up by district and islands councils in Scotland.

Rates and community charge

In 1989–90 a total of £1,190,904,000 was received from non-domestic rates of local government in Scotland. The average non-domestic rate level was 76.6p. Total non-domestic water rate income was £17,368,000 and the average non-domestic water rate levied was 5.1p. Non-domestic sewerage rate income was £81,814,000 and the average non-domestic sewerage rate levied was 5.7p. Total metered water income was £69,688,000 and the average metered water rate levied was 29.1p.

A total of £984,385,000 was received from the community charge of local government in Scotland and the average personal community charge levied was £280.39. The community water charge receipts were £70,316,000 and the average community water charge levied was £20.39.

Provisional figures for 1990–91 show total receipts from non-domestic rates of £1,187,000 and £1,062,000 from the community charge. The average non-domestic rate per £ levied for 1990–91 was 57.3p and the average personal community charge payable in Scotland was £306.37.

Local Commissioner

The Commissioner for Local Administration in Scotland is responsible for investigating complaints from members of the public who claim to have suffered injustice as a consequence of maladministration in local government (*see* page 338).

NORTHERN IRELAND

For the purpose of local government Northern Ireland has a system of 26 single-tier district councils. There are 566 members of the councils, elected for periods of four years at a time on the principle of proportional representation.

The district councils all have the same three main roles. These are:

(a) an executive role in which the councils are responsible for a wide range of local services including the provision of recreational, social, community, and cultural facilities; environmental health; consumer protection; the enforcement of building regulations; the promotion of tourist development schemes; street cleansing; refuse collection and disposal; litter prevention; and miscellaneous licensing and registration provisions, including dog control;

(b) a representative role in which they nominate representatives to sit as members of the various statutory bodies responsible for the administration of regional services such as education and libraries, health and personal social services, drainage, fire and electricity; and

(c) a consultative role in which they act as the media through which the views of local people are expressed on the operation in their area of other regional services, notably planning, roads, and conservation (including water supply and sewerage services) provided by those departments of central government which have an obligation, either statutorily or otherwise, to consult the district councils about proposals affecting their areas.

POLITICAL COMPOSITION OF LOCAL COUNCILS
(as at end May 1991)

Abbreviations: *A.* = Liberal/SDP Alliance; *C.* = Conservative; *Com.* = Communist; *Dem.* = Democrat; *Grn.* = Green; *Ind.* = Independent; *Ind.C.* = Independent Conservative; *Ind.Lab.* = Independent Labour; *Lab.* = Labour; *Lib.* = Liberal; *Lib.Dem.* = Social and Liberal Democrat; *MK* = Mebyon Kernow; *NP* = Non-Political/Non-Party; *PC* = Plaid Cymru; *RA* = Ratepayers'/Residents' Associations; *SDP* = Social Democratic Party; *SNP* = Scottish National Party.

ENGLAND

County Councils

Avon ....*Lab.* 36, *C.* 33, *Lib. Dem.* 7.
Bedfordshire........*C.* 34, *Lab.* 26, *Lib. Dem.* 11, *Ind. Lab.* 2.
Berkshire ....*C.* 38, *Lab.* 19, *Lib. Dem.* 14, *Ind.* 2, *Ind.C.* 1, *Lib.* 1, *RA* 1.
Buckinghamshire ...*C.* 49, *Lab.* 12, *Lib. Dem.* 6, *Ind.* 2, *Lib.* 1, *SDP* 1.
Cambridgeshire .....*C.* 45, *Lab.* 21, *Lib. Dem.* 10, *Ind.* 1.
Cheshire ....*Lab.* 32, *C.* 29, *Lib. Dem.* 10.
Cleveland ....*Lab.* 48, *C.* 19, *Lib. Dem* 10.
Cornwall ....*Lib. Dem.* 29, *Ind.* 25, *C.* 14, *Lab.* 8, *Lib.* 2, *MK* 1.
Cumbria............*C.* 37, *Lab.* 37, *Lib. Dem.* 7, *Ind.* 2.
Derbyshire ....*Lab.* 51, *C.* 26, *Lib. Dem.* 3, *Ind.* 2 (2 Vac.).
Devon..............*C.* 56, *Lab.* 13, *Lib. Dem.* 11, *Ind.* 2, *SDP* 2, *Lib.* 1.

Dorset ....*C.* 43, *Lib. Dem.* 22, *Lab.* 6, *Ind.* 5, *Ind. C.* 1.
Durham ....*Lab.* 57, *C.* 7, *Lib. Dem.* 4, *Ind.* 4.
East Sussex ....*C.* 38, *Lab.* 17, *Lib. Dem.* 15.
Essex ....*C.* 56, *Lab.* 26, *Lib. Dem.* 15, *Ind.* 1.
Gloucestershire .....*C.* 23, *Lib. Dem.* 22, *Lab.* 16, *Others* 1, (1 Vac.).
Hampshire ....*C.* 57, *Lib. Dem.* 25, *Lab.* 18, *Ind.* 1, (1 Vac.).
Hereford and
Worcester ....*C.* 38, *Lab.* 22, *Lib. Dem.* 11, *Ind.* 4, *Ind. Lib.* 1.
Hertfordshire ....*C.* 45, *Lab.* 27, *Lib. Dem.* 5.
Humberside ....*Lab.* 42, *C.* 30, *Lib. Dem.* 3.
Isle of Wight ....*Lib. Dem.* 26, *C.* 14, *Ind.* 2.
Kent ....*C.* 54, *Lab.* 25, *Lib. Dem.* 20.
Lancashire ....*Lab.* 50, *C.* 42, *Lib. Dem.* 7.
Leicestershire ......*C.* 41, *Lab.* 32, *Lib. Dem.* 11, (1 Vac.).
Lincolnshire ....*C.* 41, *Lab.* 19, *Lib.* 13, *Ind.* 3.
Norfolk ....*C.* 46, *Lab.* 28, *Lib. Dem.* 9, (1 Vac.).

Northamptonshire . . *C.* 34, *Lab.* 31, *Lib. Dem.* 2, *Ind.* 1.

Northumberland . . . . *Lab.* 39, *C.* 17, *Lib. Dem.* 9, *Ind.* 1.

North Yorkshire . . . . *C.* 46, *Lab.* 21, *Lib. Dem.* 20, *Ind.* 6, *SDP* 3.

Nottinghamshire. . . . . *Lab.* 50, *C.* 35, *Lib. Dem.* 3.

Oxfordshire . . . . *C.* 33, *Lab.* 23, *Lib. Dem.* 13, *Grn.* 1.

Shropshire . . . . *C.* 30, *Lab.* 24, *Lib. Dem.* 9, *Ind.* 3.

Somerset . . . . *C.* 31, *Lib. Dem.* 18, *Lab.* 6, *Ind.* 2.

Staffordshire . . . . . . *Lab.* 50, *C.* 29, *Lib. Dem.* 2, *RA* 1.

Suffolk . . . . *C.* 46, *Lab.* 27, *Lib. Dem.* 4, *Ind.* 3.

Surrey . . . . *C.* 55, *Lib. Dem.* 10, *Lab.* 7, *Ind.* 2, *RA* 2.

Warwickshire . . . . . *C.* 31, *Lab.* 24, *Lib. Dem.* 4, *Ind.* 3, *RA* 1.

West Sussex . . . . *C.* 45, *Lib. Dem.* 17, *Lab.* 9.

Wiltshire . . . . *C.* 35, *Lab.* 18, *Lib. Dem.* 17, *Ind.* 2, *SDP* 2, *Lib.* 1.

Metropolitan District Councils
GREATER MANCHESTER

Bolton . . . . *Lab.* 42, *C.* 14, *Lib. Dem.* 3, *Ind. Lab.* 1.

Bury . . . . *Lab.* 29, *C.* 18, *SDP* 1.

Manchester . . . . *Lab.* 85, *Lib. Dem.* 9, *C.* 5.

Oldham . . . . *Lab.* 42, *Lib. Dem.* 16, *C.* 2.

Rochdale . . . . *Lab.* 33, *Lib. Dem.* 15, *C.* 12.

Salford . . . . *Lab.* 56, *C.* 4.

Stockport . . . . *Lib. Dem.* 25, *C.* 17, *Lab.* 17, *Ind.* 3.

Tameside . . . . *Lab.* 52, *C.* 4, (1 Vac.).

Trafford . . . . *C.* 34, *Lab.* 25, *Lib. Dem.* 3, *Ind. Lab.* 1.

Wigan . . . . *Lab.* 63, *Lib. Dem.* 6, *C.* 2, *Ind. Lab.* 1.

MERSEYSIDE

Knowsley . . . . *Lab.* 62, *C.* 3, *Ind. Lab.* 1.

Liverpool . . . . *Lab.* 43, *Lib. Dem.* 27, *C.* 2, *Lib.* 1, *SDP* 1, *Others* 1.

St Helens . . . . *Lab.* 30, *Lib. Dem.* 15, *C.* 5, *Others* 4.

Sefton . . . . *Lab.* 27, *C.* 22, *Lib. Dem.* 20.

Wirral . . . . *Lab.* 34, *C.* 24, *Lib. Dem.* 7.

SOUTH YORKSHIRE

Barnsley . . . . *Lab.* 62, *C.* 2, *Ind.* 2.

Doncaster . . . . *Lab.* 55, *C.* 8.

Rotherham . . . . *Lab.* 65, *C.* 1.

Sheffield . . . . *Lab.* 70, *C.* 11, *Lib. Dem.* 6.

TYNE AND WEAR

Gateshead . . . . *Lab.* 60, *Lib. Dem.* 5, *C.* 1.

Newcastle upon
Tyne . . . . *Lab.* 64, *Lib. Dem.* 10, *C.* 4.

North Tyneside . . . . . *Lab.* 38, *C.* 15, *Lib.* 7.

South Tyneside . . . . . *Lab.* 56, *Lib. Dem.* 2, *C.* 1, *RA* 1.

Sunderland . . . . *Lab.* 64, *C.* 8, *Lib. Dem.* 3.

WEST MIDLANDS

Birmingham . . . . *Lab.* 71, *C.* 38, *Lib. Dem.* 12, *Ind.* 2.

Coventry . . . . *Lab.* 46, *C.* 8.

Dudley . . . . *Lab.* 43, *C.* 29.

Sandwell . . . . *Lab.* 51, *C.* 15, *Lib.* 6.

Solihull . . . . *C.* 23, *Lab.* 16, *Lib. Dem.* 6, *RA* 6.

Walsall . . . . *Lab.* 33, *C.* 17, *Lib. Dem.* 8, *Ind.* 2.

Wolverhampton . . . . *Lab.* 35, *C.* 22, *Lib. Dem.* 3.

WEST YORKSHIRE

Bradford . . . . *Lab.* 53, *C.* 35, *Lib. Dem.* 2.

Calderdale . . . . *Lab.* 28, *C.* 21, *Lib. Dem.* 5.

Kirklees . . . . *Lab.* 47, *C.* 12, *Lib. Dem.* 11, *Ind.* 2.

Leeds . . . . *Lab.* 68, *C.* 21, *Lib. Dem.* 9, *Ind.* 1.

Wakefield . . . . *Lab.* 59, *C.* 3, *Ind. Lab.* 1.

Non-Metropolitan District Councils
(* one-third of councillors of Councils so denoted retire each year, except in those years when County Council elections are held)

*Adur . . . . *Lib. Dem.* 22, *C.* 14, *Ind.* 2, *Lab.* 1.

Allerdale . . . . *Lab.* 31, *C.* 11, *Ind.* 7, *Ind. C.* 4, *Lib. Dem.* 2.

Alnwick . . . . *Lib. Dem.* 15, *C.* 7, *Ind.* 5, *Lab.* 2.

*Amber Valley . . . . . *Lab.* 22, *C.* 18, *Ind.* 3.

Arun . . . . *C.* 36, *Lib. Dem.* 12, *Lab.* 7, *Grn.* 1.

Ashfield . . . . *Lab.* 32, *C.* 1.

Ashford . . . . *C.* 29, *Lib. Dem.* 11, *Lab.* 5, *Ind.* 1, *Others* 3.

Aylesbury Vale . . . . *C.* 29, *Lib. Dem.* 22, *Ind.* 6, *Lab.* 1.

Babergh . . . . *C.* 15, *Ind.* 10, *Lab.* 6, *Lib. Dem.* 5, *Others* 5, (1 Vac.).

*Barrow-in-Furness . *Lab.* 18, *C.* 17, *Ind.* 3.

*Basildon . . . . *Lab.* 21, *C.* 17, *Lib. Dem.* 4.

*Basingstoke and
Deane . . . . *C.* 30, *Lab.* 15, *Lib. Dem.* 11, *NP* 3.

*Bassetlaw . . . . *Lab.* 29, *C.* 16, *Ind.* 3, *Ind. Lab.* 1, *Lib. Dem.* 1.

*Bath . . . . *C.* 24, *Lib. Dem.* 13, *Lab.* 11.

Berwick-upon-
Tweed . . . . *Lib. Dem.* 11, *Ind.* 6, *C.* 1, *Lab.* 1, *Others* 3.

Beverley . . . . *C.* 31, *Lib.* 19, *Lab.* 2, *Ind.* 1.

Blaby . . . . *C.* 30, *Lib. Dem.* 4, *Ind.* 3, *C.* 1, *Lab.* 1.

*Blackburn . . . . *Lab.* 39, *C.* 17, *Lib. Dem.* 3.

Blackpool . . . . *Lab.* 27, *C.* 12, *Lib. Dem.* 5.

Blyth Valley . . . . . . *Lab.* 28, *Lib. Dem.* 19.

Bolsover . . . . *Lab.* 34, *RA* 2, *Ind.* 1.

Boothferry . . . . *C.* 18, *Lab.* 12, *Ind.* 5.

Boston . . . . *C.* 10, *Ind.* 8, *Lib.* 8, *Lab.* 8.

Bournemouth . . . . . . *Lib. Dem.* 27, *C.* 20, *Lab.* 6, *Ind.* 3.

Bracknell Forest . . . *C.* 32, *Lab.* 7, *Lib. Dem.* 1.

Braintree . . . . *C.* 23, *Lab.* 21, *Lib. Dem.* 6, *RA* 4, *Ind.* 2.

Breckland . . . . *C.* 33, *Lab.* 8, *Ind.* 5, *Lib. Dem.* 1, *Others* 16.

*Brentwood . . . . *Lib. Dem.* 20, *C.* 17, *Lab.* 2.

Bridgnorth . . . . *C.* 11, *Ind.* 8, *Lib. Dem.* 4, *Ind. Lab.* 2, *NP* 2, *Lab.* 1, *Others* 5.

*Brighton . . . . *Lab.* 29, *C.* 15, *Ind. Lab.* 4.

*Bristol . . . . *Lab.* 44, *C.* 18, *Lib. Dem.* 5, (1 Vac.).

*Broadland . . . . *Ind. C.* 26, *Ind.* 8, *Lib. Dem.* 8, *Lab.* 7.

Bromsgrove . . . . *C.* 26, *Lab.* 14, *Lib. Dem.* 1.

*Broxbourne . . . . *C.* 35, *Lab.* 5, *Lib. Dem.* 2.

Broxtowe . . . . *C.* 28, *Lab.* 15, *Lib. Dem.* 5.

*Burnley . . . . *Lab.* 38, *C.* 8, *Lib. Dem.* 4.

*Cambridge . . . . *Lab.* 25, *C.* 10, *Lib. Dem.* 7.

*Cannock Chase . . . . *Lab.* 30, *C.* 5, *Lib. Dem.* 4, *Grn.* 1, *Ind. Lib. Dem.* 1, (1 Vac.).

Canterbury . . . . *Lib. Dem.* 23, *C.* 19, *Lab.* 7.
Caradon . . . . *Ind.* 23, *Lib. Dem.* 9, *C.* 5, *RA* 3, *Lab.* 1.
*Carlisle . . . . *Lab.* 32, *C.* 17, *Lib.* 1, *Ind.* 1.
Carrick . . . . *Lib. Dem.* 24, *C.* 8, *Ind.* 8, *Lab.* 4, *Ind. C.* 1.
Castle Morpeth . . . . *Ind. Lab.* 9, *Lib. Dem.* 9, *Lab.* 9, *C.* 7.
Castle Point . . . . *C.* 36, *Lab.* 3.
Charnwood . . . . *C.* 34, *Lab.* 15, *Lib. Dem.* 2, *Ind.* 1.
Chelmsford . . . . *C.* 29, *Lib. Dem.* 21, *Ind.* 3, *Lab.* 2.
*Cheltenham . . . . *Lib. Dem.* 24, *C.* 8, *Ind.* 3, *Lab.* 3, *Others* 3.
*Cherwell . . . . *C.* 28, *Lab.* 18, *Lib. Dem.* 3, *Ind. C.* 2, *Ind.* 1.
*Chester . . . . *C.* 23, *Lab.* 21, *Lib. Dem.* 14, *Ind.* 2.
Chesterfield . . . . *Lab.* 31, *Lib. Dem.* 11, *C.* 5.
Chester-le-Street . . . *Lab.* 27, *Ind.* 4, *C.* 1, *Ind.* 1, *Lib.* 1.
Chichester . . . . *C.* 34, *Lib. Dem.* 14, *Ind.* 2.
Chiltern . . . . *C.* 39, *Lib. Dem.* 9, *RA* 2.
*Chorley . . . . *Lab.* 24, *C.* 17, *Ind. C.* 3, *Lib. Dem.* 2, *Ind.* 1.
Christchurch . . . . . . *C.* 13, *Ind.* 12.
Cleethorpes . . . . *Lab.* 16, *C.* 12, *Lib. Dem.* 11, *Ind.* 1.
*Colchester . . . . *Lib. Dem.* 28, *C.* 19, *Lab.* 11, *RA* 2.
*Congleton . . . . *Lib. Dem.* 23, *C.* 14, *Lab.* 8.
Copeland . . . . *Lab.* 28, *C.* 20, *Ind.* 3.
Corby . . . . *Lab.* 23, *Lib. Dem.* 2, *C.* 1, *Ind.* 1.
Cotswold . . . . *Ind.* 16, *C.* 9, *Lib. Dem.* 3, *Others* 16.
*Craven . . . . *C.* 12, *Lib. Dem.* 12, *Ind.* 7, *Lab.* 3.
*Crawley . . . . *Lab.* 24, *C.* 7, *Lib. Dem.* 1.
*Crewe and . . . . *Lab.* 30, *C.* 23, *Lib. Dem.* 2, *Ind.* Nantwich 1, *Ind. Lab.* 1.
Dacorum . . . . *C.* 38, *Lab.* 16, *Lib. Dem.* 4.
Darlington . . . . *Lab.* 30, *C.* 18, *Ind.* 2, *Lib. Dem.* 2.
Dartford . . . . *C.* 25, *Lab.* 20, *RA* 2.
*Daventry . . . . *C.* 18, *Lab.* 13, *Ind.* 2, *Lib. Dem.* 2.
*Derby . . . . *C.* 22, *Lab.* 22.
Derbyshire Dales . . . *C.* 24, *Lib. Dem.* 9, *Lab.* 3, *Ind. C.* 2, *Ind.* 1.
Derwentside . . . . *Lab.* 38, *Ind.* 14, *C.* 2.
Dover . . . . *C.* 28, *Lab.* 21, *Lib. Dem.* 4.
Durham . . . . *Lab.* 28, *Lib. Dem.* 15, *Ind.* 6.
Easington . . . . *Lab.* 43, *Ind.* 4, *Ind. Lab.* 4, *Lib. Dem.* 4.
*Eastbourne . . . . *Lib. Dem.* 16, *C.* 12, *Ind. C.* 1, *Lab.* 1.
East . . . . *Ind.* 10, *C.* 6, *Lib. Dem.* 4, *Ind.* Cambridgeshire . . . *C.* 1, *Lab.* 1, *Others* 15.
East Devon . . . . *C.* 41, *Lib. Dem.* 11, *Ind.* 3, *Grn.* 2, *Ind. C.* 1, *Lib.* 1, *Others* 1.
East Dorset . . . . *C.* 19, *Lib. Dem.* 13, *RA* 2, *Ind.* 1, (1 *Vac.*).
East Hampshire . . . . *Lib. Dem.* 20, *C.* 16, *Ind.* 6.
East Hertfordshire . *C.* 32, *Lib. Dem.* 12, *Ind.* 3, *Lab.* 2, *RA* 1.
*Eastleigh . . . . *Lib. Dem.* 29, *C.* 18, *Lab.* 7.
East Lindsey . . . . *Ind.* 43, *C.* 8, *Lib. Dem.* 5, *Lab.* 4.
East . . . . *C.* 24, *Lab.* 9, *Lib. Dem.* 3.
Northamptonshire.
East Staffordshire . . *Lab.* 23, *C.* 19, *Lib. Dem.* 4.
East Yorkshire . . . . . *C.* 16, *Ind.* 13, *Lab.* 5, *Lib. Dem.* 5, *SDP* 3, (1 *Vac.*).
Eden . . . . *Ind.* 24, *RA* 8, *Lib. Dem.* 4, *Ind. C.* 1.

*Ellesmere Port and . . . . *Lab.* 31, *C.* 10.
Neston
*Elmbridge . . . . *C.* 26, *RA* 16, *Lab.* 9, *Lib. Dem.* 9.
*Epping Forest . . . . . . *C.* 31, *Lab.* 13, *RA* 9, *Lib. Dem.* 2, *SDP* 2, *Ind.* 1, *Ind. C.* 1.
Epsom and Ewell . . . *RA* 30, *Lib. Dem.* 6, *Lab.* 3.
Erewash . . . . *Lab.* 27, *C.* 22, *Ind.* 2, *Lib. Dem.* 1.
*Exeter . . . . *Lab.* 18, *C.* 11, *Lib. Dem.* 6, *Lib.* 1.
*Fareham . . . . *C.* 28, *Lib. Dem.* 9, *Lab.* 4, *Ind.* 1.
Fenland . . . . *C.* 28, *Lab.* 6, *Ind.* 4, *Lib. Dem.* 3.
Forest Heath . . . . . . *C.* 12, *Ind.* 9, *Lib. Dem.* 3, *Lab.* 1.
Forest of Dean . . . . . *Lab.* 25, *Ind.* 9, *Lib. Dem.* 6, *C.* 3, *Ind. C.* 1, *Others* 5.
Fylde . . . . *C.* 23, *RA* 9, *Ind.* 6, *Lib. Dem.* 4, *Others*, 13.
Gedling . . . . *C.* 38, *Lab.* 15, *Lib. Dem.* 3, *Ind.* 1.
*Gillingham . . . . *C.* 17, *Lib. Dem.* 15, *Lab.* 10
Glanford . . . . *C.* 17, *Ind.* 11, *Grn.* 3, *NP* 3.
*Gloucester . . . . *Lab.* 17, *C.* 8, *Lib. Dem.* 7, *Ind.* 1.
*Gosport . . . . *Lib. Dem.* 17, *C.* 7, *Lab.* 4, *RA* 2.
Gravesham . . . . *C.* 22, *Lab.* 22.
*Great Grimsby . . . . . *Lab.* 30, *C.* 12, *Lib. Dem.* 2, *Ind.* 1.
*Great Yarmouth . . . *Lab.* 32, *C.* 15, *Lib. Dem.* 1.
Guildford . . . . *C.* 19, *Lib. Dem.* 19, *Lab.* 6, *Ind.* 1.
*Halton . . . . *Lab.* 44, *Lib. Dem.* 7, *C.* 2.
Hambleton . . . . *C.* 24, *Ind.* 13, *Lib. Dem.* 5, *SDP* 3, *Lab.* 2.
Harborough . . . . *C.* 18, *Lib. Dem.* 12, *Ind.* 4, *Lab.* 3.
*Harlow . . . . *Lab.* 32, *C.* 6, *Lib. Dem.* 3, (1 *Vac.*).
*Harrogate . . . . *Lib. Dem.* 28, *C.* 22, *Lab.* 5, *SDP* 2, *Grn.* 1, *Ind.* 1, *Lib.* 1.
*Hart . . . . *C.* 15, *Lib. Dem.* 12, *Ind.* 8.
*Hartlepool . . . . *Lab.* 30, *C.* 11, *Lib. Dem.* 5, *Ind.* 1.
*Hastings . . . . *C.* 12, *Lab.* 10, *Lib. Dem.* 9, *Others* 1.
*Havant . . . . *C.* 19, *Lab.* 12, *Lib. Dem.* 5, *Ind.* 3, *RA* 3.
*Hereford . . . . *Lib. Dem.* 20, *Lab.* 5, *C.* 2.
*Hertsmere . . . . *C.* 22, *Lab.* 12, *Lib. Dem.* 4, *Ind* 1.
High Peak . . . . *Lab.* 16, *C.* 15, *Lib. Dem.* 10, *Ind.* 3.
Hinckley and . . . . . . *C.* 21, *Lib. Dem.* 10, *Lab.* 3.
Bosworth
Holderness . . . . *Ind.* 20, *Lib. Dem.* 7, *NP* 4.
Horsham . . . . *C.* 28, *Lib. Dem.* 16, *Ind.* 2.
Hove . . . . *C.* 21, *Lab.* 6, *Lib. Dem.* 3.
*Huntingdonshire . . *C.* 41, *Lab.* 5, *Lib. Dem.* 5, *Ind* 2.
*Hyndburn . . . . *Lab.* 34, *C.* 9, *Lib. Dem.* 3, *Ind* 1.
*Ipswich . . . . *Lab.* 37, *C.* 11.
Kennet . . . . *C.* 16, *Ind.* 11, *Lib. Dem.* 9.
Kerrier . . . . *Lib. Dem.* 16, *Lab.* 12, *Ind.* 7, *C* 5, *Lib.* 1.
Kettering . . . . *Lab.* 20, *C.* 11, *Lib. Dem.* 8, *Ind* 6.
King's Lynn and . . . . *C.* 33, *Lab.* 16, *Lib. Dem.* 5, *Ind* West Norfolk . . . . . 4.
*Kingston upon Hull *Lab.* 58, *C.* 1, *Lib. Dem.* 1.
Kingswood . . . . *Lab.* 26, *C.* 18, *Lib. Dem.* 5, *Ind* 1.

Lancaster ....Lab. 24, C. 15, Ind. 14, Lib. Dem. 7.

Langbaurgh on Tees Lab. 32, C. 20, Lib. Dem. 7.

Leicester ....Lab. 37, C. 13, Lib. Dem. 6.

*Leominster ....Ind. 16, Lib. Dem. 7, C. 6, Ind. C. 3, Lab. 2, Grn. 1, (1 Vac.).

Lewes ....Lib. Dem. 27, C. 18, Ind. 3.

Lichfield ....C. 37, Lab. 15, Ind. Lab. 3, Ind. 1.

*Lincoln ....Lab. 31, C. 2.

Luton ....Lab. 28, C. 11, Lib. Dem. 9.

*Macclesfield ......C. 31, Lib. Dem. 14, Lab. 10, RA 3, Ind. 1, (1 Vac.).

*Maidstone ....Lib. Dem. 23, C. 20, Lab. 8, Ind. 4.

Maldon ....C. 13, Ind. 9, Lib. Dem. 6, Ind. C. 1, Lab. 1.

Malvern Hills ......Ind. 18, Lib. Dem. 16, C. 14, Lab. 2, Grn. 1.

Mansfield..........Lab. 38, C. 5, Lib. Dem. 2, (1 Vac.).

Medina............C. 18, Lib. Dem. 13, Ind. 3, Lab. 2.

Melton ....C. 18, Lib. Dem. 8.

Mendip............Lib. Dem. 23, C. 13, Ind. 4, Lab. 3.

Mid Bedfordshire ..C. 40, NP 5, Lab. 3, Lib. Dem. 3, Ind. 2.

Mid Devon ....Ind. 27, Lib. Dem. 9, Lib. 2, Lab. 1, Others 1.

Middlesbrough ....Lab. 38, C. 9, Lib. Dem. 5, Ind. 1.

Mid Suffolk ....C. 17, Lib. Dem. 10, Lab. 8, Ind. 5.

*Mid Sussex ....C. 34, Lib. Dem. 13, Ind. 5, Lab. 2.

*Milton Keynes .....Lab. 25, C. 13, Lib. Dem. 7, Ind. 1.

*Mole Valley ....Lib. Dem. 15, C. 13, Ind. 12, Lab. 1.

Newark and Sherwood ....Lab. 28, C. 19, Lib. Dem. 4, Ind. 3.

Newbury ....Lib. Dem. 24, C. 20, Ind. 1.

*Newcastle under Lyme ....Lab. 39, C. 9, Lib. Dem. 8.

New Forest ....Lib. Dem. 29, C. 23, Ind. 6.

Northampton ......Lab. 21, C. 18, Lib. Dem. 4.

Northavon ....Lib. Dem. 25, C. 20, Lab. 11, Ind. 1.

*North Bedfordshire C. 21, Lab. 16, Lib. Dem. 13, Ind. 3.

North Cornwall ....Ind. 30, Lib. Dem. 5, Lab. 2, C. 1.

North Devon ......Lib. Dem. 26, Ind. 16, C. 2.

North Dorset ......Ind. 21, Lib. Dem. 12.

NE Derbyshire .....Lab. 35, C. 12, Ind. 3, Lib. Dem. 3.

*North Hertfordshire C. 26, Lab. 18, RA 3, Lib. Dem. 2, Ind. 1.

North Kesteven ....C. 10, Lab. 10, NP 7, Lab. 6, Lib. Dem. 5, Ind. C. 1.

North Norfolk .....C. & Ind. All. 24, Ind. 7, Lab. 6, Lib. Dem. 5, Others 4.

North Shropshire ..NP 28, C. 5, Lab. 4, Ind. 3.

N. Warwickshire ...Lab. 20, C. 12, Ind. 1, Lib. Dem. 1.

NW Leicestershire .Lab. 24, C. 12, Ind. 4.

North Wiltshire ....Lib. Dem. 29, C. 24, Ind. 4, Lab. 3.

*Norwich ....Lab. 36, Lib. Dem. 9, C. 3.

Nottingham ....Lab. 37, C. 17, Ind. 1.

*Nuneaton and Bedworth ....Lab. 36, C. 9.

*Oadby & Wigston ..Lib. Dem. 19, C. 7.

Oswestry ....C. 8, Ind. 8, Lab. 6, Lib. 3.

*Oxford ....Lab. 37, C. 9, Lib. Dem. 5.

Pendle ....Lab. 26, Lib. 20, C. 5.

*Penwith ....Lab. 12, C. 10, Ind. 7, Lib. Dem. 3, Ind. Lab. 1, MK 1.

*Peterborough ......Lab. 23, C. 19, Lib. 5, Lib. Dem. 1.

Plymouth ....Lab. 41, C. 19.

Poole ....Lib. Dem. 16, C. 13, (1 Vac.).

*Portsmouth........C. 17, Lab. 15, Lib. Dem. 4, Grn. 1, Ind. 1.

*Preston ....Lab. 34, C. 17, Lib. Dem. 6.

*Purbeck ....C. 10, Ind. 6, Lib. Dem. 4, Lib. 1, (1 Vac).

*Reading ....Lab. 29, C. 10, Lib. Dem. 4, Others 2.

*Redditch ....Lab. 20, C. 9.

*Reigate and Banstead ....C. 24, Lab. 12, Lib. Dem. 8, Ind. 2, RA 2.

Restormel ....Lib. Dem. 23, Ind. 13, C. 2, Lab. 1.

Ribble Valley ......C. 24, Lib. Dem. 13, Ind. 1, Lab. 1.

Richmondshire ....Ind. 27, Lib. Dem. 3, C. 1, Ind. C. 1, Others, 2.

Rochester upon Medway ....C. 21, Lab. 21, Lib. Dem. 8.

*Rochford ....Lib. Dem. 19, C. 11, Lab. 8, RA 2.

*Rossendale ....Lab. 25, C. 11.

Rother ....C. 20, Lib. Dem. 16, Ind. 6, Lab. 3.

*Rugby.............C. 20, Lab. 17, RA 6, Ind. 3, Lib. Dem. 2.

*Runnymede ....C. 26, Lab. 9, RA 6, Grn. 1.

Rushcliffe ....C. 43, Lib. Dem. 6, Lab. 5.

*Rushmoor ....C. 30, Lib. Dem. 9, Lab. 6.

Rutland ....Ind. 9, C. 6, Lib. Dem. 4, (1 Vac.).

Ryedale ....Lib. Dem. 20, Ind. 14, C. 6, Lab. 2.

*St Albans.........C. 27, Lib. Dem. 20, Lab. 9, Ind. 1.

St Edmundsbury ...C. 26, Lab. 11, Lib. Dem. 5, Ind. 2, (1 Vac.).

Salisbury ....C. 31, Ind. 9, Lib. Dem. 9, Lab. 5, RA 4.

Scarborough ....Lab. 16, C. 15, Ind. 10, Lib. Dem. 8.

*Scunthorpe ....Lab. 33, C. 5, SDP 2.

Sedgefield ....Lab. 33, Lib. Dem. 7, Ind. 5, C. 2, Others 2.

Sedgemoor ....C. 26, Lab. 12, Lib. Dem. 7, Ind. 4.

Selby.............C. 22, Lab. 13, Ind. 10, Lib. Dem. 3.

Sevenoaks ....C. 31, Ind. 11, Lib. Dem. 11.

Shepway ....Lib. Dem. 33, C. 18, Lab. 3, Ind. 2.

*Shrewsbury and Atcham ....Lab. 21, C. 19, Lib. Dem. 8, Ind. 1.

*Slough ....Lab. 30, Lib. 5, C. 4.

*Southampton.......Lab. 31, A. 9, C. 9.

*South Bedfordshire. C. 34, Lab. 11, Lib. Dem. 6, Ind. 2.

South Bucks. ......C. 30, Ind. 10, Lib. Dem. 1.

*South Cambridgeshire ... C. 27, Ind. 21, Lab. 5, Lib. Dem. 1.

South Derbyshire ..Lab. 20, C. 12, Ind. C. 2.

*Southend-on-Sea ...C. 24, Lib. Dem. 9, Lab. 6.

South Hams ....C. 23, Ind. 8, Lib. Dem. 4, Ind. C. 1, Lab. 1, Others 7.

*South Herefordshire Ind. 31, C. 6, Lib. Dem. 2.

South Holland .....Ind. 15, Lab. 9, C. 5, Ind. 1, Others 9.

South Kesteven ....C. 25, Lab. 13, Ind. 10, Lib. Dem. 8, Lib. 1.

*South Lakeland ....C. 17, Lib. Dem. 15, Lab. 6, Others 15.

South Norfolk .....A. 22, C. 22, Ind. 3.

South Northants. . *C*. 28, *Ind*. 9, *Lab*. 2, *Lib. Dem*. 1.

South Oxfordshire . *C*. 29, *Lib. Dem*. 8, *Ind*. 5, *Lab*. 5.

South Ribble . . . . *C*. 33, *Lab*. 15, *Lib. Dem*. 6.

South Shropshire . . *NP* 13, *C*. 6, *Ind*. 6, *Lib. Dem*. 3, *Ind. C*. 1, *Lab*. 1, *Others* 13.

South Somerset . . . . . *Lib. Dem*. 41, *C*. 14, *Ind*. 5.

South Staffordshire . *C*. 37, *Lab*. 8, *Ind*. 3, *Lib. Dem*. 1.

South Wight . . . . . . *Lib. Dem*. 12, *C*. 7, *Ind*. 5.

Spelthorne . . . . *C*. 33, *Lab*. 4, *Lib. Dem*. 3.

Stafford . . . . *C*. 29, *Lab*. 18, *Lib. Dem*. 13.

Staffordshire . . . . *RA* 23, *Ind. C*. 14, *Lab*. 9, *Ind*.

Moorlands . . . . 6, *Lib. Dem*. 4.

*Stevenage . . . . *Lab*. 35, *Lib. Dem*. 2, *C*. 1, *SDP* 1.

Stockton-on-Tees . . *Lab*. 26, *C*. 17, *Lib. Dem*. 11, *Ind. Lab*. 1.

*Stoke-on-Trent . . . . *Lab*. 58, *C*. 2.

*Stratford-upon- . . *C*. 27, *Lib. Dem*. 19, *Ind*. 6, *Lab*.
Avon . . . . 2, *Others* 1.

*Stroud . . . . *Lab*. 19, *C*. 15, *Lib. Dem*. 12, *Grn*. 6, *Ind*. 3.

Suffolk Coastal . . . . . *C*. 37, *Ind*. 8, *Lab*. 7, *Lib. Dem*. 3.

Surrey Heath . . . . . . *C*. 31, *Lib. Dem*. 4, *Lab*. 1.

*Swale . . . . *Lab*. 19, *C*. 18, *Lib. Dem*. 12.

*Tamworth . . . . *Lab*. 21, *C*. 9.

*Tandridge . . . . *Lib. Dem*. 19, *C*. 15 *Lab*. 7, *Ind*. 1.

Taunton Deane . . . . *Lib. Dem*. 29, *C*. 13, *Lab*. 7, *Ind*. 4.

Teesdale . . . . *Ind*. 21, *Lab*. 7, *C*. 2, *Lib. Dem*. 1.

Teignbridge . . . . *Ind*. 24, *C*. 19, *Lib. Dem*. 11, *Lab*. 4.

Tendring . . . . *Lib. Dem*. 21, *C*. 18, *Lab*. 11, *RA* 4, *Ind*. 3, *Ind. C*. 2, *Others* 1.

Test Valley . . . . *C*. 28, *Lib. Dem*. 13, *Ind*. 2, *NP* 1.

Tewkesbury . . . . *Ind*. 19, *C*. 7, *Lib. Dem*. 6, *Lab*. 2, (2 Vac.).

*Thamesdown . . . . . . *Lab*. 35, *C*. 9, *Lib. Dem*. 5, *Ind*. 1.

Thanet . . . . *C*. 29, *Lab*. 14, *Ind*. 9, *Lib. Dem*. 2.

*Three Rivers . . . . *C*. 19, *Lib. Dem*. 19, *Lab*. 10.

*Thurrock . . . . *Lab*. 33, *C*. 6.

*Tonbridge and
Malling . . . . *C*. 32, *Lib. Dem*. 17, *Lab*. 6.

*Torbay . . . . *Lib. Dem*. 21, *C*. 12, *Lab*. 2, *Ind*. 1.

Torridge . . . . *NP* 18, *C*. 5, *Ind*. 4, *Lab*. 4, *Lib. Dem*. 4, *Grn*. 1.

*Tunbridge Wells . . . *C*. 26, *Lib. Dem*. 15, *Lab*. 5, *Ind*. 1, (1 Vac.).

Tynedale . . . . *C*. 17, *Lab*. 14, *Lib. Dem*. 9, *Ind*. 7.

Uttlesford . . . . *C*. 25, *Lib. Dem*. 10, *Ind*. 6, *Lab*. 1.

Vale of White . . . . . . *C*. 29, *Lib. Dem*. 18, *Ind*. 2, *Lab*.
Horse . . . . 2.

Vale Royal . . . . *Lab*. 32, *C*. 24, *Lib. Dem*. 3, *Ind*. 1, *RA* 1.

Wansbeck . . . . *Lab*. 44, *Lib*. 2.

Wansdyke . . . . *C*. 23, *Lab*. 20, *Ind*. 3, *Lib. Dem*. 1.

Warrington . . . . *Lab*. 42, *Lib. Dem*. 9, *C*. 8.

Warwick . . . . *C*. 24, *Lab*. 10, *Lib. Dem*. 8, *RA* 3.

*Watford . . . . *Lab*. 22, *C*. 11, *Lib. Dem*. 3.

*Waveney . . . . *Lab*. 27, *C*. 14, *Lib. Dem*. 6, *Ind*. 1.

Waverley . . . . *C*. 29, *Lib. Dem*. 28, *Lab*. 2.

Wealden . . . . *C*. 44, *Lib. Dem*. 11, *Ind*. 3.

Wear Valley . . . . . . *Lib. Dem*. 28, *Lab*. 8, *Ind*. 4.

Welling . . . . *C*. 19, *Lab*. 11, *Ind*. 3, *Lib*. 1.

*Welwyn Hatfield . . . *Lab*. 26, *C*. 21.

West Devon . . . . *Ind*. 17, *Lib. Dem*. 6, *C*. 5, *Grn*. 1, *Lab*. 1.

West Dorset . . . . *C*. 18, *NP* 14, *Lib. Dem*. 11, *Lab*. 5, *Ind*. 4, *Ind. C*. 1, *SDP* 1 (1 Vac.).

*West Lancashire . . . . *Lab*. 27, *C*. 26, *Lib. Dem*. 2.

*West Lindsey . . . . . . *C*. 12, *Ind*. 10, *Lib. Dem*. 9, *Lab*. 6.

*West Oxfordshire . . *Ind*. 24, *C*. 11, *Lib. Dem*. 7, *Lab*. 6, (1 Vac.).

West Somerset . . . . . *Ind*. 22, *C*. 5, *Lab*. 3, *Lib. Dem*. 1, (1 Vac.).

West Wiltshire . . . . *Lib. Dem*. 21, *C*. 9, *Ind*. 3, *Lib*. 3, *Lab*. 2, *Others* 2.

*Weymouth and . . . . *Lab*. 12, *C*. 9, *Ind*. 7, *Lib. Dem*.
Portland . . . . 7.

*Winchester . . . . *C*. 25, *Lib. Dem*. 23, *Lab*. 6, (1 Vac.).

Windsor and
Maidenhead . . . . . *C*. 26, *Lib. Dem*. 25, *RA* 7.

*Woking . . . . *C*. 15, *Lib. Dem*. 14, *Lab*. 5, *Ind*. 1.

*Wokingham . . . . *C*. 35, *Lib. Dem*. 17, *Lab*. 2.

Woodspring . . . . *C*. 35, *Lib. Dem*. 14, *Ind*. 4, *Lab*. 4, *Grn*. 1, (1 Vac.).

*Worcester . . . . *Lab*. 24, *C*. 10, *Ind. Lab*. 1, *Lib. Dem*. 1.

*Worthing . . . . *C*. 24, *Lib. Dem*. 12.

Wrekin . . . . *Lab*. 33, *C*. 10, *Lib. Dem*. 2, *Ind*. 1.

Wychavon . . . . *C*. 32, *Lib. Dem*. 10, *Lab*. 6, *Ind*. 1.

Wycombe . . . . *C*. 38, *Lib. Dem*. 10, *Lab*. 9, *Ind*. 2, *RA* 1.

Wyre . . . . *C*. 32, *Lab*. 17, *Lib. Dem*. 5, *Ind*. 1, *RA* 1.

*Wyre Forest . . . . *Lab*. 22, *Lib. Dem*. 10, *C*. 8, *Ind*. 2.

*York . . . . *Lab*. 35, *C*. 6, *Lib. Dem*. 4.

Greater London Boroughs

Barking and
Dagenham . . . . *Lab*. 44, *RA* 3, *Lib*. 1.

Barnet . . . . *C*. 38, *Lab*. 18, *Lib. Dem*. 3, (1 Vac.).

Bexley . . . . *C*. 35, *Lab*. 18, *Lib. Dem*. 9.

Brent . . . . *C*. 31, *Lab*. 26, *Lib. Dem*. 6, *Democratic Lab*. 2, *Ind*. 1.

Bromley . . . . *C*. 43, *Lab*. 11, *Lib. Dem*. 6.

Camden . . . . *Lab*. 42, *C*. 15, *Lib. Dem*. 2.

City of Westminster . *C*. 45, *Lab*. 15.

Croydon . . . . *C*. 41, *Lab*. 29.

Ealing . . . . *C*. 40, *Lab*. 30.

Enfield . . . . *C*. 35, *Lab*. 31.

Greenwich . . . . *Lab*. 44, *C*. 12, *SDP* 4, *Lib*. 2.

Hackney . . . . *Lab*. 46, *C*. 6, *Lib. Dem*. 6, *Ind. Lab*. 1, *Ind. Lib*. 1.

Hammersmith and
Fulham . . . . *Lab*. 28, *C*. 22.

Haringey . . . . *Lab*. 43, *C*. 16.

Harrow . . . . *C*. 32, *Lab*. 13, *Lib. Dem*. 11, *Ind. C*. 4, *Ind*. 3.

Havering . . . . *Lab*. 25, *C*. 19, *RA* 13, *Lib. Dem*. 6.

Hillingdon . . . . *C*. 35, *Lab*. 34.

Hounslow . . . . *Lab*. 44, *C*. 15, *Lib. Dem*. 1.

Islington . . . . *Lab*. 49, *Lib. Dem*. 3.

Kensington and
Chelsea . . . . *C*. 39, *Lab*. 14, (1 Vac.).

Kingston upon
Thames . . . . *C*. 25, *Lib. Dem*. 17, *Lab*. 7, (1 Vac.).

Lambeth . . . . *Lab*. 40, *C*. 20, *Lib. Dem*. 4.

Lewisham . . . . *Lab*. 58, *C*. 6, *Lib. Dem*. 3.

Merton............*Lab.* 29, *C.* 22, *Ind.* 5, *Ind. Lab.* 1.
Newham ....*Lab.* 55, *C.* 3, *Lib. Dem.* 2.
Redbridge ....*C.* 42, *Lab.* 18, *Lib. Dem.* 3.
Richmond upon
Thames ....*Lib. Dem.* 48, *C.* 4.
Southwark ....*Lab.* 36, *Lib. Dem.* 21, *C.* 6, (1 Vac.).
Sutton ....*Lib. Dem.* 32, *C.* 18, *Lab.* 6.
Tower Hamlets......*Lib. Dem.* 29, *Lab.* 21.
Waltham Forest.....*Lab.* 30, *C.* 16, *Lib. Dem.* 11.
Wandsworth........*C.* 48, *Lab.* 13.

WALES
County Councils

Clwyd ....*Lab.* 33, *Ind.* 16, *C.* 9, *Radical* 7, (1 Vac.).
Dyfed ....*Ind.* 33, *Lab.* 27, *PC* 4, *Lib. Dem.* 3, *Ind. Lab.* 1, *Lib.* 1, *RA* 1.
Gwent ....*Lab.* 55, *C.* 7, *Ind.* 1.
Gwynedd...........*Ind.* 28, *Lab.* 14, *PC* 11, *Lib. Dem.* 5, *Others* 4.
Mid Glamorgan .....*Lab.* 65, *PC* 5, *Ind.* 2, *Lib. Dem.* 1, *RA* 1.
Powys............*Ind.* 38, *Lab.* 5, *Lib. Dem.* 3.
South Glamorgan ..*Lab.* 43, *C.* 13, *Lib. Dem.* 5, *PC* 1.
West Glamorgan ....*Lab.* 44, *C.* 6, *Ind.* 6, *Lib. Dem.* 2, *PC* 1, *Others* 2.

District Councils

Aberconwy ....*Lab.* 11, *Lib. Dem.* 10, *C.* 9, *Ind.* 6, *PC* 1, *Others* 4.
Alyn & Deeside ....*Lab.* 28, *C.* 8, *Ind.* 4, *Lib. Dem.* 2, *PC* 1.
Arfon ....*Ind.* 14, *PC* 14, *Lab.* 8, *Lib. Dem.* 2, *Others* 1.
Blaenau Gwent .....*Lab.* 31, *RA* 5, *Ind.* 3, *PC* 2, *C.* 1, *Lib.* 1, (1 Vac.).
Brecknock..........*Ind.* 29, *Lab.* 13, *Lib. Dem.* 2.
Cardiff ....*Lab.* 39, *C.* 16, *Lib. Dem.* 9 *Ind.* 2.
Carmarthen ....*Ind.* 27, *Lab.* 6, *PC* 2, *Lib. Dem.* 1, *RA* 1.
Ceredigion ....*Ind.* 31, *Lib. Dem.* 9, *PC* 3, *Lab.* 1.
Colwyn ....*Ind.* 12, *Lib. Dem.* 12, *C.* 7, *Lab.* 3.
Cynon Valley ....*Lab.* 26, *PC* 10, *Ind.* 1, *Others* 1.
Delyn ....*Ind.* 24, *Lab.* 12, *Lib. Dem.* 3, *PC* 2, *C.* 1.
Dinefwr ....*Lab.* 16, *Ind.* 11, *PC* 3, *NP* 1, (1 Vac.).
Dwyfor.............*PC* 7, *Others* 22.
Glyndŵr ....*Ind.* 25, *Lab.* 7, *Lib. Dem.* 2, *PC* 1.
Islwyn ....*Lab.* 30, *PC* 5.
Llanelli ....*Lab.* 20, *Lib. Dem.* 3, *Grn.* 2, *Ind.* 2, *Ind. Lab.* 1, *PC* 1, *Others* 6.
Lliw Valley ....*Lab.* 22, *Ind.* 6, *PC* 4, *C.* 1.
Meirionnydd ....*PC* 13, *Lab.* 4, *Others* 24.
Merthyr Tydfil.....*Lab.* 21, *RA* 6, *Ind.* 3, *PC* 1, *Others* 3.
Monmouth ....*C.* 22, *Lab.* 14, *Ind.* 3, *Lib. Dem.* 1.
Montgomeryshire ...*Ind.* 36, *Lab.* 4, *Lib. Dem.* 4, *C.* 1, *PC* 1.
Neath ....*Lab.* 25, *PC* 5, *SDP* 2, *Com.* 1, *Ind.* 1.
Newport ....*Lab.* 40, *C.* 7.
Ogwr ....*Lab.* 39, *C.* 8, *Ind. Lab.* 1, *Lib. Dem.* 1.

Port Talbot ....*Lab.* 24, *RA* 4, *Ind.* 1, *Lib. Dem.* 1, *SDP* 1.
Preseli ....*Ind.* 34, *Lab.* 2, *C.* 1, *Lib. Dem.* Pembrokeshire .... 1, (2 Vac.).
Radnorshire ....*Ind.* 28, *Lab.* 5.
Rhondda ....*Lab.* 29, *RA* 3, *PC* 1.
Rhuddlan ....*Ind.* 21, *Lab.* 11.
Rhymney Valley ....*Lab.* 27, *PC* 13, *Ind.* 3, *RA* 2, *Others* 1.
South Pembrokeshire *NP* 25, *Lab.* 2, *PC* 2, (1 Vac.).
Swansea............*Lab.* 31, *C.* 8, *Lib. Dem.* 6, *Ind.* 5, *Grn.* 1.
Taff-Ely ....*Lab.* 19, *PC* 14, *C.* 2, *Lib. Dem.* 2, *RA* 1, *SDP* 1.
Torfaen ....*Lab.* 36, *Lib. Dem.* 4, *Ind.* 2, *C.* 1, *Com.* 1.
Vale of Glamorgan ..*Lab.* 23, *C.* 18, *Ind.* 3, *RA* 3, *Ind.* 1.
Wrexham Maelor ...*Lab.* 28, *Lib. Dem.* 5, *C.* 4, *Ind.* 3, *NP* 3, *Lib.* 1, *PC* 1.
Ynys Môn ....*NP* 22, *PC* 8, *Lab.* 5, *Ind.* 3, *C.* 1.

SCOTLAND
Regional and Islands Councils

Borders ....*Ind.* 13, *Lib. Dem.* 6, *C.* 2, *SNP* 2.
Central ....*Lab.* 22, *SNP* 6, *C.* 5, *Ind.* 1.
Dumfries & ....*Ind.* 17, *Lab/Ind. Lab.* 11, *SNP* Galloway .... 3, *Lib. Dem.* 2, *C.* 1, *Others* 1.
Fife ....*Lab.* 30, *Lib. Dem.* 10, *C.* 2, *SNP* 2, *Com.* 1, *Ind.* 1.
Grampian ....*Lab.* 17, *SNP* 14, *C.* 12, *Lib. Dem.* 10, *Ind.* 3, *Ind. Lab.* 1.
Highland ....*Ind.* 34, *Lab.* 10, *Lib. Dem.* 3, *Ind. Lib. Dem.* 2, *SNP* 2, *C.* 1, *Grn.* 1.
Lothian ....*Lab.* 34, *C.* 12, *Lib. Dem.* 2, *SNP* 1.
Orkney ....*NP* 24.
Shetland ....*Ind.* 15, *Lab.* 2, *Others* 7, (1 Vac.).
Strathclyde.........*Lab.* 90, *C.* 5, *Lib. Dem.* 4, *Ind.* 3, *SNP* 1.
Tayside ....*Lab.* 18, *C.* 14, *SNP* 10, *Lib. Dem.* 2, *Ind.* 1, *Ind. Lab.* 1.
Western Isles ....*Ind.* 30.

District Councils

Aberdeen...........*Lab.* 27, *Lib. Dem.* 14, *C.* 9, *SNP* 2.
Angus..............*SNP* 13, *C.* 6, *Ind.* 1, *Others* 1.
Annandale & ....*Ind.* 8, *SDP* 7, *Lab.* 1, *Lib.* 1.
Eskdale
Argyll & Bute.......*Ind.* 8, *Lib. Dem.* 4, *C.* 3, *SNP* 3, *Lab.* 1, *Others* 7.
Badenoch and ....*Ind.* 11.
Strathspey
Banff & Buchan .....*NP* 9, *SNP* 8, *Ind.* 1.
Bearsden and ....*C.* 6, *Lib. Dem.* 2, *Ind.* 1, *Lab.* 1.
Milngavie
Berwickshire ....*C.* 9, *Ind.* 2, *A.* 1.
Caithness ....*Ind.* 13, *Lab.* 2, *Lib.* 1.
Clackmannan ....*Lab.* 10, *C.* 1, *SNP* 1.
Clydebank ....*Lab.* 11, *C.* 1.
Clydesdale..........*Lab.* 9, *SNP* 4, *Ind.* 2, *C.* 1.
Cumbernauld ....*Lab.* 6, *SNP* 6.
& Kilsyth
Cumnock and ....*Lab.* 8, *Ind. Lab.* 1, *Lib. Dem.* Doon Valley ...... 1.
Cunninghame ....*Lab.* 24, *C.* 4, *Ind.* 2.
Dumbarton ....*Lab.* 7, *C.* 4, *SNP* 3, *Ind.* 1, *NP* 1.

Dundee ....*Lab.* 29, *C.* 10, *SNP* 5.
Dunfermline........*Lab.* 25, *C.* 3, *Lib. Dem.* 3, *SNP* 3.
East Kilbride ....*Lab.* 12, *C.* 2, *Ind.* 2.
East Lothian.......*Lab.* 12, *C.* 4, *SNP* 1.
Eastwood..........*C.* 8, *Ind.* 1, *Lab.* 1, *Lib. Dem.* 1, *RA* 1.
Edinburgh.........*Lab.* 32, *C.* 22, *Lib. Dem.* 5, *SNP* 3.
Ettrick and
   Lauderdale ....*Ind.* 14, *Lab.* 1, *SNP* 1.
Falkirk ....*Lab.* 20, *SNP* 10, *C.* 3, *Ind. Lab.* 2, *Ind.* 1.
Glasgow...........*Lab.* 59, *C.* 4, *Lib. Dem.* 2, *Ind. Lab.* 1.
Gordon.............*Ind.* 8, *Lib. Dem.* 6, *Ind. Lib.* 2.
Hamilton ....*Lab.* 15, *Lib. Dem.* 2, *C.* 1, *Ind. Lab.* 1, *SNP* 1.
Inverclyde.........*Lab.* 12, *Lib. Dem.* 7, *C.* 1.
Inverness ....*Ind.* 14, *Lab.* 12, *Lib. Dem.* 2.
Kilmarnock and
   Loudoun ....*Lab.* 13, *C.* 3, *SNP* 2.
Kincardine and
   Deeside ....*Ind.* 6, *Lib. Dem.* 3, *C.* 2, *SNP* 1.
Kirkcaldy ....*Lab.* 32, *Ind.* 3, *Lib. Dem.* 2, *SNP* 2, *C.* 1.

Kyle and Carrick ....*Lab.* 16, *C.* 7, *Ind. C.* 1, *Ind. Lab.* 1.
Lochaber ....*Ind.* 7, *Lab.* 6, *Ind. Lab.* 1, *NP* 1.
Midlothian ....*Lab.* 14, *C.* 1.
Monklands ....*Lab.* 18, *SNP* 2.
Moray ....*Ind.* 8, *SNP* 8, *Lab.* 2.
Motherwell ....*Lab.* 22, *SNP* 3, *C.* 2, *Ind.* 2, *NP* 1.
Nairn ....*Ind.* 9, *C.* 1.
Nithsdale...........*Lab.* 12, *Ind.* 7, *SNP* 5, *C.* 4.
North East Fife .....*Lib. Dem.* 12, *C.* 4, *Ind.* 2.
Perth and Kinross ...*C.* 11, *SNP* 9, *Lab.* 5, *Ind.* 2, *Lib. Dem.* 2.
Renfrew...........*Lab.* 31, *C.* 6, *SNP* 5, *Lib. Dem.* 2, *Lib.* 1.
Ross & Cromarty ....*Ind.* 17, *Lab.* 2, *SNP* 2, *C.* 1.
Roxburgh ....*Ind.* 7, *Lib. Dem.* 4, *NP* 2, *C.* 1, *SNP* 1, *Others* 1.
Skye & Lochalsh ....*Ind.* 10, *Lib. Dem.* 1.
Stewartry ....*Ind.* 3, *Others* 9.
Stirling ....*C.* 10, *Lab.* 10.
Strathkelvin........*Lab.* 12, *C.* 2, *A* 1.
Sutherland ....*Ind.* 14.
Tweeddale..........*Ind.* 7, *C.* 1, *Lab.* 1, *SNP* 1.
West Lothian ......*Lab.* 12, *SNP* 9, *Ind.* 3.
Wigtown ....*NP* 11, *SNP* 2, *Lab.* 1.

THE KINGDOM OF ENGLAND

Position and extent.—The Kingdom of England lies between 55° 46' and 49° 57' 30" N. latitude (from a few miles north of the mouth of the Tweed to the Lizard), and between 1° 46' E. and 5° 43' W. (from Lowestoft to Land's End). England is bounded on the north by the Cheviot Hills; on the south by the English Channel; on the east by the Straits of Dover (Pas de Calais) and the North Sea; and on the West by the Atlantic Ocean, Wales and the Irish Sea. It has a total area of 50,363 sq. miles (130,439 sq. km): land 50,070 sq. miles (129,681 sq. km); inland water 293 sq. miles (758 sq. km).

Population.—The population at the 1981 Census was 46,362,836 (males 22,520,723; females 23,842,113). The preliminary report on the 1991 Census put the population at 46,161,000. The average density of the population in 1981 was 915 per square mile.

Flag.—The cross of St George, the patron saint of England (*cross gules in a field argent*), has been used since the 13th century.

Relief.—There is a marked division between the upland and lowland areas of England. In the extreme north the Cheviot Hills (highest point, *The Cheviot*, 2,674 ft) form a natural boundary with the Kingdom of Scotland. Running south from the Cheviots, though divided from them by the Tyne Gap, is the Pennine range (highest point, *Cross Fell*, 2,930 ft), the main orological feature of the country. The Pennines culminate in the Peak District of Derbyshire (*Kinder Scout*, 2,088 ft). West of the Pennines are the Cumbrian mountains, which include *Scafell Pike* (3,210 ft), the highest peak in England, and to the east are the Yorkshire Moors, their highest point being *Urra Moor* (1,490 ft).

In the west, the foothills of the Welsh mountains extend into the bordering English counties of Shropshire (the *Wrekin*, 1,334 ft; *Long Mynd*, 1,694 ft) and Hereford and Worcester (the Malvern Hills—*Worcestershire Beacon*, 1,394 ft). Extensive areas of high land and moorland are also to be found in the southwestern peninsula formed by Somerset, Devon and Cornwall: principally Exmoor (*Dunkery Beacon*, 1,704 ft), Dartmoor (*High Willhays*, 2,038 ft) and Bodmin Moor (*Brown Willy*, 1,377 ft). Ranges of low, undulating hills run across the south of the country, including the Cotswolds in the Midlands and south-west, the Chilterns to the north of Greater London, and the North (Kent) and South (Sussex) Downs of the south-east coastal areas.

The lowlands of England lie in the Vale of York, East Anglia and the area around the Wash, the lowest-lying being the Cambridgeshire Fens in the valleys of the Great Ouse and the River Nene, which are below sea-level in places; since the 17th century extensive drainage has brought much of the Fens under cultivation. The North Sea coast between the Thames and the Humber, low-lying and formed of sand and shingle for the most part, is subject to erosion and defences against further incursion have been built along many stretches.

Hydrography.—The *Severn* is the longest river in Great Britain, rising in the north-eastern slopes of Plinlimmon (Wales) and entering England in Shropshire with a total length of 220 miles (354 km) from its source to its outflow into the Bristol Channel, where it receives on the east the Bristol Avon, and on the west the Wye, its other tributaries being the Vyrnwy, Tern, Stour, Teme and Upper (or Warwickshire) Avon. The Severn is tidal below Gloucester, and a high bore or tidal wave sometimes reverses the flow as high as Tewkesbury (13¼ miles above Gloucester). The scenery of the greater part of the river is very picturesque and beautiful, and the Severn is a noted salmon river, some of its tributaries being

famous for trout. Navigation is assisted by the Gloucester and Berkeley Ship Canal (16¼ miles), which admits vessels of 350 tons to Gloucester. The Severn Tunnel was begun in 1873 and completed in 1886 at a cost of £2,000,000 and after many difficulties from flooding. It is 4 miles 628 yards in length (of which 2¼ miles are under the river). The Severn road bridge between Haysgate, Gwent, and Almondsbury, Glos., with a centre span of 3,240 ft, was opened in 1966.

The longest river wholly in England is the *Thames*, with a total length of 215 miles (346 km) from its source in the Cotswold hills to the Nore, and is navigable by ocean-going ships to London Bridge. The Thames is tidal to Teddington (69 miles from its mouth) and forms county boundaries almost throughout its course; on its banks are situated London, Windsor Castle, the home of the Sovereign, Eton College, the first of the public schools, and Oxford, the oldest university in the kingdom.

Of the remaining English rivers those flowing into the North Sea are the Tyne, Wear, Tees, Ouse and Trent from the Pennine Range, the Great Ouse (160 miles), which rises in Northamptonshire, and the Orwell and Stour from the hills of East Anglia. Flowing into the English Channel are the Sussex Ouse from the Weald, the Itchen from the Hampshire Hills, and the Axe, Teign, Dart, Tamar and Exe from the Devonian hills. Flowing into the Irish Sea are the Mersey, Ribble and Eden from the western slopes of the Pennines and the Derwent from the Cumbrian mountains. The English Lakes, noteworthy for their picturesque scenery and poetic associations, lie in Cumbria, the largest being *Windermere* (10 miles long), *Ullswater* and *Derwentwater*.

Islands.—The *Isle of Wight* is separated from Hampshire by the Solent; total area 147 sq. miles, population about 126,600. The climate is mild and healthy, making the island a popular holiday resort. The capital, Newport, stands at the head of the estuary of the Medina, Cowes (at the mouth) being the chief port. Other centres are Ryde, Sandown, Shanklin, Ventnor, Freshwater, Yarmouth, Totland Bay, Seaview and Bembridge.

Lundy (= Puffin Island), 11 miles NW of Hartland Point, Devon, is about two miles long and about half a mile broad (average), with a total area of about 1,116 acres, and a population of about 20; it became the property of the National Trust in 1969 and is now principally a bird sanctuary.

(*See also* The Isles of Scilly, p. 619.)

Climate.—England has a generally mild and temperate climate. Because of the prevailing south-westerly winds, the weather day to day is variable, being affected mainly by depressions moving eastwards across the Atlantic Ocean. This maritime influence means that the west of the country tends to experience wetter but also milder weather than the east. Rainfall also increases with altitude, the mountainous areas of the north and west having more rain than the lowlands of the south and east. Rain is fairly well distributed throughout the year in all areas but, on average, the driest months are March to June, and the wettest September to January.

The mean annual temperature reduced to sea-level varies from 11°C in the south-west to 9°C near Berwick-on-Tweed. In winter, temperatures tend to be higher in the south and west than in the east, while the warmest in summer are the south and inland areas. Latitude for latitude the mean annual temperature is lower in the east; the decrease of mean temperature with height is about 0·6°C per 100 metres.

EARLY INHABITANTS

Prehistoric Man.—Archaeological evidence suggests that England has been inhabited since at least the Palaeolithic period, though the extent of the various Palaeolithic cultures was dependent upon the degree of glaciation. The succeeding Neolithic and Bronze Age cultures have left abundant remains throughout the country, the best-known of these being the henges and stone circles of Stonehenge (ten miles north of Salisbury, Wilts.) and Avebury (Wilts.), both of which are believed to have been of religious significance. In the latter part of the Bronze Age the Goidels, a people of Celtic race, and in the Iron Age other Celtic races of Brythons and Belgae, invaded the country and brought with them Celtic civilization and dialects, place names in England bearing witness to the spread of the invasion over the whole kingdom.

The Roman Conquest.—The Roman conquest of Gaul (57–50 BC) brought Britain into close contact with Roman civilization, but although Julius Caesar raided the south of Britain in 55 BC and 54 BC, conquest was not undertaken until nearly 100 years later. In AD 43 the Emperor Claudius dispatched Aulus Plautius, with a well-equipped force of 40,000, and himself followed with reinforcements in the same year. Success was delayed by the resistance of Caratacus (Caractacus), the British leader from AD 48–51, who was finally captured and sent to Rome, and by a great revolt in AD 61 led by Boudicca (Boadicea), Queen of the Iceni; but the south of Britain was secured by AD 70, and Wales and the area north to the Tyne by about AD 80.

In AD 122, the Emperor Hadrian visited Britain and built a continuous rampart, since known as Hadrian's Wall, from Wallsend to Bowness (Tyne to Solway). The work was entrusted by the Emperor Hadrian to Aulus Platorius Nepos, legate of Britain from AD 122 to 126, and it was intended to form the northern frontier of the Roman Empire.

The Romans administered Britain as a Province under a Governor, with a well-defined system of local government, each Roman municipality ruling itself and surrounding territory, while London was the centre of the road system and the seat of the financial officials of the Province of Britain. Colchester, Lincoln, York, Gloucester and St Albans stand on the sites of five Roman municipalities, and Wroxeter, Caerleon, Chester, Lincoln and York were at various times the sites of legionary fortresses. Well-preserved Roman towns have been uncovered at (or near) Silchester (*Calleva Atrebatum*), ten miles south of Reading, Wroxeter (*Viroconium Cornoviorum*), near Shrewsbury, and St Albans (*Verulamium*) in Hertfordshire.

Four main groups of roads radiated from London, and a fifth (the Fosse) ran obliquely from Lincoln through Leicester, Cirencester and Bath to Exeter. Of the four groups radiating from London, one ran SE to Canterbury and the coast of Kent, a second to Silchester and thence to parts of western Britain and south Wales, a third (later known as Watling Street) ran through Verulamium to Chester, with various branches, and the fourth reached Colchester, Lincoln, York and the eastern counties.

In the fourth century Britain was subject to raids along the east coast by Saxon pirates, which led to the establishment of a system of coast defence from the Wash to Southampton Water, with forts at Brancaster, Burgh Castle (Yarmouth), Walton (Felixstowe), Bradwell, Reculver, Richborough, Dover, Lympne, Pevensey and Porchester (Portsmouth). The Irish (Scoti) and Picts in the north were also becoming more aggressive; from about AD 350

incursions became more frequent and more formidable. As the Roman Empire came under attack increasingly towards the end of the fourth century, many troops were removed from Britain for service in other parts of the Empire. The island was eventually cut off from Rome by the Teutonic conquest of Gaul, and with the withdrawal of the last Roman garrison early in the fifth century, the Romano-British were left to themselves.

Saxon Settlement.—According to legend, the British King Vortigern called in the Saxons to defend him against the Picts, the Saxon chieftains being Hengist and Horsa, who landed at Ebbsfleet, Kent, and established themselves in the Isle of Thanet; but the events during the one and a half centuries between the final break with Rome and the re-establishment of Christianity are unclear. However, it would appear that in the course of this period the raids turned into large-scale settlement by invaders traditionally known as Angles (England north of the Wash and East Anglia), Saxons (Essex and southern England) and Jutes (Kent and the Weald), which pushed the Romano-British into the mountainous areas of the north and west, Celtic culture outside Wales and Cornwall surviving only in topographical names. Various kingdoms were established at this time which attempted to claim overlordship of the whole country, hegemony finally being achieved by Wessex (capital, Winchester) in the ninth century. This century also saw the beginning of raids by the Vikings (Danes), which were resisted by Alfred the Great (871–899), the greatest of the Wessex kings, who fixed a limit to the advance of Danish settlement by the Treaty of Wedmore (878), giving them the area north and east of Watling Street, on condition that they adopt Christianity.

In the tenth century the Kings of Wessex recovered the whole of England from the Danes, but subsequent rulers were unable to resist a second wave of invaders. England paid tribute (*Danegeld*) for many years, and was invaded in 1013 by the Danes and ruled by Danish kings from 1016 until 1042, when Edward the Confessor was recalled from exile in Normandy. In 1066 Harold Godwinson (brother-in-law of Edward and son of Earl Godwin of Wessex) was chosen King of England. After defeating (at Stamford Bridge, Yorkshire, September 25) an invading army under Harald Hadraada, King of Norway (aided by the outlawed Earl Tostig of Northumbria, Harold's brother), Harold was himself defeated at the Battle of Hastings on October 14, 1066, and the Norman conquest secured the throne of England for Duke William of Normandy, a cousin of Edward the Confessor.

Christianity reached the Roman province of Britain from Gaul in the third century (or possibly earlier); Alban, traditionally Britain's first martyr, was put to death as a Christian during the persecution of Diocletian (June 22, 303), at his native town Verulamium; and the Bishops of Londinium, Eboracum (York), and Lindum (Lincoln) attended the Council of Arles in 314. However, the Anglo-Saxon invasions submerged the Christian religion in England until the sixth century when conversion was undertaken in the north from 563 by Celtic missionaries from Ireland led by St Columba, and in the south by a mission sent from Rome in 597 which was led by St Augustine, who became the first archbishop of Canterbury. England appears to have been converted again by the end of the seventh century and followed, after the Council of Whitby in 663, the practices of the Roman Church, which brought the kingdom into the mainstream of European thought and culture.

ENGLISH COUNTIES AND SHIRES
LORD LIEUTENANTS AND HIGH SHERIFFS

County or Shire	Lord Lieutenant	*High Sheriff, 1991–92
Avon	Sir John Wills, Bt., TD	A. M. Reid
Bedfordshire............	S. C. Whitbread	Mrs J. Skelton
Berkshire	J. R. Henderson, CVO, OBE	L. Moss, CBE
Buckinghamshire	Cdr. the Hon. J. T. Fremantle	Maj. C. J. Prideaux
Cambridgeshire	M. B. M. Bevan	A. H. Duberly
Cheshire	Sir William Bromley-Davenport	Sir Richard Baker-Wilbraham, Bt.
Cleveland	The Rt. Hon. the Lord Gisborough	M. T. D'Arcy
Cornwall	The Rt. Hon. the Viscount Falmouth	D. C. Treffry, OBE
Cumbria................	Maj. Sir Charles Graham, Bt.	I. C. Carr
Derbyshire	Col. P. Hilton, MC	H. F. Harpur-Crewe
Devon..................	Lt.-Col. the Rt. Hon. the Earl of Morley	A. L. Sayers, CBE
Dorset	The Rt. Hon. the Lord Digby	E. W. Ludlow
Durham	D. J. Grant, CBE	Sir Anthony Milbank, Bt.
East Sussex	Adm. Sir Lindsay Bryson, KCB	R. H. Petley
Essex	Adm. Sir Andrew Lewis, KCB	M. W. Clark, CBE
Gloucestershire	Col. Sir Martin Gibbs, KCVO, CB, DSO, TD	P. R. H. Clifford
Greater London	Field Marshal the Lord Bramall, GCB, OBE, MC	W. S. C. Richards
Greater Manchester	Col. J. B. Timmins, OBE, TD	Maj. D. G. Wilson, OBE
Hampshire	Lt.-Col. Sir James Scott, Bt.	R. R. Mackenzie
Hereford and Worcester	Capt. T. R. Dunne	D. E. Bulmer
Hertfordshire...........	S. A. Bowes Lyon	R. E. H. Edmonds
Humberside	R. A. Bethell	R. Marriott
Isle of Wight...........	The Rt. Hon. the Lord Mottistone, CBE	D. F. Campbell
Kent...................	The Rt. Hon. Robin Leigh-Pemberton	D. M. Holman
Lancashire	S. Towneley	J. R. Holt
Leicestershire	T. G. M. Brooks	R. T. Constable-Maxwell
Lincolnshire............	Capt. H. N. Neville	H. S. Sharpley, OBE
Merseyside	H. E. Cotton	Mrs J. Wotherspoon, OBE
Norfolk	T. J. Colman	T. R. E. Cook
Northamptonshire	J. L. Lowther, CBE	Lady Juliet Townsend, LVO
Northumberland	The Rt. Hon. the Viscount Ridley, TD	P. J. Cookson
North Yorkshire	Sir Marcus Worsley, Bt.	Sir John Ropner, Bt.
Nottinghamshire........	Sir Andrew Buchanan, Bt.	Lt.-Col. G. E. Vere-Laurie
Oxfordshire	Sir Ashley Ponsonby, Bt., MC	J. Blackwell
Shropshire	J. R. S. Dugdale	L. R. Jebb
Somerset	Col. G. W. F. Luttrell, MC	I. C. Macdonald
South Yorkshire	J. H. Neill, CBE, TD	I. S. Porter
Staffordshire	Sir Arthur Bryan	J. L. Jones
Suffolk	Sir Joshua Rowley, Bt.	Miss M. M. P. MacRae
Surrey	R. E. Thornton, OBE	Col. J. W. T. A. Malcolm
Tyne and Wear	Sir Ralph Carr-Ellison, TD	M. J. Scott
Warwickshire	The Rt. Hon. the Viscount Daventry	Maj. R. P. G. Dill
West Midlands	The Rt. Hon. the Earl of Aylesford	B. W. Tanner
West Sussex	His Grace the Duke of Richmond and Gordon	M. D. Sugden
West Yorkshire	The Rt. Hon. the Lord Ingrow, OBE, TD	I. A. Ziff
Wiltshire...............	Field Marshal Sir Roland Gibbs, GCB, CBE, DSO, MC	C. E. Eliot-Cohen

* High Sheriffs are nominated by the Queen on November 12 and come into office after Hilary Term.

COUNTY COUNCIL AREAS AND POPULATIONS

County Council	Administrative headquarters	Area (*hectares*)	Population Census 1991p	Total demand upon collection fund 1991 £
Avon	Avon House North, St James Barton, Bristol	134,628	919,800	552,700,000
Bedfordshire........	*Bedford	123,468	514,200	330,371,000
Berkshire	†Reading	125,901	716,500	447,964,000
Buckinghamshire ...	*Aylesbury	188,279	619,500	385,900,000
Cambridgeshire	†Cambridge	340,181	640,700	373,200,000
Cheshire	*Chester	233,325	937,300	582,000,000
Cleveland	Municipal Buildings, Middlesbrough	59,079	541,100	405,480,000
Cornwall	*Truro	356,442‡	469,300	276,300,000
Cumbria............	The Courts, Carlisle	682,451	486,900	305,949,000
Derbyshire	County Offices, Matlock	263,098	914,600	557,042,000
Devon..............	*Exeter	671,096	998,200	573,362,000
Dorset	*Dorchester	265,433	645,200	335,800,000
Durham	*Durham	243,369	589,800	358,253,000
East Sussex	Pelham House, St Andrews Lane, Lewes	179,530	670,600	383,236,713
Essex	*Chelmsford	367,167	1,495,600	854,058,000
Gloucestershire	†Gloucester	264,270	520,600	298,500,000
Hampshire	The Castle, Winchester	378,022	1,511,900	846,790,000
Hereford and Worcester	*Worcester	392,650	667,800	364,691,000
Hertfordshire	*Hertford	163,601	951,500	558,251,000
Humberside	*Beverley, N. Humberside	351,256	835,200	567,000,000
Isle of Wight	*Newport, IOW	38,063	126,600	76,837,000
Kent...............	*Maidstone	373,063	1,485,100	850,000,000
Lancashire	*Preston	306,957	1,365,100	902,257,000
Leicestershire	*Leicester	255,297	860,500	539,739,710
Lincolnshire........	County Offices, Lincoln	591,791	573,900	335,000,000
Norfolk	*Norwich	537,482	736,400	417,944,760
Northamptonshire ..	*Northampton	236,721	572,900	347,924,000
Northumberland	*Morpeth	503,165	300,600	177,315,000
North Yorkshire	*Northallerton	831,236	698,700	378,200,000
Nottinghamshire....	*Nottingham	216,090	980,600	625,700,000
Oxfordshire	*Oxford	260,798	553,800	313,455,000
Shropshire	The Shirehall, Shrewsbury	349,013	401,600	242,400,000
Somerset	*Taunton	345,233	459,100	274,743,480
Staffordshire	County Buildings, Stafford	271,616	1,020,300	586,591,300
Suffolk	*Ipswich	379,664	629,900	352,100,000
Surrey	*Kingston upon Thames	167,924	998,000	533,640,000
Warwickshire	†Warwick	198,052	477,000	275,100,000
West Sussex	*Chichester	198,935	692,800	354,600,000
Wiltshire...........	*Trowbridge	347,883	553,300	312,233,000

p preliminary.　　　* County Hall.　　　† Shire Hall.　　　‡ Including Isles of Scilly.

CHIEF EXECUTIVES, TREASURERS AND CHAIRMEN

County Council	Chief Executive	County Treasurer	Chairman of County Council
Avon	B. D. Smith	D. G. Morgan	D. Pearce
Bedfordshire........	V. F. Phillips	B. Phelps	K. L. White
Berkshire...........	A. J. Allen	D. J. Bowles	W. A. Wiseman
Buckinghamshire ...	C. M. Garrett	H. R. H. Spring-thorpe	Mrs G. M. M. Miscampbell, OBE
Cambridgeshire	A. G. Lister	D. Prince‡	R. E. Burke
Cheshire	M. E. Pitt	J. E. H. Whiteoak	K. Maynard
Cleveland	B. Stevenson	P. Riley†	E. Wood
Cornwall	G. K. Burgess	S. F. Nicol	D. L. C. Roberts
Cumbria............	J. E. Burnet	R. Wirth	Mrs N. W. Wrightson
Derbyshire	J. S. Raine*	R. C. Beard	J. S. Heathcote
Devon..............	R. D. Clark	B. J. Weston	F. A. C. Pinney, OBE
Dorset	P. K. Harvey	A. P. Peel	Sir Stephen Hammick, Bt.
Durham	K. W. Smith°	J. Kirkby	G. W. Terrans
East Sussex	R. M. Beechey	M. R. Hancock	H. A. Hatcher
Essex	R. W. Adcock	K. D. Neale	P. E. White
Gloucestershire	M. Honey	J. R. Cockroft	F. B. Wilton
Hampshire	A. R. Hodgson	J. E. Scotford	R. T. Millard
Hereford and Worcester	G. A. Price	G. A. Price	R. J. Carrington, OBE
Hertfordshire	B. Briscoe	B. Ogley	H. T. D. Marwood
Humberside	J. A. Parkes	G. T. Southern‡	Mrs S. Salingar
Isle of Wight	J. S. Horsnell	J. B. W. Proctor	K. A. G. Lacey
Kent	P. R. Sabin	P. Martin‡	Mrs B. Trench
Lancashire	G. W. Johnson	D. Morgan	D. W. Nelson
Leicestershire	vacant	R. Hale	Dr A. N. Strachan
Lincolnshire........	R. J. D. Procter	D. G. Barrett	W. H. Rawson
Norfolk	B. J. Capon	C. A. Boar‡	F. H. Rockcliffe
Northamptonshire ..	A. J. Greenwell, CBE	D. W. Cleggett‡	T. G. Fordyce
Northumberland	T. P. Urwin	K. Morris	W. C. Brown
North Yorkshire....	R. A. Leyland	D. Martin	Mrs A. Harris
Nottinghamshire....	M. T. Lyons	R. Latham	G. E. Miller
Oxfordshire	J. Harwood	J. T. Vokins	B. Morgan
Shropshire	M. Suter	M. N. Davis	Mrs J. A. Hayward
Somerset	B. M. Tanner	C. N. Bilsland	H. Hobhouse
Staffordshire	B. A. Price	B. Smith	J. O'Leary
Suffolk	P. F. Bye	P. B. Atkinson	J. P. Patton
Surrey	D. J. Thomas	R. Wolstenholme	A. J. Brigstocke
Warwickshire	I. G. Caulfield	J. P. Hunt	L. V. Rouch
West Sussex	B. Fieldhouse	D. P. Rigg	M. H. Long, CBE
Wiltshire...........	I. A. Browning	A. F. Gould	Mrs M. Salisbury

* County Director. ° Principal Executive Officer. ‡Director of Finance. †County Finance Officer.

Residuary Bodies

GREATER LONDON, (*see* page 598).

GREATER MANCHESTER.—The residuary body was wound up in October 1989.

MERSEYSIDE.—The residuary body was wound up on March 31, 1990.

TYNE AND WEAR.—The residuary body was wound up in October 1988.

WEST MIDLANDS.—The residuary body was wound up in March 1991.

SOUTH YORKSHIRE.—The residuary body was wound up in July 1989.

WEST YORKSHIRE.—The residuary body was wound up in March 1991.

METROPOLITAN BOROUGH AND CITY COUNCILS

Councils accorded CITY status are in SMALL CAPITALS.

Metropolitan Council	Population Census 1991p	Community charge per head 1991 £	Chief Executive	Mayor (a) Lord Mayor 1991–92
Greater Manchester	2,454,800			
Bolton	253,300	405·34	B. Collinge	G. Riley
Bury	172,200	295·92	D. J. Burton	H. Taylor
MANCHESTER	406,900	431·88	G. Hainsworth	(a) G. Chadwick
Oldham	211,400	408·00	C. Smith	R. Semple, MBE
Rochdale	196,900	249·00	J. F. D. Pierce	B. Ashworth
SALFORD	217,900	300·00	R. C. Rees, OBE	J. Murphy
Stockport	276,800	310·18	A. L. Wilson	T. Jackson
Tameside	211,700	270·00	M. Greenwood	Ms L. Eason
Trafford	205,700	205·00	W. A. Lewis	Mrs L. Burton
Wigan	301,900	267·60	S. M. Jones	J. Horrocks
Merseyside	1,376,800			
Knowsley	149,100	284·60	D. G. Henshaw	Mrs F. Clarke
LIVERPOOL	448,300	333·95	P. Bounds	(a) T. Smith
St Helens	175,300	260·97	F. Kendall	L. Tucker
Sefton	282,000	282·00	vacant	S. C. Whitby
Wirral	322,100	304·00	A. White	R. G. Patterson
South Yorkshire	1,248,500			
Barnsley	217,300	179·64	J. A. Edwards	T. Naylor
Doncaster	284,300	337·51	C. B. Jeynes	W. R. Gillies
Rotherham	247,100	229·00	J. Bell	O. Hartley
SHEFFIELD	499,700	217·00	Mrs P. Gordon	(a) Ms D. Askham
Tyne and Wear	1,087,000			
Gateshead	196,500	226·00	L. N. Elton	H. Dinning
NEWCASTLE UPON TYNE	263,000	456·20	G. N. Cook	(a) T. J. Marr
North Tyneside	188,800	284·50	‡‡E. D. Nixon	J. W. Conway
South Tyneside	151,900	220·00	S. Clark	J. Forsyth Harper
Sunderland	286,800	215·00	G. P. Key	D. J. Thompson
West Midlands	2,499,300			
BIRMINGHAM	934,900	406·00	R. M. W. Taylor	(a) B. Turner
COVENTRY	292,500	294·00	I. Roxburgh	(a) D. H. Edwards
Dudley	300,400	275·00	A. V. Astling	G. Tromans
Sandwell	282,000	319·00	Miss A. C. Griffin	A. Handley
Solihull	194,100	252·00	J. Scampion	C. J. Trinnick
Walsall	255,600	285·00	D. C. Winchurch	A. G. Davies
Wolverhampton	239,800	415·00	N. H. Perry, PH.D.	S. S. Durha
West Yorkshire	1,984,700			
BRADFORD	449,100	223·00	R. Penn	(a) S. J. Collard
Calderdale	187,300	177·36	M. Ellison	T. McElroy
Kirklees	367,600	239·00	R. V. Hughes	J. Brooke
LEEDS	674,400	269·00	J. P. Smith	(a) R. D. Feldman
WAKEFIELD	306,300	209·00	R. Mather	G. Andrews

‡‡ Director of Administrative Services.

NON-METROPOLITAN DISTRICT COUNCILS

Councils accorded CITY status are in SMALL CAPITALS, those with Borough status are distinguished by having § prefixed.

District Council	Population Census 1991p	Community charge per head 1991 £	Chief Executive (*Clerk)	Chairman 1991–92 (a) Mayor (b) Lord Mayor
Adur, West Sussex	57,400	265·00	F. M. G. Staden	Mrs J. H. Robinson
Allerdale, Cumbria	96,300	207·95	A. G. Perry	Mrs J. Minto
Alnwick, Northumberland	108,029	211·66	L. St Ruth	R. Elliott
§Amber Valley, Derbyshire	26,509	393·68	F. W. Ellis	A. Stringer
Arun, West Sussex	127,700	218·59	A. S. Potts	D. L. Whittaker
Ashfield, Nottinghamshire	106,800	245·00	S. Beedham	B. Chance

p preliminary.

District Council	Population Census 1991p	Community charge per head 1991 £	Chief Executive (*Clerk)	Chairman 1991–92 (a) Mayor (b) Lord Mayor
§Ashford, Kent	90,900	174·00	E. H. W. Mexter	(a) R. Harrington
Aylesbury Vale, Bucks.	143,600	245·00	B. J. Quoroll	W. G. Lapham
Babergh, Suffolk	78,500	234·88	D. C. Bishop	C. M. Spence
§Barrow-in-Furness, Cumbria	71,900	276·00	R. H. McCulloch	(a) Mrs R. Hamezeian
Basildon, Essex	157,500	316·10	J. C. Rosser°	D. Marks
§Basingstoke and Deane, Hants.	140,400	329·00	D. W. Pilkington, RD	(a) R. A. O'Bee
Bassetlaw, Notts.	103,000	281·00	R. D. Blair	P. Mace
BATH, Avon	79,900	244·67	N. C. Abbott	(a) D. Lovelace
§Berwick-upon-Tweed, Northumberland	26,400	358·10	J. V. Picking	(a) J. J. D. Richardson
§Beverley, Humberside	109,500	286·00	W. J. H. Thomas	(a) A. Ramshaw
§Blaby, Leics.	81,900	227·85	E. Hemsley†	G. M. Redfern
§Blackburn, Lancs.	132,800	287·00	G. L. Davies	(a) G. Bramley-Haworth
§Blackpool, Lancs.	144,500	294·00	D. Wardman	(a) J. Smith
§Blyth Valley, Northumberland	78,000	295·00	D. Crawford	(a) E. G. Tolhurst
Bolsover, Derbys.	69,000	212·49	vacant	Mrs C. M. Burns
§Boothferry, Humberside	63,100	244·00	J. W. Barber	(a) R. F. Jarred
§Boston, Lincs.	52,600	355·00	P. M. Walsh	(a) E. A. Napier
§Bournemouth, Dorset	154,400	208·00	K. Lomas	(a) L. F. Bennett
§Bracknell Forest, Berks.	93,800	240·00	A. J. Targett	(a) E. Thompson
§Braintree, Essex	115,700	220·00	C. R. Daybell	J. Perks
§Breckland, Norfolk	105,200	235·36	J. B. Heath	G. W. G. Whittworth
§Brentwood, Essex	68,600	229·00	C. P. Sivell	J. Shawcross
§Bridgnorth, Salop	49,700	210·73	A. L. Bain	C. J. Lea
§Brighton, East Sussex	133,400	255·50	G. Jones	(a) J. Townsend
BRISTOL, Avon	370,300	369·00	M. Robinson	(b) P. Abraham
§Broadland, Norfolk	104,500	228·37	J. H. Bryant	L. Woolf
Bromsgrove, Hereford and Worcs.	89,800	224·17	R. P. Bradshaw	Mrs P. M. Barnsley
§Broxbourne, Herts.	79,500	360·51	M. J. Walker	(a) N. J. H. Ames
§Broxtowe, Notts.	104,600	265·00	M. Brown	(a) J. Booth
§Burnley, Lancs.	89,000	209·00	B. Whittle	(a) Mrs I. Cooney
CAMBRIDGE	101,000	329·00	R. Hammond	(a) P. Cowell
Cannock Chase, Staffs.	87,400	408·00	M. G. Kemp	R. F. Bagguley
CANTERBURY, Kent	127,100	194·00	C. Gay	(a) J. Purchese
Caradon, Cornwall	75,800	235·65	D. J. Newell	E. R. Distin
CARLISLE, Cumbria	99,800	297·00	R. S. Brackley	(a) Miss E. Coleman
Carrick, Cornwall	82,700	244·37	P. M. Talbot	D. L. G. Hocking
§Castle Morpeth, Northumberland	49,700	304·34	M. Cole	(a) J. Turnbull
Castle Point, Essex	84,200	215·00	B. Rollinson	Mrs V. C. Elworthy
§Charnwood, Leics.	140,500	257·08	R. M. Holroyd	(a) Mrs M. P. Mason
§Chelmsford, Essex	150,000	230·99	R. M. C. Hartley	(a) D. Pyman
§Cheltenham, Glos.	85,900	416·40	C. Nye	(a) J. H. Pennington
Cherwell, Oxon.	115,900	388·51	G. J. Handley	D. E. Jelfs
CHESTER, Cheshire	115,000	308·00	P. F. Durham	(a) S. R. Proctor
§Chesterfield, Derbyshire	99,700	263·00	D. R. Shaw	(a) W. Jepson
Chester-le-Street, Co. Durham	51,600	268·93	J. A. Greensmith	Mrs S. Hubbard
§Chichester, West Sussex	100,300	160·90	C. E. Evans	H. N. Allen
Chiltern, Bucks.	88,700	249·50	D. G. Sainsbury	P. T. Lole
§Chorley, Lancs.	96,500	291·32	J. W. Davies	(a) B. J. Hodson
§Christchurch, Dorset	40,500	216·00	C. H. Dewsnap	(a) E. N. Spreadbury
§Cleethorpes, Humberside	67,500	295·12	P. Daniel	(a) J. Winn
§Colchester, Essex	141,100	208·18	J. Cobley	(a) R. P. Spendlove
§Congleton, Cheshire	82,900	295·64	D. N. Mills	(a) T. J. Howkins
§Copeland, Cumbria	70,700	371·00	R. G. Smith	(a) Ms M. Woodburn
Corby, Northants.	52,300	250·00	T. J. Simmons	J. Hazel
Cotswold, Glos.	73,000	385·37	D. A. Sketchley	D. F. S. Goodman
Craven, North Yorks	49,700	171·41	H. H. Crabtree††	R. Walker
Crawley, West Sussex	87,100	188·00	M. D. Sander	(a) W. J. Pye
§Crewe and Nantwich, Cheshire	101,800	310·37	R. Mather	(a) Mrs D. M. Hassall
§Dacorum, Herts.	129,200	225·00	K. Hunt	(a) F. Seely
§Darlington, Co. Durham	96,700	275·00	H. R. C. Owen	(a) Mrs R. Fishwick
§Dartford, Kent	78,400	207·55	C. R. Shepherd	(a) A. A. E. Gillingham
Daventry, Northants.	61,600	244·36	R. J. Symons, RD	J. Shepherd

p preliminary. ° Town Manager. † Finance and General Manager. †† Head of Paid Service.

District Council	Popula-tion Census 1991p	Community charge per head 1991 £	Chief Executive (*Clerk)	Chairman 1991–92 (a) Mayor (b) Lord Mayor
Derby........................	214,000	270·00	R. H. Cowlishaw	(a) J. H. Keith
Derbyshire Dales..............	67,700	271·00	D. Wheatcroft	Mrs O. M. Allen
Derwentside, Co. Durham......	84,800	276·00	N. F. Johnson	K. Murray-Hethering-ton
Dover, Kent	102,600	192·69	J. P. Moir, TD	P. A. Watkins
Durham......................	85,000	277·00	C. G. Firmin	(a) D. Bell
Easington, Co. Durham	96,300	330·94	T. Robinson†	A. Lockyear
§Eastbourne, East Sussex	83,200	274·00	vacant	(a) M. Skilton
East Cambridgeshire	59,300	355·20	T. T. G. Hardy	H. J. Brooks
East Devon	106,200	242·35	F. J. Vallender	W. J. Thorne
East Dorset	77,200	253·15	A. Breakwell	Mrs G. M. Prowse
East Hampshire	101,100	223·27	B. P. Roynon	Mrs E. V. Bulmer
East Hertfordshire	114,200	228·94	D. J. Anstey	R. A. Martin
§Eastleigh, Hants.............	103,200	245·00	vacant	(a) M. Buckingham
East Lindsey, Lincs.	115,600	357·16	vacant	G. S. Gillett
East Northamptonshire........	65,700	215·00	R. K. Heath	R. S. Clifton
East Staffordshire	96,200	244·00	F. W. Saunders	A. Dean
§East Yorkshire, Humberside ...	83,700	247·00	J. H. Gibson	(a) T. Brown
Eden, Cumbria	46,300	205·00	I. W. Bruce	E. S. C. Wooff
§Ellesmere Port and Neston, Cheshire	78,800	309·00	S. Ewbank	(a) E. E. Lalley
§Elmbridge, Surrey	109,900	338·50	D. W. L. Jenkins	(a) Mrs D. M. Mitchell
Epping Forest, Essex..........	113,100	248·27	A. V. Hackman	W. Axon
§Epsom and Ewell, Surrey	67,000	467·00	D. J. Smith	(a) B. J. R. Kibble
§Erewash, Derbyshire.........	104,000	274·00	R. M. Fletcher	(a) W. G. Camm
Exeter, Devon	101,100	237·00	B. Frowd	(a) A. Fry
§Fareham, Hants.	97,300	365·00	O. D. Ellis	(a) Cdr. M. G. Harper, OBE
Fenland, Cambs.	72,900	230·00	E. S. Thompson	Mrs J. Southwell
Forest Heath, Suffolk	57,200	217·00	S. W. Catchpole	G. Jaggard
Forest of Dean, Glos...........	74,200	403·79	P. R. Starling	B. W. Hobman
§Fylde, Lancs.................	70,100	184·00	J. P. Johnson	(a) L. Rigby
§Gedling, Notts.	107,600	270·22	W. Brown	(a) Mrs M. Roach
§Gillingham, Kent............	93,300	146·00	J. A. McBride	(a) Mrs E. A. Cutting
§Glanford, Humberside	70,000	250·00	D. D. H. Cameron	(a) Mrs C. M. Parks
Gloucester	91,800	260·87	G. Garbutt	(a) T. B. Wathen
§Gosport, Hants.	72,800	386·00	M. S. Friend	(a) A. R. Herridge
§Gravesham, Kent	90,000	153·00	E. V. J. Seager	(a) F. Gibson
§Great Grimsby, Humberside ...	88,900	291·00	R. S. G. Bennett	(a) Mrs K. P. Bell
§Great Yarmouth, Norfolk	85,900	161·00	K. G. Ward	B. R. Walker
§Guildford, Surrey	121,500	246·00	D. T. Watts	(a) Mrs D. Bellerby, MBE
§Halton, Cheshire	121,400	325·00	R. Turton	(a) Mrs O. Smith
Hambleton, North Yorks.	77,600	190·30	C. Spencer	C. A. Thompson
Harborough, Leics.	66,200	264·78	J. Ballantyne	J. R. Morgan
Harlow, Essex................	73,500	319·00	D. Byrne°	D. Burnham
§Harrogate, North Yorks.	141,000	252·00	vacant	(a) Dr E. S. N. Hazel
Hart, Hants.	78,700	219·13	M. W. Tyler	Mrs R. Flowers
§Hartlepool, Cleveland	88,200	297·00	B. J. Dinsdale	(a) T. Lloyd
§Hastings, East Sussex	78,100	274·00	R. A. Carrier	(a) Miss J. S. Fabian
§Havant, Hants................	117,400	229·30	D. E. Ridley	(a) J. W. Cook
Hereford	49,800	211·00	C. E. S. Willis	(a) M. Turbutt
§Hertsmere, Hertfordshire	86,100	368·71	J. N. Pearson	(a) Mrs G. Ferguson
§High Peak, Derbyshire........	83,800	262·53	R. P. H. Brady	(a) J. E. G. Boote
§Hinckley and Bosworth, Leics..	93,600	238·00	A. J. Cleary	(a) D. Bill
§Holderness, Humberside	49,900	427·50	A. Johnson	(a) C. H. Buck
Horsham, West Sussex	107,300	196·00	M. J. Pearson	Mrs S. E. van den Bergh
§Hove, East Sussex	82,500	336·97	J. P. Teasdale	(a) Mrs A. R. Buttimer
Huntingdonshire, Cambs.......	140,700	196·27	T. J. Gee	Mrs H. W. Sneden
§Hyndburn, Lancs.	76,500	243·00	M. J. Wedgeworth	(a) J. Culshaw
§Ipswich, Suffolk	115,500	309·47	J. D. Hehir	(a) K. Wilson
Kennet, Wilts.	67,500	212·66	P. L. Owens	G. A. Taylor
Kerrier, Cornwall	86,400	247·40	G. G. Cox	Mrs T. L. Jones
§Kettering, Northants.	75,200	369·50	T. P. Williams	(a) W. J. Faller
§King's Lynn and W. Norfolk ...	128,400	176·00	A. E. Pask	(a) Mrs E. Kemp
Kingston upon Hull, Humberside	242,200	230·00	A. B. Wood	(b) D. Woods
Kingswood, Avon	87,100	258·50	A. Smith	(a) L. Bishop
Lancaster, Lancs.	125,600	279·00	W. Pearson	(a) Mrs D. Henderson

p preliminary.   † Principal Chief Officer.   ° General Manager.

District Council	Popula-tion Census 1991p	Community charge per head 1991 £	Chief Executive (*Clerk)	Chairman 1991–92 (a) Mayor (b) Lord Mayor
§Langbaurgh-on-Tees, Cleveland	141,700	330·90	K. Abigail	(a) A. F. Harvison
LEICESTER	270,600	319·00	I. Farookhi	(b) C. Grundy
Leominster, Hereford and Worcs.	39,000	195·10	G. R. Chilton	T. C. A. Edwards
Lewes, East Sussex	85,400	245·09	C. W. Mann	J. O. Cornwell
Lichfield, Staffs.	90,700	376·23	J. T. Thompson	Mrs B. L. Constable
LINCOLN	81,900	364·00	C. J. Thomas	(a) A. R. Toofany
§Luton, Beds.	167,300	249·75	J. C. Southwell	(a) M. B. Guha
§Macclesfield, Cheshire	147,000	420·66	B. W. Longden	(a) K. S. Smith
§Maidstone, Kent	133,200	218·28	J. D. Makepeace	(a) Ms D. Parvin
Maldon, Essex	50,800	205·00	T. K. Griffin	Mrs M. J. Peel
Malvern Hills, Hereford and Worcs.	87,000	367·00	M. J. Jones	J. L. Foot
Mansfield, Notts.	98,800	295·00	R. P. Goad	A. Haynes
§Medina, Isle of Wight	70,100	195·46	J. Sprake‡‡	(a) Mrs A. Leigh
§Melton, Leics.	44,500	256·61	P. J. G. Herrick°	(a) I. J. Skerritt
Mendip, Somerset	95,300	268·13	G. Jeffs	O. Pippard
Mid Bedfordshire	108,000	405·81	C. A. Tucker	F. W. Jakes
Mid Devon	63,600	250·75	R. G. Greensmith	Mrs S. M. Meads
§Middlesbrough, Cleveland	141,100	309·00	J. R. Foster	(a) E. Bolland
Mid Suffolk	77,100	230·00	H. McFarlane	B. R. P. Siffleet
Mid Sussex	118,800	205·10	B. J. Grimshaw	P. Bailey
§Milton Keynes, Bucks.	172,300	299·00	M. J. Murray	(a) W. Harnett
Mole Valley, Surrey	77,400	254·00	A. A. Huggins	D. C. Keys
Newark and Sherwood, Notts.	103,400	258·64	R. G. Dix	H. Whelan
Newbury, Berks.	136,400	238·49	P. E. McMahon	G. Pickersgill
§Newcastle under Lyme, Staffs.	117,400	408·00	E. Wetherell	(a) Mrs B. Cox
New Forest, Hants.	157,000	173·00	P. A. D. Hyde	J. E. Coles
§Northampton	178,200	226·00	R. J. B. Morris	(a) D. Edwards
Northavon, Avon	129,600	258·01	F. Maude	C. E. Horton
§North Bedfordshire	132,100	403·74	L. W. Gould	(a) Mrs J. Lennon
North Cornwall	73,700	343·38	D. H. Westwell	H. S. Medland
North Devon	85,100	243·74	R. D. Hall	J. Milton
North Dorset	52,200	199·60	A. J. Bridgeman	G. A. Pitt-Rivers, OBE
North East Derbyshire	95,600	278·62	Mrs C. A. Gilbey	F. Hopkinson
North Hertfordshire	108,600	227·11	J. S. Philip	Mrs L. Faulkner
North Kesteven, Lincs.	78,400	204·96	S. M. Peatfield	E. A. Robertson
North Norfolk	90,400	178·64	T. V. Nolan	Mrs H. C. Barrow
North Shropshire	52,400	222·00	K. Flood	J. Hodnett
§North Warwickshire	59,800	313·12	D. Monks	(a) D. Forwood
North West Leicestershire	79,400	268·40	J. E. White	B. W. Hall
North Wiltshire	109,600	226·73	H. Miles	A. S. R. Jackson
NORWICH, Norfolk	120,700	276·91	J. R. Packer	(b) P. Moore
NOTTINGHAM	261,500	295·00	E. F. Cantle	(b) A. C. White
§Nuneaton and Bedworth, Warwickshire	115,300	336·00	J. Walton‡‡	(a) R. D. Hicks
§Oadby and Wigston, Leics.	51,500	287·00	vacant	(a) P. R. Upton
§Oswestry, Shropshire	33,600	399·47	D. A. Towers	(a) Mrs E. C. Lloyd-Williams
OXFORD	109,000	482·91	R. S. Black	(b) A. Pope
§Pendle, Lancs.	82,700	218·00	F. Wood	(a) Mrs K. Shore
Penwith, Cornwall	59,400	225·00	M. J. Furneaux†	T. H. E. Laity
PETERBOROUGH, Cambs.	148,800	267·59	W. E. Samuel	(a) G. R. Ridgway
PLYMOUTH, Devon	238,800	240·00	M. S. Boxall	(b) Mrs C. E. Easton, OBE
§Poole, Dorset	130,900	171·62	I. K. D. Andrews*	(a) E. Hogg
PORTSMOUTH, Hants.	174,700	179·00	R. Trist	(b) B. C. Read
§Preston, Lancs.	126,200	314·14	A. Owens	(a) Miss M. Rawcliffe
Purbeck, Dorset	42,600	170·00	P. B. Croft	A. I. F. McDonald
§Reading, Berks.	122,600	323·68	G. Filkin	(a) R. Dimmick
§Redditch, Hereford and Worcs.	76,900	261·50	D. H. Phipps	(a) Mrs M. Tillsley, MBE
§Reigate and Banstead, Surrey	114,900	270·00	C. T. Pollard	(a) A. J. Kay
§Restormel, Cornwall	88,300	224·00	D. Brown	(a) A. I. Rabey
§Ribble Valley, Lancs.	51,000	270·31	O. Hopkins	(a) A. Kay
Richmondshire, North Yorks.	43,800	191·80	M. F. Tooze	R. V. Cross
ROCHESTER UPON MEDWAY, Kent	142,000	50·00	R. I. Gregory	(a) Mrs J. W. B. Esterson
Rochford, Essex	74,400	224·00	P. W. Hughes	Mrs E. M. Hart

p preliminary.   ‡‡ Borough General Manager.   ° Borough Secretary.   † Director of Central Services.

District Council	Popula-tion Census 1991p	Community charge per head 1991 £	Chief Executive (*Clerk)	Chairman 1991–92 (a) Mayor (b) Lord Mayor
§Rossendale, Lancs.	64,000	260·00	J. S. Hartley	(a) G. Pearson
Rother, East Sussex	80,200	372·00	D. F. Powell	A. J. A. Lutman
§Rugby, Warwicks.	83,400	427·00	J. S. R. Lawton	(a) J. G. Rowe
§Runnymede, Surrey	71,500	198·00	T. N. Williams	(a) Mrs M. J. Marshall
§Rushcliffe, Notts.	94,900	253·01	J. Saxton	(a) R. Gardner
§Rushmoor, Hants.	80,400	218·00	D. Hartley	(a) B. L. Willcox
Rutland, Leics.	32,400	254·04	K. R. Emslie	C. H. Forsyth
Ryedale, North Yorks.	90,000	206·54	D. Cudworth	C. S. Scott
St ALBANS, Herts.	122,400	240·00	E. A. Hackford	(a) Mrs P. Hughes
§St Edmundsbury, Suffolk	89,100	239·22	G. R. N. Toft	(a) F. S. Jefson
Salisbury, Wilts.	103,200	205·00	D. R. J. Rawlinson	Mrs P. Spencer
§Scarborough, North Yorks.....	107,800	181·80	J. M. Trebble	(a) Mrs M. Don
§Scunthorpe, Humberside	60,500	269·00	I. M. Hutchinson	(a) Mrs T. M. Towndrow
Sedgefield, Co. Durham	89,200	216·39	A. J. Roberts	K. Howard
Sedgemoor, Somerset	97,000	241·26	D. D. Tremlett	Mrs J. M. Hooper
Selby, North Yorks.	88,200	204·90	J. C. Edwards	H. A. C. Stroud
Sevenoaks, Kent	106,100	190·90	B. C. Cova, MBE	Mrs L. Williams
Shepway, Kent...............	89,200	200·00	R. H. Summers	P. L. Huxley-Williams
§Shrewsbury and Atcham	90,900	256·50	D. Bradbury	(a) C. V. Forbes
§Slough, Berks.	98,600	330·00	A. Bhattacharya*	(a) R. Chauhan
SOUTHAMPTON, Hants.	194,400	255·00	E. A. Urquhart	(a) B. Welch
South Bedfordshire............	106,800	256·66	T. D. Rix	N. B. Costin
South Bucks.	60,300	220·89	S. R. Jobson	B. W. Learmount
South Cambridgeshire	118,100	204·53	B. J. Hancock	J. B. H. Impey
South Derbyshire	71,000	295·45	T. Day	F. W. Aldridge
§Southend-on-Sea, Essex	153,700	208·00	D. Moulson*	(a) S. G. Ayre
South Hams, Devon	77,300	373·49	F. G. Palmer	G. P. Heywood
South Herefordshire...........	51,200	321·33	A. Hughes	Mrs A. Carter
South Holland, Lincs.	66,000	217·20	C. J. Simpkins	W. D. Skells
South Kesteven, Lincs.	107,200	195·00	K. R. Cann	Mrs M. D. Clark
South Lakeland, Cumbria	101,900	269·70	A. F. Winstanley*	H. S. Lewis
South Norfolk	101,400	230·00	A. G. T. Kellett	Mrs J. M. Rawlence
South Northamptonshire	68,800	226·45	K. Whitehead	H. Wreschner
South Oxfordshire	130,900	309·00	R. Watson	T. C. Lester
§South Ribble, Lancs.	99,800	286·67	J. B. R. Leadbetter	(a) T. G. Hanson
South Shropshire	37,800	229·87	G. C. Biggs	A. H. Coles, TD
South Somerset	139,400	260·60	M. Usher	Mrs G. Garratt
South Staffordshire	103,900	206·93	G. J. Haywood	W. A. Winsper
§South Wight, IOW	56,400	238·00	D. W. Jaggar	(a) H. D. Howe
§Spelthorne, Surrey	87,100	247·00	M. B. Taylor	(a) Mrs K. V. Mackey
§Stafford	117,000	234·00	J. K. M. Krawiec*	(a) S. Glaister
Staffordshire Moorlands	94,000	230·35	A. W. Law	H. L. Richardson
§Stevenage, Herts.	73,700	433·20	H. L. Miller	(a) R. W. F. Fowler
§Stockton-on-Tees, Cleveland ..	170,200	300·28	F. F. Theobalds*	(a) M. O'Brien
STOKE-ON-TRENT, Staffs.	244,800	272·00	S. W. Titchener	(b) Mrs L. Wall
Stratford-upon-Avon, Warwicks...................	103,600	259·65	I. B. Prosser	E. I. Mulligan
Stroud, Glos...................	108,300	436·41	R. M. Ollin	G. S. Reeves
Suffolk Coastal	106,800	230·41	T. K. Griffin	Flt. Lt. D. V. Donnelly
§Surrey Heath	78,300	252·50	N. M. Pughe	(a) Ms T. Craig-Heath
§Swale, Kent.................	113,700	192·74	W. Croydon, CBE	(a) K. Evans
§Tamworth, Staffs.	68,900	246·00	G. Morrell	(a) K. Lewis
Tandridge, Surrey.............	75,000	278·54	C. W. Rockall	R. V. Page
§Taunton Deane, Somerset	93,300	238·62	P. F. Berman	(a) N. P. Cavill
Teesdale, Co. Durham..........	24,200	309·66	C. E. Fell	Mrs P. D. Austin
Teignbridge, Devon	107,100	259·60	P. B. Young	D. J. Bowles
Tendring, Essex	125,100	202·00	D. Mitchell-Gears	Mrs J. P. R. Molyneaux
§Test Valley, Hants.	99,000	176·00	G. Blythe	(a) J. G. Patten
§Tewkesbury, Glos.............	87,400	240·00	R. A. Wheeler	(a) J. W. Threadingham
§Thamesdown, Wilts.	167,200	260·00	D. M. Kent	(a) E. Smith
Thanet, Kent	121,300	172·83	I. G. Gill	Mrs M. Mortlock
Three Rivers, Herts.	74,100	275·21	A. Robertson	Ms C. Boardman
§Thurrock, Essex	124,300	266·00	K. Barnes	(a) Mrs K. Price
§Tonbridge and Malling, Kent ..	99,100	187·76	T. Thompson	(a) R. Barnes
§Torbay, Devon	122,500	240·00	D. P. Hudson	(a) W. Dolman
Torridge, Devon	52,100	206·00	R. K. Brasington	R. D. Bradford
§Tunbridge Wells, Kent........	98,300	106·20	R. J. Stone	(a) J. E. Scholes

p preliminary.

District Council	Population Census 1991p	Community charge per head 1991 £	Chief Executive (*Clerk)	Chairman 1991–92 (a) Mayor (b) Lord Mayor
Tynedale, Northumberland	58,400	436·93	A. Baty	H. J. C. Herron
Uttlesford, Essex	63,900	210·00	K. Ivory	D. Collins
Vale of White Horse, Oxon......	109,200	265·39	D. J. Heavens°	J. Francis
Vale Royal, Cheshire	111,100	287·00	W. R. T. Woods	(a) T. Carter
Wansbeck, Northumberland	60,100	212·25	A. G. White	J. Dodds
Wansdyke, Avon	78,700	284·01	P. May‡	L. Bedborough
Warrington, Cheshire	179,500	293·57	M. I. M. Sanders	(a) S. Williams
Warwick	114,900	400·89	M. J. Ward	R. R. Coombes
Watford, Herts.	72,100	294·00	D. Plank	(a) M. S. Chhina
Waveney, Suffolk	105,500	251·19	M. Berridge	Mrs R. E. Ford
Waverley, Surrey	111,500	260·17	G. W. Nuttall	(a) Mrs B. Ames
Wealden, East Sussex	127,700	232·09	D. R. Holness	Mrs E. M. Gabriel
Wear Valley, Co. Durham	62,100	356·00	F. A. Dobson†	L. M. Almond
Wellingborough, Northants....	71,100	129·00	W. B. Veal	G. P. Timms
Welwyn Hatfield, Herts.	91,600	308·00	D. Riddle	F. Clark
West Devon	44,400	260·00	J. S. Ligo	(a) R. A. Cook
West Dorset	86,300	336·16	R. C. Rennison	M. J. Pengelly
West Lancashire	106,600	259·50	B. A. Knight	A. Toal
West Lindsey, Lincs.	72,200	347·01	R. W. Nelsey	M. G. Leaning
West Oxfordshire	88,700	228·00	N. J. B. Robson	T. A. Titherington
West Somerset	34,100	243·06	H. Close	J. Lynn, OBE, MVO
West Wiltshire..............	105,900	378·71	D. G. Latham	Mrs M. Stacey
Weymouth and Portland, Dorset	61,000	240·00	M. N. Ashby	(a) Mrs I. M. Sanderson
WINCHESTER, Hants.	95,700	211·94	D. H. Cowan	(a) Capt. R. J. Bates, RN
Windsor and Maidenhead, Berks......................	128,700	287·00	R. G. Blacker	(a) Miss U. Badger
Woking, Surrey	84,000	259·68	P. Russell	(a) R. L. Williams
Wokingham, Berks.	136,300	262·77	N. B. J. Gurney	J. V. E. Trimming
Woodspring, Avon	174,300	304·00	C. A. Stephens	W. Lavelle
WORCESTER	81,000	257·00	R. G. Grant	(a) R. Turner
Worthing, West Sussex	94,100	193·07	M. J. Ball	(a) H. R. Braden, CMG
Wrekin, Shropshire	137,100	281·43	D. G. Hutchinson	J. C. Minor
Wychavon, Hereford and Worcs.	99,800	217·00	T. du Sautoy	G. E. Moore
Wycombe, Bucks..............	154,500	226·67	R. J. Cummins	Mrs P. Priestley
Wyre, Lancs.................	99,700	259·00	M. Brown	(a) G. W. Roper
Wyre Forest, Hereford and Worcs.	93,400	255·00	A. S. Dick	B. C. Moule
YORK, North Yorks.	100,600	184·00	J. Cairns	(b) A. Cowen

p preliminary.   °Director of Administration.   ‡General Manager.   †Managing Director.

PRINCIPAL ENGLISH CITIES

BIRMINGHAM

BIRMINGHAM (West Midlands) is Britain's second city and the largest metropolitan district in the country. It is a focal point in national communications networks with a rapidly expanding International Airport. The generally accepted derivation of 'Birmingham' is the *ham* or dwelling-place of the *ing* or the family of *Beorma*, presumed to have been a Saxon. During the Industrial Revolution the town grew into a major manufacturing centre. In 1889 Birmingham was granted City status.

Despite the decline in manufacturing, Birmingham is still a major hardware trade and motor component industry centre. Recent development includes the National Exhibition Centre and the Aston Science Park. An Urban Development Agency has been set up.

The principal buildings are the Town Hall, built in 1832–34; the Council House (1879); Victoria Law Courts (1891); the University (1909); the 13th century Church of St Martin (rebuilt 1873); the Cathedral (formerly St Philip's Church) (1711) and the Roman Catholic Cathedral of St Chad (1839–41).

BRADFORD

BRADFORD (West Yorkshire), 192 miles NNW of London, is the administrative centre of the Metropolitan District of Bradford. The District covers an area of 91,444 acres and lies on the southern edge of the Yorkshire Dales National Park, including within its boundaries the village of Haworth, home of the Brontë sisters, and Ilkley Moor.

Originally a Saxon township, Bradford received a market charter in 1251 but developed only slowly until the industrialization of the textile industry brought rapid growth during the 19th century. The prosperity of that period is reflected in much of the city's architecture, particularly the public buildings—City Hall (1873), Wool Exchange (1867), St George's Hall (Concert Hall, 1853), Cartwright Hall

(Art Gallery, 1904) and Technical College (1882). Other chief buildings are the Cathedral (15th century) and Bolling Hall (14th century).

Textiles still play an important part in the city's economy but industry is now more broadly based, including engineering and micro-electronics. The city has a strong banking, insurance and building society sector, and a growing tourism industry.

BRISTOL

BRISTOL (Avon) is the largest non-metropolitan district in population in the country, and lies 119 miles W. of London. The present municipal area is 10,954 hectares.

Bristol's commercial port systems constitute the largest municipally owned port in the country. The Avonmouth dock complex and Royal Portbury Dock handle import and export cargoes. Principal imports include cocoa, timber, metals, animal feeding stuffs, oil products, chemicals, vehicles and molasses. The Royal Portbury Dock, opened in August 1977, is capable of accommodating up to six vessels of 70,000 d.w.t.

The chief buildings include the 12th century Cathedral (with later additions), with Norman chapter house and gateway, the 14th century Church of St Mary Redcliffe, Wesley's Chapel, Broadmead, the Merchant Venturers' Almshouses, the Council House (1956), Guildhall, Exchange (erected from the designs of John Wood in 1743), Cabot Tower, the University and Clifton College. The Roman Catholic Cathedral at Clifton was opened in 1973.

The Clifton Suspension Bridge, with a span of 702 feet over the Avon, was projected by Brunel in 1836 but was not completed until 1864. Brunel's SS *Great Britain*, the first ocean-going propeller-driven ship, is now being restored in the City Docks from where she was launched in 1843. The docks themselves have been extensively restored and redeveloped.

Bristol was a Royal Borough before the Norman Conquest. The earliest form of the name is *Bricgstow*. In 1373 it received from Edward III a charter granting it county status.

CAMBRIDGE

CAMBRIDGE, a settlement far older than its ancient University, lies on the River Cam or Granta, 51 miles north of London. It has an area of 10,060 acres.

The city is a county town and regional headquarters. Its industries include electronics, flour milling, cement making and the manufacture of scientific instruments. Among its open spaces are Jesus Green, Sheep's Green, Coe Fen, Parker's Piece, Christ's Pieces, the University Botanic Garden, and the Backs, or lawns and gardens through which the Cam winds behind the principal line of college buildings. East of the Cam, King's Parade, upon which stand Great St Mary's Church, Gibbs' Senate House and King's College Chapel with Wilkins' screen, joins Trumpington Street to form one of the most beautiful throughfares in Europe.

University and college buildings provide the outstanding features of Cambridge architecture but several churches (especially St Benet's, the oldest building in the City, and St Sepulchre's, the Round Church) also are notable. The modern Guildhall (1939) stands on a site of which at least part has held municipal buildings since 1224.

CANTERBURY

CANTERBURY, the Metropolitan City of the Anglican Communion, has a history going back to prehistoric times. It was the Roman *Durovernum*

Cantiacorum and the Saxon *Cant-wara-byrig* (stronghold of the men of Kent). Here in 597 St Augustine began the conversion of the English to Christianity when Ethelbert, King of Kent, was baptized.

Of the Benedictine St Augustine's Abbey, burial place of the Jutish Kings of Kent (whose capital Canterbury was) only extensive ruins remain. St Martin's Church, on the eastern outskirts of the City, is stated by Bede to have been the place of worship of Queen Bertha, the Christian wife of King Ethelbert, before the advent of St Augustine.

In 1170 the rivalry of Church and State culminated in the murder in Canterbury Cathedral, by Henry II's knights, of Archbishop Thomas Becket, whose shrine became a great centre of pilgrimage as described by Chaucer in his *Canterbury Tales*. After the Reformation pilgrimages ceased, but the prosperity of the City was strengthened by an influx of Huguenot refugees, who introduced weaving. The Elizabethan poet and playwright Christopher Marlowe was born and reared in Canterbury, and there are literary associations also with Defoe, Dickens Joseph Conrad and Somerset Maugham.

The Cathedral, with architecture ranging from the 11th to 15th centuries, is world famous. Modern pilgrims are attracted particularly to the Martyrdom, The Black Prince's Tomb, the Warriors' Chapel and the many examples of medieval stained glass.

The medieval City Walls are built on Roman foundations and the 14th century West Gate is one of the finest buildings of its kind in the country.

The 1,000 seat Marlowe Theatre is the base for the Canterbury International Festival of the Arts each autumn.

CARLISLE

CARLISLE is situated at the confluence of the River Eden and River Caldew, 309 miles north west of London and about ten miles from the Scottish border. It has an area of 254,955 acres, and was granted a charter in 1158.

The city stands at the western end of Hadrian's Wall and dates from the original Roman settlement of *Luguvalium*. Granted to Scotland in the 10th century, Carlisle is not included in the Domesday Book. William Rufus reclaimed the area in 1092 and the Castle and city walls were built to guard Carlisle and the western border; the Citadel is a Tudor addition to protect the south of the city. Until the Union of the Crowns in 1603, Carlisle changed hands several times and was frequently besieged. During the Civil War the city remained Royalist; in 1745 it supported the Young Pretender.

The Cathedral, originally a 12th century Augustinian priory, was enlarged in the 13th and 14th centuries after the diocese was created in 1133. To the south is a restored Tithe Barn and nearby the 18th century church of St Cuthbert, the third to stand on a site dating from the 7th century.

Carlisle is the major shopping, commercial and agricultural centre for the area, and industries include the manufacture of metal goods, biscuits and textiles. However, the largest employer is the services sector, notably in retailing and transport. The city has an important communications position at the centre of a network of major roads, as an important stage on the main west coast rail services, and with its own airport at Crosby.

CHESTER

CHESTER is situated on the River Dee, 189 miles north west of London. The city administers an area of 173 square miles and was granted Borough and City status in 1974.

Chester's recorded history dates from the 1st century when the Romans founded the fortress of *Deva*. The city's name is derived from the Latin *castra* (a camp or encampment). During the Middle Ages, Chester was the principal port of north-west England but declined with the silting of the Dee estuary and competition from Liverpool. The city was also an important military centre, notably during Edward I's Welsh campaigns and the Elizabethan Irish campaigns. During the Civil War, Chester supported the King and was besieged from 1643–46. Chester's first charter was granted *c.* 1175 and the city was incorporated in 1506. The office of Sheriff is the earliest created in the country (*c.* 1120s), and the Mayor also enjoys the title 'Admiral of the Dee'.

The city's architectural features include the city walls (an almost complete two-mile circuit), the unique Rows (covered galleries above the street level shops), the Victorian Gothic Town Hall (1869), the Castle (rebuilt 1788 and 1822) and numerous half-timbered buildings. The Cathedral was a Benedictine abbey until the Dissolution. Remaining monastic buildings include the chapter house, refectory and cloisters and there is a modern free-standing bell tower. The Norman church of St John the Baptist was a Cathedral church in the early Middle Ages.

Chester is primarily a regional service centre and has considerable tourist appeal. In 1984 the city was awarded Development Area status which has attracted a range of nationally-known companies to expand or locate in Chester.

COVENTRY

COVENTRY (West Midlands) is 92 miles NW of London, and an important industrial centre, producing cars, machine tools, agricultural machinery, man-made fibres, composite materials and telecommunications equipment.

The city owes its beginning to Leofric, Earl of Mercia and his wife Godiva who, in 1043, founded a Benedictine monastery. The guildhall of St Mary dates from the 14th century, three of the city's churches date from the 14th and 15th centuries and 16th century almshouses may still be seen. Coventry's first cathedral was destroyed at the Reformation, its second in the 1940 blitz (its walls and spire remain) and the new cathedral designed by Sir Basil Spence, consecrated in 1962, now draws innumerable visitors.

Coventry is the home of the University of Warwick and its Science Park, the rapidly-expanding Westwood Business Park and the Museum of British Road Transport.

DERBY

DERBY stands on the banks of the River Derwent, 127 miles NNW of London, and covers an area of 30 square miles. The name Derby dates back to 880 when the Danes settled in the locality and changed the original Saxon name of 'Northworthy' to 'Deoraby'.

Derby has a wide range of industries: its products include aero engines, lawn mowers, pipework, specialized mechanical engineering equipment, textiles, chemicals, plastics and the Royal Crown Derby porcelain. The city is an established railway centre, the site of British Rail's Technical Centre with its research laboratories.

Buildings of interest include St Peter's Church and the Old Abbey Building (14th century), the Cathedral (1525), St Mary's Roman Catholic Church (1839) and the Industrial Museum, formerly the Old Silk Mill (1721). The traditional city centre is complemented by the new Eagle Centre and 'out-of-centre' retail developments. In addition to the Derby

Playhouse, the Assembly Rooms are a multi-purpose venue.

The first charter granting a Mayor and Aldermen was that of Charles I in 1637. Previous charters date back to 1154. It was granted City status in 1977.

DURHAM

The city of DURHAM is a district in the county of Durham and covers an area of 73 square miles. The city is a major tourist attraction in the county because of its prominent Norman Cathedral and Castle set high on a wooded peninsula overlooking the River Wear. The Cathedral was founded as a shrine for the body of St Cuthbert in 995. The present building dates from 1093 and among its many treasures is the tomb of the Venerable Bede (673–735). Durham's Prince Bishops had unique powers up to 1836, being lay rulers as well as religious leaders. As a palatinate Durham could have its own army, nobility, coinage and courts. The Castle was the main seat of the Prince Bishops for nearly 800 years; it is now used as a college by the University.

The University, founded on the initiative of Bishop William Van Mildert, is England's third oldest. Its students live in 14 colleges spread across the city.

Among other buildings of interest is the Guildhall in the Market Place which dates originally from the 14th century. Much work has been carried out to conserve this area, forming part of the city's major contribution to the Council of Europe's Urban Renaissance Campaign. Annual events include Durham's Regatta in June (claimed to be the oldest rowing event in Britain) and the Annual Gala (formerly Durham Miners' Gala) in July.

In the past 20 years the economy of Durham has undergone a significant change with the replacement of mining as the dominant feature by 'white collar' employment. Although still a predominantly rural area, the industrial and commercial sector is growing and a wide range of manufacturing and service industries are based on industrial estates in and around the City area.

EXETER

EXETER lies on the River Exe 170 miles SW of London and 10 miles from the sea. It covers an area of 11,661 acres and was granted a Royal Charter by Henry II.

The Romans founded *Isca Dumnoniorum* in the 1st century AD, and in the 3rd century a stone wall (most of which remains) was built, providing protection against Saxon, and then Danish invasions. After the Conquest, the city led resistance to William in the west, until reduced by siege. The Normans built the motte and bailey castle of Rougemont, the gatehouse and one tower of which remain, although the rest was pulled down in 1784. The first bridge across the Exe was built in the 13th century. The city's role as a port declined due to the silting of the river, but was somewhat restored by the construction in the 1560s of the first ship canal in England. Exeter was the Royalist headquarters in the West during the Civil War.

The diocese of Exeter was established by Edward the Confessor in 1050, although a church existed on the Cathedral site in the early 10th century. A new cathedral was built in the 12th century but the present building was begun *c.*1275 in the Gothic style, although incorporating the Norman towers, and completed about a century later with the West Front. The Guildhall dates from the 12th century and there are many other medieval buildings in the city, as well as architecture in the Georgian and Regency styles (Custom House, The Quay). Damage suffered by bombing in 1942 led to the redevelopment of the city centre.

Exeter's prosperity from medieval times was based on trade in wool and woollen cloth (commemorated by Tuckers Hall), which remained at its height until the late 18th century when export trade was hit by the French Wars. Subsequently Exeter has developed as an administrative and commercial centre, notably in the distributive trades, light manufacturing industries and tourism.

KINGSTON UPON HULL

HULL (officially 'Kingston upon Hull') lies in the mostly rural County of Humberside, at the junction of the River Hull with the Humber, 22 miles from the North Sea and 205 miles N. of London. The municipal area is 17,535 acres.

Hull is one of the great seaports of the United Kingdom. It has docks covering a water area of 172 acres, equipped to handle cargoes by unit-load techniques, and is a departure point for car ferry services to continental Europe. There is a great variety of industry and service industries, as well as increasing tourism and conference business.

The city, restored after very heavy air raid damage during World War II, has good office and administrative buildings, its municipal centre being the Guildhall, its educational centre the University of Hull and its religious centre the Parish Church of the Holy Trinity. The old Town area is being renovated and includes a new marina and shopping complex. Just west of the city is the Humber Bridge, the world's longest single span suspension bridge, which was officially opened by HM The Queen in July 1981.

Kingston upon Hull was so named by Edward I. City status was accorded in 1897 and the office of Mayor raised to the dignity of Lord Mayor in 1914.

LEEDS

LEEDS (West Yorkshire), a Metropolitan District from April 1, 1974, is a junction for road, rail, canal and air services and an important commercial centre, situated in the lower Aire Valley, 195 miles by road NNW of London. The metropolitan area is 138,915 acres.

The main manufacturing industries are mechanical engineering, printing, publishing and clothing. However, 65 per cent of employment is in services, notably professional and scientific, particularly education and medicine, distributive trades, finance and banking.

The principal buildings are the Civic Hall (1933), the Town Hall (1858), the Municipal Buildings and Art Gallery (1884) with the Henry Moore Gallery (1982), the Corn Exchange (1863) and the University. The Parish Church (St Peter's) was rebuilt in 1841; the 17th century St John's Church has a fine interior with a famous English Renaissance screen; the last remaining 18th century church is Holy Trinity, Boar Lane (1727). Kirkstall Abbey (about 3 miles from the centre of the city), founded by Henry de Lacy in 1152, is one of the most complete examples of Cistercian houses now remaining. Temple Newsam, birthplace of Lord Darnley, was acquired by the Council in 1922. The present house was largely rebuilt by Sir Arthur Ingram in about 1620. Adel Church, about 5 miles from the centre of the city, is a fine Norman structure.

Leeds was first incorporated by Charles I in 1626. The earliest forms of the name are *Loidis* or *Ledes*, the origins of which are obscure.

LEICESTER

LEICESTER is situated geographically in the centre of England, 100 miles N. of London. The City dates back to pre-Roman times and was one of the five Danish *Burhs*. In 1589 Queen Elizabeth I granted a Charter to the City and the ancient title was confirmed by Letters Patent in 1919. Under local government reorganization Leicester's area remained unchanged at 18,141 acres, and it retains its designation as a City.

The principal industries of the city are hosiery, knitwear, footwear manufacturing and engineering. The growth of Leicester as a hosiery centre increased rapidly from the introduction there of the first stocking frame in 1670 and today it has some of the largest hosiery factories in the world,with much of the output being exported.

The principal buildings in the city are the Town Hall, the New Walk Centre, the University, Leicester Polytechnic, De Montfort Hall, one of the finest concert halls in the provinces seating over 2,750 people, and the Granby Halls, a major indoor sports facility. The ancient Churches of St Martin (now Leicester Cathedral), St Nicholas, St Margaret, All Saints, St Mary de Castro, and buildings such as the Guildhall, the 14th century Newarke Gate, the Castle and the Jewry Wall Roman site still exist. The Haymarket Theatre, an integral part of a large shopping and car-parking complex, was opened in 1973.

LINCOLN

Situated 143 miles N. of London and 40 miles inland on the River Witham, LINCOLN derives its name from a contraction of *Lindum Colonia*, the settlement founded in AD 48 by the Romans to command the crossing of Ermine Street and Fosse Way. Sections of the 3rd century Roman city wall can be seen, including an extant gateway (Newport Arch), and excavations have discovered traces of a sewerage system unique in Britain. The Romans also drained the surrounding fenland and created a canal system, laying the foundations of Lincoln's agricultural prosperity, and also of the city's importance in the medieval wool trade as a port and Staple town. As one of the Five Boroughs of the Danelaw, Lincoln was an important trading centre in the 9th and 10th centuries and medieval prosperity from the wool trade lasted until the 14th century, enabling local merchants to build parish churches (of which three survive), and attracting in the 12th century a Jewish community (Jew's House and Court, Aaron's House). However, the removal of the Staple to Boston in 1369 heralded a decline from which the city only recovered fully in the 19th century when improved fen drainage made Lincoln agriculturally important, and improved canal and rail links led to industrial development, mainly in the manufacture of machinery, components and engineering products.

The Castle was built shortly after the Conquest and is unusual in having two mounds; on one motte stands a Keep (Lucy's Tower) added in the 12th century. The Cathedral was begun c.1073 when the first Norman bishop moved the see of Lindsey to Lincoln, but was mostly destroyed by fire and earthquake in the 12th century. Rebuilding was begun by St Hugh and completed over a century later. The Wren library contains manuscripts including one of the four surviving originals of the Magna Charta. Other notable architectural features of the city are the 12th century High Bridge, the oldest in Britain still to carry buildings, and the Guildhall situated above the 15th–16th century Stonebow gateway.

LIVERPOOL

LIVERPOOL (Merseyside) on the right bank of the River Mersey, 3 miles from the Irish Sea and 210 miles NW of London, is the UK's fourth most important port and the foremost for the Atlantic trade. The municipal area of 27,864 acres includes 2,840 acres in the bed of the river Mersey. Tunnels link Liverpool with Birkenhead and Wallasey.

There are 2,100 acres of dockland on both sides of the river and the Gladstone and Royal Seaforth Docks can accommodate the largest vessels afloat. Annual tonnage of cargo handled is approximately 10,500,000 tonnes. The main imports are crude oil, grain, ores, edible oils, timber, containers and break-bulk cargo. Liverpool Free Port, Britain's largest, was opened in 1984.

Liverpool was created a free borough in 1207 and a city in 1880. From the early 18th century it expanded rapidly with the growth of industrialization and Atlantic trade. Surviving buildings from this date include the Bluecoat Chambers (1717, formerly the Bluecoat School), the Town Hall (1754, rebuilt to the original design 1795), and buildings in Rodney Street, Canning Street and the suburbs. Notable from the 19th and 20th centuries are the Anglican Cathedral, built from the designs of Sir Giles Gilbert Scott (the foundation stone was laid in 1904, and the building was completed only in 1980), the Catholic Metropolitan Cathedral (designed by Sir Frederick Gibberd, consecrated 1967) and St George's Hall (1838–54), regarded as one of the finest modern examples of classical architecture. The recently refurbished Albert Dock (designed by Jesse Hartley) contains the Merseyside Maritime Museum and Tate Gallery, Liverpool. In 1852 an Act was obtained for establishing a public library, museum and art gallery: as a result Liverpool had one of the first public libraries in the country. The Brown, Picton and Hornby libraries now form one of the country's major libraries. The Victoria Building of Liverpool University, the Royal Liver, Cunard and Mersey Docks & Harbour Company buildings at the Pier Head, the Municipal Buildings and the Philharmonic Hall are other examples of the City's fine buildings. Britain's first International Garden Festival was held in Liverpool in 1984.

MANCHESTER

MANCHESTER (the *Mamucium* of the Romans, who occupied it in AD 78) is 189 miles NW of London and covers about 43 square miles.

Manchester is a commercial and industrial centre with a population engaged in the engineering, chemical, clothing, food processing and textile industries. Banking, insurance and a growing leisure industry are among the prime commercial activities. The city is connected with the sea by the Manchester Ship Canal, opened in 1894, 35½ miles long, and accommodating ships up to 15,000 tons. Manchester Airport handles more than 10 million passengers yearly.

The principal buildings are the Town Hall, erected in 1877 from the designs of Alfred Waterhouse, RA, together with a large extension of 1938; the Royal Exchange (1869, enlarged 1921) the Central Library (1934); Heaton Hall; the 17th century Chetham Library; the Rylands Library (1899), which includes the Althorp collection; the University precinct; the 15th century Cathedral (formerly the parish church); G-MEX and the Free Trade Hall. Manchester is the home of the Hallé Orchestra, the Royal Northern College of Music, the Royal Exchange Theatre and seven public art galleries. Metrolink, the new light rail system, opens in 1992.

The town received its first charter of incorporation in 1838 and was created a city in 1853. The title of city was retained under local government reorganization.

NEWCASTLE UPON TYNE

NEWCASTLE UPON TYNE (Tyne and Wear) a Metropolitan District on the north bank of the River Tyne, is 8 miles from the North Sea, 272 miles N. of London and has an area of 27,640 acres. A Cathedral and University City, it is the administrative, commercial and cultural centre for north-east England and the principal port. It is an important manufacturing centre with a wide variety of industries.

The principal buildings include the Castle Keep (12th century), Black Gate (13th century), Blackfriars (13th century), West Walls (13th century), St Nicholas's Cathedral (15th century, fine lantern tower), St Andrew's Church (12th–14th century), St John's (14th–15th century), All Saints (1786 by Stephenson), St Mary's Roman Catholic Cathedral (1844), Trinity House (17th century), Sandhill (16th century houses), Guildhall (Georgian), Grey Street (1834–39), Central Station (1846–50), Laing Art Gallery (1904), University of Newcastle Physics Building (1962) and Medical Building (1985), Civic Centre (1963), Central Library (1969) and Eldon Square Shopping Development (1976). Open spaces include the Town Moor (927 acres) and Jesmond Dene. Eight bridges span the Tyne at Newcastle.

The City derives its name from the 'new castle' (1080) erected as a defence against the Scots. In 1400 it was made a County, and in 1882 a City.

NORWICH

NORWICH (Norfolk) is an ancient City 110 miles NE of London. It grew from an early Anglo-Saxon settlement near the confluence of the Rivers Yare and Wensum, and now serves as provincial capital for the predominantly agricultural region of East Anglia. The name is thought to relate to the most northerly of a group of Anglo-Saxon villages or 'wics'. The present City has an area of 9,655 acres. The City's first known Charter was granted in 1158 by Henry II.

Norwich serves its surrounding area as a market town and commercial centre, banking and insurance being prominent among the City's businesses. From the 14th century until the Industrial Revolution, Norwich was the regional centre of the woollen industry, but now the biggest single industry is financial services and principal trades are engineering, printing, shoemaking, double glazing, and the production of chemicals, clothing, confectionery and other foodstuffs. Norwich is accessible to seagoing vessels by means of the River Yare, entered at Great Yarmouth, 20 miles to the east.

Among many historic buildings are the Cathedral (completed in the 12th century and surmounted by a 15th century spire 315 feet in height), the Keep of the Norman Castle (now a museum and art gallery), the 15th century flint-walled Guildhall (now a tourist information centre), some thirty medieval parish churches, St Andrew's and Blackfriars' Halls, the Tudor houses preserved in Elm Hill and the Georgian Assembly House. The University of East Anglia has been established in Norwich on a spacious site at Earlham on the City's western boundary and received its first students in 1963.

NOTTINGHAM

NOTTINGHAM stands on the River Trent, 124 miles NNW of London in one of the most valuable coalfields of the country connected by canal with the Atlantic and the North Sea. The municipal area is 18,364 acres.

The principal industries are hosiery, lace, bleaching, dyeing and spinning, tanning, engineering and cycle works, brewing and the manufacture of tobacco, chemicals, furniture, typewriters and mechanical products.

The chief buildings are the 17th century Nottingham Castle (restored in 1878, and now the City Museum and Gallery of Art), Wollaton Hall (1580–88) owned by the City Council and now a Natural History Museum, St Mary's, St Peter's, and St Nicholas's Churches, the Roman Catholic Cathedral (Pugin, 1842–44), the Council House (1929), the Guildhall and Court House (1888), Shire Hall, Albert Hall, the University and Polytechnic, Newstead Abbey, home of Lord Byron, the Theatre Royal (1865), the Playhouse (1963) and the Royal Concert Hall (1982).

Snotingaham or *Notingeham*, 'the village or home of the sons of Snot' (the Wise), is the Anglo-Saxon name for the Celtic *Tuigogobauc*, 'Cave Homes'. The City possesses a Charter of Henry II, and was created a City in 1897. Under local government reorganization, the style of City was reaccorded from April, 1974.

OXFORD

OXFORD is a University City, an important industrial centre, and a market town, with an area of 8,785 acres. Industry played a minor part in Oxford until the motor industry was established in 1912.

It is for its architecture that Oxford is of most interest to the visitor, its oldest specimens being the reputed Saxon tower of St Michael's church, the remains of the Norman castle and city walls and the Norman church at Iffley. It is chiefly famous however for its Gothic buildings, such as the Divinity Schools, the Old Library at Merton College, William of Wykeham's New College, Magdalen College and Christ Church and many other college buildings. Later centuries are represented by the Laudian quadrangle at St John's College, the Renaissance Sheldonian Theatre by Wren, Trinity College Chapel, and All Saints Church; Hawksmoor's mock-Gothic at All Souls College, and the 18th century Queens' College. In addition to individual buildings, High Street and Radcliffe Square, just off it, both form architectural compositions of great beauty. Most of the Colleges have gardens, those of Magdalen, New College, St John's (designed by 'Capability' Brown) and Worcester being the largest.

PLYMOUTH

PLYMOUTH is situated on the borders of Devon and Cornwall at the confluence of the Rivers Tamar and Plym, 210 miles from London, with an area of 19,572 acres. The city has a long maritime history; it was the home port of Sir Francis Drake and the starting point for his circumnavigation of the world, as well as the last port of call for the *Mayflower* when the Pilgrim Fathers sailed for the New World in 1620. Today Plymouth is host to many international yacht races. The Barbican harbour area has many Elizabethan buildings, and on Plymouth Hoe stands the first lighthouse to be built on the Eddystone Rocks, 13 miles offshore.

Following extensive war damage, the city centre, comprising a large shopping centre, municipal offices, law courts and public buildings, has been rebuilt. The main employment is provided at the Naval Base, though many new industrial firms and service industries have become established in the post-war period and the city is a growing tourism centre. In 1982 the Theatre Royal was opened. In conjunction with the Cornwall County Council, the Tamar Bridge was constructed linking the City by road with Cornwall.

PORTSMOUTH

PORTSMOUTH occupies Portsea Island, Hampshire, with boundaries extending to the mainland. It has an area of 15½ sq. miles and is 70 miles SW of London.

Portsmouth is a centre of industry and commerce, including many high technology and manufacturing industries. It is the UK headquarters of several major international companies. HM Naval Base still has a substantial work force, although this has decreased in recent years. The commercial port and Continental Ferry Port is owned and run by the City Council, and carries passengers and vehicles to France.

A major port since the 16th century, Portsmouth is also a thriving seaside resort catering for thousands of visitors and day-trippers annually. Among many historic attractions are Lord Nelson's flagship, HMS *Victory*, the Tudor warship *Mary Rose*, Britain's first 'ironclad', HMS *Warrior*, the D-Day Museum, Charles Dickens' birthplace at 393 Old Commercial Road, the Royal Naval and Royal Marine museums, Southsea Castle (built by Henry VIII), the Round Tower and Point Battery, which for hundreds of years have guarded the entrance to Portsmouth Harbour, Fort Nelson on Portsdown Hill and the Sealife Centre.

ST ALBANS

Twenty-five miles NW of London and situated on the River Ver, ST ALBANS' origins stem from the major Roman town of *Verulamium*. Named after the first Christian martyr in Britain, who was executed here, St Albans has developed around the Norman Abbey and Cathedral Church (consecrated 1115), built partly of materials from the old Roman city. The museums house Iron Age and Roman artefacts and the Roman Theatre, unique in Britain, has a stage as opposed to an amphitheatre. Archaeological excavations in the city centre continue also to reveal evidence of pre-Roman, Saxon and medieval occupation.

The town's significance grew to the extent that it was a signatory and venue for the drafting of the Magna Charta. It was also the scene of major riots during the Peasants' Revolt, the French King John was imprisoned there after the Battle of Poitiers, and heavy fighting took place during the Wars of the Roses.

Previously controlled by the Abbot, the town achieved a Royal Charter in 1553 and City status in 1877. The street market, first established in 1553, is still an important feature of the city, as are many hotels and inns which survive from the days when St Albans was an important coach stop. Tourist attractions include historic churches and houses, and a 15th century clock tower.

The city now contains a wide range of firms, with special emphasis on micro-technology and electronics, particularly in the medical field. In addition, it is the home of the Royal National Rose Society, and of Rothamsted Park, the agricultural research centre.

In 1974 the City and District of St Albans was formed, taking in the town of Harpenden and many villages, and it now covers an area of 63 square miles.

SHEFFIELD

SHEFFIELD (South Yorkshire), the centre of the special steel and cutlery trades, is situated 159 miles NNW of London, at the junction of the Sheaf, Porter, Rivelin and Loxley valleys with the River Don.

Sheffield has an area of 91,000 acres (nearly 150 square miles), including 4,619 acres of publicly owned arks and woodland. Though its cutlery, silverware and plate have long been famous, Sheffield has other and now more important industries—special and alloy steels, engineering, tool-making and financial. Research in glass, metallurgy and other fields is carried out.

The parish church of St Peter and St Paul, founded in the 12th century, became the Cathedral Church of the Diocese of Sheffield in 1914. The Roman Catholic Cathedral Church of St Marie (founded 1847) was created Cathedral for the new diocese of Hallam in 1980. Parts of the present building date from c.1435. The principal buildings are the Town Hall (1897, 1923 and 1977), the Cutlers' Hall (1832), the University 1905 and recent extensions, including 19-storey Arts Tower), City Hall (1932), Graves Art Gallery (1934), Mappin Art Gallery and the Crucible Theatre. The restored 19th century Lyceum theatre opened in 1990.

Sheffield was created a city in 1893 and on April 1, 1974 became a Metropolitan District Council incorporating Stocksbridge and most of the Wortley Rural area, and retained city status.

Master Cutler (1991–92) *of the Company of Cutlers in Hallamshire*, Dr J. T. Harvey.

SOUTHAMPTON

SOUTHAMPTON is the leading British deep-sea port on the Channel and is situated on one of the finest natural harbours in the world. The first Charter was granted by Henry II and Southampton was created a county of itself in 1447. In February 1964, The Queen granted city status by Royal Charter. The city has an area of 12,071 acres excluding tidal waters.

There have been Roman and Saxon settlements on the site of the city, which has been an important port since the time of the Conquest due to its natural deepwater harbour. The oldest church is St Michael's (1070) which has a black tournai marble font and an unusually tall spire built in the 18th century as a landmark for navigators of Southampton Water. Other buildings and monuments within the city walls are the Tudor House, God's House Tower, Bargate Museum, the Tudor Merchants Hall, the Weighhouse, West Gate, King John's House, Long House, Wool House, the ruins of Holy Rood Church, St Julien's Church and the Mayflower Memorial. The medieval town walls, built for artillery, are among the most complete in Europe. Public open spaces total over 1,000 acres in extent and comprise 9 per cent of the city's area. The Common covers an area of 328 acres in the central district of the city and is mostly natural parkland.

STOKE-ON-TRENT

STOKE-ON-TRENT (Staffordshire), familiarly known as The Potteries, stands on the River Trent 157 miles N. of London. The present municipal area is 22,916 acres (36 square miles) and the city is the main centre of employment for the population of North Staffordshire. It is the largest clayware producer in the world (china, earthenware, sanitary goods, refractories, bricks and tiles) and has a considerable coal mining output drawn from one of the richest coalfields in Western Europe. The city has steelworks, foundries, chemical works, engineering plants, rubber works, paper mills, and a very wide range of manufactures. Extensive reconstruction has been carried on in recent years.

The City was formed by the federation in 1910 of the separate municipal authorities of Tunstall, Burslem, Hanley, Stoke-upon-Trent, Fenton, and Longton, all of which are now combined in the present City of Stoke-on-Trent.

WINCHESTER

WINCHESTER, the ancient capital of England, is situated on the River Itchen 65 miles SW of London and 12 miles N. of Southampton. Since local government reorganization in 1974, the style of City has been accorded to the whole of the new district of Winchester, which embraces an area of 162,921 acres of mid-Hampshire.

Winchester is rich in architecture of all types but the Cathedral takes pride of place. The longest Gothic cathedral in the world, it was built in 1079–93 and exhibits examples of Norman, Early English and Perpendicular styles. Winchester College, founded in 1382, is one of the most famous public schools, the original building (of 1393) remaining largely unaltered. St Cross Hospital, another great medieval foundation, lies 1 mile south of the city. The Almshouses were founded in 1136 by Bishop Henry de Blois, and Cardinal Henry Beaufort added a new Almshouse of 'Noble Poverty' in 1446. The Chapel and dwellings are of great architectural interest, and visitors may still receive the 'Wayfarer's Dole' of bread and ale.

Recent excavations have done much to clarify the origins and development of Winchester. Part of the forum and several of the streets of the Roman town have been discovered; and excavations in the Cathedral Close have uncovered the entire site of the Anglo-Saxon cathedral (known as the Old Minster) and parts of the New Minster, built by Alfred's son Edward the Elder, and the burial place of the Alfredian dynasty. The original burial place of St Swithun, before his remains were translated to a site in the present cathedral, was also uncovered.

Excavations in other parts of the City have thrown much light on Norman Winchester, notably on the site of the Royal Castle, adjacent to which the new Law Courts have been built, and in the grounds of Wolvesey Castle, where the great house built by Bishops Giffard and Henry de Blois in the 12th century has been uncovered.

YORK

The City of YORK is a District in the County of North Yorkshire, and is an archiepiscopal seat.

The recorded history of York dates from AD 71, when the Roman Ninth Legion established a base under Petilius Cerealis which later became the fortress of *Eburacum*. In Anglo-Saxon times the city was the royal and ecclesiastical centre of Northumbria, and was captured by a Viking army in AD 866, after which it became the capital of the Viking kingdom of Jorvik. By the 14th century the city had become a great mercantile centre, mainly owing to its control of the wool trade, and was used as the chief base against the Scots. Under the Tudors its fortunes declined, though Henry VIII made it the headquarters of the Council of the North. Recent excavations on many sites, including Coppergate, have greatly expanded knowledge of Roman, Viking and medieval urban life.

With its development as a railway centre in the 19th century the commercial life of York expanded. The principal industries are the manufacture of chocolate, railway coaches, scientific instruments, and sugar.

The City is rich in examples of architecture of all periods. The earliest church was built in AD 627 and, in the 12th to 15th centuries, the present Minster was built in a succession of styles. Other examples within the city are the medieval city walls and gateways, churches and guildhalls. Domestic architecture includes the Georgian mansions of The Mount, Micklegate and Bootham. Its museums include York Castle Museum, the National Railway Museum and the Jorvik Viking Centre.

THE CORPORATION OF LONDON

The City of London is the historic centre at the heart of London known as 'the square mile' around which the vast metropolis has grown over the centuries. The City's residential population is 5,300 (1981 Census). The civic government is carried on by the Corporation of the City of London through the Court of Common Council, a body consisting of the Lord Mayor, 24 other Aldermen and 132 Common Councilmen. The legal title of the Corporation is 'the Mayor and Commonalty and Citizens of the City of London'.

The City is the financial and business centre of London and includes the head offices of the principal banks, insurance companies and mercantile houses, in addition to buildings ranging from the historic interest of the Roman Wall and the 15th century Guildhall, to the massive splendour of St Paul's Cathedral and the architectural beauty of Wren's spires.

The City of London was described by Tacitus in AD 62 as 'a busy emporium for trade and traders'. Under the Romans it became an important administration centre and hub of the road system. Little is known of London in Saxon times when it formed part of the kingdom of the East Saxons. In 886 Alfred recovered London from the Danes and reconstituted it a burgh under his son-in-law. In 1066 the citizens submitted to William the Conqueror who in 1067 granted them a charter, which is still preserved, establishing them in the rights and privileges they had hitherto enjoyed.

The Mayoralty

The Mayoralty was probably established about 1189, the first Mayor being Henry Fitz Ailwyn who filled the office for 23 years and was succeeded by Fitz Alan (1212–14). A new charter was granted by King John in 1215, directing the Mayor to be chosen annually, which has ever since been done, though in early times the same individual often held the office more than once. A familiar instance is that of 'Whittington, thrice Lord Mayor of London' (in reality four times, 1397, 1398, 1406, 1419); and many modern cases have occurred. The earliest instance of the phrase 'Lord Mayor' in English is in 1414. It was used more generally in the latter part of the 15th century and became invariable from 1535 onwards. At Michaelmas the Liverymen in Common Hall choose two Aldermen who have served the office of Sheriff for presentation to the Court of Aldermen, and one is chosen to be Lord Mayor for the following mayoral year.

Lord Mayor's Day

The Lord Mayor of London was previously elected on the feast of St Simon and St Jude (October 28), and from the time of Edward I, at least, was presented to the King or to the Barons of the Exchequer on the following day, unless that day was a Sunday. The day of election was altered to October 16 in 1346, and after some further changes was fixed for Michaelmas Day in 1546, but the ceremonies of admittance and swearing-in of the Lord Mayor continued to take place on October 28 and 29 respectively until 1751. In 1752, at the reform of the Calendar the Lord Mayor was continued in office until November 8, the 'New Style' equivalent of October 28. The Lord Mayor is now presented to the Lord Chief Justice at the Royal Courts of Justice on the second Saturday in November to make the final declaration of office, having been sworn in at Guildhall on the preceding day. The procession to the Royal Courts of Justice is popularly known as the Lord Mayor's Show.

Representatives

Aldermen are mentioned in the 11th century and their office is of Saxon origin. They were elected annually between 1377 and 1394, when an Act o Parliament of Richard II directed them to be chosen for life.

The Common Council, elected annually on the firs Friday in December, was, at an early date, substitute for a popular assembly called the *Folkmote*. At firs only two representatives were sent from each ward but the number has since been greatly increased.

Officers

Sheriffs were Saxon officers; their predecessor were the *wic-reeves* and *portreeves* of London an Middlesex. At first they were officers of the Crown and were named by the Barons of the Exchequer; bu Henry I (in 1132) gave the citizens permission to choose their own Sheriffs, and the annual election o Sheriffs became fully operative under King John' charter of 1199. The citizens lost this privilege, as fa as the election of Sheriff of Middlesex was concerned by the Local Government Act, 1888; but the Livery men continue to choose two Sheriffs of the City o London, who are appointed on Midsummer Day an take office at Michaelmas.

The Recorder was first appointed in 1298. Th office of Chamberlain is an ancient one, the firs contemporary record of which is 1237. The Tow Clerk (or Common Clerk) is mentioned in 1274 an the Common Serjeant in 1291.

Activities

The work is assigned to a number of committee which present reports to the Court of Commo Council. These Committees are: City Lands an Bridge House Estates, Policy and Resources, Coa Corn and Rates Finance, Planning and Communica tions, Central Markets, Billingsgate and Leadenha Markets, Spitalfields Market, Police, Port and Cit of London Health and Social Services, Libraries, Ar Galleries and Records, Boards of Governors o Schools, Music (Guildhall School of Music an Drama), Establishment, Housing, Gresham (Cit side), Hampstead Heath Management, Epping Fores and Open Spaces, West Ham Park, Privileges, Barb can Residential and Barbican Centre (Barbican Art and Conference Centre).

The City's estate, in the possession of which th Corporation of London differs from other municipa ities, is managed by the City Lands and Bridge Hous Estates Committee, the Chairmanship of whic carries with it the title of 'Chief Commoner'. *Chair man* (1991), T. A. Donelly, MBE.

The Honourable the Irish Society (The Iris Chamber, Guildhall Yard, London EC2V 5AE. *Sec* B. E. Manning), which manages the Corporation' estates in Ulster, consists of a Governor and fiv other Aldermen, the Recorder, and 19 Commo Councilmen, of whom one is elected Deputy Gover nor.

The Lord Mayor 1990–91*

The Rt. Hon. the Lord Mayor (1990–91), Sir Alexande Graham, GBE.
  Secretary, Rear-Adm. A. J. Cook, CB.

The Sheriffs 1991–92

R. N. Young (*Alderman, Bread Street*) and J. R Perring, TD; *elected*, June 24, 1991; *assumed office* September 27, 1991.

Officers

Recorder, L. J. Verney, TD, QC (1990).
Chamberlain, B. P. Harty (1983).
Town Clerk, S. Jones (1991).
Common Serjeant, R. Lymbery, RD, QC (1990).

* The Lord Mayor for 1991–92 was elected o Michaelmas Day. *See* **Stop-press.**

The Aldermen

Aldermen	Ward	Born	CC	Ald.	Shff.	Lord Mayor
Cdr. Sir Robin Gillett, Bt., GBE, RD	Bassishaw	1925	1965	1969	1973	1976
Sir Peter Gadsden, GBE	Farringdon Wt.	1929	1969	1971	1970	1979
Sir Christopher Leaver, GBE	Dowgate	1937	1973	1974	1979	1981
Dame Mary Donaldson, GBE	Coleman St	1921	1966	1975	1981	1983
Sir Alan Traill, GBE	Langbourn	1935	1970	1975	1982	1984
Sir Allan Davis, GBE	Cripplegate	1921	1971	1976	1982	1985
Sir David Rowe-Ham, GBE	Bridge	1935	....	1976	1984	1986
Sir Greville Spratt, GBE, TD	Castle Baynard	1927	....	1978	1984	1987
Sir Christopher Collett, GBE	Broad Street	1931	1973	1979	1985	1988
Sir Hugh Bidwell, GBE	Billingsgate	1934	....	1979	1986	1989
Sir Alexander Michael Graham, GBE	Queenhithe	1938	1978	1979	1986	1990

All the above have passed the Civic Chair

Brian Garton Jenkins	Cordwainer	1935	....	1980	1987	....
Francis McWilliams	Aldersgate	1926	1978	1980	1988	....
Paul Henry Newall, TD	Walbrook	1934	1980	1981	1989	....
Christopher Rupert Walford	Farringdon Wn.	1935	....	1982	1990	....
Roderic Neil Young	Bread Street	1933	1980	1982	....	....
Roger William Cork	Tower	1947	1978	1983	....	....
Bryan Edward Toye	Lime Street	1938	....	1983	....	....
Richard Everard Nichols	Candlewick	1938	1983	1984	....	....
Peter Anthony Bull	Cheap	1937	1968	1984	....	....
Sir Peter Keith Levene, KBE	Portsoken	1941	1983	1984	....	....
Leonard John Chalstrey	Vintry	1931	1981	1984	....	....
Clive Haydn Martin, OBE, TD	Aldgate	1935	....	1985	....	....
David Howarth Seymour Howard	Cornhill	1945	1972	1986	....	....
James Michael Yorrick Oliver	Bishopsgate	1940	1980	1987	....	....

The Common Council of London

Deputy.—Each Common Councilman so described serves as Deputy to the Alderman of her/his Ward.

Anstee, N. J. (1987) .... *Aldersgate*
Archibald, W. W. (1986) .... *Cornhill*
Arthur, G. F. (1988) .... *Farringdon Wt.*
Ballard, K. A., MC (1969) .... *Castle Baynard*
Balls, *Deputy* H. D. (1970) .... *Cripplegate Wt.*
Barker, J. A. (1981) .... *Cripplegate Wt.*
Barnes, H. M. F. (1986) .... *Coleman Street*
Beale, M. J. (1979) .... *Lime Street*
Bird, J. L. (1977) .... *Bridge*
Biroum-Smith, P. L. (1988) .... *Dowgate*
Blackwood, C. D. (1990) .... *Farringdon Wt.*
Block, S. A. A. (1983) .... *Cheap*
Bramwell, F. M. (1983) .... *Langbourn*
Brighton, R. L. (1984) .... *Portsoken*
Brooks, W. I. B. (1988) .... *Billingsgate*
Brown, *Deputy* D. T. (1971) ...... *Walbrook*
Cann, T. J. (1988) .... *Cripplegate Wn.*
Cassidy, M. J. (1989) .... *Coleman Street*
Catt, B. F. (1982) .... *Farringdon Wn.*
Challis, G. H., CBE (1978) .... *Langbourn*
Chandler, *Deputy* E. G., CBE (1982) .. *Cornhill*
Clements, *Deputy* G. E. I. (1960) .. *Farringdon Wt.*
Cohen, Mrs C. M. (1986) .... *Lime Street*
Cole, Lt.-Col. Sir Colin, KCVO, TD (1964) .... *Castle Baynard*
Cope, Dr J. (1963) .... *Farringdon Wt.*
Coven, *Deputy* Mrs E. O., CBE (1972) .... *Dowgate*
Currie, Miss S. E. M. (1985) .... *Cripplegate Wt.*
Daily-Hunt, R. B. (1989) .... *Cripplegate*
David, C. P. (1984) .... *Aldgate*
Delderfield, D. W. (1982) .... *Aldersgate*
de Silva, D., QC (1980) .... *Farringdon Wt.*
Donnelly, T. A., MBE (1982) .... *Bread Street*
Duckworth, *Deputy* H., CBE (1960) .. *Lime Street*
Dunitz, A. A. (1984) .... *Portsoken*
Durnin, J. C. (1976) .... *Cordwainer*
Edwards, R. D. K. (1978) .... *Bassishaw*
Eskenzi, A. N. (1970) .... *Farringdon Wn.*
Evans, Mrs J. (1975) .... *Farringdon Wt.*

Eve, R. A. (1980) .... *Cheap*
Everett, K. M. (1984) .... *Candlewick*
Falk, F. A., TD (1984) .... *Farringdon Wt.*
Farrow, M. W. W. (1987) .... *Bishopsgate*
Farthing, R. B. C. (1981) .... *Aldgate*
Fell, J. A. (1982) .... *Queenhithe*
FitzGerald, R. C. A. (1981) .... *Bread Street*
Floyd-Ewin, *Deputy* Sir David, LVO, OBE (1963) .... *Castle Baynard*
Frankenberg, P. B. (1989) .... *Cordwainer*
Frappell, *Deputy* C. E. (1973) ...... *Bread Street*
Fraser, W. B. (1981) .... *Vintry*
Frazer, C. M. (1986) .... *Farringdon Wt.*
Galloway, A. D. (1981) .... *Broad Street*
Gass, *Deputy* G. J. (1967) .... *Coleman Street*
Ginsburg, S. (1990) .... *Bishopsgate*
Gold, R. (1965) .... *Castle Baynard*
Gowman, Miss A. (1991) .... *Dowgate*
Graves, A. C. (1985) .... *Bishopsgate*
Harding, N. H. (1970) .... *Farringdon Wn.*
Hardwick, Dr P. B. (1987) .... *Aldgate*
Hart, *Deputy* M. G. (1970) .... *Bridge*
Haynes, J. E. H. (1986) .... *Cornhill*
Henderson, *Deputy* J. S., OBE (1975) .. *Langbourn*
Henderson-Begg, M. (1977) .... *Coleman Street*
Holland, *Deputy* J. (1972) .... *Aldgate*
Horlock, *Deputy* H. W. S. (1969) .... *Farringdon Wn.*
Humphrays, Mrs R. (1976) .... *Cripplegate Wt.*
Ide, W. R. (1972) .... *Castle Baynard*
Jackson, L. St J. T. (1978) .... *Bassishaw*
Jennings, I. G. (1988) .... *Cripplegate Wn.*
Keep, Mrs B. (1987) .... *Cripplegate Wn.*
Kellett, Mrs M. W. F. (1986) ...... *Tower*
Kemp, D. L. (1984) .... *Coleman Street*
Knowles, S. K. (1984) .... *Candlewick*
Lamport, J. C. (1987) .... *Cripplegate Wt.*
Langmead, A. D. G., TD (1982) ...... *Tower*
Lawrence, Dr W. O., TD (1979) ...... *Bridge*
Lawson, G. C. H. (1971) .... *Portsoken*
McAuley, *Deputy* C. (1957) .... *Bread Street*

MacLellan, A. P. W. (1989)........*Walbrook*
McNeil, I. D. (1977) ....*Lime Street*
Malins, J. H. (1981) ....*Farringdon Wt.*
Martin, R. C. (1986)................*Queenhithe*
Mayhew, Miss J. (1986) ....*Queenhithe*
Mills, A. P. (1969)..................*Bassishaw*
Minshull-Fogg, J., TD (1986) ......*Walbrook*
Mitchell, C. R. (1971)..............*Castle Baynard*
Mizen, *Deputy* D. H. (1979) ....*Broad Street*
Mobsby, D. J. L. (1985) ....*Billingsgate*
Morgan, *Deputy* B. L., CBE (1963) ...*Bishopsgate*
Moss, A. D. (1989) ....*Tower*
Murkin, *Deputy* C. H., OBE (1969) ...*Vintry*
Nash, *Deputy* Mrs J. C. (1983) ......*Aldersgate*
Neary, J. E. (1982) ....*Aldgate*
Newman, Mrs P. B. (1989) ....*Aldersgate*
Northall-Laurie, P. D. (1975).......*Walbrook*
Olson, A. H. F. (1972)..............*Dowgate*
Owen, Mrs J. (1975)................*Langbourn*
Owen-Ward, J. R. (1983)...........*Bridge*
Packard, Brig. J. J. (1972) ....*Cripplegate Wn.*
Pembroke, *Deputy* Mrs A. M. F.
  (1978) ....*Cheap*
Ponsonby of Shulbrede, The Lady
  (1981) ....*Farringdon Wt.*
Pulman, G. A. G. (1983) ....*Tower*
Ratner, R. A., TD (1981) ....*Broad Street*
Reed, *Deputy* J. L., MBE (1967) .....*Farringdon Wn.*
Revell-Smith, P. A., CBE (1959) .....*Vintry*
Rigby, P. P. (1972) ....*Farringdon Wn.*

Rigg-Milner, Mrs A. I. (1990) ....*Cripplegate Wt.*
Robinson, Mrs D. C. (1989).........*Bishopsgate*
Rodgers, Miss E. H. L. (1987) ......*Vintry*
Roney, E. P. T., CBE (1974) ....*Bishopsgate*
Samuel, *Deputy* Mrs I. (1971)........*Portsoken*
Saunders, *Deputy* R. (1975) ....*Candlewick*
Savory, M. B. (1980) ....*Broad Street*
Scriven, R. G. (1984) ....*Candlewick*
Sellon, S. A., TD, OBE (1990) ....*Cordwainer*
Shalit, D. M. (1972) ....*Farringdon Wn.*
Sharp, *Deputy* Mrs I. M. (1974) .....*Queenhithe*
Shindler, *Deputy* A. B. (1966) ......*Billingsgate*
Simpson, A. S. J. (1987).............*Aldersgate*
Smithers, H. J. (1986) ....*Billingsgate*
Snyder, M. J. (1986)................*Cordwainer*
Spanner, J. H., TD (1984)...........*Broad Street*
Stitcher, *Deputy* G. M., CBE (1966) ...*Farringdon Wt.*
Swan, N. E. B. (1985)...............*Coleman Street*
Taylor, J. A. F., TD (1991) ....*Bread Street*
Walsh, S. (1989) ....*Farringdon Wt.*
Webb, C. J. (1986)..................*Bishopsgate*
White, J. W. (1986) ....*Cornhill*
Williams, G. M. E. (1985) ....*Aldersgate*
Willoughby, P. J. (1985) ....*Bishopsgate*
Wilmot, *Deputy* R. T. D. (1973) ......*Cordwainer*
Wilson, A. B., CBE (1984)...........*Cheap*
Wixley, G. R. A., TD (1964) ....*Bassishaw*
Woodward, *Deputy* C. D., OBE (1971) *Cripplegate Wn.*
Wooldridge, F. D. (1988)............*Farringdon Wn.*

THE CITY GUILDS (LIVERY COMPANIES)

The Livery Companies of the City of London derive their name from the assumption of a distinctive dress or livery by their members in the 14th century. The order of precedence, omitting extinct companies, is given in parentheses after the name of each company.

Liverymen of the Guilds (22,572 in number) are entitled to vote at elections in Common Hall.

The Twelve Great Companies
(in order of civic precedence)

MERCERS *(1)*. *Hall*, Ironmonger Lane, EC2V 8HE. *Livery*, 250.—*Clerk*, G. M. M. Wakeford; *Master*, J. J. Fenwick.
GROCERS *(2)*. *Hall*, Princes Street, EC2R 8AD. *Livery*, 335.—*Clerk*, C. G. Mattingley, CBE; *Master*, J. Trotter.
DRAPERS *(3)*. *Hall*, Throgmorton Street, EC2N 2DQ. *Livery*, 250.—*Clerk*, R. C. G. Strick; *Master*, A. E. Woodall.
FISHMONGERS *(4)*. *Hall*, London Bridge, EC4R 9EL. *Livery*, 361.—*Clerk*, M. R. T. O'Brien; *Prime Warden*, J. P. Gough.
GOLDSMITHS *(5)*. *Hall*, Foster Lane, EC2V 6BN. *Livery*, 273.—*Clerk*, R. D. Buchanan-Dunlop, CBE; *Prime Warden*, Dr C. E. Gordon Smith, CB.
MERCHANT TAYLORS *(6)*. *Hall*, 30 Threadneedle Street, EC2R 8AY. *Livery* 330.—*Clerk*, Capt. D. A. Wallis, RN; *Master*, D. R. G. Marler.
SKINNERS *(7)*. *Hall*, 8 Dowgate Hill, EC4R 2SP. *Livery*, 360.—*Clerk*, Capt. D. H. Dyke, CBE, LVO, RN; *Master*, Sir Michael Colman, Bt.
HABERDASHERS *(8)*. *Hall*, Staining Lane, EC2V 7DD. *Livery*, 320.—*Clerk*, Capt. M. E. Barrow, DSO, RN; *Master*, D. E. K. Elliott.
SALTERS *(9)*. *Hall*, 4 Fore Street, EC2Y 5DE. *Livery*, 150.—*Clerk*, Col. M. P. Barneby; *Master*, J. R. D. Scriven.
IRONMONGERS *(10)*. *Hall*, Shaftesbury Place, Barbican, EC2Y 8AA. *Livery*, 210.—*Clerk*, J. A. Oliver; *Master*, J. M. Y. Oliver.
VINTNERS *(11)*. *Hall*, Upper Thames Street, EC4V 3BJ. *Livery*, 324.—*Clerk*, Brig. G. Read, CBE; *Master*, J. S. V. Davy.

CLOTHWORKERS *(12)*. *Hall*, Dunster Court, Mincing Lane, EC3R 7AH. *Livery*, 185.—*Clerk*, C. M. Mowll; *Master*, R. N. Horne.

Other City Guilds
(in alphabetic order)

ACCOUNTANTS, CHARTERED *(86)*. *Livery*, 340.—*Clerk*, G. H. Kingsmill, The Grove, Hinton Parva, Swindon SN4 0DH; *Master*, R. G. Wilkes, CBE, TD.
ACTUARIES *(91)*. *Livery*, 170.—*Clerk*, P. D. Esslemont, 16A Cadogan Square, SW1X 0JU; *Master*, K. E. Ayers.
AIR PILOTS AND AIR NAVIGATORS, GUILD OF *(81)*. *Livery*, 400.—*Grand Master*, HRH The Prince Philip, Duke of Edinburgh, KG, KT; *Clerk*, Gp Capt J. W. Tritton, 291 Gray's Inn Road, WC1X 8QF; *Master*, Capt. D. R. Mauleverer.
APOTHECARIES, SOCIETY OF *(58)*. *Hall*, Black Friars Lane, EC4V 6EJ. *Livery*, 1,250.—*Clerk*, Maj. J. C. O'Leary; *Master*, Prof. T. W. A. Glenister.
ARBITRATORS *(93)*. *Livery*, 190.—*Clerk*, B. W. Vigrass, OBE, VRD, 75 Cannon Street, EC4N 5BH; *Master*, A. B. Shurden.
ARMOURERS AND BRASIERS *(22)*. *Hall*, 81 Coleman Street, EC2R 5BJ. *Livery*, 120.—*Clerk*, Lt.-Col. R. R. F. Cowe; *Master*, R. M. Moody.
BAKERS *(19)*. *Hall*, Harp Lane, EC3R 6DP. *Livery*, 420.—*Clerk*, P. F. Wilson, DFC; *Master*, L. R. Springett.
BARBERS *(17)*. *Hall*, Monkwell Square, EC2Y 5BL. *Livery*, 220.—*Clerk*, Col. A. B. Harfield, CBE; *Master*, Sir William Slack.

BASKETMAKERS (52). *Livery*, 500.—*Clerk*, D. J. Farrier, 5 The Spinney, Warren Road, Purley, Surrey CR8 1AB; *Prime Warden*, A. K. Brown, MBE.

BLACKSMITHS (40). *Livery*, 285.—*Clerk*, R. C. Jorden, 27 Cheyne Walk, Grange Park, N21 1DB; *Prime Warden*, B. F. Land.

BOWYERS (38). *Livery*, 98.—*Clerk*, A. Black, CBE, 2 Serjeant's Inn, Fleet Street, EC4Y 1LL; *Master*, R. Cork.

BREWERS (14). *Hall*, Aldermanbury Square, EC2V 7HR. *Livery*, 132.—*Clerk*, Rear-Adm. M. L. T. Wemyss, CB; *Master*, T. F. F. B. Young.

BRODERERS (48). *Livery*, 148.—*Clerk*, P. J. C. Crouch, 11 Bridge Road, East Molesey, Surrey KT8 9EU; *Master*, C. C. Gotto.

BUILDERS MERCHANTS (88). *Livery*, 200.—*Clerk*, Ms S. Robinson, 14 Charterhouse Street, EC1M 6AX; *Master*, E. B. Carter.

BUTCHERS (24). *Hall*, 87 Bartholomew Close, EC1A 7EB. *Livery*, 700.—*Clerk*, A. H. Emus; *Master*, R. E. Stedman.

CARMEN (77). *Livery*, 475.—*Clerk*, Lt.-Col. G. T. Pearce, MBE, 35–37 Ludgate Hill, EC4M 7JN; *Master*, E. R. Britt.

CARPENTERS (26). *Hall*, 1 Throgmorton Avenue, EC2N 2JJ. *Livery*, 150.—*Clerk*, Capt. K. G. Hamon, RN; *Master*, H. M. F. Barnes.

CHARTERED SECRETARIES AND ADMINISTRATORS (87). *Livery*, 228.—*Hon. Clerk*, G. H. Challis, CBE, The Irish Chamber, Guildhall Yard, EC2V 5AE; *Master*, H. R. Harris.

CLOCKMAKERS (61). *Livery*, 286. *Hall*, St Dunstan's House, Carey Lane, EC2V 8AA.—*Clerk*, Air Cdre B. G. Frow, DSO, DFC; *Master*, C. L. Clarke.

COACHMAKERS AND COACH-HARNESS MAKERS (72). *Livery*, 430.—*Clerk*, Maj. W. H. Wharfe, 149 Banstead Road, Ewell, Epsom, Surrey KT17 3HL; *Master*, D. J. Burrell.

COOKS (35). *Livery*, 75.—*Clerk*, M. C. Thatcher, 35 Great Peter Street, SW1P 3LR; *Master*, H. E. Taylor.

COOPERS (36). *Hall*, 13 Devonshire Square, EC2M 4TH. *Livery*, 260.—*Clerk*, J. A. Newton; *Master*, A. R. Eustace.

CORDWAINERS (27). *Livery* 140.—*Clerk*, Cdr. C. Shears, CVO, OBE, Eldon Chambers, 30 Fleet Street, EC4Y 1AA; *Master*, J. J. B. Skinner.

CURRIERS (29). *Livery*, 100.—*Clerk*, Gp Capt F. J. Hamilton, Kestrel Cottage, East Knoyle, Salisbury, Wilts. SP3 6AD; *Master*, M. S. Chesterton.

CUTLERS (18). *Hall*, Warwick Lane, EC4M 7GR. *Livery*, 100.—*Clerk*, K. S. G. Hinde, TD; *Master*, G. W. Walker.

DISTILLERS (69). *Livery*, 256.—*Clerk*, H. B. Dehn, 71 Lincoln's Inn Fields, WC2A 3JF; *Master*, J. M. Broadbent.

DYERS (13). *Hall*, Dowgate Hill, EC4R 2ST. *Livery*, 130.—*Clerk*, J. R. Chambers; *Prime Warden*, M. W. N. Rowlandson.

ENGINEERS (94). *Livery*, 283.—*Clerk*, Cdr. B. D. Gibson, 1 Carlton House Terrace, SW1Y 5DB; *Master*, P. J. C. Crocker.

ENVIRONMENTAL CLEANERS (97). *Hall*, Mark Lane, EC3. *Livery*, 154.—*Clerk*, S. J. Holt; *Master*, G. A. Newell.

FAN MAKERS (76). *Hall*, St Botolph's Hall, Bishopsgate, EC2M 3TL. *Livery*, 217.—*Clerk*, Lt.-Col. I. R. P. Green; *Master*, H. D. E. Woods.

FARMERS (80). *Hall*, 3 Cloth Street, EC1A 7LD. *Livery*, 300.—*Clerk*, C. M. Taylor; *Master*, R. J. Upton.

FARRIERS (55). *Livery*, 375.—*Clerk*, H. W. H. Ellis, 37 The Uplands, Loughton, Essex IG10 1NQ; *Master*, J. G. Barsham.

FELTMAKERS (63). *Livery*, 186.—*Clerk*, Lt.-Col. C. J. Holroyd, Providence Cottage, Chute Cadley, Andover, Hants. SP11 9EB; *Master*, P. S. Wingfield.

FLETCHERS (39). *Hall*, 3 Cloth Street, EC1A 7LD. *Livery*, 105.—*Clerk*, J. R. Garnett; *Master*, F. N. Steiner.

FOUNDERS (33). *Hall*, 1 Cloth Fair, EC1A 7HT. *Livery*, 170.—*Clerk*, A. J. Gillett; *Master*, B. D. Farmer.

FRAMEWORK KNITTERS (64). *Livery*, 225.—*Clerk*, C. J. Eldridge, Apothecaries' Hall, Black Friars Lane, EC4V 6EL; *Master*, M. Chapman.

FRUITERERS (45). *Livery*, 240.—*Clerk*, Cdr. M. T. H. Styles, Denmead Cottage, Chawton, Alton, Hants. GU34 1SB; *Master*, D. L. Hounen.

FUELLERS (95). *Livery*, 250.—*Clerk*, Wg Cdr. H. F. C. Squire, OBE, 4 Maycross Avenue, Morden, Surrey SM4 4DA; *Master*, G. Stokes.

FURNITURE MAKERS (83). *Livery*, 260.—*Clerk*, Wg Cdr. G. Acklam, MBE, 30 Harcourt Street, W1H 2AA; *Master*, M. H. T. Jourdan.

GARDENERS (66). *Livery*, 247.—*Clerk*, Col. N. G. S. Gray, 25 Luke Street, EC2A 4AR; *Master*, R. C. Balfour, MBE.

GIRDLERS (23). *Hall*, Basinghall Avenue, EC2V 5DD. *Livery*, 81.—*Clerk*, E. B. Fleming; *Master*, P. V. Straker.

GLASS-SELLERS (71). *Livery*, 180.—*Hon. Clerk*, B. J. Rawles, 43 Aragon Avenue, Thames Ditton, Surrey KT7 0PY; *Master*, V. E. Emms.

GLAZIERS AND PAINTERS OF GLASS (53). *Hall*, 9 Montague Close, SE1 9DD. *Livery*, 280.—*Clerk*, P. R. Batchelor; *Master*, A. R. Fisher.

GLOVERS (62). *Livery*, 300.—*Clerk*, Gp Capt D. G. F. Palmer, OBE, Glovers, Tismans Common, Rudgwick, W. Sussex RH12 3DU; *Master*, D. M. Anderson.

GOLD AND SILVER WYRE DRAWERS (74). *Livery*, 350.—*Clerk*, J. R. Williams, 50 Cheyne Avenue, E18 2DR; *Master*, D. J. Kaye.

GUNMAKERS (73). *Livery*, 249.—*Clerk*, F. B. Brandt, The Proof House, 48–50 Commercial Road, E1 1LP; *Master*, A. McMillan of Cleghorn.

HORNERS (54). *Livery*, 410.—*Clerk*, Dr E. M. Hunt, 11 Hobart Place, SW1W 0HL; *Master*, D. S. du Parc Braham.

INNHOLDERS (32). *Hall*, College Street, Dowgate Hill, EC4R 2SY. *Livery*, 123.—*Clerk*, J. R. Edwardes Jones; *Master*, M. Vass.

INSURERS (92). *Hall*, 20 Aldermanbury, EC2V 7HY. *Livery*, 343.—*Clerk*, V. D. Webb; *Master*, R. C. W. Bardell, OBE.

JOINERS AND CEILERS (41). *Livery*, 132.—*Clerk*, D. A. Tate, Parkville House, Bridge Street, Pinner, Middx. HA5 3JD; *Master*, B. P. Smith.

LAUNDERERS (89). *Hall*, 9 Montague Close, SE1 9DD. *Livery*, 192.—*Clerk*, P. E. Coombe; *Master*, J. A. Dunn.

LEATHERSELLERS (15). *Hall*, 15 St Helen's Place, EC3A 6DQ. *Livery*, 150.—*Clerk*, Capt. N. MacEacharn, CBE, RN; *Master*, J. R. A. Chard.

LIGHTMONGERS (96). *Livery*, 117.—*Clerk*, S. H. Birch, 53 Leithcote Gardens, SW16 2UX; *Master*, B. J. Castlo.

LORINERS (57). *Livery*, 360.—*Clerk*, J. R. Williams, 50 Cheyne Avenue, E18 2DR; *Master*, HRH The Princess Royal, GCVO, FRS.

MARKETORS (90). *Livery*, 176.—*Clerk*, B. F. Catt, 42 Tottenham Lane, N8 7EA; *Master*, G. Darby.

MASONS (30). *Livery*, 111.—*Clerk*, H. J. Maddocks, 9 New Square, WC2R 3QN; *Master*, R. G. St J. Rowlandson.

MASTER MARINERS, HONOURABLE COMPANY OF (78). HQS *Wellington*, Temple Stairs, WC2R 2PN. *Livery*, 350.—*Clerk*, J. A. V. Maddock; *Admiral*, HRH The Duke of Edinburgh, KG, KT; *Master*, P. F. Mason.

MUSICIANS (50). *Livery*, 270.—*Clerk*, M. J. G. Fletcher, 1 The Sanctuary, Westminster, SW1P 3JT; *Master*, H. Willis.

NEEDLEMAKERS (65). *Livery*, 250.—*Clerk*, M. G. Cook, 17 Southampton Place, WC1A 2EH; *Master*, D. A. Foster.

PAINTER STAINERS (28). *Hall*, 9 Little Trinity Lane, EC4V 2AD. *Livery*, 400.—*Clerk*, Wg Cdr. B. C. Pratt; *Master*, C. Fisher.

PATTENMAKERS (70). *Livery*, 250.—*Clerk*, P. Merritt, 25 Wellesley Road, W4 4BU; *Master*, J. P. H. M. S. Cunynghame.

PAVIORS (56). *Livery*, 275.—*Clerk*, R. F. Coe, Cutlers' Hall, Warwick Lane, EC4M 7BR; *Master*, D. S. Little.

PEWTERERS. (16). *Hall*, Oat Lane, EC2V 7DE. *Livery*, 110.—*Clerk*, Maj. J. M. Halford, RM; *Master*, C. G. Grant.

PLAISTERERS (46). *Hall*, 1 London Wall, EC2Y 5JU. *Livery*, 208.—*Clerk*, H. Mott; *Master*, H. J. W. Warrell.

PLAYING CARDS, MAKERS OF (75). *Livery*, 150.—*Clerk*, M. J. Smyth, 6 The Priory, Godstone, Surrey RH9 8NL; *Master*, P. M. C. Cregeen.

PLUMBERS (31). *Livery*, 310.—*Clerk*, Col. E. M. P. Hardy, 3rd Floor, 21 Fleet Street, EC4Y 1AA; *Master*, R. D. Mann.

POULTERS (34). *Hall*, Armourers' Hall, 81 Coleman Street, EC2R 5BJ. *Livery*, 180.—*Clerk*, Lt.-Col. R. R. F. Cowe; *Master*, D. Kemp.

SADDLERS (25). *Hall*, 40 Gutter Lane, EC2V 6BR. *Livery*, 70.—*Clerk*, Gp Capt K. M. Oliver; *Master*, D. J. Sexrell-Watts.

SCIENTIFIC INSTRUMENT MAKERS (84). *Hall*, 9 Montague Close, SE1 9DD. *Livery*, 230.—*Clerk*, F. G. Everard; *Master*, C. S. den Brinker.

SCRIVENERS (44). *Livery*, 202.—*Clerk*, H. J. W. Harman, The Galleria, Station Road, Crawley, W. Sussex RH10 1HY; *Master*, E. Clements.

SHIPWRIGHTS (59). *Livery*, 500.—*Clerk*, Gp Capt R. C. Olding, CBE, DSC, Ironmongers' Hall, Barbican, EC2Y 8AA; *Permanent Master*, HRH The Duke of Edinburgh, KG, KT; *Prime Warden*, R. A. H. Arnold.

SOLICITORS (79). *Livery*, 411.—*Clerk*, Miss S. H. Robinson, TD, 14 Charterhouse Square, EC1M 6AX; *Master*, R. H. V. Dixon.

SPECTACLE MAKERS (60). *Livery*, 330.—*Clerk*, C. J. Eldridge, Apothecaries' Hall, Black Friars Lane, EC4V 6EL; *Master*, Mrs A. C. A. Silk.

STATIONERS AND NEWSPAPER MAKERS (47). *Hall*, Ave Maria Lane, EC4M 7DD. *Livery*, 450.—*Clerk*, Capt. P. Hames, RN; *Master*, W. C. Young.

SURVEYORS, CHARTERED (85). *Livery*, 325.—*Clerk*, Mrs A. L. Jackson, 16 St Mary-at-Hill, EC3R 8EE; *Master*, M. G. Clark, TD.

TALLOW CHANDLERS (21). *Hall*, 4 Dowgate Hill, EC4R 2SH. *Livery*, 180.—*Clerk*, Brig. W. K. L. Prosser, CBE, MC; *Master*, Sir Peter Cazalet.

TIN PLATE WORKERS Alias Wire Workers (67). *Livery*, 250.—*Clerk*, S. J. Holt, Whitehorns, Rannoch Road, Crowborough, E. Sussex TN6 1RA; *Master*, J Hertel.

TOBACCO PIPE MAKERS AND TOBACCO BLENDERS (82) *Livery*, 174.—*Clerk*, I. J. Kimmins, Bouverie House 154 Fleet Street, EC4A 2HX; *Master*, Dr I. Redstone

TURNERS (51). *Livery*, 165.—*Clerk*, R. G. Woodward, DSC, 33a Hill Avenue, Amersham, Bucks. HP6 5BX *Master*, M. Simmonds.

TYLERS AND BRICKLAYERS (37). *Livery*, 130.—*Clerk* F. A. G. Rider, 6 Martin Lane, Cannon Street EC4R 0DP; *Master*, C. J. N. Ward.

UPHOLDERS (49). *Livery*, 200.—*Clerk*, W. R. Wallis Charrington House, The Causeway, Bishops Stort ford CH23 2EW; *Master*, A. Kinsey.

WAX CHANDLERS (20). *Hall*, Gresham Street, EC2' 7AD. *Livery*, 100.—*Clerk*, T. Wood; *Master*, J. H Sleeman.

WEAVERS (42). *Livery*, 125.—*Clerk*, J. G. Ouvry, The Sanctuary, Westminster, SW1P 3JT; *Uppe Bailiff*, J. G. Bevan.

WHEELWRIGHTS (68). *Livery*, 271.—*Clerk*, M. R. Francis, Greenup, Milton Avenue, Gerrards Cross Bucks. SL9 8QW; *Master*, R. W. Codling.

WOOLMEN (43). *Livery*, 150.—*Clerk*, F. Allen, Hol lands, Hedsor Road, Bourne End, Bucks. SL8 5EE *Master*, R. V. Proctor.

PARISH CLERKS (*No livery*). (*Members*, 99).—*Clerk*, D. Hebblethwaite, General Synod Office, Churc House, Great Smith Street, SW1P 3NZ; *Maste Preb. A. R. Royall.

WATERMEN AND LIGHTERMEN (*No livery*). (Cra Owning Freemen, 324).—*Hall*, 16 St Mary-at-Hil EC3R 8EE.—*Clerk*, W. A. A. Wells, TD; *Master*, G. P. Crowden.

NOTE.—In certain companies the election of Mast or Prime Warden for the year does not take place t the autumn. In such cases the Master or Prim Warden for 1990–91 is given.

LONDON BOROUGHS

CITY or Borough (§Inner London Borough)	Municipal Offices	Population Census 1991p	Community charge per head 1991 £	Chief Executive (a) Town Clerk (b) Managing Director	Mayor or (a) Lord Mayor
Barking and Dagenham....	°Dagenham, RM10 7BN	139,900	170·00	(a) D. C. J. Farr	R. A. J. Patient
Barnet	†The Burroughs, Hendon, NW4 4BG	283,000	247·00	M. M. Caller	L. Pym
Bexley	‡Bexleyheath, Kent DA6 7LB	211,200	202·00	T. Musgrave	A. Catterall
Brent	†Forty Lane, Wembley, HA9 9EZ	226,100	328·00	C. Wood	T. Taylor
Bromley........	°Bromley, BR1 3UH	281,700	190·00	N. T. Palk	P. Jones, TD
§Camden	†Euston Road, NW1 2RU	170,500	300·00	J. Smith	J. Turner
§CITY OF WESTMINSTER	City Hall, Victoria Street, SW1E 6QP	181,500	176·00	(b) M. C. Montacute	(a) Dame Shirley Porter, DBE
Croydon........	Taberner House, Park Lane, Croydon CR9 3JS	299,600	180·00	R. Jefferies	J. Walker
Ealing	°Uxbridge Road, W5 2HL	263,600	255·00	Ms J. Hunt	W. Hammett
Enfield	°Enfield, EN1 3XA	248,900	248·00	B. A. McAndrew	J. A. Wyatt
§Greenwich	†Wellington Street, SE18 6PW	200,800	242·00	C. Roberts	T. Claridge
§Hackney	†Mare St, E8 1EA	164,200	322·00	J. White	G. Ross
§Hammersmith and Fulham ..	†King St, W6 9JU	136,500	247·00	vacant	Miss J. Caruana
Haringey	°Wood Green, N22 4LE	187,300	419·00	G. Singh	F. Knight
Harrow	°Harrow, HA1 2UH	194,300	253·00	A. G. Redmond	D. Green
Havering	†Romford, RM1 3BD	224,400	229·00	D. R. Bradley	D. R. O'Flynn
Hillingdon......	°Uxbridge, UB8 1UW	225,800	215·00	P. Johnson	K. Abel
Hounslow	°Lampton Rd., Hounslow, TW3 4DN	193,400	285·00	R. Kerslake	B. Han
§Islington	†Upper St, N1 2UD	155,200	376·19	E. W. Dear	Ms J. Herbert
§Kensington and Chelsea (RB)..	†Hornton St, W8 7NX	127,600	189·00	R. A. Taylor	Mrs F. Taylor
Kingston upon Thames (RB)..	Guildhall, Kingston upon Thames KT1 1EU	130,600	239·00	R. McCloy	D. Smedley
§Lambeth	†Brixton Hill, SW2 1RW	220,100	425·89	H. Ouseley	J. Singh
§Lewisham	†Catford, SE6 4RU	215,300	168·00	T. Hanafin	J. P. Dowd
Merton.........	Crown House, London Rd., Morden, SM4 5DX	161,800	269·00	W. A. McKee	P. McCabe
Newham	†East Ham, E6 2RP	200,200	304·00	D. Stevenson	A. Singh
Redbridge	†Ilford, IG1 1DD	220,600	255·00	G. U. Price	R. B. R. Hill
Richmond upon Thames	°York Street, Twickenham, TW1 3BZ	154,600	279·00	R. L. Harbord	K. MacKinney
§Southwark	†Peckham Rd., SE5 8UB	196,500	189·00	Ms A. Whyatt	D. McCarthy
Sutton	‡St Nicholas Way, Sutton, SM1 1EA	164,300	259·50	Ms P. Hughes	Ms L. O'Connell
§Tower Hamlets.	†Patriot Square, E2 9LN	153,500	147·00	A. Golding, T. Herbert	B. Blandford
Waltham Forest.	†Forest Rd., Walthamstow, E17 4JF	203,400	296·50	A. Tobias	E. G. Sizer
§Wandsworth...	†Wandsworth, SW18 2PU	237,500	0·00	G. K. Jones	Mrs A. Graham

p preliminary. RB Royal Borough. °Civic Centre. †Town Hall. ‡Civic Offices.

GREATER LONDON SERVICES

The abolition of the Greater London Council on April 1, 1986, led to the bulk of its work being passed to the London Boroughs, government departments and government-appointed bodies, and to joint boards and committees.

The London Residuary Body (LRB) was established by the Local Government Act, 1985, which abolished the GLC. Its brief was to wind up the affairs of the GLC within a maximum life of five years.

With the Government's abolition of the Inner London Education Authority, the London Residuary Body has been given the task of dealing with residual ILEA affairs as it dealt with the GLC. Its reponsibilities include closing ILEA's accounts, disposing of about 200 surplus ILEA pieces of property and land, paying redundancy to ILEA staff and temporarily taking over services such as school transport, adult education, and the payment of grants. This will prolong the life of the LRB for up to three years beyond ILEA's abolition, until March 31, 1993.

The boroughs and successor bodies finance the LRB. In February 1991 the LRB announced a levy of £15 million on London's 12 inner boroughs and the City of London, to pay for the education-related services it took over from ILEA. Nearly £700 million will have been distributed amongst the boroughs by the end of 1991.

LONDON RESIDUARY BODY, Globe House, Temple Place, WC2R 3HP (071-633 5000).
Chairman, Sir Godfrey Taylor.
Board Secretary, J. Howes.
Director of Finance, D. Judd.

Solid waste disposal

Responsibility for the disposal of London's household, commercial and civic amenity refuse lies with 16 waste disposal authorities.

There are four statutory bodies—*West London Waste Authority* (Brent, Ealing, Harrow, Hillingdon Hounslow, Richmond upon Thames), *North London Waste Authority* (Barnet, Camden, Enfield, Hackney Haringey, Islington, Waltham Forest), *East London Waste Authority* (Barking and Dagenham, Havering Newham, Redbridge) and *Western Riverside Waste Authority* (Hammersmith and Fulham, Kensington and Chelsea, Lambeth, Wandsworth).

Twelve boroughs are waste disposal authorities in their own right and eleven of them have come together in voluntary groupings—*Central London Group* (City of London, City of Westminster, Tower Hamlets), *South London Group* (Bromley, Croydon Kingston upon Thames, Merton, Sutton) and *South East London Group* (Greenwich, Lewisham, Southwark). The twelfth, Bexley, liaises with Kent County Council.

The London Waste Regulation Authority regulates and controls waste management activities in both the public and private sectors.

LONDON WASTE REGULATION AUTHORITY, Hampton House, 20 Albert Embankment, SE1 7TJ (Tel: 071 587 3074).

Fire Service

The authority for London's fire service is the London Fire and Civil Defence Authority (LFCDA) The Fire Brigade is organized into five Area Commands, which coincide with borough boundaries The LFCDA's responsibilities also include petroleum licensing.

LONDON FIRE AND CIVIL DEFENCE AUTHORITY, London Fire Brigade Headquarters, 8 Albert Embankment SE1 7SD (Tel: 071-582 3811).

ROMAN NAMES OF ENGLISH TOWNS AND CITIES

Bath	*Aquae Sulis*	Lincoln	*Lindum*
Canterbury	*Durovernum Cantiacorum*	London	*Londinium*
Carlisle	*Luguvalium*	Manchester	*Mamucium*
Chelmsford	*Caesaromagus*	Newcastle upon	
Chester	*Deva*	Tyne	*Pons Aelius*
Chichester	*Noviomagus Regnensium*	Pevensey	*Anderetium*
Cirencester	*Corinium Dobunnorum*	Rochester	*Durobrivae*
Colchester	*Camulodunum*	St Albans	*Verulamium*
Doncaster	*Danum*	Salisbury	
Dorchester	*Durnovaria*	(Old Sarum)	*Sorviodunum*
Dover	*Dubris*	Silchester	*Calleva Atrebatum*
Exeter	*Isca Dumnoniorum*	Winchester	*Venta Belgarum*
Gloucester	*Glevum*	Wroxeter	*Viroconium Cornoviorum*
Leicester	*Ratae Corieltauvorum*	York	*Eburacum*

LONDON AND ITS ENVIRONS
(For National Art Galleries and Museums in London, *see* Index.)

Adelphi, Strand, WC2.—Adelphi Terrace and district commemorate the four Adam brothers, James, John, Robert and William, who laid out the district (formerly Durham House) at the close of the 18th century, though few 18th century buildings now remain. Four of the streets were formerly called after the brothers but are now Adam Street, John Adam Street, Robert Street and Durham House Street. In the neighbourhood of the Adelphi was York House, built by the Duke of Buckingham in 1625 (the Water Gate of which still stands in Embankment Gardens), the commemorative streets being Charles Street, Villiers Street, Duke Street, Buckingham Street.

Alexandra Palace and Park, Wood Green, N22 4AY.—Set in 200 acres of parkland. The Victorian Palace was severely damaged by fire in 1980 but has been restored and developed and was reopened in January 1988. Alexandra Palace provides modern facilities for exhibitions, sports, conferences and leisure activities. There is an ice rink, open daily.

Baltic Exchange, St Mary Axe, EC3.—The world market for the chartering of cargo ships. The present Exchange was built in 1903 and the new wing opened by The Queen on November 21, 1956.

Bank of England, Threadneedle Street, EC2.— The Bank of England, founded in 1694, has always been closely connected with the Government. The present building, completed in 1939 to the designs of Sir Herbert Baker, incorporates features reminiscent of the earlier architects, Sampson (1734), Sir Robert Taylor (1765) and Sir John Soane (1788).

Bank of England Museum (entrance in Bartholomew Lane).—The Museum charts the Bank's history since the granting of the Royal Charter in 1694. Open Mon.-Fri. 10–5, Sat., Sun. and Bank Hols. 11–5. Admission free.

Banqueting House, Whitehall, SW1A 2ER.—The only important building left of the great Palace of Whitehall. The previous banqueting house was burnt down in 1619, and replaced by the present structure designed by Inigo Jones. In 1635 it was enriched with Rubens' ceiling paintings. Charles I was executed on a scaffold set up just in front of the present entrance. Open Mon.-Sat. 10–5. Closed Sun., Bank Hols. Admission (1991) £1·50, concessions £1·35.

Barbican Centre, Silk Street, EC2Y 8DS.— Owned, funded and managed by the Corporation of London, the Barbican Centre was opened on March 3, 1982 by The Queen, and is the largest complex of its kind in western Europe. It houses the 1,166 seat Barbican Theatre, the London base of the Royal Shakespeare Company, along with a smaller 200 seat studio theatre (The Pit), and the 2,026 seat Barbican Hall, the home of the London Symphony Orchestra. There are also three cinemas, an art gallery, a sculpture court, a large lending library, facilities for trade exhibitions and conferences, and bars and restaurants.

Blackheath, SE10.—272 acres of parkland. Morden College, founded in 1695 as a home for 'decayed Turkey merchants', is near the SE corner. The building was designed by Wren and its chapel doors have carvings attributed to Grinling Gibbons. Not open to the public. Concerts and poetry recitals are held at Rangers House, a villa built *c*.1700 which houses the Suffolk collection of English portraits from Larkin to Lely, and the Dolmetsch Collection of musical instruments. Open daily 10–5 (Nov.–Jan. 10–4). Closed Good Friday, Dec. 24, 25. Admission free.

Bridges.—The bridges over the Thames (from east to west) are: *Tower Bridge* (built by the Corporation of London and opened in 1894), with its bascules, operated now by new electrically-run machinery, walkway, opened to the public in 1982, and museum, opened in 1983; *London Bridge* (opened after rebuilding in 1831 by Rennie; the new London Bridge was completed in 1973 and opened by The Queen on March 16, 1973); *Southwark Bridge* (opened in 1819; also by Rennie. Rebuilt by the Corporation of London, 1922); *Blackfriars Bridge* (opened in 1769, rebuilt 1869, and widened by the Corporation of London in 1909); *Waterloo Bridge* (Rennie), opened in 1817, commanding a fine view of western London, rebuilt by LCC and reopened 1944; *Hungerford Bridge*, 1863 (railway bridge with a footbridge); *Westminster Bridge* (built in 1750 and then presenting a view that inspired Wordsworth's sonnet; rebuilt and re-opened in 1862; width, 84 ft.); *Lambeth Bridge* (built 1862, rebuilt 1932) leading from Lambeth Palace to Millbank; *Vauxhall Bridge* (built in 1811–16, rebuilt in 1906), leading to Kennington Oval; *Chelsea Bridge,* leading from Chelsea Hospital to Battersea Park (reconstructed and widened, 1937) and *Albert Bridge* (1873); *Battersea Bridge* (opened in 1890); *Wandsworth Bridge* (opened in 1873; rebuilt and re-opened in 1940); *Putney Bridge* (built 1729, rebuilt 1884, widened in 1933), where the Oxford and Cambridge Boat Race starts for Mortlake; *Hammersmith Bridge* (rebuilt 1887); *Barnes Bridge* (for pedestrians only, 1933); *Chiswick Bridge* (opened in 1933); *King Edward VII Bridge,* Kew (rebuilt in 1902, opened 1903), leading to the Royal Botanic Gardens, Kew; *Twickenham Lock Bridge; Twickenham Bridge* (opened 1933); *Richmond Bridge* (opened in 1777); *Kingston Bridge* (built 1828 and widened 1914) and *Hampton Court Bridge* (rebuilt 1933).

Buckingham Palace, SW1A 1AA.—Purchased by King George III in 1762 from the heir of the Duke of Buckingham, the Palace has been the London home of the Sovereign since Queen Victoria's accession in 1837. It was altered by Nash for King George IV, and refronted in stone (part of the Queen Victoria Memorial) by Sir Aston Webb in 1913.

The Queen's Gallery, containing a changing selection of the finest pictures and works of art from all parts of the royal collection, was opened to the public on July 25, 1962. Open Tues.-Sat. and Bank Holidays 10.30–5, Sun. 2–5. Admission charges are payable; enter from Buckingham Palace Road.

The Royal Mews is open to visitors on Wed. and Thurs. throughout the year (except in Ascot Week), 2–4. Admission charges are payable at the entrance.

Canonbury Tower, N1.—The largest remaining part of a 16th century house originally built by the Priors of St Bartholomew, and since 1952 used as the headquarters of a non-professional theatre company. Contains the 'Spencer' and 'Compton' oak-panelled rooms. Other relics of Canonbury House can be seen nearby.

Catholic Central Library, St Francis Friary, 47 Francis Street, SW1P 1QR.—Founded as a private library in 1914, it was taken over in 1959 by the Franciscan Friars of the Atonement. It is an up-to-date lending and research library of over 55,000 volumes and 150 periodicals, for the general reader, student and ecumenist. Books are sent by post when required. Open Mon.-Fri. 10–5, Sat. 10–1.30.

Cemeteries.—In *Kensal Green Cemetery,* North Kensington, W10 (70 acres), are tombs of Thackeray,

Trollope, Sydney Smith, Wilkie Collins, Tom Hood, George Cruikshank, John Leech, Leigh Hunt, I. K. Brunel and Charles Kemble. In *Highgate Cemetery*, N6, are the tombs of George Eliot, Herbert Spencer, Faraday and Marx. Guided tours only, £2. In *Abney Park Cemetery*, Stoke Newington, N16, the tomb of General Booth, founder of the Salvation Army, and memorials to many Nonconformist divines are to be found. In the *South Metropolitan Cemetery*, Norwood, SE27, are the tombs of Sir Henry Bessemer, Sir Hiram Maxim, Mrs Beeton, Sir Henry Tate and Joseph Whitaker, FSA (*Whitaker's Almanack*). In the churchyard of the former *Marylebone Chapel* are buried Charles Wesley and his son Samuel Wesley (musician). The chapel itself was demolished in 1949. **Crematoria.**—*Ilford* (City of London); *Norwood*; *Hendon*; *Streatham Park*; *Finchley* (St Marylebone) and *Golders Green* (12 acres), near Hampstead Heath, with 'Garden of Rest' and memorials to famous men and women.

Cenotaph, Whitehall, SW1.—(Literally 'empty tomb'.) Monument erected 'To the Glorious Dead', as a memorial to all ranks of the sea, land and air forces who gave their lives in the service of the Empire during the First World War. Designed by Sir Edwin Lutyens. Erected as a temporary memorial in 1919 and replaced by a permanent structure in 1920. Unveiled by King George V on Armistice Day, 1920. An additional inscription was added after the Second World War to commemorate those who gave their lives in that conflict.

Charterhouse, Sutton's Hospital, Charterhouse Square, EC1M 6AN.—A Carthusian monastery from 1371–1537, when it came into the possession of Sir Edward (later first Lord) North, who sold it in 1565 to the fourth Duke of Norfolk. After Norfolk's execution in 1572 following the Ridolfi Plot (hatched at Charterhouse), it was eventually granted by Queen Elizabeth I in 1587 to Norfolk's second son, Thomas Howard, later Earl of Suffolk. In 1611 he sold it to Thomas Sutton, who endowed it as a hospital for aged men 'of gentle birth' and a school for poor scholars (removed to Godalming in 1872). The buildings are partly 15th but mainly 16th and 17th century. Parts of the building were damaged by bombing in 1941 but have been largely restored and now accommodate some 30 pensioners. Roger Williams, founder and governor of Rhode Island, was a scholar of the foundation. Among other famous pupils were John Wesley, Lord Baden-Powell, the poets and writers Crashaw, Lovelace and Thackeray, and more recently Lord Beveridge. Visitors are shown round on Wednesdays at 2.15 (April–July). Admission £1·50.
Master, E. E. Harrison, FSA.
Registrar and Clerk to the Governors, Lt.-Col. I. Macdonald.

Chelsea Physic Garden, 66 Royal Hospital Road, SW3 4HS.—A garden of general botanical research, maintaining a wide range of rare and unusual plants. The garden was established in 1673 by the Society of Apothecaries. Open on Wed. and Sun. p.m. during summer months. All enquiries to the Curator at above address.

City Business Library (Corporation of London), 106 Fenchurch Street, EC3M 5JB. Open Mon.-Fri. 9.30-5.00. Public Information, tel: 071-480 7638.

College of Arms or Heralds' College, Queen Victoria Street, EC4V 4BT.—Her Majesty's Officers of Arms (Kings, Heralds and Pursuivants of Arms) were first incorporated by Richard III, and granted Derby House on the site of the present College building by Philip and Mary. The building now in use dates from 1671–88. The powers vested by the Crown in the Earl Marshal (The Duke of Norfolk)

with regard to State ceremonial are largely exercised through the College, which is also the official repository of English pedigrees and all Arms granted to subjects of The Queen, except in Scotland and (since 1988) Canada. Enquiry may be made to the Officer on duty in the Public Office, Mon.-Fri. 10–4.

The Heralds Museum at the Tower of London (admission charge included in the Tower's own charge) aims to explain what heraldry is about and traces its development over the centuries to its application and use in modern times. Open April–Oct.

Commonwealth Institute, Kensington High Street, W8 6NQ.—A cultural and educational centre opened on November 6, 1962, by The Queen, replacing the former Imperial Institute opened in 1893 in Kensington. A distinctive feature of the building is its paraboloid copper-sheathed roof. The Institute contains, in 60,000 square feet arranged in three floors of circular galleries, a visual representation of the history, geography and ways of life of the Commonwealth countries and dependencies, as well as educational resource, information and conference centres, and a restaurant and craft/bookshop (*see* p. 343).
Open Mon.-Sat. 10–5, Sun. 2–5. Admission free. Closed Christmas Eve, Christmas Day, Boxing Day, New Year's Day, Good Friday and May Day.

Courtauld Institute Galleries, Somerset House, Strand, WC2R 0RN.—The galleries of the University of London contain the Lee collection and the Gambier–Parry collections (14th century to 18th century old masters); the important Courtauld collection of Impressionist and Post-Impressionist paintings; the Roger Fry collection and the Witt and Spooner collections (old master drawings and English water-colours). A major bequest, the Princes Gate collection of old master paintings and drawings, was received in July 1978, and the Alastair Hunter bequest of modern British works was received in 1983. The galleries moved to Somerset House from Woburn Square in June 1990. Open weekdays 10–6, Sun. 2–6. Admission £3, concessions £1·50.
Dir., D. L. A. Farr, CBE.

Design Museum, Butlers Wharf, SE1 2YD.—Comprising a study collection, temporary exhibitions, a review of new products, a library and a lecture theatre, the Museum attempts to increase the understanding of design by explaining how mass-produced consumer objects work and why they look as they do. Open Tues.-Sun. and Bank Hols. 11.30-6.30. Admission £3, concessions £2.

Downing Street.—Number 10 Downing Street, SW1, is the official town residence of the Prime Minister, No. 11 of the Chancellor of the Exchequer and No. 12 is the office of the Government Whips. The street was named after Sir George Downing, Bt., soldier and diplomatist, who was MP for Morpeth from 1660 to 1684.
Chequers, a Tudor mansion in the Chilterns, about three miles from Princes Risborough, was presented together with a maintenance endowment by Lord and Lady Lee of Fareham in 1917 to serve, from January 1, 1921, as a country residence for the Prime Minister of the day, the Chequers estate of 700 acres being added to the gift by Lord Lee in 1921. The mansion contains a famous collection of Cromwellian portraits and relics.

Dulwich, SE21.—Contains *Dulwich College* (founded by Edward Alleyn in 1619) and the *Dulwich Picture Gallery*, built by Sir John Soane to house the collection bequeathed by the artist Sir Francis Bourgeois. The gallery, which is England's oldest public art gallery, was damaged in the Second World

War but rebuilt with the aid of a grant from the Pilgrim Trust and reopened in 1953. Open daily (not Mon.); Sun., afternoons only. *Dulwich Village* retains many of the rural characteristics of the pre-suburban period.

Eltham, SE9.—Contains remains of 13th–15th century *Eltham Palace,* the birthplace of John of Eltham (1316), son of Edward II. The hall, built by Edward IV, has a hammer-beam roof of chestnut. In the churchyard of St John the Baptist is the tomb of Thomas Doggett, the comedian and founder of the Thames Watermen's championship (Doggett's Coat and Badge).

Ely Place, Holborn Circus, EC1.—Previously the site of the London house of the Bishop of Ely, Ely Place is a private street (built in 1773) whose affairs are administered by Commissioners under a special Act of Parliament. The 14th century chapel is now St Etheldreda's (RC) Church.

Fulham Palace, Bishop's Avenue, Fulham, SW6.—The courtyard is 16th century, the remainder 18th and 19th century. Former residence of the Bishop of London.

Geffrye Museum, Kingsland Road, E2 8EA.—The Museum is housed in a building erected originally as almshouses in 1713. The exhibits are displayed in a series of period rooms dating from 1600 to 1939, showing the development of decorative art and design. A display of woodworking tools focuses on furniture-making, and the museum has an interesting picture collection. Events and temporary exhibitions are held. Special arrangements exist for children visiting the Museum in school parties (which must be booked in advance) and in their leisure time. Open on Tues.–Sat. 10–5, Sun. 2–5. Closed on Christmas Eve, Christmas Day, Boxing Day, New Year's Day and Good Friday and on Mondays except Bank Holidays. Admission free.
Director, vacant.

George Inn, Borough High Street, SE1.—Near London Bridge Station. Given to the National Trust in 1937. Last galleried inn in London, built in 1677. Open during licensed hours.

Greenwich, SE10.—*Greenwich Hospital* (since 1873, the Royal Naval College) was built by Charles II, largely from designs by John Webb, and by Queen Anne and William III, from designs by Wren. It stands on the site of an ancient royal palace, and of the more recent *Palace of Placentia,* an enlarged edition of the palace, constructed by Humphrey, Duke of Gloucester (1391–1447), son of Henry IV. Henry VIII, Queen Mary I and Queen Elizabeth I were born in the Royal Palace (which reverted to the Crown in 1447) and King Edward VI died there. In the principal quadrangle is a marble statue of George II by Rysbreeck. (For National Maritime Museum, *see* Index.) *Painted Hall* and *Chapel,* open daily (not Thurs.) 2.30–5. Visitors are also admitted to Sunday Service in the Chapel at 11 a.m., summer and winter, except during College vacations. *Greenwich Park* (196¼ acres) was enclosed by Humphrey, Duke of Gloucester, and laid out by Charles II, from the designs of Le Nôtre. *The Queen's House,* begun in 1616, was designed for Anne of Denmark by Inigo Jones. Open Mon.–Sat. 10–6, Sun. 2–6. Adm. charge. On a hill in Greenwich Park is the former Royal Observatory (founded 1675). Part of its buildings at Greenwich have been taken over by the Maritime Museum and named *Flamstead House,* after John Flamsteed (1646–1719), first Astronomer Royal. Astronomical and navigational equipment is exhibited, and the time ball and zero meridian of longitude can also be seen.

The Parish church of Greenwich (*St Alfege*) was rebuilt by Hawksmoor (Wren's pupil) in 1728, and restored after severe damage during the Second World War. General Wolfe and Thomas Tallis are buried in the church. Henry VIII was christened in the former church. *Charlton House* was built in the early 17th century (1607–1612) for Adam Newton, tutor to Prince Henry, brother to Charles I. It is largely in the Jacobean style of architecture. *Cutty Sark,* the last of the famous tea clippers, which has been preserved as a memorial to ships and men of a past era, is fully restored and re-rigged, with a museum of sail on board. Open weekdays 11–5 (summer 11–6), Sundays and Boxing Day 2.30–5. The yacht *Gipsy Moth IV* in which Sir Francis Chichester sailed single-handed round the world, 1966–67, is preserved alongside the *Cutty Sark.*

Guildhall, Gresham Street, City, EC2.—Scene of civic government for the City for more than a thousand years. Built *c.*1440; façade built 1788–9; damaged in the Great Fire, 1666, and by incendiary bombs, 1940. The main hall and crypt (the most extensive medieval crypt in London) have been restored. Events in Guildhall include the annual election of Lord Mayor, election of Sheriffs, receptions in honour of Sovereigns and Heads of State, and the meetings of the Court of Common Council (*see* Corporation of London). Open weekdays and Sun. (May to Sept.) 10–5. Admission free.
Keeper of the Guildhall, J. H. Lucioni.

The *Guildhall Library* (reference) and the Library and Museum of the Clockmakers' Company are housed in new premises. Library open Mon.–Sat. 9.30–5, Museum open Mon.–Fri. 9.30–4.45. Admission free (entrance in Aldermanbury). The Library contains plans of London, 1570; Deed of Sale with Shakespeare's signature; first, second and fourth folios of Shakespeare's plays etc. (*See also* **City Business Library.**)

Hampton Court Palace, East Molesey, Surrey.—Sixteenth-century palace built by Cardinal Wolsey, with additions by Sir Christopher Wren for William and Mary. Beautiful gardens with maze and grape vine (planted in 1769). State Apartments and collection of pictures. Tennis Court, built by King Henry VIII in 1530. Collection of Mantegna paintings. Gardens open daily until dusk, Maze and Palace open mid March–mid Oct. daily 9.30–6 (Mon. 10.15–6), mid Oct.–March 9.30–4.30. Admission charge.

Honourable Artillery Company's Headquarters, City Road, EC1Y 2BQ.—The HAC received its charter of incorporation from Henry VIII in 1537, and has occupied its present ground since 1641. The Armoury House dates from 1735. The present castellated barracks date from 1860. Four of its members who emigrated in the 17th century, founded in 1638 the Ancient and Honorable Artillery Company of Massachusetts. The HAC is the senior regiment of the Territorial Army Volunteer Reserves, and maintains a headquarters, four squadrons, a gun troop, and two companies of the Home Service Force.
Chief Exec., Capt. G. C. Lloyd, CBE, RN.

Horniman Museum and Library, London Road, Forest Hill, SE23 3PQ.—The Museum was presented in 1901 to the London County Council by F. J. Horniman, MP. With the adjoining gardens, it is now an independent charitable trust. The Museum has three main departments: ethnography, musical instruments and natural history. In the ethnography department the large collections include exhibits illustrating man's progress in the arts and crafts from prehistoric times. The natural history department includes an aquarium. Reference library (not Mon.). Education Service (adults and schoolchildren). Free

concerts and lectures (autumn and spring). Special exhibitions. Open Mon.–Sat. 10.30–6, Sun. 2–6 (not Christmas). Admission free.
Director, D. M. Boston, OBE.

Horse Guards, Whitehall, SW1.—Archway and offices built about 1753. The mounting of the guard (Life Guards, or the Blues and Royals) at 11 a.m. (10 a.m. on Sundays) and the dismounted inspection at 4 p.m. are picturesque ceremonies. Only those on the Lord Chamberlain's list may drive through the gates and archway into *Horse Guard's Parade* (230,000 sq. ft.), where the Colour is 'trooped' on The Queen's Official Birthday.

The Houses of Parliament, Westminster, SW1.— An ordinance issued in the reign of Richard II stated that 'Parliament shall be holden or kepid wheresoever it pleaseth the King' and to the present day the Sovereign summons Parliament to meet and prescribes the time and place of meeting. The royal palace of Westminster, originally built by Edward the Confessor (Westminster Hall (*q.v.*) being added by William Rufus), was the normal place of Parliament from about 1340. St Stephen's Chapel was used from about 1550 for the meetings of the House of Commons, which had previously been held in the Chapter House or Refectory of Westminster Abbey. The House of Lords met in an apartment of the royal palace.

The fire of 1834 destroyed much of the palace and the present Houses of Parliament were erected on the site from the designs of Sir Charles Barry and Augustus Welby Pugin between 1840 and 1867. The Chamber of the House of Commons was destroyed by bombing in 1941 and a new Chamber designed by Sir Giles Gilbert Scott was used for the first time on Oct. 26, 1950.

The Victoria Tower of the House of Lords is about 330 ft. high, and when Parliament is sitting the Union Flag flies by day from its flagstaff. *The Clock Tower* of the House of Commons is about 320 ft. high and contains 'Big Ben', the hour bell said to be named after Sir Benjamin Hall, First Commissioner of Works when the original bell was cast in 1856. This bell, which weighed 16 tons 11 cwt., was found to be cracked in 1857. The present bell (13½ tons) is a recasting of the original and was first brought into use in July 1859. The dials of the clock are 23 ft. in diameter, the hands being 9 ft. and 14 ft. long (including balance piece). A light is displayed from the Clock Tower at night when Parliament is sitting.

For security reasons tours of the Houses of Parliament are available only to those who have made advance arrangements through a Member or Peer.

Admission to the Strangers' Gallery of the House of Lords is arranged by a Peer or by queue via St Stephen's Entrance. Admission to the Strangers' Gallery of the House of Commons is by Members' order (Members' orders should be sought several weeks in advance), or by queue via St Stephen's Entrance. Queues are usually shorter after 6 p.m., Mon.–Thurs. Overseas visitors may obtain cards of introduction from their Embassy or High Commission.

Inns of Court.—The *Inner* and *Middle Temple*, south of Fleet Street, EC4, and north of Victoria Embankment, to which the gardens extend, have occupied (since the early 14th century) the site of the buildings of the Order of Knights Templars. *Inner Temple Hall* (rebuilt in 1955 after bomb damage) is open Mon.–Fri. 10.30–11.30 and 3–4 on application to Treasurer's Office during law sittings. *Middle Temple Hall* (1562–70) is open when not in use, Mon.–Fri. 10–12 and 3–4. Closed on public holidays. In Middle Temple Gardens (not open to the public) Shakespeare

(*Henry VI*, Part I) places the incident which led to the 'Wars of the Roses' (1455–85).

Temple Church, EC4, was restored in 1958 after severe damage by bombing. The nave formed one of five remaining round churches in England (the others being at Cambridge, Northampton, Little Maplestead (Essex) and Ludlow Castle). Open weekdays 10–4.— Services: 8.30 and 11.15 a.m. except in August and September. *Master of the Temple*, Rev. Canon J. Robinson.

Lincoln's Inn, from Chancery Lane to Lincoln's Inn Fields, WC2, occupies the site of the palace of a former Bishop of Chichester and of a Black Friar monastery. Records show the Society as being in existence in 1422. The Hall and Library Buildings are of 1845, although the Library is first mentioned in 1474, the old Hall early 16th century and the Chapel was rebuilt c.1619–23. Halls open by appointment, Chapel and Gardens, Mon.–Fri. 12–2.30. Tours weekdays mid March–mid Sept. 9.30–11.30, £2. Chapel services Sun. 11.30 a.m. during Law Terms. *Lincoln's Inn Fields* (7 acres). The Square, laid out by Inigo Jones, contains many fine old houses with handsome interiors.

Gray's Inn, Holborn/Gray's Inn Road, WC1. Early 14th century. Hall (1556–60). Chapel (largely rebuilt after bomb damage in the Second World War). Services 11.15 a.m. (during Law Dining Terms only. Holy Communion 1st Sunday in every month except Aug.–Sept. Public welcome. Gardens open to the public Mon.–Fri. The Inn has been completely restored to its former beauty with gracious red brick buildings overlooking squares and gardens. Strong Elizabethan associations.

No other 'Inns' are active, but what remains of *Staple Inn* is worth visiting as a relic of Elizabethan London; though heavy damage was done by a flying bomb, it retains a picturesque gabled front on Holborn (opposite Gray's Inn Road). *Clement's Inn* (near St Clement Danes' Church), *Clifford's Inn*, Fleet Street and *Thavies Inn*, Holborn Circus, are all rebuilt. *Serjeant's Inn*, Fleet Street (damaged by bombing and another (demolished 1910) of the same name in Chancery Lane, were composed of Serjeants-at-Law, the last of whom died in 1922.

Jewish Museum, Woburn House, Tavistock Square, WC1H 0EP (Tel: 071-388 4525).—Opened in 1932, the Museum contains a rich collection of ceremonial art, portraits and antiquities, illustrating Jewish life, history and religion. Open Tues.–Thurs. and Sun. (and Fri. in summer) 10–4, Fri. in winter 10–12.45. Closed on public and Jewish holidays Group visits by arrangement with Secretary.

Kensington Palace, W8 4PX.—The original house was bought by William III in 1689 and enlarged by Christoper Wren. The State Apartments contain pictures and furniture from the royal collections. A suite of rooms devoted to the memory of Queen Victoria is also shown and there is a display of royal wedding dresses. The *Court Dress Collection* is also open, and includes three restored rooms: the Red Saloon, the Teck Saloon and the room where Queen Victoria is said to have been born in 1819. Both open weekdays 9–5.30, Sun. 11–5.30. Admission £3·75, concessions £2·80, £2·50.

Kenwood, NW3 7JR.—Nearly 200 acres forming the northern part of Hampstead Heath. Open air symphony concerts each summer. The Iveagh Bequest, in an Adam villa, includes valuable paintings and furniture. Recitals and poetry readings in the Orangery. House open daily, except Good Friday and Dec. 24, 25. Times vary seasonally. Admission free.

Kew, Surrey.—A favourite home of the early Hanoverian monarchs. Kew House, the residence of Frederick, Prince of Wales, and later of his son

George III, was pulled down in 1803, but the earlier Dutch House, now known as *Kew Palace*, survives. It was built in 1631 and acquired by George III as an annexe to Kew House in 1781. Open April–Sept., 11–5.30. The famous Kew Gardens (*see* Index) were originally laid out as a private garden for Kew House for George III's mother in 1759 and were much enlarged in the 19th century, notably by the inclusion of the grounds of the former Richmond Lodge. *Queen Charlotte's Cottage* is also open at the weekends.

Kneller Hall, Twickenham, TW2 7DU.—Royal Military School of Music. A band of up to 120 instrumentalists gives concerts in the grounds on Wednesdays in June and July, commencing at 8 p.m. Admission charge. Season tickets and party bookings available.

Lambeth Palace, SE1.—The official residence of the Archbishop of Canterbury, on the south bank of the Thames; the oldest part is 13th century, the house itself being early 19th century. For leave to visit the historical portions, applications should be made by letter to the Archbishop's Chaplain.

Livery Companies' Halls.—The principal Companies (*see* Index) have magnificent halls but admission to view them has generally to be arranged beforehand. The following are among the finest or more interesting. *Goldsmiths' Hall,* Foster Lane. The present hall was completed in 1835, and contains some magnificent rooms. *Fishmongers' Hall,* London Bridge (built 1831–3), restored after severe bomb damage, also contains fine rooms. *Apothecaries' Hall,* Black Friars Lane, was rebuilt in 1670 after the Great Fire, and has library, hall and kitchen which are good examples of the period. *Vintners' Hall,* Upper Thames Street, was also rebuilt after the Great Fire, and its hall has late 17th century panelling. The Watermen and Lightermen's Company is not, strictly speaking, a livery company, but its *Hall,* in St Mary-at-Hill, is a good example of a smaller 18th century building, with pilastered façade. It was completed in 1780. *Stationers' Hall,* in Stationers' Hall Court, behind Ludgate Hill, has a particularly fine carved screen; its façade dates from 1800. *Barbers' Hall,* Monkwell Street, with a Hall attributed to Inigo Jones, was completely destroyed by bombing, but has been rebuilt. The new hall was built some 30 ft. from the old site to enable one of the bastions and part of the wall of the Roman fort to remain exposed to view.

Lloyd's, Lime Street, EC3M 7HA.—Society of private underwriters which evolved during the 18th century from Lloyds Coffee House. Housed in the Royal Exchange for 150 years and in Leadenhall Street and Lime Street from 1928–1986. The present building was opened for business in May 1986, and houses the Lutine Bell. Underwriting is on four floors with a total area of 114,000 sq. ft. A visitors' gallery is open Mon.–Fri. for pre-booked groups, and incorporates an exhibition showing the history and operation of the insurance market at Lloyd's.

London Planetarium, Marylebone Road, NW1 5LR.—Open daily (except Christmas Day), star show and 'space trail' 10.20–5. Admission charge.

London Transport Museum, Covent Garden, WC2E 7BB.—Housed in the former Flower Market, the Museum contains a collection of buses, trams, trolley-buses, trains, working displays and London Transport paraphernalia. There is a research library and lecture theatre. Open daily 10–6 (except Dec. 24, 25, 26). Admission £3, concessions £1·50.

Lord's Cricket Ground, St John's Wood Road, NW8 8QN.—The headquarters (since 1814) of the Marylebone Cricket Club, the premier cricket club in England (founded 1787), Lord's is the scene of some of the principal matches of the season and Middlesex County headquarters. Real tennis court and squash courts in building behind members' pavilion.

The MCC Museum is open on match days (Mon.-Sat. 10.30–5, Sun. 1–5). Admission £1, concessions 50p. Conducted tours on most days throughout the year can be arranged in advance with the Tours Manager.

Madame Tussaud's, Marylebone Road NW1 5LR.—Waxwork exhibition. Open daily (except Christmas Day) 10–5.30. Admission charge.

Mansion House, City, EC4.—(Built 1739–53, reconstructed 1930–31.) The official residence of the Lord Mayor; the Egyptian Hall and Ballroom are the chief attractions. Group visits only by arrangement with the Principal's Assistant.

Markets.—The London markets (administered by the Corporation of the City of London) provide foodstuffs for 8,500,000 to 9,000,000 people. *Central Meat, Fish, Fruit, Vegetable, and Poultry Markets,* Smithfield (built 1866) (now moved) the largest meat market in the world and site of St Bartholomew's Fair from 9th to 19th century; *Leadenhall Market* (meat and poultry), built 1881, part recently demolished; *Billingsgate* (fish), Thames Street, built 1875, part recently demolished, a market site for over 1,000 years (moved to the Isle of Dogs in Jan. 1982); *Spitalfields,* E1 (vegetables, fruit, etc.), enlarged 1928 (moved to Leyton, May 1991); *London Fruit Exchange,* Brushfield Street, built by Corporation of London 1928–29; *Covent Garden* (vegetables, fruit, flowers, etc.), (now moved to Nine Elms) established under a charter of Charles II, in 1661; *Borough Market,* SE1 (vegetables, fruit, flowers, etc.).

Marlborough House, Pall Mall, SW1A 2AF.—Built by Wren for the first Duke of Marlborough and completed in 1711, the house finally reverted to the Crown in 1835. Prince Leopold lived there until 1831, and Queen Adelaide from 1837 until her death in 1849. In 1863 it became the London house of the Prince of Wales and was the London home of Queen Mary until her death in 1953. The Queen's Chapel, Marlborough Gate, begun in 1623 from the designs of Inigo Jones for the Infanta Maria of Spain, and completed for Queen Henrietta Maria, is open to the public for services on Sundays at 8.30 a.m. and 11.15 a.m. between Easter Day and end July (*see* **St James's Palace** for winter services in The Chapel Royal). In 1959 Marlborough House was given by The Queen as a centre for Commonwealth government conferences and it was opened as such in March 1962.

London Monument (commonly called The Monument), Monument Street, EC3.—Built from designs of Wren, 1671–77, to commemorate the Great Fire of London, which broke out in Pudding Lane on September 2, 1666. The fluted Doric column is 120 ft. high (the moulded cylinder above the balcony supporting a flaming vase of gilt bronze is 42 ft. in addition), and is based on a square plinth 40 ft. high, with fine carvings on the west face (making a total height of 202 ft.). Splendid views of London from gallery at top of column (311 steps). Open April–Sept., Mon.–Fri. 9–6, Sat. and Sun. 2–6. Oct.–March, Mon.–Sat. 9–4. Closed Christmas Day, Boxing Day and Good Friday. Admission charge.

Monuments (sculptor's name in parenthesis).—*Albert Memorial,* South Kensington; *Royal Air Force,* Victoria Embankment; *Beaconsfield,* Parliament Square; *Beatty, Jellicoe* and *Cunningham,* Trafalgar Square; *Belgian Gratitude* (Reginald Blomfield), Victoria Embankment; *Boadicea* (or Boudicca), Queen of the Iceni (Thomas Thornycroft), Westminster Bridge; *Brunel* (Marochetti), Victoria Embankment; *Burghers of Calais* (Rodin), Victoria Tower Gardens,

Westminster; *Burns*, Embankment Gardens; *Carlyle* (Boehm), Cheyne Walk, Chelsea; *Cavalry*, Hyde Park; *Edith Cavell* (Frampton), St Martin's Place; *Cenotaph* (Lutyens), Whitehall; *Charles I*, Trafalgar Square; *Charles II*, inside the Royal Exchange; *Churchill*, Parliament Square; *Cleopatra's Needle* (68½ ft. high, c.1500 BC, erected on the Thames Embankment in 1877–8; the Sphinxes are Victorian); *Clive*, Whitehall; *Captain Cook* (Brock), The Mall; *Crimean*, Broad Sanctuary; *Oliver Cromwell* (Thornycroft), outside Westminster Hall; *Lord Dowding* (Faith Winter), between Australia House and St Clement Danes, Strand; *Duke of Cambridge*, Whitehall; *Duke of York* (124 ft.), Carlton House Terrace; *Edward VII* (Mackennal), Waterloo Place; *Elizabeth I* (1586, oldest outdoor statue in London; from Ludgate), Fleet Street; *Eros* (Shaftesbury Memorial) (Gilbert), Piccadilly Circus; *Marechal Foch*, Grosvenor Gardens; *Charles James Fox*, Bloomsbury Square; *George III*, Cockspur Street; *George IV* (Chantrey), riding without stirrups, Trafalgar Square; *George V*, Old Palace Yard; *George VI*, Carlton Gardens; *Gladstone*, facing Australia House, Strand; *Guards'* (Crimea), Waterloo Place; (Great War), Horse Guards' Parade; *Haig* (Hardiman), Whitehall; *Irving* (Brock), N. side of National Portrait Gallery; *James II*, Trafalgar Square; *Samuel Johnson*, opposite St Clement Danes; *Kitchener*, Horse Guards' Parade; *Abraham Lincoln*, Parliament Square; *Milton*, St Giles, Cripplegate; *The Monument* (see above); *Mountbatten*, Foreign Office Green; *Nelson* (170 ft. 2 in.), Trafalgar Square, with Landseer's lions (cast from guns recovered from the wreck of the *Royal George*); *Florence Nightingale*, Waterloo Place; *Palmerston*, Parliament Square; *Peel*, Parliament Square; *Pitt* (Chantrey), Hanover Square; *Portal*, Embankment Gardens; *Prince Consort*, Holborn Circus; *Raleigh*, Whitehall; *Richard Coeur de Lion* (Marochetti), Old Palace Yard; *Roberts*, Horse Guards' Parade; *Franklin D. Roosevelt* (Reid Dick), Grosvenor Square; *Royal Artillery* (South Africa), The Mall; (Great War), Hyde Park Corner; *Captain Scott* (Lady Scott), Waterloo Place; *Shackleton*, Kensington Gore; *Shakespeare*, Leicester Square; *Smuts* (Epstein), Parliament Square; *Sullivan*, Victoria Embankment; *Trenchard*, Victoria Embankment; *Victoria Memorial*, in front of Buckingham Palace; *George Washington* (Houdon copy), Trafalgar Square; *Wellington*, Hyde Park Corner; *Wellington* (Chantrey) riding without stirrups, Royal Exchange; *John Wesley*, City Road; *William III*, St James's Square; *Wolseley*, Horse Guards' Parade.

Percival David Foundation of Chinese Art, 53 Gordon Square, WC1H 0PD.—Set up in 1950, the Foundation contains the collection of Chinese ceramics formed by Sir Percival David and his important library of books on Chinese art. To these was added a gift from the Hon. Mountstuart Elphinstone of part of his collection of Chinese monochrome porcelains. The Foundation is administered on behalf of the University of London by the School of Oriental and African Studies. Galleries, Mon.–Fri. 10.30–5. Closed weekends and Bank Holidays. Library available to ticket holders only; applications in writing to the *Curator*, Miss R. Scott.

Port of London.—The Port of London covers the tidal portion of the River Thames from Teddington to the seaward limit (Tongue light vessel), a distance of 150 km. The governing body is the Port of London Authority (PLA), whose head office is at International House, World Trade Centre, E1 9UN.

The enclosed dock at Tilbury is wholly-owned by the PLA and is 40 km below London Bridge. The docks perform every type of cargo-handling operation. Tilbury is principally used by vessels to and from Australia, North and South America, India,

Middle and Far East, Scandinavia, USSR and continental Europe.

Passenger vessels and cruise liners can be handled at moorings at Greenwich, Tower Bridge and Tilbury Passenger Landing Stage. The latter provides accommodation for liners at all states of the tide.

Prince Henry's Room, 17 Fleet Street, EC4.— Early 17th century timber-framed house containing fine room on first floor with panelling and moulded plaster ceiling. Includes an exhibition on Samuel Pepys and the London in which he lived. Open Mon.– Fri. 1.45–5, Sat 1.45–4.30. Closed Christmas Day, Good Friday and Bank Holidays. Admission free. Available for morning or evening lettings on application to The Town Clerk, Guildhall, EC2.

Richmond, Surrey.—Contains the red brick gateway of Richmond Palace (Henry VII, 1485–1509) and buildings of the Jacobean, Queen Anne, and early Georgian periods, including *White Lodge* in Richmond Park, the former home of Queen Mary's mother (the Duke of Windsor was born there, June 23, 1894), and now the home of the Royal Ballet Lower School. The *Star and Garter* Home for Disabled Soldiers, Sailors, and Airmen (the Women's Memorial of the Great War) was opened by Queen Mary in 1924. *Richmond Park* (2,469 acres) contains herds of fallow and red deer.

Roman London.—Although visible remains from this period are few, excavations carried out in the City on sites due for redevelopment often reveal Roman features. Sections of the city wall are the most striking remains to be seen of Roman *Londinium*, although even these are largely medieval because of the Roman wall being rebuilt during the medieval period. Sections may be seen near the White Tower in the Tower of London; at Tower Hill; at Coopers' Row; at All Hallows, London Wall, its vestry being built on the remains of a semi-circular Roman bastion; at St Alphage, London Wall, showing a striking succession of building repairs from the Roman until the late medieval period, and at St Giles, Cripplegate. Excavations in the Cripplegate area have revealed that a Roman fort was built there c. AD 100–120. It was later incorporated into the city wall when this was built c. AD 200.

The administrative centre of the Roman city was the great forum and basilica, more than 165 metres square, sections of which have been encountered during excavations in the area of Leadenhall, Gracechurch Street and Lombard Street. Excavations during the past few years have revealed Roman activity along the river. Traces of a massive riverside wall, built in the late Roman period, have been found and a succession of Roman timber quays have been excavated along Lower and Upper Thames Street, helping to prove that Roman London was a thriving commercial centre.

Other major buildings are the *Provincial Governor's Palace* in Cannon Street; remains of a bath-building, preserved in Lower Thames Street; and the *Temple of Mithras* in Walbrook. The fine sculptures from this temple are displayed in the Museum of London (*see* Index) where many other relics from the Roman City may be seen. There is also an Ordnance Survey map of Roman London.

Royal Albert Hall, Kensington Gore, SW7 2AP.— The elliptical hall, one of the largest in the world, was completed in 1871, and since 1941 has been the venue each summer for the Promenade Concerts founded in 1895 by Sir Henry Wood. Other events include pop concerts, sporting events, conferences and banquets for up to 2,500 people. *Chief Exec.*, P. Deuchar.

Royal Exchange, EC3V 3LS.—Founded by Sir Thomas Gresham, 1566, opened as 'The Bourse' and proclaimed 'The Royal Exchange' by Queen Elizabeth I, 1571, rebuilt 1667–69 and 1842–44. The building is occupied by Guardian Royal Exchange Assurance and by the London International Financial Futures Exchange. It is administered by the Gresham Committee.

Clerk, Mercers' Hall, Ironmonger Lane, EC2.

Royal Geographical Society, Kensington Gore, SW7 2AR.—Map room open to public, admission free. Advice for scientific expeditions abroad, by appointment only.

Royal Hospital, Chelsea, Royal Hospital Road, Chelsea, SW3 4SL. Founded by Charles II, in 1682, and built by Wren; opened in 1692 for old and disabled soldiers. Open Mon.–Sat. 10–12, daily 2–4. The extensive grounds include the former Ranelagh Gardens, and are the venue for the Chelsea Flower Show held each May by the Royal Horticultural Society.

Governor, General Sir Roland Guy, GCB, CBE, DSO.

Lieut.-Governor and Secretary, Maj.-Gen. A. L. Watson, CB.

Royal Opera House, Covent Garden, WC2E 7DD.—Home of The Royal Ballet (1931), The Royal Opera (1946) and the Birmingham Royal Ballet (1990), formerly Sadler's Wells Royal Ballet (1946), the Royal Opera House is the third theatre to be built on the site, opening May 15, 1858: the first was opened Dec. 7, 1732. The season of the resident companies runs mid Sept.–Aug.

General Director, J. Isaacs.

St James's Palace, in Pall Mall, SW1.—Built by Henry VIII; the Gatehouse and Presence Chamber remain; later alterations were made by Wren and Kent. The Chapel Royal is open for services on Sundays at 8.30 a.m. and 11.15 a.m. between the beginning of October and Good Friday (*see* **Marlborough House** for summer services in The Queen's Chapel). Representatives of Foreign Powers are still accredited 'to the Court of St James's'. *Clarence House* (1825) in the palace precinct is the home of The Queen Mother.

St Paul's Cathedral, EC4M 8AD.—Built 1675–1710, cost £747,660. The cross on the dome is 365 ft. above the ground level, the inner cupola 218 ft. above the floor. 'Great Paul' in the south-west tower weighs nearly 17 tons. Organ by Father Smith (enlarged by Willis and rebuilt by Mander) in a case carved by Grinling Gibbons (who also carved the choir stalls). The choir and high altar were restored in 1958 after war damage and the North Transept in 1962. The American War Memorial Chapel was consecrated in November, 1958. The chapel of the Most Excellent Order of the British Empire in the Crypt of the Cathedral was dedicated in 1960. Nave and transepts free. The following parts open weekdays 9–4.15. Admission: Ambulatory, £1; Crypt, Treasury and historical display, £2; whispering gallery, stone gallery, £2·50 (Children £1).—Services: Sundays, 8, 10.30, 11.30 and 3.15. Weekdays, 7.30, 8, 12.30 and 5.

Sherlock Holmes Museum, 239 Baker Street, NW1 6XE.—Looks at the 'life and times' of Sherlock Holmes as portrayed by Sir Arthur Conan Doyle. Run by the Sherlock Holmes International Society. Open Mon.–Fri., 10–6; weekend by appointment. £5, conc. £3.

Sir John Soane's Museum, 13 Lincoln's Inn Fields, WC2A 3BP.—The house and galleries, built 1812–24, are the work of the founder, Sir John Soane (1753–1837) and contain his collections, arranged as he left them, in pursuance of an Act procured by him in 1833. Exhibits include the Sarcophagus of Seti 1 (*c.*1290 BC), Classical vases and marbles, Hogarth's *Rake's Progress* and *Election* series, paintings by Canaletto, Reynolds, Turner, Lawrence, etc., and sculpture by Chantrey, Flaxman, etc. Soane's library of 8,000 volumes, and collection of 40,000 architectural drawings are available for study by appointment. Open Tues.–Sat. 10–5. Closed Bank Holidays. Tours must be booked in advance.

Curator, P. Thornton, FSA.

Somerset House, Strand, WC2, and Victoria Embankment, WC2.—The beautiful river façade (600 ft. long) was built in 1776–86 from the designs of Sir William Chambers; the eastern extension, which houses part of King's College, was built by Smirke in 1829. Somerset House was the property of Lord Protector Somerset, at whose attainder in 1552 the palace passed to the Crown, and it was a royal residence until 1692.

South Bank, SE1.—The arts complex on the south bank of the River Thames includes the South Bank Centre, owned and managed by the South Bank Board, and consisting of the 2,903-seat *Royal Festival Hall* (opened in 1951 for the Festival of Britain), a major venue for concert and ballet seasons, with the adjacent 1,056-seat *Queen Elizabeth Hall* and 368-seat *Purcell Room,* accommodating smaller-scale performances.

The *National Film Theatre* (opened 1958), administered by the British Film Institute, has three auditoria showing almost 2,000 films a year. The London Film Festival is held here every November.

The *National Theatre* opened in 1976 and stages classical, modern, new and neglected plays in its three auditoria: the 1,160-seat Olivier theatre (open stage), the 890-seat Lyttelton theatre (proscenium stage) and the experimental Cottesloe theatre (adaptable stage) which seats up to 400.

The *Museum of the Moving Image* charts the history of the moving image in cinema and television from the earliest devices through to disc technology. Open daily 10–6 (not Dec. 24–26). Admission £4·95, concessions £4·20 and £3·50.

Southwark Cathedral, SE1 9DA.—Mainly 13th century, but the nave is largely rebuilt. The tomb of John Gower (1330–1408) is between the Bunyan and Chaucer memorial windows in the north aisle; Shakespeare's effigy backed by a view of Southwark and the Globe Theatre in the south aisle; the altar screen (erected 1520) has been restored; the tomb of Bishop Andrews (died 1626) is near the screen. The Early English Lady Chapel (behind the choir), restored 1930, was the scene of the Consistory Courts of the reign of Mary (Gardiner and Bonner) and is still used as a Consistory Court. John Harvard, after whom Harvard University is named, was baptized here in 1607, and the Chapel by the North Choir Aisle is his memorial chapel. Open 8.30–6, admission free.—Services: Sundays, 11, 3. Weekdays, 12.30, 12.45, 5.30 (sung on Tuesdays and Fridays), Saturdays, 12 noon.

Stock Exchange, EC2.—The market floor of the new Stock Exchange building in London opened for trading in June, 1973. Since 'Big Bang' in 1986, the floor has been used solely by the London Traded Options Market. A tower, 331 feet high, and the new Market replace the complex of buildings started in 1801 on the same site. The new building is the headquarters of the Stock Exchange, following the amalgamation of all the Stock Exchanges in Great Britain and Ireland on March 25, 1973.

Information on how the Exchange works can be obtained from Public Information, The London Stock Exchange, Old Broad Street, EC2N 1HP (tel: 071-588 2355).

Thames Embankments.—The *Victoria Embankment*, on the north side (from Westminster to Blackfriars), was constructed by Sir Joseph William Bazalgette for the Metropolitan Board of Works, 1864–70 (the seats, of which the supports of some are a kneeling camel, laden with spicery, and of others a winged sphinx, were presented by the Grocers' Company and by Rt. Hon. W. H. Smith, MP, in 1874); the *Albert Embankment*, on the south side (from Westminster Bridge to Vauxhall), 1866–69; the *Chelsea Embankment*, 1871–74. The total cost exceeded £2,000,000. Bazalgette (1819–91) also inaugurated the London main drainage system, 1858–65. A medallion has been placed on a pier of the Victoria Embankment to commemorate the engineer of the Thames waterside improvements ('*Flumini vincula posuit*'). County Hall includes an embankment on the Surrey side.

Thames Flood Barrier.—Officially opened in May 1984, though first used in Feb. 1983, the barrier consists of ten rising sector gates which span 570 yards from bank to bank of the Thames at Woolwich Reach. When not in use the gates lie horizontally, allowing shipping to navigate the river normally; when the barrier is closed, the gates turn through 90 degrees to stand vertically more than 50 feet above the river bed. The barrier took eight years to complete and can be raised within about 30 minutes.

Thames Tunnels.—The *Rotherhithe Tunnel*, opened in 1908 at a cost of £1,506,914, connects Commercial Road, E14, with Lower Road, Rotherhithe; it is 1 mile 332 yards long, of which 474 yards are under the river. The first *Blackwall Tunnel* (vehicles) opened in 1897 at a cost of £1,323,663, connects East India Dock Road, Poplar, with Blackwall Lane, East Greenwich. A second tunnel (for southbound vehicles only) was opened in 1967 at a cost of £9,750,000 and the old tunnel was improved at a cost of £1,350,000 and made one-way northbound. Both tunnels are now for vehicles only. The relative lengths of the tunnels measured from East India Dock Road to the Gate House on the south side are 6,215 ft. (old tunnel) and 6,152 ft. *Greenwich Tunnel* (pedestrians only), opened in 1902 at a cost of £180,000, connects the Isle of Dogs, Poplar, with Greenwich. It is 406 yards long. The *Woolwich Tunnel* (pedestrians only), opened in 1912 at a cost of £86,000, connects North and South Woolwich below the passenger and vehicular ferry from North Woolwich Station, E16, to High Street, Woolwich, SE18. The tunnel is 552 yards long.

Tower Bridge Walkway and Museum, SE1 2UP.—Owned by the Bridge House Trust of the Corporation of London and open daily April–Oct. 10-6·30, Nov.–March 10-4·45. Admission £2·50, concessions £1. Attractions include exhibitions, video, the observation platform and walkway, engine rooms, working models and souvenir gift shop.

Tower of London, EC3.—Admission to a general view of the Tower, the White Tower, the History, Oriental, Ordnance and 18th–19th century Galleries, the Royal Armouries (National Museum of Arms and Armour), and the Wall Walk Phases I and II.

The White Tower is the oldest and central building of the Royal Palace and Fortress of the Tower of London. It was built at the order of William I and constructed by Gundulph, Bishop of Rochester, in the years 1078–98. The Inner Wall, with thirteen towers, was constructed by Henry III in the 12th century. The moat was extended and completed by Richard I and the wharf is first mentioned in 1228. The Outer Wall was completed in the reign of Edward I and now incorporates six towers and two bastions. The last Monarch to reside in the Tower of London was James I. The Crown Jewels came to the Tower

in the reign of Henry III. All coinage used in Great Britain was minted in the Outer Ward of the Tower of London until 1810 when the Royal Mint was formed. The Tower of London has had a military garrison since 1078. The Chapel Royal of St John the Evangelist, within the White Tower (1080–1088) is the oldest Norman church in London. The chapel of St Peter ad Vincula was built in the early 16th century.

Open weekdays March–Oct., 9.30–6, Nov.–Feb., 9.30–5; Sundays, March–Oct., 2–6. Tower closed Christmas Eve, Christmas Day, Boxing Day, New Year's Day and Good Friday. On Sundays throughout the year (except August) the public is admitted to Holy Communion, 9.15 a.m. and Morning Service, 11 a.m. Admission £6 (reduced rate when Jewel House closed for cleaning in February); various concessions.

Constable, Field Marshal Sir John Stanier, GCB, MBE.
Lieutenant, Lt.-Gen. Sir Derek Boorman, KCB.
Resident Governor and Keeper of the Jewel House, Maj.-Gen. C. Tyler, CB.
Master of the Armouries, G. Wilson.
Chaplain at the Chapel Royal of St Peter ad Vincula, Rev. N. A. Hood.

Waltham Abbey (or Waltham Holy Cross), Essex.—The Abbey ruins, 'Harold's' Bridge (14th century), the nave of the former cruciform Abbey Church c.1120 and the traditional burial place of King Harold II (1066), and a Guild Chapel of Edward II, with crypt below, which houses a visitors centre with permanent exhibition. New evidence of four former churches on the site, and the shape of the east end of Harold's church, have been revealed in recent excavations. Lee Valley Regional Park Authority has a country centre in the Abbey grounds. At Waltham Cross, one mile from the Abbey, is one of the crosses (partly restored) erected by Edward I to mark a resting place of the corpse of Queen Eleanor on its way to Westminster Abbey. (Ten crosses were erected, but only those at Geddington, Northampton and Waltham survive; 'Charing' Cross originally stood near the spot now occupied by the statue of Charles I at Whitehall.)

Wellington Museum, Apsley House, 149 Piccadilly, at Hyde Park Corner, W1.—Known as 'No. 1 London', Apsley House was designed by Robert Adam for Lord Bathurst, the first Baron Apsley, and built 1771–78. It was bought in 1817 by the Duke of Wellington, who in 1828–29 employed Benjamin Wyatt to enlarge it, face it with Bath stone and add the Corinthian portico. The museum contains many fine paintings, sculptures, services of porcelain and silver plate and personal relics of the 1st Duke of Wellington (1769–1852). The House was given to the nation by the 7th Duke and was first opened to the public in 1952, under the administration of the Victoria and Albert Museum. Open daily 11–5. Closed Mon., Christmas Eve, Christmas Day, Boxing Day and New Year's Day. Admission £2, concessions £1.

Westminster Abbey, SW1.—Built 1050–1745. Chapel of Henry VII, Chapter House and Cloisters; King Edward the Confessor's shrine, AD 1269, tombs of kings and queens (Henry III, Edward I, Edward III, Henry V, Mary Queen of Scots, Elizabeth I), and many other monuments and objects of interest, including the grave of 'The Unknown Warrior' and Poets' Corner. The Coronation Chair encloses the 'Stone of Scone', which was removed from Scotland by Edward I in 1296. Open on weekdays 9.20–6 (9.20–7.45 Wed.). Admission to the Royal Chapels, Poets' Corner, Quire and Statesmen's Aisle £3, concessions £1·50/60p. Last admission Mon.–Fri. 4 p.m., Sat. 5 p.m. Wed. 6–8 p.m. free. Nave open on Sundays between services.—Services: Sundays, 8, 10, 11.15, 3, 6.30 (generally preceded by an organ recital). Monday–Friday, 7.30, 8, 12.30, 5. Saturdays, 8, 9.20, 3.

Westminster Cathedral, Ashley Place, SW1P 1QW.—Built 1895–1903 from the designs of J. F. Bentley. The campanile is 283 feet high. Cathedral open 6.45 a.m.–8 p.m.—Masses: Sundays, 7, 8, 9, 10.30 (sung), 12, 5.30 and 7; Solemn Vespers and Benediction 3.30. Monday–Friday, 7, 8, 8.30, 9, 10.30, 12.30, 1.05 and 5.30 (sung). Morning Prayer 7.40, Vespers 5. Saturdays 7, 8, 8.30, 9, 10.30 (sung), 12.30 and 6, Morning Prayer 7.40, Vespers 5.30. Holy days of obligation, Low Masses 7, 8, 8.30, 9, 10.30, 12.30, 1.05, 5.30 (sung) and 7.

Westminster Hall, SW1A 0AA.—The only part of the old Palace of Westminster to survive the fire of 1834, Westminster Hall is adjacent to and incorporated in the Houses of Parliament. Westminster Hall was built by William Rufus from 1097–99 and altered by Richard II, 1394–99. It is about 240 ft. long, 68 ft. wide and 92 ft. high; the hammerbeam roof of carved oak dates from 1396–98. The Hall was the scene of the trial of Charles I. Westminster Hall is included on the route followed by those who have arranged a visit to the Houses of Parliament with their MP.

Whitechapel Art Gallery, Whitechapel High Street, E1 7QX.—Opened in 1901; administered by a charitable trust. There is no permanent collection; temporary exhibitions, mainly of modern art, are presented, and community and educational projects are run. Open Tues.–Sun. 11–5; Wed. 11–8.

Wimbledon Lawn Tennis Museum, SW19 5AE.—Exhibits include fashion, trophies, replicas and memorabilia representing the history of lawn tennis. A theatre shows films of great matches. Open Tues.–Sat. 11–5, Sun. 2–5. Admission £1·50, concessions £1/75p.

Windsor Castle (begun by William the Conqueror, AD 1066–87).—The Castle precincts are open daily. Admission free. The State Apartments of Windsor Castle are open throughout the year unless The Queen is in residence. Admission charge. *Queen Mary's Dolls' House* and the *Exhibition of The Queen's Presents and Royal Carriages* can be seen on the same days as the State Apartments; admission charge. When the State Apartments are closed, the other exhibitions remain open to the public. The *Albert Memorial Chapel* is open throughout the year (closed on Sundays). Admission free. A fee is charged to visit *St George's Chapel.*

The *Royal Mausoleum,* Frogmore Gardens, Home Park, is open annually on two days in early May in conjunction with the opening of Frogmore Gardens in aid of the National Gardens Scheme. Also open on the Wednesday nearest to May 24 (Queen Victoria's birthday). Admission free.

Zoological Gardens, Regent's Park, NW1.—(Opened in 1828). Open daily (except Christmas Day) March–Oct. 9–6 or dusk (Bank Holidays and associated Suns. Easter–Aug. and Suns. July 12–Sept. 13, 9–7). Oct.–March opens 10. Admission £5·30, various concessions. Aquarium and Children's Zoo free.

[London Tourism Board and Convention Bureau.—Tourist Information Centre, Victoria Station Forecourt, SW1V 1JU. (071–730 3488).]

PARKS, SPACES AND GARDENS

The principal parks and open spaces in the Metropolitan area are maintained as under:—

By the Crown

BUSHY PARK (1,099 acres).—Adjoining Hampton Court, contains an avenue of horse-chestnuts enclosed in a fourfold avenue of limes planted by William III. 'Chestnut Sunday' (when the trees are in full bloom with their 'candles') is usually about May 1 to 15.

GREEN PARK (49 acres), W1.—Between Piccadilly and St James's Park with Constitution Hill, leading to Hyde Park Corner.

GREENWICH PARK (196½ acres), SE10.

HAMPTON COURT GARDENS (54 acres).

HAMPTON COURT GREEN (17 acres).

HAMPTON COURT PARK (622 acres).

HYDE PARK (341 acres).—From Park Lane, W1, to Kensington Gardens, W2, containing the Serpentine. Fine gateway at Hyde Park Corner, with Apsley House, the Achilles Statue, Rotten Row and the Ladies' Mile. To the north-east is the Marble Arch, originally erected by George IV at the entrance to Buckingham Palace and re-erected in the present position in 1851.

KENSINGTON GARDENS (275 acres), W2.—From the western boundary of Hyde Park to Kensington Palace, containing the Albert Memorial.

KEW, ROYAL BOTANIC GARDENS *see* p. 357.

REGENT'S PARK and PRIMROSE HILL (464 acres), NW1.—From Marylebone Road to Primrose Hill surrounded by the Outer Circle and divided by the Broad Walk leading to the Zoological Gardens.

RICHMOND PARK (2,469 acres).

ST JAMES'S PARK (93 acres), SW1.—From Whitehall to Buckingham Palace. Ornamental lake of 12 acres. The original suspension bridge built in 1857 was replaced in 1957. The Mall leads from the Admiralty Arch to the Queen Victoria Memorial and Buckingham Palace, Birdcage Walk from Storey's Gate, past Wellington Barracks, to Buckingham Palace.

By the Corporation of London

ASHTEAD COMMON, Surrey (500 acres).

BURNHAM BEECHES and FLEET WOOD, Bucks. (540 acres).—Purchased by the Corporation for the benefit of the public in 1880, Fleet Wood (65 acres) being presented in 1921.

COULSDON COMMON, Surrey (133 acres).

EPPING FOREST (6,000 acres).—Purchased by the Corporation and thrown open to the public in 1882. The present forest is 12 miles long by 1 to 2 miles wide, about one-tenth of its original area.

FARTHING DOWN, Surrey (121 acres).

HAMPSTEAD HEATH (789 acres), NW3.—Including Golders Hill (36 acres) and Parliament Hill (271 acres), this was transferred to the Corporation on April 1, 1989.

HIGHGATE WOOD (70 acres).

KENLEY COMMON, Surrey (138 acres).

QUEEN'S PARK, Kilburn (30 acres).

RIDDLESDOWN, Surrey (90 acres).

SPRING PARK, West Wickham (51 acres).

WEST HAM PARK (77 acres).

WEST WICKHAM COMMON, Kent (25 acres).

WOODSEDON AND WARLIES PARK ESTATE, Waltham Abbey (740 acres).

Also smaller open spaces within the City of London, including FINSBURY CIRCUS GARDENS.

THE PRINCIPALITY OF WALES

Position and extent.—The Principality of Wales (*Cymru*) occupies the extreme west of the central southern portion of the island of Great Britain, with a total area of 8,018 sq. miles (20,768 sq. km): land 7,968 sq. miles (20,638 sq. km); inland water 50 sq. miles (130 sq. km). It is bounded on the north by the Irish Sea, on the south by the Bristol Channel, on the east by the English counties of Cheshire, Shropshire, Hereford and Worcester, and Gloucestershire, and on the west by St George's Channel. Across the Menai Straits is the Welsh island of *Ynys Môn* (Anglesey) (276 sq. miles), communication with which is facilitated by the Menai Suspension Bridge (1,000 ft. long) built by Telford in 1826, and by the tubular railway bridge (1,100 ft. long) built by Stephenson in 1850. Holyhead harbour, on Holy Isle (NW of Anglesey), provides accommodation for ferry services to Dublin (70 miles).

Population.—The population at the Census of 1981 was 2,791,851 (males 1,352,639; females 1,439,212). The preliminary report of the 1991 census put the population at 2,798,500. The average density of population in 1981 was 343 per square mile.

Relief.—Wales is a country of extensive tracts of high plateau and shorter stretches of mountain ranges deeply dissected by river valleys. Lower-lying ground is largely confined to the coastal belt and the lower parts of the valleys. The highest mountains are those of Snowdonia in the north-west (*Snowdon*, 3,559 ft), Berwyn (*Aran Fawddwy*, 2,971 ft), Cader Idris (*Pen y Gadair*, 2,928 ft), Dyfed (*Plynlimon*, 2,467 ft), and the Black Mountain, Brecon Beacons and Black Forest ranges in the south-east (*Carmarthen Van*, 2,630 ft, *Pen y Fan*, 2,906 ft, *Waun Fâch*, 2,660 ft).

Hydrography.—The principal river rising in Wales is the *Severn* (*see* p. 575), which flows from the slopes of Plynlimon to the English border. The *Wye* (130 miles) also rises in the slopes of Plynlimon. The *Usk* (56 miles) flows into the Bristol Channel, through Gwent. The *Dee* (70 miles) rises in Bala Lake and flows through the Vale of Llangollen, where an aqueduct (built by Telford in 1805) carries the Pontcysyllte branch of the Shropshire Union Canal across the valley. The estuary of the Dee is the navigable portion, 14 miles in length and about five miles in breadth, and the tide rushes in with dangerous speed over the 'Sands of Dee'. The *Towy* (68 miles), *Teifi* (50 miles), *Taff* (40 miles), *Dovey* (30 miles), *Taf* (25 miles) and *Conway* (24 miles), the last named broad and navigable, are wholly Welsh rivers.

The largest natural lake in Wales is *Bala* (Llyn Tegid) in Gwynedd, nearly four miles long and about one mile wide; *Lake Vyrnwy* is an artificial reservoir, about the size of Bala, and forms the water supply of Liverpool; and Birmingham is supplied from a chain of reservoirs in the Elan and Claerwen valleys.

Welsh language.—According to the 1981 Census results, the percentage of persons of three years and over able to speak Welsh was:

Clwyd	18·7	Powys	20·2
Dyfed	46·3	S. Glamorgan	5·8
Gwent	2·5	W. Glamorgan	16·4
Gwynedd	61·2		
Mid Glamorgan	8·4	**Wales**	18·9

The 1981 figure represents a slight decline from 20·8 per cent in 1971 (1961, 26 per cent; 1951, 28·9 per cent).

Flag.—A red dragon on a green and white field (*per fess argent and vert a dragon passant gules*). The flag was augmented in 1953 by a royal badge on a shield encircled with a riband bearing the words *Ddraig Goch Ddyry Cychwyn* and imperially crowned. Only the unaugmented flag is flown on Government offices in Wales and, where appropriate, in London. Both flags continue to be used elsewhere.

EARLY HISTORY

Celts and Romans.—The earliest inhabitants of whom there is any record appear to have been subdued or exterminated by the Goidels (a people of Celtic race) in the Bronze Age, and a further invasion of Celtic Brythons and Belgae followed in the ensuing Iron Age. The Roman conquest of southern Britain and Wales was for some time successfully opposed by Caratacus (Caractacus or Caradog), chieftain of the Catuvellauni and son of Cunobelinus (Cymbeline). South-east Wales was subjugated and the legionary fortress at Caerleon-on-Usk established by about AD 75–77: the conquest of Wales was completed by Agricola about AD 78. Communications were opened up by the construction of military roads from Chester to Caerleon-on-Usk and Caerwent, and from Chester to Conwy (and thence to Carmarthen and Neath). Christianity was introduced during the Roman occupation, in the fourth century.

The Anglo-Saxon attacks.—The Anglo-Saxon invaders of southern Britain drove the Celts into the mountain stronghold of Wales, and into Strathclyde (Cumberland and SW Scotland) and Cornwall, giving them the name of *Waelisc*, or Welsh (= foreign). The West Saxons' victory of Deorham (AD 577) isolated Wales from Cornwall and the battle of Chester (AD 613) cut off communication with Strathclyde and northern Britain. In the eighth century the boundaries of the Welsh were further restricted by the annexations of Offa, King of Mercia, and counter-attacks were largely prevented by the construction of an artificial boundary from the Dee to the Wye (Offa's Dyke). In the ninth century Rhodri Mawr (844–78) united the country and successfully resisted further incursions of the Saxons by land and raids of Norse and Danish pirates by sea, but at his death his three provinces of Gwynedd (N.), Powys (Mid.) and Deheubarth (S.) were divided among his three sons—Anarawd, Mervyn and Cadell. Cadell's son Hywel Dda ruled a large part of Wales and codified its laws but the provinces were not united again until the rule of Llewelyn ap Seisyllt (husband of the heiress of Gwynedd) from 1018 to 1023.

The Norman Conquest.—After the Norman conquest of England, William I created Palatine counties along the Welsh frontier, and the Norman barons began to make encroachments into Welsh territory. The Welsh princes recovered many of their losses, however, during the civil wars of Stephen's reign and in the early 13th century Owen Gruffydd, prince of Gwynedd, was the dominant figure in Wales. Under Llywelyn ap Iorwerth (1194–1240) the Welsh united in powerful resistance to English incursions and Llywelyn's privileges and *de facto* independence were recognized in Magna Carta. His grandson Llywelyn ap Gruffydd, was the last native prince; he was killed in 1282 during hostilities between the Welsh and English, allowing Edward I of England to establish his authority over the country. On February 7, 1301, Edward of Caernarvon, son of Edward I was created Prince of Wales, a title which has subsequently been borne by the eldest son of the sovereign.

Strong Welsh national feeling continued, expressed in the early 15th century in the rising led by Owain Glyndŵr, but the situation was altered by the accession to the English throne in 1485 of Henry VII of the Welsh House of Tudor. Wales was politically assimilated to England under the Act of Union of 1535, which extended English laws to the Principality and gave it parliamentary representation for the first time.

Eisteddfod.—The Welsh are a distinct nation, with a language and literature of their own, and the national bardic festival (Eisteddfod), instituted by Prince Rhys ap Griffith in 1176, is still held annually (for date, *see* p. 10). These *Eisteddfodau* (sessions) form part of the *Gorsedd* (assembly), which is believed to date from the time of Prydian, a ruling prince in an age many centuries before the Christian era.

LORD LIEUTENANTS AND HIGH SHERIFFS

County	Lord Lieutenant	High Sheriff, 1991–92
Clwyd...................	Sir William Gladstone, Bt.	Capt. P. Davies-Cooke
Dyfed	D. C. Mansel Lewis	Sir Geraint Evans, Kt, CBE
Gwent	R. Hanbury-Tenison	A. T. Beverley-Jones
Gwynedd	R. E. Meuric Rees, CBE	Capt. R. G. Lewis-Jones
Mid Glamorgan	M. A. McLaggan	Lt.-Col. D. Cox, LVO, MBE
Powys...................	M. L. Bourdillon	The Hon. Mrs E. S. J. Legge-Bourke
South Glamorgan	Capt. N. Lloyd-Edwards	M. J. Clay
West Glamorgan	Lt.-Col. Sir Michael Llewellyn, Bt.	Dr E. Roberts

WELSH COUNTY COUNCILS

AREAS AND POPULATIONS

County Council	Administrative Headquarters	Area (*hectares*)	Population Census 1991p	Total demand upon collection fund 1991 £
Clwyd............	Shire Hall, Mold	243,015	401,900	71,302,000
Dyfed	County Hall, Carmarthen	576,575	341,600	53,225,005
Gwent	County Hall, Cwmbran	137,652	432,300	64,720,105
Gwynedd	County Offices, Caernarfon	386,331	238,600	35,986,848
Mid Glamorgan ...	County Hall, Cathays Park, Cardiff	101,749	526,500	79,543,000
Powys............	County Hall, Llandrindod Wells	507,716	116,500	17,079,000
South Glamorgan .	County Hall, Atlantic Wharf, Cardiff	41,622	383,300	58,897,000
West Glamorgan ..	County Hall, Swansea	81,960	357,800	57,480,000

p preliminary.

COUNTY OFFICIALS AND CHAIRMEN

County Council	Chief Executive *County Clerk	County Treasurer	Chairman of County Council
Clwyd............	M. H. Phillips, CBE	A. Dalby	R. W. Squire
Dyfed	W. J. Phillips	H. Morse	D. G. E. Davies
Gwent	M. J. Perry	J. P. Walsh	H. W. Herbert
Gwynedd	H. V. Thomas	T. D. Heald	G. A. Williams
Mid Glamorgan ...	D. H. Thomas*	L. D. James	L. J. Rees
Powys............	A. J. Barnish	A. J. Barnish	A. Smith
South Glamorgan .	M. Boyce	R. G. Tettenborn	Rev. R. H. Morgan
West Glamorgan ..	A. G. Corless	S. G. Dunster	B. T. G. Ludlam

WELSH DISTRICT COUNCILS

Those accorded City Status are shown in Small Capitals; those with Borough Status are distinguished by having § prefixed.

District	Population Census 1991p	Community charge per head 1991 £	Chief Executive	Chairman 1991–92 (a) Mayor (b) Lord Mayor
§Aberconwy, Gwynedd	54,100	117·70	J. E. Davies	(a) J. Knowles
Alyn and Deeside, Clwyd	71,700	110·85	W. E. Rogers	R. K. Evans
§Arfon, Gwynedd	54,600	99·90	D. L. Jones	(a) J. F. Thomas
§Blaenau Gwent, Gwent	74,700	71·99	R. Leadbeter	(a) D. Davies
§Brecknock, Powys	41,300	102·74	R. O. Doylend	(a) E. Meredith
Cardiff, South Glamorgan	272,600	139·37	R. E. Paine	(b) J. Sainsbury
Carmarthen, Dyfed	54,800	216·00	R. R. Morgan	D. C. Phillips
Ceredigion, Dyfed	63,600	62·40	D. Morgan	C. Jones
§Colwyn, Clwyd	54,900	137·00	W. N. Breeze	(a) Mrs B. L. Taylor
§Cynon Valley, Mid Glamorgan	63,600	252·00	T. B. Roberts	(a) D. T. Hancock
§Delyn, Clwyd	66,200	264·52	P. J. McGreevy	(a) M. Doran
§Dinefwr, Dyfed	38,000	48·45	E. W. Harries	(a) H. G. Jones
Dwyfor, Gwynedd	28,600	252·90	E. M. Royles	T. J. Williams
Glyndŵr, Clwyd	41,500	96·55	J. H. Parry	J. D. Williams
§Islwyn, Gwent	64,900	81·00	B. Bird	(a) A. J. Dance
§Llanelli, Dyfed	73,500	115·26	D. B. Parry-Jones	(a) H. J. Evans
§Lliw Valley, West Glamorgan	61,700	66·46	J. C. Howells	(a) W. J. Evans
Meirionnydd, Gwynedd	33,400	96·65	G. W. Hughes	D. Roberts
§Merthyr Tydfil, Mid Glamorgan	59,300	101·15	R. V. Morris	(a) D. R. Tovey
§Monmouth, Gwent	75,000	108·66	G. Cummings	(a) R. L. Norris
Montgomeryshire, Powys	52,000	222·30	N. J. Bardsley	D. Wyn Jones
§Neath, West Glamorgan	64,100	62·33	S. Penny	(a) W. R. Williams
§Newport, Gwent	129,900	135·00	C. Tapp	(a) H. Williams
§Ogwr, Mid Glamorgan	130,500	73·63	J. G. Cole	(a) C. E. Evans
§Port Talbot, West Glamorgan	49,900	257·00	I. K. Lewis	(a) K. V. B. Johnson
Preseli Pembrokeshire, Dyfed	69,600	80·51	I. W. R. David	W. S. Rees
Radnor, Powys	23,200	92·30	G. C. Read	J. L. Davies
§Rhondda, Mid Glamorgan	76,300	248·00	G. Evans	(a) J. D. May
§Rhuddlan, Clwyd	54,000	139·86	E. O. Lake	(a) F. Selby
Rhymney Valley, Mid Glamorgan	101,400	93·87	P. A. Bennett	M. Thomas
South Pembrokeshire, Dyfed	42,100	73·43	G. H. James	Mrs R. R. Hayes
Swansea, West Glamorgan	182,100	135·00	A. K. B. Boatswain	(b) B. G. Owen
§Taff-Ely, Mid Glamorgan	95,400	46·14	D. Gethin	(a) I. G. Jenkins
§Torfaen, Gwent	88,200	258·00	M. B. Mehta	(a) D. J. Rex
§Vale of Glamorgan, South Glamorgan	110,700	245·91	J. R. Gau	(a) H. J. Holmes
§Wrexham Maelor, Clwyd	113,600	101·30	R. J. Dutton	(a) C. Williams
§Ynys Môn (Isle of Anglesey), Gwynedd	67,800	99·00	E. L. Gibson	(a) G. O. Parry

p preliminary.

PRINCIPAL WELSH CITIES

CARDIFF

Cardiff (South Glamorgan), at the mouth of the Rivers Taff, Rhymney and Ely, is the capital city of Wales and one of Britain's major administrative, commercial and business centres. It has many industries, including steel and cigars, and is a flourishing port with a substantial and varied trade. There are many fine buildings in the civic centre started early this century, including the City Hall, the National Museum of Wales, University Buildings, Law Courts, Welsh Office, County Hall, Police Headquarters and the Temple of Peace and Health. Also in the city are Llandaff Cathedral, the Welsh National Folk Museum at St Fagans, Cardiff Castle, the New Theatre, the Sherman Theatre and the Cardiff College of Music and Drama. New buildings include St David's Hall, a 2,000-seat concert and conference hall, and the Welsh National Ice Rink.

SWANSEA

Swansea (*Abertawe*) is a city and a seaport of West Glamorgan. The Gower peninsula was brought within the City boundary under local government reform in 1974. The trade of the port includes coal, patent fuel, ores, and the import and export of oil. The municipal area is 60,511 acres.

The principal buildings are the Norman Castle (rebuilt *c.* 1330), the Royal Institution of South Wales, founded in 1835 (including Library), the University College at Singleton, and the Guildhall, containing the Brangwyn panels. New buildings include the Industrial and Maritime Museum, the new Maritime Quarter and Marina and the leisure centre. Swansea was chartered by the Earl of Warwick, *c.*1158–1184, and further charters were granted by King John, Henry III, Edward II, Edward III and James II, Cromwell (two) and the Marcher Lord William de Breos.

THE KINGDOM OF SCOTLAND

Position and extent.—The Kingdom of Scotland occupies the northern portion of the main island of Great Britain and includes the Inner and Outer Hebrides, and the Orkney, Shetland, and many other islands. The Kingdom lies between 60° 51′ 30″ and 54° 38′ N. latitude and between 1° 45′ 32″ and 6° 14′ W. longitude, its southern neighbour being the Kingdom of England, with the Atlantic Ocean on the north and west, and the North Sea on the east The greatest length of the mainland (Cape Wrath to the Mull of Galloway) is 274 miles, and the greatest breadth (Buchan Ness to Applecross) is 154 miles. The customary measurement of the island of Great Britain is from the site of John o' Groats house, near Duncansby Head, Caithness, to Land's End, Cornwall, a total distance of 603 miles in a straight line and (approximately) 900 by road. The total area of the Kingdom is 30,414 sq. miles (78,772 sq. km): land 29,761 sq. miles (77,080 sq. km); inland water 653 sq. miles (1,692 sq. km).

Population.—The population (1981 Census) was 5,130,735 (males 2,466,437; females 2,664,298). The preliminary report of the 1991 Census put the population at 4,957,289. The average density of the population in 1981 was 168 persons per square mile.

Relief.—There are three natural orographic divisions of Scotland. The southern uplands have their highest points in Merrick (2,766 ft), Rhinns of Kells (2,669 ft), and Cairnsmuir of Carsphairn (2,614 ft), in the west; and the Tweedsmuir Hills in the east Hartfell 2,651 ft, Dollar Law 2,682 ft, Broad Law 2,756 ft). The central lowlands, formed by the valleys of the Clyde, Forth and Tay, divide the southern uplands from the northern Highlands, which extend almost from the extreme north of the mainland to the central lowlands, and are divided into a northern and a southern system by the Great Glen. The Grampian Mountains, which entirely cover the southern Highland area, include in the west Ben Nevis (4,406 ft), the highest point in the British Isles, and in the east the Cairngorm Mountains (Cairn Gorm 4,084 ft, Braeriach 4,248 ft, Ben Macdui 4,296 ft). The north-western Highland area contains in the mountains of Wester and Easter Ross Carn Eige (3,880 ft) and Sgurr na Lapaich (3,775 ft).

Created, like the central lowlands, by a major geological fault, the Great Glen (60 miles long) runs between Inverness and Fort William, and contains Loch Ness, Loch Oich and Loch Lochy. These are linked to each other and to the north-east and south-west coasts of Scotland by the Caledonian Canal, providing a navigable passage between the Moray Firth and the Inner Hebrides.

Hydrography.—The western coast of Scotland is fragmented by peninsulas and islands, and indented by fjords (sea-lochs), the longest of which is Loch Fyne (42 miles long) in Argyll. Although the east coast tends to be less fractured and lower, there are several great drowned inlets (firths), e.g. Firth of Forth, Firth of Tay, Moray Firth, as well as the Firth of Clyde in the west.

The lochs are the principal hydrographic feature of the Kingdom. The largest in the Kingdom and in Great Britain is Loch Lomond (27 square miles), in the Grampian valleys; the longest and deepest is Loch Ness (24 miles long and 800 feet deep), in the Great Glen; and Lochs Shin (20 miles long) and Maree in the northern Highlands.

The longest river in Scotland is the Tay (117 miles/188 km), noted for its salmon. It flows into the North Sea, with Dundee on the estuary, which is spanned by the Tay Bridge (10,289 ft) opened in 1887 and the Tay Road Bridge (7,365 ft) opened in 1966. Other noted salmon rivers are the Dee (90 miles) which

flows into the North Sea at Aberdeen, and the Spey (110 miles), the swiftest flowing river in the British Isles, which flows into Moray Firth. The Tweed, which gave its name to the woollen cloth produced along its banks, marks in the lower stretches of its 96-mile course the border between Scotland and England.

The most important river commercially is the Clyde (106 miles), formed by the junction of the Daer and Portrail water, which flows through the city of Glasgow to the Firth of Clyde. During its course it passes over the picturesque Falls of Clyde, Bonnington Linn (30 ft), Corra Linn (84 ft), Dundaff Linn (10 ft) and Stonebyres Linn (80 ft), above and below Lanark. The Forth (66 miles), upon which stands Edinburgh, the capital, is spanned by the Forth (Railway) Bridge (1890), which is 5,330 feet long, and the Forth (Road) Bridge (1964), which has a total length of 6,156 feet (over water) and a single span of 3,000 feet.

The highest waterfall in Scotland, and the British Isles, is Eas a'Chùal Aluinn with a total height of 658 feet (200 m), which falls from Glas Bheinn in Sutherland. The Falls of Glomach, on a head-stream of the Elchaig in Wester Ross, have a drop of 370 feet.

Gaelic language.—According to the 1981 Census, 82,620 people, mainly in the Highlands and western coastal regions, were able to speak, read or write the Scottish form of Gaelic.

Flag.—The cross of St Andrew, the patron saint of Scotland (saltire argent in a field azure).

THE SCOTTISH ISLANDS

The Hebrides did not become part of the Kingdom of Scotland until 1266, when they were ceded to Alexander III by Magnus of Norway. Orkney and Shetland fell to the Scottish Crown as a pledge for the unpaid dowry of Margaret of Denmark, wife of James III, in 1468, the Danish claims to suzerainty being relinquished in 1590 when James VI married Anne of Denmark.

Orkney.—The Orkney Islands (total area 375½ sq. miles) lie about six miles north of the mainland, separated from it by the Pentland Firth. Of the 90 islands and islets (holms and skerries) in the group, about one-third are inhabited. The total population at the 1981 Census was 19,040; the 1981 populations of the islands shown here include those of smaller islands forming part of the same civil parish.

Mainland	14,299	Shapinsay	345
Eday	154	South Ronaldsay	1,188
Hoy and Graemsay	80	Stronsay	462
Papa Westray	94	Walls and Flotta	761
Rousay and Egilsay	264	Westray	741
Sanday and North Ronaldsay	652		

The islands are rich in Pictish and Scandinavian remains, the most notable being the Stone Age village of Skara Brae, the burial chamber of Maeshowe, the many brochs (Pictish towers) and St Magnus Cathedral. Scapa Flow, between the Mainland and Hoy, was the war station of the British Grand Fleet from 1914–19 and the scene of the scuttling of the surrendered German High Seas Fleet (June 21, 1919).

Most of the islands are low-lying and fertile, and farming (principally beef cattle) is the main industry. Flotta, to the south of Scapa Flow, is now the site of the oil terminal for the Piper, Claymore and Tartan fields in the North Sea.

Capital: Kirkwall (pop. 6,881) on Mainland.

Shetland.—The Shetland Islands (total area 551 sq. miles; population at the 1981 Census 27,271) lie about 50 miles north of the Orkneys, with Fair Isle about half way between the two groups. Out Stack, off Muckle Flugga, one mile north of Unst, is the most northerly part of the British Isles (60° 51' 30" N. lat.). There are over 100 islands, of which 16 are inhabited. Populations at the 1981 census were:

Mainland	22,184	Muckle Roe	101
Bressay	335	Out Skerries	79
East and West Burra,		Papa Stour	29
and Trondra	930	Unst	1,206
Fair Isle	69	Whalsay	1,026
Fetlar	102	Yell	1,168
Foula	39		

Shetland's many archaeological sites include Jarlshof, Mousa and Clickhimin, and its long connection with Scandinavia has resulted in a strong Norse influence on its place-names and dialect.

Industries include fishing, knitwear and farming. In addition to the fishing fleet there are fish processing factories, while the traditional handknitting of Fair Isle and Unst is supplemented now with machine knitted garments. Farming is mainly crofting, with sheep being raised on the moorland and hills of the islands. Latterly the islands have become an important centre of the North Sea oil industry, with pipelines from the Brent and Ninian fields running to the terminal at Sullom Voe, the largest of its kind in Europe. Lerwick is the main centre for supply services for offshore oil exploration and development.

Capital.—Lerwick (pop. 7,901) on Mainland.

The Hebrides.—Until the closing years of the 13th century the Hebrides included other Scottish islands in the Firth of Clyde, the peninsula of Kintyre (Argyllshire), the Isle of Man, and the (Irish) Isle of Rathlin. The origin of the name is stated to be the Greek *Eboudai*, latinized as *Hebudes* by Pliny, and corrupted to its present form. The Norwegian name *Sudreyjar* (Southern Islands) was latinized as *Sodorenses*, a name that survives in the Anglican bishopric of Sodor and Man.

There are over 500 islands and islets, of which about 100 are inhabited, though mountainous terrain and extensive peat bogs mean that only a fraction of the total area is under cultivation. Stone, Bronze and Iron Age settlement has left many remains, including those at Callanish on Lewis, and Norse colonization has influenced language, customs and place-names. Occupations include farming (mostly crofting and stock-raising), fishing and the manufacture of tweeds and other woollens. Tourism is also an important factor in the economy.

The **Inner Hebrides** lie off the west coast of Scotland and relatively close to the mainland. The largest and best-known is *Skye* (area 643 sq. miles; pop. 8,139; chief town, Portree), which contains the Cuillin Hills (*Sgurr Alasdair* 3,257 ft), the Red Hills (*Beinn na Caillich* 2,403 ft) as well as *Bla Bheinn* (3,046 ft) and *The Storr* (2,358 ft). Skye is also famous as the refuge of the Young Pretender in 1746. Other islands in the Highland Region include *Raasay* (pop. 182) *Rum*, *Eigg* and *Muck*. Islands in the Strathclyde Region include *Arran* (pop. 4,726) containing *Goat Fell* (2,868 ft); *Coll and Tiree* (pop. 933); *Colonsay and Oronsay* (pop. 137); *Islay* (area 235 sq. miles; pop. 3,997); *Jura* (area 160 sq. miles; pop. 239) with a range of hills culminating in the Paps of Jura (*Beinn-an-Oir*, 2,576 ft, and *Beinn Chaolais*, 2,477 ft); *Mull* (area 367 sq. miles; pop. 2,605; chief town Tobermory) containing *Ben More* (3,171 ft).

The **Outer Hebrides**, separated from the mainland by the Minch, now form the Western Isles Islands Council area (area 1,119 sq. miles; population at the 1981 Census 31,842). The main islands are *Lewis with Harris* (area 770 sq. miles, pop. 23,390), whose chief town, Stornoway (pop. 13,409), is the administrative headquarters; *North Uist* (pop. 1,454); *South Uist*

(pop. 2,223); *Benbecula* (pop. 1,988) and *Barra* (pop. 1,232). Other inhabited islands include *Bernera* (292) *Berneray* (134), *Eriskay* (219), *Grimsay* (206), *Scalpa* (461) and *Vatersay* (108).

EARLY HISTORY

Prehistoric Man.—The Picts, believed to be o non-Aryan origin, seem to have inhabited the whol of northern Britain and to have spread over the north of Ireland. Remains are most frequent ir Caithness and Sutherland and the Orkney Islands Celts arrived from Belgic Gaul during the latter par of the Bronze Age and in the early Iron Age, an except in the extreme north of the mainland and ir the islands, the civilization and speech of the peopl were definitely Celtic at the time of the Roma invasion of Britain.

The Roman Invasion.—In AD 79–80 Julius Agri cola extended the Roman conquests in Britain b advancing into *Caledonia* and building a line o fortifications across the isthmus between the Forth and Clyde, but after a victory at *Mons Graupius* h was recalled. Hadrian's Wall, mostly complete by A 130, marked the frontier until about AD 143 when the frontier moved north to the Forth–Clyde isthmus and was secured by the Antonine Wall. From abou AD 155 the Antonine Wall was damaged by frequen attacks and by the end of the second century the northern limit of Roman Britain had receded t Hadrian's Wall.

The Scots.—After the withdrawal (or absorption of the Roman garrison of Britain there were man years of tribal warfare between the Picts and Scots (the Gaelic tribe then dominant in Ireland), the Brythonic Waelisc (Welsh) of Strathclyde (south west Scotland and Cumberland), and the Anglo Saxons of Lothian. The Waelisc were isolated from their kinsmen in Wales by the victory of the Wes Saxons at Chester (613), and towards the close of the ninth century the Scots under Kenneth Macalpine became the dominant power in Caledonia. In the reign of Malcolm I (943–954) Strathclyde was brough into subjection, the English lowland kingdom (Loth ian) being conquered by Malcolm II (1005–1034) From the late 11th century until the middle of the 16th there were constant wars between Scotland and England, the outstanding figures in the struggle being William Wallace, who defeated the English a Stirling Bridge (1297) and Robert Bruce, who wor the victory of Bannockburn (1314). James IV and many of his nobles fell at the disastrous battle o Flodden (1513).

The Jacobite Revolts.—In 1603 James VI o Scotland succeeded Elizabeth I on the throne o England (his mother, Mary Queen of Scots, was the great-granddaughter of Henry VII), his successors reigning as Sovereigns of Great Britain, although political union of the two countries did not occur until 1707. After the abdication (by flight) in 1688 o James VII and II, the crown devolved upon William III (grandson of Charles I) and Mary (daughter o James VII and II). In 1689 Graham of Claverhouse roused the Highlands on behalf of James VII and II but died after a military success at Killiecrankie. After the death of Anne (second daughter of James VII and II) the throne devolved upon George I (great grandson of James VI and I). In 1715, armed risings on behalf of James Stuart (the Old Pretender) led to the indecisive battle of Sheriffmuir, but the Jacobite movement died down until 1745, when Charles Stuart (the Young Pretender) defeated the Royalist troops at Prestonpans and advanced to Derby in England (1746). From Derby, the adherents of 'James VIII and III' (the title claimed for his father by Charles Stuart) fell back on the defensive, and the movement was finally crushed at Culloden (April 16, 1746).

LORD LIEUTENANTS IN SCOTLAND

Region	Title	Name
Borders	Berwickshire	Maj.-Gen. Sir John Swinton, KCVO, OBE
	Roxburgh, Ettrick and Lauderdale	The Duke of Buccleuch and Queensberry, KT, VRD
	Tweeddale	Lt.-Col. A. M. Sprot of Haystoun, MC
Central	Clackmannan	The Earl of Mar and Kellie
	Stirling and Falkirk	Lt.-Col. J. Stirling of Garden, CBE, TD
Dumfries & Galloway	Dumfries	Capt. J. G. M. Home, TD
	The Stewartry of Kirkcudbright	Sir Michael A. R. Y. Herries, OBE, MC
	Wigtown	Maj. E. S. Orr Ewing
Fife	Fife	The Earl of Elgin and Kincardine, KT
Grampian	Aberdeenshire	Capt. C. A. Farquharson
	Banffshire	J. A. S. McPherson, CBE
	Kincardineshire	The Viscount of Arbuthnott, DSC, FRSE
	Morayshire	Capt. Sir Iain Tennant, KT
Highland	Caithness	The Viscount Thurso
	Inverness	Lt.-Cdr. L. R. D. Mackintosh of Mackintosh, OBE
	Nairn	The Earl of Leven and Melville
	Ross and Cromarty	Capt. R. W. K. Stirling of Fairburn, TD
	Sutherland	Maj.-Gen. D. Houston.
Lothian	East Lothian	Sir Hew Hamilton-Dalrymple, Bt., KCVO
	Midlothian	Sir John Dutton Clerk of Penicuik, Bt., CBE, VRD
	West Lothian	The Earl of Morton
Strathclyde	Argyll and Bute	The Marquess of Bute
	Ayr and Arran	Maj. R. Y. Henderson, TD
	Dunbartonshire	Brig. D. D. G. Hardie, TD
	Lanarkshire	Col. The Lord Clydesmuir, KT, CB, MBE, TD
	Renfrewshire	Maj. J. D. M. Crichton Maitland
Tayside	Angus	The Earl of Airlie, KT, GCVO, PC
	Perth and Kinross	Maj. Sir David Butter, KCVO, MC
Orkney	Orkney	Brig. M. G. Dennison
Shetland	Shetland	M. M. Shearer
Western Isles	Western Isles	The Earl Granville, MC

NOTE.—The Lord Provosts of the four city districts of Aberdeen, Dundee, Edinburgh and Glasgow are Lord Lieutenants for those districts *ex officio*.

PRECEDENCE IN SCOTLAND

THE SOVEREIGN.

The Prince Philip, Duke of Edinburgh.

The Lord High Commissioner to the General Assembly (while that Assembly is sitting).

The Duke of Rothesay (eldest son of the Sovereign).

The Sovereign's younger sons.

The Sovereign's cousins.

Lords Lieutenant of Counties, Lord Provosts of Counties of Cities, and Sheriffs Principal (successively—within their own localities and during holding of office).

Lord Chancellor of Great Britain.

Moderator of the General Assembly of the Church of Scotland.

The Prime Minister.

Keepers of the Great Seal and of the Privy Seal (successively—if Peers).

Hereditary Lord High Constable of Scotland.

Hereditary Master of the Household.

Dukes (successively) of England, Scotland, Great Britain and United Kingdom (including Ireland since date of Union).

Eldest sons of Dukes of the Blood Royal.

Marquesses, in same order as Dukes.

Dukes' eldest sons.

Earls, in order as Dukes.

Younger sons of Dukes of Blood Royal.

Marquesses' eldest sons.

Dukes' younger sons.

Keepers of the Great Seal and of the Privy Seal (successively if not Peers).

Lord Justice General.

Lord Clerk Register.

Lord Advocate.

Lord Justice Clerk.

Viscounts, in order as Dukes.

Earls' eldest sons.

Marquesses' younger sons.

Lord-Barons, in order as Dukes.

Viscounts' eldest sons.

Earls' younger sons.

Lord-Barons' eldest sons.

Knights of the Garter.

Privy Counsellors.

Senators of College of Justice (Lords of Session).

Viscounts' younger sons.

Lord-Barons' younger sons.

Sons of Life Peers.

Baronets.

Knights of the Thistle.

Knights Grand Cross, Grand Commander, and Knight Commanders, as in England.

Solicitor-General for Scotland.

Lord Lyon King of Arms.

Sheriffs Principal (except as shown in first column).

Knights Bachelor.

Sheriffs.

Companions of Orders, as in England.

Commanders of Royal Victorian and British Empire Orders.

Eldest sons of younger sons of Peers.

Companions of Distinguished Service Order.

Lieutenants of Royal Victorian Order.

Officers of British Empire Order.

Baronets' eldest sons.

Knights' eldest sons successively (from Garter to Bachelor).

Members, Royal Victorian Order.

Members, British Empire Order.

Baronets' younger sons.

Knights' younger sons.

Queen's Counsel.

Barons-feudal.

Esquires.

Gentlemen.

SCOTTISH REGIONAL AND ISLANDS COUNCILS
AREA AND POPULATION

Region	Administrative Headquarters	Area (*hectares*)	Population Census 1991p	Regional community charge per head 1991 £	Community water charge per head 1991 £
Borders	Newtown St Boswells	471,253	102,649	125·00	˙30·00
Central	Stirling	263,455	267,964	187·00	15·00
Dumfries and Galloway	Dumfries	639,561	147,064	132·00	32·00
Fife	Glenrothes	131,201	339,284	198·00	21·00
Grampian	Aberdeen	869,772	493,155	136·00	39·00
Highland	Inverness	2,539,759	209,419	132·00	35·00
Lothian	Edinburgh	171,595	723,678	310·00	26·00
Orkney	Kirkwall	97,581	19,450	2·00	53·00
Shetland	Lerwick	143,268	22,017	0·93	44·07
Strathclyde	Glasgow	1,350,283	2,218,229	173·00	29·00
Tayside	Dundee	749,165	385,271	189·00	26·00
Western Isles	Stornoway, Lewis	289,798	29,109	26·00	51·00

CHIEF EXECUTIVES, DIRECTORS OF FINANCE AND CONVENERS

Region	Chief Executive	Director of Finance	Convener
Borders	K. J. Clark, CBE	P. Jeary	The Earl of Minto
Central	D. Sinclair	S. C. Craig	Mrs A. Wallace
Dumfries and Galloway	N. W. D. McIntosh, CBE	J. C. Stewart	D. R. Robinson
Fife	Dr J. A. Markland	A. E. Taylor	R. Gough, CBE
Grampian	A. G. Campbell	A. McLean	R. Middleton
Highland	R. H. Stevenson	J. W. Bremner	D. J. McPherson
Lothian	G. M. Bowie	D. B. Chynoweth	E. Milligan
Orkney	R. H. Gilbert	R. H. Gilbert	J. A. Tait
Shetland	M. E. Green	vacant	E. Thomason, OBE
Strathclyde	Sir Robert Calderwood	A. Gillespie	D. Sanderson
Tayside	R. W. Black	I. B. McIver	G. W. Buckman
Western Isles	Dr G. Macleod	D. G. Macleod	Rev. D. Macaulay, OBE

p preliminary.

PRINCIPAL SCOTTISH CITIES

ABERDEEN

ABERDEEN, 130 miles north-east of Edinburgh, received its charter as a Royal Burgh from William the Lion in 1179. Scotland's third largest city, Aberdeen is the second largest Scottish fishing port and the main European centre for offshore oil exploration. It is also an ancient university town and distinguished research centre. Other industries include engineering, shipbuilding, food processing, textiles, paper manufacturing and chemicals. Places of interest: King's College and Visitor Centre, St Machar's Cathedral, Brig o' Balgownie, Duthie Park and Winter Gardens, the Kirk of St Nicholas, Mercat Cross, Marischal College and Museum of Human History, Provost Skene's House, Art Gallery, James Dun's House (children's museum), Satrosphere Hands-On Discovery Centre, and Provost Ross's House (maritime museum).

DUNDEE

DUNDEE, a Royal Burgh, is situated on the north bank of the Tay estuary. The city's port and dock installations are important to the offshore oil industry and the airport also provides servicing facilities. Principal industries include textiles, computers and other electronic industries, lasers, printing, tyre manufacture, food processing, carpets, engineering and clothing manufacture. Six sites have Enterprise Zone status, including the Technology Park, airport and port. The unique City Churches—three churches under one roof, together with the 15th century St Mary's Tower—are the most prominent architectural feature. RRS *Discovery*, the ship which took Captain Scott to the Antarctic and which was built in Dundee in 1901, is berthed in Victoria Dock.

EDINBURGH

EDINBURGH is the capital and seat of government in Scotland. The city is built on a group of hills and contains in Princes Street one of the most beautiful thoroughfares in the world. The principal buildings are the Castle, which includes St Margaret's Chapel, the oldest building in Edinburgh, and near it, the Scottish National War Memorial; the Palace of Holyroodhouse; Parliament House, the present seat of the judicature; two universities (Edinburgh and Heriot-Watt); St Giles' Cathedral (restored 1879–83) St Mary's (Scottish Episcopal) Cathedral (Sir Gilbert Scott); the General Register House (Robert Adam) the National and the Signet Libraries; the National Gallery; the Royal Scottish Academy; and the National Portrait Gallery.

GLASGOW

GLASGOW, a Royal Burgh, is the principal commercial and industrial centre in Scotland. The city occupies the north and south banks of the Clyde, formerly one of the chief commercial estuaries in the world. The principal industries include engineering, electronics, finance, chemicals and printing. The city has also developed recently as a tourism and conference centre. The chief buildings are the 13th century Gothic Cathedral, the University (Sir Gilbert Scott), the City Chambers, the Royal Concert Hall, Pollok House, the School of Art (Mackintosh), Kelvingrove Art Galleries, the Burrell Collection museum and the Mitchell Library. The city is home to the Scottish National Orchestra, Scottish Opera and Scottish Ballet.

SCOTTISH DISTRICT COUNCILS

District	Administrative Headquarters	Popula-tion Census 1991p	District community charge per head 1991 £	Chief Executive	Chairman (a) Convener (b) Provost (c) Lord Provost
Aberdeen City (5)	Aberdeen	201,099	91·00	D. MacDonald	(c) R. A. Robertson
Angus (9)	Forfar	92,881	30·00	P. B. Regan	(b) B. M. C. Milne
Annandale and Eskdale (3).........	Annan	36,805	40·00	J. A. Whitecross	(a) F. Park
Argyll and Bute (8) ...	Lochgilphead	66,987	65·00	M. A. J. Gossip, CBE	W. R. Hunter
Badenoch and Strathspey (6)......	Kingussie	12,941	10·00	Mrs J. M. Fraser	J. A. McCook
Banff and Buchan (5) .	Banff	82,949	40·00	R. M. Blackburn	(a) W. R. Cruick-shank
Bearsden and Milngavie (8)	Bearsden	39,552	53·00	I. C. Laurie	(b) Mrs J. Cameron
Berwickshire (1)	Duns	18,781	9·00	R. A. Christie	Capt. J. Evans
Caithness (6).........	Wick	26,111	5·00	A. Beattie	(a) J. M. Young, OBE
Clackmannan (2)	Alloa	47,209	90·00	I. F. Smith	(a) W. G. Watt
Clydebank (8)	Clydebank	44,658	100·00	J. T. McNally	(b) D. S. Grainger
Clydesdale (8)	Lanark	57,078	69·00	P. W. Daniels	(a) Mrs E. Logan
Cumbernauld and Kilsyth (8)	Cumbernauld	61,042	38·00	J. Hutton	(b) Ms R. McKenna
Cumnock and Doon Valley (8)	Cumnock	41,998	41·00	D. T. Hemmings, OBE	(a) E. Ross
Cunninghame (8).....	Irvine	134,676	80·00	B. Devine	(a) J. Carson
Dumbarton (8)	Dumbarton	75,973	118·00	A. Nisbet	(b) W. Petrie
Dundee City (9)	Dundee	165,548	80·00	vacant	(c) T. Mitchell
Dunfermline (4)	Dunfermline	125,529	46·00	G. Brown	(b) J. Cameron
East Kilbride (8).....	East Kilbride	81,339	88·00	D. J. Liddell	(b) Ms H. Biggins
East Lothian (7)......	Haddington	82,995	66·00	M. Duncan	G. M. Wanless
Eastwood (8)	Giffnock	58,322	19·00	M. D. Henry	(b) Mrs J. Y. Macfie
Edinburgh City (7) ...	Edinburgh	421,213	108·00	S. Lowenburg	(c) Rt. Hon. Eleanor T. McLaughlin
Ettrick and Lauderdale (1)	Galashiels	33,939	23·00	C. M. Anderson	(b) A. L. Tulley, MBE
Falkirk (2)	Falkirk	139,038	21·00	W. Weir	(b) D. Goldie
Glasgow City (8)	Glasgow	654,542	95·00	T. J. Monaghan	(c) Rt. Hon. Susan Baird, CBE
Gordon (5)...........	Inverurie	73,968	23·00	M. C. Barron	(b) J. Lawrence
Hamilton (8).........	Hamilton	103,139	75·00	A. Baird	(b) R. Gibb
Inverclyde (8)........	Greenock	88,054	59·00	I. C. Wilson, OBE	(b) F. A. McGlone
Inverness (6).........	Inverness	62,647	5·00	B. Wilson	(b) A. G. Sellar
Kilmarnock and Loudoun (8)	Kilmarnock	78,558	51·00	R. W. Jenner	(b) J. Mills
Kincardine and Deeside (5).........	Stonehaven	52,625	4·00	T. Hyder	(a) D. J. Mackenzie, MBE
Kirkcaldy (8)........	Kirkcaldy	144,574	47·00	D. A. Watt§	(a) R. King, OBE
Kyle and Carrick (8) ..	Ayr	113,572	89·50	I. R. D. Smillie†	(b) D. MacNeill
Lochaber (6)	Fort William	20,803	35·00	D. A. B. Blair	D. P. MacFarlane
Midlothian (7)	Dalkeith	77,969	54·00	T. Muir	(a) D. Lennie
Monklands (8)	Coatbridge	101,151	76·00	M. V. P. Hart	(b) E. Cairns
Moray (5)............	Elgin	82,514	16·00	L. Morgan	(a) E. Aldridge
Motherwell (8)	Motherwell	140,320	54·00	J. Bonomy	(b) J. Armstrong
Nairn (6)	Nairn	10,680	8·00	A. M. Kerr†	(b) S. A. Macarthur
Nithsdale (3)	Dumfries	56,616	40·00	T. Orr	(b) E. D. Gibson
North-East Fife (4) ...	Cupar	69,181	36·00	R. G. Brotherton	Dr C. R. Sneddon
Perth and Kinross (9) .	Perth	126,842	38·00	J. E. D. Cormie	(b) A. Murray
Renfrew (8)	Paisley	193,622	89·00	A. I. Cowe*	(b) G. Murray
Ross and Cromarty (6)	Dingwall	49,953	32·00	R. Mair	(a) G. D. Finlayson, OBE
Roxburgh (1).........	Hawick	34,615	20·00	K. W. Cramond	G. Yellowlees
Skye and Lochalsh (6).	Portree	12,541	13·00	D. H. Noble	J. F. Munro
Stewartry (3)	Kirkcudbright	23,600	21·00	J. C. Howie	(a) J. Nelson
Stirling (2)	Stirling	81,717	85·00	G. Bonner	(a) J. Hendry
Strathkelvin (8)......	Kirkintilloch	83,616	77·00	C. Mallon	(b) R. M. Coyle
Sutherland (6)	Golspie	13,743	17·00	J. Allison†	D. I. MacRae
Tweeddale (1)	Peebles	15,314	16·00	G. H. T. Garvie	M. A. R. Maher
West Lothian (7)	Bathgate	141,501	33·00	A. M. Linkston	(d) D. McCauley
Wigtown (3)	Stranraer	30,043	33·00	A. Geddes	J. Brown

p preliminary.　　‡ Town Clerk.　　§ General Manager.　　† Director of Administration.
　　　　　　　　　　　　* Managing Director.

REGIONS.—(1) Borders; (2) Central; (3) Dumfries and Galloway; (4) Fife; (5) Grampian; (6) Highland; (7) Lothian; (8) Strathclyde; (9) Tayside.

NORTHERN IRELAND

The usually resident population of Northern Ireland according to the 1981 Census was 1,556,039 (males, 761,882; females, 794,157) compared with a total population of 1,536,065 at the Census of 1971. (NB. This revised figure takes account of the population effect of non-enumerated households, estimated at 74,000 persons.) In 1981 the number of persons in the various religious denominations (expressed as percentages of the total usually resident population) were: Roman Catholic, 28·0; Presbyterian, 22·9; Church of Ireland, 19·0; Methodist, 4·0; others 7·6; not stated, 18·5.

Northern Ireland has a total area of 5,452 sq. miles (14,121 sq. km): land, 5,206 sq. miles (13,483 sq. km); inland water and tideways, 246 sq. miles (638 sq. km). There was a density of population of 282 persons per sq. mile in 1981. The population, mid-1990 estimate, was 1,589,400.

CONSTITUTION AND GOVERNMENT

As part of the United Kingdom, Northern Ireland is subject to the same fundamental constitutional provisions which apply to the rest of the United Kingdom. However, the Northern Ireland Constitution Act 1973 and the Northern Ireland Act 1982 provide for a measure of devolved government in Northern Ireland. This arrangement was last in force in January 1974, following agreement between the Northern Ireland political parties to form a power-sharing Executive. However, this arrangement collapsed in May 1974 and there has been no devolution since.

In the interim Northern Ireland continues to be governed by direct rule under the provisions of the Northern Ireland Act 1974. This allows Parliament to approve all laws for Northern Ireland and places the Northern Ireland departments under the direction and control of the Secretary of State for Northern Ireland.

Attempts have been made by successive governments to find a means of restoring a widely acceptable form of devolved government to Northern Ireland. A 78-member Assembly was elected by proportional representation in 1982. However, four years later it was dissolved after it ceased to discharge its responsibilities of making proposals for the resumption of devolved government and of monitoring the work of the Northern Ireland Departments.

In spring 1991 further dialogue between Government and the constitutional political parties in Northern Ireland was established as a means of exploring the extent of the common ground which exists between them regarding the future of Northern Ireland and its relationship with the United Kingdom and the Republic of Ireland. (*See also* **Events of the Year**.)

FLAG.—The white star in the centre of the flag of Northern Ireland (*cross gules in a field argent*) has six points representing the counties of Northern Ireland. It encloses a red hand and stands below a crown.

THE PRIVY COUNCIL

R. J. Bailie (1971); D. W. Bleakley (1971); R. H. Bradford (1969); W. Craig (1963); J. Dobson (1969); W. K. Fitzsimmons (1965); Lt.-Col. the Lord Glentoran (1953); Sir Edward Jones (1965); Mr Justice Kelly (1969); H. V. Kirk (1962); Capt. W. J. Long (1966); Lord Lowry (1971); R. W. B. McConnell (1964); W. B. McIvor, OBE (1971); W. J. Morgan (1961); The Lord Moyola (1966); Sir Ivan Neill (1950); Sir Robert Porter, QC (1969); Lord Rathcavan (1969); R. Simpson (1969); J. D. Taylor (1970); H. W. West (1960).

FINANCE

Taxation in Northern Ireland is largely imposed and collected by the United Kingdom Government. After deducting the cost of collection and of Northern Ireland's contributions to the European Economic Community the balance, known as the Attributed Share of Taxation, is paid over to the Northern Ireland Consolidated Fund. Northern Ireland's revenue is insufficient to meet its expenditure and is supplemented by a grant in aid.

	1990–91*	1991–92**
	£	£
Public income.....	4,634,142,005	4,991,300,000
Public expenditure	4,634,431,979	4,991,200,000

* Outturn   ** Estimate

PRODUCTION

Industries.—The products of the engineering, shipbuilding and aircraft industries, which employed 28,600 persons in 1985, were valued at £856 million. The textile industries, employing about 10,500 persons, produced products valued at approximately £273 million. The food and drink industry, employing about 20,000 persons, produced goods valued at £2,575 million.

Minerals.—1,308 persons were employed in mining and quarrying operations in Northern Ireland in 1989 and the minerals raised (19,239,241 tonnes) were valued at £34,260,152.

COMMUNICATIONS

Seaports.—The total tonnage handled by Northern Ireland ports in 1990 was 16·4m. Regular ferry, freight and container services operate to ports in Great Britain and Europe from 18 ports including Belfast, Coleraine, Larne, Londonderry and Warrenpoint.

Road and rail transport.—The Northern Ireland Transport Holding Company is largely responsible for the supervision of the subsidiary companies, Ulsterbus and Citybus (which operate the public road passenger services) and Northern Ireland Railways. Road freight services are also provided by a large number of hauliers operating competitively under licence.

Air transport.—Belfast International Airport is run by Northern Ireland Airports Ltd, a subsidiary of the Northern Ireland Transport Holding Company and provides scheduled and chartered services on domestic and international routes.

Scheduled services also operate from Belfast Harbour Airport to 13 British destinations and from Eglinton, Co. Londonderry, to Manchester, Glasgow and Dublin.

BELFAST

BELFAST, the administrative centre of Northern Ireland, is situated at the mouth of the River Lagan at its entrance to Belfast Lough. The city grew, owing to its easy access by sea to Scottish coal and iron, to be a great industrial centre.

The principal buildings are of a relatively recent date and include the Parliament Buildings at Stormont, the City Hall, the Law Courts, the Public Library and the Museum and Art Gallery.

Belfast received its first charter of incorporation in 1613 and was created a city in 1888; the title of Lord Mayor was conferred in 1892.

LONDONDERRY

LONDONDERRY, situated on the River Foyle, was reputedly founded in 546 by St Columba. Londonderry (formerly *Derry*) has important associations with the City of London. The Irish Society, under its royal charter of 1613, fortified the city and was for long closely associated with its administration. The city is famous for the great siege of 1688–9, when for 105 days the town held out against the forces of James II until relieved by sea. The city walls are still intact and form a circuit of almost a mile around the old city. Interesting buildings are the Protestant Cathedral of St Columb's (1633) and the Guildhall, reconstructed in 1912 and containing a number of beautiful stained glass windows, many of which were presented by the livery companies of London.

COUNTIES OF NORTHERN IRELAND

Counties and ‡County Boroughs	Area* sq. miles	Lord Lieutenant	High Sheriff, 1991
ntrim....................	1,093	Sir Richard Dobbs, KCVO	M. D. Stewart-Moore
elfast City‡..............	25	Col. J. E. Wilson, OBE	J. A. Coggle
rmagh	484	The Earl of Caledon	J. D. Thompson
own	945	Col. W. S. Brownlow	N. C. W. Clarke
ermanagh	647	The Earl of Erne	V. Chambers
ondonderry†	798	Col. M. W. McCorkell, OBE, TD	R. S. McCulloch, OBE
ondonderry City‡........	3·4	J. T. Eaton, TD	Mrs E. P. Harvey, MBE
yrone..................	1,211	The Duke of Abercorn	W. R. McAusland

† Excluding the City of Londonderry.   * Excluding inland waters and tideways.

DISTRICT AND BOROUGH COUNCILS

District and §Borough Councils	Population (June 30, 1990)	Net Annual Value £	Council Clerk	Mayor (†) or Chairman 1991
Antrim, Co. Antrim	47,600	6,362,603	S. J. Magee	†J. Graham
Ards, Co. Down	65,400	7,470,883	D. J. Fallows	†R. J. Shannon
Armagh, Co. Armagh ...	49,100	4,943,784	D. R. D. Mitchell	W. G. McCartney
Ballymena, Co. Antrim .	57,300	7,866,221	M. G. Rankin	†S. Spence
Ballymoney, Co. Antrim	24,100	2,477,733	W. J. Williamson, MBE	†J. A. Gaston
Banbridge, Co. Down ...	32,100	3,449,325	R. Gilmore	A. McKelvey
Belfast, Co. Antrim and Co. Down	295,100	53,222,756	S. McDowell	N. Dodds (*Lord Mayor*)
Carrickfergus, Co. Antrim..............	31,000	4,743,000	R. Boyd	†W. A. Haggan
Castlereagh, Co. Down ..	58,100	7,769,123	J. White	†M. E. Anderson
Coleraine, Co. Londonderry	48,600	7,563,546	W. E. Andrews	†Mrs E. T. Black
Cookstown, Co. Tyrone .	27,700	3,014,601	N. Barnes*	S. A. Glasgow
Craigavon, Co. Armagh .	78,200	10,237,174	E. A. McKinley	†J. W. Trueman
Derry, Co. Londonderry	100,500	11,433,842	J. Keanie	†Mrs M. Bradley
Down, Co. Down	57,900	5,756,394	S. Byrne	S. Quinn
Dungannon, Co. Tyrone	43,800	4,331,581	W. J. Beattie	J. Cavanagh
Fermanagh, Co. Fermanagh	50,600	5,155,784	G. Burns, MBE	C. McClaughry
Larne, Co. Antrim......	29,000	3,286,632	G. McKinley	Mrs R. G. Armstrong
Limavady, Co. Londonderry	29,900	2,734,987	J. K. Stevenson	†J. Dolan
Lisburn, Co. Antrim and Co. Down.............	98,700	12,696,795	M. S. Fielding	†W. J. McAllister
Magherafelt, Co. Londonderry	33,200	3,331,632	W. R. S. McMaster MBE	R. A. Montgomery
Moyle, Co. Antrim	15,000	1,422,865	R. G. Lewis	A. G. Kane
Newry and Mourne, Co. Down and Co. Armagh .	89,700	7,921,301	K. O'Neill	A. Moffett
Newtownabbey, Co. Antrim..............	72,900	10,844,347	J. Campbell	†K. Robinson
North Down, Co. Down .	72,600	9,059,619	J. McKimm	†D. Vitty
Omagh, Co. Tyrone	45,800	4,237,465	J. P. McKinney	C. McFarland
Strabane, Co. Tyrone ...	35,700	3,016,813	Dr R. Eakin	E. Turner
Northern Ireland	1,589,400	204,950,806		

NOTE.—Since the reorganization of local government, rates in Northern Ireland are collected by the Department of the Environment and consist of two rates, a regional rate made by the Department of Finance and a district rate made by individual District Councils.

THE ISLE OF MAN
(ELLAN VANNIN)

The Isle of Man is an island situated in the Irish Sea, in lat. 54° 3'–54° 25' N. and long. 4° 18'–4° 47' W., nearly equidistant from England, Scotland and Ireland. Although the early inhabitants were of Celtic origin, the Isle of Man was part of the Norwegian Kingdom of the Hebrides until 1266, when this was ceded to Scotland Subsequently granted to the Stanleys (Earls of Derby) in the 15th century and later to the Dukes of Atholl, it was brought under the direct administration of the Crown in 1765. The island forms the bishopric of Sodor and Man.

The total land area is 141,263 acres (221 sq. miles). The report on the 1986 Census showed a resident population of 64,282 (males, 30,782; females, 33,500). In 1989 births numbered 871 and deaths 988. The main language in use is English. There are no remaining native speakers of Manx Gaelic but around 200 people are able to speak the language.

CAPITAL, ΨDouglas. Population (1986), 20,368; ΨCastletown (3,019) is the ancient capital; the other towns are ΨPeel (3,660) and ΨRamsey (5,778).

FLAG.—Three legs in white and gold armed conjoined on a red ground.

TYNWALD DAY.—July 5.

LEGISLATURE AND GOVERNMENT

The Isle of Man is a self-governing Crown dependency, having its own parliamentary, legal and administrative system; the Crown is responsible for international relations and defence. The Lieutenant-Governor is the Queen's personal representative in the island.

The legislature, Tynwald, is the oldest parliament in the world in continuous existence. It has two branches—the Legislative Council and the House of Keys. The Council consists of the Bishop of Sodor and Man, the Attorney-General (who does not have a vote) and eight members chosen by the House of Keys. The House of Keys consists of 24 members, elected by universal adult suffrage. The branches sit separately to consider legislation and sit together, as Tynwald Court, for other parliamentary purposes.

The presiding officer in Tynwald Court is the President of Tynwald, elected by the members, who also presides over sittings of the Legislative Council. The presiding officer of the House of Keys is Mr Speaker, who is elected by members of the House.

The principal members of the Manx Government are the Chief Minister and nine departmental ministers, who comprise the Council of Ministers.

ECONOMY

Most of the income generated in the island is earned in the services sector with financial and business services being considerably larger than the traditional industry of tourism. Manufacturing industry is also a major generator of income whilst the island's other traditional industries of agriculture and fishing now play a smaller role in the economy.

Under the terms of the island's special relationship with the European Community the Island has free access to EC markets.

A twenty-acre Freeport has been developed adjacent to the main airport at Ronaldsway.

The island's unemployment rate is approximately 1 per cent and price inflation is around 7 per cent per annum.

FINANCE

The island's Budget for 1991–92 provided for gross expenditure of £269,256,660. The principal sources of Government revenue are taxes on income and expenditure. Income tax is payable at a rate of 15 per cent on the first £26,000 of taxable income of resident individuals and 20 per cent on the balance. The rate of income tax is 20 per cent on the whole taxable income of non-residents and companies. By agreement with the United Kingdom Government, the island keeps most of its rates of indirect taxation (Value Added Tax and duties) the same as those in the United Kingdom, but this agreement may be terminated by either party. A reciprocal agreement on national insurance benefits and pensions exists between the Governments of the Isle of Man and the United Kingdom. Taxes are also charged on property (rates), but these are comparatively low.

The major Government expenditure items are health, social security and education, which account for 53 per cent of the Government budget. The island makes a voluntary annual contribution to the United Kingdom for defence and other external services.

Although the island has a special relationship with the European Community it neither contributes money to nor receives funds from the EC Budget.

Lieutenant-Governor, His Excellency Air Marshal Sir Laurence Jones, KCB, AFC.
   ADC to the Lieutenant-Governor, Capt. C. M. Dawson.
President of Tynwald, The Hon. Sir Charles Kerruish, OBE.
Speaker, House of Keys, The Hon. G. V. H. Kneale, CBE.
His Honour the First Deemster and Clerk of the Rolls, J. W. Corrin.
Clerk of Tynwald, Secretary to the House of Keys, and Counsel to the Speaker, Prof. T. St J. N. Bates.
Attorney-General, T. W. Cain, QC.
Chief Minister, The Hon. M. R. Walker.
Chief Secretary, J. F. Kissack.
Chief Financial Officer, J. A. Cashen.

THE CHANNEL ISLANDS

The Channel Islands, situated off the north-west coast of France (at distances of from ten to thirty miles) are the only portions of the Dukedom of Normandy now belonging to the Crown, to which they have been attached ever since the Conquest. They consist of Jersey (28,717 acres), Guernsey (15,654 acres), and the dependencies of Guernsey—Alderney (1,962 acres), Brechou (74), Great Sark (1,035), Little Sark (239), Herm (320), Jethou (44) and Lihou (38)—a total of 48,083 acres, or 75 square miles. In 1986 the population of Jersey was 80,212; and of Guernsey, 54,380; Alderney, 2,000 and Sark, 604.

GOVERNMENT

The islands are Crown dependencies with their own legislative assemblies (the States in Jersey, Guernsey and Alderney, and the Court of Chief Pleas in Sark), and systems of local administration and of law, and their own courts. Acts passed by the States require the sanction of The Queen-in-Council. The British Government is responsible for defence and international relations.

In both Bailiwicks the Lieutenant-Governor and

Commander-in-Chief, who is appointed by the Crown, is the personal representative of the Queen and the channel of communication between the Crown (via the Privy Council) and the insular government. The Bailiffs of Jersey and Guernsey, also appointed by the Crown, are President of the States and of the Royal Courts of their respective islands. The government of each Bailiwick is conducted by committees appointed by the States. Justice is administered by the Royal Courts of Jersey and Guernsey, each consisting of the Bailiff and 12 elected Jurats.

Each Bailiwick constitutes a deanery under the jurisdiction of the Bishop of Winchester (*see* Index).

ECONOMY

A mild climate and good soil have led to the development of intensive systems of agriculture and horticulture, which form a significant part of the economy of the Channel Islands. Equally important are invisible earnings, principally from the tourist trade and from banking and finance, the low rate of income tax (20p in the £ in Jersey and Guernsey; no tax of any kind in Sark) and the absence of super-tax and death duties making the Channel Islands a popular tax-haven. Principal exports are agricultural produce and flowers; imports are chiefly machinery, manufactured goods, food, fuel and chemicals. Trade with the UK is regarded as internal trade.

British currency is legal tender in the Channel Islands but each Bailiwick issues its own coins, and some notes, of the same values as those of the UK. They also issue their own postage stamps; UK stamps are not valid.

LANGUAGE

The official languages are English and French, but French is gradually being supplanted by English, which is the language in daily use. In country districts of Jersey and Guernsey and throughout Sark a Norman-French *patois* is also in use, though to a declining extent.

CHIEF TOWNS.—ΨSt Helier on the south coast of Jersey; ΨSt Peter Port, on the east coast of Guernsey, and St Anne on Alderney.

JERSEY

Lieutenant-Governor and Commander-in-Chief of Jersey, His Excellency Air Marshal Sir John Sutton, KCB (1990).

Secretary and ADC, Cdr. D. M. L. Braybrooke, LVO.
Bailiff of Jersey, Sir Peter Crill, CBE.
Deputy Bailiff, V. A. Tomes.
Attorney-General and Receiver-General, P. M. Bailhache, QC.
Solicitor-General, T. C. Sowden, QC.
Greffier of the States, R. S. Gray.
States Treasurer, G. M. Baird.

Year to Dec. 31:	1989	1990
Revenue	£295,967,172	£327,059,999
Revenue expenditure	228,530,891	258,931,630
Capital expenditure	38,675,000	60,673,000
Public debt	−1,270,440	174,640

FLAG.—A white field charged with a red saltire, and coat of arms.

GUERNSEY AND DEPENDENCIES

Lieutenant-Governor and Commander-in-Chief of the Bailiwick of Guernsey and its Dependencies, His Excellency Lt.-Gen. Sir Michael Wilkins, KCB, OBE, *apptd.* 1990.
Secretary and ADC, Capt. D. P. L. Hodgetts.
Bailiff of Guernsey, Sir Charles Frossard.
Deputy Bailiff, G. M. Dorey.
HM Procureur and Receiver-General, de V. G. Carey, QC.
HM Comptroller, A. C. K. Day, QC.
States Supervisor, F. N. Le Cheminant.

Year to Dec. 31:	1989	1990
Revenue	£129,639,543	£138,532,424
Expenditure	112,025,191	126,047,752

FLAG.—White, bearing a red cross of St George, with an argent a cross gules superimposed on the cross.

Alderney

President of the States, J. Kay-Mouat.
Clerk of the States, D. V. Jenkins.
Clerk of the Court, A. Johnson.

Sark

Seigneur of Sark, J. M. Beaumont.
The Seneschal, L. P. de Carteret.
The Greffier, J. P. Hamon.

Brechou, Lihou and Jethou are leased by the Crown. Herm is leased by the States of Guernsey.

THE ISLES OF SCILLY

There are about 140 islands and skerries in the Scillies group (total area, 6 square miles) situated 28 miles south-west of Land's End, of which only five are inhabited: St Mary's, St Agnes, Bryher, Tresco and St Martin's. The population is 1,978. The entire group has been designated a Conservation Area, a Heritage Coast, and an Area of Outstanding Natural Beauty, and has been given National Nature Reserve status by the Nature Conservancy Council because of its unique flora and fauna. Tourism and the winter/spring flower trade for the home market form the basis of the economy of the Isles. The island group is a recognized rural development area.

The islands are administered by the Council of the Isles of Scilly, a 21-member non-political body, which combines the powers and duties of a County Council and a District Council under the Local Government

Act 1972 and the Isles of Scilly Orders 1978. Legislation is specifically applied to the Isles of Scilly by Special Order. The Council is responsible for education, fire services, highways, planning and social services, and Cornwall County Council provides other services on an agency basis; the police service is administered by the Devon and Cornwall Police Authority, of which the Council is a member. The Isles are part of the St Ives electoral division.

Administrative Headquarters, Town Hall, St Mary's, Isles of Scilly, TR21 0LW.
Chairman of the Council, H. R. Duncan.
Clerk and Chief Executive, P. S. Hygate (*acting*).
Chief Technical Officer, B. M. Lowen.

COUNTRIES OF THE WORLD

No complete survey of many countries has yet been achieved and consequently accurate area figures are not always available. Similarly, many countries have not recently, or have never, taken a census. The areas of countries given below are derived from estimated figures published by the United Nations. The conversion factors used are: (i) to convert square miles to square km, multiply by 2·589988; (ii) to convert square km to square miles, multiply by 0·3861022.

Population figures for countries are derived from the most recent estimates available. Accurate and up-to-date data for the populations of capital cities are scarce, and definitions of cities' extent differ. The figures given below are the latest estimates available, and where it is known that the figure applies to an urban agglomeration this is indicated.

AFRICA

COUNTRY	AREA Sq. miles	AREA Sq. km	POPULATION	CAPITAL	POPULATION OF CAPITAL
Algeria...............	919,595	2,381,741	24,597,000	Ψ Algiers	3,250,000
Angola	481,354	1,246,700	9,767,000	Ψ Luanda	2,000,000
Benin	43,484	112,622	4,591,000	Ψ Porto Novo......	208,258
Botswana	224,607	581,730	1,300,000	Gaborone	125,000
Burkina	105,869	274,200	8,763,000	Ouagadougou	400,000
Burundi..............	10,747	27,834	5,302,000	Bujumbura	215,243
Cameroon	183,569	475,442	11,540,000	Yaoundé	635,670
Cape Verde Islands	1,557	4,033	369,000	Ψ Praia	57,748*
Central African Rep. ...	240,535	622,984	2,841,000	Bangui	473,817
Chad	495,755	1,284,000	5,538,000	Ndjaména........	402,000
Comoros..............	838	2,171	503,000	Moroni	17,267*
Congo................	132,047	342,000	1,941,000	Brazzaville	596,200*
Côte d'Ivoire.........	124,503	322,463	12,098,000	Ψ Abidjan	3,500,000
Djibouti	8,494	22,000	395,000	Ψ Djibouti........	200,000
Egypt	386,662	1,001,449	53,080,000	Cairo	14,000,000
Equatorial Guinea	10,830	28,051	420,000	Ψ Malabo	34,980
Ethiopia	471,778	1,221,900	49,513,000	Addis Ababa	1,739,130
Gabon................	103,347	267,667	1,133,000	Ψ Libreville	251,000
Gambia	4,361	11,295	835,200	Ψ Banjul (u.a.) ...	109,986
Ghana	92,100	238,537	14,753,900	Ψ Accra (u.a.)	1,781,100
Guinea	94,926	245,857	6,706,000	Ψ Conakry	763,000
Guinea-Bissau	13,948	36,125	966,000	Ψ Bissau	109,214*
Kenya	224,961	582,646	24,872,000	Nairobi	1,400,000
Lesotho	11,720	30,355	1,700,000	Maseru	288,951*
Liberia	43,000	111,369	2,508,000	Ψ Monrovia	425,000
Libya	679,362	1,759,540	4,385,000	Ψ Tripoli.........	1,000,000
Madagascar	226,669	587,041	11,603,000	Antananarivo	1,000,000
Malawi..............	45,747	118,484	8,022,000	Lilongwe........	233,973*
Mali	478,791	1,240,000	8,960,000	Bamako..........	646,163*
Mauritania	397,955	1,030,700	1,970,000	Nouakchott	500,000
Mauritius	790	2,045	1,090,000	Ψ Port Louis	138,413
Mayotte	144	372	67,000	Mamoundzou	12,000
Morocco	172,414	446,550	27,575,000	Ψ Rabat	1,123,000
Western Sahara	102,703	266,000	174,000	Laayoune	96,784*
Mozambique	309,495	801,590	15,326,000	Ψ Maputo	1,150,000
Namibia	318,261	824,292	1,500,000	Windhoek........	110,000
Niger	489,191	1,267,080	6,895,000	Niamey	410,000
Nigeria	356,669	923,768	109,175,000	Ψ Lagos	3,000,000
Réunion.............	969	2,510	596,600	St Denis	117,072
Rwanda	10,169	26,338	6,989,000	Kigali	156,000
St Helena............	47	122	5,544	Ψ Jamestown	1,330
Ascension I.	34	88	1,206	Ψ Georgetown	..
Tristan da Cunha ...	38	98	306	Ψ Edinburgh	..
São Tomé & Príncipe ..	372	964	116,000	Ψ São Tomé	25,000
Senegal	75,750	196,192	7,172,000	Ψ Dakar	1,000,000
Seychelles	108	280	67,378	Ψ Victoria	24,733
Sierra Leone..........	27,699	71,740	4,047,000	Ψ Freetown	469,776
Somalia	246,201	637,657	7,339,000	Ψ Mogadishu	1,000,000
South Africa..........	471,445	1,221,031	34,492,000	Pretoria (u.a.) ... { Ψ Cape Town (u.a.) .. Khartoum (u.a.) ..	822,925 1,911,521 3,000,000
Sudan...............	967,500	2,505,813	24,485,000	Mbabane	38,290
Swaziland	6,704	17,363	763,000	Dodoma	85,000
Tanzania	364,900	945,087	24,802,000	Ψ Lomé	366,476
Togo	21,925	56,785	3,349,000	Ψ Tunis	1,394,749
Tunisia	63,170	163,610	7,990,000	Kampala (u.a.) ...	750,000
Uganda	91,259	236,036	17,804,000	Kinshasa.........	2,778,281*
Zaire	905,567	2,345,409	34,491,000	Lusaka (u.a.)	1,000,000
Zambia	290,586	752,614	7,804,000	Harare	681,000
Zimbabwe	150,804	390,580	9,122,000		

*latest census result　Ψ seaport　u.a. urban agglomeration

AMERICA

COUNTRY	AREA Sq. miles	AREA Sq. km	POPULATION	CAPITAL	POPULATION OF CAPITAL
North America					
Canada...............	3,849,646	9,970,537	25,309,330*	Ottawa (u.a.)......	819,263*
Greenland...........	840,004	2,175,600	55,558	ѱGodthab.........	..
Mexico...............	761,605	1,972,547	84,275,000	Mexico City (u.a.).	18,748,000
St Pierre and Miquelon	93	242	6,500	ѱSt Pierre.........	..
United States.........	3,618,787	9,372,614	248,709,873*	Washington, DC ..	606,900
Central America and the West Indies					
Anguilla	35	91	8,000	The Valley.......	500
Antigua and Barbuda..	170	440	80,200	ѱSt John's........	30,000
Aruba	75	193	62,500	ѱOranjestad.......	20,000
Bahamas	5,380	13,935	254,000	ѱNassau...........	171,000*
Barbados	166	431	256,000	ѱBridgetown......	7,466
Belize	8,867	22,965	183,200	Belmopan........	5,000
Bermuda	20	53	60,000	ѱHamilton	2,000
Cayman Islands	100	259	28,080	ѱGeorge Town.....	12,921
Costa Rica	19,575	50,700	3,000,000	San José (u.a.)....	1,068,206
Cuba...............	42,804	110,861	10,608,000	ѱHavana.........	2,100,000
Dominica	290	751	81,300	ѱRoseau.........	11,000
Dominican Republic ...	18,816	48,734	7,019,000	ѱSanto Domingo (u.a.)	1,313,172*
Grenada.............	133	344	102,000	ѱSt George's......	10,000
Guadeloupe..........	687	1,779	386,600	ѱBasse-Terre	15,778
Guatemala	42,042	108,889	8,935,000	Guatemala City...	1,300,000
Haiti...............	10,714	27,750	5,609,000	ѱPort au Prince....	1,000,000
Honduras	43,277	112,088	4,951,000	Tegucigalpa	640,900
Jamaica	4,244	10,991	2,415,100	ѱKingston (u.a.) ..	696,300
Martinique	425	1,102	359,800	ѱFort de France....	100,576
Montserrat	38	98	13,000	ѱPlymouth	3,000
Netherlands Antilles ..	371	961	191,000	ѱWillemstad	50,000
Nicaragua	50,193	130,000	3,745,000	Managua	615,000
Panama	29,762	77,082	2,370,000	ѱPanama City	1,063,565
Puerto Rico	3,435	8,897	3,658,000	ѱSan Juan (u.a.) ...	1,816,300
St Christopher and Nevis	101	261	50,000	ѱBasseterre	15,000
St Lucia	238	616	148,000	ѱCastries.........	56,147
St Vincent and the Grenadines	150	388	110,000	ѱKingstown	33,694
El Salvador	8,124	21,041	5,500,000	San Salvador (u.a.)	2,000,000
Trinidad and Tobago ..	1,981	5,130	1,263,000	ѱPort of Spain	59,649
Turks and Caicos Is. ...	166	430	9,000	ѱGrand Turk	4,500
Virgin Islands:—					
British	59	153	10,985*	ѱRoad Town......	2,479
US................	132	342	112,000	ѱCharlotte Amalie .	11,756
South America					
Argentina	1,068,302	2,766,889	32,370,298*	ѱBuenos Aires.....	2,955,002
Bolivia	424,165	1,098,581	7,193,193	La Paz...........	1,000,000
Brazil...............	3,286,488	8,511,965	150,368,000	Brasilia	1,567,709
Chile................	292,258	756,945	12,961,000	Santiago	4,172,293
Colombia	439,737	1,138,914	31,193,000	Bogotá...........	4,176,769
Ecuador	109,484	283,561	10,490,000	Quito	1,387,887
Falkland Islands	4,700	12,173	2,121*	ѱStanley	1,643*
French Guiana........	35,135	91,000	114,900	ѱCayenne	38,135
Guyana	83,000	214,969	1,024,000	ѱGeorgetown	187,056
Paraguay............	157,048	406,752	4,157,287	Asunción (u.a.) ...	729,307*
Peru	496,225	1,285,216	22,332,100	Lima (u.a.)	6,415,000
South Georgia	1,580	4,092	..		
Suriname............	63,037	163,265	410,000	ѱParamaribo (u.a.) .	182,100
Uruguay	68,037	176,215	3,077,000	ѱMontevideo	1,355,312
Venezuela	352,144	912,050	19,246,000	Caracas (u.a.).....	4,000,000

*latest census result   ѱ seaport   u.a. urban agglomeration

ASIA

| COUNTRY | AREA | | POPULATION | CAPITAL | POPULATION OF CAPITAL |
	Sq. miles	Sq. km			
Afghanistan	250,000	647,497	15,814,000	Kabul............	2,000,000
Bahrain	240	622	503,000	Ψ Manama	121,986*
Bangladesh	55,598	143,998	110,300,000	Dhaka	6,000,000
Bhutan	18,147	47,000	1,483,000	Thimphu	15,000
Brunei	2,226	5,765	249,000	Bandar Seri Begawan.......	58,000
Cambodia	69,898	181,035	8,055,000	Ψ Phnom Penh	500,000
China[1]	3,705,408	9,596,961	1,130,000,000	Beijing (Peking) (u.a.)	10,370,000
Taiwan	13,800	35,742	20,182,486	Taipei	2,702,678
Hong Kong	416	1,074	5,812,300	Ψ Victoria	..
India................	1,269,346	3,287,590	843,930,861*	Delhi	6,220,000
Indonesia	735,358	1,904,569	179,136,000	Ψ Jakarta	7,885,519
Iran	636,296	1,648,000	55,000,000	Tehran	6,000,000
Iraq................	167,925	434,924	18,279,000	Baghdad	3,205,665
Israel[2]	8,019	20,770	4,882,000	Jerusalem........	506,200
Japan	145,834	377,708	123,116,000	Tokyo (u.a.)	11,935,700
Jordan	37,738	97,740	4,103,000	Amman	1,100,000
Korea DPR (North)....	46,540	120,538	22,419,000	Pyongyang	1,500,000
Korea Rep. of (South) ..	38,025	98,484	42,380,000	Seoul	9,991,089
Kuwait	6,880	17,818	2,048,000	Ψ Kuwait (city)	400,000
Laos	91,429	231,800	3,972,000	Vientiane	120,000
Lebanon.............	4,015	10,400	2,897,000	Ψ Beirut	702,000
Macao	6	16	448,000	Ψ Macao	..
Malaysia	127,317	329,749	16,958,000	Kuala Lumpur....	1,103,200
Maldives	115	298	206,000	Ψ Malé............	46,334
Mongolia	604,250	1,565,000	2,043,000	Ulan Bator	530,000
Myanmar (Burma)	261,218	676,552	40,810,000	Ψ Rangoon (u.a.)...	3,973,872
Nepal	54,342	140,747	18,442,000	Kathmandu	235,160
Oman	82,030	212,457	1,422,000	Ψ Muscat	400,000
Pakistan	307,374	746,045	108,678,000	Islamabad (u.a.)..	350,000
Philippines	115,831	300,000	60,097,000	Ψ Manila	1,856,375
Qatar	4,247	11,000	422,000	Ψ Doha	220,000
Saudi Arabia	830,000	2,149,640	14,435,000	Riyadh	1,500,000
Singapore	241	626	3,004,200	..	..
Sri Lanka	25,332	65,610	16,806,000	Ψ Colombo	643,000
Syria...............	71,498	185,180	11,719,000	Damascus	1,343,000
Thailand	198,457	514,000	55,888,398	Ψ Bangkok	5,400,000
Turkey (in Asia)	292,261	756,953	44,485,734*	Ankara	3,196,460
United Arab Emirates .	32,278	83,600	1,546,000	..	..
Vietnam	127,242	329,556	65,682,000	Hanoi	1,089,000
Yemen	203,850	527,696	7,770,000	Sana'a	427,150

*latest census result   Ψ seaport   u.a. urban-agglomeration

[1] Including Tibet.
[2] Including East Jerusalem, the Golan Heights and Israeli citizens on the West Bank.

THE LARGEST CITIES OF THE WORLD*

	Population		Population
MEXICO CITY, Mexico	18,748,000	Moscow, USSR	8,879,000
CAIRO, Egypt	14,000,000	Ψ Bombay, India	8,202,000
Ψ Shanghai, China	12,760,000	Ψ JAKARTA, Indonesia	7,885,519
TOKYO, Japan	11,935,700	Ψ New York, USA	7,322,564
BEIJING, China	10,370,000	Manila, Philippines	6,720,050
São Paulo, Brazil	10,063,110	Rio de Janiero, Brazil..............	6,603,388
SEOUL, South Korea	9,991,089	Karachi, Pakistan	6,500,000
Ψ Calcutta, India	9,194,018	Ψ LONDON, UK	6,377,900
PARIS, France.....................	9,060,000	DELHI, India	6,220,000

* In most cases figures refer to urban agglomerations.

EUROPE

COUNTRY	AREA		POPULATION	CAPITAL	POPULATION OF CAPITAL
	Sq. miles	Sq. km			
Albania	11,099	28,748	3,410,000	Tirana	232,500
Andorra	175	453	50,000	Andorra La Vella .	16,151
Austria	32,374	83,849	7,791,000	Vienna	1,486,963
Belgium	11,781	30,513	9,928,000	Brussels (u.a.)	970,501
Bulgaria	42,823	110,912	8,992,316	Sofia	1,136,875
Cyprus	3,572	9,251	698,800	Nicosia	168,800
Czechoslovakia	49,370	127,869	15,639,000	Prague...........	1,209,149
Denmark	16,629	43,069	5,135,000	Ψ Copenhagen (u.a.).	1,495,736
Faroe Is.	540	1,399	47,485	Ψ Thorshavn	
Finland	137,851	337,032	4,962,000	Ψ Helsinki	488,777
France	211,208	547,026	56,556,000	Paris (u.a.)	9,060,000
Germany	137,738	365,755	78,700,000	Berlin	3,268,300
Gibraltar	2	6	30,861	Ψ Gibraltar	
Greece	50,944	131,944	10,256,000*	Athens (u.a.)	3,096,775*
Hungary	35,919	93,030	10,375,000*	Budapest..........	2,016,132*
Iceland	39,768	103,000	253,482	Ψ Reykjavik (u.a.) ..	95,811
Ireland, Republic of....	27,136	70,283	3,523,401*	Ψ Dublin	477,675*
Italy	116,304	301,225	57,517,000	Rome (u.a.)	2,828,692
Liechtenstein	61	157	28,452	Vaduz	4,874
Luxembourg	998	2,586	378,400	Luxembourg	77,500
Malta and Gozo	122	316	352,430	Ψ Valletta	9,196
Monaco	0·4	1	28,000	Monaco-Ville	1,234
Netherlands	15,770	40,844	15,009,000	Ψ Amsterdam (u.a.) .	1,034,562
Norway[1]	125,181	324,219	4,227,000	Ψ Oslo	454,927
Poland	120,725	312,677	38,200,000	Warsaw...........	1,655,063
Portugal[2].............	35,553	92,082	10,467,000	Ψ Lisbon	2,128,000
Romania	91,699	237,500	23,152,000	Bucharest........	1,975,508
San Marino...........	23	61	23,240	San Marino	
Spain[3]	194,897	504,782	39,054,000	Madrid (u.a.)	4,731,224
Sweden	173,732	449,964	8,493,000	Ψ Stockholm (u.a.)..	1,461,618
Switzerland	15,943	41,293	6,673,900	Berne	134,400
Turkey (in Europe)	9,121	23,623	6,942,780*		
United Kingdom[4]	94,227	244,046	55,701,000*	Ψ London (u.a.)	6,377,900*
England.............	50,363	130,439	46,161,000*		
Wales	8,018	20,768	2,798,500*	Ψ Cardiff	272,600*
Scotland	30,414	78,772	4,957,289*	Ψ Edinburgh	421,213*
Northern Ireland	5,452	14,121	1,569,971*	Ψ Belfast (u.a.)......	295,223*
USSR[5]	2,150,975	5,571,000	286,700,000	Moscow	8,879,000
Vatican City State	0·2	0·44	1,000	Vatican City	
Yugoslavia	98,766	255,804	23,690,000	Belgrade..........	1,455,000

*latest census result Ψ seaport *u.a.* urban agglomeration

[1] Excludes Svalbard and Jan Mayen Is. (approx. 24,101 sq. miles (62,422 sq. km.) and 3,000 population).

[2] Includes Madeira (314 sq. miles) and the Azores (922 sq. miles).

[3] Includes Balearic Is., Canary Is., Ceuta and Melilla.

[4] Includes Isle of Man (227 sq. miles (588 sq. km.), 64,282 population), and Channel Is. (75 sq. miles (195 sq. km.), 137,196 population).

[5] Includes USSR in Asia.

OCEANIA

COUNTRY	AREA		POPULATION	CAPITAL	POPULATION OF CAPITAL
	Sq. miles	Sq. km			
Australia.............	2,967,909	7,686,848	17,086,200	Canberra.........	303,200
Norfolk Island	14	36	1,977*	Ψ Kingston.........	..
Fiji	7,055	18,274	738,000	Ψ Suva.............	75,000
French Polynesia	1,544	4,000	189,000	Ψ Papeete	22,967
Guam	212	549	138,089	Agaña	..
Kiribati	281	728	68,000	Tarawa	17,921
Marshall Is.	70	181	43,000	Majuro	20,000
Micronesia, Fed. States of.	271	701	100,000	Kolonia	6,000
Nauru	8	21	9,000	Ψ Nauru	..
New Caledonia.......	7,358	19,058	163,000	Ψ Noumea	65,110
New Zealand.........	103,736	268,676	3,307,084*	Ψ Wellington (u.a.)..	324,600
Cook Islands	91	236	17,185*	Avarua	..
Niue	100	259	2,267	Alofi.............	..
Ross Dependency†...	286,696	750,310	..	..	..
Northern Mariana Is ..	184	476	21,777	Saipan	19,156
Palau	192	497	14,000	Koror...........	8,100
Papua New Guinea ...	178,260	461,691	3,593,000	Ψ Port Moresby	141,500
Pitcairn Islands	1·9	5	65	..	..
Samoa, Eastern (US)...	76	197	38,200	Ψ Pago Pago	3,075
Samoa, Western.......	1,097	2,842	169,000	Ψ Apia	33,100*
Solomon Islands.......	10,983	28,446	317,000	Ψ Honiara	30,499*
Tonga	270	699	119,000	Ψ Nuku'alofa	30,000
Tuvalu	10	25	9,000	Ψ Funafuti	2,856
Vanuatu	4,706	12,190	155,000	Ψ Port Vila	19,400
Wallis and Futuna Is..	106	274	12,000	Ψ Mata-Utu	..

*latest census result   Ψ seaport   *u.a.* urban agglomeration

† Includes permanent shelf ice.

WORLD POPULATION

The total population of the world in mid-1989, was estimated at 5,201 million, compared with 3,019 million in 1960 and 2,070 million in 1930.

Continent, etc	Area		Estimated population, mid-1989
	Sq. miles '000	Sq. km '000	
Africa.........	11,704	30,313	628,000,000
North America[1]	8,311	21,525	274,000,000
Latin America[2]	7,933	20,547	439,000,000
Asia[3].........	10,637	27,549	3,052,000,000
Europe[4]	1,915	4,961	497,000,000
USSR	8,649	22,402	286,000,000
Oceania[5]	3,286	8,510	26,100,000
Total........	52,435	135,807	5,201,000,000

[1] Includes Greenland and Hawaii.
[2] Mexico and the remainder of the Americas south of the USA.
[3] Includes European Turkey, excludes USSR.
[4] Excludes European Turkey and USSR.
[5] Includes Australia, New Zealand and the islands inhabited by Micronesian, Melanesian and Polynesian peoples.
Source: *UN Demographic Yearbook 1989* (pub. 1991).

A United Nations report (*The Future Growth of World Population*) in 1958, pointed out that the population of the world had increased since the beginning of the 20th century at an unprecedented rate: in 1850 it was estimated at 1,094,000,000 and in 1900 at 1,500,000,000, an increase of 42 per cent in 50 years. By 1925 it had risen to 1,907,000,000—23 per cent in 25 years—and by 1950 it had reached 2,500,000,000, an increase of 31 per cent in 25 years. Levels of population and the trend in distribution of the population by continents as forecast for the year 2000 were:—

Continents, etc.	2000	
	Estimated population	per cent
Africa....................	517,000,000	8·2
North America............	312,000,000	5·0
Latin America†...........	592,000,000	9·4
Asia (excluding USSR)....	3,870,000,000	61·8
Europe (including USSR)..	947,000,000	15·1
Oceania	29,000,000	0·5
World	6,267,000,000	100

† Mexico and the remainder of the Americas south of USA.

THE COMMONWEALTH

The Commonwealth is a free association of the 50 sovereign independent states listed below together with their associated states and dependencies.

ANTIGUA AND BARBUDA	NAURU
AUSTRALIA	NEW ZEALAND
BAHAMAS	NIGERIA
BANGLADESH	PAKISTAN
BARBADOS	PAPUA NEW GUINEA
BELIZE	SAINT CHRISTOPHER
BOTSWANA	AND NEVIS
BRUNEI	SAINT LUCIA
CANADA	SAINT VINCENT AND THE
CYPRUS	GRENADINES
DOMINICA	SEYCHELLES
GAMBIA, THE	SIERRA LEONE
GHANA	SINGAPORE
GRENADA	SOLOMON ISLANDS
GUYANA	SRI LANKA
INDIA	SWAZILAND
JAMAICA	TANZANIA
KENYA	TONGA
KIRIBATI	TRINIDAD AND TOBAGO
LESOTHO	TUVALU
MALAWI	UGANDA
MALAYSIA	UNITED KINGDOM
THE MALDIVES	VANUATU
MALTA	WESTERN SAMOA
MAURITIUS	ZAMBIA
NAMIBIA	ZIMBABWE

Area and Population.—The total surface area of the independent Commonwealth is estimated at 29,293,000 sq. km (1989), about a quarter of the world total. The total population of the Commonwealth is estimated to be about one quarter of the world total. In 1989 this amounted to 1,435,484,000 (UN estimate). Details of the areas and populations of the member states and dependencies appear in the following pages.

History and Government.—The status and relationship of member nations was first defined by the Inter-Imperial Relations Committee of the 1926 Imperial Conference, under the chairmanship of Lord Balfour, in what came to be known as the Balfour Declaration: 'They are autonomous communities . . . equal in status, in no way subordinate one to another in any aspect of their domestic or external affairs, though united by a common allegiance to the Crown and freely associated as members of the British Commonwealth of Nations.' This formula was given legal substance by the Statute of Westminster 1931.

The concept of a group of countries owing allegiance to a single Crown changed in 1949 when India decided to become a republic, and her continued membership of the Commonwealth was agreed by the other members on the basis of her 'acceptance of The King as the symbol of the free association of its independent member nations and as such the Head of the Commonwealth'. Member nations agreed at the time of the accession of Queen Elizabeth II to recognize Her Majesty as the new Head of the Commonwealth. The position is not vested in the British Crown.

Most members of the Commonwealth are parliamentary democracies.

Queen Elizabeth II is head of state of 17 member countries of the Commonwealth: Antigua and Barbuda, Australia, the Bahamas, Barbados, Belize, Britain, Canada, Grenada, Jamaica, Mauritius, New Zealand, Papua New Guinea, St Christopher and Nevis, Saint Lucia, Saint Vincent and the Grenadines, Solomon Islands and Tuvalu. In each of these countries (except Britain) The Queen is personally represented by a Governor-General, who holds in all essential respects the same position in relation to the administration of public affairs in the realm as is held by Her Majesty in Britain (with the exception of certain constitutional functions which are performed by The Queen personally). The Governor-General is appointed by The Queen on the advice of the Government of the country concerned.

Twenty-seven member countries are republics: Bangladesh, Botswana, Cyprus, Dominica, The Gambia, Ghana, Guyana, India, Kenya, Kiribati, Malawi, The Maldives, Malta, Namibia, Nauru, Nigeria, Pakistan, Seychelles, Sierra Leone, Singapore, Sri Lanka, Tanzania, Trinidad and Tobago, Uganda, Vanuatu, Zambia and Zimbabwe. In Malaysia, the head of state is elected from among the nine hereditary Malay rulers and holds office for five years. Brunei, Lesotho, Tonga, and Swaziland have their own monarchs. Western Samoa has a head of state whose functions are analogous to those of a constitutional monarch.

Membership of the Commonwealth is subject only to the approval of existing members. Two countries, Nauru and Tuvalu, are special members, with the right to participate in all functional Commonwealth meetings and activities, but not to attend meetings of Commonwealth heads of government.

Consultation.—Commonwealth heads of government meet every two years to discuss international developments and to consider co-operation among members. These meetings, the successors to the pre-war Imperial Conferences, have grown in importance as they are the only regular forum of leaders from both developed and developing countries, constituting a broad sample of the world community. Decisions are reached by consensus, and the views of the meeting are set out in a communiqué.

In addition, there are annual meetings of finance ministers, and frequent meetings of ministers and officials in the fields of trade, education, health, law, science, agriculture, labour and employment, and youth affairs.

Defence.—The Commonwealth is not a military alliance and members make their own defence arrangements in the light of their particular requirements. Some are parties to multi-lateral treaties, for example ANZUS and NATO. Various members of the Commonwealth co-operate with each other in combined exercises, joint research organizations and exchanges of personnel and training facilities.

Law.—English common law forms the basis of the legal system in many Commonwealth countries, although in most cases it has been adapted by local statute to suit individual needs and circumstances. There are countries where other systems have been adopted—for example, the law of Quebec Province and of Mauritius is founded on that of France, and Roman Dutch law forms the basis in Sri Lanka and Lesotho.

The Judicial Committee of the Privy Council sitting in London hears appeals from a number of territories of which The Queen is head of state including Antigua and Barbuda, the Bahamas, Barbados, Belize, Jamaica, Mauritius, New Zealand, St Christopher and Nevis, St Lucia, St Vincent and the Grenadines, Tuvalu, the Channel Islands, the Isle of Man and the dependent territories. Appeals from Brunei are referred by the Sultan to the Judicial Committee and the Committee also hears appeals from five republics in the Commonwealth: Dominica, The Gambia, Kiribati, Singapore, and Trinidad and Tobago.

Citizenship and Nationality.—Each member of the Commonwealth defines the citizenship and nationality of its own people and determines the status of other Commonwealth nationals within its own boundaries. Members of the Commonwealth differentiate, to a greater or lesser degree, as regards the grant of privileges, between citizens of the Commonwealth and aliens. The Republic of Ireland, which in 1949 ceased to be a member of the Commonwealth, is not regarded by the other Commonwealth nations as a foreign country nor her citizens as foreigners.

Finance and Development.—Complete financial autonomy is enjoyed by all members of the Commonwealth. In some countries, customs tariffs are lower for merchandise of Commonwealth origin than for imports from foreign countries. Developing countries, including those in the Commonwealth, obtain preference for exports of industrial goods and some agricultural exports from the developed countries under the Generalised Scheme of Preferences (GSP). Many smaller Commonwealth countries are also party to the Lomé Convention which accords preferential access to the European Community. Many former Commonwealth preferences have been replaced by these arrangements.

British aid for the development needs of the Commonwealth countries and dependent territories are dealt with under the provisions of the Overseas Aid Act 1966, administered by the Overseas Development Administration. This Act succeeds the former Colonial Development and Welfare Acts. Those countries which are party to the Lomé Convention also receive aid under that Convention from the European Community.

Commonwealth Secretariat. Marlborough House, Pall Mall, SW1Y 5HX (Tel: 071 839 3411).— This was established by decision of Commonwealth heads of government in 1965, and is the main agency for multi-lateral communication between Commonwealth governments on issues relating to the Commonwealth as a whole. It promotes consultation and disseminates information on matters of common concern, organizes meetings and conferences, coordinates Commonwealth activities and provides technical assistance for economic and social development through the Commonwealth Fund for Technical Cooperation.
Secretary General, Chief Emeka Anyaoku.

Commonwealth Institute, *see* Index.

Dependent Territories and Associated States.—Britain, Australia and New Zealand have a number of dependent territories. New Zealand also has two associated states; the Cook Islands (since 1965) and Niue (since 1974). These are self-governing states in association with New Zealand, which remains responsible for their external affairs and defence.

Member States of the Commonwealth
(with dates of independence)

1867*	Canada
1901*	Australia
1907*	New Zealand
1947	India (Republic, 1950)
	Pakistan (Republic, 1956)
1948	Sri Lanka (Republic, 1972)
1957	Ghana (Republic, 1960)
	Federation of Malaya (Federation of Malaysia since 1963—indigenous monarchy)
1960	Cyprus (Republic on independence; joined Commonwealth 1961)
	Nigeria (Republic, 1963)
1961	Sierra Leone (Republic, 1971)
	Tanganyika (Republic, 1962; united 1964 with Zanzibar as Tanzania)

1962	Western Samoa (Republic on independence; joined Commonwealth 1970)
	Jamaica
	Trinidad and Tobago (Republic, 1976)
	Uganda (Republic, 1967)
1963	Kenya (Republic, 1964; Second Republic, 1971)
	Singapore (as State in Federation of Malaysia; seceded as Republic, 1965)
1964	Malawi (Republic, 1966)
	Malta (Republic, 1974)
	Zambia (Republic on independence)
1965	The Gambia (Republic, 1970)
	Maldives (Republic, 1968; joined Commonwealth as a Special Member 1982; full member 1985)
1966	Guyana (Republic, 1970)
	Botswana (Republic on independence)
	Lesotho (indigenous monarchy)
	Barbados
1968	Mauritius
	Nauru (Republic on independence—Special Member)
	Swaziland (indigenous monarchy)
1970	Tonga (indigenous monarchy)
1971	Bangladesh (Republic on independence; joined Commonwealth 1972)
1973	Bahamas
1974	Grenada
1975	Papua New Guinea
1976	Seychelles (Republic on independence)
1978	Solomon Islands
	Tuvalu (Special Member)
	Dominica (Republic on independence)
1979	Saint Lucia
	Kiribati (Republic on independence)
	Saint Vincent and the Grenadines (joined as a Special Member; became a full member 1985)
1980	Zimbabwe (Republic on independence)
	Vanuatu (Republic on independence)
1981	Belize
	Antigua and Barbuda
1983	Saint Christopher and Nevis
1984	Brunei (indigenous monarchy)
1990	Namibia (Republic on independence)

* These are the effective dates of independence, given legal effect by the Statute of Westminster 1931.

(The above member states are realms of Queen Elizabeth II unless otherwise stated.)

Countries which have left the Commonwealth

1949	Republic of Ireland
1961	South Africa
1972	Pakistan (rejoined 1989)
1987	Fiji

ANTIGUA AND BARBUDA
(State of Antigua and Barbuda)

AREA, POPULATION, ETC.—Antigua and Barbuda comprises the islands of Antigua (108 sq. miles (279 sq. km)), Barbuda (62 sq. miles (160 sq. km)) 25 miles north of Antigua, and Redonda ($\frac{1}{2}$ sq. mile; 1·2 sq. km) 25 miles south-west of Antigua. Antigua is part of the Leeward Islands in the Eastern Caribbean and lies 17° 3′ N. and 61° 48′ W. It is distinguished from the rest of the Leeward group by its absence of high hills and forest, and a drier climate than most of the West Indies. Barbuda, formerly a possession of the Codrington family, is very flat, mainly scrub-covered with a large lagoon. Antigua was first settled by the English in 1632, and was granted to Lord Willoughby by Charles II. The total population (official estimate

1988) is 80,200; Antigua had a population of 78,800, Barbuda 1,400, and Redonda was uninhabited.

CAPITAL.—ΨSt John's. Population, 30,000. The town of Barbuda is Codrington.

CURRENCY.—East Caribbean dollar (EC$) of 100 cents.

FLAG.—Inverted triangle (centred on a red field) divided horizontally into three bands of black over blue over white; rising sun device in gold on black band.

NATIONAL ANTHEM.—Fair Antigua and Barbuda.

NATIONAL DAY.—November 1 (Independence Day).

GOVERNMENT

Antigua became internally self-governing in 1967 and fully independent on November 1, 1981, as a constitutional monarchy with HM The Queen as Head of State, represented by the Governor-General. There is a Senate of 17 appointed members and a House of Representatives elected every five years. The Attorney-General may be appointed.

The Antigua Labour party led by Mr Vere Bird won the general election of March 9, 1989 and a fourth successive term of office.

Governor-General, Sir Wilfred Ebenezer Jacobs, GCMG, GCVO, OBE, QC.

Cabinet
(as at July 18, 1991)

Prime Minister, Rt. Hon. Dr Vere C. Bird, sen.
Legal Affairs and Attorney-General, Hon. Keith Ford, QC.
Finance and Trade, Hon. Molwyn Joseph.
Home Affairs and Social Services, Hon. Christopher O'Marde.
Economic Development, Industry and Tourism, Hon. Dr Rodney Williams.
Agriculture, Fisheries, Lands and Housing, Hon. Hilroy Humphreys.
Education, Culture, and Youth Affairs, Hon. Bernard Percival.
Labour and Health, Hon. Adolphus Freeland.
Public Utilities, Transportation and Energy, Hon. Robin Yearwood.
Public Works and Communications, Hon. Eustace Cochrane.

HIGH COMMISSION FOR
ANTIGUA AND BARBUDA
15 Thayer Street, W1M 5LD
[071–486 7073]

High Commissioner, His Excellency James Thomas (1987).

ECONOMY

Tourism is the main sector of the economy. Tourism and related services account for 60 per cent of GDP and employ 40 per cent of the workforce; Antigua was one of the first Caribbean islands to attract tourists.

For many years sugar was the dominant crop but is now produced only for local consumption. Agricultural production includes livestock, sea island cotton, mixed market gardening and fishing.

FINANCE

	1989*	1990*
Revenue	EC$236,720,991	EC$249,560,916
Expenditure (recurrent)	263,579,351	271,730,204
*estimated		

Trade with UK

	1989	1990
Imports from UK	£23,954,000	£17,890,000
Exports to UK	3,447,000	2,931,000

BRITISH HIGH COMMISSION
11 Old Parham Road (PO 483), St. John's
[St John's 462 0008/9]

High Commissioner, (resides at Bridgetown, Barbados).
Resident Representative, I. D. Marsh (*First Secretary*).

THE COMMONWEALTH OF AUSTRALIA
AREA AND POPULATION

States	Estimated area (sq. km)	Estimated resident population June 30, 1990p
States		
New South Wales (NSW)	801,600	5,827,400
Queensland (Qld.)	1,727,200	2,906,800
South Australia (SA)	984,000	1,439,200
Tasmania (Tas.)	67,800	456,700
Victoria (Vic.)	227,600	4,380,000
Western Australia (WA)	2,525,500	1,633,900
Territories		
Australian Capital Territory (ACT)	2,400	285,000
Northern Territory (NT)	1,346,200	157,300
Total	7,682,300	17,086,200

p preliminary

Inter-Censal Increases, 1961–1986

Year of Census	Inter-censal increase	Net immigration during period	
1961	(b) 1,521,656	1954–1961	584,754
1966	1,051,231	1961–1966	395,485
1971 (a)	(c) 1,156,140	1966–1971	521,139
1976 (a)	965,818	1971–1976	281,074
1981 (a)	890,177	1976–1981	370,865
1986 (a)	1,095,090	1981–1986	449,960

(a) Based on Census counts, place of usual residence, adjusted for under-enumeration, and including an estimate of Australian residents temporarily overseas on Census night.
(b) Excludes full-blood Aboriginals.
(c) Based on 1971 Census figure as enumerated.

Population of Aboriginal and Torres Strait Islander Origin

	June 1986	
	Number	Percentage of state population
States		
New South Wales	59,011	1·1
Queensland	61,268	2·4
South Australia	14,291	1·1
Tasmania	6,716	1·5
Victoria	12,611	0·3
Western Australia	37,789	2·7
Territories		
Australian Capital Territory	1,220	0·5
Northern Territory	34,739	22·4
Total	227,645	1·5

Births, Deaths, Marriages and Divorces
(Year ended June 30)

	1987	1988	1989
Births......	242,797	246,200	250,853
Deaths	116,139	120,463	124,232
Marriages ..	110,690	114,350	120,121
Divorces† ..	39,725	41,007	41,383

†year ended December 31

Migration
(Year ended June 30)

	1988	1989	1990
Permanent arrivals ..	143,470	145,320	121,320
Permanent departures	20,470	21,650	27,860

PHYSICAL FEATURES

Australia, including Tasmania, comprises a land area of 7,682,300 sq. km lying between latitudes 10°41′S (Cape York) and 43°39′S (South East Cape, Tasmania) and longitudes 113°09′E (Steep Point) and 153°39′E (Cape Byron). The latitudinal distance between Cape York and South East Cape is about 3,680 kilometres and the longitudinal distance between Steep Point and Cape Byron is about 4,000 kilometres. (The latitudinal distance between Cape York and the most southerly point on the mainland South Point, Wilson's Promontory, is about 3,180 kilometres.)

Australia has three major landforms: the western plateau, the interior lowlands and the eastern uplands. The western half of the continent consists mainly of a great plateau of altitude 300–600 metres. The interior lowland includes the channel country of south-west Queensland (drainage to Lake Eyre) and the Murray-Darling river system to the south. The eastern uplands consist of a broad belt of varied width extending from north Queensland to Tasmania and composed largely of tablelands, ranges and ridges with only limited mountain areas above 1,000 metres. The highest point is Mt. Kosciusko (2,228 m) and the lowest, Lake Eyre (− 15 m).

Australia's large area and latitudinal range have resulted in climatic conditions ranging from the alpine to the tropical. Two-thirds of the continent is arid or semi-arid although good rainfalls (over 800 mm annually) occur in the northern monsoonal belt under the influence of the Australian–Asian monsoon and along the eastern and southern highland regions under the influence of the great atmospheric depressions of the Southern Ocean. The effectiveness of the rainfall is greatly reduced by marked alternations of wet and dry seasons, unreliability from year to year, high temperatures and high potential evaporation.

Fifty per cent of the area of Australia has a medium rainfall of less than 300 mm per year and 80 per cent has less than 600 mm. Extreme minimum temperatures are not as low as those recorded in other continents because of the absence of extensive mountain masses and because of the expanse of ocean to the south. However, extreme maxima are comparatively high, reaching 50°C over the inland, mainly due to the great east–west extent of the continent in the vicinity of the Tropic of Capricorn.

Only one-third of the Australian land mass drains directly to the ocean, mainly on the coastal side of the Main Divide and inland with the Murray-Darling system. With the exception of the Murray-Darling system, most rivers draining to the ocean are comparatively short and account for the majority of the country's average annual discharge.

GOVERNMENT

The Commonwealth of Australia was constituted by an Act of the Imperial Parliament dated July 9, 1900, and was inaugurated January 1, 1901. The government is that of a Federal Commonwealth within the British Commonwealth of Nations, the executive power being vested in the Sovereign (through the Governor-General), assisted by a Federal Ministry of Ministers of State. Under the Constitution the Federal Government has acquired and may acquire certain defined powers as surrendered by the States, residuary legislative power remaining with the States. The right of a State to legislate on any matter is not abrogated except in connection with matters exclusively under Federal control, but where a State law is inconsistent with a law of the Commonwealth the latter prevails to the extent of the inconsistency.

CURRENCY.—Australian dollar ($A) of 100 cents.

FLAG.—The British Blue Ensign, consisting of a blue flag, with the Union Flag occupying the upper quarter next the staff, differenced by a large white star (representing the six States of Australia and the Territories of the Commonwealth) in the centre of the lower quarter next the staff and pointing direct to the centre of the St George's Cross in the Union Flag and five white stars, representing the Southern Cross, in the fly.

NATIONAL ANTHEM.—Advance Australia Fair.

NATIONAL DAY.—January 26 (Australia Day).

Governor-General and Staff

Governor-General, His Excellency the Hon. Bill Hayden, AC, *born* January 23, 1933; *assumed office*, February 16, 1989.

Official Secretary, R. D. Sturkey.

Deputy Official Secretary, Mrs L. Lawless.

Cabinet
(as at July 7, 1991)

Prime Minister, Hon. Robert Hawke, AC.

Deputy PM and Health, Housing and Community Services, Hon. Brian Howe.

Treasurer, Hon. John Kerin.

Immigration, Local Government and Ethnic Affairs, Hon. Gerry Hand.

Attorney-General, Hon. Michael Duffy.

Defence, Senator Hon. Robert Ray.

Industrial Relations, Senator Hon. Peter Cook.

Transport and Communications, Hon. Kim Beazley.

Finance, Hon. Ralph Willis.

Foreign Affairs and Trade, Senator Hon. Gareth Evans.

Administrative Services, Senator Hon. Nick Bolkus.

Industry, Technology and Commerce, Senator Hon. John Button.

Primary Industries and Energy, Hon. Simon Crean.

Social Security, Senator Hon. Graham Richardson.

Employment, Education and Training, Hon. John Dawkins.

Arts, Sport, the Environment, Tourism and Territories, Hon. Roslyn Kelly.

Trade Negotiations, Hon. Neal Blewett.

Junior Ministers

Land Transport, Hon. Robert Brown.

Justice and Consumer Affairs, Senator Hon. Michael Tate.

Small Business and Customs, Hon. David Beddall.

Veterans' Affairs, Hon. Benjamin Humphreys.

Aboriginal Affairs, Hon. Robert Tickner.

Shipping and Aviation Support, Senator Hon. Bob Collins.

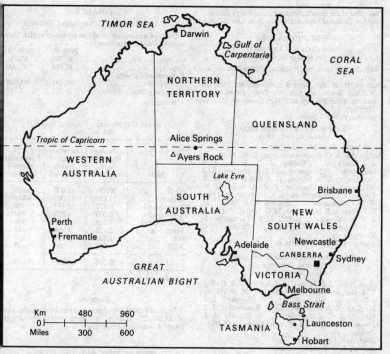

Aged, Family and Health Services, Hon. Peter Staples.
Higher Education and Employment Services, Hon.
  Peter Baldwin.
Defence Science and Personnel, Hon. Gordon Bilney.
Local Government, Hon. Wendy Fatin.
Resources, Hon. Alan Griffiths.
Arts, Tourism and Territories, Hon. David Simmons.
Science and Technology, Hon. Ross Free.

AUSTRALIAN HIGH COMMISSION
Australia House, Strand, London, WC2B 4LA
[071–379 4334]
High Commissioner, His Excellency The Hon.
  Richard Smith.
Deputy High Commissioner, R. Greet.
Official Secretary, D. Connors.
Ministers, Ms K. Campbell (Political); P. Tormey
  (Economic); E. F. Delofski (Economic).
Defence Adviser and Head of Defence Staff, Air Cdre
  B. Lane.

BRITISH HIGH COMMISSION
Commonwealth Avenue, Canberra
ACT 2600
[Canberra (06) 270 6666]
High Commissioner, His Excellency Brian L. Barder
  (1991).
Deputy High Commissioner, Head of Chancery, I.
  Mackley, CMG.
Defence and Naval Adviser and Head of British
  Defence Liaison Staff, Cdre A. C. G. Wolstenholme.
Counsellor, T. N. Young (Director, Trade Promotion).
First Secretaries, D. Moorhouse (Management); D.

Blunt, LVO; G. Minter, MVO (Commercial, Agricul-
  ture); W. C. Patey; M. R. Eastburn (Information);
  M. R. Maiden (Defence Exports); G. Burrows
  (Defence Research); K. Harding.
Military Adviser, Col. C. D. McCarthy.
Air Adviser, Gp. Capt. J. G. Sheldon.
Consuls-General, B. S. Jones, LVO (Brisbane); S. D. R.
  Brown (Melbourne); L. W. Boyes (Perth); R. S.
  Reeve (Sydney).
Cultural Adviser and British Council Representative,
  M. C. Foot, OBE, Edgecliff Centre, 203–233 New
  South Head Road (PO Box 88), Edgecliff, Sydney
  2027.

THE LEGISLATURE

Parliament consists of The Queen, the Senate and the House of Representatives. The Constitution provides that the number of members of the House of Representatives shall be, as nearly as practicable, twice the number of Senators. Members of the Senate are elected for six years by universal suffrage, half the members retiring every third year. Each of the six States returns an equal number of 12 Senators, and the Australian Capital Territory and the Northern Territory two each. The House of Representatives, similarly elected for a maximum of three years, contains members proportionate to the population, with a minimum of five members for each State. There are now 148 members in the House of Representatives, including one member for the Northern Territory and two for the Australian Capital Territory.

President of the Senate, Senator Hon. Kerry Sibraa.
Speaker, House of Representatives, Hon. Leo McLeay.

THE JUDICATURE

HIGH COURT OF AUSTRALIA
(as at May 31, 1991)

Chief Justice, Hon. Sir Anthony Frank Mason, AC, KBE.

Justices, Hons. Sir Gerard Brennan, AC, KBE; Sir William Deane, AC, KBE; Sir Daryl Dawson, AC, KBE, CB; John Toohey, AC; Mary Gaudron; Michael McHugh, AC.

Registrar, F. W. D. Jones.

FEDERAL COURT OF AUSTRALIA
(as at June 1, 1991)

Chief Justice, Hon. M. E. J. Black.

Judges, Hons. C. A. Sweeney, CBE; R. M. Northrop; J. A. Keely; J. F. Gallop; J. D. Davies; J. S. Lockhart; I. F. Sheppard, AO; T. R. Morling; K. J. Jenkinson; A. R. Neaves; B. A. Beaumont; M. R. Wilcox; J. E. J. Spender; P. R. A. Gray; C. W. Pincus; J. C. S. Burchett; J. A. Miles; D. M. Ryan; W. M. C. Gummow; R. S. French; M. R. Einfeld; M. L. Foster; A. B. Nicholson; M. C. Lee; H. W. Olney; J. W. von Doussa; D. G. Hill; M. F. O'Loughlin; D. F. O'Connor; T. J. Higgins; J. H. Phillips; P. C. Heerey.

Registrar, J. T. Howard, RFD, ED.

SUPREME COURT OF THE AUSTRALIAN CAPITAL TERRITORY
(as at May 31, 1991)

Judges, Hons. J. A. Miles (*Chief Justice*); J. F. Gallop; T. J. Higgins (*Resident Judges*); R. M. Northrop; J. D. Davies; J. S. Lockhart; I. F. Sheppard; T. R. Morling; K. J. Jenkinson; B. A. Beaumont; M. R. Wilcox; J. E. J. Spender; C. W. Pincus; M. L. Foster; D. M. Ryan; J. W. von Doussa (*Additional Judges*).

Master, A. E. Hogan.

Registrar, A. G. Towill.

SUPREME COURT OF THE NORTHERN TERRITORY
(as at May 31, 1990)

Chief Justice, Hon. K. J. A. Asche.

Judges, Hons. J. A. Nader; Sir William Kearney; P. J. Rice; B. J. Martin; D. N. Angel.

Master, P. G. Lefevre.

DEFENCE

A single Department of Defence was created in 1973, following the abolition of the Departments of the Navy, Army and Air, though the separate identities of the three services have been retained. The defence research and development elements of the former Department of Supply, along with other research groups on the three services, were incorporated in 1978 into the Defence, Science and Technology Organization. The Chief of Defence Force Staff is responsible for command of the Defence Force through the three Service Chiefs of Staff and is also the principal military adviser to the Minister.

The Secretary to the Department of Defence is responsible to the Minister for Defence for advice on policy, resources and organization.

Total defence expenditure was $A 8,476,271 in 1989–90.

The personnel strengths of the Permanent Defence Force at June 30, 1990 were:—

	Males	Females
Navy	13,737	1,919
Army	27,716	2,617
Air Force	18,624	3,228
Total	60,177	7,764

FINANCE

COMMONWEALTH GOVERNMENT FINANCE

Outlays and revenue of the Commonwealth Government were ($Amillion):

	1989–90	1990–91†
Current outlays	85,305	93,242
Capital outlays	11,813	12,009
Revenue and grants received	97,491	101,498
Financing transactions	−372	3,754

†estimate

STATE GOVERNMENT FINANCE 1989–90*
($A million)

State	Outlay (current and capital)	Revenue and grants received	Financing transactions
NSW	20,990	19,605	1,385
Victoria	17,420	13,902	3,519
Queensland	9,857	10,197	−339
S. Australia	5,660	4,829	830
W. Australia	7,011	6,112	899
Tasmania	2,122	1,955	167
NT	1,384	1,227	157
ACT	942	990	−48
Total	65,386	58,817	6,570

* preliminary

BANKING

In June 1990 the trading banks had total liabilities of $A268,022 million including total deposits of $A183,430 million securities.

PRODUCTION AND INDUSTRY

In 1985, 63·6 per cent of the Australian land area consisted of agricultural establishments, with the remainder being urban areas, State forests, mining leases and unoccupied land. Crop-growing areas constituted up to 4·32 per cent of the total agricultural establishments, emphasizing the relative importance of the livestock industries in Australia (sheep in the warm, temperate, semi-arid lands and beef cattle in the tropics).

The wide range of climatic and soil conditions over the agricultural regions of Australia has resulted in a diversity of crops being grown throughout the country. Generally, cereal crops (excluding rice and sorghum) are grown in all States over wide areas, while other crops are confined to specific locations in a few States. However, scanty or erratic rainfall, limited potential for irrigation and unsuitable soils or topography have restricted intensive agriculture.

Mines and Minerals.—Significant mineral resources comprise bauxite, coal, copper, crude petroleum, gems, gold, ilmenite, iron ore, lead, limestone, manganese, nickel, rutile, salt, silver, tin, tungsten, uranium, zinc and zircon. Recently, geological exploration has significantly increased the mineral resources of the nation and a number of oilfields are in production.

In 1988–89, value added by the mining industry was $A12,480.1m. In 1987–88 mine production of black coal was 167,761,000 tonnes, crude oil (including condensate) was 31,297 megalitres and natural gas 14,751 gigalitres. Production of principal metals was:—

Iron ore	102,202,000 tonnes
Copper	241,706* ,,
Lead-Zinc concentrate	178,694 ,,
Gold	64,780* kg

*1985–86 figures

Gross Value of Agricultural Commodities 1989–90p
($A million)

	Total
Crops	9,961·3
Livestock slaughterings and other disposals	5,718·7
Livestock products	7,809·8
Total agriculture	23,508·7

p preliminary

Livestock Numbers at March 31, 1990
(Thousands)

	Total
Cattle	23,191
Sheep	170,297
Pigs	2,706
Poultry	56,990

Gross Value of Crops 1989–90p

	Total
Cereals for grain	3,994·8
Cotton	740·1
Crops for hay	116·9
Fruit and nuts	1,413·2
Legumes for grain	306·3
Nursery production	449·9
Oilseeds	84·9
Peanuts	16·1
Sugar cane for crushing........	882·7
Tobacco	72·2
Vegetables....................	1,357·0
Pastures and grasses...........	527·2
Total crops	9,961·3

p preliminary

Manufactures.—In 1988–89 there were in Australia 31,249 industrial establishments, employing 1,072,634 persons; wages paid amounted to $A25,599m; and turnover $A151,857m.

TRADE

	1988–89	1989–90
Imports	$A47,039m	$A51,323m
Exports	43,522m	48,746m

Of Australia's total exports in the year 1989–90, the largest category was metalliferous ores and metal scrap, worth $A7,188·9m. This was followed by coal, coke and briquettes, $A5,942·2m; textile fibres and their wastes, $A4,680·5m; and non-ferrous metals, $A3,880·2m. Cereals and cereal preparations to the value of $A3,607m were exported, and meat and meat preparations worth $A2,881·4m.

The largest category of Australia's imports was road vehicles, worth $A5,061·7m. This was followed by miscellaneous manufactured articles, $A6,680·1m; office and automatic data processing machines, $A3,557·1m; general industrial machinery and equipment, $A2,975·1m; specialized machinery for particular industries, $A2,757·0m; and electrical machinery, $A2,716·7m.

In 1989–90, 26·2 per cent of Australia's total exports went to Japan. The USA received 10·8 per cent, Republic of Korea 5·5, New Zealand 5·3, Singapore 4·0, Taiwan 3·7, UK 3·6 and Hong Kong 2·7.

Of Australia's total imports in 1989–90, 24·1 per cent came from the USA, 19·2 from Japan, 6·7 West Germany, 6·5 UK, 4·2 New Zealand, 3·8 Taiwan and 3·2 Italy.

Trade with UK

	1989	1990
Imports from UK	£1,711,241,000	£1,645,620,000
Exports to UK ..	864,965,000	1,039,080,000

COMMUNICATIONS

Railways.—There are six government owned railways systems, operated by the State Rail Authority of NSW, Victorian Railways, Queensland Government Railways, Western Australian Government Railways, the State Transport Authority of Southern Australia, and the Australian National Railways Commission. The ANRC incorporates the former Commonwealth Railways system, and the Tasmanian and non-metropolitan South Australian railways (urban rail services in Southern Australia remain the responsibility of the State Transport Authority). In 1989 there were 35,763 route-kilometres open.

Gross earnings 1988–89 were:	$A million
New South Wales	1,114·1
Victoria	n.a.
Queensland	1,107·1
South Australia*	17·6
Western Australia	306·2
ANRC	315·8
Total	n.a.

*Includes urban rail operations only.

In 1988–89 there were 417m rail passenger journeys on government railways and 179m tonnes of goods and livestock carried.

Shipping.—Total arrivals and departures of vessels engaged in overseas trade at the various Australian ports in 1988–89 were: arrivals 11,831 (455,162,000 deadweight tonnes); departures 11,727 (448,130,000 deadweight tonnes).

Broadcasting and Television.—On June 30, 1984, the Australian Broadcasting Corporation operated 144 stations. Privately owned commercial broadcasting stations totalled 137. On June 30, 1984, 276 national and 152 commercial television and translator stations were in operation.

Motor Vehicles.—At June 30, 1990, there were 9,776,600 motor vehicles registered in Australia and 304,000 motor cycles.

Civil Aviation.—Figures for domestic and overseas services in 1989–90p are as follows:

	Domestic	Overseas
Paying passengers ...	9,878,000	n.a.
Freight (tonnes)	99,000	n.a.

p=preliminary

FEDERAL CAPITAL

CANBERRA is the capital of Australia. It is situated in the Australian Capital Territory which has an area of 939 sq. miles (2,395 sq. km) and was acquired from New South Wales in 1911. Canberra, which is the seat of the federal government, had a population (estimated) at June 30, 1989, of 303,200. Apart from Parliament House, the city also contains other national institutions, such as the Australian War Memorial, National Library, Royal Australian Mint and the Australian National University. Most Government departments have their headquarters in

Canberra. An artificial lake is a central feature of this planned city, based on Walter Burley Griffin's design.

THE NORTHERN TERRITORY

The Northern Territory has a total area of 519,770 sq. miles (1,346,200 sq. km), and lies between 129°–138° east longitude and 11°–26° south latitude. The estimated population in the Northern Territory at June 30, 1991 was 157,300, of which about a quarter are Aboriginals.

The administration was taken over by the Commonwealth on January 1, 1911 from the government of the State of South Australia.

The Northern Territory (Self-Government) Act 1978 established the Northern Territory as a body politic as from July 1, 1978, with Ministers having control over and responsibility for Territory finances and the administration of the functions of government as specified by the Federal Government by regulations made pursuant to the Act. Proposed laws passed by the Legislative Assembly in relation to a transferred function require the assent of the Administrator. Proposed laws in all other cases may be assented to by the Administrator or reserved by the Administrator for the Governor General's pleasure. The Governor General may disallow any laws assented to by the Administrator within six months of the Administrator's assent.

The Northern Territory has federal representation electing one member to the House of Representatives and two members to the Senate.

Seat of Administration.—Darwin.

Administrator, His Hon. the Honourable J. H. Muirhead, AC, QC.

THE MINISTRY
(as at June 30, 1991)

Chief Minister, Minister for Police, Fire and Emergency Services, Hon. Marshall Perron.

Deputy Chief Minister, Treasurer, Minister for Mines and Energy, Hon. Barry Coulter.

Attorney-General, Minister for Health and Community Services, Hon. Daryl Manzie.

Education and Arts, Employment and Training, Hon. Shane Stone.

Industries and Development, Hon. Steve Hatton.

Transport and Works, Hon. Fred Finch.

Primary Industry and Fisheries, Conservation, Correctional Services, Hon. Mike Reed.

Tourism, Sport, Recreation and Ethnic Affairs, Local Government, Hon. Roger Vale.

Lands and Housing, Hon. Max Ortmann.

Various Aboriginal Land Trusts hold title to land previously called Reserves, totalling about one-fifth of the Northern Territory.

The Aboriginal Land Rights (NT) Act of 1976 provides for the investigation and determination of Aboriginal traditional claims to vacant Crown land or land already owned by or on behalf of Aboriginals. Successful land claims to date have increased Aboriginal ownership to 34 per cent of the Northern Territory whilst a further 13 per cent is the subject of claims.

A number of major Aboriginal communities previously administered by Church Mission Societies and the Federal Government are now controlled by the Aboriginal people themselves, through local Aboriginal Councils. A recent phenomenon is the voluntary movement of some Aboriginals to their traditional homeland areas where they feel that their culture will be better preserved.

ECONOMY

Northern Territory's economy is based on the exploitation of its natural resources of minerals, land, fisheries and tourist attractions. Following the introduction of a number of government measures designed to expand and diversify primary production, the Territory's agricultural and horticultural industries are also beginning to contribute an increasing amount to Territory rural output. The beef cattle industry continues to be the major user of pastoral lands.

Mining has played a major part in the development of the Northern Territory and in 1990 total value of production was $A1·5 billion. The Territory is a leading uranium producer, extracting 3,290,069 kg of uranium oxide in 1990 with a value of $A255 million. In 1990 more than 2·1 million tonnes of manganese was sold, with a total value of about $A199 million. Gold production for 1990 was estimated at $A278 million. The value ex mines of bauxite sales exceeded $A278 million and alumina production was valued at $A189 million. The value of oil and gas production for 1990 was $A358 million.

Tourism is of importance to the Territory's economy. It is a major growth industry and generates over $A430 million annually.

COMMUNICATIONS

The Northern Territory has three main ports—Darwin, managed by the Darwin Port Authority, and the private mining ports of Gove and Groote Eylandt.

The standard gauge rail link between Southern Australia and Alice Springs was officially opened in October 1980. The link between Alice Springs and Darwin is provided by a fully co-ordinated rail-road service.

The main population centres are linked by the Stuart Highway, which connects Alice Springs to Darwin via Tennant Creek and Katherine. Of special interest to the Northern Territory is the operation of 'road trains'. These are basically massive trucks hauling two or three trailers, having a net capacity of about 100 tonnes and measuring up to 45 metres in length.

AUSTRALIAN EXTERNAL TERRITORIES

ASHMORE AND CARTIER ISLANDS

Ashmore Islands (known as Middle, East and West Islands) and Cartier Island are situated in the Indian Ocean some 850 km and 790 km west of Darwin respectively. The islands lie at the outer edge of the continental shelf. They are small and low and are composed of coral and sand. Vegetation consists mainly of grass. Turtles are plentiful at certain times of the year and beche-de-mer is abundant. The islands are uninhabited.

Great Britain took formal possession of the Ashmores in 1878 and Cartier was annexed in 1909. By Imperial Order in Council of July 23, 1931 the islands were placed under the authority of the Commonwealth of Australia, and were accepted in 1933 under the name of the Territory of Ashmore and Cartier Islands. The territory was annexed to the Northern Territory of Australia. With the granting of self-government to the Northern Territory on July 1, 1978 responsibility for the administration of Ashmore and Cartier Islands became a direct responsibility of the Commonwealth Government. In 1983 Ashmore Reef was declared a national nature reserve.

In accordance with an agreement between the governments of Indonesia and Australia, Indonesian fishermen who have traditionally plied the area may engage in limited fishing activity within the territory but are prohibited from taking any products from the nature reserve. They can land to collect water from West Island.

THE AUSTRALIAN ANTARCTIC TERRITORY

The Australian Antarctic Territory was established by an Order in Council, dated February 7, 1933, which placed under the government of the Commonwealth of Australia all the islands and territories, other than Adélie Land, which are situated south of the latitude 60° S. and lying between 160° E. longitude and 45° E. longitude. The Order came into force on August 24, 1936, after the passage of the Australian Antarctic Territory Acceptance Act 1933. The boundaries of Terre Adélie were definitely fixed by a French Decree of April 1, 1938, as the islands and territories south of 60° S. latitude lying between 136° E. longitude and 142° E. longitude. The Australian Antarctic Territory Act 1954 declared that the laws in force in the Australian Capital Territory are, so far as they are applicable, in force in the Australian Antarctic Territory. The territory is administered by the Antarctic Division of the Department of Science, which, since its inception in 1947, has organized yearly expeditions to Antarctica, known as Australian National Antarctic Research Expeditions (ANARE).

On February 13, 1954 ANARE opened Mawson Station in Mac-Robertson Land at latitude 67° 36′ S. and longitude 62° 53′ E. Scientific research conducted at Mawson includes upper atmosphere physics, cosmic ray physics, meteorology, earth sciences, biology and medical science. Mawson is also a centre for coastal and inland exploration.

Davis Station was opened on the coast of Princess Elizabeth Land on January 13, 1957, at latitude 68° 35′ S. and longitude 77° 58′ E. Scientific programmes carried out at Davis include meteorology, biology, upper atmosphere physics, with field investigations in biology.

Casey Station, on the coast of Wilkes Land at latitude 66°17′S and longitude 110°32′E, was established in 1969 to replace the American-built Wilkes Station a few miles away. A new station 0·7 miles away was opened in 1988. Scientific research conducted out of Casey includes glaciology (deep ice drilling), meteorology, upper atmosphere physics and botanical studies.

Since 1948 ANARE has operated a station on Macquarie Island, a dependency of Tasmania, situated at 54° 30′ S. and 158° 57′ E., about 900 miles north of the Antarctic Continent.

Summer stations have been established in the Bunger Hills, 200 miles west of Casey, at Cape Denison in Commonwealth Bay, in the Larsemann Hills and on Heard Island.

CHRISTMAS ISLAND

Until the end of 1957 a part of the then Colony of Singapore, Christmas Island was administered as a separate colony until October 1, 1958, when it became an Australian territory. It is situated in the Indian Ocean about 1,408 km NW of North West Cape in Western Australia, and has an area of 135 sq. km. Population (estimated, June 30, 1990) is 1,300, consisting of former employees of the Phosphate Mining Corporation, and present employees of the Christmas Island Administration, the Christmas Island Services Corporation, and their families. There is no indigenous population.

The island is densely wooded and had extensive deposits of phosphates, the extraction of which has traditionally been the major economic activity. An Australian Government company, the Phosphate Mining Corporation of Christmas Island, which carried out the mining operation ceased operating in 1987. Extensive deposits of low grade phosphate ore still remain but alternative economic development is

being encouraged. The principal current development is a hotel complex.

The Administrator is responsible to the Australian Minister for Arts, Sport, the Environment, Tourism and Territories in Canberra. The Christmas Island Local Assembly is presently chaired by the Administrator and has nine elected members. The Assembly is responsible for directing the operations of the Christmas Islands Services Corporation, which was established in 1984 to provide municipal functions and services.

Deputy to the Administrator, A. Mitchell.

COCOS (KEELING) ISLANDS

The Cocos (Keeling) Islands were declared a British possession in 1857. All land in the islands was granted to George Clunies-Ross and his heirs by Queen Victoria in 1886. In 1955 the islands, which had been governed through the British colonies of Ceylon (from 1878), the Straits Settlements (1886) and Singapore (1903), were accepted as a Territory of Australia.

In 1978 the Australian Government purchased all Clunies-Ross land and property interests except for the family home and grounds. In 1979 ownership of the kampong area of Home Island was transferred to the Cocos (Keeling) Islands Council, the local government body established in 1979. Title to most of the remaining land purchased from Clunies-Ross in 1978 was transferred to the Council in 1984.

The Cocos (Keeling) Islands Act 1955 provides the legal framework for the present political and administrative arrangements in the territory. On April 6, 1984, the Cocos community, in a UN supervised Act of Self-Determination, chose to integrate with Australia. The Government's major commitment was that living standards would reach comparable mainland levels by 1994. The Commonwealth Grants Commission monitors the progress.

The islands are two separate atolls (North Keeling Island and, 24 km to the south, the main atoll) comprising some 27 small coral islands with a total area of about 14 sq. km, situated in the Indian Ocean in latitude 12° 5′ South and longitude 96° 53′ East. The main islands of the southern atoll are West Island (the largest, about 9 km from north to south) on which are the administrative centre, the aerodrome, and the Australia-based employees of government departments; Home Island, where the Cocos Malay community and the Clunies-Ross family live; Direction Island, Horsburgh and South Island.

The territory has no viable economic base at present. In 1986–87 the copra industry suffered severe losses and in 1987 ceased production. Tourism is being developed as a likely successor to the copra industry.

The climate is equable and pleasant, being usually under the influence of the south-east trade winds for about three-quarters of the year. A weekly air charter service operates between Perth, the Cocos (Keeling) Islands and Christmas Island. Population (June 30, 1990), 618. The islands are administered by the Australian Government through the Department of the Arts, Sport, the Environment, Tourism and Territories in Canberra. All proposed Ordinances, Regulations and By-laws for the islands must be submitted to the Islands Council (est. 1979) for its consideration.

Administrator, Barry Cunningham.

CORAL SEA ISLANDS TERRITORY

The Coral Sea Islands Territory lies east of Queensland between the Great Barrier Reef and longitude 156° 06′ E., and between latitudes 12° and 24° S. It comprises scattered islands, spread over a sea area of 780,000 sq. km. The islands are formed mainly of coral and sand. Some have grass or scrub cover but most are extremely small, with no permanent fresh water.

There is a manned metereological station in the Willis Group but the remaining islands are uninhabited. Large populations of sea birds nest and breed in the area, and two national nature reserves were designated in the Territory in 1982.

The Australian Government bases its claim to the islands on numerous acts of sovereignty since early this century and enacted the Coral Sea Islands Act 1969 which declares the islands a territory of the Commonwealth of Australia. The Department of the Arts, Sport, the Environment, Tourism and Territories, Canberra, is responsible for the administration of the territory.

HEARD ISLAND AND McDONALD ISLANDS

The Heard and McDonald islands, about 4,100 km south-west of Fremantle, comprise all the islands and rocks lying between 52° 30′ and 53° 30′ S. latitude and 72° and 74° 30′ E. longitude. Sovereignty over the islands was transferred by the UK to the Commonwealth of Australia in 1947. The Heard Island and McDonald Islands Act 1953 provides for the government of the islands as one territory. Under this Act the law operating there is that of the Australian Capital Territory. The islands are administered by the Department of the Arts, Sport, the Environment, Tourism and Territories. Under the Environment Protection and Management Ordinance 1987, a permit system regulates entry to the territory and a range of activities there.

NORFOLK ISLAND

Norfolk Island is situated in the South Pacific Ocean at latitude 29° 02′ S. and longitude 167° 57′ E., being about 1,676 km NE of Sydney and 1,063 km north of Auckland. It is about 8 km long by 5 km wide, with an area of 3,455 hectares. The climate is mild and sub tropical. Resident population at the 1986 Census was 1,977.

The island, discovered by Capt. Cook in 1774, served as a penal colony from 1788 to 1814 and 1825 to 1855. In 1856, 194 descendants of the *Bounty* mutineers accepted an invitation to leave Pitcairn and settle on Norfolk Island, which led to Norfolk Island becoming a separate settlement under the jurisdiction of the Governor of NSW. In 1897 Norfolk Island became a dependency of NSW, and in 1914, pursuant to the Norfolk Island Act 1913, a territory of Australia. From that date, Norfolk Island has been regarded as an integral part of Australia.

In 1979 Norfolk Island gained a substantial degree of self-government, enabling the island to run its affairs to the greatest practical extent. Wide powers are exercised by a nine-member Legislative Assembly. The Act preserves the Commonwealth's responsibility for Norfolk Island as a territory under its authority, with the Minister for the Arts, Tourism and Territories as the responsible Minister.

The island is a popular tourist resort, and a large proportion of the population depends on tourism and its ancillaries for employment. In 1989–90 there were 23,201 tourist arrivals on the Island. Regular air services operate from mainland Australia and New Zealand.

The seat of government and administration offices are in Kingston.

Administrator, H. B. MacDonald, AM.

AUSTRALIAN STATES

NEW SOUTH WALES

The State of New South Wales is situated entirely between the 28th and 38th parallels of S. lat. and 141st and 154th meridians of E. long., and comprise an area of 309,433 sq. miles (801,427 sq. km) (exclusive of 939 sq. miles of Australian Capital Territory which lies within its borders).

POPULATION.—Preliminary estimated resident population at June 30, 1989 was 5,761,900.

Births, deaths and marriages of usually resident population were:

	1988	1989p
Births	85,901	87,27
Deaths	44,067	42,69
Marriages	38,810	44,37

p preliminary

Annual rate per 1,000 of estimated resident population in 1988:—Births 14·8; Deaths 7·8; Marriage 7·2. Deaths under 1 year per 1,000 live births, 9·0.

Religions

The members of the Roman Catholic Church in New South Wales, according to the Census of 1986 numbered 1,529,176, Anglican Church 1,519,806, Uniting (including Methodist) 327,360, Presbyterian 227,663, Orthodox 165,659, Baptist 67,187, Lutheran 31,890, other Christian 288,865, Muslim 57,551, Hebrew 28,236 and other religions 57,079. The religion of 1,101,409 persons was either not stated in the census schedules or was stated as 'none'.

PHYSIOGRAPHY

Natural features divide the State into four main zones extending from north to south: the Coastal Districts; the Tablelands, which form the Great Dividing Range between the coastal districts and the plains; the Western Slopes of the Dividing Range and the Western Plains. The highest points are Mounts Kosciusko, 7,314 ft., and Townsend, 7,251 ft. The western portion of the State is watered by the rivers of the Murray-Darling system. The Darling the major part of whose 1,712 miles is in NSW, and the Murrumbidgee, 981 miles, are both tributaries of the Murray, part of which forms the boundary between the States of New South Wales and Victoria.

Climate.—New South Wales is situated entirely in the temperate zone. At Sydney the average mean shade temperature is 18° C. Rainfall varies widely over the State diminishing from an annual average of about 2,000 mm in parts of the north coast to about 200 mm in the far north-west.

GOVERNMENT

New South Wales was first colonized as a British possession in 1788, and after progressive settlement a partly elective legislature was established in 1843. In 1855 responsible government was granted, the present Constitution being founded on the Constitution Act of 1902. New South Wales federated with the other States of Australia in 1901. The executive authority of the State is vested in a Governor (appointed by the Crown), assisted by a Council of Ministers.

GOVERNOR

Governor of New South Wales, His Excellency Rear Adm. Peter Sinclair, AO, RAN, *assumed office* August 1990.

Lt. Governor and Chief Justice of NSW, The Hon. Mr Justice Gleeson, AO.

THE MINISTRY
(as at June 30, 1991)

Premier, Treasurer, and Minister for Ethnic Affairs, Hon. N. F. Greiner.

Deputy Premier, Minister for Roads, Public Works, Hon. W. T. J. Murray.

Attorney-General, Minister for Consumer Affairs, Arts, Hon. P. E. J. Collins.

Agriculture and Rural Affairs, Hon. I. M. Armstrong, OBE.

Conservation and Land Management, Hon. G. B. West.

Housing, Hon. J. J. Schipp.

Environment, Hon. T. J. Moore.

State Development, Tourism, Hon. M. R. Yabsley.

Police and Emergency Services, Vice-President of Executive Council, Hon. E. P. Pickering.

Sport, Recreation and Racing, and Minister Assisting the Premier, Hon. G. Souris.

Health and Community Services, Hon. J. P. Hannaford.

School Education and Youth Affairs, Hon. V. A. Chadwick.

Transport, Hon. B. G. Baird.

Hospital Management, Hon. R. A. Phillips.

Planning, Energy, Hon. R. J. Webster.

Industrial Relations, Further Education, Training and Employment, Hon. J. J. Fahey.

Natural Resources, Hon. I. R. Causley.

Local Government Co-operatives, Hon. G. B. P. Peacocke.

Courts Administration and Corrective Services, Hon. T. A. Griffiths.

Chief Secretary, Minister for Administrative Services, Hon. A. M. Cohen.

AGENT-GENERAL IN LONDON

Agent-General, N. E. W. Pickard, 75 King William Street, EC4N 7HA.

THE LEGISLATURE

The Legislative Council consists of 42 members, elected by popular vote and the Legislative Assembly consists of 99 members elected for a maximum period of four years.

President of the Legislative Council, Hon. M. Willis, MLC.

Speaker, Legislative Assembly, Hon. K. R. Rozzoli, MP.

THE JUDICATURE

The judicial system includes a Supreme Court, Industrial Commission, District Court, Land and Environment Court, Compensation Court, and Local Courts (Magistrates).

Chief Justice, Supreme Court, The Hon. Mr Justice Gleeson, AO.

President, Court of Appeal, Hon. Mr Justice Kirby, CMG.

EDUCATION

Education.—Education is compulsory between the ages of 6 and 15 years. It is non-sectarian and free at all government schools. The enrolment in July 1988 in 2,204 government and 856 non-government schools was 1,038,600. The six universities had an enrolment of 71,902 students at April 30, 1988. In addition, there were 61,077 students enrolled in advanced education courses (predominantly in colleges of advanced education) in 1988. Students enrolled in technical and further education colleges in 1988 numbered 474,051.

PRODUCTION AND INDUSTRY

Livestock and Livestock Products.—A large area is suitable for sheep-raising, the principal breed of sheep being the merino, which was introduced in 1797.

Mining Industry.—The principal minerals are coal, lead, zinc, gold, rutile, copper and zircon. The total value of minerals extracted in 1987–88 was $A3,222 million. The average number of persons employed in the mining industry during 1987–88 was 22,761. In 1987–88, 76,268,000 tonnes of coal were produced.

Manufacturing Industry.—In 1987–88 there were 15,906 manufacturing establishments (employing four or more persons). The number of persons employed at June 30, 1988 was 379,000. Production of raw steel in 1989–89 was 5,259,000 tonnes.

TOWNS

ΨSydney, the State capital and the largest city in Australia, stands on the shores of Port Jackson. Sydney Harbour extends inland for 21 km; the total area of water is about 55 sq. km.

The preliminary estimated resident population at June 30, 1988 of the Sydney Statistical Division was 3,596,000. The Newcastle and Wollongong Statistical subdivisions contain populations of 422,100 and 235,300 respectively.

The populations of principal municipalities located outside the boundaries of these statistical areas are: Albury 39,610, Dubbo 31,290, Greater Taree 36,960, Hastings 42,220, Lismore 38,130, Orange 32,520, Shoalhaven 59,470, Tamworth 33,830, Wagga Wagga 50,930.

LORD HOWE ISLAND

Lord Howe Island, which is part of New South Wales, is situated 702 kilometres north-east of Sydney. Lat. 31° 33′ 4″ S., Long. 159° 4′ 26″ E. Area 6·37 sq. miles (16·5 sq. km.). Population, June 30, 1987, 290. The island is of volcanic origin with Mount Gower reaching an altitude of 866 m. The affairs of the Island are administered by the Lord Howe Island Board.

QUEENSLAND

This State, situated in lat. 9° 14′–29° S. and long. 138°–153° 30′ E., comprises the whole north-eastern portion of the Australian continent.

Queensland possesses an area of 666,798 sq. miles (1,727,000 sq. km).

POPULATION.—At June 30, 1990 the estimated resident population numbered 2,906,900.

Births, Deaths and Marriages were:

	1989	1990
Births	40,769	43,843
Deaths	18,910	20,637
Marriages	19,098	19,393

p preliminary

Annual rate per 1,000 of estimated resident population in 1990 was:—Births 15·3; Deaths 6·7; Marriages 6·8. Deaths under 1 year per 1,000 live births, 8·0.

Religions

At the Census of 1986, there were 640,867 Anglican, 628,906 Catholics, 255,287 Uniting Church, 120,239 Presbyterians, 56,910 Lutherans, 30,089 Baptists, and 211,316 other Christians.

PHYSIOGRAPHY

The Great Dividing Range on the eastern coast of the continent produces a similar formation to that of New South Wales, the eastern side having a narrow slope to the coast and the western a long and gradual slope to the central plains, where the Selwyn Range divides the land into a northern and southern watershed.

GOVERNMENT

Queensland was constituted a separate colony with responsible government in 1859, having previously formed part of New South Wales. The executive authority is vested in a Governor (appointed by the Crown), aided by an Executive Council of 18 members.

GOVERNOR

Governor of Queensland, His Excellency Hon. Sir Walter Benjamin Campbell, AC, QC.

EXECUTIVE COUNCIL
(HE the Governor presides)
(as at May 30, 1991)

Premier, Minister for Economic and Trade Development, and the Arts, Hon. W. K. Goss.
Deputy Premier, Minister for Housing and Local Government, Hon. T. J. Burns.
Police and Emergency Services, Hon. T. M. Mackenroth.
Treasurer, Hon. K. E. De Lacy.
Tourism, Sport and Racing, Hon. R. J. Gibbs.
Transport, Minister Assisting the Premier on Economic and Trade Development, Hon. D. J. Hamill.
Employment, Training and Industrial Relations, Hon. N. G. Warburton.
Resource Industries, Hon. K. H. Vaughan.
Primary Industries, Hon. E. D. Casey.
Health, Hon. K. V. McElligott.
Education, Hon. P. J. Braddy.
Environment and Heritage, Hon. P. Comben.
Attorney-General, Hon. D. M. Wells.
Family Services and Aboriginal and Islander Affairs, Hon. A. M. Warner.
Justice and Corrective Services, Hon. G. R. Milliner.
Administrative Services, Hon. R. T. McLean.
Business, Industry and Regional Development, Hon. G. N. Smith.
Land Management, Hon. A. G. Eaton.

AGENT-GENERAL IN LONDON

Agent-General, R. T. Anderson, 392 Strand, WC2R 0LZ.

THE LEGISLATURE

Parliament consists of a Legislative Assembly of 89 members, elected by all persons aged 18 years and over. The Assembly, as at June 30, 1990, was composed of: Australian Labor Party, 54; National Party of Australia, 26; Liberal Party of Australia, 9.
Speaker, Hon. D. Fouras.
Chairman of Committees, C. B. Campbell.
Leader of the Opposition, T. R. Cooper.

THE JUDICATURE

There are a Supreme Court; District Courts; Children's Courts; an Industrial Court; a Land Court and a Medical Assessment Tribunal; a Local Government Court; the Industrial Conciliation and Arbitration Commission; Inferior Courts at all the principal towns, presided over by Stipendiary Magistrates; a Small Claims Tribunal; Small Debts Court; a Licensing Court and a Mining Warden's Court.
Chief Justice, Supreme Court, Hon. J. M. Macrossan.

EDUCATION

Primary education is compulsory, secular and free between the ages of 6 and 15. At July, 1990, there were 1,065 government primary schools, 72 primary/ secondary, and 173 secondary schools with 249,561 primary students, and 141,688 secondary students.

Post-secondary education involves technical and further education (TAFE) and higher education. During 1988, 118,785 students were enrolled in TAFE courses, excluding 71,502 enrolled in adult education courses. At April 30, 1989, there were 38,962 full-time, 16,007 part-time, and 11,218 external students enrolled in higher education courses.

PRODUCTION AND INDUSTRY

Forestry.—Total Australian grown timber processed in 1989–90 amounted to 1,529,057 cubic metres (gross volume measure).

Minerals.—There are rich deposits of both metallic and non-metallic minerals. Coal is mined extensively in Central Queensland and on a lesser scale in the Ipswich district.

Manufacturing.—In 1988–89 there were 4,841 establishments with four or more workers, employing 133,743 persons, and producing goods and services worth $A 20,091 million. Much of the production was the processing of foodstuffs, minerals and chemical, petroleum and coal products. Included in other factory production were the products from engineering, transport equipment, timber, basic and fabricated metal, cement, paper and textile mills and oil refineries.

CAPITAL.—ΨBrisbane, is situated on the Brisbane River, which is navigable by large vessels to the city, over 23 kilometres from Moreton Bay. The estimated resident population of the Brisbane Statistical Division at June 30, 1990 was 1,301,658. This area includes the cities of Brisbane (749,527), Ipswich (75,955), Logan (148,320) and Redcliffe (49,803).

Other cities with population over 30,000 at June 30, 1990, are: ΨTownsville 84,138; Gold Coast 138,061; Toowoomba 82,438; ΨRockhampton 59,505; ΨCairns 43,631; ΨCaloundra 48,304; ΨThuringowa 37,337; Ψ Bundaberg 33,300.

SOUTH AUSTRALIA

The State of South Australia is situated between 26° and 38° S. lat. and 129° and 141° E. long., the total area being 380,070 sq. miles (984,376 sq. km).

POPULATION.—At June 30, 1990, the resident population was estimated to be 1,439,200.

Births, deaths and marriages were:

	1989	1990p
Births	19,703	20,014
Deaths	11,362	10,948
Marriages	9,776	9,669

p preliminary

Annual rate per 1,000 of estimated resident population in 1989 was:—Births 13·8; Deaths 8·0; Marriages 6·9. Deaths under 1 year per 1,000 live births, 7·5.

Religions

Religion is free and receives no State aid. At the Census, 1986, the persons belonging to the principal religious denominations were as follows: Catholic 267,137; Anglican 242,722; Uniting Church 176,980; Lutheran 64,851; Orthodox 37,149; Baptist 21,415; Presbyterian 18,566; Church of Christ 16,629; and Pentecostal 14,997.

PHYSIOGRAPHY

The most important physical features of South Australia are broad plains, divided longitudinally by four great secondary features, which form barriers to east-west movement, and which have thus largely determined the direction of roads and railways, the sites of towns and villages and the manner of distribution of the population. These four barriers are Spencer Gulf, Gulf St Vincent, the Mt. Lofty-Flinders Ranges and the River Murray.

The north-western portion of the State is mostly desert, while north of latitude 32° S. the country is unpromising by comparison with the fertile land which surrounds the hill country of the east. The Murray, which flows for some 400 miles through the south-eastern corner, is the only river of importance.

The lack of rivers and fresh-water lakes in the settled areas has necessitated the building of a number of reservoirs, which are supplemented by pipelines from the River Murray.

Climate.—The mean annual temperature at

Adelaide is 17·1°C, the winter temperature (June–August) averaging 11·9°C, and the summer (November–March) 22·3°C. During the summer months the maximum temperature at times exceeds 40°C, but is associated with a relatively low humidity. The average annual rainfall at Adelaide is 21 inches.

GOVERNMENT

South Australia was proclaimed a British Province in 1836, and in 1851 a partially elective legislature was established. The present Constitution rests upon a Law of Oct. 24, 1856, the executive authority being vested in a Governor appointed by the Crown, aided by a Council of 13 Ministers.

GOVERNOR

Governor of South Australia, Her Excellency the Hon. Dame Roma Mitchell, AC, DBE (1991).

Lt. Governor, The Hon. Sir Condor Laucke, KCMG (1982).

THE MINISTRY
(as at July 1, 1991)

Premier, Treasurer, and Minister of State Development, Hon. John Bannon.

Deputy Premier, Minister of Family and Community Services, the Aged, Hon. Donald Hopgood.

Attorney General, Minister of Crime Prevention, Corporate Affairs, Hon. Christopher Sumner.

Industry, Trade and Technology, Agriculture, Fisheries and Ethnic Affairs, Hon. Lynn Arnold.

Education and Children's Services, Hon. Gregory Crafter.

Transport, Finance and Correctional Services, Hon. Frank Blevins.

Tourism and Consumer Affairs, Small Business, Hon. Barbara Wiese.

Housing and Construction, Public Works, Recreation and Sport, Hon. Kym Mayes.

Environment and Planning, Water Resources, Lands, Hon. S. Lenehan.

Emergency Services, Mines and Energy, Forests, Hon. J. Klunder.

Labour, Occupational Health and Safety, Marine, Hon. R. Gregory.

Local Government, State Services and the Arts, Hon. J. Levy.

Employment and Further Education, Youth Affairs, Aboriginal Affairs, and assisting Ethnic Affairs, Hon. M. Rann.

AGENT-GENERAL IN LONDON

Agent-General, G. Walls, South Australia House, 50 Strand, WC2N 5LW.

THE LEGISLATURE

Parliament consists of a Legislative Council of 22 members elected for 8 years, one-half retiring every four years; and a House of Assembly of 47 members, elected for a maximum duration of four years. Election is by ballot, with universal adult suffrage for both the Legislative Council and the House of Assembly.

The representation in the House of Assembly is 20 Labor, 19 Liberals, and 2 Labor Independents.

President of the Legislative Council, Hon. G. L. Bruce.
Speaker of the House of Assembly, Hon. N. T. Peterson.

THE JUDICATURE

Law and Justice.—The Supreme Court is presided over by the Chief Justice and 13 Puisne Judges.

EDUCATION

Education at the primary and secondary level is available at Government schools controlled by the Education Department and at non-government schools, most of which are denominational. In 1990 there were 706 government schools with 184,868 students, and 185 independent schools with 57,867 students. Tertiary education is available through universities, colleges of advanced education, and technical and further education.

The two universities had, in 1989, a total enrolment of 16,069 full-time students.

CAPITAL.—ΨAdelaide, the chief city and capital, estimated resident population on June 30, 1990, 1,049,873 inclusive of suburbs. Other centres (with 1989 populations) are: ΨWhyalla (26,706); ΨMt. Gambier (22,194); ΨPort Pirie (15,210); ΨPort Augusta (15,752); and ΨPort Lincoln (12,941).

TASMANIA

Tasmania is an island state of Australia situated in the Southern ocean off the south-eastern extremity of the mainland. It is separated from the Australian mainland by Bass Strait and incorporates King Island and the Furneaux group of islands which are in the Strait. It lies between 40° 38′–43° 39′ S. lat. and 144° 36′–148° 23′ E. long., and contains an area of 26,383 sq. miles (68,331 sq. km). Macquarie Island, situated at 54° 30′ S. and 158° 57′ E., about 900 miles north of the Antarctic Continent, is a dependency of Tasmania.

POPULATION.—The estimated resident population at June 30, 1989 was 456,600.

Births, deaths and marriages were:

	1989	1990p
Births	6,809	6,921
Deaths	3,626	3,579
Marriages	3,140	3,113
p preliminary		

Annual rate per 1,000 of estimated resident population in 1990 was:—Births 15·4; Deaths 7·9; Marriages 6·6. Deaths under 1 year per 1,000 live births, 9·1.

Religions

In 1986 there were 154,748 members of the Anglican Church of Australia, 80,479 Catholics, 36,724 Uniting Church of Australia, 12,084 Presbyterians and 8,092 Baptists.

PHYSIOGRAPHY

The surface of the country is generally hilly and wooded, with mountains from 1,500 to 5,300 ft. in height, and expanses of level, open plains. There are numerous rivers, the South Esk, Gordon, Derwent and Huon being the largest. At Hobart the mean maximum temperature ranges from about 12°C in winter to 21°C in summer, the mean minimum from 5°C to 11°C. The western side of the island is very wet, the eastern side being much drier.

GOVERNMENT

The island was first settled by a British party from New South Wales in 1803, becoming a separate colony in 1825. In 1851 a partly elective legislature was inaugurated, and in 1856 responsible government was established. In 1901 Tasmania became a State of the Australian Commonwealth. The State executive authority is vested in a Governor (appointed by the Crown), but is exercised by Cabinet Ministers responsible to the Legislature, of which they are members.

GOVERNOR

Governor of Tasmania, His Excellency Gen. Sir Phillip Bennett, AC, KBE, DSO.

THE MINISTRY
(as at June 4, 1991)

Premier, Treasurer, Minister for State Development, Finance, Hon. M. W. Field.

Deputy Premier, Attorney-General, Minister for Justice, Environment and Planning, Hon. P. J. Patmore.

Employment, Industrial Relations and Training, Education and the Arts, and Minister assisting the Premier on Youth Affairs, Hon. M. A. Aird.

Administrative Services and Consumer Affairs, Construction, and Minister assisting the Premier on the Status of Women, Hon. F. M. Bladel.

Tourism, Sport and Recreation, Parks, Wildlife and Heritage, Hon. H. N. Holgate.

Community Services, Roads and Transport, Hon. J. L. Jackson.

Primary Industry, Forests , Hon. D. E. Llewellyn.

Resources and Energy, Police and Emergency Services, Hon. M. W. Weldon.

Health, Minister assisting the Premier on Multicultural Affairs, and on Aboriginal Affairs, Hon. J. C. White.

THE LEGISLATURE

Parliament consists of two Houses, a Legislative Council of 19 members, elected for six years (three retiring annually, in rotation, except in every sixth year, when four retire) and a House of Assembly of 35 members, elected by proportional representation for four years in five seven-member constituencies, the electors for both Houses being all Tasmanians of 18 years and over who have resided continuously in the State for at least six months. Elections for the Assembly are held every four years.

The election of May 13, 1989 resulted in a 'hung parliament' with 17 Liberal, 13 Labor and 5 Independent members. The Government was formed by the Labor Party in alliance with the Independents. The state of the parties in the Legislative Council following the election was Independent 18, Labor 1. *Speaker of the House of Assembly,* Hon. M. R. Polley. *President of the Legislative Council,* Hon. G. A. Shaw.

THE JUDICATURE

The Supreme Court of Tasmania, with civil, criminal ecclesiastical, admiralty and matrimonial jurisdiction, was established by Royal Charter on October 13, 1823.

Local Courts are held before Commissioners who are legal practitioners. Courts of General Sessions, constituted by a chairman who is a Justice of the Peace and at least one other Justice, are established in the municipalities and Courts of Petty Sessions are constituted by Magistrates sitting alone, or by two or more justices. A single justice may hear and determine certain matters.

Chief Justice, Supreme Court, Hon. Sir Guy Green, KBE.

EDUCATION

Government schools are of three main types: primary, secondary and secondary colleges. On July 1, 1990 there were 65,349 students enrolled in 250 government schools. There were also 66 independent schools with an enrolment of 19,030. The University of Tasmania at Hobart, established 1890, had 4,249 full-time students and 1,628 part-time (including external) students in 1990. The Tasmanian State Institute of Technology, offering degree and diploma courses, was established in 1972. In 1990 4,192 students were enrolled.

PRODUCTION AND INDUSTRY

Electrical Energy.—Tasmania, the smallest Australian state, ranks fourth as a producer of electrical energy—most of it derived from water power, with a total installed generator capacity of 2,315,000 kW at June 30, 1989. By reason of its low-cost electrical energy, Tasmania has large plants producing ferromanganese and newsprint. A large aluminium plant is situated at Bell Bay and Tasmania is the source of the bulk of Australian requirements of zinc and fine papers. The Hydro-Electric Commission has completed a network of 26 stations including a dual machine oil fired station at Bell Bay. Work is continuing on three hydro-electric developments in the remote western region of the State, which will increase the installed generator capacity to 2·54 million kW.

Forestry.—The quantity of timber (excluding firewood) of various species cut in 1989–90 was 4,567,900 cubic metres, including 3,619,300 cubic metres for woodchip and wood-pulp.

Minerals.—The chief ores mined are those containing copper, tin, iron, silver, zinc and lead.

Manufactures.—The chief manufactures for export are refined metals, preserved fruit and vegetables, butter, cheese, textiles, paper, confectionery, wood chips and sawn timber. In 1988–89, 962 manufacturing establishments employed 7,532 persons, including working proprietors.

CAPITAL.—ΨHobart, founded 1804. Population (June 30, 1990), (metropolitan area) 183,550. Other towns (with population at June 30, 1990) are Ψ Launceston (metropolitan area) (93,520), ΨDevonport (25,500), Burnie-Somerset (21,300), Ulverstone (14,610).

VICTORIA

The State of Victoria comprises the south-east corner of Australia, at the part where its mainland territory projects farthest into the southern latitudes; it lies between 34°–39° S. latitude and 141°–150° E. longitude. Its extreme length from east to west is about 493 miles, its greatest breadth is about 290 miles, and its extent of coast-line is about 1,043 geographical miles, including the length around Port Phillip Bay, Western Port and Corner Inlet, the entire area being 87,876 sq. miles (227,597 sq. km).

Population.—The estimated resident population at June 30, 1990 was 4,379,900.

Births, deaths and marriages were:

	1989p	1990p
Births	63,327	67,166
Deaths	31,385	32,521
Marriages	30,670	30,456

p preliminary

Annual rate per 1,000 of estimated resident population in 1989 was:—Births 14·8; Deaths 7·5; Marriages 7·1. Deaths under 1 year per 1,000 live births 6·4.

Religions

At the Census in 1986, members of the Catholic Church numbered 1,104,044, Anglican 715,414, Uniting (union of Presbyterian, Congregationalist and Methodist) 280,262, Presbyterian 138,000, Orthodox 177,565, and Baptist 39,784. The number of persons who did not state their religion was 589,132.

PHYSIOGRAPHY

The Australian Alps and the Great Dividing Range pass through the centre of the State, and divide it into a northern and southern watershed, the latter sloping down to the ocean and containing, especially in the south-east, well-wooded valleys. The length of the Murray River, which forms part of the northern boundary of Victoria, is about 1,196 miles along the Victorian bank. Melbourne, the capital city, stands upon the Yarra River, which rises in the southern slopes of the Dividing Range.

GOVERNMENT

Victoria was originally known as the Port Phillip District of New South Wales and was created separate colony in 1851, with a partially elective legislature. In 1855 Responsible Government was conferred. The executive authority is vested in a Governor, appointed by the Crown, aided by an Executive Council of Ministers.

The Legislative Assembly (elected October 1, 1988) consists of Australian Labor Party 46, Liberal Party 33, and National Party 9.

Governor of Victoria, His Excellency Rev. Dr John Davis McCaughey, AC, *assumed office* Feb. 18, 1986.

Lt. Governor, The Hon. Sir John McIntosh Young, KCMG, AO (1974).

THE MINISTRY
(as at June, 1991)

Premier, Minister responsible for Women's Affairs, Hon J. Kirner.

Deputy Premier, Attorney-General, Minister for the Arts, Major Projects, Hon J. Kennan.

Manufacturing and Industry Development, Gaming, and responsible for Ports, Hon D. White.

Ethnic, Municipal and Community Affairs, Hon C. Hogg.

Agriculture, Hon I. Baker.

Tourism, Conservation and Environment, Hon S. Crabb.

Health, Hon M. Lyster.

Planning and Housing, Hon A. McCutcheon.

Consumer Affairs, Aboriginal Affairs, Hon B. Mier.

Labour, Hon N. Pope.

Education and Training, Hon B. Pullen.

Treasurer, Hon T. Roper.

Small Business, Hon J. Harrowfield.

Police and Emergency Services, Corrections, Hon M. Sandon.

Community Services, and responsible for Child Care, Hon K. Setches.

Finance, Hon A. Sheehan.

Transport, Hon P. Spyker.

Sport and Recreation, Hon N. Trezise.

AGENT-GENERAL IN LONDON

Agent-General, L. T. Baldock, Victoria House, Melbourne Place, Strand, WC2B 4LG.

THE LEGISLATURE

Parliament consists of a Legislative Council of 44 members, elected for the 22 Provinces for two terms of the Legislative Assembly, one-half retiring every four years at a General Election; and a Legislative Assembly of 88 members, elected for a maximum duration of four years. Voting is compulsory.

President of the Legislative Council, Hon. A. J. Hunt.

Speaker of the Legislative Assembly, Hon. Dr K. A. Coghill.

THE JUDICATURE

There is a Supreme Court with a Chief Justice and 23 Puisne Judges, a County Court and Magistrates' Courts.

Chief Justice, Supreme Court, Hon. Sir John McIntosh Young, KCMG, AO.

Chief Judge, County Court, Hon. G. R. D. Waldron, AO.

EDUCATION

Primary education is compulsory, secular and free between the ages of 6 and 15. At July 12, 1989, there were 2,059 government schools, attended by 527,700 students. In addition there are technical and further education institutions and colleges of advanced education.

At July 12, 1989, 257,407 pupils attended non-government schools.

There are four state-aided universities.

PRODUCTION AND INDUSTRY

Minerals.—Minerals raised include oil and natural gas, brown coal, limestone, clays and stone for construction material. Production of brown coal in 1988–89 was valued at $A1,144,834,000.

Crude Oil and Natural Gas.—In 1965 natural gas was first discovered in commercial quantities in the offshore waters of the Gippsland Basin in eastern Victoria and in 1966–67, three more valuable oilfields were located in the same general area. These fields are still the largest yet found in Australia. Production from Victorian natural gas and crude oil fields during 1989 was 5,244,959 Mg. litres.

Secondary Industry.—At June 30, 1989 there were 9,771 manufacturing establishments in which total employees numbered 367,376.

CAPITAL.—ΨMelbourne had a resident population at June 30, 1989, estimated at 3,039,100. Other urban centres are ΨGeelong 148,980; Ballarat 80,090; Bendigo 67,920; Shepparton-Mooroopna 39,700; ΨWarrnambool 24,480; Wodonga 25,800.

WESTERN AUSTRALIA

Includes all that portion of the continent west of 129° E. long., the most westerly point being in 113° 9′ E. long. and from 13° 44′ to 35° 8′ S. lat. Its extreme length is 1,480 miles, and 1,000 miles from east to west; total area 975,920 sq. miles (2,527,621 sq. km).

POPULATION.—At June 30 1990 the estimated resident population was 1,633,900.

Births, deaths and marriages were:

	1989	1990p
Births	25,123	25,019
Deaths	9,513	9,567
Marriages	10,578	10,739

p preliminary

Annual rate per 1,000 of estimated resident population in 1989 was:—Births 15·7; Deaths 6·0; Marriages 6·7. Deaths under 1 year per 1,000 live births, 7·8.

Religions

Census of 1986—Anglican Church 371,302, Roman Catholics 347,695, Uniting Church 82,876, and Presbyterians 31,641.

PHYSIOGRAPHY

Large areas of the State, for some hundreds of miles inland, are hilly and even mountainous, although the altitude, so far as ascertained, rises nowhere above that of Mount Meharry (4,097 ft.) in the north-west division or that of Bluff Knoll (3,640 ft.) in the Stirling Range in the south-west. The Darling and Hamersley ranges of the west have a seaward slope to the Indian Ocean, into which flow many streams, notably the Preston, Collie, Murray, Swan, Murchison, Gascoyne, Ashburton, Fortescue and De Grey. In the north the Fitzroy flows from the King Leopold ranges into the Indian Ocean, and the Drysdale and Ord into the Timor Sea. The greater portion of the State may be described as an immense tableland, with an average elevation of 1,000 to 1,500 ft. above sea-level. The climate is one of the most temperate in the world. Of the total area two-thirds is suitable for pastoral purposes.

GOVERNMENT

Western Australia was first settled by the British in 1829, and in 1870 it was granted a partially elective legislature. In 1890 responsible government was granted, and the administration vested in a Governor, a Legislative Council, and a Legislative Assembly. The present constitution rests upon the

Constitution Act 1889, the Constitution Acts Amendment Act 1899, and amending Acts. The Executive is vested in a Governor appointed by the Crown and aided by a Council of responsible Ministers.

Governor of Western Australia, His Excellency the Hon. Sir Francis Burt, AC, KCMG, QC.

Lt. Governor and Administrator, Hon. D. K. Malcolm.

THE MINISTRY
(as at February 27, 1991)

Premier, Treasurer, Minister for the Family, Women's Interests, Hon. Dr Carmen Lawrence.

Deputy Premier, Minister for State Development, Goldfields, Hon. I. F. Taylor.

Attorney-General, Minister for Corrective Services, Leader of the Government in the Legislative Council, Hon. J. M. Berinson.

Education, Employment and Training, The Arts, Hon. E. K. Hallahan.

Environment, Leader of the House in the Legislative Assembly, Hon. R. J. Pearce.

Health, Hon. K. J. Wilson.

Transport, Racing and Gaming, Tourism, Hon. P. A. Beggs.

Agriculture, Water Resources, North-West, Hon. E. F. Bridge.

Mines, Fisheries, Mid-West, and assisting the Minister for State Development, Hon. G. L. Hill.

Police, Emergency Services, Sport and Recreation, Hon. G. J. Edwards.

Productivity and Labour Relations, Consumer Affairs, Hon. Y. D. Henderson.

Lands, Planning, Justice, Local Government, South-West, Hon. D. L. Smith.

Fuel and Energy, Microeconomic Reform, Parliamentary and Electoral Reform, Seniors, and assisting the Minister for Women's Interests, Hon. Dr J. Watson.

Community Services, Hon. E. S. Ripper.

Housing, Construction, Services, Heritage, Hon. J. A. McGinty.

AGENT-GENERAL IN LONDON

Agent-General, D. Fischer, Western Australia House, 115 Strand, WC2R 0AJ.

THE LEGISLATURE

Parliament consists of a Legislative Council and a Legislative Assembly, elected by adult suffrage subject to qualifications of residence and registration. The qualifying age for electors for both the Legislative Council and Legislative Assembly is 18 years. There are 34 members in the Legislative Council elected for a period of four years. The Legislative Assembly has 57 members, who are elected for a term of four years. The Legislative Assembly (elected February 4, 1989) is composed of Australian Labor Party 31, Liberal Party 20, National Party of Australia 6.

President of the Legislative Council, Hon. C. E. Griffiths.

Speaker of the Legislative Assembly, Hon. M. Barnett.

THE JUDICATURE

Chief Justice, Hon. D. K. Malcolm.

Senior Puisne Judge, Hon. A. R. A. Wallace.

Puisne Judges, Hons. P. F. Brinsden; G. A. Kennedy; W. P. Pidgeon; B. W. Rowland; E. M. Franklyn; P. L. Seaman; R. D. Nicolson; T. A. Walsh; D. A. Ipp; H. A. Wallwork; M. J. Murray.

EDUCATION

In 1990 there were 760 government and 244 non-government primary and secondary school campuses with 215,311 and 69,575 full-time students respectively. The principal higher education institutions

are the University of Western Australia (10,815 enrolments in 1990), Murdoch University (6,223), Curtin University (16,642) and Edith Cowan University (14,641).

PRODUCTION AND INDUSTRY

Manufacturing Industries.—There were 3,439 manufacturing establishments operating in the State at June 30, 1989. The total number of persons employed (including working proprietors) by these establishments at the end of June 1989 was 74,500.

Forestry.—The forests contain some of the finest hardwoods in the world. The total quantity of sawn timber produced during 1989–90 was 324,083 cubic metres.

Minerals.—The State has large deposits of a wide range of minerals, many of which are being mined or are under development for production. The ex-mine value of all minerals (excluding construction materials, clays and limestone) produced during 1988–89 was $A6,243,729,000.

CAPITAL.—ΨPerth, on the right bank of the Swan River estuary, 12 miles from Fremantle. Estimated resident population (June 30, 1990) of Perth Statistical Division, including the port of ΨFremantle, 1,193,130.

THE BAHAMAS
(The Commonwealth of The Bahamas)

AREA, POPULATION, ETC.—The Bahama Islands are an archipelago lying in the North Atlantic Ocean between 20° 55′–25° 22′ N. lat. and 72° 35′–79° 35′ W. long. They extend from the coast of Florida on the north-west almost to Haiti on the south-east. The group consists of 700 islands, of which 30 are inhabited and 2,400 cays comprising an area of more than 5,832 sq. miles. The population (Census 1990) is 254,000. The principal islands include: Abaco, Acklins, Andros, Berry Islands, Bimini, Cat Island, Crooked Island, Eleuthera, Exumas, Grand Bahama, Harbour Island, Inagua, Long Island, Mayaguana, New Providence (on which is located the capital, Nassau), Ragged Island, Rum Cay, San Salvador and Spanish Wells. San Salvador was the first landfall in the New World of Christopher Columbus on October 12, 1492.

The Bahamas were settled by British subjects when the islands were deserted. The ownership of The Bahamas was taken over in 1782 by the Spanish, but the Treaty of Versailles in 1783 restored them to the British.

CAPITAL.—ΨNassau, population (Census 1990) 171,000.

CURRENCY.—Bahamian dollar (B$) of 100 cents.

FLAG.—Horizontal stripes of aquamarine, gold and aquamarine, with a black equilateral triangle on the hoist.

NATIONAL ANTHEM.—March on, Bahamaland.

NATIONAL DAY.—July 10 (Independence Day).

GOVERNMENT

The Bahamas gained independence on July 10 1973. The Head of State is HM Queen Elizabeth II, represented in the islands by a Governor General. There is a Senate of 16 members and an elected House of Assembly of 49 members.

Governor-General, His Excellency Sir Henry Milton Taylor (1988).

Cabinet
(as at June 21, 1991)

Prime Minister and Minister of Tourism, Rt. Hon. Sir Lynden Pindling, KCMG.

Deputy PM, Minister of Foreign Affairs and of Public Personnel, Hon. Sir Clement Maynard.
National Security and Government Leader in the House of Assembly, Hon. Darrell Rolle.
Finance, Hon. Paul L. Adderley.
Works and Lands, Hon. Philip M. Bethel.
Employment and Immigration, Hon. Alfred T. Maycock.
Transport and Leader of the Senate, Senator Hon. Peter J. Bethell.
Housing and National Insurance, Hon. George W. Mackey.
Agriculture, Trade and Industry, Hon. Perry Christie.
Health, Hon. E. Charles Carter.
Education, Hon. Dr Bernard J. Nottage.
Youth, Sports and Community Affairs, Hon. Dr Norman Gay.
Consumer Affairs, Hon. Vincent A. Peet.
Local Government, Hon. Marvin B. Pinder.
Attorney-General, Senator Hon. Sean G. McWeeney.

President of the Court of Appeal, Kenneth Henry.
Chief Justice, J. C. Gonsalves-Sabola.

BAHAMAS HIGH COMMISSION
Bahamas House, 10 Chesterfield Street, W1X 8AH
[071–408 4488]

High Commissioner, Her Excellency Dr Patricia Rodgers (1988).

ECONOMY

Tourism is the economic mainstay of The Bahamas, employing about two-thirds of the labour force. It provides about two-thirds of Government revenue and about half the country's foreign exchange earnings. The second main industry is international banking and trust business. The Bahamas' absence of any direct taxation and internal stability have enabled the country to become one of the world's leading financial centres.

Agricultural production is mainly of fresh vegetables, fruit, meat and eggs for the domestic market, and crawfish, mostly for export. There are large reserves of aragonite, and reserves of limestone and salt, all of which are being commercially exploited. Freeport is the country's leading industrial centre, with a pharmaceutical and chemicals plant, an oil trans-shipment and storage terminal, and port and bunkering facilities. There are also a brewery and a rum distillery on New Providence.

EDUCATION

Education is compulsory between the ages of 5 and 14. More than 59,500 students are enrolled in Ministry of Education and independent schools in New Providence and the Family Islands.

COMMUNICATIONS

The main ports are Nassau (New Providence), Freeport (Grand Bahama), Mathew Town (Inagua). International air services are operated from Abaco, Bimini, Eleuthera, Exuma, Grand Bahama and New Providence. About 50 smaller airports and landing strips facilitate services between the islands, the services being mainly provided by Bahamasair, the national carrier. There are roads on the larger islands, and roads are under construction on the smaller islands. There are no railways. Wireless and telephone services are in operation to all parts of the world.

FINANCE AND TRADE

	1989p	1990p
Public revenue	B$448·1m	B$489·1m
Expenditure	561·6m	532·1m
p provisional		

The imports are chiefly foodstuffs, manufactured articles, building materials, vehicles and machinery, chemicals and petroleum. The chief exports are rum, petroleum, hormones, salt, crawfish and aragonite.

Trade with UK

	1989	1990
Imports from UK	£22,543,000	£22,917,000
Exports to UK	17,681,000	15,053,000

BRITISH HIGH COMMISSION
PO Box N-7516, Nassau
[Nassau 325-7471]

High Commissioner, His Excellency Michael E. J. Gore, CBE (1991).
Deputy High Commissioner, R. G. Church (*Head of Chancery*).

BANGLADESH
(Ghana Praja Tantri Bangladesh)

AREA, POPULATION, CLIMATE, ETC.—The People's Republic of Bangladesh consists of the territory which was formerly East Pakistan (the old province of East Bengal and the Sylhet district of Assam), covering an area of 55,598 sq. miles (143,998 sq. km) in the region of the Gangetic delta, and has a population (estimate 1989) of 110,300,000.

The country is crossed by a network of navigable rivers, including the eastern arms of the Ganges, the Jamuna (Brahmaputra) and the Meghna, flowing into the Bay of Bengal. The climate is tropical and monsoon: hot and extremely humid during the summer, and mild and dry during the short winter. The rainfall is heavy, varying from 50 inches to 135 inches in different districts and the bulk of it falls during monsoon season from June to September.

CAPITAL.—Dhaka, population (estimate) 6,000,000.
CURRENCY.—Taka (Tk) of 100 poisha.
FLAG.—Red circle on a bottle-green ground.
NATIONAL ANTHEM.—Amar Sonar Bangla.
NATIONAL DAY.—March 26 (Independence Day).

GOVERNMENT

Prior to becoming East Pakistan, the territory had been part of British India. It acceded to Pakistan in October 1947, which became a Republic on March 23, 1956.

By a proclamation of March 26, 1971, Bangladesh purported to secede from the central government, and a government-in-exile was set up which formally declared independence on April 17. Bangladesh achieved its independence on December 16, 1971, following the conclusion of the Indo-Pakistan war. Pakistan and Bangladesh accorded one another mutual recognition in February 1974.

From 1975 a non-political administration ran the country under martial law. A Presidential election was held in June 1978 and President Zia was elected. Martial law was subsequently lifted. Zia was assassinated in May 1981 in an unsuccessful coup. He was replaced by Justice Abdus Sattar, who won presidential elections in October 1981, but was overthrown in a coup in 1982, led by the then Chief of Army Staff, Gen. Ershad. Following elections held in May 1986, which were boycotted by several opposition parties, a civilian cabinet was appointed and Gen. Ershad was elected as President in October 1986. Further elections, again boycotted by the opposition, were held in March 1988. Popular unrest forced Gen. Ershad's resignation on December 6, 1990. A caretaker government was formed and parliamentary elections were held on February 27, 1991. The Bangladesh Nationalist Party (BNP) won the largest number of seats but failed to gain a majority. After gaining support from Islamic deputies, the BNP leader, Begum Khaleda Zia, was sworn in as Prime Minister on March 19.

On August 7, 1991, Parliament approved a constitutional amendment reverting Bangladesh to parliamentary rule after 16 years of presidential government; the amendment will be put to a referendum in September. President Shahabuddin will resign as executive President and a new figurehead president will be elected to replace him.

Acting President, Mr Justice Shahabuddin Ahmed.

Cabinet
(as at March 1991)

Prime Minister, and Minister for Information, Mineral Resources, Establishment, Home Affairs, Begum Khaleda Zia.
Law and Justice, Mirza Golam Hafiz.
Education, Dr Badruddoza Chowdhury.
Agriculture, Irrigation, Flood Control and Water Resources, Maj.-Gen. Majedul Huq (retd.).
Foreign Affairs, A. S. M. Mustafizur Rahman.
Finance and Planning, Saifur Rahman.
Local Government, Rural Development and Co-operatives, Abdus Salam Talukder.
Communication, Col. Oli Ahmed (retd.).
Commerce, M. Keramat Ali.
Shipping, M. K. Anwar.
Industry, Shamsul Islam Khan.
Health and Family Planning, Chowdhury Kamal Ibne Yusuf.

BANGLADESH HIGH COMMISSION
28 Queen's Gate, SW7 5JA
[071–584 0081]

High Commissioner, His Excellency M. M. Rezaul Karim (1991).

RELIGION

The faith of over 90 per cent of the population is Islam. Islam has been constitutionally declared the state religion of Bangladesh.

LANGUAGE

The state language is Bengali. Use of Bengali is compulsory in all government departments. English, however, is understood and is used widely as an unofficial second language.

EDUCATION

Primary education is free and planned to be universal by the year 2000. There are about 46,144 primary schools, mostly managed by the Government. There are about 10,576 secondary schools and 947 colleges offering general and technical education. There are nine universities including two for engineering and technology, one for agriculture and another for Islamic education and research. In 1990 the literacy rate was estimated to be 24 per cent (of which 31 per cent male and 16 per cent female).

TRANSPORT AND COMMUNICATIONS

Principal seaports are Chittagong and Mongla. The Bangladesh Shipping Corporation has been set up by the Government to operate the Bangladesh merchant fleet. The principal airports are Dhaka (Zia International) and Chittagong. The international airline, Bangladesh Biman, serves Europe, the Middle East, South and South-East Asia, and an internal network.

There are about 6,880 miles of roads in Bangladesh; 4,724 miles are metalled. There are 2,798 miles of railway track.

Radio Bangladesh is the main national broadcasting service. A television service was introduced in 1965 and colour transmissions began in 1980.

ECONOMY

Bangladesh is a principal producer of raw jute. Other agricultural products are rice, tea, oil seeds, pulses and sugar cane. The chief industries are jute, cotton, tea, leather, pharmaceuticals, fertilizer, sugar, prawn fishing, natural gas and garment manufacture. Remittances sent home by Bangladeshi workers abroad have been of considerable support to the economy in recent years.

Aid

Bangladesh is a major recipient of bilateral and multilateral development aid. The total annual development plan for 1991–92 is budgeted at US$2,095 million of which US$1,797 million will be financed from external sources.

Trade with UK

	1989	1990
Imports from UK	£78,270,000	£70,534,000
Exports to UK	52,527,000	72,515,000

BRITISH HIGH COMMISSION
Abu Bakr House, Plot 7, Road 84, Gulshan Dhaka,
PO Box 6079
[Dhaka 600133/7]

High Commissioner, His Excellency Colin Henry Imray, CMG (1989).
Deputy High Commissioner, G. Finlayson.

British Council Representative, J. Mayatt, 5 Fuller Road (PO Box 161), Dhaka 2.

BARBADOS

AREA, ETC.—Barbados, the most easterly of the Caribbean islands, is situated in latitude 13° 14' N. and longitude 59° 37' W. The island has a total area of 166 sq. miles, (430 sq. km), the land rising in a series of tablelands marked by terraces to the highest point, Mt. Hillaby (1,116 ft.). It is nearly 21 miles long by 14 miles broad. The climate is equable with annual average temperature 26·6°C (79·8°F) and rainfall varying from a yearly average of 75 inches in the high central district to 50 inches in some of the low-lying coastal areas.

POPULATION.—The population of Barbados (1989 UN estimate) was 256,000. There are eleven administrative areas (parishes): St Michael, Christ Church, St Andrews, St George, St James, St John, St Joseph, St Lucy, St Peter, St Philip and St Thomas.

CAPITAL.—Ψ Bridgetown (population, estimated April, 1980, 7,466) in the parish of St Michael. There are three other towns, Oistins in Christ Church, Holetown in St James and Speightstown in St Peter.

CURRENCY.—Barbados dollar (BD$) of 100 cents.

FLAG.—Three vertical stripes, dark blue, gold and dark blue, with a trident head on gold stripe.

NATIONAL ANTHEM.—In Plenty and in Time of Need.

NATIONAL DAY.—November 30 (Independence Day).

GOVERNMENT

The first inhabitants of Barbados were Arawak Indians but the island was uninhabited when first settled by the British in 1627. It was a Crown Colony from 1652 until it became an independent state within the Commonwealth on November 30, 1966. The Legislature consists of the Governor General, a Senate and a House of Assembly. The Senate comprises 21 Senators appointed by the Governor General, of whom 12 are appointed on the advice of the Prime Minister, two on the advice of the Leader of the Opposition and seven by the Governor General at his discretion to represent religious, economic or social interests in the Island or such other interests as the Governor General considers ought to be represented. The House of Assembly comprises 28 members elected every five years by adult suffrage. The last General Election took place on January 22, 1991 and, as a result, seats in the House of Assembly were distributed as follows: Democratic Labour Party 18, Barbados Labour Party 10.

Governor General, Dame Nita Barrow, GCMG, DA (1990).

Cabinet
(as at January, 1991)

Prime Minister, Minister of Finance and Economic Affairs, Civil Service, Rt. Hon. L. Erskine Sandiford.
Deputy Prime Minister, Leader of the House of Assembly, Minister of International Transport, Telecommunications and Immigration, Transport and Works, Hon. Philip M. Greaves, QC.
Attorney-General and Minister of Foreign Affairs, Hon. Maurice A. King.
Health, Hon. Brandford M. Taitt.
Housing and Lands, Hon. E. Evelyn Greaves.
Minister of State, Ministry of Finance and Economic Affairs, Hon. Harold A. Blackman.
Labour, Consumer Affairs and the Environment, Hon. Warwick O. Franklyn.
Tourism and Sports, Hon. Wesley W. Hall.
Justice and Public Safety, Hon. Keith Simmons.
Education, Hon. Cyril V. Walker.
Community Development and Culture, Hon. David J. H. Thompson.
Agriculture, Food and Fisheries and Leader of the Senate, Sen. Hon. L. V. Harcourt Lewis.
Trade, Industry and Commerce, Hon. Dr Carl Clarke.

BARBADOS HIGH COMMISSION
1 Great Russell Street, WC1B 3NH
[071–631 4975]

High Commissioner, new appointment awaited.

JUDICATURE

There is a Supreme Court of Judicature consisting of a High Court and a Court of Appeal. In certain cases a further appeal lies to the Judicial Committee of the Privy Council. The Chief Justice and Puisne Judges are appointed by the Governor-General on the recommendation of the Prime Minister and after consultation with the Leader of the Opposition.
Chief Justice, The Hon. Sir Denys Ambrose Williams.

EDUCATION

Primary and secondary education is free in Government schools. There are 105 primary schools, 21 Government secondary schools and 15 approved Government secondary schools.

COMMUNICATIONS

Barbados has some 965 miles of roads, of which about 917 miles are asphalted. The Grantley Adams International airport is situated at Seawell, 12 miles from Bridgetown, and frequent scheduled services connect Barbados with the major world air routes. Bridgetown, the only port of entry, has a deep-water harbour with berths for eight ships, but oil is pumped ashore at Spring Gardens and at an Esso installation on the West Coast. Barbados has a colour television service, three radio broadcasting services, and a wired broadcasting service.

FINANCE

	1989–90*
Current revenue	BD$960,700,000
Current expenditure	1,050,500,000
Capital expenditure	231,000,000

* estimated.

ECONOMY

The economy of the island is based on tourism, sugar and light manufacturing. In 1990, 432,092 tourists visited Barbados and 362,611 cruise ship passengers. Chief exports are sugar and its by-products, chemicals, electronic components and clothing.

Trade with UK

	1989	1990
Imports from UK	£38,136,000	£35,811,000
Exports to UK	22,304,000	24,294,000

BRITISH HIGH COMMISSION
Lower Collymore Rock, PO Box 676,
Bridgetown
[Bridgetown 436 6694]

High Commissioner, His Excellency Emrys Thomas Davies, CMG (1991).

BELIZE

AREA, ETC.—Belize lies on the east coast of Central America, bounded on the north and north-west by Mexico, and on the west and south by Guatemala. The total area (including offshore islands) is about 8,867 sq. miles (22,965 sq. km.), with a length and breadth of 174 miles and 68 miles respectively. The climate is sub-tropical, with a mean annual temperature of 20°C, but is tempered by sea breezes. There are two dry seasons, the main one from March to May and the other (the Maugre season) from August to September. The country is occasionally affected by hurricanes.

The coastal areas are mostly flat and swampy but the country rises gradually towards the interior. The northern and western districts are hilly, and in the south the Maya Mountains and the Cockscombs form the backbone of the country, reaching a height of 3,800 feet at Victoria Peak.

POPULATION.—The population is 183,000 (1990 estimate), of which the main racial groups are Creole, Mestizo (Maya-Spanish) and Carib, plus a number of East Indian and Spanish descent. The races are now heavily inter-mixed. The majority of the population is Christian, about 60 per cent Catholic and most of the remainder Protestant.

CAPITAL.—Belmopan (estimated population, 1990, 5,000). The largest city and the former capital is ΨBelize City (population, 1980 census, 39,771). Other towns are Corozal (6,899), San Ignacio (5,616), Dangriga (6,661), Orange Walk (8,439), Punta Gorda (2,396).

CURRENCY.—Belize dollar (BZ$) of 100 cents. The Belize dollar is tied to the US dollar—BZ$2 = US$1.

FLAG.—Blue ground with red band along top and

bottom edges, and in centre a white disc containing the coat of arms surrounded by a green garland.

NATIONAL ANTHEM.—Land of the Free.

NATIONAL DAY.—September 21 (Independence Day).

GOVERNMENT

The early history of Belize is little known, although the numerous ruins in the area indicate that it was heavily populated by the Maya Indians. The first British settlement was established in 1638 but was subject to repeated attacks by the Spanish, who claimed sovereignty over the area, until the decline of Spanish power in the Americas in the 19th century. In 1862 the area was recognized by Britain as a colony and called British Honduras. On June 1, 1973 the colony was officially renamed Belize, and was granted independence on September 21, 1981. The long-standing territorial dispute with Guatemala, which had delayed independence earlier, remains unresolved despite efforts to reach a settlement.

The Queen is Head of State, represented in Belize by a Governor General, who is a citizen of the country, appointed in consultation with the Prime Minister of Belize. There is a National Assembly, comprising a House of Representatives (28 members elected for five years) and a Senate (eight members appointed by the Governor General). Executive power is vested in the Cabinet, which is responsible to the National Assembly.

In elections held in September 1989, the People's United Party defeated the incumbent United Democratic Party.

Governor General, Her Excellency Dame Minita Elmira Gordon, GCMG, GCVO.

The Cabinet
(as at December, 1990)

Prime Minister and Minister of Finance, Home Affairs and Defence, Trade and Commerce, Rt. Hon. George Price.

Deputy PM and Minister of Industry and Natural Resources, Hon. Florencio Marin.

Foreign Affairs, Economic Development, Education, Hon. Said Musa.

Housing, Co-operatives, Hon. Valdemar Castillo.

Works, Hon. Samuel Waight.

Health, Urban Development, Hon. Dr Theodore Aranda.

Attorney General, Minister of Tourism and the Environment, Hon. Glenn Godfrey.

Social Services, Community Development, Hon. Remijio Montejo.

Agriculture and Fisheries, Hon. Michael Espat.

Labour, Public Service and Local Government, Hon. Leopoldo Briceño.

Energy and Communications, Hon. Carlos Diaz.

Ministers of State, Finance, Home Affairs and Defence, Trade and Commerce, Hon. Ralph Fonseca, Hon. Daniel Silva.

Minister of State, Foreign Affairs, Economic Development, Education, Hon. Vildo Marin.

Minister of State, Industry and Natural Resources, Hon. Guadalupe Pech.

Minister of State, Energy and Communications, Hon. Miguel Ruiz.

BELIZE HIGH COMMISSION
10 Harcourt House, 19A Cavendish Square,
W1M 9AD
[071-499 9728]

High Commissioner, His Excellency Robert Leslie (1991).

ECONOMY

About 42 per cent of the population is engaged in agriculture. Corn (maize), rice, red kidney beans, root crops and fruit are the main food crops, although main agricultural exports are sugar, bananas and citrus products. The country is more or less self-sufficient in fresh beef, pork and poultry, but processed meat and dairy products are imported. About 25 per cent of timber production (mostly mahogany) is exported, and there is a large US market for lobster, conch and scale fish. Tourism is also a valuable source of income.

FINANCE

	1990–91
Revenue	BZ$215·8 m
Expenditure	205·8 m
Surplus	10·0 m

TRADE

	1988	1989
Total imports	BZ$361·9 m	BZ$431·4 m
Total exports	232·5 m	248·1 m

Trade with UK

	1989	1990
Imports from UK	£11,842,000	£12,439,000
Exports to UK	24,272,000	22,734,000

EDUCATION

Education is compulsory from 5 to 14 years of age. In 1985 primary education was provided by 225 schools, most of which are government aided. Enrolment totalled 38,512. Secondary education is provided by 29 secondary and post-secondary institutions with an enrolment of 7,441. A University College of Belize has been established. The Government also offers scholarships for students to go abroad. There is an extra-mural faculty of the University of the West Indies, with a resident tutor.

COMMUNICATIONS

There is a government-operated radio service but no official television service in the country. An automatic telephone service operated by Belize Telecommunications Ltd covers the whole country.

The principal airport is at Belize City and various airlines operate international flights to US and other Central American states. The main port is also Belize City, where construction of deep water quays was recently completed. There are 1,865 miles of road, including four main highways, but there is no railway system.

BRITISH HIGH COMMISSION
PO Box 91, Belmopan
[Belmopan 2146/7]

High Commissioner, His Excellency David McKilligin (1991).

Deputy High Commissioner, H. Morgan.

BOTSWANA
(The Republic of Botswana)

AREA, ETC.—Botswana (formerly the British Protectorate of Bechuanaland) lies between latitudes 18° and 26° S. and longitudes 20° and 28° W. and is bounded by the Cape and Transvaal Provinces of South Africa on the south and east, by Zimbabwe, the Zambezi and Chobe (Linyanti) Rivers on the north and north-east and by Namibia on the west.

Botswana has a total area of 224,607 sq. miles (581,730 sq. km). The climate of the country is generally sub-tropical, but varies considerably with latitude and altitude. A plateau at a height of about 4,000 feet divides Botswana into two main topographical regions. To the east of the plateau streams flow into the Marico, Notwani and Limpopo Rivers; to the west lies a flat region comprising the Kgalagadi Desert, the Okavango Swamps and the Northern State Lands area. Large areas of the country support only herds of game. Elephant numbers have been estimated at 15–30,000.

POPULATION.—Botswana has an estimated population (1991) of 1,300,000. The eight principal Botswana tribes are Bakgatla, Bakwena, Bangwaketse, Bamalete, Bamangwato, Barolong, Batawana and Batlokwa. The principal languages in use in Botswana are Setswana and English.

CAPITAL.—Gaborone, estimated population 125,000. Other centres are Francistown (60,000), Lobatse (25,000), and Selebi-Phikwe (46,000).

CURRENCY.—Pula (P) of 100 thebe.

FLAG.—Horizontal bands of blue, white, blue, with a black stripe on the white band.

NATIONAL ANTHEM.—Fatshe La Rona.

NATIONAL DAY.—September 30.

GOVERNMENT

On September 30, 1966, Bechuanaland became a Republic within the Commonwealth under the name Botswana. The President of Botswana is Head of State and appoints as Vice President a member of the National Assembly who is his principal assistant and leader of Government business in the National Assembly. The Assembly consists of the President, 34 members elected on a basis of universal adult suffrage, four specially elected members, the Attorney-General (non-voting) and the Speaker. Presidential and legislative elections are held every five years. There is also a 15-member House of Chiefs.

President, His Excellency Dr Q. K. J. Masire, *sworn in* October 10, 1989 for a second five-year term.

Cabinet
(as at February 1991)

Vice President, Local Government and Lands, Peter Mmusi.
Presidential Affairs, Public Administration, Lt.-Gen. Mompati Merafhe.
Finance and Development Planning, Festus Mogae.
External Affairs, Dr Gaositwe Chiepe.
Mineral Resources and Water, Archibald Mogwe.
Commerce and Industry, Ponatshego Kedikilwe.
Agriculture, Daniel Kwelagobe.
Works and Communications, Chapson Butale.
Health, Kebatlemang Morake.
Education, Ray Molomo.
Home Affairs, Patrick Balopi.
Assistant Ministers: Finance, David Magang; *Local Government and Lands*, Ronald Sebego, Michael Tshipinare; *Agriculture*, Geoffrey Oteng.

BOTSWANA HIGH COMMISSION
6 Stratford Place, WIN 9AE
[071–499 0031]

High Commissioner, Her Excellency Mrs Margaret Nasha (1989).

ECONOMY

Botswana is predominantly a pastoral country. The national herd is normally around 3 million cattle and 1 million sheep and goats but recent drought conditions have reduced the number of cattle to around 2·5 million.

Cattle rearing accounts for about 85 per cent of agricultural output and livestock products, particularly beef, are a major source of foreign exchange earnings. The Government has a number of programmes to improve land use and cattle and crop production, and schemes to provide financial assistance for farmers.

Mineral extraction and processing is now the major source of income for the country following the opening of large mines for diamonds and copper-nickel. Botswana is one of the largest producers of diamonds in the world. Large deposits of coal have been discovered and are being mined on a small scale. Much of the country has yet to be fully prospected. Manufacturing industry is growing and will continue to do so as communications improve but it is still a small sector of the economy.

EDUCATION

There are over 654 primary schools (enrolment approx. 308,840), 146 community junior secondary schools (enrolment approx. 48,624) and 23 government and government-aided senior secondary schools (enrolment 19,308). There are four teacher training establishments (total enrolment 1,365), two colleges of education (enrolment 340), one polytechnic with 558 students and the University of Botswana with 2,862 undergraduates. Further expansion of the technical education system is planned via a network of vocational training centres.

COMMUNICATIONS

The railway from Cape Town to Zimbabwe passes through eastern Botswana. The main roads in the country are the north-south road, which closely follows the railway, and the road running east-west that links Francistown and Maun. A new road from Nata to Kazungula provides a direct link to Zambia from Botswana. Air services are provided on a scheduled basis between the main towns.

FINANCE

	1990–91	1991–92e
Revenue	P3,318 m	P3,183 m
Expenditure	2,899 m	3,318 m
e = estimate		

TRADE

Principal exports are diamonds, copper-nickel matte, and beef and beef products.

	1989p	1990
Imports	P2,136 m	P3,483 m
Exports	3,613 m	3,262 m
p preliminary		

Trade with UK

	1989	1990
Imports from UK	£34,682,000	£24,777,000
Exports to UK	13,135,000	18,854,000

BRITISH HIGH COMMISSION
Private Bag 0023, Gaborone
[Gaborone 352841]

High Commissioner, His Excellency Brian Smith, OBE (1989).
British Council Representative, T. A. Jones, MBE.

BRUNEI
(Negara Brunei Darussalam)

Brunei is situated on the north-west coast of the island of Borneo, total area of 2,226 sq. miles (5,765 sq. km), population (UN estimate 1989) 249,000 of whom

68 per cent are of Malay, 18 per cent Chinese and 5 per cent other indigenous races. The country has a humid tropical climate.

CAPITAL.—Bandar Seri Begawan, with a population of 58,000 (1981).

CURRENCY.—Brunei dollar (B$) of 100 sen. It is fully interchangeable with the currency of Singapore.

FLAG.—Yellow, with diagonal bands of white over narrow black band (from top by staff), with red device on diagonal bands.

NATIONAL ANTHEM.—Ya Allah Lanjutkan Lah Usia Duli Tuanku (O God, long live our Majesty the Sultan).

NATIONAL DAY.—February 23.

GOVERNMENT

In 1959, the Sultan of Brunei promulgated the first written Constitution, which provides for a Privy Council, a Council of Ministers and a Legislative Council. On January 1, 1984 Brunei resumed full independence. A ministerial system of government was established at independence, the seven Ministers being appointed by the Sultan and responsible to him. The Sultan presides over the Privy Council and the Council of Ministers. The Legislative Council was disbanded in February 1984.

Sultan, HM Sultan Haji Hassanal Bolkiah Mu'izzaddin Waddaulah, Sultan and Yang Di-Pertuan, *acceded* 1967, *crowned* August 1, 1968.

The Council of Ministers
(as at July 26, 1991)

Prime Minister, Minister of Defence, HM The Sultan.
Foreign Affairs, HRH Prince Mohammed.
Finance, HRH Prince Jefri.
Special Adviser to the Sultan and Minister for Home Affairs, Pehin Dato Haji Isa.
Education, Pehin Dato Abdul Aziz.
Law, Pengiran Bahrin.
Industry and Primary Resources, Pehin Dato Abdul Rahman.
Religious Affairs, Pehin Dato Mohammed Zain.
Development, Pengiran Dato Dr Ismail.
Culture, Youth and Sports, Pehin Dato Haji Hussein.
Health, Dato Dr Johar.
Communications, Dato Haji Zakaria.

BRUNEI DARUSSALAM HIGH COMMISSION
49 Cromwell Road, SW7 2ED
[071–581 0521]

High Commissioner, Pengiran Dato Haji Mustapha (1990).

FINANCE

	1988
Revenue	B$2,487 m
Expenditure	2,721 m

Trade with UK

	1989	1990
Imports from UK	£264,371,000	£224,562,000
Exports to UK	186,110,000	158,516,000

BRITISH HIGH COMMISSION
Hong Kong and Shanghai Bank Building (3rd floor)
Bandar Seri Begawan
[Bandar Seri Begawan 222231]

High Commissioner, His Excellency Adrian Sindall (1991).

British Council Representative, J. Semple, PO Box 3049, Bandar Seri Begawan 1930.

CANADA
AREA AND POPULATION

Provinces or Territories (with official contractions)	Area (sq. miles)	Population Census 1986
Alberta (Alta.)	255,285	2,365,825*
British Columbia (BC)	365,944	2,883,365*
Manitoba (Man.)	250,945	1,063,015*
New Brunswick (NB)	28,355	709,440*
Newfoundland and Labrador (Nfld.)	156,648	568,350
Nova Scotia (NS)	21,425	873,175*
Ontario (Ont.)	412,578	9,101,690*
Prince Edward Island (PEI)	2,185	126,645
Quebec (Que.)	594,855	6,532,460*
Saskatchewan (Sask.)	251,864	1,009,615*
Yukon Territory (YT)	186,660	23,505
Northwest Territories (NWT)	1,322,900	52,240
Total	3,849,646	25,309,330*

Area figures include land and water area.
*Excludes 1986 Census data for one or more incompletely enumerated Indian reserves or Indian settlements.

Of the total immigration of 212,166 in 1990, 11,628 were from the Caribbean, 7,959 from the United Kingdom and Ireland, and 5,960 from the United States of America.

Mother Tongues of the Population

	1986
Single Responses	
English	15,334,085
French	6,159,740
Non-Official Languages	2,860,570
Cree	57,645
Inuktitut	21,050
Ojibway	16,380
Multiple Responses	
English and French	332,610
English and non-official language(s)	525,720
French and non-official language(s)	36,310
English, French and non-official language(s)	46,585
Non-official languages	13,715
Total Population	25,309,330

PHYSIOGRAPHY

Canada was originally discovered by Cabot in 1497, but its history dates only from 1534, when the French took possession of the country. The first permanent settlement at Port Royal (now Annapolis), Nova Scotia, was founded in 1605, and Quebec was founded in 1608. In 1759 Quebec was captured by the British forces under General Wolfe, and in 1763 the whole territory of Canada became a possession of Great Britain by the Treaty of Paris of that year. Nova Scotia was ceded in 1713 by the Treaty of Utrecht, the Provinces of New Brunswick and Prince Edward Island being subsequently formed out of it. British Columbia was formed into a Crown colony in 1858, having previously been a part of the Hudson Bay Territory, and was united to Vancouver Island in 1866.

Canada occupies the whole of the northern part of the North American Continent (with the exception

of Alaska), from 49° North latitude to the North Pole, and from the Pacific to the Atlantic Ocean. In Eastern Canada, the southernmost point is Middle Island in Lake Erie, at 41° 41′.

Relief.—The relief of Canada is dominated by the mountain ranges running north and south on the west side of the Continent, by the pre-Cambrian shield on the east, with, in between, the northern extension of the North American Plain. From the physiographic point of view Canada has six main divisions. These are: (1) Appalachian-Acadian Region, (2) the Canadian Shield, (3) the St Lawrence-Great Lakes Lowland, (4) the Interior Plains, (5) the Cordilleran Region and (6) the Arctic Archipelago. The first region occupies all that part of Canada lying south-east of the St Lawrence. In general, the relief is an alternation of highlands and lowlands and is hilly rather than mountainous. The great Canadian Shield comprises more than half the area. The interior as a whole is an undulating, low plateau (general level 1,000 to 1,500 feet), with the more rugged relief lying along the border between Northern Quebec and Labrador. Throughout the whole area water or muskeg-filled depressions separate irregular hills and ridges, 150 to 200 feet in elevation. Newfoundland, an outlying portion of the shield, consists of glaciated, low rolling terrain broken here and there by mountains.

The flat relief of the St Lawrence-Great Lakes lowland varies from 500 feet in the east to 1,700 feet south of Georgian Bay. The most striking relief is provided by the eastward facing scarp of the Niagara escarpment (elevation 250 to 300 feet). The interior plains, comprising the Pacific Provinces, slope eastward and northward a few feet per mile. The descent from west to east is made from 5,000 feet to less than 1,000 feet in three distinct levels, with each new level being marked by an eastward facing conteau or scarp. Five fairly well-developed topographic divisions mark out the Cordilleran region of western Canada. These are: (1) coastal ranges, largely above 5,000 feet with deep fjords and glaciated valleys, (2) the interior plateau, around 3,500 feet and comparatively level, (3) the Selkirk ranges, largely above 5,000 feet, (4) the Rocky Mountains with their chain of 10,000 to 12,000 feet peaks, and (5) the Peace River or Tramontane region with its rolling diversified country.

The Arctic Archipelago, with its plateau-like character has an elevation between 500 and 1,000 feet, though in Baffin Land and Ellesmere Island the mountain ranges rise to 8,500 and 9,500 feet. Two tremendous waterway systems, the St Lawrence and the Mackenzie, providing thousands of miles of water highway, occupy a broad area of lowland with their dominant axis following the edge of the shield.

Climate.—The climate of the eastern and central portions presents greater extremes than in corresponding latitudes in Europe, but in the south-western portion of the Prairie Region and the southern portions of the Pacific slope the climate is milder. Spring, summer and autumn are of about seven to eight months' duration, and the winter four to five months.

GOVERNMENT

The Constitution of Canada had its source in the British North America Act of 1867 which formed a Dominion, under the name of Canada, of the four provinces of Ontario, Quebec, New Brunswick and Nova Scotia; to this federation the other provinces have subsequently been admitted. Under this Act Canada came into being on July 1, 1867, and under the Statute of Westminster, which received the royal assent on December 11, 1931, Canada and the provinces were exempted (in common with other self-governing Dominions of the Commonwealth of Na-

tions) from the operation of the Colonial Laws Validity Act, the Statute of Westminster having removed all limitations with regard to the legislative autonomy of the Dominions, except that the British North America Act could be amended in important respects only by Acts of the British Parliament.

Provinces admitted since 1867 are: Manitoba (1870), British Columbia (1871), Prince Edward Island (1873), Alberta and Saskatchewan (1905) and Newfoundland (1949).

The election of a separatist Parti Quebecois government in Quebec in 1976, led to a referendum in 1980 on whether the province should conduct negotiations with the federal government on a new 'sovereignty-association'; the proposal was rejected.

Agreement was reached in November 1981 between the federal and provincial governments (except Quebec) to patriate the Constitution so that it was amendable only in Canada. The inclusion in the Constitution of a Charter of Rights was also agreed. At the request of the Canadian Parliament, legislation was passed at Westminster and the Constitution formally patriated on April 17, 1982.

To reconcile Quebec to the new constitution the Canadian federal government and the ten provincial governments signed the Meech Lake Accord on June 3, 1987. This transfered certain powers to the provinces and specifically recognized Quebec as 'a distinct society'. The provincial legislatures of Manitoba and Newfoundland refused to approve the Accord by the deadline for its ratification on June 22, 1990. Following the collapse of the Accord, the Belanger-Campeau Commission was established. In March 1991, it recommended that Quebec conduct a referendum on its sovereignty by October 26, 1992, if a renewed federalism had not been offered by the federal government.

Executive power is vested in a Governor General appointed by the Sovereign on the advice of the Canadian Ministry, and aided by a Privy Council.

CURRENCY.—Canadian dollar (C$) of 100 cents.

FLAG.—Red maple leaf with 11 points on white square, flanked by vertical red bars one half the width of the square.

NATIONAL ANTHEM.—O Canada.

NATIONAL DAY.—July 1 (Dominion Day).

Governor General

Governor General and Commander-in-Chief, His Excellency the Rt. Hon. Ramon John Hnatyshyn, PC, CC, CMM, CD, QC.

Secretary to the Governor General, J. A. LaRocque.

The Cabinet
(as at April 21, 1991)

Prime Minister, Rt. Hon. Brian Mulroney

Minister responsible for Constitutional Affairs, President of Queen's Privy Council, Rt. Hon. Joe Clark

Fisheries and Oceans, Minister for the Atlantic Canada Opportunities Agency, Hon. John Crosbie.

Deputy Prime Minister, Minister of Finance, Hon. Don Mazankowski.

Public Works, Hon. Elmer Mackay.

Energy, Mines and Resources, Hon. Jake Epp.

Secretary of State, Hon. Robert de Cotret

Communications, Hon. Perrin Beatty

Industry, Science and Technology, International Trade, Hon. Michael Wilson

Minister of State and Government House Leader, Hon. Harvie Andre

National Revenue, Hon. Otto Jelinek

Indian Affairs and Northern Development, Hon. Tom Siddon

Western Economic Diversification, Minister of State (Grains and Oilseeds), Hon. Charles Mayer

Agriculture, Hon. Bill McKnight
Health and Welfare, Hon. Benoit Bouchard
Defence, Hon. Marcel Masse
External Affairs, Hon. Barbara McDougall
Veterans Affairs, Hon. Gerald Merrithew
Minister of State (Employment and Immigration), Minister of State (Seniors), Hon. Monique Vezina
Forestry, Hon. Frank Oberle
Government Leader in the Senate, Hon. Lowell Murray
Supply and Services, Hon. Paul Dick
Minister of State (Fitness, Youth and Amateur Sport), Deputy House Leader, Hon. Pierre Cadieux
Environment, Hon. Jean Charest
Minister of State (Small Business and Tourism), Hon. Tom Hockin
External Relations and Minister of State (Indian Affairs and Northern Development), Hon. Monique Landry
Employment and Immigration, Hon. Bernard Valcourt
Minister of State (Multiculturalism and Citizenship), Hon. Gerry Weiner
Solicitor-General, Hon. Doug Lewis
Consumer and Corporate Affairs and Minister of State (Agriculture), Hon. Pierre Blais
Minister of State (Finance and Privatization), Hon. John McDermid
Minister of State (Transport), Hon. Shirley Martin
Associate Defence Minister, Minister Responsible for the Status of Women, Hon. Mary Collins
Minister of State (Science and Technology), Hon. William Winegard
Justice Minister and Attorney-General, Hon. Kim Campbell
Transport, Hon. Jean Corbeil
President of Treasury Board, Minister of State (Finance), Hon. Gilles Loiselle
Labour, Hon. Marcel Danis
Minister of State (Environment), Hon. Pauline Browes

CANADIAN HIGH COMMISSION
Macdonald House, 1 Grosvenor Square, W1X 0AB
[071–629 9492]

High Commissioner, His Excellency Frederik Eaton (1991).
Deputy High Commissioner, Gaétan Lavertu.
Ministers, J. T. Boehm (*Political and Public Affairs*); R. J. L. Berlet (*Commercial/Economic*).
Minister-Counsellor, R. Girard (*Immigration*).

BRITISH HIGH COMMISSION
80 Elgin Street, Ottawa K1P 5K7
[Ottawa 237 1530]

High Commissioner, His Excellency Brian James Proetel Fall, CMG.
Deputy High Commissioner, P. M. Newton.
Counsellors, R. T. Fell (*Economic and Commercial*); M. G. B. Greig.
Defence and Military Adviser, Brig. T. D. V. Bevan.
Naval Adviser, Capt. P. J. Bootherstone, DSC.
Air Adviser, Gp Capt J. R. Legh-Smith.
First Secretaries, V. Welborn (*Administration*); A. Jordan; I. D. Kydd (*Commercial*); N. Penrhys-Evans; D. Scrafton.
Cultural Affairs and British Council Representative, M. Evans.
British Council Representative in Quebec, S. Dawbarn, c/o British Consulate General, 1155 University Street, Montreal, Quebec H3B 3A7.

THE LEGISLATURE

Parliament consists of a Senate and a House of Commons. The Senate consists of 107 members, nominated by the Governor General (age limit 75),

the seats being distributed between the various provinces. Each Senator must be at least thirty years old, a resident in the province for which he is appointed, a natural-born or naturalized subject of the Queen, and the owner of a property qualification amounting to $4,000. The Speaker of the Senate is chosen by the Government of the day.

The House of Commons has 295 members and is elected every five years at longest. Representation by provinces is at present as follows: Newfoundland 7, Prince Edward Island 4, Nova Scotia 11, New Brunswick 10, Quebec 75, Ontario 99, Manitoba 14, Saskatchewan 14, Alberta 26, British Columbia 32, Yukon 1, Northwest Territories 2.

THE SENATE

The state of the parties in the Senate as at June 1991 was Progressive Conservatives 53, Liberals 48, Independent 5, Reform 1.
Speaker of the Senate, Hon. Guy Charbonneau, QC.
Clerk of the Senate and Clerk of the Parliaments, Gordon Barnhart.

THE HOUSE OF COMMONS

The state of parties in the House of Commons as at April 11, 1991, was Progressive Conservatives 159, Liberals 81, New Democratic Party 44, Independent 10, Reform Party 1.
Speaker of the House of Commons, Hon. John A. Fraser.
Deputy Speaker, Andrée Champagne.
Clerk of the House of Commons, Robert Marleau.

THE JUDICATURE

The Judicature is administered by judges following the Civil Law in Quebec Province and Common Law in other Provinces. Each Province has its Court of Appeal. All Superior, County and District Court Judges are appointed by the Governor General, the others by the Lieutenant Governors of the Provinces.

The highest federal court is the Supreme Court of Canada, composed of a Chief Justice and eight puisne judges, which exercises general appellate jurisdiction throughout Canada in civil and criminal cases, and which usually holds three sessions each year. There is one other federally constituted Court, the Federal Court of Canada, which has jurisdiction on appeals from its Trial Division, from Federal Tribunals and reviews of decisions and references by Federal Boards and Commissions. The Trial Division has jurisdiction in claims by or against the Crown, its officers or servants or Federal bodies. It also deals with inter-Provincial and Federal-Provincial disputes.

SUPREME COURT OF CANADA

Chief Justice of Canada, Rt. Hon. A. Lamer, PC.
Puisne Judges, Hons. G. V. LaForest; Claire L'Heureux-Dube; J. Sopinka; C. Gonthier; P. Cory; Beverley McLachlin; W. A. Stevenson; F. Iacobucci.

FEDERAL COURT OF CANADA

Chief Justice, vacant.
Associate Chief Justice, Hon. J. A. Jerome.
Appeal Division Judges, Hons. L. Pratte; D. V. Heald; P. M. Mahoney, PC; L. Marceau; J. K. Hugesson; A. J. Stone; M. MacGuigan; Alice Desjardins; R. Décary; A. M. Linden.
Trial Division Judges, Hons. J.-E. Dubé; P. U. C. Rouleau; F. C. Muldoon; B. L. Strayer; Barbara J. Reed; P. Denault; Y. Pinard; L. M. Joyal; B. Cullen; L. A. Martin; M. A. Teitelbaum; W. A. MacKay.

VITAL STATISTICS

BIRTHS, DEATHS AND MARRIAGES 1989

Province	Births	Deaths	Marriages
Alberta	43,351	13,854	19,888
British Columbia .	43,769	22,997	25,170
Manitoba........	17,321	8,819	7,800
New Brunswick ..	9,667	5,496	5,254
Newfoundland ...	7,762	3,718	3,905
Nova Scotia	12,533	7,516	6,828
Ontario	145,338	70,907	80,377
PEI	1,937	1,089	1,019
Quebec..........	92,373	48,308	33,325
Saskatchewan ...	16,651	7,920	6,637
Yukon	480	95	214
NW Territories	1,479	249	223
Total......	392,661	190,965	190,640

Canada's birth rate per 1,000 population (1989) 15·0; Death Rate 7·3; Marriage Rate 7·3. Divorces 80,716 in 1989.

FINANCE

Federal Government gross general revenue and expenditure was:—

	1989–90	1990–91
Total Revenue	C$118,896 m	C$128,894 m
Total Expenditure.....	149,320 m	159,285 m

DEBT

	1988–89	1989–90
Gross Public Debt	C$382,219 m	C$408,483 m
Net Public Debt	325,989 m	354,439 m

Banking.—There were 67 chartered banks on Dec. 31, 1990, with assets of C$472,725 m (booked in Canada). Deposits were C$359,485 m. of which C$219,256 m. were personal savings.

NATIONAL DEFENCE

The Minister of National Defence has the control and management of the Canadian Armed Forces and all matters relating to National Defence establishments and works for the defence of Canada.

The Canadian Forces are organized on a functional basis to reflect the major commitments assigned by the government and are formed into National Defence Headquarters and five major Commands reporting to the Chief of the Defence Staff. The roles of the five Commands are: *Mobile Command*—Provision of ground forces for the protection of Canadian territory, combat forces in Canada for support of overseas commitments, and forces for support of United Nations or other peace-keeping operations. *Maritime Command*—Provision of sea forces for the defence of Canada, anti-submarine defence in support of NATO. Maritime Command also has operational control of Maritime aircraft. *Air Command*—Provision of operationally ready air forces to national, continental and international commitments. *Canadian Forces Communications Command*—Manages, operates and maintains strategic communications for the Canadian Forces. *Canadian Forces Europe*—Canadian Forces allocated to support NATO in Europe consisting of land and air elements.

National Defence expenditure for the fiscal year 1990–91 was estimated at C$12,260 million. Canadian Armed Forces strength at March 1991: 87,319 authorized force.

EDUCATION

Education is under the control of the Provincia Governments, the cost of the publicly controlle schools being met by local taxation, aided by provir cial grants. In 1990–91 there were 15,507 publicl controlled elementary and secondary schools wit 5,129,100 pupils. Of these, 1,369 were private schoo with 239,700 pupils; 387 federal schools with 49,60 pupils and 21 special schools for the blind and dea with 2,460 pupils.

In 1990–91 there were 69 degree-granting univer sities with a full-time enrolment of 532,100, as well a 324,400 students in 201 other post-secondary, non university institutions.

PRODUCTION

Agriculture.—About 7 per cent of the total lan area of Canada is farmed land. Over half of this i under cultivation, the remainder being predomi nantly classified as unimproved pasture. More tha 80 per cent of the land now cultivated is found in th prairie region of western Canada.

Farm cash receipts from the sale of farm product in 1990 were C$21,687m. Livestock and anima products contributed C$11,294m; field crop C$8,485m.

Grain crop production ('000 tonnes):

	1989	1990p
Wheat	24,578·0	31,798·4
Oats	3,546·3	3,506·5
Barley	11,666·4	13,520·7
Rye	873·4	939·0
Flaxseed	497·6	935·3
Canola	3,095·8	3,324·7
Total.................	44,257·5	54,024·6

p = preliminary

Livestock.—In July 1990 the livestock include 12,248,800 cattle, 10,393,500 pigs, 759,200 sheep an lambs and 21,303,000 chickens (layers).

Fur Production.—Canada in 1989–90 produce pelts valued at C$52m. Wild life pelts made up 42· per cent of the total, with a value of C$22m.

Fisheries.—The marketed value of catches in 198 was C$2,989m (preliminary).

Forestry.—About 43 per cent of the total land are is considered as inventoried forest area. The valu of shipments and other revenue from forestry relate industries in 1988 was: logging $9,079m; sawmill an planing mill products $9,376m; shingle and shak $237m; veneer and plywood $1,120m; and paper an allied products $26,732m.

Minerals.—In 1988, Canada was the world's larges producer of zinc and uranium, and the second larges of asbestos, potash, nickel, cobalt, gypsum and tita nium concentrate. The country is also rich in man other minerals, including gold, silver, copper, lea molybdenum, platinum group metals, elemental sul phur, aluminium and cadmium (refined production)

	1989	1990p
	('000 tonnes)	
Copper	704·4	779·6
Nickel	195·6	196·6
Lead	268·9	224·0
Molybdenum........	13·5	13·5
Zinc	1,272·9	1,285·4
Iron Ore............	39,445·0	36,443·0
Asbestos............	701·0	665·0
Gypsum	8,196·0	8,202·0
Cement	12,591·0	11,252·0
Lime	2,552·0	2,404·0
Salt	11,057·0	11,097·0
Potash	7,014·0	7,015·0

p preliminary

Production of gold was 164,991,000 grams in 1990 and of silver 1,400,000 kg. Uranium production in 1990 was 9,458,000 kilograms.

TRADE

Merchandise imports into Canada in 1990 were valued at C$136,224m and merchandise exports (including re-exports) at C$148,664m. The main exports in 1989 were passenger automobiles and chassis, motor vehicle parts (except engines), trucks, truck tractors and chassis, wood pulp and similar pulp, newsprint paper, softwood lumber, crude petroleum and other telecommunications and related equipment (excluding televisions, radio sets, phonographs). Trade with the USA accounts for 69·9 per cent of total trade in merchandise, although efforts are being made to develop alternative markets. Value of trade with Canada's six largest trading partners in 1990 was as follows (C$'000):

Country	Imports	Domestic Exports*
United States	87,895	105,279
Japan	9,523	8,196
United Kingdom	4,842	3,403
Germany	3,837	2,219
Korea, Rep. of	2,254	1,541
France	2,449	1,234
*Excluding re-exports		

Trade with UK

	1989	1990
Imports from UK	£2,165,731,000	£1,901,939,000
Exports to UK	2,174,334,000	2,259,099,000

COMMUNICATIONS

Railways.—The total track of railways in operation on Dec. 31, 1989, was 89,104 km. In 1989 freight transportation was 249 billion tonne-kilometres, and the balance of property accounts at end 1989 was C$18,808m.

Shipping.—The registered shipping on Jan. 1, 1989 including inland vessels, was 40,988 vessels with gross tonnage 5,200,816. The volume of international shipping handled at Canadian ports in 1989 was 159,069,062 metric tonnes loaded and 80,317,729 metric tonnes unloaded.

Canals.—The bulk of canal shipping in Canada is handled through the two sections of the St Lawrence Seaway, which provide access to the Great Lakes to ocean-going ships. In 1990, transits on the Montreal-Lake Ontario section numbered 2,768 for a total of 36,655,939 cargo tonnes; transits in the Welland Canal section numbered 3,577 for a total of 39,397,900 cargo tonnes. Principal commodities carried were iron ore, wheat, corn, barley, soybeans, fuel oil, manufactured iron and steel, coal and coke.

Civil Aviation.—The number of passengers carried in 1989 (all major Canadian carriers) was 37,176,000; 1,700,620,000 tonne-km of freight was carried in 1989.

Motor Vehicles.—Total motor vehicle registrations numbered 16,719,529 in 1989.

Post.—Post office revenue in the fiscal year 1990–91 was C$3,739 m.; total expenditure C$3,664 m.

(Financial and economic statistics supplied by Statistics Canada.)

FEDERAL CAPITAL

OTTAWA, the federal capital, 111 miles west of Montreal and 247 miles north-east of Toronto, is a city on the south bank of the Ottawa river. The city was chosen as the capital of the Province of Canada in 1857 and was later selected as the site of the Dominion capital. Ottawa contains the Parliamentary Buildings, the Public Archives, Royal Mint, several national museums, the National Art Gallery and the Dominion Observatory.

Manufacturing is also carried on, medical advancement, high technology (communications, defence), printing and publishing being of greatest importance. Ottawa is connected with Lake Ontario by the Rideau Canal. The City population was 300,763 at the Census of 1986; and Metropolitan Ottawa 819,263. In 1990 the Ottawa Metropolitan population was estimated to be 863,900.

YUKON TERRITORY

The area of the Territory is 186,660 sq. miles (483,450 sq. km), with a population (1990 preliminary estimate) of 29,149. Minerals and tourism are the chief industries, followed closely by transportation, communications and other utilities industry.

Seat of Government, Whitehorse, population (1990 preliminary estimate) 20,477.

The Yukon Act 1970, as amended, provides for the administration of the Territory by a Commissioner acting under instructions from time to time given by the Governor-in-Council or the Minister of Indian Affairs and Northern Development. Legislative powers, analogous to those of a provincial government, are exercised by a Legislative Assembly of 16 members elected from electoral districts in the Territory. The Executive Council of the Assembly consists of the government leader as chairman and four elected members.

Commissioner, J. K. McKinnon.

EXECUTIVE COUNCIL
(as at 1991)

Premier, Minister of the Executive Council Office, Finance, Hon. Tony Penikett.

Education, Government Services, responsible for the Public Service Commission and the Workers' Compensation Board, Hon. Piers McDonald.

Justice, responsible for the Yukon Liquor Corporation and the Women's Directorate, Hon. Margaret Joe.

Renewable Resources, Tourism, Hon. Art Webster.

Community and Transportation Services, responsible for the Yukon Development Corporation, Hon. Maurice Byblow.

Health and Social Services, responsible for the Yukon Housing Corporation, Hon. Joyce Hayden.

NORTHWEST TERRITORIES

The area of the Northwest Territories is 1,322,900 sq. miles (3,426,320 sq. km), with a population (1990 preliminary estimate) of 53,801. The chief industry is mining, with a total value of $956,897,000 in 1988. Lead, zinc, gold, silver, oil exploration and natural gas contributed about 36 per cent of the 1988 GDP of the Northwest Territories.

The Northwest Territories are subdivided into the districts of Mackenzie, Keewatin and Franklin.

Seat of Government, Yellowknife, population (1990 preliminary estimate) 13,698.

The Northwest Territories Act 1979, as amended, provides for a Legislative Assembly of 24 elected members, of which the Executive Council under the chairmanship of the government leader is the senior decision-making body of the government in the Territory.

Commissioner, D. L. Norris.

Government Leader, Minister responsible for the Executive, Minister of Intergovernmental Affairs, responsible for the NWT Science Institute and for the Devolution Office/Audit Bureau, Hon. Dennis Patterson.

Minister of Culture and Communications, Renewable Resources, Associate Minister of Aboriginal Rights and Constitutional Development, Hon. Titus Allooloo.

House Leader, Minister of Finance, Justice, responsible for Public Utilities Board, Hon. Michael Ballantyne.

Health, Energy, Mines and Petroleum Resources, Public Works, responsible for NWT Power Corporation, Hon. Nellie Cournoyee.

Deputy Government Leader, Minister of Education, Personnel, responsible for Aboriginal Rights and Constitutional Development, Hon. Stephen Kakfwi.

Social Services, Safety and Public Services, responsible for Worker's Compensation Board, and for Women's Directorate and Youth, Hon. Jeannie Marie-Jewell.

Government Services, responsible for the NWT Housing Corporation, Municipal and Community Affairs, Hon. Tom Butters.

Economic Development and Tourism, Transportation, responsible for the Highway Transport Board, Hon. Gordon Wray.

CANADIAN PROVINCES

ALBERTA

Area and Population.—The Province of Alberta has an area of 661,185 sq. km (255,285 sq. miles), including about 6,485 sq. miles of water (16,796 sq. km), with a population (April 1991) of 2,513,100.

Government.—The Government is vested in a Lieutenant Governor and Legislative Assembly composed of 83 members, elected for five years, representing 83 electoral districts in the Province. At a provincial election held on March 20, 1989, the Progressive Conservative Party took 59 seats, the New Democratic Party 16 seats and the Liberal Party 8 seats.

Lt. Governor, The Hon. Gordon Towers.

Premier, President of Executive Council, Hon. Don Getty

Deputy Premier and Minister of Federal and Intergovernmental Affairs, Government House Leader, Hon. Jim Horsman.

Provincial Treasurer, Hon. Dick Johnston.

Transportation and Utilities, Hon. Al Adair.

Forestry, Lands and Wildlife, Hon. LeRoy Fjordbotten.

Economic Development and Trade, Hon. Peter Elzinga.

Energy, Hon. Rick Orman.

Agriculture, Hon. Ernie Isley.

Health, Hon. Nancy Betkowski.

Attorney-General, Hon. Ken Rostad.

Technology, Research and Telecommunications, Hon. Fred Stewart.

Public Works, Supply and Services, Hon. Ken Kowalski.

Career Development and Employment, Hon. Norm Weiss.

Education, Hon. Jim Dinning.

Tourism, Hon. Don Sparrow.

Labour, Hon. Elaine McCoy.

Consumer and Corporate Affairs, Hon. Dennis Anderson.

Family and Social Services, Hon. John Oldring.

Associate Minister of Family and Social Services, Hon. R. Brassard.

Occupational Health and Safety, Workers' Compensation Board, Hon. Peter Trynchy.

Advanced Education and Deputy House Leader, Hon. John Gogo.

Recreation and Parks, Hon. Steve West.

Associate Minister of Agriculture, Hon. Shirley McClellan.

Municipal Affairs, Hon. Ray Speaker.

Environment, Hon. Ralph Klein.

Solicitor-General, Hon. Dick Fowler.

Culture and Multiculturalism, Hon. Doug Main.

Agent-General in London, Mary LeMessurier, Alberta House, 1 Mount Street, W1Y 5AA.

Court of Appeal of Alberta, Chief Justice, Hon. J. H. Laycraft.

Court of Queen's Bench of Alberta, Chief Justice, Hon. W. K. Moore.

Associate Chief Justice, Hon. T. H. Miller.

The total GDP at factor cost in 1989 (preliminary figures) amounted to C$66,748 million. Preliminary estimates for mineral production in 1990 came to C$19,338,662,000. Of this total, crude oil amounted to C$11,394,359,000, and natural gas and its by-products to C$6,836,675,000.

Manufacturing.—The total value of manufacturing shipments (1990) was C$18,952,317,000. Number of industrial establishments 2,966 (1988), total employees 63,532 (1988). The leading industrial products are refined petroleum and coal products, meat and meat products, chemicals and chemical products, fabricated metal products, non-metallic mineral products and primary metals.

	1989–90	1990–91
Revenue	C$9,720 m	C$11,420 m
Expenditure	12,044 m	12,200 m
Deficit	2,324 m	780 m

NOTE: The Budgetary revenue figure does not include funds allocated to the Alberta Heritage Savings Trust Fund.

CAPITAL.—Edmonton—city population (1990) 605,538, metropolitan area, 823,555. Other centres are Calgary (692,885), Lethbridge (60,614), Red Deer (56,922), Medicine Hat (42,929), St Albert (40,707), Fort McMurray (33,698).

BRITISH COLUMBIA

Area and Population.—British Columbia has a total area estimated at 947,790 sq. km (365,944 sq. miles), with a population (June 1990) of 3,131,700.

Government.—The Government consists of a Lieutenant Governor and an Executive Council together with a Legislative Assembly of 69 members.

The Social Credit Party formed a government after a General Election on October 22, 1986. The present standing in the Assembly is Social Credit Party 41, New Democratic Party 25, vacant 3.

Lt. Governor, His Honour Dr David See-Chai Lam.

Premier, Hon. Rita Johnston.

Advanced Education, Training and Technology, Hon. Peter Dueck.

Agriculture, Fisheries and Food, Hon. Larry Chalmers.

Attorney-General, Hon. Russell Fraser.

Development, Trade and Tourism, Hon. Howard Dirks.

Education, Hon. Stanley Hagen.

Energy, Mines and Petroleum Resources, Hon. Jack Weisgerber.

Environment, Hon. Dave Mercier.

Finance and Corporate Relations, Hon. John Jansen.

Forests, Hon. Claude Richmond.

Health, and responsible for Seniors, Hon. Bruce Strachan.

Labour and Consumer Services, Hon. James Rabbitt.

Lands and Parks, Hon. Dave Parker.

Municipal Affairs, Recreation and Culture, Hon. Graham Bruce.

Native Affairs, Hon. John Savage.

Provincial Secretary, and responsible for Multiculturalism and Immigration, Hon. Elwood Veitch.

Social Services and Housing, Hon. Norm Jacobsen.

Solicitor-General, Hon. Ivan Messmer.

Transportation and Highways, Hon. Lyall Hanson.

Women's Programs, Government Services and responsible for Families, Hon. Carol Gran.

Agent-General in London, G. Gardom, QC, British Columbia House, 1 Regent Street, SW1 4NR.

THE JUDICATURE

Court of Appeal, Chief Justice of British Columbia, Hon. A. McEachern.

Supreme Court, Chief Justice, Hon. W. A. Esson.

Associate Chief Justice, Hon. D. H. Campbell.

FINANCE

	1990–91	1991–92
Estimated Revenue	C$15,308·0 m	C$16,150·0 m
Estimated Expenditure	15,293·0 m	16,565·0 m
Net Guaranteed Debt ..	6,117·1 m	5,663·3 m

ECONOMY

Production and Industry.—Manufacturing activity is based largely on the processing of the output of the logging, mineral, fishing and agriculture industries. The principal manufacturing centres are Vancouver, New Westminster, Victoria, North Vancouver, Kelowna and Prince George. Forestry and forest-based industries form the most important economic activity, accounting for approximately 40 per cent of total production. British Columbia is the leading province of Canada in the quantity and value of its timber and sawmill products. Mining, the second most important non-service economic activity, is based on copper, zinc, lead, iron concentrates, molybdenum, coal, natural gas, crude petroleum, asbestos, gold and silver. Molybdenum production is approximately 99 per cent of the Canadian total.

The production levels for important industries were estimated for 1990 as follows:—

Lumber	33,514,700 cu. metres
Paper	2,993,700 tonnes
Pulp	6,604,500 tonnes
Coal	25,180,200 tonnes
Natural Gas	11,800,000,000 cu. metres

Mineral production for 1990 was valued at C$3,962·9 million.

The most important agricultural products are livestock, eggs and poultry, fruits and dairy products. Salmon accounts for approximately 60 per cent of the value of fisheries. Other species include halibut, herring, sole, cod, flounder, perch, tuna and shellfish. In 1990 farm cash receipts were valued at C$1,185·7 million.

The economy is dependent upon markets outside the province for the disposal of most of the products of industry. An estimated 55–60 per cent of production is exported to foreign markets. Manufacturing shipments in 1990 were valued at C$24,544·3 million.

Transport.—The Province has deep water harbours which are well serviced by railways and modern highways. Vancouver is the base for regular scheduled air routes to other parts of Canada, the United States, Europe, Mexico, South America, Hawaii, Fiji, Australia, Japan, Hong Kong and the Middle East.

CAPITAL.—ΨVictoria, metropolitan population (1990) 280,364. ΨVancouver, metropolitan population (1990) 1,535,301, possesses one of the finest natural harbours in the world, servicing a variety of vessels, including large bulk cargo carriers. Other principal cities are Prince George, Kamloops, Kelowna and Nanaimo.

MANITOBA

Area and Population.—Manitoba, originally the Red River settlement, is the central province of Canada. The province has a considerable area of prairie land but is also a land of wide diversity combining 645 kilometres (401 miles) of coastline on Hudson Bay, large lakes and rivers covering an area of 101,592 sq. km (39,225 sq. miles) and pre-cambrian rock which covers about three-fifths of the province. The total area is 649,947 sq. km (250,946 sq. miles), with a population (1990 estimate) of 1,089,900.

Government.—The Lieutenant Governor is The Queen's personal representative in Manitoba. There is a Legislative Assembly of 57 members, of which the Executive Council of Ministers are all members.

The Progressive Conservatives formed a minority government after a General Election held on September 11 1990. The standing in the House at June 30, 1991 was: Progressive Conservatives 30, New Democratic Party 20, Liberal 7.

Lt. Governor, His Honour George Johnson.

EXECUTIVE COUNCIL
(as at July 1991)

Premier, President of the Executive Council and Minister of Federal-Provincial Relations, Hon. Gary A. Filmon.

Natural Resources, Hon. Harry J. Enns.

Deputy Premier, Minister for Rural Development, Northern and Native Affairs, Hon. James E. Downey.

Health, Hon. Donald W. Orchard.

Highways and Transportation, Hon. Albert Driedger.

Finance and Government House Leader, Hon. Clayton S. Manness.

Family Services, Hon. Harold Gilleshammer.

Environment, Hon. James G. Cummings.

Attorney-General, Minister for Constitutional Affairs and Corrections, Hon. James C. McCrae.

Co-operative, Consumer and Corporate Affairs, Hon. Linda McIntosh.

Industry, Trade and Tourism, Hon. Eric Stefansen.

Agriculture, Hon. Glen M. Findlay.

Education and Training, Hon. Leonard Derkach.

Urban Affairs and Housing, Hon. James A. Ernest.

Culture, Heritage and Citizenship, Multiculturalism and Status of Women, Hon. Bonnie E. Mitchelson.

Government Services and Seniors, Hon. Gerald Ducharme.

Energy and Mines, Hon. Harold J. Neufeld.

Labour, Hon. Darren Thomas Praznik.

THE JUDICATURE

Court of Appeal, Chief Justice, Hon. Richard J. Scott.

Queen's Bench Division, Chief Justice, Hon. B. Hewak.

Associate Chief Justices, Hon. J. J. Oliphant (*QBD*), Hon. A. C. Hamilton (*Family Division*).

ECONOMY

Finance.—The projected revenue for the province in the fiscal year 1991–92 was C$4,917 million while expenditures were forecast at C$5,241 million.

Agriculture.—The total land area in Manitoba is 135,342,565 acres, of which 19,126,517 acres are in occupied farms. The gross value of agriculture production in 1990 was estimated at C$2,400 million.

Manufactures.—Manufacturing enterprises employed about 55,000 persons on average in 1990. The chief manufacturing centres are Winnipeg, Brandon, Selkirk and Portage la Prairie. The largest manufacturing industry is the food and beverage industry, followed by the machinery and metal fabricating industries.

CAPITAL.—Winnipeg, population 647,100 (1990 estimate). Other cities are Brandon (39,366), Thompson (14,379), Portage la Prairie (13,522) and Flin Flon (7,708).

NEW BRUNSWICK

Area and Population.—New Brunswick is situated between 45°–48° N. lat. and 63° 47′–69° W. long. and comprises an area of 73,439 sq. km (28,355 sq. miles), with a population (Jan. 1991) of 725,600. It was first colonized by British subjects in 1761, and in 1783 by inhabitants of New England, who had been dispossessed of their property in consequence of their loyalty to the British Crown. New Brunswick entered Confederation in 1867.

Government.—Government is administered by a Lieutenant Governor, an Executive Council, and a Legislative Assembly of 58 members elected by the people. The present Legislative Assembly of the Province was elected on Oct. 13, 1987 and has 58 members, all of whom are from the Liberal Party.

Lt. Governor, His Honour Gilbert Finn.

EXECUTIVE
(as at June 5, 1991)

Premier, Hon. Frank McKenna.
Justice, Hon. James Lockyer.
Transportation, Hon. Sheldon Lee.
Agriculture, Hon. Alan Graham.
Commerce and Technology, Hon. Allan Maher (*acting*).
Health and Community Services, Hon. Raymond Frenette.
Minister of State for Childhood Services, Hon. Jane Barry.
Education, Hon. Shirley Dysart.
Advanced Education and Training, Hon. Russell King.
Labour, Hon. Michael McKee.
Finance, Hon. Allan Maher.
Environment, Hon. Vaughn Blaney.
Municipal Affairs, Hon. Hubert Seamans.
Fisheries and Aquaculture, Hon. Denis Losier.
Tourism, Recreation and Heritage, Hon. Roland Beaulieu.
Chairman, Board of Management, Hon. Gérald Clavette.
Supply and Services, Hon. Bruce Smith.
Natural Resources and Energy, Hon. Morris Green.
Minister of State for Mines, Hon. Edmond Blanchard.
Income Assistance, Hon. Laureen Jarrett.
Housing, Hon. Peter Trites.
Minister responsible for Intergovernmental Affairs, Hon Aldéa Landry.
Speaker of the House, Hon. Frank Branch.
Solicitor-General, Hon. Joseph-Conrad Landry.
Chairman, NB Electric Power Commission, Hon. Al Lacey.

THE JUDICATURE

Court of Appeal, Chief Justice, Hon. S. G. Stratton.
Queen's Bench Division, Chief Justice, Hon. G. A. Richard.

ECONOMY

Finance.—The estimated revenue for the year ending March 31, 1990, was C$3,583,343,864 and ordinary expenditure, $3,470,788,271.

Manufactures.—New Brunswick's largest manufacturing group, in terms of shipments, is the paper and allied industries, followed by the food and wood industries. Together these industries accounted in 1990 for 55·1 per cent of the total value of manufacturing shipments of C$6,279 million. Saint John has a major ice-free port and is the principal manufacturing centre of the Province.

Agriculture.—Total land area 27,633 sq. miles; farms numbered 3,554 and averaged 284 acres each in 1986. Dairy products and potatoes are the leading agricultural products. Both industries together accounted for 49·7 per cent of total farm cash receipts in 1990. Farm cash receipts in 1990 totalled C$275,846,000.

Fisheries.—Fishing is an important industry, employing about 7,800 fishermen. The chief commercial fish are lobsters, herring, tuna, crab and cod. Landings reached 153,046 tonnes valued at C$99,548,000 in 1990.

Minerals.—Extensive zinc, lead and copper deposits are now being mined in the north-eastern part of the province with New Brunswick being the third largest producer of zinc in Canada. A lead smelter, fertilizer plant and port facilities have been constructed at Belledune. Canada's only primary antimony producer is located at Lake George. There is exploration and development near Sussex and Salt Springs, where potash production continues to escalate. A potash terminal has been built at the port of St John. Coal is mined at Grand Lake and exploration for other deposits is being undertaken. Total mineral production was valued at C$886,094,000 in 1990.

Tourism.—Tourism is of increasing value to the economy.

CAPITAL.—Fredericton, population (1986) 65,768. Other cities are ΨSaint John (121,265); Moncton (102,084); Bathurst (34,895); Edmundston (22,614); Campbellton (17,418).

NEWFOUNDLAND AND LABRADOR

Area and Population.—The Island of Newfoundland is situated between 46° 37′–51° 37′ N. latitude and 52° 44′–59° 30′ W. longitude, on the north-east side of the Gulf of St Lawrence, and is separated from the North American continent by the Straits of Belle Isle on the NW and by Cabot Strait on the SW. The island is about 510 km long and 508 km broad and is triangular in shape. It comprises an area of 111,390 sq. km (43,008 sq. miles), with a population (1986 Census) (inclusive of Labrador) of 568,349.

Labrador forms the most easterly part of the North American continent, and extends from Point St Charles, at the north-east entrance to the Straits of Belle Isle, on the south, to Cape Chidley, at the eastern entrance to Hudson's Straits on the north. It has an area of 294,328 sq. km (113,641 sq. miles) with a population (1986 Census) of 28,741. Labrador is noted for its cod fisheries and also possesses valuable salmon, herring, trout and seal fisheries.

Government.—On March 31, 1949 Newfoundland became the 10th Province of the Dominion of Canada. The Government is administered by a Lieutenant Governor, aided by an Executive Council and a Legislative Assembly of 52 members elected for a term of five years. A General Election was held on April

20, 1989. The standings in the current House of Assembly are: Liberals 33; Progressive Conservatives 18, New Democrats 1.

Lt. Governor, His Honour James A. McGrath.

EXECUTIVE
(as at June 4, 1991)

Premier, Hon. Clyde Wells.
Council and Treasury Board President, Hon. Winston Baker.
Fisheries, Hon. Walter Carter.
Employment and Labour Relations, Hon. Roger Grimes.
Health, Hon. Chris Decker.
Justice, Hon. Paul Dicks.
Social Services, Hon. Bill Hogan.
Forestry and Agriculture, Hon. Graham Flight.
Development, Hon. Chuck Furey.
Mines and Energy, Hon. Rex Gibbons.
Works, Services and Transportation, Hon. Dave Gilbert.
Municipal and Provincial Affairs, Hon. Eric Gullage.
Environment and Lands, and responsible for the Status of Woman, Hon. Patt Cowan.
Finance, Hon. Hubert Kitchen.
Education, Hon. Philip Warren.
Speaker of the House of Assembly, Hon. Thomas Lush.
Clerk of the Executive Council, H. H. Stanley.

THE JUDICATURE

Court of Appeal, Chief Justice, Hon. Noel H. A. Goodridge.
Trial Division, Chief Justice, Hon. T. A. Hickman.

ECONOMY

Finance.—The estimated gross capital and current account revenues for 1991–92 are C$3,042,251,000 and the gross current and capital account expenditures C$3,514,010,300.

Production and Industry.—The main primary industries are fishing, forestry and mining. In 1986 shipments of fish products were valued at C$732 million. In 1990 newsprint shipments from the three pulp and paper mills were valued at C$482 million, mining plus structural materials shipments were estimated at C$862 million, of which C$696 million was from the two iron ore mines in Labrador. Total manufacturing shipments were valued at C$1,494 million in 1990. The hydro-electric plant on the Churchill river is the largest underground plant in the world, with a capacity of 5,225,000 Kw.

Petroleum and Natural Gas.—Over 139 wells have been drilled off Newfoundland since 1965. Discovery of oil was made in 1979 on the Grand Banks. Oil production is expected to begin in the 1990s, with a peak production of 110,000 barrels of oil a day. In 1990 offshore exploration expenditure was approximately C$36 million

Transport.—The Province is connected to mainland Canada by a ferry service from North Sydney, Nova Scotia to Port aux Basques and Argentina. An official agreement on June 20, 1988 signified the end of the railway in Newfoundland. Transport between various points on the island is by highway but the south coast and Labrador still rely on the coastal boat service.

CAPITAL.—St John's (population 1986 Census, Greater St John's 161,901) is North America's oldest city, and thus of historical interest and is the seat of the provincial legislature, the site of most provincial and federal government offices and the principal port for the island of Newfoundland. Newfoundland's second city of Corner Brook (population 1986 Census, 22,719) is situated on the west coast, its principal industry being its pulp and paper mill.

NOVA SCOTIA

Area and Population.—Nova Scotia is a peninsula between 43° 25′–47° N. lat. and 59° 40′–66° 25′ W. long., and is connected to New Brunswick by a low fertile isthmus about 28 km wide. It comprises an area of 55,490 sq. km (21,425 sq. miles), including 2,650 sq. km of lakes and rivers and 10,424 km of shoreline. No place is more than 56 km from the Atlantic Ocean. Population (June 1990 estimate) 894,200.

Government.—The Government consists of a Lieutenant Governor and a 52-member elected Legislative Assembly, from which the Executive Council is selected. The state of the parties in Feb. 1991 was Conservatives 26, Liberals 22, New Democratic Party 2, Independent 1, and 1 vacant.

The Lieutenant Governor represents The Queen and is appointed by the Governor-in-Council.

Lt. Governor, His Honour Lloyd R. Crouse, PC.

EXECUTIVE COUNCIL
(as at Feb. 26, 1991)

Premier, Minister for Intergovernmental Affairs, Hon. Donald W. Cameron.
Deputy Premier, Minister for Industry, Trade and Technology, Hon. Thomas J. McInnis.
Finance, Hon. Greg Kerr.
Health and Fitness, Hon. George Moody.
Attorney-General, Solicitor-General, Provincial Secretary, Hon. Joel R. Matheson, QC.
Tourism and Culture, Hon. Terence R. B. Donahoe, QC.
Education, Hon. Ronald C. Giffin, QC.
Environment, Hon. John G. Leefe.
Fisheries, Hon. Guy LeBlanc.
Municipal Affairs, Hon. Brian Young.
Consumer Affairs, Hon. Donald P. McInnes.
Agriculture and Marketing, Hon. George Archibald.
Lands and Forests, Hon. Dr Charles W. MacNeil.
Government Services, Hon. Neil LeBlanc.
Community Services, Hon. Marie Dechman.
Labour, Hon. Leroy Legere.

Speaker of the House of Assembly, Hon. Ronald S. Russell.
Clerk of the Executive Council, H. F. G. Stevens, QC.

Nova Scotia Trade and Investment Office, Raymond Vaudry, 14 Pall Mall, SW1Y 5LU.

THE JUDICATURE

Supreme Court, Appeal Division, Chief Justice, Hon. L. O. Clarke.
Trial Division, Chief Justice, Hon. Constance R. Glube.

ECONOMY

Finance.—The revenue for the fiscal year ending March 31, 1990 was C$3,687,995 and expenditure was C$3,773,894.

Manufacturing.—Manufacturing constitutes the most important goods producing sector of the economy. Manufacturing plants provide employment for 9·9 per cent of the labour force.

Utilities.—Electric power in Nova Scotia is supplied by the Nova Scotia Power Corporation, a Crown corporation. The Corporation's generating stations, which are predominantly coal fired have a nameplate capacity of 1,964,305 kilowatts.

Petroleum Activity.—By mid-1988 a total of 125 wells had been completed off-shore since drilling began in 1967, the drilling being done by five major operations. There was one well drilled onshore in 1989–90.

Mining.—The total value of mineral production in 1989 (preliminary) was estimated at C$499 million.

Dollar value of coal production was C$200 million, and salt production C$63,176,000.

Fishing.—A total of 463,181 tonnes of fish and shellfish was harvested in 1990 for a landed value of C$427 million.

Forestry.—Forest lands total 10,000,000 acres or 73 per cent of the land area. About 71 per cent of forest land is privately owned. Forest based industries employed an average of 9,000 in 1989.

Tourism.—Between May 15 and October 31, 1990, about 1·15 million visitors spent about C$300 million in the Province.

CAPITAL.—ΨHalifax, including the neighbouring city of Dartmouth, has a population of 178,820. The harbour, ice-free all year round, is the main Atlantic winter port of Canada. Other cities and towns include ΨSydney (27,754), ΨGlace Bay (20,467), Amherst (9,671) and New Glasgow (10,022).

Cape Breton Island

This has been part of Nova Scotia since 1819. It is the centre of the steel manufacturing and coal mining industries, and is also noted for its lakes and coastal scenery, making it a tourist attraction in Canada.

ONTARIO

Area and Population.—The Province of Ontario contains a total area of 1,068,572 sq. km (412,578 sq. miles), with a population (1990 estimate) of 9,877,400.

Government.—The Government is vested in a Lieutenant Governor and a Legislative Assembly of 130 members elected for five years.

After the last election on September 6, 1990, there were 73 New Democrats, 36 Liberals, 20 Progressive Conservatives and 1 Independent.

Lt. Governor, His Honour Lincoln Alexander, PC, QC.

EXECUTIVE COUNCIL
(as at July 17, 1991)

Premier and President of the Council, and Minister of Intergovernmental Affairs, Hon. Bob Rae.
Deputy Premier, Treasurer and Minister of Economics, Hon. Floyd Laughren.
Labour, Hon. Bob Mackenzie.
Transportation, Hon. Ed Philip.
Natural Resources, with responsibility for Native Affairs, Hon. C. J. (Bud) Wildman.
Housing, Municipal Affairs, Hon. Dave Cooke.
Colleges and Universities, Skills Development, Hon. Richard Allen.
Environment, with responsibility for the Greater Toronto Area, Hon. Ruth Grier.
Mines, with responsibility for Francophone Affairs, Hon. Gilles Pouliot.
Correctional Services and Solicitor General, with responsibility for the Anti-Drug Strategy, Hon. Mike Farnan.
Attorney-General, Hon. Howard Hampton.
Northern Development, and Government House Leader, Hon. Shelley Martel.
Consumer and Corporate Affairs, Hon. Marilyn Churley.
Financial Institutions, Hon. Brian Charlton.
Community and Social Services, Hon. Zanana Akande.
Education, Hon. Marion Boyd.
Agriculture and Food, Hon. Elmer Buchanan.
Energy, Hon. Jenny Carter.
Chairman of the Management Board of Cabinet, Minister of Government Services and Health, Hon. Frances Lankin.
Culture and Communications, Hon. Rosario Marchese.
Tourism and Recreation, Hon. Peter North.
Industry, Trade and Technology, Hon. Allan Pilkey.

Revenue, Hon. Shelley Wark-Martyn.
Citizenship, with responsibility for Human Rights, the Disabled, Seniors and Race Relations, Hon. Elaine Ziemba.
Minister without Portfolio, Hon. Shirley Coppen.
Minister without Portfolio, with responsibility for Women's Issues, Hon. Anne Swarbrick.

THE JUDICATURE

Chief Justice of Ontario, Hon. C. L. Dubin.
Chief Justice of the High Court, Hon. F. W. Callaghan.

ECONOMY

Agriculture.—Ontario has the highest total of agricultural production in Canada with a gross value of C$5,550 million and a total net farm income of C$809 million.

Forestry.—Productive forested lands cover 39.9 million hectares. Paper and allied industries are by far the most important sector of Ontario's forest industry.

Minerals.—Ontario's natural resources include 15 basic minerals, such as copper, iron ore, zinc, sulphur, gold, nickel and platinum. Total value of the mineral production in 1988 was estimated at C$7,200 million.

Energy.—Total electrical energy generated in Ontario in 1990 was 136,744 million kWh.

Manufacture.—Ontario is the chief manufacturing province in Canada, producing 50 per cent of all manufactured goods. During 1990 Ontario's exports totalled C$74,414 million, an increase in value of C$6,989 million over 1989.

CAPITAL.—ΨToronto (metropolitan, estimate 1990 2,147,600) has a wide range of manufacturing and service industries and is a centre of education, business and finance. Other major urban areas are Ottawa, the national capital (311,094); ΨHamilton (307,160), with iron and steel industry, metal fabrication, machinery, electrical and chemical industries; London (285,357), a business and manufacturing centre; ΨWindsor (193,160); Kitchener (152,771) and Sudbury (89,543).

PRINCE EDWARD ISLAND

Area and Population.—Prince Edward Island lies in the southern part of the Gulf of St Lawrence between 46°–47° N. lat. and 62°–64° 30′ W. long. It is about 225 km in length, and from 6 to 64 km in breadth; its area is 5,659 sq. km (2,185 sq. miles), and its population (1989) 130,000.

Government.—The Government is vested in a Lieutenant Governor, an Executive Council, and a Legislative Assembly of 32 members elected for a term of up to five years, 16 as Councillors and 16 as Assemblymen. After the election of May 29, 1989 there were 30 Liberals and 2 Progressive Conservatives.

Lt. Governor, Her Honour Marion L. Reid.

EXECUTIVE COUNCIL
(as at June 1, 1991)

Premier, President of the Executive Council, Minister of Justice and Attorney General, Hon. Joseph A. Ghiz, QC.
Finance, Environment, Hon. Gilbert R. Clements.
Community and Cultural Affairs, Fisheries and Aquaculture, Hon. Leonce Bernard.
Industry, Hon. Robert Morrissey.
Health and Social Services, Hon. Wayne Cheverie, QC
Transportation and Public Works, Hon. Gordon MacInnis.
Agriculture, Hon. Keith Milligan.
Education, Hon. Paul Connolly.
Energy and Forestry, Hon. Barry Hicken.
Tourism and Parks, Hon. Nancy Guptill.
Labour, Hon. Roberta Hubley.

Speaker of the Legislative Assembly, Hon. Edward W. Clark.

THE JUDICATURE

Appeal Division, Chief Justice, Hon. Norman H. Carruthers.
Trial Division, Chief Justice, Hon. K. R. MacDonald.

ECONOMY

Finance.—The ordinary revenue of the Province in 1989–90 was C$656·6 million and the expenditure C$654·3 million.

Agriculture.—Approximately 48 per cent of the total area of the Province is farmland. The value of farm cash receipts in 1989 was C$253.8 million, of which 46·9 per cent was from the sale of potatoes. Dairy, beef and hogs are also important agriculture products.

Fisheries.—Fish landings were valued at C$72.4 million in 1989 of which 63·7 per cent was of lobster.

Manufacturing.—The total value of manufacturing shipments was C$366.1 million in 1989, of which 69·4 per cent was in the food products industries and 21·4 per cent in the fish products industries.

Tourism.—A major summer economic activity is tourism. Non-resident tourists spent C$98.3 million in the Province in 1989.

Education.—A university and a college of applied arts and technology were established in 1969, estimated full- and part-time enrolment for 1989–90 being 3,181 (University of Prince Edward Island), and 912 for the college of applied arts and technology (Holland College).

CAPITAL.—ΨCharlottetown (30,000), on the shore of Hillsborough Bay, which forms a good harbour.

QUEBEC

Area and Population.—The Province of Quebec contains an area estimated at 1,540,667 sq. km (594,855 sq. miles) with a population (June 1989 estimate) of 6,688,700.

Government.—The Government of the Province is vested in a Lieutenant Governor, a Council of ministers and a National Assembly of 125 members elected for five years. At September 1989, there were 92 Liberals, 29 Parti Quebecois, and 4 Equality members.

Lt. Governor, His Honour Gilles Lamontagne.

EXECUTIVE
(as at February, 1991)

Prime Minister, Hon. Robert Bourassa.
Deputy Premier, Energy and Resources, Regional Development, Hon. Lise Bacon.
Recreation, Fish and Game, Hon. Gaston Blackburn.
Manpower, Income Security, Hon. André Bourbeau.
Labour, Jun. minister for Cultural Communities, Hon. Normand Cherry.
International Affairs, Hon. John Ciaccia.
Forests, Hon. Albert Côté.
Health, Social Services and Elderly People, Electoral Reform, Hon. Marc-Yvan Côté.
Supply and Services, Hon. Robert Dutil.
Transport, Hon. Sam Elkas.
Communications, Hon. Lawrence Cannon.
Cultural Communities and Immigration, Hon. Monique Gagnon-Tremblay.
Treasury Board, Hon. Daniel Johnson.
Finance, Hon. Gérard D. Levesque.
Jun. minister for Transport, Hon. Robert Middlemiss.
Agriculture, Fisheries and Food, Regional Development, House Leader, Hon. Yvon Picotte.
Environment, Hon. Pierre Paradis.
Municipal Affairs, Public Security, Hon. Claude Ryan.

Justice, Intergovernmental Affairs, Hon. Gil Rémillard.
Responsible for La Francophonie, Hon. Guy Rivard.
Jun. minister for Finance, Hon. Louise Robic.
Cultural Affairs, Hon. Lisa Frulla-Hébert.
Higher Education and Science, Hon. Lucienne Robillard.
Revenue, Jun. minister for Mines and for Regional Development, Hon. Raymond Savoie.
Jun. minister for Native Affairs, Hon. Christos Sirros.
Industry, Trade and Technology, Hon. Gérald Tremblay.
Industry, Trade and Technology, Hon. Gérald Tremblay.
Jun. minister for the Status of Women and for the Family, Hon. Violette Trépanier.
Tourism, Hon. André Vallerand.
Jun. minister for Agriculture, Fisheries, Food, Hon. Yvon Vallières.
Education, Michel Pagé.

Agent-General in London, vacant, 59 Pall Mall, SW1Y 5JH.

THE JUDICATURE

Court of Appeal, Chief Justice of Quebec, Hon. Claude Bisson.
Superior Court, Chief Justice of Quebec (Montreal), Hon. Pierre F. Coté.

ECONOMY

Finance.—The revenue for the year 1987–88 was C$28,363,891,000; expenditure amounted to C$30,738,141,000.

Production and Industry.—The principal manufacturing centres are Montreal, Montreal East, Quebec, Trois-Rivières, Sherbrooke, Shawinigan Drummondville and Lachine. Forest lands cover 779,256 sq. km, of which 556,044 sq. km are productive.

Total estimated value of shipments in the manufacturing industries in 1989 was C$73,994 million. Value of 1989 shipments in the chief industries was accounted for by food, C$9,239 million; paper and allied industries, C$8,032 m; primary metal industries, C$7,131 m, and transport equipment, C$6,866 m.

Agriculture and Fisheries.—In 1989 total farm receipts were:

Crops	C$679,360,000
Livestock and livestock products	2,484,134,000
Other farm receipts	509,675,000

In 1989 79,101 tonnes of fish, to the value of C$79,467,000 were landed.

Mineral Production.—Minerals to the value of C$2,721,380,000 were mined in 1988. This included copper, $145,127,000; asbestos, C$190,285,000; and gold, C$562,868,000.

CAPITAL.—ΨQuebec. Population (Census 1986) 164,580; historic city visited annually by thousands of tourists, and one of the great seaport towns of Canada. ΨMontreal (1,015,420) is the commercial metropolis. Other important cities are Laval (284,164); Verdun (60,246), Sherbrooke (74,438), Montreal-Nord (90,303) and La Salle (75,621).

SASKATCHEWAN

Area and Population.—The Province of Saskatchewan lies between Manitoba to the east and Alberta to the west and has an area of 652,324 sq. km (251,864 sq. miles) (of which the land area is 570,269 sq. km, or 220,182 sq. miles), with a population (estimated 1988) of 1,012,800. Saskatchewan extends along the Canada–USA boundary for 632 km (393 miles) and northwards for 1,224 km (761 miles). Its northern width is 440 km (276 miles).

Government.—The Government is vested in the Lieutenant Governor, with a Legislative Assembly of

64 members. There is an Executive Council of 15 members. The Legislative Assembly is elected for five years and the state of the parties in June 1991 was: Progressive Conservative 33; New Democratic Party 26; Independent 1; vacancies 4.

Lt. Governor, Her Honour Sylvia O. Fedoruk.

EXECUTIVE COUNCIL
(as at June, 1991)

Premier, President of the Council, Minister of Agriculture and Food, Hon. Grant Devine.

Deputy Premier, Health, Hon. George McLeod.

Agriculture and Food, Hon. Harold Martens (*associate minister*).

Attorney-General, Minister of Justice, Provincial Secretary, Hon. Gary Lane.

Community Services, Hon. Jack Wolfe.

Economic Diversification and Trade, Hon. Grant Schmidt.

Economic Diversification and Trade, Hon. John Gerich (*associate minister*).

Human Resources, Labour and Employment, Hon. Jack Klein.

Education, Hon. Ray Meiklejohn.

Energy and Mines, Indian and Metis Affairs, Hon. Rick Swenson.

Environment and Public Safety, the Family, Hon. Beattie Martin.

Finance, Hon. Lorne Hepworth.

Highways and Transportation, Hon. Sherwin Petersen.

Parks and Renewable Resources, Hon. Lorne Kopelchuk.

Rural Development, Hon. Neal Hardy.

Social Services, Hon. Bill Neudorf.

THE JUDICATURE

Court of Appeal, Chief Justice, Hon. E. D. Bayda.

Queen's Bench, Chief Justice, Hon. D. K. MacPherson.

Provincial Court, Chief Judge, Hon. B. P. Carey.

Agent-General in London.—P. Rousseau, 16 Berkeley Street, W1X 5AE.

Finance.—Consolidated Fund and Heritage combined revenue for year ending March 1992 is C$4,554,200,000 and combined expenditure C$4,819,266,000.

CAPITAL.—Regina. Population (1990 estimate), 178,792. Other cities: Saskatoon (183,579), Moose Jaw (34,770); Prince Albert (33,671) and Yorkton (16,094).

CYPRUS
(Kypriaki Dimokratia/Kibris Cumhuriyeti)

AREA AND CLIMATE.—Cyprus with an area of 3,572 sq. miles (9,251 sq. km), is the third largest island in the Mediterranean Sea. Its greatest length is 140 miles and greatest breadth 60 miles, situated at latitude 35°N. and longitude 33° 30′E. It is about 40 miles distant from the nearest point of Asia Minor, 60 miles from Syria and 240 miles from Port Said.

Cyprus has a Mediterranean climate with a hot dry summer and a variable warm winter, while the intermediate seasons are short and transitional.

POPULATION.—In 1990 the population (estimate) was 698,800. There are two major communities, Greek Cypriots (80·1 per cent) and Turkish Cypriots (18·6 per cent); and minorities of Armenians, Maronites and others.

CAPITAL.—Nicosia, near the centre of the island, with a population of 168,800 (in the Government controlled area); the other principal towns are ΨLimassol, ΨFamagusta, ΨLarnaca, Paphos and Kyrenia.

CURRENCY.—Cyprus pound (C£) of 100 cents.

FLAG.—Gold map of Cyprus on a white ground, surmounting crossed olive branches (green).

NATIONAL ANTHEM.—Ode to Freedom.

NATIONAL DAY.—October 1 (Independence Day).

GOVERNMENT

Cyprus passed under British administration from 1878. Cyprus was formally annexed to Great Britain in November 1914, on the outbreak of war with Turkey. From 1925 to 1960 it was a Crown Colony administered by a Governor, assisted by an Executive Council and also for a time by a partly-elected Legislative Council. Following the launching in April 1955 of an armed campaign by EOKA in support of union with Greece, a state of emergency was declared in November 1955, which lasted for four years. After a meeting at Zürich between the Prime Ministers of Greece and Turkey, a conference was held in London and an agreement was signed on February 19, 1959 between the United Kingdom, Greece, Turkey and the Greek and Turkish Cypriots which provided that Cyprus would be an independent Republic.

Under the Cyprus Act 1960, the island became an independent sovereign republic on August 16, 1960. The constitution provided for a Greek Cypriot President and a Turkish Cypriot Vice-President elected for a five-year term by the Greek and Turkish communities respectively. The House of Representatives, elected for five years by universal suffrage of each community separately, was to consist of 35 Greek and 15 Turkish members. The 1960 Constitution proved unworkable in practice and led to intercommunal troubles. The UN Peace Keeping Force in Cyprus (UNFICYP) was set up in March 1964; its mandate was last renewed on June 15, 1990.

In July 1974, mainland Greek officers of the Greek Cypriot National Guard launched a coup d'état against President Makarios and installed a former EOKA member, Nikos Sampson, in his place. Turkey reserved to itself the right to maintain constitutional order and the independence and territorial integrity of the island, invaded Northern Cyprus and occupied over a third of the island. In February 1975 a 'Turkish Federated State of Cyprus' under Mr Rauf Denktash was declared in this area, its constitution being approved by referendum in July 1975. In November 1983 a 'Declaration of Statehood' was issued which purported to establish the 'Turkish Republic of Northern Cyprus'. The declaration was condemned by the UN Security Council and only Turkey has recognized the new 'state'. In May 1985 a referendum in the north of Cyprus approved a constitution for the 'Turkish Republic of Northern Cyprus': in June 1985 Mr Denktash was elected President of the 'state' and a General Election was held. Mr Denktash was re-elected in April 1990, and a General Election was held in May 1990.

Since 1974 attempts to reach a settlement have focused on intercommunal talks under the auspices of the UN.

A general election was held for the Cyprus House of Representatives on May 19, 1991, resulting in the parties gaining the following number of seats: Democratic Rally-Liberal Party 20; AKEL (Communist) 18; Democratic Party (Centre) 16; EDEK (Socialist) 7.

President, George Vassiliou, *elected* February 21 1988.

Council of Ministers
(as at May 31, 1990)

Foreign Affairs, George Iacovou.

Interior, Christodoulos Veniamin.

Finance, George Syrimis.

Education, Christophoros Christofides.

Justice, Nicos Papaioannou.
Defence, Andreas Aloneftis.
Communications and Works, Pavlos Savvides.
Health, Panicos Papageorghiou.
Commerce and Industry, Takis Nemitsas.
Labour and Social Insurance, Iacovos Aristidou.
Agriculture and Natural Resources, Andreas Gavrie-
lides.

CYPRUS HIGH COMMISSION
93 Park Street, W1Y 4ET
[071-499 2810]

High Commissioner, His Excellency Angelos Ange-
lides (1990).

ECONOMY

Although agriculture still occupies a prime position
in the Cyprus economy it is unlikely to expand
further. Main products are citrus fruits, grapes and
vine products, potatoes and other vegetables. Manufacturing, construction, distribution and other service industries are other major employers. Tourism is
the main growth industry with over 1·2 million long-
stay tourists producing C£490 million in foreign
exchange earnings in 1989. Over 5,000 foreign firms
and individuals have registered as offshore companies
in Cyprus, which supports Cyprus' claim to be a
centre for Middle East trade.

Britain continues to be the country's most important trading partner, taking some 23·4 per cent of its
exports in 1989 and supplying 11·4 per cent of its
imports. Cyprus is seeking to diversify its export
markets and until recently sold almost half its exports
to the Middle East. However, these traditional
markets are now drying up, and Cyprus is looking
more towards Europe. A Customs Union between
Cyprus and the EC came into force in January 1988.

There is a large visible trade deficit (C£737·2
million in 1989), which is offset by invisible earnings,
particularly from tourism. The current account in
1989 showed a deficit of C£72·8 m, which includes the
cost of one aircraft amounting to C£80·7 m.

FINANCE

	1988	1989
Total Revenue	C£535·0 m	C£632·7 m
Ordinary Expenditure	598·4 m	663·8 m

TRADE

	1988	1989
Imports	C£866·8 m	C£1,130·3 m
Exports (including re-exports)	330·9 m	393·0 m

Trade with UK

	1989	1990
Imports from UK	£173,092,000	£204,857,000
Exports to UK	145,047,000	154,065,000

BRITISH HIGH COMMISSION
Alexander Pallis Street (PO Box 1978)
Nicosia
[Nicosia 02-473131]

High Commissioner, His Excellency David John
Michael Dain (1990).

British Council Representative, C. Mogford, PO Box
5654, 3 Museum Street, Nicosia.

BRITISH SOVEREIGN AREAS

The United Kingdom retained full sovereignty and
jurisdiction over two areas of 99 square miles in all—
Akrotiri–Episkopi–Paramali and Dhekelia–Perga-
mos–Ayios Nicolaos–Xylophagou—and use of roads
and other facilities. The British Administrator of
these areas is appointed by The Queen and is
responsible to the Secretary of State for Defence.

Administrator of the British Sovereign Areas, Air
Vice-Marshal A. F. C. Hunter, CBE, AFC.

DOMINICA
(The Commonwealth of Dominica)

AREA, POPULATION, ETC.—Dominica, the loftiest of
the Lesser Antilles, lies in the Windward Group,
between 15° 12' and 15° 39' N. lat. and 61° 14' and 61°
29' W. long., 95 miles S. of Antigua. It is about 29
miles long and 16 broad comprising an area of 289 sq.
miles (748·5 sq. km). The island is of volcanic origin
and very mountainous, and the soil is very fertile.
The temperature varies, according to the altitude,
from 13°–29°C. The climate is healthy. The population is 81,000 (1989 estimate).

CAPITAL.—ΨRoseau, on the south-west coast, population 11,000. The other principal town is Portsmouth, population 2,220.

CURRENCY.—East Caribbean dollar (EC$) of 100
cents.

FLAG.—Green ground with a cross overall of
yellow, white and black stripes, and in the centre a
red disc charged with a Sisserou parrot in natural
colours within a ring of 10 green stars.

NATIONAL ANTHEM.—Dominica Day Song.
NATIONAL DAY.—November 3 (Independence Day).

GOVERNMENT

The island was discovered by Columbus in 1493,
when it was a stronghold of the Caribs, who remained
virtually the sole inhabitants until the French
established settlements in the 18th century. It was
captured by the British in 1759 but passed back and
forth between France and Britain until 1805, after
which British possession was not challenged. From
1871–1939 Dominica was part of the Leeward Islands
Colony, then from 1940 the island was a unit of the
Windward Islands group. Internal self-government
from 1967 was followed on November 3, 1978 by
independence as a republic with the name The
Commonwealth of Dominica. Executive authority is
vested in the President, who is elected by the House
of Assembly for not more than two terms of five years.
Parliament consists of the President and the House
of Assembly (representatives elected by universal
adult suffrage) and nine Senators, who may be
appointed by the President or elected. Parliament
has a life of five years.

At the general election of May 1990, the Dominica
Freedom Party won 11 seats, the Dominica United
Workers' Party 6, and the Labour Party of Dominica
the remaining 4.

President, His Excellency Sir Clarence Seignoret,
GCB, OBE.

Cabinet
(as at June 1991)

*Prime Minister, Minister for Finance and Economic
Affairs*, Hon. M. Eugenia Charles.
Legal Affairs, Information and Public Relations, Hon.
Jenner Armour.
External Affairs and OECS Unity, Hon. Brian
Alleyne.
Trade, Industry and Tourism, Hon. Charles Maynard.
Education and Sports, Hon. Rupert Sorhaindo sen.
Community Development and Social Affairs, Hon.
Henry George.
Health and Social Security, Hon. Allan Guye.

Labour and Immigration, Hon. Heskeith Alexander.
Communications, Works and Housing, Hon. Alleyne Carbon.
Agriculture, Hon. Maynard Joseph.
Minister without Portfolio, Prime Minister's Office, Hon. Dermott Southwell sen.
Parliamentary Secretary in the Ministry of Agriculture, Trade, Industry and Tourism, Hon. Ossie Walsh.
Parliamentary Secretary in the Ministry of Communications, Works and Housing, Hon. Clem Shillingford.

HIGH COMMISSION FOR THE COMMONWEALTH OF DOMINICA
1 Collingham Gardens, SW5 0HW
[071–370 5194/5]

High Commissioner, His Excellency Franklin A. Baron (1986) (resident in Roseau).
Minister Counsellor (London), Ashworth Elwin.

FINANCE

	1985–86 revised	1986–87 estimated
Recurrent Revenue ...	EC$83·6 m	EC$88·2 m
Recurrent Expenditure	81·1 m	91·6 m
Capital Revenue	37·9 m	49·3 m
Capital Expenditure ...	45·3 m	57·2 m

ECONOMY

Agriculture is the principal occupation, with tropical and citrus fruits the main crops. Products for export are bananas, lime juice, lime oil, bay oil, copra and rum. Forestry and fisheries are being encouraged. The only commercially exploitable mineral is pumice, used chiefly for building purposes. Manufacturing consists largely of the processing of agricultural products.

TRADE

	1988
Imports	US$87·55 m
Exports	55·55 m

Trade with UK

	1989	1990
Imports from UK	£8,727,000	£9,707,000
Exports to UK	23,709,000	23,483,000

BRITISH HIGH COMMISSION
High Commissioner, (resides at Bridgetown, Barbados).

THE GAMBIA
(The Republic of the Gambia)

AREA, POPULATION, ETC.—The Gambia takes its name from the Gambia River, which it straddles for over 200 miles inland from the west coast of Africa. It is a narrow strip, surrounded by the Republic of Senegal, except at the coast, lying between 13° 10′–13° 45′ N. and 13° 90′–16° 50′ W. The area is 4,361 sq. miles (11,295 sq. km), of which one-fifth is the river. The climate is typically Sahelian, with a dry season between October and May and heavy rainfall during the months of July and August (32–40 inches a year).

The population comprises mainly Wolof, Mandinka and Fula peoples who originally migrated there from the north and east. Population (1989 estimate) was 835,000.

The Gambia River basin was part of the region dominated in the 10th–16th centuries by the strong Songhai and Mali kingdoms centred on the upper Niger. The first recorded Europeans to reach the Gambia River were the Portuguese in 1447. In 1588 Queen Elizabeth I gave the first charter to English merchants to trade along the river. Merchants from France, Courland (now part of Latvia) and the Netherlands also established trading posts there. The English presence was strongly challenged by the French, who were dominant further north up the coast, but in 1783 the Treaty of Versailles acknowledged English rights. In 1816, after the Napoleonic Wars, and in order to enforce abolition of the slave trade, the British stationed a garrison on a low sandy island called Banjul at the river mouth. Renamed Bathurst, this became the capital of a small British-administered colony, initially under the Governor of Sierra Leone. Negotiations with France continued sporadically until 1889 when it was agreed that the British rights along the upper river should extend 10 km on either bank. British administration was extended from the Colony to this Protectorate. The Gambia became independent within the Commonwealth on February 18, 1965, and a Republic on April 24, 1970.

The Gambia's relationship with Senegal has always been an important factor in political and economic policy. Moves towards a closer association were accelerated after an abortive coup in The Gambia in July 1981 was put down with the help of Senegalese troops. In February 1982 the Senegambia Confederation was formally instituted based on certain joint institutions and integration of policies, with each country remaining sovereign and independent. However, following disagreements it was decided to dissolve the confederation, and formal dissolution took place on December 31, 1989. A treaty of friendship and co-operation was signed with Senegal in January 1991.

CAPITAL.—ψBanjul. Population (1983 Census) of the island of Banjul was 44,536, and of adjacent Kombo St Mary district 102,858. Total population of Banjul/Kombo St Mary, 147,394.

CURRENCY.—Dalasi (D) of 100 butut.

FLAG.—Horizontal stripes of red, blue and green separated by narrow white stripes.

NATIONAL ANTHEM.—For The Gambia, Our Homeland.

NATIONAL DAY.—February 18 (Independence Day).

GOVERNMENT

The constitution is democratic and Parliamentary with an executive President elected for five years. The House of Representatives has 35 elected members, five elected Chiefs Representatives and up to eight nominated members plus the Attorney-General (ex officio). The Vice-President and other Ministers are appointed by the President. Parliament must be dissolved after five years. The last general election were held in March 1987. The present state of the parties for elected members is PPP (People's Progressive Party) 31; NCP (National Convention Party) 5.

President and Cabinet
(as at 1991)

President and Minister of Defence, His Excellency Alhaji Sir Dawda Kairaba Jawara, GCMG.
Vice-President and Minister of Education, Youth, Sports and Culture, Hon. Bakary Bunja Darbo.
Attorney-General and Minister of Justice, Hon. Hassan B. Jallow.
Finance and Economic Affairs, Hon. Saihou Sabally.
External Affairs, Hon. Alhaji Omar Sey.
Interior, Hon. Lamin Kiti Jabang.
Agriculture and Natural Resources, Hon. Omar Jallow.

Local Government and Lands, Hon. Landing Jallow Sonko.
Water Resources, Forestry and Fisheries, Hon. Sarjo Touray.
Health, Environment, Labour and Social Welfare, Hon. Mrs Louise A. N'Jie.
Works and Communications, Hon. Matthew Yaya Baldeh.
Trade, Industry and Employment, Hon. Mbemba Jatta.
Information and Tourism, Hon. Alkali James Gaye.

Chief Justice, Hon. E. Olayinka Ayoola.
Speaker, Alhaji Hon. M. B. N'Jie.

GAMBIA HIGH COMMISSION
57 Kensington Court, W8 5DG
[071-937 6316]

High Commissioner, His Excellency Horace R. Monday, jun. (1987).

COMMUNICATIONS

There is an international airport at Yundum, 17 miles from Banjul, with scheduled services flying to other West African states and to the UK and Belgium. Banjul is the main port. Internal communication is by road and river. There is no railway system. There are two broadcasting stations and a UHF telephone service linking Banjul with the principal towns in the provinces. There is no television service.

EDUCATION

There are 24 secondary schools (eight high and 16 technical) with a total enrolment of 15,635 students. Two High Schools provide A-level education. Gambia College provides post-secondary courses in education, agriculture, public health and nursing. There are seven vocational training institutions with a total enrolment of 1,400. Higher education and advanced training courses are taken outside The Gambia, currently by over 200 students.

PRODUCTION

Seventy-five per cent of the population depend for their livelihood on agriculture (40 per cent of GDP). The chief product, groundnuts, is also the most important export item, forming over 80 per cent of all domestic exports. Other crops are rice, millet, sorghum, maize and cotton. Fishing and livestock industries are being developed. Thirty per cent of the country's basic food requirements are imported. There are no significant deposits of minerals. Manufactures are limited to groundnut processing, minor metal fabrications, paints, furniture, soap and bottling. Tourism is developing quickly, with 98,248 visitors in 1987–88. The entrepôt trade through The Gambia, re-exporting imported goods to neighbouring countries, is an important element in the national economy.

FINANCE

	1990–91*
Recurrent Revenue	D623,000,000
Recurrent Expenditure	633,000,000
* Estimate.	

Over 80 per cent of capital expenditure comes from external aid grants and loans. In 1987–88 there was a GDP growth rate of 5·4 per cent.

TRADE

	1987–88	1988–89
Total imports	D844,900,000	D940,000,000
Total exports	576,600,000	311,400,000

Trade with UK

	1989	1990
Imports from UK	£16,583,000	£17,815,000
Exports to UK	2,340,000	3,158,000

BRITISH HIGH COMMISSION
48 Atlantic Road, Fajara (PO Box 507), Banjul
[Banjul 95133]

High Commissioner, His Excellency Alan J. Pover, CMG (1991).

GHANA
(The Republic of Ghana)

AREA.—Ghana (formerly known as the Gold Coast) is situated on the Gulf of Guinea, between 3° 07′ W. long. and 1° 14′ E. long. (about 334 miles), and extends 441 miles north from Cape Three Points (4° 45′ N.) to 11° 11′ N. It is bounded on the north by Burkina, on the west by the Côte d'Ivoire, on the east by Togo, and on the south by the Atlantic Ocean. Although a tropical country, Ghana is cooler than many countries within similar latitudes. Ghana has a total area of 92,099 sq. miles (238,537 sq. km).

POPULATION.—The population was estimated to be 14,753,900 in 1990. Almost all Ghanaians are Sudanese Negroes, although Hamitic strains are common in northern Ghana. The official language is English. The principal indigenous language group is Akan, of which Twi and Fanti are the most commonly used. Ga, Ewe and languages of the Mole–Dagbani group are common in certain regions.

CAPITAL.—ΨAccra. Population of the Greater Accra Region (including Tema) was (1990 estimate) 1,781,100. Other towns are Kumasi, Tamale, ΨSekondi-Takoradi, ΨCape Coast, Sunyani, Ho, Koforidua, Tarkwa and ΨWinneba.

CURRENCY.—Cedi of 100 pesewas.

FLAG.—Equal horizontal bands of red over gold over green; five-point black star on gold stripe.

NATIONAL ANTHEM.—Hail the Name of Ghana.

NATIONAL DAY.—March 6 (Independence Day).

GOVERNMENT

There is no recorded history of the Gold Coast region before the coming of Europeans in the fifteenth century. The constituent parts of the State came under British administration at various times, the original Gold Coast Colony (the coastal and Southern areas) being first constituted in 1874; Ashanti in 1901; and the Northern Territories Protectorate in 1901. The territory of Trans-Volta-Togoland, part of the former German colony of Togo, was mandated to Britain by the League of Nations after the First World War, and remained under British administration as a United Nations Trusteeship after the Second World War. After a plebiscite in May 1956, under the auspices of the United Nations, the territory was integrated with the Gold Coast Colony.

The former Gold Coast Colony and associated territories became the independent state of Ghana and a member of the British Commonwealth on March 6, 1957 and adopted a Republican constitution on July 1, 1960. Since 1966 Ghana has experienced long periods of military rule divided by short-lived civilian governments. A coup in June 1979 led to the formation of an Armed Forces Revolutionary Council chaired by Flt. Lt. Jerry Rawlings. Civilian rule was restored in September 1979 but overthrown on December 31, 1981, when another coup brought back into power Flt. Lt. Rawlings.

Provisional National Defence Council

Chairman and Head of State, Flt. Lt. Jerry Rawlings.

Chairman, National Commission for Democracy, Mr Justice D. F. Annan.

Education and Culture, Dr Mary Grant.

Defence, Alhaji Mahamad Iddrissu.

General Officer Commanding, Maj.-Gen. W. M. Mensah-Wood.

Chairman of the Committee of Secretaries, P. V. Obeng.

Chairman, National Development Planning Committee, Lt.-Gen. A. Quainoo.

Labour, Ebo Tawiah.

Security and Foreign Affairs, Capt. Kojo Tsikata (retd).

PNDC Secretaries
(as at July 1991)

Agriculture, Cdr. S. G. Obimpeh.

Finance and Economic Planning, Dr Kwesi Botchwey.

Foreign, Obed Y. Asamoah.

Fuel and Power, Ato Ahwoi.

Health, Col. Osei-Owusu.

Industries, Science and Technology, Capt. K. Butah.

Information, Kofi Totobi Quakyi.

Interior Agency, Nana Akuoko Sarpong.

Justice and Attorney-General, G. Tanoh.

Transport and Communications, Kwame Peprah.

Local Government and Rural Development, Kwamena Ahwoi.

Mobilization and Social Welfare, D. S. Boateng.

Roads and Highways, Col. R. Commey.

Trade and Tourism, Huudu Yahaya.

Lands and Natural Resources, J. A. Danso.

Works and Housing, K. Ampratwum.

Youth and Sports, K. Saarah Mensah.

GHANA HIGH COMMISSION
104 Highgate Hill, N19
[081-342 8686]

High Commissioner, His Excellency K. B. Asante (1990).

PRODUCTION, ETC.

Agriculture.—Agriculture forms the basis of Ghana's economy, employing 70 per cent of the working population. Crops of the Forest Zone include cocoa, which is the largest single source of revenue, rice and a variety of other foodstuff crops grown on mixed-crop farms. Fruits such as avocado pears, oranges and pineapples are grown. Cassava is the most important crop of the Coastal Savannas Zone, of the lower Volta area. Production of pulses such as groundnuts is widespread. Near the Togo border oil palms, yams, maize, cassava, fruit and vegetables are produced. Livestock is raised in the uncultivated areas. The Northern Savanna Zone is Ghana's principal cattle rearing area and other livestock production there is important for home consumption. Corn and millet crops are produced in the far north and maize, yams, rice and groundnut crops in more southerly parts of the Zone.

Attempts are being made to diversify agricultural production, with cash crops being extensively cultivated for export and to provide raw materials for local industry.

Fisheries.—Fishing is important in coastal areas and in the Volta itself. However production cannot meet demand and there are considerable imports of fish products. About 80 per cent of home supply is obtained from sea fisheries, but production from the Volta Lake and other inland fisheries is increasing.

Mineral Production.—The area within a 60 mile radius of Dunkwa produces 90 per cent of Ghana's mineral exports. Manganese production from Nsuta ranks among the world's highest and gold, industrial diamonds and bauxite are also produced. Some 30,000 persons are employed by the mining companies.

Manufactures.—Examples of the small-scale traditional industries are tailoring, goldsmithing and carpentry. Priority has been given in recent years to the establishment of a number of 'Pioneer Industries' including timber products, vehicle and refrigerator assembly, cigarettes, boatbuilding, food processing cotton textiles, clothing, footwear, printing and other light industries. A modern industrial complex is growing in the Accra-Tema area.

Volta River Project.—Since 1966 the Volta Dam at Akosombo has generated hydro-electric power for the processing of bauxite and fed a power transmission network for the Accra-Kumasi-Takoradi area Electricity is now also sent to Togo and Benin.

COMMUNICATIONS

Accra Airport is an international airport and Ghana Airways Corporation is the national airline There are also internal airports at Takoradi, Kumasi Sunyani, and Tamale.

There are 20,000 miles of motorable roads, of which 2,335 miles are bitumenized. There are 600 miles of railway, linking Accra and the principal ports of Takoradi and Tema with their hinterlands, and with each other.

Takoradi Harbour consists of seven quay berths— one is leased specially for manganese exports. Tema Harbour has 10 berths for larger ocean going vessels and the largest dry dock on the West African coast. An oil berth has also been built to serve the Ghana refinery which has been constructed at Tema.

Trade with UK

	1989	1990
Imports from UK	£121,076,000	£162,057,000
Exports to UK	92,208,000	105,118,000

Principal exports are cocoa, timber and gold Principal imports are road vehicles, manufacturing equipment, petroleum and raw materials.

BRITISH HIGH COMMISSION
PO Box 296, Osu Link, Accra
[Accra 221665]

High Commissioner, His Excellency Anthony Michael Goodenough, CMG (1989).

British Council Representative, J. M. Day, Liberia Road (PO Box 771), Accra, and an office in Kumasi

GRENADA
(The State of Grenada)

AREA, POPULATION, ETC.—Grenada is situate between the parallels of 12° 13′–11° 58′ N. lat. and 61 20′–61° 35′ W. long., and is about 90 miles north of Trinidad, 68 miles SSW of St Vincent, and about 12 miles SW of Barbados. The island is about 21 miles in length and 12 miles in breadth, with an area of 13 sq. miles (344 sq. km). Also included in the territory of Grenada are some of the Grenadines islets, the largest of which is Carriacou, 13 square miles in area The population is estimated at 102,000 (1989 UN estimate). The country is mountainous and very picturesque, and the climate is healthy.

CAPITAL.—St George's (population 10,000) lies on the south-west coast, and possesses a good harbour.

CURRENCY.—East Caribbean dollar (EC$) of 100 cents.

FLAG.—Rectangle formed of yellow triangles top and bottom, and green triangles at side, with yellow five-pointed star on red circle in centre, and a nutmeg

in green triangle nearest the fly; all on a red ground with three yellow five-pointed stars at top and bottom.
NATIONAL DAY.—February 7 (Independence Day).

GOVERNMENT

Grenada was discovered by Columbus in 1498, and named Conception. It was originally colonized by the French, and was ceded to Great Britain by the Treaty of Versailles in 1783. It became an Associated State in 1967 and an independent nation within the Commonwealth on February 7, 1974.

The government of Sir Eric Gairy was overthrown on March 13, 1979 by the New Jewel Movement and a People's Revolutionary Government was set up. Disagreements within the PRG led, in October 1983, to violence and the death of the Prime Minister, whose government was replaced by a Revolutionary Military Council. These events prompted the intervention of Caribbean and US forces. The Governor General installed an advisory council to act as an interim government until a General Election was held, on December 3, 1984. A phased withdrawal of US forces was completed by June 1985.

The Queen is Head of State and is represented by a Governor General. Legislative power is vested in a bicameral parliament consisting of an elected House of Representatives and a 13-member Senate. The most recent General Election was held in March 1990. Nicholas Brathwaite of the National Democratic Congress was sworn in as Prime Minister on March 16, 1990.

Governor-General, Sir Paul Scoon, GCMG, GCVO, OBE (1978).

Cabinet
(as at Jan. 1991)

Prime Minister, Minister for External Affairs, Security, Information, Personnel and Management Services, Carriacou and Petit Martinique Affairs, Rt. Hon. Nicholas Brathwaite, OBE.

Finance, Economic Planning, Trade, and Industry, Hon. George Brizan.

Attorney-General, Minister for Legal Affairs, Local Government, Dr the Hon. Francis Alexis.

Agriculture, Lands, Foods and Fisheries, Hon. Phinsley St Louis.

Communications, Works, Public Utilities, Sen. the Hon. Tillman Thomas.

Tourism, Civil Aviation, Women's Affairs, Hon. Joan Purcell.

Health, Housing, the Environment, Hon. Michael Andrew.

Labour, Co-operatives, Social Security, Community Development, Hon. Edzel Thomas.

Education, Culture, Youth Affairs, Sports, Sen. the Hon. Carlyle Glean.

GRENADA HIGH COMMISSION
1 Collingham Gardens, SW5 0HW
[071–373 7808]

High Commissioner, His Excellency Lynton C. Noel (1990).

ECONOMY

The economy is principally agrarian, with cocoa, nutmegs and bananas the major crops. Fruit and vegetables are grown and a little livestock raised for domestic consumption. The fishing industry is being developed. Manufacturing is mostly confined to processing agricultural products.

Tourism has prospered since the opening in 1984 of the Point Salines International Airport. British Airways began regular weekly flights in April 1987.

A hotel expansion programme is planned. The number of cruise ships visiting Grenada in 1988 was 234.

Total value of imports in 1988 was EC$248·6 million. Principal domestic exports for 1988 were nutmeg (EC$31·3m), cocoa (EC$8·75m), mace (EC$7·3m) and fruit (EC$3·8m).

Trade with UK

	1989	1990
Imports from UK	£9,058,000	£7,822,000
Exports to UK	5,924,000	4,778,000

BRITISH HIGH COMMISSION
14 Church Street, St George's
[St George's 440-3222]

High Commissioner, (resides at Bridgetown, Barbados).

Resident Representative, A. H. Drury (*First Secretary*).

GUYANA
(The Co-operative Republic of Guyana)

AREA, POPULATION, ETC.—Guyana, the former colony of British Guiana, which includes the Counties of Demerara, Essequibo and Berbice, is situated on the north-east coast of South America, bordering on Venezuela, Brazil and Suriname. It has a total area of 83,000 sq. miles (214,969 sq. km), and a population estimate (1989) of 1,024,000. There are three distinct areas. (1) A narrow alluvial coastal belt 10 to 40 miles deep, the eastern part of which is intensively cultivated and contains some 90 per cent of the population. Much of this is below the level of the sea and is drained and irrigated by an intricate system of canals constructed by the Dutch. (2) A mountainous area of dense rain forest behind the coastland, still partly unexplored, which reaches its highest point at Mount Roraima (9,000 ft.) on the junction of the Guyana–Brazil–Venezuela borders. (3) The open savanna country of the Rupununi in the south-west where cattle ranching is practised and oil deposits have been discovered.

The entire country is intersected by numerous large rivers, though these are of limited navigational use because of rapids and waterfalls, the most notable of which are the Kaieteur Fall on the Potaro River with a sheer drop of 741 ft., the Horse Shoe Falls on the Essequibo and the Marina Fall on the Ipobe River.

Climate.—The two dry seasons normally last from mid February to end April, and from mid August to end November. In the August–October period it is hot. The mean temperature is 27°C, the usual extremes being 21°C and 32°C. In the interior the mean temperature is higher: 28°C, its extremes ranging from 19°C to 40°C. The yearly rainfall is subject to marked variation, its mean on the coast lands averaging about 90 inches with an average of 58 inches on the savannas.

CAPITAL.—ΨGeorgetown. Estimated population, including environs, 185,000. Other towns are: Linden (29,000); ΨNew Amsterdam (23,000); Corriverton (17,000).

CURRENCY.—Guyana dollar (G$) of 100 cents.

FLAG.—Red triangle with black border, pointing from hoist to fly, on a yellow triangle with white border, all on a green field.

NATIONAL ANTHEM.—Dear Land of Guyana.

NATIONAL DAYS.—May 26 (Independence Day); February 23 (Republic Day).

GOVERNMENT

Guyana became independent on May 26, 1966, with a Governor-General appointed by The Queen. It became a Co-operative Republic on February 23, 1970. Under the Independence Constitution the Prime Minister and Cabinet were responsible to a National Assembly elected by secret ballot every five years. The last election under this Constitution was in 1973 and the term of that Assembly was later extended to October 1980.

A new Constitution was passed into law in February 1980 and promulgated in October 1980. It provides for an Executive President, a National Assembly of 65 members, and also for a National Congress of Local Democratic Organs responsible for local government. The Supreme Congress of the People consists of all members of these two assemblies.

The electoral system is a proportional representation or 'single list' system, each voter casting his vote for a party list of candidates. The voting age is 18. A general election is scheduled for the end of 1991.

Executive President, H. Desmond Hoyte, *took office* Aug. 1985, *sworn in* Dec. 12, 1985 for five-year term.

Cabinet
(as at July 29, 1991)

The Executive President.
Prime Minister and Minister of Health, Hamilton Green.
Deputy PM and Minister of Public Works, Communications and Regional Development, Robert Corbin.
Deputy PM and Minister of Trade, Tourism and Industry, Winston Murray.
Finance, Carl Greenidge.
Attorney-General and Minister of Legal Affairs, Keith Massiah.
Senior Minister of Trade, Tourism and Industry, Dharamdeo Sawh.
Senior Minister of Public Works, Communications and Regional Development, Richard Kranenburg.
Senior Minister of Labour, Human Services and Social Security, Rabbian Ali-Khan.
Minister of Labour, Human Services and Social Security, Jean Persico.
Education and Cultural Development, Deryck Bernard.
Minister in the Office of the President, Gowkarran Sharma.
Minister in the Office of the President responsible for the Public Service, Faith Harding.

GUYANA HIGH COMMISSION
3 Palace Court, Bayswater Road, W2 4LP
[071-229 7684]

High Commissioner, His Excellency Cecil Stanley Pilgrim (1986).

JUDICATURE

The Supreme Court of Judicature consists of a Court of Appeal and a High Court. There are also Courts of Summary Jurisdiction. The Court of Appeal consists of the Chancellor as President, the Chief Justice and such number of Justices of Appeal as may be prescribed by Parliament.

The High Court consists of the Chief Justice, as President, and nine Puisne Judges. It is a court with unlimited jurisdiction in civil matters and exercises exclusive jurisdiction in probate, divorce and admiralty, and certain other matters.
Chancellor, K. M. George.
Chief Justice, R. Harper.

PRODUCTION, ETC.

The economy is based almost entirely on the main export items of sugar, rice, bauxite and alumina. Diamonds and gold are also mined, timber and rum are produced and there is some cattle ranching. The fishing industry is being expanded. Industry is fairly small-scale.

COMMUNICATIONS

Georgetown and New Amsterdam are the principal ports, though bauxite ships also sail to Linden, on the River Demerara, and Everton, on the River Berbice. There are no public railways and the few roads are confined mainly to the coastal areas. Air transport is the easiest form of communication between the coast and the interior. There is a state-owned radio broadcasting station which operates two channels and a fledgling television service.

EDUCATION

The Government assumed total control of the education system in September 1976 and made education free from nursery to university level. The Government trains teachers for primary and secondary schools at its own institutions.

Approximately 1,800 students were enrolled at the University of Guyana in degree programmes and certificate and diploma courses in 1990.

There are several technical and vocational institutions, as well as some 30 adult education schools (with an enrolment of 13,500). There are also a number of technical and vocational institutions not under the aegis of the Ministry of Education.

Trade with UK

	1989	1990
Imports from UK	£13,216,000	£15,294,000
Exports to UK	54,523,000	53,892,000

BRITISH HIGH COMMISSION
44 Main Street (PO Box 10849),
Georgetown
[Georgetown 65881/4]

High Commissioner, His Excellency Robert Douglas Gordon (1990) (also Ambassador to Suriname).

INDIA
(The Republic of India)

AREA AND CLIMATE.—The Republic of India has an area of 1,269,346 sq. miles (3,287,590 sq. km), composed of three well-defined regions: the mountain range of the Himalayas, the Indo–Gangetic plain, and the Southern Peninsula. The main mountain ranges are the Himalayas in the north (over 29,000 feet) and the Western and Eastern Ghats (over 8,000 feet). Major rivers include the Ganges, Indus, Krishna, Godavari and Mahanadi.

There are four seasons: the cold season (December–March); the hot season (April–May); the rainy season (June–September); and the season of the retreating SW monsoon (October–November). Temperatures vary over the whole country, between averages of about 10°C and 33°C, reaching over 38°C in some parts during the hot season. There are similar variations in rainfall, from only a few inches a year falling in the western Thar Desert to over 400 inches in Meghalaya.

POPULATION.—India is the second most populous country in the world. The population at the 1991 Census was 843,930,861, of which more than 20 per cent was urban. The majority of the population is Hindu (82 per cent), the rest being Muslim (11 per cent), Christian (2·5 per cent), Sikh (1·8 per cent), Buddhist (0·7 per cent) and Jain (0·5 per cent). The official languages are Hindi in the Devanagari script

nd English, though 14 regional languages also are
ecognized for adoption as official State languages.

HISTORY.—The Indus civilization was fully devel-
ped by c2500 BC but collapsed c1750 BC, subsequently
eing replaced by an Aryan civilization spread from
ae west. The first Arab invasions of the north-west
gan in the seventh century and Muslim, Hindu
nd Buddhist states developed until the establish-
ent of the Mogul dynasty in 1526. The British East
dia Company established settlements throughout
e 17th century; clashes with the French and native
rinces led to the British government taking control
the company in 1784. The separate dominions of
dia and Pakistan became independent within the
ommonwealth in 1947 and India became a Republic
1950.

CAPITAL.—Delhi (population in 1981 was 6,220,000).
pulations of other principal cities (1981 figures)
ere Ahmedabad 2,124,000; Bangalore 2,914,000;
Bombay (Mumbai) 8,202,000; ΨCalcutta 9,166,000;
yderabad 2,566,000; Kanpur 1,685,000; Lucknow
007,000; ΨMadras 4,277,000; Pune 1,685,000.

CURRENCY.—Indian rupee (Rs) of 100 paisa.

FLAG.—The National Flag is a horizontal tricolour
ith bands of deep saffron, white and dark green in
qual proportions. In the centre of the white band
ppears an Asoka wheel in navy blue.

NATIONAL ANTHEM.—Jana-gana-mana.

NATIONAL DAY.—January 26 (Republic Day).

GOVERNMENT

The Constitution of India came into force in 1950.
xecutive power is vested in the President, who is
ected for a five year term by an electoral college
nsisting of the elected members of the Union and
tate Legislatures. He appoints the Prime Minister
nd, on the latter's advice, the Ministers, and can
smiss them. The Council of Ministers is collectively
sponsible to the *Lok Sabha* (Lower House). The
ice-President is ex-officio chairman of the *Rajya*
abha (Upper House).

Legislative power rests with the President, the
ajya Sabha (which has up to 250 members) and the
ok Sabha (which has up to 544 members). Twelve
embers of the Rajya Sabha are nominated by the
resident, the rest are indirectly elected representa-
ves of the State and Union Territories. They hold
fice for six years. The 525 members of the Lok Sabha
presenting the States are directly elected by
niversal adult franchise, and 17 representatives of
e Union Territories are chosen, for a maximum
rm of five years. Subject to the provisions of the
nstitution, the Union Parliament can make laws
r the whole of India and the State legislatures for
eir respective units.

The Supreme Court consists of the Chief Justice
d not more than 17 other judges, appointed by the
esident. It is the highest court in respect of all
nstitutional matters and the final Court of Appeal.

esident of the Republic of India, Ramaswami
Venkataraman, *elected* July 16, 1987.
ice-President, Shankar Dayal Sharma.

Cabinet
(as at September 1991)

*rime Minister, Minister of Personnel, Public Griev-
ances, Science and Technology, Electronics, Atomic
Energy, Chemical and Fertilizers, Rural Develop-
ment, Civil Supplies and Public Distribution, Space,
Ocean Development and Industry*, P. V. Narasimha
Rao.

nance, Dr Manmohan Singh.

efence, Sharad Pawar.

griculture, Balram Jakhar.

uman Resources Development, Arjun Singh.

Urban Development, Sheila Kaul.

Railways, C. K. Jaffer Sharief.

Petroleum and Natural Gas, B. Shankaranand.

Law, Justice and Company Affairs, K. Vijaya Bhas-
kara Reddy.

Home Affairs, S. B. Chavan.

External Affairs, Madhavsinh Solanki.

Welfare, Sitaram Kesri.

Health and Family Welfare, M. L. Fotedar.

Water Resources, V. C. Shukla.

Civil Aviation and Tourism, Madhav Rao Scindia.

Parliamentary Affairs, Ghulam Nabi Azad.

In addition there are 14 ministers of state (independent charge), 21 ministers of state and seven
deputy ministers, making a total of 58 in the Council
of Ministers.

INDIAN HIGH COMMISSION
India House, Aldwych, WC2B 4NA
[071–836 8484]

High Commissioner, His Excellency Dr L. M. Singhvi
(1991).

Deputy High Commissioner, K. V. Rajan.

STATES AND TERRITORIES OF THE UNION

There are 25 States and seven Union Territories.
Each State is governed by a Governor appointed by
the President who holds office for five years, and a
Council of Ministers. All States have a Legislative
Assembly, and some have also a Legislative Council,
elected directly by adult suffrage for a maximum
period of five years. The judges of the High Court of
a State are appointed by the President.

The Union Territories are administered, except
where otherwise provided by Parliament, by the
President acting through an Administrator or Lieutenant Governor, or other authority appointed by
him.

DEFENCE

The supreme command of the armed forces is vested
in the President. Administrative and operational
control resides in the Army, Navy and Air Headquarters under the supervision of the Ministry of Defence.

The Army has five Commands, Southern, Eastern,
Northern, Western and Central.

The Indian Navy consists of two aircraft-carriers,
a number of frigate squadrons, including some of the
latest type of anti-submarine and anti-aircraft frigates, a squadron of anti-submarine patrol vessels,
minesweeping squadrons, conventional type submarines and a submarine depot ship. A Naval
aviation wing and a hydrographic office have also
been set up. India has started building her own naval
craft.

The Indian Air Force is organized in seven major
formations, the Western, Eastern, Central, Southern
and South Western Air Commands, and the Training
and Maintenance Commands. Aircraft in use include
SU-7, Hunter, Gnat, MiG 21 and MiG 23, Canberra
bomber, Jaguar and Mirage-2000, helicopter and
training planes.

PRODUCTION

Agriculture.—Agriculture is the chief industry,
supporting about 70 per cent of the population, and
providing nearly 40 per cent of the Gross Domestic
Product. The area under cultivation has been
increased by irrigation schemes, but most holdings
are less than five acres. Production has grown by
three per cent each year since 1951, remaining
slightly ahead of the two per cent increase necessary

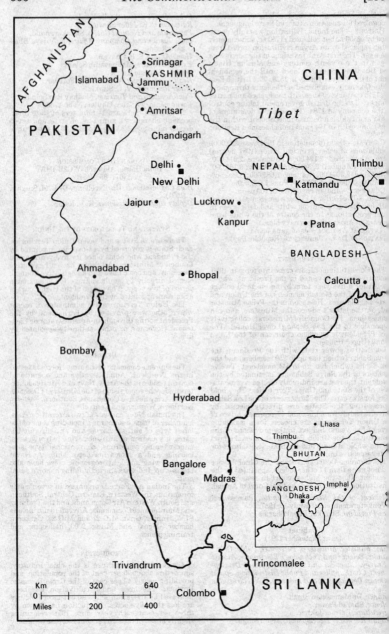

States and Territories (Capitals)	Area (sq. km)	Population (1981 Census)	Governor	Chief Minister
States				
Andhra Pradesh (Hyderabad) ..	275,100p	53,549,673	K. Kant	N. Janardhan Reddy
Arunachal Pradesh (Itanagar) .	83,700p	631,839	S. Dwivedy	Gegong Apang
Assam (Dispur)	78,400	19,896,843†	D. D. Thakur	Hiteshwar Saika
Bihar (Patna)..................	173,900p	69,914,734	M. S. Quershi	L. P. Yadav
Goa (Panaji)..................	3,701	1,000,000†	K. A. Khan	vacant
Gujarat (Gandhinagar)........	196,000p	34,085,799	Sarup Singh	Chimanbhai Patel
Haryana (Chandigarh)	44,200p	12,922,618	D. L. Mandal	Bhajan Lal
Himachal Pradesh (Shimla)	55,700	4,280,818	V. Verma	Shanta Kumar
Jammu and Kashmir* (Srinagar/Jammu)	222,200p	5,987,389	Girish Chandra Saxena	(Governor's rule)
Karnataka (Bangalore)	191,800	37,135,714	B. P. Singh	S. Rangarappa
Kerala (Trivandrum)	38,900p	25,453,680	B. Rachiah	K. Karunakaran
Madhya Pradesh (Bhopal)	443,500p	52,178,844	K. M. Ali	Sunderlal Patwa
Maharashtra (Bombay-Mumbai)	307,700p	62,784,171	C. Subramaniam	S. Naik
Manipur (Imphal)	22,300	1,420,953	C. Panigrahi	R. K. Ranvir Singh
Meghalaya (Shillong)	22,400p	1,335,819	M. Dighe	B. B. Lyngdoh
Mizoram (Aizawl)	21,100	493,757	S. Kaushal	Lal Thanhawla
Nagaland (Kohima)	16,600	774,930	C. Panigrahi	Vamuzo
Orissa (Bhubaneswar)	155,700	26,370,271	Y. D. Sharma	J. B. Patnaik
Punjab (Chandigarh)	50,400	16,788,915	Surindra Nath	(President's rule)
Rajasthan (Jaipur)	342,200	34,261,862	D. P. Chattopa- dhyaya	Bhairon Singh Shek- hawat
Sikkim (Gangtok)	7,100	316,385	Adm. R. H. Tahiliani	N. B. Bhandari
Tamil Nadu (Madras)..........	130,100p	48,408,077	Bhishma Marain Singh	J. Jayalalitha
Tripura (Agartala)	10,500	2,053,058	R. Reddy	S. R. Majumdar
Uttar Pradesh (Lucknow)......	294,400p	110,862,013	B. S. Reddy	Kalyan Singh
West Bengal (Calcutta)	88,800p	54,580,647	Prof. N. Hasan	Jyoti Basu
Union Territories				
Andaman and Nicobar Is. (Port Blair)................	8,200	188,741	*Lt. Governor* Lt.-Gen. R. S. Dyal	
Chandigarh	100	451,610	Surindra Nath	
Dadra and Nagar Haveli (Silvassa)	500	103,676	K. A. Khan	
Daman and Diu	112	51,602†	K. A. Khan	
Delhi	1,500	6,220,406	Markandey Singh	
Lakshadweep (Kavaratti)......	30	40,249	S. P. Agrawal	
Pondicherry..................	500	604,471	Harswarup Singh	S. Vaithalingam

p provisional figure   † estimated figure

*Jammu and Kashmir is an area disputed between India, Pakistan and China, all three controlling a part of the territory. The area figure includes those parts occupied by Pakistan and China, which are claimed by India, but the population figure excludes the population of these areas, where the census was not taken. The state's capital is at Srinagar in summer and Jammu in winter.

to keep pace with the rising population. Food crops occupy three-quarters of the total cropped area and production of food grains amounted to 143 million tonnes in 1986–87 but declined to 138 million tonnes in 1987–88 owing to severe drought. In 1988–89 foodgrains production was expected to reach about 169 million tonnes following good rains. The main food crops are rice, cereals (principally wheat) and pulses. The major cash crops include sugar cane, jute, cotton and tea. Other products include oil seeds, spices, groundnuts, tobacco, rubber and coffee. Livestock is raised, principally for dairy purposes or for the hides: cattle (an estimated 181 million), goats (71 million), sheep (41 million) and pigs (9·9 million).

Industry.—India's major industries are based on the exploitation and processing of her mineral resources, principally coal, oil and iron. The coal industry, nationalized in the early 1970s, reached an output in 1988–89 of 195 million tonnes. Production

of crude oil, from the main fields in Assam and from offshore drilling was about 32·2 million tonnes in 1988–89. Steel production is mainly in the hands of the public sector, with five public and one private sector integrated steel plants producing 12·4 million tonnes of ingot steel in 1986–87. The engineering industry, heavy and light, is also primarily in the hands of the public sector. The manufacture of chemicals, fertilizers, petrochemicals, motor vehicles and commercial vehicles has been expanded.

Other principal manufactures are those derived from agricultural products, textiles, jute goods, sugar, leather, which along with tea, fish, and iron ore and concentrates, are India's major exports.

Faced with the need to obtain loans from the World Bank and assistance from the IMF, India has abandoned centralized planning, after 40 years; subsidies are to be cut, state corporations privatized and the economy opened up to foreign companies.

FINANCE

The budget estimates for 1989–90, placed current expenditure (on revenue account) at Rs.596,420 million. Current revenue (excluding States' shares) was estimated at Rs.518,950 million.

Trade with UK

	1989	1990
Imports from UK	£1,382,436,000	£1,264,189,000
Exports to UK	701,985,000	799,438,000

COMMUNICATIONS

Civil Aviation.—Four international airports—Palam (Delhi), Sahar (Bombay), Dum Dum (Calcutta), Meenambakkam (Madras)—are managed by the International Airports Authority. The other 87 aerodromes are controlled and operated by the Civil Aviation Department of the Government. The national airlines are Indian Airlines (internal) and Air India (international).

Railways.—The railways are grouped into nine administrative zones, Southern, Central, Western, Northern, North-Eastern, North-East Frontier, Eastern, South-Eastern and South-Central.

Gross traffic receipts (1989–90), crores of rupees, 10,633. Working expenses, 9,788. Net railway revenues, 945.

Ports.—The chief seaports are Bombay (Mumbai), Calcutta, Haldia, Madras, Mormugao, Cochin, Visakhapatnam, Kandla, Paradip, Mangalore and Tuticorin. There are 139 minor working ports with varying capacity.

Shipping.—On November 30, 1988, 377 ships totalling 5,590,752 gross tons were on the Indian Register.

BRITISH HIGH COMMISSION
Chanakyapuri, New Delhi, 21, 1100–21.
[New Delhi 601371]

High Commissioner, His Excellency Sir David Goodall, GCMG (1987).

Minister for Cultural Affairs and British Council Representative in India, R. Arbuthnott, CBE. Offices also at *Bombay, Calcutta* and *Madras*. There are British Council libraries at these four centres and British libraries at *Ahmedabad, Bangalore, Bhopal, Hyderabad, Lucknow, Patna, Pune, Ranchi* and *Trivandrum*.

JAMAICA

AREA, POPULATION, ETC.—Jamaica is situated in the Caribbean Sea south of the eastern extremity of Cuba and lies between latitudes 17° 43′ and 18° 32′ North, and longitude 76° 11′ and 78° 21′ West. Jamaica is 4,244 sq. miles (10,991 sq. km) in area and is divided into three counties (Surrey, Middlesex and Cornwall) and 14 parishes. The greatest length from east to west (Morant Point to Negril Point) is 146 miles and the extreme breadth 51 miles.

The topography consists mainly of coastal plains, divided by the Blue Mountain Range in the east, and the hills and limestone plateaux which occupy the central and western areas of the interior. The central chain of high peaks of the Blue Mountains is over 6,000 feet above sea level, and the Blue Mountain Peak, the highest of these, reaches an elevation of 7,402 feet.

At December 31, 1989 Jamaica's population was estimated to be 2,392,300.

CAPITAL.—The seat of government is ΨKingston, the largest town and seaport (estimated population of the Corporate area of Kingston and St Andrew in 1982, 696,300). Other main towns are ΨMontego Bay, Ocho Rios, Spanish Town, Mandeville and May Pen.

CURRENCY.—Jamaican dollar (J$) of 100 cents.

FLAG.—Gold diagonal cross forming triangles o green at top and bottom, triangles of black at hois and in fly.

NATIONAL ANTHEM.—Jamaica, Land We Love.

NATIONAL DAY.—First Monday in August (Inde pendence Day).

GOVERNMENT

The island was discovered by Columbus on May 4 1494, and occupied by the Spanish from 1509 unt 1655 when a British expedition, sent out by Olive Cromwell, under Admiral Penn and General Vena bles, attacked the island, which capitulated after token resistance. In 1670 it was formally ceded t England by the Treaty of Madrid.

Jamaica became an independent state within th Commonwealth on August 6, 1962. The Legislatur consists of a Senate of 21 nominated members and House of Representatives consisting of 60 member elected by universal adult suffrage. The Constitutio provides for a Leader of the Opposition.

At the General Election of February 9, 1989, th People's National Party won 45 seats and the Jamaic Labour Party won 15.

Governor General, His Excellency Howard Feli Hanlon Cooke, *apptd* 1991.

Cabinet
(as at June 10, 1991)

Prime Minister, Rt. Hon. Michael Manley.
Deputy Prime Minister, Minister of Finance, Deve opment and Planning, Hon. P. J. Patterson, QC.
Public Service, Dr the Hon. Kenneth McNeil.
Foreign Affairs and Foreign Trade, Senator the Hor David Coore, QC.
Information and Culture, Senator Dr the Hon. Pau D. Robertson.
Industry, Production and Commerce, Hon. Hug Small, QC.
Minister for Justice and Attorney-General, Senato the Hon. Carl Rattray, QC.
Agriculture, Hon. Seymour Mullings.
Labour, Welfare and Sport, Hon. Portia Simpson.
Construction, Hon. O. D. Ramtallie.
Public Utilities and Transport, Hon. Robert Pickers gill.
Education, Senator the Hon. Carlyle Dunkley.
Local Government, Hon. Ralph Brown.
Mining and Energy, Hon. Horace Clark.
National Security, Hon. K. D. Knight, QC.
Health, Hon. Easton Douglas.
Youth and Community Development, Dr the Hor Douglas Manley.
Tourism, Senator the Hon. Frank Pringle.

JAMAICAN HIGH COMMISSION
1–2 Prince Consort Road, SW7 2BZ
[071–823 9911]

High Commissioner, Her Excellency Mrs Ellen Gra Bogle (1987).

JUDICATURE

Acting Chief Justice and Keeper of Records, Hon. I. D Rowe.
Judges of the Court of Appeal, Hons. J. S. Kerr, R. C C. White, J. Campbell, M. L. Wright.

COMMUNICATIONS

There are several excellent harbours, Kingsto being the principal port. The island has 2,944 mile of main roads and over 7,000 miles of subsidiary road

There are two international airports capable of handling the largest civil jet aircraft, the Norman Manley International Airport on the south coast serving Kingston, and Sangster Airport on the north coast serving the major tourist areas. In addition there are licensed aerodromes at Port Antonio, Ocho Rios, Mandeville and Negril. There are 16 privately owned, seven public and two military airstrips.

Air Jamaica, the national airline, operates international services; Trans-Jamaica Airlines operates scheduled internal services.

ECONOMY

Jamaica is a popular tourist resort, attracting 1,236,000 visitors during 1990. Actual foreign exchange receipts from tourism amounted to US$750m in 1990.

Alumina, bananas, bauxite and sugar are the four major Jamaican exports. Earnings from sugar in 1990 amounted to US$73m, bauxite US$103m, alumina US$611·2m and bananas US$33·8m. Less traditional exports include garments, processed food products, limestone and ornamental horticultural products.

FINANCE

	1989	1990
Revenue	US$2,083·0m	US$2,401·6m
Expenditure	2,219·7m	2,537·5m

TRADE

	1989	1990
Total imports	US$1,826·3m	US$1,850·7m
Total exports	970·3m	1,126·1m

Trade with UK

	1989	1990
Imports from UK	£61,355,000	£58,702,000
Exports to UK	95,516,000	136,535,000

BRITISH HIGH COMMISSION
PO Box 575, Trafalgar Road, Kingston 10
[Kingston 926 9050]

High Commissioner, His Excellency Derek Francis Milton, CMG (1989).

British Council Representative in the Caribbean, Gillian Roche, 3rd Floor, First Life Building, 64 Knutsford Boulevard, Kingston 5.

KENYA
(Jamhuri ya Kenya)

AREA, POPULATION, ETC.—Kenya is bisected by the equator and extends approximately from latitude 5° N. to latitude 4° S. and from longitude 34° E. to 41° E. From the coast of the Indian Ocean in the east, the borders of Kenya are with Somalia in the east and Ethiopia and Sudan in the north and north-west. To the west lie Uganda and Lake Victoria. On the south is Tanzania. The total area is 224,961 sq. miles (582,646 sq. km), including 5,171 square miles of water. The country is divided into eight provinces (Central, Coast, Eastern, Nairobi, Nyanza, North Eastern, Rift Valley, Western). The population is 24,872,000 (1989 N estimate). The main tribal groups are the Kikuyu, Luhya, Luo, Kalenjin, Kamba and Masai. The official languages are Swahili, which is generally understood throughout Kenya, and English; numerous indigenous languages are also spoken.

CAPITAL.—Nairobi, population 1,400,000 (1989 estimate).

CURRENCY.—Kenya shilling (Ksh) of 100 cents.

FLAG.—Three equal horizontal bands of black over red over green; red and white spears and shield device in centre.

NATIONAL ANTHEM.—Kenya, Land of the Lion.

NATIONAL DAY.—December 12 (Independence Day).

GOVERNMENT

Kenya became an independent state and a member of the British Commonwealth on December 12, 1963, after six months of internal self-government. Kenya became a Republic on December 12, 1964. In 1982 the Government introduced amendments to the constitution and election law, making the country a one-party state. The Kenya African National Union (KANU) is the sole legal political organization. There is a uni-cameral National Assembly of 202 members. The government continues to reject calls for political pluralism.

President and C.-in-C. Armed Forces, Hon. Daniel T. arap Moi, *took office*, October 14, 1978, returned for a third five-year term on February 29, 1988.

Cabinet
(as at June 10, 1990)

Vice-President and Minister for Finance, Hon. Prof. George Saitoti.
Environment and Natural Resources, Hon. Dr Njoroge Mungai.
Lands, Housing and Physical Planning, Hon. Darius Mbela.
Water Development, Hon. John Okwanyo.
Home Affairs and National Heritage, Hon. Davidson Kuguru.
Planning and National Development, Hon. Dr Z. Onyonka.
Transport and Communications, Hon. J. J. Kamotho.
Energy, Hon. N. K. Biwott.
Local Government, Hon. William Ntimama.
Foreign Affairs and International Co-operation, Hon. Wilson Ndolo Ayah.
Commerce, Hon. Arthur K. Magugu.
Tourism and Wildlife, Hon. Katana Ngala.
Culture and Social Services, Hon. James Njiru.
Agriculture, Hon. Maina Wanjigi.
Health, Hon. Mwai Kibaki.
Public Works, Hon. Timothy Mibei.
Co-operative Development, Hon. John Cheruiyot.
Labour, Hon. Phillip Masinde.
Education, Hon. Peter Oloo Aringo.
Information and Broadcasting, Hon. Nahashon Kanyi.
Livestock Development, Hon. Jeremiah Nyagah.
Industry, Hon. John Kyalo.
Research, Science and Technology, Hon. George Muhoho.
Supplies and Marketing, Hon. Wycliffe Musalia Mudavadi.
Technical Training and Applied Technology, Hon. Prof. Sam K. Ongeri.
Manpower Development and Employment, Hon. Dalmas Otieno.
Reclamation and Development of Arid, Semi-Arid and Waste Land, Hon. George Ndoto.
Regional Development, Hon. Onyango Midika.
Attorney-General, Hon. Amos Wako.

KENYA HIGH COMMISSION
45 Portland Place, W1N 4AS
[071–636 2371]

High Commissioner, Her Excellency Dr Sally Kosgei (1987).

PRODUCTION

Agriculture provides about 52 per cent of total export earnings (excluding processed oil products). The great variation in altitude and ecology provide conditions under which a wide range of crops can be grown. These include wheat, barley, pyrethrum, coffee, tea, sisal, coconuts, cashew nuts, cotton, maize and a wide variety of tropical and temperate fruits and vegetables. The total area of well-farmed land on which concentrated mixed farming can be practised is small and the remainder is arid or semi-arid country but population pressure and the need to increase agricultural production for export has led to attempts to develop such areas.

Prospecting and mining are carried on in some parts of the country, the principal minerals produced being soda ash, salt and limestone.

Hydro-electric power has been developed, particularly on the Upper Tana River. Kenya is now almost self-sufficient in electric power generation but the connection with Owen Falls in Uganda is still in being.

There has been considerable industrial development over the last 15 years and Kenya has a wide variety of industries processing agricultural produce and manufacturing an increasing range of products from local and imported raw materials. New industries have recently come into being such as steel, textile mills, dehydrated vegetable processing and motor tyre manufacture as well as many smaller schemes which have added to the country's already considerable consumer goods. There is an oil refinery in Mombasa supplying both Kenya and Uganda, and a fuel pipeline now connects Mombasa and Nairobi.

COMMUNICATIONS

The Kenya Railways Corporation has 1,300 miles of railway open to traffic. There are also 31,000 miles of road, of which 2,700 are bitumen surfaced. Transborder links with Tanzania were re-opened in 1985 with rail services for freight and steamer services for passengers and freight.

The principal port is Mombasa, operated by the Kenya Ports Authority.

International air services operate from airports at Nairobi and Mombasa.

TRADE

Principal exports are coffee and tea, which account for 33 per cent of total export earnings. Also exported are fruit, vegetables, and crude animal and vegetable material. Petroleum products account for about 37 per cent of imports; other imports are manufactured goods, particularly machinery, transport equipment, metals, pharmaceuticals and chemicals.

Trade with UK

	1989	1990
Imports from UK	£208,464,000	£223,080,000
Exports to UK	154,313,000	149,474,000

BRITISH HIGH COMMISSION
Bruce House, Standard Street, PO Box 30465
Nairobi
[Nairobi 335944]

High Commissioner, His Excellency Sir Roger Tomkys, KCMG (1990).

British Council Representative, T. Edmundson, (PO Box 40751) ICEA Building, Kenyatta Avenue, Nairobi. There are offices at *Kisumu* and *Mombasa*.

KIRIBATI
(Ribaberikin Kiribati)

AREA, POPULATION, ETC.—Kiribati, the former Gilbert Islands, became an independent Republic in 1979. Kiribati comprises 36 islands—the Gilbert Group (17) including Banaba, formerly Ocean Island; the Phoenix Islands (8); and the Line Islands (11)—situated in the south west central Pacific around the point at which the International Date Line cuts the Equator. The total land area of 281 sq. miles (728 sq. km) is spread over some 2 million square miles of ocean. Few of the atolls are more than half a mile in width or more than 12 feet high. The vegetation consists mainly of coconut palms, breadfruit trees and pandanus. The population (UN estimate 1989) is 68,000, and predominantly Christian.

CAPITAL.—Tarawa, population estimated at 17,921.
CURRENCY.—Kiribati uses the Australian dollar ($A) of 100 cents.
FLAG.—Red, with blue and white wavy lines in base, and in the centre a gold rising sun and a flying frigate bird.
NATIONAL ANTHEM.—Teirake Kain Kiribati (Stand Kiribati).
NATIONAL DAY.—July 12 (Independence Day).

GOVERNMENT

The President is Head of State as well as Head of Government and is elected nationally. There is an elected House of Assembly (41 members); executive authority is vested in the Cabinet.

Cabinet
(as at July 8, 1991)

President and Minister of Foreign Affairs and International Trade, HE Teatao Teannaki.
Vice-President and Minister of Finance and Economic Planning, Hon. Taomati T. Iuta.
Health, Family Affairs and Social Welfare, Hon. Baitika Toum.
Line and Phoenix Development, Hon. Boanereke Boanereke.
Home Affairs and Rural Development, Hon. Binata Tetaeka.
Transport, Communications and Tourism, Hon. Inatoa Tebania.
Education, Science and Technology, Hon. Anterea Kaitaake.
Commerce, Industry and Employment, Hon. Remuera Tateraka.
Works and Energy, Hon. Teaiwa Tenieu.

HONORARY CONSULATE

c/o Faith House, 7 Tufton Street, SW1P 3QN

Honorary Consul, Hon. Maurice Chandler, CBE.

ECONOMY

Most people still practise a semi-subsistence economy, the main staples of their diet being coconut and fish.

Estimated recurrent revenue for 1988 is $A24·9m. The principal imports are foodstuffs, consumer goods, machinery and transport equipment. The principal exports are copra, which earned $A4,203,000, and fish, income from which was around $A1,606,000 in 1988. Total value of exports in 1988 was $A6,670,000.

COMMUNICATIONS

Air communication exists between most of the islands, and is operated by Air Tungaru, a statutory corporation. Air Marshall Islands operate a weekly

ervice between Majuro, Tarawa, Funafuti and
Tandi, and Air Nauru between Tarawa, Nauru and
Tandi. Inter-island shipping is operated by a statu-
ory corporation, the Shipping Corporation of Kiri-
ati.

SOCIAL WELFARE

The Government maintains a teacher training
college and a secondary school. Five junior secondary
schools are maintained by missions. Throughout
he Republic there are about a hundred primary
chools. The total enrolment of children of school
ge is about 16,000. The Marine Training School at
arawa trains seamen for service with overseas
hipping lines. There is a general hospital at Tarawa.
he other inhabited islands have dispensaries.

Trade with UK

	1989	1990
nports from UK	£378,000	£604,000
xports to UK	26,000	21,000

BRITISH HIGH COMMISSION
PO Box 61, Bairiki, Tarawa
[Bairiki 21327]

igh Commissioner, His Excellency Derek White
(1990).

LESOTHO
('Muso oa Lesotho)

Lesotho is a landlocked mountainous state entirely
urrounded by the Republic of South Africa. Of the
otal area of 11,720 sq. miles (30,355 sq. km), a belt
etween 20 and 40 miles in width lying across the
vestern and southern boundaries and comprising
bout one-third of the total is classed as lowlands,
eing between 5,000 and 6,000 ft. above sea level. The
emaining two-thirds are classed as foothills and
ighlands, rising to 11,425 ft. The population (UN
stimate 1989) is 1,700,000.
CAPITAL.—Maseru, population (1986 Census)
8,951.
CURRENCY.—Loti (M) of 100 lisente.
FLAG.—Diagonally white over blue over green
vith the white of double width, and an assegai and
nobkerrie on a Basotho shield in brown in the upper
oist.
NATIONAL ANTHEM.—Pina ea Sechaba.
NATIONAL DAY.—October 4 (Independence Day).

GOVERNMENT

Lesotho (formerly Basutoland) became a constitu-
onal monarchy within the Commonwealth on
ctober 4, 1966. The independence constitution was
uspended in January 1970, when the country was
overned by a Council of Ministers, until the
stablishment of a nominated National Assembly in
pril 1974. The Government was overthrown in
anuary 1986, and executive and legislative powers
ere conferred upon the King, to be advised by the
filitary Council and Council of Ministers, led by
faj.-Gen. Justin Lekhanya. In March 1990 King
foshoeshoe III's powers were formally revoked and
ested in the Chairman of the Council of Ministers.
1 November 1990 the King was deposed and replaced
y his son, who assumed the title of Letsie III. Maj.-
en. Lekhanya was overthrown in a coup on April
0, 1991, led by Col. Elias Ramaema. Elections are
romised for 1992.
The country is divided into eleven administrative
istricts. In each district there is a District Secretary
ho co-ordinates all Government activity in the
rea, working in co-operation with hereditary chiefs.

ead of State, HM King Letsie III.

Military Council

Chairman, HE Col. Elias P. Ramaema.
Members, HE Brig. Benedict M. Lerotholi; HE Col.
Jacob M. Jane; HE Lt.-Col. Ernest M. Mokete; HE
Lt.-Col. Tseliso Lehohla; HE Lt.-Col. Maoabi Moth-
ibeli.

Council of Ministers
(as at May 30, 1991)

Chairman of the Council of Ministers, HE Col. Elias
Ramaema.
Finance, Planning and Economic Development, Hon.
Abel. L. Thoahlane.
Foreign Affairs, Information and Broadcasting, Hon.
Lt.-Col. Pius T. Molapo.
Water, Energy and Mining, Hon. Col. Alexander L.
Jane.
Works, Transport and Communications, Hon. Col.
Valentius M. Mokone.
Highlands Water, Hon. Major Reentseng Habi.
Education, Hon. Dr L. B. B. J. Machobane.
Justice, Prisons, Law and Constitutional Affairs, Hon.
Albert K. Maope.
Trade and Industry, Hon. Chief Moletsane Moko-
roane.
Tourism, Sports and Culture, Hon. Chief Lechesa
Mathealira.
Minister in the Office of the Military Council, Hon.
Patrick J. Molapo.
*Interior, Chieftainship Affairs and Rural Develop-
ment*, Hon. Chief Mphosi Matete.
Health, Hon. William M. Khuele.
Employment, Social Welfare and Pensions, Hon.
Leonard P. Mothakathi.

JUDICIARY

The Lesotho Courts of Law consist of the Court of
Appeal, the High Court, Magistrates' Courts, Judicial
Commissioners' Court, Central and local Courts.
Magistrates' and higher courts administer the laws
of Lesotho. They also adjudicate appeals from the
Judicial Commissioner's and Subordinate Courts.
Chief Justice, Hon. B. P. Cullinan.

LESOTHO HIGH COMMISSION
10 Collingham Road, SW5 0NR
[071–373 8581]

High Commissioner, His Excellency M. K. Tsekoa
(1989).

EDUCATION

Most schools are mission-controlled, the Government providing grants for salaries and buildings.
There are over 1,000 primary and over 100 secondary
schools; few areas lack a school and there is a high
literacy rate of about 70 per cent. Increasing emphasis
is being laid on agricultural and vocational education. The National University of Lesotho at Roma
was established in 1975.

COMMUNICATIONS

A tarred road of 110 miles links Maseru to several
of the main lowland towns, and this is being extended
in the south of the country. The mountainous areas
are linked by 1,300 miles of gravelled and earth roads
and tracks. Roads link border towns in South Africa
with the main towns in Lesotho. Maseru is connected
by rail with the main Bloemfontein–Natal line of the
South African Railways. Scheduled international
air services are operated daily between Maseru and
Johannesburg and other scheduled international
flights are to Gaborone, Harare, Manzini and Maputo.
There are around 30 airstrips. Internal scheduled

services are operated by the Lesotho Airways Corporation.

The telephone network is fully automated in all urban centres. Radio telephone communication is used extensively in the remote rural areas.

PRODUCTION

The economy of Lesotho is based on agriculture and animal husbandry, and the adverse balance of trade (mainly consumer and capital goods) is offset by the earnings of the large numbers of the population who work in South Africa. Apart from some diamonds, Lesotho has few natural resources and only small-scale industrial development. The Lesotho National Development Corporation was set up to promote the development of industry, mining, trade and tourism. Work has commenced on the Highlands Water Scheme designed to provide water for the Vaal industrial zone in South Africa and hydro-electricity for Lesotho. Drilling is being carried out for oil. A National Park has been established at Sehlabathebe in the Maluti mountains. A number of light manufacturing and processing industries have recently been established.

FINANCE AND TRADE

The main sources of revenue are customs and excise duty. Estimates of expenditure and revenue (1986) are recurrent revenue M241·2 million; recurrent expenditure M265·3 million; capital revenue M144 million; capital expenditure M198 million.

Trade with UK

	1989	1990
Imports from UK	£795,000	£642,000
Exports to UK	734,000	1,288,000

BRITISH HIGH COMMISSION
PO Box 521, Maseru
[Maseru 313961]

High Commissioner, His Excellency John Coates Edwards, CMG (1988).

British Council Representative, D. Bates, Hobson's Square, PO Box 429, Maseru 100.

MALAWI
(Dziko La Malawi)

AREA, POPULATION, ETC.—Malawi comprises Lake Malawi (formerly Lake Nyasa) and its western shore, with the high tableland separating it from the basin of the Luangwa River, the watershed forming the western frontier with Zambia; south of the lake, Malawi reaches almost to the Zambezi and is surrounded by Mozambique, the frontier lying on the west on the watershed of the Zambezi and Shire Rivers, and to the east on the Ruo, a tributary of the Shire, and Lakes Chiuta and Chirwa. This boundary reaches the eastern shore of Lake Malawi and extends up to the mid-point of the lake for about half its length where it returns to the eastern and northern shores to form a frontier with Tanzania. Malawi has a total area of 45,747 sq. miles (118,484 sq. km). The population according to the Census held in 1987 was 7,982,607. According to a UN estimate (1989), the population was 8,022,000. The official languages are Chichewa and English.

CAPITAL.—Lilongwe, population (1987) 175,000. The city of Blantyre in the Southern Region, incorporating Blantyre and Limbe (population (1987) 289,000), is the major commercial and industrial centre. Other main centres are: Mzuzu, Thyolo,

Mulanje, Mangochi, Salima, Dedza and Zomba, t former capital.

CURRENCY.—Kwacha (K) of 100 tambala.

FLAG.—Horizontal stripes of black, red and gree with rising sun in the centre of the black stripe.

NATIONAL ANTHEM.—O God Bless Our Land Malawi.

NATIONAL DAY.—July 6 (Independence Day).

GOVERNMENT

Malawi (formerly Nyasaland) became a republic July 6, 1966, having assumed internal self-gover ment on February 1, 1963, and achieved independen on July 6, 1964. There is a Cabinet consisting of t Life President and other Ministers. The Parliame consists of 112 members, each elected by univers suffrage. Under the 1981 Amendment to the Cons tution, the Life President has the power to nomina as many Members of Parliament as he wishes. Bei a one-party state (the Malawi Congress Party), elected members are required to be members of t Party. The Parliament, which usually meets thr times a year, is presided over by a Speaker.

President, Minister of External Affairs, Agricultu Justice, Works, Supplies, Dr H. Kamuzu Ban elected 1966, *sworn in as President for Life*, July 1971.

Cabinet
(as at May 31, 1991)

Trade, Industry and Tourism, Hon. Robson Chirwa

Transport and Communications, Hon. Dalton Ka pola.

Health, Hon. Dr H. Ntaba.

Finance, Hon. Louis Chimango.

Labour, Hon. Wadson Bini Deleza.

Education and Culture, Hon. Michael Mlambala.

Local Government, Hon. E. C. Katola Phiri.

Community Services, Hon. M. M. Mwakikunga.

Forestry and Natural Resources, Hon. Stanfo Demba.

Minister without Portfolio, Hon. Maxwell Pashane

JUDICIARY

Chief Justice, Hon. F. L. Makuta.

MALAWI HIGH COMMISSION
33 Grosvenor Street, W1X 0DE
[071–491 4172]

High Commissioner, His Excellency P. T. S. Kandi (1990).

EDUCATION

Primary education is the responsibility of lo authorities in both urban and rural areas, althou policy, curricula and inspection are the responsibil of the Ministry of Education and Culture. T Ministry is also responsible for secondary scho technical education and primary teacher traini Religious bodies, with Government assistance, s play an important part in these fields. The Univers of Malawi was opened in 1965 and has five constitue colleges. The total number of students in 1988 was 1·2 million in primary schools, 28,000 in seconda schools and 2,330 at university.

COMMUNICATIONS

A single-track railway runs from Mchinji on Zambian border, through Lilongwe and Salima Lake Malawi (itself served by two passenger an number of cargo boats) through to Blantyre. T route south to the Mozambique port of Beira severed at the Zambesi, but the route to Nacala in Mozambique has recently re-opened. There are 12,215 km of roads in Malawi of which about 21·8 per cent are bituminised.

There is an international airport 26 km from Lilongwe, which handles regional and inter-continental flights.

FINANCE
(excluding Development Account)

	1987–88	1988–89
Revenue	K583m	K752m
Expenditure	823m	1071m

ECONOMY

The economy is largely agricultural, with maize the main subsistence crop. Tobacco, sugar, tea, groundnuts and cotton are the main cash crops and principal exports. There are two sugar mills and total production in 1989 was 157m kg. A number of light manufacturing industries have been established, mainly in agricultural processing, clothing/textiles and building materials.

TRADE

	1987	1988
Imports	K654m	K1080m
Exports	602m	742m

Trade with UK

	1989	1990
Imports from UK	£30,604,000	£33,575,000
Exports to UK	27,890,000	24,666,000

BRITISH HIGH COMMISSION
(PO Box 30042), Lilongwe 3
[Lilongwe 731544]

High Commissioner, His Excellency Nigel Wenban Smith (1990).

British Council Representative, S. Newton, PO Box 30222, Lilongwe 3. There is also a library at *Blantyre*.

MALAYSIA
(Persekutuan Tanah Malaysia)

AREA, POPULATION, ETC.—Malaysia, comprising the 11 states of peninsular Malaya plus Sabah and Sarawak, forms a crescent well over 1,000 miles long between latitudes 1° and 7° N. and longitudes 100° and 119° E. It occupies two distinct regions—the Malay peninsula which extends from the isthmus of Kra to the Singapore Strait and the north-west coastal area of the island of Borneo. Each is separated from the other by the South China Sea. The total area of Malaysia, including the Federal Territories of Kuala Lumpur and Labuan, is about 127,317 sq. miles, (329,749 sq. km), with a population of 16,921,300 (1988 Census), 16,958,000 UN estimate (1989).

The principal racial groups are the Malays, the Chinese and those of Indian and Sri Lankan origin, as well as the indigenous races of Sarawak and Sabah. Bahasa Malaysia (Malay) is the sole official language, but English, various dialects of Chinese, and Tamil are also widely spoken. There are a few indigenous languages widely spoken in Sabah and Sarawak.

RELIGION.—Islam is the official religion of Malaysia, each Ruler being the head of religion in his State, though the Heads of State of Sabah and Sarawak are not heads of the Muslim religion in their States. The Yang di-Pertuan Agung is the head of religion in Melaka and Penang. The Constitution guarantees religious freedom.

CLIMATE.—The year is commonly divided into the south-west and north-west monsoon seasons. Rainfall averages about 100 inches throughout the year. The average daily temperature throughout Malaysia varies from 21° C to 32° C, though in higher areas temperatures are lower and vary widely.

CAPITAL.—Kuala Lumpur was proclaimed Federal Territory on February 1, 1974. Its population (1985) is 1,103,200.

CURRENCY.—Malaysian dollar (ringgit) (M$) of 100 sen.

FLAG.—Equal horizontal stripes of red (7) and white (7); 14 point yellow star and crescent in blue canton.

NATIONAL ANTHEM.—Negara-Ku.

NATIONAL DAY.—August 31 (*Hari Kebangsaan*).

STATES OF THE FEDERATION

The 13 States of the Federation of Malaysia (State capitals in brackets) and their populations at the 1988 Census are:

ΨJohore (Johore Bahru)	2,007,300
Kedah (Alor Setar)	1,353,500
Kelantan (Kota Bahru)	1,150,400
ΨMelaka (Melaka)	560,700
Negri Sembilan (Seremban)	694,100
ΨPahang (Kuantan)	1,001,200
ΨPenang (Georgetown)	1,103,200
Perak (Ipoh)	2,143,200
Perlis (Kangar)	179,700
ΨSabah (Kota Kinabalu)	1,371,000
ΨSarawak (Kuching)	1,591,000
ΨSelangor (Shah Alam)	1,878,300
ΨTerengganu (Kuala Terengganu)	705,200

FEDERAL TERRITORIES

The two Federal Territories and their population at the 1988 Census are:

Kuala Lumpur	⎫
Labuan	⎭ 1,182,700

GOVERNMENT

The Federation of Malaya became an independent country within the Commonwealth on August 31, 1957, as a result of an agreement between HM The Queen and the Rulers of the Malay States. On September 16, 1963 the Federation was enlarged by the accession of the states of Singapore, Sabah (formerly British North Borneo) and Sarawak, and the name of Malaysia was adopted from that date. On August 9, 1965 Singapore seceded from the Federation.

The Constitution was designed to ensure the existence of a strong Federal Government and also a measure of autonomy for the State Governments. It provides for a constitutional Supreme Head of the Federation (HM the *Yang di-Pertuan Agung*) to be elected for a term of five years by the Rulers from among their number, and for a Deputy Supreme Head (HRH *Timbalan Yang di-Pertuan Agung*) to be similarly elected. The Malay Rulers are either chosen or succeed to their position in accordance with the custom of the particular state. In other states of Malaysia choice of the Head of State is at the discretion of the Yang di-Pertuan Agung after consultation with the Chief Minister of the State.

The Federal Parliament consists of two houses, the Senate and the House of Representatives. The Senate (*Dewan Negara*) consists of 68 members, under a President (*Yang di-Pertua Dewan Negara*), 26 elected by the Legislative Assemblies of the States (two from each) and 42 appointed by the Yang di-Pertuan Agung. The House of Representatives (*Dewan Rak-*

yat), consists of 180 members. Members are elected on the principle of universal adult suffrage with a common electoral roll.

The Constitution provides that each State shall have its own Constitution not inconsistent with the Federal Constitution, with the Ruler or Governor acting on the advice of an Executive Council appointed on the advice of the Chief Minister and a single chamber Legislative Assembly. The State Secretary, the State Legal Adviser and the State Financial Officer sit in the Executive Council as *ex-officio* members. The Legislative Assemblies are fully elected on the same basis as the Federal Parliament.

Dr Mahathir Muhammad won a third term in office in a general election held on October 21, 1990.

Supreme Head of State, HM Sultan Azlan Muhibuddin Shah Ibni-Almarhum Sultan Yusuff Izzuddin Ghafarullahu-Lahu Shah (Sultan of Perak), sworn in April 26, 1989.

Deputy Supreme Head of State, HRH Tuanku Jaafar Ibni Al-Marhum Tuanku Abdul Rahman (Yang Dipertuan Besar of Negeri Sembilan).

Ministry
(as at March 15, 1991)

Prime Minister, Minister of Home Affairs, Hon. Datuk Seri Dr Mahathir Muhammad.

Deputy Prime Minister, Minister for Rural Development, Hon Abdul Ghafar Baba.

Transport, Hon. Datuk Seri Dr Ling Liong Sik.

Energy, Telecommunications and Posts, Hon. Datuk Seri S. Samy Vellu.

Primary Industries, Hon. Datuk Seri Dr Lim Keng Yaik.

Works, Hon. Datuk Leo Moggie Anak Irok.

International Trade and Industry, Hon. Datuk Seri Rafidah Aziz.

Education, Hon. Datuk Dr Haji Sulaiman bin Haji Daud.

Agriculture, Hon. Datuk Seri Sanusi bin Junid.

Finance, Hon. Datuk Seri Anwar bin Ibrahim.

Domestic Trade and Consumer Affairs, Hon. Datuk Haji Abu Hassan bin Haji Omar.

Health, Hon. Datuk Lee Kim Sai.

Foreign Affairs, Hon. Datuk Abdullah bin Haji Ahmad Badawi.

Defence, Hon. Datuk Sri Haji Mohd Najib bin Tun Haji Abdul Razak.

Information, Hon. Datuk Mohamed bin Rahmat.

Culture, Arts and Tourism, Hon. Datuk Sabbaruddin bin Chik.

National Unity and Community Development, Hon. Datuk Napsiah binti Omar.

Public Enterprises, Hon. Datuk Dr Mohammad Yusof bin Haji Mohamed Nor.

Human Resources, Hon. Datuk Lim Ah Lek.

Science, Technology and Environment, Hon. Law Hieng Ding.

Housing and Local Government, Hon. Dr Ting Chew Peh.

Land and Co-operative Development, Hon. Tan Sri Datuk Haji Sakaran bin Dandai.

Justice, Hon. Syed Hamid bin Syed Jaafar Albar.

Youth and Sports, Sen. the Hon. Haji Annuar bin Musa.

NOTE.—Tunku/Tengku, Tun, Tan Sri, and Datuk are titles. Tunku/Tengku is equivalent to Prince. Tun denotes membership of a high Order of Malaysian Chivalry and Tan Sri and Datuk (Datuk Seri in Perak and Datu in Sabah) are each the equivalent of a knighthood. The wife of a Tun is styled Toh Puan, that of a Tan Sri is styled Puan Sri and of a Datuk, Datin. The honorific Tuan or Encik is equivalent to Mr and the honorific Puan is equivalent to Mrs. Al-Haj or Haji indicates that the person so named has made the pilgrimage to Mecca.

MALAYSIAN HIGH COMMISSION
45 Belgrave Square, SW1X 8QT
[071–235 8033]

High Commissioner, His Excellency Tan Sri Wan Sidek (1990).

JUDICATURE

The Judicial System consists of a Supreme Court and two High Courts, one in Peninsular Malaysia and one for Sabah and Sarawak (sitting alternately in Kota Kinabalu and Kuching).

The Supreme Court comprises a President, the two Chief Justices of the High Courts and other judges. It possesses appellate, original and advisory jurisdiction.

Each of the High Courts consists of a Chief Justice and not less than four other judges. The Federal Constitution allows for a maximum of twelve such judges for Malaya and eight for Borneo. In Peninsular Malaysia the Subordinate Courts consist of the Sessions Courts and the Magistrates' Courts. In Sabah/Sarawak the Magistrates' Courts constitute the Subordinate Courts.

DEFENCE

The Malaysian Armed Forces consist of the Army, Navy and Air Force, together with volunteer forces for each arm. The defence of the country is largely borne by the army in its role of providing defence against external threat and counter-insurgency operations and also to assist the police in the performance of public order duties. The Royal Malaysian Navy (RMN) has the responsibility of defending the 3,000 miles of the country's coastline and maintaining constant patrol of the seas that separate Sabah and Sarawak from the mainland. The Royal Malaysian Air Force (RMAF) is capable of providing close strategic and tactical support to the army and police in the defence and internal security of the country.

FINANCE

	1988	1989
Revenue	M$22·0 billion	M$24·7 billion
Expenditure	25·9 billion	29·7 billion

PRODUCTION AND TRADE

Malaysia is the largest exporter of natural rubber, tin, palm oil and tropical hardwoods. Other major export commodities are manufactured and processed products, petroleum, oil, and other minerals, palm kernel oil, tea and pepper.

Manufacturing has overtaken agriculture as the largest single contributor to the economy.

Exports of major commodities were (percentage of total exports):

	1988	1989
Manufactured goods	48·5	54·1
Agriculture	33·4	28·3
Minerals	16·7	16·9

Another commodity which is produced throughout Malaysia is rice, the staple food, and efforts are being made to achieve self-sufficiency.

Imports consist mainly of machinery and transport equipment, manufactured goods, foods, mineral fuels, chemicals and inedible crude materials.

	1988	1989
Imports	M$42·8 billion	M$60·9 billion
Exports	54·4 billion	67·8 billion

Trade with UK

	1989	1990
Imports from UK	£441,762,000	£601,909,000
Exports to UK	676,258,000	775,667,000

BRITISH HIGH COMMISSION
185 JLN Ampang
(PO Box 11030), 50732 Kuala Lumpur
[Kuala Lumpur 03–2482122]

High Commissioner, His Excellency Sir John Nicholas Teague Spreckley, KCVO, CMG (1986).

British Council Representative, Dr G. Howell, PO Box 10539, Jalan Bukit Aman, Kuala Lumpur 50916; offices at *Kota Kinabalu* (Sabah) and *Kuching* (Sarawak), and a library in *Penang.*

THE MALDIVES
(Divehi Jumhuriya)

AREA, POPULATION, ETC.—The Maldives are a chain of coral atolls, some 400 miles to the south-west of Sri Lanka, stretching from just south of the equator for about 600 miles to the north. There are about 20 coral atolls comprising over 1,200 islands, 202 of which are inhabited. Total area of the islands is 115 sq. miles (298 sq. km). No point in the entire chain of islands is more than 8 feet above sea-level. The population of the islands (UN estimate 1989) is 206,000. The people are Sunni Muslims and the Maldivian (Dhivehi) language is akin to Elu or old Sinhalese.

CAPITAL.—ΨMalé, population (1985) 46,334. There is an international airport at Malé.

CURRENCY.—Rufiyaa of 100 laaris.

FLAG.—Green field bearing a white crescent, with wide red border.

NATIONAL ANTHEM.—Qawmee Salaam.

NATIONAL DAY.—July 26.

GOVERNMENT

Until 1952 the islands were a Sultanate under the protection of the British Crown. Internal self-government was achieved in 1948 and full independence in 1965. In 1982 the Republic of The Maldives became a special member of the Commonwealth, and a full member in 1985.

The Maldives form a Republic which is elective. There is a Parliament (the *Citizens' Majlis*) with representatives elected from all the atolls. The life of the Majlis is five years. The Government consists of a Cabinet, which is responsible to the Majlis.

President, His Excellency Maumoon Abdul Gayoom, *elected* 1978, 1983, *re-elected* September 1989 (also *Minister of Defence and National Security, and Minister of Finance*).

Cabinet
(as at June 30, 1990)

Foreign Affairs, Hon. Fathulla Jameel.
Justice, Hon. Mohamed Rasheed Ibrahim.
Home Affairs and Sports, Hon. Umar Zahir.
Education, Hon. Abdulla Hameed.
Health and Welfare, Hon. Abdul Sattar Moosa Didi.
Fisheries and Agriculture, Hon. Abbas Ibrahim.
Atolls Administration, Hon. Ilyas Ibrahim.
Trade and Industries, vacant.
Tourism, Hon. Abdulla Jameel.
Public Works and Labour, Hon. Abdulla Kamaludeen.
Planning and Environment, Hon. Ismail Shafeen.
Transport and Shipping, Ahmed Zahir.
Minister at the President's Office and Acting Attorney-General, Hon. Mohamed Zahir Hussain.

PRODUCTION

The vegetation of the islands is coconut palms with some scrub. Hardly any cultivation of crops is possible and nearly all food to supplement the basic fish diet has to be imported. The principal industry is fishing and considerable quantities of fish are exported to Japan. Dried fish is exported to Sri Lanka, where it is a delicacy. The tourist industry is expanding rapidly (131,000 visitors in 1987). Maldives Shipping Ltd has a fleet of some 30 merchant ships.

Trade with UK

	1989	1990
Imports from UK	£3,412,000	£3,458,000
Exports to UK	5,224,000	6,573,000

BRITISH HIGH COMMISSION
High Commissioner, (resides at Colombo, Sri Lanka).

MALTA
(Repubblika Ta'Malta)

AREA, POPULATION, ETC.—Malta lies in the Mediterranean Sea, 58 miles from Sicily and about 180 miles from the African coast, about 17 miles in length and 9 miles in breadth, and having an area of 94·9 square miles. Malta includes also the adjoining islands of Gozo (area 25·9 sq. miles), Comino and minor islets. The estimated population in 1989 was 352,430. The Maltese are mainly Roman Catholic.

The Maltese language is of Semitic origin and held by some to be derived from the Carthaginian and Phoenician tongues. Maltese and English are the official languages of administration and Maltese is ordinarily the official language in all the courts of law and the language of general use in the islands.

Malta was in turn held by the Phoenicians, Carthaginians, Romans and Arabs. In 1090 it was conquered by Count Roger of Normandy. In 1530 it was handed over to the Knights of St John, who made it a stronghold of Christianity. In 1565 it sustained the famous siege, when the last great effort of the Turks was successfully withstood by Grandmaster La Valette. The Knights expended large sums in fortifying the island and carrying out many magnificent works, until they were expelled by Napoleon in 1798. The Maltese rose against the French garrison soon afterwards, and the island was subsequently blockaded by the British fleet. The Maltese people freely requested the protection of the British Crown in 1802 on condition that their rights and privileges would be preserved and respected. The islands were finally annexed to the British Crown by the Treaty of Paris in 1814.

Malta was again closely besieged in the last war. From June 1940, to the end of the war, 432 members of the garrison and 1,540 civilians were killed by enemy aircraft, and about 35,000 houses were destroyed or damaged. The island was awarded the George Cross in 1942.

CAPITAL.—ΨValletta. Population (Census 1989), 9,196. Valletta Grand Harbour is very deep and large vessels can anchor alongside the shore. It is an important port of call and ship repairing centre for vessels, being half-way between Gibraltar and Port Said.

CURRENCY.— Maltese lira (LM) of 100 cents and 1,000 mils.

FLAG.—Two equal vertical stripes, white at the hoists and red at the fly. A representation of the George Cross is carried edged with red in the canton of the white stripe.

NATIONAL ANTHEM.—L-Innu Malti.

NATIONAL DAY.—September 21 (Independence Day).

GOVERNMENT

On September 21, 1964 Malta became an independent state within the Commonwealth; on December 13, 1974, Malta became a republic within the Commonwealth.

Elections are held for the unicameral Parliament of 69 members every five years by a system of proportional representation. Seats are obtained by the highest number of votes in the respective districts. The party with the highest number of votes forms the government, with extra members being co-opted if necessary.

President.—Dr Vincent Tabone, *took office* April 4, 1989.

Cabinet
(as at July 12, 1991)

Prime Minister, Hon. Dr Edward Fenech Adami.
Deputy PM and Minister of Foreign Affairs and Justice, Hon. Dr Guido De Marco.
Education and the Interior, Hon. Dr Ugo Mifsud Bonnici.
Social Policy, Hon. Dr Louis Galea.
Finance, Hon. Dr G. Bonello Du Puis.
Infrastructure Development, Hon. Michael Falzon.
Agriculture and Fisheries, Hon. Lawrence Gatt.
Tertiary Sector Development, Hon. Dr Emmanuel Bonnici.
Gozo, Hon. Anton Tabone.
Economic Affairs, Hon. John Dalli.

MALTA HIGH COMMISSION
16 Kensington Square, W8 5HH
[071–938 1712]

High Commissioner, His Excellency Saviour Stellini (1991).

EDUCATION

In June 1990 there were 118 government primary schools with 37,016 pupils and 43 secondary schools and new lyceums, with a total of 24,800 pupils.

The government also runs 27 technical/trade schools (with an enrolment of 6,880 students). Schools of art, music, secretarial studies, catering, nursing and dramatic art are sponsored by the government. Tertiary education is available at the University of Malta, which had 2,525 students in 1990.

A number of private schools offer more or less the same facilities that exist in Government schools. All state education is free.

AGRICULTURE

Agriculture plays a significant role in the economy. There are 3,000 full time farmers and about 14,000 part time farmers. Crop production consists mainly of tomatoes, potatoes, onions, cabbages and cauliflowers, and fruit. Grape is the largest fruit crop. Flowers and cuttings are produced for export markets.

INDUSTRY

The island's leading industry is the state-owned Malta Drydocks, employing about 4,300 people. The main port of Grand Harbour handled traffic of 13,140,007 tonnes in 1990.

At the end of 1990 manufacturing firms employed some 31,961 people. The wide range of produce includes food processing, textiles and clothing, plastics and chemical products, electronic equipment and components. The gross output of the manufacturing industry in 1990 was LM517 million, of which LM328·8 million were export sales.

Tourism has assumed primary importance, with over 871,675 tourists visiting the island in 1990, and

Marsamxett Harbour is being further developed by the extension of a yacht centre. Gross income from this industry stood at LM157·4 million.

FINANCE

	1989	1990
Revenue	LM291,779,000	LM385,606,000
Expenditure	320,744,000	381,690,000

TRADE

The principal imports for home consumption are foodstuffs (mainly wheat, meat and bullocks, milk and fruit), fodder, beverages and tobacco, fuels, chemicals, textiles and machinery (industrial, agricultural and transport). The chief domestic exports are processed food, electronics, textiles, and other manufactures.

	1989	1990
Imports	LM515,000,000	LM617,500,000
Exports	294,200,000	357,000,000

Trade with UK

	1989	1990
Imports from UK	£132,287,000	£141,298,000
Exports to UK	42,194,000	50,541,000

BRITISH HIGH COMMISSION
7 St Anne Street, Floriana
[233134/8]

High Commissioner, His Excellency Peter Wallis, CMG (1991).

British Council Representative, G. Graves, 89 Archbishop Street, Valletta.

MAURITIUS

AREA, POPULATION, ETC.—Mauritius is an island group lying in the Indian Ocean, 550 miles east of Madagascar, between 57° 17′–57° 46′ E. long. and 19° 58′–20° 33′ S. lat., and comprising with its dependencies an area of 790 square miles (2,045 sq. km). The population (December 1989 estimate, excluding Rodrigues and the outer islands) was 1,047,532, made up of Asiatic races (Hindus 52·6 per cent, Muslims 16·5 per cent), and persons of European (mainly French) extraction, mixed and African descent (28·3 per cent).

English is the official language but French may be used in the Legislative Assembly and lower law courts. However, Creole is the mostly commonly used language.

CLIMATE.—Mauritius enjoys a sub-tropical maritime climate, with a wide range of rainfall and temperature resulting from the mountainous nature of the island. Humidity is rather high throughout the year and rainfall is sufficient to maintain a green cover of vegetation, except for a brief period in the driest districts.

CAPITAL.—ΨPort Louis, population (1985) 138,272; other centres are Beau Bassin-Rose Hill (93,059); Curepipe (64,072); Vacoas-Phoenix (55,330) and Quatre Bornes (65,405).

CURRENCY.—Mauritius rupee of 100 cents.

FLAG.—Red, blue, yellow and green horizontal stripes.

NATIONAL ANTHEM.—Glory to the Motherland.

NATIONAL DAY.—March 12.

GOVERNMENT

Mauritius was discovered in 1511 by the Portuguese; the Dutch visited it in 1598 and named it Mauritius, after Prince Maurice of Nassau. From 1638 to 1710 it was held as a small Dutch colony and in 1715 the French took possession but did not settle it until 1721. Mauritius was taken by a British Force in 1810. A British garrison remained on the island until June 1960. The French language and French law were preserved under British rule.

A Crown Colony for 158 years, Mauritius became an independent state within the Commonwealth on March 12, 1968. The Constitution defined by Order in Council in 1964 was slightly altered in 1966 on the recommendation of the Banwell Commission, the effect being to increase the membership of the Legislative Assembly to 70, 62 elected by block voting in multi-member constituencies (including two members for Rodrigues) and eight specially-elected members. Of the latter, four seats go to the 'best loser' of whichever communities in the island are underrepresented in the Assembly after the General Election and the four remaining seats are allocated on the basis of both party and community. The Constitution provides for the appointment of a Governor General who acts on the advice of the Council of Ministers, collectively responsible to the Legislative Assembly.

In the August 1987 General Election, the Mouvement Socialiste Mauricien (MSM), allied with the Labour Party (MLP), the Parti Mauricien Social Democrate and the Organisation du Peuple Rodriguais (OPR), defeated the Mouvement Militant Mauricien and formed the Government, with a majority of 22 seats. The Parti Mauricien Social Democrate left the alliance in August 1988. In September 1990, the Labour Party left the governing coalition and was replaced by the Mouvement Militant Mauricien. A general election has been called for September 1991.

Governor General, His Excellency Sir Veerasamy Ringadoo, GCMG, QC.

Council of Ministers
(as at September, 1990)

Prime Minister, Minister of Defence and Internal Security, Finance, Information, Internal and External Communications and the Outer Islands, Rt. Hon. Sir Aneerood Jugnauth, KCMG, QC.

Deputy PM, Minister for Health, Hon. Prem Nababsing.

Deputy PM, Minister of Economic Planning and Development, Dr the Hon. Beergoonath Ghurburun.

External Affairs, Hon. Jean-Claude de l'Estrac.

Education, Arts and Culture, Hon. Armoogum Parsuramen.

Trade and Shipping, Hon. Dwarkanath Gungah.

Energy, Water Resources and Postal Services, Hon. Mahyendrah Utchanah.

Housing and Justice, Hon. Jayen Cuttaree.

Social Security and Reform Institutions, Hon. Viswanath Sajadah.

Labour and Industrial Relations, Women's Rights and Family Welfare, Hon. Sheilabai Bappoo.

Youth, Sports and Tourism, Hon. Michael Glover.

Rodrigues, Hon. Serge Clair.

Co-operatives, Hon. Jagdishwar Goburdhun.

Agriculture, Fisheries and Natural Resources, Hon. Murlidas Dulloo.

Industry and New Technology, Hon. Cassam Uteem.

Works, Hon. Ramduthsing Jaddoo.

Local Government, Hon. Regis Finnette.

Civil Service Affairs and Employment, Hon. Kailash Ruhee.

Environment, Hon. Swaley Kasenally.

MAURITIUS HIGH COMMISSION
32–33 Elvaston Place, SW7 5NW
[071–581 0294]

High Commissioner, His Excellency Dr Boodhun Teelock (1989).

EDUCATION

Primary education is free and in 1987 was provided for 137,935 children at 273 primary schools. Although education is not compulsory it is estimated that about 90 per cent of children of primary age attend school. At post-primary level there were a total of 69,825 students attending secondary schools; fees and teachers' salaries in the private secondary schools are paid by government. There are a number of training facilities offering training in engineering and mechanical trades, nursing, building, seamanship, hotel and catering etc. The College of Education trains primary school teachers. The Institute of Education is responsible for training secondary school teachers and for curriculum development. The University of Mauritius consists of Schools of Agriculture, Administration, Law and Industrial Technology. Estimated expenditure on education in 1989–90 was Rs.1,054,800,000.

COMMUNICATIONS

Port Louis, on the NW coast, handles the bulk of the island's external trade. A bulk sugar terminal capable of handling the total crop began operating in 1980. The international airport is located at Plaisance in the south-east of the island about 5 miles from Mahébourg. There are six daily newspapers and five weeklies, mostly in French, and two Chinese daily papers and one weekly paper. The Mauritius Broadcasting Corporation has a monopoly of radio broadcasting in the country; television was introduced in 1965. There is a satellite communications ground station near Port Louis.

PRODUCTION

In September 1989 the manufacturing sector employed 107,758, while the sugar industry employed 42,099.

About 55 per cent of the total sugar crop is produced on a plantation scale, while smaller owners (cultivating less than 10 acres) cultivate about 24 per cent of the land under cane. Tea and tobacco are also grown commercially but on a smaller scale than sugar.

	1988	1989
	tonnes	
Sugar	634,224	568,301
Tea (manufactured)	6,857	5,500
Tobacco (leaves)	970	1,058

In 1989 production of molasses, mainly for export, was 177,000 tonnes. Other products include alcohol, rum, denatured spirits, perfumed spirits and vinegar.

The bulk of the island's requirements in manufactured products still has to be imported. However, the Mauritius Export Processing Zone (MEPZ) scheme, introduced in 1971, has attracted investment from overseas and the number of export-orientated enterprises has risen from ten in 1971 to 563 at the end of 1989, employing 88,650 people. The biggest firms are in clothing manufacture, particularly woollen knitwear, but the range of goods produced includes toys, plastic products, leather goods, diamond cutting and polishing, watches, television sets and telephones.

Tourism is a major source of income for Mauritius, with an estimated 265,300 tourists in 1989. Earnings from tourism in 1989 are estimated to be Rs2,830 million. The neighbouring French island of Réunion is the most important source of tourists, followed closely by mainland France.

FINANCE

The main sources of Government revenue are private and company income tax, customs and excise duties, mainly on imports, but also on sugar exports.

	1988–89	1989–90*
Public revenue	Rs.7,193m	Rs.8,283m
Public expenditure (recurrent)	7,655m	8,290m
* estimate		

TRADE

Most foodstuffs and raw materials have to be imported from abroad. Apart from local consumption (about 36,500 tonnes per annum), the sugar produced is exported, mainly to Britain.

	1988	1989
Total imports	Rs.17,460m	Rs.20,217m
Total exports	13,854m	15,517m

Trade with UK

	1989	1990
Imports from UK	£43,528,000	£50,746,000
Exports to UK	216,190,000	233,936,000

BRITISH HIGH COMMISSION
King George V Avenue, Floreal
[Floreal 6865795/9]

High Commissioner, His Excellency Michael Edward Howell, CMG, OBE.

British Council Representative, M. Bootle, PO Box 111, Foondun Building, 2nd Floor, Royal Road, Rose Hill.

RODRIGUES AND DEPENDENCIES OF MAURITIUS

Rodrigues, formerly a dependency but now part of Mauritius, is about 350 miles east of Mauritius, with an area of 40 square miles. Population (1989) 37,538. Cattle, salt fish, sheep, goats, pigs, maize and onions are the principal exports. The island is administered by an Island Commissioner.
Island Commissioner, Claude Wong So.

The islands of Agalega and St Brandon are dependencies of Mauritius. Total population (1989) 500. Other small islands, formerly Mauritian dependencies, have since 1965 constituted the British Indian Ocean Territory (*see* p. 705).

NAMIBIA
(The Republic of Namibia)

AREA, POPULATION, ETC.—Namibia stretches from the southern border of Angola (lat. 17° 23′ S.) to the northern (Orange River) and north-western borders of the Cape Province of the Republic of South Africa; and from the Atlantic Ocean in the west to Botswana in the east. The average rainfall over 70 per cent of the country is below 400 mm per annum.

Namibia has an area of 318,261 sq. miles (824,292 sq. km), including the area of Walvis Bay (434 sq. miles) which is claimed by Nambia but remains under South African sovereignty. The population was estimated at 1,500,000 in 1990 and the main population groups are: Ovambo (587,000), Kavango (110,000), Damara (89,000), Herero (89,000), Whites (78,000), Nama (57,000), Coloured (48,000), Caprivians (44,000), Bushmen (34,000), Rehoboth Baster (29,000), Tswana (7,000).

CAPITAL.—Windhoek (population, 1987 estimate, 110,000). The only port of any size is ΨWalvis Bay.

CURRENCY.—South African rand (R) of 100 cents is legal tender.

FLAG.—Blue (above) and green; divided by diagonal red stripe bordered by white; golden sun on blue band near staff.

NATIONAL DAY.—March 21 (Independence Day).

GOVERNMENT

A German protectorate from 1880 to 1915, Namibia, as South West Africa, was administered until the end of 1920 by the Union of South Africa. Under the terms of the Treaty of Versailles, the territory was entrusted to South Africa with full powers of administration and legislation over the territory. After the dissolution of the League of Nations and in the absence of a trusteeship agreement, South Africa informed the United Nations that it would continue to administer South West Africa.

On June 21, 1971 the International Court of Justice at The Hague delivered an advisory opinion as requested by the UN Security Council on the legal consequences for states of the continued presence of South Africa in Namibia (South West Africa). It was the Court's majority opinion that the continued presence of South Africa was illegal, and that it was to withdraw its administration from Namibia immediately, putting an end to its occupation of the territory. The South African Government rejected this opinion, but accepted the principle that the territory should attain independence.

Following the failure of constitutional talks (known as the Turnhalle Conference) begun in 1975, the five Western members of the UN Security Council in 1977 drew up a plan, later incorporated into Security Council Resolution 435, for a peaceful settlement.

After a series of talks between Cuba, Angola, South Africa and the USA, agreement was reached in December 1988 for the withdrawal over 27 months of Cuban troops in Angola in exchange for South African withdrawal from Namibia leading to Namibian independence under UN Security Council Resolution 435. Implementation of Resolution 435 began on April 1, 1989. The UN Secretary General sent his Special Representative to Namibia to oversee the seven-month run-up to elections and a 4,500 strong United Nations Transition Assistance Group (UNTAG) was deployed to monitor South African troop withdrawal and the conduct of the parties.

Elections for 72 seats in Namibia's first nationally elected body took place under UN supervision on November 7–11, 1989. Of voters registered, 95·9 per cent took part. Seats were allocated to parties according to the percentage of the vote won. The South West Africa People's Organization (SWAPO) won 41 seats with 57·32 per cent of the vote, the Democratic Turnhalle Alliance won 21 seats with 28·55 per cent, the United Democratic Front won 4 seats, Action Christian National 3, Namibia Patriotic Front 1, Federal Convention of Namibia 1, and Namibia National Front 1.

The National Assembly met for the first time on November 21, 1989 at the legislative building in Windhoek (the Tintenpalast). The Independence Constitution was adopted unanimously on February 9, 1990, and independence was declared on March 21, 1990. Namibia joined the Commonwealth upon independence.

Now constitutionally defined as a multiparty, secular, democratic republic, Namibia has an executive President as Head of State who exercises the functions of government with the assistance of a Cabinet headed by a Prime Minister. Legislative authority lies with the National Assembly, which is the lower house of a bicameral parliamentary structure; an upper house (National Council) representing Regional Councils is to be created in 1992. The main function of the National Council will be to review and consider legislation from the National Assembly. Under a system of proportional representation, elections to the National Assembly are to take place every five years, or earlier if decided by the President. Members of the National Council will hold their seats for six years.

President, Sam Nujoma.

Cabinet
(as at July 25, 1991)

Prime Minister, Hage Geingob.
Home Affairs, Hifikepunye Pohamba.
Foreign Affairs, Theo-Ben Gurirab.
Defence, Peter Mueshihange.
Finance, Otto Hermgel.
Education, Culture and Sport, Nahas Angula.
Information and Broadcasting, Hidipo Hamutenya.
Health and Social Services, Dr Nicky Iyambo.
Labour, Public Service and Manpower Development, Hendrik Witbooi.
Mines and Energy, Andimba Toivo Ya Toivo.
Justice, Ngarikutuke Tjiriange.
Local Government and Housing, Dr Libertine Amathila.
Agriculture, Fisheries, Water and Rural Development, Gert Hanekom.
Trade and Industry, Ben Amathila.
Wildlife and Conservation, and Tourism, Nico Bessinger.
Works, Transport, and Communication, Richard Kapelwa.
Lands Resettlement and Rehabilitation, Marco Hausiku.

NAMIBIA HIGH COMMISSION
34 South Molton Street, W1Y 2BP
[071-408 2333]

High Commissioner, His Excellency Veiccoh K. Nghiwete (1991).

ECONOMY

Mining (mainly diamonds and uranium), agriculture and fisheries account for over 40 per cent of Namibia's GDP. Most of the labour force is employed in the agricultural sector.

Trade with UK

	1989	1990
Imports from UK	£4,264,000	£4,246,000
Exports to UK	4,568,000	349,000

BRITISH HIGH COMMISSION
116A Leutwein Street, Windhoek
[Windhoek 223022]

High Commissioner, His Excellency Francis Neville Richards (1990).

British Council Representative, J. Utley, PO Box 24224, 14 Van Rhijn Street, Windhoek 9000.

REPUBLIC OF NAURU

The Republic of Nauru is an island of 8·2 sq. miles (21 sq. km) in size, situated in 166° 55′ E. longitude and 0° 32′ S. of the Equator. It had a population (Census May 1983) of 8,042 (Nauruans 4,964; other Pacific Islanders 2,134; Asians 682; Caucasians 262). The UN estimated a total population of 9,000 in 1989. About 43 per cent of Nauruans are adherents of the Nauruan Protestant Church and there is a Roman Catholic Mission on the island. The main languages are English and Nauruan.

CURRENCY.—Nauru uses the Australian dollar ($A) of 100 cents as legal tender.

FLAG.—Twelve-point star (representing the 12 original Nauruan tribes) below a gold bar (representing the Equator), all on a blue ground.

NATIONAL DAY.—January 31 (Independence Day).

GOVERNMENT

From 1888 until the First World War Nauru was administered by Germany, in 1920 becoming a British mandated territory under the League of Nations administered by Australia. A Trusteeship superseding the Mandate was approved in 1947 by the UN and Nauru continued to be administered by Australia until it became independent on January 31, 1968. It was announced in November 1968 that a limited form of membership of the Commonwealth had been devised for Nauru at the request of its Government.

Parliament has eighteen members including the Cabinet and Speaker. Voting is compulsory for all Nauruans over 20 years of age, except in certain specified instances. Elections are held every three years. The Cabinet is chosen by the President and comprises not fewer than five nor more than six members including the President.

President and Minister for External Affairs, Internal Affairs, Island Development and Industry, Civil Aviation Authority and the Public Service, His Excellency Hon. Bernard Dowiyogo.

Cabinet
(as at June 30, 1991)

Works and Community Services and Minister Assisting the President, Hon. Vinson Detenamo.
Finance, Hon. Kinza Clodumar.
Health and Education, Hon. Vinci Clodumar.
Justice, Hon. Nimes Ekwona.

JUDICIARY

A Supreme Court of Nauru is presided over by the Chief Justice. The District Court, which is subordinate to the Supreme Court, is presided over by a Resident Magistrate. Both the Supreme Court and the District Court are Courts of Record. The Supreme Court exercises both original and appellate jurisdiction.

EDUCATION AND WELFARE

Nauru has a hospital service and other medical and dental services. There is also a maternity and child welfare service. Education is available in 9 primary and 2 secondary schools on the island with a total enrolment of about 1,600 pupils receiving primary education and 500 secondary education.

PRODUCTION, ETC.

The only fertile areas are the narrow coastal belt and local requirements of fruit and vegetables are mostly met by imports. The economy is heavily dependent on the extraction of phosphate, of which the island has one of the world's richest deposits. About 1·5 million tonnes of phosphate are mined each year, providing employment for over 1,000 people. The industry has been run since 1970 by the Nauru Phosphate Corporation. Considerable investments have been made abroad with the royalties on phosphate exports to provide for a time when production declines.

The Nauru Pacific Line owns six ships; the Government-owned Air Nauru normally operates air services throughout the Pacific region and to Australia, New Zealand, Japan, Singapore and the Philippines.

Trade with UK

	1989	1990
Imports from UK	£549,000	£1,145,000
Exports to UK	662,000	54,000

BRITISH HIGH COMMMISSION
British High Commissioner, (resides at Suva, Fiji).

NEW ZEALAND

AREA AND POPULATION

Islands	Area (Sq. miles)	Population at Census March 4, 1986†
(a) Exclusive of Island Territory		
North Island	44,281	2,441,615
South Island	58,093	865,469
Stewart Island	670	531*
Chatham Islands	372	755*
Minor Islands		
Inhabited—		
Kermadec Islands	13	5(d)*
Campbell Island	44	10(d)*
Uninhabited—		
Three Kings	3	..
Snares	1	..
Solander	⅓	..
Antipodes	24	..
Bounty	⅓	..
Auckland	234	..
Total	103,736	3,307,084
(b) Island Territory		
Tokelau	5	1,690 (e)
(c) Niue¶	100	2,531 (f)
Cook Islands¶	93	17,185 (g)
Ross Dependency	175,000	

* Included in North Island and South Island totals.
† Excluding members of the Armed Forces overseas—979 in 1981; 1,247 in 1986.
¶ The Cook Islands have had complete internal self-government since August 4, 1965, as has Niue since October 19, 1974, but Cook Islanders and Niueans remain New Zealand citizens.
(a) November 2, 1981. (b) January 1, 1981. (c) December 1, 1981. (d) March 31, 1983. (e) October 10, 1986. (f) September 29, 1986. (g) December 1, 1986.

Vital Statistics

	1988	1989
Births	57,546	58,091
Deaths	27,408	27,042
Marriages	23,485	22,733

Infant mortality per 1,000 live births in 1989, 10·77.

Races

	1981	1986
European	2,696,568	2,612,958
Maori	279,084	294,201
Chinese	18,480	19,206
Polynesian (other than NZ Maori)	88,827	90,612

Religions

	1981 per cent	1986 per cent
Church of England	25·7	24·0
Presbyterian	16·7	18·0
Roman Catholic	14·3	15·2
Methodist	4·7	4·7
Baptist	1·6	2·1

PHYSIOGRAPHY

New Zealand consists of a number of islands of varying size in the South Pacific Ocean, and has also administrative responsibility for the Ross Dependency in Antarctica. The two larger and most important islands, the North and South Islands of New Zealand, are separated by only a relatively narrow strait. The remaining islands are very much smaller and, in general, are widely dispersed over a considerable expanse of ocean. The boundaries, inclusive of the most outlying islands and dependencies, range from 33° to 53° South latitude, and from 162° East longitude to 173° West longitude.

Geographical features.—The two principal islands have a total length of 1,040 miles, and a combined area of 102,344 sq. miles (265,069 sq. km). A large proportion of the surface is mountainous in character. The principal range is the Southern Alps, extending over the entire length of the South Island and having its culminating point in Mount Cook (12,349 ft). The North Island mountains include several volcanoes, two of which are active, others being dormant or extinct. Mt. Ruapehu (9,175 ft) and Mt. Ngauruhoe (7,515 ft) are the most important. Of the numerous glaciers in the South Island, the Tasman (18 miles long by 1¼ wide), the Franz Josef and the Fox are the best known. The North Island is noted for its hot springs and geysers. For the most part the rivers are too short and rapid for navigation. The more important include the Waikato (270 miles in length), Wanganui (180), and Clutha (210). Lakes (Taupo, 234 sq. miles in area; Wakatipu, 113; and Te Anau, 133) are abundant.

In addition to North and South Islands:—

Chatham Islands, comprising Chatham, Pitt, South East Islands and some rocky islets, in 44°S. lat. and 176° 20′ W. long., have a combined area of 965 sq. km (373 sq. miles). They lie 700 km SE of Wellington, and are largely uninhabited.

Stewart Island, largely uninhabited, lies 30 km S. of South Island and has an area of 1,746 sq. km (674 sq. miles).

The Kermadec Group (population normally 9 or 10) between 29° 10′ to 31° 30′ S. lat., and 177° 45′ to 179° W. long., includes Raoul or Sunday, Macaulay, Curtis

Islands, L'Esperance, and some islets. All the inhabitants are government employees at a meteorological station. Campbell Island (used as a weather station).

The Three Kings (discovered by Tasman on the Feast of the Epiphany), in 34° 9' S. lat. and 172° 8' 8" E. long. Auckland Islands, about 290 miles south of Bluff Harbour, in 50° 32' S. lat. and 166° 13' E. long. Antipodes Group, 40° 41' 15" S. lat. and 178° 43' E. long. Bounty Islands, 47° 4' 43" S. lat., 170° 0' 30" E. long. Snares Islands and Solander. All these islands are uninhabited.

Climate.—New Zealand has a moist-temperate marine climate, but with abundant sunshine. A very important feature is the small annual range of temperature which permits some growth of vegetation, including pasture, all the year round. Very little snow falls on the low levels even in the South Island. The mean temperature ranges from 15° C in the North to about 9° C in the South. Rainfall over the more settled areas in the North Island ranges from 35 to 70 inches and in the South Island from 25 to 45 inches. The total range is from approximately 13 to over 250 inches.

CAPITAL.—ΨWellington, in the North Island (estimated population March 1989, Wellington urban area, 324,600.

Other large urban areas; ΨAuckland 850,900; ΨChristchurch 301,500; ΨDunedin 106,400; Hamilton 104,100; Ψ Napier-Hastings 107,700.

CURRENCY.—New Zealand dollar (NZ$) of 100 cents.

FLAG.—Blue ground, with Union Flag in top left quarter, four five-pointed red stars with white borders on the fly. On June 20, 1968, a naval ensign bearing the Southern Cross was adopted, replacing the British white ensign.

NATIONAL ANTHEM.—God Save The Queen/God Defend New Zealand.

NATIONAL DAY.—February 6 (Waitangi Day).

GOVERNMENT

The discoverers and first colonists of New Zealand were Polynesian people, ancestors of the Maori of today. Whether there was a single colonization, several, or many, is not known but the 9th century is generally considered to be the date of the first settlement. By the 13th or 14th century early exploration was over and there were well established Maori settlements.

The first European to discover New Zealand was a Dutch navigator, Abel Tasman, who sighted the coast on December 13, 1642 but did not land. It was the British explorer James Cook who circumnavigated New Zealand and landed in 1769. Traders, whalers and sealers made up the majority of Europeans in New Zealand from the end of the 18th century until the late 1830s, when the proportion of permanent European settlers became significant.

Largely as a result of increased British emigration, the country was annexed by the British Government in 1840. The British Lieutenant Governor, William Hobson, RN, proclaimed sovereignty over the North Island by virtue of the Treaty of Waitangi, signed by him and many Maori chiefs, and over the South Island and Stewart Island by right of discovery.

On May 3, 1841 New Zealand was, by letters patent, created a separate colony distinct from New South Wales. Organized colonization on a large scale commenced in 1840 with the New Zealand company's settlement at Wellington. On September 26, 1907 the designation was changed to 'The Dominion of New Zealand'. The Constitution rests upon the Constitution Act of 1852, and other Imperial statutes such as the Bill of Rights. A 1986 Constitution Act brought a number of statutory constitutional provisions. The Statute of Westminster was formally adopted by New Zealand in 1947. The executive authority is entrusted

to a Governor-General appointed by the Crown and aided by an Executive Council, within a Legislature consisting of one chamber, the House of Representatives.

Governor-General

Governor-General and Commander-in-Chief of New Zealand, Her Excellency Dame Catherine Tizard, GCMG, DBE, *sworn in,* November 1990.

The Executive Council
(as at June 21, 1991)
The Governor-General

Prime Minister, Minister in Charge of the New Zealand Security Intelligence Service, Rt. Hon. J. B. Bolger.

Deputy PM, Minister of External Relations and Trade, Foreign Affairs, Hon. D. C. McKinnon.

Labour, Immigration, State Services, Pacific Island Affairs, Hon. W. F. Birch.

Finance, Hon. Ruth Richardson.

Attorney-General, Hon. Paul East.

Agriculture, Forestry, Hon. John Falloon.

State-Owned Enterprises, Fisheries, Railways, Works and Development, Hon. D. L. Kidd.

Commerce, Hon. Philip Burdon.

Health, the Environment, and Research, Science and Technology, Hon. Simon Upton.

Police, Tourism, Recreation and Sport, Hon. John Banks.

Social Welfare, Women's Affairs, Hon. Jenny Shipley.

Defence, Local Government, Hon. Warren Cooper.

Justice, Disarmament and Arms Control, Arts and Culture, Hon. Douglas Graham.

Education, Hon. Dr Lockwood Smith.

Employment, Hon. Maurice McTigue.

Transport, Statistics, Lands, Hon. Rob Storey.

Maori Affairs, Hon. Winston Peters.

Conservation, Science (DSIR), Hon. Denis Marshall.

Housing, Energy, Hon. John Luxton.

Revenue, Customs, Hon. Wyatt Creech.

NEW ZEALAND HIGH COMMISSION
New Zealand House, Haymarket, SW1Y 4TQ
[071–930 8422]

High Commissioner, His Excellency Bryce Harland (1985).

Deputy High Commissioner, J. P. Larkindale.

Minister, D. Walker (*Commercial*).

Head, Defence Staff, Cdre J. G. Leonard.

LEGISLATURE

Parliament consists of a House of Representatives consisting of 97 members elected for three years. There are four Maori electorates. Women have been entitled to vote since 1893, and to be elected Members of the House of Representatives since the passing of the Women's Parliamentary Rights Act 1919. Following the General Election of October 27, 1990, the state of the parties in Parliament was National 67, Labour 29 and New Labour 1.

Speaker of the House of Representatives, Hon. Robin Gray.

JUDICATURE

The judicial system comprises a High Court and a Court of Appeal; also District Courts having both civil and criminal jurisdiction.

Chief Justice, Rt. Hon. Sir Thomas Eichelbaum, GBE, PC.

President, Court of Appeal, Rt. Hon. Sir Robin Cooke, KBE.

Judges, Rt. Hons. Sir Ivor Richardson; M. E. Casey; Hons. Hardie-Boys; Gault; McKay.

High Court Judges, Hons. Jeffries; Barker; Sinclair; Holland; Thorp; Greig; Wallace; Gallen; Tompkins; Henry; Heron; Williamson; Ellis; Smellie; Wylie; McGechan; Doogue; Tipping; Anderson; Gault; Robertson; Thomas; Temm; Fraser; Fisher; Penlington; Neazor.

High Court Administrative Divn., Hons. Jeffries; Holland; Tompkins.

Chief Judge, Labour Court, T. G. Goddard.

POLICE

On March 31, 1989 the strength of the New Zealand Police Force was 5,328 of all ranks, equivalent to 1 for every 625 of the population. Total police expenditure for the year 1988–89 was NZ$484,940,000.

DEFENCE

The Governor-General, representing the Crown, is Commander-in-Chief of the armed forces. Executive power, however, is vested in the Cabinet. The Chief of Defence Force (CDF) heads the New Zealand Defence Force (NZDF). The Chief of Naval Staff, Chief of General Staff and Chief of Air Staff are directly responsible to the CDF. The Secretary of Defence is the chief executive of the Defence Office, and the CDF and the Secretary of Defence are both directly responsible to the Minister of Defence.

Annual defence expenditure for the year 1989–90 was about 5 per cent of total net government expenditure. At August 31, 1989 the total number of armed forces personnel was 12,397.

FINANCE

Into the Consolidated Account (New Zealand's main public account) are paid the proceeds of income tax, goods and services tax, customs and excise duties and other taxes, also interest, profits from trading undertakings, and departmental receipts. Revenue from taxation is also paid into the National Roads Fund principally from a tax on motor spirits and registration and licence fees for motor vehicles.

Revenue and expenditure including the National Roads Fund for year ended March 31:

	1988	1989
Revenue	NZ$29,871·7m	NZ$32,150·6m
Expenditure (net)	30,476·8m	32,151·2m

Taxation receipts in 1988–89 for all purposes amounted to NZ$22, 863·9 million (an average of NZ$6,807 per head of population).

Gross expenditure includes:

	1988	1989
Debt services	NZ$6,945·7m	NZ$4,883·6m
Education	3,179·3m	3,637·9m
Health	3,397·1m	3,652·6m
Social welfare	7,190·8m	8,234·4m
Defence	1,278·5m	1,390·8m
Other	8,485·4m	10,351·9m
Total	30,476·8m	32,151·2m

BANKING

The New Zealand financial system comprises a central bank (the Reserve Bank of New Zealand), registered banks and a range of other financial institutions. The number of registered banks is presently 20.

The Reserve Bank is the sole issuer of notes and coin.

EDUCATION

Schools are free and attendance is compulsory between the ages of 6 and 15. At July 1988 there were 398,189 pupils attending public primary schools, and 12,053 pupils attending registered private primary

schools. The secondary education of boys and girls is carried on in 315 state secondary schools, 35 area high schools and 18 registered private secondary schools. The total number of pupils receiving full-time secondary education in July 1988 was 233,603 and in addition there were 103,646 students attending technical classes. Almost all the students attending technical classes are part-time. There are seven universities with a total of 72,313 students in 1988. The university system is co-ordinated by the University Grants Committee.

PRODUCTION AND INDUSTRY

Agricultural Production

	Year ended March	
	1986–87	1987–88
	NZ$(million)	
Gross output	6,902	7,352
Sheep	646	690
Wool	1,215	1,373
Cattle	974	935
Dairy products	1,130	1,294
Fruit, nuts, oilseeds	531	578
Agricultural services	474	538
Sales of live animals	607	590

Agricultural and Pastoral Production

	1988	1989
*Wheat, metric tons	206,000	135,000
*Wool, metric tons	346,000	341,000
†Butter, metric tons	242,000	246,000
†Cheese, metric tons	128,000	128,000
‡Stock Slaughtered—		
Lambs	30,414,000	30,302,000
Sheep	7,927,000	9,757,000
Cattle	2,222,000	2,289,000
Calves	981,000	876,000
Pigs	782,000	781,000

* Year ended June 30
† Year ended May 31
‡ Year ended September 30

Forestry.—The output of sawn timber for 1989 was 1,877,000 cubic metres, of which 1,802,000 cubic metres represented exotic varieties, mainly radiata pine.

Livestock.—Livestock on farms at June 30, 1989 included 3,302,377 dairy cattle, 4,526,056 beef cattle and 411,334 pigs. Sheep numbered 60,568,653.

Minerals.—Non-metallic minerals such as coal, clay, limestone and dolomite are both economically and industrially more important than metallic ones. Coal output in 1988 was 2,400,000 tonnes (provisional). Of the metals, the most important is ironsand. Natural gas deposits in Taranaki are being used for electricity generation and as a premium fuel, piped to all the major North Island centres.

TRADE

	1987–88	1988–89
Imports (v.f.d.)	NZ$10,625·1m	NZ$11,401·7m
Exports (f.o.b.)	12,451·5m	14,905·4m

Trade with UK

	1989	1990
Imports from UK	£399,295,000	£439,608,000
Exports to UK	436,772,000	483,615,000

New Zealand produce exported to the UK in the 12 months ending June 1989, included butter and cheese valued at NZ$292,702,000; wool NZ$133,280,000; lamb NZ$272,262,000; hides, skins and leather NZ$55,224,000.

COMMUNICATIONS

Railways.—The national railway system is owned and operated by the New Zealand Railways Corporation. In March 1989, there were 4,776 route km of Government railway in operation.

Motor Vehicles.—At March 31, 1988 there were 2,217,259 licensed motor vehicles.

Shipping.—During 1989 the vessels entered from overseas ports numbered 3,741 (gross tonnage 30,940,000) and those cleared for overseas 3,730 (gross tonnage 30,190,000).

Civil Aviation—Domestic flights in 1988 carried 4,125,000 passengers and 39,300 tonnes of freight. International flights carried 3,340,000 passengers, 127,981 tonnes of freight and 4,529 tonnes of mail.

BRITISH HIGH COMMISSION
Reserve Bank of New Zealand Building,
2 The Terrace (PO Box 1812), Wellington 1
[Wellington 4726-049]

High Commissioner, His Excellency David Joseph Moss, CMG (1990).

Deputy High Commissioner, I. C. Orr.

Defence Adviser, Capt. M. Matthews, RN.

First Secretaries, Mrs E. Blackwell (*Agriculture and Food*); P. Rogan (*Commercial*); J. R. Setterfield (*Chancery, Information*); R. Leadbeater (*Consular/ Management*).

British Council Representative, D. J. F. King.

BRITISH CHAMBER OF COMMERCE FOR AUSTRALIA AND NEW ZEALAND, PO Box 141, Manuka, ACT 2603, Australia; UK OFFICE, Suite 615, 6th Floor The Linen Hall, 162–168 Regent Street, W1R 5TB.

TERRITORIES

TOKELAU (OR UNION ISLANDS)

A group of atolls (Fakaofo, Nukunonu and Atafu) (population 1,690 at October 10, 1986), proclaimed part of New Zealand as from January 1, 1948.

THE ROSS DEPENDENCY

The Ross Dependency, placed under the jurisdiction of New Zealand by Order in Council dated July 30, 1923, is defined as all the islands and territories between 160° E. and 150° W. longitude which are situated south of the 60° S. parallel. The Ross Dependency includes Edward VII Land and portions of Victoria Land. Since 1957 a number of research stations have been established in the Dependency.

ASSOCIATED STATES

COOK ISLANDS

Included in the boundaries of New Zealand since June 1901, the group consists of the islands of Rarotonga, Aitutaki, Mangaia, Atiu, Mauke, Mitiaro, Manuae, Takutea, Palmerston, Penrhyn or Tongareva, Manihiki, Rakahanga, Suwarrow, Pukapuka or Danger and Nassau. The total population of the group was 17,185 at December 1, 1986. The chief industries of the Cook Islands are tourism, financial services and the production of fruit juice, clothing, copra, bananas, citrus fruit and pulp, and pearl shell. The trade is chiefly with New Zealand, Australia, Japan, the UK and the USA. The New Zealand Government continues to give financial aid to the Cook Islands.

The Queen has a representative on the islands, as does the New Zealand government. Since August 4, 1965, the islands have enjoyed complete internal self-government, executive power being in the hands of a Cabinet consisting of the Premier and five other ministers. The new Constitution Act was passed by the New Zealand Parliament in November 1964, but did not come into force until it had been endorsed by the 22-member Legislative Assembly of the Cook Islands, elected in April 1965.

The New Zealand citizenship of the Cook Islanders is embodied in the Constitution, and assurances have been given that the changed status of the islands will in no way affect the consideration of subsidies or the right of free entry into New Zealand for exports from the group.

HM Representative, Apenera Short, OBE.

New Zealand Representative, T. Caughley.

NIUE

The population of Niue was estimated at 2,267 at March 31, 1989.

A New Zealand Representative is stationed at Niue, which since October 1974 has been self-governing in free association with New Zealand, which is responsible for external affairs and defence, and continues to give financial aid. Executive power is in the hands of a Premier and a Cabinet of three drawn from the Assembly of 20 members. The Assembly is the supreme lawmaking body.

New Zealand Representative, K. Meyer.

NIGERIA
(Federal Republic of Nigeria)

AREA, POPULATION, ETC.—The Republic of Nigeria is situated on the west coast of Africa. It is bounded on the south by the Gulf of Guinea, on the west by the Republic of Benin, on the north by Niger and on the east by Cameroon. It has an area of 356,669 sq. miles (923,768 sq. km), with a population (UN estimate 1989) of 109,175,000. The population is almost entirely African. The main ethnic groups are Hausa/Fulani, Yoruba and Ibo, and the principal languages are English, Hausa, Yoruba and Ibo. Over half the population are Muslim, these being concentrated in the north and west. In the southern areas in particular there are many Christians.

A belt of mangrove swamp forest 10–60 miles in width lies along the entire coastline. North of this there is a zone 50–100 miles wide of tropical rain forest and oil-palms. North of this the country rises and the vegetation changes to open woodland and savanna. In the extreme north the country is semi-desert. There are few mountains, but in Northern Nigeria the central plateau rises to an average level of 4,000 feet. The Niger, Benue, and Cross are the main rivers.

The climate varies with the types of country described above, but Nigeria lies entirely within the tropics and temperatures are high. The rainy season is from about April to October; rainfall varies from under 25 inches a year in the extreme north to 172 inches on the coast line. During the dry season the *harmattan* wind blows from the desert; it is cool and laden with fine particles of dust.

CAPITAL.—ΨLagos, estimated population, 3,000,000. Other important towns are Ibadan, Kaduna, Kano, Benin City, Enugu and ΨPort Harcourt. Movement of Federal Ministries to a new capital at Abuja has begun.

CURRENCY.—Naira (N) of 100 kobo.

FLAG.—Three equal vertical bands, green, white and green.

NATIONAL ANTHEM.—Arise, O Compatriots.

NATIONAL DAY.—October 1 (Republic Day).

GOVERNMENT

The Federation of Nigeria attained independence as a member of the Commonwealth on October 1, 1960 and became a republic in 1963. On January 15, 1966 the military took power, suspended the Constitution and dissolved the legislature. In 1979 civil rule was restored under a new constitution similar to that of the United States after elections at National and State level. After similar elections in 1983 the new administration was removed by the military on December 31, this regime itself being overthrown in August 1985. A 28-member Armed Forces Ruling Council (AFRC) was sworn in on August 30; it currently has 19 members. It is the country's most senior decision-making body. The Council of Ministers is the third most senior body after the AFRC and the National Council of States, which comprises the 21 State Governors.

Originally regional in structure, the Federation was divided into 12 states in 1967. It was divided again into 19 states in 1976, and a further two states were created in 1987.

On May 3, 1989 Gen. Babangida promulgated the new draft constitution paving the way for a return to civilian rule by 1992. He also announced that a ban on political parties was to be lifted, leading to the formation in October 1989 of two new parties, the Social Democratic Party and the National Republican Convention. Local elections were held in December 1990.

Head of State, Commander-in-Chief of the Armed Forces, Chairman of the Armed Forces Ruling Council, Maj.-Gen. Ibrahim Babangida.
Vice-President, Vice-Adm. Augustus Aikhomu (retd.).

Council of Ministers
(as at November, 1990)

Agriculture and Natural Resources, Dr Shettima Mustapha.
Aviation, T. O. Graham-Douglas.
Budget and Planning, Chu Okongwu.
Communications, Olawale Adeniji-Ige.
Culture and Social Welfare, Maj.-Gen. Y. Y. Kure (retd.).
Defence and Chief of Defence Staff, Lt.-Gen. Sanni Abacha.
Education, Babs Fafunwa.
Employment, Labour and Productivity, Bonu Shariff Musa.
External Affairs, Maj.-Gen. Ike Nwachukwu (retd.).
Federal Capital Territory, Maj.-Gen. M. Gado Nasko.
Finance and Economic Planning, Abubakar Alhaji.
Health, Koye Ransome Kuti.
Industry, Air Vice-Marshal Mohammed Yahaya (retd.).
Information, Chief Alex Akinyele.
Internal Affairs, Maj.-Gen. A. B. Mamman (retd.).
Justice; Attorney-General, Prince Bola Ajibola.
Mines, Power and Steel, Air Vice-Marshal Nura Imam (retd.).
Petroleum Resources, Jibril Aminu.
Youth and Sports, Air Cmdre. Anthony Ikazobor (retd.).
Science and Technology, Gordian Ezekwe.
Trade, S. J. Ukpanah.
Transport, Cdre. Lamba Dung Gwom (retd.).
Works and Housing, Brig. M. T. Kontagora (retd.).
Special Duties, Tunji Olagunju.
Water Resources, Abubakar Hashidu.
Minister of State for External Affairs, Zakari Ibrahim.
Minister of State for Police Affairs, Sumaila Gwarzo.

NIGERIA HIGH COMMISSION
56–57 Fleet Street, EC4Y 1JU
[071–353 3776]

High Commissioner, His Excellency Mr George Dove-Edwin (1986).

EDUCATION

A programme was introduced in September 1976 intended to achieve universal primary education. Numbers of pupils in 1982–83 were: 15·4 million in primary schools, 3·5 million in secondary schools, 53,766 in polytechnics and 88,636 in universities There are 24 universities.

COMMUNICATIONS

The Nigerian railway system, which is controlled by the Nigerian Railway Corporation, is the most extensive in West Africa. There are 2,178 route miles of lines. The principal international airlines operating from Lagos, Kano and Port Harcourt bring Nigeria within about six hours of the Western European capitals. There are also services to other parts of Africa and to the United States. A network of internal air services connects the main centres The principal seaports are served by a number of shipping lines, including the Nigerian National Line A nationwide television and radio network is being developed, with each State eventually having its own television and radio station. There is a network of meteorological reporting stations.

PRODUCTION AND INDUSTRY

Nigeria was a predominantly agricultural country until the early 1970s with agriculture contributing over 60 per cent of export revenue and 45 per cent of GNP. Tin and calumbite mining on the Jos plateau, textiles and coal mining were also important. The major exports were ground nuts, palm products, tin, cocoa, rubber and timber. Recently oil has provided over 90 per cent of exports revenue and agricultural exports have greatly declined. Though agriculture still employs half the labour force it contributes only 20 per cent of GNP, exceeded by trading and oil. The construction sector is twice as large as the manufacturing sector and industries dependent on imported raw materials such as vehicle assembly have faltered recently. Three oil refineries are in operation at Port Harcourt, Warri and Kaduna. A steel plant has been opened near Warri and a larger one is being completed at Ajaokuta. Other projects include natural gas liquifaction, petro-chemicals, fertilizers and several power stations plus the Abuja Federal Capital. Several large irrigation schemes have been completed and more are planned.

TRADE

Oil revenues have been falling since 1981 and are now restricted by an OPEC production quota and lower prices to half their peak level. In March 1982 imports curbs and payments restrictions were introduced but exchange reserves fell and debts increased. Austerity measures were introduced, and continue, while the present Government attempts to stimulate greater self-reliance in the economy by encouraging non-oil exports and the use of local rather than imported raw materials.

Trade with UK

	1989	1990
Imports from UK ...	£388,777,000	£499,838,000
Exports to UK	129,406,000	297,436,000

BRITISH HIGH COMMISSION
11 Eleke Crescent, Victoria Island, Lagos
[Lagos 619531]

High Commissioner, His Excellency Christopher Macrae, CMG (1991).

British Council Representative, Jim Whittell, OBE, 11 Kingsway Road, Ikoyi (PO Box 3702), Lagos. Branch offices at *Enugu, Kaduna* and *Kano City.*

PAKISTAN
(Islami Jamhuriya-e-Pakistan)

AREA, POPULATION, ETC.—The Islamic Republic of Pakistan is situated in the north-west of the Indian sub-continent, bordered by Iran, Afghanistan, China, the disputed territory of Kashmir, and India. It covers a total area of 803,950 sq. km. Running through Pakistan are five great rivers, the Indus, Jhelum, Chenab, Ravi and Sutlej. The upper reaches of these rivers are in Kashmir, and their sources in the Himalayas.

The Census in 1981 showed a population figure of 83,780,000 (1989 UN estimate, 108,678,000). Of these, about 95 per cent are Muslims, about 1 per cent Hindus, 3·5 per cent Christians, and 0·5 per cent Buddhists.

CAPITAL.—Islamabad, population 350,000. ΨKarachi (estimated population 6,500,000) is the largest city and seaport; Lahore has a population of about 3,500,000.

CURRENCY.—Pakistan rupee of 100 paisa.

FLAG.—Dark green ground, with white vertical stripes at the mast, the green portion bearing a white crescent in the centre and a five-pointed heraldic star.

NATIONAL ANTHEM.—Quami Tarana.

NATIONAL DAYS.—March 23 (Pakistan Day), August 14 (Independence Day).

GOVERNMENT

Pakistan was constituted as a Dominion under the Indian Independence Act 1947, which received Royal Assent on July 18, 1947. Until 1972 when East Pakistan seceded, Pakistan consisted of two geographical units, West and East Pakistan, which were separated by about 1,100 miles of Indian territory.

Pakistan became a Republic on March 23, 1956, when a Parliamentary Constitution came into force. On October 7, 1958, however, this Constitution was abrogated and Pakistan came under martial law.

The first general elections held in Pakistan on a basis of 'one man, one vote', were held in December 1970 and January 1971. The Awami League in East Pakistan, led by Sheikh Mujibur Rahman, and the Pakistan People's Party in West Pakistan, led by Zulfikar Ali Bhutto, won large majorities. Following the elections there was total disagreement between the two main parties on the question of a new Constitution for Pakistan, Sheikh Mujibur insisting on complete autonomy for East Pakistan. The proposed opening of the National Assembly at Dacca on March 25, 1971, was postponed and civil war broke out. East Pakistan seceded by unilateral declaration the following day. Fighting continued until December 1971 when a ceasefire was arranged, and 'The Democratic Government of Bangladesh' was formally proclaimed on April 17, 1972.

Following general elections in March 1977 and allegations of vote-rigging, the armed forces under Gen. Zia-ul-Haq assumed power on July 5, 1977 and imposed martial law throughout the country. The military government scheduled new general elections for October 1977, but these were postponed. Gen. Zia declared himself President on September 16, 1978. In December 1984 Gen. Zia got a five-year mandate as a civilian President through a national referendum. Martial law was lifted on December 30, 1985. On May 29, 1988, Zia dissolved the National Assembly and the Cabinet and announced fresh elections. A caretaker cabinet was announced on June 9. Zia was killed in a plane crash on August 17, 1988, and the Senate Chairman, Ghulam Ishaq Khan, assumed the office of President. The Pakistan People's Party won the election to the National Assembly and Benazir Bhutto became Prime Minister on December 2, 1988. The legislature then elected President Ghulam Ishaq Khan as the President. In August 1990, the President dissolved the National Assembly and dismissed the Bhutto cabinet. Elections were held on October 24, 1990 and won by the Islamic Democratic Alliance, led by Mian Muhammad Nawaz Sharif.

President, Ghulam Ishaq Khan, *elected* December 12, 1988 *for a four-year term.*

Prime Minister, Minister of Defence, Foreign Affairs, Mian Muhammad Nawaz Sharif.

Ministers
(as at June 30, 1991)

Communications, Ghulam Murtaza Khan Jatoi.
Railways, Mir Hazar Khan Bijarani.
Production, Islam Nabi.
Housing and Works, Syed Tariq Mahmood.
Narcotics Control, Rana Chandar Singh.
Youth Affairs, Syed Ali Gohar Shah.
Finance and Economic Affairs, Sartaj Aziz.
Environment and Urban Affairs, Sardar Yaqub Khan Nasser.
Industries, Chaudhry Shujat Hussain.
Local Government and Rural Development, vacant.
Education, Syed Fakhar Imam.
Commerce, Malik Muhammad Naeem Khan.
Petroleum and Natural Resources, Chaudhry Nisar Ali Khan.
Planning and Development, Chaudhry Hamid Nasir Chatta.
Health, Syed Tasneem Nawaz Gardezi.
Food and Agriculture, Lt.-Gen. Abdul Majid Malik (retd.).
Labour, Manpower and Overseas Pakistanis, Sardar Mehtab Abbasi.
Adviser to the Prime Minister, Roedad Khan.
Adviser to the Prime Minister on Information and Broadcasting, Sheikh Rashid Ahmed.
Minister of State for Law, Justice and Parliamentary Affairs, Ch. Amir Hussain.
Minister of State for Sports, Mohammad Ajmal Khan.
Adviser to the Prime Minister for Population Planning, Syeda Abida Hussain.

HIGH COMMISSION FOR PAKISTAN
35 Lowndes Square, SW1X 9JN
[071–235 2044]

High Commissioner, His Excellency Humayun M. Khan (1990).

EDUCATION

Formal education in Pakistan is organized into five stages. These are five years of primary education (5–9 years), three years of middle or lower secondary (general or vocational), two years of upper secondary, two years of higher secondary (intermediate) and two to five years of higher education in colleges and universities. Education is free to upper secondary level. It was expected that primary education would become universal for boys by mid-1985 and for girls by mid-1988.

At primary level enrolment had increased to 6·5 million in 1984–85, and the number of schools to 75,000. At the middle level enrolment had increased to 1·7 million in 1984–85, and the number of schools to 6,200. At the upper secondary level enrolment increased to 570,000 in 1984–85.

Provincial governments are responsible for the total financial support of the government institutions and for grants to non-government institutions. But policy making is authorized by the national government, which makes annual grants. In 1986, 24 per cent of adults were estimated as being literate.

COMMUNICATIONS

The main seaport is Karachi. The main airport at Karachi occupies an important position on international trunk routes and is equipped with modern facilities and equipment. Pakistan International Airlines operates air services between the principal cities within the country as well as abroad.

Post and telegraph facilities are available to every country in the world.

FINANCE

The 1991–92 Budget anticipated net federal revenues of Rs.258·3 billion.

PRODUCTION

Pakistan's economy is chiefly based on agriculture. The principal crops are cotton, rice, wheat, sugar cane, maize and tobacco. There are large deposits of rock salt. Pakistan has one of the longest irrigation systems in the world. The total area irrigated is 33 million acres.

Pakistan also produces hides and skins, leather, wool, fertilizers, paints and varnishes, soda ash, paper, cement, fish, carpets, sports goods, surgical appliances and engineering goods, including switch-gear, transformers, cables and wires.

TRADE

Pakistan imported manufactured goods and raw materials to the value of US$5,792 million in 1986–87 and exported mainly agricultural products valued at US$3,498 million. Principal imports are petroleum products, machinery, fertilizers, transport equipment, edible oils, chemicals and ferrous metals. Principal exports are raw cotton, cotton yarn and cloth, carpets, rice, petroleum products, synthetic textiles, leather, and fish.

Trade with UK

	1989	1990
Imports from UK	£233,532,000	£251,841,000
Exports to UK	216,110,000	236,448,000

BRITISH HIGH COMMISSION
Diplomatic Enclave, Ramna 5,
PO Box 1122, Islamabad
[Islamabad 822131/5]

High Commissioner, His Excellency Sir Nicholas Barrington, KCMG, CVO (1987).

There is a British Consulate-General at *Karachi* and a Consulate at *Lahore*.

British Council Representative, L. Phillips, PO Box 1135, Islamabad. There are offices at *Karachi, Lahore* and *Peshawar*.

PAPUA NEW GUINEA

AREA, POPULATION, ETC.—Papua New Guinea extends from the equator to Cape Baganowa in the Louisiade Archipelago at 11° S. latitude and from the border with Irian Jaya to 160° E. longitude. The total area of Papua New Guinea is 178,260 sq. miles, (461,691 sq. km), of which approximately 152,420 sq. miles form the mainland, on the island of New Guinea. The country has many island groups, principally the Bismarck Archipelago, a portion of the Solomon Islands, the Trobriands, the D'Entrecasteaux Islands and the Louisade Archipelago. The main islands of the Bismarck Archipelago are New Britain, New Ireland and Manus. Bougainville is the largest of the Solomon Islands within Papua New Guinea.

Papua New Guinea lies within the tropics and has a typically monsoonal climate. Temperature and humidity are uniformly high throughout the year.

The average rainfall is about 80 inches per year but there are wide variations—from 47 inches at Port Moresby to over 200 inches in mountainous western areas.

The population in 1989 (UN estimate) was 3,593,000

CAPITAL.—ΨPort Moresby. Estimated population (1985), 139,300. Other major towns are Lae, Rabaul Madang, Wewak, Goroka and Mount Hagen.

CURRENCY.—Kina (K) of 100 toea.

FLAG.—A rectangle divided diagonally from the top of the hoist to the bottom of the fly, the upper segment scarlet and containing a soaring yellow bird of paradise. The lower segment is black charged with five white five-pointed stars representing the Southern Cross.

NATIONAL ANTHEM.—Arise All You Sons.

NATIONAL DAY.—September 16 (Independence Day).

GOVERNMENT

New Guinea was sighted by Portuguese and Spanish navigators in the early sixteenth century, but remained largely isolated from the rest of the world. In 1884 a British Protectorate was proclaimed over the southern coast of New Guinea (Papua) and the adjacent islands. British New Guinea, as the Protectorate was called, was annexed outright in 1888. In 1906 the Territory of British New Guinea was placed under the authority of the Commonwealth of Australia. Also in 1884 Germany had formally taken possession of certain northern areas, which later came to be known as the Trust Territory of New Guinea. In 1914 the German areas were occupied by Australian troops and remained under military administration until 1921, when the League of Nations conferred on Australia a mandate for their government.

New Guinea was administered under the Mandate and Papua under the Papua Act until the invasion by the Japanese in 1942 when the civil administration was suspended until the surrender of the Japanese in 1945.

The first House of Assembly for the whole country met in 1964 and included an elected majority and ten nominated official members. After 1970 there was a gradual assumption of powers by the Papua New Guinea Government, culminating in formal self-government in December 1973. Final reserve powers held by Australia over defence and foreign relations were relinquished to Papua New Guinea in March 1975, and Papua New Guinea achieved full independence on September 16, 1975.

Elections are held every five years. The Parliament comprises 109 elected Members, 20 from Regional electorates, the remainder from Open electorates. There are 19 provinces, which have their own provincial governments with certain legislative and administrative powers.

A secessionist movement, the Bougainville Revolutionary Army (BRA), began an insurrection on Bougainville in 1989. In March 1990 the Papua New Guinean security forces withdrew from the island and the BRA declared an independent republic in May 1990. In January 1991, a peace accord was signed between the two sides in Honoria, the Solomon Islands; the question of Bougainville's future status was deferred.

Governor General, His Excellency Sir Serei Eri, GCMG.

National Executive Council
(as at November, 1990)

Prime Minister, Rt. Hon. Rabbie Namaliu.
Deputy PM and Minister for Public Service, Ted Diro.
Finance and Planning, Paul Pora.
Civil Aviation, Bernard Vogae.

Communications, Brown Sinamoi, CMG.
Labour and Employment, Tony Ila.
Justice, Bernard Narokobi.
Lands, Kala Swokin.
Police, Mathias Ijape.
Provincial Affairs, John Momis.
Administrative Services, Paul Kamod.
Education, Jack Genia.
Environment and Conservation, Jim Yer Waim.
Foreign Affairs, Rt. Hon. Sir Michael Somare, CH.
Forests, Karl Stack.
Health, Robert Suckling.
Home Affairs, Mathew Bendumb.
Defence, Arnold Marsipal.
Culture and Tourism, G. Beona.
Trade and Industry, Galera Kwarara.
Housing, Michael Singan.
Minerals and Energy, Patterson Lowa.
Corrective Institutions, Tom Pais.
Transport, Anthony Temu.
Works, Paul Wanjik.
Fisheries and Marine Resources, Akoka Doi.
Agriculture and Livestock, Tenda Lau.
Ministers of State Assisting the Prime Minister, John Giheno; Jack Genia.

PAPUA NEW GUINEA HIGH COMMISSION
3rd Floor, 14 Waterloo Place, SW1Y 4AR
[071–930 0922/7]

High Commissioner, His Excellency Noel Lebi (1991).

COMMUNICATIONS

Road communications are very limited, the most important road being that linking Lae with the populous highlands.

Air Niugini (the national airline) and Qantas operate regular air services between Port Moresby and Australia. Air Niugini also operates services to Manila (Philippines), Honiara (Solomon Islands), Jayapura (Indonesia), Honolulu and Singapore. Internal air services are operated by Air Niugini, Douglas Airways, and Talair.

Several shipping companies operate cargo services between Papua New Guinea and Australia, Europe, the Far East and USA. There are very limited cargo and passenger services between Papua New Guinea main ports, outports, plantations and missions.

Papua New Guinea is linked by international cable to Australia, Guam, Hong Kong, Kota Kinabalu, the Far East and USA. Telecommunications are widely available.

ECONOMY

Until the 1970s the Papua New Guinea economy was based almost entirely on agriculture. At the beginning of the 20th century copra plantations formed the basis of the cash economy. Further crops which have been introduced over the years are cocoa, tea, coffee, palm oil, rubber, groundnuts, spices and timber. A variety of commercial agricultural developments now co-exist with the traditional informal rural economy. Government expenditure is still reliant on Australian budgetary support, to the extent of just under 30 per cent in 1983.

In 1972, Bougainville Copper Pty Ltd (BCL) began mining in the North Solomons Province, producing copper, silver and gold. The Bougainville Copper Mine closed indefinitely in May 1989 but is now scheduled to reopen. There are extensive mineral deposits throughout Papua New Guinea, including nickel, chromite, bauxite and possibly commercial deposits of oil and gas. The most important new development is the exploitation of large copper and gold deposits on the Ok Tedi, in the Western Province.

In 1984 the Papua New Guinea economy was influenced by good prices for agricultural commodities, offset by low prices for copper and gold. New developments to promote export crops and increase employment, typically involving foreign investment, are planned for the future.

Industry includes processing of primary products, and brewing, bottling and packaging, paint, plywood, and metal manufacturing and the construction industries.

Although the formal economy is still dominated by non-Papua New Guineans, the participation of Papua New Guineans is increasing.

Trade with UK

	1989	1990
Imports from UK	£15,822,000	£8,793,000
Exports to UK	47,839,000	34,849,000

BRITISH HIGH COMMISSION
PO Box 4778, Boroko, Port Moresby
[Port Moresby 212500]

High Commissioner, His Excellency John Westgarth Guy, OBE (1991).

ST CHRISTOPHER AND NEVIS
(The Federation of St Christopher and Nevis)

The State of St Christopher and Nevis is located at the northern end of the Eastern Caribbean. It comprises the islands of St Christopher (St Kitts) (68 sq. miles) and Nevis (36 sq. miles); combined population (UN estimate 1989) 50,000.

St Christopher, lat. 17° 18′ N. and long. 62° 48′ W. was the first island in the British West Indies to be colonized (1623). The central area of the island is forest-clad and mountainous, rising to the 3,792 ft. Mount Liamuiga.

Nevis, lat. 17° 10′ N. and long. 62° 35′ W. is separated from the southern tip of St Christopher by a strait two miles wide and is dominated by the central Nevis Peak, 3,232 ft.

CAPITAL—ΨBasseterre (estimated population, 15,000). Chief town of Nevis is ΨCharlestown (population 1,200), which is a port of entry.

CURRENCY.—East Caribbean dollar (EC$) of 100 cents.

FLAG—Three diagonal bands, green, black and red; each colour separated by a stripe of yellow. Two white stars on the black band.

NATIONAL ANTHEM.—Oh Land of Beauty.

NATIONAL DAY.—September 19 (Independence Day).

GOVERNMENT

The Territory of St Christopher and Nevis became a State in Association with Britain on February 27, 1967. The State of St Christopher and Nevis became an independent nation on September 19, 1983, with a new constitution under which Great Britain relinquished its responsibility for defence and external affairs. Under the new Constitution, The Queen is Head of State, represented in the islands by the Governor General. There is a central Cabinet Government with a Ministerial system, the Head of which is the Prime Minister of St Christopher and Nevis, and a National Assembly located on St Christopher. The National Assembly is composed of the Speaker, three senators, nominated by the Prime Minister and the Leader of the Opposition, and 11 elected representatives. On Nevis there is a Nevis Island Administration, the Head being styled Premier of Nevis, and a Nevis Island Assembly of five elected and three nominated members.

Governor General, His Excellency Sir Clement Athelston Arrindell, GCMG, GCVO, QC (1983).

Cabinet
(as at June 5, 1991)

Prime Minister and Minister of Finance, Home Affairs and Foreign Affairs, Rt. Hon. Dr Kennedy A. Simmonds.
Deputy PM and Minister of Labour and Tourism, Hon. Michael O. Powell.
Education, Youth and Community Affairs, Communications, Works and Community Affairs, Communications, Works and Public Utilities, Hon. Sydney E. Morris.
Agriculture, Lands, Housing and Development, Hon. Hugh C. Heyliger.
Health and Women's Affairs, Hon. Constance Mitcham.
Trade and Industry, Hon. Fitzroy P. Jones.
In Ministry of Finance, Hon. Richard L. Caines.
Attorney-General, Hon. S. W. Tapley Seaton, CVO.
Cabinet Secretary, C. Farier.

St Kitts High Commission
10 Kensington Court, W8 5DL
[071-937 9522]

High Commissioner for the Eastern Caribbean States, His Excellency Richard Gunn (1987).

Finance

	1989	1990
Revenue	EC$91,508,604	EC$96,900,000
Expenditure	84,427,961	94,100,000

Economy

The economy of the islands has been based on sugar for over three centuries. Tourism and light industry are now being developed. The economy of Nevis centres on small peasant farmers, but a sea-island cotton industry is being developed for export.

Communications

Basseterre is a port of registry and has deep water harbour facilities. Golden Rock airport, on St Kitts, can take most large jet aircraft; Newcastle airstrip on Nevis can take small aircraft and has night landing facilities.
The sea ferry route from Basseterre to Charlestown is 11 miles.

Trade with UK

	1989	1990
Imports from UK	£5,887,000	£6,477,000
Exports to UK	4,866,000	4,513,000

British Representative, (resides at Antigua), Ian Marsh.

ST LUCIA

St Lucia, the second largest of the Windward group, situated in 13° 54′ N. lat. and 60° 50′ W. long., at a distance of about 21 miles N. of St Vincent, and 24 miles S. of Martinique, is 27 miles in length, with an extreme breadth of 14 miles. It comprises an area of 238 sq. miles (616 sq. km), with an estimated population (1989) of 148,000. It possesses perhaps the most interesting history of all the smaller islands. Fights raged hotly around it, and it constantly changed hands between the English and the French. It is mountainous, its highest point being Mt. Gimie (3,145 ft) and for the most part it is covered with forest and tropical vegetation.

CAPITAL.—ΨCastries (estimated population 198: 55,000) is recognized as being one of the finest por in the West Indies on account of its reputation as safe anchorage in the hurricane season.
CURRENCY.—East Caribbean dollar (EC$) of 10 cents.
FLAG.—Blue, bearing in centre a device of yello over black over white triangles having a commo base.
NATIONAL ANTHEM.—Sons and Daughters of Sair Lucia.
NATIONAL DAY.—February 22 (Independence Day

Government

St Lucia became independent within the Common wealth on February 22, 1979. The Head of State i The Queen, represented in the island by a St Lucia Governor General, and there is a bicameral legisla ture. The Senate has 11 members, six appointed b the ruling party, three by the Opposition and two b the Governor General. The House of Assembly which has a life of five years, has 17 elected Member and a Speaker, who may be elected from outside th House.

Acting Governor General, His Excellency Stanislau James, CMG, OBE.

Cabinet
(as at June 5, 1991)

Prime Minister, Minister of Finance, Foreign Affairs Development and Home Affairs, Rt. Hon. John G M. Compton.
Deputy PM and Minister of Trade, Industry an Tourism, Hon. George Mallet.
Communications, Works and Transport, Hon. Gre gory Avril.
Health, Housing, Information and Broadcasting, Hor Romanus Lansiquot.
Youth, Community Development, Social Affairs, Spor Hon. Stephenson King.
Attorney-General and Minister for Legal Affairs, Hor Senator Parry Husbands.
Agriculture, Lands, Fisheries and Co-operatives, Hor Ferdinand Henry.
Education and Culture, Hon. Louis George.

St Lucia High Commission
10 Kensington Court, W8 5DL.
[071-937 9522]

High Commissioner for the Eastern Caribbean State: His Excellency Richard Gunn (1987).

Economy

The economy is mainly agrarian, with manufactur ing based on the processing of agricultural product Principal crops are bananas, coconuts, cocoa, man goes, avocado pears, breadfruit, spices, root crop such as cassava and yams, and citrus fruit. Attempt are being made to diversify the economy, in particula through greater industrialization; tourism is also o increasing importance, with 204,000 visitors to th island in 1989.
The principal exports are bananas, coconut prod ucts (copra, edible oils, soap), cardboard boxes, beer and textile manufactures. The chief imports ar flour, meat, machinery, building materials, moto vehicles, cotton piece goods, petroleum and fertilizers

Trade with UK

	1989	1990
Imports from UK	£19,601,000	£17,573,00
Exports to UK	48,746,000	55,737,00

OFFICE OF THE BRITISH HIGH COMMISSION
Columbus Square, PO Box 227, Castries
[Castries 22484]

High Commissioner, (resides at Bridgetown, Barbados).
Resident Representative, P. T. Rouse, MBE.

ST VINCENT
AND THE GRENADINES

The territory of the State of St Vincent includes certain of the Grenadines, a chain of small islands stretching 40 miles across the Caribbean Sea between Grenada and St Vincent, some of the larger of which are Bequia, Canouan, Mayreau, Mustique, Union Island, Petit St Vincent and Prune Island. The whole territory extends 150 sq. miles (388 sq. km).

The main island, St Vincent, is situated between 13° 6' and 14° 35' N. latitude and 61° 6' and 61° 20' W. longitude, approximately 21 miles south-west of St Lucia and 100 miles west of Barbados. The island is 18 miles long and 11 miles wide at its extremities comprising an area of 133 sq. miles (344 sq. km), and a population (1989 UN estimate) of 110,000.

CAPITAL.—ΨKingstown, estimated population 33,694.

CURRENCY.—East Caribbean dollar (EC$) of 100 cents.

FLAG.—Three vertical bands, of blue, yellow and green, with three green diamonds in the shape of a 'V' mounted on the yellow band.

NATIONAL ANTHEM.—St Vincent, Land So Beautiful.

NATIONAL DAY.—October 27 (Independence Day).

GOVERNMENT

St Vincent was discovered by Christopher Columbus in 1498. It was granted by Charles I to the Earl of Carlisle in 1627 and after subsequent grants and a series of occupations alternately by the French and English, it was finally restored to Britain in 1783.

St Vincent achieved full independence within the Commonwealth as St Vincent and the Grenadines on October 27, 1979.

St Vincent has a constitution under which there is a Governor General who is Her Majesty's Representative. Except where otherwise provided, the Governor General is required to act in accordance with the advice of the Prime Minister.

The House of Assembly consists of 15 elected members and four Senators appointed by the Government and two by the Opposition. It is presided over by a Speaker elected by the House from within or without it. All 15 seats were won by the governing New Democratic Party at the election held on May 16, 1989.

Governor-General, His Excellency Sir David Jack, GCMG, MBE, *sworn in* September 20, 1989.

Cabinet
(as at April, 1991)

Prime Minister, Minister of Finance and Foreign Affairs, Rt. Hon. James Mitchell.
Attorney-General and Minister of Justice, Hon. Parnell Campbell, CVO.
Culture, Education, Youth and Women's Affairs, Hon. John Horne.
Agriculture, Industry and Labour, Hon. Allan Cruickshank.
Trade and Tourism, Hon. Herbert Young.
Health and the Environment, Hon. Burton Williams.

Housing, Local Government, Community Development and Social Welfare, Hon. Louis Jones.
Communications and Works, Hon. Jeremiah Scott.
Ministers of State, Hon. Mrs Yvonne Gibson (*Education, Youth and Women's Affairs*); Hon. Jonathan Peters (*Foreign Affairs*); Stuart Nanton (*Trade and Tourism*).

ST VINCENT AND THE GRENADINES
HIGH COMMISSION
10 Kensington Court, W8 5DL
[071-937 9522]

High Commissioner for the Eastern Caribbean States, His Excellency Richard Gunn (1987).

ECONOMY

This is based mainly on agriculture but the tourist and manufacturing industries have been expanding. The main products are bananas, arrowroot, coconuts, cocoa, spices and various kinds of food crops. The main imports are foodstuffs (meat, rice, beverages), textiles, lumber, cement and other building materials, fertilizers, motor vehicles and fuel.

Trade with UK

	1989	1990
Imports from UK	£11,075,000	£9,514,000
Exports to UK	31,570,000	37,906,000

OFFICE OF THE BRITISH HIGH COMMISSION
Granby Street (PO Box 132), Kingstown
[St Vincent 71701]

High Commissioner, (resides at Bridgetown, Barbados).
Resident Representative, G. Greaves.

SEYCHELLES
(The Republic of Seychelles)

The Republic of Seychelles, in the Indian Ocean, consists of 115 islands with a total land area of 176 sq. miles, spread over 400,000 square miles of ocean. There is a relatively compact granitic group, 32 islands in all, with high hills and mountains (highest point about 2,972 ft.), of which Mahé is the largest and most populated (90 per cent of the population live on Mahé; and the outlying coralline group, for the most part only a little above sea-level. Although only 4° S. of the Equator, the climate is pleasant though tropical. The population was estimated (mid 1990) to be 67,378.

CAPITAL.—ΨVictoria (population, 1982, 24,733), on the north-east side of Mahé.

CURRENCY.—Seychelles rupee (Rs) of 100 cents.

FLAG.—Red over green, divided by wavy white band.

NATIONAL ANTHEM.—Fyer Seselwa (Proud Seychellois).

NATIONAL DAY.—June 5.

GOVERNMENT

Proclaimed as French territory in 1756, the Mahé group began to be settled as a dependency of Mauritius from 1770, was captured by a British ship in 1794, changed hands several times between 1803 and 1814, when it was finally assigned to Great Britain. By Letters Patent of September, 1903, these islands, together with the coralline group, were formed into a separate Colony. On June 29, 1976, the islands became an independent republic within the Commonwealth. A coup d'état took place on June 5, 1977.

A new constitution making Seychelles a one-party

state came into force in June 1979. The executive power lies with the President, who is elected by universal suffrage for a five year term. Legislative power lies with the President and the People's Assembly which has 23 elected members and two nominated by the President.

President, France Albert René, *assumed office* June 5, 1977; *elected* June 26, 1979; *re-elected* June 18, 1984, and June 12, 1989.

Council of Ministers
(as at July 18, 1991)

Defence, Environment, Legal Affairs, Industry, The President.
Finance, James Michel.
Tourism and Transport, Jacques Hodoul.
Administration and Manpower, Joseph Belmont.
Community Development, Esme Jumeau.
Planning and External Relations, Danielle de St Jorre.
Health, Ralph Adam.
Agriculture and Fisheries, Jeremie Bonnelame.
Employment and Social Affairs, William Herminie.
Education, Simone Testa.
Information, Culture and Sports, Sylvette Frichot.

SEYCHELLES HIGH COMMISSION
Box No. 4PE, 111 Baker Street, 2nd Floor, Eros House, W1M 1FE
[071–224 1660]

Acting High Commissioner, Sylvester Radegonde.

ECONOMY

The economy is based on tourism, fishing, small-scale agriculture and manufacturing, and the re-export of fuel for aircraft and ships.

Deep sea tuna fishing by foreign fleets under licence, improved trans-shipment and other port facilities at Victoria, exports from a tuna canning factory opened in 1987 and the export of fresh and frozen fish, attract growing revenues.

TRADE

	1989	1990
Imports	Rs.925,771,000	Rs.991,500,000
Exports	67,789,000	73,200,000
Re-exports	109,407,000	131,200,000

The principal imports are foodstuffs, beverages, tobacco, mineral fuels, manufactured items, building materials, machinery and transport equipment.

Trade with UK

	1989	1990
Imports from UK	£10,741,000	£14,955,000
Exports to UK	993,000	8,353,000

BRITISH HIGH COMMISSION
Victoria House, PO Box 161,
Victoria, Mahé
[Victoria 23225]

High Commissioner, His Excellency Guy William Pulbrook Hart, OBE (1989).

SIERRA LEONE
(The Republic of Sierra Leone)

AREA, POPULATION, ETC.—Sierra Leone, with a total land area of 27,699 sq. miles (71,740 sq. km.), is on the west coast of Africa, between Guinea and Liberia. A Census of December 1985 put the population at 3,700,000. The 1989 UN estimate was 4,047,000. The southern half of Sierra Leone is inhabited by peoples whose languages fall into the Mende group; the northern half by the Temne, and smaller groups such as the Limba, Loko, Koranko and Susu.

CAPITAL.—ΨFreetown (population at 1985 Census, 470,000).

CURRENCY.—Leone (Le) of 100 cents.

FLAG.—Three horizontal stripes of leaf green, white and cobalt blue.

NATIONAL ANTHEM.—High We Exalt Thee, Realm of the Free.

NATIONAL DAY.—April 27 (Independence Day).

GOVERNMENT

The origins of the country date back to the late 18th century when a project was begun to settle destitute Africans from England on Freetown peninsula. In 1808 the settlement was declared a Crown Colony and became the main base in West Africa for enforcing the 1807 Act outlawing the slave trade. The Colony was also used as a settlement for Africans from North America and the West Indies, and great numbers of Africans rescued from slave ships also settled there.

In 1896 a Protectorate was declared over the hinterland. In 1951 a new Constitution was set up that united the colony of Freetown and the Protectorate and on April 27, 1961 Sierra Leone became a fully independent state within the Commonwealth. On April 19, 1971 a Republican Constitution was adopted and Dr Siaka Stevens became the first Executive President. In June 1978 Sierra Leone became a one-party state, following approval by Parliament and a Referendum. The first General Election under the one party system was held on May 1, 1982. The Parliament comprises 105 elected members and ten Paramount Chiefs, plus ten nominated members.

The government has come under increasing pressure to introduce political reform.

President, His Excellency Maj.-Gen. Joseph Saidu Momoh, *sworn in* November 28, 1985.

Cabinet
(as at 1991)

President and Minister of Defence with responsibility for Public Services, His Excellency Maj.-Gen. J. S. Momoh.
First Vice-President, Hon. Abu Bakarr Kamara.
Second Vice-President, Hon. Salia Jusu Sheriff.
Finance, Hon. Tommy Taylor-Morgan.
Attorney-General and Minister of Justice, Hon. Dr Abdulai Conteh.
Foreign Affairs, Hon. Abdul Karim Koroma.
Economic Planning and National Development, Hon. Dr Sheka Kanu.
Agriculture, Natural Resources and Forestry, Hon. M. O. Bash-Taqi.
Trade, Hon. Joseph Bandabla Dauda.
Education, Cultural Affairs and Sports, Hon. Dr Moses Dumbuya.
Transport and Communications, Hon. Philipson Kamara.
Mines, Hon. Birch Conteh.
Health, Hon. Dr Wiltshire Johnson.
Works, Hon. J. E. Laverse.
Energy and Power, Hon. Dr Shekou Sesay.
Information and Broadcasting, Hon. V. J. V. Mambu.
Tourism, Hon. Abdul Iscandari.
Internal Affairs, Hon. Ahmed Sesay.
Rural Development, Social Services and Youth, Hon. Alhaji Musa Kabia.
Industry and State Enterprises, Hon. Ben Kanu.
Labour, Hon. M. L. Sidique.
Lands, Housing and Environment, Hon. Dominic Musa.

Ministers of State, Hon. E. R. Ndomahina (*Leader of the House*); Hon. Maj.-Gen. M. Sheku Tarawallie (*Force Cdr.*); Hon. James Bambay Kamara (*Inspector General of Police*); Hon. E. T. Kamara (*Party Affairs*).

SIERRA LEONE HIGH COMMISSION
33 Portland Place, W1N 3AG
[071–636 6483]

High Commissioner, His Excellency Caleb B. Aubee (1987).

COMMUNICATIONS

Since the phasing out of the railway system in 1974 the road network has been developed considerably and there are now 5,000 miles of roads in the country, over 2,000 miles being surfaced. A bridge has been constructed over the Mano River linking Sierra Leone and Liberia.

The Freetown international airport is situated at Lungi, across the Sierra Leone River from Freetown. The main port is Freetown, which has one of the largest natural harbours in the world, and where there is a deep water quay providing about six berths for medium sized ships. There are smaller ports at Pepel, Bonthe and Niti.

Radio is operated by the Department of Broadcasting of the Sierra Leone Government. There are two shortwave transmitting and receiving stations in Freetown. Broadcasts are made in several of the more important indigenous languages in addition to English. There is also a weekly broadcast in French.

EDUCATION

In 1989 there were 2,554 primary schools in Sierra Leone and 201 secondary schools. Technical education is provided in the two Government Technical Institutes, situated in Freetown and Kenema, in two Trade Centres and in the technical training establishments of the mining companies. Teacher training is carried out at the university, six colleges in the Provinces and in the Milton Margai Training College near Freetown. The University of Sierra Leone (1967), consists of Fourah Bay College (1827), the Institute of Public Administration and Management (1980), the College of Medicine and Allied Health Sciences (1988) and Njala University College (1964).

PRODUCTION AND TRADE

On the Freetown peninsula, farming is largely confined to the production of cassava and garden crops, such as maize and vegetables, for local consumption. In the hinterland, the principal agricultural product is rice, which is the staple food of the country, and cash crops such as cocoa, coffee, palm kernels, and ginger.

The economy depends largely on mineral exports; mainly diamonds, gold, bauxite and rutile. Diamond exports provided Le1,254·5m in 1989. Total imports for 1989 were to the value of Le10,901·8m and exports were Le8,269·5m.

Trade with UK

	1989	1990
Imports from UK	£20,402,000	£21,365,000
Exports to UK	15,899,000	7,011,000

BRITISH HIGH COMMISSION
Standard Bank of Sierra Leone Building
Lightfoot Boston Street, Freetown
[Freetown 23961]

High Commissioner, His Excellency David Keith Sprague, MVO (1991).

British Council Representative, Theresa Harvey, PO Box 124, Tower Hill, Freetown.

SINGAPORE

AREA, POPULATION, ETC.—The Republic of Singapore consists of the island of Singapore and 58 islets, covering a total area of 626·4 sq. km. Singapore island is 26 miles long and 14 miles in breadth and is situated just north of the Equator off the southern extremity of the Malay Peninsula, from which it is separated by the Straits of Johore. A causeway, carrying a road, railway and a water pipeline, crosses the three-quarters of a mile to the mainland. The highest point of the island is 581 feet above sea level. The climate is hot and humid and there are no clearly defined seasons. Rainfall averages 240 cm a year and temperature ranges from 24°–32° C (76°–89° F).

In 1990, the population was 3,002,800, which comprised 2,239,700 Chinese, 406,200 Malays, 230,000 Indians (including those of Pakistani, Bangladeshi and Sri Lankan origin) and 126,900 from other ethnic groups. Malay, Mandarin, Tamil and English are the official languages. At least 8 Chinese dialects are used.

CURRENCY.—Singapore dollar (S$) of 100 cents.
FLAG.—Horizontal bands of red over white; crescent with five five-point stars on red band near staff.
NATIONAL ANTHEM.—Majulah Singapura.
NATIONAL DAY.—August 9.

GOVERNMENT

Singapore, where Sir Stamford Raffles had first established a trading post under the East India Company in 1819, was incorporated with Penang and Malacca to form the Straits Settlements in 1826. The Straits Settlements became a Crown Colony in 1867. Singapore fell into Japanese hands in 1942 and civil government was not restored until 1946, when it became a separate colony. Internal self-government and the title 'State of Singapore' were introduced in 1959. Singapore became a state of Malaysia when the Federation was enlarged in September 1963, but left Malaysia and became an independent sovereign state within the Commonwealth on August 9, 1965. Singapore adopted a Republican constitution from that date, the Yang di-Pertuan Negara being re-styled President. There is a Cabinet collectively responsible to a fully-elected Parliament of 81 members.

After the General Election of September 3, 1988 the People's Action Party (PAP) had 80 seats in Parliament. The other seat was taken by the Singapore Democratic Party (SDP). Lee Kuan Yew resigned as Prime Minister on November 26, 1990, and was replaced by Goh Chok Tong.

President (Head of State), Wee Kim Wee, *re-elected* August 1989 for a second five-year term.

Cabinet
(as at November 28, 1990)

Prime Minister and Minister for Defence, Goh Chok Tong.
Senior Minister, PM's Office, Lee Kuan Yew, GCMG, CH.
Deputy PM, Ong Teng Cheong.
Deputy PM and Minister for Trade and Industry, Lee Hsien Loong.
National Development, S. Dhanabalan.
Education, Dr Tony Tan Keng Yam.
Environment, Dr Ahmad Mattar.
Communications and Information, Dr Yeo Ning Hong.
Law and Home Affairs, Prof. S. Jayakumar.

Finance, Dr Richard Hu Tsu Tau.
Labour, Lee Yock Suan.
Foreign Affairs and Community Development, Wong Kan Seng.
Information and Arts (acting), George Yeo.
Health, Yeo Cheow Tong.

Speaker of Parliament, Tan Soo Khoon.

SINGAPORE HIGH COMMISSION
9 Wilton Crescent, SW1X 8SA
[071–235 8315]

High Commissioner, His Excellency Abdul Aziz Mahmood (1988).

COMMUNICATIONS

Singapore is one of the largest and busiest seaports in the world, with deep water wharves and ship repairing facilities. Ships also anchor in the roads, unloading into lighters. In 1988, 90,600,000 freight tonnes of seaborne cargo was discharged and 64,100,000 freight tonnes loaded. More than 700 shipping lines use the port, with 44,600 ship arrivals in 1990. The international airport is at Changi, in the east of the island. There are 25·75 km of metric gauge railway connected to the Malaysian rail system by the causeway across the Straits of Johore, and 2,760 km of roads. There are both wireless and wired broadcasting services carrying commercial advertising. There are three television channels. The Singapore Broadcasting Authority Corporation was established in February 1980.

ECONOMY

Historically Singapore's economy was largely based on the sale and distribution of raw materials from surrounding countries and on entrepot trade in finished products. However, new manufacturing industries have been successfully introduced, including ship building and repairing, iron and steel, textiles, footwear, wood products, micro-electronics, scientific instruments, detergents, confectionery, pharmaceuticals, petroleum products, etc. Singapore has also become a financial centre with 139 commercial banks and 67 merchant banks established in the Republic, and an oil-refining centre.

In September 1988 it was announced that Singapore had been promoted by the World Bank to the 'high income' bracket of countries earning at least US$6,000 per capita annually.

Finance (estimates)

	1989	1990
Revenue	S$15,508·9m	S$16,424·7m
Expenditure	10,626·4m	13,257·1m

Trade

	1989	1990
Total imports	S$96,863·7m	S$109,805·8m
Total exports	87,116·5m	95,205·8m

Trade with UK

	1989	1990
Imports from UK	£773,866,000	£1,040,188,000
Exports to UK	903,248,000	1,021,148,000

BRITISH HIGH COMMISSION
Tanglin Road, Singapore 1024
[Singapore 4739333]

High Commissioner, His Excellency Gordon Duggan (1990).

British Council Representative, A. Webster, 30 Napier Road, Singapore 1025.

SOLOMON ISLANDS

Forming a scattered archipelago of mountainou islands and low-lying coral atolls, the Solomon Island stretches about 900 miles in a south-easterly directio from Bougainville, in Papua New Guinea, to th Santa Cruz islands. The archipelago covers an are of about 249,000 square nautical miles while the lan area is 10,938 sq. miles (28,446 sq. km). Solomo Islands lies between the east longitudes 155° 30′ an 170° 30′ and between south latitudes 5° 10′ and 12° 45′ The six biggest islands are: Choiseul, New Georgia Santa Isabel, Guadalcanal, Malaita and Makira. The are characterized by precipitous, thickly-foreste mountain ranges intersected by deep, narrow valley and vary between 90 to 120 miles in length an between 20 to 30 miles in width.

The total population was 285,176 at the 1986 Censu The 1989 UN estimate was 317,000. English is th official language; there are over 80 local languages.

CAPITAL.—ΨHoniara, population (1986), 30,499.

CURRENCY.—Solomon Islands dollar (SI$) of 10 cents.

FLAG.—Blue over green divided by a diagona yellow band, with five white stars in the top lef quarter.

NATIONAL ANTHEM.—God Bless our Solomo Islands.

NATIONAL DAY.—July 7 (Independence Day).

GOVERNMENT

The origin of the present Melanesian inhabitant is uncertain. European discovery of the islands bega in the mid-16th century and continued intermit tently for about 300 years, when the inauguration o sugar plantations in Queensland and Fiji (whic created a need for labour) and the arrival o missionaries and traders led to increased Europea interest in the region. Great Britain declared a Protectorate in 1893 over the Southern Solomons adding the Santa Cruz group in 1898 and 1899, the islands of the Shortland groups were transferred by treaty from Germany to Great Britain in 1900.

The Solomon Islands achieved internal self-govern ment in 1976, and became independent in July 1978 The Solomon Islands is a constitutional monarchy The Queen being represented locally by the Governor General. Legislative power is vested in a unicamera National Parliament of 38 members, elected for a four-year term. The executive authority is exercise by the Cabinet.

A government of political personalities was forme in October 1990.

Governor-General, His Excellency Sir George Lep ping, GCMG, MBE.

Cabinet
(as at October 1990)

Prime Minister, Hon. Solomon Mamaloni.
Deputy PM and Minister for Home Affairs, Hon. Sir Baddeley Devesi, GCMG, GCVO.
Agriculture and Lands, Hon. G. Luialamo.
Education and Human Resource Development, Hon S. Alasia.
Finance and Economic Planning, Hon. Christophe Columbus Abe.
Foreign Affairs and Trade Relations, Rt. Hon. Sir Peter Keniloria, KBE.
Health and Medical Services, Hon. Nathaniel Supa.
Housing and Government Services, Hon. A. Kemak eza.
Natural Resources, Hon. E. Alebua.
Police and Justice, Hon. A. Laore.
Post and Communications, Ben Gale Faitoa.
Provincial Government, Hon. A. Qurusu.

Tourism and Aviation, Hon. Victor Ngele.
Works and Public Utilities, Hon. A. Maetia.
Commerce and Primary Industries, Hon. M. Maina.

DIPLOMATIC REPRESENTATION

High Commissioner, His Excellency Wilson Ifunaoa, CMG (resident in Honiara, Solomon Islands).

HONORARY CONSULATE

19 Springfield Road, SW19 7AL
[081–946 5552]

Honorary Consul, E. E. Nielsen.

JUDICIARY

The High Court of Solomon Islands, constituted by the Solomon Islands Independence Order, consists of a Chief Justice and not fewer than two nor more than three Puisne Judges. The Court of Appeal Act was enacted on May 8, 1978.

COMMUNICATIONS

A new international air service was started by Solomon Airlines in June 1990. Services are operated from Honiara to Brisbane, Sydney, Auckland, Port Moresby, Vila and Nadi (Fiji). In addition there is a weekly Qantas flight Brisbane–Honiara–Brisbane and Air Niugini flight Port Moresby–Honiara–Port Moresby.

There are about 52 miles of secondary and minor roads in the urban areas of Honiara, Auki and Gizo. About 18 miles of road in and around Honiara and one mile in Gizo are bitumen sealed, the remainder being coral or gravel surfaced. In the rural areas there are some 800 miles of road, including those in private plantations, forestry areas and roads built and maintained by councils.

Telekom, a company jointly owned by Cable and Wireless Limited and Solomon Islands Government, operates the international and domestic telephone circuits from a ground station in Honiara via the Intelsat Pacific Ocean communication satellite.

FINANCE AND TRADE

The main imports are foodstuffs, consumer goods, machinery and transport materials. Principal exports are timber, fish, copra, and palm oil. Fisheries exports for 1989 totalled SI\$65·3m, timber SI\$41·3m and copra SI\$21m. Other exports include cocoa and marine shells.

Trade with UK

	1989	1990
Imports from UK	£1,088,000	£523,000
Exports to UK	6,404,000	6,903,000

BRITISH HIGH COMMISSION

Telekom House, Mendana Avenue, (PO Box 676),
Honiara
[Honiara 21705]

High Commissioner, His Excellency Raymond F. Jones (1991).

SRI LANKA
(Sri Lanka Prajatantrika Samajawadi Janarajaya)

AREA, CLIMATE, ETC.—Sri Lanka (formerly Ceylon) is an island in the Indian Ocean, off the southern tip of the peninsula of India and separated from it by a narrow strip of shallow water, the Palk Strait. Situated between 5° 55′–9° 50′ N. latitude and 79° 42′–81° 52′ E. longitude, it has an area of 25,332 sq. miles (65,610 sq. km), including 33 square miles of inland water. Its greatest length is from north to south, 270 miles; and its greatest width 140 miles, no point in Sri Lanka being more than 80 miles from the sea.

Forests, jungle and scrub cover the greater part of the island, often being intermingled. In areas over 2,000 feet above sea level grasslands (*patanas* or *talawas*) are found. One of the highest peaks in the central massif is Adam's Peak (7,360 ft), a place of pilgrimage for Buddhists, Hindus and Muslims.

The climate of Sri Lanka is warm throughout the year, with a high relative humidity. In the hills the climate is more temperate. Rainfall is generally heavy, with marked regional variations. The two main monsoon seasons are mid-May to September (south-west) and November to March (north-east).

POPULATION.—The population at the 1981 census was 14,800,001. (A 1989 UN estimate gave a figure of 16,806,000.) Of these 74 per cent were Sinhalese, 12·6 per cent Sri Lankan Tamils, 5·6 per cent Indian Tamils, 7·1 per cent Sri Lankan Moors and 0·7 per cent Burghers, Malays and others. The religion of the great majority of inhabitants is Buddhism, introduced from India, according to ancient Sinhalese chronicles, in 247 BC. After Buddhism (69·3 per cent), Hinduism has the largest following (15·5 per cent); 7·6 per cent of the population are Muslims and 7·5 per cent are Christians. The national languages are Sinhalese, Tamil and English.

CAPITAL.—ΨColombo, population (1981) 585,776. 1984 estimate 643,000. Other principal towns are ΨJaffna (118,215), Kandy (101,281), ΨGalle (77,183), ΨNegombo (51,376) and ΨTrincomalee (44,913).

CURRENCY.—Sri Lankan rupee (Rs) of 100 cents.

FLAG.—On a dark red field, within a golden border, a golden lion passant holding a sword in its right paw, and a representation of a *bo*-leaf, issuing from each corner; and to its right, two vertical stripes of saffron and green also placed within a golden border, to represent the minorities of the country.

NATIONAL ANTHEM.—Namo Namo Matha (We all stand together).

NATIONAL DAY.—February 4 (Independence Commemoration Day).

GOVERNMENT

Early in the sixteenth century the Portuguese landed in Ceylon and founded settlements, eventually conquering much of the country. Portuguese rule in Ceylon lasted 150 years, but in 1658, following a twenty-year period of decline, Portuguese rule gave way to that of the Dutch East India Company which was to exploit Ceylon with varying fortunes until 1796.

The Maritime Provinces of Ceylon were ceded by the Dutch to the British on February 16, 1798, becoming a British Crown Colony in 1802 under the terms of the Treaty of Amiens. With the annexation of the Kingdom of Kandy in 1815, all Ceylon came under British rule.

On February 4, 1948 Ceylon became a self-governing state and a member of the British Commonwealth of Nations. A republican Constitution was adopted on May 22, 1972, providing for a unicameral legislature, the National State Assembly, which has a six year term, and the country was renamed the Republic of Sri Lanka (meaning 'Resplendent Island'). On September 5, 1978 a new Constitution introduced the title the Democratic Socialist Republic of Sri Lanka and a system of proportional representation. Legislative power is exercised by Parliament, the executive power being exercised by the President.

A Bill providing for the holding of the Provincial

Council elections was passed on January 22, 1988. President Jayewardene issued a proclamation on September 8, 1988, merging the Northern and Eastern Provinces, as envisaged under the Indo-Sri Lanka Agreement. The Eelam People's Revolutionary Liberation Front (EPRLF) gained a clear majority in the Northern-Eastern Provincial Council, while the ruling United National Party (UNP) gained an absolute majority in elections to the seven other newly formed Provincial Councils.

In the General Election of February 15, 1989 the United National Party gained a decisive victory. The results were as follows: United National Party 125 seats, Sri Lanka Freedom Party 67, Independent Tamils 14, Tamil United Liberation Front 10, Sri Lanka Muslim Congress 3, United Socialist Alliance 3, Mahajana Eksath Peramuna 3.

The rebellion by secessionist Tamil groups in the north-east of the country continues.

President, His Excellency Ranasinghe Premadasa, elected Dec. 20, 1988, sworn in Jan. 2, 1989 (also Minister of Buddha Sasana, Policy Planning and Implementation).

Cabinet
(as at March, 1991)

Prime Minister and Minister of Finance, Defence, Hon. D. B. Wijetunge.
Transport and Highways, Hon. Wijayapala Mendis.
Justice, Hon. A. C. S. Hameed.
Environment and Parliamentary Affairs, Hon. M. Vincent Perera.
Education and Higher Education, Hon. Lalith Athulathmudali.
Public Administration, Provincial Councils and Home Affairs, Hon. Festus Perera.
Tourism and Rural Industrial Development, Hon. S. Thondaman.
Industries, Science and Technology, Hon. Ranil Wickramasinghe.
Lands, Irrigation and Mahaweli Development, Hon. Gamini Athukorale.
Fisheries and Aquatic Resources, Hon. Joseph Michael Perera.
Cultural Affairs and Information, Hon. W. J. M. Lokubandara.
Posts and Telecommunications, Hon. A. M. S. Adhikari.
Youth Affairs and Sports, Hon. C. Nanda Mathew.
Trade and Commerce, Hon. A. R. Munsoor.
Handlooms and Textile Industries, Hon. U. B. Wijekoon.
Health and Women's Affairs, Hon. Renuka Herath.
Reconstruction, Rehabilitation and Social Welfare, Hon. P. Dayaratne.
Housing and Construction, Hon. B. Sirisena Cooray.
Plantation Industries, Hon. Rupasena Karunatilleke.
Foreign Affairs, Hon. Harold Herat.
Food and Co-operatives, Hon. Weerasinghe Mallimarachchi.
Agricultural Development and Research, Hon. Dharmadasa Banda.
Power and Energy, Hon. K. D. M. Chandra Bandara.
Ports and Shipping, Hon. Alick Aluvihare.
Labour and Vocational Training, Hon. G. M. Premachandra.

HIGH COMMISSION FOR THE DEMOCRATIC
SOCIALIST REPUBLIC OF SRI LANKA
13 Hyde Park Gardens, W2 2LU
[071–262 1841]

High Commissioner, His Excellency Gen. D. S. Attygalle, LVO (1990).

THE JUDICATURE

The Judicial System provides for a Supreme Court a Court of Appeal, a High Court and other Courts o First Instance.

COMMUNICATIONS

There are over 15,660 miles of motorable roads i Sri Lanka and a government-run railway system with 984 miles of lines.

There is a satellite earth station at Padukka, in south-west Sri Lanka, which provides telecommunication links via satellite with any part of the globe.

The principal airports are at Katunayake, 19 miles north of Colombo, and Ratmalana, nine miles south of the capital. Air Lanka operates on 76 flights weekly to the Gulf States, the Maldives, Western Europe and throughout the Far East.

PRODUCTION

Agriculture.—The staple products of the island are tea, rubber, copra, spices and gems. There is increasing emphasis on local production of food, especially rice, and plans for the large-scale production of sugar cane, cotton and citrus fruits.

Industry.—Factories are established for the manufacture or processing of ceramic ware, vegetable oils and by-products, paper, tobacco, tanning and leather goods, plywood, cement, chemicals, sugar, flour, salt textiles, ilmenite, tiles, tyres, fertilizers, clothing jewellery and hardware and there is a petroleum refinery.

Trade with UK

	1989	1990
Imports from UK	£92,465,000	£88,496,000
Exports to UK	63,527,000	63,362,000

BRITISH HIGH COMMISSION
Galle Road, Kollupitiya (PO Box 1433),
Colombo 3
[Colombo 27611/9]

High Commissioner, new appointment awaited.

British Council Representative, R. A. Jarvis, 49 Alfred House Gardens, Colombo 3. Library also in *Kandy.*

SWAZILAND
(Umbuso we Swatini)

AREA, POPULATION, ETC.—Surrounded by South Africa on its northern, western and southern borders and by Mozambique to the east, this small land-locked country is geographically and climatically divided into three principal areas. The broken mountainous Highveld along the western border with an average altitude of 4,000 feet is densely forested mainly with conifers and eucalyptus; the Middleveld, averaging about 2,000 feet, is a mixed farming area including cotton and pineapples; and the Lowveld in the east which was mainly scrubland until the introduction of large sugar cane plantations west of the Lubombo mountain range and the Mozambique border. Four rivers, the Komati, Usutu, Mbuluzi and Ngwavuma, flow from west to east. The total area of Swaziland is 6,704 sq. miles (17,363 sq. km), and the population (UN estimate 1989) is 763,000.

CAPITAL.—Mbabane (population 1986, 38,290), the headquarters of the government, is situated at an average altitude of 3,800 ft. Other main townships are: Manzini (estimated population, 30,000), Big Bend, Mhlambanyati, Mhlume, Nhlangano, Pigg's Peak and Simunye.

CURRENCY.—Lilangeni (E) of 100 cents. South African currency is also in circulation. Swaziland is a member of the Common Monetary Area and its unit of currency *Emalangeni* (singular *Lilangeni*) has a par value with the South African Rand.

FLAG.—Five horizontal bands, crimson, bearing shield and spears device, bordered by narrow yellow bands; blue bands at top and foot.

NATIONAL ANTHEM.—Elwatini.

NATIONAL DAY.—September 6 (Independence Day).

GOVERNMENT

The Kingdom of Swaziland came into being on April 25, 1967, under a new internal self-government constitution and became an independent kingdom, headed by HM Sobhuza II, in membership of the Commonwealth on September 6, 1968.

A new Constitution was introduced in 1978, under which the King, assisted by his appointed Cabinet, holds considerable executive, legislative and judicial authority. In addition, there is a bicameral legislative body comprising a Senate and a House of Assembly. Each of the 40 traditional Tinkhundla (chieftaincies) elects two members to the electoral college who elect 40 members to the House of Assembly. The King appoints ten members to the House of Assembly, making 50 in all, who then elect ten members (not of their own number) to the Senate. To these are added ten senators appointed by the King, bringing the full membership of the Senate to 20. All political parties are banned under the 1978 Constitution.

Head of State, HM King Mswati III, *inaugurated* April 25, 1986.

Cabinet
(as at 1991)

Acting Prime Minister, Hon. Obed Dlamini.
Labour and Public Service, Hon. Sen. Ben Sibandze.
Commerce, Industry and Tourism, Hon. Sen. Douglas Ntiwane.
Natural Resources, Prince Nqaba.
Foreign Affairs, Hon. Sen. George M. Mamba.
Justice, Hon. D. A. Zonke.
Education, Hon. Chief Sipho Shongwe.
Health, Dr Fanny Friedman.
Works and Communications, Hon. Sen. Wilson Mkhonta.
Finance, Hon. Sibusiso Dlamini.
Interior and Immigration, Hon. Sen. Senzenjani Shabalala.
Agriculture, Hon. Sipho Mamba.

KINGDOM OF SWAZILAND HIGH COMMISSION
58 Pont Street, SW1X 0AE
[071–581 4976/8]

High Commissioner, His Excellency Mboni N. Dlamini (1988).

COMMUNICATIONS

Swaziland's railway is about 150 miles long and runs from Ngwenya in the west to the Mozambique border near Goba in the east, and thence to the Mozambique port of Maputo. A southern link from Phuzumoya in central Swaziland joins up with the South African railway network to Richards Bay. A rail link from Mpaka in central Swaziland to the north-west border opened in 1986 and provides a link to Komatipoort.

Most passenger and goods traffic is carried by privately-owned motor transport services. There are daily scheduled air services by Royal Swazi National Airways to Johannesburg and scheduled routes to Durban, Harare, Lusaka, Gaborone, Nairobi and Dar es Salaam. International telecommunications and television services are provided through a satellite earth station opened in 1983. There is also a national telephone network through a series of microwave links.

FINANCE

In the 1989–90 budget, total expenditure, including debt repayment, was projected at E447,000,000. A surplus of E12,500,000 was predicted due to increase in revenue.

Manufacturing was announced to have replaced agriculture as the dominant sector in 1988.

Trade with UK

	1989	1990
Imports from UK	£1,358,000	£2,719,000
Exports to UK	31,368,000	34,473,000

BRITISH HIGH COMMISSION
Allister Miller Street, Mbabane
[Mbabane 42581]

High Commissioner, His Excellency Brian Watkins (1990).

TANZANIA
(Jamhuri ya Mwungano wa Tanzania)

AREA, ETC.—Tanganyika, the mainland part of the United Republic of Tanzania (Tanganyika and Zanzibar), occupies the east-central portion of the African continent, between 1°–11° 45′ S. lat. and 29° 20′–40° 38′ E. long. It is bounded on the N. by Kenya and Uganda; on the SW by Lake Malawi, Malawi and Zambia; on the S. by Mozambique; on the W. it is bounded by Rwanda, Burundi and Zaire; on the E. the boundary is the Indian Ocean. Tanzania has an area of 364,900 sq. miles (945,087 sq. km). The greater part of the country is occupied by the Central African plateau from which rise, among others, Mt. Kilimanjaro (19,340 ft), the highest point on the continent of Africa, and Mt. Meru (14,974 ft). The Serengeti National Park, which covers an area of 6,000 sq. miles in the Arusha, Mwanza and Mara Regions, is famous for its variety and number of species of game.

POPULATION.—The UN estimated the total population of Tanzania to be 24,802,000 in 1989. Africans form a large majority, while Europeans, Asians, and other non-Africans form the minority. The African population consists mostly of tribes of mixed Bantu race. Swahili is the national and official language. The use of English is widespread both for educational and government purposes.

Zanzibar.—Formerly ruled by the Sultan of Zanzibar, and a British Protectorate until December 10, 1963. Zanzibar consists of the islands of Zanzibar, Pemba and Latham. The surface area is 2,461 sq. km, and the population (UN estimate 1989), is 643,000. ΨZanzibar (population, 133,000) is the chief town and seaport of the island.

CAPITAL.—Dodoma (population 85,000 1985 estimate). The economic and administrative centre is Ψ Dar es Salaam (population 1,096,000 1985 estimate). Other towns (1985 population) are ΨTanga (172,000), Mwanza (252,000), Mbeya (194,000).

CURRENCY.—Tanzanian shilling of 100 cents.

FLAG.—Green (above) and blue; divided by diagonal black stripe bordered by gold, running from bottom (next staff) to top (in fly).

NATIONAL ANTHEM.—Mungu Ibariki Afrika (God Bless Africa).

NATIONAL DAY.—April 26 (Union Day).

GOVERNMENT

Tanganyika became an independent state and a member of the British Commonwealth on December 9, 1961, and a Republic, within the Commonwealth, on December 9, 1962, with an executive President, elected by universal suffrage as the Head of State and Head of the Government. On December 10, 1963, Zanzibar became an independent state within the Commonwealth and on April 26, 1964, Tanganyika united with Zanzibar to form the United Republic of Tanzania.

Tanzania became a one-party state on July 10, 1965 but with the Tanganyika African National Union (TANU) and the Afro-Shirazi Party (ASP) remaining the ruling parties in Tanganyika and Zanzibar respectively. On February 5, 1977 these two parties merged to form the Chama Cha Mapinduzi (CCM) (Revolutionary Party).

A new constitution was introduced on April 26, 1977 and revised in October 1984. There is a President and two Vice-Presidents, one the President of Zanzibar and the other the Prime Minister. The President may only serve two five year terms and if he comes from Zanzibar the Prime Minister will be the First Vice-President and must come from Tanganyika. If the President comes from Tanganyika the President of Zanzibar will be the First Vice President. In a presidential election a single presidential candidate nominated by the CCM has to obtain an affirmative majority of the votes cast, failing which a fresh candidate must be nominated. The National Assembly contains 255 members, of whom 130 are elected from mainland constituencies and 50 from Zanzibar, 25 are ex-officio, 15 nominated and 35 indirectly elected. The Speaker may either be elected from among the members or be an additional member. Constituency members are elected by popular vote at a general election held at a maximum of five-yearly intervals in which the CCM nominates two candidates to contest each seat.

A new constitution was also approved in 1984 for Zanzibar providing for an elected President and House of Representatives. Although Zanzibar has its own government and Chief Minister, Tanganyika is governed by the government of the Union. Overall policy is decided by the CCM whose chairman is President Mwinyi.

President of the United Republic, HE Hon. Ali Hassan Mwinyi, *b.* 1925; *elected* Oct. 27, 1985; re-elected Oct. 28, 1990.
First Vice-President of the United Republic and Prime Minister, Hon. John Malecela.
Second Vice-President of the United Republic and President of Zanzibar, HE Salmin Amour.

Cabinet
(as at November, 1990)

Defence, The President.
Foreign Minister, Hon. Hassan Diria.
Agriculture and Livestock Development, Co-operatives, Hon. Anna Abdallah..
Communications and Transport, Hon. Jackson Makwetta.
Works, Hon. Nalaila Kiula.
Education, Hon. Charles Kabeho.
Energy, Minerals and Water, Hon. Lt.-Col. Jakaya Kikwete.
Finance, Hon. Steven Kibona.
Health, Hon. Prof. Philemon Sarungi.
Home Affairs, Hon. Augustine Mrema.
Industries and Trade, Hon. Cleopa D. Msuya.
Information and Broadcasting, Hon. Benjamin Mkapa.
Labour and Youth Development, Hon. Joseph Rwegasira.
Regional Development and Local Government, Hon. Joseph Warioba.
Lands, Housing and Urban Development, Hon. Marcel B. Komanya.
Community Development, Women and children, Hon. Anna Makinda.

Tourism, Natural Resources, Environment, Hon. Abubakar Mugumia.
Science, Technology and Higher Education, Hon. Dr William Shija.
Minister without Portfolio, and CCM Vice Chairman, Hon. Rashid M. Kawawa.

TANZANIA HIGH COMMISSION
43 Hertford Street, W1Y 7TF
[071–499 8951]

High Commissioner, His Excellency Ali S. Mchumo (1991).

EDUCATION

All Tanzanian secondary schools are expected to include practical subjects in the basic course. All who receive secondary (or equivalent) education are called up for a period of National Service. The school system is administered in Swahili but the Government is making efforts to improve English standards for the purposes of secondary and higher education. For higher education Tanzanian students go to the University of Dar es Salaam, Sokoine University of Agriculture in Morogoro, other East African universities, or to universities and colleges outside East Africa, including Britain.

COMMUNICATIONS

The main port is Dar es Salaam, and there are other ports on the coast at Tanga, Mtwara, Zanzibar, Mkoani and Wete, in addition to Mwanza, Musoma and Bukoba on Lake Victoria and Kigoma on Lake Tanganyika. Coastal shipping services connect the mainland to Zanzibar, and lake services are operated on Lake Tanganyika and Lake Malawi with neighbouring countries.

The principal international airports are Dar es Salaam and Kilimanjaro. Other airports include Zanzibar, Arusha, Mwanza and Tanga.

There are two railway systems: one connecting Dar es Salaam to Zambia, and the second having two main lines running from Dar es Salaam, one to northern Tanzania and Kenya and the other to Lake Tanganyika and Victoria.

PRODUCTION AND TRADE

The economy is based mainly on the production and export of primary produce and the growing of foodstuffs for local consumption. The islands of Zanzibar and Pemba produce a large part of the world's supply of cloves and clove oil; and coconuts, coconut oil and copra are also produced. The mainland's chief export crops are coffee, cotton, sisal, tea, tobacco, cashew nuts and diamonds. The most important minerals are diamonds. Hides and skins are another valuable export. Industry is at present largely concerned with the processing of raw material for either export or local consumption. There are also secondary manufacturing industries, including factories for the manufacture of leather and rubber footwear, knitwear, razor blades, cigarettes and textiles, and a wheat flour mill.

Trade with UK

	1989	1990
Imports from UK	£93,036,000	£84,694,000
Exports to UK	22,641,000	25,575,000

BRITISH HIGH COMMISSION
Hifadhi House, Samora Avenue (PO Box 9200),
Dar es Salaam
[Dar es Salaam 29601]

High Commissioner, His Excellency John Thorold Masefield, CMG. (1989).
British Council Representative, N. H. Ross, Ohio Samora Avenue, (PO Box 9100), Dar es Salaam.

TONGA
(Kingdom of Tonga)

Tonga, or the Friendly Islands, comprises a group of islands situated in the Southern Pacific some 450 miles to the ESE of Fiji, with an area of 270 sq. miles (699 sq. km), and population (1989 UN estimate) of 19,000. The largest island, Tongatapu, was discovered by Tasman in 1643. Most of the islands are of coral formation, but some are volcanic (Tofua, Kao and Niuafoou or 'Tin Can' Island). The limits of the group are between 15° and 23° 30′ S., and 173° and 177° W.

CAPITAL.—ΨNuku'alofa (population estimate 60,000), on Tongatapu.

CURRENCY.—Pa'anga (T$) of 100 seniti.

FLAG.—Truncated red cross on rectangular white ground (next staff) on a red field.

NATIONAL ANTHEM.—E, 'Otua Mafimafi (Oh, Almighty God Above).

NATIONAL DAY.—June 4 (Independence Day).

GOVERNMENT

The Kingdom of Tonga is an independent constitutional monarchy within the Commonwealth. Prior to June 4, 1970 it had been a British-protected state for 70 years. The constitution provides for a Government consisting of the Sovereign, a privy council which functions as a cabinet, a legislative assembly and a judiciary. The legislative assembly includes the King, privy council, nine hereditary nobles and nine popularly elected representatives (who hold office for three years). The most recent election took place on February 15, 1990.

Head of State, HM King Taufa'ahau Tupou IV, GCMG, GCVO, KBE, acceded Dec. 16, 1965.

Heir, HRH Crown Prince Tupouto'a.

Cabinet
(as at June 1991)

Prime Minister, Minister of Agriculture, Fisheries, Forests, and Marine, HRH Prince Fatafehi Tu'ipelehake, KBE.

Acting Deputy Prime Minister, Minister of Labour, Commerce and Industries, Baron Vaea of Houma.

Education, Works, Civil Aviation, Hon. Dr Hu'akavameiliku.

Police, Prisons and Fire Services, Hon. 'Akau'ola.

Health, Hon. Dr S. Tapa.

Foreign Affairs and Defence, HRH Crown Prince Tupouto'a.

Finance, Hon. J. Cecil Cocker.

Attorney-General, Minister of Justice, Hon. Tevita P. Tupou.

Minister without Portfolio, Hon. Ma'afu Tuku'i'aulahi.

Acting Minister of Lands, Survey, and Natural Resources, Hon. Dr S. Ma'afu Tupou.

Governor of Ha'apai, Hon. Fakafanua.

Acting Governor of Vava'u, Hon. Tu'i'afitu.

TONGA HIGH COMMISSION
36 Molyneux Street, W1H 6AB
[071-724 5828]

High Commissioner, His Excellency S. M. Tuita (1989).

ECONOMY

The economy is primarily agricultural; the main crops are coconuts, bananas, vanilla, yams, taro, cassava, groundnuts and other fruits. Fish is an important staple food though recent shortfalls have led to canned fish being imported. Industry is based on the processing of agricultural produce, and the manufacture of foodstuffs, clothing and sports equipment. The principal exports are copra, other coconut products, tropical root crops, bananas, knitwear, leather goods and fibreglass boats.

TRADE

	1985	1989
Total imports	T$58,900,000	T$68,334,194
Total exports	7,700,000	11,517,597

Trade with UK

	1989	1990
Imports from UK	£831,000	£1,296,000
Exports to UK	28,000	239,000

BRITISH HIGH COMMISSION
PO Box 56, Nuku'alofa
[Nuku'alofa 21020]

High Commissioner, His Excellency William Lawson Cordiner (1990).

TRINIDAD AND TOBAGO
(The Republic of Trinidad and Tobago)

AREA, POPULATION, ETC.—Trinidad, the most southerly of the West Indian islands, lies close to the north coast of S. America, the nearest point being Venezuela, 7 miles distant. The island is situated between 10° 2′–11° 12′ N. lat. and 60° 30′–61° 56′ W. long., and is about 50 miles in length by 37 miles in width, with an area of 1,864 sq. miles (4,827 sq. km). Two mountain systems, the Northern and Southern Ranges, stretch across almost its entire width and a third, the Central Range, lies diagonally across its middle portion; otherwise the island is mostly flat. The climate is tropical with temperatures averaging 82° F (27·8° C) by day and 74° F (23·3° C) by night, and a rainfall averaging 82 inches a year. There is a well-marked dry season from January to May, and a wet season from June to December broken by a short dry season (the *Petite Careme*) in September and October.

Tobago (population *c*.45,200) lies between 11° 9′ and 11° 21′ N. lat. and between 60° 30′ and 60° 50′ W. long., 19 miles north-east of Trinidad. The island is 32 miles long at its widest point, and 11 wide, and has an area of 116 sq. miles (300 sq. km). It is a popular tourist resort. It was ceded to the British Crown in 1814 and amalgamated with Trinidad in 1888.

In 1989 the population of Trinidad and Tobago was estimated by the UN to be 1,263,000.

Other Islands.—Corozal Point and Icacos Point, the NW and SW extremities of Trinidad, enclose the Gulf of Paria. West of Corozal Point lie several islands, of which Chacachacare, Huevos, Monos and Gaspar Grande are the most important.

CAPITAL.—ΨPort of Spain (population approximately 59,649 in 1985) is the administrative centre of the islands. About 33 miles south of the capital is San Fernando (population approximately 34,300 in 1985), a town of growing importance which is emerging as the industrial centre of Trinidad, and which is in close proximity to a number of large industrial plants. The main town of Tobago is ΨScarborough.

CURRENCY.—Trinidad and Tobago dollar (TT$) of 100 cents.

FLAG.—Black diagonal stripe bordered with white stripes, running from top by staff, all on a red field.

NATIONAL DAYS.—August 31 (Independence Day); September 24 (Republic Day).

GOVERNMENT

Trinidad was discovered by Columbus in 1498, was colonized in 1532 by the Spaniards, capitulated to the British under Abercromby in 1797, and was ceded to Britain under the Treaty of Amiens (March 25, 1802).

Tobago was discovered by Columbus in 1498. Dutch colonists arrived in 1632; Tobago subsequently changed hands numerous times until it was ceded to the British Crown by France in 1814 and amalgamated with Trinidad in 1888.

The Territory of Trinidad and Tobago became an independent state and a member of the British Commonwealth on August 31, 1962, and a Republic in 1976. The President is elected for five years by all members of the Senate and the House of Representatives. The House of Representatives has 36 members, elected by universal adult suffrage, and the Senate has 31, of whom 16 are appointed on the advice of the Prime Minister, six on the advice of the Leader of the Opposition and nine at the discretion of the President. Legislation was passed in Sept. 1980 which afforded Tobago a degree of self-administration through the 12-member Tobago House of Assembly.

President, His Excellency Noor Mohammed Hassanali.

Cabinet
(as at June 1991)

Prime Minister and Minister for Finance and the Economy, Hon. Arthur Robinson.
Finance, Hon. Selby Wilson.
Justice and National Security, Hon. Joseph Toney.
Environment and National Service, Hon. Lincoln Myers.
Education, Hon. Gloria Henry.
External Affairs and International Trade, Hon. Sahadeo Basdeo.
Health, Hon. Selwyn Richardson.
Industry, Enterprise, and Tourism, Hon. Dr Bhoendradatt Tewarie.
Labour, Employment and Manpower Resources, Hon. Dr Albert Richards.
Energy, Hon. Herbert Atwell.
Planning and Mobilization, Hon. Winston Dookeran.
Youth, Sports, Culture and Creative Arts, Hon. Jennifer Johnson.
Works, Infrastructure and Decentralization, Hon. Carson Charles.
Attorney General, Hon. Anthony Smart.
Social Development and Family Services, Hon. Dr Emmanuel Hosein.
Settlements and Public Utilities, Hon. Pamela Nicholson.
Food Production and Marine Exploitation, Hon. Brinsley Samaroo.

HIGH COMMISSION OF THE REPUBLIC OF
TRINIDAD AND TOBAGO
42 Belgrave Square, SW1X 8NT
[071–245 9351]

High Commissioner, His Excellency Mr Justice Ulric Cross (1990).

EDUCATION

The education system provides for free education at all state-owned and government-assisted denominational schools and certain faculties at the University of the West Indies. In addition there are various private teaching establishments. Attendance is compulsory for children aged 6–12 years, after which attendance at free secondary schools is determined by success in the common entrance examination at 11 years. There are three technical institutes, two teachers' training colleges, and one of the three branches of the University of the West Indies located in Trinidad, at the St Augustine campus. medical teaching complex was built at Mt. Hope, a operates in collaboration with the University of t West Indies.

COMMUNICATIONS

There are some 6,436 km of all-weather roads i Trinidad and Tobago. The only general cargo port Port of Spain but there are specialized port faciliti elsewhere for landing crude oil, loading refiner products and sugar, and for storing and transmittir bauxite and cement. Regular shipping services ca here and many inter-island craft use the por Another rapidly growing port is at Port Lisas whei new industries powered by local natural gas ar located.

International scheduled airlines, including th national airline, Trinidad and Tobago Airwa (BWIA) Corporation, use Piarco International Ai port outside Port of Spain. The airline also flie between Piarco and Crown Point Airport in Tobago

Three commercial broadcasting stations and on commercial television station operate in Trinida and Tobago. The internal telephone system and th external telephone and telegraph connections ar operated by part-state-owned companies.

PRODUCTION

Trinidad and Tobago's main source of revenue i from oil. Production of domestic crude was 55 barrels in 1990. Trinidad has large reserves of natur gas, and reserves are estimated to be in the region o 100 years at the current rates of production. An integrated steel plant, an anhydrous ammonia plan and a methanol plant have been constructed at Poin Lisas.

Fertilizers, tyres, clothing, soap, furniture an foodstuffs are manufactured locally while moto vehicles, radios, TV sets, and electro-domestic equip ment are assembled from parts, mainly from Japan.

Finance

	1989	1990
Revenue	TT$4,972·5m	TT$5,645·2r
Expenditure	5,776·0m	5,816·2r

TRADE

	1989	1990
Imports	TT$5,190·4m	TT$5,361·8n
Exports	6,706·9m	8,842·0n

Trade with UK

	1989	1990
Imports from UK	£45,881,000	£49,894,00
Exports to UK	37,426,000	45,058,00

BRITISH HIGH COMMISSION
Furness House, 90 Independence Square
(PO Box 778) Port of Spain
[Port of Spain 6252861]

High Commissioner, His Excellency Sir Martir Berthoud, KCVO, CMG.

TUVALU

Tuvalu comprises nine coral atolls situated in th South West Pacific around the point at which th International Date Line cuts the Equator. The tot land area is about 10 sq. miles. Few of the atolls ar more than 12 ft above sea level or more than half a mile in width. The vegetation consists mainly of coconut palms. The resident population in 1985 was 8,229, but it is estimated that about 1,500 Tuvaluans work overseas, mostly in Nauru, or as seamen. The UN estimated that the population was 9,000 in 1989. The people are almost entirely Polynesian. The principal languages are Tuvaluan and English. The entire population is Christian and is predominantly Protestant.

CAPITAL.—ΨFunafuti, estimated population 2,856. The capital has a grass strip airfield from which a service operates regularly to Fiji and Kiribati, and is also the only port.

CURRENCY.—Tuvalu uses the Australian dollar ($A) of 100 cents as legal tender. In addition there are Tuvalu dollar and cent coins in circulation.

FLAG.—Blue ground with Union Flag in top left quarter and nine five-pointed gold stars in the fly.

NATIONAL ANTHEM.—Tuvalu Mo Te Atua (Tuvalu for the Almighty).

NATIONAL DAY.—October 1 (Independence Day).

GOVERNMENT

Tuvalu, formerly the Ellice Islands, formed part of the Gilbert and Ellice Islands Colony until October 1, 1975, when separate constitutions came into force. Separation from the Gilbert Islands was implemented on January 1, 1976.

On October 1, 1978 Tuvalu became fully independent as a sovereign state within the Commonwealth. The Constitution provides for a Prime Minister and four other Ministers who must be members of the 12-member elected Parliament. The Prime Minister presides at meetings of the Cabinet, which consists of the five Ministers, and is attended by the Attorney General. Local government services are provided by elected Island Councils.

Governor-General, His Excellency the Rt. Hon. Toaripi Lauti.

Cabinet
(as at June 30, 1991)

Prime Minister, Rt. Hon. Bikenibeu Paeniu.

Minister for Finance and Commerce, Hon. Dr Alesana Seluka.

Natural Resources and Home Affairs, Hon. Tomu Sione, OBE.

Works and Communications, Hon. Ionatana Ionatana, CVO, OBE.

Health, Education and Community Affairs, Hon. Naama Latasi.

Secretary to Government, Tauaasa Taafaki.

Attorney-General, David Ballantyne.

EDUCATION AND WELFARE

There are eight primary schools in Tuvalu and a church secondary school run jointly with the Government. A maritime training school started in 1979 now caters for 60 boys per annum.

There is a 30-bed hospital at Funafuti. All islands are served by a dispensary and a primary school.

ECONOMY

Most people still practise a subsistence economy, the main staples of their diet being coconuts and fish. The main imports are foodstuffs, consumer goods and building materials. The only export is copra, though philatelic sales provide a major source of revenue and handicraft sales are increasing. However, Tuvalu is almost entirely dependent on foreign aid.

Trade with UK

	1989	1990
Imports from UK	£162,000	£506,000
Exports to UK	—	—

BRITISH HIGH COMMISSION
British High Commissioner, (resides at Suva, Fiji).

UGANDA
(Republic of Uganda)

AREA, POPULATION, ETC.—Situated in Eastern Africa, Uganda is flanked by Zaire, Sudan, Kenya and on the south by Tanzania and Rwanda. Large parts of Lakes Victoria, Edward and Albert (Mobutu) are within its boundaries, as are Lakes Kyoga, Kwania, George and Bisina (formerly Salisbury) and the course of the River Nile from its outlet from Lake Victoria to the Sudan frontier post at Nimule. Uganda has an area of 91,259 sq. miles (236,036 sq. km) (water and swamp 16,400 sq. miles) and population (1990 estimate) of 17,500,000. The official language is English. The main local vernaculars are of Bantu, Nilotic and Hamitic origins. Ki-Swahili is generally understood in trading centres.

Despite its tropical location, the climate is tempered by its situation some 3,000 ft. above sea level, and well over that altitude in the highlands of the Western and Eastern Regions. In South Uganda, temperatures seldom rise above 85° F (29° C) or fall below 60° F (15° C). The rainfall averages about 50 inches a year. Uganda has three National Parks and a fourth (Lake Mburo) has been designated.

CAPITAL.—Kampala (estimated population of Greater Kampala, 1990, 750,000). Other principal towns are Jinja (45,000), Mbale (28,000) and Masaka (29,000).

CURRENCY.—Uganda shilling of 100 cents.

FLAG.—Six horizontal stripes of black, yellow and red (repeated) with a crested crane emblem on a white orb in the centre.

NATIONAL ANTHEM.—Oh Uganda.

NATIONAL DAY.—October 9 (Independence Day).

GOVERNMENT

Uganda became an independent state and a member of the Commonwealth on October 9, 1962, after some 70 years of British rule. A Republic was instituted on September 8, 1967, under an executive President, assisted by a Cabinet of Ministers.

Early in 1971 an army coup took place and Maj.-Gen. Idi Amin, the Army Commander, proclaimed himself Head of State. In 1979, following risings and military intervention by Tanzania, President Amin was overthrown. Following elections in 1980, Dr Milton Obote became President. A military coup on July 27, 1985 ousted Dr Obote and installed a military council which attempted to negotiate a power-sharing agreement with the National Resistance Movement led by Yoweri Museveni. However, the National Resistance Army captured Kampala in late January 1986, securing control of the rest of the country in the following few months. Yoweri Museveni was sworn in as President in January 1986; subsequently the Prime Minister and a National Resistance Council (NRC) were appointed. The NRC acts as a legislative body with an interim mandate to form a constitution. Since the most recent elections in February 1989 it consists of 210 elected and 68 presidentially appointed members. In October 1989 the NRC voted to extend its term of office by five years from January 26, 1990. A new Constitution is being drafted.

President, Yoweri Museveni, *sworn in* Jan. 29, 1986.
Vice-President, Dr Samson Kisseka.

Cabinet
(as at May 30, 1991)

Minister of Defence, The President.
Internal Affairs, The Vice-President.
Prime Minister, George Cosma Adyebo.
1st Deputy PM, Eriya Kategaya.
2nd Deputy PM and Minister for Foreign Affairs, Paul Ssemogerere.
3rd Deputy PM, Abu Bakar Mayanja.
Finance, Dr Crispus Kiyonga.
Planning and Economic Development, Joshua Mayanja-Nkangi.
Agriculture, Mrs Victoria Ssekitoleko.
Industry and Technology, E. T. S. Adriko.
Commerce, Paul Etiang.
Local Government, Jaberi Bidandi-Ssali.
Animal Industries and Fisheries, Prof. George Mondo Kagonyera.
Youth, Culture and Sports, Ibrahim Mukiibi.
Public Services and Cabinet Affairs, Tom Rubale.
Information and Broadcasting, Kintu Musoke.
Education, Amanya Mushega.
Land and Surveys, Ben Okello Luwum.
Water and Mineral Development, Henry Kajura.
Justice and Attorney-General, George Kanyeihamba.
Constitutional Affairs, Sam Njuba.
Co-operatives and Marketing, James Wapakabulo.
Labour, Stanislaus Okurut.
Transport and Communications, Dr Ruhakana-Rugunda.
Energy, Richard Kaijuka.
Tourism and Wildlife, Samuel Sebageraka.
Works, Daniel Serwano Kigozi.
Health, Zak Kaheru.
Housing and Urban Development, John Ssebana-Kizito.
Environmental Protection, Moses Kintu.
Relief and Social Rehabilitation, Adoko Nekyon.
Minister without Portfolio, David Kibirango.

UGANDA HIGH COMMISSION
Uganda House, 58–59 Trafalgar Square, WC2N 5DX
[071–839 5783]

High Commissioner, His Excellency Prof. George Kirya (1990).

EDUCATION

Education is a joint undertaking by the Government, local authorities and, to some extent, voluntary agencies. In 1988 it was estimated that Uganda had 7,905 primary schools with an enrolment of 2,638,100 children. Secondary schools numbered 774 with 240,834 students enrolled; and 7,291 students in various technical training institutions.

The national university is Makerere University, Kampala, founded as a trade school in 1921 and becoming an independent university in 1970. There are universities at Mbale and Mbarara; the Uganda Martyrs University is to open in October 1991.

COMMUNICATIONS

There is an international airport at Entebbe, with direct flights to destinations in Africa and Europe. There are eight other airfields in Uganda. Having no sea coast, Uganda is heavily dependent upon rail and road links to Mombasa and Dar es Salaam for its trade. Over 5,000 km of the country's dilapidated roads are currently being rehabilitated. A railway network joins the capital to the western, eastern and northern centres.

TRADE, ETC.

The principal export earner is coffee (over 90 per cent of all exports), which earned US$264 million in 1988. Attempts are being made to increase production of cotton and tea for export. Hydro-electricity is produced from the Owen Falls power station which generated 564 kW in 1988, 110 kW of which was exported to Kenya. The principal food crops are plantains, bananas, cassava, sweet potatoes, potatoes, maize and sorghum.

Trade with UK

	1989	1990
Imports from UK	£39,218,000	£39,506,000
Exports to UK	20,985,000	12,124,000

BRITISH HIGH COMMISSION
10–12 Parliament Avenue, PO Box 7070, Kampala
[Kampala 257054/9]

High Commissioner, His Excellency Charles A. K. Cullimore (1989).
British Council Representative, Stan Moss, OBE.

VANUATU
(Ripablik Blong Vanuatu)

AREA, POPULATION, ETC.—Vanuatu, the former Anglo-French Condominium of the New Hebrides, is situated in the South Pacific Ocean, between 13° and 21° S. and 166° and 170° E. It includes 13 large and some 70 small islands, of coral and volcanic origin, including the Banks and Torres Islands in the North, and has a total land area of 4,706 sq. miles (12,190 sq. km). The principal islands are Vanua Lava, Espiritu Santo, Maewo, Pentecost, Ambae, Malekula, Ambrym, Epi, Efate, Erromango, Tanna and Aneityum. Most islands are mountainous and there are active volcanoes on several. The climate is oceanic tropical, moderated by the south-east trade winds which blow between May and October. At other times winds are variable and cyclones may occur. Temperatures range between 17° C and 28° C with annual rainfall averaging 90 in. to the south and 155 in. to the north.

Provisional results of a national census which took place in May 1989 show a population of 142,630. About 95 per cent of the population are Melanesian the rest being made up largely of Micronesians, Polynesians and Europeans. The national language is Bislama, but English and French are also official languages.

SEAT OF ADMINISTRATION—ΨPort Vila, Efate, population (1989) 19,400. The only other town is Luganville (population, 1989, 6,900), on Espiritu Santo.

CURRENCY.—Vatu of 100 centimes.

FLAG.—Red over green with a black triangle in the hoist, the three parts being divided by fimbriations of black and yellow, and in the centre of the black triangle a boar's tusk overlaid by two crossed fern leaves.

NATIONAL ANTHEM.—Nasonal sing sing blong Vanuatu.

NATIONAL DAY.—July 30 (Independence Day).

GOVERNMENT

The Condominium of the New Hebrides became an independent republic within the Commonwealth under the name of Vanuatu on July 30, 1980.

Parliament consists of 46 members elected for a term of four years. A Council of Chiefs advises on matters of custom. Executive power is held by the

Prime Minister (elected from and by parliament) and a Council of Ministers who are responsible to parliament. The President is elected for a five-year term by the presidents of the 11 regional councils and the members of parliament.

President, His Excellency Frederick Karlomuana Timakata, *elected* 1989.

Council of Ministers
(as at June 30, 1991)

Prime Minister and Minister of Planning, Information, Aviation and Public Service, Hon. Father Walter Lini, CBE.
Finance, Housing and Tourism, Hon. S. J. Regenvanu.
Lands, Minerals and Rural Water Supply, Hon. W. Mahit.
Foreign Affairs, Education and Judicial Services, Hon. D. Kalpokas.
Health, Hon. J. M. Chilia.
Agriculture, Forestry and Fisheries, Hon. J. Hopa.
Home Affairs, Hon. I. Abbil.
Trade, Commerce, Industry, Co-operatives and Energy, Hon. H. Qualao.
Transport, Public Works, Hon. E. Natapei.

Chief Justice, vacant.
Attorney-General, S. Hakwa.
High Commissioner to Great Britain, vacant (resident in Port Vila, Vanuatu).

Economy

Most of the population is employed on plantations or in subsistence agriculture. Subsistence crops include yams, taro, manioc, sweet potato and breadfruit; principal cash crops are copra, cocoa and coffee. Large numbers of cattle are kept on the plantations and beef is the second largest export after copra.

Principal exports are copra, meat (frozen, tinned and chilled), timber and cocoa.

Tourism is an important revenue earner, and the absence of direct taxation has led to growth in the finance and associated industries.

Trade with UK

	1989	1990
Imports from UK	£363,000	£1,796,000
Exports to UK	52,000	47,000

BRITISH HIGH COMMISSION
PO Box 567, Port Vila
[Vila 23100]

High Commissioner, His Excellency John Thompson, MBE (1988).

WESTERN SAMOA
(Malotuto'atasi o Samoa i Sisifo)

AREA, ETC.—Western Samoa lies in the south Pacific Ocean between latitudes 13° and 15° S. and longitudes 171° and 173° W. It consists of the islands of Savai'i (662 sq. miles) and of Upolu, which, with seven other islands (Apolima, Manono, Fanuatapu, Namua, Nuutele, Nuulua and Nuusafee) has an area of 435 sq. miles (1,714 sq. km). All the islands are mountainous. Upolu, the most fertile, contains the harbours of ΨApia and ΨSaluafata, and Savai'i the harbour of ΨAsau.

POPULATION.—The population at the 1981 census was 158,130, the largest numbers being on Upolu (114,980) and Savai'i (43,150); a 1989 UN estimate put the figure at 169,000. The Samoans are a Polynesian people, though the population also includes other Pacific Islanders, Euronesians, Chinese and Europeans. The main languages spoken are Samoan and English. The islanders are Christians of different denominations.

CAPITAL.—ΨApia, on Upolu (population, 1981 census, 33,100). Robert Louis Stevenson died and was buried at Apia in 1894.

CURRENCY.—Tala (WS$) of 100 sene.

FLAG.—Five white stars (depicting the Southern Cross) on a quarter royal blue at top next staff, and three quarters red.

NATIONAL ANTHEM.—The Banner of Freedom.

NATIONAL DAY.—January 1 (Independence Day).

GOVERNMENT

Formerly administered by New Zealand (latterly with internal self-government), Western Samoa became, on January 1, 1962 the first fully-independent Polynesian State. The State was treated as a member country of the Commonwealth until its formal admission on August 28, 1970.

The 1962 Constitution provides for a Head of State to be elected by the 47-member Legislative Assembly, the *Fono,* for a five year term. However, it was decided that initially two of the four Paramount chiefs should jointly hold the office of Head of State for life. When one of the chiefs died in April 1963, Malietoa Tanumafili II became the holder of the office of Head of State for life. The Head of State's functions are analogous to those of a constitutional monarch. Executive government is carried out by a Cabinet of Ministers.

Suffrage, previously confined to 20,000 *Matai* (the male heads of extended families), was made universal following a referendum held in October 1990. After elections held on March 7, 1991, the seats in the *Fono* were as follows: Human Rights Protection Party 30; Samoan National Development Party 13; Independents 4.

Head of State, HH Malietoa Tanumafili II, GCMG, CBE (April 15, 1963).
Deputy Head of State, Hon. Mataafa Faasuamaleaui Puela.

Cabinet
(as at May 1991)

Prime Minister, Minister for Foreign Affairs, Hon. Tofilau Eti Alesana.
Finance, Hon. Tuilaepa Sailele.
Justice, Hon. Fuimanono Lotomau.
Education, Hon. Fiame Naomi.
Health, Hon. Sala Vaimili Uili II.
Post and Telecommunications, Hon. Toi Aukuso.
Agriculture, Hon. Jack Netzler.
Public Works, Hon. Leafa Vitale.
Lands and Environment, Hon. Faasooatuloa Pati.

WESTERN SAMOA HIGH COMMISSION
Avenue Franklin D. Roosevelt 95
1050 Brussels
(6608454)

High Commissioner, His Excellency Afamasaga Toleafoa (1990).

ECONOMY

Agriculture is the basis of Western Samoa's economy, the principal cash crops (and exports) being coconuts (copra), cocoa and bananas. Other agricultural exports include coffee, timber, tropical fruits and seeds. Efforts are being made to develop fishing on a commercial scale. Manufacturing is very small in scope and concerned largely with processing agricultural products, but is being encouraged by the Government. Tourism is increasing rapidly.

Trade with UK

	1989	1990
Imports from UK	£296,000	£427,000
Exports to UK	1,376,000	295,000

BRITISH HIGH COMMISSION

High Commissioner, (resides at Wellington, New Zealand).

ZAMBIA
(Republic of Zambia)

AREA, POPULATION, ETC.—The Republic of Zambia lies on the plateau of Central Africa between the longitudes 22° E. and 33° 33′ E. and between the latitudes 8° 15′ S. and 18° S. It has an area of 290,586 sq. miles (752,614 sq. km) within boundaries 3,515 miles in length and a population (UN estimate, 1989) of 7,804,000.

With the exception of the valleys of the Zambezi, the Luapula, the Kafue and the Luangwa Rivers, and the Luano valley, elevations vary from 3,000 to 5,000 feet above sea level, but in the north-east the plateau rises to occasional altitudes of over 6,000 feet.

Although Zambia lies within the tropics, and fairly centrally in the African land mass, its elevation relieves it from extremely high temperatures and humidity.

CAPITAL.—Lusaka, situated in the Central Province. Population (1989 estimate) 1 million. Other centres are Livingstone, Kabwe, Chipata, Mazabuka, Mbala, Kasama, Solwezi, Mongu, Mansa, Ndola, Luanshya, Mufulira, Chingola, Chililabombwe, Kalulushi and Kitwe, the last six towns being the main centres on the Copperbelt.

CURRENCY.—Kwacha (K) of 100 ngwee.

FLAG.—Green with three small vertical stripes, red, black and orange (next fly); eagle device on green above stripes.

NATIONAL ANTHEM.—Stand and Sing of Zambia, Proud and Free.

NATIONAL DAY.—October 24 (Independence Day).

GOVERNMENT

At the dissolution of the Federation of Rhodesia and Nyasaland, on December 31, 1963, Northern Rhodesia (as Zambia was then known) achieved internal self-government under a new constitution. Zambia became an independent republic within the Commonwealth on October 24, 1964, 75 years after coming under British rule and nine months after achieving internal self-government.

In July 1973, a new Constitution was introduced, making the United National Independence Party (UNIP) the only party. In July 1990 it was announced that a referendum on introducing a multi-party system would be held in August 1991. After continued pressure from the Movement for Multiparty Democracy, set up in July 1990, and other opposition groups, the referendum was cancelled and multiparty and presidential elections were called for October 1991.

President, Dr Kenneth David Kaunda, *assumed office* Oct. 24, 1964; *re-elected*, Dec. 1973, Dec. 1978, Oct. 1983 and Oct. 1988.

Cabinet
(as at April, 1991)

Prime Minister and Minister for Co-operatives, Gen. Hon. Malimba Masheke.

UNIP Secretary General, Hon. A. Grey Zulu.

Secretary of State for Defence and Security, Hon. Ale? K. Shapi.

Defence, vacant.

Home Affairs, Gen. the Hon. Kingsley Chinkuli.

Agriculture, Hon. Justin J. Mukando.

Water, Lands and Natural Resources, Hon. Mavi Muyunda.

Foreign Affairs, Gen. the Hon. Benjamin Mibenge.

Attorney-General and Minister for Legal Affairs, Hon Frederick M. Chomba.

Information and Broadcasting Services, Hon. Arnol? Simuchimba.

Commerce and Industry, Hon. Rabson Chongo.

Finance, vacant.

Mines, Hon. Bernard N. Fumbelo.

Power, Transport and Communications, Brig. Gen the Hon. Enos Haimbe.

Tourism, Hon. Pickson Chitambala.

Higher Education, Science and Technology, Prof. the Hon. Lameck K. H. Goma.

General Education, Youth and Sport, Dr the Hon. E? Mwanang'onze.

Health, Hon. Jeremiah Chijikwa.

Labour, Social Development and Culture, Hon. Lav? Mulimba.

Works and Supply, Hon. Haswell Mwale.

ZAMBIA HIGH COMMISSION
2 Palace Gate, W8 5NG
[071–589 6655]

High Commissioner, His Excellency Edward Lubind? (1989).

JUDICATURE

There is a Chief Justice appointed by the President all other judges being appointed on the recommen dation of the Judicial Service Commission consistin of the Chief Justice, the chairman of the Publi Service Commission, a senior Justice of Appeal an one Presidential nominee.

PRODUCTION

Principal products are maize, sugar, groundnuts cotton, livestock, vegetables and tobacco.

Mineral production was valued at K8,390,765,00? in 1987, of which copper production (of 483,10? tonnes) accounted for K6,870,386,000.

FINANCE AND TRADE

Gross Domestic Product (current prices) wa K18,079·8m in 1987. GDP per capita (current prices was K2,486·9.

	1986	1987
Imports	K4,447,687	K6,627,47?
Exports	3,074,357	8,058,59?

Trade with UK

	1989	1990
Imports from UK	£119,057,000	£92,832,00?
Exports to UK	21,565,000	19,308,00?

BRITISH HIGH COMMISSION
Independence Avenue (PO Box 50050), Lusaka
[Lusaka 228955]

High Commissioner, His Excellency Peter Hinch cliffe, CMG (1990).

British Council Representative, G. Ness, Heroes Place Cairo Road, (PO Box 34571), Lusaka. There is als? a library in Ndola.

ZIMBABWE
(Republic of Zimbabwe)

AREA, POPULATION, ETC.—Zimbabwe, the former Southern Rhodesia (named after Cecil Rhodes) comprising eight provinces (Manicaland, Masvingo, Matabeleland North, Matabeleland South, Midlands, Mashonaland West, Central and East), lies south of the Zambezi river. The political neighbours are Zambia and Mozambique on the N., South Africa and Botswana on the S. and W., and Mozambique on the E. It has a total area of 150,804 sq. miles (390,580 sq. km), and a population (UN estimate 1989) of 9,122,000.

CAPITAL.—Harare (formerly Salisbury) situated on the Mashonaland plateau, population (July 1983) 681,000. Bulawayo—the largest town in Matabeleland, population (July 1983) 429,000. Other centres are, Chitungwiza, Mutare, Gweru, Kadoma, Kwe Kwe, Masvingo and Hwange.

CURRENCY.—Zimbabwe dollar (Z$) of 100 cents.

FLAG.—Seven horizontal stripes (green, gold, red, black, red, gold, green) with white triangle at the hoist containing the Zimbabwe bird superimposed on red five-point star.

NATIONAL ANTHEM.—Ishe Komborerai Africa.

NATIONAL DAY.—April 18 (Independence Day).

GOVERNMENT

Southern Rhodesia was granted responsible government in 1923. An illegal declaration of independence on November 11, 1965 was finally terminated on December 12, 1979. Following elections in February 1980 the country obtained independence on April 18, 1980 as the Republic of Zimbabwe, a member of the British Commonwealth.

A Constitutional Amendment Bill designed to replace the 20 reserved white seats with nominated members from any race, was approved in September 1987. On October 30, 1987 a Constitutional Amendment Bill was passed providing for the creation of an executive presidency. On December 30, 1987 Robert Mugabe was elected by MPs and Senators as the first President. The Bill provides for a President to be popularly elected every six years. The President has the power to appoint a Cabinet and to veto parliamentary bills.

A merger agreement between the ZANU (PF) and ZAPU parties was signed on December 22, 1987 with a view to the eventual creation of a one-party state. The new party is known as ZANU-PF.

The latest general election was held in March 1990. ZANU-PF won 116 of the 120 elective seats, and the legislature became unicameral, comprising a House of Assembly of 160 members.

Executive President, Hon. Robert Gabriel Mugabe, elected Dec. 30, 1987, re-elected March 1990.

Cabinet
(as at June 12, 1991)

The President.

Vice-President, Hon. Simon Muzenda.

Vice-President, Hon. Dr Joshua Nkomo.

Senior Minister, Political Affairs, Hon. Didymus Mutasa.

Senior Minister, Finance, Economic Planning and Development, Hon. Dr Bernard Chidzero.

Senior Minister for Local Government, Rural and Urban Development, Hon. Joseph Msika.

Foreign Affairs, Hon. Dr Nathan Shamuyarira.

Justice, Legal and Parliamentary Affairs, Hon. Emmerson Munangagwa.

Defence, Hon. Richard Hove.

Higher Education, Hon. David Karimanzima.

Education and Culture, Hon. Fay Chung.

Home Affairs, Hon. Moven Mahachi.

Public Construction and National Housing, Hon. Enos Chikowore.

Lands, Agriculture and Rural Settlement, Hon. Dr Witness Mangwende.

Information, Posts and Telecommunications, Hon. Victoria Chitepo.

Labour, Manpower Planning and Social Welfare, Hon. John Nkomo.

Industry and Commerce, Hon. Kumbirai Kangai.

Energy, Water Resources Development, Hon. Dr Herbert Ushewokunze.

Mines, Hon. Chris Anderson.

Transport and National Supplies, Hon. Dennis Norman.

Health, Hon. Dr Timothy Stamps.

Community and Co-operative Development, Hon. Joyce Mujuru.

Environment and Tourism, Hon. Herbert Murerwa.

Attorney-General, Hon. Patrick Chinamasa.

In addition, there are nine Ministers of State.

HIGH COMMISSION OF THE REPUBLIC OF ZIMBABWE
Zimbabwe House, 429 Strand, WC2R 0SA
[071-836 7755]

High Commissioner, S. C. Chiketa (1990).

EDUCATION

Since independence, a policy of free primary education and accelerated expansion at secondary level has resulted in rapidly expanding enrolment. In 1986 there were 2,260,367 primary school and 545,841 secondary school pupils in both Government and Government aid schools. Over 80 per cent of schools are government aided schools. The University of Zimbabwe was founded in 1955.

ECONOMY

The country is endowed with minerals, water, forests, wildlife and other resources. The agricultural sector is well developed with both commercial and communal farmers. Tobacco remains the most important crop in terms of export and maize the most important for domestic consumption. Other crops include wheat, cotton, and sugar. Beef is exported to the EC. Production can be severely affected by drought.

The manufacturing sector has a high degree of inter-dependency and many industries depend on the agricultural sector for their raw materials. Industry is dependent on vital imports e.g. fuel oil, steel products and chemicals, as well as heavy machinery and items of transport. The mining sector, although contributing a relatively small portion to GDP (7·6 per cent in 1984) is important to the economy as a foreign exchange earner (26 per cent of total in 1984). Almost all mineral production is exported. Gold is the most important mineral, others are asbestos, silver, nickel, copper, chrome ore, tin, iron ore and cobalt. There is a successful ferro-chrome industry and a substantial steel works which has been heavily subsidized by Government.

A high domestic budget deficit combining with a high external debt service ratio has put the economy into decline. The 1986–87 drought made this worse.

GOVERNMENT FINANCE

	1984–85	1985–86
Revenue	Z$2,212·3m	Z$2,616·2m
Expenditure	2,923·0m	3,307·8m

Trade with UK

	1989	1990
Imports from UK	£87,013,000	£83,718,000
Exports to UK	85,792,000	86,280,000

BRITISH HIGH COMMISSION
Stanley House, Jason Moyo Avenue,
(PO Box 4490), Harare
[Harare 793781]

High Commissioner, His Excellency Kieran Prende
gast, CMG (1989).
British Council Representative, P. L. Elborn, OBE, 2
Jason Moyo Avenue, (PO Box 664), Harare.

British Dependent Territories, etc.

ANGUILLA

Anguilla is a flat coralline island, about 16 miles in length, 3½ miles in breadth at its widest point and its area is about 35 sq. miles (91 sq. km). It lies approximately 18° N. latitude and 63° W longitude, to the north of the Leeward Islands group.

The island is covered with low scrub and fringed with some of the finest white coral-sand beaches in the Caribbean. The climate is pleasant and healthy with temperatures in the range of 24-30° C throughout the year. The population (UN estimate 1989) is about 8,000.

CAPITAL.—The Valley (population 500).
CURRENCY.—East Caribbean dollar (EC$) of 100 cents.

GOVERNMENT

Anguilla has been a British colony since 1650. For most of its history it has been linked administratively with St Christopher, but three months after the Associated State of Saint Christopher (St Kitts)-Nevis-Anguilla came into being in 1967 the Anguillans repudiated government from St Kitts. A Commissioner was installed in 1969 and in 1976 Anguilla was given a new status and separate constitution. Final separation from St Kitts and Nevis was effected on December 19, 1980 and Anguilla reverted to a British Dependency. A new Constitution was introduced in 1982, providing for a Governor, an Executive Council comprising four elected Ministers and two ex-officio members (Attorney General and Permanent Secretary, Finance), and an 11-member legislative House of Assembly presided over by a Speaker.

The 1982 Constitution (Amendment) Order 1990 came into operation on May 30, 1990. Among the new constitutional provisions are a Deputy Governor (who replaces the Permanent Secretary (Finance) in the Executive Council and the Legislature), a Parliamentary Secretary, Leader of Opposition and Deputy Speaker.

Governor, His Excellency B. G. J. Canty, OBE (1989).
Deputy Governor, vacant.

Executive Council
(as at July 30, 1991)

Chief Minister and Minister of Home Affairs, Tourism and Economic Development, Hon. Emile Gumbs.
Lands, Agriculture and Fisheries, Health, Hon. Eric Reid.
Communications, Public Utilities and Works, Hon. Kenneth Harrigan.
Finance, Education and Community Development, Hon. Osbourne Fleming.
Attorney-General, Hon. Kurt De Freitas.

ECONOMY

Low rainfall limits agricultural output and export earnings are mainly from sales of lobsters. Tourism has developed rapidly in recent years and accounts for most of the island's economic activity. In 1989 there were 28,761 tourists and a further 43,044 day visitors.

FINANCE

	1988	1989
Revenue	EC$27,602,700	EC$32,530,30
Expenditure	23,046,900	28,725,60

Trade with UK

	1989	1990
Imports from UK	£1,962,000	£1,853,00
Exports to UK	1,402,000	122,00

ASCENSION
See St Helena

BERMUDA

The Bermudas, or Somers Islands, are a cluster about 100 small islands (about 20 of which an inhabited) situated in the west of the Atlantic Ocean in 32° 18′ N. lat. and 64° 46′ W. long., the nearest poir of the mainland being Cape Hatteras in Nort Carolina, about 570 miles distant. The colony derive its name from Juan Bermudez, a Spaniard, wh sighted it before 1515, but no settlement was mad until 1609 when Sir George Somers, who wa shipwrecked there on his way to Virginia, colonize the islands.

The total area is approximately 20·59 sq. miles (5 sq. km), which includes 2·3 sq. miles leased to th USA. The civil population is approximately 60,00 (1990 estimate).

CAPITAL.—ΨHamilton (population 1990, 2,000).
CURRENCY.—Bermuda dollar of 100 cents.

GOVERNMENT

Internal self-government was introduced on Jur 8, 1968. There is a Senate of 11 members and a elected House of Assembly of 40 members. Th Governor retains responsibility for external affair defence, internal security and the police, althoug administrative matters for the Police Service hav been delegated to the Minister of Home Affairs.

At the General Election of February 9, 1989 th United Bermuda Party gained 22 seats, the Progre sive Labour Party 15 and Independents 2.

Governor and Commander-in-Chief, His Excellenc Sir Desmond Langley, KCVO, MBE (1988).
Deputy Governor, John Kelly, MBE.

Cabinet
(as at June 1991)

Premier, Hon. Sir John Swan, KBE.
Minister of Delegated and Legislative Affairs, Hor Sir John Sharpe.
Health, Social Services and Housing, Hon. Quinto Edness.
Telecommunications, Hon. Sir Charles T. M. Collis.
Labour and Home Affairs, Hon. J. Irving Pearman.
Education, Hon. Gerald D. E. Simons.
Deputy Premier and Minister of the Environmen Hon. A. F. Cartwright DeCouto.

Works and Engineering, Dr the Hon. Clarence Terceira.
Youth, Sport and Recreation, Hon. Harry W. Soares.
Community and Cultural Affairs , Hon. Leonard O. Gibbons.
Tourism, Hon. C. V. Jim Woolridge.
Transport, Hon. Ralph Marshall.
Finance, Dr the Hon. David Saul.
Management and Information Services, Hon. Michael Winfield.

President of the Senate, Hon. A. S. Jackson, MBE.
Speaker of the House of Assembly, Hon. D. Wilkinson.
Chief Justice, Hon. Sir James R. Astwood.
Puisne Judges, Hon. L. Austin Ward, QC; Hon. M. Ward; Hon. D. Hull.

ECONOMY

Locally manufactured concentrates, perfumes, cut flowers and pharmaceuticals are now the colony's leading exports. Little food is produced except vegetables and fish, other foodstuffs being imported.

The islands' economic structure is based on tourism, the major industry, and international company business, attracted by the low level of taxation and sophisticated telecommunications system. In 1989 a total of 549,624 visitors arrived by air and cruise ship. Cruise ships dock at Hamilton, Somerset and St George's.

EDUCATION

Free elementary education was introduced in 1949. Free secondary education was introduced in 1965 for those children who were below the upper limit of the statutory school age of 16 (from 1969 onwards).

FINANCE

	1989–90	1990–91
Public revenue	$307,439,000	$342,000,000
Public expenditure	274,738,000	306,081,000

Trade with UK

	1989	1990
Imports from UK	£77,122,000	£28,114,000
Exports to UK	4,517,000	12,849,000

THE BRITISH ANTARCTIC TERRITORY

The British Antarctic Territory was designated in 1962 and consists of the areas south of 60°S. latitude which were previously included in the Falkland Islands Dependencies. The territory lies between longitudes 20° and 80°W., south of latitude 60°S. and includes the South Orkney Islands, the South Shetland Islands, the mountainous Antarctic Peninsula (highest point Mount Jackson, 13,620ft, in Palmer Land) and all adjacent islands, and the land mass extending to the South Pole. The territory has no indigenous inhabitants and the British population consists of the scientists and technicians who man the British Antarctic Survey stations. The number averages about 60 to 70 in winter, but increases considerably in the summer months with the arrival of field workers. Argentina, Brazil, Chile, China, Poland, USA, USSR and Uruguay also have scientific stations in the territory.

The first two British Antarctic Survey stations were established in the South Shetland Islands in 1944, and by 1956 the number of stations had risen to twelve. Due to the completion of field work in some areas and increased mobility, the number has now

been reduced to five. These are Signy (Signy Island, S. Orkney Islands), Faraday (Argentine Islands, Graham Coast), Rothera (Adelaide Island), Halley (Caird Coast) and, in summer only, Fossil Bluff (George VI Sound). Fifteen other stations have been established but are at present unoccupied.

The territory is administered by a Commissioner, resident in London.

Commissioner, Merrick Stuart Banker-Bates.

THE BRITISH INDIAN OCEAN TERRITORY

The British Indian Ocean Territory was established by an Order in Council in 1965 and included islands formerly administered from Mauritius and the Seychelles. After the independence of both, the territory was redefined in 1976 as comprising only the islands of the Chagos Archipelago.

The Chagos Archipelago consists of six main groups of islands situated on the Great Chagos Bank and covering some 21,000 sq. miles (54,389 sq. km). The largest and most southerly of the Chagos Islands is Diego Garcia, a sand cay with a land area of about 17 square miles approximately 1,100 miles east of Mahé, used as a joint naval support facility by Britain and USA.

The other main island groups of the archipelago, Peros Banhos (29 islands with a total land area of 4 sq. miles) and Salomon (11 islands with a total land area of 2 sq. miles) are uninhabited. The islands have a typical tropical maritime climate, with average temperatures between 25°C and 29°C in Diego Garcia, and rainfall in the whole archipelago of 90–100 inches a year.

Trade with UK

	1989	1990
Imports from UK	£2,246,000	£689,000
Exports to UK	506,000	118,000

Commissioner and Administrator, T. T. Harris.

THE BRITISH VIRGIN ISLANDS

The Virgin Islands are a group of islands at the eastern extremity of the Greater Antilles, divided between Great Britain and the USA. Those of the group which are British number 46, of which 11 are inhabited, and have a total area of about 59 sq. miles, (153 sq. km). The principal are Tortola, the largest (situated in 18° 27′ N. lat. and 64° 40′ W. long., area, 21 sq. miles), Virgin Gorda (8¼ sq. miles), Anegada (15 sq.miles) and Jost Van Dyke (3½ sq. miles). The 1980 Census showed a total population of 10,985: Tortola (9,119); Virgin Gorda (1,443); Anegada (169); Jost Van Dyke (136); and other islands (82). A 1989 UN estimate gave a total figure of 13,000. Apart from Anegada, which is a flat coral island, the British Virgin Islands are hilly, being an extension of the Puerto Rico and the US Virgin Islands archipelago. The highest point is Sage Mountain on Tortola which rises to a height of 1,780 feet.

The islands lie within the trade winds belt and possess a pleasant and healthy sub-tropical climate. The average temperature varies from 22°–28°C in winter and 26°–31°C in summer. The summer heat is tempered by sea breezes and the temperature usually falls by about 6°C at night. Average rainfall is 53 inches.

CAPITAL.—ΨRoad Town, on the south-east of Tortola. Population 2,479.

CURRENCY.—The US dollar (US$) of 100 cents is legal tender.

GOVERNMENT

Under the 1977 Constitution the Governor, appointed by the Crown, remains responsible for defence and internal security, external affairs and the civil service but in other matters acts in accordance with the advice of the Executive Council. The Executive Council consists of the Governor as Chairman, one ex officio member (the Attorney-General), the Chief Minister and three other ministers. The Legislative Council consists of a Speaker chosen from outside the Council, one ex officio member (the Attorney-General), and nine elected members returned from nine one-member electoral districts.

Governor, His Excellency (John) Mark (Ambrose) Herdman, CBE, LVO (1986).
Deputy Governor, E. Georges, OBE.
Financial Secretary, R. Mathavious.

The Executive Council
(as at June 30, 1991)

Chairman, The Governor.
Chief Minister and Minister of Finance, Hon. H. Lavity Stoutt.
Natural Resources and Labour, Hon. Ralph O'Neal, OBE.
Communications and Works, Hon. Terrance Lettsome.
Health, Education and Welfare, Hon. Louis Walters, MBE.
Attorney-General, Hon. Donald Trotman.

Puisne Judge (resident), Justice Lloyd J. Williams.

COMMUNICATIONS

The principal airport is on Beef Island, linked by bridge to Tortola, and an extended runway of 3,600 ft enables larger aircraft to call. There is a second airfield on Virgin Gorda and a third on Anegada. There are direct shipping services to the United Kingdom and the United States and fast passenger services connect the main islands by ferry.

FINANCE

	1988	1989
Revenue	US$32,629,000	US$41,400,000
Expenditure	31,038,000	40,600,000

ECONOMY

Tourism is the main industry but the financial centre is growing steadily in importance. Other industries include a rum distillery, three stone-crushing plants and factories manufacturing concrete blocks and paint. The major export items are fresh fish, gravel, sand, fruit and vegetables: exports are largely confined to the US Virgin Islands. Chief imports are building materials, machinery, cars and beverages.

Trade with UK

	1989	1990
Imports from UK	£6,727,000	£4,454,000
Exports to UK	1,170,000	1,205,000

THE CAYMAN ISLANDS

The Cayman Islands, between 79° 44' and 81° 26' W. and 19° 15' and 19° 46' N., consist of three islands, Grand Cayman, Cayman Brac, and Little Cayman, with a total area of 100 sq. miles (259 sq. km). About 150 miles south of Cuba, the islands are divided from Jamaica, 180 miles to the south-east, by the Cayman Trench, the deepest part of the Caribbean. The nearest point on the US mainland is Miami in Florida, 450 miles to the north. Cooled by trade winds, the annual average temperature and rainfall is 27·2° C and 50·7 inches, respectively.

The colony derives its name from the Carib word for the crocodile, 'Caymanas', which appeared in the log of the first English visitor to the Cayman Islands, Sir Francis Drake. Although tradition has it that the first settlers arrived in 1658, the first recorded settlers arrived in 1666–71. The first recorded permanent settlers followed the first land grant by Britain in 1734. The islands were placed under direct control of Jamaica in 1863. When Jamaica became independent in 1962, the islands opted to remain under the British Crown.

Population (estimate 1990) 28,080, of which the vast majority live on Grand Cayman.

CAPITAL.—ΨGeorge Town, in Grand Cayman, population (1989) 12,921.

CURRENCY.—Cayman Islands dollar (CI$) of 100 cents, which is fixed at CI$ = US$1·20.

GOVERNMENT

The constitution provides for a Governor, a Legislative Assembly and an Executive Council, and effectively allows a large measure of self-government. Unless there are exceptional reasons, the Governor accepts the advice of the Executive Council, which comprises three official members and four others elected from the 12 elected members of the Assembly. The official members also sit in the Assembly. The Governor has responsibility for the police, civil service, defence and external affairs. The Governor handed over the presidency of the Legislative Assembly to the Speaker on February 15, 1991. The normal life of the Assembly is four years, with a general election next due in November 1992.

Governor, His Excellency Alan James Scott, CVO, CBE (1987).

Executive Council
(as at June 30, 1991)

President, The Governor.
Financial Secretary, Hon. T. C. Jefferson, OBE.
Attorney-General, Hon. R. W. Ground, QC.
Administrative Secretary, Hon. J. L. Hurlston, MBE.
Member for Tourism, Aviation and Trade, Hon. W. N. Bodden, OBE.
Member for Education, Environment, Recreation and Culture, Hon. B. O. Ebanks, OBE.
Member for Health and Social Services, Hon. D. E. Miller.
Member for Communications, Works and Agriculture, Hon. L. H. Pierson.

LONDON OFFICE
Cayman Islands Government Office,
100 Brompton Road, SW3 1EX
[071–581 9418]

Government Representative, T. Russell, CMG, CBE.

ECONOMY

Based on a complete absence of direct taxation, the Cayman Islands have been successfully promoted over the past 25 years as an offshore financial centre. With representation from 60 countries, there were, at the end of 1990, 546 banks and trust companies, of which local offices were maintained by 78. In addition, there were 360 licensed insurance companies and 22,368 registered companies at the end of 1990.

Promotion of tourism, with an emphasis on scuba diving, has also been successful. There were 253,158 visitors by air and 361,712 cruise ship callers in 1990.

The two industries support a heavy imbalance in

trade resulting from the need to import most of what is consumed and used on the islands, and have created a thriving local economy in which the GNP reached US$715·2m (US$26,160 per capita) in 1990. Import duty and fees from financial centre operations have provided revenue enabling the government to undertake heavy investment in education (which is provided free to all 4–16 year olds), health and other social programmes.

FINANCE

	1990	1991*
Revenue	CI$101·8m	CI$110·2m
Expenditure	103·0m	109·7m
*estimated		

TRADE

	1989	1990
Total imports	CI$215·6m	CI$239·7m
Total exports	2·1m	3·1m

Trade with UK

	1989	1990
Imports from UK	£5,174,000	£13,394,000
Exports to UK	8,693,000	2,262,000

FALKLAND ISLANDS

The Falkland Islands, the only considerable group in the South Atlantic, lie about 300 miles east of the Straits of Magellan, between 52° 15′–53° S. lat. and 57° 40′–62° W. long. They consist of East Falkland (area 2,610 sq. miles; 6,759 sq. km), West Falkland (2,090 sq. miles; 5,413 sq. km) and upwards of 100 small islands in the aggregate. Mount Usborne (E. Falkland), the loftiest peak, rises 2,312 feet above the level of the sea.

The climate is cool. At Stanley the mean monthly temperature varies between 9° C in January and 2° C in July. The islands are chiefly moorland.

The Falklands were sighted first by Davis in 1592, and by Hawkins in 1594; the first known landing was by Strong in 1690. A settlement was made by France in 1764; this was subsequently sold to Spain, but the latter country recognized Great Britain's title to a part at least of the group in 1771. After Argentina declared independence from Spain, the Argentine government in 1820 proclaimed its sovereignty over the Falklands and a settlement was founded in 1826. The settlement was destroyed by the Americans in 1831. In 1833 occupation was resumed by the British for the protection of the seal-fisheries, and the islands were permanently colonized as the most southerly organized colony of the British Empire. Argentina continued to claim sovereignty over the islands (known to them as las Islas Malvinas), and in pursuance of this claim invaded the islands on April 2, 1982 and also occupied South Georgia. A Task Force despatched from Great Britain recaptured South Georgia on April 25, and after landing at San Carlos Bay on May 21, recaptured the islands from the Argentines, who surrendered on June 14, 1982. A British naval and military presence remains in the area.

The population, excluding the British garrison, was 2,121 at March 5, 1991.

CHIEF TOWN.—ΨStanley, population 1,643 (1991). Stanley is about 8,103 miles distant from England.

CURRENCY.—Falkland pound of 100 pence.

GOVERNMENT

Under the 1985 Constitution, the Governor is advised by an Executive Council consisting of three elected members of the Legislative Council and two ex-officio members, the Chief Executive and the Financial Secretary. The Legislative Council consists of eight elected members and the same two ex-officio members.

Governor and Chairman of the Executive Council, His Excellency William Hugh Fullerton, CMG (1988).
Chief Executive, R. Sampson.
Financial Secretary, J. Buckland-James.
Commander, British Forces, Falkland Islands, Air Vice-Marshal P. G. Beer, CBE, LVO.
Attorney General, D. G. Lang, QC.

LONDON OFFICE
Falkland Islands Government Office,
Falkland House, 14 Broadway, SW1H 0BH
[071-222 2542]

Government Representative, Miss S. Cameron.

FINANCE

	1988–89	1990
Public Revenue	£42,115,250	£44,060,260
Expenditure	32,608,380	35,911,730

ECONOMY

The economy was formerly based solely on agriculture, principally sheep-farming with a little dairy farming for domestic requirements and crops for winter fodder. Since the establishment of an interim conservation and management zone around the islands and the consequent introduction on February 1, 1987 of a licensing regime for vessels fishing within the zone the economy has diversified and income from the associated fishing activities is now the largest source of revenue. Chief imports are provisions, alcoholic beverages, timber, clothing and hardware.

Trade with UK

	1989	1990
Imports from UK	£10,200,000	£11,309,000
Exports to UK	5,375,000	4,817,000

GIBRALTAR

Gibraltar is a rocky promontory, 2¾ miles in length, three-quarters of a mile in breadth and 1,396 ft. high at its greatest elevation, near the southern extremity of Spain, with which it is connected by a low isthmus. It is about 14 miles distant from the opposite coast of Africa. The town stands at the foot of the promontory on the W. side. In a total area of 2½ sq. miles (6 sq. km), the population at the end of 1990 stood at 30,861.

CURRENCY.—Gibraltar pound of 100 pence.

GOVERNMENT

Gibraltar was captured in 1704, during the war of the Spanish Succession, by a combined Dutch and English force, under Sir George Rooke, and was ceded to Great Britain by the Treaty of Utrecht, 1713. Several attempts have been made to retake it, the most celebrated being the great siege of 1779–83, when General Eliott, afterwards Lord Heathfield, held it for three years and seven months against a combined French and Spanish force.

The Constitution of Gibraltar, approved in 1969, made formal provision for certain domestic matters to devolve on Ministers appointed from among elected members of the House of Assembly then set up to replace the former Legislative Council. The House of Assembly consists of an independent Speaker, 15 elected members, the Attorney-General and the Financial and Development Secretary.

Governor and Commander-in-Chief, His Excellency Admiral Sir Derek Reffell, KCB.
Flag Officer, Gibraltar, and Admiral Superintendent, HM Naval Base, Gibraltar, Rear-Adm. G. W. R. Biggs.
Deputy Governor, A. Carter.
Financial and Development Secretary, P. Brooke.
Attorney-General, K. Harris.
Chief Justice, A. Kneller.
Chief Minister, J. Bossano.
Speaker, Mayor R. J. Peliza, OBE.

ECONOMY

Gibraltar enjoys the advantages of an extensive shipping trade and is a popular shopping centre. The chief sources of revenue are the port dues, the rent of the Crown estate in the town, and duties on consumer items. The free port tradition of Gibraltar is still reflected in the low rates of import duty. The gradual change from a fortress city to a holiday centre has led to a flourishing tourist trade.

A total of 3,395 merchant ships (58,057,883 gross registered tons aggregate) entered the port during 1990. Of these 2,521 were deep-sea ships (57,593,017 gross registered tons aggregate). In addition 4,950 yachts called at the port. There are 49·9 km of roads.

EDUCATION

Education is compulsory and free for children between the ages of 4 and 15 whose parents are ordinarily resident in Gibraltar. Scholarships are available for higher education in Britain. The total enrolment in Government schools was 4,612 in December 1990.

FINANCE AND TRADE

	1988–89	1989–90
Revenue	£82,125,000	£87,716,000
Expenditure	81,904,000	90,158,000

	1988	1989
Total imports	£144,717,000	£200,493,000
Total exports	46,093,000	76,138,000

Trade with UK

	1989	1990
Imports from UK	£69,350,000	£69,073,000
Exports to UK	4,560,000	5,048,000

HONG KONG

Hong Kong, consisting of a number of islands and of a portion of the mainland (Kowloon and the New Territories), on the south-eastern coast of China, is situated at the eastern side of the mouth of the Pearl River, between 22° 9′ and 22° 37′ N. lat. and 113° 52′–114° 30′ E. long. The total area of the territory (including recent reclamation) is 416 sq. miles (1,074 sq. km) with a population which at the end of 1990 was 5·8 million.

The island of Hong Kong is about 11 miles long and from two to five miles broad, with a total area of 29 sq. miles; at the eastern entrance to the harbour it is separated from the mainland by a narrow strait.

CLIMATE.—Hong Kong's climate is sub-tropical, tending towards the temperate for nearly half the year. The mean monthly temperature ranges from 16° C to 29° C. The average annual rainfall is 2,225 mm, of which nearly 80 per cent falls between May and September. Tropical cyclones passing at various distances from Hong Kong occur between June and October, causing high winds and heavy rain.

CAPITAL.—ΨVictoria, situated on the island of Hong Kong, is about 81 miles SE of Canton and 40 miles E. of the Portuguese province of Macao at the other side of the Pearl River. It lies along the northern shore of the island and faces the mainland the harbour (23 sq. miles water area) lies between the city and the mainland.

CURRENCY.—Hong Kong dollar (HK$) of 100 cents.

GOVERNMENT

The island was first occupied by Great Britain in January, 1841, and formally ceded by the Treaty of Nanking in 1842. Kowloon was subsequently acquired by the Peking Convention of 1860, and the New Territories, consisting of a peninsula in the southern part of the Guangdong province together with adjacent islands, by a 99-year lease signed June 9, 1898.

Hong Kong is administered by the Hong Kong Government, at the head of which is the Governor, and its administration has developed from the basic pattern applied to all British-governed territories overseas. Under the terms of the Joint Declaration of the British and Chinese Governments, which entered into force on May 27, 1985, Hong Kong will become with effect from July 1, 1997, a Special Administrative Region of the People's Republic of China. However, the social and economic systems in the SAR will remain unchanged for 50 years.

The Governor governs aided by an Executive Council, consisting of four ex-officio and ten appointed members, and a Legislative Council, which consists of three ex-officio and seven official members, 20 appointed members, 12 elected by the Electoral College and 14 by the functional constituencies. The first direct elections for 18 of the 60 Legislative Council seats are to be held in September 1991.

There is also an Urban Council which provides services relating to public health and sanitation, culture and recreation in the urban area. A Regional Council was also set up in 1986 to provide similar services in the New Territories. Eleven of the 36 Regional Council seats and 14 of the 40 Urban Council seats were directly elected for the first time in May 1991. Both Councils are financially autonomous. China is demanding an increasing voice in Hong Kong affairs as the handover in 1997 approaches.

Governor, His Excellency Sir David Wilson, KCMG (1987).
Chief Justice, The Hon. Sir Ti Liang Yang.
Chief Secretary, Hon. Sir David Ford, KBE, LVO.
Commander, British Forces, Maj.-Gen. P. R. Duffell CBE, MC.
Financial Secretary, Hon. N. W. H. McLeod.
Attorney-General, Hon. J. F. Mathews, CMG
Secretary for the Civil Service, Hon. E. B. Wiggham.
Planning, Environment and Lands, Hon. G. Barnes CBE.
Transport, Hon. Michael M. K. Leung.
Education and Manpower, Hon. John C. C. Chan LVO, OBE.
Economic Services, Hon. Mrs Anson Chan.
Home Affairs, Hon. Peter K. W. Tsao, CBE, CPM.
Health and Welfare, Hon. Mrs Elizabeth C. L. Wong ISO.
Security, Hon. A. P. Asprey, OBE, AE.
Monetary Affairs, D. A. C. Nendick, CBE.
Recreation and Culture, James So, OBE.
Treasury, K. Y. Yeung.
Trade and Industry, T. H. Chau.
Constitutional Affairs, Michael M. Y. Suen.
Works, Kenneth W. K. Kwok, OBE.

British Council Representative, T. Buchanan, Easey Commercial Building, 225 Hennessy Road, Wanchai, Hong Kong.

LONDON OFFICE
Hong Kong Government Office
6 Grafton Street, W1X 3LB
[071-499 9821]

Commissioner, John Yaxley, CBE (1989).

COMMUNICATIONS

Hong Kong, one of the world's finest natural harbours, possesses excellent wharves. The Kwai Chung container terminal has 12 berths. A pier at the Ocean Terminal can accommodate large liners and cargo vessels up to 290 metres length and 10 metres draught. Mooring buoys in the harbour are available to vessels of up to 12 metres draught. Available dockyard facilities include three floating drydocks, the largest being capable of docking vessels up to 150,000 tonnes deadweight. In 1990 some 20,363 ocean-going vessels and 99,460 river-trade vessels called at Hong Kong and loaded and discharged more than 89 million tonnes of cargo.

Hong Kong International Airport, Kai Tak, situated to the east of the Kowloon peninsula, is regularly used by over 43 international airlines, providing some 1,750 frequent scheduled passenger and cargo services each week. During 1990, over 105,782 aircraft on international flights arrived and departed, carrying 18·5 million passengers and 801,939 tonnes of freight. A new international airport is to be built on reclaimed land off Lantau Island.

EDUCATION

In September 1990 there were 1,887 day schools with 1,145,953 pupils. Free education for children up to the age of 15 was made compulsory in 1979. Post-secondary education is provided by two universities, two polytechnics, the Hong Kong Baptist College and two approved post-secondary colleges. The Hong Kong Polytechnic and City Polytechnic of Hong Kong have about 10,495 and 6,434 full-time students respectively. There are also eight technical institutes and four teacher-training colleges.

FINANCE

	1988–89	1990–91
Public revenue	HK$72,658m	HK$82,429m
Public expenditure	53,796m	71,366m

TRADE AND INDUSTRY

The manufacturing sector is the mainstay of Hong Kong's economy, contributing about 18·3 per cent to the GDP and accounting for about 28 per cent of total employment. Up to 90 per cent of Hong Kong's manufacturing output is eventually exported.

Hong Kong's manufacturing industries produce light consumer goods, such as electronics, plastics, electrical products, watches and clocks, which accounted for 33 per cent of Hong Kong's total domestic exports in 1989. The corresponding share of textiles and clothing, Hong Kong's traditional leading industries, was 39 per cent in 1990.

Diversification in terms of products and markets continues to be the main feature of recent industrial development, as are industrial partnerships with overseas companies. The economy of Hong Kong is based on export rather than the domestic market. In 1990, the total value of visible trade (including domestic exports, re-exports and imports) amounted to 235 per cent of the GDP. Hong Kong's visible trade account attained in 1990 a deficit of HK$2,656 million. Taking visible and invisible trade together, there was a combined surplus of HK$29,364 million, compared with HK$40,047 million in 1989. In 1990, Hong Kong's principal customers for its domestic products,

in order of value of trade, were USA, China, the Federal Republic of Germany, the United Kingdom, Japan, Singapore and Taiwan. China was its principal supplier.

TRADE

	1989	1990
Total Exports	HK$570,509m	HK$639,874m
Total Imports	562,781m	642,530m

Trade with UK

	1989	1990
Imports from UK	£1,111,517,000	£1,238,023,000
Exports to UK	2,036,976,000	1,972,154,000

MONTSERRAT

Situated in 16° 45′ N. lat. and 61° 15′ W. long., 27 miles SW of Antigua, the island is about 11 miles long and seven wide, with an area of 38 sq. miles (98 sq. km), and a population (UN estimate 1989), of 13,000. Discovered by Columbus in 1493, it was settled by Irishmen in 1632, conquered and held by the French for some time, and finally assigned to Great Britain in 1783. Fertile and green, it is volcanic with several hot springs. About two-thirds of the island is mountainous, the rest capable of cultivation.

CHIEF TOWN.—ΨPlymouth, population 3,000.
CURRENCY.—East Caribbean dollar (EC$) of 100 cents.

GOVERNMENT

A Ministerial system was introduced in Montserrat in 1960. The Executive Council is presided over by the Governor and is composed of four elected members (the Chief and three other Ministers) and two ex-officio members (the Attorney-General and the Financial Secretary). The four Ministers are appointed from the members of the political party holding the majority in the Legislative Council. The Legislative Council consists of the Speaker, two ex-officio members (the Attorney General and the Financial Secretary), two nominated unofficial members and seven elected members.

Governor, His Excellency David Taylor (1990).

Executive Council
(as at June 6, 1991)

President, The Governor.
Chief Minister and Minister of Finance, Hon. J. A. Osborne.
Communications and Works, Hon. J. B. Chalmers.
Education, Health and Community Services, Hon. V. K. Jeffers.
Agriculture, Trade, Lands and Housing, Hon. N. Tuitt.
Attorney-General, S. A. Moore.
Financial Secretary, C. T. John, OBE.

Speaker of the Legislative Council, Dr the Hon. H. A. Fergus, OBE.

ECONOMY

The economy is dominated by tourism, related construction activities, offshore business services and specializations in telecommunications and media services. The chief export in 1988 was light fixtures assembled on the island, but increased efforts are directed at the expansion of the sea-island cotton market, upgrading agriculture and agro-processing, and some data processing.

FINANCE

	1989	1990
Revenue	EC$35,049,330	EC$39,138,570
Expenditure	34,308,150	38,155,890

Trade with UK

	1989	1990
Imports from UK	£3,092,000	£3,515,000
Exports to UK	494,000	425,000

PITCAIRN ISLANDS

Pitcairn, a small volcanic island, 1·9 sq. miles (5 sq. km), in area, is the chief of a group of islands situated about midway between New Zealand and Panama in the South Pacific Ocean at longitude 130° 06′ W. and latitude 25° 04′ S.

The island rises in cliffs to a height of 1,100 feet and access from the sea is possible only at Bounty Bay, a small rocky cove, and then only by surf boats. Mean monthly temperatures vary between 66°F (19°C) in August and 75°F (24°C) in February and the average annual rainfall is 80 inches. With an equable climate, the island is very fertile and produces both tropical and sub-tropical trees and crops.

First settled in 1790 by the Bounty mutineers and their Tahitian companies, Pitcairn was left uninhabited in 1856 when the entire population was resettled on Norfolk Island. The present community, numbering 56 (June 1991), are descendants of two parties who, not wishing to remain on Norfolk, returned to Pitcairn in 1859 and 1864 respectively.

Pitcairn became a British settlement under the British Settlement Act, 1887, and was administered by the Governor of Fiji from 1952 until 1970, when the administration was transferred to the British High Commission in New Zealand and the British High Commissioner was appointed Governor. The local Government Ordinance of 1964 provides for a Council of ten members of whom six are elected.

Governor of Pitcairn, Henderson, Ducie and Oeno Islands, His Excellency David Joseph Moss, CMG (*British High Commissioner to New Zealand*).
Island Magistrate and Chairman of Island Council, J. Warren.
Education Officer and Government Adviser, A. R. Washington.

The islanders live by subsistence gardening and fishing, and their limited monetary needs are satisfied by the manufacture of wood carvings and other handicrafts which are sold to passing ships and to a few overseas customers. Other than small fees charged for gun and driving licences there are no taxes and Government revenue is derived almost solely from the sale of postage stamps. Communication with the outside world is maintained by cargo vessels travelling between New Zealand and Panama which call at irregular intervals; and by means of telephone links with New Zealand.

The New Zealand Ministry of Education provides assistance in recruiting a teacher for the sole-charge school. Education is compulsory between the ages of five and fifteen. Secondary education in New Zealand is encouraged by the Administration which provides scholarships and bursaries for the purpose. Medical care is provided by a registered nurse when a doctor is not present. Since 1887 the islanders have all been adherents of the Seventh Day Adventist Church.

The other three islands of the group (Henderson lying 105 miles ENE of Pitcairn, Oeno lying 75 miles NW and Ducie lying 293 miles E.) are all uninhabited. Henderson Island is occasionally visited by the Pitcairn Islanders to obtain supplies of 'miro' wood which is used for their carvings. Oeno is visited for excursions of about a week's duration every two years or so.

ST HELENA

Probably the best known of all the solitary islands in the world, St Helena is situated in the South Atlantic Ocean, 955 miles S. of the Equator, 702 SE of Ascension, 1,140 from the nearest point of the African Continent, 1,800 from the coast of South America, 1,694 from Cape Town (transit 5 days), in 15° 55′ S. lat. and 5° 42′ W. longitude. It is 10¼ miles long, 6¼ broad, and encloses an area of 47 sq. miles (122 sq. km), with a population of 5,544 (1987).

St Helena is of volcanic origin, and consists of numerous rugged mountains, the highest rising to 2,700 feet, interspersed with picturesque ravines. Although within the tropics, the south-east 'trades' keep the temperature mild and equable. St Helena was discovered by the Portuguese navigator, Juan da Nova Castella, in 1502 (probably on St Helena's Day) and remained unknown to other European nations until 1588. It was used as a port of call for vessels of all nations trading to the East until it was annexed by the Dutch in 1633. It was never occupied by them, however, and the English East India Company seized it in 1659. In 1834 it was ceded to the Crown. During the period 1815 to 1821 the island was lent to the British Government as a place of exile for the Emperor Napoleon Bonaparte who died in St Helena on May 5, 1821. It was formerly an important station on the route to India, but its prosperity decreased after the construction of the Suez Canal. Since the collapse of the New Zealand flax industry in 1965, there have been no significant exports. ψSt James's Bay, on the north-west of the island, possesses a good anchorage. There is as yet no airport or airstrip.

CAPITAL.—ψJamestown. Population (1987) 1,330.
CURRENCY.—St Helena pound (£) of 100 pence.

GOVERNMENT

The government of St Helena is administered by a Governor, with the aid of a Legislative Council, consisting of a Speaker, three ex-officio members (Chief Secretary, Financial Secretary and Attorney-General) and twelve elected members. Five committees of the Legislative Council are responsible for general oversight of the activities of government departments and have in addition a wide range of statutory and administrative functions. The Governor is also assisted by an Executive Council of the three ex-officio members and the Chairmen of the Council committees.

Governor, His Excellency A. N. Hoole, OBE (1991).
Chief Secretary, M. Hone, MBE.
Financial Secretary, M. Rosling.
Attorney-General, D. Jeremiah.
Chief Medical Officer, Dr N. Nichol.
Director of Agriculture and Natural Resources, C. Lomas.
Chief Education Officer, B. George.
Director of Works, vacant.
Chief Social Services and Employment Officer, vacant.

FINANCE AND TRADE

	1988–89	1989–90
Local revenue	£2,379,200	£2,410,900
Budgetary	3,543,100	3,904,300
Recurrent expenditure ..	5,905,800	6,104,700
Development aid	1,117,900	1,480,700
Total imports	4,466,000	6,156,500
Total exports	101,000	257,300

Trade with UK

	1989	1990
Imports from UK	£7,208,000	£7,429,000
Exports to UK	504,000	555,000

ASCENSION

The small island of Ascension lies in the South Atlantic (7° 56′ S., 14° 22′ W.) some 700 miles north-west of the island of St Helena. It is a rocky peak of purely volcanic origin, the highest point (Green Mountain) some 2,817 ft. is covered with lush vegetation. Ascension Island Services operate a farm of some 10 acres on the mountain, producing vegetables and livestock. The island is famous for turtles, which land on the beaches from January to May to lay their eggs. It is also a breeding area for the sooty tern, or wideawake, large numbers of which settle on the south-western coastal section every eighth month to hatch their eggs. Other wildlife on the island includes feral donkeys and cats, rabbits and francolin partridge. All wildlife except rabbits and cats is protected by law. The ocean surrounding the island contains shark, barracuda, tuna, bonito and many other fish.

Ascension is said to have been discovered by Juan da Nova Castella, on Ascension Day, 1501, and two years later was visited by Alphonse d'Albuquerque, who gave the island its present name. It was uninhabited until the arrival of Napoleon in St Helena in 1815 when a small British naval garrison was stationed on the island. It remained under the supervision of the Board of Admiralty until 1922, when it was made a dependency of St Helena by Royal Letters Patent.

The British Foreign Secretary appoints the Administrator who is responsible to the Governor resident in St Helena. There is a small Police Force and Post Office. The British organizations through Ascension Island Services (AIS) provide and operate various common services for the island (school, hospital, public works etc).

Ascension Island is a main relay point of the coaxial submarine cable system laid between South Africa, Portugal and the United Kingdom, which is operated by the South Atlantic Cable Company. Cable & Wireless PLC operates the international telephone and cable services and maintains an internal telephone service. The BBC opened its Atlantic relay station broadcasting to Africa and South America in 1967.

The resident population in March 1990 totalled 1,029, of whom 728 were from St Helena, 184 from the UK, 112 from the USA and 5 from the Republic of South Africa. The residents consist of the employees and families of the British organizations, of the contractors of the US Air Force (Computer Sciences Raytheon) and of the St Helena Government.

British forces returned to the island in April 1982 in support of operations in the Falkland Islands. At present there are over 100 RAF/PSA personnel on the island supporting the air link to the Falklands.
CAPITAL.—Georgetown.

Administrator, B. N. Connelly.

TRISTAN DA CUNHA

Tristan da Cunha is the chief of a group of islands of volcanic origin lying in lat. 37° 6′ S. and long. 12° 2′ W., discovered in 1506 by a Portuguese admiral (Tristão da Cunha), after whom they are named. They have a total area of 38 sq. miles (98 sq. km). Population (1990) 290 islanders. The main island, with a peak rising to 6,760 ft., is about 1,500 miles W. of the Cape of Good Hope, 3,600 miles NE of Cape Horn, and about 1,320 miles SSW of St Helena. It was

the resort of British and American sealers from the middle of the 18th century, and in 1760 a British naval officer visited the group and gave his name to Nightingale Island. On August 14, 1816 the group was annexed to the British Crown and a garrison was placed on Tristan da Cunha, but this force was withdrawn in 1817. William Glass, a corporal of artillery (died 1853), remained at his own request with his wife and two children. This party, with five others, formed a settlement. In 1827 five women from St Helena, and afterwards others from Cape Colony, joined the party.

The islands form a dependency of St Helena, being administered by the Foreign and Commonwealth Office through a resident Administrator, with headquarters at the settlement of Edinburgh. Under a new constitution introduced in 1969, he is advised by an elected Island Council of eight members of whom one must be a woman, and three appointed members, with universal suffrage at 18.

In October, 1961 a volcano, believed to have been extinct for thousands of years, erupted and the danger of further volcanic activity led to the evacuation of inhabitants to the United Kingdom. An advance party returned to Tristan da Cunha in the spring of 1963, and subsequently the main body of the islanders returned to the island.

A boat harbour was completed in 1967. The first freezing factory was re-established in 1966. There are no taxes on Tristan, income being derived from royalties paid by the fishing company and from the sale of stamps and handicrafts. The Camogli Hospital was opened early in 1971 and a new school in 1975.
CAPITAL.—Edinburgh.

Administrator, Bernard Pauncefort, OBE.

INACCESSIBLE ISLAND is a lofty mass of rock with sides two miles in length; the island is the resort of penguins and sea-fowl. Cultivation was started in 1937, but has been abandoned.

THE NIGHTINGALE ISLANDS are three in number, of which the largest is 1 mile long and ½ mile wide, and rises in two peaks, 960 and 1,105 ft. above sea-level respectively. The smaller islands, Stoltenhoff and Middle Isle, are little more than huge rocks. Seals, innumerable penguins, and vast numbers of sea-fowl visit these islands.

GOUGH ISLAND (or Diego Alvarez), in 40° 20′ S. and 9° 44′ W., lies about 250 miles SSE of Tristan da Cunha. The island is about 8 miles long and 4 miles broad, with a total area of 40 square miles, and has been a British possession since 1816. The island is the resort of penguins and sea-elephants and has valuable guano deposits. There is no permanent population, but there is a meteorological station maintained on the island by the South African Government and manned by South Africans.

SOUTH GEORGIA AND THE SOUTH SANDWICH ISLANDS

South Georgia is an island 800 miles east-south-east of the Falkland group, with an area of 1,450 sq. miles. The population comprises an army unit at King Edward Point, and staff of the British Antarctic Survey at Bird Island, in the north-west of S. Georgia.

The South Sandwich Islands lie some 470 miles SE of South Georgia. The group is a chain of uninhabited, actively volcanic islands about 150 miles long, with a wholly Antarctic climate.

The present constitution came into effect on October 3, 1985. It provides for a Commissioner who, for the time being, shall be the officer administering the Government of the Falkland Islands.

Commissioner for South Georgia and the South Sandwich Islands, William Hugh Fullerton, CMG (1988).

TURKS AND CAICOS ISLANDS

The Turks and Caicos Islands are situated between 21° and 22° N. latitude and 71° and 72° W. longitude, about 100 miles north of the Dominican Republic and 50 miles south-east of the Bahamas of which they are geographically an extension. There are over 30 islands of which eight are inhabited covering an estimated area of 166 sq. miles (430 sq. km). The principal is Grand Turk. The population in 1988 was estimated to be 14,000 (Grand Turk 4,500).

The Islands lie in the trade wind belt. The average temperature varies from 24°–27° C in the winter and 29°–32° C in the summer and humidity is generally low. Average rainfall is 21 inches per annum.

GOVERNMENT

A new Constitution was introduced in 1988, providing for an enlarged Executive Council and Legislative Council. The Executive Council is presided over by the Governor and comprises the Chief Minister and four elected Ministers, together with the Chief Secretary, the Attorney General and the Financial Secretary ex-officio.

At the General Election of April 3, 1991, the People's National Party won 8 seats and the People's Democratic Movement 5 seats in the Legislative Council.

Governor, His Excellency Michael John Bradley, CMG, QC (1987).

Executive Council
(as at June 4, 1991)

President, The Governor.
Chief Secretary, Hon. A. P. Fabian.
Attorney-General, Hon. G. Gatland.
Financial Secretary, Hon. A. Robinson, MBE.
Members, Hon. W. Misick (*Chief Minister*); Hon. A. Durham; Hon. A. Smith; Hon. R. Hall; Hon. M. Misick.

The principal airports are on the islands of Grand Turk, Providenciales and South Caicos. There are direct shipping services to the USA (Miami). There is an air service between Miami, Providenciales and Grand Turk, and between South Caicos and the Bahamas. An internal air service provides a twice daily service between the principal islands. A comprehensive telephone and telex service is provided by Cable and Wireless (WI) Ltd

The most important industries are fishing, tourism and offshore finance.

FINANCE

	1988–89	1989–90*
Local Revenue	US$17,222,903	US$21,095,740
Expenditure	16,843,099	20,763,035
Budgetary Aid	237,000	Nil
*estimate		

Trade with UK

	1989	1990
Imports from UK	£731,000	£1,719,000
Exports to UK	74,000	8,000

FOREIGN COUNTRIES

he following articles have been revised with the ssistance of the various governments or of the 3ritish representatives at foreign capitals and of the oreign and Commonwealth Office in London, whom he Editor thanks. The Editor is also greatly indebted o the Embassies and Consulates-General in London or their help.

AFGHANISTAN
(Da Afghanistan Jamhuriat)

resident of the Republic of Afghanistan, Gen. Dr Mohammad Najibollah.

ice Presidents, Abdul Rahim Hatif, Col.-Gen. Mohammad Aslam Rafi, Abdul Hamid Mohtat, Abdul Wahed Sorabi, Mohammad Eshaq Tokhi.

COUNCIL OF MINISTERS
(as at July 1991)

rime Minister, Fazal Hag Khaliqyar.

eputy Prime Ministers, Dr Abdul Wahed Sorabi, Dr Nehmatullah Pazhwak, Abdol Qayum Nurzay, Mohammed Sarwar Mangal, Mahboobullah Koshani.

eputy Prime Minister for Economic Affairs, Abdol Samad Salim.

eputy Prime Minister for Social and Cultural Affairs, Mohammad Anwar Arghandiwal.

ducation and Training, Masoma Esmati Wardak.

ustice, Prof. Gholam Mahaynodin Darez.

ublic Health, Prof. Mehr Mohammad Ejazi.

oreign Affairs, Abdul Wakil.

nternal Affairs, Dr Raz Mohammad Paktin.

ocial Security, Saleha Faruq Etemadi.

inance, Mohammad Hakim.

efence, Gen. Mohammad Aslam Watanjar.

tate Security, Gen. Gholam Faruq Yaqubi.

slamic Affairs and Endowments, Mohammad Sediq Saylani.

tatistics, Dr Mohammad Nazir Shahedi.

order Affairs, Sarjang Zazai.

griculture (and Land Reform), Mohammad Ghofran.

ight Industries and Foodstuffs, Dr Mohammad Anwar Dost.

onstruction Affairs, Dr Faqir Mohammad Nekzad.

lanning, Ghalan Mayhodin Shahbaz.

ines and Industries, Abdol Samad Salah.

ommerce, Zakim Shah.

ivil Aviation and Tourism, Dr Wadir Safi.

ommunications, Sayed Naseem Alawi.

ater and Electricity, Mir Abdol Rahim.

nformation and Culture, Abdol Bashir Roygar.

igher and Vocational Education, Dr Prof. Mohammad Anwar Shamas.

eturnees Affairs, Fateh Mohammad Tarin.

ehabilitation and Rural Development, Hayatollah Azizi.

ransport, Lt.-Gen. Khalilollah.

inisters without Portfolio, Nur Ahmed Berits, Dr Faqir Mohammad Yaqubi, Dr Shah Wali, Sayed Ekram Paygir.

Hezb-e-Watan
(Homeland Party)

hairman, Gen. Dr Mohammad Najibollah.

ice Chairmen, Suleiman Laeq, Farid Ahmed Mazdak, Najmuddin Kawiani, Nazar Mohammad.

xecutive Council of the Central Council, Dr Raz Mohammad Paktin, Sultan Ali Keshtmand, Suleiman Laeq, Abdul Wakil, Gen. Gholam Faruq Yaqubi, Farid Ahmad Mazdak, Gen. Mohammad Aslam Watanjar, Gen. Mohammad Aslam Rafi,

Mahmud Barialay, Najmuddin Kawiani, Nazar Mohammad (*Full Members*); Sayed Ekram Paygir, Abdol Qodus Ghorbandi (*Alternate Members*).

EMBASSY OF THE REPUBLIC OF AFGHANISTAN
31 Prince's Gate, SW7 1QQ
[071–589 8891]

Minister-Counsellor and Chargé d'Affaires, Taza Khan Wial.

Afghanistan lies to the N. and W. of Pakistan. Its ancient name was Aryana, by which title it is referred to by Strabo, the Greek geographer who lived in the 1st century BC. The estimated area is 250,000 sq. miles (647,497 sq. km), and the population 15,814,000 (1989 UN estimate). It is estimated that over four million have become refugees in Pakistan and over one million in Iran since the Soviet invasion. The population is very mixed. The most numerous race is the Pushtuns who predominate in the south and west, the Tadjiks, a Persian-speaking people, Uzbeks and Turkomans in the north, Hazaras in the centre, Baluchis in the south-west and Nuristanis, who live near the Chitral border. All are Sunni Muslims, except the Hazaras and Kizilbashes, who belong to the Shia sect.

Afghanistan is bounded on the W. by Iran, on the S. by Pakistan, on the N. by the USSR, and on the E. by Pakistan and China.

Mountains, chief among which are the Hindu Kush, cover three-quarters of the country, the elevation being generally over 4,000 feet. There are three great river basins, the Oxus, Helmand, and Kabul. The climate is dry, with extreme temperatures.

Government.—The constitutional monarchy, introduced by the 1964 Constitution, was overthrown by a coup on July 17, 1973. The country was ruled by Presidential decree until February 1977 when a constitution was approved by a *Loya Jerga* (Grand Tribal Council). Mohammad Daoud was elected President of the Republic but was overthrown on April 27, 1978 by the Armed Forces and power was handed to the People's Democratic Party of Afghanistan (PDPA). In December 1979 Soviet troops invaded Afghanistan and installed Babrak Karmal as Secretary General of the PDPA, President of the Revolutionary Council and Head of State. Karmal was replaced as Secretary General of the PDPA by Najibollah in May 1986. A peace agreement in April 1988 led to the withdrawal of Soviet troops which was completed by February 1989. A new Constitution, approved in November 1987, provides for a President, a Council of Ministers, a National Assembly and a Senate.

President Najibollah declared a State of Emergency on February 19, 1989 and the Supreme Council for the Defence of the Homeland was established to take control of the country's affairs. The State of Emergency was lifted and the Supreme Council disbanded on May 4, 1990. A new Prime Minister and Cabinet were appointed, and changes to the 1987 Constitution were ratified by a *Loya Jerga*.

Following a Second Party Congress in late June 1990, the PDPA was renamed Hezb-e-Watan (Homeland Party) and its Politburo and Central Committee were abolished and replaced by an Executive Council and Central Council. Najibollah was elected Chairman of the Party for a four-year term.

Sibgbatullah Mojaddedi was elected President of an interim government-in-exile on February 23, 1989.

Afghanistan is divided into 30 provinces each under a centrally appointed governor.

Judiciary.—The Constitution introduced in 1965

provided for the creation of a legal code, and for a new structure of courts, consisting of a lower court in each *woleswali* (sub province), and a court of appeal in each province, with a Supreme Court in Kabul. The complete separation of executive and judiciary in this constitution was abolished by Presidential Decree in July 1973. In late 1976 and early 1977 new Penal and Civil Codes were published. The 1987 Constitution and recent amendments leave the judicial system largely untouched.

Defence.—The Army numbers about 50,000 but is subject to desertion. Men between the ages of 18 and 40 are liable to four years' military service. A small air force is maintained. All military and air force equipment is now of Russian pattern. There is no precise figure of Mujahidin strength.

Production.—Agriculture and sheep raising are the principal industries. There are generally two crops a year, one of wheat (the staple food), barley, or lentils, the other of rice, millet, maize, and dal. Sugar beet and cotton are grown. Afghanistan is rich in fruits. Sheep, including the Karakuli, and transport animals are bred. Silk, woollen and hair cloths and carpets are manufactured. Salt, silver, copper, coal, iron, lead, rubies, lapis lazuli, gold, chrome, barite, uranium, and talc are found.

Main roads run from Kabul to Kandahar, Herat, Maimana via Mazari-Sharif and Faizabad via Khanabad. The road from Kabul to the north was shortened by the completion in 1964 of the Salang pass. Roads cross the border with Pakistan at Chaman and via the Khyber Pass, and there are roads from Herat to the Russian and Iranian borders. A network of minor roads fit for motor traffic in fine weather links up all important towns and districts.

In 1982 the Afghan and Soviet shores of the River Oxus were linked by a road and rail bridge which joins the Afghan port of Hairatan and the Soviet port of Termez. A network of internal air services operates between the main towns.

Language and Literature.—The principal languages of the country are Dari (a form of Persian) and Pushtu, although a number of minority languages are also spoken in various provinces. All schoolchildren learn both Persian and Pushtu. Education is free and nominally compulsory, elementary schools having been established in most centres; there are secondary schools in large urban areas and two universities, one in Kabul (established 1932) and one in Jalalabad (established early 1970s).

Trade.—Exports are mainly Persian lambskins (Karakul), dried fruits, nuts, cotton, raw wool, carpets, spice and natural gas, while the imports are chiefly oil, cotton yarn and piece goods, tea, sugar, machinery and transport equipment.

Trade with UK

	1989	1990
Imports from UK	£5,376,000	£7,816,000
Exports to UK	4,813,000	9,194,000

CAPITAL.—Kabul (1988, 1,424,400). The chief commercial centres are Kabul and Kandahar (225,500). Other provincial capitals are (UN estimates) Herat (177,300), Mazar-i-Sharif (130,600), Jalalabad (55,000).
CURRENCY.—Afghani (Af) of 100 puls.
FLAG.—Black, red and green horizontal stripes with a device in top left-hand corner.
NATIONAL ANTHEM.—Soroud-e-Melli.
NATIONAL DAY.—April 27.

BRITISH EMBASSY
Karte Parwan, Kabul
[Kabul 30511/3]

Staff were withdrawn from post in February 1989.

ALBANIA
(Republika Shqipërisë)

President, Ramiz Alia.

COUNCIL OF MINISTERS
(as at June 12, 1991)

Chairman of the Council of Ministers, Ylli Bufi.
Vice-Chairman of the Council of Ministers and Minister of economy, Gramoz Pashko.
Vice-Chairman of the Council of Ministers, Zydi Pepa.
Foreign Affairs, Muhamet Kapllani.
Defence, Perikli Teta.
Public Order, Bajram Yzeiri.
Justice, Shefqet Muci.
Finances, Genc Ruli.
Mining and Energy Sources, Drini Mezini.
Industry, Jordan Misja.
Food, Vilson Ahmeti.
Agriculture, Nexhmedin Dumani.
Foreign Economic Relations, Fatos Nano.
Home Trade and Tourism, Agim Mero.
Construction, Emin Mysliu.
Transports, Fatos Bitincka.
Education, Maqo Lakrori.
Culture, Youth, and Sports, Prec Zogaj.
Health, Sabit Broka.
Chairman of State Control Commission, Alfred Karamuco.
Chairman of the Committee of Science and Technology, Petrit Skende.
State Secretary of Economy, Leontiev Cuci.
State Secretary of Agriculture, Resmi Osmani.
State Secretary of Education, Paskal Milo.

Situated on the Adriatic Sea, Albania is bounded on the north and east by Yugoslavia and on the south by Greece. The area of the Republic is estimated at 11,099 sq. miles (28,748 sq. km), with a population (1989 estimate) of 3,202,000.

Albania was under Turkish suzerainty from 1468 until 1912, when independence was declared. After a period of unrest, a republic was declared in 1925, and in 1928 a monarchy. The King went into exile in 1939 when the country was occupied by the Italians. Albania was liberated in November 1944. Elections in 1945 resulted in a Communist-controlled Assembly; the King was deposed in absentia and a republic declared in January 1946.

From 1946 to 1991 Albania was a one-party Communist state. In March 1991 multi-party elections were held and were won by the Socialist Party (the renamed Albanian Worker's Party). Following labour unrest, a coalition government was formed in June 1991. (*See also* **Events of the Year**.)

Much of the country is mountainous and nearly a half is covered by forest. There are fertile areas along the Adriatic coast and the Koritza Basin and there have been land reclamation and irrigation programmes. The main crops are wheat, maize, sugar beet, potatoes and fruit.

All industry is nationalized. The principal industries are agricultural product processing, textiles, oil products and cement. Exports include crude oil minerals (bitumen, chrome, nickel, copper), tobacco, fruit and vegetables. The government is now committed to liberalization of the economy.

Trade with UK

	1989	1990
Imports from UK	£1,957,000	£413,000
Exports to UK	605,000	9,000

CAPITAL.—Tirana, population (1988) 232,500.
CURRENCY.—Lek (Lk) of 100 qindarka.

FLAG.—Black two-headed eagle surmounted by yellow outline star, all on a red field.

NATIONAL DAY.—January 11.

The United Kingdom resumed diplomatic relations with Albania in May 1991.

ALGERIA
(Al-Jumhuriya al-Jazairiya ad-Dimuqratiya ash-Shabiya)

President of State, Secretary-General of the Party, Chadli Bendjedid, *elected,* Feb. 1979, *re-elected,* Jan. 1984 and Dec. 1988.

GOVERNMENT
(as at June 1991)

Prime Minister, Sid Ahmed Ghozali.
National Defence, Khaled Nezzar.
Foreign Affairs, Lakhdar Brahimi.
Minister assisting the PM, responsible for Relations with the Assembly, Aboubakr Belkaid.
Interior and Local Government, Abdelatif Rahal.
Justice, Ali Benflis.
Economy, Hocine Benissad.
Energy, Nordine Ait Laoussine.
Education, Ali Benmohamed.
Labour and Social Affairs, Mohamed Salah Mentouri.
Industry and Mines, Abdenour Keramane.
Posts and Telecommunications, Mohamed Serradj.
Veterans, Brahim Chibout.
Information and Culture, Chikh Bouamrane.
Religious Affairs, M'Hamed Benredouane.
Health, Nafissa Lalliam.
Universities, Djillali Liabes.
Transport, Mourad Belguedj.
Agriculture, Mohamed Elyes Mesli.
Equipment and Housing, Mustapha Harrati.
Vocational Training and Employment, Mohamed Boumahrat.
Youth and Sports, Leila Aslaoui.
Deputy Ministers, Ali Haroun (*Human Rights*); Cherif Hadj Slimane (*Research, Technology and Environment*); Abdelmadjid Tebboune (*Local Government*); Ali Benouari (*Treasury*); Mourad Medelci (*Budget*); Ahmed Fodil Bey (*Trade*); Lakhader Bayou (*PMI*).
Secretary General of the Government, Kamel Leulmi.

ALGERIAN EMBASSY
54 Holland Park, W11 3RS
[071–221 7800]

Ambassador Extraordinary and Plenipotentiary, His Excellency Abdelkrim Gheraieb (1989).

Algeria lies between 8° 45′ W. to 12° E. longitude 27° 6′ N. to a southern limit about 19° N. and has an area of 919,595 sq. miles (2,381,741 sq. km). The population (1987 Census) was 22,971,558. A 1989 UN estimate gives a figure of 24,597,000.

Government.—Algiers surrendered to a French force on July 5, 1830, and Algeria was annexed to France in 1842. From 1881 the three northern departments of Algiers, Oran and Constantine formed an integral part of France. The Southern Territories of the Sahara, formerly a separate colony, became an integral part of Algeria on the attainment of independence. An armed rebellion led by the Muslim Front de Liberation Nationale (FLN) against French rule broke out on November 1, 1954. French control of Algeria came to an end when President de Gaulle declared Algeria independent on July 3, 1962; by October 1963 all agricultural land held by foreigners had been expropriated and by 1965 more than 80 per cent of the French population had left Algeria.
Ben Bella was elected President of the Republic in

September 1963, but was deposed; a Council of the Revolution presided over by Col. Boumediène assumed power on June 19, 1965. A new constitution was established by referendum on November 19, 1976, and in December 1976 President Boumediène was elected for a six-year term of office. Elections for a national popular assembly were held in February 1977. Following President Boumediène's death in December 1978, Chadli Bendjedid was elected President in February 1979. A new Constitution was agreed by referendum in February 1989 which moves Algeria away from a one-party socialist system to a more pluralist political system. Local elections, held in June 1990, were won by the opposition Islamic Salvation Front. Following extensive unrest, the government declared a state of siege in June 1991 and postponed multi-party elections until the end of the year.

Development in Algeria is regulated by a series of national development plans. The 1980–84 Plan concentrated on housing, water supply and agriculture. The 1985–89 Plan continued with these objectives and also included food and processing industries. Agrarian reform started in 1987. The 4,000 state farms have been broken up into 23,000 units. Following riots in October 1988, economic reform was speeded up and now endorses the industrial and financial sectors. The aim is to decentralize planning and devolve management. The private sector is also receiving official encouragement.

Algeria's main industry is the hydrocarbons industry. Oil and natural gas are pumped from the Sahara to terminals on the coast before being exported; the gas is first liquefied at liquefaction plants at Skikda and Arzew, although pipelines serve Libya and Italy direct.

Other major industries being developed include a steel industry, motor vehicles, building materials, paper making, chemical products and metal manufactures. Most major industrial enterprises are still under State control.

Trade with UK

	1989	1990
Imports from UK	£74,368,000	£73,831,000
Exports to UK	177,546,000	259,959,000

Algeria's main exports are crude oil and liquefied natural gas. Principal imports from the United Kingdom are capital plant, equipment for industrial use and foodstuffs.

Algeria has a rapidly expanding network of roads

and railways. Considerable sums are also being spent on the development of the State airline, the national shipping company and telecommunications.

CAPITAL.—ΨAlgiers, population 3,250,000 (approx). It is one of the principal ports of the Mediterranean as well as an important industrial centre. Other towns include ΨOran; Constantine; ΨAnnaba; Blida; Setif; Sidi-Bel-Abbès; Tlemcen; ΨMostaganem; ΨSkikda; ΨBejaia and Tizi Ouzou.

CURRENCY.—Algerian dinar (DA) of 100 centimes.

FLAG.—Red crescent and star on vertically divided green and white background.

NATIONAL ANTHEM.—Qassaman.

NATIONAL DAY.—November 1.

BRITISH EMBASSY
7 Chemin Capitaine Slimane Hocine,
El-Mouradia, Algiers
[Algiers 605601]

Ambassador Extraordinary and Plenipotentiary, His Excellency Christopher Charles Richard Battis- combe (1990).

Cultural Attaché, British Council Representative, D. Munro, 6 Avenue Souidani Boudjemaa, Algiers.

ANDORRA
(Principat d'Andorra)

Viguier Français, Jean-Pierre Courtois.
Viguier Episcopal, Francesc Badia.
Head of Government, Oscar Ribas Reig.

A small, neutral principality (formed by a treaty in 1278), situated on the southern slopes of the Pyrenees between Spain and France, with an approximate area of 175 sq. miles (453 sq. km), and population (UN estimate 1989) of 50,000, less than one-quarter of whom are native Andorrans. It is surrounded by mountains of 6,500 to 10,000 feet. Andorra is divided into seven Parishes, each of which has four Council- lors elected by vote to the Valleys of Andorra Council of twenty-eight. The Council appoints the head of the executive government, who designates the mem- bers of his government. Constitutionally, the sover- eignty of Andorra is vested in two co-Princes, the President of the French Republic and the Spanish Bishop of Urgel. These two co-princes can veto certain decisions of the Council of the Valleys but cannot impose their own decisions without the consent of the Council. They are represented by Permanent Delegates of whom one is the French Prefect of the Pyrenees Orientales Department at Perpignan and the other is the Spanish Vicar-General of the Diocese of Urgel. They are in turn represented in Andorra la Vella by two resident Viguiers known as the Viguier Français and the Viguier Episcopal, who have a joint responsibility for law and order and overall administration policy, together with judicial powers as members of the Supreme Court.

The language of the country is Catalan, but French and Spanish (Castilian) are also spoken. The Budget is expressed in pesetas. The estimated national revenue (1989) was US$800 million, with a per capita income of US$16,567. The climate is cold for six months, but mild in spring and summer. Potatoes are produced in the highlands and tobacco in the valleys. The mountain slopes have been developed for skiing, and it is estimated that 10,000,000 tourists visit the valleys during the year. The economy is largely based on tourism, commerce, tobacco, construction and forestry; a third of the country is classified as forest in which pine, fir, oak, birch and box-tree predomi- nate. Andorra has negotiated a customs union with the European Community which came into force on July 1, 1991.

A good road into the valleys from Spain is open all year round, and that from France is closed only occasionally in winter. An airport at Seo d'Urgell just outside Andorra provides very limited air connections. There are two radio stations in An- dorra, one privately-owned and one operated by a French Government corporation. Both pay dues to the Council of the Valleys.

Trade with UK

	1989	1990
Imports from UK	£10,493,000	£15,763,000
Exports to UK	236,000	9,000

CAPITAL.—Andorra la Vella (population 16,000).

CURRENCY.—French francs and Spanish pesetas are both in use.

FLAG.—Three vertical bands, blue, yellow, red. Andorran coat of arms frequently imposed on central (yellow) band but not essential.

NATIONAL DAY.—September 8.

HM Consul-General, D. Joy, CBE (resident in Barce- lona, Spain) (Tel. 3–4199044).

ANGOLA
(República Popular de Angola)

President, Jose Eduardo Dos Santos.

COUNCIL OF MINISTERS
(as at March 6, 1991)

Interior, Lt.-Gen. Francisco Magalhaes Paiva.
Territorial Administration, Lopo do Nascimento.
Defence, Col.-Gen. Pedro Tonha.
Foreign Affairs, Col. Pedro de Castro Van-Dunem.
Planning, Fernando José Franca van Dunem.
Trade, Ambrosio Silvestre.
Industry, Justino Fernandes.
Justice, Dr L. M. Dias.
Petroleum, J. L. Landoite.
Health, Flavio Joao Fernandes.
Labour and Social Security, Diogo Jorge de Jesus.
Public Works, J. H. Garcia.
Fisheries, Francisco Jose Ramos Da Cruz.
Agriculture, Isaac Dos Anjos.
Transport and Communications, Col. Antonio Paulo Kassoma.
Education, Antonio da Silva Neto.
Finance, Aguinaldo Jaime.
Youth and Sport, Marcolino Jose Carlos Moco.
Information, B. de Cardosa.

EMBASSY OF THE PEOPLE'S REPUBLIC OF ANGOLA
10 Fife Road, SW14 7EL
[081-876 0435]

Ambassador Extraordinary and Plenipotentiary, His Excellency José Primo (1991).

Angola, which has an area of 481,354 sq. miles (1,246,700 sq. km), lies on the western coast of Africa: its population in 1990 was estimated at 9,767,000.

After a Portuguese presence of five centuries, and an anti-colonial war since 1961, Angola became independent on November 11, 1975 in the midst of civil war. Soviet-Cuban military assistance to the Popular Movement for the Liberation of Angola (MPLA) enabled it to defeat its rivals early in 1976. However, the MPLA government remained under pressure from the UNITA guerrilla movement (led by Dr Jonas Savimbi) which by the late 1980s was operating freely. On August 8, 1988 it was announced that a ceasefire between South African, Cuban and Angolan forces had taken place pending talks on withdrawal of South African troops from Angola. The ceasefire agreement was signed, and came into effect, on August 22. In December 1988 an agreement providing for the withdrawal of the 50,000 Cuban troops by July 1991 was signed in New York. On May 31, 1991 a peace agreement was signed between the government and UNITA. Multi-party elections are to take place in the autumn of 1992.

The MPLA, a Marxist-Leninist party, was the sole legal party until early 1991 when a multi-party system was adopted. The Constitution provides for a President, who appoints a Council of Ministers to assist him, and a National People's Assembly.

Angola has valuable oil and diamond deposits and exports of these two commodities account for over 90 per cent of total exports.

Principal agricultural crops are cassava, maize, bananas, coffee, palm oil and kernels, cotton and sisal. Coffee, sisal, maize and palm oil are exported; exports also include mahogany and other hardwoods from the tropical rain forests in the north of the country.

Trade with UK

	1989	1990
Imports from UK	£24,785,000	£29,284,000
Exports to UK	1,286,000	5,142,000

CAPITAL.—ΨLuanda, population estimate 1990, 2 million.

CURRENCY.—Kwanza (Kz) of 100 lwei.

FLAG.—Red and black with a yellow star, machete and cog-wheel.

NATIONAL ANTHEM.—Angola Avante.

NATIONAL DAY.—November 11 (Independence Day).

BRITISH EMBASSY
Rua Diogo Caõ 4 (Caixa Postal 1244), Luanda
[Luanda 334582/3]

Ambassador Extraordinary and Plenipotentiary, His Excellency John Gerard Flynn (1990).

ARGENTINA
(República Argentina)

President, Dr Carlos Saúl Menem, *took office* July 8, 1989.

Vice President, Dr Eduardo Alberto Dunalde.

CABINET
(as at August 15, 1991)

Interior, José Luis Manzano.
Foreign Affairs, Dr Guido Di Tella.
Labour, Jorge Diaz.
Economy and Public Works, Dr Domingo Cavallo.
Education, Dr Antonio Salonia.
Defence, Dr Antonio Ermán González.
Health and Social Welfare, Dr Avelino Porto.
Justice, Leon Arslanaim.

EMBASSY FOR ARGENTINA
53 Hans Place, SW1X 0LA
[071–584 6494]

Ambassador Extraordinary and Plenipotentiary, His Excellency Mario Cámpora (1990).

Argentina occupies the greater portion of the southern part of the South American Continent, and extends from Bolivia to Cape Horn, a total distance of nearly 2,300 miles; its greatest breadth is about 930 miles. It is bounded on the north by Bolivia, on the north-east by Paraguay, Brazil and Uruguay, on the south-east and south by the Atlantic, and on the west by Chile, from which it is separated by the Cordillera de los Andes. On the west the mountainous Cordilleras, with their plateaux, extend from the northern to the southern boundaries; on the east are the great plains.

The Republic consists of 23 provinces and one federal district (Buenos Aires), comprising in all an area of 1,068,302 sq. miles (2,766,889 sq. km.), with a population (Census 1991) of 32,370,298.

Government.—The estuary of La Plata was discovered in 1515 by Juan Díaz de Solís, but it was not until 1536 that Pedro de Mendoza founded Buenos Aires. This city was abandoned and later re-founded by Don Juan de Garay in 1580. In 1810 Spanish rule was defied, and in 1816, after a long campaign of liberation conducted by General José de San Martín, the independence of Argentina was declared by the Congress of Tucumán.

In 1946 Juan Domingo Perón became President until overthrown in 1955. There followed eighteen years of political and economic instability, and eventually in 1973, Perón was recalled from exile. Elected President he died within a year and was succeeded by his widow, Vice President María Estela Martínez de Perón. However, warring factions in the Perónist movement and increasing terrorist activity eventually led to a coup by the armed forces on March 24, 1976. A Junta, consisting of the three commanders of the Armed Forces, was established with one of their number as President. Following the Falkland Islands defeat in 1982 the President, Gen. Galtieri, resigned and the Army appointed Gen. Bignone as President. The Navy and Air Force withdrew from the Junta but this was reconstituted shortly afterwards. Elections for a civilian government to replace the military one were held on October 30, 1983 and the Radical Party's candidate, Raúl Alfonsín, was elected President. Presidential elections in May 1989 were won by the Peronist candidate Carlos Menem. The government has embarked upon privatization of several state-owned corporations.

Agriculture.—Of a total land area of approximately 700 million acres, farms occupy about 425 million. About 60 per cent of the farmland is pasture, 10 per cent annual crops, 5 per cent permanent crops and the remaining 25 per cent forest and wasteland. A large proportion of the land is still held in large estates devoted to cattle raising but the number of small farms is increasing. The principal crops are wheat, maize, oats, barley, rye, linseed, sunflower seed, alfalfa, sugar, fruit and cotton. Argentina is pre-eminent in the production of beef, mutton and wool, and pastoral and agricultural products provide about 85 per cent of Argentina's exports.

Mineral Production.—Oil is found in various parts of the Republic and the production of oil is of first importance to Argentina's industries and, to some extent, to its economic and financial development. Total petroleum output for 1986 was 450,000 b.p.d. There is a refinery in San Lorenzo (Santa Fé province). Natural gas is also produced in a number of provinces.

Coal, lead, zinc, tungsten, iron ore, sulphur, mica and salt are the other chief minerals being exploited. There are small worked deposits of beryllium, manganese, bismuth, uranium, antimony, copper, kaolin, arsenate, gold, silver and tin. Coal is produced at the Rio Turbio mine in the province of Santa Cruz. The output of other materials is not large but greater attention is now being paid to the development of these natural resources, especially copper for which the Government and private companies are carrying out exploration.

Industries.—Meat-packing is one of the principal industries; flour-milling, sugar-refining, and the wine industry are also important. In recent years progress has been made by the textile, plastic and machine tool industries and engineering, especially in the production of motor vehicles and steel manufactures.

Communications.—There are 25,386 miles of railways, which are State property. Plans are in hand for complete re-organization of the railways in order to improve their operating efficiency and reduce a very large financial deficit. The combined national and provincial road network totals approximately 137,000 miles of which 23,180 miles are surfaced. There are air services between Argentina and all the neighbouring republics, Europe, Asia, Canada, the USA and South Africa.

Defence.—The Army consists of four corps organized into 12 brigades, including mountain, jungle, airborne and armoured troops. It numbers about 40,000, including about 10,000 conscripts who serve for between six months and one year.

The Navy consists of 1 aircraft carrier, 6 destroyers, 7 corvettes, 4 submarines, 6 minesweepers and ancillary craft. Strength is about 20,000.

The Air Force consists of 9 brigades and a training force, with a strength of 15,000.

Education.—Education is compulsory for the 7 grades of primary school (6 to 13). Secondary schools (14 to 17+) are available in and around Buenos Aires and in most of the important towns in the interior of the country. Most secondary schools are administered by the Central Ministry of Education in Buenos Aires, while primary schools are administered by the Central Ministry or by Provincial Ministries of Education. Private schools, of which there are many, are also loosely controlled by the Central Ministry. The total number of universities is over 50 with 24 national, 25 private and a small number of provincial universities.

Language and Literature.—Spanish is the language of the Republic and the literature of Spain is accepted as an inheritance by the people. There is little indigenous literature before the break from Spain, but all branches have flourished since the latter half of the nineteenth century. About 450 daily newspapers are published in Argentina, including 7 major ones in the city of Buenos Aires. The

English language newspaper is the *Buenos Aires Herald* (daily). There are several other foreign language newspapers.

Trade with UK

	1989	1990
Imports from UK	£13,585,000	£35,953,000
Exports to UK	98,490,000	144,205,000

CAPITAL.—ΨBuenos Aires, population (1990), metropolitan area 2,955,002; with suburbs, 10,881,381. Other large towns are: ΨRosario (1,071,384), Córdoba (1,134,086), ΨLa Plata (630,260), ΨMar del Plata (503,779), San Miguel de Tucumán (603,331), ΨSanta Fé (329,814) and Mendoza (706,909).

CURRENCY.—Austral (A) of 100 cents.

FLAG.—Horizontal bands of blue, white, blue; gold sun in centre of white band.

NATIONAL ANTHEM.—Oíd Mortales! (Hear, oh mortals!).

NATIONAL DAY.—May 25.

BRITISH EMBASSY
Dr Luis Agote 2412, 1425 Buenos Aires

Ambassador Extraordinary and Plenipotentiary, His Excellency The Hon. Humphrey Maud, CMG (1990).

BRITISH CHAMBER OF COMMERCE, Av. Corrientes 457, 10 piso, 1043 Buenos Aires.

AUSTRIA
(Republik Österreich)

President of the Republic of Austria, Dr Kurt Waldheim, *born* 1918; *elected* June 8, 1986.

CABINET
(as at July, 1991)

Chancellor, Dr Franz Vranitzky (SPÖ).
Vice-Chancellor, Minister for Federalism and Administrative Reform, Josef Riegler (ÖVP).
Women's Affairs, Johanna Dohnal (SPÖ).
Foreign Affairs, Dr Alois Mock (ÖVP).
Economic Affairs, Dr Wolfgang Schüssel (ÖVP).
Employment and Social Affairs, Josef Hesoun (SPÖ).
Finance, Ferdinand Lacina (SPÖ).
Health, Consumer Protection and Sport, Harald Ettl (SPÖ).
Interior, Dr Franz Löschnak (SPÖ).
Justice, Dr Nikolaus Michalek (Indep.)
Defence, Dr Werner Fasslabend (ÖVP).
Agriculture and Forestry, Dr Franz Fischler (ÖVP).
Environment, Youth and Family Affairs, Ruth Feldgrill-Zankel (ÖVP).
Education and Arts, Dr Rudolf Scholten (SPÖ).
Public Economy and Transport, Dr Rudolf Streicher (SPÖ).
Science and Research, Dr Erhard Busek.
Ministers of State, Dr Peter Jankowitsch (SPÖ) *(European Questions)*; Dr Peter Kostelka (SPÖ) *(Public Service)*; Dr Günter Stummvoll (ÖVP) *(Finance)*; Dr Maria Fekter (ÖVP) *(Economic Affairs, Construction and Tourism)*.

SPÖ: Socialists; ÖVP: People's Party (Conservatives).

AUSTRIAN EMBASSY
18 Belgrave Mews West, SW1X 8HU
[071–235 3731]

Ambassador Extraordinary and Plenipotentiary, His Excellency Dr Walter F. Magrutsch (1987).

Austria is a country of central Europe bounded on the north by Czechoslovakia, on the south by Italy and Yugoslavia, on the east by Hungary, on the north-west by the Federal Republic of Germany and on the west by Switzerland and Liechtenstein. Its area is 32,367 sq. miles (83,855 sq. km), and its population is 7,791,000 (official estimate 1990).

Government.—The Republic of Austria comprises nine provinces (Vienna, Lower Austria, Upper Austria, Salzburg, Tyrol, Vorarlberg, Carinthia, Styria and Burgenland) and was established in 1918 on the break-up of the Austro-Hungarian Empire. On March 13, 1938, as a result of the *Anschluss*, Austria (*Österreich*) was incorporated into the *Deutsches Reich* under the name *Ostmark*. After the liberation of Vienna in 1945, the Republic of Austria was reconstituted within the frontiers of 1937 and a freely-elected Government took office on December 20, 1945. The country was divided at this time into four zones occupied respectively by the UK, USA, USSR and France, while Vienna was jointly occupied by the four Powers. On May 15, 1955 the Austrian State Treaty was signed in Vienna by the Foreign Ministers of the four Powers and of Austria. This Treaty recognized the re-establishment of Austria as a sovereign, independent and democratic state, having the same frontiers as on January 1, 1938.

There is a national assembly of 183 Deputies. After the elections of October 7, 1990, the Socialists formed a coalition with the People's Party. The state of the parties in the Nationalrat (Lower House) was:

Socialist Party (Social Democrat)	80
People's Party (Conservative)	60
Freedom Party (Liberal)	33
Green Party	10

In the Bundesrat (Upper House) in March 1990 the People's Party held 30 seats, the Socialist Party 29 and the Liberal Party 5.

Religion and Education.—The predominant religion is Roman Catholic. Education is free and compulsory between the ages of 6 and 15 and there are good facilities for secondary, technical and professional education. There are 12 state-maintained universities and six colleges of art.

Language and Literature.—The language of Austria is German, but the rights of the Slovene- and Croat-speaking minorities in Carinthia, Styria and Burgenland are protected.

Communications.—Internal communications in Austria are partly restricted because of the mountainous nature of the country, although there has been an extensive programme to increase the number of motorways (*Autobahn*), many of which are tunnelled through the mountains. There were, in 1990, 14,663 km of main roads, including a network of Autobahn between major cities which also links up with the West German and Italian networks. The railways in Austria (ÖBB) are state-owned and in 1989 had 5,641 km of track, 57·4 per cent of which is electrified. Of the 425 km of waterways, 350 km are navigable and there is considerable trade through the Danube ports by both local and foreign shipping. There are six commercial airports catering for 7,004,141 passengers in 1989.

Tourism.—In 1989, 18,201,763 tourists visited Austria. Foreign exchange receipts from tourism were Schilling 123,220 million—a major contribution to the balance of payments.

PRODUCTION AND INDUSTRY

The origin of Gross Domestic Product in 1989 was as follows (in AS billion):

Agriculture and forestry	52·9
Manufacturing and mining	454·7
Energy and water supply	50·7
Construction	113·8
Commerce, hotels, restaurants	267·4
Transport and communications	100·6
Asset management	269·8
Other services and producers	295·2
Import duties and other items	66·7

The total value of GDP in 1989 was Schilling 1,671·7 billion.

Agriculture.—The arable land produces wheat, rye, barley, oats, maize, potatoes, sugar beet, turnips, and miscellaneous crops. Many varieties of fruit trees flourish and the vineyards produce excellent wine. The pastures support horses, cattle and pigs. Timber forms a valuable source of Austria's indigenous wealth, about 45 per cent of the total land area consisting of forest areas. Coniferous species predominate (75 per cent of afforested area).

FINANCE

	1988	1989
	Schilling, million	
Federal Budget:		
Revenue	451,343	477,583
Expenditure	568,904	602,300
Gross Budget Deficit...	117,561	124,717

TRADE

Main exports are processed goods (iron and steel, textiles, paper and cardboard products), machinery and transport equipment, other finished goods (including clothing), raw materials and foodstuffs. Main imports are machinery and transport equipment, processed goods, chemical products, foodstuffs, fuel and energy.

	1988	1989
	Schilling, million	
Imports	451,441	514,686
Exports	383,212	429,310

Over 80 per cent of all trade is with other European countries, EC countries accounting for about 67 per cent, Eastern Europe for about 6 per cent and EFTA members for 7 per cent.

Trade with UK

	1989	1990
Imports from UK	£598,099,000	£705,850,000
Exports to UK	933,971,000	957,789,000

CAPITAL.—Vienna, on the Danube, population 1,531,346. Other larger towns are Graz (243,166), Linz (199,910), Innsbruck (117,287), Salzburg (139,426), and Klagenfurt (87,321).

CURRENCY.—Schilling of 100 Groschen.

FLAG.—Horizontal stripes of red, white, red, with eagle crest on white stripe.

NATIONAL ANTHEM.—Land der Berge, Land am Strome (Land of mountains, land on the river).

NATIONAL DAY.—October 26.

BRITISH EMBASSY
Jauresgasse 12, 1030 Vienna
[Vienna 7131575]

Ambassador Extraordinary and Plenipotentiary, His Excellency Brian Lee Crowe, CMG (1989).

Counsellor, Consul General and Head of Chancery, R. P. Nash, LVO.

Counsellors, M. H. McMillan, OBE; P. A. S. Wise; J. Franklin.

First Secretaries, S. J. O'Flaherty; S. G. Ratcliffe (*Commercial*); J. Moorby, MBE (*HM Consul*); A. N. King, LVO (*Administration*); R. Dear (*Chancery/ Information*).

Defence Attaché, Lt.-Col. P. W. L. Hughes, MBE.

There is a British Consular Office at *Vienna*, and Honorary Consulates at *Bregenz, Graz, Innsbruck* and *Salzburg*.

British Council Representative, John Green, OBE, Schenkenstrasse 4, A-1010 Vienna.

BAHRAIN
(Dawlet al-Bahrein)

Amir, HH Shaikh Isa bin Sulman Al Khalifa, GCMG, *born* 1932; *acceded* Dec. 16, 1961.
Crown Prince and C.-in-C., *Bahrain Defence Force*, HE Shaikh Hamad bin Isa Al Khalifa, KCMG.

CABINET
(as at February 3, 1991)

Prime Minister, HE Shaikh Khalifa bin Sulman Al Khalifa.
Foreign Affairs, Shaikh Mohammed bin Mubarak Al Khalifa.
Defence, Maj.-Gen. Shaikh Khalifa bin Ahmed Al Khalifa.
Justice and Islamic Affairs, Shaikh Abdullah bin Khalid Al Khalifa.
Development and Industry, and Cabinet Affairs, Yusuf Ahmad Shirawi.
Education, Dr Ali Fakhro.
Health, Jawad Salim Al-Arayyed.
Transportation, Ibrahim Mohammed Humaidan.
Interior, Shaikh Mohammed bin Khalifa Al Khalifa.
Information, Tariq Abdulrahman Al Moayed.
Labour and Social Affairs, Shaikh Khalifa bin Sulman bin Mohammed Al Khalifa.
Works, Power and Water, Majid Jawad Al-Jishi.
Housing, Shaikh Khalid bin Abdullah Al Khalifa.
Finance and National Economy, Ibrahim Abdul Karim.
Commerce and Agriculture, Habib Ahmed Kassim.
Minister of State, Legal Affairs, Dr Hussain Al-Baharna.

EMBASSY OF THE STATE OF BAHRAIN
98 Gloucester Road, SW7 4AU
[071–370 5132]

Ambassador Extraordinary and Plenipotentiary, His Excellency Karim Ebrahim Alshakar (1990).

Area and Population.—Bahrain consists of a group of low-lying islands situated about half-way down the Gulf, some 20 miles off the east coast of Arabia. The largest of these, Bahrain island itself, is about 30 miles long and 10 miles wide at its broadest. The capital, Manama, is situated on the north shore of this island. The next largest, Muharraq, with the town and Bahrain International Airport, is connected to Manama by a causeway 1¼ miles long.

The population (1990 estimate) is 503,000, of whom 68·4 per cent are Bahraini. About 35 per cent of the Bahrainis are Sunni Muslims, the remaining 65 per cent being Shias; the ruling family and many of the most prominent merchants are Sunnis.

Climate.—The climate is humid all the year round, with rainfall of about 3 in. concentrated in the mild winter months, December to March; in summer, May to October, temperatures can exceed 110°F (44°C).

Government.—Bahrain has been a fully independent state since 1971. Government takes the form of a constitutional monarchy, in which traditional consultative procedures continue to play an important role.

Economy.—The largest sources of revenue are oil production and refining. The Bahrain field, discovered in 1932, is wholly owned by the Bahrain National Oil Co. Production in 1988 stood at about 42,000 b.p.d. The Sitra refinery derives about 70 per cent of its crude oil by submarine pipeline from Saudi Arabia. Bahrain also has a half share with Saudi Arabia in the profits of the offshore Abu Sa'afa field. A reservoir of unassociated gas has recently been developed on Bahrain island.

Heavy industry is currently limited to the Aluminium Bahrain (ALBA) smelter, producing 183,000 tonnes in 1988; the Gulf Petrochemical Industrie Co. (GPIC) producing 375,000 tonnes of ammonia an 395,000 tonnes of methanol in 1988, the Gulf Aluminium Rolling Mill (GARMCO), and the Arab Shipbuilding and Repair Yard (ASRY), operating dry doc facilities up to 500,000 tons.

There are a number of small to medium size industrial units.

The state has developed as a financial centre. Apar from commercial banks, led by the National Bank o Bahrain, the Standard Chartered Bank, the British Bank of the Middle East and the Bank of Bahrai and Kuwait, many international banks have bee licensed as offshore banking units; there are als money brokers and merchant banks.

Trade with UK

	1989	1990
Imports from UK	£138,529,000	£127,309,00
Exports to UK	61,018,000	48,459,00

Communications.—Bahrain International ai port is one of the main air traffic centres of the Gul it is the headquarters of Gulf Air, and a stoppin point on routes between Europe and Australia an the Far East for other airlines. A causeway linkin Bahrain to Saudi Arabia was opened in Novembe 1986.

A world-wide telephone and telex service, b satellite and cable, is operated by Bahrain Telecom munications Company.

CAPITAL.—ΨManama, population (1981 Censu 121,986. In 1990, it was estimated that 32 per cent o Bahrain's population lives in Manama.

CURRENCY.—Bahrain dinar (BD) of 1,000 fils.

FLAG.—Red, with vertical serrated white bar ne× to staff.

NATIONAL DAY.—December 16.

BRITISH EMBASSY
21 Government Avenue,
Manama 306, PO Box 114
[Manama 534404]

Ambassador Extraordinary and Plenipotentiary, H Excellency John Alan Shepherd, CMG (1988).
First Secretaries, W. I. Rae, MBE (*Commercial an Head of Chancery and Consul*); J. C. A. Rundall.
Second Secretary, D. J. Holder (*Commercial*).
Third Secretary, S. Harrison.

British Council Representative, J. Wright, We⟨ Wing, A A'ali Building, Building No. 146, S⟨ Salman Highway, Manama 356.

BELGIUM
(Royaume de Belgique)

King of the Belgians, HM King Baudouin, KG, *bo⟨ Sept. 7, 1930; *succeeded* July 17, 1951, on t⟨ abdication of his father, King Leopold III, aft⟨ having acted as Head of the State since August 1 1950; *married* Dec. 15, 1960, Doña Fabiola de Mo⟨ y Aragòn.
Heir Presumptive, HRH Prince Albert, *born* June⟨ 1934, *brother* of the King; *married* July 2, 195⟨ Donna Paola Ruffo di Calabria, and has *issue* Prin⟨ Philippe Léopold Louis Marie, *b.* April 15, 196⟨ Princess Astrid Josephine-Charlotte Fabrizia Eli⟨ abeth Paola Marie, *b.* June 5, 1962; Prince Lauren⟨ *b.* Oct. 20, 1963.

CABINET
(as at June 1991)

Prime Minister, Dr Wilfried Martens (CVP).
Deputy PM and Minister for the Brussels Region, ar⟨

Institutional Reform (French sector), Philippe Moureaux (PS).

eputy PM and Minister for Economic Affairs and Planning, and National Education (Flemish sector), Willy Claes (SP).

eputy PM and Minister of Communications, and Institutional Reform (Dutch sector), Jean-Luc Dehaene (CVP).

eputy PM and Minister of Justice, and the Middle Classes, Melchior Wathelet (PSC).

eputy PM and Minister for the Budget and Scientific Policy, Hugo Schiltz (VU).

oreign Affairs, Mark Eyskens (CVP).

inance, Philippe Maystadt (PSC).

oreign Trade, Robert Urbain (PS).

osts and Telecommunications, Marcel Colla (SP).

cial Affairs, Philippe Busquin (PS).

efence, Guy Coëme (PS).

terior, Modernization of Public Services and National Scientific and Cultural Institutions, Louis Tobback (SP).

o-operation and Development, André Geens (VU).

ensions, Gilbert Mottard (PS).

mployment and Work, Luc Vanden Brande (CVP).

ivil Service, Raymond Langendries (PSC).

VP—Christian Social Party (Flemish); PS—Socialist Party (Francophone); SP—Socialist Party (Flemish); PSC—Christian Social Party (Francophone); VU—Flemish Peoples' Union.

BELGIAN EMBASSY
103 Eaton Square, SW1W 9AB
[071–235 5422]

mbassador Extraordinary and Plenipotentiary, His Excellency Herman Dehennin (1991).

inister Counsellor, L. Willems.

inister Counsellor (Economic), J. Maricou.

ilitary, Naval and Air Attaché, Capt. G. H. A. Busard.

A Kingdom of western Europe, with a total area of ,781 sq. miles (30,513 sq. km), and a population 989) of 9,928,000 (Greater Brussels 971,000; Flanders 722,000; Wallonia 3,169,000, of whom 66,000 are erman-speaking). The majority of Belgians are oman Catholics. The Kingdom of Belgium is unded on the N. by the Netherlands, on the S. by rance, on the E. by the Federal Republic of Germany d Luxembourg, and on the W. by the North Sea.

Belgium has a frontier of 898 miles, and a seaboard 41 miles. The Meuse and its tributary, the Sambre, vide it into two distinct regions, that in the west ing generally level and fertile, while the table-land the Ardennes, in the east, has for the most part a or soil. The polders near the coast, which are otected by dykes against floods, cover an area of 3 sq. miles. The highest hill, Signal de Botranges, ses to a height of 2,276 feet, but the mean elevation the whole country does not exceed 526 feet. The incipal rivers are the Scheldt and the Meuse.

Government.—The kingdom formed part of the ow Countries (Netherlands) from 1815 until October , 1830, when a National Congress proclaimed its dependence, and on June 4, 1831, Prince Leopold of oburg was chosen hereditary king. The separation om the Netherlands and the neutrality and inviolility of Belgium were guaranteed by a Conference the European Powers, and by the Treaty of London pril 19, 1839), the famous 'Scrap of Paper,' signed Austria, France, Great Britain, Prussia, The etherlands, and Russia. On August 4, 1914 the ermans invaded Belgium, in violation of the terms the treaty. The kingdom was again invaded by ermany on May 10, 1940. The whole kingdom entually fell and was occupied by Nazi troops until erated by the Allies in September 1944.

According to the Constitution of 1831 the form of government is a constitutional representative and hereditary monarchy with a bicameral legislature, consisting of the King, the Senate and the Chamber of Deputies. The parliamentary term is four years.

The last general election was held on December 13, 1987. The results were as follows (seats):

Chamber of Deputies: CVP 43; PS 40; SP 32; PVV (Flemish Freedom and Progress Party) 25; PRL (Liberal Reform Party (Francophone)) 23; PSC 18; VU 16; Agalev (Flemish Environmental Party) 6; Ecolo (Francophone Ecology Party) 3; FDF (Francophone Democratic Front) 3; Vlaams Blok (Flemish Nationalist Party) 2.

Senate: CVP 22; PS 20; SP 17; PRL 12; PVV 11; PSC 9; VU 8; Ecologists 5; FDF 1; Vlaams Blok 1.

Besides these directly elected representatives the Senate also includes 51 members who are elected by the Provincial Councils and 26 who are co-opted in the proportions of the directly elected seats. HRH Prince Albert is a *sénateur de droit*.

Regional Governments.—The 1980 regionalization law made provision for the establishment of three Regional Community Parliaments (Assemblies) with executive councils which were set up in November 1981 and became effective in January 1982. The executives are autonomous from the central government, and their members are elected by the members of the Assemblies to whom they are responsible. They prepare Bills within the limits of their regional/community competences, and once these Bills have been passed by the regional assembly and published in the *Moniteur Belge*, they have the force of law.

The Flemish Community Assembly (186 members) and Executive (a President and 8 Regional Ministers) covers the provinces of Antwerp, East and West Flanders, Limbourg and the Flemish *arrondissements* (Halle, Vilvoorde, Leuven) in the province of Brabant, and is also responsible for the Flemish population of Brussels. The Walloon Regional Assembly (104 members) and Executive (a President and 6 Regional Ministers) covers the provinces of Hainaut, Liège, Luxembourg and Namur, and the *arrondissement* of Nivelles in the province of Brabant. The French Community Assembly (132 members) and Executive (a President and 3 Community Ministers) has no fixed territory but is responsible for the Francophone population of Brussels and, in concert with the Walloon Regional Assembly, deals with certain Walloon regional affairs. The German-speaking community (about 66,000) also has an Assembly, which gained autonomy in 1984. It is based in Eupen.

Since June 1989 there has been a 75-member Brussels Regional Council with a 5-member Executive: 2 Flemings, 2 Francophones and a President.

An Arbitration Court was set up in 1984 to resolve conflicts between laws made by the various legislative bodies.

Language and Literature.—Belgium is divided between those who speak Dutch (the Flemings) and those who speak French (the Walloons). Dutch is spoken in the provinces of West Flanders, East Flanders, Antwerp, Limburg, and the northern half of Brabant, and French in the provinces of Hainault, Namur, Luxembourg, Liège and the southern half of Brabant. Dutch is recognized as the official language in the northern areas and French in the southern (Walloon) area and there are guarantees for the respective linguistic minorities. Brussels is officially bi-lingual. There is a small German-speaking area (Eupen and Malmedy) along the German border, east of Liège.

The literature of France and the Netherlands is supplemented by an indigenous Belgian literary activity, in both French and Dutch. Maurice Maeterlinck (1862–1949) was awarded the Nobel Prize for Literature in 1911. Emile Verhaeren (1855–1916) was a poet of international standing. Of contemporary Belgian writers, perhaps the most celebrated was Georges Simenon (1903–89). There are 39 daily newspapers in Belgium (23 in French, 15 in Dutch and 1 in German).

Education.—The nursery schools provide free education for the 2½ to 6 age group. There are over 8,000 primary schools (6 to 12 years) of which approximately 5,000 are administered by the local Communities, on authority delegated to them by the State. The remainder are free institutions (predominantly Roman Catholic). There are more than 1,100 secondary schools offering a general academic education slightly over half of which are free institutions (predominantly Roman Catholic but subsidized by the State) and the remainder official institutions. The official school leaving age is 18.

Production.—Belgium is a manufacturing country. With no natural resources except coal, production of which has now ceased, industry is based largely on the processing for re-export of imported raw materials. Gross National Product per capita in 1988 was BFr.520,600. Principal industries are steel and metal products, chemicals and petrochemicals, textiles, glass, and foodstuffs.

FINANCE

	1988	1989
Budget		
Revenue	BFr.1,505,500m	BFr.1,037,000m
Expenditure	1,901,600m	1,409,600m

TRADE

External trade figures relate to Luxembourg as well as Belgium since the two countries formed an Economic Union in 1921.

	1987	1988
Total Imports	US$83,523m	US$92,250m
Total Exports	83,288m	92,103m

Trade with UK (Belgium and Luxembourg)

	1989	1990
Imports from UK	£4,872,641,000	£5,648,625,000
Exports to UK	5,700,534,000	5,732,427,000

Communications.—In 1983, there were 3,920 kilometres of normal gauge railways operated by the Belgian National Railways, of which 1,763 kilometres were electrified. The Belgian National Light Railways (SNCV) also operated 27,671 kilometres of regular bus routes.

Ship canals include Ghent-Terneuzen (18 miles, of which half is in Belgium and half in the Netherlands) which permits the passage to Ghent of ships up to 60,000 tons; the Canal of Willebroek Rupel-Brussels (20 miles, by which ships drawing 18 ft reach Brussels from the sea; opened in 1922); and Bruges (from Zeebrugge on the North Sea to Bruges, 6½ miles). The Albert Canal (79 miles), links Liège with Antwerp; it was completed in 1939 and accommodates barges up to 1,350 tons. The modernization of the port of Antwerp is well advanced. Inland waterway approaches to Antwerp are also to be improved. The river Meuse from the Dutch to the French frontiers, the river Sambre between Namur and Monceau, the river Scheldt from Antwerp to Ghent and the Brussels-Charleroi Canal are being widened or deepened to take barges up to 1,350 tons. Most of the maritime trade of Belgium is carried in foreign shipping.

In 1986 there were 14,260 km of trunk roads of which about 1,550 km were motorways.

The Belgian National Airline Sabena operates regular services between Brussels and London, and many continental centres, as well as overseas services to Northern and Central America, Africa, Middle East, Far East, etc. Many foreign airlines call at Brussels.

CAPITAL.—Brussels, had a population (1989) of 970,501. Other towns are ΨAntwerp, the chief port (473,082); ΨGhent (230,822); Liège (199,020); Charleroi (208,021); Bruges (117,653); ΨOstend (68,370); Malines (75,514).

CURRENCY.—Belgian franc of 100 centimes (centimen).

FLAG.—Three vertical bands, black, yellow, red.

NATIONAL ANTHEM.—La Brabançonne.

NATIONAL DAY.—July 21 (Accession of King Leopold I, 1831).

BRITISH EMBASSY
Britannia House, 28 rue Joseph II,
1040 Brussels
[Brussels 2179000]

Ambassador Extraordinary and Plenipotentiary, His Excellency Robert (Robin) James O'Neill, CMG (1989).

Counsellors, N. M. McCarthy, OBE (*Head of Chancery*); B. Attewell (*Commercial*).

Defence and Military Attaché, Col. K. Woodrow.

Naval and Air Attaché, Wing Cdr. B. A. Horton.

There are British Consular Offices at *Brussels, Antwerp* and *Liège*.

British Council Representative to Belgium and Luxembourg, K. McGuinness.

BRITISH CHAMBER OF COMMERCE FOR BELGIUM AND LUXEMBOURG (INC.), 30 rue Joseph II, 1040 Brussels

BENIN
(République du Benin)

President and Head of the Armed Forces, HE Nicéphore Soglo.

CABINET
(as at July 29, 1991)

The President.

Minister of State and Secretary General to the President, Desire Vieyra.

Defence, Florentin Feliho.

Interior, Public Security and Territorial Administration, Richard Adjaho.

Foreign Affairs and Co-operation, Théodore Hollo.

Finance, Paul Dossou.

Planning and Statistics, Robert Tagnon.

ural Development and Co-operatives, Mama Adamou N'Diaye.

ublic Works and Transport, Florentin Mito-Baba.

ndustry, Small and Medium Enterprises, Sylvain Ladikpo.

nergy, A. Houessou.

nformation and Communications, Paulin Hountondji.

Jational Education, Karim Dramane.

'outh and Sports, Théophile Natta.

'ivil Service, Antoine Gbegan.

mployment and Social Affairs, Véronique Attoyo.

ublic Health, Véronique Lawson.

nvironment, Eustache Sarré.

'arliamentary Relations, Marius Francisco.

Jandicrafts and Tourism, Bernard Houégnon.

ustice, Yves Yéhouessi.

'ulture, Mr Alabi.

EMBASSY OF THE REPUBLIC OF BENIN
87 Avenue Victor Hugo, 75116 Paris, France
[Paris 45009882]

Ambassador Extraordinary and Plenipotentiary (designate), His Excellency Cyrille Sagbo (resident in Paris).

HONORARY CONSULATE
16 The Broadway, Stanmore, Middlesex HA7 4DW
[Tel. 081–951 8800]

Jonorary Consul, L. Landau.

A republic situated in West Africa, between 2° and ' W. and 6° and 12° N., Benin (formerly known as ahomey) has a short coastline of 78 miles on the ulf of Guinea but extends northwards inland for 37 miles. It is flanked on the west by Togo, on the orth by Burkina and Niger and on the east by Jigeria. It is divided into four main regions running orizontally: a narrow sandy coastal strip, a succesion of inter-communicating lagoons, a clay belt and sandy plateau in the north. It has an area of 43,484 q. miles (122,622 sq. km), and a population of 4,591,000 JN 1989 estimate). The official language is French. lthough poor in resources, Benin is one of the most eavily populated areas in West Africa, with a high tandard of education.

Government.—The first treaty with France was igned by one of the kings of Abomey in 1851 but the ountry was not placed under French administration ntil 1892. Benin became an independent republic ithin the French Community in December 1958; ll independence outside the Community was proaimed on August 1, 1960. In October 1963 a popular evolution led to the fall of the government and the rmy held power until a civilian government was rmed. In subsequent years successive governments ere overthrown by the military after only short erms in office until a coup d'état on October 26, 1972 rought to power a Marxist-Leninist Military Revoitionary Government, headed by Lt.-Col. Kerekou.

In response to mounting unrest, the government greed to drop Marxism-Leninism as the official leology in December 1989. Following a 'National onference of Active Forces of the Nation,' the onstitution was revoked on March 1, 1990 and the ountry's official name was changed from the People's epublic of Benin to the Republic of Benin. The evolutionary National Assembly (legislature) was issolved and replaced by a High Council of the epublic (HCR). This, in conjunction with a new 15-ember civilian government, is implementing a olitical transition programme; a new pluralistic onstitution was adopted by referendum in December 990. Legislative and presidential elections were held February and March 1991. Nicéphore Soglo was vorn in as the new President on April 4, 1991 and ppointed a provisional government.

Trade.—The principal exports are cotton, palm products, ground nuts, shea-nuts, and coffee. Small deposits of gold, iron and chrome have been found; oil production started in 1983.

Trade with UK

	1989	1990
Imports from UK	£7,294,000	£6,130,000
Exports to UK	356,000	1,197,000

CAPITAL.—ΨPorto Novo, population (1982 estimate) 208,258. Principal commercial town and port, ΨCotonou (487,020).

CURRENCY.—Franc CFA of 100 centimes.

FLAG.—Green, with five-pointed red star in the top left corner.

NATIONAL DAY.—November 30.

British Ambassador (resident in Lagos, Nigeria).

BHUTAN
(Druk-yul)

King of Bhutan, HM Jigme Singye Wangchuk, *born* Nov. 11, 1955; *succeeded his father*, July 1972; *crowned*, June 2, 1974.

Heir, Crown Prince Jigme Gesar Namgyal Wangchuk, *designated*, Oct. 31, 1988.

COUNCIL OF MINISTERS
(as at June 30, 1991)

Chairman of Council of Ministers, HM The King.

HM Representative in Ministry of Finance, HRH Ashi Sonam Chhoden Wangchuk.

HM Representative in Ministry of Agriculture, HRH Ashi Dorji W. Wangchuk.

Home Affairs, HRH Namgyel Wangchuk.

Finance, Dorji Tshering.

Foreign Affairs, Dawa Tshering.

Communications, Social Services and Tourism, Dr T. Tobgyal.

Trade and Industries, Om Pradhan.

Deputy Minister of Defence, Chief Operations Officer of Royal Bhutan Army, Maj.-Gen. Lam Dorji.

Speaker of the National Assembly, Chief Justice, Sangye Penjor.

Bhutan is a small Himalayan Kingdom situated between Tibet (to the north) and India (to the west, south and east). The total area is about 18,147 sq. miles (47,000 sq. km), with a mountainous northern region which is infertile and sparsely populated, a central zone of upland valleys where most of the population and cultivated land is found, and in the south the densely forested foothills of the Himalayas, which are mainly inhabited by Nepalese settlers and indigenous tribespeople.

The population of Bhutan is estimated at 1,483,000 (UN estimate 1989), about three-quarters of whom are Buddhists. The remainder (mostly the Nepali Bhutanese) are Hindu. The official language, for administrative and religious purposes, is Dzongkha, a variant of Tibetan, which functions as a lingua franca amongst a variety of languages and dialects. It is government policy to make the study of Dzongkha compulsory in schools, although English is the medium of instruction and has become widely used within the administration.

In 1949 a treaty was concluded with the Government of India under which the Kingdom of Bhutan agreed to be guided by the advice of the Government of India in regard to its external relations. It has its own diplomatic representatives and is a member of the UN and other international and regional organizations. It also receives from the Government of India an annual payment of Rs500,000 as compensation for portions of its territory annexed by the British Government in India in 1864.

Government.—Bhutan has a 150-member National Assembly which meets twice a year. The ten-member Royal Advisory Council, nominated by the King and the National Assembly, acts as a consultative body when the National Assembly is not in session. The King is also assisted by a Council of Ministers. There are no political parties.

Economy.—The sixth 5-year Plan (1987–92) has a projected expenditure of Nu9,485m. Economic emphasis is on the infrastructure, especially roads and telecommunications. The economy is based on agriculture and animal husbandry, which engage over 90 per cent of the workforce in what is largely a self-sufficient rural society. The principal food crops are rice, wheat, maize and barley. Vegetables and fruit are also produced. Bhutan is the world's largest producer of cardamon, which forms its principal export to countries other than India. Mineral resources include dolomite and small amounts of coal, which are exported to India. A modest industrial base is being developed. A distillery and cement, chemicals and food processing plants are in production; a forestry industries complex is being expanded. Tourism and postage stamps are increasingly important sources of foreign exchange. Over 90 per cent of foreign trade is with India. Principal exports are agricultural products, timber, cement and coal; main imports are textiles, cereals and consumer goods. Bhutan's airline, Druk Air, flies between Paro and Calcutta.

Trade with UK

	1989	1990
Imports from UK	£363,000	£778,000
Exports to UK	328,000	111,000

CAPITAL.—Thimphu, population estimate (1987) 15,000.

CURRENCY.—Ngultrum of 100 chetrums. Indian currency is also legal tender.

FLAG.—Saffron yellow and orange-red divided diagonally, with dragon device in centre.

NATIONAL DAY.—December 17.

BOLIVIA
(República de Bolivia)

President of the Republic, Jaime Paz Zamora, *inaugurated,* August 6, 1989.
Vice President, Luis Ossio Sanjines.

CABINET
(as at August 12, 1991)

Foreign Affairs, Carlos Iturralde Ballivian.
Interior and Justice, Carlos Saavedra Bruno.
Minister of the Presidency, Gustavo Fernandez Saavedra.
Defence, Adm. Alberto Sainz Klinski.
Finance, David Blanco Zavala.
Planning and Co-ordination, Samuel Doria Medina.
Education and Culture, Hedim Cespedes Cossio.
Transport and Communications, Willy Vargas Vacaflor.
Industry, Commerce and Tourism, Leopoldo Lopez Cossio.
Labour, Oscar Zamora Medinacelli.
Public Health and Social Security, Mario Paz Zamora.
Mining and Metallurgy, Gonzalo Valda Cardenas.
Agriculture, Mauro Bertero Gutierrez.
Energy and Hydrocarbons, Herbert Muller Costas.

Urban Development and Housing, Fernando Kieffe Guzman.
Information, Mario Rueda Pena.

BOLIVIAN EMBASSY
106 Eaton Square, SW1W 9AD
[071–235 2257/4248]

Ambassador Extraordinary and Plenipotentiary, H Excellency Gen. Gary Prado Salmon (1990).

The land-locked Republic of Bolivia extends b tween lat. 10° and 23° S. and long. 57° 30′ and 69° 45′ \ It has an area estimated at 424,165 sq. miles (1,098,5% sq. km), with a population (UN estimate 1989) 7,193,000. The Republic derives its name from i liberator, Simon Bolivar (1783–1830).

The chief topographical feature is the great centr plateau (65,000 square miles) over 500 miles in lengt at an average altitude of 12,500 feet above sea leve between the two great chains of the Andes, whic traverse the country from south to north. The tot length of the navigable streams is about 12,000 mile the principal rivers being the Itenez, Beni, Mamo. and Madre de Dios.

Language and Literature.—The official la guage of the country is Spanish, but many of tl Indian inhabitants (about two-thirds of the popul tion) speak Quechua or Aymará, the two linguist groups being more or less equal in numbers.

The Roman Catholic religion was disestablished i 1961. Elementary education is compulsory and fr and there are secondary schools in urban centr Provision is also made for higher education; addition to St Francisco Xavier's University Sucre, founded in 1624, there are six other unive sities, the largest being the University of San Andr at La Paz. There are nine principal daily newspape in Bolivia.

Production.—Mining, natural gas, petroleum ar agriculture are the principal industries. The ancie silver mines of Potosí are now worked chiefly for ti but gold, partly dug and partly washed, is obtaine on the Eastern Cordillera of the Andes; the t output is one of the largest in the world, and togeth with other minerals (copper, antimony, lead, zir asbestos, wolfram, bismuth salt and sulphur), provid over half of Bolivia's exports.

In 1982 Bolivia produced 1·4 million cubic metr of oil, sufficient for internal consumption. G; (currently providing about a quarter of Bolivia export income) is piped to Argentina and there a plans to build a pipeline to São Paulo, Brazil. Bolivia agricultural produce consists chiefly of rice, barle oats, wheat, sugar-cane, maize, cotton, indigo, rubbe cacao, potatoes, cinchona bark, medicinal herb brazil nuts etc.

Transport and Communications.—There a 2,200 miles of railways in operation including tl lines from Corumbá to Santa Cruz (312 miles). The are about 10,950 miles of telegraphs, and microwa\ telephone communications between La Paz, San Cruz, Cochabamba, Oruro and Sucre. Most oth towns have radio/telephone communication with tl main cities. There is direct railway communicatio to the sea at Antofagasta (32 hours), Arica (10 hours and Mollendo (2 days), and also to Buenos Aires (days). Communication with Peru is by road from I Paz via Copacabana and thence to the railhead Puno.

Commercial aviation in Bolivia is conducted I the national airline, Lloyd Aereo Boliviano ar Transporte Aereo Militar between the major towr and Lloyd Aereo Boliviano and a number of foreip airlines provide international flights to the US/ South and Central America and Europe.

Bolivia is without a coastline, having been depriv

of the ports of Tocopilla, Cobija, Mejillones and Antofagasta by the Pacific War of 1879–1884.

FINANCE

The economy has deteriorated since 1977, with disappointing petroleum reserves, a large external debt, and the collapse of world tin prices in 1985. Tin prices began to increase once more from April 1989. The peso was replaced in January 1987 with the Boliviano of 1,000,000 old pesos in an effort to stem inflation. The inflation rate at the end of 1988 was about 20 per cent. Gross Domestic Product in 1987 was US$4,640 m.

Trade with UK

	1989	1990
Imports from UK	£6,148,000	£6,234,000
Exports to UK	17,666,000	12,387,000

Mineral exports represent about 94 per cent of these totals. A large part of Bolivia's minerals are shipped to UK for smelting and re-export, but Bolivia is now developing her own smelters and will in future be exporting metals. The chief imports are wheat and flour, iron and steel products, machinery, vehicles and textiles.

CAPITAL.—La Paz (Population, 1,000,000). Other large centres are Cochabamba (250,000), Oruro (180,000), Santa Cruz (380,000), Potosí (90,000), Sucre, the legal capital and seat of the judiciary (80,000) and Tarija (45,000).

CURRENCY.—Boliviano ($b) of 100 centavos.

FLAG.—Three horizontal bands; red, yellow, green.

NATIONAL ANTHEM.—Bolivianos, El Hado Propicio Oh Bolivia, our long-felt desires).

NATIONAL DAY.—August 6 (Independence Day).

BRITISH EMBASSY
Avenida Arce 2732–2754,
(Casilla 694) La Paz
[La Paz 329401/4]

Ambassador Extraordinary and Plenipotentiary, His Excellency Richard Michael Jackson, CVO (1991).

First Secretary, A. W. Shave (*Commercial and Deputy Head of Mission*).

There is an Honorary Consulate at *Santa Cruz*.

BRAZIL
(República Federativa do Brasil)

President, Fernando Collor de Mello, *inaugurated* March 15, 1990.

Vice President, Itamar Franco.

CABINET
(as at July 25, 1991)

Labour, Antonio Rogério Magri.

Social Action, Margarida Procópio.

Education, Carlos Chíarelli.

Justice, Jarbas Passarinho.

Air Force, Brig. Sócrates de Costa Monteiro.

Army, Gen. Carlos Tinoco Ribeiro Gomes.

Navy, Adm. Mário Cesar Flores.

Infrastructure, Joao Santana.

Economy, Marcilio Marques Moreira.

Foreign Affairs, Jose Francisco Rezek.

Agriculture, Antonio Cabrera.

Health, Dr Alceni Guerra.

Environmental Secretariat, Jose Lutzenberger.

Internal Revenue, Carlos Alberto Guimaraes Marcial.

Federal Police, Romeu Tuma.

Governor of Central Bank, Francisco Gros.

Government Leader in Chamber of Deputies, Ricardo Fiuza.

BRAZILIAN EMBASSY
32 Green Street, W1Y 4AT
[071–499 0877]

Ambassador Extraordinary and Plenipotentiary, His Excellency Paulo-Tarso Flecha de Lima (1990).

There is also a Brazilian Consulate-General in *London* and honorary consular offices at *Cardiff* and *Glasgow*.

Area and Population.—Brazil, discovered in 1500 by Portuguese navigator Pedro Alvares Cabral, is bounded on the north by the Atlantic Ocean, the Guianas, Colombia and Venezuela; on the west by Peru, Bolivia, Paraguay, and Argentina; on the south by Uruguay; and on the east by the Atlantic Ocean. Brazil extends between lat. 5° 16′ N. and 33° 45′ S. and long. 34° 45′ and 73° 59′22″ W. The Republic comprises an area of 3,286,488 sq. miles (8,511,965 sq. km), with a population (official estimate 1990) of 150,368,000.

The northern States of Amazonas and Pará are mainly wide, low-lying, forest-clad plains. The central states of Mato Grosso are principally plateau land and the eastern and southern States are traversed by successive mountain ranges interspersed with fertile valleys. The principal ranges are Serra do Mar, the Serra da Mantiqueira and the Serra do Espinhaco along the east coast. The River Amazon with a total length of some 4,000 miles has tributaries which are themselves great rivers, and flows from the Peruvian Andes to the Atlantic. Its principal northern tributaries are the Rio Branco, Rio Negro, and Japurá; its southern tributaries are the Juruá, Purus, Madeira and Tapajós, while the Xingú meets it within 200 miles of its outflow into the Atlantic. The Tocantins and Araguaia flow northwards from Mato Grosso and Goiás to the Gulf of Pará. The Parnaiba flows from Piaui into the Atlantic. The São Francisco rises in the South of Minas Gerais and flows to the eastern coast. The Paraguai, rising in the south-west of Mato Grosso, flows through Paraguay to its confluence with the Paraná, which rises in the mountains of that name and divides Brazil from Paraguay.

Government.—Brazil was colonized by Portugal in the early part of the sixteenth century, and in 1822 became an independent empire under Dom Pedro, son of the refugee King Joao VI of Portugal. On November 15, 1889, Dom Pedro II, second of the line, was dethroned and a republic was proclaimed.

The Federative Republic of Brazil is made up of the Federal District and 26 States.

The constitution of October 1988 draws on the same conceptual basis as that of the United States, and envisages an equal distribution of power between the executive, the legislature and the judiciary. Under the existing constitutional provisions the President, who heads the executive, is directly elected for a five-year term.

The Congress consists of a Senate (three Senators per State elected for an eight-year term) and a Chamber of Deputies which is elected every four years. (The number of Deputies per State depends upon the State's population). Each State has a Governor, and a Legislative Assembly with a four-year term.

Production.—There are large and valuable mineral deposits including iron ore (hematite), manganese, bauxite, beryllium, chrome, nickel, tungsten, cassiterite, lead, gold, monazite (containing rare earths and thorium) and zirconium. Diamonds and precious and semi-precious stones are also found. The mineral wealth is being exploited to an increasing

extent. The iron ore deposits of Minas Gerais are exceeded by those of the Amazon region, principally in the Carajás areas where deposits are estimated at 35,000 million tonnes. Mining operations began in February 1985.

Electric power production in 1989 was 243,034 Gwh. In the same year, the total output of steel was 24,600 million tonnes and production of oil was 34·6 million cubic metres.

Agriculture production was (tonnes):

	1989
Black Beans	2,327,973
Cassava	23,701,158
Cocoa	394,616
Coffee	1,412,000
Cotton	1,797,446
Maize	26,568,776
Peanuts	155,913
Potatoes	2,134,807
Rice	11,043,228
Soya	24,085,193
Tobacco	448,689
Wheat	5,295,335

Defence.—The peace-time strength of the Army is 192,000. The strength of the Navy is 49,000. The Air Force has a strength of 50,700.

Education.—Primary education is compulsory and is the responsibility of State governments an municipalities. At this level approximately 12 p cent attend private schools. Secondary education largely the responsibility of State and municip governments, although a small number of very o foundations (the Pedro II Schools) remain und direct federal control. Over 33 per cent of all pupi at this level attend private schools. Higher educatic is available in Federal, State, municipal and priva universities and faculties.

Language and Literature.—Portuguese is th language of the country, but Italian, Spanish, Ge man, Japanese and Arabic are also spoken minorities, and newspapers of considerable circul tion are produced in those languages.

Public libraries have been established in urba centres and there is a flourishing national press wit widely circulated daily and weekly newspapers.

Communications.—In 1989 there were 1,663,9 km of highways. The route-length of railways in 19 was 29,833 km. Internal air services are high developed. There are 21,944 miles of navigable inla waterways. During 1988, 8,709 vessels entered Rio Janeiro and Santos, the two leading ports.

FINANCE

	1989	1990
Revenue	NCz$515,193m	Cr$3,146,420
Expenditure	529,882m	3,146,420

In 1989 Brazil's total external public debt stood at U.S.$112,000 million.

TRADE

Principal imports are fuel and lubricants, machinery, chemicals, wheat, metals and metal manufactures. Principal exports are coffee, iron ore, soya, meat, steel and orange juice. In 1987 the Brazilian automobile industry produced 920,300 vehicles. Of these, 339,900 vehicles were exported.

	1988	1989
Total imports	US$16,055m	US$18,263m
Total exports	33,786m	34,406m

Trade with UK

	1989	1990
Imports from UK	£338,634,000	£328,234,000
Exports to UK	817,545,000	719,849,000

CAPITAL.—Brasilia (inaugurated on April 21, 1960). Population (1990 estimate) 1,567,709. Other important centres are São Paulo (10,063,110); the former capital ΨRio de Janeiro (6,603,388); Belo Horizonte ѕ,114,429); ΨRecife (1,287,623); ΨSalvador ѕ,804,438); ΨPorto Alegre (1,272,121); ΨFortaleza ѕ,582,414); and Belem (1,116,578).
CURRENCY.—Cruzeiro (BRC) of 100 centavos.
FLAG.—Green, with yellow lozenge in centre; blue where with white band and stars in centre of lozenge.
NATIONAL ANTHEM.—Ouviram do Ipirangas Marens Placidas (From peaceful Ypiranga's banks).
NATIONAL DAY.—September 7 (Independence Day).

BRITISH EMBASSY
Setor de Embaixadus Sul, Quadra 801, Conjunto K, 70.408 Brasilia DF
[Brasilia 225–2710]

Ambassador Extraordinary and Plenipotentiary, His Excellency Michael John Newington, CMG (1987).

There are British Consulates-General at *Rio de Janeiro* and *São Paulo*.

British Council Representative, Raymond Newberry, OBE, SCR, 708/9-BLF Nos 1/3 (Caixa Postal 04), 70.740 Brasilia DF. Regional Directors in *Recife, Rio de Janeiro* and *São Paulo*.

BRITISH AND COMMONWEALTH CHAMBER OF COMMERCE IN SÃO PAULO, Rua Barão de Itapetininga 275, 7th Floor, 01042, São Paulo (*Postal Address*, PO Box 421, 01000 São Paulo) and Rua Real Grandeza 99, 1281 Rio de Janeiro.

BULGARIA
(Narodna Republika Bulgaria)
COUNCIL OF STATE

President, Zhelyu Zhelev, *elected* August 1, 1990.

COUNCIL OF MINISTERS
(as at December 20, 1990)

Chairman (Prime Minister), Dimitur Popov.
Deputy Chairmen, Alexander Tomov, Viktor Vulkov, Dimitur Ludzhev.
Finance, Ivan Kostov.
Industry, Trade and Services, Ivan Pushkarov.
Foreign Economic Relations, Atanas Paparizov.
Transport, Veselin Pavlov.
Justice, Pencho Penev.
Defence, Gen. Yordan Mutafchiev.
Foreign Affairs, Viktor Vulkov.
Internal Affairs, Khristo Danov.
Agriculture, Boris Spirov.
Environment, Dimitur Vodenicharov.

Labour and Social Welfare, Emiliya Maslarova.
Health, Ivan Chernozemski.
Education, Matey Mateev.
Science and Higher Education, Georgi Fotev.
Culture, Dimo Dimov.

EMBASSY OF THE REPUBLIC OF BULGARIA
186–188 Queen's Gate, SW7 5HL
[071–584 9400/9433]

Ambassador Extraordinary and Plenipotentiary, Ivan Stancioff (1991).

The Republic of Bulgaria is bounded on the north by Romania, on the west by Yugoslavia, on the east by the Black Sea, and on the south by Greece and Turkey. The total area is 42,823 sq. miles (110,912 sq. km), with an estimated population of 8,992,316 in 1989. The largest religion of the Bulgarians is the Bulgarian Orthodox Church.

A Principality of Bulgaria was created by the Treaty of Berlin (July 13, 1878) and in 1885 Eastern Roumelia was added to the newly-created principality. In 1908 the country was declared to be an independent kingdom. In 1912–13 a successful war of the Balkan League against Turkey increased the size of the kingdom, but in August 1913, a short campaign against the remaining members of the League reduced the acquired area, and led to the surrender of Southern Dobrudja to Romania. In October 1915, Bulgaria entered the War on the side of the Central Powers by declaring war on Serbia. Involved in the defeats of 1918, Bulgaria made an unconditional surrender to the Allied Powers in September 1918, and in November 1919, signed the Treaty of Neuilly, which ceded to the Allies the Thracian territories (later handed over to Greece) and some territory on the western frontier to Yugoslavia.

Nazi troops entered the country on March 3, 1941, and occupied Black Sea ports, but Bulgaria was not at war with the Soviet Union. On August 26, 1944, the government declared Bulgaria to be neutral in the Russo-German war and sought terms of peace from Great Britain and the United States. The Soviet Union refused to recognize the so-called neutrality and called upon Bulgaria to declare war against Germany, and no satisfactory reply being received on September 5 1944, the USSR declared war on Bulgaria. Bulgaria then asked for an armistice and on September 7 declared war on Germany, hostilities with USSR ending on September 10. The armistice with the Allies was signed in Moscow, October 28, 1944. The Peace Treaty with Bulgaria was signed on February 22, 1947, and came into force on September 15, 1947. It recognized the return of Southern Dobrudja to Bulgaria.

On September 9, 1944 a coup d'état gave power to the Fatherland Front, a coalition of Communists, Agrarians, Social Democrats and officers and intellectuals. In August 1945, the main body of Agrarians and Social Democrats left the Government. On September 8, 1946 a referendum was held, which led to the abolition of the monarchy and the setting up of a Republic.

The post-war political scene was dominated by the Communist Party (BCP), led since 1954 by Todor Zhivkov. After he was forced to resign in November 1989, further leadership changes and reforms culminated, in January 1990, in the National Assembly voting to abolish the BCP's constitutional guarantee of power. Multi-party elections to a 400-seat Grand National Assembly (parliament), due to draw up a new Constitution by the end of 1991, were held in June 1990. The BCP, renamed the Bulgarian Socialist Party in April, emerged as the majority party. In August, the former leader of the opposition Union of Democratic Forces (UDF), Dr Zhelyu Zhelev, was elected President.

A BSP-dominated government, led by Andrey Lukanov, was formed in September 1990, but was brought down two months later by a combination of industrial strikes and opposition pressure. A multi-party government was formed in December 1990, led by Dimitur Popov. It has now begun to implement a radical programme of economic and political reform, against the background of economic decline and rising unemployment. A new constitution, enshrining democracy and the free market, was adopted by the Grand National Assembly on July 12, 1991.

Production.—Until 1939 Bulgaria was a predominantly agricultural country, but has since pursued an elaborate programme of industrialization. About 90 per cent of the country's agriculture has been turned over to co-operatives, and a smaller proportion mechanized. The principal crops are wheat, maize, beet, tomatoes, tobacco, oleaginous seeds, fruit, vegetables and cotton. The livestock includes cattle, sheep, goats, pigs, horses, asses, mules and water buffaloes.

There is now a substantial engineering industry and considerable production of ferrous and non-ferrous metals. In 1989 production of electricity was 44,324 million kilowatt-hours, of steel 2,899,000 tons and of coal 35,801,000 tons.

Bulgaria's heavy industry includes the Kremikovtsi Steel Plant near Sofia and the steel mill at Pernik, the chemical complex at Devnia, the petro-chemical plant at Bourgas and various other chemical and metallurgical works situated around the country. The Soviet-designed nuclear power station at Kozlodui, comprising four reactors, each with a capability of producing 800 million kilowatt-hours and a fifth, 1,000 MW unit, accounts for over 40 per cent of Bulgaria's electrical generating capacity.

Defence.—The peacetime strength of the ground forces is at present estimated to be 100,000. The term of conscription was reduced from two years to 18 months in 1991.

Education.—Free basic education is compulsory for children from 7 to 15 years inclusive. Government policy emphasizes the need to democratize the education system, to remove the former ideological basis and to encourage private education. There are three universities (at Sofia, Plovdiv and Veliko Turnovo) and 21 higher educational establishments.

Language and Literature.—Bulgarian is a Southern Slavonic tongue, closely allied to Serbo-Croat and Russian with local admixtures of modern Greek, Albanian and Turkish words. The alphabet is Cyrillic.

Finance.—Planned public expenditure for 1991 was 70,476·5 million leva, while the internal budget deficit was expected to reach 7,509·5 m leva.

TRADE

Since 1989, political and economic developments in Bulgaria and in some of her principal trading partners have had a substantial impact on the volume and pattern of foreign trade. In 1988, 79 per cent of Bulgaria's foreign trade was within the CMEA, including approximately 57 per cent with the Soviet Union. Trade with both the former CMEA member countries and with the industrialized West declined sharply in 1990. Figures for the first quarter of 1991 indicate that over 38 per cent of Bulgaria's exports by value went to the developed industrial centres, some 35 per cent to the former CMEA and 26 per cent to the developing countries. The Soviet Union retains its position as Bulgaria's largest supplier, accounting for approximately 50 per cent of Bulgarian imports by value. The principal imports are fuels, minerals and metals, engineering goods and industrial equipment. The principal exports are engineering goods and industrial equipment, industrial

consumer goods, chemicals and fuels, minerals and metals.

Trade with UK

	1989	1990
Imports from UK	£86,209,000	£32,787,000
Exports to UK	34,272,000	3,003,000

CAPITAL.—Sofia, population (1989), 1,136,875, at the foot of the Vitosha Range, the capital and commercial centre is on the main railway line to Istanbul, 338 miles from the Black Sea port of ΨVarna (316,897); ΨBourgas (224,081) is also a Black Sea port. Other important trading and industrial centres are Plovdiv (374,004), Rousse (210,219), Pleven (168,014), Stara Zagora (186,736), Pernik (120,335), Sliven (149,643), Yambol (98,651), Khaskovo (116,808) and Tolbukhin (112,582).

CURRENCY.—Lev of 100 stotinki.

FLAG.—3 horizontal bands, white, green, red.

NATIONAL DAY.—March 3.

BRITISH EMBASSY
Boulevard Marshal Tolbukhin 65–67, Sofia
[Sofia 879575]

Ambassador Extraordinary and Plenipotentiary, His Excellency Richard Thomas, CMG (1989).
British Council Representative, David Stokes, Todor Strashimirov 7, Sofia.

BURKINA FASO
(République Démocratique Populaire de Burkina Faso)

President of the Popular Front, Head of State, Minister of Defence and Security, Capt. Blaise Compaoré, assumed office, October 1987.

COUNCIL OF MINISTERS
(as at June 18, 1991)

Minister of State responsible for Government Coordination, Roch Christian Marc Kabore.
Finance and Planning, Frédéric Assomption Korsaga.
Industry, Commerce and Mines, Thomas Sanon.
Justice, Benoît Lompo.
Popular Defence and Security, Lassane Ouangrawa.
Agriculture and Animal Husbandry, Albert Djigma.
Health, Social Action and the Family, Kanidou Naboho.
External Relations, Prosper Vokouma.
Transport and Communications, Daprou Kambou.
Employment, Works and Social Security, Salif Diallo.
Civil Service and Administrative Reform, Juliette Bonkoungou.
Information and Culture, Béatrice Damiba.
Primary Education and Literacy, Alice Tiendrebeogo.
Secondary and Higher Education, Scientific Research, Mouhoussine Nacro.
Environment and Tourism, Maurice Dieudonné Bonanet.
Living Conditions, Housing and Town Planning, Joseph Kabore.
Territorial Administration, Jean Léonard Campaoré.
Water, Sabné Kouanda.
Youth and Sports, Kilimité Théodore Hien.
Minister in the Office of the Presidency, Idriss Zampaligre.
Minister, Secretary General of the Government and the Council of Ministers, Noélie Victoire Kone.

EMBASSY OF BURKINA FASO
16 Place Guy d'Arezzo, 1060 Brussels, Belgium
[Brussels 3459911]

Ambassador Extraordinary and Plenipotentiary (designate), His Excellency Salifou Rigobert Kongo (resident in Brussels).

HONORARY CONSULATE
5 Cinnamon Row, Plantation Wharf, SW11 3TW
[071–738 1800]

Honorary Consul, S. G. Singer.

Burkina Faso (formerly Upper Volta) is an inland savanna state in West Africa, situated between 9° and 15°N. and 2°E. and 5°W. with an area of 105,869 sq. miles (274,200 sq. km), and a population of 8,509,000 (UN estimate 1988). It has common boundaries with Mali on the west, Niger and Benin on the east and Togo, Ghana and the Côte d'Ivoire on the south. The largest tribe is the Mossi whose king, the Moro Naba, still wields a certain moral influence.

Burkina Faso was annexed by France in 1896 and between 1932 and 1947 was administered as part of the Colony of the Ivory Coast. It decided on December 11, 1958 to remain an autonomous republic within the French Community; full independence outside the Community was proclaimed on August 5, 1960. The official language is French.

The 1960 constitution provided for a presidential form of government with a single chamber National Assembly, but in January 1966 the Army assumed power. A new constitution allowing for a partial return to civilian rule but with the Army still in effective control was adopted in 1970, but in 1974 this was suspended. Full legislative and presidential elections were held again in 1978. Following a number of military coups, Capt. Blaise Compaoré took power in October 1987, also by coup. The present government, a broad-based coalition (the Popular Front), held a congress in March 1990 which decided to appoint a committee to draft a 'Constitution leading to democratization'. The Constitution was adopted by referendum on June 2, 1991. Presidential elections are scheduled for November and legislative elections for December 1991.

Trade.—The 1988 Budget totalled Franc CFA 90,300 million.

The principal industry is the rearing of cattle and sheep and the chief exports are livestock, groundnuts, millet and sorghum. Small deposits of gold, manganese, copper, bauxite and graphite have been found. Trade in 1987 was valued at imports, CFA 130,527 m, exports, CFA 46,593 m.

Trade with UK

	1989	1990
Imports from UK	£4,647,000	£6,557,000
Exports to UK	954,000	967,000

CAPITAL.—Ouagadougou (400,000). Other principal towns; Bobo-Dioulasso (211,538) and Koudougou (30,000).

CURRENCY.—Franc CFA.

FLAG.—Equal bands of red over green, with a yellow star in centre.

NATIONAL DAY.—August 4.

British Ambassador (resident in Abidjan, Côte d'Ivoire).

BURUNDI
(République de Burundi)

President and Minister for National Defence, Major Pierre Buyoya, *elected* Sept. 9, 1987, *sworn in* Oct. 2, 1987.

COUNCIL OF MINISTERS
(as at February 12, 1991)

Prime Minister, Adrien Sibomana.
Foreign Affairs and Co-operation, Cyprien Mbonimpa.
Agriculture and Animal Husbandry, Jumaine Hussein.

Finance, Gerard Niyibigira.
Rural Development and Handicrafts, Gabriel Toyi.
Justice, Sebastien Ntahuga.
Interior, Libere Bararunyeretse.
Commerce and Industry, Astere Girukwigomaba.
Transport, Posts and Telecommunications, Lt.-Col. Simon Rusuku.
Public Works and Urban Development, Evariste Simbarakiye.
Energy and Mines, Bonaventure Bangurambona.
Public Health, Norbert Ngendabanyikwa.
Civil Service, Charles Karikurubu.
Labour and Social Policy, Julie Ngiriye.
Women's Advancement and Social Protection, Victoire Ndikumana.
Communication, Culture and Sports, Frederick Ngenzebuhoro.
Tourism, Land Use and Environment, Louis Nduwimana.
Higher Education and Scientific Research, Gilbert Midende.
Primary and Secondary Education, Gamariel Ndarunzaniye.
Professional Training and Youth, Adolphe Nahayo.
Secretaries of State, Salvator Sahinguvu (*Planning*); Fridolin Hatungimana (*Economic Planning*); Laurent Kagimbi (*Interior*).

EMBASSY OF THE REPUBLIC OF BURUNDI
Square Marie Louise 46, 1040 Brussels, Belgium
[Brussels 2304535]

Ambassador Extraordinary and Plenipotentiary, His Excellency Julien Nahayo (1989) (resident in Brussels).

Formerly a Belgian trusteeship under the United Nations, Burundi was proclaimed independent on July 1, 1962. Situated on the east side of Lake Tanganyika, the State has an area of 10,747 sq. miles (27,834 sq. km) and a population (UN estimate 1989) of 5,302,000. The majority of the population are of the Hutu ethnic group, but power rests in the hands of the minority Tutsi ethnic group.

Burundi became independent as a constitutional monarchy but this was overthrown on November 28, 1966 and the country became a republic. On Nov. 1, 1976, the government of President Micombero was overthrown and a Supreme Revolutionary Council led by Col. Jean-Baptiste Bagaza took power. In 1980 the SRC was replaced by a political bureau and central committee as part of a process of political normalization, which continued with elections to the National Assembly, a 65-member legislature. In September 1987 the government of President Bagaza was overthrown by a Military Committee of National Redemption led by Major Pierre Buyoya. The Party of National Unity and Progress (UPRONA), the sole ruling party, has adopted a National Unity Charter which seeks to unify the Hutu and Tutsi tribal groups; the Charter was approved by a referendum in February 1991.

The chief crop is coffee, representing about 80 per cent of Burundi's export earnings. Cotton is the second most important crop. Mineral, tea, hide and skin exports are also important.

Trade with UK

	1989	1990
Imports from UK	£2,738,000	£2,804,000
Exports to UK	1,974,000	224,000

CAPITAL.—Bujumbura (formerly Usumbura), with 215,243 (1987 estimate) inhabitants. Kitega (18,000 inhabitants) is the only other sizeable town. Official languages are Kirundi, a Bantu language, and French. Kiswahili is also used.

CURRENCY.—Burundi franc of 100 centimes.

FLAG.—White diagonal cross on green and red quarters, with a circular white panel in the centre.

NATIONAL DAY.—July 1.

British Ambassador (resident in Kinshasa, Zaire).

CAMBODIA

SUPREME NATIONAL COUNCIL

Members, Prince Sihanouk (S); Hun Sen (SOC); Dit Munti (SOC); Nor Nam Hong (SOC); Ieng Mouly (KPNLF); Im Chhunlim (SOC); Khieu Samphan (KR); Norodam Ranariddh (S); Sin Sen (SOC); Son Sann (KPNLF); Son Sen (KR); Tea Banh (SOC).

KPNLF: Khmer People's National Liberation Front, KR: Khmer Rouge, S: Sihanoukist, SOC: State of Cambodia.

NATIONAL GOVERNMENT OF CAMBODIA

President, Prince Norodom Sihanouk, *resigned* July 1988 *and again in* Aug. 1989 *after previously resuming the Presidency in* Feb. 1989.
Vice-President responsible for Foreign Affairs, Khieu Samphan.
Prime Minister, Son Sann.

STATE OF CAMBODIA

Head of State, Heng Samrin.
Chairman of Council of Ministers, Hun Sen.

Area and Population.—Situated between Thailand and the south of Vietnam and extending from the border with Laos on the north to the Gulf of Thailand, Cambodia covers an area of 69,898 sq. miles, (181,035 sq. km). It has a population (UN estimate 1989) of 8,055,000. The climate is tropical monsoon with a rainy season from May to October.

Fifty per cent of the total land area is forest or jungle. Around the Tonlé Sap lake in the centre of the country and along the Mekong river, which traverses the country, there is ample fertile land for the support of the population in times of peace.

History.—Once a powerful kingdom, which, as the Khmer Empire, flourished between the tenth and fourteenth centuries, Cambodia became a French protectorate in 1863 and was granted independence within the French Union as an Associate State in 1949. Full independence was proclaimed on November 9, 1953. From 1955 the political life of the country was dominated by Prince Norodom Sihanouk, first as King, then as Head of Government after he had abdicated in favour of his father and finally (following his father's death in 1960) as Head of State. On March 18, 1970, during his absence from the country, Prince Sihanouk was deposed as Head of State by a vote of the National Assembly. A Republic was declared on October 9, 1970 and the name of the country changed to the Khmer Republic.

In April 1970 a Civil War began between communist insurgents and government forces. In April 1975 Phnom Penh fell to the North Vietnamese-backed Khmer Rouge. Prince Sihanouk returned to Cambodia on September 9, as nominal Head of State. However, a new Constitution was promulgated in 1976 and elections to a People's Representative Assembly were held in March. Prince Sihanouk resigned as Head of State in April, and Khieu Samphan was elected President of the State Presidium. A government led by Pol Pot, the leader of the Khmer Rouge (Communist) party, was appointed and the state was renamed Democratic Kampuchea. During the years of Khmer Rouge rule hundreds of thousands of Cambodians died or fled into exile. In December 1978 Vietnamese troops invaded Cambodia in support of an uprising. The Cambodian capital,

Phnom Penh, fell on January 7, 1979. The following day the Cambodian National United Front for National Salvation established a People's Revolutionary Council, recognized by Vietnam, USSR and by other, chiefly Soviet-aligned, countries. The state was renamed The People's Republic of Kampuchea (PRK).

With strong support from the Vietnamese army the PRK gained control of most of the country, containing the challenge from the guerrilla forces of the Coalition Government of Democratic Kampuchea (CGDK), which was formed in June 1982 by the Khmer Rouge and two non-communist groups. Following the final withdrawal of Vietnam's main fighting units in September 1989, the resistance forces have regained ground inside Cambodia.

Encouraged by the five permanent members of the UN Security Council and other interested parties, the four Cambodian factions have agreed to the general principles of a peace settlement, including the ending of external military support and the holding of free and fair elections under international supervision. In September 1990, the four Cambodian factions established a Supreme National Council, as provided for in the Permanent Five draft agreement, to embody Cambodian sovereignty and to help finalize and implement a comprehensive settlement. The first meeting took place in Bangkok on September 17. A temporary ceasefire began on May 1, 1991 and became permanent on June 23. Major differences remain between the SOC (the name adopted by the PRK in 1989) and the National Government of Cambodia (the name adopted by the CDGK in February 1990) over the terms of any peace agreement.

Economy.—Cambodia has an economy based on agriculture, fishing and forestry, the bulk of its people being rice-growing farmers. In addition to rice, which is the staple crop, the major products are rubber, livestock, maize, timber, pepper, palm sugar, fresh and dried fish, kapok, beans, soya and tobacco. Rice and rubber used to be the main exports though production was brought to a standstill by the hostilities. Following the Khmer Rouge victory, the populations of Phnom Penh and other towns were forcibly evacuated to the country to work on the land, and re-establish the plantations producing such crops as cotton, rubber and bananas. Following the Vietnamese invasion of 1978 the towns were repopulated and commerce revived; currency was reintroduced. Factories, in particular textile mills, iron smelting works and cement works were put back in production.

Trade with UK

	1989	1990
Imports from UK	£530,000	£478,000
Exports to UK	219,000	56,000

Communications.—The country had over 5,000 kilometres of roads, of which nearly half were hard-surfaced and passable in the rainy season, although now in a state of disrepair. There are two railways, one from Phnom Penh to the Thai border; the other from Phnom Penh to Kampot and Kompong Som, but operations and repairs are hindered by the continuing fighting. Phnom Penh is on a river capable of receiving ships of up to 2,500 tons all the year round. The deep water port at Kompong Som on the Gulf of Thailand can receive ships up to 10,000 tons. The port is linked to Phnom Penh by a modern highway.

Religion and Education.—The state religion was Buddhism of the 'Little Vehicle'. The constitution guaranteed religious freedom, but in practice Buddhism was suppressed by the Khmer Rouge. There has been some revival recently and Buddhism has been re-established as the state religion. There were also small Muslim and Christian communities, but many members of them died or fled the country during Khmer Rouge rule. The national language is Khmer. In the years preceding the civil war considerable efforts were devoted to the development of education and new schools, colleges and technical institutes had been established. Until April 1975 there was a Buddhist University in Phnom Penh, and several residential teachers' training colleges were in operation. However, most of the country's educated elite died under the Khmer Rouge regime, which closed all institutions of higher education. The university was re-opened in 1988.

CAPITAL.—Phnom Penh, population 500,000 (1983 estimate).

CURRENCY.—Riel of 100 sen.

FLAG.—(NGC) Horizontal stripes of blue, wide red stripe bearing emblem (Temple of Angkor Wat with three towers in white), and blue. (SOC) A rectangle with the upper half red and lower half blue, with five golden towers in the centre.

NATIONAL DAY.—(NGC) April 17; (SOC) January 7.

CAMEROON
(République du Cameroun)

President, Head of State, Government and Commander in Chief of the Armed Forces, His Excellency Paul Biya, *acceded* Nov. 6, 1982, *elected* Jan. 14, 1984, *re-elected* April 24, 1988, *sworn in* May 13, 1988.

MINISTRY
(as at August, 1991)

Prime Minister, Sadou Hayatou.
Minister Delegate at the Presidency Responsible for Defence, Eduard Akame Mfoumou.
Territorial Administration, Andre Tsoungui.
Social and Women's Affairs, Aissatou Yaou.
Agriculture, John Niba Ngu.
Minister for Special Duties at the Presidency, Ogork Ebot Ntui.
Industrial and Commercial Development, Rene Owona.
National Education, Prof. Joseph Mbui.
Livestock, Fisheries and Animal Industries, Dr Hamadjoda Adjoudji.
Higher Education, Computer Services and Scientific Research, Prof. Joseph Owona.
Finance, Justin Ndioro A Yombo.
Public Service and State Control, Garga Haman Adji.
Information and Culture, Augustin Kontchou Kouemegni.
Youth and Sports, Ibrahim Mbombo Njoa.
Justice, Mr Moutome.
Mines, Water Resources and Energy, Francis Nkwain.
Planning and Regional Development, Tchouta Moussa.
Posts and Telecommunications, Oumarou Sanda.
External Relations, Jacques-Roger Booh Booh.
Public Health, Prof. Joseph Mbede.
Public Works and Transport, Paul Tessa.
Labour and Social Welfare, Jean Baptiste Bokam.
Town Planning and Housing, Henri Eyebe Ayissi.

EMBASSY OF THE REPUBLIC OF CAMEROON
84 Holland Park, W11 3SB
[071–727 0771]

Ambassador Extraordinary and Plenipotentiary, His Excellency Dr Gibering Bol-Alima (1987).

The Republic of Cameroon lies on the Gulf of Guinea between Nigeria to the west, Chad and the Central African Republic to the east and Congo and Gabon and Equatorial Guinea to the south. It has an area of 183,569 sq. miles, (475,442 sq. km) and a population of 11,540,000 (UN estimate 1989).

The whole territory was administered by Germany from 1884 to 1916. From 1916 to 1959, the former East Cameroon was administered by France as a League of Nations (later UN) trusteeship. On January 1, 1960 it became independent as the Republic of Cameroon. The Republic was joined on October 1, 1961 by the former British administered trust territory of the Southern Cameroons, after a plebiscite held under United Nations auspices. Cameroon became a Federal Republic with separate East and West Cameroon state governments. Subsequently, after a plebiscite held in May 1972, Cameroon became a unitary Republic and a one-party state; after extensive unrest, multi-party elections have been promised by the end of 1991.

Cameroon is the only country in Africa where French and English are both official languages enjoying equal status, and the government's declared long-term objective is to achieve complete bilingualism and biculturalism.

The main economic emphasis is on agricultural development, both through encouraging small-scale peasant agriculture, and through the development of large-scale agro-industrial complexes, with the aim of making the country agriculturally self-sufficient and a major food exporter.

Principal products are cocoa, coffee, bananas, cotton, timber, ground-nuts, aluminium, rubber and palm products. There is an aluminium smelting plant at Edéa with an annual capacity of 50,000 tons. Oil is now also one of Cameroon's principal products with an estimated production of 7·31 m. tonnes during 1989.

TRADE

	1987	1988
	CFA million	
Total imports	526,186	378,726
Total exports	487,849	468,683

Trade with UK

	1989	1990
Imports from UK	£24,838,000	£20,652,000
Exports to UK	11,362,000	8,241,000

CAPITAL.—Yaoundé, population estimate (1986) 653,670. Ψ Douala (1,029,736) is the commercial centre.

CURRENCY.—Franc CFA of 100 centimes.

FLAG.—Vertical stripes of green, red and yellow with single five-pointed yellow star in centre of red stripe.

NATIONAL ANTHEM.—O Cameroun, Berceau de Nos Ancêtres (O Cameroon, thou cradle of our forefathers).

NATIONAL DAY.—May 20.

BRITISH EMBASSY
Avenue Winston Churchill, BP 547
Yaoundé
[Yaoundé 220545]

Ambassador Extraordinary and Plenipotentiary, His Excellency William E. Quantrill (1991).
British Council Representative, Harley Brookes, Immeuble Christo, Rue Charles de Gaulle (BP 818), Yaoundé.

CAPE VERDE
(República de Cabo Verde)

President, António Mascarenhas Monteiro *assumed office*, March 22, 1991.

COUNCIL OF MINISTERS
(as at January, 1991)

Prime Minister and Minister of Defence, Carlos Veiga.
Foreign Affairs, Jorge Fonseca.

Justice and Public Administration, Eurico Monteiro.
Finance and Planning, José Veiga.
Economy, Transport and Communications, Manuel Chantre.
Rural Development and Fisheries, António Rosario.
Education, Manuel Faustino.
Health and Social Development, Luis Leite.
Public Works, Teófilo Silva.

EMBASSY OF THE REPUBLIC OF CAPE VERDE
44 Konninginnegracht, 2514 AD, The Hague, The Netherlands
[The Hague 469623]

Ambassador Extraordinary and Plenipotentiary, His Excellency Luis Monteiro da Fonseca (1989).

Cape Verde, off the west coast of Africa, consists of two groups of islands, Windward (Santo Antão, São Vicente, Santa Luzia, São Nicolau, Boa Vista and Sal) and Leeward (Maio, São Tiago, Fogo and Brava) with a total area of 1,557 sq. miles (4,033 sq. km). The population (UN estimate 1989) was 369,000, the majority of whom are Roman Catholic.

The islands, colonized *c.*1460, achieved independence from Portugal on July 5, 1975 under the nationalist party of Guinea Bissau and Cape Verde. A federation of the islands with Guinea Bissau was planned (till 1879 Guinea-Bissau and the islands were a single administrative unit) but this was dropped following the 1980 coup in Guinea Bissau.

The Republic was a one-party (the PAICV) state until the constitution was amended in September 1990. Multi-party elections, held on January 14, 1991, were won by the opposition Movement for Democracy (MPD) which won 56 seats in the 79-seat National Assembly. The MPD leader, António Mascarenhas Monteiro was elected as President on February 17, 1991.

The islands have had little rain since 1969, and agriculture is mostly confined to irrigated inland valleys, the chief products being bananas and coffee (for export), maize, sugarcane and nuts. Fish and shellfish are important exports. Salt is obtained on Sal, Boa Vista and Maio; volcanic rock is also mined for export. The main ports are Praia and Mindelo, and there is an international airport on Sal.

Trade with UK

	1989	1990
Imports from UK	£2,301,000	£1,537,000
Exports to UK	178,000	336,000

CAPITAL.—Ψ Praia, population (1980) 57,748.
CURRENCY.—Escudo Caboverdiano of 100 centavos.
FLAG.—Horizontal band of yellow over green, with a vertical red band in the hoist charged with a black star over a garland of maize sheaves, two corn cobs and a clam shell.
NATIONAL DAY.—July 5 (Independence Day).

British Ambassador (resident in Dakar, Senegal).

CENTRAL AFRICAN REPUBLIC
(République Centrafricaine)

President and General of the Armed Forces, Gen. André Kolingba, *assumed office* Sept. 1, 1981, *re-elected* Nov. 21, 1986.

COUNCIL OF MINISTERS
(May 1991)

Prime Minister, Edouard Frank.
Economy, Finance, Planning and International Co-operation, Thierry Bingaba.
Social Security and Territorial Administration, Ismaila Nimaga.
Justice, Jean Kpwoka.

Foreign Affairs, Laurent Gomina-Pampali.
Primary, Secondary and Technical Education, Youth and Sports, Etienne Goyemide.
Higher Education, Jean-Marie Bassia.
Transport and Civil Aviation, Pierre Gonifei Gai-bounanou.
Civil Service, Labour, Social Security and Professional Training, Christian-Bernard Yamole.
Public Health and Social Affairs, Genevieve Lombilo.
Rural Development, Casimir Amakpio.
Posts and Telecommunications, Jean Tchombego.
Public Works and Territorial Development, Dieu-donné Nana.
Energy, Mines, Geology and Water Resources, Edouard Akapekabou.
Water, Forests, Fish, Wildlife and Tourism, Raymond Mbitikon.
Trade, Industry, Small and Medium Enterprises, Auguste Tene Koezoua.
Minister in charge of the General Secretariat and Relations with Parliament, Timothée Marboua.
Communications, Arts and Culture, Tony Da Sylva.

EMBASSY OF THE CENTRAL AFRICAN REPUBLIC
30 rue des Perchamps, 75016, Paris
[Paris 42244256]

Ambassador Extraordinary and Plenipotentiary, new appointment awaited.

The Republic lies just north of the Equator between the Cameroon Republic, the Republic of Chad, the southern part of Sudan and Zaire. The Republic has an area of 240,535 sq. miles (622,984 sq. km), and a population (UN estimate 1989) of 2,841,000.

On December 1, 1958 the French colony of Ubanghi Shari elected to remain within the French Community and adopted the title of the Central African Republic. It became fully independent on August 17, 1960. The first President of the Central African Republic, David Dacko, held office from 1960 until January 1, 1966, when he was replaced by the then Col. Bokassa after a coup d'état. On Dec. 4, 1976, President Bokassa proclaimed himself Emperor and a new constitution was introduced, the country being known as the Central African Empire. On Sept. 20, 1979 Emperor Bokassa was deposed by David Dacko in a bloodless coup and the country reverted to a republic. President Dacko surrendered power on September 1, 1981 to army commander Gen. André Kolingba in a bloodless coup. In September 1985 President Kolingba dissolved the Military Committee for National Recovery (CMRN) and appointed a civilian-dominated cabinet. Moves towards democratization have been made and in November 1986, a referendum was held whereby voters approved a new Constitution and the establishment of a one-party state.

Economy.—In an effort to revive an ailing economy, the Government launched a structured adjustment programme in 1986, streamlining the civil service, increasing tax revenues, and reducing price controls. Cotton, diamonds, coffee and timber are the major exports.

Trade with UK

	1989	1990
Imports from UK	£1,630,000	£1,669,000
Exports to UK	418,000	58,000

CAPITAL.—Bangui, near the border with Zaire, population (1984 estimate) 473,817.
CURRENCY.—Franc CFA of 100 centimes.
FLAG.—Four horizontal stripes, blue, white, green, yellow, crossed by central vertical red stripe with a yellow five-pointed star in top left-hand corner.
NATIONAL DAY.—December 1.

British Ambassador, (resident in Yaoundé, Cameroon).

CHAD REPUBLIC
(Republique du Tchad)

Head of State, Idriss Déby.

COUNCIL OF MINISTERS
(as at July 8, 1991)

Prime Minister, Jean Alingue Bawoyeu.
Security and Interior, Maldom Bada Abbas.
Public Works and Transport, Nadjita Beassoumal.
External Relations, Ahmad Soungui.
Defence, Djibrine Dassert.
Planning and Co-operation, Hassan Fadoul Kittir.
Justice, Youssouf Togoimi.
Rural Development, Bambe Dansala.
Economy and Finance, Gali Gatta Ngothe.
Mines, Energy and Water Resources, Habib Doutoum.
Livestock and Animal Resources, Mahamat Zene Ali Fadel.
Information, Culture and Tourism, Mahamat Saleh Ahmat.
National Education, Abderamane Koko.
Public Health and Social Affairs, Mahamat Malloum Kadre.
Post and Telecommunications, Djidi Bichara.
Civil Service and Labour, Koumbaria Laomaye Mekonyo.
Reforms, Mboumi Malloum.

EMBASSY OF THE REPUBLIC OF CHAD
Boulevard Lambermont 52, 1030 Brussels, Belgium
[Brussels 2151975]

Ambassador Extraordinary and Plenipotentiary, His Excellency Abdoulaye Lamana (1987) (resident in Brussels).

Situated in north-central Africa, the Chad Republic extends from 23° N. latitude to 7° N. latitude and is flanked by the Republics of Niger and Cameroon on the west, by Libya on the north, by the Sudan on the east and by the Central African Republic on the south. It has an area of 495,755 sq. miles (1,284,000 sq. km) and a population (UN estimate 1989) of 5,538,000.

Chad became a member state of the French Community on November 28, 1958, and was proclaimed fully independent on August 11, 1960. On April 14, 1962, a new Constitution was adopted involving a presidential-type regime. This was suspended on April 13, 1975 when President Tombalbaye was killed in a military coup. The country was run by a Supreme Military Council, under General Felix Malloum until his overthrow in February 1979. A Transitional Government of National Unity, headed by Goukouni Oueddei, was replaced in June 1982 by the government of Hissène Habre. A ceasefire between Chad and Libya was agreed in Sept. 1987 and on October 3, 1988 they reopened diplomatic relations. The ceasefire was reaffirmed and they said that they would settle the Aouzou dispute peacefully, respecting UN and OAU charters. On September 1, 1990 Chad and Libya presented their territorial claims for the Aouzou Strip to the International Court of Justice.

In December 1990 Idriss Déby launched a successful coup in Chad and the Habré government fell. Déby has announced that he will adopt a multi-party system in Chad and that a national conference will be held in 1992 to draw up a constitution and to organize presidential and general elections.

About 90 per cent of the workforce is occupied in agriculture, fishing and forestry. There is an oilfield in Kanem and salt is mined around Lake Chad, but the most important activities are cotton growing (mostly in the south) and animal husbandry (in central areas). Raw cotton and meat are the main exports.

Trade with UK

	1989	1990
Imports from UK	£3,463,000	£1,567,000
Exports to UK	822,000	369,000

CAPITAL.—Ndjaména (formerly known as Fort Lamy) south of Lake Chad (402,000).
CURRENCY.—Franc CFA of 100 centimes.
FLAG.—Vertical stripes, blue, yellow and red.
NATIONAL DAY.— April 13.

British Ambassador (resident in Yaoundé, Cameroon).
Honorary Consul, E. Abtour, BP877, Avenue Moukhtar Ould Dada, Ndjaména.

CHILE
(República de Chile)

President of the Republic, Patricio Aylwin Azócar, assumed office March 11, 1990.

CABINET
(as at July 4, 1991)

Interior, Enrique Krauss.
Foreign Affairs, Enrique Silva Cimma.
Defence, Patricio Rojas.
Trade and Industry, Carlos Ominami.
Finance, Alejandro Foxley.
Education, Ricardo Lagos.
Justice, Francisco Cumplido.
Public Works, Carlos Hurtado.
Agriculture, Juan Agustin Figueroa.
National Properties, Luis Alvarado.
Labour, Rene Cortazar.
Public Health, Jorge Jimenez.
Mining, Juan Hamilton.
Housing, Alberto Etchegaray.
Transport, German Correa.
General Secretary of Government, Enrique Correa.
General Secretary of Presidency, Edgardo Boeninger.
Central Planning, Sergio Molina.
National Commission for Energy, Jaime Toha.
Corporation for Promotion of Production (CORFO), Rene Abeliuk.

EMBASSY OF CHILE
12 Devonshire Street, W1N 2DS
[071–580 6392/7]

Ambassador Extraordinary and Plenipotentiary, His Excellency German Riesco (1990).

A state of South America lying between the Andes and the shores of the South Pacific, Chile extends coastwise from just north of Arica to Cape Horn south, between lat. 17° 15′ and 55° 59′ S. and long. 66° 30′ and 75° 48′ W. Extreme length of the country is about 2,800 miles, with an average breadth, north of 41°, of 100 miles. The great chain of the Andes runs along its eastern limit, with a general elevation of 5,000 to 15,000 feet above sea level; but numerous summits attain a greater height. The chain lowers considerably towards its southern extremity. The Andes form a boundary with Argentina, and at the head of the pass where the international road from Chile to Argentina crosses the frontier, has been erected a statue of Christ the Redeemer, 26 feet high, made of bronze from old cannon, to commemorate the peaceful settlement of a boundary dispute in 1902. There are no rivers of great size, and none of them is of much service as a navigable highway. In the north the country is arid. The total area of the Republic is 292,258 sq. miles (756,945 sq. km), with a population (UN estimate 1989) of 12,961,000.

Among the island possessions of Chile are the Juan Fernandez group (three islands) about 360 miles distant from Valparaiso. One of these islands is the reputed scene of Alexander Selkirk's (Robinson Crusoe) shipwreck. Easter Island (27° 8' S. and 109° 28' W.), about 2,000 miles distant in the South Pacific Ocean, contains stone platforms and hundreds of stone figures, the origin of which has not yet been determined. The area of the island is about 45 sq. miles (116·5 sq. km).

Chile is divided into 12 regions and the Metropolitan Area. The disputed boundary with Argentina in the Beagle Channel was settled by a treaty ratified in May 1985.

The Chilean population has four main sources: indigenous Araucanian Indians, Fuegians, and Changos; Spanish settlers and their descendants; mixed Spanish Indians; and European immigrants. Only the few remaining indigenous Indians and some originally Bolivian Indians in the north are racially separate. Following extensive intermarriage there is no distinction among the remainder.

Government.—Chile was discovered by Spanish adventurers in the 16th century and remained under Spanish rule until 1810, when a revolutionary war, culminating in the Battle of Maipu (April 5, 1818), achieved the independence of the nation.

At a general election held in September 1970, the Marxist candidate Dr Allende was elected President by a narrow margin. After severe industrial unrest and widespread violent incidents, Allende was overthrown on September 11, 1973 in a coup carried out by leaders of the Armed Forces and National Police.

After a national plebiscite, the Constitution of 1925 was replaced early in 1981 and General Pinochet was sworn in as President, to serve until 1989. Pinochet was defeated in a plebiscite of October 5, 1988 regarding his term of office being extended for a further eight years. He resisted calls for his resignation. Another plebiscite on July 30, 1989 was held on changes to the 1980 Constitution. Presidential and Congressional elections were held in December 1989. Patricio Aylwin was elected President of the Republic for four years, thus beginning a gradual transition to full democracy.

Executive power is held by the President, legislative power is exercised by a Parliament which comprises an Upper Chamber of 47 Senators and a Lower Chamber of 120 Deputies.

Production.—Cereals, legumes, sugar beet, vegetables, fruit, tobacco, hemp and vines are grown extensively (especially in the central zone) and livestock accounts for nearly 40 per cent of agricultural production. Sheep farming predominates in the extreme south. There are large timber tracts in the central and southern zones of Chile, some types of which are exported, along with wood derivatives such as cellulose and pulp. Industrial-scale fishing, which exceeded 6·5 million tonnes in 1989, makes Chile the fifth largest nation in terms of catch. The principal end product is fish meal.

The mineral wealth is considerable, the country being particularly rich in copper-ore, iron-ore and nitrates. Chile also produces iodine, manganese ore, coal, mercury, molybdenum, zinc, lead and a small quantity of gold. Uranium is also said to have been discovered in small quantities. The rainless north is the scene of the only commercial production of nitrate of soda (Chile saltpetre) from natural resources in the world. The country has also large deposits of high grade sulphur, but mostly around high extinct volcanoes in the Andes Cordillera, difficult of access. Oil was struck in Magallanes (Tierra del Fuego) in 1945, and oil and natural gas are produced in the Magallanes area from on- and off-shore wells. This domestic production, now declining, covers less than 30 per cent of total oil requirement, and imported crude oil is refined at Concon and San Vicente in the central part of the country. There is a steel plant at Huachipato, near Concepción.

Provisional production figures for 1990 were:

Coal (tonnes)	2,515,189
Copper (tonnes)	1,603,205
Crude oil (cu. metres)	1,137,900
Natural gas (cu. metres)	4,198,300,000
Steel ingots (tonnes)	760,100*

* = 1989

Industry is based on the processing of mineral, forestry, fish and agricultural products, and the manufacture of consumer goods.

Communications.—Chilean ships have a virtual monopoly in the coastwide trade, though, with the improvement of the roads, an increasing share of internal transportation is moving by road and rail. The Chilean mercantile marine numbers 73 vessels (of over 100 tons gross) with a total deadweight tonnage of 820,965 (1990).

There are 6,575 miles of railway track. A metre-gauge line (the Longitudinal) runs from La Calera, just north of Santiago, to Iquique; however, road transport has caused considerable reduction in rail traffic along this route. The wide gauge railway runs from Valparaiso through La Calera, 60 miles inland, and after passing through Santiago ends at Puerto Montt.

With the completion of a section of 435 miles from Corumba, Brazil, to Santa Cruz, Bolivia, the Trans-Continental Line will link the Chilean Pacific port of Arica with Rio de Janeiro on the Atlantic. Another line from Antofagasta to Salta (Argentina) was opened in 1948.

Chile is served by over 20 international airlines. Domestic traffic is carried by Linea Aerea Nacional (LAN) and LADECO, which also operate internationally, and smaller regional carriers.

Chile's road system is about 65,000 kilometres in length.

Defence.—Military service is compulsory, but not all those who are liable are required. Recruitment for the Navy is mostly voluntary, but there are some conscripts. The Navy consists of 1 cruiser, 10 destroyers, frigates and escorts, 6 patrol vessels and FPBs and 4 submarines. There is a support force of transports, tankers, 1 submarine depot ship and ancillary small craft. The strength of the Navy is 28,000 (3,000 conscripts) including men of the Marine Force. The Army's total strength is 53,000, which includes 3,000 officers and 30,000 conscripts (2 years). In addition there is a police force of Carabineros of 28,000 officers and men. The Air Force total strength is 15,000 with a strength of 120 aircraft.

Education.—Elementary education is free, and has been compulsory since 1920. There are eight universities (three in Santiago, two in Valparaiso, one each in Antofagasta, Concepción and Valdivia). The religion is Roman Catholic.

Language and Literature.—Spanish is the language of the country, with admixtures of local words of Indian origin. Recent efforts have reduced illiteracy and have thus afforded access to the literature of Spain, to supplement the vigorous national output. The Nobel Prize for Literature was awarded in 1945 to Señorita Gabriela Mistral, for Chilean verse and prose, and in 1971 to the poet Pablo Neruda. There are over 100 newspapers and a large number of periodicals.

FINANCE

	1987	1988
Total revenue	US$8,469·8 m	US$8,967·1 m
Total expenditure	8,421·6 m	9,452·4 m

Foreign debt at December 31, 1990 was US$18,602 million, including Central Bank obligations with the IMF of US$1,151 million.

TRADE

	1989	1990
Total imports	US$6,734·2 m	US$7,272·1 m
Total exports	8,190·4 m	8,580·3 m

Trade with UK

	1989	1990
Imports from UK	£96,003,000	£128,056,000
Exports to UK	193,280,000	222,469,000

The principal exports are metallic and non-metallic minerals (copper represented 45·5 per cent of total export earnings in 1990), sawn timber, cellulose and other wood derivatives, some metal products, fish products, vegetables, fruit and wool. The principal imports are sugar and other food products, industrial raw materials, machinery, equipment and spares, oil fuels, lubricants and transportation equipment.

CAPITAL.—Santiago, population 4,132,293 (Greater Santiago). Other large towns are:—ΨValparaiso (500,000), Concepción (170,000), Temuco (110,000), Ψ Antofagasta (110,000), Chillán (79,461), ΨTalcahuano (75,643), Talca (75,354); ΨValdivia (70,000), ΨIquique (50,000), ΨPunta Arenas (50,000). Punta Arenas on the Straits of Magellan, is the southernmost city in the world.

CURRENCY.—Chilean peso of 100 centavos.

FLAG.—Two horizontal bands, white, red; in top sixth a white star on blue square, next staff.

NATIONAL ANTHEM.—Canción Nacional de Chile.

NATIONAL DAY.—September 18 (National Anniversary).

BRITISH EMBASSY
Avenida El Bosque Norte 0125, Casilla 72-D,
Santiago
[Santiago 2319771]

Ambassador Extraordinary and Plenipotentiary, His Excellency Richard A. Nielson, CMG, LVO (1990).
Counsellor, Head of Chancery and Consul-General, R. Lavers.
Defence Attaché, Capt. J. Finnigan, RN.
Air Attaché, Gp. Capt. B. Hall.

BRITISH CONSULAR OFFICES

There are British Consular Offices at *Arica, Concepción, Santiago, Punta Arenas, Valparaiso.*

BRITISH COUNCIL

Cultural Attaché and British Council Representative, W. Campbell, Eliodoro Yañez 832, Santiago, Casilla 15-T Tajamar. The Council supplies books to the libraries of the Instituto Chileno-Britanico in *Santiago, Viña del Mar/Valparaiso* and *Concepción.*

BRITISH-CHILEAN CHAMBER OF COMMERCE
Av. Suecia 155-C, Casilla 536, Santiago

CHINA
(Zhonghua Renmin Gongheguo—
The People's Republic of China)

President of the People's Republic of China, Yang Shangkun, *elected* April 1988.
Vice President, Wang Zhen.
Chairman of the Standing Committee of the Seventh National People's Congress, Wan Li.
Chairman of the Central Military Commission, Jiang Zemin.

STATE COUNCIL
(as at July 15, 1991)

Premier, Li Peng.
Vice-Premiers, Yao Yilin; Tian Jiyun; Wu Xueqian; Zhu Rongji; Zou Jiahua.

State Councillors, Li Tieying; Qin Jiwei; Wang Bingqian; Song Jian; Wang Fang; Zou Jiahua; Li Guixian; Chen Xitong; Chen Junsheng; Qian Qichen.

MINISTERS:
Aeronautics and Astronautics Industry, Lin Zongtang.
Agriculture, Liu Zhongyi.
Chemical Industry, Gu Xiulian.
Civil Affairs, Cui Naifu.
Commerce, Hu Ping.
Communications, Huang Zhendong.
Construction, Hon Jie.
Culture, He Jingzhi.
Energy Resources, Huang Yicheng.
Finance, Wang Bingqian.
Foreign Affairs, Qian Qichen.
Foreign Economic Relations and Trade, Zheng Tuobin.
Forestry, Gao Dezhan.
Geology and Mineral Resources, Zhu Xun.
Justice, Cai Cheng.
Labour, Ruan Chongwu.
Light Industry, Zeng Xianlin.
Machine Building and Electronics Industry, He Guangyuan.
Materials, Liu Suinian.
Metallurgical Industry, Qi Yuanjing.
National Defence, Qin Jiwei.
Personnel, Zhao Dongwan.
Posts and Telecommunications, Yang Taifang.
Public Health, Chen Minzhang.
Public Security, Tao Siju.
Radio, Film and Television, Ai Zhisheng.
Railways, Li Senmao.
State Security, Jia Chunwang.
Supervision, Wei Jianxing.
Textile Industry, Wu Wenying.
Water Resources, Yang Zhenhuai.

MINISTERS IN CHARGE OF STATE COMMISSIONS

Education, Li Tieying.
Family Planning, Peng Peiyun.
Nationalities Affairs, Ismail Amat.
Physical Culture and Sports, Wu Shaozu.
Planning, Zou Jiahua.
Restructuring Economy, Chen Jinhua.
Science, Technology and Industry for National Defence, Ding Henggao.
Science and Technology, Song Jian.
Auditor General, Lu Peijian.
Secretary General, Luo Gan.

President of the People's Bank of China, Li Guixian.

THE CHINESE COMMUNIST PARTY

General Secretary, Jiang Zemin.
The Politburo Standing Committee, Jiang Zemin; Li Peng; Qiao Shi; Yao Yilin; Li Ruihuan; Song Ping.
The Politburo of the Central Committee, Wan Li; Tian Jiyun; Qiao Shi; Jiang Zemin; Li Tieying; Li Ruihuan; Li Ximing; Yang Rudai; Yang Shangkun; Wu Xueqian; Song Ping; Yao Yilin; Qin Jiwei; Li Peng (*full members*); Ding Guangen (*alternate member*).
The Secretariat of the Central Committee, Li Ruihuan; Ding Guangen; Qiao Shi; Yang Baibing (*full members*); Wen Jiabao (*alternate member*).
The Advisory Commission, Chen Yun (*Chairman*); Bo Yibo; Song Renqiong (*Vice Chairmen*).
The Discipline Inspection Commission, Secretary, Qiao Shi; *Deputy Secretaries*, Chen Zuolin; Li Zhengting; Xiao Hongda.
Membership, 50,320,000 (1991).

EMBASSY OF THE PEOPLE'S REPUBLIC OF CHINA
49–51 Portland Place, W1N 3AH
[071–636 9375]

Ambassador Extraordinary and Plenipotentiary, His
Excellency Ma Yuzhen (1991).

Area and Population.—The area of China is
3,705,408 sq. miles, (9,596,961 sq. km). A nationwide
census (the fourth) was held in July 1990, which
recorded a total population of 1,130,000,000.

China is anxious to control the growth of the
population and has introduced stringent policies
intended to result in a population of 1,250 million by
the year 2000. About 6 per cent of the population
belong to around 55 ethnic minorities. Among the
largest are the Zhuang of Guangxi, the Uygurs of
Xinjiang, the Tibetans and the Mongols.

THE PROVINCES OF CHINA
(1989 estimated population figures)

Anhui	54,690,000
Beijing	10,370,000
Fujian	28,960,000
Gansu	21,720,000
Guangdong	60,250,000
Guangxi Zhuang Autonomous Region	41,510,000
Guizhou	31,690,000
Hainan	6,280,000
Hebei	58,810,000
Heilongjiang	35,100,000
Henan	82,310,000
Hubei	52,590,000
Hunan	60,090,000
Jiangsu	65,350,000
Jiangxi	36,950,000
Jilin	24,030,000
Liaoning	38,760,000
Nei Monggol Autonomous Region	21,220,000
Ningxia Hui Autonomous Region	4,550,000
Qinghai	4,440,000
Shaanxi	31,910,000
Shandong	81,600,000
Shanghai	12,760,000
Shanxi	27,930,000
Sichuan	107,060,000
Tianjin	8,560,000
Tibet Autonomous Region	2,160,000
Xinjiang Uygur Autonomous Region	14,540,000
Yunnan	36,480,000
Zhejiang	42,080,000
Armed Forces	3,000,000*

* = 1990 estimate

Government.—On October 10, 1911, the party of
reform forced the Imperial dynasty to a 'voluntary'
abdication, and a Republic was proclaimed at Wu-
chang.

On September 30, 1949 the Chinese People's Political Consultative Conference (CPPCC) met in Beijing
(Peking) and appointed the National People's Government Council under the Chairmanship of Mao Zedong
(Mao Tse-tung). On October 1, Mao proclaimed the
inauguration of the Chinese People's Republic.

The regime was recognized by all the Communist
bloc countries in quick succession, and soon after by
the Asian countries of the Commonwealth, the
United Kingdom and by a number of other
countries. Others, led by the United States, continued to recognize the Chiang Kai-shek regime of
Taiwan as the rightful Government of China. In
1971 the People's Republic won acceptance into the
United Nations on the expulsion of Taiwan. Since
then many more countries have accorded recognition.

A new Constitution was adopted in December 1982,
under which the National People's Congress is the
highest organ of state power. It is elected for a term
of five years and is supposed to hold one session a
year. It is empowered to amend the Constitution,
make laws, select the President and Vice-President
and other leading officials of the state, approve the
national economic plan, the state budget and the final
state accounts, and to decide on questions of war and
peace. The State Council is the highest organ of the
state administration. It is composed of the Premier,
the Vice Premiers, the State Councillors, heads of
Ministries and Commissions, the Auditor General
and the Secretary General. Command over the armed
forces is vested in the Central Military Commission,
of which Jiang Zemin is the Chairman.

Deputies to congresses at the primary level are
'directly elected' by the voters 'through a secret
ballot after democratic consultation'. This is now
extended to county level. These Congresses elect the
Deputies to the Congress at the next higher level.
Deputies to the National People's Congress are
elected by the People's Congresses of the provinces,
autonomous regions and municipalities directly under the Central Government, and by the armed forces.

Local government is conducted through People's
Governments at provincial, municipal and county
levels. Autonomous regions, prefectures and counties exist for national minorities and are described as
self-governing. The system prevailing is that found
elsewhere, i.e. People's Congresses and People's
Governments. Beijing, Shanghai and Tianjin continue to come directly under the central government.

Following the deaths of Mao Zedong and Zhou En-
lai in 1976, the disgraced Vice-Premier Deng Xiaoping
was recalled. At the 11th Party Congress in 1977
Deng was elected Vice-Chairman and has since
become the dominant force within the Party by
eliminating leftist influence, rehabilitating fallen
leaders and adjusting Maoist policies to permit
economic liberalization. Deng's policies were reaffirmed at the 12th Congress in 1982. The Congress
also elected a new Party leadership dominated by
Deng and his supporters. The post of Chairman of
the Party was abolished. The Party leader now holds
the post of General Secretary. The 13th Party
Congress in 1987 reaffirmed open-door policies. Most
of the old revolutionary generation were removed,
in elections, from the top posts.

Student-led pro-democracy demonstrations
throughout April and May ended on June 3–4, 1989
when the People's Liberation Army took control of
Beijing, killing thousands of protesters.

Armed Forces.—All three military arms in China
are parts of the People's Liberation Army (PLA). The
size of this body has not been formally given, but it is
estimated that China has approximately 3 million
men under arms, with a further 12 million (or perhaps
many more) reserves who take part in militia
activities. In 1955 compulsory military service was
introduced for all men between the ages of 18 and 40.
This service was on a selective basis. The present
length of service for those conscripted is three years
in the Army, four years in the Air Force and the
Navy. The rank structure, abolished in 1965, was
reinstated in 1988.

Religion.—The indigenous religions of China are
Confucianism (which includes ancestor worship),
Taoism (originally a philosophy rather than a religion) and, since its introduction in the first century
of the Christian era, Buddhism. There are also
Chinese Muslims (officially estimated at about 12
million) and Christians (unofficially estimated at
about 50 million). Religious freedoms, severely curtailed during the Cultural Revolution, are reviving
slightly under more liberal policies. Ethnic unrest in
Buddhist Tibet and Muslim Xinjiang could threaten
such liberalization.

Education.—The Cultural Revolution caused considerable disruption to the educational system and

since 1976 attempts have been made to raise academic standards. Primary education now lasts five years, and enrolment (1988) was 143,903,000 including kindergarten. Secondary education lasts five years (three years in junior middle school and two years in senior middle school). There were 47,600,000 middle school pupils in 1988. There are 220 million illiterates; efforts are being made to expand secondary education, particularly in the rural areas. Particular attention is being paid to higher education where there are over 1,000 universities, colleges and institutes with an enrolment (1988) of 2 million students. In May 1985 the Central Committee of the Party announced the abolition of free higher education except for teacher training, and the aim of providing all children with junior secondary education within 10 years.

Language and Literature.—The Chinese language has many dialects, notably Cantonese, Hakka, Amoy, Foochow, Changsha, Nanchang, Wu (Shanghai) and the northern dialect. The Common Speech or *Putonghua* (often referred to as Mandarin) which is being taught throughout the country is based on the northern dialect. The Communists have promoted it as the national language and made intensive efforts to propagate it throughout the country. Since the most important aspect of this policy is the use of the spoken language in writing, the old literary style and ideographic form of writing has fallen into disuse.

In 1956, after some 4 years of study, the Government decided to introduce 230 simplified characters with a view to making reading and writing easier. The list was enlarged and there are now over 2,000 simplified characters in use. In January 1956 all Chinese newspapers and most books began to appear with the characters printed horizontally from left to right, instead of vertically reading from right to left, as previously.

In February 1958 the National People's Congress adopted a system of romanization, known as pinyin, using 25 of the letters of the Latin alphabet (not v). This has been used within the country largely for assisting schoolchildren and others to learn the pronunciation of characters in Putonghua, and is now used for Chinese names in foreign-language publications.

Chinese literature is one of the richest in the world. Paper has been employed for writing and printing for nearly 2,000 years. The Confucian classics which formed the basis of the traditional Chinese culture date from the Warring States period (4th–3rd centuries BC) as do the earliest texts of the rival tradition, Taoism. Histories, philosophical and scientific works, poetry, literary and art criticism, novels and romances survive from most periods. Many have been translated into English. In the past all this considerable literature was available only to a very small class of literati, but with the spread of literacy in the 20th century, a process which has received enormous impetus since the Communists took over in 1950, the old traditional literature has been largely superseded by modern works of a popular kind and by the classics of Marxism and modern developments from them.

The most important among the newspapers and magazines are the *People's Daily* and the twice-monthly *Qiushi*, which replaced *Red Flag* as the CCP's mouthpiece in August 1989.

Production and Industry.—China is essentially an agricultural and pastoral country: peasants constitute about 80 per cent of the population. People's communes gave way to townships as the basic level of State administration in rural districts under the 1982 Constitution.

New agricultural policies, designed to give greater incentives to the rural population, have meant that the responsibility for agricultural production has been devolved down to individual households, whereas previously work was generally assigned on a collective basis.

Wheat, barley, maize, millet and other cereals, with peas and beans, are grown in the northern provinces, and rice and sugar in the south. Rice is the staple food of the inhabitants. Cotton (mostly in valleys of the Yangtze and Yellow Rivers), tea (in the west and south), with hemp, jute and flax, are the most important crops.

Livestock is raised in large numbers. Silkworm culture is one of the oldest industries. Cottons, woollens and silks are manufactured in large quantities. The mineral wealth of the country is great. Coal, iron ore, tin, antimony, wolfram, bismuth and molybdenum are abundant. Oil is produced in several northern provinces, particularly in Heilongjiang and Shandong, and off-shore deposits are being sought in co-operation with Western and Japanese companies.

The Chinese State Statistical Bureau issues production figures annually. The following are of note for 1990:

Grain (tons)	435,000,000
Pork, beef, mutton (tons)	25,040,000
Tea (tons)	536,000
Cotton (tons)	4,470,000
Timber (cu. metres)	54,000,000
Crude oil (tons)	138,000,000
Steel (tons)	66,040,000
Electric power (kWh)	618 billion
Machine tools	117,800
Motor vehicles	509,100

The State Statistical Bureau valued the national income for 1990 at Yuan 1,430 billion, an increase of 4·8 per cent over 1989. The Gross National Product in 1990 was Yuan 1,740 billion, a 5 per cent increase over 1989. The total value of agricultural output rose by 6·9 per cent over the 1989 figure to Yuan 738·2 billion. The total value of industrial output rose by 7·6 per cent to Yuan 2,385·1 billion in 1990.

In 1982 China set itself the aim of quadrupling the 1980 gross agricultural and industrial output value by the year 2000. The focus of its reform programme was switched to industry in 1984. Wide-ranging reforms have been introduced to make the industrial sector more efficient by narrowing the scope of central planning and broadening enterprise decision-making, material incentives and the role of the market.

Foreign trade and external economic relations have expanded quickly since the open-door policy, adopted in the late 1970s. The principal articles of export are animals and animal products, oil, textiles, ores, metals, tea and manufactured goods. The principal imports are motor vehicles, machinery, chemical fertilizer plants, aircraft, books, paper and paper-making materials, chemicals, metals and ores, and dyes.

Trade with UK

	1989	1990
Imports from UK	£417,911,000	£465,585,000
Exports to UK	530,720,000	583,425,000

Communications.—Of the total area of China over half consists of tableland and mountainous areas where communications and travel are generally difficult. The country has more than 53,187 kilometres of railway trunk and branch lines and some 1,014,300 kilometres of highway (1989). In addition, internal civil aviation has been developed, with routes now totalling more than 471,900 kilometres. As a result the communications network now covers most of the country.

In the past where roads did not exist the principal means of communication east to west was provided by the rivers, the most important of which are the

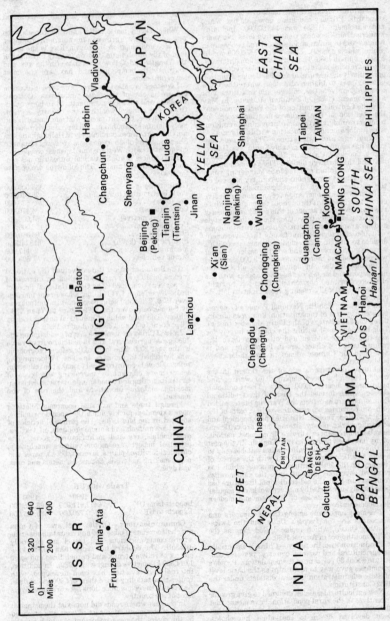

Yangtze (Changjiang) (3,400 miles long), the Yellow River (Huanghe) (2,600 miles long) and the West River (Xihe) (1,650 miles). These, together with the network of canals connecting them are still much used, but their overall importance is less than it was. Coastal port facilities are being improved and the merchant fleet expanded. In the past 10 years great progress has been made in developing postal services and telecommunications. It is claimed that 95 per cent of all rural townships are on the telephone and that postal routes reach practically every production brigade headquarters.

CAPITAL.—Beijing (Peking), population (metropolitan area, 1989) 10,370,000 (excluding temporary residents).

Population of major cities in 1989:

ΨShanghai	12,670,000*	Harbin	2,800,000
Tianjin	5,700,000	Chengdu	2,780,000
Shenyang	4,500,000	Xian	2,710,000
Wuhan	3,710,000	Nanjing	2,470,000
Guangzhou		Taiyuan	1,900,000
(Canton)	3,540,000	Kunming	1,500,000
Chongqing	2,960,000	Lanzhou	1,480,000

* = metropolitan area

CURRENCY.—The currency is called Renminbi (RMB). The unit of currency is the yuan of 10 jiao or 100 fen.

FLAG.—Red, with large gold five-point star and four small gold stars in crescent, all in upper quarter next staff.

NATIONAL ANTHEM.—March of the Volunteers.

NATIONAL DAY.—October 1 (Founding of People's Republic).

BRITISH EMBASSY
11 Guang Hua Lu,
Jian Guo Men Wai, Beijing
[Beijing 521961/5]

Ambassador, His Excellency Sir Robin McLaren, KCMG (1991).
Counsellors, D. Coates (*Political*); A. Kerfoot (*Commercial*); A. D. Johnson, CBE (*Cultural, and British Council Representative*).
Defence, Military and Air Attaché, Col. C. A. Lees.
First Secretaries, Dr J. E. Hoare (*Head of Chancery and Consul General*); G. R. Duff (*Administration and Consul*); P. Davies (*Chancery and Consul*); P. Clark (*Chancery*); J. Riordan (*Chancery*); L. Bristow-Smith (*Commercial*); J. E. Rogan (*Chancery*); J. M. Candlish (*Energy*); J. Stoddart (*Cultural ELO*); Dr G. Alexander (*Cultural/Science*).
There is also a Consulate-General in *Shanghai*.

TIBET

Tibet is a plateau seldom lower than 10,000 feet, which forms the northern frontier of India (boundary imperfectly demarcated), from Kashmir to Burma, but is separated therefrom by the Himalayas. The area is estimated at 463,000 square miles with a population of 2,160,000 in 1989.

From 1911 to 1950, Tibet was virtually an independent country though its status was never officially so recognized. In October 1950, Chinese Communist forces invaded Eastern Tibet. On May 23, 1951 an agreement was reached whereby the Chinese army was allowed entry into Tibet. A Communist military and administrative headquarters was set up. In 1954 the Government of India recognized that Tibet was an integral part of China, in return for the right to maintain trade and consular representation there.

A series of revolts against Chinese rule over several years culminated on March 17, 1959 in a rising in Lhasa. Heavy fighting continued for several days before the rebellion was suppressed by Chinese troops and military rule imposed. The Dalai Lama fled to India where he and his followers were granted political asylum. On March 28, 1959 the Tibetan government was dissolved. In its place the 16-member Preparatory Committee for the Tibetan Autonomous Region, originally set up in 1955 with the Dalai Lama as Chairman, was to administer Tibet under the State Council; the Preparatory Committee was to have the Panchen Lama as Acting Chairman.

In December 1964 the Dalai Lama was declared to be a traitor, and both he and the Panchen Lama were dismissed. The position of Acting Chairman of the Preparatory Committee was assumed by Ngapoi Ngawang Jigmi. This move marked the end of the period of co-operation by the Chinese Government with the traditional religious authorities, and the eclipse of the latter. The Preparatory Committee completed its work with the setting up of Tibet as an Autonomous Region of China on Sept. 9, 1965. The Panchen Lama was rehabilitated as an official of the CPPCC, but died in 1989. The Chinese have invited the Dalai Lama to return from exile, but suggested negotiations between the Chinese and the Dalai Lama have failed to materialize. Sporadic outbursts of unrest continue in Tibet.

TAIWAN (REPUBLIC OF CHINA)
(Chung-hua Min-kuo)

President, Lee Teng-hui, *elected*, Jan. 13, 1988, re-elected May 20, 1990.
Vice-President, Li Yuan-zu.
Premier, Hau Pei-tsun.

An island of some 13,800 sq. miles, (35,742 sq. km), in the China Sea, Taiwan, formerly Formosa, lies 90 miles east of the Chinese mainland in latitude 21° 45′N.–25° 56′N. The population (20,182,486 in 1989), is almost entirely Chinese in origin. About 2,000,000 mainlanders came to the island with Chiang Kai-shek in 1947–49.

The territories administered by the Chinese Nationalists include the Pescadores Islands (50 sq. miles), some 35 miles west of Taiwan, as well as Quemoy (68 sq. miles) and Matsu (11 sq. miles) which are only a few miles from the mainland. Settled for centuries by the Chinese, the island was administered by Japan from 1895 to 1945. General Chiang Kai-shek withdrew to Taiwan in 1949, towards the end of the war against the Communist regime, accompanied by 500,000 Nationalist troops, after which the territory continued under his presidency until his death on April 5, 1975. A mutual defence treaty between the United States and Taiwan Governments was signed in 1954 but this was terminated when the United States recognized the People's Republic of China on January 1, 1979. Martial law was lifted in July 1987, after 38 years. Chiang Kai-shek's son Chiang Ching-kuo died in January 1988 and was succeeded by Vice-President Lee Teng-hui, a native Taiwanese.

On April 30, 1991, President Lee announced that the 'period of Communist rebellion' on the Chinese mainland was over, thus granting *de facto* recognition of the People's Republic; the announcement also ended emergency measures which had frozen political life on Taiwan since 1949. Power is being shifted away from mainlanders to native Taiwanese. Elections for a reformed National Assembly are scheduled for the end of 1991.

The eastern part of the main island is mountainous and forest covered. Mt. Morrison (Yu Shan) (13,035 ft.) and Mt. Sylvia (Tz'ukaoshan) (12,972 ft.) are the highest peaks. The western plains are watered by many rivers and the soil is very fertile, producing sugar, rice, sweet potatoes, tea, bananas, pineapples and tobacco. Mineral resources are meagre. Taiwan produces one tenth of its coal needs and some natural gas. There are important fisheries. The principal seaports ΨKeelung and ΨKaohsiung are situated in the northern and southern sections of the island.

Trade with UK

	1989	1990
Imports from UK	£407,432,000	£430,643,000
Exports to UK	1,351,695,000	1,211,968,000

CAPITAL.—Taipei, population (1989), 2,702,678. Other towns are ΨKaohsiung (1,374,231); Tainan (667,622); Taichung (730,376); and ΨKeelung (348,672).

CURRENCY.—New Taiwan dollar (NT$) of 100 cents.

FLAG.—Red, with blue quarter at top next staff, bearing a twelve-point white sun.

NATIONAL DAY.—October 10.

COLOMBIA
(República de Colombia)

President, César Gaviria Trujillo, *assumed office*, August 7, 1990.

CABINET
(as at August 1991)

Interior, Humberto de la Calle.
Foreign Affairs, Luis Fernando Correa.
Justice, Fernando Carrillo Flores.
Finance and Public Credit, Rudolph Hommes Rodriguez.
Defence, Gen. Oscar Botero.
Agriculture, María del Rosario Sintes Ulloa.
Economic Development, Ernesto Samper Pizano.
Mines and Energy, Luis Fernando Vergara.
Education, Alfonso Valdivieso.
Labour and Social Security, Francisco Posada de la Peña.
Health, Camilo González Possa.
Communications, Alberto Casas Santamaría.
Public Works and Transport, Juan Felipe Gavira.
Attorney-General, Carlos Gustavo Arrieta.
Comptroller General of the Republic, Manuel Francisco Becerra Barney.
Deputy Minister of Foreign Affairs, Rodrigo Pardo.

COLOMBIAN EMBASSY
3 Hans Crescent, SW1X 0LR
[071–589 9177]

Ambassador Extraordinary and Plenipotentiary, His Excellency Dr Virgilio Barco Vargas (1990).

The Republic of Colombia lies in the extreme northwest of South America, having a coastline on both the Caribbean Sea and Pacific Ocean. It is situated between 4° 13′ S. to 12° 30′ N. lat. and 68° to 79° W. long., with an area of 439,737 sq. miles (1,138,914 sq. km), and a population (UN estimate 1989) of 31,193,000.

The country is divided into a narrow coastal strip in the west and extensive plains in the east by the Cordillera de los Andes. The Eastern Cordillera consists of a series of vast tablelands. This temperate region is the most densely peopled portion of the Republic. The principal rivers are the Magdalena, Guaviare, Cauca, Atrato, Caquetá, Putumayo and Patia.

Government.—The Colombian coast was visited in 1502 by Christopher Columbus, and in 1536 a Spanish expedition under Jiménez de Quesada penetrated to the interior and established on the site of the present capital a government which continued under Spanish rule until the revolt of the Spanish-American colonies of 1811–1824. In 1819 Simór Bolívar (1783–1831) established the Republic of Colombia, consisting of the territories now known as Colombia, Panama, Venezuela and Ecuador. In 1829-1830 Venezuela and Ecuador withdrew from the association of provinces, and in 1831 the remaining territories were formed into the Republic of New Granada. In 1858 the name was changed to the Granadine Confederation and in 1861 to the United States of Colombia. In 1866 the present title was adopted. In 1903 Panama seceded from Colombia, and became a separate Republic.

During the early 1950s Colombia suffered a period of virtual civil war between the supporters of the traditional political parties, the Conservatives and the Liberals. From 1957–1974 the country was governed under the 'National Front' agreement with the presidency alternating between the two parties every four years and ministerial posts being shared equally by the parties. The alternation of the presidency was ended in 1974 and parity in appointments in 1978. Thereafter, the constitution lays down that Government portfolios and administrative appointments shall be divided among the two majority parties in Congress in an adequate and equitable manner. However, after a General Election in 1986, the Liberal Party won a large majority. Elections to a constitutional convention were held in November 1990, in which the former guerrilla movement M19 gained 30 per cent of the vote, ending the dominance of the traditional parties. The Convention began meeting in February and a new constitution was promulgated on July 4, 1991.

Defence.—The Army's strength is some 100,000. The Navy, with 14,000 personnel including 6,000 marines, has four frigates, one sail training ship, two submarines and a number of patrol boats. The Air Force, with 6,000 personnel, is equipped with Mirage fighters, 837B's, C47's and a number of support helicopters.

Production.—Much of Colombia's natural resources in coal, natural gas and hydro-electricity remain largely unexploited. Development of coal is being given priority but no new hydro projects are likely to be started for the next 4–5 years. Annual coal production is increasing from the recent peak of 5·5 million tonnes now that the Cerrejón Norte coalfield is being fully worked. This is essentially for export. Proven coal reserves stand at 16,000 million tonnes. Estimated natural gas reserves are 3,788,000 million cu. ft., with daily use at 381,772 million B.t.u. Proven crude oil reserves stand at 1,300 million barrels. Colombia is again a net exporter of oil. In 1987 exports averaged 152,000 b.p.d. and were expected to rise to 282,000 b.p.d. by 1989.

The hydrocarbon sector accounts for over half of the mining output with precious metals (gold, platinum and silver) and iron ore accounting for the remainder. Other mineral deposits include nickel (a processing plant started operating in 1982), bauxite, copper, gypsum, limestone, phosphates, sulphur and uranium. Colombia is also the world's largest producer of emeralds and has deposits of other precious and semi-precious stones.

Because of the range of climate, a wide variety of crops can be grown, and the country is close to self-sufficiency in food. The principal agriculture product is coffee (Colombia is second only to Brazil as the world's largest coffee producer) and other major cash crops are sugar, bananas, cut flowers and cotton. Cattle are raised in large numbers, and meat and cured skins and hides are also exported.

Industry.—The Government has encouraged diversification to reduce dependence on coffee as the major export and this has led to the growth of new export-orientated industries, particularly textiles, paper products and leather goods. Stimulus to the economy has been provided by large loans from the World Bank and IADB for project development, particularly in the power sector (in which hydroelectric projects have predominated) and for telecommunications.

Communications.—The massive ranges of the Andes make surface transport difficult therefore air transport is used extensively. There are daily passenger and cargo air services between Bogotá and all the principal towns, as well as daily services to the USA, frequent services to other countries in South America, and to Europe. The 'Atlantic Railway' links the departmental lines running down to the river, and completes the connection between Bogotá and Santa Marta. Although the railways generally are in a poor state there are about 2,600 miles of rail in use at present. The total road network (1985) consists of 105,201 km of roads of all types, of which 21,800 km are classified as main trunk and transversal roads.

Large appropriations have been made for modernization of the country's telecommunication system. There are 485 radio stations (1983) and two national television channels with several regional ones.

Language and Literature.—Spanish is the language of the country and education has been free since 1870. Great efforts have been made in reducing illiteracy and estimates (1980) put the literacy rate at 77·6 per cent of those over 10 years of age. In addition to the National University with headquarters at Bogotá there are 26 other universities. There is a flourishing press in urban areas and a national literature supplements the rich inheritance from the time of Spanish rule.

Roman Catholicism is the established religion.

TRADE

Colombia's principal export is still coffee although other products, principally bananas, cut flowers, clothing and textiles, ferro-nickel and coal are important exports. Principal trading partners are USA, the EC and Latin America.

Trade with UK

	1989	1990
Imports from UK	£61,733,000	£60,469,000
Exports to UK	70,715,000	82,507,000

CAPITAL.—Bogotá, population (1985 census) 3,967,988. Bogotá is an inland city in the Eastern Cordilleras, at an elevation of 8,600 to 9,000 ft. above sea level. Other centres are Medellin (1,500,000); Cali (1,350,000); ΨBarranquilla (900,000); ΨCartagena (530,000); Bucaramanga (350,000); ΨBuenaventura (130,000) is the country's major port.

CURRENCY.—Colombian peso of 100 centavos.

FLAG.—Broad yellow band in upper half, surmounting equal bands of blue and red.

NATIONAL ANTHEM.—Oh gloria inmarcesible.

NATIONAL DAY.—July 20 (National Independence Day).

BRITISH EMBASSY
Torre Propaganda Sancho, Calle 98 No. 9–03 Piso 4,
Bogotá
[Bogota 2185111]

Ambassador Extraordinary and Plenipotentiary, His Excellency Keith E. H. Morris, CMG, (1990).

There are British Consular Offices at *Barranquilla, Bogotá, Cali* and *Medellin.*

British Council Representative, J. Coope, Calle 87 No. 12–79, Bogotá DE.

COLOMBO-BRITISH CHAMBER OF COMMERCE, Apartado Aereo 054 728, Calle 106 No. 25-41, Bogotá DE.

THE COMOROS
(Republique Fédérale Islamique des Comores)

Head of State, President Said Mohamed Djohar, *sworn in* March 20, 1990.

COUNCIL OF GOVERNMENT
(as at June 1991)

Ministers of State:
Transport, Tourism and Immigration, Said Ali Youssouf.
Ministers:
Production, Industry, Ali Mroudjae.
Foreign Affairs and Co-operation, Dr Mtara Maecha.
Finance, Economy, Abdallah Ahmed Sourette.
Environment, Post and Telecommunications, Said Hassane Said Hachim.
Health and Population, Houmadi Kaambi.
Justice, Said Attoumane.
Interior, Mohamed Taki Mboreha.
Education, Arbabidine Mohamed.
Information, Culture, Adamou Mohamed.
Secretaries of State:
Commerce and Crafts, Mouhtare Rachid.
Islamic Affairs, Daoud Attoumane.

The Comoro archipelago includes the islands of Great Comoro, Anjouan, Mayotte and Moheli and certain islets in the Indian Ocean with an area of 838 sq. miles (2,171 sq. km) and a population (UN estimate 1989) of 503,000, most of whom are Muslim. The islanders voted for independence from France in December 1974 and three islands became independent on July 6, 1975. (The island of Mayotte was against independence and has remained under French administration.)

On October 1, 1978 the three islands voted in a referendum to adopt a new Constitution which provides for a President, directly elected for a six year term. The Council of Government, consisting of a Prime Minister and up to nine other Ministers, is appointed by the President. There is a 42-member Federal Assembly elected for 5 years. Each island is administered by a Governor, assisted by up to four Commissioners whom he appoints, and has an elected Legislative Council. The latest elections took place in March 1990, following the assassination of the former President, Ahmed Abdallah Abderrahman, in December 1989.

The most important products are vanilla, copra, cloves and essential oils, which are the principal exports; cacao, sisal and coffee are also cultivated. Great Comoro is well forested and produces some timber.

Trade with UK

	1989	1990
Imports from UK	£419,000	£236,000
Exports to UK	60,000	54,000

CAPITAL.—Moroni, on Great Comoro (pop. 17,267).

CURRENCY.—Comorian franc of 100 centimes. The Comoros also use the Franc CFA of 100 centimes.

FLAG.—Green ground with a crescent and four stars all in white in the half by the hoist.

NATIONAL DAY.—July 6 (Independence Day).

British Ambassador, (resident in Mauritius).

CONGO
(République du Congo)

President, Gen. Denis Sassou-Nguesso, *appointed* 1979, *re-elected*, July 30, 1984 *and* July 30, 1989.

TRANSITIONAL GOVERNMENT
(as at June 17, 1991)

President of the Transitional Government, Mgr. Ernest Nkombo.
Prime Minister, Minister of Mines and Energy, National Defence, Andre Milongo.
Finance, Economy and Planning, Edouard Ebouka Babakas.
Foreign Affairs and Co-operation, Jean Blaise Kololo.
Interior and Decentralization, Alexis Gabou.
Justice, Administrative Reform, Martin Mbemba.
Transport and Civil Aviation, Jacques Okoko.
Primary and Secondary Education, Mr Tsomambe.
Industry and Tourism, Mr Kakoula-Kady.
Social Affairs, Mrs Fouty.
Trade and Small and Medium Enterprises, Clément Mierassa.
Agriculture and Livestock, Célestin Nkoua Gongara.
Communications and responsible for relations with the Superior Council, Government Spokesman, Guy Menga.
Youth and Sports, Jean Pierre Mberry.
Labour and Social Security, Mr Guimbi.
Culture and Arts, Antoine Letembet-Ambily.
Higher Education, Science and Technology, Mr Manzengue Younous.
Public Health, Mr Ndouna.
Public Works, Construction, Town Planning and Housing, Mr Demba-Tello.
Minister responsible for Mines, Energy and Hydrocarbons, Camille Dellho.
Fisheries and Forestry, Mr Boula.

EMBASSY OF THE REPUBLIC OF CONGO
37 bis rue Paul Valery, 75116 Paris, France
[Paris 45006057]

Ambassador Extraordinary and Plenipotentiary, His Excellency Jean-Marie Ewengue (1986).

HONORARY CONSULATE
Livingstone House, 11 Carteret Street, SW1H 9DJ
[071–222 7575]

Honorary Consul and Head of Mission, L. Muzzu.

The Republic lies on the Equator between Gabon on the west and Zaire on the east, the River Congo and its tributary the Ubangui forming most of the eastern boundary of the state. The Congo has a short Atlantic coastline. The area of the Republic of Congo is 132,047 sq. miles (342,000 sq. km), with a population of 1,941,000 (UN estimate 1989). Formerly the French colony of Middle Congo, it became a member state of the French Community on November 28, 1958, and was proclaimed fully independent on August 17, 1960.

In 1968, conduct of affairs was assumed by a National Council of Army officers. The Parti Congolais du Travail (PCT) was created by the Congress of December 29–31, 1969 and the People's Republic of the Congo was established. After popular pressure, the PCT abandoned its monopoly of power and renounced Marxism in July 1990. A transitional government was formed in January and a national conference of all political forces convened in February 1991. The national conference suspended the constitution, stripping President Sassou-Nguesso of all powers; a new constitution is to be put to a referendum in autumn 1991 and elections are to follow.

Congo has its own oil deposits, producing about 8

million tonnes annually. It also produces lead, zinc and gold. The principal agricultural products are timber, cassava, sugar cane and yams. Imports are mainly of machinery.

Trade with UK

	1989	1990
Imports from UK	£8,258,000	£9,211,000
Exports to UK	3,442,000	2,563,000

CAPITAL.—Brazzaville (600,000); Ψ Pointe Noire (350,000).
CURRENCY.—Franc CFA of 100 centimes.
FLAG.—Red, with hammer and hoe in wreath of leaves in top corner.
NATIONAL DAY.—August 15.
British Ambassador, (resident in Zaire).

COSTA RICA
(República de Costa Rica)

President, Rafael Angel Calderón Fournier, *took office,* May 8, 1990.

MINISTERS
(as at August 8, 1991)

Vice Presidents, G. Serrano Pinto; A. López Echandi.
Minister for the Presidency, R. Méndez Mata.
Foreign Affairs and Worship, B. Niehaus Quesada.
Interior and Police, L. Fishman Zonzinski.
Justice, Elizabeth Odio Benito.
Public Security, V. E. Herrera Alfaro.
Finance, T. Vargas Madrigal.
Agriculture, J. R. Lizano Sáenz.
Economy, Industry and Commerce, G. Fajardo Salas.
Natural Resources, Energy and Mines, H. Bravo Trejos.
Public Works and Transport, G. Madriz de Mezerville.
Education, H. Herrera Araya.
Health, C. Castro Charpentier.
Culture, Youth and Sports, Aida de Fishman.
Labour and Social Security, Carlos Monge Rodríguez.
Planning, H. Fallas Venegas.
Housing and Urban Development, C. Zawadzki Wojtasiak.
Foreign Trade, R. Rojas López.
Science and Technology, O. Morales Matamores.
Information and Press, Guillermo Fernández.

COSTA RICAN EMBASSY
Flat 1, 14 Lancaster Gate, W2 3LH
[071–723 1772/9630]

Ambassador Extraordinary and Plenipotentiary, his Excellency Luis Rafael Tinoco Alvarado (1991).

The Republic of Costa Rica in Central America extends across the isthmus between 8° 17′ and 11° 10′ N. lat. and from 82° 30′ to 85° 45′ W. long., has an area of 19,575 sq. miles (50,700 sq. km), and a population (1990 estimate) of 3,000,000. The population is basically of European stock, in which Costa Rica differs from most Latin American countries. The Republic lies between Nicaragua and Panama and between the Caribbean Sea and the Pacific Ocean. The coastal lowlands by the Caribbean Sea and Pacific have a tropical climate but the interior plateau, with a mean elevation of 4,000 feet, enjoys a temperate climate.

For nearly three centuries (1530–1821) Costa Rica formed part of the Spanish American dominions, the seat of government being at Cartago. In 1821 the country obtained its independence, although from 1824 to 1839 it was one of the United States of Central America.

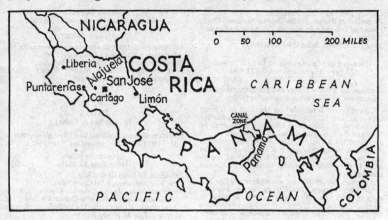

On December 1, 1948, the Army was abolished, the President declaring it unnecessary.

Economy.—Agriculture is the chief industry and the principal products are coffee, bananas, sugar and cattle (for meat), all of which are important exports. Other crops are cocoa, rice, maize, potatoes, hemp, pineapple, casava, ginger, chaw chaw, melon and flowers. Industrial activity is principally in the manufacturing sector and manufactured goods are the largest category of exports. The main goods are foodstuffs, textiles and clothing, plastic goods, pharmaceuticals, fertilizers and electrical equipment. Tourism is of growing importance.

Communications.—The chief ports are Limón, on the Atlantic coast, through which passes most of the coffee exported, and Caldera on the Pacific coast, currently under construction with Japanese aid. The railway system is nationalized. About 500 miles of railroad are open. LACSA is the national airline, operating flights throughout Central and South America, the Caribbean and USA, besides internal flights to local airports by SANSA.

Language, etc.—Spanish is the language of the country. Education is compulsory and free. The literacy rate is the highest in Latin America.

FINANCE

	1988
Revenue	₡54,200·0m
Expenditure	58,790·3m

TRADE

The chief exports are manufactured goods and other products, coffee, bananas, cocoa and sugar. The chief imports are machinery, including transport equipment, manufactures, chemicals, fuel and mineral oils and foodstuffs.

	1990	1991*
Total imports ...	US$2,026.2m	US$1,932.8m
Total exports ...	1,369.4m	1,505.2m
* preliminary		

Trade with UK

	1989	1990
Imports from UK	£12,780,000	£14,556,000
Exports to UK	24,113,000	17,468,000

CAPITAL.—San José, population (estimate 1989) 1,068,206; Alajuela (519,351); Cartago (328,259); Heredia (235,700); Guanacaste (234,962); ψ Puntarenas (326,163); ψ Limón (209,731). (Populations shown are of provinces, cantons and districts.)

CURRENCY.—Costa Rican colón (₡) of 100 céntimos.

FLAG.—Five horizontal bands, blue, white, red, white, blue (the red band twice the width of the others with emblem near staff).

NATIONAL ANTHEM.—Himno Nacional de Costa Rica.

NATIONAL DAY.—September 15.

BRITISH EMBASSY
Apartado 815, Edificio Centro Colon 1007, San José
[San José 215566]

Ambassador Extraordinary and Plenipotentiary and Consul-General, His Excellency William Marsden, CMG (1989).

CÔTE D'IVOIRE
(République de Côte d'Ivoire)

President, Félix Houphouët-Boigny, *elected* for five years in 1960; *re-elected* 1965, 1970, 1975, 1980, 1985 and 1990.

CABINET
(as at November 30, 1990)

Prime Minister, Minister of Economy and Finance, Alassane D. Ouattara.

Ministers assisting the PM; Daniel Kablan Duncan (*Economy, Finance, Trade and Planning*); Guy-Alain Emmanuel Gause (*Raw Materials*).

Defence, Leon Konan Koffi.

Foreign Affairs, Amara Essy.

Interior and Security, Emile Constant Bombet.

Justice, Jacqueline Lohoues-Oble.

National Education, Vamoussa Bamba.

Scientific Research and Professional and Technical Education, Alassane Salif N'Diaye.

Agriculture and Animal Resources, Lambert Kouassi Konan.

Industry, Mines and Energy, Yed Esaie Angoran.

Health and Social Welfare, Frederic F. Alain Ekra.

Communication and Government Spokesman, Auguste Severin Miremont.

Equipment, Transport and Tourism, Adama Coulibaly.

Environment, Construction and Town Planning, Ezan Akele.

Employment and Civil Service, Patrice Kouame.

Culture, Henriette Dagri Diabate.
Promotion of Women, Claire Therese Elisabeth Grah.
Posts and Telecommunications, Yao Nicholas Kouassi Akon.
Youth and Sports, Rene Djedjemel Diby.

EMBASSY OF THE REPUBLIC OF CÔTE D'IVOIRE
2 Upper Belgrave Street, SW1X 8BJ
[071–235 6991]

Ambassador Extraordinary and Plenipotentiary, His Excellency Yao Gervais Attoungbre (1989).

Côte d'Ivoire is situated on the Gulf of Guinea between 5° and 10° N. and 3° and 8° W. and is flanked on the west by Guinea and Liberia, on the north by Mali and Burkina and on the east by Ghana. It has an area of 124,503 sq. miles (322,463 sq. km)—tropical rain forest in the southern half and savanna in the northern—and a population of 11,613,000 (UN estimate, 1988) divided into a large number of ethnic and tribal groups.

Although French contact was made in the first half of the 19th century, Côte d'Ivoire became a colony only in 1893 and was finally pacified in 1912. It decided on December 5, 1958 to remain an autonomous republic within the French Community; full independence outside the Community was proclaimed on August 7, 1960. Special agreements with France, covering financial and cultural matters, technical assistance, defence, etc., were signed in Paris on April 24, 1961. The official language is French.

Côte d'Ivoire has a presidential system of government modelled on that of the United States and the French Fifth Republic. The single Chamber National Assembly has 175 members. Although the Constitution provides for a multi-party system, it was not until May 1990 that any party other than the ruling PDCI party was authorized. Defeating an opposition candidate, President Houphouët-Boigny was re-elected for a further five-year term in October 1990; the PDCI won multi-party elections held in November 1990. Amid allegations of electoral fraud, opposition protests continue.

BUDGET

	1990
Current Expenditure	CFA609,400 billion
Investment and Equipment...	129,600 billion

Trade.—The principal exports are coffee, cocoa, timber, palm oil, pineapples, bananas, and cotton. There are a few deposits of diamonds and minerals including manganese and iron.

TRADE

	1988	1989
Imports	US$1,907m	US$1,781m
Exports	2,354m	2,588m

Trade with UK

	1989	1990
Imports from UK ..	£29,434,000	£26,941,000
Exports to UK	65,943,000	69,849,000

CAPITAL.—ΨAbidjan (population, 3,500,000) which is also the main port. In March 1983 the National Assembly ratified a decision to transfer the political and administrative capital from Abidjan to Yamoussoukro.
CURRENCY.—Franc CFA of 100 centimes.
FLAG.—Three vertical stripes, orange, white and green.
NATIONAL ANTHEM.—L'Abidjanaise.
NATIONAL DAY.—December 7.

Immeuble Les Harmonies, 01 BP 2581,
Abidjan 01
[Abidjan 226850]

Ambassador Extraordinary and Plenipotentiary, Her Excellency Margaret I. Rothwell (1990).
Head of Chancery and Consul, D. Flanagan.
First Secretary (Education) and British Council Representative, C. Stevenson.

CUBA
(Republica de Cuba)

President of Council of State and Head of Government, Dr Fidel Castro Ruz, *appointed* November 2, 1976.

COUNCIL OF STATE
(as at June 30, 1991)

President, Dr Fidel Castro Ruz.
First Vice-President, Raúl Castro Ruz.
Vice-Presidents, Juan Almeida Bosque; Osmany Cienfuegos Gorriarán; José Ramón Machado Ventura; Pedro Miret Prieto; Carlos Rafael Rodriguez.
Secretary, José M. Miyar Barrueco.

COUNCIL OF MINISTERS

President, Dr Fidel Castro Ruz.
First Vice-President, Raúl Castro Ruz.
Vice-Presidents, Dr Carlos Rafael Rodríguez; Pedro Miret Prieto; José Ramón Fernández Alvarez; Osmany Cienfuegos Gorriarán; Antonio Esquivel Yedra; Joel Domenech Benítez; Antonio Rodriguez Maurell; Jaime Crombet Hernández-Baquero; Aldofo Diaz Suárez; Lionel Soto Prieto.
Secretary, Osmany Cienfuegos Gorriarán.
Presidents of State Committees: Antonio Rodriquez Maurell (*Central Planning Board*); Hector Rodriguez Llompart (*National Bank*); Ernesto Melendez Bachs (*Economic Co-operation*); Rodrigo J. Garcia Leon (*Finance*); Francisco Linares Calvo (*Labour and Social Security*); Sonia Rodriguez Cardona (*Material and Technical Supply*); Arturo Guzman Pascual (*Prices*); Ramón Darias Rodés (*Standardization*); Fidel Emilio Vasco Gonzalez (*Statistics*).
Ministers, Carlos Pérez León (*Agriculture*); Marcos J. Portal Leon (*Basic Industry*); Manuel Castillo Rabasa (*Communications*); Homero Crabb (*Construction*); José M. Cabañe Alvarez (*Construction Materials Industry*); Armando Enrique Hart Davalos (*Culture*); Manuel Vila Sosa (*Domestic Trade*); Luis Ignacio Gomez Gutierrez (*Education*); Jorge A. Fernandez Cuervo-Vinent (*Fishing*); Alejandro Roca Iglesias (*Food Industry*); Isidoro Octavio Malmierca Peoli (*Foreign Relations*); Ricardo Cabrisas Ruiz (*Foreign Trade*); Fernando Vecino Alegret (*Higher Education*); Gen. Abelardo Colomé Ibarra (*Interior*); Carlos Amat Fores (*Justice*); Eddie Fernandez Boada (*Light Industry*); Julio Jesus Teja Pérez (*Public Health*); Raul Castro Ruz (*Revolutionary Armed Forces*); Roberto Ignacio Gonzalez Planas (*Steel Industry*); Juan Ramon Herrera Machado (*Sugar Industry*); Gen. Senén Casas Regueiro (*Transport*); Jose Alberto Naranjo Morales; Joaqin Benavides Rodrioguez (*Ministers without Portfolio*).

EMBASSY OF THE REPUBLIC OF CUBA
167 High Holborn, WC1V 6PA
[071–240 2488]

Ambassador Extraordinary and Plenipotentiary, Her Excellency Maria A. Flores (1990).
Councillor, M Martinez-Moles Cifrian.

Cuba, the largest island in the Caribbean, lies between 74° and 85° W. long., and 19° and 23° N. lat.

with a total area of 42,804 sq. miles (110,861 sq. km). The country is divided into 14 provinces. The population in June 1990 was 10,608,000.

The island of Cuba was visited by Christopher Columbus during his first voyage, on Oct. 27, 1492, and was then believed to be part of the western mainland of India. Early in the 16th century the island was conquered by the Spanish, to be used later as a base of operations for the conquest of Mexico and Central America, and for almost four centuries Cuba remained under a Spanish Captain-General. (The island was under British rule for one year, 1762–1763, when it was returned to Spain in exchange for Florida.) Separatist agitation culminated in the closing years of the 19th century in open warfare. In 1898 the government of the United States intervened and on April 20, 1898, demanded the evacuation of Cuba by the Spanish forces. A short Spanish–American war led to the abandonment of the island, which was occupied by US troops. Cuba was under US military rule from January 1, 1899 until May 20, 1902, when an autonomous government was inaugurated with an elected President, and a legislature of two houses.

A revolution led by Dr Fidel Castro overthrew the Government of General Batista on January 1, 1959. In October 1965 the Communist Party of Cuba was formed to succeed the United Party of the Socialist Revolution. It is the only authorized political party. The new Socialist Constitution came into force on February 24, 1976 and indirect elections to the National Assembly of People's Power were subsequently held.

Production.—The Government has carried out programmes of land and urban reform and of nationalization; by March 1968, virtually all industrial and commercial enterprises were nationalized. About 85 per cent of the cultivated land is in state farms or state-controlled co-operatives. Private smallholders, who own the remainder, have to sell all their produce to the state.

Although efforts are being made to diversify the economy, sugar is still its mainstay and principal source of foreign exchange. In 1989–90 the harvest was 8·04 million tons. Cuba's other main exports are oil, nickel, seafood, citrus fruits, tobacco and rum.

The tourism industry has expanded since 1986. In 1990 340,000 tourists visited Cuba generating US$250 million in gross income.

The demise of socialism in eastern Europe has disrupted Cuba's traditional pattern of trade. A limited one-year trade agreement, instead of the normal five-year one, was signed with the USSR at the end of 1990. The new agreement envisages a transition to hard currency dealings.

There are 12,700 km of railway track, of which 5,000 km are in public service. In 1986 there were 13,247 km of road. At present scheduled international air services run to North, Central and South American countries and Europe.

Language and Literature.—Spanish is the language of the island. English, formerly widely understood, is now spoken less. Education is compulsory and free. In 1964 illiteracy was officially declared to be completely eliminated. The press and broadcasting and television are under the control of the Government.

	1987	1988
	Pesos million	
Imports	7,611·5	7,579·4
Exports	5,401·0	5,518·3

Trade with UK

	1989	1990
Imports from UK	£53,255,000	£37,568,000
Exports to UK	34,388,000	30,294,000

CAPITAL.—ΨHavana, population estimate (1986) 2,100,000; other towns are ΨSantiago (429,800), Santa Clara (198,800), Camagüey (279,800), Holgüin (254,300), and ΨCienfuegos (124,600).

CURRENCY.—Cuban peso of 100 centavos.

FLAG.—Five horizontal bands, blue and white (blue at top and bottom) with red triangle, close to staff, charged with 5-point star.

NATIONAL ANTHEM.—Al Combate, Corred Bayameses (To battle, men of Bayamo).

NATIONAL DAY.—January 1 (Day of Liberation).

BRITISH EMBASSY
Edificio Bolívar, Cárcel 101–103,
e Morro y Prado, Apartado 1069, Havana.
[Havana 623071]

Ambassador Extraordinary and Plenipotentiary, His Excellency A. Leycester S. Coltman (1991).

Counsellor, N. R. Jarrold (*Deputy Head of Mission*).

First Secretary, R. Daly (*Commercial and HM Consul*).

CZECHOSLOVAKIA
(Česká a Slovenská Federativní Republika)

President, Václav Havel, *elected* December 29, 1989, *re-elected* July 7, 1990.

Federal Government
(as at July 1, 1991)

Prime Minister, Marián Čalfa.

Deputy Prime Ministers, Jiří Dienstbier (*also Minister for Foreign Affairs*); Jozef Mikloško; Pavel Rychetsky; Václav Valeš.

Transport, Jiří Nezval.

Finance, Václav Klaus.

Defence, Luboš Dobrovský.

Labour and Social Affairs, Petr Miller.

Telecommunications, Emil Ehrenberger.

Interior, Ján Langoš.

Foreign Trade, Jozef Bakšay.

Economy, Vladimír Dlouhý.

Environment, Josef Vavroušek.

Strategic Planning, Pavel Hoffmann.

Inspection, Květoslava Kořínková.

EMBASSY OF THE CZECH AND SLOVAK
FEDERATIVE REPUBLIC
25 Kensington Palace Gardens, W8 4QY
[071–229 1255]

Ambassador Extraordinary and Plenipotentiary, His Excellency Dr Karel Duda (1990).

Area and Population.—Czechoslovakia, formerly part of the Austro-Hungarian Empire, declared its independence on October 28, 1918 (Czechoslovak Independence Day). It has an area of 49,370 sq. miles (127,869 sq. km). The population (UN estimate 1989) is 15,639,000.

Government.—The Communist Party came to power in Czechoslovakia in February 1948, and remained in power until December 1989.

In 1968 the Czechoslovak Communist Party, under the then General Secretary Alexander Dubček, embarked on a reform programme leading to proposals for economic reform, the democratization of the country's political life, greater guarantees of fundamental liberties and the establishment of a federal system.

The implications for the internal development of the other communist regimes in Eastern Europe and the Soviet Union alarmed the Soviet Union. On the night of August 20, Czechoslovakia was invaded by Soviet, Polish, East German, Hungarian and Bulgarian troops, the capital and all major towns being occupied. The Czechoslovak leadership was forced to modify its policies and to legalize the presence of Soviet troops on Czechoslovak territory. With the exception of the federal system of government, the reforms of 1968 were abandoned when Gustáv Husák became leader of the Communist party in April 1969 (President 1975–89).

Opposition to Communist Party rule gathered pace in the late 1980s encouraged by the political and economic reforms taking place in the Soviet Union and other Eastern bloc countries. An upsurge in mass street protests in November 1989 led to the resignation of the Communist Party Central Committee. The Communist Party was forced to concede its monopoly of power and on December 10 a new government was appointed in which only half the Ministers were Communist Party members. Gustáv Husák resigned as President and was replaced by Václav Havel.

Free elections were held in June 1990 in which the Civic Forum movement and its Slovak sister movement, Public Against Violence, obtained over 50 per cent of the vote. The new government, appointed in June 1990, comprises a coalition of Civic Forum/Public Against Violence and the Christian Democratic Movement. Although Civic Forum split into two parties in February 1991, both remain in the government. The government's attempts to proceed with the conversion to a market economy are hampered by continued debate over a new constitution which will satisfy both Czechs and Slovaks.

Under the present constitution, Czechoslovakia (renamed the Czech and Slovak Federative Republic in April 1990) consists of the Czech Republic and the Slovak Republic, each of which has its own government responsible to its legislative body—the National Council. Areas such as the constitution, defence, foreign affairs and currency are the responsibility of the federal administration. The Federal Government is responsible to the Federal Assembly, which is composed of two Chambers, the Chamber of the People, whose deputies are elected throughout the federation, and the Chamber of the Nations, consisting of an equal number of Czech and Slovak deputies.

The Economic System.—Under Communist rule industry was state-owned and nearly all agricultural land was cultivated by state or co-operative farms. An economic reform programme was begun in 1990 aimed at producing a free-market economy in Czechoslovakia. New laws passed in the spring of 1990 provided a legal basis for private enterprise, joint ventures and foreign investment.

Production.—Czechoslovakia is not rich in minerals, although significant quantities of coal and lignite are mined. Principal agricultural products are sugar-beet, potatoes and cereal crops; the timber industry is also very important. The country. has long been highly industrialized, and machinery, industrial consumer goods and raw materials are major exports.

Language and Literature.—Czech and Slovak are the official languages, each having its own literature. The Reformation gave a wide-spread impulse to Czech literature, the writings of Jan Hus (martyred in 1415 as a religious and social reformer) familiarizing the people with Wyclif's teaching. This impulse endured to the close of the 17th century when Jan Amos Komensky or Comenius (1592–1670) was expelled from the country. Under Austrian rule and with the persistent pursuit of Germanization, there was a period of stagnation until the national revival in the first half of the 19th century. Authors of international reputation include Jaroslav Hašek (1883–1923), Jaroslav Seifert (1901–1986, Nobel Prize for Literature, 1985), Václav Havel (b. 1936) and Milan Kundera (b. 1929).

Education.—Education is compulsory and free for all children from the ages of 6 to 16. There are five universities in Czechoslovakia of which the most famous is Charles University in Prague (founded 1348), the others being situated at Bratislava, Brno, Olomouc and Košice. In addition there are a considerable number of other institutions of university standing, technical colleges, agricultural colleges, etc.

Trade with UK

	1989	1990
Imports from UK	£131,418,000	£133,158,000
Exports to UK	156,649,000	135,988,000

CAPITAL.—Prague (Praha), on the Vltava (Moldau), the former capital of Bohemia with a population (1985) of 1,190,576. Other towns are Brno (Brünn), capital of Moravia (381,000), Bratislava (Pressburg), capital of Slovakia (401,000), Ostrava (324,000), Košice (214,000) and Plzeň (Pilsen) (174,000).

CURRENCY.—Koruna (Kčs) or Czechoslovak crown of 100 Haléřů (Heller).

FLAG.—Two equal horizontal stripes, white (above) and red; a blue triangle next to staff.

NATIONAL ANTHEM.—Kde Domov Můj (Where is my Motherland) (Czech); Nad Tatrom sa blýska (Storm over the Tatras) (Slovak).

NATIONAL DAYS.—May 9, July 5, October 28.

BRITISH EMBASSY
Thunovská 14, 11800 Prague 1
[Prague 533347]

Ambassador Extraordinary and Plenipotentiary, His Excellency David Brighty, CMG, CVO (1991).
Counsellor, J. S. Lang (*Head of Chancery*).
Defence and Military Attaché, Col. W. J. Chesshyre.
Air Attaché, Wing Cdr. B. Blackford.
Cultural Attaché, W. Jefferson (*British Council Representative*).

DENMARK
(Kongeriget Danmark)

Queen, Margrethe II, eldest daughter of King Frederik IX, *born* April 16, 1940, *succeeded* Jan. 14, 1972, *married* June 10, 1967, Count Henri de Monpezat (Prince Henrik of Denmark) and *has issue* Crown Prince Frederik *born* May 26, 1968; and Prince Joachim, *born* June 7, 1969.

CABINET
(as at December 17, 1990)

Prime Minister, Poul Schlüter (C).
Foreign Affairs, Uffe Ellemann-Jensen (V).
Finance, Henning Dyremose (C).
Economic and Fiscal Affairs, Anders Fogh Rasmussen (V).
Defence, Knud Enggaard (V).
Education and Research, Bertel Haarder (V).
Justice, Hans Engell (C).
Interior and Nordic Affairs, Thor Pedersen (V).
Housing, Svend Erik Hovmand (V).
Agriculture, Laurits Toernæs (V).
Cultural Affairs, Grethe Rostbøll (C).
Environment, Per Stig Møller (C).
Social Affairs, Else Winther Anderson (V).
Ecclesiastical Affairs and Communications, Torben Rechendorff (C).
Transport, Kaj Ikast (C).
Fisheries, Kent Kirk (C).
Labour, Knud Erik Kirkegaard (C).
Industry and Energy, Anne Birgitte Lundholt (C).
Health, Ester Larsen (V).

C: Conservative Party; V: Venstre (Liberals).

ROYAL DANISH EMBASSY
55 Sloane Street, SW1X 9SR
[071–333 0200]

Ambassador Extraordinary and Plenipotentiary, His
Excellency R. A. Thorning-Petersen (1989).
Minister Counsellors, F. N. Christensen; P. Essemann
(*Commercial*); F. A. Axmark (*Press and Culture*);
C. Søndergaard (*Economic and Consular Affairs*).
Defence Attaché, Capt. S. Lund.

Area and Population.—A Kingdom of Northern
Europe, consisting of the islands of Zeeland, Funen,
Lolland, etc., the peninsula of Jutland, and the
outlying island of Bornholm in the Baltic, the Faröes
and Greenland. Denmark is situated between 54° 34′
and 57° 45′ N. lat., 8° 5′–15° E. 12′ long., with an area
of 16,629 sq. miles (43,069 sq. km), and a population
(official estimate 1990) of 5,135,000.

Government.—Under the Constitution of the
Kingdom of Denmark Act of June 5, 1953, the
legislature consists of one chamber, the *Folketing*, of
not more than 179 members, including 2 for the
Faröes and 2 for Greenland. The voting age is 18.

The coalition government of Poul Schlüter was
formed in December 1990 after the General Election
on December 12.

Education is free and compulsory. Special schools
are numerous, commercial, technical and agricultural predominating. There are universities at
Copenhagen (founded in 1479), Aarhus (1933), Odense
(1966), Roskilde (1972) and Aalborg (1974). A further
university at Esbjerg is planned.

Language and Literature.—The Danish language is akin to Swedish and Norwegian. Danish
literature, ancient and modern, embraces all forms of
expression, familiar names being Hans Christian
Andersen (1805–1875), Søren Kierkegaard (1813–
1855) and Karen Blixen (1885–1962). Some 48 newspapers are published in Denmark; two daily papers
are published in Copenhagen.

Production and Industry.—Of the labour force,
in 1988, 1·8 per cent was engaged in agriculture,
fishing, forestry, etc.; 27·5 per cent in manufacturing,
building and construction; 15·4 per cent in commerce,
0·2 per cent in liberal professions and 53·2 per cent in
administration, transport and the financial services.
The chief agricultural products are pigs, cattle, dairy

products, poultry and eggs, seeds, cereals and sugar
beet; manufactures are mostly based on imported raw
materials but there are also considerable imports of
finished goods.

Communications.—Mercantile marine (ships
above 100 gross tonnage) at beginning of 1988, totalled
618 ships. In 1985 there was 2,471 km of state-owned
railway and 494 km of privately-owned railway
systems.

FINANCE (BUDGET ESTIMATES)

	1988	1989
Revenue	Kr201,280m	Kr221,008m
Expenditure	212,823m	222,179m

Denmark's balance of payments on current account
showed a deficit for 1988 of Kr12,200 million (1987,
Kr20,700 million).

TRADE

The principal imports are industrial raw materials,
consumer goods, construction inputs, machinery,
raw materials, vehicles and textile products. The
chief exports are miscellaneous manufactured articles, agricultural and dairy products.

	1988	1989
Total Imports	Kr178,269m	Kr194,567m
Total Exports	187,381m	204,834m

Trade with UK

	1989	1990
Imports from UK	£1,209,220,000	£1,413,713,000
Exports to UK	2,229,340,000	2,278,569,000

CAPITAL.—ΨCopenhagen, population (1988)
467,850; Greater Copenhagen 1,495,736. ΨAarhus
259,493; ΨOdense 174,948; ΨAalborg 154,547; Ψ
Esbjerg 81,480; ΨRanders 61,094; ΨKolding 57,128;
ΨHelsingør 56,754; ΨHorsens 54,940; Ψ Vejle 50,879;
Roskilde 48,996; ΨFredericia 45,992.
CURRENCY.—Danish krone (Kr) of 100 øre.
FLAG.—Red, with white cross.
NATIONAL ANTHEM.—Kong Kristian.
NATIONAL DAY.—April 16 (The Queen's Birthday).

BRITISH EMBASSY
36–40 Kastelsvej, DK-2100 Copenhagen
[Copenhagen 264600]

Ambassador Extraordinary and Plenipotentiary, His
Excellency Nigel Christopher Ransome Williams,
CMG (1989).
Counsellors, Y. S. Astley (*Head of Chancery*); A.
Layden (*Commercial*).
Defence Attaché, Cmdr. R. Woolgar, RN.

There are Consulates at *Aabenraa, Aalborg, Aar-
hus, Esbjerg, Fredericia, Herning, Odense, Rønne*
(Bornholm); at *Tórshavn* (Faröe Islands); and *Nuuk*
(Godthåb) (Greenland).

British Council Representative, Michael Holcroft,
Møntergade 1, 1116 Copenhagen K.

Outlying Parts of the Kingdom

THE FARÖES, or Sheep Islands (540 sq. miles; 1,399
sq. km; pop. (1990) 47,485), capital, Tórshavn, are
governed by a *Lagting* of 26 members, a *Landsstyre* of
four members which deals with special Faröes affairs,
and send two representatives to the *Folketing* at
Copenhagen. On Sept. 14, 1946 the Lagting, with the
consent of the Danish Government, for its own
guidance held a plebiscite on the Faröes. About one-
third of the electors did not, however, take part in
the voting; of the rest a little more than half the
votes cast were in favour of separation from Denmark
and the establishment of a republic. At the subsequent general election for the Lagting a great
majority voted in favour of remaining part of the
Kingdom of Denmark with a certain measure of home

rule and in 1948 the Faröes received this. The Faröes are not part of the EC.
Prime Minister, Alti Dam.

Trade with UK

	1989	1990
Imports from UK	£6,353,000	£7,882,000
Exports to UK	31,042,000	34,396,000

GREENLAND (total area 2,175,600 sq. km, of which approx. 16 per cent is ice-free) with a population (1990) of 55,558, is divided into three provinces (West, North and East). Greenland (capital, Nuuk (Godthåb)) has a *Landsraad* of 17 members and sends two representatives to the *Folketing* at Copenhagen. Greenland attained a status of internal autonomy on May 1, 1979. The trade of Greenland is mainly under the management of the Grønlands Handel. Following a plebiscite Greenland negotiated its withdrawal from the EC, but without discontinuing relations with Denmark, and left on February 1, 1985.

Mineral and oil prospecting revealed deposits of lead, zinc, iron ore, oil, gas and uranium. Commercial exploitation of these resources has already begun. The United States of America has acquired certain rights to maintain air bases in Greenland.
Premier, Lars Emil Johansen.

Trade with UK

	1989	1990
Imports from UK	£1,487,000	£2,256,000
Exports to UK	3,793,000	10,322,000

DJIBOUTI
(Jumhouriyya Djibouti)

President, Hassan Gouled Aptidon, *elected* 1977, *re-elected* 1981 and 1987.

CABINET
(as at May 1991)

Prime Minister, Barkat Gourad Hamadou.
Justice and Islamic Affairs, Ougure Hassan Ibrahim.
Foreign Affairs and Co-operation, Moumin Bahdon Farah.
Interior, Posts and Telecommunications, Ahmed Bulaleh Barreh.
Defence, Ismail Ali Youssouf.
Finance and National Economy, Moussa Bouraleh Robleh.
Ports and Shipping, Ahmed Aden Youssouf.
Commerce, Transport and Tourism, Ahmed Ibrahim Abdi.
Education, Omar Chirdon Abass.
Youth and Sports and Culture, Hussein Barkad Siraj.
Public Health, Mohammed Djama Elabe.
Labour, Elaf Orbis Ali.
Civil Service and Administrative Reform, Souleiman Farah Lodon.
Public Works, Construction and Housing, Ibrahim Idris Mohamed.
Industry, Salem Abdou Yaya.
Agriculture and Rural Development, Mohamed Moussa Chehem.

EMBASSY OF THE REPUBLIC OF DJIBOUTI
26 rue Emile Ménier, 75116 Paris, France
[Paris 47274922]

Ambassador Extraordinary and Plenipotentiary, His Excellency Ahmed Omar Farah (1991).

Formerly known as French Somaliland and then the French Territory of the Afars and the Issas, the Republic of Djibouti became independent on June 27, 1977. Djibouti is situated on the north-east coast of Africa (i.e. the Horn of Africa) and has an area of 8,494 sq. miles (22,000 sq. km.). It has a population

(UN estimate 1989) of 395,000. The climate is harsh and much of the country is semi-arid desert. The most recent elections to the 65-member Chamber of Deputies took place in April 1987. The sole legal party is *Rassemblement Populaire pour le Progrès* (RPP—the Popular Rally for Progress). The French continue to maintain an army, navy and air force bases. Djibouti has an excellent port, international airport and a railway line runs to Addis Ababa.

Trade with UK

	1989	1990
Imports from UK	£10,656,000	£14,962,000
Exports to UK	489,000	174,000

CAPITAL.—Ψ Djibouti, population (1985) 200,000.
CURRENCY.—Djibouti franc of 100 centimes.
FLAG.—Blue over green with white triangle in the hoist containing a red star.
NATIONAL DAY.—June 27 (Independence Day).

BRITISH CONSULATE
PO Box 81, 9–11 Rue de Geneve, Djibouti
Honorary Consul, P. Lievin.

DOMINICAN REPUBLIC
(República Dominicana)

President, Dr Joaquin Balaguer, *took office*, Aug. 16. 1986, *re-elected* May 16, 1990.
Vice-President, Carlos Morales Troncoso.

CABINET
(as at July 1, 1991)

Presidency, Dr Noe Sterling Vazquez.
Finance, Marte de Barrios.
Foreign Affairs, Joaquín Ricardo.
Education and Culture , Pedro Gil Iturbides.
Agriculture, Agronomo Nicolas Concepción.
Labour, Rafael Alburquerque.
Public Health and Social Welfare, Dr Manuel A. Bello.
Industry and Trade, Rafael Bello Andino.
Sports, Physical Education and Recreation, Cristobal Marte.
Tourism, Andres Venderhorst.
Interior and Police, Dr Atilio Guzman Fernandez.
Armed Forces, Lt.-Gen. Hector Garcia Tejeda.

EMBASSY OF THE DOMINICAN REPUBLIC
2 rue Georges Ville, 75116 Paris, France
[Paris 45018881]

Ambassador Extraordinary and Plenipotentiary, new appointment awaited.

HONORARY CONSULATE GENERAL
539 Martins Building, Water Street,
Liverpool L2 3TE
[051–236 0722]

Honorary Consul-General, T. V. Anthony.
Honorary Vice-Consul, Mrs Hilary Gatenby.

There are also Consular Offices at *Birmingham, Cardiff, Grimsby, London* (6 Queen's Mansions, Brook Green, W6 7EB), and *Plymouth*.

The Dominican Republic, formerly the Spanish portion of the island of Hispaniola, is the oldest settlement of European origin in America. The western part of the island forms the Republic of Haiti. The island lies between Cuba on the west and Puerto Rico on the east and the Republic covers an area of 18,816 sq. miles (48,734 sq. km), with a population (1984 Census) of 6,416,000. A 1989 UN estimate gives a figure of 7,019,000. The climate is tropical in the lowlands and semi-tropical to temperate in the higher altitudes.

Spanish is the language of the Republic.

Government.—Santo Domingo was discovered by Christopher Columbus in December 1492, and remained a Spanish colony until 1821. In 1822 it was subjugated by the neighbouring Haitians who remained in control until 1844 when the Dominican Republic was proclaimed. The country was occupied by American marines from 1916 until the adoption of a new Constitution in 1924. From 1930 until May 30, 1961 (when he was assassinated) Generalissimo Rafael Trujillo ruled the country.

President Juan Bosch held office from December 1962 to September 1963, when he was deposed by a military junta. A revolt in favour of ex-President Bosch in April 1965 developed into civil war lasting until September the same year when a provisional President was elected. On June 1, 1966 Dr Joaquin Balaguer was elected President and in November 1966 a new Constitution was introduced.

Executive power is vested in the President, who is elected by direct vote and serves for four years. The President forms his cabinet without reference to the Congress.

Legislative power is exercised by the Congress, which has a term of four years concurrent with the Presidency. The Upper Chamber is the Senate of 27 senators, one for each province and one for Santo Domingo. The lower is the Chamber of Deputies which has 120 members, one for each 50,000 inhabitants in each province, with the provision that no province has less than two members. Judicial power is exercised by the Supreme Court of Justice.

Communications.—According to local classification there are 2,932 miles of first class and 1,392 miles of second class and inter-communal roads in the Republic. There is a direct road from Santo Domingo to Port-au-Prince, the capital of Haiti, but that part of it in the border area has fallen into disuse. The frontier has been closed since September 1967, except for that section crossed by the main road linking the two capitals. A telephone system connects practically all the principal towns of the republic and there is a telegraph service with all parts of the world. There are more than 90 commercial broadcasting stations and six television stations.

The Republic is served by two national and six foreign airlines, and an international airport 18 miles to the east of the capital is in operation. Another has been built near Puerto Plata on the north coast.

Economy.—Sugar, coffee, cocoa, and tobacco are the most important crops. Other products are peanuts, maize, rice, bananas, molasses, salt, cement, ferro-nickel, gold, silver, cattle, sisal products, honey and chocolate. There is a growing number of light industries producing beer, tinned foodstuffs, glass products, textiles, soap, cigarettes, construction materials, plastic articles, shoes, papers, paint, rum, matches, peanut oil and other products.

FINANCE

	1986
Expenditure	RD$2,251m
Revenue	2,113m

TRADE

The chief imports are machinery, food stuffs, iron and steel, cotton textiles and yarns, mineral oils (including petrol), cars and other motor vehicles, chemical and pharmaceutical products, electrical equipment and accessories, construction material, paper and paper products, and rubber and rubber products. The chief exports are sugar, coffee, cocoa, tobacco, chocolate, molasses, bauxite, ferro-nickel and gold. Tobacco and tobacco manufactures are the principal exports to the UK.

	1984	1985
Imports	RD$1,459,000,000	RD$1,285,900,000
Exports	1,211,100,000	739,300,000

Trade with UK

	1989	1990
Imports from UK	£25,519,000	£19,668,000
Exports to UK	11,223,000	17,440,000

CAPITAL.—Ψ Santo Domingo, population of the Capital District (1981 census) 1,313,172. Other centres, with populations (1981 census): Santiago de los Caballeros (550,372); La Vega (385,043); San Francisco De Macoris (235,544); San Juan (239,957); San Cristóbal (446,132).

CURRENCY.—Dominican Republic peso (RD$) of 100 centavos.

FLAG.—Red and blue, with white cross bearing an emblem at centre.

NATIONAL ANTHEM.—Quisqueyanos Valientes, Alcemos (Brave men of Quisqueya, let's raise our song).

NATIONAL DAY.—February 27 (Independence Day, 1844).

British Ambassador, (resident in Caracas, Venezuela).

ECUADOR
(Republica del Ecuador)

President, Rodrigo Borja Cevallos, *took office* Aug. 10, 1988.

Vice President, Luis Parodi.

CABINET
(as at June 1991)

Interior and Police, César Verduga.
Foreign Affairs, Diego Cordovéz.
Education and Culture, vacant.
Social Welfare, Raul Baca.
Public Health, Plutarco Naranjo.
Agriculture and Livestock, Alfredo Saltos.
Public Works and Communications, Raúl Carrasco.
Finance and Public Credit, Pablo Better.
Industry, Commerce and Integration, Juan Falconí.
Energy, Donald Castillo.
Defence, Gen. Jorge Félix (retd.).
Labour and Human Resources, Roberto Gomez.
Secretary General of Administration, Gonzalo Ortiz.

EMBASSY OF ECUADOR
Flat 3B, 3 Hans Crescent, SW1X 0LS
[071–584 1367/2648]

Ambassador Extraordinary and Plenipotentiary, His Excellency Jose Antonio Correa (1989).

Area and Population.—Ecuador is an equatorial state of South America, the mainland extending from lat. 1° 38′ N. to 4° 50′ S., and between 75° 20′ and 81° W. long., comprising an area reduced by boundary settlements with Peru (January 1942) to about 109,484 sq. miles (283,561 sq. km).

The Republic of Ecuador is divided into 21 provinces. It has a population (UN estimate 1989) of 10,490,000, mostly descendants of the Spanish, aboriginal Indians, and Mestizoes. The territory of the Republic extends across the Western Andes, the highest peaks in Ecuador being Chimborazo (20,408 ft.) and Ilinza (17,405 ft.) in the Western Cordillera; and Cotopaxi (19,612 ft.) and Cayambe (19,160 ft.) in the Eastern Cordillera. Ecuador is watered by the Upper Amazon, and by the rivers Guayas, Mira, Santiago, Chone, and Esmeraldas on the Pacific coast. There are extensive forests.

Government.—The former Kingdom of Quito was conquered by the Incas of Peru in the latter part of the 15th century. Early in the 16th century Pizarro's conquests led to the inclusion of the present territory of Ecuador in the Spanish Vice-royalty of Quito. The independence of the country was achieved in a revolutionary war which culminated in the battle of Mount Pichincha (May 24, 1822).

After seven years of military rule, Ecuador returned to democracy in 1979. The present constitution, introduced in 1978, provides for an elected President and Vice-President who serve for a four year term. Neither may stand for re-election. There is a Chamber of Representatives with 71 members elected every four years, 12 of whom are elected on a national basis and the rest by the provinces. The Chamber meets for two months every year (Aug.-Oct.) but can be convoked at any time for extraordinary sessions. Four Legislative Commissions meet through the year.

Voting is compulsory for all literate and (since 1980) voluntary for all illiterate citizens over the age of 18. Seventeen political parties took part in the 1988 elections.

Agriculture and Industry.—Agriculture is the most important sector of the economy, supporting nearly 50 per cent of the population (particularly the poorest) and contributing 14·5 per cent of the Gross Domestic Product and 19·5 per cent of exports. The main products for export are fish (mainly shrimps, tuna and sardines), which had become the largest agricultural export by early 1982; bananas, which provide a third of agricultural exports; cocoa and coffee. Other important crops are sugar, corn, soya, rice, cotton, African palm (for oil), vegetables, fruit and timber, the temperate crops being produced mostly in the highlands.

The economy was transformed by the discovery in 1972 of major oil fields in the Oriente area, and oil accounted for two-thirds of 1981 export earnings. The economy grew rapidly in the 1970s but is now faced with reduced growth, due mainly to the fall in the price of oil. The oil deposits in the Oriente are estimated at between 10,000 and 15,000 million barrels, and further exploration and development is taking place. The oil is evacuated by a trans-Andean pipeline to the port of Balao (near Esmeraldas City).

Communications.—There are 23,256 km of permanent roads and 5,044 km of roads which are only open during the dry season. There are about 750 miles of railway, including the railway from Quito to Guayaquil. Ten commercial airlines operate international flights, linking Ecuador with major foreign cities and there are internal services between all important towns.

Defence.—The standing Army has a strength of about 50,000. There is an Air Force of some 120 aircraft of various kinds and 3,000 personnel. The Navy is 4,500 strong.

Language, etc.—Spanish is the principal language of the country but Quechua is also a recognized language and is spoken by the majority of the Indian population. As a result of an intensive national education programme more than 75 per cent of the population are now literate. Elementary education is free and compulsory. There are ten universities (three at Quito, three at Guayaquil, and one each at Cuenca, Machala, Loja and Portoviejo), polytechnic schools at Quito and Guayaquil and eight technical colleges in other provincial capitals. Two daily newspapers are published at Quito and four at Guayaquil.

Finance.—The estimated government budget in 1986 was: revenue 186,824 million sucres; expenditure 216,466 million sucres.

TRADE

Import licences are required for all merchandise and these are issued by the Central Bank of Ecuador.

Manufactured goods and machinery are the main imports.

	1987	1988
Imports	US$2,229·0m.	US$1,713·5m.
Exports	1,998·6m.	2,192·9m.

Trade with UK

	1989	1990
Imports from UK	£29,410,000	£30,155,000
Exports to UK	19,319,000	19,572,000

CAPITAL.—Quito, population (1991 estimate) 1,387,887; Ψ Guayaquil (1,531,229) is the chief port; Cuenca (332,117).

CURRENCY.—Sucre of 100 centavos.

FLAG.—Three horizontal bands, yellow, blue and red (the yellow band twice the width of the others); emblem in centre.

NATIONAL DAY.—August 10 (Independence Day).

BRITISH EMBASSY
Av. Gonzalez Suarez, 111 (Casilla 1701 314),
Quito
[Quito 560670]

Ambassador Extraordinary and Plenipotentiary, His Excellency Frank Basil Wheeler, CMG (1989).

There are British Consular Offices at *Cuenca, Galapagos* and *Guayaquil.*

British Council Representative, Desmond Lauder, Av. Amazonas 1646 (Casilla 17078829), Quito.

The GALÁPAGOS (Giant Tortoise) ISLANDS forming the province of the Archipelago de Colón, were annexed by Ecuador in 1832. The archipelago lies in the Pacific, about 500 miles from Saint Elena peninsula, the most westerly point of the mainland. There are 12 large and several hundred smaller islands with a total area of about 3,000 sq. miles and an estimated population (1982) of 6,119. The capital is San Cristobal, on Chatham Island. Although the archipelago lies on the equator, the temperature of the surrounding water is well below equatorial average owing to the Antarctic Humboldt Current. The province consists for the most part of National Park Territory, where unique marine birds, iguanas, and the giant tortoises are conserved. There is some local subsistence farming; the main industry, apart from tourism, is tuna and lobster fishing.

EGYPT
(Al-Jumhuriyal Misr al-Arabiya)

President, Muhammad Hosni Mubarak, *elected*, Oct. 13, 1981, *re-elected* 1987.

COUNCIL OF MINISTERS
(as at July 1991)

Prime Minister, Dr Atef Muhammad Naguib Sidqi.
Presidential Assistant, Muhammad Abdul Halim Abu Ghazala.
Defence and Military Production, Gen. Hussein Tantawy.
Deputy PM for External Relations, Minister of State for Emigration and Expatriates, Dr Boutros Yussef Boutros-Gali.
Deputy PM and Minister of Planning and International Co-operation, Dr Kamal Ahmed al-Ganzuri.
Deputy PM and Minister of Agriculture and Land Reclamation, Dr Yussif Amin Wali.
Foreign Affairs, Amer Mousa.
Economy and Foreign Trade, Dr Yussri Ali Mustafa.
Finance, Dr Muhammad Ahmed el-Razzaz.
Interior, Maj.-Gen. Mohammed Abdul Halim Mousa.
Oil and Mineral Wealth, Dr Hamdy El Bambi.

Tourism and Civil Aviation, Fouad Abdul Latif Sultan.

Justice, Farouq Saif al-Nasr.

Culture, Farouq Hosni.

Industry, Muhammad Mahmoud Abdul Wahhab.

Parliamentary and Shura Council Affairs, Dr Ahmed Salama.

Supply and Internal Trade, Dr Mohammed Galaleddin Abdul-Dahab.

Public Works and Water Resources, 'Issam Abdul Hamid Radi.

Manpower and Vocational Training, Assem Abdul Haq.

Education, Dr Hussein Kamal Baha El-Din.

Transport, Communications and Marine Transport, Suliman Metwalli Suliman.

Scientific Research, Dr Adel Abul-Hamid 'Ezz.

Health, Dr Mohammed Ragheb Dawidar.

Information, Muhammad Safwat al-Sharif.

Cabinet Affairs and Administrative Development, Dr 'Atif Mohammad 'Ebeid.

Religious Affairs (Waqfs), Dr Muhammad Ali Mahgoub.

Social Affairs and Social Insurance, Dr Amal Abdul Rahim Osman.

Electricity and Energy, Mohammad Mahir Osman Abaza.

Housing, New Communities and Public Utilities, Hasaballah Mohammad al-Kafrawi.

Local Government, Dr Mahmmoud Sherif.

Ministers of State, Gamal al-Sayyid Ibrahim (*Military Production*); Dr Mouris Makramallah (*International Co-operation*).

EMBASSY OF THE ARAB REPUBLIC OF EGYPT
26 South Street, W1Y 8EL
[071–499 2401]

Ambassador Extraordinary and Plenipotentiary, His Excellency Mohamed I. Shaker (1988).

Area and Population.—The total area of Egypt is 386,662 sq. miles (1,001,449 sq. km), only three per cent of which is cultivated land, with a population (UN estimate 1989) of 53,080,000.

There are three distinct elements in the native population. The largest, or 'Egyptian' element, is a Hamito-Semitic race, known in the rural districts as *Fellahin* (*fellâh*—ploughman, or tiller of the soil). A second element is the *Bedouin,* or nomadic Arabs of the Western and Arabian deserts, of whom about one-seventh are real nomads, and the remainder semi-sedentary tent-dwellers on the outskirts of the cultivated end of the Nile Valley and the Fayûm. The third element is the *Nubian* of the Nile Valley between Aswân and Wadi-Halfa of mixed Arab and Negro blood. Over 90 per cent of the population are Muslims of the Sunni denomination, and most of the rest Coptic Christians.

The territory of Egypt comprises (1) Egypt Proper, forming the N.E. corner of the African continent, divisible into (*a*) the valley and delta of the Nile, (*b*) the Western Desert, and (*c*) the Arabian or Eastern Desert; (2) The Peninsula of Sinai, forming part of the continent of Asia; and (3) a number of islands in the Gulf of Suez and Red Sea, of which the principal are Jubal, Shadwan, Gafatin and Zeberged (or St John's Island). This territory lies between 22° and 32° N. lat. and 24° and 37° E. long. The northern boundary is the Mediterranean, and in the south Egypt is conterminous with the Sudan. The western boundary runs from a point on the coast 10 kilometres N.W. of Sollûm to the latitude of Siwa and thence due S. along the 25th meridian. The E. boundary follows a line drawn from Rafa on the Mediterranean (34° 15' E. long.) to the head of the Gulf of 'Aqaba.

Physical Features.—The country is mainly flat but there are mountainous areas in the south-west, along the Red Sea coast and in the south of the Sinai peninsula, rising in some places to peaks of over 6,000 ft. The highest mountain in Egypt is Mt. Catherina (8,668 ft). Most of the land is desert but the Nile valley and delta are covered by silt 20–30 feet deep, and areas of desert are increasingly being reclaimed by irrigation and fertilization.

The Nile has a total length of 4,145 miles. In the 960 miles of its course through Egypt it receives not a single tributary stream. The river formerly had a regular yearly rise and fall of about 13 feet at Cairo, but since the completion of the Aswan High Dam in 1965 (about a mile upstream from the smaller Aswan Dam, built around the turn of the century), there has been no flood downstream of the dam and the water level remains almost constant throughout the year. The area of fertile land, a 5–15 mile wide strip in the Nile valley and some 6,000 square miles of the Nile delta, has been increased by the opening of the Aswan Dam. This has allowed the reclamation of about 1,300,000 acres, and a further 700,000 acres have been converted from basin to perennial irrigation. Westward from the Nile Valley stretches the Western desert, containing some depressions, whose springs irrigate small areas known as Oases, of which the principal, from SE to NW, are known as Kharga, Dakhla, Farafra, Baharia and Siwa.

In the Eastern Desert between the Nile and the mountains along the Red Sea coast, are plateaux of sandstones and limestones, dissected by wadis (dry water-courses), often of great length and depth, with some wild vegetation and occasional wells and springs.

History.—The unification of the Kingdoms of Lower and Upper Egypt under the Pharaohs *c.* 3100 BC marked the establishment of the Egyptian state, with Memphis as its capital. Egypt was ruled for nearly 2,800 years by a succession of Pharaonic dynasties (31 in all), which built the pyramids at Gizeh. The oldest of these is that of Zoser, built *c.* 2700 BC, and the highest the Great Pyramid of Cheops, at 451 feet; nearby is the Sphinx, 189 feet long. A period of Hellenic rule began in 332 BC, after the conquest of Egypt by Alexander the Great, followed by a period of rule by Rome (30 BC to AD 324) and then by the Byzantine Empire. In AD 640 Egypt was subjugated by Arab Muslim invaders, becoming a province of the Eastern Caliphate. In 1517 the country was incorporated in the Ottoman Empire under which it remained until early in the 19th century.

A British Protectorate over Egypt declared on Dec. 18, 1914, lasted until Feb. 28, 1922, when Sultan Ahmed Fuad was proclaimed King of Egypt. In July 1952, following a military coup d'état, King Farouk abdicated in favour of his infant son, who became King Ahmed Fuad II. In June 1953 however, Gen. Neguib's military council deposed the young King, and Egypt became a Republic.

In 1956, as a result of Egypt's trade agreements with Communist countries, Britain and USA withdrew offers of financial aid and in retaliation President Nasser seized the assets of the Suez Canal Company. Egyptian occupation of the Canal Zone while repulsing an Israeli attack was used as a pretext for military action by Britain and France in support of their Suez Canal Company interests. A ceasefire and Anglo-French withdrawal were negotiated by the UN.

The Israeli invasion of 1956 overran the Sinai peninsula but six months later Israel withdrew and a UN peace-keeping force was established in the area. However, mounting tension culminated in a second invasion of Sinai (the Six Day War of June 1967) and occupation of the peninsula by Israel. Egypt's attempt to recapture the territory (the Yom Kippur War of October 1973) was unsuccessful but Sinai was returned to Egypt in April 1982, under the treaty of 1979 which resulted from the Camp David talks between President Sadat and the Israeli Prime Minister Menachem Begin and formally terminated a 31-year old state of war between the two countries. President Mubarak came to power on October 13, 1981 after the assassination of President Sadat by Muslim fundamentalists.

Egypt has benefited considerably, both economically and politically, from its participation in the Gulf War; it has now been fully rehabilitated in the Arab world and has had large amounts of its international debt written off.

Government.—The Constitution of 1971 provides for an executive President who appoints Ministers to the Cabinet. The President determines policy which the Cabinet implements and Ministers are responsible to him. The Legislature consists of the People's Assembly (454 members, 444 of whom are elected, the remaining 10 nominated by the President); the Shura Council, or Consultative Assembly (258 members) has an advisory role. Religious courts were abolished in 1956 and their functions transferred to the national court system. The ruling National Democratic Party won general elections, boycotted in the major opposition parties, held in November and December 1990.

Agriculture.—Despite increasing industrialization, agriculture remains the most important economic activity, employing over 45 per cent of the labour force and contributing to 17 per cent of the country's exports. Agricultural output has been increased as a result of land reclamation programmes and the introduction of more efficient methods, e.g. the change from basin to perennial irrigation which yields 2–3 crops per year instead of one, the pivotal sprinkling irrigation system which uses water more efficiently, and the increasing mechanization and use of fertilizers. Egypt is still a net importer of foodstuffs, especially grain, and a food security programme has been set up with the aim of achieving self-sufficiency through the use of more advanced technology. Estimates suggest that an additional 3 million acres of land could be reclaimed by the end of the century.

The main cash crop is cotton, of which Egypt is one of the world's main producers. Other important summer crops are maize, rice and sugar cane. Important winter crops are wheat and beans. Citrus fruit and other fruits and vegetables are also grown.

Energy.—With its considerable reserves of petroleum and natural gas in Sinai, the Nile Delta and the Western Desert, and the hydro-electric power produced by the Aswan and High Dams, Egypt is self-sufficient in energy. Electricity has been provided to almost all of the country and there are plans to extend the natural gas network to all major cities.

Industry.—The production of petroleum provides Egypt with its major export (60–65 per cent of total exports), and supports a growing refining industry. Steel production is another important heavy industry. The major manufacturing industries are in food processing, motor cars and electrical goods, chemical products and yarns and textiles.

FINANCE

	1986–87	1987–88
Estimated revenue	£E12·4m	£E14·2m
Total expenditure	19·9m	21·7m

TRADE

The main imports are wheat and flour, wood and trucks. The main exports are crude petroleum, cotton, cotton yarn, oranges, rice and cotton textiles.

	1986–87
Imports	£E7·8m
Exports	2·6m

Trade with UK

	1989	1990
Imports from UK	£296,272,000	£290,262,000
Exports to UK	212,727,000	145,323,000

Communications.—The road and rail networks link the Nile Valley and Delta with the main development areas to east and west of the river.

The Suez Canal was re-opened in 1975 and a two-stage development project begun to widen and deepen the canal to allow the passage of larger shipping and to permit two-way traffic. Port Said and Suez have been reconstructed and the port of Alexandria is being improved.

CAPITAL.—Cairo (population, estimated in 1986 at 14,000,000), stands on the E. bank of the Nile, about 14 miles from the head of the Delta. Its oldest part is the fortress of Babylon in old Cairo, with its Roman bastions and Coptic churches. The earliest Arab building is the Mosque of 'Amr, dating from AD 643, and the most conspicuous is the Citadel, built by Saladin towards the end of the 12th century and containing in its walls the Mosque of Mohamed Ali built in the 19th century.

ΨAlexandria (estimated population in 1986 of 5,000,000), founded 332 BC by Alexander the Great, was for over 1,000 years the capital of Egypt and a centre of Hellenic culture which vied with Athens herself. Its great *pharos* (lighthouse), 480 feet high, with a lantern burning resinous wood, was one of the Seven Wonders of the World. Other towns are: Ismailia (400,000); ΨPort Said (285,000); Mansura (120,000); Asyût (300,000); Faiyûm (180,000); Tanta (150,000); Mahalla el Kubra (130,000); ΨSuez; ΨDamietta (100,000).

CURRENCY.—Egyptian pound (£E) of 100 piastres and 1,000 millièmes.

FLAG.—Horizontal bands of red, white and black, with an eagle in the centre of the white band.

NATIONAL DAY.—July 23 (Anniversary of Revolution in 1952).

BRITISH EMBASSY
Ahmed Ragheb Street, Garden City, Cairo
[Cairo 354–0850]

Ambassador Extraordinary and Plenipotentiary, His Excellency Sir James Adams, KCMG (1987).

EQUATORIAL GUINEA
(República de Guinea Ecuatorial)

President of the Supreme Military Council and Minister of Defence, Brig.-Gen. Teodoro Obiang Nguema Mbasogo, *took office*, Aug. 1979, *re-elected* June 1989.

MINISTERS
(as at December 1990)

Prime Minister, Cristino Seriche Bioko.
Deputy PM, Education, Youth and Sport, Isidoro Eyi Monsuy Andeme.
Minister of State, Minister Secretary-General to the Presidency, Casto Nvono Akhele.
Ministers of State at the Presidency, Eloy Elo Nve Mbengono; Alejandro Evuna Asangono.
Minister Deputy Secretary-General to the Presidency, Martin Nka Esono Nsing.
Minister of State, Economy, Trade and Planning, Marcelino Nguemo Ongueme.
Justice, Silvestre Siale Sale Bileka.
Public Works, Urban Development and Transport, Alejandro Envoro Ovono.
Agriculture, Fishing and Forestry, Anatolio Nolong Mba.
Industry and Energy, Francisco Pascual Obama Asue.
Labour and Social Development, Antonio Pascual Oko Ebobo.
Ministers Delegate:
Economic and Financial Affairs, Antonio Fernando Nve Ngu.
Mines and Hydrocarbons, Juan Olo Mba Nseng.
Culture, Tourism and Handicrafts, Leandro Mbomio Nsue.
Foreign Affairs and Co-operation, Santiago Eneme Ovono.
National Defence, vacant.
Territorial Administration and Communications, Segundo Munoz Italo.
Health, Alejandro Masoko Bengono.
Women's Development, Purificaçion Angue Ondo.

Equatorial Guinea (formerly Spanish Guinea) consists of the island of Biogo (formerly Macias Nguema), in the Bight of Biafra about 20 miles from the west coast of Africa, Pagalu Island (formerly Annobon) in the Gulf of Guinea, the Corisco Islands (Corisco, Elobey Grande and Elobey Chico) and Rio Muni, a mainland area between Cameroon and Gabon. It has a total area of 10,830 sq. miles (28,051 sq. km), and a population (UN estimate 1989) of 341,000.

Government.—Formerly colonies of Spain, the territories now forming the Republic of Equatorial Guinea were constituted as two provinces of Metropolitan Spain in 1960, became autonomous in 1964 and fully independent in 1968. Serious disorders in Rio Muni early in 1969 caused many of the Spanish community to leave.

In August 1979, President Macias was deposed by a revolutionary military council headed by his nephew Col. T. Obiang Nguema. The first parliamentary elections since 1968 were held in August 1983, under a new constitution approved by a referendum in August 1982. The most recent elections to the 41-member National Assembly took place in July 1988. All candidates were nominated by the President and elected unopposed for a five-year term.

Economy.—The chief products are cocoa, coffee and wood (which is exported almost entirely from Rio Muni). Production has declined and except for cocoa, there is little commercial agriculture and the economy is now heavily dependent on outside aid, principally from Spain. Equatorial Guinea entered the 'Franc zone' in 1985.

Trade with UK

	1989	1990
Imports from UK	£640,000	£1,159,000
Exports to UK	2,000	10,000

CAPITAL.—ΨMalabo on the island of Bioco, population (1983 estimate) 34,980. ΨBata is the principal town and port of Rio Muni.

CURRENCY.—Franc CFA of 100 centimes.

FLAG.—Three horizontal bands, green over white over red; blue triangle next staff; coat of arms in centre of white band.

NATIONAL DAY.—October 12.

British Ambassador, (resident in Yaoundé, Cameroon).

BRITISH CONSULATE
World Bank Compound, Apartado 801, Malabo
[Tel. Malabo 2400]

Honorary Consul, vacant.

ESTONIA
See p. 856

ETHIOPIA
(Hebretesebawit Ityopia)

President, Meles Zenawi.

CABINET
(as at June 11, 1991)

Prime Minister, Tamirat Layne.
Justice, Shiferaw Wolde Michael.
Information, Dima Nego.
Foreign Affairs, Seyoum Mesfin.
Health, Dr Adanech Kidane Mariam.
Education, Ibsa Gutema.
Industry, Bekele Tadessa.
Interior, Kuma Demeksa.
Mines and Energy, Isedin Ali.
Commerce, Ahmed Hussen.
State Farms, Hassan Abdella.
Defence, Seye Abraha.
Agriculture and Environmental Protection, Segeye Asfaw.
Housing and Construction, Aragaw Tirunab.
Culture and Sports, Lieule Selassie Timamo.
Labour and Social Affairs, Dr Legaso Gidada.
Transport, Belachaw Mekbib.
Finance, Wolde Miriam Girma.

EMBASSY OF THE PEOPLE'S DEMOCRATIC
REPUBLIC OF ETHIOPIA
17 Prince's Gate, SW7 1PZ
[071–589 7212]

Ambassador Extraordinary and Plenipotentiary, new appointment awaited.

Area and Population.—Ethiopia is in northeastern Africa, bounded on the north-west by the Sudan, on the south by Kenya, on the east by Djibouti and the Republic of Somalia, and on the north-east by the Red Sea. The area is 471,778 sq. miles (1,221,900 sq. km), with a population (UN estimate 1989) of 49,513,000. About one-third are of Semitic origin (Amharas and Tigrayans) and the remainder mainly Oromos (about 40 per cent of the population), Somalis and Afar.

Ethiopia has a large central plateau (average

height, 6,000–7,000 ft.) which rises to nearly 15,000 ft. at Ras Dashan in the north. The plateau drops to the Nile basin in the west and the Red Sea in the east. To the north (Eritrea) and east (Ogaden) the land is mostly desert. The chief river is the Blue Nile, issuing from Lake Tana; the Atbara and many other tributaries of the Nile also rise in the Ethiopian highlands.

Those of Semitic origin (Amharas and Tigrayans), and many of the Oromos, are Christians of the Ethiopian Orthodox Church, which was formerly led by the head of the Coptic Church, the Patriarch at Alexandria. Since 1959, however, the Ethiopian Church has been autocephalous; the present Patriarch, Abuna Merkurios, was enthroned in Sept. 1988. The Afar people, who inhabit lowland Eritrea, Wollo, Hararghe and Bale provinces, and the Somalis, in the south-east, are Muslim. The Falashas, adherents of Judaism, formerly found principally in Gonder and Tigray provinces, were airlifted to Israel in 1984–5 and 1991.

History.—The basic Hamitic culture was heavily influenced by Semitic immigration from Arabia in the centuries about the time of Christ. Christianity was introduced in the fourth century. The empire expanded sporadically, attaining a zenith in the sixth century under the Axum rulers, but subsequently checked by Islamic expansion from the east. Modern Ethiopia dates from 1855 when Theodore succeeded in establishing supremacy over the various tribes. The last Emperor was Haile Selassie who reigned from 1930, though in exile from 1936–1941 during the Italian occupation. After considerable military and civil unrest the armed forces assumed power in September 1974 and deposed the Emperor. After ten years of military rule, a Workers' Party on the Soviet model was formed in September 1984, with Mengistu Haile Mariam as General Secretary.

The civilian government of the People's Democratic Republic of Ethiopia was established under a new constitution in Sept. 1987 with Lt.-Col. Mengistu being elected the first President. Armed insurgencies by the Eritrean People's Liberation Front (EPLF) and the Ethiopian People's Revolutionary Democratic Front (EPRDF), originating in Tigray, brought down Mengistu's government in May 1991. At a national conference, held in July, an 81-member Transitional Council was formed, comprising the EPRDF and a number of other opposition groups. The transitional government, headed by Meles Zenawi, is to prepare the country for elections under a new constitution within two years.

Eritrea.—Eritrea was administered by Great Britain from the end of the Second World War until September 15, 1952, when it was federated with Ethiopia. It was incorporated as a province of Ethiopia in 1962. An armed campaign for independence started in 1962 and gathered momentum throughout the 1970s and 1980s. By May 1991, the EPLF had established complete control of the territory; the central government has granted Eritrea a referendum on secession in exchange for access to the sea via the port of Assab.

Production and Industry.—The principal pursuit is agriculture, which accounts for approximately 40 per cent of GDP, 85 per cent of exports and 80 per cent of total employment. Land was nationalized in 1975 and tenants given rights of use to the land they had tilled; large private holdings became state farms. The major food crops are teff, maize, barley, sorghum, wheat, pulses and oil seeds. Coffee, the principal export crop, generates over 50 per cent of the country's export earnings.

Famine conditions, which attracted world attention in 1984–85, again prevail in 1991. As before, the situation has been exacerbated by guerrilla activity and the recent civil war.

Manufacturing industry accounts for less than ? per cent of GDP and is heavily dependent on agriculture. Ethiopia's known, but as yet largely unexploited, natural resources include gold, platinum, copper and potash. Traces of oil and natural gas have been found.

Communications.—With the aid of loans from the IBRD, China and the African Development Bank, a network of roads has been built in rural areas and link the major cities with each other, and with the Sudanese and Kenyan borders and the Red Sea coast. Transport links have suffered during the secessionist wars and under the heavy burden of famine relief traffic. The two roads to the north have been usable only under heavy military escort in Tigray and Eritrea. There is a railway link from Addis Ababa to Djibouti although this has been vulnerable to guerrilla activity. The narrow gauge line in Eritrea has been closed by conflict. Ethiopian Airlines maintain regular services from Addis Ababa to many provincial towns. External services are operated throughout Africa and to Europe.

Defence.—Ethiopia's considerable military force (over 300,000 men) failed to contain the rebel forces and are now in disarray, pending reorganization by the post-Mengistu government.

Education.—Elementary education is provided without religious discrimination by Government schools in the main centres of population; there are also Mission schools, and cadet-schools for the Army, Navy, Air Force and Police. Government secondary schools are found mainly in Addis Ababa, but also in most of the provincial capitals. The National University (founded 1961) co-ordinates the institutions of higher education (University College, Engineering, Building and Theological Colleges in Addis Ababa, Agricultural College at Alemaya, near Harar, and Public Health Centre in Gondar, etc.). It is intended to develop the provincial colleges to university level and status.

Amharic is the official language of instruction, with English as the first foreign language and main language of instruction from secondary level upwards. Arabic is taught in Koran Schools; and Ge'e (the ancient Ethiopic) in Christian Church Schools which abound.

FINANCE

	1987–88
Revenue	US$1,709·5
Expenditure	2,226·4

TRADE

The chief imports by value are machinery and transport equipment, manufactured goods and chemicals (from UK); the principal exports by value being coffee, oilseeds, hides and skins, and pulses.

	1987–88
Total Imports	US$1,083·6m
Total Exports	393·7m

Trade with UK

	1989	1990
Imports from UK	£44,148,000	£41,403,000
Exports to UK	12,772,000	19,465,000

CAPITAL.— Addis Ababa (population, 1985 estimate, 1,464,901), also capital of the province of Shoa; Asmara (population 275,000) is the capital of the Province of Eritrea. Dire Dawa is the most important commercial centre after Addis Ababa and Asmara, Massawa and ΨAssab are the two main ports. There are ancient architectural remains at Aksum, Gondar, Lalibela and elsewhere.

CURRENCY.—Ethiopian birr (EB) of 100 cents.

FLAG.—Three horizontal bands: green, yellow, red.

NATIONAL ANTHEM.—Ityopya, Ityopya Kidemi.

NATIONAL DAY.—September 12 (People's Revolution Day).

BRITISH EMBASSY

Fikre Mariam Abatechan Street (PO Box 858)
Addis Ababa
[Addis Ababa 612354]

Ambassador Extraordinary and Plenipotentiary, His Excellency Michael John Carlisle Glaze, CMG (1990).

British Council Representative, B. Nightingale, Artistic Building, Adwa Avenue (PO Box 1043), Addis Ababa. There is also a library in *Asmara*.

FIJI
(Matanitu Ko Fiti—Republic of Fiji)

President, Ratu Sir Penaia Ganilau, GCMG, KCVO, KBE, DSO, *appointed* Dec. 5, 1987.

CABINET
(as at August 12, 1991)

Prime Minister, Home Affairs and Foreign Affairs, Ratu Sir Kamisese Mara, GCMG, KBE.

Deputy PM, Minister for Defence, Maj.-Gen. Sitiveni Rabuka.

Deputy PM, Minister for Finance and Economic Planning, Josefata Kamikamica.

Fijian Affairs and Rural Development, Col. Vatiliai Navunisaravi.

Education, Youth and Sport, Filipe Bole, CBE.

Primary Industries and Co-operatives, Viliame Gonelevu.

Trade and Commerce, Berenado Vunibobo.

Health, Apenisa Kurisaqila.

Infrastructure and Public Utilities, vacant.

Attorney-General and Justice, Sailosi Kepa.

Tourism, Civil Aviation and Energy, David Pickering, CBE.

Indian Affairs, Mrs Irene Jai Narayan.

Forests, Ratu Ovini Bokini.

Employment and Industrial Relations, Taniela Veitata.

Women and Social Welfare, Adi Finau Tabakaucoro.

Housing and Urban Development, Tomasi Vakatora.

Lands and Mineral Resources, Ratu William Toganivalu.

Information, Broadcasting, Television and Telecommunications, Ratu Inoke Kubuabola.

EMBASSY OF THE REPUBLIC OF FIJI

34 Hyde Park Gate, SW7 5BN
[071-584 3661/2]

Ambassador Extraordinary and Plenipotentiary, His Excellency Brig.-Gen. Ratu Epeli Nailatikau, LVO, OBE (1988).

Area, Population, etc.—Fiji is made up of about 332 islands and over 500 islets (including numerous atolls and reefs) in the South Pacific Ocean, about 1,100 miles north of New Zealand. About 100 islands are permanently inhabited. The gross area of the group, which extends 300 miles from east to west, and 300 north to south, between 15° 45'—21° 10' S. lat. and 176° E.—178° W. long. is 7,055 sq. miles (18,274 sq. km). The International Date Line has been diverted to the east of the island group. The largest islands are Viti Levu and Vanua Levu. The main groups of islands are Lomaiviti, Lau and Yasawas. Most of the larger islands are mountainous with sharp peaks and crags, but also have conspicuous areas of flat land and many of the rivers have built extensive deltas. The climate is tropical, without extremes of heat and temperatures rarely exceed 32° C and seldom fall below 15° C.

The population (Census 1986) was 715,373, comprising 48·6 per cent Indians, 46·2 per cent Fijians, and 5·2 per cent other races. A UN estimate (1989) gives a total figure of 738,000.

Government.—Fiji was a British colony from 1874 until October 10, 1970 when it became an independent state and a member of the Commonwealth.

A coalition of the left under Dr Timoci Bavadra defeated the Alliance Party of Ratu Sir Kamisese Mara in a General Election on April 12, 1987. The new Government, drawing its support mainly from the Indian population, was overthrown in a military coup on May 14 by Lt.-Col. Sitiveni Rabuka. In the wake of the constitutional crisis an Advisory Council of 19 members was set up by the Governor General as an interim government to consider constitutional reform.

A second coup occurred on September 25, 1987. On October 7 Rabuka declared Fiji to be a republic; the Governor General resigned on October 15 and Fiji's Commonwealth membership lapsed. An Executive Council of Ministers, with Rabuka at its head, assumed control until December 5 when Ratu Sir Penaia Ganilau was appointed President. The President called upon Ratu Sir Kamisese Mara to form another interim administration to work for a resolution to the political crisis.

A new constitution, promulgated on July 25, 1990, established the political dominance of the minority Melanesian community within the judiciary and a bicameral parliament; an amnesty was granted to participants in the 1987 coups. Elections due to be held in 1991 have been postponed until boundary changes have been completed in 1992.

FINANCE

	1987	1988
Public Income	F$342m	F$358m
Public Expenditure	416m	399m

Economy.—The economy is primarily agrarian, with about 600,000 acres under cultivation. The principal cash crop is sugar cane, which is the main export, followed by coconuts, ginger and copra. A variety of other fruit, vegetables and root crops are also grown, and self-sufficiency in rice is a major aim. Forestry, fishing and beef production are being encouraged in order to diversify the economy. The processing of agricultural, marine and timber products are the main industries, along with gold mining. A policy of tax concessions for export-oriented manufacturing has encouraged expansion of the garment industry.

Tourism is also a major factor in the economy, second only to sugar as a money-earner.

TRADE

	1988	1989
Total Imports ...	F$570,700,000	F$961,870,139
Total Exports ...	493,800,000	598,201,244

Trade with UK

	1989	1990
Imports from UK	£10,221,000	£8,168,000
Exports to UK	69,558,000	61,863,000

The chief imports are foodstuffs, machinery, mineral fuels, chemicals, beverages, tobacco and manufactured articles. Chief exports are sugar, coconut oil, gold, lumber, garments, molasses, ginger and canned fish.

Communications.—Fiji is one of the main aerial crossroads in the Pacific, providing services to New Zealand, Australia, Tonga, Western Samoa, Vanuatu, the Solomon Islands, Kiribati, Tuvalu, New Caledonia and American Samoa.

Fiji has three ports of entry, at Suva, Lautoka and Levuka.

CAPITAL.—ΨSuva, on the island of Viti Levu. Population (1985) 75,000.

CURRENCY.—Fiji dollar (F$) of 100 cents.

FLAG.—Light blue ground with Union flag in top left quarter and the shield of Fiji in the fly.

NATIONAL ANTHEM.—God Bless Fiji.

NATIONAL DAY.—October 10 (Fiji Day).

BRITISH EMBASSY
Victoria House, 47 Gladstone Road,
PO Box 1355, Suva
[Suva 311033]

Ambassador Extraordinary and Plenipotentiary, His Excellency (Alexander Basil) Peter Smart, CMG (1989).

FINLAND
(Suomen Tasavalta)

President, Dr Mauno Koivisto, *born,* 1923, *elected,* Jan 26, 1982, *re-elected,* March 1, 1988.

CABINET
(as at April 4, 1991)

Prime Minister, Esko Aho (CP).

Deputy Prime Minister, Minister of Labour and Minister at the Ministry of Finance, Ilkka Kanerva (NCP).

Foreign Affairs, Paavo Vayrynen (CP).

Social Affairs and Health, Eeva Kuuskoski (CP).

Foreign Trade, Pertti Salolainen (NCP).

Transport and Communications, Ole Norrback (SPP).

Defence, Elisabeth Rehn (SPP).

Trade and Industry, Kauko Juhantalo (CP).

Justice, Hannele Pokka (CP).

Interior, Mauri Pekkarinen (CP).

Finance, Iiro Viinanen (NCP).

Education, Riitta Uosukainen (NCP).

Cultural Affairs, Tytti Isohookana-Asunmaa (CP).

Environment, Sirpa Pietikainen (NCP).

Housing, Pirjo Rusanen, (NCP).

Development Co-operation, Toimi Kankaanniemi (FCU).

Agriculture and Forestry, Martti Pura (CP).

NCP: National Coalition Party, CP: Centre Party, FCU, Finnish Christian Union.

FINNISH EMBASSY AND CONSULATE
38 Chesham Place, SW1X 8HW
[071–235 9531]

Ambassador Extraordinary and Plenipotentiary, His Excellency Leif Blomquist (1991).

Minister Counsellor, J. Leino.

Counsellors, Dr H. Markala; A. Puura-Märkälä.

Defence Attaché, Cdr. P. Kaskeala.

Area and Population.—A country situated on the Gulfs of Finland and Bothnia, with a total area of 137,851 sq. miles (337,032 sq. km), of which 65 per cent is forest, 8 per cent cultivated land and 9 per cent lakes. The population (1989) is 4,954,484; population density is 16 inhabitants per square km. The population is predominantly Lutheran.

The Aland Archipelago (Ahvenanmaa), a group of small islands at the entrance to the Gulf of Bothnia covers about 572 square miles, with a population (December 1985) of 23,600 (95·2 per cent Swedish speaking). The islands have a semi-autonomous status.

Government.—Under the Constitution there is a single Chamber (*Eduskunta*) composed of 200 members, elected by universal suffrage. The legislative power is vested in the Chamber and the President. The highest executive power is held by the President who is elected for a period of six years.

The present government came into office in April 1990, the first government not to include left-wing parties for 25 years. The four parties in the coalition are the National Coalition Party (conservative), the Centre Party, the Swedish People's Party of Finland and the Finnish Christian Union Party.

Defence.—By the terms of the Peace Treaty (February 10, 1947) with UK and USSR, the Army is limited to a force not exceeding 34,400. The Navy is limited to a total of 10,000 tons displacement with personnel not exceeding 4,500. The Air Force including naval air arm, is limited to 60 machines with a personnel not exceeding 3,000. Bombers or aircraft with bomb-carrying facilities are expressly forbidden. The Defence Forces contain a cadre of regular officers and NCO's, but their bulk is provided by conscripts who serve for 8–11 months. Total strength of trained and equipped reserves is over 700,000, 16,500 of whom have served in the UN peacekeeping force.

Education.—Primary education (co-educational

comprehensive school) is compulsory for children from 7 to 16 years, and free of charge. In the autumn of 1986, there were 678,463 in comprehensive schools and 113,117 in vocational institutions of senior level. There are 21 universities or other schools of academic level, and enrolment was (1985) 92,230.

Language and Literature.—There are two official languages in Finland. 93·6 per cent of the population speak Finnish as their first language, 6·2 Swedish (1986). The remaining 0·2 per cent speak other languages (mainly Lapps who number about 2,500 and live in the far north). Both Finnish and Swedish are used for administration and education; newspapers, books, plays and films appear in both languages.There is a vigorous modern literature. F. E. Sillanpää, who died in 1964, was awarded the Nobel prize for Literature in 1939. In 1988 there were 103 daily newspapers (12 Swedish).

Production and Industry.—Finland is a highly industrialized country producing a wide range of capital and consumer goods. Timber and the products of the forest-based industries remain the backbone of the economy, but the importance of the metalworking, shipbuilding and engineering industries has been growing. The textile industry is well developed and Finland's glass, ceramics and furniture industries enjoy international reputations. Other important industries are rubber, plastics, chemicals and pharmaceuticals, footwear, foodstuffs and electronic equipment. The Finnish economy has been adversely affected by declining trade with eastern Europe and the Soviet Union.

Communications.—There are 9,000 kilometres of railroad, a railway connection with Sweden and USSR, passenger boat connection with Sweden, Federal Republic of Germany, Poland and USSR. Vessels on the London to Leningrad route call at Helsinki. There are also passenger/cargo services between Britain and Helsinki, Kotka and other Finnish ports. External civil air services are maintained by most European airlines. The merchant fleet at the end of 1986 totalled 1,900,000 tons gross.

TRADE

The principal imports are raw materials, machinery and manufactured goods. In 1988 more than half of all industrial production was exported. The value of exports was broken down as follows: paper 33·4 per cent, wood 8·2 per cent, metal and engineering products 31 per cent, basic metal industry 8·3 per cent, chemicals 9 per cent, textiles and clothing 4·6 per cent.

	1987	1988
Total Imports	Mk86,696m	Mk88,192m
Total Exports	87,564m	90,861m

Trade with UK

	1989	1990
Imports from UK ..	£925,784,000	£1,041,739,000
Exports to UK	1,893,163,000	1,775,766,000

CAPITAL.—ΨHelsinki (Helsingfors), population (1986) 485,626; other towns are Tampere (Tammerfors), 169,153; ΨTurku (Åbo), 161,508; Espoo (Esbo), 156,851; Vantaa (Vanda), 143,986; ΨOulu (Oleåborg), 97,329; Lahti (Lahtis), 94,467; ΨPori (Björneborg), 78,365.

CURRENCY.—Markka (Mk) of 100 penniä.

FLAG.—White with blue cross.

NATIONAL DAY.—December 6 (Independence Day).

BRITISH EMBASSY
Itäinen Puistotie 17, 00140 Helsinki
[Helsinki 661293]

Ambassador Extraordinary and Plenipotentiary, His Excellency Neil Smith (1989).

Counsellor (Commercial), N. A. Thorne.

First Secretaries, V. J. Henderson (*Head of Chancery*); R. M. F. Kelly; W. Hamilton; R. Norton.

Defence, Naval, Military and Air Attaché, Lt.-Col. F. A. B. Clement.

There are British Consular offices at *Helsinki, Jyväskylä, Kotka, Kuopio, Oulu, Pori, Tampere, Turku, Vaasa* and *Mariehamn*.

British Council Representative, G. Coe, Erottajankatu 7B, 00130 Helsinki 13.

FRANCE
(La République Française)

President of the French Republic, François Mitterrand, *elected* May 10, 1981, *re-elected* May 8, 1988.

COUNCIL OF MINISTERS
(as at May 16, 1991)

Prime Minister, Edith Cresson.
National Education, Lionel Jospin.
Economy, Finance and the Budget, Pierre Beregovoy.
Foreign Affairs, Roland Dumas.
Civil Service and Modernization of the Administration, Jean-Pierre Soisson.
Urban Affairs and Town and Country Planning, Michel Delebarre.
Justice, Henri Nallet.
Defence, Pierre Joxe.
Interior, Philippe Marchand.
Culture and Communication and Government Spokesman, Jack Lang.
Agriculture and Forestry, Louis Mermaz.
Social Affairs and Integration, Jean-Louis Bianco.
Labour, Employment and Vocational Training, Martine Aubry.
Public Works, Housing, Transport and Space, Paul Quiles.
Co-operation and Development, Edwige Avice.
Overseas Departments and Territories, Louis Le Pensec.
Research and Technology, Hubert Curien.
Relations with Parliament, Jean Poperen.
Youth and Sports, Frederique Bredin.
Environment, Brice Lalonde.

FRENCH EMBASSY
58 Knightsbridge, SW1X 7JT
[071–235 8080].

Ambassador Extraordinary and Plenipotentiary, His Excellency Bernard Dorin (1991).

Area and Population.—France extends from 42° 20' to 51° 5' N. lat., and from 7° 85' E. to 4° 45' W. long. Its area is estimated at 211,208 sq. miles (547,026 sq. km), divided into 95 departments, including the island of Corsica, in the Mediterranean, off the west coast of Italy. The population, according to preliminary 1990 census results, is 56,555,700.

POPULATION OF THE REGIONS 1990
(Names of Departments in brackets)

Alsace (Bas-Rhin, Haut-Rhin)	1,622,000
Aquitaine (Dordogne, Gironde, Landes, Lot-et-Garonne, Pyrénées-Atlantiques)	2,793,500
Auvergne (Allier, Cantal, Haute-Loire, Puy-de-Dôme)......................	1,318,200
Basse-Normandie (Calvados, Manche, Orne)	1,390,500
Bourgogne (Côte-d'Or, Nièvre, Saône-et-Loire, Yonne)	1,608,500
Bretagne (Côtes-du-Nord, Finistère, Ille-et-Vilaine, Morbihan)	2,792,800
Centre (Cher, Eure-et-Loir, Indre, Indre-et-Loire, Loir-et-Cher, Loiret)	2,369,200
Champagne-Ardenne (Ardennes, Aube, Marne, Haute-Marne)	1,345,700

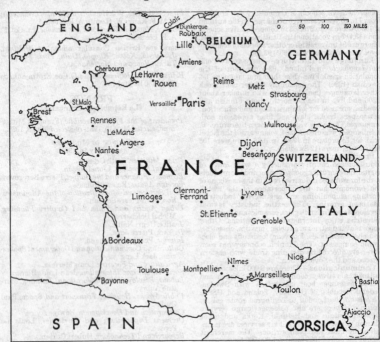

Corse (Corse-du-Sud, Haute-Corse) 240,200
Franche-Comté (Doubs, Haute-Saône, Jura, Territoire-de-Belfort) 1,097,100
Haute-Normandie (Eure, Seine-Maritime) 1,736,400
Île-de-France (Essonne, Hauts-de-Seine, Seine-et-Marne, Seine-St-Denis, Val-de-Marne, Val-d'Oise, Ville de Paris, Yvelines) 10,650,600
Languedoc-Roussillon (Aude, Gard, Hérault, Lozère, Pyrénées-Orientales) 2,109,800
Limousin (Corrèze, Creuse, Haute-Vienne) 723,800
Lorraine (Meurthe-et-Moselle, Meuse, Moselle, Vosges)...................... 2,303,700
Midi-Pyrénées (Ariège, Aveyron, Haute-Garonne, Gers, Lot, Hautes-Pyrénées, Tarn, Tarn-et-Garonne)............... 2,427,400
Nord-Pas-de-Calais (Nord, Pas-de-Calais) 3,960,000
Pays de la Loire (Loire-Atlantique, Maine-et-Loire, Mayenne, Sarthe, Vendée) ... 3,058,000
Picardie (Aisne, Oise, Somme) 1,809,600
Poitou-Charentes (Charente, Charente-Maritime, Deux-Sèvres, Vienne) 1,594,700
Provence-Alpes-Côte d'Azur (Alpes-de-Haute-Provence, Alpes-Maritime, Bouches-du-Rhône, Haute-Alpes, Var, Vaucluse) 4,260,000
Rhône-Alpes (Ain, Ardèche, Drôme, Isère, Loire, Rhône, Savoie, Haute-Savoie) .. 5,344,000

Archaeology, etc.—There are dolmens and menhirs in Brittany, prehistoric remains and cave drawings in Dordogne and Ariège, and throughout France various megalithic monuments erected by primitive tribes, predecessors of Iberian invaders from Spain (now represented by the Basques), Ligurians from northern Italy and Celts or Gauls from the valley of the Danube. Julius Caesar found Gaul 'divided into three parts' and described three political groups—Aquitanians south of the Garonne, Celts between the Garonne and the Seine and Marne, and Belgae from the Seine to the Rhine. Roman remains are plentiful throughout France in the form of aqueducts, arenas, triumphal arches, etc., and the celebrated Norman and Gothic Cathedrals, including Notre Dame in Paris, and those of Chartres, Reims, Amiens (where Peter the Hermit preached the First Crusade for the recovery of the Holy Sepulchre), Bourges, Beauvais, Rouen, etc., have survived invasions and bombardments with only partial damage, and many of the renaissance and the seventeenth and eighteenth century chateaux survived the French Revolution.

Language and Literature.—French is the official language. The work of the French Academy, founded by Richelieu in 1635, has established *le bon usage*, equivalent to 'The Queen's English' in Great Britain. French authors have been awarded the Nobel Prize for Literature on twelve occasions, including R. F. A. Sully-Prudhomme (1901), Anatole France (1921), André Gide (1947), François Mauriac (1952), Albert Camus (1957), Jean Paul Sartre (1964) and Claude Simon (1985).

GOVERNMENT

Parliament consists of the National Assembly of 577 deputies (555 for Metropolitan France and 22 for the overseas departments and territories) and the Senate composed of 319 Senators (296 for Metropolitan France; 13 for the overseas departments and territories and 10 for French dependencies). The normal session of Parliament is confined to 5½ months each year and it may also meet in extraordinary session for 12 days at the request of the Prime Minister or a majority of the Assembly.

The Prime Minister is appointed by the President, as is the Cabinet on the Prime Minister's recommendation. They are responsible to Parliament, but as the executive is constitutionally separate from the legislature Ministers may not sit in Parliament.

A Constitutional Council is responsible for supervising all elections and referenda and must be consulted on all constitutional matters and before the President of the Republic assumes emergency powers.

DEFENCE

The personnel of the Defence Forces in 1990 totalled 460,000; numbers are to be reduced. National nuclear forces include medium-range ballistic missiles, submarine-launched ballistic missiles and *Mirage* IV medium bombers. The Army has a variety of new French-made equipment in service, including medium tanks, field and anti-aircraft SP guns, trucks and radio equipment.

EDUCATION

The educational system is highly centralized and is administered by the Ministry of National Education. Local administration comprises 25 Territorial Academies, with inspecting staff for all grades, and Departmental Councils presided over by the *Préfet*, and charged especially with primary education.

Primary and secondary education are compulsory, free and secular, the school age being from 6 to 16. Schools may be single-sex or co-educational. Primary education is given in nursery schools, primary schools and *collèges d'enseignement général* (4-year secondary modern course); secondary education in *collèges d'enseignement technique, collèges d'enseignement secondaire* and *lycées* (7-year course leading to one of the five *baccalauréats*). Special schools are numerous.

There are many *Grandes Ecoles* in France which award diplomas in many subjects not taught at university, especially applied science and engineering. Most of these are state institutions but have a competitive system of entry, unlike the universities. There are universities in twenty-four towns in France, two or three in some major provincial towns, and thirteen in Paris and the immediate surrounding district.

In 1989 enrolment in pre-school and primary schools was 6,894,000; in secondary schools 5,394,000, and in post-secondary education 1,428,000.

COMMUNICATIONS

Roads.—The length of roads in use at the end of 1987 was 805,000 km of which 6,400 km were motorways.

Railways.—The system of railroads in France is very extensive. The length of lines open for traffic at the end of 1989 was 34,322 km, of which 12,430 km were electrified.

Shipping.—The French mercantile marine consisted in 1990 of 223 ships of over 100 tons gross, of which 30 were passenger vessels (223,000 tons gross), 55 tankers (2,110,000 tons gross) and 138 cargo vessels (1,536,000 tons gross). The principal rivers of France are the Seine, Loire, Garonne, and Rhône.

ECONOMY

Budget.—Government expenditure (ordinary and capital) by function in the 1989 general Budget, was:

	F million
Agriculture and Forestry	36,485
Co-operation and Development	7,758
Culture and Communications	10,333
Defence	172,856
Economy, Finance and Budget	562,289
Education	186,831
Equipment and Housing	54,734
Foreign Affairs	11,426
Industry, Local Planning and Tourism	20,784
Interior	57,471
Justice	14,425
Labour and Employment	75,256
Overseas Departments	2,411
Prime Ministerial	3,451
Research and Technology	32,421
Solidarity, Health, Social Protection	35,780
Transport and the Sea	51,660
Veterans	26,735
Youth and Sports	2,312
Other	1,533
Total	1,366,951

PRODUCTION

Agriculture.—Approximately 30,813,000 hectares of land is used for agricultural purposes, 13,932,000 hectares is forested. Production in 1988 included wheat, 29,038,500 tonnes; sugar-beet, 28,588,090 tonnes; maize, 14,698,670 tonnes; barley, 9,883,200 tonnes; and potatoes 5,772,870 tonnes.

The vine is extensively cultivated, regions famous for their wines including Bordeaux, Burgundy and Champagne. Production of wine in 1988 was 72,488,400 hectolitres. Cognac, liqueurs and cider are also important products.

Energy.—France produces its own oil, the greater part coming from fields in the Landes area, but is a net importer of crude oil, for processing by its important oil-refining industry. Natural gas is produced in the foothills of the Pyrenees. Electricity production was 408,300 m kW in 1989.

Industry.—France's heavy industries include oil-refining and the production of iron and steel, and aluminium. In 1989 production of steel was 19,300,000 tonnes and cement 25,900,000 tonnes. Other important industries produce chemicals, tyres, aluminium, textiles, paper products and processed food. Engineering products include motor vehicles, and television and radio sets.

TRADE

The principal imports are raw materials for the heavy and manufacturing industries (e.g. oil, minerals, chemicals), machinery and precision instruments, agricultural products and vehicles. Raw materials, semi-manufactured and manufactured goods are also France's principal exports. Other member countries of the EC are France's main trading partners.

TOTAL TRADE

	1988	1989
Imports	F1,208,500m	F1,408,000m
Exports	1,217,000m	1,425,000m

Trade with UK

	1989	1990
Imports from UK	£9,461,648,000	£10,885,803,000
Exports to UK	10,785,429,000	11,758,481,000

CAPITAL.—Paris, on the Seine. Population (census 1990) 2,147,000 (town); 9,060,000 (incl. suburbs).

The largest conurbations (populations 1982) are ΨMarseilles (1,087,000); Lyons (1,262,000); Toulouse (608,000); Lille (950,000) and ΨBordeaux (685,000).

The chief towns of Corsica are ψAjaccio (55,279) and ψBastia (45,081).

CURRENCY.—French franc of 100 centimes.

FLAG.—The tricolour, three vertical bands, blue, white, red (blue next to flagstaff).

NATIONAL ANTHEM.—La Marseillaise.

NATIONAL DAY.—July 14 (Bastille Day, 1789).

BRITISH EMBASSY

35 rue du Faubourg St Honoré, 75383 Paris Cedex 08 [Paris 42 66 91 42]

Ambassador Extraordinary and Plenipotentiary, His Excellency Sir Ewen Alastair John Fergusson, KCMG (1987).

Minister, J. R. Young.

Defence and Air Attaché, Air Cdre C. R. Adams, AFC.

Counsellor and Head of Chancery, J. M. Macgregor.

Consul-General, M. Hunt.

BRITISH CONSULAR OFFICES

There are British Consulates-General in Metropolitan France at *Bordeaux, Lille, Lyons, Marseilles* and *Paris.*

BRITISH COUNCIL

Representative in Paris, D. Ricks, 9 rue de Constantine, 75007 Paris.

FRANCO-BRITISH CHAMBER OF COMMERCE
8 rue Cimarosa, 75116 Paris

President, R. Lyon.
Vice-President, B. Cordery, OBE.

OVERSEAS DEPARTMENTS

Legislation passed in December 1982 by the French Parliament granted greater powers of self-government to four of the five overseas departments—French Guiana, Guadeloupe, Martinique and Réunion. These former colonies had enjoyed departmental status since 1947 and the status of regions of France since 1974. Elections to their new directly-elected Assemblies were held in each department in 1983 and the Assemblies will operate in parallel with the existing, indirectly constituted Regional Councils. The French government is represented by a Commissioner (a Prefect in French Guiana).

French Guiana.—Situated on the north-eastern coast of South America, French Guiana is flanked by Suriname on the west and by Brazil on the south and east. Area, 34,749 sq. miles (90,000 sq. km). Population (1990) 114,900. Capital, ψCayenne (38,135). Under the administration of French Guiana is a group of islands (St Joseph, Ile Royal and Ile du Diable), known as Iles du Salut. On Devil's Isle, Captain Dreyfus was imprisoned from 1894 to 1899.

Prefect, J.-P. Lacroix.

Guadeloupe.—A number of islands in the Leeward Islands group of the West Indies, consisting of the two main islands of Guadeloupe (or Basse-Terre) and Grande-Terre, with the adjacent islands of Marie-Galante, La Désirade and Iles des Saintes, and the islands of St Martin and St Barthélemy over 150 miles to the north-west. Area, 687 sq. miles (1,779 sq. km). Population (1990) 386,600. Capital ψBasse Terre (15,778) in Guadeloupe. Other towns are ψPointe à Pitre (23,889) on Grande-Terre and ψGrand Bourg (6,611) in Marie Galante.

Commissioner, J-P. Proust.

Martinique.—An island situated in the Windward Islands group of the West Indies, between Dominica in the north and St Lucia in the south. Area, 425 sq. miles (1,102 sq. km). Population (1990) 359,800. Capital ψFort de France (100,576). Other towns are ψTrinité (11,214) and ψMarin (6,104).

Commissioner, J.-C. Roure.

Réunion.—Réunion, which became a French pos-

session in 1638, lies in the Indian Ocean, about 569 miles east of Madagascar and 110 miles S.W. of Mauritius. Area, 969 sq. miles (2,510 sq. km). Population (1990 estimate) 596,600. Capital, St Denis (109,072).

Commissioner, D. Constantin.

Also lying in the Indian Ocean adjacent to Madagascar are the smaller, uninhabited islands of Bassas da India, Europa, Iles Glorieuses, Juan de Nova and Tromelin, which are administered from Réunion.

TERRITORIAL COLLECTIVITÉS

Mayotte.—Area, 144 sq. miles (372 sq. km). Population (1987 estimate) 67,000. Capital, Mamoundzou (12,000). Part of the Comoros Islands group, Mayotte remained a French dependency when the other three islands became independent as the Comoros Republic in 1975. Since 1976 the island has been a *collectivité territoriale,* an intermediate status between Overseas Department and Overseas Territory.

Commissioner, A. Khider.

St Pierre and Miquelon—Area 93 sq. miles (242 sq. km). Population (1987) 6,500. Two small groups of islands off the coast of Newfoundland. Became a *collectivité territoriale* in June 1985.

Commissioner, J.-P. Marquie.

OVERSEAS TERRITORIES

French Polynesia.—Five archipelagos in the south Pacific, comprising the Society Islands (Windward Islands group includes Tahiti, Moorea, Makatea, Mehetia, Tetiaoro, Tubuai Manu, etc; Leeward Islands group includes Huahine, Raiatea, Tahaa, Bora-Bora, Maupiti, etc.), the Tuamotu Islands (Rangiroa, Hao, Turéia, etc.), the Gambier Islands (Mangareva, etc.), the Tubuai Islands (Rimatara, Rurutu, Tubuai, Raivavae, Rapa, etc.) and the Marquesas Islands (Nuku-Hiva, Hiva-Oa, Fatu-Hiva, Tahuata Ua Huka, etc.). Area, 1,544 sq. miles (4,000 sq. km) Population (1988 census) 189,000. Capital, ψPapeete (24,200) in Tahiti. Economy based on tourism and exports of copra, coffee, vanilla, citrus fruits and cultured pearls.

High Commissioner, J. Montpezat.

New Caledonia.—A large island in the Western Pacific, 700 miles E. of Queensland. Dependencies are the Isles of Pines, the Loyalty Islands (Mahé, Lifou Urea, etc.), the Bélep Archipelago, the Chesterfield Islands, the Huon Islands and Walpole. New Caledonia was discovered in 1774 and annexed by France in 1854; from 1871 to 1896 it was a convict settlement A referendum in 1987 on the question of independence for New Caledonia was boycotted by the indigenous Kanaks, and New Caledonia therefore voted to remain French. However, a new independence referendum has been promised for 1998. Area, 7,358 sq miles (19,058 sq. km). Population (1989 census 164,200. Capital ψNoumea (66,100). It is one of the world's largest producers of nickel.

High Commissioner, B. Grasset.

Southern and Antarctic Territories.—Created in 1955 from the former Réunion dependencies, the territory comprises the islands of Amsterdam (25 sq miles) and St Paul (2·7 sq. miles), the Kerguelen Islands (2,700 sq. miles) and Crozet Islands (116 sq miles) archipelagos and Adélie Land (116,800 sq miles) in the Antarctic continent. The only population are members of staff of the scientific stations.

Wallis and Futuna Islands.—Two groups o islands (the Wallis Archipelago and the Iles de Hoorn in the central Pacific, N.E. of Fiji. Area, 106 sq. mile (274 sq. km). Population (1987 estimate) 12,000 Capital, Mata-Utu on Uvea, the main island of the Wallis group.

THE FRENCH COMMUNITY

The Constitution of the fifth French Republic promulgated on Oct. 6, 1958, envisaged the establishment of a French Community of States. A number of the former French states in Africa have seceded from the Community but for all practical purposes continue to enjoy the same close links with France as those that remain formally members of the French Community. With the exception of Guinea, all the former French colonies are closely linked to France by a series of financial, technical and economic agreements.

FRANCOPHONE COUNTRIES

In the following countries French is either the official or national language or the language of instruction; where there is another national language the name of it is shown after the name of the country:—Algeria (*Arabic*); Belgium (*Flemish*); Benin; Burkina; Burundi (*Kirundi*); Cambodia (*Khmer*); Cameroon (*English*); parts of Canada (in Quebec, parts of Ontario and New Brunswick) (*English*); Central African Republic (*Sangho*); Chad; Congo; Côte d'Ivoire; France; Gabon; Guinea; Haiti (*Creole*); Laos (*Laotian*); Lebanon (*Arabic*); Luxembourg (*German and Letzeburgesch*); Madagascar (*Malagasy*); Mali; Morocco (*Arabic*); Mauritania (*Arabic*); Niger; Rwanda (*Kinyarwanda*); Senegal; Switzerland (1,000,000 French speaking); Togo; Tunisia (*Arabic*); Vietnam (*Vietnamese*); Zaire. French is also spoken in the Overseas Departments (*see* above).

GABON
(République Gabonaise)

President, El Hadj Omar Bongo, *assumed office,* Dec. 1967, *re-elected,* Feb. 1973, Dec. 1979 and Nov. 1986.

COUNCIL OF MINISTERS
(as at June 1, 1991)

Prime Minister, Casimir Oyé Mba.
Public Works, Construction and Territorial Administration, Zacharie Myboto.
Justice, Keeper of the Seals, Michel Anchouey.
Foreign Affairs and Co-operation, Ali Bongo.
Commerce, Consumption and Industry, Relations with Parliament, André Dieudonné Berre.
Town Planning, Housing, Adrien Nkoghe Essingone.
National Defence, War Veterans, Public Security and Immigration, Martin Fidèle Magnaga.
Territorial Administration and Local Collectives, Antoine Mboumbou-Miyakou.
Civil Service and Administrative Reform, Paulette Moussavou.
Finance, Budget and State Holdings, Paul Toungui.
Planning and Economic Development, Marcel Doupamby-Matoka.
Information, Posts and Telecommunications, and Government Spokesman, Jean Rémy Pendy-Bouyiki.
Mines, Hydrocarbons, Energy and Hydraulic Resources, Jean Ping.
National Education, Higher Education and Scientific Research, Marc Ropivia.
Public Health, Population, Social Affairs and National Solidarity, Eugène Kakou Mayaza.
Employment, Human Resources and Professional Training, Serge Mba.
Agriculture, Livestock and Rural Economy, Emmanuel Ondo Methogo.
Water, Forests and Environment, Eugène Capito.
Youth, Sports, Culture and Popular Education, in charge of Francophone Affairs, Pierre Claver Nzeng.
Transport, Jerome Ngoua Bekalé.

State Control and Para-Public Sector Reform, Jean-Baptiste Obiang Etoughe.
Tourism, National Parks and Leisure, Pépin Mongoskodji.
Small and Medium-Sized Enterprises and Handicrafts, Victor Mapangou Moucani Mietsa.

EMBASSY OF THE REPUBLIC OF GABON
27 Elvaston Place, SW7 5NL
[071–823 9986]

Ambassador Extraordinary and Plenipotentiary, Vincent Boulé (1991).

Gabon lies on the Atlantic coast of Africa at the Equator and is flanked on the north by Equatorial Guinea and Cameroon and on the east and south by the People's Republic of Congo. It has an area of 103,347 sq. miles (267,667 sq. km) and a population (UN estimate 1989) of 1,133,000.

Gabon elected on November 28, 1958 to remain an autonomous republic within the French Community and was proclaimed fully independent on August 17, 1960. The Constitution provides for an Executive President directly elected for a seven-year term, who appoints the Council of Ministers. There is a unicameral National Assembly comprising 120 members.

Following widespread unrest, a national conference was called in March 1990 and delegates forced President Bongo to legalize opposition parties. Several rounds of multi-party elections were held in September, October and November 1990 and eventually won by the ruling Parti democratique gabonais (PDG), amid allegations of fraud. The PDG formed a coalition government with several opposition parties but retained the most important portfolios.

Gabon's economy remains heavily dependent on oil, and, to a much lesser extent, other mineral resources, including manganese and uranium. Gabon has considerable timber reserves (particularly Okoumé) although production in this industry has stagnated in recent years.

The economy, which experienced considerable growth in real terms from the mid-1970s onwards, had since 1986 been adversely affected by the fall in oil prices. Revenue is expected to increase in the 1990s following major oil exploitation at Rabi-Kounga.

Gabon is a full member of OPEC.

Trade with UK

	1989	1990
Imports from UK	£14,945,000	£17,563,000
Exports to UK	2,389,000	1,809,000

CAPITAL.—ΨLibreville (251,000).
CURRENCY.—Franc CFA of 100 centimes.
FLAG.—Horizontal bands, green, yellow and blue.
NATIONAL ANTHEM.—La Concorde.
NATIONAL DAY.—August 17.

British Ambassador, (resident in Zaire).

FEDERAL REPUBLIC OF GERMANY
(Bundesrepublik Deutschland)

Federal President, Dr Richard von Weizsäcker, *born* 1920, *elected President of West Germany* May 22, 1984, *re-elected* May 23, 1989, *sworn in,* July 1, 1989, *for five years.*

CABINET
(as at January 17, 1991)

Federal Chancellor, Dr Helmut Kohl (CDU).
Foreign Affairs and Deputy Chancellor, Hans Dietrich Genscher (FDP).
Federal Chancellery, Rudolf Seiters (CDU).
Interior, Dr Wolfgang Schäuble (CDU).

Justice, Dr Klaus Kinkel (Independent).
Finance, Dr Theodor Waigel (CSU).
Economy, Jürgen Möllemann (FDP).
Agriculture, Ignaz Kiechle (CSU).
Labour and Social Affairs, Dr Norbert Blüm (CDU).
Defence, Dr Gerhard Stoltenberg (CDU).
Health, Gerda Hasselfeldt (CSU).
Women and Youth, Dr Angela Merkel (CDU).
Family and Elderly, Hannelore Rönsch (CDU).
Transport, Dr Günther Krause (CDU).
Environment, Dr Klaus Töpfer (CDU).
Posts and Telecommunications, Dr Christian Schwarz-Schilling (CDU).
Housing and Construction, Dr Irmgard Adam-Schwätzer (FDP).
Research, Dr Heinz Riesenhuber (CDU).
Education, Dr Rainer Ortleb (FDP).
Economic Co-operation, Carl-Dieter Spranger (CSU).

CDU: Christian Democratic Union; CSU: Christian Social Union; FDP: Free Democratic Party.

EMBASSY OF THE FEDERAL REPUBLIC OF GERMANY
23 Belgrave Square, SW1X 8PZ
[071–235 5033]

Ambassador Extraordinary and Plenipotentiary, His Excellency Baron Hermann von Richthofen (1988).

Minister Plenipotentiary, Helmut Wegner.
Minister-Counsellor, Dr Klaus-Peter Klaiber, CMG.
First Counsellors, F. Gröning (*Head of Press Dept.*); Dr R. Huber (*Head of Economic Dept.*); Dr J. Bakenhus (*Defence Research*); D. Greineder (*Scientific Affairs*); Dr R. Peters (*Agriculture*).

Area and Population.—The area of the Federal Republic is approximately 138,000 square miles (357,050 km²). The estimated population of the Federal Republic (on unification) was 78,700,000. The distribution of the population among the *Länder* at the end of 1990 was:

Baden-Württemberg	9·5m
Bavaria	11·2m
Berlin	3·4m
Brandenburg	2·6m
Bremen	0·65m
Hamburg	1·6m
Hesse	5·6m
Lower Saxony	7·2m
Mecklenburg–Western Pomerania	2·1m
North Rhine Westphalia	16·9m
Rhineland Palatinate	3·7m
Saarland	1·1m
Saxony	4·9m

Saxony Anhalt.........................	3·0m
Schleswig-Holstein	2·6m
Thuringia	2·5m

Vital Statistics.—There were 11·4 live births per 1,000 inhabitants in the Federal Republic in 1990 (West Germany only).

History.—The term 'deutsch' (German) probably began to be used in the 8th century and initially described the language spoken in the eastern part of the Frankish realm which reached its apogee in Charlemagne's reign, subsequently being divided into an eastern and western realm whose political and linguistic borders coincided. Then the term was transferred from the language to its speakers, and ultimately to the region they lived in. The first German realm was the Holy Roman Empire, established in AD 962 when Otto I of Saxony was crowned Emperor. The Empire endured until 1806, but from as early as the 12th century the achievement of a national state was prevented by territorial fragmentation into small principalities and dukedoms, the gradually increasing autonomy of their rulers weakening the central power.

The Holy Roman Empire was replaced by a loose association of the individual sovereign states known as the German Confederation, which survived until 1866 when it was dissolved and replaced by the Prussian-dominated North German Federation. Prussia, directed by its Prime Minister (later Chancellor) Otto von Bismarck, had translated its earlier economic predominance amongst the German states into political hegemony by the annexation of the duchies of Schleswig and Holstein from Denmark in 1864 and a decisive defeat of Austria in 1866 (the Seven Weeks' War) which ended Austrian influence over German politics. After the Franco-Prussian War of 1870–71 resulted in the defeat of France and the cession of Alsace and Lorraine, the south German principalities united with the northern federation to form a second German Empire, the King of Prussia being proclaimed Emperor at Versailles on January 18, 1871.

Germany's defeat in the 1914–18 War led to the abdication of the Emperor and the princes, and the country became a Republic. The 1919 Treaty of Versailles returned Alsace and Lorraine to France, large areas in the east of the country were lost to the newly created state of Poland, and all German colonies placed under the administration of other countries. The world economic crisis of 1929 led to the collapse of the Weimar Republic and the subsequent rise to power of the National Socialist movement of Adolf Hitler, who became Chancellor in 1933.

After concluding a Treaty of Non-Aggression with Soviet Russia in August 1939, Germany invaded Poland (Sept. 1, 1939), thus precipitating World War II, which lasted until 1945. Hitler committed suicide on April 30, 1945. On May 8, 1945, the unconditional surrender of all German forces was accepted by representatives of the Western Allied and Soviet Supreme Commanders.

THE POST WAR PERIOD.—After the unconditional surrender, the Four Powers (France, UK, USA, USSR) assumed supreme authority in Germany. Policy was agreed at the Potsdam Conference (July/August 1945) between the UK, USA and USSR. Germany was divided into American, French, British and Soviet zones of occupation. Supreme authority was exercised by the Commanders-in-Chief, each in his own zone of occupation and, in matters affecting Germany as a whole, jointly through the Control Council comprising the four Commanders. Berlin was placed under the joint administration of the Four Occupying Powers.

No central German government was permitted but several German central administrations were estab-

lished as support organs for the Control Council. A peace treaty with Germany was envisaged as concluding the occupation period. However, quadripartite control failed when differences with the USSR over the implementation of the Postdam Agreement could not be resolved; and against a background of growing international tension, the USSR withdrew from the Control Council in March 1948. The rift divided Germany *de facto* into East and West.

The Federal Republic of Germany (FRG) was created out of the three Western zones in 1949 when, following general elections, a federal government took office in Bonn. A Communist government was meanwhile established in the Soviet zone (henceforth the German Democratic Republic (GDR)). The Bonn/Paris Conventions in May 1955 terminated the occupation regime in West Germany and restored federal German autonomy subject to the reservation of Three Power rights and responsibilities relating to Berlin and to Germany as a whole, including the reunification of Germany and a peace settlement. The GDR became an ostensibly sovereign state in the same year.

In August 1961 the Soviet zone was sealed off, and the Berlin Wall was built along the zonal boundary, partitioning the western sectors of the city from the eastern.

In the course of the Brandt government's policy of Ostpolitik, normalizing relations with eastern Europe, the FRG established relations of a special kind with the GDR in 1972. This step did not constitute recognition by the FRG of the GDR, which in international law would have conceded the *de jure* division of Germany (as the GDR maintained). The FRG, however, recognized the GDR as a separate and independent state (the two states/one nation theory). The status of Berlin as a city under Four Power occupation remained unchanged, although the GDR claimed East Berlin as its capital and held West Berlin to be a separate political entity.

Soviet-initiated reform in eastern Europe during the late eighties brought unrest to the GDR. The mass exodus of its citizens via the open borders to the west culminated in the opening of the Berlin Wall in November 1989 and the collapse of Communist government there. The 'Treaty on the Final Settlement with respect to Germany', concluded between the FRG, GDR and the four former occupying powers on September 12, 1990, unified Germany with effect from October 3, 1990 as a fully sovereign state and NATO member occupying the territory of the former two Germanies and Berlin. Economic and monetary union preceded formal union on July 1, 1990. Unification is constitutionally the accession of Berlin and the five re-formed *Länder* of the GDR to the FRG which remains in being. The first government of the new Germany took office in January 1991 following the first all-German elections since 1933 on December 2, 1990. Early setbacks revealed the formidable problems of translating German unity into political, social and economic reality.

Government.—The Basic Law provides for a President, elected for a five-year term, a Lower House (*Bundestag*), with a four-year term of office, elected by direct universal suffrage, and an Upper House (*Bundesrat*) composed of 68 delegates of the *Länder*, without a fixed term of office.

The results of the elections held for the Bundestag on December 2, 1990, were as follows:

Party	Seats
Christian Democratic Union	258
Social Democrats	239
Christian Social Union	51
Free Democrats	79
Democratic Socialists	17
The Greens/Alliance 90	8

The Prime Ministers of the *Länder* governments in July 1991, were:

Ministers-President

Baden-Württemberg.—Erwin Teufel (CDU).
Bavaria.—Max Streibl (CSU).
Berlin.—Eberhard Diepgen (CDU) (*Governing Mayor*).
Brandenburg.—Manfred Stolpe (SPD).
Bremen.—Klaus Wedemeier (*Mayor*) (SPD).
Hamburg.—Henning Voscherau (*First Mayor*) (SPD).
Hesse.—Hans Eichel (SPD).
Lower Saxony.—Gerhard Schröder (SPD).
Mecklenburg-Western Pomerania.—Alfred Gomolka (CDU).
North Rhine-Westphalia.—Johannes Rau (SPD).
Rhineland-Palatinate.—Rudolf Scharping (SPD).
Saarland.—Oskar Lafontaine (SPD).
Saxony.—Kurt Biedenkopf (CDU).
Saxony-Anhalt.—Werner Münch (CDU).
Schleswig-Holstein.—Björn Engholm (SPD).
Thuringia.—Josef Duchac (CDU).

Law and Justice.—Judicial authority is exercised by the Federal Constitutional Court, the Federal courts provided for in the Basic Law and the courts of the Länder.

The death sentence has been abolished.

Economy

Despite the division of Germany, which cut off from the Federal Republic the main food-producing areas of eastern Germany and some of the principal centres of light industry, the Federal Republic restored Germany's position as the main industrial power on the Continent. It is the most economically powerful member of the European community.

The immediate impact of unification, however, was to impose a severe strain on the federal economy. Massive government investment in the former GDR (estimated at DM150 billion for 1991) resulted in the first federal budgetary and trade deficits for ten years, tax increases, rising interest rates and serious inflationary pressures (high by German standards, at over 4 per cent in July 1991). Boom conditions were, however, experienced in the West. The gross national product in 1990 was estimated at DM2443·8 billion, representing a 4·6 per cent growth over 1989. Unemployment also fell sharply as industrial production and sales of services rose to meet the new demand generated in the former GDR.

In East Germany the immediate price of integration has been high. In particular, the task of transforming eastern Germany into a market economy brought a drastic fall in output (down by two-thirds since 1989), a similar rise in unemployment and estimates of 20 per cent inflation as consumer subsidies are cut and wages increase rapidly to West German levels. Also, the unexpected loss of East Germany's traditional trading outlets in eastern Europe following currency reform in July 1990 left East German goods without an effective market. Financing East German recovery is expected to require government funding at present levels for at least the next ten years.

Industrial Production.—The Federal Republic has a predominantly industrial economy. Principal industries are coal mining, iron and steel production, machine construction, the electrical industry, the manufacture of steel and metal products, chemicals and textiles, and the processing of foodstuffs. The index of industrial net production adjusted for irregularities of the calendar (1985 = 100) is as follows:

West Germany	1989	1990
Mining	85·9	85·1
Manufacturing industry	112·4	118·3
(i) Basic materials	108·9	110·9
(ii) Capital goods	116·2	123·0
(iii) Consumer goods	110·5	118·1
(iv) Foodstuffs	105·4	119·7
Power (electricity and gas)	108·6	111·8
Construction	118·2	124·1
Total industry	111·7	117·7

Annual production figures were:

West Germany	1989	1990
	Tonnes '000	
Hard coal	71,428	70,159
Brown coal	109,811	107,525
Crude petroleum	3,772	3,606
Pig iron	31,360	28,875
Raw steel	40,700	38,055
Rolled steel	31,697	29,728
Fuel oils	29,370	30,780
Petrol	20,068	21,424
Chemical fibres	837	838
Cement	28,494	30,433

East Germany	1989	1990
	Tonnes '000	
Brown coal	301,058	246,400
Cement	12,229	7,228
Rolled steel	9,383	—
Chemical fibres	192	132

Agriculture.—In 1990 total area of farmland was 14m hectares, of which 7·2m hectares (West Germany only) were arable land. Forest areas cover 7·4m hectares (West Germany only).

Crop yields were (tonnes):

West Germany	1988	1989
	Tonnes '000	
Rye	1,579·0	1,797·0
Wheat	11,922·2	11,065·0
Barley	9,587·2	9,757·0
Oats	2,038·5	1,552·0
Potatoes	7,433·7	7,811·0
Sugar beet	18,590·0	20,767·0
Rape seed	—	1,377·0

East Germany		1989
Rye		2,103·0
Wheat		3,477·0
Barley		4,683·0
Oats		476·0
Potatoes		9,167·0
Sugar beet		6,220·0
Rape seed		419·0

Milk production in 1989 was 24,243,000 tonnes (West Germany) and 9,300,000 tonnes (East Germany). Total yield of fisheries in 1989 (West Germany) was 166,495 tonnes, valued at DM230,776,000.

Labour.—Labour figures, in annual averages, were:

West Germany	1989	1990
Employment	27,729,000	28,453,000
Unemployed	2,038,000	1,883,000
Foreign workers	1,678,000	—

East Germany		1990
Employment		8,115,378
Unemployed		642,182
Short-time workers		1,795,264

Finance

East and West Germany	1991	1992
	DM billion	
Expenditure	410·33	422·44
Revenue	312·00	338·00

The 1991 plan included expenditure of DM122·6 billion on social welfare, DM52·5 billion on defence, DM35·5 billion on transport and DM13·9 billion on agriculture.

TRADE

West Germany	1989	1990
	DM million	
Total imports	506,465	550,628
Total exports	641,041	642,785

Of 1990 imports, 10·7 per cent were foodstuffs, 6·1 per cent raw materials and 70·5 per cent manufactured goods. Main trading partners in 1990 were (figures shown as percentage of total trade):

	Imports	Exports
France	11·8	13·0
Netherlands	10·2	8·4
Italy	9·4	9·3
USA	6·7	7·3
Belg./Lux.	7·2	7·4
UK	6·7	8·5
Japan	6·0	2·7

Trade with UK

	1989	1990
Imports from UK ..	£11,110,623,000	£13,169,405,000
Exports to UK	20,005,276,000	19,907,062,000

Communications (West Germany only). At the end of 1989 the state-owned railways of the Federal Republic (*Deutsche Bundesbahn*) measured 27,500 kilometres of which 11,400 kilometres were electrified, and the privately owned railways totalled approximately 2,904 kilometres. In 1988 the railways handled 315·4 million tonnes of goods. Classified roads measured 173,652 kilometres in 1989, of which motorways were 8,721 kilometres. The total number of motor vehicles registered at the beginning of 1990 was 34 million. Ocean-going shipping under the German flag in Dec. 1988, amounted to 4,034,000 tons gross. Inland waterways handled 233·3m tonnes of goods in 1988.

Social Welfare.—There is compulsory insurance against sickness, accident, old age and unemployment. Children's allowances, child rearing benefits and parental leave of absence are available in respect of all children. Pension schemes for widows and orphans of public servants are in operation. Public assistance is given to persons unable to earn their living, or with insufficient income to maintain a decent standard of living.

Education.—School attendance is compulsory for all children and juveniles between the ages of 6 and 18 and comprises nine years full-time compulsory education at primary and main schools (*Grund-und Hauptschulen*) and three years of compulsory vocational education on a part-time basis. In1988 (West Germany only) there were 20,713 primary and main schools (*Grund-und Hauptschulen*) with 3,652,565 pupils. Secondary modern schools (*Realschulen*) numbered 2,580 with 875,049 pupils. There were 2,867 other general secondary schools (*Gymnasien* including *Gesamtschulen*) with 1,820,559 pupils.

There were also 2,770 special schools (*Sonderschulen*) for physically and mentally handicapped and socially maladjusted children in the Federal Republic with 247,965 pupils.

The secondary school leaving examination (*Abitur*) entitles the holder to a place of study at a university or another institution of higher education.

Children below the age of 18 who are not attending a general secondary or a full-time vocational school have compulsory day-release at a vocational school. In 1988 (West Germany only) there were 2,728 full and part-time vocational schools (*Berufsschulen*) with 1,786,300 pupils and 277 vocational extension schools (*Berufsaufbauschulen*) with 8,709 pupils, 2,333 full-time vocational schools (*Berufsfachschulen*) with 285,254 pupils, 993 schools for secondary technical studies (*Fachoberschulen/Fachgymnasien*) with 200,174 students.

In 1989–90 there were a total of 1,508,241 students at institutions of higher education, of whom 1,019,507 were attending universities. The largest universities are in Munich, Berlin, Hamburg, Bonn and Cologne.

Language and Literature.—Modern (or New High) German has developed from the time of the Reformation to the present day, with differences of dialect in Austria and Alsace and in the German-speaking cantons of Switzerland. The literary language is usually regarded as having become fixed by Luther and Zwingli at the Reformation, since which time many great names occur in all branches, notably philosophy, from Leibnitz (1646–1716) to Kant (1724–1804), Fichte (1762–1814), Schelling (1775–1854) and Hegel (1770–1831); the drama from Goethe (1749–1832) and Schiller (1759–1805) to Gerhart Hauptmann (1862–1946); and in poetry, Heine (1797–1856). German authors have received the Nobel Prize for Literature on seven occasions—Theodor Mommsen (1902), R. Eucken (1908), P. Heyse (1909), Gerhart Hauptmann (1912), Thomas Mann (1929), N. Sachs (1966) and Heinrich Böll (1972).

Religion (West Germany only).—In 1987 there were 25·2 million Protestants in the Federal Republic, 26·2 million Roman Catholics, and 1·6 million Muslims. The number of Jews was 27,711 in 1988.

CAPITAL.—Berlin. By decision of the Bundestag, the seat of government is to be transferred from Bonn, Federal Germany's post-war provisional capital to the historical capital, Berlin. The move will take many years to complete. The *Bundesrat* (upper house) will remain in Bonn.

The population of the principal cities and towns in the Federal Republic in 1989 was:

Berlin	3,268,300	Duisburg	527,400
Hamburg	1,603,000	Dresden	501,000
Munich	1,211,600	Hanover	498,500
Cologne	937,500	Nuremberg ..	480,000
Essen	620,600	Chemnitz....	299,200
Frankfurt am		Bonn	280,000
Main	625,300	Rostock	253,000
Dortmund ...	587,300	Magdeburg ..	250,600
Düsseldorf...	569,600	Halle........	242,000
Stuttgart....	562,700	Erfurt........	217,200
Leipzig	548,400	Potsdam......	142,900
Bremen	535,000		

CURRENCY.—Deutsche Mark (DM) of 100 Pfennig.

FLAG.—Horizontal bars of black, red and gold.

NATIONAL ANTHEM.—Einigkeit und Recht und Freiheit (Unity and right and freedom).

NATIONAL DAY.—May 23.

BRITISH EMBASSY

Friedrich-Ebert-Allee 77, 5300 Bonn 1
[Bonn 23 40 61]

Ambassador Extraordinary and Plenipotentiary, His Excellency Sir Christopher Leslie George Mallaby, KCMG (1988).

Minister, Miss L. P. Neville Jones, CMG.

Counsellors, C. Budd, CMG (*Political*); B. H. Dinwiddy; Miss A. Walker (*Defence Supply*); D. S. Broucher (*Economic*); R. F. Escritt (*Science and Technology*); P. V. Rollitt (*Management*); J. Franklin (*Labour*).

First Secretaries, J. I. Link; R. E. Brinkley; R. W. Barnett; V. Evans; D. J. Grieg; J. Drake; P. Cunningham; S. Wordsworth.

Legal Adviser, P. Waterworth.

Defence Attaché, Brig. A. P. Sims.

Military Attaché, Lt.-Col. J. D. Colson.

Naval Attaché, Capt. J. McLees.

Asst. Naval Attaché, Lt.-Cdr. J. Apps.
Air Attaché, Air Cdre W. M. Craghill.
Head of Visa Section (Düsseldorf), M. Carbine.
Chaplain, Rev. J. Newsome.

BERLIN OFFICE
Olympic Stadium, Hanns-Braun Strasse,
1000 Berlin 19
International Trade Centre, Georgenstrasse,
1028 Berlin

Minister and Head of Mission, M. St. E. Burton, CMG, CVO.
Counsellors, Sir John Ramsden, Bt. (*Deputy Head of Mission*); M. J. Reynolds.
First Secretaries, R. M. Sands (*Management*); H. R. Mortimer (*Political*); O. J. Traylor; P. J. Laing (*Political*); B. Brett Rooks (*Information*); A. R. Nuttall (*Director of Trade Promotion for Eastern Germany*); D. J. Peate, OBE (*Commercial*); R. H. Sharpe (*Economic*).

There are British Consulates-General at *Berlin, Düsseldorf, Frankfurt, Hamburg, Munich* and *Stuttgart.*

BRITISH COUNCIL
Representative, M. Ward, Hahnenstrasse 6, 5000 Cologne 1. Offices at *Berlin, Hamburg* and *Munich* and British Council libraries at all four centres.

BRITISH CHAMBER OF COMMERCE
Neumarkt 14, D-5000 Köln 1

Director, Herr Heumann.

GREECE
(Elliniki Dimokratia)

President of the Hellenic Republic, Constantine Karamanlis, *elected* May 4, 1990.

CABINET
(as at August 8, 1991)

Prime Minister, Minister for the Aegean, Constantine Misotakis.
Deputy PMs, Tzannis Tzannetakis; Athanassios Kanellopoulos.
Minister of State, Mikis Theodorakis.
Minister to the PM, Miltiades Evert.
Foreign Affairs, Antonis Samaras.
Interior, Nikolaos Kleitos.
National Defence, Ioannis Varvitsiotis.
National Economy, Efthymios Christodoulou.
Finance, Ioannis Paleokrassas.
Merchant Marine, Aristotelis Pavlidis.
Agriculture, Sotiris Kouvelas.
Labour, Aristides Kalantzakos.
Health, Welfare and Social Security, George Sourlas.
Justice, Michalis Papaconstantinou.
Education and Religious Affairs, Georg Souflias.
Culture, Anna Psarouda-Benaki.
Public Order, Theodore Anagnostopoulos.
Macedonia and Thrace, Panayiotis Hadzinikolaou.
Environment, Town Planning and Public Works, Achileas Karamanlis.
Industry and Commerce, Andreas Andrianopoulos.
Transport and Communications, Nikolaos Gelestathis.
Tourism, Ioannis Kefaloyannis.

EMBASSY OF GREECE
1A Holland Park, W11 3TP
[071–727 8040]

Ambassador Extraordinary and Plenipotentiary, His Excellency George D. Papoulias (1990).
Defence Attaché, Capt. H. Zevelakis.

There are Honorary Consulates at *Belfast, Birmingham, Edinburgh, Falmouth, Glasgow, Leeds* and *Southampton.*

A maritime state in the south-east of Europe, bounded on the N. by Albania, Yugoslavia and Bulgaria, on the S. and W. by the Ionian and Mediterranean seas, and on the E. by Turkey, with an estimated area of 50,944 sq. miles (131,944 sq. km). Population (1991 Census) is 10,256,464.

The main areas of Greece are: *Macedonia* (which includes Mt. Athos and the island of Thasos), *Thrace* (including the island of Samothrace), *Epirus*, *Thessaly, Continental Greece* (which includes the island of Euboea and the Sporades or 'scattered islands' of which the largest is Skyros), the *Peloponnese* (or *Morea*), the *Dodecanese* or *Southern Sporades* (12 islands occupied by Italy in 1911 during the Italo-Turkish War and ceded to Greece by Italy in 1947) consisting of Rhodes, Astypalaia, Karpathos, Kassos, Nisyros, Kalymnos, Leros, Patmos, Kos, Symi, Khalki and Tilos, the *Cyclades* (a circular group numbering about 200, with a total area of 923 sq. miles; the chief islands are Syros, Andros, Tinos, Naxos, Paros, Santorini, Milos and Serifos), the *Ionian Islands* (Corfu, Paxos, Levkas, Ithaca, Cephalonia, Zante and Cerigo), the *Aegean Islands* (Chios, Lesbos, Limnos and Samos). In *Crete* there was for over 1,500 years (3000 to 1400 BC) a flourishing civilization which spread its influence far and wide throughout the Aegean, and the ruins of the palace of Minos at Knossos afford evidence of astonishing comfort and luxury. Greek civilization emerged about 1300 BC and the poems of Homer, the blind poet of Chios, which were probably current about 800 BC, record the 10-year struggle between the Achaeans of Greece and the Phrygians of Troy (1194–1184 BC).

Language and Literature.—The spoken language of modern Greece is descended by a process of natural development from the Common Greek of Alexander's empire. *Katharevousa*, a conservative literary dialect evolved by Adamantios Corais (Diamant Coray), who lived and died in Paris (1748–1833) and used for official and technical matters, has been phased out. Novels and poetry are mostly composed in *dimotiki*, a progressive literary dialect which owes much to John Psycharis (1854–1929). The poets Solomos, Palamas, Cavafis, Sikelianos, Seferis and Elytis have won a European reputation.

Religion.—Over 97 per cent of the people are adherents of the Greek Orthodox Church, which is the State religion, all others being tolerated and free from interference. The Church of Greece recognizes the spiritual primacy of the Œcumenical Patriarch of Constantinople, but is otherwise a self-governing body administered by the Holy Synod under the Presidency of the Archbishop of Athens and All Greece. It has no jurisdiction over the Church of Crete, which has a degree of autonomy under the Œcumenical Patriarch, nor over the Monastic Community of Mount Athos and the Church in the Dodecanese, both of which come directly under the Œcumenical Patriarch.

Government.—A military coup on April 21, 1967, suspended parliamentary government and, following an unsuccessful royal counter-coup on December 13, 1967, King Constantine went into voluntary exile in Rome. On June 1, 1973 the monarchy was abolished and a republic established under the Presidency of George Papadopoulos.

The overthrow of Archbishop Makarios, President of Cyprus, on July 15, 1974, by a military coup led by Greek officers of the Cypriot National Guard caused an international crisis, in the wake of which the heads of the Greek armed forces decided, on July 23, to relinquish power. Konstantinos Karamanlis, Prime Minister between 1955 and 1963, returned from his self-imposed exile in Paris to form a provisional Government, and the first elections for ten years were held on November 17, 1974.

The constitutional position of the King, who was still in exile, remained unsettled until December 8, when by a referendum, the Greek people rejected 'crowned democracy' by 69·2 per cent to 30·8 per cent and Greece became a republic. A new constitution came into force on June 11, 1975.

The unicameral 300-member Chamber of Deputies is elected for a four-year term by universal adult suffrage under a system of proportional representation. The most recent general election was held on April 8, 1990.

Defence.—The strength of the Army is 130,000 backed up by some 50,000 in the National Guard. The Navy consists of 19,500 men and is equipped with a fleet of destroyers, submarines, patrol boats and amphibious warfare vessels, mostly of US, French, Dutch and German origin. The Air Force consists of 25,000 men and is equipped with aircraft disposed in 14 combat squadrons supported by the necessary transport, training, helicopter and reconnaissance squadrons. National service is 2 years on average.

Communications.—The 2,650 kilometres of Greek railways are state-owned with the exception of the Athens–Piraeus Electric Railway. Greek roads total somewhat over 35,500 kilometres, of which about 25 per cent are classified as national highways and just under 30,000 km are classified as provincial roads. The road connection with Albania was reopened in 1985.

On Dec. 31, 1986 the Greek mercantile fleet numbered 2,138 ships with a total tonnage of 24,792,516 tons gross. On the same day Greek-owned ships over 100 tons gross and registered under foreign flags numbered 276 with a total tonnage of 5,176,347 tons gross. Athens has direct airline links with Australasia, North America, most countries in Europe, Africa and the Middle East.

Education is free and compulsory from the age of 6 to 15 and is maintained by state grants. There are six universities, Athens, Salonika, Patras, Thrace, Ioannina and Crete. There are several other institutes of higher learning, mostly in Athens.

Production.—Though there has in recent years been a substantial measure of industrialization, agriculture still employs about a quarter of the working population. The most important agricultural products are tobacco, wheat, cotton, sugar and rice. The most important of the fruit trees are the olive,

peach, vine, orange, lemon, fig, almond and currant-vine, and now exports of Greek fresh fruit and vegetables have established themselves as an important contributor to the economy and have considerable growth potential. Currants, grown mainly around Patras, remain one of Greece's main exports, the United Kingdom being the principal purchaser.

The principal minerals mined in Greece are nickel, bauxite, iron ore, iron pyrites, manganese magnesite, chrome, lead, zinc and emery, and prospecting for petroleum is being carried on. Oil refineries are in operation near Athens and at Salonika, where there is also a petro-chemical plant. The chief industries are textiles (cotton, woollen and synthetics), chemicals, cement, glass, metallurgy, shipbuilding, domestic electrical equipment and footwear. In recent years new factories have been opened for the production of aluminium, nickel, iron and steel products, tyres, chemicals, fertilizers and sugar (from locally-grown beet). Food processing and ancillary industries have also grown up throughout the country. The development of the country's electric power resources, irrigation and land reclamation schemes and the exploitation of Greece's lignite resources for fuel and industrial purposes are also being carried out. Tourism has developed rapidly, but is now slowing down.

TRADE

	1986	1987
Total imports ...	Drs 1,587,214·0m	Drs 1,758,951·1m
Total exports ...	789,994·6m	880,958·2m

Trade with UK

	1989	1990
Imports from UK	£571,409,000	£682,887,000
Exports to UK	395,086,000	400,476,000

CAPITAL.—Athens, population (including ΨPiraeus and suburbs), 3,096,775 (1991 Census). Other large towns are (1981) ΨSalonika (706,180); ΨPatras (154,596); ΨVolos (107,407); Larissa (102,426); and ΨKavalla (56,705).

Larger towns in the islands are: in Crete—ΨHeraklion or Candia (102,398), ΨCanea (47,451), and ΨRethymnon (18,190); in the Ionian Islands—ΨCorfu (36,901); in the Dodecanese—ΨRhodes (41,425); in the Cyclades—ΨSyros Hermoupolis (13,877); in Lesbos—ΨMytilene (24,991); in Chios—ΨChios (24,070).

CURRENCY.—Drachma of 100 leptae.

FLAG.—Blue and white stripes with a white cross on a blue field in the canton.

NATIONAL ANTHEM.—Imnos Eis Tin Eleftherian (Hymn to Freedom).

NATIONAL DAY.—March 25 (Independence Day).

BRITISH EMBASSY
1 Ploutarchou Street, 10675 Athens
[Athens 7236211/9]

Ambassador Extraordinary and Plenipotentiary, His Excellency Sir David Miers, KBE, CMG (1989).

Deputy Head of Mission and Consul-General, R. N. Culshaw, MVO.

Counsellors, W. V. Fell; Dr J. L. Munby (*Cultural Affairs*).

Defence and Military Attaché, Brig. G. Bulloch.

Naval and Air Attaché, Capt. J. J. Pearson.

Hon. Attaché, Elizabeth Bayard French (*Director, British School of Archaeology*).

BRITISH CONSULAR OFFICES

There are British Consular Offices at *Athens, Corfu, Samos, Rhodes, Salonika, Heraklion* (Crete), *Syros* and *Volos.*

BRITISH COUNCIL
17 Plateia Philikis Etairias (PO Box 3488)
Kolonaki Square, Athens 10210

Representative, Dr J. L. Munby.
There is also an office at *Salonika* and British Council libraries at both centres.

BRITISH-HELLENIC CHAMBER OF COMMERCE
25 Vas. Sofias Avenue, GR-106 74 Athens
[72 10 361]

GUATEMALA
(República de Guatemala)

Head of State, President Jorge Serrano Elias, *inaugurated*, January 1991.

CABINET
(as at June 1991)

Minister of Government, Fernando Hurtado Prem.
Foreign Affairs, Alvaro Arzu Irigoyen.
National Defence, General Luís Enrique Mendoza García.
Finance, Richard Aitkenhead Castillo.
Communications, Alvaro Heredia.
Education, María Luisa Beltranena Padilla.
Agriculture, Adolfo José Boppel Carrera.
Economy, Juan Luís Mirón.
Public Health and Social Welfare, Dr Miguel Angel Montepeque Contreras.
Labour and Social Welfare, Dr Mario Solorzano Martínez.
Energy and Mines, Carlos Leonel Hurtarte Castro.
Special Affairs, Antulio Castillo Barajas.
Urban and Rural Development, Manolo Bendfeldt Alejos.
Culture and Sport, Roberto Tomás Ogarrio Marín.

EMBASSY OF GUATEMALA
13 Fawcett Street, SW10 9HN
[071–351 3042]

Ambassador Extraordinary and Plenipotentiary, His Excellency Dr Erwin Blandon (1987).

Guatemala, in Central America, is situated in N. lat. from 13° 45′ to 17° 49′, and in W. long. from 88° 12′ 49″ to 92°13′ 43″, and has an area of 42,042 sq. miles (108,889 sq. km.), and a population (UN estimate 1989) of 8,935,000.

The Republic is divided into 22 departments, and is traversed from W. to E. by an elevated mountain chain, containing several volcanic summits rising to 13,000 feet above sea level; earthquakes are frequent. The country is well watered by numerous rivers; the climate is hot and malarial near the coast, temperate in the higher regions. The rainfall in the capital averages 57 in. per annum. The chief seaports are San José de Guatemala and Champerico on the Pacific and Santo Tomás de Castilla and Puerto Barrios on the Atlantic side.

Language and Literature.—Spanish is the language of the country, but 40 per cent of the population speak an Indian language. Since the establishment of the university in the capital, education has received a marked impulse and the high figure of illiteracy is being reduced. The national library contains about 80,000 volumes in Spanish.

Government.—The constitutionally elected president, Gen. Miguel Ydigoras Fuentes, was overthrown on March 31, 1963 by the Army, which handed executive and legislative powers to the Minister of Defence, Col. Enrique Peralta Azurdia. Elections for a new Congress and for President and Vice-President took place on March 6, 1966. The constitution was suspended 'for as long as the situation demands'

following a military coup in March 1982. An amnesty for guerrillas was unsuccessful and the Army was fully occupied dealing with the proliferating subversive groups throughout the country.

Elections for a Constituent Assembly were held on July 1, 1984, as promised by Gen. Mejía Víctores when he overthrew Gen. Ríos Montt in 1983. The Assembly drew up a new Constitution, promulgated in June 1985, and a new electoral law, paving the way for presidential, governmental and municipal elections which were won by the Christian Democratic Party. Presidential elections, held in November 1990, were won by Jorge Serrano Elias, the leader of the Solidarity Action Movement (MAS). MAS failed to win Congressional elections and a government of national unity was formed.

Finance.—The Central Government revenue in 1988 was Quetzales 2,500 million, and expenditure Quetzales 3,000 million.

TRADE

	1988
Imports (c.i.f.)	US$1,557·0 m
Exports (f.o.b.)	1,033·8 m

Trade with UK

	1989	1990
Imports from UK	£52,324,000	£17,551,000
Exports to UK	6,950,000	42,034,000

The principal export is coffee, other articles being manufactured goods, sugar, bananas, cotton, beef and essential oils. The chief imports are petroleum, vehicles, machinery and foodstuffs.

CAPITAL.—Guatemala City, population estimate, 1,300,000. Quezaltenango has a population of over 100,000. Other towns are ΨPuerto Barrios (23,000), Mazatenango (21,000), and Antigua (30,000).

CURRENCY.—Quetzal (Q) of 100 centavos.
FLAG.—Three vertical bands, blue, white, blue; coat of arms on white stripe.
NATIONAL ANTHEM.—Guatemala Feliz (Guatemala be praised).
NATIONAL DAY.—September 15.

BRITISH EMBASSY
Centro Financiero Torre II (7th Floor), Seventh Avenue 5–10 Zone 4, Guatemala City
[Guatemala City 321601]

Ambassador Extraordinary and Plenipotentiary, His Excellency Justin Nason, OBE (1990).

GUINEA
(République de Guinée)

President, Gen. Lansana Conté, *took power*, April 3, 1984.

COUNCIL OF MINISTERS
(as at June 1991)

Regional Ministers, Lt.-Col. Abou Camara (*Maritime Guinea*); Cmdt. Kissi Camera (*Upper Guinea*); Lt.-Col. Henri Tofani (*Middle Guinea*); Cmdt. Ibrahima Sory Diallo (*Forest Region*).
Foreign Affairs, Cmdt. Jean Traore.
Ministers of the Presidency, Cmdt. Abdourahmane Diallo (*National Defence*); Réné Alsény Gomez (*Secretary-General*); Hervé Vincent Bangoura (*Information, Culture and Tourism*); Cmdt. Henry Foulah (*Economy and Finance*).
Planning and International Co-operation, Ibrahima Sylla.
Economy and Finance, Edouard Benjamin.
Administrative Reform and Civil Service, Mamouna Bangoura.
Interior and Decentralization, Alhassane Conde.

Agriculture and Livestock, Koly Aboubacar Kourouma.
Natural Resources and the Environment, Cmdt. Mohamed Lamine Traore.
Posts and Telecommunications, Capt. Fassou Jean Claude Kourouma.
Town Planning and Housing, Dr Bana Sidibe.
Public Health and Population, Dr Madigbè Fofana.
Transport and Public Works, Cmdt. Ibrahima Diallo.
Trade, Industry and Handicrafts, Ousmane Sylla.
National Education, responsible for Higher Education and Scientific Research, Mamadi Diawara.
Justice, Cmdt. Facinet Toure.
Social Affairs and Employment, Bassirou Barry.
Youth and Sports, Capt. Gbago Zoumanigui.

EMBASSY OF THE REPUBLIC OF GUINEA
51 rue de la Faisanderie, 75016 Paris, France
[Paris 47048148]

Ambassador Extraordinary and Plenipotentiary, His Excellency Marcel Martin (1991).

Formerly part of French West Africa, Guinea has a coastline on the Atlantic Ocean between Guinea-Bissau and Sierra Leone and in the interior is adjacent to Senegal, Mali, Côte d'Ivoire, Liberia and Sierra Leone. Area, 94,926 sq. miles (245,857 sq. km). The population (UN estimate 1989) is 6,706,000, mostly the Fullah, Malinké and Soussou tribes.

Government.—Guinea was separated from Senegal in 1891 and administered by France as a separate colony until 1958. In a referendum held in Sept. 1958, Guinea rejected the new French Constitution and on October 2, 1958 became an independent republic governed by a Constituent Assembly. M. Sékou Touré, Prime Minister in the Territorial Assembly, assumed office as head of the new Government, and was elected President in 1961.

Under a provisional constitution, adopted in November 1958, powers of government are exercised by a president assisted by the Cabinet. The President, eligible for a term of seven years and for re-election, is head of state and of the armed forces. President Sékou Touré died in March 1984; a few days later there was a military coup. Guinea is now ruled by a military government, which is directed by a Military Committee for National Recovery (CMRN). A new constitution, providing for the end of military rule and the introduction of a two-party system within five years, was approved by referendum in December 1990.

Production, etc.—The principal products of Guinea are bauxite, alumina, iron-ore, palm kernels, millet, rice, coffee, bananas, pineapples and rubber. At Sangaredi in the mountainous hinterland, where the rivers Senegal, Gambia and Niger have their sources, large deposits of bauxite are mined. Deposits of iron ore, gold, diamonds and uranium have also been discovered. Principal imports are cotton goods, manufactured goods, tobacco, petroleum products, sugar, rice, flour and salt; exports, bauxite, alumina, iron-ore, diamonds, coffee, hides, bananas, palm kernels and pineapples.

Trade with UK

	1989	1990
Imports from UK	£20,402,000	£11,368,000
Exports to UK	15,899,000	11,508,000

CAPITAL.—ΨConakry (763,000). Other towns are Kankan, which is connected with Conakry by a railway, Kindia, N'Zérékoré, Mamou, Siguiri and Labé.
CURRENCY.—Guinea franc of 100 centimes.
FLAG.—Three vertical stripes of red, yellow and green.

NATIONAL DAY.—October 2 (Anniversary of Proclamation of Independence).

British Ambassador (resident in Dakar, Senegal).

GUINEA-BISSAU
(República da Guiné-Bissau)

President of the Council of State (Head of State), Minister of Defence, Interior, Brig.-Gen. João Bernardo Vieira, *took power, Nov. 1980; elected for a five-year term, June 1989.*

COUNCIL OF MINISTERS
(as at July 1991)

First Vice President, Minister of State for the Armed Forces, Col. Iafai Camara.
Second Vice President, Minister of Justice, Vasco Cabral.
Minister of State for Rural Development and Agriculture, Carlos Correia.
Minister of State for Social Affairs, Carmen Pereira.
Minister of State for Economy and Finance, Manuel Santos.
Minister of State at the Presidency, Fidelis Cabral de Almada.
Women's Affairs, Francisca Pereira.
Natural Resources and Industry, Filinto de Barros.
Foreign Affairs, Julio Semedo.
Civil Service, Labour, Mario Cabral.
Commerce and Tourism, Luis Oliveira Sanca.
Fisheries, Freire Monteiro.
International Co-operation, Bernardino Cardoso.
Public Health, Henriqueta Godinho Gomes.
Transport, Avito Jose da Silva.
Public Works, Construction and Town Planning, Alberto Antonio Voss Lima Gomes.
Information and Telecommunications, Mussa Djassi.
Regional Ministers, Mario Mendes (*Eastern Province*); Vasco Salvador Corneia (*Southern Province*); Zeca Martins (*Northern Province*).
Minister-Governor of the Central Bank, Pedro Godinho Gomes.
Education, Alexandre Funtado.

EMBASSY OF THE REPUBLIC OF GUINEA-BISSAU
Avenue Franklin Roosevelt 70,
1050 Brussels, Belgium
(Brussels 6470890)

Ambassador Extraordinary and Plenipotentiary, new appointment awaited.

Guinea-Bissau, formerly Portuguese Guinea, lies in Western Africa, between Senegal and Guinea; it has an area of 13,948 sq. miles (36,125 sq. km), and has a population (UN estimate 1989) of 966,000. The main ethnic groups are the Balante, Malinké, Fulani, Mandjako and Pepel.

Guinea-Bissau achieved independence on September 24, 1974. Luis Cabral was ousted in a coup led by Maj. (now Brig.-Gen.) Vieira in November 1980. Following the coup the Assembly was suspended, and a Revolutionary Council was established. Under a new constitution adopted in April 1984 the Revolutionary Council became a 15-member Council of State, and a parliament was set up. The ruling African Party for the Independence of Guinea and Cape Verde (PAIGC) voted to introduce a multiparty system in January 1991; elections, under Portuguese supervision, are to be held in 1992.

Economy.—The country produces rice, coconuts, ground-nuts and palm oil products. Cattle are raised, and there are bauxite deposits in the south.

Trade with UK

	1989	1990
Imports from UK	£1,185,000	£924,000
Exports to UK	29,000	833,000

CURRENCY.—Guinea-Bissau peso of 100 centavos.
FLAG.—Horizontal bands of yellow over green with vertical red band in the hoist charged with a black star.
NATIONAL DAY.—September 24 (Independence Day).

British Ambassador, (resident in Dakar, Senegal).

HAITI
(République d'Haiti)

President, Jean-Bertrand Aristide, *sworn in* February 7, 1991.

CABINET
(as at June, 1991)

Prime Minister, Minister for Defence, Interior, René Preval.
Justice, Karl Auguste.
Foreign Affairs and Worship, Denise Jean-Louis.
Economy and Finance, Marie-Michele Rey.
National Education, Youth and Sports, Lesley Voltaire.
Information and Co-ordination, Marie-Laurence Lassegue.
Public Health and Population, Daniel Henrys.

Agriculture, National Resources and Rural Development, François Sevrain.
Social Affairs, Myrtho Céleston.
Public Works, Transport and Communications, Frantz Verella.
Planning, External Co-operation and Civil Service, Renaud Bernardin.
Commerce and Industry, Jean François Chamblain.

The London Embassy of the Republic of Haiti closed on March 30, 1987.

The Republic of Haiti occupies the western third of the island of Hispaniola, which, after Cuba, is the largest island in the West Indies.

The area of the Republic, including off-shore islands, is 10,714 sq. miles (27,750 sq. km) (of which about three-quarters is mountainous), with a population (UN estimate 1989) of 5,609,000.

Climate.—The climate is tropical with comparatively little difference in the temperatures between the summer (March–Oct.) and the winter (Nov.–Feb.). Humidity is high, especially in the autumn.

Language.—Following the new constitution of March 1987 both French and Creole are regarded as the official languages of Haiti. French is the language of the government and the press, but it is only spoken by the educated minority. The usual language of the people is Creole.

Government.—Haiti was a French colony under the name of Saint-Domingue from 1697. The slave

population, estimated at 500,000, revolted in 1791 under the leadership of Toussaint L'Ouverture, who was born a slave and made himself Governor General of the colony. He capitulated to the French in 1802 and died in captivity in 1803. Resistance was continued by Jean Jacques Dessalines, also a former Negro slave, who, on January 1, 1804, declared the former French colony to be an independent state. It was at this time that the name Haiti, an aboriginal word meaning mountainous, was adopted. Dessalines became Emperor of Haiti, but was assassinated in 1806.

Dr Duvalier was installed as President in 1957 and held the position until his death in 1971. He was succeeded as President for life on the same day by his son, Jean Claude Duvalier, whom he had nominated as his successor. President Duvalier fled to France in February 1986 in the face of sustained popular unrest, and a council headed by Gen. Henri Namphy assumed power. In March 1987, by popular referendum, a new Constitution was agreed and Presidential elections scheduled for November; these were aborted following violence in the capital. The elections held in January 1988 were boycotted by a number of leading candidates but Leslie Manigat eventually won after a very low turnout. President Manigat was inaugurated in February 1988, but he and his government were ousted on June 19 by Gen. Henri Namphy. Manigat was deported to the Dominican Republic and Namphy set up a military government until he in turn was replaced in a coup by Lt.-Gen. Prosper Avril on September 18, 1988. Following growing government opposition in 1990, Prosper Avril resigned on March 10. The presidency devolved upon Ertha Pascal-Trouillot, advised by a 19-member Council of State. Father Jean-Bertrand Aristide, leader of the National Front for Change and Democracy, won a free presidential election, held on December 16, 1990.

Production.—In recent years measures for agricultural rehabilitation have been taken with the aim of a gradual restoration of productivity, which had declined after the ending of the colonial plantation system. The main project is a scheme for the irrigation of more than 70,000 acres of the Artibonite valley.

Coffee accounts for about 32 per cent of total exports, worth approximately US$55 million in 1986. Cocoa is the second largest export earner at US$4·5 million. Corn, 110,000 tonnes (1985), sorghum, 108,000 tonnes (1985), and rice are also grown. Increased production of tropical fruits and vegetables is being encouraged.

Industry.—Export assembly industries account for about 30 per cent of the total manufacturing industry in Haiti, employing an estimated 40,000 people. Items such as leather goods, textiles, electronic components and sports equipment are manufactured, using imported raw materials, for re-export, primarily to the USA Principal imports are raw materials for the export assembly sector, foodstuffs, machinery, vehicles, mineral oils and textiles.

Communications.—The main roads are asphalted and secondary roads are fair. Internal air services are maintained between the capital and the principal provincial towns. International air-services connect Port-au-Prince with the USA and other Caribbean and South American cities. The principal towns and villages are connected by telephone and/or telegraph. The telephone company is state owned (51 per cent) and the service both in Port-au-Prince and Inter-urban has been greatly improved. External telegraph, telephone and postal services are normal. There are several commercial radio stations and two television stations at Port-au-Prince.

Regular passenger liner services to New York have ceased, but cruise ships call occasionally. Freight sailings are frequent for the USA, Canada, Europe, Latin America (except Cuba) and the main Caribbean ports.

Education.—Education is free but estimates of illiteracy are as high as 85 per cent.

Trade with UK

	1989	1990
Imports from UK	£6,566,000	£6,807,000
Exports to UK	803,000	1,271,000

CAPITAL.—Ψ Port-au-Prince. Population estimated at about 1 million. Other centres are: Ψ Cap Haitien (54,691); Gonaives (36,736); Les Cayes (27,222); Jérémie (25,117); St Marc (20,504); Jacmel (16,449); Ψ Port de Paix (21,733).

CURRENCY.—Gourde of 100 centimes.

FLAG.—Horizontal blue over red with national arms on a white square in the centre.

NATIONAL ANTHEM.—La Dessalinienne.

NATIONAL DAY.—January 1.

British Ambassador, (resident in Kingston, Jamaica).

HOLY SEE
see VATICAN CITY STATE

HONDURAS
(Republica de Honduras)

President of the Republic, Rafael Leonardo Callejas, *assumed office*, January 27, 1990.

CABINET
(as at September 1991)

Interior and Justice, Francisco Cardona Arguelles.
Foreign Affairs, Mario Carias Zapata.
Defence, Col. Alvaro Antonio Romero.
Education, Jaime Martinez Guzman.
Finance, Benjamin Villanueva.
Economy, Ramon Medina Luna.
Communications, Public Works and Transport, Mauricio Membreno.
Health, Dr Cesar Castellanos.
Labour and Social Security, Rodolfo Rosales Abella.
Natural Resources, Mario Nufio Gamero.
Culture and Tourism, Sonia Canales De Mendieta.
Economic Planning, Manlio Martinez Cantor.
Director of National Agrarian Institute, Juan Ramon Martinez.

EMBASSY OF HONDURAS
115 Gloucester Place, W1H 3PJ
[071–486 4880]

Ambassador Extraordinary and Plenipotentiary, His
Excellency Carlos Zeron (1991).

Honduras, in Central America, lies between lat. 13°
and 16° 30′ N. and long. 83° and 89° 41′ W. with a
seaboard of about 375 miles on the Caribbean Sea and
an outlet, consisting of a small strip of coast 63 miles
in length on the Pacific. Its frontiers are contiguous
with those of Guatemala, Nicaragua and El Salvador.

The Republic contains a total area of approximately
43,277 sq. miles (112,088 sq. km) and is very mountainous, being traversed by the Cordilleras, with peaks
rising to 1,500 and 2,400 metres above sea level. Most
of the soil is poor and acidic, except for the coastal
plains of the north and some areas of the interior.
Rainfall is seasonal, May to October being wet and
November to April dry. Three-quarters of the territory is covered by pine forests which contribute to
much of the country's wealth in natural resources.
The population, estimated at 4,951,000 by the UN, is
of mixed Spanish and Indian blood. Garifunas in
Northern Honduras are of West Indian origin.

The language of the country is Spanish, although
English is the first language of many in the islands
and on the north coast. Primary and secondary
education is free, primary education being compulsory, and the Government has launched a campaign
to eradicate illiteracy.

Government.—Originally discovered and settled
by the Spanish at the beginning of the sixteenth
century Honduras formed part of the Spanish American Dominions for nearly three centuries until 1821
when independence was proclaimed. Under military
government from 1972–81, and after two terms of
Liberal administration, the most recent legislative
election in November 1989 was won by the Partido
Nacional (National Party). The new Government
took office in January 1990.

The Republic is divided into 18 departments, the
newest of which, Gracias a Dios, formed in 1957, is
now the home of thousands of Miskito Indian refugees
from Nicaragua.

Production.—Agriculture is mainly confined to
the large and fertile valleys on the wide Caribbean
plain, and the extensive valleys found in the Comay-
agua and Olancho regions of the interior. Reaching
inland from the Caribbean towards the eastern border
with Nicaragua a vast tropical forest area called the
Mosquitia provides valuable reserves of timber. Lead,
zinc and silver are mined on a small scale.

The chief exports are coffee, bananas and timber,
the most important woods being pine, mahogany and
cedar. Cattle raising and the exporting of frozen
meat is an important industry, and exports of shrimps
and lobsters are increasing. Other products are
tobacco, beans, maize, rice, cotton, palm oil, sugar
cane, cement and tropical fruits. There are large
tracts of uncultivated land.

Communications.—There are about 1,004 km of
railway in operation, chiefly to serve the banana
plantations and the Caribbean ports. There are
17,947 km of roads, of which 2,173 are paved, excluding
some 250 km of new major highways recently inau-

gurated. Improvements are being made and new roads built. There are 33 smaller airstrips and three international airports, Tegucigalpa, San Pedro Sula and La Ceiba.

ΨThe chief ports are Puerto Cortes, Tela and La Ceiba on the north coast, through which passes the bulk of the trade with the United States and Europe. Puerto Castilla is being developed as a deep-water container port, and San Lorenzo is also experiencing rapid growth.

TRADE

	1987	1988
	Lempiras	
Imports	2,646·1m	2,786·2m
Exports	1,986·9m	2,057·5m

Trade with UK

	1989	1990
Imports from UK	£5,518,000	£7,345,000
Exports to UK	12,121,000	11,661,000

CAPITAL.—Tegucigalpa, population (1987 estimate) 640,900; other towns are San Pedro Sula (429,300), ΨLa Ceiba (66,000), ΨPuerto Cortes (42,100), Choluteca (64,500) and ΨTela (27,800).

CURRENCY.—Lempira of 100 centavos.

FLAG.—Three horizontal bands, blue, white, blue (with five blue stars on white band).

NATIONAL ANTHEM.—Tu Bandera Es Un Lampo De Cielo (Your flag is a heavenly light).

NATIONAL DAY.—September 15.

BRITISH EMBASSY
Apartado Postal 290, Tegucigalpa
[Honduras 32–0612/18]

Ambassador Extraordinary and Plenipotentiary, His Excellency Peter John Streams, CMG (1989).

HUNGARY
(Magyar Köztársaság)

President, Arpad Göncz, *sworn in* August 3, 1990.

CABINET
(as at June 1991)

Prime Minister, Dr József Antall.
Interior, Dr Péter Boross.
Agriculture, Elemér Gergácz.
Justice, Dr István Balsai.
Industry and Commerce, Dr Péter Bod.
Environmental Protection, Sandor Keresztes.
Transport and Communications, Csaba Siklés.
Foreign Affairs, Géza Jeszenszky.
Defence, Lajos Für.
Labour, Dr Gyula Kiss.
Education and Culture, Dr Bertalan Andrásfalvy.
Public Welfare, László Surján.
International Economic Relations, Béla Kádár.
Finance, Mihály Kupa.
Minister without Portfolio, Ferenc Mádl.
State Secretaries:
International Economic Relations, László Bogár.
Finance, Katalin Botos.
PM's Office, Géza Entz, Gyorgy Matolcsi, Dr Miklós Palós.
Justice, Dr Tamás Isépy.
Foreign Affairs, Tamás Katona.
Social Welfare, Dr András Keleman.
Transport, Telecommunications, Zsolt Rajkai.
Agriculture, László Sarossy.
Labour, Tamás Szabó.
Environment, Mrs László Tarján.

EMBASSY OF THE REPUBLIC OF HUNGARY
35 Eaton Place, SW1X 8BY
[071–235 4048/7191]

Ambassador Extraordinary and Plenipotentiary, His Excellency Tibor Antalpéter (1990).

Counsellors, A. Gerelyes (*Consul*); T. Vajda (*Press*); E. Sziklai (*Commercial*).

Defence, Military and Air Attaché, Col. P. Szücs.

Area and Population.—The area of Hungary is 35,919 sq. miles (93,030 sq. km) with a population (1990) of 10,375,000.

Government.—Hungary, reconstituted a kingdom in 1920 after having been declared a republic on November 17, 1918, joined the Anti-Comintern Pact in February 1939 and entered the 1939–45 War on the side of Germany in 1941. On January 20, 1945 a Hungarian provisional government of liberation, which had been set up during the preceding December, signed an armistice under the terms of which the frontiers of Hungary were withdrawn to the limits existing in 1937, set under the Treaty of Trianon in 1919.

After the liberation, a coalition of the Smallholder, National Peasant, Social Democrat and Communist parties carried out major land reform and mines, heavy industry, banks and schools were nationalized. By 1949 the Communists had succeeded in gaining a monopoly of power. A campaign was opened to collectivize agriculture and by 1952 practically the entire economy had been 'socialized'. The Party formulated policy and the function of the Government was mainly executive.

The period from July 1956 to the outbreak of the national revolution on October 23 was marked by growing ferment in intellectual circles and increased discord within the Party. The withdrawal of Soviet troops from the country and free elections were among the demands put forward. Fighting broke out on the night of October 23 between demonstrators, who had been joined by large numbers of factory workers, and the State Security Police. Soviet forces intervened in strength early the next morning. By October 30 Soviet troops had withdrawn from Budapest and on November 3 an all-party coalition government under Imre Nagy was formed. This government was overthrown and the revolution suppressed as the result of a renewed attack by Soviet forces on Budapest in the early hours of November 4. The formation of a new Hungarian Revolutionary Worker Peasant Government under the leadership of Mr Kádár was announced.

From 1963, the government gradually introduced economic reforms and some political liberalization. Kádár was forced to resign in May 1989. In October 1989 the National Assembly (*Országgyülés*) approved an amended Constitution which described Hungary as an independent, democratic state. Multi-party elections took place in March and April 1990. The majority of seats were won by the Hungarian Democratic Forum, followed by the Alliance of Free Democrats. In May 1990 a coalition government was installed. The former ruling Communist Party, reconstituted as the Hungarian Socialist Party, is now in opposition.

Economy.—Since 1968 the Hungarian economy had been run according to a system which allowed more decentralized decision-making than in some other eastern European countries, although central control in vital areas such as the allocation of fuels and raw materials remained. The government has embarked upon the privatization of State-owned concerns and the return of nationalized land to its former owners.

Industrialization has made considerable progress in the last decade and now produces 68 per cent of national income. Industry is mainly based on imported raw materials but Hungary has its own coal (mostly brown), bauxite, considerable deposits of natural gas (some not yet under full exploitation), some iron ore and oil. Output figures in 1985 (1,000 tons): coal 24,042; bauxite 2,815; rolled steel 2,860; crude oil 2,000; cement 3,678. Natural gas production totalled 7,441 million cubic metres.

Agriculture still occupies an important place in the Hungarian economy. In 1990 ten and a half per cent of the entire land area was owned by state farms and a further 63·8 per cent was within co-operative farms. Co-operative farms will remain a feature of Hungarian agriculture. Production in 1989 was (tons):

Maize	6,700,000
Wheat	6,500,000
Sugar beet	5,300,000
Barley	854,000
Rye	261,000
Oats	145,000

Although there was a 1·8 per cent drop in GDP in 1989, per capita real income increased by about 2 per cent.

Religion and Education.—About two-thirds of the population are Roman Catholics, and the remainder mostly Calvinist. There are five types of schools under the Ministry of Education: kindergartens 3–6, general schools 6–14 (compulsory), vocational schools (15–18), secondary schools (15–18), universities and adult training schools (over 18).

Language and Literature.—Magyar, or Hungarian, is one of the Finno-Ugrian languages. Hungarian literature began to flourish in the second half of the sixteenth century. Among the greatest writers of the nineteenth and twentieth centuries are Mihály Vörösmarty (1800–1855), Sándor Petőfi (1823–1849), János Arany (1817–1882), Imre Madach (1823–1864), Kálmán Mikszáth (1847–1910), Endre Ady (1877–1918), Attila József (1905–1937), Mihály Babits (1883–1941) and Dezső Kosztolányi (1885–1936).

TRADE

	1989 Forints
Imports	523,200m
Exports	571,300m

Trade with UK

	1988	1990
Imports from UK	£117,947,000	£121,837,000
Exports to UK	105,221,000	102,741,000

CAPITAL.—Budapest, on the Danube; population (1985) 2,072,000. Other large towns are: Miskolc (212,000); Debrecen (210,000); Szeged (181,000) and Pécs (175,000).

CURRENCY.—Forint of 100 fillér.

FLAG.—Red, white, green (horizontally).

NATIONAL ANTHEM.—Isten Aldd Meg A Magyart (God Bless the Hungarians).

NATIONAL DAYS—March 15, August 20, October 23.

BRITISH EMBASSY
Harmincad Utca 6, Budapest V
[Budapest 118–2888]

Ambassador Extraordinary and Plenipotentiary, His Excellency John Allan Birch, CMG (1989).

Counsellor and Deputy Head of Mission, H. J. Pearce.

Defence and Military Attaché, Col. W. Ibbetson.

Air Attaché, Wg.-Cdr. M. Gaynor.

First Secretary and British Council Representative, Dr J. Grote.

Consul, F. A. Blogg.

ICELAND
(Island)

President, Vigdís Finnbogadóttir, *born* 1930, *elected* June 29, 1980, *re-elected,* July 1984 and June 1988.

CABINET
(as at April 30, 1991)

Prime Minister, Minister for the Statistical Bureau of Iceland, David Oddsson (IP).

Foreign Affairs and Trade, Jón Baldvin Hannibalsson (SDP).

Finance, Fridrik Sophusson (IP).

Fisheries, Justice and Ecclesiastical Affairs, Thorsteinn Pálsson (IP).

Education and Culture, Ólafur Einarsson (IP).

Social Affairs, Jóhanna Sigurthardóttir (SDP).

Health and Social Security, Sighvatur Björgvinsson (SDP).

Commerce, Industry and Nordic Co-operation, Jón Sigurthsson (SDP).

Agriculture and Communications, Halldór Blöndal (IP).

Environmental Affairs, Eidur Gudnason (SDP).

IP: Independence Party; SDP: Social Democrat Party.

EMBASSY OF ICELAND
1 Eaton Terrace, SW1W 8EY
[071–730 5131]

Ambassador Extraordinary and Plenipotentiary, His Excellency Helgie Ágústsson (1989).

Iceland is a large volcanic island in the North Atlantic Ocean, extending from 63° 23′ to 66° 33′ N. lat., and from 13° 22′ to 24° 35′ W. long., with an estimated area of 39,768 sq. miles (103,000 sq. km). The population was 253,482 on December 1, 1989.

Iceland was uninhabited before the ninth century, when settlers came from Norway. For several centuries a form of republican government prevailed, with an annual assembly of leading men called the *Althing,* but in 1241 Iceland became subject to Norway, and later to Denmark. During the colonial period, Iceland maintained its cultural integrity but a deterioration in the climate, together with frequent volcanic eruptions and outbreaks of disease, led to a serious fall in the standard of living and to a decline in the population to little more than 40,000. In the nineteenth century a struggle for independence began which led first to home rule for Iceland under the Danish Crown (1918), and later to complete independence under a republican form of rule in 1944.

Government.—The parliamentary (*Althing*) elections in April 1991 gave the Independence Party 28 seats, Progressives 13, Social Democratic Party 10, People's Alliance 9 and Women's Alliance 6. David Oddsson formed a new coalition government on April 30, 1991.

Language and Literature.—The ancient Norraena (or Northern tongue) presents close affinities to Anglo-Saxon and as spoken and written in Iceland today differs little from that introduced into the island in the ninth century. There is a rich literature with two distinct periods of development, from the mid-11th to the late 13th century and from the early 19th century to the present.

Production.—Iceland has considerable resources of hydro-electric and geothermal energy. It is estimated that exploited water power (4,000 Gigawatt hours/a) represents only about 9 per cent of that economically exploitable, whereas only 5 per cent of the estimated 80,000 Gigawatt hours/a of available geothermal power has so far been harnessed. Energy-intensive heavy industry includes an aluminium smelter, a nitrogen fertilizer factory, a diatomite plant and a ferro-silicone plant.

The principal exports are frozen fish fillets, salt fish, stock fish, fresh fish on ice, frozen scampi, fishmeal and oil, skins and aluminium; the imports consist of almost all the necessities of life, the chief items being petroleum products, transport equipment, textiles, foodstuffs, animal feeds, timber, and alumina.

At January 1, 1990, the mercantile marine consisted of 622 vessels of under 100 gross tons and 345 ships of 100 gross tons and over; a total of 967 vessels (178,314 gross tons), of which 842 (116,011 gross tons) are decked fishing vessels. There are regular shipping services between Reykjavík and Felixstowe, Humber ports and the Continent.

A regular air service is maintained between Glasgow and London and Reykjavík. There are also air services from the island to Scandinavia, USA, Germany, France and Luxembourg.

Road communications are adequate in summer but greatly restricted by snow in winter. Only roads in town centres and key highways are metalled, the rest being of gravel, sand and lava dust. The climate and terrain make first-class surfaces for highways out of the question. There are no railways.

FINANCE

	1988	1989
Revenue	Kr63,091m	Kr77,100m
Expenditure	55,198m	67,651m

TRADE

	1988	1989
Exports	Kr61,674m	Kr80,072m
Imports	68,971m	80,250m

Trade with UK

	1989	1990
Imports from UK	£69,497,000	£88,537,000
Exports to UK	196,678,000	259,438,000

CAPITAL.—ΨReykjavík, population (Dec. 1, 1989), 95,811.

Other centres in approximate order of importance are ΨAkureyri, Kópavogur, ΨHafnarfjörður, Keflavík, Westmann Islands, Akranes, Isafjördur and ΨSiglufjördur.

CURRENCY.—Icelandic króna (Kr) of 100 aurar.

FLAG.—Blue, with white-bordered red cross.

NATIONAL ANTHEM.—O Gud Vors Lands (Our Country's God).

NATIONAL DAY.—June 17.

BRITISH EMBASSY
Laufásvegur 49, Reykjavik
[Reykjavik 15883/4]

Ambassador Extraordinary and Plenipotentiary and Consul-General, His Excellency Sir Richard Radford Best, KCVO, CBE (1989).

Deputy Head of Mission, Second Secretary and Consul, A. Mehmet, MVO.

BRITISH CONSULAR OFFICES

There are Consular Offices at *Akureyri* and *Reykjavík.*

INDONESIA
(Republik Indonesia)

President, General Suharto, *born* June 9, 1921. *Acting President*, March 12, 1967; *confirmed as President*, March 28, 1968, *re-elected for a term of 5 years*, March 1973, March 1978, March 1983 and March 1988.

Vice-President, Lt.-Gen. Sudharmono, *elected* March 1988.

CABINET
(as at June 30, 1991)

Co-ordinating Ministers, Adm. Sudomo (*Political and Security Affairs*); Dr Radius Prawiro (*Economy, Finance, Industry and Development Supervision*); Gen. Supardjo Rustam (*Public Welfare*).

Ministers, Gen. Rudini (*Internal Affairs*); Ali Alatas (*Foreign Affairs*); Gen. L. B. Murdani (*Defence and Security*); Lt.-Gen. Ismail Saleh (*Justice*); Mr Harmoko (*Information*); Dr J. B. Sumarlin (*Finance*); Dr Arifin Siregar (*Trade*); Mr Hartarto (*Industry*); Mr Wardoyo (*Agriculture*); Air Vice Marshal Ginandjar Kartasasmita (*Mines and Energy*); Radinal Mochtar (*Public Works*); Maj.-Gen. Azwar Anas (*Communications*); Maj.-Gen. Bustanil Arifin (*Co-operatives*); Cosmas Batubara (*Manpower*); Lt.-Gen. Sugiarto (*Transmigration*); Gen. Susilo Sudarman (*Tourism, Posts and Telecommunications*); Prof. Fuad Hassan (*Education and Culture*); Dr Adhyatma (*Health*); Haji Munawir Sjadzali (*Religious Affairs*); Prof. Haryati Subadio (*Social Affairs*); Hasjrul Harahap (*Forestry*).

Ministers of State, Maj.-Gen. Murdiono (*State Secretary*); Dr Saleh Afif (*National Development Planning*); Siswono Judo Husodo (*Housing*); Prof. Emil Salim (*Population and Environment*); Sarwono Kusumaatmadja (*Administrative Reform*); Prof. B. J. Habibie (*Research and Technology*); Mrs A. Sulasikin Murpratomo (*Women's Affairs*); Akbar Tandjung (*Sport and Youth Affairs*).

INDONESIAN EMBASSY
38 Grosvenor Square, W1X 9AD
[071–499 7661]

Ambassador Extraordinary and Plenipotentiary, His Excellency Teuku Mohammad Hadi Thayeb (1990).

Minister, Rhousdy Soeriaatmadja (*Deputy Chief of Mission*).

Situated between latitudes 6° North and 11° South and between longitudes 95° and 141° East, Indonesia comprises the islands of Java, Madura, and Sumatra, the Riouw-Lingga Archipelago (which with Karimon, Anambas, Natuna Islands, Tambelan, and part of Sumatra, forms the province of Riau), the islands of Bangka and Billiton, part of the island of Borneo (Kalimantan), Sulawesi (formerly Celebes) Island, the Molucca Islands (Ternate, Tidore, Halmahera, Buru, Seram, Banda, Timor-Laut, Larat, Bachiam, Obi, Kei, Aru, Babar, Leti and Wetar), the island of Bali and the islands of Lombok, Sumbawa, Sumba,

Flores, Timor and others comprising the provinces of East and West Nusa Tenggara and the western half of the island of New Guinea (Irian Jaya), with a total area of 735,358 sq. miles (1,904,569 sq. km), and a population (UN estimate 1989) of 179,136,000.

From the early part of the 17th century much of the Indonesian Archipelago was under Netherlands rule. Following the World War 1939–45, during which the Archipelago was occupied by the Japanese, a strong nationalistic movement manifested itself and after sporadic fighting the formal transfer of sovereignty by the Netherlands of all the former Dutch East Indies except western New Guinea took place on December 27, 1949.

Western New Guinea became part of Indonesia in 1963 under the name West Irian (now Irian Jaya), this interpretation being confirmed in an 'Act of Free Choice' in July 1969, of which the United Nations took note in November 1969. Following a unilateral declaration of independence by the Fretilin in November 1975, Indonesia took over the former Portuguese colony of East Timor, which in July 1976 was declared the 27th province of Indonesia.

Following a three-week period of unrest and violent student demonstrations the Minister of the Army, General Suharto, took over effective political power in March 1966.

General Suharto was made Acting President with full powers, on March 11, 1967, and on March 28, 1968 appointed full President for a period of five years.

In the general election of April 1987, Golkar obtained 299 seats, the Muslim United Development Party 61 seats and the Indonesian Democratic Party 40 seats. President Suharto was subsequently re-elected in March 1988.

Production.—Nearly 70 per cent of the population of Indonesia is engaged in agriculture and related production. Copra, kapok, nutmeg, pepper and cloves are produced, mainly by smallholders; palm oil, sugar, fibres and cinchona are produced by large estates. Rubber, tea, coffee and tobacco are also produced by both in large quantities. Rice is a traditional staple food for the people of Indonesia and the islands of Java, Sulawesi and Sumatra are important producers. Production has risen rapidly in recent years to 25 million tons and the country is now self sufficient.

Oil and liquefied natural gas are the most important assets, the export of which constitutes around 80 per cent of Indonesia's export earnings but more recent developments have underscored the vulnerability of the economy to depressed international markets and weak oil prices. Timber is the second largest foreign exchange earner after oil. Strenuous efforts have been made to develop non-oil exports, and, although these recently reached about 56 per cent, they have since fallen back to below 50 per cent of total exports but, in real terms, their value continues to rise.

Indonesia is rich in minerals, particularly tin, of which the country is the world's third biggest producer; petroleum, coal, nickel and bauxite are the other principal products; there are also considerable deposits of gold, silver, manganese phosphates and sulphur. Aid to Indonesia is channelled through the Inter-Governmental Group on Indonesia (IGGI). Indonesia received about US$4·6 billion in 1991.

Indonesia's Fifth Development Programme started in 1984 and its main objectives are the diversification of the economy to reduce dependence on crude oil, with particular emphasis on agriculture and manufacturing.

Trade with UK

	1989	1990
Imports from UK	£184,032,000	£194,274,000
Exports to UK	273,102,000	327,877,000

Principal exports to the United Kingdom are rubber, timber, non-ferrous metals, clothing, tea, coffee, spices, vegetable oils and fats, and crude oil for refinement. Imports from the United Kingdom are mainly of machinery, transport equipment, electrical equipment and chemicals.

Transport.—In Java a main railway line connects Jakarta with Surabaya in the east of Java and there are several branches. In Sumatra the important towns of Medan, Padang and Palembang are the centres of short railway systems.

Sea communications in the archipelago are maintained by the state-run shipping companies Djakarta-Lloyd (ocean-going) and Pelni (coastal and inter-island) and other small concerns. Transport by small craft on the rivers of the larger islands plays an important part in trade. Air services in Indonesia are operated by Garuda Indonesian Airways and other local airlines, and Jakarta is served by various international services. There are approximately 50,000 miles of roads.

CAPITAL.—ΨJakarta (population 6,503,449). Other important centres are: (Java) ΨSurabaya (2,027,913), ΨSemarang (1,026,671), Bandung (1,462,637); (Sumatra) Palembang (787,187), Medan (1,378,955); (Sulawesi), ΨUjung Pandang (formerly *Makassar*) (709,038); (Kalimantan) Banjarmasin (381,286), ΨPontianak (304,778), ΨBalikpapan (280,675); (Moluccas) Ambon (208,898); (Bali) Denpasar, Singaraja (for whole island 2,174,105); (Nusa Tenggara) Kupang (329,371); (Irian Jaya) Jayapura (107,164).

CURRENCY.—Rupiah (Rp) of 100 sen.

FLAG.—Equal bands of red over white.

NATIONAL ANTHEM.—Indonesia Raya (Great Indonesia).

NATIONAL DAY.—August 17 (Anniversary of Proclamation of Independence).

BRITISH EMBASSY
Jalan M. H. Thamrin 75, Jakarta 10310
[Jakarta 330904]

Ambassador Extraordinary and Plenipotentiary, His Excellency Roger Carrick, CMG, LVO (1990).

BRITISH CONSULAR OFFICES

There are British Consular Offices at *Jakarta*, *Medan* and *Surabaya*.

British Council Representative, Howard Thompson, OBE, S Widjojo Centre, Jalan Jenderal Sudirman, 71, Jakarta 12190. There are also libraries at *Bandung* and *Medan*.

INDONESIA BRITAIN ASSOCIATION

c/o Mr R. A. M. Ramsay, Lippo Life Building, 7th Floor, Jl. HR Rasuna Said, Jakarta 12910.

IRAN
(Jomhori-e-Islami-e-Iran)

Leader of the Islamic Republic, Ayatollah Seyed Ali Khamenei, *appointed* June 1989.

President, Hojjatoleslam Ali Akbar Hashemi Rafsanjani, *elected* July 28, 1989.

CABINET
(as at June 30, 1991)

Agriculture, Issa Kalantari.
Commerce, Abdol-Hossein Vahaji.
Construction Crusade, Gholamreza Forouzesh.
Higher Education, Mostafa Moin.

Defence and Armed Forces Logistics, Akbar Torkan.
Economy and Finance, Mohsen Nourbakhsh.
Education, Mohammad Ali Najafi.
Energy, Bizhan Namdar Zanganeh.
Islamic Guidance, Mohammad Khatami.
Foreign Affairs, Ali Akbar Velayati.
Health, Reza Malekzadeh.
Heavy Industries, Mohammad Hadi Nezhad-Hossein-ian.
Housing and Urban Development, Serajuddin Kazerouni.
Industries, Mohammad Reza Nematzadeh.
Intelligence, Ali Fallahian.
Interior, Abdollah Nouri.
Justice, Esmail Shoushtari.
Labour and Social Affairs, Hossein Kamali.
Mines and Metals, Mohammad Hossein Mahloujchi.
Oil, Gholamreza Aghazadeh.
Posts, Telephones and Telegraphs, Mohammad Gharrazi.
Roads and Transport, Mohammad Saidi-Kia.

EMBASSY OF THE ISLAMIC REPUBLIC OF IRAN
27 Prince's Gate, SW7 1PX
[071–584 8101]

Charge d'Affaires, S. Sh. Khareghani.

Area and Population.—Iran has an area of 636,296 sq. miles (1,648,000 sq. km), with a population of around 55 million. It is mostly an arid table-land, encircled, except in the east, by mountains, the highest in the north rising to 18,934 ft. The central and eastern portion is a vast salt desert.

The Iranians are mostly Shi'ah Muslims but among them are Zoroastrians, Bahais, Sunni Muslims and Armenian and Assyrian Christians. Emigration has much reduced the once substantial Jewish community.

Language and Literature.—Persian, or Farsi, the language of Iran, and of some other areas formerly under Persian rule, is an Indo-European tongue with many Arabic elements added; the alphabet is mainly Arabic, with writing from right to left. Among the great names in Persian literature are those of Abu'l Kásim Mansúr, of Firdausi (AD 939–1020), Omar Khayyám, the astronomer-poet (died AD 1122), Muslihu'd-Din, known as Sa'di (born AD 1184) and Shems-ed-Din Muhammad, or Hafiz (died AD 1389).

Government.—Iran was ruled from the end of the 18th century by Shahs of the Qajar Dynasty. A nationalist movement became active in December 1905, and in August 1906, the Shah, Muzaffer-ud-Din, granted a Constitution. After the war of 1914–18, the subsequent troubles and the signature of the Soviet-Iranian Treaty of 1921, a vigorous Prime Minister, Reza Khan, re-established general order. On Oct. 31, 1925, the last representative of the Qajar Dynasty, Sultan Ahmed Shah was deposed in his absence by the National Assembly, which handed over the government to the Prime Minister, Reza Khan, who was elected Shah on Dec. 13, 1925 by the Constituent Assembly, and took the title Reza Shah Pahlavi. On September 16, 1941 Reza Shah abdicated in favour of the Crown Prince, who ascended the throne under the title of Mohammed Reza Shah Pahlavi.

Following widespread and persistent opposition to his regime, the Shah departed from Iran in January 1979. Ayatollah Khomeini, the main spiritual leader of the Shi'ah Muslims, returned to Iran from exile on February 1. Following a national referendum, Iran was declared an Islamic Republic on April 1, 1979. A new constitution, providing for a President, Prime Minister and Consultative Assembly, and also for overall leadership by Ayatollah Khomeini, was approved by referendum in December 1979. The government's severe measures suppressed violent opposition. In June 1989 Khomeini died and President Khamenei was appointed Leader of the Islamic

Republic. Rafsanjani was elected President in July 1989, and the post of prime minister was abolished.

Iran was at war with Iraq following the Iraqi invasion of Iran in September 1980. International efforts to end the fighting focused on United Nations Security Council Resolution 598 of July 1987, and a ceasefire came into effect on August 20, 1988. In August 1990 Iraq accepted Iran's conditions for settling the conflict, including return to the 1975 border, but a formal peace treaty has not been signed.

Defence.—The Army has a strength of about 250,000 men, in 4 armoured divisions, 6 infantry divisions and one airborne brigade. The Air Force has a strength of about 35,000, with some 120 combat aircraft. The Navy has a strength of about 20,000 and consists of 3 destroyers, 3 frigates, 4 corvettes, 5 minesweepers, and patrol boats, support ships, landing craft and hovercraft. The Islamic Revolutionary Guards Corps numbers about 250,000 men. Total armed forces personnel including paramilitary forces number nearly one million.

Education.—Since 1943 primary education has been compulsory and free, but there is some absenteeism, particularly outside the towns. There are 22 universities in Iran (eight in Tehran, 14 in the provinces). The educational system has been reformed following the revolution.

Agriculture.—Although accounting for 20 per cent of GDP, this has suffered from a lack of investment during the Iran–Iraq war, and from recent drought in the central and western regions. Under the current Five-Year Development Plan, an attempt is being made to reduce Iran's dependence on food imports.

Wheat is the principal crop; other important crops are barley, rice, cotton, sugar beet, fruit, nuts and vegetables. Wool is also a major product. There are extensive forests in the north and west, the conservation of which is a continuing problem.

Industry.—Apart from oil, the principal industrial products are carpets, textiles, sugar, cement and other construction materials, ginned cotton, vegetable oil and other food products, leather and shoes, metal manufactures, pharmaceuticals, motor vehicles, fertilizers and plastics. Industrial output was severely curtailed by the 1979 revolution, as a result of which many industrialists left the country, and by the Iran–Iraq war, but the private sector is now being encouraged again and prospects for industry are quite good.

Energy.—The oilfields, which lie in south-western Iran, were nationalized in 1951. From 1957 until the 1979 revolution a consortium of eight oil companies (one British, one French, one Dutch, and five US) was responsible for the production, refining and sale of oil. In July 1979 the National Iranian Oil Company assumed full control of the oil industry. In addition to that extracted from the onshore wells, oil is also produced from a number of off-shore oilfields. Oil production is approximately 3 million b.p.d., of which some 2·3 million b.p.d. is exported. Iran is a member of OPEC.

Communications.—Tehran is at the centre of a network of highways linking the capital with other major towns, the ports and the frontiers with Turkey, USSR, Afghanistan and Pakistan, and with the Caspian Sea. The Trans-Iranian Railway runs from Bandar Turcoman, on the Caspian Sea, via Tehran to Bandar Khomeini, on the Persian Gulf. Other lines link Tehran with Tabriz and with Mashad. There are also railways from Tabriz to Julfa and from Zahedan to Quetta, and a branch line from Ahwaz to Khorramshahr. An extension from Qom to Kerman is now in operation, as is one from Bandar Turcoman to Gorgan. The Iranian rail system is linked to the Turkish system via Van. There is an international airport at Tehran (Mehrabad), and airports at all the major provincial centres. The national airline, Iranair, is government-owned and operates international and domestic routes.

FINANCE

	1990
Revenue	Rials 4,009,700m
Expenditure	5,595,800m

TRADE

Some 90 per cent of Iran's export earnings come from oil, though an effort is being made to increase non-oil exports. The level of finance for imports depends largely on the international oil price, but with foreign investment being encouraged and restrictions on the private sector eased, the market has become more buoyant over the last two years.

Imports into Iran consist mainly of industrial and agricultural machinery, motor vehicles and motor vehicle components for assembly, iron and steel (including manufactures), electrical machinery and goods, meat, various other foods, and certain textile fabrics and yarns. The principal exports, apart from oil, are cotton, carpets, dried fruit, nuts, hides and skins, mineral ores, wool, gums, caviare, cumin seed and spices. Germany and Japan are Iran's leading suppliers.

Trade with UK

	1989	1990
Imports from UK ...	£257,149,000	£384,713,000
Exports to UK	250,548,000	279,135,000

CAPITAL.—Tehran, population (1989 estimate) 10 million. Other large towns are Tabriz, Isfahan, Meshed, Shiraz, Resht, Kerman, Hamadan, Yazd, Kermanshah and Ahwaz.

CURRENCY.—Rial of 100 dinars.

FLAG.—Equal horizontal bands of green, white and red; with an emblem of the Islamic Republic.

NATIONAL ANTHEM.—Sorood-e Jomhoori-e Eslami.

NATIONAL DAY.—February 11.

BRITISH EMBASSY
143 Ferdowsi Avenue, PO Box 11365-4474
Tehran 11344
[Tehran 675011]

Charge d'Affaires, D. N. Reddaway, MBE.

IRAQ
(Al-Jumhouriya al-'Iraqia)

President, Prime Minister, Chairman of the Revolutionary Command Council, Saddam Hussein, *assumed Office* July 16, 1979.
Vice President, Taha Yassin Ramadhan.

CABINET
(as at April 1991)

Prime Minister, Dr Saadoun Hammadi.
Deputy PMs, Tariq Aziz; Muhammad Hamza al Zubaidi.
Interior, Ali Hassan al Majid.
Foreign Affairs, Ahmad Hussain Khudayir.
Agriculture and Irrigation, Abdul Wahab Mahmud Abdullah al Sabbagh.
Minister of State, Arshad Ahmad Muhammad al Zibari.
Waqafs (Religious Endowments) and Religious Affairs, Abdullah Fadhil Abbas.
Planning, Samal Majid Faraj.
Minister of State for Military Affairs, Gen. Abdul Jabbar Khalil Shansal.
Trade, Dr Mohammad Mahdi Salih.
Industry and Military Industrialization, Acting Oil Minister, Gen. Amir Hammoudi al Saadi.
Labour and Social Affairs, Dr Umid Midat Mubarak.
Health, Dr Abdul Sallam Muhammad Said.
Minister of State for Foreign Affairs, Muhammad Saiid Kazim al Sahhaf.
Defence, Gen. Hussein Kamil Hasan.
Culture and Information, Hamid Yousif Hammadi.
Justice, Shabib Lazim al Maliki.
Education, Hikmat Abdullah al Bazzaz.
Higher Education and Scientific Research, Dr Abdur Razzaq Qasim al Hashimi.
Housing and Reconstruction, Mahmoud Dhgiyab al Ahmad.
Finance, Majid Abd Jafar.
Transport and Communications, Abdul Sattar Ahmad al Ma'ini.
Minister of State for Oil Affairs, Umama Abdur Razzaq Hummadi al Hithi.

IRAQI DIPLOMATIC MISSION IN LONDON

Since Iraq's breach of diplomatic relations with Britain in February 1991, the Jordanian Embassy has handled Iraqi interests in this country.

Area, etc.—Traversed by the Rivers Euphrates and Tigris, Iraq extends from Turkey on N. and N.E. to the Gulf on the S. and SE and from Iran on E. to Syria and Arabian Desert on W., the approximate position being between 37¼° to 48¼° E. long., and 37¼° to 30° N. lat. (*see* MAP, p. 778). The area of Iraq is 167,925 sq. miles (434,924 sq. km), of which 37 per cent is desert land. About 35 to 40 per cent of the remainder is potentially cultivable either by rainfall or by irrigation.

The Euphrates (which has a total length of 1,700 miles from its source to its outflow in the Persian Gulf) is formed by two arms, of which the Murad Su (415 miles) rises in eastern Erzurum, and flows westwards to a junction with the Kara Su, or Frat Su (275 miles); the other arm rises in the north-west of Erzurum in the Dumlu Dagh. The River Tigris has a total length of 1,150 miles from its source to its junction with the Euphrates at Qurna, 70 miles from the Gulf, and rises in two arms south of the Taurus mountains, in Kurdistan, uniting at Til, where the boundaries of the districts of Diarbekir, Van and Bitlis conjoin.

Population.—At the Census of October 1987 Iraq had a total population of 16,278,316. A 1989 UN estimate gives a figure of 18,279,000.

Language.—The official language is Arabic. Minority languages include Kurdish (about 15 per cent), Turkic and Aramaic.

Antiquities.—In 1944 excavations at Tell Hassuna, near Shura (on the Tigris in north Iraq) unearthed abundant traces of culture dating back to 5000 BC. Excavations in 1948 at Tel Abu Shahrain, south of 'Ur of the Chaldees,' confirm Eridu's claim to be the most ancient city of the Sumerian world. Hillah, the ancient city on the left bank of the Shatt el Hillah, a branch of the Euphrates, about 70 miles south of Baghdad, is near the site of Babylon and the 'house of the lofty-head' or 'gate of the god' (Tower of Babel). Mosul Governorate covers a great part of the ancient kingdom of Assyria, the ruins of Nineveh, the Assyrian capital, being visible on the banks of the Tigris, opposite Mosul. Qurna, at the junction of the Tigris and Euphrates, is traditionally supposed to be the site of the Garden of Eden.

Government.—Under the Treaty of Lausanne (1923), Turkey renounced sovereignty over Mesopotamia. A provisional Arab Government was set up in November 1920, and in August 1921 the Emir Faisal was elected King of Iraq. The country was a monarchy until July, 1958, when King Faisal II was assassinated. From 1958 Iraq has been under Presidential rule.

According to the Constitution, the highest state authority is the Revolutionary Command Council (RCC), which elects the President from among its own members. The President appoints the Council of Ministers. Legislative authority is shared by the RCC and the 250-member National Assembly, which is elected every four years by universal adult suffrage. Following general elections in April 1989 the Arab Ba'ath Socialist Party holds the majority of the Assembly seats, the remainder being held by the state-sponsored National Progressive Patriotic Front.

Iraq invaded Kuwait on August 2 1990. The subsequent announcement of annexation was declared void by the UN Security Council. In August 1990 Iraq accepted Iran's conditions for a peace treaty, thus formally ending hostilities in which the two states had been involved since September 1980.

Following the allied victory in Kuwait in February 1991, rebellion against the government broke out in both Kurdish northern Iraq and Shiite southern Iraq. Although the revolt was suppressed by the end of April, the plight of the resultant Kurdish refugees led Western governments to set up a security zone in northern Iraq to protect them. Allied forces were withdrawn in July. The Kurds have since established a *de facto* state in certain northern areas. (See **Events of the Year** for further details.)

Communications and Trade.—Facilities at the port of Basra have been improved but the port has not been used since the outbreak of hostilities with Iran in September 1980. Continuous dredging of the Shatt-al-Arab has also been suspended by hostilities and the channel has seriously silted. The port of Um Qasr near the Kuwaiti border has been developed for freight and sulphur handling and a container terminal is ready for operation but not in use due to the port's proximity to the war zone. All external borders, except that of Jordan, are closed to Iraqi traffic.

There is an international airport at Baghdad. Iraqi Airways provided scheduled flights between Baghdad and London, and other international airlines operated to Europe. Iraqi Republican Railways provided regular passenger and goods services between Basra, Baghdad and Mosul. There is also a metre gauge line connecting Baghdad with Khanaqin, Kirkuk and Arbil.

Iraqi communications were greatly affected by the Gulf War; large numbers of bridges were destroyed and the railway system extensively disrupted.

Agriculture and Industry.—Apart from the valuable revenues to be derived from oil, agricultural development makes a valuable contribution to the wealth of the country and two harvests can usually be gathered in the year. Production fluctuates from year to year according to rainfall. The Government's concern with agricultural development is shown in the large financial allocations made to the sector. Salinity and soil erosion, caused by a high water table, inadequate irrigation and drainage and traditional farming methods, are the major problems now being addressed by development planners.

Increasing industrialization is taking place but industrial production has been greatly reduced because of war damage.

Iraq's major industry is oil production. It was nationalized on June 1, 1972 and accounts for approximately 98 per cent of the total government revenue and 45 per cent of the Gross National Product. Production was some 3·5 million barrels per day in 1979 but the effects of war damage on the Basra terminals and the closure of the trans-Syria pipeline reduced production until new pipelines were built via Turkey and Saudi Arabia. Total revenues from oil were estimated at $11,000–14,000 million in 1988.

In August 1990, the UN imposed mandatory economic sanctions on Iraq, including a world-wide ban on its oil exports. Sanctions were modified in August 1991 to allow the sale of 20 per cent of pre-war oil production; the proceeds are to be allocated to a special UN account for the purchase of food and other essential supplies, and for the funding of war reparations.

Trade with UK

	1989	1990
Imports from UK	£450,495,000	£293,393,000
Exports to UK	55,175,000	101,557,000

The principal imports are iron and steel, cement and other building materials, mechanical and electrical machinery, motor vehicles, textiles and clothing, essential foodstuffs, grain, tinned foods and raw industrial materials. The chief exports are crude petroleum, dates, raw wool, raw hides and skins and raw cotton.

CAPITAL.—Baghdad. Population of the governorate (Census 1977) 3,205,645. Other towns of importance are Ψ Basra, Mosul and Kirkuk.

CURRENCY.—Iraqi dinar (ID) of 1,000 fils.

FLAG.—Horizontal stripes of red, white and black, with three green stars on the white stripe.

NATIONAL DAY.—July 17 (Revolution Day).

BRITISH DIPLOMATIC REPRESENTATION

The British Embassy was closed in January 1991.

IRELAND

Position and Extent.—Ireland lies in the Atlantic Ocean, to the W. of Great Britain, and is separated from Scotland by the North Channel and from Wales by the Irish Sea and St George's Channel. The area of the island is 32,588 sq. miles (84,402 sq. km), and its geographical position between 51° 26′ and 55° 21′ N. latitude and from 5° 25′ to 10° 30′ W. longitude. The greatest length of the island, from N.E. to S.W. (Torr Head to Mizen Head), is 302 miles, and the greatest breadth, from E. to W. (Dundrum Bay to Annagh Head), is 174 miles. On the N. Coast of Achill Island (Co. Mayo) are the highest cliffs in the British Isles, 2,000 feet sheer above the sea. Ireland is occupied for the greater part of its area by the Central Plain, with an elevation 50 to 350 ft. above mean sea level, with isolated mountain ranges near the coastline. The principal mountains, with their highest points, are the Sperrin Mountains (Sawel 2,240 ft.) of County Tyrone; the Mountains of Mourne (Slieve Donard

2,796 ft.) of County Down, and the Wicklow Mountains (Lugnaquilla 3,039 ft.); the Derryveagh Mountains (Errigal 2,466 ft.) of County Donegal; the Connemara Mountains (Twelve Pins 2,695 ft.) of County Galway; Macgillicuddy's Reeks (Carrantuohill 3,414 ft., the highest point in Ireland); and the Galtee Mountains (3,018 ft.) of County Tipperary, and the Knockmealdown (2,609 ft.) and Comeragh Mountains (2,470 ft.) of County Waterford. The principal river of Ireland (and the longest in the British Isles) is the Shannon (240 miles), rising in County Cavan and draining the central plain; the Shannon flows through a chain of loughs to the city of Limerick, and thence to an estuary on the western Atlantic seaboard. The Slaney flows into Wexford Harbour, the Liffey to Dublin Bay, the Boyne to Drogheda, the Lee to Cork Harbour, the Blackwater to Youghal Harbour, and the Suir, Barrow and Nore, to Waterford Harbour. As in Scotland, the principal hydrographic feature is the Loughs, of which Lough Neagh (150 sq. miles) in the north-east is the largest in Ireland and the British Isles, others being the Shannon Chain of Allen, Boderg, Forbes, Ree and Derg, and the Erne Chain of Gowna, Oughter, Lower Erne, and Erne; Melvin, Gill, Gara and Conn in the north-west; and Corrib and Mask (joined by a hidden channel) in the west. In County Kerry, to the east of Macgillicuddy's Reeks, are the famous lakes of Killarney.

Primitive Man.—Although little is known concerning the earliest inhabitants of Ireland, there are many traces of neolithic man throughout the island; a grave containing a polished stone axehead assigned to 2,500 BC was found at Linkardstown, Co. Carlow, in 1944, and the use of bronze implements appears to have become known about the middle of the 17th century BC. In the later Bronze Age a Celtic race of Goidels appears to have invaded the island, and in the early Iron Age Brythons from South Britain are believed to have effected settlements in the south-east, while Picts from North Britain established similar settlements in the north. Towards the close of the Roman occupation of Britain, the dominant tribe in the island was that of the Scoti, who afterwards established themselves in Scotland.

History.—According to Irish legends, the island of Ierne was settled by a Milesian race, who came from Scythia by way of Spain, and established the Kingdom of Tara, about 500 BC. The supremacy of the Ardri (high king) of Tara was acknowledged by eight lesser kingdoms (Munster, Connaught, Ailech, Oriel, Ulidia, Meath, Leinster and Ossory) ruled by descendants of the eight sons of Miled. The basalt columns on the coast of Antrim, eight miles from Portrush, known as the Giant's Causeway, are connected with the legendary history of Ireland as the remnants of a bridge built in the time of Finn M'Coul (Fingal) to connect Antrim with Scotland (Staffa).

Hibernia was visited by Roman merchants but never by Roman legions, and little is known of the history of the country until the invasions of *Northmen* (Norwegians and Danes) towards the close of the 8th century AD. The Norwegians were distinguished as Findgaill (White Strangers) and the Danes as Dubgaill (Black Strangers), names which survive in Fingall, MacDougall and MacDowell, while the name of the island itself is held to be derived from the Scandinavian *Ira-land* (land of the Irish), the names of the Provinces being survivals of Norse dialect forms (Ulaids-tir, Laiginstir, Mumans-tir and Kun-nak-tir). The outstanding events in the encounters with the Northmen are the *Battle of Tara* (980), at which the Hy Neill king Maelsechlainn II defeated the Scandinavians of Dublin and the Hebrides under the king Amlaib Cuarán; and the *Battle of Clontarf* (1014) by which the Scandinavian power was completely broken. After Clontarf the supreme power was disputed by the O'Briens of Munster, the O'Neills of Ulster, and the O'Connors of Connaught, with varying fortunes. In 1152 Dermod MacMurrough (Diarmit MacMurchada), the deposed king of Leinster, sought assistance in his struggle with Rauidhri O'Connor (the high king of Ireland), and visited Henry II, the Norman king of England. Henry authorized him to obtain armed support in England for the recovery of his kingdom, and Dermod enlisted the services of Richard de Clare, the Norman Earl of Pembroke, afterwards known as *Strongbow*, who landed at Waterford (Aug. 23, 1170) with 200 knights and 1,000 other troops for the reconquest of Leinster, where he eventually settled, after marriage with Dermod's daughter. In 1172 (Oct. 18) Henry II himself landed in Ireland. He received homage from the Irish kings and established his capital at Dublin. The invaders subsequently conquered most of the island and a feudal government was created. In the 14th and 15th centuries, the Irish recovered most of their lands, while many Anglo-Irish lords became virtually independent, royal authority being confined to the Pale, a small district round Dublin. Though, under Henry VII, Sir Edward Poynings, as Lord Deputy, had passed at the *Parliament of Drogheda* (1494) the act later known as *Poynings' Law*, subordinating the Irish Legislature to the Crown, the Earls of Kildare retained effective power until, in 1534, Henry VIII began the reconquest of Ireland. Parliament in 1541 recognized him as King of Ireland and by 1603 English authority was supreme.

REPUBLIC OF IRELAND
(Poblacht Na hEireann)

President, Mary Robinson, *born* 1944, *assumed office*, Dec. 3, 1990.

CABINET
(as at July 3, 1991)

Taoiseach and Minister for the Gaeltacht, Charles J. Haughey (FF).
Tánaiste and Minister for Marine, John Wilson (FF).
Foreign Affairs, Gerry Collins (FF).
Finance, Albert Reynolds (FF).
Industry and Commerce, Des O'Malley (PD).
Labour, Bertie Ahern (FF).
Justice, Ray Burke (FF).
Energy, Bobby Molloy (PD).
Defence, Brendan Daly (FF).
Agriculture and Food, Michael O'Kennedy (FF).
Social Welfare, Michael Woods (FF).
Environment, Padraig Flynn (FF).
Health, Rory O'Hanlon (FF).
Education, Mrs Mary O'Rourke (FF).
Attorney General, John Murray (FF).
Tourism, Transport and Communications, Seamus Brennan (FF).

The present coalition Government was formed by the Fianna Fail Party (FF) and the Progressive Democrat Party (PD) following a general election on June 15, 1989.

IRISH EMBASSY
17 Grosvenor Place, SW1X 7HR
[071-235 2171]

Ambassador Extraordinary and Plenipotentiary, His Excellency Joseph Small (1991).

Area and Population.—The Republic has a land area of 27,136 sq. miles (70,283 sq. km), divided into the four Provinces of *Leinster* (Carlow, Dublin, Kildare, Kilkenny, Laoighis, Longford, Louth, Meath, Offaly, Westmeath, Wexford and Wicklow); *Munster* (Clare, Cork, Kerry, Limerick, Tipperary

and Waterford); *Connacht* (Galway, Leitrim, Mayo, Roscommon and Sligo); and part of *Ulster* (Cavan, Donegal and Monaghan).

The preliminary population of the Republic in 1991 census was 3,523,401. Figures also showed 52,954 births, 17,490 marriages and 31,818 deaths in the year 1990 (provisional).

GOVERNMENT

The Constitution.—The constitution, approved by a plebiscite on July 1, 1937, came into operation on December 29, 1937. The Constitution declares the national territory to be the whole island of Ireland, its islands and the territorial seas. Pending the reintegration of the national territory, and without prejudice to the right of the Parliament and the Government established by the Constitution to exercise jurisdiction over the whole of the national territory, the laws enacted by that Parliament shall have the like area and extent of application as those of the Irish Free State, which did not include the six counties of Northern Ireland.

The Irish language, being the national language, is the first official language. The English language is recognized as a second official language.

The President (*Uachtarán na hEireann*) is elected by direct vote of the people for a period of seven years. A former or retiring President is eligible for a second term. The President summons and dissolves Dáil Éireann on the advice of the Head of the Government (*Taoiseach*). She signs and promulgates laws. The supreme command of the Defence forces is vested in her, its exercise being regulated by law. She has the power of pardon. The President, in the exercise and performance of certain of her constitutional powers and functions, is aided and advised by a Council of State.

The National Parliament (*Oireachtas*) consists of the President and two Houses: a House of Representatives (*Dáil Éireann*) and a Senate (*Seanad Éireann*).

Dáil Éireann is composed of 166 members elected by adult suffrage on a basis of proportional representation by means of the single transferable vote. All citizens, and such other persons in the state as may be determined by law, who have reached the age of 18 years and are not disqualified by law have the right to vote. Each Dáil may continue for a period not exceeding five years from the date of election.

Seanad Eireann is composed of 60 members, of whom 11 are nominated by the Taoiseach and 49 are elected; six by institutions of higher education, and 43 from panels of candidates, established on a vocational basis.

Members of Dáil are paid an allowance of IR£28,894 per annum (and members of Seanad IR£16,754). They are allowed travelling facilities between Dublin and their constituencies and are, subject to certain restrictions, granted free telephone and postal facilities from Leinster House and allowances for overnight stays in Dublin.

The executive authority is exercised by the Government subject to the Constitution. The Government is responsible to the Dáil, meets and acts as a collective authority, and is collectively responsible for the Departments of State administered by the Ministers.

The Taoiseach is appointed by the President on the nomination of the Dáil. The other members of the government are appointed by the President on the nomination of the Taoiseach with the previous approval of the Dáil. The Taoiseach appoints a member of the Government to be the *Tánaiste*, who acts for all purposes in the place of the Taoiseach in the event of the death, permanent incapacitation, or temporary absence of the Taoiseach. The Taoiseach, the Tánaiste and the Minister for Finance must be members of the Dáil. The other members of the Government must be members of the Dáil or the Seanad, but not more than two may be members of the Seanad.

The result of the general election on June 15, 1989 was as follows: Fianna Fáil 77; Fine Gael 55; Labour 15; Workers' Party 7; Progressive Democrats 6; Independent 6. Total membership including the *Ceann Comhairle* (Chairman), 166.

JUDICIAL SYSTEM

The judicial system comprises Courts of First Instance and a Court of Final Appeal called the Supreme Court (*Cúirt Uachtarach*). The Courts of First Instance include a High Court (*Ard-Chúirt*) and Courts of local and limited jurisdiction, with a right of appeal as determined by law. The High Court alone has original jurisdiction to consider the question of the validity of any law having regard to the provisions of the Constitution. The Supreme Court has appellate jurisdiction from all decisions of the High Court, with such exceptions and subject to such regulations as may be prescribed by law.

Chief Justice, Hon. Thomas A. Finlay .... IR£75,251
President of the High Court, Hon. Liam
  Hamilton .... IR£67,525
Judges, Supreme Court, Hons. Anthony
  Hederman; Niall J. McCarthy; Hugh
  O'Flaherty; Seamus Egan .... IR£64,765
Judges, High Court, Hons. Rory O'Han-
  lon; Declan Costello; Ronan Keane;
  Mella Carroll; Henry D. Barron; Fran-
  cis D. Murphy; Kevin Lynch; Robert
  Barr; Gerard Lardner; John J. Blay-
  ney; Richard Johnson; Vivian Lavan;
  Frederick Morris; Susan Denham; Paul
  Carney. .... IR£59,798
Attorney-General, John Murray.

RELIGION
(Census of 1981)

Catholic	3,204,476
Church of Ireland	95,366
Presbyterians	14,255
Methodists	5,790
Others	123,518
Total	3,443,405

DEFENCE

Establishments provide at present for a Permanent Defence Force of approximately 17,977 all ranks, including the Air Corps and the Naval Service. Recruitment is on a voluntary basis. Minimum term of enlistment is three years in the Permanent Defence Force followed by six years in the Reserve Defence Force. Establishments also provide for a Reserve Defence Force of 22,110 all ranks. Recruitment is also on a voluntary basis; minimum term of enlistment is three years. The Defence Estimate for the year ending December 31, 1991 provides for an expenditure of IR£317,435,000.

FINANCE

	1990* IR£m	1991† IR£m
Total Current Revenue	8,269	8,775
Total Current Expenditure .	8,421	9,019
Current Revenue		
Customs	114	125
Excise Duties	1,674	1,750
Capital Taxes	71	87
Stamp Duties	271	271
Income Tax	3,024	3,184
Income Levy	—	—

Corporation Tax	474	527
Value-Added Tax........	1,979	2,090
Agricultural Levies (EC) .	10	11
Motor Vehicle Duties	161	179
Employment and Training		
Levy	125	134
Total Tax Revenue	7,903	8,358
Non-Tax Revenue	366	417

*Provisional out-turn
†Post-Budget estimate

	1990* IR£m	1991† IR£m
Current Expenditure		
Debt Service	2,300	2,409
Industry and Labour	209	241
Agriculture	253	247
Fisheries	17	19
Forestry	9	6
Tourism	24	25
Roads and Transport	18	22
Sanitary Services	2	3
Health	1,197	1,233
Education	1,205	1,130
Social Welfare	1,547	1,690
Housing	13	9
Subsidies	168	169
Defence	345	362
Garda	296	315
Prisons	68	74
Legal, etc.	50	50
Other	716	1,030
Total (excluding Local Loans		
Fund Subsidies)	8,437	9,034
Add back:		
Local Loans Fund Subsidies	—	—
Total (including Local Loans		
Fund Subsidies)	8,437	9,034

*Provisional out-turn
†Post-Budget estimate
Note: The figures do not take account of Departmental balances.
The Gross Debt at end 1988 was IR£24,611·2 million.

EDUCATION

Primary education is directed by the state, with the exception of 69 private primary schools with an enrolment of 8,651 in 1989–90.

There were 3,359 state-aided primary schools with an enrolment of 552,182

In 1989–90 there were 491 recognized secondary schools with 213,617 pupils under private management (mainly religious orders), and 252 vocational schools with 85,205 pupils. Vocational schools are controlled by 38 statutory local Vocational Education Committees. There were 16 state comprehensive schools in 1989–90 with a total enrolment of 8,842 students, and 47 community schools with an enrolment of 31,297 students. There were also other miscellaneous second-level schools and the total full-time enrolment at second-level for 1989–90 was 342,364.

Third-level education is catered for by seven University Colleges, and also by third-level courses offered by the Technical Colleges and Regional Technical Colleges and other miscellaneous third-level institutions. There were 65,949 full-time third-level students in 1989–90, of whom 35,477 were attending university courses.

The estimated state expenditure on education in 1991, excluding administration and inspection, is first-level education IR£474,242,000; second-level education IR£443,872,000. The vote for third-level education amounted to IR£196,224,000.

MINERALS AND FISHERIES

Minerals.—Metal content of ores raised (1990): lead, 35,200 tonnes; zinc, 166,500 tonnes; silver 8,800,000 grammes.

Sea Fisheries.—An estimated 7,750 persons were employed in the fisheries in 1987. Total value of all fish landed in 1989 was IR£89·3 million.

COMMUNICATIONS

Railways.—In the year ended December 31, 1989, there were 1,944 km of railway; 24,595,000 passengers and 3,067,000 tonnes of merchandise were conveyed; the receipts were IR£133,464,000 and expenditure IR£126,269,000. These figures are in respect of railway working by *Iarnród Eireann.*

Road Motor Services.—In 1989 road motor vehicles carried 222,120,473 passengers, the gross receipts being IR£128,812,697.

Shipping.—In 1989 the number of ships with cargo which arrived at Irish ports was 12,928 (25,940,000 net registered tons); of these 2,567 (5,662,000 net registered tons) were of Irish nationality.

CIVIL AVIATION

Shannon Airport, 15 miles W. of Limerick, is on the main transatlantic air route. In 1990 the airport handled 1,628,765 passengers.

Dublin Airport, 6 miles N. of Dublin, serves the cross-channel and European services operated by the Irish national airline Aer Lingus and other airlines. In 1990 the airport handled 5,509,483 passengers.

Cork Airport, 5 miles S. of Cork serves the cross Channel and European services operated by Aer Lingus and other airlines. In 1990 the airport handled 708,078 passengers.

Trade with UK

	1989	1990
Imports from UK	£4,714,780,000	£5,311,539,000
Exports to UK	4,279,202,000	4,498,571,000

OVERSEAS TRADE

	1989	1990
Imports	IR£12,284,265,785	IR£12,479,481,307
Exports	14,597,040,802	14,342,996,541
Trade balance .	2,312,775,017	1,863,515,234

PRINCIPAL ARTICLES

Principal imports 1990

	IR£
Live animals	54,986,000
Food, drink and tobacco............	1,220,559,000
Petrol and petroleum products	643,989,000
Chemicals	1,554,140,000
Machinery	3,505,775,000
Transport equipment	976,233,000
Metal and manufactures	787,496,000
Textiles and clothing	952,852,000
Paper, paperboard and manufactures	399,458,000
Professional, scientific etc. goods....	308,107,000

Principal exports 1990

	IR£
Live animals	201,645,000
Meat and meat preparations	823,136,000
Other food, drink and tobacco	2,161,483,000
Machinery and transport equipment	4,488,051,000
Clothing, headgear and footwear ...	291,633,000
Textiles	416,531,000
Metal ores and scrap	235,619,000
Metal and manufactures	391,752,000
Non-metallic mineral manufactures .	172,608,000
Chemicals	2,274,398,000
Professional, scientific etc., goods ...	544,062,000

CAPITAL.—ΨDublin (*Baile Atha Cliath*) is a City and County Borough on the River Liffey at the head of Dublin Bay. In April 1991 the population (1991 Census, preliminary) was 477,675.

Other county boroughs, with their preliminary population figures at the 1991 Census, are ΨCork (127,024); ΨLimerick (52,040); ΨWaterford (40,345); and Ψ Galway (50,842).

FLAG.—Equal vertical stripes of green, white and orange.

NATIONAL ANTHEM.—Amhrán na BhFiann (The Soldier's Song).

NATIONAL DAY.—March 17 (St Patrick's Day).

BRITISH EMBASSY
31 Merrion Road, Dublin 4
[Dublin 695211]

Ambassador Extraordinary and Plenipotentiary, His Excellency David E. S. Blatherwick, CMG, OBE (1991).

Counsellor and Head of Chancery, J. Thorp.

First Secretaries, D. F. B. Edye (*Commercial*); I. R. Whitting (*Economic*); T. A. Gallagher (*Political/ Information*); G. Fergusson; D. Harris.

British Council Representative, Dr Ken Churchill, 22 Lower Mount Street, Dublin 2.

ISRAEL
(Medinat Israel)

President of Israel, Chaim Herzog, *born* 1918, *elected* 1983, *re-elected* Feb. 20, 1988, *inaugurated*, May 8, 1988.

CABINET
(as at June 30, 1991)

Prime Minister and acting Minister for Labour, Social Affairs, Environment, Yitzhak Shamir.
Deputy PM, Foreign Affairs, David Levy.
Deputy PM, Industry and Trade, Moshe Nissim.
Defence, Moshe Arens.
Interior, Arye Der'i.
Agriculture, Rafael Eitan.
Education and Culture, Zevulun Hammer.
Transport, Moshe Katsav.
Economy and Planning, David Magen.
Justice, Dan Meridor.
Police, Ronni Milo.
Finance, Yitzhak Moda'i.
Science and Technology, Energy and Infrastructure, Yuval Ne'eman.
Health, Ehud Olmert.
Tourism, Gideon Patt.
Immigrant Absorption, Yitzhak Haim Peretz.
Communications, Raphael Pinchasi.
Religious Affairs, Avner Hai Shaki.
Construction and Housing, Ariel Sharon.
Minister without Portfolio, Rehavam Ze'evi.

EMBASSY OF ISRAEL
2 Palace Green, Kensington, W8 4QB
[071–937 8050]

Ambassador Extraordinary and Plenipotentiary, His Excellency Yoav Biran (1988).

Area and Population.—Israel lies on the western edge of the continent of Asia at the eastern extremity of the Mediterranean Sea, between lat. 29° 30′–33° 15′ N. and longitude 34° 15′–35° 40′ E. Its political neighbours are Lebanon on the North, Syria on the North and East, Jordan on the East and the Egyptian province of Sinai on the South West.

The area is estimated at 8,019 sq. miles (20,770 sq. km). The population (estimate 1990) including East Jerusalem, the Golan Heights and Israeli citizens in

the other Occupied Territories is 4,882,000. During the upheavals of 1948–49 a large number of Arabs left the country as refugees and settled in neighbouring countries.

Hebrew and Arabic are the official languages of Israel. Arabs are entitled to transact all official business with Government Departments in Arabic, and provision is made in the *Knesset* for the simultaneous translation of all speeches into Arabic.

Physical Features.—Israel comprises four main regions: (a) the hill country of Galilee and Judea and Samaria, rising in places to heights of nearly 4,000 ft.; (b) the coastal plain from the Gaza strip to North of Acre, including the plain of Esdraelon running from Haifa Bay to the south-east, and cutting in two the hill region; (c) the Negev, a semi-desert triangular-shaped region, extending from a base south of Beersheba, to an apex at the head of the Gulf of 'Aqaba; and (d) parts of the Jordan valley, including the Hula Region, Tiberias and the south-western extremity of the Dead Sea. The principal river is the Jordan, which rises from three main sources in Israel, the Lebanon and Syria, and flows through the Hula valley and the canals which have replaced Lake Hula, drained in 1958. Between Hulata and Tiberias (Sea of Galilee) the river falls 926 ft. in 11 miles and becomes a turbulent stream. Lake Tiberias is 696 ft. below sea-level and liable to sudden storms. Between it and the Dead Sea the Jordan falls 591 ft. The other principal rivers are the Yarkon and Kishon. The largest lake is the Dead Sea (shared

between Israel and Jordan); area 393 sq. miles, 1,286 feet below sea-level, 51·5 miles long, with a maximum width of 11 miles and a maximum depth of 1,309 ft.; it receives the waters of the Jordan and of six other streams, and has no outlet, the surplus being carried off by evaporation. The water contains an extraordinarily high concentration of mineral substances. The highest mountain peak is Mount Meron, 3,962 ft. above sea-level, near Safad, Upper Galilee.

Climate.—The climate is variable, similar to that of Lower Egypt, but modified by altitude and distance from the sea. The summer is hot but tempered in most parts by daily winds from the Mediterranean. The winter is the rainy season lasting from November to April, the period of maximum rainfall being January and February.

Antiquities.—The following are among the principal historic sites in Israel: *Jerusalem*: the Church of the Holy Sepulchre: the Al Aqsa Mosque and Dome of the Rock, standing on the remains of the Temple Mount of Herod the Great, of which the Western (wailing) Wall is a fragment; the Church of the Dormition and the Coenaculum on Mount Zion; Ein Karem: Church of the Visitation, Church of St John the Baptist. *Galilee*: The Sea; Church and Mount of the Beatitudes, ruins of Capernaum and other sites connected with the life of Christ. *Mount Tabor*: Church of the Transfiguration. *Nazareth*: Church of the Annunciation and other Christian shrines associated with the childhood of Christ. There are also numerous sites dating from biblical and medieval days, such as Ascalon, Caesarea, Atlit, Massada, Megiddo and Hazor. Other antiquities in the West Bank of Jordan and the Golan Heights at present occupied by Israel can now be visited from Israel. In accordance with the terms of the peace treaty signed between Egypt and Israel on March 26, 1979, Israel withdrew in April 1982 to the pre-1967 boundary, returning the Sinai area to Egyptian sovereignty.

Government.—There is a Cabinet and a single-chamber Parliament (*Knesset*) of 120 members. A general election is held at least once every four years. The last General Election, held in November 1988, resulted in the formation of a 'national unity' coalition government. Disputes between Labour and Likud, the two main partners, led to the collapse of the coalition in March 1990. The present cabinet represents a coalition between Likud, four religious parties and three right-wing nationalist parties.

Immigration.—The Declaration of Independence of May 14, 1948, laid down that 'the State of Israel will be open to the immigration of Jews from all countries of their dispersion.' The Law of Return, passed by the *Knesset* on July 5, 1950, provides that an immigrant visa shall be granted to every Jew who expresses his desire to settle in Israel. From the establishment of the State until 1988, about 1·8 million immigrants had entered Israel from over 100 different countries. Since 1990, a further 250,000 Jews have arrived in Israel from the Soviet Union, eastern Europe, and Ethiopia.

Education.—Elementary education for all children from 5 to 15 years is free, though secondary education is not compulsory. The law also provides for working youth, age 15–18 who for some reason have not completed their primary education, to be exempted from work in order to do so.

In 1985–86 enrolment in all educational establishments was 1,383,838: kindergartens 277,200; elementary education 622,056; secondary education 348,262; post-secondary 98,420.

Finance.—Government expenditure in 1989 was 25,953,000,000 new Shekels at market prices. GNP at market prices was 81,880,000,000 new Shekels.

COMMUNICATIONS

Railways and Roads.—Israel State Railways started operating in August 1949. Towns now served are Haifa, Tel Aviv, Jerusalem, Lod, Nahariya, Beersheba, Dimona, Ashdod and intermediate stations. In 1986 the total railway network amounted to 528 km. There were 12,823 km of paved road and in 1986 819,102 licensed vehicles.

Shipping.—Israel's merchant marine had reached a total of 2,805,000 tons deadweight by December 1985.

The chief ports are Haifa, a modern harbour, with a depth of 30 ft. alongside the main quay; the harbour on the Red Sea at Eilat, inaugurated in September 1965, has a capacity of 10,000 tons a day; Acre has an anchorage for small vessels; the deep-water port at Ashdod, 20 miles south of Tel Aviv, which started operations at the end of 1965, handled 8,006,000 tons of cargo in 1986. In the same year Israel's three main ports handled 17,048,000 tons of cargo.

Civil Aviation.—In 1986, 3,098,000 passengers passed through Ben Gurion airport, of which 230,146 arrived by charter flight.

PRODUCTION AND INDUSTRY

Agriculture.—The country is generally fertile and climatic conditions vary so widely that a large variety of crops can be grown, ranging from temperate crops, such as wheat and cherries, to subtropical crops such as sorghum, millet and mangoes. The famous 'Jaffa' orange is produced in large quantities mostly in the coastal plain for export; high-profit

export crops such as strawberries and cut flowers are increasingly important. The citrus yield during the 1985–86 season was 1,308,700 tons. Specialized glasshouse crops for export, such as flowers, tomatoes and strawberries, are becoming increasingly popular and exports of flowers in 1985 earned US$75,454,000. Olives are cultivated, mainly for the production of oil used for edible purposes and for the manufacture of soap. The main winter crops are wheat and barley and various kinds of pulses, while in summer sorghum, millet, maize, sesame and summer pulses are grown. Large areas of seasonal vegetables are planted. Beef, cattle and poultry farming have been developed and the production of mixed vegetables and dairy produce has greatly increased. Tobacco and medium staple cotton are now grown. Fishing production (mostly from fish farms) was 14,958 tons in 1985–86. All kinds of summer fruits such as figs, grapes, plums and apples are produced in increasing quantities for local consumption. Water supply for irrigation is the principal limiting factor to greater production. The area under cultivation is 4,370,000 dunams, of which 2,370,000 is under irrigation. The Israel land measure is the *dunam*, equivalent to 1,000 square metres (approximately a quarter of an acre).

Industry.—In value polished diamonds account for about one quarter of Israel's total exports. Amongst the most important exporting industries are textiles, foodstuffs, chemicals (mainly fertilizers and pharmaceuticals). Metal-working and science-based industries are highly sophisticated and technologically advanced. These include the aircraft and military industries. Other important manufacturing industries include plastics, rubber, cement, glass, paper and oil refining.

TRADE

The principal imports are foodstuffs, crude oil, machinery and vehicles, iron, steel and manufactures thereof, and chemicals. The principal exports are citrus fruits and by-products, polished diamonds, plywood, cement, tyres, minerals, finished and semi-finished textiles.

	1988	1989
Imports	US$12,287·2m	US$12,736·5m
Exports	9,445·4m	10,334·9m

Trade with UK

	1989	1990
Imports from UK	£502,411,000	£567,712,000
Exports to UK	479,840,000	506,106,000

CAPITAL.—Most of the Government departments are in Jerusalem, population (1984) 506,200. A resolution proclaiming Jerusalem as the capital of Israel was adopted by the *Knesset* on January 23, 1950. It is not, however, recognized as the capital by the United Nations. Other principal towns (1986) were ΨTel Aviv and district (1,624,100); ΨHaifa and district (393,000) and Beersheba and district (115,000).

CURRENCY.—New Shekel of 100 agora.

FLAG.—White, with two horizontal blue stripes, the Shield of David in the centre.

NATIONAL ANTHEM.—Hatikvah (The Hope).

THE OCCUPIED TERRITORIES

As a result of the 1967 war, Israel gained control of East Jerusalem, the Gaza Strip and the West Bank of the Jordan River; East Jerusalem was subsequently annexed by Israel, although this move has not gained international recognition. Extreme Jewish groups began a programme of settlement in the Occupied Territories, later encouraged by the Israeli government. This heightened tension with the resident Palestinian population, now estimated at 1,450,000, whose protests were paralleled by Palestinian Liberation Organization attacks around the world. Frustration at the continued Israeli occupation led to the start of the *Intifada* in 1987, a campaign of sustained unrest in the Occupied Territories.

BRITISH EMBASSY
192 Hayarkon Street, Tel Aviv
[Tel Aviv 5249171]

Ambassador Extraordinary and Plenipotentiary, His Excellency Mark Elliott, CMG (1988).

Counsellor, T. R. V. Phillips (*Head of Chancery, Consul-General and Counsellor*).

Defence and Military Attaché, Col. J. R. Andrew, OBE.

British Council Representative, P. Sandiford, 140 Hayarkon Street, Tel Aviv 61032.

There is a library in *Tel Aviv* and in *West Jerusalem*.

ISRAEL-BRITISH CHAMBER OF COMMERCE, 76 IBN Guirol Street, Tel Aviv 64162.

ITALY
(Repubblica Italiana)

President of the Italian Republic, Francesco Cossiga, *born* 1928, *sworn in*, July 3, 1985.

COUNCIL OF MINISTERS
(as at April 17, 1991)

Prime Minister, Acting Minister of State Participation, Culture, Giulio Andreotti (DC).

Deputy PM, Acting Minister of Justice, Claudio Martelli (PSI).

Foreign Affairs, Gianni de Michelis (PSI).

Interior, Vincenzo Scotti (DC).

Treasury, Sen. Guido Carli (DC).

Budget, Paolo Cirino Pomicino (DC).

Finance, Rino Formica (PSI).

Defence, Virginio Rognoni (DC).

Education, Ricardo Misasi (DC).

Public Works, Sen. Gianni Prandini (DC).

Agriculture, Giovanni Goria (DC).

Transport, Carlo Bernini (DC).

Posts and Telecommunications, Carlo Vizzini (PSDI).

Industry, Guido Bodrato (DC).

Labour, Franco Marini (DC).

Foreign Trade, Vito Lattanzio (DC).

Merchant Marine, Ferdinando Facchiano (PSDI).

Health, Francesco de Lorenzo (PLI).

Tourism, Carlo Tognoli (PSI).

Environment, Sen. Giorgio Ruffolo (PSI).

South (Mezzogiorno), Calogero Mannino (DC).

Civil Protection, Nicola Capria (PSI).

Social Affairs, Sen. Rosa Jervolino Russo (DC).

Relations with Parliament, Egidio Sterpa (PLI).

Urban Areas, Carmelo Conte (PSI).

Community Affairs, Pier Luigi Romita (PSDI).

Scientific Research, Prof. Antonio Ruberti (PSI).

Regional Affairs and Institutional Reforms, Mino Martinazzoli (DC).

Public Administration, Remo Gaspari (DC).

Immigration, Margherita Boniver (PSI).

DC: Christian Democrat Party; PSI: Socialist Party; PLI: Liberal Party; PSDI: Social Democratic Party.

ITALIAN EMBASSY
14 Three Kings Yard, Davies Street, W1Y 2EH
[071–629 8200]

Ambassador Extraordinary and Plenipotentiary, His Excellency Giacomo Attolico (1991).

Minister-Counsellor, Livio Muzi-Falconi.

First Counsellors, A. V. de Mohr; F. Pigliapoco; N. Cappello; L. Visconti di Modrone; S. Ronca.

There are also consular offices in *Bedford, Edinburgh* and *Manchester*.

Italy is a Republic in the south of Europe, consisting of a peninsula, the large islands of Sicily and Sardinia, the island of Elba and about 70 other small islands. Italy is bounded on the N. by Switzerland and Austria, on the S. by the Mediterranean, on the E. by the Adriatic and Yugoslavia, and on the W. by France and the Ligurian and Tyrrhenian Seas. The total area is about 116,304 sq. miles (301,225 sq. km).

The peninsula is for the most part mountainous, but between the Apennines, which form its spine, and the east coastline are two large fertile plains: Emilia/Romagna in the north and Apulia in the south. The Alps form the northern limit of Italy, dividing it from France, Switzerland, Austria and Yugoslavia. Mont Blanc (15,771 ft.), the highest peak, is in the French Pennine Alps, but partly within the Italian borders are Monte Rosa (15,217 ft.), Matterhorn (14,780 ft.) and several peaks from 12,000 to 14,000 ft.

The chief rivers are the Po (405 miles), which flows through Piedmont, Lombardy and the Veneto, and the Adige (Trentino and Veneto) in the north, the Arno (Florentine Plain) and the Tiber (flowing through Rome to Ostia).

Population.—In February 1986 Italy's population was 57,193,708. A 1989 UN estimate gives a figure of 57,557,000.

Government.—Italian unity was accomplished under the House of Savoy, after a struggle from 1848 to 1870, in which Mazzini (1805–72), Garibaldi (1807–82) and Cavour (1810–61) were the principal figures. It was completed when Lombardy was ceded by Austria in 1859 and Venice in 1866, and through the evacuation of Rome by the French in 1870. In 1871 the King of Italy entered Rome, and that city was declared to be the capital.

Benito Mussolini, known as *Il Duce* (The Leader), was continuously in office as Prime Minister from October 30, 1922 until July 25, 1943, when the Fascist regime was abolished. He was captured by Italian partisans while attempting to escape across the Swiss frontier and killed on April 28, 1945.

In fulfilment of a promise given in April 1944 that he would retire when the Allies entered Rome, a decree was signed on June 5, 1944, by King Victor Emmanuel III under which Prince Umberto, the King's son, became Lieutenant General of the Realm. The King remained head of the House of Savoy and retained the title King of Italy until his abdication on May 9, 1946, when he was succeeded by the Crown Prince.

A general election was held on June 2, 1946 together with a referendum on the future of the monarchy. The result showed a majority in favour of replacing the monarchy with a Republic. The Royal Family left the country on June 13, and on June 28, 1946, a provisional President was elected.

Constitution.—The constitution of the Republic of Italy, approved by the Constituent Assembly on December 22, 1947, provides for the election of the President by an electoral college which consists of the two Houses of Parliament (the Chamber of Deputies and the Senate) sitting in joint session together with three delegates from each region (one in the case of the Valle d'Aosta). The President, who must be over 50 years of age, holds office for seven years. He has numerous carefully defined powers, the main one of which is the right to dissolve one or both Houses of Parliament, after consultation with the Speakers. With 50 governments since 1947, there is growing public pressure for constitutional reform.

Defence.—The Army has around 260,000 men, whom 210,000 are conscripts. In addition, the para-military *Carabinieri* force, which is part of the Army, has around 110,000 men. The Army, which has three Corps concentrated in the north, is equipped with Leopard 1 and M60 tanks and M113 armoured

personnel carriers. There is also a parachute brigade, five alpine brigades, a missile brigade, and a Light Aviation Arm with over 300 helicopters. The Navy consists of one helicopter carrier, 2 cruisers, 4 destroyers, 9 submarines, 23 frigates and corvettes and 15 mine warfare ships. Manpower strength is around 50,000. The Air Force has some 80,000 men and 400 combat aircraft. It is largely a tactical air force, equipped with Tornado, F104 and G91 aircraft, but also has transport, anti-submarine and helicopter search and rescue units. There is a large Reserve force of ex-conscripts under the age of 35.

REGIONS OF ITALY

Rome and Central Italy.—Rome was founded, according to legend, by Romulus in the year now known as 753 BC. It was the focal point of Latin civilization and dominion under the Republic and afterwards under the Roman Empire, and became the capital of Italy when the Kingdom was established in 1871. The capital is concerned mainly with tourism and government, but its importance as a business centre is steadily increasing, and it is reportedly the third largest industrial centre in the country.

Lombardy and Milan.—In the Lombardy region are to be found some 15·7 per cent of Italy's commercial

and banking services and some 21·9 per cent of the manufacturing industry. The whole range of Italian industry is represented, most important being the steel, machine tool and motor car factories.

Turin and Piedmont.—Turin between 1861 and 1865 was Italy's first capital as the home of the Piedmontese Royal Family. Now it is the headquarters of Europe's largest manufacturer of motor cars, produces 75 per cent of Italy's motor vehicles and over 80 per cent of its roller bearings. Turin is also Italy's second largest steel producing city. Piedmont is the centre of the Italian textile industry based mainly on Biella.

Genoa and the Ligurian Riviera.—Genoa has been one of Europe's major ports since the Middle Ages, and handles one-third of Italy's foreign trade. About 80 per cent of the goods handled are imports.

Venice and the North-East.—Venice is primarily a tourist attraction of unique beauty. It was founded in the middle of the 5th century by refugees from the mainland fleeing attacks, and by the 16th century it was one of the strongest and richest states of Europe, dominating Eastern Mediterranean trade. It lost its independence in 1797 when Napoleon handed it over to Austria. Industry (paper and stationery, mechanical equipment, consumer goods, electrical appliances, woollens) is now developing in the Venice area, particularly on the autostrada linking Venice with Verona, Vicenza, Padua and in the areas around Treviso and Pordenone. Near Trieste, is the modern Monfalcone shipyard.

Tuscany, Emilia and Romagna.—Florence, the capital of Tuscany, was one of the greatest cities in Europe from the 11th to the 16th centuries, and the cradle of the Renaissance. Under the Medici family in the 15th century flourished many of the greatest names in Italian art, including Filippo Lippi, Botticelli, Donatello and Brunelleschi and in the 16th century great Florentine artists like Michelangelo and Leonardo da Vinci. These regions were the agricultural centre of Italy but the post-war period has seen the development of large industrial centres at Bologna, Florence, Modena, Pistoia and Ravenna. The footwear industry is based in Florence, textiles in Prato, reproduction furniture at Cascina and Poggibonsi, ceramics at Sassuolo, and glass and pottery at Empoli and Montelupo. Bologna is an important centre for the food industry.

Naples and the toe of Italy.—Naples, formerly the capital and administrative centre of the Kingdom of Naples and Sicily, remains the dominant city in the area, but it is beset with great problems of unemployment and the need for modernization. Around it, however, helped by Government incentives, industry is slowly developing, northwards to Caserta, southwards to Salerno and eastwards to Benevento.

Puglia.—Bari has always been a commercial centre and now industrial development is also taking place in the areas of Taranto, Brindisi and Foggia. At Taranto there are a highly-mechanized steel-works and a modern oil refinery. The Bari industrial zone has factories producing electronic and pneumatic valves, specialized vehicle bodies and tyres, etc. The main industry of Brindisi is a petro-chemical plant. At Foggia there is a textile factory.

Sicily.—The main source of income is agriculture, particularly citrus fruits, almonds and tomatoes. Oil in small quantities has been found off the southern shore of the island and drilling continues, while onshore there are growing oil-refining, natural gas and petrochemical industries. Small and medium sized industries, benefiting from the Government's incentives, are developing, and tourism is bringing an increasing amount of revenue to the island.

Sardinia.—Sardinia is an autonomous region, with its capital at Cagliari. Six main industrial development areas have been officially designated. The major industries are aluminium production (there is a smelting plant at Porto Vesme), petrochemicals, lead and zinc mining; and the tourist industry is flourishing.

Economy

Italian gross domestic product in 1989 was US$859,996 million. One of the economy's major problems is the large budget deficit which is now nearing ten per cent of GDP. The rate of inflation in 1989 was 6·5 per cent.

Industry.—The general index of industrial production (1980=100) stood at +2·7 per cent in 1985–86. The state-owned sector of Italian industry is important, dominated by the holding companies IRI (mechanical, steel, airlines), ENI (petro-chemicals) and ENEL (electricity).

Mineral Production.—Italy is generally poor in mineral resources but since the war deposits of natural methane gas and small deposits of oil have been discovered and rapidly exploited. Production of lignite has also increased. Other minerals produced in significant quantities include iron ores and pyrites, mercury (over one-quarter of the world production), lead, zinc and aluminium. Marble is a traditional product of the Massa Carrara district.

Agriculture.—Agriculture accounted for 5·2 per cent of gross domestic product in 1984. The agricultural labour force was 2,242,000 in 1986.

Tourist Traffic.—In 1987 an estimated 52 million foreign tourists visited Italy, spending an estimated L15,782,808 million.

Communications.—The main railway system is state-run by the *Ferrovia dello Stato*. A network of motorways (*autostrade*) covers the country, built and operated mainly by the IRI state-holding company and ANAS the state highway authority. Alitalia, the principal international and domestic airline, is also state-controlled by the IRI group. Other smaller companies, including ATI (an Alitalia subsidiary) and Air Mediterranea operate on domestic routes. The Italian mercantile marine totalled 7,587,117 tons in December 1985.

Foreign Trade

The balance of trade in 1987 showed a deficit of 11,138 billion lira, compared with 3,722 billion lira in 1986.

The main markets for Italian exports in 1987 were the OECD countries, which accounted for almost 80 per cent of the total, and the EC markets with 56 per cent of the total. Imports came principally from the Federal Republic of Germany, France and the USA.

Trade with UK

	1989	1990
Imports from UK ..	£4,630,896,000	£5,612,751,000
Exports to UK	6,701,683,000	6,735,496,000

Language and Literature.—Italian is a Romance language derived from Latin. It is spoken in its purest form in Tuscany, but there are numerous dialects, showing variously French, German, Spanish and Arabic influences. Sard, the dialect of Sardinia is accorded by some authorities the status of a distinct Romance language. Italian literature (in addition to Latin literature, which is the common inheritance of Western Europe) is one of the richest in Europe particularly in its golden age (Dante, 1265–1321 Petrarch, 1304–1374; Boccaccio, 1313–1375) and in the renaissance (Ariosto, 1474–1533; Machiavelli 1469–1527; Tasso, 1544–1595). Modern Italian literature has many noted names in prose and verse notably Manzoni (1785–1873), Carducci (1835–1907 and Gabriele d'Annunzio (1864–1938). The Nobe Prize for Literature has been awarded to Italia authors on five occasions—G. Carducci (1906), Sig nora G. Deledda (1926), Luigi Pirandello (1934 Salvatore Quasimodo (1959) and Eugenio Montal (1975). In 1987, there were 72 daily newspaper published in Italy, of which 14 were published i Rome and seven in Milan.

Education.—Education is free and compulsor between the ages of 6 and 14; this comprises five yea at primary school and three in the 'middle school', which there are about 8,000. Pupils who obtain th middle school certificate may seek admission to an 'senior secondary school', which may be a lyceu with a classical or scientific or artistic bias, or a institute directed at technology (of which there a eight different types), trade or industry (includir vocational schools), or teacher-training. Courses the lyceums and technical institutes usually last f five years and success in the final examinatic qualifies for admission to university. There are state and 14 private universities, some of ancie foundation; those at Bologna, Modena, Parma an Padua were started in the 12th century. Universi education is not free, but entrants with high qualifications are charged reduced fees according a sliding scale. In general, schools, lyceums a universities are financed by local taxation and centr government grants.

ISLANDS.—*Pantelleria Island* (part of Trapani Province) in the Sicilian Narrows, has an area of 31 sq. miles and a population of 9,601. The *Pelagian Islands* (Lampedusa, Linosa and Lampione) are part of the Province of Agrigento and have an area of 8 sq. miles, pop. 4,811. The Tuscan Archipelago (including Elba), area 293 sq. km, pop. 31,861; Pontine Archipelago (including Ponza, area 10 sq. km, pop. 2,515); Flegrean Islands (including Ischia, area 60 sq. km, pop. 51,883); Capri; Eolian Islands (including Lipari, area 116 sq. km, pop. 18,636); Tremiti Islands (area 3 sq. km, pop. 426).

CAPITAL.—Rome. Population of the commune (1986) 2,821,420.

1986 estimates of the population of the communes of the principal cities and towns are Milan 1,511,193; ΨNaples 1,204,959; Turin 1,034,007; ΨGenoa 733,990; Bologna 436,570; Florence 429,865; Sicily, ΨPalermo 719,960; *Sardinia*, ΨCagliari 223,021.

CURRENCY.—Lira of 100 centesimi.
FLAG.—Vertical stripes of green, white and red.
NATIONAL ANTHEM.—Inno di Mameli.
NATIONAL DAY.—June 2.

BRITISH EMBASSY
Via XX Settembre 80A, 00187 Rome
[Rome 482–5441]

Ambassador Extraordinary and Plenipotentiary, His Excellency Sir Stephen Egerton, KCMG (1989).
Ministers, T. C. Wood, CMG; J. R. Goldsack, MBE (FAO).
Defence and Military Attaché, Brig. A. R. Jones.
Naval Attaché, Capt. W. C. McKnight, LVO.
Air Attaché, Group-Capt. A. R. Tolcher, RAF.
Counsellors, J. P. Watson (*Political*); G. M. Gowlland, LVO (*Political/Management*); C. R. L. de Chassiron (*Commercial/Economic*).
First Secretaries, C. W. G. Edmonds-Brown (*Management*); D. J. Hollamby (*Social Affairs*); N. K. Darroch (*Economic*); G. Roberts (*Consul*); H. Kershaw (*Commercial*); M. E. Smith (*Agriculture and Environment*); Miss K. Coombs (*Information*); R. J. C. Allen (*Political*); J. A. Towner (*Economic*); J. Ashton (*Political*).
Second Secretaries, A. A. Jones; C. J. Ley (*Management*).

There are British Consular Offices at *Milan, Rome, Naples, Genoa, Florence, Venice, Trieste, Brindisi, Bari* and *Turin*.

British Council Representative, Keith Hunter, OBE, Palazzo del Drago, Via Quattro Fontane 20, 00184 Rome.

There are *British Council Offices* at *Milan* and *Naples*, each with a library.

BRITISH CHAMBER OF COMMERCE, Via San Paolo 7, 20121 Milan.

JAPAN
(Nihon Koku—Land of the Rising Sun)

Emperor of Japan, His Imperial Majesty the Emperor Akihito, *born* December 23, 1933; *succeeded* January 8, 1989; *enthroned* November 12, 1990; *married* April 10, 1959, Miss Michiko Shoda, and has *issue* Prince Naruhito Hironomiya (*Crown Prince*), *born* February 23, 1960, Prince Akishino, *born* November 30, 1965, and Princess Sayako, *born* April 18, 1969.

CABINET
(as at June 10, 1991)

Prime Minister, Toshiki Kaifu.
Justice, Megumu Sato.
Foreign Affairs, Taro Nakayama.

Finance, Ryutar Hashimoto.
Education, Yutaka Inoue.
Health and Welfare, Shin'ichiro Shimojo.
Agriculture, Forestry and Fisheries, Motoji Kondo.
International Trade and Industry, Eiichi Nakao.
Transport, Kanezo Muraoka.
Posts and Telecommunications, Katsutsugu Sekiya.
Labour, Sadatoshi Ozato.
Construction, Yuji Otsuka.
Home Affairs, Akira Fukida.

MINISTERS OF STATE

Chief Cabinet Secretary, Misoji Sakamoto.
Director-General of Management and Co-ordination Agency, Man Sasaki.
Director-General of Hokkaido and Okinawa Development Agencies, Yoichi Tani.
Director-General of Defence Agency, Yukihiko Ikeda.
Director-General of Economic Planning Agency, Michio Ochi.
Director-General of Science and Technology Agency, Akiko Santo.
Director-General of Environment Agency, Kazuo Aichi.
Director-General of National Land Agency, Mamoru Nishida.

EMBASSY OF JAPAN
101–104 Piccadilly, W1V 9FN
[071-465 6500]

Ambassador Extraordinary and Plenipotentiary, His Excellency Hiroshi Kitamura (1991).
Ministers, Shotaro Miyake (*Financial*); Hikoharu Kure (*Commercial*).
Counsellors, Yukio Takeuchi; Hiroyasu Ando (*Information and Cultural*); Makoto Mizutani (*Economic*); Sakura Shiga (*Financial*); Shoji Miyamoto (*Agricultural*); Dr Niro Tode (*Medical Attaché*); Satoru Kanazawa (*Transport*); Hitoshi Tanaka (*Political*).
Defence Attaché, Capt. Isamu Kyoda.

Area and Population.—Japan consists of four large islands: *Honshū* (or Mainland), 230,448 sq. km (88,839 sq. m), *Shikoku*, 18,757 sq. km (7,231 sq. m), *Kyūshū*, 42,079 sq. km (16,170 sq. m), *Hokkaido*, 78,508 sq. km (30,265 sq. m), and many small islands situated in the North Pacific Ocean between longitude 128° 6′ East and 145° 49′ East and between latitude 26° 59′ and 45° 31′ N., with a total area of 145,834 sq. miles (377,708 sq. km), and a population estimated by the UN in 1989 at 123,116,000. In 1988 the birth rate was 10·8 per 1,000, and the death rate 6·5 per 1,000.

Physiography.—The coastline exceeds 17,000 miles and is deeply indented, so that few places are far from the sea. The interior is very mountainous, and crossing the mainland from the Sea of Japan to the Pacific is a group of volcanoes, mainly extinct or dormant. Mount Fuji, the loftiest and most sacred mountain of Japan, about 60 miles from Tokyo, is 12,370 ft. high and has been dormant since 1707, but there are other volcanoes which are active, including Mount Aso in Kyūshū. There are frequent earthquakes, mainly along the Pacific coast near the Bay of Tokyo. Japan proper extends from sub-tropical in the south to cool temperate in the north. Heavy snowfalls are frequent on the western slopes of Hokkaidō and Honshū, but the Pacific coasts are warmed by the Japan current. There is a plentiful rainfall and the rivers are short and swift-flowing offering abundant opportunities for the supply of hydro-electric power.

Government.—According to Japanese tradition, Jimmu, the first Emperor of Japan, ascended the throne on February 11, 660 BC. Under the *Meiji* constitution of February 11, 1889, the monarchy was hereditary in the male heirs of the Imperial house.

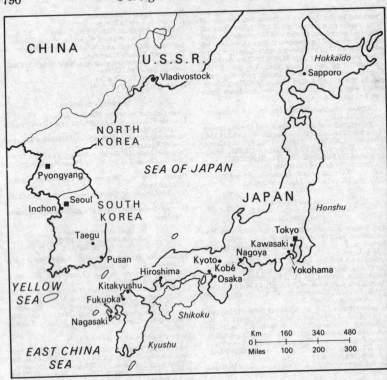

After the unconditional surrender to the Allied Nations (August 14, 1945), Japan was occupied by Allied forces under General MacArthur (September 15, 1945). A Japanese peace treaty conference held in San Francisco in September 1951 led to 48 nations signing the treaty, which became effective on April 28, 1952. Japan then resumed her status as an independent power.

A new constitution came into force on May 3, 1947. Legislative authority rests with the Diet, which is bicameral, consisting of a House of Representatives and a House of Councillors, both Houses being composed of elected members. Executive authority is vested in the Cabinet which is responsible to the Legislature.

The conservatives have governed Japan almost without interruption since World War II. Since 1955, when it was formed, the Liberal Democratic Party has maintained an absolute majority in the House of Representatives. In June 1991 the strength of the Parties was: Liberal Democratic Party 286; Japan Socialist Party 139; Komeito 46; Japan Communist Party 16; Democratic Socialist 14; Independents, 6; Social Democratic Federation 4; others 1.

The House of Councillors, whose powers are subordinate to the House of Representatives, re-elects half of its members every three years. In June 1991 the strength of the Parties was: Liberal Democratic Party 109; Japan Socialist Party 73; Komeito 21; Other, 19; Japan Communist Party 14; Democratic Socialist 10; Independent 5.

Agriculture and Livestock.—Owing to the mountainous nature of the country not more than one-sixth of its area is available for cultivation. The forest land includes Cryptomeria japonica, Pinus massoniana, Zeikowaskeaki, and Paulownia imperialis, in addition to camphor trees, mulberry, vegetable wax tree and a lacquer tree which furnishes the celebrated lacquer of Japan. The soil is only moderately fertile, but intensive cultivation secures good crops. Tobacco, tea, potato, rice, wheat and other cereals are all cultivated; rice is the staple food of the people, about 10,627,000 tonnes being produced in 1987. Fruit is abundant, including the mandarin, persimmon, loquat and peach; European fruits such as apples, strawberries, pears, grapes and figs are also produced. There is a small-scale beef industry and pigs and chickens are widely reared.

Minerals.—The country has mineral resources including gold and silver, and copper, lead, zinc, iron, chromite, white arsenic, coal, sulphur, petroleum, salt and uranium, but iron ore, coal and crude oil are among the principal post-war imports to supply deficiencies at home.

Industry.—Japan is the most highly industrialized nation in the Far East, with the whole range of modern light and heavy industries, including motor vehicles, electronics, metals, machinery, chemical textiles (cotton, silk, wool and synthetics), cement, pottery, glass, rubber, lumber, paper, oil refining and shipbuilding. The labour force of Japan in 1988 (average) was 61,700,000, of which around 2·5 per cent were unemployed. Of the total labour force, over 15 per cent are over 65 and this rate is increasing. Industrial, manufacturing and services workers numbered 53,430,000 and agricultural, forestries and fisheries workers 5,090,000 in 1985.

Communications.—There were 1,120,051 km of road and 44,297 km of rail road (steam and electric) in 1984. Also new Shinkansen (bullet train) tracks are currently being expanded. Japan National Railways was privatized on April 1, 1987 and is known as Japan Railways (JR). There are six regional companies and one goods company. The merchant fleet had a shipping capacity of 38·5 million gross tons in 1986. The opening in 1988 of the Seikan rail tunnel and the Seto Ohashi rail bridge means that the four major islands are now linked for the first time.

Armed Forces.—After the unconditional surrender of August, 1945 the Imperial Army and Navy were disarmed and disbanded.

Although the Constitution of Japan prohibits the maintenance of armed forces, internal security forces came into being in 1950, and 1952. In July 1954, the mission of the forces was extended to include the defence of Japan against direct and indirect aggression.

The defence budget allocated for the fiscal year 1986–87 amounted to Yen 3,343,549 million, equivalent to 6·18 per cent of the General Account budget. The authorized uniformed strength was: Ground Self-Defence Force (GSDF) 180,000 (Reserve 43,000); Maritime Self-Defence Force (MSDF) 43,897 (Reserve 600); Air Self-Defence Force (ASDF) 46,204. Actual strengths of all three services are slightly below their authorized figure.

The GSDF is organized into five regional Armies, totalling thirteen Divisions, one of which is an Armoured Division. Major equipment includes tanks, APCs, towed and SP guns and rocket launchers, Hawk AA missiles, and 425 aircraft. Equipment is now largely manufactured in Japan.

The MSDF has 164 warships and auxiliaries including four DDH, four TARTAR-equipped GMDs, 42 destroyers, 14 submarines and 99 others, 205 fixed-wing aircraft and 97 helicopters.

The ASDF has 820 aircraft including 375 trainers; 43 transports and 75 support aircraft (including helicopters). There are 6 groups of Nike SAM missiles and one training unit of Patriot.

Religion.—All religions are tolerated. The principal religions of Japan are Mahayana Buddhism and Shinto. About 1 per cent of Japanese are Christians.

Education.—Under the Education Law of 1947, education at elementary (six year course) and lower secondary (three year course) schools is free, compulsory and co-educational. The (three year) upper secondary schools are attended by 94 per cent of the age group. They have courses in general, agricultural, commercial, technical, mercantile marine, radio-communication and home-economics education, etc. Of the population aged between 18 and 21, 33 per cent were enrolled in higher education in 1984. There are two- or three-year junior colleges and four-year universities. Some of the universities have graduate schools. In 1987 there were 1,003 universities and junior colleges, the vast majority of which are privately maintained. The most prominent universities are the seven state universities of Tokyo, Kyoto, Tohoku (Sendai), Hokkaido (Sapporo), Kyushu (Fukuoka), Osaka and Nagoya, and the two private universities, Keio and Waseda.

Language and Literature.—Japanese is said to be one of the Uro-Altaic group of languages and remained a spoken tongue until the fifth–seventh centuries AD, when Chinese characters came into use. Japanese who have received school education (99·8 per cent of the population) can read and write the Chinese characters in current use (about 1,800 characters) and also the syllabary characters called Kana. English is the best known foreign language. It is taught in all middle and high schools and universities. There are 125 daily newspapers in Japan.

FINANCE

The Budget for the financial year 1990 for revenue and expenditure on the general account was Yen 66,236,700 million.

PRODUCTION AND TRADE

Being deficient in natural resources, Japan has had to develop a complex foreign trade. Principal imports in 1988 consisted of mineral oils (20·5 per cent), raw materials (8·7 per cent) e.g. metal ores and scrap, 4·5 per cent, timber, 3·8 per cent, foodstuffs (15·5 per cent) (e.g. wheat and sugar), machinery (14·2 per cent), chemicals (7·9 per cent) and textiles (5·7 per cent).

Principal exports consist of non-electric machinery (21·2 per cent), motor vehicles (18·4 per cent), electric machinery and appliances (18·4 per cent), steel (5·8 per cent), chemicals (4·5 per cent), textile goods (2·6 per cent) and ships (1·5 per cent).

FOREIGN TRADE

	1987	1988
	(US$'000)	
Total imports	149,515,113	187,353,686
Total exports	229,221,230	264,916,803

Trade with UK

	1989	1990
Imports from UK ..	£2,259,823,000	£2,631,326,000
Exports to UK	7,108,441,000	6,761,592,000

CAPITAL.—Tokyo, population (December 1989) 11,718,720. The other chief cities had the following populations:
ΨOsaka (2,633,000); ΨNagoya (2,152,000); ΨYokohama (3,197,000); Kyoto, the ancient capital (1,471,000); ΨKobé (1,464,000); Kita-Kyushu (1,034,000); Sapporo (1,652,000); ΨKawasaki (1,159,000); ΨFukuoka (1,220,000).

CURRENCY.—Yen of 100 sen.

FLAG.—White, charged with sun (red).

NATIONAL ANTHEM.—Kimigayo.

NATIONAL DAY.—December 23 (the Emperor's Birthday).

BRITISH EMBASSY

No. 1 Ichiban-cho, Chiyoda-ku, Tokyo 102
[Tokyo 3265–5511]

Ambassador Extraordinary and Plenipotentiary, His Excellency Sir John Stainton Whitehead, KCMG, CVO (1986).

Minister, E. J. Field, CMG (*Deputy Head of Mission*); J. E. W. Kirby (*Financial*).

Counsellors, P. Dimond (*Commercial*); C. Humfrey (*Economic*); G. H. Fry (*Head of Chancery*); Dr R. Hinder (*Science and Technology*); C. Loughlin (*Atomic Energy*); R. Seeley (*Chancery*); J. Kirby (*Financial*); D. Pragnell, LVO, OBE (*Management*).

First Secretaries, N. Hook, MVO, S. Plater (*Commercial*); D. H. Powell, M. Everest-Phillips (*Chancery*); J. Alderson, P. Madden, S. McNeil-Ritchie, S. J. Smith (*Economic*); T. Salusbury (*Science and Technology*); R. E. Coghlan (*Information*); Mrs S. Hogwood, MBE (*Consul*).

Defence and Naval Attaché, Capt. C. Crawford.

Air Attaché, Gp. Capt. A. Terrett.

There is a British Consulate-General at *Osaka* and Honorary Consulates at *Fukuoka, Hiroshima* and *Nagoya.*

British Council Representative, R. P. Joscelyne, 2 Kagurazaka 1-Chome, Shinjuku-ku, Tokyo 162. There is also an office and library in *Kyoto.*

BRITISH CHAMBER OF COMMERCE

No. 16 Kowa Building, 1–9–20 Akasaka, Minato-ku, Tokyo 107.

JORDAN
(Al-Mamlaka al Urduniya al-Hashemiyah)

King of the Jordan, Hussein, GCVO, *born* November 14, 1935, *succeeded* on the deposition of his father, King Talal, Aug. 11, 1952, *assumed constitutional powers,* May 2, 1953, on coming of age.

Crown Prince, Prince Hassan, third son of King Talal of Jordan, *born* 1948, *appointed Crown Prince,* April 1, 1965.

CABINET
(as at June 19, 1991)

Prime Minister and Minister of Defence, Taher Masri.
Deputy PM and Minister of Transport and Communications, Ali Al-Suhimat.
Waqf and Islamic Affairs, Ra'-if Najem.
Foreign Affairs, Dr Abdullah Al-Nusour.
Education, Dr Eid Al-Duhayat.
Higher Education, Dr Mohamed Al-Hamori.
Finance, Basil Jardaneh.
Planning, Dr Ziad Fariz.
Tourism and Antiquities, Abdul Karim Al-Kabariti.
Labour and Prime Ministry Affairs, Abdul-Karim Al-Daghmi.
Energy and Mineral Resources, Thabet Al-Taher.
Information and Culture, Dr Khalid Al-Karaki.
Public Works and Housing, Saad Hayall Al-Soroor.
Minister of State for Parliamentary Affairs, Abdul Salam Frihat.
Municipal and Rural Affairs and the Environment, Saleem Al-Zubi.
Social Development, Dr Aouni Al-Basheer.
Water and Irrigation, Samir Qa'war.
Minister of State for Prime Ministry Affairs, Mohammed Faris Al-Tarawneh.
Minister of State, Jamal Hadethah Al-Khrisha.
Interior, Jaudat Al-Suboul.
Justice, Tayseer Kana'an.
Agriculture, Dr Subhi Al-Qassem.
Industry and Trade and Supply, Ali Abu Al-Raghib.
Health, Dr Mamdoh Al-Abadi.
Youth, Saleh Irshedat.

EMBASSY OF THE HASHEMITE KINGDOM OF JORDAN
6 Upper Phillimore Gardens, W8 7HB
[071-937 3685/7]

Ambassador Extraordinary and Plenipotentiary, new appointment awaited.
Minister Counsellor, Dr Abdulla Madadha.
Defence Attaché, Brig. H. Al-Rusan.
Service Office: 16 Upper Phillimore Gardens, W8. (071–937–9611).

Area and Population.—The Hashemite Kingdom of the Jordan, which covers 37,738 sq. miles (97,740 sq. km), is bounded on the north by Syria, on the west by Israel, on the south by Saudi Arabia and on the east by Iraq. Since the hostilities of June 1967, that part of the country lying to the west of the Jordan River has been under Israeli occupation. The majority of the population are Sunni Muslims and Islam is the religion of the State; freedom of belief is, however, guaranteed by the Constitution. Total population on

the East Bank of the Jordan was estimated (1988) t₀ be 2,910,000.

History.—After the defeat of Turkey in the Firs₀ World War the Amirate of Transjordan was estab₀ lished in the area east of the River Jordan as a stat₀ under British mandate. The mandate was terminate₀ after the Second World War and the Amirate, sti₀ ruled by its founder, the Amir Abdullah, became th₀ Hashemite Kingdom of Jordan. Following the 194₀ war between Israel and the Arab States, that part ₀ Palestine remaining in Arab hands (but excludin₀ Gaza) was incorporated into the Hashemite Kingdom King Abdullah was assassinated in 1951; his son Tal₀ ruled briefly but abdicated in favour of the presen₀ King, Hussein, in 1952.

All of Jordan west of the River has been unde₀ Israeli occupation since 1967. In 1988 Jordan severe₀ its legal and administrative ties with the occupie₀ West Bank, but did not formally renounce sover₀ eignty over the area. As a result of the wars of 194₀ and 1967 there are about 991,000 refugees an₀ displaced persons living in East Jordan, about 200,00₀ of whom live in refugee and displaced persons cam₀ established by the UN Relief and Works Agenc₀ (UNRWA). In addition there are some 300,00₀ entirely self-supporting Palestinian members of th₀ East Jordanian community.

Government.—The present constitution of th₀ Kingdom came into force in 1952. It provides for ₀ senate of 40 members (all appointed by the King) an₀ an elected House of Representatives. Until 1988, th₀ House of Representatives had 60 members represen₀ ing both the East and West Banks. Legislation passe₀ in 1989 stipulated that in future elections, seat₀ would be contested on the East Bank only. The firs₀ parliamentary elections since 1967 to the new 8₀ member House of Representatives took place i₀ November 1989.

The King appoints the members of the Council ₀ Ministers. Crown Prince Hassan normally acts a₀ Regent when King Hussein is away from Jordan.

Production and Industry.—The main agricu₀ tural areas are the Jordan Valley, the hills overlook₀ ing the valley and the flatter country to the south ₀ Amman and around Madaba and Irbid, thoug₀ several large farms, which depend for irrigation o₀ water pumped from deep aquifers, have been estab₀ lished in the Southern desert area. The rest of th₀ country is desert and semi-desert. The principa₀ crops are wheat, barley, vegetables, olives and fru₀ (mainly grapes and citrus fruits). Agricultural pr₀ duction has increased considerably in recent year₀ due to improvements in production and irrigatio₀ techniques, and exports to Europe and elsewhere ar₀ increasing.

Important industrial products are raw phosphate (1988: 5·6 million tons) and potash (1988: 1·3 millio₀ tons), most of which is exported. The Trans-Arabia₀ oil pipeline (Tapline) runs through North Jordan o₀ its way from the eastern province of Saudi Arabia t₀ the Lebanese port of Sidon. A branch pipelin₀ together with oil trucked by road from Iraq, feeds ₀ refinery at Zerqa (production 1988: 2·3 million ton₀ which meets most of Jordan's requirements fo₀ refined petroleum products. Sufficient reserves ₀ natural gas have been discovered in the north-east t₀ produce electricity for the national grid (generator₀ were commissioned in May 1989). Despite extensiv₀ efforts no significant reserves of oil have been found

Tourism has steadily developed. Internationa₀ class hotels cater for businessmen and tourists i₀ Amman and Aqaba. A spa hotel has been opened b₀ hot springs close to the Dead Sea and a hotel comple₀ is planned at the Dead Sea.

Communications.—The trunk road system ₀ good. Amman is linked to Aqaba, Damascus, Baghda₀ and Jeddah by roads which are of considerabl importance in the overland trade of the Middle East. The former Hejaz Railway enters Jordan from Syria east of Ramtha and runs through Zerqa and Amman to Ma'an with a spur to the top of the Ras al-Naqb escarpment. It is little used, mainly for freight between Amman and Damascus. The Aqaba railway carries phosphate rock from the mines of al Hasa and al Abiad to Aqaba. A total of 2,583 vessels called at Aqaba in 1988, and 20,096,200 tons of cargo were handled. The Royal Jordanian Airline operates from Amman to Aqaba and has an extensive network of routes to the Middle East, Europe, North America and the Far East.

FINANCE

	1987	1988
	(JD'000)	
Revenue	869,969	917,562
Expenditure	965,808	1,045,680
Surplus/Deficit	−95,839	−128,118

Trade with UK

	1989	1990
Imports from UK	£110,684,000	£109,483,000
Exports to UK	18,462,000	14,788,000

CAPITAL.—Amman, population (1988 estimate) 1,100,000.

CURRENCY.—Jordanian dinar (JD) of 1,000 fils.

FLAG.—Black, white and green horizontal stripes, surcharged with white seven-point star on red triangle.

NATIONAL ANTHEM.—Long Live the King.

NATIONAL DAY.—May 25 (Independence Day).

BRITISH EMBASSY
Abdoun (PO Box 87),
Amman
[Amman 823100]

Ambassador Extraordinary and Plenipotentiary, His Excellency P. H. C. Eyers, CMG, LVO.

Counsellors, H. G. Hogger (*Deputy Head of Mission and Consul-General*); M. S. Allen.

Defence Attaché, Col. P. A. Goddard.

First Secretaries, M. J. H. Tobin (*Consul and Management*); T. Ellis (*Commercial and Development*).

British Council Representative, M. Roddis, Rainbow Street, (PO Box 634), Jebel Amman, Amman.

KOREA

Korea is situated between 124° 11″ and 130° 57′ E. long., and between 33° 7′ and 43° 1″ N. lat. It has an area of 84,565 sq. miles (219,022 sq. km), with a population (UN estimate 1989) of 64,799,000, of whom about 42 million live south of the present dividing line. The southern and western coasts are fringed with innumerable islands, of which the largest, forming a province of its own, is Cheju.

History.—The last native dynasty (Yi) ruled from 1392 until 1910, in which year Japan formally annexed Korea. The country remained an integral part of the Japanese Empire until the defeat of Japan in 1945, when it was occupied by troops of the USA and the USSR, the 38th parallel being fixed as the boundary between the two zones of occupation. The US Government endeavoured to reach agreement with the Soviet Government for the creation of a Korean Government for the whole country and the withdrawal of all Russian and American troops. These efforts met with no success, and in September 1947 the US Government laid the whole question of the future of Korea before the General Assembly of the United Nations. The Assembly in November 1947 resolved that elections should be held in Korea for a National Assembly under the supervision of a temporary Commission formed for that purpose by the United Nations and that the National Assembly when elected should set up a Government. The Soviet Government refused to allow the Commission to visit the Russian Occupied Zone and in consequence it was only able to discharge its function in that part of Korea which lies to the south of the 38th parallel.

A general election was held on May 10, 1948, and the first National Assembly met in Seoul on May 31. The Assembly passed a constitution on July 12, and on August 15, 1948 the Republic was formally inaugurated and American Military Government came to an end.

Meanwhile in the Russian-occupied zone north of the 38th parallel the Democratic People's Republic had been set up with its capital at Pyongyang; a Supreme People's Soviet was elected in September 1948, and a Soviet-style Constitution adopted.

The Korean War.—The country remained effectively divided into two along the line of the 38th parallel until June 1950, when the North Korean forces invaded South Korea. In response to Security Council recommendations that United Nations members should furnish assistance to repel the attack, 16 nations, including the USA and the UK, came to the aid of the Republic of Korea. China entered the war on the side of North Korea in November, 1950. The fighting was ended by an Armistice Agreement signed on July 27, 1953. By this Agreement (which was not signed by the representatives of the Republic of Korea) the line of division between North and South Korea remained in the neighbourhood of the 38th parallel. Talks between North and South Korea on the reunification of the country have taken place intermittently.

Language and Literature.—Despite the great cultural influence of the Chinese, Koreans have developed and preserved their own cultural heritage. The Korean language is of the Ural-Altaic Group. Its script, Hangul, was invented in the 15th century; prior to this Chinese characters alone were used. Also invented around this time was the first metal movable printing type.

REPUBLIC OF KOREA
(Daehanminkuk)

President, Roh Tae Woo, *took office* February 24, 1988.

CABINET
(as at May 29, 1991)

Prime Minister, Chung Won Shik.
Economic Planning Board, Choi Gak Joong.
Foreign Affairs, Lee Sang Ock.
Home Affairs, Lee Sang Yeon.
Finance, Rhee Yong Man.
Justice, Kim Ki Choon.
Defence, Lee Jong Koo.
Education, Yoon Hyoung Sup.
Youth and Sports, Park Chul Un.
Agriculture and Fisheries, Cho Kyung Shik.
Energy and Resources, Jin Nyum.
Environment, Kwon Ui Hyak.
Trade and Industry, Lee Bong-Suh.
Construction, Lee Jin Seol.
Health and Social Affairs, Ahn Pil Joon.
Labour, Choe Byung Yul.
Transport, Lim In Taik.
Communications, Song Eon Jong.
Culture, Lee O Young.
Information, Choi Chang Yun.
Government Administration, Lee Yun Taek.
Science and Technology, Kim Jin Hyun.
National Unification, Choi Ho Joong.

First Minister for Political Affairs, Kim Dong Young.
Second Minister for Political Affairs, Lee Kye Soon.
Director, Office of Legislation, Choi Sang Yop.
Director, Patrons and Veterans' Administration, Min Kyung Bae.
Director, National Security Planning Agency, Suh Dong Kwon.

KOREAN EMBASSY
4 Palace Gate, W8 5NF
[071–581 0247]

Ambassador Extraordinary and Plenipotentiary, His Excellency Dr Hong Koo Lee (1991).
Minister, Keun Bae Choi.

The Republic of Korea has been officially recognized by the Governments of the United States, France, United Kingdom, and most other countries but, until recently, not by any Communist bloc country. Since 1989 diplomatic relations have been established with all eastern European countries except Albania.

Government.—Following extensive political unrest in 1987, a new Constitution was adopted in February 1988. The President, who is Head of State, Chief of the Executive and Commander-in-Chief of the Armed Forces, is directly elected for a single term of five years. He appoints the Prime Minister with the consent of the National Assembly, and members of the State Council (Cabinet) on the recommendation of the Prime Minister. The President is also empowered to take wide-ranging measures in an emergency, including the declaration of martial law, but must obtain the agreement of the National Assembly. The National Assembly of 299 members is directly elected for a four-year term.

The most recent elections to the National Assembly were held in April 1989. The Democratic Justice Party (DJP) failed to achieve an overall majority despite emerging as the largest single party. In February 1990 the DJP merged with two opposition parties to form the Democratic Liberal Party, which now holds the majority.

Armed Forces.—The Republic of Korea has an army of about 650,000, a small navy mostly for coastal patrol and protection duties, an air force with about 500 combat aircraft and a marine corps which is incorporated in the navy. About five per cent of the nation's GNP is currently spent on defence.

Education and Religion.—Primary education is compulsory for six years from the age of seven. Secondary and higher education is extensive. The national illiteracy rate is among the lowest in Asia.

There is freedom of religion. Buddhism has the most followers (13 million) followed by Protestantism (8 million) and Confucianism (4·7 million). Catholics number 2·2 million.

Agriculture and Fisheries.—The soil is fertile but the arable land is limited by the mountainous nature of the country. Staple agricultural products are rice, barley and other cereals, beans, tobacco and hemp. Fruit growing and sericulture are also practised. Ginseng, a medicinal root much used by both the Chinese and Koreans, forms a useful source of revenue. The Korean fishing industry is a major contributor to both food supply and exports.

Minerals.—The Republic of Korea is deficient in mineral resources, except for deposits of coal on the east coast and tungsten. There are some prospects of discovering oil in the sea between Korea and Japan.

Finance.—The budget for 1990 totals Won 22,689,000. Since the beginning of 1962 a series of successful five-year plans resulted in real economic growth averaging around 10 per cent a year. The sixth economic development plan (1987–91) envisages a growth rate of 7·5 per cent. Annual per capita GNP is US$4,400 (1989).

Trade and Industry.—Since the 1960s the Republic of Korea has industrialized rapidly on the basis of greatly expanded exports. Important exports include cars, electrical and electronic equipment, footwear, ships, railway rolling stock and iron and steel products.

TRADE

	1989	1990
Imports	US$56,312m	US$65,091m
Exports	61,409m	63,236m

Trade with UK

	1989	1990
Imports from UK	£493,945,000	£620,690,000
Exports to UK	1,164,723,000	963,829,000

Communications and Transport.—In 1989 there were 37,493 km of paved road. Seoul and Pusan have subway systems and there are national railway and airline systems. Korean Air operates regular flights to Europe, the United States, the Middle East and South East Asia. Pusan and Inchon are the major ports with Pusan serving the industrial areas of the south-east. Inchon, 28 miles from Seoul, serves the capital, but development and operation at Inchon are hampered by a tidal variation of 9–10 metres.

CAPITAL.—Seoul, population (Nov. 1987) 9,991,089. Other main centres are Ψ Pusan (3,654,097), Taegu (2,165,954) and Ψ Inchon (1,526,435).

CURRENCY.—Won of 100 jeon.

FLAG.—White, with red over blue device in centre, three black parallel bars, some broken, in each quarter.

NATIONAL ANTHEM.—Aegukka.

NATIONAL DAY.—August 15 (Independence Day).

BRITISH EMBASSY
No. 4, Chung-Dong, Chung-Ku, Seoul 100
[Seoul 735–7341/3]

Ambassador Extraordinary and Plenipotentiary, His Excellency David John Wright, LVO (1990).
Counsellor, P. Longworth (*Commercial*).
Defence and Military Attaché, Brig. D. P. de C. Morgan.
First Secretaries, W. Morris (*Head of Chancery and Consul*); D. M. Grey (*Commercial/Information*).

There is an Honorary British Consul at *Pusan*.

British Council Representative, T. White, MBE, Anglican Church Annex, 3–7 Chung Dong, Choong-ku, Seoul.

BRITISH CHAMBER OF COMMERCE, c/o Chartered Bank, 1st and 2nd Floors, Samsung Building, 50, 1-Ka Ulchi Ro, Chung-Ku, Seoul.

DEMOCRATIC PEOPLE'S
REPUBLIC OF KOREA
(Chosun Minchu-chui Inmin Kongwa-guk)

Politburo of the Central Committee, Kim Il-sung; Kim Chong-il; O Chin-u (*full members and members of the presidium*); Yi Chong-ok; Pak Song-chol; So Chol; Kim Yong-nam; Yon Hyong-muk; Kye Ung-tae; Kang Song-san; So Yun-sok; Chon Pyong-ho; Choe Kwang; Han Song-yong (*full members*). Cho Se-ung; Chong Chun-ki; Hyon Mu-kwang; Yi Son-sil; Kang Hui-won; Kim Pok-sin; Hong Si-hak; Hong Song-nam; Choe Tae Pok; Kim Chol-man; Choe Yong-nim (*alternate members*).
Secretariat of the Central Committee, Kim Il-sung (*General Secretary*); Kim Chong-il; Hwang Chang yop; So Kwan-hui; Pak Nam-ki; Kim Chung-nin; Kye Ung-tae; Chon Pyong-ho; Choe Tae-pok; Han Song-yong; Yun Ki-pok; Kim Yong-sun.

The area of North Korea is 46,540 sq. miles (120,538 sq. km), with a population of 21,902,000 (UN estimate 1988). North Korea is rich in minerals and industry has been developed, but the economy has stagnated in recent years because of poor planning and a shortage of foreign exchange. The armed forces are believed to number about 890,000 men.

Government.—The Constitution of the Democratic People's Republic of Korea provides for a Supreme People's Assembly, presently consisting of 687 deputies, which is elected every four years by universal suffrage. The Assembly elects a President, and the Central People's Committee. In turn, the Central People's Committee directs the Administrative Council which implements the policy formulated by the Committee. The Administrative Council (51 members), formally the government of North Korea, includes the Prime Minister and various ministers. In practice however, the country is ruled by the Communist Party which elects a Central Committee; this in turn appoints a Politburo. The senior ministers of the Administrative Council are all members of the Communist Central Committee and the majority are also members of the Politburo. Kim Il-sung was elected President for a fifth four-year term on May 24, 1990.

Trade with UK

	1989	1990
Imports from UK	£3,087,000	£4,774,000
Exports to UK	1,095,000	373,000

CAPITAL.—Pyongyang, approximate population, 1,500,000.

CURRENCY.—Won of 100 chon.

FLAG.—Broad red horizontal band bordered by white lines bearing a five-point red star on a white disc in centre; blue horizontal bands at top and bottom.

NATIONAL DAY.—September 8.

NATIONAL ANTHEM.—A Chi Mun Bin No Ra I Gang San (Shine bright, oh dawn, on this land so fair).

KUWAIT
(Dowlat al- Kuwait)

Amir, HH Sheikh Jabir al-Ahmad al Jabir Al-Sabah, *born* 1928; acceded Jan. 1, 1978.

CABINET
(as at April 22, 1991)

Prime Minister, Saad al-Abdullah al-Salim Al-Sabah.
Deputy Prime Minister and Minister for Foreign Affairs, Sheikh Salim al-Sabah al-Salim.
Minister of State for Municipal Affairs, Dr Ibrahim Majid al-Shahin.
Interior, Sheikh Ahmad al-Hamud al-Jabir.
Planning, Dr Ahmad Ali al-Jassar.
Electricity and Water, Ahmad Muhammad Salih al-Adasani.
Information, Badr Jasim al-Ya'qub.
Communications, Habib Jawhar Hayat.
Petroleum, Dr Hamud Abdullah al-Raqubath.
Education, Sulayman Sa'dun al-Badr.
Minister of State for Cabinet Affairs, Dari Abdullah al-Uthman.
Commerce and Industry, Abdullah Hasan al-Jarallah.
Public Works, Abdullah Yusuf al-Qutami.
Health, Dr Abdul Wahhab Sulayman al-Fawzan.
Defence, Sheikh Ali Sabah al-Salim.
Higher Education, Dr Ali Abdullah al-Shamlan.
Justice and Legal Affairs, Ghazi Ubayd al-Sammar.
Waqf and Islamic Affairs, Muhammad Saqar al-Ma'usharji.
Minister of State for Housing, Muhammad Abd al-Muhsin al-Usfur.

Finance, Nasir Abdullah al-Rawdan.
Social Affairs and Labour, Sheikh Nuwwaf al-Ahmad al-Jabir.

EMBASSY OF THE STATE OF KUWAIT
45–46 Queen's Gate, SW7 5JN.
[071–589 4533]

Ambassador Extraordinary and Plenipotentiary, His Excellency Ghazi M. A. Al-Rayes (1980).

Area and Population.—Kuwait extends along the shore of the Persian Gulf from Iraq to Saudi Arabia, with an area of 6,880 sq. miles (17,818 sq. km). Kuwait has a dry, desert climate with a summer season extending from April to September. The mean temperature varies between 29–45°C in summer, and 8–18°C in winter. Humidity rarely exceeds 60 per cent except in July and August. At the 1985 census the population was 1,695,128, of which about 42 per cent were Kuwaiti citizens, the remainder being other Arabs, Iranians, Indians and Pakistanis. The total European and American population was about 12,500. The gross population growth rate is 6·4 per cent, a growth rate of 3·5 per cent for Kuwaiti citizens. The population was estimated at over 800,000 in June 1991.

The official language is Arabic, and English is widely spoken as a second language. Islam is the official religion, though religious freedom is constitutionally guaranteed.

Government.—Although Kuwait had been independent for some years, the 'exclusive agreement' of 1899 between the Sheikh of Kuwait and the British Government was formally abrogated by an exchange of letters dated June 19, 1961.

Under the Constitution legislative power is vested in the Amir and the 50-member National Assembly, and executive power in the Amir and the Cabinet. The sixth National Assembly was dissolved in July 1986. Elections to a new National Assembly took place in June 1990.

A new National Council was then established with an additional 25 members appointed by the Amir. Having boycotted the elections, the opposition maintained their demands for a new National Assembly. Iraq invaded Kuwait on August 2, 1990 and a government-in-exile was established in Saudi Arabia. In October 1990, the Kuwaiti Prime Minister confirmed the al-Sabahs' commitment to the 1962 constitution. Kuwait was liberated in February 1991. The restored government has promised elections in October 1992. (*See also* Events of the Year.)

Education, etc.—As a result of considerable oil revenues, the Kuwait Government embarked on a large scale development scheme and plans for social services. Education and medical treatment are free. New hospitals and schools continue to be built. Kuwait University was opened in 1966, and in 1987–88 had 15,602 students. In 1987–88 there were over 489,000 pupils at government and private schools.

Public Utilities.—Kuwait has a domestic water supply from water distillation plants which operate on natural gas from the oil fields. These plants can produce over 118,000,000 gallons of fresh water daily. Total water storage capacity, in reservoirs and water towers, amounts to over 1,201 million gallons. A natural source of fresh water, discovered at Raudhatain in the north of the State, has been developed to produce up to 3,000,000 gallons per day for at least 20 years and a pipeline has been built to carry the water to Kuwait town.

Electricity is produced by six power stations in Kuwait. Production in 1987 was 18,092 million Kwh.

Communications.—Ships of British, Dutch, Kuwaiti and other lines make regular calls at Kuwait. Several international and Middle Eastern airlines operate regular air services, and other companies make non-scheduled flights to Kuwait under charter. There is a network of dual-carriageway roads and more are under construction. Telecommunications and postal services are conducted by the Kuwait Government, which has built an earth satellite station.

Both public utilities and communications were severely damaged during the Iraqi occupation.

Finance.—Expected revenue for the financial year 1989–90 was KD2,230·5 m and expenditure KD3,549·1 m. Oil revenues constitute about 90 per cent of total revenue. There are a large number of investment banks in some of which the Government holds equity. The banking system is controlled by the Central Bank of Kuwait.

Production.—The GDP of Kuwait in 1987 was estimated at KD5,444·5 million.

Despite the desert terrain, 8·4 per cent of land is under cultivation, fruit and vegetables being the main crops. Shrimp fishing is becoming important.

The government of Kuwait began to participate in the ownership of the British- and American-owned Kuwait Oil Company in 1974 and an agreement was signed in November 1975 which brought 100 per cent government ownership. After a reorganization of the national oil industry in 1980, all the business was taken over by the Kuwait Petroleum Corporation.

The centre of Kuwait oil production is at Burgan, south of Kuwait City. Oil is also lifted in the Kuwait/Saudi Arabia Partitioned Zone (Wafra) south of the state. Oil is exported through a specially constructed port at Mina al Ahmadi.

Oil installations were extensively damaged during the Iraqi occupation. Oil exports were resumed in July 1991 but production was only 115,000 barrels per day, ten per cent of the pre-war total.

Trade.—Oil constitutes Kuwait's major export. Non-oil exports include chemical fertilizers, ammonia and other chemicals, metal pipes, shrimps and building materials; re-exports accounted for 73 per cent of non-oil exports in 1982. Major trading partners are Asian countries, followed by EC countries and Arab states.

Trade with UK

	1989	1990
Imports from UK	£228,711,000	£181,480,000
Exports to UK	150,364,000	108,970,000

CAPITAL.— Ψ Kuwait, population (excluding suburbs) 400,000.

CURRENCY.—Kuwaiti dinar (KD) of 1,000 fils.

FLAG.—Three horizontal stripes of green, white and red, with black trapezoid next to staff.

NATIONAL DAY.—February 25.

BRITISH EMBASSY
PO Box Safat 2,
Arabian Gulf Street, Kuwait
[Kuwait 2403326]

Ambassador Extraordinary and Plenipotentiary, His Excellency Michael Weston, CVO (1990).

Counsellor, L. E. Walker.

First Secretaries, R. D. Lamb (*Political*); L. Banks (*Consul*); P. Wallis (*Political*); A. Young.

British Council Representative, Dr N. Taylor, 2 al Arabi Street, (PO Box 345), Mansouriyah.

LAOS
(Satharanarath Pasathipatai Pasason Lao)

President, Kaysone Phomvihane.
President of the Supreme People's Assembly, Nouhak Phoumsavan.

COUNCIL OF MINISTERS
(as at August 1991)

Prime Minister, Gen. Khamtai Siphandon.
Deputy PM and Minister for Economy, Planning and Finance, Khamphoui Keoboualapha.
Foreign Affairs, Phoune Sipraseuth.
National Defence and Supreme Commander of the Lao People's Army, Lt.-Gen. Choummali Saignason.
Minister, and Head of the Office of the Party Central Committee and of the Office of the Council of Ministers, Maisouk Saisompheng.
Minister to the PM's Office, Chanmi Douangboutdi.
Interior, Asang Laoli.
Justice, Kou Souvannamethi.
Public Health, Kambou Sounisai.
Agriculture and Forestry, Inkong Mahavong.
Industry and Handicraft, Soulivong Daravong.
Communications, Transport, Posts and Construction, Bouathong.
Trade and Tourism, vacant.
Education and Sport, Lt.-Gen. Saman Vignaket.
Economic Relations with Foreign Countries, Phao Bounaphon.
Information and Culture, Son Khamvanvongsa.
Chairwoman of the State Bank, Pani Yathotou.
Chairman of the Party and State Inspection Committee, Maychantan Sengmani.
Chairman of the Nationalities Committee, Nhiavu Lobliayo.
Science and Technology, Souli Nanthavong.

Position and Extent.—The People's Democratic Republic of Laos is in the northerly part of Indo-China, lying between China and Vietnam, on the north and east, and Myanmar (Burma) and Thailand on the west. Laos has a common boundary with Cambodia to the south. The area of the country is 91,429 sq. miles (231,800 sq. km), with a population (UN estimate 1989) of 3,972,000.

Government.—The Kingdom of Lane Xang, the Land of a Million Elephants, was founded in the 14th century, but broke up at the beginning of the 15th century into the separate kingdoms of Luang Prabang and Vientiane and the Principality of Champassac, which together came under French protection in 1893. In 1945 the Japanese executed a coup and suppressed the French administration. Under a Constitution of 1947 Laos became a constitutional monarchy under King Sisvang Vong of the House of Luang Prabang, and an independent sovereign state in 1949. The next twenty-five years in Laos were marked by power struggles and civil war.

The Lao People's Democratic Republic was proclaimed in December 1975 following victory by the communist Lao Patriotic Front and the abdication of the King. A President and Council of Ministers were installed, and a 45-member Supreme People's Council was appointed to draft a Constitution. A draft Constitution was approved by the People's Supreme Assembly in August 1991. The Lao People's Revolutionary Party (LPRP) is the sole legal political organization.

Economy.—There is no significant industrial base in Laos, an estimated 85 per cent of the work force being engaged in agriculture, largely concerned with rice cultivation. Rice production in 1984 amounted to 1·3 million tonnes, thus rendering the country theoretically self-sufficient in this staple food.

In 1984, exports amounted to US$36·2m and imports to US$98·4m. Hydro-electric power was 88·3 per cent of exports, timber 8·5 per cent and coffee 1·2 per cent. Clearing agreements have been signed with certain socialist countries and the trade gap is largely financed by foreign aid, of which some 60 per cent is provided by socialist countries.

Laos' economic performance so far has been poor and shows no signs of early recovery. The free market rate for the dollar is much higher than the official rate and prices of consumer items continue to increase.

Trade with UK

	1989	1990
Imports from UK	£908,000	£1,261,000
Exports to UK	1,369,000	54,000

CAPITAL.—Vientiane, population (estimated 1984) 120,000.

CURRENCY.—Kip (K) of 100 at.

FLAG.—Blue background with a central white circle, framed by two horizontal red stripes.

NATIONAL DAY.—December 2.

British Ambassador, resident in Bangkok, Thailand.

LATVIA
See pp. 856–7

LEBANON
(Al-Jumhouriya al-Lubnaniya)

President of the Republic of Lebanon, Elias Hrawi, November 25, 1989.

CABINET
(as at June 30, 1991)

Prime Minister, Omar Karame.
Deputy PM and Minister of Defence, Michel Murr.
Foreign Affairs, Fares Bouez.
Justice, Khatchik Babikian.
Health and Social Affairs, Jamil Kebbeh.
Labour, Michel Sassin.
Posts and Telecommunications, Georges Saadeh.
Finance, Ali al-Khalil.
Education and Fine Arts, Boutros Harb.
Hydroelectric Resources, Muhammad Yussef Beydoun.
Economy and Trade, Marwan Hamadeh.
Information, Albert Mansour.
Agriculture, Mohsen Dalloul.
Minister of State for Administrative Reform, Zaher al-Khatib.
Public Works and Transport, Nadim Salim.
Industry and Oil, Muhammad Jarudi.
Interior, Maj. Gen. Sami al-Khatib.
Minister of State for Land, Sea and Air Transport Affairs, Shawki Fakhoury.
Minister of State for Environmental Affairs, Agop Zukhatarian.
Housing and Co-operatives, Muhammad Beydoun.
Tourism, Talal Arslan.
Ministers of State, Nabih Berri; Nazih Bizri; Walid Jumblatt; Nicola Khoury; Asad Hardan; Abdullah al-Amine; Roger Dib; Sleimane Tony Frangieh; Elie Hobeika.

LEBANESE EMBASSY IN LONDON
21 Kensington Palace Gardens, W8 4QM
[071–229 7265/6]

Ambassador Extraordinary and Plenipotentiary, His Excellency Mahmoud Hammoud (1990).
Consular Section, 15 Palace Gardens Mews, W8 (071–727 6696)

Area and Population.—Lebanon forms a strip about 120 miles in length and varying in width from 30 to 35 miles, along the Mediterranean littoral, and extending from the Israel frontier on the south to the Nahr al Kebir (15 miles north of Tripoli) on the north; its eastern boundary runs down the Anti-Lebanon range and then down the Great Central depression, the *Beqaa*, from which flow the rivers Orontes and Litani. It is divided into five districts, North Lebanon, Mount Lebanon, Beirut, South Lebanon and Beqaa. The seaward slopes of the mountains have a Mediterranean climate and vegetation. The inland range of Anti-Lebanon has the characteristics of steppe country. There is a mixed Arabic-speaking population of Christians, Muslims and Druses. The total area of Lebanon is 4,015 sq. miles, (10,400 sq. km), population (UN estimate 1989) 2,897,000.

Government.—Lebanon became an independent state in September 1920, administered under French mandate until November 22, 1943. Powers were transferred to the Lebanese Government from January 1944, and French troops were withdrawn in 1946.

In April 1975, serious fighting broke out in Beirut between members of the predominantly Christian Phalangist Party and mainly Muslim militias later supported by Palestinian guerrillas based in Lebanon; clashes continued between various parties until 1990.

In the autumn of 1976 the Arab Deterrent Forces, composed mainly of Syrian troops, imposed an effective ceasefire. In March 1978 Israeli forces invaded but withdrew some months later, handing over their positions, except for a belt in the south, to the UN Interim Force in Lebanon (UNIFIL). In the summer of 1982 Israeli forces again invaded the country, penetrating as far as Beirut. Following negotiations, Palestine Liberation Organization guerrillas left Beirut for various Arab countries. Although the bulk of Israeli troops withdrew from southern Lebanon in 1985, a buffer zone controlled by Israeli-backed Christian militias has been established along the Israeli-Lebanon border. Syrian forces are deployed in west Beirut and in the north and the east of the country.

In September 1988 outgoing President Gemayel appointed a transitional Christian-led military government under Gen. Michel Aoun to replace the Muslim-led government of Selim al-Hoss. Each party claimed to represent the constitutional government of Lebanon, and refused to accept the other's authority.

The Taif Accord 'for national conciliation', drawn up by an Arab League-appointed committee, gained the approval of a majority of Lebanese MPs in October 1989, but was rejected by Michel Aoun, who insisted on an immediate Syrian troop withdrawal. Following an outbreak of devastating fighting between Gen. Aoun and the dominant Christian militia, the Lebanese Forces, the Lebanese Government acted with the backing of Syrian troops to oust Gen. Aoun in October 1990. A new Government, which included the main militia leaders, was formed in December 1990. Since then the Government has moved to clear the militias from the Greater Beirut area and has restored its authority throughout the former Christian enclave. The Lebanese Army has now moved into surrounding areas. In May Lebanon and Syria signed a Treaty of Brotherhood, Co-operation and Co-ordination aimed at regulating the relationship between the two countries, as laid down in the Taif Accord. (*See also* **Events of the Year**.)

Production.—Fruits are the most important products and include citrus fruit, apples, grapes, bananas and olives. There is some light industry, mostly for the production of consumer goods, but most factories were adversely affected by the civil war. Reconstruction is now under way.

Communications.—The railways are not functioning as a result of the civil war. There is an international airport at Beirut, served by the national carrier MEA, Air France, Cyprus Air and some other Arab and European airlines. An internal service operates from Beirut to Tripoli. Operations have in the past been disrupted by fighting in the city.

Archaeology, etc.—Lebanon has some important historical remains, notably Baalbek (Heliopolis) which contains the ruins of first to third century Roman temples and Jbeil (Byblos), one of the oldest continuously inhabited towns in the world, and ancient Tyre.

Language and Literature.—Arabic is the official language, and French and English are also widely used.

Education.—There are six universities in Beirut, the American and the French Universities established in the last century, and the Lebanese National University, the Beirut University College, the Kaslik Saint Esprit University, the University of Balamond and the Arab University which are recent foundations in the early stages of development. There are several institutions for vocational training, and there is a good provision throughout the country of primary and secondary schools, among which are a great number of private schools. Education at all levels has been severely disrupted by the civil war.

Finance.—No reliable statistics have been published for some time. The country is known to have a deficit, and the Lebanese pound has lost much of its value against foreign currencies. At its May 1990 summit meeting, the Arab League agreed to set up an international fund for Lebanon's reconstruction, but progress in establishing the fund was halted by the Kuwait crisis.

Trade.—Principal imports are gold and precious metals, machinery and electrical equipment, textiles and yarns, vegetable products, iron and steel goods, and motor vehicles. There has been a gradual decline in the overall amount of imports, as a result of continued instability.

Principal exports include gold and precious metals, fruits and vegetables, textiles, building materials, furniture, plastic goods, foodstuffs, tobacco and wine.

At one time there was a considerable transit trade through Beirut into the Arab hinterland. Lebanon is the terminal for two oil pipe lines, one formerly belonging to the Iraq Petroleum Company, debouching at Tripoli, the other belonging to the Trans Arabian Pipeline Company, at Sidon. These lines have not functioned for some years.

Trade with UK

	1989	1990
Imports from UK	£48,474,000	£53,266,000
Exports to UK	11,054,000	6,249,000

CAPITAL.— ΨBeirut (population 702,000). Other towns are ΨTripoli (175,000), Zahlé (46,800), ΨSidon (24,740), ΨTyre (14,000).

CURRENCY.—Lebanese pound (£L) of 100 piastres.

FLAG.—Horizontal bands of red, white and red with a green cedar of Lebanon in the centre of the white band.

NATIONAL ANTHEM.—Kulluna Lil Watan Lil'ula Lil'alam (We all belong to the homeland).

NATIONAL DAY.—November 22.

BRITISH EMBASSY
Shamma Building, Raouché, Ras Beirut, Beirut
[Beirut 812849]

Ambassador Extraordinary and Plenipotentiary, His Excellency David Tatham, CMG (1989).

LIBERIA
(Republic of Liberia)

There are two competing claims to the leadership of Liberia: that of Interim President Amos Sawyer of the Interim Government of National Unity (IGNU), based in Monrovia and supported by ECOMOG (Economic Community of West African States Ceasefire Monitoring Group); and that of Charles Taylor, leader of the National Patriotic Reconstruction Assembly Government (NPRAG), supported by the National Patriotic Front of Liberia (NPFL) and based in Gbarnga, which controls a large part of the territory of Liberia. In June agreement was reached between the two sides that elections would be held under international supervision within six months.

EMBASSY OF THE REPUBLIC OF LIBERIA
2 Pembridge Place, W2 4XB
[071–221 1036]

Chargé d'Affaires, Rudolf P. Von Ballmoos.

An independent republic of West Africa, occupying that part of the coast between Sierra Leone and the Côte d'Ivoire, which is between the rivers Mano in the N.W. and Cavalla in the SE, a distance of about 350 miles, with an area of about 43,000 sq. miles (111,369 sq. km), and extending to the interior to latitude 8° 50', a distance of 150 miles from the seaboard. It was founded by the American Colonization Society in 1822 as a colony for freed American slaves, and has been recognized since 1847 as an independent state. The population at the Census of 1974 was 1,481,524; a 1989 UN estimate put the figure at 2,508,000. The official language is English. Over 16 ethnic languages are spoken.

William V. S. Tubman, President since 1944, died in 1971 and was succeeded by Dr Tolbert. The Constitution was suspended following a military coup on April 12, 1980, during which Tolbert was killed. M/Sgt. Samuel Doe assumed power as chairman of a military council. A new constitution was endorsed by a referendum in July 1984. Doe and his party, the National Democratic Party of Liberia (NDPL) won the elections held in October 1985, amid allegations of electoral fraud and a civilian government was formally installed in January 1986.

A rebel incursion launched in December 1989 by the National Patriotic Front of Liberia (NPFL) led by Charles Taylor developed into a full-scale civil war. By July 1990 most members of the government had left the country, and foreigners were airlifted to safety by US Marines. A five-nation ECOWAS peacekeeping force landed in Monrovia in an effort to end the conflict but in September President Doe was killed, having refused to step down. The Interim Government (IGNU) was formed in August in Banjul, The Gambia, and arrived in Monrovia in November. A ceasefire agreement was signed in Bamako, Mali on November 28, 1990 as efforts to reach a political settlement continued.

Communications.—The artificial harbour and free port of Monrovia was opened on July 26, 1948. There are nine ports of entry, including three river ports. Robertsfield International Airport is under NPFL control and not in use. Spriggs Payne airfield, on the outskirts of Monrovia, is used for internal flights.

Economy.—In December 1990 the UN launched an appeal for $13·8 m in emergency aid to finance the enormous task of reconstruction. Of the country's 2·5 million population an estimated 500,000 to 1 million are refugees in neighbouring countries and it is estimated that up to 20,000 have died. Liberia is receiving relief aid from a number of countries including the United Kingdom, the EC and various international agencies.

TRADE

Trade.—Before the unrest began principal exports were iron ore, crude rubber, timber, uncut diamonds, palm kernels, cocoa and coffee, but the civil war has resulted in the suspension of most economic activity.

Trade with UK

	1989	1990
Imports from UK	£15,148,000	£8,639,000
Exports to UK	12,776,000	13,240,000

CAPITAL, ΨMonrovia, population estimate (1984) 425,000. Other ports are ΨBuchanan, ΨGreenville (Sinoe) and ΨHarper (Cape Palmas).

CURRENCY.—Liberian dollar (L$) of 100 cents.

FLAG.—Alternate horizontal stripes (5 white, 6 red), with 5-pointed white star on blue field in upper corner next to flagstaff.

NATIONAL ANTHEM.—All Hail, Liberia, Hail.

NATIONAL DAY.—July 26.

BRITISH EMBASSY

The British Embassy in Monrovia was closed in March 1991.

LIBYA
(Al-Jamahiriya Al-Arabiya Al-Libya Al-Shabiya Al-Ishtirakiya Al-Uthma)

Leader of the Revolution and Supreme Commander of the Armed Forces, Col. Muammar al-Gadaffi.

SECRETARIAT OF THE GENERAL PEOPLE'S CONGRESS
(as at May 31, 1991)

Secretary, Abd al-Raziq Sawsa.

Assistant Secretary, Mahmud Hamid al-Khafifi.

Secretary (Affairs of People's Congresses), Abd al-Hamid al-Fayturi Ammar.

Secretary (Affairs of People's Committees), Sulayman Sasi al-Shuhumi.

Secretary (Affairs of Professional Congresses), Bashir Huwayj Humaydi.

GENERAL PEOPLE'S COMMITTEE

Secretary-General, Abu Zayd 'Umar Durda.

Foreign Liaison, Ibrahim Muhammad Bishari.

Petroleum, Abdullah Salem al-Badri.

Communications and Transport, Izz al-Din al-Hinshari.

Higher Education, Ibrahim Misbah Bukhzam.

Planning and Economy, Umar Mustafa al Muntasir.

Health, Dr Zaydan Badr Zaydan.

Strategic Industries, Jadallah Azzuz al-Talhi.

Treasury, Muhammad al Madani al Bukhari.

Information and Culture, Al Milad Abu Jaziyah.

Marine Wealth, Miftah Muhammad Ku'aybah.

Vocational Training, Ma'tuq Muhammad Ma'tuq.

Scientific Research, Nuri al-Fayturi al Madani.

Agrarian Reform and Land Reclamation, Abd al-Majid al-Qa'ud.

Justice, Ibrahim Muhammad Bakkar.

Education, Madani Ramadhan Abu al-Tuwayrat.

Light Industries, Dr Fathi Hamad bin Shatwan.

Electricity, Jum'a Salim al-Arbash.

Amenities and Public Works, Dr Salim Ahmad Funayr.

Social Security, Ishma'il Miftah bin Sharadah.

Youth and Sport, Bukhari Salim Hawdah.

Supervision and Follow-Up, Ammar al-Mabruk Litayf.

Arab Maghreb Union, Muhammad al-Zarruq Rajab.

Integration with Egypt, Muhammad Mahmud al-Hijazi.

Integration with Sudan, Jum'a al-Mahdi al-Fazzani.

LIBYAN DIPLOMATIC MISSION IN LONDON

Following the break of diplomatic relations with Libya in April 1984, the Royal Embassy of Saudi Arabia has handled Libyan interests in Britain.

Libya, on the Mediterranean coast of Africa, is bounded on the East by Egypt and Sudan, on the South by the Republics of Chad and Niger, and on the West by Algeria and Tunisia. It consists of the three former provinces of Tripolitania, Cyrenaica and the Fezzan, with a combined area of 679,362 sq. miles (1,759,540 sq. km) and a population (UN estimate 1988) of 4,232,000. The people of Libya are principally Arab with some Berbers in the west and some Tuareg tribesmen in the Fezzan. Islam is the official religion of Libya, but other religions are tolerated. The official language is Arabic.

Vast sand and rock deserts, almost completely barren, occupy the greater part of Libya. The southern part of the country lies within the Sahara Desert. There are few rivers and as rainfall is irregular outside parts of Cyrenaica and Tripolitania, good harvests are rare. The ancient ruins in Cyrenaica, at Cyrene, Ptolemais (Tolmeta) and Apollonia, are outstanding, as are those at Leptis Magna, 70 miles east, and at Sabratha, 40 miles west of Tripoli. An Italian expedition found in the SW of the Fezzan a series of rock-paintings more than 5,000 years old.

Government.—Libya was occupied by Italy in 1911–12 in the course of the Italo-Turkish War, and under the Treaty of Ouchy (October 1912) the sovereignty of the province was transferred by Turkey to Italy. In 1939 the four Provinces of Libya (Tripoli, Misurata, Benghazi and Derna) were incorporated in the national territory of Italy as *Libia Italiana*. After the Second World War Tripolitania and Cyrenaica were placed provisionally under British and the Fezzan under French administration, and in conformity with a resolution of the UN General Assembly in November 1949, Libya became on December 24, 1951 the first independent state to be created by the United Nations. The monarchy was overthrown by a revolution in September 1969, and the country was declared a republic. It was ruled by the Revolutionary Command Council (RCC) under the leadership of Colonel Muammar Gadaffi.

In March 1977 a new form of direct democracy, the 'Jamahiriya' (state of the masses) was promulgated and the official name of the country was changed to Socialist People's Libyan Arab Jamahiriya. At local level authority is now vested in about 1,500 Basic and 14 Municipal People's Congresses which appoint Popular Committees to execute policy. Officials of these congresses and committees, together with representatives from unions and other organizations, form the General People's Congress, which normally meets for about a week early each year. In addition, a number of extraordinary sessions are held throughout the year. This is the highest policy-making body in the country. The General People's Congress appoints its own General Secretariat and the General People's Committee, whose members head the 13 government departments which execute policy at national level. The Secretary of the General People's Committee has functions similar to those of a Prime Minister.

Since a reorganization in March 1979 neither Col. Gadaffi nor his former RCC colleagues have held formal posts in the administration. Gadaffi continues to hold the ceremonial title 'Leader of the Revolution'.

Communications.—Besides the coastal road running from the Tunisian frontier through Tripoli to Benghazi, Tobruk and the Egyptian border, which serves the main population centres, main roads now link the provincial centres, and the oil-producing areas of the south with the coastal towns. There are airports at Tripoli and Benghazi (Benina), Tobruk, Mersa Brega, Sebha, Ghadames and Kufra regularly used by commercial airlines, and military airfields near Tobruk, near Tripoli and at Al Watiya, south of Zuara.

Production and Industry.—Agriculture is confined mainly to the coastal areas of Tripolitania and

Cyrenaica, where barley, wheat, olives, almonds, citrus fruits and dates are produced, and to the areas of the oases, many of which are well supplied with springs supporting small fertile areas. Among the important oases are Jaghbub, Ghadames, Jofra, Sebha, Murzuq, Brak, Ghat, Jalo and the Kufra group in the South-East. The main industry is oil and gas production. There are pipelines from Zelten to the terminal at Mersa Brega, from Dahra to Ras-es-Sider, from Amal to Ras Lanuf and from the Intisar field to Zuetina. Since 1984 average production of crude oil has been about 1·2 million barrels per day. A major petrochemical complex has been built at Ras Lanuf where a refinery and ethylene plant began operations in early 1985. The construction of an iron and steel plant at Misurata has been completed. Economic constraints have delayed some projects, particularly since Libya decided in 1983 to go ahead with a major irrigation scheme, the 'Great Man-Made River'.

Exports from Libya are dominated by crude oil, but some wool, cattle, sheep and horses, olive oil, and hides and skins are also exported. Principal imports are foodstuffs, including sugar, tea and coffee, and most constructional materials and consumer goods. In recent years the private sector has been virtually eliminated and Libya is now a state trading country with imports controlled by state monopolies. In early 1988, however, reforms were implemented which have allowed a small private sector to be re-established.

Libya has technical assistance agreements with a number of countries, and also employs large numbers of foreign labourers and experts.

Trade with UK

	1989	1990
Imports from UK	£239,191,000	£244,850,000
Exports to UK	104,546,000	151,605,000

CAPITAL.—ΨTripoli, population estimate (1991) 1,000,000. The principal towns are: ΨBenghazi (500,000); ΨMisurata (200,000); Sirte (100,000).
CURRENCY.—Libyan dinar (LD) of 1,000 dirhams.
FLAG.—Libya uses a plain emerald green flag.
NATIONAL DAY.—September 1.

BRITISH EMBASSY

Diplomatic relations between the UK and Libya were broken in April 1984. British interests are currently handled by the British Interests Section of the Italian Embassy, Sharia Uahram 1, (PO Box 4206), Tripoli.

LIECHTENSTEIN
(Fürstentum Liechtenstein)

Prince, Hans Adam II, *born* Feb. 14, 1945; *succeeded* November 13, 1989; *married* July 30, 1967, Countess Marie Kinsky; and has *issue*, Prince Alois, *b.* June 11, 1968; Prince Maximilian, *b.* May 16, 1969; Prince Constantin, *b.* March 15, 1972; Princess Tatjana, *b.* April 10, 1973.

MINISTRY
(as at June 30, 1991)

Prime Minister, Hans Brunhart (*Head of Government 'Presidium', Foreign Affairs, Education, Finance, Construction*).
Deputy PM, Dr Herbert Wille (*Interior, Agriculture, Forestry and Environment, Culture, Youth and Sport, Justice*).
Government Councillors, René Ritter (*Economy*), Dr Peter Wolff (*Social and Health Services*), Wilfried Büchel (*Communications*).

Liechtenstein is represented in diplomatic and consular matters in the United Kingdom by the Swiss Embassy.

Liechtenstein is a principality on the Upper Rhine, between Vorarlberg (Austria) and Switzerland, with an area of 61 sq. miles (158 sq. km), and a population in 1989 of 28,452. The language of the principality is German.

At the General Election on March 5, 1989 the Patriotic Union Party won 13 seats and Progressive Citizens' Party 12.

The main industries are high and ultra-high vacuum engineering, semi-conductor industry, roller bearings, fastenings and securing systems, artificial teeth, heating and hot water equipment, synthetic fibres, woollen and homespun fabrics.

FINANCE

	1989	1990
Revenue	F371,867,639	F405,409,370
Expenditure	367,249,600	400,801,399
(F = Swiss francs)		

CAPITAL.—Vaduz, population (1990) 4,874.
CURRENCY.—Swiss franc of 100 rappen (or centimes).
FLAG.—Equal horizontal bands of blue over red; gold crown on blue band near staff.
NATIONAL ANTHEM.—Oben am Jungen Rhein (High on the Rhine).
NATIONAL DAY.—August 15.

British Consul General, T. Bryant (*office at* Dufourstrasse 56, 8008 Zürich).

LITHUANIA
See p. 857

LUXEMBOURG
(Grand-Duché de Luxembourg)

Grand Duke, HRH Jean, *born* Jan. 5, 1921, *married*, April 9, 1953, Princess Joséphine-Charlotte of Belgium, and has *issue*, three sons and two daughters; *succeeded* (on the abdication of his mother) Nov. 12, 1964.
Heir Apparent, Prince Henri, *born* April 16, 1955 *married* February 14, 1981, Maria Teresa Mestre and has *issue*, Prince Guillaume, *b.* Nov. 11, 1981; Prince Felix, *b.* June 3, 1984; Prince Louis, *b.* Aug. 3, 1986; Princess Alexandra, *b.* Feb. 2, 1991.

CABINET
(as at June 7, 1991)

Christian Socialists:
President of the Government, Minister of State Minister of the Treasury and Cultural Affairs, Jacques Santer.
Interior, Housing and Town Planning, Jean Spautz.
The Family and Middle Classes, and Tourism, Fernand Boden.
Budget, Finance and Labour, Jean-Claude Juncker.
Education, Justice and the Civil Service, Marc Fischbach.
Agriculture and Viticulture, Rene Steichen.

Socialists:
Vice-President of the Government, Minister of Foreign Affairs, Foreign Trade and Aid, and Defence, Jacques Poos.
Health, Social Security, Sport and Youth, Johny Lahure.
Economy and Trade, Transport and Public Works, Robert Goebbels.

Environment, Territorial Administration, Posts and Telecommunications and Energy, Alex Bodry.
State Secretary for Social Security, Health, Sport and Youth, Mady Delvaux.
State Secretary for Foreign Affairs, Overseas Trade, Aid and Defence, Georges Wohlfart.

EMBASSY OF LUXEMBOURG
27 Wilton Crescent, SW1X 8SD
[071–235 6961]

Ambassador Extraordinary and Plenipotentiary, His Excellency Edouard Molitor (1989).

Luxembourg is a Grand Duchy in western Europe, bounded by the Federal Republic of Germany, Belgium, and France. The area is 998 sq. miles (2,586 sq. km), the population (1990) 378,400, nearly all Roman Catholics. The country is well wooded, with many deer and wild boar. The language is Letzeburgesch but French is the official language; most speak German.

Established as an independent state under the sovereignty of the King of the Netherlands as Grand Duke by the Congress of Vienna in 1815, Luxembourg formed part of the Germanic Confederation 1815–66, and was included in the German 'Zollverein'. In 1867 the Treaty of London declared it a neutral territory. On the death of the King of the Netherlands in 1890 it passed to the Duke of Nassau. The territory was invaded and overrun by the Germans at the beginning of the war in 1914, but was liberated in 1918. By the Treaty of Versailles, 1919, Germany renounced its former agreements with Luxembourg and in 1921 an economic union was made with Belgium. The Grand Duchy was again invaded and occupied by Germany on May 10, 1940. The constitution of the Grand Duchy was modified on April 28, 1948, and the stipulation of permanent neutrality was then abandoned. Luxembourg is now a signatory of the Brussels and North Atlantic Treaties, and also a member of the European Communities. Luxembourg is a member of the Belgium-Netherlands-Luxembourg Customs Union (Benelux 1960).

The Court of the European Communities has its seat in Luxembourg, as does the Secretariat of the European Parliament, the European Investment Bank, the European Audit Court and the European Monetary Co-operation Fund.

There is a Chamber of 60 Deputies, elected by universal suffrage for five years. Legislation is submitted to the Council of State.

The Grand Duchy possesses an important iron and steel industry. Government revenue for 1990 was estimated at LF 97,300 million, expenditure LF 94,500 million. The Luxembourg franc has at present the same value as the Belgian franc.

There are 272 km of railway.

Trade with UK (Belgium and Luxembourg)

	1989	1990
Imports from UK	£4,872,641,000	£5,648,625,000
Exports to UK	5,700,534,000	5,732,427,000

CAPITAL.—Luxembourg, population (1987) 77,500, is a dismantled fortress.

CURRENCY.—Luxembourg franc (LF) of 100 centimes. Belgian currency is also legal tender.

FLAG.—Three horizontal bands, red, white and blue.

NATIONAL ANTHEM.—Ons Hémécht (Our homeland).

NATIONAL DAY.—June 23.

BRITISH EMBASSY
14 Boulevard F. D. Roosevelt, L-2450 Luxembourg
[Luxembourg 29864]

Ambassador Extraordinary and Plenipotentiary, Her Excellency Juliet Jeanne Campbell, CMG (1988).

MADAGASCAR
(Repoblika Demokratika n'i Madagaskar)

At the time of going to press (September) the situation in Madagascar was one of confusion. After several months of strikes and protests, President Ratsiraka was reported to have relinquished executive powers to a new prime minister, Guy Razanamasy, but was unwilling to leave office. Meanwhile, the main opposition group, the Forces Vives, had already established a rival government with Gen. Jean Rakotoharison (retd.) as head of state and Albert Zafy as Prime Minister. The Forces Vives have promised a new democratic constitution, and parliamentary and presidential elections within 18 months of its promulgation. Neither government is reported to exercise much control over the country.

EMBASSY OF THE DEMOCRATIC REPUBLIC OF
MADAGASCAR
4 avenue Raphael, 75016 Paris, France
[Paris 45046211]

Ambassador Plenipotentiary and Extraordinary, His Excellency François de Paul Rabotoson (1987) (resident in Paris).

HONORARY CONSULATE OF THE DEMOCRATIC
REPUBLIC OF MADAGASCAR
16 Lanark Mansions, Pennard Road, W12 8DT
[081-746 0133]

Honorary Consul, Stephen Hobbs.

Madagascar lies 240 miles off the east coast of Africa and is the fourth largest island in the world. It has an area of 226,669 sq. miles (587,041 sq. km), and a population (UN estimate 1989) of 11,603,000. The people are of mixed Polynesian, Arab and African origin. The official languages are Malagasy and French. There are sizeable French, Chinese and Indian communities.

Government.—Madagascar (known from 1958 to 1975 as the Malagasy Republic) became a French protectorate in 1895, and a French colony in 1896 when the former queen was exiled. Republican status was adopted on October 14, 1958, and independence was proclaimed on June 26, 1960.

The post-independence civilian government was replaced by a military government in January 1975 and the following month martial law was declared. A Supreme Council of the Revolution of 18 members under Capitaine de Frégate (now Admiral) Didier Ratsiraka was established on June 15, 1975.

In December 1975 a new constitution was approved in a referendum, which vested executive power in the President. He appoints a Council of Ministers to assist him, with the guidance of the Revolutionary Supreme Council. There is a 137-member National People's Assembly elected for a five-year term by universal suffrage.

Revised agreements with France, signed on June 4, 1973, provided for the withdrawal of the French forces stationed in the country after independence. The French naval base at Diégo Suarez (now called Antsiranana) was turned into a civilian ship repair yard. Madagascar also withdrew from the Franc Zone. France has recognized Madagascar's claim to the islands of Juan de Nova, Glorieuses, Isle de l'Europe, Bassa da India and Tromelin which had remained integral parts of the French Republic after independence.

Economy.—The island's economy is still largely based on agriculture, which accounts for three-quarters of its exports. Development plans have placed emphasis on increasing agricultural and livestock production, the improvement of communications, the exploitation of mineral deposits and the creation of small industries.

TRADE

	1985	1986
Imports	US$ 400·54m	US$ 441·54m
Exports	274·23m	351·18m

Trade with UK

	1989	1990
Imports from UK	£3,352,000	£16,093,000
Exports to UK	5,866,000	5,952,000

CAPITAL.—Antananarivo, population estimate 1,000,000. Other main towns are the chief port ΨToamasina (55,000); Ψ Mahajanga (50,000); Fianarantsoa (47,000); Ψ Antsiranana (41,000).

CURRENCY.—Franc Malgache (Malagasy franc) (FMG) of 100 centimes.

FLAG.—Equal horizontal bands of red (above) and green, with vertical white band by staff.

NATIONAL DAY.—June 26 (Independence Day).

BRITISH EMBASSY
BP 167, Antananarivo
[Antananarivo 277 49]

Ambassador Extraordinary and Plenipotentiary, His Excellency Dennis Oldgrieve Amy, OBE (1990).
Second Secretary, C. G. R. Poole.

MALI
(République du Mali)

MINISTERS OF THE TRANSITIONAL GOVERNMENT
(as at April 5, 1991)

Prime Minister, Soumana Sacko.
Economy and Finance, Bassary Toure.
Rural Development and Environment, Sy Maimouna Ba.
National Education, Issa N'Diaye.
Defence and Internal Security, Lt.-Col. Tiécouré Doumbia.
Justice, Mamadou Ouattara.
Mines, Hydraulics and Energy, Kadari Bamba.
Planning and International Co-operation, Bakary Mariko.
Foreign Affairs, Sqn.-Ldr. Souleymane Sidibe.
Public Health, Social Action and Advancement of Women, Sy Oumou Louise Sidibe.
Communication and Culture, Government Spokesman, Ousmane Traore.
Civil Service and Labour, Daba Diawara.
Transport and Public Works, Lt.-Col. Cheick Diarra.
Territorial Administration, Cmdt. Lamine Diabira.

EMBASSY OF THE REPUBLIC OF MALI
Avenue Molière 487, 1060 Brussels, Belgium
[Brussels 3457432]

Ambassador Extraordinary and Plenipotentiary, His Excellency Lamine Keita (1987) (resident in Brussels).

The Republic of Mali, an inland state in north-west Africa, has an area of 478,791 sq. miles (1,240,000 sq. km), and a population (UN estimate 1989) of 7,960,000. The principal rivers are the Niger and the Senegal.

Formerly the French colony of Soudan, the territory elected on November 24, 1958 to remain as an autonomous republic within the French Community. It associated with Senegal in the Federation of Mali which was granted full independence on June 20, 1960. The Federation was effectively dissolved on August 22 by the secession of Senegal. The title of the Republic of Mali was adopted in September 1960.

Government.—The regime of Modibo Keita was overthrown on Nov. 19, 1968 by a group of Army officers who formed a National Liberation Committee and appointed a Prime Minister. Moussa Traoré

assumed the functions of Head of State. A new civil constitution came into being in 1979.

After several months of pro-reform protests and strikes, often leading to bloody riots, President Traoré was overthrown in March 1991 by troops led by Lt.-Col. Amadou Toumani Toure. A joint civilian military National Reconciliation Committee, later replaced by the Transitional Committee for the Salvation of the People, suspended the constitution and dissolved the Mali People's Democratic Union (UPDM), formerly the sole, ruling party. A transitional government was formed under Soumana Sacko in April. In August, a new constitution was approved by a national conference and is to be put to a referendum; free elections have been promised.

Economy.—Mali's principal exports are groundnuts (raw and processed), cotton fibres, meat and dried fish. The Republic rejoined the CFA Franc Zone on June 1, 1984.

Trade with UK

	1989	1990
Imports from UK	£7,102,000	£8,819,000
Exports to UK	2,305,000	1,835,000

CAPITAL.—Bamako (600,000). Other towns are Gao, Kayes, Mopti, Sikasso, Segou and Timbuktu (all regional capitals).

CURRENCY.—Franc CFA of 100 centimes.

FLAG.—Vertical stripes of green (by staff), yellow and red.

NATIONAL DAY.—September 22.

British Ambassador, resident in Dakar, Senegal.

MAURITANIA
(République Islamique de Mauritanie)

President, Prime Minister, Minister of Defence, Col. Maaouya Ould Sidi Ahmed Taya, *took power Dec.* 12, 1984.

GOVERNMENT MINISTERS
(as at February 1991)

Interior, Posts and Telecommunications, Cmdt. Cheikh Sidy Ahmed Ould Baba.
Equipment and Transport, Col. Diang Oumar Arouna.
Foreign Affairs and Co-operation, Hosny Ould Didy.
Justice, Sow Samba Sow.
Planning and Employment, Mouhamedou Ould Michel.
Economy and Finance, Sidi Muhammad Ould Boubaker.
Culture and Islamization, Didy Ould Bou Naamah.
Industry and Mining, Blahy Ould Maaghaya.
Health and Social Affairs, Abdou-Rahamar. Abou Ould Moine.
Fisheries and Maritime Economy, Ahmed Ould Khalifa Ould Dyidou.
Information, Muhammad Lamine Ould Ahmed.
Civil Service, Sports, Muhammad Ould Al-Haymir.
Trade and Tourism, Soumare Oumar.
National Education, Al-Moukhtar Ould Haye.
Rural Development, Cmdt. Muhammad Ould Sidi Ahmed Lekhal.
Energy and Water Supply, Moustapha Ould Abdou-Rahman.
State Control, Al-Yassa Ould Soueid'Ahmed.

EMBASSY OF THE ISLAMIC REPUBLIC OF MAURITANIA
5 rue de Montevideo, Paris XVIe, France
[Paris 45048854]

Ambassador Extraordinary and Plenipotentiary, His Excellency Muhammad Al-Hanchi Ould Muhammad Saleh (1989) (resident in Paris).

Mauritania lies on the north-west coast of Africa immediately to the north of Senegal. It is bounded on the east by the Republic of Mali. To the north it is bounded by Morocco and the Western Sahara. Area 397,955 sq. miles (1,030,700 sq. km). The population (UN estimate 1989) is 1,970,000. The official languages are French and Arabic.

The Republic of Mauritania elected on November 28, 1958 to remain within the French Community as an autonomous republic. It became fully independent on November 28, 1960. In 1972 Mauritania broke with the Franc Zone.

Mauritania and Morocco took possession of the Western Sahara territory in February 1976 when Spain formally relinquished all right to it and in April 1976 agreed on a new frontier dividing the territory between them. In August 1979, Mauritania relinquished all claim to the southern sector of the Western Sahara after a three-year war against the Polisario front guerrilla army.

Since a military coup deposed the first President in 1978, Mauritania has been ruled by a Military Committee for National Salvation (CMSN).

Having previously rejected reform, in April 1991 President Taya announced a political amnesty, a referendum on the constitution and the calling of multi-party elections thereafter for a reconvened Senate and National Assembly. The constitution was approved by a large majority in July. Conflict continues between the Arab-dominated government and the African minority in the south of the country.

Mauritania's main source of potential wealth lies in rich deposits of iron ore around Zouérate, in the north of the country.

Trade with UK

	1989	1990
Imports from UK	£7,102,000	£2,997,000
Exports to UK	15,387,000	14,525,000

CAPITAL.—Nouakchott (500,000).
CURRENCY.—Ouguiya of 5 khoums.
FLAG.—Yellow star and crescent on green ground.
NATIONAL DAY.—November 28.

British Ambassador, resident in Rabat, Morocco.

MEXICO
(Estados Unidos Mexicanos)

President (1988–94), Carlos Salinas de Gortari, *elected*, June 4, 1988, *took office*, Dec. 1, 1988.

THE CABINET
(as at August 8, 1991)

Interior, Fernando Gutiérrez Barrios.
Foreign Affairs, Fernando Solana Morales.
Finance and Public Credit, Dr Pedro Aspe Armella.
Defence, Gen. Antonio Riviello Bazán.
Navy, Adm. Luis Carlos Ruano Angulo.
Budget and Planning, Dr Ernesto Zedillo Ponce de León.
Energy, Mines and Parastatal Industries, Fernando Hiriart Balderrama.
Trade and Industrial Development, Dr Jaime Serra Puche.
Agriculture and Water Resources, Carlos Hank González.
Communications and Transport, Andrés Caso Lombardo.
Education, Manuel Bartlett Díaz.
Urban Development and Ecology, Patricio Chirinos C.
Health, Dr Jesús Kumate Rodríguez.
Labour and Social Security, Arsenio Farell Cubillas.
Agrarian Reform, Victor Cervera Pacheco.

Tourism, Pedro Joaquin Coldwell.
Fisheries, María de los Angeles Moreno.
Attorney-General, Ignacio Morales Lechuga.
Attorney-General of Federal District, vacant.
Comptroller-General, María Elena Vazquez Nava.
Mayor of Mexico City, Manuel Camacho Solís.

MEXICAN EMBASSY
8 Halkin Street, SW1X 7DW
[071–235 6393/6]

Ambassador Extraordinary and Plenipotentiary, His Excellency Bernardo Sepulveda (1989).

Area and Population.—Mexico occupies the southern part of the continent of North America, with an extensive seaboard to both the Atlantic and Pacific Oceans, extending from 14° 33′ to 32° 43′ N. lat. and 86° 46′ to 117° 08′ W. long., and comprising one of the most varied zones in the world. It contains 31 states and the federal district of Mexico, making in all 32 political divisions, covering an area of 761,605 sq. miles (1,972,547 sq. km). At the 1990 Mexican General Census, the total population was 81,140,922; a 1989 UN estimate gives a figure of 84,275,000.

The two great ranges of North America, the Sierra Nevada and Rocky Mountains, are prolonged from the north to a convergence towards the narrowing isthmus of Tehuantepec, their course being parallel to the west and east coasts. The surface of the interior consists of an elevated plateau between the two ranges, with steep slopes both to the Pacific and Atlantic (Gulf of Mexico). In the west is the peninsula of Lower California, with a mountainous surface, separated from the mainland by the Gulf of California. The Sierra Nevada, known in Mexico as the Sierra Madre, terminates in a transverse series of volcanic peaks, from Colima on the west to Citlaltepetl (El Pico de Orizaba) on the east. The low-lying lands of the coasts form the *Tierra Caliente*, or tropical regions (below 3,000 ft.), the higher levels form the *Tierra Templada*, or temperate region (from 3,000 to 6,000 ft.), and the summit of the plateau with its peaks is known as *Tierra Fria*, or cold region (above 6,000 ft.). The main rivers are the Rio Grande del Norte which forms part of the northern boundary, and is navigable for about 70 miles from its mouth in the Gulf of Mexico, and the Rio Grande de Santiago, the Rio Balsas and Rio Papaloapan. The largest fresh-water lakes are Chapala (70 miles long and 20 miles wide), and Pátzcuaro.

History and Archaeology.—The present Mexico and Guatemala were once the centre of a remarkable indigenous civilization, which flowered in the periods from AD 500 to 1100 and AD 1300 to 1500 and collapsed before the little army of Spanish adventurers under

Hernán Cortés in the years following 1519. Pre-Columbian Mexico was divided between different but connected Indian cultures, each of which has left distinctive archaeological remains: the best-known of these are Chichén Itzá, Uxmal, Bonampak and Palenque, in Yucatán and Chiapas (Maya); Teotihu-acon, renowned for the Pyramid of the Sun (216 feet high) in the Valley of Mexico (Teotihuacáno); Monte Albán and Mitla, near Oaxaca (Zapotec); El Tajín in the state of Veracruz (Totonac); and Tula in the state of Hidalgo (Toltec). The last and most famous Indian culture of all, the Aztec, based on Tenochtitlán, suffered more than the others from the Spanish and very few Aztec monuments remain.

A few years after the conquest, the Spanish built Mexico City on the ruins of Tenochtitlán, and appointed a Viceroy to rule their new dominions, which they called New Spain. The country was largely converted to Christianity, and a distinctive colonial civilization, representing a marriage of Indian and Spanish traditions, developed and flour-ished, notably in architecture and sculpture. In 1810 a revolt began against Spanish rule. This was finally successful in 1821, when a precarious independence was proclaimed. Friction with the United States in Texas led to the war of 1845–48, at the end of which Mexico was forced to cede the northern provinces of Texas, California and New Mexico. In 1862 Mexican insolvency led to invasion by French forces which installed Archduke Maximilian of Austria as Em-peror. The empire collapsed with the execution of the Emperor in 1867 and the austere reformer, Juárez, restored the republic. Juárez's death was followed by the dictatorship of Porfirio Diaz, which saw an enormous increase of foreign, particularly British and United States, investment in the country. In 1910 began the Mexican Revolution which reformed the social structure and the land system, curbed the power of foreign companies and ushered in the independent industrial Mexico of today. In 1986 Mexico joined GATT and began a liberalization programme of large-scale privatization and adminis-trative reform.

Government.—Under the Constitution of 1917 (as subsequently amended), Congress consists of a Senate of 64 members, elected for six years, and of a Chamber of Deputies, at present numbering 500, elected for three years. Presidents, who wield full executive powers, are elected for six years; they cannot be re-elected.

There are nine political parties registered in Mexico, of which the largest and most influential is the Partido Revolucionario Institucional (PRI) which has for more than 60 years constituted the governing party, despite constant allegations of electoral fraud. The main opposition parties are Partido de Acción Nacional (PAN) and Partido de la Renovación Democratica (PRD).

Communications.—Veracruz, Tampico and Coatzacoalcos are the chief ports of the Atlantic, and Guaymas, Mazatlán, Puerto Lázaro Cárdenas, Aca-pulco, Salina Cruz and Puerto Madero on the Pacific. Work is proceeding on the reorganization and re-equipment of the whole system; help in this has been forthcoming from the World Bank, the Export-Import Bank and private sources in the United States. Total track length of the railways was 240,186 kms in 1990.

Mexico City may be reached by at least three highways from the United States, and from the south from Yucatán as well as on two principal highways from the Guatemalan border.

International telegraph services to the United States frontier are provided by the government-owned Mexican Telegraph Company and then through the United States to Canada and Europe.

Teléfonos de México, now privatized, controls about 98 per cent of all telephone services. Satélite Latinoamericano (SATELAT) is a joint government private sector venture disseminating television pro grammes to Latin America through Intelsat IV satellite facilities leased by the Mexican Government

There are 1,113 airports and landing fields i Mexico, of which eighteen are equipped to handl long-distance flights. There are 166 airline com panies, including two of the major, now private national airlines—Mexicana de Aviación and Aero méxico. The total number of air passengers in 199 was 21,825,000.

Production.—The principal agricultural crops ar maize, beans, rice, wheat, sugar cane, coffee, cotton tomatoes, chili, tobacco, chick-peas, groundnut sesame, alfalfa, vanilla, cocoa and many kinds of fruit both tropical and temperate. The maguey, or Mexica cactus, yields several fermented drinks, mezcal an tequila (distilled) and pulque (undistilled). Anothe species of the same plant supplies sisal-hemp (hene quen). The forests contain mahogany, rosewood ebony and chicle trees. Agriculture employs ar estimated 20 per cent of the working population.

The principal industries are mining and petroleum although there has been considerable expansion o both light and heavy industries. Exports of manufac tured goods now average about 56 per cent of tota exports. The steel industry expanded steadily unti recently and current production is around 6·5m tons The mineral wealth is great, and principal mineral are gold, silver, copper, lead, zinc, quicksilver, iror and sulphur. Substantial reserves of uranium have been found. In the non-metals sector, Mexico contin ues to produce 25 per cent of the world's supply o fluorspar.

The total proven petroleum reserves were 72 billion barrels in 1983. Daily production of natural gas is approximately 3 billion cubic feet. Oil reserves have increased substantially due to important discoveries in the Gulf of Campeche. A new refinery at Tula State of Hidalgo, is the nation's largest; and new refineries in Monterrey, State of Nuevo Leon, and Salina Cruz, State of Oaxaca, are under construction

Textile production is led by the artificial fibres sector, which comprised 66 per cent of the industry's output in 1983.

Defence.—Supreme command is vested in the President, exercised through the Ministries of Def ence (for Army and Air Force) and Marine.

The country is divided into 36 zones. The Army has some 100,000 men.

The Navy has a strength of about 35,000 officers and men including the Naval Air Force and Marines.

The Air Force has an approximate strength of 8,00 officers and men and 100 combat aircraft. There is a Parachute Brigade consisting of three Parachute battalions (approx. 2,000 men).

Language and Literature.—Spanish is the offi-cial language of Mexico and is spoken by about 95 per cent of the population. In addition to Spanish, there are five basic groups of Indian languages spoken in Mexico. The 1970 Census showed that of the 3,111,415 inhabitants speaking an Indian language, 25·7 per cent spoke Náhuatl; 14·6 per cent Maya; 9·1 per cent Zapotec; 7·1 per cent Otomí; 7·5 per cent Mixtec and 36 per cent one or other of the 59 dialects derived from these basic languages. The poet Octavio Paz won the Nobel Prize for Literature in 1991.

Education.—Education is divided into primary, secondary and superior levels. In 1990 there were 18,061,000 in the first level, 6,599,000 in the second and 1,236,000 in the third.

Trade with UK

	1989	1990
Imports from UK	£205,130,000	£262,952,000
Exports to UK	165,295,000	172,144,000

Major imports include computers, auto assembly material, electrical parts, auto and truck parts, powdered milk, corn and sorghum, transport, sound-recording and power-generating equipment, chemicals, industrial machinery, pharmaceuticals and specialized appliances. Principal exports include oil, automobiles, auto engines, fruits and vegetables, shrimps, coffee, computers, cattle, glass, iron and steel pipes, and copper.

CAPITAL.—Mexico City, estimated population of metropolitan area (1990) 14,776,000. Other cities (with 1986 population estimates) are:

Guadalajara .	2,884,000	Puebla	1,455,000
Monterrey...	2,549,000	León	956,000
Torréon	876,000	Ciudad	
San Luis		Juarez	798,000
Potosì	659,000	Mérida	666,000

CURRENCY.—Peso of 100 centavos.

FLAG.—Three vertical bands in green, white, red, with the Mexican emblem (an eagle on a cactus devouring a snake) in the centre.

NATIONAL ANTHEM.—Mexicanos, Al Grito De Guerra (Mexicans, to the war cry).

NATIONAL DAY.—September 16 (Proclamation of Independence).

BRITISH EMBASSY
Calle Río Lerma 71, Colonia Cuauhtémoc,
06500 Mexico City, DF
[Mexico City 207 20 89]

Ambassador Extraordinary and Plenipotentiary, His Excellency Sir Michael Keith Orlebar Simpson-Orlebar, KCMG (1989).

There are British Consular Offices at *Mexico City, Acapulco, Guadalajara, Mérida, Monterrey, Tampico, Veracruz, Oaxaca,* and *Cuidad Juarez.*

British Council Representative.—Dr Brian Lavercombe, Maestro Antonio Caso 127, Col. San Rafael (PO Box 30-588), Mexico 06470 DF.

BRITISH CHAMBER OF COMMERCE, British Trade Centre, Rio de la Plata 30, Col. Cuauhtemoc, CP 06500, Mexico City DF.—*Manager,* Stephen Grant.

MONACO
(Principauté de Monaco)

Sovereign Prince, HSH Rainier III Louis-Henri-Maxence Bertrand, *born* May 31, 1923, *succeeded* May 9, 1949; *married* April 19, 1956, Miss Grace Patricia Kelly (died Sept. 14, 1982) and *has issue* Prince Albert Alexandre Louis Pierre, *born* March 14, 1958, Princess Caroline Louise Marguerite, *born* January 23, 1957; and Princess Stephanie Marie Elisabeth, *born* Feb. 1, 1965.

President of the Crown Council, Jean-Charles Marquet.
President of the National Council, Jean-Charles Rey.

Minister of State, Jacques Dupont, *appointed* 1991.

CONSULATE GENERAL OF MONACO
4 Audley Square, W1Y 5DR
[071–629 0734]

Consul-General, I. B. Ivanovic.

A small principality on the Mediterranean, with land frontiers joining France at every point, Monaco is divided into the districts of Monaco-Ville, La Condamine, Fontvielle and Monte Carlo. The principality comprises a narrow strip of country about 2 miles long (area approx. 195 hectares), with approximately 27,063 inhabitants (1989) and a yearly average of over 250,000 visitors.

The principality, ruled by the Grimaldi family since the late 13th century, was abolished during the French Revolution and re-established in 1815 under the protection of the Kingdom of Sardinia. In 1861 Monaco came under French protection. The 1962 Constitution, which can be modified only with the approval of the National Council, maintains the traditional hereditary monarchy and guarantees freedom of association, trade union freedom and the right to strike. Legislative power is held jointly by the Prince and a uni-cameral, 18 member National Council elected by universal suffrage. Executive power is exercised by the Prince and a four-member Council of Government, headed by a Minister of State. The judicial code is based on that of France.

The whole available ground is built over, so that there is no cultivation, though there are some notable public and private gardens. Monaco has a small harbour (30 ft. alongside quay) and the import duties are the same as in France.

CAPITAL.—Monaco-Ville, population (1982) 1,234.

CURRENCY.—Monaco uses the French franc of 100 centimes as legal tender.

FLAG.—Two equal horizontal stripes, red over white.

NATIONAL ANTHEM.—Hymne Monegasque.

NATIONAL DAY.—November 19.

HM Consul-General, John Illman (1990), resident in Marseilles, France.

MONGOLIA
(Mongolian People's Republic—
Bugd Nairamdakh Mongol Ard Uls)

President, Punsalmaagiyn Ochirbat.
Vice President, Radnaasumbereliyn Gonchigdorji.

CABINET
(as at May 30, 1991)

Prime Minister, Dashiyn Byambasuren.
First Deputy PM, Davaadorjiyn Ganbold.
Deputy PMs, Dambiyn Dorligyav; Choyjilsurengiyn Purevdorj.
Defence, Maj.-Gen. Shagalyn Jadambaa.
Agriculture, Dandzangiyn Radnaaragchaa.
Education, Nonovyn Urtnasan.
Foreign Relations, Tserenpiliyn Gombosuren.
Finance, Ayuurdzanyn Badzarhuu.
National Development, Jamyangiyn Batsuur.
Trade and Industry, S. Bayarbaatar.
Labour, Choyjamtsyn Badamhaamb.
Justice, Jugneegiyn Amarsanaa.
Health and Policy Plans, Pagvajavyn Nyamdavaa.
State Control Committee for Nature and the Environment, Dzardin Batjargal.

EMBASSY OF THE MONGOLIAN PEOPLE'S REPUBLIC
7 Kensington Court, W8 5DL
[071–937 0150]

Ambassador Extraordinary and Plenipotentiary, new appointment awaited.

Area and Population.—The Mongolian People's Republic is a large and sparsely populated country to the north of China. Its area is 604,250 sq. miles (1,565,000 sq. km). Its population (1989) is about 2,043,000. However, this total constitutes only part of the Mongolians of Asia, a number of whom are to be found in China and in the neighbouring regions of the Soviet Union (especially the Mongolian Buryat Autonomous Region).

Mongolia, which is almost nowhere below 1,000 metres above sea level, forms part of the Central Asiatic Plateau and rises towards the west in the high mountains of the Mongolian Altai and Khanggai Ranges. The Khentai Mountain Range, situated to the north-east of the capital Ulan Bator, is less high. The Gobi region covers much of the southern half of the country. It contains some sand deserts, but between these less hospitable areas there is semi-desert which provides pasture for great numbers of sheep, goats, camels and horses (the latter is still the characteristic means of transport for the rural population) and some cattle. In the steppe areas to the north pasturage is better and livestock more abundant. Even further north, in the better watered provinces, grain, fodder and vegetable crops are increasingly grown. There are several long rivers and many lakes, but good water is scarce since much of the lake water is salty. The climate is harsh, with a short mild summer giving way to a long winter when temperatures can drop as low as minus 50°C.

Government.—Mongolia, under Genghis Khan the conqueror of China and much of Asia, was for many years a buffer state between Tsarist Russia and China, although it was under general Chinese suzerainty. The outbreak of the Chinese Revolution in 1911 led to a declaration of autonomy under Chinese suzerainty which was confirmed by the Sino-Russian Treaty of Kiakhta (1915), but cancelled by a unilateral Chinese declaration in 1919. Later the country became a battleground of the Russian civil war, and Soviet and Mongolian troops occupied Ulan Bator in 1921; this was followed by another declaration of independence. However, in 1924 the Soviet Union in a Treaty with China again recognized the latter's sovereignty over Mongolia; but this was never properly exercised because of China's pre-occupation with internal affairs, and later by the war with Japan.

The Mongolian People's Republic was formally established in 1924. Under the Yalta Agreement, Chiang Kai-shek agreed to a plebiscite, held in 1945, in which the Mongolians declared their desire for independence and this was formally recognized by Nationalist China. The country entered the United Nations in 1961.

The Mongolian People's Revolutionary Party (MPRP) has been the ruling party since 1924. A series of demonstrations in favour of political and economic reform began in December 1989 and led to changes in the MPRP leadership in March 1990. The MPRP's constitutionally guaranteed monopoly of power was subsequently relinquished, and the introduction of a multi-party system was approved by the Great People's Hural. In May 1990 the formation of a Small Hural was approved. While the Great Hural is still the supreme body the Small Hural is now the permanent legislative body. The MRRP won the first multi-party elections, held in July and August 1990. Since then, and following Moscow's lead, Mongolia has embarked on an ambitious programme of political and economic reforms. A coalition government was formed in October 1990.

Production, etc.—The total of Mongolia's live-stock was 25 million in 1991. Traditionally the Mongolians lead a nomadic life tending flocks of sheep, goats and horses, cows and camels. With the coming of the Communist regime and especially since 1952, great efforts have been made to settle the population, but a proportion still live nomadically or semi-nomadically in the traditional *ger* (circular tent). The pastoral population was collectivized at the end of the 1950s into huge *negdels* (co-operatives) and state farms which have hastened the process of settlement, but within these the herdsmen and their families still move with their *gers* from pasture to pasture as the seasons change. The country, and three city districts (Ulan Bator, Darkhan and Erdenet), is today divided into 18 *aimaks* (provinces) and beneath these into 258 *somons* (districts), and these

form the basis of the State organization of the country.

Membership of the Communist bloc brought Mongolia considerable quantities of aid from other Socialist countries, especially massive assistance from the Soviet Union, but this has now been halted. The aid hastened industrialization while it lasted. For although the economy remains predominantly based on the herds of animals, and the principal exports of the country are still animal by-products (especially wool, hides and furs) and cattle, factories serving the needs of the country have been started up and the coal and electricity industries are being developed to provide an industrial base. A joint Mongolian/Soviet enterprise for copper and molybdenum mining was opened in 1978, at Erdenet in northern Mongolia. It is now in full production and processes 16 million tonnes of ore annually. Coal production in 1980 was 4·5 m tons, and had risen to 8·04 m tons by 1990.

Ulan Bator, which contains over a quarter of the country's population, is the main seat of industry. The second largest industrial centre is at Darkhan north of the capital, near the Soviet frontier. Its industries include lime, cement and building materials, a flour mill and a power station. Choibalsan, in the east, is also being developed industrially. Communication is still difficult in the country as there are very few tarmac roads. The trans-Mongolian railway, following the line of the old north-south trade route, was opened in 1955 and links Mongolia with both China and Russia. Mongolia's fundamental difficulty is its very small population and labour force.

Foreign trade was formerly dominated by the Soviet Union and other eastern bloc countries. Following the collapse of the CMEA, trade with western countries, Japan and South Korea is increasing. The country is facing transitional problems in its attempt to establish a market economy by the end of 1991, such as food and fuel shortages, and unemployment; since January 1991, trade is no longer in transferable roubles but in hard currency, causing particular strain. Mongolia joined the IMF, the World Bank and the Asian Development Bank in February 1991.

Trade with UK

	1989	1990
Imports from UK	£979,000	£1,636,000
Exports to UK	405,000	1,674,000

CAPITAL.—Ulan Bator, population (1989) 530,000.
CURRENCY.—Tugrik of 100 möngö.
FLAG.—Vertical tri-colour red, blue, red and in the hoist the traditional Soyombo symbol in gold.
NATIONAL DAY.—July 11 (Anniversary of the Mongolian People's Republic).

BRITISH EMBASSY
30 Enkh Taivny Gudamzh (PO Box 703),
Ulan Bator 13
[Ulan Bator 51033/4]

Ambassador Extraordinary and Plenipotentiary, His Excellency A. B. N. Morey (1989).
Second Secretary, J. L. Hartley (*Head of Chancery*).

MOROCCO
(Al-Mamlaka Al-Maghrebia)

King, HM King Hassan II (Moulay Hassan Ben Mohammed), *born* July 9, 1929; *acceded* February 26, 1961.
Heir, Crown Prince Sidi Mohamed, *born* August 21, 1963.

MINISTERS
(as at August 1991)

Prime Minister, Azeddine Laraki.
Ministers of State, Hadj M'hamid Bahnini; Moulay Ahmed Alaoui.
Justice, Moulay Mustapha Belarbi Alaoui.
Interior and Information, Driss Basri.
Foreign Affairs and Co-operation, Abdellatif Filali.
National Education, Prof. Taieb Chkili.
Health, Tayeb Bencheikh.
Religious Endowments and Islamic Affairs, Abdelkebir Alaoui M'Daghri.
Public Works, Vocational and Executive Training, Mohamed Kabbaj.
Finance, Mohamed Berrada.
Tourism, Abdelkadar Benslimane.
Handicrafts and Social Affairs, Mohamed Abied.
Transport, Mohamed Bouamoud.
Energy and Mines, Mohamed Fettah.
Youth and Sport, Abdellatif Semlali.
Fisheries and Merchant Shipping, Bensalem Smili.
Secretary General of the Government, Abbès Kaissi.
Culture, Mohamed Benaissa.
Housing, Abderrahmane Boufettass.
Posts and Telecommunications, Mohamed Laensar.
Agriculture and Agricultural Reform, Othman Demnati.
Trade and Industry, Abdellah Al Azmani.
Employment, Hassan Abbadi.
Overseas Trade, Hassan Abouyoub.
Prime Minister's Office, Moulay Zine Zahidi (*Economic Affairs*); Khali Hanna Ould Errachid (*Saharan Affairs*); Rachidi Ghazouani (*Planning*); Abdeslem Baraka (*Relations with Parliament*); Abderrahim Ben Abdeljalil (*Administrative Affairs*).

EMBASSY OF THE KINGDOM OF MOROCCO
49 Queen's Gate Gardens, SW7 5NE
[071–581 5001/4]

Ambassador Extraordinary and Plenipotentiary, His Excellency Khalil Haddaoui (1991).
Military, Naval and Air Attaché, Col. M. Jabrane.

Area and Population.—Morocco is situated in the north-western corner of the African continent between latitude 27° 40′–36° N. and longitude 1°–13° W. with an area estimated at 172,414 sq. miles (446,550 sq. km), and a population (1990 estimate) of 27,575,000. It is traversed in the north by the Rif mountains and in a general SW to NE direction, by the Middle Atlas, the High Atlas, the Anti-Atlas and the Sarrho ranges. The northern flanks of the Middle and High Atlas mountains are well wooded but their southern slopes, exposed to the dry desert winds, are generally arid and desolate. The north-westerly point of Morocco is the peninsula of Tangier which is separated from the continent of Europe by the narrow strait of Gibraltar. The Jebel Mousa dominates the promontory and, with the rocky eminence of Gibraltar, was known to the ancients as the Pillars of Hercules, the western gateway of the Mediterranean.

Western Sahara.—Formerly the Spanish Sahara, the territory was split between Morocco and Mauritania in 1976 after Spain withdrew in Dec. 1975. In 1979 Mauritania renounced its claim to its share of the territory, which was added by Morocco to its area. Morocco's annexation has been opposed by Polisario guerrillas, who want the territory to become an independent state. On August 30, 1988, Morocco and the Polisario Front accepted a UN peace plan. Under the plan a ceasefire is to come into effect, and a referendum to determine the future of the area will be held in January 1992.

Climate.—The climate of Morocco is generally good and healthy, especially on the Atlantic coast (where a high degree of humidity is, however, prevalent), the country being partially sheltered by the Atlas mountains from the hot winds of the Sahara. The rainy season may last from November to April. The plains of the interior are intensely hot in summer. Average summer and winter temperatures for Rabat are 27°C and 7°C.

Government.—Morocco became an independent sovereign state in 1956, following joint declarations made with France on March 2, 1956, and with Spain on April 7, 1956. The Sultan of Morocco, Sidi Mohammad ben Youssef, adopted the title of King Mohammad V.

Following serious disturbances in Casablanca in March 1965, attempts were made by King Hassan, in consultation with all political parties, to form a government of national union. These efforts were unsuccessful and on June 7, 1965 the King proclaimed a 'state of exception' and suspended Parliament. Assuming himself the office of Prime Minister, he announced the formation of a new government and indicated that constitutional changes were to follow. A revised constitution was approved by a national referendum on July 24, 1970 and brought into effect soon after. It was superseded by another constitution, also approved by a national referendum, on March 1, 1972. This provides that not only political parties, but trade unions, chambers of commerce and professional bodies will participate in the organization of the state and representation of the people; specifies that the King is the supreme representative of the people; makes changes in the composition of the Regency Council and the Sovereign's rights and establishes a unicameral legislature. The Chamber has 306 members, 204 elected by direct universal suffrage (including 5 representing overseas workers) and 102 members elected by electoral colleges representing local government, industry, agriculture and working class groups. There were elections in September 1984 and the new Parliament began its six year term on October 12. A new government was named in April 1985 which included members of three political parties, though over half the portfolios went to non-political appointees. The term of the current Chamber of Representatives has been extended by two years, following a referendum held in December 1989.

Defence.—The Moroccan army, formed in 1956, is about 200,000 strong. A Moroccan air force was formed in 1959 and a navy in 1960. Their strengths are about 13,500 and 8,000 respectively. The armed forces possess quantities of French, Spanish and American equipment, including aircraft, as well as a little Soviet-supplied hardware.

Production and Trade.—Morocco's main sources of wealth are agricultural and mineral. The Five Year Plan (1981–85) for economic development placed particular emphasis on social improvement. Other priority sectors were industrial development, fisheries, agriculture and tourism. The next development plan (1987 onwards) is similar to the last. The world recession and high energy prices, coupled with a fall in the price of phosphates and poor harvests due to low rainfall have created problems for the economy since the end of the 1970s. However, rains in the winter of 1985–86 ended the long drought and the 1986 harvest was good. Similarly the fall in oil prices, the value of the dollar and interest rates have helped.

Agriculture employs more than 40 per cent of the working population and accounts for about 36 per cent of Morocco's exports. The main agricultural exports are fruit and vegetables. Cork and wood-pulp are the most important commercial forest products. Esparto grass is also produced. There is a fishing industry and substantial quantities of canned fish, mainly sardines and fishmeal, are exported. Manufacturing industries are centred in Casablanca, Fez, Tangier and Safi.

Morocco's mineral exports are phosphates, fluorite, barite, manganese, iron ore, lead, zinc, cobalt, copper and antimony. Morocco possesses nearly three-quarters of the world's estimated reserves of phosphates. There are oil refineries at Mohammedia and Sidi Kacem handling about four million tonnes of crude oil per year, but no significant quantities of hydrocarbons have been found.

Tourism is of increasing importance to the Moroccan economy with development concentrated in Agadir and Marrakesh.

Morocco's main import requirements are petroleum products, motor vehicles, building materials, agricultural and other machinery, chemical products, sugar, green tea and other foodstuffs.

	1987	1988
Imports	DH 1,066,711,000	DH 1,154,867,000
Exports	627,664,000	870,246,000

Trade with UK

	1989	1990
Imports from UK	£84,475,000	£118,599,000
Exports to UK	96,138,000	106,425,000

Communications.—The railway runs south from Tangier to Sidi Kacem. From this junction, one line runs eastwards through Fez to Oujda, and another continues southwards, through Rabat and Casablanca, to Marrakesh. A line running due south from Oujda skirts the Morocco-Algeria frontier and reaches Bouarfa. Moroccan railroads cover 1,250 miles and traction is electric or diesel. An extensive network of well-surfaced roads covers all the main towns in the kingdom.

There are air services between Casablanca, Tangier, Agadir (seasonal), Marrakesh and London, and also between Tangier and Gibraltar connecting with London. Royal-Air-Maroc operates internal services.

Language.—Arabic is the official language. Berber is the vernacular mainly in the mountain regions. French and Spanish are also spoken mainly in the towns. In 1984 there were seven Arabic and five French daily newspapers.

Education.—There are government primary, secondary and technical schools. At Fez there is a theological university of great repute in the Muslim world. There is a secular university at Rabat. Schools for special denominations, Jewish and Catholic, are permitted and may receive government grants. American schools operate in Rabat and Casablanca.

Capital.—ΨRabat population (including Salé) 1,123,000. Regional capitals, with municipal population figures as at 1989, are: ΨCasablanca (2,904,000); Marrakesh (1,425,000); Fez (933,000); Oujda (895,000); Meknes (1,425,000); Ψ Agadir (700,000). The towns of Fez, Marrakesh and Meknes were capitals at various times in Morocco's history.

Currency.—Dirham (DH) of 100 centimes.

Flag.—Red, with green pentagram (the Seal of Solomon).

National Day.—March 3 (Anniversary of the Throne).

BRITISH EMBASSY
17 Boulevard de la Tour Hassan (BP 45), Rabat
[Rabat 720905]

Ambassador Extraordinary and Plenipotentiary, His Excellency John Esmond Campbell Macrae, CMG (1990).
First Secretary, S. R. H. Pease (*Head of Chancery/Commercial, and Consul*).
Defence Attaché, Lt.-Col. C. Le Hardy.
Vice Consul (Tangier) W. W. Page.

There is a British Consulate-General/Commercial Office at *Casablanca* and an Honorary Consul at *Agadir.*

British Council Representative, J. Weston, BP 427, 3 rue Tanger, Rabat.

BRITISH CHAMBER OF COMMERCE, 1st Floor, 18 Boulevard Zerktouni, Casablanca (Tel: 256920).

MOZAMBIQUE
(República de Moçambique)

President, Joaquim Alberto Chissano, *sworn in* November 1986.

COUNCIL OF MINISTERS
(as at July 8, 1991)

Prime Minister, Mario da Graca Machungo.
Foreign Affairs, Pascoal Mocumbi.
National Defence, Alberto Joaquim Chipande.
Chief of Staff of the Armed Forces, Lt.-Gen. Antonio Hama Thai.
Co-operation, Jacinto Veloso.
Minister in the Presidency, Feliciano Gundana.
State Administration, Jose Oscar Monteiro.
Education, Aniceto dos Muchangos.
Interior, Manuel Antonio.
Security, Mariano de Araujo Matsinha.
Transport and Communications, Armando Emilio Guebuza.
Finance, Abdul Magid Osman.
Health, Dr Leonardo Simao.
Information, Rafael Maguni.
Construction and Water, Joao Salomao.
Trade, Daniel Gabriel Tembe.
Agriculture, Alexandre Jose Zandamela.
Industry and Energy, Antonio Branco.
Mineral Resources, John Kachamila.
Justice, Ossumane Ali Dauto.
Culture, Jose Mateus Muaria Catupa.
Labour, Aguiar Jonassane Mazula.

EMBASSY OF THE REPUBLIC OF MOZAMBIQUE
21 Fitzroy Square, W1P 5HJ
[071-383 3800]

Ambassador Extraordinary and Plenipotentiary, His Excellency Armando Alexandre Panguene (1988).

Area and Population.—The People's Republic of Mozambique lies on the east coast of Africa, and is bounded by Swaziland in the south, South Africa in the south and west, Zimbabwe in the west, Zambia and Malawi in the north-west and Tanzania in the north. It has an area of 309,495 sq. miles (801,590 sq km), with a population estimated at 15,200,000 (1989). The official language is Portuguese.

Government.—Mozambique, discovered by Vasco de Gama in 1498, and colonized by Portugal, achieved complete independence from Portugal on June 25 1975. The date had been agreed in September 1974 by Portugal and Frelimo (Frente de Libertação de Moçambique), the Marxist liberation movement. Frelimo ceased to be a Marxist-Leninist party in July 1989, but it still has Socialist beliefs.

In August 1990 President Chissano announced government plans to adopt a multi-party system. The new democratic constitution came into force on November 30, 1990, enshrining freedom of association and the free market. The official name of the country was changed from The People's Republic of Mozambique to the Republic of Mozambique. The legislative assembly has between 200 and 250 members. Elections have been postponed until 1992.

Negotiations with the rebel Mozambique National Resistance (MNR) continue to end the war which has devastated much of the country.

The basis of the economy is subsistence agriculture, but there is an industrial sector based mainly in Beira and Maputo. After giving priority to the development of collective farms and state enterprises in all sectors, the government is now encouraging the private sector and foreign investment, particularly in agriculture and consumer goods production. Main exports are sugar, cashew nuts, prawns, copra, cotton, tea and sisal. There are substantial coal deposits in Tete province. Mozambique has a range of aid and co-operation agreements with a number of countries in eastern Europe and in the West. An agreement of non-aggression and good neighbourliness with South Africa was signed on March 16, 1984 (the Nkomati Accord).

Trade with UK

	1989	1990
Imports from UK	£20,268,000	£28,992,000
Exports to UK	14,582,000	10,709,000

CAPITAL.—Ψ Maputo, estimated population (1990), 1,150,000. Other main ports are Ψ Beira and Ψ Nacala.
CURRENCY.—Metical (MT) of 100 centavos.
FLAG.—From top, three lateral bands of green, black and yellow separated by white stripes, and red half diamond pointing to centre of flag over which is superimposed a yellow star, book, and crossed rifle and hoe.
NATIONAL DAY.—June 25 (Independence Day).

BRITISH EMBASSY
Av. Vladimir I Lenine 310, CP 55, Maputo
[Maputo 420111/2/5/6/7]

Ambassador Extraordinary and Plenipotentiary, Her Excellency Maeve Geraldine Fort, CMG (1989).

British Council Representative, C. ffrench Blake.

MYANMAR (BURMA)
(Pyidaungsu Myanma Naingngandaw)
STATE LAW AND ORDER RESTORATION COUNCIL
(SLORC)
(as at June 30, 1991)

Chairman of SLORC, Prime Minister and Minister for Defence and Foreign Affairs, Gen. Saw Maung.
Vice-Chairman of SLORC, Gen. Than Shwe.
Energy and Mines, Vice-Adm. Maung Maung Khin.
Transport and Communications, Social Welfare and Labour, Lt.-Gen. Tin Tun.
Home and Religious Affairs, Information and Culture, Lt.-Gen. Phone Myint.
Construction, Co-operatives, Lt.-Gen. Aung Ye Kyaw.
Industry, Lt.-Gen. Sein Aung.
Livestock and Fisheries, Agriculture and Forests, Lt.-Gen. Chit Swe.
Trade and Planning, Finance, Brig. Abel.
Health and Education, Col. Pe Thein.
Secretaries, Maj.-Gen. Khin Nyunt, Maj.-Gen. Tin Oo.

EMBASSY OF THE UNION OF MYANMAR
19A Charles Street, Berkeley Square, W1X 8ER
[071–499 8841]

Ambassador Extraordinary and Plenipotentiary, His Excellency U Tin Hlaing (1989).

Area and Population.—The Union of Myanmar (Burma) forms the western portion of the Indo-Chinese district of the continent of Asia, lying between 9° 58′ and 28° N. latitude and 92° 11′ and 101° 9′ E. longitude, with an extreme length of approximately 1,200 miles and an extreme width of 575 miles. It has a sea coast on the Bay of Bengal to the south and west and a frontier with Bangladesh along the Naaf River (defined in 1964) and India to the north-west (defined in 1967). In the north and east the frontier with China was determined by a treaty with the People's Republic in October 1960, and has since been demarcated; there is a short frontier with Laos in the east, while the long finger of Tenasserim stretches southward along the west coast of the Malay Peninsula, forming a frontier with Thailand to the east. The total area of the Union is 261,218 sq. miles (676,552 sq. km), with a population (UN estimate 1989) of 40,810,000.

Physical Features.—There are four natural divisions. Arakan (with the Chin Hills region), the Irrawaddy basin, Tenasserim, including the Salween basin and extending southwards to the Myanmar-Thailand peninsula, and the elevated plateau on the east. Mountains enclose the Union on three sides, the highest point being Hka-kabo Razi (19,296 ft.) in the northern Kachin hills. Mt. Popa, 4,981 ft., in the Myingyan district is an extinct volcano and a well-known landmark in central Myanmar. The principal river systems are the Kaladan-Lemro in Arakan, the Irrawaddy-Chindwin and the Sittang in central Myanmar, and the Salween which flows through the Shan Plateau.

Races, Language and Religions.—The indigenous inhabitants who entered the country from the north and east are of similar racial types and speak languages of the Tibeto-Burman, Mon-Khmer and Thai groups. The three important non-indigenous elements are Indians, Chinese and those from the former East Pakistan. Burmese is the official language, but minority languages include Shan, Karen, Chin, Kayah and the various Kachin dialects. English is spoken in educated circles. Buddhism is the religion of 85 per cent of the people, with 5 per cent Animists, 4 per cent Muslims, 4 per cent Hindus and less than 3 per cent Christians.

Government.—The Union of Burma (the name was officially changed to the Union of Myanmar in June 1989) became an independent republic outside the British Commonwealth on January 4, 1948 and remained a parliamentary democracy for 14 years. On March 2, 1962 the army took power and suspended the parliamentary Constitution. A Revolutionary Council of senior officers under General Ne Win took measures to create a Socialist State.

In January 1974 a new Constitution was adopted under which the highest authority was the People's Assembly with a Council of State, the senior executive body being the Council of Ministers.

After months of popular demonstrations and rioting and a series of Presidents throughout the summer of 1988, Gen. Saw Maung, leader of the armed forces, assumed power in September 1988. The People's Assembly, the Council of State and the Council of Ministers were abolished and replaced by the State Law and Order Restoration Council (SLORC) headed by Gen. Saw Maung as Prime Minister. The Constitution was effectively abrogated.

A People's Assembly Election Law was published in March 1989 committing the SLORC to hold multi-party elections. These were held on May 27 1990, resulting in a majority for the National League for Democracy (NLD). The SLORC has refused to transfer power to a civilian government and large numbers of NLD members have been detained, including their leader, Aung San Suu Kyi. A 'National Coalition Government of the Union of Burma', led by Sein Winn, was established in December 1990 at Manerplaw on the Thai border by NLD members and other opposition groups.

Political Divisions.—Myanmar is comprised of seven states (Chin, Kachin, Karen, Kayah, Mon, Rakhine, Shan) and seven divisions (Irrawaddy, Magwe, Mandalay, Pegu, Rangoon, Sagaing, Tenasserim).

Education.—The literacy rate is high compared to other Asian countries. There is no caste system and women engage freely in social intercourse and play an important part in agriculture and retail trade.

Most children attend primary school, and about four million are currently enrolled; in middle and high schools, 11 million. There are three universities, at Rangoon, Mandalay and Moulmein, and in 1986–87 the numbers graduating were 9,981. A number of autonomous institutes of university standard award their own degrees. Under the universities are three affiliated Degree Colleges and the Workers' College, Rangoon. There are also 14 two-year colleges affiliated to the universities, spread throughout the country.

There are three teachers' training institutes for middle and primary schools, and 13 teachers' training schools for primary only. Seven government technical institutes offer post-secondary technical training courses and 14 technical high schools train semi-skilled tradesmen. Six agricultural institutes offer training courses in agriculture and veterinary science; nine agricultural high schools train semi-skilled agriculturists. There are 34 vocational schools for weaving, handicrafts, etc.

Finance.—The chief sources of revenue are profits on state trading, income-tax, customs duties, commercial taxes and excise duties; the chief heads of expenditure are defence, education and police. The budget estimates for 1990–91 were: Revenue K38,270 million; Expenditure, K48,670 million.

Production, Industry and Commerce.—Three-quarters of the population depend on agriculture; the chief products are rice, oilseeds (sesamum and groundnut), maize, millet, cotton, beans, wheat, grain, rice, sugarcane, tobacco, jute and rubber. Rice was for many years the mainstay of the economy, but in 1985 teak overtook rice. The quantity of teak available for export in 1989 was 180,000 tons; the quantity of rice and by-products available for export was 160,000 tons.

Myanmar is rich in minerals, including petroleum, lead, silver, tungsten, zinc, tin, wolfram and gem-stones. Of these, petroleum products are the most important. Oil is now being produced from oilfields in Myanaung, Prome and Shwepyitha and at Chauk, Yenangyaung, Mann, and Letpando. Production of crude oil in 1986–87 totalled 10,103,000 US barrels. There is a refinery at the main oilfield, Chauk, another at Syriam near Rangoon and a third at Mann. There has been a steady decline in oil production in recent years and the country is no longer self-sufficient. Onshore exploration continues. There has also been some offshore oil exploration on a small scale. Major reserves of natural gas have been discovered in the Martaban Gulf, which Myanmar is hoping to develop.

All industrial activity of any size is in the public sector. Under development plans, projects completed or under construction with overseas financial and technical assistance include the production of cement, bricks and tiles, sheet glass, steel sections, jute bags and twine, cotton yarns, cotton and cotton mixture cloth, pharmaceuticals, sugar, paper, plywood, urea fertilizers, soda ash, tractors and tyres; also a hydro-electric scheme and various irrigation works.

Faced with a serious foreign exchange shortage, Myanmar was included in the UN's list of Least Developed Countries in December 1987.

Trade with UK

	1989	1990
Imports from UK	£12,217,000	£15,951,000
Exports to UK	3,484,000	4,582,000

Communications.—The Irrawaddy and its chief tributary, the Chindwin, form important waterways, the main stream being navigable beyond Bhamo (900 miles from its mouth) and carrying much traffic.

The chief seaports are Rangoon, Moulmein, Akyab and Bassein.

The railway network covers 2,764 route miles, extending to Myitkyina, on the Upper Irrawaddy. There were 2,452 miles of Union highways and 11,767 miles of other main roads in 1982–83. The airport at Mingaladon, about 13 miles north of Rangoon, only handles limited international air traffic.

CAPITAL.—The chief city of lower Myanmar and the seat of the government of the Union is ΨRangoon (Yangon). Population (1983): Rangoon District 3,973,872; city population 2,458,712.

Mandalay is the chief city of upper Myanmar, population (1983): Mandalay district 4,580,923; city 532,985; Moulmein of 219,991 and Bassein of 144,092. Pagan, on the Irrawaddy, SW of Mandalay, contains many sacred buildings.

CURRENCY.—Kyat (K) of 100 pyas.

FLAG.—The Union flag is red, with a canton of dark blue, inside which are a cogwheel and two rice ears surrounded by 14 white stars.

NATIONAL DAY.—January 4.

BRITISH EMBASSY
80 Strand Road (Box No. 638), Rangoon
[Rangoon 81700]

Ambassador Extraordinary and Plenipotentiary, His Excellency Julian Hartland-Swann (1990).
Deputy Head of Mission, First Secretary (Commercial) and Consul, C. S. M. Shelton.
Cultural Attaché and British Council Representative, Ralph Isaacs, MBE.

NEPAL

Sovereign, HM King Birendra Bir Bikram Shah Dev, *born* Dec. 28, 1945; *succeeded* Jan. 31, 1972; *crowned* Feb. 24, 1975; *married,* Feb. 1970, HM Queen Aishwara Rajya Laxmi Devi Shah.
Heir, HRH Crown Prince Dipendra Bir Bikram Shah Dev, *born* June 27, 1971.

COUNCIL OF MINISTERS
(as at May 29, 1991)

Prime Minister, Minister of Defence, Foreign Affairs, Royal Palace Affairs, Girija Prasad Koirala.
Water Resources and Communications, Basudev Risal.
Housing and Physical Planning, Bal Bahadur Rai.
Land Reform and Management, Jagannath Acharya.
Labour and Social Welfare, Shiekh Idris.
Education, Culture and Tourism, Ramhari Joshi.
Forests, Soil Conservation and Agriculture, Shailaja Acharya.
Home Affairs, Sher Bahadur Deupa.
Local Development, Ram Chandra Paudyal.
Industries, Dundi Raj Shastri.
Supplies, Chiranjivi Wagle.
General Administration, Maheswor Prasad Singh.
Law and Justice, and Parliamentary Affairs, Taranath Bhat.
Works and Transport, Khum Bahadur Khadka.
Commerce, Gopal Man Shrestha.
Ministers of State, Dr Ram Baran Yadav (*Health*); Mahesh Acharya (*Finance*).

ROYAL NEPALESE EMBASSY
12A Kensington Palace Gardens, W8 4QU
[071–229 1594/6231]

Ambassador Extraordinary and Plenipotentiary, His Excellency Maj.-Gen. Bharat Kesher Simha (1988).
Counsellor, Badri Prasad Khanal.

Area and Population.—Nepal lies between India and the Tibet Autonomous Region of China on the slopes of the Himalayas, and includes Mount Everest (29,078 ft). It has a total area of 54,342 sq. miles (140,747 sq. km), and a population estimated by the UN (1989) at 18,442,000.

The country comprises three distinct horizontal formations. In the south, joining the Indian plains, is the Terai, a fair proportion of which was covered with jungle. It has recently been more widely cultivated but wild life is preserved in parts. The region represents 23 per cent of the total land area and nearly 44 per cent of the population live there. The central belt of the country is hilly, but with many fertile valleys, leading up to the snowline at about 14,000 feet. The hills account for 42 per cent of the area of the country and about 48 per cent of the population. The remainder of the country, the Himalayan region, consists of high mountains which are sparsely inhabited. The country is drained by three great river systems rising within and beyond the Himalayan mountain ranges and eventually flowing into the Ganges in India.

The inhabitants are of mixed stock, with Mongolian characteristics prevailing in the north and Indian in the south. The official religion is Hinduism: 89·5 per cent of the population are Hindus and 6 per cent are Buddhist. Gautama Buddha was born in Nepal.

History and Government.—The country was originally divided into numerous hill clans and petty principalities, but Nepal emerged as a nation in the middle of the 18th century when its component parts were unified by the warrior Raja of Gorkha, Prithvi Narayan Shah, who founded the present Nepalese dynasty. In 1846 power was seized by Jung Bahadur Rana after a massacre of nobles, and he was the first of a line of hereditary Rana Prime Ministers who ruled Nepal for 104 years. During this time the role of the monarchs was mainly ceremonial.

In 1950–51 a revolutionary movement achieved its aim of breaking the hereditary power of the Ranas and restoring the monarchy to its former position. After ten years, during which various parties and individuals tried their hand at government, King Mahendra proscribed all political parties and assumed direct powers on December 16, 1960, with the object of leading a united country to democracy. In 1962 he introduced a new Constitution embodying a tiered, partyless system of panchayat (council) democracy.

Mass agitation for political reform led in April 1990 to the lifting of the ban on political parties and the abolition of the Panchyat system. An interim government was appointed. A new constitution was promulgated on November 9, 1990, establishing a multi-party, parliamentary system of government and a constitutional monarchy. The monarch retained joint executive power with the Council of Ministers. A bicameral legislature was set up, consisting of a 205-member House of Representatives and a 60-member National Council, including 10 royal nominees. Elections, held on May 12, 1991, were won by the Nepali Congress Party.

Economy.—Nepal exports carpets, jute, handicrafts, garments, hides and skins, medicinal herbs, cardamom, pulses etc., and imports textiles, machinery and parts, transport equipment, medicine, construction materials etc. Tourism is the single largest commercial earner of foreign exchange (US$55·9 million in 1986–87).

The budget for the fiscal year 1988–89 was estimated at NRs. 19,520·2 million, of which NRs. 6,152,139 million was allocated to regular and NRs. 13,368,061 million to development expenditures. Revenue was estimated at NRs. 9,300 million, foreign aid and grants NRs. 8,890·2 million, and domestic borrowing NRs. 1,330 million.

Trade with UK

	1989	1990
Imports from UK	£7,802,000	£4,099,000
Exports to UK	8,306,000	7,039,000

Communications.—Kathmandu is connected with India by a road, the mountain section of which was built by India under the Colombo Plan, and to Tibet by a road to Kodari on the border which was built by the Chinese and opened on May 26, 1967. The Indian-aided Sunauli-Pokhara road (128 miles) was inaugurated in April 1972, and a road between Pokhara and Kathmandu, constructed by the Chinese, was opened in 1973. A link road between Mugling and Naryanghat, completed by the Chinese in 1981, has further improved communications between Kathmandu and the Terai. The East–West Highway (Mahendra Raj Marg) running along the entire length of the country is complete except for the Banbasa-Mahahali section. The total length of roads in Nepal in 1987–88 was 6,525 km. British assistance has included major road projects, agriculture, education and forestry.

Telecommunication services, both domestic and international, are available from the Central Telegraph Office or hotels. There are international subscriber dialling facilities from Nepal to 35 countries. Nepal television was introduced in 1984.

Royal Nepal Airlines operates an extensive network of domestic flights, and there are international flights to Britain, India, Pakistan, Bangladesh, Myanmar, Singapore, Thailand, West Germany, and the Middle East.

CAPITAL.—Kathmandu, population (1981) 235,000. Other towns of importance are Biratnagar (94,000), Lalitpur (81,000) and Bhaktapur (50,500) and Pokhara (48,500).

CURRENCY.—Nepalese rupee of 100 paisa.

FLAG.—Double pennant of crimson with blue border on peaks; white moon with rays in centre of top peak; white quarter sun, recumbent in centre of bottom peak.

NATIONAL ANTHEM.—May Glory Crown Our Illustrious Sovereign.

NATIONAL DAY.—February 18 (National Democracy Day).

BRITISH EMBASSY
Lainchaur Kathmandu, PO Box 106
[Kathmandu 410583]

Ambassador Extraordinary and Plenipotentiary, His Excellency Timothy George, CMG (1990).

First Secretary, Dr A. R. Hall (*Deputy Head of Mission and Consul*).

Defence and Military Attaché, Col. M. G. Allen.

Vice-Consul, L. C. Craig.

British Council Representative, R. P. Hale, (PO Box 640), Kantipath, Kathmandu.

THE NETHERLANDS
(Koninkrijk der Nederlanden)

Queen of the Netherlands, Her Majesty Queen Beatrix Wilhelmina Armgard, KG, GCVO, *born* Jan. 31, 1938; *succeeded,* April 30, 1980, upon the abdication of her mother Queen Juliana; *married* March 10, 1966, HRH Prince Claus George Willem Otto Frederik Geert of the Netherlands, Jonkheer van Amsberg; and has *issue,* Prince Willem Alexander, *b.* April 27, 1967; Prince Johan Friso, *b.* Sept, 25, 1968; Prince Constantijn Christof, *b.* Oct. 11, 1969.

CABINET
(as at July 1991)

Prime Minister, Ruud F. M. Lubbers (CDA).

Minister of General Affairs, Deputy PM and Minister of Finance, W. Kok (PvdA).
Home Affairs, Mrs C. J. Dales (PvdA).
Foreign Affairs, H. van der Broek (CDA).
Development Co-operation, J. Pronk (PvdA).
Defence, A. L. ter Beek (PvdA).
Economic Affairs, Dr J. E. Andriessen (CDA).
Antillian Affairs and Justice, Prof. E. H. M. Hirsch Ballin (PvdA).
Agriculture and Fisheries, P. Bukman (CDA).
Education and Science, Prof. Dr J. M. M. Ritzen (PvdA).
Social Affairs and Employment, Dr B. de Vries (CDA).
Transport and Public Works, Mrs H. May-Weggen (CDA).
Housing, Physical Planning and Environment, J. G. M. Alders (PvdA).
Welfare, Health and Culture, Mrs H. d'Acona (PvdA).

CDA: Christian Democratic Appeal; PvdA: Labour Party.

ROYAL NETHERLANDS EMBASSY
38 Hyde Park Gate, SW7 5DP
[071–584 5040]

Ambassador Extraordinary and Plenipotentiary, His Excellency Johan Bernard Hoekman (1990).
Ministers Plenipotentiary, E. J. P. Roberts; A. J. Quanjer.
Counsellors, H. W. de Boer; P. A. Hamoen; G. J. Schulten; R. J. van Vollenhouen.
First Secretaries, O. D. Kervers; P. A. Menkveld.
Defence, Naval and Air Attaché, Capt. W. F. L. van Leeuwen.
Military Attaché, Col. G. C. W. Soetermeer.

Area and Population.—The Kingdom of the Netherlands is a maritime country of western Europe, situated on the North Sea, in lat. 50° 46′–53° 34′ N. and long. 3° 22′–7° 14′ E., consisting of 12 provinces (Eastern and Southern Flevoland being amalgamated to form the twelfth province) and containing a total area of 15,770 sq. miles (40,844 sq. km). The population (1990 estimate) is 15,009,000. The live birth rate in 1990 was 195 per 1,000 of the population, and the death-rate was 127.

The land is generally flat and low, intersected by numerous canals and connecting rivers. The principal rivers are the Rhine, Maas, Yssel and Scheldt.

Language and Literature.—Dutch is a West-Germanic language of Saxon origin, closely akin to Old English and Low German. It is spoken in the Netherlands and the northern part of Belgium. It is also used in the Netherlands Antilles. Afrikaans, one of the two South African languages, has Dutch as its origin, but differs from it in grammar and pronunciation. There are six national papers, four of which are morning papers, and there are many regional daily papers.

Government.—In 1815 the Netherlands became a constitutional Kingdom under King William I, a Prince of Orange-Nassau, a descendant of the house which had taken a leading part in the destiny of the nation since the 16th century. The States-General consists of the *Eerste Kamer* (First Chamber) of 75 members, elected for four years by the Provincial Council; and the *Tweede Kamer* (Second Chamber) of 150 members, elected for four years by voters of 18 years and upwards. Members of the *Tweede Kamer* are paid. The most recent election to the Second Chamber was held in September 1989, and resulted in the formation of a centre-left coalition.

Production.—The chief agricultural products are potatoes, wheat, rye, barley, sugar beet, cattle, pigs, milk and milk products, cheese, butter, poultry, eggs, beans, peas, vegetables, fruit, flower bulbs, plants and cut flowers and there is an important fishing industry. Among the principal industries are engineering, both

mechanical and electrical, electronics, nuclear en ergy, petro-chemicals and plastics, road vehicle aircraft and defence equipment, shipbuilding repai steel, textiles of all types, electrical appliances, met ware, furniture, paper, cigars, sugar, liqueurs, bee clothing etc.

Of a total GNP of US$219·6 billion in 1989, industr accounted for around 21 per cent, agriculture for per cent and mining 3 per cent.

Defence.—The armed forces are almost entirel committed to NATO. All ground and air units ar assigned to the NATO Central Region, and nava forces to the Atlantic and Channel commands. Tota armed forces number some 102,000, which includ 45,000 conscripts and 1,700 women. In addition ther are over 155,000 reservists. There is compulsor military service of 14–17 months.

Education.—Primary and secondary education i given in both denominational and state schools, th denominational schools being eligible for state assis ance on equal terms with the state schools. Attend ance at primary school is compulsory. The princip universities are at Leiden, Utrecht, Groninge Amsterdam (2), Nijmegen and Rotterdam, and ther are technical universities at Delft (polytechnic) Eindhoven (polytechnic), Enschede (polytechnic) an Wageningen (agriculture). Illiteracy is practicall non-existent.

Communications.—The total extent of navigabl rivers including canals, was 4,845 km at Jan. 1, 1985 and of metalled roads 97,189 km. In 1985 the tota length of the railway system amounted to 2,867 km of which 1,810 km were electrified. The mercantil marine in January 1985 consisted of 550 ships of tota 3,461,000 gross registered tons. The total length o air routes covered by KLM (Royal Dutch Airlines) i 1985 was 370,640 km.

FINANCE

	1989
Budget Revenue	Guilders 147,000m
Budget Expenditure	170,000m

TRADE

The Dutch are traditionally a trading nation. Entrepot trade, banking and shipping are of particular importance to the economy. The geographical position of the Netherlands, at the mouths of the Rhine, Meuse and Scheldt, brings a large volume of transit trade to and from the interior of Europe to Dutch ports.

Principal trading partners are the Federal Republic of Germany and Belgium/Luxembourg. UK supplied 9·2 per cent of Netherlands imports in 1988 and took 7·7 per cent of the Netherlands exports.

Excluding the construction industry, the index of industrial production in the Netherlands (1980 = 100) was 109 in 1989. Inflation was 1·3 per cent in 1989.

	1989	1990
	Guilders	
Imports	221,400m	232,000m
Exports	229,400m	234,000m

Trade with UK

	1989	1990
Imports from UK	£6,515,325,000	£7,516,576,000
Exports to UK	9,585,699,000	10,483,576,000

CAPITAL.—ΨAmsterdam, population 1,031,000 (urban agglomeration).

SEAT OF GOVERNMENT, The Hague (Den Haag or, in full, 's-Gravenhage), population 443,456.

Other principal cities ΨRotterdam 571,081; Utrecht, 229,969; Eindhoven, 191,675; Haarlem 151,025; Groningen 168,119; Tilburg 153,812.

CURRENCY.—Netherlands guilder or florin of 100 cents.

FLAG.—Three horizontal bands of red, white and blue.

NATIONAL ANTHEM.—Wilhelmus.

BRITISH EMBASSY
Lange Voorhout 10, The Hague, 2514 ED
[The Hague 364 5800]

Ambassador Extraordinary and Plenipotentiary, His Excellency Sir Michael Romilly Heald Jenkins, KCMG (1988).

Counsellors, R. P. Flower (*Deputy Head of Mission*); A. D. Sprake (*Commercial/Agriculture*).
Defence and Naval Attaché, Capt. M. Bickley, RN.
Military and Air Attaché, Lt.-Col. P. Cook.
First Secretary and Head of Chancery, P. J. Sullivan.

There is a Consulate-General at Amsterdam.

British Council Representative, J. Andrews, Keizersgracht 343, 1016 EH Amsterdam.

NETHERLANDS-BRITISH CHAMBER OF COMMERCE, The Dutch House, 307–308 High Holborn, WC1V 7LS.
UK OFFICE IN THE HAGUE, Holland Trade House, Bezuidenhoutseweg 181, 2594 AH The Hague.

OVERSEAS TERRITORIES

ARUBA covers an area of 75 sq. miles (193 sq. km) with a population (1988 estimate) of 62,500. The island of Aruba was from 1828 part of the Dutch West Indies and from 1845 part of the Netherlands Antilles. On January 1, 1986 it became a separate territory within the Kingdom of the Netherlands. The 1983 Constitutional Conference agreed that Aruba's separate status would last for ten years from 1986, after which the island would become fully independent.

The economy of Aruba is based largely on tourism. In 1986 there were over 180,000 tourists.

Governor, F. B. Tromp.
Prime Minister, Nelson Oduber.

Trade with UK

	1989	1990
Imports from UK	£12,751,000	£11,386,000
Exports to UK	653,000	50,000

CAPITAL.—ΨOranjestad (population 20,000); and Sint Nicolaas (17,000).
CURRENCY.—Aruban florin.

NETHERLANDS ANTILLES comprise certain islands in the West Indies (Curaçao, Bonaire, part of St Martin, St Eustatius, and Saba). The islands cover an area of 308 sq. miles (800 sq. km) with a population (UN 1989 estimate) of 191,000. The Netherlands Antilles (which have a federal parliament) are largely self-governing under the terms of the Realm Statute which took effect on December 29, 1954.

The economy of the Netherlands Antilles is based on small manufacturing industries. The soil is too poor to permit large-scale agriculture and most products for consumption, and industrial raw materials must be imported.

Governor, Dr Jaime Saleh.
Prime Minister, Mrs Maria Liberia Peters.

Trade with UK

	1989*	1990*
Imports from UK	£19,396,000	£23,800,000
Exports to UK	5,115,000	43,552,000

*Curaçao

CAPITAL.—ΨWillemstad (on Curaçao) (pop. 50,000).
CURRENCY.—Netherlands Antilles guilder of 100 cents.

NICARAGUA
(República de Nicaragua)

President, Minister of Defence, Violeta Barrios de Chamorro, *inaugurated* April 25, 1990.
Vice-President, Virgilio Godoy.

COUNCIL OF MINISTERS
(as at August 1991)

Minister to the Presidency, Antonio Lacayo.
External Relations, Enrique Dreyfus.
Interior, Carlos Hurtado.
Finance, Emilio Pereira.
Foreign Co-operation, Erwin Krugger.
Construction and Transport, Jaime Icalbalceta Mayorga.
Health, Ernesto Salmerón.
Agriculture, Roberto Rondón Sacasa.
Labour, Francisco Rosales.
Economics and Planning, Dr Silvio de Franco Montalzon.
Education, Humberto Belli Pereira.

EMBASSY OF NICARAGUA
8 Gloucester Road, SW7 4PP
[071–584 4365]

Ambassador Extraordinary and Plenipotentiary, Roberto Parreles (1990).

Nicaragua is the largest state of Central America, with a long seaboard on both the Atlantic and Pacific Oceans, situated between 10° 45'–15° N. lat. and 83° 40'–87° 38' W. long., containing an area of 50,193 sq. miles (130,000 sq. km). It has a population (UN estimate 1989) of 3,745,000 of whom about three-quarters are of mixed blood. Another 15 per cent are white, mostly of pure Spanish descent and the remaining 10 per cent are West Indians or Indians. The latter group includes the Mosquitos, who live on the Atlantic coast and were formerly under British protection.

Government.—The eastern coast of Nicaragua was touched by Columbus in 1502, and in 1518 was overrun by Spanish forces under Davila, and formed part of the Spanish Captaincy-General of Guatemala until 1821, when its independence was secured. In 1927 Augusto Cesar Sandino began a guerrilla war against the occupation of Nicaragua by US Marines, which continued until they were expelled in 1933. Sandino was assassinated by Anastasio Somoza, Director of the National Guard, and in 1936 Somoza assumed the Presidency. He was succeeded in power by his sons Luis and Anastasio Somoza, until 1979 when the family and the National Guard were overthrown by guerrillas of the Sandinista National Liberation Front. A Junta of National Reconstruction subsequently took power. Elections for President, Vice-President and a National Assembly were held in November 1984, and in January 1985 they replaced the Junta and the Council of State.

After ten years in power, the Sandinistas lost their parliamentary majority in elections held in February 1990. A coalition of former opposition parties, Unión Nacional de Opositora (UNO) now holds the majority.

Agriculture and Industry.—The country is mainly agricultural. The major crops are cotton, coffee (30 per cent of total export earnings), sugar cane, tobacco, sesame and bananas. Beans, rice, maize and ipecacuanha, livestock and timber production are also important. However, fishing, forestry, grain and cattle production have been hit by the civil war in the main growing areas. Nicaragua possesses deposits of gold and silver.

Communications.—There are 252 miles of railway, all on the Pacific side and approximately 5,500 miles of telegraph. There are 51 radio stations and two television stations in Managua. An automatic telephone system has been installed in the capital and extended to all major cities. A ground station for satellite communication was inaugurated in 1973. Transport except on the Pacific slope, is still attended with difficulty but many new roads have either been opened or are under construction. The Inter-American Highway runs from the Honduras frontier in the north to the Costa Rican border in the south; the inter-oceanic highway runs from the Corinto on the Pacific coast via Managua to Rama, where there is a natural waterway to Bluefields on the Atlantic. The country's main airport is at Managua. The chief port is Corinto on the Pacific.

Language and Literature.—The official language of the country is Spanish and the majority profess Catholicism, although the English language and the Moravian Church are widespread on the Atlantic coast. There are three daily newspapers published at Managua, apart from the official Gazette (*La Gaceta*). A national literacy campaign in 1980 has reduced illiteracy to 12 per cent. There are universities at León and Managua.

Trade with UK

	1989	1990
Imports from UK	£6,985,000	£6,515,000
Exports to UK	918,000	1,899,000

Considerable quantities of foodstuffs are imported as well as cotton goods, jute, iron and steel, machinery and petroleum products. The chief exports are cotton, coffee, beef, gold, sugar, cottonseed and bananas.

CAPITAL.—Managua, population 615,000. The centre was almost totally destroyed in the earthquake of December 1972. León, 158,577; Granada, 72,640; Masaya, 78,308; Chinandega, 144,291.

CURRENCY.—Córdoba (C$) of 100 centavos.

FLAG.—Horizontal stripes of blue, white and blue, with the Nicaraguan coat of arms in the centre of the white stripe.

NATIONAL DAY.—September 15.

NATIONAL ANTHEM.—Salve A Ti Nicaragua (Hai Nicaragua).

BRITISH EMBASSY
PO Box A-169, El Reparto 'Los Robles', Primera Etapa, Entrada Principal de la Carretera a Masaya Managua, Nicaragua.
[Managua 70034]

British Ambassador and Consul-General, (resident i San José, Costa Rica).

NIGER
(République du Niger)

President, Minister of Defence, Brig.-Gen. Ali Saibou

MINISTERS
(as at March 1991)

Prime Minister, Aliou Mahamidou.
Foreign Affairs and Co-operation, Mahamane San Bako.
Social and Women's Affairs, Moumouni Aissata.
Youth, Sport and Culture, Capt. Abdoulrahaman Seydou.
Interior, Abara Djika.
Education, Lt.-Col. Issa Amsa.
Health, Lt.-Col. Ousmane Gazere.
Equipment, Maj. Issaka Ousmane.
Transport and Tourism, Cmdt. Hamadou Mouss Gros.
Agriculture and Livestock, Adamou Souna.
Finance, Wassalke Boukari.
Planning, Almoustapha Soumaila.
Mining and Energy, Abdou Insa.
Water and the Environment, Karadji Ayarga.
Minister-Delegate to the Presidency in charge o Administrative Reform, Mamane Boukari.
Justice, Keeper of the Seals, Ali Bandiere.
Civil Service and Employment, Dagra Mamadou.
Communication, Khamed Abdoulaye.
Economic Promotion, Nassirou Sabo.
Higher Education, Research and Technology, Abou bacar Adamou.

EMBASSY OF THE REPUBLIC OF NIGER
154 rue de Longchamp, 75116, Paris
[Paris 45048060]

Ambassador Extraordinary and Plenipotentiary, Hi Excellency Sandi Yacouba (1990).

Situated in west central Africa, between 12° and 24° N. and 0° and 16° E., Niger has common boundaries with Algeria and Libya in the north, Chad, Nigeria Benin, Mali and Burkina.

It has an area of about 489,191 sq. miles (1,267,000 sq km), with a population (UN estimate, 1989) o 6,895,000. Apart from a small region along the Nige Valley in the south-west near the capital the country is entirely savanna or desert. The main ethnic group are the Hausa (54 per cent) in the south, the Songha and Djerma in the south-west, the Fulani, th Beriberi–Manga, and the nomadic Tuareg in th north. The official language is French.

The first French expedition arrived in 1891 and the country was fully occupied by 1914. It decided on December 18, 1958 to remain an autonomous republi within the French Community; full independence outside the Community was proclaimed on August 3 1960.

The constitution of Niger, adopted on November 8 1960, provided for a presidential system of government, modelled on that of the United States and the French Fifth Republic, and a single Chamber Nation al Assembly. In April 1974 Lt.-Col. Seyni Kountche seized power, suspended the Constitution, dissolved the National Assembly, and suppressed all political organizations. He then set up a Supreme Military Council with himself as President. President Kountché died on November 10, 1987 and was succeeded peacefully by his cousin, Col. Ali Saibou, who restored a measure of normal political life.

In August 1991, a national conference of all groups voted to suspend the constitution and stripped President Saibou of all powers; he remains nominal head of state until the formation of an interim government and the calling of multi-party elections. Temporary control of the security forces was vested in Prof. André Salifou, chairman of the national conference.

Finance.—The 1989 General Budget allocation was CFA 220,100 million.

Trade.—The cultivation of ground-nuts and the production of livestock are the main industries and provide two of the main exports. A company formed by the Government, the French Atomic Energy Authority and private interests is exploiting uranium deposits at Arlit, and this is the main export. There is also some oil exploration.

Trade with UK

	1989	1990
Imports from UK	£6,862,000	£10,780,000
Exports to UK	1,472,000	1,161,000

CAPITAL.—Niamey, population 410,000.

CURRENCY.—Franc CFA of 100 centimes.

FLAG.—Three horizontal stripes, orange, white and green with an orange disc in the middle of the white stripe.

NATIONAL DAY.—December 18.

British Ambassador, (resident in Abidjan, Côte d'Ivoire).

NORWAY
(Kongeriket Norge)

King, HM Harald V, GCVO, *born* Feb. 21, 1937; *succeeded,* Jan. 17, 1991, on death of his father King Olav V; *married* Aug. 29, 1968, Sonja Haraldsen, and has *issue,* Prince Haakon Magnus (*see below*), and Princess Martha Louise, *born* Sept. 22, 1971.

Heir-Apparent, HRH Prince Haakon Magnus, *born* July 20, 1973.

CABINET
(as at November 3, 1991)

Prime Minister, Gro Harlem Brundtland.
Foreign Affairs, Thorvald Stoltenberg.
Petroleum and Energy, Finn Kristensen.
Defence, Johan Jørgen Holst.
Local Government, Kjell Borgen.
Labour and Government Administration, Tove Strand Gerhardsen.
Agriculture, Gunhild Øyangen.
Justice, Kari Gjesteby.
Fisheries, Oddrunn Pettersen.
Industry, Ole Knapp.
Environment, Thorbjørn Berntsen.
Transport and Communications, Kjell Opseth.
Health and Social Affairs, Tove Veierød.
Church, Education and Research, Gudmund Hernes.
Trade and Shipping, Eldrid Nordbø.
Family and Consumer Affairs, Matz Sandman.
Cultural Affairs, Åse Kleveland.
Finance, Sigbjørn Johnsen.
Development Co-operation, Grete Faremo.

(Some of the Ministries are being reorganized, which may result in changes in their titles).

ROYAL NORWEGIAN EMBASSY
25 Belgrave Square, SW1X 8QD
[071–235 7151]

Ambassador Extraordinary and Plenipotentiary, His Excellency Kjell Eliassen (1989).

Minister-Counsellor, Jon Bech.

Counsellors, Paul Moe (*Press and Cultural*); Marius Hauge (*Fisheries*); vacant (*Economic*); Viggo Smestad (*Commercial*).

First Secretaries, J. A. Knutsen (*Political*); W. Kirkebye (*Consul*); L. Engesaeth (*Economic*).

Second Secretaries, Katja Nordgaard (*Press, Information and Cultural*).

Area and Population.—Norway is a kingdom in the northern and western portion of the Scandinavian peninsula, and was founded in AD 872. It is 1,752 km in length, its greatest width about 430 km. The length of the coastline is 2,542 km, and the frontier between Norway and the neighbouring countries is 2,542 km (Sweden 1,619 km, Finland 727 km and USSR 196 km). It is divided into 19 counties (*fylker*) and comprises an area of 149,282 sq. miles (386,638 sq. km), of which Svalbard and Jan Mayen have a combined area of 24,101 sq. km, with a total population (April 1989) of 4,224,606.

The Norwegian coastline is extensive, deeply indented with numerous fjords, and fringed with an immense number of rocky islands. The surface is mountainous, consisting of elevated and barren tablelands, separated by deep and narrow valleys. At the North Cape the sun does not appear to set from the second week in May to the last week in July, causing the phenomenon known as the Midnight Sun; conversely, there is no apparent sunrise from about November 18 to January 23. During the long winter nights are seen the multiple coloured Northern Lights or Aurora Borealis, which have a maximum intensity in a line crossing North America from Alaska to Labrador and Northern Europe to the Arctic coast and Siberia.

Language and Literature.—Old Norse literature is among the most ancient and richest in Europe. Norwegian in both its present forms is closely related to other Scandinavian languages. Independence from Denmark (1814) and resurgent nationalism led to the development of 'new Norwegian' based on dialects, which now has equal official standing with 'bokmål', in which Danish influence is more obvious. This was formed in the time of the Reformation, and Ludvig Holberg (1684–1754) is regarded as the father of Norwegian literature, though the modern period begins with the patriotic and romantic writings of Henrik Wergeland (1808–1845). Some of the famous names are Henrik Ibsen (1828–1906), Bjørnstjerne Bjørnson (1832–1910), Nobel Prizewinner in 1903, and the novelists Jonas Lie (1833–1908), Alexander Kielland (1849–1906), Knut Hamsun (1859–1952) and Sigrid Undset (1882–1949), the latter two also Nobel Prizewinners. In 1990 there were 155 daily newspapers.

Government.—From 1397 to 1814 Norway was united with Denmark, and from November 4, 1814 with Sweden, under a personal union which was dissolved on June 7, 1905, when Norway regained complete independence. Under the constitution of May 17, 1814, the *Storting* (Parliament) itself elects one-quarter of its members to constitute the *Lagting* (Upper Chamber), the other three-quarters forming the *Odelsting* (Lower Chamber). Legislative questions alone are dealt with by both parts in separate sittings.

A minority Labour government replaced the previous three-party, centre-right coalition government, which collapsed in October 1990 because of a dispute over whether to apply for membership of the European Community.

Production.—The cultivated area is about 8,636 sq. km (2·3 per cent of total surface area); forests cover nearly 25 per cent; the rest consists of highland pastures or uninhabitable mountains.

The Gulf Stream pours from 140 to 170 million cubic feet of warm water per second into the sea around Norway and causes the temperature to be higher than the average for the latitude. It brings shoals of herring and cod into the fishing grounds, making it possible to cultivate potatoes and barley in latitudes which in other countries are perpetually frozen. In normal years the quantity of fish caught by Norwegian fishing vessels is greater than that of any other European country except USSR. In 1987 the total catch amounted to 1,867,720 tonnes.

The chief industries are manufactures, agriculture and forestry, fisheries, mining, production of metals and ferro-alloys and shipping. Also in recent years industries providing both manufactured products and services for the development of North Sea oil and gas resources have assumed growing importance. In 1988, the total workforce was 2,163,000 of which 324,000 persons were employed in Norwegian industry. Manufactures are aided by great resources of hydro-electric power. Actual production in 1988 amounted to 110,063 Gwh.

Defence.—Norway is a member of the North Atlantic Treaty Organization, and the Headquarters of Allied Forces, Northern Europe, is situated near Oslo. The period of compulsory national service is 15 months (without refresher training) in the Navy and Air Force, and 12 months (with refresher training) in the Army.

Education from 7 to 16 is free and compulsory in the 'basic schools' maintained by the municipalities with state grants-in-aid. The majority of the pupils receive post-compulsory schooling at 'upper secondary' schools, colleges of education (19), regional colleges akin to polytechnics (12), universities (4) and other university-level specialist institutions.

Communications.—The total length of railways open at the end of 1988 was 4,070 km, excludin private lines. There are 87,603 km of public roads i Norway (including urban streets). At the end of 198 2,893,639 road motor vehicles were registered.

Scheduled internal air services are operated b Scandinavian Airlines System (SAS) on behalf of De Norske Luftfartselskap (DNL), by Braathens Sout American and Far East Airtransport (SAFE), and b Wideróes Flyveselskap AS.

The Mercantile Marine, 1988, consisted of 1,53 vessels of 12,921,932 gross tons (vessels above 10 gross tons, excluding fishing boats, floating whalin factories, tugs, salvage vessels, icebreakers and sim lar types of vessel).

FINANCE

	1987	1988
Total Revenue	K321,677,000	K342,900,00
Total Expenditure	282,648,000	309,717,00

TRADE

	1987	1988
Total imports	K211,794m	K217,455r
Total exports	199,731m	213,117n

Trade with UK

	1989	1990
Imports from UK	£1,056,506,000	£1,289,789,00
Exports to UK	3,637,119,000	4,235,348,00

The chief imports are raw materials, motor ve hicles, chemicals, motor spirit, fuel and other oils coal, ships and machinery; together with manufac tures of silk, cotton and wool. The exports consis chiefly of crude oil and gas, manufactured goods, fis and products of fish (as canned fish, whale oils), pul paper, iron ore and pyrites, nitrate of lime, stone calcium carbide, aluminium, ferro-alloys, zinc, nickel cyanamides, etc.

CAPITAL.—ΨOslo (including Aker), populatio (Jan. 1987) 450,808. Other towns are ΨTrondheir 135,542; ΨBergen 209,912; ΨStavanger 96,316 ΨKristiansand 63,637; ΨDrammen 51,807; ΨTroms 49,358.

CURRENCY.—Krone of 100 øre.

FLAG.—Red, with white-bordered blue cross.

NATIONAL ANTHEM.—Ja, Vi Elsker Dette Lande (Yes, we love this country).

NATIONAL DAY.—May 17 (Constitution Day).

BRITISH EMBASSY
Thomas Heftyesgate 8, 0244 Oslo 2
[Oslo 55 24 00]

Ambassador Extraordinary and Plenipotentiary, Hi Excellency David John Edward Ratford, CM (1990).
Counsellors, A. J. K. Bailes (*Deputy Head of Missio and Consul General*); Dr C. P. Burdess, LV (*Economic and Commercial*).
First Secretaries, J. Venning; A. L. Wotton (*Economi and Commercial*); R. H. Tonkin (*Management*); T R. Bevan.
Defence and Air Attaché, Wg Cdr. J. C. W. Marshall.
Naval Attaché, Cdr. S. S. Pearson.
Military Attaché, Lt.-Col. W. R. de W. Lash.

BRITISH CONSULAR OFFICES

There is a British Consular Office at *Oslo* an Honorary Consulates at *Bergen, Tromsø, Alesund Kristiansund, Stavanger, Trondheim, Kristiansand Haugesund* and *Harstad.*

British Council Representative, D. N. Constable Fridtjof Nansens Plass 5,0160, Oslo 1.

TERRITORIES

SVALBARD. The Svalbard Archipelago lies betweer

74°–81° N. lat. and between 10°–35° E. long., with an estimated area of 24,295 square miles. The archipelago consists of a main island, known as Spitsbergen (15,200 sq. miles); North East Land, closely adjoining and separated by Hinlopen Strait; the Wiche Islands, separated from the mainland by Olga Strait; Barents and Edge Islands, separated from the mainland by Stor Fjord (or Wybe Jansz Water); Prince Charles Foreland, to the W.; Hope Island, to the SE; Bear Island (68 square miles) 127 miles to the S.; with many similar islands in the neighbourhood of the main group.

By Treaty (Feb. 9, 1920) the sovereignty of Norway over the Spitsbergen (Pointed Mountain) Archipelago was recognized by other nations, and on August 14, 1925 Norway assumed sovereignty. In September 1941 Allied forces (British, Canadian and Norwegian) landed on the main island. After destruction of the accumulated stocks of coal and dismantling of mining machinery and the wireless installation, the Norwegian inhabitants (about 600) were evacuated to a British port and the Russians (about 1,500) to the USSR. After the war the Norwegian mining plants were rebuilt. In addition to those engaged in coal-mining, the archipelago is also visited by hunters for seals, foxes and polar bears.

South Cape is 355 miles from the Norwegian coast. Ice Fjord is 520 miles from Tromsø, 650 miles from Murmansk, and 1,300 miles from Aberdeen. Transit from Tromsø to Green Harbour takes 2–3 days; from Aberdeen 5–6 days.

JAN MAYEN, an island in the Arctic Ocean (70° 49′–71° 9′ N. lat. and 7° 53′–9° 5′ W. long.) was joined to Norway by law of February 27, 1930.

Norwegian Antarctic Territories

BOUVET ISLAND (54° 26′ S. lat. and 3° 24′ E. long.) was declared a dependency of Norway by law of Feb. 27, 1930.

PETER THE FIRST ISLAND (68° 48′ S. lat. and 90° 35′ W. long.), was declared a dependency of Norway by resolution of Government, May 1, 1931.

PRINCESS RAGNHILD LAND (from 70° 30′ to 68° 40′ S. lat. and 24° 15′ to 33° 30′ E. long.) has been claimed as Norwegian since February 17, 1931.

QUEEN MAUD LAND.—On January 14, 1939 the Norwegian Government declared the area between 20° W. and 45° E., adjacent to Australian Antarctica, to be Norwegian territory.

OMAN
(The Sultanate of Oman)

Sultan, Prime Minister, Minister of Foreign Affairs, Defence and Finance, HM Qaboos Bin-Said, *succeeded* on deposition of Sultan Said bin Taimur, July 23, 1970.

COUNCIL OF MINISTERS
(as at June 30, 1991)

Personal Representative of HM The Sultan, HH Sayyid Thuwainy bin Shihab Al Said.
Deputy PM for Security and Defence, HH Sayyid Fahr bin Taimur al Said.
Deputy PM for Legal Affairs, HH Sayyid Fahad bin Mahmood al Said.
Deputy PM for Financial and Economic Affairs, HE Qais bin Abdul Munem al Zawawi.
National Heritage and Culture, HH Sayyid Faisal bin Ali al Said.
Agriculture and Fisheries, HE Mohammed bin Abdallah bin Zaher al Hinai.
Electricity and Water, HE Shaikh Mohammed bin Ali Al Qatabi.

Labour and Vocational Training, HE Sayyid al Mutasim bin Hamoud al Busaidi.
Water Resources, HE Khalfan bin Nasser al Wahaibi.
Justice, Awqaf and Islamic Affairs, HE Sayyid Hilal bin Saud bin Hareb al Busaidi.
Health, HE Dr Ali bin Mohammed bin Moosa.
Petroleum and Minerals, HE Said bin Ahmed bin Said al Shanfari.
Housing, HE Malik bin Suleiman al Mammari.
Civil Services, HE Ahmed bin Abdul Nabi Macki.
Communications, HE Shaikh Hamoud bin Abdullah al Harthy.
Education and Youth Affairs, HE Yahya bin Mahfoodh al Mantheri.
Interior, HE Sayyid Badr bin Saud bin Hareb al Busaidi.
Information, HE Abdul Aziz bin Mohammed al Rawas.
Minister of State and Wali of Dhofar, HE Sayyid Mussallan Bin Ali al Busaidy.
Environment, HH Sayyid Shabib bin Taimur bin Faisal al Said.
Regional Municipalities Affairs, HE Shaikh Amor bin Shuwain al Hosni.
Minister of State for Foreign Affairs, HE Yousuf bin al Alawi bin Abdullah.
Commerce and Industry, HE Salim bin Abdullah al Ghazali.
Social Affairs, HE Shaikh Mustahail bin Ahmed al Mashani.
Posts, Telegraphs and Telephones, HE Ahmed bin Sweidan al Baluchi.
Secretary General at the Ministry of Defence, HE Saif bin Hamad al Batashi.

EMBASSY OF THE SULTANATE OF OMAN
44A/B Montpelier Square, SW7 1JJ
[071–584 6782/3/4]

Ambassador Extraordinary and Plenipotentiary, His Excellency Abdulla Mohammed Al-Dhahab (1990).

The independent Sultanate of Oman lies at the eastern corner of the Arabian Peninsula. Its seaboard is nearly 1,000 miles long and extends from near Tibat on the west coast of the Musandam Peninsula round to Ras Darbat Ali, with the exception of the stretch between Dibba and Kalba on the east coast which belongs to Sharjah and Fujairah of the United Arab Emirates. Ras Darbat Ali marks the boundary between the Sultanate and the southern border of the Republic of Yemen. The Sultanate extends inland to the borders of the Rub al Khali, or Empty Quarter of the Arabian Desert.

The area of Oman has been estimated at 82,030 sq. miles (212,457 sq. km), and the population (UN estimate 1989) is 1,422,000. The inhabitants of the north are for the most part Arab but there are large communities of Hindus, Khojas and Baluch, in addition to Omanis of Zanzibari origin. In Dhofar there is also a large proportion of Omanis of Zanzibari origin around Salalah, but in the mountains the inhabitants are either of pure Arab descent or belong to tribes of pre-Arab origin, the Qarra and Mahra, who speak their own dialects of semitic origin.

Physically and historically modern Oman can be split into two main parts, the north and the south, divided by a large tract of desert. Northern Oman has three main sections. The Batinah, the coastal plain, varies in width from 30 miles in the neighbourhood of Suwaiq to almost nothing at Muscat where the mountains descend abruptly to the sea. The plain is fertile, with date gardens extending over its full length of 150 miles. The Hajjar is a mountain spine running from north-west to south-east, reaching nearly 10,000 feet in height on Jabal Akhdar. For the most part the mountains are barren, but numerous valleys penetrate the central massif of Jabal Akhdar and in these there is considerable cultivation irrigated by wells or a system of underground canals called *falajs* which tap the water table. The two plateaus leading from the western slopes of the mountains, the Dhahirah in the north and the Sharqia in the south-east, also have centres of settlements and cultivation. They fall from an average height of 1,000 feet into the sands of the Empty Quarter. The north is separated from the south by nearly 400 miles of inhospitable country crossed by one trunk road, the only land link. Dhofar, the southern province, is the only part of the Arabian Peninsula to be touched by the south-west monsoon. Temperatures are more moderate than in the north and sugar cane and coconuts are grown on the coastal plain, while cattle are bred on the mountains.

Government.—A Consultative Council for the State was established by Sultanic decree on October 18, 1981. The Council is a nominated body consisting of 55 members (36 representing the public and 19 representing the government). The Council's jurisdiction is confined to economic affairs and social development. There are plans for a new body.

Commerce and Trade.—Trade is mainly with the UAE, UK, Japan, the Netherlands, USA, Federal Republic of Germany, France and India. Total imports for the year 1988 were OR846,430,275. Chief imports were machinery, cars, building materials, food and telecommunications equipment.

Trade with UK

	1989	1990
Imports from UK	£298,974,000	£272,072,000
Exports to UK	84,009,000	89,446,000

Production.—Petroleum Development (Oman) Ltd (owned 60 per cent by Oman Government and 34 per cent by Shell) began exporting oil in 1967. Concessions (off and on shore) are held by several major international companies. The current level of oil production is about 650,000 barrels per day, planned to increase to 700,000.

Development.—For many years the Sultanate was a poor country with a total annual income of less than £1,000,000. The advent of oil revenues since 1967 and the change of regime in 1970 led to the initiation of a wide-ranging development programme, especially concerned with health, education and communications. New hospitals have been completed in the main provincial centres and there are now nearly 50 hospitals with around 3,400 beds; 759 schools, with 327,131 pupils, were in operation in 1989. A gas turbine power station operates at Rusail, where there is also a 200 plot industrial estate. There is a power station and a desalination plant near Muscat and flour, animal feed, cement and copper production facilities.

Communications.—Since 1972 ships have been using Port Qaboos at Matrah, where eight deep water berths have been constructed as part of the new harbour facilities.

A modern telecommunications service to the main population centres and an international service are operated by the General Telecommunications Organization. There are good tarmac roads linking most main population centres of the country with the coast and with the towns of the UAE. There is now over 4,000 km of asphalted road in the Sultanate.

CAPITAL.—Ψ Muscat, estimated population 400,000. The commercial centre has grown around Mutrah, 3 miles away and the main port, and Ruwi. The main towns on the northern coast are ΨSur, ΨBarka and ΨSohar. The main town of Dhofar is Salalah.

CURRENCY.—Rial Omani (OR) of 1,000 baiza.

FLAG.—Red, green and white with crossed daggers in red sector.

NATIONAL DAY.—November 18.

BRITISH EMBASSY
PO Box 300, Muscat
[Muscat 738501/5]

Ambassador Extraordinary and Plenipotentiary, ▮
  Excellency Sir Terence Clark, KBE, CMG, CVO (199
Counsellor, N. H. S. Armour (*Deputy Head of Missio*
Defence Attaché, Brig. M. Bremridge, MC.
Naval and Air Attaché, Cdr. K. Harris, OBE, R.N
First Secretaries, B. Baldwin; N. H. Bates.

British Council Representative, R. A. Steedman, ▮
  Box 7090, Mutrah, Oman.

PANANA
PANAMA
(República de Panama)

President, Guillermo Endara Galimany, *sworn*
  December 27, 1989.
First Vice-President, Dr Ricardo Arias Calderon.
Second Vice-President and Minister of Planning a▮
  Political Economy, Guillermo Ford Boyd.

CABINET
(as at July 1, 1991)

Foreign Affairs, Dr Julio Linares.
Treasury and Finance, Dr Mario Galindo.
Government and Justice, Juan B. Chevalier.
Agricultural Development, Dr Ezequiel Rodriguez.
Commerce and Industry, Roberto Alfaro.
Labour and Social Welfare, Jorge Rosas.
Health, Dr Guillermo Rolla Pimental.
Housing, Guillermo E. Quijano.
Education, Marco A. Alarcon.
Presidency, Julio Harris.
Public Works, Alfredo Arias.

EMBASSY OF THE REPUBLIC OF PANAMA
119 Crawford Street, W1H 1AF
[071–487 5633]

Ambassador Extraordinary and Plenipotentiary, H▮
  Excellency Teodoro F. Franco (1990).

There are also Consular Offices at *Liverpool* a▮
London (24 Tudor Street, EC4Y 0JD).

Panama lies on the isthmus of that name whi▮ connects N. and S. America. The area of the Repub▮ is 29,762 sq. miles (77,082 sq. km), the populati▮ (Census 1990) 2,315,047. Spanish is the official la▮ guage.

Government.—After a revolt in November 19▮ Panama declared its independence from Colomb▮ and established a separate Government. After 19▮ control of Panama was increasingly taken over ▮ Gen. Omar Torrijos, Commander of the Nation▮ Guard, following a military coup. In 1972 Gener▮ Torrijos was designated as 'Leader of the Revolutio▮ with wide overriding powers. In October 1978 ▮ withdrew from the government, and Dr Aristid▮ Royo was elected President by the Assembly ▮ Representatives. In a Presidential election in Ma▮ 1984, Dr Nicolas Barletta was elected president. ▮ resigned in September 1985 after disagreements wi▮ military leaders and was succeeded by his Vic▮ President, Eric Arturo Delvalle. An attempt ▮ February 1988 by President Delvalle to remove Ge▮ Noriega as Commander of the Defence Forces faile▮ Noriega ousted Delvalle and replaced him wi▮ Manuel Solis Palma. Presidential elections were he▮ in May 1989, but Noriega annulled the results, whi▮ had appeared to give victory to the opposition. A U▮ military invasion on December 20, 1989 followe▮ Noriega's formal assumption of power as Head ▮ State on December 15. Guillermo Endara, believed ▮ have won the May elections, was installed a▮ President following the ousting of General Norieg▮

'anama is still suffering from physical destruction
nd political instability caused by the US invasion.

Legislative power is vested in a unicameral Legis-
ative Assembly of 67 members; executive power is
eld by the President, assisted by two elected Vice-
residents and an appointed Cabinet. Elections are
eld every five years under a system of universal and
ompulsory adult suffrage.

Economy.—The soil is moderately fertile, but
early one-half of the land is uncultivated. The chief
rops are bananas, sugar, coconuts, cacao, coffee and
ereals. The shrimping industry plays an important
ole in the Panamanian economy. A railway 47 miles
n length joins the Atlantic and Pacific oceans.

Education is compulsory and free from 7 to 15
ears.

TRADE

Imports are mostly manufactured goods, machin-
ry, lubricants, chemicals and foodstuffs; exports are
ananas, petroleum products, shrimps, sugar, meat
nd fishmeal.

Republic of Panama	1988	1989
Imports	US$712·3m	US$796·0m
Exports	283·0m	297·3m

Colon Free Zone		
Imports	US$1,843m	US$243·8m
Exports	2,119m	249·9m

Trade with UK†

	1989	1990
Imports from UK	£32,875,000	£35,552,000
Exports to UK	6,818,000	4,056,000

† Including Colon Free Zone.

The Panama Canal Zone.—With effect from Oct.
, 1979 the Canal Zone (647 sq. miles) was disestab-
ished, with all areas of land and water within the
one reverting to Panama. By the 1977 treaty with
he USA, the USA is allowed the use of operating
ases for the Panama Canal, together with several
ilitary bases, but the Republic of Panama is
overeign in all such areas. Control of the Canal will
evert to Panama in the year 2000.

CAPITAL.—ΨPanama City, population (1990)
,064,221.

CURRENCY.—Balboa of 100 centésimos. US$ notes
re also in circulation.

FLAG.—Four quarters; white with blue star (top,
ext staff), red (in fly), blue (below, next staff) and
hite with red star.

NATIONAL ANTHEM.—Alcanzamos Por Fin La Vic-
oria (Victory is ours at last).

NATIONAL DAY.—November 3.

Dependencies of Panama.—Taboga Island (area
sq. miles) is a popular tourist resort some 12 miles
rom the Pacific entrance to the Panama Canal.
'ourist facilities have also been developed in the Las
'erlas Archipelago in the Gulf of Panama, particu-
arly on the island of Contadora. There is a penal
ettlement at Guardia on the island of Coiba (area 19
q. miles) in the Gulf of Chiriqui.

BRITISH EMBASSY

Torre Swiss Bank, Calle 53 (Apartado 889 Zona 1),
Panama City, Panama 1
[Panama City 69–0866]

Ambassador Extraordinary and Plenipotentiary, His
Excellency John Grant MacDonald, CBE (1990).
Defence, Naval, Military and Air Attaché, Lt.-Col. T.
A. Glen.

There is a British consular office at *Panama City.*

PARAGUAY
(República del Paraguay)

President, General Andrés Rodriguez, *elected* May 1,
1989.

CABINET MINISTERS
(as at August 1991)

Foreign Affairs, Dr Alexis Frutos Vaesken.
Interior, Gen. Orlando Machuca Vargas.
Finance, Juan José Díaz Perez.
Education and Worship, Angel Roberto Seifart.
Agriculture and Livestock, Raul Torres Segovia.
Public Works and Communications, Gen. Porfirio
Pereira Ruiz Diaz.
Defence, Gen. Angel Juan Souto Hernandez.
Public Health and Social Welfare, Cynthia Prieto
Conti.
Justice and Labour, Hugo Estigarribia Elizeche.
Industry and Commerce, Ubaldo Scavone.
Without portfolio, Dr Juan Ramón Cháves.

EMBASSY OF PARAGUAY
Braemar Lodge, Cornwall Gardens, SW7 4AQ
[071–937 1253]

Ambassador Extraordinary and Plenipotentiary, His
Excellency Antonio Espinoza.

Area and Population.—Paraguay is an inland
subtropical state of South America, situated
between Argentina, Bolivia and Brazil.

The area is estimated at 157,048 sq. miles (406,752 sq.
km), with a population (1990 estimate) of 4,157,287.

Paraguay is a country of grassy plains and dense
forest, the soil being marshy in many parts and liable
to floods; while the hills are covered for the most part
with immense forests. The streams flowing into the
Alto Paraná descend precipitously into that river.
In the angle formed by the Paraná-Paraguay confluence are extensive marshes, one of which, known as
Neembucú, or endless, is drained by Lake Ypoa, a
large lagoon, south-east of the capital. The Chaco,
lying between the rivers Paraguay and Pilcomayo
and bounded on the north by Bolivia, formed the
subject of a long-standing dispute with that country
and led to war between Paraguay and Bolivia from
1932 to 1935. The Chaco is a flat plain, rising
uniformly towards its western boundary to a height
of 1,140 feet; it suffers much from floods and still more
from drought, but the building of dams and reservoirs
has converted part of it into good pasture for cattle
raising.

Government.—In 1535 Paraguay was settled as a
Spanish possession. In 1811 it declared its independence of Spain.

The constitution provides for a two-chamber
parliament consisting of a 36-member Senate and a
72-member Chamber of Deputies. Two-thirds of the
seats in each chamber are allocated to the majority
party and the remaining one-third shared among the
minority parties in proportion to the votes cast.
Voting is compulsory for all citizens over 18.

The President is elected for five years and may be
re-elected for a further term. He appoints the Cabinet,
which exercises all the functions of government.
During parliamentary recess it can govern by decree
through the Council of State, the members of which
are representative of the Government, the armed
forces and various other bodies.

Gen. Alfredo Stroessner, dictator from 1954, was
overthrown by Gen. Andrés Rodriguez in February
1989. Gen. Rodriguez was elected President in May
1989. There are moves towards reform; in May 1991,
the first free municipal elections were held.

Production.—About three-quarters of the population are engaged in agriculture and cattle raising.
Cassava, sugar cane, soya, corn, cotton and wheat

are the main agricultural products. The forests contain many varieties of timber which find a good market abroad. Paraguay's hydroelectric power station at Acaray produced 1,118 kWh in 1985 of which a surplus was exported to Argentina and Brazil.

At Itaipú the largest hydroelectric dam in the world, a joint project by Paraguay and Brazil, was inaugurated in 1982. It is expected to be completed in 1991 when it will have a capacity of over 12 million kW. Work is also under way on a hydroelectric project with Argentina at Yacyretá which it is hoped will be in operation by the end of the decade.

Communications.—A railway, 985 miles in length, connects Asunción with Buenos Aires. The journey takes 55 hours. Train ferries enable the run to be accomplished without break of bulk. River steamers also connect Buenos Aires and Asunción (3–5 days). This service is liable to cancellation without warning when the river is low or in flood. There are direct shipping services to Asunción from Britain, Western Europe and the USA. Eight airlines operate services from Asunción.

There are 27,741 km (1990) of asphalted roads in Paraguay, connecting Asunción with São Paulo (26 hrs) via the Bridge of Friendship and Foz de Yguazú and with Buenos Aires (24 hrs) via Puerto Pilcomayo, and about 4,050 miles of earth roads in fairly good condition, but liable to be closed or to become impassable in wet weather. A 1,000 km road, of which 300 km are paved, links Asunción with the Bolivian border. There are services to Buenos Aires, São Paulo and Paranagua, a port on the Brazilian coast.

Defence.—There is a permanent military force of about 25,000 all ranks, most of whom are conscripts doing their military service; and about 6,500 armed police (again mostly conscripts). Three gunboats and a number of small armed launches patrol inland waters.

Language and Literature.—Spanish is the official language of the country but outside the larger towns Guarani, the language of the largest single unit of original Indian inhabitants, is widely spoken. Four daily and five weekly newspapers are published in Asunción.

Education.—Education is free and compulsory. In 1990 there were 4,641 government primary schools with 694,972 pupils and 27,477 teachers. There were 809 secondary schools with 155,339 pupils and 8,112 teachers. The National University in Asunción had 20,343 students in 1984. The Catholic University had 10,971 students.

BUDGET 1990

	Central Government	Decentralized Bodies
Expenditure	Gs815·6m	Gs1,600·5m

Trade.—Total value of imports in 1989 was US$660,778,000. The chief imports were machinery (US$211·6m); fuels and lubricants (US$115·0m); transport and accessories (US$61·7m); and drinks and tobacco (US$45·5m). Total value of exports in 1989 was US$660,778,000. The chief exports were soya bean (US$382·9m); cotton fibres (US$306·9m); meat (US$96·1m); and coffee (US$40·3m).

Trade with UK

	1989	1990
Imports from UK	£19,282,000	£32,035,000
Exports to UK	8,898,000	10,077,000

CAPITAL.—Asunción, about 1,000 miles up the River Paraguay from Buenos Aires. Population (1985 census) 729,307; other centres are Ciudad del Este (98,491); Encarnación (31,445); Concepción (25,607); P. Juan Caballero (41,475).

CURRENCY.—Guaraní (Gs) of 100 céntimos.

FLAG.—Three horizontal bands, red, white, b with the National seal on the obverse white band a the Treasury seal on the reverse white band.

NATIONAL ANTHEM.—Paraguayos, Republica Muerte (Paraguayans, republic or death).

NATIONAL DAY.—May 15.

BRITISH EMBASSY
Calle Presidente Franco 706,
(PO Box 404), Asunción
[Asunción 444472]

Ambassador Extraordinary and Plenipotentiary c Consul-General, His Excellency Michael A. Dibben (1991).

PERU
(República del Peru)

President of the Republic, Alberto Fujimori, *assun office* July 28, 1990.
First Vice-President, Máximo San Román.
Second Vice-President, Carlos García.

CABINET
(as at August 27, 1991)

Prime Minister and Minister of Foreign Affairs, Carlos Torres y Torres Lara.
Economy and Finance, Dr Carlos Boloña Behr.
Interior, Gen. Adolfo Alvarado Fournier.
Justice, Dr Augusto Antoniolli Vasquez.
Defence, Gen. Jorge Torres Aciego.
Education, Oscar de la Puente Raygada.
Health, Dr Victor Yamamoto Miyakawa.
Labour and Social Promotion, Dr Alfonso de Heros Perez Albela.
Agriculture, Enrique Rossl Link.
Housing and Construction, Guillermo del Solar Ro]
Energy and Mines, Fernando Sanchez Albavera.
Transport and Communications, Jaime Yoshiyam
Fisheries, Jaime Augustin Sobero Taira.
Industry, Commerce, Tourism and Integration, E] Victor Joy Way.

PERUVIAN EMBASSY
52 Sloane Street, SW1X 9SP
[071–235 1917/2545]

Ambassador Extraordinary and Plenipotentia Felipe Valdivieso-Belaúnde (1989).
Minister, Gilbert Chauny.
Counsellor, Julio Florián.

Area and Population.—Peru is a maritime public of South America, situated between 0° 00′ and 18° 21′ 00″ S. latitude and between 68° 39′ 27″ a 81° 20′ 13″ W. longitude. The area of the Republic 496,225 sq. miles (1,285,216 sq. km), with a populati (1990 estimate) of 22,332,100.

Physical Features.—The country is travers throughout its length by the Andes, running para to the Pacific coast, the highest points in Peru be] Huascaran (22,211 ft), Huandoy (20,855 ft), Ausang (20,235 feet), Misti volcano (18,364 ft), Hualcan (20, ft), Chachani (19,037 ft), Antajasha (18,020 ft), Pic] pichu (17,724 ft), and Mount Meiggs (17,583 ft).

There are three main regions, the *Costa*, west the Andes, the *Sierra* or mountain ranges of] Andes, which include the Punas or mountainc wastes below the region of perpetual snow and] *Montaña*, or *Selva*, which is the vast area of jun] stretching from the eastern foothills of the Andes the eastern frontiers of Peru. The coastal area, lyi] upon and near the Pacific, is not tropical, thou] close to the Equator, being cooled by the Humbo] Current.

In the mountains, where most of the Indians li] are to be found minerals in great richness a variety, and cattle, sheep, llamas and alpacas are bred there.

Language.—Spanish, the language of the original Spanish stock from which the governing and professional classes are mainly recruited, was formerly the only official language of the country. However, in May 1975, Quechua was declared the second official language. Quechua and Aymará are widely spoken by more than half the population of the country.

Government.—Peru was conquered in the early 16th century by Francisco Pizarro (1478–1541). He subjugated the Incas (the ruling caste of the Quechua Indians), who had started their rise to power some 500 years earlier, and for nearly three centuries Peru remained under Spanish rule. A revolutionary war of 1821–1824 established its independence, declared on July 28, 1821. The constitution rests upon the fundamental law of October 18, 1856 and is that of a democratic Republic. The current constitution was drawn up and approved in July 1979.

Peru is afflicted by rampant inflation, drug-inspired violence and insurgency; the main guerrilla movements are the Maoist Sendero Luminoso (Shining Path) and the Movimiento Revolucionario Tupac Amaru (MRTA). Large areas of the country are under states of emergency.

Production.—The chief products of the coastal belt are cotton, sugar and petroleum. There are large tracts of land suitable for cultivation and stock raising on the eastern slopes of the Andes, and in the mountain valleys maize, potatoes and wheat are grown. The jungle area is a source of timber and petroleum. Other major crops are fruit, vegetables, rice, barley, grapes and coffee. Mineral exports include lead, zinc, copper, iron ore and silver. Peru is normally the world's largest exporter of fishmeal.

Communications.—In recent years the coastal and sierra zones have been opened up by means of roads and air routes and there is air communication, as well as communication by protracted land routes, with the tropical and little known eastern zones which lie east of the Andes towards the borders of Brazil. The completion in 1944 of the trunk road of the Andean Highway from the Pacific port of Callao, via Lima to Pucallpa, the river port on the Ucayali, forms a link between the Pacific, the Amazon and the Atlantic. The Panamerican Highway runs along the Peruvian coast connecting it with Ecuador and Chile. The Inter-Ocean Corridor linking the port of Matarani and Buenos Aires will be opened soon.

The first railway was opened in 1850 and the 2,400 miles of track are now administered by the Government. There is also steam navigation on the Ucayali and Huallaga, and in the south on Lake Titicaca. Air services are maintained throughout Peru, and many international services call at Lima.

Defence.—The Army has a nominal strength of 80,000, the navy 25,000 and airforce 15,000. All services are based on conscription. The army is reportedly greatly depleted due to desertion. There is also a paramilitary National Police.

Education.—Education is compulsory and free for both sexes between the ages of 5 and 16.

Trade.—Import trade of Peru in 1989 totalled US$2,370 million and exports US$1,159 million.

Trade with UK

	1989	1990
Imports from UK	£29,707,000	£29,233,000
Exports to UK	125,538,000	96,654,000

The principal imports are machinery and chemicals and pharmaceutical products. The chief exports are minerals and metals, fishmeal, sugar, cotton and coffee.

CAPITAL.—Metropolitan Lima (including ΨCallao), population estimate (1990) 6,415,000. Other

major cities are: Arequipa (712,279) and Lambayeque (625,553).

CURRENCY.—Nuevo Sol 100 cents.

FLAG.—Three vertical bands, red, white, red; coat of arms on white band.

NATIONAL ANTHEM.—Somos Libres, Seámoslo Siempre (We are free, let us remain so forever).

NATIONAL DAY.—July 28 (Anniversary of Independence).

BRITISH EMBASSY

Natalio Sánchez 125 Piso 12, Plaza Washington (PO Box 854), Lima 1.
[Lima 334738]

Ambassador Extraordinary and Plenipotentiary, His Excellency Keith Haskell, CMG, CVO (1990).

First Secretary, F. R. C. Thomson (*Deputy Head of Mission and Consul*).

Defence Attaché, Col. C. H. Van der Noot, MBE.

There is a British Consular Office at *Lima* and Honorary Consulates in *Arequipa, Cusco, Iquitos, Piura* and *Trujillo*.

British Council Representative, J. Harvey, PO Box No. 14-0114, Calle Alberto Lynch 110, San Isidro, Lima 27.

THE PHILIPPINES
(Repúblika ng Pilipinas)

President, Corazon C. Aquino, *assumed office* February 25, 1986.

CABINET SECRETARIES
(as at August 1991)

Foreign Affairs, Raul Manglapus.
Finance, Jesus Estanislao.
Justice (acting), Silvestre Bello.
Agriculture, Senen Bacani.
Public Works and Highways, Jesus de Jesus.
Education, Culture and Sports, Isidro Cariño.
Labour and Employment, Ruben Torres.
Health, Alfredo Bengzon.
Trade and Industry, Peter Garrucho.
Social Welfare and Development, Mita Pardo de Tavera.

Agrarian Reform, Benjamin Leung.
Local Government, Luis Santos.
Tourism (acting), Rafael Alunan.
Environment and Natural Resources, Fulgenio Factóran.
Budget and Management, Guillermo Carague.
Transport and Communications (acting), Arturo Corona.
National Defence (acting), Benato de Villa.
Executive Secretary, Catalino Macaraig Jr.
Science and Technology, Ceferino Follosco.
Director-General, National Economic and Development Authority, Cayetano Paderanga.
Head, Presidential Management Staff, Hermino Coloma.
Presidential Adviser on National Security, Rafael Illeto.
Executive Secretary, Franklin Drilon.
Press Secretary, Tomas Gomez.

EMBASSY OF THE PHILIPPINES
9A Palace Green, W8 4QE
[071–937 1600/9]

Ambassador Extraordinary and Plenipotentiary, His Excellency Manuel T. Yan (1991).
Deputy Chief of Mission and Consul General, Edmundo Libid.
Commercial Counsellor, S. Ileto.

Area and Population.—The Philippines are situated between 21° 20′–4° 30′ N. Lat. and 116° 55′–126° 36′ E. long., and are distant about 500 miles from the south-east coast of the continent of Asia. (For MAP, see p. 776).

The total land area of the country is 115,831 sq. miles (300,000 sq. km). There are eleven larger islands and 7,079 other islands.

The principal islands are:—

	sq. miles		sq. miles
Luzon	40,422	Mindoro	3,759
Mindanao	36,538	Leyte	2,786
Samar	5,050	Cebu	1,703
Negros	4,906	Bohol	1,492
Palawan	4,550	Masbate	1,262
Panay	4,446		

Other groups in the Republic are the Sulu islands (capital, Jolo), Babuyanes and Batanes; the Catanduanes; and Culion Islands.

The population of the Philippines (UN estimate 1989) is 60,097,000.

The inhabitants, known as Filipinos, are basically of Malay stock, with a considerable admixture of Spanish and Chinese blood in many localities, and about 90 per cent of them are Christians, predominantly Roman Catholics. Most of the remainder are Muslims, in the south, and Animists and pagans, mainly in the north. There is a Chinese minority estimated at 500,000, and other much smaller foreign communities, notably Spanish, American and Indian.

Government.—The Portuguese navigator Magellan came to the Philippines in 1521 and was slain by the natives of Mactan, a small island near Cebu. In 1565 Spain undertook the conquest of the country which was named Filipinas, after the son of the King of Spain, and in 1571 the city of Manila was founded by the conquistador Legaspi, who subdued the inhabitants of almost all the islands, their conversion being undertaken by the Augustinian friars in Legaspi's train. In 1762 Manila was occupied by a British force, but in 1764 it was restored to Spain. In the Spanish-American War of 1898, Manila was captured by American troops with the help of Filipinos and the Islands were ceded to the United States by the Treaty of Paris of December 10, 1898. Despite a rebellion against the US government

between 1899 and 1902, the Americans remained control of the country until 1946.

The Republic of the Philippines came into existen on July 4, 1946 with a presidential form of governme based on the American system.

Ferdinand Marcos was President from 1965 to 19 Although he gained a majority of votes in the offic count of a Presidential election in February 1986, t election was marred by widespread electoral abu and his rival, Mrs Corazon Aquino, launched a ser of non-violent civil disturbance actions which gain wide support. On February 25, Marcos, his fam and aides left for Hawaii. Mrs Aquino took over President and has so far survived several attempts overthrow her.

A new Constitution was approved by referend in February 1987. Legislative authority is vested a bicameral elected Congress comprising a House Representatives of up to 250 members and a member Senate. Elections to the Congress were h in May and the new Constitution came into force July 27, 1987.

There is unrest in many of the islands due insurgency. Muslim insurgents, the Moro Natior Liberation Front, operate in western Mindanao a the Sulu archipelago. Most of the current activity due to the Communist New People's Army, whicł strongest in eastern Mindanao, Negros, Samar, Bic the mountains of northern Luzon, and Bataan.

Language and Literature.—The official la guages are Filipino and English. Filipino, the tional language, is based on Tagalog, one of Malay–Polynesian languages and the language of part of Luzon surrounding Metro Manila. Filipin spoken by 29·66 per cent of the total number households, but local languages and dialects a strong and Cebuano is spoken by 24·20 per cent total households. English, which is the language government and of instruction in secondary a university education, is spoken by at least 44 per ce of the population. Spanish, which ceased to be official language in 1973, is now spoken by a ve small minority; 89 per cent of the population a literate.

Education.—Secondary and higher education extensive and there are 37 private universit recognized by the Government, including the Dom ican University of Santo Tomas (founded in 161 there are also 296 state-supported colleges a universities, including the University of the Phil pines, founded 1908.

Roads and Railways.—The highway system c ered 161,709 kilometres in 1985 and there was a to of 1,120,172 registered road vehicles. The Philipp National Railway operates 740 km of track on Lu: Island.

Shipping.—There are 94 ports of entry in Philippines and 164,404 vessels of various ty totalling 50,467,000 tons, are engaged in inter-isla traffic.

Civil Aviation.—There 82 national airports a 137 privately operated airports. Philippine Air Li have regular flights throughout the Far East, to USA and Europe, in addition to inter-island servic

TRADE

	1987	1988
Total imports .	US$6,736,969,000	US$8,159,378,
Total exports .	5,720,238,000	6,994,425,

Trade with UK

	1989	1990
Imports from UK	£137,367,000	£158,030,0
Exports to UK	233,128,000	220,706,0

The Philippines is a predominantly agricultu country, the chief products being rice, coconu maize, sugar-cane, abaca (manila hemp), fruits, tobacco and lumber. There is, however, an increasing number of manufacturing industries and it is the policy of the Government to diversify its economy.

Principal exports are sugar, coconut oil, copper concentrate, lumber and copra.

CAPITAL.—ΨManila, on the island of Luzon, estimated population (1984): City area 1,728,441; Manila with suburbs (incl. Quezon City, Pasay City, Caloocan City, Makati, Parañaque, San Juan Mandaluyong and Navotas) 6,720,050. The next largest cities are (1989 estimate) ΨCebu (613,184), ΨDavao (819,525), Ψ Iloilo (287,711), ΨZamboanga (433,328), and Bacolod (328,648).

CURRENCY.—Philippine peso (P) of 100 centavos.

FLAG.—Equal horizontal bands of blue (above) and red; gold sun with three stars on a white triangle next staff.

NATIONAL ANTHEM.—Pambansang Awit.

NATIONAL DAY.—June 12 (Independence Day).

BRITISH EMBASSY
Locsin Building, 6752 Ayala Avenue,
Corner Makati Avenue, Makati, Metro Manila
(PO Box 1970)
[Manila 816-7116]

Ambassador Extraordinary and Plenipotentiary, His Excellency Keith Gordon MacInnes, CMG (1987).

Counsellor, A. Collins.

Defence Attaché, Col. J. P. Clough.

First Secretaries, D. Curran (*Political*); R. Cork (*Commercial*).

British Council Representative, N. Bisset, 7, 3rd Street, New Manila, PO Box AC 168, Cubao, Quezon City, Metro Manila.

POLAND
(Rzeczpospolita Polska)

President, Lech Walesa, *elected* December 9, 1990 *for a six-year term.*

COUNCIL OF MINISTERS
(as at January 1991)

Prime Minister, Jan Krzysztof Bielecki.

Labour and Social Policy, Michal Boni.

Justice, Wieslaw Chrzanowski.

Minister, Head of Central Planning Office, Jerzy Eysymontt.

Regional Planning and Construction, Adam Glapinski.

National Education, Prof. Robert Glebocki.

National Defence, Piotr Kolodziejczyk.

Foreign Economic Relations, Dariusz Ledworowski.

Ownership Transformation, Dr Janusz Lewandowski.

Internal Affairs, Dr Henryk Majewski.

Environmental Protection, National Resources and Forestry, Dr Maciej Nowicki.

Art and Culture, Marek Rostworoski.

Foreign Affairs, Prof. Krzysztof Skubiszewski.

Health and Social Welfare, Wladyslaw Sidorowicz.

Communications, Jerzy Slezak.

Agriculture and Food Economy, Adam Tanski.

Transport and Shipping, Ewaryst Waligorski.

Industry, Prof. Andrzej Zawislak.

Minister, Head of the Office of the Council of Ministers, Krzysztof Zabinski.

Finance, Leszek Balcerowicz.

EMBASSY OF THE REPUBLIC OF POLAND
47 Portland Place, W1N 3AG
[071–580 4324]

Ambassador Extraordinary and Plenipotentiary, His Excellency Tadeusz de Virion (1990).

Area and Population.—Poland adjoins Germany in the west, the boundary being formed by the rivers Oder and Neisse, Czechoslovakia in the south, and the USSR in the east. (The present frontiers were established at the end of the Second World War.) To the north is the Baltic Sea. The country has an area of 120,725 sq. miles (312,677 sq. km), and a population (official estimate 1990) of 38,200,000. Roman Catholicism is the religion of 95 per cent of the inhabitants.

Government.—The Polish Commonwealth ceased to exist in 1795 after three successive partitions in 1772, 1793 and 1795, in which Prussia, Russia and Austria shared. The Republic of Poland (reconstituted within the limits of the old Polish Commonwealth) was proclaimed at Warsaw in November, 1918, and its independence guaranteed by the signatories of the Treaty of Versailles.

German forces invaded Poland on September 1, 1939; on September 17, Russian forces invaded eastern Poland, and on September 21, 1939 Poland was declared by Germany and Russia to have ceased to exist. A line of demarcation was established between the areas occupied by German and Russian forces. At the end of the war a Coalition Government was formed in which the Polish Workers' Party played a large part. In December 1948, the Polish Workers' Party and the Polish Socialist Party fused in the new Polish United Workers' Party (PUWP). A new Constitution modelled on the Soviet Constitution of 1936 was adopted in July 1952, and was modified in February 1976. It changed the title of the country to the Polish People's Republic (*Polska Rzeczpospolita Ludowa*).

In July 1980 steep rises in food prices but static wages led to widespread strikes. The strikes continued throughout August, obliging the government to agree to allow independent trade unions, the right to strike, the easing of censorship and other political and economic demands. The independent trade union movement, Solidarity, led by Lech Walesa, became a powerful force but many of its leaders, including Walesa, were detained and union activity suspended when martial law was declared in December 1981. Initially there was some passive resistance to martial law, which was suspended in December 1982 and finally lifted in July 1983.

Solidarity continued as an underground movement until 1988 when a wave of strikes and the call for the legalization of Solidarity resulted in talks between Walesa and the PUWP early in 1989. By April plans for political and economic reforms had been drawn up. These included the restoration of the legal status of Solidarity (April 17); the introduction of a bicameral parliamentary system comprising an upper house (Senate) and lower house (Sejm), and an Executive Presidency; multi-party parliamentary elections were held in the summer of 1989.

General Jaruzelski was elected President by Poland's MPs on July 20, and on August 20, 1989 Tadeusz Mazowiecki became the first non-communist Prime Minister since 1945. Under the new constitution the Prime Minister can appoint all members of the Council of Ministers.

In December 1989 Poland's official title was changed from the Polish People's Republic to the Republic of Poland. The PUWP, since August 1989 no longer the ruling party, disbanded in January 1990. Lech Walesa was elected President in December 1990. Jan Bielecki became Prime Minister in January 1991, following a period of rapid introduction of the market economy. Disagreement over a post-Communist constitution continues. Parliamentary elections are scheduled for October 1991.

Education.—Elementary education (ages 7–15) is compulsory and free. Secondary education is optional and free. There are universities at Kraków, Warsaw, Poznan, Lódź, Wroclaw, Lublin and Toruń and a considerable number of other towns.

Language and Literature.—Polish is a western Slavonic tongue (*see* USSR), the Latin alphabet being used. Polish literature developed rapidly after the foundation of the University of Kraków (a printing press was established there in 1474 and there Copernicus died in 1543). A national school of poetry and drama survived the dismemberment and the former era of romanticism, whose chief Polish exponent was Adam Mickiewicz, was followed by realistic and historical fiction, including the works of Henryk Sienkiewicz (1846–1916), Nobel Prize-winner for Literature in 1905; Boleslaw Prus (1847–1912); and Stanislaw Reymont (1868–1925), Nobel Prize-winner in 1924.

Production and Industry.—On January 3, 1946, a decree was issued to provide for the nationalization of mines, petroleum resources, water, gas and electricity services, banks, textile factories and large retail stores. Until recently over 99 per cent of Polish industry was stated to be 'socialized', but 68 per cent of agricultural land was privately farmed. Legislation passed in July 1990 provides a framework for 80 per cent of the economy to be transferred from the state to the private sector.

Trade with UK

	1989	1990
Imports from UK	£196,446,000	£221,536,000
Exports to UK	330,163,000	357,164,000

CAPITAL.—Warsaw, on the Vistula, population (1989) 1,655,063. Other large towns are Lódz (851,690); Kraków (748,356); Wroclaw (642,234); Poznan (588,715); Gdansk (464,649); Szczecin (412,000); Katowice (367,041); Bydgoszcz (380,385).

CURRENCY.—Zloty of 100 groszy.

FLAG.—Equal horizontal stripes of white (above) and red.

NATIONAL ANTHEM.—Jeszcze Polska Nie Zginela (Poland has not yet been destroyed).

NATIONAL DAY.—May 3.

BRITISH EMBASSY
No. 1 Aleja Róz, 00-556 Warsaw
[Warsaw 281001]

Ambassador Extraordinary and Plenipotentiary, His Excellency Michael J. Llewellyn-Smith, CMG (1991).
Counsellor, G. G. Wetherell (*Deputy Head of Mission*).
Defence and Air Attaché, Gp. Capt. A. Harris.
Naval and Military Attaché, Lt.-Col. A. Cumings.

British Council Representative, Charles Chadwi OBE, Al. Jerozolimskie 59, 00–697 Warsaw.

PORTUGAL
(República Portuguesa)

President of the Republic, Dr Mario Soares, *electe* February 16, 1986, *re-elected,* January 13, 1991.

MINISTERS
(as at June 30, 1991)

Prime Minister, Anibal Cavaco Silva.
Minister at the PM's office, Defence, Joaquim Fe nando Nogueira.
Justice, Dr Alvaro Laborinho Lucio.
Parliamentary Affairs, Manuel Dias Loureiro.
Finance, Miguel Beleza.
Planning and Territorial Administration, Luis V ente de Oliveira.
Internal Administration, Manuel Pereira.
Foreign, João de Deus Pinheiro.
Agriculture, Fisheries and Food, Arlindo Marques Cunha.
Industry and Energy, Luis Mira Amaral.
Education, Roberto Carneiro.
Public Works, Transport and Communications, Jo quim Ferreira do Amaral.
Health, Arlindo Gomes de Carvalho.
Employment and Social Security, José Silva Peneda
Trade and Tourism, Fernando Faria de Oliveira.
Youth, Albino Couto dos Santos.
Environment and Natural Resources, Carlos Borre Azores, Mario Pinto.
Madeira, Lino Miguel.

PORTUGUESE EMBASSY
11 Belgrave Square, SW1X 8PP
[071–235 5331]

Ambassador Extraordinary and Plenipotentiary, H Excellency Antonio Vaz-Pereira (1989).
Minister Counsellor, Francisco Seixas-da-Costa.

Area and Population.—Continental Portug occupies the western part of the Iberian Peninsu covering an area of 34,317 sq. miles (88,880 sq. km). lies between 36° 58′–42° 12″ N. lat. and 6° 11′ 48″–9° 2 45″ W. long., being 362 miles in length from N. to and averaging about 117 in breadth from E. to The population (UN estimate 1989) is 10,467,0 (including the Azores and Madeira).

Language and Literature.—Portuguese is Romance language with admixtures of Arabic ar other idioms. It is the language of Portugal ar Brazil, and is the *lingua franca* of Angola, Moza bique, Cape Verde, São Tomé and Principe, Ea Timor and Guinea-Bissau. Portuguese language ar literature reached the culminating point of the development in the *Lusiadas* (dealing with t voyage of Vasco da Gama) and other works Camoens (Camões) (1524–80). There are four morni and three evening daily newspapers in Lisbon ar three morning papers in Oporto, and six main week newspapers.

Government.—From the eleventh century un 1910 the government of Portugal was a monarc and for many centuries included the Vice-Royalty Brazil, which declared its independence in 1822. 1910 an armed rising in Lisbon drove King Manuel and the royal family into exile, and the Nation Assembly of August 21, 1911 sanctioned a republica form of government. A period of great politic instability ensued until eventually the milita stepped in. The Constitution of 1933 gave form expression to the corporative 'Estado Novo' (Ne State) which was personified by Dr Salazar, Prin Minister 1932–68. Dr Caetano succeeded Salazar

Prime Minister in 1968 but his failure to liberalize the regime or to conclude the wars in the African colonies resulted in his government's overthrow by a military coup on April 25, 1974. The next two years were characterized by great political turmoil with no fewer than six provisional governments between April 1974 and July 1976 but with the failure of an attempted coup by the extreme left in November 1975 the situation began to become more stable.

Constitutional reforms introduced in 1982 have reduced the President's scope for day-to-day intervention in government but the decision to dissolve the Assembly is still largely the President's. The revisions also ended the military's capacity for political interference, and created two new organs of state, the Constitutional Tribunal and the Council of State, to advise the President. Further constitutional reforms were made in 1989. The President, elected for a five-year term by universal adult suffrage, appoints the Prime Minister. Legislative authority is vested in the 250-member Assembly of the Republic, elected by a system of proportional representation for a term of up to four years.

In the General Election held on July 19, 1987, the Social Democratic Party (PSD) won 148 of the 250 seats; the Socialist Party (PS) 60 seats; the Communist Party (PCP) 31 seats, the Democratic Renewal Party (PRD) 7 seats and the Christian Democrats (CDS) 4 seats.

Defence.—Most physically fit males are liable for military service but conscription is becoming increasingly selective as the armed forces were greatly reduced following the end of the colonial wars, and reorganized and re-equipped for a conventional national defence role. The present strength of the Army is about 43,000. One brigade is earmarked for NATO service. The Navy consists of about 14,800 officers and men, including 2,500 marines, manning about 60 craft of various types. The present serving strength of the Air Force is about 12,600, (including 2,200 paratroops) and about 80 combat aircraft plus helicopters and transport and training aircraft. Changes to the size and structure of the armed forces are expected to take place in 1991–92.

Education is free and compulsory for nine years from the age of 6. Secondary education is mainly conducted in state lyceums, commercial and industrial schools, but there are also private schools. There are also military, naval, technical, polytechnic and other special schools. There are old established universities at Coimbra (founded in 1290), Oporto and Lisbon. New universities have been established at Lisbon, Braga, Aveiro, Vila Real, Faro, Evora and in the Azores.

Communications.—There is an international airport at Portela, about 5 miles from Lisbon, and the airport of Pedras Rubras near Oporto is also used for scheduled international services. There are direct flights between London and Manchester and Faro in the Algarve.

Agriculture.—The chief agricultural products are cork, cereals, rice, vegetables, olives, figs, citrus fruits, almonds, timber, port wine and table wines. There are extensive forests of pine, cork, eucalyptus and chestnut covering about 20 per cent of the total area of the country.

Minerals.—The principal mineral products are pyrites, wolfram, tin, iron ores, copper and sodium and calcium minerals.

Industry.—The country is so far only moderately industrialized, but is fairly rapidly extending its industries. The principal manufactures are textiles, clothing and footwear, machinery (including electric machinery and transport equipment), foodstuffs (tomato concentrates and canned fish), chemicals, fertilizers, wood, cork, furniture, cement, glassware and pottery. There is a modern steelworks, and two

modern and very large shipbuilding and repair yards at Lisbon and Setúbal working mainly for foreign ship-owners. There are several hydro-electric power stations and a new thermal power station.

Finance.—Portugal is a member of the European Monetary Agreement, the World Bank, the International Monetary Fund and the International Finance Corporation. The country has substantial gold and foreign exchange reserves.

Trade.—The principal imports are cereals, meat, raw and semi-manufactured iron and steel, industrial machinery, chemicals, crude oil, motor vehicles and raw materials for textiles.

The principal exports are textiles, footwear, timber, cork, electrical and other machinery, and chemicals.

	1988	1989
Total imports	£6,164,627m	£11,535,432m
Total exports	4,230,727m	7,738,209m

Trade with UK

	1989	1990
Imports from UK ..	£915,682,000	£1,033,268,000
Exports to UK	1,040,706,000	1,176,161,000

The British share of the Portuguese market was 7·4 per cent in 1989 and the UK was the third largest market for Portuguese exports.

CAPITAL.—ΨLisbon, population estimate (1989) 2,128,000. ΨOporto 1,683,000.

CURRENCY.—Escudo (Esc) of 100 centavos.

FLAG.—Vertical band of green (next staff) and square of red, bearing arms of the Republic, framed.

NATIONAL ANTHEM.—A Portuguesa.

NATIONAL DAY.—June 10.

BRITISH EMBASSY
35–37 Rua de S. Domingos à Lapa,
1200 Lisbon
[Lisbon 3961191]

Ambassador Extraordinary and Plenipotentiary, His Excellency Hugh James Arbuthnott, CMG (1989).

There are British Consulates in *Oporto*, *Portimão*, *Funchal* (Madeira) and *Ponta Delgada* (Azores).

British Council Representative, J. Mallon, OBE, Rua de Sao Marçal 174, 1294 Lisbon.

BRITISH PORTUGUESE CHAMBER OF COMMERCE, Rua da Estrela 8, 1200 Lisbon and Rua Sa de Bandeira 784–20E, Frente, 4000 Oporto.

MADEIRA AND THE AZORES

Madeira and The Azores are two administratively autonomous regions of Portugal, having locally elected Assemblies and Governments.

MADEIRA is a group of islands in the Atlantic Ocean about 520 miles south-west of Lisbon, and consists of Madeira, Porto, Santo and three uninhabited islands (Desertas). The total area is 314 sq. miles (813 sq. km), with a population of 271,400 (1989). ΨFunchal in Madeira, the largest island (270 square miles), is the capital, with a population of 44,111; Machico (10,905).

THE AZORES are a group of nine islands (Flores, Corvo, Terceira, São Jorge, Pico, Faial, Graciosa, São Miguel and Santa Maria) in the Atlantic Ocean, with a total area of 922 sq. miles (2,387 sq. km), and a population of 255,100 (1989). ΨPonta Delgada, on São Miguel, is the capital of the group; population is 137,700. Other ports are ΨAngra, in Terceira (55,900) and ΨHorta (16,300).

MACAO

Macao, situated at the mouth of the Pearl River, comprises a peninsula and the islands of Coloane and Taipa, having an area of six sq. miles (15·5 sq. km), with a population (UN estimate 1988) of 439,000. Portuguese trade with China began early in the 16th century and Macao became a Portuguese colony in 1557; in a Sino-Portuguese treaty of 1887 China recognized Portugal's sovereignty over, and government of, Macao. In 1974 Portugal changed Macao's status from that of an Overseas Province to 'a territory under Portuguese administration'. Following the Sino-British Joint Declaration on Hong Kong in 1984, Sino-Portuguese negotiations on the transfer of administration began on June 30, 1986. The agreement on the transfer of the administration of Macao to the Chinese authorities was signed on April 13, 1987. Macao will become a 'special administrative region' of China when transferred on December 20, 1999.

Macao is subject to Portuguese constitutional law but otherwise enjoys administrative, economic and financial autonomy. The Governor is appointed by the Portuguese President and since 1976 there has been a 17-member legislative assembly, which has a three-year term. The assembly comprises 14 elected deputies appointed by the Governor. A new electoral system which came into effect February 28, 1984 gave equal voting rights to all residents, thus enfranchising the Chinese population.

Macao's major industry is textile manufacturing which accounts for 62 per cent of all exports. Port Macao is served by British, Portuguese and Dutch shipping lines and has regular services to Hong Kong, some 35 miles away.

Governor, Rocha Vieira.

Trade with UK

	1989	1990
Imports from UK	£7,498,000	£11,398,000
Exports to UK	45,299,000	44,809,000

QATAR
(Dawlat Qatar)

Head of State, HH Sheikh Khalifa bin Hamad Al Thani, GCMG, GCB, the Amir of Qatar, *assumed power* February 22, 1972.
Heir Apparent, Minister of Defence and Commander-in-Chief of Armed Forces, HH Sheikh Hamad bin Khalifa Al Thani, KCMG.

COUNCIL OF MINISTERS
(as at May 31, 1991)

Interior, HE Sheikh Abdullah bin Khalifa Al Thani.
Finance and Petroleum, HE Sheikh Abdulaziz bin Khalifa Al Thani.
Foreign Affairs, HE Mubarak Ali Al Khater.
Education, HE Abdulaziz Abdullah Turki.
Justice, HE Sheikh Ahmed bin Saif Al Thani.
Economy and Commerce HE Sheikh Hamad bin Jassim bin Hamad Al Thani.
Industry and Public Works, HE Ahmed Mohamed Ali Al Subai.
Municipal Affairs and Agriculture, temporary Minister for Electricity and Water, HE Sheikh Hamad bin Jassim bin Jabor Al Thani.
Labour, Social Affairs and Housing, HE Abdulrahman Saad Al Derham.
Communications and Transport, HE Abdulla bin Saleh Al Mana.
Public Health, HE Sheikh Khaled bin Mohamed bin Ali Al Thani.
Information and Culture, HE Sheikh Hamad bin Suhaim Al Thani.
Amiri Diwan Affairs, HE Dr Issa Ghanim Al Kuwari.

EMBASSY OF THE STATE OF QATAR
27 Chesham Place, SW1X 8HG
[071–235 0851]
Ambassador Extraordinary and Plenipotentiary, H Excellency Abdul Rahman Abdulla Al-Wohaib (1989).

The state of Qatar covers the peninsula of Qatar from approximately the northern shore of Khor a Odaid to the eastern shore of Khor al Salwa. Th area is about 4,247 sq. miles (11,000 sq. km), with population (UN estimate 1989) of 422,000. The grea majority of the population is concentrated in th urban district of the capital Doha. Only a sma minority still pursue the traditional life of the sem nomadic tribesmen and fisherfolk.

Until 1971, Qatar was one of the nine independen Emirates in the Arabian Gulf with special treat relations with the UK. In that year, with th withdrawal of British forces from the area, thes special treaty relations were terminated. On April 2 1970 a provisional constitution for Qatar was pro claimed, providing for the establishment of a Counc of Ministers and for the formation of a Consultativ Council to assist the Council of Ministers in runnir the affairs of the State. There are no political partie or legislature. Qatar is a member of the Arab Leagu as well as of the United Nations.

Production.—Although Qatar is a desert country there are gardens and smallholdings near Doha an to the north and encouragement is being given to th development of agriculture.

The Qatar General Petroleum Corporation is th state-owned company controlling Qatar's interest in oil, gas and petrochemicals. The corporation i responsible for Qatar's oil production onshore an offshore. The production level for Qatar agreed i OPEC is currently 371,000 b.p.d. Explorations con tinue for further oil. The large reserves of natur gas in the North Field are expected to come int production by 1991. A 50,000 b.p.d. oil refinery wa commissioned in 1984 to increase domestic refiner capacity.

Current industries include a steel mill, a fertilize plant, a cement factory, a petrochemical complex an two natural gas liquids plants. With the exception the cement works, which is at Umm Bab, all thes industries are at Umm Said, about 30 miles south Doha. There are tentative plans for new industr including an aluminium smelter, a second ammoni plant and a methanol plant, downstream of the Nort Field. Qatar is also expanding its infrastructur including electrical generation and water distilla tion, roads, houses, and government buildings, a though reduced demand for crude oil in internation markets has led to a downturn in the economy and slower rate of development than hitherto.

Communications.—Regular air services connec Qatar with Bahrain and the United Arab Emirate Kuwait, Muscat, Saudi Arabia, Jordan, Syria, Leba non, Egypt, the Indian sub-continent, Africa an Europe. The Qatar Broadcasting Service transmit on medium, shortwave, and VHF. Regular televisio transmissions in colour began in 1974 and a secon channel opened in 1982.

Trade with UK

	1989	1990
Imports from UK	£89,256,000	£98,504,00
Exports to UK	4,342,000	5,004,00

CAPITAL.—ΨDoha, population (estimated) 220,00 Other towns include Khor, Dukhan, Wakra ar ΨUmm Said.
CURRENCY.—Qatar riyal of 100 dirhams.
FLAG.—White and maroon, white portion neare the mast; vertical indented line comprising 17 angle divides the colours.
NATIONAL DAY.—September 3.

BRITISH EMBASSY
PO Box 3, Doha
[Doha 421991]

Ambassador Extraordinary and Plenipotentiary, His
Excellency Graham Boyce, CMG (1990).
First Secretary, J. G. Rice (*Commercial*).
Second Secretary, R. Davis (*Consul and Administration*).
Attaché, P. D. G. Cook (*Commercial*).
Vice Consul, F. A. Drayton.

British Council Representative, J. Shorter, Ras Abu
Aboud Road (PO Box 2992), Doha.

ROMANIA
(România)

President of the Republic, Ion Iliescu, *elected*, May 20,
1990.

COUNCIL OF MINISTERS
(as at May 30, 1991)

Prime Minister, Petre Roman.
*Minister of State and Minister of Economy and
Finance*, Eugen Dijmărescu.
*Minister of State for the Quality of Life and Social
Protection*, Dan Mircea Popescu.
*Minister, Assistant to the Prime Minister for Reform
and Relations with Parliament*, Adrian Severin.
Foreign Affairs, Adrian Năstase.
National Defence, Lt.-Gen. Constantin Nicolae Spiroiu.
Interior, Doru Viorel Ursu.
Industry, Victor Stănculescu.
Justice, Victor Babiuc.
Education and Science, Gheorghe Stefan.
Labour and Social Protection, Mihnea Marmeliuc.
Agriculture and Food, vacant.
Trade and Tourism, Constantin Fota.
Transport, Traian Băsescu.
Public Works and Physical Planning (*acting*), Doru
Pană.
Culture, Andrei Gabriel Pleşu.
Communications, Andrei Chirică.
Health, Bogdan Marinescu.
Environment, Valeriu Eugen Pop.
Youth and Sports (*acting*), B. N. Niculescu Duvăz.
Budget at the Ministry of Economy and Finance,
Florian Bercea.
Without Portfolio, Ion Aurel Stoica.
Secretaries of State, Andrei Tugulea (*Education and
Science*); Valeriu Pescariu (*Agriculture and Food*).

EMBASSY OF ROMANIA
4 Palace Green, W8 4QD
[071–937 9666]

Ambassador Extraordinary and Plenipotentiary, His
Excellency Sergiu Celac (1991).
Chargé d'Affaires, Nicu Bujlr.

Area and Population.—Romania is a republic of
south-eastern Europe, formerly the classical *Dacia*
and *Scythia Pontica*, having its origin in the union
of the Danubian principalities of Wallachia and
Moldavia under the Treaty of Paris (April 1856). The
area of Romania is 91,699 sq. miles (237,500 sq. km)
and the population (UN 1989 estimate) is 23,152,000.

Government.—The principalities remained separate entities under Turkish suzerainty until 1859,
when Prince Alexandru Ion Cuza was elected Prince
of both, still under the suzerainty of Turkey.
Prince Cuza abdicated in 1866 and was succeeded by
Prince Charles of Hohenzollern-Sigmaringen, in
whose successors the crown was vested. By the
Treaty of Berlin (July 13, 1878) the principality was
recognized as an independent state, and part of the

Dobrudja (which had been occupied by the Romanians) was incorporated. On March 27, 1881 it was
recognized as a Kingdom.

The outcome of the War of 1914–18 added Bessarabia, the Bukovina, Transylvania, the Banat and
Crisana-Maramures, these additions of territory
being confirmed in the Treaty of St Germain, 1919,
and the Treaty of Petit Trianon, 1920.

On June 27, 1940, in compliance with an ultimatum
from USSR, Bessarabia and Northern Bukovina were
ceded to the Soviet Government, and in August 1940
Romania ceded to Bulgaria the portion of southern
Dobrudja taken from Bulgaria in 1913.

Romania became 'The Romanian People's Republic'
in December 1947, on the abdication of King Michael.
A new Constitution, modelled on the Soviet Constitution of 1936, was adopted unanimously on September 24, 1952, by the Grand National Assembly. A new
Constitution was approved by the Grand National
Assembly in 1965 when the name of the state was
changed to the Socialist Republic of Romania. The
Constitution stated that the leading political force of
society was the Romanian Communist Party.

A revolution in December 1989 led to the overthrow
of Nicolae Ceauşescu, President since 1967, and the
collapse of his government. A provisional government was formed which abolished the leading role of
the Communist Party, promised free elections and
changed the country's name to Romania. In May
1990 presidential and parliamentary elections took
place under a system of universal adult suffrage and
proportional representation. The National Salvation
Front won 66 per cent of the vote. There is a Senate
of 119 members and a 387-member Assembly of
Deputies. A new government was formed in June
1990.

Agriculture.—Wallachia, Moldavia and Transylvania are potentially among the most fertile areas in
Europe, and agriculture and sheep and cattle raising
are the principal industries of Romania, although
extreme weather conditions can have adverse effects
on crops. These are principally cereal crops, legumes
and other vegetables, flax and hemp. Vines and fruits
are also grown. The forests of the mountainous
regions are extensive, and the timber industry is
important.

Socialization of agriculture was completed when
collectivization was achieved in the spring of 1962.
Since December 1989 agricultural workers have been
allocated plots of land and are allowed to sell their
produce on the open market. One third of the arable
land is now farmed independently. Of the remaining
6 million hectares, one third belongs to state farms
and two-thirds to co-operative farms. A law on land
privatization was adopted in early 1991, allowing for
private ownership of plots up to 10 hectares in size.
Allocation is to take place in November 1991.

Natural Resources and Industry.—Before the
war petroleum and agriculture were the backbone of
the Romanian economy but rapid industrialization
since 1948 has meant that they no longer hold the
same dominant position. There are plentiful supplies
of natural gas, together with various mineral deposits
including coal, iron ore, bauxite, lead, zinc, copper
and uranium in quantities which allow a substantial
part of the requirements of industry to be met from
local resources. Production of crude oil was put at
about 9,400,000 tonnes in 1988.

The economy has faced increasing problems since
the late 1970s, the result of over investment in
energy-intensive heavy industry and neglect of
agriculture, which has led to food shortages. The
effects of these policies were aggravated by the
international recession and by high interest rates,
and Romania was severely in debt by the early 1980s.
The Ceauşescu government sought to alleviate the
situation by reducing borrowing and cutting imports.

The formerly centrally-planned economy is being transformed into a market economy under the new government. Thirty per cent of state property is to be distributed in the form of vouchers or shares to the population. The rest is to be sold off. Foreign investment and ownership of up to 100 per cent of enterprises is now permitted. Industrial output declined sharply in 1990–91.

Language and Religion.—Romanian is a Romance language with many archaic forms and with admixtures of Slavonic, Turkish, Magyar and French words. There is wealth of folk-songs and folklore, transmitted orally through many centuries and collected in the 19th century. The leading religion is that of the Romanian Orthodox Church; the Roman Catholics and some Protestant denominations are of importance numerically. There is a Hungarian minority of around 2·5 million, and a dwindling German minority of around 150,000.

Education is free and nominally compulsory. There are universities at Bucharest, Iasi, Cluj, Timişoara, Craiova and Braşov, polytechnics at Bucharest, Timişoara, Cluj, Braşov, Galati and Iasi, two commercial academies at Bucharest and Braşov, and agricultural colleges at Bucharest, Iasi, Cluj, Craiova and Timişoara.

Communications.—In 1979 there were 11,113 km of railway open for traffic. The mercantile marine had a gross tonnage of 13,220,000 tons in 1979. The principal ports are Constanta (on the Black Sea), Sulina (on the Danube Estuary), Galati, Braila, Giurgiu and Turnu Severin. The Danube and the Black Sea are linked by a canal completed in 1984. Romania is a member of the Danube Commission whose seat is at Budapest.

TRADE

In 1990 imports were 4,374m roubles and $5,132m. The trade deficit was 700m roubles and $1,200m. Imports are chiefly semi-manufactured goods, raw materials, machinery and metals; export consists principally of maize, wheat, barley, oats, petroleum, timber, cattle, meat, machines and industrial equipment.

Trade with UK

	1989	1990
Imports from UK	£38,141,000	£85,879,000
Exports to UK	117,685,000	61,215,000

CAPITAL.—Bucharest, on the Dimbovita, population 1,961,189. Other large towns are:

Braşov 290,722		ψ Galati 254,636	
Constanţa 284,801		Craiova 243,117	
Cluj-Napoca ...270,820		Ploieşti......215,500	
Iasi 265,176		ψ Brăila........214,561	
Timişoara 261,950			

CURRENCY.—Leu (*plural* Lei) of 100 bani.
FLAG.—Three vertical bands, blue, yellow, red.
NATIONAL ANTHEM.—Trei Culori (Three colours).
NATIONAL DAY.—August 23 (Liberation Day, 1944).

BRITISH EMBASSY
24 Strada Jules Michelet, Bucharest
[Bucharest 111634/5/6]

Ambassador Extraordinary and Plenipotentiary, His Excellency Michael William Atkinson, CMG, MBE (1989).
Counsellor, Deputy Head of Mission, C. J. Ingham.
Defence, Naval and Military Attaché, Lt.-Col. P. A. Crocker.
Cultural Attaché and British Council Representative, C. C. Henning.

RWANDA
(Republika y'u Rwanda)

President, Maj.-Gen. Juvénal Habyarimana, *assumed office*, July 5, 1973, *elected*, Dec. 24, 1978, *re-elected*, Dec. 19, 1983 and Dec. 17, 1988.

MINISTERS
(as at June 1991)

Agriculture, Livestock and Forests, James Gazana.
Economy and Consumption, François Nzabahimana.
Finance, Benoît Ntigulirwa.
Industry and Crafts, Col. Aloys Nsekalije.
Public Works, Energy and Water, Joseph Nzirorera.
Transport and Communications, Hidesonse Hijaniro.
Health and Social Affairs, François Xavier Nsengumuremyi.
Primary and Secondary Education, Daniel Mbangura.
Higher Education and Scientific Research, Constantin Cubahiro.
Youth, Sports and Co-operative Societies, André Ntagerura.
Interior and Community Development, Faustin Myunyazesa.
Civil Service and Vocational Training, Charles Nyandwi.
Justice, Sylvestre Nsanzimana.
Institutional Relations, vacant.
Planning, Callixte Nzabonimana.
Foreign Affairs and International Co-operation, Dr Casimir Bizimungu.
Minister at the Presidency, Siméon Nteziryayo; Lt.-Col. Augustin Ndindiliyimana (*Defence*); Enoch Ruhigira (*Civil Service*).

EMBASSY OF THE REPUBLIC OF RWANDA
1 avenue des Fleurs, Woluwe Saint Pièrre, Brussels 1150, Belgium
[Brussels 7630702]

Ambassador Extraordinary and Plenipotentiary, new appointment awaited.

Rwanda, formerly part of the Belgian-administered trusteeship of Ruanda-Urundi, has an area of 10,169 sq. miles (26,338 sq. km), and a population (UN estimate 1989) of 6,989,000, mainly of the Hutu tribe, with Tutsi and Twa minorities.

A referendum held in September 1961 showed the majority of the population were opposed to the retention of the monarchy which was accordingly abolished on October 2, 1961. Rwanda became an independent Republic on July 1, 1962, with Gregoire Kayibanda as Head of State and Head of the Government. He was deposed in 1973, and replaced by a military government under Maj.-Gen. Juvénal Habyarimana.

In October 1990, Rwanda was invaded by the Rwandan Patriotic Front, composed of members of the minority Tutsi tribe in exile in Uganda. Attempts to reach a binding cease-fire have so far failed. The MRND (National Revolutionary Movement for Development), renamed the National Republican Movement for Democracy and Development, ended its monopoly of power in April 1991. A new multi-party constitution was promulgated in July 1991, introducing the post of prime minister and restricting the tenure of the president; elections have yet to be announced.

Coffee (accounting for 90 per cent of Rwanda's export earnings in 1989), tea and sugar are grown. Tin, hides, bark of quinine and extract of pyrethrum flowers are also exported.

The National University of Rwanda is situated at two campuses, Butare and Ruhengeri.

In 1987 total imports were valued at US$351·7m; total exports, US$112·3m.

Trade with UK

	1989	1990
Imports from UK	£1,790,000	£1,915,000
Exports to UK	2,991,000	2,128,000

CAPITAL.—Kigali (156,000).
CURRENCY.—Rwanda franc of 100 centimes.
FLAG.—Three vertical bands, red, yellow and green with letter R on yellow band.
NATIONAL DAY.—July 1.

British Ambassador (resident in Kinshasa, Zaire).

EL SALVADOR
(República de El Salvador)

President, Alfredo Felix Cristiani Burkard, *elected* March 19, 1989, *assumed office* June 1, 1989.
Vice-President, Francisco Merino.

CABINET
(as at September 3, 1991)

Minister of the Presidency, Dr Oscar Santamaría.
Foreign Affairs, Dr Manuel Pacas Castro.
Planning, Mirna Lievano de Márquez.
Interior, Col. Juan Antonio Martínez Varela.
Justice, Dr René Hernández Valiente.
Finance, Dr Rafael Alvarado Cano.
Economy, Arturo Zablah.
Education, Cecilia Gallardo do Cano.
Defence, Gen. René Emilio Ponce.
Labour and Social Security, Mauricio González.
Agriculture and Livestock, Antonio Cabrales.
Public Health and Social Welfare, Dr Lisandro Vásquez Sosa.
Works, Mauricio Stubig.
Secretary of Information, Mauricio Sandoval.

EMBASSY OF EL SALVADOR
5 Great James Street, WC1N 3DA
[071-430 2141]

Ambassador Extraordinary and Plenipotentiary, His Excellency Dr Maurico Rosales-Rivera (1986).

Area and Population.—The Republic of El Salvador extends along the Pacific coast of Central America for 160 miles with a general breadth of about 50 miles, and contains an area of 8,124 sq. miles (21,041 sq. km), with a population (1989 estimate) of 5,500,000. The population density is one of the highest in the world with 253 inhabitants per square km. It is divided into 14 Departments.

The surface of the country is very mountainous, many of the peaks being extinct volcanoes. The highest are the Santa Ana volcano (7,700 ft.) and the San Vicente volcano (7,200 ft.). Much of the interior has an average altitude of 2,000 feet. The climate varies from tropical to temperate. The lowlands along the coast are generally hot, but towards the interior the altitude tempers the severity of the heat. There is a wet season from May to October, and a dry season from November to April. Earthquakes have been frequent in the history of El Salvador, the most recent being that of October 10, 1986, when considerable damage was done to San Salvador.

The principal river is the Rio Lempa. There is a large volcanic lake (Ilopango) a few miles to the east of the capital, while farther away and to the west lies the smaller lake of Coatepeque, which appears to have been formed in a vast crater flanked by the Santa Ana volcano.

Government.—El Salvador was conquered in 1526 by Pedro de Alvarado, and formed part of the Spanish vice-royalty of Guatemala until 1821.

After two years of government by a junta headed by José Napoleon Duarte, elections for a Constituent Assembly were held in March 1982, ending decades of military rule. Presidential elections, although boycotted by the guerrilla movement (Farabundo Martí National Liberation Front (FMLN)), were held in March 1984 and won by Duarte, the Christian Democrat leader over the Nationalist Republican Alliance (ARENA) candidate. Alfredo Cristiani (ARENA) won the presidential elections in March 1989.

In elections to an enlarged 84-seat Legislative Assembly, held on March 10, 1991 and boycotted by the FMLN, ARENA won the largest number of seats (39) but failed to gain a majority. Negotiations continue between the government and the FMLN in an attempt to end the violence of both right and left; in May 1991 the UN established the UN Observers for El Salvador (ONUSAL) which will monitor the implementation of any human rights agreement.

Agriculture.—The principal cash crops are coffee, which is grown principally on the slopes of the volcanoes, cotton, which is cultivated on the coastal plains, and sugarcane and shrimps. (However, cotton and sugar production have decreased as a result of the civil war.) Also cultivated are maize, sesame, indigo, rice, balsam, etc. In the lower altitudes towards the east, sisal is produced and used in the manufacture of coffee and cereal bags. Land reforms, announced in March 1980, have largely been implemented. The Salvadorean Coffee Company, sugar exports and the banking system are nationalized but President Cristiani is in the process of privatizing these industries and introducing competition.

Industry.—Existing factories make textiles, clothing, constructional steel, furniture, cement and household items. In 1989 GDP amounted to US$4,808 million (US$874 per capita). El Salvador is a member of the Central American Common Market. The first trade zone was inaugurated in November 1974 and others are planned.

Education.—The illiterate rate has risen to 68·1 per cent (1985) since 1980 when the figure was 30·5 per cent. Primary education is nominally compulsory, but the number of schools and teachers available is too small to enable education to be given to all children of school age.

Language and Literature.—The language of the country is Spanish. There are five daily newspapers published at the capital, and four in the provinces.

Communications.—The Executive Autonomous Port Commission (CEPA) administers the port of Cutuco, at La Union and the principal port of Acajutla, and the railways through FENADESAL. There is a railway line between San Salvador and Guatemala City and Puerto Barrios on the Caribbean coast but it is subject to interruption. The roads are paved and in good condition but some bridges are temporary structures following guerrilla action. There are good roads between Acajutla and the capital (60 miles), and between the capital and Guatemala City. The Pan-American Highway from the Guatemalan frontier follows this route and continues to the Honduran frontier. The El Salvador international airport can receive jet aircraft with daily flights to other Central American capitals, Mexico, and five US cities.

There are post and telegraph offices throughout the country. There are 100 broadcasting stations and six television stations.

BUDGET

	1988
Revenue	₡2,843·8m
Expenditure	₡3,042·2m

Trade with UK

	1989	1990
Imports from UK	£9,594,000	£10,415,000
Exports to UK	2,133,000	1,261,000

There is foreign exchange control. There is also a parallel market in US dollars.

Chief exports are coffee, cotton, sugar, shrimps, sisal (in the form of bags used for exporting coffee, sugar, etc.), balsam, meat, towels, hides and skins. The chief imports are chemicals, fertilizers, pharmaceutical goods, petroleum, manufactured goods, industrial and electronic machinery and equipment, vehicles and consumer goods.

CAPITAL.—San Salvador. Estimated population of metropolitan area, 2,000,000. Other towns are Santa Ana (417,000), San Miguel (157,838), Ψ La Union (Cutuco), Ψ La Libertad and Ψ Acajutia.

CURRENCY.—El Salvador colón (₡) of 100 centavos.

FLAG.—Three horizontal bands, light blue, white, light blue; coat of arms on white band.

NATIONAL ANTHEM.—Saludemos La Patria Orgullosos (Let us proudly hail the Fatherland).

NATIONAL DAY.—September 15.

BRITISH EMBASSY
PO Box 1591, San Salvador

British Ambassador, (resident in Tegucigalpa, Honduras).

Chargé d'affaires a.i., I. R. MURRAY, OBE (*First Secretary*).

SAN MARINO
(Repubblica di San Marino)

Regents, Two 'Capitani Reggenti'.

CONSULATE GENERAL IN LONDON
166 High Holborn, WC1V 6TT
[071–836 7744]

Consul-General, The Lord Forte.

A small Republic in the hills near Rimini, on the Adriatic, founded, it is stated, by a pious stonecutter of Dalmatia in the 4th century. The Republic resisted Papal claims and those of neighbouring dukedoms during the 15th–18th centuries, and its integrity and sovereignty is recognized and respected by Italy. The area is approximately 23 sq. miles (61 sq. km.), the population (1990) is 23,240.

The Republic is governed by a State Congress of ten members, under the presidency of two Heads of State, who are elected at six-monthly intervals. The Great and General Council, a legislative body of 60 members, is elected by universal suffrage for a term of five years. A Council of Twelve forms in certain cases a Supreme Court of Justice. A coalition government of the Communist Party and the Christian Democratic Party was returned to power in the general election of May 1988.

The city of San Marino, on the slope of Monte Titano, has three towers, a fine church and Government palace, a theatre and museums. The principal products are wine, cereals, and cattle, and the main industries are tourism, ceramics, lime, concrete, cotton yarns, colour and paints.

CURRENCY.—San Marino and Italian currencies are in circulation.

FLAG.—Two horizontal bands, white, blue (with coat of arms of the Republic in centre).

NATIONAL DAY.—September 3.

British Consul-General, Miss M. L. Croll (resident in Florence, Italy).

SÃO TOMÉ AND PRÍNCIPE
(República Democrática de São Tomé e Príncipe)

President, Miguel Trovoada.

COUNCIL OF MINISTERS
(as at July 1991)

Prime Minister, Daniel Lima dos Santos Daio.
Foreign Affairs and Co-operation, Alda Bandeira.
Defence and Internal Order, Albertino Braganca.
Economy and Finance, Norberto Costa Allegre.
Justice, Labour and Public Administration, Olegario Pires Tiny.
Social Infrastructure and Environment, Oscar Aguiar Sacramento e Sousa.
Information, Armindo Aguiar.
Príncipe, Sylvestre Umbelina.

EMBASSY OF THE DEMOCRATIC REPUBLIC OF SÃO TOMÉ AND PRINCIPE
42 avenue Brugman, Brussels 1060, Belgium
[Brussels 3475375]

Ambassador Extraordinary and Plenipotentiary, new appointment awaited.

HONORARY CONSULATE
42 North Audley Street, W1A 4PY
[071–499 1995]

Honorary Consul, Mr Wilder.

The islands of São Tomé and Príncipe are situated in the gulf of Guinea, off the west coast of Africa. They have an area of 372 sq. miles (964 sq. km), and a population (UN estimate 1989) of 116,000.

Following Portugal's decision to grant independence, a transitional government was installed in December 1974, and the islands became independent on July 12, 1975.

A multi-party constitution was approved by referendum in August 1990. The Movement for the Liberation of São Tomé and Príncipe (MLSTP), which had been the sole legal party since independence, was defeated by the opposition Democratic Convergence Party (PCD) in legislative elections held on January 20, 1991. Miguel Trovoada, an independent, was elected President on March 3, 1991.

Cacao is the main product.

Trade with UK

	1989	1990
Imports from UK	£819,000	£879,000
Exports to UK	4,000	114,000

CAPITAL.—ΨSão Tomé (25,000).

CURRENCY.—Dobra of 100 centavos.

FLAG.—Horizontal stripes of green, yellow, green, the yellow of double width and bearing two black stars; and a red triangle in the hoist.

NATIONAL DAY.—July 12 (Independence Day).

British Ambassador (resident in Luanda, Angola).

British Consulate, c/o Hull Blythe (Angola)Ltd., BP 15, São Tomé.

Honorary Consul, J. Gomes.

SAUDI ARABIA
(Al Mamlaka al Arabiya as-Sa'udiyya)

Custodian of the Two Holy Mosques and King of Saudi Arabia, HM King Fahd bin Abdul Aziz, *born*, 1921, *ascended the throne* June 1, 1982.

Crown Prince, HRH Amir Abdullah bin Abdul Aziz.

COUNCIL OF MINISTERS
(as at September 5, 1991)

Prime Minister, HM King Fahd bin Abdul Aziz.

First Deputy Prime Minister and Commander of the National Guard, HRH Prince Abdullah bin Abdul Aziz.

Second Deputy Prime Minister, Defence and Aviation, HRH Prince Sultan bin Abdul Aziz.

Public Works and Housing, HRH Prince Mit'ab bin Abdul Aziz.
Interior, HRH Prince Naif bin Abdul Aziz.
Foreign Affairs, HRH Prince Saud al-Faisal bin Abdul Aziz.
Finance and National Economy, Muhammad Aba al-Khail.
Agriculture and Water, Dr Abdul Rahman bin Abdul Aziz bin Hassan Al al-Shaikh.
Municipal and Rural Affairs, Muhammad al-Shaikh.
Justice, Sheikh Mohammed bin Ibrahim al Jubeir.
Commerce, Dr Sulaiman al-Solaim.
Communications, Dr Hussain Mansouri.
Petroleum and Mineral Resources, Hisham Nazer.
Planning, Abdul Wahab al-Attar.
Labour and Social Affairs, Dr Mohamed Ali al-Faiz.
Information, Ali Sha'er.
Health, Faisal bin Abdul Aziz al Hejailan.
Pilgrimage and Endowments, Abdul Wahhab Ahmed Abdul Wasi.
Education, Dr Abdul Aziz Al-Abdullah al-Khuwaiter.
Higher Education, Khalid al-Angari.
Posts, Telegraphs and Telecommunications, Dr Alawi Darwish Kayyal.
Industry and Electricity, Abdul Aziz al-Zamil.

ROYAL EMBASSY OF SAUDI ARABIA
30 Belgrave Square, SW1X 8QB
[071–917 3000]

Ambassador Extraordinary and Plenipotentiary, His Excellency Sheikh Nasser Almanqour, GCVO (1980).
Ministers Plenipotentiary, Ibrahim M. Mosly; Saud Ahmed M. Alyahya, LVO; Abdullah O. Barry, LVO.

The Kingdom of Saudi Arabia is a personal union of two countries, the Sultan of Nejd becoming also King of the Hejaz. Great Britain recognized Abdul Aziz Ibn Saud as an independent ruler, King of the Hejaz and of Nejd and its Dependencies, by the Treaty of Jeddah (May 20, 1927). The name was changed to the Kingdom of Saudi Arabia in September 1932.

The total area of the Kingdom is about 830,000 sq. miles (2,149,640 sq. km), with a population (UN estimate 1989) of 14,435,000. Islam is the established and only permitted religion.

In the 18th century Nejd was an independent state governed from Diriya (now in ruins, 25 km from Riyadh) and the stronghold of the Wahhabis, a puritanical Islamic sect. It subsequently fell under Turkish rule; in 1913 Abdul Aziz Ibn Saud threw off Turkish rule and captured the Turkish province of Al Hasa. In 1920 he captured the Asir, and in 1921, by force of arms, he added to his dominions the Jebel Shammar territory of the Rashid family. In 1925 he completed the conquest of the Hejaz.

Saudi Arabia comprises almost the whole of the Arabian peninsula, with the exception of the Republic of Yemen in the extreme south, Oman and the UAE in the south-east and Qatar in the east. In the north-west it borders Jordan and in the north-east Iraq and Kuwait, while to the west lies the Red Sea and to the east the Gulf. The Nejd ('Plateau'), now the Central Province, extends over the centre of the peninsula, including the Nafud and Dahna deserts. The Hejaz ('the Boundary'), now the Western Province, extends along the Red Sea coast to Asir and contains the holy towns of Mecca and Medina. The former, about 60 km east of Jeddah, is the birthplace of the Prophet Mohammed, and contains the Great Mosque, within which is the Kaaba or sacred shrine of the Muslim religion. This is the focus of the annual Hajj ('Pilgrimage'), performed by 1·4 million in 1990. Medina Al Munawwarah ('The City of Light'), some 300 km north of Mecca, is celebrated as the first city to embrace Islam and as the Prophet Mohammed's burial place (he died there on Rabia 12, AH 11, corresponding to June 7, AD 632).

Asir ('Inaccessible') is named for its mountainous terrain, and, with the coastal plain of the Tihama, lies along the southern Red Sea coast from Hejaz to the border with Yemen. It is the only region to enjoy substantial rainfall. Water supplies are, however, supplemented by dams and irrigation. The east and south-east of the country are lower-lying and largely desert. Outside the manufacturing centres which have grown up around some of the towns, most of the population are engaged in agriculture. The productivity of traditional dryland farming is increasingly supplemented by irrigation.

Industry.—Oil was first found in commercial quantities in Dhahran, near Dammam, in 1938. Total production of crude oil peaked at 9·9 million b.p.d. in 1980, and in 1986 was 4·8 million b.p.d. About 97 per cent of the total is extracted by the Arabian–American Oil Company. Recoverable reserves stood at about 167 billion barrels at the end of 1986, equivalent to about 95 years' production at the 1986 rate. Aramco's 66-year lease will terminate in 1999 but the company was effectively nationalized in 1980.

The government actively encourages the establishment of manufacturing industries in the country. Industries have developed in the fields of construction materials, metal fabrication, simple machinery and electrical equipment, food and beverages, chemicals and plastics. Investment in industrial gases, intermediate petrochemicals, light engineering and machinery is encouraged. Two industrial poles have been established at Jubail and Yanbu, financed by the state agency Saudi Arabian Basic Industries Corporation. Linked by gas and oil pipelines, both are to have petrochemical complexes producing, initially, ethylene and methanol; six of the seven plants now on-stream are joint ventures with American and Japanese companies. Complete new cities are being built at each pole: Jubail will eventually house 300,000 and Yanbu 190,000. The state agency Petromin operates three domestic refineries and two lubricant plants and the last of three joint-venture export refineries came on-stream in 1986. Total refining capacity is now approximately 1,950,000 b.p.d.

Communications.—The railway from the port of Dammam to the oilfields at Abqaiq and through Hofuf to Riyadh was opened in 1951, and a direct Dammam-Riyadh line opened in 1985. An extension to Jeddah via Medina and the reopening of the Hejaz railway are planned. Metalled roads connect all the cities and main towns; the network consisted of 28,500 km in 1985. The principal port of the Gulf is Dammam which has 39 berths and an annual capacity of 9·1 million tons. Jeddah is the centre of commercial traffic on the Red Sea and has 51 piers, giving an annual capacity of 17 million tons. The government-owned Saudi Arabian Airlines (Saudia) operate scheduled services to 19 domestic airports. There are international airports at Dhahran, Jeddah and Riyadh. Work on the new King Fahd International Airport in Eastern Province has yet to be completed. Saudia have an extensive overseas operation, and a large number of international airlines operate into the country. Telecommunications are being rapidly expanded. The government is a major participant in the Arab Satellite Communications Organization.

Education.—With the exception of a few schools for expatriate children, all schools are government supervised and segregated for boys and girls. By mid-1985 there were a total of 1,692,300 schoolchildren in 5,323 primary and 1,219 intermediate and 418 secondary schools. There are universities in Jeddah, Mecca, Riyadh (branches in Abha and Qassim), Dammam (branch at Hofuf) and Dhahran, and there are Islamic universities in Medina and Riyadh. In addition there is great emphasis on vocational training, provided at 24 literacy and artisan skill training centres and 21 more advanced industrial, commercial and agricultural education institutes. Education in government-owned institutes is free at all levels.

Finance and Trade.—Oil remains the main source of receipts in the balance of payments. As a result, government revenues are markedly affected by oil prices and volume of production. The 1990 budget provided for expenditure of SR143,000 million (36 per cent on defence), and a revenue of SR25,000 million.

The leading suppliers of imports are USA, Japan, West Germany, the UK, Italy and France and the chief customers for exports are Japan, France, USA and Singapore. There is a total ban on the importation of alcohol, pork products, firearms and items regarded as non-Islamic or pornographic.

	1988	1989
Total imports	SR81,582m	SR79,219m
Total exports	88,896m	103,892m

Trade with UK

	1989	1990
Imports from UK	£2,432,941,000	£2,012,585,000
Exports to UK	502,416,000	794,633,000

CAPITAL.—Riyadh, population (1990) about 1·5 million. Other major centres are Jeddah (estimated population 1 million), Buraydah, Dammam, Hofuf, Mecca, Medina and Tabuk.

CURRENCY.—Saudi riyal (SR) of 20 qursh or 100 halala.

FLAG.—Green oblong, white Arabic device in centre: 'There is no God but God and Muhammad is the Prophet of God,' and a white scimitar beneath the lettering.

NATIONAL ANTHEM.—Long live our beloved King.

BRITISH EMBASSY
PO Box 94351, Riyadh 11693
[Riyadh 488 0077]

Ambassador Extraordinary and Plenipotentiary, His Excellency Sir Alan Gordon Munro, KCMG (1989).

Counsellors, D. J. Plumbly, CMG (*Deputy Head of Mission*); C. Wilton (*Commercial*).

Defence and Military Attaché, Brig. M. J. Holroyd Smith, OBE.

Air Attaché, Wing Cdr. G. Margiotta.

Naval Attaché, Cdr. T. Waddington.

First Secretaries, M. D. K. Halsey (*Chancery*); P. O. Gooderham (*Economic*); H. Formstone (*Commercial*); C. H. Woodland (*Consul General*); D. G. Lloyd (*Commercial*).

Consul General, Jeddah, H. J. Tunnell, PO Box 393,

Jeddah 21411. There is also a trade office in Dhahran.

British Council Representative, Clive Smith, OBE, Olaya Main Road, Al Mousa Centre, Tower B (PO Box 58012), Riyadh 11594. There is also an office in *Jeddah*.

SENEGAL
(République du Sénégal)

President and Head of Government, Abdou Diouf, installed, Jan. 1, 1981, *elected for a second five-year term*, Feb. 28, 1988.

MINISTERS
(as at April 7, 1991)

Prime Minister, Habib Thiam.

Minister of State, Abdoulaye Wade.

Economy, Finance and Planning, Famara Ibrahima Sagna.

Armed Forces, Médoune Fall.

Guardian of the Seals, Minister of Justice, Serigne Lamine Diop.

Foreign Affairs, Djibo Leyti Ka.

Interior, Madieng Khary Dieng.

National Education, André Sonko.

Equipment, Transport and the Sea, Robert Sagna.

Rural Development and Hydraulics, Cheikh Abdoul Khadre Cissokho.

Industry, Trade and Handicrafts, Alassane Dialy Ndiaye.

Tourism and Environment, Jacques Baudin.

Town Planning and Housing, Amath Dansokho.

Labour and Vocational Training, Ousmane Ngom.

Communication, Moctar Kebe.

Health and Social Action, Assane Diop.

Culture, Moustapha Ka.

African Economic Integration, Jean-Paul Diaz.

Youth and Sports, Abdoulaye Makhtar Diop.

Women, Children and the Family, Ndioro Ndiaye.

There are 12 junior ministers.

EMBASSY OF THE REPUBLIC OF SENEGAL
11 Phillimore Gardens, W8 7QG
[071–937 0925/6]

Ambassador Extraordinary and Plenipotentiary, His Excellency Seydou Madani Sy (1991).

Senegal lies on the west coast of Africa between Mauritania in the north, Mali in the east, and Guinea-Bissau and Guinea in the south. The Gambia lies entirely within Senegal, except for its sea-coast. (For MAP, *see* p. 770.) Senegal has an area of 75,750 sq. miles (196,192 sq. km), and a population (UN estimate 1989) of 7,172,000.

Formerly a French colony, Senegal elected in November 1958 to remain within the French Community as an autonomous republic. In March 1963 (after an attempted coup d'état by the then Prime Minister in the previous December) a new constitution was approved giving executive powers to the President, on the lines of the present French constitution. The process of political liberalization continued; there are now 16 political parties officially recognized. Six parties contested the General Election in February 1988. The Parti Socialiste (PS) took 103 seats and the Parti Démocratique Sénégalais (PDS) 17. A new government, including members of the opposition, was formed in April 1991. A border dispute continues with Mauretania and there is an insurgent separatist movement in the southern Casamance region.

In 1982, after an attempted coup in The Gambia in July 1981 had been put down with the aid of

Senegalese troops, the Senegambia Confederation was established, but this collapsed in 1989.

Senegal's principal exports are groundnuts (raw and processed) and phosphates. Tourism is also of growing importance as a revenue earner.

Trade with UK

	1989	1990
Imports from UK	£13,448,000	£14,884,000
Exports to UK	6,820,000	5,002,000

CAPITAL—ΨDakar (1,000,000).

CURRENCY.—Franc CFA of 100 centimes.

FLAG.—Three vertical bands, green, yellow and red; a green star on the yellow band.

NATIONAL DAY.—April 4.

BRITISH EMBASSY
BP 6025, Dakar
[Dakar 237392]

Ambassador Extraordinary and Plenipotentiary, His Excellency Roger Campbell Beetham, LVO (1990).

First Secretary, R. S. Dewar (*Head of Chancery and Consul*).

Second Secretary, Viscount Glentworth.

Third Secretary, K. J. Lynch (*Vice Consul*).

British Council Representative, A. Malamah-Thomas, 34–36 Blvd. de la Republique, Immeuble Sonatel, BP 6232, Dakar.

SOMALIA
(Jamhuuriyadda Diimoqraadiga ee Soomaaliya)

President, Ali Mahdi Mohammed.

First Vice President, Abdalqadir Mohammed Aden Gobeh.

Second Vice President, Omar Maalin Mahamud.

At the time of going to press, the situation in Somalia was confused. In July 1991 the United Somali Congress (USC), which had formed an interim administration in Mogadishu in February, met representatives of the rival Somali Salvation Democratic Front (SSDF), the Somali Patriotic Movement (SPM) and the Somali Democratic Movement (SDM) and agreed on the formation of a new coalition government. Acting President Ali Mahdi Mohammed, leader of the USC, was recognized by the other clan-based factions as President of Somalia. Each faction was assigned a number of portfolios in the new government but appointments have yet to be completed. In the north of the country, the Somali National Movement (SNM) refused to participate in negotiations and formed a government under SNM leader, and acting President, Abourahman Ahmed Ali. Ex-President Siad Barre remains at large in the south of the country.

EMBASSY OF THE SOMALI DEMOCRATIC REPUBLIC
60 Portland Place, W1N 3DG
[071–580 7148]

Ambassador Extraordinary and Plenipotentiary, His Excellency Ali Hassan Ali (1990).

The Somali Democratic Republic occupies part of the north-east horn of Africa, with a coast-line on the Indian Ocean extending from the boundary with Kenya (2° South latitude) to Cape Guardafui (12° N.); and on the Gulf of Aden to the boundary with Djibouti. Somalia is bounded on the west by Djibouti, Ethiopia and Kenya and covers an area of approximately 246,201 sq. miles (637,657 sq. km). The population, of which a large proportion is nomadic, is 7,339,000 (UN estimate 1989).

Government.—The Somali Democratic Republic, consisting of the former British Somaliland Protectorate and the former Italian trust territory of Somalia, was established on July 1, 1960. British rule in Somaliland lasted from 1887 until 1960 except for a short period in 1940–41 when the Protectorate was occupied by Italian forces. Somalia, formerly an Italian colony, was occupied by British forces in 1941. In 1950 it was placed under Italian administration by a resolution of the UN; this trusteeship lasted until independence. Following the assassination of President Shermake on October 15, 1969, the armed forces, assisted by the police, took over the Government without resistance and a Revolutionary Council under Siad Barre assumed control of the country. In July 1990 a referendum on a new Constitution, to be followed by multi-party elections, was promised but Siad Barre was overthrown in January 1991 by rebel movements. One group, the United Somali Congress (USC), took control in Mogadishu; the city was extensively damaged and property looted.

Following a dispute with Ethiopia over territory, which lasted many years, a peace agreement between the two countries was signed on April 3, 1988 in Mogadishu.

Civil war broke out in May 1988 between the Government and the opposition Somali National Movement (SNM) in the north of the country. With the downfall of Siad Barre, the SNM took control of the north and in May 1991 declared unilateral independence as the 'Somaliland Republic'.

Economy.—Livestock raising is the main occupation in Somalia and there is a modest export trade in livestock on the hoof, skins and hides. Italy, the Gulf States and Saudi Arabia import the bulk of the banana crop, the second biggest export.

Trade with UK

	1989	1990
Imports from UK	£10,508,000	£11,865,000
Exports to UK	508,000	510,000

CAPITAL.—ΨMogadishu, population (estimated 1987), 1,0Ѿ,000. Other towns are Hargeisa (20,000), Boroma (65,000), ΨKisimayu (60,000), ΨBerbera (15,000) and Burao (15,000).

CURRENCY.—Somali shilling of 100 cents.

FLAG.—Five-pointed white star on blue ground.

NATIONAL DAY.—October 21.

British Diplomatic Representation, The British Embassy in Mogadishu was closed temporarily in January 1991.

SOUTH AFRICA
(Republiek van Suid-Afrika)

State President, Frederick Willem de Klerk, *sworn in* September 20, 1989.

CABINET
(as at August 30, 1991)

Constitutional Affairs, Gerrit Viljoen.

Housing and Works, Water Affairs and Forestry, Gen. Magnus Malan.

Transport, Posts and Telecommunications, Dr Piet Welgemoed.

Public Enterprises and Economic Co-ordination, Dawie de Villiers.

Justice and Chairman of the Ministers' Council, Kobie Coetsee.

Correctional Services and Budget, Adriaan Vlok.

Education and Training, Sam de Beer.

National Health and Welfare, Dr Rina Venter.

Law and Order, Hernus Kriel.

Defence, Roelf Meyer.

Planning, Provincial Affairs, National Housing and Local Government, Leon Wessels.

Administration, Education and Culture, Piet Marais.
Foreign Affairs, Pik Botha.
Public Works, Land Affairs and Development Aid,
  Jacob de Villiers.
Agriculture, A. I. van Niekerk.
Finance, Barend du Plessis.
National Education and Environment, Louis Piennar.
Regional Development and State Expenditure, Amie
  Venter.
Home Affairs, Gene Louw.
Mineral and Energy Affairs, George Bartlett.
Manpower, Eli Louw.
Trade, Industry and Tourism, Org Marais.

EMBASSY OF THE REPUBLIC OF SOUTH AFRICA
South Africa House, Trafalgar Square, WC2N 5DP
[071–930 4488]

Ambassador Extraordinary and Plenipotentiary, His
  Excellency K. D. S. Durr (1991).
Minister, R. W. Carter.
Minister (Trade), P. M. Pullen.

Area and Population.—The Republic, comprising
the Provinces of the Cape of Good Hope, Natal, the
Transvaal and the Orange Free State, occupies the
southernmost part of the African continent from the
courses of the Limpopo, Molopo and Orange Rivers
(34° 50′ 22″ S.) to the Cape of Good Hope, with the
exception of Lesotho, Botswana and Swaziland, and
part of Mozambique. It has a total area of 471,445 sq.
miles (1,221,031 sq. km).

The official population estimate for 1990, excluding
Bophuthatswana, Ciskei, Transkei and Venda, was
30,788,000, comprising 21,600,000 Blacks, 5,018,000
Whites, 3,214,000 Coloureds, and 956,000 Indians.
These figures are not thought to be accurate; the UN
(1989) estimate for all of South Africa is 34,492,000.

The southernmost province contains many parallel
ranges, which rise in steps towards the interior. The
south-western peninsula contains the famous Table
Mountain (3,582 ft.), while the Great Swartberg and
Langeberg run in parallel lines from west to east of
the Cape Province. Between these two ranges and
the Roggeveld and Nuweveld ranges to the north is
the Great Karoo Plateau, which is bounded on the
east by the Sneeuberg, containing the highest summit
in the province (Kompasberg, 7,800 ft.). In the east
are ranges which join the Drakensberg (11,000 ft.)
between Natal and the Orange Free State.

The Orange Free State presents a succession of
undulating grassy plains with occasional hills or
kopjes. The Transvaal is also mainly an elevated
plateau with parallel ridges in the Magaliesberg and
Waterberg ranges of no great height. The eastern
province of Natal has pastoral lowlands and rich
agriculture land between the slopes of the Drakensberg and the coast, the interior rising in terraces as
in the southern provinces. The Orange, with its
tributary the Vaal, is the principal river of the south,
rising in the Drakensberg and flowing into the
Atlantic between Namibia and the Cape Province.
The Limpopo, or Crocodile River, in the north, rises
in the Transvaal and flows into the Indian Ocean
through Mozambique. Most of the remaining rivers
are furious torrents after rain, with partially dry
beds at other seasons.

Government.—The self-governing colonies of the
Cape of Good Hope, Natal, the Transvaal and the
Orange River Colony became united on May 31, 1910
under the South Africa Act 1909, in a legislative
union under the name of the Union of South Africa,
the four colonies becoming provinces of the Union.

A new Constitution came into effect in September
1984 which provided for an executive President and
a three-chamber Parliament: the House of Assembly
(178 members) representing Whites, the House of

Representatives (85 members) representing Coloureds, and the House of Delegates (45 members)
representing Indians. The majority black population
has no representation. There is joint parliamentary
responsibility for 'general' affairs (foreign policy,
defence, finance, law and order, justice, transport,
manpower, commerce and industry, agriculture), and
each chamber has separate responsibility for the
'own' affairs of the population group it represents
(housing, social welfare, health, education, local
government and some aspects of agriculture). Disputes between the chambers may be referred by the
President to the President's Council (60 members—
20 White, 10 Coloured, 5 Indian elected by their
respective chambers, 15 nominated by the President,
10 nominated by Opposition parties).

The President is chosen by an 88-member electoral
college (in the proportion 4 White : 2 Coloured : 1
Indian) of the majority parties of the three chambers.
The President appoints the Cabinet from all three
communities, and also appoints each community's
ministerial council for 'own' affairs.

Elections to the House of Assembly last took place
on September 6, 1989. Party representation is as
follows: National Party 104; Conservative Party 41;
Democratic Party 32; vacant 1.

Apartheid.—From 1948, South Africa's social and
political structure was based on the policy of racial
segregation, apartheid. Opposition protests at this
policy culminated in demonstrations at Sharpeville,
near Johannesberg, in 1960, in which 69 protesters
were shot dead by police; the African National
Congress and other opposition groups were subsequently banned. Largely as a result of world protests,
South Africa left the Commonwealth and became a
republic on May 31, 1961.

As part of its policy of apartheid, the government
established a number of black 'homelands'. Six areas,
(Gazankulu, Lebowa, KwaNdbele, KaNgwane,
Qwaqwa and KwaZulu) are now designated as self-
governing states. A further four (Bophuthatswana,
Ciskei, Transkei and Venda) are regarded as independent republics by the South African government
but are not recognized as such by the UN. Most
homelands are now in the process of re-integrating
into South Africa.

A new wave of opposition to apartheid climaxed in
1976 with uprisings in Soweto, in which hundreds of
blacks, including many schoolchildren, were shot
dead while protesting at the introduction of Afrikaans as the compulsory medium of instruction.

The promulgation of the new Constitution in 1984
coincided with rioting in the black townships and
the continuing unrest led to the declaration on July
20, 1985 of a state of emergency in 36 districts. A
nationwide state of emergency was declared on June

[2, 1986; it was renewed annually until it was finally lifted in the Cape, Transvaal and Orange Free State provinces in June 1990, and in Natal in October 1990.

In September 1989, F. W. de Klerk replaced F. W. Botha as President of South Africa and accelerated the process of reform. In February 1990, the ban on the ANC and restrictions on other anti-apartheid groups were lifted; Nelson Mandela, the main ANC political detainee, was also released. In 1991 apartheid was effectively abolished with the repeal in March of the Land Acts, restricting land ownership by race, and the Group Areas Act, restricting residence by race; the Population Registration Act, classifying people by race, was repealed in June. Negotiations continue between various groups to establish a non-racial democracy. Talks are hampered by fierce, inter-communal fighting, chiefly between members of the ANC and the Zulu-based *Inkatha* Freedom Party.

Communications.—The previously state-owned and controlled South African Transport Services has been privatized. Independent companies now operate the national railway system, the principal harbours, most long-distance passenger and freight road transport services, the South African Airways airline and a network of pipelines for petroleum products.

There are international airports at Johannesburg (Jan Smuts), Durban (Louis Botha) and Cape Town (D. F. Malan), with another under construction at La Mercy, Natal. South African Airways operates international services to Europe, South America, the Far East and the Middle East, as well as to neighbouring countries, and it is the principal operator of domestic flights.

The largest sea-port is Durban, Natal. Other major ports are Cape Town, Port Elizabeth, East London, Saldanha Bay and Mossel Bay in Cape Province and Richards Bay, Natal.

Production.—Mining is of great importance to the South African economy. Minerals to the value of R37,899·4 million were produced in 1990. Principal minerals produced are: gold, coal, diamonds, copper, iron ore, manganese, lime and limestone, and chrome ore. South Africa is the world's largest producer of gold.

Agriculture, forestry and fishing account for about 5 per cent of GDP. Over 50 per cent of land is pasture so livestock farming is widespread with meat and wool important products. Principal crops are maize, sugar-cane, fruits and vegetables, wheat, sorghum, sunflower seed and groundnuts. Cotton is widely grown because of its suitability to the climate, and viticulture is also widespread.

Industries, concentrated most heavily around Johannesburg, Pretoria and the major ports, process foodstuffs, metals and non-metallic mineral products, and also produce beverages and tobacco, motor vehicles, chemicals and chemical products, machinery, textiles and clothing, and paper and paper products.

Trade.—Principal exports are: gold, base metals and metal products, diamonds, food (especially fruit), chemicals, machinery and transport equipment, and wool. Principal imports are: machinery, chemicals, motor vehicles, metals and metal products, food, inedible raw materials and textiles.

Trade with UK

	1989	1990
Imports from UK	£1,038,242,000	£1,113,397,000
Exports to UK	884,607,000	1,078,546,000

Finance.—Estimated revenue for 1988–89 was R47,460 million, and estimated expenditure was R56,556 million.

Capital.—The administrative seat of the Government is Pretoria, Transvaal; population (1985 esti-

mate) 822,925; the seat of the legislature is ΨCape Town, population (1985) 1,911,521. Other large towns (1985 figures) are Johannesburg, Transvaal (1,609,408); ΨDurban, Natal, the largest seaport (634,301); ΨPort Elizabeth, Cape (651,993); Bloemfontein, capital of Orange Free State (232,984); ΨEast London, Cape (167,992); and Pietermaritzburg, capital of Natal (192,417).

Currency.—Rand (R) of 100 cents.

Flag.—Three horizontal stripes of equal width; from top to bottom, orange, white, blue; in the centre of the white stripe, the old Orange Free State flag hanging vertical, towards the pole the Union Flag horizontal, away from the pole the old Transvaal Vierkleur, all spread full.

National Anthem.—Die Stem Van Suid-Afrika (The Call of South Africa).

National Day.—May 31.

BRITISH EMBASSY
255 Hill Street, Pretoria
[Pretoria 433121]
91 Parliament Street, Cape Town (Jan.–June)
[Cape Town 4617220]

Ambassador Extraordinary and Plenipotentiary, His Excellency Anthony Reeve, CMG (1991).
Counsellor, Deputy Head of Mission, J. Poston.
First Secretaries, R. J. Sawers; G. D. Adams; P. Haggie; A. E. Gay (*Administration*).

Cultural Attaché and British Council Representative, W. L. Radford, 76 Juta Street, (PO Box 30637), Braamfontein 2017, Johannesburg (Tel. 339 3715).

There are British Consular Offices at *Cape Town*, *Johannesburg* and *Durban*; and Honorary Consuls at *Port Elizabeth* and *East London*.

SPAIN
(España)

Head of the Spanish State, King Juan Carlos I de Borbón y Borbón, KG, born Jan. 5, 1938, *acceded to the throne*, Nov. 22, 1975, *married* May 14, 1962, Princess Sophie of Greece *and has issue*, Infante Felipe Juan Pablo Alfonso y Todos los Santos (Prince of Asturias, *and heir to the throne*), *born* Jan. 30, 1968; Infanta Elena Maria Isabel Dominga, *born* Dec. 20, 1963; and Infanta Cristina Federica Victoria Antonia, *born* June 13, 1965.

CABINET

(as at March 11, 1991)

Prime Minister, Felipe González Márquez.
Deputy PM, Narcís Serra Serra.
Foreign Affairs, Francisco Fernández Ordóñez.
Justice, Tomás de la Quadra-Salcedo Fernández del Castillo.
Defence, Julián García Vargas.
Economy and Finance, Carlos Solchaga Catalán.
Interior, José Luis Corcuera Cuesta.
Public Works and Town Planning and Transport, José Borrell Fontelles.
Education and Science, Javier Solana Madariaga.
Labour and Social Security, Luis Martínez Noval.
Industry and Energy, Commerce and Tourism, Claudio Aranzadi Martínez.
Agriculture, Food and Fisheries, Pedro Solbes Mira.
Public Administration, Juan Manuel Eguiagaray Ucelay.
Culture, Jordi Solé Tura.
Health and Consumer Affairs, Julián García Valverde.
Relations with the Cortes and Government Secretariat, Virgilio Zapatero Gómez.
Social Affairs, Matilde Fernández Sanz.

Government Spokeswoman, Rosa Conde Gutiérrez del Alamo.

SPANISH EMBASSY
24 Belgrave Square, SW1X 8QA
[071-235 5555]

Ambassador Extraordinary and Plenipotentiary, His Excellency Felipe de la Morena (1990).
Minister-Counsellor, Marques de Torregrosa.

Area and Population.—Situated in the south-west of Europe, between 36°–43° 45′ N. lat. and 4° 25′ E.–9° 20′ W. long., Spain is bounded on the south and east by the Mediterranean, on the west by the Atlantic and Portugal, and on the north by the Bay of Biscay and France, from which it is separated by the Pyrenees. Continental Spain occupies about eleven-thirteenths of the Iberian peninsula, the remaining portion forming the Republic of Portugal. Its coast-line extends 1,317 miles, 712 formed by the Mediterranean and 605 by the Atlantic, and it comprises a total area of 194,897 sq. miles (504,782 sq. km), with a population (UN estimate 1989) of 38,811,000.

Physical Features.—The interior of the Iberian Peninsula consists of an elevated tableland surrounded and traversed by mountain ranges—the Pyrenees, the Cantabrian Mountains, the Sierra Guadarrama, Sierra Morena, Sierra Nevada, Montes de Toledo, etc. The principal rivers are the Duero, the Tajo, the Guadiana, the Guadalquivir, the Ebro and the Miño.

Government.—Spain was a monarchy until April 1931, when King Alfonso XIII left the country and a Republic was proclaimed. A Provisional Government, drawn from the various Republican and Socialist parties, was formed. On July 18, 1936 a counter-revolution broke out in many military garrisons in Spanish Morocco and spread rapidly throughout Spain. The principal leader was General Francisco Franco Bahamonde, leader of the Military-Fascist fusion, or *Falange*. On March 29, 1939 the Civil War was declared to have ended, the Popular Front Governments in Madrid and Barcelona surrendering to the Nationalists (as General Franco's followers were then named). On June 5, 1939 the Grand Council of the *Falange Española Tradicionalista y de las Juntas Ofensivas Nacional-Sindicalistas*, met at Burgos to legislate for the reorganization of the country under the presidency of General Franco.

On July 22, 1969, General Franco nominated Prince Juan Carlos (Alfonso) of Bourbon (grandson of the late King Alfonso XIII) to succeed him as head of state at his death or retirement. The nomination was approved in the *Cortes* by a large majority. Following the death of General Franco on November 20, 1975, Juan Carlos acceded to the throne.

Under the Constitution drawn up in 1977–78 there is a bicameral *Cortes* comprising a 350-member Congress of Deputies elected for four years by universal adult suffrage, and a Senate consisting of directly elected representatives of the provinces, islands, autonomous regions, and Ceuta and Melilla. At the General Election on October 29, 1989, PSOE (Spanish Socialist Workers' Party) won 175 seats, and the PP (Popular Party) 107.

Regions.—Since the promulgation of the 1978 Constitution, 17 autonomous regions have been established, with their own parliaments and governments. These are Andalucia, Aragon, Asturias, Balearics, the Basque country, Canaries, Castilla-La Mancha, Castilla-Leon, Cantabria, Cataluña, Extremadura, Galicia, Madrid, Murcia, Navarre, La Rioja and Valencia.

Defence.—Army: There are in Spain 1 armoured, 1 mechanized, 1 motorized and 2 mountain divisions; 1 artillery brigade, 2 cavalry brigades, 1 air-transportable brigade, 1 helicopter brigade, 1 coastal artillery brigade. The *Guardia Civil* operates as a gendarmerie in the rural areas under the control of the Ministry of Defence.

The active Spanish Navy consists of 1 aircraft carrier, 4 destroyers, 14 frigates and corvettes, 12 minesweepers, 5 major amphibious vessels, 8 submarines, 12 fast patrol craft, 6 hydrographic vessels, 1 tanker, and many smaller patrol craft and auxiliaries. The Navy also has 50 helicopters and 22 Harrier aircraft.

The Air Force is divided geographically into three regions covering Spain, plus an Air Zone for the Canaries. There are also functional Combat, Tactical and Transport Commands. The Air Force consists of 2 attack squadrons, 8 air defence squadrons, 1 maritime squadron, 7 transport squadrons, 3 search and rescue squadrons, training squadrons and 1 fire-fighting squadron.

Spain became a member of NATO in May 1982. Continued membership (linked to non-military integration) was confirmed in a referendum in March 1986. The present government has initiated reorganization of the military structure.

Education.—Education is free for all those aged 6–18, and compulsory up to the age of 14. Under the 1985 Education Law, private schools (30 per cent of primary and 60 per cent of secondary schools) will have to fulfill certain criteria to receive government maintenance grants.

There are 33 public sector universities, the oldest of which, Salamanca, was founded in 1218. Other ancient foundations are Valladolid (1346), Barcelona (1430), Zaragoza (1474), Santiago (1495), Valencia (1500), Seville (1505), Madrid (1508), Granada (1531), Oveido (1604). Private universities are Deusto in Bilbao, Navarra in Pamplona, one in Madrid and one in Salamanca. Student numbers in the universities in 1989–90 totalled 1,067,874.

Language and Literature.—Castilian is the language of more than three-quarters of the population of Spain. Basque, reported to have been the original language of Iberia, is spoken in Vizcaya, Guipuzcoa and Alava. Catalan is spoken in Provençal Spain, and Galician, spoken in the north-western provinces, is akin to Portuguese; the governments of these regions actively encourage use of their local languages.

The literature of Spain is one of the oldest and richest in the world, the *Poem of the Cid*, the earliest of the heroic songs of Spain, having been written about AD 1140. The outstanding writings of its golden age are those of Miguel de Cervantes Saavedra (1547–1616), Lope Felix de Vega Carpio (1562–1635) and Pedro Calderón de la Barca (1600–1681). The Nobel Prize for Literature has five times been awarded to Spanish authors—J. Echegaray (1904), J. Benavente (1922), Juan Ramón Jimenez (1956), Vicente Aleixandre (1977) and Camilo José Cela (1989).

Production and Industry.—The expansion of the Spanish economy and accession to the EC have led to changes in Spanish agriculture. It accounts for over 5 per cent of GDP and employs over 13 per cent of the working population (down from 28 per cent in 1970). Between 1970 and 1985 the net value of agricultural production increased by 56 per cent in real terms.

The country is generally fertile, and well adapted to agriculture and the cultivation of heat-loving fruits—olives, oranges, lemons, almonds, pomegranates, bananas, apricots, tomatoes, peppers, cucumbers and grapes. The agricultural products include wheat, barley, oats, rice, hemp and flax. The orange crop is exported mainly to Germany, France and the United Kingdom. The vine is cultivated widely; in the southwest, Jerez, the well-known sherry and tent wines are produced. The fishing industry is important.

Spain's mineral resources of coal, iron, wolfram, copper, zinc, lead and iron ores are variously exploited. Output of coal in 1988 was 15·5 million tonnes; output of steel (1988) 11·9 million tonnes.

The principal goods produced are cars, steel, ships, manufactured goods, textiles, chemical products, footwear and other leather goods. In 1988 an estimated 54,172,000 tourists visited Spain.

TRADE

	1988	1989
	million pesetas	
Imports	7,039,516	8,458,300
Exports	4,686,376	5,257,600

The balance of payments on current account showed a deficit of US$10,410 million in 1989 and reserves stood at US$44,697 million.

Trade with UK†

	1989†	1990*
Imports from UK	£3,227,793,000	£3,750,143,000
Exports to UK	2,846,543,000	2,884,691,000

† Including Canary Islands.
* Excluding the Canary Islands, Ceuta and Melilla.

The principal imports are cotton, tobacco, cellulose, timber, coffee and cocoa, food products, fertilizers, dyes, machinery, motor vehicles and agricultural tractors, wool and petroleum products. The principal exports include cars, petroleum products, iron ore, cork, salt, vegetables, fruits, wines, olive oil, potash, mercury, pyrites, tinned fruit and fish, tomatoes and footwear.

CAPITAL.—Madrid, population (1986) 4,731,224. Other large cities are ΨBarcelona (4,597,429), ΨValencia (2,078,812), Seville (1,594,250), Zaragoza (824,781), ΨMálaga (1,137,782), Bilbao (1,179,148); Murcia (1,006,788).

CURRENCY.—Peseta of 100 céntimos.

FLAG.—Three horizontal bands, red, yellow and red, with coat of arms on yellow band.

NATIONAL ANTHEM.—Marcha Real Española.

NATIONAL DAY.—October 12.

BRITISH EMBASSY
Calle Fernando el Santo, 16, Madrid 4
[Madrid 319 0200]

Ambassador Extraordinary and Plenipotentiary, His Excellency Robin Fearn, CMG (1989).

Minister, I. V. Roberts.

Counsellors, D. Ridgway (*Commercial*); A. Longrigg (*Economic and Community Affairs*).

Defence and Naval Attaché, Capt. S. N. G. Sloot, LVO, RN.

Head of Political Section, G. C. Gillham.

There are Consulates General in *Madrid, Barcelona, Bilbao;* Consulates in *Tenerife, Alicante, Seville, Malaga, Palma de Mallorca, Las Palmas*; Vice Consulates in *Algeciras, Ibiza*; Honorary Consulates in *Arecife, Santander, Menorca, Tarragona, Vigo.*

British Council Representative, B. Vale, OBE, Plaza Santa Barbara 10, 28004 Madrid. There is a branch library in *Barcelona.*

BRITISH CHAMBER OF COMMERCE, Plaza de Santa Barbara 10, 1st Floor, 28004 Madrid, also Paseo de Gracia 11, Barcelona 7 and Alameda de Mazarredo 5, Bilbao 1.

The BALEARIC ISLES form an archipelago off the east coast of Spain. There are four large islands (Majorca, Minorca, Ibiza and Formentera), and seven smaller (Aire, Aucanada, Botafoch, Cabrera, Dragonera, Pinto and El Rey). The islands were occupied by the Romans after the destruction of Carthage and provided contingents of the celebrated Balearic slingers. The total area is 1,935 sq. miles (5,011 sq. km), with a population of 685,088. The archipelago forms a province of Spain, the capital being ΨPalma in Majorca, pop. 304,422; ΨMahon (Minorca), pop. 22,926.

The CANARY ISLANDS are an archipelago in the Atlantic, off the African coast, consisting of seven islands and six mostly uninhabited islets. The total area is 2,807 sq. miles (7,270 sq. km), with a population of 1,444,626. The Canary Islands form two Provinces of Spain.—*Las Palmas* (Gran Canaria, Lanzarote (38,500), Fuerteventura (19,500) and the islets of Alegranza, Roque del Este, Roque del Oeste, Graciosa, Montaña Clara and Lobos), with seat of administration at ΨLas Palmas (366,454) in Gran Canaria, where major oil companies have installations for re-fuelling shipping; and *Santa Cruz de Tenerife* (Tenerife, La Palma (76,000), Gomera (31,829), and Hierro (10,000)), with seat of administration at ΨSanta Cruz in Tenerife, population estimate 190,784.

ISLA DE FAISANES is an uninhabited Franco-Spanish condominium, at the mouth of the Bidassoa in La Higuera bay.

ΨCEUTA is a fortified post on the Moroccan coast, opposite Gibraltar. The total area is 5 sq. miles (13 sq. km), with a population of 70,864.

ΨMELILLA is a town on a rocky promontory of the Rif coast, connected with the mainland by a narrow isthmus. Melilla has been in Spanish possession since 1492. Population 58,449. Ceuta and Melilla are parts of Metropolitan Spain.

OVERSEAS TERRITORIES

Spanish settlements on the Moroccan seaboard are:—

Peñon de Alhucemas, the bay of that name includes six islands: population 366.

Peñon de la Gomera (or *Peñon de Velez*) is a fortified rocky islet about 40 miles west of Alhucemas Bay; population 450.

The *Chaffarinas* (or *Zaffarines*) are a group of three islands near the Algerian frontier, about two miles north of Cape del Agua; population 610.

The protectorate of Spanish Morocco was incorporated in Morocco on the latter's independence in 1956. Ifni, the former enclave in Morocco, was incorporated by treaty on June 30, 1969, and the Spanish Sahara came under joint Moroccan and Mauritanian control in November 1975.

SUDAN
(Al-Jamhuryat es-Sudan Al-Democratia)

CABINET
(as at May 31, 1991)

Prime Minister and Minister for Defence, Lt.-Gen. Omar Hassan Ahmad al-Bashir.

Deputy PM and Minister of Interior, Maj.-Gen. Zubir Mohammed Saleh.

Presidential Affairs, Lt.-Col. Tayib Ibrahim Mohammed Khayr.

Foreign Affairs, Ali Sahlul.

Justice and Attorney General, Hassan Ismail al-Billi.

Culture and Information, Abdullah Mohammed Ahmed.

Finance and National Economic Planning, Abdel Rahim Mahmoud Hamdi.

Agriculture and Natural Resources, Ahmad Ali al-Genief.

National Guidance and Orientation, Abdella Deng Danyal.

Local Government and Co-ordination of Provincial Affairs, Natali Yanku Ambu.

Irrigation, Yacoub Abu Shura Musa.

Energy and Mining, Abdel Munim Khujali.

Industry, Dr Taj Al Sir Mustafa.

Education, Abdul Basit Sabdarat.

Housing, Construction and Public Utilities, Osman Abdul Gadir Abdul Latif.

Higher Education, Dr Ibrahim Ahmed Omer.

Transport and Communications, Col. Salah Ed Din Karer.

Labour and Social Security, George Kinga.

Commerce, Co-operation and Supply, Faruq al-Bushra.

Health and Social Welfare, Dr Hussein Abu Salih.

EMBASSY OF THE REPUBLIC OF THE SUDAN
3 Cleveland Row, SW1A 1DD
[071-839 8080]

Ambassador Extraordinary and Plenipotentiary, His Excellency El Rasheed Abushama (1989).

Area and Population.—Sudan extends from the southern boundary of Egypt, 22° N. lat., to the northern boundary of Uganda, 3° 36′ N. lat., and reaches from the Republic of Chad about 21° 49′ E. (at 12° 45′ N.) to the north-west boundary of Ethiopia in 38° 35′ E. (at 18° N.). On the east lie the Red Sea and Ethiopia; on the south lie Kenya, Uganda and Zaire; and on the west the Central African Republic, Chad, and Libya. The greatest length from north to south is approximately 1,300 miles, and east to west 950 miles.

The White Nile enters from Uganda at Nimule as the Bahr el Jebel, and leaves Sudan at Wadi Halfa. The Blue Nile flows from Lake Tana on the Ethiopian Plateau. Its course in Sudan is nearly 500 miles long, before it joins the White Nile at Khartoum. The next confluence of importance is at Atbara where the main Nile is joined by the River Atbara. Between Khartoum and Wadi Halfa lie five of the six cataracts.

The estimated area is about 967,500 sq. miles (2,505,813 sq. km), with a population of 24,484,000 (UN estimate 1989). Arab and Nubian peoples populate the northern and central two-thirds of Sudan, Nilotic and Negro peoples the southern third. Arabic is the official language and Islam the state religion, although the Nilotics of the Bahr el Ghazal and Upper Nile Valleys are generally Animists or Christians.

Government.—The Anglo-Egyptian Condominium over Sudan which had been established in 1899 ended when the Sudan House of Representatives, on December 19, 1955, voted unanimously a declaration that Sudan was a fully independent sovereign state. A Republic was proclaimed on January 1, 1956, and

was recognized by Great Britain and Egypt, Supreme Commission being sworn in to take ove sovereignty. Sudan was under military rule fron November 1958 until 1964 when a new civilia Cabinet was appointed. Government of the countr was taken over on May 25, 1969 by a ten-ma. revolutionary council headed by Col. Gaafa Mohamed El Nimeri. In February 1972 an agreemen was signed at Addis Ababa which brought to an en nearly 17 years of insurrection and civil war in th six southern provinces, and which recognized south ern regional autonomy within a unified Sudanes State. Insurrection broke out again in 1983. In Apr 1985 the Army command assumed power after popula demonstrations, deposed Nimeri and appointed a transitional government. In May 1986 power wa transferred to a civilian regime following multi-part elections.

The third military coup since Sudan's independ ence took place on June 30, 1989 when the governmen of Sadiq al Mahdi was overthrown by Brig.-Gen Omar Hassan Ahmad al-Bashir. The Constitutio was suspended and parliament was replaced by a 15 member ruling junta who have de facto control ove a cabinet of 21 ministers.

Education.—School education is free for mos children, but not compulsory, beginning with si years primary education, followed by three year secondary education at general secondary schools the more academic higher secondary schools o vocational schools. The medium of instruction i Arabic. English is taught as the principal foreig language in all schools.

Khartoum University has ten faculties. There is branch of Cairo University in Khartoum, an Islam University at Omdurman and universities at Wa Medani and Juba.

In addition to the universities there are variou technical post-secondary institutes as well as profes sional and vocational training establishments.

Production.—The principal grain crops are dur (great millet) and wheat, the staple food of the peopl in Sudan. Sesame and ground-nuts are other import ant food crops, which also yield an exportable surplu and a promising start has been made with castor seed The principal export crop is cotton. Traditionally major producer of long-staple cotton, Sudan has i recent years grown more short and medium-stapl cotton. These grades now account for more than hal total production. Production in 1987–88 is estimate to have been around 837,000 bales. Sudan als produces the bulk of the world's supply of gum arabic Sugar is an increasingly important crop, althoug Sudan still has to achieve self sufficiency in it production. Livestock is the mainstay of the nomadi Arab tribes of the desert and the Negro tribes of th swamp and wooded grassland country in the south Production has, however, been affected by drought famine and flooding.

Sudan's agriculture production provided employ ment for over 60 per cent of the labour force an contributed 37 per cent to GDP in 1986–87. It is base on large and medium sized public sector irrigatio projects with small scale private irrigation scheme providing mostly fruit and vegetables. Mechanize and traditional agriculture is practised in areas o sufficient rainfall.

The manufacturing sector contributed less than 8 per cent to GDP in 1986–87 and provided employmen for 4 per cent of the work force. The main manufac turing enterprises are concentrated in the areas o food processing, textiles, shoes, cigarettes and batter ies.

Communications.—The railway system, ad versely affected by the civil war, has a route length of about 3,200 miles, linking Khartoum with Wad Halfa, Karima, Port Sudan, Wad Medani, Sennar, E

Damazin, Kosti, El Obeid and Nyala. Nile river services between Khartoum and Juba have been interrupted by the southern insurrection. Port Sudan is the country's main seaport. Sudan Airways fly services from Khartoum to many parts of the Sudan and to other African states, Europe and the Middle East.

FINANCE

	[1986–87]
Revenue	£S2,741·1m
Expenditure	6,100·7m
Deficit	2,527·6m
Deficit financing	2,527·6m

TRADE

	1989*
Total imports	US$14,532·0m
Total exports	651·5m
*estimates	

Trade with UK

	1989	1990
Imports from UK	£60,602,000	£63,670,000
Exports to UK	9,532,000	9,016,000

The principal exports are cotton, livestock, gum arabic and other agricultural produce. The chief imports are petroleum goods and other raw materials, machinery and equipment, transport and equipment, medicines and chemicals.

CAPITAL.—Khartoum. The town contains many mosques, a Catholic cathedral and an Anglican cathedral, and the university with extensive government buildings. The combined population of Khartoum, Khartoum North and Omdurman (excluding refugees and displaced people) · is estimated at 3,000,000.

CURRENCY.—Sudanese pound (£S) of 100 piastres and 1,000 millièmes.

FLAG.—Three horizontal stripes of red, white and black with a green triangle next to the hoist.

NATIONAL ANTHEM.—Nahnu Djundullah (We are the army of God).

NATIONAL DAY.—January 1 (Independence Day).

BRITISH EMBASSY
(PO Box 801)
Khartoum
[Khartoum 70760/7]

Ambassador Extraordinary and Plenipotentiary, His Excellency Alan John Ramsay, CMG (1990).

Counsellor, Head of Chancery and Consul General, F. X. Gallagher.
Defence and Military Attaché, vacant.

British Council Representative, A. Thomas, 14 Abu Sinn Street (PO Box 1253), Khartoum.

SURINAME
(Nieuwe Republick van Suriname)

President, Johan Kraag.
Vice President, Prime Minister, Minister for Finance, Jules Wijdenbosch.

EMBASSY OF THE REPUBLIC OF SURINAME
2 Alexander Gogelweg, The Hague, The Netherlands
[The Hague 650844]

Ambassador Extraordinary and Plenipotentiary, His Excellency Cyril Bisoendat Ramkisor (1990) (resident in The Hague).

Suriname is situated on the north coast of South America and is bounded by French Guiana in the east, Brazil in the south and Guyana in the west. It has an area of 63,037 sq. miles (163,265 sq. km), with a population (UN 1989 estimate) of 398,000.

Formerly known as Dutch Guiana, Suriname remained part of the Netherlands West Indies until November 25, 1975, when it achieved complete independence. Suriname had received autonomy in domestic affairs under the Realm Statute which took effect on December 29, 1954. The civilian government was ousted in February 1980 by the military who appointed a predominantly civilian Cabinet in 1982.

According to the Constitution approved by referendum in September 1987, a National Assembly of 51 members elects the President. The Army remains the 'vanguard of the people'. President Shankar was overthrown in a military coup, instigated by Lt.-Col. Desi Bouterse, in December 1990; Johan Kraag, a supporter of Bouterse, was installed as President. Elections to the National Assembly were held on May 25, 1991. The New Front for Democracy and Development, a coalition comprising opposition groups, won 30 of the 51 seats, but failed to gain the necessary two-thirds majority to appoint the president. At the time of going to press the situation remained unclear.

Suriname has large timber resources. Rice and sugar cane are the main crops. Bauxite is mined, and is the principal export. In 1987, GDP amounted to US$1,080 million. Principal trading partners are the Netherlands, USA and Norway.

TRADE

	1985
Imports	US$359·5m
Exports	337·3m

Trade with UK

	1989	1990
Imports from UK	£6,777,000	£10,564,000
Exports to UK	16,366,000	10,094,000

CAPITAL.—ΨParamaribo, population (1971) 110,000.

CURRENCY.—Suriname guilder of 100 cents.

FLAG.—Horizontal stripes of green, white, red, white, green, with a five-pointed yellow star in the centre.

NATIONAL DAY.—November 25.

British Ambassador (resident in Georgetown, Guyana).
British Consulate, c/o VSH United Buildings, Van't Hogerhuystraat, PO Box 1300, Paramaribo.
Honorary Consul, J. J. Healy, MBE.

SWEDEN
(Konungariket Sverige)

King of Sweden, HM Carl XVI Gustaf, *born* April 30, 1946, *succeeded* September 15, 1973, *married* June 19, 1976 Fräulein Silvia Renate Sommerlath and has *issue*, Crown Princess Victoria Ingrid Alice Désirée, Duchess of Västergötland, *born* July 14, 1977; Prince Carl Philip Edmund Bertil, Duke of Värmland, *born* May 13, 1979; Princess Madeleine Thérèse Amelie Josephine, Duchess of Hälsingland and Gästrikland, *born* June 10, 1982.

COUNCIL OF MINISTERS
(as at June 30, 1991)

Prime Minister, Ingvar Carlsson.
Justice, Laila Freivalds.
Foreign Affairs, Sten Andersson.
Agriculture, Mats Hellström.
Finance, Allan Larsson.
Housing, Ulf Lönnqvist.
Labour, Mona Sahlin.
Education and Culture, Bengt Göransson.
Industry and Energy, Rune Molin.
Health and Social Affairs, Ingela Thalén.
Immigration, Majlis Lööw.
Environment, Birgitta Dahl.
Public Sector, and Wages and Salaries, Bengt K. A. Johánsson.
Foreign Trade, Anita Gradin.
Defence, Roine Carlsson.
Health and Social Affairs, Ingela Thalén.
Communications, Georg Andersson.
Aid, Lena Hjelm-Wallén.
Youth, Equality and Ecclesiastical Affairs, Margot Wallström.
Education (Deputy Minister), Göran Persson.
Finance (Deputy Minister), Erik Åsbrink.

A general election was scheduled to be held on September 15, 1991.

SWEDISH EMBASSY
11 Montagu Place, W1H 2AL
[071-724 2101]

Ambassador Extraordinary and Plenipotentiary, His Excellency Lennart Eckerberg (1991).
Minister Plenipotentiary, P. O. Jödahl.
Counsellors, L.-O. Lundberg (*Press*); P. Bruce (*Commodities*); P. Järborg (*Consular and Administration*); R. Angeby (*Political*).
Defence and Naval Attaché, Cmdr. J. Bring.
Military and Air Attaché, Col. E. J. Hjelm.
Trade Commissioner, M. Nilsson (73 Welbeck Street, W1M 8AN.).

Area and Population.—Sweden occupies the eastern area of the Scandinavian peninsula in NW Europe and comprises 24 local government districts, (*Län*), with a total area of 173,732 sq. miles (449,964 sq. km), and population of 8,493,000 (1989 UN estimate). In 1986 the birth rate was 12·2 per 1,000 inhabitants, the death rate 11·1 per 1,000 inhabitants and infant mortality rate was 6·8 per 1,000 live births.

Government.—Sweden is a constitutional monarchy, with the monarch retaining purely ceremonial functions as Head of State. Under the Act of Succession of June 6, 1809 (with amendments) the throne is hereditary in the House of Bernadotte. (A 1979 amendment vested the succession in the monarch's eldest child, irrespective of sex.) Jean-Baptiste Jules Bernadotte, Prince of Ponte Corvo, a Marshal of France, was invited to accept the title of Crown Prince, with succession to the throne. He succeeded Charles XIII in 1818.

There is a unicameral Diet (*Riksdag*) of 349 members elected by universal suffrage for three years. The Council of Ministers (*Statsråd*) is responsible to the *Riksdag*. In the General Election held in September 1988, the following seats were won: Social Democrats 156; Moderates 66; Liberals 44; Centre 42; Communists 21; Green Party 20.

On July 1, 1991 Sweden applied to join the European Community.

Production and Industry.—The country's industrial prosperity is based on an abundance of natural resources in the form of forests, mineral deposits and water power. The forests are extensive, covering about half the total land surface, and sustain flourishing timber, pulp and paper milling industries. The mineral resources include iron ore, lead, zinc, sulphur, granite, marble, precious and heavy metals (the latter not exploited) and extensive deposits of low grade uranium ore. Industries based on mining principally iron and steel, aluminium and copper are important but it is the general engineering industry that provides the basis of Sweden's exports. Growth areas are largely in the specialized machinery and systems and chemical industries. The relative importance of agriculture has declined and in 1988 only 4 per cent of the population was engaged in farming.

Apart from water power Sweden has no significant indigenous resources of conventional hydrocarbon fuels and relies to a high degree upon imported oil. Much of Sweden's electricity is generated by nuclear power but as a result of a referendum in 1980 the nuclear programme is to be discontinued by 2010. Small supplies of natural gas are imported from Denmark into southern Sweden, with the pipeline being extended to Gothenburg.

Communications.—The total length of Swedish railroads is 11,745 km. The road network is over 400,000 km in length.

The mercantile marine amounted on December 31, 1985 to 2,619,625 gross tonnage. The Board of Civil Aviation under the control of the Ministry of Communications handles civil aviation matters. Regular domestic air traffic is maintained by the Scandinavian Airlines System and by Linjeflyg. Regular European and inter-continental air traffic is maintained by the Scandinavian Airlines System.

Defence.—Based on the policy of non-alignment in peace leading to neutrality in war Sweden maintains a 'total defence' intended to make an attack on her costly. Total defence includes peace time organizations for civil, economic and psychological defence as well as universal conscription of men aged 18–47. Some 50,000 national servicemen are called up for 5–15 months training each year and most are recalled every fourth year for refresher training. On mobilization the Army strength total 4 armoured brigades, 1 mechanized brigade and 1 infantry and winter warfare brigades. The Navy has 12 submarines, 30 fast attack craft, a number of mine craft and auxiliaries and 5 coast artillery units. The Air Force has modern supersonic aircraft of Swedish manufacture forming a standing force of 200 air defence, 100 attack and 55 reconnaissance with support aircraft and a modern air defence radar system. Facilities exist for rapid dispersal from main bases in war.

Religion.—The state religion is Lutheran Protestant, to which over 95 per cent of the people officially adhere.

Language and Literature.—Swedish belongs with Danish and Norwegian, to the North Germanic language group. Swedish literature dates back to King Magnus Eriksson, who codified the old Swedish provincial laws in 1350. With his translation of the Bible, Olaus Petri (1493–1552) formed the basis for the modern Swedish language. Literature flourished during the reign of Gustavus III, who founded the Swedish Academy in 1786. Notable Swedish writers include Almquist (1795–1866), Strindberg (1849–1912) and Lagerlöf (1858–1940), Nobel Prize Winner in 1909.

Contemporary authors include Lagerquist (1891–1974), Nobel Laureate in 1951, Martinson (1904–78) and Johnson (1900–76), Nobel Laureates jointly in 1974. The Swedish scientist Alfred Nobel (1833–96) founded the Nobel Prizes for literature, science and peace.

Education.—Tuition within the state system, which is maintained by the state and by local taxation, is free. It provides 9 years' compulsory schooling from the age of 7 to 16 in the comprehensive elementary schools; further education of 2–4 years' duration in the upper secondary schools; a unified higher education system administered in six regional areas containing one of the universities—Uppsala (founded 1477); Lund (1668); Stockholm (1878); Gothenburg (1887); Umeå (1963) and Linköping (1967). At present there are 33 institutions of higher education including three technical universities in Stockholm, Gothenburg and Luleå, and the Karolinska Institute in Stockholm, which specializes in medicine and dentistry.

FINANCE

	1990–91	1991–92
	Kronor	
Revenue	407,900m	454,928m
Expenditure	408,200m	455,526m

TRADE

	1989	1990
	Kronor	
Imports	315,061·0m	322,854m
Exports	332,144·9m	339,772m

Trade with UK

	1989	1990
Imports from UK	£2,350,122,000	£2,712,775,000
Exports to UK	3,747,600,000	3,594,547,000

Sweden's main imports from Britain, accounting for 10 per cent of total imports in 1990, are engineering products, semi-manufactures and chemical products. Britain's main imports from Sweden are paper and board, road vehicles, machinery, wood, steel and pulp.

CAPITAL.—ΨStockholm. Population (1985): City 659,030; Greater Stockholm, 1,435,474; ΨGothenburg (Göteborg) (425,495); ΨMalmö (229,936); Uppsala (154,859).

CURRENCY.—Swedish krona of 100 øre.

FLAG.—Yellow cross on a blue ground.

NATIONAL ANTHEM.—Du Gamla, Du Fria (Thou ancient, thou freeborn).

NATIONAL DAY.—June 6 (Day of the Swedish Flag).

BRITISH EMBASSY
Skarpögatan 6–8, 115 27 Stockholm
[Stockholm 6670140]

Ambassador Extraordinary and Plenipotentiary, His Excellency R. L. B. Cormack, CMG (1991).
British Council Representative, Dr S. M. Lewis.

There are British Consular Offices at *Stockholm* and *Gothenburg*, and Honorary Consuls at *Gävle, Gothenburg* and *Malmö*.

BRITISH-SWEDISH CHAMBER OF COMMERCE, Grevgatan 34, 11453 Stockholm.

SWITZERLAND
(Schweizerische Eidgenossenschaft—
Confédération Suisse—Confederazione
Svizzera.)

FEDERAL COUNCIL

President of the Swiss Confederation (1991) *and Head of Home Affairs*, Flavio Cotti.

Vice President (1991) *and Head of Foreign Affairs*, René Felber.
Military, Kaspar Villiger.
Transport, Energy and Communications, Adolf Ogi.
Economic Affairs, Jean-Pascal Delamuraz.
Finance, Otto Stich.
Justice and Police, Arnold Koller.

EMBASSY OF SWITZERLAND
16–18 Montagu Place, W1H 2BQ
[071–723 0701]

Ambassador Extraordinary and Plenipotentiary, His Excellency Franz E. Muheim (1989).
Minister, C. M. W. Faessler.
Counsellor, J. Bucher (*Economic and Financial*).
Defence, Military, Naval and Air Attaché, Maj.-Gen. G. de Loës.
Consul General and Head of Administration, E. Jaun.

There is a Swiss Consulate-General in *Manchester*.

Area and Population.—Switzerland, the Helvetia of the Romans, is a federal republic of central Europe, situated between 45° 50′–47° 48′ N. lat. and 5° 58′–10° 3′ E. long. It is composed of 23 Cantons, three subdivided, making 26 in all, and comprises a total area of 15,943 sq. miles (41,293 sq. km), with a population (December 31, 1989) of 6,673,900. In 1989 there were 81,180 live births, 60,882 deaths and 45,066 marriages. Of the total population in 1980, 44·3 per cent was Protestant, 47·6 per cent Roman Catholic, 3·2 per cent other religions and 4·9 per cent without religion.

Physical Features.—Switzerland is the most mountainous country in Europe. The Alps, covered with perennial snow and from 5,000 to 15,217 feet in height, occupy its southern and eastern frontiers, and the chief part of its interior; the Jura mountains rise in the north-west. The Alps occupy 61 per cent, and the Jura mountains 12 per cent of the country. The Alps are a crescent-shaped mountain system situated in France, Italy, Switzerland, Bavaria and Austria, covering an area of 80,000 square miles from the Mediterranean to the Danube (600 miles). The highest peak, Mont Blanc, Pennine Alps (15,782 ft.) is partly in France and Italy; Monte Rosa (15,217 ft.) and Matterhorn (14,780 ft.) are partly in Switzerland and partly in Italy. The highest wholly Swiss peaks are Dufourspitze (15,203 ft.), Finsteraarhorn (14,026), Aletschhorn (13,711), Jungfrau (13,671), Mönch (13,456), Eiger (13,040), Schreckhorn (13,385), and Wetterhorn (12,150) in the Bernese Alps, and Dom (14,918), Weisshorn (14,803) and Breithorn (13,685).

The Swiss lakes are famous for their beauty and include Lakes Maggiore, Zürich, Lucerne, Neuchâtel, Geneva, Constance, Thun, Zug, Lugano, Brienz and the Walensee. There are also many artificial lakes.

Government.—The legislative power is vested in a Parliament consisting of two Chambers, a National Council (*Nationalrat*) of 200 members, and a States Council (*Ständerat*) of 46 members; both Chambers united are called the Federal Assembly. Members of the National Council are elected for four years, elections taking place in October. The executive power is in the hands of a Federal Council (*Bundesrat*) of seven members, elected for four years by the Federal Assembly and presided over by the President of the Confederation. Each year the Federal Assembly elects from the Federal Council the President and the Vice-President. Not more than one of the same canton may be elected member of the Federal Council; on the other hand, there is a tradition that Italian and French-speaking areas should between them be represented on the Federal Council by at least two members.

Defence.—All Swiss males must undertake military service in the Army or the Air Force, which is part of the Army. Swiss Army equipment includes some British items, such as Centurion tanks, Bloodhound missiles, Vampire and Hunter aircraft, the Medium Girder Bridge, the Rapier guided missile, the Hawk aircraft plus 3 watchman radars and the IMFS trunk communication system.

Production and Industry.—Agriculture is followed chiefly in the valleys and all over the Mittelland, where cereals, flax, hemp, and tobacco are produced, and nearly all temperate zone fruits and vegetables as well as grapes are grown. Dairying and stock-raising are the principal industries, about 3,000,000 acres being under grass for hay and 2,000,000 acres pasturage. The forests cover about one-quarter of the whole surface. The chief manufacturing industries comprise engineering and electrical engineering, metal-working, chemicals and pharmaceuticals, textiles, watchmaking, woodworking, foodstuffs and footwear. Banking, insurance and tourism are major industries.

Communications.—There were in 1988 5,020 km of railway tracks (Swiss Federal Railways, 2,990 km; Swiss privately owned railways 2,030 km). At the end of 1989 the number of telephones amounted to 3,785,000 and the network was fully automatic throughout the country. At the same time there were 2,629,200 licensed radio receivers and 2,385,300 television receivers.

At the end of 1989 the total length of motorways was 1,495 km. The number of motor vehicles licensed in 1989 was 3,809,000.

A merchant marine, established in 1941, consisted at June 1990 of 20 vessels with a total gross tonnage of 287,487 tonnes. In 1989, goods handled at Basle Rhine ports amounted to 8,845,162 tonnes. In 1987, 163 lake and river vessels (excluding the Rhine) transported 10,608,200 passengers and 500 tonnes of freight. Swiss airlines have a network covering 347,009 km (1989) and in 1989 carried 8,507,511 passengers. Swissair, the state airline, flies to and from the airports at Zürich, Geneva and Basle.

Education.—Education is controlled by cantonal and communal authorities: there is no central organization. Primary education is free and compulsory. School age varies, generally 7 to 14. Secondary education, age 12–15 for boys and girls. Schools are numerous and well-attended, and there are many private institutions. Special schools make a feature of commercial and technical instruction. Universities are Basle (founded 1460), Berne (1834), Fribourg (1889), Geneva (1873), Lausanne (1890), Zürich (1832), and Neuchâtel (1909), and the technical universities of Lausanne and Zürich and the commercial university of St Gall.

Language and Literature.—There are four official languages: French, German, Italian and Romansch. German is the dominating language in 19 of the 26 cantons; French in Fribourg, Jura, Geneva, Neuchâtel, Valais and Vaud; Italian in Ticino, and Romansch in parts of the Grisons.

Many modern authors, alike in the German school and in the Suisse Romande, have achieved international fame. Karl Spitteler (1845–1924) and Hermann Hesse (1877–1962) were awarded the Nobel Prize for Literature, the former in 1919, the latter in 1946.

FINANCE

	1989*	1990
Revenue	SFr28,031m	SFr30,324m
Expenditure	27,555m	29,850m
*estimate		

TRADE

The principal imports are machinery, electrical and electronic equipment, textiles, motor vehicles, non-ferrous metals, chemical elements, clothing, food, medicinal and pharmaceutical products. The principal exports are machinery, chemical elements, non-

ferrous metals, watches, electrical and electronic equipment, textiles, dyeing, tanning and colouring equipment. Switzerland is a member of EFTA.

	1988	1989
Total Imports	SFr82,398,669m	SFr95,209m
Total Exports	74,063,586	84,268m

Trade with UK†

	1989	1990
Imports from UK	£2,245,354,000	£2,358,528,000
Exports to UK	4,125,731,000	4,252,783,000
†(Including Liechtenstein)		

CAPITAL.—Berne, population (1989) 134,400 (city). Other large towns are (1989) Zürich (342,900), Basl (169,600), Geneva (165,400), Lausanne (122,600), Win terthur (85,200), St Gallen (73,200), Lucerne (59,100).
CURRENCY.—Swiss franc of 100 centimes or rappen
FLAG.—Red, with white cross.
NATIONAL ANTHEM.—Trittst im Morgenrot Dahe (Radiant in the morning sky).
NATIONAL DAY.—August 1.

BRITISH EMBASSY
Thunstrasse 50, 3000 Berne 15
[Berne 445021]

Ambassador Extraordinary and Plenipotentiary, His Excellency Christopher William Long, CMG (1988).
Counsellors, C. C. Bright; C. W. Wainwright.
First Secretary, P. Cole.
Second Secretaries, Dr J. Mitchiner; P. A. Chatt.
Defence, Naval and Military Attaché, Lt.-Col. W. R Thatcher.
Air Attaché, Wing. Cdr. H. W. Hughes.
Attaché, P. C. Albrecht (*Commercial*).

BRITISH CONSULAR OFFICES

There is a Consular Section at the Embassy in Berne; Consulates-General at *Zürich* and *Geneva* and Consular offices at *Lugano* and *Montreux*. The Directorate of British Export Promotion in Switzerland is in the Consulate-General Office in *Zürich*.

BRITISH-SWISS CHAMBER OF COMMERCE, Freiestrasse 155, 8032 Zürich.
SWISS-BRITISH SOCIETIES:
  Berne.—*President*, Dr H. Beriger.
  Zürich.—*President*, J.-P. Müller.
  Basle.—*President*, Dr C. Grey.

SYRIA
(Al-Jamhouriya Al-Arabia as-Souriya)

President, Lt.-Gen. Hafez el Assad, *b.* 1930, *assumed office* March 14, 1971, *re-elected*, Feb. 1978, March 13, 1985.
Vice-Presidents, Abdul Halim Khaddam, Rifaat Al Assad, Zuhair Mashariqa.

MINISTERS
(as at May 31, 1991)

Prime Minister, Mahmoud Al Zubi.
Deputy PM and Minister for Defence, Gen. Mustafa Tlass.
Deputy PM for Public Services, Mahmoud Qaddur.
Deputy PM for Economic Affairs, Dr Salim Yassin.
Education, Ghassan Halabi.
Higher Education, Kamal Sharaf.
Interior, Mohammad Harbah.
Transport, Yusuf al-Ahmed.
Information, Mohammad Salman.
Local Administration, Ahmed Diab.
Supply and Internal Trade, Hassan Saqqa.
Economy and Foreign Trade, Mohammad al-Imadi.
Culture, Najah al-Attar.
Foreign Affairs, Farooq ash-Shar'.
Tourism, Adnan Quli.
Health, Iyad al-Shatti.
Waqfs (Religious Endowments), Abdel-Majid Tarabulsi.
Irrigation, Abd ar-Rahman Madani.
Electricity, Kamil al-Baba.
Oil and Mineral Resources, Antonios Habib.
Construction, Marwan Farra.
Housing and Utilities, Mohammad Nur Antabi.
Agriculture and Agrarian Reform, Mohammad Ghabbash.
Finance, Khaled al-Mahayni.
Industry, Antoine Jubran.
Communications, Murad Quwatli.
Justice, Khalid Ansari.
Presidential Affairs, Wahib Fadil.
Labour and Social Affairs, Haydar Buzu.

EMBASSY OF THE SYRIAN ARAB REPUBLIC
8 Belgrave Square, SW1X 8PH
[071–245 9012]

Ambassador Extraordinary and Plenipotentiary, His Excellency Mohammed al Khoder.

Area and Population.—Syria is in the Levant, covering a portion of the former Ottoman Empire. Bounded by the Mediterranean and Lebanon on the W., Israel and Jordan on the SW, Iraq on the E. and Turkey on the N., it has an estimated area of 71,498 sq. miles (185,180 sq. km), and a population (UN 1989 estimate) of 11,719,000, most of whom are Arabic-speaking and Muslim. The Orontes flows northwards from the Lebanon range across the northern boundary to Antakya (Antioch, Turkey). The Euphrates crosses the northern boundary near Jerablus and flows through north-eastern Syria to the boundary of Iraq.

Archaeology, etc.—The region is rich in historical remains. Damascus (Dimishq ash-Sham) is said to be the oldest continuously inhabited city in the world (although Aleppo disputes this claim), having existed as a city for over 4,000 years. It is situated on the river Barada, in an oasis at the eastern foot of the Anti-Lebanon, and at the edge of the wide sandy desert which stretches to the Euphrates. The city contains the Omayed Mosque, the Tomb of Saladin, and the 'street which is called Straight' (Acts 9:11), while to the north-east is the Roman outpost of Dmeir and further east is Palmyra.

On the Mediterranean coast at Amrit are ruins of the Phoenician town of Marath, where the well has

been found and is being excavated and also ruins of Crusaders' fortresses at Markab, Sahyoun, and Krak des Chevaliers. At Tartous (also on the coast) the cathedral of Our Lady of Syria, built by the Knights Templars in the 12th and 13th centuries has been restored as a museum. One of the oldest alphabets in the world has been discovered at Ugarit (Ras Shamra), a Phoenician village near the port of Latakia.

Hittite cities dating from 2000 to 1500 BC, have recently been explored on the west bank of the Euphrates at Jerablus and Kadesh.

Government.—Syria, which had been under French mandate since the 1914–18 war, became an independent republic during the 1939–45 war. The first independently elected Parliament met on August 17, 1943, but foreign troops were in part occupation until April 1946. Syria remained an independent republic until February 1958, when it became part of the United Arab Republic. It seceded from the United Arab Republic on September 28, 1961.

A new Constitution was promulgated in March 1973: this declared that Syria is a 'democratic, popular socialist State', and that the Arab Socialist Renaissance (Ba'ath) Party, which has been the ruling party since 1963, is 'the leading party in the State and society'. Elections to the expanded 250-seat Peoples' Council in May 1990 resulted in a large majority for the Ba'ath Party, which won 134 seats; its National Progressive Front allies (Arab Socialist Union, Socialist Unionist Movement, Arab Socialist Party, Syrian Communist Party) together won 32 seats. The Independents won 84.

Production and Industry.—Agriculture is the principal source of production; wheat and barley are the main cereal crops, but the cotton crop is the highest in value. Tobacco is grown in the maritime plain in Sahel, the Sahyoun and the Djebleh district of Latakia. Large new areas are coming under irrigation and cultivation in the north-east of the country as a result of the Thawra dam. Skins and hides, leather goods, wool and silk, textiles, cement, vegetable oil, glass, soap, sugar, plastics and copper and brass utensils are produced. There are an increasing number of light assembly plants as Syria's industrialization programme develops. Oil has been found at Karachuk and other parts in the north-eastern corner of the country and production of high quality reserves is proceeding in the region of Deir ez Zor. Syria produces nearly 400,000 barrels of oil per day at present. A pipeline has been built to the Mediterranean port of Banias, via Homs. Two oil refineries are in production at Homs and Banias. Syria also has deposits of phosphate and rock salt, and produces asphalt.

Language and Literature.—Arabic is the principal language, but Kurdish, Turkish and Armenian are spoken among significant minorities and a few villages still speak Aramaic, the language spoken by Christ and the Apostles. There are three daily newspapers and several periodicals in Arabic published in Damascus, and also a daily newspaper in English. English has taken over from French as the main foreign language, especially among the young.

Education.—Education in Syria is under state control and, although a few of the schools are privately owned, they all follow a common system and syllabus. Elementary education is free at state schools, and is compulsory from the age of seven. Secondary education is not compulsory and is free only at the state schools. Because of the shortage of places, entry to these state schools is competitive. Damascus University, founded in 1924, has nine faculties and a Higher Teachers' Training College. The number of students has risen to over 60,000. There are also about 20,000 students at Aleppo University (founded 1961), over 10,000 at Tishrin University, Latakia (founded 1975) and 6,000 at

Ba'ath University, Homs. Approximately 10 per cent of all students receive scholarships, and at the present time Palestinian refugees are admitted free. The rest pay fees.

Communications.—Although railway lines run from Damascus to both Beirut and Amman, train services go only to Amman, as much of the Lebanese line has been dismantled. A track has been opened connecting Homs with Damascus. A track links Homs, Hamah, Aleppo, Deir ez Zor and Qamishliye to the Iraq frontier. Branch lines connect the ports of Tartous and Latakia to the system and another line runs from Aleppo down Euphrates valley to Deir ez Zor and thence north to Qamishliye, with a branch going to the Euphrates Dam. All the principal towns in the country are connected by roads which vary from modern dual carriageways to narrow country lanes. An internal air service operates between all major towns. The main international airport is at Damascus and there are also flights to Eastern Europe, Turkey, Greece and Armenia from Aleppo.

Trade.—The principal imports are foodstuffs (fruit, vegetables, cereals, meat and dairy products, tea, coffee and sugar), mineral and petroleum products, yarn and textiles, iron and steel manufactures, machinery, chemicals, pharmaceuticals, fertilizers and timber. Exports include raw cotton, oil, cereals, fruit, phosphates, cement, livestock and dairy products, other foodstuffs, textiles and raw wool.

Trade with UK

	1989	1990
Imports from UK	£38,537,000	£38,245,000
Exports to UK	65,256,000	85,874,000

Capital.—Damascus, population (estimated) 1,168,000. Other important towns are Aleppo, Homs and Hama, and the principal port is ΨLatakia.

Currency.—Syrian pound (S£) of 100 piastres.

Flag.—Red over white over black horizontal bands, with two green stars on central white band.

National Day.—April 17.

British Embassy

Quartier Malki, 11 rue Mohammad Kurd Ali,
Imm. Kotob, Damascus
[Damascus 712561]

Ambassador Extraordinary and Plenipotentiary, His Excellency Andrew F. Green, cmg.

THAILAND
(Prathes Thai)

King, HM Bhumibol Adulyadej, *born* 1927; *succeeded his brother* June 9, 1946; *married* Princess Sirikit Kitiyakara, April 28, 1950; *crowned* May 5, 1950; and has *issue*, Princess Ubolratana, *born* April 6, 1951; Crown Prince Vajiralongkorn, *born* July 28, 1952; Princess Sirindhorn, *born* April 2, 1955; Princess Chulabhorn *born* July 4, 1957.

Cabinet
(as at July 1991)

Prime Minister, Anand Panyarachun.
Deputy Prime Ministers, Dr Snoh Unakul; Meechai Ruchuphan; Gen. Pow Sarasin.
Ministers in the Office of the PM, Kasem Kasemsri; Phaichitr Uathavikul; Meechai Viravaidya; Khu-nying Saisuree Chutikul.
Defence, Adm. Prapat Krisanachan.
Finance, Suthee Singhasaneh.
Interior, Gen. Issarapong Noonpackdee.
Foreign Affairs, Arsa Sarasin.

Agriculture and Co-operatives, Anat Arbhabhirama.
Transport and Communications, Nukul Prachuab-moh.
Commerce, Amaret Sila-On.
Industry, Sippanondha Ketudat.
Education, Dr Kaw Sawasdipanicha.
Public Health, Dr Pairote Ningsanonda.
Science, Technology and Energy, Dr Sanga Sabhasri.
Justice, Prapasna Uaychai.
University Affairs, Dr Kasem Suwanagul.

Royal Thai Embassy in London
29–30 Queen's Gate, SW7 5JB
[071–589 0173]

Ambassador Extraordinary and Plenipotentiary, His Excellency Sudhee Prasasvinitchai (1986).

Area and Population.—The Kingdom of Thailand, formerly known as Siam, has an area of 198,457 sq. miles (514,000 sq. km), with a population (1989) of 55,888,393. The population growth rate averages 2·4 per cent per year. Thailand has a common boundary with Malaysia in the south, is bounded on the west by Myanmar (Burma) and on the north-east and east by Laos and Cambodia. Although there is no common boundary between Thailand and China, the Chinese province of Yunnan is separated from the Thai northern border only by a narrow stretch of Burmese and Laotian territory.

Thailand is divided geographically into four regions: central, north-eastern, northern and southern. The capital, Bangkok, is situated in the south of the central plain area. To the north-east there is a plateau area and to the north-west mountains. The south of Thailand consists of a narrow mountainous peninsula. The principal rivers are the Chao Phraya in the central plains, and the Mekong on the northern and north-eastern borders.

Language and Religion.—Thai is basically a monosyllabic, tonal language, a branch of the Indo-Chinese linguistic family, but its vocabulary has been strongly influenced by Sanskrit and Pali. It is written in an alphabetic script derived from ancient Indian scripts. The principal religion is Buddhism. In 1988 94·37 per cent of the population were Buddhists, 3·95 per cent were Muslims, 0·53 per cent Christians and 1·15 per cent other religions.

Government.—Thailand became a Constitutional Monarchy in 1932. The Constitution promulgated in December 1978 provides for a National Assembly consisting of a 261-member Senate appointed by the monarch and a 347-member House of Representatives elected by universal adult suffrage for a term of four years.

The civilian government of Gen. Chatichai Choon-havan was overthrown by a military coup on February 23, 1991. On March 6, 1991 the King approved an interim government, led by Anand Panyarachun; the interim constitution stipulates that elections must be held within one year.

Education.—Primary education is compulsory and free and secondary education in government schools is free. In 1988 there were 37,696 schools and training colleges, with a total of 10,699,132 pupils and 562,028 teachers. Private universities and colleges are playing an increasing role in higher education. In 1984 the government agreed to upgrade four private colleges to universities. Out of 43 universities and other similar higher institutes of learning, 21 are private and attended by some 53,708 students. In 1986 their total enrolment was 171,438 students.

Agriculture and Industry.—The agricultural sector provides just under half the national income and employs 67·5 per cent of the labour force, which in 1985 was estimated at 26·8 million. Rice remains the most important crop, accounting for 60 per cent of the area planted. After rice the main crops are sugar, maize, rubber, tobacco, kenaf and jute. In recent years the production of livestock and poultry, especially pigs and chickens for export, has gained importance. There is a large fishing industry with more than 20,000 vessels registered. Fish farming is popular in many inland areas. A ban on hardwood export has resulted in the decline of the forestry industry.

The discovery of onshore oil and offshore gas in the late 1970s ushered in a new economic era. Crude oil production which began in 1983 stood at around 1·85 million tonnes in 1989, or about 15 per cent of the country's needs. In 1988, 212,641 million cubic feet of natural gas was produced. The predicted surplus of natural gas has led the Government to designate an area on the east coast as the future centre of the petrochemical industry. Another energy resource becoming more important is lignite which is found mainly in the north and is being used increasingly for electricity production.

Mineral resources are mainly tin, tungsten, lead, antimony and iron. Among these, tin is the most important. In addition, about 60,000 tons of zinc ingots a year are expected to be produced by a zinc refinery which was opened in early 1984.

Industry is divided into two main categories: service and manufacturing. Since 1982 tourism has replaced rice as the country's top foreign exchange earner. There were 4,231,000 overseas visitors in 1988, generating an estimated 31,768 million baht for the country. The banking system is large and contributes much to the economy, especially employment. There are over 1,800 bank branches in the country employing some 72,000 workers.

Since 1960 the government has actively promoted industrial investments by means of tax relief and other incentives to local and foreign investors; in 1985, 74·6 per cent of this investment was in Thai projects. Most of the industries established under this scheme in early years were import-substituting. However, there has been an increasing shift to export-oriented industries, taking advantages of low-wage labour and available domestic resources. Manufacturing now accounts for about 21·8 per cent of the national income. Crops contribute 12·1 per cent of GDP.

Communications.—The importance of rivers and canals as the traditional mode of transportation has been replaced by highways and roads. The existing road and highway network, totalling 34,701 kilometres in 1984, reaches all parts of the country. Most of the smaller towns and bigger villages are now served by paved roads.

Navigable waterways have a length of about 1,100 km in the dry season and 1,600 km in the wet season. About 3,825 km of state-owned railways were open to traffic in 1984. Main lines run from Bangkok to Aranya Prathet on the Cambodian border via Korat to Ubon and to Nong Khai, the ferry terminal on the River Mekong opposite Vientiane, capital of Laos; to Chiang Mai and to Hat Yai, whence lines go down the eastern and western sides of the Malay peninsula, via Sungei Galok and Penang respectively, to Singapore. A new line to Sattahip on the east coast is being constructed.

Bangkok is an important international air centre and has direct flights to most of the world's major cities. The airports at Chiang Mai, Phuket and Hat Yai also receive international flights. Most major provincial towns have airports. Thai International and Thai Airways merged in April 1988. Now named THAI, the airline is state-owned.

Thailand has an extensive network of telecommunications services, and the telephone service though still poor is being improved. All major cities and towns are linked by direct long-distance calls. Thailand has two mobile telephone networks, AMPS (urban), and NMT (rural) presently covering only the central area but expanding rapidly.

There are two important ports in the country. Bangkok, which is a river port, can serve vessels up to 27 ft. draught. The deep-sea port at Sattahip caters for larger vessels. Phuket and Songkhla deep water ports have already been completed and are the first to be managed privately under a ten-year concession. Construction of Laem Chabang deep water port started in 1988.

TRADE

Thailand's main exports are rice, tapioca and tapioca products, garments, rubber, integrated circuit boards, precious stones, pearls and other ornaments, maize, canned sea food, fabrics, sugar and tin. Main imports are crude oil, chemicals and pharmaceuticals, electrical and non-electrical machinery and spare parts, industrial machinery, iron and steel, diesel oil and other fuel oil, vehicle and transport equipment.

	1989	1990
	Bhat	
Total imports	650·7bn	829·0bn
Total exports	509·9bn	590·0bn

Trade with UK

	1989	1990
Imports from UK	£427,484,000	£416,648,000
Exports to UK	443,144,000	484,276,000

CAPITAL.—ΨBangkok, at the mouth of the River Chao Phraya, population (1985) 5,400,000. Other centres are Chiang Mai, Phitsanuloke, Chon Buri, Korat, Khon Kaen, Surat Thani, Hat Yai and ΨPhuket but none approaches Bangkok in size or importance.

CURRENCY.—Baht of 100 satang.

FLAG.—Five horizontal bands, red, white, dark blue, white, red (the blue band twice the width of the others).

NATIONAL ANTHEM.—Sanrasern Phra Barami.

NATIONAL DAY.—December 5 (The King's Birthday).

BRITISH EMBASSY
Wireless Road, Bangkok 10330
[Bangkok 253 0191]

Ambassador Extraordinary and Plenipotentiary, His Excellency Michael Ramsay Melhuish, CMG (1989).

British Council Representative, Dr P. Moss, 428 Rama 1 Road, Siam Square Soi, Pathumwan, Bangkok 10330.

BRITISH CHAMBER OF COMMERCE,
BP Building 18th Floor, Unit 1810
54 Asoke Road (Sukhumvit 21) Bangkok 10110

TOGO
(République Togolaise)

President, Gen. Gnassingbé Eyadéma, *born* 1937, *assumed office*, April 14, 1967; *re-elected for seven-year term*, Dec. 23, 1986.

CABINET
(as at May 1991)

Defence, Gen. Yao Mawulikplimi Amegi.
Interior and Security, Yao Komlanvi.
Justice, Yagninim Bitoktipou.
Planning and Mines, Barry Moussa Barque.
Rural Development, Koudjolou Dogoh.

Minister Delegate to the Presidency (Information),
Gbegnon Amegboh.
Equipment, Posts and Telecommunications, Souley-
mane Galo.
National Education and Scientific Research, Yao
Amelavi Amela.
Public Health, Aissah Agbetra.
Youth, Sports and Culture, Mensah Agbeyomé Kodjo.
Foreign Affairs and Co-operation, Yaovi Adodo.
Industry and State Enterprises, Koffi Djondo.
Technical Instruction and Professional Training,
Koffi Edoh.
Economy and Finance, Komla Alipui.
Labour and Civil Service, Dahuku Pere.
Environment and Tourism, Inoussa Bouraima.
Information, Kwaovi Benyi Johnson.
Trade and Transport, Komlanvi Kloutse.

EMBASSY OF TOGO
30 Sloane Street, SW1X 9NE.

The Embassy of Togo is scheduled to close by
December 1991.

The Republic is situated in West Africa between
0°–2° W. and 6°–11° N., with a coastline 35 miles long
on the Gulf of Guinea, and extends northward inland
for 350 miles. It is flanked on the west by Ghana, on
the north by Burkina and in the east by Benin. It
has an area of 21,925 sq. miles (56,785 sq. km), and a
population (UN estimate 1989) of 3,349,000, including
people of several African races. The official language
is French; Ewe is spoken by about 47 per cent.

The first President of Togo, Sylvanus Olympio,
assassinated on January 13, 1963, was succeeded by
Nicolas Grunitzky, who was himself overthrown by
an army coup d'état on January 13, 1967. On April
14, 1967, the Commander-in-Chief of the Togolese
army, Lt. Col. (later promoted General) Eyadéma
named himself President.

President Eyadema has come under increasing
popular pressure to introduce reforms. In October
1990 the Rassemblement du peuple togolais (RPT),
the sole legal party, approved plans for a new
constitutional conference after pro-democracy riots.
Bloody riots again broke out in March 1991 in protest
at the slow pace of reform, and in April the
government was forced to concede a political amnesty, the introduction of a multi-party constitution
and a national conference. In August 1991 the
national conference stripped President Eyadema of
all powers, banned the RPT and elected Kokou
Koffigoh as Prime Minister of an interim government.
At the time of going to press (August), the political
situation was unclear.

Production and Trade.—Although the economy
of Togo remains largely agricultural, exports of
phosphates have superseded agricultural products as
the main source of export earnings. Other exports
include palm kernels, copra and manioc. The production of phosphates entirely for export was taken over
completely by the government in February 1974.

Trade with UK
	1989	1990
Imports from UK	£15,009,000	£13,038,000
Exports to UK	2,022,000	3,545,000

CAPITAL.—ΨLomé, population (1983) 366,476.
CURRENCY.—Franc CFA of 100 centimes.
FLAG.—Five alternating green and yellow horizon-
tal stripes; a quarter in red at top next staff bearing
a white star.
NATIONAL DAY.—January 13 (National Liberation
Day).

BRITISH EMBASSY
British Ambassador (resident in Accra, Ghana).

TUNISIA
(Al-Djoumhouria Attunusia)

President, Zine el-Abidine Ben Ali *took office* Nov. 7,
1987, *re-elected* April 2, 1989.

CABINET
(as at February 20, 1991)

Prime Minister, Hamed Karoui.
Justice, Abderrahim Zouari.
Director of Presidential Office, Mohamed el Jeri.
Foreign Affairs, Habib ben Yahia.
Defence, Habib Boulares.
Interior, Abdallah Kallel.
Economy, Sadok Rabah.
Finance, Mohamed Ghannouchi.
Planning and Regional Development, Mustapha
Nabli.
Agriculture, Mouldi Zouaoui.
Public Estates, Mustapha Bouaziz.
Equipment and Housing, Ahmed Friaa.
Transport, Faouzi Belkahia.
Tourism and Handicrafts, Mohamed Jegham.
Communications, Habib Lazreg.
Education and Science, Mohamed Charfi.
Culture, Moncer Rouissi.
Health, Daly Jazy.
Social Affairs, Ahmed Smaoui.
Professional Training and Employment, Taoufik
Cheikrouhou.
Youth and Childhood Welfare, Mohamed Saad.
Secretary General of the Government, Mohamed Habib
Hadj Said.

TUNISIAN EMBASSY
29 Prince's Gate, SW7 1QG
[071–584 8117]

Ambassador Extraordinary and Plenipotentiary, His
Excellency Dr Abdelaziz Hamzaoui (1991).

Area and Population.—Tunisia lies between
Algeria and Libya and extends southwards to the
Sahara Desert, with a total area of 164,150 sq. km,
and a population (UN estimate 1989) of 7,990,000.

Government.—A French Protectorate from 1881
to 1956, Tunisia became an independent sovereign
state with the signing on March 20, 1956 of an
agreement whereby France recognized Tunisia's
independence and right to conduct its own foreign
policy and to form an army.

Following a first general election held on March
25, 1956, a Constituent Assembly met for the first
time on April 8. On July 25, 1957 the Constituent
Assembly abolished the monarchy and elected M.
Bourguiba first President of the Republic. On June
1, 1959 the Constitution was promulgated and on
December 7, 1959 the National Assembly held its first
session. In March 1975 the National Assembly
proclaimed M. Bourguiba as President for life. On
November 7, 1987 M. Bourguiba was deposed and
succeeded by President Zine el-Abidine Ben Ali.
Presidential and legislative elections were held in
April 1989. The RCD (Rassemblement Constitution-
nel Democratique) won all 141 seats in the National
Assembly. Seven political parties contested the
election. President Ben Ali was re-elected with 99
per cent of the vote.

The country is divided into 23 regions (*gouvernor-
ats*) each administered by a governor.

Production, Trade, etc.—The valleys of the
northern region support large flocks and herds, and
contain rich agricultural areas, in which wheat,
barley, and oats are grown. Vines and olives are
extensively cultivated.

The chief exports are crude oil, phosphates, olive
oil, finished textiles, and fruit. The chief imports are
machinery and equipment, foodstuffs, petroleum

products, and textiles. Some oil has been discovered and crude oil production in 1989 was 4·8 million tons. Gas has also been discovered off the east coast but exploitation is not viable at present. Tourists numbered almost 3 million in 1989.

	1988	1989
Total Imports	TD3,167,000	TD4,150,000
Total Exports	2,055,000	2,762,000

France remains the main trading partner, supplying 27·6 per cent of the country's imports and purchasing 22·9 per cent of Tunisia's exports.

Trade with UK

	1989	1990
Imports from UK	£31,148,000	£40,800,000
Exports to UK	43,266,000	40,959,000

Tunisia became an associate member of the EC early in 1969, and signed a new agreement with the EC in 1976. Textile exports are the main foreign exchange earner after tourism.

CAPITAL.—Ψ Tunis, connected by canal with La Goulette on the coast, had a population (1984) of 1,394,749. The ruins of ancient Carthage lie a few miles from the city. Other towns of importance are: Ψ Sfax (577,992); Ψ Sousse (322,491); Ψ Bizerta (394,670); Kairouan; Gabes; Menzel Bourguiba.

CURRENCY.—Tunisian dinar of 1,000 millimes.

FLAG.—Red crescent and star in a white orb, all on a red ground.

NATIONAL ANTHEM.—Himat Al Hima.

NATIONAL DAY.—March 20.

BRITISH EMBASSY
5 Place de la Victoire, Tunis 1015 RP
[Tunis 245100]

Ambassador Extraordinary and Plenipotentiary and Consul-General, His Excellency Stephen Peter Day, CMG (1987).

First Secretary, A. Holmes, MBE (*Deputy Head of Mission*).

Second Secretary, C. Innes-Hopkins (*Commercial and Consul*).

British Council Representative, D. Handforth.

TURKEY
(Türkiye Cumhuriyeti)

President, Turgut Özal, *elected for a seven-year term,* October 31, 1989.

GOVERNMENT
(as at June 23, 1991)

Prime Minister, Mesut Yilmaz.
Deputy PM, Ekrem Pakdemirli.
Ministers of State, Fahrettin Kurt; Mustafa Tasar; Imren Aykut; Vehbi Dincerler; Kamran Inan; Ilhan Akuzum; Cengiz Tuncer; Sabahettin Aras; Ersin Kocak; Mehmet Cevik; Cenap Gurpinar; Birsel Sonmez; Ali Talip Ozdemir.
Justice, Sakir Seker.
National Defence, Barlas Dogu.
Interior, Mustafa Kalemli.
Foreign Affairs, Safa Giray.
Finance and Customs, Adnan Kahveci.
National Education, Avni Akyol.
Public Works and Housing, Husamettin Oruc.
Health, Yasar Eryilmaz.
Transport, Ibrahim Ozdemir.
Agriculture, Forestry and Village Affairs, Ilker Tuncay.
Labour and Social Security, Metin Emiroglu.
Industry and Commerce, Rustu Kazim Yucelen.

Energy and Natural Resources, Muzaffer Arici.
Culture, Gokhan Maras.
Tourism, Bulent Akarcali.

TURKISH EMBASSY
43 Belgrave Square, SW1X 8PA
[071–235 5252]

Ambassador Extraordinary and Plenipotentiary, His Excellency Nurver Nures (1989).

Area and Population.—People of Turkic stock are to be found scattered throughout a wide belt extending from China through the Soviet Union, Afghanistan and Iran to Turkey, and into Bulgaria.

Turkey itself extends from Edirne (Adrianople) to Transcaucasia and Iran, and from the Black Sea to the Mediterranean, Syria and Iraq. Total population at the Census of 1985 was 51,428,514, of which 6,942,780 were in Europe and 44,485,734 in Asia. A 1989 UN estimate gives a total figure of 56,741,000.

Turkey in Europe consists of Eastern Thrace, including the cities of Istanbul and Edirne, and is separated from Asia by the Bosporus at Istanbul and by the Dardanelles—about 40 miles in length with a width varying from 1 to 4 miles—the political neighbours being Greece and Bulgaria on the west.

Turkey in Asia comprises the whole of Asia Minor or Anatolia and extends from the Aegean Sea to the western boundaries of Georgia, Soviet Armenia and Iran, and from the Black Sea to the Mediterranean and the northern boundaries of Syria and Iraq.

Government.—On October 29, 1923 the National Assembly declared Turkey a Republic and elected Gazi Mustafa Kemal (later known as Kemal Ataturk) President. In 1945 a multi-party system was introduced but in 1960 the government was overthrown by the Turkish Armed Forces. A new Constitution was adopted in July 1961 and, after a general election, a civilian government took office. Civilian governments remained in power until September 1980 when mounting problems with the economy and terrorism led to a military takeover. A civilian technocratic government was appointed later that month.

A new Constitution, extending the powers of the President, was approved by a referendum on November 7, 1982. It provided for the separation of powers between the legislature, executive and judiciary, and the holding of free elections to the unicameral Grand National Assembly, which now has 500 members elected every five years. Following the General Election in November 1983 the military leadership handed over power to a newly elected civilian government.

The Motherland Party, led by Turgut Özal, won general elections held in November 1987; the next election is scheduled for October 1991. There is continued Kurdish unrest in the south-east of the country; Kurds are estimated to constitute one-sixth of the population.

Turkey is divided for administrative purposes into 73 *il* with subdivisions into *ilçe* and *nahiye*. Each *il* has a governor (*vali*) and elective council.

Religion and Education.—Islam ceased to be the state religion in 1928. However, 98·99 per cent of the population are Muslim. The main religious minorities, which are concentrated in Istanbul and on the Syrian frontier, are Greek Orthodox, Armenian, Syriani Christian, and Jewish. Education is free, secular and compulsory at primary level. There are elementary, secondary and vocational schools.

There are 27 universities in Turkey, including four in Istanbul, four in Ankara, two in Izmir, and one each in Erzurum and Trabzon.

Language and Literature.—Until 1926, Turkish was written in Arabic script, but in that year the Roman alphabet was substituted for use in official correspondence and in 1928 for universal use, with

Arabic numerals as used throughout Europe. The revolution of 1908 led to the introduction of native literature free from foreign influences and adapted to the requirements of the people. The leading Turkish newspapers are centred in Istanbul and Ankara, although most provincial towns have their own daily papers. There are foreign language papers in French, Greek, Armenian and English and numerous magazines and weeklies.

Agricultural Production.—In 1985 agricultural production accounted for some 16 per cent of the gross domestic product at constant factor prices. About 50 per cent of the working population are in the rural sector. Estimated production figures for the principal crops in 1989 were ('000 tons):

Wheat	16,200	Olives	650
Barley	4,500	Tea (wet leaves)	660
Rice	183	Hazelnuts	471
Tobacco	253	Citrus fruit	1,388
Sugar beet	11,000	Grapes and figs	3,638

With the important exception of wheat, which is mostly grown on the arid central Anatolian plateau, most of the crops are grown on the fertile littoral. Tobacco, sultana and fig cultivation is centred around Izmir, where substantial quantities of cotton are also grown. The main cotton area is in the Cukurova plain around Adana. The forests which lie between the littoral plain and the Anatolian plateau contain beech, pine, oak, elm, chestnut, lime, plane, alder, box, poplar and maple. In 1987 26 per cent of the land area was forest.

Industry.—After agriculture, Turkey's most important industry is based on the considerable mineral wealth which is, however, comparatively unexploited. The main export minerals are chromite and boron. Production in 1989 was (tons):

Coal	6,259,000
Lignite	50,926,000
Crude petroleum	2,868,000
Crude iron	3,523,000
Boron minerals	1,884,000

The bulk of the country's requirements in sugar, cotton, woollen and silk textiles, and cement, is produced locally, while other industries contributing substantially to local needs include vehicle assembly, paper, glass and glassware, iron and steel, leather and leather goods, sulphur refining, canning and rubber goods, soaps and cosmetics, pharmaceutical products, prepared foodstuffs and a host of minor industries.

Steep rises in oil prices from 1973 onwards led to a succession of economic crises culminating in January 1980 in the introduction of an economic stability programme. Exports have since risen dramatically, topping US$11,846 million in 1988. Inflation, however, remains high (68 per cent in 1989). GNP growth for 1989 was about 3·4 per cent and unemployment remains high.

COMMUNICATIONS

Railways.—The network is a nationalized one, run by the State Railways Administration. The total length of lines in operation (1989) is 10,369 km.

Roads.—At the end of 1988 there were 58,712 km of roads (31,048 of which were national).

The Bosporus is spanned by two bridges; plans are being drawn up for a third fixed link between the two continents.

Shipping.—By the end of 1988 the number of ships over 18 gross tons was 3,805.

Civil Aviation.—The state airline (THY) operates all internal services and has services to Europe and the Middle East. Most of the leading European airlines operate services to Istanbul and some also to Ankara.

FINANCE

	1990
Estimated expenditure	TL64,400·4 billion
Estimated revenue	53,860·0 billion

TRADE

	1988	1989
Total imports ...	US$14,339·7m	US$15,762·6m
Total exports ...	11,662·1m	11,627·3m

The main imports are machinery, crude oil and petroleum products, iron and steel, vehicles, medicines and dyes, chemicals, fertilizers and electrical appliances. Agricultural commodities (cotton, tobacco, fruits, nuts, livestock) represent 47 per cent of total exports. Other exports are minerals, textiles, glass and cement.

Trade with UK

	1989	1990
Imports from UK	£434,562,000	£606,829,000
Exports to UK	533,769,000	550,803,000

CAPITAL.—Ankara (Angora), an inland town of Asia Minor, about 275 miles ESE of Istanbul, with a population (1980) of 3,196,460. Ankara (or Ancyra) was the capital of the Roman Province of *Galatia Prima*, and a marble temple (now in ruins) dedicated to Augustus, contains the *Monumentum* (*Marmor*) *Ancyranum*, inscribed with a record of the reign of Augustus Caesar.

ΨIstanbul (4,870,747), the former capital, was the Roman city of Byzantium. It was selected by Constantine the Great as the capital of the Roman Empire about AD 328 and renamed Constantinople. Istanbul contains the celebrated church of St Sophia, which, after becoming a mosque, was made a museum in 1934. It also contains Topkapi, former Palace of the Ottoman Sultans, which is also a museum.

Other cities are ΨIzmir (1,968,614); Adana (1,467,346); Bursa (1,161,553); Gaziantep (387,093) and Eskişehir (543,733).

CURRENCY.—Turkish lira (TL) of 100 kurus.

FLAG.—Red, with white crescent and star.

NATIONAL ANTHEM.—Istikâl Marşi (The Independence March).

NATIONAL DAY.—October 29 (Republic Day).

BRITISH EMBASSY

Sehit Ersan Caddesi 46/A, Cankaya, Ankara
[Ankara 1274310/4]

Ambassador Extraordinary and Plenipotentiary, His Excellency Sir Timothy Lewis Achilles Daunt, KCMG (1986).

Counsellor, Deputy Head of Mission, W. B. McCleary
First Secretaries, S. N. Evans (*Political*); R. H. J Ashton (*Chancery*); D. T. Healy (*Commercial*); J M. Brown (*Management*); A. J. Mounford, Ms R L. Varley (*Cultural Affairs*).

Defence and Military Attaché, Brig. R. D. H. H Greenwood.

Naval and Air Attaché, Wing Cdr. A. Campbell.

BRITISH CONSULAR OFFICES

There is a British Consulate-General at *Istanbul,* a Vice-Consulate at *Izmir* and Honorary British Consulates at *Antalya, Bodrun, Iskenderun, Mersin* and *Marmaris.*

British Council Representative, Colin Perchard, OBE, Kirklangic Sokak 9, Gazi Osman Pasa, Ankara 06700. There is also a centre and library at *Istanbul* BRITISH CHAMBER OF COMMERCE OF TURKEY INC. Mesrutiyet Caddessi No. 34, Tepebasi Beyoğlu Istanbul (Postal Address, PO Box 190 Karaköy Istanbul).

UNION OF SOVIET SOCIALIST REPUBLICS
(Soyuz Sovetskikh Sotsialisticheskikh Respublik)

President of the USSR, Mikhail Sergevich Gorbachev, *elected* March 15, 1990.

STATE COUNCIL
(as at September 6, 1991)

A. Akaev; N. Dementei; M. Gorbachev; I. Karimov; L. Kravchuk; K. Makhkamov; A. Mutalibov; N. Nazarbayev; S. Niyazov; L. Ter-Petrosian; B. Yeltsin.

ALL UNION MINISTERS
(as at September 9, 1991)

Foreign Affairs, B. Pankin.
Interior, Col.-Gen. V. Barannikov.
KGB, V. Bakatin.
Defence, Marshal Y. Shaposhnikov.

At the time of going to press, the situation in the Soviet Union was one of flux in the aftermath of the failed coup of August 19, 1991. A new union treaty which was to have been signed in August was abandoned and replaced by interim arrangements, approved by an extraordinary Congress of People's Deputies on September 5, 1991, until a new treaty can be negotiated.

The interim arrangements consist of a State Council, a two-chamber parliament and an interim economic committee. The State Council, which will govern the country, will include the Soviet President and the leaders of the participating republics. It will directly control foreign affairs, defence, and security. Decrees issued by the State Council automatically become Soviet law.

The Parliament, the Union Supreme Soviet, will consist of an upper chamber, the Council of Republics, comprising 20 directly elected delegates from each participating republic, except Russia which will have 52 in recognition of various autonomous areas within its borders. Each republic will have one vote. The lower chamber, the Council of the Union, will contain existing members of the old Supreme Soviet; the Congress of People's Deputies, although formally still in existence, has been effectively abolished.

An inter-republican economic committee will handle international trade, inter-republican transport, economic reforms and other economic issues. The interim arrangements are voluntary; the rights of republics to secede from the Soviet Union have been recognized with the proviso that outstanding issues are resolved and international treaties recognized. The Baltic states, Moldova (Moldavia) and Georgia are expected to participate only in the economic arrangements.

EMBASSY OF THE USSR
13 Kensington Palace Gardens, W8 4QX
[071–229 3628]

Ambassador Extraordinary and Plenipotentiary, new appointment awaited.

AREA AND POPULATION

The total area of the USSR is 8,649,461 sq. miles (22,402,000 sq. km); the total population (January 1, 1989) 286,700,000. The proportion of women to men is 53 to 47. In 1987 the birth-rate was 19·0 and the mortality rate, 10·2. In 1987, 66 per cent of the population lived in urban areas.

Area and population (1989) of the constituent republics or former republics of the USSR with their date of incorporation into the Union:

Republic	Sq. miles	Population
Armenia (1936)	11,306	3,305,000
Azerbaijan (1936)	33,436	7,021,000
Belorussia (1922)	80,300	10,152,000
Estonia (1940)	17,413	1,566,000
Georgia (1936)	26,911	5,401,000
Kazakhstan (1936)	1,049,155	16,464,000
Kyrgyzstan (1936)	76,642	4,258,000
Latvia (1940)	24,695	2,667,000
Lithuania (1940)	26,173	3,675,000
Moldova (1940)	13,912	4,335,000
RSFSR (1922)	6,593,391	147,022,000
Tadjikistan (1936)	54,019	5,093,000
Turkmenistan (1924)	188,417	3,523,000
Ukraine (1922)	252,046	51,471,000
Uzbekistan (1924)	172,742	19,810,000

Before the outbreak of the Second World War (1941–45 in USSR), the USSR consisted of 11 Republics. In August 1940, the major part of Bessarabia ceded by Romania in June was joined to the Moldavian ASSR to form a Moldavian SSR. The same month, the three independent Baltic States, Estonia, Latvia and Lithuania, were forcibly incorporated into the Soviet Union. In October 1944 Tannu-Tuva, until the Second World War a nominally independent state lying to the north-west of Outer Mongolia, became the autonomous province of Tuva and in 1961, the Autonomous Republic of Tuva, within the RSFSR.

In July 1956 the Karelo-Finnish Republic (formed in 1940 from the Karelian ASSR and land ceded by Finland) reverted to the status of an Autonomous (*Karelian*) Republic within the RSFSR.

Main Nationalities
(1989 Census)

In 1989 the most numerous national groups of the USSR were: Russian, 145 million and Ukrainian, 44 million. There are between 6 and 16 million Kazakhs, Tatars, Belorussians, and Uzbeks. Azerbaidjani, Armenians and Georgians number between 3·4 and 6·7 million each group. There are some 2·0 to 3·3 million Lithuanians, Kirghizians, Turkomans, Germans, Romanians and Tadjiks. In each of the following nationality groups the population numbers between 1·12 and 2·06 millions: Chuvashes, Latvians, Poles, Mordovians, Bashkirs, Estonians, Dagestanis and Jews.

The 1989 census revealed a marked difference between the growth rates of individual nationalities; while the Slav nations showed an annual increase of under one per cent, certain Central Asian and Caucasian (mostly Muslim) nations recorded an annual net growth of 2·5 to 3·5 per cent.

Chronological System.—On February 14, 1918 the Soviet government adopted the Gregorian calendar. In 1981 Summer Time was introduced between April 1 and October 1, but there are some geographical anomalies in its application. The country is divided into 11 time zones.

LANGUAGE, LITERATURE AND ARTS

Russian is a branch of the Slavonic family of languages which is divided into the following groups: *eastern*, including Russian, Ukrainian and White Russian; *western*, including Polish, Czech, Slovak and Sorbish (or Lusatian Wendish); and *southern*, including Serbo-Croat, Slovene, Macedonian and Bulgarian. The western group and part of the southern group are written in the Latin alphabet, the others in the Cyrillic, said to have been instituted by SS. Cyril and Methodius in the ninth century and largely based on the Greek alphabet. Before the westernization of Russia under Peter the Great (1682–1725), Russian literature consisted mainly of folk ballads (*byliny*), epic songs, chronicles and works

Map as at mid-September 1991

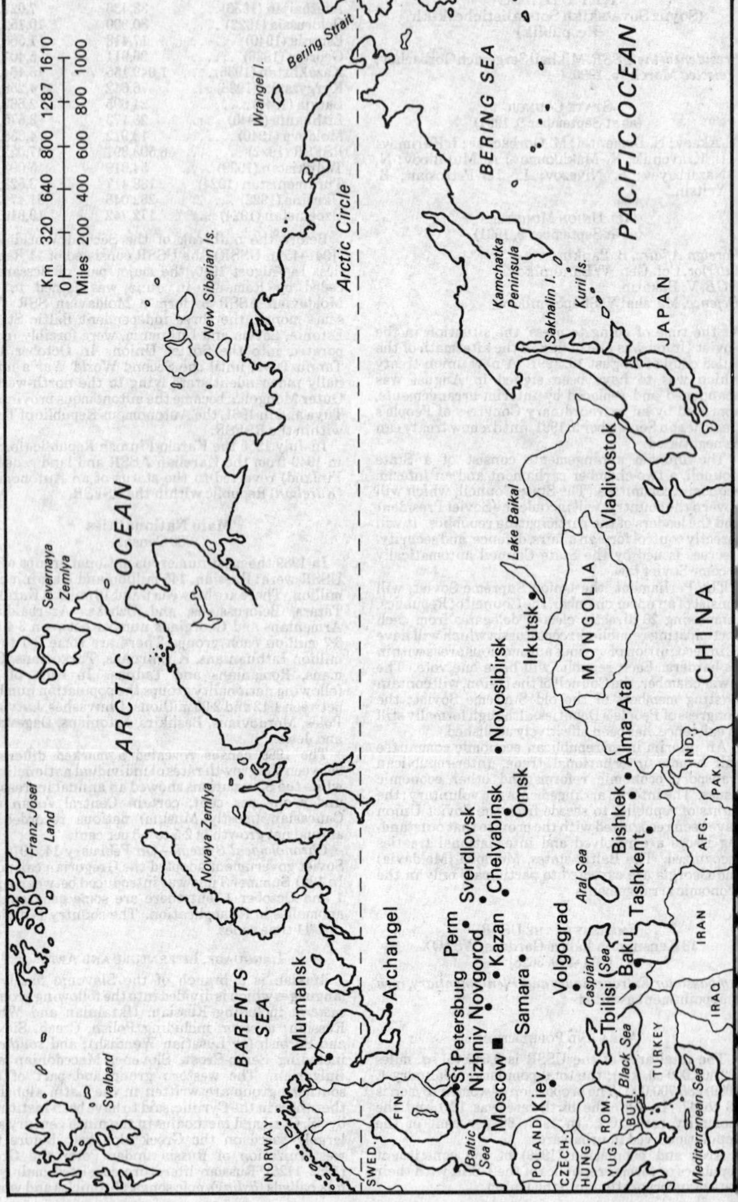

f moral theology. The eighteenth and particularly he nineteenth centuries saw a brilliant development f Russian poetry and fiction. Romantic poetry eached its zenith with Alexander Pushkin (1799– 837) and Mikhail Lermontov (1814–41). The 20th entury produced great poets like Alexander Blok 1880–1921), the 1958 Nobel Prize laureate Boris 'asternak (1890–1960), Vladimir Mayakovsky (1893– 930) and Anna Akhmatova (1888–1966). Realistic iction is associated with the names of Nikolai Gogol 1809–52), Ivan Turgenev (1818–83), Fedor Dostoyev-ky (1821–81) and Leo Tolstoy (1828–1910), and later vith Anton Chekhov (1860–1904), Maxim Gorky 1868–1936), Ivan Bunin (1870–1953) and Alexander iolzhenitsyn (b. 1918).

Great names in music include Glinka (1804–57), 3orodin (1833–87), Mussorgsky (1839–81), Rimsky-Korsakov (1844–1908), Rubinstein (1829–94), Tchai-iovsky (1840–93), Rakhmaninov (1873–1943), ikriabin (1872–1915), Prokofiev (1891–1953), Stravin-ky (1882–1971) and Shostakovich (1906–75).

GOVERNMENT

On October 7, 1977 a new Constitution was adopted o replace the 1936 Constitution. Amendments to the 977 Constitution were adopted on December 1, 1988, reating a new parliamentary structure and amend-ng electoral procedures. Further amendments fol-owed.

A new supreme representative body, a 2,250-nember Congress of People's Deputies, held its naugural session in May 1989. Partly superseding he former USSR Supreme Soviet, the Congress was o convene once or twice a year to decide on onstitutional, political and socio-economic ques-ions. Elections to the Congress were to be held every ive years. The reorganized bicameral 542-member supreme Soviet is responsible for all legislative and dministrative matters. Its members are elected by nd from the Congress of People's Deputies.

The Congress on March 13, 1990 approved the reation of the post of President of the USSR. M. S. 3orbachev was elected on March 15 for a five-year erm. Thereafter, Presidents were to be elected by niversal direct suffrage by secret ballot. The Presi-ent's executive powers included the appointment of he Chairman and members of the Council of Minis-ers (subject to ratification by Congress), declaring var in the event of an attack on the USSR, imposing emporary presidential rule with the agreement of a inion republic, and issuing decrees which were inding throughout the USSR.

In December 1990, a Cabinet of Ministers with a 'rime Minister replaced the Council of Ministers nd its Chairman. A Security Council, chaired by he President, replaced the shortlived Presidential 'ouncil in March 1991.

In March 1990 the Congress of People's Deputies bolished the Communist Party's guaranteed monop-ly of power.

A referendum was held on March 17, 1991, when oviet citizens were asked, 'Do you think it necessary o preserve the Union of Soviet Socialist Republics s a renewed federation of equal sovereign republics n which human rights and liberties will be fully uaranteed for all nationalities?'; a slightly different rording was used in Kazakhstan and additional uestions posed in some areas. Eighty per cent voted n favour, although the referendum was boycotted by he Baltic states, Armenia, Georgia and Moldova.

The imminent signing of a new union treaty, evolving greater powers to the republics, was the retext for a coup on August 19, 1991, nominally led y Vice President Gennadi Yanayev. Lack of firm upport in the armed forces and security forces and opular resistance in Moscow and Leningrad led to he collapse of the coup on August 21 and the restoration of President Gorbachev. The Communist Party was suspended throughout the Soviet Union on August 29, 1991. New interim constitutional arrangements have been introduced.

DEFENCE

Defence expenditure in the USSR for 1988 was set officially at 20,244 million roubles (or 4·6 per cent of total budget). It was later admitted that this covered only manpower costs, not weapon procurement, etc. The overall defence budget for 1989 was officially stated to be 77,300 million roubles (15·6 per cent of the total Soviet budget). For 1990 the official budget was 70,975 million roubles (14·5 per cent of the total budget). A further reduction was promised for 1991. In the event, the officially declared budget for 1991 was 96·6 billion roubles, an ostensible 36 per cent increase but officially claimed as an 8·3 per cent decrease in real terms because of large price increases for defence goods from January 1991.

The basic military service is two years in the Army or Air Force or three years in the Navy though an experiment is under way, at first in the Navy, involving a shorter period and different terms of service.

The total size of the Soviet regular forces was estimated at the beginning of 1989 to be about 5,130,000, excluding some 1,135,000 Border Guard, internal security, railway and construction troops (mainly uniformed civilians), but including some 1,500,000 command and general support troops not otherwise listed. Individual force levels are con-stantly changing.

Late in 1988 it was announced that within the next two years there would be unilateral cuts in Soviet conventional forces of 500,000 men and 10,000 tanks. About half of these cuts had been made by early 1991. Withdrawals of Soviet forces from Hungary and Czechoslovakia have been completed. Those from Poland should be completed in 1992 and from eastern Germany by 1994. All combatant forces will have left Mongolia this year and remaining auxiliary units during 1992. By 1995 it is planned that there will be no Soviet forces based or located outside Soviet territory.

The position, before Soviet unilateral cuts and withdrawals began, was as follows:

Operational ICBMs, i.e. Inter-Continental Ballistic Missiles, totalled about 1,450. SLBMs numbered 978. The number of MRBMs and IRBMs deployed was 383. The operational personnel of the Strategic Rocket Forces totalled 287,000 (not including 123,500 as-signed from Air and Navy).

The total strength of all Soviet air elements (including helicopters) was some 19,500. Of these, 10,000 can be classified as combat aircraft. The total strength of the Air Forces, excluding the Naval Air Force (68,000) and the bomber forces of the Aviation Armies (108,000), was about 450,000. The total personnel of the separate Air Defence Command, now merged with the Air Defence Troops of the Ground Forces, was estimated at 630,000.

The total size of the Soviet Ground Forces was estimated at 1,596,000.

The total personnel strength of the Soviet Navy and Naval Air Force was 437,000. In total tonnage, it is the second largest navy in the world, and its main strength lies in the submarine fleet. In mid-1989 there were 69 strategic nuclear and 280 tactical/attack submarines, with a further 19 converting to other roles including SSN, and 55 attack submarines in reserve.

The Soviet Navy has 264 major surface combat vessels, including five aircraft carriers, 37 cruisers and 52 destroyers and some 171 frigates, with 24 varied destroyers and 23 frigates in store. The landbased Naval Air Force comprised about 1,040 combat aircraft, including 355 bombers, and some 300 helicopters.

The para-military forces numbered 570,000, including 230,000 border troops formerly of the KGB and 340,000 internal security troops. There are also DOSAAF members (claimed active membership, 80 million) who participate in such activities as athletics, flight training, shooting, parachuting and pre-military training.

Minister of Defence, Marshal Y. Shaposhnikov.
Chief of General Staff, Army Gen. V. N. Lobov.

On May 14, 1955 a Treaty of Friendship, Mutual Assistance and Co-operation was signed in Warsaw between the Soviet Union and its European associates (Bulgaria, East Germany, Hungary, Poland, Romania, and Czechoslovakia) (and Albania which formally left the Pact in September 1968) to serve as a counterpoise to NATO. A united military command was set up in Moscow. The Treaty (Warsaw Pact), due to have expired in June 1985, was extended by Protocol in its existing form for a further 20 years at a meeting of Pact leaders in Warsaw on April 26, 1985.

In the wake of East–West detente and the recent political changes in eastern Europe, including the election of democratic governments and German unification, the Pact's role as a military organization was recognized to be over. Following a decision of the Pact's Political Consultative Committee in Budapest on February 25, 1991, all Warsaw Pact military structures were dissolved with effect from March 31, 1991. A Protocol dissolving the Pact was signed at a final meeting of the Political Consultative Committee, held in Prague on July 1, 1991. This must be ratified by the parliaments of all member countries before the Pact is legally terminated.

INDUSTRY AND AGRICULTURE

One of the most remarkable aspects of the Soviet economy has been the transformation of an essentially agricultural country into the second-strongest industrial power in the world. The 1988 output amounted to 163 million tonnes of steel, 116 million tonnes of rolled metal, 772 million tonnes of coal, 624 million tonnes of crude oil, 139 million tonnes of cement, 1,705,000 million kW/h of electricity and 1,300,000 cars.

Agricultural development has been slower, mainly owing to lack of incentives among peasants organized in collective farms. Repeated droughts, such as in 1980-81, were a contributing factor to a shortage of grain. The 1988 harvest was 195 million tonnes. Stock breeding has also suffered from the general mismanagement of farming, and from shortages of fodder in recent years. The livestock at January 1, 1989 included 41,500,000 cows, 77,400,000 pigs and 147,300,000 sheep and goats. Besides *kolkhozy* (collective farms) and *sovkhozy* (state farms) a significant contribution to agricultural production is made by the private plots cultivated by individual peasants. The cultivation of these plots is encouraged by the Soviet authorities. The level of productivity remains very low. Forests cover nearly 40 per cent of the whole area of the Union and form a considerable source of wealth.

Trade with UK

	1989	1990
Imports from UK	£681,599,000	£606,013,000
Exports to UK	833,369,000	917,691,000

COMMUNICATIONS

European Russia is relatively well served by railways, St. Petersburg and Moscow being the two main focal points of rail routes. The centre and south have a good system of north-south and east-west lines, but the eastern part (the Volga lands), traverse as it is by trunk lines between Europe and Asia whic enter Siberia via Sverdlovsk, Chelyabinsk, Magnit gorsk and Ufa, lacks north-south routes. In Asi there are still large areas of the USSR, notably in th far north and Siberia, with few or no railway. Railways built since 1928 include the Turkestar Siberian line (*Turksib*) which has made possible large-scale industrial exploitation of Kazakhstan, number of lines within the system of the Tran Siberian Railway (Magnitogorsk-Kartaly-Troits Sverdlovsk-Kurgan, Novosibirsk-Proyektnaya, etc. which are of great importance for the industria development in the east, the Petropavlovsk-Kara ganda-Balkhash line which has made possible th development of the Karaganda coal basin and of th Balkhash copper mines, and the Moscow-Donbas trunk line. In the northern part of European Russi the North Pechora Railway has been complete while in the Far East a recently completed secon Trans-Siberian line (the Baikal-Amur Railway) partially in use; it follows a more northerly alignmen than the earlier Trans-Siberian and terminates i the Pacific port of Sovetskaya Gavan.

Sea Ports and Inland Waterways.—The most im portant ports (Odessa, Nikolayev, Batumi, Taganro Rostov, Kerch, Sevastopol and Novorossiisk) li around the Black Sea and the Sea of Azov. Th northern ports (St. Petersburg, Murmansk an Archangel) are, with the exception of Murmansl icebound during winter. Several ports have bee built along the Arctic Sea route between Murmans and Vladivostok and are in regular use every summer The far eastern port of Vladivostok, the Pacific nava base of the USSR, is kept open by icebreakers all th year round. Inland waterways, both natural an artificial, are of great importance in the countr although some of them are icebound in winter (fro 2½ months in the south to 6 months in the north The great rivers of European Russia flow outward from the centre, linking all parts of the plain wit the chief ports, an immense system of navigabl waterways which carried about 690 million tons o freight in 1988. They are supplemented by a syste of canals which provide a through traffic between th White, Baltic, Black and Caspian Seas. The mo notable are the White Sea-Baltic Canal, the Moscow Volga Canal and the Volga-Don Canal linking th Baltic and the White Seas in the north to the Caspia the Black Sea and the Sea of Azov in the south.

CURRENCY.—Rouble of 100 kopeks.

FLAG.—Red, with five-pointed star above hamme and sickle.

NATIONAL DAY.—November 7 (commemorating th October Bolshevik Revolution of 1917).

NATIONAL ANTHEM.—Soyuz Nerushimy Respubl Svobodnykh (Indissoluble union of free republics).

BRITISH EMBASSY

Naberezhnaya Morisa Toreza 14, Moscow 72
[Moscow 2318511]

Ambassador Extraordinary and Plenipotentiary, H Excellency Sir Rodric Braithwaite, KCMG (1988).
Minister and Deputy Head of Mission, D. B. C. Loga CMG.

There is a Consular Section attached to th Embassy.

UNION REPUBLICS

In its 1977 Constitution, the USSR is described a a 'unitary federal multi-national state, formed as result of the free self-determination of nations ar the voluntary union of equal Soviet Socialist Repu lics'. Each union republic has a Constitution ar state structure modelled broadly on that of th

entral administration, and, in theory, always had
he freedom to secede.

Almost all the union republics have taken steps
wards greater autonomy since 1989.

ARMENIA

President, Levon Ter-Petrosyan.
Prime Minister, V. Manukyan.

Armenia occupies the south-western part of Trans-
aucasia; it was formed in 1920. In 1922 it joined the
ranscaucasian Federation, and on its liquidation in
936 became a Union Republic. In the south it borders
1 Turkey. It is a mountainous country consisting
several vast tablelands surrounded by ridges. The
pulation and the economic life are concentrated in
he low-lying part of Armenia, the Aras valley and
he Erevan hollow; the climate is continental, dry
1d cold, but the Araks valley has a long, hot and dry
ummer. Irrigation is essential for agriculture.
dustrial and fruit crops are grown in the low-lying
stricts, grain in the hills. Armenia is traditionally
oted for its wine. There are large copper ore and
olybdenum deposits and other minerals. The Ar-
enian Church centred in Etchmiadzin is the oldest
tablished Christian Church, Christianity having
en recognized as the state religion in AD 300.

Nearly 90 per cent of the population is Armenian
ith Azerbaijani (5 per cent) and Russian (2 per cent)
inorities.

Armenia's Supreme Soviet passed a declaration of
dependence in March 1991. A referendum on
dependence is to be held in September 1991. There
ve been clashes on the border with Azerbaijan.

CAPITAL.—Erevan. Population, 1,186,000 (1988).

AZERBAIJAN

resident, Ayaz Mutalibov.
rime Minister, G. A. Gasanov.

Azerbaijan occupies the eastern part of Transcau-
sia, on the shore of the Caspian Sea, and borders on
an. It was formed in 1920. Between 1922 and 1936
formed part of the Transcaucasian Federation. In
36 it became a Union Republic. It includes the
akhichevan Autonomous Republic and the Na-
rno-Karabakh Autonomous Province.

The north-eastern part of the Republic is taken up
the south-eastern end of the main Caucasus ridge,
s south-western part by the smaller Caucasus hills,
ld its south-eastern corner by the spurs of the
ilysh Ridge. Its central part is a depression irrigated
the Kura and by the lower reaches of its tributary
raks. Sheltered by the mountains from the humid
est winds blowing from the Black Sea, Azerbaijan
is a continental climate. The land requires artificial
rigation. Industry is dominated by oil and natural
s extraction and related chemical and engineering
dustries centred in Baku and Sumgait. A large
wer station on the Araks was completed in 1969, in
njunction with Iran. Azerbaijan is also important
a cotton growing area. The Azerbaijani (Turkic)
ake up more than three-quarters of the population
the Republic, Armenians about 8 per cent, and
issians 8 per cent. Fighting continues in the
menian enclave of Nagorno-Karabakh.

CAPITAL.—Ψ Baku. Population 1,772,000 (1988).

BELORUSSIA

esident, Nikolai Dementei.
ime Minister, V. F. Kebich.

Belorussia, lying in the western part of the
ropean area of the USSR, was formed early in 1919.
now consists of six provinces (Brest, Gomel,

Grodno, Minsk, Mogilev and Vitebsk). Belorussians
make up four-fifths of the population, with Russians
(13 per cent) and Poles (4 per cent) coming next. It is
largely a plain with many lakes, swamps and marshy
land. Since the revolution of 1917 agriculture has
been greatly developed, thanks to draining of swamps.
Most of the Republic's industry is also of recent
growth. Woodworking is of great importance, but
engineering has been greatly extended with several
major plants built in Gomel and Minsk.

The main rivers are the upper reaches of the
Dnieper, of the Niemen and of the Western Dvina.

The Belorussian Supreme Soviet declared its
sovereignty in July 1990. Independence was declared
in August 1991.

CAPITAL.—Minsk. Population 1,583,000 (1988).

GEORGIA

President, Zviad Gamsakhurdia.
Prime Minister, V. Gugushvilli.

Georgia, occupying the north-western part of
Transcaucasia, lies on the shore of the Black Sea and
borders in the south-east on Turkey. It was formed
in 1921; in 1922 it joined the Transcaucasian Federation which, in its turn, adhered to the USSR in the
same year. After the liquidation of the Transcaucasian SFSR in 1936 Georgia became a Union Republic.
It contains two Autonomous Republics (Abkhazia
and Adjaria) and the South Osetian Autonomous
Province. The latter was abolished by Georgian law
in December 1990, although this was not recognized
by the central government. Georgia is a country of
mountains, with the Greater Caucasus in the north
and the Lesser Caucasus in the south. A relatively
low-lying land between these two ridges is divided
into two parts by the Surz Ridge: Western Georgia
with a mild and damp climate and Eastern Georgia
with a more continental and dry climate. The Black
Sea shore and the Rioni lowland are subtropical in
their climatic character. The most important mineral
deposits are manganese (Chiatura), coal (Tkibuli and
Tkvarcheli) and oil (Kakhetia). Georgia is a leading
producer of manganese in the USSR. There are also
many oil refineries. Viniculture, tea and tobacco-
growing are the three main agricultural industries.
The Black Sea harbours many famous holiday resorts.
Georgians make up 68·8 per cent of the population,
the remainder being largely composed of Armenians
(14·7 per cent), Russians, Azerbaijanis and Osetians.

In March 1990 the Georgian Supreme Soviet
declared illegal the treaties of 1921–22 by which
Georgia had joined the Soviet Union. The republic's
Constitution was amended to abolish the Communist
Party's guaranteed monopoly of power. Multi-party
elections were held in October and November 1990;
Zviad Gamsakhurdia was elected President in No-
vember 1990.

CAPITAL.—Tbilisi (Tiflis), population 1,211,000
(1987).

KAZAKHSTAN

President, Nursultan Nazarbaev.
Prime Minister, U. K. Karamanov.

Kazakhstan stretching from the lower reaches of
the Volga and the Caspian in the west to the Altai
and Tienshan in the east, and bordering on China,
was formed in 1920 as an autonomous republic (under
the name of the Kazakh ASSR) within the RSFSR,
and was constituted a Union Republic in 1936. It
consists of 17 Provinces: Aktyubinsk, Alma-Ata,
Chimkent, Dzhambul, Dzhezkazgan, East-Kazakhs-
tan, Guryev, Karaganda, Kokchetav, Kustanay,

Kzyl-Orda, North-Kazakhstan, Pavlodar, Semipalatinsk, Taldy-Kurgan, Tselinograd and Uralsk.

Kazakhstan is a country of arid steppes and semi-deserts, flat in the west, hilly in the east and mountainous in the south-east (Southern Altai and Tienshan). The climate is continental and very dry. The main rivers are the (Upper) Irtysh, the Ural, the Syr-Darya and the Ili. Kazakhstan is very rich in minerals: copper in Kounrad and Dzhezkazgan, lead and zinc in the Altai and Karatau mountains, iron ore in Radryg and Lisakovsk, coal in Ekibastuz and Karaganda and oil and natural gas in the Mangyshlak peninsula. Major centres of metal industry exist in the Altai Mountains, in Chimkent, north of the Balkhash Lake and in Central Kazakhstan. Stock-raising is highly developed, particularly in the central and south-western parts of the Republic. Grain is grown in the north and north-east and cotton in the south and south-east.

The Kazakhs (a Turkic people) are in a minority in the Republic named after them; they constitute only 42 per cent of its population, Russians make up 38 per cent and Ukrainians 4 per cent.

CAPITAL.—Alma-Ata (formerly Verny). Population 1,134,000 (1988). Karaganda, a major mining centre, had a population (1987) of 633,000.

KYRGYZSTAN

President, Askar Akaev.
Prime Minister, N. Isanov.

Kyrgyzstan occupies the north-eastern part of Soviet Central Asia and borders in the south-east on China. In 1924 a Kara-Kirghiz Autonomous Province was formed within the RSFSR. In 1926 it became a Kirghiz Autonomous Republic, and in 1936 a Union Republic. It contains two provinces, Issyk-Kul and Osh. The republic's name was changed to Kyrgyzstan in December 1990. Kyrgyzstan is a mountainous country, the major part being covered by the ridge of the Central Tienshan, while mountains of the Pamir-Altai system occupy its southern part. There are a number of spacious mountain valleys, the Alai, Susamyr, the Issyk-Kul lake and others. The majority of the population is concentrated in plains, lying at the foot of mountains—Chu, Talass, part of the Ferghana Valley where agriculture prospers. Crops include sugar beet and cotton, and sheep are important in the mountains. Industry is being developed and some mining is done. The Kirghiz constitute 52·4 per cent of the population, the Russians 21·5 per cent. The Uzbeks (in Eastern Ferghana) amount to 12·9 per cent.

CAPITAL.—Bishkek (formerly Frunze). Population 646,000 (1988).

MOLDOVA

President, Mircea Snegur.
Prime Minister, V. T. Muravsky.

Moldova (formerly Moldavia), occupying the south-western corner of the USSR, borders in the west on Romania with the Pruth forming the frontier. In 1918, Romania seized the Russian Province of Bessarabia, but in 1940 the USSR forced Romania to give back Bessarabia, the major part of which was merged with the Moldavian ASSR (formed in 1924) to create the Moldavian SSR. In June 1990 the republic's Supreme Soviet voted to change the name to the SSR Moldova. In May 1991 the name was changed to the Republic of Moldova.

The northern part of the Republic consists of flat steppe lands, now all under plough. Some forests skirt the Dniester. Further south, around Kishinev, there are woody hills and further south again, low-lying steppe lands. The climate is moderate. The main river is the Dniester, navigable along the whol[e] course.

The main industry is agriculture (vinicultur[e] fruit-growing and market-gardening). Industry insignificant in both parts of Moldova, but th[e] Republic has the densest population in the USSR Romanians make up 64 per cent of the population with Ukrainians (14·2 per cent), and Russians (12 per cent) next.

On June 23, 1990 the Supreme Soviet adopted declaration of sovereignty. Independence was de[-] clared in August 1991 with the aim of eventu[al] reunion with Romania; this is resisted by the Dnest[er] Russian and Gauguz Turkish regions, which hav[e] both declared independence from Moldova.

CAPITAL.—Kishinev (Chisinau). Populatio[n] 684,000 (1988).

RUSSIA

(The Russian Soviet Federal Socialist Republic)

President, Boris Yeltsin.
Chairman of the Council of Ministers, I. S. Silaev.

Russia, the largest and the most powerful of th[e] Republics, occupies the major half of the Europea[n] part of the USSR and the major northern portion its Asiatic part and makes up 77 per cent of the tot[al] territory of the USSR with 53 per cent of the tot[al] population. About 83 per cent of the population a[re] Russians. The Muslim Tatars are the largest mino[r-] ity, with 4 per cent of the population.

Russia comprises 16 Republics (Bashkir, Burya[t] Checheno-Ingush, Chuvash, Daghestan, Kabardi[n] Balkar, Kalmyk, Karelian, Komi, Mari, Mordovia[n] North Osetian, Tatar, Tuva, Udmurt and Yakut); s[ix] regions (Altai, Khabarovsk, Krasnodar, Krasno[y-] arsk, Maritime and Stavropol) containing in the turn five autonomous provinces; 49 provinces (Amu[r] Archangel, Astrakhan, Belgorod, Bryansk, Chel[y-] abinsk, Chita, Irkutsk, Ivanovo, Kaliningrad, K[a-] luga, Kamchatka, Kemerovo, Kirov, Kostrom[a] Kurgan, Kursk, Lipetsk, Magadan, Moscow, Mu[r-] mansk, Nizhny Novgorod, Novgorod, Novosibirs[k] Omsk, Orel, Orenburg, Penza, Perm, Pskov, Rosto[v] Ryazan, St Petersburg, Sakhalin, Samara, Sarato[v] Smolensk, Sverdlovsk, Tambov, Tomsk, Tula, Tve[r] Tyumen, Ulyanovsk, Vladimir, Volgograd, Volog[da] Voronezh and Yaroslavl).

There are three principal geographic areas: a lo[w] lying flat Western part stretching eastwards up the Yenisei and divided in two by the Ural ridge; a[n] eastern part, between the Yenisei and the Pacifi[c] consisting of a number of tablelands and ridges, an[d] a southern mountainous part. Climatically, Russ[ia] extends from Arctic and tundra belts to the su[b-] tropical in the south. It has a very long coast-lin[e] including the longest Arctic coastline in the wor[ld] (about 17,000 miles). The most important rivers a[re] the Volga, the Northern Dvina and the Pechora, th[e] Neva, the Don and the Kuban in the European par[t] and in the Asiatic part, the Ob, the Irtysh, th[e] Yenisei, the Lena and the Amur, and, further nort[h] Khatanga, Olenek, Yana, Indigirka, Kolyma an[d] Anadyr. Lakes are abundant, particularly in th[e] north-west. The huge Baikal Lake in Eastern Siber[ia] is the deepest lake in the world. There are also tw[o] large artificial water reservoirs within the Great[er] Volga canal system, the Moscow and Rybinsk 'Seas[.]

Government.—As reforms to the Soviet Cons[ti-] tution in 1988 made possible, Russia has adopted two-tier legislative structure comprising its ow[n] Congress of People's Deputies as well as a bicamer[al] Supreme Soviet, whose chairman and members a[re] to be elected by Congress. The RSFSR's Congress People's Deputies, convened in May 1990, issued declaration of sovereignty on June 12, 1990. Th[e] epublic's first presidential elections were held on June 12, 1991.

Minerals.—The Republic has some of the richest mineral deposits in the world. Coal is mined in the Kuznetsk area, in the Urals, south of Moscow, in the Donets basin (its Eastern part lies in Russia) and in the Pechora area in the North. Oil is produced in the Northern Caucasus, in the area between the Volga and the Ural and in Western Siberia, which also has large deposits of natural gas. Coal and gas deposits in Siberia and the Far East (especially Yakutia) are currently being developed, now that some deposits in the western parts of the USSR are approaching exhaustion. The Ural mountains contain a unique assortment of minerals—high-quality iron ore, manganese, copper, aluminium, gold, platinum, precious stones, salt, asbestos, pyrites, coal, oil, etc. Iron ore is also mined near Kursk, Tula, Lipetsk, in several areas in Siberia and in the Kola Peninsula. Non-ferrous metals are found in the Altai, in Eastern Siberia, in the Northern Caucasus, in the Kuznetsk-Basin, in the far east and in the far north. Nine-tenths of all USSR forests are located in Russia.

Production and Industry.—The vast area of the Republic and the great variety in climatic conditions cause great differences in the structure of agriculture from north to south and from west to east. In the far north reindeer breeding, hunting and fishing are predominant. Further south, timber industry is combined with grain growing. In the southern half of the forest zone and in the adjacent forest-steppe zone, the acreage under grain crops is far larger and the structure of agriculture more complex. An extensive programme of land improvement mainly involving this zone aims to double its total agricultural output by 1990. In the eastern part of this zone, between the Volga and the Urals, cericulture is predominant (particularly summer wheat), followed by cattle breeding. Beyond the Urals is another important grain-growing and stock-breeding area in the southern part of the Western-Siberian plain. The southern steppe zone is the main wheat granary of the USSR, containing also large acreages under barley, maize and sunflower. In the extreme south cotton is now cultivated. Vine, tobacco and other southern crops are grown on the Black Sea shore of the Caucasus.

Industrially, Russia occupies the first place among the Soviet Republics. Moscow and St. Petersburg are still the two largest industrial centres in the country, but new industrial areas are being developed in the Urals, the Kuznetsk basin, and more recently in Siberia and the Far East. Most of the oil produced in the USSR comes from Russia; half the annual output comes from Tyumen Oblast in Western Siberia. All industries are represented in Russia, including iron and steel and engineering.

CAPITAL.—Moscow. Population 8,879,000 (1988). Moscow, founded about AD 1147 by Yuri Dolgoruki, became first the centre of the rising Moscow principality and in the 15th century, the capital of the whole of Russia (Muscovy). In 1325 it became the seat of the Metropolitan of Russia. In 1703 Peter the Great transferred the capital to the newly-built St Petersburg, but on March 14, 1918, Moscow was again designated as the capital. ΨSt. Petersburg (before the first World War St Petersburg, from 1914–1924 Petrograd, and from 1924–91 Leningrad) has a population of 4,948,000 (January 1, 1987).

Other towns with populations (January 1, 1987) exceeding 1,000,000 are:—

Nizhny-Novgorod (Gorky)	1,425,000
Novosibirsk (Novonikolayevsk)	1,423,000
Sverdlovsk (Yekaterinburg)	1,331,000
Samara (Kuibyshev)	1,280,000
Omsk	1,134,000
Chelyabinsk	1,119,000
Ufa	1,092,000
Perm (Molotov)	1,075,000
Kazan	1,068,000
Rostov-on-Don	1,004,000

TADJIKISTAN

President, Kakhar Makhkamov.
Prime Minister, I. Khaeev.

Tadjikistan lies in the extreme south-east of Soviet Central Asia and borders in the south on Afghanistan and in the east on China. It was originally formed in 1924 as an Autonomous Republic within the Uzbek SSR and became a Union Republic in 1929. It includes the Gorno-Badakhshan Autonomous Province and the Kulyab, Kurgan-Tyubinsk and Khodzhent Provinces.

The country is mountainous; in the east lie the Pamir highlands with the highest point in the USSR, Pik Kommunizma (24,590 feet), in the centre the high ridges of the Pamir-Altai system. Plains are formed by wide stretches of the Syr-Darya valley in the north and of the Amu-Darya in the south.

Like the other Central Asiatic Republics, Tadjikistan is a cotton-growing country. Its climatic conditions favour the cultivation of Egyptian cotton. Irrigation is of great importance. Of the population 58·8 per cent are Tadjiks (linguistically and culturally akin to the Persians), 23 per cent Uzbeks, and 10·4 per cent Russians.

In August 1990 it was reported that the Supreme Soviet of Tadjikistan had issued a declaration of sovereignty; independence was declared in September 1991.

CAPITAL.—Dushanbe (formerly Stalinabad; Dyushambe). Population, 596,000 (1988).

TURKMENISTAN

President, Saparmurad Niyazov.
Prime Minister, Kh. Akhmedov.

Turkmenistan occupies the extreme south of Soviet Central Asia, between the Caspian and the Amu-Darya, and borders in the south on Iran and Afghanistan. It was formed in 1924 and contains five Provinces: Ashkhabad, Chardjou, Krasnovodsk, Mary and Tashauz. The country is a low-lying plain, fringed by hills in the south. Ninety per cent of the plain is taken up by the arid Kara-Kum desert. Of all Central-Asiatic Republics, Turkmenistan is the lowest and driest. The cultivation of cotton, stock-raising and mineral extraction are the principal industries. The republic produces about 16 per cent of the Soviet Union's natural gas, as well as astrakhan furs and carpets. Most of the arable land is artificially irrigated. The oil and salt industries are of old standing. There are also some fisheries in the Caspian.

Turkomans make up 68·4 per cent of the population, Russians 12·6 per cent, and Uzbeks 8·5 per cent.

In August 1990 it was reported that Turkmenistan had declared itself a sovereign national state.

CAPITAL.—Ashkhabad (formerly Askhabad, Poltoratsk). Population 390,000 (1988).

UKRAINE

President, Leonid Kravchuk.
Prime Minister, V. P. Fokin.

This Republic, second largest in population, lying in the south-western part of the European half of the USSR, was formed in December 1917. Ukrainians make up nearly 75 per cent of the population, with 21 per cent Russians. It consists of 25 provinces—

Cherkassy, Chernigov, Chernovtsy, Crimea, Dnepropetrovsk, Donetsk, Ivano-Frankovsk, Kharkov, Kherson, Khmelnitsky, Kiev, Kirovograd, Lugansk, Lvov, Nikolayev, Odessa, Poltava, Rovno, Sumy, Ternopol, Transcarpathia, Vinnitsa, Volhynia, Zaporozhye and Zhitomir. The Crimea voted to become an autonomous republic within the Ukraine in September 1991.

Physical Features.—The larger part of the Ukraine forms a plain with small elevations. The Carpathian mountains lie in the south-western part of the Republic. The climate is moderate, with relatively mild winters (particularly in the south-west) and hot summers. The main rivers are the Dnieper with its tributaries, the Southern Bug and the Northern Donets (a tributary of the Don).

Production and Industry.—The main centre of Soviet coal mining and iron and steel industry is situated in the southern part of the Ukraine. In 1980, the Ukraine provided 36 per cent of the total Soviet steel, 51 per cent of iron ore and 27 per cent of coal. The engineering and chemical industries are also of importance. The central forest-steppe region (mainly on the right bank of the Dnieper) is the greatest sugar-producing area in the USSR. The Ukraine also leads in grain-growing and stock-raising.

There are large deposits of coal and salt in the Donets Basin, of iron ore in Krivoy Rog and near Kerch in the Crimea, of manganese in Nikopol, and of quicksilver in Nikitovka.

In July 1990 the Ukrainian Supreme Soviet issued a declaration of sovereignty, stating its intention to become a neutral state, but making no mention of secession from the Soviet Union. The Ukraine declared its independence in August 1991, subject to a referendum in December when elections are also scheduled to take place.

CAPITAL (since 1934).—Kiev, one of the oldest cities in the USSR, founded in the 6th–7th century AD, was the capital of the Russian State from 865 to 1240. Population (1988) 2,577,000. Other towns are:—

Kharkov	1,587,000
Dnepropetrovsk (Yekaterinoslav)	1,182,000
Ψ Odessa	1,141,000
Donetsk (Stalino; Yuzovka, i.e. Hughesovka)	1,090,000

UZBEKISTAN

President and Prime Minister, Islam Karimov.
Vice President, Sh. R. Mirsaidov.

Uzbekistan was formed in 1924 and consists of the Kara-Kalpak Autonomous Republic and of 12 provinces (Andizhan, Bokhara, Dzhizak, Ferghana, Kashka-darya, Khorezm, Namangan, Navoi, Samarkand, Surkhan-darya, Syr-darya and Tashkent). It lies between the high Tienshan Mountains and the Pamir highlands in the east and south-east and sandy lowlands in the west and north-west. The major part of the territory is a plain with huge waterless deserts and several large oases, which form the main centres of population and economic life. The largest is the Ferghana valley, watered by the Syr-darya. Other oases include Tashkent, Samarkand, Bokhara and Khorezm. The climate is continental and dry. Minerals include gold, natural gas, oil, copper, lead, zinc and coal.

The Uzbeks, a Turkic people, make up 68·7 per cent of the population, the Russians 10·8 per cent, Tatars 4·2 per cent and Kazakhs 4 per cent.

There are major agricultural and textile machinery plants and several chemical combines. Uzbekistan is the main cotton-growing area of the USSR producing more than 60 per cent of all Soviet cotton. Irrigation has always been of decisive importance in this area, and the Soviet Government has done much in this field, including the construction of the Great Ferghana Canal (230 miles).

In June 1990 the Supreme Soviet of Uzbekistan adopted a declaration of sovereignty within 'a renewed Soviet federation'. Independence was declared in August 1991.

CAPITAL.—Tashkent. Population 2,210,000 (1988). Samarkand (population (1987) 388,000) contains the Gur-Emir (Tamerlane's Mausoleum), completed AD 1400 by Ulugbek, Tamerlane's astronomer-grandson, and a 15th-century observatory.

BALTIC STATES

The independence of the Baltic republics was recognized by a decree of the Soviet State Council on September 6, 1991.

ESTONIA

President, Arnold Ruutel.
Prime Minister, E. Savisaar.

Estonia, formerly a Baltic province of the Russian Empire, was proclaimed an independent republic in 1918. In 1940, it was forcibly incorporated into the USSR. It lies on the shores of the Baltic and of the Finnish Gulf in the north and of the Gulf of Riga in the south-west. Some 800 islands, among them Dagö and Ösel, form part of Estonian territory.

The country forms a low-lying plain with many lakes, among them the Chud (or Pskov) Lake, on the border with Russia. Forests take up about one-fifth of the territory. Agriculture and dairy-farming are the chief industries, rye, oats, barley, flax and potatoes being the chief crops, and butter, bacon and eggs the chief products of dairy farming. There are important manufactures, including textiles, engineering, shipbuilding, woodworking etc.

The population consists of Estonians (61·5 per cent) and Russians (30·3 per cent).

In November 1989 the Estonian Supreme Soviet declared Estonia's 1940 annexation illegal. In February 1990 the guaranteed leading role of the Communist Party was abolished, and in May 1990, following multi-party elections to the Supreme Soviet in March, the formal title 'Republic of Estonia' was reinstated. Estonia declared its renewed independence in August 1991.

CAPITAL.—Ψ Tallinn (formerly Reval). Population, 484,000 (1988).

LATVIA

President, Anatolijs Gorbunovs.
Prime Minister, I. Godmanis.

Latvia, lying on the shores of the Baltic and of the Gulf of Riga, was formerly a Baltic Province of the Russian Empire. It was proclaimed an independent state in 1918 and was forcibly incorporated into the USSR in August 1940.

The surface of the country is generally flat interspersed by occasional chains of hills. The climate is moderately continental. The main rivers are the lower reaches of the Western Dvina and its tributaries. Forests occupy 20 per cent of the total territory.

The Latvians make up 51·8 per cent of the Republic's population, Russians 33·8 per cent and Belorussians 4·5 per cent.

Latvian industry was always highly developed with shipbuilding, engineering, chemical industry textile industry, wood-working and dairying being the chief occupations. Both Riga and Liepaja (Libava Libau) are important sea-ports.

In January 1990 the Latvian Supreme Soviet amended the Constitution to abolish the Communist Party's guaranteed leading role. In May 1990 following multi-party elections to the Supreme Soviet in March, a resolution was passed proclaiming Latvia's independence from the Soviet Union. The formal title, Republic of Latvia, was reinstated.

CAPITAL.—Ψ Riga. Population, 913,000 (1988).

LITHUANIA

President, Vytautas Landsbergis.
Prime Minister, G. Vagnorius.

Lithuania, formerly a Baltic Province of the Russian Empire, was declared an independent republic at Vilna in 1918 and was forcibly incorporated into the USSR in August 1940. The Republic forms a plain with a large number of lakes and swamps. The forests occupy 19 per cent of the whole area. The main river is the Niemen with its tributaries.

The chief industries are agriculture and forestry, the chief products being rye, oats, wheat, barley, flax, sugar-beet and potatoes.

The Lithuanians make up four-fifths of the population, Russians and Poles, 7–9 per cent each.

Following the abolition in December 1989 of the Communist Party's constitutionally guaranteed monopoly of power in Lithuania, multi-party elections to the Supreme Soviet (subsequently renamed the Supreme Council) were held in February and March 1990. A majority of seats were won by candidates affiliated to the nationalist Sajudis (Popular Front for Perestroika) movement.

On March 11, 1990 Lithuania became the first union republic to declare unilaterally its independence from the Soviet Union.

CAPITAL.—Vilnius (Vilna). Population 579,000 (1988).

UNITED ARAB EMIRATES
(Al-Imarat Al-Arabiya Al-Muttahida)

President, Shaikh Zayed bin Sultan al Nahyan (*Abu Dhabi*).
Vice-President, Shaikh Maktoum bin Rashid al Maktoum (*Dubai*).

COUNCIL OF MINISTERS
(as at November 1990)

Finance and Industry, Shaikh Hamdan bin Rashid al Maktoum.
Defence, Shaikh Mohammed bin Rashid al Maktoum.
Interior, Maj. Gen. Hamouda bin Ali.
Foreign Affairs, Rashid Abdullah al Noami.
Communications, Mohammed Saeed al Mualla.
Planning, Shaikh Humaid bin Ahmed al Mualla.
Islamic Affairs and Endowments, Shaikh Mohammed bin Ahmed al Khazraji.
Water and Electricity, Humaid bin Nasser al Oweis.
Economy and Commerce, Saeed Ghobash.
Agriculture and Fisheries, Saeed al Ragabani.
Labour and Social Affairs, Saif al Jarwan.
Minister of State for Cabinet Affairs, Saeed al Ghaith.
Information and Culture, Khalfan bin Mohammed al Roumi.
Education, Hamad Abdul Rahman al Madfa.
Minister of State for Financial and Industrial Affairs, Ahmed bin Humaid al Tayer.
Minister of State for Foreign Affairs, Shaikh Hamdan bin Zayed al Nahyan.
Minister of State for Supreme Council Affairs, Shaikh Mohammed bin Saqr bin Mohammed al Qassimi.
Higher Education, Shaikh Nahyan bin Mubarak al Nahyan.
Justice, Dr Abdullah bin Omran Taryam.
Health, Ahmed bin Saeed al Badi.
Petroleum and Mineral Resources, Yousuf bin Omeir bin Yousuf.

Public Works and Housing, Rakad bin Salem bin Rakad.
Youth and Sports, Shaikh Faisal bin Khaled bin Mohammed al Qassimi.

EMBASSY OF THE UNITED ARAB EMIRATES
30 Prince's Gate, SW7 1PT
[071–581 1281]

Ambassador Extraordinary and Plenipotentiary, Dr Khaifa Mohamed Sulaiman, GCVO (1988).

Area and Population.—The approximate area of the UAE is 32,278 sq. miles (83,600 sq. km), and the population (UN estimate 1989) is 1,546,000.

The United Arab Emirates (formerly the Trucial States) is composed of seven emirates (Abu Dhabi, Ajman, Dubai, Fujairah, Ras al Khaimah, Sharjah and Umm al Qaiwain) which came together as an independent state on December 2, 1971 when they ended their individual special treaty relationships with the British Government (Ras al Khaimah joined the other six on February 10, 1972). Six of the emirates lie on the shore of the Gulf between the Musandam peninsula in the east and the Qatar peninsula in the west while the seventh, Fujeirah, lies on the Gulf of Oman.

Government.—The British Government, by virtue of a treaty made in 1892, had been responsible for the external affairs of the emirates through the British Political Resident in the Persian Gulf and the British Political Agents in each emirate, but on independence the Union Government assumed full responsibility for all internal and external affairs apart from some internal matters that remained the prerogative of the individual emirates. Overall authority lies with the Supreme Council of the seven emirate rulers, each of whom is an absolute monarch in his own territory. The President and Vice-President are elected by the Supreme Council from among its members. The President appoints the Council of Ministers.

Security in the area is maintained by the UAE Armed Forces. The Ministry of Defence is located in Dubai with a general headquarters in Abu Dhabi. Most of the separate police forces have also been merged.

Revenue is chiefly derived from oil, re-exports and customs dues on imports.

Trade with UK

	1989	1990
Imports from UK	£571,421,000	£664,724,000
Exports to UK	165,003,000	181,486,000

CURRENCY.—UAE dirham of 100 fils.
FLAG.—Horizontal stripes of green over white over black with vertical red stripe in the hoist.
NATIONAL DAY.—December 2.

Abu Dhabi

Abu Dhabi is the largest emirate of the UAE in area, stretching from Khor al Odaid in the west to the borders with Dubai in the Jebel Ali area. It includes six villages in the Buraimi oasis, the other three being part of the Sultanate of Oman, and a number of settlements in the Liwa Oasis system. Following negotiations with Saudi Arabia, some adjustment of the border has now been made in the Khor al Odaid region, but the agreement has not yet been ratified. The population of the Emirate is now about 670,000

The Abu Dhabi government controls oil, gas and petrochemical operations in the emirate through the Supreme Petroleum Council. This body in turn issues instructions to the Abu Dhabi National Oil Company (ADNOC) which has majority shareholdings in the several oil operating and gas treatment companies.

ADNOC also has majority shareholdings in oil industry-related companies covering drilling, refining, distribution, chemical manufacture and investment. Offshore production began in 1962, the most important fields being Umm Shaif and Lower Zakum, near Das Island, site of a large associated gas liquefaction plant. The Upper Zakum field came on stream in late 1982, and four other offshore fields are being developed, one near Abu Dhabi city and three near Delma. Production of oil onshore began in 1963 from the Murban field. A large onshore associated gas liquefaction project based at Ruwais started production in 1981. Other large natural gas finds in recent years will consolidate Abu Dhabi's position as a holder of some of the largest reserves of natural gas in the world. Abu Dhabi's crude oil production in 1989 was approximately 1·47 million barrels per day.

With its oil wealth the emirate has seen a decade of growth (which is currently slowing down), not only at Abu Dhabi, now a modern city of about 450,000 people, but also at Al Ain in the Buraimi Oasis and at the new petro-chemical city at Ruwais. An international airport opened in 1982 at Abu Dhabi and another is under construction at Al Ain. There are airfields at Das Island and Jebel Dhanna. The port and harbour on Abu Dhabi island are now completed and there are port facilities at Ruwais.

Ajman and Umm al Qaiwain

Ajman and Umm al Qaiwain are the smallest emirates, having populations of around 64,000 and 29,000 respectively. Both lie on the Gulf coast although Ajman has two inland enclaves at Manama and Masfut. Exploration work continues in both Emirates for oil and gas but so far only Umm Al Qaiwain has experienced any success, with the offshore discovery of natural gas, but the field has yet to be commercially developed. The discovery of onshore gas in nearby Sharjah has increased hopes of similar discoveries in both Ajman and Umm Al Qaiwain.

Dubai

Dubai is the second largest emirate both in size and in population, which is about 419,000. The town of Dubai is the main port for the import of goods into the UAE and has a wide re-export trade to the other Gulf States. Dubai's prosperity was established by this trade long before the discovery of oil. Oil was discovered in 1966 and production began in September 1969. The producer in Dubai's offshore oilfields is Dubai Petroleum Company, operated by CONOCO. Production is in excess of 350,000 b.p.d. In 1982 an ARCO-Britoil joint venture discovered an extensive gas and condensate field onshore. A small amount of condensate is produced from the onshore Margam field.

Oil income has been used to finance Dubai's infrastructure, and major construction projects include an international airport, a dry dock complex and an international trade and exhibition centre. There is also a 66 berth port at Jebel Ali, forming the heart of an industrial complex which includes an aluminium smelter with an associated de-salination plant and a gas processing plant. The port and its immediate area is a free trade zone which is expected to attract more industry.

Fujairah

Fujairah, with a population of 40,000, is the most remote of the seven emirates lying on the Gulf of Oman coast, and only connected by a metal road to the rest of the country since the end of 1975. Largely agricultural, its population is spread between the slopes of the inland Hajar mountain range and the town of Fujairah itself, together with a number of smaller settlements on the comparatively fertile plain on the coast. Although exploration work continues, there have been no hydrocarbon discoveries in the emirate. However, there are some chrome and other mineral deposits. Fujairah has a new general cargo port.

Ras al Khaimah

Ras al Khaimah has a population of 116,000 of whom more than half live in the town. An ancient sea-port, near to which archaeological remains have been found, Ras al Khaimah is developing as the most agricultural of the emirates, producing vegetables, dates, fruit and tobacco. In 1982 Ras al Khaimah announced the discovery of oil and gas offshore and this field currently produces approximately 5,000 b.p.d. An industrial area has been developed to the north of the emirate, which includes two cement works. Ras al-Khaimah has an international airport and has also expanded its port. A new international airport is nearing completion. A new trade centre has been completed and it is hoped that more industry will be attracted to the emirate.

Sharjah

Sharjah, with a population of approximately 269,000, has declined from its former position as principal town in the area. It became the third oil producing emirate in the summer of 1974, following the discovery of oil offshore. The field declined over the years and by 1982 was yielding less than 6,000 b.p.d. However, new oil and gas discoveries were made in 1982 in the northern emirates and production now stands at about 50,000 b.p.d. Sharjah is well connected by metalled roads to all the other northern emirates. It experienced a construction boom in the mid-1970s including an ambitious layout of roads and flyovers within the town. A new container port has been constructed on the Gulf of Oman at Khor Fakkan. The international airport was officially opened in 1979.

BRITISH EMBASSIES
PO Box 248, Abu Dhabi
[Abu Dhabi 326600]

Ambassador Extraordinary and Plenipotentiary, His Excellency Graham Stuart Burton, CMG (1990).
British Council Representative, Dr P. Clark.

PO Box 65, Dubai
[Dubai 521070]

Counsellor and Consul General, R. A. M. Hendrie.
British Council Representative, A. Swales, PO Box 1636, Dubai.

UNITED STATES OF AMERICA

Physiography

The conterminous States of the Republic occupy nearly all that portion of the North American Continent between the Atlantic and Pacific Oceans, in latitude 25° 07′–49° 23′ North and longitude 66° 57′–124° 44′ West, its northern boundary being Canada and the southern boundary Mexico. The separate State of Alaska reaches a latitude of 71° 23′ N., at Point Barrow (2,502 miles from the US geographic centre).

The general coastline of the 50 States has a length of about 2,069 miles on the Atlantic, 7,623 miles on the Pacific, 1,060 miles on the Arctic, and 1,631 miles on the Gulf of Mexico.

The principal river is the mighty Mississippi-Missouri-Red, traversing the whole country from north to south, and having a course of 3,710 miles to its mouth in the Gulf of Mexico, with many large affluents, the chief of which are the Yellowstone, Platte, Arkansas, and Ohio rivers. The rivers flowing into the Atlantic and Pacific Oceans are comparatively small; among the former may be noticed the Hudson, Delaware, Susquehanna, Potomac, James, Roanoke and Savannah; of the latter, the Columbia-Snake, Sacramento, and Colorado. The Nueces, Brazos, Trinity, Pearl, Mobile-Tombigbee-Alabama, Apalachicola-Chattahoochee, Suwannee and Colorado of Texas fall into the Gulf of Mexico, also the Rio Grande, a long river partly forming the boundary with Mexico. The areas of the water-basins have been estimated as follows:—Rivers flowing to the Pacific, 647,300 square miles; to the Atlantic, 488,877; and to the Gulf of Mexico, 1,683,325 square miles, of which 1,234,600 are drained by the Mississippi-Missouri-Red. The chain of the Rocky Mountains separates the western portion of the country from the remainder, communications being carried on over certain elevated passes, several of which are now traversed by railroads and major highways; west of these, bordering the Pacific coast, the Cascade Mountains and Sierra Nevada form the outer edge of a high tableland, consisting in part of stony and sandy desert and partly of grazing land and forested mountains, and including the Great Salt Lake, which extends to the Rocky Mountains. In the Eastern States (which form the more settled and most thickly inhabited portion of the country) large forests of valuable timber still exist, the remnants of the forests which formerly extended over all the Atlantic slope, but into which great inroads have been made. The highest point is Mount McKinley (Alaska), 20,320 ft. above sea level and the lowest point of dry land is in Death Valley (Inyo, California), 282 ft. below sea-level.

AREA AND POPULATION

	Area 1980 (sq. miles)	Population*
	Total	Census 1980
The United States (a)...	3,618,770	226,545,805
Puerto Rico	3,515	3,196,520
Outlying areas under US jurisdiction	1,176	368,856
Territories	459	235,927
Guam	209	105,979
US Virgin Islands ..	132	96,569
American Samoa...	77	32,297
Midway Is.	2	453
Wake I.	3	302
Canton I. and Enderbury I.	27	—
Johnston Atoll (b) .	0·5	327
Other (c)	9	—
Pacific Islands Trust Territory (excluding N. Mariana Is.)	533	116,149
Northern Mariana Is.	184	16,780
Population abroad (d) ..		995,546
Armed Forces		515,408
Total	3,543,924	231,106,727

(a) The 50 States and the Federal District of Columbia.
(b) Formerly listed as Johnston and Sand Island. Sand Island uninhabited at time of enumeration.
(c) Navassa, Baker, Howland and Jarvis Islands, Kingman Reef, and Palmyra Atoll.
(d) Excludes US citizens temporarily abroad on private business.
* According to the 1990 Census, the total population of the United States was 248,709,873; data for the outlying areas were not available at the time of going to press.

Immigrants by Place of Birth, 1971-90

(1971-76, year ends June 30; from 1977, year ends September 30)

Place of Birth	1971-80	1990*
Europe	801,300	112,401
Asia	1,633,800	338,581
North America	1,645,000	957,558
Canada	114,800	16,812
Mexico	637,200	679,068
West Indies	759,800	115,351
Central America ..	132,400	146,202
South America	284,400	85,819
Africa	91,500	35,893
Australia	14,300	1,754
New Zealand	5,300	829
Other countries	17,700	3,648
TOTAL..........	4,493,300	1,533,900

From 1820 to 1989, 55,009,566 immigrants were admitted to the United States.
* Figures for 1990 include 880,372 legalization applicants who gained permanent residence status.

Resident Population by Race 1990
(in thousands)

White	199,686
Black	29,986
American Indian*	1,959·2
Chinese	1,645·5
Filipino	1,406·8
Japanese	847·6
Asian Indian	815·4
Korean	798·8
Vietnamese.............................	614·5
Other Asian or Pacific Islander	1,145
Hispanic origin**	22,354
Cuban	1,043·9
Mexican............................	13,495·9
Puerto Rican	2,727·8
Other Hispanic	5,086·4
All other races	9,804·8
TOTAL..............................	248,704·9

* Includes Eskimo and Aleut.
** Persons of Spanish origin may be of any race.

Registered Births and Deaths

	Live Births		Deaths	
Calendar Year	Number	Rate per 1,000	Number	Rate per 1,000
1985	3,760,561	15·8	2,086,440	8·7
1986	3,756,547	15·6	2,105,361	8·7
1987	3,809,394	15·7	2,123,323	8·7
1988	3,909,510	15·9	2,167,999	8·8
1989*	4,021,000	16·2	2,155,000	8·7
1990*	4,179,000	16·7	2,162,000	8·6

Sample base was 100 per cent.
Note.—Figures tabulated are for the United States. Deaths exclude foetal deaths. Rates are based on the population as estimated on July 1.
* Provisional.

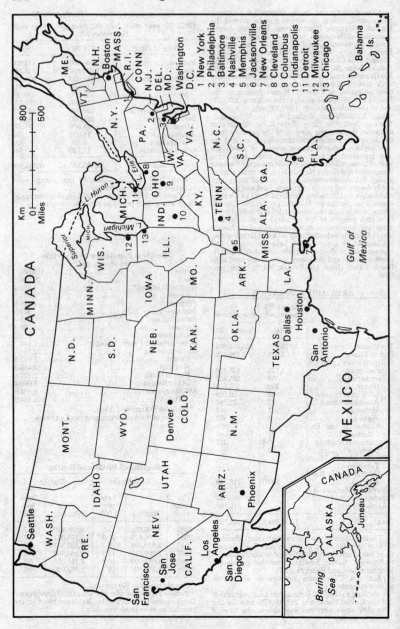

THE UNITED STATES

State (with date and *order* of admission)	Land area sq. m.	Population, (1990 Census)	Capital	Governor (term of office in years, and expiry year)
Alabama (Ala.) (1819) *(22)*	50,767	4,040,587	Montgomery	Harold G. Hunt *(R)* (4—1995)
Alaska (1959) *(49)*	570,833	550,043	Juneau	Walter Hickel *(I)* (4—1994)
Arizona (Ariz.) (1912) *(48)*	113,508	3,665,228	Phoenix	Fife Symington *(R)* (4—1995)
Arkansas (Ark.) (1836) *(25)*	52,078	2,350,725	Little Rock	Bill Clinton *(D)* (4—1995)
California (Calif.) (1850) *(31)*	156,299	29,760,021	Sacramento	Pete Wilson *(R)* (4—1995)
Colorado (Colo.) (1876) *(38)*	103,595	3,294,394	Denver	Roy Romer *(D)* (4—1995)
Connecticut (Conn.)§(1788) *(5)*	4,872	3,287,116	Hartford	Lowell Weicker *(I)* (4—1995)
Delaware (Del.) § (1787) *(1)*	1,932	666,168	Dover	Michael N. Castle *(R)* (4—1993)
Florida (Fla.) (1845) *(27)*	54,153	12,937,926	Tallahassee	Lawton Chiles *(D)* (4—1995)
Georgia (Ga.) § (1788) *(4)*	58,056	6,478,216	Atlanta	Zell Miller *(D)* (4—1995)
Hawaii (1959) *(50)*	6,425	1,108,229	Honolulu	John D. Waihee III *(D)* (4—1994)
Idaho (1890) *(43)*	82,412	1,006,749	Boise	Cecil D. Andrus *(D)* (4—1995)
Illinois (Ill.) (1818) *(21)*	55,645	11,430,602	Springfield	James R. Thompson *(R)* (4—1995)
Indiana (Ind.) (1816) *(19)*	35,932	5,544,159	Indianapolis	Evan Bayh *(D)* (4—1993)
Iowa (1846) *(29)*	55,965	2,776,755	Des Moines	Terry Branstad *(R)* (4—1995)
Kansas (Kan.) (1861) *(34)*	81,778	2,477,574	Topeka	Joan Finney *(D)* (4—1995)
Kentucky (Ky.) (1792) *(15)*	39,669	3,685,296	Frankfort	Wallace G. Wilkinson *(D)* (4—1992)
Louisiana (La.) (1812) *(18)*	44,521	4,219,973	Baton Rouge	Buddy Roemer *(R)* (4—1995)
Maine (Me.) (1820) *(23)*	30,995	1,227,928	Augusta	John R. McKernan, Jr. *(R)* (4—1995)
Maryland (Md.)§ (1788) *(7)*	9,837	4,781,468	Annapolis	William D. Schaefer *(D)* (4—1995)
Massachusetts (Mass.)§(1788)*(6)*	7,824	6,016,425	Boston	William Weld *(R)* (4—1995)
Michigan (Mich.) (1837) *(26)*	56,954	9,295,297	Lansing	John Engler *(R)* (4—1995)
Minnesota (Minn.) (1858) *(32)*	79,548	4,375,099	St Paul	Anne Carlson *(R)* (4—1995)
Mississippi (Miss.) (1817) *(20)*	47,233	2,573,216	Jackson	Ray Mabus *(D)* (4—1992)
Missouri (Mo.) (1821) *(24)*	68,945	5,117,073	Jefferson City	John Ashcroft *(R)* (4—1993)
Montana (Mont.) (1889) *(41)*	145,388	799,065	Helena	Stan Stephens *(R)* (4—1993)
Nebraska (Neb.) (1867) *(37)*	76,644	1,578,385	Lincoln	Ben Nelson *(D)* (4—1995)
Nevada (Nev.) (1864) *(36)*	109,894	1,201,833	Carson City	Robert J. Miller *(D)* (4—1995)
New Hampshire (NH)§ (1788) *(9)*	8,993	1,109,252	Concord	Judd Gregg *(R)* (2—1993)
New Jersey (NJ)§ (1787) *(3)*	7,468	7,730,188	Trenton	James S. Florio *(D)* (4—1994)
New Mexico (NM) (1912) *(47)*	121,335	1,515,069	Santa Fé	Bruce King *(D)* (4—1995)
New York (NY)§ (1788) *(11)*	47,377	17,990,455	Albany	Mario M. Cuomo *(D)* (4—1995)
North Carolina (NC)§ (1789) *(12)*	48,843	6,628,637	Raleigh	James G. Martin *(R)* (4—1993)
North Dakota (ND) (1889) *(39)*	69,300	638,800	Bismarck	George A. Sinner *(D)* (4—1993)
Ohio (1803) *(17)*	41,004	10,847,115	Columbus	George Voinovich *(R)* (4—1995)
Oklahoma (Okla.) (1907) *(46)*	68,655	3,145,585	Oklahoma City	David Walters *(D)* (4—1995)
Oregon (Ore.) (1859) *(33)*	96,184	2,842,321	Salem	Neil Goldschmidt *(D)* (4—1995)
Pennsylvania (Pa.)§ (1787) *(2)*	44,888	11,881,643	Harrisburg	Robert P. Casey *(D)* (4—1995)
Rhode Island (RI)§ (1790) *(13)*	1,055	1,003,464	Providence	Bruce Sundlun *(D)* (2—1993)
South Carolina (SC)§ (1788) *(8)*	30,203	3,486,703	Columbia	Carroll A. Campbell, Jr. *(R)* (4—1995)
South Dakota (SD) (1889) *(40)*	75,952	696,004	Pierre	George S. Mickelson *(R)* (4—1995)
Tennessee (Tenn.) (1796) *(16)*	41,155	4,877,185	Nashville	Ned R. McWherter *(D)* (4—1995)
Texas (1845) *(28)*	262,017	16,986,510	Austin	Anne Richards *(D)* (4—1995)
Utah (1896) *(45)*	82,073	1,722,850	Salt Lake City	Norman H. Bangerter *(R)* (4—1993)
Vermont (Vt.) (1791) *(14)*	9,273	562,758	Montpelier	Richard Snelling *(R)* (2—1993)
Virginia (Va.)§ (1788) *(10)*	39,704	6,187,358	Richmond	L. Douglas Wilder *(D)* (4—1994)
Washington (Wash.) (1889) *(42)*	66,511	4,866,692	Olympia	Booth Gardner *(D)* (4—1993)
West Virginia (W. Va.) (1863)*(35)*	24,119	1,793,477	Charleston	Gaston Caperton *(D)* (4—1993)
Wisconsin (Wis.) (1848) *(30)*	54,426	4,891,769	Madison	Tommy Thompson *(R)* (4—1995)
Wyoming (Wyo.) (1890) *(44)*	96,989	453,588	Cheyenne	Michael Sullivan *(D)* (4—1995)
Dist. of Columbia (DC) (1791)	63	606,900	..	†

OUTLYING TERRITORIES AND POSSESSIONS*

American Samoa	76	32,395	Pago Pago	Peter Tali Coleman *(D)* (4—1993)
Guam	209	105,816	Agaña	Joseph Ada *(R)* (4—1991)
Marshall Is.	70	31,042	Majuro	..
Fed. States of Micronesia	271	73,160	Kolonia	..
Northern Mariana Is.	184	16,780	Saipan	Lorenzo I. DeLeon Guerrero *(R)* (4—1994)
Palau	192	12,177	Koror	..
Puerto Rico	3,421	3,187,570	San Juan	R. Hernandez-Colon *(PDP)*(4—1993)
Virgin Is.	132	95,591	Charlotte Amalie	Alexander Farrelly *(D)* (4—1991)

§ The 13 Original States. *D.*—Democratic Party. *I.*—Independent. *PDP.*—Popular Democratic party. *R.*—Republican Party.
† The capital territory is governed by Congress through a Commissioner and City Council.
* Population figures are 1986 estimates.

Marriage and Divorce

Laws of marriage and of divorce are within the exclusive jurisdiction of each State. Each State legislature enacts its own laws prescribing rules and qualifications pertaining to marriage and its dissolution.

Year	Marriages	Per 1,000 Pop.§	Estimated Divorces	Per 1,000 Pop.§
1985	2,412,625	10·1	1,190,000	5·0
1986	2,407,099	10·0	1,178,000	4·9
1987	2,403,378	9·9	1,116,000	4·8
1988	2,395,926	9·7	1,167,000	4·7
1989*	2,404,000	9·7	1,163,000	4·7
1990*	2,448,000	9·8	1,175,000	4·7

§ Population as estimated on July 1.
* Provisional.

Largest Cities 1990 Census

Ψ New York, NY	7,322,564
Ψ Los Angeles, California	3,485,398
Ψ Chicago, Illinois	2,783,726
Ψ Houston, Texas	1,630,533
Ψ Philadelphia, Pennsylvania	1,585,577
Ψ San Diego, California	1,110,549
Ψ Detroit, Michigan	1,027,974
Dallas, Texas	1,006,877
Phoenix, Arizona	983,403
San Antonio, Texas	935,933
San Jose, California	782,248
Ψ Indianapolis, Indiana*	741,952
Ψ Baltimore, Maryland	736,014
Ψ San Francisco, California	723,959
Jacksonville, Florida*	672,971
Columbus, Ohio	632,910
Ψ Milwaukee, Wisconsin	628,088
Memphis, Tennessee	610,337
Washington, DC	606,900
Ψ Boston, Massachusetts	574,283
Ψ Seattle, Washington	516,259
El Paso, Texas	515,342
Nashville-Davidson, Tennessee*	510,784
Ψ Cleveland, Ohio	505,616

Ψ Seaport　*consolidated city

CAPITAL

In 1790 Congress ratified the cession of 100 sq. miles by the States of Maryland and Virginia as a site for a Federal City to be the national capital of the United States. In 1791 it was decided to name the capital Washington and in 1793 the foundation-stone of the Capitol building was laid. In 1800 the seat of Government was removed to Washington, which was chartered as a city in 1802. In 1846 the Virginia portion was retroceded and the present area of the District of Columbia (with which the City of Washington is considered co-extensive) is 63 sq. miles, with a resident population (mid-1989 estimate) of 604,000.

The District of Columbia is governed by an elected mayor and City Council.

The City of Washington is situated on the west central edge of Maryland, opposite the State of Virginia, on the left bank of the Potomac at its confluence with the Anacostia. The population of the metropolitan area in 1988 was estimated at 3,734,200.

GOVERNMENT

The United States of America is a Federal Republic consisting of 50 States and one Federal District (of which 13 are original states, seven were admitted without previous organization as territories, and 30 were admitted after such organization), and of organized Territories. Hawaii formally entered the Union as the 50th State on August 21, 1959, from which date the flag of the United States has 13 stripes and 50 stars in 9 horizontal rows of six and five alternately.

NATIONAL ANTHEM.—The Star-Spangled Banner.
NATIONAL DAY.—July 4 (Independence Day).

THE CONSTITUTION.—By the Constitution of Sept. 17, 1787 (to which ten amendments were added on Dec. 15, 1791 and eleventh to twenty-sixth, Jan. 8, 1798, Sept. 25, 1804, Dec. 18, 1865, July 28, 1868, March 30, 1870, Feb. 25, 1913, May 31, 1913, Jan. 16, 1920, Aug. 26, 1920, Feb. 6, 1933, Dec. 5, 1933, Feb. 26, 1951, March 29, 1961, Jan. 23, 1964, Feb. 10, 1967 and June 30, 1971), the government of the United States is entrusted to three separate authorities—the Executive, the Legislative, and the Judicial.

THE EXECUTIVE

The executive power is vested in a President, who is elected every four years. The mode of electing the President is as follows:—Each State elects (on the first Tuesday after the first Monday in November of the year preceding the year in which the Presidential term expires), a number of electors, equal to the whole number of Senators and Representatives to which the State may be entitled in the Congress; but no Senator or Representative, or anyone holding office under Government, shall be appointed an elector. The electors for each State meet in their respective States on the first Monday after the second Wednesday in December following, and there vote for a President by ballot. The ballots are then sent to Washington, and opened on the sixth day of January by the President of Senate in presence of Congress, and the candidate who has received a majority of the whole number of electoral votes cast is declared President for the ensuing term. If no one has a majority, then from the highest on the list (not exceeding three) the House of Representatives elects a President, the votes being taken by States, the representation from each State having one vote. There is also a Vice-President, who, on the death of the President, becomes President for the remainder of the term. Under the XXth Amendment to the Constitution the terms of the President and Vice-President end at noon on the 20th day of January of the years in which such terms would have ended if the Amendment had not been ratified, and the terms of their successors then begin. In case of the removal or death of both President and Vice-President, a statute provides for the succession. Under the XXIInd Amendment to the Constitution, the tenure of the Presidency is limited to two terms.

Executive duties:—(1) He is Commander-in-Chief of the Army and of the Navy (and of the Militias when they are in Federal service), and he commissions all officers therein. (2) With the consent of the Senate, he appoints the Cabinet officers and all the chief (and many minor) officials. (3) He exercises a general supervision over the whole Federal Administration and sees that the Federal Laws are duly carried out. Should disorder arise in any state which the authorities thereof are unable to suppress, the aid of the President is invoked. (4) He controls the foreign policy of the Republic, and has power, 'by and with the Advice and Consent of the Senate, to make Treaties, provided two-thirds of the senators present concur.' The declaration of war rests with Congress. (5) He makes recommendation of a general nature to Congress, and when laws are passed by Congress he may return them to Congress with a veto. But if a measure so vetoed is again passed by both Houses of

THE PRESIDENTS OF THE UNITED STATES OF AMERICA

Name (*with Native State*)	Party	Born	Inaug.	Died	Age
George Washington, *Va.*	Fed.	1732, Feb. 22	1789	1799, Dec. 14	67
John Adams, *Mass.*	,,	1735, Oct. 30	1797	1826, July 4	90
Thomas Jefferson, *Va.*	Rep.	1743, April 13	1801	1826, July 4	83
James Madison, *Va.*	,,	1751, Mar. 16	1809	1836, June 28	85
James Monroe, *Va.*	,,	1758, April 28	1817	1831, July 4	73
John Quincy Adams, *Mass.*	,,	1767, July 11	1825	1848, Feb 23	80
Andrew Jackson, *SC*	Dem.	1767, Mar. 15	1829	1845, June 8	78
Martin Van Buren, *NY*	,,	1782, Dec. 5	1837	1862, July 24	79
William Henry Harrison†, *Va.*	Whig	1773, Feb. 9	1841	1841, April 4	68
John Tyler (*a*), *Va.*	,,	1790, Mar. 29	1841	1862, Jan. 17	71
James Knox Polk, *NC*	Dem.	1795, Nov. 2	1845	1849, June 15	53
Zachary Taylor†, *Va.*	Whig	1784, Nov. 24	1849	1850, July 9	65
Millard Fillmore (*a*), *NY*	,,	1800, Jan. 7	1850	1874, Mar. 8	74
Franklin Pierce, *NH*	Dem.	1804, Nov. 23	1853	1869, Oct. 8	64
James Buchanan, *Pa.*	,,	1791, April 23	1857	1868, June 1	77
Abraham Lincoln†§, *Ky.*	Rep.	1809, Feb. 12	1861	1865, April 15	56
Andrew Johnson (*a*), *NC*	,,	1808, Dec. 29	1865	1875, July 31	66
Ulysses Simpson Grant, *Ohio*	,,	1822, April 27	1869	1885, July 23	63
Rutherford Birchard Hayes, *Ohio*	,,	1822, Oct. 4	1877	1893, Jan. 17	70
James Abram Garfield†§, *Ohio*	,,	1831, Nov. 19	1881	1881, Sept. 19	49
Chester Alan Arthur (*a*), *Vt.*	,,	1830, Oct. 5	1881	1886, Nov. 18	56
Grover Cleveland, *NJ*	Dem.	1837, Mar. 18	1885	1908, June 24	71
Benjamin Harrison, *Ohio*	Rep.	1833, Aug. 20	1889	1901, Mar. 13	67
Grover Cleveland, *NJ*	Dem.	1837, Mar. 18	1893	1908, June 24	71
William McKinley†§, *Ohio*	Rep.	1843, Jan. 29	1897	1901, Sept. 14	58
Theodore Roosevelt (*a*), *NY*	,,	1858, Oct. 27	1901	1919, Jan. 6	60
William Howard Taft, *Ohio*	,,	1857, Sept. 15	1909	1930, Mar. 8	72
Woodrow Wilson, *Va.*	Dem.	1856, Dec. 28	1913	1924, Feb. 3	67
Warren Gamaliel Harding†, *Ohio*	Rep.	1865, Nov. 2	1921	1923, Aug. 2	57
Calvin Coolidge (*a*), *Vt.*	,,	1872, July 4	1923	1933, Jan. 5	60
Herbert Clark Hoover, *Iowa.*	,,	1874, Aug. 10	1929	1964, Oct. 20	90
Franklin Delano Roosevelt†‡, *NY*	Dem.	1882, Jan. 30	1933	1945, April 12	63
Harry S. Truman (*a*), *Missouri*	,,	1884, May 8	1945	1972, Dec. 26	88
Dwight David Eisenhower, *Texas*	Rep.	1890, Oct. 14	1953	1969, Mar. 28	78
John Fitzgerald Kennedy, *Mass.*†§	Dem.	1917, May 29	1961	1963, Nov. 22	46
Lyndon Baines Johnson (*a*), *Texas*	,,	1908, Aug. 27	1963	1973, Jan. 22	64
Richard Milhous Nixon, *California*	Rep.	1913, Jan. 9	1969	..	..
Gerald Rudolph Ford (*b*), *Nebraska*	,,	1913, July 14	1974	..	..
James Earl Carter, *Georgia*	Dem.	1924, Oct. 1	1977	..	..
Ronald Wilson Reagan, *Illinois*	Rep.	1911, Feb. 6	1981	..	..
George Herbert Walker Bush, *Mass.*	,,	1924, June 12	1989	..	..

† Died in office. (*a*) Elected as Vice-President. § Assassinated.
‡ Re-elected Nov. 5, 1940, the first case of a third term; re-elected for a fourth term Nov. 7. 1944.
(*b*) Appointed under the provisions of the 25th Amendment.

Congress by two-thirds majority in each House, it becomes law, notwithstanding the objection of the President. The President must be at least 35 years of age and a native citizen of the United States.

President of the United States, GEORGE HERBERT WALKER BUSH, *born* June 12, 1924, *sworn in* January 20, 1989. Republican.
Vice-President, DAN QUAYLE, *born* Feb. 4, 1947, *sworn in* Jan. 20, 1989.

THE CABINET

Secretary of State, James Baker.
Secretary of the Treasury, Nicholas Brady.
Secretary of Defence, Richard Cheney.
Attorney General, Richard Thornburgh.
Secretary of the Interior, Manuel Lujan.
Secretary of Agriculture, Edward Madigan.
Secretary of Commerce, Robert Mosbacher.
Secretary of Labour, Lynn Martin.
Secretary of Health and Human Services, Dr Louis Sullivan.
Secretary of Housing and Urban Development, Jack Kemp.

Secretary of Transportation, Samuel Skinner.
Secretary of Energy, James Watkins.
Secretary of Education, Andrew Lamar Alexander.
Secretary of Veterans' Affairs, Edward Derwinski.

Other senior positions:
Director of CIA, vacant.
Director, Office of National Drug Control Policy, Bob Martinez.
White House Chief of Staff, John Sununu.
National Security Adviser, Brent Scowcroft.
Director, Office of Management and Budget, Richard Darman.
Administrator, Environmental Protection Agency, William Reilly.
US Trade Representative, Carla Hills.

UNITED STATES EMBASSY
24 Grosvenor Square W1A 1AE
[071-499 9000]

Ambassador Extraordinary and Plenipotentiary, The Honourable Raymond G. H. Seitz (1991).
Minister, Hon. Ronald Woods.
Minister for Economic Affairs, Mrs Ann R. Berry.

Minister Counsellors, Norbert J. Krieg (*Consular Affairs*); Nicholas Baskey (*Administrative Affairs*); Terrence Flannery (*acting*) (*Commercial Affairs*); James P. Rudbeck (*Agricultural Affairs*); Bruce G. Burton (*Political Affairs*); Charles E. Courtney (*Public Affairs*); Lester P. Slezak (*Political/Labour Affairs*); Jeffrey Lutz (*Scientific and Technical Affairs*).

Defence and Naval Attaché, Capt. Peter Baxter.
Army Attaché, Col. David Smith.
Air Attaché, Col. Chester Garrison.

THE CONGRESS

The Legislative power is vested in two Houses, the Senate and the House of Representatives, the President having a veto power, which may be overcome by a two-thirds vote of each House. The Senate is composed of two Senators from each State, elected by the people thereof for the term of six years, and each Senator has one vote. Representatives are chosen in each State, by popular vote, for two years. The average number of persons represented by each Congressman is 1 for 575,000. The Senate consists of 100 members. The House of Representatives consists of 435 Representatives, a resident commissioner from Puerto Rico and a delegate from American Samoa, the District of Columbia, Guam and the Virgin Islands. By the XIXth Amendment, sex is no disqualification for the franchise. The Bureau of the Census estimated that there were 185,105,411 persons of voting age, excluding members of the armed forces overseas, as of November 1990.

THE 102ND CONGRESS

President of the Senate, Dan Quayle (*Vice President of the United States*).
Speaker of the House of Representatives, Thomas S. Foley, *Washington.*
Secretary of the Senate, Walter J. Stewart, *District of Columbia.*
Clerk of the House of Representatives, Donnald K. Anderson, *California.*

Members of the 102nd Congress were elected on November 8, 1990. The 102nd Congress is constituted as follows:
Senate.—Democrats 57; Republicans 43; Total 100.
House of Representatives.—Democrats 267; Republicans 166; Independent 1; Vacancies 1. Total 435 (July 1, 1991).

THE JUDICATURE

The Federal Judiciary consists of three sets of Federal Courts: (1) The Supreme Court at Washington, DC, consisting of a Chief Justice and eight Associate Justices, with original jurisdiction in cases affecting Ambassadors, etc., or where a State is a party to the suit, and with appellate jurisdiction from inferior Federal Courts and from the judgments of the highest Courts of the States. (2) The United States Courts of Appeals, dealing with appeals from District Courts and from certain federal administrative agencies, and consisting of 168 Circuit Judges within 13 circuits. (3) The 94 United States District Courts served by 575 District Court Judges.

The Supreme Court

US Supreme Court Building, Washington
DC, 20543

Chief Justice, William H. Rehnquist, *Ariz., born* Oct. 1, 1924, *appointed* 1986.

ASSOCIATE JUSTICES

Name	Born	Apptd
Byron R. White, *Colo.*	1917	1962
Harry Blackmun, *Minn.*	1908	1970
John Paul Stevens, *Ill.*	1920	1975
Sandra Day O'Connor, *Ariz.*	1930	1981
Antonin Scalia, *Va.*	1936	1986
Anthony M. Kennedy, *Calif.*	1936	1988
David H. Souter, *NH.*	1939	1990

Clerk of the Supreme Court, William K. Suter.

CRIMINAL STATISTICS
(Number of offences)

	1989	1990
Murder and Non-negligent Manslaughter	21,500	23,438
Forcible Rape	94,504	102,555
Robbery	578,326	639,271
Aggravated Assault	951,707	1,054,863
Burglary	3,168,170	3,073,909
Larceny—Theft	7,872,442	7,945,670
Thefts of Motor Vehicles	1,564,800	1,635,907
Total	14,251,449	14,475,613

DEFENCE

Department of Defence

Secretary of Defence (*in the Cabinet*), Richard B. Cheney.
Secretary of the Army, Michael P. W. Stone.
Secretary of the Navy, H. L. Garrett.
Secretary of the Air Force, D. B. Rice.
Chairman, Joint Chiefs of Staff, Gen. Colin Powell.
Vice Chairman, Adm. David E. Jeremiah.

The Department of Defence includes the Secretary of Defence as its head, the Deputy Secretary of Defence, the Defence staff offices, the Joint Chiefs of Staff and the Joint Staff, the three military departments and the military services within those departments, the unified and specified commands, and other Department of Defence agencies as the Secretary of Defence establishes to meet specific requirements. The Defence staff offices and the joint Chiefs of Staff, although separately organized, function in full coordination and co-operation. They include the offices of the Director of Defence Research and Engineering, the Assistant Secretaries of Defence, the General Counsel of the Department of Defence and such other staff offices as the Secretary of Defence may establish. The Joint Chiefs of Staff, as a group, are directly responsible to the Secretary of Defence for the functions assigned to them. Each member of the Joint Chiefs of Staff, other than the Chairman and Vice Chairman, is responsible for keeping the Secretary of his military department fully informed on matters considered or acted upon by the Joint Chiefs of Staff.

Each military department is separately organized under its own Secretary and functions under the direction, authority and control of the Secretary of Defence.

Commanders of unified and specified commands are responsible to the President and the Secretary of Defence for the accomplishment of military missions assigned to them.

Unified Defence Commands

COMMANDERS-IN-CHIEF

US European Command, Brussels.—Gen. John R. Galvin (*US Army*).
US Southern Command, Quarry Heights, Panama Canal Zone.—Gen. George A. Joulwan (*US Army*).
US Atlantic Command, Norfolk, Virginia.—Adm. Leon Edney (*US Navy*).

US Pacific Command, Hawaii.—Adm. Huntington Hardisty (*US Navy*).
US Space Command, Gen. Donald J. Kutyna (*USAF*).
Strategic Air Command, Omaha.—Gen. John T. Chain (*USAF*).
US Transportation Command, Gen. Hansford T. Johnson (*USAF*).
US Special Operations Command, Florida.—Gen. Carl W. Stiner (*US Army*).
US Central Command, Gen. Joseph Hoar (*USMC*).
* A specified command.

Army.—The US Army had a strength on January 28, 1991, of 744,039.
Chief of the Staff of the Army, Gen. Carl E. Vuono.
Navy.—The strength of the Navy on January 28, 1991 was 576,124 active duty personnel.
Chief of Naval Operations, Adm. Frank B. Kelso II.
Marine Corps.—Established 1775. Strength on January 28, 1991 was 200,358 active duty personnel.
Commandant, Gen. Alfred M. Gray.
Air.—The United States Air Force was established as a separate organization on September 18, 1947. In March 1961 the Air Force was assigned primary responsibility for the Department of Defence space development programmes and projects. On January 28, 1991, there were 529,287 officers and airmen on active duty.
Chief of Staff of the US Air Force, Gen. John Lowe.

FINANCE

The Budget
(US$ billions)

Receipts by Source	1989 (actual)	1990 (estimated)
Individual income taxes .	445·7	489·4
Corporation income taxes	103·6	112·0
Social insurance taxes and contributions	359·4	385·4
Excise taxes	34·1	36·2
Estate and gift taxes	8·7	9·3
Customs duties	16·3	16·8
Miscellaneous	22·8	24·4
TOTAL...................	990·7	1,073·5
Outlays by Function		
National defence	303·6	296·3
International affairs	9·6	14·6
Income security	136·0	146·6
Health	48·4	57·8
Medicare	85·0	96·6
Social security	232·5	248·5
Veterans' benefits and services	30·1	28·9
Education, training, employment and social services	36·7	37·7
Commerce and housing credit	27·7	22·7
Transportation	27·6	29·2
Natural resources and environment	16·2	17·5
Energy	3·7	3·2
Community and regional development	5·4	8·8
Agriculture	16·9	14·6
Net interest	169·1	175·6
General science, space and technology	12·8	14·1
General government.....	9·1	10·6
Administration of justice	9·4	10·5
Undistributed offsetting receipts	−37·2	−36·5
TOTAL...................	1,142·6	1,197·2

Social Welfare Expenditure

Total expenditure by programme was (US$ millions):

	1987	1988
Social insurance	412,862	432,195
Education	204,549	219,368
Public aid	110,981	120,375
Health and medical	48,371	52,540
Veterans' programmes	28,051	29,254
Other social welfare	15,278	15,480
Housing	13,174	16,556
TOTAL.................	833,265	885,766

Expenditure per capita was:

Social insurance	US$1,662	US$1,724
Education	826	878
Public aid	448	482
Health and medical	195	210
Veterans' programmes	112	116
Other social welfare	62	62
Housing	53	66
TOTAL.................	3,359	3,538

Public Debt

At the end of September 1990 the total gross federal debt of the United States stood at US$3,266,073 million.

Cost of Living in USA

The Consumer Price Index for all urban consumers (CPI-U) with prices collected in 91 areas across the USA was measured for the year 1990 at 130·7 (1982–84 = 100), versus 124·0 for 1989.

Gross National Product by Industry

Gross National product by industry in 1989 was (US$ millions):

Domestic industries	5,163,200
Private industries	4,561,000
Agriculture, forestry, fisheries	113,500
Mining............................	80,300
Construction	247,700
Manufacturing	966,000
Durable goods....................	541,000
Nondurable goods................	425,000
Transportation and public utilities..	460,900
Transportation	171,500
Communication	133,700
Electric, gas, and sanitary services	155,600
Wholesale trade	339,500
Retail trade.......................	486,000
Finance, insurance, and real estate .	896,700
Services	970,500
Government and government enterprises	619,300
Rest of the world...................	37,600
TOTAL gross national product	5,200,800

GNP, national and personal income in 1990 were (US$ million):—

Gross national product	5,465,100
Net national product	4,889,500
National income	4,418,400
Personal income	4,645,500
Disposable personal income...........	3,946,100
Personal saving	180,100

Personal consumption expenditure in 1990 was US$3,657,300 million, of which durable goods accounted for US$480,300 million, non-durable goods US$1,193,700 million and services US$1,983,300 million.

Currency

The US unit of currency is the dollar ($) of 100 cents.

AGRICULTURE AND LIVESTOCK

The total number of farms in 1990 was 2,143,150, with a total area of land in farms of 987,721,000 acres, and an average acreage per farm of 461 acres. The total number of people employed on farms during the week of January 6–12, 1991 was 2,612,000, of whom 339,000 were unpaid workers, 706,000 hired workers and 168,000 agricultural service workers.

Principal crops are corn for grain, soybeans, wheat hay, cotton, tobacco, grain sorghums, potatoes, oranges and barley.

Livestock on farms on Jan. 1, 1989 and 1990 was:—

	1989	1990
All cattle	99,180,000	99,337,000
Milk cows	10,212,000	10,149,000
Sheep and lambs...	10,858,000	11,368,000
Hogs and pigs	55,469,000	53,852,000
Chickens	356,105,000	355,790,000

Gross income from farming in 1989 was US$170,060 million, of which cash receipts from marketing were US$159,173 million and government payments US$10,887 million. Cash income from all crops in 1989 was US$75,449 million and from livestock and livestock products US$83,724 million.

NONFUEL MINERALS

The value of nonfuel raw mineral production in the United States in 1989 totalled an estimated US$32,316 million compared with US$30,045 million in 1988.

Trading Figures

	1988	1989
Imports	US$33,904m	US$36,000m*
Exports	19,597m	18,496m

* estimate.

Production Figures

('000 tonnes)

	1989	1990e
Aluminium	4,030	4,000
Iron Ore	59,000	53,900
Phosphate rock	49,817	46,000
Zinc Ore	276	530
Refined Copper	1,954	2,030
Refined Lead	1,137	1,170

e = estimate

ENERGY

Energy Overview

(Quadrillion (10^{15}) Btu)

	1989	1990
Production	66.06	67.55
Coal	21.34	22.46
Natural Gas	17.78	18.16
Crude Oil................	16.12	15.46
Consumption	81.34	81.49
Petroleum	34.21	33.64
Coal	18.94	19.09
Natural Gas	19.38	19.42
Imports	14.18	13.84
Crude Oil................	12.30	12.43
Petroleum	3.03	2.67
Exports	4.77	4.91
Coal	2.56	2.70

LABOUR

Employment and Unemployment.—The civilia labour force was 125,004,000 in May 1990. The numbe of employed persons was 118,350,000. This include self-employed, wage and salary-earners, and unpai family workers. Unemployment was estimated a 6,653,000 in May 1990 (5.3 per cent) (it was 5.2 pe cent in May 1989).

Wages.—In March 1990, gross average weekl earnings in industry ranged from US$812.59 per wee in malt beverage industry (43.2 hours and US$18.8 average hourly earnings) to US$122.00 in eating an drinking places (25.0 hours and US$4.88 averag hourly earnings). The average for all manufacturin was US$436.71 compared with US$426.81 in Marc 1989.

On April 1, 1990, the minimum wage set by federa law became US$3.80 an hour. The law requires a least time and a half of an employee's regular rate o pay for all hours over 40 a week for most covere workers.

EXTERNAL TRADE

	1989	1990
	US$ million	
General imports:		
c.i.f. value	493,352.0	516,946
customs value.........	473,396.5	495,259
Exports and re-exports:		
f.a.s. value†	363,765.5	392,975
Trade balance:		
f.a.s. exports: c.i.f.		
imports	−129,586.5	−123,970
f.a.s. exports: customs		
imports	−109,631.0	−102,283

† Excluding military aid.

Exports by Principal Commodities of Domesti Origin, 1990

Commodity	Valu
	US$ millio
Food and live animals................	29,280
Grain and cereal preparations	12,636
Beverages and tobacco	7,118
Crude materials (inedible) except fuel .	26,985
Mineral fuels, lubricants, etc..........	12,174
Oils and fats (animal and vegetable) ...	1,190
Chemicals and products	38,983
Machinery and transport equipment ..	172,521
Other manufactured goods	70,955
Unclassified commodities	15,326

US Imports by Principal Commodities, 1988*

Commodity	Valu
	US$ millio
Food and live animals................	24,004
Fish and fish preparations..........	5,521
Vegetables and fruit	6,684
Coffee and tea	3,643
Beverages and tobacco	4,973
Crude materials (inedible), except fuels	15,846
Mineral fuels, lubricants, etc..........	68,741
Oils and fats (animal and vegetable) ...	870
Chemicals and products	23,663
Machinery and transport equipment ..	213,305
Other manufactured goods	148,521
Unclassified commodities	17,020

* c.i.f. value.

US Foreign Trade by Principal Areas and Countries, 1990

Area/Country	Exports and Re-exports to	General Imports from
	US$ million	
Africa	7,950·8	16,997·9
Asia	120,256·8	217,155·2
Japan	48,584·6	93,069·6
Taiwan	11,482·4	23,829·6
Korea, Rep. of	14,398·7	19,287·0
Oceania	9,964·2	6,263·1
Australia	8,534·7	4,792·8
Europe	117,237·4	115,700·5
EC	98,023·5	95,466·3
S. & Central America	121,432·3	132,696·9
Canada	82,966·5	93,780·6
Mexico	28,375·5	30,796·7
S. America	15,612·2	28,172·5

Trade with UK

	1989	1990
Imports from UK ...	£12,098,549,000	£12,998,506,000
Exports to UK	12,888,890,000	14,357,516,000

COMMUNICATIONS

Railways

Data on Class I line-haul railroads (US$ thousands)

	1987	1988
Operating		
Revenues	26,662,482	27,999,839
Freight	25,797,002	27,154,961
Passenger	93,559	84,677
Total operating		
expenses	23,878,116	24,889,015
Net working		
capital	34,081	− 217,182
Average number of		
employees	248,526	236,891

Roads

In 1989 there were 3·88 million miles of public roads and streets in the United States, of which 3·12 million miles were in rural areas and 753,777 miles were in urban areas. Surfaced roads and streets account for 90·4 per cent of the total.

An estimated total of US$67,718 million was spent in 1989 for roads and streets in the United States. Capital outlay accounts for 49·2 per cent of the total expenditure; 29·1 per cent was spent for maintenance, and 7·9 per cent for administration; 9·5 per cent for highway police and safety; and 4·2 per cent for interest on highway bonds.

Motor Vehicles and Taxation.—The number of motor vehicles registered in 1989 in the United States was 187,260,547, an increase of 1·6 per cent over the 1988 total.

Accidents.—In 1989 there were 45,555 deaths caused by motor vehicle accidents. The death rate per 100,000,000 vehicle-miles of travel was 2·16 in 1989 compared with 2·32 in 1988.

Shipping

The ocean-going Merchant Marine of the US on April 1, 1991 consisted of 630 vessels of 1,000 gross tons and over, of which 401 were privately owned and 229 were government-owned ships. There were 40 ships in the National Defence Reserve Fleet of inactive government-owned vessels.

Air Transport

According to preliminary figures, United States domestic and international scheduled airlines in 1988 carried 455,000,000 passengers over 423,300,000,000 revenue passenger miles. Air cargo ton-miles were distributed as follows: freight and express 9,632,000,000; and air mail 1,837,000,000.

Total operating revenues of all US scheduled airlines were US$63,384,000,000 in 1988.

Total operating expenses rose to US$59,923,000,000 in 1988. Scheduled operations showed a net operating profit of US$3,461,000,000 in 1988, compared with a net operating profit of US$2,431,000,000 in 1987.

EDUCATION

State School Systems

All the 50 States and the District of Columbia have compulsory school attendance laws. In general, children are obliged to attend school from 7 to 16 years of age. Officers of local administrative units, usually known as truant or attendance officers, are charged with enforcing the compulsory attendance laws.

In the autumn of 1989, 45,881,000 children were enrolled in regular elementary and secondary day schools in the United States, of whom 5·4 million or 11·7 per cent attended private schools.

The following percentages of the school-age population were estimated to be enrolled in school in the autumn of 1989: 96 per cent of 5- and 6-year-olds; 99 per cent of 7- to 13-year-olds; 95 per cent of 14- to 17-year-olds, and 34 per cent of 18- to 24-year-olds.

During the 1988–89 school year, the average daily attendance in regular public elementary and secondary day schools was 37,282,000. In the 1988–89 school year 2,456,000 students graduated from regular public high schools, 268,000 graduated from private high school. In addition some 25,000 graduated from evening schools and adult education programmes, and an estimated 357,000 received high school equivalency certificates. Public school teachers numbered 2,356,000, with an average salary of US$31,331.

Most of the revenue for public elementary and secondary school purposes comes from Federal, State, and local governments. Less than 0·5 per cent comes from gifts and from tuition and transportation fees. Revenue receipts during 1988–89 amounted to US$191,210,000,000; 6·2 per cent from the Federal Government, 47·7 per cent from State governments, and 46·1 per cent from local sources. Estimated current expenditure in the 1988–89 school year was US$172,932 million; for sites, buildings, furniture and equipment expenditures, US$13,000 million; for interest on school debt US$3,200 million.

Institutions of Higher Education

In the autumn of 1989, total enrolment in universities, colleges, professional schools, and two-year schools numbered 13,458,000.

Degrees conferred during the academic years 1987–88 and 1988–89 were:—

Degree	1987–88	1988–89
Bachelor's	994,829	1,017,669
First-Professional	70,735	70,758
Master's	299,317	309,762
Doctorates	34,870	35,759

During 1988–89 the major fields for bachelor's degrees were business and management (246,659), social sciences (107,714), education (96,988) and engineering (85,723). First-profession degrees in law (35,567) and medicine (15,454) predominated. Master's degrees were heavily concentrated in education (82,238) and business and management (73,154). The most popular fields of study for doctorates were education (6,783) and engineering (4,533).

During the 1988–89 academic year, the approximately 3,500 colleges and universities employed about 769,000 (full-time and part-time) instructional faculty. Total expenditures for colleges and universities during the 1988–89 academic year were US$134,600 million.

Particulars of some of the universities (with opening autumn enrolment figures, 1989) are: *Harvard* (24,509 students, including 11,298 women), founded at Cambridge, Mass. on Oct. 28, 1636, and named after John Harvard of Emmanuel College, Cambridge, England, who bequeathed to it his library and a sum of money in 1638; *Yale* (10,975 students, including 4,848 women), founded at New Haven, Connecticut, in 1701; *Bowdoin*, Brunswick, Me. (founded 1794; 1,372 students including 589 women); *Brown*, Providence, RI (founded 1764; 7,643 students, including 3,475 women); *Columbia*, New York, NY (founded 1754; 17,532 students, including 8,005 women); *Cornell* (founded at Ithaca, NY, 1865; 20,595 students, including 8,800 women); *Dartmouth*, Hanover, NH (founded 1769, 4,861 students, including 1,952 women); *Georgetown*, Washington, DC (founded 1789; 11,494 students, including 5,663 women); *North Carolina*, Chapel Hill, NC (founded in 1789; 23,619 students, including 13,326 women); *Pennsylvania*, Philadelphia, Pa. (founded 1740; 22,016 students, including 9,892 women); *Princeton*, NJ (founded 1746; 6,466 students and 2,435 women); and *William and Mary*, Williamsburg, Va. (founded 1693; 7,542 students, including 4,035 women).

WEIGHTS AND MEASURES

The weights and measures in common use in the United States are of British origin, and date back to the American Revolution when practically all th standards were intended to be equivalent to tho used in England at that period. Divergencies in the weights and measures were, however, quite commo due no doubt to the fact that the system of weigh and measures in England was not itself well esta lished, and hence the copies brought to the Unite States were often adjusted to different standard Because of these discrepancies, the system of weigh and measures in the United States (US inch-poun system) is not identical with the British system.

The US ton (short) = 2,000 pounds (British Imperi ton = 2,240 pounds, or 1 US long ton). The U gallon = 231 cubic inches (277·42 cubic inches in UH or 128 fluid ounces (160 fluid ounces in UK). In th British system the units of dry measure are the san as those of liquid measure. In the United States thes two are not the same, the gallon and its subdivision being used in the measurement of liquids, while th bushel, with its subdivisions, is used in the measur ment of certain dry commodities. The US gallon divided into 4 liquid quarts and the US bushel in 32 dry quarts.

In 1971, a study recommended a concerted, c ordinated, but voluntary national effort to make th International System of Units (SI) the predomina form of measurement in the United States. I December 1975, legislation was passed which esta lished the United States Metric Board to co-ordina voluntary conversion to the metric system. Sin 1982 this function has been assumed by the Office Metric Programmes of the US Department of Con merce.

TERRITORIES, ETC. OF THE UNITED STATES

The territories and the principal islands and island groups under the sovereignty of the United States of America comprise the Commonwealth of Puerto Rico, the Commonwealth of the Northern Mariana Islands, and the following territories: Guam, American Samoa, US Virgin Islands, Johnston Atoll, Midway Islands, Wake Islands.

Johnston Atoll (formerly Johnston and Sand Islands) comprises two small islands, less than 1 sq. mile in area, to the south-west of Hawaii which are administered by the US Air Force. The two Midway Islands (area, 3 sq. miles), at the western end of the Hawaiian chain, are administered by the US Navy. The Wake Islands have an area of about 3 sq. miles and an average elevation of less than 3 metres. They lie about 2,300 miles west of Hawaii and are administered by the US Air Force.

Under the terms of a Treaty of Friendship between the United States and Kiribati, signed in 1979 and subsequently ratified by the US Senate, the United States renounced its claim to Canton and Enderbury Islands.

There are certain small guano islands, rocks, or keys which, in pursuance of action taken under the Act of Congress, August 18, 1856, subsequently embodied in Sections 5570–5578 of the Revised Statutes are considered as appertaining to the United States. Responsibility for territorial affairs generally is centred in the Office of the Assistant Secretary, Territorial and International Affairs, Dept. of the Interior, Washington DC. Puerto Rico was removed from the Department of the Interior's administrative jurisdiction with the acquisition of Commonwealth status in 1952.

THE COMMONWEALTH OF PUERTO RICO

Puerto Rico (Rich Port) is an island of the Greater Antilles group in the West Indies, and lies between

17° 50′–18° 30′ N. lat. and 65° 30′–67° 15′ W. long., wit a total area of 3,421 sq. miles (8,860 sq. km), and a estimated population (UN 1989) of 3,658,000. Th majority of the inhabitants are of Spanish descer and Spanish is the official language. The island i about 111 miles from west to east, and 36 miles fro north to south. The capital is 1,600 miles distant fro New York, and 1,000 miles from Miami.

Puerto Rico was discovered in 1493 by Christophe Columbus and explored by Ponce de Léon in 1508. I continued as a Spanish possession until October 1 1898, when the United States took formal possessio as a result of the Spanish-American War. It wa ceded by Spain to the United States by the Treat ratified on April 11, 1899.

The Constitution approved by the Congress ar the President of the United States, which came int force on July 25, 1952, establishes the Commonwealt of Puerto Rico with full powers of local governmen Legislative functions are vested in the Legislativ Assembly, which consists of two elected houses; th Senate of 27 members (two from each of eigh senatorial districts and 11 at large) and the House Representatives of 51 members (one from each of 4 representative districts and 11 at large). Membershi of each house may be increased slightly to accommo date minority representatives. The term of th Legislative Assembly is four years. The selection the Secretary of State must be approved also by th House of Representatives.

The Governor is popularly elected for a term four years. A Supreme Court of seven members appointed by the Governor, with the advice an consent of the Senate. The Governor appoints al Judges. Residents of Puerto Rico are US citizen Puerto Rico is represented in Congress by a Reside Commissioner, elected for a term of four years, wh has a seat in the House of Representatives, but not vote, although he has a right to vote on thos committees of which he is a member.

Preliminary 1983 figures for the Commonwealth overnment's budget were Receipts, US$4,948 million (of which US$1,180 million were transfers from e Federal Government) and Expenditures, S$4,111 million (including payments of US$135 illion to the Federal Government). Manufacturing dded US$5,765 million to net Commonwealth income 1983 (preliminary figures), trade US$1,743 million, nance, insurance and real estate US$1,841 million nd agriculture US$435 million. Principal crops are gar cane, coffee, vegetables, fruits and tobacco. lost valuable areas of manufacturing are chemicals d allied products, metal products and machinery. ublic and private schools are established throughut—enrolment in 1985–86 was 686,914. Enrolment private colleges and universities for 1985–86 was ,402.

CAPITAL.—ΨSan Juan, population of the municiality (1984), 1,816,300; Other major towns are: Ponce (234,500); ΨMayagüez (209,800); and ΨArebo (163,300).

overnor, Rafael Hernández Colón.

TRADE

	1985	1986
otal Imports	US$10,113 m	US$10,108 m
otal Exports	10,543 m	11,588 m

Trade with UK

	1989	1990
nports from UK	£79,851,000	£69,593,000
xports to UK	117,628,000	123,087,000

GUAM

Guam, the largest of the Ladrone or Mariana lands in the North Pacific Ocean, lies in 13° 26′ N. t. and 144° 39′ E. long., at a distance of about 1,506 iles east of Manila. The area of the island is stimated at 209 sq. miles (541 sq. km), with an stimated population (1989) of 138,089.

The Guamanians are of Chamorro stock mingled ith Filipino and Spanish blood. The Chamorro nguage belongs to the Malayo-Polynesian family, it has had considerable admixture of Spanish. hamorro and English are the official languages and ost residents are bilingual.

Guam was occupied by the Japanese in December 41 but was recaptured and occupied throughout by S forces before the end of July, 1944. Under the rganic Act of Guam of August 1, 1950 (Public Law 0 of the 81st Congress), Guam has statutory powers self-government, and Guamanians are United tates citizens. A 21-member unicameral legislature elected biennially. The Governor and Lieutenant overnor are popularly elected. A non-voting Delete is elected to serve in the US House of Representives. There is also a District Court of Guam, with iginal jurisdiction in cases under federal law. Guam's two main sources of revenue are tourism nd US military spending.

CAPITAL.—Agaña. Port of entry, ΨApra.

overnor, Joseph F. Ada.
t. Governor, Frank Blas.

AMERICAN SAMOA

American Samoa consists of the island of Tutuila, nu'u, Ofu, Olesega, Ta'u, Rose and Swains Islands, ith a total area of 76 sq. miles (197 sq. km) and an stimated population of 38,200 in 1989.

Tutuila, the largest of the group, has an area of 52 uare miles and contains a magnificent harbour at Pago Pago, the capital. The remaining islands have area of about 24 square miles. Tuna and copra are e chief exports.

American Samoans are US nationals, but some have acquired citizenship through service in the United States armed forces or other naturalization procedure.

The 1960 Constitution grants American Samoa a measure of self-government, with certain powers reserved to the US Secretary of the Interior. There is a bicameral legislature with popularly elected Representatives and Governors, and a popularlyelected Governor. A non-voting Delegate is elected to serve in the US House of Representatives.

The constitution of American Samoa designates the village of Fagatogo as the seat of government.

Governor, Peter Tali Coleman.
Lt. Governor, Galea'i Poumele.

VIRGIN ISLANDS

Purchased by the United States from Denmark for the sum of US$25 million, and proclaimed January 25, 1917. The total area of the islands is 132 sq. miles (342 sq. km), with an estimated population (1988) of 106,000. There are three main islands, St Thomas (28 sq. miles), St Croix (84 sq. miles), St John (20 sq. miles) and about 50 small islets or cays, mostly uninhabited.

The government of the Virgin Islands is organized under the provisions of the Revised Organic Act of the Virgin Islands, enacted by the Congress of the United States on July 22, 1954. Legislative power is vested in the Legislature of the Virgin Islands, a unicameral body composed of 15 senators popularly elected for two-year terms. Virgin Islanders are citizens of the United States. From the elections of November 1970, the Governor has been popularly elected. A non-voting Delegate is elected to serve in the US House of Representatives. A referendum is to take place in June 1991 to determine the future political status of the islands.

The Virgin Islands are now a favourite tourist area in the Caribbean.

CAPITAL.—ΨCharlotte Amalie on St Thomas. Population (1980) 11,756.

Governor, Alexander Farrelly.
Lt. Governor, Derek M. Hodge.

NORTHERN MARIANA ISLANDS

The land area of the Northern Mariana Islands is 184 sq. miles (476 sq. km) with an estimated population (1988) of 21,777. Saipan, the government seat and commerce centre, has an estimated population of 19,156 (1988).

A law enacted by Congress on March 24, 1976 provides a Covenant to establish a Commonwealth of the Northern Mariana Islands. The provisions of the Covenant became fully effective upon termination of the Trusteeship Agreement on November 3, 1986. Most of the residents became US citizens. There is a popularly elected bicameral legislature and a popularly elected Governor.

Governor, Lorenzo D. L. Guerrero.
Lt. Governor, Benjamin M. Manglona.

MARSHALL ISLANDS

The land area of the Marshall Islands is 70 sq. miles (181 sq. km), with an estimated population of 43,000.

In May 1979 Constitutional Government was installed in the Marshall Islands which provides for a bicameral legislature comprising a Senate and a House of Assembly. A Compact of Free Association with the United States was signed on June 25, 1983, becoming law on January 14, 1986. This allows the Marshall Islands self government and vests in the

United States full responsibility for the defence of the Marshall Islands for 15 years. The UN Security Council voted to terminate UN trust status in December 1990; the Marshall Islands are expected to be admitted to the UN as an independent state in September 1991.

CAPITAL.—Majuro, population 20,000.

President, Amata Kabua.

FEDERATED STATES OF MICRONESIA

The Federated States of Micronesia comprise the four states of Kosrae, Ponape, Truk and Yap, which have a combined area of 271 sq. miles (701 sq. km) and an estimated population of 100,000 in 1988.

Constitutional government was installed in the Federated States of Micronesia in May 1979 and provides for a unicameral 14-member National Congress comprising members from the four states. Each state also elects its own Governor and legislature.

A Compact of Free Association with the United States was signed in October 1982, becoming law on January 14, 1986. The Federated States enjoy full self-government and the responsibility for their defence is vested fully in the United States for 15 years. The UN Security Council voted to terminate UN trust status in December 1990; the Federated States are expected to be admitted to the UN as an independent state in September 1991.

CAPITAL.—Kolonia, on Ponape. Estimated population 6,000.

President of the Federated States of Micronesia, Bailey Olter.
Vice President, Joseph Nena.

REPUBLIC OF PALAU

Palau consists of more than 200 Pacific Ocean islands of which eight are permanently inhabited. The Palau archipelago stretches over 400 miles. The land area is 191 sq. miles (494 sq. km), with an estimated population of 14,000. The major island is Koror with a population of 8,100.

Palau and the USA signed a Compact of Free Association in August 1982, which, when approved by a two-thirds majority of the voters of Palau, will recognize the Republic of Palau to be a self-governing state. The USA is responsible for financial support, and for the defence of Palau for 50 years. The Compact is incompatible with the ban on nuclear weapons in the constitution. The status of Palau remains unclear.

Constitutional government was installed in Palau in January 1981 and provides for a bicameral legislature. The President and Vice President are directly elected.

President, Ngiratkel Etpison.
Vice President, Kuniwo Nakamura.

THE PANAMA CANAL

As a result of the Panama Canal Treaty, 1977, the Canal Zone was disestablished, with all areas of land and water within the former Canal Zone reverting to Panama with effect from October 1, 1979. Under the treaty, the United States is allowed the use of operating areas for the Panama Canal, together with several military bases, although the Republic of Panama is sovereign in all such areas. The Panama Canal Commission, an arm of the US Government, will continue to operate the canal until the year 2000.

TOTAL OCEAN GOING COMMERCIAL TRAFFIC

Fiscal Year	No. of Transits	Canal, Net Tons	Cargo Tons
1982	14,009	202,956,182	185,452,332
1983	11,707	169,577,417	145,590,759
1984	11,230	162,399,908	140,470,818
1985	11,515	168,990,073	138,643,243
1986	11,925	182,791,695	139,945,181
1987	12,230	186,488,707	148,690,380
1988	12,234	191,566,065	156,482,641
1989	11,989	185,825,532	151,636,113
1990	11,941	181,604,590	157,072,979

The canal is fifty statute miles long (44·08 nautica miles), and the channel is from 500 to 1,000 feet wid at the bottom. It contains 12 locks in twin flights three steps at Gatun on the Atlantic side, one step a Pedro Miguel and two at Miraflores on the Pacifi side. Each lock chamber is 1,000 feet long and 110 fee wide. Transit from sea to sea takes on average 8 t 10 hours. The least width is in Gaillard Cut, and th greatest in Gatun Lake.

BRITISH EMBASSY
3100 Massachusetts Avenue NW
Washington DC 20008
[Washington DC 462 1340]

Ambassador Extraordinary and Plenipotentiary, H Excellency Sir Robin Renwick, KCMG, (1991).
Ministers, D. Peretz (*Economic*); C. V. Balmer (*De ence Equipment*); C. J. R. Meyer, CMG (*Comme cial*); A. M. Wood, CMG; P. Lo (*Hong Kong Econom and Trade Affairs*).
Head of British Defence Staff and Defence Attach Air Vice Marshal Peter Dodworth, OBE, AFC.
Naval Attaché, Rear-Adm. A. P. Hoddinott, OBE.
Military Attaché, Brig. E. F. G. Burton.
Air Attaché, Air Cdre R. G. Peters.
Counsellors, R. Ralph, CVO (*Head of Chancery*); A. Smith (*Admin. and HM Consul-General*); Brown (*Economic*); D. J. Hall (*Commercial*); R. Graham-Harrison (*Overseas Development*); P. Leung (*Hong Kong Commercial Affairs* R. J. Griffins (*Civil Aviation and Shipping*); A. R. Allcock (*Science, Technology and Energy*); W. Browne (*Information*); J. D. N. R. Clibborn; J. Limbert (*Defence Supply*); K. R. Tebbit; P. Torry (*External Affairs*); R. J. Nicholls; E. Ma ningham-Buller; L. N. Large (*Defence, Science an Equipment*); J. D. Hansen.
Cultural Attaché and British Council Representativ G. Tindale, OBE.

There are British Consulates General in *Atlant Boston, Chicago, Houston, Los Angeles, New Yor* and *San Francisco*.
There are British Consulates in *Anchorage, Clev land, Dallas, Kansas City, Miami, New Orlean Norfolk, Philadelphia, Portland, St Louis, Seattle an Puerto Rico*.

BRITISH-AMERICAN CHAMBER OF COMMERCE, 27 Madison Avenue, New York 10016; UK OFFICE, Suit 201, High Holborn, WCIV 6RR.

URUGUAY
(República Oriental del Uruguay)

President, Dr Luis Alberto Lacalle, *took office* March 1, 1990.
Vice President, Dr Gonzalo Aguirre Ramírez.

CABINET
(as at August 12, 1991)

Interior, Dr Juan Andrés Ramírez.
Foreign Affairs, Dr Héctor Gros Espiell.
Economy and Finance, Enrique Braga.
Transport and Public Works, Wilson Elso Goñi.
Public Health, Dr Carlos del Piazzo.
Labour and Social Security, Carlos Cat.
Livestock, Agriculture and Fisheries, Alvaro Ramos.
Education and Culture, Dr Guillermo García Costa.
National Defence, Dr Mariano R. Brito.
Industry and Energy, Dr Augusto Montesdeoca.
Tourism, José Villar.
Housing, Territorial Regulation and Environment, Raul Lago.
Planning and Budget Office, Conrado Hughes Alvarez.

EMBASSY OF THE ORIENTAL REPUBLIC OF URUGUAY
48 Lennox Gardens, SW1X 0DL
[071–584 8192; *Consulate* 071–589 8735]

Ambassador Extraordinary and Plenipotentiary, His Excellency Dr Luis Alberto Solé-Romeo (1987).

Area and Population.—The smallest Republic in South America, on the east coast of the Rio de la Plata situated in lat. 30°–35° S. and long. 53° 15′–57° 42′ W., with an area of 68,037 sq. miles (176,215 sq. km), and a population (UN estimate 1989) of 3,077,000, almost entirely white and predominantly of Spanish and Italian descent. Many Uruguayans are Roman Catholics. There is complete freedom of religion and no church is established by the state.

Physical Features.—The country consists mainly of undulating grassy plains. The principal chains of hills are the Cuchilla del Haedo, which cross the Brazilian boundary and extend southwards to the Cuchilla Grande of the south and east. In no case do the peaks exceed 2,000 feet.

The principal river is the Rio Negro (with its tributary the Yi), flowing from north-east to south-west into the Rio Uruguay. The boundary river Uruguay is navigable from its estuary to Salto, about 200 miles north, and the Negro is also navigable for a considerable distance. Smaller rivers are the Cuareim, Yaguaron, Santa Lucia, Queguay and the Cebollati.

The summer is warm, but the heat is often tempered by the breezes of the Atlantic. The winter is, on the whole, mild, but cold spells, characterized by winds from the South Polar regions, are experienced in June, July and August. Rainfall is regular throughout the year, but there are occasional droughts. Floods also occur.

Government.—Uruguay—or the *Banda Oriental*, as the territory lying on the eastern bank of the Uruguay River was then called—resisted all attempted invasions of the Portuguese and Spanish until the beginning of the 17th century, and 100 years later the Portuguese settlements were captured by the Spanish. From 1726 to 1814 the country formed part of Spanish South America and underwent many vicissitudes during the wars of independence. In 1814 the armies of the Argentine Confederation captured the capital and annexed the province, and it was afterwards annexed by Portugal and became a province of Brazil. In 1825, the country threw off Brazilian rule. This action led to war between Argentina and Brazil which was settled by the mediation of the United Kingdom, Uruguay being declared an independent state in 1828. In 1830 a Republic was inaugurated.

According to the Constitution the President appoints a council of 11 ministers and a Secretary (Planning and Budget Office), and the Vice-President presides over Congress. The legislature consists of a Chamber of 99 deputies and a Senate of 30 members (plus the Vice-President), elected for five years by a system of proportional representation. General elections held in November 1984 marked the return to civilian rule after 11 years of presidential rule with military support. The first fully free presidential and legislative elections since 1971 were held in November 1989, and were won by the Partido Nacional Blanco.

The Republic is divided into 19 Departments each with a chief of police and a Departmental Council.

Production and Industry.—Wheat, barley, maize, linseed, sunflower seed and rice are cultivated. The wealth of the country is obtained from its pasturage, which supports large herds of cattle and sheep. There are just over 9 million cattle and just under 24 million sheep. In addition to wool, meat packing, other foodstuffs (citrus, wine, beer), fishing and textile industries are of importance.

The development of local industry continues and, in addition to the greatly augmented textile industry, marked expansion in local production is notable in respect of tyres, sheet-glass, three-ply wood, cement, leather-curing, beet-sugar, plastics, household consumer goods, edible oils and the refining of petroleum and petroleum products.

Mineral Deposits.—There are some ferrous minerals, not extracted at present. Non-ferrous exploited minerals include clinker, dolomite, marble and granite.

Communications.—There are about 9,899 km of national highways, and about 12,083 km of telegraph and 48,375 miles of telephone communications.

There are about 2,987 km of standard gauge railway in use in Uruguay. Passenger rail services were cancelled in January 1988. Services are now limited to cargo transport. A State Autonomous Entity was formed to administer the railway systems purchased by the Government from four British companies in 1948.

An airline, PLUNA, which is owned by the state, runs daily services to southern Brazil, Paraguay and Argentina, and two flights a week to Spain. The principal capitals of the interior and a limited freight service are connected to Montevideo by TAMU, another state-owned airline, using principally military aircraft and personnel. International passenger and freight services are maintained by American, South American and European airlines. The international airport of Carrasco lies 12 miles outside Montevideo.

Education.—Primary education is compulsory and free, and technical and trade schools and evening courses for adult education are state controlled. There are about 322,053 pupils in the 2,362 state schools. The university at Montevideo (founded in 1849) has about 18,000 students enrolled in its ten faculties.

Language and Literature.—Spanish is the language of the Republic. Five daily newspapers are published in Montevideo with an estimated total circulation of 150,000. Most of them are distributed throughout the country.

FINANCE

	1988	1989
	pesos	
Revenue	456,675·2 m	753,573 m
Expenditure	510,651·4 m	918,442 m

The external debt at June 1990 was US$6,117·3 million. Central Bank reserves (December 1989) were US$1,017 million.

TRADE

	1988	1989
Total exports .	US$1,404,527 m	US$1,598,800 m
Total imports .	1,176,945 m	1,195,900 m

The major exports are meat and by-products, wool and by-products, hides and bristle and agricultural products. The principal imports are raw materials, construction materials, oils and lubricants, automotive vehicles, kits and machinery. Principal trading partners are Brazil, USA and Argentina.

Trade with UK

	1989	1990
Imports from UK	£26,119,000	£31,192,000
Exports to UK	52,185,000	51,859,000

The principal export items to the UK are wool and beef, the main imports are chemicals, machinery, raw materials, metals and beverages.

CAPITAL.—ΨMontevideo, population (1984) 1,355,312. Other centres are Salto, ΨPaysandu, Mercedes, Minas, Melo, and Rivera.

CURRENCY.—New Uruguayan peso of 100 centésimos.

FLAG.—Four blue and five white horizontal stripes surcharged with sun on a white ground in the top corner, next flagstaff.

NATIONAL ANTHEM.—Orientales, La Patria O La Tumba (Uruguayans, the fatherland or death).

NATIONAL DAY.—August 25 (Declaration of Independence, 1825).

BRITISH EMBASSY
Calle Marco Bruto 1073, Montevideo 11300
[Montevideo 623650]

Ambassador Extraordinary and Plenipotentiary, His Excellency Donald Lamont (1991)
First Secretaries, A. T. Lovelock (*Deputy Head of Mission and Consul*); R. J. Hutchings (*Chancery/ Information*).

There is a British Consular Office at *Montevideo*.

ANGLO-URUGUAYAN CULTURAL INSTITUTE, San José 1426, Montevideo. There are branch Institutes throughout Uruguay.

BRITISH-URUGUAYAN CHAMBER OF COMMERCE, Avenida Labertador Brig. Gen., Lavalleja 1641, P2-OF 201, Montevideo.

VATICAN CITY STATE
(Stato della Città del Vaticano)

Sovereign Pontiff, His Holiness Pope John Paul II (Karol Wojtyla), *born* at Wadowice (Krakow, Poland), May 18, 1920, *elected* Pope (in succession to Pope John Paul I), Oct. 16, 1978.
Secretary of State, Cardinal Angelo Sodano, *appointed* December, 1990.

APOSTOLIC NUNCIATURE
54 Parkside, SW19 5NI
[081–946 1410]

Apostolic Pro Nuncio, His Excellency Archbishop Luigi Barbarito (1986).
Counsellor, Mgr. Ramero Ingles Molinar.

The office of the ecclesiastical head of the Roman Catholic Church (Holy See) is vested in the Pope, the Sovereign Pontiff. For many centuries the Sovereign Pontiff exercised temporal power, but by 1870 the Papal States had become part of unified Italy. The temporal power of the Pope was in suspense until the treaty of February 11, 1929, which recognized the full and independent sovereignty of the Holy See in the City of the Vatican. The area of the Vatican City is 108 acres and its population in 1989 was about 1,000.

Trade with UK

	1989	1990
Imports from UK	£955,000	£461,000
Exports to UK	24,000	16,000

CURRENCY.—Italian currency is legal tender.

FLAG.—Square flag; equal vertical bands of yello (next staff), and white; crossed keys and triple crow device on white band.

NATIONAL DAY.—October 22 (Inauguration present Pontiff).

BRITISH EMBASSY TO THE HOLY SEE
91 Via Condotti, 00187 Rome
[Rome 678 9462]

Ambassador Extraordinary and Plenipotentiary, H Excellency Andrew Eustace Palmer, CMG, CV (1991).
First Secretary, P. J. McCormick.

VENEZUELA
(La Republica de Venezuela)

President, Carlos Andrés Pérez, *elected* Dec. 4, 198 *inaugurated*, Feb. 2, 1989.

COUNCIL OF MINISTERS
(as at August, 1991)

Interior, Alejandro Izaguirre.
Foreign Affairs, Armande Durán.
Finance, Roberto Pocaterra.
Defence, Gen. Fernando Ochoa Antich.
Transport and Communications, Roberto Smith.
Urban Development, Luis Penzini Fleury.
Energy and Mines, Celestino Armas.
Environment and Natural Resources, Enrique Col menares Finol.
Health and Social Welfare, Pedro Páez Camargo.
Agriculture and Livestock, Jonathan Coles.
Education, Gustavo Rossen.
Labour, Jesús Rubin Rodríguez.
The Family, Marisela Padron.
Justice, Alfredo Ducharne.
Presidential Secretariat, Beatrice Rangel.
Science and Technology, Dulce Arnao de Uzcátegui.
Culture, José Antonio Abreu.
Co-ordination and Planning, Miguel Rodríguez.
Minister, President of the Venezuelan Investmen Fund, Gerver Torres.

VENEZUELAN EMBASSY
1 Cromwell Road, SW7 2HW
[071–584 4206/7]

Ambassador Extraordinary and Plenipotentiary, H Excellency Dr Francisco Kerdel-Vegas, CBE (1988)

Area and Population.—A South American Re public, situated approximately between 0° 45′ S. lat and 12° 12′ N. lat. and 59° 45′–73° 09′ W. long Venezuela consists of one Federal District, 20 state and two territories. It has a total area of 352,144 sq miles (912, 050 sq. km) and a population (UN estimat 1989) of 19,246,000.

Venezuela lies on the north of the South America continent, and is bounded on the north by the Caribbean Sea, west by the Republic of Colombia, eas by Guyana, and south by Brazil. Included in the are of the Republic are 72 islands off the coast, with total area of about 14,650 square miles, the larges being Margarita, which is politically associated wit Tortuga, Cubagua and Coche to form the state o Nueva Esparta. Margarita has an area of about 40 square miles.

Physical Features.—The Eastern Andes from the south-west cross the border and reach to the Carib bean coast, where they are prolonged by the Maritim Andes of Venezuela to the Gulf of Paria on the north east. The main range is known as the Sierra Nevada de Merida, and contains the highest peaks in the country in Pico Bolivar (16,411 feet) and Picacho d la Sierra (15,420 feet). Near the Brazilian border the

Sierras Parima and Pacaraima, and on the eastern border the Sierras de Rincote and de Usupamo, enclose the republic with parallel northward spurs, between which are valleys of the Orinoco tributaries. The slopes of the mountains and foothills are covered with dense forests, but the basin of the Orinoco is mainly llanos, or level stretches of open prairie, with occasional woods.

The principal river is the Orinoco, with innumerable affluents, the main river exceeding 1,600 miles in length from its rise in the southern highlands of the republic to its outflow in the deltaic region of the north-east. The Orinoco is navigable for large steamers from its mouth for 700 miles, and by smaller vessels as far as the Maipures cataract, some 200 miles farther up-stream. Dredging operations have opened the Orinoco to ocean-going ships, of up to 40 ft. draft, as far as Ciudad Guayana (about 150 miles up-stream). The upper waters of the Orinoco are united with those of the Rio Negro (a Brazilian tributary of the Amazon) by a natural river or canal, known as the Casiquiare.

The coastal regions of Venezuela are much indented and contain many lagoons and lakes, of which Maracaibo, with an area of 8,296 square miles, is the largest lake in South America. Other lakes are Zulia (290 square miles), south-west of Maracaibo, and Valencia (216 square miles) about 1,400 ft. above sea-level in the Maritime Andes.

The climate is tropical and, except where modified by altitude or tempered by sea breezes, is unhealthy, particularly in the coastal regions and in the neighbourhood of lowland streams and lagoons. The hot, wet season lasts from April to October, the dry, cooler season from November to March.

Government.—The Republic of Venezuela gained independence from Spain in 1830. According to the 1961 Constitution, executive power is held by the President, who also appoints the Council of Ministers. Legislative power is exercised by a bicameral National Congress, comprising a 196-member Chamber of Deputies and a Senate of 49 elected members plus the former Presidents of constitutional governments as life members. The President and National Congress are directly elected for concurrent five-year terms. The most recent elections were held in December 1988.

Language and Literature.—Spanish is the language of the country. There are 61 daily newspapers

in Venezuela, of which ten are published in Caracas, and about 60 to 70 weekly news magazines. There is also a large number of fortnightly, monthly and quarterly publications.

Education is free and compulsory between the ages of 7 and 13. There are ten universities in Venezuela, five in Caracas and the others in Maracaibo, Mérida, Valencia, Cumaná and Barquisimeto.

Production and Industry.—Products of the tropical forest region include orchids, wild rubber, timber, mangrove bark, balata gum and tonka beans; of agricultural areas, cocoa beans, coffee, cotton, rice, maize, sugar, sesame, groundnuts, potatoes, tomatoes, other vegetables, sisal and tobacco. There is an extensive beef and dairy farming industry. Despite substantial improvements in agriculture, Venezuela is heavily reliant upon food imports, which constitute about 60 per cent of total consumption. The government has embarked on a policy of economic reform and privatization.

The principal industry is that of petroleum, which in 1986 contributed 83 per cent of Venezuela's foreign exchange income. Daily production in the oilfields (nationalized 1976) has steadily declined since 1973 in line with Venezuela's conservation policies, reaching 1·7m b.p.d. in 1986 (compared with 3·366m in 1973) but has since recovered to around 2·5m. There are refineries at Punta Cardon, Amuay, Caripitó, San Lorenzo, Puerto La Cruz, Tucupeido, El Chaure and El Palito. Development of the Orinoco heavy oil belt is now moving ahead with the inauguration of the Lagovén continuous steam injection pilot plant at El Jobo in southern Monagas. It has been estimated conservatively that there might exist recoverable resources of 70,000 million barrels in the Orinoco region.

Aluminium is the second highest source of foreign exchange after petroleum. The Venezuelan state now holds the majority stake in both the principal producing companies, Venalum and Alcasa, and is moving towards a consolidation of the aluminium industry, with both companies sharing their resources and adopting general policies of marketing and procurement of supplies.

Rich iron ore deposits in eastern Venezuela have been developed. The government-owned steel mill at Matanzas in the Guayana uses local iron ore and obtains its electric power from hydro-electric installations on the Caroni River. It produces seamless steel tubes, billets, wire and profiles. A mill at Ciudad Guayana for the production of centrifugally-cast iron pipe came into operation at the end of 1970, with an annual capacity of 30,000 tons.

Other industries include petrochemicals, gold, diamonds and asbestos; textiles, clothing and footwear; plastics; manufacture or preparation of foodstuffs, alcoholic and non-alcoholic beverages; manufacture of paper, cement, glass, tyres, cigarettes, soap, animal feeding concentrates, simple steel products, tins, jewellery, rope, furniture, sacks, paint and motor-vehicle assembly; preparation of pharmaceutical goods; pearl fishing, sanitary ware, electric home appliances, pumps, toys, agricultural machinery, bicycles, electronic components, cosmetics and many others.

Communications.—There are about 62,449 km of roads, 22,975 km of them paved. The state has now acquired all but a very few of the railway lines, whose total length is only some 372 kilometres. Road and river communications have made railways of negligibile importance in Venezuela except for carrying iron ore in the south-east. However, the government is restoring the Puerto Cabello-Barquisimeto line and expanding it to Turén in the agricultural heartland of Venezuela. A new line connecting Caracas with La Guaira and the Litoral is planned, and in 1983 the Caracas Metro came into operation.

British, US and European airlines provide Venezuela with a wide range of services. There are three Venezuelan airlines which between them have a comprehensive network of internal lines and also connect Caracas with the United States, Central and South America, the Caribbean and Europe. Foreign vessels are not permitted to engage in the coast trade. The telegraph, radio-telegraph and radio-telephone services are state-owned. There are four television stations in Venezuela, all in Caracas. Two are government controlled.

TRADE

	1987	1988
Total imports	US$8,711 m	US$10,472 m
Total exports	10,843 m	10,365 m

Trade with UK

	1989	1990
Imports from UK	£124,672,000	£204,921,000
Exports to UK	111,072,000	101,717,000

CAPITAL.—Caracas, population around 4,000,000. Other principal towns are ΨMaracaibo (1·7 m), Barquisimeto (504,000), Valencia (495,000), Maracay (322,000), San Cristobal (230,000), Cumaná (155,000) and Ciudad Guayana (250,000).

CURRENCY.—Bolivar (BS) of 100 céntimos.

FLAG.—Three horizontal bands, yellow, blue, red (with seven white stars on blue band and coat of arms next staff on yellow band).

NATIONAL ANTHEM.—Gloria Al Bravo Pueblo (Glory to the brave people).

NATIONAL DAY.—July 5.

BRITISH EMBASSY
Apartado 1246, Caracas 1010-A
[Caracas 7511022]

Ambassador Extraordinary and Plenipotentiary, His Excellency Giles Eden FitzHerbert, CMG (1987).
Counsellor, M. Hickson (*Deputy Head of Mission*).
Defence Attaché, Capt. W. McLaren, RN.
British Council Representative, Dr V. A. Atkinson.

There are British Consular Offices at *Caracas, Maracaibo* and *Mérida*.

BRITISH-VENEZUELAN CHAMBER OF COMMERCE, Apartado 5713, Caracas 1010. Torre Británica, Piso 11, Letra E, Av. José Félix Sosa, Altamira Sur, Caracas 1060.

VIETNAM
(Công Hòa Xã Hội Chu Nghĩa Việt Nam)

COUNCIL OF STATE
(as at August 10, 1991)

Chairman, Vo Chi Cong.

COUNCIL OF MINISTERS

Chairman, Vo Van Kiet.
Vice-Chairmen, Phan Van Khai; Vo Nguyen Giap; Nguyen Kanh; Tran Duc Luong.
National Defence, Doan Khue.
Foreign Affairs, Nguyen Manh Cam.
Interior, Bui Thieu Ngo.
Chairman of the State Planning Commission, Do Quoc Sam.
Chairman of the State Commission for Co-operation and Investment, Dao Ngoc Xuan.
Chairman of the State Science Commission, Dang Huu.
Chairman of the State Inspection Commission, Nguyen Ky Cam.
Chairman of the State Commission for Prices, Phan Van Tiem.

Finance, Hoang Quy.
Director General of the State Bank, Cao Si Kiem.
Commerce, Le Van Triet.
Labour, War Invalids and Social Affairs, Tran Dinh Hoan.
Building, Ngo Xuan Loc.
Communications, Transport and Posts and Telegraphs, Bui Danh Luu.
Heavy Industry, Tran Lam.
Energy, Vu Ngoc Hai.
Light Industry, Dang Vu Chu.
Agriculture and Food Industry, Nguyen Cong Tan.
Forestry, Phan Xuan Dot.
Water Conservancy, Nguyen Canh Dinh.
Marine Products, Nguyen Tien Trinh.
Culture, Information, Sport and Tourism, Tran Hoan.
Public Health, Pham Song.
Education and Training, Tran Hong Quan.
Justice, Phan Hien.
Mountain Regions and Nationalities, Hoang Minh Thang.

VIETNAMESE COMMUNIST PARTY

Politburo of the Central Committee, Do Muoi (*General Secretary*); Le Duc Anh; Voa Van Kiet; Dao Duy Tung; Doan Khue; Vu Oanh; Le Phuoc Tho; Pham Van Kai; Bui Thien Ngo; Nong Duc Manh; Phan The Duyet; Nguyen Duc Binh; Vo Tran Chi (*full members*).

EMBASSY OF THE SOCIALIST REPUBLIC OF VIETNAM
12–14 Victoria Road, W8 5RD
[071–937 1912]

Ambassador Extraordinary and Plenipotentiary, His Excellency Chau Phong (1990).

Vietnam, with an area of 127,242 sq. miles (329,556 sq. km), and an estimated population (UN 1989) of 65,682,000, is bordered on the north by China and the west by Laos and Cambodia.

Government.—Following the end of the war in Vietnam in 1975, and the establishment of a Provisional Revolutionary Government to administer South Vietnam, a National Assembly representing the whole of Vietnam was elected on April 25, 1976. The Assembly met in Hanoi on June 24, and on July 2 approved the reunification of North and South Vietnam under the name of the Socialist Republic of Vietnam. The national flag, anthem and capital of North Vietnam were unanimously adopted for the Socialist Republic, and Saigon was renamed Ho Chi Minh City.

Effective power lies with the ruling party, the Vietnamese Communist Party (VCP), its highest executive body being the Central Committee, elected by a Party Congress on a national basis.

The Seventh Party Congress of the VCP in June 1991 elected a new Central Committee. It is the Politburo and the Secretariat of the Central Committee which exercises real power and rules Vietnam.

Economy.—During recent years, Vietnam's economy has faced considerable problems. These include serious agricultural losses because of adverse weather, attempts to collectivize agriculture in the south, major reductions in western aid (as a result of Vietnam's invasion and occupation of neighbouring Cambodia), border hostilities with China, and the continued allocation of resources to military expenditure. Efforts to integrate the economies of the north and south have not been very successful.

Vietnam's overall economic position is not good. Vietnam has been in default of repayments to the international banking world from the IMF to major commercial and merchant banks and therefore has received very few long term credits. Some attempted reforms of the economic system in 1985, including devaluation and a currency change, had adverse

effects and inflation increased rapidly in late 1985 and early 1986. Assistance from the Soviet Union (estimated at US$2·3 billion p.a. in 1987) has declined. However, economic reforms were instituted in the wake of the Sixth Party Congress (1986) and have begun to take effect. Inflation is down to single figures per month; the exchange rate has been rationalized, subsidies removed and much greater economic activity allowed. The effective creation of free market conditions for agricultural production and petty trading since 1989 has led to a significant improvement in agricultural production, with Vietnam becoming a major rice exporter. Foreign investment is being actively encouraged and is beginning to have effect but the amount of western and international agency investment and aid will remain limited until Vietnam is judged to have made a suitable contribution to the solution of the Cambodian problem.

Trade with UK

	1989	1990
Imports from UK	£4,108,000	£5,802,000
Exports to UK	1,711,000	1,443,000

CAPITAL.—Hanoi, population (1989) 1,089,000. Other cities are Ho Chi Minh City (3,169,000) and Hai Phong (456,000).

CURRENCY.—Dông of 10 hao or 100 xu.

FLAG.—Red, with yellow five-point star in centre.

NATIONAL ANTHEM.—Tien Quan Ca (The troops are advancing).

NATIONAL DAY.—September 2.

BRITISH EMBASSY
16 Pho Ly Thuong Kiet, Hanoi
[Hanoi 4252510]

Ambassador Extraordinary and Plenipotentiary, His
Excellency Peter Keegan Williams (1990).

REPUBLIC OF YEMEN
(Al-Jamhuriya Al-Yamaniya)

President, Gen. Ali Abdullah Saleh, *elected* May 22,
1990.
Vice President, Ali Salim al-Beedh.
Members of Presidential Council, Qadi Abdel-Karim
al-Arashi; Abdel Aziz Abdel Ghani; Salim Salih
Mohammed.

COUNCIL OF MINISTERS
(as at June 1991)

Prime Minister, Haider Abu Bakr al-Attas.
First Deputy PM, Dr Hassan Mohammed Makki.
Deputy PM, Minister for Internal Affairs, Brig.-Gen.
Mujahid Yahya Abu Shawarib.
Deputy PM, Security and Defence, Brig.-Gen. Salih
Ubayd Ahmed.
*Deputy PM, Development of Manpower and Admin-
istrative Reform*, Mohammed Haider Masdus.
Construction, Abdullah Hussayn al-Kurshumi.
Foreign Affairs, Abdullah al-Karim Ali al-Iryani.
Expatriates' Affairs, Brig.-Gen. Salih Munassar as-
Siyayli.
Industry, Mohammed Said al-Attar.
Oil and Mineral Resources, Salih Abu Bakr Bin
Hussain.
Supply and Trade, Fadl Mohsin Abdullah.
Legal Administration, Mohammed Said Abdullah
Muhsin.
Electricity and Water, Abdul-Wahhab Mahmud Ab-
dul-Hamid.
Civil Service and Administrative Reform, Mohammed
al-Khadim al-Wajih.
Planning and Development, Faraj Bin Ghanim.
Telecommunications, Ahmad Mohammed al-Unsi.
Legal Affairs, Ismail Ahmad al-Wazir.
Waqfs (Religious Affairs) and Guidance, Muhsin
Mohammed al-Ulufi.
Securities and Social Affairs, Ahmad Mohammed
Luqman.
Culture and Tourism, Hasan Ahmad al-Lawzi.
Youth and Sports, Mohammed Ahmad al-Kabab.
Education, Mohammed Abdullah al-Jayfi.
Justice, Abdul Wasi Ahmed Sallam.
Information, Mohammed Ahmed Jirghum.
Transport, Salih Abdullah Muthanna.
Fisheries, Salim Mohammad Jubran.
Housing and Urban Planning, Mohammed Ahmed
Salman.
Finance, Alawi Salih al-Salami.
Public Health, Mohammed Ali Muqbil.
Agriculture and Water Resources, Sadiq Amin Abu
Ras.
Interior and Security, Col. Ghalib Motahar al-Qomesh.
Defence, Brig.-Gen. Haytham Qasim Tahir.
Labour and Vocational Training, Abdul Rahman
Dhiban.
Higher Education and Scientific Research, Ahmad
Salim al-Qadi.

In addition there are four Ministers of State.

EMBASSY OF THE REPUBLIC OF YEMEN
41 South Street, W1Y 5PD
[071–629 9905]

Ambassador Extraordinary and Plenipotentiary, new
appointment awaited.

Area and Population.—The Republic of Yemen
comprises that area of the Arabian peninsula formerly occupied by the Yemen Arab republic (North
Yemen) and the People's Democratic Republic of
Yemen (South Yemen). Bounded on the west by
the Red Sea, on the north by Saudi Arabia, on the
east by Oman and on the south by the Gulf of Aden,
Yemen has an estimated area of 203,850 sq. miles
(527,969 sq. km) and an estimated combined population (1990) of 12,500,000. Included in the state are the
offshore islands of Perim and Kamaran in the Red
Sea, and Socotra in the Gulf of Aden.

The highlands and central plateau, and the highest
portions of the maritime range of what was South
Yemen, form the most fertile part of Arabia, with
abundant but irregular rainfall. The area of North
Yemen is largely composed of mountains and desert,
and rainfall is generally scarce.

Government.—Turkish occupation of North
Yemen (1872–1918) was followed by the rule of the
Hamid al-Din dynasty until a revolution in 1962
overthrew the monarchy and the Yemen Arab
Republic was declared. The People's Republic of
South Yemen was set up in November 1967 when the
British government ceded power to the National
Liberation Front, thus bringing to an end 129 years
of British rule in Aden and some years of protectorate
status in the hinterland. The name was changed to
the People's Democratic Republic of Yemen in
November 1970. Negotiations towards merging the
two states began in 1979.

A draft joint Constitution, proposing the establishment of a unified multi-party state, was published by
the leaders of North and South Yemen in December
1989. Unification was proclaimed on May 22, 1990
following ratification the previous day by both
parliaments. The constitution was approved by
referendum on May 16, 1991. Elections are to be held
at the end of 1992.

A five-member Presidential Council comprising
former senior government figures of the separate
states was formed for the period of transition. The
former President of North Yemen was declared
President of the unified state, with the former
President of South Yemen becoming Prime Minister.
The parliament of the unified state, the House of
Representatives, comprises 270 members, 159 of which
were former members of North Yemen's government,
and 111 of South Yemen's.

Economy and Production.—Exports include cotton, coffee, hides and skins. Agriculture is the main
occupation of the inhabitants. This is largely of a
subsistence nature, sorghum, sesame and millets
being the chief crops, with wheat and barley widely
grown at the higher elevations. Oil has been produced
at Marib since December 1987; production averages
250,000 b.p.d. and is expected to reach 400,000 b.p.d.
by 1992. A new field is being developed at Shabwa in
what used to be South Yemen. There is a refinery at
Aden. The Aden Free Zone was opened in May 1991
and could help Aden recover its old commercial
importance in the region.

Trade with U.K.
(North Yemen)

	1989	1990
Imports from UK	£41,653,000	£51,946,000
Exports to UK	1,598,000	33,698,000

(South Yemen)

	1989	1990
Imports from UK	£17,246,000	£18,889,000
Exports to UK	5,029,000	2,540,000

CAPITAL.—Sana'a, population (1986) 427,150.
Ψ Aden (270,000) is the other main city and the
former capital of South Yemen.

CURRENCY.—Yemeni dinar (YD) of 1,000 fils and
Riyals of 100 fils are both legal tender (1 Dinar = 26
Riyals).

FLAG.—Horizontal bands of red, white and black.
NATIONAL DAY.—May 22.

BRITISH EMBASSY
PO Box 1287, Sana'a
[Sana'a 275584]

Ambassador Extraordinary and Plenipotentiary, His
Excellency Mark Anthony Marshall, CMG (1987).
First Secretary, G. Kirby (*Deputy Head of Mission
and Aid*).

There is a British Consulate at *Aden*.

British Council Representative, A. Lewis, Beit Al-
Mottahar, Al-Bonia Street, Harat Handhal (PO
Box 2157), Sana'a.

YUGOSLAVIA
(Socijalistička Federativna Republika Jugoslavije)

THE PRESIDENCY

President of the Presidency (1991–92), Stipe Mesić
(*Croatia*).
Vice-President of the Presidency (1991–92), Branko
Kostic (*Montenegro*).
Members of the Presidency, Janez Drnovšek *Slov-
enia*); Borisav Jović (*Serbia*); Jugoslav Kostić
(*Vojvodina*); Sejdo Bajramovic (*Kosovo*); Vasil
Tupurkovski (*Macedonia*); Bogić Bogićević (*Bos-
nia and Hercegovina*).

FEDERAL EXECUTIVE COUNCIL
(as at May 1991)

President (Federal Prime Minister), Ante Markovic.
Vice-President, Aleksandar Mitrovic.
Foreign Affairs, Budimir Lončar.
National Defence, Veljko Kadijević.
Internal Affairs, Petar Gracanin.
Finance, Branko Zekan.
Foreign Trade, Franc Horvat.
Trade and General Economic Affairs, Nazmi Mustafa.
Justice and Organization of Federal Administration,
Vlado Kambovski.
Agriculture, Stevo Mirjanic.
Transport and Communications, Joze Slokar.
*Labour, Health and Social Security, Questions con-
cerning War Veterans and Disabled Veterans*,
Radisa Gacic.
Energy and Industry, Stevan Santo.

President of the SFRY Assembly, Slobodan Gligori-
jević.

EMBASSY OF THE SOCIALIST FEDERAL
REPUBLIC OF YUGOSLAVIA
5–7 Lexham Gardens, W8 5JU
[071–370 6105]

Ambassador Extraordinary and Plenipotentiary,Svet-
ozar Rikanovic (1989).

Area and Population.—The area of Yugoslavia is
estimated at 98,766 sq. miles (255,804 sq. km). The
population (UN estimate 1989) is 23,690,000; the latest
Census (April 1981) broke down the population into
8,140,000 Serbs, 4,430,000 Croats, 1,750,000 Slovenes,
1,730,000 Albanians, 1,341,000 Macedonians and
1,220,000 'Yugoslavs', as well as a variety of other
minorities.

Government.—Yugoslavia is a federation comprising the Republics of Serbia, Bosnia and Hercegovina, Croatia, Montenegro, Macedonia and Slovenia.
On November 29, 1945, the Constituent Assembly of
Yugoslavia at a joint session of the Skupština and
the House of Nationalities, proclaimed Yugoslavia a
Republic. The official name of the country, 'The
Socialist Federal Republic of Yugoslavia', was
adopted by the 1963 Constitution.

Several amendments to the Constitution were
made in 1971. The most important formed a new
ruling body called the Presidency, which has eight
members, one from each Republic and Autonomous
Province. Since the death of President Tito in May
1980, its members take it in turns according to a fixed
order of succession to become President of the
Presidency of the Republic for a period of 12 months
each.

A new Constitution was proclaimed in 1974 followed by the reconstitution of the Federal Assembly
into two chambers consisting of the Federal Chamber
(220 delegates) and the Republican/Provincial Chamber (88 delegates). A new Federal Executive Council
(i.e. government) was also formed. The current
Council was elected in March 1989. The first election
of the SFRY Presidency since President Tito's death
occurred in May 1984; each new member has a five-
year mandate.

Yugoslavia has been gradually unravelling since
the death of Tito with the Catholic, western-looking,
more prosperous republics of Slovenia and Croatia
breaking away from the other predominantly Orthodox and Muslim, Balkan republics of the rest of
Yugoslavia; Communism has now been widely rejected. Efforts by the Federal Presidency and international mediators to end inter-communal conflict
and negotiate a new federal or confederal structure
for the country have so far failed and at the time of
going to press (September) Yugoslavia was in a state
of confusion.

Republics.—Bosnia-Hercegovina is bounded by
Serbia, Montenegro and Croatia. It has a population
of 4·1 million, of whom some 40 per cent are Muslims,
32 per cent Serbs and 18 per cent Croats. The capital
is Sarajevo. Results for the elections, held in
November and December 1990 for the 240-seat bicameral Assembly, were: the (Muslim) Party of Democratic Action 86 seats, the (Serbian) Democratic
Party 72, and the Croat Democratic Union 44.
President, Alija Izetbegovic.

Croatia is bounded by Slovenia, Hungary, Serbia
and Bosnia-Hercegovina; it includes the Adriatic
coastline of Istria and Dalmatia. It has a population
of 4·7 million of whom 75 per cent are Croats and
some 12 per cent Serbs. The capital is Zagreb.
Elections held in April and May 1990 for the three-
chamber *Sabor* were won by the Croat Democratic
Union. Croatia declared its independence on June
25, 1991. For some months members of the Serbian
minority had refused to recognize Croatian moves
towards independence and began a guerrilla war
against local security forces. From July they were
reported to be being supported by units of the federal
army; at the time of going to press (September),
Serbian irregulars (Chetniks) and federal troops had
occupied up to a third of Croatian territory and
controlled the Serb enclaves in the east and south of
the republic.
President, Franjo Tudjman.

Macedonia is a landlocked republic bounded by
Serbia, Bulgaria, Greece and Albania. It has a
population of 2·1 million, of whom 67 per cent are
Macedonian and 20 per cent Albanian. The capital is
Skopje. Multi-party elections were held in November
and December 1990 for the 120-seat Assembly.
President, Kiro Gligorov.

Montenegro is bounded by Bosnia-Hercegovina,
Serbia, Albania and the Adriatic. It has a population
of 650,000, of whom 68 per cent are Montenegrins, 13
per cent Muslim and 6 per cent Albanian. The capital
is Titograd. The League of Communists won multi-
party elections, held in December 1990 for the 125-
seat assembly. Montenegro is an ally of Serbia.
President, Momir Bulatovic.

Serbia shares frontiers with all the Yugoslav
republics except Slovenia, as well as with Hungary,

Romania and Bulgaria. The capital is Belgrade. It has a population of 9·8 million, of whom 66 per cent are Serbs. It includes the provinces of Kosovo, of great historic importance to Serbs, and Vojvodina; the autonomy of both was ended in September 1990. Kosovo, with its capital at Priština, is predominantly Albanian (90 per cent). Vojvodina, with its capital at Novi Sad, has a large Hungarian minority (21 per cent). The Socialist Party of Serbia (formerly the League of Communists) won multi-party elections for the 250-seat National Assembly, held in December 1990. Serbia has traditionally been the dominant republic in Yugoslavia.

President, Slobodan Milosevic.

Slovenia is bounded by Italy, Austria, Hungary and Croatia. It has a population of 2 million, of whom over 90 per cent are Slovene. The capital is Ljubljana. The United Democratic Opposition (Demos) won multi-party elections held in April 1990. Slovenia declared its independence on June 25, 1991. Attacks by the federal army followed but failed to coerce the republic and troops began to be withdrawn in July.

President, Milan Kucan.

Defence.—The Army, Navy and Air Force on a peace footing consisted of 180,000 officers and men. With the outbreak of inter-communal fighting, the armed forces are now reduced and are manned largely by Serbs.

Religion.—The three main religions are the Orthodox, Catholic and Islamic, and freedom to practise is constitutionally guaranteed.

Education.—Eight years' elementary education is compulsory and all education is free. There are 18 universities.

Language and Literature.—The language mainly used throughout Yugoslavia and in the Federal Government is Serbo-Croat but Slovenian and Macedonian (also South Slav tongues) and Albanian, Bulgarian, Romanian, Italian, Slovak, Ruthenian, Hungarian and Turkish are also spoken in certain areas. There is, however, no official language since all are constitutionally equal, except in the Armed Forces where Serbo-Croat is obligatory. In Serbia, Macedonia and Montenegro, the Cyrillic script is used and in the rest of the country the Latin. There are four Serbian daily newspapers in Belgrade, two Slovene dailies in Ljubljana, two Croat dailies in Zagreb, and many other dailies published in other towns. There are also many local newspapers and radio programmes in the different 'minority' languages.

Production and Industry.—The share of industry in Gross Domestic Product (average annual rate in real terms of 6·5 per cent in 1981) is now 40 per cent, while agriculture is 14 per cent. In industry the high level of investment of recent years is being cut back and present efforts are directed towards development of high priority areas such as mining, energy resources and transport and communications. Agricultural policy is directed towards substantially increased production, to make the country self-sufficient and to provide significant exports of foodstuffs. Some 80 per cent of land is still privately owned.

The main crops are wheat, maize, sugar beet, sunflower and soya. Yields in 1988 were (tons): wheat 6·3m; maize 7·7m; sugar beet 4·6m. According to Yugoslav official estimates, the livestock population in 1988 was approximately as follows: 4,881,000 cattle; 7,824,000, sheep; 8,323,000, pigs; 78,589,000 poultry.

Minerals are an important source of wealth particularly in the central and south-eastern regions. Production in 1988 included the following (tons):—

Coal	72,590,000
Coke	3,208,000
Iron ore	5,545,000
Pig iron	2,916,000
Steel	4,485,000
Crude oil	3,681,000

Smaller quantities of copper, zinc and mercury are produced.

Communications.—In 1984 there were 9,279 km of standard and narrow gauge railway and approximately 116,600 km of classified roads. In 1987 there were 3,909,000 telephones in use in the country. The principal ports on the long Adriatic seaboard of Yugoslavia are Rijeka, Bakar, Šibenik, Split, Zadar, Kardeljeva (formerly Ploče), Dubrovnik, Bar, Kotor (Cattaro) and Koper. The Danube forms a great commercial highway and the tributary rivers Sava and Tisa provide other shipping routes.

FINANCE

	1987	1988
Revenue	US$20,451m	US$22,953m
Expenditure	US$19,203m	20,466m

Trade with UK

	1989	1990
Imports from UK	£219,866,000	£260,972,000
Exports to UK	202,450,000	189,421,000

CAPITAL.—Belgrade, population (1981) 1,455,000. Other towns are Zagreb (763,000); Skopje (503,000); Ljubljana (253,000); Sarajevo (447,000); Novi Sad (169,000); Priština (1971) (153,000); Ψ Split (152,000); Ψ Rijeka (133,000); Titograd (95,000).

CURRENCY.—Yugoslav new dinar of 100 paras.

FLAG.—Five-point red star outlined by narrow yellow stripe, on a ground of three horizontal bars, blue, white and red.

NATIONAL ANTHEM.—Hej, Slaveni, Jošte Živi Reč Naših Dedova (Oh! Slavs, our ancestors' words still live).

NATIONAL DAY.—November 29.

BRITISH EMBASSY
General Ždanova 46, Belgrade
[Belgrade 645055]

Ambassador Extraordinary and Plenipotentiary, His Excellency Peter E. Hall, CMG, (1989).
Counsellor, M. J. Robinson.
Defence and Military Attaché, Col. E. D. Powell-Jones.
Naval and Air Attaché, Wg. Cdr. R. Parker.

There are British Consular Offices at *Belgrade, Dubrovnik, Split* and *Zagreb.*

British Council Representative, P. Early, Generala Ždanova 34-Mezanin, (Post Fah 248), 11001 Belgrade.

ZAIRE
(République du Zaïre)

President of the Republic and National Security, Marshal Mobutu Sésé Séko, *born* Oct. 30, 1930; *assumed office* November 25, 1965; *elected* Nov. 5, 1970; *re-elected for third term,* July 28, 1984.

EXECUTIVE COUNCIL
(as at June 1991)

Prime Minister, Mulumba Lukoji.
Deputy PM in charge of Institutional Reforms, Kisimba Ngoy.
Deputy PM in charge of Administration of the Land and Decentralization, Mozagba Ngbuka.
Deputy PM in charge of Economy and Industry, Malu Biakalua.
Foreign Affairs, Inonga Lokungo L'Ome.
Defence, Territorial Security and Veterans, Mavua Mudima.

Justice, Muyabu Nkulu.

Finance, Ilunga Ilunkamba.

Planning and Territorial Development, Bombito Botomba.

Budget, Mananga Ma Pholo.

Press and Information, Banza Mukalay Nsungu.

International Co-operation, Ngongo Kamanda.

Agriculture, Rural Affairs and Community Development, Onyembe Pene Mbutu.

External Trade, Mulamba Musambay.

Mining, Mushobekwa Kalimba Wa Katana.

Energy, Mulangala Luakabwanga.

Small and Medium Enterprises, Mimpiya Akan.

Public Works, Town Planning and Housing, Nyindu Kitenge.

Transport and Communications, Kimasi Matuiku Basaula.

Land Affairs, Kabange Ntabala Mualim.

Higher and University Education, Payanzo Ntsomo.

Scientific Research, Kambayi Bwatsha.

Primary, Secondary and Professional Education, Koli Elombe Mutukuo.

Health, Mboso Nkodia Pwanga.

Environment and Nature Conservation, Katende Ngunza.

Public Office, Muduka Inyanza.

Social Affairs, Longelo Muyangandu.

Employment and Social Security, Kwete Minga.

Women's and Family Affairs, Mitheo Lola Mara Tumba.

Posts and Telecommunications, Kitenge Yezu.

Culture, Arts and Tourism, Mutuza Kaba.

Relations with Parliament, Bashala Kantu Wa Milandu.

Youth, Sport and Leisure, Tangelo Okito.

EMBASSY OF THE REPUBLIC OF ZAIRE
26 Chesham Place, SW1X 8HG
[071–235 6137]

Ambassador Extraordinary and Plenipotentiary, His Excellency Liloo Nkema (1991).

Situated between long. 12°–31° E. and lat. 5° N.–13° S., the Republic of Zaire comprises an area of 905,567 sq. miles (2,345,409 sq. km), with a population (1985 Census) of 34,671,607. A 1989 UN estimate gives a figure of 34,491,000.

Climate.—Apart from the coastal district in the west which is fairly dry, the rainfall averages between 60 and 80 inches. The average temperature is about 27°C, but in the south the winter temperature can fall nearly to freezing point. Extensive forest covers the central districts.

Government.—The State of the Congo, founded in 1885, became a Belgian Colony in November 1908, and was administered by Belgium until independence in 1960, when it became the Democratic Republic of the Congo. In October 1971 the name changed to the Republic of Zaire.

Mobutu Sésé Seko, formerly Commander-in-Chief of the Congolese National Army, came to power in a coup in 1965, and was elected President in 1970. Legislative power is vested in a unicameral National Legislative Council, elected for a five-year term by compulsory, direct and universal suffrage. All candidates are proposed by the sole legal political party, Mouvement Populaire de la Révolution (MPR). In 1980 a MPR central committee was formed with powers to overrule the National Legislative Council.

Following mounting social tension, political reforms were announced in April 1990. They include the separation of the roles of head of state and head of government, and the gradual introduction of a three-party system. A transitional government was appointed in May 1990. After mounting opposition

pressure, President Mobutu called a national conference, intended to draft a new constitution, in April 1991; the conference convened in August.

Provinces.—There are 11 regions, each under a Governor and provincial administration (names of capitals in brackets) Bas-Zaire (Matadi); Bandundu (Bandundu); Equateur (Mbandaka); Haut-Zaire (Kisangani); Kinshasa (Kinshasa); Maniema (Kindu); Nord-Kivu (Goma); Sud-Kivu (Bukavu); Shaba, formerly Katanga (Lubumbashi); East Kasai (Mbuji-Mayi); West Kasai (Kananga).

Language, Religion and Education.—The population is composed almost entirely of Bantu groups, divided into semi-autonomous tribes, each speaking a Bantu tongue. Minorities include Sudanese, Nilotes, Pygmies and Hamites, as well as refugees from Angola.

Swahili, a Bantu dialect with an admixture of Arabic, is the nearest approach to a common language in the east and south, while Lingala is the language of a large area along the river and in the north, and Kikongo of the region between Kinshasa and the sea. French is the language of administration.

The National University of Zaire has campuses in Kinshasa, Kisangani and Lubumbashi.

Production.—The cultivation of oil palms is widespread, palm oil being the most important agricultural cash product though it is no longer exported. Coffee, rubber, cocoa and timber are the most important agricultural exports. The production of cotton, pyrethrum and copal fell sharply on independence but is now increasing. The country is rich in minerals, particularly Shaba (ex-Katanga) province. Copper is widely exploited, and industrial diamonds and cobalt are also produced. Oil deposits are exploited off the Zaire estuary and reef-gold is mined in the north-east of the country.

There is a wide variety of small secondary industries, the main products being foodstuffs, beverages, tobacco, textiles, leather, wood products, cement and building materials, matallurgy, small river craft and bicycles. There are large reserves of hydro-electric power and the huge Inga dam on the river Zaire supplies electricity to Matadi, Kinshasa and Shaba.

The chief exports are copper, crude oil, coffee, diamonds, rubber, cobalt, gold, cassiterite, zinc and other metals.

Communications. There are approximately 20,500 km of roads (earth-surfaced) of national importance, and 6,000 km of railways. The country has four international and 40 principal airports.

Trade with UK

	1989	1990
Imports from UK	£28,419,000	£23,801,000
Exports to UK	9,069,000	7,337,000

CAPITAL.—Kinshasa (formerly Leopoldville), population (1985 Census) 2,778,281. Principal towns, Lubumbashi (formerly Elisabethville) (403,623); Kisangani (formerly Stanleyville) (310,705); Likasi (146,394); Kananga (601,239); ψ Matadi (143,598); and Mbandaka (134,495).

CURRENCY.—Zaïre of 100 makuta.

FLAG.—Dark brown hand and torch with red flame in yellow roundel on green background.

NATIONAL DAY.—November 24.

BRITISH EMBASSY
Avenue des Trois 'Z', Gombe, Kinshasa
[Kinshasa 34775/8]

Ambassador Extraordinary and Plenipotentiary, His Excellency Roger Westbrook, CMG (1991).

There are British Consulates at *Lubumbashi, Goma* and *Kisangani.*

CURRENCIES OF THE WORLD
and Exchange Rates against £ sterling

NOTE: Franc CFA = Franc de la Communauté financière africaine; Franc CFP = Franc des Comptoirs français du Pacifique.

Country	Monetary Unit	Average Rate to £ September 3, 1990	Average Rate to £ September 3, 1991
Afghanistan	Afghani (Af) of 100 puls	Af 99·25	Af 99·25
Albania	Lek (Lk) of 100 qindarka	Lk 9·9194	Lk 10·0850
Algeria..............	Algerian dinar (DA) of 100 centimes	DA 16.4868	DA 30·5920
Andorra..............	French and Spanish currencies are both in use	—	—
Angola	Kwanza (Kz) of 100 lwei	Kz 58·403	Kz 99·8395
Antigua and Barbuda..	East Caribbean dollar (EC$) of 100 cents	EC$ 5·0584	EC$ 4·5510
Argentina	Austral (A) of 100 centavos or 1,000 pesos	A 11749·95	A 16767·5
Aruba..............	Aruban florin	Florins 3·3536	Florins 3·0170
Australia.............	Australian dollar ($A) of 100 cents	$A 2·30125	$A 2·1485
Austria	Schilling of 100 Groschen	Schilling 20·825	Schilling 20·695
Azores	Currency is that of Portugal	Esc 261$30	Esc 252$00
Bahamas	Bahamian dollar (B$) of 100 cents	B$ 1·8730	B$ 1·6850
Bahrain..............	Bahrain dinar (BD) of 1,000 fils	BD 0·7067	BD 0·6343
Balearic Isles	Currency is that of Spain	Pesetas 184·75	Pesetas 183·00
Bangladesh	Taka (Tk) of 100 poisha	Tk 65·00	Tk 57·60
Barbados	Barbados dollar (BD$) of 100 cents	BD$ 3·7682	BD$ 3·39
Belgium	Belgian franc (or frank) of 100 centimes (centiemen)	Francs 60·85	Francs 60·55
Belize	Belize dollar (BZ$) of 100 cents	BZ$ 3·747	BZ$ 3.3710
Benin	Franc CFA	Francs 497·25	Francs 499·63
Bermuda	Bermuda dollar of 100 cents	$ 1·8730	$ 1·6850
Bhutan	Ngultrum of 100 chetrum (Indian currency is also legal tender)	Ngultrum 33·00	Ngultrum 43·25
Bolivia	Boliviano ($b) of 100 centavos	$b 6·0139	$b 6·1099
Botswana	Pula (P) of 100 thebe	P 3·4750	P 3·4730
Brazil	Cruzeiro (BRC) of 100 centavos	BRC 134·023	BRC 664·475
British Virgin Islands .	US dollar (US$) (£ sterling and EC$ also circulate)	US$ 1·8730	US$ 1·6850
Brunei	Brunei dollar of 100 sen (fully interchangeable with Singapore currency)	$ 3·3085	$ 2·8948
Bulgaria	Lev of 100 stotinki	Leva 5·5416	Leva 31·014
Burkina..............	Franc CFA	Francs 497·25	Francs 499·63
Burundi..............	Burundi franc of 100 centimes	Francs 325·20	Francs 290·50
Cambodia	Riel of 100 sen	Riel 861·58	Riel 1348·40
Cameroon	Franc CFA	Francs 497·25	Francs 499·63
Canada..............	Canadian dollar (C$) of 100 cents	C$ 2·1585	C$ 1·9225
Canary Islands........	Currency is that of Spain	Pesetas 184·75	Pesetas 183·00
Cape Verde	Escudo Caboverdiano of 100 centavos	Esc 128$71	Esc 125$70
Cayman Islands	Cayman Islands dollar (CI$) of 100 cents	CI$ 1·5550	CI$ 1·3990
Central African Republic	Franc CFA	Francs 497·25	Francs 499·63
Chad................	Franc CFA	Francs 497·25	Francs 499·63
Chile................	Chilean peso of 100 centavos	Pesos 561·44	Pesos 594·70
China................	Yuan of 10 jiao or 100 fen	Yuan 8·9023	Yuan 9·0773
Colombia	Colombian peso of 100 centavos	Pesos 975·68	Pesos 1048·40
Comoros..............	Comorian franc of 100 centimes (Franc CFA also in circulation)	Francs 497·25	Francs 499·63
Congo................	Franc CFA	Francs 497·25	Francs 499·63
Costa Rica	Costa Rican colón (₡) of 100 céntimos	₡ 176·17	₡ 225·02
Côte d'Ivoire..........	Franc CFA	Francs 497·25	Francs 499·63
Cuba	Cuban peso of 100 centavos	Pesos 1·4922	Pesos 2·2515
Cyprus	Cyprus pound (C£) of 100 cents	C£ 0·8401	C£ 0·8050
Czechoslovakia	Koruna (Kčs) of 100 haléru	Kčs 30·32	Kčs 51·45
Denmark	Danish krone of 100 øre	Kroner 11·3500	Kroner 11·3575
Djibouti	Djibouti franc of 100 centimes	Francs 325·00	Francs 295·00
Dominica	East Caribbean dollar (EC$) of 100 cents	EC$ 5·0584	EC$ 4·5510
Dominican Republic ...	Dominican Republic peso (RD$) of 100 centavos	RD$ 20·4039	RD$ 21·3720
Ecuador	Sucre of 100 centavos	Sucres 1636·43	Sucres 1835·75

Country	Monetary Unit	Average Rate to £ September 3, 1990	Average Rate to £ September 3, 1991
Egypt	Egyptian pound (£E) of 100 piastres or 1,000 millièmes	£E 5·105	£E 5·57
Equatorial Guinea	Franc CFA	Francs 497·25	Francs 499·63
Ethiopia	Ethiopian birr (EB) of 100 cents	EB 3·8510	EB 3·4595
Falkland Islands	Falkland pound of 100 pence	(at parity with £ sterling)	
Faroe Islands	Currency is that of Denmark	Kroner 11·3500	Kroner 11·3575
Fiji	Fiji dollar (F$) of 100 cents	F$ 2·6941	F$ 2·5082
Finland	Markka (Mk) of 100 penniä	Mk 6·9712	Mk 7·1528
France	Franc of 100 centimes	Francs 9·9450	Francs 9·9925
French Guiana........	Currency is that of France	Francs 9·9450	Francs 9·9925
French Polynesia	Franc CFP	Francs 177·00	Francs 180·00
Gabon	Franc CFA	Francs 497·25	Francs 499·63
Gambia	Dalasi (D) of 100 butut	D 15·8048	D 15·9045
Germany	Deutsche Mark (DM) of 100 Pfennig	M 2·9675	DM 2·9400
Ghana	Cedi of 100 pesewas	Cedi 629·516	Cedi 637·50
Gibraltar	Gibraltar pound of 100 pence	(at parity with £ sterling)	
Greece	Drachma of 100 leptae	Drachmae 292·75	Drachmae 324·425
Greenland	Currency is that of Denmark	Kroner 11·3500	Kroner 11·3575
Grenada............	East Caribbean dollar (EC$) of 100 cents	EC$ 5·0584	EC$ 4·5510
Guadeloupe..........	Currency is that of France	Francs 9·9450	Francs 9·9925
Guam	Currency is that of USA	US$ 1·8730	US$ 1·6850
Guatemala	Quetzal (Q) of 100 centavos	Q 8·4714	Q 8·5370
Guinea	Guinea franc of 100 centimes	Francs 562·05	Francs 505·65
Guinea-Bissau	Guinea-Bissau peso of 100 centavos	Pesos 1217·77	Pesos 1095·55
Guyana	Guyana dollar (G$) of 100 cents	G$ 83·39	G$ 214·05
Haiti	Gourde of 100 centimes	Gourdes 9·3675	Gourdes 8·4275
Honduras	Lempira of 100 centavos	Lempiras 9·1817	Lempiras 8·9610
Hong Kong	Hong Kong dollar (HK$) of 100 cents	HK$ 1·45452	HK$ 13·0685
Hungary	Forint of 100 fillér	Forints 120·6295	Forints 128·68
Iceland..............	Icelandic króna (Kr) of 100 aurar	Kr 108·80	Kr 103·25
India................	Indian rupee (Rs) of 100 paisa	Rs 33·00	Rs 43·25
Indonesia	Rupiah (Rp) of 100 sen	Rp 3522·10	Rp 3311·75
Iran	Rial of 100 dinars	Rials 126·50	Rials 113·10
Iraq................	Iraqi dinar (ID) of 1,000 fils	ID 0·6060	ID 0·5936
Ireland, Republic of....	Punt (IR£) of 100 pence	IR£ 1·1060	IR£ 1·0995
Israel	Shekel of 100 agora	Shekels 3·877	Shekels 3·9120
Italy	Lira of 100 centesimi	Lire 2207·25	Lire 2130·00
Jamaica	Jamaican dollar (J$) of 100 cents	J$ 12·8125	J$ 17·53
Japan	Yen of 100 sen	Yen 268·75	Yen 230·25
Jordan	Jordanian dinar (JD) of 1,000 fils	JD 1·2302	JD 1·1482
Kenya	Kenya shilling (Ksh) of 100 cents	Ksh 43·68	Ksh 48·9638
Kiribati	Australian dollar ($A) of 100 cents	$A 2·30125	$A 2·1485
Korea, North	Won of 100 jun	Won 1·8173	Won 1·6350
Korea, South	Won of 100 jeon	Won 1348·15	Won 1236·90
Kuwait	Kuwaiti dinar (KD) of 1,000 fils	n/a	KD 0·49105
Laos	Kip (K) of 100 at	K 1130·18	K 1179·85
Lebanon............	Lebanese pound (L£) of 100 piastres	L£ 2009·7	L£ 1503·10
Lesotho............	Loti (M) of 100 lisente	M 4·8312	M 4·8408
Liberia	Liberian dollar (L$) of 100 cents	L$ 1·8730	L$ 1·6850
Libya	Libyan dinar (LD) of 1,000 dirhams	LD 0·5193	LD 0·4895
Liechtenstein	Swiss franc of 100 Rappen (or centimes)	Francs 2·4650	Francs 2·5825
Luxembourg	Luxembourg franc (LF) of 100 centimes (Belgian currency is also legal tender)	LF 60·85	LF 60·55
Macao	Pataca of 100 avos	Pataca 15·0221	Pataca 13·5130
Madagascar	Franc malgache (FMG) of 100 centimes	FMG 2265·75	FMG 2218·00
Madeira..............	Currency is that of Portugal	Esc 261·30	Esc 252·00
Malawi..............	Kwacha (K) of 100 tambala	K 5·0175	K 4·8130
Malaysia	Malaysian dollar (ringgit) (M$) of 100 sen	M$ 5·0357	M$ 4·6882
Maldives	Rufiyaa of 100 laaris	Rufiyaa 17·9912	Rufiyaa 16·9660
Mali	Franc CFA	Francs 497·25	Francs 499·63
Malta	Maltese lira (LM) of 100 cents or 1,000 mils	LM 0·5770	LM 0·5640
Martinique	Currency is that of France	Francs 9·9450	Francs 9·9925
Mauritania	Ouguiya (UM) of 5 khoums	UM 154·5263	UM 145·90
Mauritius	Mauritius rupee of 100 cents	Rs 26·85	Rs 27·00
Mayotte	Currency is that of France	Francs 9·9450	Francs 9·9925
Mexico	Peso of 100 centavos	Pesos 3414·49	Pesos 5132·15

Country	Monetary Unit	Average Rate to £ September 3, 1990	Average Rate to £ September 3, 1991
Monaco	French franc of 100 centimes	Francs 9·9450	Francs 9·9925
Mongolia	Tugrik of 100 möngö	Tugriks 6·2865	Tugriks 5·4500
Montserrat	East Caribbean dollar (EC$) of 100 cents	EC$ 5·0584	EC$ 4·5510
Morocco	Dirham (DH) of 100 centimes	DH 15·4294	DH 14·95
Mozambique	Metical (MT) of 100 centavos	1722 MT 19	2549 ML 75
Myanmar (Burma)	Kyat (K) of 100 pyas	K 11·5102	K 10·5879
Namibia	South African rand (R) of 100 cents	R 4·8312	R 4·8408
Nauru	Australian dollar ($A) of 100 cents	$A 2·30125	$A 2·1485
Nepal	Nepalese rupee of 100 paisa	Rs 54·9479	Rs 71·95
Netherlands	Gulden (guilder) or florin of 100 cents	Guilders 3·3425	Guilders 3·3125
Netherlands Antilles . .	Netherlands Antilles guilder of 100 cents	Guilders 3·3536	Guilders 3·0170
New Caledonia	Franc CFP	CFP 177·00	Francs 180·00
New Zealand	New Zealand dollar (NZ$) of 100 cents	NZ$ 3·0425	NZ$ 2·9345
Nicaragua	Córdoba (C$) of 100 centavos	C$ 1798560	C$ 8·4275
Niger	Franc CFA	Francs 497·25	Francs 499·63
Nigeria	Naira (N) of 100 kobo	N 14·80	N 18·4560
Norway	Krone of 100 øre	Kroner 11·4575	Kroner 11·5050
Oman	Rial Omani (OR) of 1,000 baiza	OR 0·7217	OR 0·6478
Pakistan	Pakistan rupee of 100 paisa	Rs 41·00	Rs 40·50
Panama	Balboa of 100 centésimos (US notes are also in circulation)	Balboa 1·8730	Balboa 1·6850
Papua New Guinea	Kina (K) of 100 toea	K 1·7625	K 1·6040
Paraguay	Guaraní (Gs) of 100 céntimos	Gs 2244·71	Gs 2217·05
Peru	New Sol of 100 cénts	Inti 72835·55	New Sol 1·3400
Philippines	Philippine peso (P) of 100 centavos	P 46·00	P 43·00
Poland	Złoty of 100 groszy	Złotys 18537·00	Złotys 19043·00
Portugal	Escudo (Esc) of 100 centavos	Esc 261·30	Esc 252·00
Puerto Rico	Currency is that of USA	US$ 1·8730	US$ 1·6850
Qatar	Qatar riyal of 100 dirhams	Riyals 6·8252	Riyals 6·1243
Réunion	Currency is that of France	Francs 9·9450	Francs 9·9925
Romania	Leu (Lei) of 100 bani	Lei 37·02	Lei 102·61
Rwanda	Rwanda franc of 100 centimes	Francs 143·82	Francs 215·84
St Christopher and Nevis	East Caribbean dollar (EC$) of 100 cents	EC$ 5·0584	EC$ 4·5510
St Helena	St Helena pound (£) of 100 pence	At parity with £ sterling	
St Lucia	East Caribbean dollar (EC$) of 100 cents	EC$ 5·0584	EC$ 4·5510
St Pierre and Miquelon	Currency is that of France	Francs 9·9450	Francs 9·9925
St Vincent and the Grenadines	East Caribbean dollar (EC$) of 100 cents	EC$ 5·0584	EC$ 4·5510
El Salvador	El Salvador colón (₡) of 100 centavos	₡ 11·9058	₡ 13·4635
San Marino	Italian currency is in circulation	Lire 2207·25	Lire 2193·00
São Tomé and Príncipe .	Dobra of 100 centavos	Dobra 188·3484	Dobra 315·20
Saudi Arabia	Saudi riyal (SR) of 20 qursh or 100 halala	SR 7·0247	SR 6·3103
Senegal	Franc CFA	Francs 497·25	Francs 499·63
Seychelles	Seychelles rupee of 100 cents	Rs 9·71	Rs 8·95
Sierra Leone	Leone (Le) of 100 cents	Le 298·00	Le 520·00
Singapore	Singapore dollar (S$) of 100 cents	S$ 3·3085	S$ 2·8948
Solomon Islands	Solomon Islands dollar (SI$) of 100 cents	SI$ 4·7575	SI$ 4·6300
Somalia	Somali shilling of 100 cents	Shillings 768·135	Shillings 4416·00
South Africa	Rand (R) of 100 cents	R 4·8312	R 4·8408
Spain	Peseta of 100 céntimos	Pesetas 184·75	Pesetas 183·00
Sri Lanka	Sri Lankan rupee of 100 cents	Rs 75·00	Rs 69·00
Sudan	Sudanese pound (£S) of 100 piastres or 1,000 millièmes	£S 21·4516	£S 19·2990
Suriname	Suriname guilder of 100 cents	Guilders 3·3442	Guilders 3·0085
Swaziland	Lilangeni (E) of 100 cents (South African currency also in circulation)	E 4·8312	E 4·8408
Sweden	Swedish krona of 100 öre	Kronor 10·8825	Kronor 10·6925
Switzerland	Swiss franc of 100 Rappen (or centimes)	Francs 2·4650	Francs 2·5825
Syria	Syrian pound (S$) of 100 piastres	S£ 39·3435	S£ 35·40
Taiwan	New Taiwan dollar (NT$) of 100 cents	NT$ 51·05	NT$ 44·95

Country	Monetary Unit	Average Rate to £ September 3, 1990	Average Rate to £ September 3, 1991
Tanzania	Tanzanian shilling of 100 cents	Shillings 369·40	Shillings 385·65
Thailand	Baht of 100 satang	Baht 48·00	Baht 42·50
Togo	Franc CFA	Francs 497·25	Francs 499·63
Tonga	Pa'anga (T$) of 100 seniti	T$ 2·30125	T$ 2·1485
Trinidad and Tobago ..	Trinidad and Tobago dollar (TT$) of 100 cents	TT$ 7·9624	TT$ 7·1635
Tunisia	Tunisian dinar of 1,000 millimes	Dinars 1·6440	Dinars 1·6335
Turkey	Turkish lira (TL) of 100 kurus	TL 5240·17	TL 7753·07
Tuvalu	Australian dollar ($A) of 100 cents	$A 2·30125	$A 2·1485
Uganda	Uganda shilling of 100 cents	Shillings 849·777	Shillings 1350·70
Union of Soviet Socialist Republics	Rouble of 100 kopeks	Roubles 1·1018	Roubles 1·0003
United Arab Emirates .	UAE dirham of 100 fils	Dirham 6·8772	Dirham 6·1790
United Kingdom	Pound sterling (£) of 100 pence	£ 1·00	£ 1·00
United States of America............	US dollar (US$) of 100 cents	US$ 1·8730	US$ 1·6850
Uruguay	New Uruguayan peso of 100 centésimos	Pesos 2348·74	Pesos 3606·60
Vanuatu	Vatu of 100 centimes	Vatu 210·50	Vatu 187·50
Vatican City State	Italian currency is legal tender	Lire 2207·25	Lire 2193·00
Venezuela	Bolívar (Bs) of 100 céntimos	Bs 91·0539	Bs 92·2560
Vietnam	Dông of 10 hào or 100 xu	Dông 8430·75	Dông 15186·35
Virgin Islands (US)....	Currency is that of USA	US$ 1·8730	US$ 1·6850
Western Samoa	Tala (WS$) of 100 sene	WS$ 4·3917	WS$ 4·0315
Republic of Yemen	Yemeni dinar (YD) of 1,000 fils	YD 0·8646	YD 0·7770
	Riyal of 100 fils	Riyals 22·482	Riyals 20·3945
Yugoslavia	Dinar of 100 paras	Dinars 20·9218	Dinars 38·1
Zaïre	Zaïre of 100 makuta	Zaïre 1266·04	Zaïre 25175·00
Zambia	Kwacha (K) of 100 ngwee	K 75·7063	K 116·45
Zimbabwe	Zimbabwe dollar (Z$) of 100 cents	Z$ 4·6975	Z$ 6·5905

DISTANCES FROM LONDON BY AIR

The list of the distances in statute miles from London, Heathrow, to various places abroad has been supplied by the publishers of *IATA/IAL Air Distances Manual*, Southall, Middx.

To	Miles	To	Miles	To	Miles
Abidjan	3,197	Detroit	3,754	Munich	588
Abu Dhabi	3,425	Dhaka	4,976	Nairobi	4,248
Addis Ababa	3,675	Doha	3,253	Naples	1,011
Aden	3,670	Dubai	3,414	Nassau	4,333
Algiers	1,035	Dublin	279	New York (J. F. Kennedy)	3,440
Amman	2,287	Durban	5,937	Nice	645
Amsterdam	230	Düsseldorf	310	Oporto	806
Ankara	1,770	Entebbe	4,033	Oslo (Fornebu)	723
Athens	1,500	Frankfurt	406	Ottawa	3,321
Auckland	11,404	Freetown	3,046	Palma, Majorca	836
Baghdad	2,551	Geneva	468	Paris	215 (Orly 227)
Bahrain	3,163	Gibraltar	1,084	Perth, Australia	9,008
Bangkok	5,928	Gothenburg (Landvetter)	664	Port of Spain, Trinidad	4,405
Barbados	4,193	Hamburg	463	Prague	649
Barcelona	712	Harare	5,156	Reykjavik	1,167
Basle	447	Havana	4,647	Rhodes	1,743
Beijing (Peking)	5,063	Helsinki (Vantaa)	1,147	Rio de Janeiro	5,745
Beirut	2,161	Hong Kong	5,990	Riyadh	3,067
Belfast	325	Honolulu	7,220	Rome (Fiumicino)	895
Belgrade	1,056	Istanbul	1,560	Salzburg	651
Berlin (Tegel)	588	Jeddah	2,947	San Francisco	5,351
Bermuda	3,428	Johannesburg	5,634	Seoul	5,507
Berne	476	Karachi	3,935	Shannon	369
Bombay	4,478	Khartoum	3,071	Singapore	6,756
Brasilia	5,452	Khartoum	4,668	Sofia	1,266
Brisbane	10,273	Kuala Lumpur	6,557	Stockholm (Arlanda)	908
Brussels	217	Kuwait	2,903	Sydney, Australia	10,568
Bucharest	1,307	Lagos	3,107	Tangier	1,120
Budapest	923	Larnaca, Cyprus	2,036	Tehran	2,741
Buenos Aires	6,915	Leningrad	1,314	Tel Aviv	2,227
Cairo	2,194	Lima	6,303	Tokyo (Narita)	5,956
Calcutta	4,958	Lisbon	972	Toronto	3,545
Canberra	10,563	Lomé	3,129	Tripoli	1,468
Cape Town	6,011	Los Angeles	5,439	Tunis	1,137
Caracas	4,639	Madrid	773	Turin (Caselle)	570
Casablanca	1,300	Malta	1,305	Valencia	82
Chicago (O'Hare)	3,941	Manila	6,685	Vancouver	4,707
Cologne	331	Marseilles	614	Venice (Tessera)	71
Colombo	5,411	Mauritius	6,075	Vienna (Schwechat)	79
Copenhagen	608	Mexico City	5,529	Warsaw	91
Dakar	2,706	Milan	609	Washington	3,66
Damascus	2,223	Montego Bay	4,687	Wellington	11,69
Dar-es-Salaam	4,662	Montevideo	6,841	Yangon (Rangoon)	5,58
Darwin	8,613	Montreal (Mirabel)	3,241	Zagreb	84
Delhi	4,180	Moscow (Sheremetievo)	1,557	Zürich	49

BALANCE OF PAYMENTS OF THE UNITED KINGDOM (£ million)

	1983	1984	1985	1986	1987	1988
Current account						
Visible trade						
Exports (fob)	60,700	70,265	77,991	72,656	79,446	80,776
Imports (fob)	62,237	75,601	81,336	82,141	90,669	101,854
Visible balance	−1,537	−5,336	−3,345	−9,485	−11,223	−21,078
Invisibles						
Credits	65,803	77,516	80,157	77,248	79,855	88,168
Debits...............................	60,479	70,348	74,062	67,787	72,814	82,241
Invisibles balance	5,325	7,168	6,095	9,462	7,042	5,927
of which:						
Services balance....................	*4,064*	*4,519*	*6,687*	*6,692*	*6,624*	*4,502*
Interest, profits and dividends balance .	*2,854*	*4,379*	*2,519*	*4,927*	*3,820*	*4,971*
Transfers balance	*−1,593*	*−1,730*	*−3,111*	*−2,157*	*−3,402*	*−3,546*
Current balance	3,787	1,832	3,750	−24	−4,182	−15,151
Transactions in external assets and liabilities*						
Investment overseas by UK residents						
Direct................................	−5,417	−6,033	−8,456	−11,730	−19,198	−20,685
Portfolio	−7,193	−9,869	−19,426	−23,072	3,323	−9,870
Total UK investment overseas	−12,611	−15,902	−27,882	−34,853	−15,875	−30,555
Investment in the UK by overseas residents						
Direct................................	3,386	−181	3,865	4,987	8,681	9,218
Portfolio	1,701	1,288	8,913	10,911	17,710	13,220
Total overseas investment in UK	5,087	1,107	12,778	15,898	26,391	22,438
Foreign currency lending abroad by UK banks	−16,162	−9,439	−20,200	−47,885	−45,684	−14,698
Foreign currency borrowing abroad by UK banks	17,192	18,648	25,306	58,361	44,277	20,301
Net foreign currency transactions of UK banks	1,030	9,209	5,106	10,476	−1,407	5,603
Sterling lending abroad by UK banks	−2,232	−4,933	−1,635	−5,955	−4,638	−4,570
Sterling borrowing and deposit liabilities abroad of UK banks	3,945	6,149	4,155	5,605	8,537	13,544
Net sterling transactions of UK banks	1,713	1,216	2,520	−350	3,899	8,974
Deposits with and lending to banks abroad by UK non-bank private sector	863	−3,213	−1,240	−2,724	−5,177	−3,644
Borrowing from banks abroad by:						
UK non-bank private sector	73	−2,215	2,618	3,817	2,109	4,137
Public corporations...................	−35	−47	64	−31	−166	−253
General government...................	78	49	87	100	104	−10
Official reserves (additions to − drawings on +)	607	908	−1,758	−2,891	−12,012	−2,761
Other external assets of:						
UK non-bank private sector and public corporations	−161	1,281	528	1,930	550	875
General government...................	−478	−743	−730	−509	−796	−891
Other external liabilities of:						
UK non-bank private sector and public corporations	−55	517	731	547	1,381	2,187
General government...................	−661	−89	−64	+78	1,468	914
Net transactions in assets and liabilities	−4,551	−7,923	−7,241	−8,572	469	7,015
Balancing item	764	6,091	4,491	8,536	3,713	8,136

Source: HMSO—Annual Abstract of Statistics 1991

* Assets: increase −/decrease +. Liabilities: increase +/decrease −.

VALUE OF UNITED KINGDOM IMPORTS (cif)
Analysis by sections and divisions (£ million)

	1986	1987	1988	1989*
Total UK imports	86,175·5	94,026·2	106,571·2	120,787·7
Food and live animals chiefly for food	8,718·6	8,723·9	9,093·4	9,762·4
Live animals chiefly for food	293·4	236·4	287·1	286·5
Meat and meat preparations	1,465·3	1,562·2	1,646·2	1,826·9
Dairy products and birds' eggs	653·2	617·8	761·2	786·4
Fish, crustaceans and molluscs, and preparations thereof	747·8	759·1	785·8	885·0
Cereals and cereal preparations	769·3	740·8	751·2	722·2
Vegetables and fruit	2,184·4	2,394·0	2,458·9	2,727·1
Sugar, sugar preparations and honey	530·3	521·2	575·7	603·6
Coffee, tea, cocoa, spices, and manufactures thereof	1,220·6	997·2	946·0	941·6
Feeding-stuff for animals (not including unmilled cereals)	527·3	506·5	557·7	582·3
Miscellaneous edible products and preparations	326·9	388·5	323·7	400·8
Beverages and tobacco	1,346·7	1,433·2	1,521·4	1,667·5
Beverages	1,007·9	1,105·4	1,196·1	1,322·1
Tobacco and tobacco manufactures	338·7	327·9	325·3	345·4
Crude materials, inedible, except fuels	4,622·4	5,183·9	5,612·2	6,097·6
Hides, skins and furskins, raw	216·4	264·1	194·2	149·2
Oil seeds and oleaginous fruit	271·3	255·0	227·5	238·9
Crude rubber (including synthetic and reclaimed)	203·5	227·1	236·3	250·2
Cork and wood	1,000·3	1,198·6	1,355·5	1,429·0
Pulp and waste paper	523·3	657·2	723·5	896·3
Textile fibres (other than wool tops) and their wastes (not manufactured into yarn or fabric)	546·9	633·5	687·9	681·2
Crude fertilizers and crude minerals (excluding coal, petroleum and precious stones)	317·1	286·6	353·6	360·8
Metalliferous ores and metal scrap	1,139·5	1,223·1	1,369·0	1,573·8
Crude animal and vegetable materials	404·1	438·6	464·7	518·1
Mineral fuels, lubricants and related materials	6,400·4	6,117·0	5,037·8	6,235·1
Petroleum, petroleum products and related materials	4,461·3	4,493·3	3,484·8	4,674·4
Coal, coke, gas and electric current	1,939·1	1,623·7	1,553·0	1,560·7
Animal and vegetable oils, fats and waxes	365·1	427·0	372·2	384·9
Total manufactured goods	62,825·3	70,995·1	83,521·1	95,128·2
Chemicals and related products	7,345·3	8,329·8	9,313·8	10,440·5
Organic chemicals	1,830·7	2,025·7	2,352·6	2,631·1
Inorganic chemicals	951·4	987·3	910·7	1,006·8
Dyeing, tanning and colouring materials	396·5	448·1	543·5	612·6
Medicinal and pharmaceutical products	679·7	786·3	877·1	1,061·6
Essential oils and perfume materials; toilet, polishing and cleansing materials	480·3	554·5	615·1	681·8
Fertilizers, manufactured	213·2	210·6	204·1	271·2
Explosives and pyrotechnic products	22·0	24·1	1,935·0	2,059·8
Artificial resins and plastic materials, and cellulose esters and ethers	1,985·2	2,415·6	910·8	996·1
Chemical materials and products, not elsewhere specified	786·4	877·5	964·9	1,119·4

* provisional.

Value of United Kingdom Imports (cif) (£ million)—*Continued*

	1986	1987	1988	1989*
Total UK imports	86,175·5	94,026·2	106,571·2	120,787·7
Manufactured goods classified chiefly by material.................................	15,328·1	16,968·7	19,673·3	21,730·4
Leather, leather manufactures, nes, and dressed furskins..................................	247·9	299·4	245·3	242·7
Rubber manufactures, nes	589·2	682·4	799·1	827·1
Cork and wood manufactures (excluding furniture)	687·8	784·6	964·9	967·0
Paper, paperboard, and articles of paper pulp, of paper or of paperboard	2,702·8	3,237·8	3,621·6	4,016·0
Textile yarn, fabrics, made-up articles, nes, and related products...........................	3,162·4	3,497·3	3,635·5	3,769·7
Non-metallic mineral manufactures, nes	2,661·7	2,747·4	3,385·4	3,567·0
Iron and steel	1,796·2	1,889·9	2,369·0	2,787·9
Non-ferrous metals	1,835·7	1,942·3	2,506·0	3,069·9
Manufactures of metal, nes	1,644·5	1,887·5	2,146·6	2,483·1
Machinery and transport equipment	28,765·7	32,808·9	40,103·2	45,899·6
Power generating machinery and equipment ...	2,237·3	2,513·3	3,046·6	3,487·3
Machinery specialized for particular industries	2,362·7	2,856·2	3,477·7	3,854·2
Metalworking machinery	645·7	567·7	804·3	950·9
General industrial machinery and equipment, nes, and machine parts, nes	2,757·2	3,014·2	3,544·7	4,167·6
Office machines and automatic data processing equipment................................	4,542·1	5,431·1	6,289·6	7,552·3
Telecommunications, sound recording and re-producing apparatus and equipment.........	2,401·6	2,800·8	3,199·6	3,692·7
Electrical machinery, apparatus and appliances, nes, and electrical parts thereof (including non-electrical counterparts, nes, of electrical household type equipment)	4,445·9	5,051·7	5,821·7	6,681·5
Road vehicles (including air cushion vehicles)..	7,938·8	8,807·4	11,255·5	13,003·4
Other transport equipment	1,434·5	1,766·4	2,663·5	2,509·7
Miscellaneous manufactured articles	11,386·1	12,887·8	14,430·8	17,057·7
Sanitary, plumbing, heating and lighting fix-tures and fittings, nes......................	216·6	254·5	336·2	371·7
Furniture and parts thereof	776·0	877·7	988·7	1,099·6
Travel goods, handbags and similar containers .	199·9	230·9	251·5	293·0
Articles of apparel and clothing accessories	2,386·1	2,777·7	3,111·4	3,542·3
Footwear	734·4	799·3	907·8	973·2
Professional, scientific and controlling instru-ments and apparatus, nes	1,790·0	1,903·2	2,025·0	2,377·9
Photographic apparatus, equipment and sup-plies and optical goods, nes, watches and clocks	1,285·6	1,357·4	1,467·0	1,616·5
Miscellaneous manufactured articles, nes	3,997·5	4,687·2	5,343·2	6,783·5
Commodities and transactions not classi-fied elsewhere	1,897·0	1,146·2	1,413·1	1,512·0

Source: HMSO—Annual Abstract of Statistics 1991

nes not elsewhere specified.   * provisional.

VALUE OF UNITED KINGDOM EXPORTS (fob)
Analysis by sections and divisions (£ million)

	1986	1987	1988	1989*
Total UK exports	72,987·7	79,848·7	81,654·9	93,249·1
Food and live animals chiefly for food	3,745·8	3,730·3	3,458·2	4,228·4
Live animals chiefly for food	299·9	325·8	254·8	265·7
Meat and meat preparations	521·9	625·9	590·4	699·6
Dairy products and birds' eggs	331·5	314·1	389·1	501·9
Fish, crustaceans and molluscs, and preparations thereof	328·9	407·2	384·4	450·0
Cereals and cereal preparations	1,177·5	831·2	674·8	951·3
Vegetables and fruit	251·7	300·3	222·3	281·3
Sugar, sugar preparations and honey	170·4	218·6	196·2	228·2
Coffee, tea, cocoa, spices and manufactures thereof	364·0	377·5	362·8	387·7
Feeding-stuff for animals (not including un-milled cereals)	139·3	155·8	176·4	228·7
Miscellaneous edible products and preparations	160·6	173·9	207·1	234·0
Beverages and tobacco	1,737·9	1,861·4	2,075·4	2,326·3
Beverages	1,331·6	1,411·6	1,575·4	1,802·2
Tobacco and tobacco manufactures	406·3	449·8	500·0	524·2
Crude materials, inedible, except fuels	1,940·9	1,926·4	2,031·6	2,264·1
Hides, skins and furskins, raw	260·2	311·5	254·8	253·9
Oil seeds and oleaginous fruit.................	155·5	86·2	41·7	37·2
Crude rubber (including synthetic and reclaimed)	183·0	180·0	193·0	211·6
Cork and wood	22·9	26·0	26·2	27·8
Pulp and waste paper	25·0	33·9	46·4	51·7
Textile fibres (other than wool tops) and their wastes (not manufactured into yarn or fabric)	373·0	397·0	439·5	498·1
Crude fertilizers and crude minerals (excluding coal, petroleum and precious stones).........	271·9	340·6	339·3	368·9
Metalliferous ores and metal scrap	538·9	451·6	593·0	711·7
Crude animal and vegetable materials	110·4	99·7	97·6	103·1
Mineral fuels, lubricants and related materials	8,671·9	8,769·0	5,817·8	5,768·1
Petroleum, petroleum products and related materials	8,207·9	8,465·8	5,575·9	5,511·8
Coal, coke, gas and electric current	464·0	303·1	241·9	256·3
Animal and vegetable oils, fats and waxes ..	105·3	263·5	88·7	83·6
Total manufactured goods	54,580·5	61,036·8	66,218·1	76,322·5
Chemicals and related products	9,676·8	10,518·6	11,331·2	12,349·6
Organic chemicals...........................	2,571·0	2,830·6	3,138·3	3,373·3
Inorganic chemicals.........................	1,123·3	1,099·6	1,105·6	1,021·4
Dyeing, tanning and colouring materials	763·2	878·9	938·7	1,063·3
Medicinal and pharmaceutical products	1,532·7	1,620·7	1,734·4	2,016·3
Essential oils and perfume materials; toilet, polishing and cleansing materials	807·7	886·4	943·2	1,003·4
Fertilizers, manufactured	67·4	85·4	90·0	105·2
Explosives and pyrotechnic products	42·8	45·7	1,113·9	1,245·0
Artificial resins and plastic materials, and cellulose esters and ethers	1,401·1	1,553·1	616·1	686·3
Chemical materials and products, not elsewhere specified	1,367·5	1,518·1	1,651·0	1,835·4

* provisional.

Value of United Kingdom Exports (fob) (£ million)—*Continued*

	1986	1987	1988	1989*
Total UK exports	72,987·7	79,848·7	81,654·9	93,249·1
Manufactured goods classified chiefly by material............................	10,977·8	11,875·8	12,714·5	14,510·2
Leather, leather manufactures, nes, and dressed furskins............................	321·5	372·9	311·4	326·5
Rubber manufactures, nes....................	611·8	678·0	715·4	801·6
Cork and wood manufactures (excluding furniture)............................	77·2	85·6	82·7	91·0
Paper, paperboard, and articles of paper pulp, of paper or of paperboard....................	824·3	971·2	1,093·7	1,239·8
Textile yarn, fabrics, made-up articles, nes, and related products........................	1,711·5	1,886·2	1,934·9	2,205·0
Non-metallic mineral manufactures, nes.......	2,549·3	2,654·3	2,974·0	3,198·6
Iron and steel............................	1,866·5	2,185·8	2,392·0	2,893·6
Non-ferrous metals........................	1,551·3	1,502·2	1,650·8	1,967·5
Manufactures of metal, nes................	1,464·5	1,539·7	1,560·0	1,786·5
Machinery and transport equipment.......	25,351·2	28,802·8	32,101·5	37,690·0
Power generating machinery and equipment...	3,251·1	3,241·5	3,884·8	4,738·9
Machinery specialized for particular industries	3,101·1	3,300·5	3,288·6	3,772·8
Metalworking machinery....................	581·2	691·1	780·3	748·8
General industrial machinery and equipment, nes, and machine parts, nes................	3,037·2	3,097·5	3,577·7	4,037·5
Office machines and automatic data processing equipment............................	3,561·9	4,483·2	5,299·4	6,115·9
Telecommunications and sound recording and reproducing apparatus and equipment.......	1,401·6	1,567·6	1,759·0	2,222·6
Electrical machinery, apparatus and appliances, nes, and electrical parts thereof (including non-electrical counterparts, nes, of electrical household type equipment)................	3,382·6	3,785·7	4,343·5	5,050·5
Road vehicles (including air cushion vehicles)..	3,953·5	4,876·8	4,992·8	6,071·0
Other transport equipment....................	3,080·9	3,758·9	4,175·5	4,932·0
Miscellaneous manufactured articles......	8,574·7	9,839·6	10,070·8	11,772·6
Sanitary, plumbing, heating and lighting fixtures and fittings, nes......................	126·3	133·0	199·4	222·3
Furniture and parts thereof................	356·3	394·7	377·6	460·8
Travel goods, handbags and similar containers .	30·6	34·8	43·9	56·3
Articles of apparel and clothing accessories	1,228·2	1,428·7	1,414·3	1,444·8
Footwear................................	167·2	186·6	210·4	227·6
Professional, scientific and controlling instruments and apparatus, nes................	2,283·7	2,328·5	2,531·6	2,793·0
Photographic apparatus, equipment and supplies and optical goods, nes, watches and clocks................................	843·3	976·2	1,004·1	1,134·6
Miscellaneous manufactured articles, nes......	3,539·2	4,357·1	4,289·5	5,433·2
Commodities and transactions not classified elsewhere	2,205·5	2,261·3	1,965·1	2,256·1

Source: HMSO—Annual Abstract of Statistics 1991

nes not elsewhere specified.   * provisional.

INTERNATIONAL ORGANIZATIONS

ASSOCIATION OF SOUTH EAST ASIAN NATIONS

70 A. Jl. Sisingamangaraja Kebayoran Baru, Jakarta, Indonesia

Formed in 1967, the main aims of the Association of South East Asian Nations (ASEAN) are the acceleration of economic growth, social progress and cultural development, the promotion of collaboration and mutual assistance in matters of common interest, and the continuing stability of the South East Asian region.

The Heads of Government of the member countries are the highest authority and give directions to ASEAN as and when necessary. The main policy-making body is the annual meeting of foreign ministers of the member countries. The members of the Association are Brunei, Indonesia, Malaysia, the Philippines, Singapore and Thailand.

Sec.-Gen., Rusli Noor (*Indonesia*).

BANK FOR INTERNATIONAL SETTLEMENTS

Centralbahnplatz 2, 4002 Basle, Switzerland

The objectives of the Bank for International Settlements (founded in 1930) are to promote the co-operation of central banks; to provide facilities for international financial operations; and to act as trustee or agent in international financial settlements entrusted to it. The London agent is the Bank of England, and the Governor of the Bank of England is a member of the Board of Directors, in which administrative control is vested.

Chairman of the Board of Directors and President of the Bank for International Settlements, B. Dennis (*Sweden*) (1991).

CAB INTERNATIONAL

Wallingford, Oxon. OX10 8DE
[0491-32111]

CAB International (formerly the Commonwealth Agricultural Bureaux) was founded in 1929. It consists of four Institutes and five editorial divisions under the control of an Executive Council comprising representatives of the countries which contribute to its funds. The functions of CABI are to provide a scientific information service, identification of pests, biological control services and mutual assistance. Each Institute and editorial division acts as an effective clearing house for the collection, collation and dissemination of information in its particular branch of agricultural science.

Director-General, D. Mentz.

CARIBBEAN COMMUNITY AND COMMON MARKET

PO Box 10827, Georgetown, Guyana

The Caribbean Community and Common Market (Caricom) was established in 1973 with three objectives: economic co-operation through the Caribbean Common Market; the co-ordination of foreign policy among the independent member states; the provision of common services and co-operation in functional matters such as health, education and culture, communications and industrial relations. The principal organs are the Conference of Heads of Government, which determines policy, and the Common Market Council of Ministers, consisting of ministers of government (usually ministers of trade) designated by each member state, which is responsible for the development and smooth running of the Common Market and for the settlement of any problems arising out of its functioning. The principal administrative arm is the Secretariat, based in Guyana.

The 13 member states are Antigua and Barbuda, The Bahamas (which is not a member of the Common Market), Barbados, Belize, Dominica, Grenada, Guyana, Jamaica, Montserrat, St Christopher and Nevis, St Lucia, St Vincent and the Grenadines and Trinidad and Tobago. The British Virgin Islands and the Turks and Caicos Islands are associate members. The Dominican Republic, Haiti, Mexico, Puerto Rico, Suriname and Venezuela have observer status.

Sec.-Gen., Roderick Rainford (*Jamaica*).

CONFERENCE ON SECURITY AND CO-OPERATION IN EUROPE

Thunovska 12, Mala, Strana, 110 00 Prague 1

The Conference on Security and Co-operation in Europe (CSCE) was launched in 1975 under the Helsinki Final Act, which established agreements between NATO members, Warsaw Pact members, and neutral and non-aligned European countries covering security in Europe; economic, scientific, technological and environmental co-operation; and humanitarian principles and co-operation. Further conferences were held at Belgrade (1977–80), Madrid (1980–83) and Vienna (1986–89).

With the end of the Cold War, it was decided that the CSCE should be revitalized to provide a new security framework for Europe. The Charter of Paris for a New Europe was signed at Paris on November 21, 1990, committing members to support for multi-party democracy, free-market economics and human rights. The signatories also undertook to enhance political consultation, agreeing on regular meetings of heads of government, ministers and officials. The CSCE is underpinned by a new institutional structure; a Secretariat (Prague), a Conflict Prevention Centre (Vienna) and an Office of Free Elections (Warsaw). The European Assembly of member parliamentarians will also be formed. In June 1991 the CSCE agreed upon new crisis prevention mechanisms to prevent violent conflict between and within member countries.

The CSCE has 35 members: Albania, Austria, Belgium, Bulgaria, Canada, Cyprus, Czechoslovakia, Denmark, Finland, France, Germany, Greece, Hungary, Iceland, Ireland, Italy, Liechtenstein, Luxembourg, Malta, Monaco, the Netherlands, Norway, Poland, Portugal, Romania, San Marino, Spain, Sweden, Switzerland, Turkey, UK, USA, USSR, the Vatican and Yugoslavia.

Director, Nils Eliasson (*Sweden*).

COUNCIL FOR MUTUAL ECONOMIC ASSISTANCE

(Disbanded June 28, 1991)

THE COUNCIL OF EUROPE

67006 Strasbourg, France

The Council of Europe was founded in 1949. Its aim is to achieve greater unity between its members to safeguard their European heritage and to facilitate their economic and social progress through discussion and common action in economic, social, cultural, educational, scientific, legal and administrative matters and in the maintenance and furtherance of human rights and fundamental freedoms.

The 25 members are Austria, Belgium, Cyprus, Czechoslovakia, Denmark, Finland, France, Germany, Greece, Hungary, Iceland, the Republic of Ireland, Italy, Liechtenstein, Luxembourg, Malta, Netherlands, Norway, Portugal, San Marino, Spain, Sweden, Switzerland, Turkey and the UK. 'Special guest status' has been granted to Bulgaria, Poland, Romania, USSR and Yugoslavia.

The organs are the Committee of Ministers, consisting of the foreign ministers of member countries, who meet twice yearly, and the Parliamentary Assembly of 192 members, elected or chosen by the national parliaments of member countries in proportion to the relative strength of political parties. There is also a Joint Committee of Ministers and Representatives of the Parliamentary Assembly.

The Committee of Ministers is the executive organ of the Council. The majority of its conclusions take the form of international agreements (known as European Conventions) or recommendations to governments. Decisions of the Ministers may also be embodied in partial agreements to which a limited number of member governments are party. Member governments accredit Permanent Representatives to the Council in Strasbourg, who are also the Ministers' Deputies. The Committee of Deputies meets every month to transact business and to take decisions on behalf of Ministers.

The Parliamentary Assembly holds three week-long sessions a year. It debates reports on, *inter alia*, political, economic, agricultural, social, educational, legal and regional planning affairs, and also reports received annually from the OECD, other European organizations and certain specialized agencies of the United Nations. Its 13 permanent committees meet, normally in private, once or twice between each public plenary session of the Assembly. The Standing Conference of Local and Regional Authorities of Europe each year brings together mayors and municipal councillors in the same numbers as the members of the Parliamentary Assembly.

One of the principal achievements of the Council of Europe is the European Convention of Human Rights (1950) under which was established the European Commission and the European Court of Human Rights. Among the other conventions and agreements which have been concluded are the European Social Charter, the European Social Security Code, and conventions on extradition, the legal status of migrant workers, conservation, and the transfer of sentenced prisoners.

Non-member states take part in certain Council of Europe activities on a regular or *ad hoc* basis; thus the Holy See and Yugoslavia participate in all the educational, cultural and sports activities. The European Youth Foundation funds events in both Eastern and Western European countries and in some outside Europe, while nationals of these countries attend courses and seminars at the European Youth Centre.

Secretary-General, Catherine Lalumière (*France*).
Permanent UK Representative, His Excellency Noël Marshall, CMG (1990).

THE ECONOMIC COMMUNITY OF WEST AFRICAN STATES
6 King George V Road, PMB 12745,
Lagos, Nigeria

The Economic Community of West African States (ECOWAS) was founded at a summit of West African heads of government at Lagos on May 28, 1975, and came into operation in January 1977. It aims to promote the cultural, economic and social development of West Africa through mutual co-operation.

Measures undertaken by ECOWAS include the gradual elimination of barriers to the movement of goods, people and services between member states and the improvement of regional telecommunications and transport. Members are committed to the creation of a single monetary zone by 1992.

The supreme authority of ECOWAS is vested in the annual summit of heads of government of all 16 member states. A Council of Ministers, two from each member state, meets biannually to monitor the organization and make recommendations to the summit. ECOWAS operates through a Secretariat, headed by the Executive Secretary. In addition there is a financial controller, an external auditor, the Disputes Tribunal and the Defence Council.

A Fund for Co-operation, Compensation and Development, situated at Lomé, Togo, finances development projects and provides compensation to member states who have suffered losses as a result of ECOWAS's policies, particularly in relation to trade liberalization.

Executive Secretary, Dr Abbas Bundu.

THE EUROPEAN BANK OF RECONSTRUCTION AND DEVELOPMENT
122 Leadenhall Street,
London EC3

The foundation of a European Bank of Reconstruction and Development (EBRD) was proposed by President Mitterrand of France on October 25, 1989. The charter of the EBRD was signed in Paris by 40 countries, the European Commission and the European Investment Bank on May 29, 1990. The EBRD was inaugurated in London on May 29, 1991.

The aim of the EBRD is to assist the transformation of the states of central and eastern Europe (Bulgaria, Czechoslovakia, Hungary, Poland, Romania, the USSR and Yugoslavia) from centrally-planned economies to free market economies, with particular regard for strengthening democratic institutions, and respect for human rights and the environment. The EBRD provides technical assistance, training and investment in: the upgrading of infrastructure (energy, telecommunications and transport); the creation of modern financial systems (efficient banks, capital markets); and the restructuring of state industries. The EBRD's assistance is weighted towards the private sector; no more than 40 per cent of its investment can be made in state-owned concerns. It works in co-operation with its members, private companies, and international organizations, such as the OECD, the IMF, the World Bank and the UN specialized agencies.

The EBRD has an initial subscribed capital of ECU10 billion. The major subscribers are: the USA, 10 per cent; Britain, France, Germany, Italy and Japan, 8·5 per cent each; central and eastern European states, 11·9 per cent (of which the USSR 6 per cent).

The EBRD has 41 members. The highest authority is the Board of Governors; each member appoints one Governor and one alternate. The Governors delegate most powers to a 23-member Board of Directors; the Directors are responsible for the EBRD's operations and are appointed by the Governors for three-year terms. The Governors also elect the President of the Board of Directors, who acts as the Bank's chief of staff, for a four-year term. A Secretary-General liaises between the Directors and EBRD staff.

President of the Board of Directors, Jacques Attali (*France*).
UK Executive Director, J. A. L. Faint.
Secretary-General, Bart le Blanc (*Netherlands*).

THE EUROPEAN COMMUNITY

The beginnings of the European Community (EC) lie in the desire following the Second World War to replace the European system of competing nation states with a new union. It was partially out of a desire to heal traditional Franco-German enmity that in May 1951 Robert Schuman, the French Foreign Minister of the time, proposed that France and West Germany pool their coal and steel industries under an independent, supranational authority. They were joined by Belgium, Luxembourg, the Netherlands and Italy and the Treaty of Paris was signed in 1951, establishing the European Coal and Steel Community (ECSC) in 1952.

The success of the ECSC led to discussions in 1955 in Messina, Italy, between the foreign ministers of its six member states on proposals for further moves towards European economic integration. As a result of these discussions the Treaty of Rome, establishing the European Economic Community, was signed on March 25, 1957. A second treaty founding the European Atomic Energy Community (EURATOM) was signed on the same day; this pledged the six signatories to co-operate in research into nuclear science, particularly in relation to nuclear energy.

The Treaty of Rome was intended to create a customs union to remove all obstacles to the free movement of capital, goods, people and services between member states. It also established a common external trade policy and common policies for agriculture and fisheries. Other articles of the treaty refer to preventing the distortion of competition within the Common Market; the co-ordination of economic policies: the harmonization of social policy sufficient to enable the functioning of the Common Market; the creation of a European Social Fund to increase employment and raise living standards; and the association of overseas countries and territories with the Community to increase mutual trade and to assist their economic and social development.

In addition, the Treaty of Rome established the Community's institutional structure; the Commission, the Council of Ministers, the Economic and Social Committee, the European Investment Bank, the Parliament and the Court of Justice. Whereas the Parliament and Court of Justice were common to all three Communities from 1958, each Community had its own executive body and Council of Ministers. The three separate executive bodies and Councils of Ministers were merged in 1967.

In May 1969, the heads of government of the Six met at the Hague and decided both to widen and to deepen the Community. In accordance with the Hague decisions, the Council of Ministers agreed in 1970 that from 1975 the Community would have its own revenue, independent of national contributions; this would be derived from customs duties and agricultural import levies collected at the EC external frontier, and a proportion of national receipts from VAT.

In June 1970, the Six invited Britain, Denmark, Ireland and Norway to open negotiations on their applications to join the EC. The four countries signed a Treaty of Accession in Brussels on January 22, 1972; Norway subsequently withdrew its application after conducting a referendum on EC entry. The enlarged Community of the Nine came into existence on January 1, 1973.

During the 1970s the EC sought to strengthen the democracies of southern Europe; this led to the admission of Greece to the EC on January 1, 1981, and Portugal and Spain on January 1, 1986. Following a plebiscite, Greenland negotiated its withdrawal from the EC and left in 1986. The unification of Germany brought the former German Democratic Republic into the EC in October 1990. Andorra joined the customs union on July 1, 1991, but does not participate in other EC institutions.

Following the completion of the Single Market in 1993, the EC is expected to undergo further enlargement. Applications for EC membership have already been received from Austria, Cyprus, Malta, Sweden and Turkey, and are expected from a number of other European states. The Commission is developing the concept of affiliate EC membership for the new democracies of eastern Europe.

The Common Agricultural Policy

The Treaty of Rome established the Common Agricultural Policy (CAP) to increase agricultural production, to provide a fair standard of living for farmers and to ensure the availability of food at reasonable prices. This aim is achieved by a number of mechanisms: Import Levies (the EC sets a target price for a particular product in the Community, the world price is monitored and if it falls below the guide price, an import levy can be imposed equivalent to the difference between the two); Intervention Purchase (if the price of a product falls below the level indicated by the Council, member states must purchase supplies of the product, provided that they are of suitable quality); Export Subsidies (the EC pays a food exporter a subsidy equivalent to the difference between the price at which the product is bought in the EC and the lower sale price on the world market).

These measures had the required aim of stimulating production but also placed increasing demands on the EC budget. To surmount this problem, the EC created the system of co-responsibility levies; farm payments to the EC by volume of product sold. This system was supplemented by national quotas for particular products, such as milk. The increase in the number of EC members and the greater use of modern technology has further increased production and exacerbated EC budgetary problems; CAP now accounts for over 50 per cent of EC expenditure. Radical reforms are currently under consideration.

European Political Co-operation

The framework for European Political Co-operation (EPC) dates from an initiative at the Hague summit in 1969. In the resultant Luxembourg Report (1970), EC foreign ministers decided to harmonize and co-ordinate their foreign policy positions and achieve common actions where possible. Although the Single European Act obliged EC members to consult each other on foreign policy and the Commission participates in deliberations, EPC is an intergovernmental system operating parallel to, but outside, the Community.

The EPC system is headed by the European Council, which provides general lines of policy. Specific policy decisions are taken by the Council of Foreign Ministers, which meets at least four times a year. The foreign minister of the state holding the EC Presidency initiates action, manages EPC and represents it abroad. He is supported by a Secretariat based in Brussels and is advised by the past and future holders of the Presidency, forming a so-called troika. The Council of Ministers is supported by the Political Committee which meets each month, or within 48 hours if there is a crisis, to prepare for ministerial discussions. A Group of Correspondents, designated diplomats in each member's foreign ministry, provides day-to-day contact.

The Single Market

Throughout the 1970s and early 1980s, EC members became increasingly concerned at the slow growth of the European economy. Although tariffs and quotas had been removed between member states, the EC was still separated into a number of national markets by a series of non-tariff barriers. It was to overcome these internal barriers to trade that the concept of the Single Market was developed. The measures to be undertaken were outlined in the Cockfield report (1985) and codified in the Single European Act (SEA), signed in 1986 and which came into force in 1987.

The SEA includes articles removing obstacles that distort the internal market: the elimination of frontier controls; the mutual recognition of professional qualifications; the harmonization of product specifications, largely by the mutual recognition of national standards; open tendering for public procurement contracts; the free movement of capital; the harmonization of VAT and excise duties; and the reduction of state aid to particular industries. The SEA changed the legislative process within the EC; particularly with the introduction of qualified majority voting in the Council of Ministers for some policy areas. The SEA also extends EC competence into the fields of technology, the environment, regional policy, monetary policy and external policy. The Single Market is to be completed on January 1, 1993 and is expected to result in at least a five per cent increase in the collective GNP of EC member states.

New Developments

EC members are currently discussing further moves towards European integration. Inter-governmental conferences on political and economic union began in December 1990 and are expected to draft two new treaties for signature at the end of 1991. The following measures are under discussion: the integration of European Political Co-operation into the EC and the extension of majority voting into foreign policy; a common policy on asylum and immigration; greater powers for the European Parliament; extending EC competence in energy, the environment, tourism, culture, education, public health, infrastructure, research and development, industrial policy, consumer protection, worker consultation, working conditions, and equal opportunities; the use of majority voting in these areas; and the establishment of a central European bank as a step towards full European monetary union.

The Legislative Process

The core of the EC policymaking process is a dialogue between the Commission, which initiates and implements policy, and the Council of Ministers, which takes policy decisions. A degree of democratic control is exercised by the European Parliament.

The original EC legislative process is known as the consultative procedure. The Commission drafts a proposal which it submits to the Council. The Council then consults the ESC and the Parliament; the Parliament may request that amendments are made. With or without these amendments, the proposal is then adopted by the Council and becomes law.

Under the Single European Act, changes were made to the EC legislative process, particularly in strengthening the role of the Parliament in the implementation of the single market, in some areas of social policy, and in research and development. In these areas the new co-operation procedure operates. The Parliament now has a second reading of proposals in these fields, and after the second reading its rejection of a proposal can only be overturned by a unanimous decision of the Council.

The Council issues the following legislation: (a) Regulations, which are binding in their entirety and directly applicable to all member states; they do not need to be incorporated into national law to come into effect; (b) Directives, which are less specific, binding as to the result to be achieved but leaving the method of implementation open to member states; a directive thus has no force until it is incorporated into national law; (c) Decisions, which are also binding but are addressed solely to one or more member states or individuals in a member state; (d) Recommendations; (e) Opinions, which are merely persuasive.

THE COUNCIL OF MINISTERS
170 rue de la Loi, 1048 Brussels, Belgium

The Council of Ministers consists of ministers from the government of each of the member states. It formally comprises the foreign ministers of the member states but in practice the minister depends on the subject under discussion; i.e. when EC environment matters are under discussion, the meeting is informally known as the Environment Council. Council decisions are taken by majority vote, qualified majority vote (in which members' votes are weighted) or by unanimity. Council meetings are prepared by the Committee of Permanent Representatives (COREPER) of the member states, which acts as the 'gatekeeper' between national governments and the supranational EC, often negotiating on proposals with the Commission during the legislative process.

The European Council, comprising the heads of government of the member states, meets twice a year to provide overall policy direction. Established in 1974, the European Council was only formally brought within the EC institutional framework with the SEA.

The Presidency of the EC is held in rotation for six-month periods, setting the agenda for and chairing all Council meetings. The Presidency serves an important function since the incumbent nation has an opportunity to pursue its own particular policy priorities. The European Council holds a summit in the country holding the Presidency at the end of its period in office. The holders of the Presidency for the years 1991–94 are:
1991 Luxembourg; The Netherlands
1992 Portugal; UK
1993 Denmark; Belgium
1994 Greece; Germany

Office of the United Kingdom Permanent Representative to the European Communities
Rond-point Robert Schuman 6, 1040 Brussels, Belgium

Ambassador and UK Permanent Representative, Sir John Kerr, KCMG, *apptd.* 1990.

THE COMMISSION
200 rue de la Loi, 1049 Brussels, Belgium

The Commission consists of 17 Commissioners, two each from France, Germany, Italy, Spain and the UK, and one each from the remaining member states. The members of the Commission are appointed for four-year renewable terms by the agreement of the member states; the President and Vice-Presidents are appointed from among the Commissioners for two-year terms, also renewable. The Commissioners pledge sole allegiance to the EC.

The Commission initiates and implements EC legislation and is the guardian of the EC treaties. It is the exponent of Community-wide interests rather than the national preoccupations of the Council. Each Commissioner is supported by advisers and oversees whichever of the 23 departments, known as Directorates-General (DGs), assigned to him. Each Directorate-General is headed by a Director-General.

Commissioners

President

Secretariat General; Legal Services; Monetary Affairs; Spokesman's Service; Joint Interpreting and Conference Service; Think Tank; Security Office, Jacques Delors (France).

Vice-Presidents

External Relations and Trade Policy; Co-operation with other European Countries, Frans Andriessen (Netherlands).

Economic and Financial Affairs; Co-ordination of Structural Instruments; Statistics Office, Henning Christophersen (Denmark).

Co-operation and Development; Fisheries, Manuel Marin (Spain).

Research and Science; Telecommunications; Information Technology and Innovation; Joint Research Centre, Filippo Maria Pandolfi (Italy).

Internal Market and Industrial Affairs; Relations with the European Parliament, Martin Bangemann (Germany).

Competition Policy; Financial Institutions, Sir Leon Brittan (UK).

Members

Environment; Nuclear Safety; Civil Protection, Carlo Ripa Di Meana (Italy).

Personnel and Administration; Energy; Euratom Supply Agency; Policy on Small and Medium-Sized Enterprises; Tourism; Social Economy, Antonio Cardoso E. Cunha (Portugal).

Mediterranean Policy; Relations with Latin America; North-South Relations, Abel Matutes (Spain).

Budget; Financial Control, Peter Schmidhuber (Germany).

Taxation; Customs Union; Questions Relating to Obligatory Levies, Christiane Scrivener (France).

Regional Policy, Bruce Millan (UK).

Audio-Visual Policy; Cultural Affairs; Information and Communication Policy; Citizens' Europe; Office for Official Publications, Jean Dondelinger (Luxembourg).

Agriculture; Rural Development, Ray MacSharry (Ireland).

Transport; Credit, Investments and Financial Instruments; Consumer Protection, Karel Van Miert (Belgium).

Social Affairs and Employment; Education and Training; Human Resources, Vasso Papandreou (Greece).

Secretary-General, D. Williamson (UK).

Director-Generals

DGI, External Relations, H. G. Krenzler.
DGII, Economic and Financial Affairs, G. Ravasio.
DGIII, Internal Market and Industrial Affairs, R. Perissich.
DGIV, Competition, C.-D. Ehlerman.
DGV, Employment, Industrial Relations and Social Affairs, J. Degimbe.
DGVI, Agriculture, G. Legras.
DGVII, Transport, E. Peña Abizanda.
DGVIII, Development, D. Frisch.
DGIX, Personnel and Administration, F. de Koster.
DGX, Audiovisual, Information, Communication and Culture, C. Flesch.
DGXI, Environment, Consumer Protection and Nuclear Safety, L. J. Brinkhorst.
DGXII, Science and Research and Development, P. Fasella.
DGXIII, Telecommunications, Information Technology and Innovation, M. Carpentier.
DGXIV, Fisheries, J. Almedia Serra.
DGXV, Financial Institutions and Company Law, G. Fitchew.
DGXVI, Regional Policies, E. L. Illarramendi.
DGXVII, Energy, C. S. Maniatopoulos.
DGXVIII, Credit and Investments, E. Cioffi.
DGXIX, Budgets, J.-P. Mingasson.
DGXX, Financial Control, L. de Moor.
DGXXI, Customs Union and Indirect Taxation, P. Wilmott.
DGXXII, Co-ordination of Structural Policies, T. O'Dwyer.
DGXXIII, Enterprise Policy, Commerce, Tourism and Social Economy, H. von Moltke.

THE EUROPEAN PARLIAMENT

The European Parliament originated as the Common Assembly of the ECSC; it acquired its present name in 1962. MEPs were initially appointed from the membership of national parliaments. Direct elections to the Parliament began in 1979. Elections to the Parliament are held on differing bases throughout the EC; British MEPs are elected on a first-past-the-post system, except in Northern Ireland which uses proportional representation. The next elections will be held in 1994.

The Parliament has 518 seats allocated as follows: France, Germany, Italy, UK, 81 each; Spain, 60; the Netherlands, 25; Belgium, Greece and Portugal, 24 each; Denmark, 16; Ireland, 15; Luxembourg, 6. An additional eighteen German non-voting MEPs represent the länder of the former East Germany. MEPs serve on 18 committees, which scrutinise draft EC legislation and particular Directorate-Generals. Plenary sessions are held in Strasbourg, committees meet in Brussels and the Secretariat is situated in Luxembourg.

The EP has gradually expanded its influence within the EC. It has general powers of supervision over and consultation with the Commission and the Council; it can dismiss the Commission by a two-thirds majority. It can reject the EC budget as a whole and alter non-compulsory expenditure not specified in the EC primary legislation. Although the EP cannot directly initiate legislation, its reports can spur the Commission into action.

The MEPs in the present Parliament sit in the following political groupings: Socialist (including the British Labour Party), 179; European People's Party (including the Official Unionist Party), 122; Liberal Democratic Reformists, 49; European Democrats (including the British Conservative Party), 34; Greens, 29; European United Left, 28; European Democratic Alliance, 22; European Right, 16; Rainbow Alliance (including Scottish National Party), 15; Coalition Left, 14; Independents (including the Democratic Unionist Party), 10.

Parliament, Palais de l'Europe, 67006 Strasbourg Cedex, France; 97–113 rue Belliard, 1040 Bruxelles, Belgium.

Secretariat, Centre Européen, Kirchberg, 2929 Luxembourg.

President, Enrique Baron Crespo (Spain).
(For a full list of British MEPs, see p. 276).

THE ECONOMIC AND SOCIAL COMMITTEE
2 rue Ravenstein, 1000 Brussels, Belgium

The Economic and Social Committee is an advisory and consultative body. The ESC has 189 members, who are nominated by member states. It is divided into three groups; employers; workers; and other interest groups such as consumers, farmers and the self-employed. It issues opinions on draft EC legislation and can bring matters to the attention of the Commission, Council and Parliament; it has a key role in providing specialist and technical input.

THE COURT OF AUDITORS
12 rue A. de Gasperi, L-1615 Luxembourg

The Court of Auditors was established in 1975 to oversee EC expenditure and replaced the former Audit Board. It has 12 members.
President, Aldo Angioi (*Italy*).

EUROPEAN COURT OF JUSTICE
L-2925 Luxembourg

The European Court superseded the Court of Justice of ECSC and is common to the three European Communities. It exists to safeguard the law in the interpretation and application of the Community treaties, to decide on the legality of decisions of the Council of Ministers or the Commission, and to determine violations of the Treaties. Cases may be brought to it by the member States, the Community institutions, firms or individuals. Its decisions are directly binding in the member countries. The thirteen judges and six advocates-general of the Court are appointed for renewable six-year terms by the member Governments in concert. During 1990, 384 new cases were lodged at the court and 193 judgments were delivered.

Composition of the Court in order of precedence, with effect from October 7, 1990:

O. Due (*President*); G. F. Mancini (*President of the 6th Chamber*); T. F. O'Higgins (*President of the 2nd Chamber*); J. C. Moitinho de Almeida (*President of the 3rd and 5th Chambers*); G. C. Rodriguez Iglesias (*President of the 1st Chamber*); M. Diez de Velasco (*President of the 4th Chamber*); F. G. Jacobs (*First Advocate-General*); Sir Gordon Slynn; C. N. Kakouris; C. O. Lenz (*Advocate-General*); M. Darmon (*Advocate-General*); R. Joliet; F. A. Schockweiler; J. Mischo (*Advocate-General*); F. Grevisse; M. Zuleeg; W. van Gerven (*Advocate-General*); G. Tesauro (*Advocate-General*); P. J. G. Kapteyn; J.-G. Giraud (*Registrar*).

COURT OF FIRST INSTANCE
L-2529 Luxembourg

Established by a Council decision of October 24, 1988, under powers conferred by the Single European Act, the Court of First Instance took up its duties in 1989 and started to exercise its functions at the end of October. It has jurisdiction to hear and determine certain categories of cases brought by natural or legal persons, in particular cases brought by European Community officials, or cases on competition law.

Composition of the Court in order of precedence, with effect from October 7, 1990:

J. L. da Cruz Vilaca (*President*); A. Saggio (*President of the 2nd Chamber*); C. Yeraris (*President of the 3rd Chamber*); R. Schintgen (*President of the 4th Chamber*); C. P. Briet (*President of the 5th Chamber*); D. P. M. Barrington; D. A. O. Edward; H. Kirschner; B. Vesterdorf; R. Garcia-Valdecasas Y Fernandez; J. Biancarelli; K. Lenaerts; H. Jung (*Registrar*).

THE EUROPEAN INVESTMENT BANK
100 Boulevard Konrad Adenauer
L-2950 Luxembourg

The European Investment Bank (EIB) was set up in 1958 under the terms of the Treaty of Rome to finance capital investment projects promoting the balanced development of the European Community.

It grants long-term loans to private enterprises, public authorities and financial institutions, to finance projects which further: the economic development of less advanced regions (Assisted Areas); improvement of European communications; environmental protection; attainment of the Community's energy policy objectives; modernization of enterprises, co-operation between undertakings in the different member states, and the activities of small and medium sized enterprises.

EIB activities have also been extended outside member countries as part of the Community's development co-operation policy, under the terms of different association or co-operation agreements with twelve countries in the Mediterranean region, five in eastern Europe and, under the Lomé Conventions, 70 in Africa, the Caribbean and the Pacific.

The Bank's total financing operations in 1990 amounted to 13,393 million ECU, of which 12,680 million were for investments in the European Community and 713 million for outside the Community. Between 1986 and 1990 the EIB had made available a total of £4,710 million ECU for investment in the UK.

The members of the European Investment Bank are the twelve member states of the Community, who have all subscribed to the Bank's capital, of 57,600 million ECU. The bulk of the funds required by the Bank to carry out its tasks are borrowed on the capital markets of the Community and non-member countries, and on the international market.

As it operates on a non-profit-making basis, the interest rates charged by the EIB reflect the cost of the Bank's borrowings and closely follow conditions on world capital markets.

The Board of Governors of the European Investment Bank consists of one government minister nominated by each of the member countries, usually the finance minister, who lay down general directives on the policy of the Bank and appoint members to the Board of Directors (21 nominated by the member states, one by the Commission of the European Communities), which takes decisions on the granting and raising of loans and the fixing of interest rates. A Management Committee, also appointed by the Board of Governors, is responsible for the day-to-day operations of the Bank.

President, Ernst-Günther Bröder.
Vice-Presidents, Lucio Izzo; Alain Prate; Miguel A. Arnedo Orbañanos; Ludovicus Meulemans; Roger Lavelle; Hans Duborg.

(The President and Vice-Presidents also preside as Chairman and Vice-Chairmen at meetings of the Board of Directors.)
UK Office: 68 Pall Mall, SW1Y 5ES (Tel: 071-839 3351).

European Community Information

The Commission maintains information offices in:
LONDON, 8 Storey's Gate, SW1P 3AT. Tel: 071-973 1992.
EDINBURGH, 9 Alva Street, EH2 4HP. Tel: 031-225 2058.
CARDIFF, 4 Cathedral Road, CF1 9SG. Tel: 0222-371631.
BELFAST, Windsor House, 9–15 Bedford Street, BT2 7EG. Tel: 0232-240708.
DUBLIN, 39 Molesworth Street, Dublin 2.
WASHINGTON, 2100 M Street NW (Suite 707), Washington DC 20037.
NEW YORK, 1 Dag Hammarskjöld Plaza, 254 East 47th Street, New York, NY 10017.
OTTAWA, Inn of the Provinces, Office Tower (Suite 1110), 350 Sparks Street, Ontario, K1R 7SA.
CANBERRA, 18 Alakana Street, Yarralumia, ACT 2600, and a number of other cities.

The UK European Parliament Information Office is at: 2 Queen Anne's Gate, London, SW1H 9AA. Tel: 071-222 0411. There are European Information Centres, set up to give information and advice to small businesses, in 24 British towns and cities. A number of universities maintain European Documentation Centres.

EUROPEAN FREE TRADE ASSOCIATION
9–11 rue de Varembé, 1211 Geneva 20, Switzerland

The European Free Trade Association (EFTA) was established on May 3, 1960, by Austria, Denmark, Norway, Portugal, Sweden, Switzerland and the UK. EFTA was subsequently joined by Finland, Iceland and Liechtenstein; Denmark and the UK left EFTA in 1972 and Portugal in 1986; all joined the EC.

The first objective of EFTA was to establish free trade in industrial goods between members; this was achieved in 1966. Its second objective was the creation of a single market in western Europe and in 1972 EFTA signed a free trade agreement with the EC covering trade in industrial goods; the remaining tariffs on industrial products were finally abolished in 1984.

In 1989 exploratory talks began on the free movement of goods, services, capital and labour throughout the EC–EFTA area. The talks also covered co-operation in education, the environment, social policy, and research and development. Formal negotiations on the establishment of a European Economic Area (EEA), encompassing all 19 EC and EFTA countries, began in 1990. These negotiations are scheduled to be concluded by the end of 1991, so that the EEA treaty can come into force at the same time as the EC single market in 1993.

In 1983 EFTA adopted a declaration outlining co-operation with Yugoslavia; similar declarations were signed in 1990 with Czechoslovakia, Hungary and Poland. EFTA has begun negotiating free trade agreements with these countries in order to assist their economic reforms. A free trade agreement is also under negotiation with Turkey.

With the applications of Austria and Sweden to the EC and the expected applications of other EFTA members, many observers predict the eventual dissolution of EFTA and its fusion with the EC.

The Council of EFTA is the principle organ of the Association. It generally meets once a fortnight at the level of heads of the permanent national delegations to EFTA and twice a year at ministerial level. The chairmanship of the Council rotates every six months. Each state has a single vote and recommendations must normally be unanimous; decisions of the Council are binding on member countries.

Secretary General, Georg Reisch (*Austria*).

EUROPEAN ORGANIZATION FOR NUCLEAR RESEARCH (CERN)
1211 Geneva 23, Switzerland

The Convention establishing the European Organization for Nuclear Research (CERN) came into force in 1954. The Organization promotes European collaboration in high energy physics of a purely scientific nature. It is not concerned with research of a military nature.

The member countries are Austria, Belgium, Denmark, Finland, France, Germany, Greece, Italy, Netherlands, Norway, Poland, Portugal, Spain, Sweden, Switzerland and the UK. The following have observer status: Turkey, Yugoslavia, the EC Commission and UNESCO.

The Council is the highest policy-making body and is made up of two delegates from each member state. There is also a Committee of the Council comprising a single delegate from each member state (who is also a Council member) and the chairmen of the scientific policy and finance advisory committees. The Council is chaired by a President who is elected by the Council in Session. The Council also elects the Director-General, the person responsible for the internal organization of CERN. The Director-General heads a workforce of approximately 3,500, including physicists, craftsmen, technicians and administrative staff. At present over 5,000 physicists use CERN's facilities.

The member countries contribute to the budget directly in proportion to their net national revenue. The 1990 budget was SFr 908 million.

President of the Council, Sir William Mitchell, CBE, FRS (*UK*).

Director-General, C. Rubbia (1989–1993).

EUROPEAN SPACE AGENCY
8–10 rue Mario Nikis, 75738 Paris, France

The European Space Agency (ESA) was set up on May 31, 1975. It was formed from two earlier space organizations—the European Space Research Organization (ESRO) and the European Launcher Development Organization (ELDO). Its aims include the advancement of space research and technology, the implementation of a long-term European space policy and the co-ordination of national space programmes.

The member countries are Austria, Belgium, Denmark, France, Federal Republic of Germany, Republic of Ireland, Italy, Netherlands, Norway, Spain, Sweden, Switzerland and the United Kingdom. Finland is an associate member and Canada a co-operating state.

The agency is directed by a Council composed of the representatives of the member states, and its chief officer is the Director-General.

Director-General, Jean-Marie Luton (1990).

FOOD AND AGRICULTURE ORGANIZATION OF THE UNITED NATIONS
Via della Terme di Caracalla, 00100 Rome, Italy

The Food and Agriculture Organization (FAO) is a specialized UN agency, established on October 16, 1945. It assists rural populations by raising levels of nutrition and living standards, and by encouraging greater efficiency in food production and distribution. In addition, it collects, analyses and disseminates information on agriculture and natural resources. FAO also advises governments on national agricultural policy and planning; its Investment Centre, together with the World Bank and other financial institutions, helps to prepare development projects. FAO's field programme covers a range of activities, including strengthening crop production, rural and livestock development, and conservation.

The FAO keeps a special watch on areas where famine can occur. The Office for Special Relief Operations channels emergency aid from governments and other agencies, and assists in rehabilitation. The Technical Co-operation Programme provides schemes for countries facing agricultural crises.

The FAO had 157 members as at January 1991. It is governed by a biennial Conference of all its members which sets the forthcoming programme and budget. The budget for 1992–3 is US$568,800,000, funded by member countries in proportion to their gross national products. The FAO also receives substantial additional funding from the UN Development Programme, donor governments and other institutions.

The Conference elects a Director-General and a 49-member Council, which governs between Conferences. Projects are administered by a Secretariat, headed by the Director-General, and five regional offices.

Director-General, Edouard Saouma (*Lebanon*).

UK Representative, J. Goldsack, MBE, British Embassy, Rome.

GENERAL AGREEMENT ON TARIFFS AND TRADE

Centre William Rappard, 154 rue de Lausanne,
1211 Geneva 21, Switzerland

Under an initiative of the UN Economic and Social Council, a committee met in 1947 to draft the charter of a new international trade organization. The charter was never ratified and the General Agreement on Tariffs and Trade (GATT), intended as an interim arrangement with effect from January 1948, became the only regime for the regulation of world trade. Never formalized, GATT has evolved rules and procedures to adapt to changing circumstances. One hundred and two states are now contracting parties and a further 28 apply its rules *de facto*; GATT thus covers nearly 90 per cent of world trade.

GATT is dedicated to the expansion of non-discriminatory international trade. It provides a common code of conduct and a forum for the discussion and solution of international trade problems, and for multilateral negotiations to reduce tariffs and other trade barriers. Special attention is given to assisting the trade of developing countries, which are exempted from some GATT provisions.

Extensions of free trade are made progressively via 'rounds' of multilateral negotiations. Seven have been completed, including the Kennedy Round (1964–67) and the Tokyo Round (1973–79). The average duties on manufactured goods have been reduced from 40 per cent in the 1940s to 5 per cent. The current Uruguay Round was launched in 1986. The 108 participating governments are conducting negotiations covering market access and new trade rules regarding tariffs, non-tariff barriers, tropical products, textiles, agriculture, etc. For the first time new multilateral rules for services, intellectual property and investment are also being discussed.

The Uruguay Round was scheduled to finish in December 1990, but has not been completed because of disagreement between the USA, other members of the Cairns Group of New World agricultural producers, and the European Community over the level of Community agricultural subsidies.

A Secretariat performs administrative and intelligence functions, as well as playing an important role in diffusing conflicts between contracting parties. A Council of Representatives convenes usually eight times a year to set the agenda for forthcoming meetings of the parties. Various standing committees and groups of experts address specific issues.

The International Trade Centre, founded in 1964 to help developing countries with export expansion, is operated jointly with the UN Conference on Trade and Development.

Director-General, A. Dunkel (*Switzerland*).
Permanent UK Representative, M. R. Morland, CMG, 37–39 rue de Vermont, 1211 Geneva 20.

INTERNATIONAL ATOMIC ENERGY AGENCY

Vienna International Centre, Wagramerstrasse 5,
PO Box 100, 1400 Vienna, Austria

The International Atomic Energy Agency (IAEA) was established on July 29, 1957 as a consequence of the UN International Conference on the Peaceful Uses of Atomic Energy held the previous year. Although it operates under the aegis of, and reports annually to, the UN, the IAEA is not a specialized agency.

The IAEA aims to accelerate and enlarge the contribution of atomic energy to peace, health and prosperity, and to ensure that any assistance provided by it or under its supervision is not used for military purposes. It establishes atomic energy safety standards and inspects their implementation. The

IAEA also encourages research and training in nuclear power. It is additionally charged with drawing up safeguards and verifying their use in accordance with the Non-Proliferation Treaty of 1968.

Together with the Food and Agriculture Organization and the World Health Organization, the IAEA established an International Consultative Group on Food Irradiation in 1983.

The IAEA had 113 members as at June 1990. A General Conference of all its members meets annually to decide policy, a programme and a budget (1990, US$162,800,000), as well as electing a Director-General and 35-member Board of Governors. The Board meets four times a year to execute policy which is implemented by the Secretariat under a Director-General.

Director-General, Hans Blix (*Sweden*).
Permanent UK Representative, G. E. Clark, CMG, Jaurésgasse 12, 1030 Vienna, Austria.

INTERNATIONAL CIVIL AVIATION ORGANIZATION

1000 Sherbrooke Street West, Montreal,
Quebec, Canada H3A 2R2

The International Civil Aviation Organization (ICAO) was established as a UN specialized agency under the Chicago Convention on International Civil Aviation on April 4, 1947. It sets international technical standards and recommended practices for all areas of civil aviation, including airworthiness, air navigation, traffic control and pilot licensing. It encourages uniformity and simplicity in ground regulations and operations at international airports, including immigration and customs control. The ICAO also promotes regional plans for ground facilities, and collects and distributes air transport statistics worldwide. It is dedicated to improving safety and to the orderly development of civil aviation throughout the world.

The ICAO had 164 members as at May 31, 1991. It is governed by an assembly of all its members which meets at least once every three years. A Council of 33 members is elected, taking into account the leading air transport nations as well as ensuring representation of less developed countries. The Council elects the President, appoints the Secretary-General and supervises the Organization through subsidiary committees, serviced by a Secretariat.

President of the Council, Dr Assad Kotaite (*Lebanon*).
Secretary-General, Dr Philippe Rochat (*Switzerland*).
UK Representative, F. A. Neal, CMG, Suite 928, 1000 Sherbrooke Street West, Montreal, Quebec, Canada H3A 3G4.

INTERNATIONAL CONFEDERATION OF FREE TRADE UNIONS

37–41 rue Montagne aux Herbes Potageres, 1000
Brussels, Belgium

Formed in 1949 the International Confederation of Free Trade Unions (ICFTU) was created to promote free trade unionism worldwide. It aims to establish, maintain and promote free trade unions, and to promote peace with economic security and social justice.

Affiliated to the ICFTU are 144 individual unions and representative bodies in 101 countries and territories. On December 7, 1990 there were nearly 100 million members.

The supreme authority of the organization is the Congress which convenes at least every four years. It is composed of delegates from the affiliated trade union organizations. The Congress elects an Executive Board of 35 members which meets at least twice a year. The Board establishes the budget and receives suggestions and proposals from affiliates as well as acting on behalf of the Confederation. The Congress also elects the General Secretary.

General Secretary, John Vanderveken.

UK Affiliate, TUC, Congress House, 23–28 Great Russell Street, WC1B 3LS.

INTERNATIONAL CRIMINAL POLICE ORGANIZATION
50 quai Achille Lignon, BP 6041, 69411 Lyon, France

The International Criminal Police Commission (Interpol) was set up in 1923 to establish an international criminal records office and to harmonize extradition procedures. In 1956 a revised Constitution was adopted and the organization adopted its present name. On October 1, 1990 the organization comprised 154 member states.

Interpol's aims are to ensure and promote mutual assistance between all criminal police authorities, and to support government agencies concerned with combating crime, whilst respecting the national sovereignty of members. Interpol is financed by annual contributions from the governments of member states.

Interpol's policy is decided by the General Assembly which meets annually; it is composed of delegates appointed by the member states. The 13-member Executive Committee is elected by the General Assembly from among the member states' delegates, and is chaired by the President, who has a four-year term of office. The permanent administrative organ is the General Secretariat, headed by the Secretary General, who is appointed by the General Assembly.

Secretary-General, Raymond Kendall, QPM (*UK*).

UK Office, Interpol Bureau, New Scotland Yard, SW1H 0BG.—*UK Representative,* W. Taylor, QPM.

INTERNATIONAL ENERGY AGENCY
Chateau de la Muette, 2 rue Andre-Pascal, 75775 Paris, France

The International Energy Agency (IEA), founded in November 1974, is an autonomous agency within the framework of the Organization for Economic Co-operation and Development (OECD). The IEA had 21 member countries at June 1990.

The IEA's objectives include improvement of energy supply and demand worldwide, increased efficiency, development of alternative energy sources and the promotion of relations between oil producing and oil consuming countries. The IEA also maintains an emergency system to alleviate the effects of severe oil supply disruptions.

The main decision-making body is the Governing Board composed of senior energy officials from member countries. Various standing groups and special committees exist to facilitate the work of the Board. The IEA Secretariat, with a staff of energy experts, carries out the work of the Governing Board and its subordinate bodies. The Executive Director is appointed by the Board.

Executive Director, Mrs Helga Steeg (*Germany*).

INTERNATIONAL FUND FOR AGRICULTURAL DEVELOPMENT
107 Via del Serafico, 00142 Rome, Italy

The establishment of the International Fund for Agricultural Development (IFAD) was proposed by the 1974 World Food Conference and IFAD began operations as a UN specialized agency in December 1977. Its purpose is to mobilize additional funds for agricultural and rural development projects in devel-

oping countries that benefit the poorest rural populations.

IFAD had 145 members as at June 1991. Membership is divided into three categories: the developed countries (OECD), the oil-exporting developing countries (OPEC) and the remaining developing countries. All powers are vested in a Governing Council of a member countries. It elects an 18-member Executive Board (with 17 alternate members) responsible for IFAD's operations. The Council elects a President who is also chairman of the Board.

President, Idriss Jazairy (*Algeria*).

INTERNATIONAL LABOUR ORGANIZATION
4 route des Morillons, 1211 Geneva 22, Switzerland

The International Labour Organization (ILO) was established in 1919 as an autonomous body of the League of Nations and became the UN's first specialized agency in 1946. The ILO aims to increase productive labour, improve working conditions and raise living standards. It sets minimum international labour standards through the drafting of international conventions. Member countries are obliged to submit these to their domestic authorities for ratification, and thus undertake to bring their domestic legislation in line with the conventions. Members must report to the ILO periodically on how these regulations are being implemented. The ILO also runs a technical assistance programme in developing countries, and conducts research and disseminates information on labour. Through its World Employment Programme, it is attempting to reduce unemployment in developing countries by assisting national and international efforts to provide productive work. It is also developing an international programme to improve working conditions.

The ILO had 149 members at May 1990. It is composed of the International Labour Conference, the Governing Body and the International Labour Office. The Conference of members meets annually, and is attended by national delegations comprising two government delegates, one worker delegate and one employer delegate. It formulates international labour conventions and recommendations, provides a forum for discussion of world labour and social problems, and approves the ILO's programme and budget (1990–1, US$330,440,000). Additional project funding is provided by the UN Development Programme, the UN Fund for Population Activities and other sources.

The 56-member Governing Body, composed of 28 government, 14 worker and 14 employer members, acts as the ILO's executive council. Ten governments, including Britain, hold seats on the Governing Body because of their industrial importance. There are also various regional conferences and advisory committees. The International Labour Office acts as a secretariat and as a centre for operations, publishing and research.

In 1960 the ILO established the International Institute for Labour Studies in Geneva as a think tank on labour and social policy.

Director-General, Michel Hansenne (*Belgium*).

UK Office, Vincent House, Vincent Square, SW1 2NB. (Tel: 071-828 6401).

INTERNATIONAL MARITIME ORGANIZATION
4 Albert Embankment, London SE1 7SR

The International Maritime Organization (IMO) was established as a UN specialized agency in 1948. Due to delays in treaty ratification it did not commence operations until March 17, 1958. Originally it was called the Inter-Governmental Maritime

onsultative Organization (IMCO) but changed its
ame in 1982.

The IMO fosters inter-governmental co-operation
n technical matters relating to international ship-
ing, especially with regard to safety at sea. It is also
harged with preventing and controlling marine
ollution caused by shipping and facilitating marine
raffic. The IMO is responsible for calling maritime
onferences and drafting marine conventions. Ad-
itionally, it provides technical aid to countries
ishing to develop their activities at sea.

The IMO had 135 members as at June 1991. It is
overned by an Assembly comprising delegates of all
ts members. It meets biennially to make policy,
ecide the budget (1990–1, US$24,906,000) and vote
n specific recommendations on pollution and mari-
me safety. It elects the Council and the Maritime
afety Committee. The Council fulfils the functions
f the Assembly between sessions and appoints the
ecretary-General. It consists of 32 members; eight
rom the world's largest shipping nations, eight from
he nations most dependent on seaborne trade, and
6 other members to ensure a fair geographical
epresentation. The Maritime Safety Committee,
vorking through various sub-committees, makes
eports and recommendations to the Council and the
ssembly. There are a number of other specialist
ubsidiary committees, including one for marine
nvironmental protection.

The IMO acts as the secretariat for the London
)umping Convention (1972) which regulates the
isposal of land-generated waste at sea.

ecretary-General, William A. O'Neil (*Canada*).

INTERNATIONAL MARITIME SATELLITE ORGANIZATION
40 Melton Street, London NW1 2EQ

Inmarsat (the International Maritime Satellite
rganization) was founded in July 1978 and began
perations on February 1, 1982. Inmarsat operates a
ystem of satellites to provide telephone, telex, data
nd facsimile transmission, as well as distress and
afety communication services to the world's ship-
ing, aviation and offshore industries.

Inmarsat comprises three bodies: the Assembly,
he Council and the Directorate. The Assembly is
omposed of representatives of all member countries,
ach with one vote. It meets every two years to
eview activities and objectives, and to make recom-
nendations to the Council. The Council is the main
ecision-making body and consists of representatives
f the 18 members with the largest investment shares.
our others who represent the interests of developing
ountries are elected to the Council on the basis of
eographical representation. The Council meets at
east three times a year and oversees the activities of
he Directorate, the permanent staff of Inmarsat.

As at May 1991 there were 64 member countries.

irector-General, Olof Lundberg (*Sweden*).

INTERNATIONAL MONETARY FUND
700 19th Street NW, Washington DC 20431, USA

The International Monetary Fund (IMF) was
stablished on July 22, 1944, at the UN Monetary and
inancial Conference held at Bretton Woods, New
lampshire. Its Articles of Agreement entered into
orce on December 27, 1945, and the IMF began
perations in May 1946. The IMF exists to promote
nternational monetary co-operation, the expansion
f world trade, and exchange stability, and to
liminate foreign exchange restrictions. The IMF
dvises members on their economic and financial
olicies; promotes policy co-ordination among the
aajor industrial countries; and gives technical

assistance in central banking, balance of payments
accounting, taxation, and other financial matters.

Upon joining the IMF, a member is assigned a
'quota', based on the member's relative standing in
the world economy and its balance of payments
position, that determines its capital subscription to
the Fund, its access to IMF resources, its voting
power, and its share in the allocation of Special
Drawing Rights (SDR's). Quotas are reviewed every
five years and adjusted accordingly. After the latest
review, it was agreed to increase quotas by 50 per
cent, from the present total of SDR 91·1 billion to
SDR 136·7 billion; ratification of the increase is
expected by the end of 1991. The SDR, an international reserve asset issued by the IMF, is calculated
daily on a basket of usable currencies and is the IMF's
unit of account; on May 1, 1991, SDR 1 equalled
US$1·35031. SDRs are allocated at intervals to
supplement members' reserves and thereby improve
international financial liquidity.

IMF financial resources derive primarily from
members' capital subscriptions, which are equivalent
to their quotas. In addition, the IMF is authorized to
borrow from official lenders. Periodic charges are
also levied on financial assistance. At the end of
March 1991, total outstanding IMF credits amounted
to SDR 25 billion; borrowings amounted to SDR 3·6
billion.

The IMF is not a bank and does not lend money; it
provides temporary financial assistance by selling a
member's SDRs or other members' currencies in
exchange for the member's own currency. The
member can then use the purchased currency to
alleviate its balance of payments difficulties. The
IMF disburses this purchased currency in four 'credit
tranches', each equal to 25 per cent of the member's
quota, either over one to three years (a stand-by
arrangement) or over three to four years (an extended
arrangement). Drawings beyond the first credit
tranch are subject to economic policy conditions. A
member is expected to repay or repurchase its
currency from the IMF within three and a quarter to
five years under a stand-by arrangement, and within
four and a half to ten years under an extended
arrangement. Repurchase is made with SDRs or
currencies acceptable to the Fund.

In addition, members with acute balance of payments problems can draw larger amounts through
the enlarged access policy. Members experiencing a
temporary balance of payments shortfall have access
to the compensatory and contingency financing
facility. The IMF also offers credits to low-income
countries engaged in economic reform through its
structural adjustment facility and enhanced structural adjustment facility.

The IMF is headed by a Board of Governors,
comprising representatives of all members, which
meets annually. The Governors delegate powers to
22 Executive Directors, six appointed and 16 elected.
The Executive Directors operate the Fund on a daily
basis under a Managing Director, whom they elect.
The appointed directors represent France, Germany,
Japan, Saudi Arabia, UK and USA.

Managing Director, Michel Camdessus (*France*).

UK Executive Director, D. Peretz, Room 11-120, IMF,
700 19th Street NW, Washington DC 20431.

INTERNATIONAL RED CROSS AND RED CRESCENT MOVEMENT
17 avenue de la Paix, 1211 Geneva, Switzerland

The International Red Cross and Red Crescent
Movement is composed of three elements. The
International Committee of the Red Cross (ICRC) is
the founding body of the Red Cross and was formed
in 1863. It is a neutral intermediary negotiating
between warring factions, working throughout the

world to protect and assist victims of armed conflict. It also ensures the application of the Geneva Conventions with regard to prisoners of war and detainees.

The League of Red Cross and Red Crescent Societies, founded in 1919, is the international federation which exists to contribute to the development of the humanitarian activities of National Societies, to co-ordinate their relief operations for victims of natural disasters, and to care for refugees outside areas of conflict. There are national Red Cross and Red Crescent Societies in 147 countries with a global membership of 250 million.

The International Conference of the Red Cross and Red Crescent meets every four years, bringing together delegates of the ICRC, the League and the National Societies, as well as representatives of nations bound by the Geneva Conventions.
President of the ICRC, Cornelio Sommaruga.
British Red Cross London, 9 Grosvenor Crescent, SW1X 7EJ.—*Director-General*, Michael R. Whitlam.

INTERNATIONAL TELECOMMUNICATIONS SATELLITE ORGANIZATION
3400 International Drive NW, Washington DC 20008–3098, USA

Formed in 1964, the International Telecommunications Satellite Organization (Intelsat) owns and operates the world-wide commercial communications satellite system. The system is composed of a network of fifteen satellites and more than 1,600 antennas which link together over 170 countries, territories and dependencies.

Intelsat provides an international telephone service; an international television service; the Intelsat Business Service (IBS); Intelnet (a digital service designed for data collection and distribution); domestic telecommunications services and the Vista service providing telecommunications to remote communities.

Each of the 120 member states contributes to the capital costs of the organization in proportion to its investment share. The investment share is based on the relative usage of the system by member countries.

There is a four-tier hierarchy. The Assembly of Parties to the agreement meets every two years to consider long-term objectives and is composed of representatives of the member governments. The Meeting of Signatories annually considers the financial, technical and operational aspects of the system. The Board of Governors has 28 members; the Executive Organ is the permanent staff of Intelsat and is headed by a Director-General who reports to the Board of Governors.
Director-General, Dean Burch (*USA*).

INTERNATIONAL TELECOMMUNICATIONS UNION
Place des Nations, 1211 Geneva 20, Switzerland

The International Telecommunications Union (ITU) was founded in Paris in 1865 as the International Telegraph Union and became a UN specialized agency in 1947. It promotes international co-operation and sets standards and regulations for telecommunications operations of all kinds. It assists the development of telecommunications and provides technical assistance to developing countries. The ITU allocates the radio frequency spectrum and registers radio frequency assignments in order to avoid harmful interference between radio stations of different countries. It also collects and disseminates telecommunications information.

The ITU had 164 members as at June 11, 1991. The supreme authority is the Plenipotentiary Conference, composed of representatives of all the members, which meets not less than once every five years. It elects the Administrative Council of 43 members which meets annually to supervise the Union and set the budget (1991, SFr130,145,000). The Conference also elects the Secretary-General, who heads the General Secretariat. Four other permanent bodies include the International Frequency Registration Board, the Telecommunications Development Bureau and two consultative committees, one for radio, and one for telephone and telegraph.
Secretary-General, Dr P. Tarjanne (*Finland*).

LEAGUE OF ARAB STATES
Maidane Al-Tahrir, Nile Cornish, Cairo, Egypt

The purpose of the League of Arab States (founded 1945) is to ensure co-operation among member states and protect their independence and sovereignty, to supervise the affairs and interests of Arab countries and to control the execution of agreements concluded among the member states. The League considers itself a regional organization and is an observer at the United Nations.

Member states are Algeria, Bahrain, Djibouti, Egypt, Iraq, Jordan, Kuwait, Lebanon, Libya, Mauritania, Morocco, Oman, Palestine, Qatar, Saudi Arabia, Somalia, Sudan, Syria, Tunisia, United Arab Emirates and the Republic of Yemen.
Secretary-General, Dr Ahmed Asmat Abdel-Meguid (*Egypt*).
UK Office— 52 Green Street, WIY 3RH.

NORDIC COUNCIL
Tyrgatan 7, Box 19506, Stockholm 10432, Sweden

The Nordic Council was established in March 195 as an advisory body on economic and social co operation, comprising parliamentary delegates from Denmark, Iceland, Norway and Sweden. It was subsequently joined by Finland (1955), and representatives from the Faröes and the Åland Islands (1969 70), and Greenland (1984).

Co-operation is regulated by the Treaty of Helsink signed in 1962. This was amended in 1971 to creat the Nordic Council of Ministers, which discusses a matters except defence and foreign affairs. Matter are given preparatory consideration by a Committee of Co-operation Ministers' Deputies and joint com mittees of officials. Decisions of the Council o Ministers, which are taken by unanimous consent are binding, although if ratification by member parliaments is required, decisions only become effee tive following parliamentary approval. The Counc of Ministers is advised by the Nordic Council, t which it reports annually. There are Ministers fo Nordic Co-operation in every member government.

The Nordic Council, comprising 89 voting delegate nominated from member parliaments and about 8 non-voting government representatives, meets an nually in plenary sessions. The full Council choose a ten-member Praesidium, comprising two delegate from each sovereign member, which conducts busi ness between sessions. A Secretariat, headed by Secretary-General, liaises with the Council of Min isters and provides administrative support, as well a acting as a publishing house and information centr The Council of Ministers has a separate Secretaria based in Copenhagen.
Secretary-General, Jostein Osnes (*Norway*).
Secretariat of Nordic Council of Ministers, Stor Strandgade 18, 1255 Copenhagen K, Denmark.

NORTH ATLANTIC TREATY ORGANIZATION
Brussels 1110, Belgium

The North Atlantic Treaty was signed on April 4, 1949, by the foreign ministers of twelve nations: Belgium, Canada, Denmark, France, Iceland, Italy, Luxembourg, the Netherlands, Norway, Portugal, the UK and USA. Greece and Turkey acceded to the treaty in 1952, the Federal Republic of Germany in 1955, and Spain in 1982.

The North Atlantic Council, chaired by the Secretary-General, is the highest authority of the Alliance and is composed of permanent representatives of the sixteen member countries. It meets at ministerial level (foreign ministers) at least twice a year. The permanent representatives (Ambassadors) head national delegations of advisers and experts. Defence matters are dealt with in the Defence Planning Committee (DPC), composed of representatives of all member countries, except France.

The Council and DPC are forums for confidential and constant inter-governmental consultation and are the main decision-making bodies within the North Atlantic Alliance. They are assisted by an international Staff, divided into five divisions: Political Affairs; Defence Planning and Policy; Defence Support; Infrastructure, Logistics and Civil Emergency Planning; Scientific Affairs.

The senior military authority in NATO, under the Council and DPC, is the Military Committee composed of the Chief of Defence of each member country except France and Iceland. The Military Committee, which is assisted by an international military staff, also meets in permanent session with permanent military representatives and is responsible for making recommendations to the Council and Defence Planning Committee on measures considered necessary for the common defence of the NATO area and for supplying guidance on military matters to the Major NATO Commanders.

The strategic area covered by the North Atlantic Treaty is divided among three Commands (European, Atlantic and Channel) and a Regional Planning Group (Canada and the United States).

The Major NATO Commanders are responsible for the development of defence plans for their respective areas, for the determination of force requirements and for the deployment and exercise of the forces under their command. The Major NATO Commanders report to the Military Committee.

At a NATO summit held in London in 1990, NATO heads of state and government redefined the goals and strategy of the Organization in the light of the end of the Cold War. At a meeting held in May 1991, defence ministers agreed to reduce overall NATO forces by up to 30 per cent and create a new rapid reaction corps under British command.

Secretary-General and Chairman of the North Atlantic Council, Manfred Wörner (*Germany*).
UK Permanent Representative, Sir Michael Alexander, KCMG.
Chairman of the Military Committee, Gen. Vigleik Eide (*Norway*).
Supreme Allied Commander, Europe, Gen. John Galvin (*US*).
Supreme Allied Commander, Atlantic, Adm. Leon Edney (*US*).
Commander-in-Chief, Channel, Adm. Sir Benjamin Bathurst, GCB (*UK*).

ORGANIZATION FOR ECONOMIC CO-OPERATION AND DEVELOPMENT
2 rue André-Pascal, 75116 Paris

Formed on September 30, 1961, the Organization for Economic Co-operation and Development (OECD) replaced the Organization for European Economic Co-operation. The OECD is the instrument for international co-operation among industrialized member countries on economic and social policies. Its objectives are to assist its member governments in the formulation and co-ordination of policies designed to achieve high, sustained economic growth while maintaining financial stability, to contribute to world trade on a multilateral basis and to stimulate members' aid to developing countries.

The following countries belong to the OECD: Australia, Austria, Belgium, Canada, Denmark, Germany, Finland, France, Greece, Iceland, Republic of Ireland, Italy, Japan, Luxembourg, the Netherlands, New Zealand, Norway, Portugal, Spain, Sweden, Switzerland, Turkey, UK and USA (Yugoslavia participates with a special status).

The Council is the supreme body of the Organization. Composed of one representative for each member country, it meets at permanent representative level under the chairmanship of the Secretary-General, or at ministerial level (usually once a year) under the chairmanship of a minister elected annually. Decisions and recommendations are adopted by mutual agreement of all members of the Council. Fourteen members of the Council are chosen annually to form an Executive Committee to assist the Council. However, most of the OECD's work is undertaken in over 200 specialized committees and working parties. Five autonomous or semi-autonomous bodies are related in varying degrees to the Organization: the Nuclear Energy Agency, the International Energy Agency, the Development Centre, the Centre for Educational Research and Innovation, and the European Conference of Ministers of Transport. These bodies, the committees and the Council are serviced by an international Secretariat headed by the Secretary-General of the Organization.

Secretary-General, Jean-Claude Paye (*France*).
UK Permanent Representative, John W. D. Gray, CMG, 19 rue de Franqueville, Paris 75116.

ORGANIZATION OF AFRICAN UNITY
PO Box 3243, Addis Ababa, Ethiopia

The Organization of African Unity (OAU) was established in 1963 and has 51 members. It aims to further African unity and solidarity, to co-ordinate political, economic, social and defence policies, and to eliminate colonialism in Africa.

The chief organs are the Assembly of heads of state or government and the Council of foreign ministers. The main administrative body is the Secretariat, based in Addis Ababa.

Secretary-General, Salim Ahmed Salim (*Tanzania*).

ORGANIZATION OF AMERICAN STATES
17th Street and Constitution Avenue NW, Washington DC 20006, USA

Originally founded in 1890 for largely commercial purposes, the Organization of American States (OAS) adopted its present name and charter in 1948. Its aims are to strengthen the peace and security of the continent; to prevent possible causes of difficulties and to ensure the pacific settlement of disputes that may arise among the member states; to provide for common action on the part of those states in the event of aggression; to seek the solution of political, judicial and economic problems that may arise among them; and to promote, by co-operative action, their economic, social and cultural development. The OAS is a regional organization within the United Nations.

Policy is determined by the annual General Assembly. Meetings of Ministers of Foreign Affairs consider urgent problems, and advise in cases of armed attack and threats to peace.

The 35 member states are Antigua and Barbuda, Argentina, Bahamas, Barbados, Belize, Bolivia, Brazil, Canada, Chile, Colombia, Costa Rica, Cuba, Dominica, Dominican Republic, Ecuador, Grenada, Guatemala, Guyana, Haiti, Honduras, Jamaica, Mexico, Nicaragua, Panama, Paraguay, Peru, St Christopher and Nevis, St Lucia, St Vincent and the Grenadines, El Salvador, Suriname, Trinidad and Tobago, USA, Uruguay and Venezuela.
Secretary-General, João Clemente Baena Soares (*Brazil*).

ORGANIZATION OF ARAB PETROLEUM EXPORTING COUNTRIES
PO Box 20501 Safat, 13066 Kuwait

The Organization of Arab Petroleum and Exporting Countries (OAPEC) was founded in 1968. The objectives of the organization are to promote co-operation in economic activities; to safeguard members' interests; to unite efforts to ensure the flow of oil to consumer markets; and to create a favourable climate for the investment of capital and expertise.

The Ministerial Council is composed of oil ministers from the member countries and meets twice a year to determine policy, to direct activities and to approve the budgets and accounts of the General Secretariat and the Judicial Tribunal. The Judicial Tribunal is composed of nine part-time judges who rule on disputes between member nations and disputes between nations and oil companies. The executive organ of OAPEC is the General Secretariat.

The member countries of OAPEC are Algeria, Bahrain, Egypt, Iraq, Kuwait, Libya, Qatar, Saudi Arabia, Syria and the United Arab Emirates. (Tunisia's membership has been inactive since 1987).
Acting Secretary-General, Abdelaziz Alwattari.

ORGANIZATION OF THE PETROLEUM EXPORTING COUNTRIES
Obere Donaustrasse 93, 1020 Vienna, Austria

The Organization of the Petroleum Exporting Countries (OPEC) was created in 1960 as a permanent intergovernmental organization with the aims of unifying and co-ordinating the pertroleum policies of members and determining the best means of protecting their interests, individually and collectively.

The supreme authority is the Conference of Ministers of Oil, Mines and Energy of member countries which meets at least twice a year and formulates policy. The Board of Governors, nominated by member countries, directs the management of OPEC and implements Conference resolutions. The Secretariat, based in Vienna, carries out executive functions under the direction of the Board of Governors.

The 13 member countries are Algeria, Ecuador, Gabon, Indonesia, Iran, Iraq, Kuwait, Libya, Nigeria, Qatar, Saudi Arabia, UAE and Venezuela.
Secretary-General, Dr Subroto (*Indonesia*).

SOUTH PACIFIC COMMISSION
BP D5, Nouméa Cedex, New Caledonia

The South Pacific Commission is a technical assistance agency with programmes in agriculture and plant protection, marine resources, rural management and technology, and community and education services. The management committee is involved with the day-to-day running of the organization and is headed by the Secretary-General. The other members are the Director and the Deputy Director of Programmes.

The South Pacific Commission was established in February 1947 following the signing of the Canberra Agreement by the governments of Australia, France,

the Netherlands, New Zealand, the UK and the USA. The aim was to promote the economic and social stability of the islands in the region.

In 1983, the South Pacific Conference adopted a resolution that the Conference's 27 governments and administrations should have full and equal membership. Since 1967 the Conférence has met annually to discuss the future policy of the Commission, to adopt the budget and to nominate the officers of the Commission.
Secretary-General, Atanraoi Baiteke (*Kiribati*).
Director of Programmes, Hélène Courte (*New Caledonia*).
Deputy Director of Programmes, Vaasatia Poloma Komiti (*Western Samoa*).

THE UNITED NATIONS
UN Plaza, New York, NY 10017, USA

The United Nations is a voluntary association of states, dedicated through signature of the UN Charter to the maintenance of international peace and security and the solution of economic, social and political problems through international co-operation. The UN is not a world government and has no right of intervention in the essentially domestic affairs of states.

The UN was founded as a successor to the League of Nations and inherited many of its procedures and institutions. The name 'United Nations' was first used in the Washington Declaration of January 1942 to describe the 26 states which had allied to fight the Axis powers. The UN Charter developed from discussions at the Moscow Conference of the foreign ministers of China, the United Kingdom, the USA and Soviet Union held in October 1943. Further progress was made in Dumbarton Oaks, Washington, between August and October 1944 during talks involving the same states. The role of the Security Council was formulated at the Yalta Conference of Churchill, Roosevelt and Stalin in January 1945. The Charter was formerly drawn up by 50 allied nations at the San Francisco Conference between April and June 26, 1945, when it was signed. Following ratification the UN came into effect on October 24, 1945, which is celebrated annually as United Nations Day. The UN flag is light blue with the UN emblem centred in white.

The principal organs of the UN are the General Assembly, the Security Council, the Economic and Social Council, the Trusteeship Council, the Secretariat and the International Court of Justice. The Economic and Social Council and the Trusteeship Council are auxiliaries, charged with assisting and advising the General Assembly and Security Council. The official languages used are Arabic, Chinese, English, French, Russian and Spanish. Deliberations at the International Court of Justice are in English and French only.

Membership is open to all countries which accept the Charter and its principle of peaceful co-existence. New members are admitted by the General Assembly on the recommendation of the Security Council. The original membership of 51 states has grown to 159:—

Afghanistan	*Belgium
Albania	Belize
Algeria	Benin
Angola	Bhutan
Antigua and Barbuda	*Bolivia
*Argentina	Botswana
*Australia	*Brazil
Austria	Brunei
Bahamas	Bulgaria
Bahrain	Burkina
Bangladesh	Burundi
Barbados	*Belorussia

Cambodia (Kampuchea)	Mongolia
Cameroon	Morocco
*Canada	Mozambique
Cape Verde	Namibia
Central African Rep.	Nepal
Chad	*Netherlands
*Chile	*New Zealand
*China	*Nicaragua
*Colombia	Niger
Comoros	Nigeria
Congo	*Norway
*Costa Rica	Oman
Côte d'Ivoire	Pakistan
Cuba	*Panama
Cyprus	Papua New Guinea
Czechoslovakia	*Paraguay
Denmark	*Peru
Djibouti	*Philippines
Dominica	*Poland
*Dominican Rep.	Portugal
*Ecuador	Qatar
*Egypt	Romania
Equatorial Guinea	Rwanda
*Ethiopia	St Christopher and
Fiji	Nevis
Finland	St Lucia
*France	St Vincent and the
Gabon	Grenadines
Gambia	*El Salvador
Germany	São Tomé and Príncipe
Ghana	*Saudi Arabia
*Greece	Senegal
Grenada	Seychelles
*Guatemala	Sierra Leone
Guinea	Singapore
Guinea-Bissau	Solomon Is.
Guyana	Somalia
*Haiti	*South Africa
*Honduras	Spain
Hungary	Sri Lanka
Iceland	Sudan
India	Suriname
Indonesia	Swaziland
Iran	Sweden
Iraq	*Syria
Ireland, Rep. of	Tanzania
Israel	Thailand
Italy	Togo
Jamaica	Trinidad and Tobago
Japan	Tunisia
Jordan	*Turkey
Kenya	Uganda
Kuwait	*Ukraine
Laos	*Union of Soviet
Lebanon	Socialist Republics
Lesotho	United Arab Emirates
Liberia	*United Kingdom
Libya	*United States of
Liechtenstein	America
Luxembourg	*Uruguay
Madagascar	Vanuatu
Malawi	*Venezuela
Malaysia	Vietnam
Maldives	Western Samoa
Mali	Yemen
Malta	*Yugoslavia
Mauritania	Zaire
Mauritius	Zambia
Myanmar (Burma)	Zimbabwe
Mexico	

*Original member (i.e. from 1945). (From October 25, 1971 'China' was taken to mean the People's Republic of China.)

A number of countries are not members, usually due to their small size and limited financial resources. Notable exceptions include Switzerland, which follows a policy of absolute neutrality, and Taiwan, which was replaced by the People's Republic of China in October 1971. The Byelorussian and Ukrainian SSRs are not sovereign states but were granted separate UN membership as a concession to Soviet fears of non-Communist domination of the UN. Permanent observer status is held by the Holy See, Monaco, North Korea, South Korea, San Marino and Switzerland. The Palestinian Liberation Organization has special observer status.

THE GENERAL ASSEMBLY
UN Plaza, New York, NY 10017, USA

The General Assembly is the main deliberative organ of the UN. It consists of all members, each entitled to five representatives but having only one vote. The annual session begins on the third Tuesday of September, when the President is elected, and usually continues until mid-December. Special sessions are held on specific issues and emergency special sessions can be called within 24 hours.

The Assembly is empowered to discuss any matter within the scope of the Charter, except when it is under consideration by the Security Council, and to make recommendations. Under the 'uniting for peace' resolution, adopted in November 1950, the Assembly may also take action to maintain international peace and security when the Security Council fails to do so because of a lack of unanimity of its permanent members. Important decisions, such as those on peace and security, the election of officers, the budget, etc., need a two-thirds majority. Others need a simple majority. The Assembly has effective power only over the internal operations of the UN itself; external recommendations are not legally binding.

The work of the General Assembly is divided among seven main committees, on each of which every member has the right to be represented : Disarmament and related security questions (assisted by a Special Political Committee); Economic and Financial; Social, Humanitarian and Cultural; Decolonization (including non-self governing territories); Administrative and Budgetary; Legal. In addition, the General Assembly appoints *ad hoc* committees to consider special issues, such as human rights, peacekeeping, disarmament and international law. All committees consider items referred to them by the Assembly and recommend draft resolutions to its plenary meeting.

The Assembly is assisted by a number of functional committees. The General Committee co-ordinates its proceedings and operations, while the Credentials Committee verifies the credentials of representatives. There are also two standing committees, the Advisory Committee on Administration and Budgetary Questions and the Committee on Contributions, which suggests the scale of members' payments to the UN.
President of the General Assembly (1991), Samir S. Shihabi *(Saudi Arabia).*

The Assembly has created a large number of specialized bodies over the years, which are supervised jointly with the Economic and Social Council. They are supported by UN and voluntary contributions from governments, non-governmental organizations and individuals. These organizations include:

The Conference on Disarmament (CD), Palais des Nations, 1211 Geneva 10, Switzerland. Established by the UN as the Committee on Disarmament in 1962, the CD is the single multilateral disarmament negotiating forum. The present title of the organization was adopted in 1984. There were 39 members as at June 1, 1991.

The Conference holds three regular sessions per year, from January to March, May to June, and July to August. The work of the Conference is conducted both in public plenary meetings and in private *ad hoc* committees set up with the consent of all members to deal with specific items of the agenda. Currently under negotiation are a ban on chemical weapons and the prevention of an arms race in outer space.
Secretary-General, HE Miljan Komatina.

UK Representative, Miss T. A. H. Solesby, CMG, 37–39 rue de Vermont, 1211 Geneva 10, Switzerland.

The United Nations Children's Fund (UNICEF), 3 UN Plaza, New York, NY 10017, USA. Established in 1947 to assist children and mothers in the immediate post-war period, UNICEF now concentrates on developing countries. It provides primary health-care and health education. In particular, it conducts programmes in oral hydration, immunization against leading diseases, child growth monitoring, and the encouragement of breast-feeding. Its operations are often conducted in co-operation with the World Health Organization (WHO).
Executive Director, James Grant (*USA*).

The United Nations Development Programme (UNDP), 1 UN Plaza, New York, NY 10017, USA. Established in 1966 from the merger of the UN Expanded Programme of Technical Assistance and the UN Special Fund, UNDP is the central funding agency for economic and social development projects around the world. Much of its annual expenditure is channelled through UN specialized agencies, governments and non-governmental organizations.
Administrator, William H. Draper III (*USA*).

The United Nations High Commissioner for Refugees (UNHCR), Centre William Rappard, 154 rue de Lausanne, PO Box 2500, 1211 Geneva 2, Switzerland. Established in 1951 to protect the rights and interests of refugees, it organizes emergency relief and longer-term solutions, such as voluntary repatriation, local integration or resettlement.
High Commissioner, Sadako Ogata (*Japan*).
UK Office, 36 Westminster Palace Gardens, SW1P 1RR (Tel : 071-222 3065).

The UN Relief and Works Agency for Palestine Refugees in the Near East (UNWRA), Vienna International Centre, Wagramerstrasse 5, PO Box 100, 1400 Vienna, Austria. Established in 1949 to bring relief to the Palestinians displaced by the Arab-Israeli conflict.
Commissioner-General, Ilter Turkman (*Turkey*).

Other bodies include :
THE UN CENTRE FOR HUMAN SETTLEMENTS (Habitat), PO Box 30030, Nairobi, Kenya.
THE UN COMMISSION FOR TRADE AND DEVELOPMENT (UNCTAD), Palais des Nations, 1211 Geneva 10, Switzerland.
THE OFFICE OF THE UN DISASTER AND RELIEF CO-ORDINATOR (UNDRO), Palais des Nations, 1211 Geneva 10, Switzerland.
THE UN ENVIRONMENT PROGRAMME (UNEP), PO Box 30552, Nairobi, Kenya.
THE UN FUND FOR POPULATION ACTIVITIES (UNFPA), 220 East 42nd Street, New York, NY 10017, USA.
THE UN INSTITUTE FOR THE ADVANCEMENT OF WOMEN (INSTRAW), PO Box 21747, Santo Domingo, Dominican Republic.
THE UN UNIVERSITY (UNU), Toho Seimei Building, 15 – 1, Shibuya, 2-Chome, Shibuya-ku, Tokyo 150, Japan.
THE WORLD FOOD COUNCIL (WFC), Via delle Terme di Caracalla, 00100 Rome, Italy.
THE WORLD FOOD PROGRAMME (WFP), Via delle Terme di Caracalla, 00100 Rome, Italy.

Budget of the United Nations
The budget adopted for the biennium 1990–1 wa US$1,983,000,000. The scale of assessment contribu tions of 88 UN members is set at the minimum 0·0 per cent. The ten largest assessments are: USA, 2 per cent; USSR (total), 11·57; Japan, 11·38; Germany 9·36; France, 6·25; UK, 4·86; Italy, 3·99; Canada, 3·09 Spain, 1·95; Netherlands, 1·65.

THE SECURITY COUNCIL
UN Plaza, New York, NY 10017, USA

The Security Council is the senior arm of the UN and has the primary responsibility for maintaining world peace and security. It consists of 15 members each with one representative and one vote. Ther are five permanent members, China, France, UK USA and USSR, and ten non-permanent members Each of the non-permanent members is elected for a two-year term by a two-thirds majority of the Genera Assembly and is ineligible for immediate re-election Five of the elective seats are allocated to Africa and Asia, one to Eastern Europe, two to Latin America and two to Western Europe and remaining countries Procedural questions are determined by a simple majority vote. Other matters require a majority inclusive of the votes of the permanent members they thus have a right of veto. The abstention of a permanent member does not constitute a veto. The presidency rotates each month by state in (English alphabetical order. Parties to a dispute, other non members and individuals can be invited to participate in Security Council debates but are not permitted to vote. In 1991 the ten non-permanent members were Côte d'Ivoire, Cuba, Romania, Yemen and Zaire (*term expires Dec. 31, 1991*); Austria, Belgium, Ecuador India and Zimbabwe (*term expires Dec. 31, 1992*).

The Security Council is empowered to settle on adjudicate in disputes or situations which threaten international peace and security. It can adopt political, economic and military measures to achieve this end. Any matter considered to be a threat to on breach of the peace or an act of aggression can be brought to the Security Council's attention by any member state or by the Secretary-General. The Charter envisaged members placing at the disposal o the Security Council armed forces and other facilities which would be co-ordinated by the Military Staf Committee, composed of military representatives o the five permanent members. The Security Council is also supported by a Committee of Experts, to advise on procedural and technical matters, and a Committee on Admission of New Members. Owing to superpower disunity, the Security Council has rarely played the decisive role set out in the Charter; the Military Staff Committee was effectively suspended from 1948 until 1990, when a meeting was convened during the Gulf Crisis on the formation and control of UN-supervised armed forces.

The Security Council has established a number of peace-keeping forces since its foundation, comprising contingents provided mainly by neutral and non-aligned UN members. Current forces include: the UN Truce Supervision Organization (UNTSO), 1948, Israel; the UN Military Observer Group in India and Pakistan (UNMOGIP), 1949; the UN Force in Cyprus (UNFICYP), 1964; the UN Disengagement Observer Force (UNDOF), 1974, Golan Heights, Syria; the UN Interim Force in Lebanon (UNIFIL), 1978; the UN Iran-Iraq Military Observer Group (UNIIMOG), 1988; the UN Angola Verification Mission (UNA-VEM), 1988; the UN Observer Group in Central America (ONUCA), 1989; the UN Iraq-Kuwait Observation Mission (UNIKOM), 1991; UN Observers for El Salvador (ONUSAL), 1991; and the UN Mission for the Referendum in Western Sahara (MINURSO), 1991.

THE ECONOMIC AND SOCIAL COUNCIL
UN Plaza, New York, NY 10017, USA

The Economic and Social Council is responsible under the General Assembly for the economic and social work of the UN and for the co-ordination of the activities of the 15 specialized agencies and other UN bodies. It makes reports and recommendations on economic, social, cultural, educational, health and related matters, often in consultation with non-governmental organizations, passing the reports to the General Assembly and other UN bodies. It also drafts conventions for submission to the Assembly and calls conferences on matters within its remit.

The Council consists of 54 members, 18 of whom are elected annually by the General Assembly for a three-year term. Each has one vote and can be immediately re-elected on retirement. A President is elected annually and is also eligible for re-election. Meetings are held biennially and decisions reached by simple majority vote of those present.

The Council has established a number of standing committees on particular issues and several commissions. Commissions include: Statistical, Human Rights, Social Development, Status of Women, Narcotic Drugs, and Population; and Regional Economic Commissions for Europe, Asia and the Pacific, Western Asia, Latin America and Africa.

THE TRUSTEESHIP COUNCIL
UN Plaza, New York, NY 10017, USA

The Trusteeship Council supervises the administration of territories within the UN Trusteeship system inherited from the League of Nations. It now consists of the USA, the only remaining administrator, and the four other permanent members of the Security Council. Meetings are held annually and decisions reached by a majority vote of those present. Ten of the original eleven trusteeships have now progressed towards independence or merged with neighbouring states. With the partial termination of the trust status for the Federated States of Micronesia in December 1990, only the Republic of Palau now remains within the system.

THE SECRETARIAT
UN Plaza, New York, NY 10017, USA

The Secretariat services the other UN organs and is headed by a Secretary-General elected by a majority vote of the General Assembly on the recommendation of the Security Council. He is assisted by an international staff, chosen to represent the international character of the organization. The Secretary-General is charged with bringing to the attention of the Security Council any matter which he considers poses a threat to international peace and security. He may also bring other matters to the attention of the General Assembly and other UN bodies and may be entrusted by them with additional duties. As chief administrator to the UN, the Secretary-General is present in person or via representatives at all meetings of the other five main organs of the UN. He may also act as an impartial mediator in disputes between member states.

The power and influence of the Secretary-General has, to a large extent, been determined by the character of the office-holder and by the state of relations between the superpowers. The thaw in these relations since the mid-1980s has increased the effectiveness of the UN, particularly in its attempts to intervene in international disputes. It helped to end the Iran-Iraq war and sponsored peace in Central America. Following Iraq's invasion of Kuwait in 1990 the UN took its first collective security action since the Korean War. A 1,400-strong observer force (UNIKOM) has been established to police a nine-mile

wide and 120-mile long buffer zone between Kuwait and Iraq. UN action to protect the Kurds in northern Iraq has widened its legal authority by breaching the prohibition on its intervention in the essentially domestic affairs of states. Currently the UN plans to set up a UN-sponsored interim government in Cambodia and is addressing the global problems of AIDS and environmental destruction.

Secretary-General, Javier Pérez de Cuellar (*Peru*) (1981–end 1991).

INTERNATIONAL COURT OF JUSTICE
The Peace Palace, 2517 KJ The Hague,
The Netherlands

The International Court of Justice is the principal judicial organ of the UN. The Statute of the Court is an integral part of the Charter and all members of the UN are *ipso facto* parties to it. The Court is composed of 15 judges, elected by both the General Assembly and the Security Council for nine-year terms which are renewable. Judges may deliberate over cases in which their country is involved. If no judge on the bench is from a country which is a party to a dispute under consideration, that party may designate a judge to participate *ad hoc* in that particular deliberation. If any party to a case fails to adhere to the judgment of the Court, the other party may have recourse to the Security Council.

President, Sir Robert Jennings (*UK*) (2000).
Vice-President, Shigeru Oda (*Japan*) (1994).
Judges, Manfred Lachs (*Poland*) (1994); Taslim Olawale Elias (*Nigeria*) (1994); Roberto Ago (*Italy*) (1997); Stephen M. Schwebel (*USA*) (1997); Mohammed Bedjaoui (*Algeria*) (1997); Ni Zhengyu (*China*) (1994); Jens Evensen (*Norway*) (1994); Nikolai K. Tarassov (*USSR*) (1997); Gilbert Guillaume (*France*) (2000); Mohammed Shahabuddeen (*Guyana*) (1997); Andrés Aguilar Mawdsley (*Venezuela*) (2000); Christopher G. Weeramantry (*Sri Lanka*) (2000); and Raymond Ranjeva (*Madagascar*) (2000).

SPECIALIZED AGENCIES

Fifteen independent international organizations, each with its own membership, budget and headquarters, carry out their responsibilities in co-ordination with the UN under agreements made with the Economic and Social Council. An entry for each appears elsewhere in the International Organizations section. They are as follows: the Food and Agriculture Organization of the UN; International Civil Aviation Organization; International Fund for Agricultural Development; International Labour Organization; International Maritime Organization; the International Monetary Fund; International Telecommunications Union; UN Educational, Scientific and Cultural Organization; UN Industrial Development Organization; Universal Postal Union; World Bank (International Bank for Reconstruction and Development, International Development Agency, International Finance Corporation); World Health Organization; World Intellectual Property Organization; World Meteorological Organization; and World Tourist Organization. The International Atomic Energy Agency and the General Agreement on Tariffs and Trade are linked to the UN but are not specialized agencies.

UK Mission to the United Nations
845 Third Avenue, New York, NY 10022, USA

Permanent Representative to the United Nations and Representative on the Security Council, Sir David Hannay, KCMG, *apptd.* 1990.
Deputy Permanent Representative, T. L. Richardson, CMG.

UK Mission to the Office of the UN and Other International Organizations in Geneva

37–39 rue de Vermont, 1211 Geneva 20,
Switzerland

Permanent UK Representative, M. R. Morland, CMG
apptd. 1990.
Deputy Permanent Representatives, G. W. Hewitt
(*Head of Chancery*); Miss A. E. Stoddart (*Economic Affairs*).

UK Mission to the International Atomic Energy Agency, the UN Industrial Development Organization and the United Nations Office at Vienna

Jaurésgasse 12, 1030 Vienna,
Austria

Permanent UK Representative, G. E. Clark, CMG
apptd. 1987.
Deputy Permanent Representative, Miss M. R. McIntosh.

UN Office and Information Centre

Ship House, 20 Buckingham Gate, SW1E 6LB
[Tel: 071-630 1981]

UNITED NATIONS EDUCATIONAL, SCIENTIFIC AND CULTURAL ORGANIZATION

7 place de Fontenoy, Paris 75700, France

The United Nations Educational, Scientific and Cultural Organization (UNESCO) was established on November 4, 1946, the consequence of an international conference held in London in 1945. It promotes collaboration among its member states in education, science, culture and communication. It aims to further a universal respect for human rights, justice and the rule of law, without distinction of race, sex, language or religion, in accordance with the UN Charter.

UNESCO runs a number of programmes to improve education and extend access to it. It provides assistance to improve the quality of the world's media and maintain cultural heritage in the face of development. It fosters research and study in all areas of the social sciences.

UNESCO had 159 member states as at June 1991. There are three associate members. The General Conference, consisting of representatives of all the members, meets biennially to decide the programme and the budget (1990–91, US$378,788,000). It elects the 51-member Executive Board, which supervises operations, and appoints a Director-General. The Director-General heads a Secretariat responsible for day-to-day functions. In most member states national commissions liaise with UNESCO to execute its programme.

The UK withdrew from UNESCO in 1985. It was granted observer status in 1986.
Director-General, Federico Mayor Zaragoza (*Spain*).

UNITED NATIONS INDUSTRIAL DEVELOPMENT ORGANIZATION

Vienna International Centre, Wagramerstrasse 5,
PO Box 300, 1400 Vienna, Austria

The United Nations Industrial Development Organization (UNIDO) was established as an organ of the UN General Assembly in 1966, replacing the Centre for Industrial Development. It became a UN specialized agency on January 1, 1986 with the aim of promoting the industrialization of developing countries, with special emphasis upon the manufacturing sector. To this end it provides technical assistance and advice, as well as help with planning.

UNIDO had 151 members as at May 1991. It is funded by the UN Development Programme, other UN bodies, governments and non-governmental organizations. A General Conference of all the members meets biennially to discuss policy, set a budget (1991–2, US$180,000,000) and elect the Industrial Development Board. This executive body is composed of 33 members from developing countries, 15 from developed countries and five from centrally planned economies. There is a subsidiary Programme and Budget Committee. A Secretariat administers UNIDO under a Director-General, appointed by the Conference.

Director-General, Domingo L. Siazon jun. (*Philippines*).
Permanent UK Representative, G. E. Clark, CMG,
British Embassy, Vienna.

UNIVERSAL POSTAL UNION

Weltpoststrasse 4, 3000 Berne 15,
Switzerland

The Universal Postal Union (UPU) was established by the Convention of Berne on October 9, 1874, taking effect from July 1875, and became a UN specialized agency in June 1947. The UPU exists to form a single postal territory of all member countries, for the reciprocal exchange of correspondence without discrimination. It also assists and advises on the improvement of postal services.

The UPU had 168 members as at June 1991. A Universal Postal Congress of all the members meets every five years to review the Convention and to elect a 40-member Executive Council (including one member from the host country) which continues the UPU's work between Congresses. The Congress also elects a 35-member Consultative Council for Postal Studies which meets annually to address specific matters. The Council, together with the Swiss government, supervises the International Bureau, a secretariat headed by a Director-General.

Funding is provided by members according to a scale of contributions drawn up by the Congress. The Council sets the annual budget (1991, SFr25,689,430) within a five-year figure decided by the Congress.
Director-General, A. C. Botto de Barros (*Brazil*).

WESTERN EUROPEAN UNION

9 Grosvenor Place, London SW1X 7HL

The Western European Union (WEU) originated as the Brussels Treaty Organization (BTO). This was established under the Treaty of Brussels, signed in 1948 by Belgium, France, Luxembourg, the Netherlands and UK, to provide collective self-defence and economic, cultural and social collaboration amongst its signatories. With the collapse of the European Defence Community and the decision of NATO to incorporate the Federal Republic of Germany into the Western security system, the BTO was modified to become the WEU in 1954 with the admission of West Germany and Italy.

Owing to the overlap with NATO and the Council of Europe, the Union became largely defunct. From the late 1970s onwards efforts were made to add a security dimension to European Political Co-operation. Opposition to these efforts from Denmark, Greece and Ireland led the remaining EC countries, all WEU members, to decide to reactivate the Union in 1984. Members committed themselves to harmonizing their views on defence and security and developing a European security identity, while bearing in mind the importance of transatlantic relations. Portugal and Spain joined the WEU in 1988.

The future of the WEU is currently under debate. Some members want the WEU to strengthen its position as a European pillar of the transatlantic alliance, others want the WEU to be absorbed into the EC as part of a unitary European defence and security policy. In 1991 a study group was established to investigate the creation of a WEU-controlled rapid deployment force. The WEU is to be reassessed in 1996.

A Council of Ministers (foreign and defence) meets biannually in the capital of the presiding country; the Presidency rotates annually. A Permanent Council of the signatories' London ambassadors and a senior British official meet regularly in London. An Enlarged Council of political directors and member defence officials was created in 1986. Both the Enlarged Committee and the Permanent Committee are chaired by the Secretary-General and serviced by the Secretariat. The Assembly of the WEU is composed of 108 parliamentarians of member states and meets twice annually in Paris to debate matters within the scope of the Brussels Treaty. A WEU Institute for Security Studies was set up in Paris in 1989.

Presidency (1991–92), Germany.

Secretary-General, Dr Willem van Eekelen (*Netherlands*).

Assembly, 43 avenue du Président Wilson, 75775 Paris Cedex 16, France.

THE WORLD BANK
1818 H Street NW, Washington DC 20433, USA

The World Bank, more formally known as the International Bank for Reconstruction and Development (IBRD), is a specialized agency of the UN, and developed from the international monetary and financial conference held at Bretton Woods, New Hampshire, in 1944. Determined to avoid the financial chaos and depression of the inter-war years, 39 nations established the IBRD on December 27, 1945, to encourage economic growth in developing countries through the provision of loans and technical assistance to their respective governments. The IBRD now has 155 members.

The Bank is owned by the governments of member countries and its capital is subscribed by its members. It finances its lending primarily from borrowing in world capital markets, and derives a substantial contribution to its resources from its retained earnings and the repayment of loans. The interest rate on its loans is calculated in relation to its cost of borrowing. Loans generally have a grace period of five years and are repayable within 20 years. The loans (including IFC loans) made by the Bank since its inception to December 31, 1990, totalled US$194,260,000,000 to 106 countries. Subscribed capital is US$136,760,000,000.

Originally directed towards post-war reconstruction in Europe, the Bank has subsequently turned towards assisting less-developed countries with the establishment of two affiliates, the International Finance Corporation (IFC) in 1956 and the International Development Association (IDA) in 1960. The IFC aids developing member countries by promoting the growth of the private sector of their economies and by helping to mobilize domestic and foreign capital for this purpose. The IFC's subscribed share capital was US$1,300,000,000 at June 30, 1990. It is also empowered to borrow up to two and half times the amount of its unimpaired subscribed capital and accumulated earnings for use in its lending programme. At June 30, 1991, the IFC had committed financing totalling more than US$8,000,000,000 in about 95 countries.

The IDA performs the same function as the World Bank but primarily to less developed countries and on terms that bear less heavily on their balance of payments than IRBD loans. Eligible countries must have a per capita gross national product of less than US$1140 (1989). Funds (called credits to distinguish them from IBRD loans) come mostly in the form of subscriptions and contributions from the IDA's richer members and transfers from the net income of the IBRD. The terms for IDA credits, which bear no interest and are made to governments only, are ten-year grace periods and 35- or 40-year maturities. By June 30, 1990, the IDA had extended development credits totalling US$58,200,000,000 to 87 countries.

The IBRD and its affiliates are financially and legally distinct but share headquarters. The IBRD is headed by a Board of Governors, consisting of one Governor and one alternate Governor appointed by each member country. Twenty-two Executive Directors exercise all powers of the Bank except those reserved to the Board of Governors. The President, elected by the Executive Directors, conducts the business of the Bank, assisted by an international staff. Membership in both the IFC (140 members) and the IDA (139 members) is open to all IBRD countries. The IDA is administered by the same staff as the Bank; the IFC has its own personnel but draws on the IBRD for administrative and other support. All share the same President.

President (IBRD, IFC, IDA), L. Preston (*USA*).

UK Executive Director, P. Coady, Room D1328, IMF, 1809 G Street NW, Washington DC 20433.

European Office, 66 avenue d'Iena, 75116 Paris, France.

Japan Office, Kokusai Building 1-1, Marunouchi 3-Chomse, Chiyoda-ku, Tokyo 100, Japan.

UK Office, New Zealand House, Haymarket, SW1Y 4TQ.

THE WORLD COUNCIL OF CHURCHES
PO Box 2100, 1211 Geneva 2
Switzerland

The World Council of Churches (WCC) was constituted in Amsterdam in 1948 to promote unity among the many different Christian churches. The 317 member churches of the WCC have adherents in more than 100 countries. With the exception of Roman Catholicism, virtually all Christian traditions are included in the WCC membership.

The policies of the Council are determined by delegates of the member churches meeting in Assembly, about every eight years; the seventh Assembly was held in Canberra, Australia, in February 1991. More detailed decisions are taken by a 151-member Central Committee which is elected by the Assembly and meets, with the eight WCC Presidents, annually. The Central Committee in turn appoints a smaller Executive Committee and also nominates commissions and working groups, to guide the various programmes.

General Secretary, Dr Emilio Castro (*Uruguay*).

WORLD FEDERATION OF TRADE UNIONS
Na Dobesce 35, Branik, Prague 4, Czechoslovakia

The World Federation of Trade Unions (WFTU) was founded in October 1945. In 1949 a number of members withdrew and founded the International Confederation of Free Trade Unions. The WFTU now has 92 affiliated federations with 188 million members.

The Congress, which is comprised of delegates from member nations, meets every five years to review WFTU's work and to elect the General Council and Bureau. The General Council is elected from members of national federations and meets three times between Congresses. Each affiliated organization has one member and one deputy. The Presidential Council of 20 members is elected by the General Council and carries out the executive work of the WFTU

General Secretary, Alexander Zharikov (*USSR*).

WORLD HEALTH ORGANIZATION
20 avenue Appia, 1211 Geneva 27,
Switzerland

The UN International Health Conference held in 1946 established the World Health Organization (WHO) as a UN specialized agency, with effect from April 7, 1948. It is dedicated to attaining the highest possible level of health for all. It collaborates with member governments, UN agencies and other bodies to develop health standards, control communicable diseases and promote all aspects of family and environmental health. It seeks to raise the standards of health teaching and training, and promotes research through collaborating research centres world-wide. Its other services include the *International Pharmacopoeia*, epidemiological surveillance, and the collation and publication of statistics. WHO activities are orientated to achieving 'Health for all by the year 2000', i.e. a level of health allowing the world's citizens to lead socially and economically productive lives.

WHO had 168 members as at May 1991. It is governed by the annual World Health Assembly of members which meets to set policy, approve the budget (1992–93 biennium, US$734,936,000), appoint a Director-General, and adopt health conventions and regulations. It also elects 31 members who designate one health-qualified person to serve in a personal capacity on the Executive Board. The Board effects the programme, suggests initiatives and is empowered to deal with emergencies. A Secretariat, headed by the Director-General, supervises the health activities of six regional offices.

Director-General, Dr H. Nakajima (*Japan*).

WORLD INTELLECTUAL PROPERTY ORGANIZATION
34 chemin des Colombettes, 1211 Geneva 20,
Switzerland

The World Intellectual Property Organization (WIPO) was established in 1967 and was intended to replace the Bureau international réuni pour la protection de la propriété intellectuelle (BIRPI). BIRPI was founded in 1893 to represent the joint secretariats of the Paris Convention for the Protection of Industrial Property (1883) and the Berne Convention for the Protection of Literary and Artistic Works (1886). Both conventions maintain separate organizations pending the formal accession of all BIRPI members to WIPO. WIPO became a UN specialized agency in 1974.

WIPO promotes the protection of intellectual property: industrial property (patented inventions and designs, scientific discoveries and trademarks, etc.); and copyright (literary, musical, cinematic and artistic works, etc.). WIPO also assists creative intellectual activity and facilitates technology transfer, particularly to developing countries. It administers various conventions, most importantly the Berne and Paris Conventions.

WIPO had 126 members as at April 30, 1991. The biennial Conference of all its members sets policy, a programme and a budget (1990–1, SFr155,399,000). A General Assembly meets simultaneously, comprising only WIPO members who are also members of BIRPI. The Assembly appoints, instructs and supervises a Director-General, who heads the International Bureau (secretariat). A Co-ordination Committee represents the organizations of the Berne and Paris Conventions.

A separate International Union for the Protection of New Varieties of Plants (UPOV), established by convention in 1961, is linked to WIPO. It has 19 members.

Director-General, Arpad Bogsch (*USA*).

WORLD METEOROLOGICAL ORGANIZATION
41 avenue Giuseppe Motta, PO Box 2400,
1211 Geneva 20, Switzerland

The World Meteorological Organization (WMO) was established as a UN specialized agency on March 19, 1951, succeeding the International Meteorological Organization which had been founded in 1874. It facilitates co-operation between the world-wide network of meteorological services, standardizes meteorological observations and data, and assists training and research. It also fosters collaboration between meteorological and hydrological services, and furthers the application of meteorology to aviation, shipping, agriculture, etc.

The WMO had 155 member states and five member territories, as at June 1, 1991. The supreme authority is the World Meteorological Congress of member states and member territories, which meets every four years to determine general policy, make recommendations and set a budget (1992–95, SFr236,100,000). It also elects 26 members of the 36-member Executive Council, the other members being the President and three Vice-Presidents of the WMO, and the Presidents of the six Regional Associations. The Council supervises the implementation of Congress decisions, initiates studies and makes recommendations on matters needing international action. The WMO functions through six Regional Meteorological Associations and eight technical commissions. The Secretariat is headed by a Secretary-General, appointed by the Congress.

Secretary-General, G. O. P. Obasi (*Nigeria*).

WORLD TOURISM ORGANIZATION
Capitan Haya 42, 28020 Madrid,
Spain

The World Tourism Organization (WTO) was established in 1975 as a UN specialized agency. It aims to develop and promote tourism in order to contribute to economic development and international understanding. The WTO provides specific countries with technical assistance to help them develop their tourist industries, as well as fostering better education and training. It also seeks to improve the security of tourists and facilities provided for them, to harmonize and codify tourism law, and to act as a tourism information centre.

There are three categories of membership: full (103 members), associate (four members), and affiliate (156 members.

The WTO is governed by a General Assembly of all members which meets biennially to agree policy and set a budget (1990–1, US$14,005,200). The 22-member Executive Council has one member elected for every five full members of the WTO, as well as non-voting single representatives for the associate members, and the Committee of Affiliated Members. The latter comprises international, inter-governmental and non-governmental bodies with a special interest in tourism, and develops its own programme within the framework of WTO actions. There are regional commissions for Africa, the Americas, Europe, the Middle East, South Asia, and East Asia and the Pacific. The UK is not a member.

Secretary-General, Antonio Enriquez Savignac (*Mexico*).

BROADCASTING

TELEVISION

The British Broadcasting Corporation (*see* pp. 301–2) is responsible for public service broadcasting in the United Kingdom. Its constitution and finances are governed by Royal Charter and by a Licence and Agreement. Its role is to provide high-quality programmes with wide-ranging appeal that educate, inform and entertain.

The Independent Television Commission (*see* page 330) is the regulator and licenser for independent television companies. The present ITV franchises for the 15 regional companies and for breakfast television expire at the end of 1992; applications for new ten-year licences were received by the ITC in May 1991 and were allocated in October 1991. Details of allocations were not available at time of going to press. A new independent national television channel is due to be established by the autumn of 1993.

All channels are broadcast in colour on 625 lines UHF from a network of transmitting stations which are owned and operated by National Transcommunications Ltd. Transmissions are available to more than 99 per cent of the population.

BBC Television

The BBC's experiments in television broadcasting started in 1929 and in 1936 the BBC began the world's first public service of high-definition television from Alexandra Palace.

The BBC broadcasts two national television services, BBC 1 (BBC Wales in Wales, BBC Scotland in Scotland, BBC Northern Ireland in Northern Ireland) and BBC 2.

Independent Television Companies

ANGLIA TELEVISION (*East of England*), Anglia House, Norwich. Tel: 0603-615151.

BORDER TELEVISION (*The Borders*), Television Centre, Carlisle. Tel: 0228-25101.

CENTRAL INDEPENDENT TELEVISION (*East and West Midlands*), Central House, Broad Street, Birmingham. Tel: 021-643 9898.

CHANNEL FOUR TELEVISION COMPANY LTD, 60 Charlotte Street, W1. Tel: 071-631 4444.

CHANNEL TELEVISION (*Channel Islands*), The Television Centre, St Helier, Jersey. Tel: 0534-73999.

GRAMPIAN TELEVISION (*North Scotland*), Queen's Cross, Aberdeen. Tel: 0224-646464.

GRANADA TELEVISION (*North-West England*), Granada TV Centre, Manchester. Tel: 061-832 7211.

HTV (*Wales and West of England*), HTV Wales, Television Centre, Cardiff CF5 6XJ. Tel: 0222-590590.

INDEPENDENT TELEVISION NEWS LTD, ITN House, 200 Gray's Inn Road, WC1. Tel: 071-833 3000.

LONDON WEEKEND TELEVISION (*London (weekends)*), London Television Centre, Upper Ground, SE1 9LT. Tel: 071-620 1620.

ORACLE TELETEXT LTD., Craven House, 25–32 Marshall Street, W1. Tel: 071-434 3121.

SCOTTISH TELEVISION (*Central Scotland*), Cowcaddens, Glasgow. Tel: 041-332 9999.

THAMES TELEVISION (*London (weekdays)*), Thames Television House, 306–316 Euston Road, NW1. Tel: 071-387 9494.

TSW (TELEVISION SOUTH WEST) (*South-West England*), Derry's Cross, Plymouth. Tel: 0752-663322.

TV-AM, Hawley Crescent, NW1. Tel: 071-267 4300.

TVS (TELEVISION SOUTH) (*South and South-East England*), Television Centre, Southampton. Tel: 0703-34211.

TYNE TEES TELEVISION (*North-East England*), The Television Centre, City Road, Newcastle upon Tyne. Tel: 091-261 0181.

ULSTER TELEVISION (*Northern Ireland*), Havelock House, Ormeau Road, Belfast. Tel: 0232-228122.

WELSH FOURTH CHANNEL AUTHORITY (Sianel Pedwar Cymru), Parc Ty Glas, Llanishen, Cardiff. Tel: 0222-747444.

YORKSHIRE TELEVISION (*Yorkshire*), The Television Centre, Leeds. Tel: 0532-438283.

INDEPENDENT TELEVISION ASSOCIATION, Knighton House, 56 Mortimer Street, W1N 8AN. Tel: 071-612 8000.—*Director*, D. Shaw.

BBC World Service

BBC World Service Television Ltd is a wholly-owned subsidiary of the BBC incorporated in March 1991 and initially financed by BBC Enterprises. The company took over responsibility for all the BBC's satellite television broadcasting services and brought together the BBC's European subscription channel, formerly known as *BBC TV Europe*, and the BBC World Service's plans for a global television news service. The result is a completely rescheduled channel which was launched in April 1991 and offers a range of programmes from BBC 1 and BBC 2, the global television news service and English language teaching programmes. The World Service Television News will also be sold in English and other languages to television channels and networks throughout the world.

Direct Broadcasting by Satellite Television

BRITISH SKY BROADCASTING, 6 Centaurs Business Park, Grant Way, Isleworth, Middx. TW7 5QD. Tel: 071-782 3000. Broadcasts five channels (*Sky 1, Sky News, Sky Sport, The Movie Channel* and *Sky Movies Plus*).

RADIO

The BBC provides both national and local radio services. The Radio Authority (*see* page 355) is the regulator and licenser for independent radio companies.

Under the Broadcasting Act 1990, the Radio Authority was empowered to allocate licences for three national radio stations. The first national licence was awarded to Classic FM in September 1991. Up to 30 new independent local radio licences were also offered by the Radio Authority in 1991.

BBC Radio

BBC Radio broadcasts five national services to the United Kingdom, Isle of Man and the Channel Islands plus a sixth tier consisting of national regional services in Wales, Scotland and Northern Ireland and local radio services in England and the Channel Islands. In Wales there are two regional services based on the Welsh and English languages respectively.

The national services are:

Radio 1: (Pop and rock music)—5 a.m.–2 a.m. daily. Frequencies: FM 98–99 MHz, coverage 92%; MW 1053 kHz/285m and 1089 kHz/275m, plus two local fillers.

Radio 2: (Light music, entertainment and sport)—24 hours a day. Frequency: FM 88-90.2 MHz, coverage 98%.

Radio 3: (Classical music, drama and documentaries, poetry, and cricket in season)—6.55 a.m.–12.35 a.m. daily. Frequencies: FM 90.2–92.4 MHz, population coverage 98%; MW (main centres of population only), 1215 kHz/247m, plus four local fillers on 1197 kHz/251m.

Radio 4: (News, documentaries, drama and entertainment)—5.50 a.m. to 12.45 a.m. daily. Frequencies: FM England, Channel Islands and Isle of Man, plus part of Wales, Scotland and Northern Ireland 92·4–95·8 MHz, coverage 98%; LW 198kHz/1515m, plus eight local fillers on MW.

Radio 5: (Speech radio for the family, with sport, education, children and youth programmes and elements of World Service)—6a.m.–12 midnight daily. Frequencies: MW 693 kHz/433m and 909 kHz/330m, plus three local fillers.

The national regional services are:

Radio Scotland: Frequencies: MW 810 kHz/370m plus two local fillers; FM 92–95 MHz, coverage 94%.

Local programmes on FM 92–95 MHz: *Radio Aberdeen* (also MW 990 kHz/303m); *Radio Highland; Radio nan Eilean; Radio nan Gaidheal; Radio Orkney; Radio Shetland; Radio Solway* (also MW 585 kHz/513m); *Radio Tweed.*

Radio Ulster: Frequencies: MW 1341 kHz/224m, plus one local filler; FM 92–95 MHz, coverage 97%.
Radio Foyle: Frequencies: MW 792 kHz/379m; FM 92–95 MHz.

Radio Wales: Frequency: MW 882 kHz/340m plus two local fillers giving coverage 96% (day) and 63% (night).
Radio Clwyd: Frequency: MW 657 kHz/457m.

Radio Cymru (Welsh-language): Frequencies: FM 92–95 MHz, coverage 91%.

BBC Local Radio Stations

There are 39 local stations serving England and the Channel Islands:

BEDFORDSHIRE, PO Box 476, Hastings Street, Luton LU1 5BA. Tel: 0582-459111. *Wavelengths:* 258/476m, 1161/630 kHz, 95·5/103·8/104·5 FM.

BERKSHIRE, Broadcasting House, 42a Portman Road, Reading, Berks. RG3 1NB. Tel: 0734-560070. Broadcasting from Jan. 1, 1992. *Wavelengths:* 94·6/95·4/104·1/104·4 FM.

BRISTOL, 3 Tyndalls Park Road, Bristol BS8 1PP. Tel: 0272-741111. *Wavelengths:* 194/227m, 1548/1323 kHz, 94·9/95·5/104·6 FM.

CAMBRIDGESHIRE, Broadcasting House, 104 Hills Road, Cambridge CB2 1LD. Tel: 0223-315970. *Wavelengths:* 207/292m, 1449/1026 kHz, 96·0/95·7 FM.

CLEVELAND, PO Box 1548, Broadcasting House, Newport Road, Middlesbrough, Cleveland TS1 5DG. Tel: 0642-225211. *Wavelengths:* 194m, 1548 kHz, 95·0/95·8 FM.

CORNWALL, Phoenix Wharf, Truro, Cornwall TR1 1UA. Tel: 0872-75421. *Wavelengths:* 476/457m, 630/657 kHz, 95·2/96·0/103·9 FM.

CUMBRIA, Hilltop Heights, London Road, Carlisle CA1 2NA. Tel: 0228-31661. *Wavelengths:* 397/206/358m, 756/1458/837 kHz, 95·2/95·6/96·1/104·2 FM.

CWR (COVENTRY AND WARWICKSHIRE RADIO), 25 Warwick Road, Coventry CV1 2FA. Tel: 0203-525341. *Wavelengths:* 94·8/103·7 FM.

DERBY, 56 St Helen's Street, Derby DE1 3HL. Tel: 0332-361111. *Wavelengths:* 269m, 1116 kHz, 104·5/94·2/95·3 FM.

DEVON, PO Box 100, St David's Hill, Exeter EX4 4DB. Tel: 0392-215651. *Wavelengths:* 351/303/206/375m, 855/990/1458/801 kHz, 103·4/96·0/95·8/94·8 FM.

ESSEX, PO Box 765, Chelmsford CM2 9AB. Tel: 0245-262393. *Wavelengths:* 392/196/412m, 765/729/1530 kHz, 103·5/95·3 FM.

GLOUCESTERSHIRE, London Road, Gloucester GL1 1SW. Tel: 0452-308585. *Wavelengths:* 498m, 603 kHz, 95·0/104·7 FM.

GLR (GREATER LONDON RADIO), 35A Marylebone High Street, W1A 4LG. Tel: 071-224 2424. *Wavelengths:* 206m, 1458 kHz, 94·9 FM.

GMR (GREATER MANCHESTER RADIO), New Broadcasting House, Oxford Road, Manchester M60 1SJ. Tel: 061-200 2000. *Wavelengths:* 206m, 1458 kHz, 95·1 FM.

GUERNSEY, Commerce House, Les Banques, St Peter Port, Guernsey. Tel: 0481-28977. *Wavelengths:* 269m, 1116 kHz, 93·2 FM.

HEREFORD AND WORCESTER, 43 Broad Street, Hereford HR4 9HH; and Hylton Road, Worcester WR2 5WW. Tel: 0905-748485. *Wavelengths:* 819 kHz (Hereford); 738 kHz (Worcester); 104·0/94·7/104·6 FM.

HUMBERSIDE, 9 Chapel Street, Hull HU1 3NU. Tel: 0482-23232. *Wavelengths:* 202m, 1485 kHz, 95·9 FM.

JERSEY, Broadcasting House, Rouge Bouillon, St Helier, Jersey. Tel: 0534-70000. *Wavelengths:* 292m, 1026 kHz, 88·8 FM.

KENT, Sun Pier, Chatham, Kent ME4 4EZ. Tel: 0634-830505. *Wavelengths:* 290/388/187m, 1035/774/1602 kHz, 96·7/104·2 FM.

LANCASHIRE, 20–26 Darwen Street, Blackburn BB2 2EA. Tel: 0254-62411. *Wavelengths:* 351/193m, 855/1557 kHz, 95·5/104·5/103·9 FM.

LEEDS, Broadcasting House, Woodhouse Lane, Leeds LS2 9PN. Tel: 0532-442131. *Wavelengths:* 388m, 774 kHz, 92·4/95·3 FM.

LEICESTER, Epic House, Charles Street, Leicester LE1 3SH. Tel: 0533-516688. *Wavelengths:* 358m, 837 kHz, 104·9 FM.

LINCOLNSHIRE, Radio Buildings, Newport, Lincoln LN1 3XY. Tel: 0522-511411. *Wavelengths:* 219m, 1368 kHz, 94·9 FM.

MERSEYSIDE, 55 Paradise Street, Liverpool L1 3BP. Tel: 051-708 5500. *Wavelengths:* 202m, 1485 kHz, 95·8 FM.

NEWCASTLE, Broadcasting Centre, Barrack Road, Fenham, Newcastle upon Tyne NE99 1RN. Tel: 091-232 4141. *Wavelengths:* 206m, 1458 kHz, 95·4/104·4/96·0 FM.

NORFOLK, Norfolk Tower, Surrey Street, Norwich NR13PA. Tel: 0603-617411. *Wavelengths:* 351/344m, 855/873 kHz, 95·1/104·4 FM.

NORTHAMPTON, PO Box 1107, Abington Street, Northampton NN1 2BE. Tel: 0604-239100. *Wavelengths:* 271m, 1107 kHz, 104·2/103·6 FM.

NOTTINGHAM, York House, Mansfield Road, Nottingham NG1 3JB. Tel: 0602-415161. *Wavelengths:* 197/189m, 1521/1584 kHz, 103·8/95·5 FM.

OXFORD, 269 Banbury Road, Oxford OX2 7DW. Tel: 0865-311444. *Wavelengths:* 202m, 1485 kHz, 95·2 FM.

SHEFFIELD, Ashdell Grove, 60 Westbourne Road, Sheffield S10 2QU. Tel: 0742-686185. *Wavelengths:* 290m, 1035 kHz, 104·1/88·6 FM.

SHROPSHIRE, 2–4 Boscobel Drive, Shrewsbury SY1 3TT. Tel: 0743-248484. *Wavelengths:* 189/397m, 1584/756 kHz, 95·0/96·0 FM.

SOLENT, Broadcasting House, Havelock Road, Southampton SO1 0XR. Tel: 0703-631311. *Wavelengths:* 300m, 999 kHz, 221m, 999 kHz, 1359 kHz, 96·1 FM.

STOKE-ON-TRENT, Conway House, Cheapside, Hanley, Stoke-on-Trent ST1 1JJ. Tel: 0782-208080. *Wavelengths:* 200m, 1503 kHz, 94·6 FM.

SUFFOLK, Broadcasting House, St Matthew's Street, Ipswich IP1 3EP. Tel: 0473-250000. *Wavelengths:* 103·9/104·6 FM.

SURREY, Broadcasting House, Guildford, Surrey GU125SF. Tel: 0483-306306. *Wavelength:* 104·6 FM.

SUSSEX, Marlborough Place, Brighton BN1 1TU. Tel: 0273-680231. *Wavelengths:* 202/258/219m, 1485/1161/1368 kHz, 95·3/104·5/104·0 FM.

WILTSHIRE SOUND, Broadcasting House, 56–58 Prospect Place, Swindon SN1 3RW. Tel: 0793-513626. *Wavelengths:* 1332/1368 kHz, 103·6/104·3/103·5 FM.

WM (WEST MIDLANDS), Pebble Mill Road, Birmingham B5 7SD. Tel: 021-414 8484. *Wavelengths:* 206/362m, 1458/828 kHz, 95·6 FM.

York, 20 Bootham Row, York YO3 7BR. Tel: 0904-641351. *Wavelengths*: 450/238m, 666/1260 kHz, 103·7/104·3/95·5 FM.

BBC World Service

The World Service broadcasts 796 hours of programmes a week in 36 languages including the English Service. Ninety-five transmitters are used, 44 of them in the UK and 51 at relay stations overseas. In addition the World Service supplies many recorded programmes to other radio stations.

World Service in English, 24 hours a day, directed to all parts of the world, and with additional streams of programmes specially designated for audiences in Africa and South Asia at appropriate peak listening times.

African Service, which broadcasts in Swahili, Somali and Hausa.

Arabic Service, on the air for nine hours a day to Middle East and North Africa.

Central European Service, in Czech, Slovak, Hungarian, Polish and Finnish.

Eastern Service, which broadcasts in Bengali, Burmese, Hindi, Nepali, Pashto, Persian, Sinhalese, Tamil and Urdu.

Far Eastern Service, in Chinese (Cantonese and Mandarin), Indonesian, Thai and Vietnamese.

French and Portuguese Service, directed to Europe and Africa.

German Service, directed to Germany, Austria, and German-speaking Switzerland.

Latin American Service, in Spanish and Portuguese.

Russian Service, on the air for six and a half hours a day in Russian to the USSR.

South-East European Service, in Bulgarian, Romanian, Serbo-Croat, Slovene, Greek and Turkish.

BBC English by Radio and Television teaches English to learners outside Britain through radio, television and a wide range of published courses.

Monitoring Service provides regional summaries and a teleprinted news service from the output of overseas radio stations.

Topical Tapes provides a variety of programmes on tape for overseas radio stations and produces the twice-weekly 'Calling the Falklands' programme.

Transcription Service produces and sells to overseas radio stations recorded programmes drawn from the whole range of BBC Radio.

Independent Local Radio Stations

Aire FM, PO Box 2000, Leeds LS3 1LR. Tel: 0532-452299. *Wavelength*: 96·3 FM.

Beacon Radio, 267 Tettenhall Road, Wolverhampton WV6 0DQ. Tel: 0902-757211. *Wavelength*: 97·2 FM.

Breeze AM, PO Box 300, Southend-on-Sea, Essex SS1 1SY. Tel: 0702-430966. *Wavelength*: 1359 kHz.

BRMB, PO Box 555, Aston Road North, Birmingham B6 4BX. Tel: 021-359 4481/9. *Wavelength*: 96·4 FM.

Brunel Classic Gold, PO Box 2000, Swindon SN4 7EX. Tel: 0793-279900; PO Box 2000, Bristol BS99 7SN. Tel: 0272-279900. *Wavelengths*: 1260 kHz (Bristol); 1161 kHz (Swindon); 936 kHz (West Wilts).

Buzz FM, 20 Augusta Street, Jewellery Quarter, Birmingham B18 6JA. Tel: 021-236 4888. *Wavelength*: 102·4 FM.

Capital Radio plc, Euston Tower, NW1 3DR. Tel: 071-388 1288. *Wavelengths*: 194m, 1548 kHz, 95·8 FM.

Central FM, PO Box 967, Stirling FK7 7RP. Tel: 0786-51188. *Wavelength*: 96·7 FM.

Chiltern Radio plc, Chiltern Road, Dunstable, Bedfordshire LU6 1HQ. Tel: 0582-666001. *Wavelengths*: 362m, 828 kHz, 97·6 FM (Luton), 379m, 792 kHz, 96·9 FM (Bedford).

Choice FM, 16–18 Trinity Gardens, SW9 8DP. Tel: 071-738 7969. *Wavelength*: 96·9 FM.

City Talk, PO Box 967, Liverpool L69 1TQ. Tel: 051-227 3045. *Wavelength*: 1548 kHz.

Classic Gold, PO Box 194, Hartshead, Sheffield S1 1GP. Tel: 0742-766766. *Wavelengths*: 1548 kHz (Sheffield and Rotherham); 1305 kHz (Barnsley); 990 kHz (Doncaster); 1278 kHz (Bradford); 1530 kHz (Huddersfield and Halifax); 1161 kHz (Humberside).

Classic Trax BCR, Russell Court, Claremont Street, Lisburn Road, Belfast BT9 6JX. Tel: 0232-438500. *Wavelength*: 96·7 FM.

CN FM (Cambridge and Newmarket), PO Box 1000, The Vision Park, Chivers Way, Histon, Cambridge CB4 4WW. Tel: 0223-235255. *Wavelength*: 103·0 FM.

Coast Classics, 15 Station Road East, Canterbury, Kent CT1 2RB. Tel: 0227-767661. *Wavelength*: 1242 kHz (Maidstone and Medway); 603 kHz (East Kent).

Cool FM, Newtownards, Co. Down BT23 4ES. Tel: 0247-815555. *Wavelength*: 97·4 FM.

Delta Radio, 11 Lower Street, Haslemere, Surrey GU27 2NY. Tel: 0428-61019. *Wavelength*: 97·1 FM.

DevonAir Radio, 35–37 St David's Hill, Exeter EX4 4DA. Tel: 0392-430703. *Wavelengths*: 666 kHz, 97·0 FM (Exeter); 96·4 FM (Torbay); 103 FM (East Devon); 954 kHz.

Downtown Radio, Kiltonga Industrial Estate, Newtownards, Co. Down BT23 4ES. Tel: 0247-815555. *Wavelengths*: 293m, 1026 kHz, 96·6/96·4/102·4 FM.

East End Radio, Greater Easterhouse Business Centre, 19 Blairtummock Road, Glasgow G33 4AN. Tel: 041-774 5335. *Wavelength*: 103·5 FM.

Echo 96, Studio 257, Stoke Road, Stoke-on-Trent. Tel: 0782-747047. *Wavelengths*: 96·4 FM (Cheshire); 96·9 FM (Stafford).

Essex Radio plc, Radio House, Clifftown Road, Southend-on-Sea, Essex SS1 1SX. Tel: 0702-333711. *Wavelengths*: 96·3 FM (Southend), 102·6 FM (Chelmsford).

First Gold Radio, Chertsey Road, Woking, Surrey GU21 5XY. Tel: 0483-740066. *Wavelength*: 1476 kHz.

Fox FM, Brush House, Pony Road, Horspath Estate, Cowley, Oxford OX4 2XR. Tel: 0865-748787. *Wavelengths*: 102·6 FM (Oxford); 97·4 FM (Banbury).

Galaxy Radio, 25 Portland Square, Bristol BS2 8RZ. Tel: 0272-240111. *Wavelength*: 97·2 FM.

GEM-AM, 29–31 Castle Gate, Nottingham NG1 7AP. Tel: 0602-581731. *Wavelengths*: 1260 kHz (Leicester); 999 kHz (Nottingham); 945 kHz (Derby).

Great North Radio, Long Rigg, Swalwell, Newcastle-upon-Tyne NE99 1BB. Tel: 091-496 0377. *Wavelengths*: 1152 kHz (Tyne and Wear); 1170 kHz (Teeside).

GWR FM (West), PO Box 2000, Bristol BS99 7SN. Tel: 0272-279900. *Wavelength*: 96·3 FM.

GWR FM (East), PO Box 2000, Swindon SN4 7EX. Tel: 0793-853222. *Wavelengths*: 96·5 FM (Marlborough); 97·2 FM (Swindon); 102·2 FM (West Wilts).

Hallam FM, PO Box 194, Hartshead, Sheffield S1 1GP. Tel: 0742-766766. *Wavelengths*: 97·4 FM (Sheffield); 96·1 FM (Rotherham); 102·9 FM (Barnsley); 103·4 FM (Doncaster).

Hereward Radio Ltd, PO Box 225, Queensgate Centre, Peterborough PE1 1XJ. Tel: 0733-46225. *Wavelengths*: 225m, 1332 kHz, 102·7 FM.

Horizon Radio, Broadcast Centre, Crownhill, Milton Keynes, Bucks. MK8 0AB. Tel: 0908-269111. *Wavelength*: 103·3 FM.

INVICTA FM, Radio House, John Wilson Business Park, Whitstable, Kent CT5 3TX. Tel: 0227-772004. *Wavelengths*: 102·8/95·9/97·0/96·1/103·1 FM.

ISLE OF WIGHT RADIO, Dodnor Park, Newport, Isle of Wight PO30 5EX. Tel: 0983-822557. *Wavelength*: 1242 kHz.

JAZZ FM, 26–27 Castlereagh Street, W1H 5YR. Tel: 071-706 4100. *Wavelength*: 102·2 FM.

KCBC (Kettering), PO Box 1530, Kettering, Northants. NN16 8PU. Tel: 0536-412413. *Wavelength*: 1530 kHz.

KFM (Stockport), Regent House, Heaton Lane, Stockport SK4 1BX. Tel: 061-480 5445. *Wavelength*: 104·9 FM.

KISS FM, Kiss House, 80 Holloway Road, N7 8JG. Tel: 071-700 6100. *Wavelength*: 100·0 FM.

LBC NEWSTALK (London Broadcasting Company Ltd), Crown House, 72 Hammersmith Road, W14 8YE. Tel: 071-603 2400. *Wavelength*: 97·3 FM.

LONDON GREEK RADIO, Florentia Village, Vale Road, N4 1TD. Tel: 081-800 8001. *Wavelength*: 103·3 FM.

LONDON TALKBACK RADIO, Crown House, 72 Hammersmith Road, W14 8YE. Tel: 071-333 0003. *Wavelength*: 1152 kHz.

MAGIC 828, PO Box 2000, Leeds LS3 1LR. Tel: 0532-452299. *Wavelength*: 828 kHz.

MARCHER SOUND/SAIN-Y-GORORAU, The Studios, Mold Road, Gwersyllt, Wrexham, Clwyd LL11 4AF. Tel: 0978-752202. *Wavelengths*: 238m, 1260 kHz.

MAX AM, Forth House, Forth Street, Edinburgh EH1 3LF. Tel: 031-556 9255. *Wavelength*: 1548 kHz.

MELLOW 1557, PO Box 1557, Colchester, Essex. Tel: 0255-675303. *Wavelength*: 1557 kHz.

MELODY RADIO, 180 Brompton Road, SW3 1HF. Tel: 071-584 1049. *Wavelength*: 104·9 FM.

MERCIA FM, Hertford Place, Coventry CV1 3TT. Tel: 0203-633933. *Wavelengths*: 97·0/102·9 FM.

METRO FM, Long Rigg, Swalwell, Newcastle upon Tyne. Tel: 091-488 3131. *Wavelengths*: 97·1/103·0 FM.

MFM, The Studios, Mold Road, Wrexham, Clwyd LL11 4AF. Tel: 0978-752202. *Wavelengths*: 103·4/97·1 FM.

MORAY FIRTH RADIO LTD, PO Box 271, Inverness IV3 6SF. Tel: 0463-224433. *Wavelengths*: 271m, 1107 kHz, 97·4 FM.

NORTHANTS RADIO, PO Box 96·6, Northampton NN1 2NR. Tel: 0733-46225. *Wavelength*: 96·6 FM.

NORTH SOUND RADIO, 45 Kings Gate, Aberdeen AB2 6BL. Tel: 0224-632234. *Wavelengths*: 290m, 1035 kHz, 96·9 FM.

OCEAN SOUND CLASSIC HITS, Radio House,, Whittle Avenue, Segensworth West, Fareham, Hants. PO15 5PA. Tel: 0489-589911. *Wavelengths*: 97·5/96·7 FM.

ORCHARD FM, Haygrove House, Shoreditch, Taunton TA3 7BT. Tel: 0823-338448. *Wavelength*: 102·6 FM.

PENNINE FM, PO Box 235, Pennine House, Forster Square, Bradford BD1 5NP. Tel: 0274-731521. *Wavelengths*: 97·5 FM (Bradford), 102·5 FM (Huddersfield, Halifax).

PICCADILLY RADIO LTD, 127-131 The Piazza, Piccadilly Plaza, Manchester M1 4AW. Tel: 061-236 9913. *Wavelengths*: 261m, 1152 kHz, 103·0 FM.

PLYMOUTH SOUND LTD, Earl's Acre, Alma Road, Plymouth PL3 4HX. Tel: 0752-27272. *Wavelengths*: 261m, 1152 kHz, 97·0 FM.

POWERFM, Radio House, Whittle Avenue, Segensworth West, Fareham, Hants. PO15 5PA. Tel: 0489-589911. *Wavelength*: 103·2 FM.

PREMIER RADIO, The Friary, Guildford, Surrey GU1 4YX. Tel: 0483-740066. *Wavelength*: 96·4 FM.

RADIO BORDERS, Tweedside Park, Galashiels TD1 3TD. Tel: 0896-59444. *Wavelengths*: 96·8/97·5/103·1/103·4 FM.

RADIO BROADLAND, St George's Plain, 47–49 Colegate, Norwich. Tel: 0603-630621. *Wavelengths*: 260m, 1152 kHz, 102·4 FM.

RADIO CITY, PO Box 967, Liverpool L69 1TQ. Tel: 051 227 5100. *Wavelength*: 96·7 FM.

RADIO CLYDE, Clydebank Business Park, Clydebank Glasgow G81 2RX. Tel: 041-306 2200. *Wavelengths* 261m, 1152 kHz, 102·5 FM.

RADIO FORTH RFM, Forth House, Forth Street Edinburgh EH1 3LF. Tel: 031-556 9255. *Wave lengths*: 97·3 FM.

RADIO HARMONY, Ringway House, Hill Street, Cov entry CV1 4AN. Tel: 0203-525656. *Wavelength* 102·6 FM.

RADIO IN TAVISTOCK, 3A North Street, Tavistock Devon PL19 4AN. Tel: 0752-227272. *Wavelength* 96·6 FM.

RADIO MERCURY, Broadfield House, Brighton Road Crawley, W. Sussex RH11 9TT. Tel: 0293-51916] *Wavelengths*: 197m, 1521 kHz, 102·7, 97·5 FM.

RADIO ORWELL LTD, Electric House, Lloyds Avenue Ipswich IP1 3HZ. Tel: 0473-216971. *Wavelengths* 257m, 1170 kHz, 97·1 FM.

RADIO TAY, PO Box 123, 6 North Islast, Dundee DD 9UF. Tel: 0382-200800. *Wavelengths*: 258m, 116 kHz, 102·8 FM (Dundee); 189m, 1584 kHz, 96·4 FM (Perth).

RADIO TFM, 74 Dovecot Street, Stockton-on-Tees Cleveland TS18 1HB. Tel: 0642-615111. *Wavelength* 96·6 FM.

RADIO WYVERN, 5–6 Barbourne Terrace, Worceste WR1 3JZ. Tel: 0905-612212. *Wavelengths*: 314m, 95 kHz, 97·6 FM (Hereford), 196m, 1530 kHz, 102·8 FM (Worcester).

RED DRAGON FM, Radio House, West Canal Wharf Cardiff CF1 5XJ. Tel: 0222-384041. *Wavelengths* 97·4/103·2 FM.

RED ROSE GOLD, PO Box 301, St Paul's Square Preston, Lancashire PR1 1YE. Tel: 0772-556301 *Wavelengths*: 301m, 999 kHz, 97·4 FM.

RTM, 19 Tavy Bridge, Thamesmead, SE2 9UG. Tel 081-311 3112. *Wavelength*: 103·8 FM.

SAXON RADIO, Long Brackland, Bury St Edmunds Suffolk IP33 1JY. Tel: 0284-701511. *Wavelengths* 240m, 1251 kHz, 96·4 FM.

SEVERN SOUND, Old Talbot House, 67 Southgat Street, Gloucester GL1 2DQ. Tel: 0452-423791 *Wavelengths*: 103·0/102·4 FM.

SIGNAL RADIO, Studio 257, Stoke Road, Stoke-on Trent. Tel: 0782-747047. *Wavelengths*: 257m, 117 kHz, 102·6 FM.

SOUND FM, Granville House, Granville Road, Leices ter LE1 7RW. Tel: 0533-551616. *Wavelength*: 103·2 FM.

SOUTH COAST RADIO, Radio House, Whittle Avenue Segensworth West, Fareham, Hants. PO15 5PA Tel: 0489-589453; Radio House, PO Box 200C Brighton BN41 2SS. Tel: 0273-430111. *Wavelengths* 1170/1557/1323 kHz.

SOUTHERN SOUND CLASSIC HITS, Radio House, PC Box 2000, Brighton BN41 2SS. Tel: 0273-430111 *Wavelengths*: 103·5 FM (Brighton); 96·9 FM (Newhaven); 102·4 FM (Eastbourne); 97·5 FM (Hastings).

SOUTH WEST SOUND, Campbell House, Bankend Road Dumfries DG1 4TH. Tel: 0387-50999. *Wavelength* 97·2 FM.

SPECTRUM INTERNATIONAL RADIO, Endeavour House Brent Cross, NW2 1JT. Tel: 081-905 5000. *Wave length*: 558 kHz.

SUNRISE FM, Chapel Street, Little Germany, Brad ford BD1 5DN. Tel: 081-905 5000. *Wavelength*: 103·2 FM.

SUNRISE RADIO, PO Box 212, Hounslow, Middx. TW3 2AD. Tel: 081-569 6666. *Wavelength*: 1413 kHz.

SUNSET RADIO, 23 New Mount Street, Manchester M4 4DE. Tel: 061-953 5353. *Wavelength*: 102·0 FM.

SWANSEA SOUND, Victoria Road, Gowerton, Swansea SA4 3AB. Tel: 0792-893751. *Wavelengths*: 257m, 1170 kHz, 96·4 FM.

'HREE COUNTIES RADIO, Old Talbot House, 67 South-gate Street, Gloucester GL1 2DQ. Tel: 0452-423791. *Wavelength*: 774 kHz.

'RENT-FM (DERBY), The Market Place, Derby DE1 3AA. Tel: 0332-292945. *Wavelength*: 102·8 FM.

'RENT-FM (NOTTINGHAM), 29–31 Castle Gate, Nottingham NG1 7AP. Tel: 0602-581731. *Wavelengths*: 96·2/96·5 FM.

'OUCH AM, PO Box 99, Cardiff CF1 5YJ. Tel: 0222-237878. *Wavelengths*: 1359 kHz (Cardiff); 1305 kHz (Newport).

'CR CLASSIC GOLD, 5–7 Southcote Road, Bournemouth BH1 3LR. Tel: 0202-294881. *Wavelengths*: 362m, 828 kHz, 102·3 FM.

10 CLASSIC GOLD RADIO, PO Box 2020, Reading, Berks. RG3 5RZ. Tel: 0734-413131. *Wavelength*: 1431 kHz.

10 FM, PO Box 210, Reading, Berks. RG3 5RZ. Tel: 0734-413131. *Wavelengths*: 97·0 FM (Reading); 102·9 FM (Basingstoke and Andover).

VIKING FM, Commercial Road, Hull HU1 2SG. Tel: 0482-25141. *Wavelength*: 96·9 FM.

WABC, 267 Tettenhall Road, Wolverhampton WV6 0DQ. Tel: 0902-757211. *Wavelengths*: 990 kHz (Wolverhampton); 1017 kHz (Shrewsbury/Telford).

WEAR FM, Forster Building, Sunderland Polytechnic, Chester Road, Tyne and Wear SR1 3SD. Tel: 091-515 2103. *Wavelength*: 103·4 FM.

WEST SOUND RADIO, Radio House, 54 Holmston Road, Ayr. Tel: 0292-283662. *Wavelengths*: 290m, 1035 kHz, 96·7 FM.

WNK, 185B High Road, Wood Green, N22 6BA. Tel: 081-889 1547. *Wavelength*: 103·3 FM.

XTRA-AM, PO Box 555, Aston Road North, Birmingham B6 4BX. Tel: 021-359 4481. *Wavelengths*: 1152 kHz (Birmingham); 1359 kHz (Coventry).

ASSOCIATION OF INDEPENDENT RADIO COMPANIES, 46 Westbourne Grove, W2 5SH. Tel: 071-727 2646.— *Director*, B. West.

THE BROADCASTING COMPLAINTS COMMISSION
Grosvenor Gardens House, 35–37 Grosvenor Gardens, SW1W 0BS
[071–630 1966]

The Broadcasting Complaints Commission's function and authority derive from the Broadcasting Act 990. Its task is to consider and adjudicate upon omplaints of unjust or unfair treatment in sound or television programmes broadcast by the BBC, S4C, he Independent Television Commission, the Radio uthority or their licensees as appropriate. This unction extends to all sound, television and cable dvertisements and teletext transmissions, and pro-rammes broadcast by the BBC's World Services.

The Members of the Commission are appointed by the Home Secretary.

Chairman, Lady Anglesey, DBE.
Members, D. Allen, CB; T. Christopher, CBE; D. Holmes; Mrs B. Wells.
Legal Adviser, Sir Basil Hall, KCB, MC, TD.
Secretary, R. D. Hewlett.

SERVICES SOUND AND VISION CORPORATION
(Incorporating BFBS)
Chalfont Grove, Gerrards Cross, Bucks. SL9 8TN
[02407–4461]

The Services Sound and Vision Corporation 3SVC) is the official organization providing the Ministry of Defence, HM Forces and their families ith radio and television broadcasting, audio-visual nd electronic training and educational support, aining film production, and entertainment. The SVC is a private limited company and registered narity with 1,100 employees and an annual turnover pproaching £40 million; financial surpluses are onated to Services' welfare.

The Corporation's radio arm (British Forces Broad-asting Service) operates stations in London, Ger-any, Gibraltar, Cyprus, the Falklands, Hong Kong, runei and Belize. BFBS provides programmes from ondon for inclusion with local input by its overseas taff, and broadcasts to overseas stations by satellite hroughout the year.

SSVC television broadcasts its own, BBC and ITV rogrammes in Germany, Cyprus and the Falkland

Islands. Up to 60 isolated detachments of HM Forces (including ships at sea and the Service Children's Education Authority schools overseas), receive daily TV programmes on cassette.

In-flight films on RAF long-haul passenger services are organized by SSVC, and Combined Services Entertainment provides stage shows to such isolated garrisons and units as the Falklands and Ascension Islands. SSVC also operates cinemas around the world. Training films are produced by SSVC's own crews and studios.

Audio-visual rentals and sales are provided through SSVC's Sound and Vision Centre shops in Germany and at home.

All SSVC services are available to other organizations and are provided to overseas governments and many UK companies.

Managing Director, A. Protheroe, CBE, TD.

PRINCIPAL NEWSPAPERS

DAILY NEWSPAPERS

National

DAILY EXPRESS, Ludgate House, 245 Blackfriars Road, SE1 9UX.

DAILY MAIL, Northcliffe House, 2 Derry Street, W8 5TT.

DAILY MIRROR, Holborn Circus, EC1P 1DQ.

DAILY SPORT, 3rd Floor, Marten House, 39–47 East Road, N1 6AH

DAILY TELEGRAPH, Peterborough Court at South Quay, 181 Marsh Wall, E14 9SR.

FINANCIAL TIMES, 1 Southwark Bridge, SE1 9HL.

THE GUARDIAN, 119 Farringdon Road, EC1R 3ER.

THE INDEPENDENT, 40 City Road, EC1Y 2DB.

MORNING STAR, 74 Luke Street, EC2A 4PY.

RACING POST, 112–120 Coombe Lane, SW20 0BA.

THE SPORTING LIFE, Orbit House, 1 New Fetter Lane, EC4A 1AR.

THE STAR, Ludgate House, 245 Blackfriars Road, SE1 9UX.

THE SUN, Virginia Street, E1 9BD.

THE TIMES, 1 Pennington Street, E1 9XN.

TODAY, 70 Vauxhall Bridge Road, SW1V 2RP.

Regional

Aberdeen—PRESS AND JOURNAL, and EVENING EXPRESS, PO Box 43, Lang Stracht, Mastrick, AB9 8AF.

Barrow-in-Furness—NORTH-WEST EVENING MAIL, Newspaper House, Abbey Road, LA14 5QS.

Bath—BATH EVENING CHRONICLE, 33–34 Westgate Street, BA1 1EW.

Belfast—BELFAST TELEGRAPH, 124–144 Royal Avenue, BT1 1EB; IRISH NEWS AND BELFAST MORNING NEWS, 113–117 Donegall Street, BT1 2GE; NEWS LETTER, 51–59 Donegall Street, BT1 2GB.

Birmingham—THE BIRMINGHAM POST, and BIRMINGHAM EVENING MAIL, PO Box 18, 28 Colmore Circus, Queensway, B4 6AX.

Blackburn—LANCASHIRE EVENING TELEGRAPH, Telegraph House, High Street, BB1 1HT.

Blackpool—WEST LANCASHIRE EVENING GAZETTE, PO Box 20, FY4 4AU.

Bolton—BOLTON EVENING NEWS, Newspaper House, Churchgate, BL1 1DE.

Bournemouth—EVENING ECHO, Richmond Hill, BH2 6HH.

Bradford—TELEGRAPH AND ARGUS, Hall Ings, BD1 1JR.

Brighton—EVENING ARGUS, Argus House, 89 North Road, BN1 4AU.

Bristol—BRISTOL EVENING POST, and WESTERN DAILY PRESS, Temple Way, BS99 7HD.

Burton-on-Trent—BURTON MAIL, 65–68 High Street, DE14 1LE.

Cambridge—CAMBRIDGE EVENING NEWS, 51 Newmarket Road, CB5 8EJ.

Cardiff—SOUTH WALES ECHO, and WESTERN MAIL, Thomson House, Havelock Street, CF1 1WR.

Cheltenham—GLOUCESTERSHIRE ECHO, 1 Clarence Parade, GL50 3NZ.

Colchester—EVENING GAZETTE, Oriel House, 43–44 North Hill, CO1 1TZ.

Coventry—COVENTRY EVENING TELEGRAPH, Corporation Street, CV1 1FP.

Darlington—NORTHERN ECHO, Priestgate, DL1 1NP.

Derby—DERBY EVENING TELEGRAPH, Northcliff House, Meadow Road, DE1 2DW.

Dundee—COURIER AND ADVERTISER, and EVENING TELEGRAPH AND POST, 7 Bank Street, DD1 9HU.

Edinburgh—THE SCOTSMAN, and EVENING NEWS, 20 North Bridge, EH1 1YT.

Exeter—EXPRESS AND ECHO, Sidwell House, Sidwell Street, EX4 6RS.

Glasgow—DAILY RECORD, 40 Anderston Quay, G3 8DA; GLASGOW HERALD, and EVENING TIMES, 195 Albion Street, G1 1QP.

Gloucester—THE GLOUCESTERSHIRE CITIZEN, St John's Lane, GL1 2AY.

Greenock—GREENOCK TELEGRAPH, 2 Crawfurd Street, PA15 1LH.

Grimsby—GRIMSBY EVENING TELEGRAPH, 80 Cleethorpe Road, DN31 3EH.

Guernsey—GUERNSEY EVENING PRESS AND STAR, PO Box 57, Braye Road, Vale.

Halifax—EVENING COURIER, PO Box 19, Courier Buildings, HX1 2SF.

Hartlepool—HARTLEPOOL MAIL, Clarence Road, TS24 8BU.

Huddersfield—HUDDERSFIELD DAILY EXAMINER, Ramsden Street, HD1 2TD.

Hull—HULL DAILY MAIL, Blundell's Corner, Beverley Road, HU3 1XS.

Ipswich—EAST ANGLIAN DAILY TIMES, and EVENING STAR, 30 Lower Brook Street, IP4 1AN.

Jersey—JERSEY EVENING POST, PO Box 582, Five Oaks, St Saviour.

Kettering—NORTHAMPTONSHIRE EVENING TELEGRAPH, Northfield Avenue, NN16 9JN.

Leeds—YORKSHIRE EVENING POST, and YORKSHIRE POST, Wellington Street, LS1 1RF.

Leicester—LEICESTER MERCURY, St George Street, LE1 9FQ.

Lincoln—LINCOLNSHIRE ECHO, Brayford Wharf East, LN5 7AT.

Liverpool—DAILY POST, and LIVERPOOL ECHO, PO Box 48, Old Hall Street, L69 3EB.

London—THE LONDON EVENING STANDARD, Northcliffe House, 2 Derry Street, W8 5HY.

Maidstone—KENT EVENING POST, New Hythe Lane, Larkfield, ME20 6SG.

Manchester—MANCHESTER EVENING NEWS, 164 Deansgate, M60 2RD.

Middlesbrough—EVENING GAZETTE, Gazette Building, Borough Road, TS1 3AZ.

Newcastle upon Tyne—EVENING CHRONICLE, and THE JOURNAL, Thomson House, Groat Market, NE1 1ED.

Newport—SOUTH WALES ARGUS, Cardiff Road, Maesglas, NP9 1QW.

Northampton—CHRONICLE AND ECHO, Upper Mounts, NN1 3HR.

Norwich—EASTERN DAILY PRESS, and EASTERN EVENING NEWS, Prospect House, Rouen Road, NR1 1RE.

Nottingham—EVENING POST, Forman Street, NG1 4AB.

Nuneaton—NUNEATON EVENING TRIBUNE, Watling House, Whitacre Road, CV11 6BJ.

Oldham—EVENING CHRONICLE, 172 Union Street, OL1 1EQ.

Oxford—OXFORD MAIL, Newspaper House, Osney Mead, OX2 0EJ.

Paisley—PAISLEY DAILY EXPRESS, Hellenic House, 87–97 Bath Street, Glasgow, G2 2DZ.

Peterborough—PETERBOROUGH EVENING TELEGRAPH, Telegraph House, Priestgate, PE1 1JW.

Plymouth—WESTERN MORNING NEWS, and EVENING HERALD, 65 New George Street, PL1 1RE.

Portsmouth—THE NEWS, The News Centre, Hilsea, PO2 9SX.

Preston—LANCASHIRE EVENING POST, Oliver's Place, Fulwood, PR2 4ZA.

Reading—EVENING POST, 8 Tessa Road, RG1 8NS.

Scarborough—SCARBOROUGH EVENING NEWS, 17–23 Aberdeen Walk, YO11 1BB.

Scunthorpe—SCUNTHORPE EVENING TELEGRAPH, Telegraph House, Doncaster Road, DN15 7RE.

Sheffield—THE STAR, York Street, S1 1PU.

South Shields—SHIELDS GAZETTE, Chapter Row, NE33 1BL.

Southampton—SOUTHERN EVENING ECHO, 45 Above Bar, SO9 7BA.

Stoke-on-Trent—EVENING SENTINEL, Sentinel House, Etruria, ST1 5SS.

Sunderland—SUNDERLAND ECHO, Pennywell Industrial Estate, SR4 9ER.

Swansea—SOUTH WALES EVENING POST, Adelaide Street, SA1 1QT.

Swindon—EVENING ADVERTISER, Newspaper House, 100 Victoria Road, SN1 3BE.

Telford—SHROPSHIRE STAR, Ketley, TF1 4HU.

Torquay—HERALD EXPRESS, Harmsworth House, Barton Hill Road, TQ2 8JN.

Weymouth—DORSET EVENING ECHO, 57 St Thomas Street, DT4 8EU.

Wolverhampton—EXPRESS AND STAR, 51–53 Queen Street, WV1 3BU.

Worcester—EVENING NEWS, Hylton Road, WR2 5JX.

York—YORKSHIRE EVENING PRESS, PO Box 29, 76–78 Walmgate, YO1 1YN.

WEEKLY NEWSPAPERS

THE EUROPEAN—Orbit House, 5 New Fetter Lane, EC4A 1AP.

THE INDEPENDENT ON SUNDAY—40 City Road, EC1Y 2DB.

THE MAIL ON SUNDAY—Northcliffe House, 2 Derry Street, W8 5TS.

NEWS OF THE WORLD—Virginia Street, E1 9XR.

THE OBSERVER—Chelsea Bridge House, Queenstown Road, SW8 4NN.

THE PEOPLE—Holborn Circus, EC1P 1DQ.

SCOTLAND ON SUNDAY—20 North Bridge, Edinburgh EH1 1YT.

SUNDAY EXPRESS—Ludgate House, 245 Blackfriars Road, SE1 9UX.

SUNDAY MAIL—40 Anderston Quay, Glasgow G3 8DA.

SUNDAY MIRROR—Holborn Circus, EC1P 1DQ.

SUNDAY NEWS—51–59 Donegall Street, Belfast BT1 2GB.

SUNDAY POST—Courier Place, Dundee DD1 9QJ.

SUNDAY SPORT—3rd Floor, Marten House, 39–47 East Road, N1 6AH.

SUNDAY TELEGRAPH—Peterborough Court at South Quay, 181 Marsh Wall, E14 9SR.

THE SUNDAY TIMES—1 Pennington Street, E1 9XW.

RELIGIOUS PAPERS

Alt. = Alternate; *M.* = Monthly; *W.* = Weekly

BAPTIST TIMES—PO Box 54, 129 The Broadway, Didcot, Oxon OX11 8XB. *W.*

CATHOLIC HERALD—Herald House, Lamb's Passage, Bunhill Row, EC1Y 8TQ. *W.*

CHALLENGE : THE GOOD NEWS PAPER—Revenue Buildings, Chapel Road, Worthing, W. Sussex BN11 1BQ. *M.*

CHRISTIAN HERALD—Herald House, 96 Dominion Road, Worthing, W. Sussex BN14 8JP. *W.*

CHRISTIAN WEEK—77–79 Farringdon Road, EC1M 3JY. *W.*

CHURCH OF ENGLAND NEWSPAPER—77–79 Farringdon Road, EC1M 3JY. *W.*

CHURCH OF IRELAND GAZETTE—36 Bachelor's Walk, Lisburn, Co. Antrim, BT28 1XN. *W.*

CHURCH TIMES—33 Upper Street, N1 0PW. *W.*

ENGLISH CHURCHMAN—Mill Lane House, Margate, Kent CT9 1ND. *Alt. W.*

THE FRIEND—Drayton House, 30 Gordon Street, WC1H 0BQ. *W.*

THE INQUIRER—1–6 Essex Street, WC2R 3HY. *Alt. W.*

JEWISH CHRONICLE—25 Furnival Street, EC4A 1JT. *W.*

JEWISH GAZETTE—27 Bury Old Road, Prestwich, Manchester M25 8EY. *W.*

JEWISH TELEGRAPH—Telegraph House, 11 Park Hill, Bury Old Road, Prestwich, Manchester M25 8HH. *W.*

LIFE AND WORK—Church of Scotland, 121 George Street, Edinburgh EH2 4QS. *M.*

METHODIST RECORDER—122 Golden Lane, EC1Y 0TL. *W.*

THE NEW DAY MAGAZINE—1st Floor, St James Building, Oxford Street, Manchester M1 6FP. *M.*

ORTHODOX NEWS—64 Prebend Gardens, W6 0XU. *Alt. M.*

REFORM—86 Tavistock Place, WC1H 9RT. *M.*

THE TABLET—48 Great Peter Street, SW1P 2HB. *W.*

THE WAR CRY—101 Queen Victoria Street, EC4P 4EP. *W.*

PERIODICALS, MAGAZINES AND REVIEWS

Alt. = Alternate; *M.* = Monthly; *Q.* = Quarterly; *W.* = Weekly

AMATEUR GARDENING—Westover House, West Quay Road, Poole, Dorset BH15 1JG. *W.*

AMATEUR PHOTOGRAPHER—Prospect House, 9–13 Ewell Road, Cheam, Surrey SM1 4QQ. *W.*

ANGLER'S MAIL—King's Reach Tower, Stamford Street, SE1 9LS. *W.*

ANTIQUARIES JOURNAL—Oxford University Press, Pinkhill House, Southfield Road, Eynsham, Oxford OX8 1JJ. *Twice a year.*

THE ANTIQUE COLLECTOR—National Magazine House, 72 Broadwick Street, W1V 2BP. *M.*

APOLLO MAGAZINE—3 St James's Place, SW1A 1NP. *M.*

ARENA—The Old Laundry, Ossington Buildings, Moxon Street, W1M 3HX. *Alt. M.*

THE ARTIST—Caxton House, 63–65 High Street, Tenterden, Kent TN30 6BD. *M.*

AUTOCAR AND MOTOR—38–42 Hampton Road, Teddington, Middx. TW11 0JE. *W.*

BELLA—2nd Floor, Shirley House, 25–27 Camden Road, NW1 9LL. *W.*

BEST—10th Floor, Portland House, Stag Place, SW1E 5AU. *W.*

BIRDS—RSPB, The Lodge, Sandy, Beds. SG19 2DL. *Q.*

BLITZ—40–42 Newman Street, W1P 3PA. *M.*

BOXING NEWS—PO Box 300, SW15 5QF. *W.*

BRAIN—Oxford University Press, Pinkhill House, Southfield Road, Eynsham, Oxford OX8 1JJ. *Alt. M.*

BRIDES & SETTING UP HOME—Vogue House, Hanover Square, W1R 0AD. *Alt. M.*

BRITISH BIRDS—Fountains, Park Lane, Blunham, Bedford MK44 3NJ. *M.*

BRITISH BOOK NEWS—The British Council, 65 Davies Street, W1Y 2AA. *M.*

THE BURLINGTON MAGAZINE—6 Bloomsbury Square, WC1A 2LP. *M.*

BUSES EXTRA—Terminal House, Station Approach, Shepperton, Middx. TW17 8AS. *M.*

CAGE AND AVIARY BIRDS—Prospect House, 9–13 Ewell Road, Cheam, Surrey SM1 4QQ. *W.*

CAMPING & CARAVANNING—11 Lower Grosvenor Place, SW1W 0EY. *M.*

CARAVAN MAGAZINE—Link House, Dingwall Avenue, Croydon CR9 2TA. *M.*

CARIBBEAN TIMES—139–149 Fonthill Road, N4 3HF. *W.*

CHAT—King's Reach Tower, Stamford Street, SE1 9LS. *W.*

CLASSICAL QUARTERLY—Oxford University Press, Pinkhill House, Southfield Road, Eynsham, Oxford OX8 1JJ. *Twice a Year.*

CLASSICAL REVIEW—Oxford University Press, Pinkhill House, Southfield Road, Eynsham, Oxford OX8 1JJ. *Twice a Year.*

CLOTHES SHOW MAGAZINE—20–26 Brunswick Place, N1 6DJ. *Alt. M.*

COAL NEWS—Hobart House, Grosvenor Place, SW1X 7AE. *M.*

COIN MONTHLY—Sovereign House, Brentwood, Essex CM14 4SE. *M.*

COIN NEWS—84 High Street, Honiton, Devon EX14 8JW. *M.*

COMPANY—72 Broadwick Street, W1V 2BP. *M.*

CONTEMPORARY REVIEW—61 Carey Street, WC2A 2JG. *M.*

COSMOPOLITAN—72 Broadwick Street, W1V 2BP. *M.*

COUNTRY HOMES AND INTERIORS—King's Reach Tower, Stamford Street, SE1 9LS. *M.*

COUNTRY LIFE—King's Reach Tower, Stamford Street, SE1 9LS. *W.*

COUNTRY LIVING—72 Broadwick Street, W1V 2BP. *Alt. M.*

THE COUNTRYMAN—23–27 Tudor Street, EC4Y 0HR. *Alt. M.*

CRICKETER INTERNATIONAL—Beech Hanger, Ashurst, Tunbridge Wells, Kent TN3 9ST. *M.*

CRIMINOLOGIST—Little London, Chichester, W. Sussex PO19 1PG. *Q.*

CYCLING WEEKLY—Prospect House, 9–13 Ewell Road, Cheam, Surrey SM1 4QQ. *W.*

DALTONS WEEKLY—CI Tower, St George's Square, New Malden, Surrey KT3 4JA. *W.*

DANCE AND DANCERS—4th Floor, Centro House, Mandela Street, NW1 0DU. *M.*

DANCING TIMES—Clerkenwell House, 45–47 Clerkenwell Green, EC1R 0BE. *M.*

DOG WORLD—9 Tufton Street, Ashford, Kent TN23 1QN. *W.*

DO IT YOURSELF—Link House, Dingwall Avenue, Croydon CR9 2TA. *M.*

ECONOMIC JOURNAL—108 Cowley Road, Oxford OX4 1JF. *Q.*

ECONOMICA—108 Cowley Road, Oxford OX4 1JF. *Alt. M.*

THE ECONOMIST—25 St James's Street, SW1A 1HG. *W.*

EDINBURGH GAZETTE (*Official*)—HMSO, PO Box 276, London SW8 5DT. *Alt. W.*

ELLE—Rex House, 4–12 Lower Regent Street, SW1Y 4PE. *M.*

EMPIRE—42 Great Portland Street, W1N 5AH. *M.*

THE ENGLISH HISTORICAL REVIEW—Longman House, Burnt Mill, Harlow, Essex CM20 2JE. *Q.*

ESQUIRE—72 Broadwick Street, W1V 2BP. *M.*

ESSENTIALS—Garden House, 57–59 Long Acre, WC2E 9JL. *M.*

EVERYWOMAN—34 Islington Green, N1 8DU. *M.*

EXCHANGE AND MART—Link House, West Street, Poole, Dorset BH15 1LL. *W.*

THE FACE—The Old Laundry, Ossington Buildings, Moxon Street, W1M 3HX. *M.*

FAMILY CIRCLE—King's Reach Tower, Stamford Street, SE1 9LS. *Thirteen times a year.*

THE FIELD—10 Sheet Street, Windsor, Berks. SL4 1BG. *M.*

GARDEN NEWS—Apex House, Oundle Road, Peterborough PE2 0UW. *W.*

GEOGRAPHICAL MAGAZINE—Hyde Park House, 5 Manfred Road, SW15 2RS. *M.*

GOLF ILLUSTRATED WEEKLY—37 Mill Harbour, E14 9TX. *Alt. W.*

GOLF MONTHLY—King's Reach Tower, Stamford Street, SE1 9LS. *M.*

GOOD HOUSEKEEPING—72 Broadwick Street, W1V 2BP. *M.*

GOOD MOTORING—Station Road, Forest Row, East Sussex RH18 5EN. *Alt. M.*

GQ—Vogue House, Hanover Square, W1R 0AD. *M.*

GRAMOPHONE—177–179 Kenton Road, Harrow, Middx. HA3 0HA. *M.*

GRANTA—44A Hobson Street, Cambridge CB1 1NL. *Q.*

GREECE AND ROME—Oxford University Press, Pinkhill House, Southfield Road, Eynsham, Oxford OX8 1JJ. *Twice a year.*

GUIDING—17–19 Buckingham Palace Road, SW1W 0PT. *M.*

HANSARD—*see* Parliamentary Debates.

HARPERS AND QUEEN—72 Broadwick Street, W1V 2BP. *M.*

HELLO—30–34 New Bridge Street, EC4V 6HH. *W.*

HIGH MAGAZINE—164 Barker Road, Leicester LE2 2LD. *M.*

HISTORY—108 Cowley Road, Oxford OX4 1JF. *Three times a year.*

HISTORY TODAY—83–84 Berwick Street, W1V 3PJ. *M.*

HOMES AND GARDENS—King's Reach Tower, Stamford Street, SE1 9LS. *M.*

HOMOEOPATHY—27A Devonshire Street, W1N 1RJ. *Alt. M.*

HORSE AND HOUND—King's Reach Tower, Stamford Street, SE1 9LS. *W.*

HOUSE AND GARDEN—Vogue House, Hanover Square, W1R 0AD. *M.*

I-D MAGAZINE—134–146 Curtain Road, EC4A 3AR. *M.*

IDEAL HOME—King's Reach Tower, Stamford Street, SE1 9LS. *M.*

ILLUSTRATED LONDON NEWS—Laurence House, 91–93 Southwark Street, SE1 0HX. *Alt. M.*

IN BRITAIN—BTA, Thames Tower, Black's Road, W6 9EL. *M.*

INTERNATIONAL AFFAIRS—Cambridge University Press, The Edinburgh Building, Shaftesbury Road, Cambridge CB2 2RU. *Q.*

IRISH POST—Lex House, 77 South Road, Southall, Middx. UB1 1SQ. *W.*

JAZZ JOURNAL INTERNATIONAL—113–117 Farringdon Road, EC1R 3BT. *M.*

JUST SEVENTEEN—52–55 Carnaby Street, W1V 1PF. *W.*

KENNEL GAZETTE—1 Clarges Street, W1Y 8AB. *M.*

LABOUR RESEARCH—78 Blackfriars Road, SE1 8HF. *M.*

THE LADY—39–40 Bedford Street, WC2E 9ER. *W.*

LAND AND LIBERTY—177 Vauxhall Bridge Road, SW1V 1EU. *Alt. M.*

LIGHT—College of Psychic Studies, 16 Queensberry Place, SW7 2EB. *Three times a year.*

LITERARY REVIEW—51 Beak Street, W1R 3LF. *M.*

LIVING—King's Reach Tower, Stamford Street, SE1 9LS. *Thirteen times a year.*

LOCAL GOVERNMENT CHRONICLE—122 Minories, EC3N 1NT. *W.*

LONDON GAZETTE (*Official*)—Room 143, HMSO, 51 Nine Elms Lane, SW8 5DR. *Five times a week.*

LONDON REVIEW OF BOOKS—Tavistock House South, Tavistock Square, WC1H 9JZ. *Alt. W.*

LONDON WEEKLY DIARY OF SOCIAL EVENTS—25 Park Row, SE10 9NL. *W.*

MAJESTY—80 Highgate Road, NW5 1PB. *M.*

MARIE CLAIRE—2 Hatfields, SE1 9PG. *M.*

MELODY MAKER (MM)—King's Reach Tower, Stamford Street, SE1 9LS. *W.*

METEOROLOGICAL MAGAZINE—HMSO, PO Box 276, SW8 5DT. *M.*

MIND—Oxford University Press, Pinkhill House, Southfield Road, Eynsham, Oxford OX8 1JJ. *Q.*

MODEL BOATS—Argus House, Boundary Way, Hemel Hempstead, Herts. HP2 7ST. *M.*

MODEL RAILWAYS—Argus House, Boundary Way, Hemel Hempstead, Herts. HP2 7ST. *M.*

MONTH—114 Mount Street, W1Y 6AH. *M.*

MONTHLY DIGEST OF STATISTICS (*Official*)—HMSO, PO Box 276, SW8 5DT. *M.*

MOTOR CYCLE NEWS—Bushfield House, Orton Centre, Peterborough PE2 0UW. *W.*

MUNICIPAL REVIEW AND AMA NEWS—35 Great Smith Street, SW1P 3BJ. *Ten times a year.*

MUSEUMS JOURNAL—34 Bloomsbury Way, WC1A 2SF. *Q.*

MUSIC AND LETTERS—Oxford University Press, Pinkhill House, Southfield Road, Eynsham, Oxford OX8 1JJ. *M.*

MY WEEKLY—80 Kingsway East, Dundee DD4 8SL. *W.*

NATURE—4 Little Essex Street, WC2R 3LF. *W.*

NAUTICAL MAGAZINE—4–10 Darnley Street, Glasgow G41 2SD. *M.*

NAVY INTERNATIONAL—Hunters Moon, Hogspudding Lane, Newdigate, Dorking, Surrey RH5 5DS. *Eleven times a year.*

NME—King's Reach Tower, Stamford Street, SE1 9LS. *W.*

NEW SCIENTIST—King's Reach Tower, Stamford Street, SE1 9LS. *W.*

NEW STATESMAN AND SOCIETY—Foundation House, Perseverance Works, 38 Kingsland Road, E2 8DQ. *W.*

NEWSWEEK INTERNATIONAL—25 Upper Brook Street, W1Y 2AB. *W.*

19—King's Reach Tower, Stamford Street, SE1 9LS. *M.*

NOTES AND QUERIES—Oxford University Press, Pinkhill House, Southfield Road, Eynsham, Oxford OX8 1JJ. *Q.*

NURSERY WORLD—The Schoolhouse Workshop, 51 Calthorpe Street, WC1X 0HH. *W.*

OPERA—1A Mountgrove Road, N5 2LU. *M.*

OPTIONS—King's Reach Tower, Stamford Street, SE1 9LS. *M.*

OUR DOGS—5 Oxford Road, Station Approach, Manchester M60 1SX. *W.*

PARENTS—Victory House, 14 Leicester Place, WC2H 7BP. *M.*

PARLIAMENTARY DEBATES (COMMONS) (Hansard)—HMSO, PO Box 276, SW8 5DT. *Daily or weekly during Session.*

PARLIAMENTARY DEBATES (LORDS) (Hansard)—HMSO, PO Box 276, SW8 5DT. *Daily or weekly during Session.*

PEOPLE'S FRIEND—80 Kingsway East, Dundee DD4 8SL. *W.*

PHILOSOPHY—Cambridge University Press, The Edinburgh Building, Shaftesbury Road, Cambridge CB2 2RU. *Q.*

PLAYS AND PLAYERS—Media House, 55 Lower Addiscombe, Croydon CR0 6TQ. *M.*

POETRY REVIEW—21 Earl's Court Square, SW5 9DE. *Q.*

POLITICAL QUARTERLY—108 Cowley Road, Oxford OX4 1JF. *Q.*

PONY—296 Ewell Road, Surbiton, Surrey KT6 7AQ. *M.*

POULTRY WORLD—Greenfield House, 69–73 Manor Road, Wallington, Surrey SM6 0DE. *M.*

PRACTICAL BOAT OWNER—Westover House, West Quay Road, Poole, Dorset BH15 1JG. *M.*

PRACTICAL CARAVAN—38–42 Hampton Road, Teddington, Middx. TW11 0JE. *M.*

PRACTICAL GARDENING—Apex House, Oundle Road, Peterborough PE3 8DZ. *M.*

PRACTICAL HOUSEHOLDER—Greater London House, Hampstead Road, NW1 7QQ. *M.*

PRACTICAL PHOTOGRAPHY—Apex House, Oundle Road, Peterborough PE3 8DZ. *M.*

PRIMA—Portland House, Stag Place, SW1E 5AU. *M.*

PRIVATE EYE—6 Carlisle Street, W1V 5RG. *Alt. W.*

PROGRESS (*Braille type*)—PO Box 173, Peterborough PE2 0WS. *M.*

PUNCH—Ludgate House, 245 Blackfriars Road, SE1 9UZ. *W.*

RACING CALENDAR—The Jockey Club, Weatherbys, Sanders Road, Wellingborough, Northants. NN8 4BX. *W.*

RADIO CONTROL MODELS AND ELECTRONICS—Argus House, Boundary Way, Hemel Hempstead, Herts. HP2 7ST. *M.*

RADIO TIMES—35 Marylebone High Street, W1M 4AA. *W.*

RAILWAY MAGAZINE—Prospect House, 9–13 Ewell Road, Cheam, Surrey SM1 4QQ. *M.*

RAILWAY WORLD—Terminal House, Station Approach, Shepperton, Middx. TW17 8AS. *M.*

READER'S DIGEST—Berkeley Square House, Berkeley Square, W1X 6AB. *M.*

RIDING—Corner House, Foston, Grantham, Lincs. NG32 2JU. *M.*

SCOTS INDEPENDENT—51 Cowans Street, Stirling FK8 1JW. *M.*

SCOTTISH FIELD—7th Floor, The Plaza Tower, East Kilbride, Glasgow G74 1LW. *M.*

SCOUTING—Baden-Powell House, Queen's Gate, SW7 5JS. *M.*

THE SEAFARER—202 Lambeth Road, SE1 7JW. *Q.*

SHE—72 Broadwick Street, W1V 2BP. *M.*

SHOOT—King's Reach Tower, Stamford Street, SE1 9LS. *W.*

SHOOTING TIMES AND COUNTRY MAGAZINE—10 Sheet Street, Windsor, Berks. SL4 1BG. *W.*

SLIMMING MAGAZINE—Victory House, 14 Leicester Place, WC2H 7BP. *Alt. M.*

THE SOCIAL AND LIBERAL DEMOCRATS NEWS—4 Cowley Street, SW1P 3NB. *W.*

SOCIOLOGICAL REVIEW—11 New Fetter Lane, EC4P 4EE. *Q.*

SPARE RIB—27 Clerkenwell Close, EC1R 0AT. *M.*

THE SPECTATOR—56 Doughty Street, WC1N 2LL. *W.*

THE STRAD—4th Floor, Centro House, Mandela Street, NW1 0DU. *M.*

TATLER—Vogue House, Hanover Square, W1R 0AD. *Ten times a year.*

TENNIS WORLD—The Spendlove Centre, Enstone Road, Charlbury, Oxon OX7 3PU. *Ten times a year.*

THIS ENGLAND—Alma House, Rodney Road, Cheltenham, Glos. GL50 1YQ. *Q.*

TIME—Time Life Building, 143 New Bond Street, W1Y 0AA. *W.*

THE TIMES EDUCATIONAL SUPPLEMENT—Priory House, St John's Lane, EC1M 4BX. *W.*

THE TIMES HIGHER EDUCATION SUPPLEMENT—Priory House, St John's Lane, EC1M 4BX. *W.*

THE TIMES LITERARY SUPPLEMENT—Priory House, St John's Lane, EC1M 4BX. *W.*

TRIBUNE—308 Gray's Inn Road, WC1X 8DY. *W.*

TROUT AND SALMON—Bretton Court, Bretton, Peterborough PE3 8DZ. *M.*

TRUE ROMANCES—2–4 Leigham Court Road, SW16 2PD. *M.*

TRUE STORY—2–4 Leigham Court Road, SW16 2PD. *M.*

TV TIMES—247 Tottenham Court Road, W1P 0AU. *W.*

VACHER'S PARLIAMENTARY COMPANION—113 High Street, Berkhamsted, Herts. HP4 2DJ. *Q.*

VANITY FAIR—Vogue House, Hanover Square, W1R 0AD. *M.*

VIZ COMIC—PO Box 1PT, Newcastle upon Tyne NE99 1PT. *Alt. M.*

VOGUE—Vogue House, Hanover Square, W1R 0AD. *M.*

THE VOICE—370 Coldharbour Lane, SW9 8PL. *W.*

WEATHER—James Glaisher House, Grenville Place, Bracknell, Berks. RG12 1BX. *M.*

WELSH NATION—51 Cathedral Road, Cardiff CF1 9HD. *Alt. M.*

WEST AFRICA—43–45 Coldharbour Lane, SE5 9NR. *W.*

WHICH?—2 Marylebone Road, NW1 4DX. *M.*

WOMAN—King's Reach Tower, Stamford Street, SE1 9LS. *W.*

WOMAN AND HOME—King's Reach Tower, Stamford Street, SE1 9LS. *M.*

WOMAN'S JOURNAL—King's Reach Tower, Stamford Street, SE1 9LS. *M.*

WOMAN'S OWN—King's Reach Tower, Stamford Street, SE1 9LS. *W.*

WOMAN'S REALM—King's Reach Tower, Stamford Street, SE1 9LS. *W.*

WOMAN'S WEEKLY—King's Reach Tower, Stamford Street, SE1 9LS. *W.*

THE WORLD TODAY—Chatham House, 10 St James's Square, SW1Y 4LE. *M.*

YACHTING MONTHLY—King's Reach Tower, Stamford Street, SE1 9LS. *M.*

YACHTING WORLD—Prospect House, 9–13 Ewell Road, Cheam, Surrey SM1 4QQ. *M.*

YACHTS AND YACHTING—196 Eastern Esplanade, Southend-on-Sea, Essex SS1 3AB. *Alt. W.*

TRADE, PROFESSIONAL AND BUSINESS JOURNALS

Alt. = Alternate;   *M.* = Monthly;   *Q.* = Quarterly
W. = Weekly

ACCOUNTANCY—40 Bernard Street, WC1N 1LD. *M.*

ACCOUNTANTS' MAGAZINE—27 Queen Street, Edinburgh EH2 1LA. *M.*

ADMINISTRATOR—38 St John's Street, EC1M 4AY *M.*

AGRICULTURE INTERNATIONAL—Yew Tree House Horne, Horley, Surrey RH6 9JP. *M.*

ANTIQUE DEALER AND COLLECTORS' GUIDE—PO Box 805, SE10 8TD. *M.*

ANTIQUES TRADE GAZETTE—17 Whitcomb Street WC2H 7PL. *W.*

ARCHITECTS' JOURNAL—33–35 Bowling Green Lane EC1A 0DA. *W.*

ARCHITECTURAL REVIEW—33–35 Bowling Green Lane, EC1A 0DA. *M.*

THE AUTHOR—84 Drayton Gardens, SW10 9SB. *Q.*

BAKERS' REVIEW—Turret House, 171 High Street Rickmansworth, Herts. WD3 1SN. *M.*

THE BANKER—102–108 Clerkenwell Road, EC1M 5SA *M.*

BANKING WORLD—Greater London House, Hampstead Road, NW1 7QQ. *M.*

THE BOOKSELLER—12 Dyott Street, WC1A 1DF. *W.*

BREWERS' GUARDIAN—10 Belgrade Road, Hampton Middx TW12 2AZ. *M.*

BRITISH BAKER—PO Box 109, Maclaren House, 19 Scarbrook Road, Croydon CR9 1QH. *W.*

BRITISH DENTAL JOURNAL—BMA House, Tavistock Square, WC1H 9JR. *Alt. W.*

BRITISH FOOD JOURNAL—MCB University Press Ltd, 62 Toller Lane, Bradford BD8 9BY. *Nine times a year.*

BRITISH JEWELLER—Wentworth House, Wentworth Street, Peterborough PE1 1DS. *M.*

BRITISH JOURNAL FOR THE PHILOSOPHY OF SCIENCE— Oxford University Press, Pinkhill House, Southfield Road, Eynsham, Oxford OX8 1JJ. *Q.*

BRITISH JOURNAL OF PHOTOGRAPHY—58 Fleet Street, EC4Y 1JU. *W.*

BRITISH MEDICAL JOURNAL—BMA House, Tavistock Square, WC1H 9JR. *W.*

BRITISH PRINTER—Maclean Hunter House, Chalk Lane, Cockfosters Road, Barnet, Herts. EN4 0BU. *M.*

BRITISH SUGAR BEET REVIEW—PO Box 26, Oundle Road, Peterborough PE2 9QU. *Q.*

BRITISH TAX REVIEW—South Quay Plaza, 183 Marsh Wall, E14 9FT. *Alt. M.*

BRITISH VETERINARY JOURNAL—24–28 Oval Road, NW1 7DX. *Alt. M.*

BUILDING TRADE & INDUSTRY—131–133 Duckmoor Road, Bristol BS3 2BH. *M.*

BUSINESS CONNECTIONS—Node Court, Drivers End, Codicote, Hitchin, Herts. SG4 8TR. *Alt. M.*

CABINET MAKER—Sovereign Way, Tonbridge, Kent TN9 1RW. *W.*

CAMPAIGN—22 Lancaster Gate, W2 3LY. *W.*

CARPET AND FLOORCOVERINGS REVIEW—Sovereign Way, Tonbridge, Kent TN9 1RW. *Alt. W.*

CATERER AND HOTELKEEPER—Quadrant House, The Quadrant, Sutton, Surrey SM2 5AS. *W.*

CHEMIST AND DRUGGIST—Sovereign Way, Tonbridge, Kent TN9 1RW. *W.*

CHEMISTRY AND INDUSTRY—14 Belgrave Square, SW1X 8PS. *Alt. W.*

CHEMISTRY IN BRITAIN—Thomas Graham House, Science Park, Milton Road, Cambridge CB4 4WF. *M.*

CHILD EDUCATION—Marlborough House, Holly Walk, Leamington Spa, Warks. CV32 4LS. *M.*

CLUB MIRROR—29–31 Lower Coombe Street, Croydon CR9 1LX. *M.*

COLLIERY GUARDIAN—Queensway House, 2 Queensway, Redhill, Surrey RH1 1QS. *M.*

COMMERCIAL MOTOR—Quadrant House, The Quadrant, Sutton, Surrey SM2 5AS. *W.*

COMPUTER SURVEY—PO Box 372, SW19 6LH. *Alt. M.*

COMPUTING—VNU House, 32–34 Broadwick Street, W1A 2HG. *W.*

CONCRETE—Framewood Road, Wexham, Slough, Berks. SL3 6PJ. *M.*

CONSTRUCTION WEEKLY—Morgan-Grampian House, Calderwood Street, SE18 6QH. *W.*

CONTAINERISATION INTERNATIONAL—72 Broadwick Street, W1V 2BP. *M.*

CONTRACT JOURNAL—Carew House, Wallington, Surrey SM6 0DX. *W.*

CONTROL AND INSTRUMENTATION—Morgan-Grampian House, 30 Calderwood Street, SE18 6QH. *M.*

CSE NEWS—Camping and Sports Equipment Ltd, Exhibition House, 4 Spring Street, W2 3RB. *M.*

DAIRY FARMER—Wharfedale Road, Ipswich IP1 4LG. *M.*

DAIRY INDUSTRIES INTERNATIONAL—Willmington House, Church Hill, Wilmington, Dartford, Kent DA2 7EF. *M.*

DESIGN—The Design Centre, 28 Haymarket, SW1Y 4SU. *M.*

DIRECTOR—Mountbarrow House, 6–20 Elizabeth Street, SW1W 9RB. *M.*

DOCK AND HARBOUR AUTHORITY—20 Harcourt Street, W1H 2AX. *M.*

DR THE FASHION BUSINESS—Greater London House, Hampstead Road, NW1 7QZ. *W.*

EDUCATION—21–27 Lamb's Conduit Street, WC1N 3NJ. *W.*

EDUCATION EQUIPMENT—Bullen Lane, East Peckham, Tonbridge, Kent TN12 5LP. *Eleven times a year.*

ELECTRICAL AND RADIO TRADING—Quadrant House, The Quadrant, Sutton, Surrey SM2 5AS. *W.*

ELECTRICAL REVIEW—Quadrant House, The Quadrant, Sutton, Surrey SM2 5AS. *W.*

ELECTRICAL TIMES—Quadrant House, The Quadrant, Sutton, Surrey SM2 5AS. *M.*

ELECTRONIC ENGINEERING—Morgan-Grampian House, 30 Calderwood Street, SE18 6QH. *M.*

ELECTRONICS WEEKLY—Quadrant House, The Quadrant, Sutton, Surrey SM2 5AS. *W.*

EMBROIDERY—PO Box 42B, East Molesey, Surrey KT8 9BB. *Q.*

THE ENGINEER—Morgan-Grampian House, 30 Calderwood Street, SE18 6QH. *W.*

ENGINEERING—28 Haymarket, SW1Y 4SU. *M.*

ENGINEER'S DIGEST—Convex House, 43 Dudley Road, Tunbridge Wells, Kent TN1 1LE. *Ten times a year.*

ESTATES GAZETTE—151 Wardour Street, W1V 4BN. *W.*

FAIRPLAY INTERNATIONAL SHIPPING WEEKLY—20 Ullswater Crescent, Coulsdon, Surrey CR5 2HR. *W.*

FARMERS WEEKLY—Greenfield House, 69–73 Manor Road, Wallington, Surrey SM6 0DX. *W.*

FIRE—Queensway House, 2 Queensway, Redhill, Surrey RH1 1QS. *M.*

FIRE AND SECURITY PROTECTION—Stanley House, 9 West Street, Epsom, Surrey KT18 7RL. *M.*

FISH FRIERS REVIEW—289 Dewsbury Road, Leeds LS11 5HW. *M.*

FISH TRADER—Queensway House, 2 Queensway, Redhill, Surrey RH1 1QS. *Alt. W.*

FLIGHT INTERNATIONAL—Quadrant House, The Quadrant, Sutton, Surrey SM2 5AS. *W.*

FOOD TRADE REVIEW—Station House, Hortons Way, Westerham, Kent TN16 1BZ. *M.*

FORESTRY AND BRITISH TIMBER—Sovereign Way, Tonbridge, Kent TN9 1RW. *M.*

FOUNDRY TRADE JOURNAL—Queensway House, 2 Queensway, Redhill, Surrey RH1 1QS. *Alt. W.*

FROZEN AND CHILLED FOODS—Queensway House, 2 Queensway, Redhill, Surrey RH1 1QS. *M.*

FUEL—PO Box 63, Westbury House, Bury Street, Guildford GU2 5BH. *M.*

FUNERAL SERVICE JOURNAL—43 Stockens Green, Knebworth, Herts. SG3 6DQ. *M.*

GAS MARKETING—Sovereign Way, Tonbridge, Kent TN9 1RW. *M.*

GAS WORLD—Sovereign Way, Tonbridge, Kent TN9 1RW. *Q.*

GIFTS INTERNATIONAL—Bullen Lane, East Peckham, Tonbridge, Kent TN12 5LP. *M.*

GLASS—Queensway House, 2 Queensway, Redhill, Surrey RH1 1QS. *M.*

THE GROCER—Broadfield Park, Crawley, West Sussex, RH11 9RJ. *W.*

THE GROWER—50 Doughty Street, WC1N 2LS. *W.*

HAIRDRESSERS' JOURNAL INTERNATIONAL—Quadrant House, The Quadrant, Sutton, Surrey SM2 5AS. *W.*

HANDY SHIPPING GUIDE—230–234 Long Lane, SE1 4QE. *W.*

HARDWARE TODAY—20 Harborne Road, Edgbaston, Birmingham B15 3AB. *M.*

HARPERS SPORTS & LEISURE—47A High Street, Bushey, Herts. WD2 1BD. *Every three weeks.*

HARPERS WINE AND SPIRIT GAZETTE—Harling House, 47–51 Great Suffolk Street, SE1 0BS. *W.*

THE HEALTH SERVICE JOURNAL—4 Little Essex Street, WC2R 3LF. *W.*

HEALTH VISITOR—BMA House, Tavistock Square, WC1H 9JR. *M.*

HEATING AND VENTILATING ENGINEER—171 High Street, Rickmansworth, Herts. WD3 1SN. *Alt. M.*

ICE CREAM AND FROZEN CONFECTIONERY—90–94 Gray's Inn Road, WC1X 8AH. *M.*

INVESTORS CHRONICLE—Greystoke Place, Fetter Lane, EC4A 1ND. *W.*

JOURNAL OF THE CHEMICAL SOCIETY—Thomas Graham House, Science Park, Milton Road, Cambridge CB4 4WF. *Five parts each M.*

THE JOURNALIST—Acorn House, 314 Gray's Inn Rd., WC1X 8DP. *M.*

JUSTICE OF THE PEACE—East Row, Little London, Chichester, W. Sussex PO19 1PG. *W.*

KNITTING AND HABERDASHERY REVIEW—Marshall's Chambers, 80A South Street, Romford RM1 1RX. *Alt. M.*

THE LANCET—46 Bedford Square, WC1B 3SL. *W.*

LAW QUARTERLY REVIEW—South Quay Plaza, 183 Marsh Wall, E14 9FT. *Q.*

THE LAW REPORTS—3 Stone Buildings, Lincoln's Inn, WC2A 3XN. *M.*

LAW SOCIETY'S GAZETTE—50 Chancery Lane, WC2A 1SX. *W.*

LEATHER—Sovereign Way, Tonbridge, Kent TN9 1RW. *M.*

THE LEGAL EXECUTIVE JOURNAL—Silbury Court, 356 Silbury Boulevard, Milton Keynes, Bucks. MK9 2LR. *M.*

LIBRARY REVIEW—62 Toller Lane, Bradford BD8 9BY. *Q.*

LITHO WEEK—38–42 Hampton Road, Teddington, Middx. TW11 0JE. *W.*

LLOYD'S LOADING LIST—Sheepen Place, Colchester, Essex CO3 3LP. *W.*

LLOYD'S SHIPPING INDEX—Sheepen Place, Colchester, Essex CO3 3LP. *Daily.*

LOCOMOTIVE JOURNAL—9 Arkwright Road, NW3 6AA. *M.*

LONDON CORN CIRCULAR—54 Wentworth Crescent, Ash Vale, Aldershot, Hants. GU12 5LF. *W.*

MACHINERY AND PRODUCTION ENGINEERING—Franks Hall, Franks Lane, Horton Kirby, Dartford, Kent DA4 9LL. *Alt. W.*

MACHINERY MARKET—6 Blyth Road, Bromley, Kent BR1 3RX. *W.*

MANAGEMENT ACCOUNTING—24–28 Oval Road, NW1 7DX. *M.*

MANAGEMENT DECISION—62 Toller Lane, Bradford BD8 9BY. *Eight times a year.*

MANAGEMENT TODAY—22 Lancaster Gate, W2 3LY *M.*

MANUFACTURING CHEMIST—Morgan-Grampian House 30 Calderwood Street, SE18 6QH. *M.*

MARKETING—22 Lancaster Gate, W2 3LY. *W.*

MATERIALS RECLAMATION WEEKLY—PO Box 109 Maclaren House, 19 Scarbrook Road, Croydon CR9 1QH. *W.*

MEAT TRADES' JOURNAL—Greater London House Hampstead Road, NW1 7QZ. *W.*

MEDICO-LEGAL JOURNAL—5 New Square, Lincoln's Inn, WC2A 3RJ. *Q.*

MEN'S WEAR—Greater London House, Hampstead Road, NW1 7QZ. *W.*

METAL BULLETIN—Park House, Park Terrace Worcester Park, Surrey KT4 7HY. *Twice a week.*

METALLURGIA—Queensway House, 2 Queensway Redhill, Surrey RH1 1QS. *M.*

MILK INDUSTRY—37 Spearpoint Gardens, Aldborough Road North, Newbury Park, Ilford, Essex IG2 7SX *M.*

MINING JOURNAL—60 Worship Street, EC2A 2HD *W.*

MINING MAGAZINE—60 Worship Street, EC2A 2HD *M.*

MODEL ENGINEER—Argus House, Boundary Way Hemel Hempstead, Herts. HP2 7ST. *Alt. W.*

MODERN RAILWAYS—Terminal House, Station Approach, Shepperton, Middx. TW17 8AS. *M.*

MOTOR BOAT AND YACHTING—Prospect House, 9–13 Ewell Road, Cheam, Surrey SM1 4QQ. *M.*

MOTOR TRADER—Quadrant House, The Quadrant Sutton, Surrey SM2 5AS. *W.*

MOTOR TRANSPORT—Quadrant House, The Quadrant, Sutton, Surrey SM2 5AS. *W.*

THE MUSICAL TIMES—4th Floor, Centro House Mandela Street, NW1 0DU. *M.*

NATIONAL BUILDER—82 New Cavendish Street, W1M 8AD. *M.*

NATURAL GAS—Sovereign Way, Tonbridge, Kent TN9 1RW. *Alt. M.*

NEW LAW JOURNAL—9–12 Bell Yard, WC2A 2JR. *W*

NUCLEAR ENGINEERING INTERNATIONAL—Quadrant House, The Quadrant, Sutton, Surrey SM2 5AS. *M.*

NURSERYMAN & GARDEN CENTRE—Bullen Lane, East Peckham, Tonbridge, Kent TN12 5LP. *Alt. W.*

NURSING TIMES & NURSING MIRROR—4 Little Essex Street, WC2R 3LF. *W.*

OFF-LICENCE NEWS—Broadfield Park, Crawley, W Sussex RH11 9RJ. *W.*

OPTICIAN—Quadrant House, The Quadrant, Sutton, Surrey SM2 5AS. *W.*

OPTOMETRY TODAY—Bridge House, 233–234 Blackfriars Road, SE1 8NW. *Alt. W.*

PACKAGING—Turret House, 171 High Street, Rickmansworth, Herts. WD3 1SN. *M.*

PACKAGING WEEK—Sovereign Way, Tonbridge, Kent TN9 1RW. *W.*

PAINT & RESIN—Turret House, 171 High Street, Rickmansworth, Herts. WD3 1SN. *Alt. M.*

PAPER—Sovereign Way, Tonbridge, Kent TN9 1RW. *Alt. W.*

PERSONNEL MANAGEMENT—57 Mortimer Street, W1N 7TD. *M.*

PHARMACEUTICAL JOURNAL—1 Lambeth High Street, SE1 7JN. *W.*

THE PHOTOGRAPHER—Fox Talbot House, Anwell End, Ware, Herts. SG12 9HN. *M.*

PHYSICS EDUCATION—Techno House, Redcliffe Way, Bristol BS1 6NX. *Alt. M.*

PHYSICS WORLD—Techno House, Redcliffe Way, Bristol BS1 6NX. *M.*

PLUMBING AND HEATING EQUIPMENT NEWS—Peterson House, Northbank, Berryhill Industrial Estate, Droitwich, Worcs. WR9 9BL. *M.*

POLICE REVIEW—South Quay Plaza 2, 183 Marsh Wall, E14 9FZ. *W.*

POWER FARMING—Greenfield House, 69–73 Manor Road, Wallington, Surrey SM6 0DE. *M.*

PRACTICAL WIRELESS—Enefco House, The Quay, Poole, Dorset BH15 1PP. *M.*

PRACTICAL WOODWORKING—King's Reach Tower, Stamford Street, SE1 9LS. *M.*

THE PRACTITIONER—Morgan-Grampian House, 30 Calderwood Street, SE18 6QH. *M.*

PRECISION TOOLMAKER—Queensway House, 2 Queensway, Redhill, Surrey RH1 1QS. *Nine times a year.*

PRINTING WORLD—Sovereign Way, Tonbridge, Kent TN9 1RW. *W.*

PRODUCT FINISHING—127 Stanstead Road, SE23 1JE. *M.*

PUBLIC LAW—8th Floor, South Quay Plaza, 183 Marsh Wall, E14 9FT. *Q.*

PUBLIC SERVICE—1 Mabledon Place, WC1H 9AJ. *M.*

QUARRY MANAGEMENT—7 Regent Street, Nottingham NG1 5BY. *M.*

QUARTERLY JOURNAL OF MEDICINE—Oxford University Press, Pinkhill House, Southfield Road, Eynsham, Oxford OX8 1JJ. *M.*

RAILWAY GAZETTE INTERNATIONAL—Quadrant House, The Quadrant, Sutton, Surrey SM2 5AS. *M.*

RATING & VALUATION REPORTER—2 Paper Buildings, Temple, EC4Y 7ET. *M.*

RESALE WEEKLY—1–23 Queen's Road West, E13 0PE. *W.*

RETAIL JEWELLER—Greater London House, Hampstead Road, NW1 7QZ. *Alt. W.*

RETAIL NEWSAGENT TOBACCONIST CONFECTIONER—Robert Taylor House, 11 Angel Gate, City Road, EC1V 2PT. *W.*

THE REVIEW—Audit House, Field End Road, Eastcote, Ruislip, Middx. HA4 9LT. *M.*

REVIEW OF ENGLISH STUDIES—Oxford University Press, Pinkhill House, Southfield Road, Eynsham, Oxford OX8 1JJ. *Q.*

SAFETY AT SEA—Queensway House, 2 Queensway, Redhill, Surrey RH1 1QS. *M.*

THE SCOTTISH FARMER—7th Floor, The Plaza Tower, East Kilbride, Glasgow G74 1LW. *W.*

SCOTTISH GROCER—10 Park Circus, Glasgow G3 6AX. *M.*

SERVICE STATION—Suite D, Overcliffe House, 55 New Road, Gravesend, Kent DA11 0AD. *M.*

SHEET METAL INDUSTRIES—Queensway House, 2 Queensway, Redhill, Surrey RH1 1QS. *M.*

SHIPPING WORLD & SHIPBUILDER—4 Hubbard Road, Houndsmill, Basingstoke, Hants. RG21 2UH. *M.*

SHOE & LEATHER NEWS—Greater London House, Hampstead Road, NW1 7QZ. *W.*

SOAP, PERFUMERY AND COSMETICS—Wilmington House, Church Hill, Wilmington, Dartford, Kent DA2 7EF. *M.*

SOLICITORS' JOURNAL—21–27 Lamb's Conduit Street, WC1N 3NJ. *W.*

SPORTS RETAILING—Bullen Lane, East Peckham, Tonbridge, Kent TN12 5RT. *Alt. W.*

THE STAGE AND TELEVISION TODAY—47 Bermondsey Street, SE1 3XT. *W.*

STRUCTURAL ENGINEER—11 Upper Belgrave Street, SW1X 8BH. *M. (Part A), Q. (Part B).*

SURVEYOR—Carew House, Wallington, Surrey SM6 0DX. *W.*

TABLEWARE INTERNATIONAL—Queensway House, 2 Queensway, Redhill, Surrey RH1 1QS. *Eleven times a year.*

TAXATION—Tolley House, 2 Addiscombe Road, Croydon, Surrey CR9 5AF. *W.*

TEACHING HISTORY—108 Cowley Road, Oxford OX4 1JF. *Q.*

TELEVISION—King's Reach Tower, Stamford Street, SE1 9LS. *M.*

TEXTILE HORIZONS—10 Blackfriars Street, Manchester M3 5DR. *M.*

TEXTILE MONTH—Caidan House, Canal Road, Timperley, Altrincham, Cheshire WA14 1TD. *M.*

TIMBER TRADES JOURNAL & WOOD PROCESSING—Sovereign Way, Tonbridge, Kent TN9 1RW. *W.*

TOBACCO—Queensway House, 2 Queensway, Redhill, Surrey RH1 1QS. *M.*

TOWN AND COUNTRY PLANNING—17 Carlton House Terrace, SW1Y 5AH. *M.*

TOWN PLANNING REVIEW—Liverpool University Press, PO Box 147, Liverpool L69 3BX. *Q.*

TOY TRADER—177 Hagden Lane, Watford, Herts. WD1 8LN. *M.*

TRADE MARKS JOURNAL—25 Southampton Buildings, WC2A 1AY. *W.*

TRAFFIC ENGINEERING AND CONTROL—29 Newman Street, W1P 3PE. *M.*

TRAVEL TRADE GAZETTE (UK and Ireland)—Morgan-Grampian House, 30 Calderwood Street, SE18 6QH. *W.*

UK PRESS GAZETTE—Maclean Hunter House, Chalk Lane, Cockfosters Road, Barnet, Herts. EN4 0BU. *W.*

ULTRASONICS—PO Box 63, Westbury House, Bury Street, Guildford, Surrey GU2 5BH. *Alt. M.*

WEEKLY LAW REPORTS—3 Stone Buildings, Lincoln's Inn, WC2A 3XN. *W.*

WELDING AND METAL FABRICATION—Queensway House, 2 Queensway, Redhill, Surrey RH1 1QS. *Ten times a year.*

WHITAKER'S BOOKS OF THE MONTH AND BOOKS TO COME—12 Dyott Street, WC1A 1DF. *M.*

WIRE INDUSTRY—110–112 Station Road East, Oxted, Surrey RH8 0QA. *M.*

WOODWORKER—Argus House, Boundary Way, Hemel Hempstead, Herts. HP2 7ST. *M.*

WORLD'S FAIR—2 Daltry Street, Oldham OL1 4BB. *W.*

REPORTING AND NEWS AGENCIES IN LONDON

THE ASSOCIATED PRESS LTD—12 Norwich Street, EC4A 4BP. (Tel: 071–353 1515).

CENTRAL PRESS FEATURES LTD—20 Spectrum House, 32 Gordon House Road, NW3 1LP. (Tel: 071–284 1433).

HAYTERS.—4–5 Gough Square, EC4A 3DE. (Tel: 071–353 0971).

PARLIAMENTARY AND EEC NEWS SERVICE.—19 Douglas Street, SW1P 4PA. (Tel: 071–233 8283).

PRESS ASSOCIATION LTD—85 Fleet Street, EC4P 4BE. (Tel: 071–353 7440).

REUTERS LTD—85 Fleet Street, EC4P 4AJ. (Tel: 071–250 1122).

UNITED PRESS INTERNATIONAL (UK) LTD—2 Greenwich View, Millharbour, E14 9NN. (Tel: 071–538 0932).

UNIVERSAL NEWS SERVICE LTD—Communications House, Gough Square, Fleet Street, EC4 4DP. (Tel: 071–353 5200).

THE PRESS COMPLAINTS COMMISSION
1 Salisbury Square, EC3Y 8AE
[071–353 1248]

The Press Complaints Commission was founded by the newspaper and magazine industry in January 1991 to succeed the Press Council (established in 1953), following the report published in June 1990 by the Committee on Privacy and Related Matters whose members had been appointed by the Government. It is a voluntary, non-statutory body set up to operate the press's self-regulation system, but the Committee on Privacy recommended that if the voluntary system is not successful the Commission should be converted into a statutory body. The Commission is funded by the industry through the Press Standards Board of Finance.

The Commission's objects are to consider, adjudicate, conciliate and resolve complaints of unfair treatment or unwarranted infringement of privacy by the press; and to ensure that the press maintains the highest professional standards, and respects and defends generally recognized freedoms, including freedom of expression, the public's right to know, and the right of the press to operate free from improper pressure.

The Commission judges newspaper and magazine conduct by a code of practice drafted by editors and agreed by the industry. The code, binding in the spirit as well as the letter, covers the obligations on newspapers and periodicals to be accurate; to publish corrections and apologies; to provide a fair opportunity to reply; to distinguish comment and conjecture from fact; and to respect privacy. It requires journalists generally to avoid misrepresentation, subterfuge, intimidation and harassment, to identify themselves when making inquiries at hospitals, and to protect confidential sources of information. The code also deals with press intrusion into grief and shock, interviewing, the photographing of children, the identification of children in sex cases, financial journalism, payments to witnesses, criminals, and their associates, and press references to race, colour, religion, sex, sexual orientation, and physical or mental handicap.

Seven of the Commission's 16 members are editors of national, regional and local newspapers and magazines, three are former editors, and six, including the Chairman, are drawn from other fields.

Chairman, Lord McGregor of Durris.

Members, W. Anderson, CBE; Lady Elizabeth Cavendish, LVO; Ms P. Chapman; D. Chipp; M. Clayton; The Lord Colnbrook, KCMG, PC; Dame Mary Donaldson, GBE; Sir Richard Francis, KCMG; M. Hastings; B. Hitchen, CBE; A. Hughes; Sir Edward Pickering; Prof. R. Pinker; Prof. L. Rees, FRCP, FRPath; R. Ridley.

Director, K. Morgan, OBE.

BOOK PUBLISHERS

More than 12,000 firms, individuals and societies have published one or more books in recent years. The list which follows is a selective one comprising, in the main, those firms whose names are most familiar to the general public. An interleaved list, *Publishers in the United Kingdom and Their Addresses*, containing some 2,000 names and addresses is published annually in April by the publishers of *Whitaker's Almanack*.

ABELARD-SCHUMANN, 7 Leicester Place, WC2H 7BP. Tel: 071–734 7521.

ALLAN (IAN), Terminal House, Station Approach, Shepperton, Middx. TW17 8AS. Tel: 0923–228950.

ALLEN (J. A.), 1 Lower Grosvenor Place, SW1W 0EL. Tel: 071–834 0090.

ALLEN (W. H.), 26 Grand Union Centre, 338 Ladbroke Grove, W10 5AH. Tel: 081–968 7554.

ANAYA PUBLISHERS, 44–50 Osnaburgh Street, NW1 3ND. Tel: 071–383 2997.

ANGUS & ROBERTSON, 77 Fulham Palace Road, W6 8JB. Tel: 081–741 7070.

APPLE PRESS, 6 Blundell Street, N7 9BH. Tel: 071–700 6700.

ARGUS BOOKS, Argus House, Boundary Way, Hemel Hempstead, Herts. HP2 7ST. Tel: 0442–66551.

ARMADA BOOKS, 77 Fulham Palace Road, W6 8JB. Tel: 081–741 7070.

ARMS & ARMOUR PRESS, 41 Strand, WC2N 5JE. Tel: 071–839 4900.

ARNOLD (EDWARD), Mill Road, Dunton Green, Sevenoaks TN13 2YA. Tel: 0732–450111.

ARROW BOOKS, 20 Vauxhall Bridge Road, SW1V 2SA. Tel: 071–973 9700.

ATHLONE PRESS, 1 Park Drive, NW11 7SG. Tel: 081–458 0888.

AURUM PRESS, 10 Museum Street, WC1A 1JS. Tel: 071–379 1252.

BBC BOOKS, 80 Wood Lane, W12 0TT. Tel: 081–576 2536.

BAILLIÈRE, Tindall, 24 Oval Road, NW1 7DX. Tel: 071–267 4466.

BANTAM BOOKS, 61 Uxbridge Road, W5 5SA. Tel: 081–579 2652.

BARKER (ARTHUR), 91 Clapham High Street, SW4 9TA. Tel: 071–622 9933.

BARRIE & JENKINS, 20 Vauxhall Bridge Road, SW1V 2SA. Tel: 071–973 9710.

BARTHOLOMEW, 12 Duncan Street, Edinburgh EH9 1TA. Tel: 031–667 9341.

BATSFORD (B. T.), 4 Fitzhardinge Street, W1H 0AH. Tel: 071–486 8484.

BENN (ERNEST), 35 Bedford Row, WC1R 4JH. Tel: 071–242 0946.

BINGLEY (CLIVE), 7 Ridgmount Street, WC1E 7AE. Tel: 071–636 7543.

BLACK (A. & C.), 35 Bedford Row, WC1R 4JH. Tel: 071–242 0946.

BLACKIE & SON, Wester Cleddens Road, Bishopbriggs, Glasgow G64 2NZ. Tel: 041–772 2311.

BLACKWELL PUBLISHERS, 108 Cowley Road, Oxford OX4 1JF. Tel: 0865–791100.

BLANDFORD PRESS, 41 Strand, WC2N 5JE. Tel: 071–839 4900.

BLOOMSBURY PUBLISHING, 2 Soho Square, W1V 5DE. Tel: 071–494 2111.

BODLEY HEAD, 20 Vauxhall Bridge Road, SW1V 2SA. Tel: 071–973 9730.

BOXTREE, 36 Tavistock Street, WC2E 7PB. Tel: 071–379 4666.

BOYARS (MARION), 24 Lacy Road, SW15 1NL. Tel: 081–788 9522.

BRACKEN BOOKS, 50 Eastcastle Street, W1N 7AP. Tel: 071–636 5070.

BRITISH MUSEUM PRESS, 46 Bloomsbury Street, WC1B 3QQ. Tel: 071–323 1234.

BROWN, SON & FERGUSON, 4 Darnley Street, Glasgow G41 2SD. Tel: 041–429 1234.

BUTTERWORTH & Co., Borough Green, Sevenoaks TN15 8PH. Tel: 0732–884567.

CALDER PUBLICATIONS, 9–15 Neal Street, WC2H 9TU. Tel: 071–497 1741.

CAMBRIDGE UNIVERSITY PRESS, The Edinburgh Building, Cambridge CB2 2RU. Tel: 0223–312393.

CAPE (JONATHAN), 20 Vauxhall Bridge Road, SW1V 2SA. Tel: 071–973 9730.

CASSELL, 41 Strand, WC2N 5JE. Tel: 071–839 4900.

CENTAUR PRESS, Fontwell, Arundel, Sussex BN18 0TA. Tel: 0243–543302.

CENTURY PUBLISHING Co., *see* Random Century Group.

CHAMBERS (W. & R.), 43 Annandale Street, Edinburgh EH7 4AZ. Tel: 031–557 4571.

CHAPMAN & HALL, 2 Boundary Row, SE1 8HN. Tel: 071–865 0066.

CHAPMAN (GEOFFREY), 41 Strand, WC2N 5JE. Tel: 071–839 4900.

CHAPMANS PUBLISHERS, 141 Drury Lane, WC2B 5TB. Tel: 071–379 9799.

CHATTO & WINDUS, 20 Vauxhall Bridge Road, SW1V 2SA. Tel: 071–973 9740.

CHIVERS PRESS, Windsor Bridge Road, Bath BA2 3AX. Tel: 0225–335336.

CHURCH HOUSE PUBLISHING, Church House, Great Smith Street, SW1P 3NZ. Tel: 071–222 9011.

CHURCHILL LIVINGSTONE, 1–3 Baxter's Place, Leith Walk, Edinburgh EH1 3AF. Tel: 031–556 2424.

COLLINS (WILLIAM), *see* HarperCollins Publishers.

CONSTABLE & Co., 3 The Lanchesters, 162 Fulham Palace Road, W6 9ER. Tel: 081–741 3663.

CONSUMERS' ASSOCIATION, 2 Marylebone Road, NW1 4DX. Tel: 071–486 5544.

CORGI BOOKS, 61 Uxbridge Road, W5 5SA. Tel: 081–579 2652.

DARTON, LONGMAN & TODD, 89 Lillie Road, SW6 1UD. Tel: 071–385 2341.

DAVID & CHARLES, Brunel House, Newton Abbot, Devon TQ12 4PU. Tel: 0626–61121.

DENT (J. M.) & SONS, 91 Clapham High Street, SW4 9TA. Tel: 071–622 9933.

DEUTSCH (ANDRE), 105 Great Russell Street, WC1B 3LJ. Tel: 071–580 2746.

DORLING KINDERSLEY, 9 Henrietta Street, WC2E 8PS. Tel: 071–836 5411.

DOUBLEDAY, 61 Uxbridge Road, W5 5SA. Tel: 081–579 2652.

DUCKWORTH & Co., 48 Hoxton Square, N1 6PB. Tel: 071–729 5986.

ELLIOT RIGHT WAY BOOKS, Kingswood Building, Kingswood, Tadworth, Surrey KT20 6TD. Tel: 0737–832202.

ENCYCLOPAEDIA BRITANNICA, Carew House, Station Approach, Wallington, Surrey SM6 0DA. Tel: 081–669 4355.

EPWORTH PRESS, Wesley Methodist Church, Christ's Pieces, Cambridge CB1 1LB. Tel: 0223–355982.

EVANS BROS, 2A Portman Mansions, Chiltern Street, W1M 1LE. Tel: 071–935 7160.

FABER & FABER, 3 Queen Square, WC1N 3AU. Tel: 071–465 0045.

FONTANA, 77 Fulham Palace Road, W6 8JB. Tel: 081–741 7070.

FOULIS (G. T.), Sparkford, Yeovil, Somerset BA22 7JJ. Tel: 0963–40635.

FOULSHAM (W.) & Co., Yeovil Road, Slough SL1 4JH. Tel: 0753–26769.

FOUNTAIN PRESS, 2 Claremont Road, Surbiton KT6 4QU. Tel: 081–390 7768.

FRENCH (SAMUEL), 52 Fitzroy Street, W1P 6JR. Tel: 071–387 9373.

FUTURA, *see* Macdonald & Co.

GEE & CO., 183 Marsh Wall, E14 9FS. Tel: 071–538 5386.

GIBBONS (STANLEY), 5 Parkside, Christchurch Road, Ringwood, Hants. BH24 3SH. Tel: 0425–472363.

GIBSON (ROBERT), 17 Fitzroy Place, Glasgow G3 7SF. Tel: 041–248 5674.

GINN & Co., Prebendal House, Parson's Fee, Aylesbury, Bucks. HP20 2QZ. Tel: 0296–88411.

GLASGOW (MARY), 131 Holland Park Avenue, W11 4UT. Tel: 071–603 4688.

GOLLANCZ (VICTOR), 14 Henrietta Street, WC2E 8QJ. Tel: 071–836 2006.

GOWER PUBLISHING CO., Croft Road, Aldershot, Hants. GU11 3HR. Tel: 0252–331551.

GRAFTON BOOKS, 77 Fulham Palace Road, W6 8JB. Tel: 081–741 7070.

GRAHAM (FRANK), 10 Blythswood North, Osborne Road, Jesmond, Newcastle NE2 2AZ. Tel: 091–281 3067.

GREEN (W.), 21 Alva Street, Edinburgh EH2 4PS. Tel: 031–225 4879.

GUINNESS PUBLISHING, 33 London Road, Enfield, Middx. EN2 6DJ. Tel: 081–367 4567.

HALE (ROBERT), 45 Clerkenwell Green, EC1R 0HT. Tel: 071–251 2661.

HAMILTON (HAMISH), 27 Wright's Lane, W8 5TZ. Tel: 071–938 3388.

HAMLYN PUBLISHING GROUP, 81 Fulham Road, SW3 6RB. Tel: 071–581 9393.

HARCOURT BRACE JOVANOVICH, 24 Oval Road, NW1 7DX. Tel: 071–267 4466.

HARPERCOLLINS PUBLISHERS, 77 Fulham Palace Road, W6 8JB. Tel: 081–741 7070.

HARRAP, 26 Market Square, Bromley BR1 1NA. Tel: 081–313 3484.

HARVESTER WHEATSHEAF, 66 Wood Lane End, Hemel Hempstead HP2 4RG. Tel: 0442–231555.

HAYNES (J. H.), Sparkford, Yeovil, Somerset BA22 7TJ. Tel: 0963–40635.

HEADLINE BOOK PUBLISHING, 79 Great Titchfield Street, W1P 7FN. Tel: 071–631 1687.

HEINEMANN (WILLIAM), 81 Fulham Road, SW3 6RB. Tel: 071–581 9393.

HMSO, PO Box 276, SW8 5DT. Tel: 071–873 0011.

HODDER & STOUGHTON, 47 Bedford Square, WC1B 3DP. Tel: 071–636 9851.

HOGARTH PRESS, 20 Vauxhall Bridge Road, SW1V 2SA. Tel: 071–973 9740.

HOLMES MCDOUGALL, 137 Leith Walk, Edinburgh EH6 8NS. Tel: 031–554 9444.

HUTCHINSON, *see* Random Century Group.

JANE'S INFORMATION GROUP, 163 Brighton Road, Coulsdon CR3 2NX. Tel: 081–763 1030.

JARROLD PUBLISHING, Barrack Street, Norwich NR3 1TR. Tel: 0603–763300.

JOHNSTON & BACON, PO Box 1, Stirling. Tel: 0786–841867.

JORDAN & SONS, 21 St Thomas Street, Bristol BS1 6JS. Tel: 0272–230600.

JOSEPH (MICHAEL), 27 Wright's Lane, W8 5TZ. Tel: 071–937 7255.

KAYE & WARD, 38 Hans Crescent, SW1X 0LZ. Tel: 071–581 9393.

KEGAN PAUL INTERNATIONAL, PO Box 256, WC1B 3SW. Tel: 071–580 5511.

KELLY'S, East Grinstead House, East Grinstead, Sussex RH19 1XB. Tel: 0342–326972.

KIMBER (WILLIAM), 77 Fulham Palace Road, W6 8JB. Tel: 081–741 7070.

KIMPTON MEDICAL, 82 Great King Street, Edinburgh EH3 6QY. Tel: 031–332 8764.

KINGSWAY PUBLICATIONS, 1 St Anne's Road, Eastbourne, E. Sussex BN21 3UN. Tel: 0323–410930.

KOGAN PAGE, 120 Pentonville Road, N1 9JN. Tel: 071–278 0433.

LADYBIRD BOOKS, Beeches Road, Loughborough LE11 2NQ. Tel: 0509–268021.

LAWRENCE & WISHART, 144A Old South Lambeth Road, SW8 1XX. Tel: 071–820 9281.

LETTS (CHARLES), 77 Borough Road, SE1 1DW. Tel: 071–407 8891.

LINCOLN (FRANCES), 5 Charlton Kings Road, NW5 2SB. Tel: 071–482 3302.

LION PUBLISHING, Peter's Way, Littlemore, Oxford OX4 5HG. Tel: 0865–747550.

LONGMAN GROUP, Burnt Mill, Harlow, Essex CM20 2JE. Tel: 0279–426721.

LUND HUMPHRIES, 16 Pembridge Road, W11 3HL. Tel: 071–229 1825.

LUTTERWORTH PRESS, PO Box 60, Cambridge CB1 2NT. Tel: 0223–350865.

MACDONALD & CO., 165 Great Dover Street, SE1 4YA. Tel: 071–334 4800.

MACDONALD & EVANS, 128 Long Acre, WC2E 9AN. Tel: 071–379 7383.

McGRAW-HILL, Shoppenhangers Road, Maidenhead, Berks. SL6 2QL. Tel: 0628–23432.

MACMILLAN PUBLISHERS, 4 Little Essex Street, WC2R 3LF. Tel: 071–836 6633.

MANDARIN, 81 Fulham Road, SW3 6RB. Tel: 071–581 9393.

MARSHALL CAVENDISH, 58 Old Compton Street, W1V 5PA. Tel: 071–734 6710.

METHODIST PUBLISHING, 20 Ivatt Way, Peterborough PE3 7PG. Tel: 0733–332202.

METHUEN LONDON, 81 Fulham Road, SW3 6RB. Tel: 071–581 9393.

MILLS & BOON, 18 Paradise Road, Richmond, Surrey TW9 1SR. Tel: 081–948 0444.

MITCHELL BEAZLEY, 14 Manette Street, W1V 5LB. Tel: 071–439 7211.

MOWBRAY, 41 Strand, WC2N 5JE. Tel: 071–839 4900.

MULLER (FREDERICK), 20 Vauxhall Bridge Road, SW1V 2SA. Tel: 071–973 9680.

MURRAY (JOHN), 50 Albemarle Street, W1X 4BD. Tel: 071–493 4361.

NATIONAL CHRISTIAN EDUCATION COUNCIL, Robert Denholm House, Nutfield, Redhill RH1 4HW. Tel: 0737–822411.

NELSON (THOMAS), Mayfield Road, Walton-on-Thames KT12 5PL. Tel: 0932–246133.

NEW ENGLISH LIBRARY, 47 Bedford Square, WC1B 3DP. Tel: 071–636 9851.

NISBET & CO., 78 Tilehouse Street, Hitchin, Herts. SG5 2DY. Tel: 0462–438331.

NOVELLO & CO., 8 Lower James Street, W1R 3PL. Tel: 071–287 5060.

OCTOPUS BOOKS, 81 Fulham Road, SW3 6RB. Tel: 071–581 9393.

OLIVER & BOYD, Longman House, Burnt Mill, Harlow, Essex CM20 2JE. Tel: 0279–426721.

O'MARA (MICHAEL) BOOKS, 9 Lion Yard, 11 Tremadoc Road, SW4 7NF. Tel: 071–720 8643.

OWEN (PETER), 73 Kenway Road, SW5 0RE. Tel: 071–373 5628.

OXFORD UNIVERSITY PRESS, Walton Street, Oxford OX2 6DP. Tel: 0865–56767.

PAN BOOKS, 18 Cavaye Place, SW10 9PG. Tel: 071–373 6070.

PELHAM BOOKS, 27 Wright's Lane, W8 5TZ. Tel: 071–937 7255.

PENGUIN BOOKS, Harmondsworth, Middx. UB7 0DA. Tel: 081–759 1984.

PERGAMON PRESS, Headington Hill Hall, Oxford OX3 0BW. Tel: 0865–794141.

PHAIDON PRESS, 140 Kensington Church Street, W8 4BN. Tel: 071–221 5656.

PHARMACEUTICAL PRESS, 1 Lambeth High Street, SE1 7JN. Tel: 071–735 9141.

PHILIP (GEORGE), 59 Grosvenor Street, W1X 9DA. Tel: 071–493 5841.

PIATKUS BOOKS, 5 Windmill Street, W1P 1HF. Tel: 071–631 0710.

PICCADILLY PRESS, 5 Castle Road, NW1 8PR. Tel: 071–267 4492.

PITKIN PICTORIALS, Healey House, Dene Road, Andover, Hants. SP10 2AA. Tel: 0264–334303.

PITMAN PUBLISHING, 128 Long Acre, WC2E 9AN. Tel: 071–379 7383.

PUTNAM & CO., 101 Fleet Street, EC4Y 1DE. Tel: 071–583 2412.

QUARTET BOOKS, 27 Goodge Street, W1P 1FD. Tel: 071–636 3992.

QUILLER PRESS, 46 Lillie Road, SW6 1TN. Tel: 071–499 6529.

RANDOM CENTURY GROUP, 20 Vauxhall Bridge Road, SW1V 2SA. Tel: 071–973 9000.

RAVETTE BOOKS, 3 Glenside Estate, Star Road, Partridge Green, Horsham, W. Sussex RH13 8RA. Tel: 0403–710392.

READER'S DIGEST, 25 Berkeley Square, W1X 6AB. Tel: 071–629 8144.

RELIGIOUS & MORAL EDUCATION PRESS, St Mary's Works, St Mary's Plain, Norwich NR3 3BH. Tel: 0603–615995.

RIDER & CO., *see* Randon Century Group.

ROUTLEDGE, 11 New Fetter Lane, EC4P 4EE. Tel: 071–583 9855.

SCM PRESS, 26 Tottenham Road, N1 4BZ. Tel: 071–249 7262.

SPCK, Holy Trinity Church, Marylebone Road, NW1 4DU. Tel: 071–387 5282.

ST ANDREW PRESS, 121 George Street, Edinburgh EH2 4YN. Tel: 031–225 5722.

SCRIPTURE UNION, 130 City Road, EC1V 2NJ. Tel: 071–782 0013.

SECKER & WARBURG, 81 Fulham Road, SW3 6RB. Tel: 071–581 9393.

SEVERN HOUSE, 35 Manor Road, Wallington, Surrey SM6 0BW. Tel: 081–773 4161.

SHEED & WARD, 2 Creechurch Lane, EC3A 5AQ. Tel: 071–283 6330.

SHELDON PRESS, Holy Trinity Church, Marylebone Road, NW1 4DU. Tel: 071–387 5282.

SIDGWICK & JACKSON, Cavaye Place, SW10 9PG. Tel: 071–373 6070.

SIMON & SCHUSTER, Wolsey House, Wolsey Road, Hemel Hempstead HP2 4SS. Tel: 0442–231900.

SINCLAIR-STEVENSON, 7 Kendrick Mews, SW7 3HG. Tel: 071–581 1645.

SMYTHE (COLIN), PO Box 6, Gerrards Cross, Bucks. SL9 8XA. Tel: 0753–886000.

SOUVENIR PRESS, 43 Great Russell Street, WC1B 3PA. Tel: 071–580 9307.

SPHERE BOOKS, 165 Great Dover Street, SE1 4YA. Tel: 071–334 4800.

SPON (E. & F. N.), 2 Boundary Row, SE1 8HN. Tel: 071–865 0066.

STEPHENS (PATRICK), Sparkford, Yeovil BA22 7JJ. Tel: 0963–40635.

STEVENS & SONS, 183 Marsh Wall, E14 9FT. Tel: 071–538 8686.

SWEET & MAXWELL, 183 Marsh Wall, E14 9FT. Tel: 071–538 8686.

THAMES & HUDSON, 30 Bloomsbury Street, WC1B 3QP. Tel: 071–636 5488.

THORSONS PUBLISHERS, 77 Fulham Palace Road, W6 8JB. Tel: 081–741 7070.

TIMES BOOKS, 77 Fulham Palace Road, W6 8JB. Tel: 081–741 7070.

UNIVERSITY OF WALES PRESS, Gwennyth Street, Cardiff CF2 4YD. Tel: 0222–231919.

UNWIN HYMAN, *see* HarperCollins Publishers.

VALLENTINE MITCHELL, 11 Gainsborough Road, E11 1RS. Tel: 081–530 4226.

VIKING, 27 Wright's Lane, W8 5TZ. Tel: 071–938 2200.

VIRAGO PRESS, 20–23 Mandela Street, NW1 0HQ. Tel: 071–383 5150.

WALKER BOOKS, 87 Vauxhall Walk, SE11 5HJ. Tel: 071–793 0909.

WARD LOCK, 41 Strand, WC2N 5JE. Tel: 071–839 4900.

WARD LOCK EDUCATIONAL CO., TR House, Christopher Road, East Grinstead, W. Sussex, RH19 3BT. Tel: 0342–318980.

WARNE (FREDERICK), 27 Wright's Lane, W8 5TZ. Tel: 071–938 2200.

WEBB & BOWER, 5 Cathedral Close, Exeter EX1 1EZ. Tel: 0392–435362.

WEIDENFELD & NICOLSON, 91 Clapham High Street, SW4 9TA. Tel: 071–622 9933.

WHITAKER (J.), 12 Dyott Street, WC1A 1DF. Tel: 071–836 8911.

WILDWOOD HOUSE, Gower House, Croft Road, Aldershot, Hants. GU11 3HR. Tel: 0252–331551.

WISDEN (JOHN), 25 Down Road, Merrow, Guildford GU1 2PY. Tel: 0483–570358.

WITHERBY (H. F. & G.), 14 Henrietta Street, WC2E 8QJ. Tel: 071–836 2006.

WOLFE PUBLISHING, 2 Torrington Place, WC1E 7LT. Tel: 071–636 4622.

WORLD'S WORK, *see* Heinemann (William).

BOOK PRODUCTION AND BOOK EXPORTS

The following figures for book production and exports are issued by the Department of Trade and Industry.

Year	Total value of books produced in UK £ million	Total value of books exported from UK £ million	Year	Total value of books produced in UK £ million	Total value of books exported from UK £ million
1975	342·4	138·6	1985	1044·0	340·9
1980	666·9	213·7	1986	1068·3	315·4
1982	759·1	232·8	1987	1191·2	342·2
1983	831·9	261·1	1988	1310·8	361·2
1984	937·2	307·3	1989	1472·8	401·4

ANNUAL REFERENCE BOOKS

ADVERTISER'S ANNUAL.—East Grinstead House, East Grinstead, W. Sussex RH19 1XE. 3v, £95·00.

ALLIED DUNBAR INVESTMENT GUIDE.—PO Box 88, Harlow, Essex CM19 5SR. £16·99.

ALLIED DUNBAR TAX GUIDE.—PO Box 88, Harlow, Essex CM19 5SR. £16·99.

ANNUAL REGISTER OF WORLD EVENTS.—PC Box 88, Harlow, Essex, CM19 5SR. £77·00.

ANTIQUE SHOPS OF BRITAIN, GUIDE TO THE.—5 Church Street, Woodbridge, Suffolk IP12 1DS. £12·95.

ART SALES INDEX.—1 Thames Street, Weybridge, Surrey KT1 8JG. £90·00.

ASSOCIATION OF CONSULTING ENGINEERS WHO'S WHO AND YEAR BOOK.—32 Vauxhall Bridge Road, SW1V 2SS. £40·00.

ASTRONOMICAL ALMANAC.—HMSO, PO Box 276, SW8 5DT. (Aug.) £15·00.

AUTOMOBILE YEAR.—Unit 6, Pilton Estate, Croydon, Surrey CR0 3RY. £27·95.

BAILY'S HUNTING DIRECTORY.—10 Sheet Street, Windsor, Berks. SL4 1BG. (Oct.) £27·50.

BANKER'S ALMANAC AND YEAR BOOK.—East Grinstead House, East Grinstead, W. Sussex RH19 1XE. (Feb.) 2 v. £170·00.

BENEDICTINE YEAR BOOK.—Ampleforth Abbey, York YO6 4EN. £1·00.

BENN'S DIRECT MARKETING SERVICES.—PO Box 20, Sovereign Way, Tonbridge, Kent TN9 1RQ. £75·00.

BENN'S HOUSEWARES, DO-IT-YOURSELF, GARDENS.—PO Box 20, Sovereign Way, Tonbridge, Kent TN9 1RQ. £42·00.

BENN'S MEDIA DIRECTORY.—PO Box 20, Sovereign Way, Tonbridge, Kent TN9 1RQ. 2v. each £90·00.

BIRMINGHAM POST AND MAIL YEAR BOOK AND WHO'S WHO.—137 Newhall Street, Birmingham B3 1SF. (Sept.) £18·50.

BRITAIN: AN OFFICIAL HANDBOOK.—HMSO, PO Box 276, SW8 5DT. (Jan.) £15·95.

BRITANNICA BOOK OF THE YEAR.—Carew House, Station Approach, Wallington, Surrey SM6 0DA. (Apr.) £48·00.

BRITISH CLOTHING INDUSTRY YEAR BOOK.—Westbury House, 701–705 Warwick Road, Solihull B91 3DA. £45·00.

BRITISH EXPORTS.—East Grinstead House, East Grinstead, W. Sussex RH19 1XB. £115·00.

BRITISH MUSIC YEAR BOOK.—241 Shaftesbury Avenue, WC2H 8EH. £12·95.

BRITISH PLASTICS AND RUBBER DIRECTORY.—Catalyst House, 159 Clapham High Street, SW4 7SS. £10·00.

BROWN'S NAUTICAL ALMANACK DAILY TIDE TABLES.—4–10 Darnley Street, Glasgow G41 2SD. (Sept.) £30·00.

BUILDING SOCIETIES YEAR BOOK.—7 Swallow Place, W1R 8AB. £46·00.

BUSES YEARBOOK.—Coombelands House, Addlestone, Weybridge, Surrey KT15 1HY. £9·95.

CARPET ANNUAL.—PO Box 20, Sovereign Way, Tonbridge, Kent TN9 1RQ. £64·00.

CATHOLIC DIRECTORY OF ENGLAND AND WALES.—18 Crosby Road North, Liverpool L22 4QF. £17·50.

CHARITIES DIGEST.—501–505 Kingsland Road, E8 4AU. £10·95.

CHEMICAL INDUSTRY DIRECTORY.—PO Box 20, Sovereign Way, Tonbridge, Kent TN9 1RQ. £105·00.

CHEMIST & DRUGGIST DIRECTORY.—PO Box 20, Sovereign Way, Tonbridge, Kent TN9 1RQ. £72·00.

CHRISTIES' REVIEW OF THE SEASON.—Musterlin House, Jordan Hill Road, Oxford OX2 8DP. (Dec.) £30·00.

CHURCH OF ENGLAND YEAR BOOK.—Church House, Dean's Yard, Westminster, SW1P 3NZ. (Jan.) £15·00.

CHURCH OF SCOTLAND YEAR BOOK.—121 George Street, Edinburgh EH2 4YN. (Apr.) £9·95.

CITY OF LONDON DIRECTORY AND LIVERY COMPANIES GUIDE.—Fairfax House, Causton Road, Colchester CO1 1RJ. £15·50.

CIVIL AVIATION REVIEW.—Coombelands House, Addlestone, Weybridge, Surrey KT15 1HY. £9·95.

CIVIL SERVICE YEAR BOOK.—HMSO, PO Box 276, SW8 5DT. (Feb.) £17·50.

COMMONWEALTH UNIVERSITIES YEAR BOOK.—36 Gordon Square, WC1H 0PF. (Sept.) £110·00.

COMMONWEALTH YEAR BOOK.—HMSO, PO Box 276, SW8 5DT. (May) £19.50.

COMPUTER USERS' YEAR BOOK.—32–34 Broadwick Street, W1A 2HG. £125·50.

CONCRETE YEAR BOOK.—Thomas Telford House, 1 Heron Quay, E14 9XF. £50·00.

CURRENT LAW YEAR BOOK.—11 New Fetter Lane, EC4P 4EE. £68·00.

DIPLOMATIC SERVICE LIST.—HMSO, PO Box 276, SW8 5DT. (April) £18·00.

DIRECTORY OF DIRECTORS.—East Grinstead House, East Grinstead, W. Sussex RH19 1XE. (Apr.) £130·00.

DIRECTORY OF OFFICIAL ARCHITECTURE AND PLANNING.—PO Box 88, Harlow, Essex CM19 5SR. £52·50.

DIRECTORY OF OPPORTUNITIES FOR GRADUATES.—Newpoint House, St James's Lane, N10 3DF. 7v. each £7·95.

DOD'S PARLIAMENTARY COMPANION.—Hurst Green, Etchingham, E. Sussex TN19 7PX. £60·00.

EDUCATION AUTHORITIES' DIRECTORY AND ANNUAL.—Derby House, Bletchingley Road, Merstham, Surrey RH1 3DN. (Jan.) £58·00.

EDUCATION YEAR BOOK.—PO Box 88, Harlow, Essex CM19 5SR. £57·50.

ELECTRICAL AND ELECTRONICS TRADES DIRECTORY.—Michael Faraday House, Six Hills Way, Stevenage, Herts. SG1 2AY. (Feb.) £60·00.

ELECTRICITY SUPPLY HANDBOOK.—Quadrant House, The Quadrant, Sutton, Surrey SM2 5AS. (Feb.) £25·00.

ENGINEER BUYERS' GUIDE.—40 Beresford Street, SE18 6BQ. £48·00.

EUROPA WORLD YEAR BOOK.—18 Bedford Square, WC1B 3JN. 2 v. £240·00.

EUROPEAN FOOD TRADES DIRECTORY.—48 Poland Street, W1V 4PP. £105·00.

EUROPEAN GLASS DIRECTORY AND BUYER'S GUIDE.—2 Queensway, Redhill, Surrey RH1 1QS. £48·50.

FAIRPLAY WORLD SHIPPING YEARBOOK.—PO Box 96, Coulsdon, Surrey CR3 2TE. £49·00.

FARM AND GARDEN EQUIPMENT DATA BOOK.—63 Ulcombe Gardens, Canterbury, Kent CT2 7QZ. £10·95.

FLIGHT INTERNATIONAL DIRECTORY OF BRITISH AVIATION.—PO Box 1315, Potters Bar, Herts. EN6 1PU. £36·00.

FROZEN AND CHILLED FOODS YEAR BOOK.—2 Queensway, Redhill, Surrey RH1 1QS. £58·30.

FURNISHING TRADE, DIRECTORY TO THE.—PO Box 20, Sovereign Way, Tonbridge, Kent TN9 1RQ. £85·00.

GAS INDUSTRY DIRECTORY.—PO Box 20, Sovereign Way, Tonbridge, Kent TN9 1RQ. (Jan.) £60·00.

GIBBONS' STAMPS OF THE WORLD CATALOGUE.—5 Parkside, Christchurch Road, Ringwood, Hants. BH24 3SH. (Oct.) 2v. each £16·50.

GOOD FOOD GUIDE.—PO Box 6, Mill Road, Dunton Green, Sevenoaks, Kent TN13 2YA. £12·95.

GOOD HOTEL GUIDE.—Brunel Road, Houndmills, Basingstoke, Hants. RG21 2XS. £12·99.

GOVERNMENT AND MUNICIPAL CONTRACTORS REGISTER.—55 High Street, Epsom, Surrey KT19 8DW. (Jan.) £45·00.

GUINNESS BOOK OF ANSWERS.—33 London Road, Enfield EN2 6DJ. £11·99.

GUINNESS BOOK OF RECORDS.—33 London Road, Enfield EN2 6DJ. (Oct.) £12·99.

HISTORIC HOUSES, CASTLES AND GARDENS IN GREAT BRITAIN AND IRELAND.—Star Road, Partridge Green, Horsham, W. Sussex RH13 8LD. (Feb.) £5·45.

HOLLIS PRESS AND PR ANNUAL.—Contact House, Lower Hampton Road, Sunbury-on-Thames, TW16 5HG. (Oct.) £79·50.

HOSPITALS AND HEALTH SERVICES YEARBOOK AND DIRECTORY OF HOSPITAL SUPPLIERS.—75 Portland Place, W1N 4AN. £62·00.

HOTEL, RESTAURANT AND CATERING SUPPLIES.—55 High Street, Epsom, Surrey KT19 8DW. £45·00.

HUTCHINS' PRICED SCHEDULES.—33 Station Road, Bexhill-on-Sea, E. Sussex TN40 1RG. £35·00.

INDEPENDENT SCHOOLS YEAR BOOK.—35 Bedford Row, WC1R 4JH. 2v. £16·50, £10·95.

INTERNATIONAL PAPER DIRECTORY, PHILIPS'.—PO Box 20, Sovereign Way, Tonbridge, Kent TN9 1RQ. £90·00.

INTERNATIONAL YEARBOOK AND STATESMAN'S WHO'S WHO.—East Grinstead House, East Grinstead, W. Sussex RH19 1XE. (Apr.) £115·00.

JANE'S ALL THE WORLD'S AIRCRAFT.—Sentinel House, 163 Brighton Road, Coulsdon, Surrey CR3 2NX. (Oct.) £125·00.

JANE'S ARMOUR AND ARTILLERY.—Sentinel House, 163 Brighton Road, Coulsdon, Surrey CR3 2NX. (Nov.) £125·00.

JANE'S CONTAINERIZATION DIRECT.—Sentinel House, 163 Brighton Road, Coulsdon, Surrey CR3 2NX. (Nov.) £125·00.

JANE'S FIGHTING SHIPS.—Sentinel House, 163 Brighton Road, Coulsdon, Surrey CR3 2NX. £125·00.

JANE'S HIGH SPEED MARINE CRAFT AND AIR CUSHION VEHICLES.—Sentinel House, 163 Brighton Road, Coulsdon, Surrey CR3 2NX. £125·00.

JANE'S INFANTRY WEAPONS.—Sentinel House, 163 Brighton Road, Coulsdon, Surrey CR3 2NX. (Aug.) £125·00.

JANE'S NAVAL WEAPON SYSTEMS.—Sentinel House, 163 Brighton Road, Coulsdon, Surrey CR3 2NX. £225·00.

JANE'S WORLD RAILWAYS.—Sentinel House, 163 Brighton Road, Coulsdon, Surrey CR3 2NX. £125·00.

JEWISH YEAR BOOK.—25 Furnival Street, EC4A 1JT. (Jan.) £12·95.

KELLY'S BUSINESS DIRECTORY.—East Grinstead House, East Grinstead, W. Sussex RH19 1XB. £130·00.

KELLY'S POST OFFICE LONDON BUSINESS DIRECTORY.—East Grinstead House, East Grinstead, W. Sussex RH19 1XB. 2v, £145·00.

KEMPE'S ENGINEERS YEAR BOOK.—40 Beresford Street, SE18 6BQ. £95·00.

KEMP'S INTERNATIONAL FILM AND TV YEAR BOOK.—Westbury House, 701–705 Warwick Road, Solihull B91 3DA. (May) £45·00.

KEMP'S INTERNATIONAL MUSIC AND RECORDING INDUSTRY YEAR BOOK.—Westbury House, 701–705 Warwick Road, Solihull B91 3DA. £25·00.

KIME'S INTERNATIONAL LAW DIRECTORY.—PO Box 88, Harlow, Essex CM19 5SR. (Dec.) £30·00.

LAXTON'S NATIONAL BUILDING PRICE BOOK.—East Grinstead House, East Grinstead, W. Sussex RH19 1XE. £61·00.

LIBRARY ASSOCIATION YEARBOOK.—7 Ridgmount Street, WC1E 7AE. (May) £29·50.

LLOYD'S LIST OF SHIPOWNERS.—71 Fenchurch Street, EC3M 4BS. (Sept.) £70·00.

LLOYD'S MARITIME DIRECTORY.—Sheepen Place, Colchester CO3 3LP. (Jan.) £125·00.

LLOYD'S NAUTICAL YEAR BOOK.—Sheepen Place, Colchester CO3 3LP. (Sept.) £30·00.

LLOYD'S REGISTER OF SHIPS.—71 Fenchurch Street, EC3M 4BS. (July). £275·00.

LONDON TRADE DIRECTORY.—3rd Floor, Albany House, Hurst Street, Birmingham B5 4BD. (Sept.) £75·00.

LYLE'S OFFICIAL ANTIQUES REVIEW.—Glenmayne, Galashiels TD1 3NR. £16·95.

LYLE'S OFFICIAL ARTS REVIEW.—Glenmayne, Galashiels TD1 3NR. £16·95.

MACMILLAN AND SILK CUT NAUTICAL ALMANACK.—Brunel Road, Houndmills, Basingstoke, Hants. RG21 2XS. £19·99.

MAGISTRATES' COURT GUIDE.—Borough Green, Sevenoaks, Kent TN15 8PH. £16·95.

MEDICAL ANNUAL.—PO Box 63, Westbury House, Bury Street, Guildford, Surrey GU2 5BH. (July). £29·50.

MEDICAL DIRECTORY.—PO Box 88, Harlow, Essex CM19 5SR. (Apr.) 2v, £125·00.

MEDICAL REGISTER.—44 Hallam Street, W1N 6AE. (Mar.) 3v. £90·00.

MIDDLE EAST AND NORTH AFRICA.—18 Bedford Square, WC1B 3JN. (Oct.) £115·00.

MILLER'S ANTIQUES PRICE GUIDE.—Sissinghurst Court, Sissinghurst, Kent TN17 2JA. £17·95.

MINING ANNUAL REVIEW.—PO Box 10, Edenbridge, Kent TN8 5NE. £42·50.

MINING INTERNATIONAL YEAR BOOK.—PO Box 88, Harlow, Essex CM19 5SR. (June) £115·00.

MOTOR INDUSTRY OF GREAT BRITAIN WORLD AUTOMOTIVE STATISTICS.—Forbes House, Halkin Street, SW1X 7DS. (Oct.) £75·00.

MOTOR SHIP DIRECTORY.—Quadrant House, The Quadrant, Sutton, Surrey SM2 5AS. £80·00.

MUNICIPAL YEARBOOK AND PUBLIC SERVICES DIRECTORY, 32 Vauxhall Bridge Road, SW1V 2SS. (Dec.) 2v. £94·00.

MUSEUMS AND GALLERIES IN GREAT BRITAIN AND IRELAND.—Star Road, Partridge Green, Horsham, W. Sussex RH13 8LD. (Nov.) £4·40.

NAUTICAL ALMANAC.—HMSO, PO Box 276, SW8 5DT. (Oct.) £13·50.

OWEN'S AFRICA BUSINESS DIRECTORY.—18 Farndon Road, Oxford OX6 2RT. £60·00.

OWEN'S GULF DIRECTORY.—18 Farndon Road, Oxford OX6 2RT. £90·00.

PACKAGING INDUSTRY DIRECTORY.—PO Box 20, Sovereign Way, Tonbridge, Kent TN9 1RQ. £56·00.

PEARS CYCLOPEDIA.—27 Wright's Lane, W8 5TZ. £13·99.

PHOTOGRAPHY YEAR BOOK.—45 The Broadway, Tolworth, Surbiton, Surrey KT6 7DW. £18·95.

POLYMERS, PAINT AND COLOUR YEAR BOOK.—2 Queensway, Redhill, Surrey RH1 1QS. £75·00.

PORTS OF THE WORLD.—Sheepen Place, Colchester, Essex CO3 3LP. £115·00.

PRINTERS' YEAR BOOK.—11 Bedford Row, WC1R 4DX. £40·00.

PRINTING TRADES DIRECTORY.—PO Box 20, Sovereign Way, Tonbridge, Kent TN9 1RQ. £79·00.

PUBLISHING, DIRECTORY OF.—Artillery House, Artillery Row, SW1P 1RT. (Oct.) £32·50.

RAC EUROPEAN HOTEL GUIDE.—PO Box 100, RAC House, Lansdowne Road, Croydon CR9 2JA. (Jan.) £7·95.

RAC HOTEL GUIDE.—PO Box 100, RAC House, Lansdowne Road, Croydon CR9 2JA. (Apr.) £10·95.

RAILWAY DIRECTORY AND YEAR BOOK.—Quadrant House, The Quadrant, Sutton, Surrey SM2 5AS. (Dec.) £39·00.

RAILWAY WORLD YEAR BOOK.—Coombelands House, Addlestone, Weybridge, Surrey KT15 1HY. £9·95.

RETAIL DIRECTORY OF THE UNITED KINGDOM.—32 Vauxhall Bridge Road, SW1V 2SS. £106·00.

RIBA DIRECTORY OF PRACTICES.—Royal Institute of British Architects, 39 Moreland Street, EC1V 8BB. (Oct.) £40·00.

ROTHMANS FOOTBALL YEAR BOOK.—Orbit House, 1 New Fetter Lane, EC4A 1AR. (Aug.) £17·95; £13·95.

ROYAL SOCIETY YEAR BOOK.—6 Carlton House Terrace, SW1Y 5AG. (Feb.) £13·75.

RUFF'S GUIDE TO THE TURF AND SPORTING LIFE ANNUAL.—Orbit House, 1 New Fetter Lane, EC4A 1AR. (Dec.) £50·00.

RUSI AND BRASSEY'S DEFENCE YEAR BOOK.—Headington Hill Hall, Oxford OX3 0BW. £38·50.

SALVATION ARMY YEAR BOOK.—117–121 Judd Street, WC1H 9NN. (April) £8·50, £3·95.

SCOTTISH CURRENT LAW YEAR BOOK.—2 St Giles Street, Edinburgh EH1 1PU. £125·00.

SCOTTISH LAW DIRECTORY.—59 George Street, Edinburgh EH2 2LQ. £29·00.

SCREEN INTERNATIONAL FILM AND TELEVISION YEAR BOOK.—6 Great Chapel Street, W1V 3AG. £31·00.

SCREEN WORLD.—Random Century House, 20 Vauxhall Bridge Road, SW1V 2SA. £16·99.

SELL'S AEROSPACE EUROPE.—55 High Street, Epsom, Surrey KT19 8DW. £55·00.

SELL'S BRITISH EXPORTERS.—55 High Street, Epsom, Surrey KT19 8DW. £40·00.

SELL'S BUILDING INDEX.—55 High Street, Epsom, Surrey KT19 8DW. £45·00.

SELL'S DIRECTORY OF PRODUCTS AND SERVICES.—55 High Street, Epsom, Surrey KT19 8DW. (July) £70·00.

SELL'S HEALTH SERVICE BUYERS GUIDE.—55 High Street, Epsom, Surrey KT19 8DW. £45·00.

SHEET METAL INDUSTRIES YEAR BOOK.—2 Queensway, Redhill, Surrey RH1 1QS. £46·50.

SOLICITORS AND BARRISTERS DIRECTORY.—Paulton House, 8 Shepherdess Walk, N1 7LB. £43·00.

SPON'S ARCHITECTS' AND BUILDERS' PRICE BOOK.—2–6 Boundary Row, SE1 8HN. £49·50.

SPON'S MECHANICAL AND ELECTRICAL SERVICES PRICES BOOK.—2–6 Boundary Row, SE1 8HN. £52·50.

STATESMAN'S YEARBOOK.—Brunel House, Houndmills, Basingstoke, Hants. RG21 2XS. (Aug.) £35·00.

STOCK EXCHANGE OFFICIAL YEAR BOOK.—Brunel House, Houndmills, Basingstoke, Hants. RG21 2XS. £165·00.

STONE'S JUSTICES' MANUAL.—Borough Green, Sevenoaks, Kent TN15 8PH. 3v. (May) £150·00.

TANKER REGISTER.—12 Camomile Street, EC3A 7BP. (May) £135·00.

TIMBER TRADES JOURNAL TELEPHONE ADDRESS BOOK.—Sovereign Way, Tonbridge, Kent TN9 1RQ. £40·00.

TRAINING DIRECTORY.—120 Pentonville Road, N1 9JN. £25·00.

TRAVEL TRADE DIRECTORY.—40 Beresford Street, SE18 6BQ. (July) £45·00.

UK KOMPASS REGISTER.—East Grinstead House, East Grinstead, W. Sussex RH19 1XD. v. 1–3, £335·00, v. 4, £165·00.

UNITED KINGDOM MINERALS YEARBOOK.—Keyworth, Nottingham NG12 5GG. £27·50.

UNIT TRUST YEAR BOOK.—7th Floor, 50–64 Broadway, SW1H 0DB. (Mar.) £60·00.

UNITED REFORMED CHURCH YEAR BOOK.—86 Tavistock Place, WC1H 9RT. (Sept.) £7·50.

VETERINARY ANNUAL.—Osney Mead, Oxford OX2 0EL. £49·50.

WATER SERVICES YEAR BOOK.—2 Queensway, Redhill, Surrey RH1 1QS. (Oct.) £43·00.

WHITAKER'S ALMANACK.—12 Dyott Street, WC1A 1DF. (Nov.) £35·50; £22·50; £11·95.

WHITAKER'S BOOKS IN PRINT.—12 Dyott Street, WC1A 1DF. (Sept.) £170·00.

WHITAKER'S PUBLISHERS IN THE UNITED KINGDOM AND THEIR ADDRESSES.—12 Dyott Street, WC1A 1DF. (Mar.) £5·00.

WHO OWNS WHOM?—Holmers Farm Way, High Wycombe, Bucks. HP12 4UL. 2v. £239·00.

WHO'S WHO.—35 Bedford Row, WC1R 4JH. £80·00.

WHO'S WHO, INTERNATIONAL.—18 Bedford Square, WC1R 4JH. (Sept.) £115·00.

WILLING'S PRESS GUIDE.—East Grinstead House, East Grinstead, W. Sussex RH19 1XE. (Feb.) 2v. £115·00.

WISDEN CRICKETERS' ALMANACK.—13–14 Eldon Way, Lineside Estate, Littlehampton, W. Sussex BN17 7HE. £20·00; £16·75.

WORLD HOTEL DIRECTORY.—PO Box 88, Harlow, Essex CM19 5SR. £69·00.

WORLD INSURANCE.—PO Box 88, Harlow, Essex CM19 5SR. £105·00.

WORLD OF LEARNING.—18 Bedford Square, WC1B 3JN. (Jan.) 2v. £150·00.

WRITERS' AND ARTISTS' YEAR BOOK.—35 Bedford Row, WC1R 4JH. (Jan.) £8·99.

THE QUEEN'S AWARDS FOR EXPORT AND TECHNOLOGY

The Queen's Award for Export Achievement and The Queen's Award for Technological Achievement were instituted by Royal Warrant in 1976. The two separate awards took the place of The Queen's Award to Industry, which had been instituted in 1965.

The awards are designed to recognize and encourage outstanding achievements in exporting goods or services from the United Kingdom and in advancing process or product technology. They differ from a personal Royal honour in that they are given to a unit as a whole—management and employees working as a team.

They may be applied for by any organization within the United Kingdom, the Channel Islands or the Isle of Man producing goods or services which meet the criteria for the awards. Eligibility is not influenced in any way by the particular activities of the unit applying, its location, or size. Units or agencies of central and local government with industrial functions, as well as research associations, educational institutions and bodies of a similar character, are also eligible, provided that they can show they have contributed to industrial efficiency.

Criteria

The criteria on which recommendations for the awards are based are:

Export Achievement—A substantial and sustained increase in export earnings to a level which is outstanding for the products or services concerned and for the size of the applicant unit's operations. Account will be taken of any special market factors described in the application. Applicants for the award will be expected to explain the basis of the achievement (e.g. improved marketing organization or new initiative to cater for export markets) and this will be taken into consideration. Export earnings considered will include receipts by the applicant unit in this country from the export of goods produced in this country, and the provision of services to non-residents. Account will be taken of the overseas expenses incurred other than marketing expenses. Income from profits (after overseas tax) remitted to this country from the applicant unit's direct investments in its overseas branches, subsidiaries or associates in the same general line of business will be taken into account, but not receipts from profits on other overseas investments or by interest on overseas loans or credits.

Technological Achievement—A significant advance, leading to increased efficiency, in the application of technology to a production or development process in British industry or the production for sale of goods which incorporate new and advanced technological qualities.

Each award is formally conferred by a Grant of Appointment and is symbolized by a representation of its emblem cast in stainless steel and encapsulated in a transparent acrylic block.

Awards are held for five years and holders are entitled to fly the appropriate award flag and to display the emblem on the packaging of goods produced in this country, on the goods themselves, on the unit's stationery, in advertising and on certain articles used by employees. Units may also display the emblem of any previous current awards during the five years.

Awards are announced on April 21 (the actual birthday of The Queen) and published formally in a special supplement to the London Gazette.

Awards Office

All enquiries about the scheme and requests for application forms (completed forms must be returned by October 31) should be made to: The Secretary, The Queen's Awards Office, Dean Bradley House, 52 Horseferry Road, London SW1P 2AG (Tel: 071-222 2277).

Awards for Export Achievement

In 1991, the Queen's Award for Export Achievement was conferred on the following concerns:

The Special Projects Division of A. P. V. Baker Ltd, Peterborough.

Agrisystems (Overseas) Ltd, Aylesbury, Bucks.

Allen Industrial Ltd, Bodelwyddan, Clwyd.

Allmakes Ltd, Abingdon, Oxon.

Arnold Designs Ltd, Stroud, Glos.

B. & H. Exchangers Ltd, Peterlee, Co. Durham.

B.H.-F. (Engineering) Ltd, Abingdon, Oxon.

BOC Cryoplants, Guildford, Surrey.

B. R. G. International Ltd, Stockport, Cheshire.

The Ballantyne Cashmere Company Ltd, Innerleithen, Peeblesshire.

Baring Securities Ltd, London E1.

Bechtel Ltd, London W6.

Bede Scientific Instruments Ltd, Bowburn, Co. Durham.

Berne Ltd, Wellingborough, Northants.

Boss Trucks Ltd, Leighton Buzzard, Beds.

Brett Martin Ltd, Mullusk, Co. Antrim.

British Aerospace (Military Aircraft) Ltd, Preston, Lancs.

British Alcan Rolled Products Ltd, Gerrards Cross, Bucks.

Bunting Biological Control Ltd, Colchester, Essex.

Burlington Slate Ltd, Coniston, Cumbria.

Burn Stewart Distillers PLC, Barrhead, Glasgow.

Cabletime Ltd, Newbury, Berks.

Cadbury Schweppes Overseas Ltd, Bournville, Birmingham.

Carrs of Sheffield (Manufacturing) Ltd, Sheffield.

Cirrus Research Ltd, Hunmanby, N. Yorks.

Coates Coatings Ltd, Witney, Oxon.

The Cobb Breeding Company Ltd, Chelmsford, Essex.

Com Dev Europe Ltd, Aylesbury, Bucks.

Combustion Developments Ltd, Bakewell, Derbyshire.

Constance Carroll Holdings Ltd, Skelmersdale, Lancs.

Corin Medical Ltd, Cirencester, Glos.

Cutting & Wear Resistant Developments Ltd, Rotherham.

Cyberscience PLC, Hoddesdon, Herts.

Delcam International Ltd, Birmingham.

Designers Guild Ltd, London W12.

Martin Dunitz Ltd, London NW1.

The Maydown Works of Du Pont (UK) Ltd, Londonderry.

Dunlopillo UK, Harrogate, N. Yorks.

Elsenham Quality Foods, Bishop's Stortford, Herts.

English Provender Company Ltd, Henley-on-Thames, Oxon.

Extravert Design Ltd, t/a Extravert by Ritva Kariniemi, London W8.

Farne Salmon & Trout Ltd, Duns, Berwickshire.

Fibreguide Ltd, Macclesfield, Cheshire.

Field Airmotive Ltd, Croydon, Surrey.

Fisher Controls—Process Instrumentation, Leicester.

Flight Link Control Ltd, Alton, Hants.

Formica Ltd, North Shields, Tyne and Wear.

Gibson Centri—Tech Ltd, Sutton Coldfield.

Glantre Engineering Ltd, Reading, Berks.

H. M. B. Subwork Ltd, Great Yarmouth, Norfolk.

Harkers Engineering Ltd, Stockton-on-Tees, Cleveland.

Helicon Yarns & Fibres, Tiverton, Devon.

Hounsfield Test Equipment Ltd, Redhill, Surrey.

House of Campbell Ltd, Kilwinning, Ayrshire.

Hurco Europe Ltd, High Wycombe, Bucks.

ICL Workstations Product Group, Bracknell, Berks.

Industrial Market Research Ltd, London W5.

The Carrongrove Mill of Inveresk Ltd, Denny, Stirlingshire.

Ironspray Ltd, Cwmbran, Gwent.

JEM Smoke Machine Company Ltd, Spilsby, Lincs.

J. P. W. Loudspeakers Ltd, Plymouth.

J. S. R. Healthbred Ltd, Driffield, N. Humberside.

Key Organics Ltd, Camelford, Cornwall.

Komatsu UK Ltd, Chester-le-Street, Co. Durham.

Lee Steel Strip Ltd, Sheffield.

Jeffrey S. Levitt Ltd, t/a Mint & Boxed, Edgware, Middx.

Leyland Daf Holdings Ltd, Preston, Lancs.

Linton Tweeds Ltd, Carlisle.

Lion Cabinets Ltd, Leeds.

Loughborough Sound Images Ltd, Loughborough, Leics.

Lowe Refrigeration Company, Carry Duff, Co. Down.

Stotfold Facility, International Cellular Subscriber Division of Motorola Ltd, Hitchin, Herts.

Power Transformers Division of NEI Peebles Ltd, East Pilton, Edinburgh.

Nautech Ltd, Portsmouth.

Newbridge Networks Ltd, Newport, Gwent.

OCLI Optical Coatings Ltd, Dunfermline, Fife.

The 'Old Bushmills' Distillery Company Ltd, Bushmills, Co. Antrim.

Oxford University Press, Oxford.

John Partridge Sales Ltd, Rugeley, Staffs.

B. A. Peters PLC, Chichester, W. Sussex.

Phosyn PLC, Pocklington, N. Humberside.

L. E. Pritchitt & Company Ltd, t/a Pritchitt Foods, Bromley, Kent.

Quatro Biosystems Ltd, Manchester.

R. K. Textiles Composite Fibres Ltd, Altrincham, Cheshire.

R. S. R. Ltd, Pentwyn, Cardiff.

Racal Survey (UK) Ltd, East Tullos, Aberdeen.

Redman Fisher Engineering Ltd, Tipton, West Midlands.

Ricardo Consulting Engineers Ltd, Shoreham-by-Sea, W. Sussex.

Rigby-Maryland (Stainless) Ltd, Liversedge, W. Yorkshire.

Robertson Geologging Ltd, Conwy, Gwynedd.

L. A. Rumbold Ltd, Camberley, Surrey.

Schmidt Manufacturing and Equipment (UK) Ltd, Sutton, Cambs.

Scientific Hospital Supplies Ltd, Liverpool.

Second Nature Ltd, London W10.

Securon (Amersham) Ltd, Amersham, Bucks.

Sinclair International Ltd, Norwich.

The Hosiery Division of John Smedley Ltd, Matlock Derbyshire.

Smith Wires Ltd, Halifax, W. Yorks.

The Medal Manufacturing Division of Spink & Son Ltd, London SW1.

Starkey's Technicast Ltd, Hull.

Steiner Group Ltd, Stanmore, Middx.

Sun Valley Poultry Ltd, Hereford.

Synon Ltd, London N1.

Technophone Ltd, Camberley, Surrey.

Temco Ltd, Cinderford, Glos.

Trafford Carpets Ltd, Manchester.

United Merchant Bar PLC, Scunthorpe, S. Humberside.

University of Surrey, Guildford, Surrey.

Vision Engineering Ltd, Woking, Surrey.

The Wayfarers UK Ltd, Aspatria, Cumbria.

Josiah Wedgwood & Sons Ltd, Stoke-on-Trent.

Weetabix Ltd, Kettering, Northants.

The Wellcome Foundation Ltd, London NW1.

Wellman Process Engineering Ltd, Smethwick, Warley, W. Midlands.

Henry Whitham & Son Ltd, Sheffield.

F. G. Wilson (Engineering) Ltd, Newtonabbey, Co. Antrim.

Yours and Mine Ltd, London N7.

ZED Instruments Ltd, West Molesey, Surrey.

Awards for Technological Achievement

In 1991 the Queen's Award for Technological Achievement was conferred on the following concerns:

AMT Holdings Ltd, Reading, Berks. (*Distributed array computer processor (jointly with the VLSI Design and Architecture Division of the Electronics Division of the Defence Research Agency)*).

Anson, Ltd, Gateshead (*Anson 'longlife' swivel joint used in steel pipe systems*).

BSH Industries Ltd, Swinton, Gtr Manchester (*Use of heated rear windscreen of cars as a radio antenna*).

Bede Scientific Instruments Ltd, Bowburn, Co Durham (*High resolution diffraction and topography systems for semiconductor characterization*).

Bio-Rad Microscience Ltd, Hemel Hempstead, Herts (*Laser Scanning microscope (jointly with The Laboratory of Molecular Biology of the MRC)*).

British Coal Technical Department, Burton-on-Trent, Staffs. (*Extraction drum for dust and frictional ignition control at coalfaces*).

The Gallium Arsenide Device Division of the Electronics Division of the Defence Research Agency, Malvern, Worcs. (*Semiconductor optoelectronic components using advanced epitaxial techniques (jointly with STC Optical Devices)*).

The VLSI Design and Architecture Division of the Electronics Division of the Defence Research Agency, Malvern, Worcs. (*Distributed array computer processor (jointly with AMT (Holding) Ltd)*).

Dowty Aerospace Gloucester Ltd, Gloucester (*Composite bladed propellers for commuter aircraft and hovercraft*).

Eschmann Bros & Walsh Ltd (Simcare), Lancing, W. Sussex (*WC-disposable colostomy bags*).

Fibreguide Ltd, Macclesfield, Cheshire (*Air-jet for intermingling of continuous synthetic yarns*).

Foseco (F.S.) Ltd, Tamworth, Staffs. ('*Solstar*' *metal casting solidification simulation system*).

GEC ALSTHOM Transmission & Distribution Projects Ltd (TaDPoLe), Stafford (*High voltage liquid cooled thyristor valve*).

GPT Payphone Systems, Liverpool (*Cashless intelligent payphone services*).

Guinness Brewing Worldwide, London NW10 (*Canned draught Guinness*).

ICI Katalco, Billingham, Cleveland (*Purification of gaseous and liquid hydrocarbons using new catalytic technology*).

ICI Pharmaceuticals, Macclesfield, Cheshire ('*Zoladex*', *a drug for treatment of prostate cancer*).

The Drug Development Section of the Institute of Cancer Research, The Royal Cancer Hospital, Sutton, Surrey (*Platinum-based anti-cancer drugs and 'carboplatin' (jointly with The Johnson Matthey Technology Centre and The Royal Marsden Hospital*).

Intelligent Applications Ltd, Livingston Village, West Lothian ('*Amethyst*' *expert computer system for engineering applications*).

Johnson Matthey Technology Centre, Reading (*Platinum-based anti-cancer drugs and 'carboplatin' (jointly with The Drug Development Section, The Institute of Cancer Research, The Royal Cancer Hospital and The Royal Marsden Hospital*).

The Laboratory of Molecular Biology of the Medical Research Council, Cambridge (*Laser scanning microscope (jointly with Bio-Rad Microscience Ltd*).

The Military Communications Division of Marconi Communication Systems Ltd, Chelmsford, Essex (*Scimitar H high-frequency combat radio*).

Oxford Magnet Technology Ltd, Eynsham, Oxford (*Active-shield magnets for magnet resonance scanners*).

The Biometrics Division of Penny and Giles Blackwood Ltd, Blackwood, Gwent (*Measurement and recording of human movement by twin axes electrogoniometers*).

Central Research Division, Pfizer Ltd, Sandwich, Kent (*Diflucan (fluconazole) for treatment of systemic fungal infections*).

Portals Ltd, Overton, Basingstoke (*Windowed thread security paper*).

Quantel Ltd, Newbury, Berks. (*Graphic paintbox creative pre-press system*).

Redland Engineering Ltd, Crawley, W. Sussex (*Cambrian interlocking slate (jointly with Redland Roof Tiles Ltd and Redland Technology Ltd*).

Redland Roof Tiles Ltd, Reigate, Surrey (*Cambrian interlocking slate (jointly with Redland Engineering Ltd and Redland Technology Ltd*).

Redland Technology Ltd, Horsham, W. Sussex (*Cambrian interlocking slate (jointly with Redland Engineering Ltd and Redland Roof Tiles Ltd*).

The Royal Marsden Hospital, London SW3 (*Platinum-based anti-cancer drugs and 'carboplatin' (jointly with The Drug Development Section of The Institute of Cancer Research, The Royal Cancer Hospital and Johnson Matthey Technology Centre*).

STC Optical Devices, Paignton, Devon (*Semiconductor optoelectronic components using advanced epitaxial techniques (jointly with The Gallium Arsenide Devices Division of the Electronics Division of the Defence Research Agency*).

Sandon Flexographic Printing Rollers Ltd, Runcorn, Cheshire (*Keyless ceramic printing roller*).

SmithKline Beecham Pharmaceuticals Research and Development, Epsom, Surrey (*'Eminase' a thrombolytic drug*).

Soil Machine Dynamics Ltd, Stocksfield, Northumberland (*Subsea cable ploughs*).

Synon Ltd, London N1 ('*Synon/2*' *computer software system*).

Systematica Ltd, Bournemouth, Dorset (*Computer-aided software engineering*).

TI Reynolds Rings Ltd, Birmingham (*Tru-form precision rings for aeroengines*).

Telsis Ltd, Fareham, Hants. (*Interactive voice equipment for automatic telephone services*).

Wood Group Production Technology Ltd, Dyce, Aberdeenshire (*Permanent downhole oilwell instrumentation*).

CLUBS

LONDON CLUBS

ALPINE (1857), 118 Eaton Square, SW1W 9AF. (Tel: 071-259 5591).—*Hon. Sec.*, Dr M. J. Esten.

ANGLO-BELGIAN (1955), 60 Knightsbridge, SW1X 7LF. (Tel: 071-235 2121).—*Sec.*, Lt.-Col. T. C. Morris, LVO.

ARMY AND NAVY (1837), 36–39 Pall Mall, SW1Y 5JN. (Tel: 071-930 9721).—*Sec.*, Col. D. O. O'Reilly.

ARTS (1863), 40 Dover Street, W1X 3RB. (Tel: 071-499 8581).—*Sec.*, Mrs J. Downing.

ARTS THEATRE (1927), 50 Frith Street, W1V 5TE. (Tel: 071-287 9236).—*Sec.*, R. Thornton.

THE ATHENAEUM (1824), 107 Pall Mall, SW1Y 5ER. (Tel: 071-930 4843).—*Sec.*, R. R. T. Smith.

AUTHORS' (1892), 40 Dover Street, W1X 3RB. (Tel: 071-499 8581).—*Sec.*, Mrs H. Ridgway.

BEEFSTEAK (1876), 9 Irving Street, WC2H 7AT. (Tel: 071-930 5722).—*Sec.*, E. Pool, MC.

BOODLE'S (1762), 28 St James's Street, SW1A 1HJ. (Tel: 071-930 7166).—*Sec.*, R. J. Edmonds.

BROOKS'S (1764), St James's Street, SW1A 1LN. (Tel: 071-493 4411).—*Sec.*, M. A. Roberts.

BUCK'S (1919), 18 Clifford Street, W1X 1RG. (Tel: 071-734 2337).—*Sec.*, Miss J. Turner.

CALEDONIAN (1891), 9 Halkin Street, SW1X 7DR. (Tel: 071-235 5162).—*Sec.*, P. J. Varney.

CANNING (1910), 42 Half Moon Street, W1Y 8DS. (Tel: 071-499 5163).—*Sec.*, T. M. Harrington.

CARLTON (1832), 69 St James's Street, SW1A 1PJ. (Tel: 071-493 1164).—*Sec.*, R. N. Linsley.

CAVALRY AND GUARDS (1893), 127 Piccadilly, W1V 0PX. (Tel: 071-499 1261).—*Sec.*, N. Walford.

CHALLONER (1949), 59–61 Pont Street, SW1 0BG—*Gen. Manager*, G. W. Jago.

CHELSEA ARTS (1891), 143 Old Church Street, SW3 6EB.—*Sec.*, Hon. D. Winterbottom.

CITY LIVERY (1914), Sion College, Victoria Embankment, EC4Y 0DN. (Tel: 071-353 2431).—*Hon. Sec.*, B. L. Morgan, CBE.

CITY OF LONDON (1832), 19 Old Broad Street, EC2N 1DS. (Tel: 071-588 7991).—*Sec.*, G. S. Chisholm.

CITY UNIVERSITY (1895), 50 Cornhill, EC3V 3PD. (Tel: 071-626 8571).—*Sec.*, Miss R. C. Graham.

EAST INDIA (1849), 16 St James's Square, SW1Y 4LH. (Tel: 071-930 1000).—*Sec.*, J. G. F. Stoy.

FARMERS (1842), 3 Whitehall Court, SW1A 2EL. (Tel: 071-930 3751).—*Sec.*, Lt.-Col. G. B. Murray.

FLYFISHERS' (1884), 24A Old Burlington Street, W1X 1RG. (Tel: 071-734 9229).—*Sec.*, Cdr. N. T. Fuller (*retd.*).

GARRICK (1831), 15 Garrick Street, WC2E 9AY. (Tel: 071-379 6478).—*Sec.*, M. J. Harvey.

GREEN ROOM (1877), 9 Adam Street, WC2N 6AA.—*Sec.*, J. Booth.

GRESHAM (1843), 15 Abchurch Lane, EC4N 7BB. (Tel: 071-626 7231).—*Acting Sec.*, P. A. Smart.

GROUCHO (1985), 45 Dean Street, W1V 5AP. (Tel: 071-439 4685).—*Company Sec.*, Ms. Z. Brand.

HUNTERS (1981), 3 London Wall Buildings, EC2M 5PD. (Tel: 071-638 0363).—*Sec.*, R. A. Sanders.

HURLINGHAM (1869), Ranelagh Gardens, SW6 3PR. (Tel: 071-736 8411).—*Sec.*, P. H. Covell.

KEMPTON PARK (1878), Kempton Park Racecourse, Sunbury-on-Thames, Middx., TW16 5AQ. (Tel: 0932-782292).—*Sec.*, Mrs C. Milburn-Lee.

KENNEL (1873), 1–5 Clarges Street, W1Y 8AB. (Tel: 071-493 6651).—*Sec.*, Maj.-Gen. M. H. Sinnatt, CB.

LANSDOWNE (1934), 9 Fitzmaurice Place, W1X 6JD. (Tel: 071-629 7200).—*Sec.*, Lt.-Cdr. T. P. Havers (*retd.*).

LONDON ROWING (1856), Embankment, Putney, SW15 1LB. (Tel: 081-788 0666).—*Hon. Sec.*, N. A. Smith.

LONDON THAMES FENCING (1848), 83 Perham Road, W14 9SY.—*Hon. Sec.*, G. Morrison.

MCC (MARYLEBONE CRICKET CLUB) (1787), Lord's Cricket Ground, NW8 8QN. (Tel: 071-289 1611).—*Sec.*, Lt.-Col. J. R. Stephenson, OBE.

NATIONAL (1845), c/o Carlton Club (*q.v.*).—*Sec.*, I. E. Nash.

NATIONAL LIBERAL (1882), Whitehall Place SW1A 2HE. (Tel: 071-930 9871).—*Sec.*, G. Snell.

NAVAL (1946), 38 Hill Street, W1X 8DP. (Tel: 071-493 7672).—*Chief Exec.*, Capt R. J. Husk.

NAVAL AND MILITARY (1862), 94 Piccadilly, W1V 0BP. (Tel: 071-499 5163).—*Sec.*, A. Hickey.

NEW CAVENDISH (1984), (formerly VAD), 44 Great Cumberland Place, W1H 8BS. (Tel: 071-723 0391).—*Sec.*, J. Malone-Lee.

ORIENTAL (1824), Stratford House, Stratford Place, W1N 0ES. (Tel: 071-629 5126).—*Sec.*, S. C. Doble.

PORTLAND (1816), 42 Half Moon Street, W1Y 7RD (Tel: 071-499 1523).—*Sec.*, R. B. Little.

PRATT'S (1841), 14 Park Place, SW1A 1LP. (Tel: 071-493 0397).—*Sec.*, Capt. P. W. E. Parry, MBE.

QUEEN'S (1886), Palliser Road, W14 9EQ.—*Sec.*, J. A S. Edwardes.

RAILWAY (1899), Keen House, 4 Calshot Street, N1 9DA.—*Hon. Sec.*, A. G. Wells.

REFORM (1836), 104–105 Pall Mall, SW1Y 5EW. (Tel: 071-930 9374).—*Sec.*, R. A. M. Forrest.

ROEHAMPTON (1901), Roehampton Lane, SW15 5LR. (Tel: 081-876 5505).—*Chief Exec.*, M. Yates.

ROYAL AIR FORCE (1918), 128 Piccadilly, W1V 0PY (Tel: 071-499 3456).—*Sec.*, P. N. Owen.

ROYAL AUTOMOBILE (1897), 89–91 Pall Mall, SW1Y 5HS. (Tel: 071-930 2345).—*Sec.*, J. N. Cranfield.

ROYAL OCEAN RACING (1925), 20 St James's Place SW1A 1NN. (Tel: 071-493 2248).—*Gen. Manager* D. J. Minords, OBE.

ROYAL OVER-SEAS LEAGUE (1910), Over-Seas House, Park Place, St James's Street, SW1A 1LR. (Tel: 071-408 0214).—*Gen. Manager*, Capt. J. Rumble.

ROYAL THAMES YACHT (1775), 60 Knightsbridge, SW1X 7LF. (Tel: 071-235 2121).—*Sec.*, Capt. A. R. Ward, CBE, RN.

ST STEPHEN'S CONSTITUTIONAL (1870), 34 Queen Anne's Gate, SW1H 9AB. (Tel: 071-222 1382).—*Sec.*, L. D. Mawby.

SAVAGE (1857), 1 Whitehall Place, SW1A 2HD. (Tel: 071-930 8118).—*Hon. Sec.*, D. Stirling.

SAVILE (1868), 69 Brook Street, W1Y 2ER. (Tel: 071-629 5462).—*Sec.*, P. Aldersley.

SKI CLUB OF GREAT BRITAIN (1903), 118 Eaton Square SW1W 9AF. (Tel: 071-245 1033).—*Sec.*, Air Vice Marshal J. M. Jones, CB (*retd.*).

THAMES ROWING (1860), Embankment, Putney, SW15 1LB. (Tel: 081-788 0676).—*Hon. Sec.*, Mrs S. Thomas

TRAVELLERS' (1819), 106 Pall Mall, SW1Y 5EP. (Tel: 071-930 8688).—*Sec.*, M. S. Allcock.

TURF (1868), 5 Carlton House Terrace, SW1Y 5AQ (Tel: 071-930 8555).—*Sec.*, Col. J. G. B. Rigby, OBE.

UNITED OXFORD AND CAMBRIDGE UNIVERSITY (1972), 71 Pall Mall, SW1Y 5HD. (Tel: 071-930 5151).—*Gen. Sec.*, D. McDougall.

UNIVERSITY WOMEN'S (1886), 2 Audley Square, W1Y 6DB. (Tel: 071-499 2268).—*Sec.*, H. Marriner.

VICTORIA (1863), 1 North Court, Great Peter Street, SW1P 3LL. (Tel: 071-222 2357).—*Sec.*, Ms H. David.

VICTORY SERVICES (1907), 63–79 Seymour Street, W2 2HF. (Tel: 071-723 4474).—*Gen. Manager*, Capt. G. F. Taylor.

WHITE'S (1693), 37–38 St James's Street, SW1A 1JG. (Tel: 071-493 6671).—*Sec.*, D. C. Ward.

WIG AND PEN (1908), 229–230 Strand, WC2R 1BA. (Tel: 071-583 7255).—*Administrator*, J. Reynolds.

CLUBS OUTSIDE LONDON

Aldershot.—ROYAL ALDERSHOT OFFICERS CLUB (1856), Farnborough Road, Aldershot, Hants. (Tel: 0252-24036).—*Sec.*, Lt.-Col. A. F. J. Channon, MBE (retd.).

Bath.—BATH AND COUNTY CLUB (1865), Queens Parade, Bath, BA1 2NJ. (Tel: 0225-423732).—*Sec.*, Mrs G. M. Jones.

Birmingham.—BIRMINGHAM CLUB (1872), Winston Churchill House, 8 Ethel Street, Birmingham B2 4BG. (Tel: 021-643 3357).—*Hon. Sec.*, T. R. Pepper.

ST. PAUL'S CLUB (1859), 34 St Paul's Square, Birmingham B3 1QZ. (Tel: 021-236 1950).—*Hon. Sec.*, J. S. Scott, TD.

Bishop Auckland.—THE CLUB (1868), 1 Victoria Avenue, Bishop Auckland, Co. Durham DL14 7JH. (Tel: 0388-603219).—*Hon. Sec.*, L. Cooke.

Bristol.—CLIFTON CLUB (1882), 22 The Mall, Clifton, Bristol BS8 4DS. (Tel: 0272-735527).—*Sec.*, H. B. Peckham.

Cambridge.—AMATEUR DRAMATIC CLUB (1855), ADC Theatre, Park Street, Cambridge CB5 9AS. (Tel: 0223-359547).—*Sec.*, Ms C. Wenban-Smith.

THE UNION (1815), Bridge Street, Cambridge CB2 1UB. (Tel: 0223-61521).—*Chief Clerk*, B. Thoday.

UNIVERSITY PITT CLUB (1835), Jesus Lane, Cambridge CB5 8BA. (Tel: 0223-355844).—*Hon. Sec.*, S. d'O. Duckworth.

Canterbury.—KENT AND CANTERBURY CLUB (1868), 17 Old Dover Road, Canterbury CT1 3JB. (Tel: 0277-462181).—*Sec.*, F. T. Bedingham.

Cheltenham.—NEW CLUB (1874), Montpellier Parade, Cheltenham GL50 1UD. (Tel: 0242-523285).—*Hon. Sec.*, J. A. Warhurst, OBE.

Chester.—CITY CLUB (1807), St Peter's Churchyard, Chester CH1 2AG.—*Sec.*, C. Hodkinson.

Chichester.—WEST SUSSEX COUNTY CLUB (1872), 5 Stirling Road, Chichester, W. Sussex PO19 2EW.—*Sec.*, Mrs P. Green.

Colchester.—THE COLCHESTER CLUB (1874), 3–5 Culver Street, Colchester, Essex CO1 1LE. (Tel: 0206-573037).—*Sec.*, D. G. Congdon.

Devizes.—DEVIZES AND DISTRICT CLUB (1932), 27 St John Street, Devizes, Wilts. SN10 1BN.—*Sec.*, D. J. J. Cox.

Durham.—COUNTY CLUB (1890), 52 Old Elvet, Durham.—*Sec.*, Mrs C. Arnot.

DURHAM UNION SOCIETY (1842), North Bailey Club, 24 North Bailey, Durham DH1 3EP. (Tel: 091-384 3724).—*Sec.*, Mrs E. M. Hardcastle.

Eastbourne.—DEVONSHIRE CLUB (1872), Hartington Place, Eastbourne, Sussex BN21 3RN.—*Hon. Sec.*, D. G. Matthews.

Exeter.—EXETER AND COUNTY CLUB (1871), 5 Cathedral Close, Exeter EX1 1EZ.—*Sec.*, Miss M. J. Toogood.

Guildford.—COUNTY CLUB, 158 High Street, Guildford GU1 3HF. (Tel: 0483-575370).—*Hon. Sec.*, R. W. D. Hemingway.

Harrogate.—THE CLUB (1857), 36 Victoria Avenue, Harrogate, N. Yorks.—*Hon. Sec.*, C. L. Leslie.

Henley-on-Thames.—LEANDER CLUB (1818), Henley-on-Thames, Oxon. RG9 2LP.—*Hon. Sec.*, K. Hylton-Smith.

PHYLLIS COURT CLUB (1906), Marlow Road, Henley, Oxon. RG9 2HT. (Tel: 0491-574366).—*Sec.*, D. M. Brockett.

Hove.—HOVE CLUB (1882), 28 Fourth Avenue, Hove, E. Sussex BN3 2PJ. (Tel: 0273-730872).—*Sec.*, Sqn. Ldr. G. A. Inverarity, DFC.

Leamington.—TENNIS COURT CLUB (1846), 50 Bedford Street, Leamington, Warks. CV32 5DT. (Tel: 0926-424977).—*Hon. Sec.*, O. D. R. Dixon.

Leeds.—LEEDS CLUB (1850), 3 Albion Place, Leeds LS1 6JL.—*Administrator*, Mrs D. Kavanagh.

Leicester.—LEICESTERSHIRE CLUB (1873), 9 Welford Place, Leicester LE1 6ZH.—*Manager*, J. A. Evans.

Liverpool.—THE ATHENAEUM (1797), Church Alley, Liverpool L1 3DD. (Tel: 051-709 7700).—*Hon. Sec.*, R. B. Brown.

Macclesfield.—OLD BOYS' AND PARK GREEN CLUB, 7 Churchside, Macclesfield, Cheshire SK10 1HG. (Tel: 0625-423292).—*Hon. Sec.*, Dr P. R. Baker.

Manchester.—ST JAMES'S CLUB, St James's House, Charlotte Street, Manchester M1 4DZ. (Tel: 061-236 2235).—*Hon. Sec.*, C. R. I. Estridge.

Newcastle upon Tyne.—NORTHERN CONSTITUTIONAL CLUB (1882), 37 Pilgrim Street, Newcastle upon Tyne NE1 6QE. (Tel: 091-232 0884).—*Hon. Sec.*, J. L. Browne.

Northampton.—NORTHAMPTON AND COUNTY CLUB (1873), George Row, Northampton NN1 1DF. (Tel: 0604-32962).—*Sec.*, Maj. G. D. Denholm, BEM(retd.).

Norwich.—NORFOLK CLUB (1770), 17 Upper King Street, Norwich NR3 1RB. (Tel: 0603-610652).—*Sec.*, A. J. M. Williamson.

Nottingham.—NOTTINGHAM AND NOTTS. UNITED SERVICES CLUB (1920), Newdigate House, Castle Gate, Nottingham NG1 6AF. (Tel: 0602-472138).—*Hon. Sec.*, A. C. Ready.

Oxford.—FREWEN CLUB (1869), 98 St Aldate's, Oxford OX1 1BT. (Tel: 0865-243816).—*Hon. Sec.*, W. H. Miller, BEM.

OXFORD UNION SOCIETY (1823), Frewin Court, Oxford OX1 3JB.—*Sec.*, S. Green.

VINCENT'S CLUB (1863), 1A King Edward Street, Oxford OX1 4HS. (Tel: 0865-722984).—*Sec.*, J. C. Leek.

Paignton.—PAIGNTON CLUB (1882), The Esplanade, Paignton, Devon TQ4 6ED. (Tel: 0803-559682).—*Hon. Sec.* P. Grafton.

Peterborough.—CITY AND COUNTIES CLUB (1867), Priestgate, Peterborough PE6 7LT.—*Sec.*, J. R. Fillingham.

Reading.—BERKSHIRE ATHENAEUM CLUB (1972), 53 Blagrave Street, Reading, Berks.—*Hon. Sec.*, W. J. Stuck.

Rye.—DORMY HOUSE CLUB (1896), Rye, E. Sussex TN31 7LD. (Tel: 0797-222338).—*Hon. Sec.*, P. G. Armitage.

Shrewsbury.—SALOP CLUB (1974), The Old House, Dogpole, Shrewsbury SY1 1EP. (Tel: 0743-362182).—*Sec.*, J. W. Rouse.

Stourbridge.—STOURBRIDGE OLD EDWARDIAN CLUB (1898), Drury Lane, Stourbridge, West Midlands DY8 1BL. (Tel: 0384-395635).—*Hon. Sec.*, J. V. Saunders.

Teddington.—ROYAL CANOE CLUB (1866), Trowlock Island, Teddington, Middx. TW11 9QZ. (Tel: 081-977 5269).—*Hon. Sec.*, Mrs J. S. Evans.

Worcester.—UNION AND COUNTY CLUB (1861), 40 Foregate Street, Worcester.—*Sec.*, M. G. Maton.

York.—YORKSHIRE CLUB (1839), 17 Museum Street, York YO1 2DW. (Tel: 0904-624116).—*Hon. Sec.*, D. E. Gabbitas.

Wales

Cardiff.—CARDIFF AND COUNTY CLUB (1866), Westgate Street, Cardiff CF1 1DA. (Tel: 0222-220846).—*Hon. Sec.*, Cdr. J. E. Payn.

Scotland

Aberdeen.—ROYAL NORTHERN AND UNIVERSITY CLUB (1979), 9 Albyn Place, Aberdeen AB1 1YE. (Tel: 0224-583292).—*Sec.*, Miss R. A. Black.

Ayr.—COUNTY CLUB (1872), Savoy Park Hotel, Ayr KA7 2XA.—*Hon. Sec.*, J. K. Templeton.

Edinburgh.—CALEDONIAN CLUB (1825), 32 Abercromby Place, Edinburgh EH3 6QE. (Tel: 031-332 6939).—*Sec.*, Mrs C. Lile.

NEW CLUB (1787), 86 Princes Street, Edinburgh EH2 2BB. (Tel: 031-226 4881).—*Sec.*, A. D. Orr Ewing.

Glasgow.—GLASGOW ART CLUB (1867), 185 Bath Street, Glasgow G2 4HU.—*Sec.*, L. J. McIntyre.

ROYAL SCOTTISH AUTOMOBILE CLUB (1899), 11 Blythswood Square, Glasgow G2 4AG. (Tel: 041-221 3850).—*Acting Sec.*, J. C. Lord.

WESTERN CLUB (1825), 32 Royal Exchange Square, Glasgow G1 3AB. (Tel: 041-221 2016).—*Sec.*, D. H. Gifford.

Northern Ireland

Belfast.—ULSTER REFORM CLUB (1885), 4 Royal Avenue, Belfast BT1 1DA. (Tel: 0232-323411).—*Sec.*, Miss M. P. Mackintosh.

Enniskillen.—FERMANAGH COUNTY CLUB (1883), 20 Church Street, Enniskillen, N. Ireland BT74 6DF.—*Hon. Sec.*, P. Little.

Channel Islands

Guernsey.—UNITED CLUB (1870), St Peter Port, Guernsey. (Tel: 0481-725722).—*Sec.*, J. G. Doggart.

Jersey.—VICTORIA CLUB (1853), Beresford Street, St Helier, Jersey. (Tel: 0534-23381).—*Sec.*, Gp Capt J. W. E. Holmes, DFC, AFC.

YACHT CLUBS

Bembridge.—BEMBRIDGE SAILING CLUB (1886), Embankment Road, Bembridge, IOW, PO35 5NR. (Tel: 0983-873087).—*Hon. Sec.*, B. J. B. Sloley.

Birkenhead.—ROYAL MERSEY YACHT CLUB (1844), Bedford Road East, Rock Ferry, Birkenhead, Merseyside L42 1LS. (Tel: 051-645 3204).—*Hon. Sec.*, C. P. Broad.

Bridlington.—ROYAL YORKSHIRE YACHT CLUB (1847), 1 Windsor Crescent, Bridlington, N. Humberside YO15 3HX. (Tel: 0262-678319).—*Sec.*, I. Harness.

Burnham-on-Crouch.—ROYAL CORINTHIAN YACHT CLUB (1872), Burnham-on-Crouch, Essex CM0 8AX (Tel: 0621-782105).—*Hon. Sec.*, K. W. Bushell.

Cowes.—ROYAL YACHT SQUADRON (1815), The Castle, Cowes, IOW, PO31 7QT. (Tel: 0983-292191).—*Sec.*, Maj. R. P. Rising, RM.

ROYAL LONDON YACHT CLUB (1838), The Parade, Cowes, IOW, PO31 7QS. (Tel: 0983-299727).—*Sec.*, Lt.-Col. R. J. Freeman-Wallace (*retd*).

Dover.—ROYAL CINQUE PORTS YACHT CLUB (1872), Waterloo Crescent, Dover, Kent CT16 1LA. (Tel: 0304-206262).—*Sec.*, T. V. Taylor.

Fishbourne.—ROYAL VICTORIA YACHT CLUB (1844) Fishbourne Lane, Ryde, IOW, PO33 4EU. (Tel: 0983-882325).—*Hon. Sec.*, Ms H. Vrba.

Fowey.—ROYAL FOWEY YACHT CLUB (1881), Fowey, Cornwall PL23 1BH. (Tel: 0726-833573).—*Hon. Sec.*, E. P. Warren.

Harwich.—ROYAL HARWICH YACHT CLUB (1843) Woolverstone, Ipswich IP9 1AT. (Tel: 0473 780319).—*Sec.*, Col. C. H. Bavin.

Kingswear.—ROYAL DART YACHT CLUB (1866), Priory Street, Kingswear, Dartmouth, Devon TQ6 0AB (Tel: 080 425-496).—*Hon. Sec.*, T. M. Goodearl.

Leigh-on-Sea.—ESSEX YACHT CLUB (1890), HQS Bembridge, Foreshore, Leigh-on-Sea, Essex SS9 1BD (Tel: 0702-78404).—*Hon. Sec.*, A. Manning.

London.—THE CRUISING ASSOCIATION (1908), Ivory House, St Katharine Dock, E1 9AT. (Tel: 071-481 0881).—*Gen. Sec.*, Mrs L. Hammett.

ROYAL CRUISING CLUB (1880), c/o Naval and Military Club, 94 Piccadilly, W1Y 8DS. (Tel: 071 499 5136).—*Hon. Sec.*, C. Buckley.

Lowestoft.—ROYAL NORFOLK AND SUFFOLK YACHT CLUB (1859), Royal Plain, Lowestoft, Suffolk NR33 0AQ. (Tel: 0502-566726).—*Hon. Sec.*, J. M. Brown.

Lymington.—ROYAL LYMINGTON YACHT CLUB (1922), Bath Road, Lymington, Hants. SO41 9SE. (Tel: 0590-672677).—*Sec.*, Gp Capt J. D. Hutchinson (*retd.*).

Plymouth.—ROYAL WESTERN YACHT CLUB (1827), Queen Anne's Battery, Plymouth PL4 0TW. (Tel: 0752-660077).—*Sec.*, Cdr. R. J. Harvey (*retd*).

ROYAL PLYMOUTH CORINTHIAN YACHT CLUB (1877), Madeira Road, Plymouth PL1 2NY. (Tel: 0752-664327).—*Hon. Sec.*, V. J. de Boo.

Poole.—EAST DORSET SAILING CLUB (1875), 352 Sandbanks Road, Poole, Dorset BH14 8HY.—*Hon. Sec.*, K. H. Okey.

PARKSTONE YACHT CLUB (1895), Pearce Avenue, Parkstone, Poole, Dorset BH14 8EH. (Tel: 0202 743610).—*Sec.*, M. C. Packham.

POOLE HARBOUR YACHT CLUB (1949), 38 Salterns Way, Lilliput, Poole, Dorset BH14 8JR. (Tel: 0202 707321).—*Sec.*, J. N. J. Smith.

POOLE YACHT CLUB (1865), New Harbour Road West, Hamworthy, Poole, Dorset BH15 4AQ. (Tel 0202-672687).—*Sec.*, Miss L. Clark.

Portsmouth.—ROYAL NAVAL CLUB AND ROYAL ALBERT YACHT CLUB (1867), 17 Pembroke Road, Portsmouth PO1 2NT. (Tel: 0705-824491).—*Sec.*, Lt.-Cdr. C. J. Howe.

Ramsgate.—ROYAL TEMPLE YACHT CLUB (1857), 6 Westcliff Mansions, Ramsgate, Kent CT11 9HY. (Tel: 0843-591766).—*Hon. Sec.*, G. F. Randell.

Southampton.—ROYAL AIR FORCE YACHT CLUB

(1932), Riverside House, Rope Walk, Hamble, Southampton SO3 5HD. (Tel: 0703-452208).—*Sec.*, Miss R. M. Clements.

ROYAL SOUTHAMPTON YACHT CLUB, 1 Channel Way, Ocean Village, Southampton SO1 1XE. (Tel: 0703-223352).—*Hon. Sec.*, R. Higgs.

ROYAL SOUTHERN YACHT CLUB (1837), Hamble, Southampton SO3 5HB. (Tel: 0703-453271).—*Sec.*, Cdr. M. Pringle.

Southend.—ALEXANDRA YACHT CLUB (1873), Clifton Terrace, Southend-on-Sea SS1 1DT.—*Hon. Sec.*, D. C. Osborn.

Torquay.—ROYAL TORBAY YACHT CLUB (1863), Beacon Hill, Torquay, Devon TQ1 2BQ. (Tel: 0803-292006).—*Sec.*, A. E. Hinkins.

Westcliff-on-Sea.—THAMES ESTUARY YACHT CLUB (1895), 3 The Leas, Westcliff-on-Sea, Essex SS0 7ST. (Tel: 0702-345967).—*Hon. Sec.*, G. R. Noble.

Weymouth.—ROYAL DORSET YACHT CLUB (1875), 11 Custom House Quay, Weymouth, Dorset DT4 8BG. (Tel: 0305-786258).—*Sec.*, Mrs J. B. Cannon.

Windermere.—ROYAL WINDERMERE YACHT CLUB (1860), Fallbarrow Road, Bowness-on-Windermere, Cumbria LA23 3DJ.—*Hon. Sec.*, M. C. Bentley.

Yarmouth.—ROYAL SOLENT YACHT CLUB (1878), Yarmouth, IOW, PO41 0NS. (Tel: 0983-760256).—*Sec.*, Mrs S. Tribe.

Wales

Beaumaris.—ROYAL ANGLESEY YACHT CLUB (1802), 6-7 Green Edge, Beaumaris, Gwynedd LL58 8AL. (Tel: 0248-810295).—*Hon. Sec.*, V. G. Keep.

Caernarvon.—ROYAL WELSH YACHT CLUB (1847), Porth-Yr-Aur, Caernarvon, Gwynedd LL55 1SW. (Tel: 0286-672599).—*Hon. Sec.*, G. Tecwyn Evans.

Penarth.—PENARTH YACHT CLUB (1880). The Esplanade, Penarth, S. Glamorgan CF6 2AU. (Tel: 0222-708196).—*Hon. Sec.*, R. S. McGregor.

Swansea.—BRISTOL CHANNEL YACHT CLUB (1875), 744 Mumbles Road, Mumbles, Swansea SA3 4EL. (Tel: 0792-366000).—*Hon. Sec.*, B. G. T. Rees.

Scotland

Dundee.—ROYAL TAY YACHT CLUB (1885), 34 Dundee Road, Broughty Ferry, Dundee DD5 1LX. (Tel: 0382-77516).—*Hon. Sec.*, T. Black.

Edinburgh.—ROYAL FORTH YACHT CLUB (1868), Middle Pier, Granton Harbour, Edinburgh, EH5 1HF. (Tel: 031-552 8560).—*Hon. Sec.*, A. R. Woods.

Glasgow.—ROYAL WESTERN YACHT CLUB (1875).—*Hon. Sec.*, D. G. M. Watson, Lochaber, 20 Barclay Drive, Helensburgh, Dunbartonshire G84 9RB.

Oban.—ROYAL HIGHLAND YACHT CLUB (1881).—*Sec.*, Mrs J. D. Carr, West Manse House, Kilchrenan, Taynuilt, Argyll PA35 1HG.

Rhu.—ROYAL NORTHERN AND CLYDE YACHT CLUB (1978), Rhu, Helensburgh, Dunbartonshire G84 8NG. (Tel: 0436-820322).—*Hon. Sec.*, B. C. Staig.

Northern Ireland

Bangor.—ROYAL ULSTER YACHT CLUB (1866), 101 Clifton Road, Bangor, Co. Down BT20 5HY. (Tel: 0247-270568).—*Hon. Sec.*, T. O'Hara.

Channel Islands

Jersey.—ROYAL CHANNEL ISLANDS YACHT CLUB (1862), Le Boulevard, Bulwarks, St Aubin, Jersey. (Tel: 0534-41023).—*Hon. Sec.*, A. K. Jackson.

SOCIETIES AND INSTITUTIONS

ABBEYFIELD SOCIETY, 186–192 Darkes Lane, Potters Bar, Herts. EN6 1AB. Tel: 0707-44845.—Housing for elderly people. 1,000 houses nationwide.—*Gen. Sec.*, Mrs P. Spratt.

ACCOUNTANTS, INSTITUTE OF CHARTERED, IN ENGLAND AND WALES (1880), PO Box 433, Chartered Accountants' Hall, Moorgate Place, EC2P 2BJ. Tel: 071-628 7060.—*Sec.*, A. J. Colquhoun.

ACCOUNTANTS, CHARTERED ASSOCIATION OF CERTIFIED (1904), 29 Lincoln's Inn Fields, WC2A 3EE.—*Sec.*, A. W. Sansom.

ACCOUNTANTS OF SCOTLAND, THE INSTITUTE OF CHARTERED (1854), 27 Queen Street, Edinburgh EH2 1LA. Tel: 031-225 5673.—*Chief Exec.*, P. W. Johnston.

ACCOUNTANTS IN IRELAND, INSTITUTE OF CHARTERED (1888), Chartered Accountants House, 87–89 Pembroke Road, Dublin 4. Tel: Dublin 680400/Belfast 321600.—*Dir.*, R. F. Hussey.

ACCOUNTANTS, INSTITUTE OF COMPANY (1974), 40 Tyndalls Park Road, Bristol BS8 1PL.—*Sec. Gen.*, B. T. Banks.

ACCOUNTING TECHNICIANS, ASSOCIATION OF (1980), 154 Clerkenwell Road, EC1R 5AD. Tel: 071-837 8600.—*Sec.*, J. Hanson.

ACE STUDY TOURS (formerly Association for Cultural Exchange), Babraham, Cambridge CB2 4AP. Tel: 0223-835055.—*Gen. Sec.*, P. B. Barnes.

ACTION RESEARCH (1952), Vincent House, North Parade, Horsham, W. Sussex RH12 2DA. Tel: 0403-210406.—*Dir. Gen.*, Mrs A. Luther.

ACTORS' BENEVOLENT FUND (1882), 13 Short's Gardens, WC2H 9AT. Tel: 071–836 6378.—*Gen. Sec.*, Mrs R. Stevens.

ACTORS' CHARITABLE TRUST (1896), 19–20 Euston Centre, NW1 3JH. Tel: 071-380 6212.—*Gen. Sec.*, Ms A. Stewart.

ACTORS' CHURCH UNION (1899), St Paul's Church, Bedford Street, WC2E 9ED. Tel: 071-836 5221.—*Senior Chaplain*, Canon W. Hall.

ACTUARIES IN SCOTLAND, THE FACULTY OF (1856), 23 St Andrew Square, Edinburgh EH2 1AQ.—*Sec.*, W. W. Mair.

ACTUARIES, INSTITUTE OF (1848), Staple Inn Hall, High Holborn, WC1V 7QJ. Tel: 071-242 0106.—*Sec. Gen.*, A. G. Tait.

ADMINISTRATIVE MANAGEMENT, INSTITUTE OF (1915), 40 Chatsworth Parade, Orpington, Kent BR5 1RW. Tel: 0689-875555.—*Chief Exec.*, Ms C. Hayhurst.

ADULT SCHOOL ORGANIZATION, NATIONAL (1899), Masu Centre, Gaywood Croft, Cregoe Street, Birmingham B15 2ED. Tel: 021-622 3400.—*Gen. Sec.*, W. J. Scarle.

ADVERTISING BENEVOLENT SOCIETY, NATIONAL (1913), 3 Crawford Place, W1H 1JB. Tel: 071-723 8028.—*Dir.*, Mrs D. Larkin.

ADVERTISING, INSTITUTE OF PRACTITIONERS IN (1927), 44 Belgrave Square, SW1X 8QS. Tel: 071-235 7020.—*Dir. Gen.*, N. Phillips.

ADVERTISING STANDARDS AUTHORITY (1962), Brook House, 2–16 Torrington Place, WC1E 7HN.—*Dir. Gen.*, Mrs M. Alderson.

AERONAUTICAL SOCIETY, ROYAL (1866), 4 Hamilton Place, W1V 0BQ. Tel: 071-499 3515.—*Dir.*, R. J. Kennett.

AFRICAN INSTITUTE, INTERNATIONAL (1926), London School of Economics, Connaught House, Houghton Street, WC2A 2AE. Tel: 071-831 3068.—*Hon. Dir.*, Prof. P. Lloyd.

AFRICAN MEDICAL AND RESEARCH FOUNDATION, 1 Waterloo Street, Clifton, Bristol BS8 4BT.—*Exec Dir.*, Mrs E. Young.

AGE CONCERN ENGLAND (1940), Astral House, 126 London Road, SW16 4ER. Tel: 081-679 8000.—*Dir* Ms S. Greengross.

AGE CONCERN NORTHERN IRELAND (1976), 6 Lowe Crescent, Belfast, BT2 7BG.—*Chief Exec.*, J. A O'Neill.

AGE CONCERN SCOTLAND (1943), 54A Fountainbridge Edinburgh EH3 9PT. Tel: 031-228 5656.—*Dir.*, M Cairns.

AGE CONCERN WALES, 4th Floor, 1 Cathedral Road Cardiff, CF1 9SD. Tel: 0222-371566.—*Chief Office* R. W. Taylor.

AGED POOR SOCIETY (1708), St Joseph's House, 4 Brook Green, W6 7BW. Tel: 071-603 9817.—*Sec* Flt. Lt. W. Watson.

AGEING, CENTRE FOR POLICY ON (1947), 25–31 Iron monger Row, EC1V 3QP. Tel: 071-253 1787.—*Dir* E. Midwinter, D.Phil.

AGEING, RESEARCH INTO (1978), 49 Queen Victori Street, EC4N 4SA. Tel: 071-236 4365.—*Dir.*, Ms E Mills.

AGRICULTURAL BENEVOLENT INSTITUTION, ROYAL (1860), Shaw House, 27 West Way, Oxford OX2 0QH Tel: 0865-724931.—*Chief Exec.*, Maj. Gen. P. L Spurgeon, CB.

AGRICULTURAL BENEVOLENT INSTITUTION, ROYAL SCOTTISH (1897), Ingliston, Edinburgh, EH28 8NB Tel: 031-333 1023. *Dir.*, I. C. Purves-Hume.

AGRICULTURAL ENGINEERS ASSOCIATION (1875) Samuelson House, Paxton Road, Orton Centre Peterborough PE2 0LT. Tel: 0733-371381.—*Dir Gen.*, J. Vowles.

AGRICULTURAL SOCIETY, EAST OF ENGLAND, East o England Showground, Peterborough PE2 0XE Tel: 0733-234451.—*Chief Exec.*, R. W. Bird, MBE.

AGRICULTURAL SOCIETY OF ENGLAND, ROYAL (1838) National Agricultural Centre, Stoneleigh Park Warks. CV8 2LZ. Tel: 0203-696969.—*Chief Exec.* R. E. Hicks.

AGRICULTURAL SOCIETY OF THE COMMONWEALTH ROYAL (1957), 55 Sleaford Street, SW8 5AB. Tel 071-627 2111.—*Hon. Sec.*, F. R. Francis, LVO, MBE.

AGRICULTURAL SOCIETY, ROYAL ULSTER (1826), The King's Hall, Balmoral Show Grounds, Belfast BT9 6GW. Tel: 0232-665225.—*Chief Exec.*, W. H Yarr.

AIR LEAGUE, THE (1909), 4 Hamilton Place, W1V 0BQ Tel: 071-491 0740.— *Sec. Gen.*, Air Cdre J. C Atkinson, CBE.

ALCOHOLICS ANONYMOUS (1947), PO Box 1, Stonebow House, Stonebow, York YO1 2NJ. Tel: 0904 644026.—*Gen. Sec.*, J. Keeney.

ALEXANDRA ROSE DAY COMMITTEE (1912), 1 Castelnau, Barnes, SW13 9RP.—*Nat. Organizing Sec.*, Mrs G. Greenwood.

ALLOTMENT AND LEISURE GARDENERS LIMITED, NATIONAL SOCIETY OF (1930), Hunters Road, Corby Northants. NN17 1JE. Tel: 0536-66576.—*Nat. Sec.*, G. W. Stokes.

ALMSHOUSES, NATIONAL ASSOCIATION OF (1946), Billingbear Lodge, Wokingham, Berks. RG11 5RU.—*Dir.*, D. M. Scott.

ALZHEIMER'S DISEASE SOCIETY (1979), 158–160 Balham High Road, SW12 9BN. Tel: 081-675 6557.—*Dir.*, Mrs N. Siba.

AMNESTY INTERNATIONAL (1961), International Secretariat, 1 Easton Street, WC1X 8DJ. Tel: 071-278 6000.—*Dir.*, D. Bull.

ANAESTHETISTS OF GREAT BRITAIN AND IRELAND, ASSOCIATION OF (1932), 9 Bedford Square, WC1B 3RA.—*Hon. Sec.*, Dr W. L. M. Baird.

ANCIENT BUILDINGS, SOCIETY FOR THE PROTECTION OF (1877), 37 Spital Square, E1 6DY. Tel: 071-377 1644.—*Sec.*, P. Venning.

ANCIENT MONUMENTS SOCIETY (1924), St Andrew-by-the-Wardrobe, Queen Victoria Street, EC4V 5DE. Tel: 071-236 3934.—*Sec.*, M. Saunders.

ANGLO-ARAB ASSOCIATION (1961), The Arab British Centre, 21 Collingham Road, SW5 0NU. Tel: 071-373 8414.—*Exec. Dir.*, A. Lee.

ANGLO-BELGIAN SOCIETY (1982).—*Hon. Sec.*, Mrs A. M. Woodhead, 45 West Common, Haywards Heath, W. Sussex RH16 2AJ. Tel: 0444-452183.

ANGLO-BRAZILIAN SOCIETY (1943), 32 Green Street, W1Y 3FD.—*Sec.*, Mrs M. J. Fyfe.

ANGLO-DANISH SOCIETY (1924), 25 New Street Square, EC4A 3LN. Tel: 0753-884846.—*Chairman*, Sir Andrew Stark, KCMG, CVO.

ANGLO-NORSE SOCIETY (1918), 25 Belgrave Square, SW1X 8QD.—*Chairman*, Mrs A. Dixon.

ANGLO-POLISH SOCIETY (1832), London HQ, c/o SPCK, 238–246 King Street, W6 0RF.—*Hon. Sec.*, Mrs K. Szymaniak.

ANGLO-THAI SOCIETY (1962).—*Hon. Sec.*, J. A. Bradstreet, 500 Grovely Lane, Birmingham B45 8PD.

ANIMAL CONCERN (SCOTLAND) (1988), 62 Old Dumbarton Road, Glasgow G3 8RE. Tel: 041-334 6014.—*Organizing Sec.*, J. F. Robins.

ANIMAL HEALTH TRUST (1942), PO Box 5, Newmarket, Suffolk CB8 7DW. Tel: 0638-661111.—*Dir.*, A. J. Higgins, Ph.D.

ANTHROPOLOGICAL INSTITUTE, ROYAL (1843), 50 Fitzroy Street, W1P 5HS. Tel: 071-387 0455.—*Dir.*, J. C. M. Benthall.

ANTHROPOSOPHICAL SOCIETY IN GREAT BRITAIN (1923), Rudolf Steiner House, 35 Park Road, NW1 6XT. Tel: 071-723 4400.—*Gen. Sec.*, N. C. Thomas.

ANTIQUARIES OF LONDON, SOCIETY OF (1717), Burlington House, Piccadilly, W1V 0HS. Tel: 071-734 0193.—*Gen. Sec.*, H. P. A. Chapman, Ph.D.

ANTIQUARIES OF SCOTLAND, SOCIETY OF (1780), Royal Museum of Scotland, Queen Street, Edinburgh EH2 1JD. Tel: 031-225 7534, ext. 327/8.—*Sec.*, Miss C. R. Wickham-Jones.

ANTI-SLAVERY INTERNATIONAL FOR THE PROTECTION OF HUMAN RIGHTS (1839), 180 Brixton Road, SW9 6AT. Tel: 071-582 4040.—*Dir.*, Miss L. Roberts.

ANTI-VIVISECTION: BRITISH UNION FOR THE ABOLITION OF VIVISECTION (1898), 16A Crane Grove, N7 8LB.—*Gen. Sec.*, C. Fisher.

ANTI-VIVISECTION SOCIETY, THE NATIONAL (1875), 261 Goldhawk Road, W12 9PE. Tel: 081-846 9777.—*Dir.*, Ms J. Creamer.

APOSTLESHIP OF THE SEA (1920), Stella Maris, 66 Dock Road, Tilbury, Essex RM18 7BX. Tel: 0375-845641.—For active and retired seafarers. *Nat. Dir.*, Rev. J. Maguire.

APOTHECARIES OF LONDON, SOCIETY OF (1617), Black Friars Lane, EC4V 6EJ.—*Clerk*, Maj. J. C. O'Leary; *Registrar*, D. H. C. Barrie.

ARBITRATORS, THE CHARTERED INSTITUTE OF (1915), International Arbitration Centre, 24 Angel Gate, City Road, EC1V 2RS. Tel: 071-837 4483.—*Sec.*, K. R. K. Harding.

ARCHAEOLOGICAL ASSOCIATION, BRITISH (1843), 24 Lower Street, Harnham, Salisbury SP2 8EY.—*Asst. Sec.*, M. Cowan.

ARCHAEOLOGICAL ASSOCIATION, CAMBRIAN (1846).—*Gen. Sec.*, R. S. Kelly, Arlwyn, 52 Upper Garth Road, Bangor, Gwynedd LL57 2SS. Tel: 0248-355966.

ARCHAEOLOGICAL INSTITUTE, ROYAL (1843), c/o Society of Antiquaries of London, Burlington House, Piccadilly, W1V 0HS.—*Sec.*, J. G. Coad.

ARCHAEOLOGY, COUNCIL FOR BRITISH (1944), 112 Kennington Road, SE11 6RE. Tel: 071-582 0494.—*Dir.*, R. K. Morris.

ARCHITECTS, THE ROYAL INSTITUTE OF BRITISH (1834), 66 Portland Place, W1N 4AD. Tel: 071-580 5533.—*Pres.*, R. MacCormac. *Dir. Gen.*, The Rt. Hon. W. Rodgers.

ARCHITECTS AND SURVEYORS, INCORPORATED ASSOCIATION OF (1925), Jubilee House, Billing Brook Road, Weston Favell, Northampton NN3 4NW. Tel: 0604-404121.—*Administrator*, B. D. Hughes.

ARCHITECTS AND SURVEYORS INSTITUTE (1926), 15 St Mary Street, Chippenham, Wilts. SN15 3JN. Tel: 0249-444504.—*Chief Exec.*, B. A. Hunt.

ARCHITECTS BENEVOLENT SOCIETY (1850), 66 Portland Place, W1N 4AD.—*Hon. Sec.*, R. J. Double.

ARCHITECTS IN SCOTLAND, ROYAL INCORPORATION OF (1922), 15 Rutland Square, Edinburgh EH1 2BE. Tel: 031-229 7545.—*Sec.*, C. A. McKean, FRSA.

ARCHITECTS REGISTRATION COUNCIL OF THE UNITED KINGDOM (1931), 73 Hallam Street, W1N 6EE. Tel: 071-580 5861.— *Registrar*, D. W. G. Smart.

ARCHITECTURAL ASSOCIATION (INC.) (1847), 34–36 Bedford Square, WC1B 3EG.—*Sec.*, E. Le Maistre.

ARCHITECTURAL HERITAGE FUND, THE (1976), 17 Carlton House Terrace, SW1Y 5AW. Tel: 071-925 0199.—*Sec.*, Lady Weir.

ARCHIVISTS, SOCIETY OF (1947).—*Exec. Sec.*, P. S. Cleary, Information House, 20–24 Old Street, EC1V 9AP. Tel: 071-253 5087 ext. 63.

ARK ENVIRONMENTAL FOUNDATION, THE (1988), 498 Harrow Road, W9 3QA. Tel: 081-968 6780.—*Chairman*, R. Boorer.

ARMY BENEVOLENT FUND (1944), 41 Queen's Gate, SW7 5HR.—*Controller*, Maj.-Gen. G. M. G. Swindells, CB.

ARMY CADET FORCE ASSOCIATION (1930), E Block, Duke of York's HQ, SW3 4RR. Tel: 071-730 9733.—*Gen. Sec.*, Brig. R. B. MacGregor-Oakford, CBE, MC.

ART, THE ROYAL CAMBRIAN ACADEMY OF (1882), Plas Mawr, High Street, Conwy, Gwynedd LL32 8DE. Tel: 0492-593413.—*Hon. Sec.* Ms A. Hind; *Curator and Sec.*, L. H. S. Mercer.

ART COLLECTIONS FUND, NATIONAL (1903), 20 John Islip Street, SW1P 4JX. Tel: 071-821 0404.—*Dir.*, Sir Peter Wakefield, KBE, CMG.

ARTHRITIS AND RHEUMATISM COUNCIL (1936), 41 Eagle Street, WC1R 4AR.—*Gen. Sec.*, J. Norton.

ARTHRITIS CARE (1949), 5 Grosvenor Crescent, SW1X 7ER. Tel: 071-235 0902.—*Sec.*, J. R. Collins.

ARTISTS, FEDERATION OF BRITISH, 17 Carlton House Terrace, SW1Y 5BD.—*Chief Exec.*, O. Warman.

ARTISTS' GENERAL BENEVOLENT INSTITUTION (1814) AND ARTISTS' ORPHAN FUND (1871), Burlington House, Piccadilly, W1V 0DJ. Tel: 071-734 1193.—*Sec.*, Mrs C. M. Rees.

ARTISTS, ROYAL SOCIETY OF BRITISH, 17 Carlton House Terrace, SW1Y 5BD.— *Sec.*, R. Morgan.

ART LIBRARIES SOCIETY, BRITAIN AND EIRE (ARLIS) (1969).—*Administrator.*, Ms S. French, 18 College Road, Bromsgrove, Worcs. B60 2NE. Tel: 0527-579298.

ART WORKERS' GUILD (1884), 6 Queen Square, WC1N 3AR. Tel: 071-837 3474.—*Sec.*, H. Krall.

ASLIB (The Association for Information Management) (1924), Information House, 20–24 Old Street, EC1V 9AP. Tel: 071-253 4488.—*Chief Exec.*, R. Bowes.

ASSISTANT MASTERS AND MISTRESSES ASSOCIATION (1978), 7 Northumberland Street, WC2N 5DA. Tel: 071-930 6441.—*Gen. Sec.*, P. Smith.

ASTHMA CAMPAIGN, NATIONAL (1927), 300 Upper Street, N1 2XX. Tel: 071-226 2260.—*Chairman*, Sir Peter Emery, MP.

ASTRONOMICAL ASSOCIATION, BRITISH (1890), Burlington House, Piccadilly, W1V 9AG. Meetings at 23 Savile Row, W1X 1AB.— *Asst. Sec.*, Miss P. M. Barber.

ASTRONOMICAL SOCIETY, ROYAL (1820), Burlington House, Piccadilly, W1V 0NL.—*Pres.*, Prof. K. A. Pounds, CBE, FRS; *Exec. Secs.*, Dr B. A. Hobbs; Dr K. A. Whaler; Prof. D. A. Williams.

ATS and WRAC BENEVOLENT FUNDS (1964), Queen Elizabeth Park, Guildford, Surrey GU2 6QH.— *Sec.*, Mrs A. H. S. Matthews.

AUDIT BUREAU OF CIRCULATIONS LTD (1931), Black Prince Yard, 207–209 High Street, Berkhamsted, Herts. HP4 1AD. Tel: 0442-870800. *Sec.*, J. Beadell.

AUTHORS, THE SOCIETY OF (1884), 84 Drayton Gardens, SW10 9SB. Tel: 071-373 6642.—*Gen. Sec.*, M. Le Fanu.

AUTOMOBILE ASSOCIATION (1905), Fanum House, Basingstoke, Hants. RG21 2EA. Tel: 0256-20123.— *Dir. Gen.*, S. Dyer.

AVICULTURAL SOCIETY (1894), c/o Bristol Zoological Gardens, Clifton, Bristol BS8 3HA. Tel: 0272-738951.—*Hon. Sec.*, G. R. Greed.

AYRSHIRE CATTLE SOCIETY OF GREAT BRITAIN AND IRELAND (1877), PO Box 8, 1 Racecourse Road, Ayr KA7 2DE. Tel: 0292-267123.—*Gen. Sec.*, S. J. Thomson.

BALTIC AIR CHARTER ASSOCIATION (1949), The Baltic Exchange, St Mary Axe, EC3A 8BU. Tel: 081-519 3909.—*Hon. Exec.*, D. Shepherd.

BALTIC EXCHANGE LTD (1903), 19–21 Bury Street, EC3A 5AU. Tel: 071-623 5501.—*Sec.*, D. J. Walker.

BALTIC EXCHANGE CHARITABLE SOCIETY (1978), 14–20 St Mary Axe, EC3A 8BU. Tel: 071-623 5501.—*Sec.*, R. T. Wheelans.

BALZAN FOUNDATION, INTERNATIONAL (1956), Piazzetta U. Giordano 4, Milan 20122, Italy. Tel: 010 392-7600 2212.—*Sec. Gen.*, Dr F. M. Tedeschi.

BANKERS, THE CHARTERED INSTITUTE OF (1879), 10 Lombard Street, EC3V 9AS. Tel: 071-623 5071.— *Sec. Gen.*, E. Glover.

BANKERS IN SCOTLAND, THE INSTITUTE OF (1875), 19 Rutland Square, Edinburgh EH1 2DE. Tel: 031-229 9869.—*Sec.*, Dr C. W. Munn.

BAPTIST MISSIONARY SOCIETY (1792), Baptist House, PO Box 49, 129 Broadway, Didcot, Oxon. OX11 8RT. Tel: 0235-512077.—*Gen. Sec.*, Rev. R. G. S. Harvey.

BAR ASSOCIATION FOR LOCAL GOVERNMENT AND THE PUBLIC SERVICE (1945).—*Chairman*, P. G. Stivadoros, 23 Wentworth Way, Bletchley, Milton Keynes MK3 7RW. Tel: 0908-682205.

BARNARDO'S (1866), Tanners Lane, Barkingside, Ilford, Essex IG6 1QG. Tel: 081-550 8822.—*Senior Dir.*, R. Singleton.

BARONETAGE, STANDING COUNCIL OF THE (1898), The Church House, Bibury, Cirencester, Glos. GL7 5NR.—*Hon. Sec.*, R. B. Snow.

BARRISTERS' BENEVOLENT ASSOCIATION, THE (1873), 14 Gray's Inn Square, WC1R 5JP. Tel: 071-242 4761.—*Sec.*, Mrs A. Ashley.

BCMS CROSSLINKS (1922), 251 Lewisham Way, SE4 1XF. Tel: 081-691 6111.—*Gen. Sec.*, Canon J. M. Ball.

BEECHAM TRUST, SIR THOMAS (1946), Denton House, Denton, Harleston, Norfolk IP20 0AA.—*Sec.*, Shirley, Lady Beecham.

BEE-KEEPERS' ASSOCIATION, BRITISH (1874), National Agricultural Centre, Stoneleigh Park, Warks. CV8 2LZ. Tel: 0203-696679.—*Gen. Sec.*, J. K. Law.

BIBLE SOCIETY, BRITISH AND FOREIGN (1804), Stonehill Green, Westlea, Swindon SN5 7DG. Tel: 0793-513713.—*Exec. Dir.*, N. Crosbie.

BIBLIOGRAPHICAL SOCIETY (1892), British Library Humanities and Social Sciences, Great Russell Street, WC1B 3DG.—*Hon. Sec.*, Dr M. M. Foot.

BIBLIOGRAPHICAL SOCIETY, EDINBURGH (1890), c/o New College Library, Mound Place, Edinburgh EH1 2LU. Tel: 031-225 8400, ext. 256.—*Hon. Sec.*, Dr M. C. T. Simpson.

BIOCHEMICAL SOCIETY (1911), 59 Portland Place, W1N 3AJ. Tel: 071-580 5530.—*Exec. Sec.*, G. D. Jones.

BIOLOGICAL COUNCIL, THE (1945), c/o Institute of Biology, 20 Queensberry Place, SW7 2DZ. Tel: 071 581 8333.—*Hon. Sec.*, Dr N. J. Lane.

BIOLOGICAL ENGINEERING SOCIETY (1960), Royal College of Surgeons, Lincoln's Inn Fields, WC2A 3PN. Tel: 071-242 7750.—*Hon. Sec.*, Dr R. E. Trotman.

BIOLOGY, THE INSTITUTE OF (1950), 20 Queensberry Place, SW7 2DZ. Tel: 071-581 8333.—*Gen. Sec.*, Dr. R. H. Priestley.

BIRD PRESERVATION, INTERNATIONAL COUNCIL FOR (BRITISH SECTION) (1922), c/o RSPB, The Lodge, Sandy, Beds. SG19 2DL. Tel: 0767-680551.—*Exec. Sec.*, A. Gammell.

BIRMINGHAM AND MIDLAND INSTITUTE (1854) and PRIESTLEY LIBRARY (1779), Margaret Street, Birmingham B3 3BS. Tel: 021-236 3591.—*Admin. J.* Hunt.

BIRTHDAY TRUST FUND, NATIONAL (1928), 27 Sussex Place, NW1 4RG. For extension of maternity services. Tel: 071-706 3903.—*Sec.*, Mrs M. C. Matthews.

BLIND, GUIDE DOGS FOR THE, *see* GUIDE DOGS FOR THE BLIND ASSOCIATION.

BLIND, INCORPORATED ASSOCIATION FOR PROMOTING THE GENERAL WELFARE OF THE (1854), 37–55 Ashburton Grove, N7 7DW.—*Chief Exec.*, G. P. Robinson.

BLIND PEOPLE, ACTION FOR (1857), 14–16 Verney Road, SE16 3DZ. Tel: 071-732 8771.—*Dir.*, A. Kent.

BLIND, NATIONAL LIBRARY FOR THE (1882), Cromwell Road, Bredbury, Stockport, Cheshire SK6 2SG. Over 400,000 volumes available. Tel: 061-494 0217.—*Dir. Gen.*, A. Leach.

BLIND, ROYAL NATIONAL COLLEGE FOR THE (1872), College Road, Hereford HR1 1EB. Tel: 0432-265275.—*Principal*, Dr M. Semple.

BLIND, ROYAL NATIONAL INSTITUTE FOR THE, *see* ROYAL NATIONAL INSTITUTE FOR THE BLIND.

BLIND, ROYAL SCHOOL FOR THE (1799), Highlands Road, Leatherhead, Surrey KT22 8NR. Tel: 0372-373086.—*Chief-Exec.*, R. M. Perkins.

BLOOD TRANSFUSION ASSOCIATION, SCOTTISH NATIONAL (1940), Erskine House, 68–73 Queen Street, Edinburgh EH2 4NH. Tel: 031-226 4488.—*Sec.*, P. C. Taylor.

BLOOD TRANSFUSION SERVICE, NATIONAL (1948), National Directorate, North Western Regional Health Authority, Gateway House, Piccadilly South, Manchester M60 7LP.—*Nat. Dir.*, Dr H. H. Gunson.

BLUE CROSS (1897), Shilton Road, Burford, Oxon. OX18 4PF. Tel: 0993-822651.—*Sec.*, A. Kennard, MBE.

BODLEIAN, FRIENDS OF THE (1925), Bodleian Library, Oxford OX1 3BG. Tel: 0865-277000.—*Sec.*, G. Groom.

BOOKSELLERS ASSOCIATION OF GREAT BRITAIN AND IRELAND (1895), 272–274 Vauxhall Bridge Road, SW1V 1BA. Tel: 071-834 5477.—*Dir.*, T. E. Godfray.

BOOK TRADE BENEVOLENT SOCIETY (1967), Dillon Lodge, The Retreat, Kings Langley, Herts. WD4 8LT. Tel: 0923-263128.—*Exec. Sec.*, Mrs A. R. Brown.

BOOK TRUST (1986), Book House, 45 East Hill, SW18 2QZ. Tel: 081-870 9055.—*Chief Exec.*, K. Mc-Williams.

BOTANICAL SOCIETY OF THE BRITISH ISLES (1836), Dept. of Botany, The Natural History Museum, Cromwell Road, SW7 5BD.—*Hon. Gen. Sec.*, Mrs M. Briggs, MBE.

BOTANICAL SOCIETY OF EDINBURGH, Royal Botanic Garden, Inverleith Row, Edinburgh EH3 5LR. Tel: 031-552 7171.—*Hon. Gen. Sec.*, Dr M. Chamberlain.

BOY SCOUTS ASSOCIATION, *see* SCOUT ASSOCIATION.

BOYS' BRIGADE, THE (1883), 1 Galena Road, W6 0LT. Membership worldwide: 400,000 in 60 countries. Tel: 081-741 4001.—*Brigade Sec.*, S. Jones.

BOYS' CLUBS, NATIONAL ASSOCIATION OF (1925), 369 Kennington Lane, SE11 5QY. Has affiliated to it 2,000 clubs. Tel: 071-793 0787.—*Nat. Dir.*, D. P. Harris.

BOYS' CLUBS OF NORTHERN IRELAND (1940), Bryson House, 28 Bedford Street, Belfast BT2 7FE. Tel: 0232-241924.—*Gen. Sec.*, K. Culbert

BREWING, INSTITUTE OF (1886), 33 Clarges Street, W1Y 8EE. Tel: 071-499 8144.—*Chief Exec.*, P. W. E. Istead.

BRIDEWELL ROYAL HOSPITAL (1553), Witley, Surrey GU8 5SG. Tel: 0428-682371. *Registrar*, Mrs J. Benyon.

BRITAIN-NEPAL SOCIETY (1960).—*Hon. Sec.*, Mrs J. Thomas, 24 Carthew Villas, W6 0BS.

BRITISH AND FOREIGN SCHOOL SOCIETY (1808), Richard Mayo Hall, Eden Street, Kingston upon Thames, Surrey KT1 1HZ. Tel: 081-546 2379.—*Sec.*, S. M. A. Banister.

BRITISH ATLANTIC COMMITTEE (1952), 5 St James's Place, SW1A 1NP.—*Dir.*, Maj.-Gen. C. J. Popham, CB.

BRITISH INSTITUTE IN EASTERN AFRICA (1959), 1 Kensington Gore, SW7 2AR. Tel: 071-584 4653.—*London Sec.*, Mrs J. Moyo.

BRITISH INSTITUTE OF ARCHAEOLOGY AT ANKARA (1948), c/o British Academy, 20–21 Cornwall Terrace, NW1 4QP.—*London Sec.*, Ms E. F. Chapman-Purchas.

BRITISH INSTITUTE OF PERSIAN STUDIES (1961), 13 Cambrian Road, Richmond, Surrey TW10 6JQ. Tel: 081-940 0647.—*Sec.*, Mrs M. E. Gueritz, MBE.

BRITISH INTERPLANETARY SOCIETY (1933), 27–29 South Lambeth Road, SW8 1SZ. Tel: 071-735 3160.—*Exec. Sec.*, S. A. Jones.

BRITISH ISRAEL WORLD FEDERATION (1919), 8 Blades Court, Deodar Road, SW15 2NU. Tel: 081-877 9010.—*Sec.*, A. E. Gibb.

BRITISH LEGION, THE ROYAL (1921), 48 Pall Mall, SW1Y 5JY. Tel: 071-973 0633.—*Gen. Sec.*, Lt.-Col. P. C. E. Creasy, OBE.

BRITISH LEGION SCOTLAND, ROYAL (1921), New Haig House, Logie Green Road, Edinburgh EH7 4HR.—*Gen. Sec.*, Brig. R. W. Riddle, OBE.

BRITISH MEDICAL ASSOCIATION (1832), BMA House, Tavistock Square, WC1H 9JP. Tel: 071-387 4499.—*Pres.*, Prof. A. C. Kennedy, FRSE; *Sec.*, Dr I. T. Field.

BRITISH RED CROSS (1870), 9 Grosvenor Crescent, SW1X 7EJ. Tel: 071-235 5454.—*Dir. Gen.*, M. Whitlam.

BRITISH SCHOOL OF ARCHAEOLOGY IN JERUSALEM (1919), The British Academy, 20–21 Cornwall Terrace, NW1 4QP. Tel: 031-650 3975.—*Dir.*, R. P. Harper.

BRUSH MANUFACTURERS' ASSOCIATION, BRITISH (1908), 35 Billing Road, Northampton NN1 5DD. Tel: 0604 22023.—*Sec.*, A. N. Nisbet.

BTCV (BRITISH TRUST FOR CONSERVATION VOLUNTEERS) (1970), 36 St Mary's Street, Wallingford, Oxon. OX10 0EU. Tel: 0491-39766.—*Chief Exec.*, R. Morley.

BUDDHIST SOCIETY, THE (1924), 58 Eccleston Square, SW1V 1PH. Tel: 071-834 5858.—*Gen. Sec.*, R. C. Maddox.

BUDGERIGAR SOCIETY, THE (1925), 49–53 Hazelwood Road, Northampton NN1 1LG.—*Gen. Sec.*, A. C. Crook.

BUILDING, CHARTERED INSTITUTE OF (1834), Englemere, Kings Ride, Ascot, Berks. SL5 8BJ. Tel: 0344-23355.—*Chief Exec.*, K. Banbury.

BUILDING SERVICES ENGINEERS, CHARTERED INSTITUTION OF (1897), Delta House, 222 Balham High Road, SW12 9BS. Tel: 081-675 5211.—*Sec.*, A. V. Ramsay.

BUILDING SOCIETIES ASSOCIATION (1936), 3 Savile Row, W1X 1AF. Tel: 071-437 0655.—*Dir. Gen.*, M. J. Boléat.

BUSINESS AND PROFESSIONAL WOMEN, UNITED KINGDOM FEDERATION OF (1938), 23 Ansdell Street, W8 5BN. Tel: 071-938 1729.—*Sec.*, Mrs P. Coney.

BUSINESS ARCHIVES COUNCIL (1934), 185 Tower Bridge Road, SE1 2UF.—*Sec. Gen.*, vacant.

BUSINESS EDUCATION, THE FACULTY OF (1872), 1 The Old School, Pant Glas, Oswestry SY10 7HS. Tel: 0691-654019.—*Gen. Sec.*, L. Garner.

CADET FORCE ASSOCIATION, COMBINED (1952), 'E' Block, The Duke of York's HQ, SW3 4RR. Tel: 071-730 9733.—*Sec.*, Brig. R. B. MacGregor-Oakford, CBE, MC.

CAFOD (CATHOLIC FUND FOR OVERSEAS DEVELOPMENT) (1962), 2 Romero Close, Stockwell Road, SW9 9TY. Tel: 071-733 7900.—*Dir.*, J. Filochowski.

CALOUSTE GULBENKIAN FOUNDATION (1956), 98 Portland Place, W1N 4ET. Tel: 071-636 5313.—*Dir.*, B. Whitaker.

CAMBRIDGE PRESERVATION SOCIETY (1929), Wandlebury Ring, Gog Magog Hills, Babraham, Cambridge CB2 4AE. Tel: 0223-243830.—*Sec.*, G. Brewster.

CAMERON FUND, THE (1971), Tavistock House North, Tavistock Square, WC1H 9JP.—*Sec.*, Mrs J. Martin.

CAMPAIGN FOR NUCLEAR DISARMAMENT (CND) (1958), 162 Holloway Road, N7 8DQ. Tel: 071-700 2393.—*Gen. Sec.*, G. Lefley.

CANCER RELIEF MACMILLAN FUND (1911), Anchor House, 15–19 Britten Street, SW3 3TZ.—*Dir.*, D. Scott.

CANCER RESEARCH CAMPAIGN, 2 Carlton House Terrace, SW1Y 5AR. Tel: 071-930 8972.—*Dir. Gen.*, D. de Peyer.

CANCER RESEARCH FUND, IMPERIAL (1902), PO Box 123, Lincoln's Inn Fields, WC2A 3PX. Tel: 071-242 0200.—*Sec.*, Miss M. J. Craggs.

CANCER RESEARCH, THE INSTITUTE OF, Royal Cancer Hospital, 17A Onslow Gardens, SW7 3AL. Tel: 071-352 8133.—*Sec.*, J. Kipling.

CANCER UNITED PATIENTS, BRITISH ASSOCIATION OF (BACUP) (1985), 121–123 Charterhouse Street, EC1M 6AA. Tel: 071-608 1785.—*Chairman*, M. Slevin.

CAREER TEACHERS, ASSOCIATION OF (1975), Hillsborough, Castledine Street, Loughborough, Leics. LE11 2DX.—*Gen. Sec.*, Miss P. Yaffé.

CARERS NATIONAL ASSOCIATION (1988), 29 Chilworth Mews, W2 3RG.—*Dir.*, Ms J. Pitkeathley.

CARNEGIE DUNFERMLINE TRUST (1903), Abbey Park House, Dunfermline KY12 7PB. Social and cultural purposes in Dunfermline. Tel: 0383-723638.—*Sec.*, F. Mann.

CARNEGIE HERO FUND TRUST (1908). Abbey Park House, Dunfermline KY12 7PB. Tel: 0383-723638.—*Sec.*, F. Mann.

CARNEGIE UNITED KINGDOM TRUST (1913), Comely Park House, Dunfermline KY12 7EJ. Tel: 0383-721445.—*Sec.*, G. Lord, OBE.

CATHEDRALS FABRIC COMMISSION FOR ENGLAND (1949), 83 London Wall, EC2M 5NA. Tel: 071-638 0971.—*Sec.*, Dr R. Gem.

CATHOLIC MARRIAGE ADVISORY COUNCIL (1946), Clitherow House, 1 Blythe Mews, Blythe Road, W14 0NW.—*Chief Exec.*, Mrs J. C. Judge.

CATHOLIC RECORD SOCIETY (1904), c/o 114 Mount Street, W1Y 6AH.—*Hon. Sec.*, Miss R. Rendel.

CATHOLIC TRUTH SOCIETY (1868), 38–40 Eccleston Square, SW1V 1PD.—*Gen. Sec.*, D. Murphy.

CATHOLIC UNION OF GREAT BRITAIN (1872), St Maximilian Kolbe House, 63 Jeddo Road, W12 9EE. Tel: 081-749 1321.—*Pres.*, The Duke of Norfolk, KG, GCVO, CB, CBE, MC; *Hon. Sec.*, Mrs J. Stuyt, MBE.

CATTLE BREEDERS' ASSOCIATION, NATIONAL.—*Sec.*, R. W. Kershaw-Dolby, Lawford Grange, Lawford Heath, Rugby, Warks. CV23 9HG. Tel: 0788-565264.

CATTLE BREEDER'S CLUB LTD, BRITISH. (1945), Lavenders, Isfield, Uckfield, E. Sussex TN22 5TX. Tel: 082 575-356.—*Sec.*, C. R. Stains.

CECIL HOUSES (Inc.) (1926), 2 Priory Road, Kew, Richmond, Surrey TW9 3DG. (Housing Association). Tel: 081-940 9828.—*Sec.*, G. Brighton.

CENTRAL BUREAU (for educational visits and exchanges) (1948), Seymour Mews House, Seymour Mews, W1H 9PE. Tel: 071-486 5101.—*Dir.* A. H. Male.

CERAMICS, INSTITUTE OF (1955), Shelton House, Stoke Road, Shelton, Stoke-on-Trent ST4 2DR.—*Pres.*, Dr D. W. F. James.

CHADWICK TRUST (1895), Department of Civil Engineering, University College London, Gower Street, WC1E 6BT. For the promotion of health and prevention of disease.—*Sec to the Trustees*, I. K. Orchardson PH.D.

CHANTREY BEQUEST (1875), Royal Academy of Arts Burlington House, Piccadilly, W1V 0DS. Tel: 071 439 7438.—*Sec.*, P. Rodgers.

CHARITIES AID FOUNDATION (1974), 48 Pembury Road Tonbridge, Kent TN9 2JD. Tel: 0732-771333.—*Dir* M. Brophy.

CHARTERED SECRETARIES AND ADMINISTRATORS, IN STITUTE OF (1891), 16 Park Crescent, W1N 4AH Tel: 071-580 4741.—*Sec.*, M. J. Ainsworth.

CHEMICAL ENGINEERS, INSTITUTION OF (1922), Th Davis Building, 165–171 Railway Terrace, Rugby Warks. CV21 3HQ. Tel: 0788-578214.—*Gen. Sec* Dr T. J. Evans.

CHEMISTRY, THE ROYAL SOCIETY OF, Burlington House, Piccadilly, W1V 0BN. Tel: 071-437 8656.—*Sec. Gen.*, Dr J. S. Gow, FRSE.

CHESHIRE (LEONARD) FOUNDATION, *see* LEONARD CHESHIRE FOUNDATION.

CHESS FEDERATION, BRITISH (1904), 9A Grand Parade St Leonards-on-Sea, E. Sussex TN38 0DD. Tel 0424-442500.—*Gen. Sec.*, Mrs G. White.

CHEST, HEART AND STROKE ASSOCIATION (1899) Tavistock House North, Tavistock Square WC1H 9JE.—*Dir. Gen.*, Sir David Atkinson, KBE.

CHILDBIRTH TRUST, NATIONAL (1956), Alexandra House, Oldham Terrace W3 6NH. Tel: 081-99 8637.—*Chief Exec.*, Ms S. Dobson.

CHILDMINDING ASSOCIATION, NATIONAL (1977), Masons Hill, Bromley, Kent BR2 9EY. Tel: 081-46 6164.—*Dir.*, Mrs J. Burnell.

CHILDREN'S HOME, NATIONAL (1869), 85 Highbury Park, N5 1UD. Tel: 071-226 2033.—*Principal*, T White, CBE.

CHILDREN'S SOCIETY, THE (1881), Edward Rudol House, Margery Street, WC1X 0JL. Tel: 071-83 4299.—*Dir.*, I. Sparks.

CHINA ASSOCIATION (1889), Swire House, 59 Buck ingham Gate, SW1E 6AJ. Tel: 071-821 3220/1.—*Exec. Dir.*, Brig. B. G. Hickey, OBE, MC.

CHIROPODISTS, SOCIETY OF (1945), 53 Welbeck Street W1M 7HE.—*Gen. Sec.*, J. G. C. Trouncer.

CHOIRS SCHOOLS ASSOCIATION (1921), York Minster School, Deangate, York YO1 2JA. Tel: 0940 625217.—*Hon. Sec.*, R. J. Shephard.

CHRISTIAN ACTION, St Peter's House, 308 Kennington Lane, SE11 5HY. Tel: 071-735 2372.—*Hon. Dir.* Rev. Canon E. James.

CHRISTIAN AID (1945), PO Box 100, SE1 7RT. Tel: 071 620 4444.—*Dir.*, Rev. M. H. Taylor.

CHRISTIAN EDUCATION COUNCIL, NATIONAL (1809) Robert Denholm House, Nutfield, Redhill RH1 4HW. Tel: 0737-822411.—*Exec. Officer*, D. Trenaman.

CHRISTIAN EDUCATION MOVEMENT (1965), Royal Buildings, Victoria Street, Derby DE1 1GW. Tel: 0332 296655.— *Gen. Sec.*, Rev. Dr S. Orchard.

CHRISTIAN EVIDENCE SOCIETY (1870), St Stephen's House, St Stephen's Crescent, Brentwood, Esse: CM13 2AT.—*Hon. Sec.*, Mrs G. M. Ryeland.

CHRISTIAN KNOWLEDGE, SOCIETY FOR PROMOTING (SPCK) (1698), Holy Trinity Church, Marylebone Road, NW1 4DU. Tel: 071-387 5282.—*Gen. Sec.*, P N. G. Gilbert.

CHRISTIANS AND JEWS, COUNCIL OF (1942), 1 Denning ton Park Road, NW6 1AX. Tel: 071-794 8178.—*Exec. Dir.*, Rev. Canon J. Richardson.

CHURCH ARMY (1882), Independents Road, SE3 9LG Tel: 081-318 1226.—*Chief Sec.*, Capt. P. Johanson.

CHURCH BUILDING SOCIETY, INCORPORATED (1818), Fulham Palace, SW6 6EA. Tel: 071-736 3054.—*Sec.*, R. H. C. Heptinstall.

CHURCH EDUCATION CORPORATION, Bedgebury School, Goudhurst, Cranbrook, Kent TN17 2SH.—*Sec.*, R. P. Gilbert.

CHURCH HOUSE, THE CORPORATION OF (1888), Dean's Yard, SW1P 3NZ. Tel: 071-222 9011.—*Sec.*, C. D. L. Menzies.

CHURCH LADS' AND CHURCH GIRLS' BRIGADE (1891), 2 Barnsley Road, Wath upon Dearne, Rotherham, S. Yorks. S63 6PY. Tel: 0709-876535.—*Gen. Sec.*, Wg Cdr. J. S. Cresswell (*retd.*).

CHURCH MISSIONARY SOCIETY (1799), 157 Waterloo Road, SE1 8UU. Tel: 071-928 8681.—*Gen. Sec.*, Rt. Rev. M. Nazir-Ali.

CHURCH MUSIC, ROYAL SCHOOL OF (1927), Addington Palace, Croydon CR9 5AD. Tel: 081-654 7676.—*Chief Exec.*, R. Lawrence.

CHURCH OF ENGLAND PENSIONS BOARD (1926), 7 Little College Street, SW1P 3SF. Tel: 071-222 2091.—*Sec.*, R. G. Radford.

CHURCH OF ENGLAND SOLDIERS', SAILORS' AND AIR-MEN'S CLUBS (1891), 1 Shakespeare Terrace, 126 High Street, Portsmouth PO1 2RH.—*Chairman*, Rear-Adm. A. G. Watson, CB.

CHURCH UNION (1859), Faith House, 7 Tufton Street, SW1P 3QN. Tel: 071-222 6952.—*Gen. Sec.*, A. Leggatt.

CHURCHES, COUNCIL FOR THE CARE OF (1921), 83 London Wall, EC2M 5NA.—*Sec.*, Dr T. Cocke.

CHURCHES FOR BRITAIN AND IRELAND, COUNCIL OF (1942), Inter-Church House, 35–41 Lower Marsh, SE1 7RL. Tel: 071-620 4444.—*Gen. Sec.*, Rev. J. P. Reardon.

CHURCHES, FRIENDS OF FRIENDLESS (1957), 12 Edwardes Square, W8 6HG. Tel: 071-602 6267.—*Hon. Sec.*, J. H. Bowles.

CHURCHES MAIN COMMITTEE (1941), Fielden House, Little College Street, SW1P 3JZ. Tel: 071-222 4984.—*Sec.*, J. D. Taylor Thompson, CB.

CHURCHES TOGETHER IN ENGLAND (1990), Inter Church House, 35-41 Lower Marsh, SE1 7RL. Tel: 071-620 4444.—*Gen. Sec.*, Canon M. Reardon.

CHURCHES TOGETHER IN SCOTLAND, ACTION OF (1990), Scottish Churches House, Kirk Street, Dunblane FK15 0AJ. Tel: 0786-823588.—*Gen. Sec.*, Rev. M. Craig.

CITIZENS' ADVICE BUREAUX, NATIONAL ASSOCIATION OF (1931), Myddelton House, 115–123 Pentonville Road, N1 9LZ. Tel: 071-833 2181.—*Chief Exec.* A. Abraham.

CITY PAROCHIAL FOUNDATION (1891), 6 Middle Street, EC1A 7PH. Tel: 071-606 6145.—*Clerk*, T. Cook.

CIVIC TRUST, THE (1957), 17 Carlton House Terrace, SW1Y 5AW. Tel: 071-930 0914.—*Dir.*, M. C. Bradshaw.

CIVIL DEFENCE, INSTITUTE OF (1938), Bell Court House, 11 Blomfield Street, EC2M 7AY. Tel: 071-588 3700.—*Hon. Gen. Sec.*, J. Lawal.

CIVIL ENGINEERS, INSTITUTION OF (1818), Great George Street, SW1P 3AA.—*Sec.*, J. C. McKenzie.

CIVIL LIBERTIES, NATIONAL COUNCIL FOR, *see* LIBERTY.

CLASSICAL ASSOCIATION (1903).—*Hon. Treas.*, R. Wallace, Dept. of Classics, University of Keele, Keele, Newcastle under Lyme, Staffs. ST5 5BG. Tel: 0782-62111, ext. 3231.

CLEAN AIR AND ENVIRONMENTAL PROTECTION, NATIONAL SOCIETY FOR (1899), 136 North Street, Brighton BN1 1RG. Tel: 0273-26313.—*Sec. Gen.*, Air Cdre J. Langston, CBE.

CLERGY ORPHAN CORPORATION (1749), 57B Tufton Street, SW1P 3QL.—*Sec.*, Miss J. Buncher.

CLERKS OF WORKS OF GREAT BRITAIN INC., INSTITUTE OF (1882), 41 The Mall, Ealing, W5 3TJ. Tel: 081-579 2917/8.—*Sec.*, A. P. Macnamara.

COACHING CLUB (1871), 8 Parthenia Road, SW6 4BD. Tel: 071-384 1165.—*Sec.*, D. H. Clarke.

COMMERCE, ASSOCIATION OF BRITISH CHAMBERS OF (1860), Sovereign House, 212 Shaftesbury Avenue, WC2H 8EW. Tel: 071-240 5831.—*Dir. Gen.*, R. G. Taylor, CBE.

COMMERCE, ASSOCIATION OF SCOTTISH CHAMBERS OF, 30 George Square, Glasgow G2 1EQ. Tel: 0333-25164.—*Dir.*, A. Moore.

COMMERCE AND INDUSTRY, LONDON CHAMBER OF (1881), 69 Cannon Street, EC4N 5AB. Tel: 071-248 4444.—*Chief Exec.*, vacant.

COMMERCE AND MANUFACTURERS, EDINBURGH CHAMBER OF (1786), 3 Randolph Crescent, Edinburgh EH3 7UD. Tel: 031-225 5851.—*Chief Exec.*, I. Brown.

COMMERCE AND MANUFACTURERS, GLASGOW CHAMBER OF (1783), 30 George Square, Glasgow G2 1EQ. Tel: 041-204 2121—*Chief Exec.*, E. Marwick.

COMMERCE, CANADA UNITED KINGDOM CHAMBER OF (1921), 3 Regent Street, SW1Y 4NZ. Tel: 071-930 7711.—*Exec. Dir.*, G. F. Bacon.

COMMERCIAL AND INDUSTRIAL EDUCATION, BRITISH ASSOCIATION FOR (BACIE) (1919), 16 Park Crescent, W1N 4AP.—*Dir.*, B. V. Murphy.

COMMERCIAL TRAVELLERS' BENEVOLENT INSTITUTION (1849).—*Sec.*, M. N. Bown, Gable End, Mill Hill Road, Arnesby, Leics. LE8 3WG. Tel: 0533-478647.

COMMISSIONAIRES, THE CORPS OF (1859). *Headquarters*, Market House, 85 Cowcross Street, EC1M 6BP. Tel: 071-490 1125. Divisions in Belfast, Birmingham, Bristol, Edinburgh, Glasgow, Leeds, Liverpool, London, Manchester, Newcastle upon Tyne.—*Commandant*, Col. R. B. Robertson.

COMMONWEALTH TRUST (linking the Royal Commonwealth Society and the Victoria League for Commonwealth Friendship), Commonwealth House, 18 Northumberland Avenue, WC2N 5BJ.—*Dir. Gen.*, Sir David Thorne.

COMPLEMENTARY AND ALTERNATIVE MEDICINE, COUNCIL FOR (1985), 179 Gloucester Place, NW1 6DX. Tel: 071-724 9103.—*Sec.*, Ms C. Daglish.

COMPLEMENTARY MEDICINE, INSTITUTE FOR (1856), 21 Portland Place, W1N 3AF.—*Dir.*, A. Baird.

COMPOSERS' GUILD OF GREAT BRITAIN (1945), 34 Hanway Street, W1P 9DE. Tel: 071-436 0007.—*Gen. Sec.*, Ms E. Yeoman.

COMPUTER SOCIETY, BRITISH (1957), 13 Mansfield Street, W1M 0BP.—*Chief Exec.*, J. R. Brookes.

CONSERVATION OF HISTORIC AND ARTISTIC WORKS, INTERNATIONAL INSTITUTE FOR (1950), 6 Buckingham Street, WC2N 6BA. Tel: 071-839 5975.—*Sec. Gen.*, Prof. H. W. M. Hodges.

CONSULTING ECONOMISTS' ASSOCIATION, INTERNATIONAL (1986), 16A Barnes High Street, SW13 9LW. Tel: 081-876 2299.—*Chairman*, J. T. Winpenny.

CONSULTING ENGINEERS, ASSOCIATION OF (1913), Alliance House, 12 Caxton Street, SW1H 0QL. Tel: 071-222 6557.—*Sec.*, Brig. H. Woodrow.

CONSULTING SCIENTISTS, ASSOCIATION OF (1958), 2-3 Bosworth House, High Street, Thorpe-le-Soken, Essex CO16 0EA. Tel: 0255-862412.—*Hon. Sec.*, W. G. Simpson.

CONSUMERS' ASSOCIATION (1957), c/o The Association for Consumer Research, 2 Marylebone Road, NW1 4DX. Tel: 071-486 5544.—*Dir.*, J. Beishon.

CONTEMPORARY APPLIED ARTS (1948), 43 Earlham Street, WC2H 9LD. Tel: 071-836 6993.—*Dir.*, Ms T. Peters.

CONVEYANCERS, COUNCIL FOR LICENSED (1986), Suite 3, Cairngorm House, 203 Marsh Wall, E14 9YT. Tel: 071-537 2953.—*Sec.*, A. Viner.

CO-OPERATIVE SOCIETIES AND ASSOCIATIONS :—

Co-operative Party, 342 Hoe Street, E17 9PX. Tel: 081-520 3580.—*Sec.*, D. Wise, OBE.

Co-operative Union Ltd (1869), Holyoake House, Hanover Street, Manchester M60 0AS. Tel: 061-832 4300.—*Chief Exec. and Gen. Sec.*, D. L. Wilkinson.

Co-operative Wholesale Society Ltd (CWS) (1863), PO Box 53, New Century House, Manchester M60 4ES. Tel: 061-834 1212.—*Chief Exec.*, Sir Dennis Landau.

Co-operative Women's Guild (1883), 342 Hoe Street, E17 9PX. Tel: 081-520 4902.—*Gen Sec.*, Mrs S. Bell.

Plunkett Foundation for Co-operative Studies (1919), 23 Hanborough Business Park, Long Hanborough, Oxford OX7 2LH. Tel: 0993-883636.—*Dir.*, E. Parnell.

COPYRIGHT COUNCIL, BRITISH (1953), 29–33 Berners Street, W1P 4AA.—*Sec.*, G. V. Adams.

CORONERS' SOCIETY OF ENGLAND AND WALES (1846).—*Hon. Sec.*, Dr J. D. K. Burton, CBE, 7 Orchard Rise, Richmond, Surrey TW10 5BX.

CORPORATE TREASURERS, ASSOCIATION OF (1979), 12 Devereux Court, WC2R 3JJ.—*Sec.*, Ms G. Pierpoint.

CORPORATE TRUSTEES, ASSOCIATION OF (1974), 2 Withdean Rise, Brighton BN1 6YN. Tel: 0273-504276.—*Sec.*, L. C. Howes.

CORRESPONDENCE COLLEGES, ASSOCIATION OF BRITISH (1955), 6 Francis Grove, SW19 4DT.—*Sec.*, Mrs M. Coren.

CORRYMEELA COMMUNITY (1965), Corrymeela House, 8 Upper Crescent, Belfast BT7 1NT. Tel: 0232-325008.—*Dir.*, Rev. J. Morrow.

COTTON GROWING ASSOCIATION, BRITISH (1904), 13 Upper High Street, Thame, Oxon. OX9 3HL. Tel: 0844-261447.—*Managing Dir.*, M. Maynard.

COUNCIL FOR THE PROTECTION OF RURAL ENGLAND (CPRE), *see* RURAL.

COUNSEL AND CARE (1954), Twyman House, 16 Bonny Street, NW1 9PG. Tel: 071-485 1550.—*Gen. Mgr.*, J. Smith.

COUNTRY HOUSES ASSOCIATION LTD (1955), 41 Kingsway, WC2B 6UB.—*Chief Exec.*, R. D. Bratby.

COUNTRY LANDOWNERS ASSOCIATION (1907), 16 Belgrave Square, SW1X 8PQ. Tel: 071-235 0511.—*Dir. Gen.*, J. Anderson.

COUNTY CHIEF EXECUTIVES, ASSOCIATION OF (1974).—*Hon. Sec.*, I. G. Caulfield, Shire Hall, Warwick CV34 4RR. Tel: 0926-412559.

COUNTY COUNCILS, ASSOCIATION OF (1890), Eaton House, 66A Eaton Square, SW1W 9BH. Tel: 071-235 1200.—*Sec.*, R. G. Wendt.

COUNTY EMERGENCY PLANNING OFFICERS' SOCIETY (1966).—*Hon. Sec.*, N. B. Knocker, OBE, Emergency Planning Dept., County Hall, Trowbridge, Wilts BA14 8JE. Tel: 0225-753641, ext. 3510.

COUNTY SECRETARIES, SOCIETY OF (1974).—*Hon. Sec.* G. D. Gordon, County Hall, Chester CH1 1SF. Tel 0244-602107.

COUNTY SURVEYORS' SOCIETY (1884).—*Hon. Sec.*, D. A. Hutchinson, County Hall, Dorchester DT1 1XJ Tel: 0305-204914.

COUNTY TREASURERS, SOCIETY OF (1903).— *Hon. Sec.* B. Smith, County Buildings, Eastgate Street, Stafford ST16 2NF. Tel: 0785-223121.

CRUEL SPORTS, THE LEAGUE AGAINST (1924), 83 Union Street, SE1 1SG. Tel: 071-407 0979.—*Exec. Dir.*, J Barrington.

CRUELTY TO ANIMALS, SOCIETY FOR THE PREVENTION OF, *see* ROYAL and SCOTTISH.

CRUELTY TO CHILDREN, SOCIETY FOR THE PREVENTION OF, *see* NATIONAL and ROYAL SCOTTISH.

CRUSE—BEREAVEMENT CARE (1959), 126 Sheen Road Richmond, Surrey TW9 1UR.—*Dir.*, A. Sandison.

CURWEN INSTITUTE (1875), 17 Primrose Avenue, Chadwell Heath, Romford RM6 4QB. Tel: 081-599 8230.—*Gen. Sec.*, H. Jones.

CWMNI URDD GOBAITH CYMRU (1922), Swyddfa'r Urdd Aberystwyth, Dyfed SY23 1EN. Tel: 0970-623744.—*Dir.*, J. E. Williams.

CYCLISTS' TOURING CLUB (1878), Cotterell House, 69 Meadrow, Godalming, Surrey GU7 3HS. Tel: 0483 417217.—*Dir.*, A. Harlow.

CYMMRODORION, THE HONOURABLE SOCIETY OF (1751), 30 Eastcastle Street, W1N 7PD.—*Hon. Sec.*, Dr T. Wyn Jones.

CYSTIC FIBROSIS RESEARCH TRUST (1964), Alexandra House, 5 Blyth Road, Bromley BR1 3RS. Tel: 081-464 7211.—*Dir.*, G. J. Edkins.

CYTUN (CHURCHES TOGETHER IN WALES) (1990), 21 St Helen's Road, Swansea SA1 4AP. Tel: 0792-460876.—*Gen. Sec.*, Rev. N. A. Davies.

DAIRY ASSOCIATION, UNITED KINGDOM (1950), Giggs Hill Green, Thames Ditton, Surrey KT7 0EL. Tel: 081-398 4101, ext. 2436.—*Sec.*, Mrs J. M. Newton.

DAIRY FARMERS, ROYAL ASSOCIATION OF BRITISH (1876), 55 Sleaford Street, SW8 5AB. Tel: 071-627 2111.—*Chief Exec.*, P. M. Gilbert.

DAIRY TECHNOLOGY, SOCIETY OF (1943), 72 Ermine Street, Huntingdon, Cambs. PE18 6EZ. Tel: 0480-450741.—*Nat. Sec.*, Mrs R. Gale.

DATA (Design and Technology Association), Smallpiece House, 27 Newbold Terrace East, Leamington Spa, Warks. CV32 4EC. Tel: 0926-315984.—*Dir.*, G. Warren.

D-DAY AND NORMANDY FELLOWSHIP (1968).—*Hon. Sec.*, Mrs L. R. Reed, 9 South Parade, Southsea, Hants. PO5 2JB. Tel: 0705-812180.

DEAF, COMMONWEALTH SOCIETY FOR THE (1959), Dilke House, Malet Street, WC1E 7JA. Tel: 071-631 5311.—*Chairman*, C. Holborow, OBE, TD, MD.

DEAF, ROYAL NATIONAL INSTITUTE FOR THE (1911), 105 Gower Street, WC1E 6AH. Tel: 071-387 8033.—*Chief Exec.*, S. Etherington.

DEAF ASSOCIATION, BRITISH (1890 *formerly* BRITISH DEAF AND DUMB ASSOCIATION), 38 Victoria Place, Carlisle CA1 1HU. Tel: 0228-48844.—*Chief Exec.*, Ms E. Wincott.

DEAF CHILDREN, ROYAL SCHOOL FOR (1792), Victoria Road, Margate, Kent CT9 1NB. Tel: 0843-227561.—*Sec.*, D. E. Downs.

DEAF PEOPLE, FOLEY HOUSE RESIDENTIAL HOME FOR (1851), Foley House, 115 High Garrett, Braintree, Essex CM7 5NU. Tel: 0376-26652.—*Dir.*, Mrs N. Hartard.

DEAF PEOPLE, ROYAL ASSOCIATION IN AID OF (1841), 27 Old Oak Road, W3 7HN. Tel: 081-743 6187.—*Chief Exec.*, Ms R. Brotherwood.

DEER MANAGEMENT SOCIETIES, THE FEDERATION OF (1975).—*Chairman.*, J. Hotchkis, Stede Court, Biddenden, Ashford, Kent TN27 8JG. Tel: 0580-291235.

DEFENCE STUDIES, ROYAL UNITED SERVICES INSTITUTE FOR (1831), Whitehall, SW1A 2ET. Tel: 071-930 5854.—*Dir.*, Gp. Capt. D. Bolton.

DENTAL ASSOCIATION, BRITISH (1880), 64 Wimpole Street, W1M 8AL. Tel: 071-935 0875.—*Sec.*, N. H. Whitehouse.

DENTAL COUNCIL, GENERAL (1956), 37 Wimpole Street, W1M 8DQ.—*Registrar*, N. T. Davies, MBE.

DENTAL HOSPITALS OF THE UNITED KINGDOM, ASSOCIATION OF (1942).—*Hon. Sec.*, Mrs P. Harrington, Birmingham Dental Hospital, St Chad's Queensway, Birmingham B4 6NN.

DESIGN AND INDUSTRIES ASSOCIATION (1915).—*Dir.*, R. Moxley, 17 Lawn Crescent, Kew Gardens, Surrey TW9 3NR.

DESIGNERS FOR INDUSTRY, FACULTY OF ROYAL (1936), RSA, 8 John Adam Street, WC2N 6EZ. Tel: 071-930 5115.—*Sec.*, C. Lucas.

DESIGNERS, THE CHARTERED SOCIETY OF (1930), 29 Bedford Square, WC1B 3EG. Tel: 071-631 1510.—*Dir.*, B. Lymbery.

DIABETIC ASSOCIATION, BRITISH (1934), 10 Queen Anne Street, W1M 0BD.—*Sec. Gen.*, Capt. D. G. Armytage, CBE, RN.

DICKENS FELLOWSHIP (1902), Dickens House, 48 Doughty Street, WC1N 2LF.—*Hon. Gen. Sec.*, A. S. Watts.

DIRECTORS OF PUBLIC HEALTH, ASSOCIATION OF (1982).—*Hon. Sec.*, Dr J. A. Sorrell, Burton District Hospital Centre, Belvedere Road, Burton upon Trent, Staffs. DE13 0RB.

DIRECTORS, INSTITUTE OF (1903), 116 Pall Mall, SW1Y 5ED. Tel: 071-839 1233.—*Dir. Gen.*, P. Morgan.

DISPENSING OPTICIANS, ASSOCIATION OF BRITISH (1925), 6 Hurlingham Business Park, Sulivan Road, SW6 3DU. Tel: 071-736 0088.—*Registrar*, D. S. Baker.

DISTRESSED GENTLEFOLKS' AID ASSOCIATION (1897), Vicarage Gate House, Vicarage Gate, W8 4AQ. Tel: 071-229 9341.—*Gen. Sec.*, N. B. M. Clack.

DISTRICT COUNCILS, ASSOCIATION OF (1974), 26 Chapter Street, SW1P 4ND. Tel: 071-233 6860.

DISTRICT SECRETARIES, ASSOCIATION OF (1974), 9 Margaret Road, Bishopsworth, Bristol BS13 9DQ. Tel: 0272-647299.—*Hon. Sec.*, M. Bull (*until Oct. 1991*).

DITCHLEY FOUNDATION, Ditchley Park, Enstone, Oxford OX7 4ER. Tel: 0608-677346.—*Dir.*, Sir John Graham, Bt., GCMG.

DOCKLAND SETTLEMENTS (1895), Rotherhithe Street, SE16 1LJ.—*Chief Exec.*, J. B. Faul.

DOMESTIC SERVANTS' BENEVOLENT INSTITUTION (1846), Royal Bank of Scotland PLC, 7 Burlington Gardens, W1A 3DD.—*Sec.*, A. J. Gibson.

DOWSERS, BRITISH SOCIETY OF (1933).—*Sec.*, M. D. Rust, Sycamore Cottage, Tamley Lane, Hastingleigh, Ashford, Kent TN25 5HW. Tel: 0233-75253.

DRAINAGE AUTHORITIES, ASSOCIATION OF (1937).—*Sec.*, D. Noble, The Mews, 3 Royal Oak Passage, High Street, Huntingdon, Cambs. PE18 6EA. Tel: 0480-411123.

DRINKING FOUNTAIN AND CATTLE TROUGH ASSOCIATION, METROPOLITAN (1859).—*Sec.* D. R. W. Randall, 105 Wansunt Road, Bexley, Kent DA5 2DN. Tel: 0322-528062.

DRIVING SOCIETY, BRITISH (1957), 27 Dugard Place, Barford, Warwick CV35 8DX. Tel: 0926-624420.—*Sec.*, Mrs J. M. Dillon.

DRUG DEPENDENCE, INSTITUTE FOR THE STUDY OF (1968), 1–4 Hatton Place, EC1N 8ND. Tel: 071-430 1991.—*Dir.*, J. Woodcock, OBE.

DUKE OF EDINBURGH'S AWARD SCHEME (1956), Gulliver House, Madeira Walk, Windsor, Berks. SL4 1EU. Tel: 0753-810753.—*Dir.*, Maj.-Gen. M. F. Hobbs, CBE.

DYERS AND COLOURISTS, SOCIETY OF (1884), Perkin House, PO Box 244, 82 Grattan Road, Bradford BD1 2JB. Tel: 0274-725138.—*Gen. Sec.*, M. Tordoff, PH.D.

EARL HAIG'S (BRITISH LEGION) APPEAL FUND, *see* BRITISH LEGION, ROYAL.

EARLY CHILDHOOD EDUCATION, BRITISH ASSOCIATION FOR (1923), 111 City View House, 463 Bethnal Green Road, E2 9QY. Tel: 071-739 7594.— *Sec.*, Mrs B. Boon.

ECCLESIASTICAL HISTORY SOCIETY (1961).—*Sec.*, Dr R. Swanson, School of History, University of Birmingham, Edgbaston B15 2TT. Tel: 021-414 5736.

ECCLESIOLOGICAL SOCIETY (1839).—*Hon. Sec. (acting)*, K. V. Richardson, 127 Marvels Lane, SE12 9PP.

EDUCATION IN ART AND DESIGN, NATIONAL SOCIETY FOR (1888), 7A High Street, Corsham, Wilts. SN13 0ES. Tel: 0249-714825.—*Gen. Sec.*, J. Steers.

EDUCATION OFFICERS, SOCIETY OF (1971), 20 Bedford Way, WC1H 0AL. Tel: 071-580 2581.—*Gen. Sec.*, D. J. Hatfield, CBE.

EDUCATION OFFICERS' SOCIETY, COUNTY (1889).—*Hon. Sec.*, S. Sharp, Education Dept., County Hall, Aylesbury, Bucks. Tel: 0296-382602.

EDUCATIONAL CENTRES ASSOCIATION (1921), Chequer Centre, Chequer Street, EC1Y 8PL.—*Gen. Sec.*, D. Delahunt.

EDUCATIONAL RESEARCH IN ENGLAND AND WALES, NATIONAL FOUNDATION FOR (1946), The Mere, Upton Park, Slough SL1 2DQ. Tel: 0753-574123.—*Dir.*, Ms C. Burstall, PH.D., D.SC.

EGYPT EXPLORATION SOCIETY (1882), 3 Doughty Mews, WC1N 2PG. Tel: 071-242 1880.—*Sec.*, Dr P. A. Spencer.

ELECTORAL REFORM SOCIETY OF GREAT BRITAIN AND IRELAND, 6 Chancel Street, SE1 0UU. Tel: 071-928 1622.—*Pres.*, Lord Blake, FBA.

ELECTRICAL ENGINEERS, INSTITUTION OF (1871), Savoy Place, WC2R 0BL. Tel: 071-240 1871.—*Sec.*, J. C. Williams, PH.D., F.ENG.

ELGAR FOUNDATION (1973).— *Sec. to the Trustees*, J. G. Hughes, 23 Meadow Hill Road, Birmingham B38 8DE. Tel: 021-458 2747.

ELGAR SOCIETY (1951).—*Sec.*, Mrs C. Holt, 20 Geraldine Road, Malvern, Worcs. WR14 3PA. Tel: 0684-568822.

ENERGY, INSTITUTE OF (1927), 18 Devonshire Street, W1N 2AU. Tel: 071-580 7124.—*Sec.*, C. Rigg, TD.

ENGINEERING COUNCIL, THE (1981), 10 Maltravers Street, WC2R 3ER. Tel: 071-240 7891.—*Sec.*, L. Chelton.

ENGINEERING DESIGNERS, INSTITUTE OF (1945), Courtleigh, Westbury Leigh, Westbury, Wilts. BA13 3TA. Tel: 0373-822801.—*Sec.*, M. J. Osborne.

ENGINEERING INDUSTRIES ASSOCIATION (1941), 16 Dartmouth Street, SW1H 9BL. Tel: 071-222 2367.—*Dir. Gen.*, Col. W. T. Williams.

ENGINEERS AND SHIPBUILDERS, NE COAST INSTITUTION OF (1884), Great North House, Sandyford Road, Newcastle upon Tyne NE1 8ND. Tel: 091-230 1515.—*Sec.*, Mrs A. J. Rainsford.

ENGINEERS, INSTITUTION OF BRITISH (1928), Royal Liver Building, 6 Hampton Place, Brighton BN1 3DD.—*Sec.*, Mrs D. Henry.

ENGINEERS, SOCIETY OF (INCORPORATED) (1854), Parsifal College, 527 Finchley Road, NW3 7BG. Tel: 071-435 5600.—*Sec.*, P. A. Lancaster.

ENGLISH ASSOCIATION, THE (1906), The Vicarage, Priory Gardens, W4 1TT. Tel: 081-995 4236.—*Sec.*, Dr R. Fairbanks-Joseph.

ENGLISH FOLK DANCE AND SONG SOCIETY (1932), Cecil Sharp House, 2 Regent's Park Road, NW1 7AY. Tel: 071-485 2206.—*Chairman*, vacant.

ENGLISH PLACE-NAME SOCIETY (1923).—*Hon. Dir.* Prof. K. Cameron, CBE, FBA, Dept. of English, The University, Nottingham NG7 2RD. Tel: 0602-484848, ext. 2892.

ENGLISH-SPEAKING UNION OF THE COMMONWEALTH, THE (1918), 37 Charles Street, W1X 8AB. Tel: 071-493 3328.—*Dir. Gen.*, H. D. Hicks, MBE.

ENTOMOLOGICAL SOCIETY OF LONDON, ROYAL (1833), 41 Queen's Gate, SW7 5HU. Tel: 071-584 8361.—*Registrar*, G. G. Bentley.

ENVIRONMENTAL HEALTH OFFICERS, INSTITUTION OF (1883), Chadwick House, Rushworth Street, SE1 0QT. Tel: 071-928 6006.—*Sec.*, T. Blunt.

ENVIRONMENT COUNCIL (1969), 80 York Way, N1 9AG. Tel: 071-278 4736.—*Chief Exec.*, S. Robinson.

EPILEPSY ASSOCIATION, BRITISH (1949), Anstey House, 40 Hanover Square, Leeds LS3 1BE. Tel: 0532-439393.—*Chief Exec.*, T. J. O'Leary.

EPILEPSY, THE NATIONAL SOCIETY FOR (1892), Chalfont Centre for Epilepsy, Chalfont St Peter, Gerrards Cross, Bucks. SL9 0RJ. Tel: 024 07-3991.—*Chief Exec.*, Col. D. W. Eking.

EQUESTRIAN FEDERATION, BRITISH (1972), Stoneleigh, Kenilworth, Warks. CV8 2LR. Tel: 0203-696697.—*Dir. Gen.*, Maj. M. Wallace.

ESPERANTO ASSOCIATION OF BRITAIN (1977), 140 Holland Park Avenue, W11 4UF. Tel: 071-727 7821.—*Hon. Sec.*, W. Green.

ESTATE AGENTS, NATIONAL ASSOCIATION OF (1962), Arbon House, 21 Jury Street, Warwick CV34 4EH. Tel: 0926-496800.—*Gen. Sec.*, A. B. Clark.

EUGENICS SOCIETY *see* GALTON INSTITUTE.

EVANGELICAL ALLIANCE (1846), Whitefield House, 186 Kennington Park Road, SE11 4BT. Tel: 071-582 0228.—*Gen. Dir.*, Rev. C. R. Calver.

EVANGELICAL LIBRARY, THE (1928), 78A Chiltern Street, W1M 2HB. Tel: 071-935 6997.—*Librarian*, S. J. Taylor.

EXECUTIVES ASSOCIATION OF GREAT BRITAIN LTD (1929), Suite 87–89, The Hop Exchange, 24 Southwark Street, SE1 1TY. Tel: 071-403 3653.—*Sec.*, Lt.-Col. J. J. Langdon-Mudge.

EXPORT, INSTITUTE OF, Export House, 64 Clifton Street, EC2A 4HB. Tel: 071-247 9812.—*Sec.*, D. J. Langham.

EX-SERVICES LEAGUE, BRITISH COMMONWEALTH (1921), 48 Pall Mall, SW1Y 5JY. Tel: 071-973 0633.—*Sec. Gen.*, Brig. M. J. Doyle, MBE.

EX-SERVICES MENTAL WELFARE SOCIETY (1919), Broadway House, The Broadway, SW19 1RL. Tel: 081-543 6333.—*Gen. Sec.*, Brig. A. K. Dixon.

FABIAN SOCIETY (1884), 11 Dartmouth Street, SW1H 9BN. Tel: 071-222 8877.—*Gen. Sec.*, S. Crine.

FAIR ISLE BIRD OBSERVATORY TRUST (1948), 21 Regent Terrace, Edinburgh EH7 5BT. Tel: 031-556 6042.—*Hon. Sec.*, Miss V. M. Thom.

FAMILY CONCILIATION COUNCIL, NATIONAL (1982), Shaftesbury Centre, Percy Street, Swindon SN2 2AZ. Tel: 0793-514055.—*Chairman*, Prof. B. Hoggett.

FAMILY HISTORY SOCIETIES, FEDERATION OF (1974).—*Administrator*, Mrs P. A. Saul, c/o The Benson Room, Birmingham and Midland Institute, Margaret Street, Birmingham B3 3BS.

FAMILY PLANNING ASSOCIATION (1939), 27–35 Mortimer Street, W1N 7RJ. Tel: 071-636 7866.—*Dir.*, Ms D. E. Massey.

FAMILY WELFARE ASSOCIATION (1869), 501–505 Kingsland Road, E8 4AU.—*Dir.*, R. E. Morley.

FAUNA AND FLORA PRESERVATION SOCIETY (1903), 1 Kensington Gore, SW7 2AR. Tel: 071-823 8899.—*Administrator*, Miss A. Hillier.

FELLOWSHIP HOUSES TRUST (1937), Clock House, 192 High Road, Byfleet, Weybridge, Surrey KT14 7RN. Tel: 0932-343172.—*Sec.*, Mrs A. J. Elliot.

FIELD ARCHAEOLOGISTS, INSTITUTE OF (1982), Metallurgy and Materials Building, University of Birmingham, Edgbaston, Birmingham B15 2TT. Tel: 021-471 2788.—*Company Sec.*, S. M. Walls.

FIELD SPORTS SOCIETY, BRITISH (1930), 59 Kennington Road, SE1 7PZ.—*Dir.*, Maj.-Gen. J. Hopkinson, CB.

FIELD STUDIES COUNCIL (1943), Preston Montford, Montford Bridge, Shrewsbury SY4 1HW. Tel: 0743-850674.—*Dir.*, A. D. Thomas.

FILM CLASSIFICATION, BRITISH BOARD OF (1912), 3 Soho Square, W1V 5DE. Tel: 071-439 7961.—*Dir.*, J. Ferman.

FILM INSTITUTE, BRITISH (1933), 21 Stephen Street, W1P 1PL. Tel: 071-255 1444.—*Dir.*, W. Stevenson.

FINANCIAL ACCOUNTANTS, INSTITUTE OF (1916), Burford House, 44 London Road, Sevenoaks, Kent TN13 1AS. Tel: 0732-458080.—*Chief Exec.*, D. Gurney.

FIRE ENGINEERS, INSTITUTION OF (1918), 148 New Walk, Leicester LE1 7QB. Tel: 0533-553654.—*Gen. Sec.*, Mrs C. E. Mackwood.

FIRE PROTECTION ASSOCIATION (1946), 140 Aldersgate Street, EC1A 4HX. Tel: 071-606 3757.—*Dir.*, A. S. Kidd.

FIRE SERVICES ASSOCIATION, BRITISH (1949), 86 London Road, Leicester LE2 0QR. Tel: 0533-542879.—*Gen. Sec.*, D. Stevens.

FIRE SERVICES NATIONAL BENEVOLENT FUND (1943), Marine Court, Fitzalan Road, Littlehampton, W. Sussex BN17 5NF. Tel: 0903-717185.—*Gen. Manager*, R. A. Spackman.

FLEET AIR ARM OFFICERS ASSOCIATION (1957), 94 Piccadilly, W1V 0BP. Tel: 071-499 0360.—*Chairman*, Capt. A. J. Leary, CBE, RN (retd).

FOLKLORE SOCIETY, c/o University College London, Gower Street, WC1E 6BT. Tel: 071-387 5894.—*Hon. Sec.*, Ms. M. Bowman.

FOOD AND FARMING INFORMATION SERVICE (1991), European Business Centre, 460 Fulham Road, SW6 1B7. Tel: 071-610 0402.

FOOD FROM BRITAIN (1983), 301–344 Market Towers, New Covent Garden Market, SW8 5NQ.—*Chairman*, P. R. Judge.

FOOD SCIENCE AND TECHNOLOGY, INSTITUTE OF (1964), 5 Cambridge Court, 210 Shepherd's Bush Road, W6 7NL. Tel: 071-603 6316.—*Exec. Sec.*, Ms H. G. Wild.

FORCES HELP SOCIETY AND LORD ROBERTS WORKSHOPS (1899), 122 Brompton Road, SW3 1JE. Tel: 071-589 3243.—*Comptroller and Sec.*, Col. A. W. Davis, MBE.

FOREIGN PRESS ASSOCIATION IN LONDON (1888), 11 Carlton House Terrace, SW1Y 5AJ.—*Sec.* Mrs D. Crole.

FORENSIC SCIENCE SOCIETY, THE (1959), Clarke House, 18A Mount Parade, Harrogate, HG1 1BX. Tel: 0423-506068.—*Hon. Sec.*, B. W. J. Rankin.

FORENSIC SCIENCES, BRITISH ACADEMY OF (1959).— *Sec. Gen.*, Dr P. J. Flynn, Anaesthetic Unit, The London Hospital Medical College, Turner Street, E1 2AD. Tel: 071-377 9201.

FORESTERS, INSTITUTE OF CHARTERED (1982), 22 Walker Street, Edinburgh EH3 7HR.—*Sec.*, Mrs M. W. Dick.

FORESTRY ASSOCIATION, COMMONWEALTH (1921), c/o Oxford Forestry Institute, South Parks Road, Oxford OX1 3RB. Tel: 0865-275072 —*Sec. (acting)*, P. J. Wood.

FORESTRY SOCIETY OF ENGLAND, WALES AND NORTHERN IRELAND, ROYAL (1882), 102 High Street, Tring, Herts. HP23 4AF. Tel: 044 282-2028.—*Dir.*, J. E. Jackson, PH.D.

FORESTRY SOCIETY, ROYAL SCOTTISH (1854), 11 Atholl Crescent, Edinburgh EH3 8HE. Tel: 031-229 8180.—*Sec.* W. B. C. Walker.

FOUNDRYMEN, INSTITUTE OF BRITISH (1904), 3rd Floor, Bridge House, 121 Smallbrook Queensway, Birmingham B5 4JP. Tel: 021-643 4523.—*Sec.*, G. A. Schofield.

FRANCO-BRITISH SOCIETY (1924), Room 636, Linen Hall, 162–168 Regent Street, W1R 5TB. Tel: 071-734 0815.—*Exec. Sec.*, Mrs M. Clarke.

FREE CHURCH FEDERAL COUNCIL (1940), 27 Tavistock Square, WC1H 9HH. Tel: 071-387 8413.—*Gen. Sec.*, Rev. D. Staple.

FREEDOM ASSOCIATION (1975), 35 Westminster Bridge Road, SE1 7JB.—*Chairman*, N. D. McWhirter, CBE.

FREEMASONS, GRAND LODGE OF ANTIENT FREE AND ACCEPTED MASONS OF SCOTLAND (1736), Freemasons' Hall, 96 George Street, Edinburgh EH2 3DH. Tel: 031-225 5304.—*Grand Master Mason of Scotland*, Brig. Sir Gregor MacGregor of MacGregor, Bt.; *Grand Sec.*, A. O. Hazel.

FREEMASONS, UNITED GRAND LODGE OF ENGLAND (1717), Freemasons' Hall, Great Queen Street, WC2B 5AZ. Tel: 071-831 9811.—*Grand Master*, HRH The Duke of Kent, KG, GCMG, GCVO; *Grand Sec.*, Cdr. M. B. S. Higham.

FREEMEN OF ENGLAND (1966).—*Sec.*, R. J. M. Bishop, 10 Wyngate Road, Hale, Altrincham, Cheshire WA15 0LZ. Tel: 061-904 9304.

FREEMEN'S GUILDS:—
City of Coventry Freemen's Guild (1946).—*Hon. Clerk*, J. H. Bradbury, 5 Adare Drive, Styvechale, Coventry CV3 6AD. Tel: 0203-501801.
Guild of Freemen of the City of London (1908), PO Box 153, 40A Ludgate Hill, EC4M 7DE. Tel: 071-223 7638.—*Clerk*, Col. D. Ivy.
Guild of Freemen of the City of York (1953).—*Hon. Clerk*, R. Lee, 29 Albemarle Road, York YO2 1EW.

FRIENDLY SOCIETIES, NATIONAL CONFERENCE OF (1887), Room 313, Victoria House, Vernon Place, WC1B 4DP. Tel: 071-242 1923.—*Sec.*, P. M. Madders.

FRIENDS OF CATHEDRAL MUSIC (1956), c/o Addington Palace, Croydon, Surrey CR9 5AD. Tel: 071-638 1621.—*Hon. Gen. Sec.*, V. Waterhouse.

FRIENDS OF THE CLERGY CORPORATION, THE (1972), 27 Medway Street, SW1P 2BD.—*Sec.*, J. M. Greany.

FRIENDS OF THE EARTH (1971), 26–28 Underwood Street, N1 7JQ. Tel: 071-490 1555.—*Dir.*, D. Gee.

FRIENDS OF THE ELDERLY AND GENTLEFOLK'S HELP (1905), 42 Ebury Street, SW1W 0LZ.—*Gen. Sec.*, Rev. J. Schofield.

FRIENDS OF THE NATIONAL LIBRARIES (1931), The British Library, WC1B 3DG. Tel: 071-323 7559.— *Hon. Sec.*, J. F. Fuggles.

FURNITURE HISTORY SOCIETY (1964), c/o Dept. of Furniture and Interior Design, Victoria and Albert Museum, SW7 2RL. Tel: 0444-413845.—*Hon. Sec.*, vacant.

GALLIPOLI ASSOCIATION (1915).—*Hon. Sec.*, J. C. Watson Smith, Earlydene Orchard, Earlydene, Ascot, Berks. SL5 9JY. Tel: 0344-26523.

GALTON INSTITUTE, THE (*formerly* The Eugenics Society) (1907), 19 Northfields Prospect, SW18 1PE. Tel: 081-874 7257.—*Gen. Sec.*, Mrs L. Brooks.

GAMBLERS ANONYMOUS (1954), PO Box 88, SW10 0EU. Tel: 081-741 4181.

GAME CONSERVANCY, THE (1969), Fordingbridge, Hants. SP6 1EF. Tel: 0425-652381.—*Dir. Gen.*, R. M. Van Oss.

GARDEN HISTORY SOCIETY (1965), 5 The Knoll, Hereford HR1 1RU. Tel: 0432-354479.—*Hon. Membership Sec.*, Mrs A. Richards.

GARDENERS' ASSOCIATION, THE GOOD (1968), Two Mile Lane, Highnam, Glos. GL2 8DW. Tel: 0452-305814.—*Hon. Dir.*, J. D. Wilkin.

GARDENERS' ROYAL BENEVOLENT SOCIETY (1839), Bridge House, 139 Kingston Road, Leatherhead, Surrey KT22 7NT. Tel: 0372-373962.—*Sec.-Administrator*, C. R. C. Bunce.

GAS CONSUMERS COUNCIL (1986), 6th Floor, Abford House, 15 Wilton Road, SW1V 1LT. Tel: 071-931 0977.—*Dir.*, I. W. Powe.

GAS ENGINEERS, INSTITUTION OF (1863), 17 Grosvenor Crescent, SW1X 7ES. Tel: 071-245 9811.—*Sec.*, D. J. Chapman.

GEMMOLOGICAL ASSOCIATION OF GREAT BRITAIN (1931), 1st Floor, 27 Greville Street, EC1N 8SU. Tel: 071-404 3334.—*Sec.*, A. Klein.

GENEALOGICAL RESEARCH SOCIETY, IRISH (1936).— *Hon. Sec.*, Miss R. McCutcheon, c/o The Challoner Club, 61 Pont Street, SW1X 0BG.

GENEALOGISTS AND RECORD AGENTS, ASSOCIATION OF (1968), 1 Woodside Close, Caterham, Surrey CR3 6AU. Tel: 0283-716587.—*Chairman*, S. W. Taylor.

GENEALOGISTS, SOCIETY OF (1911), 14 Charterhouse Buildings, Goswell Road, EC1M 7BA. Tel: 071-251 8799.—*Dir.*, A. J. Camp.

GENERAL PRACTITIONERS, ROYAL COLLEGE OF (1952), 14 Princes Gate, Hyde Park, SW7 1PU.—*Gen. Administrator*, Mrs S. Irvine.

GENTLEPEOPLE, GUILD OF AID FOR (1904), 10 St Christopher's Place, W1M 6HY. Tel: 071-935 0641.—*Sec.*, Mrs G. A. Burgess.

GEOGRAPHICAL ASSOCIATION, 343 Fulwood Road, Sheffield S10 3BP. Tel: 0742-670666.—*Sen. Administrator*, Miss F. Soar.

GEOGRAPHICAL SOCIETY, ROYAL (1830), 1 Kensington Gore, SW7 2AR. Tel: 071-589 5466.—*Pres.*, Sir Crispin Tickell, GCMG, KCVO.

GEOGRAPHICAL SOCIETY, ROYAL SCOTTISH (1884), 10 Randolph Crescent, Edinburgh EH3 7TU. Tel: 031-225 3330.—*Sec.*, A. B. Cruickshank.

GEOLOGICAL SOCIETY (1807), Burlington House, Piccadilly, W1V 0JU. Tel: 071-434 9944.—*Pres.*, Prof. A. L. Harris; *Exec. Sec.*, R. M. Bateman.

GEOLOGISTS' ASSOCIATION (1858), Burlington House, Piccadilly, W1V 9AG. Tel: 071-434 9298.—*Hon. Gen. Sec.*, Mrs M. E. Pugh.

GEOLOGISTS, THE INSTITUTION OF (1977), Burlington House, Piccadilly, W1V 9AG.—*Sec.*, Dr J. A. Seymour.

GEORGIAN GROUP (1937), 37 Spital Square, E1 6DY. Tel: 071-377 1722.—*Sec.*, R. White.

GIFTED CHILDREN, NATIONAL ASSOCIATION FOR (1966), Park Campus, Boughton Green Road, Northampton NN2 7AL. Tel: 0604-792300.—*Dir.*, M. Short.

GILBERT AND SULLIVAN SOCIETY (1924).—*Hon. Sec.*, Miss B. Dove, 31A Kenmere Gardens, Wembley, Middx. HA0 1TD.

GINGERBREAD, AN ASSOCIATION FOR ONE PARENT FAMILIES (1970), 35 Wellington Street, WC2E 7BN. Tel: 071-240 0953.—*Chief Exec.*, Ms P. Gostyn.

GIRL GUIDES ASSOCIATION (1910), 17–19 Buckingham Palace Road, SW1W 0PT. Tel: 071-834 6242.—*Chief Commissioner*, Mrs A. F. Garside; *Gen. Sec.*, Miss M. W. Hayter.

GIRLS' BRIGADE, THE, Girls' Brigade House, 62 Foxhall Road, Didcot, Oxon. OX11 7BQ. Tel: 0235-510425.—*Brigade Sec. for England and Wales*, Miss D. M. Cosser.

GIRLS' FRIENDLY SOCIETY AND TOWNSEND FELLOWSHIP (1875), 126 Queens Gate, SW7 5LQ. Tel: 071-589 9628.—*Gen. Sec.*, Miss H. G. Smith.

GIRLS' VENTURE CORPS AIR CADETS (1964), Redhill Aerodrome, Kings Mill Lane, South Nutfield, Redhill RH1 5JY. Tel: 0737-823345.—*Sec. Gen.*, Miss H. P. Prosper.

GLASS ENGRAVERS, THE GUILD OF (1975).—*Sec.*, Mrs K. Coleman, 49 Crediton Hill, NW6 1HS. Tel: 071-794 0644.

GLASS TECHNOLOGY, SOCIETY OF (1916), Thornton, 20 Hallam Gate Road, Sheffield S10 5BT. Tel: 0742-663168.—*Hon. Sec.*, W. Simpson.

GLIDING ASSOCIATION, BRITISH (1930), Kimberley House, Vaughan Way, Leicester LE1 4SE.—*Gen. Sec.*, B. Rolfe.

GOAT SOCIETY, BRITISH (1879), 34–36 Fore Street, Bovey Tracey, Newton Abbot, Devon TQ13 9AD. Tel: 0626-833168.—*Sec.*, Mrs S. Knowles.

GRAPHIC FINE ART, SOCIETY OF (1919), 9 Newburgh Street, W1V 1LH.—*Sec.*, Ms J. Caesar.

GRAPHOLOGISTS, THE BRITISH INSTITUTE OF (1983), 4th Floor, Bell Court House, 11 Blomfield Street, EC2M 7AY.—*Chairman*, Dr C. Molander.

GREAT BRITAIN-USSR SOCIETY, THE (1959), 14 Grosvenor Place, SW1X 7HW. Tel: 071-235 2116.—*Dir.*, J. C. Q. Roberts.

GREEK INSTITUTE (1969), 34 Bush Hill Road, N21 2DS. Tel: 081-360 7968.—*Dir.*, Dr K. Tofallis.

GREEN PARTY, THE (1973), 10 Station Parade, Balham High Road, SW12 9AZ. Tel: 081-673 0045.—*Office Manager*, J. Bishop.

GREENPEACE UK (1971), Canonbury Villas, N1 2PN. Tel: 071-354 5100.—*Exec. Dir.*, Lord Melchett.

GROCERS ASSOCIATION, BRITISH INDEPENDENT (1890), Federation House, 17 Farnborough Street, Farnborough, Hants. GU14 8AG. Tel: 0252-515001.—*Nat. Sec.*, A. Taylor.

GUIDE DOGS FOR THE BLIND ASSOCIATION (1931), Alexandra House, Park Street, Windsor, Berks SL4 1JR. Tel: 0753-855711.—*Dir. Gen.*, J. C. Oxley

GULBENKIAN FOUNDATION, *see* CALOUSTE GULBENKIAN FOUNDATION.

HAEMOPHILIA SOCIETY, THE (1950), 123 Westminster Bridge Road, SE1 7HR.—*Sec.*, D. G. Watters.

HAKLUYT SOCIETY (1846), c/o Map Library, The British Library, Great Russell Street, WC1B 3DG. Tel: 0986-86359.—*Joint Hon. Secs.*, Dr W. F. Ryan; Mrs S. Tyacke.

HANSARD SOCIETY FOR PARLIAMENTARY GOVERNMENT, THE (1944), 16 Gower Street, WC1E 6DP. Tel: 071-323 1131.—*Dir.*, D. Harris.

HARD OF HEARING, BRITISH ASSOCIATION OF THE (1948), 7–11 Armstrong Road, W3 7JL. Tel: 081-743 1110.—*Chairman*, P. J. Phillips.

HARVEIAN SOCIETY OF EDINBURGH (1782), Dept. of Medicine, The Royal Infirmary, Edinburgh EH3 9YW.—*Joint Secs.*, Dr A. D. Toft; A. B. MacGregor.

HARVEIAN SOCIETY OF LONDON (1831), 11 Chandos Street, W1M 0EB. Tel: 071-580 1043.—*Exec. Sec.*, Maj. T. Tudor-Williams.

HEAD TEACHERS, NATIONAL ASSOCIATION OF (1897).—*Gen. Sec.*, D. M. Hart, OBE, 1 Heath Square, Boltro Road, Haywards Heath, W. Sussex RH16 1BL. Tel: 0444-458133.

HEALTH AUTHORITIES AND TRUSTS, NATIONAL ASSOCIATION OF (1974), Birmingham Research Park, Vincent Drive, Birmingham B15 2SQ. Tel: 021-471 4444.—*Dir.*, P. Hunt.

HEALTH CARE ASSOCIATION, BRITISH (1931), The Courtyard, Allerton Park, Knaresborough, N Yorks. HG5 0SE. Tel: 0423-331295.—*Nat. Sec.*, G. K. Waite.

HEALTH EDUCATION, INSTITUTE OF (1962).—*Hon. Sec.*, Prof. L. Baric, PH.D., 14 High Elm Road, Hale Barns, Altrincham, Cheshire WA15 0HS. Tel: 061-980 8276.

HEALTH, GUILD OF (1904), Edward Wilson House, 26 Queen Anne Street, W1M 9LB. Tel: 071-580 2492.—*Nat. Dir.*, W. R. Booth.

HEALTH SERVICES MANAGEMENT, INSTITUTE OF (1902) 75 Portland Place, W1N 4AN. Tel: 071-580 5041.—*Dir.*, Ms P. Charlwood.

HEART FOUNDATION, BRITISH (1963), 14 Fitzhardinge Street, W1H 4DH. Tel: 071-935 0185.—*Dir. Gen.*, Maj.-Gen. L. F. H. Busk, CB.

HEDGEHOG PRESERVATION SOCIETY, BRITISH (1982), Knowbury House, Knowbury, Ludlow, Shropshire SY8 3LQ.—*Founder.*, A. H. Coles.

HELLENIC STUDIES, SOCIETY FOR THE PROMOTION OF (1879), 31–34 Gordon Square, WC1H 0PP. Tel: 071-387 7495.—*Sec.*, Dr L. Rodley.

HELP THE AGED (1960), St James's Walk, EC1R 0BE. Tel: 071-253 0253.—*Dir. Gen.*, Col. J. Mayo, OBE.

HERALDIC AND GENEALOGICAL STUDIES, INSTITUTE OF (1961), 79–82 Northgate, Canterbury, Kent CT1 1BA.—*Registrar.*, Ms J. Carter.

HERALDRY SOCIETY, THE (1947), 44–45 Museum Street, WC1A 1LY. Tel: 071-340 2172.—*Sec.*, Mrs M. Miles, MBE.

HERALDRY SOCIETY OF SCOTLAND (1977).—PO Box 1, Roslin, Midlothian EH25 9TB.

HERPETOLOGICAL SOCIETY, BRITISH (1947), c/o Zoological Society of London, Regent's Park, NW1 4RY. Tel: 081-452 9578.—*Sec.*, Mrs M. Green.

HIGHWAYS AND TRANSPORTATION, INSTITUTION OF (1930), 3 Lygon Place, Ebury Street, SW1W 0JS. Tel: 071-370 5245.—*Sec.*, Dr M. R. Cragg.

HISPANIC AND LUSO BRAZILIAN COUNCIL (1943), Canning House, 2 Belgrave Square, SW1X 8PJ.—*Dir. Gen.*, Sir Kenneth James, KCMG.

HISTORICAL ASSOCIATION, THE (1906), 59A Kennington Park Road, SE11 4JH. Tel: 071-735 3901.—*Sec.*, Mrs M. Stiles.

HISTORICAL SOCIETY, ROYAL (1868), University College London, Gower Street, WC1E 6BT. Tel: 071-387 7532.—*Pres.*, Prof. F. M. L. Thompson; *Exec. Sec.*, Mrs J. N. McCarthy.

HOMEOPATHIC ASSOCIATION, BRITISH (1902), 27A Devonshire Street, W1N 1RJ. Tel: 071-935 2163.—*Gen. Sec.*, Mrs E. Segall.

HONG KONG ASSOCIATION (1961), Swire House, 59 Buckingham Gate, SW1E 6AJ. Tel: 071-821 3220.—*Exec. Dir.*, Brig. B. G. Hickey, OBE, MC.

HOROLOGICAL INSTITUTE, BRITISH (1858), Upton Hall, Upton, Newark, Notts. NG23 5TE. Tel: 0636-813795.—*Sec.*, W. M. G. Evans.

HOROLOGICAL SOCIETY, ANTIQUARIAN (1953), New House, High Street, Ticehurst, Wadhurst, E. Sussex TN5 7AL. Tel: 0580-200155.—*Sec.*, Mrs. M. A. Collins.

HORSE SOCIETY, BRITISH (1947) (incorporating The Pony Club), British Equestrian Centre, Kenilworth, Warks. CV8 2LR. Tel: 0203-696697.—*Chief Exec.*, Col. T. Eastwood.

HOSPITAL FEDERATION, INTERNATIONAL (1947), 4 Abbotts Place, NW6 4NP. Tel: 071-372 7181.—*Dir. Gen.*, Dr E. N. Pickering.

HOSPITAL SATURDAY FUND, THE (1873), 192–198 Vauxhall Bridge Road, SW1V 1EE. Tel: 071-828 0836.—*Chief Exec.*, K. R. Bradley.

HOSPITAL SAVING ASSOCIATION, THE, Hambleden House, Andover, Hants. SP10 1LQ. Tel: 0264-353211.—*Gen. Sec.*, J. A. Young.

HOSPITALITY ASSOCIATION, BRITISH (1907), 40 Duke Street, W1M 6HR. Tel: 071-499 6641.—*Chief Exec.*, R. Lees, CB, MBE.

HOTEL, CATERING AND INSTITUTIONAL MANAGEMENT ASSOCIATION (1971), 191 Trinity Road, SW17 7HN.—*Dir.*, Miss E. Gadsby.

HOUSE OF ST BARNABAS-IN-SOHO (1846), 1 Greek Street, W1V 6NQ. For homeless women in London. Tel: 071-437 1894.—*Dir.*, D. G. Saunders.

HOUSING, INSTITUTE OF, Octavia House, Westwood Business Park, Westwood Way, Coventry CV4 8JP. Tel: 0203-694433.—*Dir.*, P. McGurk.

HOUSING AID SOCIETY, CATHOLIC (1956), 189A Old Brompton Road, SW5 0AR.—*Dir.*, Ms R. Rafferty.

HOUSING AND TOWN PLANNING COUNCIL, NATIONAL (1900), 14–18 Old Street, EC1V 9AB. Tel: 071-251 2363.—*Dir.*, R. Walker.

HOUSING ASSOCIATION FOR OFFICERS' FAMILIES (1916), Alban Dobson House, Green Lane, Morden, Surrey SM4 5NS.—*Gen. Sec.*, J. B. Holt.

HOVERCRAFT SOCIETY, THE (1971), 24 Jellicoe Avenue, Alverstoke, Gosport, Hants. PO12 2PE.—*Chairman*, B. J. Russell.

HOWARD LEAGUE FOR PENAL REFORM, THE (1866), 708 Holloway Road, N19 3NL.—*Dir.*, Ms F. Crook.

HUGUENOT SOCIETY OF GREAT BRITAIN AND IRELAND (1885), The Huguenot Library, University College, Gower Street, WC1E 6BT. Tel: 071-380 7094.—*Sec.*, Mrs M. Bayliss.

HUMANE RESEARCH TRUST, (1974), Brook House, 29 Bramhall Lane South, Bramhall, Cheshire SK7 2DN. Tel: 061-439 8041.—*Chairman*, R. MacAlastair Brown.

HYDROGRAPHIC SOCIETY (1972), c/o Polytechnic of East London, Longbridge Road, Dagenham, Essex RM8 2AS. Tel: 081-597 1946.—*Hon. Sec.*, V. J. Abbott.

HYMN SOCIETY OF GREAT BRITAIN AND IRELAND (1936).—*Sec.*, Rev. M. Garland, St Nicholas Rectory, Glebe Fields, Curdworth, Sutton Coldfield, W. Midlands B76 9ES. Tel: 0675-470384.

INDEPENDENT BRITAIN, CAMPAIGN FOR AN (1976), 81 Ashmole Street, SW8 1NF. Tel: 081-340 0314.—*Hon. Sec.*, Sir Robin Williams, Bt.

INDEPENDENT SCHOOL BURSARS' ASSOCIATION (1933).—*Sec.*, D. J. Bird, Woodlands, Closewood Road, Denmead, Portsmouth PO7 6JD. Tel: 0705-264506.

INDEPENDENT SCHOOLS CAREERS ORGANIZATION (1942), 12A–18A Princess Way, Camberley, Surrey GU15 3SP. Tel: 0276-21188.—*Dir.* G. W. Searle.

INDEPENDENT SCHOOLS INFORMATION SERVICE (ISIS) (1972), 56 Buckingham Gate, SW1E 6AG. Tel: 071-630 8793.—*Dir.*, D. J. Woodhead.

INDEPENDENT SCHOOLS JOINT COUNCIL (1974), 35–37 Grosvenor Gardens, SW1W 0BS. Tel: 071-630 0144.—*Gen. Sec.*, Dr A. G. Hearnden.

INDEXERS, SOCIETY OF (1957).—*Sec.*, Mrs C. Troughton, 16 Green Road, Birchington, Kent CT7 9JZ. Tel: 0843-41115.

INDUSTRIAL CHRISTIAN FELLOWSHIP (1877).—*Nat. Sec.*, D. Arthur, Dukes Meadow, 1 One Tree Lane, Beaconsfield, Bucks. HP9 2BU.

INDUSTRIAL EDITORS, BRITISH ASSOCIATION OF, (1949), 3 Locks Yard, High Street, Sevenoaks, Kent, TN13 1LT. Tel: 0732-459331.—*Chief Exec.*, C. Pedersen.

INDUSTRIAL MANAGERS, INSTITUTION OF (1931), Rochester House, 66 Little Ealing Lane, W5 4XX.—*Chief Exec.*, G. J. Rawlings, OBE.

INDUSTRIAL MARKETING RESEARCH ASSOCIATION (IMRA) (1963), 11 Bird Street, Lichfield, Staffs. WS13 6PW. Tel: 0543-263448.—*Exec. Officer*, M. Berry.

INDUSTRIAL SOCIETY, THE (1918), Robert Hyde House, 48 Bryanston Square, W1H 7LN. Tel: 071-262 2401.—*Dir.*, Mrs R. Chapman.

INDUSTRY AND PARLIAMENT TRUST, 1 Buckingham Place, SW1E 6HR. Tel: 071-976 5311.—*Dir.*, F. R. Hyde-Chambers.

INDUSTRY TRAINING ORGANIZATIONS, NATIONAL COUNCIL OF (1988), 5 George Lane, Royston, Herts. SG8 9AR. Tel: 0763-247285.—*Administrator*, Mrs D. Wilson.

INFANT DEATHS, THE FOUNDATION FOR THE STUDY OF (1971), 35 Belgrave Square, SW1X 8PS. Tel: 071-235 0965.—*Sec. Gen.*, Mrs J. Epstein.

INFORMATION SCIENTISTS, INSTITUTE OF (1958), 44–45 Museum Street, WC1A 1LY. Tel: 071-831 8003.—*Exec. Sec.*, Mrs S. A. Carter.

INNER WHEEL CLUBS IN GREAT BRITAIN AND IRELAND, ASSOCIATION OF (1934), 51 Warwick Square, SW1V 2AT. Tel: 071-834 4600.—*Gen. Sec.*, Miss J. Dobson.

INSURANCE AND INVESTMENT BROKERS' ASSOCIATION, BRITISH, BIIBA House, 14 Bevis Marks, EC3A 7NT. Tel: 071-623 9043.—*Dir. Gen.*, J. C. T. Hackett.

INSURANCE BROKERS REGISTRATION COUNCIL, 15 St Helen's Place, EC3A 6DS. Tel: 071-588 4387.—*Registrar*, Miss E. J. Rees.

INSURANCE INSTITUTE, CHARTERED (1897), 20 Aldermanbury, EC2V 7HY. Tel: 071-606 3835.—*Dir.
Gen.*, Dr D. E. Bland.

INSURERS, ASSOCIATION OF BRITISH (1985), 51–55
Gresham Street, EC2V 7BB. Tel: 071-600 3333.—
Chief Exec., M. A. Jones.

INTERCON (INTERCONTINENTAL CHURCH SOCIETY)
(1823), 175 Tower Bridge Road, SE1 2AQ. Tel: 071-
407 4588.—*Gen. Sec.*, Rev. Canon D. R. Irving.

INTERNATIONAL AFFAIRS, ROYAL INSTITUTE OF (1920),
Chatham House, 10 St James's Square, SW1Y 4LE.
Tel: 071-957 5700.—*Dir.*, Prof. L. Martin.

INTERNATIONAL FRIENDSHIP LEAGUE (1931), 3 Cres-
wick Road, W3 9HE.—*Sec.*, Mrs B. Macdonald.

INTERNATIONAL LAW ASSOCIATION (1873), Charles
Clore House, 17 Russell Square, WC1B 5DR. Tel:
071-323 2978.—*Hon. Sec. Gen.*, B. Mauleverer, QC.

INTERNATIONAL POLICE ASSOCIATION (British Section) (1950), 1 Fox Road, West Bridgford, Nottingham NG2 6AJ. Tel: 0602-813638.—*Chief Exec.
Officer*, K. H. Robinson.

INTERNATIONAL SHIPPING FEDERATION (1909), 30–32
St Mary Axe, EC3A 8ET. Tel: 071-283 2922.—*Sec.*,
D. A. Dearsley.

INTERNATIONAL STUDENTS HOUSE (1962), 229 Great
Portland Street, W1N 5HD.—*Sec.*, W. R. Murray.

INTERNATIONAL TIN RESEARCH INSTITUTE (1932),
Kingston Lane, Uxbridge, Middx. UB8 3PJ. Tel:
0895-72406.—*Dir.*, Dr B. T. K. Barry.

INTERNATIONAL VOLUNTARY SERVICE (1920), 162 Upper New Walk, Leicester LE1 7QA.—*Gen. Secs.*, P.
Ticher; D. T. Huggins.

INTERSERVE (*formerly* BMMF) (1852), Whitefield
House, 186 Kennington Park Road, SE11 4BT. Tel:
071-735 8227.—*Gen. Dir.*, A. M. S. Pont.

INTER VARSITY CLUBS, ASSOCIATION OF (1946), 26
Chesswood Road, Worthing, W. Sussex
BN11 2AD.—*Sec.*, M. A. Rooke-Matthews.

INVALID CHILDREN'S AID NATIONWIDE (I CAN) (1888),
10 Bowling Green Lane, EC1R 0BD. Tel: 071-253
9111.—*Dir.*, B. J. Jones.

INVALIDS-AT-HOME (1966).—*Hon. Sec.*, Mrs E. Pierce,
23 Farm Avenue, NW2 2BJ.

INVISIBLES, BRITISH (1983), Windsor House, 39 King
Street, EC2V 8DQ. Tel: 071-600 1198.—*Dir. Gen.*,
Hon. A. Wright.

INVOLVEMENT AND PARTICIPATION ASSOCIATION
(1884), 87–95 Tooley Street, SE1 2RA. Tel: 071-403
6018.—*Dir.*, B. C. Stevens.

IRAN SOCIETY (1936), 2 Belgrave Square, SW1X 8PJ.
Tel: 071-235 5122.—*Hon. Sec.*, J. R. H. James, OBE.

JACQUELINE DU PRE MEMORIAL FUND (1988), 14 Ogle
Street, W1P 7LG. Tel: 071-436 3173.—*Chairman*,
Lord Goodman, CH.

JAPAN ASSOCIATION (1950), Swire House, 59 Buckingham Gate, SW1E 6AJ. Tel: 071-821 3220.—*Exec.
Dir.*, Brig. B. G. Hickey, OBE, MC.

JERUSALEM AND THE MIDDLE EAST CHURCH ASSOCIA-
TION, THE (1887), The Old Gatehouse, Castle Hill,
Farnham, Surrey GU9 0AE. Tel: 0252-726994.—
Sec., Mrs V. Wells.

JEWISH HISTORICAL SOCIETY OF ENGLAND (1893), 33
Seymour Place, W1H 5AP. Tel: 081-723 4044.—
Hon. Sec., C. M. Drukker.

JEWISH WELFARE BOARD (1859).—*Exec. Dir.*, M. I.
Carlowe, 221 Golders Green Road, NW11 9DW.

JEWISH YOUTH, ASSOCIATION FOR (1899), A.J.Y.
House, 50 Lindley Street, E1 3AX. Tel: 071-790
6407.—*Exec. Dir.*, M. Shaw.

JEWS, CHURCH'S MINISTRY AMONG THE (1809), 30c
Clarence Road, St Albans, Herts. AL1 4JJ. Tel:
0727-833114.—*Gen. Dir.*, Rev. J. M. V. Drummond.

JOURNALISTS, THE CHARTERED INSTITUTE OF (1883),
Suite 2, Dock Offices, Surrey Quays, Lower Road,
SE16 2XL. Tel: 071-252 1187.—*Dir.*, W. Tadd.

JUSTICE (British Section of the International Commission of Jurists) (1957), 95A Chancery Lane,
WC2A 1DT. Tel: 071-405 6018.—*Dir.*, Ms L. Levin.

JUSTICES' CLERKS' SOCIETY (1839), The Court House,
Homer Road, Solihull, W. Midlands B91 3RD. Tel:
021-705 8101.—*Hon. Sec.*, A. R. Heath.

KING EDWARD'S HOSPITAL FUND FOR LONDON (THE
KING'S FUND) (1897), 14 Palace Court, W2 4HT.
Tel: 071-727 0581.—*Dir.*, Dr J. Ivey Bufford.

KING GEORGE'S FUND FOR SAILORS (1917), 1 Chesham
Street, SW1X 8NF. Tel: 071-235 2884.—*Dir. Gen.*,
Hon. H. Lawson.

KIPLING SOCIETY, THE (1927), 2nd Floor, Schomberg
House, 80–82 Pall Mall, SW1 5HF. Tel: 0428-
652709.—*Hon. Sec.*, N. Entract.

LADIES IN REDUCED CIRCUMSTANCES, SOCIETY FOR
THE ASSISTANCE OF (1886), Lancaster House, 25
Hornyold Road, Malvern, Worcs. WR14 1QQ.—
Sec., Miss H. C. Grahamslaw.

LANDSCAPE INSTITUTE (1929), 6–7 Barnard Mews,
SW11 1QU. Tel: 071-738 9166.—*Registrar*, P. R.
Broadbent, OBE.

LAND-VALUE TAXATION AND FREE TRADE, INTERNA-
TIONAL UNION FOR, 177 Vauxhall Bridge Road,
SW1V 1EU. Tel: 071-834 4266.—*Pres.*, Mrs B. P.
Sobrielo.

LANGUAGE LEARNING, ASSOCIATION FOR (1990), 16
Regent Place, Rugby CV21 2PN. Tel: 0788-
546443.—*Gen. Sec.*, Mrs C. Wilding.

LAW REPORTING FOR ENGLAND AND WALES, INCOR-
PORATED COUNCIL OF (1865), 3 Stone Buildings,
Lincoln's Inn, WC2A 3XN. Tel: 071-242 6471.—
Sec., B. Symondson.

LEAGUE OF THE HELPING HAND (1908), Baileys, Church
Street, Charlbury, Oxford OX7 3PR. Tel: 0608-
810411.—*Sec.*, Mrs D. R. Colvin.

LEAGUE OF WELLDOERS (1893), 119–121 Limekiln
Lane, Liverpool L5 8SN. Tel: 051-207 1984—*Warden and Sec.*, K. H. Stanton.

LEATHER AND HIDE TRADES' BENEVOLENT INSTITU-
TION (1860), 60 Wickham Hill, Hurstpierpoint,
Hassocks, W. Sussex BN6 9NP. Tel: 0273-843488.—
Sec., Mrs G. M. Stapleton, MBE.

LEGAL EXECUTIVES, INSTITUTE OF (1892), Kempston
Manor, Kempston, Bedford MK42 7AB. Tel: 0234-
841000.—*Sec. Gen.*, L. A. Evans.

LEONARD CHESHIRE FOUNDATION (1955), Leonard
Cheshire House, 26–29 Maunsel Street, SW1P 2QN.
Tel: 071-828 1822.—*Dir.*, J. Stanford.

LEPROSY MISSION, THE (England and Wales) (1874),
Goldhay Way, Orton Goldhay, Peterborough,
PE2 0GZ.—*Chairman*, Dr D. Moore.

LEUKAEMIA RESEARCH FUND (1962), 43 Great Ormond
Street, WC1N 3JJ. Tel: 071-405 0101.—*Dir.*, D. L.
Osborne.

LIBERTY (formerly NATIONAL COUNCIL FOR CIVIL
LIBERTIES) (1934), 21 Tabard Street, SE1 4LA. Tel:
071-403 3888.—*Gen. Sec.*, A. Puddephatt.

LIBRARY ASSOCIATION (1877), 7 Ridgmount Street,
WC1E 7AE. Tel: 071-636 7543.—*Chief Exec.*, G.
Cunningham.

LIFEBOATS, see ROYAL NATIONAL LIFEBOAT INSTITU-
TION.

LIGHT HORSE BREEDING SOCIETY, NATIONAL (1885), 96 High Street, Edenbridge, Kent TN8 5AR. Tel: 0732-866277.—*Sec.*, G. W. Evans.

LINGUISTS, INSTITUTE OF (1910), 24A Highbury Grove, N5 2EA. Tel: 071-359 7445.—*Gen. Sec.*, W. Hedley.

LINNAEAN SOCIETY OF LONDON (1788), Burlington House, Piccadilly, W1V 0LQ. Tel: 071-434 4479.—*Exec.-Sec.*, Dr J. C. Marsden.

LIONS CLUBS INTERNATIONAL (British Isles and Ireland) (1949), 5 Vine Terrace, The Square, Harborne, Birmingham B17 9PU. Tel: 021-428 1909.—*Gen. Sec.*, P. Jay.

LLOYD'S, 1 Lime Street, EC3M 7HL. Tel: 071-623 7100.—*Chief Exec.*, A. Lord, CB.

LLOYD'S PATRIOTIC FUND (1803), Lloyd's, Lime Street, EC3M 7HA. Tel: 071-623 7100, ext. 5062.—*Sec.*, Mrs J. H. Bright.

LOCAL AUTHORITY CHIEF EXECUTIVES, SOCIETY OF (1974).—*Hon. Sec.*, S. Jones, County Hall, Glenfield, Leicester LE3 8RA. Tel: 0533-656220.

LOCAL COUNCILS, NATIONAL ASSOCIATION OF (1947), 108 Great Russell Street, WC1B 3LD. Tel: 071-637 1865.—*Sec.*, J. Clark.

LOCAL GOVERNMENT INTERNATIONAL BUREAU (1913), *also* COUNCIL OF EUROPEAN MUNICIPALITIES AND REGIONS (British Section) (1951), 35 Great Smith Street, SW1P 3BJ. Tel: 071-222 1636.—*Sec. Gen.*, P. N. Bongers.

LONDON APPRECIATION SOCIETY (1932), 17 Manson Mews, SW7 5AF. Tel: 071-370 1100.—*Hon. Sec.*, H. L. B. Peers, PH.D.

LONDON BOROUGHS ASSOCIATION (1964), 23 Buckingham Gate, SW1E 6LB. Tel: 071-834 6935.—*Sec.*, J. Hall.

LONDON CITY MISSION (1835), 175 Tower Bridge Road, SE1 2AH. Tel: 071-407 7585.—*Gen. Sec.*, Rev. D. M. Whyte.

LONDON COURT OF INTERNATIONAL ARBITRATION (1892), 30–32 St Mary Axe, EC3A 8ET. Tel: 071-626 7962.—*Pres.*, The Rt. Hon. Sir Michael Kerr; *Registrar*, B. W. Vigrass, OBE, VRD.

LONDON FLOTILLA (1937).—*Hon. Sec.*, Lt. Cdr. P. A. G. Norman RD, RNR, Marden Rise, 81 Lower Road, Fetcham, Leatherhead, Surrey KT22 9HG. Tel: 0372-453059.

LONDON LIBRARY, THE (1841), 14 St James's Square, SW1Y 4LG.—*Librarian*, D. Matthews.

LONDON MAGISTRATES' CLERKS' ASSOCIATION (1889).—*Hon. Sec.*, J. V. Mulreany, c/o Marylebone Magistrates Court, 181–183 Marylebone Road, NW1 5QJ. Tel: 071-706 1261.

LONDON PLAYING FIELDS SOCIETY, THE (1890) (incorporating Greater London Playing Fields Association), Boston Manor Playing Field, Boston Gardens, Brentford, Middx. TW8 9LR.—*Sec.*, T. W. Syms.

LONDON SOCIETY, THE (1912), 4th Floor, Senate House, Malet Street, WC1E 7HU.—*Hon. Sec.*, Mrs B. Jones.

LORD'S DAY OBSERVANCE SOCIETY, THE (1831), 6 Sherman Road, Bromley, Kent BR1 3JH. Tel: 081-313 0456.—*Gen. Sec.*, J. G. Roberts.

LORD'S TAVERNERS, THE (1950), 1 Chester Street, SW1X 7HP. Tel: 071-245 6466.—*Dir.*, Capt. J. A. R. Swainson, OBE, RN.

LOTTERIES COUNCIL, THE (1979), 81 Mansel Street, Swansea SA1 5TT.—*Hon. Sec.* J. H. Solly.

MAGISTRATES' ASSOCIATION, THE (1920), 28 Fitzroy Square, W1P 6DD. Tel: 071-387 2353.—*Sec.*, T. R. P. Rudin.

MAIL USERS' ASSOCIATION (1976), 3 Pavement House, The Pavement, Hay-on-Wye HR3 5BU. Tel: 0497-821357.—*Chairman*, J. Blackwell.

MALAYSIAN RUBBER PRODUCERS' RESEARCH ASSOCIATION (1938), Tun Abdul Razak Laboratory, Brickendonbury, Hertford SG13 8NL. Tel: 0992-584966.—*Dir.*, Dr C. S. L. Baker.

MALCOLM SARGENT CANCER FUND FOR CHILDREN (1968).—*Gen. Administrator*, Miss S. Darley, OBE, 14 Abingdon Road, W8 6AF. Tel: 071-937 4548.

MALONE SOCIETY (for the publication of scholarly editions and facsimiles of early English dramatic texts).—*Exec. Sec.*, Prof. J. Creaser, Royal Holloway and Bedford New College, Egham Hill, Egham, Surrey TW20 0EX.

MANAGEMENT, BRITISH INSTITUTE OF (1947), 3rd Floor, 2 Savoy Court, Strand, WC2R 0EZ. Tel: 071-497 0580.—*Dir. Gen.*, P. Benton.

MANAGEMENT AND PROFESSIONAL STAFFS, ASSOCIATION OF (1972), Parkgates, Bury New Road, Prestwich, Manchester M25 8JX. Tel: 061-773 8621.—*Exec. Sec.*, Mr A. J. Casey.

MANAGEMENT SERVICES, INSTITUTE OF, 1 Cecil Court, London Road, Enfield, Middx. EN2 6DD. Tel: 081-363 7452.—*Sec.*, Ms K. Teeluck.

MANORIAL SOCIETY OF GREAT BRITAIN (1906), 104 Kennington Road, SE11 6RE. Tel: 071-735 6633.—*Hon. Chairman*, R. A. Smith.

MANPOWER SOCIETY (1969).—*Administrator*, Mrs M. P. Bradney, Old Rickyard, School Lane, Newton Burgoland, Leics. LE6 1SL. Tel: 0530-270965.

MARIE CURIE MEMORIAL FOUNDATION (1948), 28 Belgrave Square, SW1X 8QG. Tel: 071-235 3325.—*Dir. Gen.*, Maj.-Gen. M. E. Carleton-Smith, CBE. *Scottish Office*, 21 Rutland Street, Edinburgh EH1 2AH.

MARINE ARTISTS, ROYAL SOCIETY OF (1939), 17 Carlton House Terrace, SW1V 4DG.—*Sec.*, M. Myers.

MARINE BIOLOGICAL ASSOCIATION OF THE UK (1884), Citadel Hill, Plymouth PL1 2PB. Tel: 0752-222772.—*Sec.*, Dr M. Whitfield.

MARINE BIOLOGICAL ASSOCIATION, SCOTTISH (1914), PO Box 3, Oban, Argyll PA34 4AD. Tel: 0631-62244.—*Dir.*, Prof. J. B. L. Matthews.

MARINE ENGINEERS, THE INSTITUTE OF (1889), The Memorial Building, 76 Mark Lane, EC3R 7JN. Tel: 071-481 8493.—*Sec.*, J. E. Sloggett.

MARINE SOCIETY, THE (1756), 202 Lambeth Road, SE1 7JW. Tel: 071-261 9535.—*Gen. Sec.*, Lt. Cdr. R. M. Frampton.

MARIO LANZA EDUCATIONAL FOUNDATION (for singers) (1976),—*Hon. Sec.*, Miss P. Barron, 7 Lionfields Avenue, Allesley Village, Coventry CV5 9GN.

MARKET AUTHORITIES, NATIONAL ASSOCIATION OF BRITISH (1948).—*Sec.*, B. Ormshaw, 19 Derwent Avenue, Milnrow, Rochdale, Lancs. OL16 3UD. Tel: 0706-57740.

MARKETING, CHARTERED INSTITUTE OF (1911), Moor Hall, Cookham, Maidenhead, Berks. SL6 9QH.—*Dir. Gen.*, T. J. Nash.

MARKET TRADERS' FEDERATION, NATIONAL (1899), Hampton House, Hawshaw Lane, Hoyland, Barnsley S74 0HA. Tel: 0226-749021.—*Gen. Sec.*, R. J. Toller.

MARK MASTER MASONS, GRAND LODGE OF (1856), Mark Masons' Hall, 86 St James's Street, SW1A 1PL.—*Grand Master*, HRH Prince Michael of Kent; *Grand Sec.*, P. G. Williams.

MARRIAGE GUIDANCE, *see* RELATE.

MASONIC BENEVOLENT INSTITUTION, ROYAL (1842), 20 Great Queen Street, WC2B 5BG. Tel: 071-405 8341.—*Sec.*, N. A. Grout.

MASONIC BENEVOLENT INSTITUTIONS IN IRELAND, 17–19 Molesworth Street, Dublin 2.—*Sec.*, M. R. McWilliam. Tel: 0001-679 6799.

MASONIC TRUST FOR GIRLS AND BOYS (1985), 31 Great Queen Street, WC2B 5AG. Tel: 071-405 2644.— *Sec.*, Col. R. K. Hind.

MASTER BUILDERS, FEDERATION OF (1941), Gordon Fisher House, 14–15 Great James Street, WC1N 3DP.—*Dir. Gen.*, W. S. Hilton.

MASTERS OF FOXHOUNDS ASSOCIATION (1881).—*Sec.*, A. H. B. Hart, Parsloes Cottage, Bagendon, Cirencester, Glos. GL7 7DU.

MASTERS OF WINE, THE INSTITUTE OF (1955), Five Kings House, 1 Queen Street Place, EC4R 1QS. Tel: 071-236 4427.—*Exec. Dir.*, D. F. Stevens.

MATERNAL AND CHILD WELFARE, NATIONAL ASSOCIATION FOR (1911), 1 South Audley Street, W1Y 6JS.—*Gen. Sec.*, W. H. L. Hedley.

MATERNITY ALLIANCE, THE (1980), 15 Britannia Street, WC1X 9JP.—*Sec.*, Ms A. Sedley.

MATHEMATICAL ASSOCIATION (1871), 259 London Road, Leicester LE2 3BE. Tel: 0533-703877.—*Exec. Sec.*, Ms H. Whitby.

MATHEMATICS AND ITS APPLICATIONS, INSTITUTE OF (1964), 16 Nelson Street, Southend-on-Sea SS1 1EF. Tel: 0702-354020.—*Registrar*, Miss C. M. Richards.

MECHANICAL ENGINEERS, INSTITUTION OF (1847), 1 Birdcage Walk, SW1H 9JJ. Tel: 071-222 7899.— *Sec.*, R. W. Mellor, CBE.

MEDIC-ALERT FOUNDATION, 17 Bridge Wharf, 156 Caledonian Road, N1 9UU. Tel: 071-833 3034.— *Sec. Gen.*, Mrs M. L. Stanton.

MEDICAL COUNCIL, GENERAL (1858), 44 Hallam Street, W1N 6AE. Tel: 071-580 7642.—*Registrar*, P. L. Towers.

MEDICAL SOCIETY OF LONDON (1773), 11 Chandos Street, W1M 0EB.—*Registrar*, Maj. T. Tudor-Williams.

MEDICAL WOMEN'S FEDERATION (1917), Tavistock House North, Tavistock Square, WC1H 9HX.— *Hon. Sec.*, Dr I. Weinreb.

MEMORIAL FUND FOR DISASTER RELIEF, 3 Throgmorton Avenue, EC2N 2WW. Tel: 071-638 6442.—*Dir.*, R. Kandt.

MEN OF THE TREES (1922), Sandy Lane, Crawley Down, W. Sussex RH10 4HS. Tel: 0342-712536.— *Exec. Sec.*, Mrs E. Sandwell.

MENTAL AFTER CARE ASSOCIATION (1879), Bainbridge House, Bainbridge Street, WC1A 1HP. Tel: 071-436 6194.—*Dir.*, B. G. Garner.

MENTAL HEALTH FOUNDATION, THE (1949), 8 Hallam Street, W1N 6DH. Tel: 071-580 0145.—*Dir. Gen.*, P. Searle.

MERCHANT NAVY WELFARE BOARD (1948), 19–21 Lancaster Gate, W2 3LN.—*Gen. Sec.*, J. I. K. Walker.

METALS, THE INSTITUTE OF (1985), 1 Carlton House Terrace, SW1Y 5DB. Tel: 071-839 4071.—*Sec.*, Dr J. A. Catterall.

METAL TRADES BENEVOLENT SOCIETY, ROYAL (1843), Kelvin House, 1 Totteridge Avenue, High Wycombe, Bucks. HP13 6XG. Tel: 0494-530430.—*Gen. Sec.*, A Whittle, MBE.

METEOROLOGICAL SOCIETY, ROYAL (1850), 104 Oxford Road, Reading, Berks. RG1 7LJ. Tel: 0734-568500.—*Exec. Sec.*, R. P. C. Swash.

METROPOLITAN AND CITY POLICE ORPHANS FUND (1870), 30 Hazlewell Road, SW15 6LH. Tel: 081-788 5140.—*Sec.*, R. Duff-Cole, BEM.

METROPOLITAN AUTHORITIES, ASSOCIATION OF (1974), 35 Great Smith Street, SW1P 3BJ. Tel: 071-222 8100.—*Sec.*, R. Brooke.

METROPOLITAN HOSPITAL-SUNDAY FUND (1872), 40 High Street, Teddington, Middx. TW11 8EW. Tel: 081-977 4154.—*Sec.*, D. A. B. Lynch.

MIDDLE EAST ASSOCIATION, THE (1961), Bury House, 33 Bury Street, SW1Y 6AX. Tel: 071-839 2137.— *Dir.-Gen.*, Sir James Craig, GCMG.

MIDWIVES, ROYAL COLLEGE OF (1881), 15 Mansfield Street, W1M 0BE. Tel: 071–580 6523.—*Gen. Sec.*, Miss R. M. Ashton, OBE.

MIGRAINE ASSOCIATION, BRITISH (1958), 178a High Road, Byfleet, Weybridge, Surrey KT14 7ED. Tel: 0932-352 468.—*Hon. Sec.*, Mrs J. Liddell.

MIGRAINE TRUST (1965), 45 Great Ormond Street, WC1N 3HZ. Tel: 071-278 2676.—*Dir.*, P. Hodgkins.

MILITARY HISTORICAL SOCIETY, National Army Museum, Royal Hospital Road, SW3 4HT. Tel: 081-460 7341.—*Hon. Sec.*, J. Gaylor.

MIND (National Association for Mental Health), 22 Harley Street, W1N 2ED. Tel: 071-673 0741.—*Dir.*, Ms R. Hepplewhite.

MINERALOGICAL SOCIETY (1876), 41 Queen's Gate, SW7 5HR.—*Hon. Gen. Sec.*, Dr M. G. Bown.

MINES OF GREAT BRITAIN, FEDERATION OF SMALL, 29 King Street, Newcastle under Lyme, Staffs. ST5 1ER. Tel: 0782-614618.—*Sec.*, R. W. Bladen.

MINIATURE PAINTERS, SCULPTORS AND GRAVERS, ROYAL SOCIETY OF (1895).—*Exec. Sec.*, Mrs S. M. Burton, Burwood House, 15 Union Street, Wells, Somerset BA5 2PU. Tel: 0749-674472.

MINIATURISTS, SOCIETY OF (1895), Castle Gallery, Castle Hill, Ilkley, W. Yorks. LS29 9DT.—*Dir.*, L. Simpson.

MISSION TO DEEP SEA FISHERMEN, ROYAL NATIONAL (1881), 43 Nottingham Place, W1M 4BX. Tel: 071-487 5101.—*Chief Exec.*, A. D. Marsden.

MISSIONS TO SEAMEN, THE (1856), St Michael Paternoster Royal, College Hill, EC4R 2RL. Tel: 071-248 5202.—*Gen. Sec.*, Rev. Canon G. Jones.

MODERN CHURCHPEOPLE'S UNION (1898). For the advancement of liberal religious thought.—*Hon. Sec.*, Rev. R. C. Truss, The Rectory, Church Square, Shepperton, Middx. TW17 9JY. Tel: 0932-220511.

MONUMENTAL BRASS SOCIETY (1887).—*Hon. Sec.*, W. Mendelsson, 57 Leeside Crescent, NW11 0HA.

MORAVIAN MISSIONS, LONDON ASSOCIATION IN AID OF (1817), Moravian Church House, 5–7 Muswell Hill, N10 3TJ. Tel: 081-883 3409.—*Sec.*, Rev. F. Linyard.

MOTHERS' UNION, THE (1876), Mary Sumner House, 24 Tufton Street, SW1P 3RB. Tel: 071-222 5533.— *Central Sec.*, Mrs M. Chapman.

MOTOR INDUSTRY, THE INSTITUTE OF THE, Fanshaws, Brickendon, Hertford SG13 8PQ.—*Sec.*, F. W. Janes.

MOUNTBATTEN MEMORIAL TRUST (1979), 1 Grosvenor Crescent, SW1X 7EF. Tel: 071-235 5231, ext. 255.— *Dir.*, J. Boyd-Brent.

MOUNTBATTEN TRUST, THE EDWINA (1960), 1 Grosvenor Crescent, SW1X 7EF. Tel: 071-235 5231, ext. 255.—*Sec.*, J. Boyd-Brent.

MULTIPLE SCLEROSIS SOCIETY (1953), 25 Effie Road, SW6 1EE.—*Gen. Sec.*, J. Walford.

MUNICIPAL ENGINEERS, ASSOCIATION OF, 1–7 Great George Street, SW1P 3AA.—*Dir.*, K. J. Marchant.

MUSEUMS ASSOCIATION (1889), 34 Bloomsbury Way, WC1A 2SF. Tel: 071-404 4767.—*Dir.*, M. Taylor.

MUSIC HALL SOCIETY, BRITISH (1963), Brodie and Middleton Ltd, 68 Drury Lane, WC2B 5SP. Tel: 071-836 3289.—*Hon. Sec.*, Mrs J. D. Masterton.

MUSICIANS BENEVOLENT FUND (1921), 16 Ogle Street, W1P 7LG. Tel: 071-636 4481.—*Sec.*, M. B. M. Williams.

MUSICIANS, INCORPORATED SOCIETY OF (1882), 10 Stratford Place, W1N 9AE. Tel: 071-629 4413.—*Chief Exec.*, N. Hoyle.

MUSICIANS OF GREAT BRITAIN, ROYAL SOCIETY OF (1738), 10 Stratford Place, W1N 9AE. Tel: 071-629 6137.—*Sec.*, Mrs M. E. Gleed, MBE.

MUSIC INFORMATION CENTRE, BRITISH (1967), 10 Stratford Place, W1N 9AE. Tel: 071-499 8567.—*Administrator*, Ms E. Yeoman.

MUSIC SOCIETIES, NATIONAL FEDERATION OF (1935), Francis House, Francis Street, SW1P 1DE. Tel: 071-828 7320.—*Dir.*, R. Jones.

MYALGIC ENCEPHALOMYELITIS ASSOCIATION (1976), 4A Corringham Road, Stanford-le-Hope, Essex SS17 0AU.—*Dir.*, S. Powell.

NATIONAL AND UNIVERSITY LIBRARIES, STANDING CONFERENCE OF (SCONUL) (1950), 102 Euston Street, NW1 2HA. Tel: 071-387 0317.—*Sec.*, Miss G. M. Pentelow.

NATIONAL BENEVOLENT INSTITUTION (1812), 61 Bayswater Road, W2 3PG. Tel: 071-723 0021.—*Sec.*, Gp. Capt. D. St J. Homer, MVO.

NATIONAL COUNCIL FOR VOLUNTARY ORGANIZATIONS (1919), 26 Bedford Square, WC1B 3HU. Tel: 071-636 4066.—*Dir.*, Ms J. Weleminsky.

NATIONAL COUNCIL OF WOMEN OF GREAT BRITAIN (1895), 36 Danbury Street, N1 8JU.—*Pres.*, Mrs E. Bavidge.

NATIONAL LISTENING LIBRARY, 12 Lant Street, SE1 1QH. Tel: 071-407 9417.—*Exec. Dir.*, G. A. Hepworth.

NATIONAL SOCIETY, THE, (1811), Church House, Great Smith Street, SW1P 3NZ. For promoting religious education. Tel: 071-222 1672.—*Gen. Sec.*, G. Duncan.

NATIONAL SOCIETY FOR THE PREVENTION OF CRUELTY TO CHILDREN (NSPCC) (1884), 67 Saffron Hill, EC1N 8RS.—*Dir.*, C. Brown.

NATIONAL TRUST, THE (1895), 36 Queen Anne's Gate, SW1H 9AS. Tel: 071-222 9251.—*Chairman*, Dame Jennifer Jenkins; *Dir. Gen.*, A. Stirling.

NATIONAL TRUST FOR SCOTLAND (1931), 5 Charlotte Square, Edinburgh EH2 4DU. Tel: 031-226 5922.—*Dir.*, L. Borley.

NATIONAL UNION OF STUDENTS (1922), Nelson Mandela House, 461 Holloway Road, N7 6LJ. Tel: 071-272 8900.—*Nat. Pres.*, S. Twigg.

NATIONAL VIEWERS' AND LISTENERS' ASSOCIATION (1964).—*Pres.*, Mrs M. Whitehouse, CBE, Ardleigh, Colchester CO7 7RH. Tel: 0206-230123.

NATIONAL WOMEN'S REGISTER (1960), 9 Bank Plain, Norwich, Norfolk NR2 4SL. Tel: 0603-765392.—*Nat. Organizer*, Ms J. Cooke.

NATION'S FUND FOR NURSES (1917), 3 Albemarle Way, EC1V 4JB. Tel: 071-490 4227.—*Administrator*, Mrs S. D. Andrews.

NATURALISTS' ASSOCIATION, BRITISH (1905).— *Hon. Mem. Sec.*, Mrs Y. H. Griffiths, 23 Oak Hill Close, Woodford Green, Essex IG8 9PH.

NATURE CONSERVATION, ROYAL SOCIETY FOR (1912), The Green, Witham Park, Lincoln LN5 7JR. Tel: 0522-544400.—*Chief Exec.*, T. S. Cordy.

NAUTICAL RESEARCH, SOCIETY FOR (1911), c/o National Maritime Museum, Greenwich, SE10 9NF. Tel: 071-873 2139.—*Hon. Sec.*, D. G. Law.

NAVAL, MILITARY AND AIR FORCE BIBLE SOCIETY (1780), Radstock House, 3 Eccleston Street, SW1W 9LZ. Tel: 071-730 2155.—*Gen. Sec.*, R. Kennedy.

NAVAL ARCHITECTS, ROYAL INSTITUTION OF (1860), 10 Upper Belgrave Street, SW1X 8BQ. Tel: 071-235 4622.—*Sec.*, J. Rosewarn.

NAVIGATION, ROYAL INSTITUTE OF (1947), 1 Kensington Gore, SW7 2AT. Tel: 071-589 5021.—*Dir.*, Rear-Adm. R. M. Burgoyne, CB.

NAVY RECORDS SOCIETY (1893), c/o Barclays Bank PLC, Murray House, 1 Royal Mint Court, EC3N 4HH.—*Hon. Sec.*, A. J. McMillan.

NEEDLEWORK, ROYAL SCHOOL OF (1872).—*Principal*, Mrs E. Elvin, Apt. 12A, Hampton Court Palace, East Molesey, Surrey KT8 9AU. Tel: 081-943 1432.

NEWCOMEN SOCIETY (1920), Science Museum, SW7 2DD. For the study of the history of engineering and technology. Tel: 071-589 1793.—*Exec. Sec.*, A. Smith.

NEW ENGLISH ART CLUB (1886), 17 Carlton House Terrace, SW1Y 5BD.—*Sec.*, W. Bowyer, RA.

NEWSPAPER EDITORS, GUILD OF BRITISH (1946), Bloomsbury House, Bloomsbury Square, 74–77 Great Russell Street, WC1B 3DA. Tel: 071-636 7014.—*Sec.*, J. K. Bradbury.

NEWSPAPER PRESS FUND (1864), Dickens House, 35 Wathen Road, Dorking, Surrey RH4 1JY. Tel: 0306-887511.—*Dir.*, P. W. Evans.

NEWSPAPER SOCIETY (1836), Bloomsbury House, Bloomsbury Square, 74–77 Great Russell Street, WC1B 3DA. Tel: 071-636 7014.—*Dir.*, D. Nisbet-Smith.

NEWSVENDORS' BENEVOLENT INSTITUTION (1839), PO Box 306, Dunmow, Essex CM6 1HY. Tel: 0371-874198.—*Dir.*, C. S. Jones.

NOISE ABATEMENT SOCIETY (1959), PO Box 8, Bromley BR2 0UH.—*Chairman*, J. Connell, OBE.

NON-SMOKERS, NATIONAL SOCIETY OF , *see* QUIT.

NORWOOD CHILD CARE (1795), Stuart Young House, 221 Golders Green Road, NW11 9DL. Tel: 081-458 3282.—*Exec. Dir.*, S. Brier.

NOTARIES' SOCIETY (1907), 7 Lower Brook Street, Ipswich, IP4 1AF. Tel: 0473-214762.—*Sec.*, A. G. Dunford.

NUCLEAR ENERGY SOCIETY, BRITISH (1962), 1–7 Great George Street, SW1P 3AA. Tel: 071-222 7722.—*Exec. Officer*, P. Bacos.

NUFFIELD FOUNDATION (1943), 28 Bedford Square, WC1B 3EG. Tel: 071-631 0566.—*Dir.*, R. Hazell.

NUFFIELD PROVINCIAL HOSPITALS TRUST (1939), 3 Prince Albert Road, NW1 7SP. Tel: 071-485 6632.—*Sec.*, Dr M. Ashley-Miller.

NUMISMATIC SOCIETY, BRITISH (1903).—*Hon. Sec.*, G. P. Dyer, Royal Mint, Llantrisant, Pontyclun, Mid Glam. CF7 8YT.

NUMISMATIC SOCIETY, ROYAL (1836), c/o Dept. of Coins and Medals, The British Museum, Great Russell Street, WC1B 3DG. Tel: 071-323 8404.—*Hon. Secs.*, J. E. Cribb; R. G. Bland.

NURSES ASSOCIATION, ROYAL BRITISH (1887), 94 Upper Tollington Park, N4 4NB. Tel: 071-272 6821.—*Vice-Pres.*, Miss M. M. Tachon.

NURSES', RETIRED, NATIONAL HOME (1934), Riverside Avenue, Bournemouth BH7 7EE.—*Chairman*, E. V. Cornell.

NURSES, ROYAL NATIONAL PENSION FUND FOR, Burdett House, 15 Buckingham Street, WC2N 6ED. Tel: 071-839 6785.

NURSING, MIDWIFERY AND HEALTH VISITING, UK CENTRAL COUNCIL FOR, 23 Portland Place, W1N 3AF. Tel: 071-637 7181.—*Registrar and Chief Exec.*, C. Ralph.

England.—Victory House, 170 Tottenham Court Road, W1P 0HA. Tel: 071-388 3131.—*Chief Exec. Officer*, A. P. Smith.

Wales.—Floor 13, Pearl Assurance House, Greyfriars Road, Cardiff CF1 3AG. Tel: 0222-395535.—*Chief Exec. Officer*, D. A. Ravey.

Scotland.—22 Queen Street, Edinburgh EH2 1JX. Tel: 031-226 7371.—*Chief Exec. Officer*, Mrs L. Mitchell.

N.Ireland—RAC House, 79 Chichester Street, Belfast BT1 4JE. Tel: 0232-238152.—*Chief Exec. Officer*, J. J. Walsh.

NURSING, ROYAL COLLEGE OF, 20 Cavendish Square, W1M 0AB.

NUTRITION FOUNDATION, BRITISH (1967), 15 Belgrave Square, SW1X 8PG. Tel: 071-235 4904.—*Dir. Gen.* Dr D. M. Conning.

NUTRITION SOCIETY (1941), Grosvenor Gardens House, 35–37 Grosvenor Gardens, SW1W 0BS.—*Hon. Sec.*, Dr R. F. Grimble.

OBSTETRICIANS AND GYNAECOLOGISTS, ROYAL COLLEGE OF (1929), 27 Sussex Place, NW1 4RG. Tel: 071-262 5425.—*Pres.*, S. Simmons; *Sec.*, P. A. Barnett.

OCCUPATIONAL SAFETY AND HEALTH, INSTITUTION OF (1946), 222 Uppingham Road, Leicester LE5 0QG. Tel: 0533-768424.—*Chief Exec.*, J. R. Barrell.

OFFICERS' ASSOCIATION, THE (1920), 48 Pall Mall, SW1Y 5JY. Tel: 071-930 0125.—*Gen. Sec.*, Brig. P. D. Johnson.

OFFICERS' PENSIONS SOCIETY LTD (1946), 15 Buckingham Gate, SW1E 6NS. Tel: 071-828 2508.—*Gen. Sec.*, Maj.-Gen. Sir Laurence New, CB, CBE.

OIL PAINTERS, ROYAL INSTITUTE OF (1883).—*Sec.*, Mrs J. Easterling, 76 Coniston Road, Bromley BR1 4JB.

OILSEED, OIL AND FEEDINGSTUFFS TRADES BENEVOLENT ASSOCIATION, 14–20 St. Mary Axe, EC3A 8BU. Tel: 071-623 5501.—*Sec.*, R. T. Wheelans.

ONE PARENT FAMILIES, NATIONAL COUNCIL FOR, 255 Kentish Town Road, NW5 2LX. Tel: 071-267 1361.—*Dir.*, Miss S. Slipman.

OPEN-AIR MISSION, THE (1853), 19 John Street, WC1N 2DL.—*Sec.*, A. J. Greenbank.

OPEN SPACES SOCIETY (1865). Commons, open spaces and footpaths preservation society. 25A Bell Street, Henley-on-Thames, Oxon. RG9 2BA. Tel: 0491-573535.—*Gen. Sec.*, Miss K. Ashbrook.

OPERATIC AND DRAMATIC ASSOCIATION, NATIONAL (1899), NODA House, 1 Crestfield Street, WC1H 8AU. Tel: 071-837 5655.—*Gen. Administrator*, B. Clarke.

OPTICAL COUNCIL, GENERAL (1958), 41 Harley Street, W1N 2DJ. Tel: 071-580 3898.—*Registrar*, R. Wilshin.

OPTOMETRISTS, BRITISH COLLEGE OF, 10 Knaresborough Place, SW5 0TG. Tel: 071-373 7765.—*Gen. Sec.*, T. H. Collingridge.

ORDERS AND MEDALS RESEARCH SOCIETY (1942).—*Gen. Sec.*, N. G. Gooding, 123 Turnpike Link, Croydon CR0 5NU. Tel: 081-680 2701.

ORIENTAL CERAMIC SOCIETY (1921), 31B Torrington Square, WC1E 7LJ. Tel: 071-636 7985.—*Sec.*, Vice-Adm. Sir John Gray, KBE, CB.

ORNITHOLOGISTS' CLUB, SCOTTISH (1936), 21 Regent Terrace, Edinburgh EH7 5BT. Tel: 031-556 6042.—*Sec.*, M. H. Murphy.

ORNITHOLOGISTS' UNION, BRITISH (1858), c/o British Museum (Natural History), Sub-dept. of Ornithology, Tring, Herts. HP23 6AP. Tel: 0442-890080.—*Hon. Sec.*, Mrs G. Bonham.

ORNITHOLOGY, BRITISH TRUST FOR (1932), The Nunnery, Nunnery Place, Thetford, Norfolk IP24 2PU. Tel: 0842-750050.—*Dir. of Services*, A. Elvin.

ORTHOPAEDIC ASSOCIATION, BRITISH (1918), The Royal College of Surgeons, 35–43 Lincoln's Inn Fields, WC2A 3PN. Tel: 071-405 6507.—*Hon. Sec.*, M. K. d'A. Benson.

OSTEOPATHIC MEDICINE, LONDON COLLEGE OF, 8–10 Boston Place, NW1 6QH.

OSTEOPOROSIS SOCIETY, THE NATIONAL (1986), PO Box 10, Radstock, Bath BA3 3YB. Tel: 0761-32472.—*Gen. Sec.*, Mrs V. Collier.

OUTWARD BOUND TRUST LTD (1941), Chestnut Field, Regent Place, Rugby, Warks. CV21 2PJ. Tel: 0788-560423.—*Dir.*, I. L. Fothergill.

OVERSEAS DEVELOPMENT INSTITUTE (1960), Regent's College, Inner Circle, Regent's Park, NW1 4NS. Tel: 071-487 7413.—*Dir.*, Dr J. Howell.

OVERSEAS SERVICE PENSIONERS' ASSOCIATION (1960), 63 Church Road, Hove, E. Sussex BN3 2BD. Tel: 0273-721630.—*Sec.*, C. D. Stenton.

OVERSEAS SETTLEMENT, CHURCH OF ENGLAND BOARD FOR SOCIAL RESPONSIBILITY (1925), Great Smith Street, SW1P 3NZ. Tel: 071-222 9011.—*Admin. Sec.*, Miss P. J. Hallett.

OXFAM (1942), 274 Banbury Road, Oxford OX2 7DZ. Tel: 0865-311311.—*Dir.*, Lord Judd of Portsea.

OXFORD PRESERVATION TRUST (1927), 10 Turn Again Lane, St Ebbes, Oxford OX1 1QL. Tel: 0865-242918.—*Sec.*, Mrs M. Haynes.

OXFORD SOCIETY (1932), 8 Wellington Square, Oxford OX1 2HY. Tel: 0865-270088.—*Sec.*, Dr H. A. Hurren.

PAEDIATRIC ASSOCIATION, BRITISH (1928), 5 St Andrew's Place, NW1 4LB. Tel: 071-486 6151.—*Hon. Sec.*, Dr R. MacFaul.

PAINTER-PRINTMAKERS, ROYAL SOCIETY OF (1880), Bankside Gallery, 48 Hopton Street, SE1 9JH. Tel: 071-928 7521.—*Sec.*, J. Winkelman.

PAINTERS IN WATER COLOURS, ROYAL INSTITUTE OF (1831), 17 Carlton House Terrace, SW1Y 5BD.—*Sec.*, R. Spurrier.

PALAEONTOGRAPHICAL SOCIETY (1847) c/o British Geological Survey, Keyworth, Nottingham NG12 5GG.—*Sec.*, S. P. Tunnicliff.

PALAEONTOLOGICAL ASSOCIATION (1957).—*Sec.*, Dr J. A. Crame, c/o British Antarctic Survey, High Cross, Madingley Road, Cambridge CB3 0ET. Tel: 0223-61188, ext. 261.

PARKINSON'S DISEASE SOCIETY (1969), 22 Upper Woburn Place, WC1H 0RA. Tel: 071-383 3513.—*Exec. Dir.*, Ms M. Baker.

PARLIAMENTARY AND SCIENTIFIC COMMITTEE (1939), 16 Great College Street, SW1P 3RX. Tel: 071-222 7085.—*Sec.*, A. Butler.

PASTORAL PSYCHOLOGY, GUILD OF (1936).—*Hon. Sec.*, Miss J. Whale, 5 Kilmeny House, 36 Arterberry Road, SW20 8AQ. Tel: 081-946 3172.

PATENT AGENTS, CHARTERED INSTITUTE OF (1882), Staple Inn Buildings, High Holborn, WC1V 7PZ. Tel: 071-405 9450.—*Sec.*, Miss M. E. Poole.

PATENTEES AND INVENTORS, INSTITUTE OF (1919), Triumph House, 189 Regent Street, W1R 7WF. Tel: 071-242 7812.—*Sec.*, J. R. Kay.

PATHOLOGISTS, ROYAL COLLEGE OF, 2 Carlton House Terrace, SW1Y 5AF. Tel: 071-930 5863.—*Sec.*, K. Lockyer.

PATIENTS ASSOCIATION (1963), 18 Victoria Park Square, E2 9PF. Tel: 081-981 5676.—*Chairman*, Rabbi Julia Neuberger.

PEACE COUNCIL, NATIONAL (1908), 88 Islington High Street, N1 8EG. Tel: 071-354 5200.—*Co-ordinators*, A. L. McLeod; L. Peck.

PEAK AND NORTHERN FOOTPATHS SOCIETY (1894). Tel: 061-790 4383.—*Hon. Gen. Sec.*, D. Taylor, 15 Parkfield Drive, Tyldesley, Manchester M29 8NR.

PEARSON'S HOLIDAY FUND, 18–20 Kingston Road, SW19 1JZ. Tel: 081-542 5550.—*Gen. Sec.*, G. P. Holloway.

PEDESTRIANS ASSOCIATION (1929), 1 Wandsworth Road, SW8 2XX. Tel: 071-735 3270.—*Chairman*, C. Myerscough.

PEN, INTERNATIONAL (1921), 9–10 Charterhouse Buildings, Goswell Road, EC1M 7AT. World association of writers. Tel: 071-253 4308.—*International Sec.*, A. Blokh.

PENSION FUNDS LTD, NATIONAL ASSOCIATION OF (1923), 12–18 Grosvenor Gardens, SW1W 0DH.—*Dir. Gen.*, M. A. Elton.

PEOPLE'S DISPENSARY FOR SICK ANIMALS (1917), Whitechapel Way, Priorslee, Telford, Shropshire TF2 9PQ. Tel: 0952-290999.—*Gen. Sec.*, M. R. Curtis, MBE.

PERFORMING RIGHT SOCIETY LTD (1914), 29–33 Berners Street, W1P 4AA. Tel: 071-580 5544.—*Chief Exec.*, M. J. Freegard.

PERIODICAL PUBLISHERS ASSOCIATION LTD (1913), Imperial House, 15–19 Kingsway, WC2B 6UN. Tel: 071-379 6268.—*Chief Exec.*, I. Locks.

PESTALOZZI CHILDREN'S VILLAGE TRUST (1959), Sedlescombe, Battle, E. Sussex TN33 0RR. Tel: 0424-870444.—*Dir.*, C. C. Wagstaff.

PETROLEUM, INSTITUTE OF (1913), 61 New Cavendish Street, W1M 8AR. Tel: 071-636 1004.—*Dir. Gen.*, A. E. H. Williams.

PHARMACEUTICAL SOCIETY OF GREAT BRITAIN, ROYAL (1841), 1 Lambeth High Street, SE1 7JN.—*Sec. and Registrar*, J. Ferguson.

PHARMACOLOGICAL SOCIETY, BRITISH (1931).—*Hon. Gen. Sec.*, Dr A. R. Green, Astra Neuroscience Research Unit, 1 Wakefield Street, WC1N 1PJ. Tel: 071-837 9242.

PHILOLOGICAL SOCIETY (1842).—*Hon. Sec.*, Prof. T. Bynon, School of Oriental and African Studies, University of London, Thornhaugh Street, WC1H 0XG. Tel: 071-637 2388, ext. 2561.

PHILOSOPHY, ROYAL INSTITUTE OF (1925), 14 Gordon Square, WC1H 0AG. Tel: 071-387 4130.—*Dir.*, Prof. A. Phillips Griffiths.

PHOTOGRAMMETRIC SOCIETY (1952).—*Hon. Sec.*, Dr A. S. Walker, Kern Instruments Ltd, Revenge Road, Lordswood, Chatham, Kent ME5 8TE.

PHOTOGRAPHY, BRITISH INSTITUTE OF PROFESSIONAL (1901), Fox Talbot House, Amwell End, Ware, Herts. SG12 9HN. Tel: 0920-464011.—*Chief Exec.*, A. M. Berkeley.

PHYSICAL RECREATION, CENTRAL COUNCIL OF (1935), Francis House, Francis Street, SW1P 1DE. Tel: 071-828 3163/4.—*Gen. Sec.*, P. Lawson.

PHYSICIANS, ROYAL COLLEGE OF (1518), 11 St Andrew's Place, NW1 4LE. Tel: 071-935 1174.—*Sec.*, D. B. Lloyd.

PHYSICIANS AND SURGEONS, ROYAL COLLEGE OF (Glasgow) (1599), 234–242 St Vincent Street, Glasgow G2 5RJ. Tel: 041-221 6072.—*Hon. Sec.*, Dr A. D. Beattie.

PHYSICIANS OF EDINBURGH, ROYAL COLLEGE OF (1681), 9 Queen Street, Edinburgh EH2 1JQ. Tel: 031-225 7324.—*Sec.*, Dr J. L. Anderton.

PHYSICS, INSTITUTE OF (1874), 47 Belgrave Square, SW1X 8QX. Tel: 071-235 6111.—*Chief Exec.*, Dr A. Jones.

PHYSIOLOGICAL SOCIETY (1876).—*Hon. Sec.*, Dr D. Cotterell, PO Box 506, Oxford OX1 3XE.

PHYSIOTHERAPY, THE CHARTERED SOCIETY OF (1894), 14 Bedford Row, WC1R 4ED. Tel: 071-242 1941.—*Sec.*, T. Simon.

PIG ASSOCIATION, BRITISH (1884), 7 Rickmansworth Road, Watford, Herts. WD1 7HE. Tel: 0923 34377.—*Chief Exec.*, G. E. Welsh.

PILGRIM TRUST, THE (1930), Fielden House, Little College Street, SW1P 3SH. Tel: 071-222 4723.—*Sec.*, Hon. A. H. Millar.

PILGRIMS OF GREAT BRITAIN, THE (1902), Savoy Hotel, WC2R 0EU.—*Hon. Sec.*, Lt. Col. S. W. Chant-Sempill, OBE, MC.

PLANT ENGINEERS, INSTITUTION OF, 77 Great Peter Street, SW1P 2EZ. Tel: 071-233 2855.—*Sec. Gen.*, R. S. Pratt.

PLASTICS AND RUBBER INSTITUTE, THE (1921), 11 Hobart Place, SW1W 0HL. Tel: 071-245 1555.—*Sec. Gen.* J. Hawkins.

PLAYING CARD SOCIETY, THE INTERNATIONAL (1972), 188 Sheen Lane, SW14 8LF.—*Sec.*, C. C. Rayner.

PLAYING FIELDS ASSOCIATION, NATIONAL (1925), 25 Ovington Square, SW3 1LQ. Tel: 071-584 6445.—*Gen. Sec.*, Mrs H. Hays.

POETRY SOCIETY (1909), 21 Earl's Court Square, SW5 9DE. Tel: 071-373 7861.—*Dir. and Gen. Sec.*, C. Green.

POLICY STUDIES INSTITUTE (1978), 100 Park Village East, NW1 3SR. Tel: 071-387 2171.—*Dir.*, W. W. Daniel.

POLIO FELLOWSHIP, BRITISH (1939), Bell Close, West End Road, Ruislip, Middx. HA4 6LP. Tel: 0895-675515.—*Gen. Sec.*, L. P. Jackson.

POLYTECHNIC AND COLLEGE TEACHERS, ASSOCIATION OF (1973), 104 Albert Road, Southsea, Hants. PO5 2SN. Tel: 0705-818625.—*Chief Exec.*, Ms C. Cheesman.

POLYTECHNICS, COMMITTEE OF DIRECTORS OF (1970), Kirkman House, 12–14 Whitfield Street, W1P 6AX. Tel: 071-637 9939.—*Sec.*, R. P. Blows.

PORTRAIT PAINTERS, ROYAL SOCIETY OF (1891), 17 Carlton House Terrace, SW1Y 5BD.—*Pres.*, D. Poole.

POST OFFICE USERS' NATIONAL COUNCIL (1970), Waterloo Bridge House, Waterloo Road, SE1 8UA. Tel: 071-928 9458.—*Sec.*, K. Hall.

POULTRY CLUB OF GREAT BRITAIN, THE (1877).—*Gen. Sec.*, Mrs E. A. Aubrey-Fletcher, Cliveden, Sandy Bank Farm, Chipping, Preston, Lancs. PR3 2GA.

PRAYER BOOK SOCIETY, THE (1975), St. James Garlickhythe, Garlick Hill, EC4V 2AL. Tel: 081-958 8769.—*Hon. Sec.*, Mrs. M. Thompson.

PRECEPTORS, COLLEGE OF, (1846), Coppice Row, Theydon Bois, Epping, Essex CM16 7DN. Tel: 0992-812727.—*Membership Officer*, A. Dixon.

PREPARATORY SCHOOLS, INCORPORATED ASSOCIATION OF, 138 Kensington Church Street, W8 4BN.—*Sec.*, J. M. C. Coates.

PRE-SCHOOL PLAYGROUPS ASSOCIATION, 61–63 Kings Cross Road, WC1X 9LL.—*Nat. Administrator*, Ms M. Lochrie.

PRESS ASSOCIATION (1868), 85 Fleet Street, EC4P 4BE.—*Sec.*, R. C. Henry.

PRESS UNION, COMMONWEALTH (1909), Studio House, 184 Fleet Street, EC4A 2DU. Tel: 071-242 1056.—*Dir.*, R. Mackichan.

PREVENTION OF ACCIDENTS, ROYAL SOCIETY FOR THE (1916), Cannon House, Priory Queensway, Birmingham B4 6BS. Tel: 021-200 2461.—*Dir. Gen.*, J. Wethered.

PRINCESS LOUISE SCOTTISH HOSPITAL (Erskine Hospital) (1916), Bishopton, Renfrewshire PA7 5PU. Tel: 041-812 1100. For disabled ex-servicemen and women.—*Commandant*, Col. W. K. Shepherd.

PRINTERS' CHARITABLE CORPORATION (1827), Victoria House, Harestone Valley Road, Caterham, Surrey CR3 6HY. Tel: 0883-345331.—*Deputy Dir.*, H. J. Court.

PRINTING HISTORICAL SOCIETY (1964), St Bride Institute, Bride Lane, EC4Y 8EE.—*Hon. Sec.*, Dr M. Smith.

PRINTING, INSTITUTE OF (1961), 8 Lonsdale Gardens, Tunbridge Wells, Kent TN1 1NU. Tel: 0892-38118/9.—*Sec.*, C. F. Partridge.

PRISON VISITORS, NATIONAL ASSOCIATION OF (1922), 46B Hartington Street, Bedford MK41 7RP. Tel: 0234-359763.—*Gen. Sec.*, Mrs A. G. McKenna.

PRIVATE LIBRARIES ASSOCIATION (1957).—*Hon. Sec.*, F. Broomhead, Ravelston, South View Road, Pinner, Middx. HA5 3YD.

PROCURATORS IN GLASGOW, ROYAL FACULTY OF (1600), 12 Nelson Mandela Place, Glasgow G2 1BT. Tel: 041-204 3213.—*Clerk*, J. H. Sinclair.

PRODUCTION CONTROL, INSTITUTE OF, Elmcroft House, Tiddington Road, Tiddington, Stratford-upon-Avon, Warks. CV37 7AQ.—*Gen. Sec.*, K. Roberts.

PRODUCTION ENGINEERS, INSTITUTION OF, Rochester House, 66 Little Ealing Lane, W5 4XX.—*Sec.*, Brig. P. V. Crooks.

PROFESSIONAL CLASSES AID COUNCIL (1921), 10 St Christopher's Place, W1M 6HY. Tel: 071-935 0641.—*Sec.*, Mrs G. A. Burgess.

PROFESSIONAL ENGINEERS, UK ASSOCIATION OF (1969), Hayes Court, West Common Road, Bromley BR2 7AU. Tel: 081-462 7755.—*Nat. Sec.*, B. Strutton.

PROFESSIONAL FOOTBALLERS' ASSOCIATION, 2 Oxford Court, Bishopsgate, Manchester M2 3WQ. Tel: 061-236 0575.—*Sec.*, G. Taylor.

PROFESSIONS SUPPLEMENTARY TO MEDICINE, COUNCIL FOR, Park House, 184 Kennington Park Road, SE11 4BU.—*Registrar*, R. Pickis.

PROTECTION OF THE UNBORN CHILD, SOCIETY FOR THE (1967), 7 Tufton Street, SW1P 3QN. Tel: 071-222 5845.—*Dir.*, Mrs P. Bowman.

PROTESTANT ALLIANCE, THE (1845), 77 Ampthill Gardens, Flitwick, Bedford MK45 1BD. Tel: 0525-712348.—*Gen. Sec.*, Rev. A. G. Ashdown.

PSORIASIS ASSOCIATION (1968), 7 Milton Street, Northampton NN2 7JG. Tel: 0604-711129.—*Nat. Sec.*, Mrs L. Henley.

PSYCHIATRISTS, ROYAL COLLEGE OF (1971), 17 Belgrave Square, SW1X 8PG. Tel: 071-235 2351.—*Sec.*, Mrs V. Cameron.

PSYCHICAL RESEARCH, SOCIETY FOR (1882), 49 Marloes Road, W8 6LA. Tel: 071-937 8984.—*Pres.*, Dr A. Gauld.

PSYCHOLOGICAL SOCIETY, THE BRITISH (1901), St Andrews House, 48 Princess Road East, Leicester LE1 7DR. Tel: 0533-549568.—*Exec. Sec.*, C. V. Newman, PH.D.

PUBLIC ADMINISTRATION, ROYAL INSTITUTE OF (1922), 3 Birdcage Walk, SW1H 9JH. Tel: 071-222 2248.—*Dir. Gen.*, D. Falcon.

PUBLIC FINANCE AND ACCOUNTANCY, CHARTERED INSTITUTE OF (1885), 3 Robert Street, WC2N 6BH. Tel: 071-895 8823.—*Dir.*, N. P. Hepworth, OBE.

PUBLIC HEALTH AND HYGIENE, THE ROYAL INSTITUTE OF (1937), 28 Portland Place, W1N 4DE. Tel: 071-580 2731/2.—*Sec.*, Gp. Capt. R. A. Smith (*retd.*).

PUBLIC HEALTH ENGINEERS, INSTITUTION OF, *see* WATER AND ENVIRONMENTAL MANAGEMENT.

PUBLIC RELATIONS, THE INSTITUTE OF (1948), The Old Trading House, 15 Northburgh Street, EC1V 0PR. Tel: 071-253 5151.—*Exec. Dir.*, J. B. Lavelle.

PUBLIC TEACHERS OF LAW, SOCIETY OF (1908).—*Hon. Sec.*, Prof. P. B. H. Birks, All Souls College, Oxford OX1 4AL. Tel: 0865-279338.

PURCHASING AND SUPPLY, INSTITUTE OF (1967), Easton House, Easton on the Hill, Stamford, Lincs. PE9 3NZ. Tel: 0780-56777.—*Dir. Gen.*, P. Thomson.

PURE WATER ASSOCIATION, NATIONAL (1960).—*Sec.*, N. Brugge, Meridan, Cae Goody Lane, Ellesmere, Shrops. SY12 9DW. Tel: 0691-623015.

QUALITY ASSURANCE, INSTITUTE OF, 10 Grosvenor Gardens, SW1 0DQ. Tel: 071-730 7154.—*Sec. Gen.*, Dr J. Davies.

QUARRIER'S HOMES (1871), Bridge of Weir, Renfrewshire PA11 3SA. Tel: 0505-612224.—*Chief Exec.*, J. Rea, OBE.

QUARRYING, INSTITUTE OF (1917), 7 Regent Street, Nottingham NG1 5BY. Tel: 0602-411315.—*Sec.*, M. J. Arthur.

QUEEN ELIZABETH'S FOUNDATION FOR THE DISABLED (1967), Leatherhead, Surrey KT22 0BN. Tel: 0372-842204.—*Dir.*, M. B. Clark, PH.D.

QUEEN VICTORIA CLERGY FUND (1897), Church House, Dean's Yard, SW1P 3NZ. Tel: 071-222 5261.—*Sec.*, C. D. L. Menzies.

QUEEN VICTORIA SCHOOL (1908), Dunblane, Perthshire FK15 0JY. Tel: 0786-822288.—*Headmaster*, J. D. Hankinson.

QUEEN'S ENGLISH SOCIETY, THE (1972).—*Hon. Membership Sec.*, M. Plumbe, 104 Drive Mansions, Fulham Road, SW6 5JH. Tel: 071-731 1664.

QUEEN'S NURSING INSTITUTE (1887), 3 Albemarle Way, EC1V 4JB. Tel: 071-490 4227.—*Dir.*, Mrs S. Andrews.

QUEKETT MICROSCOPICAL CLUB (1865).—*Hon. Business Sec.*, A. V. Dodge, 61 Pewley Way, Guildford GU1 3PZ. Tel: 0483-67986.

QUIT (National Society of Non-Smokers) (1926), 102 Gloucester Place, W1H 3DA. Tel: 071-487 2858.—*Dir.*, Ms S. Wilson.

RADAR (THE ROYAL ASSOCIATION FOR DISABILITY AND REHABILITATION) (1977), 25 Mortimer Street, W1N 8AB.—*Dir.* B. Massie, OBE.

RADIOLOGISTS, ROYAL COLLEGE OF (1934), 38 Portland Place, W1N 3DG. Tel: 071-636 4432.—*Sec.*, A. J. Cowles.

RADIOLOGY, BRITISH INSTITUTE OF (1897), 36 Portland Place, W1N 4AT. Tel: 071-580 4085.—*Gen. Sec.*, Ms M-A. Piggott.

RAILWAY AND CANAL HISTORICAL SOCIETY.—*Hon. Sec.*, G. H. R. Gwatkin, 17 Clumber Crescent North, The Park, Nottingham NG7 1EY. Tel: 0602 414844.

RAILWAY BENEVOLENT INSTITUTION (1858), 67 Ashbourne Road, Derby DE3 3FS. Tel: 0332-363067.—*Dir.*, R.B. Boiling.

RAINER FOUNDATION (1876), 227–239 Tooley Street, SE1 2JX. Helps young people at risk or in need; administers the Intermediate Treatment Fund on behalf of the government.—*Dir.*, R. Kay.

RAMBLERS' ASSOCIATION (1935), 1–5 Wandsworth Road, SW8 2XX. Tel: 071-582 6878.—*Dir.*, A. Mattingly.

RANFURLY LIBRARY SERVICE (1954), 2 Coldharbour Place, 39–41 Coldharbour Lane, SE5 9NR. Tel: 071-733 3577.—*Dir.*, Mrs S. Harrity.

RARE BREEDS SURVIVAL TRUST LTD. (1973), National Agricultural Centre, Kenilworth, Warks. CV8 2LG. Tel: 0203-696551.—*Exec. Dir.*, L. Alderson.

RATHBONE SOCIETY, THE (1919), 1st Floor, Princess House, 105–107 Princess Street, Manchester M1 6DD. Tel: 061-236 5358.—*Chief Exec.*, Ms A. Weinstock.

RECORD SOCIETY, SCOTTISH (1897), Dept. of Scottish History, University of Glasgow, Glasgow G12 8QQ. Tel: 041-339 8855, ext. 5682.—*Hon. Sec.*, Dr J. Kirk.

RECORDS ASSOCIATION, BRITISH (1932), 18 Padbury Court, E2 7EH. Tel: 071-729 1415.—*Hon. Sec.*, J. Davies.

RED CROSS SOCIETY, BRITISH, *see* BRITISH RED CROSS.

RED POLL CATTLE SOCIETY (1888), The Market Hill, Woodbridge, Suffolk IP12 4DU. Tel: 0394-380643.—*Sec.*, P. Ryder-Davies.

REFRIGERATION, INSTITUTE OF (1899), Kelvin House, 76 Mill Lane, Carshalton, Surrey SM5 2JR. Tel: 081-647 7033.—*Sec.*, M. J. Horlick.

REFUGEE COUNCIL, BRITISH (1981), Bondway House, 3–9 Bondway, SW8 1SJ. Tel: 071-582 6922.—*Dir.*, A. Dubs.

REGIONAL STUDIES ASSOCIATION (1965), Wharfdale Projects, 15 Micawber Street, N1 17TB. Tel: 071-490 1128.—*Dir.*, Mrs S. Hardy.

REGULAR FORCES EMPLOYMENT ASSOCIATION (1885), 25 Bloomsbury Square, WC1A 2LN. Tel: 071-637 3918.—*Gen. Manager*, Maj.-Gen. D. T. Crabtree, CB.

RELATE: MARRIAGE GUIDANCE (1938), Herbert Gray College, Little Church Street, Rugby, Warks. CV21 3AP. Tel: 0788-573241.—*Dir.*, D. French.

RENT OFFICERS, INSTITUTE OF (1966).—*Hon. Sec.*, M. R. Webber, Musgrave House, Musgrave Row, Exeter EX4 3TW. Tel: 0392-72321.

RESEARCH DEFENCE SOCIETY (1908), Grosvenor Gardens House, Grosvenor Gardens, SW1W 0BS.—*Exec. Dir.*, Dr M. Matfield.

RESIDENTS' ASSOCIATIONS, NATIONAL UNION OF (1921).—*Hon. Gen. Sec.*, Mrs B. Reith, 35 Clement Way, Upminster, Essex RM14 2NX.

RETAIL BOOK, STATIONERY AND ALLIED TRADES EMPLOYEES' ASSOCIATION (1919), 8–9 Commercial Road, Swindon SN1 5RB. Tel: 0793-615811.—*Gen. Sec.*, J. Windust.

RETIREMENT PENSIONS ASSOCIATIONS, NATIONAL FEDERATION OF (1938), 14 St Peter Street, Blackburn BB2 2HD. Tel: 0254-52606.—*Gen. Sec.*, R. Stansfield.

REVENUES, RATING AND VALUATION INSTITUTE OF (1882), 41 Doughty Street, WC1N 2LF. Tel: 071-831 3505.—*Dir.*, C. Farrington.

RICHARD III SOCIETY (1924), 4 Oakley Street, SW3 5NN.—*Sec.*, Miss E. M. Nokes.

ROAD SAFETY OFFICERS, INSTITUTE OF (1971).—*Sec.*, E. M. Marsh, 31 Dyers Close, West Buckland, Wellington, Somerset TA21 9JU. Tel: 0823-663833.

ROAD TRANSPORT ENGINEERS, INSTITUTE OF (1945), 1 Cromwell Place, SW7 2JF. Tel: 071-589 3744.—*Exec. Sec.*, A. F. Stroud.

ROMAN STUDIES, SOCIETY FOR PROMOTION OF (1910), 31–34 Gordon Square, WC1H 0PP. Tel: 071-387 8157.—*Sec.*, Dr H. M. Cockle.

ROTARY INTERNATIONAL IN GREAT BRITAIN AND IRELAND (1914), Kinwarton Road, Alcester, Warks. B49 6BP. Tel: 0789-765411.—*Sec.*, G. S. Large.

ROUND TABLES OF GREAT BRITAIN AND IRELAND, NATIONAL ASSOCIATION OF (1927), Marchesi House, 4 Embassy Drive, Calthorpe Road, Edgbaston, Birmingham B15 1TP. Tel: 021-456 4402.—*Gen. Sec.*, R. H. Renold.

ROYAL AFRICAN SOCIETY (1901), 18 Northumberland Avenue, WC2N 5BJ. Tel: 071-930 1662.—*Sec.*, Mrs L. Allan.

ROYAL AIR FORCE BENEVOLENT FUND (1919), 67 Portland Place, W1N 4AR. Tel: 071-580 8343.—*Controller*, Air Chief Marshal Sir Thomas Kennedy, GCB, AFC.

ROYAL AIR FORCES ASSOCIATION (1943), 43 Grove Park Road, W4 3RX. Tel: 081-994 8504.—*Sec. Gen.*, M. G. Tomkins, MBE.

ROYAL ALEXANDRA AND ALBERT SCHOOL (1758), Gatton Park, Reigate, Surrey RH2 0TW. Tel: 0737-642576.—*Sec.*, Capt. A. J. Walsh, RN.

ROYAL ALFRED SEAFARERS' SOCIETY (1865), Weston Acres, Woodmansterne Lane, Banstead, Surrey SM7 3HB. Tel: 0737-352231.—*Gen. Sec.*, J. H. Moore.

ROYAL ARMOURED CORPS WAR MEMORIAL BENEVOLENT FUND (1946), c/o RHQ RTR, Bovington, Dorset BH20 6JA. Tel: 0929-403331.—*Sec.*, Maj. R. Clooney.

ROYAL ARTILLERY ASSOCIATION, Artillery House, Old Royal Military Academy, SE18 4DN. Tel: 081-319 4052.—*Gen. Sec.*, Lt.-Col. M.J. Darmody.

ROYAL ASIATIC SOCIETY (1823), 60 Queen's Gardens, W2 3AF. Tel: 071-724 4741/2.—*Sec.*, Miss L. Collins.

ROYAL CALEDONIAN SCHOOLS (1815), Aldenham Road, Bushey, Herts. WD2 3TS.—*Master*, Capt. D. F. Watts, RN.

ROYAL CELTIC SOCIETY (1820), 23 Rutland Street, Edinburgh EH1 2RN. Tel: 031-228 6449.—*Sec.*, J. G. Cameron.

ROYAL CHORAL SOCIETY (1871), International House, 2–4 Wendell Road, W12 9RT. Tel: 081-740 4273.—*Gen. Manager*, M. Heyland.

ROYAL ENGINEERS ASSOCIATION, RHQ Royal Engineers, Brompton Barracks, Chatham, Kent ME4 4UG. Tel: 0634-847005.—*Controller*, Maj. C. F. Cooper, MBE, (retd.).

ROYAL ENGINEERS, THE INSTITUTION OF (1875), Brompton Barracks, Chatham, Kent ME4 4UG. Tel: 0634-842669.—*Sec.*, Lt. Col. F. R. Beringer.

ROYAL HIGHLAND AND AGRICULTURAL SOCIETY OF SCOTLAND (1784), Edinburgh Exhibition and Trade Centre, Ingliston, Edinburgh EH28 8NF. Tel: 031-333 2444.—*Sec.*, J. R. Good.

ROYAL HORTICULTURAL SOCIETY (1804), PO Box 313, SW1P 2PE. Tel: 071-834 4333.—*Sec.*, D. P. Hearn.

ROYAL HOSPITAL AND HOME, PUTNEY (1854), West Hill, SW15 3SW. Tel: 081-788 4511.—*Chief Exec.*, Col. B. E. Blunt.

ROYAL HUMANE SOCIETY (1774), Brettenham House, Lancaster Place, WC2E 7EP. Tel: 071-836 8155.—*Sec.*, Maj. A. J. Dickinson.

ROYAL INSTITUTION, THE (1799), 21 Albemarle Street, W1X 4BS. Tel: 071-409 2992.—*Dir.*, Prof. P. Day, FRS; *Sec.*, Prof. D. C. Bradley, FRS.

ROYAL LIFE SAVING SOCIETY, UK (1891), Mountbatten House, Studley, Warks. B80 7NN.—*Dir.*, Ms C. J. Godsall.

ROYAL LITERARY FUND (1790), 144 Temple Chambers, Temple Avenue, EC4Y 0DT. Tel: 071-353 7150.—*Sec.*, Mrs F. M. Clark.

ROYAL MEDICAL BENEVOLENT FUND (1836), 24 King's Road, SW19 8QN. Tel: 081-540 9194.—*Sec.*, Mrs G. A. R. Wells.

ROYAL MEDICAL SOCIETY (1737), Students Centre, 5-5 Bristo Square, Edinburgh EH8 9AL. Tel: 031-650 2672.—*Sec.*, Ms A. Fullarton.

ROYAL MICROSCOPICAL SOCIETY (1839), 37–38 St Clements, Oxford OX4 1AJ. Tel: 0865-248768.—*Administrator*, P. B. Hirst.

ROYAL MUSICAL ASSOCIATION (1874).—*Sec.*, P. Owens, 135 Purves Road, NW10 5TH.

ROYAL NATIONAL INSTITUTE FOR THE BLIND (1868), 224 Great Portland Street, W1N 6AA. Tel: 071-388 1266.—*Dir. Gen.*, I. Bruce.

ROYAL NATIONAL LIFEBOAT INSTITUTION (1824), West Quay Road, Poole, Dorset BH15 1HZ. Tel: 0202-671133.—*Chairman*, M. Vernon.

ROYAL NAVAL AND ROYAL MARINES CHILDREN'S TRUST (1834), HMS *Nelson*, Portsmouth, PO1 3HH. Tel: 0705-817435.—*Sec.*, Mrs M. Bateman.

ROYAL NAVAL ASSOCIATION (1950), 82 Chelsea Manor Street, SW3 5QJ. Tel: 071-352 6764.—*Gen. Sec.*, Capt. J. W. Rayner.

ROYAL NAVAL BENEVOLENT SOCIETY (1739), 1 Fleet Street, EC4Y 1BD. Tel: 071-353 4080, ext. 471.—*Sec.*, Capt. M. Murray, RN (retd.).

ROYAL NAVAL BENEVOLENT TRUST (1922), 1 High Street, Brompton, Gillingham, Kent ME7 5QZ. Tel: 0634-842743.—*Gen. Sec.*, Lt.-Cdr. D. C. Lawrence (retd.).

ROYAL NAVY OFFICERS, ASSOCIATION OF (1920), 70 Porchester Terrace, W2 3TP. Tel: 071-402 5231.—*Sec.*, Lt.-Cdr. I. M. P. Coombes.

ROYAL OVER-SEAS LEAGUE (1910), Over-Seas House, Park Place, St James's Street, SW1A 1LR. Tel: 071-408 0214.—*Dir. Gen.*, R. F. Newell.

ROYAL PATRIOTIC FUND CORPORATION (1854), Golden Cross House, Duncannon Street, WC2 4JR.—*Sec.*, Brig. T. G. Williams, CBE.

ROYAL PHILATELIC SOCIETY, LONDON, THE (1869), 41 Devonshire Place, W1N 1PE. Tel: 071-486 1044.—*Gen. Sec.*, Miss M. Simmonds.

ROYAL PHOTOGRAPHIC SOCIETY (1853), Milsom Street, Bath BA1 1DN. Tel: 0225-462841.—*Sec.*, Ms A. Nevill.

ROYAL PINNER SCHOOL FOUNDATION, 110 Old Brompton Road, SW7 3RB. Tel: 071-373 6168.—*Sec.*, D. Crawford.

ROYAL SAILORS' RESTS (1876), 2A South Street, Gosport, Hants. PO12 1ES. Tel: 0705-589551.—*Sec.*, A. A. Lockwood.

ROYAL SCOTTISH SOCIETY FOR PREVENTION OF CRUELTY TO CHILDREN (1884), Melville House, 41 Polwarth Terrace, Edinburgh EH11 1NU.—*Gen. Sec.*, A. M. M. Wood, OBE.

ROYAL SIGNALS INSTITUTION (1950), 56 Regency Street, SW1P 4AD.—*Sec.*, Col. A. N. de Bretton-Gordon.

ROYAL SOCIETY FOR ASIAN AFFAIRS (1901), 2 Belgrave Square, SW1X 8PJ. Tel: 071-235 5122.—*Sec.*, Miss M. FitzSimons.

ROYAL SOCIETY FOR THE encouragement OF ARTS, MANUFACTURES AND COMMERCE (RSA) (1754), 8 John Adam Street, WC2N 6EZ. Tel: 071-930 5115.—*Chief Exec.*, C. Lucas.

ROYAL SOCIETY FOR THE PREVENTION OF CRUELTY TO ANIMALS (1824), Causeway, Horsham, W. Susse. RH12 1HG. Tel: 0403-64181.—*Chief Exec.*, A. J Richmond, CB.

ROYAL SOCIETY FOR THE PROTECTION OF BIRDS (1889) The Lodge, Sandy, Beds. SG19 2DL. Tel: 0767 680551.—*Chief Exec.*, Ms B. Young.

ROYAL SOCIETY OF HEALTH, THE (1876), RSH House 38A St George's Drive, SW1V 4BH. Tel: 071-630 0121.—*Sec.*, D. Goad.

ROYAL SOCIETY OF LITERATURE (1823), 1 Hyde Parl Gardens, W2 2LT. Tel: 071-723 5104.—*Sec.*, Mrs P M. Schute.

ROYAL SOCIETY OF MEDICINE (1805), 1 Wimpole Street W1M 8AE. Tel: 071-408 2119.—*Exec. Dir.*, R. N Thomson.

ROYAL SOCIETY OF ST GEORGE, (1894), Dartmouth House, 37 Charles Street, W1X 8AB. Tel: 071-499 5430.—*Chairman*, J. Minshull-Fogg, TD.

ROYAL STAR AND GARTER HOME FOR DISABLEI SAILORS, SOLDIERS AND AIRMEN (1916), Richmond Surrey TW10 6RR. Tel: 081-940 3314.—*Comman dant*, Brig. M. W. H. Branch (retd.).

ROYAL STATISTICAL SOCIETY (1834), 25 Enford Street W1H 2BH. Tel: 071-723 5882.—*Exec. Sec.*, D. W Harding.

ROYAL TANK REGIMENT BENEVOLENT FUND (1919) RHQ RTR Centre, Bovington, Dorset BH20 6JA Tel: 0929-403331.—*Regimental Sec.*, Maj. R. Cloo ney (retd.).

ROYAL TELEVISION SOCIETY (1927), Tavistock House East, Tavistock Square, WC1H 9HR. Tel: 071-387 1970.—*Hon. Sec.*, A. Pilgrim.

ROYAL UNITED KINGDOM BENEFICENT ASSOCIATION (1863), 6 Avonmore Road, W14 8RL. Tel: 071-602 6274.—*Dir.*, W. Rathbone.

RURAL ENGLAND, COUNCIL FOR THE PROTECTION OF (CPRE) (1926), Warwick House, 25–27 Buckingham Palace Road, SW1W 0PP. Tel: 071-976 6433.—*Dir.* A. Purkis.

RURAL SCOTLAND, ASSOCIATION FOR THE PROTECTION OF (1926), Charleston, Dalguise, Dunkeld, PH8 0JX Tel: 035 02-8712.—*Dir.*, R. L. Smith, OBE.

RURAL WALES, CAMPAIGN FOR THE PROTECTION OI (1928), Tŷ Gwyn, 31 High Street, Welshpool, Powys SY21 7JP. Tel: 0938-556212.—*Dir.*, Dr N. Caldwell

SAILORS' FAMILIES' SOCIETY, THE (1821), Newland Hull HU6 7RJ. Tel: 0482-42331.—*Gen. Sec.*, Lt.-Cdr. C. G. R. Streatfeild-James.

SAILORS' SOCIETY, BRITISH (1818), Orchard Place Southampton, SO9 7SS. Tel: 0703-337333.—*Gen Sec.*, G. Chambers.

ST DEINIOL'S LIBRARY (1902), Hawarden, Deeside Clwyd CH5 3DF. Tel: 0244-532350.—*Warden ana Chief Librarian*, Rev. Dr P. J. Jagger.

ST DUNSTAN'S, PO Box 4XB, 12–14 Harcourt Street W1A 4XB. For men and women blinded on war service. Tel: 071-723 5021.—*Sec.*, W. C. Weisblatt.

ST JOHN AMBULANCE (1887), 1 Grosvenor Crescent, SW1X 7EF. Tel: 071-235 5231.—*Exec. Dir.*, T. Gauvain.

SALES AND MARKETING MANAGEMENT, INSTITUTE OF (1966), 31 Upper George Street, Luton LU1 2RD Tel: 0582-411130.—*Dir. Gen.*, K. Williams.

SALMON AND TROUT ASSOCIATION (1903), Fishmongers' Hall, London Bridge, EC4R 9EL. Tel: 071-283 5838.—*Dir.*, Col. J. Ferguson.

SALTIRE SOCIETY (1936), 9 Fountain Close, 22 High Street, Edinburgh EH1 1TF. Tel: 031-556 1836.—*Administrator*, Miss K. Austin.

SAMARITANS, THE (1953), 17 Uxbridge Road, Slough, Berks. SL1 1SN. Tel: 0735-532713. Tel. numbers in local telephone directories.—*Chief Exec.*, S. Armson.

SAMUEL PEPYS CLUB (1903).—*Sec.*, P. L. Gray, 26 Gloucester Street, Faringdon, Oxon. SN7 7HY. Tel: 0367-242537.

SANE: SCHIZOPHRENIA A NATIONAL EMERGENCY (1986), 5th Floor, 120 Regent Street, W1R 5FE. Tel: 071-494 4840.—*Exec. Dir.*, Ms M. Wallace.

SAVE BRITAIN'S HERITAGE (1975), 68 Battersea High Street, SW11 3HX.—*Sec.*, Ms M. Watson-Smyth.

SAVE THE CHILDREN FUND, THE (1919), Mary Datchelor House, 17 Grove Lane, SE5 8RD. Tel: 071-703 5400.—*Dir. Gen.*, N. J. Hinton, CBE.

SCHIZOPHRENIA FELLOWSHIP, NATIONAL (1970), 28 Castle Street, Kingston upon Thames, Surrey KT1 1SS. Tel: 081-547 3937.—*Chief Exec.*, M. Eede.

SCHOOL LIBRARY ASSOCIATION (1937), Liden Library, Barrington Close, Liden, Swindon SN3 6HF. Tel: 0793-617838.—*Exec. Sec.*, Ms V. Fea.

SCHOOL NATURAL SCIENCE SOCIETY (1903).—*Hon. Gen. Sec.*, Miss D. S. Jackson, 153 Fernside Avenue, Hanworth, Middx. TW13 7BQ.

SCHOOLMASTERS, SOCIETY OF (1798).—*Sec.*, Mrs M. S. Freeburn, 29 Corrib Court, Fox Lane, N13 4BG.

SCHOOLMISTRESSES AND GOVERNESSES BENEVOLENT INSTITUTION (1843), Queen Mary House, Manor Park Road, Chislehurst, Kent BR7 5PY. Tel: 081-468 7997.—*Dir.*, R. W. Hayward.

SCIENCE AND LEARNING, SOCIETY FOR THE PROTECTION OF (1933), 20–21 Compton Terrace, NI 2UN.—*Sec.*, Ms E. Fraser.

SCIENCE AND TECHNOLOGY, BRITISH ASSOCIATION FOR THE PROMOTION OF (1831), Fortress House, 23 Savile Row, W1X 1AB. Tel: 071-494 3326.—*Exec. Sec.*, Dr P. Briggs.

SCIENCE EDUCATION, ASSOCIATION FOR (1963), College Lane, Hatfield, Herts. AL10 9AA. Tel: 0707-267411.—*Gen. Sec.*, Dr D. S. Moore.

SCOTCH WHISKY ASSOCIATION, THE (1919), 20 Atholl Crescent, Edinburgh EH3 8HF. Tel: 031-229 4383.—*Dir. Gen.*, Col. H. F. O. Bewsher, OBE.

SCOTTISH CHURCH HISTORY SOCIETY (1922).—*Hon. Sec.*, Rev. C. G. F. Brockie, Grange Manse, 51 Portland Road, Kilmarnock, Ayrshire KA1 2EQ. Tel: 0563-25311.

SCOTTISH CORPORATION, THE ROYAL (1611), 37 King Street, WC2E 8JS.—*Chief Exec.*, Wg. Cdr. A. Robertson.

SCOTTISH COUNTRY DANCE SOCIETY, ROYAL (1923), 12 Coates Crescent, Edinburgh EH3 7AF. Tel: 031-225 3854.—*Sec.*, Mrs J. A. Moore.

SCOTTISH GENEALOGY SOCIETY (1953), Library and Family History Centre, 15 Victoria Terrace, Edinburgh EH1 2JL. Tel: 031-220 3677.—*Hon. Sec.*, Miss J. P. S. Ferguson.

SCOTTISH HISTORY SOCIETY (1886).—*Hon. Sec.*, Dr N. MacDougall, Dept. of Scottish History, St Salvator's College, University of St Andrews, Fife KY16 9AJ.

SCOTTISH LANDOWNERS' FEDERATION (1906).—*Dir.*, S. Fraser, 25 Maritime Street, Edinburgh EH6 5PN. Tel: 031-555 1031.

SCOTTISH LAW AGENTS SOCIETY.—*Sec.*, R. M. Sinclair, 3 Albyn Place, Edinburgh EH2 4NQ. Tel: 031-225 7515.

SCOTTISH LIFE OFFICES, ASSOCIATED (1841), 23 St Andrew Square, Edinburgh EH2 1AQ.—*Sec.*, W. W. Mair.

SCOTTISH NATIONAL INSTITUTION FOR THE WAR BLINDED (1915), Gillespie Crescent, Edinburgh EH10 4HZ. Tel: 031-229 1456.—*Sec.*, J. B. M. Munro.

SCOTTISH NATIONAL WAR MEMORIAL (1927), The Castle, Edinburgh EH1 2YT. Tel: 031-226 7393.—*Sec.*, T. C. Barker.

SCOTTISH SECONDARY TEACHERS' ASSOCIATION (1946), 15 Dundas Street, Edinburgh EH3 6QG. Tel: 031-556 5919.—*Gen. Sec.*, A. A. Stanley.

SCOTTISH SOCIETY FOR THE PREVENTION OF CRUELTY TO ANIMALS (1950), 19 Melville Street, Edinburgh EH3 7PL. Tel: 031-225 6418.—*Chief Exec.*, J. Morris, CBE.

SCOTTISH SOCIETY FOR THE PROTECTION OF WILD BIRDS (1927), Foremount House, Kilbarchan, Renfrewshire PA10 2EZ. Tel: 050 57-2419.—*Sec.*, Dr J. A. Gibson.

SCOTTISH WILDLIFE TRUST (1964), Cramond House, Kirk Cramond, Cramond Glebe Road, Edinburgh EH4 6NS.—*Dir.*, D. J. Hughes Hallett.

SCOUT ASSOCIATION, THE (1907), Baden-Powell House, Queen's Gate, SW7 5JS. Tel: 071-584 7030.—*Chief Scout*, W. G. Morrison; *Chief Exec. Commissioner*, A. E. N. Black, OBE.

SCRIBES AND ILLUMINATORS, THE SOCIETY OF (1921), 54 Boileau Road, SW13 9BL. Tel: 081-748 9951.

SCRIPTURE GIFT MISSION INCORPORATED (1888), Radstock House, 3 Eccleston Street, SW1W 9LZ. Tel: 071-730 2155.—*Gen. Sec.*, R. Kennedy.

SCRIPTURE UNION (1867), 130 City Road, EC1V 2NJ. Tel: 071-782 0013.—*Gen. Dir.*, Rev. D. M. S. Cohen.

SCULPTORS, ROYAL SOCIETY OF BRITISH (1904), 108 Old Brompton Road, SW7 3RA. Tel: 071-373 5554.—*Pres.*, Ms P. Davidson Davis.

SEA CADETS, (1895), 202 Lambeth Road, SE1 7JF. Tel: 071-928 8978.—*Gen. Sec.*, Cdr. G. J. A. Shaw, OBE (*retd.*).

SEAMEN'S BOYS' HOME, BRITISH (1863), Berry Head Road, Brixham, Devon TQ5 9AE. Tel: 0803-882129.—*Sec.*, Capt. E. M. Marks, RD, RNR.

SEAMEN'S CHRISTIAN FRIEND SOCIETY (1846), PO Box 60, Wilmslow, Cheshire SK9 1QX. Tel: 0625-586300.—*Administrator*, M. J. Wilson.

SEAMEN'S PENSION FUND, ROYAL (1919), 65 High Street, Ewell, Epsom, Surrey KT17 1RX.—*Sec.*, B. Barker.

SECONDARY HEADS ASSOCIATION (1978), 130 Regent Road, Leicester LE1 7PG. Tel: 0533-471797.—*Gen. Sec.*, J. Sutton.

SECULAR SOCIETY LTD, NATIONAL (1866), 702 Holloway Road, N19 3NL.—*Gen. Sec.*, T. Mullins.

SELDEN SOCIETY (1887), Faculty of Laws, Queen Mary and Westfield College, Mile End Road, E1 4NS. To encourage the study and advance the knowledge of the history of English law. Tel: 071-975 5136.—*Sec.*, V. Tunkel.

SELF EMPLOYED AND SMALL BUSINESSES, NATIONAL FEDERATION OF (1974), Parliamentary Office, 140 Lower Marsh, SE1 7AE. Tel: 071-928 9272.—*Nat. Chairman*, W. Knox.

SENSE (The National Deaf-Blind and Rubella Association) (1955), 311 Grays Inn Road, WC1X 8AT. Tel: 071-278 1005.—*Chief Exec.*, R. Clark.

SHAFTESBURY HOMES AND *Arethusa* (1843), 3 Rectory Grove, SW4 0EG.—*Dir.*, Capt. N. C. Baird-Murray, CBE, RN.

SHAFTESBURY SOCIETY, THE (1844), 18–20 Kingston Road, SW19 1JZ. Tel: 081-542 5550. Cares for physically and mentally handicapped, elderly and socially deprived people.—*Chief Exec.*, G. Holloway.

SHELLFISH ASSOCIATION OF GREAT BRITAIN (1904), Fishmongers' Hall, London Bridge, EC4R 9EL. Tel: 071-283 8305.—*Dir.*, E. Edwards, ph.D.

SHELTER (1966), 88 Old Street, EC1V 9HU.—*Dir.*, Ms S. McKechnie.

SHERLOCK HOLMES SOCIETY OF LONDON (1951).—*Hon. Sec.*, Cdr. G. S. Stavert, MBE (*retd.*), 3 Outram Road, Southsea, Hants. PO5 1QP. Tel: 0705-812104.

SHIPBROKERS, INSTITUTE OF CHARTERED (1911), 24 St Mary Axe, EC3A 8DE. Tel: 071-283 1361.—*Sec.*, J. H. Parker.

SHIRE HORSE SOCIETY (1878), East of England Showground, Peterborough PE2 0XE. Tel: 0733-390696.—*Sec.*, S. A. Stagg.

SHRIEVALTY ASSOCIATION (1971), Express Buildings, 17–29 Parliament Street, Nottingham NG1 2AQ. Tel: 0602-350350.—*Sec.*, R. Bullock.

SIGHT SAVERS (Royal Commonwealth Society for the Blind) (1950), PO Box 191, Haywards Heath, W. Sussex RH16 4YF. Tel: 0444-412424.—*Exec. Dir.*, A. W. Johns, CMG, OBE.

SIMPLIFIED SPELLING SOCIETY (1908).—*Chairman*, C. J. H. Jolly, Clare Hall, Chapel Lane, Chigwell, Essex IG7 6JJ. Tel: 081-501 0405.

SIR OSWALD STOLL FOUNDATION (1916), 446 Fulham Road, SW6 1DT. Tel: 071-385 2110.—*Dir.*, R. C. Brunwin.

SMALL FARMERS' ASSOCIATION, THE (1979), PO Box 18, Woodbridge, Suffolk IP13 0QP.—*Chairman*, J. Morford.

SOCIALIST PARTY OF GREAT BRITAIN (1904), 52 Clapham High Street, SW4 7UN. Tel: 071-622 3811.—*Gen. Sec.*, P. Hope.

SOCIAL RESPONSIBILITY AND EDUCATION, QUAKER, Friends House, Euston Road, NW1 2BJ. Tel: 071-387 3601.—*Gen. Sec.*, Ms B. Smith.

SOCIAL WORKERS, BRITISH ASSOCIATION OF (1970), 16 Kent Street, Birmingham B5 6RD.—*Gen. Sec.*, D. N. Jones.

SOLDIERS' AND AIRMEN'S SCRIPTURE READERS ASSOCIATION, THE (1838), Havelock House, Barrack Road, Aldershot, Hants. GU11 3NP. Tel: 0252-310033.—*Gen. Sec.*, Lt. Col. K. W. Sear (*until Jan. 1992*).

SOLDIERS', SAILORS' AND AIRMEN'S FAMILIES ASSOCIATION (1885), 19 Queen Elizabeth Street, SE1 2LP.—*Controller*, Maj.-Gen. C. R. Grey, CBE; *Sec.*, Mrs B. R. Best, OBE.

SOLDIERS, SAILORS AND AIRMEN'S HELP SOCIETY, *see* FORCES HELP SOCIETY.

SOLDIERS' WIDOWS, ROYAL CAMBRIDGE HOME FOR (1851), 82–84 Hurst Road, East Molesey, Surrey KT8 9AH. Tel: 081-941 1531.—*Superintendent*, Mrs A. M. Webb.

SOLICITORS IN THE SUPREME COURTS OF SCOTLAND, SOCIETY OF (1784).—*Sec.*, A. R. Brownlie, OBE, 2 Abercromby Place, Edinburgh EH3 6JZ. Tel: 031-556 4070.

SOROPTIMIST INTERNATIONAL OF GREAT BRITAIN AND IRELAND (1923), 127 Wellington Road South, Stockport SK1 3TS. Tel: 061-480 7686.—*Exec. Officer*, Ms K. Hindley.

SOS SOCIETY, THE, *see* 2CARE.

SOUTH AMERICAN MISSIONARY SOCIETY (1844), Allen Gardiner House, Pembury Road, Tunbridge Wells, Kent TN2 3QU. Tel: 0892-538647.—*Gen. Sec.*, Rt. Rev. J. W. H. Flagg.

SOUTH WALES INSTITUTE OF ENGINEERS (1857), Empire House, Mount Stuart Square, Cardiff CF1 6DN. Tel: 0222-481726.—*Hon. Sec.*, R. E. Lindsay.

SPASTICS SOCIETY, THE (1952), 12 Park Crescent, W1N 4EQ. Tel: 071-636 5020.—*Chief Exec.*, R. Limb.

SPEAKERS CLUBS, THE ASSOCIATION OF (1971).—*Nat. Sec.*, F. W. P. Dawkins, 3 Leawood Croft, Holloway, Matlock, Derbyshire DE4 5BD. Tel: 0629-534619.

SPINA BIFIDA AND HYDROCEPHALUS, ASSOCIATION FOR (ASBAH), 42 Park Road, Peterborough PE1 2UQ. Tel: 0733-555988.—*Exec. Dir.*, A. Russell.

SPORTS MEDICINE, INSTITUTE OF (1963), Burlington House, Piccadilly, W1V 0LQ. Tel: 071-287 5269.—*Hon. Sec.*, Dr W. T. Orton.

SPURGEON'S CHILD CARE (1867), 30 Mill Street, Bedford MK40 3HD. Tel: 0234-261843.—*Dir.*, D. C. Culwick.

STATISTICIANS, INSTITUTE OF (1948), 43 St Peters Square, Preston PR1 7BX. Tel: 0772-204237.—*Sec.*, D. A. Holland.

STATUTE LAW SOCIETY (1968), Onslow House, 9 The Green, Richmond, Surrey TW9 1PU. Tel: 081-940 0017.—*Hon. Sec.*, N. Frudd.

STEWART SOCIETY (1899), 48 Castle Street, Edinburgh EH2 3LX. Tel: 031-225 3912.—*Hon. Sec.*, Mrs M. Walker.

STRATEGIC PLANNING SOCIETY, THE (1967), 17 Portland Place, W1N 3AF. Tel: 071-636 7737.—*Gen. Sec.*, G. A. Goodridge.

STRATEGIC STUDIES, THE INTERNATIONAL INSTITUTE FOR (1958), 23 Tavistock Street, WC2E 7NQ. Tel: 071-379 7676.—*Dir.*, F. Heisbourg.

STRUCTURAL ENGINEERS, INSTITUTION OF (1908), 11 Upper Belgrave Street, SW1X 8BH. Tel: 071-235 4535.—*Sec.*, D. J. Clark.

STUDENT CHRISTIAN MOVEMENT (1889), 186 St Paul's Road, Balsall Heath, Birmingham B12 8LZ. Tel 021-440 3000.—*Gen. Sec.*, Rev. T. E. McClure.

SUFFOLK HORSE SOCIETY (1878), The Market Hill, Woodbridge, Suffolk IP12 4DU. Tel: 0394-380643.—*Sec.*, P. Ryder-Davies.

SURGEONS OF EDINBURGH, ROYAL COLLEGE OF (1505) Nicolson Street, Edinburgh EH8 9DW. Tel: 031 556 6206.—*Sec.*, Prof. A. G. D. Maran.

SURGEONS OF ENGLAND, ROYAL COLLEGE OF (1800) 35–43 Lincoln's Inn Fields, WC2A 3PN. Tel: 071 405 3474.—*Sec.*, R. H. E. Duffett.

SURVEYORS, ROYAL INSTITUTION OF CHARTERED (1868), Surveyor Court, Westwood Way, Coventry CV4 8JE. Tel: 071-222 7000.—*Sec. Gen.*, M. Patti son.

SUSSEX CATTLE SOCIETY (1887), Station Road, Robertsbridge, E. Sussex TN32 5DG.—*Manager*, Miss S. G. Kennedy.

SWEDENBORG SOCIETY (1810), 20–21 Bloomsbury Way WC1A 2TH. Tel: 071-405 7986.—*Sec.*, Ms M. G Waters.

TALKING BOOKS FOR THE HANDICAPPED AND HOSPITAL PATIENTS, *see* NATIONAL LISTENING LIBRARY.

TAVISTOCK INSTITUTE OF HUMAN RELATIONS (1947) The Tavistock Centre, Belsize Lane, NW3 5BA Tel: 071-435 7111.—*Sec.*, N. Barnes.

TAXATION, INSTITUTE OF (1930), 12 Upper Belgrave Street, SW1X 8BB. Tel: 071-235 9381.—*Sec.*, R. J Ison.

TEACHERS OF HOME ECONOMICS, NATIONAL ASSOCIATION OF (1896), Hamilton House, Mabledon Place WC1H 9BJ. Tel: 071-387 1441.—*Gen. Manager*, P G. Higgins.

TEACHERS OF MATHEMATICS, ASSOCIATION OF (1952) 7 Shaftesbury Street, Derby DE3 8YB. Tel: 0332 46599.—*Hon. Sec.*, Ms C. Hopkins.

TEACHERS OF THE DEAF, BRITISH ASSOCIATION OF (1977).—*Hon. Sec.*, Ms S. Dowe, Icknield High School HIU, Riddy Lane, Luton LU3 2AH.

TEACHERS' UNION, ULSTER (1919), 94 Malone Road, Belfast BT9 5HP. Tel: 0232-662216.—*Gen. Sec.*, D. Allen.

TELECOMMUNICATIONS USERS' ASSOCIATION (1965), 48 Percy Road, N12 8BU.—*Chief Exec.*, Ms V. Peters.

TEMPERANCE SOCIETIES:—

British National Temperance League (1834), Room 4, Shirley House, 31 Psalter Lane, Sheffield S11 8YL. Tel: 0742-500713.—*Sec.*, L. Swales.

Church of England National Council for Social Aid, 38 Ebury Street, SW1W 0LU. Tel: 071-730 6175.—*Gen. Sec.*, Rev. E. W. F. Agar.

Division of Social Responsibility of the Methodist Church (1932), 1 Central Buildings, Westminster, SW1H 9NH.—*Gen. Sec.*, Rev. B. Duckworth.

National United Temperance Council (1880), 123 Regent Street, W1R 7HA. Tel: 071-934 9058.—*Gen. Sec.*, Rev. B. Kinman.

Order of the Sons of Temperance (1855), 5 Ashbourne Road, Derby, DE3 3FQ. Tel: 0332-41672.—*Sec.*, D. Newbury.

Royal Naval Temperance Society (1876) (auxiliary of Royal Sailors' Rests), 2A South Street, Gosport, Hants. PO12 1ES. Tel: 0705-589551.—*Sec.*, A. A. Lockwood.

Social Responsibility Dept., General Assembly of Unitarian and Free Christian Churches, Essex Hall, 1–6 Essex Street, WC2R 3HY.—*Hon. Sec.*, Rev. B. Packer.

United Kingdom Alliance (1863), New Gallery, 123 Regent Street, W1R 7HA. Tel: 071-734 9058.—*Gen. Sec.*, Rev. B. Kinman.

TEMPLETON FOUNDATION (1973), 16 Kingfisher Lane, Turners Hill, Crawley, W. Sussex RH10 4QP. Tel: 0342-715750.—*UK Rep.*, Mrs N. Pearse.

TERRENCE HIGGINS TRUST (1982), 52–54 Grays Inn Road, WC1X 8JU. Tel: 071-831 0330.—*Chairman*, M. Taylor.

TERRITORIAL, AUXILIARY AND VOLUNTEER RESERVE ASSOCIATIONS, COUNCIL OF (1908), The Chapel, Duke of York's HQ, SW3 4SG. Tel: 071-730 6122.—*Sec.*, Maj.-Gen. M. Matthews, CB.

TEXTILE INSTITUTE, THE (1910), International HQ, 10 Blackfriars Street, Manchester M3 5DR. Tel: 061-834 8457.—*Gen. Sec.*, R. G. Denyer.

THEATRE ASSOCIATION, BRITISH (1919), Cranbourn Mansions, Cranbourn Street, WC2H 7AG.—*Administrator*, R. Haddon.

THEATRE RESEARCH, SOCIETY FOR (1948), c/o The Theatre Museum, 1E Tavistock Street, WC2E 7PA.—*Joint Hon. Secs.*, Ms E. Cottis; Ms F. Dann.

THEATRES TRUST, THE (1976), 10 St Martin's Court, WC2N 4AJ. Tel: 071-836 8591.—*Chairman*, Sir David Crouch; *Dir.*, J. Earl.

THEATRICAL FUND, ROYAL (1839), 11 Garrick Street, WC2E 9AR. Tel: 071-836 3322.—*Sec.*, J. Berkeley.

THEATRICAL LADIES' GUILD OF CHARITY (1892), 49 Endell Street, WC2H 9AJ. Tel: 071-497 3030.—*Admin. Sec.*, Mrs K. Nichols.

THEOSOPHICAL SOCIETY IN ENGLAND (1875), 50 Gloucester Place, W1H 3HJ. Tel: 071-935 9261.—*Gen. Sec.*, Miss I. H. Hoskins.

THISTLE FOUNDATION, THE (1945), 27A Walker Street, Edinburgh EH3 7HX. Tel: 031-225 7282.—*Dir.*, P. Croft.

THOMAS CORAM FOUNDATION FOR CHILDREN (formerly The Foundling Hospital) (1739), 40 Brunswick Square, WC1N 1AZ. Tel: 071-278 2424.—*Dir. and Sec.*, C. P. Masters.

TIDY BRITAIN GROUP (1953), The Pier, Wigan WN3 4EX. Tel: 0942-824620.—*Dir. Gen.*, Prof. G. Ashworth, CBE.

TOC H (1915), Headquarters, 1 Forest Close, Wendover, Aylesbury, Bucks. HP22 6BT. Tel: 0296-623911.—*Exec. Sec.*, S. Casimir.

TOURIST BOARD, ENGLISH, Thames Tower, Black's Road, W6 9EL.—*Chief Exec.*, M. Medlicott.

TOURIST BOARD, NORTHERN IRELAND, St Anne's Court, North Street, Belfast BT1 1ND. Tel: 0232-231221.—*Chief Exec.*, E. Friel.

TOURIST BOARD, SCOTTISH (1969), 23 Ravelston Terrace, Edinburgh EH4 3EU.—*Chief Exec.*, T. M. Band.

TOURIST BOARD, WALES, Brunel House, 2 Fitzalan Road, Cardiff CF2 1UY.—*Chief Exec.*, P. Loveluck.

TOWN AND COUNTRY PLANNING ASSOCIATION (1899), 17 Carlton House Terrace, SW1Y 5AS. Tel: 071-930 8903.—*Dir.*, D. Hall.

TOWN PLANNING INSTITUTE, ROYAL (1914), 26 Portland Place, W1N 4BE. Tel: 071-636 9107.—*Sec. Gen.*, D. Fryer.

TOWNSWOMEN'S GUILDS, (1929), Chamber of Commerce House, 75 Harborne Road, Birmingham B15 3DA. Tel: 021-456 3435.—*Nat. Sec.*, Ms R. Styles.

TOYNBEE HALL, The Universities' Settlement in East London (1884), 28 Commercial Street, E1 6LS. Tel: 071-247 6943.—*Warden and Chief Exec.*, A. L. Williams, OBE.

TRADE, NATIONAL CHAMBER OF (1897), Enterprise House, 59 Castle Street, Reading, Berks. RG1 7SN. Tel: 0734-566744.—*Chief Exec.*, B. Tennant.

TRADE MARK AGENTS, INSTITUTE OF (1934), 4th Floor, Canterbury House, 2–6 Sydenham Road, Croydon CR0 9XE. Tel: 081-686 2052.—*Sec.*, Mrs M. J. Tyler

TRADING STANDARDS ADMINISTRATION, THE INSTITUTE OF (1881), 4–5 Hadleigh Business Centre, 351 London Road, Hadleigh, Essex SS7 2BT.—*Dir. of Admin. and PR*, Mrs G. Jordan.

TRANSLATION AND INTERPRETING, INSTITUTE OF (1986), 318A Finchley Road, NW3 5HT. Tel: 071-794 9931.—*Chairman*, R. Fletcher.

TRANSPORT ADMINISTRATION, INSTITUTE OF (1944), 32 Palmerston Road, Southampton SO1 1LL. Tel: 0703-631380.—*Dir.*, Wg Cdr. P. F. Green.

TRANSPORT, CHARTERED INSTITUTE OF (1919), 80 Portland Place, W1N 4DP.—*Dir. Gen.*, R. P. Botwood.

TRANSPORT CONSULTATIVE COMMITTEE, CENTRAL (1948), 1st Floor, Golden Cross House, Duncannon Street, WC2N 4JF. Tel: 071-839 7338.—*Sec.*, M. Patterson.

TRAVEL AGENTS, ASSOCIATION OF BRITISH (ABTA) (1950), 55–57 Newman Street, W1P 4AH. Tel: 071-637 2444.—*Pres.*, J. Dunscombe.

TREE COUNCIL (1974), 35 Belgrave Square, SW1X 8XN. Tel: 071-235 8854.—*Dir.*, R. Osborne.

TROPICAL MEDICINE AND HYGIENE, ROYAL SOCIETY OF (1907), Manson House, 26 Portland Place, W1N 4EY. Tel: 071-580 2127. *Hon. Secs.*, Dr D. C. Barker; Dr S. G. Wright.

TURNER SOCIETY (1975), BCM Box Turner, WC1N 3XX.— *Chairman*, E. Shanes.

2CARE (formerly The SOS Society) (1929), 13 Harwood Road, SW6 4QP. Tel: 071-371 0118. Residential homes for the elderly, psychiatric rehabilitation centres.—*Chief Exec.*, Miss E. C. R. O'Sullivan.

UFAW (Universities Federation for Animal Welfare) (1926), 8 Hamilton Close, South Mimms, Potters Bar, Herts. EN6 3QD. Tel: 0707 58202.—*Sec.*, Lt.-Col. T. J. Reynolds.

UNIT TRUST ASSOCIATION (1959), 65 Kingsway, WC2B 6TD.—*Chief Exec.*, A. C. Smith.

UNITED NATIONS ASSOCIATION OF GREAT BRITAIN AND NORTHERN IRELAND (1945), 3 Whitehall Court, SW1A 2EL. Tel: 071-930 2931.—*Dir.*, M. C. Harper.

UNITED REFORMED CHURCH HISTORY SOCIETY (1972), 86 Tavistock Place, WC1H 9RT. Tel: 071-837 7661.—*Hon. Sec.*, Rev. Dr C. Orchard.

UNITED SOCIETY FOR CHRISTIAN LITERATURE (1799), Robertson House, Leas Road, Guildford, Surrey GU14 4QW. Tel: 0483-577877.—*Gen. Sec.*, Rev. A. Gilmore.

UNITED SOCIETY FOR THE PROPAGATION OF THE GOSPEL (USPG) (1701), Partnership House, 157 Waterloo Road, SE1 8XA. Tel: 071-928 8681.—*Sec.*, Canon P. Price.

UNIVERSITIES CENTRAL COUNCIL ON ADMISSIONS (1961), PO Box 28, Cheltenham, Glos. GL50 3SA. Tel: 0242-222444—*Gen. Sec.*, P. A. Oakley, MBE.

UNIVERSITIES OF THE UNITED KINGDOM, COMMITTEE OF VICE-CHANCELLORS AND PRINCIPALS OF THE (1918), 29 Tavistock Square, WC1H 9EZ. Tel: 071-387 9231.—*Sec.*, T. U. Burgner.

UNIVERSITY WOMEN, BRITISH FEDERATION OF (1907), Crosby Hall, Cheyne Walk, SW3 5BA. Tel: 071-352 5354.—*Sec.*, Mrs A. B. Stein.

VALUERS AND AUCTIONEERS, INCORPORATED SOCIETY OF (1968), 3 Cadogan Gate, SW1X 0AS. Tel: 071-235 2282.—*Sec.*, H. Whitty.

VEGAN SOCIETY, THE (1944), 7 Battle Road, St Leonards-on-Sea, E. Sussex TN37 7AA. Tel: 0424-427393.—*Gen. Sec.*, R. Farhall.

VEGETARIAN SOCIETY OF THE UNITED KINGDOM LTD, Parkdale, Dunham Road, Altrincham, Cheshire WA14 4QG. Tel: 061-928 0793.—*Dir.*, C. Cottom.

VENEREAL DISEASES, MEDICAL SOCIETY FOR THE STUDY OF (1922).—*Hon. Sec.*, Dr M. J. Godley, Royal Berkshire Hospital, Reading RG1 5AN. Tel: 0734-877206.

VERNACULAR ARCHITECTURE GROUP (1953).—*Hon. Sec.*, R. Meeson, 16 Falna Crescent, Coton Green, Tamworth, Staffs. B79 8JS. Tel: 0827-69434.

VETERINARY ASSOCIATION, BRITISH (1881), 7 Mansfield Street, W1M 0AT. Tel: 071-636 6541.—*Chief Exec.*, J. H. Baird.

VETERINARY SURGEONS, ROYAL COLLEGE OF, 32 Belgrave Square, SW1X 8QP (1844).—*Registrar*, A. R. W. Porter, CBE.

VICTIM SUPPORT (1979), Cranmer House, 39 Brixton Road, SW9 6DZ. Tel: 071-735 9166.—*Dir.*, Ms H. Reeves, OBE.

VICTORIA CROSS AND GEORGE CROSS ASSOCIATION, Room 04, Archway Block South, Old Admiralty Building, Whitehall, SW1A 2BE.—*Chairman*, Rear-Adm. B. C. G. Place, VC, CB, DSC.

VICTORIA INSTITUTE, THE (Philosophical Society of Great Britain), Latchell Hall, Latchett Road, E18 1DL. Tel: 081-505 5224.—*Hon. Treas.*, B. H. T. Weller.

VICTORIAN SOCIETY (1958), 1 Priory Gardens, Bedford Park, W4 1TT. Tel: 081-994 1019.—*Sec.*, Mrs T. Sladen.

VICTORY (SERVICES) ASSOCIATION LTD AND CLUB (1907), 63–79 Seymour Street, W2 2HF. Tel: 071-723 4474.—*Gen. Manager*, G. F. Taylor.

VIKING SOCIETY FOR NORTHERN RESEARCH (1892), University College London, Gower Street, WC1E 6BT. Tel: 071-387 7050.—*Hon. Sec.*, Prof. M. P. Barnes.

VITREOUS ENAMELLERS, INSTITUTE OF (1935), Ripley, Derby DE5 3EB. Tel: 0773-743136.—*Sec.*, J. D. Gardom.

VOLUNTARY AGENCIES, NATIONAL COUNCIL FOR (1919), 26 Bedford Square, WC1B 3HU. Tel: 071-636 4066.—*Gen. Sec.*, Ms J. Weleminsky.

VSO (Voluntary Service Overseas) (1958), 317 Putney Bridge Road, SW15 2PN. Tel: 081-780 2266.—*Dir.*, D. Green.

WAR ON WANT (1952), 37–39 Great Guildford Street, SE1 0ES. Tel: 071-620 0111.—*Dir.*, G. Allheddie.

WATER AND ENVIRONMENTAL MANAGEMENT, INSTITUTION OF (1987), 15 John Street, WC1N 2EB. Tel: 071-831 3110.—*Exec. Dir.*, H. R. Evans.

WATERCOLOUR SOCIETY, ROYAL (1804), Bankside Gallery, 48 Hopton Street, SE1 9JH. Tel: 071-928 7521.—*Pres.*, C. Bartlett; *Sec.*, M. Spender.

WELDING INSTITUTE, THE, Abington Hall, Cambridge CB1 6AL.—*Chief Exec.*, A. B. M. Braithwaite.

WELFARE OFFICERS, INSTITUTE OF (1945), 254 The Corn Exchange, Hanging Ditch, Manchester M4 3ES.—*Sec.*, Mrs M. Maclean-Ives.

WELLCOME TRUST (1936), 1 Park Square West, NW1 4LJ.—*Dir.*, Dr P. O. Williams.

WELLS, H. G., SOCIETY (1961). *Hon. Sec.*, Ms S. Hardy, English Dept., Nene College, Moulton Park, Northampton NN2 7AL. Tel: 0604-715000.

WESLEY HISTORICAL SOCIETY (1893).—*Gen. Sec.*, Dr E. D. Graham, 34 Spiceland Road, Northfield, Birmingham B31 1NJ. Tel: 021-475 4914.

WEST INDIA COMMITTEE (1750), Commonwealth House, 18 Northumberland Avenue, WC2N 5RA.—*Dir.*, D. A. Jessop.

WEST LONDON MISSION (1887), 19 Thayer Street, W1M 5LJ. Tel: 071-935 6179.—*Supt.*, Rev. D. S. Cruise.

WILDFOWL AND WETLANDS TRUST (1946), The New Grounds, Slimbridge, Gloucester GL2 7BT. Tel: 0453-890333.—*Dir. Gen.*, Dr B. Bertram.

WILDLIFE ARTISTS, SOCIETY OF (1962), 17 Carlton House Terrace, SW1Y 5AH.—*Hon. Sec.*, K. J. Wood.

WILLIAM MORRIS SOCIETY AND KELMSCOTT FELLOWSHIP (1918), Kelmscott House, 26 Upper Mall, W6 9TA. Tel: 081-741 3735.—*Hon. Sec.*, J. Purkis.

WINE AND SPIRIT ASSOCIATION OF GREAT BRITAIN AND NORTHERN IRELAND (c. 1825), Five Kings House, 1 Queen Street Place, EC4R 1XX.—*Dir.*, R. H. Insoll.

WOMEN, CAREERS FOR (1933), 4th Floor, 2 Valentine Place, SE1 8QH. Tel: 071-401 2280.—*Dir.*, Miss K. M. Menon.

WOMEN, SOCIETY FOR PROMOTING THE TRAINING OF (1859).—*Sec.*, Rev. B. Harris, The Rectory, Bent Lane, Warburton, Lymm, Cheshire WA13 7TQ. Tel: 092 575-4716.

WOMEN ARTISTS, SOCIETY OF (1855), Westminster Gallery, Westminster Central Hall, Storey's Gate, SW1H 9NU.—*Pres.*, Ms B. Tate.

WOMEN'S ENGINEERING SOCIETY (1920), Imperial College of Science and Technology, Dept. of Civil Engineering, Imperial College Road, SW7 2BU. Tel: 071-589 5111, ext. 4731.—*Sec.*, Ms G. Maxwell.

WOMEN'S INSTITUTES, NATIONAL FEDERATION OF (1915), 104 New Kings Road, SW6 4LY. Tel: 071-371 9300.—*Gen. Sec.,* Ms H. Mayall.

WOMEN'S INSTITUTES OF NORTHERN IRELAND, FEDERATION OF (1932), 209–211 Upper Lisburn Road, Belfast BT10 0LL. Tel: 0232-301506.—*Gen. Sec.,* Mrs I. A. Sproule.

WOMEN'S INTERNATIONAL LEAGUE FOR PEACE AND FREEDOM (British Section) (1915), 157 Lyndhurst Road, Worthing, W. Sussex BN11 2DG.—*Chair,* Ms M. Miller.

WOMEN'S NATIONAL CANCER CONTROL CAMPAIGN (1964), 1 South Audley Street, W1Y 5DQ. Tel: 071-729 4688.—*Administrator,* Ms J. Harding.

WOMEN'S ROYAL NAVAL SERVICE BENEVOLENT TRUST (1942), 1A Chesham Street, SW1X 8NL.—*Gen. Sec.,* Mrs J. Y. Ellis.

WOMEN'S ROYAL VOLUNTARY SERVICE (WRVS) (1938), 234–244 Stockwell Road, SW9 9SP. Tel: 071-416 0146.—*National Chairman,* Hon. Mrs M. Corsar.

WOMEN'S RURAL INSTITUTES, SCOTTISH (1917), 42 Heriot Row, Edinburgh EH3 6ES.—*Gen. Sec.,* Mrs E. Nicol.

WOMEN'S TRANSPORT SERVICE (1907), FANY HQ (E Block), Duke of York's HQ, SW3 4RX. Tel: 071-730 2058.—*Corps Commander,* Mrs A. Whitehead

WOODLAND TRUST, THE (1972), Autumn Park, Dysart Road, Grantham, Lincs. NG31 6LL. Tel: 0476-74297.—*Exec. Dir.,* J. D. James.

WOOD PRESERVING ASSOCIATION, BRITISH (1930), 6 The Office Village, 4 Romford Road, E15 4EA. Tel: 081-519 2588.—*Sec.,* M. J. Tuck.

WORKERS' EDUCATIONAL ASSOCIATION, Temple House, 9 Upper Berkeley Street, W1H 8BY.—*Gen. Sec.,* R. Lochrie.

WORKING MOTHERS ASSOCIATION, THE (1985), 77 Holloway Road, N7 8JZ.—*Dir.,* Ms L. Daniels.

WORLD EDUCATION FELLOWSHIP (1921), 33 Kinnaird Avenue, W4 3SH. Tel: 081-994 7258.—*Gen. Sec.,* Mrs R. Crommelin.

WORLD ENERGY COUNCIL (1924), 34 St James's Street, SW1A 1HD. Tel: 071-930 3966.—*Sec. Gen.,* I. D. Lindsay.

WORLD MISSION, COUNCIL FOR (1977), Livingstone House, 11 Carteret Street, SW1H 9DL.—*Gen. Sec.,* vacant.

WORLD SHIP SOCIETY (1946).—*Sec.,* S. J. F. Miller, 35 Wickham Way, Haywards Heath, W. Sussex RH16 1UJ. Tel: 0444-413066.

WORLD SOCIETY FOR THE PROTECTION OF ANIMALS (1981), Park Place, 10 Lawn Lane, SW8 1UD. Tel: 071-793 0540.—*Dir. Gen.,* G. Walwyn, CVO.

WORLD-WIDE EDUCATION SERVICE (1888), 10 Barley Mow Passage, W4 4PH.—*Asst. Dir.,* Mrs T. Mulder-Reynolds.

WORLD WIDE FUND FOR NATURE—UK (1961), Panda House, Weyside Park, Godalming, Surrey GU7 1XR. Tel: 0483-426444.—*Dir.,* G. J. Medley, OBE.

WRITERS TO HM SIGNET, SOCIETY OF (1532), 16 Hill Street, Edinburgh EH2 3LD. Tel: 031-226 6703.—*Clerk,* A. M. Kerr.

YEOMANRY BENEVOLENT FUND (1902), 10 Stone Buildings, Lincoln's Inn, WC2A 3TG. Tel: 071-831 6727.—*Sec.,* Mrs C. W. Chrystie.

YORKSHIRE AGRICULTURAL SOCIETY (1837), Great Yorkshire Showground, Hookstone Oval, Harrogate HG2 8PW. Tel: 0423-561536.—*Sec.-Gen.,* Lt.-Col. M. G. A. Young.

YORKSHIRE SOCIETY, THE (1812), 27 Kensington Park, Milford-on-Sea, Hants. SO41 0WD. Tel: 0590-

644725. Educational trust making grants to students of all ages.—*Sec.,* G. G. Prince, TD.

YOUNG FARMERS' CLUBS, NATIONAL FEDERATION OF, The YFC Centre, National Agricultural Centre, Kenilworth, Warks. CV8 2LG. Tel: 0203-696544.—*Sec.,* Ms P. Shields.

YOUNG MEN'S CHRISTIAN ASSOCIATION (YMCA) (1844), National Council of YMCAs, 640 Forest Road, E17 3DZ. Tel: 081-520 5599.—*Nat. Sec.,* C. J. Naylor.

YOUNG WOMEN'S CHRISTIAN ASSOCIATION OF GREAT BRITAIN (YWCA) (1855), 52 Cornmarket Street, Oxford OX1 3EJ.—*Exec. Dir.,* Miss F. E. Sharples.

YOUTH CLUBS, NORTHERN IRELAND ASSOCIATION OF (1944), Hampton, Glenmachan Park, Belfast BT4 2PJ. Tel: 0232-760067.—*Dir.,* G. Johnston.

YOUTH CLUBS UK (1911), Keswick House, 30 Peacock Lane, Leicester LE1 5NY. Tel: 0533-629514.—*Chief Exec.,* D. Stickels.

YOUTH HOSTELS ASSOCIATION (ENGLAND AND WALES) (1930), Trevelyan House, 8 St Stephens Hill, St Albans, Herts. AL1 2DY. Tel: 0727-55215.—*Chief Exec.,* A. G. F. Chinneck.

YOUTH HOSTELS ASSOCIATION OF NORTHERN IRELAND (1931), Bradbury Buildings, 56 Bradbury Place, Belfast BT7 1RU. Tel: 0232-324733.—*Hon. Sec.,* N. O'Reilly.

YOUTH HOSTELS ASSOCIATION, SCOTTISH (1931), 7 Glebe Crescent, Stirling FK8 2JA. Tel: 0786-51181.—*Gen. Sec.,* J. Martin.

ZOO CHECK (1984), Cherry Tree Cottage, Coldharbour, Dorking, Surrey RH5 6HA.—*Chairman,* W. Travers.

ZOOLOGICAL SOCIETY OF LONDON (1826), Regent's Park, NW1 4RY. *Managing Dir.,* A. Y. Grant.

ZOOLOGICAL SOCIETY OF SCOTLAND, ROYAL (1913), Scottish National Zoological Park, Murrayfield, Edinburgh EH12 6TS. Tel: 031-334 9171.—*Dir.,* R. J. Wheater, FRSE.

LOCAL HISTORY AND ARCHAEOLOGICAL SOCIETIES

England

Bedfordshire.—SOUTH BEDFORDSHIRE ARCHAEOLOGICAL SOCIETY. *Hon. Sec.* D. H. Kennett, 27 Lords Lane, Bradwell, Great Yarmouth, Norfolk NR31 8NY.

Berkshire.—BERKSHIRE ARCHAEOLOGICAL SOCIETY. *Hon. Sec.,* L. J. Over, 43 Laburnham Road, Maidenhead, Berks. SL6 4DE. Tel: 0628-31225.

   NEWBURY DISTRICT FIELD CLUB. *Hon. Sec.,* Mrs P. M. Jermyn, 30 Butson Close, Newbury, Berks. RG14 5JQ.

Buckinghamshire.—BUCKINGHAMSHIRE ARCHAEOLOGICAL SOCIETY. *Hon. Sec.,* Dr R. P. Hagerty, County Museum, Church Street, Aylesbury, Bucks. HP20 2QP.

Cambridgeshire.—CAMBRIDGE ANTIQUARIAN SOCIETY. *Hon. Sec.,* Dr M. Hesse, 39 Highsett Hills Road, Cambridge CB2 1NZ. Tel: 0223-355515.

Cheshire.—CHESTER ARCHAEOLOGICAL SOCIETY. *Sec.,* Dr D. J. P. Mason, Ochr Cottage, Porch Lane, Hope Mountain, Caergwrle, Clwyd LL12 9LS.

Cornwall.—CORNWALL ARCHAEOLOGICAL SOCIETY. *Hon. Sec.,* Mrs A. Cooke, Pentrelew, Flushing, Falmouth, Cornwall TR11 5UD. Tel: 0326-74288.

Cumberland and Westmorland.—CUMBERLAND AND WESTMORLAND ANTIQUARIAN AND ARCHAEOLOGICAL SOCIETY. *Hon. Sec.,* R. Hall, 2 High Tenterfell, Kendal, Cumbria LA9 4PG. Tel: 0539-721000.

Derbyshire.—DERBYSHIRE ARCHAEOLOGICAL SOCIETY. Hon. Sec., M. E. Burrows, 2 Millers Court, Edward Street, Derby DE1 3BN. Tel: 0332-49447.

Devonshire.—DEVON ARCHAEOLOGICAL SOCIETY, Royal Albert Memorial Museum, Queen Street, Exeter EX4 3RX.—Hon. Sec., Miss D. M. Griffiths.

Dorset.—DORSET NATURAL HISTORY AND ARCHAEOLOGICAL SOCIETY, Dorset County Museum, Dorchester DT1 1XA. Tel: 0305-262735. Sec., R. Peers.

Durham.—DURHAM AND NORTHUMBERLAND ARCHITECTURAL AND ARCHAEOLOGICAL SOCIETY. Hon. Sec., R. Daniels, 56 Welldeck Road, Hartlepool, Cleveland TS26 8JS.

Essex.—ESSEX SOCIETY FOR ARCHAEOLOGY AND HISTORY, Hollytrees Museum, High Street, Colchester CO1 1UG. Tel: 0206-271458. Sec., N. P. Wickenden.

Gloucestershire.—BRISTOL AND GLOUCESTERSHIRE ARCHAEOLOGICAL SOCIETY, Hon. Sec., D. J. H. Smith, FSA, 22 Beaumont Road, Gloucester GL2 0EJ. Tel: 0452-302610.

Hampshire.—HAMPSHIRE FIELD CLUB AND ARCHAEOLOGICAL SOCIETY. Hon. Sec., Dr M. A. Hicks, King Alfred's College, Winchester, Hants. SO22 4NR. Tel: 0962-841515.

Herefordshire.—WOOLHOPE NATURALISTS' FIELD CLUB. Hon. Sec., J. W. Tonkin, FSA, Chy an Whyloryon, Wigmore, Leominster, Herefordshire HR6 9UD. Tel: 056 886-356.

Hertfordshire.—EAST HERTFORDSHIRE ARCHAEOLOGICAL SOCIETY. Hon. Sec., Mrs M. C. Readman, 1 Marsh Lane, Stanstead Abbots, Ware, Herts. SG12 8HH. Tel: 0920-870664.

ST ALBANS AND HERTFORDSHIRE ARCHITECTURAL AND ARCHAEOLOGICAL SOCIETY. Hon. Sec., B. E. Moody, 24 Rose Walk, St Albans, Herts. AL4 9AF.

Isle of Wight.—ISLE OF WIGHT NATURAL HISTORY AND ARCHAEOLOGICAL SOCIETY. Hon. Sec., Mrs T. Goodley, Ivy Cottage, New Barn Lane, Shorwell, Newport, IOW, PO30 3JQ. Tel: 0983-740711.

Kent.—KENT ARCHAEOLOGICAL SOCIETY. Hon. Gen. Sec., A. C. Harrison, FSA, Prings Cottage, Pilgrims Road, Upper Halling, Rochester ME2 1HR. Tel: 0634-240745.

Lancashire.— HISTORIC SOCIETY OF LANCASHIRE AND CHESHIRE. Hon. Sec., Mrs G. M. Wyatt, 302 Prescot Road, Aughton, Ormskirk, Lancs. L39 6RR. Tel: 0695-423425.

Leicestershire.—LEICESTERSHIRE ARCHAEOLOGICAL AND HISTORICAL SOCIETY, The Guildhall, Leicester LE1 5FQ. Hon. Sec., Dr A. D. McWhirr.

London and Middlesex.—CITY OF LONDON ARCHAEOLOGICAL SOCIETY. Hon. Sec., Ms M. Andrews, 19 Hawes Road, Bromley, Kent BR1 3JS. Tel: 071-832 7367.

LONDON AND MIDDLESEX ARCHAEOLOGICAL SOCIETY. Hon. Sec., M. Curtis, 3 Cedar Drive, Pinner, Middx. HA5 4DD. Tel: 081-879 7109.

Norfolk.—NORFOLK AND NORWICH ARCHAEOLOGICAL SOCIETY. Hon. Gen. Sec., R. Bellinger, 30 Brettingham Avenue, Norwich NR4 6XG. Tel: 0603-55913.

Northumberland and Tyne and Wear.—SOCIETY OF ANTIQUARIES OF NEWCASTLE UPON TYNE, Black Gate, Castle Garth, Newcastle upon Tyne NE1 1RQ. Tel: 091-261 5390. Sec., D. Cutts.

SUNDERLAND ANTIQUARIAN SOCIETY. Hon. Sec., Mrs V. M. Stevens, 16 Grizedale Court, Seaburn Dene, Sunderland SR6 8JP. Tel: 091-548 7541.

Oxfordshire.—OXFORDSHIRE ARCHITECTURAL AND HISTORICAL SOCIETY, Museums and Archives Services, Fletchers House, Park Street, Woodstock OX7 1SN. Tel: 0993-811456. Hon. Sec., D. Dawson.

Shropshire.—SHROPSHIRE ARCHAEOLOGICAL AND HISTORICAL SOCIETY. Chairman, J. B. Lawson, Westcott Farm, Pontesbury, Shrewsbury SY5 0SQ.

Somerset.—SOMERSET ARCHAEOLOGICAL AND NATURAL HISTORY SOCIETY, Taunton Castle, Taunton, Somerset TA1 4AD. Hon. Sec., B. Watkin.

Staffordshire.—CITY OF STOKE-ON-TRENT MUSEUM ARCHAEOLOGICAL SOCIETY, City Museum and Art Gallery, Hanley, Stoke-on-Trent ST1 3DW. Tel: 0782-202173. Chairman, E. E. Royle.

Suffolk.—SUFFOLK INSTITUTE OF ARCHAEOLOGY AND HISTORY. Hon. Sec., E. A. Martin, Oak Tree Farm, Finborough Road, Hitcham, Ipswich IP7 7LS. Tel: 0449-741266.

Surrey.—SURREY ARCHAEOLOGICAL SOCIETY, Castle Arch, Guildford, Surrey GU1 3SX. Tel: 0483-32454. Hon. Secs., Mr and Mrs K. D. Graham.

Sussex.—SUSSEX ARCHAEOLOGICAL SOCIETY, Barbican House, High Street, Lewes, E. Sussex BN7 1YE. Exec. Sec., D. P. White.

Warwickshire.—BIRMINGHAM AND WARWICKSHIRE ARCHAEOLOGICAL SOCIETY, c/o Birmingham and Midland Institute, Margaret Street, Birmingham B3 3BS. Tel: 021-236 3591. Hon. Sec., A. J. Wilson.

Wiltshire.—WILTSHIRE ARCHAEOLOGICAL AND NATURAL HISTORY SOCIETY, The Museum, 41 Long Street, Devizes SN10 1NS. Tel: 0380-727369. Sec., G. G. Brown.

Worcestershire.—WORCESTERSHIRE ARCHAEOLOGICAL SOCIETY. Hon. Sec., Mrs G. Grice, 91 Hallow Road, Worcester WR2 6DF. Tel: 0905-422310.

Yorkshire.—YORKSHIRE ARCHAEOLOGICAL SOCIETY. Hon. Sec., P. B. Davidson, Claremont, 23 Clarendon Road, Leeds LS2 9NZ. Tel: 0532-457910.

HALIFAX ANTIQUARIAN SOCIETY. Hon. Sec., J. A. Hargreaves, 7 Hyde Park Gardens, Haugh Shaw Road, Halifax HX1 3AH. Tel: 0422-352126.

THORESBY SOCIETY. Hon. Sec., D. M. Watson. Claremont, 23 Clarendon Road, Leeds LS2 9NZ.

Channel Islands

SOCIETE JERSIAISE, Archaeological Section, La Hougue Bie Museum, Grouville, Jersey. Hon. Sec., Ms J. D. Aubin.

Scotland

AYRSHIRE ARCHAEOLOGICAL AND NATURAL HISTORY SOCIETY. Hon. Sec., Dr T. Mathews, 10 Longlands Park, Ayr KA7 4RJ. Tel: 0292-41915.

DUMFRIESSHIRE AND GALLOWAY NATURAL HISTORY AND ANTIQUARIAN SOCIETY. Hon. Sec., 13 Douglas Terrace, Lockerbie, Dumfriesshire DG11 2DZ.

HAWICK ARCHAEOLOGICAL SOCIETY. Hon. Sec., I. W. Landles, Orrock House, Stirches Road, Hawick, Roxburghshire TD9 7HF. Tel: 0450-75546.

INVERNESS FIELD CLUB. Hon. Sec., Miss I. McLean, 6 Drumblair Crescent, Inverness IV2 4RG.

Wales

Dyfed.—CEREDIGION ANTIQUARIAN SOCIETY. Hon. Sec., I. M. Jones, Dolau-gwyn, Dole, Bow Street, Dyfed SY24 5AE.

Gwynedd.—ANGLESEY ANTIQUARIAN SOCIETY. Hon. Sec., S. C. G. Caffell, 1 Fronheulog Sling, Tregarth, Bangor LL57 4RD.

Powys.—POWYSLAND CLUB. Hon. Sec., W. Hughes, Pennant, Abermule, Montgomery SY15 6NB.

NATIONAL ACADEMIES OF SCHOLARSHIP

THE BRITISH ACADEMY (1901)
20–21 Cornwall Terrace, NW1 4QP
[071-487 5966]

The British Academy is an independent, self-governing learned society for the promotion of historical, philosophical and philological studies. It supports advanced academic research in the humanities and social sciences, and is the recognized channel outside the universities for the Government's support of research in the humanities and social sciences.

The Fellowship of the Academy is limited to 350 under the age of 70. The Fellows are scholars who have attained distinction in one of the branches of study that the Academy exists to promote. Candidates must be nominated by existing Fellows. At June 12, 1991 there were 575 Fellows, 16 Honorary Fellows, and 300 Corresponding Fellows overseas.

President, Dr A. J. P. Kenny, FBA.
Treasurer, Dr E. A. Wrigley, FBA.
Foreign Secretary, Prof. J. B. Trapp, FBA.
Publications Officer, Prof. D. E. Luscombe, FBA.
Secretary, P. W. H. Brown.

THE FELLOWSHIP OF ENGINEERING (1976)
2 Little Smith Street, SW1P 3DL
[071-222 2688]

The Fellowship of Engineering is the United Kingdom national academy of engineering. It is an independent, self-governing body whose object is the pursuit, encouragement and maintenance of excellence in the whole field of engineering, in order to promote the advancement of the science, art and practice of engineering for the benefit of the public.

Election to the Fellowship is by invitation only from nominations supported by the body of Fellows. Fellows are chosen from among chartered engineers of all disciplines. The Royal Charter states that the total number of Fellows should not exceed 1,000 at any one time. At July 16, 1991 there were 861 Fellows, three Honorary Fellows and 41 Foreign Members. The Duke of Edinburgh is the Senior Fellow and the Duke of Kent is a Royal Fellow.

President, Sir William Barlow, F.Eng.
Past Presidents, Sir Denis Rooke, CBE, FRS, F.Eng.; The Viscount Caldecote, KBE, DSC, F.Eng.
Senior Vice President, R. Malpas, CBE, F.Eng.
Vice Presidents, Dr J. Alvey, CB, F.Eng.; Dr J. A. Gaffney, CBE, F.Eng.; B. F. Street, F.Eng.
Hon. Treasurer, G. A. Lee, F.Eng.
Hon. Secretaries, R. Garrick, CBE, F.Eng. *(Mechanical Engineering)*; D. G. M. Roberts, CBE, F.Eng. *(Civil Engineering)*; Dr T. B. McCrirrick, CBE, F.Eng *(Electrical Engineering)*; Dr G. S. G. Beveridge, F.Eng, FRSE *(Process Engineering)*; J. C. McKenzie, F.Eng. *(Overseas Affairs)*; B. W. Manley, F.Eng. *(Education, Training and Competence to Practise)*.
Executive Secretary, G. A. Atkinson.

THE ROYAL ACADEMY (1768)
Burlington House, W1V 0DS
[071-439 7438]

The Royal Academy of Arts is an independent, self-governing society devoted to the encouragement and promotion of the fine arts.

Membership of the Academy is limited to 50 Royal Academicians and 30 Associates, all being painters, engravers, sculptors or architects. Candidates are nominated and elected by the existing Academicians. There is also a limited class of honorary membership and there were 10 honorary members as at mid-1991.

President, Sir Roger de Grey, KCVO, PRA.
Treasurer, Sir Philip Powell, CH, OBE, RA.

Keeper, Prof. N. Adams, RA.
Secretary, P. Rodgers.

THE ROYAL SCOTTISH ACADEMY (1838)
The Mound, Edinburgh EH2 2EL
[031-225 6671]

The Scottish Academy was founded in 1826 to arrange exhibitions for contemporary paintings and to establish a society of fine art in Scotland. The Academy was granted a Royal Charter in 1838.

Members are elected from the disciplines of painting, sculpture, architecture and printmaking. Elections are from nominations put forward by the existing membership. At mid-1991 there were 13 Senior Academicians, 35 Academicians, 44 Associates, two non-resident Associates and 20 Honorary Members.

President, W. J. L. Baillie, PRSA.
Secretary, J. Knox, RSA.
Treasurer, I. McKenzie Smith, RSA.
Librarian, P. Collins, RSA.
Administrative Secretary, W. T. Meikle.

THE ROYAL SOCIETY (1660)
6 Carlton House Terrace, SW1Y 5AG
[071-930 2170]

The Royal Society is the United Kingdom's national academy of science. It is an independent, self-governing body under a Royal Charter, promoting and advancing all fields of physical and biological sciences, of mathematics and engineering, medical and agricultural sciences, their applications and place in society.

Election to Fellowship of the Royal Society is limited to those distinguished for original scientific work. Each year up to 40 new Fellows and six Foreign Members are elected from the most distinguished scientists. In addition, the Council can recommend for election members of the Royal family and, on average, one person each year for conspicuous service to the cause of science. At July 8, 1991, there were 1,095 Fellows and 101 Foreign Members.

President, Sir Michael Atiyah, FRS.
Treasurer, Sir Robert Honeycombe, FRS.
Biological Secretary, Prof. B. K. Follett, FRS.
Physical Secretary, Sir Francis Graham-Smith, FRS.
Foreign Secretary, Sir Anthony Epstein, CBE, FRS.
Executive Secretary, Dr P. T. Warren.

THE ROYAL SOCIETY OF EDINBURGH (1783)
22–24 George Street, Edinburgh EH2 2PQ
[031-225 6057]

The Royal Society of Edinburgh is Scotland's premier learned society. The Society was founded by Royal Charter in 1783 for 'the advancement of Learning and Useful Knowledge', and its principal role is the promotion of scholarship in all its branches. It provides a forum for broadly-based interdisciplinary activity in Scotland, including organizing public lectures, conferences and specialist research seminars; providing advice to Parliament and government; administering a range of research fellowships held in Scotland; and publishing learned journals.

Fellows are elected by ballot after being nominated by at least four existing Fellows. At July 2, 1991 there were 947 Ordinary Fellows and 64 Honorary Fellows.

President, Sir Alastair Currie, FRCP, FRCPE, FRCPG, FRCSE, FRCPath.
Treasurer, The Lord Balfour of Burleigh.
General Secretary, Dr C. D. Waterston.
Executive Secretary, Dr W. Duncan.

THE RESEARCH COUNCILS

The Government funds basic and applied civil science research mostly through the five research councils, which are supported by the Department of Education and Science. The councils conduct research through their own establishments (listed below) and by supporting selected research, study and training in universities and other higher education establishments. They also receive income for research commissioned by government departments and the private sector.

AGRICULTURAL AND FOOD RESEARCH COUNCIL

AFRC Institute for Animal Health
Director of Research, Prof. F. J. Bourne, ph.d., Compton, Newbury, Berks. RG16 0NN.

COMPTON LABORATORY, Compton, Newbury, Berks. RG16 0NN.—*Head of Division in Charge*, Dr P. Jones.

HOUGHTON LABORATORY, Houghton, Huntingdon, Cambs. PE17 2DA.—*Head of Lab.* (*acting*), L. N. Payne, ph.d., d.sc.

PIRBRIGHT LABORATORY, Ash Road, Woking, Surrey GU24 0NF.—*Head of Lab.* (*acting*), Dr A. I. Donaldson.

AFRC AND MRC NEUROPATHOGENESIS UNIT, Ogston Building, West Mains Road, Edinburgh EH9 3JF.—*Head of Unit*, vacant.

AFRC Institute of Animal Physiology and Genetics Research
Director of Research, R. B. Heap, ph.d., sc.d., frs, Babraham Hall, Babraham, Cambridge CB2 4AT.

CAMBRIDGE RESEARCH STATION, Babraham, Cambridge CB2 4AT.—*Head of Station*, Dr R. G. Dyer.

EDINBURGH RESEARCH STATION, Roslin, Midlothian EH25 9PS.—*Head of Station*, Prof. G. Bulfield, ph.d.

AFRC Institute of Arable Crops Research
Director of Research (*acting*), Prof. T. Lewis. Rothamsted Experimental Station, Harpenden, Herts. AL5 2JQ.

LONG ASHTON RESEARCH STATION, Long Ashton, Bristol BS18 9AF.—*Director*, Prof. P. R. Shewry.

ROTHAMSTED EXPERIMENTAL STATION, Harpenden, Herts. AL5 2JQ.—*Head of Station*, Prof. T. Lewis, ph.d., d.sc.

BROOM'S BARN EXPERIMENTAL STATION, Higham, Bury St Edmunds, Suffolk IP28 6NP.—*Head of Station*, T. H. Thomas, ph.d., d.sc.

AFRC Silsoe Research Institute
Director of Research, Prof. B. J. Legg, Wrest Park, Silsoe, Bedford MK45 4HS.

AFRC Institute of Food Research
Director of Research, D. L. Georgala, cbe, ph.d., Shinfield, Reading RG2 9AT.

NORWICH LABORATORY, Colney Lane, Norwich NR4 7UA.—*Head of Lab.*, Prof. P. Richmond, d.sc.

READING LABORATORY, Shinfield, Reading RG2 9AT.—*Head of Lab.*, Prof. B. E. B. Moseley, ph.d.

AFRC Institute of Grassland Environmental Research
Director of Research, Prof. J. L. Stoddart, ph.d., d.sc., Plas Gogerddan, Aberystwyth, Dyfed SY23 3EB.

Plant Science and Plant Breeding Division:
WELSH PLANT BREEDING STATION, Plas Gogerddan, Aberystwyth, Dyfed SY23 3EB.—*Director and Head of Division*, D. Wilson, ph.d.

Grassland and Ruminant Division:
NORTH WYKE RESEARCH STATION, Okehampton, Devon EX20 2SB.—*Officer in Charge*, R. D. Sheldrick, obe.

AFRC Institute of Plant Science Research
Director, Prof. R. B. Flavell, John Innes Institute, Colney Lane, Norwich NR4 7UH.

JOHN INNES INSTITUTE, Colney Lane, Norwich NR4 7UH.—*Director*, Prof. R. B. Flavell.

IPSR CAMBRIDGE LABORATORY, Colney Lane, Norwich NR4 7UH.—*Head*, C. N. Law, ph.d.

IPSR NITROGEN FIXATION LABORATORY, University of Sussex, Brighton BN1 9RQ.—*Head*, Prof. B. E. Smith, ph.d.

AFRC COMPUTING DIVISION, West Common, Harpenden, Herts. AL5 2JE.—*Head of Division*, A. Windram.

SCOTTISH AGRICULTURAL RESEARCH INSTITUTES

HANNAH RESEARCH INSTITUTE, Ayr KA6 5HL.—*Director*, Prof. M. Peaker.

MACAULAY LAND USE RESEARCH INSTITUTE, Craigiebuckler, Aberdeen AB9 2QJ; Bush Estate, Penicuik, Midlothian EH26 0PY.—*Director*, Prof. T. J. Maxwell, ph.d.

MOREDUN RESEARCH INSTITUTE, 408 Gilmerton Road, Edinburgh EH17 7JH.—*Director*, I. D. Aitken, ph.d.

ROWETT RESEARCH INSTITUTE, Greenburn Road, Bucksburn, Aberdeen AB2 9SB.—*Director*, Prof. W. P. T. James.

SCOTTISH CROP RESEARCH INSTITUTE, Invergowrie, Dundee DD2 5DA; Pentlandfield, Roslin, Midlothian EH25 9RF.—*Director*, Prof. J. Hillman, ph.d., fls, frse.

SCOTTISH AGRICULTURAL STATISTICS SERVICE, University of Edinburgh, James Clerk Maxwell Building, The King's Buildings, Mayfield Road, Edinburgh EH9 3JZ.—*Director*, R. A. Kempton.

ECONOMIC AND SOCIAL RESEARCH COUNCIL

CAMBRIDGE GROUP FOR THE HISTORY OF POPULATION AND SOCIAL STRUCTURE, 27 Trumpington Street, Cambridge CB2 1QA.—*Director*, Dr R. Schofield.

CENTRE FOR ECONOMIC PERFORMANCE, London School of Economics, Houghton Street, WC2A 2AE.—*Director*, Prof. R. Layard.

CENTRE FOR EDUCATIONAL SOCIOLOGY, University of Edinburgh, 7 Buccleuch Place, Edinburgh EH8 9LW.—*Director*, Prof. D. Raffe.

CENTRE FOR HEALTH ECONOMICS, University of York, Heslington, York YO2 5DD.—*Director*, Prof. A. Maynard.

CENTRE FOR HOUSING RESEARCH, 25 Bute Gardens, Hillhead, The University, Glasgow G12 8LE.—*Director*, Dr D. MacLennan.

CENTRE FOR RESEARCH IN ETHNIC RELATIONS, University of Warwick, Gibble Hill Road, Coventry CV4 7AL.—*Director*, Dr M. Anwar.

CENTRE FOR SCIENCE TECHNOLOGY AND ENERGY POLICY, Science Policy Research Unit, University of Sussex, Mantell Building, Falmer, Brighton BN1 9RF.—*Director*, Prof. G. Oldham.

SOCIAL WORK RESEARCH CENTRE, University of Stirling, Stirling FK9 4LA.—*Director*, Prof. Juliet Cheetham.

CENTRE FOR SOCIO-LEGAL STUDIES, Wolfson College, University of Oxford, Oxford OX2 6UD.—*Director*, D. Harris.

ESRC DATA ARCHIVE, University of Essex, Wivenhoe Park, Colchester, Essex CO4 3SQ.—*Director*, vacant.

INDUSTRIAL RELATIONS RESEARCH UNIT, School of Industrial Business Studies, University of Warwick, Gibble Hill Road, Coventry CV4 7AL.—*Director*, Prof. K. Sisson.

MRC/ESRC SOCIAL AND APPLIED PSYCHOLOGY UNIT, Department of Psychology, University of Sheffield, Sheffield S10 2TN.—*Director*, Prof. P. Warr.

NORTHERN IRELAND ECONOMIC RESEARCH CENTRE, 46–48 University Road, Belfast BT7 1NJ.—*Director*, Dr G. Gudgin.

RESEARCH CENTRE IN HUMAN COMMUNICATION, University of Edinburgh, 2 Buccleuch Place, Edinburgh EH8 9LW.—*Director*, Prof. K. Stenning.

RESEARCH CENTRE IN MICRO-SOCIAL CHANGE, University of Essex, Wivenhoe Park, Colchester, Essex CO4 3SQ.—*Director*, Prof. A. Coxon.

RESEARCH UNIT IN HEALTH AND BEHAVIOURAL CHANGE, University of Edinburgh, 17 Teviot Place, Edinburgh EH1 2QR.—*Director*, Dr D. McQueen.

CENTRE FOR FISCAL POLICY, The Institute for Fiscal Studies, 7, Ridgmount Street, WC1E 7AE.—*Director*, Prof. R. Blundell.

CENTRE FOR SOCIAL AND ECONOMIC RESEARCH ON THE GLOBAL ENVIRONMENT, University of East Anglia, Norwich NR4 7TJ.—*Director*, R. Kerry Turner.

MEDICAL RESEARCH COUNCIL

NATIONAL INSTITUTE FOR MEDICAL RESEARCH, Mill Hill, NW7.—*Director*, J. Skehel, PH.D., FRS.

CLINICAL RESEARCH CENTRE, Watford Road, Harrow, Middlesex.—*Director*, Dr K. E. Kirkham.

Research Units

ANATOMICAL NEUROPHARMACOLOGY UNIT, Mansfield Road, Oxford OX1 3TH.—*Director*, Prof. A. D. Smith, D.Phil.

APPLIED PSYCHOLOGY UNIT, 15 Chaucer Road, Cambridge CB2 2EF.—*Director*, A. D. Baddeley, PH.D.

MRC BIOCHEMICAL AND CLINICAL MAGNETIC RESONANCE UNIT, University Dept. of Biochemistry, South Parks Road, Oxford OX1 3QU.—*Director*, Prof. G. K. Radda, D.phil., FRS.

BIOSTATISTICS UNIT, 5 Shaftesbury Road, Cambridge CB2 2BW.—*Director*, N. E. Day, PH.D.

BLOOD GROUP UNIT, University College, London, Wolfson House, 4 Stephenson Way, NW1 2EH.—*Director*, Patricia Tippett, PH.D.

BLOOD PRESSURE UNIT, Western Infirmary, Glasgow G11 6NT.—*Director*, A. F. Lever, FRCP, FRSE.

BRAIN METABOLISM UNIT, University Dept. of Pharmacology, 1 George Square, Edinburgh EH8 9JZ.—*Director*, G. Fink, MD, D.phil.

CELL MUTATION UNIT, University of Sussex, Falmer, Brighton BN1 9RR.—*Director*, Prof. B. A. Bridges, PH.D.

CELLULAR IMMUNOLOGY UNIT, Sir William Dunn

School of Pathology, Oxford OX1 3RE.—*Director*, Dr A. F. Williams, PH.D.

CHILD PSYCHIATRY UNIT, Institute of Psychiatry, De Crespigny Park, Denmark Hill, SE5 8AF.—*Director*, Prof. M. Rutter, CBE, MD, FRCP.

CLINICAL ONCOLOGY AND RADIOTHERAPEUTICS UNIT, MRC Centre, Hills Road, Cambridge CB2 2QH.—*Hon. Director*, Prof. N. M. Bleehen, FRCP, FRCR.

CLINICAL PHARMACOLOGY UNIT, University Department of Clinical Pharmacology, Radcliffe Infirmary, Woodstock Road, Oxford OX2 6HE.—*Hon. Director*, Prof. D. G. Grahame-Smith, FRCP.

COGNITIVE DEVELOPMENT UNIT, 17 Gordon Street, WC1.—*Director*, Prof. J. Morton, PH.D.

MRC COLLABORATIVE CENTRE, 1–3 Burtonhole Lane, Mill Hill, NW7 1AD.—*Director*, C. C. G. Hentschel, PH.D.

CYCLOTRON UNIT, Hammersmith Hospital, Du Cane Road, W12.—*Director*, K. I. Gibson, PH.D.

DENTAL RESEARCH UNIT, London Hospital Medical College, 30–32 Newark Street, E1 2AA.—*Director*, Prof. N. W. Johnson, PH.D.

DUNN NUTRITION UNIT, Downhams Lane, Milton Road, Cambridge.—*Director*, R. G. Whitehead, PH.D.

ENVIRONMENTAL EPIDEMIOLOGY UNIT, Southampton General Hospital, Southampton SO9 4XY.—*Director*, Prof. D. J. P. Barker, MD, PH.D, FRCP.

EPIDEMIOLOGY AND MEDICAL CARE UNIT, Northwick Park Hospital, Watford Road, Harrow, Middx.—*Director*, T. W. Meade, DM, FRCP.

EPIDEMIOLOGY UNIT (SOUTH WALES), Llandough Hospital, Penarth, South Glamorgan CF6 1XX.—*Director*, P. C. Elwood, MD, FRCP.

EXPERIMENTAL EMBRYOLOGY AND TERATOLOGY UNIT, St George's Hospital Medical School, Cranmer Terrace, SW170RE.—*Director*, D. G. Whittingham, D.SC.

HUMAN BIOCHEMICAL GENETICS UNIT, Galton Laboratory, University College London, Wolfson House, 4 Stephenson Way, NW1.—*Hon. Director*, D. A. Hopkinson, MD.

HUMAN GENETICS UNIT, Western General Hospital, Crewe Road, Edinburgh EH4 2XU.—*Director*, Prof. H. J. Evans, PH.D, FRSE.

MRC HUMAN MOVEMENT AND BALANCE UNIT, Institute of Neurology, National Hospital, Queens Square, WC1.—*Director*. Prof. C. D. Marsden, FRS.

IMMUNOCHEMISTRY UNIT, University Department of Biochemistry, South Parks Road, Oxford OX1 3QU.—*Director*, K. B. M. Reid, PH.D.

INSTITUTE OF HEARING RESEARCH, University of Nottingham, Nottingham NG7 2RD.—*Director*, M. P. Haggard, PH.D.

MRC LABORATORIES, THE GAMBIA, Fajara, near Banjul, The Gambia.—*Director*, B. M. Greenwood, CBE, MD, FRCP.

MRC LABORATORIES, JAMAICA, University of the West Indies, Mona, Kingston, Jamaica.—*Director*, Prof. G. R. Serjeant, CMG, MD, FRCP.

MRC/LRF LEUKAEMIA UNIT, Royal Postgraduate Medical School, Du Cane Road, W12 0NN.—*Hon. Director*, Prof. L. Luzzatto, MD, FRCP.

MAMMALIAN DEVELOPMENT UNIT, University College London, Wolfson House, 4 Stephenson Way, NW1.—*Director*, Anne McLaren, D.Phil., FRS.

MEDICAL SOCIOLOGY UNIT, 6, Lilybank Gardens, Glasgow, G12 8QQ.—*Director*, Sally Macintyre, PH.D.

LABORATORY OF MOLECULAR BIOLOGY, Hills Road, Cambridge CB2 2QH.—*Director*, Sir Aaron Klug, PH.D., FRS.

MOLECULAR HAEMATOLOGY UNIT, John Radcliffe Hospital, Headington, Oxford OX3 9DU.—*Director*, Prof. D. J. Weatherall, MD, FRCP, FRS.

MRC MOLECULAR IMMUNOPATHOLOGY UNIT, University Medical School, Hills Road, Cambridge

CB2 2QH.—*Director*, Prof. P. J. Lachmann, PRCpath., FRS.

MOLECULAR NEUROBIOLOGY UNIT, University Medical School, Hills Road, Cambridge CB2 2QH.—*Director*, Prof. E. A. Barnard.

MRC MUSCLE AND CELL MOTILITY UNIT, Division of Biomolecular Sciences, King's College, 26–29 Drury Lane, WC2B 5RL.—*Hon. Director*, Prof. R. M. Simmonds, ph.D.

NEUROCHEMICAL PATHOLOGY UNIT, Newcastle General Hospital, Westgate Road, Newcastle upon Tyne NE4 6BE.—*Director*, Prof. J. A. Edwardson, ph.D.

NEUROLOGICAL PROSTHESES UNIT, Institute of Psychiatry, 1 Windsor Walk, De Crespigny Park, SE5.—*Hon. Director*, Prof. G. S. Brindley, MD, FRCP, FRS.

AFRC/MRC NEUROPATHOGENESIS UNIT, Ogston Building, West Mains Road, Edinburgh.—*Director*, vacant.

MRC PROTEIN FUNCTION AND DESIGN UNIT, Dept. of Chemistry, University of Cambridge, Lensfield Road, Cambridge CB2 1EW.—*Director*, A. R. Fersht, ph.D., FRS.

MRC PROTEIN PHOSPHORYLATION UNIT, Dept. of Biochemistry, University of Dundee, Dundee DD1 4HN.—*Director*, Prof. P. Cohen, ph.D., FRS, FRSE.

RADIOBIOLOGY UNIT, Chilton, Didcot, Oxon. OX11 0RD—*Director*, Prof. G. E. Adams, ph.D., D.SC.

REPRODUCTIVE BIOLOGY UNIT, Centre for Reproductive Biology, 37 Chalmers Street, Edinburgh EH3 9EW.—*Director*, D. W. Lincoln, D.SC.

SOCIAL AND APPLIED PSYCHOLOGY UNIT, Dept. of Psychology, University of Sheffield S10 2TN.—*Director*, P. B. Warr, ph.D.

SOCIAL (AND COMMUNITY) PSYCHIATRY UNIT, Institute of Psychiatry, De Crespigny Park, Denmark Hill, SE5.—*Director*, Prof. J. P. Leff, MD, FRCPsych.

TOXICOLOGY UNIT, MRC Laboratories, Woodmansterne Road, Carshalton, Surrey SM5 4EF.—*Director*, Dr L. Smith.

TUBERCULOSIS AND RELATED INFECTIONS UNIT, Hammersmith Hospital, Du Cane Road, W12 0HS.—*Director*, Dr J. Ivanyi, MD, ph.D.

VIROLOGY UNIT, Institute of Virology, Church Street, Glasgow G11 5JR.—*Hon. Director*, Prof. J. H. Subak-Sharpe, CBE, ph.D, FRSE.

NATURAL ENVIRONMENT RESEARCH COUNCIL

Research Institutes and Units

BRITISH ANTARCTIC SURVEY, Madingley Road, Cambridge CB3 0ET. Tel: 0223–61188.—*Director*, Dr D. J. Drewry.

BRITISH GEOLOGICAL SURVEY, Nicker Hill, Keyworth, Nottingham NG12 5GG. Tel: 06077–6111.—*Director*, Dr P. Cook.

INSTITUTE OF OCEANOGRAPHIC SCIENCES, Deacon Laboratory, Wormley, nr. Godalming, Surrey GU8 5UB. Tel: 042868–4141.—*Director*, Dr C. Summerhayes.

PLYMOUTH MARINE LABORATORY, Prospect Place, The

Hoe, Plymouth PL1 3DH; Citadel Hill, Plymouth PL1 2PB. Tel: 0752–222772.—*Director*, B. L. Bayne, ph.D.; *Assistant Director*, Dr P. N. Claridge.

PROUDMAN OCEANOGRAPHIC LABORATORY, Bidston, Birkenhead L43 7RA. Tel: 051–653 8633.—*Director*, B. S. McCartney, ph.D.

SEA MAMMAL RESEARCH UNIT, c/o British Antarctic Survey. Tel: 0223–311354.—*Head of Unit*, J. Harwood, ph.D.

INSTITUTE OF HYDROLOGY, Maclean Building, Crowmarsh Gifford, Wallingford, Oxon. OX10 8BB. Tel: 0491–38800.—*Director*, Prof. W. B. Wilkinson.

INSTITUTE OF TERRESTRIAL ECOLOGY (NORTH), Bush Estate, Penicuik, Midlothian EH26 0QB. Tel: 031–445 4343.—*Director*, Prof. O. W. Heal.

INSTITUTE OF TERRESTRIAL ECOLOGY (SOUTH), Monks Wood Experimental Station, Abbots Ripton, Huntingdon PE17 2LS. Tel: 04873–381/8.—*Director*, Dr T. M. Roberts.

INSTITUTE OF VIROLOGY AND ENVIRONMENTAL MICROBIOLOGY, Mansfield Road, Oxford OX1 3SR. Tel: 0865–512361.—*Director*, Prof. D. H. L. Bishop.

INSTITUTE OF FRESHWATER ECOLOGY, The Ferry House, Far Sawrey, Ambleside, Cumbria LA22 0LP. Tel: 09662–2468/9.—*Director*, Prof. J. G. Jones.

DUNSTAFFNAGE MARINE LABORATORY, PO Box 3, Oban, Argyll PA34 4AD. Tel: 0631–62244.—*Director*, Prof. J. B. L. Matthews.

UNIT OF COMPARATIVE PLANT ECOLOGY, Dept. of Animal and Plant Biology and Ecology, Sheffield University, Sheffield S10 2TN. Tel: 0742–768555.—*Head of Unit*, Prof. J. P. Grime.

INTERDISCIPLINARY CENTRE FOR POPULATION BIOLOGY, Imperial College, Silwood Park, Ascot, Berks. SL5 7PY. Tel: 0344–23911.—*Director*, Prof. J. Lawton.

JAMES RENNELL CENTRE FOR OCEAN CIRCULATION, Gamma House, Chilworth Research Centre, Chilworth, Southampton SO1 7NS. Tel: 0703–766766.—*Head of Centre*, Dr R. Pollard.

NERC UNIT FOR THEMATIC INFORMATION SYSTEMS, Dept. of Geography, Reading University, Whiteknights, PO Box 227, Reading RG6 2AB. Tel: 0734–318741.—*Officer in Charge*, Prof. R. Gurney.

SCIENCE AND ENGINEERING RESEARCH COUNCIL

Research Establishments

DARESBURY LABORATORY, Keckwick Lane, Daresbury, Warrington, Cheshire WA4 4AD.—*Director*, Prof. A. J. Leadbetter. (The Nuclear Structure Facility at Daresbury is due to close at the end of 1992.)

ROYAL GREENWICH OBSERVATORY, Madingley Road, Cambridge CB3 0EZ.—*Director*, Prof. A. Boksenberg, FRS.

ROYAL OBSERVATORY, EDINBURGH, Blackford Hill, Edinburgh EH9 3HJ.—*Director* (*acting*), Dr P. Murdin.

RUTHERFORD APPLETON NUCLEAR PHYSICS LABORATORY, Chilton, Didcot, Oxon OX11 0QX.—*Director*, Dr P. R. Williams.

INDUSTRIAL AND TECHNOLOGICAL RESEARCH ASSOCIATIONS

The following are members of the Association of Independent Research and Technology Organizations (AIRTO), PO Box 330, Cambridge CB5 8DU.

AIRCRAFT RESEARCH ASSOCIATION LTD, Manton Lane, Bedford MK41 7PF. Tel: 0234–350681.—*Chief Exec.*, Dr J. E. Green.

ADVANCED MANUFACTURING TECHNOLOGY RESEARCH INSTITUTE, Hulley Road, Macclesfield, Cheshire SK10 2NE. Tel: 0625–425421.—*Chief Exec.*, vacant.

BCIRA INTERNATIONAL CENTRE FOR CAST METALS TECHNOLOGY, Alvechurch, Birmingham B48 7QB. Tel: 0527–66414.—*Director*, Dr S. W. Radcliffe.

BHR GROUP LTD (BRITISH HYDRO-MECHANICS RESEARCH GROUP), Cranfield, Bedford MK43 0AJ. Tel: 0234–750422.—*Chief exec.*, I. Cooper.

BICERI—THE BRITISH INTERNAL COMBUSTION ENGINE RESEARCH INSTITUTE LTD, 111–112 Buckingham Avenue, Slough SL1 4PH. Tel: 0753–27371.—*Chief Exec.*, Dr C. Ashley, CBE.

BNF FULMER CENTRE, Wantage Business Park, Denchworth Road, Wantage, Oxon. OX12 9BJ. Tel: 0235–772992.—*Chief Exec.*, Dr W. H. Bowyer.

BRITISH CERAMIC RESEARCH LTD, Queen's Road, Penkhull, Stoke-on-Trent ST4 7LQ. Tel: 0782–45431.—*Chief Exec.*, Dr N. E. Sanderson.

BRITISH GLASS, Northumberland Road, Sheffield S10 2UA. Tel: 0742–686201.—*Research Director*, Dr G. J. Copley.

BRITISH LEATHER CONFEDERATION, Leather Trade House, Kings Park Road, Moulton Park, Northants. NN3 1JD. Tel: 0604–494131.—*Director*, Dr R. L. Sykes, OBE.

BRITISH MARITIME TECHNOLOGY LTD, Orlando House, 1 Waldegrave Road, Teddington, Middx. TW11 8LZ. Tel: 081–943 5544.—*Chief Exec.*, D. Goodrich.

BRITISH TEXTILE TECHNOLOGY GROUP, Shirley Towers, Didsbury, Manchester M20 8RX; Wira House, West Park Ring Road, Leeds LS16 6QL. Tel: 061–445 8141.—*Managing Dir.*, Dr D. N. Munro.

BUILDING SERVICES RESEARCH AND INFORMATION ASSOCIATION, Old Bracknell Lane West, Bracknell, Berks. RG12 4AH. Tel: 0344–426511.—*Chief Exec.*, G. J. Baker.

CAMBRIDGE CONSULTANTS LTD (*Product and process development of technology applications in business*), Science Park, Milton Road, Cambridge CB4 4DW. Tel: 0223–420024.—*Managing Dir.*, Dr J. P. Auton.

CAMPDEN FOOD AND DRINK RESEARCH ASSOCIATION, Chipping Campden, Glos. GL55 6LD.

CIRIA (THE CONSTRUCTION INDUSTRY RESEARCH AND INFORMATION ASSOCIATION), 6 Storey's Gate, SW1P 3AU. Tel: 071–222 8891.—*Dir. Gen.*, Dr P. L. Bransby.

CUTLERY AND ALLIED TRADES RESEARCH ASSOCIATION, Henry Street, Sheffield S3 7EQ. Tel: 0742–769736.—*Dir. of Research*, R. C. Hamby.

ERA TECHNOLOGY LTD (*Electronic and electrical engineering*), Cleeve Road, Leatherhead, Surrey KT22 7SA. Tel: 0372–374151.—*Chief Exec.*, M. J. Withers.

FURNITURE INDUSTRY RESEARCH ASSOCIATION, Maxwell Road, Stevenage, Herts. SG1 2EW. Tel: 0438–313433.—*Chief Exec.*, D. M. Heughan.

INVERESK RESEARCH INTERNATIONAL LTD (*Pharmaceutical, veterinary, agricultural and chemical product evaluation*), Musselburgh, Midlothian EH21 7UB. Tel: 0875–614545.—*Managing Dir.*, Dr I. P. Sword.

LAMBEG INDUSTRIAL RESEARCH ASSOCIATION (*Textiles*), Lambeg, Lisburn, Co. Antrim, N. Ireland BT27 4RJ. Tel: 0846–662255.—*Dir.*, B. B. Robinson.

LEATHERHEAD FOOD RESEARCH ASSOCIATION, Randalls Road, Leatherhead, Surrey KT22 7RY. Tel: 0372–376761.—*Dir.*, Dr M. P. J. Kierstan.

MOTOR INDUSTRY RESEARCH ASSOCIATION, Watling Street, Nuneaton, Warks. CV10 0TU. Tel: 0203–348541.—*Managing Dir. (acting)*, P. F. Willmer.

THE NATIONAL COMPUTING CENTRE LTD, Oxford Road, Manchester M1 7ED. Tel: 061–228 6333.—*Chief Exec.*, J. Lloyd.

INTERNATIONAL RESEARCH AND DEVELOPMENT LTD (*Electronics and mechanical and electrical engineering*), Fossway, Newcastle upon Tyne NE6 2YD. Tel: 091–265 0451.—*Managing Dir.*, P. R. Whitehouse.

PAINT RESEARCH ASSOCIATION, 8 Waldegrave Road, Teddington, Middx. TW11 8LD. Tel: 081–977 4427.—*Managing Dir.*, J. A. Bernie.

PERA INTERNATIONAL (*Multi-disciplinary research, design, development and consultancy*), Melton Mowbray, Leics. LE13 0PB. Tel: 0664–501501.—*Dir. Gen.*, R. A. Armstrong.

PIRA INTERNATIONAL (*Paper and board, printing, publishing and packaging*), Randalls Road, Leatherhead, Surrey KT22 7RU. Tel: 0372–376161.—*Managing Dir.*, B. W. Blunden.

RAPRA TECHNOLOGY LTD (*Polymer materials*), Shawbury, Shrewsbury SY4 4NR. Tel: 0939–250383.—*Chief Exec.*, Dr M. Copley.

RICARDO GROUP PLC (*Consulting engineers*), Bridge Works, Shoreham-by-Sea, W. Sussex BN43 5FG. Tel: 0273–455611.—*Managing Dir.*, C. Ross.

SATRA FOOTWEAR TECHNOLOGY CENTRE, Satra House, Rockingham Road, Kettering, Northants. NN16 9JH. Tel: 0536–410000.—*Chief Exec.*, J. G. Butlin, OBE.

SHIPOWNERS REFRIGERATED CARGO RESEARCH ASSOCIATION, 140 Newmarket Road, Cambridge CB5 8HE. Tel: 0223–65101.—*Technical Dir.*, R. D. Heap.

SIRA LTD (*Instrumentation and systems technology*), South Hill, Chislehurst, Kent BR7 5EH. Tel: 081–467 2636.—*Managing Dir.*, R. A. Brook.

SMITH ASSOCIATES LTD (*System engineering consultancy*), Surrey Research Park, Guildford, Surrey GU2 5YP. Tel: 0483–505565.—*Chairman*, Dr B. G. Smith.

SPRING RESEARCH AND MANUFACTURERS' ASSOCIATION, Henry Street, Sheffield S3 7EQ. Tel: 0742–760771.—*Dir.*, D. Saynor.

TIMBER RESEARCH AND DEVELOPMENT ASSOCIATION, Stocking Lane, Hughenden Valley, High Wycombe, Bucks. HP14 4ND. Tel: 0240–243091.—*Dir.*, C. J. Gill.

WATER RESEARCH CENTRE, PLC, Henley Road, Medmenham, PO Box 16, Marlow, Bucks. SL7 2HD. Tel: 0491–571531.—*Managing Dir.*, M. J. Rouse.

THE WELDING INSTITUTE, Abington Hall, Abington, Cambridge CB1 6AL. Tel: 0223–891162.—*Chief Exec.*, A. B. M. Braithwaite, OBE.

EMPLOYERS' AND TRADE BODIES

CONFEDERATION OF BRITISH INDUSTRY

Centre Point, 103 New Oxford Street, WC1A 1DU
[071–379 7400]

The Confederation of British Industry was founded in August 1965 and is an independent non-party political body financed by industry and commerce. It exists primarily to ensure that the Government understands the intentions, needs and problems of British business. It is the recognized spokesman for the business viewpoint and is consulted as such by the Government.

The CBI represents, directly and indirectly, some 250,000 companies. All the major nationalized industries are in membership and thereby able to work with the CBI on problems that are the concern of all management.

The governing body of the CBI is the 400-strong Council, which meets monthly in London under the chairmanship of the President. It is assisted by some 27 expert standing committees which advise on the main aspects of policy. There are 13 Regional Councils and offices covering the administrative regions of England, Wales, Scotland and Northern Ireland. There is also an office in Brussels.

President, Sir Brian Corby.
Director-General, J. Banham.
Secretary, M. W. Hunt.

ADVERTISING ASSOCIATION, Abford House, 15 Wilton Road, SW1V 1NJ. (Tel: 071–828 2771).—*Dir. Gen.*, R. L. Wade.

AEROSPACE COMPANIES LTD, SOCIETY OF BRITISH, 29 King Street, SW1Y 6RD. (Tel: 071–839 3231).—*Dir.*, Sir Barry Duxbury, KCB, CBE.

BAKERS, FEDERATION OF, 20 Bedford Square, WC1B 3HF.—*Dir.*, A. Casdagli, CBE.

BANKERS' ASSOCIATION, BRITISH, 10 Lombard Street, EC3V 9EL. (Tel: 071–623 4001).—*Sec.-Gen.*, Lord Inchyra.

BLIND AND DISABLED INC., NATIONAL ASSOCIATION OF INDUSTRIES FOR THE, Triton House, 43A High Street South, Dunstable, Beds. LU6 3RZ. (Tel: 0582-606796).—*Hon. Sec.*, G. J Entwistle.

BREWERS' SOCIETY, 42 Portman Square, W1H 0BB. (Tel: 071–486 4831).—*Dir. Gen.*, A. G. Tilbury, CBE.

BUILDING EMPLOYERS' CONFEDERATION, 82 New Cavendish Street, W1M 8AD. (Tel: 071–580 5588).—*Dir. Gen.*, J. Owens.

BUILDING MATERIAL PRODUCERS, NATIONAL COUNCIL OF, 26 Store Street, WC1E 7BT. (Tel: 071–323 3770).—*Dir. Gen.*, N. M. Chaldecott, OBE.

BUS AND COACH COUNCIL, Sardinia House, 52 Lincoln's Inn Fields, WC2A 3LZ. (Tel: 071–831 7546).—*Dir. Gen.*, Mrs A. V. M. Palmer, MBE.

CHEMICAL INDUSTRIES ASSOCIATION LTD., Kings Buildings, Smith Square, SW1P 3JJ. (Tel: 071–834 3399).—*Dir. Gen.*, J. C. L. Cox.

CLOTHING INDUSTRY ASSOCIATION LTD, BRITISH, British Apparel Centre, 7 Swallow Place, W1R 7AA.—*Dir.* J. R. Wilson.

DAIRY TRADE FEDERATION, 19 Cornwall Terrace, NW1 4QP. (Tel: 071–486 7244).—*Dir. Gen.*, J. P. Price.

ELECTROTECHNICAL AND ALLIED MANUFACTURERS' ASSOCIATIONS, FEDERATION OF BRITISH (BEAMA), Leicester House, 8 Leicester Street, WC2H 7BN.—*Dir. Gen.*, J. G. Gaddes.

ENGINEERING EMPLOYERS' FEDERATION, Broadway House, Tothill Street, SW1H 9NQ. (Tel: 071–222 7777).—*Dir. Gen.*, P. Brighton.

FARMERS' UNION, NATIONAL (NFU), Agriculture House, Knightsbridge, SW1X 7NJ. (Tel: 071–235 5077).—*Dir. Gen.*, D. Evans.

FARMERS' UNION OF SCOTLAND, NATIONAL, 17 Grosvenor Crescent, Edinburgh EH12 5EN. (Tel: 031–337 4333).—*Chief Exec.*, D. S. Johnston, OBE.

FARMERS' UNION, ULSTER, Dunedin, 475–477 Antrim Road, Belfast BT15 3DA. (Tel: 0232–370222).—*Gen. Sec.*, J. V. Smyth.

FINANCE HOUSES ASSOCIATION, 18 Upper Grosvenor Street, W1X 9PB. (Tel: 071–491 2783).—*Dir.*, N. A. D. Grant, CBE.

FOOD AND DRINK FEDERATION, 6 Catherine Street, WC2B 5JJ. (Tel: 071–836 2460).—*Dir. Gen.*, M. P. Mackenzie.

FREIGHT TRANSPORT ASSOCIATION LTD., Hermes House, 157 St John's Road, Tunbridge Wells, Kent TN4 9UZ. (Tel: 0892–26171).—*Dir.-Gen.*, G. Turvey.

INSURERS, ASSOCIATION OF BRITISH, 51–55 Gresham Street, EC2V 7HQ. (Tel: 071–600 3333).—*Chief Exec.*, M. A. Jones.

KNITTING INDUSTRIES FEDERATION LTD., 7 Gregory Boulevard, Nottingham NG7 6NB. (Tel: 0602-621081).—*Dir.*, J. P. Harrison.

LEATHER CONFEDERATION, BRITISH, Leather Trade House, Kings Park Road, Moulton Park, Northampton NN3 1JD. (Tel: 0604–494131).—*Dir.*, R. L. Sykes, OBE, PH.D.

LEATHER PRODUCERS' ASSOCIATION, Leather Trade House, Kings Park Road, Moulton Park, Northampton NN3 1JD. (Tel: 0604–494131).—*Nat. Sec.*, J. Purvis.

MANAGEMENT CONSULTANCIES ASSOCIATION, 11 West Halkin Street, SW1X 8JL. (Tel: 071–235 3897).—*Exec. Dir.*, B. O'Rorke.

MARINE INDUSTRIES FEDERATION, BRITISH, Meadlake Place, Thorpe Lea Road, Egham, Surrey TW20 8HE. (Tel: 0784–473377).—*Chief Exec.*, P. V. Wagstaffe.

MOTOR MANUFACTURERS AND TRADERS LTD., SOCIETY OF, Forbes House, Halkin Street, SW1X 7DS. (Tel: 071–235 7000).—*Dir.*, S. R. Foster.

NEWSPAPER PUBLISHERS ASSOCIATION LTD., 34 Southwark Bridge Road, SE1 9EU. (Tel: 071–928 6928).—*Dir.*, J. E. Lepage.

OFFICE SYSTEMS AND STATIONERY FEDERATION, BRITISH, 6 Wimpole Street, W1M 8AS. (Tel: 071–637 7692).—*Dir.*, D. F. Hall.

PAPER AND BOARD INDUSTRY FEDERATION, BRITISH, Papermakers House, Rivenhall Road, Westlea, Swindon SN5 7BE. (Tel: 0793–886086).—*Dir. Gen.*, W. J. Bartlett.

PLASTICS FEDERATION, BRITISH, 5 Belgrave Square, SW1X 8PD. (Tel: 071–235 9483).—*Dir.*, D. R. Jones.

PORTS FEDERATION, BRITISH, Victoria House, Vernon Place, WC1B 4LL. (Tel: 071–242 1200).—*Managing Dir.* J. Sharples.

PRINTING INDUSTRIES FEDERATION, BRITISH, 11 Bedford Row, WC1R 4DX. (Tel: 071–242 6904).—*Dir. Gen.*, C. Stanley.

PUBLISHERS ASSOCIATION, 19 Bedford Square, WC1B 3HJ. (Tel: 071–580 6321).—*Chief Exec.*, C. Bradley.

RADIO CONTRACTORS LTD, ASSOCIATION OF INDEPENDENT, Radio House, 46 Westbourne Grove, W2 5SH. (Tel: 071–727 2646).—*Chief Exec.*, B. West.

RETAIL CONSORTIUM, Bedford House, 69–79 Fulham High Street, SW6 3JW. (Tel: 071–371 5185).—*Dir. Gen.*, J. N. W. May.

RETAIL NEWSAGENTS, NATIONAL FEDERATION OF, Yeoman House, Sekforde Street, EC1R 0HD. (Tel: 071–253 4225).—*Chief Exec.*, K. E. J. Peters.

ROAD FEDERATION LTD, BRITISH, Pillar House, 194–202 Old Kent Road, SE1 5TG. (Tel: 071–703 9769).—*Dir.*, P. J. Witt.

ROAD HAULAGE ASSOCIATION LTD., Roadway House, 35 Monument Hill, Weybridge, Surrey KT13 8RN. (Tel: 0932–841515).—*Dir. Gen.*, D. B. H. Colley, CB, CBE.

RUBBER MANUFACTURERS' ASSOCIATION LTD, BRITISH, 90–91 Tottenham Court Road, W1P 0BR.—*Dir.*, G. C. Gullan.

SHIPPING, GENERAL COUNCIL OF BRITISH, 30–32 St Mary Axe, EC3A 8ET. (Tel: 071–283 2922).—*Dir. Gen.*, Sir Nicholas Hunt, GCB, LVO.

SPORTS AND ALLIED INDUSTRIES FEDERATION LTD, BRITISH, 23 Brighton Road, Croydon CR2 4EA. (Tel: 081–681 1242).—*Chief Exec.*, L. F. Standen.

TELEVISION ASSOCIATION, INDEPENDENT, Knighton House, 56 Mortimer Street, W1N 8AN. (Tel: 071–636 6866).—*Dir.*, D. Shaw.

TEXTILE CONFEDERATION, BRITISH, British Apparel and Textiles Centre, 7 Swallow Place, W1R 7AA. (Tel: 071–491 9702).—*Dir.*, C. M. Purvis.

TIMBER GROWERS' UNITED KINGDOM, Admel House, 24 High Street, SW19 5DX. (Tel: 081–944 6340).—*Chief Exec.*, A. J. Murray.

TIMBER MERCHANTS' ASSOCIATION, BRITISH, Stocking Lane, Hughenden Valley, High Wycombe, Bucks. HP14 4JZ. (Tel: 024 024–3602).—*Sec.*, R. T. Allcorn.

TIMBER TRADE FEDERATION, Clareville House, 26–27 Oxendon Street, SW1Y 4EL. (Tel: 071–839 1891).—*Dir. Gen.*, A. A. Lockyer, LVO.

UK OFFSHORE OPERATORS ASSOCIATION LTD., 3 Hans Crescent, SW1X 0LN. (Tel: 071–589 5255).—*Dir. Gen.*, Dr H. W. D. Hughes, OBE.

UK PETROLEUM INDUSTRY ASSOCIATION LTD., 9 Kingsway, WC2B 6XH.—*Dir. Gen.*, Dr I. D. G. Berwick.

WHOLESALE AND INDUSTRIAL DISTRIBUTORS, FEDERATION OF, The Old Post Office, Dunchideock, Exeter EX2 9TU. (Tel: 0392–832559).—*Dir.*, J. Hussey.

TRADE UNIONS

TRADES UNION CONGRESS (TUC)
Congress House, 23–28 Great Russell Street,
WC1B 3LS
[071–636 4030]

The Trades Union Congress, founded in 1868, is a voluntary association of trade unions, the representatives of which meet annually to consider matters of common concern to their members. The Congress has met annually since 1871 and in recent years has met normally on the first Monday in September, its sessions extending through the succeeding four days. Congress is constituted by delegates of the affiliated unions on the basis of one delegate for every 5,000 members, or fraction thereof, on whose behalf affiliation fees are paid. Affiliated unions (in 1990–91) totalled 74 with an aggregate membership of 8,188,448 (women's membership, 2,827,113).

The main business of the annual Congress is to consider the report of its General Council dealing with the activities of the Congress year, along with motions from affiliated societies on questions of policy and organization.

The standing committees of the General Council are serviced by a full time staff appointed by the General Secretary, who is himself elected by Congress and who remains in office until the age of 65, subject to decision of Congress or the General Council.

Through the General Council and its committees the trade union movement maintains systematic relations with the Government and government departments, with the Confederation of British Industry and with a large number of other bodies. It is represented on the National Economic Development Council, the Health and Safety Commission, the council of the Advisory Conciliation and Arbitration Service and a number of other bodies.

Among powers vested in the General Council by consent of the unions in Congress is the responsibility of intervening in disputes and differences between affiliated organizations; if possible this is done through informal conciliation meetings under TUC auspices but where necessary a Disputes Committee is formed consisting of one member of the General Council and two senior officials of unions not involved in the dispute. This investigates the matter concerned and issues its findings.

Unions retain full control of their own affairs and the only sanctions which Congress can apply are suspension or exclusion from membership.

Chairman (1991–92), R. Bickerstaffe (NUPE).
General Secretary, N. D. Willis.

SCOTTISH TRADES UNION CONGRESS
16 Woodlands Terrace, Glasgow G3 6DF
[041–332 4946]

The Congress was formed in 1897 and acts as a national centre for the trade union movement in Scotland. In 1991 it consisted of 54 unions with a membership of 829,763 and 42 directly affiliated Trades Councils. The majority of the unions organize throughout Britain and affiliate on their membership in Scotland.

The Annual Congress in April elects a 35-member General Council on the basis of 7 industrial sections.

Chairperson, Ms J. McKay.
General Secretary, C. Christie.

TRADES UNIONS AFFILIATED TO TUC

A list of the trades unions affiliated to the Trades Union Congress at September 1, 1991. The number of members of each union is shown in parenthesis.

AMALGAMATED ASSOCIATION OF BEAMERS, TWISTER
AND DRAWERS (HAND AND MACHINE), THE (405), 2
Every Street, Nelson, Lancs. BB9 7NE. (Tel: 0282
64181).—*Gen. Sec.*, A. Brindle.

AMALGAMATED ENGINEERING UNION (AEU) (702,228
110 Peckham Road, SE15 5EL. (Tel: 071
703 4231).—*Gen. Sec.*, G. H. Laird, CBE.

AMALGAMATED SOCIETY OF TEXTILE WORKERS AN
KINDRED TRADES (2,300), Foxlowe, Market Plac
Leek, Staffs. ST13 6AD. (Tel: 0538–382068).—*Ger
Sec.*, A. Hitchmough.

ASSOCIATED SOCIETY OF LOCOMOTIVE ENGINEERS AN
FIREMEN (ASLEF) (18,000), 9 Arkwright Road, NW
6AB. (Tel: 071–431 0275).—*Sec.*, D. Fullick.

ASSOCIATION OF CINEMATOGRAPH, TELEVISION AN
ALLIED TECHNICIANS, *see* p. 972.

ASSOCIATION OF FIRST DIVISION CIVIL SERVANT
(10,796), 2 Caxton Street, SW1H 0QH. (Tel: 071–22
6242).—*Gen. Sec.*, Ms E. Symons.

ASSOCIATION OF UNIVERSITY TEACHERS (31,000
United House, 1 Pembridge Road, W11 3JY. (Tel
071–221 4370).—*Gen. Sec.*, Ms D. Warwick.

BAKERS, FOOD AND ALLIED WORKERS' UNION (36,000
Stanborough House, Great North Road, Stanbor
ough, Welwyn Garden City, Herts. AL8 7TA. (Tel
0707–260150).—*Gen. Sec.*, J. R. Marino.

BANKING, INSURANCE AND FINANCE UNION (171,101
Sheffield House, 1B Amity Grove, SW20 0LG. (Tel
081–946 9151).—*Gen. Sec.*, L. A. Mills.

BRITISH ACTORS' EQUITY ASSOCIATION (44,269),
Harley Street, W1N 2AB. (Tel: 071–637 9311).—
Gen. Sec., I. McGarry.

BRITISH AIR LINE PILOTS ASSOCIATION, THE (7,684
81 New Road, Harlington, Hayes, Middx. UB3 5BC
(Tel: 081–759 9331).—*Gen. Sec.*, vacant.

BRITISH ASSOCIATION OF COLLIERY MANAGEMEN
THE (7,370), BACM House, 317 Nottingham Roac
Old Basford, Nottingham NG7 7DP. (Tel: 0602
785819).—*Gen. Sec.*, J. D. Meads.

BROADCASTING, ENTERTAINMENT AND CINEMATC
GRAPH TECHNICIANS' UNION (BECTU) (60,000), 181
185 Wardour Street, W1V 4BE. (Tel: 071–439 7585
111 Wardour Street, W1V 4AY. (Tel: 071–43
8506).—*Gen. Sec.*, D. A. Hearn. *See also* p. 972.

CARD SETTING MACHINE TENTERS' SOCIETY (92), 3
Greenton Avenue, Scholes, Cleckheaton, W. York:
BD19 6DT. (Tel: 0274–670022).—*Sec.*, G. Priestley

CERAMIC AND ALLIED TRADES UNION, THE (28,863
Hillcrest House, Garth Street, Stoke-on-Trent ST
2AB. (Tel: 0782–272755).—*Gen. Sec.*, A. W. Clowes

CIVIL AND PUBLIC SERVICES ASSOCIATION, TH
(122,670), 160 Falcon Road, SW11 2LN. (Tel: 071
924 2727).—*Gen. Sec.*, J. N. Ellis.

COMMUNICATION MANAGERS' ASSOCIATION (19,500
Hughes House, Ruscombe Road, Twyford, Readin
RG10 9JD. (Tel: 0734–342300).—*Gen. Sec.*, T. I
Deegan.

CONFEDERATION OF HEALTH SERVICE EMPLOYEE
(COHSE) (203,311), Glen House, High Street, Bar
stead, Surrey SM7 2LH. (Tel: 0737–353322).—*Ger
Sec.*, H. MacKenzie.

EDUCATIONAL INSTITUTE OF SCOTLAND, THE (46,489
46 Moray Place, Edinburgh EH3 6BH. (Tel: 031
225 6244).—*Gen. Sec.*, J. B. Martin.

ELECTRICAL AND PLUMBING INDUSTRIES UNION (4,000
Park House, 64–66 Wandsworth Common Nortl
Side, SW18 2SH. (Tel: 081–874 0458).—*Gen. Sec.*, a
Aitkin.

ENGINEERING AND FASTENERS TRADE UNION (430), 42 Galton Road, Warley, West Midlands, B67 5JU. (Tel: 021–429 2594).—*Gen. Sec.*, J. Burdis.

ENGINEERS' AND MANAGERS' ASSOCIATION (41,000), Station House, Fox Lane North, Chertsey, Surrey KT16 9HW. (Tel: 0932–564131).—*Gen. Sec.*, D. A. Cooper.

FILM ARTISTES' ASSOCIATION (2,114), 61 Marloes Road, W8 6LE. (Tel: 071–937 4567).—*Sec.*, M. Reynel.

FIRE BRIGADES UNION, THE (47,801), Bradley House, 68 Coombe Road, Kingston upon Thames, Surrey KT2 7AE. (Tel: 081–541 1765).—*Gen. Sec.*, K. Cameron.

FURNITURE, TIMBER AND ALLIED TRADES UNION (38,349), Fairfields, Roe Green, NW9 0PT. (Tel: 081–204 0273).—*Gen. Sec.*, C. A. Christopher.

GENERAL UNION OF ASSOCIATIONS OF LOOM OVER-LOOKERS, THE (698), Overlookers Institute, 9 Wellington Street, St Johns, Blackburn, Lancs. BB1 8AF. (Tel: 0254–51760).—*Pres.*, E. Macro.

GMB (formerly GENERAL, MUNICIPAL, BOILERMAKERS AND ALLIED TRADES UNION (865,000), 22–24 Worple Road, SW19 4DF. (Tel: 081–947 3131).—*Gen. Sec.*, J. Edmonds.

GRAPHICAL, PAPER AND MEDIA UNION (300,000), 63–67 Bromham Road, Bedford MK40 2AG. (Tel: 0234–351521).—*Gen. Sec.*, A. D. Dubbins. *See also* p. 972.

HEALTH VISITORS' ASSOCIATION SECTION (Manufacturing, Science and Finance Union) (15,000), 50 Southwark Street, SE1 1UN. (Tel: 071–378 7255).—*Gen. Sec.*, Ms C. Burns. *See also* p. 972.

HOSPITAL CONSULTANTS AND SPECIALISTS ASSOCIATION, THE (2,360), The Old Court House, London Road, Ascot, Berks. SL5 7EN. (Tel: 0344–25052).—*Chief Exec.*, S. J. Charkham.

INLAND REVENUE STAFF FEDERATION (51,409), Douglas Houghton House, 231 Vauxhall Bridge Road, SW1V 1EH. (Tel: 071–834 8254).—*Gen. Sec.*, C. Brooke.

INSTITUTION OF PROFESSIONALS, MANAGERS AND SPECIALISTS (91,524), 75–79 York Road, SE1 7AQ. (Tel: 071–928 9951).—*Gen. Sec.*, W. Brett.

IRON AND STEEL TRADES CONFEDERATION, THE (56,000), Swinton House, 324 Gray's Inn Road, WC1X 8DD. (Tel: 071–837 6691).—*Gen. Sec.*, R. L. Evans. *See also* p. 972.

MANUFACTURING, SCIENCE AND FINANCE UNION (MSF) (653,000), Park House, 64–66 Wandsworth Common North Side, SW18 2SH. (Tel: 081–871 2100).—*Gen. Sec.*, R. Lyons.

MILITARY AND ORCHESTRAL MUSICAL INSTRUMENT MAKERS' TRADE SOCIETY (43), 2 Whitehouse Avenue, Boreham Wood, Herts. WD6 1HD.—*Gen. Sec.*, F. McKenzie.

MUSICIANS' UNION (40,395), 60–62 Clapham Road, SW9 0JJ. (Tel: 071–582 5566).—*Gen. Sec.*, D. Scard.

NATIONAL AND LOCAL GOVERNMENT OFFICERS' ASSOCIATION (NALGO) (744,453), 1 Mabledon Place, WC1H 9AJ. (Tel: 071–388 2366).—*Gen. Sec.*, A. Jinkinson. *See* p. 972.

NATIONAL ASSOCIATION OF COLLIERY OVERMEN, DEPUTIES AND SHOTFIRERS (6,395), Simpson House, 48 Nether Hall Road, Doncaster DN1 2PZ. (Tel: 0302–368015).—*Sec.*, P. McNestry.

NATIONAL ASSOCIATION OF CO-OPERATIVE OFFICIALS (4,454), Coronation House, Arndale Centre, Manchester M4 2HW. (Tel: 061–834 6029).—*Gen. Sec.*, L. W. Ewing.

NATIONAL ASSOCIATION OF LICENSED HOUSE MANAGERS (11,000), 9 Coombe Lane, SW20 8NE. (Tel: 081–947 3080).—*Gen. Sec.*, J. Madden.

NATIONAL ASSOCIATION OF PROBATION OFFICERS (7,279), 3–4 Chivalry Road, SW11 1HT. (Tel: 071–223 4887).—*Sec.*, W. L. Beaumont.

NATIONAL ASSOCIATION OF SCHOOLMASTERS/UNION OF WOMEN TEACHERS (NAS/UWT) (166,331), Hillscourt Education Centre, Rose Hill, Rednal, Birmingham B45 8RS. (Tel: 021–453 6150).—*Gen. Sec.*, N. De Gruchy.

NATIONAL ASSOCIATION OF TEACHERS IN FURTHER AND HIGHER EDUCATION (80,000), 27 Britannia Street, WC1X 9JP. (Tel: 071–837 3636).—*Gen. Sec.*, G. Woolf.

NATIONAL COMMUNICATIONS UNION (151,523), Greystoke House, 150 Brunswick Road, W5 1AW. (Tel: 081–998 2981).—*Gen. Sec.*, A. I. Young.

NATIONAL GRAPHICAL ASSOCIATION 1982 (NGA '82), *see* p. 972.

NATIONAL LEAGUE OF THE BLIND AND DISABLED, THE (2,681), 2 Tenterden Road, N17 8BE. (Tel: 081–808 6030).—*Sec.*, M. A. Barrett.

NATIONAL UNION OF CIVIL AND PUBLIC SERVANTS (NUCPS) (113,488), 124–130 Southwark Street, SE1 0TU. (Tel: 071–928 9671).—*Gen. Sec.*, L. Christie.

NATIONAL UNION OF DOMESTIC APPLIANCES AND GENERAL OPERATIVES, THE (3,000), 6–8 Imperial Buildings, Corporation Street, Rotherham, S. Yorks. S60 1PB. (Tel: 0709–382820).—*Gen. Sec.*, A. McCarthy.

NATIONAL UNION OF HOSIERY AND KNITWEAR WORKERS, *see* p. 972.

NATIONAL UNION OF INSURANCE WORKERS (18,057), 27 Old Gloucester Street, WC1N 3AF. (Tel: 071–405 6798).—*Gen. Sec.*, K. Perry.

NATIONAL UNION OF JOURNALISTS (NUJ) (32,206), Acorn House, 314–320 Gray's Inn Road, WC1X 8DP. (Tel: 071–278 7916).—*Gen. Sec.*, J. Eccleston (*acting*).

NATIONAL UNION OF KNITWEAR, FOOTWEAR AND APPAREL TRADES (60,000), The Grange, Northampton Road, Earls Barton, Northampton NN6 0JH. (Tel: 0604–810326).—*Gen. Sec.*, G. Browett. *See also* p. 972.

NATIONAL UNION OF LOCK AND METAL WORKERS (5,004), Bellamy House, Wilkes Street, Willenhall, W. Midlands WV13 2BS. (Tel: 0902–366651).—*Gen. Sec.*, M. Bradley.

NATIONAL UNION OF MARINE, AVIATION AND SHIPPING TRANSPORT OFFICERS, THE (18,470), Oceanair House, 750–760 High Road, E11 3BB. (Tel: 081–989 6677).—*Gen. Sec.*, J. Newman.

NATIONAL UNION OF MINEWORKERS (NUM) (53,112), Holly Street, Sheffield S1 2GT. (Tel: 0742–766900).—*Sec.*, P. E. Heathfield.

NATIONAL UNION OF PUBLIC EMPLOYEES (NUPE) (578,992), Civic House, 20 Grand Depot Road, SE18 6SF. (Tel: 081–854 2244).—*Sec.*, R. K. Bickerstaffe. *See also* p. 972.

NATIONAL UNION OF RAIL, MARITIME AND TRANSPORT WORKERS (RMT) (120,000), Unity House, Euston Road, NW1 2BL. (Tel: 071–387 4771).—*Gen. Sec.*, J. Knapp. *See also* p. 972.

NATIONAL UNION OF SCALEMAKERS (779), Queensway House, 57 Livery Street, Birmingham B3 1HA. (Tel: 021–236 8998).—*Gen. Sec.*, A. F. Smith.

NATIONAL UNION OF SEAMEN, *see* p. 972.

NATIONAL UNION OF TAILORS AND GARMENT WORKERS, *see* p. 972.

NATIONAL UNION OF TEACHERS (NUT) (183,605), Hamilton House, Mabledon Place, WC1H 9BD. (Tel: 071–388 6191).—*Gen. Sec.*, D. McAvoy.

NATIONAL UNION OF THE FOOTWEAR, LEATHER AND ALLIED TRADES, *see below.*

NORTHERN CARPET TRADES' UNION (1,010), 22 Clare Road, Halifax HX1 2HX. (Tel: 0422–360492).—*Gen. Sec.*, K. Edmondson.

PATTERN WEAVERS SOCIETY (61), 38 St Paul's Road, Kirkheaton, Huddersfield HD5 0EY. (Tel: 0484–424988).—*Gen. Sec.*, K. Bradley.

POWER LOOM CARPET WEAVERS' AND TEXTILE WORKERS' UNION, THE (2,400), Carpet Weavers Hall, Callows Lane, Kidderminster, Worcs. DY10 2JG. (Tel: 0562–823192).—*Gen. Sec.*, R. White.

PRISON OFFICERS' ASSOCIATION, THE (25,795), Cronin House, 245 Church Street, N9 9HW. (Tel: 081–803 0255).—*Gen. Sec.*, D. Evans.

ROSSENDALE UNION OF BOOT, SHOE AND SLIPPER OPERATIVES, THE (2,329), Taylor House, 7 Tenterfield Street, Waterfoot, Rossendale, Lancs. BB4 7BA. (Tel: 0706–215657).—*Gen. Sec.*, M. Murray.

SCOTTISH PRISON OFFICERS' ASSOCIATION (3,900), 21 Calder Road, Edinburgh EH11 3PF. (Tel: 031–443 8105).—*Gen. Sec.*, W. Goodall.

SCOTTISH UNION OF POWER-LOOM OVERLOOKERS (70), 3 Napier Terrace, Dundee DD2 2SL. (Tel: 0382–612196).—*Sec.*, J. D. Reilly.

SHEFFIELD WOOL SHEAR WORKERS' UNION (17), 50 Bankfield Road, Malin Bridge, Sheffield S9 4RD. (Tel: 0742–333688).—*Sec.*, J. H. R. Cutler.

SOCIETY OF GRAPHICAL AND ALLIED TRADES 1982 (SOGAT '82), *see below.*

SOCIETY OF SHUTTLEMAKERS (20), 211 Burnley Road, Colne, Lancs. BB8 8JD. (Tel: 0282–866716).—*Gen. Sec.*, L. Illingworth.

SOCIETY OF TELECOM EXECUTIVES (27,151), 1 Park Road, Teddington, Middx. TW11 0AR. (Tel: 081–943 5181).—*Gen. Sec.*, S. Petch.

TRANSPORT AND GENERAL WORKERS' UNION (TGWU) (1,270,776), Transport House, Smith Square, SW1P 3JB. (Tel: 071–828 7788).—*Gen. Sec.*, R. Todd (until March 1992).

TRANSPORT SALARIED STAFFS' ASSOCIATION (39,000), Walkden House, 10 Melton Street, NW1 2EJ. (Tel: 071–387 2101).—*Gen. Sec.*, R. A. Rosser.

UNION OF COMMUNICATION WORKERS, THE (202,500), UCW House, Crescent Lane, SW4 9RN. (Tel: 071–622 9977).—*Gen. Sec.*, A. D. Tuffin.

UNION OF CONSTRUCTION, ALLIED TRADES AND TECHNICIANS (UCATT) (258,616), UCATT House, 177 Abbeville Road, SW4 9RL. (Tel: 071–622 2442).—*Sec.*, A. Williams.

UNION OF SHOP, DISTRIBUTIVE AND ALLIED WORKERS (USDAW) (361,789), Oakley, 188 Wilmslow Road, Fallowfield, Manchester M14 6LJ. (Tel: 061–224 2804).—*Sec.*, D. G. Davies.

UNITED ROAD TRANSPORT UNION (20,000), 76 High Lane, Chorlton, Manchester M21 1FD. (Tel: 061–881 6245).—*Gen. Sec.*, F. Griffin.

WIRE WORKERS' SECTION (Iron and Steel Trades Confederation) (4,500), Prospect House, Alma

Street, Sheffield S3 8SA. (Tel: 0742–721674).—*No Sec.*, A. M. Ardron. *See also below.*

WRITERS' GUILD OF GREAT BRITAIN, THE (1,800), 43 Edgware Road, W2 1EH. (Tel: 071–723 8074).—*Ger Sec.*, W. J. Jeffrey.

YORKSHIRE ASSOCIATION OF POWER LOOM OVERLOOK ERS (519), 20 Hallfield Road, Bradford BD1 3RG (Tel: 0274–727966).—*Gen. Sec.*, A. D. Barrow.

Mergers, etc, 1990–91

The Association of Cinematograph, Television an Allied Technicians (ACTT) amalgamated with th Broadcasting and Entertainments Trade Allianc (BETA) to form the Broadcasting, Entertainmen and Cinematograph Technicians' Union in Septem ber 1990.

The Health Visitors Association became a section c the Manufacturing, Science and Finance Union i August 1990.

The National Graphical Association 1982 (NGA '8: and the Society of Graphical and Allied Trade 1982 (SOGAT '82) amalgamated to form the Graph ical, Paper and Media Union (GPMU) in Septembe 1991.

The National Union of Hosiery and Knitwear Work ers amalgamated with the National Union of th Footwear, Leather and Allied Trades to form th National Union of Knitwear, Footwear and A parel Trades in January 1991.

The National Union of Railwaymen and the Nationa Union of Seamen amalgamated to form the N tional Union of Rail, Maritime and Transpor Workers (RMT) in September 1990.

The National Union of Tailors and Garment Worker amalgamated with GMB in March 1991.

The Wire Workers Union became a section of th Iron and Steel Trades Confederation in April 199

Mergers under consideration

The Civil and Public Services Association (CPSA and the National Union of Civil and Publ: Servants (NUCPS) were balloted on a possibl amalgamation on October 25, 1991.

Negotiations are still taking place between th Confederation of Health Service Employee (COHSE), the National and Local Governmen Officers' Union (NALGO) and the National Unior of Public Employees (NUPE) about the possibl amalgamation of the three unions.

Negotiations are taking place between the Nationa Union of Mineworkers and the Transport an General Workers Union about the possible ama gamation of the two unions.

Expelled from the TUC, September 1988 :

ELECTRICAL, ELECTRONIC, TELECOMMUNICATION AN PLUMBING UNION (EETPU) (367,411), Hayes Cour West Common Road, Bromley BR2 7AU. (Tel: 081 462 7755).—*Gen. Sec.*, P. Gallagher.

BEQUESTS TO CHARITY 1990–91

The alphabetical list below represents some of the principal charitable bequests from Wills published since the last edition. As prior bequests, expenses and inheritance tax are all deducted from the net figures given, the exact amounts left to charities are not known.

Nearly one in five of the estates listed include bequests to the National Trust. Among their largest legacies is the residue of the estate of Kathleen Collot; the residue of the estate of William Straw, which included a property in Worksop known as Gentleman's Gardens; the residue of the estate of Brian Heap; and the residue of the estate of Harry Fletcher.

There are nearly as many bequests to hospitals in the list. Arthur Armitage left the residue of his estate to Wakefield Health Authority, to provide medical equipment for patients under the care of the consultants at Pinderfields Hospital so that they could live in the community; Doris Macklin left the residue of her estate to the London Hospital for nephritis research. Henry Kemp left the bulk of his estate between his local church and the Bassetlaw Hospice at Worksop; and Caroline Robertson left half the residue of her estate to such charities as her trustees thought fit, preference to be given to the Barnsley Hospice Appeal and the Friends of Barnsley Hospital. Other bequests not listed include those of Isa Miles who left most of her £518,098 estate to equip two wards in any hospital established in the vicinity of Whitchurch, Bristol, within ten years of her death, and Dorothy Sutor who left nearly all her £534,301 estate to Moorfields Eye Hospital for research (but not any involving animals).

Animal charities still figure prominently in the list. The Feline Advisory Bureau received the residue of the estate of Grahame Budgen, but only if they procured a centrally-heated home for his cats Kara and Shan and a number of other conditions for their well-being. Other specific bequests for pets included the sum of £10,000 for the upkeep of Csoki, the parrot of Victoria Brown (listed below), while others not listed include £8,000 for the upkeep of any dog belonging to Marjorie Greenwood, of Inkberrow in Worcestershire, and £10,000 for the upkeep of two cats belonging to Sarah Hawker, of Bispham, Lancs.

Other charitable estates not listed below include Max Wall, the comedian, who left one-third of the residue of his £189,650 estate between Age Concern and 'Mentally Handicapped Children Blind and Deaf Children'. Jill Bennett, the actress, left the residue of her £582,530 estate to her mother if she survived her, otherwise to Battersea Dogs Home (her mother predeceased her). Dame Eva Turner, the Oldham-born opera singer, left a number of large bequests and the residue of her £574,731 estate between the Royal Northern School of Music, Manchester, the Royal College of Music, Manchester, and the Royal Academy of Music, London, all for singing scholarships.

Dinah Geraldine **Albright**, of Ledbury, Hertfordshire £3,382,271
(the residue equally between the Friends of the Poor and Gentlefolk's Help, Gloucester Diocesan Board of Finance, National Trust and the Albright Charitable Trust)

Arthur **Armitage**, of Ossett, W. Yorks £833,579
(the remainder to Wakefield Health Authority to establish the A. Armitage Trust for Pinderfields Hospital)

Frank Harvey **Ayling**, of Warnham, W. Sussex £2,109,864
(the residue to the Salvation Army)

Charles Gilbert **Baker**, of Worthing, W. Sussex £602,493
(£5,000 and one-third of the residue each to the Friends of Highgate School Society, London, and the Multiple Sclerosis Society, and £1,000 and one-third of the residue to the Psoriasis Association)

Barbara Mary **Barton**, of Wilmington, Honiton, Devon £1,044,197
(the residue equally between the Chest, Heart and Stroke Association, National Kidney Research Fund, Imperial Cancer Research Fund, Arthritis Care, SPANA, and the International Centre for Conservation Education, Guiting Power, Glos.)

Florence Annie **Bent**, of Llandudno, Gwynedd £751,847
(one-third of the residue each to the Salvation Army and the Christie Hospital, Manchester)

Lieselotte **Berkovitch**, of Lyndhurst Gardens, London NW3 . . . . £1,262,525
(11/225ths of the residue to the Jewish Welfare Board, 10/225ths of the residue each to the Friends of the Hebrew University of Jerusalem, Belsize Square, Synagogue, NW3, Jewish Blind Society, British Na'amat and B'nai Brith Housing Society, London, and 5/225ths of the residue to the Association of Baltic Jews in Great Britain)

Peter John **Blyth**, of Leigh Woods, Bristol £1,749,439
(the residue to the Friends of the Elderly)

Victoria Maisie **Brown**, of Oakhill Park, London NW3 . . . . £2,565,129
(the sum needed to provide a Tyne class or similar lifeboat and one-third of the residue to the RNLI, and one-third of the residue each to the Blue Cross and PDSA)

Grahame Howard **Budgen**, of Upper Bentley, Redditch, Worcs £1,047,457
(the residue to the Feline Advisory Bureau on condition they look after his cats)

Doreen Edith **Burgess**, of Burford, Oxon £2,289,978
(the residue equally between the John Masefield Cheshire Home, Burcot, Sue Ryder Foundation, Nettlebed, and the Convent of the Poor Sisters of Nazareth, Oxford)

Phyllis Vera **Caine**, of Worthing, W. Sussex £698,915
(the residue equally between St Barnabas Home, Worthing, Imperial Cancer Research Fund, Leukaemia Research Fund and the Nuffield Nursing Home Trust)

Michael Richard **Anstruther-Gough-Calthorpe**, of Petersham Place, London SW7 . . . . £3,112,929
(the residue to the Maranatha Christian Fellowship)

Violet Armstrong **Clay**, of Poole, Dorset . . . £715,760
(the residue equally between the Institute of Psycho-Analysis, Help the Aged and the Mental Health Foundation)

Mary Dugdale **Clayton**, of Edington, Westbury, Wilts £1,367,779
(certain china and half the residue to the National Trust)

Kathleen **Collot**, of Newtown, Powys . . . £1,880,377
(the residue equally between the Montgomeryshire Wildlife Trust and the National Trust)

Rose Aveline **Corbin**, of Brighton, E. Sussex £1,668,730
(the residue equally betweeen the Spastics Society, World Wide Fund for Nature and Barnardo's)

Lt.-Cdr. Francis Paul Usborne **Croker**, RN (retd), of
Southsea, Hants. £727,387
(the residue equally between the British Red
Cross Society and Salvation Army)

Edith Marjorie **Crow**, of Sidmouth,
Devon..................................£2,932,425
(one-quarter of the residue each to the Patrick
Charitable Trust and the Patrick Foundation)

Annie **Cufflin**, of Leasingham, Lincs £624,014
(the residue equally between the Bransby Home
of Rest for Horses, PDSA, National Canine
Defence League and Cats Protection League)

Philip Norman **Cutner**, of Henley-on-Thames,
Oxon................................£1,063,218
(£100,000 each to the Royal College of Surgeons
of Edinburgh, Royal College of Surgeons of
England and the Faculty of Medicine at Edinburgh University, and the residue, on the death
of his wife, equally between them)

Louise Margaret **Darkin**, of Farnham, Surrey £792,434
(one-sixth of the residue each to the Distressed
Gentlefolk's Aid Association and Guide Dogs for
the Blind Association, and one-twelfth of the
residue each to the PDSA, Battersea Dogs Home,
SPANA, Wood Green Animal Shelter, Brooke
Hospital for Animals, Blue Cross, Home of Rest
for Horses, Aylesbury, and Pine Ridge Dog
Sanctuary, Ascot)

Marjorie Annie **Davis**, of Newick, E. Sussex £2,133,189
(the residue to the Cheshire Foundation)

Esmond Samuel **De Beer**, CBE, FBA, of Stoke
Hammond, Bucks £842,295
(46 per cent of the residue to the Charities Aid
Foundation, 5 per cent of the residue each to the
London Library, National Art Collections Fund,
Friends of the National Libraries, Bodleian
Library, Oxford, British Academy and the Saxl
Fund of London University, and 3 per cent of the
residue each to Mill Hill School, London, New
College, Oxford, University College, London,
Durham University, Institute of Historical Re-
search at London University, Jewish Lads Bri-
gade, Save the Children Fund and National
Trust)

Philip Joseph **Fawdry**, of Henley-on-Thames,
Oxon..................................£640,984
(the residue equally between the Stonyhurst
Association Charitable Trusts and the Roman
Catholic Diocese of Birmingham)

Launa Dorothy **Fennamore**, of Plymouth,
Devon................................£714,029
(the residue to the National Trust for the upkeep
of Saltram House and Park, Plymouth)

Lady Frances Mary **Fermor**, of Sidmouth,
Devon................................£694,357
(the residue to the Geological Society, London)

Harry Walter **Fletcher**, of Esher,
Surrey £2,839,620
(the residue equally between the National Trust,
Princess Alice Hospice, Esher, and Salvation
Army)

Dr Ian Corbet **Fletcher**, of Woolton Hill,
Hants..................................£832,797
(the residue equally between the Children's
Society, NSPCC, Barnardo's and Multiple Sclerosis Society)

Kathleen Hope **Fraser**, of Ham Common, Surrey £582,784
(the residue to the Royal College of Physicians
for a scholarship to assist needy post-graduates)

Dr Ivan Joseph **Freedman**, of Sloane Avenue,
London SW3..........................£971,156
(his entire estate equally between the Imperial

Cancer Research Fund and Greater London
Fund for the Blind)

Eliza Agnes **Golding**, of Waterloo, Liverpool..................................£1,421,42ː
(£5,000 and half the residue to the Wood Green
Animal Shelter and half the residue to the
RSPCA)

Florence Elizabeth **Goodacre**, of North Chailey, E.
Sussex £680,51ː
(the residue to the New District Hospital,
Haywards Heath)

Marjorie Louise **Grahl**, of Gloucester £634,00ː
(the residue equally between the Royal Hospital
and Home for Incurables, London SW15, and the
RNIB)

Roger James **Green**, of Lyndhurst Road, London
NW3................................£1,573,05ː
(8 per cent of the residue each to Great Ormond
Street Hospital, Save the Children Fund, Children's Society, Cheshire Foundation, the Seek-
ers Trust and College of Psychic Studies, 7 per
cent each to Barnardo's and Salvation Army, 6
per cent to the NSPCC, 5 per cent to Greenpeace,
4 per cent to the Guide Dogs for the Blind
Association, 3 per cent to St Joseph's Hospice,
London E8, and 2 per cent each to the Marie
Curie Memorial Foundation and the Fellowship
of Friends)

Brian Burton **Heap**, of Bowdon, Greater
Manchester..........................£1,518,36ː
(the residue to the National Trust)

William **Hinchcliff**, of Upton, Wirral......£700,94ː
(the residue equally between the Royal Commonwealth Society for the Blind, RNIB and National
Trust)

George Palmer **Holt**, of Llanycil, Bala, Gwynedd................................£2,036,90ː
(the residue to the National Art Collections
Fund)

Sybil Dorothea **Howard**, MBE, of Esher, Surrey £926,33ː
(the residue equally between the National Trust
and RNIB)

Gladys Beatrice **Hudson**, of Kingston upon Thames,
Surrey £610,37ː
(the residue to the Injured Jockeys Fund)

Shirley **Hughes** of Cambridge £803,031
(the residue to the British Dental Association
for a research prize or scholarship)

John Lewis **Hunt**, of Dalbury, Lees, Derbyshire..............................£1,236,081
(the residue equally between the Derby Scanner
Appeal, RSPB, Imperial Cancer Research Fund
and British Diabetic Association)

Dorothy **Jacobs**, of Weymouth Street, London
W1..................................£703,93ː
(the residue for such charitable purposes as her
executors decide)

Bessie Anne **Jenkins**, of Cross Inn, Llanon,
Dyfed................................£1,343,79ː
(her entire estate equally between Bronglais
General Hospital, Aberystwyth, and Aberaeron
Cottage Hospital)

Ethel **Johnson**, of Thirsk, N. Yorks.......£858,04ː
(£7,100 and one-fifth of the residue to St Mary's
Parish Church, Thirsk, £1,000 and one-fifth of
the residue to the League of Friends of Lambert
Memorial Hospital, Thirsk, and one-fifth of the
residue each to the British Red Cross Society,
Missions to Seamen and Leukaemia Research
Fund)

Ivor Hilton **Jones**, of Kingston upon Thames,
Surrey £1,121,31ː
(the residue equally between the National Society for Cancer Relief, RNLI and British Heart
Foundation)

Eleanor Thelma **Joseph**, of Edgware, Middx. £618,150
(her entire estate equally between the World Wide Fund for Nature and RSPCA)

John Michael **Kahn**, of Iffley, Oxford £963,605
(the residue to the Save the Children Fund)

Henry **Kemp**, of Grove, Retford, Notts .. £1,639,407
(the residue equally between the Bassetlaw Hospice, Worksop, and Grove Church)

Doris Annie **Macklin**, of Felixstowe, Suffolk £962,529
(the residue to the London Hospital for research into nephritis)

Mavis Clare **Marlowe**, of Formby, Merseyside £740,102
(5/14ths of the residue to the Crusade Against All Cruelty to Animals, and 1/14th of the residue each to the National Anti-Vivisection Society, Animal Welfare Trust, International League for the Protection of Horses, Council of Justice to Animals, the Fund for the Replacement of Animals in Medical Experiments, Universities Federation for Animal Welfare, Animal Aid and the National Canine Defence League)

Dorothy Prestwich **Maslin**, of Sutton, Surrey £1,629,110
(the residue, after a life interest, to such charitable institutions as her executor thinks fit)

Kathleen Myfanwy **Matthison**, of Uplands, Swansea £1,106,512
(the residue equally between Oxfam, RSPCA, NSPCC, Distressed Gentlefolk's Aid Association, Guide Dogs for the Blind Association, RNLI, Multiple Sclerosis Society and the National Trust)

Eileen Margaret **Minchin**, of Beaconsfield, Bucks £816,315
(the residue equally between the British Union for the Abolition of Vivisection, RSPCA, Wood Green Animal Shelter, Home of Rest for Horses, Aylesbury, International League for the Protection of Horses, Blue Cross, Donkey Sanctuary, Sidmouth, National Trust, Battersea Dogs Home and RNIB)

Philip **Moss**, of Lewes, E. Sussex £1,526,342
(the residue for such charitable institutions or objects as his executor selects)

Agnes Muriel Barrow **Musson**, of Felixstowe, Suffolk £651,899
(1/17th of the residue each to Prescot Parish Church, Merseyside, St Ann's Church, Liverpool, NSPCC, Distressed Gentlefolk's Aid Association, Friends of the Clergy Corporation, RNIB, British Deaf Association, St Dunstan's, Institute of Cancer Research, Church Army, RNLI, RSPB, RSPCA, British Naturalists Association, Men of the Trees, and Wildfowl Trust, and 1/34th of the residue each to St Peter and St Paul's Church, Old Felixstowe, and St Andrew's Church, Felixstowe)

Sir Joseph **Nickerson**, of Rothwell, Lincs £7,479,207
(£75,000 to the Joseph Nickerson Rothwell Memorial Trust, £50,000 to the Joseph Nickerson Rothwell Young Persons Project, and certain property and bequests to the Joseph Nickerson Charitable Foundation)

Joyce **Owen**, of Didsbury, Manchester..... £629,400
(the residue equally between the Humane Education Society Convalescent Home, Wilmslow, Mabel Spur Cat Foundation, Wilmslow, Link Centre for Deafened People, Eastbourne, Guide Dogs for the Blind Association, British Deaf Association, National Society for Cancer Relief, PDSA, Save the Children Fund and Cats Protection League)

Edward **Partridge**, of Cobham, Surrey .. £1,841,361

(one-quarter of the residue to the Yehudi Menuhin School, Stoke D'Abernon, one-fifth to Guildford Diocesan Board of Finance, for their Aided Day Schools, one-eighth each to the Wood Green Animal Shelter and the Royal Horticultural Society, and one-tenth each to the Church of England Pensions Board, Corporation of the Sons of the Clergy, and the Agricola Club, Wye College, Ashford, Kent)

Hilda Mary **Pearce**, of Stedham, Midhurst, W. Sussex £621,265
(the residue equally between the Methodist Homes for the Aged, RUKBA, Distressed Gentlefolk's Aid Association, RNIB, Marie Curie Memorial Foundation and British Heart Foundation)

William Aubrey **Pegrum**, of Lyme Regis, Dorset £672,090
(the residue to the Marie Curie Memorial Foundation)

Doris Elsie **Penfold**, of Seaford, E. Sussex £1,035,438
(the residue equally between the Imperial Cancer Research Fund, National Trust and the Arthritis and Rheumatism Council)

Neville Jabez Egan **Pluck**, of Bentley, Ipswich £1,171,725
(one-third of the residue to the National Trust)

Evret George **Porter**, of Shropham, Norfolk £1,124,645
(one-fifth of the residue to the RNLI, for the Lowestoft Lifeboat, 3/20ths each to the Imperial Cancer Research Fund, Salvation Army, NSPCC, Save the Children Fund and Barnardo's, and 1/20th to the Norfolk Branch of the Farmers Benevolent Fund)

Gladys Isobel **Potts**, of Gosforth, Tyne and Wear £768,990
(the residue to the Northumberland Cheshire Homes)

Gladys **Reed**, of Godalming, Surrey £1,958,140
(the residue, as to the income for 10 years and then the capital, equally between ASBAH, Multiple Sclerosis Society, Spastics Society, Muscular Dystrophy Group, Cystic Fibrosis Research Trust, Mencap, Imperial Cancer Research Fund, RNIB and British Deaf Association)

Caroline Amelia **Robertson**, of Barnsley, S. Yorks £1,256,077
(half the residue to Edinburgh University and half for such charities as her trustees think fit, preference being given to the Barnsley Hospice Appeal and the Friends of Barnsley Hospital)

Eileen **Rogers**, of Ashbourne, Derbys. £673,519
(the residue equally between the Nightingale Continuing Care Unit, Derby, PDSA, Missions to Seamen, Queen Alexandra Hospital Home, Worthing, Imperial Cancer Research Fund, RNID, NSPCC, RSPCA, RNLI and Age Concern England)

Florence Elizabeth **Siebel**, of Winthorpe, Notts £1,166,184
(the residue to create a charity for the relief of elderly ill people living within 12 miles of Newark Town Hall)

Dr Hugh MacDonald **Sinclair**, of Sutton Courtenay, Oxon £1,385,350
(the residue to the International Nutrition Foundation)

Dorothea Ann **Smelt**, of Branksome Park, Dorset £1,146,366
(the residue equally between the RSPCA, Hampshire and Dorset Animal Home, Barnardo's, PDSA, RNLI, Save the Children Fund, Cancer Research Campaign and Mencap)

Francis William **Snelson**, of Richmond, Surrey £937,142
(the residue equally between the Humanist

Housing Association, Marie Curie Memorial Foundation, Oxfam and the Friends Service Council)

Willy **Soldan**, of Enfield, Middx £851,038
(the residue equally between Oxfam, Save the Children Fund, Marie Curie Memorial Foundation, National Trust and Abbeyfield Society)

Gladys Irene **Spencer**, of East Dean, Eastbourne £2,063,853
(3/14ths of the residue each to the RSPCA and British Heart Foundation, one-seventh to the Imperial Cancer Research Fund and 1/14th each to the National Association of the League of Hospital Friends, Abbeyfield Society, NSPCC, National Kidney Research Fund, Spastics Society and Salvation Army)

Margaret Max **Spencer**, of Branksome, Dorset £922,157
(£250 and the residue to the National Trust)

Marianne Sybil **Stewart**, of Beyton, Suffolk £885,497
(the residue equally between the WRVS, Distressed Gentlefolk's Aid Association, Sue Ryder Foundation and Save the Children Fund)

Pamela Mary **Fox-Strangways**, of Galmpton, Devon £752,736
(the residue equally between the South Devon Animal Shelter, Donkey Sanctuary, Sidmouth, PDSA, Cats Protection League, 'Anglo-Italian Society' and RSPB)

William **Straw**, of Worksop, Notts £1,507,024
(the residue to the National Trust)

Hon. John Douglas **Stuart**, of Shawfield Street, London SW3 .... £1,651,973
(20 per cent of the residue each to the National Hospital for Nervous Diseases, London, National Art Collections Fund, King Edward VII Hospital for Officers, London, and the Cancer Relief MacMillan Fund, and 10 per cent of the residue each to the Guide Dogs for the Blind Association and St Luke's Nursing Home, Sheffield)

Ernest Bartlett **Taylor**, of Witney, Oxon £1,715,824
(£750,000 for such charitable purposes as his trustees select)

Rose Violet Edith **Teasdale**, of Highcliffe, Dorset £957,282
(one-quarter of the residue each to the RNIB, Florence Nightingale Hospital, London, and RAF Benevolent Fund, and one-twelfth each to York Minster, Stoke Mandeville Hospital, and Gifford House, Worthing)

Iris Winifred **Thomas**, of Epping, Essex . £1,091,527
(one-eighth of the residue each to Mencap, Guide Dogs for the Blind Association, St Joseph's Hospice, London E8, and St Francis Hospice, Havering-atte-Bower)

Arthur William **Trigg**, of Walton-on-Thames, Surrey £1,006,28
(the residue equally between the British Heart Foundation and the Royal College of Surgeons)

Johannes **Van Lohuizen**, of Cambridge ... £675,13
(his home, library and other effects to the Ancient India and Iran Trust and 10 per cent of the residue to support this bequest, and 90 per cent of the residue for charitable purposes for the advancement of education in the area of South and South-East Asian art history)

Constance Gertrude **Ward**, of Repton, Derbys. £864,76
(the residue to Help the Aged, Guildford, Surrey, part to be used for a Gifted Housing Scheme in or near Repton)

Sally, Duchess of **Westminster**, of Wickwar, Avon £1,308,84
(half the residue for such charities in Cheshire as the 6th Duke of Westminster decides)

Marjory Constance **Whayman**, of Romford, Essex £1,355,37
(1/50th of the residue each to the Migraine Trust, British Heart Foundation, Arthritis and Rheumatism Council, Cancer Research Campaign, and St Francis Hospice, Havering-atte-Bower)

Margaret Mercie **Wynn-Williams**, of Upper Richmond Road, London SW15 .... £628,56
(the residue to the National Trust)

Geoffrey **Wilson**, of Tenterden, Kent £1,496,70
(the residue equally between the RSPCA, NSPCC, RNLI, Guide Dogs for the Blind Association and Cancer Research Campaign)

Maurice **Winston**, of Brighton, E. Sussex .. £779,78
(£125,000 to the Royal Sussex County Hospital, Brighton, for the General Surgical Department, and £75,000 and 75 parts of the residue for its Cardiology Department; £40,000 and 40 parts of the residue to the Tarner Home, Brighton; £25,000 and 25 parts of the residue each to the Save the Children Fund, Barnardo's and Imperial Cancer Research Fund; £20,000 and 20 parts of the residue each to St Barnabas Hospice, Worthing, Help the Aged and the Arthritis and Rheumatism Council; £10,000 and ten parts of the residue each to the Jewish Old Age Home, Brighton, the Worthing, Littlehampton and District Branch of the Spastics Society, Salvation Army, Cancer Relief MacMillan Fund, Multiple Sclerosis Society, Alzheimers Disease Society, Cystic Fibrosis Research Trust, Leukaemia Research Fund and Abbeyfield Society; £5,000 and five parts of the residue to Copper Cliff Hospice, Brighton)

Anne Elizabeth Phoebe Cynthia **Zur Nedden**, of Stapeley, Cheshire £782,37
(the residue to the RSPCA, for a home and refuge with a clinic at Stapeley)

THE NOBEL PRIZES

For prize winners for the years 1901–1987, *see* earlier editions of WHITAKER'S ALMANACK.

The Nobel Prizes are awarded each year from the income of a trust fund established by the Swedish scientist Alfred Nobel, the inventor of dynamite, who died on December 10, 1896, leaving a fortune of £1,750,000. The prizes are awarded to those who have contributed most to the common good in the domain of:

  (a) Physics, awarded by the Royal Swedish Academy of Sciences;
  (b) Chemistry, awarded by the Royal Swedish Academy of Sciences;
  (c) Physiology or Medicine, awarded by the Karolinska Institute;
  (d) Literature, awarded by the Swedish Academy of Arts;
  (e) Peace, awarded by a five-person committee elected by the Norwegian Storting;
  (f) Economic Sciences (instituted 1969), awarded by the Royal Swedish Academy of Sciences.

The first awards were made in 1901 on the fifth anniversary of Nobel's death. The prizes are awarded every year on December 10, the anniversary of Nobel's death.

The Trust is administered by the board of directors of the Nobel Foundation, Stockholm, consisting of five members and three deputy members. The Swedish Government appoints a chairman and a deputy chairman, the remaining members being appointed by the awarding authorities.

Prize	1988	1989	1990
PHYSICS	Dr L. Lederman (American) Dr M. Schwartz (American) Dr J. Steinberger (American)	Prof. N. Ramsey (American) Prof. H. Dehmelt (American) Prof. W. Paul (W. German)	Prof. J. Friedman (American) Prof. H. Kendall (American) Prof. R. Taylor (Canadian)
CHEMISTRY	Dr J. Deisenhofer (W. German) Dr R. Huber (W. German) Dr H. Michel (W. German)	Prof. T. Cech (American) Prof. S. Altman (American)	Prof. E. Corey (American)
PHYSIOLOGY OR MEDICINE	Sir James Black (British) Dr G. Elion (American) Dr G. Hitchings (American)	Prof. J. M. Bishop (American) Prof. H. E. Varmus (American)	Dr J. Murray (American) Dr E. D. Thomas (American)
LITERATURE	N. Mahfouz (Egyptian)	C. José Cela (Spanish)	O. Paz (Mexican)
PEACE	United Nations peacekeeping forces	HH the Dalai Lama of Tibet (Tibetan)	Pres. M. Gorbachev (Russian)
ECONOMICS	Prof. M. Allais (French)	T. Haavelmo (Norwegian)	Prof. H. Markowitz (American) Prof. M. Miller (American) Prof. W. Sharpe (American)

The awards have been distributed as follows:

PHYSICS.—American 55; British 20; German 19 (1948–90, W. German 8); French 9; Russian 7; Dutch 6; Swedish 4; Austrian 3; Danish 3; Italian 3; Japanese 3; Chinese 2; Swiss 2; Canadian 1; Indian 1; Irish 1; Pakistani 1.

CHEMISTRY.—American 36; German 27 (1948–90, W. German 10); British 23; French 7; Swedish 4; Swiss 4; Canadian 2; Dutch 2; Argentinian 1; Austrian 1; Belgian 1; Czech 1; Finnish 1; Hungarian 1; Italian 1; Japanese 1; Norwegian 1; Russian 1.

PHYSIOLOGY/MEDICINE.—American 67; British 22; German 12 (1948–90, W. German 4); French 7; Swedish 7; Danish 5; Swiss 5; Austrian 4; Belgian 4; Italian 3; Australian 2; Canadian 2; Dutch 2; Hungarian 2; Russian 2; Argentinian 1; Japanese 1; Portuguese 1; S. African 1; Spanish 1.

LITERATURE.—French 12; American 9; British 8; Swedish 7; German 6 (1948–90, W. German 1); Italian 5; Spanish 5; Danish 3; Norwegian 3; Russian 3; Chilean 2; Greek 2; Irish 2; Polish 2; Swiss 2; Australian 1; Belgian 1; Colombian 1; Czech 1; Egyptian 1; Finnish 1; Guatemalan 1; Icelandic 1; Indian 1; Israeli 1; Japanese 1; Mexican 1; Nigerian 1; Yugoslav 1; Stateless 1.

PEACE.—American 17; Institutions 16; British 9; French 9; Swedish 5; German 4 (1948–90, W. German 1); Belgian 3; Swiss 3; Argentinian 2; Austrian 2; Norwegian 2; Russian 2; S. African 2; Canadian 1; Costa Rican 1; Danish 1; Dutch 1; Egyptian 1; Irish 1; Israeli 1; Italian 1; Japanese 1; Mexican 1; Polish 1; Tibetan 1; Vietnamese 1; Yugoslav 1.

ECONOMICS.—American 18; British 5; Norwegian 2; Swedish 2; Dutch 1; French 1; Russian 1.

BRITISH CURRENCY

COIN

Gold Coins
†One hundred pounds £100
†Fifty pounds £50
†Twenty-five pounds £25
†Ten pounds £10
Five pounds £5
Two pounds £2
Sovereign £1
Half-Sovereign 50p

Silver Coins
‡*Maundy Money*
Fourpence 4p
Threepence 3p
Twopence 2p
Penny 1p

Nickel-Brass Coins
Two pounds £2
One pound £1

Cupro-Nickel Coins
Crown £5 (1990)
50 pence 50p
Crown 25p
20 pence 20p
10 pence 10p
§5 pence 5p

Bronze Coins
2 pence 2p
1 penny 1p

†Britannia gold bullion coins, introduced in October 1987.

‡Gifts of special money distributed by the Sovereign annually on Maundy Thursday to the number of aged poor men and women corresponding to the Sovereign's own age.

§New 5 pence coin introduced on June 27, 1990.

Gold Coin

Gold ceased to circulate during the First World War. An Order of April 27, 1966, made it illegal for UK residents to continue holding more than four gold coins minted after 1837, or to acquire such coins unless they had been licensed as genuine collectors by the Bank of England. This Order was revoked on April 1, 1971, by the Exchange Control (Gold Coins Exemption) Order, 1971, whereby residents of the United Kingdom, Channel Islands and the Isle of Man may freely buy and sell and hold gold coins.

The 1971 Order was revoked on April 15, 1975, by the Exchange Control (Gold Coins Exemption) Order, 1975. Under this Order, Section 1 of the Exchange Control Act 1947 (which prohibits dealings in gold or foreign currency except with Treasury permission) was exempted for gold coins minted in or before 1837. The import of gold coins minted after 1837 was prohibited except by authorized dealers in gold with individual import licences from the Department of Trade and Industry, and dealing between other UK residents was restricted to coins already held in the UK.

Under an amendment, dated December 16, 1977, the exemptions contained in the 1975 Order were extended to cover gold coins minted in or before 1937.

The 1975 controls over the import of and dealing in gold coins were abolished on June 13, 1979 under the Exchange Control (Gold Coins Exemption) Order

1979, and gold coins, with certain exceptions,* may now be imported and exported without restriction.

On April 1, 1982 the Government introduced VAT (currently 17·5 per cent) on sales of all gold coin.

Silver Coin

Prior to 1920 silver coins were struck from sterling silver, an alloy of which 925 parts in 1,000 were silver. In 1920 the proportion of silver was reduced to 500 parts. From January 1, 1947 all 'silver' coins, except Maundy money, have been struck from cupro-nickel, an alloy of copper 75 parts and nickel 25 parts, except for the 20p, composed of copper 84 parts, nickel 16 parts. Maundy coins continue to be struck from sterling silver.

Bronze Coin

Bronze, introduced in 1860 to replace copper, is currently an alloy of copper 97 parts, zinc 2·5 parts and tin 0·5 part. These proportions have been subject to slight variations in the past.

The 'remedy' is the amount of variation from standard permitted in weight and fineness of coins when first issued from the Mint.

Legal tender

Gold, dated 1838 onwards, if not below least current weight, is legal tender to any amount. £5 (Crown 1990), £2 and £1 coins are legal tender to any amount; 50p and 20p coins are legal tender up to £10; 10p and 5p coins are legal tender up to £5, and bronze coins are legal tender for amounts up to 20p. Farthings ceased to be legal tender on December 31, 1960, the halfpenny on August 1, 1969, the halfcrown on January 1, 1970, the threepence and penny on August 31, 1971, the sixpence on June 30, 1980 and the decimal halfpenny on December 31, 1984. Also, the old 5p ceased to be legal tender after December 31, 1990.

The decimal system was introduced on February 15, 1971. Since 1982 the word 'new' in 'new pence' displayed on decimal coins has been dropped.

The Channel Islands and the Isle of Man issue their own coinage, which are legal tender only in the island of issue. (For denominations, *see* p. 979).

---

*Gold coins which are more than fifty years old and valued at a sum in excess of £8,000 cannot be exported without specific authorization from the Department of Trade and Industry.

Denomination	Metal	Standard weight (g)	Standard diameter (cm)
Penny	bronze	3·56400	2·0320
2 pence	bronze	7·12800	2·5910
5p	cupro-nickel	3·25	1·80
10 pence	cupro-nickel	11·31036	2·8500
20 pence	cupro-nickel	5·0	2·14
25p Crown	cupro-nickel	28·27590	3·8608
50 pence	cupro-nickel	13·5	3·0
£1	copper/nickel/zinc	9·5	2·25
£2	copper/nickel/zinc	15·98	2·84
£5 Crown	cupro-nickel	28·28	3·861

BANKNOTES

Bank of England notes are currently issued in denominations of £5, £10, £20 and £50 for the amount of the Fiduciary Note Issue, and are legal tender in England and Wales.

The old white notes for £10, £20, £50, £100, £500 and £1,000, which were issued until April 22, 1943, ceased to be legal tender in May 1945, and the old white £5 note in March 1946.

The white £5 note issued between October 1945 and September 1956, the £5 notes issued between 1957 and 1963, bearing a portrait of Britannia and the first series to bear a portrait of the Queen, issued between 1963 and 1971, ceased to be legal tender on March 14, 1961, June 27, 1967 and September 1, 1973 respectively. The series of £1 notes issued during the years 1928 to 1960 and the 10s. notes of the same type issued from 1928 to 1961—those without the royal portrait—ceased to be legal tender on May 29 and October 30, 1962 respectively. The £1 note first issued in March 1960 (bearing on the back a representation of Britannia) and the £10 note first issued in February 1964 (bearing a lion on the back) both bearing a portrait of the Queen on the front ceased to be legal tender on June 1, 1979. The £1 note first issued in 1978 ceased to be legal tender on March 11, 1988. The 10s. note was replaced by the 50p coin in October 1969, and ceased to be legal tender on November 21, 1970. Bank notes which are no longer legal tender are payable when presented at the Head Office of the Bank of England in London.

The first of the present D series of Bank notes was a £20 note issued on July 9, 1970. This was followed by the £5 note on November 11, 1971, £10 note on February 20, 1975, £1 note on February 9, 1978 and £50 note on March 20, 1981. The £1 coin was introduced on April 21, 1983 to replace the £1 note. The predominant identifying feature of each note is the portrayal on the back of a prominent figure from Britain's history, namely:

£5	The Duke of Wellington
£10	Florence Nightingale
£20	William Shakespeare
£50	Sir Christopher Wren

A new series of notes was introduced in June 1990 when a new £5 was issued, followed by a £20 note in June 1991. This new E series will eventually replace the D series. The historical figures portrayed in this series are:

£5	George Stephenson
£10	Charles Dickens
£20	Michael Faraday
£50	Sir John Houblon

The £10 and £50 notes will be issued over the next few years.

Note Circulation

Note circulation is highest at the two peak spending periods of the year—around Christmas and during the summer holiday period. A peak of £18,412 million was reached immediately prior to Christmas 1990, a 4·8 per cent increase on the previous year.

The proportion of the total value of notes in circulation of £1 notes at end February 1991 compared with the previous year, remained constant at 0·4 per cent. £5 notes fell from 10·2 per cent to 8·9 per cent. £10 notes decreased from 39·1 per cent to 37·8 per cent. £20 and £50 notes increased from 29·2 per cent and 15·3 per cent to 31·5 per cent and 15·4 per cent respectively.

On February 28, 1991 the values of notes in circulation were:

£1	£60,669,003
£5	£1,372,619,705
£10	£5,810,062,000
£20	£4,847,563,740
£50	£2,374,598,850

OTHER BANK NOTES

Scotland.—Bank notes are issued by three Scottish banks. The Royal Bank of Scotland and the Bank of Scotland issue notes for £5, £10, £20 and £100. The Royal Bank of Scotland also issues £1 notes. The Clydesdale Bank issues notes for £5, £10, £20, £50, £100. Scottish notes are not legal tender in Scotland but they enjoy there a status equal to that of the Bank of England note.

Northern Ireland.—Bank notes are issued by four banks in Northern Ireland. The Northern Bank and the Ulster Bank issue notes for £5, £10, £20, £50 and £100. The Allied Irish Bank and the Bank of Ireland issue notes for £5, £10, £20 and £100. Northern Irish notes are not legal tender in Northern Ireland but they circulate widely and enjoy a status comparable to that of Bank of England notes.

Channel Islands.—The States of Jersey issues its own currency notes and coinage. The note denominations are for £1, £5, £10, £20 and £50. Seven denominations of coins are issued: 1p, 2p, 5p, 10p, 20p, 50p and £1. The States of Guernsey issues its own currency notes and coinage. The notes are for £1, £5, £10 and £20. The denomination of coins are 1p, 2p, 5p, 10p, 20p, 50p, £1 and £2.

The Isle of Man.—The Isle of Man Government issues notes for £1, £5, £10, £20 and £50. Although these notes are only legal tender in the Isle of Man they are accepted at face value in branches of the clearing banks in the United Kingdom. The Isle of Man issues coins for 1p, 2p, 5p, 10p, 20p, 50p, £1, £2 and £5.

Although none of the series of notes specified above is legal tender in the United Kingdom they are generally accepted by the banks irrespective of their place of issue. At one time the banks made a commission charge for handling Scottish and Irish notes but this was abolished some years ago.

SLANG TERMS FOR MONEY
(Reproduced from *Whitaker's Almanack* 1891)

In addition to the ordinary terms there are others which, although puzzling to a foreigner, are tolerably well understood in this country. In Scotland, a man who flies 'kites' may not be worth a 'bodle', and in England not worth a 'mag'—coins which no one ever saw. Such a man will toss you for a 'bob'. He, of course, would be shunned by the lady who lost a 'pony' on last year's 'Oaks', and by her husband who lost a 'monkey' on the 'Derby' at Epsom a day or two previously. A gentleman who is worth a 'plum' (£100,000) need never be short of 'tin'; while the outcast who begs a few 'coppers' in order to procure a bed generally has no 'blunt'. The following words are commonly in use:

A Joey = 4d.	Half a Bull = 2s. 6d.	A Pony = £25.	Browns = Copper or bronze.
A Tanner = 6d.	A Bull = 5s.	A Monkey = £500.	Tin = Money generally.
A Bob = 1s.	A Quid = £1.	A Kite = An accommodation Bill.	Blunt = Silver, or money in general.

THE LONDON STOCK EXCHANGE

Old Broad Street, EC2N 1HP

[071-588 2355]

The International Stock Exchange of the United Kingdom and Republic of Ireland Ltd serves the needs of government, industry and investors by providing facilities for raising capital and a central market place for securities trading. There are 7,158 securities listed on the London Stock Exchange, which have a value of approximately £2,195,212·7 million. In 1990 securities worth some £1,666,637·9 million changed hands. This central market place covers not only government stocks (called gilts) and UK and overseas company shares (called equities and fixed interest stocks) but other investment instruments such as traded options on equities and indices.

Big Bang

During 1986 the London Stock Exchange went through the greatest period of change in its two hundred year history. In March 1986 it opened its doors for the first time to overseas and corporate membership of the Exchange, allowing banks, insurance companies and overseas securities houses to become members of the Exchange and to buy existing member firms. On October 27, 1986, three major reforms took place, changes which became known as 'Big Bang':

(1) abolition of scales of minimum commissions, allowing clients to negotiate freely with their brokers about the charge for their services

(2) abolition of the separation of member firms into brokers and jobbers. Under the new system, firms are broker/dealers, able to act as agents on behalf of clients; to act as principals buying and selling shares for their own account; and to become registered market makers, making continuous buying and selling prices in specific securities

(3) the introduction of the Stock Exchange Automated Quotations (SEAQ) system. Market makers input their buying and selling prices into SEAQ, which displays the competing quotations on a composite page onscreen. For all but the smallest, least frequently traded UK companies, the volume of shares traded is also updated continuously throughout the day.

Of all these changes, the implementation of SEAQ has had perhaps the most visible effect. Dealing in stocks and shares now takes place via the telephone in the firms' own dealing rooms, rather than face to face on the floor of the Exchange. The new systems also provide increased investor protection. All deals taking place via the Exchange's SEAQ system are recorded on a database which can be used to resolve disputes or to carry out investigations.

Members of the London Stock Exchange buy and sell shares on behalf of the public, as well as institutions such as pension funds or insurance companies. In return for transacting the deal, the broker will charge a commission, which is usually based upon the value of the transaction. The market makers, or wholesalers, in each security do not charge a commission for their services, but will quote the broker two prices, a price at which they will buy and a price at which they will sell. It is the middle of these two prices which is published in lists of Stock Exchange prices in newspapers.

Regulatory Bodies

On November 12, 1986 members of the Exchange agreed to merge with members of the international broking community in London, based outside the Exchange, in order to form two new bodies—the International Stock Exchange of the United Kingdom and Republic of Ireland Ltd and the Securities Association Ltd These two regulatory bodies have been formed under the provisions of the Financial Services Act 1986, which requires investment businesses to be authorized and regulated by a self regulating organization (SRO) of which the Securities Association is one. The Act also requires business to be conducted through a registered investment exchange (RIE). The London Stock Exchange is an RIE, regulating four main markets: UK equities, international equities, gilts and options.

Primary Markets

The Exchange serves the needs of industry by providing a mechanism where they can raise capital for development and growth through the issue of listed securities. For a company entering the market for the first time there are two possible Stock Exchange markets, depending upon the size, history and requirements of the company. The first is the listed market, which exists for well-established companies which must comply with stringent criteria relating to all aspects of their operations. At present, companies coming to this market require a three-year trading record with a minimum of 25 per cent of the shares held in public hands. The Unlisted Securities Market was established in 1980 with less rigorous entry requirements designed with the smaller and newer company in mind. Companies at present are required to provide a two-year trading record and a minimum of 10 per cent of the shares must be in public hands.

Once admitted to the Exchange, all companies are obliged to keep their shareholders informed of their progress, making announcements of a price-sensitive nature through the Exchange's company announcements department.

The International Stock Exchange has its headquarters in London, and administrative centres around the UK and the Republic of Ireland. At present there are some 5,178 individual members and 402 member firms.

The Governing Board

The interests of the membership of the London Stock Exchange are reflected in the governing Board, whose members are responsible for overall policy and the strategic direction of the Exchange. The three strategic business units; Primary Markets (responsible for the Exchange's functions as a competent authority for listing in the United Kingdom), Trading Markets (responsible for the Exchange's functions as a recognized investment exchange for a variety of trading markets) and Settlement Services (responsible for the Exchange's clearing house functions), are represented on the Board by their respective board chairmen. The Board also consists of representatives drawn from Stock Exchange member firms, listed companies, investors and other major users, elected at the annual general meeting, and the Government Broker, the Chief Executive and up to five senior executives of the Stock Exchange.

Chairman, A. C. Hugh Smith.
Chief Executive of Stock Exchange, P. J. Rawlins.

INSURANCE

Authorization of Insurance Companies

Section Three of the Insurance Companies Act 1982 empowers the Department of Trade and Industry (Insurance Division, 10–18 Victoria Street, SW1H 0NN) to authorize corporate bodies to transact insurance in the United Kingdom provided they comply with the financial and other regulations detailed in the Act.

At the end of 1990 there were 839 insurance companies with authorization to transact one or more classes of insurance business in the UK.

Regulation of Insurance Companies

Under the Financial Services Act 1986, the Securities and Investments Board (SIB) is empowered to make, monitor and enforce rules about the conduct of investment business.

The SIB has, in turn, set up a number of self-regulating organizations dealing with different sectors of the investment market. Insurance companies offering long-term contracts like life insurance, pensions, unit trusts and annuities can either obtain authorization directly from SIB or from the main SRO dealing with the marketing of life insurance and pensions, the Life And Unit Trust Regulatory Organization (LAUTRO), Centre Point, 103 New Oxford Street, WC1A 1QH. It is possible that insurers may also need authorization from other SROs, for example, the Investment Management Regulatory Organization (IMRO), Centre Point, 103 New Oxford Street, WC1A 1QH.

Association of British Insurers

Ninety per cent of the world-wide business of insurance companies is transacted by the 450 members of the Association of British Insurers. This trade association has represented both life and general insurers since 1985 when it replaced the British Insurance Association, the Life Offices Association and other such organizations.

GENERAL INSURANCE

1990 was a year of record losses with UK companies recording an overall underwriting loss just under £5,000 million. An indication of the troubled year ahead came in January and early February 1990 with the worst-ever storms and floods leading to claims for £2,081 million, the largest UK loss in history, dwarfing the £1,050 million cost of the storm in October 1987.

The rest of the year continued in similar vein, with total fire claims exceeding £1 billion for the first time, theft claims rising to £597 m (34 per cent up on 1989) and a second consecutive dry summer causing claims for subsidence to rise to £500 million, five times the previous average. These losses have forced insurers drastically to revise premium rates, with many predicting increases of around 30 per cent, particularly for home and motor policies.

BRITISH INSURANCE COMPANIES IN 1990

The following insurance company figures refer to members of the Association of British Insurers, and also to certain non-members.

World-wide General Business Trading Result

	1988 £m	1989 £m	1990 £m
Net written premiums	21,902	25,247	25,518
Underwriting profit/loss for one year account business			
Motor	−374	−778	−1,413
Fire and Accident	−643	−643	−2,669
Transfer to profit and loss account for other business			
Marine, Aviation, Transport	+29	−174	−382
Other	−106	−375	−524
Total underwriting result	−568	−1,970	−4,988
Investment income	2,918	3,546	3,506
Overall trading profit	2,350	1,575	−1,482
Profit as a % of premium income	+10·7	+6·2%	−5·8%

World-wide General Business Underwriting Result

	1989				1990			
	UK	USA	Other	Total	UK	USA	Other	Total
Fire and Accident								
Premiums (£m)	7,947	1,997	3,011	12,954	8,805	1,689	3,017	13,511
Profit/loss (£m)	−19·4	−363·8	−331·9	−715·1	−1,939·5	−236·3	−493·6	−2,669·5
% of premiums	−0·2	−18·2	−11·0	−5·5	−22·0	−14·0	−16·4	−19·8
Motor								
Premiums (£m)	4,539	1,369	2,323	8,231	4,839	1,203	2,387	8,428
Profit/loss (£m)	−276·7	−170·5	−322·9	−770·1	−904·3	−184·2	−324·6	−1,413·1
% of premiums	−6·1	−12·5	−13·9	−9·4	−18·7	−15·3	−13·6	−16·8

Net Premium Income by Territory 1990

	UK £m	Other EC countries £m	USA £m	Other overseas £m	Total (world-wide) £m	Increase %
Fire and Accident (non-motor)	9,352	1,279	1,768	3,039	15,438	+0·9
Motor...........................	4,905	1,102	1,204	1,314	8,525	+2·6
Marine, Aviation and Transport	1,162	151	131	111	1,555	−5·3
Total general business	**15,419**	**2,532**	**3,103**	**4,464**	**25,518**	**+1·1**
Ordinary long-term	32,140	1,995	1,824	2,776	38,735	+11·1
Industrial long-term	1,363	—	—	—	1,363	+0·7
Total long-term business	**33,503**	**1,995**	**1,824**	**2,776**	**40,097**	**+10·7**
TOTAL...................	48,922	4,527	4,927	7,240	65,615	+6·8

Claims Statistics

	1989	1990
Fire claims		
Commercial fires	£591·5 m	£784·6 m (+32·6%)
Domestic fires	£200·9 m	£220·6 m (+9·8%)
Theft claims		
Commercial theft (inc. money)	£167.9 m	£232·9 m (+38·7%)
Domestic theft	£276·4 m	£363·9 m (+31·7%)

LLOYD'S OF LONDON

Lloyd's of London is an incorporated society of private underwriters who provide an international market for almost any type of insurance. Ships, aircraft, oil rigs, cargo of all descriptions, motor cars, civil engineering projects, fire, personal accident and third party liability are a few random examples of the everyday risks placed at Lloyd's which currently earn a premium income of over £6,000 million for underwriters each year. Three-quarters of this business comes from outside Britain and makes a valuable contribution to the country's balance of payments.

A policy is subscribed at Lloyd's by private individuals with unlimited liability. A specialist underwriter accepts risks at Lloyd's on behalf of members (often referred to as 'names') grouped in a syndicate. There are currently over 28,000 members in some 444 syndicates of varying sizes, some with over two thousand names and each managed by an underwriting agent approved by the Council of Lloyd's.

Lloyd's membership today is drawn from many sources. Industry, commerce and the professions are strongly represented while many members work at Lloyd's either for brokerage firms or for underwriting agencies.

Underwriting membership of Lloyd's is open to men and women of any nationality provided that they meet the stringent financial requirements of the Society, or Corporation, of Lloyd's. Assets of up to £250,000 have to be shown and a deposit lodged with the Corporation as security for underwriting liabilities. This deposit, which must be in the form of approved securities, is determined at 30 per cent of the member's annual premium income.

Lloyd's is incorporated by Act of Parliament and governed by a Council of 28 members, twelve of whom are elected from and by underwriting members working at Lloyd's and eight from and by the external membership. Eight Council members are nominated by the Council, subject to confirmation by the Governor of the Bank of England.

The Council is a legislative body responsible for deciding on major policy matters, for regulating the Lloyd's market, for the election of new underwriting members, and for establishing the requirements of membership and the rules governing the financial security to be provided by those doing business at Lloyd's.

The Council's 'working' members form the Committee of Lloyd's, an executive body which is responsible for putting the Council's directives into effect, managing the Society's affairs, and administering the Lloyd's market on a day-to-day basis.

The Corporation is a non-profit-making body chiefly financed by its members' subscriptions. It provides the premises, administrative staff and services enabling Lloyd's underwriting syndicates to conduct their business. It does not, however, assume corporate liability for the risks accepted by its members, who remain responsible to the full extent of their personal means for their underwriting affairs.

Lloyd's syndicates have no direct contact with the public. All business is transacted through some 254 firms of insurance brokers accredited by the Corporation of Lloyd's. In addition, non-Lloyd's brokers in the UK when guaranteed by Lloyd's brokers, are able to deal directly with Lloyd's motor syndicates, a facility which has made the Lloyd's market more accessible to the insuring public.

Lloyd's also provides the most comprehensive shipping intelligence service available in the world. Shipping and other information received from Lloyd's agents, shipowners, news agencies and other sources throughout the world, is collated and distributed to newspapers, radio and television services, as well as to maritime and commercial interests in general. This information is published by Lloyd's of London Press Ltd and distributed worldwide. *Lloyd's List* is London's oldest daily newspaper and contains news of general commercial interest as well as shipping information. *Lloyd's Shipping Index*, also published daily, lists some 25,000 ocean-going vessels in alphabetical order and gives the latest known report of each.

Latest results

Like the insurance companies, the Lloyd's market suffered heavy losses in 1988 (the latest reported year), with many commentators expecting worse to come. For the first time in twenty-one years Lloyd's final global result was an overall loss of £510 million. Much of this loss has been caused by the need to strengthen reserves for legal liability claims, mainly from the USA. The much publicized result of these losses is that some Lloyd's 'names' have been called upon to make good the deficit from their own funds. These problems, together with a number of well-publicized scandals, have led to a number of writs, litigation and 'names' resigning from Lloyd's. The heavy losses have also provoked suggestions that the unlimited financial liability of 'names' should be restricted in some way. This would fundamentally alter the nature of membership of Lloyd's, which has always made it clear that a 'name' is financially committed 'to the last cufflink'.

Lloyd's Global Accounts
(as at December 31, 1990)

Year of account	1987 £'000	1988 £'000
Gross premiums	6,154,604	5,899,545
Premiums in respect of reinsurance ceded	1,959,696	2,185,891
Net premiums	4,194,908	3,713,654
Reinsurance premiums received from previous accounts	4,656,086	4,862,115
	8,850,994	8,575,769
Gross claims	5,617,587	7,532,872
Reinsurance recoveries	2,718,352	4,462,662
Net claims	2,899,235	3,070,210
Reinsurance premiums paid to close the accounts ...	5,540,054	6,054,797
	8,439,289	9,125,007
Underwriting result	411,705	(549,238)
Gross investment income	607,536	615,195
Gross investment appreciation	188,063	173,477
Gross investment return	795,599	788,672
Profit/(Loss) on currency exchange	14,532	5,673
	810,131	794,345
Result before syndicate expenses	1,221,836	245,107
Syndicate expenses	341,055	391,297
Closed year of account loss/profit	880,781	(146,190)
Names' personal expenses	371,618	363,483
(Loss attributable) profit available to Names before tax	509,163	(509,673)

Lloyd's Membership Syndicates and Brokers 1983–1990

	1983	1984	1985	1986	1987	1988	1989	1990
Membership	21,601	23,438	26,050	28,944	31,484	33,532	31,329	28,770
Of which Brokers........	272	265	261	258	258	275	260	254

Lloyd's Results 1988

Year of Account	Marine		Non-Marine		Aviation		Motor	
	1987	1988	1987	1988	1987	1988	1987	1988
	£m	£m	£m	£m	£m	£m	£m	£m
Net premiums..............	1,466·9	1,263·5	1,820·4	1,583·8	428·3	320·9	479·3	545·5
Underwriting result.........	146·9	(609·4)	8·7	(154·0)	176·0	112·2	80·1	102·0
Gross investment return	228·7	179·7	428·4	461·3	91·4	73·5	47·1	74·1
Closed year of account profit .	291·9	(551·3)	281·9	149·3	246·2	154·2	60·8	101·7

INSURANCE BROKERS

The Insurance Brokers Registration Act 1977 empowers the Insurance Brokers Registration Council (15 St Helens Place, EC3A 6DS) as the statutory body responsible for the registration of insurance brokers. The Council is responsible for the registration and training of insurance brokers, conduct of business, and discipline, and it lays down rules relating to such matters as accounting practice, staff qualifications, advertising, etc.

It is possible to act as an insurance intermediary without being registered with the IBRC but unregistered intermediaries are forbidden to use the words 'Insurance Broker' as a title.

IBRC Registered Brokers

	1991
Registered individuals	16,272
Limited Companies registered	3,112
Sole traders and partnerships...........	1,427
(containing 2,233 partners and directors)	

THE EUROPEAN COMMUNITY AND 1992

In 1986 the European Community's Heads of Government signed the Single European Act, which set out a programme of over 300 EC directives which are intended to achieve the removal of barriers to a free market within the community.

Progress on the establishment of a single European insurance market was very slow. Sir Leon Brittan, the EC Commissioner responsible for financial services and competition, outlined in November 1989 plans to introduce a number of directives which will help insurance catch up with other financial sectors in the preparation for a single European market.

In November 1989 Sir Leon announced his proposals for a 'single licence' system (already applying to banks and investment services) for the insurance sector. He also announced a very ambitious timetable for draft directives to give effect to these plans. The single licence concept envisages the supervisor in the insurer's home country carrying out all the financial supervision necessary. This would mean a UK insurer, authorized by the Department of Trade, would automatically satisfy the supervisory authority in all other EC countries. Sir Leon's proposals were published in the Non-Life Framework Directive on July 20, 1990. A comparable life framework directive was published in February 1991.

July 1990 saw the Non-Life Services Directive become operative. This made cross-frontier buying of non-life insurance possible. This had little effect in the UK, Netherlands, and, to some extent, Belgium, as they had an open insurance market already. In some of the remaining EC countries, before this directive was approved, it was not legally possible for even large insurance buyers to arrange cover outside their own borders.

Although the broad brush approach now being adopted by the EC Commission has accelerated moves towards a single European market in insurance, there is no prospect of it being fully in place before the end of 1992.

INVISIBLE EARNINGS OF INSURANCE

	1988	1989
Insurance	£3,772 m	£2,927 m

LIFE INSURANCE AND PENSIONS

Life Insurance in 1990

Despite an 11 per cent rise in total premium income to £40,000 million, 1990 was an extremely difficult year for life insurers. First, there were the effects of the recession. In any period of tighter money and rising unemployment there is a marked fall in the proportion of the average family's income available to buy life insurance. The year also saw a reduction in the level of demand for personal pensions. This was expected as it reflects the large number of people who had already opted out of SERPS in favour of a personal pension in earlier years when the DSS rebates were greater.

A further factor was the year-long slump in the housing market. The popularity of the endowment mortgage in the past had ensured a steady flow of business for life insurers which dried to a trickle with the stagnation of the housing market.

Despite the problems of the year, life insurance remained the most popular savings vehicle for the smaller investor.

Individual Pensions—New Business 1989–90

Personal (or self-employed) pensions	New annual premiums £m			New single premiums £m			DSS rebates* £m	
	Non-linked	Linked	Total	Non-linked	Linked	Total	Non-linked	Linked
1989								
1st quarter	120	126	246	194	112	305	236	230
2nd quarter	167	189	356	283	233	516	318	307
3rd quarter	101	124	225	262	226	488	80	141
4th quarter	96	122	218	372	282	654	80	113
1990								
1st quarter	109	153	262	385	354	739	88	106
2nd quarter	129	178	307	497	377	874	98	129
3rd quarter	94	136	230	371	364	736	80	100
4th quarter	146	137	282	365	385	750	118	118
12 months to:								
December 1989	484	562	1,046	1,111	853	1,963	714	791
December 1990	478	603	1,082	1,618	1,480	3,098	384	453

The figures given for total years are taken from the annual returns which are completed in the following year and therefore are more accurate than the total of the four quarters.
* The figures shown here are the best estimate of the current year's DSS rebates and incentives to be received under policies effected in the quarter, whether received or not.

Premium Income for World-wide Long-Term Insurance Business

	1988 £m	1989 £m	1990 £m
Ordinary Branch:			
Yearly premiums for life insurances, annuities and pensions in the UK	12,585	15,094	17,137 (+12·7%)
Single premiums for life insurances, annuities and pensions in the UK	8,044	12,772	14,692 (+12·3%)
Premiums for permanent health and other long-term insurances in the UK	226	270	311 (+16·3%)
Overseas premium income	4,845	6,289	6,595 (+4·5%)
Industrial Branch:			
Premium Income (UK only)	1,351	1,353	1,363 (+0·7%)

(Percentages shown are increases of 1990 figures over those for 1989).

World-wide Long-Term Insurance Business—Outgo

	1988 £m	1989 £m	1990 £m
Ordinary Branch:			
Total payments made to UK policyholders	13,998	15,984	19,141 (+19·2%)
Total payments made to overseas policyholders	2,213	3,308	3,219 (−2·8%)
Industrial Branch:			
Total payments made to UK policyholders	1,435	1,687	1,962 (+16·3%)

NB: Payments to policyholders includes death claims, maturities, annuities, surrenders (including planned cashing-in of linked and other similar savings policies and surrenders of bonus and bonuses in cash), refunds under pension schemes and payments under PHI and other long-term contracts.

Investments of insurance companies

In 1990, even their investment income was not enough to offset the underwriting losses of the general insurers. Below is a table of the types of investments of the insurance companies.

Investment of funds	Long-term business		General business	
	1989 £m	1990 £m	1989 £m	1990 £m
Index-linked British Government securities ...	4,220	3,592	134	225
British Government authority securities (excluding those in line 1)	29,086	27,395	5,665	5,233
Other government, provincial and municipal stocks	6,706	7,542	7,043	7,525
Debentures, loan stocks, preference and guaranteed stocks and shares	22,913	23,064	8,753	6,761
Ordinary stocks and shares	145,226	123,812	16,184	12,820
Mortgages	13,738	13,371	1,988	2,102
Real property and ground rents	42,585	37,888	4,324	4,130
Other invested assets	13,824	18,886	7,219	8,022
'Net current assets'	144	2,672	5,904	6,038
Total net assets	277,442	258,223	57,214	52,856
Gross income for year on investment holdings (gross of tax and interest paid)	15,415	17,391	3,893	3,913
Interest payable in year	447	601	358	406

DIRECTORY OF INSURANCE COMPANIES

The class of Insurance undertaken is shown in the second column as follows: A—Accident (which includes Motor, Employers' Liability, etc.); F—Fire (including Burglary); L—Life; M—Marine; and Re—Reinsurance.

A number of offices are now included in a Group—the initials of which appear after the name. The main Groups are as follows—ES—Eagle Star; CU—Commercial Union; GRE—Guardian Royal Exchange; GA—General Accident; NU—Norwich Union; R—Royal; SA—Sun Alliance & London.

Est.	Nature of Business	Name of Company	Address
1961	L	Abbey Life	80 Holdenhurst Road, Bournemouth BH8 8AL
1951	AFM Re	Albion	9–13 Fenchurch Buildings, EC3M 5HR
1824	AFLM	Alliance Assurance .... SA	1 Bartholomew Lane, EC2N 2AB
1965	L	Allied Dunbar	Allied Dunbar Centre, Swindon
1921	L	American Life	2–8 Altyre Road, Croydon CR9 2LG
1960	AF	Ansvar	31 St Leonards Road, Eastbourne BN21 3UR
1808	AFM	Atlas .... GRE	Royal Exchange, EC3V 3LS
1849	L	Australian Mutual Provident ..	A.M.P. House, Dingwall Rd., Croydon CR9 2AD
1925	AFL Re	Avon	Arden Street, Stratford-upon-Avon CV37 6WA
1905	AF	Baptist	1 Merchant Street E3 4LY
1965	L	Barclays	94 St Paul's Churchyard, EC4
1894	AFM	Bedford General	Zurich House, Stanhope Road, Portsmouth
1925	AFLM Re	Black Sea and Baltic	65 Fenchurch Street, EC3M 4EV
1959	AFLM	Bradford	North Park, Halifax HX1 2TU
	L	Britannia Life	190 West George Street, Glasgow
1866	AFL	Britannic	Moor Green, Moseley, Birmingham B13 8QF
1863	M	British & Foreign Marine .... R	New Hall Place, Liverpool
1878	Engineering	British Engine .... R	Longridge House, Manchester M60 4DT
1854	AFLM	British Equitable .... GRE	Royal Exchange, EC3V 3LS
1896	L	British Life Office	Reliance House, Mount Ephraim, Tunbridge Wells, Kent TN4 8BL
1908	FM	British Oak .... GRE	Royal Exchange, EC3V 3LS
1881	A	Builders' Accident	31 & 32 Bedford Street, Strand, WC2
1805	L	Caledonian .... GRE	Royal Exchange, EC3V 3LS
1934	AFM	Cambrian .... GRE	Royal Exchange, EC3V 3LS
1847	L	Canada Life	Canada Life House, Potters Bar, Herts. EN6 5BA
1963	L	Cannon Lincoln	1 Olympic Way, Wembley HA9 0NB
1903	AFM	Car & General .... GRE	Royal Exchange, EC3V 3LS
1922	AFMex-motor	Chemists' Mutual	321 Chase Road, Southgate, N14
	AL	Cigna Services UK	PO Box 42, Greenock, Renfrewshire PA15 1AB
	L	Citibank Life	Perrymount Road, Haywards Heath, W. Sussex RH16 3TP
1862	L	City of Glasgow Friendly	200 Bath Street, Glasgow G2 4HJ
1824	L	Clerical, Medical Group	10–14 John Adam Street, WC2N 6HA
1873	L	Colonial Mutual	24 Ludgate Hill, EC4P 4BD
1861	AFLMRe	Commercial Union	St Helen's, 1 Undershaft, EC3P 3DQ

Est.	Nature of Business	Name of Company	Address
1871	L	Confederation	Lytton Way, Stevenage, Herts SG1 2NN
1891	AF	Congregational and General	Currer House, Currer Street, Bradford BD1 5BA
1867	AFLM	Co-operative	Miller Street, Manchester M60 0AL
1905	AFLM Re	Cornhill	32 Cornhill, EC3V 3LJ
1900	L	Crown Financial Management	Crown House, Crown Square, Woking GU21 1XW
1899	A	Crusader	Woodhatch, Reigate, Surrey RH2 8BL
1908	AFM	Dominion	52–54 Leadenhall Street, EC3A 2AQ
1904	AFLM Re	Eagle Star	60 St Mary Axe, EC3A 8JQ
1887	AFL	Ecclesiastical	Beaufort House, Brunswick Road, Gloucester
1901	AFL	Economic	Economic House, 25 London Road, Sittingbourne, ME10 1PE
1880	AFM	Employers' Liability .... CU	St Helen's, 1 Undershaft, EC3
1932	Animal Ins.	Equine and Livestock	PO Box 100, Ouseburn, York YO5 9SZ
1762	L	Equitable Life	4 Coleman Street, EC2R 5AP
1844	L	Equity & Law	Amersham Road, High Wycombe, Bucks HP13 5AL
1802	AFM	Essex & Suffolk .... GRE	Royal Exchange, EC3V 3LS
1925	A	Federation	29 Linkfield Lane, Redhill, Surrey RH1 1JH
1890	AF	Fine Art & General .... CU	St Helen's, 1 Undershaft, EC3
1832	L	Friends' Provident	Pixham End, Dorking, Surrey
1899	L	FS Assurance	190 West George Street, Glasgow
1885	AFM Re	General Accident	Pitheavlis, Perth, Scotland
1837	LRe	General Accident Life	2 Rougier Street, York YO1 1HR
1910	AF	Gresham Fire & Accident	11 Queen Victoria Street, EC4N 4XP
1848	L	Gresham Life	2–6 Prince of Wales Road, Bournemouth
1840	AFM	Guarantee Society .... GA	36–37 Old Jewry, EC2
1821	L	Guardian Assurance ..... GRE	Royal Exchange, EC3V 3LS
1821	ALFM Re	Guardian Royal Exch. .... GRE	Royal Exchange, EC3V 3LS
1908	AFM	Hibernian	Haddington Road, Dublin 4
1960	L	Hill Samuel	NLA Tower, Addiscombe Road, Croydon
1932	FL	Ideal	Pitmaston, Birmingham, 13
1935	LAFM Re	Insurance Corporation of Ireland	Burlington Road, Dublin 4
1939	L	Irish Life	Lower Abbey Street, Dublin 2
1880	AF	Iron Trades	Iron Trades House, 21–24 Grosvenor Place, SW1V 7JA
1838	L	LAS Group	10 George Street, Edinburgh EH2 2YH
1896	L	Laurentian Life	Laurentian House, Barnwood, Glos GL4 7RZ
1836	AFLM Re	Legal and General	Temple Court, 11 Queen Victoria Street, EC4N 4TP
1970	L	Liberty Life	Liberty House, Station Road, New Barnet
1890	AF	Licenses & General	15 Bonhill Street, EC2A 4BY
1918	AFM	Liverpool Marine & General	4–5 King William Street, EC4
1843	L	Liverpool Victoria Friendly	Victoria House, Southampton Row, WC1B 4DB
1890	AFM	Local Government Guarantee ... GRE	Royal Exchange, EC3V 3LS
1836	AFM Re	Lombard Continental Insurance	77 Gracechurch Street, EC3
1894	AFM	London & Edinburgh	The Warren, Worthing, W. Sussex BN14 9QD
1919	AFM	London & Lancashire	New Hall Place, Liverpool
1869	L	London & Manchester	Winslade Park, Exeter, Devon EX5 1DS
1860	AFM	London & Provincial Marine ... GA	Lloyd's Building, Lime Street, EC3
1862	AFM	London & Scottish .... CU	St Helen's, 1 Undershaft, EC3
1869	AFM Re	London Guar. & Reinsurance	4 Colston Avenue, Bristol
1806	L	London Life	100 Temple Street, Bristol
1961	L	M & G Assurance	M & G House, Victoria Road, Chelmsford
1887	L	Manufacturers Life	St George's Way, Stevenage
1836	M	Marine	34–36 Lime Street, EC3
1864	M	Maritime	Surrey Street, Norwich
1884	L	Med., Sickness, Ann. and Life.	7–10 Chandos Street, Cavendish Square, W1A 2LN
1907	Re	Mercantile & General	Moorfields House, Moorfields, EC2Y 9AL
1970	L	Merchant Investors MI Group	91 Wimpole Street, W1M 7DA
1871	M	Merchants' Marine .... CU	St Helen's, 1 Undershaft, EC3
1872	AF	Methodist	Brazennose House, Brazennose Street, Manchester M2 5AS
1852	L	MGM Assurance	MGM House, Heene Road, Worthing BN11 2DY
1940	AFM	Minster	Minster House, Arthur Street, EC4
1906	AF	Motor Union .... GRE	Royal Exchange, EC3V 3LS
1903	AFL	Municipal Mutual	25–27 Old Queen Street, Westminster, SW1
1890	FL	Nalgo Insurance Association	137 Euston Road, NW1 2AU

Est.	Nature of Business	Name of Company	Address
1863	Fidelity Guar.	Natl. Guaran. & Suretyship CU	St Helen's, 1 Undershaft, EC3
1894	AF	National Ins. & Guarantee Cor. .	Heron House, 145 City Road, EC1
1830	L	National Mutual Life	The Priory, Hitchin, Herts. SG5 2DW
1835	L	National Provident Institution .	N.P. House, Tunbridge Wells, Kent TN1 2UE
1864	Machinery	National Vulcan Eng. Ins. Group . . . . SA	Empire House, St Martin's-le-Grand, EC1
1921	Naval Officers' risks, etc.	Navigators & General . . . . . . ES	113 Queens Road, Brighton BN1 3XN
1935	L	NEL Britannia	Milton Court, Dorking, Surrey RH4 3LZ
1914	AF	NEM Insurance	Station Road, Swindon, Wilts. SN1 1DF
1910	AFL Re	NFU Mutual	Tiddington Road, Stratford-upon-Avon CV37 7BJ
1869	L	N.M. Financial Management . . .	Enterprise House, Isambard Brunel Road, Portsmouth PO1 2AW
1809	AFLM	North British & Mercantile CU	St Helen's, 1 Undershaft, EC3
1836	AFLM	Northern . . . . CU	St Helen's, 1 Undershaft, EC3
1797	AFM Re	Norwich Union Fire	Surrey Street, Norwich
1808	L	Norwich Union Life	Surrey Street, Norwich
1871	AFM	Ocean Accident . . . . CU	St Helen's, 1 Undershaft, EC3
1859	M	Ocean Marine . . . . CU	St Helens, Undershaft, EC3
1931	AFM Aviation	Orion	Orion House, Bouverie Road West, Folkestone, Kent CT20 2RW
1886	AFM Re	Palatine	77 Leadenhall Street, EC3
1864	AFLM Re	Pearl	Pearl House, Thorpe Wood, Peterborough
1958	L Sickness A	Permanent	7–10 Chandos Street, Cavendish Square, W1
1782	AFLM	Phoenix . . . . SA	1 Bartholomew Lane, EC2N 2AB
1987	L	Prolific Life and Pensions	Bridge Mills, Stramongate, Kendal LA9 4UB
1969	L	Property Growth	Leon House, High Street, Croydon
1877	L	Provident Life Association	Provident Way, Basingstoke, Hampshire RG21 2SZ
1840	L	Provident Mutual Life	25–31 Moorgate, EC2R 6BA
1903	F	Provincial	Stramongate, Kendal, Cumbria LA9 4BE
1848	AFLM Re	Prudential	1 Stephen Street, W1P 2AP
1986	L	Prudential Holborn	30 Old Burlington Street, W1
1849	AF	Railway Passengers . . . . CU	St Helen's, 1 Undershaft, EC3
1864	AFL	Refuge	Refuge House, Alderley Road, Wilmslow, Cheshire SK9 1PF
1881	AFM	Reliance Marine . . . . GRE	Royal Exchange, EC3V 3LS
1911	L	Reliance Mutual	Reliance House, Mount Ephraim, Tunbridge Wells, Kent
1918	AF	Road Transport & General GA	Pitheavlis, Perth
1720	AF	Royal Exchange	Royal Exchange, EC3V 3LS
1971	L	Royal Heritage Life	Royal Ins. House, Business Park, Peterborough PE2 6GG
1845	L	Royal Life	PO Box 30, New Hall Place, Liverpool L69 3HS
1850	L	Royal Liver Friendly	Royal Liver Building, Pier Head, Liverpool L3 1HT
1861	AFL	Royal London	Royal London House, Middleborough, Colchester CO1 1RA
1887	L	Royal Nat. Pension Fund for Nurses	Burdett House, 15 Buckingham Street, Strand WC2N 6ED
1909	F	Salvation Army	117–121 Judd Street, WC1H 9NN
1963	L	Save and Prosper	1 Finsbury Avenue, EC2M
1826	L	Scottish Amicable	150 St Vincent Street, Glasgow G2 5NQ
1881	Engineering	Scottish Boiler . . . . GA	Pitheavlis, Perth, Scotland
1831	L	Scottish Equitable	28 St Andrew Square, Edinburgh EH2 1YF
1919	AFM	Scottish General . . . . GA	100 West Nile Street, Glasgow G2
1852	L	Scottish Legal	95 Bothwell Street, Glasgow G2
1881	L	Scottish Life	19 St Andrew Square, Edinburgh EH2 2YA
1883	L	Scottish Mutual	109 St Vincent Street, Glasgow G2 5HN
1837	L	Scottish Provident Institution .	6 St Andrew Square, Edinburgh EH2 2YA
1824	AFLM	Scottish Union & National NU	Surrey Street, Norwich
1815	L	Scottish Widows'	15 Dalkeith Road, Edinburgh EH16 5BU
1875	AFM	Sea . . . . SA	1 Bartholomew Lane, EC2
1904	L	Sentinel Life	2 Eyre Street Hill, EC1
1964	L	Stalwart Assurance	Stalwart House, 142 South Street, Dorking RH4 2EV
1825	L	Standard Life	3 George Street, Edinburgh EH2 2X2
1891	AFM	State Assurance . . . . GRE	Royal Exchange, EC3V 3LS
1710	AFLM	Sun Alliance and London	1 Bartholomew Lane, EC2N 2AB

Est.	Nature of Business	Name of Company	Address
1710	AFM	Sun Insurance Office ....SA	1 Bartholomew Lane, EC2N 2AB
1810	L	Sun Life Assurance Group	107 Cheapside, EC2V 6DU
1865	L Re	Sun Life of Canada	Basing View, Basingstoke, Hants. RG21 2DZ
1891	AL	Swiss Pioneer Life.............	16 Crosby Road North, Waterloo, Liverpool L22 0NY
1936	FL	Teacher's Assurance	12 Christchurch Road, Bournemouth BH1 3LW
1869	L	Tunstall & District	Station Chambers, Tunstall, Stoke-on-Trent ST6 6DU
1867	M	Ulster Marine .... GA	Pitheavlis, Perth
1714	AFM	Union Assurance.......... CU	St Helen's, 1 Undershaft, EC3
1835	AFM	Union Ins. Soc. of Canton GRE	Royal Exchange, EC3V 3LS
1863	M	Union Marine	4–5 King William Street, EC4
1908	AFL	United Friendly...............	42 Southwark Bridge Road, SE1
1963	L	UK Life Assurance	U.K. House, Worthing Road, Horsham
1825	L	University	4 Coleman Street, EC2R 5AP
1919	Re	Victory Reinsurance	Castle Hill Avenue, Folkestone, Kent CT20 2TF
1911	AF	Welsh Insurance Corp'n. ... CU	St Helen's, 1 Undershaft, EC3
1841	AFLRe	Wesleyan Assurance	Colmore Circus, Birmingham, B4 6AR
1912	AFLM	Western Australian	Swan Court, Mansel Road, Wimbledon, SW19
1886	AF	West of Scotland .... CU	26 George Street, Edinburgh 2
1865	AF	White Cross .... CU	St Helen's, 1 Undershaft, EC3
1963	AL	Windsor Life	Windsor House, Telford, Salop TF3 4NB.
1894	AFM	World Marine & General ... CU	Dunster House, Mark Lane, EC3
1872	AFM Re	Zurich	Zurich House, Stanhope Road, Portsmouth

EXPECTATION OF LIFE

(Interim figures)

	England and Wales		Scotland		Northern Ireland	
	Life Table, 1986–88		Life Table, 1986–88		Life Table, 1986–88	
Age	Males	Females	Males	Females	Males	Females
0............	72·4	78·1	70·3	76·5	70·6	76·7
5............	68·3	73·8	66·2	72·1	66·4	72·5
10............	63·4	68·9	61·2	67·2	61·5	67·6
15............	58·4	63·9	56·3	62·2	56·6	62·6
20............	53·6	59·0	51·5	57·3	51·8	57·7
25............	48·8	54·1	46·8	52·4	47·1	52·8
30............	44·0	49·2	42·0	47·5	42·4	47·9
35............	39·2	44·3	37·3	42·6	37·6	43·1
40............	34·5	39·5	32·6	37·8	32·9	38·3
45............	29·8	34·8	28·0	33·1	28·3	33·5
50............	25·3	30·2	23·7	28·6	23·9	28·9
55............	21·1	25·7	19·6	24·2	19·8	24·5
60............	17·2	21·5	16·0	20·2	16·0	20·4
65............	13·7	17·6	12·8	16·5	12·8	16·5
70............	10·7	14·0	10·0	13·1	10·0	13·0
75............	8·2	10·8	7·7	10·2	7·7	9·9
80............	6·2	8·0	5·8	7·6	5·7	7·2
85............	4·7	5·7	4·3	5·4	4·0	5·1

Source: HMSO—Annual Abstract of Statistics 1991

MUTUAL SOCIETIES

FRIENDLY SOCIETIES IN GREAT BRITAIN

Friendly societies are voluntary mutual organizations, the main purposes of which are the provision of relief or maintenance during sickness, unemployment or retirement, and the provision of life assurance. Many of the older traditional societies complement their business activities by social activity and a general care for individual members in ways normally outside the scope of a purely commercial organization. There are three main categories of friendly societies: societies with separately registered branches, commonly called orders; centralized societies, which conduct business directly with members (having no separately registered branches); and collecting societies. Collecting societies conduct industrial assurance business and are subject to the requirements of the Industrial Assurance Acts in addition to the Friendly Societies Acts. Industrial assurance is life assurance, the premiums in respect of which are payable at intervals of less than two months and are received by means of collectors who make house-to-house visits for the purpose.

Long before the term 'friendly society' came into use, the seeds of voluntary mutual insurance had been sown in the ancient religious and trade guilds. Guilds had become widespread in Britain by the 14th century. By then, the purely charitable character of the original guilds had largely changed with the emergence of numerous small institutions adopting primitive mutual insurance methods of a regular flat rate contribution to insure relief when sick or in old age and a payment to the widow in the event of death. The present register of friendly societies includes several societies which have been in existence for upwards of 200 years, the oldest, operating in Scotland, being the Incorporation of Carters in Leith, established as long ago as 1555.

The first Act for the encouragement and protection of friendly societies in this country was not passed until 1793, but various amending Acts were passed during the next century as the result of the recommendations of successive select committees (including a Royal Commission in 1871). For example, it was not until the 1829 Act that all registered friendly societies were required to keep proper records of individual sickness and mortality amongst their members, which data enabled the construction of standard actuarial tables showing the expected (average) duration of sickness at successive ages, and also (with data from the Census) the corresponding mortality rates.

The rules and other documents of societies deposited with local justices passed into the custody of the Registrar of Friendly Societies following the Act of 1846. Those relating to some societies no longer on the register have been transferred to the Public Record Office for permanent preservation.

The Friendly Societies Act 1974 allows other specific classes (described below) to be registered thereunder, but tax exemption is enjoyed only by registered friendly societies. The limit on premiums for tax-exempt life and endowment policies was increased to £150 per annum by section 49 of the Finance Act 1990.

Proposals for new legislation for friendly societies were set out in a Green Paper issued in 1990. These would enable societies to incorporate and to carry out a wider range of activities through subsidiaries, while retaining their mutual constitution and continuing their unique combination of business and caring mutual support. The Government has announced its intention to bring forward legislation in a future session of Parliament and a Bill is in preparation following consultation with representative bodies. The legislation is not expected to be enacted before mid-1992 and could be affected by the outcome of a General Election.

In addition to friendly societies there are three other main classes of society which may be registered under the Friendly Societies Act 1974: benevolent societies, working men's clubs and specially authorized societies. Benevolent societies are established for any charitable or benevolent purpose, to provide the same type of benefits as would be permissible for a friendly society, but in contrast the benefits must be for persons who are not members instead of, or in addition to, members. Working men's clubs provide social and recreational facilities for members. Specially authorized societies are registered for any purpose authorized by the Treasury as a purpose to which some or all of the provisions of the 1974 Act ought to be extended. Examples are societies for the promotion of science, literature and the fine arts, or to enable members to pursue an interest in sports and games.

The principal statistics at the end of 1989 are given in the table below.

	Orders and branches	Collecting societies	Other centralized societies	Benevolent societies	Working men's clubs	Specially authorized societies		Other
						Loan	Others	
Number of societies	2,024 (a)	31	431	81	2,404	9	141	1
Number of members 000's	431 (b)	14,574 (c)	2,754	279	2,078 (d)	14	94	—
Total benefits paid £000's	5,925 (b)	185,755	172,693	6,256	Not applicable	Not applicable	41	—
Total funds £000's	186,357 (b)	2,449,366	2,217,346	26,176	141,877 (d)	412	11,813	5

(a) 20 orders, 2,004 branches   (b) 1988 figures   (c) Assurances   (d) 1985 figures

INDUSTRIAL AND PROVIDENT SOCIETIES IN GREAT BRITAIN

The familiar 'Co-op' societies are amongst the wide variety which are registered under the Industrial and Provident Societies Act 1965. This consolidating Act which, like the Friendly Societies Act, is administered by the Chief Registrar of Friendly Societies, provides for the registration of societies and lays down the broad framework within which they must operate. Internal relations of societies are governed by their registered rules.

Registration under the Act confers upon a society corporate status by its registered name with perpetual succession and a common seal, and limited liability. A society qualifies for registration if it is carrying on an industry, business or trade, and it satisfies the Registrar either (a) that it is a bona fide co-operative society, or (b) that in view of the fact that its business is being, or is intended to be, conducted for the benefit of the community, there are special reasons why it

should be registered under the Act rather than as a company under the Companies Act.

The Credit Unions Act 1979 added a new class of society registerable under the 1965 Act. It also made provision for the supervision of these savings and loan bodies. Unlike other classes, where the role of the Registry is solely that of a registration authority, it is for credit unions the prudential supervisor, seeking to encourage the prudent safekeeping of investors' money.

During 1989 the number of registered societies of all classes increased by 372 to 11,243. The largest single group was the 4,497 housing societies. The largest group in terms of turnover was that consisting of the retail societies, which includes those trading under the 'Co-op' sign, with sales (in 1989) of £4,406 million. The principal statistics at the end of 1989 are given in the table below.

	Retail	Wholesale and productive	Agricultural	Fishing	Social and recreational clubs	General service	Housing	Credit unions	Total
Number of societies	210	219	1,098	100	3,784	1,132	4,497	203	11,243
Number of members 000's	7,588	757	389	8	2,948	258	143	40	12,131
Funds of members £000's	974,374	510,009	222,023	5,950	171,866	4,584,341	7,477,290	11,682	13,957,535
Total assets £000's	1,951,652	1,008,612	550,589	12,480	344,260	5,210,254	13,587,101	12,355	22,677,303

BUILDING SOCIETIES IN THE UNITED KINGDOM

The most significant event for the building societies in recent times was the passage of the Building Societies Act 1986, most of the provisions of which came into effect on January 1, 1987. The Act gave building societies a completely new legal framework, the first since the initial comprehensive building society legislation in 1874. The new Act replaced both the 1962 Act and the 1967 Act covering Northern Ireland, and therefore applies to societies based throughout the United Kingdom.

The 1986 Act made provision for a Building Societies Commission to promote the protection of shareholders and depositors, the financial stability of societies, and to administer the system of regulation of building societies provided under the Act. The First Commissioner and Chairman of the Commission is also Chief Registrar of Friendly Societies (*see* Index). Much of the Act is concerned with the powers of control of the Commission and provision in relation to the management of societies, accounts, audit and so on. But the greatest impact flowed from the new powers which societies could adopt, leading to an increased range of services which they might provide. There were also some significant changes in relation to members' rights.

Under the 1962 Act, raising funds to make loans was the only purpose for which a building society could exist. Under the 1986 Act that has only to be its principal purpose. The constitutional provisions include the right of members to have access to the register of members, entitlement to have notices of meetings and to vote, and the right of members to have a resolution circulated.

In addition to traditional mortgage business, the power of societies to lend in respect of shared ownership, index-linked and equity-linked schemes is given. Societies may also lend the deposit, lend on registered land before the borrower is registered as the owner and on other equitable interests. Provision is also made for societies to make advances secured on land outside the United Kingdom. Larger societies were able, for the first time, to make unsecured loans, and make loans on mobile homes.

Under the 1962 Act building societies could only hold land for the purposes of running their business. The 1986 Act gave building societies power to hold and develop land as a commercial asset. However, the land has to be primarily for residential purposes, or adjoining land, or for purposes incidental to the holding of residential land.

Detailed provisions were contained in the Act for an investor protection scheme similar to those in the Banking Act of 1979. The level of protection given is 90 per cent of accounts up to £10,000.

Societies were also empowered to offer for the first time the following services:—

(a) Money transmission services
(b) Foreign exchange services
(c) Making or receiving of payments as agents
(d) Management, as agents, of mortgage investments
(e) Management, as agents, of land (larger societies only)
(f) Arranging for the provision of services relating to the acquisition or disposal of investments for individuals.
(g) Establishment and management of personal equity plans.
(h) Arranging for the provision of credit to individuals.
(i) Establishment and management of unit trust schemes for the provision of pensions (through a subsidiary).
(j) Establishment and administration of pension schemes.
(k) Arranging for the provision of insurance of any description.
(l) Giving advice on insurance of any description.
(m) Estate agency service (through a subsidiary).
(n) Surveys and valuations of land.
(o) Conveyancing services.

Technical problems emerged in relation to these services and in June 1988 Parliament made Orders which allowed societies to have the power to own up to 100 per cent of a life assurance company, 15 per cent of a general insurance company, 100 per cent of a stockbroking company and to offer an additional range of financial services including executorship and trusteeship, hire purchase and leasing and safe deposit facilities. The Orders also included an increase in the limit on unsecured personal loans from £5,000 to £10,000.

Societies must belong to an ombudsman scheme for the investigation of complaints. Matters to be covered by the scheme include operation of share and deposit accounts, loans (but not the making of new loans), money transmission services, foreign exchange services, agency payments and receipts, and the provision of credit. Grounds for complaint include breach of the Act or contract, unfair treatment or maladministration, and where the complainant has suffered pecuniary loss or expense or inconvenience. A society must agree to be bound by decisions of the adjudicator unless it agrees to give notice to its members and the public of its reasons for not doing so. For address of the Building Societies Ombudsman scheme, see Index.

On mergers, the main difference is that borrowers have a vote. For a merger to be approved at least 50 per cent of borrowers who exercise their right to vote must vote in favour, as well as 75 per cent of qualifying share investors who vote. Provision is also made for a society to convert to company status. During 1989 the Abbey National became the first building society to complete the process of conversion to a company. During the year ended 31 March 1991 ten mergers between societies were completed but no society announced an intention to convert.

BUILDING SOCIETIES, 1980–1990

Year	Number of societies	Number of share holders 000's	Number of depositors 000's	Number of borrowers 000's	Share balances £m	Deposit balances £m
1980	273	30,636	915	5,383	48,915	1,742
1981	253	33,388	995	5,490	55,463	2,539
1982	227	36,609	1,094	5,643	64,977	3,447
1983	206	37,713	1,202	5,928	75,180	5,610
1984	190	39,385	1,550	6,317	88,078	8,426
1985	167	39,997	2,150	6,659	102,331	10,751
1986	151	40,563	2,850	7,025	115,538	16,864
1987	138	41,953	3,648	7,182	129,948	20,575
1988	131	43,816	4,306	7,369	149,791	26,529
1989	126	36,805	4,490	6,699	143,359	30,533
1990	117	36,948	4,299	6,724	160,538	40,696

Year	Mortgage balances £m	Total assets £m	Advances during year		Average mortgage rate %	Average share rate %
			Number 000's	Amount £m		
1980	42,437	53,793	936	9,503	14·92	10·34
1981	48,875	61,815	1,096	12,005	14·01	9·19
1982	56,691	73,033	1,320	14,971	13·32	8·77
1983	67,490	85,868	1,513	19,357	11·05	7·26
1984	81,879	102,688	1,657	23,767	11·83	7·71
1985	96,751	120,764	1,678	26,508	13·46	8·65
1986	115,644	140,603	2,058	35,885	12·07	7·75
1987	130,905	160,098	1,889	35,848	11·64	7·42
1988	153,015	188,844	2,080	47,375	11·25	7·04
1989	151,492	187,012	1,585	42,032	13·65	9·32
1990	175,745	216,848	1,397	43,081	15·12	10·53

SOCIETIES WITH TOTAL ASSETS EXCEEDING £1 MILLION AT END OF
FINANCIAL YEAR 1990

Year Established	* Name of Society (abbreviated) and Head Office	Share investors	Total assets £'000
1985	Alliance and Leicester, 49 Park Lane, London W1Y 4EQ	2,640,196	18,401,800
1853	Barnsley, Regent Street, Barnsley, South Yorks S70 2EH	27,251	140,519
1953	Bath Investment and Bldg. Soc., 20 Charles Street, Bath BA1 1HY	12,205	42,817
1881	Bedford Crown, 117 Midland Road, Bedford MK40 1DE.................	3,232	13,466
1866	Beverley, 57 Market Place, Beverley, N. Humberside, HU17 8AA	5,669	26,749
1914	Bexhill-on-Sea, 2 Devonshire Square, Bexhill-on-Sea, Sussex TN40 1AE ...	2,714	14,890
1889	Birmingham Midshires, PO Box 81, 35–49 Lichfield Street, Wolverhampton WV1 1EL	661,993	3,652,200
1851	Bradford and Bingley, PO Box 2, Bingley, West Yorks. BD16 2LW	2,040,802	9,047,661
1850	Bristol and West, Broad Quay, Bristol BS99 7AX	762,098	5,646,612
1856	Britannia, Newton House, Cheadle Road, Leek, Staffs. ST13 5RG	1,094,157	7,422,844
1907	Buckinghamshire, High Street, Chalfont St Giles, Bucks. HP8 4QB	5,969	38,554
1850	Cambridge, 32 St Andrew's Street, Cambridge CB2 3AR	32,000	232,980
1960	Catholic, 7 Strutton Ground, London SW1P 2HY	3,202	18,369
1899	Century, 23 Albany Street, Edinburgh EH1 3QW	1,076	8,694
1875	Chelsea, Thirlestaine Hall, Thirlestaine Road, Cheltenham, Glos. GL53 7AL....	205,371	2,089,520
1850	Cheltenham and Gloucester, Barnett Way, Gloucester GL4 7RL	913,426	11,570,900
1845	Chesham, 12 Market Square, Chesham, Bucks. HP5 1ER	8,047	51,307
1870	Cheshire, Castle Street, Macclesfield, Chesire SK11 6AH	216,812	905,584
1861	Cheshunt, 100 Crossbrook Street, Waltham Cross, Herts. EN8 8JJ	53,665	419,800
1859	Chorley and District, 49–51 St Thomas's Road, Chorley, Lancs. PR7 1JL ...	7,285	43,239
1946	City and Metropolitan, 219 High Street, Bromley, Kent BR1 1PR	10,587	82,151
1859	Clay Cross Benefit, 42 Thanet Street, Clay Cross, Chesterfield S45 9JT	3,136	11,935
1884	Coventry, PO Box 9, High Street, Coventry CV1 5QN	397,024	2,002,201
1850	Cumberland, 38 Fisher Street, Carlisle CA3 8RQ	132,812	410,346
1946	Darlington, Tubwell Row, Darlington, Co. Durham DL1 1NX	37,700	201,836
1859	Derbyshire, Duffield Hall, Duffield, Derby DE5 1AG	276,128	1,182,166
1858	Dudley, Dudley House, Stone Street, Dudley DY1 1NP	14,388	59,495
1869	Dunfermline, 12 East Port, Dunfermline, Fife KY12 7LD	112,950	547,935
1857	Earl Shilton, 22 The Hollow, Earl Shilton, Leicester LE9 7NB	9,357	44,824
1980	Ecology, 18 Station Road, Cross Hills, Keighley, West Yorks BD20 7EH ...	1,987	6,222
1865	Furness, 51–55 Duke Street, Barrow-in-Furness LA14 1RT	58,641	275,751
1911	Gainsborough, 26 Lord Street, Gainsborough, Lincs. DN21 2DB	4,203	17,138
1852	Greenwich, 279–283 Greenwich High Road, London SE10 8NL	28,120	133,970
1853	Halifax, Trinity Road, Halifax, West Yorks HX1 2RG	8,348,205	54,145,900
1866	Hampshire, Anchor House, Kingston Crescent, Portsmouth, Hants. PO2 8BX....	13,909	95,311
1854	Hanley Economic, 42 Cheapside, Hanley, Stoke-on-Trent, Staffs. ST1 1EX .	27,069	133,873
1953	Harpenden, 14 Station Road, Harpenden, Herts. AL5 4SE	8,462	35,742
1890	Haywards Heath, 33 Boltro Road, Haywards Heath, W. Sussex RH16 1BQ .	19,648	114,974
1863	Heart of England, Olympus Avenue, Tachbrook Park, Warwick CV34 6NQ	192,602	920,051
1865	Hinckley and Rugby, Upper Bond Street, Hinckley, Leics. LE10 1DG	40,365	219,602
1855	Holmesdale B., 43 Church Street, Reigate, Surrey RH2 0AE	6,784	50,986
1853	Ilkeston P., 24–26 South Street, Ilkeston, Derby DE2 5HQ.............	4,056	14,604
1849	Ipswich, 44 Upper Brook Street, Ipswich IP4 1DP	28,632	140,916
1888	Kent Reliance, Reliance House, Manor Road, Chatham, Kent ME4 6AF ...	45,347	207,782
1852	Lambeth, 118–120 Westminster Bridge Road, London SE1 7AX	42,247	481,015
1872	Lancastrian, Sadler Street, Middleton, Manchester M24 3UJ	48,427	279,991
1853	Leamington Spa, Leamington House, Milverton Hill, Leamington Spa, Warks. CV32 5FE	122,044	1,461,233
1875	Leeds and Holbeck, 105 Albion Street, Leeds LS1 5AS	248,349	1,827,810
1848	Leeds P., Permanent House, The Headrow, Leeds LS1 1NS	3,220,383	14,648,700
1863	Leek United, 50 St Edward Street, Leek, Staffs. ST13 5DH	46,289	243,753
1876	Londonderry Provident, 7 Castle Street, Londonderry BT48 6HQ	986	4,065
1867	Loughborough P., 6 High Street, Loughborough, Leics. LE11 2PY	11,757	70,053
1922	Manchester, 18–20 Bridge Street, Manchester M3 3BU	7,927	61,516
1870	Mansfield, Regent House, Regent Street, Mansfield, Notts. NG18 1SS	16,575	82,423
1870	Market Harborough, Welland House, The Square, Market Harborough, Leics. LE16 7PD	25,819	168,465
1860	Marsden, 6–20 Russell Street, Nelson, Lancs. BB9 7NJ	37,100	194,232
1874	Melton Mowbray, 39 Nottingham Street, Melton Mowbray, Leics. LE13 1NR	28,686	151,647
1966	Mercantile, 75 Howard Street, North Shields, Tyne and Wear NE30 1AQ..	18,820	107,828
1880	Mid-Sussex, Mid-Sussex House, 66 Church Road, Burgess Hill, Sussex RH15 9AU	5,468	23,658
1869	Monmouthshire, John Frost Square, Newport, Gwent NP9 1PX	16,700	108,507

* P. = Permanent; B. = Benefit. The words 'Building Society' are the last words in every society's name.

Year Estab- lished	Name of Society (abbreviated) and Head Office	Share investors	Total assets £'000
1866	Mornington, 158 Kentish Town Road, London NW5 2BT	19,206	188,522
1869	National and Provincial, Provincial House, Bradford BD1 1NL	1,636,250	9,272,000
1896	National Counties, Waterloo House, 147–153 High Street, Epsom, Surrey KT19 8EN	18,094	305,834
1884	Nationwide Anglia, Chesterfield House, Bloomsbury Way, London WC1V 6PW	6,249,831	31,124,838
1856	Newbury, 17–20 Bartholomew Street, Newbury, Berks. RG14 5LY	28,393	189,069
1863	Newcastle, Grainger Chambers, Hood Street, Newcastle upon Tyne NE1 6JP	126,428	852,062
1877	North of England, 57 Fawcett Street, Sunderland SR1 1SA	241,697	1,008,367
1850	Northern Rock, Northern Rock House, Gosforth, Newcastle upon Tyne NE3 4PL	713,259	3,420,397
1860	Norwich and Peterborough, Peterborough Business Park, Lynchwood, Peterborough PE2 0FZ	197,860	1,157,864
1850	Nottingham, 5–13 Upper Parliament Street, Nottingham NG1 2BX	130,889	539,139
1935	Nottingham Imperial, Imperial Building, 29 Bridgeford Road, West Bridgeford, Nottingham NG2 6AU	6,865	28,675
1877	Penrith, 7 King Street, Penrith, Cumbria CA11 7AR	6,874	38,986
1846	Portman, Portman House, Richmond Hill, Bournemouth, Dorset BH2 6EP	453,033	2,444,370
1896	Portsmouth, Churchill House, Winston Churchill Avenue, Portsmouth PO1 2EP	99,231	860,796
1860	Principality, PO Box 89, Principality Buildings, Queen Street, Cardiff CF1 1UA	220,781	908,683
1914	Progressive, 33–37 Wellington Place, Belfast BT1 6HH	33,862	210,426
1849	Saffron Walden, Herts. and Essex, 1A Market Street, Saffron Walden, Essex CB10 1HX	31,525	173,955
1937	St Pancras, 200 Finchley Road, London NW3 6DA	10,676	91,470
1846	Scarborough, Prospect House, 442/444 Scalby Road, Scarborough, Yorks. YO12 6EE	59,388	348,674
1848	Scottish, 23 Manor Place, Edinburgh EH3 7XE	16,414	85,208
1879	Shepshed, Bull Ring, Shepshed, Loughborough, Leics. LE12 9QD	6,359	25,142
1853	Skipton, 59 High Street, Skipton, Yorks. BD23 1DN	233,652	2,223,463
1876	Southdown, 40–42 Friars Walk, Lewes, East Sussex BN7 2LW	137,049	782,973
1877	Stafford Railway, 4 Market Square, Stafford ST16 2JH	7,515	35,858
1902	Staffordshire, Jubilee House, PO Box 66, 84 Salop Street, Wolverhampton WV3 0SA	169,277	740,790
1875	Standard, 64 Church Way, North Shields, Tyne and Wear NE29 0AF	2,153	13,198
1850	Stroud and Swindon, Rowcroft, Stroud, Glos. GL5 3BG	84,766	481,908
1861	Sun, 13 Tempest Hey, Liverpool L2 2AD	645	1,203
1903	Surrey, Sentinel House, 10–12 Massetts Road, Horley, Surrey RH6 7DE	9,290	73,781
1923	Swansea, 11 Cradock Street, Swansea SA1 3EW	3,115	22,335
1966	Teachers, Allenview House, Wimborne, Dorset BH21 1AG	9,498	104,844
1901	Tipton and Coseley, 57–60 High Street, Tipton, West Midlands DY4 8HG	15,095	64,147
1848	Town and Country, 215 Strand, London WC2R 1AY	222,459	2,224,139
1855	Tynemouth, 53–55 Howard Street, North Shields, Tyne and Wear NE30 1AF	6,265	40,387
1863	Universal, 41 Pilgrim Street, Newcastle upon Tyne NE1 6BT	25,646	140,795
1924	Vernon, 19 St Petersgate, Stockport, Cheshire SK1 1HF	20,553	90,442
1849	West Bromwich, 374 High Street, West Bromwich, West Midlands B70 8LR	280,971	1,022,607
1882	West Cumbria, Cumbria House, Murray Road, Workington CA14 2AD	6,545	29,599
1847	Woolwich Corporate Headquarters, Watling Street, Bexley Heath, Kent DA6 7RR	2,809,602	18,195,200
1885	Yorkshire, Yorkshire House, Westgate, Bradford BD1 2AU	682,918	3,586,116

THE COST OF LIVING

The first cost-of-living index to be calculated in Great Britain was the one which took July 1914 as 100 and was based on the pattern of expenditure of working class families in 1904. Since 1947 the Index of Retail Prices has superseded the cost-of-living index, although the older term is still often popularly applied to it. This index is designed to reflect the month-by-month changes in the average level of retail prices of goods and services purchased by the 'majority' of households in the United Kingdom, including practically all wage-earners and most small and medium salary-earners. For spending coming within the scope of the index, a representative list of items is selected and the prices actually charged for these items are collected at regular intervals. In working out the index figure, the price changes are 'weighted'—that is, given different degrees of importance—in accordance with the pattern of consumption of the average family.

A more widely used guide when considering changes in the average level of prices of all consumer goods and services, particularly over a number of years, is the consumer price index, now renamed the consumers' expenditure deflator. This index, which has been calculated back to 1938, covers the expenditure of all consumers as defined for national income purposes, and compares the price of goods and services actually purchased in a given year with the prices of the same goods and services in a base year.

During 1973 the Central Statistical Office constructed an annual index of prices of consumer goods and services over the period 1914 to 1972. This index has been constructed by linking together the pre-war cost of living index for the period 1914–1938, the consumers' expenditure deflator for the period 1938 and 1946–62* and the General Index of Retail Prices for the period 1962–1972.

In August 1979, the tax and price index (TPI) was introduced in order to provide a statistic which incorporates the effects of direct and indirect taxation, as well as prices, on taxpayers. The TPI is not directly concerned with the purchasing power of money, however, but with the purchasing power of pre-tax income. The General Index of Retail Prices thus retains its function of measuring the changes in the prices of goods and services purchased by households (from their post-tax income), and therefore as an indicator of the purchasing power of money.

* There are no official figures for 1939–45.

	Long Term Index of Consumer Goods and Services (Jan. 1987 = 100)	Comparable Purchasing Power of £1 in 1990
1914............	2·8	45·04
1915............	3·5	36·08
1920............	7·0	18·01
1925............	5·0	25·22
1930............	4·5	28·02
1935............	4·0	31·53
1938............	4·4	28·66
1946............	7·4	17·04
1950............	9·0	14·01
1955............	11·2	11·26
1960............	12·6	10·01
1965............	14·8	8·52
1970............	18·5	6·82
1971............	20·3	6·21
1972............	21·7	5·81
1973............	23·7	5·32
1974............	27·5	4·59
1975............	34·2	3·69
1976............	39·8	3·17
1977............	46·1	2·74
1978............	50·0	2·52
1979............	56·6	2·23
1980............	66·8	1·89
1981............	74·8	1·55
1982............	81·2	1·49
1983............	84·9	1·41
1984............	89·2	1·33
1985............	94·6	1·29
1986............	97·8	1·24
1987............	101·9	1·18
1988............	106·9	1·09
1989............	115·2	1·07
1990............	126·1	1·00

By employing this table an annual purchasing power of the pound index may be derived by taking the inverse of the price index. So, for example, if the purchasing power of the pound is taken to be 100p in 1972, then its comparable purchasing power in 1990 would be:

$$100 \times \frac{21·7}{126·1} = 17·2p$$

It should be noted that these figures can only be approximate.

INTEREST RATES – MORTGAGE AND SHARE

The interest rates prevailing on mortgage lending and share investment vary to a degree from society to society and in relation to the type or amount of loan or investment. General rate changes are made in response to market conditions and the predominant rates in recent years, with the dates of change, are given below.

The interval between the payments or compounding of interest is crucial in determining the competitiveness of particular societies' accounts. In order to make a true comparison of interest rates, the annual percentage rate or APR, which should appear in all advertisements and leaflets, must be used.

	May 1988	Aug. 1988	Oct. 1988	Jan. 1989	Feb. 1990	April 1990	Oct. 1990	Feb. 1991	May 1991
Mortgages %	9·50–9·80	11·50	12·75	13·50	14·50	15·40	15·00	14·50	12·95
Ordinary shares %	3·50	4·75	5·65	6·15	6·75	7·00	7·00	7·00	7·00

BANKING IN BRITAIN

The main institutions within the British banking system are the Bank of England (the central bank, see p. 301), the clearing banks (the major retail banks), the merchant banks, the overseas banks and the discount houses.

The clearing banks are Abbey National, Bank of Scotland, Barclays, Clydesdale, Co-operative, Coutts, Girobank, Lloyds, Midland, National Westminster, The Royal Bank of Scotland Group, the TSB and the Yorkshire Bank.

Deposit-taking institutions may be broadly divided into the monetary sector which is predominantly banks and is supervised by the Bank of England, and those institutions outside the monetary sector of which the most important are the building societies and the National Savings Bank. The Banking Act 1987 established a single category of authorized institutions eligible to carry out banking business.

There follows a list of authorized institutions as at August 23, 1991.

AUTHORIZED INSTITUTIONS

* In administration
** Provisional liquidator appointed

INCORPORATED IN UK
(Including partnerships formed
under the law of any part of the UK)

ABC International Bank PLC
ANZ Grindlays Bank PLC
ANZ Merchant Bank Ltd
Abbey National PLC
Abbey National Treasury Services PLC
Adam & Company PLC
Afghan National Credit & Finance Ltd
Airdrie Savings Bank
Aitken Hume Bank PLC
Ak International Bank Ltd
Albaraka International Bank Ltd
Alexanders Discount PLC
Alliance Trust (Finance) Ltd
Allied Trust Bank Ltd
Anglo Irish Asset Finance PLC
Anglo-Romanian Bank Ltd
Anglo Yugoslav Bank Ltd
Henry Ansbacher & Co. Ltd
Assemblies of God Property Trust
Associates Capital Corporation Ltd
Avco Trust Ltd

BNL Investment Bank PLC
Banca Novara (UK) Ltd
Banco Hispano Americano Ltd
Bank Leumi (UK) PLC
Bank of America International Ltd
Bank of Boston Ltd
Bank of Cyprus (London) Ltd
Bank of Scotland
Bank of Tokyo International Ltd
Bank of Wales PLC
Bankers Trust International PLC
Banque Belge Ltd
Banque de la Méditerranée (UK) Ltd
Banque Nationale de Paris PLC
The Baptist Union Corporation Ltd
Barclays Bank PLC
Barclays Bank Trust Company Ltd
Barclays de Zoete Wedd Ltd
Baring Brothers & Co. Ltd
Belmont Bank Ltd
Benchmark Bank PLC
Beneficial Bank PLC
Birmingham Capital Trust PLC
Boston Safe Deposit and Trust Company (UK) Ltd

*British and Commonwealth Merchant Bank PLC
The British Bank of the Middle East
British Credit Trust Ltd
The British Linen Bank Ltd
British Railways Savings Company Ltd
Brown, Shipley & Co. Ltd
Bunge Finance Ltd

Caledonian Bank PLC
Cater Allen Ltd
*Chancery PLC
The Charities Aid Foundation Money Management Company Ltd
Chartered Trust PLC
Chartered WestLB Ltd
Charterhouse Bank Ltd
Chase Investment Bank Ltd
Chesterfield Street Trust Ltd
Citibank Trust Ltd
Citicorp Investment Bank Ltd
City Merchants Bank Ltd
City Trust Ltd
Clive Discount Company Ltd
Close Brothers Ltd
Clydesdale Bank PLC
Clydesdale Bank Finance Corporation Ltd
Combined Capital Ltd
Commercial Bank Trust PLC
Commercial Bank of London PLC
Confederation Bank Ltd
Consolidated Credits Bank Ltd
Co-operative Bank PLC
Coutts & Co.
Craneheath Securities Ltd
Credito Italiano International Ltd
Credit Suisse Financial Products

DG Investment Bank Ltd
Daiwa Europe Bank PLC
Dalbeattie Finance Co. Ltd
Darlington Merchant Credits Ltd
Dartington & Co. Ltd
Davenham Trust Ltd
Deacon Hoare & Co. Ltd
Den norske Bank PLC
The Dorset, Somerset & Wilts. Investment Society Ltd
Dryfield Finance Ltd
Dunbar Bank PLC
Duncan Lawrie Ltd

East Trust Ltd
Eccles Savings and Loans Ltd
*Edington PLC
English Trust Company Ltd
Enskilda Securities-Skandinaviska Enskilda Ltd
Equatorial Bank PLC
Everett Chettle Associates
Exeter Bank Ltd

FIBI Bank (UK) Ltd
Fairmount Trust Ltd
Family Finance Ltd
FennoScandia Bank Ltd
Financial & General Bank PLC
James Finlay Bank Ltd
First Interstate Capital Markets Ltd
First National Bank PLC
First National Commercial Bank PLC
The First Personal Bank PLC
Robert Fleming & Co. Ltd
Ford Credit PLC
Foreign & Colonial Management Ltd
Forward Trust Ltd
Robert Fraser & Partners Ltd
Frizzell Banking Services Ltd

Gartmore Money Management Ltd

Gerrard & National Ltd
Girobank PLC
Goldman Sachs Ltd
Goode Durrant Bank PLC
Granville Trust Ltd
Gresham Trust PLC
Greyhound Bank PLC
Guinness Mahon & Co. Ltd

HFC Bank PLC
Habibsons Bank Ltd
Hambros Bank Ltd
Hampshire Trust PLC
The Hardware Federation Finance Co. Ltd
Harrods Bank Ltd
Harton Securities Ltd
Havana International Bank Ltd
The Heritable & General Investment Bank Ltd
Hill Samuel Bank Ltd
Hill Samuel Personal Finance Ltd
C. Hoare & Co.
Julian Hodge Bank Ltd
Holdenhurst Securities PLC
Hongkong Bank London Ltd
Humberclyde Finance Group Ltd
Hungarian International Bank Ltd

3i PLC
3i Group PLC
IBJ International Ltd
Independent Trust and Finance Ltd
International Mexican Bank Ltd
Iran Overseas Investment Bank Ltd
Italian International Bank PLC

Japan International Bank Ltd
Jordan International Bank PLC
Leopold Joseph & Sons Ltd

KDB International (London) Ltd
King & Shaxson Ltd
Kleinwort Benson Ltd
Kleinwort Benson Investment Management Ltd

LTCB International Ltd
Lazard Brothers & Co. Ltd
Lloyds Bank PLC
Lloyds Bank (BLSA) Ltd
Lloyds Bowmaker Ltd
Lloyds Merchant Bank Ltd
Lombard Bank Ltd
Lombard & Ulster Ltd
Lombard North Central PLC
London Arab Investment Bank Ltd
London Scottish Bank PLC
Lordsvale Finance PLC

McDonnell Douglas Bank Ltd
McNeill Pearson Ltd
Manchester Exchange and Investment Bank Ltd
W. M. Mann & Co. (Investments) Ltd
Manufacturers Hanover Ltd
Marks and Spencer Financial Services Ltd
Mase Westpac Ltd
Matheson Bank Ltd
Matlock Bank Ltd
Meghraj Bank Ltd
Mercantile Credit Company Ltd
Mercury Provident PLC
Merrill Lynch International Bank Ltd
The Methodist Chapel Aid Association Ltd
Midland Bank PLC
Midland Bank Finance Corporation Ltd
Midland Bank Trust Company Ltd
Minories Finance Ltd
Minster Trust Ltd
Samuel Montagu & Co. Ltd
Morgan Grenfell & Co. Ltd
Moscow Narodny Bank Ltd
Mount Banking Corporation Ltd

Municipal Mutual Bank PLC
Mutual Trust and Savings Ltd
Mynshul Bank PLC

NIIB Group Ltd
NWS Bank PLC
National Guardian Mortgage Corporation Ltd
The National Mortgage Bank PLC
National Westminster Bank PLC
NatWest Investment Bank Ltd
The Nikko Bank (UK) PLC
Noble Grossart Ltd
Nomura Bank International PLC
Northern Bank Ltd
Northern Bank Executor & Trustee Company Ltd
Norwich General Trust Ltd
Nykredit Mortgage Bank PLC

Omega Trust Co. Ltd

PaineWebber International Bank Ltd
Panmure Gordon Bankers Ltd
People's Bank Ltd
Philadelphia National Ltd
Pointon York Ltd
The Private Bank and Trust Company Ltd
Property Lending Bank PLC
Provincial Bank PLC

Ralli Investment Company Ltd
R. Raphael & Sons PLC
Rathbone Bros. & Co. Ltd
Rea Brothers Ltd
Reliance Bank Ltd
Riggs AP Bank Ltd
N. M. Rothschild & Sons Ltd
Roxburghe Bank Ltd
Royal Bank of Canada Europe Ltd
The Royal Bank of Scotland PLC
Royal Trust Bank
RoyScot Trust PLC

Sanwa International PLC
Saudi International Bank (Al-Bank Al-Saudi Al-Alami Ltd)
Schroder Leasing Ltd
J. Henry Schroder Wagg & Co. Ltd
Scotiabank (UK) Ltd
Scottish Amicable Money Managers Ltd
Seccombe Marshall & Campion PLC
Secure Homes Ltd
Security Pacific Trust Ltd
Shire Trust Ltd
Singer & Friedlander Ltd
Smith & Williamson Securities
Société Générale Merchant Bank PLC
Southsea Mortgage & Investment Co. Ltd
Standard Chartered Bank
Standard Chartered Bank Africa PLC
Sterling Bank & Trust Ltd
Svenska International PLC

TSB Bank PLC
TSB Bank Northern Ireland PLC
TSB Bank Scotland PLC
Tyndall & Co. Ltd

UBAF Bank Ltd
UCB Bank PLC
ULC Trust Ltd
Ulster Bank Ltd
Unibank PLC
Union Discount Company Ltd
The United Bank of Kuwait PLC
United Dominions Trust Ltd
Unity Trust Bank PLC

WPZ Bank (UK) Ltd
Wagon Finance Ltd
S. G. Warburg & Co. Ltd
S. G. Warburg Discount Ltd

Western Trust & Savings Ltd
Whiteaway Laidlaw Bank Ltd
Wimbledon & South West Finance Co. PLC
Wintrust Securities Ltd
Woodchester Bank UK PLC

Yamaichi Bank (UK) PLC
Yorkshire Bank PLC
H. F. Young & Co. Ltd

INCORPORATED OUTSIDE THE UK

(Including partnerships or other unincorporated associations formed under the law of any member state of the European Community other than the UK)

AIB Capital Markets PLC
AIB Finance Ltd
ASLK—CGER Bank
Algemene Bank Nederland NV
Allied Bank of Pakistan Ltd
Allied Banking Corporation
Allied Irish Banks PLC
American Express Bank Ltd
Amsterdam-Rotterdam Bank NV
Anglo Irish Bank Corporation PLC
Arab African International Bank
Arab Bank PLC
Arab Banking Corporation BSC
Arab National Bank
Ashikaga Bank Ltd
Australia & New Zealand Banking Group Ltd

BSI—Banca della Svizzera Italiana
Banca CRT–Cassa di Risparmio di Torino
Banca Commerciale Italiana
Banca Nazionale dell'Agricoltura SpA
Banca Nazionale del Lavoro
Banca Popolare di Milano
Banca Serfin SNC
Banco Bilbao–Vizcaya
Banco Central, SA
Banco de la Nación Argentina
Banco de Sabadell
Banco di Napoli
Banco di Roma SpA
Banco di Santo Spirito
Banco di Sicilia
Banco do Brasil SA
Banco do Estado de São Paulo SA
Banco Español de Crédito SA
Banco Espirito Santo e Comercial de Lisboa
Banco Exterior Internacional SA
Banco Mercantil de São Paulo SA
Banco Nacional de México SNC
Banco Nacional Ultramarino SA
Banco Português do Atlântico
Banco Real SA
Banco Santander
Banco Totta & Açores SA
Bancomer SNC
Bangkok Bank Ltd
Bank Julius Baer & Co. Ltd
Bank Bumiputra Malaysia Berhad
Bank für Gemeinwirtschaft AG
Bank Handlowy w Warszawie SA
Bank Hapoalim BM
Bank Mees & Hope NV
Bank Mellat
Bank Melli Iran
Bank Negara Indonesia 1946
Bank of America NT & SA
Bank of Baroda
The Bank of California NA
Bank of Ceylon
Bank of China
**Bank of Credit and Commerce International SA

The Bank of East Asia Ltd
Bank of India
The Bank of Ireland
Bank of Montreal
The Bank of New York
Bank of New Zealand
The Bank of Nova Scotia
Bank of Oman Ltd
Bank of Seoul
The Bank of Tokyo Ltd
The Bank of Yokohama Ltd
Bank Saderat Iran
Bank Sepah-Iran
Bank Tejarat
Bankers Trust Company
Bankorp Ltd
Banque Arabe et Internationale d'Investissement
Banque Bruxelles Lambert SA
Banque de l'Orient Arabe et d'Outre-Mer
Banque Française de l'Orient
Banque Française du Commerce Extérieur
Banque Indosuez
Banque Internationale à Luxembourg SA
Banque Nationale de Paris
Banque Paribas
Banque Worms
Bayerische Hypotheken-und Wechsel-Bank AG
Bayerische Landesbank Girozentrale
Bayerische Vereinsbank AG
Beirut Riyad Bank SAL
Belgolaise SA
Berliner Bank AG
Berliner Handels-und Frankfurter Bank
Byblos Bank SAL

CBI-TDB Union Bancaire Privée
CIC-Union Européenne, International et Cie
Caisse Nationale de Crédit Agricole
Canadian Imperial Bank of Commerce
Canara Bank
Cassa di Risparmio delle Provincie Lombarde
The Chase Manhattan Bank NA
Chemical Bank
The Chiba Bank Ltd
Cho Hung Bank
Christiania Bank og Kreditkasse
The Chuo Trust & Banking Co. Ltd
Citibank NA
Commercial Bank of Korea Ltd
Commerzbank AG
Commonwealth Bank of Australia
Confederacion Española de Cajas de Ahorros
Continental Bank, National Association
CoreStates Bank NA
Crédit Commercial de France
Crédit du Nord
Crédit Lyonnais
Crédit Lyonnais Bank Nederland NV
Crédit Suisse
Creditanstalt-Bankverein
Credito Italiano
Cyprus Credit Bank Ltd
The Cyprus Popular Bank

The Dai-Ichi Kangyo Bank Ltd
The Daiwa Bank Ltd
Den Danske Bank Aktieselskab
Den norske Bank A/S
Deutsche Bank AG
Deutsche Genossenschaftsbank
The Development Bank of Singapore Ltd
Discount Bank and Trust Company
Dresdner Bank AG

Fidelity Bank NA
First Bank of Nigeria Ltd
First City, Texas–Houston NA
First Commercial Bank

First Interstate Bank of California
The First National Bank of Boston
The First National Bank of Chicago
Fleet Bank of Massachusetts NA
French Bank of Southern Africa Ltd
The Fuji Bank Ltd

Generale Bank
Ghana Commercial Bank
Girozentrale und Bank der österreichischen Spar-
kassen AG
Gota Bank
Gulf International Bank BSC

Habib Bank AG Zurich
Habib Bank Ltd
Hamburgische Landesbank Girozentrale
Hanil Bank
Harris Trust and Savings Bank
Hessische Landesbank-Girozentrale
The Hokkaido Takushoku Bank Ltd
The Hokuriku Bank Ltd
The Hongkong and Shanghai Banking Corporation
Ltd

The Industrial Bank of Japan Ltd
The Investment Bank of Ireland Ltd
Istituto Bancario San Paolo di Torino

Jyske Bank

Kansallis-Osake-Pankki
Keesler Federal Credit Union
Korea Exchange Bank
Korea First Bank
Kredietbank NV
The Kyowa Saitama Bank Ltd

The Long-Term Credit Bank of Japan Ltd

Malayan Banking Berhad
Manufacturers Hanover Trust Company
Mellon Bank NA
Merchants National Bank & Trust Company of
Indianapolis
Middle East Bank Ltd
The Mitsubishi Bank Ltd
The Mitsubishi Trust and Banking Corporation
The Mitsui Taiyo Kobe Bank Ltd
The Mitsui Trust & Banking Co. Ltd
Monte dei Paschi di Siena
Morgan Guaranty Trust Company of New York
Multibanco Comermex SNC

NBD Bank NA
NCNB National Bank of North Carolina
NMB Postbank Groep NV
National Australia Bank Ltd
National Bank of Abu Dhabi
National Bank of Canada
The National Bank of Dubai Ltd
National Bank of Egypt
National Bank of Greece SA
The National Bank of Kuwait SAK
The National Commercial Bank
National Bank of Pakistan
NedPerm Bank Ltd
The Nippon Credit Bank Ltd
Nordbanken
Norddeutsche Landesbank Girozentrale
The Norinchukin Bank
The Northern Trust Company

Österreichische Länderbank AG
Oversea-Chinese Banking Corporation Ltd
Overseas Trust Bank Ltd
Overseas Union Bank Ltd

Philippine National Bank
Postipankki Ltd

Qatar National Bank SAQ

The R&I Bank of Western Australia Ltd
Rabobank Nederland (Coöperatieve Centrale Raiffei-
sen-Boerenleenbank BA)
**Rafidain Bank
Raiffeisen Zentralbank Osterreich AG
Republic National Bank of New York
Reserve Bank of Australia
The Riggs National Bank of Washington DC
Riyad Bank
Royal Bank of Canada

Saudi American Bank
Scandinavian Bank (Skandinaviska Enskilda Ban-
ken)
Security Pacific National Bank
Shanghai Commercial Bank Ltd
The Siam Commercial Bank Ltd
Société Générale
Sonali Bank
State Bank of India
State Bank of New South Wales Ltd
State Bank of South Australia
State Street Bank and Trust Company
Südwestdeutsche Landesbank Girozentrale
The Sumitomo Bank Ltd
The Sumitomo Trust & Banking Co. Ltd
Svenska Handelsbanken
SwedBank
Swiss Bank Corporation
Swiss Volksbank
Syndicate Bank

TC Ziraat Bankasi
The Thai Farmers Bank Ltd
The Tokai Bank, Ltd
The Toronto-Dominion Bank
The Toyo Trust & Banking Company Ltd
Turkish Bank Ltd
Türkiye Iş Bankasi AŞ

Uco Bank
Ulster Investment Bank Ltd
Union Bank of Finland Ltd
Union Bank of Nigeria Ltd
Union Bank of Norway
Union Bank of Switzerland
Unitas Bank Ltd
United Bank Ltd
United Mizrahi Bank Ltd
United Overseas Bank (Banque Unie pour les Pays
d'Outre Mer)
United Overseas Bank Ltd

Volkskas Bank Ltd

Westdeutsche Landesbank Girozentrale
Westpac Banking Corporation

The Yasuda Trust & Banking Co. Ltd

Zambia National Commercial Bank Ltd
Zivnostenská Banka National Corporation

Bank base rates 1990–91

1990	Sept.	15·0%	1991	Apr. 12	12·0%
	Oct. 8	14·0%		May 24	11·5%
1991	Feb. 13	13·5%		July 12	11·0%
	Feb. 27	13·0%			

BANKING HOURS

Weekdays

ENGLAND AND WALES.—Monday–Friday 9.30–3.30*; *City of London town clearers*, 9.30–3.00.
SCOTLAND.—Banking hours in Scotland are: Monday–Wednesday, Friday, 9.15–4.45; Thursday, 9.15–5.30†.
NORTHERN IRELAND.—Open four days per week 10.00–3.30; Open 9.30–5.00 one day per week.

Saturdays

ENGLAND AND WALES.—(Selected branches open): *Barclays* 9.30–12.00; *Lloyds* 9.30–12.30; *Midland* 9.30–3.30;
 National Westminster 9.30–12.30; *TSB* 9.30–12.30.
SCOTLAND.—CLOSED.
NORTHERN IRELAND.—Closed.

* Still the minimum banking hours but many banks are experimenting with longer hours (usually 9.15–6.00).
† Hours can vary from branch to branch.

THE CLEARING BANKS, 1990

Bank Group	Profit/loss before taxation £m	Profit/loss after taxation £m	Total assets £m	Number of UK branches
Abbey National	582	377	46,496	687
Bank of Scotland	134·1	86·1	22,095·2	523
Barclays	760	428	134,887	2,600
Clydesdale	70·24	44·31	4,618	350
†Co-operative	18·68	10·89	2·70	110
†Coutts & Co.	15	9·8	3,513·5	19
*Girobank	21·7	15·1	2,389·2	20,000
Lloyds	591	292	55,202	2,100
Midland	11	−177	59,636	1,910
†National Westminster	404	198	116,200	3,116
The Royal Bank of Scotland Group	262·2	169·6	30,100	908
*Yorkshire Bank	92·12	58·37	4,599	256

* Nine months only
† 1990 figures

BANKING SERVICES

Association for Payment Clearing Services (APACS)
Mercury House, Triton Court, 14 Finsbury Square, EC2A 1BR.
[071–7116200]

APACS was set up by the banks in 1985 to manage the payment clearing systems and oversee money transmission in the UK.

Three operational clearing companies operate under the aegis of APACS. They are:

BACS LTD, De Havilland Road, Edgware, Middx. HA8 5QA.—Provides an automated service for inter-bank clearing of payment and collection transactions in the UK (e.g. standing orders, direct debits). *Chief Exec.*, A. E. Robinson.

CHEQUE AND CREDIT CLEARING CO. LTD., Mercury House, Triton Court, 14 Finsbury Square, EC2A 1BR.—Operates bulk clearing systems for inter-bank cheques and paper credit items. *Chief Inspector*, E. W. Stubbs.

CHAPS AND TOWN CLEARING CO. LTD., Mercury House, Triton Court, 14 Finsbury Square, EC2A 1BR.—Provides same-day clearing for high value cheques and electronic funds transfer. *Chief Inspector*, E. W. Stubbs.

APACS also oversees the London currency clearings and the cheque card and eurocheque schemes in the UK.

Membership of APACS and the operational clearing companies is open to any appropriately regulated financial institution providing payment services and meeting the relevant membership criteria. As at June 1991 APACS had 21 members, comprising the major banks and building societies.
Head of Public Affairs, R. Tyson-Davies.

Committee of London and Scottish Bankers
10 Lombard Street, EC3V 9EL
[071-623 4001]

The Committee consists of the Chairmen of Barclays, Lloyds, Midland, National Westminster, Standard Chartered, Bank of Scotland, Royal Bank of Scotland and the TSB Group, and meets regularly to discuss matters of common interest. It was subsumed into the British Bankers Association in April 1991.
Secretary-General, The Lord Inchyra.

FINANCIAL OMBUDSMEN

The following Ombudsmen schemes are non-statutory.

The Office of the Banking Ombudsman
Citadel House, 5–11 Fetter Lane, EC4A 1BR
[071-583 1395]

The purpose of the Banking Ombudsman scheme is to investigate complaints from bank customers dissatisfied with the banking services of member banks. The Scheme was set up in 1985 and became operational on Jan. 1, 1986. The Scheme has 27 member banks who fund it and in addition there are 22 designated associates. There is a eight-member Council who appoint the Ombudsman, give guidance on the performance of his duties, monitor his terms of reference, prepare the budget and approve the annual report. The Ombudsman and his staff are responsible to the Council.
The Banking Ombudsman, L. Shurman.

The Office of the Building Societies Ombudsman
Grosvenor Gardens House, 35–37 Grosvenor Gardens, SW1X 7AW
[071-931 0044]

The purpose of the Building Societies Ombudsman scheme, which came into operation on July 1, 1987, is to investigate complaints from building society customers about the services of building societies belonging to the scheme. All building societies belong to the scheme and it is funded by contributions from the members. The Ombudsman is appointed by and responsible to an independent Ombudsman Council.
The Building Societies Ombudsman, S. Edell.

The Insurance Ombudsman Bureau
31 Southampton Row, WC1B 5HJ
[071-242 8613]

The purpose of the Insurance Ombudsman scheme is to settle disputes between insurance policyholders and unit trust investors and member insurance companies. The scheme came into operation in March 1981 for insurance matters and October 1988 for unit trust matters, and is funded by contributions from the member companies. Over 325 companies are members of the scheme. An independent Council appoints and supervises the work of the Ombudsman.
The Insurance Ombudsman, Dr J. T. Farrand.
Deputy Ombudsman, L. Slade.

THE NATIONAL DEBT

Net central government borrowing each year represents an addition to the National Debt. At the end of March 1990 the National Debt amounted to some £192,500 million of which about £6,700 million was in currencies other than sterling. Of the £185,900 million sterling debt, £125,600 million consisted of gilt-edged stock; of this, 30 per cent had a maturity of up to five years, 42 per cent a maturity of over five years and up to 15 years and 28 per cent a maturity of over 15 years or undated. The remaining sterling debt was made up mainly of national savings (£29,100 million), certificates of tax deposits, Treasury bills, and Ways and Means advances (very short-term internal government borrowing).

Sizable Trust Funds have been established over the past fifty years for the purpose of reducing the National Debt. The National Fund was established in 1927 with an original gift of £499,878. At March 31, 1990 it was valued at £72,653,490; it is administered by Baring Brothers & Co. Ltd The Elsie Mackay Fund was established in 1929 with an original gift of £527,809 to run for 45–50 years. It was wound up on January 19, 1979, when it was valued at £4,902,864. The John Buchanan Fund was established in 1932 with gifts totalling £36,702 to run for 50 years. It was wound up on February 28, 1982, when it was valued at £204,138.

NATIONAL SAVINGS

Ordinary and Investment Accounts

National Savings Bank.—On May 31, 1991, there were about 15,722,000 active accounts with the sum of approximately £1,465 million due to depositors in Ordinary accounts and about 4,857,000 active accounts with the sum of approximately £8,615·5 million due to depositors in Investment accounts.

Interest is earned at 5 per cent per year on each Ordinary account for every complete calendar month in which the balance is £500 or more, provided the account is kept open for the whole of 1991 (December 31, 1990—January 1, 1992); and at 2·5 per cent per year for other months or for accounts opened or closed during 1991. The minimum deposit is £5; maximum balance £10,000 plus interest credited. On May 31, 1991 the average amount held in Ordinary accounts was approximately £93.

The Investment account pays a higher rate of interest (the current rate can be found at any post office). The minimum deposit is £5; maximum balance £25,000 plus interest credited. On May 31, 1991 the average amount held in Investment accounts was approximately £1,774.

Premium Bonds

Premium Bonds are a Government security which were first introduced on November 1, 1956. Premium Bonds enable savers to enter a regular draw for tax-free prizes, whilst retaining the right to get their money back. A sum equivalent to interest on each bond is put into a prize fund and distributed by weekly and monthly prize draws. (The rate of interest is 6·5 per cent a year from July 1, 1988). The prizes are drawn by ERNIE (electronic random number indicator equipment) and are free of all UK income tax and capital gains tax.

Bonds are in units of £1, with a minimum purchase of £100; above this, purchases must be in multiples of £10, up to a maximum holding limit of £10,000 per person. The exception to this is that the minimum purchase by parents, guardians and grandparents for children under 16 are £10. Winners of £50 prize warrants will be invited to return their prize warrants to the Bonds and Stock Office if they wish to reinvest. This transaction cannot be done through the Post Office. Bonds can only be held in the name of an individual and not by organizations.

Bonds become eligible for prizes once they have been held for three clear calendar months following the month of purchase. Each £1 unit can win only one prize per draw, but it will be awarded the highest for which it is drawn. Bonds remain eligible for prizes until they are repaid. When a holder dies, bonds remain eligible for prizes up to and including the twelfth monthly draw after the month in which the holder dies.

By April 1991 bonds to the value of £4,950 million had been sold. Of these £2,620 million had been cashed, leaving £2,329 million still invested. By the April 1991 prize draw, 37 million prizes totalling £2,180 million had been distributed since the first prize draw in June 1957.

Income Bonds

National Savings Income Bonds were introduced in 1982. They are particularly suitable for those who want to receive regular monthly payments of interest while preserving the full cash value of their capital. The Bonds are sold in multiples of £1,000. The minimum holding is £2,000 and the maximum £25,000.

Interest is calculated on a day-to-day basis and paid monthly. Interest is taxable, but is paid without deduction of tax at source. The Bonds have a guaranteed life of ten years, but may be repaid at par

before maturity on giving three months' notice. repayment of a bond is made within the first year purchase, interest from the date of purchase to t date of repayment is earned at half rate. If the so or sole surviving holder dies, however, no form period of notice is required and there is no loss interest for repayment made within the first year.

Net investment in National Savings Income Bon was £9,026 million at the end of April 1991.

Indexed Income Bonds

Indexed Income Bonds were withdrawn from sa on August 28, 1987. Existing holders will continue receive monthly income in accordance with t prospectus.

Children's Bonus Bonds

Children's Bonus Bonds (Series A) were introduce in July 1991. They can be bought for any child und 16 and will go on growing in value until he or she 21. The Bonds are sold in multiples of £25. T minimum holding is £25, the maximum £1,000 p child (excluding interest and bonuses). Bonds f children under 16 must be held by a parent guardian.

Children's Bonus Bonds (Series A) earn 5 per ce a year over five years. A substantial bonus (47·36 p cent) of the purchase price is added at the fif anniversary. This is equal to 11·84 per cent a ye compound. All returns are totally exempt from U income tax. No interest is earned on Bonds cashe in before the first anniversary of purchase. Bonus are only payable if the Bond is held until the ne bonus date. Bonds over five years old continue earn interest and bonuses until the holder is 21, whe they should be cashed in. If Bonds are not cashed on the holder's 21st birthday, they earn no intere after that birthday.

Capital Bonds

National Savings Capital Bonds (Series A) we introduced in January 1989, and replaced by Series in July 1990. Series B was replaced by Series C April 1991. For personal savers Capital Bonds offe capital growth over five years with guarantee returns at fixed rates. The interest is taxable eac year (for those who pay income tax) but is n deducted at source. The minimum purchase is £10 with larger purchases in multiples of £100. There a maximum holding limit of £100,000 for Series bonds and any subsequent series.

Capital Bonds will be repaid in full with all intere gained at the end of five years. Early repayment ma be obtained at three months notice. No interest earned on Bonds repaid in the first year.

Deposit Bonds

National Savings Deposit Bonds were withdraw from sale on November 19, 1988. All Deposit Bon purchased on or before that date may continue to held until the tenth anniversary of purchase. The will continue to earn interest until then.

Yearly Plan

The National Savings Yearly Plan was introduce on July 2, 1984. It offers a guaranteed tax-free retur Applicants agree to make 12 monthly payment leading to the issue of a Yearly Plan Certificate. Th maximum guaranteed rate of interest is earned if th Certificate is held for a full four years. Applicatio may be made by any individuals aged 7 or over; the name of children under 7; and by not more tha two trustees for a sole beneficiary.

Payments must be made on the same date every month by standing order from a bank or other acceptable account. Only one payment may be made in any one month and must be in multiples of £5. Minimum monthly contribution is £20, maximum £200. Net investment in National Savings Yearly Plan was £513,800,000 at April 31, 1991.

Gilts on the National Savings Stock Register

Government stock or 'Gilts' are Stock Exchange securities issued by the Government. They usually have a life of between five and 20 years and most pay a guaranteed fixed rate of interest twice a year throughout this period. When they reach the end of this period they are 'redeemed' (which means repaid) at their face value.

The National Savings Stock Register enables investors to buy and sell Gilts by post. It is now possible to have most new issues of Gilts registered on the National Savings Stock Register. Interest on Gilts held on the National Savings Stock Register, although taxable, is paid in full without deduction of tax at source.

National Savings Certificates

The amount, including accrued interest, index-linked increase or bonus remaining to the credit of investors in National Savings Certificates on April 30, 1991 was approximately £883·9 million. In 1990–91, approx. £2,199 million was subscribed and £3,261 million (excluding interest, index-linked increase or bonus) was repaid. Interest, index-linked increase, bonus or other sum payable is free of UK income tax (including investment income surcharge) and capital gains tax.

Issue and maximum holding (in units)	Unit cost £	Value after		Interest per unit
		Years	£ p	
Index-Linked Retirement Issue (June 2, 1975–Nov. 15, 1980) (120)	10			Unlike conventional issues where interest is accrued periodically, the repayment value of Index-Linked Certificates, subject to their being held a year, is related to the movement of the UK General Index of Retail Prices.** N.B. Certificates of the Retirement Issue were on sale only to men aged 65 years and over and women aged 60 years and over, but may now be transferred to anyone.
nd Index-Linked Issue (Nov. 17, 1980–June 29, 1985) (1,000)	10			The repayment value, subject to their being held a year, is related to the movement of the UK General Index of Retail Prices.** N.B. Certificates of the 2nd Index-Linked Issue were made available to anyone, regardless of age, from September 7, 1981.
rd Index-Linked Issue (July 1, 1985–July 31, (1986) (200)	25			The repayment value, subject to their being held for one year, is related to the movement of the UK General Index of Retail Prices.** In addition, there is guaranteed extra interest of 2·5 per cent for the 1st year, 2·75 per cent for the 2nd year, 3·25 per cent for the 3rd year, 4·0 per cent for the 4th year and 5·25 per cent for the 5th year. This interest is worth 3·54 per cent compound over a full five years.
th Index-Linked Issue (Aug. 1, 1986–June 30, 1990) (200)	25			The repayment value, subject to their being held for one year, is related to the movement of the UK General Index of Retail Prices.** In addition, there is guaranteed extra interest of 3·0 per cent for the 1st year, 3·25 per cent for the 2nd year, 3·5 per cent for the 3rd year, 4·5 per cent for the 4th year, and 6·0 per cent for the 5th year. This interest is worth 4·04 per cent compound over a full five years.
Thirty-second....... (Nov. 12, 1986–March 10, 1987) (200)	25	5	38·03	After 1 year, £1·63 is added, during 2nd year, 50p per completed 3 months, during 3rd year, 62p per completed 3 months, during 4th year, 77p per completed 3 months and during 5th year, 96p per completed 3 months.*
Thirty-third........ (May 1, 1987–July 21, 1988) (40, plus special facilities to hold up to a further 200)	25	5	35·06	After 1 year, the repayment value increases by 5·5 per cent for ordinarily held 33rd Issue. However, 33rd Reinvestment Certificates earn interest during the 1st year at the rate of 5·5 per cent per annum for each 3 month period. Thereafter all 33rd Issue earn 5·75 per cent after 2 years, 6·0 per cent after 3 years, 6·5 per cent after 4 years and 7·0 per cent after 5 years.*
Thirty-fourth....... (July 22, 1988–June 16, 1990) (40, plus special facilities to hold up to a further 400.)	25	5	35·89	After 1 year, the repayment value increases by 6·0 per cent for ordinarily held 34th Issue. However, 34th Reinvestment certificates earn interest during the 1st year at the rate of 6·0 per cent per annum for each 3 month period. Thereafter, all 34th Issue earn 6·25 per cent after two years, 6·5 per cent after 3 years, 7·0 per cent after 4 years, and 7·5 per cent after 5 years.*

Issue and maximum holding (in units)	Unit cost £	Value after		Interest per unit
		Years	£ p	
Thirty-fifth .... (June 18, 1990–March 14, 1991) (40, plus special facilities to hold up to a further 400)	25	5	39·36	After 1 year, the repayment value increases by 6·5 per cent for ordinarily held 35th Issue. However, 35th Issue Reinvestment Certificates earn interest during the first year at the rate of 6·5 per cent per annum. Thereafter, all 35th Issue earn 7 per cent after two years; 7·75 per cent after three years; 8·5 per cent after four years and 9·5 per cent after five years.
5th Index-linked Issue (July 2, 1990–) (200, plus special facilities to hold up to a further 400)	25			The repayment value, subject to their being held for one year is related to the movement of the UK General Index of Retail Prices. In addition there is guaranteed extra interest which is paid from the date of purchase for each full year the certificates are held. For the first year the return is the Retail Price Index (RPI) only. For the second, RPI plus 0·5 per cent for the third RPI plus 1 per cent; for the fourth RPI plus 2· per cent and at the fifth anniversary RPI plus 4·5 per cent.
Thirty-sixth .... (April 2, 1991–) (200, plus special facilities to hold up to a further 400)	25	5	37·59	After 1 year, the repayment increases by 5·5 per cent for ordinarily held 36th Issue. However, 36th Issue Reinvestment Certificates earn interest during the first year at the rate of 5·5 per cent per annum. Thereafter, all 36th Issue earn 6·0 per cent after two years, 6·75 per cent after three years, 7·5 per cent after four years and 8·5 per cent after five years.

*As announced by the Treasury.

†From June 1982, savings certificates of the 7th to 14th, 16th, 18th, 19th, 21st, 23rd to 31st Issues will be extended on General Extension Rates as they reach the end of their existing extension periods. The percentage interest rate is determined by the Treasury and any change in this General Extension Rate will be applicable from the 1st of the month following its announcement.

Under the new system, a certificate earns interest for each complete period of three months beyond the expiry of the previous extension terms. Within each three-month period interest is calculated separately for each month at the rate applicable from the beginning of that month. The interest for each month is one twelfth of the annual rate (i.e. it does not vary with the number of days in the month) and is capitalized annually on the anniversary of the date of purchase. The current rate of interest under the General Extension Rate is displayed on special posters at most post offices.

**Index-linked certificates of the 1st and 2nd Issues were eligible for an annual supplement of 1·5 per cent for the year to August 1, 1989. There have been six previous annual supplements of 2·4 per cent for 1982–83 and 1983–84 and 3 per cent for 1984–85, 1985–86, 4 per cent for 1986–87 and 3 per cent for 1987–88. No further bonuses will be payable. At the fifth anniversary there is a bonus of 4 per cent of the purchase price and at the tenth anniversary there is a second bonus of 4 per cent of the full fifth anniversary value. All supplements and bonuses are fully index-linked once earned.

TAXATION

INCOME TAX

ncome tax is charged on the total income of ndividuals for a year of assessment commencing on April 6 and ending on the following April 5. The ates of tax and the calculation of liability will requently differ, sometimes substantially, as between one year of assessment and another. The following nformation is confined to the year of assessment 991–92, ending on April 5, 1992.

Liability to income tax is determined by establishng the taxable income for a year of assessment. The ncome will be reduced by an individual's personal allowances and other reliefs. The first £23,700 of axable income remaining is assessable to income tax at the basic rate of 25 per cent, with any excess over this amount taxable at the higher rate of 40 per cent.

The two rates apply to the assessment of both earned and investment income. Indeed, there is little distinction between the two classes, although the eceipt of earned income may produce an entitlement o some allowances not available against investment ncome.

The tables on the following two pages show the ncome tax payable for 1991–92 by an individual on the amount of income specified, after deducting the personal allowance and married couple's allowance also, where appropriate. Elderly persons over the age of 74 years may pay less tax. The taxpayer may also be entitled to transitional allowances and other reliefs which reduce the tax payable below the amount hown by the tables.

Trustees administering settled property are hargeable to income tax at the basic rate of 25 per cent. Where the trustees retain discretionary powers, or income is accumulated, there will also be iability to the additional rate of 10 per cent. Companies residing in the United Kingdom are not iable to income tax but suffer corporation tax on ncome, profits and gains.

The charge to income tax broadly arises on all axable income accruing from sources in the United Kingdom. Individuals who are resident in this erritory may also become liable on income arising overseas. An individual is resident in the United Kingdom if he or she normally resides here. Persons not normally residing in the United Kingdom may become resident if they visit this territory for periods which average three months or more throughout a period of years, or are present for at least 183 days in a particular year. The existence of a place of abode n the United Kingdom may be sufficient to indicate esidence if visits of any duration are made during the year of assessment.

Income arising overseas will often incur liability o foreign taxation. If that income is also chargeable o United Kingdom income tax, excessive liability could well arise. The United Kingdom has concluded double taxation agreements with many overseas erritories and these ensure that the same slice of ncome is not doubly assessed. In the absence of such an agreement, foreign tax suffered can usually be elieved under the domestic code when calculating iability to United Kingdom income tax.

Independent taxation

For many years the income of a married woman living with' her husband was treated as that of the ausband for income tax purposes. This did not generally apply in the year of marriage and it emained possible for the couple to exercise the right of separate assessment or for the wife to be separately assessed as a single person on her earned income. However, the husband was usually responsible for submitting income tax returns, for discharging income tax on the combined incomes and dealing generally with taxation matters.

This practice ceased to apply on April 6, 1990, with the introduction of independent taxation. From this date a husband and wife are independently taxed, with each entitled to a personal allowance. In most situations any unused personal allowance available to one spouse cannot be transferred to the other. A married man 'living with' his wife can obtain a married couple's allowance. This allowance must, if possible, be set against the husband's income but where that income is insufficient any balance of the married couple's allowance may be transferred to the wife.

Each spouse may obtain other allowances and reliefs where the underlying conditions are satisfied. Income must be accurately allocated between a husband and wife by reference to the individual beneficially entitled to that income. Where income arises from jointly-held assets this must be apportioned equally between husband and wife. However, in those cases where the beneficial interests in jointly-held assets are not equal, a special declaration can be made to apportion income by reference to the actual interests in that income.

Income taxable

Income tax is assessed and collected under several Schedules. Each Schedule determines the extent of liability and establishes the amount to be included in taxable income. In some instances the actual income arising in a year of assessment will be charged to income tax for that year. A different basis of assessment may arise for income taxable under Cases I to V of Schedule D. Frequently, income assessable under these Cases will be that arising in a previous year or period but there are special rules where a new source is acquired or an existing source discontinued.

Following the withdrawal of income tax liability for most commercial woodlands in the United Kingdom, Schedule B ceased to apply from April 6, 1988. The contents of the remaining schedules are shown below.

Schedule A.—Tax is charged on annual profits arising from the ownership or occupation of land in the United Kingdom. This will include rents, ground rents and other income from land. Expenditure incurred by the landlord on maintenance, repairs, insurance and management can be subtracted from the annual profits. This Schedule does not include profits from farming, market gardening or woodlands, nor does it extend to mineral rents and royalties. Premiums arising on the grant of a lease for a period not exceeding fifty years are assessed to income tax as rent. However, the amount of the taxable premium may be reduced by 2 per cent for each complete year, after the first year, of the leasing period. Income from furnished lettings is assessable under Case VI of Schedule D, unless an option is exercised for such income to be assessed under Schedule A. Where income arises from furnished holiday lettings, additional expenditure may be included in calculating income chargeable to tax. Income from furnished holiday lettings is treated as earned income.

Schedule C.—This Schedule is confined to interest or dividends on government or public authority funds and certain payments made out of the public revenues of overseas countries.

Single Persons and Married Women

Income	Persons under 65		Persons 65 or over*	
	Income tax	Average rate	Income tax	Average rate
£	£	per cent	£	per cent
4,000	176	4·4	—	—
5,000	426	8·5	245	4·9
6,000	676	11·3	495	8·3
7,000	926	13·2	745	10·6
8,000	1,176	14·7	995	12·4
9,000	1,426	15·8	1,245	13·8
10,000	1,676	16·8	1,495	15·0
12,000	2,176	18·1	1,995	16·6
14,000	2,676	19·1	2,558	18·3
16,000	3,176	19·9	3,176	19·9
18,000	3,676	20·4	3,676	20·4
20,000	4,176	20·9	4,176	20·9
25,000	5,426	21·7	5,426	21·7
30,000	7,127	23·8	7,127	23·8
40,000	11,127	27·8	11,127	27·8
50,000	15,127	30·3	15,127	30·3
60,000	19,127	31·9	19,127	31·9
100,000	35,127	35·1	35,127	35·1

* Persons aged 75 or over suffer rather less tax on income falling below £16,000 on this table.

Schedule D.—This Schedule is divided into six Cases, as follows:

Cases I and II.—Profits arising from trades, professions and vocations, including farming and market gardening. Capital expenditure incurred on assets used for business purposes will often produce an entitlement to capital allowances which reduce the profits chargeable. These profits may also be reduced following the submission of claims for loss relief and other matters.

Case III.—Interest on government stocks not taxed at source (e.g. War Loan and British Savings Bonds), interest on National Savings Bank deposits and discounts. Interest up to £70 on ordinary National Savings Bank deposits is exempt from income tax. The exemption applies to both husband and wife separately. Interest on National Savings Bank Special Investment accounts is not exempt.

Cases IV and V.—Interest from overseas securities, rents, dividends and all other income accruing outside the United Kingdom. Assessment is based on the full amount of income arising, whether remitted to the United Kingdom or retained overseas, but individuals who are either not domiciled in the United Kingdom or who are ordinarily resident overseas may be taxed on a remittance basis. Overseas pensions are taxable but the amount arising may be reduced by 10 per cent for assessment purposes.

Case VI.—Sundry profits and annual receipts not assessed under any other Case or Schedule. These may include insurance commissions, post-cessation receipts and numerous other receipts specifically charged under Case VI.

Schedule E.—All emoluments from an office or employment are assessable under this Schedule. There are three Cases, as follows:

Case I.—This applies to all emoluments of an individual resident and ordinarily resident in the United Kingdom.

Case II.—Of application where the individual is not resident or not ordinarily resident and extends to emoluments for duties undertaken in the United Kingdom.

Case III.—Applies in rare situations to other emoluments remitted to the United Kingdom.

Although earnings for overseas duties may be assessable under Case I where the employee is residen and ordinarily resident in the United Kingdom, a deduction of 100 per cent may be available, which reduces the overseas assessable earnings to nil. Thi deduction can be obtained where duties are performe overseas for a continuous period reaching or exceed ing 365 days and is confined to earnings from th overseas activity.

For years up to and including that ending on Apr 5, 1989, alternative methods could be used to calculat the emoluments for a year of assessment. However these methods were discontinued and replaced by new 'receipts' basis. Liability is now governed by th date of receipt.

Where emoluments are assessable under Case I o Case II, the date of receipt, and therefore the year o assessment into which the receipt falls, will compris the earlier of:

(a) the date of payment;

(b) the date entitlement arises.

In the case of company directors it is the earliest o the two dates given above with the addition of th following three which establish the time of receipt:

(c) the date emoluments are credited in the com pany's books;

(d) where emoluments for a period are determine after the end of that period, the date o determination;

(e) where emoluments for a period are determine in that period, the last day of that period.

The emoluments assessable under Schedule] include all salaries, wages, director's fees and othe money sums. In addition, there are a wide range o benefits which must be added to taxable emoluments These include the provision of living accommodatio on advantageous terms and advantages arising from the use of vouchers.

Further taxable benefits accrue to directors an employees receiving emoluments of £8,500 or more ir the year of assessment. These benefits include th reimbursement of expenses, the availability of moto cars for private motoring, the provision of petrol c other fuel for private motoring, the provision o interest free loans, and other benefits provided at th employer's expense. The cost of providing a limite range of child care facilities may be excluded.

Married Men

Income	Couples under 65		Couples 65 or over*	
	Income tax	Average rate	Income tax	Average rate
£	£	per cent	£	per cent
6,000	246	4·1	—	—
7,000	496	7·1	156	2·2
8,000	746	9·3	406	5·1
9,000	996	11·1	656	7·3
10,000	1,246	12·5	906	9·1
12,000	1,746	14·6	1,406	11·7
14,000	2,246	16·0	1,969	14·1
16,000	2,746	17·2	2,719	17·0
18,000	3,246	18·0	3,246	18·0
20,000	3,746	18·7	3,746	18·7
25,000	4,996	20·0	4,996	20·0
30,000	6,439	21·5	6,439	21·5
40,000	10,439	26·1	10,439	26·1
50,000	14,439	28·9	14,439	28·9
60,000	18,439	30·7	18,439	30·7
100,000	34,439	34·4	34,439	34·4

Persons aged 75 or over suffer rather less tax on income falling below £18,000 on this table.

In arriving at the amount to be assessed under Schedule E, all expenses incurred wholly, exclusively and necessarily in the performance of the duties may be deducted. This includes fees and subscriptions paid to certain professional bodies and learned societies. Fees paid to managers by entertainers, actors and others assessable under Schedule E may be deducted, up to a maximum of 17·5 per cent of earnings.

Compensation for loss of office and other sums received on the termination of an office or employment are assessable to tax. However, the first £30,000 may usually be excluded with only the balance remaining chargeable.

Earnings received from an approved profit-related pay scheme are exempt from income tax.

Schedule F.—This Schedule is concerned with company dividends and distributions. A United Kingdom resident company paying a dividend or making a distribution must account to the Inland Revenue for advance corporation tax at the rate equal to one third of the sum paid to shareholders in 1991–92. A shareholder residing in the United Kingdom receives the dividend or distribution, together with a tax credit equal to the amount of advance corporation tax. The dividend or distribution is regarded as having suffered income tax, equal to the tax credit, at the basic rate, and where the shareholder is not liable, or not fully liable, at this rate a repayment can be obtained. Individuals liable at the higher rate of 40 per cent will incur further liability. Some payments made by an unquoted trading company to redeem or purchase its own shares are not treated as distributions.

Building society interest and bank interest.—For many years a special composite rate tax scheme applied to payments of building society interest and, more recently, to most payments of bank interest made to individuals. Interest of this nature incurred no liability to basic rate income tax in the hands of the depositor, nor could tax be recovered by a depositor not liable to income tax. The actual interest received was 'grossed up' at the rate of one third to establish the amount of total income received by a depositor liable at the higher rate of 40 per cent.

A composite rate scheme was not compatible with a system of independent taxation as a spouse entitled to a personal allowance, but with little income, could not obtain repayment of composite rate tax. There-

fore the composite tax scheme ceased to apply on April 6, 1991. From this date most payments of building society and bank interest are received after the deduction of income tax at the basic rate. However, those not liable to income tax at the basic rate may arrange to receive interest gross, with no tax being deducted on payment.

Income not taxable

This includes interest on National Savings Certificates, most scholarship income, bounty payments to members of the armed services and annuities payable to the holders of certain awards. Dividend income arising from investments in personal equity plans may be exempt from tax. Income received under most maintenance agreements and court orders made after June 30, 1988 will not be liable to tax. Nor will payments made under many deeds of covenant executed after March 14, 1988 be recognized for tax purposes, unless the recipient is a charity. Interest arising after December 31, 1990 on a Tax Exempt Special Savings Account (TESSA) opened with a building society or bank will be exempt from tax, if the account is maintained throughout a five-year period.

Social security benefits

Many social security benefits are not liable to income tax. These include family income supplement, long-term sickness benefit, child benefit, war widow's pension, mobility allowance and numerous others. Among the limited range of benefits which are taxable is the retirement pension, widow's allowance, widowed mother's allowance, and unemployment benefits. Short-term sickness benefit and maternity pay payable by an employer is also chargeable to tax.

Pay as you earn

The Pay As You Earn system is not an independent form of taxation but has been designed to collect income tax by deduction from most emoluments. When paying emoluments to employees an employer is usually required to deduct income tax and account for that tax to the Inland Revenue. In many cases this deduction procedure will fully exhaust the individual's liability to income tax, unless there is other income. The date of 'receipt' used for assessment purposes (*see* above) also identifies the date of 'payment' when establishing liability for PAYE.

Allowances

The previous system of conferring personal and other allowances was substantially amended for 1990–91 and future years by the introduction of independent taxation. The available allowances for 1991–92 are outlined below.

Personal allowance.—Each individual receives a basic personal allowance of £3,295. This is increased to £4,020 for individuals over the age of 64 on April 5, 1992, and further increased to £4,180 for those over the age of 74 on the same date. The increased allowance is available for those who died during the year of assessment but who would otherwise have achieved the appropriate age not later than April 5, 1992.

The amount of the increased personal allowance for older taxpayers will be reduced by one-half of total income in excess of £13,500. This reduction in the allowance will continue until it has been reduced to the basic personal allowance of £3,295.

Apart from limited transitional matters mentioned below, any unused part of the personal allowance of one spouse cannot be transferred to the other.

Married couple's allowance.—A married man who was 'living with' his wife at any time in the year ending on April 5, 1992, is entitled to a married couple's allowance. The basic allowance is £1,720. This may be increased to £2,355 if either the husband or the wife is 65 years or over at any time in the year ending on April 5, 1992. A further increase to £2,395 can be obtained where either party to the marriage was 75 or over on April 5, 1992. Where an individual would otherwise have reached either age by April 5, 1992, but who died earlier in the year, the increased allowance is given.

The amount of the increased married couple's allowance may be reduced where the income of the husband (excluding the income of the wife) exceeds £13,500. The reduction will comprise:

(a) one-half of the husband's total income in excess of £13,500, less

(b) the amount of any reduction made when calculating the husband's increased personal allowance.

This reduction in the married couple's allowance cannot reduce that allowance below the basic amount of £1,720.

If husband and wife were married during 1991–92 the married couple's allowance of £1,720, or any increased sum, must be reduced by one-twelfth for each complete month commencing on April 6, 1991, and preceding the date of marriage.

Where a husband cannot utilize all or any part of the married couple's allowance due to an absence of income, he may transfer the unused portion to his wife. The decision whether or not to transfer remains with the husband and he cannot be compelled to act.

Additional personal allowance.—An allowance of £1,720 is available to a single person who has a qualifying child resident with him or her in 1991–92. The allowance can also be obtained by a married man whose wife is totally incapacitated by physical or mental infirmity throughout the year.

A 'qualifying child' for 1991–92 must be born during the year, be under the age of 16 years at the commencement of the year, or be over the age of 16 at the commencement of the year and either receiving full-time instruction at a university, college, school or other educational establishment or undergoing training for a trade, profession or vocation throughout a minimum period of two years. It is also necessary that the child is the claimant's own or, i not such a child, was either born during 1991–92 or under the age of 18 at the commencement of the year and maintained by the claimant at his or her own expense during the whole of the succeeding twelve month period.

Only one additional personal allowance of £1,720 can be obtained by an individual notwithstanding the number of children involved. Where an unmarried couple are living together as husband and wife it is not possible for both to obtain the additional personal allowance.

Widow's bereavement allowance.—For the year of assessment in which a husband dies his surviving widow may obtain a widow's bereavement allowance which is £1,720 for 1991–92. It is a requirement that the parties were 'living together' immediately before the husband's death. A similar allowance will be available in the year following death, unless the widow remarried in the year of death. No widow's bereavement allowance can be obtained for future years.

Blind person's allowance.—An allowance of £1,080 is available to an individual if at any time during the year ending on April 5, 1992, he or she was registered as blind on a register maintained by a local authority. If the individual is 'living with' a wife or husband, any unused part of the blind person's allowance can be transferred to the other spouse.

Transitional allowances.—There are three limited transitional allowances which are intended to ensure that the introduction of independent taxation does not increase liability to income tax. These allowances comprise:

(a) an increased personal allowance available to a wife where the husband cannot fully use that allowance in 1991–92;

(b) a special personal allowance available to a husband where his wife falls into a higher age group, namely over 64 or over 74;

(c) a married couple's allowance available to a separated husband not 'living with' his wife if the separation occurred before April 6, 1990.

Life assurance relief

Life assurance deduction relief is limited to premiums paid on policies made before March 14, 1984. No relief is available for policies issued after this date. Where the terms of a policy made before March 14, 1984 are subsequently varied or extended to produce increased benefits, future premiums paid may no longer qualify for relief.

When paying premiums under a qualifying policy made before March 14, 1984, the payer will deduct and retain income tax at the rate of 12·5 per cent. The ability to retain deductions made in this manner is not affected by the payer's liability to income tax on taxable income. No restriction to the deduction procedure arises if aggregate premiums paid during a year of assessment do not exceed £1,500 (calculated before deducting tax). Should premiums exceed this amount, relief will be confined to £1,500 or one-sixth of total income, whichever is the greater. Where sums deducted exceed the maximum limit, the excess must be accounted for to the Inland Revenue.

Other deductions

In addition to personal and other allowances which reduce taxable income, further deductions may be available to an individual. These include payments of interest.

In some instances interest paid by a business proprietor may be included when calculating profits chargeable to income tax under Case I or Case II of Schedule D. Many private individuals cannot obtain relief in this manner and must satisfy stringent requirements before relief will be forthcoming. In general terms, before interest can qualify for relief it must be annual, as opposed to short, interest or paid to a bank, stockbroker or discount house. Relief will not be available to the extent that interest exceeds a reasonable commercial rate and no relief is forthcoming for interest on an overdraft.

For 1991–92 relief will be available on the following payments:

(a) Interest on a loan to purchase, develop or improve an interest in land owned by the individual and used as the only or main residence of that individual. 'Land' includes large houseboats and also caravans used for a similar purpose. No relief is available for interest on loans applied after April 5, 1988 for the development or improvement of land, unless the work involves the construction of a new building. Relief is available for interest paid on a loan applied to acquire a property which is the only or main residence of a dependent relative, a separated spouse or a divorced former spouse, but only where that person occupied the property before April 6, 1988. Relief may also be forthcoming for interest on a loan used to acquire some other property, perhaps to be used as the only or main residence on retirement, by an individual who is compelled to occupy property by reason of his or her work. If the loan, or aggregate of several loans, exceeds £30,000, relief is restricted to interest on that amount. Where two or more persons apply loans after July 31, 1988 to acquire interests in a single building, those persons cannot, collectively, obtain relief for interest on more than £30,000 in relation to that building. For interest paid after April 5, 1991, relief is confined to income tax at the basic rate. There can be no relief at the higher rate in excess of 25 per cent.

(b) Interest on a loan to purchase or improve an interest in land which is let or available for letting at a commercial rent. This interest is only capable of being deducted from rental income.

(c) Interest on a loan made to acquire an interest in a close company or in a partnership, or to advance money to such a person.

(d) Interest on a loan to a member of a partnership to acquire machinery or plant for use in the partnership business.

(e) Interest on a loan to an employed person to acquire machinery or plant for the purposes of his/her employment.

(f) Interest on a loan made for the purpose of contributing capital to an industrial co-operative.

(g) Interest on a loan applied for investment in an employee-controlled company.

(h) Interest on a loan made to elderly persons for the purchase of an annuity where the loan is secured on land. If the loan exceeds £30,000, relief is limited to interest on this amount. This relief also is restricted to income tax at the basic rate for payments made after April 5, 1991.

(i) Interest on a loan to personal representatives to provide funds for the payment of capital transfer tax or inheritance tax.

Relief for many payments of mortgage interest is obtained through a special scheme known as MIRAS (mortgage interest relief at source). This applies to interest paid to a building society, bank, insurance company and certain other persons. When making payments of this nature the payer will deduct and retain income tax at the basic rate. This will provide the payer with full relief at the basic rate and no other relief will be necessary. Qualifying payments of interest outside the MIRAS scheme continue to produce relief by deduction from income chargeable to income tax at the basic rate. Where mortgage interest is payable by a husband and/or his wife 'living together', the parties may allocate the interest payment between themselves in whatever manner is most tax efficient. With the withdrawal of relief at the higher rate little advantage now arises from this facility.

Many employees pay contributions to an approved occupational pension scheme. The amount of their contributions may be deducted when establishing emoluments assessable under Schedule E. Relief should also be available for any additional voluntary contributions paid.

Self-employed individuals and those receiving earnings not covered by an occupational pension scheme may contribute under personal pension scheme arrangements. These individuals may also pay premiums under retirement annuity schemes, if the arrangements were concluded before July 1, 1988. Contributions paid under both headings may obtain income tax relief, subject to maximum limits.

Subject to a maximum of £40,000 in any one year the cost of subscribing for shares in an unquoted company may qualify as a deduction from taxable income under the Business Expansion Scheme. Many requirements must be satisfied before this relief can be obtained, but husband and wife may each take advantage of the £40,000 annual maximum.

CAPITAL GAINS TAX

A person is chargeable to capital gains tax on chargeable gains which accrue to him or her during a year of assessment ending on April 5. The application of the tax has been amended substantially in recent years and the following information is confined to the year of assessment 1991–92, ending on April 5 1992.

Liability extends to persons who are either resident or ordinarily resident for the year but special rules apply where a person permanently leaves the United Kingdom or comes to this territory for the purpose of acquiring residence. Non-residents are not liable to capital gains tax unless, exceptionally, they carry on a business in the United Kingdom through a branch or agency.

Chargeable gains accruing to companies are assessable to corporation tax and not to capital gains tax.

Capital gains tax is chargeable on the total of chargeable gains which accrue to a person in a year of assessment, after subtracting allowable losses arising in the same year. Unused allowable losses brought forward from some earlier year may be offset against current chargeable gains but in the case of individuals this must not reduce the net chargeable gains for 1991–92 below £5,500. It is possible to utilize trading losses in this manner for 1991–92 and future years where those losses have not been offset against income.

Rate of tax

Where the net chargeable gains accruing to an individual during 1991–92 do not exceed £5,500 there will be no liability to capital gains tax. If the net gains exceed £5,500 the excess is chargeable at the taxpayer's marginal rate of income tax. This is achieved by adding to the amount of income chargeable to income tax the excess net chargeable gains. The rate attributable to this top slice will disclose the rate of capital gains tax payable, which may be at 25 per cent, 40 per cent or a combination of the two. Although income tax rates are used, capital gains tax remains a separate tax.

Capital gains tax for 1991–92 normally falls due for payment on or before December 1, 1992. If the return or other information recording chargeable gains is delayed, interest may become chargeable.

Husband and wife

For 1989–90 and earlier years only one aggregate annual exemption was available for a husband and wife 'living together'. In addition, apart from the year of marriage, chargeable gains of a married woman 'living with' her husband were assessed and charged on the husband, unless an election for separate assessment was made. This election did not reduce the aggregate tax payable but merely apportioned liability between the spouses on an equitable basis.

This treatment of a married woman's gains ceased to apply on April 6, 1990. For the future, each spouse is independently assessed on his or her gains, with each being separately entitled to the annual exemption of £5,500 for 1991–92.

No liability to capital gains tax arises from the transfer of assets between spouses 'living together'.

Disposal of assets

Before liability to capital gains tax can arise a disposal, or deemed disposal, of an asset must take place. This occurs not only where assets are sold or exchanged but applies on the making of a gift. There is also a disposal of assets where any capital sum is derived from assets, for example, where compensation is received for loss or damage to an asset.

The date on which a disposal must be treated as having taken place will determine the year of assessment into which the chargeable gain or allowable loss falls. In those cases where a disposal is made under an unconditional contract, the time of disposal will be that when the contract was entered into and not the subsequent date of conveyance or transfer. A disposal under a conditional contract or option is treated as taking place when the contract becomes unconditional or the option is exercised. Disposals by way of gift are undertaken when the gift becomes effective.

Valuation of assets

The amount actually received as consideration for the disposal of an asset will be the sum from which very limited outgoings must be deducted for the purpose of establishing the gain or loss. In some cases, however, the consideration passing will not accurately reflect the value of the asset and a different basis must be used. This applies, in particular, where an asset is transferred by way of gift or otherwise than by a bargain made at arm's length. Such transactions are deemed to take place for a consideration representing market value, which will determine both the disposal proceeds accruing to the

transferor and the cost of acquisition to the transferee.

Market value represents the price which an asset might reasonably be expected to fetch on a sale in the open market. In the case of unquoted shares or securities it is to be assumed that the hypothetical purchaser in the open market would have available all the information which a prudent prospective purchaser of shares or securities might reasonably require if he were proposing to purchase them from a willing vendor by private treaty and at arm's length. This is an important consideration as the amount of information deemed to be available to a hypothetical purchaser may materially affect the price 'reasonably' offered in an open market situation. The market value of unquoted shares or securities will usually be established following negotiations with the Shares Valuation Division of the Capital Taxes Office.

Special rules apply to determine the market value of shares quoted on the Stock Exchange.

Deduction for outgoings

Once the actual or notional disposal proceeds have been determined it only remains to subtract eligible outgoings for the purpose of computing the gain or loss. There is the general rule that any outgoings deducted, or which are available to be deducted, when calculating income tax liability must be ignored. Subject to this, deductions will usually be limited to:

(a) the cost of acquiring the asset, together with incidental costs wholly and exclusively incurred in connection with the acquisition;

(b) expenditure incurred wholly and exclusively on the asset in enhancing its value, being expenditure reflected in the state or nature of the asset at the time of the disposal, and any other expenditure wholly and exclusively incurred in establishing, preserving or defending title to, or a right over, the asset; and

(c) the incidental costs of making the disposal.

Where the disposal concerns a leasehold interest having less than 50 years to run, any expenditure falling under (a) and (b) must be written off throughout the duration of the lease. This recognizes that a lease is a wasting asset which, at the termination of the leasing period, will retain no value.

Assets held on March 31, 1982

Where the disposal of assets held on March 31, 1982 takes place after April 5, 1988, the actual cost of acquisition will not usually enter into the calculation of gain. It is to be assumed that such assets were acquired on March 31, 1982 for a consideration representing market value on that date. The increase in value, if any, occurring before March 31, 1982 will not be assessable to capital gains tax.

Indexation allowance

An indexation allowance will be available when calculating the chargeable gain or allowable loss. This allowance is based on percentage increases in the retail prices index between the month of March 1982, or if later the month in which expenditure is incurred, and the month of disposal. The increase is applied to the items of expenditure in (a) and (b) above to determine the amount of the indexation allowance. However, if the asset was acquired before March 31, 1982 and the disposal occurs after April 5, 1988, the allowance will be based on market value at March 31, 1982.

The amount of the indexation allowance will be

subtracted from the gain, or added to the loss, to calculate the chargeable gain or allowable loss arising on disposal.

Exemptions

There is a general exemption from liability to capital gains tax where the net gains of an individual for 1991–92 do not exceed £5,500. From April 6, 1990, this general exemption applies separately to a husband and to his wife where the parties are 'living together'.

The disposal of many assets will not give rise to chargeable gains or allowable losses and these include:

(a) private motor cars;
(b) government securities;
(c) loan stock and other securities (but not shares);
(d) options and contracts relating to securities within (b) and (c);
(e) National Savings Certificates, Premium Bonds, Defence Bonds and National Development Bonds;
(f) currency of any description acquired for personal expenditure outside the United Kingdom;
(g) decorations awarded for valour;
(h) betting wins and pools, lottery or games prizes;
(i) compensation or damages for any wrong or injury suffered by an individual in his/her person or in his/her profession or vocation;
(j) life assurance and deferred annuity contracts where the person making the disposal is the original beneficial owner;
(k) dwelling-houses and land enjoyed with the residence which is an individual's only or main residence;
(l) tangible movable property, the consideration for the disposal of which does not exceed £6,000;
(m) certain tangible movable property which is a wasting asset having a life not exceeding 50 years;
(n) assets transferred to charities and other bodies;
(o) works of art, historic buildings and similar assets;
(p) assets used to provide maintenance funds for historic buildings;
(q) assets transferred to trustees for the benefit of employees.

Dwelling-houses

Exemption from capital gains tax will usually be available for any gain which accrues to an individual from the disposal of, or of an interest in, a dwelling-house or part of a dwelling-house which has been his/her only or main residence. The exemption extends to land which has been occupied and enjoyed with the residence as its garden or grounds. Some restriction may be necessary where the land exceeds half a hectare.

The gain will not be chargeable to capital gains tax if the dwelling-house, or part, has been the individual's only or main residence throughout the period of ownership, or throughout the entire period except for all or any part of the last three years (or two years for disposals before March 19, 1991). A proportionate part of the gain will be exempt if the dwelling-house has been the individual's only or main residence for part only of the period of ownership. In the case of property acquired before March 31, 1982, the period of ownership is treated as commencing on this date.

Where part of the dwelling-house has been used exclusively for business purposes, that part of the gain attributable to business use will not be exempt. It will be comparatively unusual for any part to be used exclusively for such a purpose, except perhaps in the case of doctors' or dentists' surgeries.

In those cases where part of a qualifying dwelling-house has been used to provide rented residential accommodation this non-personal use may frequently be ignored when calculating exemption from capital gains tax, unless relatively substantial sums are involved.

Dwellings occupied by dependent relatives or separated or divorced former spouses, may also qualify for the exemption, but only where occupation commenced before April 6, 1988.

Roll-over relief

Persons carrying on business will often undertake the disposal of an asset and use the proceeds to finance the acquisition of a replacement asset. Where this situation arises a claim for roll-over relief may be available. The broad effect of such a claim is that all or part of the gain arising on the disposal of the old asset may be disregarded. The gain or part is then subtracted from the cost of acquiring the replacement asset. As this cost is reduced, any gain arising from the future disposal of the replacement asset will be correspondingly increased, unless of course a further roll-over situation then develops.

It remains a requirement that both the old and the replacement asset must be used for the purpose of the taxpayer's business. Relief will only be available if the acquisition of the replacement asset takes place within a period commencing twelve months before, and ending three years after, the disposal of the old asset, although the Board of Inland Revenue retain a discretion to extend this period where the circumstances were such that it was impossible for the taxpayer to acquire the replacement asset before the expiration of the normal time limit.

Whilst many business assets qualify for roll-over relief there are exceptions.

Gifts

The gift of an asset is treated as a disposal made for a consideration equal to market value, with a corresponding acquisition by the transferee at an identical value. For gifts made by individuals and trustees before March 14, 1989, a wide-ranging claim for hold-over relief was available where the transferee was resident in the United Kingdom.

In the case of gifts made subsequently, hold-over relief is limited to the transfer of certain assets only. The more important of these comprise:

(a) assets used for the purposes of a trade or similar activity carried on by the transferor or his/her family company;
(b) shares or securities of a trading company which is neither quoted on a stock exchange nor dealt in on the Unlisted Securities Market;
(c) shares or securities of a trading company which is quoted or listed but which is the transferor's family company;
(d) many interests in agricultural property qualifying for 50 per cent or 30 per cent inheritance tax relief;
(e) assets involved in transactions which are lifetime transfers for inheritance tax purposes, other than potentially exempt transfers.

The effect of the claim is similar to that following a claim for roll-over relief, but adjustments will be necessary where some consideration is given for the transfer, the asset has not been used for business purposes throughout the period of ownership, or not all assets of a company are used for business purposes.

Retirement relief

Retirement relief is available to an individual who disposes by way of sale or gift of the whole or part of a business. It does not necessarily follow that the isolated disposal of assets will represent the disposal of the whole or part of a business. The main condition for granting this relief is that throughout a period of at least one year the business has been owned either by the individual or by a trading company in which the individual retained a sufficient shareholding interest. The relief extends also to cases where an individual disposes by way of sale or gift of shares or securities of a company. It must be demonstrated that the company was a trading company, that the individual retained a sufficient shareholding interest, and that he/she was engaged as a full-time working director.

An individual who has attained the age of 55 years at the time of a disposal may obtain retirement relief up to a maximum of £375,000 for disposals taking place after March 18, 1991. The amount of this relief must be reduced if the conditions have not been satisfied throughout a ten-year period. With a single exception no retirement relief can be obtained if the disposal occurs before the individual's 55th birthday. This exception arises where an individual is compelled to retire early on the grounds of ill-health. The normal retirement relief may then be obtained. Any retirement relief must be subtracted from the net gains arising on disposal, leaving the balance remaining, if any, chargeable to capital gains tax in the normal manner.

Death

No capital gains tax is chargeable on the value of assets retained at the time of death. However, the personal representatives administering the deceased's estate are deemed to acquire those assets for a consideration representing market value on death. This ensures that any increase in value occurring before the date of death will not be chargeable to capital gains tax. If a legatee or other person acquires an asset under a will or intestacy no chargeable gain will accrue to the personal representatives, and the person taking the asset will also be treated as having acquired it at the time of death for its then market value.

INHERITANCE TAX

Throughout a period of some 90 years estate duty was payable on the value of an individual's estate at the time of death. Liability did not extend to lifetime gifts other than those made shortly before death and a limited range of further gifts where the donor continued to retain some benefit from the assets gifted. Estate duty ceased to apply for deaths occurring after March 12, 1975 following the introduction of capital transfer tax. This tax was not limited to the value of an estate at the time of death but applied to many gifts made during lifetime. Although the broad framework of capital transfer tax remains, very substantial changes were introduced for events occurring after March 17, 1986. In recognition of these changes the tax was renamed inheritance tax and now bears many characteristics of the former estate duty.

The nature and scope of inheritance tax is outlined below, but the comments made have little application

to events occurring before 18 March 1986 when capital transfer tax applied.

Liability to inheritance tax may arise on a limited range of lifetime gifts and other dispositions and also on the value of assets retained, or deemed to be retained, at the time of death. An individual's domicile at the time of any gift or on death is an important matter. Domicile will generally be determined by applying normal rules, but special considerations may be necessary where an individual was previously domiciled in the United Kingdom but subsequently acquired a domicile of choice overseas. Where a person was domiciled in the United Kingdom at the time of a disposition or on death the location of assets is immaterial and full liability to inheritance tax arises. Individuals domiciled outside the United Kindom are, however, chargeable to inheritance tax only on transactions affecting assets located in the United Kingdom.

The assets of husband and wife are not merged for inheritance tax purposes. Each spouse is treated as a separate individual entitled to receive the benefit of his or her exemptions, reliefs and rates of tax. Where husband and wife retain similar assets, special 'related property' provisions may require the merger of those assets for valuation purposes only.

Lifetime gifts and dispositions

Gifts and dispositions made during lifetime fall under four broad headings, namely:

(a) dispositions which are not transfers of value;
(b) exempt transfers;
(c) potentially exempt transfers; and
(d) chargeable transfers.

Dispositions which are not transfers of value.—Several lifetime transactions are not treated as transfers of value and may be entirely disregarded for inheritance tax purposes. These include transactions not intended to confer gratuitous benefit, the provision of family maintenance, the waiver of the right to receive remuneration or dividends, and the grant of agricultural tenancies for full consideration.

Exempt transfers.—Certain other transfers are treated as exempt transfers and incur no liability to inheritance tax. The main exempt transfers are listed below:

Transfers between spouses.—Transfers between husband and wife are usually exempt. However, if the transferor is, but the transferee spouse is not, domiciled in the United Kingdom, transfers will be exempt only to the extent that the total does not exceed £55,000. Unlike the requirement used for income tax and capital gains tax purposes, it is immaterial whether husband and wife are living together.

Annual exemption.—The first £3,000 of gifts and other dispositions made in a year ending on April 5 is exempt. If the exemption is not used, or not wholly used, in any year the balance may be carried forward to the following year only. The annual exemption will only be available for a potentially exempt transfer (*see* p. 1013) if that transfer subsequently becomes chargeable by reason of the donor's death.

Small gifts.—Outright gifts of £250 or less to any person in one year ending April 5 are exempt.

Normal expenditure.—A transfer made during lifetime and comprising normal expenditure is exempt. To obtain this exemption it must be shown that:

(a) the transfer was made as part of the normal expenditure of the transferor;
(b) taking one year with another, the transfer was made out of income; and

(c) after allowing for all transfers of value forming part of normal expenditure the transferor was left with sufficient income to maintain his or her usual standard of living.

Gifts in consideration of marriage.—These are exempt if they satisfy certain requirements. The amount allowed will be governed by the relationship between the donor and a party to the marriage. The allowable amounts comprise:

(a) gifts by a parent—£5,000;
(b) gifts by a grandparent—£2,500;
(c) gifts by a party to the marriage—£2,500;
(d) gifts by other persons—£1,000.

Gifts to charities.—Gifts to charities are exempt from liability.

Gifts to political parties.—Gifts to political parties which satisfy certain requirements are generally exempt.

Gifts for national purposes.—Gifts made to an extensive list of bodies are exempt from liability. These include, among others:

(a) the National Gallery;
(b) the British Museum;
(c) the National Trust;
(d) the National Art Collections Fund;
(e) the Nature Conservancy Council;
(f) the Historic Buildings and Monuments Commission for England;
(g) any local authority;
(h) any university or university college in the United Kingdom.

A number of other gifts made for the public benefit are also exempt.

Potentially exempt transfers.—Lifetime gifts and dispositions which are neither to be ignored nor comprise exempt transfers incur possible liability to inheritance tax. However, relief is available for a range of potentially exempt transfers. These comprise gifts made by an individual to:

(a) a second individual;
(b) trustees administering an accumulation and maintenance trust; or
(c) trustees administering a disabled person's trust.

The accumulation and maintenance trust mentioned in (b) must provide that on reaching a specified age, not exceeding twenty-five years, a beneficiary will become absolutely entitled to trust assets or obtain an interest in possession in the income of those assets.

Further additions were made to the list of potentially exempt transfers for transactions taking place after March 16, 1987. These affect settled property administered by trustees where an individual, or individuals, retain an interest in possession. The transfer of assets to, the removal of assets from, or the rearrangement of interests in such property comprise potentially exempt transfers if the person transferring an interest and the person benefiting from the transfer are both individuals.

No immediate liability to inheritance tax will arise on the making of a potentially exempt transfer. Should the donor survive for a period of seven years, immunity from liability will be confirmed. However, the donor's death within the seven-year *inter vivos* period produces liability, as explained later, if the amounts involved are sufficiently substantial.

Chargeable transfers.—Any remaining lifetime gifts or dispositions which are neither to be ignored nor represent exempt transfers or potentially exempt transfers, incur liability to inheritance tax. The range of such chargeable transfers is severely limited and is broadly confined to transfers made to or affecting certain trusts, transfers to non-individuals and transfers involving companies.

Gifts with reservation

A lifetime gift of assets made at any time after March 17, 1986 may incur additional liability to inheritance tax if the donor retains some interest in the subject matter of the gift. This may arise, for example, where a parent transfers a dwelling-house to a son or daughter and continues to occupy the property or to enjoy some benefit from that property. The retention of a benefit may be ignored where it is enjoyed in return for full consideration, perhaps a commercial rent, or where the benefit arises from changed circumstances which could not have been foreseen at the time of the original gift. The gift with reservation provisions will not usually apply to most exempt transfers.

There are three possibilities which may arise where the donor reserves or enjoys some benefit from the subject matter of a previous gift and subsequently dies, namely:

(a) If no benefit is enjoyed within a period of seven years before death there can be no further liability.
(b) If the benefit ceased to be enjoyed within a period of seven years before the date of death the original donor is deemed to have made a potentially exempt transfer representing the value of the asset at the time of cessation.
(c) If the benefit is enjoyed at the time of death the value of the asset must be included in the value of the deceased's estate on death.

It must be emphasized that the existence of a benefit enjoyed at any time within a period of seven years before death will establish liability on gifts with reservation, notwithstanding that the gift may have been made many years earlier, providing it was undertaken after March 17, 1986.

Death

Immediately before the time of death an individual is deemed to make a transfer of value. This transfer will comprise the value of assets forming part of the deceased's estate after subtracting most liabilities. Any exempt transfers may, however, be excluded. These include transfers for the benefit of a surviving spouse, a charity and a qualifying political party, together with bequests to approved bodies and for national purposes.

Death may also trigger three additional liabilities, namely:

(a) A potentially exempt transfer made within the period of seven years ending on death loses its potential status and becomes chargeable to inheritance tax.
(b) The value of gifts made with reservation may incur liability if any benefit was enjoyed within a period of seven years preceding death.
(c) Additional tax may become payable for chargeable lifetime transfers made within seven years before death.

Valuations

The valuation of assets is an important matter as this will establish the value transferred for lifetime dispositions and also the value of a person's estate at the time of death. The value of property will represent the price which might reasonably be expected from a sale in the open market. This price cannot be reduced on the grounds that, should the whole property be placed on the market simultaneously, values would be depressed.

In some cases it may be necessary to incorporate the value of 'related property'. This will include property comprised in the estate of the transferor's spouse and certain property previously transferred to charities. The purpose of the related property valuation rules is not to add the value of the property to the estate of the transferor. Related property must be merged to establish the aggregate value of the respective interests and this value is then apportioned, usually on a *pro rata* basis, to the separate interests.

The value of shares and securities quoted on the Stock Exchange will be determined by extracting figures from the daily list of official prices.

Where quoted shares and securities are sold within a period of twelve months following the date of death, a claim may be made to substitute the proceeds for the value on death. This claim will only be beneficial if the gross proceeds realized are lower than market value at the time of death. A similar claim may be available for interests in land sold within a period of three years following death.

Relief for assets

Special relief is made available for certain assets, notably woodlands, agricultural property and business property. The effect of this relief is summarized below:

Woodlands.—Where woodlands pass on death the value will usually be included in the deceased's estate. However, an election may be made in respect of land in the United Kingdom on which trees or underwood is growing to delete the value of those assets. Relief is confined to the value of trees or underwood and does not extend to the land on which they are growing. Liability to inheritance tax will arise if and when the trees or underwood are sold on a future occasion.

Agricultural property.—Relief is available for the agricultural value of agricultural property. Such property must be occupied and used for agricultural purposes and relief is confined to the agricultural value.

The value transferred, either on a lifetime gift or on death, must be determined. This value may then be reduced by a percentage. A higher 50 per cent deduction will be available if the transferor retained vacant possession or could have obtained that possession within a period of twelve months following the transfer. The increased deduction of 50 per cent may also be available for certain agricultural property held on March 9, 1981. In other cases, notably including land let to tenants, a lower deduction of 30 per cent is available.

It remains a requirement that the agricultural property was either occupied by the transferor for the purposes of agriculture throughout a two-year period ending on the date of the transfer, or was owned by him/her throughout a period of seven years ending on that date and occupied for agricultural purposes.

Business property.—Where the value transferred is attributable to relevant business property, that value may be reduced by a percentage. The reduction in value applies to:

(a) property consisting of a business or an interest in a business;

(b) shares or securities of a company, whether quoted or unquoted, which provided the transferor with control of the company immediately before the transfer. Control for this purpose may include that created by related property;

(c) unquoted shares or securities not falling within (b) which provided the transferor with more than 25 per cent of voting rights;

(d) other unquoted shares or securities not falling within (c);

(e) any land, building, machinery or plant which, immediately before the transfer, was used wholly or mainly for the purposes of a business carried on by a company of which the transferor had control;

(f) any land, building, machinery or plant which, immediately before the transfer, was used wholly or mainly for the purposes of a business carried on by a partnership of which the transferor was a partner; and

(g) any land, building, machinery or plant which, immediately before the transfer, was used wholly or mainly for the purposes of a business carried on by the transferor and was then settled property in which he retained an interest in possession.

For property falling within (a) or (b) the deduction is 50 per cent. A similar deduction is available for property in (c), if the event occurs after March 16, 1987. A reduced deduction of 30 per cent applies to property in (d) to (g).

It is a general requirement that the property must have been retained for a period of two years before the transfer or death and restrictions may be necessary if the property has not been used wholly for business purposes. The same slice of property cannot obtain both business property relief and the relief available for agricultural property.

Calculation of tax payable

The calculation of inheritance tax payable adopts the use of a cumulative total. Each chargeable lifetime transfer is added to the total with a final addition made on death. The top slice added to the total for the current event determines the rate at which inheritance tax must be paid. However, the cumulative total will only include transfers made within a period of seven years before the current event and those undertaken outside this period must be excluded. Although inheritance tax was only introduced on March 18, 1986, the seven-year cumulative total will include chargeable lifetime gifts made before that date, subject to the seven-year limitation.

Lifetime chargeable transfers.—The value transferred by the limited range of lifetime chargeable transfers must be added to the seven-year cumulative total to calculate the amount of inheritance tax due. The tax is imposed at one-half of the rate shown below. However, if the donor dies within a period of seven years from the date of the chargeable lifetime transfer, additional tax may be due. This is calculated by applying tax at the full rate (in substitution for the one-half rate previously used). The amount of tax is then reduced to a percentage by applying tapering relief. This percentage is governed by the number of years from the date of the lifetime gift to the date of death and is as follows:

Period of years before death	Percentage
Not more than 3	100
More than 3 but not more than 4	80
More than 4 but not more than 5	60
More than 5 but not more than 6	40
More than 6 but not more than 7	20

Should this exercise produce liability greater than that previously paid at the one-half rate on the lifetime transfer, additional tax, representing the difference, must be discharged. Where the calculation shows an amount falling below tax paid on the lifetime transfer, no additional liability can arise nor will the deficiency become repayable.

Potentially exempt transfers.—Where a potentially exempt transfer loses immunity from liability, due to the donor's death within the seven-year *inter vivos* period, the value transferred becomes liable to inheritance tax. Liability is calculated by applying the full rate shown below, reduced to the percentage governed by tapering relief if the original transfer occurred more than three years before death.

Death.—The final addition to the seven-year cumulative total will comprise the value of an estate on death. Inheritance tax will be calculated by applying the full rate shown below. No tapering relief can be obtained.

Rates of tax

In earlier times there were several rates of inheritance tax which progressively increased as the value transferred grew in size. However, for events taking place after March 14, 1988, a nil rate applies to the initial slice. The size of this slice has been increased on several occasions and for events occurring after April 5, 1991 is £140,000. Any excess is charged at the single positive rate of 40 per cent.

Only one-half of the 40 per cent rate (namely 20 per cent) will be applicable for chargeable lifetime transfers.

It must be anticipated that the above rate and rateband will be amended on future occasions.

Payment of tax

Inheritance tax usually falls due for payment six months after the end of the month in which the chargeable transaction takes place. Where a transfer, other than that made on death, occurs after April 5 and before the following October 1, tax falls due on the following April 30, although there are some exceptions to this general rule.

Inheritance tax attributable to the transfer of certain land, controlling shareholding interests, unquoted shares, businesses and interests in businesses, together with agricultural property, may usually be satisfied by instalments spread over ten years. Except in the case of non-agricultural land, where interest is charged on outstanding instalments, no liability to interest arises where tax is paid on the due date. In all cases, delay in the payment of tax may incur liability to interest.

Settled property

Complex rules apply to establish inheritance tax liability on settled property. Where a person is beneficially entitled to an interest in possession, that person is effectively deemed to own the property in which the interest subsists. It follows that where the interest comes to an end during the beneficiary's lifetime and some other person becomes entitled to the property or interest, the beneficiary is treated as having made a transfer of value. However, for events taking place after March 16, 1987 this will usually comprise a potentially exempt transfer. No liability will arise where the property vests in the absolute ownership of the previous beneficiary. The death of a person entitled to an interest in possession will require the value of the underlying property to be added to the value of the deceased's estate.

In the case of other settled property where there is no interest in possession (e.g. discretionary trusts), liability to tax will arise on each ten-year anniversary of the trust. There will also be liability if property ceases to be held on discretionary trusts before the first ten-year anniversary date is reached or between anniversaries. The rate of tax suffered will be governed by several considerations, including previous dispositions made by the settlor, transactions concluded by the trustees, and the period throughout which property has been held in trust.

Accumulation and maintenance settlements which require assets to be distributed, or interests in income to be created, not later than a beneficiary's twenty-fifth birthday may be exempt from any liability to inheritance tax.

CORPORATION TAX

Profits, gains and income accruing to companies resident in the United Kingdom incur liability to corporation tax. Non-resident companies are immune from this tax unless they carry on a trade in the United Kingdom through a permanent establishment, branch or office. Companies residing outside the United Kingdom may be liable to income tax at the basic rate on other income arising in the United Kingdom, perhaps from letting property. The following comments are confined to companies resident in the United Kingdom and have little application to those residing overseas.

Liability to corporation tax is governed by the profits, gains or income for an accounting period. This is usually the period for which financial accounts are made up, and in the case of companies preparing accounts to the same accounting date annually will comprise successive periods of twelve months.

Rate of tax

The amount of profits or income for an accounting period must be determined on normal taxation principles. The special rules which apply to individuals where a source of income is acquired or discontinued are ignored and consideration is confined to the actual profits or income for an accounting period.

The rate of corporation tax is fixed for a financial year ending on March 31. Where the accounting period of a company overlaps this date and there is a change in the rate of corporation tax, profits and income must be apportioned.

For earlier years the full rate of corporation tax was 52 per cent but this rate was progressively reduced as follows:

Financial year		Per cent
12 months ending	March 31, 1984	50
,,	March 31, 1985	45
,,	March 31, 1986	40
,,	March 31, 1987, 1988, 1989 and 1990	35
,,	March 31, 1991	34
,,	March 31, 1992	33

Small companies rate

Where the profits of a company do not exceed stated limits, corporation tax becomes payable at the small companies rate. It is the amount of profits and not the size of the company which governs the application of this rate.

The level of profits which a company may derive without losing the benefit of the small companies rate has been frequently changed. In recent years the following small companies rate applies where profits do not exceed £250,000 for the year ending March 31, 1992, £200,000 for the year ending March 31, 1991,

£150,000 for the year ending March 31, 1990 or £100,000 for earlier years:

Financial year		Per cent
12 months ending	March 31, 1984	38
„	March 31, 1985 and 1986	30
„	March 31, 1987	29
„	March 31, 1988	27
„	March 31, 1989, 1990	
	1991 and 1992	25

If profits do exceed £250,000 for the year to March 31, 1992 but fall below £1,250,000, marginal small companies rate relief applies. The broad effect of marginal relief is that the first £250,000 of profits is taxed at the appropriate small companies rate. Profits falling in the margin then incur liability at the marginal rate of 35 per cent. Different upper limits and marginal rates applied for earlier years. However, where the accounting period of a company overlaps March 31, profits must be apportioned to establish the appropriate rate for each part of those profits.

The lower limit of £250,000 and the upper limit of £1,250,000 applies for a period of twelve months in duration and must be proportionately reduced for shorter periods. Some restriction in the small companies rate and the marginal rate may be necessary if there are two or more associated companies, namely companies under common control.

For accounting periods commencing after March 31, 1989, the small companies rate is not available for close investment-holding companies. These are mainly investment companies, other than those receiving most of their income from letting land and property.

Capital gains

Chargeable gains arising to a company are calculated in a manner similar to that used for individuals. However, companies cannot obtain the annual exemption of £5,500, nor are they assessed to capital gains tax. In place of this tax companies suffer liability to corporation tax on chargeable gains.

For disposals taking place before March 17, 1987 only a fraction of the chargeable gain was assessable to corporation tax at the full rate. The fraction selected ensured that companies effectively suffered corporation tax at the rate of 30 per cent on the full chargeable gain. A different approach is adopted for disposals taking place after this date. The full chargeable gain, and not a fraction, is assessable to corporation tax. However, unlike the previous system, the chargeable gain is treated as ordinary profit, thereby obtaining the benefit of the small companies rate where figures are sufficiently low.

Distributions

Dividends and other qualifying distributions made by a United Kingdom resident company are not satisfied after deduction of income tax. However, when making a distribution a company is required to account to the Inland Revenue for an amount of advance corporation tax. For distributions made in the year ending April 5, 1992, the amount of advance corporation tax will represent one-third of the distribution. Thus a cash dividend of £75 paid to a shareholder will also require satisfaction of advance corporation tax amounting to £25.

Advance corporation tax accounted for in this manner for distributions made in an accounting period may usually be set against a company's corporation tax liability for the same period. Some restrictions are imposed on the amount which can be offset but any surplus can be carried forward, or

carried backwards, and set against corporation tax due for other accounting periods.

A United Kingdom resident shareholder receiving a qualifying distribution also obtains a tax credit, which for the year ending April 5, 1992, is equal to one-third of the distribution made. Therefore the total income of the individual comprises the aggregate of the distribution and the tax credit. If the individual is not liable, or not fully liable, to income tax at the basic rate, all or part of the tax credit can be refunded by the Inland Revenue. Individuals with substantial incomes incur liability to income tax at the higher rate of 40 per cent on the aggregate of the distribution and the tax credit, although as tax is deemed to have been suffered at the rate of 25 per cent the additional liability will be limited to the excess of 15 per cent.

Payment of tax

Corporation tax, less any relief for advance corporation tax, usually falls due for payment nine months following the end of the accounting period to which the tax relates. Companies which were carrying on business before 1966 may have a later due and payable date, but this is gradually being amended to achieve a common nine-month period for all companies.

Interest

On making many payments of interest a company is required to deduct income tax at the basic rate and account for the tax deducted to the Inland Revenue. The gross amount of interest paid will usually comprise a charge on income to be offset against profits on which corporation tax becomes payable.

Groups of companies

Each company within a group is separately charged to corporation tax on profits, gains and income. However, where one group member realizes a loss, other than a capital loss, a claim may be made to offset the deficiency against profits of some other member of the same group.

Claims are also available to avoid the payment of advance corporation tax on distributions, or the deduction of income tax on the payment of interest, for transactions between members of a group of companies. The transfer of capital assets from one member of a group to a fellow member will incur no liability to tax on chargeable gains.

VALUE ADDED TAX

Unlike income tax, capital gains tax, inheritance tax and corporation tax, which are collected and administered by the Inland Revenue, value added tax is the responsibility of Customs and Excise. Value added tax is charged on the value of supplies made in the United Kingdom by a registered trader and extends both to the supply of goods and to the supply of services. Liability also arises on the value of goods imported into the United Kingdom.

Registration

All traders, including professional men and women, together with companies, making taxable supplies of a value exceeding stated limits are required to register for value added tax purposes. Taxable supplies represent the supply of goods and services potentially chargeable with value added tax. The limits which govern mandatory registration are amended annually but from March 20, 1991, an unregistered trader must register:

(a) at any time, if there are reasonable grounds for believing that the value of taxable supplies in the next 30 days will exceed £35,000; or

(b) at the end of any month if the value of taxable supplies in the last 12 months then ending has exceeded £35,000.

Liability to register under (b) may be avoided if it can be shown that the value of supplies in the period of 12 months then beginning will not exceed £33,600. There may, however, be liability to register immediately where a business is taken over from another trader as a 'going concern'.

Where the limits governing mandatory registration have been exceeded it is necessary for the trader to notify Customs and Excise. Failure to provide prompt notification may have unfortunate results as the person concerned will be required to account for value added tax from the proper registration date.

A trader whose taxable supplies do not reach the mandatory registration limits may apply for voluntary registration. This step may be thought advisable to recover input tax or to compete with other registered traders.

A registered trader may submit an application for de-registration if the value of taxable supplies subsequently falls. From May 1, 1991, an application for de-registration can be made if the value of taxable supplies for the year beginning on the application date is not expected to exceed £33,600.

Input tax

A registered trader will both suffer tax (input tax) when obtaining goods or services for the purposes of his business and also become liable to account for tax (output tax) on the value of goods and services which he supplies. Relief can usually be obtained for input tax suffered, either by setting that tax against output tax due or by repayment. Most items of input tax can be relieved in this manner but there are exceptions including the prohibition of relief for the cost of business entertaining. Where a registered trader makes both exempt supplies and also taxable supplies to his customers or clients there may be some restriction in the amount of input tax which can be recovered.

Output tax

When making a taxable supply of goods or services a registered trader must account for output tax, if any, on the value of the supply. Usually the price charged by the registered trader will be increased by adding value added tax but failure to make the required addition will not remove liability to account for output tax.

Exempt supplies

No value added tax is chargeable on the supply of goods or services which are treated as exempt supplies. These include the provision of burial and cremation facilities, insurance, finance and education. The granting of a lease to occupy land or the sale of land will usually comprise an exempt supply, but there are numerous exceptions. In particular, the sale of new non-domestic buildings or certain buildings used by charities, constructed after April 1, 1989, can no longer be treated as exempt supplies.

From August 1, 1989 a taxable person may elect to tax rents and other supplies of buildings and agricultural land not used for residential or charitable purposes.

Exempt supplies do not enter into the calculation of taxable supplies which governs liability to mandatory registration. Such supplies made by a registered trader may, however, limit the amount of input tax which can be relieved. It is for this reason that the election available from August 1, 1989 may be useful.

Rates of tax

Two rates of value added tax applied since June 18, 1979, namely:

(a) a zero, or nil, rate; and

(b) a standard rate of 15 per cent.

However, the standard rate was increased to 17·5 per cent for supplies made after March 31, 1991.

Although no tax is due on a zero-rated supply, this does comprise a taxable supply which must be included in the calculation governing liability to register.

Zero-rating

A large number of supplies are zero-rated, including, among others:

(a) the supply of many items of food and drink for human consumption. This does not include ice creams, chocolates, sweets, potato crisps and alcoholic drinks. Nor does it extend to supplies made in the course of catering, for example, at a wedding reception or other social function, or to items supplied for consumption in a restaurant or cafe. Whilst the supply of cold items, for example sandwiches, for consumption away from the supplier's premises, is zero-rated, the supply of hot food, for example fish and chips, is not;

(b) animal feeding stuffs;

(c) sewerage and water, unless supplied for industrial purposes;

(d) books, brochures, pamphlets, leaflets, newspapers, maps and charts;

(e) talking books for the blind and handicapped and wireless sets for the blind;

(f) electricity, gas and coal, but supplies are now limited to domestic use;

(g) supplies of services, other than professional services, when constructing a new domestic building or a building to be used by a charity. The supply of materials for such a building is also zero-rated, together with the sale or the grant of a long lease for these buildings. Before April 1, 1989 this applied to most new buildings but subsequently it is limited to domestic buildings and buildings used by charities. Alterations to some protected buildings are also zero-rated;

(h) the transportation of persons in a vehicle, ship or aircraft designed to carry not less than twelve persons;

(i) supplies of drugs, medicines and other aids for the handicapped;

(j) supplies of clothing and footwear for young persons;

(k) exports.

This list is not exhaustive but indicates the wide range of supplies which may be zero-rated.

Collection of tax

Registered traders submit value added tax returns for accounting periods. Each accounting period is three months in duration but arrangements can be made to submit returns on a monthly basis. The return will show both the output tax due for supplies made by the trader in the accounting period and also the input tax for which relief is claimed. If the output tax exceeds input tax the balance must be remitted with the value added tax return. Where input tax suffered exceeds the output tax due the registered trader may claim recovery of the excess from Customs and Excise.

This basis for collecting tax explains the structure of value added tax. Where supplies are made between registered traders the supplier will account for an amount of tax which will usually be identical to the tax recovered by the person to whom the supply is made. However, where the supply is made to a person who is not a registered trader there can be no recovery of input tax and it is on this person that the final burden of value added tax eventually falls.

Tax on imports into the United Kingdom must be satisfied at the time of importation or perhaps later where special arrangements have been agreed.

An optional scheme will be made available for registered traders having an annual turnover of taxable supplies not exceeding £300,000 (or £250,000 before April 1, 1991). Such traders may, if they wish, render returns annually. Nine equal payments of value added tax will be paid on account, with a final balancing payment accompanying submission of the return.

Bad debts

Many retailers operate special retail schemes for calculating the amount of value added tax due. These schemes are, broadly, based on the volume of consideration received in an accounting period. Should a customer fail to pay for goods or services supplied, there will be no consideration on which value added tax falls to be calculated.

To avoid the problem of bad debts incurred by traders not operating a special retail scheme, an optional system of cash accounting is available. This scheme, confined to traders with annual taxable supplies not exceeding £300,000, enables returns to be made on a cash basis, in substitution for the normal supply basis. Traders using such a scheme will not, of course, include bad debts in the calculation of cash receipts.

Where neither the cash accounting arrangements nor the special retail scheme applies, output tax falls due on the value of the supply and liability is not affected by failure to receive consideration. For some time limited relief was available for bad debts where a trader became insolvent. In future, however, where a debt is more than 12 months old and is written off in the supplier's books, relief for bad debts will be forthcoming. This first applied to supplies made after April 1, 1989 with the earliest relief given after April 1, 1991.

Other special schemes

In addition to the schemes for retailers, there are several special schemes applied to calculate the amount of value added tax due and which also limit the ability to recover input tax. These schemes apply to the supply of second-hand motor cars, motor cycles, caravans, boats, electronic organs, aircraft and firearms, together with works of art, antiques and collectors' pieces.

STAMP DUTIES

Stamp duty is a tax on documents. There are a number of separate duties, under different heads of charge. The Finance Act 1990 included provisions abolishing all the stamp duty charges on transactions in shares from a date to be fixed by Treasury order. The Finance Act 1991 removed the stamp duty charges on documents relating to all other types of property except land and buildings, again from a date to be specified (expected to be early in 1992). In the list of documents which follows, those which will be affected by the above provisions are indicated with an asterisk*.

Agreement for Lease, *see* **Leases.**

Agreement for Sale of Property.—Charged with *ad valorem* duty as if an actual conveyance on sale, with certain exceptions, e.g. agreements for the sale of land, stocks and shares, goods, wares or merchandise, or a ship (*see* S. 59 (1), Stamp Act 1891). If *ad valorem* duty is paid on an agreement in accordance with this provision, the subsequent conveyance or transfer is not chargeable with any *ad valorem* duty and the Commissioners will upon application either place a denoting stamp on such conveyance or transfer or will transfer the *ad valorem* duty thereto. Further, if such an agreement is rescinded, not performed, etc., the Commissioners will return the *ad valorem* duty paid.

Agreement under seal, subject to
exemptions 50p

Assignment:
By way of sale—*see* **Conveyance.**
By way of gift—*see* **Voluntary Disposition.**

Assurance—*see* **Insurance Policies.**

* Bearer Instrument:
Inland bearer instrument, i.e. share warrant, stock certificate to bearer or any other instrument to bearer by which stock can be transferred, issued by a company or body formed or established in UK .... 1·5%
Overseas bearer instrument, i.e. such an instrument issued in Great Britain by a company formed out of the UK .... 1·5%

Bill of sale, Absolute, *see* **Conveyance on Sale.**

Capital Duty.—This was charged at 1 per cent on every £100 or fraction of £100 of the actual value of assets contributed by the members of a company provided the place of effective management of the company was in Great Britain, or its registered office was in Great Britain but the place of its effective management was outside the EC (Finance Act 1973).
The tax was abolished by the Finance Act 1988 in respect of transactions entered into on or after March 16, 1988.

Contract, *see* **Agreement.**

* Contract or Grant for Payment of a Superannuation Annuity.—For every £10 or fractional part of £10 .... 5p

Conveyance or Transfer on Sale (in the case of a Voluntary Disposition, *see* below) of any property (except stock or marketable securities), where the Conveyance or Transfer contains a certificate of value certifying that the transaction does not form part of a larger transaction or a series of transactions in respect of which the aggregate amount or value of the consideration exceeds £30,000 . *nil*
Exceeds £30,000 (for every £100 or fraction of £100)..................................... £1
If the Conveyance or Transfer on Sale does not contain the appropriate statement, duty at the full rate of £1 for every £100 or fraction of £100 will be payable whatever the amount of the consideration.
However, if the consideration does not exceed £500, and the instrument does not contain a certificate of value, there are graduated duties ranging from 50p to £5.
Conveyances to charities are exempt from duty under this head provided the instrument is stamped with a denoting stamp.

Conveyance or Transfer of any other kind.—Fixed duty 50p
However, under the Stamp Duty (Exempt Instruments) Regulations 1987, instruments which would otherwise fall under this head are exempt from stamp duty provided that the document is duly certified. The certificate must contain a sufficient description of the category into which the instrument falls, and must be signed by the transferor, his solicitor or agent. 'I/We hereby certify that this instrument falls within category ... in the Schedule to the Stamp Duty (Exempt Instruments) Regulations 1987.'

Covenant.—For original creation and sale of any annuity, *see* **Conveyance.**

Declaration of Trust, not being a Will or Settlement 50p

Demise, *see* **Lease**

Duplicate or Counterpart.—Same duty as original, but not to exceed 50p

Gift, *see* **Voluntary Disposition.**

* Guarantee.—If under seal 50p

Insurance Policies, Life.—
Exceeding £50 and not exceeding £1,000, for every £100 or part of £100 .... 5p
Exceeding £1,000, for every £1,000 or any fractional part of £1,000.................. 50p
Made after August 1, 1966 for period not exceeding two years 5p

The Finance Act 1989 abolished this charge for policies made after December 31, 1989.

Leases (including Agreements for Leases).—
Lease or tack for any definite term less than a year of any furnished dwelling-house or apartments where the rent for such term exceeds £500 .... £1

Of any lands, tenements, etc., in consideration of any rent, according to the following table:

Annual rent not exceeding	*Term not exceeding			Term exceeding 100 years
	7 years	35 years	100 years	
£	£ p	£ p	£ p	£ p
5	Nil	0·10	0·60	1·20
10	Nil	0·20	1·20	2·40
15	Nil	0·30	1·80	3·60
20	Nil	0·40	2·40	4·80
25	Nil	0·50	3·00	6·00
50	Nil	1·00	6·00	12·00
75	Nil	1·50	9·00	18·00
100	Nil	2·00	12·00	24·00
150	Nil	3·00	18·00	36·00
200	Nil	4·00	24·00	48·00
250	Nil	5·00	30·00	60·00
300	Nil	6·00	36·00	72·00
350	Nil	7·00	42·00	84·00
400	Nil	8·00	48·00	96·00
450	Nil	9·00	54·00	108·00
500	Nil	10·00	60·00	120·00
Exceeding £500, for every £50 or fraction of £50	0·50	1·00	6·00	12·00

*If the term is indefinite the same duty is payable as if the term did not exceed seven years.

Where a consideration other than rent is payable, the same rule applies where the consideration does not exceed £30,000 as under Conveyance or Transfer on Sale (except stock or marketable securities) provided that any rent payable does not exceed £300 a year and a certificate of value is included in the Conveyance or Transfer.

Leases to charities are exempt from duty under this head provided the instrument is stamped with a denoting stamp.

Mortgages.—Exempt.

Receipts for Salaries, Wages and Superannuation, and other like allowances.— Exempt.

* **Transfer of Stock and Shares by sale** .... 0·5%

* **Unit Trust Instrument.**—Any trust instrument of a unit trust scheme, for every £100 or fraction of £100, of the amount or value of the property subject to the trusts created or recorded by the instrument 25p
By the Finance Act 1989, the transfer of units in certain authorized unit trusts is no longer subject to duty.

Voluntary Disposition *inter vivos* 50p

The Commissioners as a general rule allow deeds etc., to be stamped after execution:—

Without Penalty, on Payment of Duty only Deeds and instruments not otherwise excepted within 30 days of first execution.
NB. Where wholly executed abroad, the period begins to run from the date of arrival here.

Penalties Enforceable on Stamping in Addition to Duty:—Instruments presented after the proper time (subject to special provisions in some cases and subject to the Commissioner's power to mitigate) a penalty equal to the duty £10

LEGAL NOTES

IMPORTANT

The purpose of these notes is to outline some of the more common parts of the law as they may affect the average person. They are believed to be correct at the time of going to press. However, the law is constantly developing and changing, and it is always best to take expert advice. Anyone who does not have a solicitor already, and is unable to find one through the recommendation of a friend, can contact the Citizens' Advice Bureau (whose address can be obtained from the telephone directory or from any post office or town hall). Each CAB has a list of solicitors in the area who deal with particular types of problem. Alternatively, assistance can be sought from The Law Society, 113 Chancery Lane, London, WC2A 1PL or The Law Society of Scotland, 26 Drumsheugh Gardens, Edinburgh, EH3 7YR.

The Legal Aid and Legal Advice and Assistance schemes exist to make the help of the trained lawyer available to everyone whatever their means. The best policy is to go to a solicitor without delay—timely advice will set your mind at rest but sitting on your rights can mean that you lose them.

It is not necessary for a dispute to have arisen before advice is sought from a solicitor; the Legal Advice and Assistance Scheme enables a solicitor to advise you on your rights, for instance under a tenancy agreement, the estate of a deceased person or in connection with matrimonial and consumer matters, and to write letters or take other steps on your behalf. Your entitlement to take advantage of the scheme depends on your means (*see* p. 1041) but a solicitor or Citizens' Advice Bureau will be able to advise about entitlement.

BRITISH CITIZENSHIP

There are three types of citizenship: British Citizenship; Citizenship of the British Dependent Territories; and British Overseas Citizenship.

Acquisition of citizenship on change of law.—The British Nationality Act 1981 which came into force on January 1, 1983 made substantial changes to the law of citizenship, which before that date did not distinguish between the three types of citizenship referred to above. Almost all persons who were then both citizens of the UK and colonies and who had a right of abode in the UK became British citizens when the Act came into force. Most UK and colonies citizens who did not have a right of abode in the UK became Citizens of the British Dependent Territories. This type of citizenship was, broadly speaking, conferred on citizens of the UK and colonies by birth, naturalization or registration in dependent territories. Dependent territories include Hong Kong, Gibraltar, the Falkland Islands, and St Helena and its dependencies. Any UK and colonies citizen who, on January 1, 1983, did not acquire either British or British Dependent Territories' Citizenship became a British Overseas Citizen.

Later acquisition of British citizenship.—British citizenship is acquired automatically by those born in the UK (including, for this purpose, the Channel Islands and the Isle of Man) who have a parent who is a British citizen or a parent who is settled in the UK. Certain other categories of children born in the UK also acquire this type of citizenship, i.e. foundlings, those whose parents subsequently settle in the UK, those who live in the UK for ten years from birth and those adopted in the UK.

A person born outside the UK may acquire British citizenship in the following ways:

- (a) if one of his/her parents is a British citizen otherwise than by descent (e.g. parent was born in the UK).

- (b) if one of his/her parents is a British citizen serving the Crown overseas.

- (c) if the Secretary of State consents to his/her registration while he/she is a minor.

- (d) if he/she is a Citizen of the British Dependent Territories, a British Overseas Citizen, a British Subject or a British Protected Person (these last two are residual categories of people who have not acquired one of the three new types of citizenship) and has been lawfully resident in the UK for five years without any time restriction.

- (e) if he/she is a British Dependent Territories Citizen who is a national of the UK for the purposes of the EC (i.e. a Gibraltarian).

- (f) if he/she is naturalized. Naturalization may be applied for only by adults and the Secretary of State has a discretion whether to permit it. The basic requirements are five years' residence, good character, sufficient knowledge of the English or Welsh language, and an intention to reside in the UK permanently. The requirements are somewhat less restrictive in the case of an applicant who is married to a British citizen.

Acquisition of British Dependent Territories and British Overseas Citizenship after the Act.—These citizenships are intended for persons connected with certain Commonwealth countries other than the UK. In the case of dependent territories the rules are very similar to those for acquiring British citizenship, except that the connection is with the dependent territory rather than with the UK. British Overseas Citizenship may be acquired by the wife and minor children of a British Overseas Citizen in certain circumstances.

Retention of nationality by persons born in or who are citizens of the Republic of Ireland.—By the Ireland Act 1949, a person who was born before December 6, 1922, in what is now the Republic of Ireland (Eire) and was a British subject immediately before January 1, 1949, is not deemed to have ceased to be a British subject unless either he/she (a) was domiciled in the Irish Free State on December 6, 1922, (b) was on or after April 10, 1935, and before January 1, 1949, permanently resident there, or (c) had before January 1, 1949 been registered as a citizen of Eire under the laws of that country.

In addition, by the British Nationality Act 1948, any citizen of Eire who immediately before January 1, 1949, was also a British subject can retain that status by submitting at any time a claim to the Home Secretary on any of the following grounds:

- (a) he/she has been in the service of the United Kingdom government;

- (b) he/she holds a British passport issued in the United Kingdom or in any colony, protectorate, United Kingdom mandated or trust territory;

- (c) he/she has associations by way of descent, residence or otherwise with any such place; or on complying with similar legislation in any of the 'dominions'.

The British Nationality Act 1981 provides that persons who have made a claim may continue to be British subjects. Any citizen of Eire who was a

British subject before January 1, 1949 and who has not yet made a claim may do so provided that:

(a) he/she is or has been in Crown service under the government of the United Kingdom; or

(b) he/she has associations by way of descent, residence or otherwise with the United Kingdom or any dependent territory.

Renunciation and resumption.—A person may cease to be a British citizen by renouncing his/her citizenship (with the consent of the Secretary of State in wartime). The renunciation is required to be registered with the Secretary of State and will be revoked if no new citizenship or nationality is acquired within six months. Once renounced, citizenship may be reacquired if the renunciation was necessary to retain or acquire some other citizenship or nationality. Similar rules as to renunciation and reacquisition apply in the case of British Dependent Territories Citizenships and of renunciation (but not reacquisition) in the case of British Overseas Citizenship.

Status of aliens.—Property may be held by an alien in the same manner as by a natural-born British subject, but he/she may not hold public office, exercise the franchise or own a British ship or aircraft. The Republic of Ireland Act 1949 declares that the Republic, though not part of HM Dominions, is not a foreign country, and any reference in an Act of Parliament to foreigners, aliens, foreign countries, etc., shall be construed accordingly.

CONSUMER LAW

The Supply of Goods and Services

(1) The Sale of Goods Act 1979 provides protection to the purchaser of goods, by implying certain terms into every contract for the sale of goods. These implied terms are:

(a) A condition that the seller will pass good title to the buyer (unless the seller agrees to transfer only such title as he or his principal has) and warranties that the goods will be free from undisclosed encumbrances, and that the buyer will enjoy quiet possession of the goods.

(b) Where there is a sale of goods by description, a condition that the goods will correspond with that description, and where the sale is by sample and description, a condition that the bulk of the goods shall correspond with both sample and description.

(c) Where the seller sells goods in the course of a business, a condition that the goods will be of merchantable quality, unless before the contract is made, the buyer has examined the goods and ought to have noticed the defect, bearing in mind the purchaser's knowledge of the goods and the extent of the examination, or unless the seller has specifically drawn the attention of the buyer to the defect. Merchantable quality means fit for the purpose for which goods of the kind are commonly bought, taking into account any description applied to them, the price and other relevant circumstances.

(d) A condition that where the seller sells goods in the course of a business, the goods are reasonably fit for any purpose made known to the seller by the buyer, unless the buyer does not rely on the seller's skill and judgment, or it would be unreasonable for him to do so.

(e) Where there is a sale of goods by sample, conditions that the bulk of the goods shall correspond with the sample in quality, that the buyer will have a reasonable opportunity of comparing the bulk with the sample, and that the goods are free from any defect rendering them unmerchantable, which would not be apparent from the sample.

For these purposes, the broad difference between a condition and a warranty is that the remedy for a breach of an implied condition may enable the buyer to reject the goods and recover damages if he has suffered loss, whereas the remedy for a breach of warranty will only enable the buyer to recover damages.

It is possible for a seller to exclude some of the above terms from a contract, subject to restrictions imposed by the Unfair Contract Terms Act 1977 as given below. These restrictions give more protection where the buyer 'deals as consumer'. In a contract of sale of goods, a buyer 'deals as consumer' where there is a sale by a seller in the course of a business, where the goods are of a type ordinarily bought for private use or consumption, and where the goods are sold to a person who does not buy or hold himself out as buying them in the course of a business. A buyer in a sale by auction or competitive tender never 'deals as consumer'.

The 1977 Act prohibits the exclusion of the implied terms given in (b) to (e) above, where the buyer 'deals as consumer'. In sales where the buyer does not 'deal as consumer', terms purporting to exclude these implied terms may be relied upon only to the extent that it would be reasonable to allow reliance. The Act provides guidelines for determining whether it would be reasonable to allow reliance. The implied terms in (a) above cannot be excluded whether the buyer 'deals as consumer' or not.

(2) Similar terms to those implied in contracts of sale of goods are implied into contracts of hire-purchase by the Supply of Goods (Implied Terms) Act 1973, and the 1977 Act limits the exclusion of these implied terms in a similar manner.

(3) Under the Supply of Goods and Services Act 1982, terms similar to those in the Sale of Goods Act relating to quiet possession, compliance with description, merchantable quality, fitness for purpose and correspondence with sample are implied into other types of contract under which ownership of goods passes (e.g. a contract for 'work and materials' such as a supply of new parts during the servicing of a motor car) and also into contracts for the hire of goods. In the case of contracts under which ownership of goods is to pass, there is also an implied condition as to title.

The 1977 Act limits the exclusion of these implied terms in a similar manner to the implied terms in the Sale of Goods Act.

(4) The Supply of Goods and Services Act 1982 also implies into a contract for the supply of services terms that the supplier will use reasonable care and skill, carry out the service within a reasonable time (unless the time is agreed) and make a reasonable charge (unless the charge is agreed).

(5) The Trade Descriptions Act 1968 provides that it is a criminal offence for a trader or businessman to apply a false trade description to any goods, or to supply or offer to supply any goods to which a false trade description has been applied. A trade description includes a description as to quantity, size, method, place and date of manufacture, other history, composition, other physical characteristics, fitness for purpose, behaviour or accuracy, testing or approval. It is also an offence to give a false indication as to the price of goods. Prosecutions are brought by trading standards inspectors.

(6) The Fair Trading Act 1973 is also designed to protect the consumer. It provides for the appoint-

ment of a Director General of Fair Trading, whose duties include keeping under review commercial activities in the UK relating to the supply of goods or services to consumers, and to collect information to discover practices that may adversely affect the economic interests of the consumer. He may refer certain consumer trade practices to the Consumer Protection Advisory Committee, or of his own initiative take proceedings against firms that are trading unfairly. He may also publish information and advice to consumers. Examples of practices which have been prohibited by virtue of references made under this Act include the use of certain void exclusion clauses in contracts for the sale of goods and hire-purchase, and advertisements by traders appearing to sell as private persons.

(7) The Consumer Protection Act 1987 makes the producer of a product liable for any damage exceeding £275 caused by a defect in that product, subject to certain defences.

(8) The Consumer Protection (Cancellation of Contracts Concluded away from Business Premises) Regulations 1987 allow consumers a seven-day period in which to cancel most contracts for supply of goods or services exceeding £35 in cost, where these contracts have been made following an unsolicited visit to the consumer's home or workplace.

Scotland

The Sale of Goods Act 1979, a consolidating Act, applies with some modification to Scotland. For example, it is not necessary in Scotland to distinguish between the words condition and warranty. The remedies of the buyer in both cases are the same, i.e. the buyer can either within a reasonable time reject the goods and treat the contract as repudiated, or retain the goods and treat the failure to perform such material part as a breach which may give rise to a claim for compensation or damages.

Consumer Credit

The Consumer Credit Act 1974 provides a system for the protection of the consumer, of licensing and control of all matters relating to the provision of credit or to the supply of goods on hire or hire-purchase, administered by the Director-General of Fair Trading. A licence is required to carry on a consumer credit or consumer hire business, or to deal in credit brokerage, debt adjusting, counselling or collecting, for which group licences are available. Any 'fit' person may apply to the Director of Fair Trading for a licence which is normally renewable after ten years. A licence is not necessary if such types of business are only transacted 'occasionally' or if exempt agreements only are involved.

For the Act's provisions to apply, the agreement must be 'regulated', i.e. be to individuals or partnerships only; must not be exempt, e.g. certain loans by local authorities or building societies; and the total credit must not exceed £15,000. The terms of a regulated agreement can be varied by the creditor, but only if the agreement gives him the right to do so and the debtor receives notice in the prescribed form.

To be enforceable the agreement must be properly executed, and the specified information must be given during the antecedent negotiations for the contract. These are conducted by the creditor, credit broker or supplier (these being the creditor's agents) and begin when the parties first begin discussions.

The agreement must state certain information such as the amount of credit, the annual percentage rate of interest, and the amount and timing of repayments.

An agreement is cancellable under the Act if representations were made in the debtor's presence during antecedent negotiations and the debtor signed

the agreement other than at the creditor's (or credit-broker's or negotiator's) place of business. Time for cancellation expires five clear days after the debtor receives a second copy of the agreement. The agreement must inform the debtor of his right to cancel and how to cancel.

Where there are arrangements or connections between the creditor and supplier, the former is generally liable for any misrepresentation or breach of contract by the latter, and will thus be liable to indemnify the debtor.

If the debtor is in arrears or is otherwise in breach of the agreement, the creditor may not enforce the agreement, e.g. by repossessing goods, without serving a default notice on the debtor. This notice will give the debtor a chance to remedy the default. Even if the default is not remedied by the debtor, if the agreement is a hire-purchase or conditional sale agreement, the creditor cannot repossess the goods without an order of the court if the debtor has paid one-third of the total price of the goods.

Where the agreement requires the debtor to make grossly exorbitant payments or is contrary to the ordinary principles of fair dealing, the Court can reopen it either at the debtor's request or during enforcement proceedings and (*inter alia*) alter the terms of the contract or set aside any obligations it imposes so as to do justice between the parties. Whether an agreement is such an extortionate credit bargain is decided by reference (*inter alia*) to interest rates prevailing at the date of agreement, the pressure for finance the debtor was under, etc.

If a credit reference agency was used to check the debtor's financial standing the creditor must give the agency's name to the debtor, who is entitled to see the agency's file on him on payment of a fee of £1.

Scotland

The Consumer Credit Act also extends to Scotland and goes far in assimilating the Scots law on this topic with English law. The Supply of Goods (Implied Terms) Act 1973 also applies to Scotland. Parts II and III only of the Unfair Contract Terms Act 1977 apply to Scotland. The Sale of Goods Act 1979, applies with some modification to Scotland.

Receipts

The law on receipts in Scotland is governed by the Prescription and Limitations (Scotland) Act 1973, which for this purpose came into force on July 25, 1976. Now, receipts need only be kept for a period of five years and if a creditor does not make a relevant claim within that period no action can be raised.

THE CROWN—PROCEEDINGS AGAINST

Before 1947, proceedings against the Crown were generally possible only by a procedure known as a petition of right, which placed the litigant at a considerable disadvantage. However, by the Crown Proceedings Act 1947, which came into operation on January 1, 1948, the Crown, in its public capacity, is largely placed in the same position as a subject, although some procedural disadvantages remain, for example, the enforcement of judgments against the Crown.

Scotland.—The Act as amended extends to Scotland and has the effect of bringing the practice of the two countries as closely together as the different legal systems will permit. While formerly actions against the Crown, when permissible, were confined to the Court of Session, proceedings may now be brought in the Sheriff Court.

The Act lays down that arrestment of money in the hands of the Crown or of a government department is competent in any case where arrestment in the hands of a subject would have been competent, but an exception is made in respect of National Savings Bank deposits. Section 2 (1) of the Law Reform (Miscellaneous Provisions) (Scotland) Act 1966 removes the privilege whereby the wages of Crown servants, other than serving members of the armed forces, are exempt from arrestment in execution.

DEATHS

Registration
(For Certificates, *see* pp. 1030–1)

England and Wales

When a death takes place, information of it must be given in person to the local Registrar of Births and Deaths, and the register signed in his/her presence, by a relative of the deceased present at the death, or in attendance during the last illness; or by some other relative of the deceased; in default of any relatives by (a) a person present at the death, or the occupier of the house in which the death happened, or (b) an inmate of the house. A person (other than a relative) registering the death must be causing the disposal of the body.

The registration must be made within five days of the death, or within the same time written notice of the death must be sent to the Registrar. If the deceased was attended during his/her last illness by a registered medical practitioner, a certificate of cause of death must be sent by the doctor to the Registrar. The doctor must give to the informant of the death a written notice of the signing of the certificate, which must be delivered to the Registrar. It is essential that a certificate for disposal should be obtained from the Registrar before the funeral and delivered to the clergyman or other person in charge of the churchyard or cemetery. No fee is chargeable for this certificate.

If the death is not registered within five days (or fourteen days if written notice of the occurrence of the death is sent to him/her), the Registrar may require any one of the above-mentioned persons to attend to register at a stated time and place. Failure to comply involves a penalty. The registration of a death is free of charge. After twelve months no death can be registered without the Registrar General's consent.

Whenever the death of a child is registered, particulars of the name and occupation of the mother are to be entered in the register.

A body must not be disposed of until: either the Registrar has given a certificate to the effect that he/she has registered or received notice of the death; or until the Coroner has made a disposal order (Births and Deaths Registration Act 1926, s. 1).

A person disposing of a body must within ninety-six hours deliver to the Registrar a notification as to the date, place, and means of the disposal of the body (*ib.*, s. 3).

Still births.—See p. 1030.

Death at sea.—The master of a British ship must record any death on board and send particulars to the Registrar General of Shipping.

Death abroad.—Consular Officers are authorized to register deaths of British subjects occurring abroad. Certificates are obtainable at the Registrar General's Office, London. If the deceased was of Scottish domicile, particulars are sent to the Registrar General for Scotland.

With regard to the registration of deaths of members of the armed forces, and deaths occurring on HM ships and aircraft, *see* the Registration of Births, etc. Act 1957.

Scotland

The Registration of Births, Deaths and Marriages (Scotland) Act 1965 supersedes provisions in former Acts.

Personal notification within eight days must be given to the Registrar of either the registration district in which the death took place, or any registration district in which the deceased was ordinarily resident immediately before his death. When a body is found and the place of death is not known, notification must be given to the Registrar of either the registration district in which the body was found or any other registration district appropriate by virtue of the preceding sentence. When a person dies (in or out of Scotland) in a ship, aircraft or land vehicle during a journey and the body is conveyed therein to any place in Scotland the death shall, unless the Registrar General otherwise directs, be deemed to have occurred at that place.

The register must be signed in the presence of the Registrar by one of the following: (a) any relative of the deceased; (b) any person present at the death; (c) the deceased's executor or other legal representative; (d) the occupier, at the time of the death, of the premises where the death took place; (e) if these fail, any other person having knowledge of the particulars to be registered. Failure to comply involves a penalty.

The medical practitioner who attended the deceased during the last illness must sign a certificate of the cause of death within seven days. If there is no such medical practitioner, any medical practitioner who is able to do so may sign the certificate. At the time of registering the death the Registrar shall, without charge, give the informant a certificate of registration, and the person to whom the certificate is given must hand it to the undertaker before cremation. A body may, however, be interred before the death is registered, in which case the undertaker must deliver a certificate of burial to the Registrar within three days.

Burial

The duty of burial is incumbent on the deceased person's executors (if any appointed); it is also a recognized obligation of the husband of a woman, the parent of a child, and also of a householder where the body lies. Funeral expenses of a reasonable amount will be repayable out of the deceased's estate in priority to any other claims. Directions as to place and mode of burial are frequently contained in the deceased's will, in some memorandum placed with private papers, or may have been communicated verbally to a relative. Consequently, steps should immediately be taken to ascertain the deceased's wishes from the above sources. If the wishes are considered objectionable, they are not necessarily enforceable; legal advice should be taken. A person may legally leave directions for the anatomical examination of his/her body. As to the place of burial, unless closed by Order in Council the parish churchyard is the normal burying place for parishioners or any person dying in the parish, but nowadays this will apply only in villages and smaller towns. In populous districts cemeteries and crematoria have been established, either by the local council or a private company, and burials will take place there in accordance with the regulations. For an exclusive right to a burial space in the churchyard, a faculty is required from the Ecclesiastical Court. Poor persons may be buried at the public expense by the local authority. As to the necessity for obtaining a Registrar's certificate or authority from the Coroner for disposal, *see* above.

Cremation

Under the Cremation Acts 1902 and 1952, regulations are made by the Home Secretary dealing fully with the cremation of a body, disposal of ashes, etc., and containing numerous essential safeguards.

If cremation is desired it is advisable for instructions to be left in writing to that effect. However, in Scotland, even if the deceased wished his/her body to be cremated or anatomically dissected, relatives can still veto his/her wishes.

To arrange for cremation, the executor or near relative should instruct the undertaker to that effect and obtain from him the forms required by statute.

INTESTACY

ENGLAND AND WALES

As regards deaths on or after March 15, 1977, the position is governed by the Administration of Estates Act 1925, as amended by the Intestates' Estates Act 1952, the Family Provision Act 1966 and Orders made thereunder. If the intestate leaves a spouse and issue, the spouse takes: (a) the 'personal chattels'; (b) £75,000 with interest at six per cent from death until payment; and (c) a life interest in half of the rest of the estate. This life interest can be capitalized at the option of the spouse. Personal chattels are articles of household use or ornament (including motor cars), not used for business purposes. The rest of the estate goes to the issue. If the intestate leaves a spouse and no issue, but leaves a parent or brother or sister of the whole blood or issue of such brothers and sisters the spouse takes: (a) the 'personal chattels'; (b) £125,000 with interest at six per cent from death until payment; and (c) half of the rest of the estate absolutely. The other half of the rest of the estate goes to the parents, equally if more than one, or, if none, to the brothers and sisters of the whole blood or issue of such brothers and sisters. If the intestate leaves a spouse, but no issue, no parents and no brothers or sisters of the whole blood or their issue, the spouse takes the whole estate absolutely.

If resident therein at the intestate's death, the surviving spouse may generally require the personal representatives to appropriate the interest of the intestate in the matrimonial home in or towards satisfaction of any absolute interest of the spouse, including the capitalized value of a life interest. In certain cases, leave of Court is required. On a partial intestacy any benefit (other than personal chattels specifically bequeathed) received by the surviving spouse under the will must be brought into account against the statutory legacy of £75,000 or £125,000, as the case may be. If there is no surviving spouse, the estate is distributed among those who survive the intestate in the following order (those entitled under earlier numbers taking to the exclusion of those entitled under later numbers):—(1) children; (2) father or mother (equally, if both alive); (3) brothers and sisters of the whole blood; (4) brothers and sisters of the half blood; (5) grandparents (equally, if more than one alive); (6) uncles and aunts of the whole blood; (7) uncles and aunts of the half blood; (8) the Crown.

In cases (1), (3), (4), (6) and (7), the persons entitled lose their interests unless they or their issue not only survive the intestate, but also attain eighteen or marry under that age, their shares going to the persons (if any) within the same group who do attain eighteen or marry. Moreover, in the same cases, succession is not *per capita*, but *per stirpes*, i.e. by stocks or families. Thus, if the intestate leaves one child and two grandchildren, being the children of a child of the intestate who predeceased the intestate, the two grandchildren represent their deceased parent and take between them one-half of the issue's share, the remaining half going to the surviving

child. Similarly, nephews and nieces represent a deceased brother, and so on.

When the deceased died partially intestate (i.e. leaving a will which disposed of only part of his/her property), the above rules apply to the intestate part.

Children must bring into account (hotchpot) any substantial advances received from the intestate during his/her lifetime before claiming any further share under the intestacy. Special hotchpot provisions apply to partial intestacy.

In respect of deaths occurring on or after April 4, 1988, Section 18 of the Family Law Reform Act 1987 provides that references to any relationship between two persons shall, unless the contrary intention appears, be construed without regard to whether or not the father and mother of either of them, or the father and mother of any person through whom the relationship is deduced, have or had been married to each other at any time.

In respect of deaths after March 1976 the provisions of the Inheritance (Provision for Family and Dependants) Act 1975 may allow other persons to claim provision out of the estate. See p. 1026.

For personal application for letters of administration, *see* p. 1027.

SCOTLAND

The Succession (Scotland) Act 1964, provides that the whole estate of any person dying intestate shall devolve without distinction between heritable and moveable property. By that Act the surviving spouse of an intestate may, as a prior right (in addition to legal rights, *see* below), claim the matrimonial home to a maximum of £65,000, or a choice of one matrimonial home if more than one (or in certain circumstances the value thereof), with its furniture and plenishings not exceeding £12,000 in value, plus the sum of £21,000 if the deceased left issue or, if no issue, the sum of £35,000. These figures apply from May 1, 1988 and may be increased from time to time by order of the Secretary of State.

The fact that a person was born illegitimate no longer has any effect in their rights of succession as against a legitimate child, by virtue of the Law Reform (Parent and Child) (Scotland) Act 1986.

Legal rights, referred to above, are:

Jus relicti(ae): the right of a surviving spouse to one half of the deceased's net moveable estate after satisfaction of prior rights if there are no surviving children, or to one-third if there are any surviving children.

Legitim: the right of surviving children to one-half of the net moveable estate of deceased parents if no surviving spouse, or one-third of the net moveable estate of deceased parents after satisfaction of prior rights where there is a surviving spouse.

There are no legal rights in heritage.

In general, the lines of succession are: (1) descendants; (2) collaterals; (3) ascendants and their collaterals, and so on in the ascending scale. The Crown is *ultimus haeres.* The right of representation, i.e. the right of the issue of a person who would have succeeded if he/she had survived the intestate, is open to any line of succession where previously it was limited to apply only when there were next of kin or the issue of predeceasing next of kin. The surviving mother of an intestate now has equal rights of succession with the surviving father, where formerly these were restricted. The intestate's maternal relations, who prior to the Act had no rights of succession, are now on an equal footing with the paternal relations. Where the intestate is survived only by parents and by brothers and sisters (collaterals), half of the estate is taken by the parents and the other half by the brothers and sisters, those of the whole blood being preferred to those of the half blood. Where, however, succession opens to collaterals (which expression can include the brothers and sisters of an ancestor of the intestate) of the half blood, they shall rank equally amongst themselves, whether related to the intestate (or his/her ancestor) through their father or their mother.

WILLS

The following notes and those on intestacy must be read subject to the provisions of the Inheritance (Provision for Family and Dependants) Act 1975, which can affect the estate of anyone dying domiciled in England and Wales after March 1976. Very broadly, a spouse, former spouse who has not remarried, a child of the deceased or one treated by the deceased as a child of his/her family, or any person maintained by him/her at his/her death may apply to the Court under the Act. If the Court thinks that the will or the law of intestacy or both do not make reasonable provision for the applicant, it may order payment out of the net estate of maintenance or a lump sum. It may also order the transfer of property or vary certain trusts, and the powers can affect property disposed of by the deceased in his/her lifetime intending to defeat the Act. It is up to the applicant to take the initiative, and the application must generally be made within six months of the grant of probate or letters of administration.

Making a Will

Every person over the age of 18 should make a will. However small the estate, the rules of intestacy (*see* above) may not reflect a person's wishes as to his/her property. In any case a will can do more than just deal with property. It can in particular appoint executors, give directions as to the disposal of the body and appoint guardians to take care of children in the event of the parents' death. For the wealthier person an appropriately drawn will can operate to reduce the burden of inheritance tax.

It is considered desirable for a will to be properly drawn up by a solicitor. Although normally the making of a will is not one of the services which can be provided under the Legal Advice and Assistance scheme, it can be provided for certain special categories of person such as the aged and infirm (*see* below).

In no circumstances should one person prepare a will for another person where the former is to take any benefit under it. This can easily lead to a suggestion of undue influence, which may cause the will to be held bad.

Assuming a lawyer is not employed, a person having resolved to make a will must remember that it is only after a person is dead, and cannot explain his/her meaning, that his/her will can be open to dispute. It is the more necessary, therefore, to express what is meant in language of the utmost clarity, avoiding the use of any word or expression that admits of another meaning than the one intended. Avoid the use of legal terms, such as heirs and issue, when the same thing may be expressed in plain language. If in writing the will a mistake be made, it is better to rewrite the whole. Before a will is executed (*see* below) an alteration may be made by striking through the words with a pen, but opposite to such alteration the testator and witnesses should write their names or place their initials. Never scratch out a word with a knife or other instrument; no alteration of any kind whatever must be made after the will is executed. If the testator afterwards wishes to change the disposition of his/her estate, it is best to make a new will, revoking the old one. The use of codicils should be left to the lawyer.

A will should be written in ink and very legibly, on a single sheet of paper. Although forms of wills must vary to suit different cases, the following forms may be found useful to those who, in cases of emergency, are called upon to draw up wills, either for themselves or others. Nothing more complicated should be attempted. The forms should be studied in conjunction with the following notes:

'This is the last will and testament of me [*Thomas Smith*] of [*Vine Cottage, Silver Street, Reading, Berks.*] which I make this [*thirteenth*] day of [*February,* 1992] and whereby I revoke all previous wills and testamentary dispositions.

1. I hereby appoint [*John Green of —— and Richard Brown of ——*] to be the executor(s) of this my will.

2. I give all my property real and personal to [*my wife Mary* or *my sons Raymond and David equally* or as the case may be].

Signed by the testator in the presence of us both present at the same time who, at his request, in his presence and in the presence of each other have hereunto set our names as witnesses.　　Thomas Smith　*Signature of Testator;*

William Jones (*signed*) of Green Gables, South Street, Reading, tailor.

Henry Morgan (*signed*) of 16 North Street, Reading, butcher.'

Should it be desired to give legacies and/or gifts of specific property, instead of giving the whole estate to one or more persons, the form above should be used with the substitution for clause 2 of the following clauses:

'2. I give to —— of —— the sum of £—— and to —— of —— the sum of £—— and to —— of —— all my books [*or as the case may require*].

3. All the residue of my property real and personal I give to —— of ——.'

Terms.—Real property includes freehold land and houses, while personal property includes debts due, arrears of rents, money, leasehold property, house furniture, goods, assurance policies, stocks and shares in companies, and the like. The words 'my money', apart from the context, will normally only include actual real money. The expression 'goods and chattels' should not be used. In giving particular property, ordinary language is sufficient, e.g. 'my house, Vine Cottage, Silver Street, Reading, Berks.'. Such specific gifts fail if not owned by the testator at his death.

Residuary legatees.—It is well in all cases where legacies or specific gifts are made, to leave to some person or persons 'the residue of my property', although it may be thought that the whole of the property has been disposed of in legacies, etc., already mentioned in the will. It should be remembered that a will operates on property owned at the time of death.

Execution of a will, and witnesses.—The testator should sign his/her name at the foot or end of the will, in the presence of two witnesses, who will immediately afterwards sign their names in the testator's and in each other's presence. A person who has been left any gift or share of residue in the will, or whose wife or husband has been left such a gift, should not be an attesting witness. Their attestation would be good, but they would forfeit the gift. It is better that a person named as executor should not be a witness. Husband and wife may both be witnesses, provided neither is a legatee. If a solicitor be appointed executor, it is lawful to direct that his/her ordinary fees and charges shall be paid; but in this case the solicitor (as an interested party) must not be a witness to the will.

It is desirable that the witnesses should be fully described, as they may possibly be wanted at some future time. If the testator should be too ill to sign, even by a mark, another person may sign the testator's name to the will for him/her, in his/her presence and by his/her direction, and in this case it should be shown that the testator knew the contents of the document. The attestation clause should therefore be worded: 'Signed by Thomas Brown, by the direction and in the presence of the testator, Thomas Smith, in the joint presence of us, who thereupon signed our names in his presence and in the presence of each other, the will having been first read over to the testator, who appeared fully to understand the same.'

Where there is any suspicion that the testator is not, by reason of age or infirmity, fully in command of his faculties it is desirable to ask his/her doctor to act as a witness (*see* Testamentary capacity below).

A blind person may make a will in braille. If the testator be blind the will should be read aloud to him/her in the presence of the witnesses, and the fact mentioned in the attestation clause. A blind person cannot witness a will.

If by inadvertence the testator should have signed his/her will without the witnesses being present, then the attestation should be: 'The testator acknowledged his signature already made as his signature to his last will and testament, in the joint presence,' etc. Any omission in the observance of these details may invalidate the will. The stringency of the law as to signature and witnessing of a will is only relaxed in favour of soldiers, sailors and airmen in certain circumstances.

Executors.—It is usual to appoint two executors, although one is sufficient; any number up to and including four may be appointed. The name and address of each executor should be given in full. An executor may be a legatee. Thus a child of full age or wife to whom the whole or a portion of the estate is left may be appointed sole executor, or one of two executors. The addresses of the executors are not essential, but it is desirable here as elsewhere, to avoid ambiguity or vagueness.

Lapsed legacies.—If a legatee dies in the lifetime of the testator, the legacy generally lapses and falls into the residue. Where a residuary legatee predeceases the testator, his/her share of the residuary estate will not generally pass to the other residuary legatees, but will pass to the persons entitled on the deceased's intestacy. In all such cases it is desirable to make a new will.

An important exception to the general rule of lapse stated above is contained in the Administration of Justice Act 1982, where there is a gift to a child or remoter issue of the testator who dies before the testator leaving issue who survive the testator. In such a case the gift will pass to the issue of the deceased child.

Testamentary capacity.—A person under the age of 18 cannot make a will (except for soldiers, sailors and airmen and then only in exceptional circumstances).

So far as mental capacity is concerned the testator must be able to understand and appreciate the nature and effect of making a will, the property of which he can dispose and the claims to which he ought to give effect. If a person is not mentally able to make a will, provision exists (under the Mental Health Act 1983) for the Court to do this for him/her.

Revocation

A later will revokes an earlier will if it expressly says so, or is completely inconsistent with it. Otherwise the earlier one is revoked only in so far as it is inconsistent with the later one. A will may also be revoked by burning, tearing or otherwise destroying the will with the intention of revoking it. Such destruction must either be by the testator or by some other person in the testator's presence and at his/her direction. It is not sufficient to obliterate the will with a pen. Marriage in every case acts as the revocation of a will, except that under the Administration of Justice Act 1982, there is a provision to the effect that if it appears from a will that at the time it was made the testator was expecting to be married to a particular person and that he/she intended that the will (or a disposition in the will) should not be revoked by the marriage to that person, the will will not be revoked by marriage to that person. The Act also provides that where after a testator has made a will the testator's marriage is terminated by a decree of divorce or nullity, any gift to a spouse shall lapse and any appointment of the spouse as executor shall be omitted from the will unless the will shows a contrary intention.

Probate or Letters of Administration

Application for probate or for letters of administration may be made in person at the Personal Application Department of the Principal Registry of the Family Division, a district probate registry or sub-registry, or a probate office, by the executors or persons entitled to a grant of administration. Applicants should bring (a) the will, if any; (b) a certificate of death; (c) particulars of all property and assets left by the deceased; and (d) a list of debts and funeral expenses.

Intending applicants, before attending at a registry or probate office, should write or telephone to the nearest probate registry or sub-registry for the necessary forms. Postal or telephone applications cannot be dealt with at the local probate offices, which are part-time only.

Certain property can be disposed of on death without a grant of probate or administration, or in pursuance of a nomination made by the deceased, provided the amount involved does not exceed £5,000. *See* The Administration of Estates (Small Payments) Act 1965.

Where to Find a Proved Will

A will proved since 1858 must have been proved either at the Principal Registry at Somerset House, or a District Registry. In the former case the original will itself is preserved at St Catherine's House, the copy of which probate has been granted is in the hands of the executors who proved the will, and another copy for Parliament is bound up in a folio volume of wills made by testators of that initial and date. The indices to these volumes may be examined at St Catherine's House and a copy of any will read. In the latter case, the original will proved in the District Registry is kept there and may be seen or a copy obtained, but a copy is sent to and filed at St Catherine's House, where also it may be seen. A general index of grants, both probates and administrations, is prepared and printed annually in lexicographical form, and may be seen at either the Principal or a District Registry. This index is usually ready by about October of the following year.

Recent deaths.—A system introduced in 1975 enables a person to discover when a grant of probate or letters of administration is made which may be invaluable to a creditor of the deceased or applicant under the Inheritance (Provision for Family and Dependants) Act 1975 (*see* p. 1026). A standing search may be made by sending a request in the form set out below to the Record Keeper at the Principal Registry of the Family Division with a small fee. The searcher will receive particulars of any grant made in the previous twelve months or the following six months, including names and addresses of the executors or administrators and the Registry in which the grant was made.

Form of search

In the High Court of Justice
Family Division
The Principal Registry (Probate)
I/We apply for the entry of a standing search so that there shall be sent to me/us an office copy of every grant of representation in England and Wales in the estate of:
Full name of deceased:
Alternative or alias name
Full address
Exact date of death

Which either has issued not more than twelve months before the entry of this application or issues within six months hereafter
Signed.—(full address).

SCOTLAND

A domiciled Scotsman, unlike a domiciled Englishman, cannot in certain circumstances dispose effectively of the entirety of his estate. If he leave a widow and children, the widow is entitled to a one-third share in the whole of the moveable estate (her *jus relictae*), and the children are entitled to another one-third share equally between them (their *legitim*). If he leave a widow but no children, or children but no widow, the *jus relictae* or *legitim* is increased to a one-half share of the net moveable estate. The remaining portion is known as the dead's part. A surviving husband and children have comparable rights (*jus relicti* and *legitim*) in the wife's estate. The dead's part is the only portion of which the testator can freely dispose. Legacies and bequests are payable only out of the dead's part. All debts are payable out of the whole estate before any division.

Pupils, i.e. a girl up to the age of twelve or a boy up to the age of fourteen, cannot make wills. Formerly a minor could dispose only of movables but since the passing of the Succession (Scotland) Act 1964, a minor has a like capacity to test on heritable property.

A will must be in writing and may be typewritten or even in pencil. A will may be either: (a) holograph, i.e. written, dated and subscribed by the testator himself/herself, in which case no witnesses are necessary; a printed form filled up by the testator or a typewritten document is not necessarily a holograph but may become so if the testator writes, in hand, at the foot of the form or document the words 'adopted as holograph' followed by his/her signature and the date. Words written on erasure or marginal additions or interlineations in holograph writings, if proved to be in the handwriting of the maker of the deed, are valid; (b) attested, i.e. signed in presence of two witnesses. It is not necessary that these witnesses should sign in the presence of one another, or even that they should see the testator signing so long as the testator acknowledges his/her signature to the witnesses.

The Conveyancing and Feudal Reform (Scotland) Act 1970, whilst altering generally the rules for the subscription of deeds, specifically (s. 44 (2)) makes no change in the rules applying to wills, which must still be signed by the testator on every page. If the testator cannot write or is blind, the will may be authenticated by a law agent, notary public or justice of the peace and two witnesses. It is better that the will be not witnessed by a beneficiary thereunder, although this circumstance will not invalidate the attestation of the will or (as it would in England) the gift. A parish minister may act as a notary for the purpose of subscribing a will in his own parish.

Wills may be registered in the Books of the Sheriffdom in which the deceased died domiciled, or in the Books of Council and Session, HM General Register House, Edinburgh. The original deed may be inspected on payment of a small fee and a certified official copy may be obtained. A Scottish will is not revoked by the subsequent marriage of the testator. The subsequent birth of a child for whom no testamentary provision has been made may revoke a will. A will may be revoked by a subsequent will, either expressly or by implication; but in so far as the two can be read together, both wills have effect. If a subsequent will is revoked, the earlier will is revived.

Confirmation

Confirmation, the Scottish equivalent of probate, is obtained in the Sheriff Court of the sheriffdom in which the deceased was domiciled at the date of his/her death or, where the deceased had no fixed domicile or died abroad, in the Commissariat of Edinburgh. Executors are either 'nominate' or 'dative'. An executor nominate is one nominated by the deceased in the will or, where such person has predeceased the testator, by the residuary beneficiary. An executor dative is one appointed by the Court in the case of intestacy or where the deceased had failed to name an executor in the will and there is no residuary beneficiary. In the former case the deceased's next-of-kin are all entitled to be declared executors dative. An inventory of the deceased's estate and a schedule of debts, together with an affidavit, must first be given up. In estates under £17,000 gross, confirmation is obtained under a simplified procedure at reduced fees.

Presumption of Survivorship

The Succession (Scotland) Act 1964 provides, by s. 31, that where two persons die in circumstances indicating that they died simultaneously or if it is uncertain which was the survivor, the younger will be deemed to have survived the elder unless the elder person left testamentary provision in favour of the younger, whom failing in favour of a third person, the younger person having died intestate (partially or wholly); but if the persons so dying were husband and wife, neither shall be presumed to have survived the other.

EMPLOYMENT

Wages and Sick Pay

Under the Wages Act 1986, subject to certain exceptions, employers may not make deductions from an employee's wages unless authorized by statute or contract or with the employee's prior written consent. There is an upper limit of one-tenth of gross pay for deductions from retail workers' wages on account of cash or stock shortages.

Under the Social Security and Housing Benefits Act 1982 as amended, an employee absent from work because of illness or injury is entitled to receive Statutory Sick Pay from the employer for a maximum period of 28 weeks in any period of three years. No payment is made for the first three days of any period of illness. The employer can recoup the payments from his National Insurance contributions.

The Equal Pay Act 1970, which extends to Scotland, prevents discrimination as regards terms and conditions of employment between men and women employed on like work in the same employment.

Particulars of Terms of Employment

Under the Employment Protection (Consolidation) Act 1978, an employer must give each full-time employee within 13 weeks of the beginning of the employment a written statement containing the following particulars of the contract between them:

(a) the date when the employment began (when continuous employment began if previous work counts as continuous with this job);
(b) the rate of remuneration (or how it is calculated);
(c) the intervals at which wages are paid;
(d) the hours of work;
(e) the employee's entitlement to holidays (including public holidays) and holiday pay;
(f) the title of the employee's job;
(g) terms relating to sickness, injury and sick pay;
(h) details of any pension scheme;
(i) the length of notice which the employee should give and receive in order to terminate the contract.

In addition, the written particulars must specify any disciplinary rules; and also must identify the person to whom the employee can apply if dissatisfied with any disciplinary decision or to seek redress of any grievance, and what further steps may ensue.

Termination of Employment

An employee may be dismissed without notice if guilty of gross breach of contract, such as disobedience to a lawful order or dishonesty. The employee is then entitled only to wages accrued due at the date of dismissal.

In other cases, the employee is entitled to reasonable notice which, under the Employment Protection (Consolidation) Act 1978, must not be less than one week if he/she has been continuously employed for four weeks, but less than two years; after two years it is two weeks' notice increasing by one week's notice for each further full year worked up to a maximum of twelve weeks' notice after twelve years' service.

An employer who wrongfully dismisses an employee (i.e. with less than the length of notice to which he/she is entitled) is generally liable to pay wages for the period of proper notice.

An employee who has a fixed term contract has no claim against his/her employer for wrongful dismissal if the contract is not renewed when it expires. He/she may, however, have a claim for a redundancy payment or compensation for unfair dismissal. If he/she is wrongfully dismissed before the contract expires, he/she is generally entitled to remuneration payable over the full period of the contract.

An employee may be entitled to a redundancy payment or to compensation for unfair dismissal if the employment has been terminated by the employer (with or without proper notice) or he/she has a fixed term contract which expires without being renewed or the employment has been terminated by the employee by reason of the employer's breach of contract.

Under the Employment Protection (Consolidation) Act 1978, an employee who satisfies the foregoing conditions and has been continuously employed for two years and who is dismissed by reason of redundancy may be entitled to a redundancy payment calculated by reference to his/her age, pay and length of service.

The Employment Protection (Consolidation) Act 1978 also enables an employee who is unfairly dismissed to complain to an industrial tribunal (generally within three months of dismissal). The onus will then be on the employer to prove that the dismissal was due to capability, conduct, redundancy, illegality or some other substantial reason justifying dismissal. The tribunal must decide whether the employer acted reasonably in dismissing the employee. If the employer fails to prove that the dismissal was due to one or more of the above five reasons, or the tribunal decides that the employer did not act reasonably in dismissing the employee, the dismissal will be unfair, in which case the tribunal can:

(a) order re-engagement or reinstatement; or
(b) award compensation consisting of a basic and a compensatory award.

For an employee to bring himself/herself within the unfair dismissal provisions, he/she must have been continuously employed for a period of two years.

All complaints of unfair dismissal are referred to a conciliation officer or the Department of Employment and a very high proportion of complaints are disposed of in this way.

FAMILY LAW
ADOPTION OF CHILDREN

In England and Wales the adoption of children is mainly governed by the Adoption Act 1976, as amended by the Children Act 1989. A court order is necessary to legalize the adoption, which, when completed, has the effect of making the adopted child the child of the adopter as if he or she had been born to the adopter in lawful wedlock, and the original rights and duties of the natural parents are thereby cut. The adopter has full rights as to custody, education etc. and the child is treated as his/hers for the purpose of any devolution of property on an intestacy occurring or under any disposition made after the adoption order. The application may be made to the High Court (Family Division) or to a county court or magistrates' court.

Orders may be made in favour of married couples, single, widowed or divorced persons, but not of one party to a marriage alone unless the other spouse cannot be found, is physically or mentally incapable of making an application, or they are separated in circumstances likely to be permanent. A person aged under 21 cannot adopt.

The child's parents or guardians must consent unconditionally to the making of the order unless the court dispenses with the consent, which it may do if the parent cannot be found or is incapable of giving consent, is withholding consent unreasonably, or has neglected or ill-treated the child.

Restrictions are placed on societies which may arrange adoptions.

An adopted person aged over 18 may apply to the Registrar General for information to enable him/her to obtain a full certificate of his/her birth, but before being supplied with the information he/she will be informed that counselling services are available to him/her. The 1989 Act provides for the creation of a new register (the Adoption Contact Registrar) in which details of those who have had their children adopted, and of adopted persons themselves, may be recorded.

An adopter and the adopted child are within the prohibited degrees for the purposes of marriage to one another.

All adoptions in Great Britain are registered in the Registers of Adopted Children kept by the

Registrars General in London and Edinburgh respectively. Certificates from these registers, including short certificates which contain no reference to adoptions, can be obtained on conditions similar to those relating to birth certificates (*see* below).

SCOTLAND

The law is consolidated in the Adoption (Scotland) Act 1978 as amended by the Children Act 1989. The law relating to fostering is consolidated in the Foster Children (Scotland) Act 1984. A petition for adoption is presented either to the Sheriff Court or the Court of Session. As in England, the petitioner(s) must be 21 or over and may be a married couple or one person who, if married, is living apart permanently from his or her spouse. The consent of the child's natural parents/guardians is required unless dispensed with, or the child is already free for adoption.

The Succession (Scotland) Act 1964 gives the adopted child the same rights of succession as a child born to the adopter in wedlock but deprives him/her of any such rights in the estates of his natural parents.

BIRTHS (REGISTRATION)

When a birth takes place, personal information of it must be given to the Registrar of Births and Deaths for the sub-district in which the birth occurred, and the register signed in his/her presence by the father or mother of the child; or, if they fail, by (a) the occupier of the house in which the birth happened; (b) a person present at the birth; or (c) the person having charge of the child. The duty of attending to the registration therefore rests firstly on the parents. The mother is responsible for the registration of the birth of an illegitimate child.

The registration is required to be made within 42 days of the birth. Failure to do this without reasonable cause involves liability to a penalty. The registration of a birth is free. In England or Wales, the informant, instead of attending before the registrar of the sub-district where the birth occurred, may make a declaration of the particulars required to be registered in the presence of any registrar. Under the National Health Service Act 1977, notice of every birth must be given by the father, or person in attendance on the mother, to the district medical officer of health by post within 36 hours of the birth. This is in addition to the registration already mentioned.

Still birth.—A still birth must be registered, and a certificate signed by the doctor or midwife who was present at the birth or who has examined the body of the child must be produced to the registrar. The certificate must, where possible, state the cause of death and the estimated duration of the pregnancy. A stillbirth may only be registered within three months of the birth.

Re-registration.—The re-registration of the birth of a person legitimated by the subsequent marriage of the parents is provided for in the Births and Deaths Registration Act 1953, as amended by the Family Law Reform Act 1987. Special provisions apply to the registration and re-registration of births of abandoned children, and the re-registration of births of illegitimate children showing the father's name; the mother must normally be party to the latter application.

Birth at sea.—The master of a British ship must record any birth on board and send particulars to the Registrar General of Shipping.

Birth abroad.—Consular officers are authorized to register births of British subjects occurring abroad.

Certificates are obtainable in due course at the Registrar General's Office, London.

The registration of births occurring out of the United Kingdom among members of the armed forces, or occurring on board HM ships and aircraft, is provided for by the Registration of Births, Deaths and Marriages (Special Provisions) Act 1957, applicable also to Scotland.

SCOTLAND

The Registration of Births, Deaths and Marriages (Scotland) Act 1965 supersedes former Acts. Personal notification within 21 days of any birth must be given to the registrar of either the registration district in which the birth took place, or any registration district in which the mother of the child was ordinarily resident at the time of the birth. In the case of a foundling child, dead or alive, when the place of birth is not known, notification must be given to the registrar of the registration district in which the child, or the body, was found, within two months from the date on which the child was found. When a child is born (in or out of Scotland) in a ship, aircraft or land vehicle during a journey and the child is conveyed therein to any place in Scotland, the birth shall, unless the Registrar General otherwise directs, be deemed to have occurred at that place.

The register must be signed in the presence of the registrar by the father or mother of the child, or, if they fail, by (a) any relative of either parent who has knowledge of the birth; (b) the occupier of the premises in which the child was, to the knowledge of that occupier, born; (c) any person present at the birth; (d) any person having charge of the child. Failure without reasonable cause involves a penalty.

The name of the father of a child born out of wedlock may be entered in the register of births at the time of registration if jointly requested by the mother and father, and the latter's name may also be recorded at a later date on declaration by both parents. A free abbreviated certificate of birth will be issued to the informant at the time of registration.

Still birth.—A still birth must be registered and a certificate, signed by the doctor or certified midwife present at the birth or who has examined the body of the child, must be produced.

Re-registration.—Provision is made for the re-registration of the birth of a person made legitimate by the subsequent marriage of the parents or whose birth entry is affected by any matter respecting place or paternity, or has been so made as to imply that he/she is a foundling.

CERTIFICATES OF BIRTHS, MARRIAGES, OR DEATHS

Certificates of births, deaths, or marriages in England and Wales can be obtained at the Office of Population Censuses and Surveys, St Catherine's House, 10 Kingsway, London WC2B 6JP, or from the Superintendent Registrar having the legal custody of the register containing the entry of which a certificate is required. Certificates of marriage can also be obtained from the incumbent of the church in which the marriage took place, or from the nonconformist minister (or other authorized person) where the marriage takes place in a registered building.

It is considered desirable when a certificate is required to consult the nearest Register Office which, if told the exact or approximate date and place of registration, will be able to advise on the best way of obtaining it, and any fees payable, which vary according to the type of certificate required and other factors.

Records of births, deaths and marriages registered in England and Wales since 1837 are kept at the Office of Population Censuses and Surveys, St Catherine's House, 10 Kingsway, London WC2B 6JP. The Society of Genealogists, 14 Charterhouse Buildings, Goswell Road, London EC1M 7BA, possesses many records of baptisms, marriages and deaths prior to 1837, including copies in whole or in part of about 4,000 parish registers.

SCOTLAND

Certificates of births, deaths or marriages registered from 1855 (when compulsory registration commenced in Scotland) can be obtained personally at the General Register Office, New Register House, Edinburgh EH1 3YT, or from the appropriate local registrar, on payment of the fee of £7·50 for a full extract entry of birth, death, or marriage (£9·50 by post), and £6·50 for an abbreviated certificate of birth (£8·50 by post). An abbreviated certificate of registration of death is issued free of charge for National Insurance purposes in certain cases. A Register of Divorces (which includes decrees of declaration of nullity of marriage) is kept by the Registrar General at the General Register Office. The fee for an extract decree is £7·50 (£9·50 by post).

There are also available at the General Register Office old parish registers of the date prior to 1855, which were formerly kept under the administration of the established Church of Scotland. An extract of an entry in these registers may be obtained on payment of the appropriate fee. A fee of £15·00 per day is payable for a general search of all the Scottish registers.

The Registration of Presumed Deaths (Prescription of Particulars) (Scotland) Regulations 1978 as read with Presumption of Death (Scotland) Act 1977 prescribe the particulars to be notified by the Clerk of Court to the Registrar General after a decree or variation order has been granted in an action of declarator of death of a missing person.

DIVORCE, SEPARATION AND ANCILLARY MATTERS

Matrimonial suits may be conveniently divided into two classes: those in which it is sought to annul the marriage because of some defect; and those in which, the marriage being admitted, it is sought to end the marriage or the duties arising from it. By virtue of the Matrimonial and Family Proceedings Act 1984, all matrimonial causes are commenced in one of the divorce county courts designated by the Lord Chancellor or in the Divorce Registry in London. If the suit becomes defended, it may be transferred to the High Court.

Nullity of Marriage

Nullity of marriage is now mainly governed as to England and Wales by the Matrimonial Causes Act 1973. A marriage is void *ab initio* if the parties were within the prohibited degrees of affinity; or were not male and female; if it was bigamous; if one of the parties was under the age of consent, i.e. 16; or, in the case of a polygamous marriage entered into outside England and Wales, if either party was at the time of the marriage domiciled in England or Wales. Where the formalities of the marriage were defective, the marriage is generally void if both parties knew of the defect (e.g. where marriage took place otherwise than in an authorized building). However, absence of the consent of parents or guardians (or of the Court or other authority, in lieu thereof) in the case of minors does not invalidate the marriage.

A marriage is voidable (i.e. a decree of nullity may

be obtained but until such time the marriage remains valid) on the following grounds:

(a) incapacity of either party to consummate;
(b) respondent's wilful refusal to consummate;
(c) that either party did not validly consent to the marriage, whether in consequence of duress, mistake, unsoundness of mind or otherwise;
(d) that either party at the time of marriage was a mentally disordered person;
(e) that at the time of marriage the respondent was suffering from communicable venereal disease;
(f) that at the time of the marriage the respondent was pregnant by another man.

In cases (e) and (f), the petitioner must have been ignorant of the grounds at the date of the marriage. In cases (c), (d), (e) and (f) proceedings must be instituted within three years of the marriage, although leave may be allowed to petition outside this period in the case of certain persons suffering from mental illness. In all cases the court shall not grant a decree where the petitioner has led the respondent to believe that he/she would not seek a decree and it would be unjust for it to be granted.

The 1973 Act provides that a decree of nullity in a voidable marriage only annuls the marriage from the date of the decree. The marriage remains valid until the decree and any children of the marriage are legitimate. Children of a void marriage are illegitimate unless the father was domiciled in England or Wales at the child's birth (or father's death, if earlier), and at the time of conception (or marriage if later) both or either of the parents reasonably believed the marriage was valid.

A spouse's insistence upon the use of contraceptives will not constitute wilful refusal to consummate within (b) above, even though there has been no normal intercourse, but it may in certain circumstances constitute unreasonable behaviour for the purpose of divorce (*see* below). Further, it has been allowed as a defence to a charge of desertion against the aggrieved party.

Judicial Separation and Divorce

The second class of suit includes a suit for judicial separation (which does not dissolve a marriage) and a suit for divorce (which, if successful, dissolves the marriage altogether and leaves the parties at liberty to marry again). Either spouse may petition for judicial separation. It is not necessary to prove that the marriage has broken down irretrievably and the five facts listed under **Divorce** below are grounds for judicial separation.

Divorce

The sole ground on which a divorce is obtained by either husband or wife is the irretrievable breakdown of the marriage. However, the court is precluded from holding that a marriage has irretrievably broken down unless it is satisfied of one or more of the following facts:

(a) that the respondent has committed adultery since the marriage and the petitioner finds it intolerable to live with the respondent;
(b) that the respondent has behaved in such a way that the petitioner cannot reasonably be expected to continue cohabitation;
(c) desertion by the respondent for two years immediately before the petition;
(d) five years' separation immediately before the petition (but only two years where the respondent consents to the decree). Matrimonial Causes Act 1973.

The foregoing is subject to a clause prohibiting any

petition for divorce (but not for judicial separation) before the lapse of one year from the date of the marriage.

Desertion may be defined as a voluntary withdrawal from cohabitation by one spouse without just cause and against the wishes of the other. Where one spouse is guilty of conduct of a serious nature which forces the other to leave, the party at fault is said to be guilty of constructive desertion.

Encouragement of reconciliation.—The 1973 Act requires the solicitor for the petitioner in certain cases to certify whether the possibility of a reconciliation has been discussed with the petitioner and whether or not the solicitor has given the petitioner the names and addresses of persons qualified to help effect a reconciliation.

A total period of less than six months during which the parties have resumed living together is to be disregarded in determining whether the prescribed period of desertion or separation has been continuous. Similar provision for effecting a reconciliation exists in relation to the other proofs of breakdown, but a petitioner cannot rely on an act of adultery by the other party if they have lived together for more than six months after discovery of that act of adultery.

Obtaining the decree nisi.—Where the suit is defended, i.e. the respondent opposes the dissolution or the fact/ground on which the petitioner seeks it, the petition will be heard by a judge in open court, the parties giving oral evidence. Where the suit is undefended, the evidence will normally take the form of a sworn written statement made by the petitioner which will be sent to the Court and read over by a District Judge. If the District Judge is satisfied that the petitioner has proved the contents of the petition, he will simply fix a date for the pronouncement of the decree nisi in open court, it being unnecessary for either party to attend. Only if the District Judge is not satisfied as above will he order that the petition be heard formally by the Judge.

Children.—(Until October 14, 1991) subject to exceptions, the decree nisi cannot be made absolute unless a Judge by order declares that he is satisfied with the proposed arrangements for the welfare of any child of the family who is under 16, or under 18 and receiving education or vocational training. If there is no dispute as to the children between the parties and the proposed arrangements for residence, education etc. are specific, an appointment will be made for the Judge to interview one or both parents informally and if satisfied he will make an order to that effect. (This will usually be on the same day as the decree nisi is pronounced.) If not, the parties are informed that it is up to them to seek a hearing before the Judge to resolve the matters in dispute.

Under the provisions of the Children Act 1989, from October 14, 1991, the Judge will not be required to make an order that he is satisfied, nor will the parents need to attend before a Judge unless there are exceptional circumstances.

Decree absolute.—Every decree of divorce or nullity is in the first instance a decree nisi, and the marriage subsists until the decree is made absolute, usually six weeks after decree nisi on the petitioner's application. After the decree absolute either party is free to remarry.

Maintenance, etc.—The court has wide powers to order either party to the marriage to make financial provision (e.g. periodical payments, a lump sum, the transfer of property) for the other party or any child of the family, having regard to the party's means, the recipient's needs and all the important aspects of the case. These so-called ancillary matters often present more difficulty than the divorce itself, especially

affecting the home, and may go on long after the marriage is dissolved. There is, however, nothing to stop financial matters being negotiated by the parties through their solicitors before the divorce goes through.

The court may, where the husband has wilfully neglected to provide reasonable maintenance for the wife or children, order the husband to make provision for them, even though no matrimonial suit is pending between the parties to the marriage, and while such an order is in force the court may also deal with custody of and access to the children.

Orders regarding Children

The Court may make orders in respect of children in connection with a suit for divorce, nullity or judicial separation (above), or with an application to the magistrates (below) whether the suit succeeds or not. In addition, if there is no other matrimonial suit involved, a parent may apply for orders under the Guardianship of Minors Acts 1971 (after October 14, 1991 under similar provisions in the Children Act 1989), and any person interested may apply to the High Court for the child to be made a ward of court.

In all cases the welfare of the child is the first and paramount consideration. The categories of child who may be covered by any particular type of proceedings differ according to the nature of those proceedings and to the nature of the particular relief sought, but it should be borne in mind that in connection with divorce, nullity and judicial separation a child which has been treated by the spouses as a child of the family may be included as a 'child of the family' as well as the children of the spouses themselves. This also applies to most maintenance cases in the magistrates' court (*see* below). It should be borne in mind that where there is financial need (because of continuing education or disability, for instance), maintenance may be ordered for children even beyond the age of majority.

Any dispute relating to the above matters should be placed in the hands of a solicitor without delay.

The Children Act 1989 introduces fundamental changes to the types of orders the courts can make, after October 14, 1991.

Separation by Agreement

Husband and wife may enter into an agreement to separate and live apart but the agreement, to be valid, must be followed by an immediate separation. It is most desirable to consult a solicitor in every such case, who will often advise obtaining a court order by consent.

Magistrates' Custody and Maintenance Orders

For many years the law relating to domestic proceedings in magistrates' courts was out of line with the divorce law which was reformed in 1969. The Domestic Proceedings and Magistrates' Courts Act 1978 took effect in early 1981 and now contains the relevant law.

A husband or wife can apply to a magistrates' court for a matrimonial order on the grounds that the other spouse: (a) has failed to pay reasonable maintenance for the applicant; (b) has failed to make a proper contribution towards the reasonable maintenance of a child of the family; (c) has deserted the applicant; or (d) has behaved in such a way that the applicant cannot reasonably be expected to live with the respondent.

If the case is proved the court can order: (a) periodical payments for the applicant; (b) periodical payments for a child of the family; or (c) a lump sum (not exceeding £1,000) for the benefit of the applicant and for any child of the family.

In deciding what orders (if any) to make, the magistrates must consider a number of guidelines which are similar to those governing financial orders on divorce. There are also special provisions relating to consent orders and separation by agreement. The court also has powers to make orders relating to a child of the family and these orders together with orders for child maintenance can be made even though the court makes no order for spouse maintenance. Other provisions of the Act relate to interim orders, and variation, discharge and revival of orders. An order may be enforceable even though the parties are living together, but in some cases it will cease to have effect if they continue to do so for six months. The hearing of matrimonial disputes is separate from ordinary court business, and the public are not admitted.

Domestic Violence

The Domestic Violence and Matrimonial Proceedings Act 1976, the Domestic Proceedings and Magistrates' Courts Act 1978 (the former not being applicable to Scotland and the latter only to a limited extent; *see* below) and the Matrimonial Homes Act 1983 have made it easier for one spouse who has been subjected to violence by the other to obtain an order to restrain further violence and if need be to have the other excluded from the home. Such orders can be obtained very quickly, and a person disobeying them is liable to be imprisoned for contempt of court. There are some differences of detail between the three Acts; in particular the 1976 Act also applies to unmarried couples. Such orders may also be obtained in the course of suits for divorce and judicial separation.

SCOTLAND

Nullity of Marriage

A declaration of nullity of marriage may be obtained on the ground of any impediment, viz., consanguinity and affinity, subsistence of a previous marriage, nonage of one of the parties, incapacity or insanity of one of the parties, or by the absence of genuine consent. The financial provisions on divorce contained in the Family Law (Scotland) Act 1985 also apply to an action for declaration of nullity of marriage.

Judicial Separation

Under the Divorce (Scotland) Act 1976, a decree of judicial separation can be obtained by proof of the same facts necessary to obtain decree of divorce, except that for the principle of irretrievable breakdown there is substituted that of grounds justifying separation. This type of action is competent in both the Court of Session and the Sheriff Court.

Divorce

Actions of divorce could formerly only be raised in the Court of Session, having jurisdiction to entertain such actions only if either of the parties to the marriage in question is domiciled in Scotland on the date when the action is begun, or was habitually resident in Scotland throughout the period of one year ending with that date. As from May 1, 1984, however, when the Divorce Jurisdiction, Court Fees and Legal Aid (Scotland) Act 1983 came into force, actions of divorce may also be raised in the Sheriff Courts provided the above conditions are complied with, and provided either party to the marriage was resident in the Sheriffdom for a period of forty days ending with the date the action was begun, or was resident in the Sheriffdom for a period of not less

than forty days ending not more than forty days before the date the action was begun.

The Scots law of divorce is now governed by the Divorce (Scotland) Act 1976, which for the purposes of divorce came into force on January 1, 1977. The sole ground of divorce is now irretrievable breakdown of the marriage. This can be established only in one of the following ways:

(a) The defending spouse has committed adultery since the date of the marriage. It is not necessary for the pursuing spouse to prove that the fact of adultery made it intolerable to live with the defending spouse.

(b) The defending spouse has behaved in such a way that the pursuing spouse cannot reasonably be expected to cohabit with him or her. It is immaterial whether or not the conduct founded upon is active or passive.

(c) The defending spouse has deserted the pursuing spouse for a continuous period of two years. There must be no question of the pursuing spouse having refused a genuine and reasonable offer to adhere. Nor is irretrievable breakdown established if cohabitation is resumed for a period of more than three months, after the two-year period has expired.

(d) There has been no cohabitation at any time during a continuous period of two years immediately preceding the action between the parties to the action, and the defending spouse consents to the divorce being granted.

(e) There has been no cohabitation at any time during a continuous period of five years, as in (d), except that on the expiry of the five-year period, the consent of the defending spouse is not required.

The facts of desertion and separation are not interrupted by the parties cohabiting for a period or periods not exceeding six months. However, such a period or periods of cohabitation would not be included in the calculation of the two-year or five-year periods.

Encouragement of reconciliation.—The burden of promoting a reconciliation between spouses in a divorce action in Scotland falls upon the Court by virtue of the 1976 Act. Where an action of divorce has been raised, it may be postponed by the Court to enable the parties to seek to effect a reconciliation, if the Court feels that there may be a reasonable prospect of such reconciliation. If the parties do cohabit during such postponement, no account shall be taken of such cohabitation if the action later proceeds.

Maintenance, etc.—The 1976 Act also provides that either party to a marriage can apply to the Court at any time prior to decree being granted for: (a) an order for interim custody of all or some of the children of the marriage under 16 years of age; (b) an order for access to all or some of the children of the marriage under 16 years of age in the custody of the other party.

The financial provisions on divorce in the 1976 Act have been superseded by the Family Law (Scotland) Act 1985, which allows either party to the marriage to apply to the court for an order for payment of a capital sum or for a periodical allowance or for an incidental order. The Act sets out principles to be applied by the Court, one of these being that the financial provisions awarded to a party who has been dependent for financial support on the other party should be given over a period of not more than three years.

The Act also defines the rights and obligations of aliment between parents and children, thereby excluding aliment between grandparents and grand-children and of children to parents, and provides that a child is entitled to aliment up to the age of eighteen or to twenty-five if in full-time further education, and for the claiming of aliment whether in connection with an action of divorce etc. or independently.

Procedure.—Appearance in Court at a Proof in an undefended divorce action has been rendered unnecessary since April 1978. A full Proof is still necessary if the action is defended in any respect. In place of court appearance, affidavits (statements sworn before a Notary Public) by the pursuer and any witnesses are lodged in the Court together with a Minute by the solicitor craving decree.

A new simplified procedure for 'do-it-yourself' divorce was introduced in January 1983 for certain divorces. Thus, if the action is based on (d) or (e) above and will not be opposed, and if there are no children under 16 and no financial claims, then the applicant can write directly to the Court of Session, Divorce Section (SP), Parliament House, Edinburgh or to the local Sheriff Court for the appropriate forms to enable him or her to proceed. The fee is £40 unless the applicant receives Income Support, Family Credit or legal advice and assistance, in which case there is no fee.

Custody of Children

In actions for divorce and separation, the Court has a discretion in awarding the custody of the children of the parties. The welfare of the children is the paramount consideration, and the mere fact that a spouse, by reason of his or her behaviour, brought about the breakdown of the marriage does not of itself preclude him or her from being awarded custody. The Children Act 1975, as amended, also applies to Scotland.

Domestic Violence

The Matrimonial Homes (Family Protection) (Scotland) Act 1981, as amended, provides that one spouse, whether or not he or she has title to the matrimonial home, can obtain an exclusion order suspending the other spouse's occupancy rights in the matrimonial home. The Court (either Court of Session or Sheriff Court) is empowered to make such an order if satisfied that it is necessary to protect the applicant or any child of the family from any conduct, actual or threatened or reasonably apprehended of the other spouse which would be injurious to the physical or mental health of the applicant or child. In making the order the Court may include a warrant for the summary ejection of the non-applicant spouse from the matrimonial home and for an interdict prohibiting him/her from entering it.

ILLEGITIMACY AND LEGITIMATION

England and Wales

The former provisions of the Affiliation Proceedings Act 1957, under which a man could be summoned to petty sessions on the application of the mother of an illegitimate child, or by the Supplementary Benefits Commission where benefit has been paid for the requirements of the child, and under which the Justices, on his being proved to be the father of the child, could make an order requiring him to pay for its maintenance and education a sum in their discretion, were replaced by extensive provisions relating to parental rights and duties in Part II of the Family Law Reform Act 1987. These provisions will, in turn, be replaced by those of the Children Act 1989 from October 14, 1991, which give the mother parental responsibility for her child when not married to the father. The father can acquire parental

responsbilitiy by agreement with her (in prescribed form) or by court order.

Prima facie every child born of a married woman during a marriage is legitimate; and this presumption can only be rebutted by strong evidence. However, under the Family Law Reform Act 1969, any presumption of law as to the legitimacy (or illegitimacy) of any person may in civil proceedings be rebutted by evidence showing that it is more probable than not that the person is illegitimate (or legitimate) and in any proceedings where paternity is in question, blood tests may be ordered. If, however, the husband and wife are separated under an Order of the Court, a child conceived by the wife during such separation is presumed not to be the husband's child.

Legitimation

The Legitimacy Act 1976 consolidates earlier legislation dating back to January 1, 1927. Where the parents of an illegitimate person marry, or have married, whether before or after that date, the marriage, if the father is at the date thereof domiciled in England or Wales, renders that person, if living, legitimate as from January 1, 1927, or from the date of the marriage, whichever last happens. Marriage legitimates a person even though the father or mother was married to a third person at the time when the illegitimate person was born. It is the duty of the parents to supply to the Registrar General information for re-registration of the birth of a legitimate child.

Declarations of Legitimacy.—A person claiming that he, his parents, or any remoter ancestor has become legitimated, may petition the High Court or the County Court for the necessary declaration.

Rights and Duties of Legitimated Persons.—A legitimated person, his/her spouse or children may take property under an intestacy occurring after the date of legitimation, or under any disposition (e.g. a will) coming into operation after such date, as if he/she had been legitimate. He/she must maintain all persons whom he/she would be bound to maintain had he/she been born legitimate, and he/she is entitled to the benefit of any Act of Parliament which confers rights on legitimate persons to recover damages or compensation. The Act specially provides that nothing therein contained is to render any person capable of succeeding to or transmitting a right to any dignity or title.

Property Rights of Illegitimate Children

By the Family Law Reform Act 1969 the rights of an illegitimate child on an intestacy were broadly equated with those of a legitimate child, and in any disposition made after December 31, 1969, any reference to children or other relatives was, unless the contrary intention appears, to be construed as including any person who is illegitimate or who is related through another person who is illegitimate. However, these provisions of the 1969 Act have been replaced by the general provision of the Family Law Reform Act 1987 (*see* p. 1025).

Scotland

The Law Reform (Parent & Child) Scotland Act 1986 implements the Scottish Law Commission' report on illegitimacy. The Act contains a general provision granting equality status to all person whatever the marital status of their parents. Th mother of an illegitimate child may raise an action of affiliation and aliment against the father, either in the Court of Session or, more usually, in the Sheriff Court. Where in any such action the Court find that the defender is the father of the child, the Court shall, in awarding expenses, or aliment, have regard to the means of the parties and the whole circumstance of the case. The Court may, upon application by the mother or by the father of any illegitimate child, or in any action for aliment for an illegitimate child, make such order as it may think fit regarding the custody of such child and the right of access thereto of either parent, having regard to the welfare of the child and to the conduct of the parents and to the wishes as well of the mother as of the father and may on the application of either parent recall or vary such order. The obligation of the mother and of the father of an illegitimate child to provide aliment for such child shall (without prejudice to any obligation attaching at common law) endure until the child attains the age of sixteen.

Legitimation

By Scottish law an illegitimate child is legitimated by and on the date of the subsequent marriage of its parents and there is no objection to there having been an impediment to the marriage of the parents at the time of the child's conception—*see* the Legitimation (Scotland) Act 1968, which came into operation on June 8, 1968, on which date thousands of existing illegitimate children were regarded as legitimated. By the Registration of Births, Deaths and Marriages (Scotland) Act 1965, a child so legitimated, who has already been registered as illegitimate, may be re-registered as legitimate. The consent of the father of an illegitimate child to its adoption is not required unless he has been awarded parental rights by the court.

MARRIAGE

Marriage According to Rites of the Church of England

Marriage by Banns

The Marriage Act 1949 prescribes audible publication according to the rubric, on three Sundays preceding the ceremony during morning service or, if there is no morning service on a Sunday on which the banns are to be published, during evening service. Where the parties reside in different parishes, the banns must be published in both. Under the Act, banns may be published and the marriage solemnized in the parish church, which is the usual place of worship of the persons to be married or either of them, although neither of such persons dwells in such parish; but this publication of banns is in addition to any other publication required by law and does not apply if the church or the residence of either party is in Wales. The Act provides specially for the case where one of the parties resides in Scotland and the other in England, the publication being then in the parish in England in which one party resides, and, according to the law and custom in Scotland, in the place where the other party resides. After the lapse of three months from the last time of publication, the banns become useless, and the parties must either obtain a licence (*see* below), or submit to the republication of banns.

Marriage by Licence

Marriage licences are of two kinds:—

Common Licence.—A common licence, dispensing with the necessity for banns, is granted by the Archbishops and Bishops through their surrogates, for marriages in any church or chapel duly licensed for marriages. A common licence can be obtained in London by application at the Faculty Office (1 The Sanctuary, Westminster, SW1) and (for marriages in London) at the Bishop of London's Diocesan Registry (1 The Sanctuary, SW1), by one of the parties about to be married. In the country they may be obtained at the offices of the Bishop's registrars, but licences

obtained at the Bishop's diocesan registry only enable the parties to be married in the diocese in which they are issued; those procured at the Faculty Office are available for all England and Wales. No instructions, either verbal or in writing, can be received, except from one of the parties. Affidavits are prepared from the personal instructions of one of the parties about to be married, and the licence is delivered to the party upon payment of a fee (*see* page 1037). Before a licence can be granted one of the parties must make an affidavit that there is no legal impediment to the intended marriage; and also that one of such parties has had his or her usual place of abode for the space of fifteen days immediately preceding the issuing of the licence within the parish or ecclesiastical district of the church in which the marriage is to be solemnized, or that the church in which the marriage is to be solemnized is the usual place of worship of the parties or one of them. In the country there may generally be found a parochial clergyman (surrogate) before whom the affidavit may be taken, and whose office it is to deliver the licence personally to the applicant. (In some dioceses it is necessary for the surrogate to procure the licence from the Bishop's registry.) The licence continues in force for three months from its date.

Special Licence.—A special licence is granted by the Archbishop of Canterbury, in special circumstances, for marriage at any place with or without previous residence in the district, or at any time, etc.; but the reasons assigned must meet with the Archbishop's approval. Application must be made to the Faculty Office. (For fee, *see* page 1037.)

Marriage under Superintendent Registrar's Certificate

A marriage may be performed in church on the Superintendent Registrar's Certificate (*see* below) without banns, provided that the incumbent's consent is obtained. One of the parties must be resident within the ecclesiastical parish of the church in which the marriage is to take place unless the church is the usual place of worship of the parties or one of them.

Marriage under Superintendent Registrar's Certificate

The following marriages may be solemnized on the authority of a Superintendent Registrar's certificate (either with or without a licence):

(a) A marriage in a registered building (e.g. a nonconformist church registered for the solemnization of marriages therein).
(b) A marriage in a register office.
(c) A marriage according to the usages of the Society of Friends (commonly called Quakers).
(d) A marriage between two persons professing the Jewish religion according to the usages of the Jews.
(e) A marriage according to the rites of the Church of England (*see* above—in this case the marriage can only be without licence).
(f) A marriage of a person who is housebound or is detained at the place where he or she normally resides (*see* p. 1037).

Notice of the intended marriage must be given as follows:

Marriage by certificate (without licence).—If both parties reside in the same registration district, they must both have resided there for seven days before the notice can be given. It may then be given by either party. If the parties reside in different registration districts, notice must be given by each to the Superintendent Registrar of the district in which he or she resides, and the preliminary residential qualification of seven days must be fulfilled by each before either notice can be given.

Marriage by certificate (with licence).—One notice only is necessary, whether the parties live in the same or in different registration districts. Either party may give the notice, which must be given to the Superintendent Registrar of any registration district in which one of the parties has resided for the period of fifteen days immediately preceding the giving of notice, but both parties must be resident in England or Wales on the day notice is given.

The notice (in either case) must be in the prescribed form and must contain particulars as to names, marital status, occupation, residence, length of residence, and the building in which the marriage is to take place. The notice must also contain or have added at the foot thereof a solemn declaration that there is no legal impediment to the marriage, and, in the case of minors, that the consent of the person whose consent to the marriage is required by law (*see* *Minors*, p. 1037) has been duly given, and that the residential qualifications mentioned above have been complied with. A person making a false declaration renders himself or herself liable to prosecution for perjury. The notice is entered in the marriage notice book.

ISSUE OF CERTIFICATE

Without licence.—The notice (or an exact copy thereof) is affixed in some conspicuous place in the Superintendent Registrar's office for 21 days next after the notice was entered in the marriage notice book. After the lapse of this period the Superintendent Registrar may, provided no impediment is shown, issue his certificate for the marriage which can then take place at any time within three months from the date of the entry of the notice.

With licence.—The notice in this case is not affixed in the office of the Superintendent Registrar. After the lapse of one whole day (other than a Sunday, Christmas Day or Good Friday) from the date of entry of the notice, the Superintendent Registrar may, provided no impediment is shown, issue his certificate and licence for the marriage, which can then take place on any day within three months from the date of entry of the notice.

SOLEMNIZATION OF THE MARRIAGE

In a registered building.—The marriage must generally take place at a building within the district of residence of one of the parties, but if the usual place of worship of either is outside the district of his or her residence, it may take place in such usual place of worship. Further, if there is not within the district of residence of one of the parties a registered building within which marriages are solemnized according to the rites and ceremonies which the parties desire to adopt in solemnizing their marriage, it may take place in an appropriate registered building in the nearest district.

The presence of a Registrar of Marriages is not necessary at marriages at registered buildings which have adopted the provisions of section 43 of the Marriage Act 1949. This section provides for the appointment of an authorized person (a person, usually the minister or an official of the building, certified by the trustees or governing body as having been duly authorized for the purpose) who must be present and must register the marriage.

The marriage must be solemnized between the hours of 8 a.m. and 6 p.m., with open doors in the presence of two or more witnesses. The parties must at some time during the ceremony make the following

declaration: 'I do solemnly declare that I know no of any lawful impediment why I, A. B., may not be joined in matrimony to C. D.' Also each of the parties must say to the other: 'I call upon these persons here present to witness that I, A. B., do take thee, C. D., to be my lawful wedded wife [or husband],' or, if the marriage is solemnized in the presence of an author ized person without the presence of a Registrar, each party may say in lieu thereof: 'I, A. B., do take thee C. D., to be my wedded wife [or husband].'

In a register office.—The marriage may be solemnized in the office of the Superintendent Registrar to whom notice of the marriage has been given. The marriage must be solemnized between the hours of 8 a.m. and 6 p.m., with open doors in the presence of the Superintendent Registrar or a Registrar of the registration district of that Superintendent Registrar, and in the presence of two witnesses. The parties must make the following declaration: 'I do solemnly declare that I know not of any lawful impediment why I, A. B., may not be joined in matrimony to C. D.,' and each party must say to the other: 'I call upon these persons here present to witness that I, A. B., do take thee, C. D., to be my lawful wedded wife [or husband].' No religious ceremony may take place in the register office, though the parties may, on production of their marriage certificate, go through a subsequent religious ceremony in any church or persuasion of which they are members.

Other cases.—If both parties are members of the Society of Friends (Quakers), or if, not being in membership, they have been authorized by the Society of Friends to solemnize their marriage in accordance with its usages, they may be married in a Friends' meeting-house. The marriage must be registered by the registering officer of the Society appointed to act for the district in which the meeting house is situated. The presence of a Registrar of Marriages is not necessary.

If both parties are Jews they may marry according to their usages in a synagogue which has a certified marriage secretary, or in a private dwelling-house at any hour; the building may be situated within or without the district of residence. The marriage must be registered by the secretary of the synagogue of which the man is a member. The presence of a Registrar of Marriages is not necessary.

Marriage under Registrar General's Licence

The main purpose of the Marriage (Registrar General's Licence) Act 1970, which came into force on January 1, 1971, is to enable non-Anglicans to be married in unregistered premises where one of the persons to be married is seriously ill, is not expected to recover and cannot be moved to registered premises.

Detained and Housebound Persons

The Marriage Act 1983 (which does not extend to Scotland) enables marriages of detained persons and housebound persons to be solemnized at their place of residence. The Act came into operation on May 1 1984.

Marriage in England or Wales when one party lives in Scotland or Northern Ireland

Notice for a marriage by a Superintendent Registrar's certificate in a register office or registered building may be given in the usual way by the party resident in England. As regards Scotland, the party there should give notice of intention to marry to the

Registrar. As regards Northern Ireland, the party there, after a residence of seven days, must give notice to the District Registrar of Marriages. Notice cannot be given for such marriages to take place by certificate with licence of the Superintendent Registrar.

Marriage of such parties may take place in a church of the Church of England after the publication of banns, or by ecclesiastical licence.

Civil Fees
(from April 1, 1991)

Marriage by Superintendent Registrar's certificate:
If both parties live in same district
In register office......................	£31·00
In a registered building when presence of Registrar is required	£42·00
If the parties live in different districts	
In register office......................	£46·00
In a registered building when presence of Registrar is required	£57·00

Marriage by Superintendent Registrar's licence:
In register office........................	£73·00
In a registered building when presence of Registrar is required	£84·00

Total fees for the preliminaries to marriage by Registrar General's licence	£15·00

Marriage of a housebound or detained person:
For attendance of Superintendent Registrar at residence of housebound or detained person to attest notice of marriage	£29·00
For attendance of Superintendent Registrar at residence of housebound or detained person	£29·00
For attendance of Registrar at residence of house-bound or detained person	£27·00

In the case of a registered building, further fees may be payable to the Minister or the authorities of the building.

Ecclesiastical Fees
(from April 1, 1990)

Marriage after Banns
Parties residing in same parish	£53·00
Parties residing in different parishes	£62·00

Marriages by Common Licence
Fee for licence (varies, but usually)......	£38·00
Fee to Church authorities for ceremony .	£47·00

Marriage on the authority of the Superintendent Registrar's certificate
Parties residing in same registration district
	£62·00
Parties residing in different districts	£77·00

Marriage by special licence
Fee payable at Faculty office	£75·00

Marriage of a housebound or detained person
For attendance of a Superintendent Registrar at residence of a housebound or detained person to attest marriage..	£29·00
For entering notice of marriage*........	£15·00

*Two notices are required to be given if the parties reside in different registration districts.
Further fees may be payable for additional facilities at the marriage, e.g. the organist's fee.
Some of the above fees may not apply to the Church in Wales.

Miscellaneous Notes

Consanguinity and affinity.—A marriage between persons within the prohibited degrees of consanguinity or affinity is void. Relaxations have, however, been made by various statutes which have now been replaced by the Marriage Act 1949 (see 1st Schedule to the Act) and the Marriage (Enabling) Act 1960. It is now permitted to contract a marriage with:

(a) Sister, aunt or niece of a former wife (whether living or not).
(b) Former wife of brother, uncle or nephew (whether living or not).
No clergyman can be compelled to solemnize any of the foregoing marriages, but he may allow his church to be used for the purpose by another minister.

The Marriage (Prohibited Degrees of Relationship) Act 1986 makes further provision with regard to the marriage of persons related by affinity, e.g. after section 1 of the Act comes into force, a marriage between a man and the daughter or grand-daughter of his former wife will not be void by reason only of that relationship if both parties have attained 21 at the time of the marriage and the younger party has not at any time before attaining 18 been a child of the family in relation to the other party.

Minors.—Persons under 18 years of age are generally required to obtain the consent of certain persons (Marriage Act 1949, section 3 and 2nd Schedule as amended by the Children Act 1989). Where both parents are living, both must consent. Where one is dead, the survivor, or, if there is a guardian appointed by the deceased parent, the guardian and the survivor must consent. (For the position where the parents of the child were not married to each other at the time of the birth, see Schedule 12, paragraph 5 to the Children Act 1989.) No consent is required in the case of an infant's second marriage. In certain exceptional cases consent may be dispensed with, e.g. the insanity of a parent.

If consent is refused the Court may, on application being made, consent to the marriage; application can be made for this purpose to the High Court, the County Court, or a court of summary jurisdiction. The Act prohibits any marriage where either party is under 16 years of age.

MARRIAGES IN SCOTLAND

According to the law of Scotland, marriage is a contract which is completed by the mutual consent of parties. The Marriage (Scotland) Act 1977, which came into force on January 1, 1978, states or restates the law in convenient form. References in this section are to that Act.

Impediments to Marriage

These are: (a) nonage, i.e. where either party is under the age of 16; (b) forbidden degrees of relationship (Section 2) as amended by the Marriage Prohibited Degrees of Relationship Act 1986; (c) subsisting previous marriage; (d) incapacity to understand the nature of the contract; (e) both parties of the same sex; (f) non-residence, i.e. if the requirements of prior residence of one or other of the parties in Scotland have not been complied with.

The Act also states the grounds on which certain marriages may be declared void, but this is amended by the Law Reform (Miscellaneous Provisions) (Scotland) Act 1980 which prevents a marriage being rendered void solely due to the failure to comply with certain formalities, provided the particulars of that marriage are entered in a register of marriages by or at the behest of an appropriate registrar.

Marriages may be regular or irregular, thus:

Regular Marriages

A regular marriage is one which is celebrated by a minister of religion or authorized registrar or other celebrant specified in the Act. The parties must submit to the District Registrar a statutory notice of intention to marry, the fee for which is £7·50 each. The Registrar will then enter the parties' names and particulars in the marriage notice book which must also show the intended date of the marriage. The Registrar must then display the notice of intention to marry in a prominent public place until the intended date, and any person claiming an interest may lodge written objections thereto with the Registrar (Section 5). The Registrar, after fourteen days of receipt of the marriage notice and on being satisfied that there are no legal impediments to the marriage, will issue to either or both parties a marriage schedule. The fourteen-day period may be shortened in exceptional circumstances. The marriage schedule must be produced to the celebrant of the marriage. The fee for the solemnization ceremony in a register office is £16. After the ceremony the marriage must be registered within three days with the Registrar General for inclusion in the Register of Births, Deaths and Marriages. Within one month of the ceremony, the fee for an extract marriage certificate is £5·00; thereafter it is £7·50.

Irregular Marriages

Since the Marriage (Scotland) Act 1939 the only form of irregular marriage to be recognized by law, marriage by habit and repute, remains competent under the 1977 Act. If the parties live together constantly as husband and wife and are held to be such by the general repute of the neighbourhood and among their friends and relations, then there may arise a presumption from which marriage can be inferred. Before such a marriage can be registered, however, a decree of declarator of marriage must be obtained from the Deputy Principal Clerk of the Court of Session. It is the duty of the Deputy Principal Clerk to register the decree as soon as it is granted.

JURY SERVICE

Every local or parliamentary elector between the ages of 18 and 70 who has resided in the United Kingdom, Channel Islands or Isle of Man for at least five years since he/she attained the age of 13 will be qualified to serve on a jury unless he/she is ineligible or disqualified.

Ineligible persons include those who have at any time been judges, magistrates and certain senior court officials, those who within the previous ten years have been concerned with the law (such as barristers and solicitors and their clerks, court officers, coroners, police, prison and probation officers); priests of any religion and vowed members of religious communities; and certain sufferers from mental illness.

Disqualified persons are those who have at any time been sentenced by a court in the United Kingdom, Channel Islands or Isle of Man, to a term of imprisonment of five years or more, or a person who in the last ten years has (a) served any part of a sentence of imprisonment, youth custody or detention; (b) been detained in a Borstal institution; (c) had passed on him/her or made in respect of him/her a suspended sentence of imprisonment or order for detention; or (d) had made in respect of him/her a community service order. A person who at any time in the last five years has been placed on probation is also disqualified.

Some others are excusable as of right. These include persons over 65, members and officers of the Houses of Parliament, full-time serving members of the armed forces, registered and practising members of the medical, dental, nursing, veterinary and pharmaceutical professions, and any person who has served on a jury in the two years before he/she is summoned. In other cases the court may excuse a juror at its discretion, e.g. where the service would be a hardship to the juror.

If a person serves on a jury knowing himself/herself to be disqualified or ineligible, he/she is liable to be fined up to £2,000 or £400 respectively.

A juror is entitled to subsistence and travelling expenses, compensation for other expenses incurred in consequence of attendance for jury service, loss of earnings and loss of national insurance benefits, but certain maximum figures (which are revised from time to time) are laid down.

A verdict of a jury must normally be unanimous but after two hours' consideration (or such longer period as the court thinks reasonable), a majority verdict is acceptable if ten jurors agree to it (or nine if the size of the jury has been reduced to ten, e.g. by illness during the trial).

Jury trial is now very unusual in civil cases but a person charged with any but the least serious crimes is entitled to be tried by a jury. The defendant may object to any juror if he/she can show that that juror ought not to be on the jury, e.g. because he/she is ineligible or is biased against him/her.

The Coroners' Juries Act 1983 (which does not extend to Scotland) makes new provision in relation to qualification to serve on coroners' juries.

SCOTLAND

It is the duty of the sheriff principal of each sheriffdom, in respect of each sheriff court district in the sheriffdom, to maintain a book (the general jury book) containing the names and designations of persons within the district who are qualified and liable to serve as jurors. The book, which is compiled from information which every householder is required to provide, is kept open for the inspection by any person, upon payment of a nominal fee, at the sheriff clerk's office for the district.

Under s.1 of the Law Reform (Miscellaneous Provisions) (Scotland) Act 1980, every man or woman between the ages of 18 and 65 who is for the time being registered as a parliamentary or local government elector and who has been ordinarily resident in the United Kingdom, the Channel Islands or the Isle of Man for any period of at least five years since attaining the age of 13 years, is qualified to serve on a jury.

Ineligible persons include those who at any time within the past ten years have been judges of the supreme courts, sheriffs and certain other senior court officials, those who at any time within the past five years have been concerned with the administration of justice (such as advocates and their clerks, solicitors, court staff, police officers, prison officers, sheriff officers, procurator fiscals, and members of parole boards and children's panels), and certain sufferers from mental illness.

The same rules for disqualified persons operate in Scotland as in England.

Those excusable as of right are members and officers of the Houses of Parliament, full-time serving members of the armed forces, registered and practising members of the medical, dental, nursing, veterinary nd pharmaceutical professions, ministers of religion nd other persons in holy orders, and any person who as attended for jury service in the past five years.

If a person serves on a jury knowing himself/herself o be disqualified or ineligible, he/she is liable to be ned up to £2,000 or £400 respectively. Jurors failing o attend without good cause are liable to a maximum ne of £200.

Part II of the Juries Act 1949 (amended by egulations following thereon and by the Law Reform Miscellaneous Provisions) (Scotland) Act 1980) ap- lies only to Scotland and provides, *inter alia*, for the ayment of travelling expenses and subsistence llowances to jurors and for loss of earnings.

The number of a jury in a civil cause in the Court f Session is twelve and in the Sheriff Court seven. n a criminal trial the number is fifteen.

LANDLORD AND TENANT

Although basically the relationship between the arties to a lease is governed by the lease itself, the osition is complicated by numerous statutory pro- isions. The few points dealt with may show the esirability of seeking professional assistance in these matters. Important provisions include the following:

(1) The Agricultural Holdings Act 1986, among ther things, regulates the length of notice necessary o determine an agricultural tenancy, the tenant's ight to remove fixtures on the land, his right to ompensation for damage done by game, for improve- nents and for disturbance, and his right to require he consent of the Agricultural Land Tribunal to the peration of a notice to quit.

(2) The Landlord and Tenant Acts 1927 and 1954, s amended: Part II of the 1954 Act gives security of enure to the tenant of most business premises, and n effect the tenant can only be ousted on one or more f the seven grounds set out in the Act. In some ases, where the landlord can resume possession, the enant is entitled to compensation.

(3) The complicated mass of legislation regarding welling-houses is embodied in the Rent Act 1977 and he Housing Act 1988.

If a tenancy of a house is within the Rent Act, the enant has a personal right to reside there, and may nly be ousted on certain grounds. Tenancies with ull Rent Act protection are known as regulated enancies. The maximum rent recoverable under uch a tenancy is the rent agreed between the andlord and tenant, unless a fair rent has been egistered, in which case that is the maximum. Application for the registration of a fair rent may be nade by either the landlord or tenant, to the local ent officer, and appeal against his decision lies to the ent assessment committee.

Since the Housing Act 1988 came into force on anuary 15, 1989, it has not generally been possible o create a new regulated tenancy, although the bove protection remains for existing regulated enancies. Tenancies granted on or after January 5, 1989 are known as assured tenancies provided hey satisfy certain conditions, which are broadly he same as those for regulated tenancies under the 977 Act. However, the rent payable by an assured enant is either that agreed with the landlord or the pen market rent fixed by the Rent Assessment Committee.

(4) The Rent Act 1974 gave tenants of dwellings et furnished the same security of tenure as those of nfurnished dwellings unless the landlord lived in art of the house. In the latter case, and in the case f a tenancy of a dwelling granted by a resident landlord after August 13, 1974, the tenancy will usually be outside full Rent Act protection, but may fall within the restricted contract provisions of the Rent Act 1977. In this event, the landlord or the tenant may apply to the Rent Tribunal for a reasonable rent to be registered and once registered, this is the maximum rent recoverable. No new restricted contracts can be created after January 15, 1989.

(5) The Protection from Eviction Act 1977, as amended by the Housing Act 1988, provides that if any person with intent to cause the residential occupier of any premises to give up the occupation thereof does any act calculated to interfere with the peace or comfort of the residential occupier or members of the household, that person shall be guilty of an offence. A further provision prevents a landlord enforcing without a court order a right to possession against a tenant who is not protected by any statute of tenure legislation, and there are special rules in such cases relating to agricultural employees.

(6) A notice to quit any dwelling-house must be given at least four weeks before it is to take effect, and must be in writing and in the prescribed statutory form.

(7) Part I of the Landlord and Tenant Act 1954 applies to most tenancies of houses for over twenty- one years at a ground rent. Where it applies, the contractual tenancy is continued until brought to an end in the manner prescribed by the Act, and in effect the landlord can only get possession on limited grounds.

Further, under the Leasehold Reform Act 1967, tenants of houses under leases for over twenty-one years at a rent less than two-thirds of the rateable value of the house are in most cases given a right to purchase the freehold or to take an extended lease for a term of fifty years, provided the tenant at the time when he/she seeks to exercise the right has been occupying the house as his/her residence for the last three years or for periods amounting to three years in the last ten years.

(8) Full Rent Act or Housing Act protection is available only if a house is let on a tenancy. If the occupier of a house has a mere licence to occupy, he/ she does not have protection. Further, even if he/she has a tenancy, he/she will not be protected if the rent payable is less than two-thirds of the rateable value of the house. For these reasons, many occupants of houses owned by farmers and occupied by farm workers did not enjoy full security of tenure. The Rent (Agriculture) Act 1976 contains detailed provi- sions conferring security of tenure on certain agri- cultural workers housed by their employers and on their successors on death.

(9) Under the Landlord and Tenant Act 1985 (which does not extend to Scotland), in a lease of a dwelling-house granted for a term of less than seven years, there is implied a covenant by the landlord (a) to keep in repair the structure and exterior of the house and (b) to keep in repair and proper working order the installations in the house for the supply of water, gas and electricity, for sanitation, and for space heating or heating water.

(10) The Housing Act 1985 gives security of tenure to many tenants of local authorities and certain other bodies. Further, and subject to certain condi- tions, such tenants may have the right to purchase their houses or to take a long lease of their flats.

(11) Tenants of flats and other dwellings are given a number of special rights by the Landlord and Tenant Act 1987, as amended by the Housing Act 1988.

SCOTLAND

A lease is a contract, the relationship of the parties being governed by the terms thereof. As is also the case in England, legislation has played an important part in regulating that relationship. Thus, what at common law was an agreement binding only the parties to the deed, becomes in virtue of the Leases Act 1449, a contract binding the landlord's successors, as purchasers or creditors, provided the following four conditions are observed: (a) the lease, if for more than one year, must be in writing; (b) there must be a rent; (c) there must be a term of expiry; and (d) the tenant must have entered into possession.

It would be impracticable to enter here upon a general discussion of this branch of the law. A few important provisions include:

(1) The Agricultural Holdings (Scotland) Act 1949 (amended by the Agriculture Act 1958), is a consolidating Act applicable to Scotland. It contains provisions similar to those in the English Act, alluded to in the preceding section.

The Small Landholders Act 1911 provided for the setting up of the Land Court, which has jurisdiction over a large proportion of agricultural and pastoral land in Scotland.

(2) In Scotland business premises are not controlled by statute to so great an extent as in England, but the Tenancy of Shops (Scotland) Act 1949 gives a measure of security to tenants of shops. This Act enables the tenant of a shop who is threatened with eviction to apply to the Sheriff for a renewal of the tenancy. If the landlord has offered to sell the subjects to the tenant at an agreed price the application for a renewal of the tenancy may be dismissed. Reference should be made to Section 1 (3) of the 1949 Act for particulars of other circumstances in which the Sheriff has a discretion to dismiss an application. The Act extends to premises held by the Crown or government departments, either as landlord or tenant.

(3) Many leases contain references to the term and quarter days in connection with the expiry of the lease payment dates or for rent reviews. At common law these days and dates are respectively Candlemas (February 2), Whitsunday (May 15), Lammas (August 1) and Martinmas (November 11). The Term and Quarter Days (Scotland) Act 1990 amends these dates to February 28, May 28, August 28 and November 28 respectively, with effect from July 13, 1991, unless, in the case of a deed executed before that date an application had been made to a Sheriff for a declaration that a date other than the statutory date should apply. Where a pre-existing deed contains a reference to a specific date instead of or in addition to a day, then it is that date which shall apply.

(4) The Housing (Scotland) Act 1987 consolidates previous legislation in regard to the extensive powers and duties to local authorities in relation to housing. Included therein is the general provision regarding the rights of public sector tenants to purchase the houses which they occupy and the restrictions regarding this right in certain circumstances where the house has been designed or adapted for occupation by the elderly. This Act also makes provision for secure tenancies for public sector tenants.

(5) The Housing (Scotland) Act 1988 creates, with certain exceptions, two new forms of tenancy for tenancies created after January 2, 1989: assured tenancies and short assured tenancies. The assured tenancy significantly reduces the concept of security of tenure and abolishes any method of regulating rent other than market forces. The short assured tenancy lasts for at least six months and if properly constituted will allow the landlord to recover possession on its expiry. Provision is made for a tenant to apply to the Rent Assessment Committee to fix a rent based on the rent a landlord might reasonably expect for a short assured tenancy of the property.

(6) For most tenancies created before January 2, 1989, the Rent (Scotland) Act 1984 will continue to apply. It defines regulated tenancies, which may be either furnished or unfurnished, and lays down the system by which a landlord or tenant may obtain from the Rent Office registration of a fair rent. The Act gives to tenants of either furnished or unfurnished lets a substantial degree of security of tenure. There are, however, certain exceptions; they do not apply to tenancies where the interest belongs to the Crown or to a government department or to a local authority, a development corporation of a new town or a housing corporation. There must be a true tenancy for the Act to apply. It does not apply to licencees such as lodgers or persons allowed to occupy houses on a grace and favour basis or to services occupiers.

The Act regulates the short tenancy, a category of let under which, on compliance with certain conditions, the landlord can be assured of recovering possession on the expiry of the stipulated period of let. The Act defines the circumstances in which generally a landlord may apply for increased rent as a consequence of having carried out improvements to the property, and also lays down the system of phasing such rent increases. On the death of a statutory successor to a tenancy, the tenancy may pass for a second time to a member of the family or a relative who has been in residence in the house for a period of at least six months. The Act further lays down the duties and functions of rent officers and rent assessment committees with regard to unfurnished accommodation and of rent tribunals for furnished accommodation.

The Secretary of State for Scotland is given power in the 1988 Act to repeal or amend those sections of the 1984 Act relating to the phasing of rent increases. The other major features of the 1988 Act are to establish Scottish Homes, and to permit public sector properties to be transferred to Scottish Homes or a landlord approved by Scottish Homes.

LEGAL AID

The Legal Aid Act 1988 (as amended) is designed to make legal aid and advice more readily available for persons of small and moderate means. The main structure of the service is contained in the Act itself and the Regulations made thereunder, administered by the Legal Aid Board.

Civil Proceedings

Legal aid is available for proceedings (including matrimonial causes) in the House of Lords, Court of Appeal, High Court, County Courts, Lands Tribunal Restrictive Practices Court, before the Commons Commissioners, and civil proceedings in magistrates courts. In any event, an application for legal aid will not be approved if it appears that the applicant would gain only a trivial advantage from the proceedings Further, proceedings wholly or partly in respect of defamation are excepted from the scheme, as are also relator actions and election petitions. It is generally not available for obtaining the decree in undefended divorce and judicial separation, although the Legal Advice and Assistance Scheme (see below) is, and legal aid is still available to deal with property custody disputes, etc., arising in the suit.

Where a person is concerned in proceedings only in a representative, fiduciary or official capacity, his, her personal resources are not to be taken into account in considering eligibility for legal aid. Apart from this, eligibility in civil proceedings depends upon an applicant's disposable income and disposable capital. The figures change frequently; particulars can be obtained from a solicitor, the Law Society or a Citizens' Advice Bureau. Disposable income is calculated by making deductions from gross income in respect of certain matters such as dependants, interest on loans, income tax, rates, rent and other matters for which the applicant must or reasonably may provide. Disposable capital is calculated by excluding from gross capital part of the value of the house in which the applicant resides, of furniture and household possessions; allowances are made in respect of dependants. Except in cases where the spouses are living apart, or have a contrary interest, any resources of a person's wife or husband are to be treated as that person's resources. These figures will be assessed by the Department of Social Security and will be referred to the Legal Aid Board, who will determine whether reasonable grounds exist for the grant of a civil aid certificate. Appeal from refusal of a certificate lies to an area committee. A person resident in England or Wales desiring legal aid should apply for a certificate to the appropriate area director for the area in which he or she resides; if resident elsewhere, application should be made to an area director in London. If a certificate is granted, the applicant may select his/her solicitor, and, if necessary, counsel from a panel. The costs of the assisted person's solicitor and counsel will be paid out of the legal aid fund. When, however, damages or property are recovered or preserved by the assisted person, the legal aid fund has a charge over them in respect of these costs less any contribution towards the costs recovered from the unsuccessful party. In matrimonial cases, maintenance is exempt, as is the first £2,500 of any property settlement. The court may order that the costs of a successful unassisted party shall be paid out of the legal aid fund.

In an urgent case, e.g. domestic violence or to restrain the kidnapping abroad of a child, legal aid may be granted without the applicant's means being fully investigated beforehand. If on a full examination later he/she is found financially ineligible, he/she is liable to pay all the costs incurred on his/her behalf.

Legal Advice and Assistance

The scheme is governed by the Legal Aid Act 1988.

Under the Legal Advice and Assistance Scheme a client may obtain such advice or assistance as is normally provided by a solicitor. If necessary, the advice of a barrister may be obtained but, with the exception of domestic proceedings in a magistrates' court and certain other proceedings (see below), the scheme does not extend to taking any step in any proceedings before any court or tribunal. Where legal aid is available for civil proceedings (see above) or in criminal cases (see below) the scheme covers work done in making application for such legal aid.

A person (other than one receiving advice and assistance at a police station or from a duty solicitor) is eligible for advice or assistance under the scheme provided his/her disposable capital and his/her disposable income do not exceed limits in force from time to time or if he/she is eligible for Income Support or Family Credit. In calculating disposable income, income tax and National Insurance contributions are deducted. For a married man or person with children or other dependants further deductions will be made from both income and capital. It is intended that the financial limits shall approximate to those

applying for legal aid in civil proceedings (see above). Except when they are separated or have conflicting interests, the means of husband and wife or cohabiting couple will be aggregated for the purpose of determining financial eligibility. As in the case of legal aid, depending on his/her means, a person may be called upon to pay a contribution towards the costs of work done for him/her. Particulars may be obtained from a solicitor, the Law Society or a Citizens' Advice Bureau.

A solicitor cannot do more than two hours' work, or three hours' in the case of divorce, etc., without leave of the area legal aid committee. The solicitor's costs are paid out of the client's contribution and any monies recovered in respect of costs or damages from another party (although this may be waived by leave of the area committee in cases of hardship) and the balance will be paid by the legal aid fund.

The Act also extends the scheme to cover the costs of a solicitor who is present within the precincts of a magistrates' court or county court and is requested by the court to advise or represent a person who is in need of help.

In April 1980 the scheme was enlarged to cover the cost of representation in domestic proceedings in a magistrates' court. It has since been extended to cover the representation of patients before Mental Health Review Tribunals. Subject to financial eligibility limits, application is made to the area or local committee for 'approval of assistance by way of representation' which will replace legal aid for such proceedings. However, the two-hour limit referred to above will not apply. An applicant who is outside the financial limits but eligible for legal aid will still have to apply for a legal aid certificate as before. Free advice and assistance, and assistance by way of representation from a duty solicitor, is also available in limited circumstances to persons appearing before a magistrates' court charged with a criminal offence.

In January 1986 the scheme was further extended to provide free advice and assistance to all suspects detained at a police station, whether arrested or merely helping police with their enquiries, and free representation for all arrested persons who are the subject of an application for a warrant of further detention under the Police and Criminal Evidence Act 1984. Such persons may instruct a solicitor of their choice or take advantage of the duty solicitor scheme which has now been extended to cover police stations.

Criminal Proceedings

The Legal Aid Act 1988 provides for legal aid in criminal proceedings, and for children and parents in care proceedings and related applications under the Children and Young Persons Act 1969. A criminal court (e.g. magistrates' court, Crown Court) has power to order legal aid to be granted where it appears desirable to do so in the interests of justice. The court shall make an order in certain cases, e.g. where a person is committed for trial on a charge of murder. However, the court may not make an order unless it appears to the court that the person's disposable income and capital are such that he/she requires assistance in meeting the costs of the particular proceedings in question. Application should be made to the appropriate court where proceedings are to take place.

An applicant shall be required to make a contribution towards the costs of his/her case if his/her disposable income and capital exceed certain prescribed limits. Persons in receipt of Income Support are automatically exempt. In order to ascertain the amount of this contribution an applicant will have to produce written evidence of his/her means. Investigation of means will be carried out by the court. Any person who falls into arrears with the payment of contribution is liable to have the order revoked.

Any practising barrister or solicitor may act for a legally aided person in criminal proceedings unless excluded by reason of misconduct. In general, where legal aid is given it will normally include representation by both counsel and solicitor. However, in connection with magistrates' courts, representation will be by solicitor alone unless the offence is a serious one.

Where any doubt arises about the grant of a legal aid order, that doubt is to be resolved in favour of the applicant. The court also has power to amend or revoke a legal aid order. Legal aid may also be granted in connection with appellate proceedings, e.g. on appeal to the Criminal Division of the Court of Appeal under the Criminal Appeal Act 1968.

SCOTLAND

Legal aid in Scotland is now governed by the Legal Aid (Scotland) Act 1986 and the Regulations made thereunder. This Act established the Scottish Legal Aid Board which has the general function of securing that legal aid and legal advice and assistance are available in accordance with the Act, and of administering the Scottish Legal Aid Fund.

Civil Proceedings

Civil legal aid is available in relation to civil proceedings in the House of Lords in appeals from the Court of Session, in the Court of Session, the Lands Valuation Appeal Court, the Scottish Land Court, the Sheriff Court, the Lands Tribunal for Scotland, the Employment Appeals Tribunal and to the European Court of Human Rights. Civil legal aid is granted if, on application to the Board, the Board is satisfied that there is *probabilis causa litigandi* and that it is reasonable in the particular circumstances of the case that legal aid should be awarded. As in England eligibility and any contribution required from an applicant is dependent on their disposable income and disposable capital. Information on current financial limits can be obtained from the Scottish Legal Aid Board, a solicitor, or a Citizens' Advice Bureau.

A person believing himself/herself to be eligible may instruct any solicitor of his/her own choice. If a court action is not immediately contemplated, application will be made for legal advice and assistance which operates in a similar manner to the legal advice and assistance scheme in England. If proceedings are contemplated then a formal application for civil legal aid will be made and there are special provisions for emergency applications in appropriate circumstances.

If proceedings are decided against a person in receipt of legal aid the court shall determine a reasonable sum in the circumstances as an appropriate award of expenses to be made against the applicant. The court may make an award out of the fund only if proceedings were instituted by the legally assisted person and the court is satisfied that the resisting party would suffer severe financial hardship unless the order is made, and if the court is satisfied that in all the circumstances it is just and equitable that an award be made. If monies are recovered by a legally assisted person these fall to be paid to the Scottish Legal Aid Board who will then determine the appropriate level of contribution from the sums received which should be made to the expenses of their litigation.

Criminal Proceedings

Legal aid in criminal causes is also administered under the Legal Aid (Scotland) Act 1986. The procedure for application for criminal legal aid is dependent on the circumstances of each case. In serious cases heard before a jury under solemn procedure it is for the court to decide whether to grant legal aid. Applications for legal aid must normally be made on the prescribed forms to the clerk of the court in question and an applicant is required to provide therein particulars of the merits of his/her case and his/her financial circumstances. In summary criminal causes, however, the procedure is dependent on whether the applicant is in custody; if so he/she is entitled to automatic free legal aid from the duty solicitor. If the applicant is not in custody and wishes to plead guilty, he/she is ineligible for full legal aid but may be entitled to criminal legal advice and assistance and in some circumstances may qualify for assistance by way of representation which will enable his/her solicitor to appear and make a plea in mitigation on his/her behalf. If he/she is not in custody and wishes to plead not guilty, he/she can apply to the Scottish Legal Aid Board for criminal legal aid on the prescribed form not later than fourteen days after the first court appearance at which he/she made the plea, and legal aid shall be granted only if the Board is satisfied that the accused cannot meet the expenses of the case without undue hardship and that it is in the interest of justice as defined by the 1986 Act.

TOWN AND COUNTRY PLANNING

The Town and Country Planning Act 1990 (consolidating earlier Acts) as amended by the Planning and Compensation Act 1991, contains far-reaching provisions affecting the liberty of an owner of land to develop and use it at will. A person has generally to get planning permission from the local planning authority before carrying out any development on the land.

Development includes:

(a) Carrying out of building, engineering, mining or other operations.

(b) Making a material change in use.

It is expressly provided that if one dwelling-house is converted into two or more dwelling-houses, this involves a material change in use.

The following do not constitute 'development':

(a) Maintaining, improving or altering the interior of a building, provided there is no material change to the exterior, with the exception that any expansion, or works begun for the expansion, of a building below ground level constitutes development.

(b) Changing the use of property within the curtilage of a dwelling-house for a purpose incidental to the use of the dwelling-house as such. (It will, however, be development if building operations are carried out.)

Application can be made to the local planning authority to determine whether or not an operation or change of use constitutes development.

Planning Permission

Application for planning permission is not always necessary, as the Secretary of State may make Development Orders giving general permission for a specified type of development, e.g. enlargement of a dwelling-house (including erection of a garage), so long as the cubic content of the original dwelling (external measurement) is not exceeded by more than

70 cubic metres or 15 per cent, whichever is greater, subject to a maximum of 115 cubic metres. However, in the case of a terraced house, the limitation is 50 cubic metres or 10 per cent, whichever is the greater, subject to the maximum of 115 cubic metres.

Appeal against refusal of permission lies to the Secretary of State and from his decision, in limited circumstances, to the High Court. If the result of the appeal is unsatisfactory, an applicant may in certain circumstances require the local authority to purchase the land.

SCOTLAND

The Town and Country Planning (Scotland) Act 1972 consolidates the statute law relating to town and country planning in Scotland.

The uses of buildings are classified by the Town and Country Planning (Use Classes) (Scotland) Order 1988. Changes in use prior to December 31, 1984 are immune from enforcement proceedings.

Development normally requires to be commenced within five years from the date of granting permission.

The 1972 Act contains provisions for an appeal to the Secretary of State against the refusal of planning permission. The decision of the Secretary of State is final.

Sections 87 and 92 of the Local Government, Planning and Land Act 1980 contain important provisions on planning applications and, unlike certain parts of this Act, extend to Scotland.

VOTERS' QUALIFICATIONS

The franchise is governed by the Representation of the People Acts 1983 and 1985. Those entitled to vote as electors at a parliamentary election in any constituency are all persons resident there on the qualifying date who, at that date and on the date of the poll, are Commonwealth citizens or citizens of the Republic of Ireland and who are not subject to any legal incapacity to vote and who on the date of the poll are at least 18 years of age. However, a person is not entitled to vote at a parliamentary election in any constituency in Northern Ireland unless he/she was resident in Northern Ireland during the whole of the period of three months ending on the qualifying date for that election. Also, no person can use his/her vote unless he/she is on the register of electors kept for the constituency. A person who is of voting age on the date of the poll at a parliamentary or local government election is entitled to vote, whether or not he/she was of voting age on the qualifying date. Accordingly, a qualified person will be entitled to be registered in a register of parliamentary electors or a register of local government electors if he/she will attain voting age within twelve months from the date on which the register is required to be published. Subject to certain conditions, the 1985 Act extends the franchise to British citizens overseas.

The register is prepared by the registration officer in each constituency in Great Britain. It is the registration officer's duty to have a house-to-house or other official inquiry made as to the persons entitled to be registered and to publish preliminary electors' lists showing the persons appearing to him/her to be entitled to be registered. Any person whose name is omitted may claim registration, and any person on the list may object to the inclusion therein of other persons' names; the registration officer determines the claims and objections.

Voters at a parliamentary or local government election must generally vote in person at the allotted polling station, except for those entitled to vote by post or at any polling station, and those for whom proxies have been appointed. Certain people can apply to be treated as absent voters at a parliamentary election and thus able to vote by post—among these are registered service voters, those unable by reason of blindness or other physical incapacity to go in person to the polling station, and those unable to go in person from their qualifying address to the polling station without making a journey by air or sea.

Unless entitled to vote by post, a person registered as a service voter may vote by proxy at a parliamentary or local government election. A proxy may also be appointed by a registered elector, where the registration officer is satisfied that the applicant's circumstances on the date of the poll are likely to be such that he/she cannot reasonably be expected to vote in person at the allotted polling station. The appointment of a person to vote as proxy at parliamentary elections has effect also for the purposes of local government elections.

THE PROBATION SERVICE

England and Wales

The Probation Service is employed in each area (55 in total) by an independent committee of justices and it provides a professional social work agency in the courts, with responsibility for a wide range of duties which include: (a) a social enquiry service for the criminal courts; (b) provision of a range of non-custodial measures involving the supervision of offenders in the community ; (c) supervisory aftercare for offenders released from custody, together with social work in penal establishments and help for the families of those serving sentences; (d) an enquiry, conciliation and supervision service in the divorce and domestic courts; (e) support for and promotion of preventive and containment measures in the community designed to reduce the level of crime and domestic breakdown. It is a direct grant service funded 80 per cent from the Home Office and 20 per cent from the relevant local authority.

Its national representative bodies are:

THE CENTRAL COUNCIL OF PROBATION COMMITTEES, 38 Belgrave Square, London SW1X 8NT (Tel: 071-245 9364). *Secretary*, I. Miles.

THE ASSOCIATION OF CHIEF OFFICERS OF PROBATION, 20–30 Lawefield Lane, Wakefield WF2 8SP (Tel: 0924–361156). *Secretary*, W. R. Weston.

THE NATIONAL ASSOCIATION OF PROBATION OFFICERS, 3–4 Chivalry Road, Battersea, London SW11 1HT (Tel: 071–223 4887). *Gen. Secretary*, W. Beaumont.

Scotland

The probation service in Scotland is a statutory duty of local authorities under s. 27 of the Social Work (Scotland) Act 1968. Social workers have to supervise and provide advice, guidance and assistance to those persons living in their area who are subject to a court's supervision order. This is done by social workers as part of their normal duties and not by a separate probation staff.

NATIONAL INSURANCE AND RELATED CASH BENEFITS

The State insurance and assistance schemes, comprising schemes of national insurance and industrial injuries insurance, national assistance, and non-contributory old age pensions came into force from July 5, 1948. The Ministry of Social Security Act 1966 replaced national assistance and non-contributory old age pensions with a scheme of non-contributory benefits, termed supplementary allowances and pensions. These, and subsequent measures relating to social security provision in Great Britain, were consolidated by the Social Security Act 1975; the Social Security (Consequential Provisions) Act 1975; and the Industrial Injuries and Diseases (Old Cases) Act 1975. Corresponding measures were passed for Northern Ireland. The Social Security Pensions Act 1975 introduced a new State pensions scheme, which came into force on April 6, 1978, and the graduated pension scheme 1961 to 1975 has been wound up, existing rights being preserved. The Pensioners' Payments and Social Security Act 1979 provided for a £10 bonus for pensioners in 1979 and for the payment of a bonus in succeeding years at levels then to be determined. The Child Benefit Act 1975 replaced family allowances (introduced 1946) with child benefit and one parent benefit.

Some of the above legislation has been superseded by the provisions of the Social Security Acts 1968 to 1991.

NATIONAL INSURANCE SCHEME

The National Insurance scheme operates under the Social Security Acts 1975 to 1991, and orders and regulations made thereunder. The scheme is financed by contributions payable by earners, employers and others (such as non-employed persons, paying voluntary contributions). It provides the funds required for paying benefits payable under the Social Security Acts out of the National Insurance Fund and not out of other public money and for the making of payments towards the cost of the National Health Service. In 1991 the Redundancy Fund was absorbed into the National Insurance Fund. The yearly Treasury supplement to the National Insurance Fund was abolished in April 1989.

CONTRIBUTIONS

Contributions are of four classes:

Class 1 contributions are earnings-related, based on a percentage of the employee's earnings.

  (a) primary Class 1 contributions are payable by employed earners and office-holders over age 16 with gross earnings at or above the lower earnings limit of £52.00 per week. For those with gross earnings at or above this level, contributions are payable on all earnings up to an upper limit of £390 per week. 'Gross earnings' include overtime pay, commission, bonus, etc., without deduction of any superannuation contributions.

Women who marry for the first time no longer have a right to elect not to pay the full contribution rate. Married women and widows who before May 12, 1977, elected not to pay contributions at the full rate retain the right to pay a reduced rate over the same earnings range, which covers industrial injuries benefits and a contribution to the National Health Service. They lose this right if, after April 5, 1978, there are two consecutive tax years in which they have no earnings on which primary Class 1 contributions are payable and in which they have not been at any time self-employed earners. No primary contributions are due on earnings paid for a period

on or after the employee's pension age, even when retirement is deferred.

  (b) secondary Class 1 contributions are payable by employers of employed earners, and by the appropriate authorities in the case of office-holders. On October 6, 1985, the upper earnings limit for employers' contributions was abolished and secondary contributions are payable on all the employee's earnings if they reach or exceed £52.00 per week.

Primary contributions are deducted from earnings by the employer and are paid, together with the employer's contributions, to the Inland Revenue along with income tax collected under the PAYE system. On October 6, 1985 several lower percentage rates of contribution for lower paid employees and their employers were introduced.

Class 2 contributions are flat-rate, paid weekly by self-employed earners over age 16. Those with earnings below £2,900 a year for the tax year 1991–92 can apply for exemption from liability to pay Class 2 contributions. People who while self-employed are exempted from liability to pay contributions on the grounds of small earnings may pay either Class 2 or Class 3 contributions voluntarily. Self-employed earners (whether or not they pay Class 2 contributions) may also be liable to pay Class 4 contributions based on profits or gains within certain limits. There are special rules for those who are concurrently employed and self-employed. Married women and widows can no longer choose not to pay Class 2 contributions. Those who elected not to pay Class 2 contributions before May 12, 1977, retain the right until there is a period of two consecutive tax years after April 5, 1978 in which they were not at any time either self-employed earners or had earnings on which primary Class 1 contributions were payable.

Class 2 contributions may be paid by direct debit through a bank or National Giro account or by stamping a contribution card.

Class 3 contributions are voluntary flat-rate contributions payable by persons over school-leaving age who would otherwise be unable to qualify for retirement pension and certain other benefits because they have an insufficient record of Class 1 or Class 2 contributions. Married women and widows who on or before May 11, 1977, elected not to pay Class 1 (full rate) or Class 2 contributions cannot pay Class 3 contributions while they retain this right.

Payment may be made by stamping a contribution card or by direct debit through a bank Giro account.

Class 4 contributions are payable by self-employed earners, whether or not they pay Class 2 contributions, on annual profits or gains from a trade, profession or vocation chargeable to income tax under Schedule D, where these fall between £5,900 and £20,280 a year. The maximum Class 4 contribution, payable on profits or gains of £20,280 or more, is £905.94.

Class 4 contributions are generally assessed and collected by the Inland Revenue along with Schedule D income tax. Self-employed persons under 16, or who at the beginning of a tax year are over pension age even where retirement is deferred, are not liable to pay Class 4 contributions. There are special rules for people who have more than one job, or who pay Class 1 contributions on earnings which are chargeable to income tax under Schedule D.

Regulations state the cases in which earners may be exempted from liability to pay contributions, and the conditions upon which contributions are credited to persons who are exempted. Leaflet NI 208 is obtainable from local social security offices.

The Secretary of State for Social Services is

empowered by the Social Security Acts to alter certain rates of contributions by order approved by both Houses of Parliament, and is required by the same enactments to make annual reviews of the general level of earnings in order to determine whether such an order should be made.

For the period April 6, 1991 to April 4, 1992 the earnings brackets determining Class 1 contributions are:

	Weekly earnings £
1	52·00— 84·99
2	85·00—129·99
3	130·00—184·99
4	185·00—390·00
5	over 390·00

Contribution rates for the period April 6, 1991 to April 5, 1992 are:

Class 1 contributions—not contracted out

Employee's rates

Earnings bracket	On first £52·00		On earnings from £52·00–£390·00	
	standard	reduced	standard	reduced
1	2	3·85	9	3·85
2	2	3·85	9	3·85
3	2	3·85	9	3·85
4	2	3·85	9	3·85
5	2*	3·85*	9	3·85

* to a maximum of £390 per week.

Class 1 contributions—contracted out
(*see also* p. 1046)

Employee's rates

Earnings bracket	On first £52·00		On earnings from £52·00–£390·00	
	standard	reduced	standard	reduced
1	2	3·85	7	3·85
2	2	3·85	7	3·85
3, 4, 5	2	3·85	7	3·85

Employer's rates

Earnings bracket	On first £52·00	On earnings from £52·00–£390·00	On any earnings over £390·00
1	4·6	0·8	0
2	6·6	2·8	0
3	8·6	4·8	0
4	10·4	6·6	0
5	10·4	6·6	10·4

	Weekly flat rate
Class 2 contributions	£5·15
Class 3 contributions	£5·05

	Percentage of profits or gains
Class 4 contributions	6·3

From October 5, 1989 there was a change in the assessment of National Insurance contributions for employees. Earnings brackets for employees' contributions were abolished and replaced by a new lower contribution rate on earnings up to and including the lower earnings limit and at a main percentage rate on earnings between the lower earnings limit up to and including the employees' upper earnings limit.

Where earnings were paid or were due to be paid before October 5, 1989, employees' contributions continued to be paid at 5, 7, and 9 per cent (plus the corresponding lower contracted out rates if appropriate) depending on the earnings bracket.

Where earnings were paid or were due to be paid on or after October 5, 1989, employees' contributions were paid at 2 per cent at the lower earnings limit (£52·00 a week or equivalent) plus 9 per cent (not contracted out) or 7 per cent (contracted out) of earnings between the lower earnings limit up to and including the employees' upper earnings limit (£390·00 a week or equivalent). Employees contributing at the reduced rate continue to pay contributions at 3·85 per cent on all earnings up to and including the employees' upper earnings limit.

The Social Security (Contributions) Act 1991 added a new class of contributions: 1A, payable in respect of car fuel by persons liable to pay secondary Class 1 contributions. It has effect with regard to the 1991–2 tax year and thereafter.

Employees earning less than the lower earnings limit continue not to pay any contributions.

There was no change in the assessment of employers' contributions.

THE STATE EARNINGS RELATED PENSION SCHEME (SERPS)

The Social Security Pensions Act 1975, which came into force in April 1978, aims to reduce reliance upon means-tested benefit in old age, in widowhood and in chronic ill-health by providing better pensions; to ensure that occupational pension schemes which are contracted out of part of the State scheme fulfil the conditions of a good scheme; that pensions are adequately protected against inflation; and that in both the State and occupational schemes men and women are treated equally. Retirement, widow's and invalidity pensions under the new scheme started to be paid in April 1979. Since April 6, 1979, flat-rate retirement and other State pensions have been augmented for employed earners by additional pensions related to earnings, but it will be twenty years before these additional pensions become payable at the full rate.

Under the scheme, retirement, invalidity and widow's pensions for employees are related to the earnings on which national insurance contributions have been paid. For employees of either sex with a complete insurance record the scheme provides a category A retirement pension in two parts, a basic and an additional pension. The basic pension corresponds to the old personal flat-rate national insurance pension. The additional pension is 1·25 per cent of average earnings between the lower weekly earnings limit for Class 1 contribution liability and the upper earnings limit for each year of such earnings under the scheme, and will thus build up to 25 per cent in twenty years.

The additional pension will be calculated in a different way for individuals who reach pension age after April 6, 1999. The changes are to be phased in over ten years. From 2010 a lifetime's earnings will be included in the calculation and for years from 1988–89 onwards the accrual rate on these surplus earnings will be 20 per cent. The accrual rate on surplus earnings for the years from 1978–79 to 1987–88 will remain at 25 per cent.

Actual earnings are to be revalued in terms of the earnings level current in the last complete tax year before pension age (or death or incapacity). Both components of pensions in payment will be uprated annually in line with the movement of prices. Graduated retirement pensions in payment, and rights to such pensions earned by people who are still working, will be brought into the annual review of benefits.

Self-employed persons pay contributions towards the basic pension. The non-employed and employees with earnings below the lower limit may contribute voluntarily for basic pension. Although no primary Class 1 contributions or Class 2 or Class 4 contributions are payable by persons who work beyond pension age (65 for men, 60 for women), the employer's liability for secondary Class 1 contributions continues if earnings are at or above the lower earnings limit. Class 4 contributions are still payable up to the end of the tax year during which pension age is reached.

Widows will get the whole of any additional pensions earned by their husbands with their widowed mother's allowances or widow's pensions; and can add to the retirement pensions earned by their own contributions any additional pensions earned by their husbands up to the maximum payable on one person's contributions. Men whose wives die when they are both over pension age can add together their own and their wives' pension rights in the same way as widows. Among the steps taken to give women equal treatment in benefit provision, the State scheme permits years of home responsibilities to reduce the number of qualifying years (since 1978) needed for retirement pension, widowed mother's allowance and widow's pension; and the 'half-test' by which a married woman who married before age 55 could not qualify for a Category A retirement pension unless she had contributed on earnings at the basic level in at least half the years between marriage and pension age have been abolished with effect from December 22, 1984. The range of short-term social security benefits and industrial injury benefits under the Social Security Act 1975 continues with only minor changes.

Contracted-Out and Personal Pension Schemes

Members of occupational pension schemes which meet the standards laid down in the Social Security Pensions Act 1975 can be contracted-out of the earnings related part of the state scheme relating to retirement and widows' benefits. Regulations made under the Act require employers to consult employees and their organizations and inform them of their intention to contract out. (Leaflets relating to pensions and guidance for employers about contracting-out are available from local social security offices.) The Act also contains provisions ensuring equal access to membership of schemes for men and women.

Until April 6, 1988, occupational pension schemes could only contract out if they promised a pension that was related to earnings. These are known as contracted-out salary related schemes. They must provide a pension that is not less than the guaranteed minimum pension (GMP), which is broadly equivalent to the state earnings related pension. However, new options have been introduced by the Social Security Act 1986. Since April 6, 1988, occupational pension schemes which promise a minimum level of contributions have also been able to contract out. These are known as contracted-out money purchase schemes. They provide a pension based on the fund built up in the scheme over the years plus the results of the way they have been invested.

In addition, since July 1988 employees whose employers do not provide a pension scheme have been able to start their own personal pension instead of staying in the state earnings related pension scheme. Since April 6, 1988, this choice has been open to all employees even if their employer does have a pension scheme. A personal pension, like a contracted-out money purchase scheme, provides a pension based on the fund built up in the scheme over the years plus the results of the way they have been invested.

The decision on whether or not an occupational pension scheme may become contracted-out lies with the Occupational Pension Board, an independent statutory body who have a general responsibility for supervising contracting-out. They also consider and approve personal pension schemes which can be used instead of state additional pension.

The State earnings related pension payable to a member of a contracted-out salary related scheme, or his widow, will be reduced by the amount of GMP payable (which in the case of a widow must be at least half of the late husband's GMP entitlement). Members of contracted-out money purchase schemes and personal pension schemes, or their widows, have no GMP entitlement as such. But the state earnings related pension payable will be reduced by an amount equivalent to a GMP (or widow's GMP).

Since April 6, 1988 contracted-out salary related schemes must also provide a widower's GMP which must be at least half of the late wife's GMP entitlement built up from April 6, 1988. (A scheme need not provide entitlement to a GMP for widowers of earners dying before April 1989.) Contracted-out money purchase schemes and personal pension schemes must provide half-rate widower's benefit.

In contracted-out schemes, both the employee and the employer pay the full ordinary rate of contribution on the first £52·00 (1991–92 figure) of earnings but earnings above that amount attract a lower rate of contribution from the employee, and from the employer where the employee's earnings are under £390·00; where the employee's earnings exceed this amount, the full ordinary rate of contribution is payable only by the employer and the employee has no liability for contributions on these earnings (*see also* p. 1045).

An employee who chooses a personal pension in place of SERPS or their employer's pension scheme must pay National Insurance contributions at the full ordinary rate (the employer's share must also be paid at the same rate). The DSS pays the difference between the lower contracted-out rate and the full ordinary rate directly into the personal pension scheme.

FINANCE

The National Insurance Fund receives all social security contributions (less only the National Health Service and Redundancy Fund and Maternity Pay Fund allocations and the National Insurance surcharge for taxation purposes) together with the Consolidated Fund supplement; and it bears the cost of all contributory benefits provided by the Social Security Acts and the cost of administration.

Approximate receipts and payments of the National Insurance Fund for the year ended March 31, 1989, were as follows:

Receipts	£'000
Balance, April 1, 1988	7,287,620
Contributions under the Social Security Acts (net of SSP)	27,393,783
Consolidated Fund Supplement	1,653,000
Income from investments	777,502
Other receipts	1,072
	37,112,977

Payments	£'000	£'000
Benefit:		
Unemployment benefit	1,106,745	
Sickness benefit	191,960	
Invalidity benefit	3,359,358	
Maternity allowance	26,870	
Widow's benefit	850,164	
Guardian's allowance and child's special allowance	1,352	

Payments	£'000	£'000
Retirement pension	19,237,593	
Disablement benefits	451,278	
Death benefit	58,610	
Other industrial injury benefits	3,695	
Pensioners' lump sum payments	109,000	
		25,396,625
Transfers to Northern Ireland		185,000
Administration		865,786
Other payments		8,253
Write offs		
Balance, March 31, 1989		10,368,808
		36,824,472

NOTE.—There have been changes to the National Insurance Fund. Payments will no longer be paid into surcharges or the Maternity Pay Fund. However, residual payments are still being paid in respect of late paid contributions for premium years.

BENEFITS

The benefits payable under the Social Security Acts are as follows:

Contributory Benefits:

Unemployment benefit.
Sickness benefit.
Invalidity pension and allowance.
Maternity allowance.
Widow's benefit, comprising widow's payment, widowed mother's allowance and widow's pension.
Retirement pensions, categories A and B.

Non-contributory Benefits:

Child benefit.
One parent benefit.
Guardian's allowance.
Invalid care allowance.
Attendance allowance.
Severe disablement allowance.
Mobility allowance.
Retirement pensions, categories C and D.
Income Support.
Family Credit.
Social Fund.

Benefits for Industrial Injuries, Disablement and Death.

Other:

Statutory sick pay.
Statutory maternity pay.

Leaflets relating to the various benefits and payments are obtainable from local social security offices.

The Social Security Acts empower the Secretary of State to increase certain rates of benefit by order approved by both Houses of Parliament, and require him to increase certain rates by such an order if an annual review shows that they have not retained their value in relation to the general level of prices obtaining in Great Britain as measured by the Retail Price Index.

The latest order providing for increases in benefit rates took effect from the week commencing April 8, 1991. It did not apply to all benefits.

CONTRIBUTORY BENEFITS

Entitlement to contributory benefits depends on contribution conditions being satisfied either by the claimant or by some other person (depending on the kind of benefit). The class or classes of contribution which for this purpose are relevant to each benefit are as follows:

Short-term benefits

Unemployment benefit	Class 1
Sickness benefit	Class 1 or 2
Maternity allowance	Class 1 or 2
Widow's payment	Class 1, 2 or 3

Other benefits

Widowed mother's allowance	
Widow's pension	
Category A retirement pension	Class 1, 2 or 3
Category B retirement pension	
Invalidity benefit	Class 1 or 2

The system of contribution conditions relates to yearly levels of earnings on which contributions have been paid. The contribution conditions for different benefits are set out in summary form in leaflets available at local social security offices.

Unemployment Benefit

Benefit is payable in a period of interruption of employment for up to 312 days (a year, excluding Sundays). Spells of unemployment and sickness not separated by more than eight weeks count as one period of interruption of employment. A person who has exhausted benefit requalifies when he has again worked as an employed earner for at least 16 hours a week for 13 weeks. These weeks need not be consecutive but must generally fall within 26 weeks prior to the date of the claim.

There are disqualifications from receiving benefit, e.g. for a period not exceeding 26 weeks if a person has lost his employment through his misconduct, or has voluntarily left his employment without just cause, or has, without good cause, refused an offer of employment or training.

Sickness Benefit

Sickness benefit is payable for up to 28 weeks of sickness in a period of interruption of employment and is then replaced by invalidity benefit (*see* below).

There are disqualifications from receiving sickness or invalidity benefit for a period not exceeding six weeks if a person has become incapable of work through his own misconduct or if he fails without good cause to attend for or submit himself to prescribed medical or other examination or treatment, or observe prescribed rules of behaviour.

Statutory sick pay (SSP) was introduced from April 6, 1983 and was payable for up to eight weeks. Since April 6, 1986, employers are responsible for paying SSP to their employees for up to 28 weeks of sickness in any period of incapacity for work. SSP replaces the employee's entitlement to State Sickness Benefit which is not payable as long as any SSP liability remains. SSP is subject to PAYE and to NI deductions. From April 6, 1991 employers can recover 80 per cent (previously 100 per cent) of the SSP they have paid out. Employees who cannot get SSP can claim State Sickness Benefit instead.

Invalidity Benefit

Normally, after 28 weeks of sickness, sickness benefit, or SSP where the underlying conditions for sickness benefit are satisfied, is replaced by an invalidity pension. In addition an invalidity allowance is payable if incapacity for work begins more than five years before pension age. The allowance varies according to the age on falling sick, and if still in payment at pension age will continue as an addition to retirement pension. From Sept. 16, 1985 invalidity allowance has been reduced or withdrawn completely if there is entitlement to an additional earnings-related pension and/or a guaranteed minimum pension.

Maternity Benefit

Statutory maternity pay (SMP) is administered by employers but there is still a state maternity allowance scheme for women who are self-employed or otherwise do not qualify for SMP.

In general, employers pay SMP to pregnant women who have been employed by them for at least six months and earned at least the lower earnings limit for the payment of NI contributions. For those who have been employed for at least two years, payment of SMP for the first six weeks is related to earnings, followed by up to twelve weeks at a standard rate of £44·50. Those who have been employed for at least six months but less than two years receive payment at standard rate only for the 18 weeks. Part-time working women also qualify for the earnings-related element if employed for at least five years. Women have some choice in deciding when to begin maternity leave but SMP is not payable for any week in which work is done.

A woman may qualify for maternity allowance (MA) if she has been working and paying contributions at the full rate for at least 26 weeks in the 52-week period which ends 15 weeks before the baby is due. She also has an element of choice in deciding when to stop work and receive MA, which is not payable for any period she works.

Widow's Benefits

Only the late husband's contributions of any class count for widow's benefit in any of its three forms.

Widow's Payment.—May be received by a woman who at her husband's death is under 60, or whose husband was not entitled to a Category A retirement pension when he died.

Widowed Mother's Allowance.—Payable to a widow if she is receiving child benefit for one of her children; if her husband was receiving child benefit; or if she is expecting her husband's baby.

Widow's Pension.—A widow may receive this pension if aged 45 or over at the time of her husband's death or when her widowed mother's allowance ends. If aged 55 or over she will receive the full widow's pension rate.

Widow's benefit of any form ceases upon remarriage.

Retirement Pension
Categories A and B

A Category A pension is payable for life to men or women on their own contributions if they are over pension age (65 for a man and 60 for a woman).

Where a person defers making a claim at 65 (60 for a woman) or later opts to be treated as if he/she had not made a claim, and does not draw a Category A pension, the weekly rate of pension is increased, when he or she finally makes a claim or reaches the age of 70 (65 for a woman), in respect of weeks when pension is forgone during the five years after reaching minimum pension age. Details of the increase in the rate of pension due to deferred retirement are given in leaflet NP46, available at social security offices. If a married man defers his own Category A pension, his wife has to defer receiving her Category B pension based on his contribution record. During this time she earns increments to the Category B pension, which is payable to her (and not her husband) when they both claim their pensions.

A Category B pension is normally payable for life to a woman on her husband's contributions when he has claimed, or is over 70, and has qualified for his own Category A pension, and she has reached 60. It is also payable on widowhood after 60 whether or not the late husband had retired and qualified for his

own pension. The weekly pension is payable at the rate of the increase for a wife while the husband is alive, and at the single person's rate on widowhood after 60. Where a woman is widowed before she reaches 60, a Category B pension is paid to her on reaching 60 at the same weekly rate as her widow's pension if she claims. If a woman qualifies for a pension of each category she receives whichever pension is the larger. Details of the increase in the rate of pension due to deferred retirement are given in leaflet NP46, available at social security offices.

The earnings rule which stated that a man aged 65 to 70, or a woman aged 60 to 65, who has qualified for pension would have it reduced if he or she earned more than a certain amount was abolished on October 1, 1989. Where an adult dependant is living with the claimant, an Adult Dependants Allowance will only be payable if the dependant's earnings do not exceed the standard rate of unemployment benefit for a single person under pensionable age (*see* below). For the purpose of the dependency rule only, earnings will include payments by way of occupational pension. The earnings of a separated spouse affect the increase of retirement pension if they exceed £31·25 a week.

Unemployment, sickness or invalidity benefit is payable to men between 65 and 70 and women between 60 and 65 who have not claimed their retirement pension and who would have been entitled to a retirement pension if they had claimed at pension age. This applies in the case of sickness and invalidity benefit if incapacity for work is the result of an industrial accident or prescribed disease. These rates of benefit for people over pension age are shown in leaflet NI 196. A retirement pension will be increased by the amount of any invalidity allowance the pensioner was getting within the period of eight weeks and one day before reaching minimum pension age but this will be offset against any Additional Pension or Guaranteed Minimum Pension. An age addition of 25p per week is payable if a retirement pensioner is aged 80 or over. (For attendance allowance and invalidity care allowance, *see* Non-contributory Benefits).

Graduated Pension

The graduated pension scheme under which national insurance contributions and retirement pensions were graduated within specified limits, according to earnings, was discontinued in April 1975 under the Social Security Act 1975. Any graduated pension which an employed person over 18 and under 70 (65 for a woman) had earned by paying graduated contributions between April 6, 1961, when the scheme started, and April 5, 1975, will be paid when the contributor claims retirement pension or at 70 (65 for a woman), in addition to any retirement pension for which he or she qualifies.

Graduated pension is at the rate of 6·81p a week for each 'unit' of graduated contributions paid by the employee (half a unit or more counts as a whole unit). A unit of contributions is £7·50 for men, and £9·00 for women, of graduated contributions paid.

A wife can get a graduated pension in return for her own graduated contributions, but not for her husband's. A widow gets a graduated addition to her retirement pension equal to half of any graduated additions earned by her late husband, plus any additions earned by her own graduated contributions. If a person defers making a claim beyond 65 (60 for a woman), entitlement may be increased by one seventh of a penny per £1 of its weekly rate for each complete week of deferred retirement, as long as the retirement is deferred for a minimum of seven weeks.

Rates of Benefits
(from week commencing April 8, 1991)

	Weekly rate £
Unemployment Benefit—standard rate:	
Person under pension age	41·40
Increase for wife/other adult dependant	25·55
Person over pension age*	52·00
Increase for wife/other adult dependant	31·25
Sickness Benefit—standard rate:	
Person under pension age	39·60
Increase for wife/other adult dependant	24·50
Person over pension age*	49·90
Increase for wife/other adult dependant	29·95
Invalidity Pension*:	
Person (under or over pension age)	52·00
Increase for wife or adult dependant	31·25
Invalidity Allowance (maximum amount payable):	
higher rate	11·10
middle rate	6·90
lower rate	3·45
Maternity Allowance	40·60
Widow's Payment (lump sum)	1,000·00
Widowed Mother's Allowance* and Widow's Pension*	52·00
Retirement pension*—*categories A and B*:	
Single person	52·00
Increase for wife or adult dependant	31·25

* These benefits attract an increase for each dependent child (in addition to child benefit) of £10·70. (£9·70 for only, elder or eldest child for whom higher rate of Child Benefit payable.)

NON-CONTRIBUTORY BENEFITS
Child Benefit

Child benefit is payable for virtually all children aged under 16, and for those aged 16–18 who are studying full-time up to and including A-level or equivalent standard. It is also payable for a short period if the child has left school recently and is registered for work or a youth training scheme.

One Parent Benefit

This benefit may be paid to a person in receipt of Child Benefit who is responsible for bringing up one or more children on his/her own. It is a flat rate non means-tested, non-contributory benefit payable for the first or only child.

Guardian's Allowance

Where the parents of a child are dead, the person who has the child in his family may claim a guardian's allowance in addition to child benefit. The allowance, in exceptional circumstances, is payable on the death of only one parent.

Invalid Care Allowance

Invalid care allowance is payable to persons of working age, who are not gainfully employed because they are regularly and substantially engaged in caring for a severely disabled person who is receiving attendance allowance (from April 1992 the middle or higher rate of disability living allowance) or constant attendance allowance with either a war or services pension, industrial disablement workman's compensation, or an allowance under the Pneumoconiosis, Byssinosis and Miscellaneous Diseases Benefit Scheme.

Mobility Allowance

The allowance is, subject to certain conditions, payable to persons who are suffering from such physical disablement that they are likely to remain unable, or virtually unable, to walk for at least a year. This includes those who are deaf and blind, and those without any legs. It can be claimed by persons between the ages of 5 and 65 (for this purpose a claim may be made up to 12 months from that birthday) and may be retained to age 80.

Severe Disablement Allowance

Persons of working age who have been continuously incapable of work for a period of at least 28 weeks but who do not qualify for a contributory invalidity pension may be entitled to severe disablement allowance. People who first become incapable of work after their 20th birthday must be at least 80 per cent disabled.

Attendance Allowance/Disability Living Allowance

Attendance allowance is payable to severely disabled people. The higher rate is paid to those in need of a great deal of attention or supervision both by day and by night. The allowance is paid at the lower rate to those whose need for attention or supervision arises either by day or by night. There is a six-month qualifying period.

Since October 1990 attendance allowance at the higher rate has also been available to people with a progressive illness likely to limit life expectancy to six months. Such people can get the allowance from the beginning of their claim.

Satisfaction of the medical criteria for an allowance is determined by the Attendance Allowance Board or a doctor acting on the Board's behalf. However, from April 1992 such decisions on attendance allowance (and on disability living allowance which will replace and extend attendance allowance for those disabled before age 65) will be taken by lay adjudication officers.

Non-contributory Retirement Pension
Categories C and D

A Category C pension is provided, subject to a residence test, for persons who were over pensionable age on July 5, 1948, and for women whose husbands are so entitled if they are over pension age, with increases for adult and child dependants. A Category D pension is provided for others when they reach 80 if they are not already getting a retirement pension of any category or if they are getting that pension at less than these rates. An age addition of 25p per week is payable if persons entitled to retirement pension are aged 80 or over.

Rates of Benefits
(from week commencing April 8, 1991)

	Weekly rate £
Child Benefit (first child)	8·25
each subsequent child	7·25
One Parent Benefit:	
First or only child of certain lone parents.........................	5·60

	Weekly rate £
Guardian's Allowance (first child)	9·70
each subsequent child............	10·70
Severe Disablement Allowance*:	
Basic rate†	31·25
Under 40	11·10
40–49...........................	6·90
50–59...........................	3·45
Increase for wife/other adult	
dependant	18·70
Mobility Allowance	29·10
Invalid Care Allowance*.............	31·25
Increase for wife/other adult	
dependant.......................	18·70
Attendance Allowance:	
higher rate	41·65
lower rate	27·80
Retirement Pension—Categories C* and D:	
Single person	31·25
Increase for wife/other adult	
dependant.......................	18·70
(not payable with Category D pension)	

*These benefits attract an increase for each dependent child (in addition to child benefit) of £9·70 for the first child and £10·70 for each subsequent child.
†The age addition applies to the age when incapacity began.

INCOME SUPPORT

Income Support is a benefit for those aged 18 and over (although certain vulnerable 16 and 17 year olds may be eligible) whose income is inadequate and who are unemployed. Others who may be eligible include people: over 60; bringing up children alone; unable to work through sickness; caring for a disabled person; or working part-time. Except in special cases Income Support is not available to those who work for more than 24 hours per week or who have a partner who works for more than 24 hours per week, or 16 hours per week from April 1992. Income Support is not payable if the claimant, or claimant and partner, have capital or savings in excess of £8,000. The rate of benefits is affected by possession of capital or savings in excess of £3,000 and may be affected by a claimant's earnings. Sums payable depend on fixed allowances laid down by law for people in different circumstances. Special rates apply for people living in board and lodging, hostels, residential care or nursing homes. Details are available from local social security offices. Income Support is payable via post offices, either by order book or, for the unemployed, by girocheque. Applications for Income Support are made on form SB1, available from post offices; Income Support claim forms, available from social security offices; or on form B1 (for the unemployed), available from unemployment benefit offices. If both partners are entitled to Income Support, either may claim it for the couple. People receiving Income Support will be able to receive Housing Benefit, help with mortgage or home loan interest and help with health care. They may also be eligible for help with exceptional expenses, from the Social Fund. Leaflet SB20 gives a detailed explanation of Income Support.

INCOME SUPPORT PREMIUMS

Income Support Premiums are additional weekly payments for those with special needs. People qualifying for more than one premium will normally only receive the highest single premium for which they qualify. However Family Premium, Disabled Child's Premium and Severe Disability Premium are payable in addition to other premiums.

People with children qualify for a Family Premium

if they have at least one child; a Disabled Child's Premium if they have a child who receives Attendance Allowance or Mobility Allowance or is registered blind; or a Lone Parent Premium if they are bringing up one or more children alone.

Long-term sick or disabled people qualify for a Disability Premium if they or their partner are receiving certain benefits because they are disabled or cannot work; are registered blind; or have been sending in doctor's statements for at least 28 weeks stating inability to work through sickness. If they are in receipt of Attendance Allowance, without anyone receiving Invalid Care Allowance for looking after them, they qualify for a Severe Disability Premium in addition to a Disability Premium.

People qualify for a Pensioner Premium if they or their partner are aged between 60 and 79, and for a Higher Pensioner Premium if they or their partner are aged 80 or over. A Higher Pensioner Premium is also payable to people aged between 60 and 79 who receive Attendance Allowance, Mobility Allowance, Invalidity Benefit or Severe Disablement Allowance, or who are registered blind. A Higher Pensioner Premium may be paid as well as a Severe Disability Premium.

Rates of Benefit
(from week commencing April 8, 1991)

	Weekly rate £
Income Support	
Single people	
aged 16–17........................	23·65
aged 18–24	31·15
aged 25 and over	39·65
aged 18 and over and a single parent.	39·65
Couples	
both under 18	47·30
one or both aged 18 or over	62·25
For each child in a family	
under 11...........................	13·35
aged 11–15	19·75
aged 16–17*.......................	23·65
aged 18 and over*.................	31·15

*if in full-time education up to A level or equivalent standard.

Premiums	
Family Premium	7·95
Disabled Child's Premium	16·65
Lone Parent Premium	4·45
Disability Premium	
Single	16·65
Couple	23·90
Severe Disability Premium	
Single............................	31·25
Couple (one person qualified)	31·25
Couple (both qualified)	62·50
Pensioner Premium	
Single	13·75
Couple	20·90
Higher Pensioner Premium	
Single............................	18·45
Couple	26·20
Enhanced Pensioner Premium	
Single............................	1·80
Couple	2·45

(payable to pensioners aged between 75 and 79 in addition to Pensioner Premium).

FAMILY CREDIT

Family Credit is a tax-free benefit for working families with children. It is not a loan and does not have to be paid back. To qualify, a family must include at least one child under 16 (under 19 if in full-time education up to A-level or equivalent standard), and the claimant, or partner, must be working for at least 24 hours per week. It does not matter which partner is working and they may be employed or self-employed. The right to Family Credit does not depend on NI contributions and the same rates of benefit are paid to one and two parent families. Family Credit is not payable if the claimant, or claimant and partner, have capital or savings in excess of £8,000. The rate of benefit is affected if capital or savings in excess of £3,000 are held. The rate of benefit payable depends upon the claimant's (and partner's) net income (excluding Child Benefit), number of children, and children's ages. Family Credit is paid for 26 weeks and the amount payable will usually remain the same throughout this period, regardless of change of circumstances. Payment is made weekly via post offices or four-weekly directly into a bank or building society account. Family Credit is claimed by post. A claim pack FC1 which includes a claim form can be obtained at a post office or social security office. In two parent families the woman should claim.

Rates of Benefit
(from week commencing April 8, 1991)

	Weekly rate £

The maximum amount will be payable where net income is no more than £62·25 per week. Where net income exceeds that amount, the maximum credit is reduced by 70 per cent of the excess and the result is the Family Credit payable. The maximum rate consists of:

Adult credit (for one or two parents)	38·30
plus for each child aged:	
under 11	9·70
11–15	16·10
16–17	20·05
18	27·95

THE SOCIAL FUND

The Social Fund helps people with expenses which are difficult to meet from regular income. Regulated Maternity, Funeral and Cold Weather payments are decided by Adjudication Officers and are not cash-limited. Discretionary Community Care Grants, and Budgeting and Crisis Loans are decided by Social Fund Officers and come out of a yearly budget which is allocated to each district (1991–92, grants £67·7 million; loans £160m).

Regulated payments

Maternity Payments.— A flat-rate payment of £100 for each baby expected, born or adopted. It is payable to people on Income Support and Family Credit and is non-repayable.

Funeral Payments.—Payable for reasonable funeral expenses incurred by people receiving Income Support, Family Credit, Housing Benefit or Community Charge Rebate. It is recoverable from the estate of the deceased.

Cold Weather Payments.—£6 for any consecutive seven days when the average temperature is 0°C or below. Paid to people on Income Support who are pensioners, disabled or parents with a child under 5. It is non-repayable.

Discretionary payments

Community Care Grants.—They are intended to help people on Income Support to move into the community or avoid institutional care; ease exceptional pressures on families; and/or meet certain essential travelling expenses. They are usually non-repayable.

Budgeting Loans.—These are interest-free loans to people who have been receiving Income Support for at least six months, for intermittent expenses that may be difficult to budget for.

Crisis Loans.—These are interest-free loans to anyone, whether receiving benefit or not, who is without resources in an emergency, where there is no other means of preventing serious risk or damage to health or safety.

Loans are normally repaid over a period of up to 78 weeks at 15, 10 or 5 per cent of Income Support (less housing costs), depending on other commitments.

Savings.—Savings over £500 (£1,000 for people aged 60 or over) are taken into account for Cold Weather, Maternity and Funeral Payments, Community Care Grants and Budgeting Loans. All savings are taken into account for crisis loans.

Appeals and Reviews.—For regulated payment there is a right of appeal to an independent Social Security Appeal and thereafter to a Social Security Commissioner. For discretionary payments there is a review system where persons can ask for a review at the local office with a further right of review to an independent Social Fund Inspector.

DETERMINATION OF CLAIMS AND QUESTIONS

With a few exceptions, claims and questions relating to Social Security benefits are decided by statutory authorities who act independently of the Department of Social Security and Department of Employment. The first of the statutory authorities, the Adjudication Officer, determines entitlement to benefit. A claimant who is dissatisfied with that decision has the right of appeal to a Social Security Appeal Tribunal. There is a further right of appeal to a Social Security Commissioner against the Tribunal's decision but leave to appeal must first be obtained. Appeals to the Commissioner must be on a point of law. Provision is also made for the determination of certain questions by the Secretary of State for Social Services.

Disablement questions are decided by adjudicating medical authorities or Medical Appeal Tribunals. Appeal to the Commissioner against a tribunal's decision is with leave and on a point of law only. Leaflet NI 246 which is available from social security offices, explains how to appeal, and leaflet NI260 is a guide to reviews and appeals.

INDUSTRIAL INJURIES, DISABLEMENT AND DEATH BENEFITS

The Industrial Injuries scheme, administered under the Social Security Act 1975 and subsequent Acts and Regulations, provides a range of benefits designed to compensate for disablement resulting from an industrial accident (i.e. an accident arising out of and in the course of an employed earner's employment) or from a prescribed disease due to the nature of a person's employment. Rates of benefit are increased periodically.

Determination of Claims and Questions.—Provision is made for the determination of certain questions by the Secretary of State for Social Security, and of 'disablement questions' by a medical board (or a single doctor) or, on appeal, by a medical appeal tribunal. An appeal on a point of law against a medical appeal tribunal decision is determined by the Social Security Commissioner. Claims for benefit and certain questions arising in connection with a claim for or award of benefit (e.g. whether the accident arose out of and in the course of the employment) are determined by an adjudication officer appointed by the Secretary of State, or a Social Security Appeal Tribunal, or in certain circumstances, on further appeal, by the Commissioners.

Special schemes under the Industrial Injuries and Diseases (Old Cases) Act 1975 provide supplementary allowances to those entitled to receive weekly payments of workmen's compensation for loss of earnings due to injury at work, or disease contracted during employment before July 5, 1948 when the Industrial Injuries scheme was introduced. Other schemes under the Act provide allowances to those who contracted slowly developing diseases during employment before July 1948 where neither workmen's compensation nor Industrial Injuries Benefits are payable. A lump sum death benefit of up to £300 may also be payable to a dependant of such a person.

Benefits

Disablement Benefit is normally payable 15 weeks (90 days) after the date of accident or onset of disease if the employed earner suffers from loss of physical or mental faculty such that the resulting disablement is assessed at not less than 14 per cent. The amount of disablement benefit payable varies according to the degree of disablement (in the form of a percentage) assessed by an adjudicating medical authority or medical appeal tribunal.

Disablement assessed at less than 14 per cent does not normally attract basic benefit except for certain chest diseases. A weekly pension is payable where the assessment of disablement is between 14 and 100 per cent (assessments of 14 to 19 per cent are payable at the 20 per cent rate). Payment can be made for a limited period or for life.

The basic rates are applicable to adults and to juveniles entitled to an increase for a child or adult dependant; other juveniles receive lower rates.

Basic rates of pension are not related to the pensioner's loss of earning power, and are payable whether he is in work or not. If disablement is assessed at one per cent or more, loss of earnings may be compensated by a reduced earnings allowance. This may be paid even if basic disablement pension is not paid because disablement is assessed at less than 14 per cent, providing there is a current disablement assessment of at least 1 per cent. However, reduced earnings allowance cannot be paid where the date of the accident or the onset of a prescribed disease was on or after October 1, 1990. There is provision also

for increases of pension if the pensioner requires constant attendance or if his disablement is exceptionally severe. A pensioner may draw SSP, sickness or invalidity benefit as appropriate, in addition to disablement pension, during spells of incapacity for work.

Death Benefit, in the form of a pension, is available for women widowed before April 11, 1988. The amount of pension depends on the widow's circumstances at the date of the death and not upon the deceased's earnings.

Regulations impose certain obligations on claimants and beneficiaries and on employers, including, in the case of claimants for disablement benefit, that of submitting themselves for medical examination.

Rates of Benefits
(from April 10, 1991)

	Weekly rate £
Disablement Benefit/Pension	
Degree of disablement—100 per cent.	84·90
90	76·41
80	67·92
70	59·43
60	50·94
50	42·45
40	33·96
30	25·47
20	16·98
Unemployability supplement*	52·00
Addition for adult dependant (subject to earnings rule)	31·25
Reduced earnings allowance (maximum)	33·96
Constant Attendance allowance (normal maximum rate)	34·00
Exceptionally severe disablement allowance	34·00
Industrial death benefit widow's pension*	
Higher permanent rate	52·00
Lower permanent rate	15·60

* These benefits attract an increase for each dependent child (in addition to child benefit) of £9·70 for the first child and £10·70 for each subsequent child.

WAR PENSIONS

War pensions are awarded under The Naval, Military and Air Forces, Etc. (Disablement and Death) Service Pensions Order 1983, which was a consolidation of the previous Royal Warrants, Orders in Council and Orders by Her Majesty.

The DSS awards war pensions to members of the armed forces in respect of the periods August 4, 1914 to September 30, 1921 and subsequent to September 3, 1939 (including present members of the armed forces). The DSS also has special schemes for the Merchant Navy, Naval Auxiliary personnel, the Ulster Defence Regiment, civil defence volunteers, civilians, Home Guard, Polish armed forces under British command and Polish resettlement forces.

War pensions for the period October 1, 1921 to September 2, 1939 are dealt with by the Ministry of Defence, which is also responsible for the Armed Forces Pension Scheme.

ELIGIBILITY AND GENERAL PROVISIONS

War disablement pension is awarded for the disabling effects of any injury, wound or disease which is attributable to, or aggravated by, conditions of service in the armed forces. It cannot be paid until the serviceman has left the armed forces.

Disablement is assessed by comparison of the disabled person's condition with that of a normal, healthy person of the same age and sex, without taking into account the disabled person's earnings or occupation, and is expressed on a percentage scale up to 100 per cent. Disablement above 20 per cent, for which a pension is awarded, is assessed in steps of 10 per cent. Maximum assessment does not necessarily imply total incapacity. For assessment of less than 20 per cent a lump sum is payable.

Dependency allowance. A 100 per cent disabled pensioner may receive an allowance of 60p a week for his wife or dependent child. Where disablement is less than 100 per cent the allowance is proportionate to the degree of disablement.

War widow's pension is awarded where death occurs as a result of service. Where a war disablement pensioner was receiving constant attendance allowance at the time of his death, or would have been receiving it if he were not in hospital, his widow has automatic entitlement to a war widow's pension, regardless of the cause of death.

Additional allowances are payable for dependent children, in addition to child benefit.

A reduced weekly rate is payable to war widows of men below the rank of Lieutenant-Colonel who are under the age of 40, without children and capable of maintaining themselves. This is increased to the standard rate at age 40.

Rank additions to disablement and widows pensions. Rank additions may be paid with war pensions where the rank held was above that of private (or equivalent).

Claims.—Where a claim is made no later than seven years after the termination of service, the claimant does not have to prove that the disablement or death on which the claim is based is related to service and receives the benefit of any reasonable doubt. Where a claim is made more than seven years after the termination of service the claimant has to show that disablement or death is related to service. However, the claim succeeds if reliable evidence is produced which raises a reasonable doubt whether disablement or death is related to service. There is no time limit for making a claim for war pension.

SUPPLEMENTARY ALLOWANCES

A number of supplementary allowances may be awarded to a war pensioner which are intended to meet the various needs which may result from disablement or death and take account of its particular effect on the pensioner. Decisions on supplementary allowances are made on a discretionary basis on behalf of the Secretary of State and there is no provision for a statutory right of appeal against them. However, war pensioners may discuss any aspect of their pension position with their local War Pensions Committees, which may be able to arrange help or make representations to the war pensions branch of the DSS.

The principal supplementary allowances are:

Unemployability supplement, with additional allowances for dependants, may be paid to a war pensioner whose pensioned disablement is so serious as to make him unemployable. In addition, an invalidity allowance may be payable if the incapacity for work began more than five years before normal retirement age.

Allowance for lowered standard of occupation may be awarded to a partially disabled pensioner whose pensioned disablement permanently prevents him from following his pre-service occupation and from doing another job of equivalent financial standard. The allowance, together with the basic war disablement pension, must not exceed pension at the 100 per cent rate.

Widow's age allowance is paid at three different rates according to age (65–69, 70–79 and over 80).

Widow's child's allowance may be paid in addition to child benefit.

Other supplementary allowances include constant attendance allowance, exceptionally severe disablement allowance, severe disablement occupational allowance, mobility supplement, treatment allowance, age allowance and education allowance.

WAR PENSIONERS ABROAD

The DSS is responsible for the payment of war pensions, and provision of necessary treatment for accepted disablement, to pensioners who reside overseas. They receive the same pension rates as war pensioners in this country and benefit from the same annual upratings.

WAR PENSIONERS AND SOCIAL SECURITY BENEFITS

When a war disablement pensioner is sick, unemployed or retired, the appropriate social security benefits are paid in addition to the war pension, unless he is entitled to unemployability supplement or severe disablement occupational allowance instead.

Any sickness, invalidity, unemployment benefit or retirement pension for which a war widow qualifies on her own contributions, and any graduated retirement benefit, or additional earnings related pension inherited from her husband, can be paid in addition to her war widow's pension or temporary allowance. A war pensioner or war widow who claims Income Support or Family Credit has the first £10 of pension disregarded. A similar provision operates for housing benefit and community charge relief; but the local authority may, at its discretion, disregard any or all of the balance. A special tax free Christmas bonus of £10.00 is payable to war disablement pensioners who are in receipt of unemployability supplement, constant attendance allowance, have retired, or are aged over 70 (65 for women); and to all war widows who do not otherwise receive this payment.

PENSIONS APPEAL TRIBUNALS

There are independent Pensions Appeal Tribunals which hear appeals against the decisions of the DSS on entitlement, and assessment of disablement, in respect of the 1939–45 War and subsequent service cases. There are now no rights of appeal in the 1914–21 War disablement cases, the great majority of which were given final assessment in the 1920s with a 12 months' right of appeal at the time. An appeal by a 1914 war widow must be made within twelve months of the date on which the rejection of the claim is notified.

WAR PENSIONERS WELFARE SERVICE

The DSS operates a war pensioners welfare service to advise and assist war pensioners and their widows on any matters affecting their welfare. Welfare officers are attached to War Pensioners' Welfare Offices located in the major towns, and work closely with central and local government agencies as well as the various ex-service organizations. The service is available on call to any war pensioner or widow who needs it. In addition the service takes the initiative in arranging regular visits in certain cases.

Rates of War Pensions and Allowances
(from week commencing April 8, 1991)

	Weekly rates £
War Disablement pension	
(for Private or equivalent rank)	
Degree of disablement:	
100 per cent	84.90
90 per cent	76.41
80 per cent	67.92
70 per cent	59.43
60 per cent	50.94
50 per cent	42.45
40 per cent	33.96
30 per cent	25.47
20 per cent	16.98
Unemployability supplement	
Personal allowance	55.25
Increase for wife/other adult dependant	31.25
Increase for first child	9.70
for other children	10·70
Allowance for lowered standard of occupation (maximum)	33.96
Widow's pension	
(widow of Private or equivalent rank)	
Standard rate	67.60
Increase for first child	13.65
for other children	14·65
Childless widow under 40	14.07

Weekly rates £	
Widow's age allowance	
Aged 65–69	7.75
70–79	14.95
80 and over	22.20

The current rates of all War Pensions and Allowances are listed in leaflet MPL154 'Rates of War Pensions and Allowances' which is obtainable from War Pensioners Welfare Offices or from The Leaflets Unit, PO Box 21, Stanmore, Middx. HA7 1AY.

NATIONAL HEALTH SERVICE
(and Local Authority Personal Social Services)

The National Health Service came into being on July 5, 1948, as a result of the National Health Service Act 1946. The Act placed a duty on the Secretary of State for Social Services to promote the establishment in England and Wales of a comprehensive health service designed to secure improvement in the mental and physical health of the people and the prevention, diagnosis and treatment of illness. The Secretary of State for Wales administers the National Health Service in Wales. There are separate Acts for Scotland and Northern Ireland, where the health services are run on very similar lines and the respective Secretaries of State are responsible to Parliament.

The National Health Service covers a comprehensive range of hospital, specialist, family practitioner (medical, dental, ophthalmic and pharmaceutical), artificial limb and appliance, ambulance, and community health services. Everyone normally resident in this country is entitled to use any of these services, there are no contribution conditions and the charges made (except those for amenity beds) are reduced or waived in cases of hardship. In addition, the Secretary of State for Social Services is responsible under the Local Authority Social Services Act 1970 for the provision by local authorities of social services for the elderly, the disabled, those with mental disorders and for families and children.

The 1980 Health Services Act led to major changes in the structure of the Health Service. Since April 1982, District Health Authorities (DHAs) are responsible for the operational management of health services and for planning within regional and national strategic guidelines. There are 190 DHAs in England and nine in Wales. Each DHA is required to arrange its services into units of management at hospital and community services level, and as many decisions as possible are delegated to unit level. Four of the London postgraduate teaching hospitals are now managed by DHAs (and eight are managed by special health authorities). Arrangements for the Family Doctor Service are administered by Family Health Services Authorities—90 in England and eight in Wales. FHSAs also contribute to the planning of health services.

The 14 Regional Health Authorities (RHAs) in England are responsible for regional planning, the allocation of resources to District Authorities, and the promotion of national policies and priorities. Performance review meetings are held annually between each hospital unit and its DHA, each DHA and its RHA, and between each RHA and Department of Health ministers, thereby strengthening authorities' accountability to Parliament, whilst respecting the essentially locally-based nature of decision making. Professional advisory machinery incorporated within the structure ensures that health authorities and their staffs make decisions in the full knowledge of expert opinion.

The NHS is financed mainly from taxation and the cost met from moneys voted by Parliament. In the United Kingdom this will amount to £32·8 billion in 1991–92. The Department of Health makes capital and revenue allocations to the RHAs and from these the RHAs meet the cost of their own services and make allocations to DHAs as well as funding Community Health Councils.

The National Health Service and Community Care Act 1990 provides for wide-ranging reforms in management and patient care. The reforms are intended to offer better health care and a greater choice of services to patients, and to encourage those working in the NHS to respond to local needs in a more specific and cost-conscious way. Reforms in the NHS have been implemented between April 1990 and April 1991, and those in community care are being implemented between April 1991 and April 1993.

THE HEALTH SERVICES
Family Doctor Service

In England and Wales the Family Doctor Service (or General Medical Services) is organized by 98 Family Health Services Authorities which also organize the general dental, pharmaceutical and ophthalmic services for their areas. There is a Family Health Services Authority for one or more District Health Authorities. In Wales the chairman and non-executive members are appointed by the Secretary of State. In England the chairman is appointed by the Secretary of State and the non-executive members by the Regional Health Authority. There are nine non-executive members—a general medical practitioner, a general dental practitioner, a community pharmacist, a nurse and five lay members.

Any doctor may take part in the Family Doctor Scheme (provided the area in which he wishes to practise has not already an adequate number of doctors) and about 29,000 general practitioners in England and Wales do so. They may at the same time have private fee-paying patients. Family doctors are paid for their Health Service work in accordance with a scheme of remuneration which includes *inter alia* a basic practice allowance, capitation fees, reimbursement of certain practice expenses and payments for out of hours work.

The National Health Service and Community Care Act 1990 enables general practitioner practices with at least 9,000 patients to apply for fund-holding status. This makes the practice responsible for its own NHS budget. In April 1991, 306 GP practices achieved fund-holding status and applications from GP practices wishing to manage their own funds from April 1992 are currently under consideration.

Everyone aged 16 or over can choose their doctor (parents or guardians choose for children under 16) and the doctor is also free to accept a person or not as he or she chooses. A person may change their doctor if they wish, by going to the surgery of a general practioner of their choice who is willing to accept them, and either handing in their medical card to register or filling in a form. When people are away from home they can still use the Family Doctor Service if they ask to be treated as temporary residents, and in an emergency, if a person's own doctor is not available, any doctor in the service will give treatment and advice.

Patients are treated either in the doctor's surgery or, when necessary, at home. Doctors may prescribe for their patients all drugs and medicines which are medically necessary for their treatment and also a certain number of surgical appliances (the more elaborate being provided through hospitals).

Dental Service

Dentists, like doctors, may take part in the National Health Service and may also have private patients. About 16,000 of the dentists available for general practice in England provide NHS general dental services. They are responsible to the Family Health Services Authorities in whose areas they provide services.

Patients are free to go to any dentist taking part in the Service and willing to accept them. Dentists are paid a capitation fee for patients registered with them who are under 18 years of age. They receive payment for items of treatment for individual adult patients and, in addition, a continuing care payment for those registered with them.

Patients are asked to pay three-quarters of the cost of NHS dental treatment. The maximum charge for a course of treatment is £200. There is no charge for arrest of bleeding, repairs to dentures, home visits by the dentist or re-opening a surgery in an emergency (in these two cases payment will be for treatment given in the normal way). The following are exempt from dental charges:

(i) young people under 18;
(ii) full time students under 19;
(iii) expectant mothers who were pregnant when accepted for treatment;
(iv) women who have had a child in the previous 12 months.

People receiving Income Support or Family Credit, and members of the same family as someone receiving Income Support or Family Credit, are automatically entitled to full remission of charges.

Leaflet AB11 available from post offices and leaflet D11 available from local social security offices explain how other people on a low income can, depending on their financial circumstances, get free treatment or help with charges.

Pharmaceutical Service

Patients may obtain medicines, appliances and oral contraceptives prescribed under the NHS from any pharmacy whose owner has entered into arrangements with the Family Health Services Authority to provide this service. Almost all pharmacy owners have done so and display notices that they dispense under the NHS; the number of these pharmacies in England and Wales at the end of 1990 was about 10,400. There are also some appliance suppliers who only provide special appliances. In country areas where access to a pharmacy may be difficult, patients may be able to obtain medicines, etc. from their doctor.

Except for contraceptives (for which there is no charge), a charge of £3·40 is payable for each item supplied unless the patient is exempt and the declaration on the back of the prescription form is completed. Exemptions cover:

(i) children under 16;
(ii) young people under 19 and still in full-time education;
(iii) men aged 65 and over;
(iv) women aged 60 and over;
(v) pregnant women;
(vi) mothers who have had a baby within the last 12 months;
(vii) people suffering from certain medical conditions;
(viii) people who receive Income Support or Family Credit;
(ix) people on low income;
(x) war pensioners (for their accepted disablements).

Prepayment certificates (£17·60 valid for four months, £48·50 valid for a year) may be purchased by those patients not entitled to exemption who require frequent prescriptions. Further information about the exemption and prepayment arrangements is given in leaflet P11.

General Ophthalmic Services

General Ophthalmic Services, which are administered by Family Practitioner Committees, form part of the ophthalmic services available under the National Health Service. The NHS sight test is available free to children under 16, full-time students under the age of 19, those people and their partners in receipt of Income Support and Family Credit, people prescribed complex lenses, the registered blind and partially sighted, diagnosed diabetic and glaucoma patients, and close relatives aged 40 or over of diagnosed glaucoma patients. Those on a low income may qualify for help with the cost.

Certain groups are automatically entitled to help with the purchase of glasses under an NHS voucher scheme: children under 16; full-time students under 19; people who are themselves or whose partners are in receipt of Income Support or Family Credit; people wearing certain complex lenses; and people whose spectacles are lost or damaged as a result of their disability, injury or illness. The value of the voucher depends on the lenses required. Vouchers may be used to help pay for the glasses or contact lenses of the patient's choice. People with a low income may claim help on form AG1. Glasses or contact lenses should not be purchased until the result of a claim is known as no refunds can be given. Booklet G11 gives further details.

Diagnosis and specialist treatment of eye conditions is available through the Hospital Eye Service as well as the provision of glasses of a special type. Testing of sight may be carried out by any ophthalmic medical practitioner or ophthalmic optician and can cost between £10 and £15. The optician must hand the prescription, and a voucher if eligible, to the patient who can take this to any supplier of glasses of his/her choice to have dispensed. However, only registered opticians can supply glasses to children and to people registered as blind or partially sighted.

Primary Health Care Services

Primary health care services include the general medical, dental, ophthalmic and pharmaceutical services and the family doctor service. They also include community services run by district health authorities, health centres and clinics, family planning outside the hospital service, and preventive activities in the community including vaccination, immunization and fluoridation. The district nursing and health visiting services include community psychiatric nursing for mentally ill people living outside hospital, and school nursing for the health surveillance of school children of all ages; ante- and post-natal care and chiropody are also an integral part of the primary health care service.

Community Child Health Services

Pre-school services, usually at child health clinics, provide regular surveillance of children's physical, mental and emotional health and development, and advice to parents on their children's health and welfare. The School Health Service provides for the medical and dental examination of schoolchildren, and advises the local education authority, the school, the parents and the pupil of any health factors which may require special consideration during the pupil's school life.

Hospitals and Other Services

The Secretary of State for Health has a duty to provide, to such extent as he/she considers necessary to meet all reasonable requirements, hospital and other accommodation; medical, dental, nursing and ambulance services; other facilities for the care of expectant and nursing mothers and young children; facilities for the prevention of illness and the care and after-care of persons suffering from illness; and such other services as are required for the diagnosis and treatment of illness. Rehabilitation services (occupational therapy, physiotherapy and speech therapy) may also be provided for those who need it and surgical and medical appliances are supplied in appropriate cases.

Specialists and consultants who take part in the

Service can engage in private practice, including the treatment of their private patients in NHS hospitals.

In a number of hospitals, accommodation is available for the treatment of private in-patients who undertake to pay the full costs of hospital accommodation and services and (usually) separate medical fees to a specialist as well. The amount of the medical fees is a matter for agreement between doctor and patient. Hospital charges for private resident patients are determined by District Health Authorities either on a local basis or in line with a central 'model' list.

Certain hospitals have accommodation in single rooms or small wards which, if not required for patients who need privacy for medical reasons, may be made available to patients who desire it as an amenity. In such cases the patients are treated in every other respect as National Health patients.

There is no charge for drugs supplied to National Health hospital in-patients but out-patients pay £3·40 per item unless they are exempt.

With certain exceptions, hospital out-patients have to pay fixed charges for dentures, contact lenses and certain appliances. Glasses may be obtained either from the hospital or an optician and the charge will be related to the type of lens prescribed and the choice of frame.

The National Health Service and Community Care Act 1990 enables hospitals to become independent of health authority control as self-governing NHS trusts run by boards of directors. The trusts derive their income principally from NHS contracts to provide services to health authorities and fund-holding general practitioners. The first 56 hospitals became trusts in April 1991, and applications from hospitals wishing to become trusts in April 1992 are currently under consideration.

Local Authority Personal Social Services

Local authorities are responsible for the organization, management and administration of the personal social services and each authority has a Director of Social Services and a Social Services Committee responsible for the social services functions placed upon them by the Local Authority Social Services Act 1970.

POSTAL SERVICES

On October 1, 1969 the Post Office ceased to be a government department. The responsibility for running postal services was transferred to a public authority called the Post Office, which also administered telecommunications in the United Kingdom. The British Telecommunications Act 1981 separated the postal and telecommunications functions and gave the Secretary of State for Trade and Industry powers to suspend the monopoly of the Post Office in certain areas and to issue licences to other bodies to provide an alternative service. Non-Post Office bodies are now permitted to transfer mail between document exchanges and to deliver letters, provided that a minimum fee of £1 per letter is charged. Charitable organizations are allowed to carry and deliver Christmas and New Year cards.

INLAND POSTAL SERVICES AND REGULATIONS

Inland Letter Post Rates

Not over	1st Class	2nd Class
60 g	24p	18p
100 g	36p	28p
150 g	45p	34p
200 g	54p	41p
250 g	64p	49p
300 g	74p	58p
350 g	85p	66p
400 g	96p	75p
450 g	£1.08	84p
500 g	£1.20	93p
600 g	£1.50	£1.15
700 g	£1.80	£1.35
750 g	£1.95	£1.40 (max)
800 g	£2.05	
900 g	£2.25	
1,000 g	£2.40	
Each extra 250 g or part thereof	60p	

Postcards travel at the same rates.

Stamps

There is a two-tier postal delivery system in the UK with 1st class letters normally being delivered the following day and 2nd class post within two days.

Postage stamps are sold in values of 1p, 2p, 3p, 4p, 5p, 6p, 10p, 18p, 20p, 24p, 28p, 29p, 30p, 32p, 34p, 35p, 39p, 50p, 75p, £1, £1.50, £2.00, and £5.00.

Books of stamps costing 50p or £1 are available from electronic vending machines at some main post offices. At post office counters books are sold containing 10 first class stamps (£2.40) and 10 second class stamps (£1.80). Rolls of 24p and 18p stamps are also sold. Mixed value rolls are only available on special order from post offices. The sale of postage stamps has been extended to outlets other than post offices, including stationers and newsagents.

Prepaid Stationery

Aerogrammes to all destinations, 32p.

Forces Aerogrammes, free to certain destinations.

Registered Letter Envelopes, printed with a £1.75 stamp (£1.55 for registration and 20p for postage), come in three sizes.

G, 156 × 95mm = £2.30
H, 203 × 120mm = £2.35
K, 292 × 152mm = £2.45

Printed postage stamps cut from envelopes, postcards, newspaper wrappers etc. may be used as stamps in payment of postage, provided that they are not imperfect or defaced.

Postal Orders

Postal Orders (British pattern) are issued and paid at nearly all post offices in the UK. They are also paid in the Irish Republic, and issued and/or paid in many other countries overseas.

Postal orders are printed with a counterfoil for denominations of 50p and £1, followed by £1 steps to £10, £15 and £20. Postage stamps may be affixed in the space provided to increase the value of the postal order by up to 49p.

Charges (in addition to the value of the postal order): Up to £1 = 25p; £2–£4 = 40p; £5–£7 = 50p; £8–£10 = 60p; £15 = 70p; £20 = 80p.

The name of the payee must be inserted on the postal order. If not presented within six months of the last day of the month of issue, orders must be sent to the local customer services manager of Post Office Counters Ltd (the address and telephone number can be found in the telephone directory), to ascertain whether the order may still be paid.

Other Services

Cash on Delivery Service.—(Inland, excluding Irish Republic and HM ships). A trade charge (amount to be collected) up to £350 can, under certain conditions, be collected from addresses and remitted to the sender of a parcel containing an invoice. Invoice values of over £50 are only collectable at Post Office premises.

Charge per parcel (exclusive of postage and registration): Customers under contract = £1.20; other customers = £1.60; COD enquiry = £1.20.

Certificate of Posting.—Issued free on request at time of posting.

Compensation.—(Inland only). Compensation up to a maximum of £24 may be paid where it can be shown that a letter or parcel was damaged or lost in the post. The onus of making up properly any parcel sent by post lies with the sender. The Post Office does not accept any responsibility for loss arising from faulty packing. No compensation may be claimed for injury or damage to a parcel unless the item was registered and covered by consequential loss insurance.

Newspaper Post.—Copies of newspapers registered at the Post Office may be posted by the publisher or their agents in wrappers open at both ends, in unsealed envelopes approved by the Post Office, or without covers and tied by string which can be removed without cutting. Wrappers and envelopes must be prominently marked 'newspaper post' in the top left-hand corner. No writing or additional printing is permitted, other than the words 'with compliments', name and address of sender, request for return if undeliverable and a reference to a page. Items receive 1st class letter service.

Newspapers posted by the public, or supplements to registered newspapers despatched apart from their ordinary publications, are transmitted under the conditions governing the 1st or 2nd class letter services.

Prohibited Articles.—Prohibitions include offensive or dangerous articles, packets likely to impede Post Office sorters, and certain kinds of advertisement.

Recorded Delivery.—The recorded delivery service provides a record of posting and delivery of inland letters. No compensation is available for money or jewellery sent by this service. Charge: 30p; advice of delivery: a further 31p.

Redirection.—(i) By agent of addressee.—Mail other than parcels, business reply and freepost items may be reposted free not later than the day after delivery (not counting Sundays and public holidays) if unopened and if original addressee's name is unobscured. Parcels may be redirected free of charge within the same time limits only if the original and substituted address are in the same local parcel delivery area (or within the London postal area). Registered packets, which must be taken to a post office, are re-registered free only up to the day after delivery.

(ii) By the Post Office.—Requests for redirection of mail should be made on printed forms obtainable from the Post Office and must be signed by the person to whom the letters are to be addressed. A fee is payable for each different surname on the application form.

Charges: Up to 1 calendar month = £3.50; Up to 3 calendar months = £7.75; Up to 12 calendar months = £18.75; Up to 12 calendar months where redirection has already been in operation for 12 months or more = £65.00.

Registration.—(Inland 1st class letters only). All packets intended for registration must be handed to the post office and a certificate of posting obtained.

Compensation in respect of money is given only if money is sent by registered letter post in one of the special envelopes sold officially (*see* **Prepaid Stationery**). Compensation cannot be paid in the case of any packet containing anything not legally transmissable by post. Compensation is paid for fragile articles only if they have been adequately packed. No compensation is paid for deterioration due to delay of perishable articles or for damage to exceptionally fragile articles. Information about charges and compensation rates is available from the local head postmaster (in London, the district head postmaster). Advice of delivery: a further 31p at time of posting.

Undelivered Mail.—Undelivered mail is returned to the sender provided the return address is indicated either on the outside of the envelope or inside. If the sender's address is not available, items not containing property are destroyed. If the packet contains something of value it is retained for up to three months. Exceptionally, items in the minimum weight step on which a rebate of postage has been allowed are destroyed unopened unless there is a return address shown on the outside of the cover. In addition, undeliverable 2nd class mail which contains newspapers, magazines or commercial advertising is destroyed.

Unpaid Mail.—All unpaid or underpaid letters are treated as 2nd class mail. The recipient is charged the amount of underpayment plus 13p per item. The same rates apply to parcels.

SPECIAL DELIVERY SERVICES

Datapost.—A guaranteed service for the delivery of documents and packages: (i) Datapost Sameday offers same-day collection and delivery in many areas; (ii) Datapost Overnight offers next day delivery nationwide. Items may be collected or handed in at post offices. There are also Datapost links with a number of overseas countries.

Express Delivery.—This service is by special messenger from the office of delivery and is available to or from the Isle of Man or the Channel Islands. Charge (in addition to postage): £1.95.

Royal Mail Special Delivery.—This service offers special messenger treatment, where necessary, to ensure next day delivery of 1st class letters and packets. The fee of £1.95 is refunded if next working day delivery is not achieved, provided that items are posted before latest recommended posting times.

Swiftair.—Express delivery of air mail letters and packets anywhere in the world. Items normally arrive at least one day in advance of normal air mail. Charge (in addition to postage): £1.95.

OVERSEAS POSTAL SERVICES AND REGULATIONS

Overseas Surface Mail Rates

Letters and Postcards

Not over			Not over		
20 g	....	28p	450 g	....	£2.44
60 g	....	48p	500 g	....	£2.70
100 g	....	69p	750 g	....	£4.00
150 g	....	92p	1,000 g	....	£5.30
200 g	....	£1.18	1,250 g	....	£6.60
250 g	....	£1.42	1,500 g	....	£7.90
300 g	....	£1.66	1,750 g	....	£9.20
350 g	....	£1.92	2,000 g	....	£10.50
400 g	....	£2.18			

Airmail Letter Rates

Europe: Letters and Postcards

Not over			Not over		
20 g	....	24p	260 g	....	£1.60
20 g non EC	..	28p	280 g	....	£1.71
40 g	....	39p	300 g	....	£1.82
60 g	....	50p	320 g	....	£1.93
80 g	....	61p	340 g	....	£2.04
100 g	....	72p	360 g	....	£2.15
120 g	....	83p	380 g	....	£2.26
140 g	....	94p	400 g	....	£2.37
160 g	....	£1.05	420 g	....	£2.48
180 g	....	£1.16	440 g	....	£2.59
200 g	....	£1.27	460 g	....	£2.70
220 g	....	£1.38	480 g	....	£2.81
240 g	....	£1.49	*500 g	....	£2.92

* Max. 2 kg.

Outside Europe: Letters

	Not over 10 g	Not over 25 g	Each extra 10 g
Zone 1	39p	57p	32p
Zone 2	39p	57p	42p

NB: Zone 1 has replaced Zones A and B, Zone 2 has replaced Zone C. (For Airmail Letter Zones outside Europe, *see* pp. 1063–5.)

Other Services

Cash on Delivery.—(Applicable to parcels only, but not to all countries, nor to British naval, military and RAF forces serving overseas.) A charge starting at £3.50 per parcel must be prepaid in addition to the postage for outward parcels. The trade charge (amount to be collected) may not exceed £1,500 but to most non-European countries the limit is lower. The addressee has also to pay on delivery, besides Customs charges if any, a further charge which is not prepayable. If the trade charge cannot be collected, special rules apply for undeliverable COD parcels.

Compensation.—If a certificate of posting is produced, compensation may be given for loss or damage in the UK to uninsured parcels to or from most overseas countries. No compensation will be paid for any loss or damage due to the action of the Queen's Enemies.

Export Restrictions.—Under Department of Trade and Industry regulations the exportation of some goods by post is prohibited except under Department of Trade licence. Enquiries should be addressed to the Export Data Branch, Overseas Trade Divisions, Department of Trade and Industry, 1 Victoria Street, London, SW1H 0ET (Tel. 071-215 5000).

Insurance.—Packets containing valuable papers, documents or articles such as jewellery can be insured as letters, or as parcels if the country of destination does not accept dutiable goods in the letter post. For HM ships abroad and also members of the Army and RAF overseas using BFPO numbers, parcels only are insurable up to £140 at a fee of £1.20.

Charges: Cover up to £150=£1.90; up to £300= £2.15; up to £450=£2.40; up to £600=£2.65; to a limit of £3.90 for £1,500 coverage.

International Reply Coupons.—Coupons are used to prepay replies to letters. They are exchangeable abroad for stamps representing the minimum surface mail letter rate from the country concerned to the UK. Charge: 60p each.

Poste Restante.—(Solely for the convenience of travellers and for three months only in any one town). A packet may be addressed to any post office, except town sub-offices, and should have the words 'Poste Restante' or 'to be called for' in the address. Redirection from a Poste Restante is undertaken for up to three months. Letters at a seaport for an expected ship are kept for two months: otherwise letters are kept for two weeks, or for one month if

originating from abroad. At the end of this period mail is treated as undeliverable, unless bearing a request for return.

Registration.—(Except for parcels and printed paper items posted in bulk). Registration is available to all countries except the British Indian Ocean Territory and the Republic of the Maldives. No compensation is payable for loss or damage to valuable articles sent in an unregistered letter. Charge in addition to postage: £1.90.

Small Packets Post.—This service permits the transmission of goods up to 1 kg to all countries, in the same mails as printed papers. (NB: to Australia, Cuba, Myanmar (Burma) and Papua New Guinea there is a limit of 500 g). Packets must be packed to enable examination by the Post Office. Registration is allowed as insurance as long as the item is packed in a way which complies with appropriate insurance regulations. A customs declaration is required.

Instructions for the disposal of undelivered packets must be given at the time of posting. A parcel which cannot be delivered will be returned to the sender at his expense.

Small Packets Post Rates

Not over		Not over	
100 g	45p	400 g	£1.35
150 g	60p	450 g	£1.50
200 g	75p	500 g	£1.65
250 g	90p	750 g	£2.30
300 g	£1.05	1,000 g	£2.95
350 g	£1.20		

WEATHERCALL SERVICE

To obtain local weather forecasts, dial the prefix code 0898 500 followed by the appropriate regional code.

Calls are charged at 34p per minute cheap rate, 45p at all other times.

MARINECALL SERVICE

To obtain information about weather conditions up to twelve miles off the coast, dial the prefix code 0898 500, followed by the appropriate area code.

Calls are charged at 34p per minute cheap rate, 45p at all other times.

PUBLIC TELECOMMUNICATIONS SERVICES

Under the British Telecommunications Act 1981 the functions of the Post Office were divided between two separate organizations. The Post Office retained control of postal services and BT (formerly British Telecom) was created to provide a telecommunications service. The Act also provided for a limited relaxation of the telecommunications monopoly. This was further advanced by the Telecommunications Act 1984, which removed BT's monopoly on running the public telecommunications system. British Telecom was privatized as a public limited company in 1984.

The Telecommunications Act 1984 also established the Office of Telecommunications (Oftel) as the independent regulatory body for the telecommunications industry. (*See also* **Government and Public Offices.**)

Public telecommunications operators

There are three licensed fixed link public telecommunications operators (PTOs) in the UK: BT, Mercury Communications Ltd and Kingston Communications (Hull) PLC. In 1988 the Government announced its intention to license up to six other operators to provide one-way satellite communications systems; during 1989 three of these operators were granted temporary licences and the Government announced that such operators could offer services throughout Europe, rather than in the UK only, as previously indicated. In November 1990, the Government began a formal review of the two major fixed link operators as part of a wider review of UK telecommunications provision and competition arrangements.

BT's obligations under its operating licence include the provision of (i) a universal telecommunications service; (ii) a service in rural areas; and (iii) essential services, such as public call boxes and emergency services.

Mercury Communications is licensed to provide national and international telephone services for residential and business customers. These services utilize the digital network created by Mercury. Mercury can also provide the following services: (i) public payphone services; (ii) national and international telex; (iii) international packet data services; (iv) electronic messaging (electronic mail and access to telex via a personal computer); (v) data network services; and (vi) nationwide radiopaging.

Private telephone services

There are over 260 private telephone companies which offer information on a variety of subjects such as the weather, stock market analysis, horoscopes, etc., on the BT network. Other services are also now available on Mercury's network.

The lines and equipment are provided by BT under condition that services adhere to the codes of practice of the Independent Committee for the Supervision of Standards of Telephone Information Practice. All services are charged at 45p per minute (peak and standard rate) or 34p per minute (cheap rate).

Mobile telephone systems

Cellular telephone network systems, in existence since 1985, allow calls to be made to and from mobile telephones. The two companies licensed by the Department of Trade and Industry to provide competing cellular telephone systems are Cellnet, jointly owned by BT and Securicor, and Racal Vodafone Ltd, owned by the Racal Electronics Group. Cellular phones can be identified by the number prefixes 0860 or 0836 and calls to them are charged at the 'm' rate.

INLAND TELEPHONES

Since December 1986 an individual customer can install an extension telephone socket or apparatus in their own home without the need to buy the items from any of the licensed public telecommunications operators. However, it is necessary to possess a special style of master-socket which must be supplied by the public network operator. Although an individual need not buy or rent an apparatus from a PTO, a telephone bought from a retail outlet must be of an approved standard compatible with the public network (indicated by a green disc on the label).

BT Charges

Exchange line rentals	Per quarter (excl. VAT)
Residential, exclusive............	£18.46
Business, exclusive	£29.90

Telephone apparatus rental	
Residential	from £3.80
Business	from £4.70
Private payphone	from £36.50

Exchange line connection and take-over charges (incl. VAT)

	Residential	Business
New customer	£163.75	£179.49
Removing customer	£140.35	£156.10
Take-over of existing lines	£0.00	£0.00
Non-simultaneous take-over of lines	£36.78	£36.78

Local and dialled national calls are charged in 4.2p units when made from ordinary lines and in 10p units when made from payphones. All charges are subject to VAT except those from payphones which are VAT inclusive. VAT charges on ordinary lines are calculated as a percentage of the total quarterly bill.

The length of time per unit depends on the distance of the call and the time of day:

Local rate*
'a' rate = up to 35 miles (56 km).
'b1' rate = frequently used routes over 35 miles (56 km).
'b' rate = over 35 miles (56 km) (incl. Channel Islands and Isle of Man).
'm' rate = dialled calls to mobile phones.
* Greater London has an exceptionally large 'local' call area.

Peak rate: Monday to Friday, 9a.m.–1p.m.
Standard rate: Monday to Friday, 8a.m.–9a.m. and 1p.m.–6p.m.
Cheap rate: Monday to Friday, 6p.m.–8a.m. All day Saturday and Sunday and also Christmas Day, Boxing Day and New Year's Day.

Dialled Call Unit Time (excl. VAT)

	Seconds per unit at 4.2p
Local rate	
Peak	57.5
Standard	80
Cheap	220
'a' rate	
Peak	27
Standard	36.15
Cheap	80.8

'b1' rate	Seconds per unit at 4.2p
Peak	23.9
Standard	32
Cheap	50.35

'b' rate	
Peak	19.2
Standard	32
Cheap	50.35

'm' rate	
Peak	7.16
Standard	7.16
Cheap	11.4

Prefixed call charges

0800 = free.

0345 = charged at the local rate.

0860, 0831 and Callstream 0077 services = charged at 'm' rate (and some 0836 calls also).

0898 = charged at 'p1' rate.

Operator-Connected Calls

Operator-connected calls from ordinary lines are generally subject to a three-minute minimum charge (and thereafter by the minute) which varies with distance and time of day. Operator-connected calls from payphones are charged in three-minute periods at the payphone tariff. For calls that have to be placed through the operator because a dialled call has failed, the charge is equivalent to the dialled rate, subject normally to the three-minute minimum.

Higher charges apply to other operator-connected calls, including special services calls and those to mobile phones, the Irish Republic and the Channel Islands.

Phonecards

Phonecards to the value of £2, £4, £10 and £20 are available from post offices and other outlets for use in specially designated public telephone boxes. Each phonecard unit is equivalent to a 10p coin in a payphone.

Special public payphones at major railway stations and airports also accept commercial credit cards.

INTERNATIONAL TELEPHONES

All UK customers have access to International Direct Dialling (IDD) and can dial direct to numbers on most exchanges in 201 countries worldwide. Details about how to make calls are given in dialling code information and in the International Telephone Guide.

For countries without IDD, calls have to be made through the International Operator. All operator-connected calls are subject to a three-minute minimum charge. Thereafter the call is charged by the minute.

Countries which can be called on IDD fall into one of 13 international charge bands depending on location. Charges in each band also vary according to the time of day; cheap rate dialled calls are available to all countries at certain times, but there is no reduced rate for operator-connected calls. Details of current international telephone charges can be obtained from the International Operator.

(For International Dialling Codes, *see* pp. 1063-65.)

OTHER TELECOMMUNICATIONS SERVICES

Telex Service.—There are now 208 countries that can be reached by the BT telex service from the UK, over 200 of them by direct dialling.

For most customers, direct dialled calls to international destinations are charged in six-second units. Units cost between 4.5p and 13.5p depending upon the country called. Calls via the BT operator are charged in one-minute steps with a three-minute minimum, plus a surcharge of £1.30 a call. Operator-connected calls are charged at between 39p and £1.60 a minute depending upon the country called.

Calls made via BT's Telex Plus store and forward facility attract normal telex charges and a handling charge of 13p for inland delivered messages and 30p for international delivered messages.

Telemessage.—Telemessages can be sent by telephone or telex within the UK for 'hard copy' delivery the next working day, including Saturdays. To achieve this, a telemessage must be telephoned/telexed before 10pm Monday to Saturday (7pm Sundays and Bank Holidays). Dial 100 (190 in London, Birmingham and Glasgow) and ask for the Telemessage Service or see the telex directory for codes.

A telemessage costs £5 for the first 50 words and £2.75 for each subsequent group of 50 words—the name and address are free. A sender's copy costs 85p. A selection of cards is available for special occasions at 80p per card. All prices are subject to VAT.

International Telemessage.—Telemessage is also available to the USA. For next working day delivery a telemessage must be filed by 10pm UK time Monday to Saturday (7pm Sundays and Bank Holidays). US addresses must include the ZIP code. Charges are £7.25 for the first 50 words and £3.60 for each subsequent group of 50 words. The name and address are free but all charges are subject to VAT.

BT SERVICES

Operator Services—100

For difficulties

For the following call services: alarm calls (booking charge £2.15); advice of duration and charge (charge 75p); charge card calls (charge 25p); freefone calls; international personal calls (charge £2.15–£4.30); transferred charge calls (charge 40p); subscriber controlled transfer. (All charges exclude VAT).

International Operator—155

Directory Enquiries:-

For numbers in the London postal area, 142.

For numbers outside the London postal area including the Irish Republic, 192.

International Directory Enquiries—153

Emergency Services—999

Services include: fire service; police service; ambulance service; coastguard; lifeboat; cave rescue; mountain rescue.

Faults—151

Telemessage—100 (190 in London, Birmingham and Glasgow).

International Telemessage—100 (190 in London, Birmingham and Glasgow). The service is only available to the USA.

International Telegrams—100 (190 in London, Birmingham and Glasgow). The service is available worldwide.

Maritime Services—100. Includes Ship's Telegram Service and Ship's Telephone Service.

BT Inmarsat Satellite Service—155

All other call enquiries—191

INTERNATIONAL POST AND TELEPHONE CODES

The table below includes airmail letter zones for countries outside Europe (1 or 2). Destinations to which European airmail letter rates apply are indicated by *e*, or by *ec* for European Community destinations (*see* p. 1059). (*Source: Post Office*)

International dialling codes are composed of four elements which are dialled in sequence: (i) the international code; (ii) the country code (*see* below); (iii) the area code; (iv) the customer's number. Calls to some countries (indicated by † below) must be made via the international operator. (*Source: BT*)

Country	Airmail zone	IDD code from UK	IDD code to UK
Afghanistan	1	†	†
Albania	e	010 355	†
Algeria	1	010 213	00p44
Andorra	ec	010 33 628	0p44
Angola	1	010 244	†
Anguilla	1	010 1 809	001 44
Antigua and Barbuda	1	010 1 809	011 44
Argentina	1	010 54	00 44
Aruba	1	010 297	†
Ascension Island	1	010 247	
Australia	2	010 61	00 11 44
Austria	e	010 43	00 44
Azores	ec	010 351	00 44
Bahamas	1	010 1 809	011 44
Bahrain	1	010 973	0 44
Bangladesh	1	010 880	00 44
Barbados	1	010 1 809	011 44
Belgium	ec	010 32	00p44*
Belize	1	010 501	†
Benin	1	010 229	00 p 44
Bermuda	1	010 1 809	1 44
Bhutan	1	010 975	00 44
Bolivia	1	010 591	00 44
Botswana	1	010 267	00 44
Brazil	1	010 55	00 44
British Virgin Islands	1	010 1 809 49	011 44
Brunei	1	010 673	00 44
Bulgaria	e	010 359	00 44
Burkina	1	010 226	
Burundi	1	010 257	90 44
Cambodia	1	†	†
Cameroon	1	010 237	00 44
Canada	1	010 1	011 44
Canary Islands	ec	010 34	07p44
Cape Verde	e	010 238	†
Cayman Islands	1	010 1 809	0 44
Central African Republic	1	010 236	†
Chad	1	010 235	†
Chile	1	010 56	00 44
China	2	010 86	00 44
Colombia	1	010 57	90 44
Comoros	1	†	†
Congo	1	010 242	00 44
Cook Islands	2	010 682	00 44
Costa Rica	1	010 506	00 44
Côte d'Ivoire	1	010 225	00 44
Cuba	1	010 53	
Cyprus	e	010 357	00 44
Czechoslovakia	e	010 42	00 44
Denmark	ec	010 45	009 44
Djibouti	1	010 253	00 44
Dominica	1	010 1 809	011 44
Dominican Republic	1	010 1 809	†
Ecuador	1	010 593	00 44
Egypt	1	010 20	00 44
Equatorial Guinea	1	010 240	†
Ethiopia	1	010 251	
Falkland Islands	1	010 500	01 44
Faroe Islands	e	010 298	009 44
Fiji	2	010 679	05 44
Finland	e	010 358	990 44
France	ec	010 33	19p44°
French Guiana	1	010 594	†
French Polynesia	2	010 689	00 44

e Europe. *ec* European Community. † Calls must be made via the international operator. *p* A pause in dialling is necessary whilst waiting for a second tone. * *p* only in Bruges, Ostende and Veurne. ° The second tone may not always be audible.

Country	Airmail zone	IDD code from UK	IDD code to UK
Gabon	1	010 241	00 44
The Gambia	1	010 220	00 44
Germany, East	e	010 37	000 44§
Germany, West	ec	010 49	00 44
Ghana	1	010 233	
Gibraltar	ec	010 350	00 44
Greece	ec	010 30	00 44
Greenland	e	010 299	009 44
Grenada	1	010 1 809	011 44
Guadeloupe	1	010 590	†
Guam	2	010 671	00 44
Guatemala	1	010 502	00 44
Guinea	1	010 224	†
Guinea-Bissau	1	010 245	†
Guyana	1	010 592	011 44
Haiti	1	010 509	†
Honduras	1	010 504	00 44
Hong Kong	1	010 852	001 44
Hungary	e	010 36	00 44
Iceland	e	010 354	90 44
India	1	010 91	00 44
Indonesia	1	010 62	00 44
Iran	1	010 98	00 44
Iraq	1	010 964	00 44
Ireland, Republic of	ec	010 353	
Dublin		0001	
Israel	1	010 972	00 44
Italy	ec	010 39	00 44
Jamaica	1	010 1 809	†
Japan	2	010 81	001 44
Jordan	1	010 962	00 44 varies
Kenya	1	010 254	000 44
Kiribati	2	010 686	09 44
Korea, North	2	010 850	†
Korea, South	2	010 82	001 44
Kuwait	1	010 965	00 44
Laos	1	†	†
Lebanon	1	010 961	00 44
Lesotho	1	010 266	00 44
Liberia	1	010 231	00 44
Libya	1	010 218	00 44
Liechtenstein	e	010 41 75	00 44
Luxembourg	ec	010 352	00 44
Macao	1	010 853	00 44
Madagascar	1	010 261	†
Madeira	ec	010 351 91	00 44*
Malawi	1	010 265	101 44
Malaysia	1	010 60	00 44
Maldives	1	010 960	
Mali	1	010 223	00 44
Malta	e	010 356	00 44
Martinique	1	010 596	†
Mauritania	1	010 222	†
Mauritius	1	010 230	
Mexico	1	010 52	98 44
Monaco	ec	010 33 93	19p44
Mongolia	2	†	†
Montserrat	1	010 1 809	†
Morocco	1	010 212	00p44
Mozambique	1	010 258	†
Myanmar	1	010 95	†
Namibia	1	010 264	091 44
Nauru	2	010 674	00 44
Nepal	1	010 977	00 44
Netherlands	ec	010 31	09p44
Netherlands Antilles	1	010 599	00 44
New Caledonia	2	010 687	00 44
New Zealand	2	010 64	00 44
Nicaragua	1	010 505	00 44
Niger	1	010 227	00 44
Nigeria	1	010 234	009 44

e Europe. *ec* European Community. † Calls must be made via the international operator. *p* A pause in dialling is necessary whilst waiting for a second tone. § From Berlin, Cottbus, Erfurt, Frankfurt (Oder), Gera, Halle, Salle, Leipzig, Magdeburg, Neubrandenburg and Suhl, dial 06 44. * Varies in some areas.

Country	Airmail zone	IDD code from UK	IDD code to UK
Norfolk Island	2	010 672	
Norway	e	010 47	095 44
Oman	1	010 968	00 44
Pakistan	1	010 92	00 44
Panama	1	010 507	00 44
Papua New Guinea	2	010 675	31 44
Paraguay	1	010 595	002 or 003 44
Peru	1	010 51	00 44
Philippines	2	010 63	00 44
Poland	e	010 48	0p044
Portugal	ec	010 351	00 44
Puerto Rico	1	010 1 809	135 44
Qatar	1	010 974	044
Réunion	1	010 262	19p44
Romania	e	010 40	
Rwanda	1	010 250	†
St Helena	1	010 290	†
St Kitts and Nevis	1	010 1 809	†
St Lucia	1	010 1 809	0 44
St Pierre and Miquelon	1	010 508	†
St Vincent and the Grenadines	1	010 1 809	0 44
El Salvador	1	010 503	00 44
Samoa, American	2	010 684	144
San Marino	ec	010 39 549	00 44
São Tomé and Príncipe	1	010 239	†
Saudi Arabia	1	010 966	00 44
Senegal	1	010 221	00p44
Seychelles	1	010 248	0 44
Sierra Leone	1	010 232	†
Singapore	1	010 65	005 44
Solomon Islands	2	010 677	00 44
Somalia	1	010 252	†
South Africa	1	010 27	09 44
Spain	ec	010 34	07p44
Sri Lanka	1	010 94	00 44
Sudan	1	010 249	†
Suriname	1	010 597	001 44
Swaziland	1	010 268	00 44
Sweden	e	010 46	009 44p
Switzerland	e	010 41	00 44
Syria	1	010 963	00 44
Taiwan	2	010 886	002 44
Tanzania	1	010 255	†
Thailand	1	010 66	001 44
Togo	1	010 228	
Tonga	2	010 676	0 44
Trinidad and Tobago	1	010 1 809	01 44
Tristan da Cunha	1	†	
Tunisia	1	010 216	00 44
Turkey	e	010 90	9p944
Turks and Caicos Islands	1	010 1 809	†
Tuvalu	2	010 688	†
Uganda	1	010 256	†
United Arab Emirates	1	010 971	00 44
Uruguay	1	010 598	00 44
USA	1	010 1	011 44
Alaska		010 1 907	
Hawaii		010 1 808	
USSR	e	010 7	810 44
Vanuatu	2	010 678	†
Vatican City State	ec	010 39 66982	
Venezuela	1	010 58	00 44
Vietnam	1	010 84	†
Virgin Islands (US)	1	010 1 809	011 44
Western Samoa	2	010 685	†
Yemen, North	1	010 967	00 44
Yemen, South	1	010 969	00 44
Yugoslavia	e	010 38	99 44
Zaire	1	010 243	00 44
Zambia	1	010 260	00 44
Zimbabwe	1	010 263	110 44

e Europe. *ec* European Community. † Calls must be made via the international operator. *p* A pause in dialling is necessary whilst waiting for a second tone.

BRITISH PASSPORT REGULATIONS

Applications for United Kingdom passports must be made on the forms obtainable at any of the Passport Offices (addresses given below) or at any main post office (except in Northern Ireland).

London.—Clive House, 70–78 Petty France, SW1H 9HD.

Liverpool.—India Buildings, Water Street, Liverpool L2 0QZ.

Newport.—Olympia House, Upper Dock Street, Newport, Gwent NP9 1XA.

Peterborough.—Passport Office, Aragon Court, Northminster Road, Peterborough PE1 1QG.

Glasgow.—3 Northgate, 96 Milton Street, Cowcaddens, Glasgow G4 0BT.

Belfast.—Passport Office, Hampton House, 47–53 High Street, Belfast BT1 2QS.

The above offices are open Monday–Friday 9 a.m. to 4.30 p.m. (9 a.m.–4 p.m. in London). The Passport Office, London, is also open for cases of special emergency (e.g. death or serious illness) arising outside normal office hours between 4 p.m. and 6 p.m. and on Saturdays between 10 a.m. and noon.

Completed application forms should be sent to one of the six passport offices, with photographs, supporting documents and the fee of £15, in the form of a cheque or postal order which should be crossed and made payable to the passport office.

A passport cannot be issued or extended on behalf of a person already abroad; such person should apply to the nearest British High Commission or Consulate.

United Kingdom passports are granted to:—
(i) British Citizens.
(ii) British Dependent Territories Citizens.
(iii) British Nationals (Overseas).
(iv) British Overseas Citizens.
(v) British Subjects.
(vi) British Protected Persons.

A passport granted to a child under 16 will normally be valid for an initial period of five years, after which it may be extended for a further five years with no extra charge. Children who have reached the age of 16 require separate passports. Their application must be signed by one of their parents.

A passport granted to a person over 16 will normally be valid for ten years and will not be renewable. Thereafter, or if at any time the passport contains no further space for visas, a new passport must be obtained.

The issue of passports including details of the holder's spouse has been discontinued, but existing family passports may be used until expiry.

A passport including particulars of the holder's spouse is not available for his/her use when he/she is travelling alone.

Completed passport applications should be countersigned by a Member of Parliament, Justice of the Peace, minister of religion, a professionally qualified person (e.g. doctor, engineer, lawyer, teacher), bank officer, established Civil Servant, police officer or a person of similar standing who has personally known the applicant for at least two years, and who is either a British Citizen, a British Dependent Territories Citizen, a British Overseas Citizen, a British subject or a citizen of a Commonwealth country. A relative must not countersign the application. The applicant's birth certificate or previous British passport, and other evidence in support of the statements made in the application must be produced.

In the case of children under the age of 16 requiring a separate passport, an application should be made by one of the parents on Form B.

If the applicant for a passport is a British national by naturalization or registration, the certificate of naturalization or registration must be produced with the application, unless the applicant holds a previous

United Kingdom passport issued after registration or naturalization.

United Kingdom passports are generally available for travel to all countries. The possession of a passport does not, however, exempt the holder from compliance with any immigration regulations in force in British or foreign countries, or from the necessity of obtaining a visa where required.

Photographs

Duplicate unmounted photographs of the applicant must be sent. These photographs should be printed on normal thin photographic paper. They should measure 45 mm by 35 mm (1·77 in. by 1·38 in.) and should be taken full face without a hat. One photograph should be certified as a true likeness of the applicant by the person who countersigns the application form.

Extension of Passports

Applications for the extension of United Kingdom passports which have been valid for less than ten years must be made on Form D.

94-page Passports

In 1973 a new type of passport became available. Intended to meet the needs of frequent travellers who fill standard passports well before the ten-year validity has expired, it contains 94 pages, is valid for ten years and costs £30.

British Visitor's Passports

A simplified form of travel document is available for British Citizens, British Dependent Territories Citizens or British Overseas Citizens wishing to pay short visits (not exceeding three months) to the following countries:

Andorra; Austria; Belgium; Bermuda; Denmark; Finland; France (including Corsica); Greece (and the Greek islands); Germany; Gibraltar; Iceland; Italy; Liechtenstein; Luxembourg; Malta; Monaco; Netherlands; Norway; Portugal (including Madeira and the Azores); San Marino; Spain (including Balearic and the Canary Islands); Sweden; Switzerland; Tunisia; Turkey; Yugoslavia.

A fee of £7·50 (£11·25 if particulars of spouse included) is charged for the issue of a British Visitor's Passport, which is valid for 12 months, cannot be amended and is not renewable. On expiry, application should be made for a new passport if required. Particulars of an applicant's spouse and/or children under 16 years can be included at the time of issue only. A child of 8 years of age and over is eligible to hold a British Visitor's Passport. Applications for, or including, a person under 18 years of age (unless married or serving in HM Forces) must be countersigned by the legal guardian.

British Visitor's Passports are obtainable by application on Form VP (from any main post office except in Northern Ireland). Applicants in England, Scotland and Wales should take the completed form in person to any main post office which will normally issue the passport without further delay; applicants in Northern Ireland to the Passport Office, Belfast, from whom application forms may also be obtained. British Visitor's Passports are not obtainable from passport offices other than Belfast.

Two recent passport photographs will be required of the applicant; photographs of his/her spouse and children included on the British Visitor's Passport are not required. Size of photographs must be 50 mm by 38 mm (2 in. × 1½ in.). They should be unmounted and must be printed on normal thin photographic paper. No visas are required on British Visitor's Passports. Applicants must also produce for the purpose of identification the documents listed on the application form.

VISAS

The visa requirements of a country may vary depending upon the purpose or the length of the visit. Visa regulations are also liable to change, sometimes at short notice, and enquiries should always be made at the Consulate or Embassy concerned (addresses and telephone numbers are given in the **Commonwealth** and **Foreign Countries** sections).

For entry for tourist purposes into the following countries a visa or permit may be required: Afghanistan; Albania; Algeria; Angola; Australia; Benin; Bhutan; Bulgaria; Burkina; Burundi; Cameroon Republic; Cape Verde; Central African Republic; Chad; China; Congo; Czechoslovakia; Djibouti; Egypt; Equatorial Guinea; Ethiopia; Gabon; Ghana; Guatemala; Guinea; Guinea Bissau; Guyana; Haiti; Hong Kong; India; Indonesia; Iran; Iraq; Jordan; Kuwait; Laos; Lebanon; Liberia; Libya; Madagascar; Mali; Mauritania; Mongolia; Mozambique; Myanmar; Nepal; Nigeria; Oman; Pakistan; Papua New Guinea; Philippines; Poland; Romania; Rwanda; Saudi Arabia; Senegal; Sierra Leone; Somali Democratic Republic; Sudan; Syria; Turkey; Uganda; USSR; Vietnam; Yemeni Republic; Zaire.

WORK AND BUSINESS OVERSEAS

A passport issued after December 31, 1982 showing the holder's national status as British citizen will secure for the holder the right to take employment or to establish himself/herself in business or other self-employed activity in another member state of the European Community (except Spain and Portugal). A passport bearing the endorsement 'holder has the right of abode in the United Kingdom' where the holder so qualifies will also secure the same right. Employment permits are required in most other countries, even for casual labour. The nearest representative of the country concerned should be consulted. Local employment offices have a booklet entitled *Working Abroad*.

Those planning to travel abroad on export business are advised to contact the Department of Trade and Industry–British Overseas Trade Board, 1 Victoria Street, London SW1H 0ET or its regional offices in London, Birmingham, Bristol, Cambridge, Leeds, Manchester, Newcastle upon Tyne and Nottingham. In Wales, contact the Welsh Office Industry Division, Cathays Park, Cardiff CF1 3NQ; in Scotland, the Scottish Office Industry Department, Alhambra House, 45 Waterloo Street, Glasgow G2 6AT; in Northern Ireland, the Industrial Development Board for Northern Ireland, Department of Economic Development, Netherleigh, Massey Avenue, Belfast BT4 2JP. These offices will send advance notification of visits to the Commercial Section of the relevant Consulate or Embassy, and can offer advice and information about the markets to be visited.

VACCINATION

In very general terms vaccination for protection against cholera, typhoid and polio are recommended for all countries outside Europe, except North America, Australia and New Zealand. Protection, in the form of tablets, is advised for malaria similarly.

Vaccination against yellow fever is essential for entry into Benin, Burkina, Cameroon, Central African Republic, Chad, Congo, Côte d'Ivoire, French Guiana, The Gambia, Ghana, Liberia, Mali, Mauritania, Niger, Panama, Rwanda, São Tomé and Príncipe, Senegal, Sierra Leone, Sudan, Tanzania, Togo and Uganda, and is recommended for most other African and South American countries. Fuller details are set out in Department of Health leaflet SA 40, *The Traveller's Guide to Health*. For up-to-date information about vaccination requirements, contact one of the following health departments: ENGLAND—Communicable Disease Surveillance Centre, 61 Colindale Avenue, London NW9 5EQ (081-200 4400).

WALES—Welsh Office, Cathays Park, Cardiff CF1 3NQ (0222-825111).

SCOTLAND—Scottish Home and Health Department, St Andrew's House, Edinburgh EH1 3DE (031-556 8501) or the Communicable Diseases (Scotland) Unit, Ruchill Hospital, Bilsland Drive, Glasgow G20 9NB (041-946 7120).

NORTHERN IRELAND—DHSS, Dundonald House, Upper Newtownards Road, Belfast BT4 3SF (0232-63939).

Your doctor should be consulted at least eight weeks before departure, and will advise you and arrange vaccinations. If children will be travelling outside Europe, North America, Australia and New Zealand the doctor should be informed, especially if they have not completed their full course of childhood immunization.

Details of free or reduced cost emergency medical treatment when visiting other European countries, Australia, British Dependent Territories, Hong Kong or New Zealand are set out in leaflet T1, available from some travel agents, local post offices or the Health Publications Unit, No. 2 Site, Manchester Road, Heywood, Lancs. OL10 2PZ.

DUTY AND TAX-FREE ALLOWANCES

You are entitled to the allowances in either of the columns below (but not both) for any category of goods, as represented by the boxes (*see* Notes on Allowances). Passengers under 17 are not, however, entitled to tobacco and drinks allowances.

Column 1	Column 2
Goods obtained duty and tax-free in the EC, or duty and tax-free on a ship or aircraft, or goods obtained outside the EC.	Goods obtained duty and tax paid in the EC.

Column 1	Column 2
Tobacco goods 200 cigarettes **or** 100 cigarillos **or** 50 cigars **or** 250 grammes of tobacco	**Tobacco goods** 300 cigarettes **or** 150 cigarillos **or** 75 cigars **or** 400 grammes of tobacco
Alcoholic drinks 2 litres of still table wine	**Alcoholic drinks** 5 litres of still table wine
plus	**plus**
1 litre over 22% vol. (e.g. spirits and strong liqueurs) **or** 2 litres not over 22% vol. (e.g. low strength liqueurs, fortified wine or sparkling wine) **or** A further 2 litres of still table wine	1·5 litres over 22% vol. (e.g. spirits and strong liqueurs) **or** 3 litres not over 22% vol. (e.g. low strength liqueurs, fortified wine, or sparkling wine) **or** A further 3 litres of still table wine
Perfume 50 grammes (60 cc or 2 fl oz)	**Perfume** 75 grammes (90 cc or 3 fl oz)
Toilet water 250 cc (9 fl oz)	**Toilet water** 375 cc (13 fl oz)
Other goods £32 worth	**Other goods** £420 worth

NB: A maximum of 50 litres of beer and 25 lighters may be imported duty-free, subject to the limitations of the 'Other goods' monetary allowance.

If you are visiting the United Kingdom for less than six months, you are also entitled to bring in, free of duty and tax, all personal effects (except tobacco goods, alcoholic drinks and perfume) which you intend to take with you when you leave.

Notes on allowances

(1) The countries of the European Community are Belgium, Denmark, France, Germany, Greece, the Irish Republic, Italy, Luxembourg, the Netherlands, Portugal, Spain (but not the Canary Islands), and the United Kingdom (but not the Channel Islands).

(2) The allowances apply only to goods carried and cleared by you at the time of your arrival.

(3) The allowances do not apply to goods brought in for sale or for other commercial purposes.

(4) Reduced allowances apply to certain persons crossing the Irish land boundary and to seamen and aircrew members.

(5) Whisky, gin, rum, brandy, vodka and most liqueurs normally exceed 22% vol. (38.8° proof) but advocaat, cassis, fraise, suze and aperitifs may be less. Fortified wines include port, sherry, vermouth and madeira. Sparkling wines include champagne, perelada, spumante and semi-sparkling wines. Still table wines include claret, Sauterne, Graves and Chianti. Burgundy, Chablis, hock and Moselle may be either sparkling or still, depending on manufacture.

(6) You may not mix goods obtained duty and tax-free or outside the EC with goods of the same category (as represented by the boxes) obtained duty and tax paid in the EC to obtain the higher allowance, e.g. you will not get the higher allowance for tobacco goods if any of the items in that category were obtained duty and tax-free or outside the EC.

(7) Where there are alternative quantities within a category of goods they may be apportioned. For example, 150 cigarettes (half allowance) plus 75 cigarillos (half allowance).

(8) One litre is approximately 1¾ pints or 35 fl oz.

(9) A cigarillo is a cigar with a maximum weight of 3 grammes.

PROHIBITED AND RESTRICTED GOODS

Customs officers are able to provide full information. This is a list of more frequently met items:

Controlled drugs (such as opium, heroin, morphine, cocaine, cannabis, amphetamines, lysergide (LSD) and barbiturates).

Firearms (including gas pistols, electric shock batons and similar weapons), ammunition and explosives (including fireworks).

Offensive weapons (including certain types of

knife, swordsticks, knuckle-dusters and other martial arts equipment).

Counterfeit currency and other counterfeit goods, such as fake watches and sports shirts; goods bearing a false indication of their place of manufacture or in breach of United Kingdom copyright.

Obscene books, magazines, films, videotapes, laser discs, computer discs and other material; horror comics.

Radio transmitters (walkie-talkies, Citizen's Band radios, cordless telephones, etc.) not approved for use in the UK.

Meat and poultry, and most of their products, including ham, bacon, sausage, paté, eggs, milk and cream. (Exception: 1 kg per passenger of fully cooked meat or poultrymeat products in cans or other hermetically-sealed containers of glass or foil).

Plants, parts thereof and plant produce, including trees and shrubs, soil, potatoes and certain other vegetables, fruit, bulbs and seeds.

Anglers' lead weights.

Animals and birds, whether alive or dead (e.g. stuffed), certain fish and fish eggs, whether live or dead, or bees; certain articles derived from rare species including furskins, ivory, reptile leather and goods made from them.

NB: Cats, dogs and other mammals, including mice, rats, guinea-pigs and gerbils, must not be landed unless a British import licence (rabies) has previously been issued.

EXPORT CONTROL

The following are some of the goods subject to export control and should be declared to the customs officer. There are formalities to be completed in respect of these goods prior to arrival at the port of exportation and further information is available through any local office of Customs and Excise (address in the telephone directory).

● Controlled drugs.
● Firearms and ammunition.
● Photographic material over 60 years old and valued at £500 or more.
● Portraits (including sculptures) of British historical personages which are over 50 years old and valued at £6,000 or more.
● Antiques, collectors' items, etc. (including paintings and other works of art) over 50 years old and valued at £30,000 or more.
● Certain archaeological material.
● Most live animals and birds, and items made from animals occurring wild in the UK.

HM COASTGUARD

Founded in 1822, originally to guard the coasts against smuggling, HM Coastguard's role today is the very different one of dedication to the guarding and saving of all life at sea. Administered by the Department of Transport, it is responsible for co-ordinating all civil marine search and rescue operations around the 2,500 mile coastline of Great Britain and Northern Ireland and 1,200 miles into the Atlantic, as well as co-operating with search and rescue organizations of neighbouring countries both in western Europe and around the Atlantic seaboard. In addition, the Service maintains a 24-hour radar watch on the Dover Strait, providing a Channel navigation information service for all shipping in one of the busiest sea lanes in the world.

Since 1978 HM Coastguard has been organized into six regions, each with a Regional Controller, operating from a Maritime Rescue Co-ordination Centre. Each region is subdivided into districts under District Controllers, operating from Maritime Rescue Sub-Centres. In all there are 21 of these centres. They are on 24-hour watch and are fitted with a comprehensive range of communications and rescue equipment. They are supported by some 350 smaller stations manned by Auxiliary Coastguards under the direction of Regulars, each of which keeps its parent centre fully informed of day-to-day casualty risk, particularly on the more remote danger spots around the coast.

Between January 1 and December 31, 1990, the 500 Regular and 4,500 Auxiliary Coastguards co-ordinated 7,076 incidents requiring search and rescue facilities, resulting in assistance being given to 13,474 persons. All distress telephone and radio calls are centralized on the 21 centres, which are on the alert for people or vessels in distress, shipping hazards and oil slicks. Using their modern telecommunications equipment and the facilities provided by British Telecom's coast radio stations, they can alert and co-ordinate the most appropriate rescue facilities; RNLI lifeboats, Royal Navy, RAF or Coastguard helicopters, fixed-wing aircraft, naval vessels, ships in the vicinity, or Coastguard shore and cliff rescue teams.

For those who regularly sail in local waters or make longer passages, the Coastguard Yacht and Boat Safety Scheme provides a valuable free service. Its aim is to give the Coastguard a record of the details of craft, their normal operating areas and their passage plans. Yacht and Boat Safety Scheme cards are available from all Coastguard stations, harbourmasters' offices, and most yacht clubs and marinas.

Members of the public who see an accident or a potentially dangerous incident on or around the coast should without hesitation dial 999 and ask for the Coastguard.

SPORT 1990–91

ALPINE SKIING
World Cup
MEN

Downhill.—F. Heinzer (Switzerland), 159 pts
Slalom.—M. Girardelli (Luxembourg), 110 pts
Giant Slalom.—A. Tomba (Italy), 152 pts
Super Giant Slalom.—F. Heinzer (Switzerland), 40 pts
Overall.—M. Girardelli (Luxembourg), 242 pts

WOMEN

Downhill.—C. Bournissen (Switzerland), 140 pts
Slalom.—P. Kronberger (Austria), 83 pts
Giant Slalom.—V Schneider (Switzerland), 105 pts
Super Giant Slalom.—C. Merle (France), 88 pts
Overall.—P. Kronberger (Austria), 312 pts

Nations Cup.—1. Austria; 2. Switzerland; 3. Germany.

World Championships 1991
(Saalbach, Austria)
MEN

Downhill.—F. Heinzer (Switzerland), 1m 54·91s

Slalom.—M. Girardelli (Luxembourg), 1m 55·38s
Giant Slalom.—R. Nierlich (Austria), 2m 29·94s
Super Giant Slalom.—S. Eberharter (Austria), 1m 26·73s

WOMEN

Downhill.—P. Kronberger (Austria), 1m 29·12s
Slalom.—V. Schneider (Switzerland), 1m 25·90s
Giant Slalom.—P. Wiberg (Sweden), 2m 07·45s
Super Giant Slalom.—U. Maier (Austria), 1m 08·72s

AMERICAN FOOTBALL 1991

XXV American Superbowl (Tampa, Florida, Jan. 27).—New York Giants beat Buffalo Bills 20–19.
World League of American Football Bowl (Wembley, June 9).—London Monarchs beat Barcelona Dragons 21–0.
American Bowl (Wembley, July 20).—Buffalo Bills beat Philadelphia Eagles 17–13.
Coca Cola League final (Alexander Stadium, Birmingham, Aug. 4).—Birmingham Bulls beat London Olympians 39–38.

ANGLING
NATIONAL COARSE CHAMPIONSHIPS

Year	Venue	No. of teams	Individual Winner	Weight kg	Team Winners	Points	Division
1990	R. Witham	89	S. Cheetham (Middle Nene)	20·390	Trevs AS	935	1
,,	Keadby Canal	85	S. Cocksey (Disley & New Mills)	9·810	Milton Keynes	803	2
,,	Royal Military Canal	84	K. Locke (Woolwich & District)	5·790	Bowlers AS	803	3
,,	R. Nene	82	M. Cheesman (Epsom)	17·350	Daiwa Goldthorpe	854	4
,,	R. Trent	98	H. Clapham (Rossington AC)	13·690	Avon Bait	1027	5
,,	Grand Union Canal	47	S. Allen/I. Walton (Staffs.)	2·840	Milton Keynes	502	Jnr

ASSOCIATION FOOTBALL
League Competitions
ENGLAND AND WALES

Division 1.—1. Arsenal 83 pts (2 points deducted—*see* Events p. 503); 2. Liverpool 76 pts. *Relegated,* Sunderland 34 pts; Derby County 24 pts.
Division 2.—1. Oldham Athletic 88 pts; 2. West Ham 87 pts; 3. Sheffield Wednesday 82 pts. *Fourth promotion place:* Notts County. *Relegated,* West Bromwich Albion 48 pts; Hull City 45 pts.
Division 3.—1. Cambridge United 86 pts; 2. Southend United 85 pts; 3. Grimsby Town 83 pts. *Fourth promotion place:* Tranmere Rovers. *Relegated,* Crewe Alexandra 44 pts; Rotherham United 42 pts; Mansfield Town 38 pts.
Division 4.—1. Darlington 83 pts; 2. Stockport County 82 pts; 3. Hartlepool United 82 pts; 4. Peterborough United 80 pts. *Fifth promotion place:* Torquay United. *No relegation.*
GM Vauxhall Conference.—*Promoted,* Barnet 87 pts. *Relegated,* Sutton United 39 pts; Fisher 30 pts.

SCOTLAND

Premier Division.—1. Rangers 55 pts; 2. Aberdeen 53 pts. *No relegation.*
Division 1.—1. Falkirk 54 pts; Airdrieonians 53 pts. *Relegated,* Clyde 27 pts; Brechin City 24 pts.
Division 2.—1. Stirling Albion 54 pts; 2. Montrose 46 pts. *No relegation.*

Cup Competitions
ENGLAND

FA Cup final 1991 (Wembley, May 8).—Tottenham Hotspur beat Nottingham Forest 2–1 a.e.t.
Rumbelows League Cup final 1991.—Sheffield Wednesday beat Manchester Utd. 1–0.
Zenith Data Systems Cup final 1991.—Crystal Palace beat Everton 4–1.
Leyland Daf Cup final 1991.—Birmingham City beat Tranmere Rovers 3–2.
FA Vase final 1991.—Gresley Rovers 4, Guiseley 4 a.e.t. *Replay.*—Guiseley beat Gresley Rovers 3–1.

FA Trophy final 1991.—Wycombe Wanderers beat Kidderminster Harriers 2–1.

Arthur Dunn Cup final 1991.—Old Carthusians 1, Old Reptonians 1 a.e.t. *Replay.*—Old Reptonians beat Old Carthusians 4–0.

Women's FA Cup final 1991.—Millwall Lionesses beat Doncaster Belles 1–0.

WALES

Welsh FA Cup final 1991 (Cardiff, May 19).—Swansea beat Wrexham 2–0.

SCOTLAND

Scottish FA Cup final 1991 (Hampden, May 8).—Motherwell beat Dundee United 4–3 a.e.t.

Skol Cup final 1990.—Rangers beat Celtic 2–1 a.e.t.

Centenary Cup Final 1990.—Dundee beat Ayr Utd. 3–2.

EUROPE

European Cup final 1991 (Bari).—Marseille 0 Red Star Belgrade 0 a.e.t. Red Star Belgrade won 5–3 on penalties.

European Cup-Winners Cup final 1991 (Rotterdam).—Manchester Utd. beat Barcelona 2–1.

UEFA Cup final 1991.— Inter Milan beat AS Roma 2–1 on agg.

Charity Shield 1990.—Liverpool and Manchester Utd. drew 1–1.

Internationals

1990		
Sept. 11	Copenhagen:	Denmark 1, Wales 0.
Sept. 12	Wembley:	England 1, Hungary 0.
1991		
Feb. 5	Belfast:	N. Ireland 3, Poland 1.
Feb. 6	Wembley:	England 2, Cameroon 0.
	Wrexham:	Wales 0, Rep. of Ireland 3.
	Ibrox Park:	Scotland 0, USSR 1.
May 1	Cardiff:	Wales 1, Iceland 0.
May 29	Radom:	Poland 0, Wales 0.
June 1	Sydney:	Australia 0, England 1.
June 3	Auckland:	New Zealand 0, England 1.
June 8	Wellington:	New Zealand 0, England 2.
June 12	Kuala Lumpur:	Malaysia 2, England 4.
Sept 11	Wembley:	England 0, Germany 1.
	Cardiff:	Wales 1, Brazil 0.

ENGLAND CHALLENGE CUP

May 21	Wembley:	England 3, USSR 1.
May 23	Old Trafford:	Argentina 1, USSR 1.
May 25	Wembley:	England 2, Argentina 2.
		1. England 2. Argentina 3. USSR

European Cup

(Qualifying Rounds)

1990		
Sept. 12	Hampden:	Scotland 2, Romania 1.
	Belfast:	N. Ireland 0, Yugoslavia 2.
Oct. 17	Wembley:	England 2, Poland 0.
	Cardiff:	Wales 3, Belgium 1.
	Hampden:	Scotland 2, Switzerland 1.
	Belfast:	N. Ireland 1, Denmark 1.
Nov. 14	Dublin:	Rep. of Ireland 1, England 1.
	L'bourg:	Luxembourg 0, Wales 1.
	Sofia:	Bulgaria 1, Scotland 1.
	Vienna:	Austria 0, N. Ireland 0.

1991		
Mar. 27	Wembley:	England 1, Rep. of Ireland 1.
	Brussels:	Belgium 1, Wales 1.
	Hampden:	Scotland 1, Bulgaria 1.
	Belgrade:	Yugoslavia 4, N. Ireland 1.
May 1	Izmir:	Turkey 0, England 1.
	Cardiff:	Wales 1, Iceland 0.
	Serravalle:	San Marino 0, Scotland 2.
	Belfast:	N. Ireland 1, Faroe Islands 1.
	Dublin:	Rep of Ireland 0, Poland 0.
June 5	Cardiff:	Wales 1, Germany 0.
Sept. 11	Berne:	Switzerland 2, Scotland 2.
	Landskrona, Sweden:	Faroe Islands 0, N. Ireland 5.

ATHLETICS, 1991

AAA/WAAA Indoor Championships

Held at Cosford, February 2–3, 1991

Men's Events

metres	min.	sec.
60—L. Christie (TVH)		6·63
200—L. Christie (TVH)		21·28
400—A. Mafe (London Irish)		47·18
800—M. Steele (Longwood)	1	49·43
1,500—M. Scruton (Sale)	3	51·98
3,000—R. Denmark (Gateshead)	7	54·83
60 hurdles—T. Kearns (Ireland)		7·73
		metres
High jump—G. Parsons (Blue Circle)		2·24
Pole vault—P. Widen (Sweden)		5·51
Long jump—V. George (USA)		7·84
Triple jump—J. Sweeney (TVH)		15·93
Shot—P. Edwards (RAF)		18·58

Women's Events

metres	min.	sec.
60—S. Douglas (Milton Keynes)		7·25
200—A. Williams (Trinidad)		24·08
400—S. Douglas (Stretford)		55·20
800—P. Fryer (Sale)	2	08·96
1,500—J. Dering (Andover)	4	13·31
3,000—S. McGeorge (Brighton)	9	05·99
60 hurdles—L-A. Skeete (Swindon)		8·19
		metres
High jump—D. Marti (Bromley)		1·94
Long jump—K. Hagger (Essex)		6·39
Triple jump—M. Griffith (Windsor)		13·07
Shot—J. Oakes (Croydon)		17·83

National Cross-Country Championships (Women)

Held at Birkenhead, February 16, 1991

	min.	sec.
1. A. Whitcombe (Parkside)	19	55
2. A. Wyeth (Parkside)	20	09
3. S. Ellis (Birchfield)	20	14
Team result: 1. Parkside, 50 pts.		

National Cross-Country Championships (Men)

Held at Luton, Feburary 23, 1991

	min.	sec.
1. R. Nerurkar (Bingley)	43	11
2. D. Lewis (Rossendale)	43	21
3. M. McLoughlin (Liverpool Pembroke)	43	29
Team result: 1. Bingley, 175 pts.		

Great Britain v. USA

Held at Glasgow, March 3, 1991

Men's Events

metres	min.	sec.
60—L. Christie (GB)		6·55
200—J. Regis (GB)		20·83
400—R. Pierre (USA)		47·55
800—M. Steele (GB)	1	48·46
1 *mile*—S. Crabb (GB)	4	00·37
3,000—M. Rowland (GB)	8	03·68
60 *hurdles*—A. Blake (USA)		7·65
3,000 *walk*—D. Fournier (USA)	11	34·24
4 × 200 *relay*—Great Britain	1	22·11
	metres	
High jump—R. Noji (USA)		2·26
Pole vault—K. Tarpenning (USA)		5·65
Long jump—J. Greene (USA)		7·68
Triple jump—D. McFadgen (USA)		16·15
Shot—R. Backes (USA)		19·91

USA 82 pts, Great Britain 68.

Women's Events

metres	min.	sec.
60—T. Neighbours (USA)		7·26
200—R. Stevens (USA)		23·67
400—R. Stevens (USA)		53·07
800—M. Rainey (USA)	2	06·35
1 *mile*—A. Hill (USA)	4	34·94
3,000—E. McColgan (GB)	8	57·82
60 *hurdles*—K. McKenzie (USA)		8·05
3,000 *walk*—V. Herazo (USA)	13	28·05
4 × 400 *relay*—USA	3	34·66
	metres	
High jump—D. Marti (GB)		1·91
Long jump—F. May (GB)		6·61
Shot—C. Price (USA)		18·56

USA 68 pts, Great Britain 59.

World Indoor Championships

Held at Seville, Spain, March 8–10, 1991

Men's Events

metres	min.	sec.
60—A. Cason (USA)		6·54
200—N. Antonov (Bulgaria)		20·67
400—D. Morris (Jamaica)		46·17
800—P. Ereng (Kenya)	1	47·08
1,500—N. Morceli (Algeria)	3	41·57
3,000—F. O'Mara (Ireland)	7	41·14
60 *hurdles*—G. Foster (USA)		7·45
5,000 *walk*—M. Shchennikov (USSR)	18	23·55
4 × 400 *relay*—Germany	3	03·05
	metres	
High jump—H. Conway (USA)		2·40
Pole vault—S. Bubka (USSR)		6·00
Long jump—D. Haaf (Germany)		8·15
Triple jump—I. Lapshin (USSR)		17·31
Shot—W. Gunthor (Switzerland)		21·17

Women's Events

metres	min.	sec.
60—I. Sergeyeva (USSR)		7·02
200—M. Ottey (Jamaica)		22·24
400—D. Dixon (USA)		50·64
800—C. Wachtel (Germany)	2	01·51
1,500—L. Rogacheva (USSR)	4	05·09
3,000—M-P. Duros (France)	8	50·69
60 *hurdles*—L. Narozhilenko (USSR)		7·88
3,000 *walk*—B. Anders (Germany)	11	50·90
4 × 400 *relay*—Germany	3	27·22
	metres	
High jump—H. Henkel (Germany)		2·00
Long jump—L. Berezhnaya (USSR)		6·84
Shot—Xinmei Sui (China)		20·54

RWA National 20 km Walk (Men)

Held at Sheffield, March 17, 1991

	hr.	min.	sec.
1. M. Easton (Surrey)	1	25	36
2. M. Rush (Lakeland)	1	26	01
3. A. Penn (Coventry)	1	26	05

Team result: 1. Coventry, 44 pts.

National 10 km Walk (Women)

Held at Sheffield, March 17, 1991

	min.	sec.
1. B. Sworowski (Sheffield)	47	23
2. H. Elleker (Sheffield)	47	26
3. V. Lupton (Sheffield)	47	30

Team result: 1. Sheffield, 6 pts.

World Cross-Country Championships

Held at Antwerp, Belgium, March 24, 1991

Men	min.	sec.
1. K. Skah (Morocco)	33	53
2. M. Tanui (Kenya)	33	54
3. S. Karori (Kenya)	33	54
Team result: 1. Kenya		38 pts.
2. Ethiopia		104 pts.
3. Spain		198 pts.
Women	min.	sec.
1. L. Jennings (USA)	20	24
2. D. Tulu (Ethiopia)	20	27
3. E. McColgan (GB)	20	28
Team result: 1. Kenya		36 pts.
2. Ethiopia		36 pts.
3. USSR		48 pts.

London Marathon
(incorporating the World Cup)

Held April 21, 1991

Men	hr.	min.	sec.
1. I. Tolstikov (USSR)	2	09	17
2. M. Matias (Portugal)	2	10	21
3. J. Huruk (Poland)	2	10	21
Team result: Great Britain	6	34	59
Women	hr.	min.	sec.
1. R. Mota (Portugal)	2	26	14
2. F. Larrieu-Smith (USA)	2	27	35
3. V. Yegorova (USSR)	2	28	18
Team result: USSR	7	30	21

RWA National 10 Miles Walk (Men)

Held at Victoria Park, London, May 11, 1991

	hr.	min.	sec.
1. I. McCombie (Cambridge H.)	1	08	17
2. M. Easton (Surrey)	1	08	36
3. D. Stone (Steyning)	1	09	39

Team result: 1. Steyning, 33 pts.

National 15 km Walk (Women)

Held at Victoria Park, London, May 11, 1991

	hr.	min.	sec.
1. = V. Lupton (Sheffield)	1	12	32
1. = B. Sworowski (Sheffield)	1	12	32
3. H. Elleker (Sheffield)	1	15	17

Team result: 1. Sheffield, 6 pts.

IAAF World Walking Cup (Lugano Trophy)

Held at San José, USA, June 1–2, 1991

Men (20 km)	hr.	min.	sec.
1. M. Shchennikov (USSR)	1	20	43
2. E. Canto (Mexico)	1	20	46
3. T. Toutain (France)	1	20	56

Team result: 1. Italy, 263 pts.

Men (50 km)	hr.	min.	sec.
1. C. Mercenario (Mexico)	3	42	03
2. S. Baker (Australia)	3	46	36
3. R. Weigel (Germany)	3	47	50

Team result: 1. Italy, 517 pts.

Women (10 km)		min.	sec.
1. I. Strakhova (USSR)		43	55
2. G. Mendoza (Mexico)		44	09
3. E. Sajko (USSR)		44	11

Team result: 1. USSR, 203 pts.

RWA National 35 km Walk (Men)

Held at Sutton Park, June 8, 1991

	hr.	min.	sec.
1. S. Philips (Ilford)	2	55	21
2. D. Thorn (Coventry)	2	56	48
3. M. Smith (Coventry)	2	59	00

Team result: 1. Coventry, 19 pts.

United Kingdom Championships

Held at Cardiff, June 8–9, 1991

Men's Events

metres	min.	sec.
100—L. Christie (TVH)		10·39
200—J. Regis (Belgrave)		21·24
400—P. Sanders (Team Solent)		47·69
800—D. Sharpe (Jarrow)	1	50·31
1,500—S. Fairbrother (Haringey)	3	48·59
3,000—P. Elliott (Rotherham)	8	07·51
5,000—I. Hamer (Swansea)	13	49·86
3,000 *steeplechase*—P. McColgan (Dundee)	8	49·54
110 *hurdles*—D. Nelson (Wolverhampton)		13·88
400 *hurdles*—M. Robertson (Wolverhampton)		50·33
10,000 *walk*—S. Partington (Boundary)	42	26·28
		metres
High jump—D. Grant (Haringey)		2·20
Pole vault—A. Ashurst (Sale)		5·15
Long jump—M. Forsythe (Ballymena)		7·81
Triple jump—V. Samuels (Wolverhampton)		16·19
Shot—P. Edwards (Walton)		18·68
Discus—P. Mardle (Wolverhampton)		54·66
Hammer—P. Head (Newham)		73·64
Javelin—G. Jenson (Haringey)		76·90

Women's Events

metres	min.	sec.
100—B. Kinch (Hounslow)		11·63
200—L. Keough (Basingstoke)		24·25
400—S. Leigh (Stevenage)		53·55
800—P. Fryer (Sale)	2	05·43
1,500—A. Wyeth (Parkside)	4	14·98
3,000—E. McColgan (Dundee)	8	59·39
100 *hurdles*—L-A. Skeete (Swindon)		13·66
400 *hurdles*—J. Parker (Essex)		57·64
5,000 *walk*—V. Lupton (Sheffield)	22	51·38
		metres
High jump—L. Haggett (Croydon)		1·85
Long jump—F. May (Derby)		6·74

Shot—J. Oakes (Croydon)		18·37
Discus—J. McKernan (Lisburn)		53·14
Javelin—S. Gibson (Notts)		60·14

Great Britain v. Germany

Held at Crystal Palace, London, June 19, 1991

Men's Events

metres	min.	sec.
100—L. Christie (GB)		10·30
200—L. Christie (GB)		20·43
400—R. Black (GB)		44·91
800—T. McKean (GB)	1	46·81
1,500—H. Fuhlbrugge (Germany)	3	44·14
3,000—R. Denmark (GB)	7	47·42
3,000 *steeplechase*—A. Fischer (Germany)	8	34·00
110 *hurdles*—A. Jarrett (GB)		13·38
400 *hurdles*—K. Akabusi (GB)		49·02
4 × 100 *relay*—Great Britain		39·05
4 × 400 *relay*—Great Britain	3	04·01
		metres
High jump—S. Smith (GB)		2·28
Pole vault—B. Zintl (Germany)		5·40
Long jump—D. Haaf (Germany)		8·04
Triple jump—R. Jaros (Germany)		17·47
Shot—S-O. Buder (Germany)		19·58
Discus—L. Riedel (Germany)		65·82
Hammer—H. Weis (Germany)		77·62
Javelin—S. Backley (GB)		88·24

Great Britain 198 pts, Germany 197.

Women's Events

metres	min.	sec.
100—S. Douglas (GB)		11·55
200—S. Knoll (Germany)		23·56
400—L. Keough (GB)		51·81
800—C. Wachtel (Germany)	1	59·72
1,500—Y. Murray (GB)	4	18·25
3,000—E. McColgan (GB)	8	41·78
100 *hurdles*—K. Patzwahl (Germany)		13·22
400 *hurdles*—S. Gunnell (GB)		55·38
4 × 100 *relay*—Great Britain		44·29
4 × 400 *relay*—Germany	3	28·35
		metres
High jump—H. Henkel (Germany)		1·96
Long jump—H. Drechsler (Germany)		7·12
Shot—A. Kumbernuss (Germany)		19·44
Discus—I. Wyludda (Germany)		68·18
Javelin—P. Felke-Meyer (Germany)		68·26

Germany 169 pts, Great Britain 133.

European Cup

Held at Frankfurt, June 29–30, 1991

Men's Events

metres	min.	sec.
100—L. Christie (GB)		10·18
200—J-C. Trouabal (France)		20·60
400—R. Black (GB)		44·91
800—T. McKean (GB)	1	45·60
1,500—P. Elliott (GB)	3	43·39
5,000—S. Antibo (Italy)	13	21·68
10,000—E. Martin (GB)	28	00·53
3,000 *steeplechase*—A. Lambruschini (Italy)	8	29·62
110 *hurdles*—C. Jackson (GB)		13·31
400 *hurdles*—K. Akabusi (GB)		48·39
4 × 100 *relay*—France		38·67
4 × 400 *relay*—Great Britain	3	00·58
		metres
High jump—D. Grant (GB)		2·30
Pole vault—G. Yegorov (USSR)		5·60

Long jump—D. Haaf (Germany)		8·30
Triple jump—R. Jaros (Germany)		17·66
Shot—U. Timmermann (Germany)		20·26
Discus—A. Horvath (Hungary)		65·24
Hammer—I. Astapkovich (USSR)		81·60
Javelin—J. Zelezny (Czechoslovakia)		82·84

Team points: USSR 114 pts, Great Britain 110·5, Germany 108, Italy 106, France 98·5, Czechoslovakia 66·5, Hungary 62, Bulgaria 52·5.

Women's Events

metres	min.	sec.
100—I. Sergeyeva (USSR)		11·29
200—I. Sergeyeva (USSR)		22·48
400—M-J. Perec (France)		49·32
800—E. Kovacs (Romania)	1	59·01
1,500—D. Melinte (Romania)	4	00·83
3,000—M. Keszeg (Romania)	8	44·47
10,000—K. Ullrich (Germany)	31	03·62
100 *hurdles*—L. Narozhilenko (USSR)		12·55
400 *hurdles*—M. Ponomaryeva (USSR)		54·42
4 × 100 *relay*—USSR		42·51
4 × 400 *relay*—USSR	3	21·77
		metres
High jump—Y. Rodina (USSR)*		1·98
Long jump—H. Drechsler (Germany)		7·20
Shot—N. Lissovskaya (USSR)		21·12
Discus—I. Wyludda (Germany)		68·82
Javelin—T. Sanderson (GB)		65·18

*Disqualified after positive drugs test.

Team points: Germany 110 pts, USSR 105, Great Britain 82, Romania 71, France 62, Poland 55, Bulgaria 46, Hungary 44.

European Cup—Combined Events

Held at Helmond, Netherlands, July 6–7, 1991

Men	pts.
1. C. Plaziat (France)	8,518
2. C. Schenk (Germany)	8,402
3. A. Blondel (France)	8,211

Team result: Germany 24,350 pts.

Women	pts.
1. P. Beer (Germany)	6,383
2. H. Tischler (Germany)	6,366
3. A. Behmer (Germany)	6,274

Team result: Germany 19,023 pts.

National 50 km Walk

Held at Basildon, July 17, 1991

	hr.	min.	sec.
1. L. Morton (Sheffield)	4	15	48
2. C. Berwick (Leicester)	4	30	53
3. M. Smith (Coventry)	4	32	17

Team result: Coventry 29 pts.

National 5,000 m Walk (Women)

Held at Basildon, July 17, 1991

	min.	sec.
1. V. Lupton (Sheffield)	22	50
2. B. Sworowski (Sheffield)	22	56
3. S. Black (Birchfield)	23	48

Team result: Sheffield 10 pts.

Great Britain v. USSR

Held at Edinburgh, July 19, 1991

Men's Events

metres	min.	sec.
100—L. Christie (GB)		10·26
200—M. Rosswess (GB)		20·55

metres	min.	sec.
400—P. Sanders (GB)		46·06
800—T. McKean (GB)	1	47·16
1,500—P. Elliott (GB)	3	38·46
3,000—G. Staines (GB)	7	44·98
3,000 *steeplechase*—I. Konovalov (USSR)	8	30·34
110 *hurdles*—A. Jarrett (GB)		13·49
400 *hurdles*—K. Akabusi (GB)		48·79
4 × 100 *relay*—Great Britain		39·37
4 × 400 *relay*—Great Britain	3	05·36
		metres
High jump—D. Grant (GB)		2·20
Pole vault—M. Tarasov (USSR)		5·40
Long jump—V. Ochkan (USSR)		8·14
Triple jump—A. Kovalenko (USSR)		16·87
Shot—S. Nikolayev (USSR)		19·85
Discus—S. Lyakhov (USSR)		61·32
Hammer—V. Sidorenko (USSR)		78·82
Javelin—S. Backley (GB)		88·46

Great Britain 217 pts, USSR 173 pts.

Women's Events

metres	min.	sec.
100—T. Alekseyeva (USSR)		11·59
200—O. Styepicheva (USSR)		22·74
400—A. Yurchenko (USSR)		51·60
800—S Masterkova (USSR)	2	00·08
1,500—K. Wade (GB)	4	09·98
3,000—Y Murray (GB)	8	36·05
100 *hurdles*—K. Morley-Brown (GB)		13·29
400 *hurdles*—T. Kurochkina (USSR)		56·68
4 × 100 *relay*—USSR		44·40
4 × 400 *relay*—USSR	3	26·24
		metres
High jump—I. Babkova (USSR)		1·93
Long jump—Y. Senchukova (USSR)		6·78
Shot—S. Krivelyova (USSR)		20·27
Discus—L. Mikhalchenko (USSR)		67·94
Javelin—I. Kostyuchenkova (USSR)		64·46

USSR 183 pts, Great Britain 125 pts.

AAA/WAAA Championships

Held at Birmingham, July 26–27, 1991

Men's Events

metres	min.	sec.
100—L. Christie (TVH)		10·14
200—J. Drummond (USA)		20·61
400—D. Redmond (Birchfield)		46·07
800—T. McKean (Bellshill AC)	1	45·67
1,500—M. Yates (Newham & EB)	3	40·88
3,000—T. Hanlon (Reebok)	8	02·11
5,000—E Martin (Basildon)	13	32·99
3,000 *steeplechase*—C. Walker (Gateshead)	8	38·02
110 *hurdles*—D. Nelson (Wolverhampton)		13·55
400 *hurdles*—M. Robertson (Wolverhampton)		49·98
10 km *walk*—I. McCombie (Cambridge)	41	24·69
		metres
High jump—H. Conway (USA)		2·31
Pole vault—T. Bright (USA)		5·50
Long jump—B. Williams (Carnock)		7·94
Triple jump—W. Banks (USA)		16·60
Shot—P. Edwards (Belgrave)		18·92
Discus—W. Reiterer (Australia)		59·56
Hammer—S. Carlin (Australia)		72·58
Javelin—M. Hill (Leeds)		84·54

Held at Cardiff, June 9, 1991

	min.	sec.
10,000m—C. Thackeray (Hallamshire)	28	37·52

Held at Stoke, Aug. 3–4, 1991

Decathlon—E. Hollingsworth (Sheffield)		7,631 pts

Women's Events

metres		min.	sec.
100—E. Ashford (USA)............			11·15
200—S. Douglas (Milton Keynes)......			23·37
400—M. Malone (USA)...............			50·89
800—P. Fryer (Sale)		2	02·19
1,500—A. Williams (Sale)............		4	08·93
3,000—Y. Murray (ESPC)		8	46·47
100 *hurdles*—S. Gunnell (Essex Ladies)			13·02
400 *hurdles*—G. Retchakan (Thurrock)			55·67
5 km *walk*—B. Sworowski (Sheffield) ..		22	29·04
			metres
High jump—D. Marti (Bromley)			1·88
Long jump—F. May (Derby Ladies) ...			6·58
Triple jump—E. Finikin (Shaftesbury Barnet)			13·46
Shot—J. Oakes (Croydon)			18·24
Discus—J. McKernan (Lisburn)			57·76
Javelin—S. Gibson (Notts.)...........			57·34

Held at Cardiff, June 8, 1991

	min.	sec.
10,000m—S. Vivod (Yugoslavia)	33	04·60

Held at Stoke, Aug. 3-4, 1991

Heptathlon—C. Court (Birchfield).....	5,875 pts

World Championships

Held at Tokyo, Japan, Aug. 24-Sept. 1, 1991

Men's Events

metres	hr.	min.	sec.
100—C. Lewis (USA)			9·86
200—M. Johnson (USA)........			20·01
400—A. Pettigrew (USA).......			44·57
800—B. Konchellah (Kenya).....		1	43·99
1,500—N. Morceli (Algeria)......		3	32·84
5,000—Y. Ondieki (Kenya)		13	14·45
10,000—M. Tanui (Kenya).......		27	38·74
Marathon—H. Taniguchi (Japan)	2	14	57
3,000 *steeplechase*—M. Kiptani (Kenya)		8	12·59
110 *hurdles*—G. Foster (USA) ...			13·06
400 *hurdles*—S. Matete (Zambia) .			47·64
20 km *walk*—M. Damilano (Italy)	1	19	37
50 km *walk*—A. Potashov (USSR)	3	53	09
4 × 100 *relay*—USA			37·50
4 × 400 *relay*—Great Britain		2	57·53
			metres
High jump—C. Austin (USA)			2·38
Pole vault—S. Bubka (USSR) ...			5·95
Long jump—M. Powell (USA) ...			8·95
Triple jump—K. Harrison (USA) .			17·78
Shot—W. Gunthor (Switzerland) .			21·67
Discus—L. Riedel (Germany)			66·20
Hammer—Y. Sedykh (USSR) ...			81·70
Javelin—K. Kinnunen (Finland) .			90·82
Decathlon—D. O'Brien (USA) ...			8,812 pts

Women's Events

metres	hr.	min.	sec.
100—K. Krabbe (Germany)			10·99
200—K. Krabbe (Germany)			22·09
400—M.-J. Perec (France)			49·13
800—L. Nurutdinova (USSR)....		1	57·50
1,500—H. Boulmerka (Algeria)...		4	02·21
3,000—T. Dorovskikh (USSR) ...		8	35·82
10,000—E. McColgan (GB).......		31	14·31
Marathon—W. Panfil (Poland)...	2	29	53
100 *hurdles*—N. Narozhilenko (USSR)........................			12·59
400 *hurdles*—T. Ledovskaya (USSR)........................			53·11
4 × 100 *relay*—Jamaica			41·94
4 × 400 *relay*—USSR		3	18·43
10 km *walk*—A. Ivanova (USSR) .		42	57

	metres
High jump—H. Henkel (Germany)....................	2·05
Long jump—J. Joyner-Kersee (USA)...................	7·32
Shot—Z. Huang (China).........	20·83
Discus—T. Kristova (Bulgaria) ..	71·02
Javelin—D. Xu (China)	68·78
Heptathlon—S. Braun (Germany)	6,672 pts

BADMINTON

WORLD CUP CHAMPIONSHIPS
(Jakarta, Indonesia, Nov. 1990)

Men's Singles.—W. Wenkai (China).
Women's Singles.—S. Kusumawardhani (Indonesia).
Men's Doubles.—R. Sidek and J. Sidek (Malaysia).
Women's Doubles.—Y. Fen and L. Caiqin (China).
Mixed Doubles.— Gunawan and R. Tendean (Indonesia).

ENGLISH NATIONAL CHAMPIONSHIPS 1991

Men's Singles.—D. Hall.
Women's Singles.—J. Bradbury.
Men's Doubles.—N. Ponting and D. Wright.
Women's Doubles.—G. Gowers and J. Muggeridge.
Mixed Doubles.—A. Goode and Ms. G. Gowers.

SCOTTISH NATIONAL CHAMPIONSHIPS 1991

Men's Singles.—K. Scott.
Women's Singles.—A. Gibson.
Men's Doubles.—R. Hogg and K. Middlemiss.
Women's Doubles.—T. Allen and E. Allen.
Mixed Doubles.—D. Travers and A. Nairn.

WELSH NATIONAL CHAMPIONSHIPS 1991

Men's Singles.—A. Spencer.
Women's Singles.—R. Edwards.
Men's Doubles.—A. Spencer and L. Williams.
Women's Doubles.—H. Tarleton and S. Williams.
Mixed Doubles.—A. Carlotti and H. Tarleton.

ALL-ENGLAND CHAMPIONSHIPS 1991

Men's Singles.—A Wiranata (Indonesia).
Women's Singles.—S. Susanti (Indonesia).
Men's Doubles.—L. Yongbo and T. Bingyi (China).
Women's Doubles.—C. So Young and H. Hye Young (S. Korea).
Mixed Doubles.—P. Joo Bong and C. Myeong Hee (S. Korea).

WORLD CHAMPIONSHIPS
(Copenhagen, May 1991)

Men's Singles.—Zhao Jianhua (China).
Women's Singles.—Tang Jiuhong (China).
Men's Doubles.—P. Joo Bong and K. Moon Soo (S. Korea).
Women's Doubles.—G. Weizhen and N. Qunhua (China).
Mixed Doubles.—P. Joo Bong and C. Myeong Hee (S. Korea).

BASKETBALL

MEN

Commonwealth Championship 1991.—England.
British Championship 1991.—England.
Nat West Trophy 1990.—Kingston beat Manchester Giants 69-59.
National Cup 1991.—Sunderland beat Leicester 88-81.
National League.—Kingston.

WOMEN

Commonwealth Championship 1991.—England.
British Championship 1991.—England.
National Cup 1991.—Sheffield Hatters beat Nottingham 79–46.
National League.—Sheffield Hatters.

BILLIARDS

World Professional Billiards Championship 1991.— M. Russell (England).
World Amateur Billiards Champion.—M. Kothari (India).
World Matchplay Championship 1991.—M. Russell (England) beat G. Sethi (India) 7–6.
UK Billiards Championship 1991.—M. Russell (England) beat G. Sethi (India) 1,839–1,538.
British Open Championship 1991.—N. Dagley beat I. Williamson 7–5.

BOWLS

MEN

NATIONAL CHAMPIONSHIPS 1991
(Worthing)

Fours final.—Wokingham (Berks.) beat Spencer, Melksham (Wilts.) 21–20.
Triples final.—Wigton (Cumbria) beat Summertown (Oxon.) 16–15.
Pairs final.—Wigton (Cumbria) beat N.P.L. (Middx) 29–16.
Singles final.—A. Allcock (Cheltenham, Glos.) beat D. G. Hobbis (Stratford-upon-Avon, Warks.) 21–3.

BRITISH ISLES INDOOR CHAMPIONSHIPS 1991
(Aberdeen)

Fours.—England
Triples.—England.
Pairs.—Scotland.
Singles.—A. Thomson (England).

World Indoor Championship 1991.—R. Corsie (Scotland).
World Indoor Pairs Championship 1991.—D. Bryant and A. Allcock (England).
UK Indoor Singles Championship 1991.—A. Thomson (England).

World Fours Champions.—Ireland.
World Triples Champions.—New Zealand.
World Pairs Champions.—New Zealand.
World Singles Champion.—D. Bryant (England).
Middleton Cup (Inter-County Championship) final 1991.—Kent beat Devon 123–107.

WOMEN

NATIONAL CHAMPIONSHIPS 1991
(Leamington Spa)

Fours final.—Middlesex beat Somerset 22–19.
Triples final.—Oxfordshire beat Somerset 23–17.
Pairs final.—Kent beat Notts. 20–18.
Singles final (four woods).—J. Evans (Hunts.) beat E. Bessell (Somerset) 21–15.
Singles final (two woods).—W. Line (Hants.) beat J. Baker (Derbyshire) 17–13.

BRITISH ISLES INDOOR CHAMPIONSHIPS 1991
(Prestwick)

Fours.—N. Ireland.
Triples.—England.
Pairs.—N. Ireland.
Singles.—M. Letham (Scotland).

World Fours Champions.—Australia.
World Triples Champions.—Australia.

World Pairs Champions.—Ireland.
World Singles Champion.—J. Ackland (Wales).

BOXING

AMATEUR BOXING ASSOCIATION (ABA) CHAMPIONSHIP WINNERS

Super-heavy (91 + kg).—K. McCormack.
Heavy (91kg).—P. Lawson.
Light-heavy (81kg).—A. Todd.
Middle (75kg).—M. Edwards.
Light-middle (71kg).—T. Taylor.
Welter (67kg).—J. Calzaghie.
Light-welter (63.5kg).—J. Matthews.
Light (60kg).—P. Ramsey.
Feather (57kg).—J. Irwin.
Bantam (54kg).—D. Hardie.
Fly (51kg).—P. Ingle.
Light-fly (48kg).—P. Culshaw.

PROFESSIONAL BOXING
(as at October 3, 1991)

WORLD BOXING COUNCIL (WBC) CHAMPIONS

Heavy.—E. Holyfield (USA).
Cruiser.—A. Wamba (France).
Light-heavy.—J. Harding (Australia).
Super-middle.—M. Galvano (Italy).
Middle.—J. Jackson (USA).
Super-welter.—T. Norris (USA).
Welter.—S. Brown (USA).
Super-light.—J. C. Chavez (Mexico).
Light.—P. Whitaker (USA).
Super-feather.—A. Nelson (Ghana).
Feather.—M. Villasana (Mexico).
Super-bantam.—D. Zaragoza (Mexico).
Bantam.—J. Tatsuyoshi (Japan).
Super-fly.—S. Moon (Korea).
Fly.—M. Kittikasem (Thailand).
Light-fly.—H. Gonzalez (Mexico).
Straw.—R Lopez (Mexico).

WORLD BOXING ASSOCIATION (WBA) CHAMPIONS

Heavy.—E. Holyfield (USA).
Cruiser.—R. Czyz (USA).
Light-heavy.—T. Hearns (USA).
Super-middle.—V. Cordoba (Panama).
Middle.—M. McCallum (Jamaica/USA).
Super-welter.—V. Pazienza (USA).
Welter.—M. Taylor (USA).
Super-light.—E. Rosario (Puerto Rico).
Light.—P. Whitaker (GB).
Super-feather.—J. Gamache (USA).
Feather.—P. Young Kyun (Korea).
Super-bantam.—L. Mendoza (Colombia).
Bantam.—L. Espinoza (Philippines).
Super-fly.—K. Galaxy (Thailand).
Fly.—K. Yong Kang (Korea).
Light-fly.—Yuh Myung Woo (Korea).
Straw.—C. Hui Young (Korea).

INTERNATIONAL BOXING FEDERATION (IBF) CHAMPIONS

Heavy.—E. Holyfield (USA).
Cruiser.—J. Warring (USA).
Light-heavy.—C. Williams (USA).
Super-middle.—D. Van Horn (USA).
Middle.—J. Toney (USA).
Super-welter.—G. F. Rosi (Italy).
Welter.—vacant.
Super-light.—J. Chavez (Mexico).
Light.—P. Whitaker (USA).
Super-feather.—B. Mitchell (S. Africa).
Feather.—M. Medina (Mexico).

Super-bantam.—W. Ncita (S. Africa).
Bantam.—O. Canizales (USA).
Super-fly.—R. Quiroga (USA).
Fly.—D. McAuley (GB).
Light-fly.—M. Carbajal (USA).
Straw.—F. L. Lookmingkwan (Thailand).

BRITISH CHAMPIONS

Heavy.—L. Lewis.
Cruiser.—D. Angol.
Light-heavy.—C. Ashley.
Super-middle.—S. O'Toole.
Middle.—H. Graham.
Light-middle.—W. Swift.
Welter.—D. Bryan.
Light-welter.—A. Holligan.
Light.—C. Crook.
Super-feather.—J. Doherty.
Feather.—C. McMillan.
Bantam.—vacant.
Fly.—F. Ampofo.

COMMONWEALTH CHAMPIONS

Heavy.—D. Williams (GB).
Cruiser.—D. Angol (GB).
Light-heavy.—G. Waters (Australia).
Super-middle.—H. Wharton (GB).
Middle.—M. Watson (GB).
Light-middle.—vacant.
Welter.—D. Boucher (Canada).
Light-welter.—A. Holligan (GB).
Light.—C. Crook (GB).
Super-feather.—H. Forde (GB).
Feather.—B. Francis (Canada).
Bantam.—R. Minus (Bahamas).
Fly.—A. Kotei (Ghana).

EUROPEAN CHAMPIONS

Heavy.—L. Lewis (GB).
Cruiser.—J. Nelson (GB).
Light-heavy.—G. Rocchigiani (Germany).
Super-middle.—J. Cook (GB).
Middle.—S. Kalambay (Italy).
Light-middle.—J. C. Fontana (France).
Welter.—P. Oliva (Italy).
Light-welter.—P. Barratt (GB).
Light.—A. Renzo (Italy).
Super-feather.—D. Londas (France).
Feather.—F. Benichou (France).
Bantam.—T. Jacob (France).
Fly.—S. Fanni (Italy).

CHESS

World Champion.—G. Kasparov (USSR).
British Championship 1991.—J. Hodgson.
Ladies.—S. Arkell.

CRICKET

TEST MATCHES

Pakistan v. New Zealand

First Test (Karachi, Oct. 10–15, 1990).—Pakistan won by an innings and 43 runs. New Zealand 196 and 194; Pakistan 433–6 dec.

Second Test (Lahore, Oct. 18–23, 1990).—Pakistan won by 9 wickets. New Zealand 160 and 287; Pakistan 373–9 dec. and 77–1.

Third Test (Faisalabad, Oct. 26–31, 1990).—Pakistan won by 65 runs. Pakistan 102 and 357; New Zealand 217 and 177.

Pakistan v. West Indies

First Test (Karachi, Nov. 15–20, 1990).—Pakistan won by 8 wickets. West Indies 261 and 181. Pakistan 345 and 98–2.

Second Test (Faisalabad, Nov. 23–25, 1990).—West Indies won by 7 wickets. Pakistan 170 and 154; West Indies 195 and 130–3.

Third Test (Lahore, Dec. 6–11, 1990).—Drawn. West Indies 294 and 173; Pakistan 122 and 242–6.

India v Sri Lanka

Test (Chandigarh, Nov. 23–27, 1990).—India won by an innings and 8 runs. India 288; Sri Lanka 82 and 198.

Australia v. England

First Test (Brisbane, Nov. 23–25, 1990).—Australia won by 10 wickets. England 194 and 114; Australia 152 and 157–0.

Second Test (Melbourne, Dec. 26–30, 1990).—Australia won by 8 wickets. England 352 and 150; Australia 306 and 197–2.

Third Test (Sydney, Jan. 4–8).—Drawn. Australia 518 and 205; England 469–8 dec. and 113–4.

Fourth Test (Adelaide, Jan. 25–29).—Drawn. Australia 386 and 314–6 dec.; England 229 and 335–5.

Fifth Test (Perth, Feb. 1–5).—Australia won by 9 wickets. England 244 and 182; Australia 307 and 120–1.

New Zealand v. Sri Lanka

First Test (Wellington, Jan. 31–Feb. 4).—Drawn. New Zealand 174 and 671–4; Sri Lanka 497–9 dec.

Second Test (Hamilton, Feb. 22–26)).—Drawn. New Zealand 296 and 374–6 dec.; Sri Lanka 253 and 344–6.

Third Test (Auckland, March 1–5).—Drawn. Sri Lanka 380 and 319; New Zealand 317 and 261–5.

West Indies v Australia

First Test (Kingston, March 1–6).—Drawn. West Indies 264 and 334–3; Australia 371.

Second Test (Georgetown, March 23–28).—West Indies won by 10 wickets. Australia 348 and 248; West Indies 569 and 31 for no wicket.

Third Test (Port of Spain, April 5–10).—Drawn. Australia 294 and 123–3; West Indies 227.

Fourth Test (Bridgetown, April 19–24).—West Indies won by 343 runs. West Indies 149 and 536–9 dec.; Australia 134 and 208.

Fifth Test (Antigua, April 27–May 2).—Australia won by 157 runs. Australia 403 and 265; West Indies 214 and 297.

England v. West Indies

First Test (Headingley, June 6–10).—England won by 115 runs. England 198 and 252; West Indies 173 and 162.

Second Test (Lords, June 20–24).—Drawn. West Indies 419 and 12–2; England 354.

Third Test (Trent Bridge, July 4–9).—West Indies won by 9 wickets. England 300 and 211; West Indies 397 and 115–1.

Fourth Test (Edgbaston, July 25–28).—West Indies won by 7 wickets. England 188 and 255; West Indies 292 and 157–3.

Fifth Test (The Oval, Aug. 8–12).—England won by 5 wickets. England 419 and 146–5; West Indies 176 and 385.

England v. Sri Lanka

Test (Lords, Aug. 22–27).—England won by 137 runs. England 282 and 364–3 dec.; Sri Lanka 224 and 285.

One-Day Internationals

New Zealand v. England

Christchurch (Feb. 9).—England won by 14 runs. England 230–7; New Zealand 216–8.

Wellington (Feb. 13).—New Zealand won by 9 runs. New Zealand 187; England 187.

Auckland (Feb. 16).—New Zealand won by 7 runs. New Zealand 224–7; England 217.

New Zealand won the series 2–1.

England v. West Indies
(Texaco Trophy)

Edgbaston (May 23–24).—England won by 1 wicket. W. Indies 173–8; England 175–9.

Old Trafford (May 25).—England won by 9 runs. England 270–4; W. Indies 261–8.

Lord's (May 27).—England won by 7 wickets. W. Indies 264–9; England 265–3.

England won Texaco Trophy 3–0.

International Cups

Sharjah Cup 1990.—Pakistan.
World Series Cup 1991.—Australia.
ICC Cup 1990.—Zimbabwe.

Australia v. England 1990–91 (Averages)

Australia Batting

Batsmen	I	NO	R	HS	Av.
D. C. Boon	9	2	530	121	75·71
G. R. J. Matthews	7	2	353	128	70·60
C. J. McDermott	2	1	67	42*	67·00
M. E. Waugh	3	0	187	138	62·33
A. R. Border	7	1	281	83*	46·83
G. R. Marsh	10	3	314	79*	44·85
L. A. Healy	7	0	175	69	25·00
M. A. Taylor	10	1	213	67*	23·66
D. M. Jones	7	0	163	60	23·28
S. R. Waugh	4	0	82	48	20·50
T. M. Alderman	5	2	34	26*	11·33
M. G. Hughes	5	0	44	30	8·80
B. A. Reid	5	2	13	5*	4.33

Played in one match: C. G. Rackemann, 9, 1.
*Not out.

Bowling

Bowlers	O	M	R	W	Av.
B. A. Reid	180·1	49	432	27	16·00
C. J. McDermott	97·4	12	360	18	20·00
M. G. Hughes	142·1	38	365	15	24·33
T. M. Alderman	148·5	33	428	16	26·75
G. R. J. Matthews	169·0	51	422	7	60·28
A. R. Border	28·0	6	82	1	82·00
S. R. Waugh	38.0	15	90	1	90·00

Also bowled: M. E. Waugh, 6-1-26-0; C. G. Rackemann, 28·5-5-109-0.

England Batting

Batsmen	I	NO	R	HS	Av.
G. A. Gooch	8	0	426	117	53·25
D. I. Gower	10	1	407	123	45·22
A. J. Lamb	6	0	195	91	32·50
M. A. Atherton	10	1	279	105	31·00
R. A. Smith	10	2	238	58	29·75
W. Larkins	6	0	141	64	23·50
A. J. Stewart	10	0	224	91	22·40
R. C. Russell	5	1	77	30*	19·25
P. A. J. DeFreitas	6	1	77	45	15·40
G. C. Small	6	1	42	15	8·40
P. C. R. Tufnell	6	4	13	8	6·50
A. R. C. Fraser	5	0	27	24	5·40
D. E. Malcolm	7	1	27	7	4·50

Played in one match: P. J. Newport, 40*, 0; C. C. Lewis, 20, 14; E. E. Hemmings, 0.
*Not out.

Bowling

Bowlers	O	M	R	W	Av.
C. C. Lewis	15·0	0	58	3	19·33
A. R. C. Fraser	143·0	31	311	11	28·27
P. A. J. DeFreitas	113·3	22	318	10	31·80
E. E. Hemmings	73·0	16	199	6	33·16
G. A. Gooch	23·0	5	69	2	34·50
P. C. R. Tufnell	140·0	47	345	9	38·33
D. E. Malcolm	223·5	42	665	16	41·56
G. C. Small	149·0	33	424	9	47·11
P. J. Newport	20·0	0	78	1	78·00

Also bowled: M. A. Atherton, 15-2-70-0.

England v. West Indies 1991 (Averages)

England Batting

Batsmen	I	NO	R	HS	Av.
R. A. Smith	7	2	416	148*	83·20
C. C. Lewis	3	1	125	65	62·50
G. A. Gooch	9	1	480	154*	60·00
M. R. Ramprakash	9	0	210	29	23·33
P. A. J. DeFreitas	8	1	134	55*	19·14
D. R. Pringle	7	0	128	45	18·28
D. V. Lawrence	3	0	47	34	15·66
R. K. Illingworth	4	2	31	13	15·50
A. J. Lamb	7	0	88	29	12·57
H. Morris	4	0	50	44	12·50
G. A. Hick	7	0	75	43	10·71
R. C. Russell	7	0	73	46	10·42
M. A. Atherton	9	0	79	32	8·77
D. E. Malcolm	3	1	9	5*	4·50
S. L. Watkin	3	0	8	6	2·66

Played in one match: A. J. Stewart, 38*, 31; I. T. Botham, 31, 4; P. C. R. Tufnell, 2, 0.
*Not out.

Bowling

Bowlers	O	M	R	W	Av.
P. A. J. DeFreitas	185·5	55	457	22	20·77
I. T. Botham	27·0	8	67	3	22·33
P. C. R. Tufnell	60·3	9	175	7	25·00
D. R. Pringle	128·1	33	322	12	26·83
S. L. Watkin	36·0	4	153	5	30·60
C. C. Lewis	79·0	30	201	6	33·50
D. V. Lawrence	78·1	7	350	10	35·00
G. A. Hick	24·0	5	95	2	47·50
R. K. Illingworth	56·4	10	213	4	53·25
D. E. Malcolm	42·3	3	180	3	60·00

Also bowled: G. A. Gooch, 8-1-14-0.

Batsmen	I	NO	R	HS	Av.
R. B. Richardson ..	10	1	495	121	55·00
I. V. A. Richards ..	8	1	376	80	53·71
D. L. Haynes	10	3	323	75*	46·14
C. L. Hooper	9	2	271	111	38·71
A. L. Logie	5	0	120	78	24·00
M. D. Marshall	7	1	116	67	19·33
P. V. Simmons	10	0	181	38	18·10
P. J. L. Dujon	7	0	89	33	12·71
C. A. Walsh	7	0	66	18	9·42
B. P. Patterson ...	5	3	11	5*	5·50
C. E. L. Ambrose ..	7	0	37	17	5·28
I. B. A. Allen	2	2	5	4*	5·00

Played in one match : C. B. Lambert, 39, 14.
*Not out.

BOWLING

Bowlers	O	M	R	W	Av.
C. B. Lambert	0·4	0	4	1	4·00
C. E. L. Ambrose ..	249·0	68	560	28	20·00
M. D. Marshall	172·1	36	442	20	22·10
B. P. Patterson ...	117·3	20	389	13	29·92
C. A. Walsh	187·0	42	493	15	32·86
I. B. A. Allen	47·0	4	180	5	36·00
C. L. Hooper	64·0	13	137	2	68·50

Also bowled : I. V. A. Richards, 5-1-6-0; P. V. Simmons, 3-0-7-0.

County Championship Table 1991

Order for 1990 in brackets	Played	Won	Lost.	Drawn	Bonus Btg.	Bonus Blng.	Points
Essex (2)	22	11	5	6	69	67	312
Warwickshire (5)	22	11	4	7	58	65	299
Derbyshire (12)	22	9	5	8	46	68	258
Nottinghamshire (13) ..	22	7	5	10	64	69	245
Surrey (9)	22	8	6	8	47	66	241
Worcestershire (4)	22	6	4	12	54	59	209
Kent (16)*	22	6	3	12	50	55	209
Lancashire (6)	22	6	9	7	60	49	205
Hampshire (3)	22	5	7	10	57	56	193
Northamptonshire (11) .	22	5	6	11	55	54	189
Sussex (17)*	22	4	3	14	57	60	189
Glamorgan (8)	22	5	5	12	50	57	187
Gloucestershire (13) ...	22	5	10	7	42	53	175
Yorkshire (10)	22	4	6	12	58	37	159
Middlesex (1)	22	3	9	10	48	63	159
Leicestershire (7)	22	3	8	11	46	53	147
Somerset (15)	22	2	5	15	66	45	143

*Kent and Sussex eight points each for a tied match.

Other Results 1991

Benson and Hedges Cup final.—Worcestershire beat Lancashire by 65 runs. Worcestershire 236–8; Lancashire 171 all out.
NatWest Trophy final.—Hampshire beat Surrey by 4 wickets. Surrey 240–5; Hants. 243–6.
Refuge Assurance Sunday League Champions.—Nottinghamshire.
Refuge Assurance Cup.—Worcestershire beat Lancashire by 7 runs. Worcestershire 235–5; Lancashire 228.
Britannic Challenge.—(*1 day*) Victoria beat Essex by 59 runs. Victoria 274–3; Essex 215. (*4 day*) Match drawn. Essex 343–9 dec.; Victoria 168 and 56–8.
Holt Cup (Minor Counties knockout final).—Staffordshire beat Devon by 4 wickets. Devon 239–8; Staffordshire 241–6.

Minor Counties Championship final.—Staffordshire beat Oxfordshire by 10 wickets. Oxfordshire 215–8; Staffordshire 216–0.
National Club Championship final.—Teddington beat Walsall by 20 runs. Teddington 217–8; Walsall 197.
National Village Championship final.—St Fagans beat Harome by 17 runs. St Fagans 169–6; Harome 152–9.
Universities.—Drawn. Cambridge University 279 and 146–7 dec.; Oxford University 145–1 dec. and 108–1.

BATTING AND BOWLING AVERAGES

First Class Batting Averages 1991

Batsmen	I	NO	R	HS	Av.
C. L. Hooper	25	9	1,501	196	93·81
S. J. Cook	42	8	2,755	210*	81·02
M. W. Gatting	39	11	2,057	215*	73·46
Salim Malik	36	9	1,972	215	73·03
G. A. Gooch	31	4	1,911	259	70·77
R. B. Richardson ..	26	5	1,403	135*	66·81
C. L. Smith	27	3	1,553	200	64·70
D. A. Leatherdale ..	6	0	379	157	63·16
T. M. Moody	34	4	1,887	210	62·90
D. W. Randall	34	9	1,567	143*	62·68
M. P. Maynard	36	6	1,803	243	60·10
A. P. Wells	36	6	1,784	253*	59·46
M. Azharuddin ...	39	5	2,016	212	59·29
I. V. A. Richards ..	18	4	817	131	58·35
G. J. Turner	8	2	349	101*	58·16
R. T. Robinson ...	37	8	1,673	180	57·69
N. R. Taylor	36	4	1,806	203*	56·43
N. Hussain	33	8	1,354	196	54·16
R. A. Smith	30	4	1,397	148*	53·73
S. T. Jayasuriya ...	11	2	482	100*	53·55
C. J. Tavare	37	7	1,601	183	53·36
H. Morris	41	7	1,803	156*	53·02
C. B. Lambert	13	2	551	116	50·09
B. C. Broad	38	3	1,739	166	49·68
N. V. Knight......	10	1	441	101*	49·00

* Not out.

First Class Bowling Averages 1991

Bowlers	O	M	R	W	Av.
Waqar Younis ...	582·0	112	1,656	113	14·65
C. E. L. Ambrose .	390·0	122	869	51	17·03
A. A. Donald	522·1	91	1,634	83	19·68
N. A. Foster	757·2	185	2,138	102	20·96
D. A. Reeve	402·1	117	957	45	21·26
G. R. Dilley	305·2	62	823	37	22·24
Wasim Akram ...	429·3	99	1,251	56	22·33
N. A. Mallender ..	349·5	76	969	42	23·07
R. J. Shastri	307·5	88	724	31	23·35
J. R. Ayling	211·1	49	595	25	23·80
O. H. Mortensen .	559·1	143	1,384	58	23·86
D. V. Lawrence ..	515·1	79	1,790	74	24·18
P. A. J. DeFreitas .	657·1	173	1,780	73	24·38
I. T. Botham	351·1	73	1,077	44	24·47
K. J. Barnett	211·1	47	496	20	24·80
K. M. Curran	436·2	110	1,204	48	25·08
P. C. R. Tufnell ...	903·4	254	2,219	88	25·21
C. C. Lewis	471·4	127	1,213	48	25·27
C. Penn	429·4	82	1,323	52	25·44
T. A. Munton	693·1	184	1,863	73	25·52
D. G. Cork	494·3	84	1,460	57	25·61
F. D. Stephenson .	714·1	158	2,010	78	25·76
M. D. Marshall...	282·1	57	782	30	26·06
C. L. Hooper	336·2	71	837	31	27·00
A. P. Igglesden...	471·0	94	1,351	50	27·02

Source for averages and County Championship:
TCCB/Bull Computer Official Statistics.

CYCLING

European Community Tour 1990.—Men, C. Marsal (France); *Women*, J. Bruyneel (Belgium).
Tour of Spain 1991.— M. Mauri (Spain).
*Giro d'Italia 1991.—*F. Chioccioli (Italy).
*Milk Race 1991.—*C. Walker (GB).
*Tour de France 1991.—*M. Indurain (Spain).
*Tour of Britain 1991.—*P. Anderson (Australia).
*Nissan Classic 1991.—*S. Kelly (Ireland).

World Professional Road Race Championship 1991.— G. Bugno (Italy).
*British Open Championship 1991.—*C. Young.
*British Road Race Championship 1991.—*B. Smith.
*British Amateur Road Race Championship 1991.—*J. Hughes.
*Scottish Provident League.—*J. Clay (Banana–Falcon).
*World Professional Cyclo-Cross Championship 1991.—*R. Simunek (Czechoslovakia).
World Amateur Cyclo-Cross Championship 1991.— T. Frischnecht (Switzerland).
*Women's World Road Race Championship 1991.—*L. van Moorsel (Holland).
Women's National Road Race Championship 1991.— M. Purvis.

EQUESTRIANISM 1991

Show Jumping

World Cup final (Gothenburg)
1. J. Whitaker on Henderson Milton (GB).
2. N. Pessoa on Special Envoy (Brazil).
3. R.-Y. Bost on Norton de Rhuys (France).

European Championships (La Baule, France)
 Individual
  1. E. Navet on Waiti Quito de Baussy (France).
  2. F. Sloothaak on Optiebeurs Walzerkoenig (Germany).
  3. J. Lansink on Optiebeurs Egano (Holland).
 Team
  1. The Netherlands.
  2. Great Britain.
  3. Switzerland.

British Jumping Derby (Hickstead)
1. M. Whitaker on Henderson Monsanta (GB).
2. Miss T. Cassan on Treffer (GB).
3. L. Beerbaum on Almox Athletico (Germany).

Three-day Eventing

European Championships (Punchestown, Ireland).
 Individual
  1. I. Stark on Glenburnie (GB).
  2. R. Walker on Jacana (GB).
  3. Miss K. Straker on Get Smart (GB).
 Team
  1. GB.
  2. Ireland.
  3. France.

Badminton Horse Trials
1. R. Powell on The Irishman II (GB).
2. I. Stark on Murphy Himself (GB).
3. Mrs H. Bell on Troubleshooter (GB).

British Open Horse Trials (Gatcombe Park)
1. Miss M. Thomson on King William (GB).
2. Miss P. Nolan on Sir Barnaby (GB).
3. Ms J. Herbert on Chaka (GB).

Burghley Horse Trials
1. M. Todd on Welton Greylag (NZ).
2. G. Watson on Chaka (Australia).
3. Miss K. Lende on Mr Maxwell (USA).

ETON FIVES 1991

*Amateur Championship (Kinnaird Cup).—*J. Reynolds and M. de Souza-Girao.
*NatWest County Championship.—*Middlesex.
*Holmwoods Schools' Championships.—*Harrow.
*Alan Barber Cup.—*Old Cholmeleians.
*League Championship (Douglas Keeble Cup).—*Old Cholmeleians.

FENCING

MEN

World Championships 1991:
 *Foil.—*I. Weissenborn (Germany).
 *Epée.—*A. Shuvalov (USSR).
 *Sabre.—*G. Kirienko (USSR).
 *Team Foil.—*Cuba.
 *Team Epée.—*USSR.
 *Team Sabre.—*Hungary.

British Championships 1991:
 *Foil.—*W. Gosbee (Salle Boston).
 *Epée.—*J. Llewellyn (Reading).
 *Sabre.—*I. Williams (London Thames).

*Sporting Record Cup.—*not fenced.
*Savage Shield.—*Reading.
*Martin Edmunds Cup.—*not fenced.
*Challenge Martini International Epée 1991.—*U. Sandergren (Sweden).
*Eden Cup final 1990.—*T. Becker (W. Germany).

WOMEN

World Championships 1991:
 *Foil.—*G. Trillini (Italy).
 *Epée.—*M. Horvath (Hungary).
 *Team Foil.—*Hungary.
 *Team Epée.—*Hungary.

British Championships 1991:
 *Foil.—*F. McIntosh (Salle Paul).
 *Epée.—*G. Usher (Meadowbank).
 *Sabre.—*S. Benny (Glastonbury).

GOLF

MEN'S CHAMPIONSHIPS

The Major Championships 1991

US Masters (Augusta, Georgia; April 11–14).—I. Woosnam (GB), 277.
US Open (Chaska, Minnesota; June 13–17).—P. Stewart (USA), 282.
The Open (Royal Birkdale; July 18–21).—I. Baker-Finch (Australia), 272.
US PGA Championship (Crooked Stick, Indiana; Aug. 8–11).—J. Daly (USA), 276.

European PGA Tour 1990

Austrian Open (Salzburg).—B. Langer (Germany), 271.
Portuguese Open (Quinto do Largo).—M. McLean (GB), 274.
Volvo Masters (Sotogrande, Spain).—M. Harwood (Australia), 286.
*Benson and Hedges Trophy (El Bosque, Spain).—J.-M. Cañizares (Spain) and Tania Abitbol (Spain).
*European PGA Tour Order of Merit 1990.—*1. I. Woosnam (Wales); 2. M. McNulty (Zimbabwe); 3. J.-M. Olazábal (Spain).

---

* mixed event.

European PGA Tour 1991

Girona Open.—S. Richardson (GB), 272.
Mediterranean Open (St Raphael, France).—I. Woosnam (GB), 279.
Balearic Open (Majorca).—G. Levenson (S. Africa), 282.
Catalan Open (Tarragona, Spain)—J.-M. Olazábal (Spain), 271.
Portuguese Open (Estela).—S. Richardson (GB), 283.
Florence Open.—A. Forsbrand (Sweden), 275.
Jersey Open.—S. Torrance (GB), 279.
International Open (St Mellion, Plymouth).—B. Langer (Germany), 286.
Madrid Open.—A. Sherborne (GB), 272.
Cannes Open.—D. Feherty (GB), 275.
Spanish Open (Madrid).—E. Romero (Argentina), 275.
Italian Open (Castelconturbia).—C. Parry (Ausralia), 279.
PGA Championship (Wentworth).—S. Ballesteros (Spain), 271.
British Masters (Woburn).—S. Ballesteros (Spain), 275.
Murphy's Cup (York).—T. Johnstone (Zimbabwe), 40 pts.
Belgian Open (Brussels).—P.-U. Johansson (Sweden), 276.
Irish Open (Killarney).—N. Faldo (GB), 283.
French Open (Paris).—E. Romero (Argentina), 281.
Monte Carlo Open.—I. Woosnam (GB), 261.
Scottish Open (Gleneagles).—C. Parry (Australia), 268.
Dutch Open (Noordwijk).—P. Stewart (USA), 267.
Scandinavian Masters (Stockholm).—C. Montgomerie (GB), 270.
English Open (The Belfry).—D. Gilford (GB), 278.
German Open (Dusseldorf).—M. McNulty (Zimbabwe), 273.
European Open (Walton Heath, Surrey)—M. Harwood (Australia), 277.
European Masters–Swiss Open (Crans-sur-Sierre).—J. Hawkes (S. Africa), 268.
Lancôme Trophy (Paris).—F. Nobilo (New Zealand), 267.
Grand Prix (Chepstow).—J.-M. Olazábal (Spain), 265.
Austrian Open (Salzburg).—M. Davis (GB), 269.
German Masters (Stuttgart).—B. Langer (Germany), 275.

Amateur Championships 1991

President's Putter (Rye).—B. Ingleby.
Halford Hewitt Cup (for public schools' old boys) (Deal).—Shrewsbury beat Lancing 3½-1½.
Berkshire Trophy (The Berkshire).—J. Bickerton, 280.
Welsh Open Strokeplay (Royal Porthcawl).—A. V. Jones, 290.
Brabazon Trophy (English Open Strokeplay) (Hunstanton).—*Equal 1.* M. Pullan (GB), 284; G. Evans (GB), 284.
Scottish Open Strokeplay (Royal Troon).—A Cottart, 295.
British Amateur (Ganton).—G. Wolstenholme (Bristol and Clifton).
Lytham Trophy (Royal Lytham & St Anne's).—G.Evans, 284.
English Amateur (Formby).—R. Willison.
Scottish Amateur (Downfield).—A. G. Lowson.
Welsh Amateur (Ashburnham).—S. Pardoe.
Universities.—Cambridge beat Oxford 10–5.

Team Events

DUNHILL CUP 1990 (St Andrews, Oct 11–14).—Ireland beat England 3½-2½.
RYDER CUP 1991 (Kiawah Island, South Carolina, Sept. 27–29).—USA beat Great Britain and Europe 14½-13½.

World Cup of Golf 1990.—Germany.
Eisenhower Trophy 1990 (world amateur team championship).—Sweden.
European Team Championship 1990.—Scotland.
Home International Championship 1990.—Ireland.
Home International Championship 1991.—Ireland.
Walker Cup 1991.—USA beat GB and Ireland 14–10.

WOMEN'S CHAMPIONSHIPS

US Women's Open 1991 (Fort Worth, Texas).—M. Mallon (USA), 283.

WPG European Tour 1990

Trophée Urban–World Championship of Women's Golf (Cély-en-Bière).—C. Gerring (USA), 278.
Ladies' Matchplay Championship (Madrid).—F. Descampe (Belgium).
AGF Open (Biarritz).—L. Davies (GB), 136.
**Benson and Hedges Trophy* (El Bosque, Spain).—Tania Abitbol (Spain) and J.-M. Cañizares (Spain).
Longines Classic (St Raphael, France).—T. Johnson (GB), 286.
European Order of Merit 1990.—1. T. Johnson (GB); 2. A. Nicholas (GB); 3. H. Alfredsson (Sweden).

WPG European Tour 1991

Valextra Classic (Rome).—L. Davies (GB), 281.
AGF Open, (Paris).—S. Strudwick (GB), 278.
Ford Ladies' Classic (Woburn).—D. Reid (GB), 280.
European Masters (Brussels).—C. Dibnah (Australia), 284.
La Manga Club Classic (Spain).—C. Dibnah (Australia), 286.
Hennessy Cup (Cologne).—H. Alfredsson (Sweden), 280.
Trophee Coconut Skol (Paris).—H. Alfredsson (Sweden), 276.
Eastleigh Classic.—D. Reid (GB), 249.
German Open (Munich).—F. Descampe (Belgium), 272.
British Open (Woburn).—P. Grice-Whittaker (GB), 284.
Swedish Open (Haninge).—L. Neumann (Sweden), 282.
Italian Open (Venice).—C. Dibnah (Australia), 272.
English Open (Tytherington).—K. Douglas (GB), 285.

Amateur Championships 1991

Welsh Championship (Royal St David's).—V. Thomas.
Scottish Championship (Carnoustie).—C. Lambert.
English Championship (Sheringham).—N. Buxton.
British Open Championship (Bristol).—J. Morley, 297.
Welsh Strokeplay (Royal Porthcawl).—M. Sutton, 224.
English Strokeplay (Ganton).—J. Morley, 301.
British Strokeplay (Pannall, Yorks.).—V. Michaud (France).

Team Championships

SOLHEIM CUP 1990 (Lake Nona, Florida, Nov. 16–18).—USA beat Europe 11½-4½.
Curtis Cup 1990 (Bernardsville, New Jersey, USA).—USA beat Great Britain and Ireland 14–4.
Espirito Santo Trophy 1990 (world amateur team championship).—USA.
Home International Championship 1990.—Scotland.
Home International Championship 1991.—Scotland.

GREYHOUND RACING 1991

Television Trophy (Wolverhampton).—Jenny's Wish.
Grand National (Birmingham).—Ideal Man and Ballycarey Dell (dead heat).
Greyhound Derby (Wimbledon).—Ballinderry Ash.
Scurry Gold Cup (Catford).—Portrun Flier.

* mixed event.

GYMNASTICS 1991

MEN

World Champion, G. Misutin (USSR).
World Individual Apparatus Champions:
  Floor, I. Korobchinski (USSR).
  Pommel Horse, V. Belenki (USSR).
  Rings, G. Misutin (USSR).
  Vault, Y. Ok Youl (S. Korea).
  Parallel Bars, Li Jing (China).
  High Bar, 1= Li Chunyang (China); R. Büchner (Germany).
World Team Champions, USSR.

British Champion, P. Bowler.
British Individual Apparatus Champions:
  Floor, J. May.
  Pommel Horse, P. Bowler.
  Rings, P. Bowler.
  Vault, P. Bowler.
  Parallel Bars, J. May.
  High Bar, 1= J. May; P. Bowler.
British Team Champions (Adam Shield), Liverpool School of Physical Education.

WOMEN

World Champion, K. Zmeskal (USA).
World Individual Apparatus Champions:
  Beam, S. Boginskaya (USSR).
  Floor, 1= C. Bontas (Romania); O. Chusovitina (USSR).
  Vault, L. Milosovici (Romania).
  Assymetric Bars, K. Gwang Suk (N. Korea).
World Team Champions, USSR.

British Champion, L. Timmins.
British Individual Apparatus Champions:
  Vault, L. Redding.
  Asymmetric Bars, R. Haynes.
  Beam, R. Roberts.
  Floor, L. Redding.
British Rhythmics Champion, V. Seifert.
British Open Club Team Champions, Heathrow.

HOCKEY

MEN

World Cup 1990 (Lahore).—Netherlands.
Champions Trophy 1990.—Australia.
Champions Trophy 1991.—Germany.

Home Countries Indoor 1991.—England.

County Championship final 1991.—Middlesex beat Kent 4–3.
National League.—Havant.
Lague Cup Final 1991.—Hounslow beat Havant 4–1.
National Club Championship final 1991.—Hounslow beat Havant 3–2.
National Indoor Club Championship final 1991.—St Albans beat Welton 5–2.
Universities.—Oxford beat Cambridge 3–1.

WOMEN

World Cup 1990 (Sydney).—Netherlands.
Typhoo Tea Cup 1991.—France beat England 2–1.
Home Countries Indoor Tournament 1991.—Scotland.
County Championship 1990.—Lancashire beat Staffordshire 2–0.
National Club Championship 1991.—Sutton Coldfield 1, Leicester 1. Sutton Coldfield won 4–3 on penalties.
National League.—Slough.
National Indoor Club Championship final 1991.—Hightown beat Slough.

HORSERACING

Horseracing in Great Britain is under the control of THE JOCKEY CLUB (incorporating the National Hunt Committee), 42 Portman Square, London, W1H 0EN. Stewards are: Marquess of Hartington (*Senior Steward*); A. J. Struthers (*Deputy Senior Steward*); Brig. A. H. Parker Bowles; Maj. M. C. Wyatt; Col. Sir Piers Bengough; Capt. W. H. Bulwer-Long; C. J. Spence.

Winning Owners 1990

Hamdan Al-Maktoum	£1,536,793
Sheikh Mohammed	1,498,151
K. Abdulla	688,462
B. Cooper	459,117
Maktoum Al-Maktoum	346,379
R. E. Sangster	343,102
HH Aga Khan	313,273
G. Leigh	294,515
C. A. B. St George	236,864
Lord Howard De Walden	202,384

Winning Trainers 1990

H. R. A. Cecil	£1,520,092
L. M. Cumani	1,006,010
M. R. Stoute	803,657
D. R. C. Elsworth	780,885
B. W. Hills	737,389
R. Hannon	653,511
J. L. Dunlop	626,793
R. Charlton	612,175
Maj. W. R. Hern	502,893
G. Harwood	457,703

Leading Breeders 1990

	Value
Capt. Macdonald-Buchanan	£459,117
Juddmonte Farms	429,248
Kilcarn Stud	386,688
Darley Stud (USA)	373,961
HH Aga Khan	346,683
G. W. Leigh	305,634
G. E. Hofmann (USA)	243,368
Lord Howard De Walden	190,542
Hesmonds Stud Ltd	183,174
Mohammed Al-Maktoum	180,352

Winning Sires 1990

	Horses	Races won	Total Value
Sadler's Wells (1981) by Northern Dancer	63	45	£1,514,272
Night Shift (1980) by Northern Dancer	41	41	900,237
Nureyev (1977) by Northern Dancer	27	18	750,581
Persian Bold (1975) by Bold Lad	68	40	705,258
Rainbow Quest (1981) by Blushing Groom	33	27	695,107
Diesis (1980) by Sharpen Up	42	32	679,011
Caerleon (1980) by Nijinsky	60	57	646,103
Kris (1976) by Sharpen Up	50	32	610,555
Known Fact (1977) by In Reality	46	26	553,126
El Gran Senor (1981) by Northern Dancer	25	22	538,302

Winning Flat Jockeys 1990

	1st	2nd	3rd	Unpl.	Total Mts.
P. Eddery	209	133	90	458	890
W. Carson	187	131	103	485	906
S. Cauthen	142	78	72	333	625
L. Dettori	136	83	73	398	691
M. Roberts	124	112	117	496	849
W. Swinburn...	111	119	108	398	736
R. Cochrane ...	109	99	98	510	816
A. Munro	89	58	56	395	598
K. Darley	80	78	69	353	580
D. McKeown ...	74	77	55	451	657

Winning National Hunt Jockeys 1990–91

	1st	2nd	3rd	Unpl.	Total Mts.
P. Scudamore ..	141	53	38	190	422
R. Dunwoody ..	127	122	77	320	646
N. Doughty	96	62	38	154	350
P. Niven	86	65	61	211	423
G. McCourt	83	84	54	214	435
M. Dwyer	81	64	51	184	380
J. Osborne	62	59	37	196	354
M. Perrett	58	27	30	157	272
C. Grant	57	41	41	209	348
S. Smith Eccles .	56	38	27	115	236

(The above statistics are the copyright of *The Sporting Life*.)

THE CLASSICS

One Thousand Guineas (1814)

(Rowley Mile, Newmarket. For three year old fillies)

Year	Winner	Betting	Owner	Jockey	Trainer	No. of Runners
1988	Ravinella.........	5–2	E. Aland........	G. Moore	Mrs C. Head ..	12
1989	Musical Bliss	7–2	Sheikh Mohammed	W. Swinburn .	M. Stoute.....	7
1990	Salsabil	6–4	H. Al-Maktoum .	W. Carson	J. Dunlop.....	10
1991	Shadayid	4–6	H. Al-Maktoum .	W. Carson	J. Dunlop.....	14

Two Thousand Guineas (1809)

(Rowley Mile, Newmarket. For three year olds)

Year	Winner	Betting	Owner	Jockey	Trainer	No. of Runners
1988	Doyoun	4–5	HH Aga Khan ..	W. Swinburn .	M. Stoute.....	9
1989	Nashwan	3–1	H. Al-Maktoum .	W. Carson	R. Hern	14
1990	Tirol	9–1	J. Horgan	M. Kinane ...	R. Hannon....	14
1991	Mystiko	13–2	Lady Beaverbrook....	M. Roberts ...	C. Brittain ...	14

Record time: 1 minute 35·84 seconds, 1990.

The Derby (1780)

(Epsom, 1½ miles. For three year olds)

The first winner was Sir Charles Bunbury's Diomed in 1780. The owners with the record number of winners are Lord Egremont, who won in 1782, 1804, 1805, 1807, 1826 (also won 5 Oaks); and the late Aga Khan, who won in 1930, 1935, 1936, 1948, 1952 (also won 2 Oaks). Other winning owners are: Duke of Grafton (1802, 1809, 1810, 1815); Mr J. Bowes (1835, 1843, 1852, 1853); Sir J. Hawley (1851, 1858, 1859, 1868); the 1st Duke of Westminster (1880, 1882, 1886, 1899); Sir Victor Sassoon (1953, 1957, 1958, 1960).

Record times are: 2 min. 33·80 sec. by Mahmoud in 1936; 2 min. 33·84 sec. by Kahyasi in 1988; 2 min. 33·9 sec. by Reference Point in 1987.

The Derby was run at Newmarket from 1915–18 and from 1940–45.

Year	Winner	Betting	Owner	Jockey	Trainer	No. of Runners
1988	Kahyasi	11–1	HH Aga Khan ..	R. Cochrane ..	L. Cumani	14
1989	Nashwan	5–4	H. Al-Maktoum .	W. Carson	R. Hern	12
1990	Quest for Fame....	7–1	K. Abdulla	P. Eddery......	R. Charlton ...	18
1991	Generous	9–1	Prince Fahd Salman	A. Munro.....	P. Cole	13

The Oaks (1779)

(Epsom, 1½ miles. For three year old fillies)

Year	Winner	Betting	Owner	Jockey	Trainer	No. of Runners
1988	Diminuendo	7–4	Sheikh Mohammed	S. Cauthen ...	H. Cecil	11
*1989	Snow Bride	13–2	S. M. Al-Maktoum.......	S. Cauthen ...	H. Cecil	9
1990	Salsabil	2–1	H. Al-Maktoum .	W. Carson	J.Dunlop	8
1991	Jet Ski Lady	50–1	J. Dunlop	C. Roche	J. Bolger	9

* The Oaks in 1989 was won by HH Aga Khan's Aliysa, but Aliysa was disqualified after a urine test found traces of a prohibited substance, and the Jockey Club awarded the race to Snow Bride.

St Leger (1776)

(Doncaster, 1 m. 6f., 127 yd. For three year olds)

Year	Winner	Betting	Owner	Jockey	Trainer	No. of Runners
1988	Minster Son	15–2	Lady Beaverbrook....	W. Carson	N. Graham ...	6
†1989	Michelozzo	6–4	C. St George	S. Cauthen ...	H. Cecil	8
1990	Snurge	7–2	M. Abib	R. Quinn	P. Cole	8
1991	Toulon	5–2	K. Abdulla	P. Eddery	A. Fabre......	10

† The 1989 St Leger was run at Ayr after the course at Doncaster was ruled unsatisfactory.

Cesarewitch (1839)
(Newmarket, 2¼ miles)

1988 Nomadic Way (3y), (7st 9lb).
1989 Double Dutch (5y), (9st 10lb).
1990 Trainglot (3y), (7st 12lb), W. Carson.

Champion Stakes (1877)
(Newmarket, 1¼ miles)

1988 Indian Skimmer (4y), (9st).
1989 Legal Case (3y), (8st 10lb).
1990 In the Grove (3y), (8st 9lb), S. Cauthen.

*Hennessy Gold Cup (1957)
(Newbury, 3¼ miles, 82 yd)

1987 Playschool (9y), (10st 8lb).
1988 Strands of Gold (9y), (10st).
1989 Ghofar (6y), (10st 2lb).
1990 Arctic Call (7y), (11st), J. Osborne.

*King George VI Chase (1937)
(Kempton, 3 miles)

1987 Nupsala (8y), (11st 10lb).
1988 Desert Orchid (9y), (11st 10lb).
1989 Desert Orchid (10y), (11st 10lb).
1990 Desert Orchid (11y), (11st 10lb), R. Dunwoody.

*Champion Hurdle (1927)
(Cheltenham, 2 miles, 200 yd)

1988 Celtic Shot (6y), (12st).
1989 Beech Road (7y), (12st).
1990 Kribensis (6y), (12st).
1991 Morley Street (7y), (12st), J. Frost.

*Queen Mother Champion Chase (1959)
(Cheltenham, about 2 miles)

1988 Pearlyman (9y), (12st).
1989 Barnbrook Again (8y), (12st).
1990 Barnbrook Again (9y), (12st).
1991 Katabatic (8y), (12st), S. McNeill.

*Cheltenham Gold Cup (1924)
(about 3¼ miles)

1988 Charter Party (10y), (12st).
1989 Desert Orchid (10y), (12st).
1990 Norton's Coin (9y), (12st).
1991 Garrison Savannah (8y), (12st), M. Pitman.

Lincoln Handicap (1965)
(Doncaster, 1 mile)

1988 Cuvee Charlie (4y), (7st 13lb).
1989 Fact Finder (5y), (7st 9lb).
1990 Evichstar (6y), (7st 10lb).
1991 Amenable (6y), (8st 1lb), Miss A. Greaves.

*Grand National (1837)
(Liverpool, about 4 miles, 856 yd)

1988 Rhyme 'N' Reason (9y), (11st).
1989 Little Polveir (12y), (10st).
1990 Mr Frisk (11y), (10st).
1991 Seagram (11y), (10st 6lb), N. Hawke.

Record times: 8 min. 47·8 sec. by Mr Frisk in 1990; 9 min. 1·9 sec. by Red Rum in 1973.

*Whitbread Gold Cup (1957)
(Sandown, 3 miles, 5 f, 25 yd)

1988 Desert Orchid (9y), (11st 11lb).
1989 Brown Windsor (7y), (10st).
1990 Mr Frisk (11y), (10st).
†1991 Docklands Express (9y), (10st 13lb), A. Tory.

† Cahervillahow finished first but after an objection and a stewards' inquiry was placed second.

Jockey Club Stakes (1894)
(Newmarket, 1½ miles)

1988 Almaarad (4y), (8st 5lb).
1989 Unfwain (4y), (8st 10lb).
1990 Roseate Tern (4y), (8st 9lb).
1991 Rock Hopper (4y), (8st 7lb), P. Eddery.

Prix du Jockey Club (1836)
(Chantilly, 1 mile, 4 f)

1988 Hours After.
1989 Old Vic.
1990 Sanglamore.
1991 Suave Dancer (9st 2lb), C. Asmussen.

Ascot Gold Cup (1807)
(Ascot, 2½ miles)

1988 Sadeem (5y), (9st).
1989 Sadeem (6y), (9st).
1990 Ashal (4y), (9st).
1991 Indian Queen (6y), (8st 13lb), W. Swinburn.

*National Hunt

Irish Sweeps Derby (1866)
(Curragh, 1½ miles. Three year olds)

1988 Kahyasi (9st).
1989 Old Vic (9st).
1990 Salsabil (8st 11lb).
1991 Generous (9st), A. Munro.

Kentucky Derby (1875)
(Louisville, Kentucky, 1¼ miles)

1988 Winning Colors.
1989 Sunday Silence.
1990 Unbridled.
1991 Strike the Gold, C. Antley.

Eclipse Stakes (1886)
(Sandown, 1¼ miles)

1988 Mtoto (5y), (9st 7lb).
1989 Nashwan (3y), (8st 8lb).
1990 Elmaamul (3y), (8st 10lb).
1991 Environment Friend (3y), (8st 10lb), G. Duffield.

King George VI and Queen Elizabeth Diamond Stakes (1952)
(Ascot, 1½ miles)

1988 Mtoto (5y), (9st 7lb).
1989 Nashwan (3y), (8st 8lb).
1990 Belmez (3y), (8st 9lb).
1991 Generous (3y), (8st 9lb), A. Munro.

Goodwood Cup (1812)
(Goodwood, about 2 miles, 5f.)

1988 Sadeem (5y), (9st 7lb).
1989 Mazzacano (4y), (9st).
1990 Lucky Moon (3y), (7st 10lb).
1991 Further Flight (5y), (9st), M. Hills.

Cambridgeshire Handicap (1839)
(Newmarket, 1 mile, 1f)

1988 Quinlan Terry (3y), (8st 5lb).
1989 Rambo's Hall (4y), (8st 6lb).
1990 Risen Moon (3y), (8st 9lb).
1991 Mellottie (6y), (9st 11lb), J. Lowe.

Prix de L'Arc de Triomphe (1920)
(Longchamp, 1½ miles)

1988 Tony Bin, (5y), (9st 4lb).
1989 Carroll House (4y), (9st 4lb).
1990 Saumarez (3y), (8st 11lb).
1991 Suave Dancer (3y), (8st 11lb), C. Asmussen.

ICE HOCKEY 1991

World Champions.—Sweden.
British Champions.—Durham Wasps.
League Champions:
   Premier Division.—Durham Wasps.
   First Division.—Humberside Seahawks.
Stanley Cup.—Edmonton Oilers.

ICE SKATING
British Championships
(Basingstoke, Nov. 1990)

Men's.—S. Cousins.
Women's.—J. Conway.
Pairs.—Miss C. Peake and A. Naylor.
Ice Dance.—Miss A. Hall and J. Blomfield.

European Championships
(Sofia, Jan. 1991)

Men's.—V. Petrenko (USSR).
Women's.—Miss S. Bonaly (France).

Pairs.—Miss N. Mishkutienok and A. Dmitriev (USSR).
Ice Dance.—Miss M. Klimova and S. Ponomarenko (USSR).

World Championships
(Munich, March 1991)

Men's.—K. Browning (Canada).
Women's.—K. Yamaguchi (USA).
Pairs.—Miss N. Mishkutienok and A. Dmitriev (USSR).
Ice Dance.—Miss I. Duchesnay and P. Duchesnay (France).

JUDO
World Championships 1991
(Barcelona, July)

MEN

Heavyweight (over 95 kg).—S. Kosorotow (USSR).
Light heavyweight (95 kg).—S. Traineau (France).
Middleweight (86 kg).—H. Okada (Japan).
Light middleweight (78 kg).—D. Lascau (Germany).
Lightweight (71 kg).—T. Koga (Japan).
Featherweight (65 kg).—G. Quellmalz (Germany).
Bantamweight (60 kg).—T. Koshino (Japan).
Openweight.—N. Ogawa (Japan).

WOMEN

Heavyweight (over 72 kg).—J. Moon (S. Korea).
Light heavyweight (72 kg), M. J. Kim (S. Korea).
Middleweight (66 kg), E. Pierantozzi (Italy).
Light middleweight (61 kg).—F. Eickhoff (Germany).
Lightweight (56 kg).—M. Blasco (Spain).
Featherweight (52 kg).—A. Giungi (Italy).
Bantamweight (48 kg).—C. Nowak (France).
Openweight.— Y. Zhuang (China).

British Championships 1990
(Crystal Palace, Dec.)

MEN

Heavyweight (over 95 kg).—J. Webb.
Light heavyweight (95 kg).—N. Kokotaylo.
Middleweight (86 kg).—S. Cross.
Light middleweight (78 kg).—K. Brown.
Lightweight (71 kg).—W. Cusack.
Featherweight (65 kg).—O. Pinnock.
Bantamweight (60 kg).—J. Newton.

WOMEN

Heavyweight (over 72 kg).—M. Bell.
Light heavyweight (72 kg).—J. Horton.
Middleweight (66 kg).—P. Robinson.
Light middleweight (61 kg).—M. Reveley.
Lightweight (56 kg).—N. Evans.
Featherweight (52 kg).—E. Summers.
Bantamweight (48 kg).—E. Bowley.

LAWN TENNIS

MAJOR CHAMPIONSHIPS 1991

Australian Open Championships (Melbourne)

Men's Singles.—B. Becker (Germany) beat I. Lendl (Czechoslovakia) 1–6, 6–4, 6–4, 6–4.

Women's Singles.—M. Seles (Yugoslavia) beat J. Novotna (Czechoslovakia) 5–7, 6–3, 6–1.

Men's Doubles.—S. Davis and D. Pate (USA) beat P. McEnroe and D. Wheaton (USA) 6–7, 7–6, 6–3, 7–5.

Women's Doubles.—P. Fendick and M. J. Fernandez (USA) beat G. Fernandez (USA) and J. Novotna (Czechoslovakia) 7–6, 6–1.

Mixed Doubles.—Miss J. Durie and J. Bates (GB) beat Miss R. White and S. Davis (USA) 2–6, 6–4, 6–4.

French Open Championships (Paris)

Men's Singles.—J. Courier (USA) beat A. Agassi (USA) 3–6, 6–4, 2–6, 6–1, 6–4.
Women's Singles.—M. Seles (Yugoslavia) beat A. Sanchez Vicario (Spain) 6–3, 6–4.
Men's Doubles.—J. Fitzgerald (Australia) and A. Jarryd (Sweden) beat R. Leach and J. Pugh (USA) 6–0, 7–6.
Women's Doubles.—G. Fernandez (USA) and J. Novotna (Czechoslovakia) beat L. Savchenko and N. Zvereva (USSR) 6–4, 6–0.
Mixed Doubles.—Miss H. Sukova and C. Suk (Czechoslovakia) beat Miss C. Vis and P. Haarhuis (Holland) 3–6, 6–4, 6–1.

All England Championships (Wimbledon)

Men's Singles.—M. Stich (Germany) beat B. Becker (Germany) 6–4, 7–6, 6–4.
Women's Singles.—S. Graf (Germany) beat G. Sabatini (Argentina) 6–4, 3–6, 8–6.
Men's Doubles.—J. Fitzgerald (Australia) and A. Jarryd (Sweden) beat J. Frana (Argentina) and L. Lavalle (Mexico) 6–3, 6–4, 6–7, 6–1.
Women's Doubles.—L. Savchenko and N. Zvereva (USSR) beat G. Fernandez (Puerto Rico) and J. Novotna (Czechoslovakia) 6–4, 3–6, 6–4.
Mixed Doubles.—Mrs P. Smylie and J. Fitzgerald (Australia) beat Miss N. Zvereva (USSR) and J. Pugh (USA) 7–6, 6–2.

US Open Championships (New York)

Men's Singles.—S. Edberg (Sweden) beat J. Courier (USA), 6–2, 6–4, 6–0.
Women's Singles.—M. Seles (Yugoslavia) beat M. Navratilova (USA) 7–6, 6–1.
Men's Doubles.—J. Fitzgerald (Australia) and A. Jarryd (Sweden) beat S. Davis and D. Pate (USA) 6–3, 3–6, 6–3, 6–3.
Women's Doubles.—P. Shriver (USA) and N. Zvereva (USSR) beat J. Novotna (Czechoslovakia) and L. Savchenko (USSR) 6–4, 4–6, 7–6.
Mixed Doubles.—Ms M. Bollegraf and T. Nijssen (Netherlands) beat Miss A. Sanchez Vicario and E. Sanchez (Spain) 6–2, 7–6.

THE GRAND SLAM CUP 1990.—P. Sampras (USA) beat B. Gilbert (USA) 3–0.

TEAM CHAMPIONSHIPS

Davis Cup 1990.—USA beat Australia 3–2.
Federation Cup 1991 (Nottingham).—Spain beat USA 2–1.
LTA County Cup 1991.—Men, Yorkshire; *Women,* Yorkshire.

NATIONAL CHAMPIONSHIPS 1990

Men's Singles.—J. Bates.
Woman's Singles.—J. Durie.
Mens Doubles.—J. Bates and A. Castle.
Women's Doubles.—J. Durie and A. Hobbs.

MOTOR CYCLING

Riders' Championship 1990.—1. W. Rainey, 255 pts; 2. K. Schwantz, 188 pts; 3. M. Doohan, 179 pts.

500 cc Grand Prix 1991

Japanese (Suzuka).—K. Schwantz (Suzuki).
Australian (Sydney).—W. Rainey (Yamaha).

United States (Laguna Seca, California).—W. Rainey (Yamaha).
Spanish (Jerez).—M. Doohan (Honda).
Italian (Misano).—M. Doohan (Honda).
West German (Hockenheim).—K. Schwantz (Suzuki).
Austrian (Salzburg).—M. Doohan (Honda).
European (Madrid).—W. Rainey (Yamaha).
Dutch (Assen).—K. Schwantz (Suzuki).
French (Le Castellet).—W. Rainey (Yamaha).
British (Donington Park).—K. Schwantz (Suzuki).
San Marino.—W. Rainey (Yamaha).
Czech (Brno).—W. Rainey (Yamaha).
Le Mans.—K. Schwantz (Suzuki).
Malaysian (Shah Alam).—J. Kocinski (Yamaha).

Riders' Championship 1991.—1. W. Rainey, 233 pts; 2. M. Doohan, 224 pts; 3. K. Schwantz, 204 pts.

Senior Manx Grand Prix.—T. Knight (Honda).
Senior TT, Isle of Man.—S. Hislop (Honda).
Junior TT, Isle of Man.—R. Dunlop (Yamaha).

MOTOR RACING

Formula One Grand Prix 1990

Japanese (Suzuka).—1. N. Piquet (Benetton); 2. R. Moreno (Benetton); 3. A. Suzuki (Larrousse).
Australian (Adelaide).—1. N. Piquet (Benetton); 2. N. Mansell (Ferrari); 3. A. Prost (Ferrari).
Drivers' Championship winner 1990.—A. Senna (McLaren), 78 pts.
Constructors' Championship winner 1990.—McLaren–Honda, 121 pts.

Formula One Grand Prix 1991

United States (Phoenix).—1. A. Senna (McLaren); 2. A. Prost (Ferrari); 3. N. Piquet (Benetton).
Brazilian (Sao Paulo).—1. A. Senna (McLaren); 2. R. Patrese (Williams); 3. G. Berger (McLaren).
San Marino (Imola).—1. A. Senna (McLaren); 2. G. Berger (McLaren); 3. J. J. Lehto (Dallara).
Monaco (Monte Carlo).—1. A. Senna (McLaren); 2. N. Mansell (Williams); 3. J. Alesi (Ferrari).
Canadian (Montreal).—1. N. Piquet (Benetton); 2. S. Modena (Tyrrell); 3. R. Patrese (Williams).
Mexican (Mexico City).—1. R. Patrese (Williams); 2. N. Mansell (Williams); 3. A. Senna (McLaren).
French (Magny-Cours).—1. N. Mansell (Williams); 2. A. Prost (Ferrari); 3. A. Senna (McLaren).
British (Silverstone).—1. N. Mansell (Williams); 2. G. Berger (McLaren); 3. A. Prost (Ferrari).
German (Hockenheim).—1. N. Mansell (Williams); 2. R. Patrese (Williams); 3. J. Alesi (Ferrari).
Hungarian (Budapest).—1. A. Senna (McLaren); 2. N. Mansell (Williams); 3. R. Patrese (Williams).
Belgian (Spa-Francorchamps).—1. A. Senna (McLaren); 2. G. Berger (McLaren); 3. N. Piquet (Benetton).
Italian (Monza).—1. N. Mansell (Williams); 2. A. Senna (McLaren); 3. A. Prost (Ferrari).
Portuguese (Estoril).—1. R. Patrese (Williams); 2. A. Senna (McLaren); 3. J. Alesi (Ferrari).
Spanish (Barcelona).—1. N. Mansell (Williams); 2. A. Prost (Ferrari); 3. R. Patrese (Williams).

MOTOR RALLYING

Lombard RAC Rally 1990.—C. Sainz and L. Moya (Spain) (Toyota).
Paris/Dakar Trans-Sahara Rally 1991.—A. Vatanen (Finland) (Citroen).
Monte Carlo Rally 1991.—C. Sainz (Spain) (Toyota).
Safari Rally 1991.—J. Kankkunen (Finland) (Lancia).
Circuit of Ireland Rally 1991.—C. McRae (Scotland) (Subaru).

Indianapolis 500 1991.—R. Mears (USA) (Penske–Chevrolet).

Le Mans 24-hour 1991.—V. Weidler (Germany), J. Herbert (GB) and B. Gachot (Belgium) (Mazda).

Birmingham Super-Prix 1991.—cancelled.

NETBALL

World Championship final 1991.—Australia beat New Zealand 53–52.

Test Matches

1990
Nov. 17 Gateshead: England 40, Australia 48
     21 Leicester: England 39, Australia 55.
     24 London Arena: England 34, Australia 60.

Internationals

1991
Jan. 26 Dublin: Rep. of Ireland 43, Wales 39.
Feb. 2 E. Kilbride: Scotland 47, N. Ireland 33.
     16 Reading: England 64, Rep. of Ireland 34.
March 16 Lisburn: N. Ireland 32, England 53.
        Cardiff: Wales 52, Scotland 45.

Inter-County Championship final 1991.—Surrey beat Birmingham 21–17.

National Clubs Championship final 1991.—Harborne beat Linden 53–49.

English Counties League Champions.—Surrey.

POLO 1991

Prince of Wales's Trophy.—Munnipore beat Sladmore 8–6.

Queen's Cup final.—Ellerston White beat Tramontana 11–5.

Gold Cup (British Championship).—Tramontana beat Ellerston White 11–7.

Coronation Cup.—New Zealand beat England 12–10.

Silver Jubilee Cup.—Prince of Wales's Team beat Hurlingham Association 7–6½.

Warwickshire Cup.—Black Bears beat Munnipore 13–11.

Cowdray Challenge Cup.—Loc Locos beat Windsor Park15–8.

Universities.—Cambridge beat Oxford 4–2.

RACKETS

World Singles Champion.—J. Male.

World Doubles Champions.—J. Male and J. Prenn.

Amateur Singles Championship 1990.—J. Male beat W. Boone 3–1.

Amateur Doubles Championship 1991.—J. Prenn and J. Male beat W. Boone and J. Snow, 4–0.

Professional Singles Championship 1991.—S. Hazell beat N. Smith 3–1.

British Open Singles Championship 1991.—J. Male beat N. Smith 4–1.

British Open Doubles Championship 1991.—N. Smith and S. Hazell beat J. Male and J. Prenn 4–3.

Noel Bruce Cup 1990.—Eton (W. Boone and M. Hue Williams) beat Harrow (J. Prenn and C. Hue Williams) 4–1.

Public Schools Doubles Championship 1991.—Clifton (J. Crane and M. Windows) beat Eton (J. Larken and A. Smith-Bingham) 4–2.

Universities 1991.—Oxford beat Cambridge 3–0.

REAL TENNIS

World Singles Champion.—W. Davies.

Professional Singles Championship 1991.—L. Deuchar beat C. Ronaldson 3–0.

Professional Doubles Championship 1991.—C. Bray and C. Lumley beat A. Phillips and K. King 2–1.

Amateur Singles Championship 1991.—J. Snow beat A. Page 3–0.

Amateur Doubles Championship 1991.—J. Snow and M. McMurrugh beat M. Howard and A. Page 3–0.

British Open Singles Championship 1990.—L. Deuchar beat J. Snow 3–0.

British Open Doubles Championship 1990.—W. Davies and L. Deuchar beat R. Fahey and P. Meares 3–0.

British Open Ladies Singles 1991.—P. Fellows beat A. Garside 2–0.

Henry Leaf Cup final 1991.—Radley (J. Male and T. Warburg) beat Lancing (A. Page and J. Scott) 2–0.

Universities 1991.—Oxford beat Cambridge 6–0.

ROWING 1991

World Championships
(Vienna, August)

MEN

Coxless pairs.—Great Britain.
Coxless fours.—Australia.
Coxed pairs.—Italy.
Coxed fours.—Germany.
Single sculls.—T. Lange (Germany).
Double sculls.—Holland.
Quad sculls.—USSR.
Eights.—Germany.

WOMEN

Coxless pairs.—Canada.
Coxless fours.—Canada.
Single sculls.—S. Laumann (Canada).
Double sculls.—Germany.
Quad sculls.—Germany.
Eights.—Canada.

Henley Royal Regatta

Grand Challenge Cup.—Leander and Star beat Dinamo and Soviet Army (USSR) by 2¼ lengths.

Ladies' Challenge Plate.—Leander and Molesey beat University of London and Oxford University by 1 length.

Henley Prize.—University of Bristol beat Imperial College, London by 3 ft.

Visitors' Cup.—Goldie A beat University of London by 1½ lengths.

Thames Challenge Cup.—University of Pennsylvania A beat University of London by 1 length.

Stewards' Challenge Cup.—Leander and Molesey beat Leander by 2 lengths.

Queen Mother Challenge Cup.—Leander and Tideway Scullers School beat Nottinghamshire County RA and London, easily.

Princess Elizabeth Cup.—Eton College beat King's School, Canterbury, by 4½ lengths.

Prince Philip Cup.—Leander and Star beat Dinamo Vilnius, Lithuania (USSR) by 2¼ lengths.

Silver Goblets and Nickall's Challenge Cup.—S. Redgrave and M. Pinsent (Leander) beat J. Robert and M. Bermudez (Natacio Banyoles, Spain), easily.

Wyfold Cup.—Nautilus beat Nottinghamshire County RA by 2¼ lengths.

Britannia Challenge Cup.—Nottinghamshire County RA beat Nottingham and Union by 5 lengths.

Double Sculls Cup.—B. Eltang (Danske Studenters, Denmark) and H. Bang (Fana, Norway) beat R. Luke and C. Skuse (Leander), easily.

Diamond Challenge Sculls.—W. van Belleghem (Ghent, Belgium) beat E. Verdonk (Koru, New Zealand), not rowed out.

National Championships
(Holme Pierrepont)

MEN

Coxed pairs.—University of London.
Coxless pairs.—Bedford B.
Coxed fours.—Nottingham County.
Coxless fours.—Goldie (Cambridge University).
Single sculls.—T. Mossop (Kingston).
Double sculls.—Molesey.
Quad sculls.—Tideway Scullers A.
Eights.—University of London/Leander/Nottingham County.

WOMEN

Coxless pairs.—Norwich/Norwich Union.
Coxless fours.—Thames Tradesmen C.
Coxed fours.—Edinburgh University/Alexandria.
Single sculls.—S. Appelboom (Mortlake Anglian Alpha).
Double Sculls.—Nottingham County.
Quad sculls.—Tideway Scullers.
Eights.—Cambridge University.

The 137th University Boat Race
(Putney-Mortlake, 4 miles 1 f, 180 yd)

Oxford beat Cambridge by 4¼ lengths, 16 m, 59 s.
(Cambridge have won 69 times, Oxford 67 and there has been 1 dead-heat. The record time is 16 m, 45 s, rowed by Oxford in 1984.)
Women's Boat Race.—Oxford beat Cambridge by 3 lengths; 17 m, 29 s.

Other Rowing Events

Oxford Torpids.—*Men*, Christ Church; *Women*, Somerville.
Cambridge Lents.—*Men*, Trinity Hall; *Women*, Emmanuel.
Oxford Summer Eights.—*Men*, University College; *Women*, Somerville.
Cambridge Mays.—*Men*, Downing; *Women*, Lady Margaret.
Head of the River.—*Men*, Leander I; *Women*, University of London/Okeanos/Norwich/Nereus/Thames Tradesmen/Triton.
Doggett's Coat and Badge (*Estab.* 1715, 277th race, London Bridge-Chelsea, 4½ miles).—L. C. Leicho (Sevenoaks).
Wingfield Sculls.—G. Pooley (Cambridge University).

RUGBY FIVES

National Singles Championship 1990.—*Men*, W. Enstone beat N. Roberts 2–0; *Women*, P. Smith beat D. Hall-Witton 1–0.
National Doubles Championships 1991.—W. Enstone and N. Roberts beat I. Fuller and D. Hebden 2–0.
Scottish Open Championships 1991.—*Singles:* N. Roberts; *Doubles:* N. Roberts and M. Hinton.
National Schools' Championships 1991.—*Singles:* J. Nelmes (Clifton). *Doubles:* Loretto.

RUGBY LEAGUE
International Matches

1990
Oct. 27 Wembley: Great Britain 19, Australia 12.
Nov. 10 Old Trafford: Great Britain 10, Australia 14.
24 Elland Road: Great Britain 0, Australia 14.
1991
Jan. 27 Perpignan: France 10, Great Britain 45.
Feb. 16 Headingley: Great Britain 60, France 4.

Domestic Competitions

Rugby League Challenge Cup final 1991. (Wembley, April 27).—Wigan beat St Helens 13–8.
Premiership Trophy final 1991. (Old Trafford, May 12).—Hull beat Widnes 14–4.
Division 2 Premiership final 1991.—Salford beat Halifax 27–20.
Stones Bitter Championship.—Wigan.
Division 2 Championship.—Salford.
Regal Trophy final 1991. (Headingley, Jan. 12).—Warrington beat Bradford Northern 12–2.
Lancashire Cup 1990.—Widnes beat Salford 24–18.
Yorkshire Cup 1990.—Castleford beat Wakefield Trinity 11–8.
Universities 1991.—Oxford beat Cambridge 24–4.

AMATEUR RUGBY LEAGUE

County Championship.—Lancashire.
National Inter-League Shield Competitions.—
Open Age.—Humberside.
Under 19.—York.
Under 17.—Castleford.
National Cup Competitions.—
Open Age.—Saddleworth Rangers.
Under 19.—Saddleworth Rangers.
National League Champions.—Leigh East.
National League Challenge Cup Winners 1991.—Millom.

RUGBY UNION
International Matches

Erratum (1991 edition, page 1088): March 17, 1990—Scotland 13, England 7.

1990
Oct. 27 Dublin: Ireland 20, Argentina 18.
Nov. 3 Twickenham: England 51, Argentina 0.
10 Edinburgh: Scotland 49, Argentina 3.
1991
Jan. 19 Cardiff: Wales 6, England 25.
Paris: France 15, Scotland 9.
Feb. 2 Edinburgh: Scotland 32, Wales 12.
Dublin: Ireland 13, France 21.
16 Twickenham: England 21, Scotland 12.
Cardiff: Wales 21, Ireland 21.
Mar. 2 Dublin: Ireland 7, England 16.
Paris: France 36, Wales 3.
16 Twickenham: England 21, France 19.
Edinburgh: Scotland 28, Ireland 25.
May 18 Connecticut: USA 12, Scotland 41.
25 New Brunswick: Canada 24, Scotland 19.
July 20 Suva: Fiji 12, England 28.
Windhoek: Namibia 15, Ireland 6.
21 Brisbane: Australia 63, Wales 6.
27 Sydney: Australia 40, England 15.
Windhoek: Namibia 26, Ireland 15.
Aug. 31 Bucharest: Romania 18, Scotland 12.
Sept. 4 Cardiff: Wales 9, France 22.
7 Twickenham: England 53, USSR 0.

The World Cup runs from Sept. 29 to Nov. 2, 1991.

Five Nations' Championship 1991

	P	W	D	L	Pts. F	Pts. A	Total
England	4	4	0	0	83	44	8
France	4	3	0	1	91	46	6
Scotland	4	2	0	2	81	73	4
Ireland	4	0	1	3	66	86	1
Wales	4	0	1	3	42	114	1

Domestic Competitions

English League.—division 1, Bath, 22 pts; *division 2*, Rugby, 20 pts; *division 3*, West Hartlepool, 21 pts; *division 4*, Otley, 22 pts (*north*); Redruth, 24 pts (*south*).

*County Championship final 1991.—*Cornwall beat Yorkshire 29–20.

Scottish League.—division 1, Boroughmuir, 23 pts; *division 2*, Watsonians, 26 pts; *division 3*, Peebles, 22 pts; *division 4*, Dumfries 22 pts; *Division 5*, Alloa, 22 pts; *division 6*, Falkirk 24 pts.

Welsh League.—premier division, Neath, 28 pts; *division 1*, Newport, 26 pts; *division 2*, Dunvant, 31 pts; *division 3*, Llandovery, 30 pts.

Pilkington Cup final 1991 (Twickenham, May 4).—Harlequins beat Northampton 25–13.

*Welsh Cup final 1991.—*Llanelli beat Pontypool 24–9.

*Hospitals' Cup final 1991.—*St Mary's beat The London 15–8.

*Services Championship 1991.—*Army beat Royal Navy 10–0; RAF beat Army 30–14; RAF beat Royal Navy 22–13.

*Universities, 1990.—*Oxford beat Cambridge 21–12.

*Middlesex Sevens 1991—*London Scottish beat Harlequins 20–16.

Women's World Cup final 1991 (Cardiff Arms Park, April 14).—USA beat England 19–6.

SHOOTING

Bisley, 122nd NRA, 1991

*Queen's Prize.—*1. C. Fitzpatrick, 293 pts; 2. C. A. Brook, 292 pts; 3. T. A. Ringer, 291 pts.

*Grand Aggregate.—*1. J. E. M. Bellringer, 595 pts; 2. P. G. Kent, 592 pts; 3. C. N. Tremlett, 589 pts.

*Prince of Wales Prize.—*1. A. G. Harrison, 75·15 pts; 2. N. P. Moxon, 75·14 pts; 3. S. H. Cox, 75·14 pts.

*St George's Vase.—*1. T. A. Ringer, 150 pts; 2. D. Coleman, 149 pts; 3. A. St G. Tucker, 149 pts.

*Allcomers Aggregate.—*1. J. E. M. Bellringer, 321·45 pts; 2. N. R. J. Brazier, 319·43 pts; 3. P. A. E. Charlton, 319·41 pts.

*National Trophy.—*1. England, 2,032·259 pts; 2. Scotland, 2,027·244 pts; 3. Ireland, 2,007·225 pts.

*Kolapore Cup.—*1. Great Britain, 1,182·164 pts; 2. Jersey, 1,169·151 pts; 3. Canada, 1,153·132 pts.

*Chancellor's Challenge Plate.—*1. Cambridge University, 1,150·130 pts; 2. Oxford University, 1,124·112 pts.

*Musketeers Cup.—*1. London University A, 586·81 pts; 2. London University B, 573·67 pts.

*Vizianagram Trophy.—*1. House of Lords, 661·31 pts; 2. House of Commons, 645·19 pts.

*County Long-Range Championship.—*1. Surrey, 291 pts; 2. Cheshire, 290 pts; 3. Berkshire, 288 pts.

*Mackinnon Challenge Cup.—*1. England, 1,139 pts; 2. Scotland, 1,125 pts; 3. Canada, 1,124 pts.

Clay Pigeon Shooting 1991

*World Cup.—*S. Clarke (GB).

*Women's World Cup.—*S. Bayley (GB).

*International Cup (Down-the-Line).—*Ireland, 7,064/7,500.

*British Open Down-the-Line Championship.—*N. Bailey, 100/299.

*Mackintosh Trophy.—*Canada, 7,371/7,500.

*British Open Skeet Championship.—*G. Digweed, 100+375.

*British Open Sporting Championship.—*G. Digweed, 89/100.

*Coronation Cup.—*J. H. Winn, 370.

SNOOKER

*World Professional Championship 1991.—*J. Parrott (England) beat J. White (England) 18–11.

*World Matchplay Championship 1990.—*J. White (England) beat S. Hendry (Scotland) 18–9.

*Scottish Masters 1990.—*S. Hendry (Scotland) beat T. Griffiths (Wales) 10–6.

*Rothman's Grand Prix 1990.—*S. Hendry (Scotland) beat N. Bond (England) 10–5.

*Dubai Classic 1990.—*S. Hendry (Scotland) beat S. Davis (England) 9–1.

*European Open 1991.—*A. Jones (England) beat M. Johnston-Allen (England) 9–7.

*Irish Masters 1991.—*S. Davies (England) beat J. Parrott (England) 9–5.

European Masters League 1991. S. Davies (England) beat J. White (England) 6–2.

*Benson and Hedges Masters 1991.—*S. Hendry (Scotland) beat M. Hallett (England) 9–8.

*UK Professional Championship 1990.—*S. Hendry (Scotland) beat S. Davis (England) 16–15.

*British Open Championship 1991.—*S. Hendry (Scotland) beat G. Wilkinson (England) 10–9.

*Mercantile Credit Classic 1991.—*J. White (England) beat S. Hendry (Scotland) 10–4.

*World Amateur Championship 1990.—*S. O'Connor (Rep. of Ireland) beat S. Lemmans (Belgium) 11–8.

*Women's World Championship 1990.—*K. Corr (England) beat S. Hill (England) 7–4.

*Women's UK Championship 1991.—*cancelled.

SPEEDWAY

1990

*British League Riders' Champion.—*H. Nielsen (Oxford).

*British League Champions.—*Reading.

*British League Knock-Out Cup Winners.—*Reading.

*National League Champions.—*Poole.

*National League Knock-out Cup Winners.—*Poole.

1991

*World Individual Championship.—*J. O. Pedersen (Denmark).

*World Pairs Championship.—*H. Nielson, J. O. Pedersen and T. Knudsen (Denmark).

*World Team Championship.—*Denmark.

*Gold Cup final.—*Berwick beat Oxford 93–87.

*British Champion.—*G. Havelock (Bradford).

SQUASH RACKETS

MEN

*World Open Championship 1991.—*R. Martin (Australia) beat Jahangir Khan (Pakistan) 3–1.

*World Team Championship 1989.—*Australia.

*European Team Championship 1991.—*England.

*European Club Championship 1991.—*Kiel (Germany).

*British Open Championship 1991.—*Jahangir Khan (Pakistan) beat Jansher Khan (Pakistan), 3–1.

*National Championship 1991.—*P. Gregory beat S. Parke 3–1.

*Scottish Open Championship 1991.—*Jahangir Khan beat C. Dittmar 3–1.

WOMEN

*World Open Championship 1990.—*S. Devoy (NZ) beat M. Le Moignan (GB).

*World Team Championship 1990.—*England.

*European Team Championship 1991.—*England.

*European Club Championship 1991.—*Victoria Club (Rotterdam).

*British Open Championship 1991.—*L. Opie beat S. Wright 3–1.

*National Championship 1991.—*M. Le Moignan beat S. Horner 3–0.

SWIMMING 1991

World Swimming Championships
(Perth, January)

MEN

50m freestyle.—T. Jager (USA).
100m freestyle.—M. Biondi (USA).
200m freestyle.—G. Lamberti (Italy).
400m freestyle.—J. Hoffmann (Germany).
1,500m freestyle.—J. Hoffmann (Germany).
*50m breaststroke.—Chen Jianhong (China).
100m breaststroke.—N. Rozsa (Hungary).
200m breaststroke.—M. Barrowman (USA).
*50m butterfly.—T. Haase (Germany).
100m butterfly.—A. Nesty (Surinam).
200m butterfly.—M. Stewart (USA).
*50m backstroke.—D. Richter (Germany).
100m backstroke.—J. Rouse (USA).
200m backstroke.—M. Lopez-Zubero (Spain).
200m medley.—T. Darnyi (Hungary).
400m medley.—T. Darnyi (Hungary).
*4 × 50m freestyle relay.—Germany.
4 × 100m freestyle relay.—USA.
4 × 100m medley relay.—USA.
4 × 200m freestyle relay.—Germany.

WOMEN

50m freestyle.—Zhuang Yong (China).
100m freestyle.—N. Haislett (USA).
200m freestyle.—H. Lewis (Australia).
400m freestyle.—J. Evans (USA).
800m freestyle.—J. Evans (USA).
*50m breaststroke.—I. Landik (USSR).
100m breaststroke.—L. Frame (Australia).
200m breaststroke.—Y. Volkova (USSR).
*50m butterfly.—Qian Hong (China).
100m butterfly.—Qian Hong (China).
200m butterfly.—S. Sanders (USA).
*50m backstroke.—Yang Wenyi (China).
100m backstroke.—K. Egerszegi (Hungary).
200m backstroke.—K. Egerszegi (Hungary).
200m medley.—Lin Li (China).
400m medley.—Lin Li (China).
*4 × 50m freestyle relay.—Germany.
4 × 100m freestyle relay.—USA.
4 × 100m medley relay.—USA.
4 × 200m freestyle relay.—Germany.

* sprint finals, outside official World Championships.

National Swimming Championships
(Leeds, August)

MEN

50m freestyle.—M. Fibbens (Barnet).
100m freestyle.—M. Fibbens (Barnet).
200m freestyle.—P. Howe (Birmingham).
400m freestyle.—P. Howe (Birmingham).
1,500m freestyle.—I. Wilson (Sunderland).
50m breaststroke.—A. Moorhouse (Leeds).
100m breaststroke.—A. Moorhouse (Leeds).
200m breaststroke.—N. Gillingham (Birmingham).
50m butterfly.—M. Fibbens (Barnet).
100m butterfly.—M. Fibbens (Barnet).
200m butterfly.—K. Crosby (Warrington).
50m backstroke.—M. Harris (Barnet).
100m backstroke.—M. Harris (Barnet).
200m backstroke.—G. Robins (Portsmouth).
200m medley.—J. Davey (Leeds).
400m medley.—A. Rolley (Portsmouth).
4 × 100m freestyle relay.—Leeds.
4 × 100m medley relay.—Portsmouth.

WOMEN

50m freestyle.—A. Sheppard (Milngavie and Bearsden).
100m freestyle.—K. Pickering (Ipswich).
200m freestyle.—R. Gilfillan (Dundee).
400m freestyle.—R. Gilfillan (Dundee).
800m freestyle.—S. Foggo (Newcastle).
50m breaststroke.—L. Coombes (Southampton).
100m breaststroke.—L. Coombes (Southampton).
200m breaststroke.—J. Hill (Cumbernauld).
50m butterfly.—N. Kennedy (Nova Centurion).
100m butterfly.—M. Campbell (Portsmouth).
200m butterfly.—H. Jepson (Kirklees).
50m backstroke.—K. Read (Barnet).
100m backstroke.—K. Read (Barnet).
200m backstroke.—K. Read (Barnet).
200m medley.—Z. Long (Beckenham).
400m medley.—Z. Long (Beckenham).
4 × 100m freestyle relay.—Nova Centurion.
4 × 100m medley relay.—City of Southampton.

TABLE TENNIS 1991

World Championships
(Chiba, Japan)

Men's Singles.—J. Persson (Sweden) beat J.-O. Waldner (Sweden) 3–0.
Women's Singles.—Deng Yaping (China) beat Li Bunhui (Korea) 2–1.
Men's Doubles.—P. Karlsson and T. von Scheele (Sweden) beat Wang Tao and Lu Lin (China) 3–2.
Women's Doubles.—Chen Zihe and Gao Jun (China) beat Qiao Hong and Deng Yaping (China) 3–1.
Mixed Doubles.—Wang Tao and Liu Wei (China) beat Xie Chaojie and Chen Zihe (China) 3–0.

English National Championships
(Stourbridge)

Men's Singles.—C. Prean beat D. Douglas 3–0.
Women's Singles.—A. Holt beat L. Lomas 3–2.
Men's Doubles.—S. Andrew and N. Mason beat S. Gibson and J. Holland 2–0.
Women's Doubles.—L. Lomas and F. Elliot beat A. Gordon and A. Holt 2–0.
Mixed Doubles.—N. Deaton and C. Xin Hua beat S. Andrew and F. Elliot 2–1.
European Nations Cup.—Germany.

VOLLEYBALL

MEN

World Championships 1990.—Italy.
British Championships 1991.—Scotland.
National League Champions.—Mizuno Malory.
National Cup Final 1991.—Polonia beat Reebok Liverpool City 3–2.

WOMEN

World Championships 1990.—USSR.
British Championships 1991.—England.
National League Champions.—Mizuno Britannia.
National Cup final 1991.—Mizuno Britannia beat Woolwich Brixton Knights 3–1.

YACHTING

BOC single-handed round-the-world race (Sept. 15, 1990–April 1991).—C. Auguin (*Groupe Sceta*) in 120 days, 22 hours, 36 minutes.
Admiral's Cup 1991.—France (*Corum Saphir/Corum Rubis/Corum Diament*), 138·75 pts.
Fastnet Race 1991.—X. Phelipon (France), *Corum Diament*.

WORLD STUDENT GAMES

Sheffield July 13–25, 1991

ATHLETICS

Men
100m, M. Bates (USA), 10·17s
200m, J. Drummond (USA), 20·58s
400m, P. O'Connor (Jamaica), 45·42s
800m, G. D'Urso (Italy), 1m 46.82s
1,500m, N. Bruton (Ireland), 3m 50·59s
5,000m, J. Maycock (GB), 13m 39·25s
10,000m, S. Freigang (Germany), 28m 15·84s
Marathon, Yung-Jo Whang (Korea), 2h 12m 40s
110m hurdles, E. Ellis (USA), 13·83s
400m hurdles, D. Adkins (USA), 49·01s
3,000m steeplechase, S. Creighton (Australia), 8m 32·30s
20km walk, R. Korzeniowski (Poland), 1h 24m 37s
4 × 100m, USA, 39·10s
4 × 400m, USA, 3m 03·65s
High jump, H. Conway (USA), 2·37m
Pole vault, I. Bagyula (Hungary), 5·80m
Long jump, A. Turner (USA), 8·18m
Triple jump, B. Wellman (Bermuda), 17·07m
Shot, A. Klimenko (USSR), 19·35m
Discus, A. Olukoju (Nigeria), 61·48m
Hammer, K. Flax (USA), 76·46m
Javelin, S. Backley (GB), 87·42m
Decathlon, S. Fritz (USA), 8,079 pts

Women
100m, C. Gaines (USA), 11·27s
200m, Huei-Chen Wang (Taiwan), 23·22s
400m, M. Malone (USA), 50·65s
800m, I. Yevseyeva (USSR), 1m 59·80s
1,500m, S. O'Sullivan (Ireland), 4m 12·14s
3,000m, I. Besliu (Romania), 8m 55·42s
10,000m, A. Letko (USA), 32m 36·87s
Marathon, M. Iwai (Japan), 2h 36m 27s
100m hurdles, M. Azyabina (USSR), 12·95s
400m hurdles, G. Tromp (Netherlands), 55·30s
10km walk, S. Essayah (Finland), 44m 04s
4 × 100m, USA, 44·45s
4 × 400m, USA, 3m 27·93s
High jump, A. Inverarity (Australia), 1·92m
Long jump, I. Kravets (USSR), 6·87m
Triple jump, Huirong Li (China), 14·20m
Shot, S. Krieleva (USSR), 19·94m
Discus, Yanling Xiao (China), 64·36m
Javelin, T. Shilolenko (USSR), 63·56m
Heptathlon, B. Clarius (Germany), 6,419 pts

SWIMMING

Men
50m freestyle, S. Caron (France), 22·97s
100m freestyle, S. Caron (France), 49·72s
200m freestyle, S. Caron (France), 1m 50·24s
400m freestyle, A. Wojdat (Poland), 3m 52·55s
1,500m freestyle, I. Wilson (GB), 15m 15·30s
4 × 100m freestyle, USA, 3m 22·73s
4 × 200m freestyle, USSR, 7m 23·28s
100m breaststroke, B. Pager (USA), 1m 03·21s
200m breaststroke, G. O'Toole (Ireland), 2m 16·75s
100m backstroke, D. Botsford (Canada), 56·40s
200m backstroke, W. Schwenk (USA), 2m 00·38s
100m butterfly, T. Li (China), 55·61s
200m butterfly, R. Carey (USA), 1m 58·36s
200m medley, G. Burgess (USA), 2m 03·90s
400m medley, T. Fujimoto (Japan), 4m 23·10s
4 × 100m medley, USA, 3m 44·33s
Water polo, USA.

Women
50m freestyle, Wenyi Yang (China), 25·92s
100m freestyle, Yong Zhuang (China), 56·26s
200m freestyle, K. Kraemer (USA), 2m 02·23s
400m freestyle, P. Noall (Canada), 4m 16·74s
800m freestyle, F. Ferrarni (Italy), 8m 43·55s
4 × 100m freestyle, China, 3m 46·41s
4 × 200m freestyle, USSR, 8m 14·48s
100m breaststroke, G. Cloutier (Canada), 1m 10·93s
200m breaststroke, S. Kuzymina (USSR), 2m 31·60s
100m backstroke, B. Bedford (USA), 1m 02·08s
200m backstroke, Lin Li (China), 2m 15·12s
100m butterfly, Xiaohong Wang (China), 1m 00·00s
200m butterfly, Xiaohong Wang (China), 2m 10·76s
200m medley, Lin Li (China), 2m 14·22s
400m medley, Lin Li (China), 4m 45·58s
4 × 100m medley, USA, 4m 11.70s

DIVING

Men
Highboard, Feilong Wu (China)
1m springboard, Wei Lan (China)
3m springboard, Li Deliang (China)

Women
Highboard, Kim Chun-Ok (N. Korea)
1m springboard, X. Yu (China)
3m springboard, Min Gao (China)

ASSOCIATION FOOTBALL

Men, South Korea

BASKETBALL

Men, USA
Women, USA

HOCKEY

Men, Great Britain
Women, Netherlands

FENCING

Men
Individual foil, D. Shevchenko (USSR)
Team foil, Italy
Individual épée, P. Kolobkov (USSR)
Team épée, Germany
Individual sabre, G. Kirienko (USSR)
Team sabre, Germany

Women
Individual foil, G. Trillini (Italy)
Team foil, Italy
Individual épée, M. Horvath (Hungary)
Team épée, Hungary

GYMNASTICS

Men
All-round, Wang Zong Sheng (China)
Floor exercises, M. Racanelli (Italy)
Pommel horse, H. Dong Huang (China)
Vault, H. Chun Yeo (S. Korea)
Horizontal bar, G-Su Pai (N. Korea)
Parallel bars, A. Kan (USSR)
Rings, Myomg Su-Sin (N. Korea)
Team, USSR

Women
All-round, E. Sazonenkova (USSR)
Floor exercises, N. Lashonova (USSR)
Beam, Choi Gyong Hui (N. Korea)
Assymetric bars, H. Gyong Choi (N. Korea)
Vault, K. Seo (Japan)
Team, North Korea
Rhythmic all-round, Gyong Hui-Li (N. Korea)
Rhythmic rope, Gyong Hui-Li (N. Korea)
Rhythmic hoop, Suk Yong-Li (N. Korea)
Rhythmic ball, Gyong Hui-Li (N. Korea)
Rhythmic clubs, Suk Yong-Li (N. Korea)

TENNIS

Men's singles, Xia Jai-Ping (China)
Women's singles, M. Endo (Japan)
Men's doubles, Chang Eui Jong/Ho Ji Seong (S. Korea)
Women's doubles, Kim Il-Soon/Lee Jung-Myung (S. Korea)
Mixed doubles, B. Hanson/S. Gilchrist (USA)

VOLLEYBALL

Men, Poland
Women, Italy

THE OLYMPIC GAMES

The modern Olympic Games have been held as follows:

I	Athens, Greece	1896
II	Paris, France	1900
III	St Louis, USA	1904
IV	London, Britain	1908
V	Stockholm, Sweden	1912
VII	Antwerp, Belgium	1920
VIII	Paris, France	1924
IX	Amsterdam, Netherlands	1928
X	Los Angeles, USA	1932
XI	Berlin, Germany	1936
XIV	London, Britain	1948
XV	Helsinki, Finland	1952
XVI	Melbourne, Australia	1956
XVII	Rome, Italy	1960
XVIII	Tokyo, Japan	1964
XIX	Mexico City, Mexico	1968
XX	Munich, West Germany	1972
XXI	Montreal, Canada	1976
XXII	Moscow, USSR	1980
XXIII	Los Angeles, USA	1984
XXIV	Seoul, South Korea	1988
XXV	Barcelona, Spain	1992
XXVI	Atlanta, USA	1996

The following Games were scheduled but did not take place owing to World Wars:

VI	Berlin, Germany	1916
XII	Tokyo, Japan, then Helsinki, Finland	1940
XIII	London, Britain	1944

WINTER OLYMPIC GAMES

I	Chamonix, France	1924
II	St Moritz, Switzerland	1928
III	Lake Placid, USA	1932
IV	Garmisch-Partenkirchen, Germany	1936
V	St Moritz, Switzerland	1948
VI	Oslo, Norway	1952
VII	Cortina d'Ampezzo, Italy	1956
VIII	Squaw Valley, USA	1960
IX	Innsbruck, Austria	1964
X	Grenoble, France	1968
XI	Sapporo, Japan	1972
XII	Innsbruck, Austria	1976
XIII	Lake Placid, USA	1980
XIV	Sarajevo, Yugoslavia	1984
XV	Calgary, Canada	1988
XVI	Albertville, France	1992
XVII	Lillehammer, Norway	1994

THE COMMONWEALTH GAMES

The Games were originally called the British Empire Games. From 1954 to 1966 the Games were known as the British Empire and Commonwealth Games, and from 1970 to 1974 as the British Commonwealth Games. Since 1978 the Games have been called the Commonwealth Games.

British Empire Games

I	Hamilton, Canada	1930
II	London, England	1934
III	Sydney, Australia	1938
IV	Auckland, New Zealand	1950

British Empire and Commonwealth Games

V	Vancouver, Canada	1954
VI	Cardiff, Wales	1958
VII	Perth, Australia	1962
VIII	Kingston, Jamaica	1966

British Commonwealth Games

IX	Edinburgh, Scotland	1970
X	Christchurch, New Zealand	1974

Commonwealth Games

XI	Edmonton, Canada	1978
XII	Brisbane, Australia	1982
XIII	Edinburgh, Scotland	1986
XIV	Auckland, New Zealand	1990
XV	Victoria, Canada	1994

SPORTS RECORDS

ATHLETICS

WORLD RECORDS
(as at September 2, 1991)

All the world records given below have been accepted by the International Amateur Athletic Federation except those marked with an asterisk* which are awaiting homologation.

Fully automatic timing to 1/100th second is mandatory up to and including 400 metres. For distances up to and including 10,000 metres, records will be accepted to 1/100th second if timed automatically, and to 1/10th if hand timing is used.

MEN'S EVENTS
Running

Distances	h	m	Time s	Name	Nation	Year
100 metres			9·86	C. Lewis	USA	1991
200 metres			19·72	P. Mennea	Italy	1979
400 metres			43·29	H.Reynolds	USA	1988
800 metres		1	41·73	S. Coe	GB	1981
1,000 metres		2	12·18	S. Coe	GB	1981
1,500 metres		3	29·46	S. Aouita	Morocco	1985
1 mile		3	46·32	S. Cram	GB	1985
2,000 metres		4	50·81	S. Aouita	Morocco	1987
3,000 metres		7	29·45	S. Aouita	Morocco	1989
5,000 metres		12	58·39	S. Aouita	Morocco	1987
10,000 metres		27	08·23	A. Barrios	Mexico	1989
20,000 metres		56	55·6	A. Barrios	Mexico	1991
21,101 metres (13 miles 196 yards 1 foot)	1	00	00·0	A. Barrios	Mexico	1991
25,000 metres	1	13	55·8	T. Seko	Japan	1981
30,000 metres	1	29	18·8	T. Seko	Japan	1981
110 metres hurdles (3 ft 6 in)			12·92	R. Kingdom	USA	1989
400 metres hurdles (3 ft 0 in)			47·02	E. Moses	USA	1983
3,000 metres steeplechase		8	05·35	P. Koech	Kenya	1989

Relay Racing

Distance	m	Time s	Nation	Year
4 × 100 metres		37·50	USA	1991
4 × 200 metres	1	19·38	Santa Monica TC	1989
4 × 400 metres	2	56·16	USA	1988
4 × 800 metres	7	03·89	GB	1982
4 × 1,500 metres	14	38·8	FRG	1977

Jumping and Throwing

	metres	ft	in	Name	Nation	Year
High jump	2·44	8	0	J. Sotomayor	Cuba	1989
Pole vault	6·10	20	0½	S. Bubka	USSR	1991
Long jump	8·95	29	4½	M. Powell	USA	1991
Triple jump	17·97	58	11½	W. Banks	USA	1985
Shot	23·12*	75	10½	R. Barnes	USA	1990
Discus	74·08	243	0	J. Schult	GDR	1986
Hammer	86·74	284	7	Y. Sedykh	USSR	1986
Javelin†	96·96	318	1	S. Raty	Finland	1991
Decathlon‡	8,847 pts.			D. Thompson	GB	1984

† New type of javelin now in force.
‡ Ten events comprising 100 m, long jump, shot, high jump, 400 m, 110 m hurdles, discus, pole vault, javelin, 1500 m.

Walking (Track)

Distance	h	m	Time s	Name	Nation	Year
20,000 metres	1	18	40	E. Canto	Mexico	1984
28,800* metres (17 miles 1576 yards)	2	00	00·0	G. Leblanc	Canada	1990
30,000 metres	2	04	55·7	G. Leblanc	Canada	1990
50,000 metres	3	41	39·00	R. Gonzalez	Mexico	1979

WOMEN'S EVENTS
Running

Distance	Time		Name	Nation	Year
	m	s			
100 metres		10·49	F. Griffith-Joyner	USA	1988
200 metres		21·34	F. Griffith-Joyner	USA	1988
400 metres		47·60	M. Koch	GDR	1985
800 metres	1	53·28	J. Kratochvilova	Czechoslovakia	1983
1,500 metres	3	52·47	T. Kazankina	USSR	1980
1 mile	4	15·61	P. Ivan	Romania	1989
3,000 metres	8	22·62	T. Kazankina	USSR	1984
5,000 metres	14	37·33	I. Kristiansen	Norway	1986
10,000 metres	30	13·74	I. Kristiansen	Norway	1986
100 metres hurdles (2 ft 9 in)		12·21	Y. Donkova	Bulgaria	1988
400 metres hurdles (2 ft 6 in)		52·94	M. Stepanova	USSR	1986

Relays

Distance	Time		Nation	Year
	m	s		
4 × 100 metres		41·37	GDR	1985
4 × 200 metres	1	28·15	GDR	1980
4 × 400 metres	3	15·17	USSR	1988
4 × 800 metres	7	50·17	USSR	1984

Jumping and Throwing

	metres	ft	in	Name	Nation	Year
High jump	2·09	6	10¼	S. Kostadinova	Bulgaria	1987
Long jump	7·52	24	8¼	G. Chistiakova	USSR	1988
Triple jump	14·95	49	0¼	I. Kravets	USSR	1991
Shot	22·63	74	3	N. Lisovskaya	USSR	1987
Discus	76·80	252	0	G. Reinsch	GDR	1988
Javelin	80·00	262	5	P. Felke	GDR	1988
Heptathlon†	7,291 pts.			J. Joyner–Kersee	USA	1988

†Seven events comprising 100 m hurdles, shot, high jump, 200 m, long jump, javelin, 800 m.

UNITED KINGDOM (NATIONAL) RECORDS
(as at September 15, 1991)
Records set anywhere by athletes eligible to represent Great Britain and Northern Ireland

Men

100 metres	9.92s	L. Christie	1991
200 metres	20.09s	J. Regis	1988
400 metres	44.50s	D. Redmond	1987
800 metres	1m 41.73s	S. Coe	1981
1,000 metres	2m 12.18s	S. Coe	1981
1,500 metres	3m 29.67s	S. Coe	1985
1 mile	3m 46.32s	S. Cram	1985
2,000 metres	4m 51.39s	S. Cram	1985
3,000 metres	7m 32.79s	D. Moorcroft	1982
5,000 metres	13m 00.41s	D. Moorcroft	1982
10,000 metres	27m 23.06s	E. Martin	1988
20,000 metres	57m 28.7s	C. Thackery	1990
20,855 metres	1h	C. Thackery	1990
25,000 metres	1h 15m 22.6s	R. Hill	1965
30,000 metres	1h 31m 30.4s	J. Alder	1970

Steeplechase

3,000 metres	8m 07.96s	M. Rowland	1988

Hurdles

110 metres	13.08s	C. Jackson	1990
400 metres	47.86s	K. Akabusi	1991

Relay

4 × 100 metres	37.98s	GB team	1990
4 × 200 metres	1m 21.29s	GB team	1989
4 × 400 metres	2m 57.53s	GB team	1991
4 × 800 metres	7m 03.89s	GB team	1982

High jump	2.36m (7ft 8¼in)	D. Grant	1991
Pole vault	5.65m (18ft 6½in)	K. Stock	1981
Long jump	8.23m (27ft 0in)	L. Davies	1968
Triple jump	17.57m (57ft 7¼in)	K. Connor	1982
Shot	21.68m (71ft 1¼in)	G. Capes	1980
Discus	64.32m (211ft 0in)	W. Tancred	1974
Hammer	77.54m (254ft 5in)	M. Girvan	1984
Javelin	91.36m (299ft 9in)	S. Backley	1991
Decathlon	8,847 points	D. Thompson	1984

Walking (track)

20,000 metres	1h 23m 26.5s	I. McCombie	1990
30,000 metres	2h 19m 18s	C. Maddocks	1984
50,000 metres	4h 05m 44.6s	P. Blagg	1990
2 hours	16 miles 315 yards	R. Wallwork	1971

Women

100 metres	11.10s	K. Cook	1981
200 metres	22.10s	K. Cook	1984
400 metres	49.43s	K. Cook	1984
800 metres	1m 57.42s	K. Wade	1985
1,500 metres	3m 59.96s	Z. Budd	1985
1 mile	4m 17.57s	Z. Budd	1985
3,000 metres	8m 28.83s	Z. Budd	1985
5,000 metres	14m 48.07s	Z. Budd	1985
10,000 metres	30m 57.07s	E. McColgan	1991

Hurdles

100 metres	12.82s	S. Gunnell	1988
400 metres	53.16s	S. Gunnell	1991

SWIMMING

WORLD RECORDS
(as at August 31, 1991)

Men

50 metres freestyle.—T. Jager (USA), 21·81s
100 metres freestyle.—M. Biondi (USA), 48·42s
200 metres freestyle.—G. Lamberti (Italy), 1m 46·69s
400 metres freestyle.—U. Dassler (GDR), 3m 46·95s
800 metres freestyle.—K. Perkins (Australia), 7m 47·85s
1,500 metres freestyle.—J. Hoffman (Germany), 14m 50·36s
100 metres breaststroke.—N. Rosza (Hungary), 1m 01·29s
200 metres breaststroke.—M. Barrowman (USA), 2m 10·60s
100 metres butterfly.—P. Morales (USA), 52·84s
200 metres butterfly.—M. Stewart (USA), 1m 55·69s
100 metres backstroke.—J. Rouse (USA), 53·93s
200 metres backstroke.—M. Lopez-Zubero (Spain), 1m 57·30s
200 metres medley.—T. Darnyi (Hungary), 1m 59·36s
400 metres medley.—T. Darnyi (Hungary) 4m 12·36s
4 × 100 metres freestyle relay.—USA, 3m 16·53s
4 × 200 metres freestyle relay.—USA, 7m 12·51s
4 × 100 metres medley relay.—USA, 3m 36·93s

Women

50 metres freestyle.—Yang Wenyi (China), 24·98s
100 metres freestyle.—K. Otto (GDR), 54·73s
200 metres freestyle.—H. Friedrich (GDR), 1m 57·55s
400 metres freestyle.—J. Evans (USA), 4m 03·85s
800 metres freestyle.—J. Evans (USA), 8m 16·22s
1,500 metres freestyle.—J. Evans (USA), 15m 52·10s
100 metres breaststroke.—S. Hörner (GDR), 1m 07·91s
200 metres breaststroke.—S. Hörner (GDR), 2m 26·71s

100 metres butterfly.—M. Meagher (USA), 57·93s
200 metres butterfly.—M. Meagher (USA), 2m 05·96s
100 metres backstroke.—K. Egerszegi (Hungary), 1m 00·31s
200 metres backstroke.—K. Egerszegi (Hungary), 2m 06·62s
200 metres medley.—U. Geweniger (GDR), 2m 11·73s
400 metres medley.—P. Schneider (GDR), 4m 36·10s
4 × 100 metres freestyle relay.—GDR, 3m 40·57s
4 × 200 metres freestyle relay.—GDR, 7m 55·47s
4 × 100 metres medley relay.—GDR, 4m 03·69s

WEIGHTLIFTING

WORLD RECORDS (TOTALS)
(as at August 31, 1991)

Class	kg		
52 kg	272·5	I. Ivanov (Bulgaria)	1989
56 kg	300	N. Shalamanov (Bulgaria)	1984
60 kg	342·5	N. Suleymanoglu (Turkey)	1988
67·5 kg	355	M. Petrov (Bulgaria)	1987
75 kg	382·5	A. Varbanov (Bulgaria)	1988
82·5 kg	405	Y. Vardanyan (USSR)	1984
90 kg	422·5	V. Solodov (USSR)	1984
100 kg	440	Y. Zakharevich (USSR)	1983
110 kg	455	Y. Zakharevich (USSR)	1988
Over 110 kg	475	L. Taranenko (USSR)	1988

SPORTS BODIES

Sports Councils.—THE SPORTS COUNCIL, 16 Upper Woburn Place, WC1H 0QP. (Tel: 071-388 1277).—*Dir. Gen.*, D. Pickup.

—THE SCOTTISH SPORTS COUNCIL, Caledonia House, South Gyle, Edinburgh EH12 9DQ. (Tel: 031-317 7200).—*Chief Exec.*, F. A. L. Alstead, CBE.

—THE SPORTS COUNCIL FOR WALES, Sophia Gardens, Cardiff CF1 9SW. (Tel: 0222-397571).—*Dir.*, L. Tatham.

—THE SPORTS COUNCIL FOR NORTHERN IRELAND, House of Sport, Upper Malone Road, Belfast BT9 5LA. (Tel: 0232-381222).—*Dir.*, J. E. Miller.

—CENTRAL COUNCIL OF PHYSICAL RECREATION, Francis House, Francis Street, SW1P 1DE. (Tel: 071-828 3163).—*Gen. Sec.*, P. Lawson.

Angling.—NATIONAL FEDERATION OF ANGLERS, Halliday House, 2 Wilson Street, Derby DE1 1PG. (Tel: 0332-362000).—*Chief Admin. Officer*, K. E. Watkins.

Archery.—GRAND NATIONAL ARCHERY SOCIETY, 7th Street, National Agricultural Centre, Stoneleigh, Kenilworth, Coventry CV8 2LG. (Tel: 0203-696631).—*Dir.*, J. S. Middleton.

Association Football.—THE FOOTBALL ASSOCIATION, 16 Lancaster Gate, W2 3LW. (Tel: 071-262 4542).—*Chief Exec.*, R. H. G. Kelly.

—FOOTBALL LEAGUE LTD, 319 Clifton Drive South, Lytham St Annes, Lancs FY8 1JG. (Tel: 0253-729421).—*Chief Exec.*, A. Sandford.

—SCOTTISH FOOTBALL ASSOCIATION, 6 Park Gardens, Glasgow G3 7YF. (Tel: 041-332 6372).—*Chief Exec.*, J. Farry.

—SCOTTISH FOOTBALL LEAGUE, 188 West Regent Street, Glasgow G2 4RY. (Tel: 041-248 3844).—*Sec.*, P. Donald.

—FOOTBALL ASSOCIATION OF WALES, Plymouth Chambers, 3 Westgate Street, Cardiff CF1 1DD. (Tel: 0222-372325).—*Sec.*, A. E. Evans.

—IRISH FOOTBALL ASSOCIATION, 20 Windsor Avenue, Belfast, Northern Ireland BT9 6EG. (Tel: 0232-669458).—*Chief Exec.*, D. I. Bowen.

—IRISH FOOTBALL LEAGUE, 96 University Street, Belfast BT7 1HE. (Tel: 0232-242888).—*Chief Exec.*, M. D. G. Brown.

—WOMEN'S FOOTBALL ASSOCIATION, 448–450 Hanging Ditch, The Corn Exchange, Manchester M4 3ES. (Tel: 061-832 5911).—*Chief Exec.*, Ms L. Whitehead.

Athletics.—BRITISH ATHLETICS FEDERATION, Edgbaston House, 3 Duchess Place, Hagley Road, Birmingham B16 8NM. (Tel: 021-456 4050).—*Gen. Sec. (acting)*, M. A. Farrell.

—AMATEUR ATHLETIC ASSOCIATION OF ENGLAND, Edgbaston House, 3 Duchess Place, Hagley Road, Birmingham B16 8NM. (Tel: 021-456 4050).—*Gen. Sec. (acting)*, D. Johnson.

Badminton.—BADMINTON ASSOCIATION OF ENGLAND LTD, National Badminton Centre, Loughton Lodge, Bradwell Road, Milton Keynes MK8 9LA. (Tel: 0908-568822).—*Chief Exec.*, G. Snowdon.

—SCOTTISH BADMINTON UNION, Cockburn Centre, 40 Bogmoor Place, Glasgow G51 4TQ. (Tel: 041-445 1218).—*Chief Exec.*, Miss A. Smillie.

—WELSH BADMINTON UNION, Third Floor, 3 Westgate Street, Cardiff CF1 1JF. (Tel: 0222-222082).—*Chief Exec.*, L. Williams.

Baseball.—BRITISH BASEBALL FEDERATION, 96 Bilsdale Grove, Southcoates Lane, Hull HU9 3US. (Tel: 0482-792337).—*Sec.*, Mrs. R. Collinson.

Basketball.—ENGLISH BASKET BALL ASSOCIATION, 48 Bradford Road, Leeds LS28 6DF. (Tel: 0532-361166).—*Sec.*, B. E. Coleman.

—SCOTTISH BASKETBALL ASSOCIATION, Caledonia House, South Gyle, Edinburgh EH12 9DQ. (Tel: 031-317 7260).—*Sec.*, Miss E. Dudgeon.

—BASKETBALL ASSOCIATION OF WALES, 327 Cowbridge Road East, Canton, Cardiff CF5 1JD. (Tel: 0222-238180).—*Administrator*, L. Beck.

Billiards.—BILLIARDS AND SNOOKER CONTROL COUNCIL, 92 Kirkstall Road, Leeds LS3 1LT. (Tel: 0532-440586).—*Chief Exec.*, D. M. Ford.

Bobsleigh.—BRITISH BOBSLEIGH ASSOCIATION, Springfield House, 7 Woodstock Road, Coulsdon, Surrey CR5 3HS. (Tel: 0737-552713).—*Sec.*, P. Pruszynski.

Bowls. BRITISH ISLES BOWLING COUNCIL, *Hon. Sec.*, R. McKay, 43 Belfast Road, Ballynure, Ballyclare, Co. Antrim BT39 9TZ. (Tel: 0960-352334).

—BRITISH ISLES INDOOR BOWLING COUNCIL, 8/2 Back Dean, Ravelston Terrace, Edinburgh EH4 3UA. (Tel: 031-343 3632).—*Sec.*, M. Conlin.

—BRITISH ISLES WOMEN'S BOWLING COUNCIL, *Hon. Sec.*, Ms N. Colling, Darracombe, The Clays, Market Lavington, Devizes, Wilts SN10 4AY.

—BRITISH ISLES WOMEN'S INDOOR BOWLS COUNCIL, *Hon. Sec.*, Ms J. Johns, 16 Windsor Crescent, Radyr, Cardiff CF4 8AE. (Tel: 0222-842391).

Boxing.—AMATEUR BOXING ASSOCIATION OF ENGLAND, Francis House, Francis Street, SW1P 1DE (Tel: 071-976 5361).—*Hon. Sec.*, J. H. Lewis.

—BRITISH BOXING BOARD OF CONTROL, 70 Vauxhall Bridge Road, SW1V 2RP. (Tel: 071-828 2133).—*Gen. Sec.*, J. Morris.

—BRITISH AMATEUR BOXING ASSOCIATION, 96 High Street, Lochee, Dundee DD2 3AY. (Tel: 0382-611412).—*Sec.*, F. Hendry.

Canoeing.—BRITISH CANOE UNION, Adbolton Lane, West Bridgford, Nottingham NG2 5AS. (Tel: 0602-821100).— *Dir.*, T. J. Bailey.

Clay Pigeon Shooting.—CLAY PIGEON SHOOTING ASSOCIATION, 107 Epping New Road, Buckhurst Hill, Essex IG9 5TQ. (Tel: 081-505 6221).—*Dir*, K. J. Murray.

Cricket.—MCC, Lords, NW8 8QN. (Tel: 071-289 1611).—*Pres.* Rt. Hon. Lord Griffiths; *Sec.*, Lt.-Col. J. R. Stephenson, OBE.

—TEST AND COUNTY CRICKET BOARD, Lord's, NW8 8QZ. (Tel: 071-286 4405).—*Chairman (1991–92)*, W. R. F. Chamberlain; *Chief Exec.*, A. C. Smith.

—CRICKET COUNCIL, Lord's, NW8 8QZ. (Tel: 071-286 4405). *Chairman*, W. R. F. Chamberlain; *Sec.*, A. C. Smith.

Croquet.—CROQUET ASSOCIATION, c/o The Hurlingham Club, Ranelagh Gardens, SW6 3PR. (Tel: 071-736 3148) *Sec.*, L. W. D. Antenen.

Cycling.—BRITISH CYCLING FEDERATION, 36 Rockingham Road, Kettering, Northants. NN16 8HG. (Tel: 0536-412211).—*Chief Exec.*, J. Hendry.

—ROAD TIME TRIALS COUNCIL, Dallacre, Mill Road, Yarwell, Peterborough PE8 6PS. (Tel: 0780-782464).—*Sec.*, D. E. Roberts.

Equestrianism.—BRITISH EQUESTRIAN FEDERATION, British Equestrian Centre, Kenilworth, Warks. CV8 2LR. (Tel: 0203-696697).—*Dir. Gen.*, Maj. M. Wallace.

Eton Fives.—ETON FIVES ASSOCIATION.—*Hon. Sec.*, M. P. Powell, Welches, Bentley, Farnham, Surrey.

Fencing.—AMATEUR FENCING ASSOCIATION, 83 Perham Road, W14 9SP. (Tel: 071-385 7442).—*Sec.*, Miss G. Kenneally.

Gliding.—BRITISH GLIDING ASSOCIATION, Kimberley House, Vaughan Way, Leicester LE1 4SE. (Tel: 0533-531051).—*Sec.*, B. Rolfe.

Golf.—ROYAL AND ANCIENT GOLF CLUB, St Andrews, Fife KY16 9JD. Tel: 0334-72112).—*Sec.*, M. F. Bonallack, OBE.

—LADIES' GOLF UNION, The Scores, St Andrews, Fife KY16 9AT (Tel: 0334-75811).—*Administrator*, Mrs A. Robertson.

Greyhound Racing.—THE NATIONAL GREYHOUND RACING CLUB LTD, 24–28 Oval Road, NW1 7DA.

(Tel: 071-267 9256).—*Senior Stipendiary Steward*, F. Melville.

Gymnastics.—BRITISH AMATEUR GYMNASTICS ASSOCIATION, Ford Hall, Lilleshall National Sports Centre, nr. Newport, Shropshire TF10 9ND. (Tel: 0952-820330).—*Sec.*, D. Minnery.

Hockey.—HOCKEY ASSOCIATION, 16 Northdown Street, N1 9BG. (Tel: 071-837 8878).—*Chief Exec.*, S. P. Baines.

— ALL ENGLAND WOMEN'S HOCKEY ASSOCIATION, 51 High Street, Shrewsbury SY1 1ST. (Tel: 0743-233572).—*Sec.*, Miss T. Morris.

—SCOTTISH HOCKEY UNION, Caledonia House, South Gyle, Edinburgh EH12 9DQ. (Tel: 031-317 7254).—*Exec. Administrator*, Ms L. Gillies.

—SCOTTISH WOMEN'S HOCKEY UNION, Caledonia House, South Gyle, Edinburgh EH12 9DQ. (Tel: 031-317 7254).—*Chief Exec.*, Ms F. Perman.

—WELSH HOCKEY ASSOCIATION, 1 White Hart Lane, Caerleon, Gwent NP6 1AB. (Tel: 0633-420326).—*Sec.*, J. G. Williams.

—WELSH WOMEN'S HOCKEY ASSOCIATION, Welsh Hockey Office, Deeside Leisure Centre, Chester Road West, Deeside, Clwyd CH5 1SA. (Tel: 0244-812311).—*Chief Exec.*, Mrs A. Humphreys.

Horse-racing.—THE JOCKEY CLUB (incorporating National Hunt Committee), 42 Portman Square, W1H 0EN (Tel: 071-486 4921).—*Chief Exec.*, C. J. M. Haines.

Ice Hockey.—BRITISH ICE HOCKEY ASSOCIATION, Second Floor Offices, 517 Christchurch Road, Boscombe, Bournemouth BH1 4AG (Tel: 0202-303946).—*Gen. Sec.*, D. Pickles.

Judo.—BRITISH JUDO ASSOCIATION, 7A Rutland Street, Leicester LE1 1RB. (Tel: 0533-559669).—*Chairman*, M. Leigh.

Lacrosse.—ENGLISH LACROSSE UNION, *Hon. Sec.*, R. Balls, 70 High Road, Rayleigh, Essex SS6 7AD.

— ALL ENGLAND WOMEN'S LACROSSE ASSOCIATION, 4 Western Court, Bromley Street, Digbeth, Birmingham B9 4AN. (Tel: 021-773 4422).—*Administrator*, Miss K. M. Howard.

Lawn Tennis.—LAWN TENNIS ASSOCIATION, The Queen's Club, W14 9EG. (Tel: 071-385 2366).—*Sec.*, J. C. U. James.

Lugeing.—THE GREAT BRITAIN LUGE ASSOCIATION, 43 Wimpole Street, W1M 7AF.—*President*, R. L. Liversedge.

Martial Arts.—MARTIAL ARTS COMMISSION, Broadway House, 15–16 Deptford Broadway, SE8 4PE. (Tel: 081-691 8711).—*Gen. Sec.*, Ms P. Mitchell.

Motor Sports.—AUTO-CYCLE UNION, Miller House, Corporation Street, Rugby, Warwicks. CV21 2DN. (Tel: 0788-540519).—*Sec. Gen.*, D. G. Coleman.

—RAC MOTOR SPORTS ASSOCIATION LTD, Motor Sports House, Riverside Park, Colnbrook, Slough SL3 0HG. (Tel: 0753-681736).—*Chief Exec.*, J. R. Quenby.

—SCOTTISH AUTO CYCLE UNION LTD, Block 2, Unit 6, Whiteside Industrial Estate, Bathgate, West Lothian EH48 2RX. (Tel: 0506-630262.)—*Sec.*, A. M. Brownlie.

Mountaineering.—BRITISH MOUNTAINEERING COUNCIL, Crawford House, Precinct Centre, Booth Street East, Manchester M13 9RZ. (Tel: 061-273 5835).—*Gen. Sec.*, D. Walker.

Multi-Sport Bodies.—BRITISH OLYMPIC ASSOCIATION, 1 Wandsworth Plain, SW18 1EH. (Tel: 081-871 2677).—*Gen. Sec.*, R. Palmer, OBE.

—COMMONWEALTH GAMES FEDERATION, Knightsbridge House, 197 Knightsbridge, SW7 1RZ. (Tel: 071-225 5555).—*Hon. Sec.*, D. M. Dixon.

—BRITISH COLLEGES SPORTS ASSOCIATION, 11 Allcock Street, Birmingham B9 4DY. (Tel: 021-766 8855).—*Hon. Admin. Sec.*, P. Rhodes.

—BRITISH POLYTECHNIC SPORTS ASSOCIATION, 11 Allcock Street, Birmingham B9 4DY. (Tel: 021-766 8855).—*Administrator*, S. Fairhall.

—BRITISH UNIVERSITIES SPORTS FEDERATION, 11 Allcock Street, Birmingham B9 4DY. (Tel: 021-766 8855).—*Gen. Sec.*, P. Rhodes.

Netball.—ALL ENGLAND NETBALL ASSOCIATION, Francis House, Francis Street, SW1P 1DE. (Tel: 071-828 2176).—*Chief Exec.*, Mrs E. M. Nicholl.

—SCOTTISH NETBALL ASSOCIATION, Kelvin Hall Sports Complex, Argyle Street, Glasgow G3 8AW. (Tel: 041-334 3650).—*Administrator*, Ms A. Murray.

—WELSH NETBALL ASSOCIATION, 82 Cathedral Road, Cardiff CF1 9LN. (Tel: 0222-237048).

Orienteering.—BRITISH ORIENTEERING FEDERATION, Riversdale, Dale Road North, Darley Dale, Matlock, Derbyshire DE4 2HX. (Tel: 0629-734042).—*Manager*, Mrs. H. Gregson.

Polo.—THE HURLINGHAM POLO ASSOCIATION, Winterlake, Kirtlington, Oxford OX5 3HG. (Tel: 0869-50044).—*Hon. Sec.*, J. W. M. Crisp.

Rackets and Real Tennis.—TENNIS AND RACKETS ASSOCIATION, c/o The Queen's Club, Palliser Road, W14 9EQ. (Tel: 071-381 4746).—*Chief Exec.*, Brig. A. D. Myrtle, CB, CBE.

Rifle Shooting.—NATIONAL RIFLE ASSOCIATION, Bisley Camp, Brookwood, Woking, Surrey GU24 0PB. (Tel: 0483-797777).—*Chief Exec.*, C. A. Ewing, OBE.

—NATIONAL SMALL-BORE RIFLE ASSOCIATION, Lord Roberts House, Bisley Camp, Brookwood, Woking GU24 0NP. (Tel: 04867-6969).—*Sec.*, Gp Capt D. King, MBE.

Rowing.—AMATEUR ROWING ASSOCIATION LTD., The Priory, 6 Lower Mall, W6 9DJ. (Tel: 081-748 3632).—*Senior Admin. Officer*, Mrs R. E. Webb.

—HENLEY ROYAL REGATTA, Regatta Headquarters, Henley-on-Thames, Oxon. RG9 2LY. (Tel: 0491-572153).—*Sec.*, R. S. Goddard.

—SCOTTISH AMATEUR ROWING ASSOCIATION, 11 Spottiswode Street, Edinburgh EH9 1EP. (Tel: 031-229 2366).—*Sec.*, N. MacFarlane.

—WELSH AMATEUR ROWING ASSOCIATION, *Hon. Sec.*, Dr G. R. H. Greaves, 30 Lady Mary Road, Cardiff CF2 5NT. (Tel: 0222-754259).

Rugby Fives.—RUGBY FIVES ASSOCIATION, 10 Lovelace Road, SE21 8JX. (Tel: 081-670 3298).—*Sec.*, Mrs J. Fuller.

Rugby League.—THE RUGBY FOOTBALL LEAGUE, 180 Chapeltown Road, Leeds LS7 4HT. (Tel: 0532-624637).—*Chief Exec.*, D. S. Oxley, OBE.

— BRITISH AMATEUR RUGBY LEAGUE ASSOCIATION, West Yorkshire House, 4 New North Parade, Huddersfield HD1 5JP. (Tel: 0484-544131).—*Chief Exec.*, M. F. Oldroyd.

Rugby Union.—RUGBY FOOTBALL UNION, Twickenham TW1 1DZ. (Tel: 081-892 8161).—*Sec.*, D. E. Wood.

—SCOTTISH RUGBY UNION, Murrayfield, Roseburn Street, Edinburgh EH12 5PJ. (Tel: 031-337 2346).—*Sec.*, I. A. L. Hogg.

—WELSH RUGBY UNION, Cardiff Arms Park, PO Box 22, Cardiff CF1 1JL. (Tel: 0222-390111).—*Sec.*, D. P. Evans.

—IRISH RUGBY FOOTBALL UNION, 62 Lansdowne Road, Dublin 4, Republic of Ireland. (Tel: 0001-684601).—*Sec.*, P. Moss.

—WOMEN'S RUGBY FOOTBALL UNION, Meadow House, Springfield Farm, Shipston-on-Stour, Warks. CV36 4HQ. (Tel: 081-994 0816).—*Sec.*, Ms R. Golby.

Skating.—NATIONAL SKATING ASSOCIATION OF GREAT BRITAIN, 15–27 Gee Street, EC1V 3RE. (Tel: 071-253 3824).—*Pres.*, C. J. L. Jones, OBE.

Skiing.—BRITISH SKI FEDERATION, 258 Main Street, East Calder, West Lothian EH53 0EE. (Tel: 0506-884343).—*Chairman*, J. Blyth.

Snooker.—BILLIARDS AND SNOOKER CONTROL COUNCIL, 92 Kirkstall Road, Leeds LS3 1LT. (Tel: 0532-440586).—*Chief Exec.*, D. M. Ford.

Speedway.—THE SPEEDWAY CONTROL BOARD, 57 Villa Crescent, Bulkington, Nuneaton CV12 9NF. (Tel: 0203-643336).—*Manager*, J. Eglese.

Squash Rackets.—SQUASH RACKETS ASSOCIATION, Westpoint, 33–34 Worple Way, W3 0RQ. (Tel: 081-746 1616).— *Chief Exec.*, R. I. Morris.

—SCOTTISH SQUASH RACKETS ASSOCIATION, Caledonia House, South Gyle, Edinburgh EH12 9DQ. (Tel: 031-317 7343).—*Sec.*, vacant.

—WELSH SQUASH RACKETS FEDERATION, 7 Kymin Terrace, Penarth, South Glamorgan CF6 1AP. (Tel: 0222-704096).—*Chairman*, A. Price.

Swimming.—AMATEUR SWIMMING ASSOCIATION, Harold Fern House, Derby Square, Loughborough, Leics. LE11 0AL. (Tel: 0509-230431).— *Sec.*, D. A. Reeves.

—SCOTTISH AMATEUR SWIMMING ASSOCIATION, Airthrey Castle, University of Stirling, Stirling FK9 4LA. (Tel: 0786-70544).—*Gen. Sec.*, W. Charles.

—WELSH AMATEUR SWIMMING ASSOCIATION, Empire Pool, Wood Street, Cardiff CF1 1PP. (Tel: 0222-342201).—*Hon. Gen. Sec.*, J. A. Jones-Pritchard.

—BRITISH SUB-AQUA CLUB, Telfords Quay, Ellesmere Port, South Wirral, Cheshire L65 4FY. (Tel: 051-357 1951).—*Chairman*, D. Ellerby.

Table Tennis.—ENGLISH TABLE TENNIS ASSOCIATION, Queensbury House, Havelock Road, Hastings TN34 1HF. (Tel: 0424-722525).—*Chief Exec.*, Miss E. Shaw.

Volleyball.—ENGLISH VOLLEYBALL ASSOCIATION, 27 South Road, West Bridgford, Nottingham NG2 7AG. (Tel: 0602-816324).—*National Dir.*, G. Bulman.

—SCOTTISH VOLLEYBALL ASSOCIATION, 48 The Pleasance, Edinburgh EH8 9TJ. (Tel: 031-556 4633).—*Chief Exec.*, N. Moody.

—WELSH VOLLEYBALL ASSOCIATION, 136 Bwlch Road, Fairwater, Cardiff CF5 9EF. (Tel: 0222-566417).—*Sec.*, S. Marshall.

Walking.—RACE WALKING ASSOCIATION. *Hon. Sec.*, Mrs B. E. M. Randle, 9 Whitehouse Close, Rectory Road, Sutton Coldfield, West Midlands B75 7SD.

Water Skiing.—BRITISH WATER SKI FEDERATION, 390 City Road, EC1V 2QA. (Tel: 071-833 2855).—*Sec.*, Ms G. Hill.

Weightlifting.—BRITISH AMATEUR WEIGHTLIFTERS ASSOCIATION. *Hon. Sec.*, W. Holland, OBE, 3 Iffley Turn, Oxford OX4 4DU.

Wrestling.—ENGLISH OLYMPIC WRESTLING ASSOCIATION, 16 Choir Street, Cambridge Industrial Estate, Salford M7 9ZD. (Tel: 061-832 9209).—*Sec.*, H. I. Jacob, OBE.

Yachting.—ROYAL YACHTING ASSOCIATION, RYA House, Romsey Road, Eastleigh, Hants. SO5 4YA. (Tel: 0703-629962).—*Sec. Gen.*, R. Duchesne, OBE.

LITERATURE 1990–91

Salman Rushdie, still living under armed guard following the death sentence pronounced on him for blasphemy against Islam in his book *The Satanic Verses*, emerged briefly from hiding for the publication of his latest work. *Haroun and the Sea of Stories* is a collection of tales written for his son Zafar, in response to the boy's demand that his father produce a book that he could understand.

The book tells the story of Haroun, who lives in a large city in the land of Alifbay with his mother Soraya and his father Rashid, a story-teller. Soraya runs away with Mr Sengupta, the clerk who lives in the room above, who had asked, 'What's the use of stories that aren't even true?', a refrain throughout the book. Rashid's source of stories dries up, as the sea that provides the liquid inspiration is threatened by pollution. The villain of the piece is Khattam-Shud, 'the Prince of Silence and the Foe of Speech', who is poisoning the sea. Drawing on a range of influences, from *The Thousand and One Nights* to *Alice's Adventures in Wonderland*, the book is an enjoyable and witty modern fable, given poignancy by Rushdie's own situation.

An apparent easing of tension encouraged Rushdie to make a few public appearances to promote the work, but the affair is by no means resolved. On *The South Bank Show*, Rushdie said of *The Satanic Verses*, 'The book did not set out to do the thing that it has been accused of, to insult and abuse, and if that is how people have read it then I am very sorry. I did not want to do that. People have said that I ought to be punished. All I can say is if punishment was the aim, I've had some . . . It is like the old Chinese curse, "May you live in interesting times". Writers should not have to live in such interesting times as I have to.'

In an article in *The Times* on December 28, 1990, Rushdie announced that, after a meeting with six Muslim scholars, he had espoused the Muslim faith and would restrict publication of *The Satanic Verses* in the future. Rushdie wrote that he had decided to affirm 'the two central tenets of Islam—the oneness of God and the genuineness of the prophecy of the Prophet Muhammad—and thus to enter into the body of Islam after a lifetime spent outside it.' He said that the scholars had agreed with him that 'the controversy over *The Satanic Verses* was based on a tragic misunderstanding, and we must all now work to explain to Muslims everywhere that neither I nor my work have ever been inimical to Islam.' Rushdie said that he had agreed that he would permit no new translations of the book, nor publish an English language paperback edition, 'while any risk of further offence remains'. He would not agree, however, to the book's total withdrawal.

Many of Rushdie's supporters in Britain were surprised by his change of heart and affirmation of the Muslim faith, and his estranged wife later denounced him bitterly in the press. Rushdie asked for the support of the Government and the Opposition to press for the lifting of the *fatwa* (religious decree), since he had received the blessing of the leader of the Sunni Muslims. However, some Muslims in Britain denounced his acceptance of faith as a 'disingenuous ploy', and demanded that he should withdraw the book. February 14, 1991, the second anniversary of the *fatwa*, was marked in Iran by renewed calls for his death: 'This edict is a particular order and no-one can cancel it . . . even if Salman Rushdie becomes the most pious person of the age he cannot be pardoned.' Events took a brutal turn in July, with the murder of Hitoshi Igarashi, Japanese translator of *The Satanic Verses*, and an attack on Ettore Capriolo, who translated the Italian edition.

Rushdie also published *Imaginary Homelands: Essays and Criticism 1981–91*. The volume included an article he wrote after a year in hiding, in which he declared, 'To put it as simply as possible: *I am not a Muslim* . . . I do not accept the charge of apostasy, because I have never in my adult life affirmed any belief.' One can but speculate at the pressures on him that led to such a radical reappraisal of his beliefs.

The Booker

The 22nd Booker Prize for Fiction was awarded to A. S. Byatt for *Possession*. The chairman of the panel of judges, Sir Denis Forman, said that the book was 'selected by a majority vote'. As he also said that 'there was strong individual support for several books on the short-list', there was once again the suggestion of compromise in the final choice. Although *Possession* was generally well regarded, there was disappointment at the Booker's failure to acknowledge the younger generation of authors or to look beyond the mainstream. At the age of 54, Antonia Byatt was the youngest of the six finalists, four of whom had been shortlisted before.

Possession is the story of the research by two academics, Roland Michell and Dr Maud Bailey, into the life of Randolph Henry Ash, Victorian man of letters. The discovery of a letter from Ash to Christabel La Motte, a little-known poet, lead the academics to a secret love affair between the writers. Byatt skilfully and convincingly constructs poems by Ash and La Motte, and builds the novel around their letters and journals. The preface is taken from Nathaniel Hawthorne's Preface to *The House of the Seven Gables*: 'The point of view in which this tale comes under the Romantic definition lies in the attempt to connect a bygone time with the very present that is flitting away from us.' *Possession* is an ambitious novel and an impressive achievement. The book also won the Irish Times Aer Lingus International Prize for Fiction, worth IR£25,000.

Penelope Fitzgerald's *The Gate of Angels* was her fourth novel to be shortlisted for the Booker. It is set in Cambridge in 1912, at the fictional college of St Angelicus, where all women are barred. Brian Moore's *Lies of Silence* is a contemporary thriller set in Northern Ireland, in which personal dilemmas are played out against a background of sectarian violence and media censorship. Beryl Bainbridge's *An Awfully Big Adventure* concerns the exploits of a repertory company staging a production of *Peter Pan* in Liverpool in 1950. The Canadian novelist Mordecai Richler was shortlisted for *Solomon Gursky was Here*, a Jewish-Canadian family saga which received the

Commonwealth Writers' Prize (A$21,000). The other finalist was John McGahern's *Amongst Women*, the story of Michael Moran, his second wife Rose and their five children; after the Republican troubles in Ireland, for Michael 'things were never so simple and clear again'. The book was reported to be the runner-up for the Booker and for the Irish Times Aer Lingus Award. Although unsuccessful in these awards, McGahern won the Irish Times Irish Fiction Award (IR£10,000) and the Hughes Irish Fiction Award (IR£2,000).

Dark Horse

The winner of the 1990 Whitbread Book of the Year was Nicholas Mosley's *Hopeful Monsters*. Mosley was the self-confessed 'dark horse of the literary world'. *Hopeful Monsters* is his 13th novel but his work is not widely known, and the novel was ignored by the literary pages of some of the leading newspapers. However, Mosley has a loyal and influential following: Malcolm Bradbury declared him 'one of our most important writers and severely underestimated by the critics'. As a Whitbread judge, Bradbury was able to rectify the error. The novel concludes a sequence of five works known by the title of the first, *Catastrophe Practice*; this consists of three plays and a novella which relate the mathematical 'catastrophe theory' to human relationships. *Hopeful Monsters* follows the relationship between Eleanor Anders, a German Jewess, and Max Ackermann, an English student of biology and physics, in the period between the two world wars. Set against a background of radical politics in Berlin, Spain, Africa and England, it ends in Los Alamos with the making of the atomic bomb. The Whitbread award to *Hopeful Monsters* should renew interest in Mosley's work, which the *Oxford Companion to English Literature* describes as 'highly intellectual, experimental and metaphysical'. Mosley received £20,250, plus £1,750 for winning the best novel category.

The other Whitbread category winners were Hanif Kureishi's *The Buddha of Suburbia* (first novel), described by the judges as 'energetic and compellingly readable'; *Daddy, Daddy* by Paul Durcan (poetry), 'wide-ranging, funny, brilliant and appalling'; *A. A. Milne: His Life* by Ann Thwaite (biography), 'written with gentleness, humour and elegance, and above all holding together as a work of literature'; and *AK* by Peter Dickinson (children's novel), 'rooted in a world which robs children of food, education and freedom'.

Other awards

The W. H. Smith Literary Award (£10,000) was awarded to Derek Walcott for his epic poem *Omeros*. Inspired by the *Iliad*, the *Odyssey* and the *Inferno*, it tells the story of Achille and Philoctete, fishermen from St Lucia, who travel the world through time. Homer is transported 'across centuries of the sea's parchment atlas', and the thrilling verse is sustained for 2,500 stanzas in rhyming hexameters. The winner of the Guardian Fiction Prize was Pauline Melville for her collection of short stories, *Shapeshifter*. Susan Kay received the Boots Romantic Novel of the Year

Award (£5,000) for *Phantom*, and Pauline Fisk received the Smarties Prize for children's books for *Midnight Blue* (£7,000, plus £1,000 for winning the aged 9–11 category). The Ian St James Prize (£12,000) was won by Annie Hedley for *Mothering Sunday*. In France, the prestigious Prix Goncourt, worth 50 francs, was won by Jean Rouaud for *Les Champs d'Honneur*.

The 1990 Nobel Prize for Literature (4 million krona or some £360,000) was awarded to a Spanish-speaking writer for the second year. Alfred Nobel decreed that the prize should be awarded to a writer 'who shall have produced in the field of literature the most outstanding work of an idealistic tendency', and the Mexican poet Octavio Paz was honoured 'for impassioned writing with wide horizons, characterized by sensuous intelligence and humanistic integrity'. His best-known works are *The Labyrinth of Solitude: Life and Thought in Mexico*; *Sun Stone* and *The Monkey Grammarian*. In a remarkable demonstration of how far-reaching the effects of *perestroika* have been in the Soviet Union, Alexander Solzhenitsyn, who was expelled from the country in 1974, was awarded the Russian State Literature Prize for *The Gulag Archipelago*.

Dickens duo

Two remarkable books inspired by Charles Dickens were shortlisted for the NCR Prize (£25,000), awarded to a work of non-fiction. However, Peter Ackroyd's massive biography of the author was displaced by Claire Tomalin's account of the life of a woman to whom Dickens was apparently devoted for some 12 years, and yet who was not even mentioned in Forster's biography of the writer. *The Invisible Woman: The Story of Nelly Ternan and Charles Dickens* is a fascinating story, pieced together from what little is known or extant. Ternan was an actress with whom Dickens was infatuated and for whom he left his wife of 22 years. Dickens denied any impropriety in the relationship—'Upon my soul and honour, there is not on this earth a more virtuous and spotless creature than this young lady'—and attempted to destroy all evidence of the affair. However, there is enough information to suggest that he set Ternan up in houses in London and Slough, and possibly in France, where it seems likely that she had a child by him. Her story was not the stuff of Dickens's own fiction, but 'a small piece of reality to set against the omissions and evasions of Victorian fiction: a complicated and resourceful young woman who was very nearly crushed by the huge weight of Dickens in her life'.

However, 'Nelly's story begins long before her meeting with Dickens and continues long after his death'. After Dickens' death, she effectively closed off that period in her life. She married George Robinson and the couple opened a school in Margate, had two children and, after the school failed, moved to London. Tomalin has pieced together a highly readable and enjoyable story from the scraps of information available, a tribute to a resolute character who defied the mores of her age and survived to begin life afresh after her relationship with one of the most famous figures of the age.

Peter Ackroyd is reported to have read every word Dickens wrote at least three times and also every word about him. Unlike Tomalin, he believes Dickens' relationship with Nelly Ternan was chaste, although Tomalin's case is better made. Ackroyd's *Dickens* is an exhaustive (nearly 1,200 pages) account of almost everything one could possibly wish to know about the writer, and much else besides: 'To see Dickens day by day, making his way, the incidents of his existence shaping his fiction just as his fiction alters his life, the same pattern of emotion and imagery rising up from letters and novels and conversations, the same momentum and the same desire for control—to see Dickens thus is to turn biography into an agent of true knowledge.'

However, for Ackroyd so to immerse himself in the works of his subject that he feels able to visualize Dickens in events and places, and to fictionalize them, is self-indulgent. He imagines Dickens entering Marshalsea Prison where he sees William Dorrit, 'very like my own father', and has Dickens' characters meeting at Greenwich fair. Ackroyd also uses the device of time shifts that he has employed in his novels *Hawksmoor* and *Chatterton*, but the device is less successful in a biography. When he creates a scene between Chatterton, Wilde and Eliot, all subjects of Ackroyd, in which they have a 'true conversation between imagined selves', and then announces that Blake will be his next biographical subject, Ackroyd is not only indulgent but pretentious. Inside *Dickens* there is a competent and slimmer biography struggling to get out.

Lives

Martin Gilbert took over the official biography of Sir Winston Churchill on the death of Churchill's son Randolph, who wrote the first two volumes. Gilbert completed his main task with the publication in 1988 of the eighth and final volume, *Never Despair—Winston Churchill 1945–65*. He has still to publish the last of the companion volumes of documents that have been appearing at intervals to supplement the main work. Meanwhile, Gilbert has published a one-volume account distilled from the main body of work, *Churchill: A Life*. This aims 'to present Churchill's own words and arguments, his thinking, his true intentions, and his precise actions'. Gilbert believes that, with the passage of time, 'Churchill's actions and aims will be seen to have been humane and far-sighted. His patriotism, his sense of fair play, his belief in democracy and his hopes for the human race were matched by formidable powers of work and thought, vision and foresight. His path was often beset by controversy, disappointment and abuse, but these never deflected him from his sense of duty and his faith in the British people.' Gilbert's mastery of his subject is such that there can be little that he has not covered, but he is an uncritical recorder of the facts who does not seek to analyse Churchill's thoughts or actions and this aspect of his work has attracted unfavourable reviews.

The publication of the third volume of Michael Holroyd's biography of George Bernard Shaw, *The Lure of Fantasy*, completed the life on which he embarked some 17 years ago. Holroyd will also be issuing supplementary volumes; a one-volume biography, a commentary on the plays and a source book of some 10,000 footnote references. Shaw does not emerge well from the latest volume, which covers the years from 1918 to his death in 1950. The triumph of *St Joan* finally won Shaw the Nobel Prize for Literature in 1926, 'a hideous calamity for me,' he wrote, 'almost as bad as my 70th birthday'. However, his support for the 'strenuous tyranny' of Mussolini and the labour camps of Stalin, and his failure to acknowledge that the concentration camps of Hitler existed are difficult to excuse, as is his endorsement of murder as an instrument of government: 'What you want to do is shoot your poor whites—every one of them. You should also shoot many of your rich whites', he told the South Africans. It is difficult to pass off such attitudes as naïvety or Shavian wit. Lady Astor's remark, on introducing William Douglas-Home to Shaw, exemplifies the mixture of affection and exasperation that Shaw induced in those who knew him: 'Come out of there, you old fool. You've written enough nonsense in your life.'

King or knot

Philip Ziegler was granted access to the royal archives to write *King Edward VIII: The Official Biography*. He was able to draw on Edward's early diaries, papers from courtiers and the Cabinet, some 22,000 letters, plus another 2,000 or so that Edward wrote to his first love, Freda Dudley Ward. Ziegler presents a convincing and rounded portrait of a man who was both immature and irresponsible. His father, George V, had been unable to establish any sort of relationship with him, and Wallis Simpson was able to dominate him and exploit his weaknesses. Ziegler refutes the charges of secret Nazi sympathies that have been laid against Edward in recent years, but also disputes that Edward would have found the popular support he believed existed had he gone against Baldwin's advice over the abdication. He also led an unreal and largely purposeless existence as Duke of Windsor after he left the throne, though Ziegler demonstrates that his period as Governor of the Bahamas proved him a competent administrator. The overall impression is of a weak and misguided man who was unable to fulfil his destiny, and who may come to be remembered for the tie knot to which he gave his name.

In *Bob Boothby: A Portrait*, Robert Rhodes James recounts the life of the rebellious Conservative MP whose personal vanity and penchant for indiscretion prevented him from reaching the highest political office. His short tenure as Parliamentary Secretary to the Minister of Food ended in disgrace when he was forced to resign for having failed to disclose a personal interest in the recovery of Czech assets. He believed Churchill, who was later to refer to him disparagingly as 'the Member for television', had made him a scapegoat over the affair.

Anthony Howard has written a biography of the man whom he succeeded as editor of the *New Stateman*. *Crossman: The Pursuit of Power* presents a portrait of an intellectual bully who accomplished little in his six years in office, but achieved posthumous fame of a kind with the publication of his diaries. Richard Crossman had wanted to 'write a book which, like Bagehot's *English Constitution*, would disclose the secret operations of British Government'. A more immediate effect has been a stream of books from retired or displaced Cabinet ministers, justifying their actions and securing their future. Tony Benn is one who has followed in Crossman's footsteps, recording the minutiae of his everyday political life. Although apparently written without an eye to posterity, Benn's diary is revealing both for his disclosure of the haphazard way in which major political decisions appear to be made, and for his belief in the necessity for Militant Tendency, trade union strife and the significance of 'the winter of discontent' in 1979. *Conflicts of Interest: Diaries 1977–80* is the fourth of Benn's volumes, heavily edited by Ruth Winstone (although serious students of the era will be reassured that 'the uncut text has been made available').

Servant or sewer?

The end of the Thatcher era was marked by two revealing and contrasting works about Bernard Ingham, her press secretary for eleven years. *Good and Faithful Servant* is Robert Harris's revealing account of how Ingham, a civil servant, apparently used his position to take over the Government's information service for party political ends. The two formed an unlikely alliance, Ingham having been a die-hard Labour supporter; however, there is no doubt that he was devoted to Mrs Thatcher. It was with good cause that she said of him, 'Bernard's marvellous ... He's the greatest'. However, his manipulation of the lobby system, which he used to attack or undermine ministers who were out of favour, was infamous. John Biffen, one of his victims, remarked that Ingham was 'the sewer, rather than the sewage', a conduit for his leader's dirty work.

The points are well-made in Ingham's own account of his career, *Kill the Messenger*. The book was submitted to the Cabinet Office for clearance, a process which many felt unnecessary, but Ingham nevertheless acceded to their request for cuts. It was reported that the printed version had to omit or tone down remarks about certain ministers and members of the European Community. Ingham's reliance on his memory, rather than notes, for his memoirs also proved to have its shortcomings. He gives an account of a lunch at which a journalist had offended him, leading Ingham to gain his revenge by thereafter withholding information from him. It transpired that the person in question had not attended the meeting, leading to an embarrassing retraction and correction.

Jeremy Paxman has written an entertaining survey of British institutions in *Friends in High Places: Who Runs Britain?* Following in the footsteps of Anthony Sampson's *The Anatomy of Britain*, Paxman looks at the army, the church, public schools, clubs, the Foreign Office and the monarchy, to examine their influence and to determine their part in the country's decline. He describes the process of examining the establishment as like 'taking apart one of those Russian dolls ... by the time you reach its heart, you have already missed the pattern of beliefs and ideas which hold it together and give it form'. To the question he poses in the title, he

concludes that 'the only plausible answer is the Prime Minister'.

Catty

Biography plumbed new depths with the publication of *Nancy Reagan: The Unauthorised Biography* by Kitty Kelley. Kelley has made a practice of demolishing those who have achieved prominence in public life in the USA, where public figures have almost no recourse to the courts for libel. Her biography of Nancy Reagan is largely a collection of gossip and rumour, in which half-truths and innuendo masquerade as facts. By contrast, *An American Life: The Autobiography of Ronald Reagan* is a positively anodyne account by the actor-turned-President.

'To publish an account of my own intimate, domestic, sexual experiences would hurt a number of people who have emotional claims on me ... and I have no desire to cause pain, or further pain, to them or myself', wrote Kingsley Amis in the preface to his *Memoirs*, explaining that he had 'already written an account of myself in twenty or more volumes, most of them called novels'. However, he had few qualms about relating the intimate experiences of others, causing pain to many people mentioned in the volume, a great number of whom were at variance with Amis in their recall of the events he described. Those who are dead came off worst, not having the protection of the laws of libel, though the friends of victims such as Roald Dahl and Malcolm Muggeridge rushed into print to defend their reputations. *Memoirs* was considered to have exceeded the bounds of good taste in its malicious and misogynist tone, but was also found wickedly funny and thoroughly entertaining.

Shifting perceptions

J. M. Coetzee's *Age of Iron* is a parable of the ending of apartheid and the death of white liberalism in South Africa. It is written as a letter from Elizabeth Curren, a woman dying of cancer, to her daughter, who has emigrated to the USA. On the day she is told that her illness is terminal, a drunken tramp takes up residence in her yard, and the novel details her relationship with him and with Bheki, the son of her maid Florence, and his friend, who are involved in the troubles in the black townships. Elizabeth has 'a gathering feeling of walking over black faces. They are dead but the spirit has not left them. They lie there heavy and obdurate, waiting for my feet to pass, waiting for me to go, waiting to be raised up again. Millions of figures of pig-iron floating under the skin of the earth. The age of iron waiting to return.' There is no place for people like her in South Africa any more, and that is the tragedy of South Africa: 'To be good in yourself is not enough'. *Age of Iron* is a beautifully written novel, eloquent and powerful in its allegory. Coetzee was awarded the Sunday Express Book of the Year Award (£20,000) for the work.

Brazzaville Beach, William Boyd's fifth novel, is also set in Africa, and concerns Dr Hope Clearwater, an ethnologist studying the behaviour of a colony of chimpanzees at the Grosso Arvoro Research Centre. Hope's husband John, a mathematician, has had a breakdown as he studies theories of erratic behaviour and attempts to find a mathematical formula for life. She 'fled to Africa to escape what happened in England and then, as the continent will, it embroiled me further'. Her observation of a rogue colony of chimps threatened the research work of the head of the centre, Professor Eugene Mallabar, putting her life at risk.

'He lies like an eyewitness' is Julian Barnes' epigraph to *Talking It Over*, the account of the relationships between Stuart, a decent and solid banker, Oliver, charming teacher of English to foreign students, and Gillian, a picture restorer. The story is told by the three main characters in turn, in monologues addressed to the reader, with occasional comments from other characters. No single version is the truth, just as Gillian states that you can only restore a painting to your perception of what it was once like. Oliver realizes that 'There is no "real" picture under there waiting to be revealed. What I have always said about life itself . . . It's just my word against everybody else's.' Occasionally, notably in the case of Oliver, whose language is overblown and unconvincing, Barnes' authorial voice intrudes too much in an otherwise enjoyable book.

Penelope Lively's *City of the Mind* is a story about London seen through its buildings as they are perceived by Matthew Holland, an architect. London is 'entirely in the mind. It is a construct of the memory and of the intellect', against which Matthew's relationships with his wife and other people are measured. Unfortunately, the concentration on architecture tends to diminish the human element in the book.

Margaret Forster's *The Battle for Christabel* is a powerful and angry work about the adoption of a child. The narrator is Isobel, whose best friend Rowena is killed in an accident, leaving five-year old Christabel effectively orphaned as her father does not know of her existence. Opening with the result of Isobel's attempt to adopt the child—'Today, I lost the battle for Christabel. I lost the whole war (this is a war story, make no mistake)'—the story then recounts her agonizing over the decision of what to do with the unwanted child and the events leading up to the adoption hearing.

Angela Carter's *Wise Children* is the exuberant tale of Dora and Nora Chance, 75-year-old former chorus girls who live in Brixton. Their natural father, famous Shakespearian actor Sir Melchior Hazard, finally acknowledges them as his offspring on his 100th birthday. His brother, Peregrine, had been more like a father to them, and is in fact the father of Melchior's supposedly legitimate children. 'It's a wise child that knows its own father' is the theme, and the book is also full of Shakespearian allusion, with its multiple sets of twins and themes of loss and regeneration.

John le Carré's *The Secret Pilgrim* consists of a collection of reminiscences, as retired spymaster George Smiley addresses students at Sarratt, the school for spies. Le Carré showed in *The Russia House* that he had adapted to the new spirit prevailing in Eastern Europe. As Smiley remarks: 'Time you rang down the curtain on yesterday's cold warrior. The new time needs new people.'

Across the water

Bret Easton Ellis's *American Psycho* recounts the life of Patrick Bateman, a serial killer. In America the book caused controversy, and its original publishers dropped it before publication as 'a matter of taste'. As its reputation preceded it to Britain, some distinguished writers, including Fay Weldon, Doris Lessing and A. S. Byatt, asked Picador not to publish it: 'The world would be a better place without such a book', claimed Byatt, a dubious premise, as the book merely exploits a curious contemporary fascination with serial killers. The film *The Silence of the Lambs* and the book on which it is based have also been a popular success. Controversy can generate sales; as Margaret Drabble commented, 'If books are banned people become even more interested'. However, it cannot ensure critical success. *American Psycho* is superficial, poorly written and devoid of literary merit.

John Updike has completed his quartet of novels about the life of Harry Angstrom, known as 'Rabbit'. In *Rabbit at Rest* the 55-year-old protagonist has retired to Florida with his wife, leaving his son Nelson to run his motor business in Pennsylvania. Unfortunately, Nelson wrecks the business through his addiction to cocaine, finally losing the prized Toyota franchise, and Rabbit succumbs to heart attacks brought on by over-indulgence in sodium-drenched snacks. Rabbit is 'helplessly falling towards death', like the victims of the Lockerbie aeroplane disaster, a powerful image that haunts the book. 'Everything falling apart: airplanes, bridges, eight years under Reagan of nobody minding the store, making money out of nothing, trusting in God.' The 'Rabbit' books have been a marvellous saga of late 20th century life in America, and the character will be sorely missed.

In *Hocus Pocus*, Kurt Vonnegut relates the memoirs of Eugene Debs Hartke, written 'in pencil on everything from brown wrapping paper to the backs of business cards'. He is awaiting trial in the prison of which he was once governor, for supposedly arranging a mass escape of prisoners from it. Set in 2001, Vonnegut's America is now dominated by the Japanese, and is described in his familiar satiric style.

William Wharton's *Last Lovers* is the touching story of Jack, an ex-computer company executive aged 49, who is now (like Wharton) painting in Paris; he meets and falls in love with Mirabelle, a blind 71-year-old, 'a young girl trapped inside an old woman's body'.

Public Lending Right

In the eighth annual payment to authors registered under the PLR scheme, the rate per loan was 1·37p. The number of registered authors increased from 17,594 to 18,976, but public library book loans dropped from 611 million to 583 million, of which 239 million were of books on the PLR register. A total of 55 authors received the maximum permissible payment of £6,000; 25 received £5,000–£6,000; 148, £2,500–£4,999; 406, £1,000–£2,499; 572, £500–£999; 3,061, £100–£499; 11,204, £1–£99; and 3,505 registered authors received no payment.

The Royal Shakespeare Company carried out its threat to close its two London stages at the Barbican Centre in November 1990, one of the low points in another difficult year for the theatre. Once again, the year consists of a litany of theatres and theatre companies under threat, of inadequate funding, of poor attendances, and of failed productions.

In the autumn of 1990, a campaign was launched by leading actors and producers to save British theatre from, in the words of Sir Peter Hall, being 'bled to death'. The causes of the crisis were identified as reduced Arts Council subsidies, the new business rates, community charge capping of local authorities, and the ending of the self-employed status of actors for income tax purposes; and the Education Reform Act was blamed for a reduction in the number of organized school visits to the theatre. These factors were exacerbated in early 1991 by the Gulf war, the recession, and the fall of the dollar against the pound, which contributed to a substantial decline in the number of tourists in the country. Tickets for even the most popular established shows, such as *Miss Saigon*, were available on the day of performance early in 1991.

However, in spite of the gloom, there were some encouraging signs and some outstanding productions and performances. The Stoll Moss Group, which controls 13 West End theatres, sold 3·5 million tickets in 1990, one million more than the previous year, and it was reported that gross revenues for West End theatres in 1990 was £178 million, £25 million up on 1989. There was concern in September 1990 over the future of the Stoll Moss theatres, which include the London Palladium, the Garrick, the Lyric and the Theatre Royal, Drury Lane, following the death of Robert Holmes à Court, who owned the group. However, Mrs Holmes à Court stated that the theatres were not for sale and that it was 'business as usual'. In April 1991 Stoll Moss invested £3 million in a computerized box office service for its theatres, to simplify and improve the purchase and booking of tickets.

Under Threat

In August 1990 the Young Vic launched an appeal to raise £100,000 for urgent repairs; without essential safety work and rewiring its licence was under threat and the theatre would have had to close. Helped by a benefit performance of *The Man Who Had All the Luck* by Arthur Miller (a playwright with whom the Young Vic have enjoyed a close and productive relationship), the theatre was able to raise the necessary funds. A subsequent appeal aims to raise a further £250,000 to restore the theatre.

The Lyric, Hammersmith was forced to reduce its output after its grant was cut by nearly £100,000, one-third of the total. The Lyric also suffered financially because its bold production of Malory's *Morte d'Arthur*, lasting seven hours and using the additional venue of St Paul's Church, had drawn audiences of less than one-sixth of the theatre's capacity.

The Almeida's future was threatened by the withdrawal of funding from the London Boroughs' Grants Committee. However, the theatre secured an Arts Council loan, and later obtained sponsorship from the American telecommunications company AT & T. Although a generous sponsor of theatre in the USA, this was AT & T's first such venture in Britain. Andrew Lloyd Webber was also reported to have donated £100,000 to the Almeida to alleviate its plight.

The Old Vic's artistic director, Jonathan Miller, resigned in October 1990 following the abrupt cancellation of his last two productions, three weeks into rehearsals. David Mirvish, son of Ed Mirvish who had bought and restored the theatre, said that it would have been 'financially irresponsible to proceed' with the plays. The Old Vic brought in the Theatr Clwyd production of J. B. Priestley's *Time and the Conways*, a period piece notable more for its dominance by the Olivier clan than its merit. Laurence Olivier's widow, Joan Plowright, starred in a production which was directed by his son Richard and also featured his daughters Tamsin and Julie Kate Olivier. Other theatres in difficulty included Sadler's Wells, reportedly £500,000 in deficit, and Greenwich, which lost local authority funding worth £45,000 and feared a similar reduction in its Arts Council grant.

Outside London, the Liverpool Playhouse, reputed to be the oldest surviving repertory theatre in the country, was £600,000 in deficit. A rescue scheme was launched, which entailed the appointment of an administrator under the terms of the Insolvency Act. One of his first moves was to cancel on the grounds of expense the scheduled production of *An Awfully Big Adventure* by Beryl Bainbridge, which was based on her novel about her experiences as an assistant stage manager in the same theatre. The Playhouse was subsequently saved from liquidation by the rescue campaign, officially launched by Environment Secretary Michael Heseltine with the aim of raising £1·5 million in five years to secure the theatre's future. Littlewoods presented £50,000 as part of a pledge of £250,000 towards the campaign, and local councils promised to increase the 1990–91 grant of £120,000 by £250,000 for 1991–92, to add to the Arts Council's grant of £527,000. Theatre impresario Bill Kenwright also offered to underwrite the theatre's debts, dependent on local authority and Arts Council funding. However, as part of the rescue scheme, 15 of the theatre's 70 staff were made redundant.

Arts Council

The whole question of Arts Council funding of theatres had been highlighted by the Royal Shakespeare Company's well-publicized withdrawal from the Barbican. As the RSC pointed out, under the Priestley Report, a special financial scrutiny carried out by the Cabinet Office's Management and Efficiency Group, the company was found to be both well managed and 'palpably underfunded'. However, the real value of its subsidy had not been maintained in subsequent years, allowing a deficit to accumulate.

Fortunately for the company, following an appraisal in December 1990, the Arts Council increased it's grant by 30 per cent. And with the change of Prime Minister in November 1990, there was evidence of a more sympathetic approach to the arts. The Arts Council's funding was increased by 11 per cent for 1991–92, with an extra 14 per cent earmarked for the theatre. The RSC received an allocation of £7·87 million for 1991–92, compared with £6 million the previous year, and an additional £1·3 million from a special enhancement fund. The fund, worth in total £22·5 million over three years, is for special cases, and the beneficiaries are required to match the funding with local authority grants. This was provided in the Barbican's case by the City of London Corporation.

Royal Shakespeare Company

Adrian Noble, the new artistic director of the RSC, wrote that, '1991 promises to be a very special year in our history . . . for the first time in years . . . a year of financial stability.' The central function of the RSC is 'to do poetry, make living the experience that poetic drama can give', he said. After several years in which the company appeared to have lost direction, Noble's regime brought a sense of optimism and a return to what the company did best, Shakespearean and classic drama, rather than costly mistakes like the ill-fated musical *Carrie*.

The departure from the Barbican was undoubtedly a low point in the RSC's history. The decision was criticized by many, who felt the company unrealistic to make demands for extra funding in times of financial stringency. It was also felt to be unfair to other employees of the Barbican Centre, to its customers and organizers of other events to be deprived of the RSC's presence and the audience it attracts. Royal Insurance Company, major sponsors of the RSC, while renewing their sponsorship of £2·1 million over the three years from 1991–93, expressed concern at the company's plight and hinted that their sponsorship was partially dependent on the company having a presence in London.

The move was designed to save the RSC £1·3 million and to prevent the £2 million deficit rising to £4·4 million. However, the chairman of the RSC council, Geoffrey Cass, warned: 'The reopening of the Barbican Theatre next March cannot be relied upon. Unless substantial help appears in the meantime, we'll be in worse trouble next year'. The closing productions at the Barbican were *Moscow Gold*, a leaden drama by Tariq Ali and Howard Brenton, and Peter Flannery's *Singer*. Claiming to be 'tackling the Everest of *perestroika*', *Moscow Gold* barely reached the foothills. One of the drama's few redeeming features was David Calder's impersonation of Gorbachev. Not only was the play an unfortunate poor note on which to close, it also appeared irresponsible of the RSC to mount a new play of such scale barely one month before closing the theatre in which it was premièred. More apt were the closing words of *Singer*: 'This is a theatre in which there's always so much else to say. If we had all night. And another day.'

The RSC's departure also marked a low point in the company's relationship with the management of the Barbican Centre, and when the RSC returned in March 1991, the City of London Corporation attempted to ensure that such a situation would not recur by attaching strict conditions to its grant. The RSC was required to commit itself to the Barbican and the Pit, to eliminate its deficit by the end of March 1994, to pay compensation for cancelled productions, and to give the City Corporation the right to hire out the theatres if the RSC suspended operations for four weeks or more.

The Barbican reopened with Terry Hands' last Stratford Shakespeare production, *Love's Labour's Lost*, which was well-received. In the Pit, Richard Nelson's *Two Shakespearean Actors*, first seen at the Swan, was based on the 19th century feud between the American tragedian Edwin Forrest and the English actor William Charles Macready. This climaxed in a riot at the Astor Place Opera House caused by their rival productions of *Macbeth*, resulting in the deaths of some 30 people and injuries to 100 more. Nelson took some historical liberties with the facts and did not realize the full dramatic potential of the situation; however, the play was certainly apposite, as American resentment of English theatrical intruders was again demonstrated by the attempts to prevent Jonathan Pryce appearing in the Broadway production of *Miss Saigon*.

The Stratford season opened at the Swan with Phyllida Lloyd's RSC debut, a much praised production of the rarely performed *The Virtuoso* by Shadwell. Written in 1676, the comedy had not been performed for some 300 years, and the playwright was best remembered for Dryden's ridiculing of him. Adrian Noble's productions of *Henry IV Parts I and II* were acclaimed as intelligent and highly impressive productions. They saw the RSC debut of Robert Stephens, whose portrayal of Sir John Falstaff was widely praised. Less successful was Griff Rhys Jones's RSC directorial debut; his *Twelfth Night* was ill-prepared and poorly done.

Terry Hands' final production as artistic director of the RSC was Chekhov's *The Seagull*, in Michael Frayn's translation. As with his final Shakespeare production, he was felt to have left on a high note; if at times his management of the company was open to criticism, he is still a director of uncommon ability.

National Theatre

The National Theatre received a 10 per cent increase in its Arts Council grant for 1991, a rise from £8·9 million to £9·8 million; however, it received nothing from the enhancement fund. As artistic director Richard Eyre pointed out, the grant took no account of the substantial maintenance costs of the South Bank theatre complex, estimated at £1 million a year. Without extra funding, he feared that the National might also have to close for part of a season.

Artistically, the National flourished, the success of its productions being matched by an increase in attendances. In 1990, the complex enjoyed an 85 per cent take-up of seats, compared with 75 per cent the previous year. David Hare's *Racing Demon*, well-received on its première in the Cottesloe, transferred to the Olivier. Alan Bennett's adaptation of Kenneth Grahame's *The Wind in the Willows*, featuring finely judged comic performances from Richard Briers and Griff Rhys Jones, also proved popular.

David Edgar's *The Shape of the Table* is an

intelligent and thoughtful look at the upheavals in eastern Europe, influenced by the circumstances of Vaclav Havel, the Czechoslovak playwright who became his country's president. Also premièred in the Cottesloe was Christopher Hampton's *White Chameleon*, a dramatized account of his childhood in Alexandria at the time of the Suez crisis. The play is a sensitive account of the development of the playwright's outlook, superficially able to adapt to his surroundings like his pet chameleon, but with no feeling of belonging.

Alan Ayckbourn's *Invisible Friends* was alleged to be his play *Woman in Mind* 'softened up' for a family audience. It tells the story of 14-year-old Lucy Baines, who escapes from her dull family through her day-dreams. However, following a fall, her imaginary friends materialize, replacing her relatives; although everything is fine at first, in typical Ayckbourn fashion a darker side to the situation soon emerges.

Brian Friel's new play *Dancing at Lughnasa* was a critical and popular success. Set in Donegal in 1936, it centres on the Mundy sisters at the time of the harvest festival, when magical pagan influences are at work. The tale is remembered by the narrator Michael, played by Gerard McSorley, who recalls an atmosphere where 'everything is simultaneously actual and illusory'. Alec McCowen joined the Abbey Theatre production at the Lyttelton, whence after a successful run, the play transferred to the Phoenix.

The National Theatre also enjoyed success with its world tour of *Richard III* with Ian McKellen and *King Lear* with Brian Cox. The tour included four dates in eastern Europe. At Prague the cast was received by President Havel, who professed himself much moved by *King Lear*; they received rapturous receptions there and at Bucharest, Leipzig and Dresden. The National also continued its successful collaboration with the Bristol Old Vic. Its co-production of Eugene O'Neill's *A Long Day's Journey Into Night*, featuring Timothy West and Prunella Scales, toured seven UK cities after its Bristol opening, before playing in the Lyttelton.

Opening the Iron Curtain

The interest in matters eastern European, as evidenced by *Moscow Gold* and *The Shape of the Table*, was matched by a cultural exchange which demonstrated the power of the theatre not only in dramatizing events but, to a lesser extent, in influencing them. Caryl Churchill began a studio exercise with final year students at the Central School of Speech and Drama. The resulting play, *Mad Forest*, was about Romania under Ceausescu, the revolution and events that followed in that country. In September 1990 the cast performed the play in Bucharest. Director Mark Wing-Davey told the Romanian press that the piece was 'about the pain that individuals go through as the result of circumstances beyond their control'. The play was reported to have had a powerful, cathartic effect on the audience, enabling them to discuss feelings that they had repressed for years under the dictatorial regime in Romania. A Romanian company hopes to produce the play in Cluj. After Bucharest, the students presented the play at the Royal Court.

At the Lyttelton, the Bulandra Theatre Company

of Bucharest performed their version of *Hamlet*. The play achieved massive success in Romania before Ceausescu's overthrow; its message of a country under a corrupt regime struck a chord with the audience, although the parallels were apparently lost on the authorities. Performed in Romanian with Ion Caramitru as the Prince, Alexandru Tocilescu's production was both a fascinating reading of the text and a mark of the universality and timelessness of Shakespeare's plays. As part of the London International Festival of Theatre, the Comedy Theatre of Bucharest also performed Shakespeare's *A Midsummer Night's Dream* at the Lyric, Hammersmith. LIFT opened in June 1991 with a production of the same play by the travelling Footsbarn company, originally from Cornwall but now based in France. LIFT featured 25 theatre companies from twelve countries, performing in twelve venues.

Exodus of Genesis

The Royal Shakespeare Company was perhaps fortunate that its financial difficulties forced it to end its involvement with *Children of God*, a musical based on the book of Genesis. The production was written and directed by John Caird, with music and lyrics by Stephen Schwartz, composer of *Godspell*. It was an expensive and short-lived flop. Before it opened, Caird was involved in a dispute with Equity. Although he was allowed to cast the black American actor Ken Page in the role of God, he was initially refused permission to cast Tokyo-based actress Hiromi Ito in the role of Aysha. The musical's scheduled opening then clashed with the UN deadline for Iraq to withdraw from Kuwait so the date was brought forward. Critical reception was generally unfavourable, regarding the show as uninspiring, unoriginal and ineffectual. The production was reported to have cost £2·2 million and involved a cast of 38 with an orchestra of 23.

By contrast, the Glasgow Citizens production of *The Gospels* by Giles Havergal, with a cast of six, was widely praised for its stunning theatricality. Also successful in the West End was Andrew Lloyd Webber and Tim Rice's *Joseph and the Amazing Technicolor Dreamcoat*. What had started out as a 20-minute end of term school concert was felt by some to have sacrificed much of its charm when inflated to two hours in length and given full West End treatment. However, the show is an enjoyable romp, and the engaging performance of Australian actor and singer Jason Donovan in the title role contributed significantly to the show's success.

The musical *Matador*, a fictionalized account of the life of a bullfighter, was short-lived. Although the staging was impressive, the songs were weak, and the plot deteriorated sharply in the second half, with the introduction of Stefanie Powers as an American film star attempting to turn the matador Domingo, played by Ian Barrowman, away from the bull ring. The Theatre Royal, Stratford East, achieved a well-deserved success with a small-scale revue celebrating the songs of the 1940s jazz musician Louis Jordan; *Five Guys Named Moe* by Clarke Peters became a West End hit and the transfer deal and royalties helped to cut the Stratford East theatre's deficit.

Stephen Sondheim's 1987 musical, *Into the Woods*, featured Julia McKenzie as a witch in a grown-up compilation of fairy tales. In spite of fine performances and good reviews, the show had limited appeal, demonstrating once again that Sondheim's appeal has not successfully crossed the Atlantic.

Two of Lionel Bart's hit musicals were revived, *Blitz!* and *Oliver!* The National Youth Theatre production of *Blitz!* appeared at the Playhouse to mark the 50th anniversary of the bombing of London during the Second World War. The Royal Shakespeare Company had hoped to stage the show but demurred, unable to match the original spectacular set. *Blitz!* had not aged well, appearing amateurish and sentimental. *Oliver!* proved the far superior show, with excellent songs and music, in the National Youth Music Theatre production at Sadler's Wells.

Born Again was Peter Hall and Jason Carr's version of Ionesco's anti-fascist drama *Rhinoceros.* 'I would hate anybody to think that we had musicalized the play, although the main characters remain', said Hall. The play received mixed reviews; although an enjoyable entertainment, with impressive rhinoceros designs by Gerald Scarfe, the original Ionesco message had been softened to become an allegory about the herd instinct and born-again Christianity. The production was perhaps too *avant garde* for the Chichester Festival Theatre, and the hoped-for London and New York transfers failed to materialize.

August Wilson's *Fences* opened at the Garrick after running at the Liverpool Playhouse. Wilson's plays dramatize the experiences of black Americans in the 20th century; *Ma Rainey's Black Bottom*, a success at the Cottesloe in 1989–90, exposes the exploitation of black performers in the 1920s. *Fences* deals with discrimination in sport. The production featured Yaphet Kotto as Troy Maxson, a garbage collector who has been unable to fulfil his potential in baseball. Kotto gave a powerful and energetic performance, making Maxson a flawed but tragic hero. However, in spite of critical approval, the play failed to find an audience in London.

Wallace Shawn's one-man show *The Fever* began life as a performance for friends in their apartments. It consisted of a 100-minute monologue, given by a man in a hotel room who is reliving a frightening experience in a totalitarian country. A confessional inspired by anger and the desire for political debate, it depicted the 'awakening of a pampered man's conscience', driven to breakdown by his ordeal. Shawn's powerful *tour de force* was performed both as 'dinner-party' theatre in the UK, before small groups of invited guests, and also on stage at the Theatre Upstairs (Royal Court) and in the National.

The sixtieth birthday of Harold Pinter was marked by new productions of a number of his plays. At The Place, Nancy Meckler directed the Shared Experience Theatre production of *The Birthday Party*, while Peter Hall directed *The Homecoming* at the Comedy, a play he directed on its première in 1965. The production marked a reconciliation between Hall and Pinter, who had fallen out in 1983 over passages in Hall's published diaries. At the Almeida, David Leveaux directed *Betrayal*, which, like many of Pinter's works, was undervalued when first performed in 1978. *The Homecoming* was succeeded at the Comedy by *The Caretaker*, directed by Pinter himself, with Donald Pleasence taking again the role of the tramp, Davies, which he had created in the original production. Pinter has not created any major new works in recent years, but a six-minute piece entitled *The New World Order* was performed at the Royal Court in July as part of the London International Festival of Theatre.

The Whitehall saw the world première of *Rick's Bar Casablanca*, the original 1942 drama on which the popular film is based. Written by Murray Burnett and Joan Alison, it featured Leslie Grantham in the role made famous by Bogart, and proved to be acceptable if dated drama. William Nicholson had achieved great success with *Shadowlands*, but his new play, *Map of the Heart*, received poor reviews and closed after three weeks. The 1950s hit farce *Sailor, Beware!* was revived at the Lyric Hammersmith but although well received, it played to one-fifth capacity audiences and failed to survive. The English Shakespeare Company also found difficulty in attracting audiences to its West End season. With half-full houses, its anticipated profits dwindled to next-to-nothing, and in an attempt to boost its finances it announced that it would replace a planned production of *All's Well That Ends Well* with Michael Bogdanov's musical version of Goethe's *Reynard the Fox*.

In Glasgow, Bill Bryden wrote and directed *The Ship*, a tribute to the city's once-famous shipbuilding industry. Staged in a disused Clydeside engine shed, with an impressive design of a ship's framework by William Dudley, this episodic drama featured Jimmy Logan and Tom Watson in a moving, if romanticized, account of the story of the shipyards. The event climaxed with a splendidly theatrical ship launching.

At Chichester, Michael Rudman resigned as artistic director after a season that had proved a partial artistic success but a commercial failure. Rudman was replaced by Patrick Garland, director from 1981 to 1984, whose first move was to cancel two scheduled productions, *The Three Musketeers* by Alexander Dumas and *Till Tomorrow* by Don MacLean.

Peter Hall's company took up residence at Jeffrey Archer's Playhouse, which invested £500,000 in Hall's productions of *Twelfth Night* and Tennessee Williams' *The Rose Tattoo*. In spite of playing to 70 per cent capacity, *Twelfth Night* was reported to have lost £100,000; *The Rose Tattoo*, featuring Julie Walters, was profitable. However, it is rumoured that Archer wants to sell the theatre. Trevor Nunn adapted and directed Shakespeare's seldom-performed *Timon of Athens* at the Young Vic to general approval.

Awards

In the London Evening Standard Drama Awards, presented in November 1990, best actor was Richard Harris (*Henry IV*); best actress, Josette Simon (*After the Fall*); best play, William Nicholson's *Shadowlands*; best director, Richard Jones (*The Illusion* and *Into the Woods*); best musical, *Into the Woods*; best comedy, *Jeffrey Bernard is Unwell* (Keith Waterhouse) and *Man of the Moment* (Alan Ayckbourn); most promising playwright, Clare McIntyre (*My Heart's a Suitcase*).

The winners of the Laurence Olivier Awards, presented by the Society of West End Theatres, were: special lifetime award, Dame Peggy Ashcroft; best actor, Sir Ian McKellen (*Richard III*); best actress, Kathryn Hunter (*The Visit*); best play, *Dancing at Lughnasa* (Brian Friel); best musical, *Sunday in the Park with George* (Stephen Sondheim); best comedy, *Out of Order* (Ray Cooney); best entertainment, *Five Guys Named Moe*; best director, Richard Jones (*Into the Woods*); best set designer, Mark Thompson (*Wind in the Willows*).

The first Sunday Times Royal National Theatre Ian Charleson Award was presented to Ian Hughes for his performance in *Tasso*. Dame Maggie Smith received the Shakespeare Prize, awarded by the FVS Foundation of Hamburg.

PRODUCTIONS

London productions between August 16, 1990, and August 15, 1991, included the following:

ALDWYCH: WC2. (1990) Sept. 19. *Private Lives* by Noël Coward, with Joan Collins, Keith Baxter, Edward Duke, Sara Crowe, dir. by Tim Luscombe, des. by Carl Toms. (1991) April 9. Shakespeare's *Coriolanus*, with Michael Pennington, Bernard Lloyd, Lynn Farleigh, June Watson, dir. by Michael Bogdanov (English Shakespeare Co. prodn). April 11. Shakespeare's *The Winter's Tale*, with Lynn Farleigh, Michael Pennington, Bernard Lloyd, James Hayes, Trilby James, dir. by Michael Bogdanov (ESC prodn).

ALMEIDA: N1. (1990) Sept. 18. *The Rehearsal* by Jean Anouilh (trans. by Jeremy Sams), with Jonathan Hyde, Nicola Pagett, Jonathan Kent, Julie Ormond, costumes des. by Jasper Conran, set des. by Anthony Ward, dir. by Ian McDiarmid. Nov. 5. *Bajazet* by Racine (trans. by Allan Hollinghurst), with Suzanne Bertish, Terence Rigby, Oliver Parker, Martin Wenner, Olwen Fouéré, des. by Chloë Obolensky, dir. by Peter Eyre. Nov. 15. *In the Solitude of the Cotton Fields* by Bernard-Marie Koltès, with Jeffery Kissoon, Jonathan Phillips, dir. by Kim Dambaek, des. by Stewart Laing. (1991) Jan. 22. *Betrayal* by Harold Pinter, with Martin Shaw, Bill Nighy, Cheryl Campbell, dir. by David Leveaux, des. by Mark Thompson. March 12. *The Lulu Plays* (*Earth Spirit* and *Pandora's Box*) by Frank Wedekind, with Joanne Whalley-Kilmer, Jonathan Kent, David King, Larry Lamb, Belinda Lang, Philip Lock, dir. by Ian McDiarmid, des. by Maria Björnson. April 30. *All for Love* by John Dryden, with James Laurenson, Diana Rigg, Angela Down, Bernard Horsfall, Alan MacNaughtan, dir. by Jonathan Kent, des. by Peter J. Davison and Sue Willmington.

AMBASSADORS: WC2. (1990) Oct. 30. *The Mystery of Irma Vep* by Charles Ludlam, with Nickolas Grace, Edward Hibbert, dir. by Maria Aitken. (1991) April 2. *My Lovely . . . Shayna Maidel* by Barbara Lebow, with Anita Dobson, Laurel Lefkow and John Burgess, dir. by Lisa Forrell.

APOLLO: W1. (1990) Oct. 31. *Bookends* by Keith Waterhouse, with Michael Hordern, Dinsdale Landern, dir. by Ned Sherrin, des. by John Gunter. (1991) March 26. *Don't Dress for Dinner* by Marc Camoletti (adapted by Robin Hawdon), with John Quayle, Su Pollard, Simon Cadell, Jane How, dir. by Peter Farago.

BARBICAN: EC2. (1990) Sept. 26. *Moscow Gold* by Tariq Ali and Howard Brenton, with David Calder, Sara Kestelman, Russell Dixon, Clive Merrison, Gabrielle Lloyd, dir. by Barry Kyle, des. by Stephanos Lazaridis. (1991) March 27. Shakespeare's *Love's Labour's Lost* (trans. from Stratford Memorial Theatre). April 10. Shakespeare's *Much Ado About Nothing*, with Susan Fleetwood, Roger Allam, John Carlisle, Alex Kingston, dir. by Bill Alexander, des. by Kit Surrey. May 1. Shakespeare's *King Lear*, with John Wood, Alex Kingston, Linda Kerr Scott, Estelle Kohler, Sally Dexter, Norman Rodway, David Troughton, Linus Roache, Ralph Fiennes, dir. by Nicholas Hytner, des. by David Fielding. June 19. Shakespeare's *The Comedy of Errors*, with Desmond Barrit, Graham Turner, Estelle Kohler, Caroline Loncq, David Waller, David Killick, dir. by Ian Judge, des. by Mark Thompson. July 11. *The Seagull* by Anton Chekhov (trans. from The Swan, Stratford).

BARBICAN PIT: (1991) March 26. *Two Shakespearean Actors* by Richard Nelson (trans. from The Swan, Stratford). April 9. *The Last Days of Don Juan* by Tirso de Molina (adapted by Nick Dear), with Linus Roache, Sally Dexter, Sylvester Morand, Paterson Joseph, Yolanda Vazquez, dir. by Danny Boyle, des. by Kandis Cook. April 29. *Edward II* by Christopher Marlowe, with Simon Russell Beale, Katy Behean, Ciaran Hinds, Grant Thatcher, dir. by Gerard Murphy, des. by Sandy Powell. June 18. Shakespeare's *Troilus and Cressida*, with Amanda Root, Ralph Fiennes, Norman Rodway, David Troughton, Ciaran Hinds, Simon Russell Beale, dir. by Sam Mendes, des. by Anthony Ward.

BLOOMSBURY: WC1. (1990) Sept. 6. *Once a Catholic* by Mary O'Malley (National Youth Theatre prodn). (1991) May 16. Shakespeare's *Antony and Cleopatra*, with Dona Croll, Jeffery Kissoon, Ben Thomas, David Webber, dir. by Yvonne Brewster, des. by Helen Turner (Talawa Theatre, trans. from Merseyside Everyman).

BOULEVARD: W1. (1990) Aug. 23. *Let My People Come* by Earl Wilson.

BUSH: W12. (1990) Aug. 28. *The Evil Doers* by Chris Hannan, with Tom Mannion, Sharon Muircroft, Alison Peebles, Lucy Aston, Douglas Henshall, dir. by Simon Usher, des. by Anthony Lamble. Nov. 9. *Dancing Attendance* by Lucy Gannon, with Barry Foster, David Beames, Cherith Mellor, dir. by Stuart Burge, des. by Annie Smart. (1991) Jan. 5. *The Pitchfork Disney* by Philip Ridley, with Rupert Graves, Tilly Vosburgh, Dominic Keating, dir. by Matthew Lloyd, des. by Moggie Douglas. April 2. *Our Own Kind* by Roy MacGregor, with Charlotte Coleman, Brian Protheroe, Kevin Whatley, Jane Horrocks, dir. by Dominic Dromgoole, des. by Vicki Mortimer.

COMEDY: WC2. (1990) Aug. 28. *Having a Ball* by Alan Bleasdale, with William Gaunt, Helen Lederer, Keith Clifford, dir. by Pip Broughton. Nov. 15. *The Boys Next Door* by Tom Griffin, with Steve Guttenberg (trans. from Hampstead). (1991) Jan. 10. *The Homecoming* by Harold Pinter, with Warren Mitchell, Greg Hicks, Cherie Lunghi, Douglas McFerran, Nicholas Woodeson, dir. by Peter Hall, des. by John Bury. June 20. *The Caretaker*, written and dir. by Harold Pinter, with Donald Pleasence, Peter Howitt, Colin Firth, des. by Eileen Diss.

DOMINION: WC1. (1991) Feb. 27. *42nd Street* with Cheryl Hall, Jenna Ward, Kenneth Nelson, Alison Mellor, dir. by Mark Bramble.

DUCHESS: WC2. (1990) Sept. 17. *Run for Your Wife* by Ray Cooney (trans. from Aldwych).

GARRICK: WC2. (1990) Sept. 24. *Fences* by August Wilson (trans. from Liverpool Playhouse). Nov. 12. *The Rehearsal* by Jean Anouilh (trans. from Almeida).

GATE: W11. (1990) Nov. 16. *Vassa Zheleznova* by Maxim Gorky (trans. by Cathy Porter), with Paola

Dionisotti, Sarah Harper, Kristin Hewson, Judy Sweeney, Lizzie McInnerny, dir. by Katie Mitchell (Classics on a Shoestring prodn).

GLOBE: W1. (1991) March 7. *Map of the Heart* by William Nicholson, with Patrick Malahide, Sinead Cusack, Frederick Treves, David Rintoul, Susan Wooldridge, dir. by Peter Woods, des. by Mark Thompson. May 13. *Same Old Moon* by Geraldine Aron, with James Ellis, dir. by Jenny Killick. Aug. 6. *When She Danced* by Martin Sherman, with Vanessa Redgrave, Oleg Menshikov, Frances de la Tour, Alison Fiske, dir. by Robert Allan Ackerman, des. by Bob Crowley.

GREENWICH: SE10. (1990) Sept. 24. *Cyrano de Bergerac* by Edmond Rostand (trans. by Patrick Garland), with Edward Petherbridge, Jason Connery, Jemma Redgrave, dir. by Matthew Francis. Nov. 12. *Miss Julie* by August Strindberg (trans. by Helen Cooper), with Lesley Manville, Barry Lynch, Janine Duvitski, dir. and des. by Tom Cairns. Dec. 17. *Gaslight* by Patrick Hamilton, with Bernard Gallagher, Stuart Calder, Robert Pickavance, Sally Edwards, Charlotte Barker, dir. by Annie Castledine, des. by Martin Johns. (1991) Feb. 12. *The Corn is Green* by Emlyn Williams, with Brendan O'Hea, Patricia Routledge, Arthur Cox, Paula Jacobs, dir. by Matthew Francis. March 21. *Victory* by Howard Barker, with Nicholas Le Prevost, Tricia Kelly, Philip Franks, Iain Mitchell, dir. by Kenny Ireland, des. by Johan Engels (Wrestling School prodn in assocn with Leicester Haymarket). June 10. *Cops* by Mark Baker, adapted and dir. by Bill Bryden, with Tony Haygarth, John Guerrasio, Gary Love. July 15. *Broadway Bound* by Neil Simon, with Toby Whithouse, Anna Massey, William Gaminara, Gary Waldhorn, Frank Middlemass, Barbara Ferris, dir. by David Taylor, des. by Simon Higlett.

HAMPSTEAD: NW3. (1990) Aug. 23. *The Day You'll Love Me* by Jose Ignacio Cabrujas, with Gillian Barge, Greg Hicks, Victoria Scarborough, Matthew Marsh, Maria Freedman, dir. by Lisa Forrell, des. by Andrew Wood. Oct. 5. *The Boys Next Door* by Tom Griffin, with Allan Corduner, Marcus D'Amico, Richard Cordery, Joseph Mydell, Jack Fortune, dir. by Rob Mulholland. Nov. 1. *Can't Stand Up for Falling Down*, written and dir. by Richard Cameron, with Joanne Wootton, Deborah Kilner, Donna Stones. Dec. 4. *What the Butler Saw* by Joe Orton, with Sheila Gish, Joseph Maher, Ben Porter, Clive Francis, Gary Olsen, dir. by John Tillinger. (1991) Jan. 29. *Imagine Drowning* by Terry Johnson, with Nabil Shaban, Sylvestra le Touzel, Douglas Hodge, Ed Bishop, Frances Barber, dir. by Richard Wilson, des. by Julian McGowan. March 15. *The Closing Number*, devised and dir. by Mladen Materic, with Phil Daniels, Denise Wong, Kate France, Tony Anthony (Shared Experience Co.). April 13. *Days of Hope*, music and lyrics by Howard Goodall, script by Renata Allen, with Nicholas Caunter, Una Stubbs, Carla Mendonca, John Turner, dir. by John Retallack. June 4. *Dickens' Women* with Miriam Margolyes, dir. by Sonia Fraser. July 16. *Four Door Saloon* by Jennifer Phillips, with Kevin McNally, Peter Jonfield, Leonard Fenton, Eleanor David, Kathy Burke, Tom Watt, dir. by Geraldine McEwan.

HAYMARKET THEATRE ROYAL: SW1. (1991) Feb. 26. *Silly Cow*, written and dir. by Ben Elton, with Dawn French, Alan Haywood, Patrick Barlow, Victoria Carling, Kevin Allen, des. by Terry Parsons.

KING'S HEAD: N1. (1990) Aug. 29. *Flare Path* by Terence Rattigan, with Andrée Evans, Robin Nedwell, Sophie Ward, Helen Blizard, Mark Aiken, dir. by Derek Goldby, des. by Tim Heywood. Nov. 13. *Rough Crossing* by Ferenc Molnar (adapted by Tom Stoppard), with Roland Curram, Kevin Moore, Ronald Allen, Robert Austin, Anita Dobson, dir. by Martin Connor.

LILIAN BAYLIS: EC1. (1991) Feb. 4. *The Pilgrim* by Almeida Garrett, adapted and dir. by Robin Midgley, with Terry Taplin, David Gwillim, Valerie Braddell, Emma D'Inverno (New Vic Theatre Touring Co.). April 23. *The Seagull* by Anton Chekhov, with Caroline Quentin, Pam Ferris, John Halstead, Roger Frost, Michael Mueller, Nicholas Clay, dir. by Mike Alfreds (Oxford Stage Co.).

LONDON PALLADIUM: W1. (1991) June 12. *Joseph and the Amazing Technicolor Dreamcoat*, lyrics by Tim Rice, music by Andrew Lloyd Webber, with Jason Donovan, David Easter, Linzi Hateley, Aubrey Woods, Nadia Strachan, dir. by Steven Pimlott.

LYRIC: Hammersmith, W6. (1990) Oct. 30. *Travels with My Aunt* by Graham Greene, adapted and dir. by Giles Havergal and Jon Pope, with Havergal, Gavin Mitchell, Derwent Watson, Patrick Hannaway, des. by Stewart Laing (Glasgow Citizens prodn). Nov. 19. Shakespeare's *Hamlet* with Timothy Walker, Peter Needham, Cathryn Bradshaw, Scott Cherry, Natasha Parry, dir. by Declan Donnellan, des. by Nick Ormerod (Cheek by Jowl prodn). (1991) Feb. 6. *Volpone* by Ben Jonson, with John Woodvine, Stephen Jameson, Gary Richmond, Gary Taylor, Lois Harvey, dir. by Tim Luscombe (ESC prodn). Feb. 7. Shakespeare's *The Merchant of Venice*, with John Woodvine, Laurence Kennedy, Piers Gibbon, Fary Raymond, Lois Harvey, Stephen Jameson, Adam Magnani, dir. by Tim Luscombe (ESC prodn). March 5. *The Winter Wife* by Claire Tomalin, with Rachel Joyce, Gabrielle Lloyd, Pamela Ruddock, Michael Irving, dir. by Patrick Sandford, des. by Tanya McCallin (Nuffield, Southampton prodn). April 20. *An Enemy of the People* by Henrik Ibsen, with Geraint Wyn Davies, Jack Carr, David Lloyd Meredith, dir. by Toby Robertson, des. by Jeremy Brooks (Theatr Clwyd prodn). May 20. *Sailor, Beware!* by Philip King and Falkland Cary, with John Cater, Sheila Steafel, Colin Hurley, Catherine Russell, Paul Venables, Jane Freeman, Richard Howard, dir. by Peter James, des. by Bernard Culshaw. July 8. Shakespeare's *A Midsummer Night's Dream*, with Serban Ionescu, Gabriela Popescu, Serban Cellea, dir. by Alexandru Darie (Comedy Theatre of Bucharest). July 20. *Brothers and Sisters* by Fydor Abramov, adapted and dir. by Lev Dodin, with Pyotr Semak, Tatyana Shestakova, Natasha Sokolova, Sergei Vlasov (Maly Theatre, Leningrad). July 24. *The Manchurian Candidate* by Richard Condon (adapted by John Lahr), with Gerard Murphy, Siân Phillips, Manning Redwood, dir. by Robin Midgley. Aug. 12. *Uncle Vanya* by Anton Chekhov (adapted by Pam Gems), with Annabel Arden, Richard Briers, Peter Egan, Patrick Godfrey, Siân Thomas, dir. by Peter Egan and Kenneth Branagh (Renaissance Co. prodn).

LYRIC STUDIO: W6. (1990) Oct. 4. *The Old Law* by Thomas Middleton and William Rowley (adapted by Max Hafler), with Max Hafler, Iona Kennedy, Ian McCurrach, Stephi Hemelryk, dir. by Tony Hegarty (Commonweal Theatre Co.). Nov. 7. *Tasso* by Goethe (trans. by Robert David MacDonald), with Ian Hughes, Thomas Lockyer, Helen Schlesinger, Peter Kenvyn, dir. by Ceri Sherlock (Actors Touring Co.). (1991) Jan. 12. *Heloise and Abelard* by Hugh Carr, with Bernard Brown, Karen Ford, dir. by Harry Landis. April. *Ghosts* by Henrik Ibsen, with Allister Bain, Francis Johnson, dir. by Alby James (Temba Co. prodn). June 11. *Augustine (Big Hysteria)*, written and dir. by Anna Furse, with James Dreyfus, Shona Morris (Paines Plough prodn).

LYRIC: Shaftesbury Avenue, W1. (1990) Oct. 17. *Other People's Money* by Jerry Sterner, with Martin

Shaw, Maria Aitken, Paul Rogers, dir. by Alan Strachan, des. by Michael Pavelka. Dec. 14. *Five Guys Named Moe* by Clarke Peters (trans. from Theatre Royal, Stratford East).

MERMAID: EC4. (1991) June 3. *Thunderbirds F.A.B.—The Next Generation*, with Paul Kent and Wayne Forester, dir. by Andrew Dawson and Gavin Robertson.

NATIONAL THEATRE: SE1. COTTESLOE: (1990) Sept. 18. *Once in a While the Odd Thing Happens*, written and dir. by Paul Godfrey, with Michael Maloney, Stephen Boxer, Julian Wadham, Hilary Dawson, Deborah Findlay, des. by Stephen Brimson Lewis. Nov. 8. *The Shape of the Table* by David Edgar, with Oliver Ford Davis, Stephen Boxer, Stratford Johns, John Ringham, Karl Johnson, dir. by Jenny Killick, des. by Dermot Hayes. Dec. 6. *Tectonic Plates*, devised and dir. by Robert Lepage. (1991) Jan. 7. *Accidental Death of an Anarchist* by Dario Fo (adapted by Alan Cumming and Tim Supple), with Alan Cumming, dir. by Tim Supple, des. by Ashley Martin Davis. Feb. 14. *White Chameleon* by Christopher Hampton, with David Birkin, Tom Wilkinson, Suzanne Burden, Saeed Jeffrey, dir. by Richard Eyre, des. by Bob Crowley. March 13. *Invisible Friends*, written and dir. by Alan Ayckbourn, with Bill Moody, Emma Chambers, Simon Chandler, Robert Hands, Claire Skinner, Mark Benton. April 25. *Black Snow* by Bulgakov (adapted by Keith Dewhurst), with Ron Cook, Paul Moriarty, Marion Bailey, Robin Bailey, Gillian Barge, dir. by William Gaskill, des. by Annie Smart. July 18. *The Coup* by Mustapha Matura, with Norman Beaton, Tony Armatrading, Lennie James, Gordon Case, Stefan Kalipha, Jeffery Kissoon, dir. by Roger Michell, des. by William Dudley.

LYTTELTON: (1990) Sept. 5. *My Children! My Africa!*, written and dir. by Athol Fugard, with John Kani, Rapulana Seiphemo, Lisa Fugard, des. by Susan Hilferty and Douglas Stein (Market Theatre, Johannesburg prodn). Sept. 20. Shakespeare's *Hamlet*, with Ion Caramitru, Ion Cocieru, Mariana Buruiana, Gina Patrichi, Ion Besoiu, dir. by Alexandru Tocilescu, des. by Jan Jitianu (Bulandra Theatre, Budapest prodn). Oct. 15. *Dancing at Lughnasa* by Brian Friel, with Alec McCowen, Anita Reeves, Brid Ni Neachtain, Rosaleen Linehan, Gerard McSorley, Stephen Dillane, Brid Brennan, Catherine Byrne, dir. by Patrick Mason, des. by Joe Vanek (Abbey Theatre, Dublin prodn). Nov. 14. *The Kingdom of Desire* with Wu Hsing-kuo and Wei Hai-ming (Contemporary Legend Theatre of Taipei). (1991) Feb. 7. *The Visit* by Friedrich Dürrenmatt (adapted by Maurice Valency), with Simon McBurney, Kathryn Hunter, Marcello Magni, dir. by Annabel Arden and Simon McBurney, des. by Rae Smith (*Théâtre de Complicité* prodn). March 5. *The Trial* by Kafka, adapted, dir. and des. by Steven Berkoff, with Antony Sher, Leonard Rossiter, Teddy Kempner, Matthew Scurfield. May 21. *A Long Day's Journey into Night* by Eugene O'Neill, with Timothy West, Prunella Scales, Sean McGinley, Stephen Dillane, Geraldine Fitzgerald, dir. by Howard Davies, des. by John Gunter (co-prodn with Bristol Old Vic). June 27. *Napoli Milionaria* by Eduardo de Filippo (trans. by Peter Tinniswood), with Clare Higgins, Ian McKellen, Antonia Pemberton, Mark Strong, dir. by Richard Eyre, des. by Anthony Ward.

OLIVIER: (1990) Dec. 12. *The Wind in the Willows* by Kenneth Grahame (adapted by Alan Bennett), with Richard Briers, Griff Rhys Jones, David Bamber, Michael Bryant, Terence Rigby, dir. by Nicholas Hytner, des. by Mark Thompson. (1991) May 9. *The Miser* by Molière (trans. by Jeremy Sams), with Charles Kay, Eleanor Bron, David Ross, Adam Kotz, Adrian Rawlins, dir. by Steven Pimlott, des. by

Ashley Martin-Davis. June 18. *The White Devil* by John Webster, with Denis Quilley, Josette Simon, Claire Benedict, Akim Mogaji, Rupert Frazer, T. P. McKenna, Tristram Jellinek, dir. and des. by Philip Prowse. Aug. 8. *The Resistible Rise of Arturolli* by Bertold Brecht (trans. by Ranjit Bolt), with Antony Sher, Michael Bryant, Nick Holder, dir. by Di Trevis, des. by Ultz.

NEW END: NW3. (1990) Sept. 26. *Fool's Mate* by Pavel Kohout, with Catherine Schell, John Baddeley, Donald Gee, dir. by Karis Mond, des. by Penny Fitt.

OLD VIC: SE1. (1990) Nov. 30. *Time and the Conways* by J. B. Priestley, with Joan Plowright, Julia Swift, Tamsin Olivier, Julie Kate Olivier, dir. by Richard Olivier, des. by Terry Parsons (Theatr Clwyd prodn). (1991) April 8. *Carmen Jones* by Oscar Hammerstein, music by George Bizet, with Damon Evans, Michael Austin, Sharon Benson, Wilhelmenia Fernandez, Gregg Baker, Karen Parks, music dir. by Henry Lewis, dir. by Simon Callow.

OPEN AIR: Regent's Park, NW1. (1991) May 28. Shakespeare's *A Midsummer Night's Dream*, with Roy Hudd, Louise Gold, Richard O'Callaghan, Jenny Galloway, Emily Raymond, Sarah-Jane Holm, dir. by Ian Talbot, des. by Paul Farnsworth (New Shakespeare Co.). June 13. Shakespeare's *Macbeth*, with Peter Woodward, Nichola McAuliffe, dir. by William Gaunt, des. by Bruno Santini. June 24. *The Boys from Syracuse* by Rodgers and Hart, with Bill Homewood, Peter Woodward, Gavin Muir, Richard O'Callaghan, Louise Gold, Jenny Galloway, dir. by Judi Dench, des. by James Merifield.

PHOENIX: WC2. (1990) Sept. 25. *Into the Woods*, music and lyrics by Stephen Sondheim, book by James Lapine, with Julia McKenzie, Imelda Staunton, Patsy Rowlands, Clive Carter, Nicholas Parsons, Mark Tinkler, dir. by Richard Jones, des. by Richard Hudson. (1991) March 25. *Dancing at Lughnasa* by Brian Friel (trans. from Lyttelton).

THE PLACE: WC1. (1990) Nov. 20. *The Birthday Party* by Harold Pinter, with Sandra Voe, John Halstead, Paul Higgins, Peter Whitman, Michael Packer, Cecilia Noble, dir. by Nancy Meckler, des. by Lucy Weller (Shared Experience Theatre prodn).

PLAYHOUSE: WC2. (1990) Sept. 10. *Blitz!* by Lionel Bart, with Jessica Stevenson, George Livings, Elizabeth Mills, Daniel Hopkins, dir. by Edward Wilson, des. by Brian Lee (National Youth Theatre prodn). (1991) Feb. 28. Shakespeare's *Twelfth Night*, with Sara Crowe, Maria Miles, Martin Jarvis, Dinsdale Landen, Eric Porter, David Ryall, Richard Garnett, Peter Lindford, dir. by Peter Hall, des. by Timothy O'Brien. June 4. *The Rose Tattoo* by Tennessee Williams, with Julie Walters, Ken Stott, Patricia Hayes, Lisa Orgolini, dir. by Peter Hall.

PRINCE EDWARD: W1. (1991) Jan. 8. *Children of God*, written and dir. by John Caird, music and lyrics by Stephen Schwartz, with Ken Page, Kevin Colson, Richard Lloyd-King, Martin Smith, Adrian Beaumont, Francis Ruffelle, des. by John Napier.

QUEEN'S: (1990) Dec. 11. *Three Sisters* by Anton Chekhov, with Vanessa Redgrave, Lynn Redgrave, Jemma Redgrave, Stuart Wilson, Phoebe Nicholls, dir. by Robert Sturua, des. by Giorgi Meskhishvili (from Yvonne Arnaud, Guildford). (1991) April 16. *Matador*, music by Michael Leander, lyrics by Edward Seago, book by Peter Jukes, with John Barrowman, Stefanie Powers, Nicky Henson, Jackie Dunn, dir. by Elijah Moshinsky, des. by William Dudley, chor. by Arlene Phillips and Rafael Aguilar.

RIVERSIDE STUDIOS: W6. (1990) Sept. 21. *Directions to Servants* by Jonathan Swift (adapted by Shuji

Terayama), with Yoshitaka Kaizu, Keitoku Takata, dir. by J. A. Seazer (Tokyo Globe Co. prodn). Oct. 24. *Mein Kampf: Farce* by George Tabori, with Jonathan Oliver, Joseph Long, Howard Goorney, Josephine Welcome, dir. by Michael Batz. Nov. 15. Shakespeare's *Macbeth* with Roy Marsden, Neil Duncan, Polly Hemingway, dir. by Malcolm Ransom, des. by Demetra Hersey (Red and Gold Theatre Co. prodn). Nov. 16. *The Clink* by Stephen Jeffreys, with Keith Osborn, Shelagh Fraser, Liz Kettle, Tony Bluto, Ric Morgan, Mark Lockyer, dir. by Anna Furse, des. by Sally Jacob (Paines Plough Co. prodn). Dec. 4. *The Real Don Juan* by José Zorrilla (adapted by Sanjit Bolt), with Jon Michie, Carla Mendonça, dir. by John Retallack, des. by Kenny Miller (Oxford Stage Co. prodn). (1991) Jan. 16. *Ines de Castro* by John Clifford, with Stuart McQuarrie, Maureen Beattie, Myra McFadyen, Alexander West, Hilary MacLean, dir. by Ian Brown (Traverse Theatre, Edinburgh prodn). March 27. *Why is Here There Everwhere Now?* by David Gale, with Mary Tamm, Julian Armstrong, Patricia England, dir. by Hilary Westlake (Lumiere & Son and Soho Theatre Co. prodn). July 5. *No One Writes to the Colonel*, adapted and dir. by Carlos Gimenez, with Anibal Grunn, Aura Rivas, José Tejera (Rajatabla Co. of Venezuela). July 11. *Guadeamus*, improvised by Maly Drama Theatre, Leningrad. July 30. *The Lady from the Sea* by Henrik Ibsen (trans. by Heidi Thomas), with Kathryn Pogson, Hugh Fraser, Peter Gowen, dir. by Jules Wright.

ROYAL COURT: SW1. (1990) Oct. 10. *Mad Forest* by Caryl Churchill, with David Mestecky, Lucy Cohu, dir. by Mark Wing-Davey. Nov. 5. *Etta Jenks* by Marlane Meyer, with Miranda Richardson, Lennie James, David Rintoul, Robin Soans, Christopher Fairbank, dir. by Max Stafford-Clark, des. by William Dudley. (1991) Jan. 9. *All Things Nice* by Sharman MacDonald, with Joanna Roth, Cara Kelly, Patti Love, Mary MacLeod, Ewan Hooper, dir. by Max Stafford-Clark. April 15. *Top Girls* by Caryl Churchill, with Cecily Hobbs, Sarah Lam, Deborah Findlay, Lesley Manville, Lesley Sharp, dir. by Max Stafford-Clark. July 18. *Spunk*, adapted and dir. by George C. Wolfe, with Stanley Wayne Mathias, Kevin Jackson, Danitra Vance. July 19. *The New World Order* by Harold Pinter, with Michael Byrne, Bill Paterson, Douglas McFerran.

ROYAL COURT THEATRE UPSTAIRS: (1990) Aug. 29. *Killing the Cat* by David Spencer, with Sean Bean, Dominic Kinnaird, Henry Stamper, Kate McLoughlin, Sally Rogers, Valerie Lilley, dir. by Sue Dunderdale, des. by Shimon Castiel (Soho Theatre Co.). Oct. 9. *Rafts and Dreams* by Robert Holman, with Natasha Pyne, Jonathan Cullen, Adie Allen, Jason Watkins, dir. by John Dove, des. by Michael Taylor. Nov. 27. *No One Sees the Video* by Martin Crimp, with Celia Imrie, Stephen Tompkinson, Adie Allen, Emer McCourt, Neil Dudgeon, dir. by Lindsay Posner, des. by Simon Vincenzi. (1991) Jan. 7. *Fever* by and with Wallace Shawn. May 20. *Getting Attention* by Martin Crimp, with Nigel Cooke, Bridget Turner, Paul Slack, Diana Hunter, dir. by Jude Kelly, des. by Rob Jones (West Yorkshire Playhouse prodn).

SADLER'S WELLS: EC1. (1991) Jan. 10. *Oliver!* by Lionel Bart, with Julian Forsyth, Philip Doghan, Irfan Ahmad, Nuala Willis, Sara Weymouth, Billy Hartman, Marcel Bruneau, dir. by Jeremy James Taylor, des. by Jason Denvir. chor. by Stuart Hopps (National Youth Theatre prodn). Feb. 12. *The King and I* by Rodgers and Hammerstein, with Susan Hampshire, Koshiro Matsumoto IX, dir. by James Hammerstein.

SHAFTESBURY: WC2. (1990) Oct. 9. *Out of Order*, written and dir. by Ray Cooney, with Donald Sinden, Michael Williams, Sandra Dickinson, Brian Murphy,

Dennis Ramsden, Wanda Ventham (Theatre of Comedy prodn). (1991) March 25. *Jeffrey Bernard is Unwell* by Keith Waterhouse, with Peter O'Toole, dir. by Ned Sherrin.

SHAW: (1990) Sept. 4. *Sir Thomas More* by Anthony Munday, Henry Chettle, Thomas Dekker, Thomas Heywood and William Shakespeare, with Ken Bones, Paul Aves, John Pine, Tim Hudson, Martin Head, Andrew Melville, dir. by Michael Walling, des. by Emma Ryott (Walling's Stage One Co.). (1991) Feb. 18. *Waterland* by Graham Swift (adapted by Richard Hogger), with Neil Caple, Paula Stockbridge, Carlene Reed, dir. by Hettie MacDonald, des. by Jane Green (Eastern Angles Theatre Co. prodn).

THEATRE ROYAL: E15. (1990) Aug. 31. *Greek Tragedy*, devised and dir. by Mike Leigh, with Evdokia Katahanas, Stan Kouros (Belvoir Street Theatre, Sydney). Oct. 22. *Five Guys Named Moe* by Clarke Peters, with Kenny Andrews, Paul J. Medford, Peter Alex Newton, Omar Okai, Clarke Peters, Dig Wayne, dir. by Charles Augins, des. by Tim Goodchild. (1991) Jan. 30. *I Thought I Heard a Rustling* by Alan Plater, with Paul Copley, Annette Crosbie, dir. by Philip Hedley. March 11. *Unlawful Killing* by Judith Cook, with Patrick Waldron, Jane Galloway, dir. by Jeff Teare, des. by Jenny Tiramani.

TRICYCLE: NW6. (1990) Oct. 8. *Factory Girls* by Frank McGuinness, with Eileen Pollock, Val Lilley, Michelle Fairley, Heather Tobias, Kathy Kiera-Clarke, Gerard O'Hare, dir. by Nicholas Kent. Nov. 22. *Just So*, music by George Stiles, lyrics by Anthony Drewe, with David Schneider, Nadia Strahan, Sharon Benso, Jenna Russell, Gary Bond, Linzi Hateley, dir. by Mike Ockrent. (1991) Jan. *A Free Country* by Jean-Claude Grumberg, with Miriam Karlin, Henry Goodman, James Grant. March 14. *Meetings* by Mustapha Matura, with Lenny Algernon-Edwards, Judith Jacob, dir. by Malcolm Frederick (Black Theatre Co-op. prodn). April 14. *The Cure at Troy* by Sophocles (adapted by Seamus Heaney), with Des McAleer, Ian McElhinney, Sean Rock, dir. by Stephen Rea, des. by Bob Crowley (Field Day Co.).

VAUDEVILLE: WC2. (1991) June 17. *70, Girls, 70* by John Kander and Fred Ebb, with Dora Bryan, Joan Savage, Pip Hinton, Shezwae Powell, dir. by Paul Kerryson.

WHITEHALL: SW1. (1991) April 10. *Rick's Bar Casablanca* by Murray Burnett and Joan Alison, with Leslie Grantham, Shelley Thompson, Edward de Souza, dir. by David Gilmore, des. by Saul Radomsky.

WYNDHAM'S: WC2. (1990) Oct. 1. *Love Letters* by A. R. Gurney, with Robert Wagner, Stefanie Powers (Oct. 22, with George Peppard, Elaine Stritch), dir. by John Tillinger. Nov. 28. *Scenes from a Marriage* by Ingmar Bergman (trans. from Chichester Minerva Theatre). (1991) Jan. 24. *What the Butler Saw* by Joe Orton (trans. from Hampstead). May 15. *The Philanthropist* by Christopher Hampton, with Edward Fox, Sarah Berger, Frank Barrie, Tim Brooke-Taylor, Jennifer Calvert, dir. by Kenneth Ives, des. by Eileen Diss.

YOUNG VIC: SE1. (1990) Nov. 12. *TO* by Jim Cartwright, with John McArdle, Sue Johnston, dir. by Andrew Hay. (1991) March 6. Shakespeare's *Timon of Athens*, with David Suchet, Barry Foster, Rudolph Walker, Jerome Flynn, dir. by Trevor Nunn, des. by John Gunter. May 7. *The Plough and the Stars* by Sean O'Casey, with Stanley Townsend, Dearbhla Molloy, John Rogan, Niamh Cusack, Judi Dench, Breffni McKenna, dir. by Sam Mendes. July 9. *Sex Please, We're Italian* by Tom Kempinski, with John Levitt, Helen Mirren, Kenneth Colley, Mossie Smith, dir. by David Thacker.

Outside London

STRATFORD MEMORIAL THEATRE: (RSC). (1990) Sept. 5. *Love's Labour's Lost*, with Ralph Fiennes, Simon Russell Beale, John Wood, Carol Royle, Amanda Root, David Troughton, dir. by Terry Hands, des. Timothy O'Brien. Nov. 7. *Richard II*, with Alex Jennings, Anton Lesser, Yolanda Vazquez, Alan MacNaughtan, David Waller, dir. by Ron Daniels, des. by Antony McDonald. (1991) April 16. *Henry IV, Part One*, with Robert Stephens, Michael Maloney, David Bradley, Owen Teale, Sylvestra le Touzel, Julian Glover, Philip Voss, Bernard Kay, dir. by Adrian Noble, des. by Bob Crowley. April 24. *Twelfth Night*, with Freddie Jones, Sylvestra le Touzel, Tim McInnerny, Ken Wynne, Bill Wallis and Terence Hillyer, dir. by Griff Rhys Jones, des. by Ultz. May 30. *Henry IV, Part Two*, with Robert Stephens, Michael Maloney, Julian Glover, dir. by Adrian Noble, des. by Bob Crowley.

THE SWAN: Stratford (RSC). (1990) Sept. 4. *Two Shakespearean Actors* by Richard Nelson, with John Carlisle, Anton Lesser, Paul Jesson, dir. by Roger Michell, des. by Alexandra Byrne. Nov. 6. *The Seagull* by Anton Chekhov (trans. by Michael Frayn), with Susan Fleetwood, Simon Russell Beale, Katy Behean, Amanda Root, Roger Allam, John Carlisle, Paul Jesson, Alfred Burke, dir. by Terry Hands, des. by Johan Engels. (1991) March 28. *The Virtuoso* by Thomas Shadwell, with Freddie Jones, Sheila Reid, Ken Wynne, Barry Lynch, Sean Murray, Saskia Reeves, Josette Bushell-Mingo, Linda Marlowe, dir. by Phyllida Lloyd, des. by Anthony Ward. April 17. *Two Gentlemen of Verona*, with Barry Lynch, Richard Bonneville, Guy Henry, Sean Murray, Richard Moore, Clare Holman, dir. by David Thacker, des. by Shelagh Keegan. June 25. *'Tis Pity She's a Whore* by John Ford, with Jonathan Cullen, Saskia Reeves, Richard Bonneville, Jonathan Hyde, Sheila Reid, Celia Gregory, Terence Wilton, Tim McInnerny, dir. by David Leveaux, des. by Kenny Miller.

CHICHESTER FESTIVAL: (1990) Sept. 3. *Born Again*, score by Jason Carr, libretto by Julian Barry and Peter Hall, with Mandy Patinkin, José Ferrer, Claire Moore, dir. by Peter Hall, des. by Gerald Scarfe, chor. by Gillian Gregory (Peter Hall Co. prodn). (1991) April 26. *Arsenic and Old Lace* by Joseph Kesselring, with Bernard Bresslaw, Peter Davison, Rosemary Harris, Elizabeth Spriggs, Geoffrey Freshwater, dir. by Annie Castledine. May 22. *Henry VIII* by William Shakespeare and John Fletcher, with Keith Michell, Tony Britton, Fiona Fullerton, Christopher Timothy, Dorothy Tutin, Benjamin Whitrow, dir. by Ian Judge, des. by Russell Craig. July 15. *Tovarich* by Jacques Deval, with Natalia Makarova, Robert Powell, Sarah Badel, Tony Britton, Rowland Davies, dir. by Patrick Garland. Aug. 15. *Preserving Mr Panmure* by Pinero, with Margaret Courtenay, Alison Fiske, Alec McCowen, Abigail McKern.

MINERVA: Chichester. (1990) Sept. 4. *Scenes from a Marriage* by Ingmar Bergman (trans. by Alan Blair), with Alan Howard, Penny Downie, dir. by Rita Russek, des. by Simon Higlett. (1991) June 5. *Point Valaine* by Noël Coward, with Sara Kestelman, Jack Klaff, Edward Petherbridge, dir. by Tim Luscombe, des. by Paul Farnsworth. July 1. *The Sisterhood* by Molière (adapted by Ranjit Bolt), with Judy Parfitt,

Isla Blair, Serena Gordon, Neil Daglish, John Quentin, Benjamin Whitrow, dir. by Tony Britton.

BRISTOL OLD VIC: (1991) Feb. 19. *A Long Day's Journey into Night* by Eugene O'Neill, with Timothy West, Prunella Scales, Sean McGinley, Stephen Dillane, Geraldine Fitzgerald, dir. by Howard Davies, des. by John Gunter (co-prodn with National Theatre).

GLASGOW CITIZENS: (1990) Oct. 7. *The Housekeeper* by Goldoni, with Julia Blalock, Angela Chadfield, Jill Spurrier, Andrew Wilde, Debra Gillett, trans. and dir. by Robert David MacDonald, des. by Michael Levine. (1991) Feb. 1. *The Gospels*, adapted and dir. by Giles Havergal, with Debra Gillett, Alastair Gilbraith, Anne Myatt, Sandy Welch, Tristram Wymark, Patrick Hannaway, des. by Michael Lancaster. April. *Mourning Becomes Electra* by Eugene O'Neill, with Glenda Jackson, Gerard Murphy, Georgina Hayle, dir. and des. by Philip Prowse.

TRAMWAY: (1990) Oct. 31. *La Tempête* by Shakespeare, with Sotigui Kouyaté, Alain Maratrat, David Bennent, dir. by Peter Brook, des. by Chloe Obolensky.

LEICESTER: HAYMARKET: (1991) May. *A Streetcar Named Desire* by Tennessee Williams, with Cheryl Campbell, Vincenzo Ricotta, Rachel Joyce, dir. by Nancy Meckler, des. by Lucy Weller.

LIVERPOOL: PLAYHOUSE: (1990) Aug. 21. *Fences* by August Wilson, with Yaphet Kotto, Adrian Lester, Tyrone Huggins, Doyle Richmond, Eddie Nestor, Sally Sagoe, dir. by Alby James, des. by Ellen Cairns. (1991) Jan. 24. *Loot* by Joe Orton, with Desmond Jordan, Brian Capron, Gabrielle Drake, Tom Radcliffe, dir. by Joanna Hole, des. by David Knapman (Co-Producers Co.).

MANCHESTER: ROYAL EXCHANGE: (1990) Sept. 13. Shakespeare's *The Tempest*, with David Horovitch, Christopher Hancock, Dan Hildebrand, Emil Wolk, Emily Raymond, dir. by Braham Murray, des. by Johanna Bryant. Nov. 26. *Death and the King's Horseman* by Wole Soyinka, with George Harris, Peter Badejo, Claire Benedict, des. by Phyllida Lloyd. (1991) Feb. 7. *Pride and Prejudice* by Jane Austen, adapted and dir. by James Maxwell, with Melanie Thaw, Rufus Sewell, Abigail Thaw, David Allister, Avril Elgar. May 16. *The Doctor's Dilemma* by George Bernard Shaw, with Jeremy Clyde, Clive Owen, Ewan Hooper, Trevor Baxter, Fiona Gillies, dir. by James Maxwell, des. by Di Seymour.

NOTTINGHAM: PLAYHOUSE: (1990) Nov. *Two-Way Mirror* by Arthur Miller, with Julie Covington, Nicholas le Prevost.

SCARBOROUGH: STEPHEN JOSEPH: (1990) Oct. 2. Shakespeare's *Othello*, with Michael Gambon, Ken Stott, Claire Skinner, Simon Dormandy, dir. by Alan Ayckbourn. (1991) May 6. *Wildest Dreams*, written and dir. by Alan Ayckbourn, with Anna Keaveney, Gary Whitaker, Isabel Lloyd, Barry McCarthy, Rebecca Lacey, Peter Laird.

SOUTHAMPTON: NUFFIELD: (1990) Oct. 23. *A Curious Accident* by Goldoni (adapted by Graham Alborough), with Michael Burrell, Billy Hartman, Elizabeth Rider, Robin McCaffrey, dir. by Jeremy Raison.

Despite the continuing recession, the consequent dwindling of commercial sponsorship and the severe financial constraints from which all British companies suffer at the present time, opera has never been more popular. From mega-spectacles such as the *Tosca* staged with a cast of hundreds at Earls Court, and *Der Ring des Nibelungen*, three-quarters of the way to completion at Covent Garden, to small-scale productions by the companies such as Travelling Opera and Opera 80 that indefatigably tour the length and breadth of the country, opera is now attracting larger audiences and reaching more people in more places than ever before. In spite of drenching rain, over 100,000 people turned out to listen to Luciano Pavarotti when the Italian tenor gave his much-publicized open-air concert in Hyde Park in July. At the other end of the spectrum is City of Birmingham Touring Opera's staging of *The Ring Saga*, a version of Wagner's *Ring* abridged to two four-hour evenings, with an orchestra reduced to 18 players, which has aroused tremendous enthusiasm wherever it has been performed. And Welsh National Opera's BP Opera Circuit production of *Hansel and Gretel*, adapted for four singers and five instrumentalists, and Scottish Opera Go Round's *Eugene Onegin*, with a company of 14, each visited from 25 to 30 arts centres, town and village halls, or small theatres in their respective regions.

Musical Chairs

Meanwhile, a complicated game of musical chairs is being played by the managements of the major companies. At the Royal Opera Paul Findlay, the opera director, will leave in 1993 after 25 years at Covent Garden; Lord Sainsbury, chairman of the board, Jeffrey Tate, principal conductor, and Robin Stapleton, chorus master, left at the end of the 1990–91 season. Tate's successor, Edward Downes, is appointed associate music director as well as principal conductor. At English National Opera the triumvirate largely responsible for the artistic excellence of the company in recent years—Peter Jonas, general director, Mark Elder, music director and David Pountney, director of productions—are leaving in 1993; no successors have so far been appointed.

Brian McMaster, general manager of Welsh National Opera since 1976, left the company in August 1991 to become director of the Edinburgh Festival; his successor at WNO will be Matthew Epstein, an American administrator of wide operatic experience. WNO is also losing its music director, Sir Charles Mackerras, who steps down in 1992 and will be succeeded by the young Italian conductor Carlo Rizzi. Another vacancy is at Scottish Opera, where Richard Mantle, managing director, resigned in May 1991.

Opera has not been a major ingredient of the Edinburgh Festival during the last few years, and it is to be hoped that the appointment of Brian McMaster as director will remedy this omission, in spite of the difficulty of providing large-scale opera in a city without a suitable theatre. The difficulty was illustrated yet again in 1991, when the Kirov Opera of Leningrad brought a cycle of works by Mussorgsky (originally put on for the 150th anniversary of the composer's birth in 1989) to Edinburgh and was only able to stage two of the productions, *Khovanshchina* and *The Marriage*. The other three, *Sorochinsky Fair*, *Salammbô* and *Boris Godunov*, had to be given in concert. The Bolshoi Opera from Moscow was also featured at the 1991 Edinburgh Festival, with stagings of Tchaikovsky's *Eugene Onegin* and Rimsky Korsakov's *Christmas Eve*. Scottish Opera unveiled its new production of Mozart's *La clemenza di Tito* at Edinburgh.

Remembering Mozart

As 1991 was the bicentenary of the death of Mozart, the first eight months of the year, not surprisingly, included a great many performances of his operas. At the 1991 Glyndebourne Festival the repertory consisted entirely of Mozart, with a new production of *Così fan tutte*, set on board a cruise liner, and of *La clemenza di Tito*, as well as revivals of *Le nozze di Figaro*, *Idomeneo*, *Don Giovanni* and last year's controversial production by Peter Sellars of *The Magic Flute*, now given in English with the dialogue mostly restored. The Buxton Festival also concentrated on Mozart, offering *The Abduction from the Seraglio* and, in a double bill, *Il sogno di Scipione* and *The Impresario*. Opera Factory staged a brand new *Marriage of Figaro* and revived its highly enjoyable production of *Così fan tutte*, set on a beach in the Caribbean. The Royal Opera could only muster a revival of its twelve-year-old staging of *Die Zauberflöte*, with promises of further Mozart performances in the new season.

The centenary of the birth of Prokofiev, on the other hand, was largely ignored. Apart from a revival of *The Love for Three Oranges* by ENO, the only Prokofiev opera to be heard was a Promenade concert performance of *The Fiery Angel* at the Royal Albert Hall.

ENO included revivals of Mozart's *The Magic Flute*, *Così fan tutte* and *Don Giovanni* in its enterprising 1990–91 season TWENTY PLUS, which otherwise consisted entirely of 20th-century operas. New productions of *Wozzeck*, *Pelléas and Mélisande* and *Peter Grimes* were given, together with two interesting double-bills that paired Delius' *Fennimore and Gerda* with Puccini's *Gianni Schicchi*, and Stravinsky's *Oedipus Rex* with Bartok's *Duke Bluebeard's Castle*. These were accompanied by revivals including Busoni's *Doctor Faustus*, Dvorak's *Rusalka* and Shostakovich's *Lady Macbeth of Mtsensk*. To obtain the financial backing required for the last-named work, individual sponsorship was invited from the members of ENO's audiences; as a result, over 1,200 donors contributed more than £87,000. TWENTY PLUS also encompassed the world première of Stephen Oliver's *Timon of Athens*, an adaptation of the tragedy by Shakespeare. Both the production and the performance were highly praised, and Oliver's score for *Timon* was admired. However, the bleakness of the subject and the absence of any female or other high voices, leading to a certain monotony, militated against a popular success.

New Works

Another world première of an opera by a British composer, Harrison Birtwistle's *Gawain*, was given a spectacular production by the Royal Opera at Covent Garden, and fared better in public and critical estimation. Based on the medieval poem *Sir Gawain and the Green Knight*, the text combined Arthurian legend with the ritual frequently to be found in Birtwistle's stage works; the music, more accessible than that of many of his earlier scores, was vocally rewarding and orchestrally rich. This change in Birtwistle's style was underlined by comparison with *Punch and Judy*, newly staged in June 1991 at the Aldeburgh Festival, where the opera received its première in 1968. An imaginative double bill at Aldeburgh paired Britten's church parable *Curlew River* with the Japanese Noh play that was its inspiration.

At Glasgow, Scottish Opera gave the world première of *The Vanishing Bridegroom*; Judith Weir's second full-length opera combined three separate folk-tales from the Scottish Highlands to form a satisfying dramatic and musical whole. After a very successful opening, *The Vanishing Bridegroom* received a single performance at Covent Garden, during a short London visit by the company that included two complete performances of Berlioz' epic *Les Troyens*, a co-production with Opera North and WNO. Scottish Opera also staged the European première of *Regina*, but Marc Blitzstein's opera, originally performed in 1949, was not considered to be of much interest. Opera Factory (Zurich) gave the British première of *Julia* by the Swiss composer Rudolf Kelterborn, at the Queen Eliabeth Hall. *Julia* is another opera that combines three separate stories with the same theme: in this case, three versions of *Romeo and Juliet*, by Shakespeare, by Gottfried Keller (whose version was adapted by Delius in *A Village Romeo and Juliet*), and a love-story set in present-day Israel.

Farewells

It had been planned that Dame Joan Sutherland should make her farewell to the opera stage at Covent Garden in December 1990 as Rosalinde in *Die Fledermaus*. In the event Sutherland took her farewell at the Sydney Opera House during October, as Queen Marguerite de Valois in Meyerbeer's *Les Huguenots*. This performance was seen on British television and also relayed on a large screen in the auditorium of Covent Garden. Though she did not sing Rosalinde, Dame Joan was one of the guest stars in the party scene of *Die Fledermaus* at the performance on New Year's Eve, together with Marilyn Horne and Luciano Pavarotti. She sang a duet from Rossini's *Semiramide* with Horne and a duet from *La traviata* with Pavarotti; then, almost 40 years after her first appearance at Covent Garden in 1952 as First Lady in *The Magic Flute*, Joan Sutherland said a final goodbye to the theatre in which she had so frequently sung, not with a florid aria from *Norma* or *Lucia di Lammermoor* or any other opera from her Bellini or Donizetti repertory, but with the song 'Home, Sweet Home'.

Two singers with almost equally long connections with the Royal Opera died during the period under review. The tenor Richard Lewis first sang at Covent Garden in 1947 in the title role of *Peter Grimes*. He created Troilus in Walton's *Troilus and Cressida*, Mark in Tippett's *Midsummer Marriage*, Achilles in the same composer's *King Priam* and sang a wide variety of roles from Hermann in *The Queen of Spades* and Don José in *Carmen* to Captain Vere in *Billy Budd* and Aaron in Schoenberg's *Moses and Aaron*. Lewis also had a long association with Glyndebourne, where he sang Nero in *The Coronation of Poppaea*, many Mozart roles, Florestan in *Fidelio*, Tom Rakewell in Stravinsky's *The Rake's Progress* and Bacchus in *Ariadne auf Naxos*.

Michael Langdon, who joined the Covent Garden chorus in 1948, became a bass principal in 1951. He created Mr Ratcliff in *Billy Budd*, the Recorder of Norwich in *Gloriana*, the He-Ancient in *The Midsummer Marriage* and, for Scottish Opera, the title role of Orr's *Hermiston*. His enormous repertory embraced French, Italian and German opera, while his finest and best-known interpretation was Baron Ochs in *Der Rosenkavalier*, which he sang all over Europe and in the USA as well as in the United Kingdom. After his retirement he became director of the National Opera Studio in London.

Though Sir Reginald Goodall died in May 1990, a memorial concert in his honour did not take place until June 1991. The ENO Orchestra, conducted by Mark Elder, paid tribute to the much-loved conductor and vocal coach at the Royal Festival Hall. The programme, designed to reflect the various facets of Goodall's career, included the Four Sea Interludes from *Peter Grimes*, whose first performance he had conducted at Sadler's Wells in 1945, as well as excerpts from Wagner's *Ring*, *The Mastersingers*, *Tristan and Isolde* and *Parsifal*, which he had prepared and conducted so superbly for both ENO and WNO. The singers, originally coached in their Wagner roles by Goodall, were Anne Evans, Alberto Remedios, Norman Bailey, John Tomlinson and Gwynne Howell. In the four decades during which Reginald Goodall worked for the Royal Opera at Covent Garden, he conducted innumerable performances of operas in the French, Italian and German repertoires and trained three generations of Wagner singers, both British and from other countries. His influence on operatic performance in the United Kingdom was incalculable.

PRODUCTIONS

In the summaries of the company activities shown below, the dates in brackets indicate the year that the current production entered the company's repertory.

ROYAL OPERA (1946)
Royal Opera House, Covent Garden, WC2E 9DD

Productions from the repertory were *Turandot* (1984), *Il barbiere di Siviglia* (1985), *Die Fledermaus* (1989), *Samson et Dalila* (1981), *Die Zauberflöte* (1979), *Boris Godunov* (1983), *Tosca* (1964), *Les Contes d'Hoffmann* (1980), *La Cenerentola* (1990) and *La fanciulla del West* (1977).
New productions were:
Oct. 4, 1990. **Siegfried** (Wagner). Conductor, Ber-

nard Haitink; *producer*, Götz Friedrich; *designer*, Peter Sykora.

Siegfried, René Kollo; *Wanderer*, James Morris; *Mime*, Alexander Oliver; *Fafner*, Willard White; *Erda*, Birgitta Svenden; *Brünnhilde*, Gwynneth Jones.

Oct. 13, 1990. Attila (Verdi). *Conductor*, Edward Downes; *producer*, Elijah Moshinsky; *designer*, Michael Yeargan.

Attila, Ruggiero Raimondi; *Odabella*, Josephine Barstow; *Ezio*, Giorgio Zancanaro, *Foresto*, Dennis O'Neill.

Nov. 21, 1990. Fidelio (Beethoven), a co-production with the Théâtre Royal de la Monnaie, Brussels. *Conductor*, Christoph von Dohnányi; *producer* Adolf Dresen; *designer*, Margit Bardy.

Leonore, Gabriela Beňačkova; *Jacquino*, Neil Archer; *Marzelline*, Marie McLaughlin; *Rocco*, Robert Lloyd; *Don Pizarro*, Monte Pedersen; *Florestan*, Josef Protschka; *Don Fernando*, Hans Tschammer.

Jan. 7. Capriccio (R. Strauss), a co-production with San Francisco Opera. *Conductor*, Jeffrey Tate; *producer*, John Cox; *designers*, Mauro Pagano (*set*), Gianni Versace (*costumes*).

The Countess Madeleine, Kiri Te Kanawa; *La Roche*, Franz Ferdinand Nentwig; *Olivier*, William Shimell; *Flamand*, David Rendall; *The Count*, Thomas Allen; *Clairon*, Anne Howells.

Feb. 4. Götterdämmerung (Wagner). *Conductor*, Bernard Haitink; *producer*, Götz Friedrich; *designer*, Peter Sykora.

Brünnhilde, Gwynneth Jones; *Siegfried*, René Kollo; *Hagen*, John Tomlinson; *Gunther*, Donald Maxwell; *Gutrune*, Kathryn Harries; *Waltraute*, Hanna Schwarz; *Alberich*, Roderick Earle.

April 26. Carmen (Bizet), a co-production with the Teatro Liceo, Barcelona. *Conductor*, Zubin Mehta; *producer*, Nuria Espert; *designers*, Gerardo Vera (*sets*), Franca Squarciapino (*costumes*).

Micaela, Leontina Vaduva; *Don José*, Luis Lima; *Carmen*, Maria Ewing; *Frasquita*, Judith Howarth; *Mercedes*, Jean Rigby; *Escamillo*, Gino Quilico.

May 30. The world première of **Gawain** (Birtwistle). *Conductor*, Elgar Howarth; *producer*, Di Trevis; *designer*, Alison Chitty; *choreographer*, Jane Gibson.

Morgan le Fay, Marie Angel; *Lady de Hautdesert*, Elizabeth Laurence; *King Arthur*, Richard Greager; *A Fool*, Omar Ebrahim; *Gawain*, François Le Roux; *Bishop Baldwin*, Kevin Smith; *The Green Knight/Bertilak de Hautdesert*, John Tomlinson.

July 5. Orfeo ed Euridice (Gluck). *Conductor*, Hartmut Haenchen; *producer*, Harry Kupfer; *designers*, Hans Schavernoch (*sets*), Eleonore Kleiber (*costumes*).

Orfeo, Jochen Kowalski; *Euridice*, Gillian Webster; *Amor*, Jeremy Budd.

English National Opera
London Coliseum, St Martin's Lane, WC2N 4ES

Productions from the repertory were *Tosca* (1987), *The Magic Flute* (1988), *Doctor Faust* (1986), *Così fan tutte* (1980), *The Love for Three Oranges* (1989), *Madam Butterfly* (1984), *Rusalka* (1983), *The Turn of the Screw* (1979), *Lear* (1989), *Salome* (1975), *Don Giovanni* (1985), *The Cunning Little Vixen* (1988) and *Lady Macbeth of Mtsensk* (1987).

New productions were:

Sept. 13, 1990. Wozzeck (Berg). *Conductor*, Mark Elder; *producer*, David Pountney; *designer*, Stefanos Lazaridis.

Wozzeck, Donald Maxwell; *Marie*, Kristine Ciesinski; *Captain*, Alan Woodrow; *Doctor*, Richard Angas;

Drum Major, John Treleaven; *Margret*, Ethna Robinson.

Sept. 27, 1990. Greek (Turnage). *Conductor*, Richard Bernas; *producer*, Jonathan Moore; *designer*, David Blight.

Mum/Waitress 2/Sphinx 1, Helen Charnock; *Wife/Doreen/Waitress 1/Sphinx 2*, Fiona Kimm; *Eddy*, Quentin Hayes; *Dad/Café Manager/Chief of Police*, Richard Suart.

Nov. 7, 1990. Fennimore and Gerda (Delius) and **Gianni Schicchi** (Puccini). *Conductor*, Charles Mackerras; *producers*, Julia Hollander (*Fennimore*), Stephen Unwin (*Schicchi*); *designer*, Ultz.

Fennimore, Sally Burgess; *Niels*, Peter Coleman-Wright; *Erik*, Adrian Martin; *Gerda*, Fiona O'Neill.

Schicci, Benjamin Luxon; *Lauretta*, Alison Hagley; *Zita*, Anne Collins; *Rinuccio*, David Maxwell-Anderson.

Nov. 30, 1990. Pelléas and Mélisande (Debussy). *Conductor*, Mark Elder; *producer*, David Pountney; *designer*, Marie-Jeanne Lecca.

Golaud, Willard White; *Mélisande*, Cathryn Pope; *Geneviève*, Anne-Marie Owens; *Arkel*, John Connell; *Pelléas*, Thomas Randle.

Jan. 23. Oedipus Rex (Stravinsky) and **Bluebeard's Castle** (Bartok). *Conductor*, Mark Elder; *producer*, David Alden; *designer*, Nigel Lowery.

Oedipus, Philip Langridge; *Creon*, Malcolm Donnelly; *Tiresias*, Richard Van Allan; *Jocasta*, Jean Rigby.

Bluebeard, Gwynne Howell; *Judith*, Sally Burgess.

April 17. Peter Grimes (Britten). *Conductor*, David Atherton; *producer*, Tim Albery; *designers*, Hildegard Bechtler (*sets*), Nicky Gillibrand (*costumes*).

Peter Grimes, Philip Langridge; *Ellen Orford*, Josephine Barstow; *Captain Balstrode*, Jonathan Summers; *Auntie*, Ann Howard; *Bob Boles*, Graeme Matheson-Bruce; *Swallow*, John Connell; *Mrs Sedley*, Anne Collins; *Ned Keene*, Jason Howard.

May 17. The world première of **Timon of Athens** (Oliver). *Conductor*, Graeme Jenkins; *producer*, Graham Vick; *designer*, Chris Dyer.

Timon, Monte Jaffe; *Lucullus*, Geoffrey Pogson; *Varro*, Paul Wilson; *Sempronius*, David Marsh; *Mutius*, Nicholas Folwell; *Apemantus*, Keith Latham; *Alcibiades*, Gregory Yurisich.

Welsh National Opera (1946)
John Street, Cardiff CF1 4SP

Productions from the repertory were *The Marriage of Figaro* (1987), *From the House of the Dead* (1982), *Salome* (1988), *Falstaff* (1988) and *La traviata* (1988).

New productions were:

Sept. 17, 1990. Carmen (Bizet). *Conductor*, John Burdekin; *producer*, André Engel; *designers*, Nick Rieti (*set*), Elisabeth Neumuller (*costumes*).

Carmen, Jean Stilwell; *Don José*, Noel Espiritu Velasco; *Micaela*, Gillian Webster; *Escamillo*, Richard Paul Fink.

Feb. 16. Count Ory (Rossini). *Conductor*, Carlo Rizzi; *producer*, Aidan Lang; *designer*, Russell Craig.

Count Ory, Bonaventura Bottone; *Countess Adele*, Janice Watson; *Isolier*, Bernadette Cullen; *Raimbaud*, Peter Savidge; *Tutor*, Peter Rose; *Ragonde*, Anne-Marie Owens.

March 4. La fanciulla del West (Puccini). *Conductor*, Julian Smith; *producer*, Petrika Ionesco; *designers*, Petrika Ionesco (*set*), Marie Louise Wallek (*costumes*).

Minnie, Suzanne Murphy; *Jack Rance*, Donald Maxwell; *Dick Johnson*, Dennis O'Neill; *Sonora*, Mark Holland.

May 25. **Rigoletto** (Verdi). *Conductor*, Carlo Rizzi; *producer*, Patrick Mason; *designer*, Joe Vanek.

Rigoletto, Richard Paul Fink; *The Duke of Mantua*, Noel Espiritu Velasco; *Gilda*, Alexandrina Pendachanska; *Sparafucile*, Alastair Miles; *Maddalena*, Marie Walshe.

Performances of the repertory were given at the New Theatre, Cardiff, and on tour at Southampton, Bristol, Swansea, Oxford, Birmingham, Liverpool, Plymouth, Manchester and the Bunkamuru Centre, Tokyo.

OPERA NORTH (1978)
Grand Theatre, New Briggate, Leeds LS1 6NU

Productions from the repertory were *La traviata* (1985), *The Threepenny Opera* (1984), *Così fan tutte* (1982), *Faust* (1986) and *Carmen* (1987).

New productions were:

Sept. 17, 1990. **Ariane and Bluebeard** (Dukas). *Conductor*, Paul Daniel; *producer*, Patrick Mason; *designer*, Joe Vanek.

Ariane, Anne-Marie Owens; *The Nurse*, Anne Collins; *Bluebeard*, Jonathan Best.

Dec. 20, 1990. **Attila** (Verdi). *Conductor*, Paul Daniel; *producer*, Ian Judge; *designers*, John Gunter (*set*), Deirdre Clancy (*costumes*).

Attila, John Tomlinson; *Odabella*, Karen Huffstodt; *Foresto*, Edmund Barham; *Ezio*, Jason Howard.

Feb. 19. **The Jewel Box** (Mozart, arr. Griffiths). *Conductor*, Elgar Howarth; *producer*, Francisco Negrin; *designer*, Tony Baker.

Aloysia, Jennifer Rhys-Davies; *Columbina*, Mary Hegarty; *Mozart*, Pamela Helen Stephen; *Arlecchino*, Barry Banks; *Dottore*, Mark Curtis; *Pantaleone*, Quentin Hayes.

May 3. **King Priam** (Tippett). *Conductor*, Paul Daniel; *producer and designer*, Tom Cairns.

King Priam, Andrew Shore; *Hecuba*, Eiddwen Harrhy; *Andromache*, Linda McLeod; *Helen*, Patricia Bardon; *Paris*, Christopher Ventris; *Achilles*, Neill Archer; *Hector*, Geoffrey Dolton; *Hermes*, Mark Curtis.

July 2. **Don Giovanni** (Mozart). *Conductor*, Paul Daniel; *producer*, Tim Albery; *designer*, Ashley Martin-Davis.

Don Giovanni, Robert Hayward; *Leporello*, John Hall; *Donna Anna*, Helen Field; *Donna Elvira*, Jane Leslie Mackenzie; *Don Ottavio*, Paul Nilon; *Zerlina*, Lynne Davies; *Massetto*, Peter Snipp; *Commendatore*, John Connell.

Performances of the repertory were given at the Grand Theatre, Leeds, and at Manchester, Nottingham, Hull, Birmingham and Sheffield.

SCOTTISH OPERA (1962)
39, Elmbank Crescent, Glasgow G2 4PT

Productions from the repertory were *Tosca* (1980), *La bohème* (1988), *The Cunning Little Vixen* (1988) and *The Barber of Seville* (1985).

New productions were:

Sept. 18 and 19. **Les Troyens** (Berlioz), a co-production with Opera North and Welsh National Opera. *Conductor*, John Mauceri; *producer*, Tim Albery; *designers*, Anthony MacDonald and Tom Cairns.

Cassandra, Katherine Ciesinski; *Chorebus*, Steven Page; *Aeneas*, Seppo Ruohonen; *Dido*, Kathryn Harries; *Anna*, Patricia Bardon; *Ascanius*, Andrea Bolton; *Iopas*, Alasdair Elliott; *Hylas*, Mark Curtis; *Narbal*, Peter Rose.

Oct. 17, 1990. The world première of **The Vanishing Bridegroom** (Weir). *Conductor*, Alan Hacker; *producer*, Ian Spink; *designer*, Richard Hudson.

Bride/Wife/Mother, Virginia Kerr; *Daughter*, Elizabeth McCormack; *Bride's Lover/Husband's Friend/Preacher*, Harry Nicoll; *Bridegroom/Husband/Father*, Peter Snipp; *Doctor/Policeman/Stranger*, Robert Poulton.

Jan. 29. **Fidelio** (Beethoven). *Conductor*, Roderick Brydon; *producer*, Stephen Wadsworth; *designers*, Derek McLane (*set*), Dunya Ramicova (*costumes*).

Leonore, Gudrun Volkert; *Marzelline*, Nerys Jones; *Rocco*, Adelbert Waller; *Jacquino*, Mark Tucker; *Don Pizarro*, Greer Grimsley; *Florestan*, Richard Brunner.

April 16. **Falstaff** (Verdi). *Conductor*, John Mauceri: *producer*, Ian Judge; *designer*, Mark Thompson.

Falstaff, Gordon Sandison; *Ford*, Steven Page; *Mistress Ford*, Maria Prosperi; *Mistress Page*, Fiona Kimm; *Nannetta*, Susannah Waters; *Fenton*, John Mark Ainsley; *Mistress Quickly*, Sarah Walker.

May 16. The European première of **Regina** (Blitzstein). *Conductor*, John Mauceri; *producer*, Robert Carsen; *designer*, Michael Levine.

Regina, Katherine Terrell; *Alexandra*, Susan Roberts; *Birdie*, Nan Christie; *Horace*, William McCue; *William*, David Morrison; *Addie*, Theresa Merritt; *Leo*, Philip Gould.

Performances of the repertory were given at the Theatre Royal, Glasgow, and on tour at Newcastle, Edinburgh, Aberdeen, Inverness, Oxford, Bradford and Covent Garden, London.

GLYNDEBOURNE FESTIVAL OPERA (1934)
Glyndebourne, Lewes, East Sussex BN8 5UU

The 1991 Festival ran from May 21 to August 23. Four of the productions were revivals: *Le nozze di Figaro* (1989), *Idomeneo* (1983), *The Magic Flute* (1990) and *Don Giovanni* (1977).

The new productions were:

May 24. **Così fan tutte** (Mozarte). *Conductor*, Simon Rattle; *producer*, Trevor Nunn; *designer*, Maria Bjørnson.

Fiordiligi, Amanda Roocroft; *Dorabella*, Suzanne Johnston; *Despina*, Gianna Rolandi; *Ferrando*, Kurt Streit; *Guglielmo*, Jake Gardner; *Don Alfonso*, Claudio Desderi.

June 28. **La clemenza di Tito** (Mozart). *Conductor*, Andrew Davis; *producer*, Nicholas Hytner; *designer*, David Fielding.

Sesto, Diana Montague; *Vitellia*, Ashley Putnam; *Annio*, Martine Mahé; *Tito*, Philip Langridge; *Servilia*, Elzbieta Szmytka; *Publio*, Peter Rose.

The Glyndebourne Touring Opera performed *La bohème*, *Così fan tutte* and *Jenufa* at Glyndebourne, Sheffield, Plymouth, Manchester, Dublin, Oxford and Southampton, between October and December 1991.

OPERA 80 (1980)

Performances of *Lucia di Lammermoor* and *The Merry Widow* were toured to Dartford, Bath, Wolverhampton and Southsea in November 1990. Performances of *The Magic Flute* and *Don Pasquale* were toured to Swindon, Exeter, Yeovil, Weston-super-Mare, Cheltenham, Poole, Crawley, Reading, Brighton, Lincoln, Darlington, Carlisle, Ulverston, Blackpool, Scunthorpe, Buxton, Cambridge, Canterbury, Ipswich, Basildon and Sadler's Wells Theatre, London, between February and June 1991.

OPERA NORTHERN IRELAND
Grand Opera House, Belfast

Sept. 21, 1990. **Tosca** (Puccini). *Conductor*, Christopher Bell; *producer*, Bliss Herbert; *designer*, Allen Charles Klein.

Tosca, Sylvie Valayre; *Cavaradossi*, Daniel Doster; *Scarpia*, Frédéric Vassar.

Sept. 22, 1990. **The Magic Flute** (Mozart). *Conductor*, Kenneth Montgomery; *producer*, Clare Venables; *designer*, Tim Reed.

Tamino, John Mark Ainsley; *Pamina*, Rosemary Joshua; *Queen of Night*, Nicola Sharkey; *Sarastro*, Stephen Richardson; *Papageno*, Geoffrey Dolton; *Papagena*, Sally-Ann Shepherdson.

March 2, 1991. **The Marriage of Figaro** (Mozart). *Conductor*, Kenneth Montgomery; *producer*, Tim Coleman; *designer*, Tim Reed.

Figaro, Robert Heiman; *Susanna*, Kathryn Magestro; *Count Almaviva*, Johannes Mannov; *Countess Almaviva*, Dagmar Schellenberg; *Cherubino*, Naria Jagusz.

OPERA FACTORY
South Bank Centre, London SE1 8XX

New productions were:

Feb. 20. **The Marriage of Figaro** (Mozart). *Conductor*, Peter Robinson; *producer*, David Freeman; *designer*, David Roger.

Figaro, Lyndon Terracini; *Susanna*, Janis Kelly; *Count Almaviva*, Geoffrey Dolton; *Countess Almaviva*, Marie Angel; *Cherubino*, Susannah Walters; *Dr Bartolo*, Tom McDonell.

Aug. 20. The British première of **Julia** (Kelterborn). *Conductor*, Brenton Langbein; *producer*, David Freeman; *designer*, David Roger.

Julia, Cynthia Grose Downing; *Romeo*, Mark Oldfield; *Sali*, David Aldred; *Ahmed*, Fabrice Raviola; *Julia's father*, Jean-Pierre Gerber; *Nurse/Sali's mother*, Rosina Maria Zoppi.

These operas, with the revival of *Così fan tutte*, were performed at the Queen Elizabeth Hall, London, and both new productions were toured to Oxford, Bath and Newcastle in August and September 1991.

MASTERS OF THE QUEEN'S/KING'S MUSIC

	Apptd.
Nicholas Lanier	1626
Louis Grabu	1666
Nicholas Staggins	1674
John Eccles	1700
Maurice Greene	1735
William Boyce	1755
John Stanley	1779
Sir William Parsons	1786
William Shield	1817
Christian Kramer	1829

	Apptd.
François (Franz) Cramer	1834
George Frederick Anderson	1848
Sir William George Cusins	1870
Sir Walter Parratt	1893
Sir Edward Elgar	1924
Sir Henry Walford Davies	1934
Sir Arnold Bax	1942
Sir Arthur Bliss	1953
Malcolm Williamson	1975

DANCE 1990–91

The dance world suffered two major losses in the first months of 1991. On February 21 Margot Fonteyn, Prima Ballerina Assoluta of the Royal Ballet, died in Panama City after a long illness, and on April 1 Martha Graham, the founding figure of contemporary dance, died in New York City at the age of 96. The influence of both women on the development of dance in Britain is incalculable.

Dame Margot Fonteyn de Arias was born Margaret Hookham in 1919. Her first serious dance study began in 1932 in Shanghai, where her father was then working, and after her return to England in 1934, she studied under Astafieva and at the Vic-Wells Ballet School. Almost immediately she began to perform with the Vic-Wells Ballet and attracted the attention of Frederick Ashton, who became the company's chief choreographer in 1935. Thus was born a creative partnership which came to define the style and quality of British ballet. Fonteyn's perfect line, innate musicality and dramatic sincerity inspired many of Ashton's greatest creations.

By the time war broke out, Fonteyn was established as the company's ballerina and had created roles in a number of Ashton ballets, including *Le Baiser de la Fée* (1935), *Apparitions* (1936), *Nocturne* (1936), *Les Patineurs* (1937) and *A Wedding Bouquet* (1937). Throughout the war she toured Britain with the company, gaining a large following and helping to popularize ballet in Britain. When the company was invited to re-open the Royal Opera House, Covent Garden in 1946, she took the leading role in *The Sleeping Beauty*. She became an international star when the company visited New York for the first time in 1949. Ashton continued to create ballets for her, *Symphonic Variations* (1946), *Scènes de Ballet* (1948), *Cinderella* (with Moira Shearer, 1948), *Daphnis and Chloe* (1951) and *Ondine* (1958) being amongst the most important.

The defection of the Soviet dancer Rudolf Nureyev in 1961 provided Fonteyn with a new partner in a partnership which was universally acclaimed and led her to postpone retirement. Ashton created *Marguerite and Armand* for them in 1963, and they danced in Nureyev's own production of *Swan Lake* in Vienna in 1964.

Other leading roles Fonteyn created included Roland Petit's *Les Demoiselles de la Nuit* (1948), *Paradise Lost* (1962) and *Pelléas et Mélisande* (1969), and Martha Graham's *Lucifer* (1975). *Lucifer* brought Fonteyn, the supreme exponent of classical dance, into contact with Martha Graham, the American dancer and choreographer who invented and codified a new dance technique which came to be used all over the world. Under Graham's influence contemporary dance flourished and became an established art form which both challenged and complemented classical dance.

Graham was born in Pennsylvania in 1894 and studied dance in Los Angeles before moving to New York in 1923; she gave her first solo performance in 1926. She began to teach and founded in 1927 the Martha Graham School of Contemporary Dance, from which her own company was established in 1929. The company toured throughout the USA,

with Graham as its director, teacher and leading dancer.

Graham's works were often dramatic and always theatrical. Although breaking new ground in many respects, Graham can be seen as a great exponent of the principle established by Mikhail Fokine in the early years of the 20th century; that dance, music and design are of equal importance in creating a credible and moving theatrical experience. Where she differed was in the quality of movement itself. The works she created were based on the back as the area of the body where movement originates, and on her precept that 'all movement into space is the result of the subtle off-balancing of the dancer's weight'. The variety and use of spirals, falls and travelling steps are unique to the Graham technique.

The Martha Graham Dance Company came to Europe in the 1950s. Their London debut was in 1954; audiences were sparse but enthusiastic and the seeds were sown for the growth of British contemporary dance. Graham returned to London in 1963 for what proved a triumphant season, at the instigation of Robin Howard. He founded the London School of Contemporary Dance in 1966 and persuaded one of Graham's leading dancers, Robert Cohan, to run it. From this came the first performances by London Contemporary Dance Theatre in 1967. Dancers in Ballet Rambert also began to take classes in Graham technique and dancers trained in the Graham technique eventually started to experiment with choreography and choreographic styles themselves. Graham's 'offspring' include Merce Cunningham and Paul Taylor in the USA, and Richard Alston and Siobhan Davies in Britain.

Martha Graham's career as a dancer lasted until 1969, and she continued to choreograph and produce works into the 1980s. She created a total of over 160 works, many with mythological or mystical themes, often seen from a self-consciously American perspective. Her most famous works include *Lamentation* (1930), *Primitive Mysteries* (1931), *Frontier* (1935), *Appalachian Spring* (1944), *Night Journey* (1947) and *Clytemnestra* (1958).

Soviet guests

Fonteyn's erstwhile partner, Rudolf Nureyev, this year celebrated the 30th anniversary of his famous 'leap to freedom' on June 17, 1961. Thanks to *glasnost* Soviet dancers no longer have to defect if they wish to dance with Western companies. In Britain, Irek Mukhamedov, the former star of the Bolshoi Ballet, has now completed his first season with the Royal Ballet, and Nina Ananiashvili and Alexei Fadeyechev, also from the Bolshoi, and Altynai Assylmuratova from the Kirov guested with the company in the past year. The Bolshoi's Victor Barikin and the Kirov's Natalya Sveshnikova joined London City Ballet, and Irina Chistiakova from the Kirov performed with the same company as a guest artist. Galina Mezentseva, a senior Kirov ballerina, joined Scottish Ballet; and Yelena Pankova, also from the Kirov, danced with English National Ballet and has now joined London City Ballet as a resident guest artist. Moscow Classical Ballet, Moscow Festival Ballet, the Russian State Ballet and other groups of Soviet dancers also visited the UK. The long-term effect of this development on dance both in the Soviet Union and the West remains to be seen.

The effect of guest artists in general on the Royal Ballet became a source of some controversy in the past year. As the company shares the Royal Opera House with the Royal Opera, there is always a shortage of performances, especially for principal dancers; when guest artists are introduced, the pressure on casting becomes enormous. Fears have been expressed that the company will become a mere backdrop for guest stars. On the other hand, some feel that guest artists have an exciting and inspiring effect. This controversy is likely to continue, as more guest performances are planned for the 1991–92 season.

Meanwhile, one of the Royal Ballet's resident stars, Darcey Bussell, received both the Evening Standard Ballet Award and the Variety Club Most Promising Newcomer Award for 1990. She also created a role in a new one-act ballet by Kenneth MacMillan, *Winter Dreams*, which is loosely based on Chekhov's play *The Three Sisters*. The season's major première was David Bintley's three-act *Cyrano*, which received its première in May to mark the Royal Ballet's 60th anniversary. The company also performed two works by Bronislava Nijinska, *Les Biches* and *Les Noces*, to mark the centenary of her birth.

Money matters

Financially, the Royal Opera House broke even on current operations in 1990–91, but this was achieved partly by redundancies and partly by increasing ticket prices to what many now feel to be an unacceptable level. The Royal Opera House still has an accumulated deficit of £1·7 million to be eliminated by 1994, and its chairman, Lord Sainsbury, resigned because he felt that he would not be able to devote sufficient time to the work involved. He was replaced by Angus Stirling.

Other companies with financial problems included London City Ballet. In spite of its successful record of fund-raising, the company announced in March that it would have to close at the end of the season unless funding were forthcoming from the Arts Council for the 1991–92 season. In the event, the company received an assurance from the Arts Council that it would 'consider positively' the needs of London City Ballet and the company decided to continue operating. Second Stride, a highly respected and inventive contemporary group, was also under threat of closure in February 1991 after the Arts Council withdrew funding. However, the Council reversed its decision in April and awarded the company a grant of £65,000, enabling it to stay open. Extemporary Dance Theatre received no such reprieve and closed in the spring after the Arts Council withdrew its funding for 1991–92.

Adventures in Motion Pictures secured its future by becoming the 'national dance company of the South West' in a £70,000 three-year deal with South West Arts. The Arts Council announced in April

that it had set aside £300,000 for five 'national dance agencies' to provide a focal point for dancers, both amateur and professional. They are located in Newcastle, Leicester, Swindon, London (The Place) and Leeds.

New starts

Most of Britain's larger companies have been operating under new conditions in the past year. Birmingham Royal Ballet (formerly Sadler's Wells) had a successful first year as resident company at the Birmingham Hippodrome and its director, Peter Wright, was elected a Fellow of the Birmingham Conservatoire for his services to ballet. He staged a new and acclaimed production of *The Nutcracker* at the Hippodrome in December 1990. Throughout the season Miyako Yoshida's performances consolidated her reputation as a ballerina of extraordinary speed, grace and musicality. The season ended on a sad note, however, with the death of the company's former director, John Field. He joined the Sadler's Wells Ballet in 1939 as a dancer and became an administrator in 1955. After leaving the Royal Ballet in 1971, Field became artistic director of the Royal Academy of Dancing and then of London Festival Ballet.

Scottish Ballet and English National Ballet were both under new directors in 1990–91. Galina Samsova was confirmed as artistic director of Scottish Ballet from January 1991, and introduced some challenging new works into the company's repertoire as well as reviving Peter Darrell's 1977 production of *Swan Lake*. English National Ballet under Ivan Nagy fared less well. The works introduced into the repertoire, including Cranko's *The Taming of the Shrew*, attracted mostly negative criticism. The performances of the company's guest artist Yelena Pankova were warmly received but also served to highlight the uneven quality of the company's dancing as a whole.

London Contemporary Dance Theatre was effectively without a director for much of the season, as Dan Wagoner returned to the USA for personal reasons after little over a year in charge. The company announced in March that Nancy Dunn would be artistic director from August 1991, with the controversial choreographer Mark Morris as artistic associate from January 1992. Jonathan Lunn, who resigned as the company's associate artistic director in January after being passed over for the directorship, returned to mount a successful season for the company at The Place in April; it served as a tribute to both Robin Howard and Martha Graham.

Rambert Dance Company had a quietly successful season, but caused some controversy by staging a London season at the Riverside Studios instead of at Sadler's Wells Theatre, its usual London venue. Although this move was apparently taken for the sake of a larger performing area, it also restricted the designs that could be used and meant that the new work by Lucinda Childs, *Four Elements*, could not be given. Moreover, the auditorium of the Riverside Studios is one-fifth that of Sadler's Wells; grave doubts were expressed about this apparent scaling-down of the company's London activities. Rambert are due to perform at the Royalty Theatre in London's West End in autumn 1991, which may prove to be a successful compromise venue. Meanwhile, Sadler's Wells Theatre continues to discuss redevelopment plans with Islington Council and English Heritage.

Northern Ballet Theatre, formerly based in Manchester, took up its new residence in Halifax with financial support worth £330,000 from the five West Yorkshire metropolitan councils. In February its artistic director, Christopher Gable, mounted a highly successful new production of *Romeo and Juliet*, with choreography by the Italian choreographer Massimo Moricone and designs by Lez Brotherston.

Two of the most welcome visitors to Britain, the Stuttgart Ballet and the Alvin Ailey Dance Company, performed in Glasgow and Bradford respectively. London received its first visit from Dutch National Ballet for many years, but although eagerly anticipated the season was widely regarded as a disappointment, largely due to the overlong and uninspiring production of *Romeo and Juliet* which was the only work performed by the company.

PRODUCTIONS

ROYAL BALLET (1931)
Royal Opera House, Covent Garden, WC2E 9DD

World premières:
Bloodlines (Nov. 29, 1990). A one-act ballet. *Choreography*, Ashley Page; *music*, Bruce Gilbert; *design*, Deanna Petherbridge. The central role was taken by Bruce Sansom.

Winter Dreams (Feb. 7). A one-act ballet. *Choreography*, Kenneth MacMillan; *music*, Tchaikovsky; *design*, Peter Farmer. The leading roles were taken by Darcey Bussell, Irek Mukhamedov, Viviana Durante, Nicola Tranah and Anthony Dowell.

Cyrano (May 2). A three-act ballet. *Choreography*, David Bintley; *music*, Wilfred Josephs; *design*, Hayden Griffin.
Cast: *Cyrano*, Stephen Jefferies; *Roxane*, Lesley Collier; *Christian*, Bruce Sansom.

Company première:
Stravinsky Violin Concerto (Nov. 29, 1990). *Choreography*, George Balanchine (1972); *music*, Stravinsky. The first cast included Darcey Bussell, Wayne Eagling, Viviana Durante and Stuart Cassidy. The solo violinist was Hagai Shaham.

Full length ballets from the repertoire were: *The Prince of the Pagodas* (MacMillan, 1989); *La Bayadère* (Makarova after Petipa, 1980); *The Nutcracker* (Ivanov/Wright, 1984); *Manon* (MacMillan, 1974); *Swan Lake* (Petipa/Ivanov, prod. Dowell, 1987).

One-act ballets from the repertoire were:
The Planets (Bintley); *Enclosure* (Tuckett); *Elite Syncopations* (MacMillan); *Raymonda Act III* (Petipa/Nureyev); *Danses Concertantes* (MacMillan); *A Month in the Country* (Ashton); *Requiem* (MacMillan); *Agon* (Balanchine); *Les Biches* (Nijinska); *Scènes de Ballet* (Ashton); *Les Noces* (Nijinska); *'Still Life' at the Penguin Café* (Bintley).

Tours: the company visited the USA for the first time since 1983, performing at the John F. Kennedy Center, Washington DC, from March 12 to 24, *The Prince of the Pagodas*, *'Still Life' at the Penguin Café*, *Scènes de Ballet* and *A Month in the Country*. It returned to dance at the Metropolitan Opera House, New York, from July 8 to 20, followed by a three-week tour to Miami Beach, Austin, Texas, and Costa Mesa, with *Swan Lake*, *Manon*, *Scènes de Ballet*, *Winter Dreams* and *'Still Life' at the Penguin Café*.

The company also took *Cyrano*, *Danses Concertantes*, *A Month in the Country* and *Raymonda Act III* to the Birmingham Hippodrome from June 17 to 22.

BIRMINGHAM ROYAL BALLET (1946)
(formerly Sadler's Wells Royal Ballet)
Birmingham Hippodrome, Thorp Street,
Birmingham B5 4AU

World premières:
Brahms Handel Variations (Oct. 30, 1990). A one-act ballet premièred as part of a Royal Gala to mark the company's first performance as resident company at the Birmingham Hippodrome. *Choreography*, David Bintley; *music*, Brahms; *design*, Maria Djurkovic.

The Nutcracker (Dec. 29, 1990). *Choreography*, Ivanov/Peter Wright; *production*, Peter Wright; *music*, Tchaikovsky; *design*, John MacFarlane. The cast included Miyako Yoshida, Petter Jacobsson, Sandra Madgwick, Galina Samsova and Joseph Cipolla.

Sacred Symphony (May 10). A one-act ballet. *Choreography*, Oliver Hindle; *music*, Andrzej Panufnik; *design*, Jan Blake.

License My Roving Hands (May 22). A one-act ballet. *Choreography*, William Tuckett; *music*, Jimi Hendrix; *design*, Candida Cook.

Company premières:
Jazz Calendar (Oct. 30, 1990). *Choreography*, Frederick Ashton (1968); *music*, Richard Rodney Bennett; *design*, Derek Jarman.

La Fin du Jour (Nov. 9, 1990). *Choreography*, Kenneth MacMillan (1979); *music*, Ravel; *design*, Ian Spurling. The first cast included Marion Tait, Miyako Yoshida, Kevin O'Hare and Mark Silver.

Symphony in Three Movements (Nov. 9, 1990). *Choreography*, George Balanchine (1972); *music*, Stravinsky. The first cast was led by Ravenna Tucker, Mark Silver, Mireille Bourgeois, Joseph Cipolla, Karen Donovan and David Yow.

Airs (May 10). *Choreography*, Paul Taylor (1978); *music*, Handel; *design*, Gene Moore.

Pavane pas de deux (May 15). *Choreography*, Kenneth MacMillan (1973); *music*, Fauré; *design*, Deborah Williams. The first cast was Marion Tait and Mark Silver.

Full length ballets from the repertoire were: *The Sleeping Beauty* (Petipa/Wright, 1984); *Swan Lake* (Petipa/ Ivanov, additional choreography by Wright, 1980); *Hobson's Choice* (Bintley, 1989); *La Fille mal gardée* (Ashton, 1960).

One-act ballets from the repertoire were: *Theme and Variations* (Balanchine); *Elite Syncopations* (MacMillan); *Valses Nobles et Sentimentales* (Ashton); *Les Rendezvous* (Ashton); *Inscape* (Lustig); *Paquita* (Petipa); and *Façade* (Ashton).

In addition to three seasons at the Birmingham Hippodrome, the company toured to Edinburgh, Glasgow, Plymouth, Manchester, Sunderland, Cardiff, Southampton and Bradford. It also returned to Sadler's Wells Theatre for a season in May, and performed at the Royal Opera House, Covent Garden, in March and August.

ENGLISH NATIONAL BALLET
Markova House, 39 Jay Mews, SW7 2ES

Company premières:
Our Waltzes (Feb. 4). *Choreography*, Vincente Nebrada (1976); *music*, Teresa Carreno; *design*, Maria Puig. The first cast included Renata Calderini and José Manuel Carreno.

The Taming of the Shrew (April 16). *Choreography*, John Cranko (1969); *music*, Scarlatti/Kurt-Heinz Stolze; *design*, Elisabeth Dalton. The first cast was led by Renata Calderini and Maurizio Bellezza.

Anne Frank (June 28). *Choreography*, Mauricio Wainrot (1985); *music*, Bartok and 'Lili Marleen'; *design*, Carlos Gallardo. The first cast included Josephine Jewkes, Renata Calderini, Dominic Hickie and Rachael Hunt.

Full length ballets from the repertoire were: *Onegin* (Cranko, 1965); *Coppélia* (Hynd, 1985); *The Nutcracker* (Schaufuss, 1986); *Giselle* (Skeaping, 1971; revived to mark the 150th anniversary of the ballet).

One-act ballets from the repertoire were: *Schéhérazade* (Fokine); *Etudes* (Lander); *Four Last Songs* (Stevenson); *Les Sylphides* (Fokine, prod. Markova); *Three Preludes* (Stevenson); *Swansong* (Bruce); *The Sanguine Fan* (Hynd); *Graduation Ball* (Lichine).

The company also performed *Le Corsaire pas de deux* (after Petipa); *Don Quixote pas de deux* (Petipa); and *Diana and Actaeon pas de deux* (Vaganova).

In addition to two seasons at the Royal Festival Hall, London and one at the London Coliseum, the company visited Plymouth, Bristol, Bradford, Southampton, Newcastle, Manchester, Nottingham, Birmingham and Oxford. A small-scale tour in the spring visited Malvern, Worthing, Barrow, Preston, Warwick, Basildon, Cambridge, Lowestoft, Exeter and Poole.

A gala in celebration of Dame Alicia Markova's 80th birthday was staged on Nov. 27, 1990 at the Palace Theatre, Manchester, in the presence of HRH The Princess of Wales. The programme was *Les Sylphides*, divertissements and *Etudes*.

The company toured to Dortmund, Germany, for one week in April. The repertoire was *Les Sylphides*, *Swansong*, *Etudes*, *Our Waltzes* and *Four Last Songs*. It also took *Giselle* to the Nervi Festival in Italy from July 10 to 13.

RAMBERT DANCE COMPANY (1926)
94 Chiswick High Road, W4 1SH

World premières:
Four Elements (Nov. 16, 1990). *Choreography*, Lucinda Childs; *score*, Gavin Bryars; *design*, Jennifer Bartlett.

Roughcut (Dec. 7, 1990). *Choreography*, Richard Alston; *score*, Steve Reich; *design*, Tim Hatley.

Slippage (April 23). *Choreography*, William Tuckett (the Frederick Ashton Memorial Commission); *score*, Dan Jones; *design*, Candida Cook.

Hiding-Game (La Chambre des Trois Paravents) (July 19, at the Aix-en-Provence Festival). *Choreography*, Herve Robbe; *score*, Kaspar T. Toeplitz; *set design*, Robin Brown; *costumes*, Allison Amin.

Company première:
Plain Song (April 12). *Choreography*, Siobhan Davies (1981); *music*, Satie; *design*, David Buckland.

Works from the repertoire were: *Doubles* (Cunningham, 1984); *Soda Lake* (Alston, 1981); *Longevity* (Lambert, 1990); *Currulao* (Page, 1990); *Dealing with Shadows* (Alston, 1990); *Signature* (Davies, 1990); *Embrace Tiger and Return to Mountain* (Tetley, 1968); *Embarque* (Davies, 1988); *Opal Loop* (Brown, 1980).

The company performed in Canterbury, Manchester, Leicester, Oxford, Newcastle (as part of the Newcastle International Dance Festival), Glasgow, Bath, Mold, Nottingham, Southampton, London (Riverside Studios), Bradford and Bristol. It also visited France in January, performing *Signature*, *Embrace Tiger and Return to Mountain*, and *Roughcut* in Bayonne and Toulouse, and *Four Elements*,

Embrace Tiger and Return to Mountain and *Roughcut* at the Paris Opéra, Palais Garnier.

The company took *Four Elements*, *Signature*, *Roughcut* and *Doubles* to the Spoleto Festival, South Carolina, USA, in May. It also performed in Italy in June at the Torinodanza Festival, Turin; the works given were *Doubles*, *Plain Song*, *Roughcut* and *Dealing with Shadows*. It performed *Les Chambres des Trois Paravents*, *Opal Loop*, *Roughcut* and *Dealing with Shadows* at the Aix-en-Provence Festival, France, on July 19–20, and as part of the Mozart Bicentennial Celebrations the company gave a performance of *Dealing with Shadows* (set to Mozart's piano sonata K331) outside Salzburg Cathedral on August 1.

LONDON CONTEMPORARY DANCE THEATRE (1967)
The Place, 17 Duke's Road, WC1H 9AB

World premières:
Beneath the Skin (Oct. 16, 1990). *Choreography*, Jonathan Lunn; *music*, Benjamin Britten; *set*, Peter Mumford; *costumes*, Belinda Ackermann.

White Heat (Oct. 30, 1990). *Choreography*, Dan Wagoner; *music*, Bartok; *design*, William Ivey Long.

Tango (Feb. 7). *Choreography*, Yael Flexer; *score*, Karri Postel; *costumes*, Nicki Gibbs. *Dancers*, Leesa Phillips and Tom Ward.

The Blue Door (March 14). *Choreography*, Jonathan Lunn; *score*, Ian Dearden; *design*, Fotini Dimou.

Rikud (April 5). *Choreography*, Liat Dror and Nir Ben Gal; *music*, Shostakovich; *design*, Liat Dror and Nir Ben Gal.

In Dream I Dream A Dream (April 9). *Choreography*, Kim Brandstrup; *score*, John Lunn; *costumes*, Fotini Dimou. The cast was led by Paul Liburd, Tom Ward, Leesa Phillips and Andrew Robinson.

The Fall (April 9). A dance film, with all the elements created by Darshan Singh Bhuller.

Company première:
Lamentation (April 5). *Choreography*, Martha Graham (1930); *music*, Zoltan Kodaly; *costume*, Martha Graham. *Dancer*, Joyce Herring (a guest from the Martha Graham Dance Company).

Other works from the repertoire were: *Something To Do* (Alston, 1969); *Forest* (Cohan, 1977); *Hang Up* (Lunn, 1987); *Cloven Kingdom* (Taylor, 1976); *Orfeo* (Brandstrup, 1989); *The Dybbuk* (Brandstrup, 1990); *Turtles All The Way Down* (Wagoner, 1989); *Goes Without Saying* (Lunn, 1989); *Harmonica Breakdown* (Dudley, 1938); *Flee As A Bird* (Wagoner, 1986); *Changing Your Mind* (Wagoner, 1974); *Interlock* (Bhuller, 1988).

The company performed in Plymouth, Coventry, Cardiff, Leeds, Bristol, Hexham, Oxford, Northampton, Canterbury, Glasgow and Newcastle upon Tyne. It also gave a season at Sadler's Wells Theatre, London, and in April it performed at The Place, London, in an eight-day season intended as a tribute to the late Robin Howard. The season, *10 to 1*, presented works by ten choreographers.

In June the company visited Prague, Bratislava and Brno in Czechoslovakia at an international festival of contemporary dance; it then performed in Cologne at a festival of modern dance. The works performed were *Cloven Kingdom*, *Orfeo*, *White Heat*, *Changing Your Mind* and *Interlock*.

THE SCOTTISH BALLET (1956)
261 West Princes Street, Glasgow G4 9EE

Company premières:
Jardin aux Lilas (Sept. 7, 1990). *Choreography*,

Anthony Tudor (1936); *music*, Ernest Chausson; *design*, after Hugh Stevenson. The cast was led by Elspeth Shaw, Kevin Horne and Fabrice Maufrais.

Forgotten Land (Sept. 7, 1990). *Choreography*, Jiri Kylian (1981); *music*, Benjamin Britten; *design*, John MacFarlane. Rebecca Fletcher, Robert Hampton, Noriko Ohara, Vincent Hantam, Cecilia Boorman and Brady Wheedon danced at the première.

Raymonda Act III (Sept. 7, 1990). *Choreography*, Petipa (1898); *music*, Glazunov; *design*, Alexandre Vasiliev. The cast was led by Noriko Ohara and Robert Hampton.

Montones I and II (first performed at a gala in Aberdeen on Sept. 25, 1990 and taken into the repertoire of SB2 in June 1991). *Choreography*, Frederick Ashton (1965 and 1966); *music*, Satie; *design*, Frederick Ashton. The dancers at the gala were Claire Mahon, Fabrice Maufrais, Muriel Valtat, Preston Clare, Paula Marshall and Michael Rolnick.

Laurencia Pas de Six (May 21). *Choreography*, Galina Samsova after Vakhtang Chaboukiani; *music*, Alexander Krein/Ludwig Minkus; *design*, Norman McDowell. Muriel Valtat, Rose Marie O'Donnell,

Roddie Patrizio, Cecilia Boorman, Preston Clare and Fabrice Maufrais danced at the première, which was given by SB2.

Five Brahms Waltzes in the manner of Isadora Duncan (June 8). *Choreography*, Frederick Ashton (1976); *music*, Brahms. The dancer at the première (SB2) was Ruth Robinson.

Full length ballets from the repertoire were: *Swan Lake* (Darrell after Petipa and Ivanov, 1977); *Romeo and Juliet* (Cranko, 1962); *The Nutcracker* (Darrell after Ivanov, 1973).

One-act ballets from the repertoire were: *Chéri* (Darrell); *Petrushka* (Vinogradov); *Three Dances to Japanese Music* (Carter); *Les Sylphides* (Fokine); *Napoli Act III* (Bournonville); *Othello* (Darrell).

The company gave performances in Glasgow, Edinburgh, Aberdeen, Dublin, Belfast, Hull, Liverpool, Sheffield, Dundee, Stirling, Kirkcaldy, Aboyne and Ayr. The small-scale touring company, SB2, visited smaller venues throughout Scotland in the spring and summer. The company also performed in Japan in November 1990 as part of the British Council's UK90 Festival. The repertoire was *Romeo and Juliet*, *Chéri* and *Petrushka*.

FILM AND CINEMA, 1990–91

The decline of the British film industry continued in 1990, with less than thirty films being made. Investment dropped from the mid-1980s peak of £270 million to £137 million. However, although it was difficult to identify any mainstream British film, cinema attendances showed an upward trend. In 1990 audiences increased to 98 million, from 84 million in 1988, and revenues rose by 12 per cent.

In spite of the continued popularity of video rentals and the increasing audience of satellite film channels, there is still a strong demand to see films in cinemas on first release. A significant trend has been the spread of multiplex cinema screens, over 400 having opened in the UK since 1985. Unfortunately, Hollywood has been the main beneficiary of the UK cinema boom, with *Ghost* and *Pretty Woman* the most popular films in 1990; the top-earning British film was *Shirley Valentine*, which was 11th, above *Memphis Belle* and *The Krays*.

Following the meeting in June 1990 between the then Prime Minister, Margaret Thatcher, and a deputation of leading figures in the British film industry, there had been hope of incentives for investment in the industry, such as tax relief, the application of the business expansion scheme to films, and the ending of double taxation for visiting artists. However, no measures were announced in the 1991 budget to help the industry, which felt that undertakings made by Mrs Thatcher had been unfulfilled.

National Film Commission

One measure that was taken as a result of the meeting included the establishment of the National Film Commission, headed by Sydney Samuelson. The commission was launched by Lord Hesketh, Trade and Industry Minister responsible for films, at the Cannes Film Festival. A grant of £3.5 million was provided to set up the new body and run it for the first four years. The commission's task will be to attract overseas film production to Britain, and to provide film-makers with 'technical services, people, locations, laboratories, contacts with local authorities or police'. The Government also set up a £5 million fund to assist British producers seeking to enter into European co-productions.

Unexpected success

In 1990, nine American films took over $100 million at the US box office, though the most popular films were not those that the studios had expected to do well. The surprise success was *Home Alone*, made by 20th Century Fox because Warner Bros turned it down. The story of an eight-year-old boy, Kevin McCallister (played by Macauley Culkin), accidentally left at home when his family go to Paris for a Christmas holiday, cost $18 million to produce and took over $215 million at the box office. Directed by Chris Columbus from a script by John Hughes, Kevin's successful attempts to fight off would-be burglars, played by Joe Pesci and Daniel Stern, struck a popular chord, especially with young audiences. *Home Alone* became the highest-grossing comedy of all time.

Ghost was also an unexpected hit, earning $212 million in 1990. It stars Patrick Swayze as a banker who is killed in a mugging. He returns from the dead to attempt to warn his girlfriend, played by Demi Moore, that her life is also in danger. He is only able to communicate with her through a fraudulent medium, Ota-Mae Brown, hilariously played by Whoopi Goldberg. *Ghost* cost some $20 million to make and was an instant success. It was directed by Jerry Zucker from a screenplay by Bruce Joel Rubin.

Wolves wins Oscars

The 63rd Academy Awards (Oscars) ceremony of the US Academy of Motion Picture Arts and Sciences was the expected triumph for Kevin Costner's epic western *Dances with Wolves*. Nominated for awards in twelve categories, the film received seven Oscars, including the most prestigious ones for best picture and best director. Costner's success was vindication of a project that had been considered at best eccentric and at worst totally misguided in Hollywood: Westerns have been out of favour since the costly failure of *Heaven's Gate*. To make a three-hour film in an unfashionable genre, with American Indians speaking in their own language with subtitles on screen, seemed to be flying in the face of conventional wisdom; furthermore, the film was Costner's directorial debut. However, Costner was more attuned to American sensibilities than his detractors. His film used the best features of Westerns, an epic scale and spectacular set pieces including battle scenes and a buffalo hunt, but viewed with hindsight. Costner himself played John J. Dunbar, who, when offered his choice of army posting, opts 'to see the frontier before it goes'. He becomes friendly with the Sioux Indians in the remote outposts in Dakota, learns their Lakota language, takes a Sioux bride (a white girl brought up by the Indians, played by Mary McDonnell) and helps the Sioux fight their enemies, the Pawnees. An essentially simple story, *Dances with Wolves* treats the Sioux with dignity, reflecting modern American guilt at an inglorious period in the country's history.

The award for best actor was a triumph for Jeremy Irons as Claus von Bulow in *Reversal of Fortune*. The film is based on the true account of the Danish aristocrat's trial, conviction and subsequent acquittal for attempting to murder his wife, a *cause célèbre* in the 1980s. Irons trod the difficult path of playing a living person with skill and subtlety. He had faced strong competition in a category that also included Kevin Costner (*Dances with Wolves*) Robert De Niro (*Awakenings*), Richard Harris (*The Field*) and Gerard Depardieu (*Cyrano de Bergerac*). *Reversal of Fortune* was directed by Barbet Schroeder, with a screenplay by Nicholas Kazan from a book by Alan Dershowitz, a Harvard professor of law who defended von Bulow.

The best actress award went to Kathy Bates for her portrayal of the obsessive Annie Wilkes in *Misery*, adapted by William Goldman from Stephen King's novel and directed by Rob Reiner. Bates plays a woman who rescues her favourite author Paul Sheldon (James Caan) from a car crash. While nursing him back to health, she discovers that in his latest novel he has killed off her favourite character, Misery Chastain, and she keeps him prisoner until he rewrites the story and resurrects the character.

Best supporting actor was Joe Pesci for his role as Tommy De Vito in Martin Scorsese's chilling tale of life in the Mafia, *GoodFellas*. Based on Nicholas Pileggi's novel *Wiseguys: Life in a Mafia Family*, and co-scripted by Pileggi and Scorsese, the film featured Ray Liotta as Henry Hill. It concerns Hill's 30-year life of crime in New York, recorded and depicted as day-to-day business. *GoodFellas* is an effective, well-made film which manages to avoid glamorizing the violence it depicts. Whoopi Goldberg was named best supporting actress for her role in *Ghost*.

Apart from Jeremy Iron's Oscar, there was a notable success for Britain in the category of best animated short film, which was awarded to Nick Park for *Creature Comforts*. The film features zoo animals made from plasticine, who are interviewed about their life in Britain. Part-funded by Channel 4, the film cost £50,000 to make. The best foreign film was *Journey of Hope* directed by Xavier Koller.

European Awards

The 1990 European Film Awards, presented in Glasgow in December, are Europe's answer to the Oscar ceremony and an attempt to promote the idea of a European film industry with an identity distinct from Hollywood. Nominations are made by the 27 participating countries for the best films in three categories, shortlists are selected by juries, and the final decisions are made by a main jury the week before the ceremony. The European Film of the Year award went to *Open Doors* (Italy), directed by Gianni Amelio. Kenneth Branagh's *Henry V* won the award for best Young European Film, and Branagh won best actor. Best actress was Carmen Maura for *Ay Carmela!* (Spain), directed by Carlos Saura. *December Bride*, directed by Thaddeus O'Sullivan (Republic of Ireland) was awarded the Special Jury prize and Andrzej Wajda received a European Lifetime Achievement Award.

British Awards

At the 22nd British Academy of Film and Television Awards (BAFTA), Martin Scorsese's *GoodFellas* won the awards for best film, best direction and best adapted screenplay. The best actor was Philippe Noiret in *Cinema Paradiso*, and best actress Jessica Tandy in *Driving Miss Daisy*. *Cinema Paradiso* also won awards for best foreign language film, best original film score (Ennio and Andrea Morricone), best original screenplay (Guiseppe Tornatore) and best supporting actor (Salvatore Cascio). Whoopi Goldberg was named best supporting actress for her role in *Ghost*. Film producer Jeremy Thomas received the Michael Balcon Award.

Major films

Oliver Sacks's account of his work at a New York hospital in 1969, when he was able temporarily to release some 20 patients from their long-term catatonic state through use of the drug L-dopa, was made into a sensitive and moving film in *Awakenings*, directed by Penny Marshall. Robin Williams gave a restrained performance as Dr Sayer, the character based on Sacks, with Robert De Niro exceptional as patient Leonard Lowe. Steven Zaillian wrote the screenplay.

The successful partnership of producer Ismail Merchant, director James Ivory and writer Ruth Prawer Jhabvala was responsible for *Mr and Mrs Bridge*, a subtle and beautifully made account of a marriage spanning 25 years. Based on two novels by Evan S. Connell, the film stars Paul Newman as a staid but successful lawyer and Joanne Woodward as his devoted wife.

Anthony Hopkins gives a chilling performance as Dr Hannibal Lecter, a cannibalistic serial killer, in *The Silence of the Lambs*, based on the novel by Thomas Harris. Directed by Jonathan Demme, this grisly and powerful thriller also stars Jodie Foster as trainee FBI agent Clarice Starling, who visits Lecter in prison to seek his help in tracking down another serial killer, nicknamed 'Buffalo Bill'. The film achieved huge success in America and Britain.

Edward Scissorhands is an oddity, a gothic fairy-tale about a boy created by an inventor (played by Vincent Price) whose untimely death leaves him with scissors instead of hands. Directed by Tim Burton, the film was an unexpected success. Johnny Depp plays the title role, with support from Dianne Wiest, Winona Ryder and Anthony Michael Hall.

Ridley Scott's *Thelma and Louise* has been described as 'the world's first feminist road movie'. It stars Geena Davis as a bored housewife who escapes from a domineering husband, and Susan Sarandon as a waitress who joins her on a weekend away. The two throw off all restraints when they are pursued by the police for shooting a man who attempted to rape one of them. Although the male characters are almost universally hostile and unsympathetic, the strength of the film is the development of the two main characters. Beautifully filmed by Ridley Scott from a screenplay by Callie Khouri, this comic and stylish adventure was a popular, if controversial, success.

After her success in *Pretty Woman*, a curiously dated reworking of the *Pygmalion* theme in which she plays a prostitute employed by businessman Richard Gere as his escort for a week, Julia Roberts became Hollywood's highest paid actress. In *Sleeping with the Enemy*, she portrays a battered wife who fakes her own death to escape her husband, played by Patrick Bergin. However, he tracks her down and destroys her new-found happiness with a drama teacher, played by Kevin Anderson. Directed by Joseph Ruben, the cast failed to rise above a contrived and implausible plot. Julia Roberts also starred in *Flatliners* with Kiefer Sutherland and Kevin Bacon, a far-fetched thriller directed by Joel Schumacher, about a group of medical students who stop their hearts (thus creating a flat line on the ECG machine) so that they can experience the afterlife.

Arachnophobia is a well-made comic thriller about a plague of killer spiders in a small American town. A young doctor, played by Jeff Daniels, moves there from the city for a better life, only to find that the previous practitioner is reluctant to give up his patients. Daniels has to overcome the townspeople's suspicions, especially when his few patients die mysteriously, and his own fear of spiders. The film was directed by Frank Marshall.

Postcards from the Edge was adapted by Carrie Fisher from her own semi-autobiographical novel and directed by Mike Nichols. It features Meryl Streep as a drug-addicted actress forced to live with her overbearing mother, played by Shirley MacLaine, as a condition of resurrecting her career.

Merrie and Mad

Two major feature films devoted to the exploits of Robin Hood appeared during the year. Patrick Bergin's portrayal in *Robin Hood* was the more worthy, the less costly (at some $15 million) but the duller of the two. Directed by John Irvin, it features Uma Thurman as Maid Marian, with Edward Fox, Owen Teale and Jurgen Prochnow. By way of contrast, *Robin Hood: Prince of Thieves*, starring Kevin Costner, is a much livelier, swashbuckling romp, and, at $50 million, over three times as expensive to produce. Directed by Kevin Reynolds, the Costner version takes greater historical liberties, for instance, Robin is accompanied home from the Crusades by a Moor, played by Morgan Freeman. Although it received a poor critical reception in the USA, the film succeeded on entertainment value, with Alan Rickman stealing scenes as a delightfully wicked Sheriff of Nottingham.

Franco Zeffirelli achieved the difficult task of introducing Shakespeare's *Hamlet* to a wider audience without compromising the essence of the play or its poetry. Mel Gibson, better known for adventures such as the *Mad Max* trilogy and the *Lethal Weapon* films, handled the part of the Prince of Denmark with skill and sensitivity. He was well supported by Glenn Close as Gertrude, Alan Bates as Claudius, Paul Scofield as the ghost and Helena Bonham-Carter as Ophelia, in a gripping and lucid film.

In *The Godfather Part III*, Coppola returned to the saga of the Corleone family after a break of some 17 years. Written by Coppola and Mario Puzo, and filmed by Gordon Willis, the film relates Mafia leader Michael Corleone's attempts to buy himself peace and redemption in his old age, after a lifetime of violent crime. Al Pacino returned to the role of Michael, with Diane Keaton again as his wife Kay and Andy Garcia as his potential heir, Vincent Mancini. Unfortunately, the plot lacked the narrative clarity of its predecessors, becoming over-complex in its interweaving of the Vatican bank scandal with Corleone family business.

Also screened

One of the year's more costly flops was *Hudson Hawks*, a feebly plotted and derivative comedy, starring Bruce Willis as a New York jewel thief. Willis also appeared in *Bonfire of the Vanities*, Brian de Palma's misguided attempt to film Tom Wolfe's satire on New York. Tom Hanks was miscast as merchant banker Sherman McCoy, and Michael Cristofer's screenplay lost the novel's satiric edge. Sydney Pollack's *Havana*, set in Cuba in 1958, was a dull and stereotyped affair, with Robert Redford as a professional card-player.

Memphis Belle was David Puttnam's response to what he saw as the excesses of *Top Gun*. Based on William Wyler's famous 1943 documentary about the 25th bombing mission over Germany of a B-17 Flying Fortress, the film was an entertaining but clichéd war film. Directed by Michael Caton-Jones from a screenplay by Monte Merrick, and co-produced by Wyler's daughter Catherine, *Memphis Belle* featured Matthew Modine, Eric Stolz and Harry Connick jun.

David Leland's *The Big Man* is based on a novel by William McIlvanney, adapted by Don McPherson. Liam Neeson plays an ex-miner imprisoned for violence during the pit strike. Embarrassed at being supported by his wife, played by Joanne Whalley-Kilmer, he takes up bare-knuckle fighting and is drawn into the Glasgow underworld. The film also featured Ian Bannen and Billy Connolly.

Gerard Dépardieu is excellent as Edmond Rostand's long-nosed hero in Jean-Paul Rappeneau's much-praised production of *Cyrano de Bergerac*. Reputed to be the most costly French language film ever made, with a large cast, numerous extras and splendid sets and costumes, the film was an international success. The cast also features Anne Brochet as Roxanne and Vincent Perez as Christian.

Cynthia Scott's *The Company of Strangers* is a moving and uplifting story about seven women, aged from 64 to 89, who have to fend for themselves after their bus breaks down. The film was improvised by a cast of amateurs and is a tribute to the dignity of old age. It was financed by the National Film Board of Canada.

Other films released during the year include: *The Field*, directed by Jim Sheridan, featuring Richard Harris, who was nominated for an Oscar for his role as Bull McCabe, an Irish farmer driven to madness and murder when the plot of land he has lovingly cultivated is threatened; *Hidden Agenda*, directed by Ken Loach and written by Jim Allen, with Brian Cox, a muddled polemic against the British presence in Northern Ireland; *Where Angels Fear to Tread*, based on E. M. Forster's novel, directed by Charles Sturridge, and featuring Helen Mirren, Rupert Graves, Helen Bonham-Carter and Judi Davis; *Ballad of the Sad Café*, based on Carson McCullers' novella and directed by Simon Callow, with Vanessa Redgrave as Miss Amelia, Keith Carradine as her husband and Cork Hubbert as her cousin Lymon, the dwarf; *Presumed Innocent*, adapted by Frank Pierson from Scott Turow's courtroom thriller, with Harrison Ford, Greta Scacchi, Raul Julia and Paul Winfield, directed by Alan J. Pakula; *Teenage Mutant Ninja Turtles*, a popular film version of the television cartoon, directed by Steve Barron with models by Jim Henson's Creative Shop; *Henry and June*, the story of the triangular relationship of Henry Miller, his wife June and the writer Anaïs Nin, featuring Fred Ward, Maria de Medeiros and Uma Thurman; *Kindergarten Cop*, directed by Ivan Reitman, with Arnold Schwarzenegger; *The Russia House*, adapted by Tom Stoppard from John le Carré's post-*glasnost* spy thriller, and directed by Fred Schepisi, featuring Sean Connery, Michelle Pfeiffer and Roy Scheider; *The Grifters*, with Anjelica Huston, directed by

Stephen Frears; *The Freshman*, written and directed by Andrew Bergman, with Marlon Brando, Matthew Broderick and Maximilian Schell.

Sequels included *Robocop 2*, directed by Irvin Kershner, with Peter Weller and Dan O'Herlihy; *Young Guns II: Blaze of Glory*, directed by Geoff Murphy, with James Coburn and William Petersen; *Rocky V*, directed by John Avildsen, with Sylvester Stallone; and *Three Men and a Little Lady*, directed by Emile Ardolino.

Festivals

At the 44th Edinburgh Film Festival, the Michael Balcon Award for the best British film went to David Hayman's *Silent Scream*. Iain Glen portrays a convicted murderer, Larry Winters, who suffers from schizophrenia, and who reveals artistic talent when transferred to Glasgow's Barlinnie Prison. Edinburgh featured the world première of Derek Jarman's *The Garden*, his thoughts on the state of England inspired by the story of the Passion and by his own garden near the nuclear power station at Dungeness on the Kent coast. The festival showed a retrospective of the films of John Landis, the American director whose output is widely available on video and frequently screened on television, and of the work of Pupi Avati, a distinguished contemporary Italian director whose films have yet to receive commercial distribution in the UK.

At Venice (*XLVII Mostra Internazionale d'Arte Cinematografica*), the Golden Lion for best film was awarded to Tom Stoppard for his film version of his 1967 play *Rosencrantz and Guildenstern Are Dead*, about the two courtiers in *Hamlet*. The film, Stoppard's directorial debut, was the first British film to win the Golden Lion since Olivier's *Hamlet* 43 years earlier. Gary Oldman and Tim Roth play the courtiers with Iain Glen as Hamlet, Richard Dreyfuss as the Player King and Donald Sumpter as Claudius. Martin Scorsese's *GoodFellas* won the Silver Lion for best director, and Jane Campion's *An Angel at My Table*, originally shot on 16mm in three parts for New Zealand television, received the Special Jury Prize. This remarkable film is based on the autobiography of the writer Janet Frame, who spent eight years in a psychiatric hospital and endured shock treatment after being wrongly diagnosed as schizophrenic. Written by Laura Jones, it features Alexia Keogh and Karen Fergusson. Venice also presented a tribute to Michael Powell which included the British Film Institute's restoration of his 1937 film *Edge of the World*.

The 34th London Film Festival was dedicated to Powell's memory. Featuring over 200 films from 40 countries, the festival opened with *Texasville*, Peter Bogdanovich's unsatisfactory sequel to his much-acclaimed *The Last Picture Show*. *Life is Sweet*, Mike Leigh's latest improvised film, was premièred at the festival. A farcical account of a family's misadventures, it features Alison Steadman, Jim Broadbent and Timothy Spall. The tenth anniversary of the Thames Silents presentations included E. A. Dupont's 1929 film *Moulin Rouge*, which was screened with a live jazz accompaniment, and Raymond Bernard's *The Chess Player*, made in 1926. The original score by Henri Rabaud was conducted by

Carl Davis. Set in Vilnius in 1776, the film concerns a mechanical chess player which has great success in Europe. However, the machine contains the leader of a crushed revolution, who is unable to stay silent when Catherine the Great cheats in a chess match. The festival closed with Bernardo Bertolucci's *The Sheltering Sky*, adapted from Paul Bowles' novel. It tells the story of a trip through Morocco in 1947 by two American travellers, played by John Malkovich and Debra Winger. Although impressively filmed, the film lacks narrative drive.

The 41st Berlin Film Festival was the first to be held in a reunited Germany. The Golden Bear was awarded to Marco Ferreri's *House of Smiles*, starring Ingrid Thulin. Maynard Eziashi won the prize for best actor for his role in *Mister Johnson*, directed by Bruce Beresford. Adapted by William Boyd from Joyce Cary's novel, it tells the story of an African clerk who copies his colonial masters in his desire to win their approval. The award for best actress went to Victoria Abril in *Lovers*, directed by Vincente Aranda, while the prize for direction was shared by Ricky Tognazzi for *Ultra* and Jonathan Demme for *The Silence of the Lambs*.

Cannes do

The 44th Cannes Film Festival was a triumph for Joel and Ethan Coen, whose *Barton Fink* won the *Palme d'Or* for best film, the prize for best direction and also for best actor (John Turturro). A comedy set in Hollywood in the 1940s, it was the third consecutive American success at Cannes. *La Belle Noiseuse*, Jacques Rivette's four-hour epic drama about a painter returning years later to resume an abandoned portrait, received the Special Jury Prize. Best actress was Irene Jacob in Krzysztof Kieslowski's *The Double Life of Veronique*, in which she played the parts of a Polish girl and a French girl. The Jury Prize was shared by Lars von Trier's *Europa* and Maroun Bagdadi's *Hors La Vie*. Peter Greenaway's *Prospero's Books*, inspired by Shakespeare's *The Tempest* and featuring John Gielgud, should have represented Britain in the main competition but was not finished in time. However, the first 17 minutes were screened, suggesting a complex and elaborate work.

Reprints

To mark the 50th anniversary of its release, a new print of Orson Welles' *Citizen Kane* was issued from the original negative. *Kane* continues to cause controversy but is still generally regarded as one of the most influential films of all time. Jean Renoir's 1938 classic *La Bête Humaine* was released. Based on Zola's novel, it stars Simone Simon and Jean Gabin in a passionate and poetic masterpiece. Michael Roemer's *The Plot Against Harry* was made in 1969 but due to adverse reaction when it was first screened, it was never generally released. However, in 1990 it appeared at several film festivals and achieved a cult appeal for its 1960s period flavour. Martin Priest plays Harry Plotnick, a numbers racketeer, in a richly characterized and sharply scripted film that well deserves its rescue from obscurity.

Samuel Beckett's *Film*, a 23-minute short made in 1965, also made a welcome reappearance. Directed by

Alan Schneider, it features a 70-year-old Buster Keaton as a man called 'O', shown only from behind as he looks at photographs of his life, until his face is revealed in the seventh photograph. A marvellous cinematic experience, *Film* received its first British screening. Robert Bresson's *A Man Escaped*, made in 1956, is based on the true story of the escape of a Frenchman, Devigny, from a Gestapo prison in Lyons in 1943. It features an amateur actor, François Leterrier, in the leading role of the prisoner, called Lt. Fontaine in the film. The film is a compulsive, intense study in human fortitude.

THE ACADEMY AWARDS 1990

Best Picture.—*Dances with Wolves.*

Best Director.—Kevin Costner, *Dances with Wolves.*

Best Actor.—Jeremy Irons, *Reversal of Fortune.*

Best Actress.—Kathy Bates, *Misery.*

Best Supporting Actor.—Joe Pesci, *GoodFellas.*

Best Supporting Actress.—Whoopi Goldberg, *Ghost.*

Best Original Screenplay.—Bruce Joel Rubin, *Ghost.*

Best Adapted Screenplay.—Michael Blake, *Dances with Wolves.*

Best Foreign Language Film.—*Journey of Hope,* Switzerland.

Best Original Score.—John Barry, *Dances with Wolves.*

Best Original Song.—Stephen Sondheim, 'Sooner or Later (I Always Get My Man)', *Dick Tracy.*

Best Cinematography.—Dean Semler, *Dances with Wolves.*

Best Art Direction.—Richard Sylbert and Rick Simpson, *Dick Tracy.*

Best Costume Design.—Franca Squarciapino, *Cyrano de Bergerac.*

Best Film Editing.—Neil Travis, *Dances with Wolves.*

Best Sound.—Russell Williams II, Jeffrey Perkins, Bill W. Benton and Greg Watkins, *Dances with Wolves.*

Best Sound Effects Editing.—Cecilia Hall and George Watters, *The Hunt for Red October.*

Special Award for Visual Effects.—*Total Recall.*

Best Make-up.—John Caglione Jnr. and Doug Drexler, *Dick Tracy.*

Best Animated Short.—Nick Park, *Creature Comforts.*

Best Short Documentary.—Steven Okazaki, *Days of Waiting.*

Best Documentary Feature.—Barbara Kopple and Arthur Cohn, *American Dream.*

Best Live Action Short.—Adam Davison, *The Lunch Date.*

Honorary Awards.—Myrna Loy and Sophia Loren.

FILM AND VIDEO CERTIFICATES

The British Board of Film Classification issues the following categories of film certificates:

U   Universal: suitable for all.

PG Parental Guidance: some scenes may be unsuitable for young children.

12 Passed only for persons of twelve years and over.

15 Passed only for persons of fifteen years and over.

18 Passed only for persons of eighteen years and over.

R18 For Restricted Distribution Only (through specially licensed cinemas or sex shops to which no one under the age of eighteen is admitted).

The classifications of video tapes differ slightly:

U   Universal: suitable for all.

Uc Universal: particularly suitable for children.

PG Parental Guidance: general viewing, but some scenes may be unsuitable for young children.

15 Suitable only for persons of 15 years and over.

18 Suitable only for persons of 18 years and over.

R18 Restricted: to be supplied only in licensed sex shops to persons of not less than 18 years.

TELEVISION 1990-91

The effects of competition and recession led to a year of upheaval for the main television organizations. The Broadcasting Act 1990 came into force in January 1991, introducing a new system of awarding franchises to the independent television companies. The BBC was told by the Government to cut costs and also faced a real drop in its licence income. And British Satellite Broadcasting, which began transmission on April 29, 1990, merged with its rival, Sky, on November 2, 1990.

The Broadcasting Act received the Royal Assent on November 1, 1990. In the later stages of its passage through Parliament, the Bill aroused controversy when Conservative MPs and peers persuaded the Government to make the Independent Television Commission, successor body to the IBA and the Cable Authority, enforce stricter guidelines on impartiality in programmes. The amendment would have made broadcasters allow equal time for opposing views to be expressed in a programme or series; even programmes expressing personal views would have had to be balanced. It was feared that this would lead to dull and uncontroversial programmes.

The chairman of the BBC wrote to the Home Secretary, 'The BBC does not believe that impartiality in programmes is an appropriate area for detailed legislation', and the IBA, which would have had to enforce the rules in its new guise as the Independent Television Commission (ITC), said the proposals were 'unworkable'. There was widespread opposition within Parliament, broadcasting and the legal profession, and the Government was forced to revise the amendment. The new draft replaced the requirement for impartiality in 'individual issues' with impartiality in 'major matters', which some still considered so vague as to encourage litigation. However, the IBA felt that it would be able to produce a 'workable code' with the new wording and the amendment was passed.

In February 1991 the House of Lords upheld the Government's ban on radio or television interviews with members of republican or loyalist paramilitary groups in Northern Ireland. The measure was introduced by Home Secretary Douglas Hurd in October 1988 and had been attacked as an infringement of free speech. However, it is of symbolic rather than practical value, as broadcasters are able to circumvent the ban by rerecording the words used by banned groups using a reporter or actor to supply the voice-over to the original film. The House of Lords said the restriction was 'of limited scope' and did not exceed the Home Secretary's powers.

Channel 3

The independent television companies, denounced by Margaret Thatcher when Prime Minister as 'the last bastion of restrictive practices', suffered an uncomfortable year as they were subjected to the full rigours of the free market economy. Advertising revenues fell substantially for the first time in a decade, and yet the companies were required to make projections of their income for more than ten years ahead in order to determine how much to bid to retain their franchises, knowing that they would be committed to paying that amount each year to the Treasury.

The Government decided that the new Channel 3 licences will be awarded for ten years from 1993 to regionally based companies on the basis of 'the highest qualifying cash bid', after applicants had satisfied a programme quality requirement. The ITC said that the 'quality threshold' would be high, and that applicants will have to ensure that their programming includes the nine categories of programmes currently covered by the ITV companies. Programmes imported from non-EC countries may not exceed 25 per cent of the total.

The ITC published an invitation to apply for licences in February 1991. The existing regional boundaries are to be maintained and there will continue to be 15 regional companies and one national breakfast-time licence. Existing companies will be able to bid for more than one licence, but not for one whose region borders their own. Companies wishing to bid for more licences than they may hold under the restrictions on cross-ownership have to list the regions in which they are interested in order of preference. After 1993, however, Channel 3 companies will be able to merge or be taken over by other companies on the stock market, raising the possibility that many smaller companies may disappear while any major ITV company that loses out in the bidding for franchises may re-emerge.

The ITC laid emphasis in its invitation to apply for licences on the importance of regional programming, requiring that 80 per cent of such programmes be made within the relevant region. It was felt that this would be some protection for the six smallest companies, Border, Channel, Grampian, TSW, Tyne Tees and Ulster, which appear the most vulnerable to superior bids but contribute least to the network. The ITC is also faced with the possibility of the main network providers, such as Central, Thames, Granada and London Weekend, being outbid for their franchises. This could have a disastrous effect on the national network. It is rumoured that if Granada, with the perennially popular *Coronation Street*, loses its franchise, the programme might be sold to satellite television or even the BBC. Changes such as this would affect the projections of advertising income on which other companies have based their franchise applications.

It is apparent that the original intention of auctioning the new franchises to the highest bidders has been subverted by the impossibility of knowing whether the companies will be able to fulfil their promises. In the past, successful bidders for licences, such as TV-am, had not always been able to live up fully to the promises that won them the licence. To avoid the embarrassment of blank screens, the ITC has two escape clauses: first, all applicants have to pass the 'quality threshold', which is by no means guaranteed; second, a lower bid may be accepted due to 'exceptional circumstances', a provision which, if invoked, could be challenged in the courts.

The closing date for the delivery of franchise applications was May 15, 1991. The ITC received 40 bids for the 16 licences, which included applications from companies bidding for more than one licence. Of the larger companies, only Central's bid was unopposed; a rival consortium collapsed shortly before the deadline, and it was rumoured that Central, aware of the fact, was able to submit a token bid of around £1 million, having previously intended to bid some £30 million. Meanwhile, the troubled TVS, which was widely perceived as one of the most vulnerable companies, revealed that it had bid £54 million to retain its franchise. Although all applicants were bound by the ITC to secrecy, under Stock Exchange rules TVS was obliged to inform its shareholders of the amount when seeking further funds from them. TVS's bid was reputed to be far in excess of those of the three other applicants for its franchise. This was considered to be a shrewd gamble on the part of TVS's new chairman, Rudolph Agnew, as it is unlikely that TVS or any other of the incumbent companies will fail to pass the quality threshold. However, there was concern that such a high bid would compromise TVS's ability to sustain its promised levels of programming, on which grounds it could be rejected. Whatever the outcome, it is nonetheless a remarkable turnaround in the fortunes of a company that had been brought to the brink of ruin by its disastrous purchase of the American production company MTM Entertainment.

Border and Scottish TV were also unopposed in their regions, but a new consortium, Carlton Communications, challenged Thames and TVS, and CP-TV, backed by Richard Branson and David Frost, challenged Anglia, Thames and TVS. Tyne Tees faced a rival bid from North East TV, a group backed by Granada and Border. Granada itself was challenged by North West TV, backed by Yorkshire, Tyne Tees and Mersey TV, the production company run by Phil Redmond which produces *Grange Hill* for the BBC and Channel 4's *Brookside*. NWTV's application was the most radical one submitted: it proposes to 'weave broadcasting into the community', offering some 50 hours a week of regional programmes, with access to the airwaves for community groups and amateur companies and an all-night free-form chat show.

HTV was disturbed that one of its three challengers was backed by Sir David Nicholas, chairman of ITN, which is owned by the ITV companies. TSW was similarly aggrieved that the challenge to it from Westcountry TV should be backed by the director-general of the CBI, John Banham, since TSW is a member of that organization.

After the franchise applications were received, the ITC allowed a six-week consultation period for comment on the prospectuses. Over 2,200 comments were received, including some from ITV companies. The ITC will announce which companies have been successful at the end of October 1991. However, informed rumour and speculation about the sizes of the bids submitted, and suggestions that established companies such as Thames and TV-am have been outbid, led to a flurry of activity on the stock market. There were substantial rises in the stocks of some companies and concern that a false market in ITV company shares was being created.

Whatever the final outcome of the latest franchise round, there was a widespread feeling that the system

was a lottery, and that the ending of the restriction on mergers in 1994 would herald more upheaval. In addition, a further major problem will confront the successful companies, as Channel 3 companies will not have the right to schedule their own programmes but will have to appoint a central scheduler. The scheduler's function will be to select from the output of the companies for the national network, subject to the approval of the ITC and the Office of Fair Trading. Should the companies be unable to agree on an acceptable networking system, the ITC may impose one on them.

Sponsorship

The ITC published new rules governing sponsorship of programmes. With effect from January 1, 1991, all programmes except news and current affairs are open to sponsorship. However, no political organizations are allowed to sponsor programmes, and companies sponsoring programmes will not be able to determine their content or time of broadcast. Sponsors will be identified at the beginning and end of programmes but may not be promoted during them. It was later announced that Unilever will back an international soap opera, *Riviera*, set in the south of France. Granada bought the UK rights for the 260-part series.

ITN

Independent Television News, which has provided news services for ITV since 1955, faced a difficult year. The Broadcasting Act required that 51 per cent of its shares be sold off, creating uncertainty about its future, and the ITC was considering licensing two news providers for Channel 3. In October 1990 ITN asked the ITV companies for a temporary injection of £6·5 million cash and to guarantee its bank loans. The company had exceeded its budget, having incurred extra expense covering the Iraqi invasion of Kuwait. Further, it had expected to be able to let off excess floor space in its new premises but because of the slump in the property market it was unable to find tenants. According to its chairman, Sir David Nicholas, ITN was 'on the verge of serious instability'.

Although the ITC's decision to award ITN the contract as sole news provider for Channel 3 gave it some confidence for the future, the ten-year £60 million a year contract is subject to review in 1995. ITN suffered further embarrassment in March 1991 when it was disclosed that the company had overspent by nearly £10 million, in addition to the expected deficit of nearly £3 million. There were serious problems with the company's internal accounting systems. Night-time news bulletins were cut and staff laid off. In June, ITN announced a pay freeze, plus a further batch of 137 compulsory redundancies. When ITN's senior newscaster, Sir Alastair Burnet, announced his retirement in August 1991 it was widely perceived as the end of an era for the troubled news station.

BBC

A report into the running of the BBC by the accountancy firm Price Waterhouse said that the Corporation was overstaffed, poorly managed and could be run more efficiently. This was endorsed by Sir John Harvey-Jones, former chairman of ICI, who had been employed by the BBC as a consultant. He said that staff could be reduced by one-third, management by half and that the BBC should concentrate on quality programming, not the pursuit of ratings. Sir John's comments caused some embarrassment as he had been the unlikely star of a BBC2 series, *Troubleshooter*, in which he looked at established British companies and advised them on how to improve their performance.

The Home Office told the BBC that it would have to cut its costs by £130 million over five years; Michael Checkland, the director-general, said that this would mean cuts in staffing of 2,800 over three years. In April 1991 the BBC's licence fee rose by £6 for a colour television to £77, an increase of 7·9 per cent, and £1.50 for a black and white television to £25.50. As the increase was below the rate of inflation, the BBC suffered a reduction in income in real terms of some £35 million. Responsibility for collection of the licence passed from the Post Office to the BBC.

In its annual report, published in July 1991, the BBC announced that staff levels would be reduced from 24,000 in March 1990 to less than 20,000 in 1993. The savings will go towards improved pay and conditions for remaining staff and for 'programme enhancement'. The BBC reported that it had lost £80 million in 1990–91, mainly due to buying leases in property.

The question of the future financing of the BBC was also raised by Professor Sir Alan Peacock at the 1990 Annual Television Festival in Edinburgh. His 1986 report on public service broadcasting had recommended replacing the licence fee by subscription services and pay as you view schemes. Sir Alan said that the Corporation, whose current charter expires in 1996, should become a private, non-profit-making foundation. He proposed that those who valued the BBC's services should subscribe voluntarily to its upkeep; like members of the Automobile Association, 'they would put their money where their mouth is, buttressed, perhaps, by the tax reliefs which would go with private contributions to charitable organizations'.

In July 1991, Michael Checkland's contract as director-general was extended by one year from March 1992; it was reported that he had sought a further three-year term. His deputy, John Birt, was appointed to succeed him from March 1993. Mr Birt said : 'The main tasks facing the BBC in the '90s are to work out what programme services the BBC can best provide in the burgeoning radio and television market-place, and to ensure that in all of its activities the BBC is as lean and efficient as any of its competitors.'

The BBC closed its famous Lime Grove studios after 41 years' use, but its new headquarters at White City for news and current affairs, costing £175 million, was postponed. It was decided to spend the money on boosting entertainment and drama to halt a slide in ratings which saw the BBC's audience share drop as low as 32 per cent.

New services

During the year the BBC launched World Service Television, a subscription service on satellite television based on its radio news service. The service was included in BBC TV Europe, a compilation of BBC1 and BBC2, available 18 hours a day in 27 countries in Europe.

The BBC also decided to look again at generating extra income through night-time subscription services, in spite of the failure of a medical service launched in October 1988 which closed in February 1990. The new service is called BBC Select and will feature up to 50 different specialist services. The first, Legal Network Television run jointly with the College of Law, was scheduled to begin transmission in September 1991.

The Sadler inquiry into cross-media promotion, set up in December 1989, criticized the BBC for using its programmes to promote its own magazines, as it 'exceeded the limit of propriety by a wide margin'. The matter was referred to the Monopolies and Mergers Commission by the Trade and Industry Secretary.

From March 1, 1991, the monopoly in programme listings enjoyed by the BBC and ITV ended. This enabled *Radio Times* and *TV Times* to carry full details of each other's services, plus satellite programmes, and also encouraged the publication of a number of competitors. A fierce circulation war ensued, with several magazines cutting cover prices in an attempt to establish themselves in the market.

Satellite

Sky Television, which began broadcasting in February 1989, and British Satellite Broadcasting, which began in April 1990, announced that they would merge on November 2, 1990. The IBA, which had granted BSB the satellite franchise in December 1986 for 15 years, was not informed of the move in advance. It had to consider whether the merger made BSB's contract null and void, and whether the new company, British Sky Broadcasting (BSkyB), could legally transmit via the DBS Marco Polo satellite commissioned by BSB. The Office of Fair Trading also said it would investigate the merger, which might be referred to the Monopolies and Mergers Commission.

The merger was also controversial because Sky had been exempt from UK restrictions on foreign and cross-media ownership; as its Astra satellite used European frequencies, it had been classified as a non-domestic service. The merger meant that Rupert Murdoch, the proprietor of News Corporation, which owns Sky, controlled half of the satellite service to the UK and five national newspapers. Under cross-media ownership regulations, newspaper owners had been restricted to a 20 per cent interest in satellite broadcasting.

On November 16, the IBA ruled that the merger breached BSB's contract, but that the contract would not be terminated until BSB subscribers had received

Sky dishes to replace their 'squarials'. It also ruled that BSkyB should stop broadcasting via the Marco Polo satellite. In December, the merger was cleared when the Trade and Industry Secretary announced that the Office of Fair Trading had found no grounds for referring it to the Monopolies and Mergers Commission.

Following the merger, BSkyB announced that it would be offering five channels, including both film channels, Sky News, and entertainment and sports channels. However, the European Commission ruled that Sky's agreement with the European Broadcasting Union granting exclusive rights to sporting events was unlawful. Eurosport was replaced by Sky Sports, covering UK sports, in April.

On financial grounds, the merger seemed logical, as Sky was losing an estimated £2·2 million a week and BSB £8 million a week. Sky had sold nearly 1 million satellite receiving dishes, and had a further 600,000 viewers on cable; BSB had sold 117,000 dishes and had a further 600,000 viewers on cable. In addition to having fewer customers, BSB had been beset by technical problems The IBA had insisted that it use the new D-MAC system, which promised high quality but proved complex, and it had suffered delays in developing its aerial receivers. Also, BSB's equipment was nearly twice as expensive as Sky's.

Reed, one of the main backers of BSB, reduced its holding in BSkyB in April, having decided not to take up its share options in a refinancing deal. The other main BSB shareholders, Granada, Pearson and Chargeurs, increased their share holdings. News Corporation maintained its 50 per cent share in the merged company by contributing both in cash and in kind (film rights) to take up its option. Dish sales, which had dropped to 17,000 in January, picked up to 50,000 in April. It was reported that in May BSkyB was losing around £6 million a week.

Standards

The Broadcasting Standards Council was placed on a statutory footing when the Broadcasting Act came into force. The BSC had originally been set up by the Government in 1988 to act as 'a focus for public concern', particularly in regard to the portrayal of sex and violence on television and radio. It had no powers to review programmes or to enforce standards.

In mid-February 1991, the BSC reported that it had rejected all 58 complaints it had so far received; 40 had concerned television and radio coverage of the Gulf war. The results of the 'attitudes to television' survey commissioned by the ITC disclosed that viewers were more offended by bad language than by sex or violence, suggesting that the BSC had no real role to perform.

The BSC received eight complaints about a brutal murder in the cult BBC2 series *Twin Peaks*, which it judged 'went beyond all reasonable limits'. 'The Council noted the protracted nature of the struggle, its sadistic quality, and the depiction of the blows inflicted on the woman victim as well as the injuries she sustained.' However, the BBC received three times as many complaints when it rescheduled *Twin Peaks* to show the world snooker championship.

The BSC also upheld 23 complaints against the Channel 4 screening of *Sex and the Censors* in the 'Banned' series, ruling that some scenes were 'wholly unacceptable', and the programme was screened too early at 9pm. The ITC concurred with the latter point, saying that the time of broadcast was a grave error of judgment. In the same 'Banned' series there were also complaints about a scene in the 1973 film, *WR: Mysteries of the Organism*, by the Yugoslav director Dusan Makavejev; although parts of the scene were electronically masked, it was considered to have gone beyond acceptable limits.

Cable

The Cable Authority, whose functions were taken over by the ITC under the Broadcasting Act, had awarded 135 franchises for cable services by the time it handed over its responsibilities; some 60,000 miles of cable should be laid by 1995, with a potential market of 14 million homes. However, Jon Davey, director-general of the Cable Authority, expressed concern in September 1990 at plans by British Telecom to use its existing cable network for broadcasting programmes. He felt that this would harm future investment in cable services; at that time only £1 billion of an estimated £6 billion had been spent on cable services.

The prospects for cable were also damaged by the BSB-Sky merger. Both had been available via cable, and the merger meant that cable television had four fewer channels to offer. The competition between the two, with separate receiving dishes required, had also offered a cost advantage to cable services which was now diminished.

Awards

In the British Academy of Film and Television Awards, Peter Jones received the award for best factual series for *The Trials of Life*, the BBC natural history series presented by David Attenborough. The best drama series was the BBC's *Oranges are not the Only Fruit*, awarded to Phillippa Giles, Beeban Kidron and Jeanette Winterson, on whose novel the series was based. Geraldine McEwan received the award for best actress for her role in the same series. Simon Gray received the writer's award, and the production team of Channel 4 News received the award for best news or outside broadcast coverage. The best light entertainment programme was *Whose Line is it Anyway?* (Channel 4, Dan Patterson and Chris Bould), and the best children's programme (drama) was Central's *Press Gang* (Steve Moffat and Sandra C. Hastie). Best children's programme (documentary or educational) was *Ipso Facto* (BBC, Madeleine Wiltshire). Best single drama was *Newshounds* (BBC, Les Blair and Sarah Curtis) and best comedy series *The New Statesman* (YTV, Laurence Marks, Maurice Gran, David Reynolds and Geoffrey Sax). The Huw Weldon Award for best arts programme was won by David Thomas for 'Bolt and Lean' (*South Bank Show*, LWT); three of the four finalists for this award were episodes of the South Bank Show. The Desmond Davis Award for Creative Contribution to Television was awarded to Ray Fitzwalter, head of current affairs at Granada. David Jason, after several unsuccessful nominations, was the popular choice for the light entertainment award for his role as Derek Trotter in the BBC series *Only Fools and Horses*. The Originality Award went to Sir John Harvey-Jones and Richard Reisz for *Troubleshooter* (BBC), and David Wallace received the Flaherty Documentary Award for *The Last African Flying Boat* (BBC). Best foreign television programme was Krystzof Kieslowski's *Ten Commandments*, and best actor was Ian Richardson in BBC's *House of Cards*. Louis Malle received a Fellowship Award, and Deborah Kerr a Special Award.

The presentation of the Richard Dimbleby Award for factual television reporting to John Pilger for *Cambodia: The Betrayal* (Central) was controversial. David Dimbleby strongly criticized the decision, saying, 'John Pilger stands for a type of polemical broadcasting that is the antithesis of everything my father believed in'. BAFTA had 'taken leave of its senses', he said. The citation praised Pilger for his 'uncompromising reporting', saying he was an 'outstanding journalist'; in his acceptance speech, he said that ' a dissenting voice is every bit as legitimate if not more so than one respective of authority'. The programme was, however, criticized by the United Nations Border Relief Operation for alleged errors of fact, including the suggestion that the UN Border Relief Operation had leased a warehouse in Thailand to the USA to store weapons for the Khmer Rouge. Pilger was also sued for libel by two men who were said in the programme to be members of the SAS and to have helped the Khmer Rouge to lay mines. They received 'very substantial' damages.

At the Royal Television Society Awards, the independent company Zenith Productions won the award for best single drama for *Shoot to Kill*, a dramatized account of the investigation by John Stalker into the alleged killing of terrorists by the RUC in Northern Ireland. The best drama series award went to *Inspector Morse*, starring John Thaw, and *Oranges are not the Only Fruit* was best drama serial. The BBC won seven news awards, including journalist of the year for foreign affairs editor John Simpson and political editor John Cole. In the American Emmy Awards, Tracey Ullman received the award for best single variety programme for *The Best of the Tracey Ullman Show*, and also a writing award. Ten Danson, star of *Cheers*, was named best comedy actor, having been nominated unsuccessfully eight times in the past. *LA Law* was named best drama series for the third time; although *Twin Peaks* received 14 nominations, it won no awards.

BOOKER PRIZEWINNERS

1969   *Something to Answer For*—P. H. Newby (Faber).
1970   *The Elected Member*—Bernice Rubens (Eyre & Spottiswoode).
1971   *In A Free State*—V. S. Naipaul (Andre Deutsch).
1972   *G*—John Berger (Weidenfeld).
1973   *The Siege of Krishnapur*—J. G. Farrell (Weidenfeld).
1974   *The Conservationist*—Nadine Gordimer (Cape).
         Holiday—Stanley Middleton (Hutchinson).
1975   *Heat and Dust*—Ruth Prawer Jhabvala (Murray).
1976   *Saville*—David Storey (Cape).
1977   *Staying On*—Paul Scott (Heinemann).
1978   *The Sea, The Sea*—Iris Murdoch (Chatto & Windus).
1979   *Offshore*—Penelope Fitzgerald (Collins).
1980   *Rites of Passage*—William Golding (Faber).
1981   *Midnight's Children*—Salman Rushdie (Cape).
1982   *Schindler's Ark*—Thomas Keneally (Hodder & Stoughton).
1983   *Life & Times of Michael K*—J. M. Coetzee (Secker & Warburg).
1984   *Hôtel du Lac*—Anita Brookner (Cape).
1985   *The Bone People*—Keri Hulme (Hodder & Stoughton).
1986   *The Old Devils*—Kingsley Amis (Hutchinson).
1987   *Moon Tiger*—Penelope Lively (Deutsch).
1988   *Oscar and Lucinda*—Peter Carey (Faber).
1989   *The Remains of the Day*—Kazuo Ishiguro (Faber).
1990   *Possession*—A. S. Byatt (Chatto & Windus).

The finalists for the 1991 prize were:
Time's Arrow—Martin Amis (Jonathan Cape); *The Van*—Roddy Doyle (Secker & Warburg); *Such a Long Journey*—Rohinton Mistry (Faber); *The Redundancy of Courage*—Timothy Mo (Chatto & Windus); *The Famished Road*—Ben Okri (Jonathan Cape); *Reading Turgenev* (from *Two Lives*)—William Trevor (Viking).

ARCHITECTURE 1990–91

NATIONAL GALLERY EXTENSION, LONDON
Architects: Venturi, Scott Brown and Associates

Important public buildings can take many years to reach fruition, but few can have taken quite so long or generated quite so much heated debate, both public and professional, as the new wing of the National Gallery. The site was occupied by Hampton's furniture store until 1940, when it was destroyed by a bomb. The government acquired the site for the National Gallery extension in 1959 but it continued as a car park, and latterly as a construction site for an underground railway extension, for many years. Not until 1982 was an architect/developer competition held. This was based on a concept of mixed commercial and gallery uses. A short list of six finalists produced no clear winner but architects Ahrends Burton and Koralek were commissioned to produce a new design. It was the unveiling of their proposals that attracted the attentions of the Prince of Wales, who condemned the design in his famous 'carbuncle' speech to the Royal Institute of British Architects in 1984.

Following the refusal of planning permission for the original design, the Sainsbury family offered to fund the extension. Robert Venturi was selected as the architect and he commenced design work on a new brief which excluded any commercial component. The new gallery was opened by HM The Queen on July 9, 1991.

The design seems to have disregarded one of the basic tenets of modernism, in that the external form and style of the elevations do not give a logical expression of the internal spaces and functions. Instead, there appears to be two buildings. One is an internal world finely tuned to the needs of the gallery directors and curators whose overriding concern is to present pictures in as near ideal conditions as a modern gallery can encompass; the other is a varied and cosmetic exterior screen wall, designed to dress up the contents in whatever style seemed most appropriate for its surroundings at the time. The exterior of the building is at times slavishly contextual and at others wilfully irrelevant or inconsistent. The architect is the author of *Complexity and Contradiction in Architecture*, and these two abstract concepts go some way towards explaining otherwise perverse features of this design.

The most important façade is that facing the open expanses of Trafalgar Square, the one which is a literal extension of the main Gallery façade. At this crucial point of juxtaposition the architect has 'celebrated' the corner of the earlier classical design with an echoing cluster of classical pilasters. They are not set with any logical relationship to the structural bays of the buildings, but are used in a purely rhythmic way to signal the critical point of tension between new and old. On moving away from this point, the classical vocabulary begins to be deliberately stripped away. Classical incidents occur further and further apart, cornice and mouldings gradually lose their details. After a last burst of energy, in the form of an attached three-quarters column emerging from one side of a pilaster, they

disappear altogether as the elevation turns the corner into Pall Mall. Even before the last quotations disappear into the smooth Portland stone face of the main south-facing elevation, the wall faces are interrupted by huge blank openings cut into the base and extending up beyond the base line of the surrounding pilasters. They are unornamented, unrelated to the proportions and placement of the classical features, and are presumably intended to be 'contradictory'.

On the Pall Mall frontage a grid of tall recessed windows sits above another blank opening, and the last vestiges of Classical ornament terminate on a vertical line away from the corner on to Whitcomb Street. No sooner does the Portland stone cladding turn this corner than it is translated into plain brickwork of a light buff colour. This is relieved only by the panelling effect of special moulded bricks introduced at movement control joints and by the continuation of the stonework in the stocky ground floor columns. The rear elevation on to Orange Street displays yet another character, with massive brick panelled walls and monumental lettering.

The most audacious transition is reserved for the south-east corner (the point of tension referred to above). Here the cluster of pilasters makes as if to turn the corner in the expected fashion but instead is instantly cut away to be replaced by a sheer curtain wall screen. This runs parallel to the side elevation of the Gallery and later reveals itself as a wall outside a wall. It encloses the main approach staircase leading up to the link and the first floor gallery spaces and provides dramatic views from inside out over the square beyond.

One could interpret the multifarious responses to the surrounding context as a sign of indecision and weakness of vision, yet each of the facades is handled with unmistakable integrity and good manners, and the transitions, though abrupt, are sensitively detailed. A considered view might be that the architect is indeed playing a finely calculated game of 'complexity and contradiction', offering a wealth of symbols and implied meanings for trained eyes, and steering a difficult middle course between frivolity and pomposity.

Whatever the opinion of the exterior, the internal sequence of gallery spaces is, by common assent, a huge success, setting off the richness of the early Italian Renaissance paintings to perfection. The architect knew from the start that his extension would house this part of the collection and he has created an appropriately austere interior evocative of a Tuscan Renaissance palace, with light grey walls, vaulted ceilings and sturdy stone columns of fine grey Tuscan pietra-serena stone.

The galleries comprise 16 separate yet interlinked rooms arranged in three linear sequences running north-south. A central axis runs through the larger gallery spaces at the centre. The smaller galleries to each side are linked by openings one to another but not through a common axis; views from room to room are seen diagonally but are controlled in length. At two points subsidiary cross-axes are opened up through the central galleries. These have been used by the gallery's curators to forge links between seemingly unrelated sections of the collection. Indeed, the entire gallery layout has been devised with the sole purpose of maximizing the impact of the pictures and appears to be supremely successful.

The major cross-axis falls across the northernmost room of each range of galleries at an odd angle arising from the alignment of the new wing with the axis of the existing building. The cross-axis forms the pivotal linking route between new and old, the grand stair arriving to one side of a central linking space that fills the gap between the two buildings.

Critical to all modern gallery design is the control and use of natural and artificial light. The design of the main galleries owes much to the influence of Sir John Soane and his Dulwich Picture Gallery (1811), with flat plaster soffits over clear glazed lantern daylights and inward-sloping ceiling soffits around the perimeter, into which the upper part of arched openings and architrave surrounds are cut. However, daylight is regarded by the modern curator as a potentially destructive medium and in the Sainsbury wing the lantern lights offer only the illusion of daylight. Above these is highly sophisticated and extensive rooftop glazing which illuminates an intermediate 'lightbox' of service space. The lightbox, through a series of automatically controlled louvres, permits a proportion of daylight to pass into the galleries below. Natural light is supplemented by a battery of fluorescent tubes placed behind the windows to simulate daylight. Rows of spotlights recessed around the perimeter of the upper ceiling are the actual light sources for the pictures themselves. The considerable presence exerted by the massive glazed roof structure on the building's exterior countenance is therefore ultimately misleading, being responsible for only a fraction of the light experienced in the galleries.

The tantalizing idiosyncracies of the exterior are secondary to the presentation of sublime works of art. Success in this respect has certainly been achieved.

AIRPORT TERMINAL BUILDING, STANSTED, ESSEX
Architect: Foster Associates

Proposals for a third London airport were first made in the 1960s but it was not until 1986 that planning permission was eventually granted for an expansion of the existing Stansted Airport. Work had started on the design of a new terminal towards the end of 1980 and the basis of the final design concept was generated early in 1981 after the initial feasibility study by Foster Associates. The new terminal was officially opened by HM The Queen on March 15, 1991, and went into public service on March 19.

The overall form of the final design is a direct response to the conflicting requirements of providing a memorable and easily assimilated image to attract the travelling public in their thousands, while minimizing the impact of a huge amount of accommodation and all its ancillary structures upon a previously rural site. Fortunately, the site available at Stansted was large enough for a terminal capable of handling eight million passengers a year while keeping all the principal arrival and departure areas on a single level.

A key component of the design was the architect's desire to eliminate as far as possible all obstructions between the passenger arriving for a flight and the jets parked on the runway. He wished to avoid the impersonal and cluttered environment of the average air terminal, where the operation of security and administrative procedures have taken much of the enjoyment out of travel, and to restore a sense of immediacy. The architect's vision of directness, simplicity and transparency has been realized with breathtaking skill. These qualities result almost entirely from the structure used to support the vast expanse of roof, and the decision to liberate the roof itself from all the debilitating effects of servicing and environmental control systems.

The primary structural system has been likened to a series of 'trees', supporting a light and airy roof canopy. Each 'tree' has a 'trunk' formed from four large steel columns, rising to a height of four storeys from a special foundation pad at the lowest floor level. These were prefabricated off-site as towers, each measuring 3·5 metres square by 17 metres high. From the top of each corner column springs a long slender branch, which slopes out as it rises to the corner of an 18 metre square section of the roof. The four topmost corners of the branches are linked by a square grid of steel members acting as the main roof support beams. Each of the branches is braced back to a central nodal point by a pair of tension rods attached by a single bolt to the point of a pyramid of steel supports on top of the main 'trunk'. Each of the 18 metre roof squares is infilled by a shallow lattice steel dome, one to each 'tree' square. A second dome spans between the edges of adjacent trees, which are spaced at twice the modular size, i.e. at 36 metre centres. All the structural members, whether solid members in compression or rods in tension, are circular in section. The overall building is a square of 11 bays by 11, and the resulting roof, 198 metres square, forms a continuous rigid structure, with no movement joints; all thermal and wind load movements are taken up by deflection in the steel members themselves.

The effect of the shallow roof domes is akin to that of a tent, held up by the undercurrent of air, and the structure almost seems designed to hold the roof down rather than up. The roof domes are not true domes, but constructed geometrically from four intersecting part cylinders, a factor which assists the actual roof construction by eliminating double curves.

The liberation of the roof from service-orientated functions and paraphernalia is rendered possible by the use of the column cluster 'trunks'. All air, light, power, safety and information functions are delivered to the main concourse level via ducts and cableways located within the service 'trunks', rising from the three-storey undercroft below the main concourse. The service 'stalks' contain air supply and return ducts (some of which double in an emergency as automatic smoke vents), a metal spiral access stairway, so that maintenance and repairs can be effected without disrupting concourse activities, and powerful uplighters fitted to the tops of the ducts to provide night-time reflected lighting off the roof canopy. Around the perimeter of each unit are located a number of secondary services, including local electrical power, hose reels, emergency lighting, illuminated signs and passenger information services such as clocks and flight information monitors. All these functions are combined into a co-ordinated and compact series of services pods, housed within and structurally supported from the column cluster 'tree trunks'.

The final component in the liberation of the roof is the syphonic rainwater disposal system, a radical alternative to the conventional clutter of outlets, penetrations and falling pipework. A system not previously used in this country, it involves the use of pipes with a smaller than normal diameter which are laid horizontally and designed to operate only at 'full bore'. This creates a syphonic action which pulls the rainwater along the pipe. The outlets are designed to come into operation only when a full head of water has been achieved. This system enables the pipes to be much smaller than normal and to run horizontally, thus making no impact upon the interior design of the roof membrane. The rainwater pipes are exposed at each bay on the side walls of the building, tapering elegantly as they approach ground level.

Freed from all services paraphernalia, the roof can be manipulated purely for aesthetic and light control purposes, diffusing daylight entering during the day and reflecting artificial lighting from below at night. At the centre of each dome is a square opening within which a smaller solid square is arranged on the diagonal, thus creating four triangular rooflights. The shape of these four openings is mirrored by four kite-like triangular perforated metal planes suspended directly below. These diffuse the light, reducing glare and reflecting a proportion of the incident daylight back up on to the ceiling surface. At night these reflector planes appear white in the beams of the uplighters concealed within the trunks, partially concealing the cold black holes of the rooflights. Although the area of glazing amounts to only three per cent of the roof area, the effect is of total permeation of daylight.

Typical of the architect's attention to detail is the detail at the eaves, where much effort has gone into expressing the structural independence of the roof from the walls. It was necessary here to solve the problem of differential movement from thermal expansion and wind load. The 12 metre high glazed wall construction had to be stabilized at the roof level, yet enable the roof to move in every direction in relation to it. The solution devised incorporates a hinged connection piece welded to the steel roof frame and linked by a sliding bar attachment to the top of the glazed wall frame. A toughened glass strip attached to the underside of the eaves allows a continuous flexible weatherproof membrane to be concealed along its bottom edge, maintaining the appearance of a clear break between wall and roof structures.

Every corner of the building is characterized by such conscientious attention to detail. The carefully organized concourse cabins house visually disruptive but essential activities such as catering and retail facilities, while the check-in desks are purpose-designed to look as though built for a lifetime of use but are in fact extremely adaptable and of modular construction. Indeed, this approach extends from the carefully considered spaces of the British Rail arrival platforms in their cathedral-like basement cavern, to the final departure lounges in the satellite buildings away from the main terminal building. The design of Stansted, based on directness of approach, has achieved simplicity and elegance, and this is a seminal building.

INFANTS SCHOOL, BISHOPSTOKE, HANTS
Architect: Hampshire County Council
Chief Architect: Colin Stansfield Smith
Project Architect: Stephen Harte

The public sector has declined over the last decade because of cost-cutting and privatization, and this has led to falling standards of architectural design and environmental quality in local public works up and down the country. Throughout the whole of this period, however, the Hampshire County Council's Architects' Department has produced buildings of great visual quality, sensitivity and stylistic variety, skilfully related to the needs of the communities which they serve through a close awareness of local conditions.

Among the most notable achievements of the Department has been their schools building programme, and the new infants school at Bishopstoke is a typical example. The name of the place conjures up a rural image but the place itself has the anonymous character of many new country suburbs. The new school is a deliberate attempt to create a point of focus in the local environment, combining dignity with a degree of excitement and visual stimulus. Its memorable and recognizable form is that of a giant tepee, with a huge sweeping roof fanning out to embrace the carefully landscaped setting. The site is at the junction of a wood and grasslands, and slopes away from the edge of the wood towards the adjacent housing, so that the building is seen against a background of hill and forest.

The 'tepee' concept has been tried on other occasions, and here involves a simple but effective planning concept which can be easily read from the outside. A tall circular hall lies at the centre of the plan, under a high, pointed, roof lit by a clear glazed conical rooflight. Curving timber rafters soar upwards into the light, while the radiating lines of steel tie rods and the pairs of vertical braces supporting light fittings add complexity and intricacy to the simple volume. The circular hall is surrounded by another drum, set eccentrically, so that at the point of widest divergence there is space for ancillary accommodation such as staff rooms and offices at first floor level, and storage areas at ground level. Around the outside of this drum, a white painted masonry structure, is the main circulation route. This is a broad top-lit curving space, that forms the social hub and focus of all activities, with half flights of stairs leading up to the nine individual classrooms which form the outermost ring of the building. These have aspects out to the west, south and east, enabling them all to enjoy the benefits of sunlight during the day.

The shape of the classrooms is irregular, with the radiating partition walls cranked at the mid-point to give the plan the effect of a rotating spiral. The irregularity of the rooms lends intimacy of scale and adds a visual interest suited to the needs of the very young. Each classroom also has a small external area immediately adjacent, protected by an overhanging wing of the spreading roof, which provides a semi-protected outside territory complementary to the internal classroom. At a half-level above each classroom is a second class area, reached via another half-flight of steps from the classroom and tucked under the slope of the roof.

These smaller areas at first floor level have a fully glazed inner wall, which is faceted on plan and overlooks the drum of the central walls. The children are therefore afforded views down into the common circulation areas and across into other class areas, as well as into the lower part of their own classroom. They can feel part of what is, to them, a substantial social community, while remaining safely enclosed within their own private territory. This understanding of the psychological as well as the physical needs of small children informs the whole design and underlies the school's success in providing a built environment capable of introducing them to life outside the home in a gentle and humane way.

Tucked into the northern segment of the plan are the kitchen and servery areas (the servery opening into the central hall which doubles as a dining room), together with music and drama facilities and a community lounge, all at ground level. Bishopstoke is typical of many schools in having a community role in addition to the children's education and the design incorporates extra facilities to accommodate community activities. At this point in the building the gently flattening slope of the roof plane is cut and lowered to reveal the structure of the principal central drum and the encircling girdle of roof glazing over the central 'street'.

The materials used are simple and appropriate to the form of the building and its setting. The topmost segment of the great sweeping form of the roof is clad in cedar wood shingles. The central and lower sections, down to the faceted projections of the generous overhanging eaves, are metal clad, the rhythm of the standing seams echoing the pattern of the glazing bars of the 'girdles' of rooflight, and set off at contrasting angles over each classroom to heighten the effect of movement and emphasize the constituent internal spaces. Walls are white block-work, clean and fresh against the green landscape setting and maximizing the reflection of daylight internally.

The school is clearly a joy to occupy and is a shining example of what vision and imagination can achieve within the rigorous context of local authority construction budgets given the will to lift ambitions above the most basic. That Hampshire should be the authority to demonstrate the possibilities is due very much to the leadership of its Chief Architect, Colin Stansfield Smith. His unique contribution both as a designer and as a catalyst for others won Colin Stansfield Smith the 1991 Royal Gold Medal for Architecture, the architectural profession's highest honour.

INTERNATIONAL CONVENTION CENTRE, CENTENARY SQUARE, BIRMINGHAM
Architects: Convention Centre Partnership
(comprising Percy Thomas Partnership and Renton Howard Wood Levin Partnership)

The new International Convention Centre in Birmingham contains a series of multi-purpose halls and convention facilities, and a world-class concert hall to house the Birmingham Symphony Orchestra.

This massive new complex is the country's largest convention centre. Located on a site between Cambridge Street and Broad Street, just outside the city's inner ring road, it links the heart of the city with its industrial heritage as part of the Broad Street development. This development has opened up new routes into the city centre, creating pedestrian routes through the central urban space, Centenary Square, and through the Convention complex to link with developments around the old Birmingham Canal. The complex boasts 11 separate halls of differing sizes and functional capabilities, a tall and spacious central Mall linking all the activities together, and an appropriately wide range of catering and other public facilities. The jewel among all these facilities is the new Symphony Hall, visually sumptuous and acoustically capable of matching the best concert halls in the world.

The early design stages for the project date from October 1983, when the City conducted a feasibility study on the Convention Centre in the area of Broad Street. In March 1984 Percy Thomas Partnership and Renton Howard Wood Levin were appointed as architects. This was followed by the appointment of Artec Inc., a New York-based company of theatre consultants and acousticians, to develop the acoustic design principles for all the halls and assist in the detailed design work. After confirmation of European Community funding, design work commenced in early 1986, continuing through the construction period into 1988, when a large team of site architects was established to co-ordinate the final designs for the main buildings and interiors. Sections of the building were completed for handover between August and December of 1990, and the fitting-out and commissioning processes culminated in the formal opening of the Convention Centre in April 1991.

The finished building, in reality a group of linked buildings, is monumental in size but manages to avoid being forbidding. It is structured in such a way as actively to encourage the movement of pedestrians through the heart of the Centre even though they may not be involved in any of the activities in the surrounding halls. The entrance to the complex is located without particular ceremony at the north-west corner of Centenary Square, where a pointed, glazed prow projects forward between the bulky volumes of the Symphony Hall to the south and the Exhibition Hall to the north. The prow is supported by four slender, blue-painted steel columns, with similar blue steel bracing spars inclined upwards from their mid-point to support the lattice edge beams of the dark-glazed canopy. By day the tinted glass conceals what is within, but drama is achieved at night when the spatial excitement of the mall and the dominating complexity of the trussed roof structure are seen to powerful effect from the square outside.

Once inside the doors, the visitor enters a world of semi-tropical trees, enticing flights of steps and escalators, bridges, balconies and huge chrome-finish pipes at all angles to the main axis, with views to further spaces beyond and below and eventually to the outside again. Cafes, shops and even a post office provide focal points for human activity in the quieter periods, but when the Centre is in full swing with a concert, exhibition or conference, the Mall becomes vast and dynamic, literally at the heart of Birmingham's cultural world.

The halls are arranged on each side of the Mall. On the left-hand side as one enters is the Symphony Hall, the largest and most magnificent of the spaces, designed to seat 2,200 people. It is intended primarily for classical concerts but has the flexibility to adapt to popular music, convention events and other forms of entertainment. Behind the hall is a suite of smaller rooms which can function either as a self-contained convention centre or house separate activities. The three smaller halls and the large Symphony Hall, together with their ancillary accommodation, form one half of the complex and line the southern side of the Mall.

On the other side of the Mall, and with its major planning grid set at 45° to the Mall, are to be found Halls 1, 3 and 4: Hall 1 has the largest raked-seat theatrical space, Hall 4 is a multi-purpose hall suitable for banqueting or exhibitions, while Hall 3 provides a further large but more basic multi-purpose hall which is self-contained and can be operated independently of the main centre. The Conference Auditorium (Hall 1) is designed to seat 1,500 people in two tiers, with direct access possible to the stage from all parts of the hall. The lower tier accommodates some 700 people and can be used without the enveloping upper tier by adjusting the lighting levels. Alternate rows of seats can also be adapted as writing tables, and the sophisticated technical back-up systems include 12 simultaneous translation booths at the sides of the hall. In addition, there is an enormous stage, capable of opening to a proscenium width of 22 metres and strong enough to support heavy loads such as cars, as well as a 56 metre high fly tower. The blue colour scheme for the seats and walls provides a cool but positive background for the many uses that this space can handle.

The centrepiece of the whole complex, upon which most care and attention to detail have been lavished, is the Symphony Hall. Like all new concert auditoria it has been subject primarily to the most rigorous of acoustic criteria, in order to provide a worthy home to a world-class orchestra. The presence nearby of railway tunnels, busy roads and potentially noisy crowds posed the first problem for the designers, who secured the requisite acoustic isolation by using techniques such as rubber mountings on the founda-

tion piles and structural isolation joints. The roof structure of the central mall was also designed to be self-supporting to avoid the possibilities of sound transfer as far as possible.

The science of acoustics has benefited greatly from new technology. The application of this to auditorium design has seen a gradual move away from the recently favoured wide-fan format of seating, which was derived more from visual criteria than acoustic, and back to the spatial proportions of nineteenth century halls.

Older halls tend to be narrower and longer on plan, taller in section and relatively smaller; their volume often corresponds approximately to a double cube. The rediscovery of the most appropriate geometric configurations of space for clarity and immediacy of sound has coincided with a growing appreciation of the value of being able to vary the given acoustic environment by means of acoustic canopies and curtains, and by openable reverberation chambers.

The reverberation chambers built into the flattened oval form of the hall are large volumes of space, comprising some 12,700 cubic metres. They are placed symmetrically immediately behind the platform and rise to the full height of the hall to join up with further chambers, located along the sides of the hall at high level. These permit the acoustics of the hall to be varied by the opening up of hinged panels which circle the top of the hall and extend downwards at each side of the platform. When fully opened the panels and chambers acting together can reputedly increase the hall's reverberation to that of a small cathedral, yet this increase in 'liveness' of the sound is achieved with no loss of clarity.

The internal layout and treatment of finishes are intended to exploit the spatial qualities of the hall and the smooth geometric lines of the curving balconies. Reflective metallic strips emphasize the flowing lines, and the warm welcoming colours of honey-brown hard-wood floors and a vibrant red for the seating and free-standing circular columns provide a homely but vibrant ambience throughout. The focal centrepiece to the rear of the platform is the new organ, manufactured in Germany, with its graceful asymetrical display of pipes in contrast to the symmetry of the hall.

Externally, the huge volumes of the principal halls are handled in a series of simply modelled forms, with faceted corners and set backs reducing the bulkiness of the composition. The architecture is competent and workmanlike rather than inspired, and offers little in the way of visual delight to passers-by. Yet the completed complex displays a sure mastery of the technical skills required to create first-class public entertainment and meeting places; a clear sense of organization in relating individual spaces to the public core and this in turn to the wider urban context, and a well thought-out response to a wide-ranging brief that required the complex to be capable of hosting almost any kind of event. The convention centre will do much to regenerate and expand cultural life in the city in the years to come.

ARCHAEOLOGY 1990–91

The Snettisham Hoard

According to a report by J. Pearson Andrew in *Coin News* for May 1991, it took a coroners' jury at King's Lynn, Norfolk, on March 7, 1991, only fifteen minutes to decide that the discovery of 63 torques or neck ornaments and associated items of precious metal were treasure trove and therefore the property of the Crown, or in this case the Duchy of Lancaster. A treasure trove verdict is usually returned when it can be demonstrated that the buried items of precious metal were deposited in the ground with the apparent intention of recovery. It may be assumed that the sheer magnificence of the material described in *Coin News* was such that it is unlikely that anyone would have abandoned the objects without intending to recover them at a later date.

The story started with a retired RAF Squadron Leader searching a field, with permission, after ploughing on the Ken Hill Estate at Snettisham, Norfolk. Four small fragments of torques and a coin were found with the use of a metal detector in 1989. In 1990 a hoard, comprising 'a mass of broken metalwork weighing 9.2 kg buried in what seems to have been a bronze vessel' was recovered. Assessment by the staff of the British Museum indicated that 'there were fragments of at least 50 torques, over 70 ingot rings/bracelets, three straight ingots and nine coins'. In November and December 1990 some three acres were investigated in detail and five more hoards were recovered, but 'no trace was discovered of a contemporary occupation of the site'.

The report by J. Pearson Andrew states that: 'four of the hoards were closely packed 'nests' of torques, each hoard being in a very small pit. All the metals were alloys in varying proportions of gold, silver and copper. The first hoard was buried in two instalments, with five silver, one silver/gold and four bronze torques on top, then a layer of earth before the lower deposit which has a massive gold/silver torque on top of five bronze torques and four ingot/bracelets.' The second, third, fourth and fifth hoards (this last being the richest) were not dissimilar in terms of composition although there were differences in the way the deposits had been made. It is reported that 'in all, the five hoards found in November 1990 produced 63 torques: 7 gold, 11 gold/silver, 6 silver/gold, 14 silver and 25 bronze'.

Although one piece from the lower deposit in the final hoard might be as old as the third century BC, it is thought likely on the evidence of the coins found with the hoards that a date 'in the first half of the first century BC, perhaps, *c.* 70 BC' could indicate a date for the deposition of the hoards which may all have been buried at the same time. There must always remain an element of doubt as to the precise reason for the burial of so much valuable material and an obvious suggestion would be for safety in time of threat. The conclusion reached by J. Pearson Andrew in the article in *Coin News* is that: 'The evidence points most strongly to the likelihood that the deposits were a veritable treasury, perhaps the possession of more than one individual, a family, or even a tribe, carefully and cunningly buried for safe keeping.'

Middle Saxon London

One of the duties which the archaeologist has to the public is to synthesize the results of a number of excavations so that knowledge of a particular period is advanced. Often this is a process drawn out over a number of years but a good example, spanning less than a decade, is encapsulated in the article by John Mills entitled *Before King Alfred: The Saxons in Town and Country* published in *Current Archaeology* Number 124 for May 1991. The article is based mainly on investigations in advance of development in central London, and the problem it addresses is, where was Middle Saxon London? While the documentary evidence of occupation in London can be taken to start with the foundation of St Paul's Cathedral in AD 604, the archaeological evidence in the City was of only late Saxon occupation. In 1984 two scholars working independently, Alan Vince and Professor Martin Biddle, both came to the conclusion that, as there was little evidence of Saxon occupation within the walls of the Roman city before the ninth century, earlier occupation must have been substantially outside those walls. In his summary John Mills says: 'Biddle suggested that Middle Saxon London comprised two elements: a trading and market settlement outside the walls, along the Strand, while the walled area of the old Roman city was occupied only by the elite, with few buildings. The latter might include St Paul's Cathedral Church, founded in 604, and possibly a Royal hall at Cripplegate. Contemporary writers probably used the name *Lundenwic* for the extra-mural settlement. Perhaps the area of the Aldwych ('the old *wic*' or town), at the junction of the Strand and Fleet Street ought to have received more attention!'

While there was little archaeological evidence to support the theory in 1984, in 1985 a major discovery was made at the Jubilee Hall next to Covent Garden. A rescue excavation there revealed a range of pits, gulleys and post holes which were taken to indicate fence lines and perhaps buildings spread out over a substantial area. An inhumation burial with a radiocarbon date of AD 630–675 was one of the earliest features. John Mills continues: 'Since then seven further excavations and a large number of watching briefs in the area have helped to confirm that Middle Saxon London was located in the vicinity of the Strand.' Of particular significance was the excavation at the National Gallery in Trafalgar Square. Mills reports that 'Test excavations in the cellars revealed three massive pits containing 5,500 animal bones and a range of artefacts including Ipswich ware, imported Badorf ware, bone combs and glass fragments'. No structures were found in the excavation but large quarry pits from which the Saxons had taken gravel suggested that the edge of the Saxon town was somewhere in the vicinity of Trafalgar Square. Dendrochronology was brought into play on the results of a small site at York Buildings on the river side of the Strand. Evidence was found of the waterfront, including some timber frontages still retaining bark which could be dated to AD 670–90. 'This may have been an embankment of brushwood at least 17 m wide, laid down on sandy foreshore and built up around oak and alder stakes driven into the ground. The revetments may have been used as a level area where vessels beached adjacent could be loaded and unloaded.' In 1989 excavations inside the basements of standing buildings at Shorts Gardens 'at the northern edge of the settlement area, have revealed extensive traces of industry, including iron-working. Eight hearths were discovered, one of which had been used for iron smithing, and there were quantities of slag and glass beads.'

Taken together a number of broad conclusions could be drawn. For example, it is reported that 'There were few sunken buildings – instead most were of timber, with wattle-and-daub walls and thatched roofs. Several sites, including Maiden Lane and Shorts Buildings, produced fragments of wall daub with whitewash.' The predominant pottery on all sites is Ipswich ware and the local chaff tempered ware, although on some sites it is noted that up to 20 per cent of the pottery appears to have been imported, mostly from northern France and the Rhineland. In addition to this, fragments of lava querns have been found which would have been imported from the Rhineland. So far as the extent of the settlement of Middle Saxon London is concerned, John Mills reports that 'Judging by the distribution of discoveries, the settlement extended 1 km along the river (from Trafalgar Square to Aldwych) and 600 m inland; whether it extended as far east as the Fleet river (i.e. the edge of the Roman city) has yet to be demonstrated. To the west the river bank at White-hall was low-lying and marshy and not so ideal for settlement.'

The end of Middle Saxon London was distinctive; Mills reports that 'by the later 9th century the site was abandoned, and occupation was transferred within the walls of the old Roman town. Ipswich ware typical of the 8th–9th century is not found within the walled city, while late Saxon Shelly wares typical of the 10th century are not found in the Strand settlement. We can even date this event precisely, for the Anglo-Saxon Chronicle records that in 886 "King Alfred occupied London" ... in part, the abandonment of the town may be related to the declining prosperity of continental trading emporia, caused by reduced silver supply and civil war. But the main reason must have been the devastating Viking raids which swept North-West Europe in the 9th century. *Lundenwic*, without walled defences, was particularly vulnerable to attack. It was raided in 842 and 871, and finally taken by the Viking Great Army in 872.'

Roman Britain

Britannia Volume XXI for 1990 includes a wide-ranging summary of work carried out on sites of the Roman period. Those of more general interest include the following. At the Castledykes marching-complex in Strathclyde another camp, some 25.5 acres in extent, has been identified from the air, with others north of the Roman fort. At Ladyward, Dumfries and Galloway, aerial survey has also found a fort on the left bank of Dryfe Water. This fort was about half an acre in extent and lay within a system of five ditches; two periods are suggested. On Hadrian's

Wall at South Shields fort, a second pair of third-century barracks was located beneath the courtyard building. The importance of drought conditions to the archaeologist was demonstrated at Brinkheugh, Northumberland, where the site of a postulated Roman bridge which carried either the Devil's Causeway or a branch from it over the River Coquet was found. It is reported that 'Masonry of the northern abutment, jointed with melted lead, survives in the river bank, and the remains of a rubble pier were noted in the river bed. Two trenches across the southern approach revealed the metalling of the road.'

Amongst the excavations at key Roman sites may be noted the excavations at 35–41 Blossom Street, York, where 'a cemetery overlay an earlier ditched enclosure, pits and rubbish dumps. A lead cremation ossuary, at least thirty-one inhumations and a mausoleum 5 m square were excavated. The mausoleum had been demolished in the Roman period and was cut by later inhumation graves.' At Ribchester, Lancs., it is reported that 'the clay and turf rampart of the first (early Flavian) fort was found to rest on a well-preserved timber strapping. Four large post-holes, *c.* 2 m deep, represented either a tower or part of the N. Gate. During demolition, three defensive ditches were buried beneath a spread of rampart material. The southern edge of the later *vicus* was bounded by the road to Kirkham, which showed several phases of metalling. To the north lay buildings marked by cobble foundations. The road overlay substantial signs of industrial activity, indicated by hearths and spreads of slag and charcoal, together with waterlogged organic material and preserved parts of timber buildings. This area was separated from the *vicus* to the north by a large vertical-sided ditch. Beside the road from the N. Gate of the second fort lay a large timber building associated with industrial features such as smelting and smithing slags. There were indications of contraction of settlement in the late Roman period when a cremation cemetery, now mostly ploughed away, encroached on the earlier inhabited area.'

Hoards of coins continue to be found with considerable frequency and among these may be noted the 1,070 antoniniani excavated at Boothsbank Farm, Greater Manchester, near the Roman road from Manchester to Wigan. The coins range in date from Gallienus to Diocletian, terminating in about AD 296. At Chalgrove, Oxon., a hoard of 3,823 billon antoniniani was found ending in about AD 274, while at Chalfont St Giles, Bucks., a hoard of about 9,000 billon antoniniani, terminating in the same year, is recorded. A hoard of 53 billon folles, ending about AD 317, is reported as being found in Milton Keynes. At Downside, Somerset, a hoard of 538 billon folles, terminating in about AD 317, is recorded and at Membury, Devon, a hoard of 236 denarii with a terminal date of about AD 43 is noted. Among the coins found in Hampshire were a hoard of 48 siliquae terminating about AD 410, at Whitchurch. It is reported that at Kingston upon Thames, Surrey 'excavation in a silted river-channel revealed much pottery and building-material, together with over 350 bronze coins, largely of the House of Constantine, some of which have been filed or hammered flat'.

At Wavendon Gate, Walton, Bucks., further excavations 'revealed at least eleven Iron Age round houses associated with ditched enclosures lying north of the second-century enclosure' previously found. For the later period 'three early Roman round houses and two first-century pottery kilns (one circular with central pedestal, the other sub-rectangular with paired rectangular pedestal)' were found. While no more cremations relating to the second-century cemetery were found, 'five of the early first century together with three undated cremations were found occurring haphazardly within both the Iron Age and Roman enclosures. Within the east side of the latter lay a pit 7 m in diameter and 3 m deep, entered by crude stone steps at the SW corner and containing waterlogged deposits which yielded three shoes and much wood, including a carved oak wheel-symbol attached to a tenon with nail-hole, evidently for fixing to some larger structure or vehicle. At the base of the pit lay a large section of elm-trunk. Close by a cockerel had been buried in a substantial stone-packed post-hole.'

Reports of aisled buildings of the Roman period during the year under review include part of an aisled building discovered during excavations at the Batten Hanger villa at Elsted in West Sussex. A previously discovered aisled barn at Barnwell, Northants., was recorded as measuring about 35 by 11 m; 'two rows of post-holes for the nave were backed to a depth of almost 2 m and suggest a substantial structure. The entrance lay at the S. end. The eastern wall was accompanied by a ditch, in the filling of which four late fourth-century pots had been deposited in a stone-lined hole. A later pit, c. 15 by 10 m, had been cut against the S. wall and also truncated the ditch.' The complex history of the aisled building at Littlecote Park Villa in Wiltshire was clarified, and at the aisled house at Shavards Farm at Meonstoke, Hants., important recovery work was undertaken. This latter aisled house is reported as being some 15 m by at least 30 m in extent and 'had been built in or after the mid third century over the burnt remains of a second-century building'. Perhaps in the early fourth century a new façade was built. 'The new SE wall had collapsed outwards, the upper part virtually intact, and the remains have been lifted by the British Museum... The fallen wall sealed late fourth-century coins and had been cut by early Saxon post-holes; it must have fallen before c. AD 500. The evident attention to architectural detail, the evidence of a clerestory, and the skilful use of contrasting colours in the choice of materials on the façade usefully clarify notions about this type of villa.'

Much important archaeological work continues to be undertaken as a result of external pressure caused by commercial development. In the City of London a further part of the Huggin Hill Baths was investigated. 'In the main room, containing over 100 *pilae*, a small area of mosaic survived. Many tiles carried the known stamp PP BR LON. In a second phase the western apse was converted into a separate room. To the west stood a massive solid foundation. The furnace lay to the north and beyond it other walls standing 3 m high revetted a terrace on which stood further walls; a 10 m length of water-pipe made of

ceramic tubes was also found in this area. The building became disused in the third century and was partly robbed. Traces of later clay and timber buildings with clay and gravel floors were found within the shell. The bath-house has been reburied in the hope of future display.' At the Stansted Airport Catering site at Takeley, Essex, it is reported that 'occupation is now thought to have started c. 75 BC with the erection of two post-built round houses and a six-post granary. About 50 BC a defensive ditch was dug and six or seven round houses surrounded by open gullies were built around the periphery, with a rectangular shrine, measuring 6 by 6.5 m, in the open centre. Occupation may have ceased c. 25 BC, but was resumed between c. AD 40 and 60 with a new round house in the NW angle and worship at the shrine attested by the deposit of over thirty brooches of Colchester types and of an onyx intaglio depicting Diomedes stealing the Palladium.'

The construction of the Brighton by-pass at Patcham, East Sussex, provided an opportunity for the investigation of the Celtic fields there. 'The system dates to the later prehistoric and Roman periods; some lynchets originated as flint banks against which soil later accumulated. A marling pit of possible Roman date and a mound yielding Iron Age and Roman sherds were also examined.' A threat of a different kind is the investigation of a site with the results remaining unpublished. At East Hill, Dartford, 'a large area of burials was stripped in a cemetery known from intermittent discoveries since 1792 and which had suffered several previous unpublished excavations. Eighty-three graves were excavated and a further 103 were visible. Of the few which yielded finds, a child's grave contained parts of a third-century colour-coated cup.' In addition, there were two lead coffins containing an adult and a child respectively as well as pottery, bronze objects and fragments of a glass vessel. 'Differences were noted both in density and in preservation between the northern and southern areas. The southern group were densely clustered, more orderly laid out and contained no grave goods and few surviving bones. This group appeared to be arranged in an arc around some focus to the east.'

Medieval Period

Amongst the extensive number of investigations relating to the Medieval period published in *Medieval Archaeology*, Volume XXXIV for 1990, may be noted the additional excavations of the deserted medieval village at Westbury, Milton Keynes, Bucks. The area will be destroyed by development and it is reported that 'The settlement appears to have been a collection of small and perhaps only loosely connected farmsteads, built around the intersection of a N.–S. and an E.–W. road. Evidence has been recovered of occupation from the 11th to 16th century, after which the site seems to have been largely abandoned. Westbury would seem to have undergone several changes of fortune during its life. There is clear evidence demonstrating both the subdivision and amalgamation of platforms, and of ploughing between building phases. Structural remains of the earlier buildings were slight, though the stone footings for a number of late Medieval timber buildings were well preserved. A wide variety of artefacts, particularly of iron and pottery, have also been recovered.'

At the site at 1–9 New Street, Chelmsford, Essex, also in advance of redevelopment, it is noted that 'Despite severe disturbance by Victorian brick buildings, the remains of 13th-century timber buildings were found, with a large pit to the rear, which produced mid 13th-century pottery. A more surprising discovery was that of Roman and early to middle Saxon pottery in the fill of a roadside ditch, which had been encroached on by the Medieval timber buildings. No Saxon settlement is known from this area of Chelmsford, although cemeteries have been found at Broomfield and Springfield.' In the City of London a series of excavations produced much interesting information. At 4 Billiter Street and 34–35 Leadenhall Street there were found pits 'filled with building rubble and large quantities of ceramic bell-mould. Documentary evidence confirms the presence of bell foundries on and around the site in the 14th and 15th centuries. Other notable finds include several complete Rouen-style baluster jugs from a barrel-lined well.' In an excavation at 21–38 Mincing Lane/85 Great Tower Street/12–18 Mark Lane 'A 13th- or 14th-century chalk-lined well was recorded. Its back fill contained a whalebone or walrus ivory book cover of 12th- or 13th-century date, with incised decoration of a griffin or winged lion.' At Skinmarket Place in Southwark there was an investigation of 'early Medieval ditches sealed by flood clays of 14th-/15th-century date. A pit cutting these clays contained two bear skeletons, probably derived from a Tudor bear-baiting ring known to have existed on the site (no trace of this was found).

At 50A Commercial Street, Hereford, a 'lost' Medieval open hall in an unlisted complex of buildings was discovered and surveyed. It is noted that 'The building is now Grade II listed. Although most of the side frames have been removed the wind-braced roof survives almost intact, even down to its smoke-louvre purlins. In style it is very similar to the surviving roof structure of the original Vicars' Choral in Castle Street, and is probably of late 14th- or 15th-century date. Structurally of two bays but stylistically divided into four by the inclusion of subsidiary trusses, the hall was almost square in plan and would have been associated with a building on the street frontage and a service wing behind. It has three sets of cusped and pierced wind braces, originally with fleurons on the cusps supporting two sets of chamfered purlins and the ridge. The trefoiled motif is carried on in the upper parts of the trusses and there is sufficient evidence to suggest a trefoiled pattern all around the upper parts of the walls.' At Waltham Cross, Herts., an excavation was undertaken at the base of the late 13th century Eleanor Cross as part of its restoration: 'the aim of the excavation was to examine the foundations of the monument and to examine whether any further steps survive. This is the only surviving Eleanor Cross to have been subject to a controlled archaeological investigation. A possible construction deposit was located and a wall foundation of sandstone pieces topped by ashlar blocks of the same Caen stone of which the Cross is built. It appears that the base of the original structure

extended a further 1.5 m beyond its present limit and that the current steps of the monument are a comparatively recent addition, probably 19th century. It is possible that the base of the Cross was altered before construction of the Falcon Inn which stood nearby and used the Cross base as part of its foundation.'

Among many excavations in medieval towns, an unusual result was obtained at one in Hull. At Blaydes Staithe in the High Street, excavations showed that successive land reclamation had moved the line of the waterfront to the east so that 'by c.1500 the site of the earlier waterfront was overlain by massive dumps of clays intermixed with organic material. Set into this new surface were two large stave-built casks or vats. Each was c.2 m in diameter and built of oak staves, bound with ash or willow hoops. They were joined at the base by a wooden pipe, which would formerly have had a sluice at one, or possibly both, ends. They appear to have been intended as live tanks for keeping freshly landed lobsters, crabs or shellfish in. The bottom 1 m or so of each cask was recessed into clay-packed pits – thereby keeping their contents cool. Fragments of Raeren stoneware were recovered from this packing.' At Guildhall Lane, Leicester, investigations were carried out into a 12th-century cellar first recorded in the 19th century. 'The building almost certainly represents the ground floor of a 12th-century town house of the "hall and cellar" type; the inserted S. wall may point to the later subdivision of the upper hall (now destroyed) to create a solar. Limited excavation has taken place in the interior of the building. Evidence for the original mortar floor survives in places; pottery from an occupation layer above this is dated to c.1150. No definite Medieval levels have been found which predate the building.'

At the ruined All Saints' Church at Beachamwell, Norfolk, the west wall, which had contained a decorated window and a coat of arms dated 1612, collapsed. The rubble was sorted through and it is reported that 'large quantities of hitherto invisible reused stonework in 14th- and 15th-century styles, with traces of burning, was recovered, and also a fragment of a late Saxon wheelheaded cross, of which only three certain and one possible examples were previously known from the county'. In advance of grave-digging, important excavations were undertaken at Eynsham Abbey in Oxfordshire and among the results may be noted that 'Early Saxon occupation is represented by a sunken featured building and stone post pits. The coin-dated backfilling of a large well presents the first securely dated mid 8th-century deposit excavated in the Oxford region. Probably for the first time from middle Saxon England, a fragment of wall face from the superstructure of a major timber framed building has been found. Preserved and protected by the depression from the settlement of the mid 8th-century well filling, this building fragment may date to the later 8th or 9th century.'

At Telford, Shropshire, Apley Castle Stables, known to contain parts of a medieval fortified and moated manor house, was investigated and it is reported that the work 'showed the Medieval house to be substantially intact. It consisted of a hall, with a two-storey service block at the low end, a solar block at the high, next to which was a first-floor chapel whose fixtures were almost intact. It still retained an ogee-headed piscina and a two-light window with ogee-heads looking down into the hall. Its large W. window looked into the solar block, which may have been a secondary Medieval addition. The chapel included remains of 14th-century wall-paintings but these had been damaged as a result of the roof being removed. The entire S. wall of the hall had been removed in the late 18th century and replaced, removing traces of the probable oriel. The N. doorway of the cross-passage survives, as does the original centrally positioned two-centred doorway into the service block. Chamfered jambs have unusual bottle or flagon stops. A second two-centred doorway in the same wall was added later. The hall was once lit by at least one large window but the original fenestration was remodelled in the 17th century. Despite later additions it is clear that this is one of the most significant Medieval houses in E. Shropshire.'

In Somerset it is noted that 'a small cast copper-alloy censer was recovered from the immediate neighbourhood of Glastonbury Abbey. The exact find spot is uncertain but it is thought to have been in Silver Street within the northern precinct of the Abbey. This casual find is an import from the Eastern Mediterranean and is thought to be of 7th-century date. The censer is an intriguing westerly outlier of E. Mediterranean workshop products which appeared in England mainly concentrated in the wealthy cemeteries of Kent and East Anglia. The Glastonbury censer may well have Christian connections.'

Post-Medieval Period

A comprehensive summary of work relating to post-medieval Britain is to be found in *Post-Medieval Archaeology* Volume 24 for 1990. Amongst the considerable variety of investigations undertaken may be noted the work at Edinburgh Castle, and in particular the report that 'Seven metres of deposits were completely removed at the Guardhouse Tattoo Store to create a new gift shop. The E. end of this area produced evidence of a large, angle-pointed bastion, the N. part of which projected northwards into what is now Princes Street Gardens. This can be dated to the later 15th/early 16th centuries. Evidence was found to suggest that each successive construction phase occurred in direct response to damage caused during the sieges of 1544, 1573, 1640 and 1650. This bastion contained an inner gateway which allowed the main access road to pass through it, before making a dog-leg S. to follow the present road-line in the E. of the Portcullis Gate. Part of the gateway survived in the outer face of the E. end wall of the bastion. This can be seen today as a 4 m-high infilled, flat, pointed archway.' There were a number of other changes in that area and discoveries elsewhere in the Castle, for example 'At the coal yard, earlier ditches were partially infilled by the construction of the spur in the mid 16th century, the N. portions finally being filled when access was realigned in the first half of the 17th century. The top backfill was cut into by at least 16 graves laid out in rows with no intercutting. These burials were of young male adults, some of whom were of above average

stature. A number of these exhibited signs of healed traumatic injuries. The cemetery is dated to *c.*1650, when Cromwell's troops were garrisoned in the Castle.'

At Plymouth, Devon, an excavation was undertaken at the Chinahouse, which is described as 'the sole survivor from a group of three large limestone warehouses erected *c.*1650 by George Rattenbury, a prominent Plymouth merchant'. It is further noted that 'The excavation confirmed that the quay warehouses and a small dwelling house adjoining the N. warehouse were probably all built in a single reclamation episode in the mid 17th century. A group of 1,643 sherds from the make-up layers of the quay contains 98 per cent unused plain Saintonge wares, principally large three-handled jugs, some smaller jugs, chaffing dishes and bichrome bowls and dishes, which must represent breakages from a ship's cargo. The Chinahouse quay and warehouses represent a remarkable investment so soon after the end of the Civil War.' The warehouses were used for a number of purposes in the 17th and 18th centuries and 'between 1768–70 the property was occupied by William Cookworthy's porcelain factory, hence the name Chinahouse. No evidence of the factory was found in the excavations. Between 1778 and 1786 the S. warehouse was demolished and at this period or a little later both the N. and W. warehouses were substantially rebuilt'.

Investigations in the City of London include work in advance of the relaying of the railway line between Blackfriars and Holborn Viaduct Stations, which took place over a considerable area of the lower Fleet Valley. 'To the N. of Ludgate Hill, parts of the Fleet Prison were excavated, including the E. perimeter wall, the rooms inside the main prison building and the courtyard. One room contained a hearth in brick and Reigate stone'. It is reported that at Thames Exchange in Upper Thames Street 'the base frame of Three Cranes Stairs was located, an important ferry terminal, which continued in use until Southwark Bridge was completed in 1819. A waterlogged pit contained several wooden bowls, two brooms, packing boxes, a basket and a ball and skittle, together with Spanish, German and English domestic pottery. Industrial ceramics used in sugar-refining were also found.' At 69 Upper Thames Street it is reported that 'foreshore deposits removed from a coffer-dam in the River Thames were systematically searched with metal-detectors and yielded large numbers of artefacts of 16th- to 18th-century date. These include small-denomination coins, a series of late 16th-century pewter tokens, a dagger, a sheet copper-alloy candlestick and part of a miniature lead cupboard, probably a toy. A large group of 16th/17th-century cloth-seals includes examples from England, France and Germany, together with many issues of London dyers; these probably derive from nearby dye-houses.'

A certain amount of work was carried out during the year on village sites and at Gooseham, Wedmore, Somerset, 'the remains of the tiny lost settlement of Gooseham have been traced in a field near Matcham. Field work suggests that four plots were originally laid out. Three cottages and gardens are shown on the 1838 tithe map. The 1851 census records three households, totalling fourteen adults and nine children. Two cottages are shown on the 1886 OS map, but were abandoned soon after. One cottage can still be clearly defined, with part of a gable end and remains of collapsed walls. A stone-lined well with paved surround, which served the community, is still used for watering cattle.' The site of a lost hamlet has also been located in Tadham Moor, Somerset, alongside Sand Drove. The hamlet was part of the post-enclosure settlement built on the peat moors and was in existence by 1841. It appears that about ten plots were originally planned, although only four buildings are shown on the 1886 OS map. The main building became the local public house (occupied by Joseph Roper, cider seller, and his family); by 1886 it was called Sand Drove Farm. The settlement was abandoned at the beginning of this century. Of the four houses, traces of the farm alone survive. The house platform, with collapsed walls of brick and rubble, two yards enclosed with a bank and ditch, and a circular stone-paved platform (probably a haystack base) remain.

A totally different kind of investigation was that undertaken at Painswick, Glos., where there was an excavation of the 'footings of a Gothic pavilion, formerly located on top of the vaulted Eagle House. It was built in the 1740s. Its E. side was shown in Thomas Robins' painting of the garden, dated 1748, and its W. side was illustrated in a slightly later

painting, also by Robins. It had been demolished by 1820. The coursed limestone dwarf walls (stabilized by buttresses) on which the superstructure had rested, was partially robbed, but enough survived to demonstrate that the pavilion itself formed an irregular hexagon. Each of its sides measured 7 ft 6 in but its N.–S. axis was longer than the W.–E. one. Pieces of ochre-plaster rendering with lathmarks on the back indicate that the pavilion was made of wood. As suggested by the paintings, its roof consisted of Welsh slates, several of which were found in the demolition layers. The pavilion can now be reconstructed with considerable accuracy by combining the artistic and the archaeological evidence.'

A contrast was the investigation of the Devon Great Consols Mine and Arsenic Works at Tavistock Hamlets in Devon. An inventory of the remains of the 19th-century copper mine and a survey of the 1921–25 arsenic work was carried out and it is noted that 'This was the richest copper mine in Europe in the mid-19th century. In the 1860s arsenic production began, and in 1869 half the world's output came from the mine. All surface structures other than a few cottages were levelled when operations ceased in 1902. The standing arsenic works was built between 1921 and 1923, and closed in 1925. The remains of most of the buildings survive, enabling the manufacturing process to be clearly traced.'

SCIENCE AND DISCOVERY

Antarctic sea-urchins.—The method of reproduction generally used by sea-urchins is to release millions of gametes into the water with the hope that a few of the resulting larvae will survive and reach adulthood. However, this procedure is definitely not followed by two new species of sea-urchin found in the Antarctic. Bruno David and Richard Moori, biologists at the University of Dijon, France, have discovered that these two Antarctic species protect their young by allowing them to develop in womb-like pouches within the shell of the female until they are about 4 mm long and have fully developed spines.

The biologists first noted what looked like skeletonal pouches in dry specimens at the Smithsonian Institution. They then examined fresh specimens from the Weddell Sea and found that the female sea-urchin produces up to five eggs, laid in individual pouches. It is thought that the male releases sperm into the water close to the female and that the female wafts the sperm towards the aperture on top of the urchin and into the pouches. The fertilized egg develops into a miniature urchin, missing out the larva stage.

The biologists have also discovered how the sea-urchin gives birth through an aperture only 1 mm across. The plates ringing the apical aperture are connected by elastic collagen tissue which allows them to fold inwards, thus opening the birth canal. The young urchins are thought to work their way up this canal using their spines.

The skeleton of the new Antarctic species is similar to that found in the ancient forms of echinoderms. The older types have either a ventral skeleton made up of an orderly arrangement of plates, or a less organized dorsal skeleton with collagen between the plates. Most sea-urchins have only the ventral skeleton but the two new species seem to have more in common with the dorsal type of skeleton.

Archaeopteryx challenged.—The *Archaeopteryx*, discovered in 1863 in the Jurassic limestones of Bavaria, is of prime importance in the theory of evolution because it was at a stage half-way through the process of evolving from a reptile or dinosaur to a bird. It had teeth and it also had feathers. Whether or not it was able to fly in the modern sense is open to debate. It is generally considered to be the oldest bird, but this accepted fact is now being questioned by finds in Texas which are thought to be 225 million years old, some 75 million years older than the *Archaeopteryx*.

Sankar Chatterjee of the Texas Tech University, in an article in The Royal Society's *Philosophical Transactions*, describes the discovery of two fossilized bird-like skeletons in a Texas quarry. The palaeontologist first reported his discovery some three years ago but it was greeted with scepticism, mainly because it had taken so long for him to prepare the paper describing the finds. The two fossils, named *Protoavis texensis* (i.e. first bird from Texas), indicate that the creatures were about the size of a pheasant but had a long bony tail. The rear portions resemble a small meat-eating dinosaur but the front parts, the skull, neckbones, forelimbs and shoulder are birdlike. According to the report, the creature could fly well

and had already developed 'flapping flight'. It also has the saddle-shaped surfaces between the vertebrae of its neck required to make the neck extremely flexible, a typically birdlike feature. Dinosaurs had two holes in the temple behind the eye socket to accommodate muscle bulges. In both the *Protavis* and modern birds, these holes have merged with the eye socket. This enables the skull to become flexible and allows movement in the upper jaw. Dinosaurs and the *Archaeopteryx* could not move their upper jaws and their skulls were rigid.

There will obviously be argument about the new find. One point will centre around the fact that the *Archaeopteryx* had feathers but the *Protoavis* definitely had not.

Ball lightning.—Throughout history there have been stories of balls of fire travelling through the air, passing through windows and generally behaving in very strange ways. Often these have been observed during thunderstorms but there have been cases when they have been seen in fair weather. They are usually described as a ball of fire about 25 cm in diameter and having a white, red or orange colour. Some scientists have been sceptical about their existence but physicists from Japan have produced the phenomenon in the laboratory, giving credence to a theory put forward in the 1950s which suggested that ball lightning was produced by a plasma discharge caused by interference between radio waves.

Y. H. Ohtsuki of Waseda University in Tokyo and H. Ofuruton of the Tokyo Metropolitan College of Aeronautical Engineering used a microwave oscillator to generate up to 5 kilowatts of microwave power at a frequency of 2.45 gigahertz. They then guided the radiation into an airfilled metal cavity 161 mm in diameter and 370 mm long. The microwaves were reflected up and down the tube, setting up standing waves with 6 antinodes. They filmed several different types of plasma discharge originating at the antinodes. One type varying in colour from white or blue to red-orange moved out of the cavity and into the waveguide through which the microwaves were being fed. When a 3 mm thick ceramic board was placed between the cavity and the waveguide, the plasma moved through the board without damaging it.

The experimenters varied the basic experiments, in one case using a 100 mm long copper bar in the cavity. The plasma balls were seen to travel along the bar. Even when a strong wind was introduced, some of the plasma balls travelled along the bar against the wind.

Brightest quasar.—British astronomers have identified what is thought to be the brightest quasar yet discovered. The object does not qualify as the most distant quasar, although it is not far short. It has a red shift of 4·7, whereas the record for the most distant quasar known at present stands at 4·89.

Richard McMahon of the Institute of Astronomy at Cambridge and Michael Irwin of the Royal Greenwich Observatory, also now at Cambridge, found the new quasar by digitizing the information on 100 photographic plates and using a computer to search the data for such objects. Each of the plates, which were taken by the UK Schmidt Telescope in Australia, shows about 250,000 objects. The astronomers picked out from the data about 50 promising objects and then used the 2·5 metre Isaac Newton Telescope in the Canary Islands to determine the red shift of each object. The quasar, BR 1202–07, has a magnitude of 17·5. The fact that it is so bright and at the same time so far away, makes it the brightest-known quasar.

If the currently accepted figure for the age of the Universe is correct (i.e. about 15 thousand million years), the quasar as we now see it is within a few thousand million years of the Big Bang, the birth of the Universe. Bright quasars are thought to be supermassive black holes in the core of newly born galaxies. As they pull matter into them, the gravitational energy is converted into intense radiation. McMahon thinks that BR 1202–07 has a mass of about ten thousand million Suns and that it is swallowing matter at the rate of 100 solar masses each year.

Because this new object is so bright, it will permit detailed study, using high dispersion spectroscopy, of the intervening clouds and galaxies. This is of prime importance in learning about the distribution of mass in the Universe.

Brightest star.—A star in the constellation of Cygnus has just been identified as the brightest star in our Galaxy. It is so bright that if it were placed at the same distance from the Sun as Proxima-Centauri, the nearest star to the Sun, it would appear several times brighter than the full Moon.

The star, VI Cygni No 12, is a blue supergiant which has a surface temperature of 13,000 K and shines at visual wavelengths with a luminosity of about 900,000 Suns. It is brighter than some complete galaxies. It is thought that the star lies in a group of more than 100 hot blue stars at a distance of some 5,700 light-years. The group is known as the Cygnus OB2 Association. Some astronomers are not sure that VI Cygni No 12 should be associated with this group and suggest that it is much nearer and therefore not so luminous. To determine the absolute brightness of a star, it is necessary to determine two quantities, its apparent brightness and its distance. The former quantity is easy to find but the determination of the latter can be a difficult exercise. Philip Massey and Anthea Thompson of Kitt Peak National Observatory have studied the Cygnus OB2 Association in detail, including VI Cygni No 12. They are convinced that the star is genuinely a member of the Association, whose distance is known from other data.

The astronomers say that there is some uncertainty about the calculations for the luminosity because the star is surrounded by a thick cloud of dust. The cloud absorbs so much light from the star that, although it is a blue supergiant, it appears red to the observer on the Earth. The astronomers say that but for the dust, the star would be visible to the naked eye. They claim that the dust cloud absorbs about 10,000 times as much light as it lets through. If this absorption is found to be overestimated, then the star's intrinsic luminosity will have been overestimated and it may lose its place on the luminosity scale. Even so, it will still be exceptionally bright, brighter than the star Rigel, the luminous blue supergiant in the constellation of Orion.

Bright Galaxy.—What is claimed to be the most luminous object in the Universe has been identified by an international team of astronomers led by Michael Rowan-Robinson of Queen Mary and Westfield College, London. It is 30,000 times brighter than the Milky Way but what is more unusual is that it emits most of its radiation at infra-red wavelengths.

The team have been trying for some time to identify galaxies which emit infra-red radiation. Their starting point was a list of such sources recorded by the Infra-red Astronomical Satellite (IRAS) launched in 1983. Amongst the faintest of these sources was an object listed as IRAS F10214 + 4724. The team found a faint visual object near this position on existing photographs and then used the William Herschel Telescope at La Palma, Canary Islands, to record its spectrum. To their surprise, they found that the object had a very high red shift, 2·286, indicating that it was a very distant object and that they were looking at it as it was when the Universe was approximately a quarter of its present age. The extreme distance makes the object the most luminous infra-red object known, the infra-red radiation exceeding the visual radiation by a factor of over 100. This raises many questions, including the basic ones of what kind of object it is and the source of the infra-red radiation. It is thought that the radiation comes from dust heated by an unseen source. Some say this must be a quasar but Rowan-Robinson believes that it is related to a starburst galaxy. In such cases, much of the gas in a galaxy is suddenly turned into young hot stars producing ultraviolet radiation. This radiation is absorbed by the surrounding dust clouds and these in turn radiate the energy away in the form of infra-red radiation.

It is hoped that these questions may be resolved by radio studies using the Very Large Array radio telescope in New Mexico. The presence of a central radio source will indicate a central quasar.

Buckminsterfullerene.—A molecule shaped like a soccer ball and consisting of 60 carbon atoms has been identified in interstellar space. It was discovered by a team of physicists and chemists led by Harry Kroto of Sussex University. This discovery was quickly followed by its identification on the Earth, where it can be found in chimneys or anywhere where there are sooty flames. The structure of the molecule is similar to the geodesic domes designed by Buckminster Fuller and the molecule has been named buckminsterfullerene, or fullerene, in his honour.

Carbon has the special property of being capable of combining with other elements to form very large molecules; organic chemistry is based on this property. Even when carbon alone is involved, the formation of large molecules with a wide range of properties is well known. On the Earth, crystalline carbon forms include graphite, in which the atoms form flat plates and which is used as a lubricant, and diamond, which has a tightlocking three dimensional structure. The fullerene molecule is constructed of carbon atoms fitting together mostly in hexagons, like chicken wire wrapped round a ball.

Fullerene was discovered in dark interstellar clouds and is believed to have been formed from stellar winds blown from the surface of ageing stars which have formed carbon in nuclear synthesis. The presence of graphite in these clouds has been known for some time. The presence of fullerene was identified by its natural vibrations, which have a frequency in the radio waveband.

There are many possible uses for the new molecule. It may turn out to be a better lubricant than graphite. When doped with a small quantity of potassium, the resulting compound behaves like a metal and has been found to be superconducting at a temperature of 19 K ($-254°C$). However, practical applications of the new compound are very limited because of the highly reactive properties of potassium. Research is being carried out with other doping materials, e.g. rubidium, and further uses for fullerene and its derivatives may be discovered in the near future.

Chiron.—When Chiron was first discovered in 1977 by Charles Kowal at the Palomar Observatory, it created much confusion in the minds of astronomers. Its orbit lay further out in the solar system than any known asteroid, between the orbits of Saturn and Uranus, yet it did not have the appearance of a comet. Subsequent research pointed to it being a comet because a huge coma of gas and dust formed around it as it moved closer to the Sun. This explanation has recently been questioned because Chiron has been found to be much larger than previously thought. Originally, it was considered to have a diameter of about 180 km and to reflect 10 per cent of the sunlight falling on it, but recent work indicates that it has a diameter of up to 372 km and that it reflects only 2·7 per cent of the incident light. This implies that it has no connection with comets and that it is just a planetesimal (a small body formed in the early stages of the solar system) that was ejected from the inner solar system when the planets were formed.

This recent work has been the result of studies carried out by American astronomers from Arizona and California, using visual and infra-red wavelengths. They suspect that Chiron may radiate heat unevenly because its pole lies in the plane of the orbit. This means that part of the surface would be in permanent darkness for considerable periods.

Astronomers from the Lowell Observatory do not support the non-comet theory and have recently published more evidence in favour of it being a comet; for example, they have detected the emission of cyanide gas from Chiron. The discovery in February 1991 by Rob McNaught of Adelaide University of another asteroid, 1991 DA, with an orbit that takes it out beyond the orbit of Uranus, adds fuel to the fire. Although this new object exhibits no features to show it is a comet, there is strong belief that it may be a rare example of a burned-out comet.

It is certain that Chiron holds more surprises and astronomers are looking forward to 1996 when Chiron approaches closest to the Sun and hence much nearer to the Earth.

Cloud Satellites of the Earth.—About 30 years ago, observational evidence was put forward for the existence of two new natural satellites of the Earth. These were not in the form usually expected for satellites but clouds of dust particles orbiting the Earth at the same distance as, but about 60° ahead and behind, the Moon. These orbiting positions are known as the L_4 and L_5 Lagrangian points, gravitationally stable positions between two bodies where it is possible for dust and small grains to collect. The existence of such satellites would not be unique to the Earth; such positions relative to the planet Jupiter are known to harbour minor planets, the so-called Trojan asteroids.

The original detections were made visually by Kazimierz Kordylewski of Krakow Observatory, Poland, but the clouds were very difficult to detect, even under ideal conditions when interference from the zodiacal light and gegenschein could be eliminated. In 1975, J. R. Roach reported that he had identified the clouds using the OSO6 satellite by observing the area opposite the Sun and watching for the clouds to pass into the Earth's shadow. Even so, there was reluctance to accept the presence of the clouds.

Recently Maciej Winiarski of Jagiellonian University claimed that he had detected the clouds photographically. He has developed techniques to detect sky brightness changes by such small amounts as 0·02 to 0·04 magnitudes. His analysis involved the study of 18 photographic plates of the L_5 region and 36 reference plates of the same region of the sky when the L_5 point was not present. After eliminating the effects of the zodiacal light, he found evidence of the clouds. They were several degrees across and wandered 10° or more from the theoretical L_5 point. Winiarski says that the cloud satellites are redder than the gegenschein and suggests that the clouds originate from lunar dust thrown clear by bombardment. This would make the material in the clouds different from the normal interplanetary dust.

Cold dark matter.—The gravitational influence it exerts on stars and galaxies suggests that over 90 per cent of the mass of the universe is in the form of non-luminous or, as it is generally called, dark matter. Over the past few years there has been much debate as to whether this dark matter is hot or cold. Recent observations made from the South Pole seem to rule out the possibility of hot dark matter, such as neutrinos moving at or near to the speed of light.

Theories supporting cold dark matter suggest that it consists of slow-moving particles that clump together in the same way as ordinary matter. Although no cold dark matter has ever been discovered, theory predicts that it exists in the form of particles called axions and photinos. Computer models show that if bright galaxies are embedded in cold dark matter, they will form clusters and chains as the Universe expands, similar to those observed. Small deviations from this model have created difficulties and some investigators have indicated that the model is not sound.

However, the theory has received a boost from the results of investigations carried out by researchers from the Canadian Institute for Theoretical Physics, the University of Oxford and the University of California at Santa Barbara. They have studied the records of cosmic background radiation made at the South Pole and compared them with the predictions for both hot and cold dark matter. The dark matter models are frequently described by a quantity known as the biassing factor. If the distribution of bright galaxies is the same as the distribution of dark matter, the factor is 1. If the distribution of bright galaxies is more clustered than the dark matter, as required by cold dark matter theories, the factor is greater than 1. In hot dark matter models, the biassing factor is much less than 1. The new cosmic background radiation studies indicate a value greater than 0·86, which rules out all the current hot dark matter theories.

More will be known about dark matter when the results from the Cosmic Background Explorer Satellite (COBE), now in orbit, become available.

Death of dinosaurs.—Each year brings further evidence to support the theory that a huge meteoroid hit the Earth and caused much damage, including wiping out the dinosaurs and other life forms, at the end of the Cretaceous period some 65 million years ago. The latest evidence is based on geological discoveries in Mexico and parts of the West Indies; of prime importance is the discovery in Haiti of glass tektites from the era. Much of the previous evidence was circumstantial because there was no direct evidence of a crater or of products formed by impact. The tektites in Haiti have provided the latter.

Past evidence derived from shocked minerals indicates that the impact associated with the boundary between the Cretaceous/Tertiary (K/T) periods occurred on continental crust, probably in or close to North America. The only known crater in the region of the right age is the Manson crater (35 km in diameter) but this had been dismissed as the relevant crater because of its small size.

Research carried out over the last decade has revealed the presence of a buried impact crater in the Yucatan province of Mexico, the Chicxulub crater with a diameter of 135 km. Shocked quartz grains as large as 1 mm found some 50 km from the rim of the crater have provided evidence in addition to the gravity and magnetic anomalies previously identified. The discovery of tektites in Haiti precisely on the K/T boundary has provided the confirming evidence for the impact.

It is now suggested that there were two impacts at the critical time, at Manson and at Chicxulub. The effect of such impacts would have been disastrous; for example, the tsunami (surface wave) produced would have been between 500 and 1,000 m high. To complicate matters further, there is evidence that the age of the 105 km diameter Popigai crater in the USSR should be reassessed from 30 to 65 million years. If the older age is found to be correct, the mass extinction of dinosaurs and other species was caused by a multiple impact, adding to the severe conditions which would have existed at the time.

Firefly flashes.—One of the most spectacular natural phenomena is the flashing in unison of huge swarms of fireflies, which can be seen in south-east Asia. To appreciate fully the phenomenon, one should imagine a very large tree with a firefly on each leaf; all the insects flash in unison every two seconds, lighting up the tree, but in between flashes the tree is in complete darkness.

The question raised is why the fireflies flash in unison. Renato Mirollo and Steven Strogatz have recently provided a mathematical proof of a conjecture first put forward by C. S. Peskin. They showed that synchrony is the rule for mathematical models in which each firefly interacts with every other. The mathematical model consists of a population of oscillators coupled together by a visual signal. In previous work the coupling was assumed to be smooth but in 1975 Peskin formulated a model where the oscillators were coupled discontinuously. His conjecture was that whatever the initial conditions, eventually all oscillators became synchronized. Mirollo and Strogatz provided the proof.

Peskin's model involved component oscillators in which the voltage built up gradually. As soon as it reached a set value, it would fire and then immediately fall to zero again. The oscillators were pulse-coupled, i.e. they would only affect a neighbour at the moment of firing. This increases the appropriate variable in each neighbour by a fixed amount, causing it to fire if it exceeded the set amount. The proof put forward by Mirollo and Strogatz shows that, regardless of the initial conditions, two oscillators will lock together, i.e. stay in phase, and will not unlock. A multiple sequence of events produces the condition that all oscillators will eventually become in phase.

There are many cases of biological oscillators which tend to work in unison, e.g. the pace-maker cells of the heart, the insulin-secreting cells of the pancreas, crickets chirping in unison, and groups of women whose menstrual periods become mutually synchronized. It appears that all the systems attain synchrony by the same mathematical mechanism of absorption.

Gold on the sea-bed.—Peter Herzig of the Aachen University of Technology in Germany and colleagues have discovered gold grains in the sulphide minerals on the sea floor in an area where a new oceanic floor is being formed. In these locations, hot fluid from hydrothermal vents mixes with cold water and the gold precipitates out. It has been known for some time that sulphide minerals deposited at ancient sites where the sea floor is spreading are important sources of metals. Theoretical studies carried out in Canada have shown that the sulphides should contain gold but until the recent discovery geologists had found it only in minute quantities, up to seven parts per million. No one had discovered gold in the form of discrete grains.

Herzig, together with Yves Fouquet of the French Institute for the Exploitation of the Sea in Brest, France, and Ulrich von Stackelberg of the Federal Institution of Geosciences and Natural Resources in Hanover, used a submersible named *Nautile* to examine the Valu Fa ridge. The ridge lies 1,100 metres under the south-western Pacific Ocean at a latitude 22°S. and west of the Tonga trench. It is part of a region known as the Lau back-arc spreading centre. At the Lau back-arc, material is added to the ocean floor much more slowly than at mid-oceanic ridges. Samples revealed microscopic grains of gold, as large as 5 micrometres across, in metallic form and not as a trace element in other minerals. The grains occur only in the sulphide samples but have an unusually high overall concentration of gold, between 12 and 20 parts per million.

Earlier investigations at mid-oceanic ridges failed to find metallic gold, possibly due to the volcanic rocks at mid-oceanic ridges having a different composition. If geologists can discover the mechanism whereby the gold is deposited, it could lead to the discovery of further deposits, possibly with even higher concentrations of the precious metal.

The little ice age.—A period in the 17th century experienced weather so severe that during some winters rivers such as the Thames froze over. Climatologists refer to the period as the little ice age. At this time very few sunspots were seen on the Sun's surface for about 50 years, a period known as the Maunder minimum. Tree rings from this period have undergone radiocarbon-14 studies (which indicate the quantity of cosmic rays coming from the Sun) and these show that the Sun's magnetic activity was also much lower than usual. One theory is that the Maunder minimum was just an extension of the normal period of low solar activity in the usual 11 year cycle, but this idea is questioned by many astronomers.

Discussion centres on the possibility of a larger than normal variation in the Sun's energy output. To explain the little ice age solely in terms of solar variability, the Sun's energy output would have to have fallen by between 0·2 and 0·5 per cent. Recent estimates of solar variability suggest a maximum of about 0·1 per cent. Work carried out in the United States on the variability of output from stars similar to the Sun has shown that of 13 stars for which monthly records have been kept, nine show a cycle similar to that of the Sun but the remaining four have remained magnetically 'flat'. If this 'flatness' can be attributed to something like the Maunder minimum, and if the magnetic activity during the Maunder minimum was much lower than that during a normal sunspot minimum, then the little ice age could be linked to a fall in solar output.

These findings are in line with other radio-carbon data which suggest that there have been similar minima during the last few thousand years, also linked with cold spells. However, research into future cold spells may be futile as man's activities may affect the climate to a far greater extent than any natural fluctuations.

Halley's Comet.—Halley's Comet travels round the Sun in a highly eccentric orbit which takes about 76 years. Its nearest approach to the Sun and Earth last occurred in 1986. Like all comets as they move away from the Sun, activity in the nucleus of Halley's Comet gradually dies down and by the time it has reached distances comparable with the orbits of Saturn and Uranus, activity is virtually nil and the comet then appears in even the largest telescopes as a faint point of light.

On February 12, 1991, Olivier Hainaut and Alain Smette of the European Southern Observatory in Chile took a routine one-hour photograph of Halley's Comet, expecting to record only a faint speck of light. Instead they found on the television screen a large patch of bright light. At first they thought they had photographed a bright nebula by mistake or recorded a ghost image of a bright star reflected in the telescope's optics. However, over the next few nights they found that the light moved along a line identical to that in which the comet was moving and they realized that something strange had happened to Halley. Measurements of the bright patch showed that the 15 km nucleus had ejected a cloud of dust with a diameter of 300,000 km. The cloud reflected sunlight, producing the bright patch, which is some 300 times brighter than that of the comet's nucleus. Ten days later, Smette used the 3·5 metre New Technology Telescope to obtain a spectrum of the cloud. It showed that the cloud consisted mainly of dust and had a complete absence of emission spectral lines of any gas.

The outburst has completely baffled astronomers. As the comet is at a distance of 14 astronomical units from the Sun, sunlight would heat the surface of the nucleus to only −200°C, so it is considered unlikely that the cause of the explosion was due to the Sun. Even the most intense burst of protons would not deliver sufficient energy to cause the eruption. The only feasible explanation put forward so far is that the comet was hit by a small object, possibly only a few metres in diameter. Close monitoring of the comet continues and may provide more clues to the cause of the outburst.

Ice age bacteria.—The discovery of a well-preserved mastodon in a peat bog in Ohio has provided an unexpected bonus for the study of life some 11,000 years ago. The remains of this four-ton animal included the well-preserved intestines and these contained, in addition to the mastodon's last meal, bacteria which scientists believe could be the oldest living organisms ever isolated.

Gerald Goldstein of the Ohio Wesleyan University has cultured bacteria called *Enterobacter cloacae* from the intestines. This bacterium is found in the gut of present-day mammals and in water. First, Goldstein had to show that the bacterium had come from the intestines and not from contamination. He was able to culture different bacteria from the area surrounding the animal but was unable to identify any enterobacter in any of the samples taken. When he checked the concentration of bacteria in the intestinal remains, he found levels so high that he was convinced that the bacterium had originated in the intestines. Goldstein thinks that the bacteria survived because of a series of fortunate circumstances. The very cold temperatures at the bottom of the bog refrigerated the remains, and in addition the area became sealed, preventing air from getting to the body. Also, because it was winter when the skeleton was uncovered, the intestines started to freeze as soon as it was dug up. Further, the scientists put the intestines into a freezer when they returned to the laboratory. Goldstein is now analysing the DNA of these bacteria and comparing them with the strain of enterobacter existing today.

The mammal's last meal consisted of shallow water plants, such as water-lilies, swamp grass and sedges, but not twigs of conifers. If this was a normal meal, it upsets the commonly-held theory that these large animals became extinct as the evergreen forests moved northwards at the end of the ice age. It is more likely that the demise was due to the draining of the wetlands in the late glacial and early post-glacial periods causing a shortage of food.

Meteorite fall in Britain.—There have been only three confirmed meteorite falls in the British Isles since the last war, the last occurring in Northern Ireland in 1969. On May 5, 1991 at 1130 UT (1230 BST), Arthur Pettifor, an 82-year-old retired civil servant, was planting out a bed of onions in his garden at Glatton, near Peterborough, when he heard a whistling, whining noise, followed by a thump. He noticed that one of the conifers forming a screening hedge was moving and that a hawthorn bush had been damaged. Under the bush he found a small stone which was lukewarm to the touch. He contacted Anglia TV, who contacted David Dewhirst at the Institute of Astronomy at Cambridge, and David Dewhirst contacted Howard Miles of the British Astronomical Association. The description of the stone given over the telephone indicated that it might be a meteorite and the Natural History Museum in London was alerted. A visit to the site by Dr Robert Hutchinson of the Museum confirmed that the stone was definitely a meteorite.

The stone measured about $100 \times 60 \times 60$ mm and weighed 767 grams. It was covered with a thin dark fusion crust and it had some poorly developed regmaglypts (thumbprints) on one surface. These are caused by fusion of the surface layers of the stone during its passage through the atmosphere. Preliminary analysis has shown it to be a stony meteorite classified as a L6 chondrite. It contains about 23 per cent iron, of which 5 per cent is nickel-iron, the rest being mainly in the silicate minerals olivine and pyroxene, common components of the basalt lavas on the Earth. Radiation studies have indicated that for over two million years the stone was part of a boulder less than a metre across, travelling round the Sun in the asteroid belt, a region lying between Mars and Jupiter.

The stone is quite a common type of meteorite, the same as those which fell at Barwell, Leicestershire, in 1965 and Bovedy, Northern Ireland, in 1969. The Glatton meteorite is now under detailed study at the Natural History Museum and fragments from it will be sent to other establishments for further tests.

Near miss for the Earth.—Most of the asteroids, or minor planets, orbit the Sun between the orbits of Mars and Jupiter. However, there are some which have strongly eccentric orbits which cause them to cross the orbit of the Earth. About 100 of these are known and they are classed as 'Apollo' objects. The most famous of these is Eros, which can approach to within 22 million kilometres of the Earth. At one time Eros was of special interest for determining the astronomical unit, the average distance of the Earth from the Sun. Another asteroid, Hermes, came within 800,000 km of the Earth in 1937, i.e. about twice the distance of the Moon. Others have since come even nearer. In March 1989 an object, 1989 FC, passed within 690,000 km of the Earth. However, these close encounters paled into insignificance on January 18, 1991 when an object passed the Earth at a distance of only 170,000 km, less than half the distance of the Moon.

The object was discovered in the constellation of Cancer by David Rabinowitz, using the 90 cm (36 inch) telescope at Kitt Peak in Arizona. He and his colleague, Jim Scotti, tracked the object for five hours. Brian Marsden of the Smithsonian Center for Astrophysics used their data to compute the orbit of the object. He calculated that a few hours after it had been discovered, the object made its closest approach to the Earth. The object, known as 1991 BA, is thought to be the smallest asteroid discovered, having a diameter of between 5 and 10 metres. No other known minor planet has come so close. If it had hit the Earth it would have produced quite a large crater and, depending on where the impact occurred, could have done tremendous damage.

The discoverers are members of the Spacewatch team who keep a constant watch on the skies for asteroids. The Earth is constantly being peppered with smaller rocks, known as meteorites, and they are of considerable scientific interest.

The Murchison meteorite.—Isotopic evidence from a study of some carbonaceous meteorites, in particular the Murchison meteorite which fell in Australia in 1969, has indicated that the grains comprising the meteorite were formed outside the solar system. The evidence is based on the unusual percentage of the isotopes of the five noble gases (helium, neon, argon, krypton and xenon) found in the grains of silicon carbide within the meteorite. Isotopes of a particular element are atoms having a fixed number of protons in their nuclei but a differing number of neutrons.

This evidence first came to light in 1978 when it was found that xenon isotopes showed signs of having undergone 'slow' neutron capture, a process thought to take place in red giant stars. At the end of 1990, it was reported that Roy Lewis and colleagues at the University of Chicago had found evidence from the noble gases to suggest that the grains were formed in several stars with slightly differing chemistries. Roberto Gallino of the Institute of Physics in Turin, Italy, and colleagues have shown theoretically that the silicon carbide grains form in the cool outer layers of carbon stars, a class of red giants. As the grains gradually drift away from the star, they are bombarded with xenon and krypton ions accelerated by the stellar wind.

A recent discovery by researchers at Chicago and Washington Universities of the high values for the ratios of aluminium-26 to aluminium-27 in some of the Murchison grains have shown that an origin in the very hot Wolf-Rayet stars or supernovae is inconsistent with modern theory. Once again the most likely source is thought to be red giants.

These studies have provided an insight into stellar atmosphere and shown that not all meteorites have origins within the solar system. A new channel for the study of the regions beyond the solar system has opened up.

Network theory.—Mathematical theory about the most efficient way of joining up a pattern of dots is exceedingly complex. Much thought has gone into the problem because the theory is used in the creation of efficient networks, applications of which are numerous and include the design of computer circuits, telephone networks and factory layouts. The efficiency of the network has financial and efficiency implications for the application. Progress in network theory has recently been made by Ding Zhu Du, a visiting Chinese mathematician at Princetown University, and Frank Hwang of AT & T Bell Laboratories.

To illustrate the problem, consider a set (P) of points (n) on a plane surface. The shortest network that connects all the points is called a Steiner minimum tree (SMT) after Jakob Steiner, the 19th century Swiss mathematician. He introduced new points called Steiner points and used these as vertices. For example, in the case of three points fixed at the corners of an equilateral triangle, the SMT could be obtained by putting a Steiner point at the centre of the triangle. The problem becomes very difficult if the number of points is large and computers are required to obtain even approximate solutions. One of these involves the use of a 'minimum spanning tree' (MST) of the set P. This is the shortest network whose vertices are precisely the points in P, no extra vertices being permitted. In the example above, the MST is the 'V' formed by joining two of the vertices to the third one. In general, the MST is longer than the SMT, but it is much easier to compute. A measure of the goodness of the MST is given by the ratio of the lengths of the SMT to that of the MST, called the Steiner ratio. Work carried out in 1968 suggested that the ratio would never fall below 0·866. By 1989, it had been proved that this was true for any set P with less than seven points. For a larger number of points the amount of computation grew rapidly but it had been possible to push up the lower bound of the ratio to 0·824. Du and Kwang, using a completely different approach, transformed the Steiner ratio conjecture into a min-max problem similar to that in game theory. They developed some important properties and then translated these properties back to the original problem. In this way they were able to show that the original conjecture was correct. The techniques used will no doubt be used to solve other optimization problems.

Oldest land dwellers.—Discoveries from the Ludlow bone bed in Shropshire have brought to light fossils of the earliest known land dwellers, with ages of 414 million years, some 20 million years older than the previously accepted oldest land creature. The animals are two centipedes and an arachnid and it is possible that these were not the first creatures to live on the land.

Andrew Jeram and Paul Selden of the University of Manchester, with Diana Edwards of the University of Wales in Cardiff, crushed rock from the Ludlow bone bed and dissolved it in acid. They identified the fossils of a *trigonotarbid arachnoid* and a centipede, as well as fossils of land plants and water dwellers such as *euripterids*. This rather odd mixture of fossils resulted from the rocks being formed on a beach or mudflat. The researchers are confident that the three animals lived on the land because present-day centipedes are land animals and trigonotarbids found in younger rocks have a respiratory system suitable only for breathing air. In addition, a study of the skeletons has shown that the legs were designed for moving on land and would have been unsuitable for underwater movement. The presence of fossils of land plants also strengthened the case for land-living creatures.

Because the creatures seem to have been part of an established ecosystem, it has been inferred that animals left the water for dry land considerably more than 414 million years ago. As one of the workers remarked 'If we have predators, they must have eaten something'.

Oldest multicellular animals.—Until recently the oldest known multicellular animals were the 'Ediacara' fauna, complex soft-bodied creatures, fossils of which have been found in more than 25 locations world-wide. The animals lived after the last Precambrian ice age. They had sizes up to a metre across, which suggested that they were not the first multicellular animals. A recent find by Canadian geologists has provided evidence to support this view.

Hans Hofmann of the University of Montreal and James Aitkin of the Geological Survey of Canada in Alberta, examined the Twitya formation in the Mackenzie Mountains of northwest Canada and found more than 100 anemone-like fossils in sandstone which is 600 million years old. The fossils were about 1 cm across. The geologists identified three types of early animals in the fossils and think that they lived in large numbers on a muddy sea bottom. It is thought that the casts are of soft animals, formed when strong submarine currents deposited sand on them. The majority of the remains are shallow hemispheres but others consist of annulae with irregular constrictions around their rims and, in one case, a distinct central spot and radial markings. Similar animals are present in the Ediacara fauna.

No precise date for the fossils has yet been given but the fact that they lay below the glacial deposits indicates that they are the oldest members of the Ediacara fauna. This find creates some uncertainty about the theory that the Ediacara fauna were able to evolve only when the Earth warmed up at the end of the Precambrian ice ages. More research is needed to clarify this problem.

The ozone layer.—The protective ozone layer in the upper atmosphere of the Earth is disappearing much more quickly than was previously thought. There is now no doubt that the ozone is being destroyed by the chlorine derived from man-made chemicals such as chlorofluorocarbons (CFCs), used for refrigeration, the manufacture of insulating foams and as a cleaning solvent in making computer chips.

The largest decrease in the amount of ozone occurs over the Antarctic during the spring, when virtually all the ozone in the lower stratosphere is removed. Because the meteorology of the Arctic region is completely different from that of the Antarctic, the loss of ozone is not nearly as great, although it is quite appreciable and the decrease has recently been recorded at much lower latitudes than previously. More important is the fact that the ozone depletion has been detected well into the late spring months, upsetting the theory that ozone depletion was significant only during the cold months. (It had been thought that warmer temperatures tended to slow down the chemical reactions in which the chlorine from the CFCs attacked the ozone.) The depletion in the late spring has important implications; it is thought that for every 1 per cent fall in ozone concentration, there is an increase of 2 per cent in the amount of solar ultraviolet radiation reaching the Earth's surface, thereby increasing the incidence of skin cancer.

To illustrate the magnitude of the problem, it is known that much of northern hemisphere above 30–35° latitude lies under a depleted ozone layer. With the growth of the depletion, scientists and many other organizations are pressing for a more rapid removal of CFC production than that agreed in the 1987 Montreal Protocol.

Planetary systems.—Some astronomers claim that the most exciting discovery of the last decade was the identification of a disc of material surrounding β-Pictoris, a star twice as massive and ten times as bright as the Sun. The disc has provided data which may throw light on the formation of and the conditions existing in the early days of the solar system. It was discovered after observations made by the Infra-red Astronomical Satellite (IRAS) revealed that the star was brighter than expected for a main sequence star. Observations from IRAS have shown that several main sequence stars are surrounded by small dust grains. Astronomers used to think that the regions around a star should be clean. It was thought that radiation pressure pushed the small dust grains free from the star's gravitational field. Another process, known as the Poynting-Robertson effect, causes small particles to spiral into the star. These two processes should sweep clean the region around a star in a few million years, leaving behind just planets, planetesimals, asteroids and comets. The dust disc of β-Pictoris should have been swept clean by now but instead it extends out to a distance of 1,000 astronomical units (AU) (an astronomical unit is the distance of the Earth from the Sun). It is therefore concluded that there must be a continual replacement of the dust grains. Likewise, studies of the gas disc or shell around the star out to a distance of 1 AU have shown for some time that plasma (matter split into ions and electrons) is falling into the star. Like the dust, this plasma must be continually replenished.

It is thought that the disc is a protoplanetary disc which has evolved part of the way towards forming planets. The dusty material is thought to be continually renewed from the debris of comet and asteroid collisions. Some of the comets which approach too close to the star are drawn into the star and become part of the infalling plasma cloud.

Recent studies have shown that some of the dust grains consist of silicates and work is now being carried out to see if the spectra of these silicates have any similarity to the spectra of similar particles from Halley's comet.

Prehistoric wine-making.—A red stain inside a pre-Bronze Age wine jar has been found to be the remnants from wine-making carried out 5,500 years ago, some 500 years earlier than the previously accepted date for the start of wine-making. An amphora found during an excavation at Godin Tepe

in the Zagros mountains of western Iran was pieced together by Virginia Badler of the University of Toronto. It was found to have a large red stain on the bottom and on one side, suggesting that it had been used for storing liquids. Badler and colleagues carried out an infra-red spectroscopic analysis of the stain and showed that it contained phenolic acid (tannin) and tartaric acid. Directly opposite the stain was a hole in the jar, a common feature as it prevented the jar from bursting after secondary fermentation. The jar dates from the Sumerian Uruk civilization, a pre-Bronze Age society thought to have carried out trade in copper and semi-precious stones with other regions of Iran and Afghanistan. The civilization existed at the period when writing was invented and irrigated agriculture was first recorded.

With the amphora were found drinking vessels and also a mud bin, which was possibly used for storing grapes. Further investigations in the area have been impossible due to war.

Previous investigations revealed charred vines and grape pips dating from 3500 BC, indicating that grapes were grown at the time the amphora was used. Sloman Katz of the University of Pennsylvania, Philadelphia, believes that wine was made by simply crushing grapes in a skin or some other storage device. The surface of the grapes contains plenty of yeast and sugar, which would be sufficient to make wine if the grapes were left for a few days.

Both Katz and Daniel Zohary of the Hebrew University of Jerusalem are currently working on the theory that fermentation preceded agriculture. Some investigators believe that barley beer may have been available as long ago as 8000 BC.

The primrose puzzle.—Biologists have puzzled for some time over the failure of a rare form of the common primrose to spread and become as common as the normal varieties when it is a form which has the advantage of being able to self-pollinate.

The flowers of the common primrose normally occur in one of two forms. The 'pin' type has a long stigma which extends just above the corolla tube, with the anthers at the base of the corolla. In the 'thrum' type the stigma is short and the anthers are at the neck of the corolla. The traditional view is that pollination occurs when insects get pollen on their bodies and transfer it between the pin and thrum varieties. The third, rare form of the common primrose is homostyle, i.e. its stigma and anthers are at the same level. In addition to being able to pollinate the pin and thrum types, this third type of primrose can self-fertilizing. Self-fertilization should give this variety an advantage over the pin and thrum types, but it has remained a relatively rare plant. It is found in the Chiltern Hills and in parts of Somerset and north Dorset, and in the forty years that this variety has been known, the number of plants has remained more or less constant.

Botanists from the Open University have monitored primroses for long periods and although bees and butterflies visited the flowers, actual pollination has never been witnessed. The insects seem to prefer other flowers such as violets. Because primroses are highly scented and particularly visible, they attract moths at night, and it is thought that moths are the main source of pollination. Laboratory experiments have shown that large moths are effective pollinators of both the pin and thrum forms, but only the pin form can be pollinated by small moths. The homostyle form sets seed equally well with or without moths. In the wild the homostyle form produces large quantities of seeds, though many of these are small. The pin and thrum forms produce few but large seeds. The larger seeds have an advantage when germinating so, contrary to expectations and general rules, the production of large quantities of small seeds by self-pollination does not result in a large increase in plants. The belief that the ability to self-pollinate is an advantage when insects are scarce is now open to question.

Second terracotta army.—The discovery nearly twenty years ago of the life-size terracotta army of China's first emperor Qin Shihuangdi in the Shaanxi province of China has led to the site becoming a leading tourist attraction. Because of its popularity plans were drawn up to construct a new airport, near the city of Xian with a new 19 km motorway to connect it to the city.

In the course of the construction of the motorway, a second terracotta army was discovered. The area was known to contain burial sites of the Han and Tang dynasties and tests were made in a wheat field some 300 metres south of the tomb of the wife of the emperor Liu Qi, known during his reign as Jing. He lived from 188 to 144 BC and both he and his wife were buried at Yangling, 22 km north-west of Xian. At a depth of 6·5 metres a small piece of broken orange pottery was found which was subsequently identified as the shoulder of a statue. The whole field was then examined in detail by a team which had worked on the Han tombs. The new site was found to cover 96,000 square metres. It contains an army of terracotta figures associated with the two tombs and housed in 24 vaults separated by about 20 metres and in rows aligned north–south. The vaults are 4 to 10 metres wide and 25 to 291 metres in length. The figures are smaller in stature but greater in number than the first terracotta army.

All the human statues consist of naked men about 50 cm high. Their bodies are painted an orange-red colour and their hair, eyebrows, beards and eyes painted black. The number of statues in each vault varies considerably but it is thought they may correspond to those of the army units they contain. One vault contains mostly cavalry. A particularly striking feature about the statues is that the figures have graceful forms and delicately sculptured faces. Each face is different in age and facial expression. None of the bodies has arms and the reason for this is a mystery. One theory is that they were movable and originally made of wood which has subsequently disintegrated, like the clothing. More than 300 statues have so far been uncovered but it is thought that thousands remain buried.

Construction of the motorway continues but a 320 metre long bridge is being constructed over the site.

The size of the Universe.—Most popular books on astronomy describe in general terms the size of the Universe and the ways in which it is measured. Very few indicate that the values quoted are open to considerable error and some can be classed only as intelligent guesses. Much greater accuracy has been obtained recently, thanks to the Hubble Space Telescope and the ring of gas expanding from supernova 1987A. Supernova 1987A exploded in 1987 in the Large Magellanic Cloud, a satellite galaxy visible in the southern hemisphere, and it has been under constant observation since then. An accurate estimate of the distance of this object can be used as a stepping stone to more accurate values for more distant objects and ultimately for the size of the universe.

The ring of gas around the supernova was not created in the explosion but was ejected from the star a few thousand years earlier, during the time that it was a red supergiant. It ejected the shell of gas in the form of a stellar wind. Later the star evolved into a blue supergiant and a faster stellar wind was ejected. This compressed the gas into a ring-like structure. This ring was first observed in August 1990 using the Hubble Space Telescope's faint objects camera, and was seen to be glowing with a temperature of 20,000°C. The angular diameter was measured at 1·66 arc-seconds. By studying the supernova in ultraviolet light over a period of three years, it was found that the UV light from the near side of the ring was recorded 80 days after the explosion, while that from the far side arrived 340 days later. From this finding it was calculated that the ring was inclined at an angle of 43° to the line of site. It was then possible to deduce a value of 1·37 light-years for the diameter of the ring. Armed with this information it was found that the supernova, and hence the Large Magellanic Cloud, was 169,000 light-years distant.

It will now be possible to estimate the Hubble Constant to within 10–15 per cent, a much more accurate value than that adopted at present. The Hubble Constant is used to estimate how fast the Universe is expanding, and from this estimates of the age and size of the Universe can be calculated.

Termite bands.—Until recently termites were considered to be a pest, but now an analysis of their behaviour has revealed that they can help farmers to increase their crop yield.

Scientists working on a dry land farming scheme in Botswana became puzzled when the sorghum and maize plants on some plots grew as much as three to eight times as fast as plants on other plots. There was also a corresponding increase in the crop. The soil of the plots was analysed and showed no differences chemically, and the method of tilling the ground was the same, but the growth and yield of the crops showed consistent variations. It was also noted that the same variation occurred with the natural vegetation outside the experimental plots. Tom Wood and Peter Brinn of the Natural Resources Institute visited the site in 1989 and they discovered that termites were responsible.

In southern Africa, termites are changing the landscape by producing termite bands, large striped patterns up to a kilometre long. The bands consist of alternate ridges and gulleys, each ridge about two metres high and separated by about 50 metres. The bands were first identified in the late 1970s but it is only now that their importance has been recognized.

The banding is produced by termites of the genus *Odontotermes*, which build horizontally instead of vertically. Why they do this is now known but it is thought that the reason is to keep their nests dry. The ridges descend sloping fields in straight lines and the troughs that separate them act as channels for water during the rainy season. It has been found that sorghum grows best half-way up a ridge, a position which may be ideal for the roots to receive the right amount of water.

Why the termites build such long ridges and in the spacing observed is not fully understood but it could be due to competition between various species or to environmental factors not yet recognized.

Triton.—Until the visit of *Voyager 2* to the vicinity of Neptune in 1989, very little was known about the planet, and even less about Triton, its largest moon. Triton is roughly the same size as our Moon but because it is so far from the Sun, it has a surface temperature of about $-237°C$. It was thought that so low a surface temperature would make Triton too cold for any surface activity to take place but the visit of *Voyager* has shown this not to be the case. The average surface temperature was found to be $-235°C$ and a thin atmosphere of nitrogen was identified. Photographs of its surface showed streaks of dark matter and also four active sites where plumes of material were being shot up to heights of about 8 km.

Any explanation has to accommodate the fact that Triton spins on its axis roughly at right angles to its orbital plane. This means that any icy material would be transferred from one pole to the other and back again every 165 years, the orbital period of Neptune around the Sun. If the dark bands were permanent features, they would be covered regularly. The geysers could be the source of the dark markings but it is difficult to find a mechanism which could activate the geysers. It has been suggested that the surface of Triton is covered with a layer of nitrogen ice about a metre thick. Dark material could be in the form of organic polymers generated by the action of UV light on the methane known to exist on the satellite. This could collect beneath the ice layer and the sunlight could penetrate it to warm the dark layer by a greenhouse effect. An increase in temperature of 4° above the average would be sufficient to increase tenfold the pressure beneath the nitrogen ice. A weakness in this ice layer would provide a location for a jet of material several kilometres in height.

An alternative explanation is the possibility that the geysers are similar to 'wind devils', atmospheric phenomena seen in hot regions on the Earth. Large dust devils have been observed on Mars, where they rise to heights of about 6 km.

Venus mapped.—The thick cloud covering Venus makes it impossible to obtain a clear visual picture of the surface of the planet. Soviet probes have managed to obtain relatively crude pictures, whilst the Americans have, over the years, gradually improved their radar scanning abilities. These improvements have borne fruit with the *Magellan* orbiting spacecraft, America's latest Venus probe. *Magellan* has been

radar scanning the planet since August 16, 1990 and has just completed its first cycle of mapping, making 1,789 orbits in 243 days (i.e. one year on Venus) and covering 84 per cent of the planet's surface. The resolution obtained was 120 metres. Some data was lost while Venus was on the far side of the Sun and mapping of the south polar regions was impossible due to the probe's orientation.

The surface of the planet consists mainly of volcanic flows, some as long as 300 km to 500 km, covering as much as 80 per cent of its surface. Some of the volcanoes rise to heights above the surrounding plane of about 4 km and some have calderas many kilometres across. Of much interest is the mountain range known as Maxwell Montes, rising some 12 km above the equivalent of sea-level. There are impact craters, for example the 32 km diameter Aurelia and the double-ringed feature known as Cleopatra, but the largest identified is a double-ringed basin 275 km in diameter. A new type of feature called a corona, of which there are examples ranging in diameter from 100 km to 2000 km, have been identified on various parts of the surface. One theory suggests that they were formed when plumes of hot rock welled up in the fluid mantle, in a similar way to hot spots on the Earth. The question of whether the planet has large-scale plate tectonics has not yet been resolved, although there is some evidence of small-scale tectonics.

Magellan started the second cycle of scans on May 16, 1991. The probe's orientation has been altered so that the areas missed in the first scan, especially the south polar regions, will be covered. The change in angle will also provide further details of features already identified in the first scan.

Volcanic gas emission and the atmosphere.— Recent measurements of the gas emission from Mount Etna have shown that the volcano is emitting carbon dioxide at a rate of at least 25 million tons a year. This amount is comparable with the output from four 1000 MW coal-fired power stations. The emission is extremely high when one considers that the average value for land-based volcanoes is 1·3 million tons; the emission from all the volcanoes along the entire 60,000 km mid-oceanic ridge amounts only to a value between 30 and 65 million tons.

The reason for this high value of carbon dioxide emission from Mount Etna is not known but it has been suggested that the volcanic emission is supplemented by the decarbonization of the limestone surrounding the volcano. However, this explanation does not explain why the amount of sulphur dioxide is also very high. Another theory suggests that the high carbon dioxide emission is characteristic of alkaline volcanic systems. It may be possible to test this by measuring the output from similar volcanoes, such as Mount Erebus and Nyiragongo.

The emission of carbon dioxide from volcanoes was an important part of the natural order before the advent of industrial processes. It balanced the removal of carbon dioxide from the atmosphere by silicate weathering, carbonate deposition and the burial of organic matter. These would have removed all the carbon dioxide from our atmosphere in 10,000 years and from the atmosphere-ocean system in

500,000 years. The global rate of carbon dioxide emission from all volcanoes is not known but it is thought to be in the region of 130–175 million tons a year, possibly half of which is needed to keep a natural balance. This is currently being augmented by carbon dioxide from burning fossil fuels, amounting to 22,000 million tons a year, plus a roughly similar amount from other human activities. So human activity is releasing carbon dioxide into the atmosphere at a rate more than 45 times the natural emission.

Voyager.—The *Voyager* mission teams have now moved out of their main operations rooms at NASA to make way for the coming *Cassini* mission to Saturn, but this does not mean that the *Voyager* probes have been written off. They are still sending back data on conditions existing in the outer regions of the solar system and the beginnings of interstellar space.

Because the probes will not make any more close visits to planets and satellites, the imaging cameras and most of the scanning instruments have been switched off. However, the particle detector, magnetic field detector and wave detector are still returning data. The scan platform is still in operation so that a spectrometer can detect ultraviolet radiation. This spectrometer is able to record wavelengths between 500 and 1200 angstroms, a region which cannot be studied from Earth-based instruments. Although these wavelengths tend to be absorbed by interstellar gas, the instrument has detected radiation from very hot white dwarf stars, which suggests that there are holes in the hydrogen clouds filling interstellar space. The discovery of strong UV emission from globular clusters shows also that although the clusters are very old, there are some young hot stars amongst the old ones.

The cosmic ray detectors have produced some surprises. They have identified sources of cosmic rays coming from the Sun, the Milky Way and intergalactic space, but in addition they have found rays coming possibly from interstellar space energized by turbulence occurring near the heliopause, the boundary between the solar wind and the interstellar medium. The abundance of the elements neon, argon and helium has agreed generally with that expected, although there have been some unexpected differences.

The two *Voyager* probes will work with the *Pioneer* probes in mapping the magnetic field in the outer regions of the solar system to provide data on the position and conditions existing at the heliopause, which the *Voyager* probes will reach about 2000 AD.

Youngest star.—A star can be defined as an object shining as a result of burning nuclear fuel in its core. Of great interest to the astronomer is the behaviour of a cloud of gas before it becomes a true star. In the past all attempts to identify such objects have had only limited success but recently a team of British, German and American astronomers, led by Colin Aspin of the Joint Astronomy Centre in Hawaii, have identified what they believe to be the youngest protostar ever found.

The object was identified in a nebula (NGC 1333) about 1,100 light-years away, in a region long recognized as one in which stars were thought to be forming. Eight years ago the infra-red satellite IRAS located seven bright spots in an arc just south of the position occupied by the optical nebula. Some of these spots have subsequently been linked to visible young stars but others appear to be surrounded by dust clouds. It is one of these, IRAS 4, the coldest of the sources, that astronomers claim is the 'youngest star'.

Aspin and colleagues have carried out further studies on the new object using the UK Infra-red Telescope (UKIRT) and the James Clerk Maxwell Telescope (JCMT), both situated on Mauna Kea in Hawaii. The JCMT studies have revealed a shell of dust thicker than any yet seen surrounding a young star, suggesting that the star is still forming. As the whirling dust cloud is drawn in by gravity, it is also heated by friction. It is thought that this process has been going on for only a few thousand years. Detailed study of IRAS 4 suggests that there might be two objects, both slightly elliptical in shape, indicating that the dust is in the form of a disc which is orbiting the centre of each of the protostars.

ASTRONOMERS ROYAL

CONSERVATION AND HERITAGE 1990-91

THE NATURAL ENVIRONMENT

From April 1991, the government agency for nature conservation, the Nature Conservancy Council (NCC), was replaced by separate bodies for England, Wales and Scotland. The reorganization formed the most controversial part of the Environment Protection Act 1990. The new bodies are English Nature, which takes over the functions of the NCC in England; the Countryside Council for Wales, which combines the functions of the NCC and the Countryside Commission within the Principality; and the Nature Conservancy Council for Scotland. The latter is an interim body. Separate legislation, enacted during 1991, combines the functions of the NCC and the Countryside Commission for Scotland to create a new heritage body for Scotland which comes into operation in 1992 (*see* below).

A fourth body, the Joint Nature Conservation Committee, was established to co-ordinate matters of British and international conservation concern, and to create common standards of practice. The Committee is funded jointly by the three national agencies, each of which has a seat on the Committee.

The reorganization of the old NCC has led to changing work ethics and practices, staff changes and shortages and an internalization of effort that most of those involved feel they could have done without. Whether it will eventually result in an improvement in nature conservation, and better relations between conservationists and landowners (now officially referred to as 'customers'), remains to be seen.

Scottish Natural Heritage.—In 1992, a new body, Scottish Natural Heritage, will take over the functions of the NCC for Scotland and the Countryside Commission for Scotland. However, conservationists fear that the ability of the NCC for Scotland or its successor to provide adequate protection for Sites of Special Scientific Interest (SSSI) in Scotland has been dealt a serious blow.

The Natural Heritage (Scotland) Act was intended to be little more than enabling legislation for the body. However, its passage occasioned a concerted attack by a group of Scottish landowners on the ability of the NCC to notify SSSIs. As a result of pressure, the Government inserted a clause providing for an independent review procedure of all SSSIs in Scotland. Owners or occupiers wishing to appeal against SSSIs on their land being notified will now be able to do so through a committee appointed by the Secretary of State for Scotland. The procedure threatens to undermine the credibility of the new body (which was not consulted about the move) and may result in a logjam of appeals that will limit Scottish Natural Heritage's ability to promote more positive and imaginative work in the field of landscape and wildlife conservation. The chairman of the NCC for Scotland, Magnus Magnusson, voiced his dismay at the prospect, and it has led to the resignation of Sir Fred Holliday, chairman of the Joint Nature Conservation Committee.

A court decision in which a Perthshire hill farmer

was awarded £568,000 compensation (plus interest and legal costs) for not developing his farm (which includes a large SSSI for agriculture and forestry, has further alarmed conservationists. The tribunal based its figures not on profits foregone, as hitherto, but on the deemed fall in the capital value of the land as a result of SSSI designation. If the case sets a precedent, Scottish Natural Heritage may be unable to afford management agreements with landowners on more than a small proportion of SSSIs in Scotland.

By contrast, in England the Environment Secretary, Michael Heseltine, has announced proposals designed to improve protection for SSSIs, notably the withdrawal of development rights for temporary recreational uses such as off-road motorcycle events and paint-ball games. He has also pledged to call in planning applications on sites designated for their national and international nature conservation importance.

Badger Bill.—A new law to improve protection for badgers comes into force in October 1991. Since 1973 it has been an offence to ill-treat a badger. However, the previous Badger Act protected the animal without also protecting its home. This loophole enabled badger-baiters to unearth sets claiming that they were searching for foxes or lost terrier dogs. An estimated 9,000 badgers are killed by badger-baiters each year (*see* p. 1153 of **Whitaker's Almanack** 1991). The Badger Act 1991 creates a new offence of 'interfering with a badger set', which includes causing dogs to enter the set and disturbing badgers occupying the set.

The Badger Bill was supported by conservation and animal welfare organizations and was introduced by Roy Hughes, MP for Newport East. It passed its third reading in the Commons in May 1991 with 100 MPs voting in favour and 19 against. A previous Bill had failed after being 'talked out' by a single objector representing hunting interests who queried the precise definition of a 'set'. The new Bill was carried after concessions to fox-hunting and farming interests. Under licence, hunts can continue to stop up sets temporarily to allow dogs to search for foxes. Sets will also continue to be blocked on Welsh hill land to control foxes. Issuing licences under the new Act is the task of English Nature in matters concerning wildlife and development, and of the Ministry of Agriculture and the Welsh Office in matters relating to stock protection and crop damage. Licences are not likely to be given to destroy sets until appropriate arrangements are made to accommodate the animals elsewhere. Nor are they likely to be issued between December and June, the period when young cubs are underground.

Countryside stewardship.—The White Paper *This Common Inheritance*, published in September 1990, disappointed conservationists. Though much concerned with energy conservation, noise reduction and pollution control, it contained few new ideas, and fewer concrete proposals, to improve protection for habitats and wildlife. The problem is urgent, for SSSIs continue to be lost or eroded through development, especially roadworks, building and peat extraction. According to a report published by the Royal Society for Nature Conservation, 687 SSSIs (14 per cent of the total) were lost or damaged between 1984 and 1987. The White Paper did, however, galvanize other political parties into putting forward their own environmental programmes, and environmental policy is likely to be a major issue at the next election.

One positive outcome of the White Paper has been a government-funded scheme called Countryside Stewardship, details of which were annnounced by the Countryside Commission in December 1990. Some £13 million has been earmarked over the next three years to encourage landowners to manage or restore key landscape features and wildlife habitats. Initially the scheme is concentrating on four kinds of landscape: chalk and limestone grasslands, lowland heaths, river valleys and other waterside landscapes, and the coast. The scheme came into operation in June 1991. However, although the scheme is well-intentioned, the resources made available to it will benefit only a fraction of the farmed countryside. Moreover, the existing separate schemes of Environmentally Sensitive Areas, Set-aside grants and the Countryside Premium Scheme threaten to produce a bureaucratic muddle, and confusion for the farmer.

Drought deepens.—A succession of dry seasons has meant water shortages in parts of eastern and central England and has had severe effect on spring-fed rivers, lakes and fens. In 1990, the National Rivers Authority identified forty 'disappearing rivers', including famous chalk streams like the Pang and the Kennet. In East Anglia the water-levels of Wicken Fen and Chippenham Fen are falling, and some of the beautiful Breckland meres dried out altogether in 1990 and 1991.

In many cases the problem has been exacerbated by boreholes and farm irrigation schemes. Redgrave and Lopham Fen in Suffolk is among the few remaining habitats of the rare and spectacularly large fen raft spider. Its value was recognized by its designation by the Government as a 'Ramsar' wetland site of international importance in February 1991. However, the springs that feed the Fen also supply water to the Suffolk Water company and the fall in water-level threatens the spiders' habitat. The cost of moving the borehole is far beyond the means of the Suffolk Wildlife Trust, which owns the Fen. The National Rivers Authority is currently considering revoking the water company's abstraction licence. In the meantime, Suffolk Water has agreed to pipe water back into the Fen as an interim measure to try to save the spiders.

Estuaries.—A growing number of development proposals, ranging from tidal barrages and boating marinas to bypasses and airports, threaten to destroy or badly damage many estuaries in England and Wales. One well-known case is that of the tidal barrage which the Government and the Cardiff Bay Development Corporation want to build across Cardiff Bay to form an amenity lake, part of a scheme intended to boost the local economy. A tidal barrage would result in the permanent flooding of tidal flats of international importance for wading birds, and

the proposal has been resisted with vigour, especially by the RSPB. A similar proposal has been made for the Usk estuary at Newport which threatens the survival of salmon and other migratory fish in that river. Developers tend to see tidal mudflats as unsightly wastes. To conservationists they are among the richest wild habitats in Britain, and one which we have an international responsibility to maintain.

In response to these threats, the RSPB and the NCC both produced major reports on estuaries in 1990–91. *Turning the Tide–A Future for Estuaries* is the RSPB's survey of the 123 principal estuaries of Britain and their use by more than two million waders and wildfowl for feeding and roosting, and as staging posts during migration. The report urges the production of a national strategy for estuaries, including the establishment of a chain of wildlife sanctuaries along the 'east Atlantic flyway' and more generous government funding for research on the biology of coastal wildlife. The RSPB believes that the Government has failed to protect estuaries and their wildlife from the assortment of dangers they face, and calls for a new Coastal and Marine Department to cut through the present confused system of management and planning.

The NCC's report *Nature conservation and estuaries in Great Britain* is a detailed national overview of our estuaries, their value for wildlife and the impacts that affect that value. It brings together an immense amount of scientific knowledge, hitherto unpublished or in specialist publications, that will provide a firm foundation for a nationwide policy of estuarine conservation if the Government can be persuaded to adopt one.

Gulf war pollution.—Oil spills in excess of 11 million barrels into the Persian Gulf during the Gulf war produced the worst oil pollution incident in history. About half of the oil, including some of the most toxic constituents, will evaporate. The rest will sink to the sea-bed or be deposited along the coast. The full ecological impact of the slick is not yet clear, but as the Gulf is an enclosed water body, oil does not disperse as quickly as in more turbulent open seas and oceans. A Natural Environment Research Council report, published in February 1991, indicates that underwater oil plumes move separately from surface slicks, thus evading surface barriers. The habitats most at risk from oil pollution include the coral reefs, mangrove swamps and sea-grass beds, nurseries for the important Gulf shrimp industry, and mudflats and islands used by around two million waders, terns and gulls each year. Thirty species of seabirds are considered at risk, including the Socotra cormorant, which is confined to the Gulf and the south Arabian coast. Marine turtles and some 6,000 sea-cows or dugongs that live in the southern Gulf are also under threat.

The International Union for the Conservation of Nature, the World Wide Fund for Nature and the United Nations Environment Programme have joined forces to co-ordinate damage assessment and wildlife protection. Bird experts from the United Kingdom have joined the Saudi oil-spill task force to identify the species most at risk and especially sensitive areas. They have also advised on the training and equipment needed for the clean-up and on long-term action. Quite apart from the oil slick, however, is the problem of human sewage and war debris, which is likely to leave its mark on the area for many years.

Mar Lodge.—Attempts to purchase for the nation the 77,000-acre estate of Mar Lodge in the Cairngorms were still unresolved in August 1991. The estate was put up for sale in January 1990 by its owner, the American businessman John Kluge, who bought it in 1989. Mar Lodge includes some of the finest scenery in the Highlands, including the high granite tops, remnants of Caledonian pine forest and the valley of the River Dee. It is regarded as a national treasure; much of the estate is already a National Nature Reserve, and the Cairngorms as a whole is also under consideration as a World Heritage Site. However, the beauty and conservation value of Mar Lodge is threatened by overgrazing and a variety of inappropriate management practices. The formerly extensive woods of its valleys and glens have virtually ceased to regenerate.

For these reasons, conservation bodies have been urging the Scottish Office to support a campaign to meet the purchase price of some £10–£13 million. The Prince of Wales has lent his support by urging Mr Kluge to accept an offer from the Crown Estate, which would then lease the estate to the Nature Conservancy Council for Scotland. This idea was turned down, but conservation charities led by the World Wide Fund for Nature and the Royal Society for the Protection of Birds have raised £5 million towards the purchase. The Scottish Office refuses to match this sum, however, asserting that it 'does not have any resources, nor is it our policy, to buy up Highland estates'. The Scottish Office continues to advocate voluntary management agreements with private owners, despite abundant evidence that this approach has failed at Mar Lodge.

Representations made to Michael Heseltine, the Environment Secretary, met a more helpful response—a promise to help find the £5 million needed to match the conservation bodies' funds. Unfortunately, the most likely means for the Department of the Environment to intervene, through the National Heritage Memorial Fund, has met further obstructions. It seems that, through an oversight in the Environment Protection Act, there is at present no allowance for the Fund to operate in Scotland or Wales.

THE BUILT ENVIRONMENT

Building preservation.—The Architectural Heritage Fund, established largely to grant-aid building preservation trusts, was able to increase its loan commitments in 1989–90 to more than £5·6 million in support of 77 projects. Its annual report, published in October 1990, anticipated a similar increase for 1990–91 as grants from the Secretary of State for Scotland and English Heritage in March 1990 helped to push the working capital from £4·6 million on April 5, 1989 to almost £5·4 million on April 5, 1990.

The Snowdonia National Park Authority is hoping to establish an independent buildings preservation trust in its area by the end of 1991. The Trust would operate on the standard BPT principle of buying properties, restoring them, selling them with covenants and ploughing back the profits into future projects. An Historic Churches Trust for Hertfordshire and Bedfordshire, designed to raise money to repair historic churches in those two counties, was planned in 1990–91. One of Glasgow's great architectural sons, Alexander or 'Greek' Thomson, is now the subject of a society dedicated to studying and celebrating his works. Plans were mooted in 1990 to establish a Society for Welsh Traditional Buildings, to be known as GWADDOL. Its initial aim would be education and campaigning, but it hopes over time to sponsor a buildings preservation trust.

Care of Cathedrals.—A new system of grant aid from central government for cathedrals was established in 1991; the amount available for grants is set at £11·5 million over three years. The first grants will be offered before the end of 1991.

To be eligible, cathedrals have to be recognized as architecturally outstanding, a description which has so far been accepted for all Anglican cathedrals except Blackburn. Six Roman Catholic cathedrals have failed the test, but as four of those fall within conservation areas they will be eligible for assistance under other schemes. Every repair grant offered to archaeologically sensitive fabric will be accompanied by a contribution to the cost of essential analytical recording. The grants, to be administered on the advice of the Cathedrals and Churches Advisory Committee of English Heritage, will be reviewed after three years.

The grants were the 'carrot' in a package which also included an element of stick, represented by the Care of Cathedrals Measure which came into force on March 1, 1991. This provides, for the first time, some external control over what Deans and Chapters can do within England's Anglican cathedrals. Henceforward, each cathedral will have its own Fabric Advisory Committee to deal with the small-scale work, but any work that will be permanent, involve demolition, disturb archaeological remains or require the sale, loan or dispersal of an object of outstanding interest will have to be referred to the Cathedrals Fabric Commission for permission. The first referral, involving the obliteration of a Clayton and Bell mural scheme with associated glass from the Chapel of English Saints at Gloucester, proved highly controversial. Consent has been refused in respect of those aspects over which the Commission has power.

One of the cases which led to the demand for the Measure was the projected sale of the Mappa Mundi from Hereford Cathedral. During 1991 it was proposed to donate it as a gift, together with the Chained Library, to a new charitable trust. The National Heritage Memorial Fund and J. Paul Getty jun. agreed to contribute towards the cost of building and endowing a new permanent home for both immediately adjacent to the Cathedral.

Conservation awards.—The 1990 Civic Trust Awards included some notable works of conversion. Among these were the restoration of the former mill at Chagford, Devon (architect: Alan van der Steen); the conversion of Ebley Mill, Stroud, Glos., to produce local authority offices (architect: Niall Phillips); the conversion and extension of Oakhill House, Hildenborough, Kent (Aukett Associates); the restoration of the Moot Hall at Aldeburgh, Suffolk (by Michael and Sheila Gooch); and the rehabilitation of courtyard buildings in the Younger Botanic Garden at Ben More, Argyll, Strathclyde (by the Properties Services Agency, Scotland).

A new award was announced in the summer of 1990 for work by ecclesiastical architects, builders and craftsmen. It will be known as the Cookson Conservation and Restoration Award and be presented for what the judges consider to be the finest work carried out at any church or ecclesiastical building in the United Kingdom.

English Heritage.—English Heritage's annual report for 1989–90, published in October 1990, showed that in the 12 months under review it spent some £87 million, of which £16·5 million went in grants to historic buildings including churches, £7·5 million on rescue archaeology, £6·9 million on historic towns, £2·9 million on ancient monuments, £0·6 million to the Merseyside Special Scheme, £15·2 million in maintaining and repairing its own properties, and £4·5 million in marketing costs. Total income from admissions, sales, membership and related activities was £8 million, an increase of 21 per cent over the previous year. By July its membership stood at 235,837, whilst 4,840,000 visits were made to its properties. By far the most popular was Stonehenge which attracted 668,393; Osborne House, with 235,840 visitors, came a poor second. The organization also received a generous financial settlement in November 1990. The Government offered the organization £89·2 million in 1991–92 (an increase of 12 per cent over the previous year) and £108·5 million by 1993–94.

A Scottish equivalent to English Heritage was established early in 1991. Historic Scotland will run Scotland's 330 historic buildings and provide repair grants on a budget of £31 million.

Historical Monuments.—The Royal Commission on the Historical Monuments of England, now recognized by the Government as the principal sponsor and co-ordinator of archaeological and architectural research, confirmed in 1990 that in future its National Archaeological Record will include information on archaeological sites in England the origins of which date from any time before 1945. Most of the National Archaeological Record's current holdings concern sites and monuments dating to before 1714. The decision means that the Record will now cover comprehensively industrial remains, defensive works, agricultural systems, canals, roads and railways, mines and quarries, parks, enclosures and gardens.

The Commission also announced a rapid survey of English hospitals, to be finished in three years and to include the publication of a report that will identify the major national developments in hospital architecture and areas where more detailed work at local level might profitably be undertaken. Efforts to move the Commission headquarters from London to Swindon continued in the course of the year although,

following an outcry, it was decided that the National Buildings Record should remain in London until the end of the century, pending further investigation into its location long-term.

Listings and threats.—The lists of statutorily protected buildings continued to expand throughout the year. Structures newly protected include: the tomb of Elizabeth Johnstone (1784) in the churchyard of St Mary Abbots, Kensington High Street, designed by Sir John Soane; the former prisoner-of-war camp at Island Farm, Merthyr Mawr, Bridgend, Mid-Glamorgan, which was the scene in March 1945 of the biggest escape attempt by German prisoners-of-war in Britain; the Secular Hall (1881) in Humberstone Gate, Leicester, the first Secular Society hall in the world; the Rudolf Steiner House (1924–6) in Park Road, NW1; the sea lock and bridge (1611) at Meon Marsh, near Titchfield, Hampshire, that survives from one of England's earliest canal navigation systems; a water-driven scythe forge of c.1840 at Blakedown, Worcestershire; and Llanaeron House in Dyfed, the most complete surviving house by John Nash in Wales.

Listing does not necessarily mean preservation in perpetuity and owners may apply for permission to demolish. The more important applications in the past year included proposals to destroy: Oakhill Park Mansion, Accrington, Lancs. (refused); the Mornington Road Methodist Church, Bingley, W. Yorks., an impressive design of 1874; Eastbrook Hall, Bradford, a splendid hall of c.1900; Burnaston House, near Derby (a Neo-Classical villa demolished to make way for a new Toyota factory); Dixon's Chimney, Shaddongate, Carlisle, the tallest mill chimney in the country (refused); the Belgrave Chapel, Darwen, Lancs., of 1847, listed Grade II* (refused); 50–51 Market Place, Doncaster, a delicate late 18th century Adamesque design (refused); All Saints Church, Hawkhurst, Kent, a mature Gilbert Scott design of 1859, where a scheme for part-demolition won approval; the Palace House Mansion in Palace Street, Newmarket, Suffolk, which incorporates the remains of the old Royal Palace of c.1670 built for Charles II (refused); five listed buildings in Ber Street and King Street, Norwich, threatened by a County Council proposal for a relief road; the Broughton Park Congregational Church (1874), Salford; the Argyle Church (1873), St Helen's Road, Swansea; and St Bride's Church, Wentloog, Gwent, a major medieval monument (refused). Probably the most audacious application was to demolish Highcliffe Castle, Christchurch, Dorset, which is listed Grade I; the application was swiftly refused.

Very few applications end up in the law courts, but two major ones did in 1990–91. The application by Lord Palumbo to demolish nine listed buildings opposite the Mansion House in the City of London in order to construct a new building by James Stirling was contested in the courts by the conservation group Save Britain's Heritage. Save was able to have the Secretary of State for the Environment's decision to grant consent overturned, but that decision was itself reversed in the House of Lords, after which Lord Palumbo chose to exercise his right to secure £120,000 costs from the small charitable organization.

Save Britain's Heritage also contested the decision by the Secretary of State not to intervene to prevent the alienation of Canova's exquisite *The Three Graces* from the tempietto at Woburn Abbey which was built to house it, after the statue was sold to an overseas buyer for £7·6 million. The court case was dropped after the Secretary of State announced that listed building consent for removal was not required given that the statue had been regarded as a fitting and not a fixture and was therefore beyond statutory control.

Museums.—A number of museums opened in 1990–91, many within historic buildings. One of London's great 'private palaces', Spencer House, was opened to the public for the first time after a comprehensive and magnificent restoration carried out by Lord Rothschild. The house, begun in 1756, was the London home of the Earls Spencer.

The National Trust saved two properties where major collections had faced dispersal. Avebury Manor, Wiltshire, is an oustanding 16th century house adjacent to the Avebury stone circles; there had been plans to make the house the centre of a theme park. A La Ronde at Topsham, Devon, is a charmingly eccentric property, listed Grade I. Built by spinster cousins in 1798, it has 16 sides and a conical dormered roof, and contains one of those museums of curiosities beloved of the 19th century.

The Hertfordshire Building Preservation Trust announced an ambitious project to conserve the forge at Much Hadham. The forge was worked by the Page family for nearly two centuries and still contains some 7,000 items and tools. Plans have been announced to create a museum within the former British Schools in Queen Street, Hitchin, Herts., which contains one of the few surviving stepped floor classrooms built on the recommendation of Matthew Arnold. The Vivat Trust launched an appeal for the repair of the belvedere (1725) near Waldershare Park at Dover. Designed either by Lord Burlington or Colen Campbell, this vast four-square tower is externally austere but offers internally the surprise of two domes.

One of the most important nonconformist chapels in Yorkshire, the former Queen Street Methodist Chapel in the centre of Huddersfield, is to be converted to provide a theatre for that city. Other museums are planned in the former Town Hall and Customs House at Fleetwood, Lancs., which was laid out at a model town by Decimus Burton in the 19th century. A Museum of Brickwork is planned at the former Bursledon Brickworks at Swanwick, Hants.

National Heritage Memorial Fund.—The annual report of the National Heritage Memorial Fund, published in October 1990, revealed expenditure of nearly £17·5 million in the year under review. The Fund exists to facilitate the purchase of treasures, artistic, architectural and natural, by parties other than itself. The report confirms just how much the Fund deserved the Government's decision, announced in November 1990, to increase its guaranteed annual income from £3 million to £12 million.

Projects assisted in 1990 included the acquisition

of Spencer family papers from Althorp by the Northamptonshire Record Office; the conservation of drawings owned by the Royal Incorporation of Architects in Scotland; the purchase by the Fitzwilliam Museum, Cambridge, of an elaborate lapis lazuli cup commissioned by William Beckford of Fonthill Abbey; the safeguarding (for £3·365 million) of the contents of Brodsworth Hall, South Yorkshire, for transfer to English Heritage, which was given the house in 1988; the acquisition of further Brunel family papers by Bristol University Library; the retention in the RIBA Drawings Collection of the 3,819 drawings by the architect George Devey which had been on loan to it since 1968; the restoration of the memorial (1611) to the first Earl Dunbar in the parish church at Dunbar that was severely damaged by fire in 1987; the purchase of eight plaster maquettes (1954) by Henry Moore for a scheme entered unsuccessfully by the architect Michael Rosenauer for the proposed Marconi House extension to the English Electric Company headquarters in the Strand; the resiting at the Jackfield Tile Museum at Ironbridge, Shropshire, of the enchanting tiled panels made by Carters of Poole in 1929 for the Babies' Ward in the West Wing of the Middlesex Hospital; the donation of the Ricketts Photographic Collection to the National Museum of Photography, Film and Television, Bradford; and the continuing conservation of the monuments and stained glass at St Nicholas's Church, Stanford-on-Avon, Northamptonshire.

Registers and recognition.—The White Paper *This Common Inheritance* laid out the Government's environmental policy. Much of it was in the nature of a review but among the proposed actions, the Government announced its intention to strengthen the legislation protecting scheduled monuments, and the preparation by English Heritage of a register of landscapes and sites (such as battlefields) which are of historic significance but where there are no longer any identifiable remains.

A less well-known EC Green Paper on the urban environment, also published in autumn 1990, suggested the introduction of Community grants for the conservation of historic buildings of European significance and the possible establishment of a Community system of recognition of the historic and cultural significance of individual buildings and parts of urban areas.

Recognition without concomitant statutory protection lay behind two further campaigns of archaeological recording in 1991. In response to a request from the General Synod, the Council for British Archaeology compiled a preliminary survey of 304 ruined churches which were certainly or probably the responsibility of parochial church councils. Appendices provided lists of 434 ruins in private ownership and 560 so-called flat sites. Meanwhile, the Churches Committee of the Council for Scottish Archaeology announced the establishment of a research project to compile an inventory that will bring together written source material about all places of Christian worship in Scotland. A print-out will eventually be stored at the National Monuments Record (Scotland) and at Restenneth Library.

COUNTRYSIDE CONSERVATION

NATIONAL PARKS
England and Wales

The ten National Parks of England and Wales were established in the 1950s under the provisions of the National Parks and Access to the Countryside Act 1949. The National Parks were set up to conserve and protect scenic landscapes from inappropriate development and to provide access to the land for public enjoyment.

The Countryside Commission is the statutory body which has the power to designate National Parks in England and the Countryside Council for Wales is responsible for National Parks in Wales. The designation of National Parks in England is considered and confirmed by the Secretary of State for the Environment, and the designation of National Parks in Wales by the Secretary of State for Wales. The designation of a National Park does not affect the ownership of the land, nor does it remove the rights of the local community. Although the parks are administered through local government, the vast majority of the land is owned by private landowners (74 per cent) or by other bodies like the National Trust (7 per cent) and the Forestry Commission (7 per cent). The National Park Authorities own only 2·3 per cent of the land in the National Parks.

Under the Local Government Act 1972, National Park Authorities (NPAs) are the authorities responsible for park administration. They also influence land use and development, and deal with planning applications.

Two-thirds of the members of each authority are appointed by the county and district councils within whose boundaries the parks lie. One-third of the members are appointed by the Secretary of State for the Environment or the Secretary of State for Wales with advice from the Countryside Commission or the Countryside Council for Wales.

In the Peak District and the Lake District the NPAs are special boards: the Peak Park Joint Planning Board and the Lake District Special Planning Board. These are autonomous authorities which are financially independent, unlike the authorities in the other eight parks which are county council committees. The NPAs appoint the National Park Officer for the National Park they administer.

Central government provides 75 per cent of the funding for the parks through the National Park Supplementary Grant. The remaining 25 per cent is supplied by the local authorities concerned. Forecast expenditure for 1991–92 was £22,126,410.

The Countryside Commission has stated that other areas are regarded as being worthy of National Parks status. A special statutory authority, the Broads Authority, was established in 1989 to develop, conserve and manage the Norfolk and Suffolk Broads (*see* **Government and Public Offices**). The other area considered worthy of designation is the New Forest and it has been the subject of a consultative report to decide upon its future.

The National Parks in England and Wales are:

Brecon Beacons (1,344 sq. km/519 sq. miles).— Designated in 1957, the park lies in Powys (66 per cent), Dyfed, Gwent and Mid Glamorgan. The park is centred on the Beacons, Pen y Fan, Corn Du and Cribyn, but also includes the valley of the Usk, the Black Mountains to the east and the Black Mountain to the west.

There are information centres at Brecon, Craig-y-nos Country Park, Abergavenny and Llandovery, a study centre at Danywenallt and a day visitor centre near Libanus.

Information Office, 7 Glamorgan Street, Brecon, Powys LD3 7DP. (Tel. 0874-624437). *National Park Officer*, M. Fitton.

Dartmoor (945 sq. km/365 sq. miles).—Designated in 1951, Dartmoor lies wholly in Devon. Dartmoor consists of moorland and rocky granite tors, and is rich in prehistoric remains.

There are information centres at Newbridge, Tavistock, Bovey Tracey, Steps Bridge, Princetown and Postbridge.

Information Office, Parke, Haytor Road, Bovey Tracey, Devon TQ13 9JQ. (Tel. 0626-832093). *National Park Officer*, N. Atkinson.

Exmoor (686 sq. km/265 sq. miles).—Designated in 1954, Exmoor lies in Somerset (71 per cent) and Devon. Exmoor is a moorland plateau inhabited by wild ponies and red deer. There are many ancient remains and burial mounds.

There are information centres at Lynmouth, County Gate, Dulverton and Combe Martin.

Information Office, Exmoor House, Dulverton, Somerset TA22 9HL. (Tel. 0398-23665). *National Park Officer*, K. Bungay.

Lake District (2,292 sq. km/885 sq. miles).—Designated in 1951, the Lake District lies wholly in Cumbria. The Lake District includes England's highest mountains (Scafell Pike, Helvellyn and Skiddaw) but it is most famous for its glaciated lakes.

There are information centres at Keswick, Waterhead, Hawkshead, Seatoller, Bowness, Grasmere, Coniston, Glenridding and Pooley Bridge, an information van at Gosforth and a park centre at Brockhole, Windermere.

Information Office, Busher Walk, Kendal, Cumbria LA9 4RH. (Tel. 0539-724555). *National Park Officer*, J. Toothill.

Northumberland (1,031 sq. km/398 sq. miles).— Designated in 1956, the Northumberland National Park lies wholly in Northumberland. The park is an area of hill country stretching from Hadrian's Wall to the Scottish Border.

There are information centres at Ingram, Once Brewed, Rothbury, Housesteads, Harbottle and Kielder, and an information caravan at Cawfields.

Information Office, Eastburn, South Park, Hexham, Northumberland NE46 1BS. (Tel. 0434-605555). *National Park Officer*, G. Taylor.

North York Moors (1,433 sq. km/553 sq. miles).— Designated in 1952, the North York Moors lie in North Yorkshire (96 per cent) and Cleveland. The park consists of woodland and moorland, and includes the Hambleton Hills and the Cleveland Way.

There are information centres at Danby, Pickering, Sutton Bank, Ravenscar, Helmsley and Hutton-le-Hole, and a day study centre at Danby.

Information Office, The Old Vicarage, Bondgate, Helmsley, York YO6 5BP. (Tel. 0439-70657). *National Park Officer*, D. Statham.

Peak District (1,404 sq. km/542 sq. miles).—Designated in 1951, the Peak District lies in Derbyshire (64 per cent), Staffordshire, South Yorkshire, Cheshire, West Yorkshire and Greater Manchester. The Peak District is composed of the gritstone moors of the 'dark peak' and the limestone dales of the 'white peak'.

There are information centres at Bakewell, Edale, Fairholmes and Castleton, and information points in the Goyt Valley and at Hartington.

Information Office, Aldern House, Baslow Road, Bakewell, Derbyshire DE4 1AE. (Tel. 0629 814321). *National Park Officer*, M. Dower.

Pembrokeshire Coast (583 sq. km/225 sq. miles). Designated in 1952, the Pembrokeshire Coast National Park lies wholly in Dyfed. The park consists of cliffs, open moorland and Skomer Island.

There are information centres at Tenby, St David's, Pembroke, Newport, Kilgetty, Haverfordwest and Broad Haven.

Information Office, County Offices, Haverfordwest, Dyfed SA61 1QZ. (Tel. 0437-764591). *National Park Officer*, N. Wheeler.

Snowdonia (2,171 sq. km/838 sq. miles).—Designated in 1951, Snowdonia lies wholly in Gwynedd. It is an area of deep valleys and rugged mountains in northern Wales.

There are information centres at Aberdovey, Bala, Betws y Coed, Blaenau Ffestiniog, Conwy, Harlech, Dolgellau and Llanberis.

Information Office, Penrhyndeudraeth, Gwynedd LL48 6LS. (Tel. 0766-770274). *National Park Officer*, A. Jones.

Yorkshire Dales (1,762 sq. km/680 sq. miles).— Designated in 1954, the Yorkshire Dales National Park lies in North Yorkshire (88 per cent) and Cumbria. The Yorkshire Dales are composed primarily of limestone overlaid in places by millstone grit. The three peaks of Ingleborough, Whernside and Pen-y-Ghent are within the park.

There are information centres at Clapham, Grassington, Hawes, Aysgarth Falls, Malham and Sedbergh.

Information Office, Yorebridge House, Bainbridge, Leyburn, North Yorkshire DL8 3BP. (Tel. 0969-50456). *National Park Officer*, R. Harvey.

Scotland and Northern Ireland

The National Parks and Access to the Countryside Act 1949 dealt only with England and Wales, and made no provision for Scotland or Northern Ireland. Although there are no national parks in these two countries, there is power to designate them in Northern Ireland under the Amenity Lands Act 1965 and the Nature Conservation and Amenity Lands Order (Northern Ireland) 1985; and in 1989 the Scottish Office asked the Countryside Commission for Scotland to report on whether national parks should be designated in Scotland.

AREAS OF OUTSTANDING NATURAL BEAUTY

England and Wales

Under the National Parks and Access to the Countryside Act 1949, provision was made for the designation of Areas of Outstanding Natural Beauty (AONBs) by the Countryside Commission. The Countryside Act 1968 further defines the role of AONBs, suggesting that they should show due regard for the interests of other land users, such as agriculture and forestry groups. The Countryside Commission continues to be responsible for AONBs in England but since April 1991 the Countryside Council for Wales has been responsible for the Welsh AONBs. Designations in England are confirmed by the Secretary of State for the Environment and those in Wales by the Secretary of State for Wales.

Although less emphasis is placed upon the provision of open-air enjoyment for the public than in the national parks, AONBs are seen as areas which are no less beautiful and require the same degree of protection to conserve and enhance the natural beauty of the countryside. This includes protecting flora and fauna, geographical and other landscape features.

In AONBs planning and management responsibilities are split between county and district councils (there are 17 which cross county boundaries). Finance for the AONBs is provided by grant-aid.

Thirty-nine Areas of Outstanding Natural Beauty have been designated since 1956. They are (with dates of foundation):

Anglesey (1967) (215 sq. km/83 sq. miles).—The designated area extends along the entire coastline of the island, except for breaks around the urban areas and in the vicinity of Wylfa.

Arnside and Silverdale (1972) (75 sq. km/29 sq. miles).—The area embraces the upper half of Morecambe Bay, the Kent estuary, and includes extensive tidal flats in the Bay.

Blackdown Hills (1991) (370 sq. km/143 sq. miles).—An area of greensand ridges of Devon and Somerset extending from Cullompton in the west to Chard in the east, south of Taunton to north of Honiton.

Cannock Chase (1958) (68 sq. km/26 sq. miles).— An area of high heathland in Staffordshire. Deer continue to roam over the Chase.

Chichester Harbour (1964) (75 sq. km/29 sq. miles).—The area extends from Hayling Island to Apuldram and includes Thorney Island.

Chilterns (1965) (833 sq. km/325 sq. miles).—Chalk downlands running from South Oxfordshire northeastwards to Bedfordshire, including the outlying group of hills beyond Luton.

Clwydian Range (1985) (156 sq. km/60 sq. miles).— A prominent ridge extending southwards from Prestatyn on the north Wales coast. Offa's Dike runs along the crest of the range.

Cornwall (1959; Camel Estuary 1983) (957 sq. km/ 370 sq. miles).—A number of separate areas including Bodmin Moor; most of the Land's End peninsula; the coast between St Michael's Mount and St Austell (with Falmouth omitted); the Fowey Estuary; in north Cornwall most of the coast to Bedruthan Steps and between Perranporth and Godrevy Towans, plus the Camel Estuary.

Cotswolds (1966; extended 1991) (1,990 sq. km/768 sq. miles).—The area of limestone hills above the Vales of Gloucester and Evesham.

Cranborne Chase and West Wiltshire Downs (1983) (960 sq. km/371 sq. miles).—A chalkland area covering parts of Wiltshire, Dorset, Hampshire and Somerset, including the wooded remnants of the ancient Chase.

Dedham Vale (1970; extended 1978) (72 sq. km/28 sq. miles).—The area on the Essex/Suffolk border, where John Constable painted.

East Devon (1963) (267 sq. km/103 sq. miles).—The coastline between Exmouth and Lyme Regis, with Sidmouth, Beer and Seaton omitted. Inland Gittisham Hill, East Hill and Woodbury and Aylebeare Commons are included.

North Devon (1960) (171 sq. km/66 sq. miles).— Includes most of the North Devon coastline, from just north of Bude to the boundary of the Exmoor National Park.

South Devon (1960) (332 sq. km/128 sq. miles).— Includes the coast between Bolt Head and Bolt Tail, Salcombe, Slapton Sands and Dartmouth, and the estuaries and valleys of the Yealm, Erme, Avon and Dart.

Dorset (1959) (1,036 sq. km/400 sq. miles).—The coastline between Lyme Regis and Poole, with the Isle of Portland and Weymouth omitted, stretching inland to include the Purbeck Hills and the downs of Hardy country.

Forest of Bowland (1964) (803 sq. km/310 sq. miles).—A moorland area mostly in Lancashire running westward from the River Ribble, with a small outlying area east of the Ribble which includes Pendle Hill.

Gower (1956) (189 sq. km/73 sq. miles).—A peninsula in West Glamorgan, South Wales, known for its coastline.

East Hampshire (1962) (391 sq. km/151 sq. miles).—A chalkland area stretching from the outskirts of Winchester to the Sussex border at a distance of about 10 miles inland.

South Hampshire Coast (1967) (78 sq. km/30 sq. miles).—14 miles of coastline between Hurst Castle and Calshot Castle, extending inland up the Beaulieu River for about six miles.

High Weald (1983) (1,450 sq. km/560 sq. miles).— The area covers parts of East and West Sussex, Kent and Surrey. It is predominantly wooded, and includes larger heathland areas like Ashdown Forest, the remnants of the old Wealden forests.

Howardian Hills (1987) (205 sq. km/79 sq. miles).— Wooded hills which rise above the Vales of York and Pickering.

Kent Downs (1968) (845 sq. km/326 sq. miles).— Running east and south-east from the Surrey border near Westerham to the coast near Dover and Folkestone, with a coastal outlier at South Foreland and a narrow strip of the old sea cliff escarpment west of Hythe overlooking Romney Marsh.

Lincolnshire Wolds (1973) (560 sq. km/216 sq. miles).—The area extends in a south-east direction from Laceby and Caistor in the north to the region of Spilsby, about ten miles west of the coast.

Lleyn (1957) (155 sq. km/60 sq. miles).—An isolated peninsula in Gwynedd.

Malvern Hills (1959) (104 sq. km/40 sq. miles).— The whole range of the Malvern Hills in the county of Hereford and Worcester, just touching Gloucestershire.

Mendip Hills (1972) (206 sq. km/80 sq. miles).— Comprising over half of the Mendip Hills, the area stretches from Bleadon Hill to the A39 road north of Wells and includes Cheddar Gorge and Wookey Hole.

Norfolk Coast (1968) (450 sq. km/174 sq. miles).— An almost continuous coastal strip three to five miles in depth from Hunstanton to Bacton, with a further small strip between Sea Palling and Winterton-on-Sea. The area includes part of the Sandringham Estate.

North Pennines (1988) (1,998 sq. km/779 sq. miles).—The northern limit of the Pennine chain and largest AONB, covering parts of Cumbria, County Durham and Northumberland.

Northumberland Coast (1958) (129 sq. km/50 sq. miles).—Stretches from just south of Berwick to Amble and includes Holy Island and the Farne Islands.

Quantock Hills (1957) (99 sq. km/38 sq. miles).—A range of sandstone hills in Somerset.

Isles of Scilly (1976) (16 sq. km/6 sq. miles).—About 140 islands and skerries in the Scillies group of which only five are inhabited. There are a number of Sites of Special Scientific Interest.

Shropshire Hills (1959) (777 sq. km/300 sq. miles).— Most of south-west Shropshire between the Welsh border and the boundary with Hereford and Worcester, including the region around Clun, the area of the Stiperstones, the Long Mynd and Wenlock Edge, with the tongues of land running north-east to the Wrekin and south towards Ludlow.

Solway Coast (1964) (107 sq. km/41 sq. miles).—A stretch of coastline in Cumbria from Maryport to the estuaries of the Rivers Eden and Esk (with Silloth omitted) backed by the Solway Plain.

Suffolk Coast and Heaths (1970) (391 sq. km/151 sq. miles).—The area includes 38 miles of coastline and parts of the Stour and Orwell estuaries, while the Deben, Alde and Blyth flow through it.

Surrey Hills (1958) (414 sq. km/160 sq. miles).—An area of hills to the east and south of Guildford, including the Hog's Back and the ridge of the North Downs.

Sussex Downs (1966) (981 sq. km/379 sq. miles).— The area includes the chalk escarpment of the South Downs from Beachy Head to the Hampshire border, and stretches down to the coast between Eastbourne and Seaford.

North Wessex Downs (1972) (1,738 sq. km/671 sq. miles).—An upland area in Hampshire, Wiltshire, Oxfordshire and Berkshire, bounded by the Marlborough and Lambourn Downs in the west, the Chiltern Hills in the east and Salisbury Plain in the south.

Isle of Wight (1963) (189 sq. km/73 sq. miles).—A number of separate areas comprising stretches of coastline, the Yar Valley, the high downland behind Ventnor and the chalk ridge which runs from Newport to Culver Cliff and Foreland.

Wye Valley (1971) (325 sq. km/125 sq. miles).—The river valley running through the counties of Gwent, Gloucestershire, and Hereford and Worcester.

Proposals for further designations include: the Tamar and Tavy Valleys, Devon/Cornwall; the Berwyn Mountains, mid-Wales; and the Nidderdale Moors, North Yorkshire.

Northern Ireland

The Department of the Environment for Northern Ireland, with advice from the Council for Nature Conservation and the Countryside, designates Areas of Outstanding Natural Beauty in Northern Ireland. At present there are nine and these cover a total area of approximately 282,395 hectares (695,166 acres).

Antrim Coast and Glens, Co. Antrim (70,600 ha/ 174,452 acres).

Causeway Coast, Co. Antrim (4,050 ha/10,000 acres).

Lagan Valley, Co. Down (2,072 ha/5,119 acres).

Lecale Coast, Co. Down (3,108 ha/7,679 acres).

Mourne, Co. Down (57,012 ha/140,876 acres).

North Derry, Co. Londonderry (12,950 ha/31,999 acres).

South Armagh, Co. Armagh (12,950 ha/31,999 acres).

Sperrin, Co. Tyrone/Co. Londonderry (101,006 ha/ 249,585 acres).

Strangford Lough, Co. Down (18,647 ha/46,077 acres).

NATIONAL SCENIC AREAS

No Areas of Outstanding Natural Beauty are designated in Scotland. However, National Scenic Areas have a broadly equivalent status.

The Countryside Commission for Scotland recognizes areas of national scenic significance. At present there are 40, covering a total area of 1,017,300 hectares (2,513,748 acres).

Development within National Scenic Areas is dealt with by the local planning authority, who are required to consult the Countryside Commission for Scotland for certain categories of development within these areas. Land management uses can also be modified in the interest of scenic conservation. The Secretary of State for Scotland has limited powers of intervention should a planning authority and the Countryside Commission for Scotland disagree.

	ha	acres
Border		
Eildon and Leaderfoot	3,600	8,896
Upper Tweeddale	12,300	30,393
Central		
Loch Lomond*	13,900	34,347
Loch Rannoch and Glen Lyon*	1,300	3,212
The Trossachs	4,600	11,367
Dumfries and Galloway		
East Stewartry Coast	5,200	12,849
Fleet Valley	5,300	13,096
Nith Estuary	9,300	22,980
Grampian		
The Cairngorm Mountains*	29,800	73,636
Deeside and Lochnagar* ...	32,200	79,566
Highland		
Assynt-Coigach	90,200	222,884
Ben Nevis and Glen Coe* ..	69,600	171,982
The Cairngorm Mountains*	37,400	92,415
The Cuillin Hills	21,900	54,115
Dornoch Firth	7,500	18,532
Glen Affric	19,300	47,690
Glen Strathfarrar	3,800	9,390
Kintail	16,300	40,277
Knoydart	39,500	97,604

	ha	acres
Kyle of Tongue............	18,500	45,713
Loch Shiel	13,400	33,111
Morar, Moidart and Ardnamurchan	15,900	39,289
North-west Sutherland	20,500	50,655
The Small Isles	15,500	38,300
Trotternish...............	5,000	12,355
Wester Ross	145,300	359,036
Orkney Islands		
Hoy and West Mainland ...	14,800	36,571
Shetland Islands		
Shetland	15,600	38,548
Strathclyde		
Ben Nevis and Glen Coe* ..	17,500	43,242
Jura	21,800	53,868
Knapdale	19,800	48,926
Kyles of Bute	4,400	10,872
Loch Lomond*	30,300	74,871
Loch na Keal, Isle of Mull ..	12,700	31,382
Lynn of Lorn	4,800	11,861
Scarba, Lunga and the Garvellachs.............	1,900	4,692
Tayside		
Ben Nevis and Glen Coe* ...	4,500	11,119
Deeside and Lochnagar* ...	7,800	19,274
Loch Rannoch and Glen Lyon*	47,100	116,384
Loch Tummel	9,200	22,733
River Earn	3,000	7,413
River Tay	5,600	13,838
Western Isles		
St Kilda	900	2,224
South Lewis, Harris and North Uist	108,600	268,351
South Uist Machair	6,100	15,073
Total	1,017,300	2,513,748

*National Scenic Areas in more than one region

PERIODS OF GESTATION OR INCUBATION

The table shows approximate periods of gestation or incubation for some common animals and birds. In some cases the periods may vary and where doubt arises professional advice should be sought.

Species	Shortest period (days)	Usual period (days)	Longest period (days)	Species	Shortest period (days)	Usual period (days)	Longest period (days)
Human.............	240	273	313	Duck.............	28	28	32
Horse	305	336	340	Chicken	20	21	22
Cow	273	280	294	Pigeon	17	18	19
Goat	147	151	155	Canary	12	14	14
Sheep	140	147–50	160	Guinea Pig	63	—	70
Pig	109	112	125	Mouse	18	—	19
Dog	55	63	70	Rat	21	—	24
Cat	53	56	63	Elephant		21–22 months	
Rabbit	30	32	35				
Goose	28	30	32	Zebra		56 weeks	
Turkey.............	25	28	28	Camel...........		45 weeks	

NATURE CONSERVATION AREAS

SITES OF SPECIAL SCIENTIFIC INTEREST

Site of Special Scientific Interest (SSSI) is a legal designation applied to land in England, Scotland or Wales which the Nature Conservancy Council for England, or for Scotland (NCC), or the Countryside Council for Wales (CCW) identifies as being of special interest because of its flora, fauna, geological or physiographical features. In some cases, SSSI are managed as nature reserves.

The NCC or CCW must notify its intention to declare the land of special interest to the local planning authority, the water and drainage authority, every owner/occupier of the land, and the Secretary of State for the Environment (or Secretary of State for Scotland or for Wales where applicable). Forestry and agricultural departments must also be notified.

Objections to the designation of SSSI can be made and ultimately heard at a full meeting of the Council of the NCCs or CCW. As a last resort a site can be purchased.

The protection of most sites depends on the co-operation of individual landowners and occupiers. Occupiers must consult the NCCs or CCW and gain written consent before they can undertake certain listed activities on the site.

As at March 31, 1991 there were 5,671 SSSI in Britain, covering 1,778,474 hectares (4,394,698 acres).

	No.	hectares	acres
England	3,536	781,526	1,931,190
Scotland	1,319	803,906	1,986,492
Wales	816	193,042	477,016

Northern Ireland

In Northern Ireland 26 Areas of Special Scientific Interest (ASSIs) have been established by the Department of the Environment for Northern Ireland. These cover a total area of 6,890 hectares (17,017 acres).

NATIONAL NATURE RESERVES

National Nature Reserves are defined in the National Parks and Access to the Countryside Act 1949 as land designated for the study and preservation of flora and fauna, or of geological or physiographical features.

The NCCs or CCW can designate as a National Nature Reserve land which is being managed as a nature reserve under an agreement with the NCC; land held and managed by the NCC; or land held and managed as a nature reserve by another approved body. The NCCs or CCW can turn to the appropriate Secretary of State to impose by-laws for the protection of the reserves from undesirable development.

As at March 31, 1991 there were 242 National Nature Reserves in Britain, covering 168,309 hectares (415,900 acres).

	No.	hectares	acres
England	128	43,270	106,922
Scotland	68	112,241	277,344
Wales	46	12,798	31,623

Northern Ireland

National Nature Reserves are established and managed by the Department of the Environment for Northern Ireland, with advice from the Council for Nature Conservation and the Countryside. There are 44 National Nature Reserves covering 4,368 hectares (10,789 acres).

LOCAL NATURE RESERVES

Local Nature Reserves are defined in the National Parks and Access to the Countryside Act 1949 as land designated for the study and preservation of flora and fauna, or of geological or physiographical features. The Act gives local authorities in England and Wales and district councils in Scotland the power to acquire, declare and manage local nature reserves in consultation with the Nature Conservancy Council. Conservation trusts can also own and manage non-statutory local nature reserves.

As at March 31, 1991 there were 195 designated Local Nature Reserve areas in Britain, covering 14,835 hectares (36,658 acres).

	No.	hectares	acres
England	221	11,010	27,206
Scotland	6	2,688	6,643
Wales	14	1,137	2,809

An additional 16.8 km of linear trails are designated as LNRs.

FOREST NATURE RESERVES

The Forestry Commission has created Forest Nature Reserves from conservation sites within the Commission's estate. These are like other nature reserves in that their purpose is to protect and conserve special forms of natural habitat, flora and fauna existing in forested areas.

The Forestry Commission has 340 SSSI on its estates and has chosen 46 as Forest Nature Reserves. They extend in size from under 50 hectares (124 acres) to 500 hectares (1,236 acres). The largest include the Black Wood of Rannoch, by Loch Rannoch; Cannop Valley Oakwoods, Forest of Dean; Culbin Forest, near Forres; Glen Affric, near Fort Augustus; Kylerhea, Skye; Pembrey, Carmarthen Bay; Starr Forest, in Galloway Forest Park; Wyre Forest, near Kidderminster.

Northern Ireland

There are 36 Forest Nature Reserves in Northern Ireland, covering 1,759 hectares (4,346 acres). They are designated and administered by the Forest Service, a division of the Department of Agriculture for Northern Ireland.

MARINE NATURE RESERVES

The Wildlife and Countryside Act 1981 gave the Secretary of State for the Environment (and the Secretaries of State for Wales and for Scotland where appropriate) power to designate Marine Nature Reserves and the Nature Conservancy Council powers to select and manage these reserves. Interested parties at a local and at a national level are consulted prior to the confirmation of an area.

Marine Nature Reserves provide protection for marine flora and fauna, and geological and physiographical features on land covered by tidal waters up to and including the limit of territorial waters. Reserves also provide opportunities for study and research.

Lundy, in the Bristol Channel, became the first statutory Marine Nature Reserve in November 1986. Skomer, Dyfed, was designated in July 1990. Other areas proposed for designation as reserves are: the Isles of Scilly; the Menai Strait; Bardsey Island and part of the Lleyn peninsula, Gwynedd; Loch Sween, Strathclyde; St Abb's Head, Berwickshire.

A number of non-statutory marine reserves have been set up by conservation groups.

HISTORIC MONUMENTS

England

The following is a select list of monuments under the control of English Heritage.

Charges for admission represent the figures obtaining in 1991–92. Concessionary rates are available for children, etc.

Annual membership passes are available at £15 for adults, £10·50 for pensioners and £7 for children upon application to English Heritage Membership Department., PO Box 1BB, W1A 1BB.

Standard hours of opening (marked *) are as follows:

Good Friday or April 1 (which-
ever is earlier)–Sept. 30   Daily 10–6
Oct. 1–Maundy Thursday or
April 1 (whichever is earlier)   Tues.–Sun. 10–4

Monuments not marked * are open from Good Friday to September only.

All monuments are closed on Christmas Eve, Christmas Day, Boxing Day and New Year's Day. Some smaller sites may close for the lunch-hour, which is normally 1–2 p.m. During the winter season, many monuments are closed on Mondays.

BATTLE ABBEY, E. Sussex. £1·90*. Remains of the abbey founded by William the Conqueror on the site of the Battle of Hastings.

BEESTON CASTLE, Cheshire. £1.60*. Thirteenth-century inner ward with gatehouse and towers, and considerable remains of large outer ward.

BOLSOVER CASTLE, Derbyshire. £1.60*. Notable for its exceptionally interesting 17th century buildings.

BOSCOBEL HOUSE, Shropshire. £2.50*. Timber-framed early 17th century hunting lodge with later alterations. Charles II's 'Royal Oak' is nearby.

BRINKBURN PRIORY, Northumberland. 95p. A house of Augustinian canons; the church (c.1200, repaired in 1858) and parts of the cloister buildings survive.

BROUGHAM CASTLE, Cumbria. 95p*. Extensive remains of the 13th century keep, and of other buildings of periods up to the 17th century.

BYLAND ABBEY, North Yorkshire. 95p*. Considerable remains of church and conventual buildings date from the abbey's foundation in 1177 by the Cistercians.

CARISBROOKE CASTLE, Isle of Wight. £2.60*. Norman castle, the prison of Charles I from 1647–1648.

CARLISLE CASTLE, Cumbria. £1.60*. Medieval castle, prison of Mary Queen of Scots. Inner and outer wards enclosing a 12th century keep.

CASTLE ACRE PRIORY, Norfolk. £1.30*. Extensive remains include the 12th century church and the prior's lodgings.

CASTLE RISING CASTLE, Norfolk. 95p*. A 12th century keep standing in a massive earthwork with its gatehouse and bridge.

CHESTERS ROMAN FORT, Northumberland. £1.60*. Fine example of a bath house.

CHYSAUSTER ANCIENT VILLAGE, Cornwall. 95p*. Romano–Cornish village, 2nd and 3rd century AD, probably on a late Iron Age site.

CLEEVE ABBEY, Somerset. £1.30*. Much of the claustral buildings survive including timber-roofed frater, but only foundations of the church.

CORBRIDGE ROMAN SITE, Northumberland. £1.60*. Excavations have revealed the central area of a Roman town and successive military bases.

DEAL CASTLE, Kent. £1.60*. The largest and most complete of the forts erected by Henry VIII for coastal defence.

DOVER CASTLE, Kent. £3.00*. One of the strongest British castles, with Roman, Saxon and Norman features.

DUNSTANBURGH CASTLE, Northumberland. 95p*. The 14th century castle standing on a cliff above the sea has a substantial gatehouse-keep.

FARLEIGH HUNGERFORD CASTLE, Somerset. 95p*. Late 14th century castle of two courts. The chapel contains fine tomb of Sir Thomas Hungerford.

FARNHAM CASTLE KEEP, Surrey. £1.30. Built by the Bishops of Winchester, the motte of the castle is enclosed by a large 12th century shell keep. Foundations of a Norman tower.

FINCHALE PRIORY, Durham. 95p* (free in winter). Benedictine priory on banks of River Wear with considerable 13th century remains.

FRAMLINGHAM CASTLE, Suffolk. £1.30*. Impressive castle (c.1200) with high curtain walls enclosing a poorhouse of 1639.

FURNESS ABBEY, Cumbria. £1.60*. Founded in 1123 by Stephen, afterwards King of England; extensive remains of church and conventual buildings.

GOODRICH CASTLE, Hereford and Worcester. £1.30*. Extensive remains of 13th and 14th century castle incorporating 12th century keep.

GRIMES GRAVES, Norfolk. 95p*. Extensive group of flint mines dating from the Neolithic period. Several shafts can be inspected.

HAILES ABBEY, Gloucestershire. £1.30*. Ruins of a Cistercian monastery founded in 1246. Museum contains some fine architectural fragments.

HELMSLEY CASTLE, North Yorkshire. £1.30*. Twelfth century keep and curtain wall with 16th century domestic buildings. Spectacular earthwork defences.

HOUSESTEADS ROMAN FORT, Northumberland. £1.60*. Excavation has exposed this infantry fort on Hadrian's Wall with its extra-mural civilian settlement.

KENILWORTH CASTLE, Warwickshire. £1.30*. One of the most extensive castles in Britain, showing many styles of building from 1155 to 1649.

LANERCOST PRIORY, Cumbria. 65p. The nave of the Augustinian priory church, c.1166, is still used and there are remains of other claustral buildings.

LINDISFARNE PRIORY, Northumberland. £1.60* (subject to tide). The bishopric of the Northumbrian kingdom destroyed by the Danes; re-established in 11th century as a Benedictine priory, now ruined.

LULLINGSTONE ROMAN VILLA, Kent. £1.30*. A large villa occupied through much of the Roman period; fine mosaics.

MIDDLEHAM CASTLE, North Yorkshire. 95p*. Childhood home of Richard III. The 12th century keep stands within later fortifications and domestic buildings.

MOUNT GRACE PRIORY, North Yorkshire. £1.60*. Carthusian monastery, founded 1398, with remains of monastic buildings.

NETLEY ABBEY, Hampshire. 95p* (weekends only in winter). Extensive remains of Cistercian abbey, founded 1239, with ruined Tudor house.

OLD SARUM, Wiltshire. 95p*. Large earthworks enclosing the excavated remains of the castle and the first Salisbury cathedral, begun in 1078.

ORFORD CASTLE, Suffolk. £1.30*. Circular keep of c.1170 and remains of coastal defence castle built by Henry II.

PENDENNIS CASTLE, Cornwall. £1.60*. Well-preserved castle erected by Henry VIII for coastal defence.

PEVENSEY CASTLE, East Sussex. £1.30*. Walls of a 4th century Roman fort enclosing remains of an 11th century castle.

PEVERIL CASTLE, Derbyshire. 95p*. In a picturesque and nearly impregnable position, this 12th century castle is defended on two sides by precipitous rocks.

PORTCHESTER CASTLE, Hampshire. £1.30*. Walls of a late Roman fort enclosing a Norman keep and an Augustinian priory church.

RECULVER TOWERS and ROMAN FORT, Kent. Adm. free. Remains of Saxon and Norman church with 12th century towers, standing in a Roman fort.

RICHBOROUGH CASTLE, Kent. £1.30*. The landing-site of the Claudian invasion in 43 AD, with massive 3rd century stone walls.

RICHMOND CASTLE, North Yorkshire. £1.30*. This 12th century keep, with 11th century curtain wall and gatehouse, commands Swaledale.

RIEVAULX ABBEY, North Yorkshire. £1.60*. Founded c.1132. Extensive remains include an early Cistercian nave and fine 13th century choir and claustral buildings.

ROCHESTER CASTLE, Kent. £1.30*. Eleventh century castle partly founded on the Roman city wall, with a square keep of c.1130.

ST AUGUSTINE'S ABBEY, Kent. 95p*. Remains of Benedictine monastery, with Norman church, on site of abbey founded by St Augustine in 598.

ST MAWES CASTLE, Cornwall. 95p*. Coastal defence castle built by Henry VIII consisting of central tower and three bastions.

SCARBOROUGH CASTLE, North Yorkshire. £1.30*. Remains of 12th century keep and curtain walls dominating the town.

STONEHENGE, Wiltshire. £1.90*. Prehistoric monument consisting of a series of concentric stone circles surrounded by a ditch and bank.

TILBURY FORT, Essex. £1.30*. One of Henry VIII's coastal forts, extended by Charles II.

TINTAGEL CASTLE, Cornwall. £1.60*. 12th century castle on cliff top. Dark Age settlement site.

TYNEMOUTH PRIORY and CASTLE, Tyne and Wear. 95p*. Remains of a Benedictine priory, founded 1090, on Saxon monastic site. Coastal batteries with reconstructed First World War magazine.

WALMER CASTLE, Kent. £2.20*. (Closed when Lord Warden is in residence.) One of Henry VIII's coastal defence castles, now the residence of the Lord Warden of the Cinque Ports.

WARKWORTH CASTLE, Northumberland. 95p*. 15th century keep amidst earlier ruins with a 14th century hermitage upstream.

WHITBY ABBEY, North Yorkshire. 95p*. 13th and 14th century Benedictine church on site of monastery founded in 657.

WROXETER ROMAN CITY, Shropshire. £1·30*. The 2nd century public baths and part of the forum remain of the Roman town of Viroconium.

Wales

The following is a select list of monuments under the control of Cadw: Welsh Historic Monuments. Charges for admission (subject to alteration) are given below. Concessionary rates are available for children, etc.

Standard hours of admission:

	Weekdays	Sundays
March 25–Oct. 26	9.30–6.30	2.00–6.30
Oct. 27–March 24	9.30–4.00	2.00–4.00

All monuments are closed on Christmas Eve, Christmas Day, Boxing Day and New Year's Day.

BEAUMARIS CASTLE, Anglesey, Gwynedd. £1.50. The finest example of the concentrically planned castle in Britain, it is still almost intact.

CAERLEON ROMAN AMPHITHEATRE, Gwent. £1·25. Late 1st century oval arena surrounded by bank for spectators.

CAERLEON ROMAN FORTRESS BATHS, Gwent. £1·25. Rare example of a legionary bath-house.

CAERNARFON CASTLE, Gwynedd. £3, family ticket £8. The most important of the Edwardian castles, built together with the town wall between 1283 and 1330.

CAERPHILLY CASTLE, Mid-Glamorgan. £1.50. Concentrically planned castle (c.1270) notable for its great scale and use of water defences.

CASTELL COCH, S. Glamorgan. £1.75. Rebuilt 1875–90 on medieval foundations.

CHEPSTOW CASTLE, Gwent. £2, family ticket £5. Fine rectangular keep in the middle of extensive fortifications.

CONWY CASTLE, Gwynedd. £2. Built by Edward I to guard the Conwy ferry.

CRICCIETH CASTLE, Gwynedd. £1.75, family ticket £5. A native Welsh castle of the early 13th century, much altered by Edward I.

DENBIGH CASTLE, Clwyd. £1·25. The remains of the castle, which dates from 1282–1322, include an unusual triangular gatehouse.

HARLECH CASTLE, Gwynedd. £2. Well preserved Edwardian castle with a concentric plan sited on a rocky outcrop above the former shore-line.

RAGLAN CASTLE, Gwent. £1.75. Extensive remains of 15th century castle with moated hexagonal keep.

ST DAVID'S, BISHOP'S PALACE, Dyfed. £1.50. Extensive remains of principal residence of Bishop of St David's dating from 1280–1350.

TINTERN ABBEY, Gwent. £1.75. Extensive remains of 13th century church and conventual buildings of this Cistercian monastery.

TRETOWER COURT, Powys. £1.50. Medieval house with remains of castle nearby.

Scotland

The following is a select list of monuments under the control of Historic Buildings and Monuments, Scottish Development Department.

Charges for admission are those obtaining in 1991. Except where indicated differently, charges are adults 80p, concessions (con.) 40p.

Standard hours of opening (marked S.) are as follows:

	Weekdays	Sundays
April–Sept.	9.30–6.00	2.00–6.00
Oct.–March	9.30–4.00	2.00–4.00

Monuments open at any reasonable time are indicated by A.

ABERLEMNO, Tayside. A. Closed in winter. Adm. free. Four Pictish stones.

ANTONINE WALL, Central and Strathclyde Regions. A. Adm. free.

ARNOL BLACKHOUSE, Western Isles. S. Closed Sun. Traditional Hebridean dwelling.

BONAWE, Strathclyde. S. Closed in winter. Mid-18th century iron-furnace. £1·20, con. 60p.

BROCH OF BIRSAY, Orkney. S. Closed Mon., Tues. a.m. in winter. Remains of the Norse period.

BROWN AND WHITE CATERTHUNS, Tayside. A. Adm. free. Iron Age hill forts.

CAERLAVEROCK CASTLE, Dumfries and Galloway. S. £1, con. 50p.

CAIRNPAPPLE HILL, Lothian. S. Closed in winter. A prehistoric ritual complex and Bronze Age cairn.

CALLANISH, Western Isles. A. Adm. free. Standing Stones.

CAMSTER CAIRNS, Highland. A. Adm. free.

CLAVA CAIRNS, Highland. A. Adm. free.

DRYBURGH ABBEY, Borders. S. £1.50, con. 75p.

EARLS AND BISHOPS PALACES, Kirkwall, Orkney. S. Closed in winter. Family ticket £4.

EDINBURGH CASTLE, including Scottish National War Memorial, Scottish United Services Museum and Historic Apartments. Open winter: Jan. 4–March 31 and Oct. 1–Dec. 31, Mon.–Sat. 9.30–4.20, Sun. 12.30–3.35. Summer: April 1–Sept. 30, Mon.–Sat. 9.30–5.05, Sun. 11–5.05. Alterations may be made to opening hours during the Tattoo, state and military events. Adm. to War Memorial, free; to all other areas £2.80, con. £1.40, family ticket £7.

EDZELL CASTLE, Tayside. S. Closed Thurs. p.m. and Fri. in winter. £1, con. 50p.

ELGIN CATHEDRAL, Grampian. S.

FORT GEORGE, Highland. S. £1.75, con. 85p, family ticket £4·50.

GLASGOW CATHEDRAL, Strathclyde. S. Adm. free.

GLENELG BROCHS, Highland. A. Adm. free.

HERMITAGE CASTLE, Borders. S.

HUNTLY CASTLE, Grampian. S. Closed Thurs. p.m. and Fri. in winter. £1·20, con. 60p

JARLSHOF, Shetland. S. Closed all winter. Remains of villages from Bronze Age to Viking times. £1·50, con. 75p.

JEDBURGH ABBEY, Borders. S. £1.50, con. 75p, family ticket £3.

KELSO ABBEY, Borders. S. Adm. free.

LINLITHGOW PALACE, Lothian. S. £1·20, con. 60p, family ticket £3.

LOANHEAD STONE CIRCLE, Grampian. A. Adm. free.

MAES HOWE, Orkney. S. £1·20, con. 60p, family ticket £3. Prehistoric tomb.

MEIGLE MUSEUM, Tayside. S. Pictish stones.

MELROSE ABBEY, Borders. S. £1.50, con. 75p, family ticket £3.

MOUSA BROCH, Shetland. A. Adm. free.

NETHER LARGIE CAIRNS, Strathclyde. A. Adm. free.

NEW ABBEY CORN MILL, Dumfries and Galloway. S. Closed Thurs. p.m., Fri. £1, con. 50p.

RING OF BROGAR, Orkney. A. Adm. free.

RUTHWELL CROSS, Dumfries and Galloway. A. Adm. free.

ST ANDREWS CASTLE AND CATHEDRAL, Fife. S. Cathedral, £1, con. 50p.

SKARA BRAE, Orkney. S. £1.50, con. 75p, family ticket £4. Prehistoric village.

SMAILHOLM TOWER, Borders. S. Closed in winter.

STIRLING CASTLE, Central. Open winter: Jan. 4–March 31 and Oct. 1–Dec. 31, Mon.–Sat. 9.30–4.20, Sun. 12.30–3.35; summer: April 1–Sept. 30, Mon.–Sat. 9.30–5.15, Sun. 10.30–4.45. £2, con. £1, family ticket £5.

TANTALLON CASTLE, Lothian. S. £1·20, con. 60p. Closed Thurs. p.m. and Fri. in winter.

THREAVE CASTLE, Dumfries and Galloway. S.

HISTORIC HOUSES AND CASTLES

Dates of opening and admission fees shown are those which obtained in 1991, and are subject to modification. Specific opening hours are not given but may be checked by telephone. Most houses have concessionary rates for certain categories of visitor.

Space permits only a selection of some of the more noteworthy houses in the UK which are open to the public. (*Property of the National Trust; Adm. admission; PM. = open in afternoons only.)

*A LA RONDE, Exmouth.—Good Friday–Oct. 31. Sun.-Thurs. Adm. £2.50. Tel. 0395–265514.

ALNWICK CASTLE, Northumberland.—April 29– Oct. 4 daily PM (not Sat. except July–Aug.). Open Bank Hol. weekends. Adm. £2.50. Tel. 0665–510777.

ALTHORP, Northampton.—Daily (not Christmas). Adm. £2.95, Weds. £3.95 (Connoisseurs' Day). Gardens 50p.

*ANGLESEY ABBEY, Cambs.—March 30–Oct. 13. Adm. £4.50. Gardens only Adm. £2.00. Tel. 0223– 811200.

ARUNDEL CASTLE, W. Sussex.—March 29–Oct. 30 daily (not Sat.). PM. Adm. charge. Tel. 0903–883136.

*BASILDON PARK, Berks.—April–Oct. (not Mon. except Bank Hols; not Tues. not Good Friday). Adm. £2.80. Grounds £1.80. Tel. 0734–843040.

BEAULIEU, Hants.—Daily (not Christmas). Adm. charge. Tel. 0590–612345. (*See also* p. 1170.)

*BELTON HOUSE, Grantham.—April–Oct. Wed.- Sun. and Bank Hol. Mons. (not Good Friday). PM. Adm. £3.50. Tel. 0476–66116.

BELVOIR CASTLE, nr. Grantham.—March 29–Oct. 1 daily (not Mon., Fri. except Bank Hols.) Rest of March, Oct., Sun. only. Adm. £3.00. Tel. 0476–870262.

BERKELEY CASTLE, Glos.—April, Sept. daily (not Mon. except Bank Hols.). PM only except May–Aug., Tues.–Sat. and Bank Hols. Oct. Sun. only. Adm. £2.90. Tel. 0453–810332.

BLAIR CASTLE, Tayside.—March 28–Oct. 25 daily (Sun. April, May and Oct PM.). Adm. £3.30. Tel. 079 681–207.

BLENHEIM PALACE, Oxon.—Mid-March–Oct. 31 daily. Adm. charge. Tel. 0993–811325.

BOUGHTON HOUSE, Northants.—July 27–Sept. 1 daily. Grounds (excl. Gardens) daily (not Fri.) April 27–Sept. 29. PM. Adm. £3.30, Grounds only, £1. Tel. 0536–515731.

BOWHILL, Selkirk.—House July 1–July 31 daily; Grounds April 28–Aug. 28 (not Fri.). daily PM. Adm. £3, Grounds only, £1. Tel. 0750–20732.

BROADLANDS, Hants.—March 28–Sept. 29 daily (not Fri. until Aug., except Good Friday). Adm. £4.50. Tel. 0794–516878.

BRONTË PARSONAGE, Haworth, West Yorks.— Daily, April–Sept. (not Christmas or Jan. 21–Feb. 8). Adm. £2.50. Tel. 0535–42323.

BROUGHTON CASTLE, Oxon.—May 19–Sept. 11 Wed., Sun. (also Thurs. in July and Aug.) and Bank Hol. Suns and Mons. PM. Adm. £2.60. Tel. 0295–262624.

*BUCKLAND ABBEY, Devon.—March 29–end Oct. daily. Nov.–March Wed., Sat., Sun. PM. Adm. £3.60. Tel. 0822–853607.

BURGHLEY HOUSE, Stamford.—Good Friday–Oct. 6 (closed Sept. 14) daily. Adm. £3.80. Tel. 0780–52451.

*CALKE ABBEY, Derbyshire.—March 30–end Oct., Sat.–Wed. PM. Adm. £3.70. Tel. 0332–863822.

CARDIFF CASTLE.—Daily (not Christmas, New Year). Adm. £2.75, Grounds £1.50. Tel. 0222–822086.

*CARLYLE'S HOUSE, Chelsea, London.—April–end Oct. Wed.–Sun. and Bank Hol. Mons. (not Good Friday). Adm. £2.20. Tel. 071–352 7087.

*CASTLE COOLE, Enniskillen.—Easter period, daily; June, July, Aug. daily (not Thurs.); Sat., Sun. and Bank Hols. in April, May, Sept. PM. Adm. £2, Grounds April–Sept. free. Tel. 0365–322690.

*CASTLE DROGO, Devon.—March 29–end Oct. daily except Fri. Adm. £3.80. Grounds £1.60. Tel. 064743– 3306.

CASTLE HOWARD, N. Yorks.—March 22–Nov. 3, daily. Adm. £5.00. Tel. 065384–333.

CAWDOR CASTLE, Inverness.—May–Oct. 6, daily. Adm. £3.20, Grounds £1.60. Tel. 06677–615.

*CHARTWELL, Kent.—Open three days each week. Times vary. Adm. £3.70, Grounds £1.50. Tel. 0732– 866368.

CHATSWORTH, Derbyshire.—March 24–Nov. 23 daily. Grounds March 24–Sept. 29, daily. Adm. charge. Tel. 0246–582204.

CHICHELEY HALL, Newport Pagnell.—March 31– May 27, Aug. Sun. and Bank Hols. PM. Adm. £2.75. Tel. 023065–252.

*CLIVEDEN, Maidenhead.—House, March 29–Oct. 31, Thurs. and Sun. PM. Gardens March–Dec. daily. Adm. £2.80, £1 extra for House. Tel. 0628–605069.

*COMPTON CASTLE, nr. Paignton.—April 2–end Oct. Mon., Wed., Thurs. daily. Adm. £2.00. Tel. 0803– 872112.

*CROFT CASTLE, Herefordshire.—Easter Bank Hol. weekend, May–Sept. Wed.–Sun., Bank Hol. Mons., April and Oct. weekends. PM. Adm. £2.40. Tel. 056885–246.

DICKENS HOUSE, London, WC1.—Daily (not Sun. and Bank Hols.). Adm. £1.50. Tel. 071–405 2127.

DR JOHNSON'S HOUSE, London, EC4.—Daily (not Sun. and Bank Hols.). Adm. £2. Tel. 071–353 3745.

DOWN HOUSE, Downe, Kent.—March–Jan. 31 (not Christmas), not Mon. (except Bank Hols.) or Fri. PM. Adm. £1·50. Tel. 0689–859119.

DRUMLANRIG CASTLE, Dumfries.—April 27–Aug. 25, daily (not Thurs.). Grounds open April 27–Sept. 29. Adm. £3, Grounds only £1. Tel. 0848–31682.

HADDON HALL, Derbyshire.—March 29–Sept. 29. Tues.–Sun., and Bank Hols. Closed Sun. in July and Aug. (except Bank Hol. weekends). Adm. £3.00. Tel. 0629–812855.

HAM HOUSE, Richmond, Surrey.—April–Aug. daily (not Mon., except Bank Hols.; not Good Friday or May 1). Garden all year (except Mon). Adm. £2, Grounds free. Tel. 081–940 1950.

*HARDWICK HALL, Derbyshire.—March 30–Oct. 31. House Wed., Thurs., Sat., Sun., Bank Hol. Mons. Garden daily to end Oct. (not Good Friday). PM. Adm. £4.50, Garden only, £1.80. Tel. 0246–850430.

HAREWOOD HOUSE, Leeds.—March 24–Oct. 31. daily. Sun. only, Feb., March, and Nov. Adm. charge. Tel. 0532–886225.

HATFIELD HOUSE, Herts.—March 25–Oct. 13 daily (not Mon. except Bank Hols., not Good Friday). PM. except Bank Hols. Grounds, times vary. Adm. £3.90. Tel. 0707–262823.

HEVER CASTLE, Kent.—March 19–Nov. 10, daily PM, except Grounds. Adm. charge. Tel. 0732–865224.

HOLKER HALL, Cumbria.—Easter Sun.–last Sun. in Oct. daily (not Sat.). Adm. charge. Tel. 05395–58328.

HOLKHAM HALL, Norfolk.—Late May–Sept. Sun.– Thurs. and Easter, Spring and Summer Bank Holidays. PM, except Bank Hols. Adm. £2. Tel. 0328– 710227.

HOPETOUN HOUSE, nr. Edinburgh.—Easter weekend, April 27–Sept. 29, daily. Adm. £3.00. Tel. 031– 331 2451.

HOUGHTON HALL, Norfolk.—Easter Sun.-Sept. 29, Sun., Thurs. and Bank Hols. PM. Adm. £3. Tel. 048-522 569.

*HUGHENDEN MANOR, High Wycombe.—April-end Oct. (not Good Friday), Wed.-Sun. and Bank Hol. Mons. PM. March, weekends only. Adm. £2.80. Tel. 0494-532580.

INVERARAY CASTLE, Argyll.—1st Sat. in April-2nd Sun. in Oct. daily (not Fri., except July-Aug.), Sun., PM. Woods open all year. Tel. 0499-2203.

JANE AUSTEN'S HOUSE, Chawton, Hants.—April-Oct. daily, Jan. and Feb. weekends, Nov., Dec. and March, Wed.-Sun. (not Christmas). Adm. £1.50. Tel. 0420-83262.

KEATS HOUSE, Hampstead, London.—All year, daily, PM (except Sat.). (Not Christmas, New Year, Good Friday, Easter Eve., May 7.) Adm. free. Tel. 071-435 2062.

KELMSCOTT MANOR, nr. Lechlade, Glos.—April-Sept., Wed. only. Thurs., Fri. by written application. Adm. £4.00.

*KINGSTON LACY HOUSE, Dorset.—March 25-Nov. 3, PM. Sat.-Wed. Adm. £4.50, Grounds only £1.40. Tel. 0202-883402.

KNEBWORTH HOUSE, Herts.—March 22-May 19, Sat., Sun., School and Bank Hols., May 25-Sept. 8 daily (not Mon.). Weekends only to Sept. 29. Adm. £3.50, Grounds only, £2. Tel. 0438-812661.

*KNOLE, Kent.—March 29-Oct. Wed.-Sat. and Bank Hol. Mons. Sun., PM. Adm. £3.00. Tel. 0732-450608.

LEEDS CASTLE, Kent.—April 1-end Oct. daily. Nov.-March, weekends only. Adm. charge. Tel. 0622-765400.

*LITTLE MORETON HALL, Cheshire.—April-Sept. 30, except Bank Hols. daily (not Tues.), March and Oct., weekends only. PM. Adm. £2.30 Weekends and Bank Hols. £2.90. Tel. 0260-272018.

LONGLEAT HOUSE, Warminster.—House daily (not Christmas). Safari Park mid-March-Oct. Adm. charge. Tel. 09853-551.

LUTON HOO, Beds.—March 26-Oct. 13, daily, PM (not Mon. except Bank Hols.). Adm. £3.70. Tel. 0582-22955.

MARBLE HILL HOUSE, Twickenham, Middx.—All year, daily (not Dec. 24, 25). Adm. free. Tel. 081-892 5115.

MICHELHAM PRIORY, E. Sussex.—March 25-Oct. 31 daily. Nov., Feb. and March, Sun. only. Adm. £2.50. Tel. 0323-844224.

*MONTACUTE HOUSE, Yeovil.—March 30-Nov. 3 daily (not Tues.). Grounds open all year. Adm. £4.00, Grounds only £2.00. Tel. 0935-823289.

*MOUNT STEWART, Co. Down.—Times vary. Adm. House, Garden, Temple £3, Garden and Temple only £2.50. Tel. 024774-387.

OSBORNE HOUSE, IOW.—June 9-Oct. 31 daily. Adm. £4.30. Tel. 0983-200022.

*OSTERLEY PARK HOUSE, Isleworth, Middx.—Daily (not Mon., May 1, Good Friday, Dec. 24-28, Jan. 1). Adm. £2, Grounds free. Tel. 081-560 3918.

*PENRHYN CASTLE, Bangor.—March 28-Nov. 3 daily (not Tues.) PM. Adm. £3.50. Tel. 0248-353084.

PENSHURST PLACE, Kent.—March 28-Sept. 29 daily (not Mon. except Bank Hols.) PM. Adm. charge. Tel. 0892-870307.

*PETWORTH HOUSE, W. Sussex.—March 29-end Oct. Tues.-Sun., Bank Hol. Mons., Good Friday. PM. Adm. £3.30. Tel. 0798-42207.

PORTMEIRION, Gwynedd.—All year daily. Adm. £2.50 (April-Sept.) £1.25 (Oct.-March). Tel. 0766-770457.

POWDERHAM CASTLE, Exeter.—May 26-Sept. 12 Sun.-Thurs. PM. Adm. £3.20. Tel. 0626-890243.

*POWIS CASTLE, Powys.—March 28-June 30, Sept. 1-Nov. 3 Wed.-Sun. and Bank Hol. Mons.; July and Aug. daily (not Mon. except Bank Hol.). Adm. charge. Tel. 0938-554336.

RABY CASTLE, Durham.—Easter (Sat.-Wed.), May 1-June 30 Wed. and Sun., July-Sept. daily (not Sat.). Also Bank Hol. Sat.-Tues., PM. Adm. charge. Tel. 0833-60202.

RAGLEY HALL, Warks.—March 30-Sept. 29 daily (not Mon., Fri.). PM. Open Bank Hols. Adm. £4.00. Tel. 0789-762090.

ROCKINGHAM CASTLE, Corby.—Easter Sunday-Sept. 30, Sun., Thurs., (also Bank Hol. Mon. and Tues. and Tues. in Aug.), PM. Adm. £3.00, Gardens only £1.50. Tel. 0536-770240.

*RUFFORD OLD HALL, Lancashire—March 30-Nov. 3 daily (not Fri.), PM. Adm. £2.30. Tel. 0704-821254.

SANDRINGHAM, Norfolk.—April 21-Sept. 30 (closed July 22-Aug. 10) Mon.-Thurs.; Sun. PM. Closed when Royal Family in residence. Adm. £2.20. Tel. 0553-772675.

SCONE PALACE, Perth.—March 29-Oct. 14, daily. Sun., PM. Adm. £3.30. Tel. 0738-52300.

SHERBORNE CASTLE, Dorset.—Easter Sat.-end Sept. Thurs., Sat., Sun. and Bank Hol. Mons. PM. Adm. charge. Tel. 0935-813182.

*SHUGBOROUGH, Staffs.—March 29-Dec. 21, daily. Adm. £6 (House, Museum, Farm; House only, £2.50). Tel. 0889-881388.

SKIPTON CASTLE, N. Yorks.—Open all year (not Christmas Day). Daily. (Sun., PM). Adm. £2.20. Tel. 0756-792442.

*SMALLHYTHE PLACE, Kent.—March 29-end Oct. Sat.-Wed. PM. Open Good Friday. Adm. £1.80. Tel. 05806-2334.

STANFORD HALL, Leics.—Easter Saturday-end Sept. Sat., Sun., Bank Hols. (Mon. and Tues.). PM. Adm. £2.50. Tel. 0788-860250.

STONELEIGH ABBEY, Warks.—Open by prior appointment only, Mon.-Fri. Tel. 0926-52116.

STONOR PARK, Oxon.—Times vary. Adm. charge. Tel. 049163-587.

*STOURHEAD, Wilts.—March 25-Nov.3, Sat.-Wed. PM. Adm. £2.50. Gardens all year, daily. Adm. House £3.50, Garden £3.50 Tel. 0747-840348.

STRATFIELD SAYE HOUSE, Reading.—May 1-last Sun. in Sept. daily (not Fri.). Grounds March-Oct. daily, Nov.-Feb. weekends only. Adm. charge. Tel. 0256-882882.

SUDELEY CASTLE, Glos.—March 28-Oct. 31 daily, PM. Adm. £4.20. Tel. 0242-602308.

SULGRAVE MANOR, Northants.—March-Dec. 31, daily (not Wed.), Closed Christmas. Adm. £2.50. Tel. 029576-205.

SYON HOUSE, Brentford, Middx.—Easter-Sept. 29 Sun.-Thurs., and Sun. in Oct. PM. Adm. charge. Tel. 081-560 0881.

*TRERICE, Cornwall.—March 29-end Oct. daily (not Tues.). Adm. £3.20. Tel. 0637-875404.

TYN-Y-RHOS HALL, and Shrine of St George, Shropshire—Sun. PM. Morning prayers 11.30. Tel. 0691-777898.

WARWICK CASTLE.—Daily (not Christmas Day). Adm. charge. Tel. 0926-495421.

WILTON HOUSE, Wilts.—March 29-Oct. 13, Tues.-Sat. and Bank Hol. Mons., Sun. PM. Adm. £4.20. Tel. 0722-743641.

WOBURN ABBEY, Beds.—March 25-Nov. 3 daily. Dec. 29-March 24, weekends only. Adm. £5.00. Tel. 0525-290666.

MUSEUMS AND ART GALLERIES OUTSIDE LONDON

(For National Art Galleries and Museums in London and Merseyside Museums, *see* Index.)

(Adm. admission; con. concessionary rates)

Barnard Castle, Co. Durham.—*The Bowes Museum.* British and European fine art from medieval period to 19th century. Fine porcelain and glass, tapestries and furniture. Music and costume galleries. English period rooms from Elizabeth I to Victoria; French decorative arts of 18th and 19th centuries; local antiquities. Temporary exhibitions. Open weekdays: May–Sept., 10–5.30, March, April, Oct., 10–5, Nov.–Feb., 10–4. Sun., 2–5 (summer); 2–4 (winter). Adm. charge.

Bath.—*Roman Baths Museum.* Roman Baths complex of 1st century AD. Open daily, 9–6. Adm. (including adjoining 18th century Pump Room), £3.25, con. £1.50. *Museum of Costume*, Assembly Rooms. Fashion from 16th century to date. Closed for repairs until 1991. *American Museum in Britain*, Claverton Manor. American decorative arts from late 17th to mid 19th centuries. Open April 1–Oct. 30, daily (not Mon.), 2–5, Bank Hol. Mons. and preceding Suns. 11–5. During winter only on application. Adm. charge. *Victoria Art Gallery*, Bridge Street. Open Mon.–Fri. 10–6, Sat. 10–5. Closed Sun., Bank Hols. Adm. free.

Beamish.—*The North of England Open Air Museum*, Beamish, Co. Durham. Re-creates Northern life *c.*1900. Local buildings have been rebuilt and furnished, including the Town with houses, shops, etc., the Colliery Village, the Railway Station and Home Farm complete with agricultural machinery, animals and exhibitions. Open daily (not Mon. in winter), summer 10–6, winter 10–5.

Beaulieu.—*National Motor Museum.* Displays of vehicles dating from 1895 to present. Open daily (not Christmas Day), 10–6 (winter, 10–5). Adm. charge.

Belfast.—*Ulster Museum*, Botanic Gardens. Collections of Irish antiquities, natural and local history, fine and applied arts. Open Mon.–Fri. 10–5, Sat. 1–5, Sun. 2–5. *Ulster Folk and Transport Museum*, Holywood. Indoor and outdoor exhibits. Open Oct.– March, weekdays 9.30–4.30, weekends 12.30–4.30 (April–Sept. 9.30–5, Sat. 10.30–6, Sun. 12–6). July, Aug. 10.30–6. Adm. £2.20, con. £1.10. *Transport Museum*, Holywood and Witham Street. History of land, sea and air transport in Ireland. Holywood site—open as for Folk Museum. Witham Street site open weekdays 10–5. Adm. 70p, children 40p. Special arrangements at Christmas and Easter.

Beverley, N. Humberside.—*Museum of Army Transport.* Exhibits include field workshop, amphibious assault landing, railway section and aircraft. Open 10–5. Closed Christmas period. Adm. charge.

Birmingham.—*City Museum and Art Gallery.* British and European masters from 14th to 20th centuries (particularly Pre-Raphaelites), sculpture, European gold, silver and jewellery, metalwork, glass, pottery and porcelain, furniture, textiles and costume, archaeology, local and natural history. Open Mon.–Sat. 9.30–5, Sun. 2–5. Closed Christmas Day, Boxing Day and New Year's Day. Adm. free.

Museum of Science and Industry, Newhall Street. From the Industrial Revolution to the present; many working machines. Open Mon.–Sat. 9.30–5, Sun. 2–5. Adm. free. Also *Aston Hall, Blakesley Hall, Birmingham Nature Centre, Sarehole Mill*, and *Weoley Castle.*

Bradford.—*Cartwright Hall*, Lister Park. British 19th and 20th century fine art. *Bolling Hall*, off Wakefield Road, a furnished period house, mainly 17th and 18th century. *Industrial Museum*, Moorside Road, illustrates the local industries and transport in an old mill, with mill owner's house. *Cliffe Castle*,

Keighley. Natural and local history, minerals and gem display, and period rooms. *Manor House*, Ilkley. Archaeology, local history and contemporary fine art. Open 10–5 (April–Sept. 10–6, except Industrial Museum). Closed Good Friday, Christmas Day, Boxing Day and Mon. (except Bank Hols.). Adm. free.

Brighton.—*The Royal Pavilion*, Palace of George IV. Chinoiserie interiors with much of the original furniture. Open daily 10–5 (June–Sept. 10–6). Closed Christmas Day and Boxing Day. Adm. charge.

Museum and Art Gallery, Church Street. Old master paintings; Willett pottery and porcelain collection, 20th century art and furniture, ethnography, archaeology, local history, musical instruments, costume gallery. Open Tues.–Sat. 10–5.45, Sun. 2–5. Closed Mon. (except Bank Hols.), Christmas Day, Boxing Day, Good Friday and Jan. 1. Adm. free.

Preston Manor, Preston Park. Thomas-Stanford: Macquoid bequests of English period furniture, china and silver. Servants quarters. Open Tues.–Sun. and Bank Hol. Mon. 10–5. Closed Christmas Day, Boxing Day, Good Friday. Adm. charge.

The Grange, Art Gallery and Museum, Rottingdean. Sussex Room, Kipling Room and collections of National Toy Museum. Open Mon., Thurs., Sat. 10–5, Tues. and Fri. 10–1, 2–5, Sun. 2–5. Closed Wed., Christmas Day, Boxing Day, Good Friday, and Jan. 1. Adm. free.

The Booth Museum of Natural History, Dyke Road. Open 10–5, Sun. 2–5. Closed Thurs., Christmas Day, Boxing Day, Good Friday, and Jan. 1. Adm. free.

Bristol.—*City Museum and Art Gallery.* Collections include Egyptology, ethnography, Bristol ceramics and the Bristol school of artists, silver, French paintings and Chinese ceramics. Glass collection. *Bristol Industrial Museum*, Prince's Wharf. Collections connected with the Bristol region's industrial history, including an early working model railway and Bristol-built aero-engines. *Maritime Heritage Centre.* Includes SS *Great Britain*, (adm. charge). Also *Red Lodge, Blaise Castle House Museum, Kings Weston Roman Villa, Georgian House* and *St Nicholas Church Museum.* Times vary, tel. 0272–223571.

Cambridge.—*Fitzwilliam Museum.* Egyptian, Greek, Near Eastern and Roman antiquities, coins and medals, medieval manuscripts, paintings and drawings, prints, sculpture, Oriental and Occidental fans, pottery and porcelain, textiles, arms and armour, medieval and renaissance objects of art, and a library. Open Tues.–Sat., Lower Galleries 10–2, Upper Galleries 2–5; Sun. 2.15–5. Closed Dec. 24–Jan. 1, Good Friday, Mon. incl. May Day Bank Hol. but not Easter and Bank Hol. Mons. Adm. free.

Canterbury.—*Royal Museum and Art Gallery*, and *Buffs Regimental Museum.* Archaeology, porcelain, prints and pictures. Open Mon.–Sat. 10–5. Adm. free. *Canterbury Heritage*, a museum of the city's history in the medieval Poor Priest's Hospital, Stour Street. Open Mon.–Sat. 10.30–5, Sun. (June–Oct.) 1.30–5. Adm. £1.20, con. 90p. *Roman Mosaic Museum.* Closed for redevelopment. *West Gate Museum.* Arms and armour and display of city gate-house with battlements.

Carlisle.—*Tullie House Museum and Art Gallery*, Castle Street. Collections of archaeology, natural and social history, fine and decorative arts in Jacobean house with Victorian and modern extensions. *Guildhall Museum*, Greenmarket. Civic and guild history and artefacts. Contact Tullie House Museum for information (Tel: 0228–34781).

Chester.—*Grosvenor Museum*, Grosvenor Street.

Roman antiquities from legionary fortress; natural history, art and folk-life. Open weekdays 10.30–5, Sun. 2–5. *Chester Heritage Centre*, St Michael's Church, Bridge Street Row. Displays Chester's history and architecture. Open weekdays 10.30–5, Sun. 2–5. Adm. charge. *King Charles Tower*, City Walls. Civil War displays. Open Mon.–Fri. 11–5, Sat. 10–5, Sun. 2–5. Adm. charge.

Colchester.—*Colchester Castle.* Local archaeological antiquities, especially from Roman Colchester. Tours of Roman vaults, castle walls, chapel and prisons, weekends April-Sept. and weekdays July-Aug. Open Mon.–Sat. 10–5, Sun. April–Sept. 2–5. Closed Good Friday and Christmas period. Adm. £1, con. 50p. *Hollytrees Museum.* 18th and 19th century costume, toys and social history. Open Mon.–Sat. 10–5. Closed Good Friday and Christmas period. Adm. free. *Natural History Museum*, All Saints Church. Open as Hollytrees. *Social History Museum*, Holy Trinity Church. Domestic life and crafts. Open as Hollytrees. *Tymperleys Clock Museum.* Open Mon.–Sat., April–Oct. 10–5. Adm. free.

Coventry.—*Herbert Art Gallery and Museum*, Jordan Well. Archaeology, natural and local history, fine and decorative arts. Open weekdays 10–5.30, Sun. 2–5. Closed Good Friday and Christmas period. *Museum of British Road Transport*, St Agnes Lane, Hales Street. Open daily 10–5. Adm. £2, children £1. *Lunt Roman Fort*, Baginton. June–Sept., 12–6 (closed Mon. and Thurs.). Adm. £1, children 50p. *Whitefriars Museum.* Open Thurs., Fri., Sat., and some Bank Hols., 10–5.

Crich, Nr. Matlock, Derbyshire—*National Tramway Museum.* Open-air working museum. Open April–Oct. weekends and Bank Hols. 10–6.30. April–Sept., open daily (not Fri. except during school holidays) 10–5.30.

Derby.—*Museum and Art Gallery*, The Strand. Archaeology, military, social history, natural history, paintings by Joseph Wright of Derby, Derby porcelain. Open Mon. 11–5, Tues.–Sat. 10–5, Sun. and Bank Hols. 2–5. *Industrial Museum*, Silk Mill, Full Street. Rolls-Royce collection of aero engines, a railway engineering gallery. Open as above. Adm. 30p. *Pickford's House*, Friargate. 18th and 19th century period room settings, social history, decorative arts, costume and textiles. Open as above. Adm. 30p.

Dorchester.—*Dorset County Museum.* Geology, archaeology, local and natural history and rural crafts of Dorset. Collection of Thomas Hardy's manuscripts, books, notebooks, drawings, etc. Open Mon.–Sat. 10–5, closed Christmas Day, Boxing Day and Good Friday. Adm. £1.50, con. 75p.

Durham.—*Light Infantry Museum and Art Gallery.* Display of County regiment's 200-year history, arts and crafts exhibitions. Open weekdays (except Mon.) 10–5, Sun. and Bank Hol. Mon. 2–5. Closed Christmas Day and Boxing Day. Adm. 70p, con. 30p. *Oriental Museum*, The University. Collections ranging from Ancient Egypt to China and Japan. Open weekdays: 9.30–5. Weekends: Nov.–Feb. closed; March–Oct., Sat. 9.30–5, Sun. 2–5. *Cathedral Treasury.* Relics of St Cuthbert, church plate, medieval seals, manuscripts and vestments. Open weekdays 10–4.30, Sun. 2–4.30. Adm. 60p, con. 10p. *Old Fulling Mill Museum.* Archaeological material from local excavations. Open Nov.–March, daily 12.30–3, April–Oct., daily 11–4. Adm. 50p, con. 25p.

Edinburgh.—*City Art Centre*, 2 Market Street. Late 19th and 20th century art, mostly Scottish, and temporary exhibitions. Open weekdays 10–5 (June–Sept. 10–6). Adm. free. *People's Story, Canongate Tolbooth*, Canongate. Courthouse and prison, now museum of Edinburgh life. Open weekdays 10–5 (June–Sept. 10–6). Adm. free. *Huntly House*, Canongate. Local history, collections of Edinburgh silver, glass and Scottish pottery. Open weekdays 10–5 (June–Sept. 10–6). Adm. free. *Lady Stair's House*, Lawnmarket. Mon.–Sat. 10–5 (June–Sept. 10–6). *Lauriston Castle*, Cramond Road South. April–Oct. daily (except Fri.), 11–5; Nov.–March, weekends only. *Museum of Childhood*, High Street. Open weekdays 10–5 (June–Sept. 10–6). Adm. free.

Exeter.—*Exeter Maritime Museum*, The Haven. Collection of boats. 'Cruel Sea' exhibition. Open daily 10–5. Adm. charge. *Royal Albert Memorial Museum and Art Gallery*, Queen Street. Fine art, Exeter silver, ceramics, ethnography, natural and local history. Open Tues.–Sat. and some Suns. in summer, 10–5.30. Adm. free. *Underground Passages*, High Street. Medieval water supply. *Rougemont House Museum.* Costume displayed in Georgian rooms. Castle Street. Open Mon.–Sat. 10–5. *St Nicholas' Priory.* Norman priory. Open Tues.–Sat. 10–5.30.

Fort William.—*West Highland Museum*, Cameron Square. Historical, natural history and folk exhibits, including those of the 1745 Rising. Daily (except Sun.) 10–1, 2–5; June and Sept. 9.30–5.30; July and Aug. 9.30–9.

Glasgow.—*Art Gallery and Museum*, Kelvingrove. Old Masters, 19th century French paintings, archaeology and natural history, collection of armour. *People's Palace*, Glasgow Green. History of city from 1175 to present. *The Burrell Collection*, Pollok Park. Textiles, furniture, ceramics, stained glass, silver and paintings, especially 19th century French. *Pollok House*, Pollok Park. Spanish paintings, furniture, silver, ceramics. *Haggs Castle Museum*, St Andrews Drive. Children's museum with activity workshops. *Provand's Lordship*, Castle Street. Oldest house in Glasgow, period furniture displays. *Rutherglen Museum*, King Street. History of former royal burgh of Rutherglen. *Museum of Transport*, Kelvin Hall. All open daily, times vary. Adm. free. Also *McLellan Galleries*, Sauchiehall Street. Major exhibition venue for large-scale temporary exhibitions. Adm. charge.

Hull.—*Ferens Art Gallery.* European art, especially Dutch 17th century, British portraits from 17th–20th centuries, Humberside marine paintings, live art space and changing exhibitions. *Wilberforce House.* Jacobean merchant's house, birthplace of Wilberforce; slavery relics, period furniture, costume and ceramics. *Streetlife.* Museum of Transport; public service vehicles from the stage-coach to the last surviving Hull tram. *Hull and East Riding Museum.* Archæology and transport; Celtic world, Iron Age Hasholme Boat, mosaics. *Town Docks Museum.* Whaling, fishing, trawling, ships and shipping. *Old Grammar School.* Hull's oldest secular building with story of Hull displays. *Spurn Lightship*, built 1927, restored 1986. Closed Mon. and Tues. in winter. All open Mon.–Sat. 10–5, Sun. 1.30–4.30.

Huntingdon.—*Cromwell Museum.* Remaining portion of the 12th century Hospital of St John; portraits of Cromwell, his family and Parliamentary notables, and Cromwelliana. Open April–Oct., Tues.–Fri. 11–5, Sat, Sun. 11–4 (closed 1–2); Nov.–March, Tues.–Fri. 1–4, Sat., Sun., as before. Closed Bank Hols. other than Good Friday. Adm. free.

Ipswich.—*Ipswich Museum.* Suffolk geology, archaeology, natural history and ethnology. Temporary exhibitions. Open Tues.–Sat. 10–5. *Christchurch Mansion.* Tudor house containing furniture, Suffolk portraits, English porcelain, pottery and glass. Collections of paintings (local artists, Gainsborough, Constable). *Wolsey Art Gallery*, temporary exhibitions. Open Tues.–Sat. 10–5, Sun. 2.30–4.30. Closed Good Friday, Dec. 24, 25, 26. Adm. free.

Leeds.—*City Art Gallery.* English watercolours. British and European painting, modern sculpture, Henry Moore gallery, Print Room. Open weekdays, 10–6, Sun. 2–5.

Temple Newsam House. Tudor/Jacobean house, furnished in style of 17th and 18th centuries; silver, European porcelain and pottery, pictures, etc. Open daily (except Mon.) 10.30–6.15, Weds. (May–Sept.) 10.30–8.30, all Bank Hols. (except Christmas). Adm. 65p, con. 30p. *Lotherton Hall*, Gascoigne art and silver collection, oriental gallery, costume collection, 19th century furniture, ceramics; park and gardens. Open daily (except Mon.) 10.30–6.15, Thurs. (May–Sept.) 10.30–8.30, all Bank Hols. (except Christmas). Adm. 65p, con. 30p. *Abbey House Museum.* Folk museum including three full-sized streets. Open Oct.–March, weekdays 10–5, Sun. 2–5 (April–Sept. 2–6). *Industrial Museum.* Open April–Sept., Tues.–Sat. 10–5, Sun. 2–5 (Oct.–March 2–4). Open Bank Hols. *City Museum.* Geology, archaeology, ethnography and natural history. Open Tues.–Fri. 9.30–5.30, Sat. 9.30–4.

Leicester.—*Leicestershire Museum and Art Gallery*, New Walk. Natural history, geology, Egyptology, 18th–20th century European paintings, ceramics, silver. *Newarke Houses*, The Newarke. Social history of Leicestershire from 1500, musical instruments, local clocks. *Jewry Wall Museum*, St Nicholas Circle. Archaeology, Roman Jewry Wall and Baths, mosaics. *Belgrave Hall*, Church Road. Queen Anne house with furniture and garden, coaches and agricultural collection. *Museum of the Royal Leicestershire Regiment*, Oxford Street. *Museum of Technology*, Corporation Road. Knitting industry and Power galleries. Horse-drawn and motor vehicles, beam engines. *Wygston's House Museum of Costume*, Applegate. Costume from 1789–present. All museums open weekdays 10–5.30, Sun. 2–5.30. Closed Christmas Day, Boxing Day and Good Friday.

Lewes.—*Museum of Sussex Archaeology*, Barbican House, near Castle. Open weekdays, 10–5.30, Sun. (April–Oct.) 11–5.30. Adm. (including Castle) £2.50, con. £1.25. *Museum of Local History*, Anne of Cleves House, Southover. Local history and folk museum. Open April–Oct., weekdays 10–5.30, Sun. 2–5.30. Adm. £1.50, con. 75p.

Lincoln.—*Usher Gallery.* Watches, miniatures, porcelain, silver, etc., Peter de Wint collection of oils and watercolours, Lincolnshire topographical drawings, *personalia* associated with Tennyson family. Open weekdays 10–5.30, Sun. 2.30–5. *City and County Museum*, The Greyfriars. Geology, natural history and archaeology of Lincolnshire. Open weekdays 10–5.30, Sun. 2.30–5. *Museum of Lincolnshire Life.* Covers the last 200 years; large agricultural collection. Open weekdays 10–5.30, Sun. 2–5.30. *National Cycle Museum*, Brayford Wharf North. Vintage cycles. Open daily, except Christmas week, 10–5.

Manchester.—*City Art Galleries*, Mosley Street and Princess Street. Old Masters, Turner, Pre-Raphaelites; sculpture, furniture, porcelain, silver. Changing exhibitions. Weekdays 10–5.45, Sun. 2–5.45. *Whitworth Art Gallery*, University of Manchester, Oxford Road. Watercolours, drawings, prints, textiles and wallpaper collections, 20th century British art. Mon.–Sat. 10–5 (Thurs. 10–9), closed Suns, Good Friday and Christmas week. Adm. free. *Museum of Science and Industry*, Liverpool Road, Castlefield. Working machinery and displays in world's oldest passenger railway station. Open daily 10–5. *Gallery of English Costume*, Platt Hall, Platt Fields, Rusholme. Exhibits from 16th century to present. Times vary. Also *Heaton Hall*, Prestwich, *Wythenshawe Hall*, Northenden. Times vary (tel: 061–236 5244).

Newcastle upon Tyne.—*Laing Art Gallery*, Higham Place. Fine art from 17th century, pottery, glass, silver and metalwork. Open Tues.–Fri. 10–5.30, Sat. 10–4.30, Sun. 2.30–5.30. *Castle Keep*, St Nicholas Street. Oct.–March, Tues.–Sun. 9.30–4.30 (April–Sept. 9.30–5). *Trinity Maritime Centre* and *Trinity House*, Broad Chare. Centre open April–Oct. Tues.–Fri. 11–4; Nov.–March, by arrangement. Trinity House, April–Nov. (chapel and entrance hall only; tour of house by appointment.) *Military Vehicle Museum*, Exhibition Park. Open daily 10–4. *Museum of Science and Engineering*, West Blandford Square. Tues.–Fri. 10–5.30, Sat. 10–4.30. *Newburn Hall Motor Museum*, Townfield Gardens. Tues.–Sun. 10–8.

Newmarket.—*National Horseracing Museum.* Six galleries of displays relating to horseracing, horses and people connected with the sport. Sporting art galleries. Equine Tours. Open April–Dec., Tues.–Sat. 10–5, Sun. 12–5. Closed Mon. except Bank Hols, July, Aug. Adm. £2.50, con. £1.50/75p.

Norwich.—*Castle Museum.* Exhibits of art (including Norwich School), archaeology, natural history, silver and glass. Open Mon.–Sat., 10–5, Sun. 2–5. *Strangers' Hall*, Charing Cross. Medieval mansion with period room settings from Tudor to Victorian times, toy display and costumes. Open Mon.–Sat. 10–5. *Bridewell Museum of Local Industries*, Bridewell Alley. Open Mon.–Sat. 10–5. *St Peter Hungate Church Museum*, Princes Street. 15th century church used for display of church art and antiquities. Open Mon.–Sat. 10–5.

Nottingham.—*Castle Museum and Art Gallery.* Paintings and drawings 17th–20th centuries. Selection of decorative arts, history of Nottingham gallery with working models and Sherwood Foresters' regimental collection. Conducted tours of Mortimer's Hole caves. Open summer, 10–5.45, winter, 10–4.45. Closed Christmas Day. Adm. free, small charge on Sun. and Bank Hols. *Industrial Museum*, Wollaton Park. Lacemaking machinery, steam engines, transport. Open Summer, Mon.–Sat. 10–6, Sun. 2–6; Winter, Wed., Sat. 10–5, Sun. 1–5. Closed Christmas Day. Adm. free, small charge on Sun. and Bank Hols. *Canal Museum*, Canal Street. History of local canals and river transport. Open Summer, Wed–Sat. 10–5.45, Sun. 1–5; Winter, Wed.–Sat. 10–5, Sun. 1–5. Adm. free. *Natural History Museum*, Wollaton Hall. Tudor building and park. Open summer 10–7, Sun. 2–5; winter 10–dusk (Sun. 1.30–4.30). Closed Christmas Day. Adm. free except Sun. and Bank Hols. *Castlegate Museum of Costumes and Textiles.* Open daily 10–5. Closed Christmas Day. Adm. free. *Brewhouse Yard Museum*, Castle Boulevard. Everyday life from the 17th century to present. Open daily 10–5. Adm. free. Closed Christmas Day. *Green's Mill and Science Centre*, Sneinton. Working windmill and interactive science centre. Open Wed.–Sun. 10–5. Closed Christmas Day. Adm. free. Also *The Lace Hall* and *Robin Hood Centre.*

Oakham.—*Rutland County Museum*, Catmos Street.—Archaeology, local history, craft tools and agricultural implements. Open Tues.–Sat. 10–1, 2–5, Sun. (April–Oct.) 2–5, and Bank Hol. Mons.

Oxford.—*Ashmolean Museum*, Beaumont Street. The University's collections of European and Oriental fine and applied arts, Classical and Near-Eastern archaeology and numismatics. Open Tues.–Sat. 10–4, Sun. 2–4. Bank Hol. Mons. 2–5. Adm. free.

Plymouth.—*City Museum and Art Gallery*, Drake Circus. Fine art including Reynolds' portraits,

Plymouth porcelain, archaeology, local and natural history. Tues.–Sat. 10–5.30, Sun. 2–5. Also Bank Holiday Mons. Adm. free. *Elizabethan House*, 32 New Street. *Merchant's House*, 33 St Andrew's Street. 16th century. *The Dome*, the Hoe. Maritime history museum.

Portsmouth.—*City Museum and Art Gallery*, Museum Road. *Cumberland House Natural Science Museum and Butterfly House*, Eastern Parade. *Southsea Castle and Museum*, Clarence Esplanade. *D-Day Museum*, Clarence Esplanade. All open daily 10.30–5.30, except Dec. 24–26. Adm. charge. *Charles Dickens' Birthplace Museum*, Old Commercial Road. Open March 1–Oct. 31, daily 10.30–5.30. Adm. charge. *Eastney Industrial Museum*, Henderson Road. Open April–Sept. weekends, Bank Hols.; Oct.–March 1st Sun. of month. Adm. charge. *Naval Heritage Area*. Tells the story of the Royal Navy using Henry VIII's *Mary Rose*, HMS *Victory* and the Victorian ironclad, HMS *Warrior* (1860). *Royal Naval Museum*. Open daily (except Christmas Day). Adm. charge.

St Albans.—*Museum of St Albans*, Hatfield Road. Story of St Albans since Roman times. Open weekdays 10–5. *Verulamium Museum*, St Michael's. Iron Age and Roman Verulamium including wall plasters, jewellery, mosaics. Open weekdays 10–5.30, Sun. 2–5.30. Closes Nov. 4–Feb. Adm. £1.60, con. 80p.

Sheffield.—*City Museum*, Weston Park. Includes the Bateman Collection of antiquities from Peak District, cutlery and old Sheffield plate, local geology and wildlife. *Mappin Art Gallery*, Weston Park. Paintings and sculpture of 18th–20th centuries (mainly British School) and contemporary works. *Abbeydale Industrial Hamlet*, Abbeydale Road South. A late 18th–early 19th century scythe and steel works with associated housing. *Kelham Island Industrial Museum*. Sheffield's industrial past. *Shepherd Wheel*, Whiteley Wood. Water-powered cutlery grinding establishment. *Bishops' House*, Meersbrook Park. Museum of local history in Tudor yeoman's house. Opening times vary (Tel: 0742–768588).

Stoke-on-Trent.—*City Museum and Art Gallery*, Bethesda Street, Hanley. Major ceramic collections. Open daily 10–5, Sun. 2–5. *Chatterley Whitfield Mining Museum*, Tunstall. Guided tours underground. *Gladstone Pottery Museum*, Longton. A working Victorian pottery.

Pottery Factory Tours are available at the following: *Royal Doulton*, Nile Street, Burslem; *Spode*, Church Street, Stoke; *Beswick*, Gold Street; *Royal Grafton China*, Marlborough Road, Longton; *Coalport*, Park Street, Fenton, *Wedgwood's*, Barlaston; *Aynsley*, Uttoxeter Road, Longton.

Stratford-upon-Avon.—*Shakespeare's Birthplace*. Period furniture, rare books, MSS and memorabilia; new Shakespeare Centre nearby. *Anne Hathaway's Cottage*, Shottery. Home of Shakespeare's wife. *Mary Arden's House*, Wilmcote. Tudor farmhouse home of Shakespeare's mother. *New Place*, where Shakespeare died. *Hall's Croft*. Shakespeare's daughter's home. *Grammar School* attended by Shakespeare. *Royal Shakespeare Theatre*. Burnt down 1926, rebuilt 1932. New *Swan Theatre*, opened in 1986.

Styal.—*Quarry Bank Mill*, Cheshire. History of the cotton industry, weaving demonstrations at water-powered cotton mill. Restored Apprentice House. Open all year. Closed Mon., Oct.–March. Open Bank Hols. Adm. £3.75, con. £2.75.

Winchester.—*City Museum*. Weekdays 10–5, Sun. 2–5 (closed Mon. in winter). *Cathedral Library* and *Triforium Gallery*. Illuminated manuscripts, sculpture, wood- and metalwork from 12th–19th centuries. Times vary. Closed Mon. morning and Suns. Adm. charge. *Cathedral Treasury*. Exhibition of silverware. Open May–Sept., daily 2.30–4.30. Adm. charge.

Worcester.—*City Museum and Art Gallery*. Natural history of Worcestershire, changing art exhibitions; also military museum. Open Mon.–Wed., Fri. 9.30–6, Sat. 9.30–5. Closed Thurs., Sun. *The Commandery*, Sidbury. Civil War centre. Weekdays 10.30–5, Sun. 1.30–5. *Tudor House Museum*, Friar Street. Local history. Mon.–Wed., Fri., Sat. 10.30–5. *Dyson Perrins Museum and Royal Worcester Porcelain Works*, Severn Street. Mon.–Fri. 9.30–5, Sat. 10–5.

York.—*Castle Museum*. Everyday life of the last three centuries. Open weekdays 9.30–5.30, Sun. 10–5.30 (closes 6.30 April–Oct., 4.45 Nov.–March). Adm. £3.35, con. £1.70. *Jorvik Viking Centre*, Coppergate. Reconstruction of Viking York. Open daily. Adm. £3.30, con. £1.65. *Yorkshire Museum and Gardens*, Museum Street, Roman Life gallery, archaeology, decorative arts, geology, natural history. Open weekdays 10–5, Sun. 1–5. Adm. charge. Gardens, Roman, Anglian and medieval ruins. Open weekdays 7.30–dusk (summer 7.30–8), Sun. 10–dusk. *The York Story*, Castlegate. Open weekdays 10–5, Sun. 1–5. Adm. 80p, con. 40p. *Art Gallery*, Exhibition Square. European paintings, 14th–20th century; watercolours and prints of Yorkshire; modern English stoneware pottery. Open weekdays 10–5, Sun. 2.30–5. Adm. free *Treasurer's House* (National Trust), Chapter House Street. Open April–Oct. 10.30–5 (closed Good Friday). Adm. £2.30, con. £1.

WILDLIFE CONSERVATION

PROTECTED SPECIES

The Wildlife and Countryside Act 1981 gives legal protection to a wide range of animals and wild plants.

Animals, etc.

Under Schedule 5 of the Act it is normally an offence to kill, injure, take, possess or sell any of the animals mentioned below (whether alive or dead) and to disturb its place of shelter and protection or to destroy that place.

† Adder (*Vipera berus*)
§ Allis shad (*alosa alosa*)
 Anemone, Ivell's Sea (*Edwardsia ivelli*)
 Anemone, Startlet Sea (*Nematosella vectensis*)
 Apus (*Triops cancriformis*)
 Bat, Horseshoe (*Rhinolophidae*, all species)
 Bat, Typical (*Vespertilionidae*, all species)
 Beetle, Rainbow Leaf (*Chrysolina cerealis*)
 Beetle, Violet Click (*Limoniscus violaceus*)
 Burbot (*Lota lota*)
* Butterfly, Adonis Blue (*Lysandra bellargus*)
* Butterfly, Black Hairstreak (*Strymonidia pruni*)
* Butterfly, Brown Hairstreak (*Thecla betulae*)
* Butterfly, Chalkhill Blue (*Lysandra coridon*)
* Butterfly, Chequered Skipper (*Carterocephalus palaemon*)
* Butterfly, Duke of Burgundy Fritillary (*Hamearis lucina*)
* Butterfly, Glanville Fritillary (*Melitaea cinxia*)
 Butterfly, Heath Fritillary (*Mellicta athalia* (or *Melitaea athalia*))
* Butterfly, High Brown Fritillary (*Argynnis adippe*)
 Butterfly, Large Blue (*Maculinea arion*)
* Butterfly, Large Copper (*Lycaena dispar*)
* Butterfly, Large Heath (*Coenonympha tullia*)
* Butterfly, Large Tortoiseshell (*Nymphalis polychloros*)
* Butterfly, Lulworth Skipper (*Thymelicus acteon*)
* Butterfly, Marsh Fritillary (*Eurodryas aurinia*)
* Butterfly, Mountain Ringlet (*Erebia epiphron*)
* Butterfly, Northern Brown Argus (*Aricia artaxerxes*)
* Butterfly, Pearl-bordered Fritillary (*Boloria euphrosyne*)
* Butterfly, Purple Emperor (*Apatura iris*)
* Butterfly, Silver Spotted Skipper (*Hesperia comma*)
* Butterfly, Silver-studded Blue (*Plebejus argus*)
* Butterfly, Small Blue (*Cupido minimus*)
 Butterfly, Swallowtail (*Papilio machaon*)
* Butterfly, White Letter Hairstreak (*Stymonidia w-album*)
* Butterfly, Wood White (*Leptidea sinapis*)
 Cat, Wild (*Felis silvestris*)
 Cicada, New Forest (*Cicadetta montana*)
** Crayfish, Atlantic Stream (*Austropotamobius pallipes*)
 Cricket, Field (*Gryllus campestris*)
 Cricket, Mole (*Gryllotalpa gryllotalpa*)
 Dolphin (*Cetacea*)
 Dormouse (*Muscardinus avellanarius*)
 Dragonfly, Norfolk Aeshna (*Aeshna isosceles*)
* Frog, Common (*Rana temporaria*)
 Grasshopper, Wart-biter (*Decticus verrucivorus*)
 Leech, Medicinal (*Hirudo medicinalis*)
 Lizard, Sand (*Lacerta agilis*)
‡ Lizard, Viviparous (*Lacerta vivipara*)

* the offence relates to 'sale' only.
** the offence relates to 'taking' and 'sale' only.
† the offence relates to 'killing and injuring' only.
‡ the offence relates to 'killing, injuring and sale'.
§ the offence relates to 'killing, injuring and taking'.

Marten, Pine (*Martes martes*)
Moth, Barberry Carpet (*Pareulype berberata*)
Moth, Black-veined (*Siona lineata* (or *Idaea lineata*))
Moth, Essex Emerald (*Thetidia smaragdaria*)
Moth, New Forest Burnet (*Zygaena viciae*)
Moth, Reddish Buff (*Acosmetia caliginosa*)
Moth, Viper's Bugloss (*Hadena irregularis*)
Mussel, Freshwater Pearl (*Margaritifera margaritifera*)
Newt, Great Crested (or Warty) (*Triturus cristatus*)
* Newt, Palmate (*Triturus helveticus*)
* Newt, Smooth (*Triturus vulgaris*)
 Otter, Common (*Lutra lutra*)
 Porpoise (*Cetacea*)
 Sandworm, Lagoon (*Armandia cirrhosa*)
 Sea-Mat, Trembling (*Victorella pavida*)
 Shrimp, Fairy (*Chirocephalus diaphanus*)
 Shrimp, Lagoon Sand (*Gammarus insensibilis*)
‡ Slow-worm (*Anguis fragilis*)
 Snail, Glutinous (*Myxas glutinosa*)
 Snail, Sandbowl (*Catinella arenaria*)
‡ Snake, Grass (*Natrix natrix* (*Natrix helvetica*))
 Snake, Smooth (*Coronella austriaca*)
 Spider, Fen Raft (*Dolomedes plantarius*)
 Spider, Ladybird (*Eresus niger*)
 Squirrel, Red (*Sciurus vulgaris*)
* Toad, Common (*Bufo bufo*)
 Toad, Natterjack (*Bufo calamita*)
 Turtle, Marine (*Dermochelyidae* and *Cheloniidae*, all species)
 Vendace (*Coregonus albula*)
 Walrus (*Odobenus rosmarus*)
 Whale (*Cetacea*)
 Whitefish (*Coregonus lavaretus*)

Plants

Under Schedule 8 of the Wildlife and Countryside Act, it is normally an offence to pick, uproot, sell or destroy any of the plants mentioned below and, unless authorized, to uproot any wild plant.

Adder's tongue, Least (*Ophioglossum lusitanicum*)
Alison, Small (*Alyssum alyssoides*)
Broomrape, Bedstraw (*Orobanche caryophyllacea*)
Broomrape, Oxtongue (*Orobanche loricata*)
Broomrape, Thistle (*Orobanche reticulata*)
Cabbage, Lundy (*Rhynchosinapis wrightii*)
Calamint, Wood (*Calamintha sylvatica*)
Catchfly, Alpine (*Lychnis alpina*)
Cinquefoil, Rock (*Potentilla rupestris*)
Club-rush, Triangular (*Scirpus triquetrus*)
Colt's-foot, Purple (*Homogyne alpina*)
Cotoneaster, Wild (*Cotoneaster integerrimus*)
Cottongrass, Slender (*Eriophorum gracile*)
Cow-wheat, Field (*Melampyrum arvense*)
Crocus, Sand (*Romulea columnae*)
Cudweed, Jersey (*Gnaphalium luteoalbum*)
Cudweed, Red-tipped (*Filago lutescens*)
Diapensia (*Diapensia lapponica*)
Eryngo, Field (*Eryngium campestre*)
Fern, Dickie's bladder (*Cystopteris dickieana*)
Fern, Killarney (*Trichomanes speciosum*)
Fleabane, Alpine (*Erigeron borealis*)
Fleabane, Small (*Pulicaria vulgaris*)
Galingale, Brown (*Cyperus fuscus*)
Gentian, Alpine (*Gentiana nivalis*)
Gentian, Fringed (*Gentianella ciliata*)
Gentian, Spring (*Gentiana verna*)
Germander, Cut-leaved (*Teucrium botrys*)
Germander, Water (*Teucrium scordium*)
Gladiolus, Wild (*Gladiolus illyricus*)
Goosefoot, Stinking (*Chenopodium vulvaria*)
Grass-poly (*Lythrum hyssopifolia*)
Hare's-ear, Sickle-leaved (*Bupleurum falcatum*)

Hare's-ear, Small (*Bupleurum baldense*)
Hawk's-beard, Stinking (*Crepis foetida*)
Heath, Blue (*Phyllodoce caerulea*)
Helleborine, Red (*Cephalanthera rubra*)
Helleborine, Young's (*Epipactis youngiana*)
Horsetail, Branched (*Equisetum ramosissimum*)
Hound's-tongue, Green (*Cynoglossum germanicum*)
Knawel, Perennial (*Scleranthus perennis*)
Knotgrass, Sea (*Polygonum maritimum*)
Lady's-slipper (*Cypripedium calceolus*)
Lavender, Sea (*Limonium paradoxum*) (*Limonium recurvum*)
Leek, Round-headed (*Allium sphaerocephalon*)
Lettuce, Least (*Lactuca saligna*)
Lily, Snowdon (*Lloydia serotina*)
Marsh-mallow, Rough (*Althaea hirsuta*)
Marshwort, Creeping (*Apium repens*)
Milk-parsley, Cambridge (*Selinum carvifolia*)
Naiad, Holly-leaved (*Najas marina*)
Orchid, Early Spider (*Ophrys sphegodes*)
Orchid, Fen (*Liparis loeselii*)
Orchid, Ghost (*Epipogium aphyllum*)
Orchid, Late Spider (*Ophrys fuciflora*)
Orchid, Lizard (*Himantoglossum hircinum*)
Orchid, Military (*Orchis militaris*)
Orchid, Monkey (*Orchis simia*)
Pear, Plymouth (*Pyrus cordata*)
Pennyroyal (*Mentha pulegium*)
Pigmyweed (*Crassula aquatica*)
Pink, Cheddar (*Dianthus gratianopolitanus*)
Pink, Childling (*Petroraghia nanteuilii*)
Ragwort, Fen (*Senecio paludosus*)
Ramping-fumitory, Martin's (*Fumaria martinii*)
Restharrow, Small (*Ononis reclinata*)
Rock-cress, Alpine (*Arabis alpina*)
Rock-cress, Bristol (*Arabis stricta*)
Sandwort, Norwegian (*Arenaria norvegica*)
Sandwort, Teesdale (*Minuartia stricta*)
Saxifrage, Drooping (*Saxifraga cernua*)
Saxifrage, Tufted (*Saxifraga cespitosa*)
Solomon's-seal, Whorled (*Polygonatum verticillatum*)
Sow-thistle, Alpine (*Cicerbita alpina*)
Spearwort, Adder's-tongue (*Ranunculus ophioglossifolius*)
Speedwell, Fingered (*Veronica triphyllos*)
Speedwell, Spiked (*Veronica spicata*)
Spurge, Purple (*Euphorbia peplis*)
Star-of-Bethlehem, Early (*Gagea bohemica*)
Starfruit (*Damasonium alisma*)
Stonewort, Foxtail (*Lamprothamnium papulosum*)
Strapwort (*Corrigiola litoralis*)
Violet, Fen (*Viola persicifolia*)
Viper's-grass (*Scorzonera humilis*)
Water-plantain, Ribbon-leaved (*Alisma gramineum*)
Wood-sedge, Starved (*Carex depauperata*)
Woodsia, Alpine (*Woodsia alpina*)
Woodsia, Oblong (*Woodsia ilvensis*)
Wormwood, Field (*Artemisia campestris*)
Woundwort, Downy (*Stachys germanica*)
Woundwort, Limestone (*Stachys alpina*)
Yellow-rattle, Greater (*Rhinanthus serotinus*)

Wild Birds

The Wildlife and Countryside Act, 1981, lays down a close season for wild birds (other than game birds) from February 1 to August 31 inclusive, each year. Exceptions to these dates are made for:

Capercaillie and (except Scotland) *Woodcock*—February 1–September 30.

Snipe—February 1–August 11.

Wild Duck and *Wild Goose* (below high water mark)—February 21–August 31.

Birds which may be killed or taken outside the close season (except on Sundays and on Christmas Day in Scotland, and on Sundays in prescribed areas of England and Wales) are the above-named and coot,

certain wild duck (gadwall, goldeneye, mallard, pintail, pochard, shoveler, teal, tufted duck, wigeon), certain wild geese (Canada, greylag, pink-footed, white-fronted (in England and Wales only)), moorhen, golden plover and woodcock.

Certain wild birds may be killed or taken at any time by authorized persons: crow, collared dove, gull (great and lesser black-backed or herring), jackdaw, jay, magpie, pigeon (feral or wood), rook, sparrow (house), and starling.

All other British birds are fully protected by law throughout the year.

CLOSE SEASONS AND TIMES

Game Birds

In each case the dates are inclusive:—

Black game–December 11–August 19 (August 31 in Somerset, Devon and New Forest).

*Grouse–December 11–August 11.

*Partridge–February 2–August 31.

*Pheasant–February 2–September 30.

*Ptarmigan–(Scotland only) December 11–August 11.

It is also unlawful in England and Wales to kill the game marked * above on a Sunday or Christmas Day.

Hunting and Ground Game

There is no statutory close-time for fox-hunting or rabbit-shooting, nor for hares; but by an Act passed in 1892 the sale of hares or leverets in Great Britain is prohibited from March 1 to July 31 inclusive under a penalty of £1. November 1 is the recognized date for the opening of the fox-hunting season, which continues till the following April.

Deer

The statutory close seasons for deer (all dates inclusive) are:

	England and Wales	Scotland
Fallow deer		
Male	May 1–July 31	May 1–July 31
Female	Mar. 1–Oct. 31	Feb. 16–Oct. 20
Red deer		
Male	May 1–July 31	Oct. 21–June 30
Female	Mar. 1–Oct. 31	Feb. 16–Oct. 20
Roe deer		
Male	Nov. 1–Mar. 31	Oct. 21–Mar. 31
Female	Mar. 1–Oct. 31	April 1–Oct. 20
Sika deer		
Male	May 1–July 31	Oct. 21–June 30
Female	Mar. 1–Oct. 31	Feb. 16–Oct. 20
Red/Sika hybrids		
Male	—	Oct. 21–June 30
Female	—	Feb. 16–Oct. 20

Angling

Close seasons (dates inclusive) are:

Coarse fishing.—Yorkshire, last day in February–May 31; South West, none; rest of country, March 15–June 15.

Game fishing.—Trout, October 1–last day of February*; Salmon, November 1–January 31*.

* The above dates are statutory close times. Particularly with salmon, migratory trout and trout, close seasons vary in accordance with local by-laws. In all cases, it is best to check with the National Rivers Authority regional office covering the area (details can be found in the local telephone directory).

THE ANTARCTIC

THE ANTARCTIC is generally defined as the area lying within the Antarctic Convergence—the zone where cold northward-flowing Antarctic sea water sinks below warmer southward-flowing water. This zone is at about lat. 50° S. in the Atlantic Ocean and lat. 55°–62° S. in the Pacific Ocean. The continent itself lies almost entirely within the Antarctic Circle, an area of about 5·5 million square miles, 99 per cent of which is permanently ice-covered. The average thickness of the ice is 7,100 ft. but in places exceeds 14,500 ft., submerging entire mountain ranges; some mountains protrude, the highest being Vinson Massif, 16,067 ft. The ice amounts to some 7·2 million cubic miles and represents more than 90 per cent of the world's fresh water.

Along one-third of the Antarctic coastline, land-ice flowing outwards forms extensive ice shelves, fragments of which break off to form tabular icebergs, leaving ice cliffs up to 150 ft. high. Much of the sea freezes in winter, forming fast ice which breaks up in summer and drifts north as pack ice. The presence of ice and continuous darkness in winter restrict access to the coastline by sea to the summer months.

The most conspicuous physical features of the continent are its high inland plateau (much of it over 10,000 ft.), the Transantarctic Mountains (which together with the large embayments of the Weddell Sea and Ross Sea mark the approximate boundary between Greater and Lesser Antarctica), and the mountainous Antarctic Peninsula and off-lying islands (which extend northwards towards South America). The continental shelf averages about 20 miles in width (half the global mean, and in places it is non-existent) and reaches exceptional depths (1,300–2,600 ft., which is 3–6 times the global mean).

Climate.—On land, summer temperatures range from just below freezing around the coast to −34° C (about −30° F) on the plateau, and in winter −20° C (about −4° F) on the coast to −65° C (about −85° F) inland. Over a large area the maxima do not exceed −15° C (+5° F).

Precipitation is scanty over the plateau but amounts to 25–76 cm (10–30 in) (water equivalent) along the coast and some scientific stations are permanently buried by snow. Some rain falls over the more northerly areas in summer. Gravity winds on the plateau slopes and cyclonic storms further north can both exceed 100 m.p.h. and gusts have been known to reach 150 m.p.h. Visibility can be reduced to zero in blizzards.

Flora and Fauna.—Although a small number of flowering plants, ferns and clubmosses occur on the sub-Antarctic islands, only two (a grass and a pearlwort) extend south of 60° S. Antarctic vegetation is dominated by lichens and mosses, with a few liverworts, algae, and fungi. Most of these occur around the coast or on islands, but lichens and some mosses also occur inland.

The only land animals are tiny insects and mites with nematodes, rotifers, and tardigrades in the mosses, but large numbers of seals, penguins, and other sea-birds go ashore to breed in the summer. The emperor penguin is the only species which breeds ashore throughout the winter. In contrast, the Antarctic seas abound with life, a wide variety of invertebrates (including krill) and fish providing food for the seals, penguins, and other birds and a residual population of whales.

Exploration and Antarctic Treaty.—In the 180 years from Captain James Cook's circumnavigation of the Antarctic in 1772–75 to the mid-1950s, about half of all expeditions to the Antarctic were British and a number made major contributions to geographical and scientific knowledge of the area. Notable were the expeditions of Sir James Clark Ross, Captain Robert Scott and Sir Ernest Shackleton.

Apart from four years during the Second World War, British Antarctic research has been continuous since 1925, and most of it is now organized and carried out by the British Antarctic Survey (a component of the Natural Environment Research Council).

The world-wide International Geophysical Year 1957–58 gave great impetus to Antarctic research, increasing the number of stations from 17 to 44 and the number of nations involved in research from four to 12 by 1957. The co-operative scientific effort proved so fruitful that the 12 nations involved pledged themselves to continue to promote scientific and technical co-operation unhampered by politics (territorial claims being left in abeyance) and agreed that the continent should be used for peaceful purposes only. These aims were embodied in the Antarctic Treaty (covering the area south of lat. 60° S., excluding the high seas but including the ice shelves), which came into force in 1961. It has since been signed by a further 27 states, 14 of which are active in the Antarctic and have therefore been accorded consultative status.

Potential resources.—Increasing pressure on the world's food and mineral supplies has stimulated the search for new sources even in the extremely hostile polar environment. Minerals have been found in great variety but not in commercially exploitable concentrations in accessible localities. There are indications that off-shore hydrocarbons could be present but mostly below great depths of stormy, ice-infested seas.

The Antarctic Treaty nations have considered the environmental implications of possible mineral exploration and exploitation. In October 1991 a Protocol was adopted by the Antarctic Treaty nations prohibiting mineral exploration, except specific mining research, in the Antarctic for 50 years. Restrictions will only be lifted if all the signatories with full voting rights agree. The agreement protects native species of plants and animals and restricts tourism, waste disposal and pollution.

Currently, the chief interest is in marine protein, including the shrimp-like krill already fished commercially by Japan, Poland and the USSR. Research to ensure rational management of stocks of this organism is being continued by international groups, but it is estimated that they could sustain a yield equal to the present total annual world fish catch.

Scientific research.—At present, five British stations are maintained in the British Antarctic Territory and at South Georgia. Two are biological stations, two geophysical observatories, and one is the centre for airborne earth sciences.

There are another 42 permanently occupied stations operated by the following nations: Argentina (6), Australia (4), Brazil (1), Chile (3), China (2), France (4), Germany (2), India (1), Japan (2), New Zealand (2), Poland (1), South Africa (3), South Korea (1), Uruguay (1), USA (3, including one at the South Pole), USSR (6).

The staff of these stations and summer field-workers are the only people present on the continent and off-lying islands. There are no indigenous inhabitants.

HALLMARKS

Hallmarks are the symbols stamped on gold, silver or platinum articles to indicate that they have been tested at an official Assay Office and that they conform to one of the legal standards. With certain exceptions, all gold, silver, or platinum articles are required by law to be hallmarked before they are offered for sale. Hallmarking was instituted in England in 1300 under a statute of Edward I.

MODERN HALLMARKS

Normally a complete modern hallmark consists of four symbols—the sponsor's mark, the assay office mark, the standard mark and the date letter. Additional marks have been authorized from time to time.

Sponsor's Mark—Instituted in England in 1363, the sponsor's mark was originally a device such as a bird or fleur-de-lis. Now it consists of the initial letters of the name or names of the manufacturer or firm. Where two or more sponsors have the same initials, there is a variation in the surrounding shield or style of letters.

Standard Mark—The standard mark indicates that the content of the precious metal in the alloy from which the article is made, is not less than the legal standard. The legal standard is the minimum content of precious metal by weight in parts per thousand, and the standards are:

Gold	916·6	(22 carat)
	750	(18 carat)
	585	(14 carat)
	375	(9 carat)
Silver	958·4	(Britannia)
	925	(sterling)
Platinum	950	

The metals are marked as follows, if they are manufactured in the United Kingdom:

GOLD—a crown followed by the millesimal figure for the standard, e.g. 916 for 22 carat (see table above).

SILVER—Britannia silver: a full-length figure of Britannia. Sterling silver: a lion passant (England) or a lion rampant (Scotland).

PLATINUM—an orb.

Gold

Britannia Silver

Sterling Silver (England)

Sterling Silver (Scotland)

Platinum

Assay Office Mark—This mark identifies the particular assay office at which the article was tested and marked. The existing assay offices in Britain are:

LONDON, Goldsmiths' Hall, EC2V 8AQ (Tel: 071-606 8971).
BIRMINGHAM, Newhall Street, B3 1SB (Tel: 021-236 6951).
SHEFFIELD, 137 Portobello Street, S1 4DS (Tel: 0742-755111).

EDINBURGH, 9 Granton Road, EH5 3QJ (Tel: 031-551 2189).

Their marks are as follows:

London

Birmingham

Gold and platinum

Silver

Sheffield

Edinburgh

Assay offices formerly existed in other towns, e.g. Chester, Exeter, Glasgow, Newcastle, Norwich and York, each having its own distinguishing mark.

Date Letter—The date letter shows the year in which an article was assayed and hallmarked. Each alphabetical cycle has a distinctive style of lettering or shape of shield. The date letters were different at the various assay offices and the particular office must be established from the assay office mark before reference is made to tables of date letters.

The following table shows specimen shields and letters used by the London Assay Office on silver articles in each period from 1498. The same letters are found on gold articles but the surrounding shield may differ. Since January 1, 1975, each office has used the same style of date letter and shield for all articles (*see* table on p. 1178).

OTHER MARKS

Foreign Goods—Since 1842 foreign goods imported into Britain have been required to be hallmarked before sale. The marks consist of the importer's mark, a special assay office mark, the figure denoting fineness (fineness mark) and the annual date letter.

The following are the assay office marks for gold imported articles. For silver and platinum the symbols remain the same but the shields differ in shape.

London   Birmingham   Sheffield   Edinburgh

Convention Hallmarks—Special marks at authorized assay offices of the signatory countries of the International Convention (Austria, Denmark, Finland, Ireland, Portugal, Norway, Sweden, Switzerland and the UK) are legally recognized in the United Kingdom as approved hallmarks. These consist of a sponsor's mark, a common control mark, a fineness mark (arabic numerals showing the standard in parts per thousand), and an assay office mark. There is no date letter.

The fineness marks are: for gold, 750 (18 carat), 585

(14 carat) and 375 (9 carat); for silver, 925 (sterling); and for platinum, 950. The common control marks are:

| *Gold* (18 carat) | *Silver* | *Platinum* |

Duty Marks—In 1784 an additional mark of the reigning sovereign's head was introduced to signify that the excise duty had been paid. The mark became obsolete on the abolition of the duty in 1890.

Commemorative Marks—There are three other marks to commemorate special events, the Silver Jubilee of King George V and Queen Mary in 1935, the Coronation of Queen Elizabeth II in 1953, and her Silver Jubilee in 1977.

London (Goldsmiths' Hall) Date Letters from 1498

	Black letter, small	1498–9 to 1517–8		Roman letter, small ...	1739–40 to 1755–6
	Lombardic	1518–9 „ 1537–8		Old English, capitals ..	1756–7 „ 1775–6
	Roman and other capitals	1538–9 „ 1557–8		Roman letter, small ...	1776–7 „ 1795–6
	Black letter, small	1558–9 „ 1577–8		Roman letter, capitals .	1796–7 „ 1815–6
	Roman letter, capitals .	1578–9 „ 1597–8		Roman letter, small ...	1816–7 „ 1835–6
	Lombardic, external cusps	1598–9 „ 1617–8		Old English, capitals ..	1836–7 „ 1855–6
	Italic letter, small	1618–9 „ 1637–8		Old English, small	1856–7 „ 1875–6
	Court hand	1638–9 „ 1657–8		Roman letter, capitals [A to M *square* shield N to Z as shown]	1876–7 „ 1895–6
	Black letter, capitals ..	1658–9 „ 1677–8		Roman letter, small ...	1896–7 „ 1915–6
	Black letter, small	1678–9 „ 1696–7		Black letter, small	1916–7 „ 1935–6
	Court hand	1697 „ 1715–6		Roman letter, capitals .	1936–7 „ 1955–6
	Roman letter, capitals	1716–7 „ 1735–6		Italic letter, small	1956–7 „ 1974
	Roman letter, small ...	1736–7 „ 1738–9		Italic letter, capitals ..	1975 „ ...

WEIGHTS AND MEASURES

SI UNITS

The Système International d'Unités (SI) is an international and coherent system of units devised to meet all known needs for measurement in science and technology. The system was adopted by the 11th Conférence Générale des Poids et Mesures (CGPM) in 1960. The British Standards describing the essential features of the International System of Units are *Specifications for SI Units* (BS 5555:1981) and *Conversion Factors and Tables* (BS 350, Part 1:1974).

The system consists of seven base units and the derived units formed as products or quotients of various powers of the base units. Together the base units and the derived units make up the coherent system of units. In the UK the SI base units, and almost all important derived units, are realized at the National Physical Laboratory and disseminated through the National Measurement System.

Base Units

Metre (m) = unit of length

Kilogram (kg) = unit of mass

Second (s) = unit of time

Ampere (A) = unit of electric current

Kelvin (K) = unit of thermodynamic temperature

Mole (mol) = unit of amount of substance

Candela (cd) = unit of luminous intensity

Derived Units

For some of the derived SI units, special names and symbols exist; those approved by the CGPM are listed below.

Hertz (Hz) = unit of frequency

Newton (N) = unit of force

Pascal (Pa) = unit of pressure, stress

Joule (J) = unit of energy, work, quantity of heat

Watt (W) = unit of power, radiant flux

Coulomb (C) = unit of electric charge, quantity of electricity

Volt (V) = unit of electric potential, potential difference, electromotive force

Farad (F) = unit of electric capacitance

Ohm (Ω) = unit of electric resistance

Siemens (S) = unit of electric conductance

Weber (Wb) = unit of magnetic flux

Tesla (T) = unit of magnetic flux density

Henry (H) = unit of inductance

Degree Celsius (°C) = unit of Celsius temperature

Lumen (lm) = unit of luminous flux

Lux (lx) = unit of illuminance

Becquerel (Bq) = unit of activity (of a radionuclide)

Gray (Gy) = unit of absorbed dose, specific energy imparted, kerma, absorbed dose index

Sievert (Sv) = unit of dose equivalent, dose equivalent index

Supplementary Units

The derived units include, as a special case, the supplementary units which may be treated as dimensionless within the SI.

Radian (rad) = unit of plane angle

Steradian (sr) = unit of solid angle

Other derived units are expressed in terms of base units and/or supplementary units. Some of the more commonly-used derived units are the following:

Unit of area = square metre (m^2)

Unit of volume = cubic metre (m^3)

Unit of velocity = metre per second ($m\,s^{-1}$)

Unit of acceleration = metre per second squared ($m\,s^{-2}$)

Unit of density = kilogram per cubic metre ($kg\,m^{-3}$)

Unit of momentum = kilogram metre per second ($kg\,m\,s^{-1}$)

Unit of magnetic field strength = ampere per metre ($A\,m^{-1}$)

Unit of surface tension = newton per metre ($N\,m^{-1}$)

Unit of dynamic viscosity = pascal second ($Pa\,s$)

Unit of heat capacity = joule per kelvin ($J\,K^{-1}$)

Unit of specific heat capacity = joule per kilogram kelvin ($J\,kg^{-1}\,K^{-1}$)

Unit of heat flux density, irradiance = watt per square metre ($W\,m^{-2}$)

Unit of thermal conductivity = watt per metre kelvin ($W\,m^{-1}\,K^{-1}$)

Unit of electric field strength = volt per metre ($V\,m^{-1}$)

Unit of luminance = candela per square metre ($cd\,m^{-2}$)

SI Prefixes

Decimal multiples and submultiples of the SI units are indicated by SI prefixes. These are as follows:

multiples	submultiples
yotta (Y) $\times 10^{24}$	deci (d) $\times 10^{-1}$
zetta (Z) $\times 10^{21}$	centi (c) $\times 10^{-2}$
exa (E) $\times 10^{18}$	milli (m) $\times 10^{-3}$
peta (P) $\times 10^{15}$	micro (μ) $\times 10^{-6}$
tera (T) $\times 10^{12}$	nano (n) $\times 10^{-9}$
giga (G) $\times 10^{9}$	pico (p) $\times 10^{-12}$
mega (M) $\times 10^{6}$	femto (f) $\times 10^{-15}$
kilo (k) $\times 10^{3}$	atto (a) $\times 10^{-18}$
hecto (h) $\times 10^{2}$	zepto (z) $\times 10^{-21}$
deca (da) $\times 10$	yocto (y) $\times 10^{-24}$

UK UNITS

The legal measures for the United Kingdom are enacted in the Weights and Measures Act 1985. The United Kingdom primary standards are the **yard** or the **metre** as the unit of measurement of length, and the **pound** or the **kilogram** as the unit of measurement of mass. Other units of measurement are defined by reference to the primary standards.

Responsibility for the maintenance of the primary standards and for the determination or redetermination of their value rests with the Secretary of State for Trade and Industry.

The definition of the UK primary standards is as follows:

YARD = 0·9144 metre

METRE is the length of the path travelled by light in vacuum during a time interval of 1/299 792 458 of a second.

POUND = 0·453 592 37 kilogram

KILOGRAM is equal to the mass of the international prototype of the kilogram

The following list shows the definitions of measures set out in Schedule 1 of the Weights and Measures Act 1985.

Measurement of Length

Imperial Units
Mile = 1760 yards
Yard (yd) = 0·9144 metre
Foot (ft) = 1/3 yard
Inch (in) = 1/36 yard

Metric Units
Kilometre (km) = 1000 metres
Metre (m) is the length of the path travelled by light in vacuum during a time interval of 1/299 792 458 of a second
Decimetre (dm) = 1/10 metre
Centimetre (cm) = 1/100 metre
Millimetre (mm) = 1/1000 metre

Measurement of Area

Imperial Units
Acre = 4840 square yards
Square Yard = a superficial area equal to that of a square each side of which measures one yard
Square foot = 1/9 square yard

Metric Units
Hectare (ha) = 100 ares
Decare = 10 ares
Are (a) = 100 square metres
Square Metre = a superficial area equal to that of a square each side of which measures one metre
Square decimetre = 1/100 square metre
Square centimetre = 1/100 square decimetre
Square millimetre = 1/100 square centimetre

Measurement of Volume

Metric Units
Cubic Metre (m³) = a volume equal to that of a cube each edge of which measures one metre
Cubic decimetre = 1/1000 cubic metre
Cubic centimetre (cc) = 1/1000 cubic decimetre
Hectolitre = 100 litres
Litre = a cubic decimetre
Decilitre = 1/10 litre
Centilitre = 1/100 litre
Millilitre = 1/1000 litre

Measurement of Capacity

Imperial Units
Gallon = 4·546 09 cubic decimetres
Quart = 1/4 gallon
Pint (pt) = 1/2 quart
Gill = 1/4 pint
Fluid ounce (fl oz) = 1/20 pint

Metric Units
Hectolitre (hl) = 100 litres
Litre (l or L) = a cubic decimetre
Decilitre (dl) = 1/10 litre
Centilitre (cl) = 1/100 litre
Millilitre (ml) = 1/1000 litre

Measurement of Mass or Weight

Imperial Units
Pound (lb) = 0·453 592 37 kilogram
Ounce (oz) = 1/16 pound
*Ounce troy = 12/175 pound

Metric Units
Tonne, metric ton (t) = 1000 kilograms
Kilogram (kg) is the unit of mass; it is equal to the mass of the international prototype of the kilogram

Hectogram (hg) = 1/10 kilogram
Gram (g) = 1/1000 kilogram
**Carat (metric) = 1/5 gram
Milligram (mg) = 1/1000 gram

*used only for transactions in gold, silver or other precious metals, and articles made therefrom.
**used only for transactions in precious stones or pearls.

Certain units of measurement may no longer be used for trade although the measure may still be used, e.g. it is legal to sell a 112 lb quantity of a commodity but it must be referred to in invoices, etc., as 112 lb, not as 1 cwt. These units are defined as follows:

Measurement of Length

Furlong = 220 yards
Chain = 22 yards

Measurement of Area

Square mile = 640 acres
Rood = 1210 square yards
Square inch = 1/144 square foot

Measurement of Volume

Cubic yard = a volume equal to that of a cube each edge of which measures one yard
Cubic foot = 1/27 cubic yard
Cubic inch = 1/1728 cubic foot

Measurement of Capacity

Bushel = 8 gallons
Peck = 2 gallons
Fluid drachm = 1/8 fluid ounce
Minim (min) = 1/60 fluid drachm

Measurement of Mass or Weight

Ton = 2240 pounds
Hundredweight (cwt) = 112 pounds
Cental = 100 pounds
Quarter = 28 pounds
Stone = 14 pounds
Dram (dr) = 1/16 ounce
Grain (gr) = 1/7000 pound
Pennyweight (dwt) = 24 grains
Ounce apothecaries = 480 grains
Drachm (ʒ1) = 1/8 ounce apothecaries
Scruple(ʒ1) = 1/3 drachm

Metric ton = 1000 kilograms
Quintal (q) = 100 kilograms

Measurement of Electricity

Units of measurement of electricity are defined by the Weights and Measures Act 1985, as follows:
An Ampere (A) is that constant current which, if maintained in two straight parallel conductors of infinite length, of negligible circular cross-section and placed 1 metre apart in vacuum, would produce between these conductors a force equal to 2×10^{-7} newton per metre of length.
An Ohm (Ω) is the electric resistance between two points of a conductor when a constant potential difference of 1 volt, applied between the two points, produces in the conductor a current of 1 ampere, the conductor not being the seat of any electromotive force.
A Volt (V) is the difference of electric potential between two points of a conducting wire carrying a constant current of 1 ampere when the power dissipated between these points is equal to 1 watt.

A WATT (W) is the power which in one second gives rise to energy of 1 joule
Kilowatt (kW) = 1,000 watts
Megawatt (MW) = one million watts

WATER MEASURES
(approximate)

1 cubic foot = 62·32 lb
1 gallon = 10 lb
1 cubic cm = 1 gram
1000 cubic cm = 1 litre; 1 kilogram
1 cubic metre = 1000 litres; 1000 kg; 1 tonne
An inch of rain on the surface of an acre (43560 sq. ft.) = 3630 cubic ft = 100·992 tons
Cisterns: A cistern 4 × 2½ feet and 3 feet deep will hold brimful 186·963 gallons, weighing 1869·63 lbs in addition to its own weight

Water for Ships

Kilderkin = 18 gallons
Barrel = 36 gallons
Puncheon = 72 gallons
Butt = 110 gallons
Tun = 210 gallons

Wine Measures

Under the Weights and Measures (Intoxicating Liquor) Order 1988, as amended by the Weights and Measures (Various Foods) (Amendment) Order 1990, still wines may be pre-packed only in the following quantities: 10, 25, 37·5, 50 and 75 cl; 1, 1·5, 2, 3, 4, 5, 6, 8, 9 and 10 litres. In addition, the 18·7 cl size is permitted for consumption on board aircraft, ships and trains or for sale duty-free, and all quantities up to and including 25 cl are allowed when for consumption on the premises of the seller.

The Intoxicating Liquor Order also provides that, with effect from January 1, 1991, sparkling wines (including champagne) may be pre-packed only in the following quantities: 12·5, 20, 37·5 and 75 cl; 1·5, 3, 4·5, 6 and 9 litres. From January 1, 1992, spirits and liqueurs may be pre-packed only in the following quantities: 2, 3, 4, 5, 7·1, 10, 20, 35, 50 and 70 cl; 1, 1·5, 2, 2·5, 3 and 4·5 litres. In addition, 1·125, 5 and 10 litres will be permitted for non-retail sales.

Bottles of Wine

Traditional equivalents in standard champagne bottles:

Magnum = 2 bottles
Jeroboam = 4 bottles
Rehoboam = 6 bottles
Methuselah = 8 bottles
Salmanazar = 12 bottles
Balthazar = 16 bottles
Nebuchadnezzar = 20 bottles
A quarter of a bottle is known as a *nip*.
An eighth of a bottle is known as a *baby*.

ANGULAR AND CIRCULAR MEASURES

60 seconds (″) = 1 minute (′)
60 minutes = 1 degree (°)
90 degrees = 1 right angle or quadrant
Diameter of circle × 3·141 6 = circumference
Diameter squared × 0·7854 = area of circle
Diameter squared × 3·141 6 = surface of sphere
Diameter cubed × 0·523 = solidity of sphere
One degree of circumference × 57·3 = radius*
Diameter of cylinder × 3·141 6; product by length or height, gives the surface
Diameter squared × 0·7854; product by length or height, gives solid content.

* Or, one radian (the angle subtended at the centre of a circle by an arc of the circumference equal in length to the radius) = 57·3 degrees.

MILLION, BILLION, ETC.

Value in the United Kingdom

Million . . . . thousand × thousand (10^6)
Billion . . . . million × million (10^{12})
Trillion . . . . million × billion (10^{18})
Quadrillion . . . . million × trillion (10^{24})

Value in USA

Million . . . . thousand × thousand (10^6)
Billion . . . . thousand × million (10^9)
Trillion . . . . million × million (10^{12})
Quadrillion . . . . million × billion US (10^{15})

The American usage of billion (i.e. 10^9) is increasingly common, and is now universally used by statisticians.

NAUTICAL MEASURES

Distance at sea is measured in nautical miles. The British standard nautical mile was 6080 feet (the length of a minute of an arc of a great circle of the earth, rounded off to a mean value to allow for the length varying at different latitudes). This measure has been obsolete since 1970 when the international nautical mile of 1852 metres was adopted by the Hydrographic Department of the Ministry of Defence as a result of a recommendation by the International Hydrographic Bureau.

The cable (600 feet or 100 fathoms) was a measure approximately one tenth of a nautical mile. Such distances are now expressed in decimal parts of a sea mile or in metres.

Soundings at sea were recorded in fathoms (6 feet). Depths are now expressed in metres on new Admiralty charts.

Speed

Speed is measured in nautical miles per hour, called knots. A ship moving at the rate of 30 nautical miles per hour is said to be doing 30 knots.

knots	m.p.h.	knots	m.p.h.
1	1·1515	9	10·3636
2	2·3030	10	11·5151
3	3·4545	15	17·2727
4	4·6060	20	23·0303
5	5·7575	25	28·7878
6	6·9090	30	34·5454
7	8·0606	35	40·3030
8	9·2121	40	46·0606

Tonnage

The tonnage of a vessel is measured in tons of 100 cubic feet.
Gross tonnage = the total volume of all the enclosed spaces of a vessel
Net tonnage = gross tonnage less deductions for crew space, engine room, water ballast and other spaces not used for passengers or cargo

DISTANCE OF THE HORIZON

The limit of distance to which one can see varies with the height of the spectator. The greatest distance at which an object on the surface of the sea, or of a level plain, can be seen by a person whose eyes are at a height of five feet from the same level is nearly three miles. At a height of 20 feet the range is increased to nearly six miles, and an approximate rule for finding the range of vision for small heights is to increase the square root of the number of feet that the eye is above the level surface by a third of itself. The result is the distance of the horizon in miles, but is slightly in excess of that in the table below, which is computed by a more precise formula. The table may be used conversely to show the distance of an object of given height that is just visible from a point on the surface of the earth or sea. Refraction is taken into account both in the approximate rule and in the table.

At a height of	the range is
5 ft	2·9 miles
20 „	5·9 „
50 „	9·3 „
100 „	13·2 „
500 „	29·5 „
1,000 „	41·6 „
2,000 „	58·9 „
3,000 „	72·1 „
4,000 „	83·3 „
5,000 „	93·1 „
20,000 „	186·2 „

TEMPERATURE SCALES

The Celsius scale is the SI name for the Centigrade scale. The Fahrenheit scale is related to it by the relationships:

$$C = (F - 32) \div 1·8$$
$$F = (C \times 1·8) + 32$$

Conversion between scales of Celsius and Fahrenheit

°C	°F	°C	°F	°C	°F
100	212	60	140	20	68
99	210·2	59	138·2	19	66·2
98	208·4	58	136·4	18	64·4
97	206·6	57	134·6	17	62·6
96	204·8	56	132·8	16	60·8
95	203	55	131	15	59
94	201·2	54	129·2	14	57·2
93	199·4	53	127·4	13	55·4
92	197·6	52	125·6	12	53·6
91	195·8	51	123·8	11	51·8
90	194	50	122	10	50
89	192·2	49	120·2	9	48·2
88	190·4	48	118·4	8	46·4
87	188·6	47	116·6	7	44·6
86	186·8	46	114·8	6	42·8
85	185	45	113	5	41
84	183·2	44	111·2	4	39·2
83	181·4	43	109·4	3	37·4
82	179·6	42	107·6	2	35·6
81	177·8	41	105·8	1	33·8
80	176	40	104	zero	32
79	174·2	39	102·2	− 1	30·2
78	172·4	38	100·4	− 2	28·4
77	170·6	37	98·6	− 3	26·6
76	168·8	36	96·8	− 4	24·8
75	167	35	95	− 5	23
74	165·2	34	93·2	− 6	21·2
73	163·4	33	91·4	− 7	19·4
72	161·6	32	89·6	− 8	17·6
71	159·8	31	87·8	− 9	15·8
70	158	30	86	−10	14
69	156·2	29	84·2	−11	12·2
68	154·4	28	82·4	−12	10·4
67	152·6	27	80·6	−13	8·6
66	150·8	26	78·8	−14	6·8
65	149	25	77	−15	5
64	147·2	24	75·2	−16	3·2
63	145·4	23	73·4	−17	1·4
62	143·6	22	71·6	−18	0·4
61	141·8	21	69·8	−19	−2·2

NOTE:—The normal temperature of the human body is 36·9 °C or 98·4 °F. The freezing point of water is 0 °C = 32 °F. The boiling point is 99·974 °C (on adoption of a new International Temperature Scale, ITS–90, from January 1, 1990) = 212 °F approximately.

On the kelvin temperature scale, the kelvin unit is 1/273·16 of the triple point of water (i.e. where ice, water and water vapour are in equilibrium). Absolute zero is zero K, the freezing point of water is 273·15 K and the boiling point is 373·124 K.

PAPER MEASURES

Writing Paper	*Printing Paper*
480 sheets = 1 ream	516 sheets = 1 ream
24 sheets = 1 quire	2 reams = 1 bundle
20 quires = 1 ream	5 bundles = 1 bale

Sizes of Writing and Drawing Papers

	inches			inches
Emperor	72 ×48	Copy or Draft .	20 ×16
Antiquarian ..	53 ×31	Demy	20 ×15½
Double		Post	19 ×15½
Elephant ...	40 ×27	Pinched Post .	18½ ×14½
Grand Eagle .	42 ×28¾	Foolscap	17 ×13½
Atlas	34 ×26	Double	
Colombier ..	34½ ×23½	Foolscap	26½ ×16½
Imperial	30 ×22	Double Post ..	30½ ×19
Elephant	28 ×23	Double Large	
Cartridge	26 ×21	Post	33 ×21
Super Royal ..	27 ×19	Double Demy .	31 ×20
Royal	24 ×19	Brief	16½ ×13½
Medium	22 ×17½	Pott	15 ×12½
Large Post	21 ×16½		

Sizes of Printing Papers

	inches			inches
Foolscap	17 ×13½	Double Large	
Double		Post	33 ×21
Foolscap	27 ×17	Demy	22½ ×17½
Quad Foolscap	34 ×27	Double Demy .	35 ×22½
Crown	20 ×15	Quad Demy ..	45 ×35
Double Crown	30 ×20	Music Demy ..	20 ×15½
Quad Crown ..	40 ×30	Medium	23 ×18
Double Quad		Royal	25 ×20
Crown	60 ×40	Super Royal ..	27½ ×20½
Post	19½ ×15½	Elephant	28 ×23
Double Post...	31½ ×19½	Imperial	30 ×22

Sizes of Brown Papers

	inches			inches
Casing	46 ×36	Imperial Cap ..	29 ×22
Double		Haven Cap ...	26 ×21
Imperial	45 ×29	Bag Cap	24 ×19½
Elephant	34 ×24	Kent Cap	21 ×18
Double Four			
Pound	31 ×21		

INTERNATIONAL PAPER SIZES

The basis of the international series of paper sizes is a rectangle having an area of one square metre, the sides of which are in the proportion of 1:√2. The proportions 1:√2 have a geometrical relationship, the side and diagonal of any square being in this proportion. The effect of this arrangement is that if the area of the sheet of paper is doubled or halved, the shorter side and the longer side of the new sheet are still in the same proportion 1:√2. This feature is useful where photographic enlargement or reduction is used, as the proportions remain the same.

Description of the A series is by capital A followed by a figure. The basic size has the description A0 and the higher the figure following the letter, the greater is the number of sub-divisions and therefore the smaller the sheet. Half A0 is A1 and half A1 is A2.

Where larger dimensions are required the A is preceded by a figure. Thus 2A means twice the size A0; 4A is four times the size of A0.

Subsidiary Series.—A series of B sizes has been devised for use in exceptional circumstances when sizes intermediate between any two adjacent sizes of the A series are needed.

In addition there is a series of C sizes which is used much less. A is for magazines and books, B for posters, wall charts and other large items, C for envelopes particularly where it is necessary for an envelope (in C series) to fit into another envelope. The size recommended for business correspondence is A4.

Long Sizes.—Long sizes (DL) are obtainable by dividing any appropriate sizes from the two series above into three, four or eight equal parts parallel with the shorter side in such a manner that the proportions mentioned in paragraph two are not maintained, the ratio between the longer and the shorter sides being greater than √2:1. In practice long sizes should be produced from the A series only.

It is an essential feature of these series that the dimensions are of the trimmed or finished size.

A Series

	mm		*mm*
A0	841 × 1189	A6	105 × 148
A1	594 × 841	A7	74 × 105
A2	420 × 594	A8	52 × 74
A3	297 × 420	A9	37 × 52
A4	210 × 297	A10	26 × 37
A5	148 × 210		

B Series

	mm		*mm*
B0	1000 × 1414	B6	125 × 176
B1	707 × 1000	B7	88 × 125
B2	500 × 707	B8	62 × 88
B3	353 × 500	B9	44 × 62
B4	250 × 353	B10	31 × 44
B5	176 × 250		

C Series / **DL**

	mm		*mm*
C4	324 × 229	DL	110 × 220
C5	229 × 162		
C6	114 × 162		

SIZES OF BOUND BOOKS

The book sizes most commonly used are listed below. Approximate centimetre equivalents are also shown. International sizes are converted to their nearest imperial size (e.g. A4 = D4; A5 = D8).

		inches	*cm*
Crown 32mo	C32	2½ × 3¾	6 × 9
Crown 16mo	C16	3¾ × 5	9 × 13
Foolscap 8vo	F8	4¼ × 6¾	11 × 17
Demy 16mo	D16	4⅜ × 5⅝	11 × 14
Crown 8vo	C8	5 × 7½	13 × 19
Demy 8vo	D8	5⅝ × 8¾	14 × 22
Medium 8vo	M8	5¾ × 9	15 × 23
Royal 8vo	R8	6¼ × 10	16 × 25
Super Royal 8vo	suR8	6¾ × 10	17 × 25
Foolscap 4to	F4	6¾ × 8½	17 × 22
Crown 4to	C4	7½ × 10	19 × 25
Imperial 8vo	Imp8	7½ × 11	19 × 28
Demy 4to	D4	8¾ × 11¼	22 × 29
Royal 4to	R4	10 × 12½	25 × 31
Super Royal 4to	suR4	10 × 13½	25 × 34
Crown Folio	Cfol	10 × 15	25 × 38
Imperial Folio	Impfol	11 × 15	28 × 38

Folio means a sheet folded in half, *quarto* (4to) folded into four, *octavo* (8vo) folded into eight. Books are usually bound up in sheets of 16 or 32 pages. Octavo books are generally printed 64 pages at a time—32 pages on each side of a sheet of quad.

A TABLE OF THE NUMBER OF DAYS FROM ANY DAY IN ONE MONTH TO THE SAME IN ANY OTHER MONTH IN ORDINARY YEARS

	Jan.	Feb.	Mar.	April	May	June	July	Aug.	Sept.	Oct.	Nov.	Dec.
January	365	31	59	90	120	151	181	212	243	273	304	334
February	334	365	28	59	89	120	150	181	212	242	273	303
March	306	337	365	31	61	92	122	153	184	214	245	275
April	275	306	334	365	30	61	91	122	153	183	214	244
May	245	276	304	335	365	31	61	92	123	153	184	214
June	214	245	273	304	334	365	30	61	92	122	153	183
July	184	215	243	274	304	335	365	31	62	92	123	153
August	153	184	212	243	273	304	334	365	31	61	92	122
September	122	153	181	212	242	273	303	334	365	30	61	91
October	92	123	151	182	212	243	273	304	335	365	31	61
November	61	92	120	151	181	212	242	273	304	334	365	30
December	31	62	90	121	151	182	212	243	274	304	335	365

CONVERSION TABLES FOR WEIGHTS AND MEASURES

NOTE.—The central figures in heavy type represent either of the two columns beside them, as the case may be.
Examples:—1 centimetre = 0·394 inch and 1 inch = 2·540 centimetres. 1 metre = 1·094 yards and 1 yard = 0·914 metre. 1 kilometre = 0·621 mile and 1 mile = 1·609 kilometres.

Block 1

Length			Area			Volume			Weight (Mass)		
Centimetres		Inches	Square centimetres		Square inches	Cubic centimetres		Cubic inches	Kilograms		Pounds
2·540	1	0·394	6·452	1	0·155	16·387	1	0·061	0·454	1	2·205
5·080	2	0·787	12·903	2	0·310	32·774	2	0·122	0·907	2	4·409
7·620	3	1·181	19·355	3	0·465	49·161	3	0·183	1·361	3	6·614
10·160	4	1·575	25·806	4	0·620	65·548	4	0·244	1·814	4	8·819
12·700	5	1·969	32·258	5	0·775	81·936	5	0·305	2·268	5	11·023
15·240	6	2·362	38·710	6	0·930	98·323	6	0·366	2·722	6	13·228
17·780	7	2·756	45·161	7	1·085	114·710	7	0·427	3·175	7	15·432
20·320	8	3·150	51·613	8	1·240	131·097	8	0·488	3·629	8	17·637
22·860	9	3·543	58·064	9	1·395	147·484	9	0·549	4·082	9	19·842
25·400	10	3·937	64·516	10	1·550	163·871	10	0·610	4·536	10	22·046
50·800	20	7·874	129·032	20	3·100	327·742	20	1·220	9·072	20	44·092
76·200	30	11·811	193·548	30	4·650	491·613	30	1·831	13·608	30	66·139
101·600	40	15·748	258·064	40	6·200	655·484	40	2·441	18·144	40	88·185
127·000	50	19·685	322·580	50	7·750	819·355	50	3·051	22·680	50	110·231
152·400	60	23·622	387·096	60	9·300	983·226	60	3·661	27·216	60	132·277
177·800	70	27·559	451·612	70	10·850	1147·097	70	4·272	31·752	70	154·324
203·200	80	31·496	516·128	80	12·400	1310·968	80	4·882	36·287	80	176·370
228·600	90	35·433	580·644	90	13·950	1474·839	90	5·492	40·823	90	198·416
254·000	100	39·370	645·160	100	15·500	1638·710	100	6·102	45·359	100	220·464

Block 2

Metres		Yards	Square metres		Square yards	Cubic metres		Cubic yards	Metric tonnes		Tons (UK)
0·914	1	1·094	0·836	1	1·196	0·765	1	1·308	1·016	1	0·984
1·829	2	2·187	1·672	2	2·392	1·529	2	2·616	2·032	2	1·968
2·743	3	3·281	2·508	3	3·588	2·294	3	3·924	3·048	3	2·953
3·658	4	4·374	3·345	4	4·784	3·058	4	5·232	4·064	4	3·937
4·572	5	5·468	4·181	5	5·980	3·823	5	6·540	5·080	5	4·921
5·486	6	6·562	5·017	6	7·176	4·587	6	7·848	6·096	6	5·905
6·401	7	7·655	5·853	7	8·372	5·352	7	9·156	7·112	7	6·889
7·315	8	8·749	6·689	8	9·568	6·116	8	10·464	8·128	8	7·874
8·230	9	9·843	7·525	9	10·764	6·881	9	11·772	9·144	9	8·858
9·144	10	10·936	8·361	10	11·960	7·646	10	13·080	10·161	10	9·842
18·288	20	21·872	16·723	20	23·920	15·291	20	26·159	20·321	20	19·684
27·432	30	32·808	25·084	30	35·880	22·937	30	39·239	30·481	30	29·526
36·576	40	43·745	33·445	40	47·840	30·582	40	52·318	40·642	40	39·368
45·720	50	54·681	41·806	50	59·799	38·228	50	65·398	50·802	50	49·210
54·864	60	65·617	50·168	60	71·759	45·873	60	78·477	60·963	60	59·052
64·008	70	76·553	58·529	70	83·719	53·519	70	91·557	71·123	70	68·894
73·152	80	87·489	66·890	80	95·679	61·164	80	104·636	81·284	80	78·737
82·296	90	98·425	75·251	90	107·639	68·810	90	117·716	91·444	90	88·579
91·440	100	109·361	83·613	100	119·599	76·455	100	130·795	101·605	100	98·421

Block 3

Kilometres		Miles	Hectares		Acres	Litres		Gallons	Metric tonnes		Tons (US)
1·609	1	0·621	0·405	1	2·471	4·546	1	0·220	0·907	1	1·102
3·219	2	1·243	0·809	2	4·942	9·092	2	0·440	1·814	2	2·205
4·828	3	1·864	1·214	3	7·413	13·638	3	0·660	2·722	3	3·305
6·437	4	2·485	1·619	4	9·844	18·184	4	0·880	3·629	4	4·409
8·047	5	3·107	2·023	5	12·355	22·730	5	1·100	4·536	5	5·521
9·656	6	3·728	2·428	6	14·826	27·276	6	1·320	5·443	6	6·614
11·265	7	4·350	2·833	7	17·297	31·822	7	1·540	6·350	7	7·716
12·875	8	4·971	3·327	8	19·769	36·368	8	1·760	7·257	8	8·818
14·484	9	5·592	3·642	9	22·240	40·914	9	1·980	8·165	9	9·921
16·093	10	6·214	4·047	10	24·711	45·460	10	2·200	9·072	10	11·023
32·187	20	12·427	8·094	20	49·421	90·919	20	4·400	18·144	20	22·046
48·280	30	18·641	12·140	30	74·132	136·379	30	6·599	27·216	30	33·069
64·374	40	24·855	16·187	40	98·842	181·839	40	8·799	36·287	40	44·092
80·467	50	31·069	20·234	50	123·555	227·298	50	10·999	45·359	50	55·116
96·561	60	37·282	24·281	60	148·263	272·758	60	13·199	54·431	60	66·139
112·654	70	43·496	28·328	70	172·974	318·217	70	15·398	63·503	70	77·162
128·748	80	49·710	32·375	80	197·684	363·677	80	17·598	72·575	80	88·185
144·841	90	55·923	36·422	90	222·395	409·137	90	19·798	81·647	90	99·208
160·934	100	62·137	40·469	100	247·105	454·596	100	21·998	90·719	100	110·231

ABBREVIATIONS

Ψ = Seaport.

A

A	Associate of.
AA	Alcoholics Anonymous; Anti-Aircraft; Automobile Association.
AAA	Amateur Athletic Association.
AB	Able-bodied seaman.
ABA	Amateur Boxing Association.
abbr(ev)	abbreviation.
ABM	Anti-ballistic missile defence system.
abr	abridged.
ac	alternating current.
a/c	account.
AC	Aircraftman; (*Ante Christum*) Before Christ; Companion, Order of Australia.
ACAS	Advisory, Conciliation and Arbitration Service.
ACT	Australian Capital Territory.
ACTT	Association of Cinematograph, Television and Allied Technicians.
AD	(*Anno Domini*) In the year of our Lord.
ADC	Aide-de-Camp.
ADC (P)	Personal ADC to The Queen.
adj	adjective.
Adj	Adjutant.
ad lib	(*ad libitum*) at pleasure.
Adm	Admiral; Admission.
adv	adverb; advocate.
AE	Air Efficiency Award.
AEA	Atomic Energy Authority.
AEM	Air Efficiency Medal.
AERE	Atomic Energy Research Establishment.
AEU	Amalgamated Engineering Union.
AFC	Air Force Cross; Association Football Club.
AFM	Air Force Medal.
AFRC	Agricultural and Food Research Council.
AFV	Armoured fighting vehicle.
AG	Adjutant-General; Attorney-General.
AGM	air-to-ground missile; annual general meeting.
AH	(*Anno Hegirae*) In the year of the Hegira.
AIDS	Acquired Immune Deficiency Syndrome.
alt	altitude.
am	(*ante meridiem*) before noon.
AM	(*Anno mundi*) In the year of the world.
amp	ampere; amplifier.
ANC	African National Congress.
anon	anonymous(ly).
ANZAC	Australian and New Zealand Army Corps.
AO	Air Officer; Officer, Order of Australia.
AOC	Air Officer Commanding.
APEX	Association of Professional, Executive, Clerical and Computer Staff.
AS	Anglo-Saxon.
ASA	Advertising Standards Authority; Amateur Swimming Association.
ASB	*Alternative Service Book.*
ASEAN	Association of South East Asian Nations.
ASH	Action on Smoking and Health.
ASLEF	Associated Society of Locomotive Engineers and Firemen.
ASLIB	Association for Information Management.
ASTMS	Association of Scientific, Technical and Managerial Staffs.
ATC	Air Training Corps.
AUC	(*ab urbe condita*) In the year from the foundation of Rome; (*anno urbis conditae*) In the year of the founding of the city.
AUT	Association of University Teachers.
AV	Audio-visual; Authorized Version.
AVR	Army Volunteer Reserve.

AWOL	Absent without leave.

B

b	born; bowled.
BA	Bachelor of Arts.
BAA	British Airports Authority; British Astronomical Association.
BAFTA	British Academy of Film and Television Arts.
BAOR	British Army of the Rhine.
Bart	Baronet.
BAS	Bachelor in Agricultural Science; British Antarctic Survey.
BB	Boys' Brigade.
BBC	British Broadcasting Corporation.
BC	Before Christ; British Columbia.
B Ch (D)	Bachelor of (Dental) Surgery.
BCL	*do*, of Civil Law.
B Com	*do*, of Commerce.
BD	*do*, of Divinity.
BDA	British Dental Association.
BDS	Bachelor of Dental Surgery.
B Ed	*do*, of Education.
BEM	British Empire Medal.
B Eng	Bachelor of Engineering.
BFI	British Film Institute.
BFPO	British Forces Post Office.
BIM	British Institute of Management.
B Litt	Bachelor of Letters *or* of Literature.
BM	*do*, of Medicine; British Museum.
BMA	British Medical Association.
B Mus	Bachelor of Music.
BOTB	British Overseas Trade Board.
Bp	Bishop.
B Pharm	Bachelor of Pharmacy.
B Phil	*do*, of Philosophy.
Br	Britain; British.
BR	British Rail.
BRCS	British Red Cross Society.
Brig	Brigadier.
Brit	Britain; British.
BSc	Bachelor of Science.
BSC	British Steel Corporation.
BSI	British Standards Institution.
BST	British Summer Time.
Bt	Baronet.
BTEC	Business and Technician Education Council.
B Th	Bachelor of Theology.
Btu	British thermal unit.
BVM	(*Beata Virgo Maria*) Blessed Virgin Mary.
BVMS	Bachelor of Veterinary Medicine and Surgery.
BWB	British Waterways Board.

C

c	(*circa*) about.
C	Celsius; Centigrade; Conservative.
CA	Chartered Accountant (*Scotland*).
CAA	Civil Aviation Authority.
CAB	Citizens' Advice Bureau.
Cantab	(of) Cambridge.
Cantuar:	of Canterbury (*Archbishop*).
CAP	Common Agricultural Policy.
Capt	Captain.
Caricom	Caribbean Community and Common Market.
Carliol:	of Carlisle (*Bishop*).
CB	Companion, Order of the Bath.
CBE	Commander, Order of the British Empire.
CBI	Confederation of British Industry.

CC   Chamber of Commerce; Companion, Order of Canada; City Council; County Council; County Court.
CCC   County Cricket Club.
C Chem   Chartered Chemist.
CD   Civil Defence; Compact Disc; Corps Diplomatique.
Cdr   Commander.
Cdre   Commodore.
CDS   Chief of the Defence Staff.
CE   Civil Engineer.
C Eng   Chartered Engineer.
Cento   Central Treaty Organization.
Cestr: of Chester (*Bishop*).
CET   Central European Time; Common External Tariff.
cf   (*confer*) compare.
CF   Chaplain to the Forces.
CFC   Chlorofluorocarbon.
CGM   Conspicuous Gallantry Medal.
CGS   Centimetre-gramme-second (*system*); Chief of General Staff.
CH   Companion of Honour.
ChB/M   Bachelor/Master of Surgery.
CI   Channel Islands; The Imperial Order of the Crown of India.
CIA   Central Intelligence Agency.
Cicestr: of Chichester (*Bishop*).
CID   Criminal Investigation Department.
CIE   Companion, Order of the Indian Empire.
cif   cost, insurance and freight.
C-in-C   Commander-in-Chief.
CIPFA   Chartered Institute of Public Finance and Accountancy.
C Lit   Companion of Literature.
CLJ   Commander, Order of St Lazarus of Jerusalem.
CM   (*Chirurgiae Magister*) Master of Surgery.
CMEA   Council for Mutual Economic Assistance.
CMG   Companion, Order of St Michael and St George.
CNAA   Council for National Academic Awards.
CND   Campaign for Nuclear Disarmament.
c/o   care of.
CO   Commanding Officer; conscientious objector.
COD   Cash on delivery.
C of E   Church of England.
COHSE   Confederation of Health Service Employees.
COI   Central Office of Information.
Col   Colonel.
Comecon   Council for Mutual Economic Assistance.
Con   Conservative.
Cpl   Corporal.
CPM   Colonial Police Medal.
CPRE   Council for the Protection of Rural England.
CPVE   Certificate of Pre-Vocational Education.
CRE   Council for Racial Equality.
CSCE   Conference on Security and Co-operation in Europe.
CSE   Certificate of Secondary Education.
CSI   Companion, Order of the Star of India.
CVO   Commander, Royal Victorian Order.

D

d   (*denarius*) penny.
DBE   Dame Commander, Order of the British Empire.
dc   direct current.
DC   District Council; District of Columbia.
DCB   Dame Commander, Order of the Bath.
D Ch   (*Doctor Chirurgiae*) Doctor of Surgery.
DCL   Doctor of Civil Law.

DCM   Distinguished Conduct Medal.
DCMG   Dame Commander, Order of St Michael and St George.
DCVO   Dame Commander, Royal Victorian Order.
DD   Doctor of Divinity.
DDS   *do,* of Dental Surgery.
DDT   dichlorodiphenyl-trichloroethane.
del   (*delineavit*) he/she drew it.
DES   Department of Education and Science.
DFC   Distinguished Flying Cross.
DFM   Distinguished Flying Medal.
DG   (*Dei gratia*) By the grace of God; Director-General.
DH   Department of Health.
DHA   District Health Authority.
DHSS   Department of Health and Social Security.
Dip Ed   Diploma in Education.
Dip H E   Diploma in Higher Education.
Dip Tech   Diploma in Technology.
DJ   Disc jockey.
DL   Deputy Lieutenant.
D Litt   Doctor of Letters *or* of Literature.
D Mus   *do,* of Music.
DNA   deoxyribonucleic acid.
DNB   *Dictionary of National Biography.*
do   (*ditto*) the same.
DoE   Department of the Environment.
DOS   Disk operating system (*computer*).
DP   Data processing.
D Ph *or*
D Phil   Doctor of Philosophy.
DPP   Director of Public Prosecutions.
Dr   Doctor.
DSc   Doctor of Science.
DSC   Distinguished Service Cross.
DSM   Distinguished Service Medal.
DSO   Companion, Distinguished Service Order.
DSS   Department of Social Security.
DTI   Department of Trade and Industry.
Dunelm: of Durham (*Bishop*).
DV   (*Deo volente*) God willing.

E

E   East.
Ebor: of York (*Archbishop*).
EC   European Community.
ECG   Electrocardiogram.
ECSC   European Coal and Steel Community.
ECU   European Currency Unit.
ED   Efficiency Decoration.
EEC   European Economic Community.
EEG   Electroencephalogram.
EETPU   Electrical, Electronic, Telecommunication and Plumbing Union.
EFTA   European Free Trade Association.
eg   (*exempli gratia*) for the sake of example.
EMS   European Monetary System.
ENEA   European Nuclear Energy Agency.
ER   (*Elizabetha Regina*) Queen Elizabeth.
ERD   Emergency Reserve Decoration.
ERM   Exchange Rate Mechanism.
ERNIE   Electronic random number indicator equipment.
ESA   European Space Agency.
ESP   Extra-sensory perception.
ESRC   Economic and Social Research Council.
ETA   Euzkadi ta Askatasuna (*Basque separatist organization*).
et al   (*et alibi*) and elsewhere; (*et alii*) and others.
etc   (*et cetera*) and the other things/and so forth.
et seq   (*et sequentia*) and the following.
Euratom   European Atomic Energy Commission.

Exon: of Exeter (*Bishop*).

F

f	(*forte*) loud.
F	Fahrenheit; Fellow of.
FA	Football Association.
FANY	First Aid Nursing Yeomanry.
FAO	Food and Agriculture Organization.
FBA	Fellow, British Academy.
FBAA	*do*, British Association of Accountants and Auditors.
FBI	Federal Bureau of Investigation.
FBIM	Fellow, British Institute of Management.
FBS	*do*, Botanical Society.
FCA	*do*, Institute of Chartered Accountants (*of England and Wales*).
FCCA	*do*, Chartered Association of Certified Accountants.
FCGI	*do*, City and Guilds of London Institute.
FCIA	*do*, Corporation of Insurance Agents.
FCIArb	*do*, Chartered Institute of Arbitrators.
FCIB	*do*, Chartered Institute of Bankers; *do*, Corporation of Insurance Brokers.
FCIBSE	*do*, Chartered Institution of Building Services Engineers.
FCII	*do*, Chartered Insurance Institute.
FCIS	*do*, Institute of Chartered Secretaries and Administrators.
FCIT	*do*, Chartered Institute of Transport.
FCMA	*do*, Chartered Institute of Management Accountants.
FCO	Foreign and Commonwealth Office.
FCP	Fellow, College of Preceptors.
FD	(*Fidei Defensor*) Defender of the Faith.
fec	(*fecit*) made this.
FEng	Fellow, Fellowship of Engineering.
ff	(*fecerunt*) made this (*pl*); (*fortissimo*) very loud.
FFA	Fellow, Faculty of Actuaries (*Scotland*); *do*, Institute of Financial Accountants.
FFAS	*do*, Faculty of Architects and Surveyors.
FGS	*do*, Geological Society.
FHS	*do*, Heraldry Society.
FHSM	*do*, Institute of Health Service Management.
FIA	*do*, Institute of Actuaries.
FIBiol	*do*, Institute of Biology.
FICE	*do*, Institution of Civil Engineers.
FICS	*do*, Institution of Chartered Shipbrokers.
FIEE	*do*, Institution of Electrical Engineers.
FIERE	*do*, Institution of Electronic and Radio Engineers.
FIFA	International Association Football Federation.
FIM	Fellow, Institute of Metals.
FIMM	*do*, Institution of Mining and Metallurgy.
FInstF	*do*, Institute of Fuel.
FInstP	*do*, Institute of Physics.
FIQS	*do*, Institute of Quantity Surveyors.
FIS	*do*, Institute of Statisticians.
FJI	*do*, Institute of Journalists.
fl	(*floruit*) flourished.
FLA	Fellow, Library Association.
FLS	*do*, Linnean Society.
FM	Field Marshal; frequency modulation.
fo	folio.
FO	Flying Officer.
fob	free on board.
FPA	Family Planning Association.
FPhS	Fellow, Philosophical Society.
FRAD	*do*, Royal Academy of Dancing.
FRAeS	*do*, Royal Aeronautical Society.
FRAI	*do*, Royal Anthropological Institute.
FRAM	*do*, Royal Academy of Music.
FRAS	*do*, Royal Astronomical Society.

FRBS	*do*, Royal Botanical Society; *do*, Royal Society of British Sculptors.
FRCGP	*do*, Royal College of General Practitioners.
FRCM	*do*, Royal College of Music.
FRCO	*do*, Royal College of Organists.
FRCOG	*do*, Royal College of Obstetricians and Gynaecologists.
FRCP	*do*, Royal College of Physicians, London.
FRCPath	*do*, Royal College of Pathologists.
FRCPE(d)	*do*, Royal College of Physicians, Edinburgh.
FRCPI	*do*, Royal College of Physicians, Ireland.
FRCPsych	*do*, Royal College of Psychiatrists.
FRCR	*do*, Royal College of Radiologists.
FRCS	*do*, Royal College of Surgeons of England.
FRCSE(d)	*do*, Royal College of Surgeons of Edinburgh.
FRCSGlas	*do*, Royal College of Physicians and Surgeons of Glasgow.
FRCSI	*do*, Royal College of Surgeons in Ireland.
FRCVS	*do*, Royal College of Veterinary Surgeons.
FREconS	*do*, Royal Economic Society.
FRGS	*do*, Royal Geographical Society.
FRHistS	*do*, Royal Historical Society.
FRHS	*do*, Royal Horticultural Society.
FRIBA	*do*, Royal Institute of British Architects.
FRICS	*do*, Royal Institution of Chartered Surveyors.
FRMetS	*do*, Royal Meteorological Society.
FRMS	*do*, Royal Microscopical Society.
FRNS	*do*, Royal Numismatic Society.
FRPharmS	*do*, Royal Pharmaceutical Society.
FRPS	*do*, Royal Photographic Society.
FRS	*do*, Royal Society.
FRSA	*do*, Royal Society of Arts.
FRSC	*do*, Royal Society of Chemistry.
FRSE	*do*, Royal Society of Edinburgh.
FRSL	*do*, Royal Society of Literature.
FRTPI	*do*, Royal Town Planning Institute.
FSA	*do*, Society of Antiquaries.
FSS	*do*, Statistical Society.
FSVA	*do*, Incorporated Society of Valuers and Auctioneers.
FT	*Financial Times*.
FTI	Fellow, Textile Institute.
FTII	*do*, Institute of Taxation.
FZS	*do*, Zoological Society.

G

GATT	General Agreement on Tariffs and Trade.
GBE	Dame/Knight Grand Cross, Order of the British Empire.
GC	George Cross.
GCB	Dame/Knight Grand Cross, Order of the Bath.
GCE	General Certificate of Education.
GCHQ	Government Communications Headquarters.
GCIE	Knight Grand Commander, Order of the Indian Empire.
GCLJ	Knight Grand Cross, Order of St Lazarus of Jerusalem.
GCMG	Dame/Knight Grand Cross, Order of St Michael and St George.
GCSE	General Certificate of Secondary Education.
GCSI	Knight Grand Commander, Order of the Star of India.
GCVO	Dame/Knight Grand Cross, Royal Victorian Order.
GDP	Gross domestic product.
Gen	General.
GHQ	General Headquarters.
GM	George Medal.

GMB	General, Municipal, Boilermakers and Allied Trades Union.
GMT	Greenwich Mean Time.
GNP	Gross national product.
GOC	General Officer Commanding.
GP	General Practitioner.
Gp Capt	Group Captain.
GSO	General Staff Officer.

H

HAC	Honourable Artillery Company.
HBM	Her/His Britannic Majesty('s).
HCF	Highest common factor; Honorary Chaplain to the Forces.
HE	Her/His Excellency; His Eminence.
HGV	Heavy Goods Vehicle.
HH	Her/His Highness; Her/His Honour; His Holiness.
HIM	Her/His Imperial Majesty.
HIV	Human Immunodeficiency Virus.
HJS	(*hic jacet sepultus*) here lies buried.
HM	Her/His Majesty('s).
HMAS	Her/His Majesty's Australian Ship.
HMC	Headmasters' Conference.
HMI	Her/His Majesty's Inspector.
HML	Her/His Majesty's Lieutenant.
HMS	Her/His Majesty's Ship.
HMSO	Her/His Majesty's Stationery Office.
HNC	Higher National Certificate.
HND	Higher National Diploma.
HOLMES	Home Office Large Major Enquiry System.
Hon	Honorary; Honourable.
hp	horse power.
HP	Hire purchase.
HQ	Headquarters.
HRH	Her/His Royal Highness.
HSE	Health and Safety Executive; (*hic sepultus est*) here lies buried.
HSH	Her/His Serene Highness.
HTR	High temperature reactor.
HWM	High water mark.

I

I	Island.
IAAS	Incorporated Association of Architects and Surveyors.
IAEA	International Atomic Energy Agency.
IATA	International Air Transport Association.
Ibid	(*ibidem*) in the same place.
IBRD	International Bank for Reconstruction and Development.
ICAO	International Civil Aviation Organization.
ICBM	Inter-continental ballistic missile.
ICFTU	International Confederation of Free Trade Unions.
ICJ	International Court of Justice.
ICRC	International Committee of the Red Cross.
Id	(*idem*) the same.
IDA	International Development Association.
ie	(*id est*) that is.
IEA	International Energy Agency.
IFAD	International Fund for Agricultural Development.
IFC	International Finance Corporation.
IHS	(*Iesus Hominum Salvator*) Jesus the Saviour of Mankind.
ILEA	Inner London Education Authority.
ILO	International Labour Office/Organization.
ILR	Independent local radio.
IMF	International Monetary Fund.
IMO	International Maritime Organization.
Inc	Incorporated.

Incog	(*incognito*) unknown, unrecognized.
INF	International Nuclear Force.
INLA	Irish National Liberation Army.
In loc	(*in loco*) in its place.
Inmarsat	International Maritime Satellite Organization.
INRI	(*Iesus Nazarenus Rex Iudaeorum*) Jesus of Nazareth, King of the Jews.
Inst	(*instant*) current month.
Intelsat	International Telecommunications Satellite Consortium.
Interpol	International Criminal Police Commission.
IOM	Isle of Man.
IOU	I owe you.
IOW	Isle of Wight.
IQ	Intelligence quotient.
IRA	Irish Republican Army.
IRC	International Red Cross.
Is	Islands.
ISBN	International Standard Book Number.
ISO	Imperial Service Order.
ITC	Independent Television Commission.
ITU	International Telecommunication Union.
ITV	Independent Television.

J

JP	Justice of the Peace.

K

K	Köchel numeration (*of Mozart's works*).
KANU	Kenyan African National Union.
KBE	Knight Commander, Order of the British Empire.
KCB	*do*, Order of the Bath.
KCIE	*do*, Order of the Indian Empire.
KCLJ	*do*, Order of St Lazarus of Jerusalem.
KCMG	*do*, Order of St Michael and St George.
KCSI	*do*, Order of the Star of India.
KCVO	*do*, Royal Victorian Order.
KG	Knight of the Garter.
KGB	(*Komitet Gosudarstvennoi Besopasnosti*) Committee of State Security (USSR).
KKK	Ku Klux Klan.
KLJ	Knight, Order of St Lazarus of Jerusalem.
ko	knock out (*boxing*).
KP	Knight, Order of St Patrick.
KStJ	Knight, Order of St John of Jerusalem.
Kt	Knight.
KT	Knight of the Thistle.
kV	Kilovolt.
kW	Kilowatt.
kWh	Kilowatt hour.

L

L	Liberal.
Lab	Labour.
Lat	Latitude.
lbw	leg before wicket.
lc	lower case (*printing*).
LCJ	Lord Chief Justice.
LCM	Least/lowest common multiple.
LD	Liberal Democrat.
LDS	Licentiate in Dental Surgery.
LEA	Local Education Authority.
LHD	(*Literarum Humaniorum Doctor*) Doctor of Humane Letters/Literature.
Lib	Liberal.
Lic	(*Licenciado*) lawyer (*Spanish*).
Lic Med	Licentiate in Medicine.
Lit	Literary.
Lit Hum	(*Literae Humaniores*) Faculty of classics and philosophy, Oxford.
Litt D	Doctor of Letters.
LJ	Lord Justice.

LLB	Bachelor of Laws.
LLD	Doctor of Laws.
LLM	Master of Laws.
LM	Licentiate in Midwifery.
LMSSA	*do*, in Medicine and Surgery, Society of Apothecaries.
loc cit	(*loco citato*) in the place cited.
log	logarithm.
Londin:	of London (*Bishop*).
Long	Longitude.
LS	(*loco sigilli*) place of the seal.
LSA	Licentiate of Society of Apothecaries.
Lsd	(*Librae, solidi, denarii*) £, shillings and pence.
LSE	London School of Economics and Political Science.
Lt	Lieutenant.
LTA	Lawn Tennis Association.
Ltd	Limited (liability).
LTh *or*	
L Theol	Licentiate in Theology.
LVO	Lieutenant, Royal Victorian Order.
LWM	Low water mark.

M

M	Member of; Monsieur.
MA	Master of Arts.
MAFF	Ministry of Agriculture, Fisheries and Food.
Maj	Major.
max	maximum.
MB/D	Bachelor/Doctor of Medicine.
MBA	Master of Business Administration.
MBE	Member, Order of the British Empire.
MC	Master of Ceremonies; Military Cross.
MCC	Marylebone Cricket Club.
MCh(D)	*do*, of (Dental) Surgery.
MDS	*do*, of Dental Surgery.
ME	Middle English.
MEC	Member of Executive Council.
MEd	Master of Education.
mega	one million times.
MEP	Member of the European Parliament.
MFH	Master of Foxhounds.
Mgr	Monsignor.
MI	Military Intelligence.
micro	one-millionth part.
milli	one-thousandth part.
min	minimum.
MIRAS	Mortgage Interest Relief at Source.
MLA	Member of Legislative Assembly.
MLC	Member of Legislative Council.
Mlle	Mademoiselle.
MLR	Minimum lending rate.
MM	Military Medal.
Mme	Madame.
MN	Merchant Navy.
MO	Medical Officer/Orderly.
MoD	Ministry of Defence.
MoT	Ministry of Transport.
MP	Member of Parliament; Military Police.
mph	miles per hour.
MR	Master of the Rolls.
MRC	Medical Research Council.
MS	Master of Surgery; Manuscript (*pl* MSS).
MSc	Master of Science.
MSF	Manufacturing, Science and Finance Union.
MTh	Master of Theology.
Mus B/D	Bachelor/Doctor of Music.
MV	Merchant Vessel; Motor Vessel.
MVO	Member, Royal Victorian Order.
MW	Medium Wave.

N

N	North.
n/a	not applicable; not available.

NAAFI	Navy, Army and Air Force Institutes.
NALGO	National and Local Government Officers' Association.
NASA	National Aeronautics and Space Administration.
NAS/UWT	National Association of Schoolmasters/ Union of Women Teachers.
NATO	North Atlantic Treaty Organization.
NB	New Brunswick; (*Nota bene*) note well.
NCO	Non-commissioned officer.
NEB	New English Bible.
NEDC	National Economic Development Council.
Nem con	(*Nemine contradicente*) no one contradicting.
NERC	Natural Environment Research Council.
nes	not elsewhere specified.
NFT	National Film Theatre.
NFU	National Farmers' Union.
NGA '82	National Graphical Association 1982.
NHS	National Health Service.
NI	National Insurance; Northern Ireland.
No	(*numero*) number.
Non seq	(*Non sequitur*) it does not follow.
Norvic:	of Norwich (*Bishop*).
NP	Notary Public.
NRA	National Rifle Association.
NS	New Style (*calendar*); Nova Scotia.
NSPCC	National Society for the Prevention of Cruelty to Children.
NSW	New South Wales.
NT	National Theatre; National Trust; New Testament.
NUCPS	National Union of Civil and Public Servants.
NUJ	*do*, of Journalists.
NUM	*do*, of Mineworkers.
NUPE	*do*, of Public Employees.
NUR	*do*, of Railwaymen.
NUS	*do*, of Seamen; *do*, of Students.
NUT	*do*, of Teachers.
NVQ	National Vocational Qualification.
NWT	Northwest Territory.
NY	New York.
NZ	New Zealand.

O

OAPEC	Organization of Arab Petroleum Exporting Countries.
OAS	Organization of American States.
OAU	Organization of African Unity.
Ob *or* obit	died.
OBE	Officer, Order of the British Empire.
OC	Officer Commanding.
ODA	Overseas Development Administration.
OE	Old English; omissions excepted.
OECD	Organization for Economic Co-operation and Development.
OED	*Oxford English Dictionary*.
Ofgas	Office of Gas Supply.
OFM	Order of Friars Minor (*Franciscans*).
Oftel	Office of Telecommunications.
OHMS	On Her/His Majesty's Service.
OM	Order of Merit.
OND	Ordinary National Diploma.
op	(*opus*) work.
OP	Opposite prompt side (*of theatre*); Order of Preachers (*Dominicans*); out of print (*books*).
op cit	(*opere citato*) in the work cited.
OPCS	Office of Population Censuses and Surveys.
OPEC	Organization of Petroleum Exporting Countries.
OS	Old Style (*calendar*); Ordnance Survey.
OSA	Order of St Augustine.
OSB	Order of St Benedict.

O St J	Officer, Order of St John of Jerusalem.
OT	Old Testament.
OTC	Officers' Training Corps.
Oxon	(of) Oxford; Oxfordshire.

P

p	page (pp pages).
p	(*piano*) softly.
PA	Personal Assistant; Press Association.
PAYE	Pay as You Earn.
pc	(*per centum*) in the hundred.
PC	Personal Computer; Police Constable; Privy Counsellor.
PCAS	Polytechnics Central Admissions System.
PCFC	Polytechnics' and Colleges' Funding Council.
PDSA	People's Dispensary for Sick Animals.
PE	Physical Education.
Petriburg:	of Peterborough (*Bishop*).
PhD	Doctor of Philosophy.
pinx(it)	he/she painted it.
pl	plural.
PLA	Port of London Authority.
PLC	Public Limited Company.
PLO	Palestine Liberation Organization.
pm	(*post meridiem*) after noon.
PM	Prime Minister.
PMRAFNS	Princess Mary's Royal Air Force Nursing Service.
PO	Petty Officer; Pilot Officer; Post Office; postal order.
POW	Prisoner of War.
pp	(*per procurationem*) by proxy.
PPS	Parliamentary Private Secretary.
PR	Proportional Representation; Public Relations.
PRA	President of the Royal Academy.
Pro tem	(*pro tempore*) for the time being.
Prox	(*proximo*) next month.
PRS	President of the Royal Society.
PRSE	*do*, of Edinburgh.
Ps	Psalm.
PS	(*Post scriptum*) postscript.
PSBR	Public sector borrowing requirement.
psc	passed Staff College.
PSV	Public Service Vehicle.
Pte	Private.
PTO	Please turn over.

Q

QARANC	Queen Alexandra's Royal Army Nursing Corps.
QARNNS	Queen Alexandra's Royal Naval Nursing Service.
QB	Queen's Bench.
QC	Queen's Counsel.
QED	(*quod erat demonstrandum*) which was to be proved.
QGM	Queen's Gallantry Medal.
QHC	Queen's Honorary Chaplain.
QHDS	Queen's Honorary Dental Surgeon.
QHNS	Queen's Honorary Nursing Sister.
QHP	Queen's Honorary Physician.
QHS	Queen's Honorary Surgeon.
QMG	Quartermaster General.
QPM	Queen's Police Medal.
QS	Quarter Sessions.
QSO	Quasi-stellar object (quasar); Queen's Service Order.
quango	quasi-autonomous non-governmental organization.
qv	(*quod vide*) which see.

R

R	(*Regina*) Queen; (*Rex*) King.

RA	Royal Academy/Academician; Royal Artillery.
RAC	Royal Armoured Corps; Royal Automobile Club.
RADA	Royal Academy of Dramatic Art.
RADC	Royal Army Dental Corps.
RAE	Royal Aerospace Establishment.
RAEC	Royal Army Educational Corps.
RAeS	Royal Aeronautical Society.
RAF	Royal Air Force.
RAM	Random-access memory (*computer*); Royal Academy of Music.
RAMC	Royal Army Medical Corps.
RAN	Royal Australian Navy.
RAOC	Royal Army Ordnance Corps.
RAPC	Royal Army Pay Corps.
RAVC	Royal Army Veterinary Corps.
RBA	Royal Society of British Artists.
RBS	Royal Society of British Sculptors.
RC	Red Cross; Roman Catholic.
RCM	Royal College of Music.
RCN	Royal Canadian Navy.
RCT	Royal Corps of Transport.
RD	Refer to drawer (*banking*); Royal Naval and Royal Marine Forces Reserve Decoration; Rural Dean.
RDI	Royal Designer for Industry.
RE	Religious Education; Royal Engineers.
REME	Royal Electrical and Mechanical Engineers.
Rep	Representative; Republican.
Rev(d)	Reverend.
RGN	Registered General Nurse.
RGS	Royal Geographical Society.
RHA	Regional Health Authority.
RHS	Royal Horticultural Society; Royal Humane Society.
RI	Rhode Island; Royal Institute of Painters in Watercolours; Royal Institution.
RIBA	Royal Institute of British Architects.
RIP	(*Requiescat in pace*) May he/she rest in peace.
RL	Rugby League.
RM	Registered Midwife; Royal Marines.
RMA	Royal Military Academy.
RMN	Registered Mental Nurse.
RN	Royal Navy.
RNIB	Royal National Institute for the Blind.
RNID	Royal National Institute for the Deaf.
RNLI	Royal National Lifeboat Institution.
RNR	Royal Naval Reserve.
RNVR	Royal Naval Volunteer Reserve.
RNXS	Royal Naval Auxiliary Service.
RNZN	Royal New Zealand Navy.
Ro	(*Recto*) on the right-hand page.
ROC	Royal Observer Corps.
Roffen:	of Rochester (*Bishop*).
ROI	Royal Institute of Oil Painters.
ROM	Read-only memory (*computer*).
RoSPA	Royal Society for the Prevention of Accidents.
RP	Royal Society of Portrait Painters.
rpm	revolutions per minute.
RRC	Lady of Royal Red Cross.
RSA	Republic of South Africa; Royal Scottish Academician; Royal Society of Arts.
RSC	Royal Shakespeare Company.
RSCN	Registered Sick Children's Nurse.
RSE	Royal Society of Edinburgh.
RSM	Regimental Sergeant Major.
RSPB	Royal Society for the Protection of Birds.
RSPCA	Royal Society for the Prevention of Cruelty to Animals.
RSV	Revised Standard Version (*of Bible*).
RSVP	(*Répondez, s'il vous plaît*) Please reply.
RSW	Royal Scottish Society of Painters in Watercolours.

RTPI	Royal Town Planning Institute.
RU	Rugby Union.
RUC	Royal Ulster Constabulary.
RV	Revised Version (*of Bible*).
RVM	Royal Victorian Medal.
RWS	Royal Water Colour Society.
RYS	Royal Yacht Squadron.

S

s	second; (*solidus*) shilling.
S	South.
SA	Salvation Army; South Africa; South America; South Australia.
SAE	Stamped addressed envelope.
Salop	Shropshire.
Sarum:	of Salisbury (*Bishop*).
SAS	Special Air Service Regiment.
SBS	Special Boat Squadron.
ScD	Doctor of Science.
SCM	State Certified Midwife.
SDLP	Social Democratic and Labour Party.
SDP	Social Democratic Party.
SEAQ	Stock Exchange Automated Quotations system.
SEN	State Enrolled Nurse.
SERC	Science and Engineering Research Council.
SERPS	State Earnings Related Pension Scheme.
SI	(*Système Internationale d'Unités*) International System of Units; Statutory Instrument.
Sic	So written.
Sig	Signature; Signor.
SJ	Society of Jesus (*Jesuits*).
SLD	Social and Liberal Democrats.
SMP	Statutory Maternity Pay.
SNP	Scottish National Party.
SOGAT	Society of Graphical and Allied Trades.
SOS	Save Our Souls (*distress signal*).
sp	(*sine prole*) without issue.
spgr	specific gravity.
SPQR	(*Senatus Populusque Romanus*) The Senate and People of Rome.
SRN	State Registered Nurse.
SS	Saints; Steamship.
SSC	Solicitor before Supreme Court (*Scotland*).
SSF	Society of St Francis.
SSP	Statutory Sick Pay.
SSSI	Site of special scientific interest.
stet	let it stand (*printing*).
STD	(*Sacrae Theologiae Doctor*) Doctor of Sacred Theology; Subscriber trunk dialling.
stp	Standard temperature and pressure.
STP	(*Sacrae Theologiae Professor*) Professor of Sacred Theology.
Sub Lt	Sub-Lieutenant.
SWAPO	South West Africa People's Organization.

T

TA	Territorial Army.
TB	Tuberculosis.
TCCB	Test and County Cricket Board.
TD	Territorial Efficiency Decoration.
temp	temperature; temporary employee.
TES	*Times Educational Supplement.*
TGWU	Transport and General Workers' Union.
TLS	*Times Literary Supplement.*
TNT	trinitrotoluene (*explosive*).
tr	transpose (*printing*).
TRH	Their Royal Highnesses.
TT	Teetotal; Tuberculin tested.
TUC	Trades Union Congress.
TVEI	Technical and Vocational Education Initiative.

U

U	Unionist.
UAE	United Arab Emirates.
uc	upper case (*printing*).
UCATT	Union of Construction, Allied Trades and Technicians.
UCCA	Universities' Central Council on Admissions.
UDI	Unilateral Declaration of Independence.
UDM	Union of Democratic Mineworkers.
UDR	Ulster Defence Regiment.
UEFA	Union of European Football Associations.
UFC	Universities' Funding Council.
UFO	Unidentified flying object.
UHF	ultra-high frequency.
UK	United Kingdom.
UKAEA	UK Atomic Energy Authority.
UN	United Nations.
UNESCO	United Nations Educational, Scientific and Cultural Organization.
UNICEF	United Nations Children's Fund.
UNIDO	United Nations Industrial Development Organization.
Unita	National Union for the Total Independence of Angola.
UPU	Universal Postal Union.
URC	United Reformed Church.
US(A)	United States (of America).
USDAW	Union of Shop, Distributive and Allied Workers.
USM	Unlisted Securities Market.
USSR	Union of Soviet Socialist Republics.

V

v	(*versus*) against.
VA	Vicar Apostolic; Victoria and Albert Order.
VAD	Voluntary Aid Detachment.
VAT	Value added tax.
VC	Victoria Cross.
VD	Venereal disease; Volunteer Officers' Decoration.
VDU	Visual display unit.
Ven	Venerable.
VHF	very high frequency.
VIP	Very important person.
Vo	(*Verso*) on the left-hand page.
VRD	Royal Naval Volunteer Reserve Officers' Decoration.
VSO	Voluntary Service Overseas.
VTOL	Vertical take-off and landing (*aircraft*).

W

W	West.
WCC	World Council of Churches.
WEA	Workers' Educational Association.
WEU	Western European Union.
WFTU	World Federation of Trade Unions.
WHO	World Health Organization.
WI	West Indies; Women's Institute.
Winton:	of Winchester (*Bishop*).
WIPO	World Intellectual Property Organization.
WMO	World Meteorological Organization.
WO	Warrant Officer.
WRAC	Women's Royal Army Corps.
WRAF	Women's Royal Air Force.
WRNS	Women's Royal Naval Service.
WRVS	Women's Royal Voluntary Service.
WS	Writer to the Signet.

Y

YMCA	Young Men's Christian Association.
YWCA	Young Women's Christian Association.

Z

ZANU	Zimbabwe African National Union.

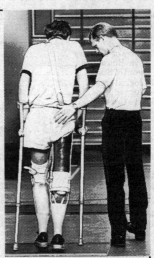

DAME ANNA NEAGLE

KENNETH MORE

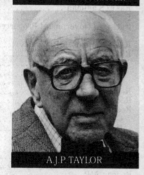
A.J.P. TAYLOR

RAY KENNEDY

PARKINSON'S DISEASE CAN BE *ANYBODY'S* DISEASE.

It's often assumed that tremors are the only symptom
of Parkinson's Disease. If only they were.
Speech difficulty; inability to swallow; a face lacking
expression; slow and clumsy movement; feet and legs
that refuse to move. They are all symptoms.
There are over 100,000 sufferers in this country alone.
There is no known cure.
Parkinson's Disease Society seeks to ease the burden
and find the cure for Parkinson's Disease.
We need *your* help. Please send a donation, a covenant
or leave us a legacy. You can even phone your
donation by Access or Visa to 071-383 3513.

HELP MAKE IT *NOBODY'S* DISEASE

Parkinson's Disease Society
22 Upper Woburn Place, London WC1H 0RA. Tel: 071-383 3513
Patron: HRH The Princess of Wales

INDEX TO ADVERTISEMENTS

STOP-PRESS

Peerage

Sir Nicolas Browne-Wilkinson created Baron Browne-Wilkinson.

Parliament

Adm. Sir Richard Thomas to be Gentleman Usher of the Black Rod in Jan. 1992.
Dafydd Wigley, MP, to be president of Plaid Cymru.
Vacant constituencies: Hemsworth, Langbaurgh.

Government and Public Offices

Ministry of Agriculture: C. R. Cann to be Deputy Secretary, Countryside, Marine, Environment and Fisheries.
Dept. of Health: G. Greenshields to be Director of Finance and Corporate Information, NHS Management Executive.
Royal Commission on the Historical Monuments of England: Miss A. Riches and R. Yorke to be members.
Lord Great Chamberlain's Office: Adm. Sir Richard Thomas to be Secretary in Jan. 1992.
Joint Nature Conservation Committee: The Earl of Selborne to be chairman.

Law Courts and Offices

Lord Brandon of Oakbrook retired September 1991.
New Lords of Appeal in Ordinary: Sir Nicolas Browne-Wilkinson, Sir Michael Mustill, Sir Gordon Slynn.
New Vice-Chancellor: Sir Donald Nicholls.
New Lord Justices of Appeal: Mr Justice Scott (Chancery Division), Mr Justice Steyn (Queen's Bench Division).
New Justice of the High Court: J. M. Chadwick (Chancery Division).
Sir Allan Green resigned as Director of Public Prosecutions.

Police

A. G. Elliott to be Chief Constable of Cumbria from Oct. 1991.

Churches

J. Brotherton to be Archdeacon of Chichester.
L. Moss to be Archdeacon of Hereford.
D. Bonser to be Bishop Suffragan of Bolton.
H. B. Taylor to be Bishop Suffragan of Selby.
Rt. Rev. Nigel McCulloch to be Bishop of Wakefield.

Local Government

Alderman Brian Jenkins to be Lord Mayor of London.
Capt. R. C. Cunningham-Jardine to be Lord Lieutenant of Dumfries and Galloway (Districts of Nithsdale and of Annandale and Eskdale).
Rev. D. Macaulay resigned as convener of the Western Isles Islands Council.

Commonwealth

Winston Peters was replaced as the New Zealand Minister for Maori Affairs by Douglas Kidd.
Sir Serei Eri resigned as Governor-General of Papua New Guinea.
Fr Lini resigned as PM of Vanuatu and was succeeded by Donald Kalpokas.

Foreign Countries

Saddoun Hammadi replaced as PM of Iraq by Muhammad Hamza al Zubaidi.
Ryutaro Hashimoto resigned as Finance Minister of Japan after a number of financial scandals.

International Organizations

Albania joined the European Bank of Reconstruction and Development.
Estonia, Latvia and Lithuania became members of the CSCE.
Estonia, Latvia, Lithuania, North Korea, South Korea, the Marshall Islands and Micronesia became members of the UN.

EVENTS

Sept. 2. A third night of rioting took place in Cardiff and in Oxford. **4.** Bank base rates were cut to 10·5 per cent. **5.** The Soviet Congress of People's Deputies approved three interim inter-republican bodies to replace the existing central government. **7.** An EC-sponsored Yugoslav peace conference opened in The Hague, chaired by Lord Carrington. **9.** Floods in Cambodia killed about 10,000 people. Rioting and looting took place in North Shields, Tyne and Wear. Tadjikistan declared independence from the Soviet Union. **11.** Riots took place in Newcastle upon Tyne. **15.** Elections to the Hong Kong Legislative Council took place. The ruling coalition won the Mauritius general election. The Social Democrats lost the general election in Sweden; a centre-right coalition took office with Carl Bildt as PM. **21.** Michael Watson underwent operations to remove a blood clot from his brain after being stopped by Chris Eubank in the final round of a title fight in London. **23.** Armenia declared independence from the Soviet Union. **24.** British hostage Jackie Mann was released in Beirut. **25.** Rioting in Bucharest led to the resignation of the Romanian government; Teodor Stolojan became the new PM. The national executive committee of the Labour Party suspended two Labour MPs, Terry Field (Liverpool Broadgreen) and Dave Nellist (Coventry South East), pending an inquiry into their alleged support of the Militant Tendency. **30.** President Aristide of Haiti was overthrown in a military coup. EC foreign ministers rejected a Dutch draft treaty for political union.

Oct. 3. The Director of Public Prosecutions, Sir Allan Green, resigned after being stopped by police for allegedly kerb-crawling. Serbia and its three allies on the Yugoslav collective presidency were accused of mounting a coup when they assumed powers to take decisions without the consent of the other four members. Nadine Gordimer won the Nobel Prize for Literature.

DEATHS

September

2. Laura Riding, American poet and writer, aged 90.
   —Alfonso Garcia Robles, diplomat, disarmament crusader and Nobel Peace Prize winner, aged 80.
3. Frank Capra, American film director, aged 94.
4. Margaret (Peggy) Ramsay, theatrical agent, aged 83.
5. Jean Rook, journalist, aged 59.

6. 8th Viscount Hawarden, aged 65.
7. Edwin McMillan, American physicist and Nobel laureate, co-discoverer of neptunium and plutonium, aged 83.
11. George Eardley, VC, MM, aged 79.
14. George Buckley, MP, Labour MP for Hemsworth since 1987, aged 56.
16. Olga Spessivtseva, Russian ballet dancer, aged 96.
   —Ernest Davies, Labour MP for Enfield 1945–50 and for East Enfield 1950–59, aged 89.
17. 5th Baron Lurgan, OBE, aged 80.
21. Richard Holt, MP, Conservative MP for Langbaurgh since 1983, aged 60.

23. Sir Yue-Kong Pao, CBE, Hong Kong shipping and property magnate, aged 72.
24. Theodore Seuss Geisel (Dr Seuss), writer of children's books, aged 87.
25. Klaus Barbie, wartime Gestapo chief in Lyons, aged 77.
26. Joe Hulme, footballer and cricketer, aged 87.
28. Roy Fuller, poet, novelist and critic, aged 79.
   Miles Davis, jazz trumpeter, aged 65.

October

2. Dimitrios I, Ecumenical Patriarch of Constantinople since 1972, aged 77.